R.A. Campbell
Aug 2, 1978

Who's Who in the Midwest

**Biographical Reference Works
Published by Marquis Who's Who**

Who's Who in America
Who Was Who in America
  Historical Volume (1607-1896)
  Volume I (1897-1942)
  Volume II (1943-1950)
  Volume III (1951-1960)
  Volume IV (1961-1968)
  Volume V (1969-1973)
  Volume VI (1974-1976)
Who Was Who in American History—Arts and Letters
Who Was Who in American History—The Military
Who Was Who in American History—Science and Technology
Who's Who in the Midwest
Who's Who in the East
Who's Who in the South and Southwest
Who's Who in the West
Who's Who of American Women
Who's Who in Government
Who's Who in Finance and Industry
Who's Who in Religion
Who's Who in American Law
Who's Who in the World
Who's Who Biographical Record—Child Development Professionals
Who's Who Biographical Record—School District Officials
World Who's Who in Science
Directory of Medical Specialists
Marquis Who's Who Publications / Index to All Books
Travelers' Guide to U.S. Certified Doctors Abroad

Who's Who
in the Midwest ®

Including Illinois, Indiana, Iowa, Kansas,
Michigan, Minnesota, Missouri, Nebraska,
North Dakota, Ohio, South Dakota, and
Wisconsin; and in Canada, Manitoba and
western Ontario

16th edition
1978-1979

MARQUIS
Who's Who

Marquis Who's Who, Inc.
200 East Ohio Street
Chicago, Illinois 60611 U.S.A.

Library of Congress Catalog Card Number 50-289
International Standard Book Number 0-8379-0716-0
Product Code Number 030189

Manufactured in the United States of America

Table of Contents

Preface

Traditionally one of the world's richest agricultural areas, the Midwest has over the past century emerged as a leader in transportation and industry. This evolution has been facilitated by its vast system of waterways that have made it possible for most of the Midwest's interior cities to be easily accessible to each other as well as to the Atlantic Ocean. Its strategic location in the heartland of America has made the Midwest the nation's center for rail transportation. The extensive network of railways emanating from the cities of the Midwest has made possible the transportation of raw materials for industry. It also has provided farmers with readily available markets for their many agricultural products. Air travel has stimulated communication and trade with other areas of the nation and has provided Midwestern manufacturers with additional outlets abroad. Increased industrialization has fostered the growth of Midwestern cities. Today over one-fourth of America's people are Midwesterners.

It, thus, becomes more difficult with each biennial edition to select the most significant individuals for inclusion in Who's Who in the Midwest. This new, Sixteenth Edition, however, represents our editors' attempts to recognize particular merit and to satisfy reference interest—to record the latest and the continuing accomplishments of individuals involved in all significant fields of endeavor in the Midwest.

Assiduously reviewed, revised, and amended, the Sixteenth Edition offers up-to-the-minute coverage of a broad range of Midwesterners based on position or individual achievement. Our editors have made every effort to present a balanced picture of achievement in the Midwest. To assure such balance in compilation of the volume, a list of essential names is made up of those men and women who are so eminent that their omission would fault the usefulness of the book. In the great majority of cases these individuals have furnished their own data, thus assuring a high degree of accuracy. In some cases where individuals have failed to supply information, Marquis staff members compile the data through careful and independent research. Sketches compiled in this manner are denoted by an asterisk. As in previous editions, biographees are given the opportunity to review pre-publication proofs of their sketches to make sure they are correct.

Marquis Who's Who editors exercise the utmost care in preparing each biographical sketch for publication. Occasionally, however, errors do occur despite all precautions taken to minimize such occurrences. All users of this directory are requested to draw the attention of the publisher to any errors found, so that corrections can be made in a later edition.

The Sixteenth Edition contains more than 18,000 names from the region embracing Illinois, Indiana, Iowa, Kansas, Michigan, Minnesota, Missouri, Nebraska, North Dakota, Ohio, South Dakota, and Wisconsin; and in Canada, Manitoba and western Ontario.

The persons sketched in this volume represent a broad spectrum of achievement in virtually every significant field of endeavor. Included are executives and officials in government, business, education, religion, the press, civic affairs, the arts, cultural affairs, law and other fields. This edition also includes significant contributors in such fields as contemporary art, music and science.

The question is often asked, "How do people get into a Who's Who volume?" Name selection is based on one fundamental principle: reference value.

Biographees of Who's Who in the Midwest can be classified into two basic categories: (1) Persons who are of regional reference importance to colleagues, librarians, researchers, scholars, the press, historians, biographers, participants in business and civic affairs, and others with specific or general inquiry needs; (2) Individuals of national reference interest who are also of such regional or local importance that their inclusion in the book is essential to its serviceability. With these names there is a minimum of duplication between this volume and Who's Who in America. In recognition of the complementary relationship between these two Marquis publications, however, this Sixteenth Edition of Who's Who in the Midwest contains a listing of all those biographees of the Midwestern region whose sketches appear in the Fortieth Edition of Who's Who in America.

In the editorial evaluation that resulted in the ultimate selection of the names in this directory, an individual's desire to be listed was not sufficient reason for inclusion; rather it was the individual's demonstrated merit that ruled. Similarly, wealth or social position was not a criterion; only occupational stature or achievement in some field affecting the development of the Midwestern region of North America influenced selection. Indeed, many of the biographees are engaged in fields marked far more by service than by monetary reward. And, of course, this volume lists worthy individuals regardless of their race or ethnic origin.

Thus, on every level, this Sixteenth Edition of Who's Who in the Midwest carries on the tradition of excellence established in 1899 with the publication of the first edition of Who's Who in America. The essence of that tradition is reflected in our unceasing effort to produce reference works that are responsive to the needs of their users throughout the world.

Standards of Admission

The foremost consideration in determining possible biographees for *Who's Who in the Midwest* is the extent of an individual's reference interest. Such reference interest is judged on either of two factors: (1) The position of responsibility held, or (2) The level of significant achievement attained.

Admissions based on the factor of position may include:

Members of the U.S. Congress

Federal judges.

Governors of states covered by this volume.

Premiers of Canadian provinces covered by this volume.

State attorneys general.

Judges of state and territorial courts of highest appellate jurisdiction.

Mayors of major cities.

Heads of the major universities and colleges.

Authors of books of more than ephemeral interest or value.

Heads of leading philanthropic, educational, cultural, and scientific institutions and associations.

Chief ecclesiastics of the principal religious denominations.

Principal officers of national and international businesses.

Others chosen because of incumbency, authorship, or membership.

Admissions based on individual achievement, on the other hand, must be decided by a judicious process of evaluating qualitative factors. To be selected on this basis, a person must have accomplished some conspicuous achievement—something that distinguishes him or her from the vast majority of contemporaries. He or she may scarcely be known in the local community but may be widely recognized in some field of endeavor. Such a person often is one whose work is better known than is his/her name.

Key to Information in this Directory

❶ WATTS, BENJAMIN GREEN,❷mfg. co. exec.;**❸**b. Youngstown, Ohio, May 21, 1932;**❹**s. William and Verna (Stevens) W.; **❺** B.S., Northwestern U., 1954, M.B.A., 1955;**❻**m. Pearl Riley, Nov. 7, 1958; **❼** children—Benjamin Allen, Melissa Anne. **❽** With Ross Bros. Mfg. Co., Chgo., 1957—, sales mgr., 1965-68, v.p. sales, 1968-70, pres., 1970-77, chmn. bd., 1977—, also dir.; instr. North Shore Community Coll., Wilmette, Ill., 1969-71. **❾** Active Boy Scouts Am.; mem. Lake County Zoning Commn., 1968—; trustee Whitlow Coll. **❿** Served with U.S. Army, 1955-56. **⓫** Recipient Outstanding Alumni award Northwestern U., 1971. **⓬** Mem. NAM, Sales and Mktg. Exec. Club, Am. Mgmt. Assn., Phi Delta Theta. **⓭**Republican. **⓮** Presbyterian. **⓯** Clubs: Masons (32 deg., Shriner), Exmoor Country (Highland Park, Ill.); Tavern, Saddle and Cycle (Chgo.). **⓰** Author: Sales Techniques in a Climbing Market, 1969. **⓱** Home: 1450 Greentree Blvd Highland Park IL 60035 **⓲** Office: 320 N. Michigan Ave Chicago IL 60611

KEY

❶ Name
❷ Occupation
❸ Vital statistics
❹ Parents
❺ Education
❻ Marriage
❼ Children
❽ Career
❾ Civic and political activities
❿ Military record
⓫ Awards and certifications
⓬ Professional and association
   memberships
⓭ Political affiliation
⓮ Religion
⓯ Clubs (including lodges)
⓰ Writings and special achievements
⓱ Home address
⓲ Office address

The biographical listings in *Who's Who in the Midwest* are arranged in alphabetical order according to the first letter of the last name of the biographee. Each sketch is presented in a uniform order as in the sample sketch above. The many abbreviations used in the sketches are explained in the Table of Abbreviations.

Table of Abbreviations

The following abbreviations and symbols are frequently used in this Directory

* Following a sketch indicates that it was researched and written by the Marquis Who's Who editorial staff and has not been verified by the biographee.

A.A. Associate in Arts
AAAL American Academy of Arts and Letters
AAAS American Association for the Advancement of Science
AAHPER American Association for Health, Physical Education and Recreation
A. and M. Agricultural and Mechanical
AAU Amateur Athletic Union
AAUP American Association of University Professors
AAUW American Association of University Women
A.B. Arts, Bachelor of
AB Alberta
ABC American Broadcasting Company
AC Air Corps
acad. academy
ACDA Arms Control and Disarmament Agency
ACLU American Civil Liberties Union
A.C.P. American College of Physicians
A.C.S. American College of Surgeons
ADA American Dental Association
a.d.c. aide-de-camp
adj. adjunct, adjutant
adj. gen. adjutant general
adm. admiral
adminstr. administrator
adminstrn. administration
adminstrv. administrative
adv. advocate
advt. advertising
A.E. Agricultural Engineer
A.E. and P., AEP Ambassador Extraordinary and Plenipotentiary
AEC Atomic Energy Commission
aero. aeronautical, aeronautic
AFB Air Force Base
AFL-CIO American Federation of Labor and Congress of Industrial Organizations
AFTRA American Federation TV and Radio Artists
agr. agriculture
agrl. agricultural
agt. agent
AGVA American Guild of Variety Artists
AIA American Institute of Architects
AID Agency for International Development
AIEE American Institute of Electrical Engineers
AIM American Institute of Management
AK Alaska
AL Alabama
ALA American Library Association
Ala. Alabama
alt. alternate
Alta. Alberta
A.M. Arts, Master of
Am. American, America
AMA American Medical Association
A.M.E. African Methodist Episcopal
Amtrak National Railroad Passenger Corporation
anat. anatomical
ann. annual
ANTA American National Theatre and Academy
anthrop. anthropological
AP Associated Press
APO Army Post Office
apptd. appointed
apt. apartment
AR Arkansas
ARC American Red Cross
archeol. archeological

archtl. architectural
Ariz. Arizona
Ark. Arkansas
Arts D. Arts, Doctor of
arty. artillery
ASCAP American Society of Composers, Authors and Publishers
ASCE American Society of Civil Engineers
ASME American Society of Mechanical Engineers
assn. association
asso. associate
asst. assistant
ASTM American Society for Testing and Materials
astron. astronomical
astrophys. astrophysical
ATSC Air Technical Service Command
AT&T American Telephone & Telegraph Company
atty. attorney
AUS Army of the United States
aux. auxiliary
Ave. Avenue
AVMA American Veterinary Medical Association
AZ Arizona

B. Bachelor
b. born
B.A. Bachelor of Arts
B. Agr. Bachelor of Agriculture
Balt. Baltimore
Bapt. Baptist
B.Arch. Bachelor of Architecture
B.A.S. Bachelor of Agricultural Science
B.B.A. Bachelor of Business Administration
BBC British Broadcasting Corporation
B.C., BC British Columbia
B.C.E. Bachelor of Civil Engineering
B.Chir. Bachelor of Surgery
B.C.L. Bachelor of Civil Law
B.C.S. Bachelor of Commercial Science
B.D. Bachelor of Divinity
bd. board
B.E. Bachelor of Education
B.E.E. Bachelor of Electrical Engineering
B.F.A. Bachelor of Fine Arts
bibl. biblical
bibliog. bibliographical
biog. biographical
biol. biological
B.J. Bachelor of Journalism
Bklyn. Brooklyn
B.L. Bachelor of Letters
bldg. building
B.L.S. Bachelor of Library Science
Blvd. Boulevard
bn. battalion
B.&O.R.R. Baltimore & Ohio Railroad
bot. botanical
B.P.E. Bachelor of Physical Education
br. branch
B.R.E. Bachelor of Religious Education
brig. gen. brigadier general
Brit. British, Britannica
Bros. Brothers
B.S. Bachelor of Science
B.S.A. Bachelor of Agricultural Science
B.S.D. Bachelor of Didactic Science
B.S.T. Bachelor of Sacred Theology
B.Th. Bachelor of Theology
bull. bulletin
bur. bureau
bus. business
B.W.I. British West Indies

CA California
CAA Civil Aeronautics Administration
CAB Civil Aeronautics Board
Calif. California
C.Am. Central America
Can. Canada
CAP Civil Air Patrol
capt. captain
CARE Cooperative American Relief Everywhere
Cath. Catholic
cav. cavalry
CBC Canadian Broadcasting Company
CBI China, Burma, India Theatre of Operations
CBS Columbia Broadcasting System
CCC Commodity Credit Corporation
CD Civil Defense
C.E. Corps of Engineers
CENTO Central Treaty Organization
CERN European Organization of Nuclear Research
ch. church
Ch.D. Doctor of Chemistry
chem. chemical
Chem. E. Chemical Engineer
Chgo. Chicago
chirurg. chirurgical
chmn. chairman
chpt. chapter
CIA Central Intelligence Agency
CIC Counter Intelligence Corps
Cin. Cincinnati
Cleve. Cleveland
climatol. climatological
clin. clinical
clk. clerk
C.L.U. Chartered Life Underwriter
C.M. Master in Surgery
C.&N.W.Ry. Chicago & Northwestern Railway
CO Colorado
Co. Company
COF Catholic Order of Foresters
C. of C. Chamber of Commerce
col. colonel
coll. college
Colo. Colorado
com. committee
comd. commanded
comdg. commanding
comdr. commander
comdt. commandant
commd. commissioned
comml. commercial
commn. commission
commr. commissioner
condr. conductor
Conf. Conference
Congl. Congregational
Conglist. Congregationalist
Conn. Connecticut
cons. consultant, consulting
consol. consolidated
constl. constitutional
constn. constitution
constrn. construction
contbd. contributed
contbg. contributing
contbr. contributor
Conv. Convention
coop., co-op. cooperative
CORDS Civil Operations and Revolutionary Development Support
CORE Congress of Racial Equality
corp. corporation
corr. correspondent, corresponding

C.&O.Ry. Chesapeake & Ohio Railway
C.P.A. Certified Public Accountant
C.P.C.U. Chartered property and casualty underwriter
C.P.H. Certificate of Public Health
cpl. corporal
C.P.Ry. Canadian Pacific Railway
C.S. Christian Science
C.S.B. Bachelor of Christian Science
CSC Civil Service Commission
C.S.D. Doctor of Christian Science
CT Connecticut
ct. court
CWS Chemical Warfare Service
C.Z. Canal Zone

d. daughter
D. Doctor
D.Agr. Doctor of Agriculture
D.A.R. Daughters of the American Revolution
dau. daughter
DAV Disabled American Veterans
D.C., DC District of Columbia
D.C.L. Doctor of Civil Law
D.C.S. Doctor of Commercial Science
D.D. Doctor of Divinity
D.D.S. Doctor of Dental Surgery
DE Delaware
dec. deceased
def. defense
Del. Delaware
del. delegate, delegation
Dem. Democrat, Democratic
D.Eng. Doctor of Engineering
denom. denomination
dep. deputy
dept. department
desc. descendant
devel. development
D.F.A. Doctor of Fine Arts
D.F.C. Distinguished Flying Cross
D.H.L. Doctor of Hebrew Literature
dir. director
dist. district
distbg. distributing
distbn. distribution
distbr. distributor
div. division, divinity, divorce
D.Litt. Doctor of Literature
D.M.D. Doctor of Medical Dentistry
D.M.S. Doctor of Medical Science
D.O. Doctor of Osteopathy
D.P.H. Diploma in Public Health
D.R. Daughters of the Revolution
Dr. Drive
D.R.E. Doctor of Religious Education
Dr.P.H. Doctor of Public Health, Doctor of Public Hygiene
D.S.C. Distinguished Service Cross
D.Sc. Doctor of Science
D.S.M. Distinguished Service Medal
D.S.T. Doctor of Sacred Theology
D.T.M. Doctor of Tropical Medicine
D.V.M. Doctor of Veterinary Medicine
D.V.S. Doctor of Veterinary Surgery

E. East
E. and P. Extraordinary and Plenipotentiary
Eccles. Ecclesiastical
ecol. ecological
ECOSOC Economic and Social Council (of the UN)
E.D. Doctor of Engineering
ed. educated

Ed.B. Bachelor of Education
Ed.D. Doctor of Education
edit. edition
Ed.M. Master of Education
edn. education
ednl. educational
EDP electronic data processing
E.E. Electrical Engineer
E.E. and M.P. Envoy Extraordinary and Minister Plenipotentiary
EEC European Economic Community
EEG electroencephalogram
EKG electrocardiogram
E.Ger. German Democratic Republic
elec. electrical
electrochem. electrochemical
electrophys. electrophysical
E.M. Engineer of Mines
ency. encyclopedia
Eng. England
engr. engineer
engring. engineering
entomol. entomological
environ. environmental
EPA Environmental Protection Agency
epidemiol. epidemiological
Episc. Episcopalian
ERDA Energy Research and Development Administration
ESSA Environmental Science Services Administration
ethnol. ethnological
ETO European Theatre of Operations
Evang. Evangelical
exam. examination, examining
exec. executive
exhbn. exhibition
expdn. expedition
expn. exposition
expt. experiment
exptl. experimental

F.A. Field Artillery
FAA Federal Aviation Administration
FAO Food and Agriculture Organization (of the UN)
FBI Federal Bureau of Investigation
FCA Farm Credit Administration
FCC Federal Communication Commission
FCDA Federal Civil Defense Administration
FDA Food and Drug Administration
FDIA Federal Deposit Insurance Administration
FDIC Federal Deposit Insurance Corporation
F.E. Forest Engineer
fed. federal
fedn. federation
fgn. foreign
FHA Federal Housing Administration
fin. financial, finance
FL Florida
Fla. Florida
FMC Federal Maritime Commission
FOA Foreign Operations Administration
found. foundation
FPC Federal Power Commission
FPO Fleet Post Office
FRS Federal Reserve System
FSA Federal Security Agency
Ft. Fort
FTC Federal Trade Commission, Federal Tariff Commission

G-1 (or other number) Division of General Staff
Ga., GA Georgia

GAO General Accounting Office
gastroent. gastroenterological
GATT General Agreement of Tariff and Trades
gen. general
geneal. genealogical
geod. geodetic
geog. geographic, geographical
geol. geological
geophys. geophysical
gerontol. gerontological
G.H.Q. General Headquarters
G.N.Ry. Great Northern Railway
gov. governor
govt. government
govtl. governmental
GPO Government Printing Office
grad. graduate
GSA General Services Administration
Gt. Great
GU Guam
gynecol. gynecological

hdqrs. headquarters
HEW Department of Health, Education and Welfare
H.H.D. Doctor of Humanities
HHFA Housing and Home Finance Agency
HI Hawaii
hist. historical, historic
H.M. Master of Humanics
homeo. homeopathic
hon. honorary, honorable
Ho. of Dels. House of Delegates
Ho. of Reps. House of Representatives
hort. horticultural
hosp. hospital
HUD Department of Housing and Urban Development
Hwy. Highway
hydrog. hydrographic

IA Iowa
IAEA International Atomic Energy Agency
IBM International Business Machines Corporation
IBRD International Bank for Reconstruction and Development
ICA International Cooperation Administration
ICC Interstate Commerce Commission
ID Idaho
IEEE Institute of Electrical and Electronics Engineers
IFC International Finance Corporation
IGY International Geophysical Year
IL Illinois
Ill. Illinois
ILO International Labor Organization
IMF International Monetary Fund
IN Indiana
Inc. Incorporated
ind. independent
Ind. Indiana
Indpls. Indianapolis
indsl. industrial
inf. infantry
info. information
ins. insurance
insp. inspector
insp. gen. inspector general
inst. institute
instl. institutional
instn. institution
instr. instructor
internat. international
intro. introduction
IRE Institute of Radio Engineers

IRS Internal Revenue Service
ITT International Telephone & Telegraph Corporation

J.B. Jurum Baccolaureus
J.C.B. Juris Canonici Bachelor
J.C.L. Juris Canonici Lector
J.D. Doctor of Jurisprudence
j.g. junior grade
jour. journal
jr. junior
J.S.D. Juris Utriusque Doctor, Doctor of Both (Canon and Civil) Laws
jud. judicial
Judge Adv. Gen. Judge Advocate General

Kans. Kansas
K.C. Knights of Columbus
K.P. Knights of Pythias
KS Kansas
K.T. Knight Templar
Ky., KY Kentucky

La., LA Louisiana
lab. laboratory
lang. language
laryngol. laryngological
LB Labrador
lectr. lecturer
legis. legislation, legislative
L.H.D. Doctor of Humane Letters
L.I. Long Island
L.I.R.R. Long Island Railroad
lit. literary, literature
Litt. B. Bachelor of Letters
Litt. D. Doctor of Letters
LL.B. Bachelor of Laws
LL.D. Doctor of Laws
LL.M. Master of Laws
Ln. Lane
L.&N.R.R. Louisville & Nashville Railroad
L.S. Library Science (in degree)
lt. lieutenant
Ltd. Limited
Luth. Lutheran

m. married
M. Master
M.A. Master of Arts
MA Massachusetts
mag. magazine
M.Agr. Master of Agriculture
maj. major
Man. Manitoba
M.Arch. Master in Architecture
Mass. Massachusetts
math. mathematical
MATS Military Air Transport Service
M.B. Bachelor of Medicine
MB Manitoba
M.B.A. Master of Business Administration
MBS Mutual Broadcasting System
M.C. Medical Corps
M.C.E. Master of Civil Engineering
mcht. merchant
M.C.S. Master of Commercial Science
M.D. Doctor of Medicine
Md., MD Maryland
M.Dip. Master in Diplomacy
mdse. merchandise
M.D.V. Doctor of Veterinary Medicine
M.E. Mechanical Engineer
ME Maine
M.E. Ch. Methodist Episcopal Church

mech. mechanical
M.Ed. Master of Education
med. medical
M.E.E. Master of Electrical Engineering
mem. member
meml. memorial
met. metropolitan
metall. metallurgical
Met. E. Metallurgical Engineer
meteorol. meteorological
Meth. Methodist
Mex. Mexico
M.F. Master of Forestry
M.F.A. Master of Fine Arts
mfg. manufacturing
mfr. manufacturer
mgmt. management
mgr. manager
M.H.A. Master of Hospital Administration
M.I. Military Intelligence
MI Michigan
Mich. Michigan
micros. microscopical
mil. military
Milw. Milwaukee
mineral. mineralogical
Minn. Minnesota
Miss. Mississippi
mktg. marketing
M.L. Master of Laws
M.L.D. Magister Legnum Diplomatic
M.Litt. Master of Literature
M.L.S. Master of Library Science
M.M.E. Master of Mechanical Engineering
MN Minnesota
mng. managing
Mo., MO Missouri
moblzn. mobilization
Mont. Montana
M.P. Member of Parliament
M.P.E. Master of Physical Education
M.P.H. Master of Public Health
M.P.L. Master of Patent Law
Mpls. Minneapolis
M.R.E. Master of Religious Education
M.S. Master of Science
MS Mississippi
M.Sc. Master of Science
M.S.F. Master of Science of Forestry
M.S.T. Master of Sacred Theology
M.S.W. Master of Social Work
MT Montana
Mt. Mount
MTO Mediterranean Theatre of Operations
mus. museum, musical
Mus.B. Bachelor of Music
Mus.D. Doctor of Music
Mus.M. Master of Music
mut. mutual

N. North
NAACP National Association for the Advancement of Colored People
NACA National Advisory Committee for Aeronautics
NAD National Academy of Design
N.Am. North America
NAM National Association of Manufacturers
NAPA National Association of Performing Artists
NARS National Archives and Record Service
NASA National Aeronautics and Space Administration
nat. national
NATO North Atlantic Treaty Organization

NATOUSA North African Theatre of Operations
nav. navigation
N.B., NB New Brunswick
NBC National Broadcasting Company
N.C., NC North Carolina
NCCJ National Conference of Christians and Jews
N.D., ND North Dakota
NDEA National Defense Education Act
NE Nebraska
N.E. Northeast
NEA National Education Association
Nebr. Nebraska
neurol. neurological
Nev. Nevada
NF Newfoundland
Nfld. Newfoundland
N.G. National Guard
N.H., NH New Hampshire
NIH National Institutes of Health
NIMH National Institute of Mental Health
N.J., NJ New Jersey
NLRB National Labor Relations Board
NM New Mexico
N.Mex. New Mexico
No. Northern
NORAD North American Air Defense
NOW National Organization for Women
N.P. Ry. Northern Pacific Railway
NRC National Research Council
N.S., NS Nova Scotia
NSC National Security Council
NSF National Science Foundation
N.T. New Testament
NT Northwest Territories
numis. numismatic
NV Nevada
NW Northwest
N.W.T. Northwest Territories
N.Y., NY New York
N.Y.C. New York City
N.Z. New Zealand

OAS Organization of American States
obs. observatory
O.D. Doctor of Optometry
OECD Organization of European Cooperation and Development
OEEC Organization of European Economic Cooperation
OEO Office of Economic Opportunity
ofcl. official
OH Ohio
OK Oklahoma
Okla. Oklahoma
ON Ontario
Ont. Ontario
ophthal. ophthalmological
ops. operations
OR Oregon
orch. orchestra
Oreg. Oregon
orgn. organization
ornithol. ornithological
OSRD Office of Scientific Research and Development
OSS Office of Strategic Services
osteo. osteopathic
otol. otological
otolaryn. otolaryngological

Pa., PA Pennsylvania
paleontol. paleontological
path. pathological
P.C. Professional Corporation

PE Prince Edward Island
P.E.I. Prince Edward Island
PEN Poets, Playwrights, Editors, Essayists and Novelists (international association)
penol. penological
P.E.O. women's organization (full name not disclosed)
pfc. private first class
PHA Public Housing Administration
pharm. Pharmaceutical
Pharm.D. Doctor of Pharmacy
Pharm.M. Master of Pharmacy
Ph.B. Bachelor of Philosophy
Ph.D. Doctor of Philosophy
Phila. Philadelphia
philol. philological
philos. philosophical
photog. photographic
phys. physical
physiol. physiological
Pitts. Pittsburgh
Pkwy. Parkway
Pl. Place
P.&L.E.R.R. Pittsburgh & Lake Erie Railroad
P.O. Post Office
P.O.B. Post Office Box
polit. political
poly. polytechnic
P.Q. Province of Quebec
P.R., PR Puerto Rico
prep. preparatory
pres. president
Presbyn. Presbyterian
presdl. presidential
prin. principal
proc. proceedings
prod. produced (play production)
prof. professor
profl. professional
prog. progressive
propr. proprietor
pros. atty. prosecuting attorney
pro tem pro tempore
psychiat. psychiatric
psychol. psychological
PTA Parent-Teachers Association
PTO Pacific Theatre of Operations
pub. publisher, publishing, public
publ. publication
pvt. private

quar. quarterly
q.m. quartermaster
Q.M.C. Quartermaster Corps
Que. Quebec

radiol. radiological
RAF Royal Air Force
RCA Radio Corporation of America
RCAF Royal Canadian Air Force
R.D. Rural Delivery
Rd. Road
REA Rural Electrification Administration
rec. recording
ref. reformed
regt. regiment
regtl. regimental
rehab. rehabilitation
rep. representative
Rep. Republican
Res. Reserve
ret. retired
rev. review, revised
RFC Reconstruction Finance Corporation

R.F.D. Rural Free Delivery
rhinol. rhinological
R.I., RI Rhode Island
R.N. Registered Nurse
roentgenol. roentgenological
ROTC Reserve Officers Training Corps
R.R. Railroad
Ry. Railway

s. son
S. South
SAC Strategic Air Command
SALT Strategic Arms Limitation Talks
S.Am. South America
san. sanitary
SAR Sons of the American Revolution
Sask. Saskatchewan
savs. savings
S.B. Bachelor of Science
SBA Small Business Administration
S.C., SC South Carolina
SCAP Supreme Command Allies Pacific
Sc.B. Bachelor of Science
S.C.D. Doctor of Commercial Science
Sc.D. Doctor of Science
sch. school
sci. science, scientific
SCLC Southern Christian Leadership Conference
SCV Sons of Confederate Veterans
S.D., SD South Dakota
SE Southeast
SEATO Southeast Asia Treaty Organization
sec. secretary
SEC Securities and Exchange Commission
sect. section
seismol. seismological
sem. seminary
sgt. sergeant
SHAEF Supreme Headquarters Allied Expeditionary Forces
SHAPE Supreme Headquarters Allied Powers in Europe
S.I. Staten Island
S.J. Society of Jesus (Jesuit)
S.J.D. Doctor Juristic Science
SK Saskatchewan
S.M. Master of Science
So. Southern
soc. society
sociol. sociological
S.P. Co. Southern Pacific Company
spl. special
splty. specialty
Sq. Square
sr. senior
S.R. Sons of the Revolution
S.S. Steamship
SSS Selective Service System
St. Saint
St. Street
sta. station
statis. statistical
S.T.B. Bachelor of Sacred Theology
stblzn. stabilization
S.T.D. Doctor of Sacred Theology
subs. subsidiary
supr. supervisor
supt. superintendent
surg. surgical
SW Southwest

TAPPI Technical Association of Pulp and Paper Industry

Tb Tuberculosis
tchr. teacher
tech. technical, technology
technol. technological
Tel.&Tel. Telephone & Telegraph
temp. temporary
Tenn. Tennessee
Ter. Territory
Terr. Terrace
Tex. Texas
Th.D. Doctor of Theology
theol. theological
Th.M. Master of Theology
TN Tennessee
tng. training
topog. topographical
trans. transaction, transferred
transl. translation, translated
transp. transportation
treas. treasurer
TV television
TVA Tennessee Valley Authority
twp. township
TX Texas
typog. typographical

U. University
UAW United Auto Workers
UDC United Daughters of the Confederacy
U.K. United Kingdom
UN United Nations
UNESCO United Nations Educational, Scientific and Cultural Organization
UNICEF United Nations International Children's Emergency Fund
univ. university
UNRRA United Nations Relief and Rehabilitation Administration
UPI United Press International
U.P.R.R. Union Pacific Railroad
urol. urological
U.S. United States
U.S.A. United States of America
USAAF United States Army Air Force
USAF United States Air Force
USAFR United States Air Force Reserve
USAR United States Army Reserve
USCG United States Coast Guard
USCGR United States Coast Guard Reserve
USES United States Employment Service
USIA United States Information Agency
USIS United States Information Service
USMC United States Marine Corps
USMCR United States Marine Corps Reserve
USN United States Navy
USNG United States National Guard
USNR United States Naval Reserve
USO United Service Organizations
USPHS United States Public Health Service
U.S.S. United States Ship
USSR Union of the Soviet Socialist Republics
USV United States Volunteers
UT Utah

VA Veterans' Administration
Va., VA Virginia
vet. veteran
VFW Veterans of Foreign Wars
V.I., VI Virgin Islands
vice pres. vice president
vis. visiting
VISTA Volunteers in Service to America
VITA Volunteers in Technical Service

vocat. vocational
vol. volunteer
v.p. vice president
vs. versus
Vt., VT Vermont

W. West
WA Washington
WAC Women's Army Corps
Wash. Washington

WAVES Women's Reserve, U.S. Naval Reserve
WCTU Women's Christian Temperance Union
W. Ger. Germany, Federal Republic of
WHO World Health Organization
WI Wisconsin
Wis. Wisconsin
WSB Wage Stabilization Board
WV West Virginia
W. Va. West Virginia
WY Wyoming
Wyo. Wyoming

YMCA Young Men's Christian Association
YMHA Young Men's Hebrew Association
YM & YWHA Young Men's and Young Women's Hebrew Association
Y.T., YT Yukon Territory
YWCA Young Women's Christian Association
yr. year

zool. zoological

Alphabetical Practices

Names are arranged alphabetically according to the surnames, and under identical surnames according to the first given name. If both surname and first given name are identical, names are arranged alphabetically according to the second given name. Where full names are identical, they are arranged in order of age—those of the elder being put first.

Surnames beginning with De, Des, Du, etc., however capitalized or spaced, are recorded with the prefix preceding the surname and arranged alphabetically, under the letter D.

Surnames beginning with Mac are arranged alphabetically under M. This likewise holds for names beginning with Mc; that is, all names beginning Mc will be found in alphabetical order after those beginning Mac.

Surnames beginning with Saint or St. all appear after names that would begin Sains, and such surnames are arranged according to the second part of the name, e.g., St. Clair would come before Saint Dennis.

Surnames beginning with prefix Van are arranged alphabetically under letter V.

Surnames containing the prefix Von or von are usually arranged alphabetically under letter V; any exceptions are noted by cross references (Von Kleinsmid, Rufus Bernhard; see Kleinsmid, Rufus Bernhard von).

Compound hyphenated surnames are arranged according to the first member of the compound.

Compound unhyphenated surnames common in Spanish are not rearranged but are treated as hyphenated names.

Since Chinese names have the family name first, they are so arranged, but without comma between family name and given name (as Lin Yutang).

Parentheses used in connection with a name indicate which part of the full name is usually deleted in common usage. Hence Abbott, W(illiam) Lewis indicates that the usual form of the given name is W. Lewis. In alphabetizing this type name, the parentheses are not considered. However if the name is recorded Abbott, (William) Lewis, signifying that the entire name William is not commonly used, the alphabetizing would be arranged as though the name were Abbott, William Lewis.

Who's Who in the Midwest

AAGESEN, LARRY KENNETH, orthodontist; b. Flint, Mich., Sept. 1, 1942; s. Kenneth Leroy and Clara Evelyn (Goodman) A.; B.S., Mich. State U., 1964; D.D.S., U. Mich., 1969, M.S., 1971; m. Jane Pamela Old, June 29, 1968; children—Leisa Wynn, Larry Kenneth, Matthew Goodman. Pvt. practice gen. dentistry, Brighton, Mich., 1968-71; pvt. practice orthodontics, Rochester, Mich., 1971—; clin. instr. restorative dentistry U. Mich., 1968-69, clin. instr. undergrad. orthodontics, 1971-73. Bd. dirs. Oakland Youth Symphony. Mem. Am. Assn. Orthodontists, ADA, Gt. Lakes, Mich. socs. orthodontists, Mich., Oakland County dental assns., Omicron Kappa Upsilon, Delta Sigma Delta, Jr. C. of C. Episcopalian. Club: Rotary. Home and Office: 961 Oakwood Dr Rochester MI 48063

AAKER, ROLAND H., ret. banker; b. Moorhead, Minn., June 22, 1901; s. Hans H. and Annette (Petersen) A.; student U. N.D., 1919; m. Constance Margurite Nelson, Jan. 17, 1925; children—Rauland Austin (Tuck), Thomas Nelson Helge. Delivery boy Fargo Forum, 1912-14; service mgr. Meyers Motor Co., East Grand Forks, Minn., 1923-27; staff mem., agt. Fleischmann Yeast Co., Grand Forks, N.D., 1927-28; div. mgr. Standard Brands Co., 1927-38; owner Central Baking Co., Inc., Mlontevideo, Minn., 1938-60; pres. Minn. Bakers Assn., 1945-46; mem. bd. Am. Retail Bakers Assn., 1946-52; exec. dir. Urban Renewal, 1962-69; chmn. bd., dir. N.W. State Bank, Montevideo, 1942-73. Mayor of Montevideo, 1944-46; chmn. Ind. Devel. Commn., Montevideo, 1950-52; aided in initiation of Eisenhower's People-to-People Program, 1953; initiated, served as dignitary chmn. Montevideo Fiesta Sister City Program with Montevideo, Uruguay, 1946-77. Mem. Nat. Assn. Housing and Redevel. Ofcls., Internat. Platform Assn., Am. Soc. Baking Engrs. Lutheran (pres. 1941-46, chmn. bldg. com. 1948-50). Clubs: Masons (32 deg.), Shriners, Odd Fellows, Elks, Mpls. Athletic. Home: Green Lake Beach Spicer MN 56288

AAMODT, MARGARET DORA, author; b. Crow Wing County, Minn., Dec. 14, 1910; d. Roy J. and Effie Louise (Thomson) Cunningham; m. Henry Oscar Aamodt, May 15, 1930; children—Myrna (Mrs. Duane Langerud), Bonnie (Mrs. Verdell Schmalle). News corr. Mason City (Iowa) Globe Gazette, 1927—, Des Moines Register and Tribune, 1942—, Northwood (Iowa) Anchor, 1942-46, Forest City (Iowa) Summit, 1947-66; news corr. Albert Lea (Minn.) Tribune, 1947-69, 71—, farm editor, 1969-71; news corr. Lake Mills (Iowa) Graphic, 1950-66, editor, 1966-69. Mem. Lake Mills (Iowa) Sr. Citizens Orgn., past sec., mem. exec. bd.; mem. Winnebago County (Iowa) bd. Area Agy. on Aging. Recipient numerous poetry and press awards. Founding fellow Internat. Poetry Soc.; mem. Midwest Fedn. Chaparral Poets (regent Iowa 1972-76, asso. editor mag.). Author: (poetry) Through Country Lanes, 1963. Home: 106 S Lincoln St Lake Mills IA 50450

AANERUD, MELVIN BERNARD, bus. devel. specialist; b. Spring Lake Park, Minn., Jan. 7, 1943; s. Bernard Melvin and Margaret Agnes (Beck) A.; B.A., U. Minn., 1964. Prodn. analyst Honeywell, Inc., New Brighton, Minn., 1966-68; plant mgr. Ault, Inc., Mpls., 1968-71; gen. mgr. Mille Lacs Reservation Bus. Enterprise, Vineland, Minn., 1971-74; bus. devel. specialist SBA, Mpls., 1974—. Pres., Columbia Hgts. Charter Commn., 1971—; chmn. Minn. Minority Bus. Opportunity Com. 1976—. Served with Signal Corps, AUS, 1964-66. Recipient Gold Key Man award Minn. Jaycees, 1971, 76, Silver Key, 1973; Columbia Heights Distinguished Service award, 1970, Columbia Hgts. Outstanding Civic Achievement award, 1970. Mem. Minn. (exec. dir. Minn. Jaycee Found. 1976—), Columbia Heights (nat. U.S. dir. 1972-73) jaycees, U. Minn. Alumni Assn. Mem. Democratic Farm Labor party. K.C. Home: 5115 7th St Columbia Heights MN 55421 Office: 12 S 6th St Minneapolis MN 55402

AARON, JAMES ETHRIDGE, educator; b. Eldorado, Ill., Oct. 8, 1927; s. Orval R. and Beulah E. (Boyd) A.; B.S., U. Ill., 1950, M.S., 1951; postgrad. Purdue U., 1955; Ed.D., N.Y. U., 1960, postgrad., 1961-63; m. Melba Marie Runyon, Aug. 21, 1951; children—Britt Le, Brian E. Tchr., supr. student and adult driver edn. program Granite City (Ill.) High Sch., 1951-56; tchr., supr. driver edn. program for tchrs. N.Y. U., N.Y.C., 1956-57; adminstr., tchr., coordinator of Safety Center, So. Ill. U., Carbondale, 1957—. Cons., State of Ill., Sec. State for Ill., Ford Motor Co.; mem. Nat. Hwy. Safety Adv. Com., 1970-73. Safety chmn. Ill. P.T.A. Served with USN, 1946-47. Recipient A.W. Whitney fellowship N.Y. U., 1956, grants U.S. Dept. Transp., 1973, State of Ill., 1972, 73. Mem. Am. Driver & Traffic Safety Edn. Assn., Higher Edn. Assn., Ill. High Sch. and Coll. Driver Edn. Assn., N.E.A., Nat. Safety Council. Author: (with A. Shafter) The Police Officer and Alcoholism, 1963; (with M. Strasser, R. Bohn, J. Eales) Fundamentals of Safety Education, 1973; (with M. Strasser) Driver and Traffic Safety Education, 1977, Driver Education—Learning to Drive Defensively, 1973, Driving Task Instruction, 1974; (with others) First Aid and Emergency Care, 1978. Home: Rural Route 4 Carbondale IL 62901

AARONS, HAROLD, tool mfg. co. exec.; b. Detroit, Jan. 17, 1895; s. Joseph and Ada (Pragnell) A.; student U. Mich., 1913-17; m. Mariam Carrington Bostwick, Nov. 24, 1924; children—Mariam (Mrs. Duncan R. McGillivray), Bradford Aarons. Advt. mgr. Kermoth Mfg. Co., 1922-30; with Barron Tool Co., Lewiston, Mich., 1939—, pres., 1941—; treas. Prodn. Assembly Systems, Inc., Lewiston, 1971—; with Aarons Sill & Caron, Inc., Lewiston, 1931—, pres., 1935. Sec. Montmorency County Planning Commn., 1969—. Served to 1st lt. U.S. Army, 1917-19. Lion (pres. 1967). Club: Curling (pres. 1960-61) (Lewiston). Home: East Hill Lewiston MI 49750 Office: Prodn Assembly Systems Inc Airport Rd Lewiston MI 49756

AARONSON, ABE LOUIS, physician; b. Phila., Aug. 26, 1905; s. Benjamin and Elizabeth (Rubenstein) A.; B.S., U. Ill., 1926, M.D., 1928, M.S., 1931; m. Rose Lovitt, Aug. 18, 1929; children—Donald W., Neil Roger. Intern, Cook County Hosp., Chgo.; asso. in medicine U. Ill., 1930-47; asst. prof. medicine Chgo. Med. Sch., 1947-58, clin. asso. prof. medicine, 1958-72, clin. prof., 1972—; attending physician allergy Mt. Sinai Hosp., Chgo. Served to maj. M.C. AUS, World War II. Fellow Am. Acad. Allergy, Am. Coll. Allergists, Am. Coll. Chest Physicians; mem. Sigma Xi, Alpha Omega Alpha, Phi Delta Epsilon (past nat. pres.). Home: 3180 Lake Shore Dr Chicago IL 60657 Office: 25 E Washington St Chicago IL 60602

AARTHUN, MARTIN, ednl. adminstr.; b. Milton, N.D., July 26, 1912; s. John and Gertrude (Anderson) A.; B.A., Concordia Coll., 1935; M.Sc. in Edn., U. N.D., 1948; m. Clara O. Rykken, July 12, 1943; children—John, Carol, Jean. Tchr., Lignite (N.D.) Pub. Sch., 1935-38, supt. schs., 1938-46; supt. schs., Grenora, N.D., 1946-56, Washburn, N.D., 1956-66; dir. surplus property N.D. Dept. Pub. Instrn., Bismarck, 1966—. Mem. NEA, N.D. Edn. Assn., Phi Delta Kappa. Lutheran. Lion (past sec., pres. Washburn). Home: 108 Cherokee Ave Bismarck ND 58501 Office: State Capitol Bismarck ND 58501

ABBASI, ALI ABDEL-WAHHAB, physician; b. Safed, Palestine, Feb. 24, 1936; s. Abdel-Wahhab S. and Fattoum (Hadidi) A.; came to U.S., 1964, naturalized, 1976; P.C.B., Damascus U., 1957, M.D., 1963; m. Lamia Murad, Oct. 5, 1966; children—Samer, Basel, Susan. Intern, Damascus U. Hosp., 1962-64; instr. Wayne State U., Detroit, 1969-73, asst. prof., 1973-77, asso. prof., 1977—; staff physician VA Hosp., Allen Park, Mich., 1971—, chief sect. endocrinology and metabolism. 1971—. Recipient AMSA-Eaton Med. Photography award, 1970, 74, 77. Fellow Royal Coll. Physicians Can., A.C.P.; mem. Mich., Wayne County med. socs., AMA, Am. Diabetes Assn., Am. Fedn. Clin. Research, Endocrine Soc. Moslem. Office: VA Hospital Allen Park MI 48101

ABBASY, IFTIKHARUL H., surgeon; b. Pakistan, Oct. 28, 1935; s. Ikramul Haque and Mumtaz Begum; came to U.S., 1964, naturalized, 1970; M.B., B.S., Dow Med. Coll., Karachi, Pakistan, 1961; m. Karen Gaye Hampton, Feb. 14, 1969; 1 dau., Shameen Ara. Intern, Civil Hosp., Karachi, Pakistan, 1961-62, St. Olaves Hosp., London, 1962-63; resident in surgery E. Ham Meml. Hosp., London, 1963, Michael Reese Hosp., Chgo., 1965-69; practice medicine specializing in gen. surgery and peripheral vascular surgery, Villa Park, Ill., 1969—; mem. staff Meml. Hosp., Elmhurst, Ill., McHenry (Ill.) Hosp., Good Samaritan Hosp., Downers Grove, Ill., Harvard (Ill.) Community Hosp. Diplomate Am. Bd. Surgery. Fellow A.C.S., Internat. Coll. Surgeons; mem. Royal Coll. Surgeons Can., AMA (Physicians's Recognition award 1974-77). Home: 244 Eggleston St Elmhurst IL 60126 Office: 10 E Central Blvd Villa Park IL 60181

ABBEY, ROBERT HARRY, guidance counselor; b. Akron, Ohio, Apr. 3, 1935; s. Earl R. and Catherine (Christopher) A.; B.A., U. Akron, 1958, M.A., 1966; m. Arlene Dietrich, Nov. 26, 1960; children—Renee, Michele. Account exec. Stalker Advt. Agy., Akron, 1958-59; tchr. Brunswick (Ohio) High Sch., 1959-65; dir. guidance Columbia Local Schs., Columbia Station, Ohio, 1965-77. Mem. Am., Ohio (pres.) sch. counselors assns., Nat., Ohio personnel and guidance assns. Home: 305 Forest Meadows Dr Medina OH 44256 Office: 14168 W River Rd Columbia Station OH 44028

ABBOTT, ALBERT CLIFFORD, surgeon; b. Stockton, Man., Can., Aug. 5, 1897; s. Albert Edward and Annie (Brown) A.; B.A., U. Man., 1917, M.D., C.M., 1921; LL.B. (hon.), U. Winnipeg, 1974; m. Mary Eileen Abbott, Jan. 1925; children—Edward Clifford Bulman, Frances (Mrs. John Gunn). U. Man. travelling scholar, 1921-22; surgeon urologist Abbott Clinic, Winnipeg, Man., 1925-70, asso. prof. surgery U. Man., Winnipeg, 1936-61, cons. med. research, 1957-61. Recipient Good Citizenship award Golden Boy, 1970; service award City of Winnipeg, 1972. Fellow Royal Coll. Surgeons (Can.), Royal Coll. Surgeons (Edinburgh), A.C.S., Internat. Coll. Surgeons (treas. 1973-74); mem. Can. Assn. Med. Clinics (pres. 1968), Winnipeg Med. Assn. (life), Cusco Med. Assn. Peru (hon.), Coll. Phys. and Surgeons (life). Clubs: Gyro, Winnipeg Winter. Home: 130 Handsart Blvd Winnipeg MB R3P 0C5 Canada Office: 1274 Osborne St Winnipeg MB Canada

ABBOTT, DEAN FREDERICK, landscape architect, urban designer; b. Yonkers, N.Y., Feb. 18, 1939; s. Frederick and Marion (Polkemus) A.; B.S., Mich. State U., 1961; M.L.A., Harvard U., 1963; children—Lance, Marisa. Designer, Zion & Breen, N.Y.C., M. Paul Friedberg, N.Y.C., 1963-64; faculty U. Ga. Sch. Environ. Design, Athens, 1964-67; designer Sasaki, Walker Assos., San Francisco, 1967-69; project mgr./designer Lawrence Halprin Assos., N.Y.C., 1969-74; cons. Ed Stone, Jr., Ft. Lauderdale, Fla., 1971-72; co-dir. New York office, 1974-76, also environ. design cons.; asso. ARTEKA, Inc., Mpls., 1977—; faculty U. Minn. Sch. Architecture and Landscape Architecture, Mpls., 1977—; vis. critic/lectr. Rutgers U., 1970—, City U. N.Y., 1973, U. Va. Archtl. Sch., Charlottesville, 1975; mem. Environ. Advisory Council, Ossining, N.Y.; environ. design cons. Design Communication Collaborative, Washington, Attic & Cellar Studios, Inc., Washington. Recipient Design and Environment award Battery Park City Urban Open Spaces Plan, N.Y.C., 1975, Com. Urban Environment award, 1975, 2d pl. for Rainbow Center Plaza Internat. Design competition, Niagara, N.Y., 1973. Registered landscape architect, Ga. Mem. Am. Soc. Landscape Architects (profl. awards jury 1975). Works include central interior space Nat. City Bank Bldg., Mpls.; urban design plan, Charlottesville, Va. Home: 13000 Harriet St Burnsville MN 55337

ABBOUD, FRANCOIS MITRY, physician; b. Cairo, Egypt, Jan. 1,, 1931; s. Mitry Y. and Asma (Habac) A.; student U. Cairo, 1948-52; M.B., B.Ch., Ein Chams U., 1955; m. Doris Evelyn Khal, June 5, 1955; children—Mary Agnese, Susan Marie, Nancy Louise, Anthony Lawrence. Came to U.S., 1955, naturalized, 1963. Intern, Demerdash Govt. Hosp., Cairo, 1955; resident Milw. County Hosp., 1955-58; Am. Heart Assn. research fellow cardiovascular labs. Marquette U., 1958-60; Am. Heart Assn. advanced research fellow U. Iowa, 1960-62, asst. prof., 1961-65, asso. prof. medicine, 1965-68, prof. medicine, 1968—, dir. cardiovascular div., 1970-76, dir. cardiovascular center, 1975—, chmn. dept. internal medicine, 1976—; attending physician at VA Hosp., Iowa City, 1963—, U. Iowa Hosps., 1961—. Recipient European Traveling fellowship French Govt., 1948, career devel. award NIH, 1962-71, award Am. Soc. Pharmacology and Exptl. Therapeutics, 1972. Fellow Am. Coll. Cardiology; mem. Assn. Univ. Cardiologists, Assn. Am. Physicians, Am. Soc. Clin. Investigation, Central Soc. for Clin. Research, Soc. Explt. Biology and Medicine, A.C.P., AMA, Am. Fedn. Clin. Research (pres. 1971-72), AAUP, Am. Physiol. Soc., Am. Soc. Pharmacology and Exptl. Therapeutics, Sigma Xi. Research and publs. in cardiovascular physiology on vascular reactivity and autonomic pharmacology in man and animals. Home: 1911 Rochester Ct Iowa City IA 52240

ABBOUD, JOSEPH THOMAS, optometrist; b. Cambridge, Mass., July 2, 1920; s. Michael T. and Helen C. (Reidy) A.; student Eau Claire State U., 1946-48; Dr. Optometry, Pa. Coll., 1952; m. Barbara Donaldson, June 22, 1946; 1 son, Jeffry. Optometrist, Rice Lake, Wis., 1953—. Mem. Wis. Bd. Examiners in Optometry, 1961-65. Chmn. Pack 28 Cub Scouts, Boy Scouts of Am., Rice Lake, Wis., 1960-61; pres. Barron County (Wis.) Cancer Soc., 1956-58; chmn, Heart Fund, Rice Lake, 1954; bd. dirs. West Central Wis. Health Planning Council, Inc.; mem. Rice Lake Sch. Health Council, 1954, 57, 60, 65; mem. Barron County Comprehensive Health Planning Council. Served with USMC, 1941-45. Fellow Am. Acad. Optometry; mem. Indianhead Optometric Soc. (pres. 1957-58), Wis. (2d v.p. 1959-60, mem. Peer Review com.; Optometrist of Yr. 1969, mem. legis. com. 1962-71), Am. optometric assns., Internat. Assn. Bds. of Examiners in Optometry (2d v.p. 1965-66, 1st v.p. 1966-67, pres. 1968-69), Rice Lake Jr. C. of C. (outstanding Wis. local pres. 1956-57), C. of C. (treas. 1960-61). Clubs: Elks, Lions (pres. 1968-69), Moose, K.C., Toastmasters. Home: 304 Hilltop Dr Rice Lake WI 54868 Office: 40 W Newton St Rice Lake WI 54868

ABBRECHT, PETER HERMAN, physiologist, educator; b. Toledo, Nov. 27, 1930; s. Hermann Richard and Paula Katherine (Schwenk) A.; B.S., Purdue U., 1952; M.S., U. Mich., 1953, Ph.D. in Chem. Engring., 1957, M.D., 1962; m. Anne Patterson Lampman, Feb. 16, 1957; children—Elaine, Brian. Sr. chem. engr. Minn. Mining & Mfg. Co., Detroit, 1956-58; intern, U. Calif. Hosp., Los Angeles, 1962-63; mem. faculty U. Mich. Med. Sch., Ann Arbor, 1963—, prof. physiology, 1972—, chmn. bioengring. program 1972—, prof. internal medicine, 1976—; resident in internal medicine U. Mich. Hosp., 1971-72, fellow in pulmonary disease, 1974-75; vis. prof. bioengring. U. Calif., San Diego, 1973; acting dir. physiology and biomed. engring. program NIGMS, NIH, 1977. Cons. NIH, NSF; mem. nat. research resources adv. council, 1975—. Recipient Outstanding Research award Mich. Heart Assn., 1960, Research Career Devel. award NIH, 1969-73. Mem. Biomed. Engring. Soc. (dir. 1970-72), Am. Physiol. Soc., Am. Soc. Artifical Internal Organs, Soc. Exptl. Biology and Medicine. Editor in chief: Internat. Jour. Biomed. Engring., 1972-74. Editorial bd. Jour. Biomechanics, Jour. Bioengring. Contbr. articles to profl. jours. Home: 1108 Meadowbrook Ave Ann Arbor MI 48103

ABDALLAH, SALAM MOHAMED, sr. research engr.; b. Cairo, July 6, 1944; s. Mohamed A. and Faridah M. (Ibraheem) A.; came to U.S., 1968, naturalized, 1977; M.S.M.E., U. of Ill., 1971; M.S. in Math. U. of Iowa, 1975, Ph.D., 1976; m. Mahasen H. Abdallah, Aug. 1, 1972; 1 child, Waleed A. Project engr. York Div. Borg-Warner Corp., Chgo., 1968-70; project engr. engring. dept. Perkins & Will Corp., Chgo., 1971-72; instr. U. Iowa, Iowa City, 1973-76, NSF postdoctoral research fellow, 1976; now sr. research engr. Owens-Corning Tech. Center, Granville, Ohio; cons. in field. NSF grantee, 1976. Mem. Am. Soc. Heating, Refrigeration, Air-conditioning Engrs., ASME, Sigma Xi. Moslem. Club: Egyptians Am. (Chgo.). Contbr. articles in field. Home: 683-B W Broadway Granville OH 43023 Office: Energy Research Lab Owens-Corning Tech Center Granville OH 43023

ABDNOR, JAMES, congressman; b. Kennebec, S.D., Feb. 13, 1923; s. Samuel and Mary (Wehby) A.; B.A. in Bus. Adminstrn., U. Neb., 1944. High sch. tchr., coach, Presho, S.D., 1948-49; farmer, rancher, Kennebec, 1950—; mem. S.D. Senate, 1956-69; lt. gov. of S.D., 1969-71; mem. 93d to 95th congresses from 2d dist. S.D. Chmn., S.D. State Cancer Crusade, 1971-73; S.D. Easter Seal chmn., 1977. Served with AUS, World War II. Mem. Am. Legion, S.D. Stockgrowers, S.D. Wheat Producers, Farm Bur., Farmers Union, Izaak Walton League, Sigma Chi. Methodist. Mason, Elk. Home: Kennebec SD 57544 Office: 1224 Longworth House Office Bldg Washington DC 20515

ABEL, ALAN WILSON, tech. editor; b. Wilkinsburg, Pa., Mar. 7, 1939; s. Raymond L. and Agnes H. (Smail) A.; B.S., U. Pitts., 1961, Ph.D., 1967. With Chem. Abstracts Service, Ohio State U., Columbus, 1967—, asso. editor, 1969-70, sr. asso. editor, 1970—. Mem. Am. Chem. Soc., Sigma Xi. Home: 3015 Stadium Dr Apt 2 Columbus OH 43202

ABEL, BILLY LARUE, educator; b. Whiteland, Ind., Sept. 25, 1921; s. Lester N. and Katherine (Pearson) A.; student Taylor U., 1941-43; A.B., Franklin Coll., 1947; M.Ed., U. Louisville, 1955; Ed.D., Ind. U., 1970; m. Dorothy La June Fay, April 23, 1943; children—Billy Lester, Dorothy Katherine. Tchr., coach high sch., Pekin, Ind., 1947-49, Paoli, Ind., 1949-51; tchr., prin. high sch., Charlestown, Ind., 1951-55; prin. high sch., Attica, Ind., 1955-58, Plainfield, Ind., 1958-66, Ben Davis High Sch., Indpls., 1966-70, Bedford (Ind.) High Sch., 1970-72; asso. prof. edn. Ind. U. Purdue U. at Indpls., 1972—. Served with USAAF, World War II. Chosen an Outstanding Christian Layman for tour Russia and Iron Curtain countries People to People Found., 1963. Mem. Nat. Assn. Secondary Sch. Prins. Methodist. Mason (32 deg.). Developer Trad-Flex, an innovation in edn. Home: 5520 Vin Rose Ln Indianapolis IN 46226 Office: 920 N Meridian St Indianapolis IN 46204

ABEL, HAROLD, univ. pres.; b. N.Y.C., July 31, 1926; s. Felix N. and Jennie (Schaefer) A.; A.B., Syracuse U., 1949, M.A., 1959, Ph.D., 1958; m. Iris Tash, Jan. 30, 1949; children—Lawrence William, Matthew Robert. Tchr. advanced mentally retarded Syracuse (N.Y.) Pub. Schs. 1950-51, intermediate mentally retarded pub. sch., Rochester, N.Y., 1951-52; asst. instr. Sch. Edn. Syracuse U., 1952-54, asst. instr. dept. psychology, 1954-56; asso. prof., prof. depts. psychology and home econs. and dir. child devel. lab. U. Nebr., 1956-65; dir. div. psycho-ednl. studies, prof. edn. U. Oreg., 1965-68, asso. dean, prof. ednl. psychology Coll. Edn., 1968-70; pres. Castleton State Coll., 1970-75, Central Mich. U., Mt. Pleasant, 1975—. Mem. Gov. Nebr. Commn. on Human Relations, 1963-65; vice chmn. Gov. Neb. Interagy. Com. on Mental Retardation, 1963-65; mem. mayor's com. on phys. handicapped, Lincoln, Nebr., 1963-65; mem. Gov. Oreg. Com. on Aging, 1967-68; mem. nat. adv. com. Project Follow-Through, 1967-69. Served with AUS, 1945-46. Mem. AAAS, Am. Psychol. Assn., Soc. Research in Child Devel., Sigma Xi, Phi Delta Kappa. Home: 524 E Bellows St Mt Pleasant MI 48858 Office: Central Mich U Mt Pleasant MI 48859

ABELE, HOMER EUGENE, judge; b. Wellston, Ohio, Nov. 21, 1916; s. Oscar A. and Margaret (Burke) A.; J.D., Ohio State U., 1953; m. Addie Riggs, Jan. 30, 1938; children—Terrell Ann (Mrs. Robert

Smith), Peter Burke, David Anderson. Started as highway patrolman State of Ohio, Van Wert, Findlay, Bellefountaine, 1941-46; admitted to Ohio bar, 1954; practiced in McArthur, Ohio, 1954-66; legislative counsel Ohio Spl. R.R. Transp. Com. Columbus, 1953-57; spl. counsel Ohio atty. gen. McArthur, 1954-58, counsel C.&O. Ry. Co., B.&O. R.R., The Twin States Mining Co., The McArthur Stone & Coal Co.; mem. 88th Congress, 10th dist. Ohio; judge Ct. Appeals 4th Dist. Ohio, 1967—, presiding judge, 1977-78; sec.-treas. Ohio Judges of Ct. of Appeals, 1977. Chmn. ct. sect. Am. Legion Buckeye Boys State. Mem. Ohio Ho. of Reps., 1949-52; asst. to Taft mgr. Republican Nat. Conv., 1952; del. Rep. Nat. Conv., 1956; mem. exec. com. Vinton County Rep. Com., 1952—, chmn. 1954-58; Rep. candidate U.S. Ho. of Reps. from 10th dist. Ohio, 1958. Served with USAAF, 1943-46. Recipient resolution of honor Ohio Senate. Mem. Am. Legion (mem. nat. com. on law and order, dist. exec. officer Ohio Hwy. Patrol sect.; dept. judge adv. 1970-71). Home: Main St McArthur OH 45651 Office: Court House McArthur OH 45651

ABELES, NORMAN, educator, psychologist; b. Vienna, Austria, Apr. 15, 1928; s. Felix and Bertha (Gronich) A.; came to U.S., 1939, naturalized, 1944; B.A., N.Y.U., 1949; M.A., U. Tex., 1952, Ph.D., 1958; m. Jeanette Bueller, Apr. 14, 1957; children—Linda, Mark. Fellow in counseling U. Tex., Austin, 1956-57; instr. Mich. State U., East Lansing, 1957-59, asst. prof., 1959-64, asso. prof., 1964-67, prof. psychology, 1968—, asst. dir. Counseling Center, 1965-71; U.S. State Dept. ednl. exchange prof. U. Utrecht, The Netherlands, 1969, vis. prof., 1975. Cons. Peace Corps., 1965-69, Social Security/Disability Hearings, 1962—. Mem. Commn. for Certification of Psychologists in Mich., 1962—, chmn., 1966-68; mem. council Nat. Register Health Service Providers in Psychology, 1974—, vice chmn., 1975—. Served with AUS, 1954-56. Recipient Fulbright-Hays grant, 1969. Diplomate Am. Bd. Profl. Psychology (mem. Midwest regional bd. 1972—, chmn., nat. trustee, 1975—). Fellow Am. Psychol. Assn. (council of reps. 1972-75, 77—, policy and planning bd. 1975—, chmn. 1976); mem. Midwestern, Mich. (legislative chmn. 1964-72, pres. 1971-72, Distinguished Psychologist award 1974) psychol. assns., Sigma Xi. Contbr. numerous articles in field to profl jours. Home: 953 Rosewood St East Lansing MI 48823

ABELL, JOSEPH RICHARD, library ofcl.; b. Wilmington, Ohio, June 7, 1932; s. Joseph Kenneth and Cleo Faye (Jones) A.; B.A., Wilmington Coll., 1954; M.S. in L.S., Western Res. U., 1955; postgrad. U. Cin., 1964. Library asst. Case Inst. Tech., 1954-55; librarian asst. history and lit. dept. Pub. Library of Cin. and Hamilton County (Ohio), 1957-61, fiction specialist, 1961-62, head history and lit. dept., 1962—. Served with AUS, 1955-57. Mem. ALA (mem. div. affiliates com. 1968), Ohio Soc. Archivists, Cin. Hist. Soc., Ohio (mem. exec. bd. 1962), Martha Kinney Cooper Ohioana (chmn. for authors Hamilton County com. 1965—) library assns., S.A.R. (chpt. pres. 1967), Soc. Colonial Wars. Episcopalian. Club: Filson. Home: 2356 Park Ave Cincinnati OH 45206 Office: Public Library of Cin and Hamilton County Cincinnati OH 45202

ABERG, ROBERT KENNETH, lawyer; b. Madison, Wis., Oct. 11, 1930; s. William Jon Per and Hebe (Leeden) A.; B.S. with honors, U. Wis., 1957, LL.B., 1959, LL.D., 1966; m. Beverly Ann Rang, May 2, 1951; children—William Karl, Cynthia. Admitted to Wis. bar, 1959, U.S. Supreme Court bar, 1972, I.R.S., 1962, U.S. Treasury, 1962; mem. firm Aberg, Bell, Blake, Metzner, Madison, Wis., 1959-76, partner, 1965-76; partner firm Aberg & Jorgensen, 1976—. Trustee Village of Shorewood Hills (Wis.), 1958-60, pres., 1961-63. Bd. dirs., treas. Wis. Natural Resources Found. Served with USAF, 1950-54. Mem. Am., Wis., Dane County bar assns. Editor, University of Wis. Law Review, 1957-58. Home: 1005 Moorland Rd Madison WI 53713 Office: 131 W Wilson St Madison WI 53703

ABLIN, RICHARD JOEL, immunologist; b. Chgo., May 15, 1940; s. Robert Benjamin and Minnie Edith (Gordon) A.; A.B., Lake Forest Coll., 1962; Ph.D. in Microbiology, State U. N.Y., Buffalo, 1967; m. Linda Lee Lutwack; 1 son, Michael David. Grad. asst. dept. biology State U. N.Y., Buffalo, 1963-65, research asst., summer 1963, research fellow, 1965-66, USPHS postdoctoral fellow dept. microbiology Sch. Medicine, lectr., lab. instr., 1966-68; instr., research asst. Rosary Hill Coll., 1965-66; research cons. program med. edn. AID, Paraguay, 1968; dir. div. immunology Millard Fillmore Hosp., Buffalo, 1968-70; head sect. immunology, renal unit, Meml. Hosp. of Springfield (Ill.), 1970-73; dir. sect. immunobiology div. urology dept. surgery Cook County Hosp. and Hektoen Inst. for Med. Research, Chgo., 1973-75, sr. sci. officer div. immunology, 1976—, sr. mem. sci. staff, clin. immunologist Cook County Hosp., 1973-75; asst. prof. medicine So. Ill. U., 1971-73; asso. prof. microbiology Univ. Health Sci./Chgo. Med. Sch., 1973-74. Chief Sangamo Nation Y-Indian Guides, Springfield, 1972-73; mgr. Skokie (Ill.) Indians' Boys' Baseball, 1973-74, 77—; cubmaster N.W. Suburban council Boy Scouts Am., 1974—, asst. scoutmaster, 1975—. Recipient Nat. Pres. Leader's Dist. award Boy Scouts Am., 1975; Named Cubmaster of Year, 1977. Fellow Am. Assn. Clin. Immunology, Allergy, Am. Coll. Cryosurgery (v.p.), Inst. Medicina Chgo.; mem. Am. Assn. Cancer Research, AAAS, Am., Chgo. assns. immunologists, Am. Fedn. Clin. Research, Am. Soc. Microbiology, Internat. Assn. Biol. Standardization, Internat. Soc. Chronobiology, Internat. Soc. Cryosurgery, Japan Soc. Low Temperature Medicine, N.Y. Acad. Sci., Reticuloendothelial Soc., Soc. Cryobiology, Soc. Protozoologists, Soc. Study Human Biology, Soc. Study Reprodn., Transplantation Soc., Am. Bd. Clin. Immunology, Allergy (diplomate), Nat. Registry Microbiologists (certified specialist in pub. health and med. lab. microbiology), Cryoimmunotherapeutic Study Group (chmn.), Sigma Xi. Jewish. Contbr. numerous articles to profl. jours. and texts; cons. editor Allergologia et Immunopathologia, 1974; editor Current Perspectives in Allergology and Immunopathology, 1974—; contbg. editor Ill. Med. Jour., 1975—; advisory editor Jour. Cancer, 1976—; asso. editor Low Temperature Medicine, 1975—; internat. editorial staff Medikon, 1974—. Home: 5055 Culver St Skokie IL 60076 Office: 1825 W Harrison St Chicago IL 60612

ABLOFF, RICHARD LEE, lawyer, psychologist; b. Wichita Falls, Tex., Dec. 26, 1945; s. Martin S. and Marian E. (Davis) A.; B.A. in Govt., So. Ill. U., 1968; J.D., U. Mo. at Kansas City, 1971, M.A. in Social Psychology (Victor Wilson scholar), 1975, M.A. in Counseling Psychology, 1976, postgrad. in counseling psychology, 1977—. Admitted to Mo. bar, 1971; asso. firm Hutson Van Horn, Schmidt & Hammett, Kansas City, Mo., 1971-72; intern U. Mo. Counseling Center, 1976-77; corrections counselor Community Treatment Center, Fed. Bur. Prisons, Dept. Justice, Kansas City, Mo., 1975-77; counselor Community Alcohol Program, Kansas City, Mo., 1977—; lectr. div. counselor edn. U. Mo., summer, 1977; cons. Mo. Div. Youth Services. Mem. Mo., Kansas City bar assns., Mo., Greater Kansas City psychol. assns., Am. Assn. Sex Educators, Counselors and Therapists, Am. Personnel and Guidance Assn., Pi Lambda Theta, Phi Kappa Phi, Phi Alpha Delta. Contbr. articles in field to profl. jours. Home: 219 W 62nd Terr Kansas City MO 64113 Office: 3515 Broadway Suite 300 Kansas City MO 64111

ABNEY, CHARLOTTE MAXINE, sch. counselor, librarian; b. Courtois, Mo., May 9, 1936; d. Grayfer Leo and Isla (Evans) A.; student (Valedictorian scholar, Delta Kappa Gamma scholar) Flat River Jr. Coll., 1953-54; B.S. in Edn. cum laude, SW Mo. State U., 1962, M.S. in Guidance and Counseling, 1970. Mgr., Abneys' Restaurant, Caledonia, Mo., 1954-55; tchr. Grandview R-II Sch., Ware, Mo., 1955-60; tchr., librarian Bismarck (Mo.) R-V Sch., 1960-67, 1969-74, counselor, librarian, 1974—; lectr. edn. and child devel.; Tchr. rep. Bd. Edn., 1972-75. Certified tchr., sch. psychol. examiner, counselor, librarian. Mem. Am. Personnel and Guidance Assn., Am. Sch. Counselors Assn., Mo., SE Mo. Dist. guidance assns., St. Francois County Edn. Assn. (sec. 1965-66), Bismarck R-V Community, Mo. State tchrs. assns., Internat. Reading Assn. (Mineral Area Chpt.), Mineral Area Math. Assn. Methodist. Home: Caledonia MO 63631 Office: Campus Dr Bismarck MO 63624

ABOUREZK, JAMES G., U.S. senator; b. Wood, S.D., Feb. 24, 1931; B.S. in C.E., S.D. Sch. Mines, 1961; J.D., U. S.D., 1966; m. Mary Ann Houlton, 1952; children—Charles Thomas, Nikki June, Paul Edwin. Admitted to S.D. bar, U.S. Supreme Ct. bar, D.C. bar; former partner firm LaFleur & Abourezk, Rapid City, S.D.; mem. 92d Congress from 2d dist. S.D.; U.S. senator from S.D., 1973—, mem. budget com.; chmn. adminstrv. practices and procedures subcom. Judiciary Com.; chmn. Indian Affairs Com., Parks and Recreation Subcom.; mem. Energy and Natural Resources Com.; chmn. Am. Indian Policy Rev. Commn. Served with USN, 1948-52. Mem. Am., S.D., D.C. bar assns., Am. Trial Lawyers Assn. Home: Rapid City SD 57701 Office: Room 3321 New Senate Office Bldg Washington DC 20510

ABRAHAM, BETTE HAVENS, psychotherapist; b. Meriden, Conn., June 19, 1946; d. John Joseph and Abina Dorothy (Walsh) Havens; B.A. with honors, Lake Erie Coll., 1968; M.A., U. N.D., 1970; m. Alden A. Abraham, Aug. 29, 1970. Tchr., Chgo. Sch. for Retarded, 1971; supr. psychology dept. London Meml. Hosp., Chgo., 1971-75; pvt. practice psychotherapy, Chgo., 1975-77, Mpls., 1977—; cons. Paul Cekan, M.D., 1975-77, Anil Godbole, M.D., 1976-77; asso. Transculture Center for Human Relations, 1974-76, Chgo. Med. Sch. Faculty, 1974-76, Ill. Psychol. Assn., 1974-77; group psychotherapist Abbott Northwestern Hosp., Mpls., 1977—. Mem. Am., Midwest, Ill., Minn. psychol. assns., Assn. for Women in Psychology, Ill. Group Psychotherapy Soc., Assn. Advancement Psychology, U. Chgo. Library Soc., ACLU, Common Cause, Center for Study of Democratic Instns. Home and office: 3526 W 28th St Minneapolis MN 55416

ABRAHAM, JOHN, real estate co. exec.; b. Detroit, Jan. 1, 1923; s. Sam and Rasheda (David) A.; student U. Toledo, Adrian Coll., U. Mich.; m. Loraine James, June 25, 1949; children—Carmen Kim, David John. Pres., Abraham Realty Co., Adrian, Mich., 1950—. Bd. dirs. Family Counseling Service, Adrian, 1965-71. Recipient Realtor of Yr. award Nat. Assn. Real Estate Appraisers, 1971. Mem. Nat. Assn. Homebuilders. Methodist (pres. bd. trustees 1969-70). Rotarian. Club: Lenawee Country. Home: 360 Alexander Dr Adrian MI 49221 Office: 4210 W Maple St Adrian MI 49221

ABRAHAMSON, JAMES ALAN, air force officer; b. Williston, N.D., May 19, 1933; s. Norval S. and Themla B. (Helle) A.; B.S. in Aeros., Mass. Inst. Tech., 1955; M.S. in Aerospace Engring., U. Okla., 1961; m. Barbara Jean Northcott, Nov. 7, 1959; children—Kelly Anne, James A. Commd. 2d lt. U.S. Air Force, 1955, advanced through grades to maj. gen., 1978; flight instr. Bryan AFB, Tex., 1957-59; spacecraft project officer, Vela nuclear detection satellite program, Los Angeles USAF Sta., 1961-64; fighter pilot Tactical Air Command, 1964; astronaut USAF Manned Orbiting Lab. Program, 1967-69; mem. staff NASC, Exec. Office of Pres., 1969-71; program dir. Maverick Program, 1971-73; comdr. 4950th test wing Wright Patterson AFB, Ohio, 1973-74; insp. gen. Air Force Systems Command, 1974-76, system program dir., multinat. F-16 program, 1976—. Decorated Legion of Merit with one oak leaf cluster, Air medal with one oak leaf cluster. Home: 610 Yount Dr Wright Patterson AFB OH 45433 Office: ASD/YP Wright Patterson AFB OH 45433

ABRAHAMSON, LEONARD, electronics co. exec.; b. Hammond, Ind., Aug. 21, 1926; s. Al and Fannie (Goldberg) A.; B.S., Northwestern U., 1956, M.B.A., 1959; m. Inez Levin, Aug. 29, 1948; children—Ellen, Tom. With Motorola, Inc., Chgo., 1952-63, mgr. adminstrv. services, 1958-61, mgr. ops. rev., 1962-63; cons. Asso. Bus. Consultants, Chgo., 1963-64; exec. v.p. Perma-Power Co., Chgo., 1964-69; v.p. operations Dynascan Corp., Chgo., 1969—. Instr. bus. adminstrn. Chgo. City Coll., 1960-64, Lake County Coll., 1974—. Chmn. Wheeling Indsl. Commn., 1958, Wheeling Recreational Program, 1959; mem. Gov.'s Commn. on Ill. Budget Rev., 1962; cons. Talent Assistance Program, 1970, dir., 1974—; affiliate Operation DARE prison rehab., 1972; vice chmn. Highland Park Human Relations Commn., 1974—. Served with USNR, 1944-46. Named Vol. of Year, TAP, 1972. Mem. Am. Mgmt. Assn., AIM. Home: 1807 Midland Ave Highland Park IL 60035 Office: 1801 Belle Plaine Ave Chicago IL 60613

ABRAM, PATRICIA JEAN, univ. adminstr.; b. Bangor, Maine, Dec. 15, 1951; d. Frank Beverly and Margaretta Celeste (Butler) Abram; B.A., U. Maine, Orono, 1974; M.Ed., Ohio U., 1976. Resident dir. Ohio U., Athens, 1974-76; student affairs coordinator U. Wis., Madison, 1976—. Ohio U. grantee, 1975-76. Mem. Nat. Assn. Student Personnel Adminstrs., Am. Personnel and Guidance Assn., Am. Coll. Personnel Assn., NOW. Democrat. Roman Catholic. Home and Office: Tripp Gatehouse Univ Wis Madison WI 53706

ABRAMS, BERNARD S., optical co. exec., optometrist; b. Lancaster, Ohio, July 11, 1929; s. Micheal L. and Dora (Silberman) A.; B.S. in Optometry, Ohio State U., 1952; postgrad. Capital U., Columbus, Ohio, 1952-54, Franklin Law U., 1959-60; m. Shirley Ann Raikin, Nov. 21, 1949; children—Joel, Marcie, Steven, David, Felice. Optometrist, Columbus; pres. Select Optical, 1952-68, optical div. KMS Industries, 1968-70; chmn. bd. B.S.A. Industries, Columbus, 1970—. Cons. ophthalmic lens to industry Ethyl Corp., Gen. Electric Corp., PPG, Inc., Frigitronics Inc. of Am., Norville Optics, Eng., Israeli Govt., Asahi Glass, Japan, Lamard, France. Mason, Lion. Inventor contact lens, thermoset plastic lenses and lens systems. Home: 220 Stanwood Rd Bexley OH 43209 Office: 6510 Huntley Rd Columbus OH 43229

ABRAMS, WALTER, physician; b. Chgo., Mar. 3, 1919; s. Samuel and Pearl (Friedman) A.; student Lewis Inst., 1936-39; B.S., U. Ill., 1942, M.D., 1943; m. Ruth Pressman, Jan. 6, 1945; children—Clifford, Glenn Lee. Intern, Michael Reese Hosp., Chgo., 1943, resident, 1946-50; pvt. practice medicine specializing in obstetrics and gynecology, Homewood, Ill., 1950—, Olympia Fields, Ill., 1955—; chmn. dept. obstetrics and gynecology Ingalls Meml. Hosp., Harvey, Ill., 1952—, pres. med. staff, 1973—. Served with USNR, 1943-46. Diplomate Am. Bd. Obstetrics and Gynecology. Fellow Am. Coll. Obstetrics and Gynecology, A.C.S., Am. Coll. Abdominal Surgeons; mem. AMA, Chgo., Ill. med. assns. Club: Idlewild Country. Home: 1000 Lake Shore Dr Chicago IL 60611 also Olympia Fields IL 60461

ABRAMSON, HERBERT FRANCIS, sch. adminstr.; b. Chgo., Dec. 16, 1930; s. Maurice P. and Rose (Harris) A.; B.S., Ind. U., 1953; M.Ed., Loyola U., 1961; postgrad. Roosevelt, Purdue, Ind. univs.; m. Sylvia Linde, June 29, 1958; children—Marcia Beth, Jacquelyn, Rachel. Tchr. pub. secondary schs., Lake Ridge, 1955—, prin. Calumet Jr. High Sch., Lake Ridge Sch. System, 1961-69; prin. Lake Jr. High Sch., 1969-74; supt. Lake Ridge Schs., Gary, 1974—. prin. Temple Israel Religious Sch., Gary. Dir. Gary Sch. Employee Fed. Credit Union. Served with AUS, 1953-55. Bd. dirs. N.W. Ind. Jewish Welfare Fedn.; bd. dirs. Temple Israel, Gary, 1971-72, pres. 1973-75; cons. Hebrew Acad. N.W. Ind. Mem. Am. Fedn. Tchrs. (past pres. No. 662), Nat. Assn. Secondary Sch. Prins., Lake County Jr. and Sr. High Prins. Assn., Ind. Assn. Pub. Sch. Supts., ACLU. Mem. B'nai B'rith. Contbr. articles to profl. jours. Home: 7210 Polk St Merrillville IN 46410 Office: 6111 W Ridge Rd Gary IN 46408

ABRAMSON, JEAN MARGARET, educator; b. Laurium, Mich., Nov. 12, 1926; d. Victor Wilbert and Lyle (Talvensaari) Abramson; Mus.B., Chgo. Musical Coll., 1948; Mus.M., U. Rochester, 1951, D. Mus. Arts, 1965. Instr. music Suomi Coll., Hancock, Mich., 1948-50; instr. piano Mary Hardin-Baylor Coll., Belton, Tex., 1952-54; faculty Wartburg Coll., Waverly, Iowa, 1954—, prof. music 1973—. Mem. AAUP, Mus. Tchrs. Nat. Assn., Iowa Mus. Tchrs. Assn., Coll. Music Soc., Delta Kappa Gamma. Lutheran. Home: 319 11th St NW Apt 4 Waverly IA 50677 Office: Wartburg College Waverly IA 50677

ABRELL, PHILLIP EUGENE, pub. exec.; b. Muncie, Ind., June 27, 1926; s. Homer Ray and Ruby May (Moody) A.; grad. Muncie pub. schs.; m. Barbra Joan Phair, Oct. 7, 1951; 1 son, Gregory Phillip. Bookkeeper, Merchants Nat. Bank, Muncie, Ind., 1947-48, chief bookkeeper, 1948; nat. bank examiner 7th Fed. Reserve Dist., Chgo., 1948-52; outside prodn. sr. buyer Oliver Corp., Battle Creek, Mich., 1952-53; customer accounts rep. Enquirer & News, Battle Creek, Mich., 1953-54, office and personnel mgr., 1954-62, bus. mgr., 1962-76; pres., pub. The Times Herald, Port Huron, Mich., 1976—. Bd. dirs. Port Huron Indsl. Devel. Corp., Michigan United Way, Port Huron United Way, Port Huron Dist. Found., Family Service Agy. Served with U.S. Army, 1945-46. Mem. Am. Newspaper Publs. Assn., Mich. Press Assn. Republican. Mason (Shriner). Club: Port Huron Golf, Rotary. Home: 2800 Riverwood Ct Port Huron MI 48060 Office: 907 6th St Port Huron MI 48060

ABRUZZO, PETER JOSEPH, ednl. adminstr.; b. Chgo., Apr. 21, 1939; s. Peter and Theresa (Cannella) A.; B.S. in Edn., No. Ill. U., 1961, M.S. in Edn., 1967; m. Nancy Jean Hall, Aug. 5, 1961; children—Lori Ann, Terri Ann, Peter Michael. Tchr., coach elementary and jr. high sch. Marquardt Dist. #15, Glen Ellyn, Ill., 1961-63, tchr., counselor, adminstr. jr. high sch., 1964-68; counselor Glenbard North High Sch., Carol Stream, Ill., 1968-71, dir. guidance services, 1971-72; adminstrv. asst., dir. guidance services Glenbard South High Sch., Glen Ellyn, 1972-75, asst. prin., 1975—. Mem. Nat., Ill. assns. secondary sch. prins., Am., Ill. personnel and guidance assns., Chgo. Suburban Dirs. Pupil Personnel Services, Tau Kappa Epsilon. Roman Catholic. Home: 2S125 Hampton Ln Butterfield Lombard IL 60148 Office: Glenbard South High School Glen Ellyn IL 60137

ABUZZAHAB, FARUK SAID, SR., psychiatrist; b. Beirut, Lebanon, Oct. 12, 1932; s. Said Salim and Nimet Mohammad (Muezzin) A.; B.S., Am. U. Beirut, Lebanon, 1955, M.D., 1959; Ph.D., U. Minn., 1968; m. Beverly Elaine Swinter, June 29, 1962; children—Nada Josephine, Mary Jennifer, Faruk Said, Jeffrey Faruk, Mark Faruk. Came to U.S., 1953, permanent resident, 1965. Rotating intern Am. U. Hosp., Beirut, 1958-59; resident psychiatry Johns Hopkins Hosp., Balt., 1959-62; practice medicine specializing in psychiatry and clin. psychopharmacology, Mpls., 1962—; mem. staff U. Minn. Hosps., St. Mary's, Fairview, Mpls.; acting med. dir. Hastings (Minn.) State Hosp., 1963—; mem. staff Meml. Hosp., Menomonie, Wis., 1974—; research fellow U. Minn., Mpls., 1962-66, instr., 1966-68, asst. prof. psychiatry and pharmacology, 1968-73, clin. asso. prof., 1973—; cons. psychiatrist St. Croix County Health Center, New Richmond, Wis., 1975—, Dunn County Health Care Center, Menominee, 1970—. Pres., clin. Psychopharmacology Consultants, 1973—; adminstr. psychopharmacology and pharmacopsychiatry funds, 1969—. Bd. dirs. Minn. Life Care Centers, 1975—. Recipient Faculty Devel. award Pharm. Mfrs. Assn. Found., 1967-69. Fellow Am. Psychiat. Assn., Am. Coll. Clin. Pharmacology; mem. Am. Soc. Clin. Pharmacology and Therapeutics, AMA, Minn. Med. Soc. (subcom. on alcoholism and drug abuse 1970—), Soc. for Biol. Psychiatry, Hennepin County Psychiat. Soc. (pres. 1976—), Collegium Internat. Neuropsychopharmacologium, Am. Coll. Clin. Pharmacology, Sigma Xi, Alpha Omega Alpha. Contbr. articles to profl. jours. Home: 2601 E Lake of the Isles Blvd Minneapolis MN 55408 Office: Suite 818 Fairview-St Mary's Med Bldg 606 S 24th Ave Minneapolis MN 55454 also Box 393 Mayo U Minn Minneapolis MN 55455

ACCOLA, LOUIS WAYNE, clergyman; b. Ames, Iowa, Sept. 16, 1937; s. Ralph Arnold and Joyce Helen (Sheldahl) A.; B.A., Luther Coll., 1959; B.D. with highest honors, Luther Theol. Sem., 1964; Th.M. with highest honors, Princeton, 1965; m. Kathleen Mae McMullen, July 3, 1976; children—Terence Steven, Hans Louis, Steven Michael. Ordained to ministry Lutheran Ch., 1965; missionary tchr., Rhodesia, 1961-63; pastor Our Savior's Luth. Ch., Waterloo, Iowa, 1965-66, Our Savior's Luth. Ch., Milw., 1966-74; dir. parish devel. div. life and mission Am. Luth. Ch., Mpls., 1974—. Mem. model parish team ministry, 1966-74; Ch. Renewal Movement leader; mem. Milw. Met. Luth. Council, 1969-70; guest lectr. Marquette U., Alverno Coll., Spencerian Coll., Milw., 1970; sec., mem. forward planning com. Am. Luth. Ch's. Milw. Conf., 1971-74; fraternal del. for Am. Luth. Ch. to 9th gen. assembly Nat. Council of Chs., Dallas, 1972; mem. Commn. on Interchurch Relations, Am. Luth. Ch. Hdqrs. Mpls., 1973-74, rep. to Inter-Luth. Commn. on Worship, 1975-77. Democrat. Author: Personal Faith for Human Crises, 1970; co-author: Parish Planning Resource Manual, 1977. Home: 8100 32d Ave N Minneapolis MN 55427 Office: 422 S 5th St Minneapolis MN 55415

ACKER, DUANE CALVIN, univ. pres.; b. Atlantic, Iowa, Mar. 13, 1931; s. Clayton and Ruth (Kimball) A.; B.S., Iowa State U., 1952, M.S., 1953; Ph.D., Okla. State U., 1957; m. Shirley Hansen, Mar. 23, 1952; children—Diane, LuAnn. Instr. animal husbandry Okla. State U., 1953-55; instr. Iowa State U., 1955-56, asst. prof., 1956-58, asso. prof. animal sci., 1958-62; asso. dean agr. Kans. State U., Manhattan, 1962-66, pres., 1975—; dean Coll. Agr. and Biol. Scis., dir. Agrl. Expt. Sta., S.D. State U., 1966-74, dir. Coop. Extension Service, 1971-74; vice chancellor for agr. and natural resources U. Nebr., 1974-75. Mem. Nat. Assn. State Univs. and Land Grant Colls., Am. Soc. Animal Sci., AAAS, Sigma Xi, Gamma Sigma Delta, Alpha Zeta, Phi Kappa Phi. Author: Animal Science Laboratory Manual, 1958; Animal Science and Industry, 1963, 2d edit., 1971; contbr. articles to animal sci., edn. and nutrition jours. Office: Pres's Office 106 Anderson Hall Kans State U Manhattan KS 66506

ACKERMAN, JERRY WILLIAM, heavy equipment mfg. co. exec.; b. Atlanta, June 10, 1935; s. Russell Tingley and Viola Mary (Diemer) A.; B.S., Coll. City N.Y., 1958; M.B.A., Kent State U., 1969; m. Mary Margaret Waldron, Oct. 4, 1958; children—Joseph William, Andrew Russell, Michael Waldron. Various sales and engring. positions, 1952-58; research engr. research and devel. div. Babcock & Wilcox, Alliance, Ohio, 1958-68, mktg. planning and research mgr., corporate mktg. dept., 1969-71, mktg. services mgr. power generation group, Barberton, Ohio, 1972-76, exploratory research mgr., Alliance, 1976—. Tech. adviser Nat. Power Survey FPC, 1973. Served with AUS, 1959. Registered profl. engr., Ohio, N.Y. Mem. Am. Mktg. Assn. Elk. Contbr. articles to profl. publs. Home: 1147 Kingsway Alliance OH 44601 Office: 1562 Beeson St Alliance OH 44601

ACKERMAN, ORA RAY, hosp. supt.; b. Mapleton, Minn., Jan. 13, 1931; s. Ora R. and Minnie T. (Quam) A.; B.S. with distinction, U. Minn., 1953, M.Ed., 1955; certificate dir. recreation, Ind. U., 1961, Ed.D., 1963; certificate recreation techniques in rehab., N.Y. U., 1966; grad. exec. devel. program, Ind. U., 1968; m. Barbara Singley, Mar. 25, 1951; children—Bruce, David, Cindy. Mental health coordinator in Cal., Md. and Ind., 1953-63; dir. edn. and activity therapy Ind. Dept. Mental Health, 1963-66; supt. Ft. Wayne (Ind.) State Hosp. and Tng. Center, 1966—; vis. prof. psychology Ind. U., Purdue-Ft. Wayne campus, 1967—. Mem. Great Lakes dist. adv. com. Nat. Recreation Assn., 1965-68; bd. dirs. Nat. Therapeutic Recreation Soc., 1966-69; mem. adv. council title IV-A, Ind. State Library, 1968—; chmn. pub. edn. com. ARC; mem. Com. Comprehensive Spl. Edn. Planning and Devel. with Pub. Schs., Hosps., Clinics and Rehab. Services; mem. Gov.'s Tech. Planning Com. for Devel. Plans for Correction Center; mem. Ind. Mental Health-Mental Retardation Planning Commn.; mem. Mental Health-Mental Retardation Steering Com. on Residential Facilities for the Mentally Retarded; pres. Allen County unit Am. Cancer Soc.; pres. Ind. div. Am. Cancer Soc., 1973-74; mem. Gov.'s Developmental Disabilities Adv. Council, 1971—. Mem. Assn. Mental Health. Adminstrs., Am. Soc. Mental Deficiency, Am. Recreation Soc., Ind. Park and Recreation Assn. Methodist (chmn. bd. 1967). Kiwanian. Contbr. profl. jours. Office: 801 E State Blvd Fort Wayne IN 46805

ACKERMAN, WALTER J., dentist; b. Herreid, S.D., Nov. 1, 1918; s. Henry and Christina (Buckenberger) A.; student U. S.D., 1953-55; B.S., U. Minn., 1957, D.D.S., 1959; m. Viola Elizabeth Papendick, Oct. 9, 1942; 1 son, Michael Alan. With Butler Bros. Mining Co., Nashwauk, Minn., 1941-42, Boeing Aircraft, Seattle, 1942-45; owner Coast to Coast Hardware Store, Dell Rapids, S.D., 1945-47; co-owner Peacock Cafe, Winner, S.D., 1947-50, Men's Clothing store, 1950-53; pvt. dental practice, Rapid City, S.D., 1959—; mem. active staff St. John's Hosp., Rapid City. Mem. Am. Soc. Dentistry for Children (state unit pres. 1964-65, Distinguished Service award S.D. unit 1966), ADA, S.D. (v.p. 1975-76, pres. 1977-78), Black Hills dental socs., VMCCA Hist. Auto Club, Soc. Preservation and Encouragement Barbershop Quartet Singing in Am. (pres. Mt. Rushmore chpt. 1976), Delta Sigma Delta (dir. dental chpt. S.D. 1972-73). Elk, Kiwanian (pres. 1972-73). Club: Black Hills Antiques (pres. 1967-68). Home: 107 N Platte St Rapid City SD 57701 Office: 2610 Jackson Blvd Rapid City SD 57701

ACORD, FRANK DONALD, r.r. exec.; b. Spring City, Utah, Apr. 1, 1916; s. Henry L. and Mary Ellen (Allred) A.; grad. high sch., 1935; m. Faun Ellen Terry, Dec. 23, 1937; children—Sherry, Connie, Susan, Vickie, Tamara, Donald F. With U.P.R.R. Co., 1936—, machinist apprentice, Cheyenne, Wyo., 1936-40, machinist, Ogden, Utah, 1940-44, foreman, 1944-50, gen. foreman, Provo, Utah, 1950-52, dist. foreman, N. Platte, Nebr., 1952-62, master mechanic, Los Angeles, 1954-56, Salt Lake City, 1956-62, Cheyenne, 1962, mech. supt., Omaha, 1962-66, asst. gen. supt. motive power & machinery, Omaha, 1966-70, gen. supt. motive power and machinery, 1970-71, chief mech. officer, 1971—. Mem. ASME, Soc. Automotive Engrs. Clubs: Engrs. Omaha, Elks. Home: 825 S 120th Ave Omaha NE 68154 Office: 1416 Dodge St Omaha NE 68179

ACOSTA-OLMEDA, JOSE GUILLERMO, pathologist; b. Mayaguez, P.R., Sept. 22, 1935; s. Francisco R. and Maria Esperanza (Olmeda) A.; B.S., U. P.R., 1956; M.D. (Am. Cyanamid Co. fellow in biochemistry), Temple U., 1959; m. Alice Mary Green, Feb. 7, 1959 (dec.); m. 2d, Karen Lee Callaway, Nov. 20, 1970; children—Francis Jose, Jose Rene, Maria Esperanza, Monica, Anita, Julianne, Jennifer Lynn. Intern, St. Charles Hosp., Toledo, 1959-60; resident in internal medicine VA Hosp., San Juan, P.R., 1960-61, resident in pathology VA Hosp., Milw., 1963-64, VA Hosp., Bronx, N.Y., 1964-67; staff pathologist VA Hosp., Syracuse, N.Y., 1967-68; practice medicine specializing in pathology; dir. labs. Illini Hosp., Silvis, Ill., 1968—; dir. lab. Jackson County Pub. Hosp., Maquoketa, Iowa, 1971—; cons. in pathology DeWitt (Iowa) Community Hosp., 1972—; asso. med. dir. Miss. Valley Regional Blood Center; asst. prof. pathology State U. N.Y., Syracuse, 1967-68. Served with M.C., U.S. Army, 1961-63. Diplomate Am. Bd. Pathology, Nat. Bd. Med. Examiners. Mem. AMA, Ill., Rock Island County med. socs., Am. Coll. Pathologists, Am. Soc. Clin. Pathologists, Internat. Acad. Pathologists, Am. Assn. Blood Banks, Assn. Advancement in Med. Instrumentation, Blackhawk Lung Assn. (pres.). Roman Catholic. Club: Rotary (East Moline, Ill.). Home: Rural Route 2 Box 70 Coal Valley IL 61240 Office: Illini Hosp 801 13th Ave Silvis IL 61282

ADAIR, CHARLES VALLOYD, physician; b. Lorain, Ohio, Apr. 20, 1923; s. Waite and Ella Jane (Robertson) A.; A.B., Hobart Coll., Geneva, N.Y., 1944; M.D., Western Res. U., 1947; m. Constance Dean, Apr. 1, 1944; children—Allen V., Richard D. Intern, then asst. resident in medicine Rochester (N.Y.) Gen. Hosp., 1947-49; fellow in medicine Univ. Hosps., Syracuse, N.Y., 1949-51; practice medicine specializing in internal medicine, Mansfield, Ohio, 1953—; mem. staffs Mansfield Gen. Hosp., Peoples Hosp., Richland Neuropsychiat. Hosp.; mem. Mansfield City Bd. Health; trustee, past pres. Mansfield lMeml. Homes. Served to capt. AUS, 1943-46, 51-53. Diplomate Am. Bd. Internal Medicine. Fellow A.C.P.; mem. Am. Soc. Internal Medicine, Am., Ohio med. assns., Richland County Med. Soc. Republican. Congregationalist. Clubs: Our, Westbrook Country, University. Home: 1010 Woodland Rd Mansfield OH 44907 Office: 480 Glessner Ave Mansfield OH 44903

ADAIR, JOHN GLENN, psychologist; b. San Antonio, Dec. 19, 1933; s. Charles Glenn and Lucie (Berlon) A.; B.S., Trinity U. Tex., 1954, M.S., 1956; Ph.D., U. Iowa, 1965; m. Carolyn Ann Johnson, Aug. 13, 1960; children—Leslie Kyle, Colin Glenn, Heidi Janelle, Joel Channing. Instr., asst. prof. Dakota Wesleyan U., 1959-63; instr. U. Iowa, 1964-65; mem. faculty U. Man., Winnipeg, Can., 1965—, prof., head dept. psychology, 1973—, bd. govs. univ., 1976-79. Served with USAF, 1956-57. NSF fellow, 1963-64; Canada Council leave fellow, 1971-72. Mem. Am., Canadian (dir. 1975-78), Midwestern psychol. assns. Author: The Human Subject, 1973. Home: 14 Tunis Bay Winnipeg MB Canada Office: Dept Psychology Univ Manitoba Winnipeg MB Canada

ADAIRE, BRUCE BOWER, beverage co. exec.; b. Providence, R.I., Mar. 23, 1937; s. William Roger and Elizabeth M. (Bower) A.; A.B., Princeton U., 1960; M.A., U. Wis., 1961; m. Marilyn Dorothy Miller, Aug. 27, 1960; children—Geoffrey Miller, Jennifer Robin. Mem. faculty Tabor Acad., Marion, Mass., summer 1960, 61; media planner J. Walter Thompson Co., N.Y.C., 1961-62, media supr., 1963-64, in London, 1964-66, account rep., 1966-68, account supr., 1968-71, v.p., 1970-71; mktg. dir. Checkerboard Farms div. Ralston Purina Co., St. Louis, 1971-72; dir. mktg. Seven-Up Internat., Inc., St. Louis, 1972—, v.p., 1973; cons. to mktg. program Washington U., St. Louis, 1973—. Mktg. bd. St. Louis Symphony Soc., 1975—; mem. adv. bd. St. Louis Priory Sch., 1974—; trustee Villa Duchesne Sch. Recipient Pub. Service award Archdiocese of N.Y. Cath. Youth Orgn., 1969; English-Speaking Union Internat. Schoolboy fellow, 1955; Woodrow Wilson fellow, 1960. Mem. Am. Mgmt. Assn., Am. Mktg. Assn., Internat. Advt. Assn. Methodist. Clubs: Woodsmill Racquet, Creve Coeur Racquet. Home: 13562 Featherstone Dr Saint Louis MO 63131 Office: 121 S Meramec St Saint Louis MO 63105

ADAM, PAUL JAMES, mech. engr.; b. Kansas City, Mo., Oct. 26, 1934; s. Paul James and Adrienne (Zimmerman) A.; B.S. in Mech. Engring., U. Kans., 1956; m. Barbara Ann Mills, Dec. 18, 1956; children—Paul James III, Blair Dodderidge II, Matthew Mills. Mech. engr. Black & Veatch, Cons. Engrs., Kansas City, Mo., 1956, 59-74, partner, asst. head power div., 1975—. Mem. Greater Univ. Fund Adv. Bd., U. Kans., 1964-66. Served to 1st lt., USAF, 1956-59. Registered profl. engr., Ariz., Fla., Minn., Mo., Ohio, Tex., Wash., Wyo. Mem. Nat., Mo. socs. profl. engrs., ASME, Am. Nuclear Soc., Atomic Indsl. Forum, Tau Beta Pi, Sigma Tau, Pi Tau Sigma, Omicron Delta Kappa, Alpha Tau Omega. Episcopalian. Club: Mission Hills Country. Office: 1500 Meadow Lake Pkwy Kansas City MO 64114

ADAMS, DONALD EARL, lawyer, judge; b. nr. Pontiac, Mich., Dec. 27, 1912; s. Jayno W. and Blanche W. (Earl) A.; A.B., U. Mich., 1934, J.D., 1936; m. Elizabeth B. Sparks, Nov. 12, 1936; 1 son, David Earl. Admitted to Mich. bar, 1936, since practiced in Pontiac, Drayton Plains; justice of the peace Waterford Twp., Mich., 1937-61; state pub. adminstr. Oakland County, Mich., 1949-51; interim atty. gen. State Mich., 1960; judge probate Oakland County, 1961-77; dir. First Fed. Savs. and Loan Assn. Oakland. Mem. Democratic State Central Com., 1949-51, 53-57; first chmn. Waterford Twp. Recreation Bd., 1951; mem. Twp. Zoning Bd. of Appeals and Waterford Twp. Bd., 1939-41, 46-47, 49-51. Mem. Oakland County Community Mental Health Services Bd., 1963-72, chmn., 1969-72; bd. dirs. Children's Charter Cts. Mich., Camp Oakland, Inc., Pontiac Boys Club. Served with USNR, World War II; now lt. comdr. Res. Mem. Am. Judicature Soc., Mich. Probate Judges Assn., State Bar Mich. (commr. 1955-61), Am. Oakland County (past sec.) bar assns., Nat. Coll. Probate Judges, Nat. Council Juvenile Ct. Judges, Navy League U.S., Oakland County Pioneer and Hist. Soc. (past pres.), Phi Beta Kappa. Presbyn. Mason, Elk. Clubs: Lions (past pres. Pontiac); Oakland County Sportmen's (past pres. bd. dirs.). Address: Box 248 Drayton Plains MI 48020

ADAMS, EDWARD LARRABEE, JR., psychology cons.; b. Ann Arbor, Mich., May 9, 1915; s. Edward Larrabee and Sarah Sager (Hardy) A.; A.B., U. Mich., 1937, M.A., 1939; M.A., U. Minn., 1949, Ph.D., 1951; m. Nita DuMar Addleman, Jan. 24, 1953; 1 dau., Susan DuMar. Instr. Culver (Ind.) Mil. Acad., 1940-41; instr., sr. counselor Duke, 1951-53; cons. psychologist partner Rohrer, Hibler, Replogle, N.Y.C. and Detroit, 1953-62; cons. psychologist, Ann Arbor, 1962—; mng. partner Adams, Madden, Moody & Fisher, Ann Arbor, 1963-76; pres. Achievement Resources, Ann Arbor, 1973—; prin. Edward L. Adams Jr. and Assos., Ann Arbor, 1962—. Served to lt. col., inf. AUS, 1941-46. Mem. Am. Psychol. Assn., Am. Personnel and Guidance Assn., Mich. Soc. Cons. Psychologists, Nat. Cons. Psychologists to Mgmt. Rotarian. Author: Career Advancement Guide, 1975. Columnist, Dr. Adams-On Careers, Detroit News, 1975—. Contbr. articles to profl. jours. Home and office: 1850 Washtenaw Ave Ann Arbor MI 48104

ADAMS, ELLIS WENTWORTH, pediatrician; b. Spokane, Wash., Nov. 26, 1913; s. Ralph Wentworth and Gertrude (Everett) A.; B.S. in Civil Engring., U. Mich., 1935; postgrad. Mich. State U., 1935-37; M.D., Duke U., 1941; m. Mary Katherine Dierberger, June 13, 1940; children—Katherine, Joan, Mary Beth. Intern, U. Rochester (N.Y.) Sch. Medicine, 1941, asst. resident in pediatrics, 1942-43, resident in pediatrics, outpatient dept., 1943-44, chief resident in pediatrics, 1944, also instr. pediatrics; practice medicine specializing in pediatrics Great Falls (Mont.) Clinic, 1944-48, Jackson, Mich., 1948—; asst. clin. prof. dept. human development Mich. State U.; chief of staff W.A. Foots Meml. Hosp., Jackson, 1960-61, Mercy Hosp., Jackson, 1965-66. Fellow Am. Acad. Pediatrics, Am. Acad. for Cerebral Palsy; mem. Jackson County (pres. 1967-68), Mich. State med. socs., AMA. Republican. Presbyterian. Club: Rotary Internat. Home: 1360 Kathmar St Jackson MI 49203 Office: 720 W Franklin St Jackson MI 49201

ADAMS, GENE, editor; b. Springfield, Mo., Nov. 3, 1923; s. Charles H. and Marguerite (Kibbe) A.; B.A., Northwestern U., 1950; m. LaVergne Kanara, Apr. 4, 1945; 1 dau., Bonnie Jean. Pub., Midwestern Baker also Chgo. Retail Baker, Chgo., 1950-53; editor, pub. Mobile Homes & Mobile Living, 1953-58; editor Splty. Salesman, Chgo., 1958-67; editor Modern Garden Center, Barrington, Ill., 1967-68; editorial dir. Selling Sporting Goods, Chgo., 1968-72; editor-in-chief Ground Water Age, Elmhurst, Ill., 1972-77; editorial dir. Scott Periodicals, 1977—. Publ. cons.; graphic and package designer; tchr. ceramics. Active Boy Scouts Am. Served with USN, 1941-45. Mem. Am. Soc. Bus. Press Editors (pres., dir.), Soc. Publ. Designers Roman Catholic. Club: Chgo. Press. Home: 810 Manchester St Westchester IL 60153 Office: 110 N York Rd Elmhurst IL 60126

ADAMS, GORDON DEWEY, surgeon; b. Red Cloud, Nebr., Mar. 26, 1932; s. James D. and Hildegarde (Swanson) A.; student Nebr. State Coll., Kearney; M.D., U. Nebr., 1956; m. Gloria J. Adams, Aug. 29, 1954;children—Jane Marie, Jeffrey Dwight, Jennifer Louise. Resident gen. surgery Wayne County Gen. Hosp., Eloise, Mich., 1959-63; surgeon Norfolk (Nebr.) Med. Group, 1963—; vice chief staff Luth. Community Hosp., Norfolk, 1967-69, chief of staff, 1969-71. Dir. Norfolk First Fed. Savs. and Loan. Mem. low rent housing authority bd., Norfolk, Nebr., 1969—; pres. Boulevard Village Low Rent Housing Authority, 1977. Bd. dirs. Nebr. div. Am. Cancer Soc., v.p. Nebr. div., 1971-72, pres. Nebr. div., 1972-73; bd. dirs. Luth. Community Hosp. Served to capt. AUS, 1957-59. Lutheran. Home: 2205 Koenigstein Norfolk NE 68701 Office: 900 Norfolk Ave Norfolk NE 68701

ADAMS, JAMES LEWIS, state legislator; b. Iron Mountain, Mich., Oct. 2, 1921; s. Lewis James and Signe (Peterson) A.; student U. Minn. extension courses; m. Edith Ann Hvambsal, Jan. 30, 1954; children—Judith Marie, Douglas James, Laura Lee. Electrician; mem. Minn. Ho. of Reps., 1954—. Served in U.S. Army, World War II, PTO. Mem. Am. Legion, VFW. Home: 4234 19th Ave S Minneapolis MN 55407

ADAMS, JOHN CARTER, accounting firm exec.; b. Bismark, N.D., Apr. 20, 1919; s. John Bennett and Olive Hazel (Procter) A.; student Wilson Jr. Coll., 1946, Walton Sch. Commerce, Chgo., 1947-48, LaSalle U., 1954-55; C.P.A., U. Ill., 1956; m. Pauline Janette Scott, Mar. 1, 1944 (div.); children—John, Judith Fitzgerald, Paul, William; m. 2d, Harriet N. Hall, May 1, 1976. With John E. Burke & Co., 1946-48, Gen. Motors Corp., 1948-51; with Wynn M. Wagner & Co. (now Wagner Sim & Co.), pub. accountants, Chgo., 1951—, partner, 1956—; v.p. Naperville (Ill.) Elderly Homes, Inc., 1972-75, pres., 1975-76, also dir.; partner Mill Ogden Venture, Mill St. Properties. Served with USAAF, 1942-46. C.P.A., Ill. Mem. Am. Inst. C.P.A.'s, Ill. Soc. C.P.A.'s. Club: Union League (Chgo.). Home: 1001 Belaire Ct Naperville IL 60540 Office: 20 N Wacker Dr Chicago IL 60606

ADAMS, JOHN ERNEST, JR., guidance counselor; b. Van Nuys, Calif., Dec. 23, 1945; s. John Ernest and Mary Margaret (Burnett) A.; B.A., Wofford Coll., 1967; M.A., Chgo. Theol. Sem., 1972; m. Nina Paulette Magid, Sept. 18, 1969. Minister, Carlisle-Gilliam's Chapel Meth. Ch., Carlisle, S.C., 1965-66; payroll clk. E.B. Hall & Co., Wilmington, Calif., 1968-69; accountant, cashier Sem. Coop. Bookstore, Inc., Chgo., 1967-72; career, residential counselor Grinnell (Iowa) Coll., 1972-73, asst. dir. career services office, 1973-74, dir. career services office, 1974—; cons. in field. Pres. bd. dirs. Jr. Achievement Grinnell, 1977—. Mem. Am. Personnel and Guidance Assn., Am. Coll. Personnel Assn., Nat. Vocat. Guidance Assn., M.W. College Placement Assn., Coll. Placement Council, Assn. for Sch., Coll. and Univ. Staffing, Great Lakes, Iowa assns. for sch., coll. and univ. staffing. Author: The Resume, A Guide, 1972; contbr. articles to profl. jours. Club: Lions. Home: 1407 Elm St Grinnell IA 50112 Office: Career Services Office Grinnell Coll 1119 Park St Grinnell IA 50112

ADAMS, JOHN MARSHALL, lawyer; b. Columbus, Ohio, Dec. 6, 1930; s. H.F. and Ada Margaret (Gregg) A.; B.A., Ohio State U., 1952, J.D. summa cum laude, 1954; m. Janet Hawk, June 28, 1952; children—John Marshall, Susan Lynn, William Alfred. Admitted to Ohio bar, 1954; mem. firm Cowan & Adams, Columbus, 1954-55; asst. city atty. City of Columbus, 1955-56; mem. firm Knepper, White, Richards & Miller, 1956-63; practiced in Columbus, 1963-74; partner firm Porter, Wright, Morris & Arthur, Columbus, 1975—. Trustee Ohio Bar Automated Research Trust. Fellow Am. Coll. Trial Lawyers; fellow, trustee Ohio Bar Found.; mem. Am., Ohio (mem. exec. com. 1975—, pres. elect 1977-78), Columbus (bd. govs. 1970-72, sec.-treas. 1972-73, pres. 1974-75) bar assns., Lawyers Club (pres. 1968-69), Order of Coif, Delta Upsilon, Phi Delta Phi. Republican. Mason. Clubs: Athletic, Scioto Country. Home: 3921 Lytham Ct Columbus OH 43220 Office: 37 W Broad St Columbus OH 43215

ADAMS, KENDALL ALFRED, marketing specialist; b. McMinnville, Oreg.; June 4, 1926; s. John and Dana Belle (Hulett) Shetterly; B.S., Oreg. State U., 1951; Ph.D., Mich. State U., 1962; m. Kathryn Frances Hildebrand, Dec. 29, 1963; children—Derek Winston, Kevin Shetterly. House mgr. Delta Tau Delta, 1950-51; grad. asst. instr. Mich. State U., 1953-54; marketing specialist Coop. Extension Service, Mich. State U., 1954-56, grad. asst. research, 1956-62; asst. prof. Ariz. State U., 1962-65; asso. prof. So. Ill. U., 1965-67; project specialist Ford Found., 1967-69; asso. prof. to prof. marketing So. Ill. U., Carbondale, 1969—; cons. to industry. Mem. Williamson County Zoning Commn., 1970-71, Carbondale Task Force, 1972-74. Served with USNR, 1942-44. Mem. Am. Marketing Assn., Am. Agrl. Econs. Assn., Beta Gamma Sigma. Club: World Trade (St. Louis). Contbr. articles to Jour. Retailing, Bus. Perspectives, Proceedings Am. Marketing Assn., Poultry Sci. Jour. Home: 1002 S Oakland St Carbondale IL 62901 Office: Marketing Dept Southern Illinois University Carbondale IL 62901

ADAMS, LESLIE, musician; b. Clev., 1932; B.Mus., Oberlin (Ohio) Coll., 1955; M.A., Calif. State U., Long Beach; Ph.D., Ohio State U., 1973. Mem. faculty Kans. U., 1970; composer: Largo For Horn and Piano, 1963, (ballet) A Kiss in Xanadu, 1954, 73; also a symphony and works for piano, horn, cello, brass ensemble, chorus; works performed, N.Y.C., 1962, 63. Winner choral composition competition Christian Arts, 1974; Piano Concerto chosen for performance Houston Symphony Symposium, 1974. Mem. Am. Choral Dirs. Assn., Am. Music Center, Pi Kappa Lambda, Phi Delta Kappa, Phi Mu Alpha Sinfonia. Contbr. to profl. jours. Address: 9409 Kempton Ave Cleveland OH

ADAMS, MAX DWAIN, chemist; b. Red Oak, Iowa, May 23, 1926; s. R. Glen and Elva (Penry) A.; B.A., Tarkio Coll., 1948; M.S., Okla. State U., 1950; Ph.D., St. Louis U., 1955; m. Jeanne Margaret Beatty, July 25, 1947; children—Victoria (Mrs. Thomas Anderson), Ross, Scott. Chemist, Mallinckrodt Chem. Co., St. Louis, 1950-52; research asso. St. Louis U., 1952-55; chemist Argonne (Ill.) Nat. Lab., 1955-73; owner M.D. Adams Assos., tech. cons., Naperville, Ill., 1973—. Served with AUS, 1944-46. Fellow Am. Inst. Chemists, AAAS; mem. Am. Chem. Soc., Am. Nuclear Soc., Research Soc. Am., N.Y. Acad. Sci., Microscopic Soc. Ill. (state v.p. 1973, pres. 1974), Sigma Xi. Contbr. articles to profl. jours. Home and office: 313 Tamarack Ave Naperville IL 60540

ADAMS, MELVIN HARRISON, SR., banker, ins. agency exec.; b. Big Springs, Nebr., Aug. 2, 1912; s. George Douglas and Mary Ann (Longfellow) A.; B.S., U. Nebr., 1933; postgrad. Grad. Sch. Banking, U. Colo., 1956, U. Okla., 1970; m. Lucille Bricker, May 29, 1934; children—Melvin Harrison, John B. Accountant, Fairmont Foods Co., 1936-40; cashier Bank of Brule (Nebr.), 1940-41, pres., 1944—; chmn. bd. Adams Banks Nebr., Brule, 1944—; owner Melvin Adams Ins. Agency, Brule, 1940—; dir. Bank of Brule, Keith County Bank & Trust Co., Ogallala, Nebr., Chase County Bank & Trust Co., Imperial, Nebr., 1st. Security Bank Sutherland, Nebr., Security State Bank Madrid, Nebr. Treas. Ednl. Service Unit, Ogallala, 1970—; exec. council Tri-Trails Council Boy Scouts Am., 1962—; bd. dirs. Ogallala Roundup Inc. Served to lt. col., inf., AUS, 1941-46. Decorated Bronze Star, Combat Inf. Badge. Mem. Am. Legion, VFW, Alpha Kappa Psi, Beta Gamma Sigma. Clubs: Lions, Masons, Shriners. Home: 502 Oak St Brule NE 69127 Office: 202 State St Brule NE 69127

ADAMS, PETER WEBSTER, investment co. exec.; b. Cleve., Jan. 1, 1939; s. Donald Croxton and Nancy (Downer) A.; B.A., Yale U., 1961; m. Anne Rounds, Oct. 22, 1962; children—Michael C., Lynne S. Vice pres. Nat. City Bank Cleve., 1961-68; exec. v.p. Alexander, Van Cleef & Woods, Cleve., 1968-75; v.p. Alliance Capital Mgmt. Corp., Cleve., 1975—; dir. Weber, Wood Medinger, Inc., MPS, Inc., Investment Mgmt. Internat. Inc., N. Am. Cts., Inc. Trustee Cleve. Area League for Nursing, 1972-76. Chartered fin. analyst, 1971. Mem. Chartered Fin. Analysts' Soc., Cleve. Soc. Security Analysts, Univ. Sch. Alumni Assn. (pres. 1976-77). Clubs: Union, Tavern, Mayfield (Cleve.). Home: 2674 Wrenford Rd Shaker Heights OH 44122 Office: 720 National City Bank Bldg Cleveland OH 44114

ADAMS, RICHARD MELVERNE, research instn. adminstr.; b. Gary, Ind., Nov. 1, 1916; s. Melvern Merritt and Freda (Schueffler) A.; B.S., U. Chgo., 1939, M.S., 1948; Ph.D., Ill. Inst. Tech., 1953; m. Marjorie Ann Albright, Feb. 23, 1944; children—Victoria Gail, Richard Merritt. Chemist, Portland Cement Assn., Chgo., 1940-42; research asso. Office Sci. Research Devel., U. Chgo., 1942-43; chemist metall lab. Manhattan Project, Chgo., 1943-46; asst. group leader Los Alamos (N.Mex.) Sci. Lab., 1946; lectr. chemistry U. Ind., Gary, 1946-49; asso. chemist Argonne (Ill.) Nat. Lab., 1949-59, sci. asst. to dir., 1959-65, asst. lab. dir., 1965—. Mem. Am. Chem. Soc., Am. Phys. Soc., Am., Korea nuclear socs., AAAS, Sigma Xi. Contbr. articles to sci. jours. Home: 4744 S Kimbark Ave Chicago IL 60615 Office: Argonne Nat Laboratory 9700 S Cass Ave Argonne IL 60439

ADAMS, ROBERT MCLEAN, mfg. co. exec.; b. Hibbing, Minn., Aug. 4, 1922; s. John William and Julia (Straub) A.; A.A.S., Blackburn Coll., 1941, D.Sc., 1971; B.S., U. Ill., 1943, M.S., 1944, Ph.D., 1950; m. Carol Margaret Johnson, Sept. 4, 1943; children—Margaret, William, Carl, John Adams. With 3M Co., St. Paul, 1949—, sales staff, 1954-58, tech. dir., 1958-68, gen. mgr. new bus. ventures div.,

1968-69, v.p. research and devel., 1969—, also dir., mem. exec. com. Mem. adv. council Inst. Tech. U. Minn., 1971; trustee Sci. Mus. of Minn., 1975—, Blackburn Coll., Carlinville, Ill., 1975—. Served to lt. (j.g.) USNR, 1944-49. Mem. Am. Chem. Soc., Minn. Acad. Sci., Ind. Research Inst. Presbyterian. Home: 10426 Ideal Ave N White Bear Lake MN 55110 Office: 3M Co 3M Center St Paul MN 55101

ADAMS, THOMAS BROOKS, advt. exec.; b. Detroit, Sept. 16, 1919; s. Andrew S. and Louise A. (Brooks) A.; B.A., Wayne State U., 1941; m. Mary E. Bryant, Mar. 22, 1945; children—Janis E., Julie A., Kathleen M. With Campbell Ewald Co., Detroit, 1945—, chmn. bd., 1968—; dir. McLouth Steel Corp., Kent-Moore Corp. Vice pres. United Found.; chmn. Wayne County Stadium Authority, 1970—. Trustee Children's Hosp. Mich., Menninger Found.; bd. dirs. Wayne State U. Alumni Fund. Served to lt. comdr. USNR, 1941-45. Decorated Navy Cross, D.F.C., Air medal; named Outstanding Young Advt. Man Year N.Y. Assn. Advt. Men and Women, 1955. Mem. Advt. Council (chmn. 1976-77, dir.). Home: 931 W Harsdale Rd Bloomfield Hills MI 48013 Office: Campbell-Ewald Co Gen Motors Bldg Detroit MI 48202

ADAMS, WAYNE BARRY, pub. relations exec.; b. Plain City, Ohio, Feb. 20, 1948; s. Paul J. and Ella (Perry) A.; B.S. in Journalism, Ohio U., 1974, postgrad., 1977—; postgrad. U. Cin., 1976-77; m. Cheryl Ann Noble, Sept. 2, 1972. Publicity asst., Ohio U. Press, Athens, 1972-74; dir. pub. relations St. Francis Hosp., Cin., 1975-77; asso. dir. Ohio U. Alumni Assn., Athens, 1977—. dist. pub. info. officer Ohio Dept. Transp., Marietta, Ohio, 1974-75. Served with USN, 1966-70; now lt. (j.g.) USNR. Mem. Pub. Relations Soc. Am., Acad. of Hosp. Pub. Relations, Am. Soc. Hosp. Pub. Relations, Nat. Wildlife Fedn., Westwood Civic Assn., Nat. Geog. Soc., Cin. Editors Soc., Council Advancement and Support of Edn. Democrat. Unitarian. Club: West Side Racket. Home: 76 S May St Athens OH 45701 Office: Lindley Hall Ohio U Athens OH 45701

ADAMS, WILLIAM LAWRESON, elec. products co. exec.; b. Gay, Mich., July 9, 1932; s. Robert Newton and Dorothy Margaret (Vertin) A.; B.S. in Elec. Engring., Mich. Tech. U., 1954; S.M. in Elec. Engring., Mass. Inst. Tech., 1956; Ph.D. in Elec. Engring., Purdue U., 1962; m. Claire Marie Belyea, June 23, 1956; children—Kathleen, Robert, Judith, Patricia, Mary, David, James, Thomas, Stephen, Daniel, Emily. Sr. design engr. Gen. Electronic Labs., Inc., Cambridge, Mass., 1956-58; instr. Purdue U., West Lafayette, Ind., 1958-62, asst. prof., 1962-63; v.p. engring. Indsl. Nucleonics Corp., Columbus, Ohio, 1963—. Cons. Addressograph Multigraph Co., 1955-63. Served to 2d lt. C.E., AUS, 1957. Mem. IEEE, Instrument Soc. Am., Am. Mgmt. Assn., Sigma Xi, Phi Eta Sigma, Tau Beta Pi, Eta Kappa Nu. Republican. Roman Catholic. Researcher on elec. properties of bulk materials. Home: 9600 Olentangy River Rd Powell OH 43065 Office: 650 Ackerman Rd Columbus OH 43202

ADAMS, WILLIAM RICHARD, archaeozoologist; b. Bloomington, Ind., Feb. 21, 1923; s. William Baker and Mildred Florence (Dingle) A.; A.B., Ind. U., 1945, M.A., 1951; m. Connie Marie, Oct. 20, 1968; children—William H., James E., Richard B., Margaret E., Scott C., Teresa M. Archaeologist, Ind. Hist. Bur., 1945-47; instr., embalmer Sch. Medicine, Ind. U., Bloomington, 1947-49; ethnozoologist Central Miss. Valley Archaeol. Expdn., St. Louis, 1949; field archaeologist Royal Ont. Museum, 1955-56; dir. Ind. Ethnozoological Lab., Bloomington, 1947—; curator Ind. U. Museums, Bloomington, 1949—, instr. ethnozoology, 1956—; pres., chmn. bd. Bloomington Nat. Bank. Mem. Ind. Bankers Assn., Independent Bankers Assn., Nat. Assn. Bank Auditors and Comptrollers, Soc. Am. Archaeology, Southwestern Archaeol. Assn., Wilderness Soc., Sierra Club, Audubon Soc., Ind. Hist. Soc., Ind. Acad. Sci., Monroe County Aux. Police. Republican. Clubs: Trowel and Brush, Elks, Ind. Police League, Ind. Chiefs Police. Office: 200 S Washington St Bloomington IN 47401

ADAMSON, GARY, mag. editor, dir. graphics; b. Springfield, Mo., Oct. 16, 1930; s. Vincel T. and Zola D. (McGuire) A.; B.A., Drury Coll., 1959; m. Millicent Winslow Ames, July 1, 1952; children—Margaret, Helen, Ames. Reporter Springfield (Mo.) Newspapers, Inc., 1953-55; news reporter KWTO-Radio, Springfield, 1955; case worker Greene County (Mo.) Juvenile Ct., 1955-57; creative dir. Newcomer Corp., 1960-63; mag. editor Falstaff Brewing Corp., St. Louis, 1963-65; editor Optimist mag., Optimist Internat., St. Louis, 1966—, also dir. graphics. Served with AUS, 1949-51. Mem. Burns Club St. Louis. Contbr. to Ency. Brit. Home: 614 Woodard Dr Kirkwood MO 63122 Office: 4494 Lindell Blvd St Louis MO 63108

ADAMSON, JOHN DOUGLAS, physician, educator; b. St. Boniface, Man., Can., Mar. 1, 1932; s. Gilberth L. and Emma M. (Richter) A.; M.D., U. Man., 1956; m. L. Gail Faulder, Oct. 19, 1957; children—Barbara, Janice, Carol, James, Shelagh, Gavin. Intern Winnipeg (Man.) Gen. Hosp., Can., 1955-56; sr. intern Toronto (Ont.) Gen. Hosp., Can., 1956-57; resident in psychiatry Douglas Hosp., Montreal, Que., Can., 1957-58; jr. asst. resident in medicine Montreal Gen. Hosp., 1958-59; asso. resident in psychiatry Strong Meml. Hosp., Rochester, N.Y., 1959-60, chief resident, 1960-61; practice medicine specializing in psychiatry, Winnipeg, 1961—; instr. Sch. of Medicine and Dentistry, U. Rochester, N.Y., 1960-61; lectr. dept. of psychiatry U. Man., Winnipeg, 1961-63, asst. prof. faculty of medicine, 1963-65, asso. prof. psychiatry, 1965—; dir. psychiat. in-patient unit Winnipeg Health Scis. Centre, 1961-65, mem. courtesy staff, 1961-62, asst. psychiatrist, 1962—, dir. psychiat. clin. investigation, 1965—; mem. Man. Rehab. courtesy staff, 1969—; coordinator psychiat. research Man. Dept. Health and Social Devel., 1965—. Chmn. profl. and tech. adv. com. Alcoholism Found. of Man., 1965-76; mem. adv. com. Man. Mental Health Research Found., 1972-74, chmn., 1974—; mem. subcom. on rehab. Dept. of Nat. Health and Welfare, Ottawa, Ont., Can., 1963-65, subcom. Mental Health Research, 1965-68. Served to sub-lt. Royal Canadian Navy Reserve, 1949-55. Isbister scholar, 1950; R.S. McLaughlin Travelling fellow, 1959-61; certified in psychiatry Royal Coll. Physicians and Surgeons Can. Mem. Canadian (mem. nucleus com. on psychotherapy, 1966-70, chmn. subcom. on tng. 1966-70, editorial bd. 1972—, sci. council 1972-76), Man. (chmn. subcom. on econs. 1964-72) psychiat. assns., Am. Psychosomatic Soc., Canadian Assn. for the Advancement of Health Scis., Canadian Assn. U. Tchrs., Soc. for Psychophysiol. Research, Canadian, Man. med. assns. Contbr. articles on psychiatry to med. jours. Home: 225 Dromore Av Winnipeg MB R3M OJ1 Canada Office: Health Sciences Centre 700 William Av Winnipeg MB R3E 0Z3 Canada

ADAMSON, JOHN RICHARD, city ofcl.; b. Iowa City, Oct. 8, 1941; s. William L. and Helen Frances (Drain) A.; B.A., U. Iowa, 1964, M.A., 1966; m. Susan Michael Mitchell, June 27, 1965; 1 dau., Michelle Suzanne. Adminstrv. asst. to city mgr. City of Iowa City, 1964-66; mgr. Village Wood Dale (Ill.), 1970-71; adminstr. Village of Carol Stream (Ill.), 1971—. Chmn. DuPage Mayor and Mgrs. Conf. Joint Purchasing Com., 1971, conf. dir., 1975—; chmn. DuKane Valley Council Planning and Econ. Devel. Commn., 1972-74, DuPage County Regional Planning Commn., 1975—; instr., Coll. of DuPage, 1972. Served to capt. AUS, 1966-70. Decorated Bronze Star medal; Army Commendation medal. Mem. Internat. (Chgo. met. area urban strategy com., dir. Chgo. met. sect. 1974-76), Am. Pub. Works Assn., Ill. city mgmt. assns., Am. Soc. Planning Ofcls., Municipal Finance Officers Assn., Phi Kappa Sigma. Home: 600 Mohican Rd Carol Stream IL 60187 Office: 415 N Gary Av Carol Stream IL 60187

ADAN, ADELBERTO, clin. scientist; b. Camaguey, Cuba, Aug. 27, 1924; s. Alberto and Blanca (Rius) Adan; B.S., B.A., Camaguey Inst. (Cuba), 1941; Pharm.D., Havana (Cuba) U., 1947; student Central Mich. U., 1965. m. Bertha Cepeda, Aug. 15, 1948; children—Adelberto J., Silvia M. Dir., Adan Pharmacy, Camaguey, Cuba, 1947-60; parasitologist Pub. Health Dept., Camaguey, Cuba, 1948-60; lab. clinician-owner Adan-Rius Clin. Lab., Camaguey, 1948-65; mem. staff Midland (Mich.) Hosp. Center, 1965-68, research scientist, 1968-77; cons. Gelman Instrument Co., Ann Arbor, Mich., 1973-74, Bay Med. Center Lab., Bay City, Mich., 1975—. Treas. Midland chpt. People to People Internat., 1975—. Mem. Am. Pharm. Assn., Am. Inst. History of Pharmacy, Brazilian Inst. History, Am. Assn. Clin. Chemistry, Assn. Clin. Biochemists, Am. Chem. Soc., Am. Assn. Clin. Pathologists. Research on plasmacitic dyscrasias and alpha fetoprotein. Home: 4318 Paine Dr Midland MI 48640 Office: Midland Hosp Center Lab 4005 Orchard Dr Midland MI 48640

ADDICKS, MENTOR CHARLES, JR., lawyer, author; b. Mpls., Dec. 28, 1939; s. Mentor C. and Rubye Gertrude (Chandler) A.; B.A., U. Minn., 1963, J.D., 1966; postgrad. United Theol. Sem. Twin Cities; m. Beverly Ruth Johnson, Dec. 29, 1962; children—Jennifer Kristen, Gregory Charles. Dir. U. Minn. Legal Aid Clinic, 1965-66; admitted to Minn. bar, 1966; asst. atty. Ramsey County, St. Paul, 1966-67; partner Meredith & Addicks, St. Paul, 1968-70; staff atty. Assn. Minn. Counties, St. Paul, 1970-73; legislative counsel League Minn. Cities, St. Paul, 1973—; pres. Addicks Machine Co., Inc., 1973—. Mem. Minn. Bar Assn., Wider Quaker Fellowship, Minn. Soc. Assn. Execs., Luth. Ch. Library Assn., Minn. Christian Writers Guild (v.p.), Minn. Assn. Commerce and Industry, Authors Guild, Phi Delta Phi, Chi Phi (pres., dir. Gamma Delta alumni assn. 1966-73). Lutheran. Mason (Shriner, 32deg.). Author: Looking Forward to a Career in Law, 1971; Handbook for Statutory Cities, 1975. Contbr. poetry to lit. mags., also devotions, book revs., articles to religious mags. Home: 19511 E Front Blvd NE Wyoming MN 55092 Office: Hanover Bldg St Paul MN 55103

ADDINGTON, LEONARD MILTON, lawyer; b. Owatonna, Minn., June 23, 1936; s. Milton Clarence and Dorothy Evelyn (Lufi) A.; student Austin Jr. Coll., 1954-56; B.A., U. Minn., 1958; LL.B., Yale, 1961; m. Mary Hammerstrom, June 1, 1968; children—David, John. Admitted to Minn. bar, 1961; mem. firm Best & Flanagan, Mpls., 1966—, partner, 1968—. Mem. Citizens League, Mpls., 1966—. Bd. dirs. Met. Med. Center, 1973—, vice chmn., 1977—. Served to lt. USNR, 1961-66. Mem. Am., Minn., Hennepin County bar assns. Episcopalian. Clubs: Minneapolis Athletic, Minikakda Country. Home: 4305 Country Club Rd Edina MN 55424 Office: 4040 IDS Center Minneapolis MN 55402

ADDIS, WINSTON CLARK, sch. supt.; b. Oswego, N.Y., Nov. 13, 1938; s. Laird Clark and Dora Ersel (Webber) A.; B.A., U. Iowa, 1960, M.A., 1964, Ph.D., 1968; m. Georgie Ann Johansen, July 23, 1961; children—Shaunda Lynn, Lisa Ann, Cameron Clark. Math. tchr. Mt. Vernon (Iowa) High Sch., 1960-63, prin., 1963-66; research asst. U. Iowa, Iowa City, 1966-67; elementary sch. prin. Durant Community Sch., Durant, Iowa, 1967-68; supr. research Milw. Pub. Schs., 1968-69; research and devel. specialist N.W. Regional Ednl. Lab., Portland, Oreg., 1969-73; supt. schs. Mt. Vernon Community Schs., 1973—. Mem. Planning and Zoning Commn., Mt. Vernon, 1973—, chmn., 1977. Mem. Am., Iowa assns. sch. adminstrs., Assn. Ednl. Data Systems, Iowa Assn. Ednl. Data Systems (dir. 1974—), Assn. for Supervision and Curriculum Devel., Am. Ednl. Research Assn., Nat. Assn. Secondary Sch. Prins., Oreg. Council for Computer Edn. (dir. 1971-73), U. Iowa Alumni Assn., Phi Delta Kappa. Democrat. Methodist. Lion. Author: (with J. Edwards, D. Richardson) Introduction to Computers, 10 vols., 1973; (with K. Breitenbucher) Administrator Training Course, 8 vols., 1974; (with Breitenbucher, Edwards, Lynch, Richardson) Computer Careers, 8 vols., 1974. Home: 707 3d Ave N Mount Vernon IA 52314

ADDISON, CORNELIUS PHILIP, surgeon; b. Grand Haven, Mich., Aug. 4, 1917; s. Cornelius John and Caroline Anna (Coon) A.; A.B., U. Calif., Berkeley, 1940; M.D., Creighton U., 1943; m. Virginia Ellen Casey, Sept. 24, 1944; children—Sharon, Michael, Brian, Constance, Barbara, Christopher, Ellen, Jon. Intern, St. Mary's Hosp., San Francisco, 1944; resident in surgery Vets. Hosp., Des Moines, 1946-50; staff surgeon Sioux Falls (S.D.) Vets. Hosp., 1950-51; practice medicine specializing in surgery, Ft. Dodge, Iowa, 1951-52, Waterloo, Iowa, 1952—. Served with AUS, 1944-46. Diplomate Am. Bd. Surgery. Fellow A.C.S.; mem. AMA, Iowa Med. Assn., Black Hawk County Med. Soc. Republican. Roman Catholic. Clubs: Elks, K.C., Sunnyside Country. Home: 1128 Ridgemont Rd Waterloo IA 50701 Office: 201 Professional Bldg Saint Francis Dr Waterloo IA 50702

ADDUCCI, JOSEPH EDWARD, gynecologist; b. Chgo., Dec. 1, 1934; s. Dominee Edward and Harriet Evelyn (Kneppreth) A.; B.S., U. Ill.; M.D., Loyola U., Chgo.; m. Mary Ann Tietje, Sept. 16, 1958; children—Christopher, Gregory, Steven, Jessica, Tobias. Intern, Cook County Hosp., Chgo., 1959-60; resident Mt. Carmel Hosp., Detroit, 1960-64; practice medicine specializing in obstetrics and gynecology Williston, N.D., 1966—; chief staff, chmn. obstetrics dept. Mercy, Good Samaritan hosps. (both Williston); obstetrician-gynecologist Craven Hagen Clinic, Williston; instr. U. N.D. Med. Sch., 1973—. Mem. N.D. Bd. Med. Examiners, 1974—; project dir. Tri County Family Planning Service; past pres. Tri County Health Planning Council. Chmn., Williams County Welfare Bd., 1966—. Served with M.C., AUS, 1964-66. Diplomate Am. Bd. Obstetrics and Gynecology. Fellow Am. Soc. Abdominal Surgeons, A.C.S., Am. Coll. Obstetrics and Gynecologists (sect. chmn. N.D.), Internat. Coll. Surgeons (regent 1972-74), Am. Fertility Soc., Soc. Gynecol. Laparopists, N.D. Obstetricians and Gynecologists Soc. (pres. 1966, 76). Elk. Home: 1717 Main St Williston ND 58801 Office: Med Center Williston ND 58801

ADDY, ALVA LEROY, mech. engr.; b. Dallas, S.D., Mar. 28, 1936; s. Alva Isaac and Nellie Amelia (Brumbaugh) A.; B.S., S.D. Sch. Mines and Tech., 1958; M.S., U. Cin., 1960; Ph.D., U. Ill., 1963; m. Sandra Ruth Turney, June 8, 1958. Engr., Gen. Electric Co., Lancaster, Calif. and Cin., 1958-60; prof. mech. engring. U. Ill., Urbana, 1963—, dir. mech. engring. lab., 1965—; aerodynamics cons. U.S. Army Missile Command, Radstone Arsenal, Ala., summers 1965—; cons. U.S. Army Research Office, 1964—; cons. in high-speed fluid dynamics to indsl. firms, 1963—; vis. research prof. U.S. Army, 1976; lectr. Von Karman Inst. Fluid Dynamics, Brussels, 1968, 73, 76. Fellow Am. Inst. Aeros. and Astronautics (asso.); mem. ASME, Soc. Engring. Edn., Sigma Xi, Pi Tau Sigma, Sigma Tau. Home: 1706 Golfview Dr Urbana IL 61801 Office: 208 Mech Engring Lab U Ill Urbana IL 61801

ADE, WALTER FRANK CHARLES, educator; b. Ottawa, Ont., Can., Oct. 24, 1910; s. Leonard Konrad and Bertha Pauline (Rhode) A.; came to U.S., 1949, naturalized, 1954; B.A. (Ellen M. Nickle Meml. fellow), Queen's U., Can., 1933; M.A., U. Toronto, 1939, B.Paed., 1943, M.Ed., 1945; Ph.D., Northwestern U., 1949; M.S. in Edn., Ind. U., 1955, Ed.D., 1960; postdoctoral diplomas, U. Erlangen-Nürnberg, 1955, U. Munich, 1956, U. Heidelberg, 1957; m. Eleanor Anne Schroeder, June 28, 1941; children—Virginia Anne (Mrs. Robert Miller), George Leonard. Lectr., U. Toronto, 1933-38, Lisgar Collegiate Inst., Ottawa, 1939-49; asso. prof. Valparaiso (Ind.) U., 1949-58, Ariz. State U., Tempe, 1958-59; prof. modern langs. and edn. Purdue U., Hammond, Ind., 1959-76, prof. emeritus, 1976—, chmn. dept. modern langs., 1959-67. Editor, Agrl. Bulls., Dept. Agr., Toronto, 1934-36; Studienprofessor, Oberrealschule mit humanistischem Gymnasium, Nördlingen/Bavaria/W.Germany, 1956-57; profl. research W.Germany, 1964-65, 67-68; profl. translator, 1966—. Examiner, Coll. Entrance English, Toronto, 1936-39; air raid warden Can., 1940-44; instr. first aid and atomic warfare Can., 1940-44; examiner German and French for naval cadets Fed. Civil Service Commn., Ottawa, 1941-43. Served as flying officer RCAF, 1943-45. P.Q. fellow in French, 1944, Northwestern U. research fellow, 1945-46, Ind. U. grad. research fellow, 1954-55, Fulbright fellow to Germany, 1955-56, Valparaiso U. travel grantee, 1957-58, Purdue Research Found. grantee, 1964-65, Purdue U. travel grantee, 1967-68. Life fellow Internat. Inst. Arts and Letters, Switzerland, Intercontinental Biog. Assn., Cambridge, Eng.; mem. Ind. Fgn. Lang. Tchrs. Assn. (sec.-treas. 1953-57), Am. Assn. Tchrs. German (sec.-treas. Ind. chpt. 1953-55), Sigma Phi Epsilon, Kappa Phi Tau. Club: Canadian (Chgo.). Author numerous books and monographs. Home: 8021 Schreiber Dr Munster IN 46321 Office: Purdue U Classroom-Office Bldg Room 246-E Woodmar at 173d St Hammond IN 46323

ADEGBILE, GIDEON SUNDAY ADEBISI, physician; b. Iree, Nigeria, May 18, 1941; s. John Bimpe and Sarah Oyefunke (Awoyemi) A.; came to U.S., 1962, naturalized, 1974; B.S. cum laude, Va. Union U., 1966; M.D., Meharry Med. Coll., 1971; m. Doris Mae Goodman, June 10, 1966; children—Lisa Aderonke, Titilayo Angel, Babalola Oluwole. Intern, Good Samaritan Hosp., Dayton, Ohio, 1971-72; emergency physician PEG, Inc., Dayton, 1972-75; community health physician Drexel Health Center, Dayton, 1972-73; practice medicine specializing in family medicine Dayton, 1973—; clin. instr. Wright State U. Sch. Medicine, 1975—; med. dir. Christel Manor Nursing Home; part-time physician City of Dayton, 1973—. Recipient certificate of appreciation Christel Manor Nursing Home, 1977. Mem. AMA, Ohio State, Nat. med. assns., Montgomery County Med. Soc., Am. Coll. Emergency Physicians, NAACP, Alpha Phi Alpha. Democrat. Baptist. Clubs: Tennis Racket. Research on drug abuse. Home: 1617 Burbank Dr Dayton OH 45406 Office: 2230 Germantown St Dayton OH 45408

ADELBERGER, WILLIAM HENRY, dentist, educator; b. Dayton, Ohio, Nov. 24, 1925; s. Henry William and Clara Bell (Pierce) A.; student Ohio State U., 1943-45; B.S., U. Miami, 1959; D.D.S. (Alpha Omega scholar), Case Western Res. U., 1963; m. Marilyn Ann Johnson, July 23, 1949; children—Susan Beth, William Henry, Robert. Partner Adelberger & Gancarz, bldg. contractors, Coral Gables, Fla., 1948-59; pvt. practice dentistry, South Miami, Fla., 1963-65, Cleve., 1965—; faculty Case Western Res. U., Sch. of Dentistry, Cleve., 1965—, asso. prof. dir. clinic, 1971—. Dental dir. maternity and infant care project Cleve. Met. Gen. Hosp., 1966-70, cons., 1972—. Recipient Key Man award Coral Gables (Fla.) Jr. C. of C., 1950; Outstanding Faculty award Case Western Res. U. Sch. Dentistry, 1968. Fellow Am. Coll. Dentists; mem. Delta Sigma Delta, Omicron Kappa Upsilon. Patentee in field. Home: 1375 Yellowstone Rd Cleveland Heights OH 44121 Office: 2123 Abington Rd Cleveland OH 44106

ADELMAN, BETSY COLLEN, rehab. adminstr.; b. Chgo., Ill., Apr. 4, 1930; d. Harold I. and Florence (Grossman) Collen; B.A., Roosevelt U., 1970, M.A., 1976; children—Cary, Grant, Skyler. Mem. staff Chgo. Town News, 1969-70; tchr. Chgo. Lighthouse for Blind, 1970-72, dir. office skills tng. programs, 1973—; tchr. visually handicapped Wright Jr. Coll., 1974, 75. Den mother Cub Scouts, 1962-68. Ill. Div. Vocat. Rehab. grantee, 1975, 77. Mem. Am. Personnel and Guidance Assn., Nat. Rehab. Assn., Nat. Rehab. Counselors Assn., Am. Assn. Workers for the Blind, Am. Rehab. Counselors Assn., Word Processing Mgmt. Assn. Chgo., Internat. Word Processing Assn., Ill. Rehab. Assn., Ill. Fedn. of Blind, Roosevelt U. Alumni Assn. Home: 8930 N Kolmar Ave Skokie IL 60076 Office: 1850 W Roosevelt Rd Chicago IL 60608

ADELMAN, RAPHAEL MARTIN, physician, hosp. adminstr.; b. Plainfield, N.J., May 4, 1915; s. Samuel and Betty (Taich) A.; D.D.S., U. Pa., 1939; M.Sc., Northwestern U., 1940; B.M., Chgo. Med. Sch., 1943, M.D., 1944; m. Charlotte Mary Koepke, Aug. 25, 1945; children—Karen Rae, Robert John. Intern Norwegian-Am. Hosp., Chgo., 1943-44; asso. in surgery Chgo. Med. Sch., 1945-50; asso. in plastic surgery to Dr. A.M. Brown, Chgo., 1946-50; gen. practice medicine, Wauconda, Ill., 1950—; chief staff St. Therese Hosp., 1963—, chief exec. com., 1965, asst. adminstr., med. dir., 1965—; v.p. med. affairs, 1973, dir., 1974—; chief sect. ear nose throat Victory Meml. Hosp., Waukegan, 1963, 65-66; med. dir. Am. Hosp. Supply Corp.; cons. physician Coll. Lake County Health Services Trust; physician cons. utilization rev. Region V. HEW, 1973-75, cons. quality and standards, 1975; physician cons. Lake County Bd. Health, 1974-76; cons. continuing med. edn. Downey VA Hosp., 1974-76; authorized agt. for Lake County, Ill. Dept. Pub. Health, 1974-76, Mem. exec. com. Lake County chpt. Am. Cancer Soc., 1963—; pres. Wauconda High Sch. Bd. Edn., 1954-60; mem. Wauconda Grade Sch. Bd. Edn., 1952-60; chmn. health and safety N.W. Dist., North Suburban council Boy Scouts Am., 1964-65, vice. chmn. N.W. dist. North Shore council, 1967, 75, mem. exec. com. Northeastern Ill. council; mem. Lake County Health Services Com., 1969—; mem. profl. adv. com. United Community Services Planning Div., 1969—; mem. exec. com., exec. bd. Evanston-North Shore Area Council, 1969; mem. mgmt. com. Lake County Mental Health Clinic, 1967-69; mem. budget and fin. com., 1968-69; group chmn. Regional Conf. on Health Care Costs, Health, Edn. and Welfare, Cleve., 1968; del. Hosp. Planning Council Chgo., 1967-69; chmn. subcom. Ill. Hosp. Licensing Bd. Com., 1969; pres. 1968-69 class U. Ala. Health Service Adminstrs. Devel. Program; chmn. Lake County (Ill.) Health Services Planning Council, Inc.; mem. regional com. Hosp. Admission Surveillance Program, State of Ill., 1972-77; mem. Lake County Drug Commn., 1972-73; mem. Lake County Bd. Health, 1973-77; chmn. orgn. and search com. for exec. dir. Lake County Health Dept.; mem. com. on search for dean univ. health scis. Chgo. Med. Sch., 1975; mem. Lake County Coroner's Adv. Commn., 1977; mem. adv. council health edn. programs Coll. Lake County, 1970-77; bd. dirs. Blumberg Blood Bank; bd. dirs. St. Therese Nurse Scholarship Fund, 1962, Lake County Health Planning Council, 1969-72. Fellow Am. Pub. Health Assn. (community health edn. accreditation panel 1975-76), AAAS, Chgo. Inst. Medicine, Royal Soc. Health, Am. Acad. Med. Adminstrs., Soc. for Acad. Achievement (life), Am. Coll. Hosp. Adminstrs.; mem. Am., Ill. (state del. 1960-63, dir.), Lake County (past pres.) acads. gen. practice, AMA, ADA, Assn. Mil. Surgeons of U.S., Ill. Hosp. Assn. (ad hoc com. emergency radio network 1969, state com. safety 1972-77), Ill. Soc. Med. Research, Ill. Med. Soc. (com. physician-hosp. relationship 1974-75), Am. Acad. Dental Radiology, Am. Acad. Family Practice (del. 1974—), Ill. Pub. Health Assn. (exec. council 1976-78), Assn. Hosp. Med. Assn. (resources com. 1976-78), Ill. Found. Med. Care (utilization rev. ednl. accreditation program com. 1973-75, ad hoc com. utilization rev. 1973-75), Am. Coll. Preventive Medicine, Sigma Xi, Alpha Omega, Phi Lambda Kappa. Home: 1202 Oak Trail Dr Libertyville IL 60048 Office: St Therese Hosp Waukegan IL 60085

ADELSTEIN, HERMAN, orthodontist; b. Cleve., Mar. 3, 1908; s. Simon and Dina (Fertel) A.; D.D.S., U. Louisville, 1930, certificate orthodontia, 1933; postgrad. Columbia, 1942, 44, U. Toronto, 1947, U. Detroit, 1948, Begg-Kesling course, 1959; m. Fannie Ruth Peskin, Oct. 7, 1934; children—Stephen, Arthur. Gen. practice dentistry, Cleveland Heights, Ohio, 1930-32, practice limited to orthodontics, 1933—; asst. clinician Mt. Sinai Hosp., 1936-39, clinician, 1940-44, clinician charge orthodontia dept., 1947-60, mem. staff, orthodontist out patient dept., 1961—, orthodontic mem. Edward Reiter Cleft Palate Team, 1948-59; orthodontic cons. Polyclinic Hosp., 1963—. Chmn., University Heights council Boy Scouts Am., 1946-47; mem. Mus. Arts Assn. Cleve. Orch., 1962-70, Cleve. Inst. Music, 1937—. Served to lt. USNR, 1944-46. Mem. Am., Ohio dental assns., Cleve. Dental Soc. (chmn. program spring meeting 1951), Am. Assn. Orthodontists, Great Lakes, Cleve. socs. orthodontists, Alpha Omega (Merit award 1965, nat. regent 1941-42, nat. chmn. 1958). Home: 31849 Gates Mills Blvd Pepper Pike OH 44124 Office: Severance Med Arts Bldg Cleveland Heights OH 44118

ADLER, ABRAHAM DAVID, accounting firm exec.; b. Steubenville, Ohio, Jan. 20, 1921; s. Isaac and Rebecca (Rubenstein) A.; student Robert Morris Coll., 1940-43; m. Shirley Katz, Dec. 2, 1944; children—Ruth G. (Mrs. Donn R. Rosensweig), Elaine J., Sidney W., Leon R., Jane A. Individual practice accounting, Steubenville, 1940-59; partner Adler, Faunce & Leonard, 1959-68; mng. partner Adler & Co., Pitts., 1968-70, Columbus, Ohio, 1970-73; mng. partner J.K. Lasser & Co., Columbus, 1973-77; partner Touche Ross & Co., Columbus, 1977—. Mem. Steubenville Bd. Edn., 1970. Served with F.A., AUS, 1942-43. C.P.A., Ohio, Pa., W.Va., La. Mem. Steubenville C. of C. (pres. 1956). Home: 380 S Merkle Rd Columbus OH 43209 Office: 250 E Broad St Columbus OH 43215

ADLER, DAVID LEO, pathologist; b. N.Y.C., Sept. 5, 1913; s. Herman and Rose (Herskovitz) A.; A.B., Ind. U., 1934, M.D., 1938; m. Mary Jane Sanders, June 27, 1939; children—David W., Philip I, Douglas R. Intern, St. Elizabeth Hosp., Dayton, Ohio, 1938-39; instr. in pathology, Sch. Medicine, U. Tex., Galveston, 1939-40, Sch. Medicine, N.Y. U., N.Y.C., 1946-47; dir. lab. Bartholomew County Hosp., Columbus, Ind., 1947-74; dir. lab. Columbus Med. Lab., 1976—; dir. lab. Indpls. Med. Lab., 1976—. Dir. ARC, 1950-70; pres. Ind. State Bd. Health, 1960-64; pres. Negro Scholarship Found., 1960-61. Served with M.C. U.S. Army, 1941-46. Recipient commendations, Ind. Gov., Ind. Bd. Health, ARC. Mem. Ind. State, Bartholomew County Med. Socs., Coll. Am. Pathologists, Am. Soc. Clin. Pathologists. Contbr. articles to profl. mags. Home: 4224 N Riverside Dr Columbus IN 47201 Office: Doctors Park Columbus IN 47201

ADLER, GERSON, corp. exec.; b. Berlin, Germany, Oct. 2, 1927; s. Max and Rosy (Lange) A.; came to U.S., 1939, naturalized, 1945; student Coll. City N.Y., 1946-56, Western Res. U., 1954-63, Rabbinical Coll. Telshe, 1950-51; m. Naomi Samuel, Aug. 1, 1950; children—Don, Samson, Nathan, Eli, Hillel, Ezra, Zahava Sarah. Owner, operator Eagle Day Camp, N.Y.C., 1948-50; dir. Hebrew Acad. Cleve., 1951-61; inventory controller Am. Greetings Corp., Cleve., 1961-62, dir. audits, 1962-65, asst. v.p., 1965-68, v.p. audit and research, 1968-71; exec. v.p. Courtland Group and affiliated cos., 1971-74; mgmt. cons. Gerson Adler and Assos., Cleveland Heights, Ohio, 1974—; pres., dir. Courtland Communications Corp.; exec. v.p. Andover Crest & Co., Inc., Courtland Capital Corp., Courtland Hosp. Systems Corp. Lectr. Am. Mgmt. Assn., 1970; cons. audit standards U.S. Gen. Accounting Office, 1970-72. Mem. Ohio Sch. Survey Commn., 1966-67; chmn. com. legislative auditor, State of Ohio, 1970-72; pres. Agudath Israel Orgn., 1961—. Chmn. bd. Rabbinical Coll. Telshe; bd. dirs. Citizens for Ednl. Freedom, Hebrew Acad. Cleve., 1952—, mem. community relations com. 1968—. Mem. Inst. Internal Auditors (pres. 1967), Cleve. Growth Assn. Address: 3595 Severn Rd Cleveland OH 44118

ADLER, SEYMOUR JACK, social work exec.; b. Chgo., Oct. 22, 1930; s. Michael L. and Sarah (Pasnick) A.; B.S., Northwestern U., 1952; M.A., U. Chgo., 1958; m. Barbara Fingold, Mar. 24, 1958; children—Susan Lynn, Karen Sandra, Michelle Lauren. Caseworker, Cook County Dept. Pub. Aid, Chgo., 1955; juvenile officer Cook County Sheriff's Office, 1955-56; U.S. probation-parole officer U.S. Dist. Ct., Chgo., 1958-68; exec. dir. Youth Guidance, Chgo., 1968-73; dir. court services Juvenile ct. Cook County, Chgo., 1973-75; exec. dir. Methodist Youth Services, Chgo., 1975—. Mem. Ill. Law Enforcement Commn., 1969-72; instr. corrections program Chgo. State U., 1972-75. Served to 1st lt. USMCR, 1952-55. Recipient Morris J. Wexler award Ill. Acad. Criminology, 1975, Meritorious Service award Chgo. City Colls., 1968. Mem. Ill. Acad. Criminology (pres. 1972), Nat. Assn. Social Workers (chmn. corrections council), Ill. Probation, Parole & Correctional Assn., Alpha Kappa Delta, Tau Delta Phi. Contbr. articles in field to profl. jours. Home: 2524 Happy Hollow Rd Glenview IL 60025 Office: 542 S Dearborn St Chicago IL 60605

ADSIT, FRANK DANIEL, mfg. co. exec.; b. St. Paul, Oct. 11, 1911; s. Frank Wilson and Elizabeth (Kearns) A.; student U. Minn., 1929-32; m. Helen M. Truhler; children—Joan (Mrs. Harold F. Mann), Michael D. Salesman, John Hancock Ins. Co., 1935-36; clk., White Store Grocery, 1932-35; candy maker Griggs Cooper Co., 1936-40; apprentice machinist Serley Mfg. Co., St. Paul, 1940-42, tool and die maker, 1940-46, mgr., 1941-46, owner, 1946—; pres. Bal-Met Corp., St. Paul, 1969—; dir. Refining Systems, Inc. Patentee in field. Home: 6213 St Croix Trail N Apt 203 Stillwater MN 55082 Office: 267 E Fillmore Ave St Paul MN 55107

ADUSS, HOWARD, orthodontist, educator; b. Bklyn., Mar. 31, 1932; s. Irving and Yvette (Rothwax) A.; B.S., Purdue U., 1954; D.D.S., Northwestern U., 1957; M.S., U. Rochester, 1962; m. Marcia Joyce Katz, Dec. 27, 1953; children—Kathy, Laura, Robert, Deborah. Prof. orthodontics U. Ill. Med. Center, Chgo., 1962—; pvt. practice orthodontics, Skokie, Ill., 1962—; cons. St. Francis Hosp., Evanston, 1970—, Cook County Hosp., Chgo., 1968—; prof. surgery Rush Presbyn. Med. Center, Chgo., 1973. Served to lt. USNR, 1957-59. NIH postdoctoral fellow, 1961-62, Office Naval Research fellow, 1960-61. Diplomate Am. Bd. Orthodontics. Fellow Am. Coll. Dentists; mem. Am. Cleft Palate Assn. (treas. 1967-69, v.p. 1972-73, pres. 1975-76), Internat. Assn. Dental Research (sec.-treas. craniofacial biology group 1969—), Sigma Xi. Contbr. to profl. publs. in field of craniofacial malformations. Home: 237 Lakeside Pl Highland Park IL 60035 Office: Univ Ill Med Center PO Box 6998 Chicago IL 60680

AFFELDT, GEORGE RICHARD, lawyer; b. Milw., Jan. 27, 1921; s. George A. and Esther R. (Blaesser) A.; B.A., U. Wis., 1943, LL.B., 1948; m. Nancy T. Fellenz, Feb. 12, 1944; children—George Richard, Mark Steven, Caryl Ann, Sue Ellen, David Arthur, Steven Andrew, John Alan. Admitted to Wis. bar, 1948; asso. Affeldt & Lichtsinn, Milw., 1948-52, partner, 1952-63; ind. practice law, Milw., 1964—; counsel Systems, Inc., Menomonee Falls, Wis., 1961—; dir. Hydro-Flo Products, Brookfield, Wis. Active Wis. Student Aid Found.; fund raising campaigns U. Wis. Found., Elevejhem Art Center, U. Wis. Bd. visitors U. Wis., 1971-77; mem. U. Wis.-Madison Athletic Bd.; bd. dirs. U. Wis. Found. Trustee, guardian various legal matters in local cts. Served with USNR, 1943-45; comdr. Res. ret. Mem. Am., Wis., Milw. (past treas., exec. com. 1966-71, pres. 1969-70) bar assns., Milw. Bar Assn. Found. (pres. 1972-74), Am. Judicature Soc., U. Wis. Alumni Club Milw. (past pres.), Wis. Alumni Assn. (dir., pres. 1977—), Central Wis. Law Alumni Assn. Methodist (mem. adminstrv. bd., trustee). Lion (pres. 1973-74). Club: National W (past pres.); Wisconsin. Home: 154 N 89th St Wauwatosa WI 53226 Office: 740 N Plankinton Ave Milwaukee WI 53203

AGGARWAL, RAJ KUMAR, educator; b. Jagraon, Punjab, India, June 27, 1947; s. Nathu Ram and Pushpa Vati Gupta; B.Tech., Indian Inst. Tech., New Delhi, 1968; M.B.A., Kent State U., 1970, D.B.A., 1975; postgrad. U. Chgo., 1972-73; m. Karen L. Blackburn, May 15, 1976. Tech. dir., dir. Agerson Electronic and Gen. Industries Ltd., New Delhi, 1966-68; grad. appointee, teaching fellow Kent (Ohio) State U., 1968-72; coordinator finance area, faculty lectr. Ind. U. N.W., Gary, 1972-74; asst. prof. finance Seton Hall U., South Orange, N.J., 1974-76; asso. prof. finance U. Toledo, 1976—. Mem. Fin. Mgmt. Assn., Fin. Execs. Inst., Am. Finance Assn., Acad. Internat. Bus., Inst. Mgmt. Sci., Am. Inst. Decision Scis., So. Internat. Devel., Beta Gamma Sigma, Delta Sigma Pi. Author: Financial Policies for the Multinational Company: The Management of Foreign Exchange, 1976; (with Inder Khera) Applications in Management Science: Cases, 1977; International Business Finance: A Selected Bibliography, 1977; contbr. articles to profl. jours. Home: 2667 Cheltenham Rd Toledo OH 43606 Office: 2801 W Bancroft St Toledo OH 43606

AGRAWAL, BHUPENDRA KISHOR, heavy machinery mfg. co. exec., indsl. engr.; b. Faizabad, India, Jan. 1, 1939; s. Gopal Kishor and Padma Vati (Rai) A.; came to U.S., 1964; B.S. in Math., Allahabad U., India, 1956; B.M.E., Rourkee U., India, 1960; M.S. in Indsl. Engring., Okla. State U., 1965; M.B.A., U. Wis., 1969; m. Sudhi Mital, Jan. 12, 1970; children—Amitabh K., Anurag K. (boys). Engr. trainee Uttar Pradesh Irrigation Dept., Allahabad, 1960-62; asst. engr. Heavy Engring. Corp., Ranchi, India, 1962-64; indsl. engr. Allis Chalmers Corp., Milw., 1965-66, sr. indsl. engr., 1966-67, mgmt. sci. analyst, 1967-68, sr. analyst, 1968-69, coordinator engring. and mfg. systems, 1969-71, mfg. cons., 1971-73, mgr. mfg. systems, 1973-76, gen. mgr., 1977—; mem. faculty dept. engring. and mgmt. U. Wis., Milw., 1969-75; cons. UN Indsl. Devel. Orgn., 1974-76. Recipient Outstanding Service award Allis Chalmers Corp., 1973; registered profl. engr., Wis. Mem. Am. Inst. Indsl. Engrs. (sr.). Office: 1126 S 70th St Milwaukee WI 53201

AGRE, COURTLAND LEVERNE, educator; b. Boyd, Minn., Sept. 11, 1913; s. Peter Cornelius and Mathilda Louise (Quaal) A.; B. Chem. Engring., U. Minn., 1934, Ph.D., 1937; m. Ellen Swedberg, Aug. 24, 1946; children—Annetta (Mrs. Gary Anderson), Peter, James, Paul, Ruth, Mark. Researcher E.I. duPont de Nemours, Wilmington, Del., 1937-41, 3M Co., St. Paul, 1942-46; prof. chemistry Augsburg Coll., Mpls., 1959—. Cons. 3M Co. Served with CAC, 1940-41. Mem. Am. Chem. Soc. (recipient Minn. award 1966). Home: 3104 40th Ave S Minneapolis MN 55406

AGRUSS, NEIL STUART, physician; b. Chgo., June 2, 1939; s. Meyer and Frances (Spector) A.; B.S., U. Ill., 1960, M.D., 1963; m. Alice Jane Goldberg, Aug. 11, 1965; children—David, Lauren, Michael. Intern, U. Ill. Hosp., Chgo., 1963-64, resident in internal medicine, 1964-65, 67-68; fellow in cardiology, Cin. Gen. Hosp., 1968-70, dir. coronary care unit, 1971-74, dir. echocardiography lab., 1972-74; dir. cardiac diagnostic labs., Central DuPage Hosp., Winfield, Ill., 1974—; asst. prof. medicine, U. Cin., 1970-74, Rush Med. Coll., 1976—. Chmn. coronary care com. Heart Assn. DuPage County, 1974—; active Congregation Etz Chaim, Lombard, Ill. Served to capt. M.C. U.S. Army, 1965-67. Diplomate Am. Bd. Internal Medicine. Fellow A.C.P., Am. Coll. Cardiology, Am. Coll. Chest Physicians, Council Clin. Cardiology, Am. Heart Assn.; mem. AMA, DuPage County, Ill. State Med. Socs., Am. Fedn. Clin. Research, Chgo. Heart Assn. Author and co-author publs. in field. Office: 454 Pennsylvania St Glen Ellyn IL 60137

AGUIAR, H. ALEXANDER, banker; b. Ecuador, Nov. 1, 1939; s. Eliseo Segundo and Victoria Ochea (Zaona) A.; B.A., Mil. Acad. Ecuador, 1958; M.A., Central U. Ecuador, 1965; Ph.D., Ohio Christian U., 1973; postgrad. San Marco, Lima, Peru, 1965-66, U. Madrid, 1966-67; m. Patricia Merubia Estabrooke, June 7, 1961; children—Debbie Jean, Alex. Came to U.S., 1969. Midwest regional dir. Spanish div. Grolier Interstate, Chgo., 1969-71; v.p., asst. to pres. Amalgamated Trust & Savs. Bank, Chgo., 1971—; dir. Minority Purchasing Council/Chgo. Community Ventures, Inc. Mem. adv. bd. Lt. Gov's. Office, 1973—, Sheriff Cook County, 1974—, WGN-TV, 1973—, WLS-TV Oiga Amigo, 1972-73, WCIU-TV, Ayda, 1972—, Merit Com.-Youth Motivation, 1974—, State Ill. Alcoholism Council, 1973—, Cath. Charities, 1974—. Bd. dirs. Esperanza Sch., Drug Abuse Council, Central States Inst. Addiction, Boys Scouts Chgo. council, Camp Fire Girls. Recient Banker of Year award Nat. Econ. Devel. Assn., 1974, Best Friends award El Rincon Community Project, 1972, William D. Saltiel award for community service Chgo. Jaycees, 1972. Mem. Mexican Am. Labor, Puerto Rican Educators Ill., Hispano Am. Jr. C. of C. (dir. 1971-74). Club: Masons. Office: 100 S State St Chicago IL 60603

AHERN, JOHN FRANCIS, educator; b. Manchester, N.H., Oct. 14, 1936; s. John F. and Mary Margaret (Devine) A.; B.S., Boston Coll., 1958; M.A. in Edn., U. Mass., 1960, Ed.D., 1969; m. Anne O'Brien, Apr. 18, 1964. Tchr., Chicopee, Mass., 1960-64, Wahconah Regional, Dalton, Mass., 1964-65; instr. U. Mass., Amherst, 1967-69; prof. U. Toledo, 1969—; vice chmn. Rossford Bd. Edn., 1976—. Served to capt. U.S. Army, 1958. Mem. Nat. Council Social Studies, Humanistic Planning Com. Democrat. Roman Catholic. Author: Ideas-A Handbook for Teaching Elementary Social Studies, 1976. Home: 30531 E River Rd Perrysburg OH 43551 Office: U Toledo Coll Edn 2801 W Bancroft St Toledo OH 43606

AHERN, JOHN JOSEPH, lawyer; b. Chgo., Aug. 13, 1925; s. Michael J. and Genevieve (Donahue) A.; student Loyola U., Chgo., 1946-47, Northwestern U., 1948-49, DePaul U., 1950; J.D., DePaul U., 1961; m. Jayne E. Sennett, Apr. 18, 1953; children—Ellen L., John Joseph, Brian P., Jeanette R., Marjorie J., Mary Beth. Patrolman, Chgo. Police Dept., 1952-59; security insp. Chgo. Bd. Edn., 1959-62; admitted to Ill. bar, 1962; mem. firm Connelly, Callahan, Ahern & Ahern, Chgo., 1963—. Chmn. inquiry panel C, Attys. Registration and Discipline Commn., Supreme Ct. Ill., 1974—. Pack com. chmn. Boy Scouts Am., 1963-64, mem. troop com., 1965-68, chmn., 1969—, chmn. family fund dri. Trailblazer dist., 1964, finance chmn., 1965. Served with USN, 1943-46, 50-52. Mem. Ill., Chgo. (mem. inquiry com. 1972—) bar assns., Am. Legion, Phi Alpha Delta. Elk. Club: Trial Lawyers (Chgo.). Home: 6329 N Hermitage Av Chicago IL 60660 Office: 77 W Washington St Chicago IL 60602 also 1737 W Devon Av Chicago IL 60660

AHERN, PAUL LEE, lawyer; b. Edina, Mo., Dec. 11, 1919; s. Francis William and Noema (Sandknop) A.; B.S., U. Denver, 1941; J.D., DePaul U., 1949; m. Elayne Kelly, June 25, 1949; children—Paul L., Mary Layne, James K., Mark T., Patrick J. Chemist E.I. duPont Co., Wilmington, Del., 1941-46; admitted to Ill. bar, 1950; lawyer Spencer, Marzall, Johnston & Cook, Chgo., 1950-52, Abbott Labs., North Chgo., 1952-61; partner Leydig, Voit, Osann, Mayer and Holt, Ltd., Chgo., 1964—. Instr. John Marshall Law Sch., Chgo., 1959—. Chmn. Lake County Red Cross, 1957-58. Alderman Lake Forest City Council, 1961-67. Pres., Lake Forest Open Lands Assn. Mem. Chgo., Am. bar assns., Am., Chgo. patent law assns. Clubs: Onwentsia Winter, (Lake Forest), Law, University (Chgo.). Home: 1350 N Green Bay Rd Lake Forest IL 60045 Office: One IBM Plaza Chicago IL 60611

AHLBERG, CLARK DAVID, univ. pres.; b. Wichita, Kans., May 23, 1918; A.B., U. Wichita, 1939; M.A. (Maxwell fellow), Syracuse U., 1942, Ph.D. in Polit. Sci., 1951, LL.D., 1969. Personnel asst. Panama Canal, 1942; mem. staff adminstrv. mgt. div. VA, 1946-47; mem. research staff sci. research bd. Exec. Office of Pres., 1947, personnel research staff Nat. Bur. Standards, 1947-48; dir. research Syracuse U., Research Office, Washington, 1949-51; asst. dean coll. engring. Syracuse (N.Y.) U., 1951-54, v.p. adminstrn. and research, 1959-68, pres. Research Corp., 1959-68, Syracuse U. Press, 1959-68; dep. dir. N.Y. State Budget Div., Albany, 1955-57, dir. of budget, 1957-59; pres. Wichita State U., 1968—. First dep. controller N.Y. State Dept. Audit and Control, Albany, 1959; cons. N.Y. State Civil Service Commn., 1959-68, N.Y. State Dept. Audit and Control, 1959-68, USPHS, 1960. Served with AUS, 1944-46. Mem. Polit. Sci. Assn., Soc. Pub. Adminstrn., Soc. Engring. Edn., Inst. Indsl. Engring. Office: Wichita State U Wichita KS 67208

AHLENIUS, WILLIAM MATHESON, lawyer; b. Chgo., July 26, 1934; s. William Hilmer and Kathryn Marcella (Trenkle) A.; A.B., U. Ill., 1955, J.D., 1961; postgrad. Georgetown U., 1957-59; m. Jacqueline LaRue Painter, June 15, 1958; children—Lisa Jo, Kristen Sue. Admitted to Ill. bar, 1961, Iowa bar, 1961; asso. firm Betty, Neuman, Heniger & McMahon, Davenport, Iowa, 1961-62; partner firm Swain, Johnson & Gard, Peoria, Ill., 1962—. Mem. faculty Ill. Inst. for Continuing Legal Edn., 1972—. Active Heart of Ill. United Fund. Mem. Peoria County Republican Central Com., 1966-70, 72—, sec., 1974—. Served with USNR, 1955-59. Mem. Am., Ill., Iowa, Peoria County bar assns., Naval res. Assn., Phi Delta Phi. Episcopalian. Club: Cleve Coeur (Peoria). Home: 1130 Multiflora Ln Peoria IL 61614 Office: 411 Hamilton Blvd Suite 1900 Peoria IL 61602

AHLERS, ANDREW WILLIAM, banker; b. nr. LeMars, Iowa, July 12, 1899; s. Henry Anthony and Wilhelmina (Lewis) A.; student parochial schs.; m. Angela Clare Buckley, June 19, 1934; children—Joan Kathryn (Mrs. Orville Portz), Mary Jean (Mrs. Gerald Portz), Delores Angeles (Mrs. Raphael Portz), Patricia Helen (Mrs. Mike Lovely), Janiece Marie (Mrs. Charles Bohlke). Engaged in farming near Remsen, Iowa, 1934-54; pres. Farmers Savings Bank, Struble, Iowa, 1940—; pres. Andrew W. Ahlers Ins. & Real Estate, Remsen, 1961—. Mem. Service Corps Ret. Execs. Mem. Plymouth County Bankers Assn., Plymouth County Realtors Assn., Remsen C. of C. (dir.). Democrat. Roman Catholic. K.C. Club: Community. Home: 620 Kennedy St Remsen IA 51050 Office: 163 S Washington St Remsen IA 51050

AHLES, SISTER MARY THEOPHANE, hosp. adminstr.; b. Bluffton, Minn., Dec. 23, 1914; d. Joseph and Elizabeth (Nett) Ahles; B.A., Mt. Mary Coll., 1943; M.H.A., St. Louis U., 1961. Tchr., 1943-59; asst. adminstr. St. Anthony Hosp., Milw., 1961-63, adminstr., 1963-66; adminstr. Trinity Meml. Hosp., Cudahy, Wis., 1966—. Mem. Wis. Council Hosp. Regulation and Approval. Mem. Found. of Trinity Meml. Hosp., Inc. Mem. Franciscan Sisters of Little Falls (Minn.). Fellow Am. Coll. Hosp. Adminstrs.; mem. Wis. Conf. Cath. Hosps. (pres. 1970—), Hosp. Council Greater Milw. (v.p. 1967-69). Club: Zonta (Milw., trustee). Address: 5900 S Lake Dr Cudahy WI 53110

AHLSTROM, RONALD GUSTIN, artist; b. Chgo., Jan. 17, 1922; s. Frederick Karl and Gertrude (Gustin) A.; ed. U. Chgo., Art Inst. Chgo.; B.F.A., 1955; m. Nancy Costa; 1 son, Arn Gustin. Exhibited work in one-man shows at Barat Coll., Lake Forest, Ill., 1958, Blackhawk Restaurant, Chgo., 1961, collages at Main Street Galleries, Chgo., 1969, Joseph Faulkner Galleries, Chgo., 1970, 71, Spiesberger Gallery, Skokie, Ill., 1975; exhibited group shows including Chgo. and Vicinity Ann., Art Inst. Chgo., 1955, 56, 59, 61, 62, 64, other shows at Art Inst. Chgo., 1957, 58, Inst. Jewish Studies, 1956, 1020 Art Center, 1957, Navy Pier, 1957, 58, Old Town Art Center, 1959, B. C. Holland Gallery, 1961, McCormick Pl. Art Gallery, 1961, 62, 63, Hyde Park Art Center, 1963, Studio 22, 1970 (all Chgo.), Charles McNider Mus., Mason City, Iowa, 1971; Touchstone Gallery, N.Y.C., 1973; exhibited in Chgo. Artists European Tour Exhibit, USIA, 1957-59, Festival of Fine Arts, Lake Forest, 1958, Soc. of Four Arts Exhibit, West Palm Beach, Fla., 1959, Eastern Mich. Coll. at Ypsilanti, 1960. Corcoran Gallery Art, Washington, 1961. Tacoma Art Mus., 1963, 5 Abstractionists, Main St. Galleries, 1968; represented in permanent collections Tacoma Art Museum, Barat Coll. Gallery, Art Inst. Chgo., Blue Cross, Chgo., Atlantic-Richfield, Chgo., Ill. Bell Telephone, Container Corp. Am., Chgo., also in numerous pvt. collections; work represented in book Collage and Found. Art (Meilach and Ten Hoor), 1964, Collage and Assemblage, Trend and Techniques (Meilach and Ten Hoor), 1973. Asst. dir. McCormick Pl. Gallery 1960-63; dir. Tacoma Art Mus., 1963—. Served with AUS, 1942-46. Recipient Clyde M. Carr Prize for Painting, 1955, Alumni of Sch. Art Inst. Prize, 1959, Jane Broadus Clark Prize, 1961 (all Art Inst. Chgo.); Singer and Sons Prize, 1957, William H. Bartels Prize, 1958 (both Navy Pier); Abel Fagan Prize. Festival Fine Arts, Lake Forest, 1958; Ford Found. purchase prize Seattle Art Mus., 1964. Unitarian. Home: 121 W Park Dr Lombard IL 60148

AHLUWALLA, MUNESHWAR SINGH, pathologist; b. Delhi, India, Aug. 5, 1935; s. Rajeshwar and Koshalya Devi (Ahluwalia) Singh; student Hindu Coll., U. Delhi (India), 1951-53; M.B., B.S., Med. Coll., Punjab U., 1958; m. Tarvinder Rekhi, June 13, 1965; children—Arlina, Jasbina, Balrina. Intern, V. J. Hosp., Amritsar also Irwin Hosp., New Delhi, 1958-59; instr. microbiology Lady Hardinge Med. Coll., New Delhi, India, 1959-60; resident pathology All India Inst. Med. Scis., New Delhi, 1960-63; resident, fellowship in hematology Cook County Hosp. also Hektoen Inst. for Med. Research, Chgo., 1963-64; postdoctoral officership in pathology All India Inst. Med. Sci., New Delhi, 1964-66; sr. pathologist Cook County Hosp., Chgo., 1966-70; research asso. in pathology Hektoen Inst. Med. Research, Chgo., 1967-70; asst. prof. pathology Chgo. Med. Sch., 1967-73; clin. asso. prof. pathology U. Ill., Abrham Lincoln Sch. Medicine, Chgo., 1976—; mem. teaching faculty Cook County Grad. Sch. Medicine, Chgo., 1966-70; staff pathologist MacNeal Meml. Hosp., Berwyn, Ill., 1970—; staff pathologist Morris (Ill.) Hosp., 1974—; coroner's physician Grundy County, Ill., 1974—. Pres., Am. Cancer Soc., Berwyn, Ill., 1976. Fellow Coll. Am. Pathologists, Am. Soc. Clin. Pathologists, Inst. Medicine of Chgo.; mem. Internat. Acad. Pathology, Am. Fedn. Clin. Research, Chgo.

Pathol. Soc., Ill. Soc. Anatomic Pathologists, Ill. Soc. Cytology, Indian Assn. Pathologists, Indian Med. Assn., South Delhi, Chgo. med. socs., AMA, Ill. State Med. Soc., Chgo. Found. Med. Care. Mason (Shriner). Home: 1239 W 39th St Downers Grove IL 60515 Office: 3249 Oak Park Ave Berwyn IL 60402

AHMAD, BASHIR, educator; b. Sialkot, Pakistan, Sept. 9, 1929; s. Shahnawaz and Maryum (Begum) Khan; came to U.S., 1955; M.A. in Diplomatic History, DePaul U., 1964, Ph.D. in Polit. Sci., 1972; M. Shamim Butt, Dec. 16, 1972. Asst. prof. polit. sci. DePaul U., Chgo., 1968—. Mem. Am., Midwest, Internat. polit. sci. assns., Internat. Studies Assn., Intercontinental Biographical Assn. (London, Eng.), Asia Soc. N.Y. (Pakistan council 1972—), Royal Soc. for India, Pakistan and Ceylon. Research in analysis of the Yalta conf. with spl. emphasis on the Far East; politics of the major powers toward the Kashmir dispute. Home: 5700 N Magnolia Ave Chicago IL 60660

AHMAD, IJAZ, pathologist; b. Pakistan, Sept. 30, 1937; s. Nazir and Begum (Bibbi) A.; B. Medicine, B. Surgery, King Edward Med. Coll., Lahore, Pakistan, 1962; m. Riffat, Apr. 28, 1969; children—Attiya, Aqeel. Intern, Mayo Hosp., Lahore, Pakistan, 1965-66; resident in hosps., Pakistan, Gt. Britain, 1966-69; resident Marymount Hosp., Cleve., 1969-70; fellow in pathology Cleve. Clinic, 1970-71; resident St. Joseph Hosp., Providence, 1971-72; chief resident Mt. Sinai Hosp., Cleve., 1972-73; pathologist Huron Rd. Hosp., Cleve., 1973—; clin. instr. pathology Case-Western Res. U., 1975—; dir. sch. med. tech. Huron Rd. Hosp., Cleve., 1974—, chmn. infectious disease com., 1976—. Diplomate Am. Bd. Pathology. Fellow Coll. Am. Pathologists, Am. Soc. Clin. Pathologists; mem. Am. Soc. Clin. Chemists (chmn. Cleve. sect. 1978), Cleve. Soc. Pathologists, Pakistan-Am. League, Islamic Center Cleve. Moslem. Contbr. article to med. jour. Home: 5179 Hickory Dr Lyndhurst OH 44124 Office: Huron Rd Hosp 13951 Terrace Rd Cleveland OH 44112

AHMED, KHALIL, biochemist, pharmacologist, educator; b. Lahore, Pakistan, Nov. 30, 1934; s. Abdul and Ghulam (Sughra) Haq; came to U.S., 1960, naturalized, 1965; B.S. with honors, Panjab U., Pakistan, 1954, M.S. with honors, 1955; Ph.D., McGill U., Montreal, Can., 1960; m. Ritva Helena Veikkamo, June 27, 1969; children—Karim, Rehana. Research asso. Wistar Inst., Phila., 1960-63; asst. prof. metabolic research Chgo. Med. Sch., 1963-67; mem. sr. staff Nat. Cancer Inst., Balt., 1967-71; research biochemist, chief toxicology research lab. VA Hosp., Mpls., 1971—; asso. prof. lab. medicine and pathology, U. Minn., Mpls., 1971-76, prof., 1977—; vis. scientist lab. of physiology, Helsinki, Finland, 1962; vis. lectr. Chgo. Med. Sch., 1968-69. Named Outstanding Citizen, Met. Chgo. Citizenship Council, 1966. Mem. Am. Chem. Soc., Am. Soc. of Pharmacology and Exptl. Therapeutics, AAAS, Biochem. Soc. of London, Am. Soc. of Biol. Chemists, Endocrine Soc., N.Y. Acad. Scis., Sigma Xi. Contbr. articles to profl. jours. Home: 2011 James Ave S Minneapolis MN 55405 Office: Mpls VA Hosp 54th St and 48th Ave S Minneapolis MN 55417

AHMED, NASIR, educator; b. Bangalore, India, Aug. 11, 1940; s. Nazir and Nurjehan (Alikhan) A.; B.S., U. Mysore (India) 1961; M.S., U. N.M., 1963, Ph.D., 1966; m. Esther Pariente, Jan. 28, 1965; 1 son. Came to U.S., 1961, naturalized, 1971. Prin. research engr. Honeywell, Inc., Mpls., 1966-68; asst. prof. elec. engring. Kans. State U., Manhattan, 1968-71, asso. prof., 1972-76, prof., 1977—. Nat. research travel grantee Ljubljana, Yugoslavia, 1971. Mem. IEEE. Author: Orthogonal Transforms for Digital Signal Processing, 1975; Computer Science Fundamentals: An Algorithmic Structured Programming Approach, 1979. Asso. editor IEEE Trans. on Electromagnetic Compatibility, 1972—. Contbr. articles to profl. jours. Home: 314 Twykingham Pl Manhattan KS 66502

AHMED, SHAFFIQ-UDDIN, educator; b. Hawrah, W. Bengal, India, Mar. 1, 1934; s. Kausaraddin and Rabeya (Ali) A.; B.E. in Metall. Engring., U. Calcutta, 1954; M.S., U. Ill., 1958; Ph.D., Case Inst. Tech., 1965; m. Ursula Schmengler, Sept. 26, 1963; 1 son, Rafiq. Mem. research staff AEC, Urbana, Ill., 1955-60, Case Inst. Tech., Cleve., 1962-63; asst. prof. Youngstown (Ohio) U., 1960-65, asso. prof., 1965-67; prof. chmn. dept. metall. engring. Youngstown State U., 1967—; dir. Ahmed & Assos., cons., Youngstown. Decorated Silver Star, 4th Bengal Engring. Platoon; named Profl. Man of Yr., Warren chpt. Am. Soc. Metals. Fellow AAAS, Am. Inst. Chemists; mem. Nat. Soc. Profl. Engrs., Am. Inst. Mining and Metall. Engrs., Verein Deutscher Eisenhuettenleute (W. Germany), Am., Indian insts. metals, Instn. Engrs. (India), Am. Soc. Engring. Edn., Am. Soc. for Metals, N.Y., Ohio acads. sci., Instn. Metallurgists London (asso.), Sigma Tau. Author several books on metallurgy, also articles in profl. jours. Home: 269 Redondo Rd Youngstown OH 44504

AHONEN, CLIFFORD JOHN, marketing cons.; b. Ironwood, Mich., Mar. 1, 1934; s. Telfield John and Helen Tina (Kuula) A.; B.B.A., U. Wis., 1959; M.B.A., Roosevelt U., 1963; postgrad. U. Chgo., 1964-65; m. Patricia Ann Doyle, Aug. 20, 1961; children—Helen, Allan, Michael, Mark. Sales engr. Richards-Wilcox Mfg. Co., Aurora, Ill., 1959-61; marketing specialist Link-Belt Co., Chgo., 1961-64; dir. long range planning Joy Mfg. Co., Michigan City, Ind., 1964-69; v.p. mktg. strategy Starcraft Co., Goshen, Ind., 1969-72; exec. v.p. Marketing Cons., Inc., Elkhart, Ind., 1972—, also dir.; faculty Goshen (Ind.) Coll., 1971-74, Southwestern Mich. Coll., Dowagiac, 1974—. Chmn. Cherokee dist. Boy Scouts Am., 1975-77. Served with U.S. Army, 1955-57. Mem. Am. Mktg. Assn. (chpt. pres. 1973), Am. Statis. Assn. Republican. Roman Catholic. Club: Sales and Advt. Home: 250 S Main St Goshen IN 46526 Office: 339 Communicana Bldg Elkhart IN 46514

AHRENDTS, HAROLD LEE, educator; b. Boone County, Nebr., Aug. 4, 1914; s. Albert W. and Clara Susan (Galloway) A.; A.B., Nebr. Wesleyan U., 1938; M.A., U. Mich., 1942; Ph.D., U. Denver, 1962; m. Norma E. Reynolds, Aug. 30, 1942; 1 son, David Harold. Faculty Nebr. State Coll., Kearney, 1943—, prof. speech, 1952—, chmn. div. fine arts 1952—; dir. lay speaking Nebr. United Meth. Conf. Profl. speaker, lectr.; spl. research speaking on William Jennings Bryan. Mem. White House Com. for Nebr. Youth; chmn. Buffalo County ARC, 1971-72. Bd. dirs. Nebr. Soc. Crippled Children, 1950. Mem. NEA, Nebr. Schoolmasters Club, Speech Assn. Am., Am. Speech and Hearing Assn., Nebr. Edn. Assn., Am. Forensic Assn., AAUP, Nat. Art Assn., Meth. Men Nat. Assn., Blue Key, Psi Chi, Theta Chi Alpha, Pi Kappa Delta, Phi Kappa Phi. Methodist (mem. nat. bd. edn.). Mason. Author: Principles of Public Speaking, 1963; Core-Knowledge Study Guide for Speech Communication, 1972; also articles in profl. and ednl. publs. Home: 2120 96th Ave Kearney NE 68847

AHRENS, CLAUDE WESLEY, recreation equipment mfg. co. exec.; b. Grinnell, Iowa, Aug. 18, 1912; s. John Wesley and Mary Blanche (Badger) A.; student Grinnell Coll., 1934-35; m. Dorothy Hey, Oct. 7, 1937; 1 son, Paul Wesley. Pres., Ahrens Seed Co., Grinnell, 1940-47; with Ahrens Mfg. Co., Miracle Recreation Co. (merged into Miracle Recreation Equipment Co., 1972), Grinnell, chmn. bd., 1972—. Operator, C & P Farms, Grinnell, 1974—. Named to Grinnell Pub. Sch. Hall of Fame, 1942; named Citizen of Year, Grinnell, 1948; recipient Corporate Citizenship citation Grinnell Coll., 1973. Mem. Iowa Mfrs. Assn. (dir. 1965—). Elk. Clubs: Grinnell Country, Grinnell; Indian Wells Country (Palm Desert, Calif.). Patentee in recreation equipment field. Home: RFD 3 Grinnell IA 50112 Office: Hwy 6 West Box 275 Grinnell IA 50112

AHRENS, ROBERT JOHN, city ofcl.; b. Oak Park, Ill., Aug. 29, 1922; s. William Robert and Anna (Fischer) A.; B.S.C., Roosevelt U., 1949, M.A. in Ednl. Adminstrn., 1956. Dir. alumni relations, asst. to pres. Roosevelt U., 1948-56, dir. continuing edn. and extension, Roosevelt U., 1962-65, v.p. for devel., 1965-67; exec. dir. Adult Edn. Council of Greater Chgo., 1956-62; exec. dir. Chgo. Commn. for Sr. Citizens, 1967-69; dir. div. sr. citizens City of Chgo. Dept. Human Resources, 1969-71; dir. Mayor's Office for Sr. Citizens and Handicapped, Chgo., 1972—. Spl. cons. transp. White House Conf. on Aging, 1971; pres. Urban Elderly Coalition, 1976—; mem. exec. com., chmn. pub. policy com. Nat. Council on Aging, 1974—. Dir. Shoreham Conf. on Continuing Edn. of Alumni, sponsored by Fund for Adult Edn. and Am. Alumni Council, 1956; bd. dirs. Adult Edn. Council Greater Chgo., 1962-73; pres. Citizens Sch. Com., 1966-68, bd. dirs. 1962-72; mem. Ill. Ednl. Council, 1969-70. Mem. founding com. ednl. TV sta. Channel 11; mem. cultural adv. com. Chgo. Mayor's Com. for Econ. and Cultural Devel., acting chmn., 1967-68; mem. Mayor's Adv. Commn. on Chgo. Sch. Bd. Nominations, 1964, 65; bd. dirs. Urban Gateways; mem. exec. bd. Auditorium Theatre Council. Served from pvt. to tech sgt., C.E., AUS, USAAF, 1942-46; ETO. Recipient Eleanor Roosevelt Key as outstanding alumnus Roosevelt U., 1960; 1969 Pub. Service award Ill. Assn. Clin. Labs.; Outstanding Pub. Service award radio sta. WIND-AM. Fellow Gerontol. Soc. U.S. Club: Cliff Dwellers (Chgo.). Home: 5201 S Cornell Ave #23A Chicago IL 60615 Office: 180 N LaSalle St Chicago IL 60601

AHSTROM, JAMES PETER, JR., physician; b. Chgo., Dec. 3, 1925; s. James Peter and Anna (Berg) A.; B.S., U. Richmond, 1946; M.B., Northwestern U., 1948, M.D., 1949; m. Harriet Jane White, Aug. 3, 1949; children—James D., Jill D. Intern, Evanston Hosp. Assn., 1949; resident VA Hosp., Hines, Ill., 1950, 52-53, USN Hosp., Oakland, Calif., 1951-52, Shriners Hosp. for Crippled Children, Chgo., 1954; practice medicine specializing in orthopaedic surgery, Oak Park, Ill., 1955—; mem. staffs West Suburban Hosp., Oak Park, Norwegian Am. Hosp., Chgo., VA Hosp., Hines, Shriners Hosp., Chgo., Oak Park (Ill.) Hosp., Good Samaritan Hosp., Downers Grove clin. asst. prof. orthopaedic surgery Abraham Lincoln Sch. Medicine, U. Ill. at the Med. Center, Chgo. Served to lt. USNR, 1950-52. Fellow A.C.S.; mem. Am. Acad. Orthopaedic Surgeons, Am. Orthopedic Assn., Am. Soc. for Surgery of Hand, Clinical Orthopaedic Soc., Chgo. Orthopaedic Soc., AMA, Phi Beta Kappa, Alpha Omega Alpha. Mason (32 deg., Shriner), Rotarian. Club: River Forest Tennis. Home: 821 Bonnie Brae River Forest IL 60305 Office: 3815 Highland Ave Suite 2M Downers Grove IL 60515

AICHNER, HARRY CLIFFORD, psychologist; b. Erie, Pa., Feb. 19, 1931; s. Harry Clifford and Hattie Angela (Heffinger) A.; A.B., Westminster (Pa.) Coll., 1952; M.S., Pa. State U., 1955. Intern, VA Hosp., Roanoke, Va., 1953-54; psychologist various community mental health facilities, Ohio, 1958—; pvt. practice psychology Springfield, Ohio, 1965-67, Ashtabula, Ohio, 1967-76, Cleve., 1976—; clinic dir., chief psychologist Ohio Mental Health Clinics, 1964-74. Served with AUS, 1956-58. Fellow Internat. Acad. Forensic Psychology; mem. Am., Ohio, Cleve. psychol. assns., AAAS, Ohio Mental Health Forum, Am. Psychology-Law Soc., Phi Kappa Tau. Address: PO Box 129 Ashtabula OH 44004

AIELLO, ALFRED, ednl. adminstr.; b. Cleve., Nov. 10, 1925; s. Peter and Mary (Critelli) A.; B.S., Western Res. U., 1950, M.A., 1952; postgrad. Bank St. Coll., 1963, Cleve. State U., 1970-71; children—Leslie Franklin, Beverly Joan. Mem. faculty Cleve. Bd. Edn., 1950—, prin. John D. Rockefeller Elementary Sch., 1976—. Tchr. WEWS-TV Cleve., 1964—; asst. dir. Western Res. U. Workshop, Cleve., 1965—; asso. clin. prof. Ohio State U.; tchr. tng. cons. Cleve. State U., 1952—; bus. mgr. Royalton Recorder, North Royalton, Ohio, 1953—; pres. Met. Co-op. Services, Inc.; treas. Crest, Inc.; dir. Roll, Inc., Hough Devel. Corp. Vice pres. Hough Area Community Council, sec., 1965, mem. exec. bd., 1965—; sec. Ohio Dept. Elementary Sch. Prins. Mem. bd. Community Action for Youth, Inc., Community Devel. Adv. Com., Thurgood Marshall Playfield Adv. Com.; mem. bd. mgrs. YMCA, Cleve., 1956—, chmn. Golden Triangle Campaign; scout master Boy Scouts Am., North Royalton, 1950-55; mem. exec. bd. Family Service Assn., Cleve., 1960-62, Bell Center Settlement House, Cleve., 1961—; mem. bd. League Park Center; exec. bd. Friendly Town, 1973; trustee Lake Erie council Girl Scouts U.S.A. 1973; pres. Inner-City Protestant Parish, 1974-75; v.p. Buckeye-Woodland Community Congress, 1975; bd. dirs. Greater Cleve. Tchr. Center, 1975—. Served with USMCR, 1944-46. Named Young Man of Yr., North Royalton Jr. C. of C., 1964. Mem. NEA, Northeast Ohio Tchrs. Assn., Northeast Ohio Tchrs. Elementary Sch. Prins. Assn. (pres.), Cleve. Elementary Prins. Assn. (pres. 1967—), Ohio, Cleve. (v.p. 1975) edn. assns., Nat. Sci. Tchrs. Assn., Ohio Assn. Elementary Sch. Prins. (exec. bd. 1971, dir., legis. com. 1974—), Cleve. Council Adminstrs. and Suprs., Council Social Studies, N. Royalton Bd. Edn. (pres. 1960-63), N. Royalton Edn. Council, NAACP, Hough Execs., Council Human Relations, N. Royalton C. of C. (sec.-treas. 1956-61), Phi Delta Kappa. Lutheran (congregation pres. 1959-64, bldg. chmn. 1966-67, chmn. bd. edn. 1967—, Sunday sch. supt. 1966—). Clubs: Kiwanis (v.p. 1960), Key (div. chmn. 1961), Schoolmasters. Author: (with Dr. Oswald J. Roders) tchr. tng. program, Cleve. State U., 1966. Author elementary sci. units, 1958-60, TV scripts elementary sci. lessons, 1960. Contbr. to book The Real Tchrs.; also articles. Home: 17920 Winslow Rd Shaker Heights OH 44122 Office: 11529 Buckeye Ave Cleveland OH 44104

AIKEN, ROGER GEORGE, energy research analyst; b. Feilding, N. Z., Jan. 12, 1933; s. Henry George and Muriel Christine; came to U.S., 1973; B.Sc., U. Canterbury, Christchurch, N.Z., 1954, B.E. with honours, 1956, M.E. with distinction, 1958; postgrad. in mech. engring., U. Minn., 1973—; m. Susan Graham Hamilton, July 14, 1962; children—Andrew Graham, David George. Engr. physics and engring. labs., Dept. Sci. and Indsl. Research, Lower Hutt, N.Z., 1958-59, Collier and Beale Ltd., Wellington, N.Z., 1959-61, Hirst Research Centre, Brit. Gen. Electric Co., Wembley, England, 1961-65, Bell No. Research, Ottawa, Ont., Can., 1965-67, transmission dept. N.Z. Post Office, Wellington, 1968, Communications Research Centre, Canadian Fed. Dept. Communications, Ottawa, Ont., 1968-73; research fellow Center for Studies of Phys. Environment, Inst. Tech., U. Minn., Mpls., 1974-76; energy research analyst research div. Minn. Energy Agy., St. Paul, 1976—. Mem. Instn. of Elec. Engrs. (U.K.), IEEE, Biomass Energy Inst. (Can.), Am. Inst. of Aero. and Astronautics, Internat. Solar Energy Soc., Phi Kappa Phi. Mem. United Ch. of Christ. Clubs: Univ., YMCA. Contbr. articles to profl. jours. and meetings. Home: 1589 Hollywood Ct St Paul MN 55108 Office: 720 American Center Bldg 150 E Kellogg Blvd St Paul MN 55101

AILES, CURTIS ALBERT, artist; b. Franklin County, Ind., July 11, 1920; s. Albert Sidney and Martha Evelyn (Abrams) A.; student comml. art Famous Artist Schs., 1960-63; m. Ethel June Saylor, Aug. 4, 1945; children—Jerome, Tobin, Pamela, James, Terry, Julia Ann. Employed as electronic technician, 1953-74; exhibited in one man and group shows: Sheldon Swope Art Gallery, Terre Haute, Ind., 1974, Hoosier Salon Art Gallery, Indpls., 1976, Mus. Art, Evansville, Ind., 1976, Brown County Art Gallery Assn., Nashville, Ind., 1977; represented in permanent collection: Fireside Art Gallery, Metamora, Ind. Served with 8th Air Force USAAF, 1942-45; ETO; German prisoner of war, 1944. Decorated D.F.C.; recipient various art awards. Mem. Am. Water Color Soc. (asso.), White Water Valley Art Assn. (past pres.), Hoosier Salon Art Assn., Brown County Art Gallery (asso.). Baptist. Home: Rural Route 5 Country Brook Connersville IN 47331

AINLEY, ROBERT WALLACE, advt. exec.; b. Perry, Ia., Aug. 18, 1922; s. Oscar Albert and Goldie (Beatty) A.; student Kemper Mil. Sch., 1940-41, State U. Ia., 1941-43; A.B., Drake U., 1947; m. Ila June Inman, Apr. 15, 1949; children—Robert Kent, Leslie Ann. With sales dept. Maytag Co., Newton, Ia., 1947-48; sales rep. Upson Co., Des Moines, 1948-54; advt. sales rep. Wallaces Farmer, Des Moines, 1954-65; advt. mgr. Prairie Farmer, Prairie Farmer Pub. Co., Chgo., 1965-75, also supr. Midwest Unit Farm Publs., Chgo., 1969-74, advt. and sales promotion mgr., 1974-75; mgr. advt. sales Farm Progress Publs., 1976—. Chgo. plans bd. mem. State Farm Mag. Advt. Bur., Indpls. Past pres. Churchill Grade Sch. PTA, Glen Ellyn, Ill.; cultural arts chmn. Hawthorn Sch. PTA, Glen Ellyn, 1973-75; pres. N.Am. Farm Show Council, 1975-76. Trustee Prairie Farmer Pension Trust, 1970-73. Served with AUS, 1943-46, 50-51. Decorated Bronze Star medal. Mem. Nat. Agrl. Marketing Assn., Chgo. Federated Advt. Club, VFW, Am. Legion, Sigma Delta Chi. Republican. Methodist. Elk. Home: 754 Colonial Dr Greenwood IN 46142 Office: 2346 S Lynhurst Dr Indianapolis IN 46241

AIRY, JOHN MADISON, agrl. cons.; b. nr. Derby, Iowa, Feb. 17, 1915; s. Delbert and Dora (Pearcy) A.; B.S. in Agronomy, Iowa State U., 1938; m. Beulah Arvinia Mundell, May 6, 1933 (dec.); children—R. Dean, H. Darlene (Mrs. Frank J. Stermole), B. Joan (Mrs. Robert L. Monroe); m. 2d, Cleo J. Graf McGlothren, Oct. 30, 1973. Farm laborer, 1933-34; with Pioneer Hi-Bred Internat. Inc., Des Moines, 1938-73, dist. sales supr., 1938-49, prodn. supr. and insp., 1939-45, prodn. mgr., 1945-65, dir. fng. sales, 1964-70, treas., dir. corporate planning, 1965-67, v.p., 1967-73, dir., 1961-73; pres. Pioneer Beef Cattle Co., 1970-73; agrl. cons., 1973—. Mem. bd. U.S. Feed Grains Council, 1965-70, cow-calf team to Europe, 1972; sec. Iowa Gov.'s Beef Cattle Task Force, 1973-74; vice chmn. Nat. Industry State Agrl. Research Council, 1972-74, chmn., 1974-76. Chmn. Iowa Gov.'s Hwy. Liaison Commn., 1961-63. Bd. dirs. Tallcorn Area council Boy Scouts Am., 1946-61. Recipient Silver Beaver award Boy Scouts Am., 1955. Mem. Am. Soc. Agronomy, Am. Soc. Animal Sci., Am. Soc. Agrl. Cons. (pres. 1976-77), Am. Nat. Cattlemen's Assn. (chmn. research com. 1972-76, legis. com. 1974-76), Beef Improvement Fedn. (dir. 1973-76), Am. Seed Trade Assn. (chmn. corn and sorghum div. 1967-68), Des Moines C. of C., Alpha Zeta, Phi Kappa Phi. Democrat. Methodist. Rotarian. Contbr. articles and chpts. to profl. publs. Developer innovative cattle breeding program. Home: 1916 68th St Des Moines IA 50322

AITKEN, WILLIAM INGLIS, lawyer; b. Lincoln, Nebr., Oct. 4, 1896; s. Martin Inglis and Clara Elizabeth (Carmody) A.; A.B., U. Neb., 1918; J.D., Harvard U., 1921; m. Helen Mary Cook, Sept. 22, 1923; children—Martha Elizabeth (Mrs. J. Taylor Greer), Mary (Mrs. R.C.L. Greer), Nancy (Mrs. H. L. Senger, Jr.). Admitted to Nebr. bar, 1921, since practiced in Lincoln; mem. firm Woods, Aitken, Smith, Greer, Overcash & Spangler, 1921—; cons. Woodman Accident & Life Co.; dir. Sahara Coal Co., Chgo. Mem. Greater Lincoln Planning Commn., 1931-35. Water Adv. Bd., 1952-53. Adv. com. of bd. dirs. Lincoln Found.; trustee U. Neb. Found., 1960—, Neb. Hist. Found., 1968—, Neb. Independent Coll. Found., 1970—. Served as 2d lt. F.A., U.S. Army, 1918-19; 2d lt. Res., 1919-24. Mem. C. of C. (dir. 1949-53), Am., Nebr., Lincoln bar assns., Newcomen Soc., Ind. Pioneers Telephone Assn., Patriarchs, Phi Gamma Delta, Alpha Kappa Psi. Republican. Congregationalist (trustee 1942-45, 47-50, chmn. bd. trustees of trust fund). Clubs: Round Table, Lincoln Country, University (Lincoln). Home: 2240 Woodsdale Blvd Lincoln NE 68502 Office: 1241 N St Lincoln NE 68508

AIYEDE, ADEBAYO OLUMUYIWA, physician; b. Lagos, Nigeria, May 2, 1932; s. Emmanuel Oke and Clementina Olabisi (Osho) A.; M.D., U. Man., 1960; m. Shirley Loretta Parris, Mar. 28, 1959; children—Bamidele, Olayinka, Afolake, Babatunde. Jr. intern St. Boniface Hosp., Winnipeg, Man., Can., 1960-61; resident in psychiatry Brandon (Man.) Mental Hosp., 1962; asst. physician to Dr. N.F. Burke, Smooth Rock Falls, Ont., Can., 1962-63; pvt. practice medicine specializing in family practice, Powassan, Ont., 1963—; mem. active courtesy staff St. Joseph's Hosp., Civic Hosp., North Bay, Ont.; owner, dir. Med. Clinic, Powassan, 1969—; physician in charge Nipissing Manor Nursing Center, 1967—; home physician Eastholme and Glow Wood Lodge, 1969—; coroner areas 17 and 18, Ont., 1973-77; chmn. Aiyede Med. Clinics Ltd., Lagos, Nigeria. Pres. Aiyede Enterprises, Ltd., 1971—, Erba Corp., Ltd., 1971—. Alt. del. Ont. Conservative Party Conv., 1971. Fellow Med. Council Gen. Practice (Nigeria); mem. Canadian, Ont. med. assns., Coll. Family Physicians (Can.), North Bay and Dist. Med. Soc., Theta Kappa Psi. Mason, Lion. Office: 217 King St Powassan ON P0H 1Z0 Canada

AJAMY, DAVID ALBERT, juvenile ct. counselor; b. Boston, Apr. 9, 1948; s. Emile James and Madeleine Mary (Dahood) A.; B.S., Eastern Mich. U., 1971, M.A., 1973; m. Bobbie Sue Trondson, July 31, 1971; children—Elizabeth Helen, James Edward. Tchr., counselor Starr Commonwealth Boys, Albion, Mich., 1971-72; paraprofl. high sch. phys. edn. Plymouth (Mich.) Community Schs., 1972-73; tchr., counselor Ypsilanti (Mich.) Area Community Schs., summer 1973; probation officer, social worker, counselor Children's Village, Oakland County Juvenile Ct., Pontiac, Mich., 1973—; testing analyst Clin. Resources, Inc., Royal Oak, Mich., 1975—; adviser J-Teens, Milford, Mich., 1976-77; pres. Maple North Housing Coop., 1974; vol. worker, lectr., cons. in field. Mem. Am., Mich. (dir.) personnel and guidance assns., Mich. Pub. Offender Counselor Assn. (pres. 1976-78), Pub. Offender Counselor Assn., Mich. Jaycees. Home: 948 Queen St Milford MI 48042 Office: 1200 N Telegraph St Pontiac MI 48053

AKCASU, ZIYAEDDIN AHMET, nuclear engr.; b. Aydin, Turkey, Aug. 26, 1925; s. Osman and Faika (Egel) A.; came to U.S., 1959; M.S., Tech. U. Istanbul, 1948; Ph.D., U. Mich., 1963; m. Melahat Turksal, July 16, 1954; children—Nur, Feza, Aydin. Asst. prof. Tech. U. Istanbul (Turkey), 1948-53, asso. prof., 1954-59; resident research asso. Argonne (Ill.) Nat. Lab., 1959-61; asst. prof. U. Mich., Ann Arbor, 1963-65, asso. prof., U. 1965-68, prof., 1968—. Served as res. officer, Turkish Army, 1953-54. Recipient Distinguished Service award U. Mich., 1965. Fellow Am. Nuclear Soc.; mem. Am. Phys. Soc., Sigma Xi, Phi Kappa Phi. Moslem. Author: (with others) Mathematical Methods in Nuclear Reactor Dynamics, 1970; contbr. articles in statis., plasma and reactor physics to sci. Jours. Home: 901 Westwood St Ann Arbor MI 48103 Office: Dept Nuclear Engineering Univ Michigan North Campus Ann Arbor MI 48109

AKE, MONTIE RALPH, hotel exec.; b. San Angelo, Tex., July 10, 1931; s. William Raleigh and Lorraine (Elliott) A.; B.S., Lamar State Coll. Tech., 1949, B.A., 1953. Trainee, front office mgr. Sheraton

Corp. Am., St. Louis, 1956-61; sales mgr. Tan-Tar-A Resort, Osage Beach, Mo., 1962-63, gen. mgr., 1963-69, v.p., 1969—. Sustaining mem. Gt. Rivers council Boy Scouts Am. Past pres., bd. dirs. Lake Ozarks Assn., 1967—. Served with AUS, 1953-55. Mem. Am. Hotel-Motel Assn. (dir.), Mo. Restaurant Assn. (dir., chmn. tourism com.), Mo. Hotel and Motel Assn., AMKO Assn. (dir.). Democrat. Presbyn. Club: Lake Valley Golf and Country. Address: Estate 37E Tan-Tar-A Golf and Tennis Resort Osage Beach MO 65065

AKE, SAM EUGENE, lab. exec.; b. Cleve., Mar. 7, 1944; s. Samuel Elwood and Virginia Louise (Malone) A.; student Fenn Coll., 1963, Kent State U., 1964; m. Susan LaBatte, Dec. 30, 1968; children—Shannon, Jennifer. With Morco, Inc., 1962; machinist City of Bedford Heights, Ohio, 1962; waste water treatment ofcl. City of Bedford, Ohio, 1963; waste water treatment insp. W.F. Schade & Assos., Cleve., 1964-67; surveyor, draftsman Pumps, Inc., Bedford, 1967-68; pres. Ake Lab., Bedford, 1968—; dir. S-T Products & Leasing, Inc.; pres. Sam Ake, Inc. Pres. Bedford Community Theatre. Served with U.S. Army, 1965-71. Mem. Bedford C. of C. Clubs: Pine Lake Trout, Millcreek Racquet, N.E. Ohio Vette. Home: 6030 Sunset St Bedford Heights OH 44146 Office: 503 Broadway Bedford OH 44146

AKERT, BENJAMIN BRUCE, pub. co. exec.; b. McCook, Nebr., July 9, 1927; s. Paul and Cyla A. (Moseley) A.; A.B., Nebr. Wesleyan Coll., 1951; M.Ed., U. Nebr., 1954; m. Jacqueline R. Harrison, Aug. 10, 1952; children—Leonard Alan, Bruce Eugene. Tchr., Whittier Jr. High Sch., Lincoln, Nebr., 1951-53, prin., 1953-54; supt. schs., Elkhorn, Nebr., 1954-57; with Scott, Foresman & Co., Glenview, Ill., 1957—, Nebr. agt., Lincoln, 1957—. Mem. Nebr. Profl. Bookmen (pres. 1961-62, 72-73, sec. 1968-69). Served with AUS, 1945-46. Address: 1800 S 51st St Lincoln NE 68506

ALADJEM, SILVIO, obstetrician, gynecologist, educator; b. Bucharest, Romania, June 16, 1928; s. Nahman and Lea (Campus) A.; came to U.S., 1964, naturalized, 1969; M.D. summa cum laude, U. Uruguay, Montevideo, 1961; m. Sonia Goldberg, Mar. 29, 1952; children—Vivien, Norman. Intern, Uruguay Pub. Health Service, Montevideo, 1961-62; resident in obstetrics and gynecology U. Uruguay, 1962-63, Cleve. Metropolitan Gen. Hosp., 1964-67; fellow in obstetrics, gynecology Western Res. U., 1967, asst. prof., attending obstetrician, gynecologist, 1969-74; instr. Med. Coll. Ga., 1967-68, asst. prof. obstetrics and gynecology, 1968-69; asso. prof. U. Ill., Chgo., 1975-76, prof., 1976—, head div. perinatal medicine, 1976—; practice medicine specializing in obstetrics and gynecology, Chgo.; cons. Nat. Found. March of Dimes, Cleve., Chgo. Diplomate Am. Bd. Obstetrics, Gynecology. Mem. Am. Coll. Obstetricians, Gynecologists (Ephraim McDowell award 1967), Am. Fertility Soc. (Carl Hartman award 1968), Soc. Gynecologic Investigations, Am. Soc. Anatomists, N.Y. Acad. Scis., Chgo. Gynecol. Soc., Chgo. Med. Soc., Ill., Am. med. assns., Perinatal Group of Ill. (pres. 1976), Phi Delta Epsilon. Democrat. Jewish. Club: B'nai B'rith (pres. local lodge 1972). Author: Risks in the Practice of Obstetrics, 1972; (with Audrey Brown) Clinical Perinatology, 1975, Perinatal Intensive Care, 1976; contbr. numerous articles to med. jours. Home: 175 E Delaware Pl Chicago IL 60611 Office: 840 S Wood St Chicago IL 60612

ALBANITO, DONALD MICHAEL, univ. adminstr.; b. Punxsutawney, Pa., Aug. 15, 1923; s. Michael and Martha (Rothermund) A.; B.S., Indiana (Pa.) U., 1949; M.A., U. Pitts., 1951; Ed.D., Ind. U., 1971; m. Goldie Dale Plymire, Aug. 1, 1947; children—Diane, Donald M., Darrell, Fred. Head accounting and finance depts. Am. Psychol. Assn., Washington, 1953-55; faculty bus. adminstrn. S.W. Mo. State Coll., Springfield, 1955-56; head bus. mgmt. and adminstrn. Bradley U., Peoria, Ill., 1956-71, dean Coll. Continuing Edn., 1971—. Mem. Ill. Gov.'s Adv. Council; pres. Luth. Found., 1975—. Served with Adj. Gen. Corps, AUS, 1944-46. Ford Found. Bus. fellow, 1962, 64; Found. for Econ. Edn. fellow, 1968. Mem. Midwest Bus. Adminstrn. Assn. (pres. 1978). Lutheran (pres. ch. 1966—). Rotarian. Contbr. articles to profl. jours. Home: 5203 N Merrimac Ave Peoria IL 61614

ALBERA, VICTOR HAROLD, anesthesiologist; b. Los Angeles, Aug. 1, 1931; s. Elmer and Eaula (Dietrich) A.; student U. Oreg., 1949-50, Denver U., 1950-52; M.D., U. Colo., 1956; m. Nellie Balocca, June 1955; children—Krista, Steven, Teresa, Cynthia, Sylvia, Lisa Jo; m. 2d, Kay Craun, Oct. 2, 1965; 1 adopted dau., Katherine. Intern, Gen. Hosp. Riverside County, Arlington, Calif., 1956-57; gen. practice medicine, Gallup, N.M., 1959-65, St. Louis, 1975—; resident anesthesia U. Colo. Med. Center, Denver, 1965-66, U. Mo., Columbia, 1966-68; sr. anesthesiologist Jewish Hosp., St. Louis, 1968-75, Faith West Hosp., 1975—; emergency room physician St. Francis Hosp., Washington, Mo., 1976—; med. examiner Coroner's Office, Franklin County, Mo.; asso. prof. anesthesia Washington U., St. Louis. Mem. com. on security 7 Pines Improvement Assn.; officer Civil Def. St. Louis County Police, 1973-76. Served to capt. M.C., USAR, 1957-59. Fellow Am. Coll. Anesthesiologists, Am. Acad. Family Practioners; mem. Am., Mo., St. Louis County socs. anesthesiologists, Am., Mo. med. assns., St. Louis County Med. Soc. Home: Route 2 Box 236 St Clair MO 63077

ALBERNAZ, JOSE GERALDO, neurosurgeron; b. Januaria, Brazil, Dec. 3, 1923; s. Carlos Lagoeiro and Maria Amelia (Gomes) A.; B.S., U. Minas Gerais, Brazil, 1940; M.S., 1946, D.Sc., 1955; Ph.D., U. Guanabara (Brazil), 1958; m. Doris Frances Sailer, June 24, 1950; children—Frances, Joyce, Marcus, Priscilla, Vanessa. Came to U.S., 1968, naturalized, 1971. Intern, St. Mary's Hosp., Huntington, W.Va., 1948-49; resident Chgo. Meml. Hosp., 1950-52, Ill. Neuropsychiat. Inst., Chgo., 1949-50, 52-53; prof., head dept. neurology and neurosurgery U. Minas Gerais, 1956-68; prof. anatomy Med. Coll. of Ohio, Toledo, 1968-72; chief neurology and neurosurgery Frederick C. Smith Clinic, Marion, Ohio, 1972—. Served with Brazilian Army, 1942-47. Diplomate Am. Bd. Neur. Surg. Rockefeller Found. fellow, 1959-60; W.K. Kellogg Found. fellow, 1952-53. Fellow A.C.S.; mem. Brazilian Soc. Neurosurgery (exec. com. 1964-74, pres. 1962-64), Pan Am. Assn. Anatomists (sec. 1970-72), Pan Am. Congress Neurology, Internat. Congress Neurosurgery (hon. v.p. 1966), AMA, Ohio, Brazilian med. assns. Lion. Author: Meningeal Tumors, 1955; Pneumoencephalography, 1958; Substantia Nigra and Gamma System, 1962. Contbr. articles to profl. jours. Home: 807 Vernon Heights Blvd Marion OH 43302 Office: 1040 Delaware Ave Marion OH 43302

ALBERT, JOHN MURRAY, paper co. exec.; b. West New York, N.J., June 3, 1923; s. Arthur Burroughs and Elene Clare (Murray) A.; B.S., Randolph Macon Coll., 1949; m. Nydia Cintron, Dec. 4, 1948; children—Elene, Theresa, John. Salesman C.G. Winans Co., Newark, 1949-58, Sealright Co., Boston, 1958-60, Atlantic Gummed Paper Corp., Cleve., 1960-71; v.p. mktg. Central Paper Co., Menasha, Wis., 1971—. Served with U.S. Army, 1943-45. Decorated 3 Battle Stars. Mem. Northeastern Wis. Sales and Mktg. Execs. Assn., Gummed Industries Assn. Roman Catholic. Clubs: North Shore Golf, Oshkosh Powerboat, Elks, P.O.P. Home: 324 Willow Ln Menasha WI 54952 Office: PO Box 330 Menasha WI 54952

ALBERT, NORMAN IRVING, physician; b. Ill., Apr. 7, 1912; M.D., Chgo. Med. Sch., 1938; m. Dorothy Trout, 1942 (dec.); 1 son, Norman Erick. Gen. practice medicine and surgery, Johnston City, Ill., 1939—; mem. staff Marion Meml. Hosp., pres., 1963—. Pres., Franklin and Williamson County Bds. Health, 1959-73; med. dir. U.S. Powder, Ordell, 1964; chmn. adv. bd. Williamson County Ill. Pub. Aid Commn.; pres. Williamson County Welfare Service Com., 1956-71; chmn. bd. Williamson County Sanatarium, 1953-73. Mem. draft, ration bds., Williamson County, World War II. Recipient Congl. Selective Service medal. Fellow Am. Geriatrics Soc., Internat. Acad. Proctology (pres. 1964-65); mem. Internat. Bd. Proctology, AMA, World Med. Assn., Ill. Acad. Gen Practice (past dir.), Williamson County Med. Soc. (pres. 1955). Club: Buck-Eye. Mason (Shriner), Odd Fellow, Elk. Asso. editor: Am. Jour. Proctology, 1965. Contbr. articles to med. jours. Home: 1414 Barham St Johnston City IL 62951 Office: 126 W Broadway Johnston City IL 62951

ALBERTI, CHARLES EDWARD, ednl. adminstr.; b. Chgo., July 14, 1945; s. Joseph J. and Gwendolyn G. (Doering) A.; B.F.A., Art Inst. Chgo., 1969; M.Ed., Loyola U., Chgo., 1971, Ph.D. (Arthur J. Schmitt scholar), 1975; m. Valerie Jean Vaughan, Aug. 14, 1970; 1 son, Leo Charlton. Asst. prin., Oak Forest (Ill.) High Sch., 1973-74; lectr. Loyola U., Chgo., 1974-77; dir. student teaching Ill. Benedictine Coll., Lisle, 1975-76; dir. grad. programs in edn. Lewis U., Lockport, Ill., 1976—; ednl. cons. Glen Ellyn (Ill.) elementary schs.; grad. asst. in art history Art Inst. Chgo., 1968-69. Fellow Midwest Philosophy of Edn. Soc., Am. Edn. Studies Assn.; mem. Nat. Philosophy of Edn. Soc., Am. Acad. Polit. and Social Scis., Phi Delta Kappa (pres. 1977-78, grantee). Author: Due Process in Discipline, 1977; editor of abstracts No. Ill. Assn. for Ednl. Research, 1977, Internal Foundations of Edn. Quar., 1973-75. Home: 1448 Blackburn Wheaton IL 60187 Office: Lewis Univ Route 53 Lockport IL 60441

ALBERTS, MARION EDWARD, physician; b. Hastings, Nebr., Mar. 14, 1923; s. Eddie and Mary Margaret (Hilbers) A.; B.A., U. Neb., 1944, M.D., 1948; m. Jeannette McDaniel, Dec. 25, 1944; children—Kathryn, Brian, Deborah, Timothy. Intern, Iowa Methodist Hosp., Des Moines, 1948-49; resident in pediatrics Raymond Blank Hosp. Children, Des Moines, 1949-50, 52-53; practice medicine specializing in pediatrics, Des Moines, 1953—; chief pediatrics Mercy Hosp., 1958—; mem. med. staff Iowa Luth. Hosp., Iowa Meth. Hosp., Broadlawns Polk County Hosp.; instr. clin. pediatrics Coll. Osteo. Medicine and Surgery, 1970—. Served to comdr. USNR, 1943-45, 50-52. Licenciate, Am. Bd. Pediatrics. Fellow Am. Acad. Pediatrics, Internat. Coll. Pediatrics; mem. AMA, Iowa Med. Soc. (sci. editor jour.), Des Moines C. of C. Republican. Presbyterian (elder). Club: Masons. Contbr. articles to profl. jours. Home: 7205 Washington Ave Des Moines IA 50311 Office: 1071 5th Ave Des Moines IA 50314

ALBERTSON, CLARENCE ELMO, chemist; b. Rockwood, Tenn., Oct. 7, 1922; s. Clarence Elmo and Eleanor Austin (Reemelin) A.; A.B., Miami U., Oxford, O., 1943; Ph.D., U. Cin., 1949; m. Helen Lucille Wolfe, Dec. 27, 1947; children—Barbara Jill, Pamela Sue, Charles Alan. Chemist, Hooker Chem. Co., Niagara Falls, N.Y., 1943-46; postdoctoral research Purdue U., Lafayette, Ind., 1949-50; chemist Robertshaw Fulton Controls Co., Pitts., 1950-51; with Borg Warner Corp., Chgo., 1951—, staff scientist, 1964-66, mgr. phys. chemistry research, 1966—. Recipient Henry Hochstetter award U. Cin., 1948. Mem. Am. Chem. Soc., Electrochem. Soc., Am. Eletroplaters Soc., Am. Soc. Lubrication Engrs., Chgo. Catalyst Club, Am. Inst. Chemists. Patentee clutch linings for automatic transmissions. Home: 240 S Monterey Ave Villa Park IL 60181 Office: Borg Warner Wolf and Algonquin Rds Des Plaines IL 60018

ALBINI, ALVO EDO, pub. relations exec.; b. Kenosha, Wis., Dec. 1, 1917; s. Julius and Filomena (Gentile) A.; B.A., U. Wis., 1940; M.S., Northwestern U., 1941; m. Eileen Rose Gamble, Sept. 14, 1946; children—Roseanna Marie, Christopher Robin. Reporter Wall Street Jour., 1941-42; financial writer Carl Byoir & Associates, 1942-44; asst. account exec. Selvage & Lee, 1944-46; advt. and sales promotion mgr. Studebaker Export Corp., 1946-54; dir. pub. relations Mahogany Assn., 1954-56; mgr. pub. relations Watch Div., Elgin Nat. Watch Co., 1956-57; ednl. services mgr. Montgomery Ward & Co., 1957-67; dir. pub. relations Loyola U., Chgo., 1967—. Mem. Pub. Relations Soc. Am., Northwestern Alumni, U. Wis. Alumni, Sigma Delta Chi. Clubs: Chicago Headline, Chicago Publicity. Home: 1026 Midway Rd Northbrook IL 60062 Office: 820 N Michigan Ave Chicago IL 60611

ALBOTT, WILLIAM LEROY, research clin. psychologists; b. Wichita, Kans., July 6, 1942; s. William Leeroy and Lillian (Humphreys) A.; B.A., Ft. Hays Coll. (Kans.), 1964, M.S., 1965; Ph.D., Ohio U., 1971; m. Carolyn Ramirez, Dec. 2, 1972; children—Cristina Sophia, Andreana Kendra. Clin., psychologist Larned (Kans.) State Hosp., 1965, Osawatomie (Kans.) State Hosp., 1966; sch. psychologist, Kankakee, Ill., 1966-68; grad. teaching asst. Ohio U., Athens, 1968-70; clin. psychol. intern Topeka State Hosp., 1970-71, dir. depts. research and edn., 1972—; pvt. practice, Topeka, 1974—; adj. faculty Wichita State U., Washburn Univs.; cons. Kans. Hwy. Patrol, Kans. Bur. Investigation; bd. dirs. Central Plains Drug Rehab Center, Inc., Certified psychologist, Kans. Mem. Am., MW, Kans. psychol. assns., Internat. Soc. for Non-Verbal Psychotherapy, AAAS, Sigma Xi. Democrat. Unitarian. Contbr. numerous articles to profl. jours.; reviewer Personality & Social Psychology Bull. Home: 1607 Boswell St Topeka KS 66604 Office: 2700 W 6th St Topeka KS 66606

ALBRECHT, EDWARD DANIEL, metals mfg. co. exec.; b. Kewanee, Ill., Feb. 11, 1937; s. Edward Albert and Mary Jane (Horner) A.; B.S. in Metall. Engring., U. Ariz., 1959, M.S., 1961, Ph.D., 1964, Metal. Engr. (hon.), 1973; m. Mignon Y. Buehler, Jan. 1, 1973; children—Renata E., Deborah J., Paul R. Research metallurgist, U. Calif. Los Alamos Lab., 1959-61; sr. physicist, project mgr. U. Calif. Lawrence Radiation Lab., Livermore, 1964-71; pres. Metall. Innovations Inc., Pleasanton, Calif., 1969-71; gen. mgr. Buehler Ltd. & Adolph I. Buehler, Inc., Evanston, Ill., 1972, v.p., gen. mgr., 1973-76, chmn., pres., 1976, also dir.; dir. Tech Met Canada Ltd. Bd. dirs. Danville (Calif.) Homeowners Inc., 1966-68; trustee Lake Forest Acad. - Ferry Hall Prep Sch. NDEA fellow, 1959-62. Fellow Am. Soc. Metals (chmn. Tucson 1961); mem. Internat. Metallographic Soc. (pres. 1973-75, dir. 1975-81), Sigma Gamm Epsilon, Delta Upsilon. Contbr. articles to profl. jours. Patentee in field. Office: PO Box 1459 Evanston IL 60204

ALBRECHT, EDWIN RAYMOND, optometrist; b. Mpls., Mar. 22, 1925; s. Otto F. and Mabel C. (Litke) A.; D. Optometry, No. Ill. Coll. Optometry, 1949; m. Loretta H. Jackelen, May 29, 1948; children—Arnold, Dianne, Linda, Karen. Pvt. practice optometry, Wabasha, Minn., 1950—, Plainview, 1952—. Served with AUS, 1943-46. Deocrated Purple Heart medal. Mem. V.F.W., Am. Legion. K.C. Home: 823 Broadway Wabasha MN 55981 Office: 155 W Main St Wabasha MN 55981

ALBRECHT, RONALD FRANK, physician; b. Chgo., Apr. 17, 1937; s. Frank William and Mabel Dorothy (Cassens) A.; A.B., U. Ill., 1958, B.S., 1959, M.D., 1961; m. Joyce Yvonne Burchfield, June 27, 1962; children—Ronald Frank II, Mark Burchfield, Meredith Ann. Intern, Cin. Gen. Hosp., 1961-62; resident anesthesiology U. Ill. Research and Ednl. Hosp., Chgo., 1962-64, attending physician, 1966-73; clin. asso. NIH, Bethesda, Md., 1964-66; practice medicine, specializing in anesthesiology, Chgo., 1966—; mem. med. staff Michael Reese Med. Center, Chgo., chmn. dept. anesthesiology, 1971—; asst. prof. anesthesiology U. Ill. Coll. Medicine, Chgo., 1966-70, clin. asso. prof., 1970-73; prof. anesthesiology U. Chgo. Sch. Medicine, 1973—. Served to lt. comdr. USPHS, 1964-66. Diplomate Am. Bd. Anesthesiology. Fellow Am. Coll. Anesthesiology; mem. AMA, Ill., Chgo. med. socs., Am., Ill. (sec. 1973—) socs. anesthesiologists, Chgo. Soc. Anesthesiologists, Internat. Anesthesia Research Soc. Presbyterian. Contbr. articles to profl. jours. Home: 28 Salem Ln Evanston IL 60203 Office: Dept Anesthesiology Michael Reese Med Center Chicago IL 60616

ALBRECHT, WILLARD HAROLD, physician; b. Middlebury, Ind., June 12, 1926; s. Aaron J. and Kathryn Rebecca (Hooley) A.; B.A., Goshen Coll., 1954; M.D., Northwestern U., 1958; m. Mary Ann McMahan, Sept. 6, 1959; children—Sharon Ruth, Mary Grace, John David, Douglas Todd. Intern Marion County Gen. Hosp., Indpls., 1958-59, resident, 1960-62, asst. dir. dept. anesthesiology, 1965—; practice medicine, Gary, Ind., 1959-60; asst. prof. anesthesiology Ind. U. Med. Sch., Indpls., 1965—; v.p., dir. Dryden Corp., Indpls., 1968—. Diplomate Am. Bd. Anesthesiology. Fellow Am. Coll. Anesthesiology; mem. Am. Soc. Anesthesiology, AMA, Ind. State Med. Assn., Marion County Med. Soc., Indpls. Soc. Anesthesiology (pres. 1967-68, 75-76), Pi Kappa Epsilon. Mem. Mennonite Ch. Home: 7400 Hollingsworth Dr Indianapolis IN 46268 Office: 1001 W 10th St Indianapolis IN 46202

ALBRIGHT, ARTHUR STANLEY, former utility co. exec.; b. Columbus, Ohio, June 13, 1889; s. James G. and Helen Isabel (Twiss) A.; M.Engring. in E.E., Ohio State U., 1912; m. Dorothe E. Becker, Sept. 5, 1916; 1 dau., Joyce (Mrs. William T. Greig). With Detroit Edison Co., elec. utility, 1912-54, controller, 1943-49, treas., 1949-53, exec. v.p., 1953-54. Mem. Thomas County (Ga.) Zoning Commn. Appeals Bd., 1960-65. Bd. dirs. Detroit Better Bus. Bur., 1950-54, pres., 1952-53. Recipient Distinguished Alumnus award Ohio State U., 1970. Decorated D.S.M. Mich. NG. Fellow IEEE; mem. Assn. Better Bus. Burs. (vice chmn. bd. dirs. 1953-54), Tau Beta Pi, Eta Kappa Nu, Phi Gamma Delta. Clubs: Masons, Rotary of Thomasville (Ga.) (hon.). Home: 504 Three Rivers N Fort Wayne IN 46802

ALBRIGHT, JOSEPH WILLIAM, army officer; b. Chillicothe, Ohio, Feb. 3, 1954; s. Herman LeRoy and Catherine Regina (Rieder) A.; B.M.E., U. Dayton, 1976; m. Marilyn Ann Miller, May 1, 1976. Commd. 2d lt. Ordnance Br., U.S. Army, 1976; accountable officer 9th Ordnance Co., Germany, 1977—. Mem. Nat. Def. Preparedness Assn., ASME, Assn. U.S. Army, Am. Soc. Heating, Refrigerating and Air-Conditioning Engrs. Home: 653 Orange St Chillicothe OH 45601 Office: Box 4846 9th Ordnance Co APO New York City NY 09059

ALBY, JAMES FRANCIS PAUL, clergyman, educator; b. Milw., July 16, 1936; s. Francis Joseph and Sara Sophie (Hansen) A.; B.A., Gallaudet Coll., 1963, M.S. in Edn., 1964; M.Div., Va. Theol. Sem., 1971. Ordained priest Episcopal Ch., 1971; priest to the deaf St. James Mission of the Deaf, Milw., 1971-76; priest asso. St. Peter's Ch., West Allis, Wis., 1972—. Tchr. high sch. hearing impaired Milw. Pub. Schs., 1972—; instr. interpreting for deaf U. Wis., Milw., 1975—; sr. high sch. boys dorm supr.-counselor St. John's Sch. for the Deaf, St. Francis, Wis., 1971-72; tchr. lang. of signs Milw. Area Tech. Coll., 1974-75; mem. adv. com. continuing edn. deaf adults, Milw., 1976—, tchr. hearing impaired Milw. Pub. Schs., 1977—. Mem. Ecumenical Clergy Assn., Nat., Wis. assns. of deaf, Am. Conf. Instrs. Deaf, Alpha Sigma Pi. Club: Lions (charter pres. Greater Milw. 1974-76). Contbr. articles to profl. jours.

ALDER, EDWIN FRANCIS, chem. co. exec.; b. Hugo, Okla., Sept. 1, 1927; s. Joseph B. and Mary Frances (Alder) A.; B.S., U. Okla., 1951, Ph.D., 1956; M.S. (Wychwood fellow), U. Chgo., 1952; postgrad. (Fulbright fellow) U. Bergen (Norway), 1953-54; m. Ann Ruth Wilson, Feb. 10, 1951; children—Gwendolyn Ann (Mrs. Jerry D. Bryant), Jan Allison, Martha Ellen, Steven Edwin. Instr., Ark. State Coll., Jonesboro, 1953, U. Okla., Norman, 1955, U. Ark., Fayetteville, 1955-57; with Eli Lilly & Co., Greenfield, Ind., 1957—, dir. agrl. research, 1966, v.p. agrl. research and devel., 1969—, v.p. research labs., 1973—. Mem. com. persistent pesticides Nat. Acad. Sci./NRC, 1968; mem. commn. on pesticides Dept. Health, Edn. and Welfare, 1969. Served with USN, 1945-48. Mem. AAAS, Am. Soc. Plant Physiologists, Scandinavian Soc. Plant Physiology, Weed Sci. Soc. Am., Phi Beta Kappa, Sigma Xi. Contbr. articles to profl. jours. Research on dinitroaniline herbicides. Home: 10140 E Troy Av Indianapolis IN 46239 Office: PO Box 708 Greenfield IN 46140

ALDERFER, WILLIAM KENNETH, historian; b. DuBois, Pa., Nov. 10, 1929; s. Clement Robinson and Katharine (Mayo) A.; student William and Mary Coll., 1947-49; B.S., U. Pa., 1951; M.A., U. Rochester, 1956; student U. Wis., 1956-58; m. Marilyn Manta Ruth, June 2, 1951;children—W. Kenneth, John M. Asst. supr. gen. accounting dept. Delco Appliance div. Gen. Motors Corp., Rochester, N.Y., 1951-55; teaching fellow U. Rochester, 1955-56; teaching asst. U. Wis., 1956-58; supr. Office Field Services, State Hist. Soc. Wis., Madison, 1958-64; dir. Mich. Hist. Soc., Lansing, 1964-67; state historian State of Ill., Springfield, 1967—. Chancellor Lincoln Acad. Ill., 1970-74, exec. dir., 1974—; mem. Ill. State Records Commn., sec., 1967—. Sec. Gov.'s Com. on Restoration of State Capitol, Lansing, Mich., 1966-67; chmn. Heritage Day, Mich. Week, 1966-67; pres. Waubesa Beach Community Center, 1961; mem. Capitol City Planning Commn., 1967—; mem. Ill. Sesquicentennial Commn., 1967-68, Ill. Bicentennial Commn., 1974-77; mem. Council Am. Assn. State and Local History, Abraham Lincoln Assn. (sec. 1967—), Ulysses S. Grant Assn. (dir. 1967—), Ill. State Hist. Soc. (exec. dir. 1967—), Am. Assn. for State and Local History (nat. awards chmn. 1973-76), Sangamon County, Vermilion County hist. socs., Chgo. Civil War Round Table, Am. Library Assn. Office: Old State Capitol Springfield IL 62707

ALDERMAN, DAVID ARDEN, mgmt. cons. co. exec.; b. Garrettsville, Ohio, Dec. 28, 1935; s. Lester Theodore and Isabelle Clara (Woodworth) A.; student Ohio State U., 1954-57, Kent State U., 1961-66; B.S. in Indsl. Mgmt., Youngstown State U., 1970; postgrad U. Akron, 1970-71; m. Peggy Ann Maggard, Apr. 6, 1957; children—Erin Jae, Craig Trenton, Lisa Renee. Project engr. ADS Machinery Corp., Warren, Ohio, 1961-67, Ajax Magnethermic Corp.,

Warren, 1968-71; pres. RARECorp., Warren, 1971—; guest lectr. Kent State U.; dir. Peppermint Prodns., Inc., Youngstown. Vice chmn. Trumbull County (Ohio) Republican Central Com., 1974-77. Mem. Soc. Profl. Mgmt. Consultants, Inst. Certification of Engring. Technicians, ASME, Nat. Mgmt. Assn., Am. Foundryman's Soc., Assn. Iron and Steel Engrs. Methodist. Clubs: Rotary, Masons, Shriners. Home: 1402 Frederick St Niles OH 44446 Office: 1620 McMyler NW Box 3037 Warren OH 44485

ALDERMAN, ROALDA JENSEN, hosp. adminstr.; b. Rochester, Minn., Apr. 23, 1930; d. Lloyd Bryan and Marvel Dora (Johannesen) Jensen; B.A., U. Chgo., 1949, M.A., 1967; postgrad. Ill. Tchrs. Coll., 1963; m. William Walter Alderman, Nov. 19, 1968; children—Bruce Donald, Karen Laurie. Dietary supr. Billings Hosp., U. Chgo., 1951-53, psychometrist Office Vocation Guidance Counsel, U. Chgo., 1950-51, 53-54; project research specialist div. hosp. and scientific orgn., asst. dir. project new fields sci. inquiry, exobiology Indsl. Relations Center, U. Chgo., 1965-68; dir. tng. Cook County Hosp., Chgo., 1968-69, dir. personnel, 1969-71, asso. hosp. dir. personal services, 1969-70; exec. adminstr. Ill. Dept. Pub. Health Hosp. and Clinics, Chgo., 1971-75; Chgo. region asst. to dep. dir. Ill. Dept. Pub. Aid, 1971-73; supt. div. alcoholism Ill. Dept. Mental Health and D/D, State Alcoholism Authority, 1975—; lectr. Grad. Sch. Pub. Health, U. Ill., 1975—. Co-founder Chel-win South Improvement Assn., 1965, sec., 1966, dir., 1965-67. Recipient State Ill. Gov.'s awards, Superior Achievement certificate, 1972, citation radio sta. WAIT, Chgo., 1975. Mem. Chgo. Hosp. Personnel Mgmt. Assn., Ill. Pub. Health Assn. (mem. membership com. 1971), Am., Ill. hosp. assns., Council State and Territorial Alcohol Authorities, Am. Coll. Hosp. Adminstrs. Home: 28 W 440 Main St Warrenville IL 60555 Office: Room 1900 188 W Randolph St Chicago IL 60601

ALDERSON, BERNITA MAE, publisher, educator; b. Sterling, Colo., Dec. 22, 1921; d. Robert Thomas and Gladys Fay (Pitchford) Alderson; student Brown's Bus. Coll., 1940; B.S., U. Ill., 1950. Sec. to advt. mgr. Baker's Mfg. Co., Springfield, Ill., 1940; dictaphone operator Springfield/Livingstone Ct. Reporting Agy., 1941; sec. Sangamon Ordnance Plant, 1942; weather observer Springfield Airport Weather Bur., 1943-45; part-time sec. Rich-or-Poor Lab., Urbana, Ill., 1945-49; tchr. Brown's Bus. Coll., Springfield, 1950, mgr., 1952-55, owner, 1955—; pres. Ill. Bus. Coll., 1963-68; tchr., sec. Terre Haute Comml. Coll., 1951; pres. Brown's Career Coll., 1969—; pub. Women of Ill. History, City Name Trails. Mem. Assn. Commerce and Industry. Home: 1529 S Douglas Ave Springfield IL 62704

ALDERTON, HARVEY RANDALL, child psychiatrist; b. Mitcham, Surrey, Eng., Aug. 29, 1927; s. Randall Frederick and Margaret (Bassett) A.; M.B.,B.S., London (Eng.) Hosp. Med. Coll., 1950; Diploma in Psychol. Medicine, Maudsley Hosp., 1957; m. Rae West, Aug. 5, 1954; children—Susan, Jennifer, Gillian. Intern, London Hosp. Med. Coll., 1950-52; resident Inst. Psychiatry, Maudsley Hosp., London, 1954-57; practice medicine specializing in child psychiatry, Toronto, Ont., Can., 1957—; staff psychiatrist Thistletown Regional Centre, Rexdale, Ont., Can., 1957-60, clin. dir., 1961-70, dir. out patient dept., 1967-70, dir. tng. and research, 1970-72, dir. psychiat. tng. and research, 1972-75; sr. staff psychiatrist Hosp. for Sick Children, 1976—; dir. East York-Leaside Child Guidance Clinic, 1960-61; faculty U. Toronto, 1958—, asso. prof. dept. psychiatry, 1970—; cons. psychiatrist North York Bd. Edn., 1972—, Powell-Brown Nursery, 1971—, Earlscourt Children's Home, 1965—. Bd. dir. Powell-Brown Nursery, 1972—, chmn. profl. adv. bd., 1972—; mem. profl. adv. bd. Earlscourt Childrens Home, 1972—. Served to capt. M.C., Royal Army, 1952-54. Fellow Royal Coll. Physicians (Can.), Am. Psychiat. Assn., A.C.P., Royal Coll. Psychiatrists; mem. Canadian, Ont. med. assns., Canadian, Ont. (sec. 1969-72) psychiat. assns. Mem. editorial bd. Canadian Psychiat. Assn. Jour., 1965-76. Contbr. articles to profl. jours. Home: 4 Meadow Height Ct Thornhill ON Canada Office: Suite 205 3995 Bathurst St Downsview ON Canada

ALDRIDGE, VICTOR E., JR., lawyer; b. nr. Indian Springs, Ind., Jan. 31, 1919; s. Victor E. and Cleta B. (Wadsworth) A.; A.B., Ind. U., 1941, J.D. with distinction, 1943; m. Sandra Anderson, Nov. 11, 1970; 1 son, Victor E. III; 1 dau. by previous marriage, Mary Victoria (Mrs. Richard M. Turner). Admitted to Ind. bar, 1943; practiced in Terre Haute, Ind., 1946—. Treas. Young Democrats Club of Vigo County, Ind., 1947-50. Bd. dirs. United Fund, Terre Haute; bd. dirs. YMCA, pres., 1965-67. Served as lt. col. AUS, 1943-46. Decorated Bronze Star medal, Purple Heart. Mem. Ind., Terre Haute (pres. 1959-60), 6th Dist. (pres. 1955-56) bar assns., Order of Coif, Phi Delta Phi, Pi Sigma Alpha, Sigma Alpha Epsilon. Mason, Elk. Club: Ind. University (pres. Terre Haute 1950). Home: 524 Deming St Terre Haute IN 47807 Office: 1200 Sycamore Bldg Terre Haute IN 47807

ALEFF, HOWARD JOSEPH, dentist; b. Sheboygan, Wis., Apr. 18, 1915; s. Joseph William and Theresa Rose (Loesing) A.; student Ripon Coll., 1933-35; D.D.S., Northwestern U., 1940; m. Phyllis Leanne Perkins, Oct. 15, 1943; children—Andrea (Mrs. David L. Nelson), Phyllis Jane (Mrs. Howard R. Mater), Howard John. Pvt. practice dentistry, Sheboygan, 1940-42, 46-47; dentist VA Hosp., Knoxville, Iowa, 1947—, chief dental service, 1969—; asso. prof. dentistry U. Iowa, Iowa City, 1971—. Dir. Marion County Savs. & Loan Assn., 1960—, Ladies Ready to Wear, Knoxville, 1962—. Bd. dirs. ARC, 1952-58, Knoxville council Boy Scouts Am., 1958-60, United Fund, 1969—. Served with AUS, 1942-46. Decorated Bronze Star, Croix de Guerre (France). Mem. ADA. Rotarian. Club: Pine Knoll Country. Home: 304 Terrace Ln Knoxville IA 50138 Office: VA Hosp Knoxville IA 50138

ALEKSANDROWICZ, FRANK JOHN, photographer; b. Erie, Pa., Sept. 17, 1921; s. John and Julia (Pawski) A.; student St. John Kanty Coll., 1941, U. Pitts., Erie Extension Sch. Journalism, 1941-42; m. Louise Andrianne, July 17, 1945. Newspaper photographer Erie (Pa.) Dispatch, 1941-42, 45-57; photographer Cleve. Press, 1957-67, columnist, 1962; free-lance comml. photography in advt., indsl. pub. relations 1967—. One-man shows at Design House, Cuyahoga Savs. and Loan, Broadview Savs. and Loan. Served with AUS, 1943-45; ETO; with AUS, 1950-51; Korea. Recipient advt. photography awards CA. Mag., N.Y. Art Dirs. Show, Chgo. Art Dirs. Show, Cleve. Soc. Communicating Arts. Mem. Nat. Press Photographers Assn., Ohio News Photographers Assn., Am. Soc. Mag. Photographers, Cleve. Soc. Communicating Arts, Sigma Delta Chi. Home: 343 Canterbury Rd Bay Village OH 44140 Office: 624 St Clair Ave NW Cleveland OH 44113

ALESCH, DANIEL JAMES, public policy researcher; b. Appleton, Wis., Apr. 21, 1939; s. Roman William and Margaret Ella (Danielsen) A.; B.S., U. Wis., 1962, M.S. in Urban and Regional Planning, 1964; M.A. in Polit. Sci., U. Calif. at Los Angeles, 1969, Ph.D., 1970; m. Jane G. Basten, June 10, 1961; children—Kirsten, Greta. Resident fellow Inst. Pub. Adminstrn., N.Y.C., 1964-65; dep. chief bur. state planning N.Y. State Office of Planning Coordination, Albany, 1965-67; research staff U. So. Calif. Sch. Pub. Adminstrn., 1967-68; social scientist The Rand Corp., Santa Monica, Calif., 1968-73, mgr. Green Bay (Wis.) office, 1973—; chmn. bd. dirs. Housing Allowance Office of Brown County, Green Bay, 1973—; lectr. pub. adminstrn. U. Calif. at Los Angeles, 1970-73, U. So. Calif., 1968-72; lectr. environ. adminstrn. U. Wis. at Green Bay, 1976—. Ford Found. fellow, 1962-64. Mem. Am. Soc. Pub. Adminstrn. Roman Catholic. Author: (with others) Urban Government for Greater Stockholm, 1968. Home: 909 Forest Hill Dr Green Bay WI 54301 Office: 630 Cherry St Green Bay WI 54301

ALEXAKOS, CONSTANTINE EVANGELOS, psychologist; b. Tripolis, Greece, Aug. 21, 1928; s. Evangelos Constantine and Penelope Athanasios (Katsavelos) A.; came to U.S., 1960, naturalized, 1973; B.A. (fellow), U. Athens (Greece), 1958; M.Ed. (scholar), Harvard, 1961; postgrad. U. Chgo., 1961-62; Ph.D., U. Wis., 1965; m. Martha Lee Schellhase, June 17, 1961; children—Peter David, Mark Jason. Research asso. U. Wis., 1965-66; asst. prof. W.Va. U. Coll. Human Resources, Morgantown, 1966-69, asso. prof. edn. and psychology, 1969-70; clin. supr. dept. psychology Woodward (Ia.) State Hosp.-Sch., 1970-71; clin. psychologist Mental Health Inst., Mt. Pleasant, Iowa, 1971-72; pvt. practice as psychologist, Chgo., 1972—. Sch. psychologist, cons. bilingual-bicultural Greek-speaking children, 1972—. Bd. dirs. White House Conf. on Children and Youth, State W.Va., 1967-69. Served with Greek Army, 1950-53. Fulbright travel grantee, 1960-61. Mem. Am., Ill. psychol. assns., Nat. Soc. for Study Edn., Chgo. Psychol. Club. Mem. Order Ahepa. Home: 4846 N Washtenaw Ave Chicago IL 60625 Office: 168 N Michigan Ave Chicago IL 60601

ALEXANDER, C. ALEX, physician, educator; b. Kerala, India, Mar. 1, 1935; s. Chandy and Sarah (Yohannan) A.; came to U.S., 1962, naturalized, 1974; M.D., U. Madras (India), 1958; M.P.H., Johns Hopkins U., 1964, Dr.P.H., 1966; m. Chimu Kalaya, Jan. 3, 1960. Intern, Plainfield, N.J., 1962-63; resident in preventive medicine Johns Hopkins U., Balt., 1964-66, asst. to asso. prof. pub. health adminstrn.; 1966-72; dir. med. affairs Provident Hosp., Balt., 1971-73; asso. prof. social and preventive medicine Med. Sch. U. Md., Balt., 1972-75; chief of staff VA Center, Dayton, Ohio, 1975—; clin. prof. community medicine Wright State U., Dayton, 1975—, asst. dean Sch. Medicine, 1975-76; cons. WHO, 1969, USPHS. Recipient Distinquished Service award Community Health Council Md., 1974; diplomate Am. Bd. Preventive Medicine. Fellow Am. Coll Preventive Medicine, Am. Pub. Health Assn., Am. Coll. Internat. Physicians (pres. elect 1977); mem. Ohio Med. Assn., Montgomery County Med. Soc., Am. Mgmt. Assn. Syrian Orthodox. Club: Dayton Racquet. Contbr. articles in field to profl. jours. Home: 1242 Ashburton Dr Dayton OH 45459 Office: VA Center Dayton OH 45428

ALEXANDER, CHARLES FREEMAN, JR., marine propulsion mfg. co. exec.; b. Kansas City, Mo., Nov. 14, 1921; s. Charles Freeman and Marjorie May (Longan) A.; B.S.M.E., B.S. in Naval Architecture and Marine Engring., U. Mich., 1943; student U.S. Navy Midshipman Sch., Columbia U., 1943; postgrad. Advanced mgmt. program Harvard U., 1976; m. Juliet Ruth Lindeman, Nov. 6, 1943; children—Charles Freeman III, Wendy L. Alexander Fitzgerald, Anne K., Lori E. Engr., Atlas Imperial Diesel Engine Co., Oakland, Calif., 1946-47, project engr. propulsion lab. U.S. Naval Air Missile Test Center, Pt. Mugu, Calif., 1947-53; asst. to v.p. engring. Mercury Marine div. Brunswick Corp., Fond du Lac, Wis., 1953, chief plant engr., 1953-64, v.p. engring., 1964-77, pres. Mercury Marine, v.p. and group exec. marine power, 1977—; pres. Brunswick Corp.; dir. Nat. Exchange Bank, Fond du Lac. Served to lt. (j.g.) U.S. Navy, 1943-46. Mem. Soc. Automotive Engrs., Am. Soc. Naval Engrs., Soc. Naval Architects and Marine Engrs., ASME, Am. Power Boat Assn. Clubs: South Hills, Elks. Patentee outboard motors and stern drives. Office: 1939 Pioneer Rd Fond du Lac WI 54935

ALEXANDER, DANIEL RICHARD, dentist; b. Bellaire, Ohio, Mar. 28, 1931; s. Andrew and Josephine (Vannelle) A.; B.S., Wheeling Coll., 1960; D.D.S., U. Pitts., 1964; m. Jane Goldsmith, Oct. 9, 1960 (dec. 1974); children—Daniel Joseph, Andrew James, Kimberly, Buffy, Gus; m. 2d, Mary Ann McGee, July, 1975. Gen. practice dentistry, Bellaire, 1964—; dir. Eastern Ohio Nat. Bank; pres. Profl. Group, Inc., 1972—. Pres., Belmont County Heart Assn., 1968-69. Served with USNR, 1952-54. Mem. Am., Eastern Ohio dental assns. Elk. Club: Belmont Hill Country (St. Clairesville, Ohio). Home: Bellview Heights Bellaire OH 43906 Office: 38th & Jefferson Sts Bellaire OH 43906

ALEXANDER, DON KENNETH, cardiologist; b. Ann Arbor, Mich., July 2, 1932; s. John Byron and Helen Edna (Hammon) A.; B.S. in Pharmacy, U. Mich., 1954, M.D., 1962; m. Caroline Anderson, Aug. 16, 1972; children—Don Kenneth, Renée, Tracy, Donna, Cherie. Intern, St. Joseph Hosp., Ann Arbor, 1962-63, resident in internal medicine, 1963-66; resident in cardiology U. Mich. Med. Center, Ann Arbor, 1966-67; practice medicine specializing in cardiology, Ann Arbor, 1967—; clin. instr. U. Mich. Med. Center. Served with USMC, 1954-56. Mem. AMA, Washtenaw Med. Soc., Mich. State Med. Soc., Am. Heart Assn. Methodist. Home: 1499 Folkstone Ct Ann Arbor MI 48105 Office: 4870 Clark Rd Ypsilanti MI 48197

ALEXANDER, DONALD WAYNE, counselor; b. Springfield, Mo., Dec. 19, 1940; s. Thomas Walker and Clara Alma A.; B.S., Southwest Mo. State U., 1972, M.S., 1975; m. Dixie Beatrice Alexander, Mar. 10, 1962; children—Carrie Kathleen, Danny Walker. Tchr. substitute, Everton, Willard, Ash Grove, Springfield, Mo., 1974-75; counselor Dade County Neighborhood Center, Greenfield, Mo., 1975-76, Greene County Neighborhood Center, Springfield, 1975-76; caseworker, counselor Mo. Div. Corrections, Fordland, 1976-77; counselor D.E. Burrell Community Mental Health Center, Springfield, Mo., 1977—. Served with USMC, 1965-67: Vietnam. Decorated Purple Heart. Mem. VFW, DAV, Am. Personnel Guidance Assn., Pub. Offender Counseling Assn., Amateur Athletic Union. Home: Rt 2 Box 181A Rogersville MO 65742 Office: 430 South Ave Springfield MO 65802

ALEXANDER, JAMES, psychoanalyst; b. Galveston, Tex., Sept. 25, 1910; s. Keeton and Daisy (Jeffrey) A.; student U. Tex., 1929-32; M.D., Baylor U., 1936; m. Ann Krumm, Dec. 23, 1939. Intern, Md. Gen. Hosp., Balt., 1936; psychiat. resident Austin (Tex.) State Hosp., 1937-39; practice psychoanalysis, Chgo., 1949—; mem. faculty Northwestern U., Chgo., 1975—, prof. psychiatry, 1975—. Served with AUS, 1942-46. Mem. Assn. Symbolic Logic, Am. Friends Austria, Am. Math. Soc., Am. Psychoanalytic Assn., Internat. Psychoanalytic Assn. Club: Germania. Contbr. articles to psychoanalytic jours. Home: 301 S Cuyler St Oak Park IL 60302 Office: 664 N Michigan Ave Chicago IL 60611

ALEXANDER, KENNETH OLIVER, economist, educator; b. Vulcan, Mich., Oct. 19, 1927; s. Oliver and Jennie (Mortier) A.; B.A., Mich. State U., 1949; Ph.D., Mass. Inst. Tech., 1957; m. Eleanor Ann Salmon, Dec. 19, 1959; children—Laura, Paul. Teaching and research asst. Mass. Inst. Tech., Cambridge, Mass., 1951-53; instr., asst. prof. Mich. State U., East Lansing, 1955-61; asso. prof. Mich. Tech. U., Houghton, 1961-64, prof., econ. coordinator, 1965—; prof., asso. dir. U. Iowa, Iowa City, 1964-65; asso. for content planning The American Economy, CBS-TV series, 1962-63. Served with USCG, 1945-47, with U.S. Army, 1953-55. Mem. Am. Econ. Assn., Indsl. Relations Research Assn., Econs. Soc. Mich. Co-author: The American Economy, 1962; contbr. numerous articles in econs. to profl. jours. Home: 212 Harris Ave Hancock MI 49930 Office: Sch Bus Mich Tech Houghton MI 49931

ALEXANDER, NANCY CAROL, counselor; b. Kirksville, Mo., Oct. 14, 1951; d. Kem Fletcher and Vivian Genevieve (Gardine) George; B.S.E., Northeast Mo. State U., 1973, M.A., 1976; houseparent Adams County Youth Home, Quincy, Ill., 1973-74; dir., counselor Macon (Mo.) County Counseling Center, 1976-77; Coordinator, counselor Muscatine (Iowa) Community Coll., 1977—. Vol. counselor, Planned Parenthood, Kirksville. Recipient Bernice B. Beggs award, 1972. Mem. Mo. Assn. Alcohol Counselors, Am. Personnel and Guidance Assn. Office: Muscatine Community Coll 152 Colorado Blvd Muscatine IA 52761

ALEXANDER, PATRICIA LOUISE, sch. adminstr.; b. Indpls., July 15, 1929; d. Jacob Michael and Dorothy Emily Leffler; B.S., Butler U., Indpls., 1964, M.S., 1966; Ed.D. (scholar), Ind. U., 1975; m. Arthur Alexander, Apr. 23, 1949; children—Frederick B., James M., Brian E. Biology tchr., counselor, dir. publns. Indpls. pub. schs., 1964-69, dean girls Thomas Carr Howe High Sch., 1969-74, asst. supr. spl. services, 1975—; pres., dir. Stopover, Inc., crisis counseling for runaways. Dir. edni. div. Greater Indpls. United Way campaign, 1976. Newspaper Fund fellow, summer 1968. Mem. AAUW, Am. Assn. Sch. Adminstrs., Nat. Assn. Secondary Sch. Prins., Ind. secondary sch. Adminstrs. and Prins., Am. Personnel and Guidance Assn., Am. Sch. Counselors Assn., Nat. Orgn. Legal Problems in Edn., Council Exceptional Children, Nat. Council Adminstrv. Women in Edn., Community Service Council, Nat. Assn. Tchrs. Young Children, Phi Kappa Phi, Phi Delta Kappa, Kappa Delta Pi. Presbyterian. Clubs: Indpls. Athletic, Athenaeum Turners. Address: 120 E Walnut St Indianapolis IN 46204

ALEXANDER, ROBERT LEE, aircraft co. exec.; b. Greensboro, N.C., May 15, 1920; s. Robert and Meta Belle A.; B.S. in Edn., Va. State Coll., 1946; M.A. in Edn., N.Y. U., 1948; m. Ruth Roberta Dabney, Aug. 25, 1946; 1 dau., Roberta Leigh. Tchr. music, civics, govt. Dunbar High Sch., Lynchburg, Va., 1947-51; supply clk. to logistics officer Wright-Patterson AFB, Dayton, Ohio, 1951-76; logistics coordinator Northrop Worldwide Aircraft Services, Inc., Dayton, 1976—; chmn. U.S. Air Force Command Logistics Career Bd.; mem. Non-Appropriated Funds Council; counselor Equal Employment Opportunity; adj. prof. Wilberforce U., Air Force Inst. Tech., Dept. Def. Sch. Logistics. Served with U.S. Army, 1943-45. Decorated Purple Heart; recipient Outstanding Service award U.S. Air Force, 1959, 66; Bronze medallion U.S. Army Logistics Center, 1959; Gold Zero Defects award U.S. Air Force, 1971, Significant Achievement award, 1972, Meritorious Service award, 1976; Proudly We Hail award Wright-Patterson AFB, 1976. Mem. Nat. Tchr. Edn. Assn., Soc. Logistics Engrs., Armed Forces Preparedness Assn., Dayton Chamber Music Soc., Alpha Phi Alpha. Republican. Clubs: Twin Base Golf (Dayton); Ky. Cols. Home: 125 Miami Dr Yellow Springs OH 45387 Office: PO Box 33352 Wright-Patterson AFB OH 45433

ALEXANDER, WILLIAM MICHAEL, lawyer; b. Omaha, June 10, 1942; s. Michael Edward and Marie Francie (Roesing) A.; B.A., Creighton U., 1966, J.D., 1972; m. Mary Catherine Wiehl, July 28, 1968; children—Mark Michael, Beth Catherine, Megan Maril. Admitted to Iowa bar, 1972, Nebr. bar, 1972; analyst, underwriter Mutual of Omaha, 1966-69; mem. firm George T. Qualley, Sioux City, Iowa, 1972-75, William M. Alexander, Laurens, Iowa, 1976-77. Mem. Laurens C. of C., Am., Iowa, Nebr. bar assns., Delta Theta Phi. Republican. Roman Catholic. Clubs: Lions, Laurens Country, K.C. Home: 301 S 2d St Laurens IA 50554 Office: 123 3d St N Laurens IA 50554

ALEXANDERSON, ELDON LUDWIG, nuclear engr.; b. Norway, Mich., Nov. 14, 1919; s. Nels Ludwig and Wilmont Esther (O'Blenes) A.; B.S., Hillsdale Coll., 1943; M.S., U. Mich., 1949; m. E. Pauline Ely, Apr. 24, 1943; children—Alvin, Marie, Steven. With Detroit Edison Co., 1946-51, 53-71, asst. supt. and reactor engr. Enrico Fermi Atomic Power Plant, Newport, Mich., 1966-71; asst. gen. mgr. Power Reactor Devel. Co., Detroit, 1971-72, gen. mgr., 1972-75, dir. nuclear engring. div. Generation Engring. Dept., 1976—; cons. GAO. Active Boy Scouts Am. Served with USAAF, 1943-46, with USAF, 1951-53. Mem. Am. Nuclear Soc. (chmn. Mich. sect. 1966-67), Engring. Soc. of Detroit. Contbr. articles to profl. jours. Home: 10 Robindale Ct Dearborn MI 48124

ALEXIS, MARCUS, educator; b. N.Y.C., Feb. 26, 1932; B.A., Bklyn. Coll., 1953; M.A. (Univ. scholar, Hinman fellow), Mich. State U., 1954; Ph.D. (Univ. fellow), U. Minn., 1959; m.; 3 children. Instr. econs. U. Minn., 1954-57; asst. prof. econs. and mktg. Macalester Coll., 1957-60; asso. prof. mktg. DePaul U., 1960-62; asso. prof. to prof. bus. adminstrn. U. Rochester, 1962-70; prof. econs. Northwestern U., Evanston, Ill., 1970—, chmn. dept., 1975—; vis. prof. U. Calif. at Berkeley, 1969-71. Vis. scholar, Ford Found. fellow Grad. Sch. Bus. Harvard, 1961-62; vis. asso. prof. U. Minn., 1962, 65. Mem. Am. Econ. Assn. (mem. com. to increase supply of minority economists 1971-74, mem. com. on honors and awards 1972—, chmn. com. status of minorities in the profession 1974—, dir. summer program for minority students 1974-77), Am. Mktg. Assn. (dir. 1968-70), Caucus Black Economists (chmn. 1969-71, mem. steering com. 1969-73). Office: Coll Arts and Scis Northwestern U Evanston IL 60201

ALFORD, GERALD DEAN, hwy. project engr.; b. Peru, Kans., Nov. 12, 1935; s. Daniel Ralph and Dorothy Lee (Chrisman) A.; student Coffeyville Coll., 1953-55; m. Janice Maxine Wiggins, Feb. 6, 1955; children—Michael Dean, Gerald Scott, Douglas Kirk, Lori Ann. With Kans. Hwy. Commn., Independence, 1956—, hwy. project engr., 1967—. Registered profl. engr., Kans. Mem. Kans. Engring. Soc., Nat. Soc. Profl. Engrs. Baptist. Home: 517 E Myrtle St Independence KS 67301 Office: Box 884 Independence KS 67301

ALFRED, KARL SVERRE, orthopedic surgeon; b. Stavanger, Norway, July 10, 1917; s. Alfred Bjarne Abrahamsen and Thora (Garpestad) Floen; student U. Va., 1935-38; M.D., L.I. Coll. Medicine, 1942; m. Amalia Leona Bombach, July 26, 1951; children—Patricia (Mrs. Dennis Alleman), Richard Lincoln, Peter Karl. Intern, Mountainside Hosp., Montclair, N.J., 1942-43; resident orthopedics Univ. Hosps., Cleve., 1947-50; practice medicine specializing in orthopedic surgery, Cleve., 1950—; chief orthopedic surgery St. Vincent Charity Hosp., Cleve., 1955—, chief of staff, 1971-75; asso. staff Euclid Gen. Hosp., Cleve.; courtesy staff Univ., St. Luke's hosps., Cleve., Geauga Community Hosp., Chardon, O.; orthopedic cons. Norfolk & Western R.R.; affiliate tchr. orthopedics Bunts Edn. Inst., Cleve. Clinic Found. Trustee St. Vincent Charity Hosp., Cleve. Served with M.C., USNR, 1943-47. Episcopalian. Mason, Rotarian. Contbr. articles to profl. jours. Home: 20 Brandywood Dr Pepper Pike OH 44124 Office: 2475 E 22d St Cleveland OH 44115

ALI, HUSSIEN, financial cons.; b. San Antonio, Nov. 22, 1948; s. Bey and Eleanor Logan Ali; B.S. in Bus. Adminstrn., Tex. So. U., 1970; m. Jackie Ali, June 6, 1973; 1 child, Waseem. V.p. sales, Good Food Inc., Cleve., 1972-75; prin. Hussien Ali & Co., 1974—. Served with U.S. Army, 1970-72. Decorated Bronze Star. Mem. Better Bus. Bur., Internat. Consumer Credit Assn., C. of C., Nat. Assn. Credit Mgmt. Democrat. Islam. Home: 216 4860647 1540E Cleveland OH 44117 Office: 1 Public Square #502 Cleveland OH 44113

ALI, MIR MASOOM, educator; b. Bangladesh, Feb. 1, 1937; s. Mir Muazzam and Azifa Khatoon (Chowdhury) A.; came to U.S., 1969; B.Sc. with honors, U. Dacca, 1956, M.Sc., 1957; M.Sc., U. Toronto, 1967, Ph.D., 1969; m. Firoza Chowdhury, June 25, 1959; children—Naheed, Fahima, Farah, Mir Ishtiaque. Research officer Ministry of Food and Agriculture, Ministry of Commerce, Central Pub. Service Commn., Govt. of Pakistan, 1958-66; teaching asst. U. Toronto (Ont., Can.), 1966-69; asst. prof. math. scis. Ball State U., Muncie, Ind., 1969-74, asso. prof., 1974—; vis. spl. lectr. U. Windsor (Can.), 1972-73. Grantee Ball State U., 1976-77, Ind. Com. for Humanities, 1976-77. Fellow Royal Statis. Soc. London; mem. Am. Statis. Assn., Inst. Math. Statistics, Am. Math. Soc., Calcutta Math. Soc. Moslem. Contbr. articles to profl. jours. Home: 3003 Riverside Ave Muncie IN 47304 Office: Ball State U Dept Mathematical Sciences Muncie IN 47306

ALIG, FRANK DOUGLAS STALNAKER, constrn. co. exec.; b. Indpls., Oct. 10, 1921; s. Clarence Schirmer and Marjory (Stalnaker) A.; student Mich. U., 1939-41; B.S., Purdue U., 1948; m. Ann Bobbs, Oct. 22, 1949; children—Douglas, Helen, Barbara. Proj. engr. Ind. State Hwy. Commn., Indpls., 1948; pres. Alig-Stark Constrn. Co., Inc., 1949-57, Frank S. Alig, Inc., 1957—; chmn. bd. Concrete Structures Corp., Indpls.; v.p., dir. Bo-Wit Products Corp., Edinburg, Ind.; pres. dir. Home Stove Realty Co.; pres, dir. Home Land Investment Co., Inc. Served with AUS, 1943-46. Mem. U.S., Ind. socs. profl. engrs., Ind. Assn. Credit Men, U.S. Ind. State, Indpls. chambers commerce. Republican. Presbyn. (deacon). Clubs: Woodstock, Dramatic, University. Home: 8080 N Pennsylvania St Indianapolis IN 46240 Office: 4849 W 96th St Indianapolis IN 46268

ALL, DAVID CLAYTON, lawyer; b. McPherson, Kans., Oct. 30, 1940; s. Wilbur L. and Marjorie E. (Clayton) A.; B.S., Kans. State U., 1962; J.D., U. Kans., 1965; m. Priscilla Ann Osborn, Oct. 30, 1965; children—Stacy Ann, Matthew David. Admitted to Kans. bar, 1966; mgmt. devel. candidate Conoco, Lincoln, Nebr., 1965-66; asso. firm Anderson & Clark, Wichita, Kans., 1966-68; mem. firm Gaines & All, Augusta, Kans., 1968—; asst. atty. Butler County, 1971; municipal judge City of Augusta, 1970-71. Bd. dirs. Augusta Med. Complex, 1973—, pres., chmn. bd., 1977-78; bd. dirs. South Central Kans. Mental Health Counciling Center, 1973—. Mem. Butler County Bar Assn. (pres. 1973), Augusta C. of C. (dir. 1972-75, v.p. 1975), Delta Tau Delta. Democrat. Mem. Christian Ch. (elder 1971, chmn. bd. 1975-77). Elk. Home: 26 Angelina Dr Augusta KS 67010 Office: 120 E 5th St Augusta KS 67010

ALLABEN, ROBERT DEWITT, surgeon, med. service adminstr.; b. Grand Rapids, Mich., Sept. 26, 1930; s. Fred Roland and Joanna Jo (Dewitt) A.; B.S., U. Mich., 1952; M.D., Wayne State U., 1956; m. Ruth Elaine Six, Aug. 29, 1952; children—Elizabeth Ann, Janet Louise, Bruce Atwood. Intern Women's Hosp., Detroit, 1956-57; resident Harper Hosp., Detroit, 1957-61; practice medicine specializing in surgery, Detroit, 1961—; mem. staff Harper, Mount Carmel, Children's, Sinai, Detroit Gen. hosps. (all Detroit); chief gen. surg. sect. lHarper Hosp., Detroit, 1969-72, vice-chief dept. of surgery, 1971-77; clin. asst. prof. surgery Wayne State U., Detroit, 1965—; chief sect. of transplation Mt. Carmel Mercy Hosp., Detroit, 1972—. Councilman Village of Quakertown, Mich., 1967-69, pres., 1971-73. Diplomate Am. Bd. Surgery. Fellow A.C.S.; mem. AMA (alt. del. 1977—), Mich. State, Wayne County med. socs., Midwest (councilor 1973—, pres. 1977-78), Pan-Pacific, Detroit (jr. councilor 1971-72) surg. assns., Detroit Acad. Surgery, Detroit Gastroenterological Soc. (pres. 1972-73), Transplantation Soc. Mich. (dir. 1974—), Detroit Surg. Soc. (sec. 1964-66), Am. Soc. Transplant Surgeons, Wayne State U. Sch. Medicine Alumni Assn. (dir. 1964-66), Detroit Cancer Club. Contbr. articles on gastroenterology and surgery to profl. jours. Home: 33000 Biddestone Ln Farmington MI 48018 Office: 18255 W McNichols Rd Detroit MI 48219

ALLAN, VERNON ARTHUR, telephone co. exec.; b. Bondurant, Iowa, Nov. 24, 1918; s. Charles G. and Mamie (Hall) A.; grad. Dale Carnegie Course, 1956; grad. Dale Carnegie Instr. Course, 1965, USITA Mgmt. Course, Univ. Kansas, 1965; m. Ada Lee Coleman, November 11, 1950. Accountant, Ia. State Telephone Co., Newton, 1938-39, cashier, 1939-40; dist. mgr. Central Carolina Telephone Co., Southern Pines, N.C., 1940-43; comml. supt. Central Mo. and Ark. Asso. Telephone Co., Warrensburg, Mo., 1945-48; comml. supt. Platte Valley Telephone Corp., Scottsbluff, Neb., 1948-52, traffic supt., 1948-52; asst. gen. mgr. United Telephone Co. of West, 1952-67, gen. mgr., 1967-70, comml. mgr., 1970-72, v.p., 1962-72, v.p. adminstrn., 1972—. Mem. bd. Longs Peak Area council Boy Scouts Am., 1951—, pres., 1967-68, also mem. bd. N. Central region, 1968—; sec. West Neb. Gen. Hosp., 1961-64, v.p., 1964-67, mem. bd., 1956-67; mem. bd. Scottsbluff Pub. Library, 1954-67, pres., 1965-67; bd. dirs. Nebr. Council on Econ. Edn. Served pvt. to 1st lt., USAAF, 1943-45; maj. Res., 1945-65, now ret. Recipient Silver Beaver award, 1956, Silver Antelope award, 1974 (both Boy Scouts Am.). Mem. Nebr. (pres. 1957-58, dir.), Rocky Mountain (dir. 1976—) telephone assns., Telephone Pioneers Am., Ind. Telephone Pioneer Assn., Res. Officers Assn., Scottsbluff C. of C. (mem. bd., v.p. 1968-69, pres. 1969-70), Am. Legion. Republican. Methodist. Mason, Elk. Clubs: Rotary, Cosmopolitan. Home: 1508 4th Ave Scottsbluff NE 69361 Office: PO Box 1112 Scottsbluff NE 69361

ALLANSON, JOHN FREDERICK, city ofcl., educator; b. Elgin, Ill., July 5, 1927; s. Robert A. and Eleanor (Deutsch) A.; B.A., cum laude, Colo. Coll., 1950; M.A., Ariz. State U., 1951; M.P.H., U. Calif. at Berkeley, 1953; m. Amy Leonora Lund, June 2, 1951; children—Sharon, Kathleen, Theresa, John D. Grad. asst. Ariz. State U., 1950-51; exec. sec. Ariz. Gov's. Conf. Children and Youth, Phoenix, 1951; health edn. cons. Ariz. Dept. Health, Phoenix, 1951-55; health edn. cons. N.Mex. Dept. Pub. Health, Santa Fe, 1955-59, coordinator sch. health, 1959-61, dir. Sch. Health div., 1961-69; health educator Kansas City Health Dept., 1969—; sch. health extension instr. U. Ariz., 1953-55, St. Michael's Coll. (Santa Fe), 1956-57, U. N.Mex., 1959—. Chmn. N.M. Coordinating Com. Sch. Health, 1957-59, Santa Fe County chpt. ARC, 1965. Served with USNR, 1945. Fellow Am. Sch. Health Assn.; mem. N.Mex. Pub. Health Assn. (past pres.), Am. Coll. Health Assn., N.Mex. Health Educators Assn., N.Mex. Congress Parents and Tchrs. (state health chmn.), N.Mex. Assn. Health, Phys. Edn. and Recreation (v.p. health 1965), Sigma Chi, Delta Omega, Delta Epsilon. Democrat. Roman Catholic. Co-author, editor with others New Mexico School Health Manual for Elementary and Secondary Schools, 1963, New Mexico School Health Evaluation Guide for Elementary and Secondary Schools, 1965. Contbr. articles to sch. health publs. Composer: (choral mass) Missa Deo Gratias, 1962. Home: 302 NE Northcrest Dr Kansas City MO 64116 Office: City Hall Kansas City MO 64116

ALLARD, DONALD JAMES, orthodontist; b. Omaha, Aug. 11, 1924; s. William Edwin and Dora Florence (Couch) A.; B.S., State U. Iowa, 1957; D.D.S., U. Iowa, 1960; certificate in orthodontics Eastman Dental Dispensary Orthodontic Center, 1963; m. Rosalie Amelia Seefeldt, Nov. 22, 1945; children—Donald James, Mary Ann (Mrs. Peter Charles Lau), Teresa (Mrs. Peter Weston Radford), Carl Christian. Dental technician Allard Dental Lab., Davenport, Iowa, 1945-54; pvt. practice dentistry, Sigourney, Iowa, 1960; clin. fellow, dental intern Eastman Dental Dispensary, 1961; pvt. practice orthodontics, Davenport, 1963—. Instr., orthodontic cons. Augustana Coll., Rock Island, Ill., Speech and Hearing Center, 1963—; cons. Ill. Services Crippled Children, 1963—; mem. courtesy med. staff St. Lukes Hosp., Davenport, 1963—. Served with USNR, 1942-46; PTO. NIH research fellow, 1962, 63, research grantee, 1962, 63. Mem. Am. Assn. Orthodontists, Am., Iowa, Scott County (sec. 1968-69) dental assns., Iowa Orthodontic Assn., Fedn. Dentaire Internationale, Iowa Pub. Health Assn. Rotarian. Clubs: Exchange, Iowa Quarterback, Outing, Davenport Country (Davenport). Home: 11 Oak Park Dr Bettendorf IA 52722 Office: 202 Profl Arts Bldg Davenport IA 52803

ALLEN, ARTHUR L., JR., computer service co. exec.; b. Dayton, Ohio, Aug. 3, 1946; s. Arthur Leroy and Rebecca Ann (Denlinger) A.; Asso. Sci., Dayton Jr. Coll., 1966; m. Frances Dianne Hale, Sept. 14, 1968; children—Ryan Michael, Amy Elaine. Systems analyst, Gen. Motors Co., Dayton, Ohio, 1968-71, Detroit, 1971-72; asst. v.p. sales Cutler-Williams Inc., Dallas, 1972-76; v.p., prin. Allen Services Corp., Vandalia, Ohio, 1976—, also dir. Served with USMCR, 1966-68; Vietnam. Office: 212 W National Rd Vandalia OH 45377

ALLEN, ARVON DALE, JR., educator; b. Greensburg, Ind., Apr. 10, 1935; s. Arvon Dale and Dorothy Verna (Thorne) A.; B.S., Ind. U., 1959, M.B.A., 1960; D. of Bus. Adminstrn. (fellow), U. Colo., 1966; m. Anita Gayle Barton, Aug. 12, 1961; children—Lori Lynn, Krista Gayle, Kirk Dale, Tanya Beth, Alysia Dawn. Labor relations rep. RCA, Bloomington, Ind., 1960-61; instr. mgmt., econs. and finance U. Evansville, Ind., 1961-63; teaching asst. prodn. mgmt. U. Colo., 1964-65; asst. prof. mgmt. and labor relations U. Louisville, 1966-67; prof. mgmt. and labor relations Kan. State U., Manhattan, 1967-74; chmn. dept. mgmt. No. Ill. U., DeKalb, 1974-75; prof. mgmt. and labor relations Seidman Grad. Sch. Bus. Grand Valley State Coll., Allendale, Mich., 1975—. Labor mgmt. arbitrator, permanent arbitrator for various firms and labor unions; cons. in the areas of leadership, worker motivation, labor relations; lectr. to profl. groups. Served with AUS, 1955-57. Fed. grantee in field. Mem. Nat. Acad. Arbitrators, Fed. Mediation and Conciliation Service, Acad. Mgmt., Indsl. Relations Research Assn., Am. Arbitration Assn., Nat. Center for Dispute Settlement, Soc. Profls. in Dispute Resolution, Southwestern Social Sci. Assn. Author: Labor Law: A Programmed Instruction Manual, 1967. Contbg. editor: Management Horizons. Contbr. articles to profl. pubs. Home: 7105 Rockhill Dr Jenison (Grand Rapids) MI 49428

ALLEN, CHARLES WILLARD, educator; b. Akron, Ind., Jan. 7, 1932; s. James Henry and Mabel Antoinette (Tripp) A.; B.S., U. Notre Dame, 1954, M.S., 1956, Ph.D., 1958; m. Teresa Carol Law, Aug. 1, 1959; children—Sean Joseph, Jamina Maria, Thane Joseph, Joslyn Maryse. Postdoctoral fellow U. Notre Dame, 1958-59, asst. prof. metallurgy, 1959-64, asso. prof., 1964-68, prof., 1968—; cons. Argonne Nat. Lab., 1972—, summer faculty asso., 1972, 74. Active Boy Scouts Am. Fulbright research scholar, 1970-71. Mem. Am. Soc. Metals, Am. Soc. Engring. Edn., Electron Microscopy Soc. Am., Am. Inst. Mining, Metall., Petroleum Engrs., Internat. Metallographic Soc., Sigma Xi, Alpha Sigma Mu, Tau Beta Pi. Contbr. articles profl. jours. Home: 533 Philip Rd Niles MI 49120 Office: Dept Metall Engring and Materials Sci Univ Notre Dame Notre Dame IN 46556

ALLEN, CLYDE ERWIN, JR., computer co. exec.; b. Mpls., Apr. 19, 1934; s. Clyde E. and Pearl B. (Peterson) A.; B.S., Gustavus Adolphus Coll., 1956; m. Lois L. Madsen, July 13, 1957; children—Paul Douglas, Mark Thomas. With North Am. Aviation, Los Angeles, 1956-57; with Univac div. Sperry Rand, St. Paul, 1957—, dir. systems software engring., 1965—. Mem. Assn. Computing Machinery. Home: 10736 James Circle Bloomington MN 55431 Office: Box 3625 Univac Park St Paul MN 55165

ALLEN, EUGENE VINCENT, security co. exec.; b. Newark, May 31, 1932; s. Raymond Peter and Alma Mary (Hagel) Dankowski; B.A. (Jewish Women's League scholar), U. Miami, 1957; postgrad. F.B.I. Acad. Law, 1957; m. Alice Francis Winnicki, Sept. 10, 1967; children—Robert, Edward, Jill, Phillip. Spl. agt. FBI, 1953-62; investigator in charge United Airlines, Chgo., 1962-64; security dir. ARA Services, Inc., Phila., 1964-65; regional mgr. The Wackenhut Corp., Chgo., 1966-68; pres. Taskpower Security, Inc., investigations and security guards, Chgo., 1968—. Cons. on loss prevention; adviser to dean City Colls. Chgo., 1973, Mayfield Coll., Chgo., 1975. Treas., Kaneland Council Govts., 1974, pres., 1975; trustee Blackberry Twp., 1974; co-founder Kaneland Concerned Citizens Assn., 1973, vice chmn., 1973—; trustee Chgo. Pops Orch., 1976; mem. Kane County Water Pollution Control Div. Steering Com., 1976. Served with USMCR, 1949-51. Decorated 3 Bronze Stars. Mem. Former F.B.I. Agts. Assn. (treas. 1972, vice chmn. 1973, chmn. 1975), Ill. Security Chiefs Assn. (treas. 1972, v.p. 1973, pres. 1975), Am. Soc. Indsl. Security (mem. exec. com. 1972, treas. 1973, chmn. 1974), Ill. Chiefs of Police Assn. Republican. Conglist. Contbr. to profl. publs. in field. Home: Rural Route 1 Oakleaf Dr Elburn IL 60119 Office: 10001 Derby Ln Westchester IL 60153

ALLEN, FRANK BENJAMIN, JR., educator; b. Mt. Vernon, Ill., Oct. 21, 1909; s. Frank Benjamin and Elizabeth L. (Mernagh) A.; B.E., So. Ill. U., 1929; M.S., U. Iowa, 1934; postgrad. U. Ill., 1936-38; m. Eleanor Marie Ruff, June 19, 1943; children—Barbara Lee, Marilyn Joyce, John Roger. Tchr. high sch. math., Ill., 1929-68; chmn. math. dept. Lyons Twp. High Sch. and Jr. Coll., La Grange, Ill., 1956-68; asso. prof. math. Elmhurst (Ill.) Coll., 1968-71, prof., 1971—, part-time, 1975—, chmn. dept. math., 1970-75, chmn. div. natural scis. and math., 1972-75. Served as capt. U.S. Army, 1943-46. Recipient Service award Central Suburban Chairmen of Math., 1975. Mem. Nat. (pres. 1962-64, Distinguished Service certi- ficate 1970), Ill. (pres. 1954-55) councils tchrs. of math., Met. Math. Club Greater Chgo. (pres. 1952-53). Republican. Presbyterian. Author: (with Pearson) Modern Algebra—A Logical Approach, 1964, Book II, 1966; (with Guyer) Basic Concepts in Geometry—An Introduction to Proof, 1973. Home: 567 Berkley Ave Elmhurst IL 60126 Office: Elmhurst Coll Elmhurst IL 60126

ALLEN, GARALD FREDRICK, chem. engr., counselor; b. Toledo, Nov. 30, 1917; s. Roy Howard and Mamie (Bacon) A.; B.A., Albion Coll., 1941, M.S., U. Iowa, 1942; M.A., Central Mich. U., 1975; m. Dorothy Helen Sessions, June 30, 1944; children—John Garald, Kathleen Sue. Chem. engr. Dow Chem. Co., Midland, Mich., 1942-74; instr. Central Mich. U., 1975—. Mem. Am. Inst. Chem. Engrs., Am. Personnel and Guidance Assn., Assn. Counselor Edn. and Supervision. Methodist. Club: Exchange. Home: 801 Crescent Dr Midland MI 48640

ALLEN, GEORGE DOUGLAS, engr.; b. Jackson, Miss., Sept. 5, 1938; s. Vernon Douglas and Ruth Lucy (Searcy) A.; B.S. in E.E., Loyola U., Los Angeles, 1962; M.S. in E.E., U. So. Calif., 1969; m. June Marie Bannister, Sept. 11, 1963; children—Desie Ann, Rusty Nardy, George Douglas. Elec. engr. Los Angeles Dept. Water and Power, 1962-72; self-employed as elec. engr., 1969-72; chief engr. Systems engring. A.B. Chance Co., Centralia, Mo., 1972—. Lectr. grad. elec. program U. So. Cal., 1969-72. Registered profl. engr., Cal. Mem. U.S. Jaycees (v.p. Crescenta, Can. chpt. 1971, sec. 1970, state dir. 1971), Phi Kappa Theta. Republican. Roman Catholic. Kiwanian (program dir. Centralia club 1973, youth chmn. 1974), Moose. Contbr. articles to profl. publs.; patentee in field. Home: Route 4 Centralia MO 65204 Office: 210 N Allen St Centralia MO 65240

ALLEN, GLEN GENE, bus. cons.; b. Topeka, Dec. 6, 1924; s. Glen and Velma (Fischer) A.; B.S. cum laude, Kans. State U., 1948, M.S., 1949; student U. Kans., 1943, U. N.C., 1945, Notre Dame U., 1944; m. Phyllis J. Scott, Aug. 4, 1946; children—Scott F., Peggy, Patti. Economist Armour & Co., Chgo., 1949-55; regional sales mgr. Ford Motor Co., Dearborn, Mich., 1955-61; research dir., sec.-treas. Agri Research, Inc., Manhattan, Kans., 1961-65; exec. dir. Theracon, Inc., Topeka, 1965-71; pres. Agri-sci. Mgmt. Co., Topeka, 1969—, Agriventures Co., Topeka, 1971—, Allen Enterprises, Topeka, 1972—, Livestock Internat., Inc., 1973—, Am. Agro-Services Co. Inc., Topeka, 1975—; dir. Livestock Market Centers Inc. Bd. govs. Livestock Merchandising Inst., 1971—. Served with USNR, 1943-45. Mem. Nat. Agrl. Advt. and Mktg. Assn., Topeka C. of C. Presbyterian. Rotarian. Home: 1285 Pembroke Ln Topeka KS 66604 Office: Box 1576 Topeka KS 66601

ALLEN, JACK B., broadcasting exec.; ed. Loyola U., Chgo.; m. Chandra Allen; 10 children. Stage mgr., asso. dir. WEKB-TV, from 1958; with Adam Young Co., to 1964; with Metro TV Sales, ABC-TV Spot Sales; sales mgr., gen. sales mgr. WXYZ-TV, Detroit, from 1970; now sta. mgr. WWJ-TV, Detroit. Home: 500 Hupp Cross Rd Birmingham MI 48010

ALLEN, JAMES CURTIS, mfg. co. exec.; b. Winston, Mo., June 7, 1922; s. Vernon and Carrie Belle (Palmer) A.; grad. Chillicothe Bus. Coll., (Mo.), 1942, Internat. Corr. Schs., 1946; m. Juanita G. Kennedy, Dec. 4, 1944; children—Daryl C., Karen A., Marti L., Jimmie, Randy. Accountant, Nat. Bellas Hess, Kansas City, Mo., 1946-48; controller Lawn-Boy div. Outboard Marine Corp., Lamar, Mo., 1948-63; sec.-treas. EFCO Corp., Monett, Mo., 1963-66; co-owner, sec-treas. F.M. Thorpe Mfg. Co., Lamar, Mo., 1966—; dir. Barton County State Bank. Pres., United Fund, 1970-71; pres. Community Betterment, 1968-70; dist. chmn. Sowemco council Boy Scouts Am., 1964-66, Arrowhead council, 1972, v.p. Mo-Kan Area council, 1975—, recipient Golden Sun award; mem. Lamar Sch. Bd., 1969-71; mem. Lamar Park Bd., 1955-73, pres., 1973—. Served with USNR, 1942-45. Recipient Outstanding Leadership award Mo. Municipal League, 1971; Distinguished Service award Kiwanis Club Monett, Mo., 1965; Leadership award Mo. Community Betterment, 1970. Mem. Lamar, Mo. chambers commerce. Methodist (chmn. bd. 1971, del. conf. 1968-71, treas. 1966—, supt. 1955-63). Mason (Shriner), Rotarian (pres. 1971-72), Kiwanian (pres. 1968). Home: 400 W 1st St Lamar MO 64759 Office: 1801 Gulf St Lamar MO 64759

ALLEN, JOHN DONALD, mgmt. cons.; b. Newton, Kans., June 16, 1936; s. Theodore Alfred and Doris Elizabeth (Sulser) A.; B.B.A., U. Houston, 1965; m. Mary Elizabeth Phillips, Sept. 2, 1960; children—Kim Elizabeth, Scot Stewart. Accounting, billing clerk Plastic Applicators, Inc., Houston, 1962-65; line haul services rep. R.E.A. Express, Inc., Atlanta, 1965-66, traveling auditor, Dallas, 1966-67, regional mgr. of revenue, credit, Kansas City, Mo., 1967-71; zone mgr. Investors Diversified Services, Kansas City, 1972; bus. mgr. Harrisonville (Mo.) Cass R-9 Sch. Dist., 1973-74; pvt. practice mgmt. cons., Overland Park, Kans., 1975—. Alderman City of Harrisonville (Mo.), 1970-74; sec. Cass R-9 Bd. Edn., Harrisonville, 1973-74. Served with U.S. Army, 1960-62. Mem. Mo. Pilots Assn. Republican. Clubs: Mason, DeMolay. Home: 1402 Edgevale Dr PO Box 7 Harrisonville MO 64701 Office: 10977 Granada Ln Overland Park KS 66211

ALLEN, JOHN EDWARD, cons. mech. chem.; b. Shinnston, W.Va., May 17, 1915; s. Edward Alburtis and Vera (Radabaugh) A.; B.S.Chem.E. in Metall. Engring., W.Va. U., 1937; m. Lucille E. Fierek, May 29, 1948; children—Mary Catherine, Judith Ann, John Edward. Blast furnace foreman Donora, Pa., works Am. Steel & Wire div. U.S. Steel Corp., 1937-42, asst. supt. Duluth, Minn., works, 1942-48; gen. supt. Central Furnaces & Docks Co., Cleve., 1948-64; pres. Boynton Engrs., Inc., Chgo., 1964-68, J. E. Allen & Assos. Inc., Chgo., Lake Forest, Ill., 1968—; pres. Ferro-Carb Agglomeration, Ltd., Internat. Mineral Recovery, Ltd. Served to 1st lt. Combat Engrs. Res., 1937-42. Mem. Eastern States Blast Furnace, Coke Oven Assn. (pres. 1955-56), Western States Blast Furnace, Coke Plant Assn., Assn. Iron, Steel Engrs., Iron, Steel Soc. Republican. Club: Exmoor Country. Contbr. articles to profl. jours.; patentee in field. Home: 606 Timber Ln Lake Forest IL 60045 Office: PO Box 690 Lake Forest IL 60045

ALLEN, LAYMAN EDWARD, educator; b. Turtle Creek, Pa., June 9, 1927; s. Layman Grant and Viola Iris (Williams) A.; student Washington and Jefferson Coll., 1945-46; A.B., Princeton, 1951; M. Pub. Adminstrn., Harvard, 1952; LL.B., Yale, 1956; m. Christine R. Patmore, Mar. 29, 1950; children—Layman G., Patricia R. Admitted to Conn. bar, 1956; fellow Center for Advanced Study in the Behavioral Scis., 1961-62; sr. fellow Yale Law Sch., 1956-57, lectr., 1957-58, instr., 1958-59, asst. prof., 1959-63, asso. prof., 1963-66; asso. prof. law U. Mich. Law Sch., Ann Arbor, 1966-71, prof., 1971—; research scientist Mental Health Research Inst., U. Mich., 1966—. Cons. legal drafting Nat. Life Ins. Co.; editor in chief Jurimetrics Jour., quarterly publ. Electronic Data Retrieval Com. of Am. Bar Assn.; newspaper corr.; editor Jour. of Conflict Resolution; operations research analyst McKinsey & Co.; orgn. and methods analyst Office of Sec. of Air Force. Trustee Center for Study of Responsive Law. Served with USNR, 1945-46. Mem. A.A.A.S., Assn. Symbolic Logic, Nat. Council Tchrs. Math., Am. Bar Assn. (Council of sect. on sci. and tech.), ACLU. Democrat. Unitarian. Author: WFF 'N Proof: The Game of Modern Logic, 1961, latest rev. edit., 1973; (with Robin B.S. Brooks, Patricia A. James) Automatic Retrieval of Legal Literature; Why and How, 1962; WFF: The Beginner's Game of Modern Logic, 1962, latest rev. edit., 1973; Equations: The Game of Creative Mathematics, 1963, latest rev. edit., 1973; (with Mary E. Caldwell) Reflections of the Communications Sciences and Law; The Jurimetrics Conference, 1965; (with J. Ross and P. Kugel) Queries 'N Theories: The Game of Science and Language, 1970, latest rev. edit., 1973; (with F. Goodman, D. Humphrey and J. Ross) On-Words: The Game of Word Structures, 1971, rev. edit., 1973. Contbr. articles in field to profl. jours. Home: 1407 Brooklyn Ave Ann Arbor MI 48104

ALLEN, LEE HARRISON, wholesale co. exec.; b. Cleve., Oct. 12, 1924; s. Horace Joseph and Eleanor Quayle (Malone) A.; B.Engring., Yale U., 1948; m. Marieke Sellenraad, Sept. 18, 1955; children—Horace, Jan, Adrian, Carel, Eleanor. With Hickman, Williams & Co., supplier raw materials to iron and steel industry, Detroit, 1948—, metallurgist, 1951-70, div. mgr., 1970—, v.p., dir., 1971-76, pres., 1976—; owner L.H. Allen & Sons, wholesale tree nursery, Frankenmuth, Mich., 1969—. Home: 71 Moross Rd Grosse Pointe Farms MI 48236 Office: 100 Renaissance Center Suite 1875 Detroit MI 48243

ALLEN, LOIS ARLENE HEIGHT (MRS. JAMES PIERPONT ALLEN), musician; b. Kenton, Ohio, Sept. 2, 1932; d. Robert Harold and Frances (Sims) Height; B.S., Ohio State U., 1954, M.A., 1958; m. James Pierpont Allen, June 14, 1953; children—Daniel Pierpont, Carole Elizabeth. Tchr. jr. and sr. high music, Upper Arlington High Sch., Columbus, O., 1954-56; high sch. music supr., Westerville, Ohio, 1956-67; tchr. music Ohio State U. Sch., 1957-59; pvt. tchr. music, Columbus, 1960—; ch. organist, choir dir. Mountview Bapt. Ch., Upper Arlington, Ohio, 1960-77; ednl. radio interviewer WOSU, 1970, 71, 72. Mem. Project Hope, Central Ohio, 1967-73; mem. sustaining bd. Maryhaven House for Alcoholic Women, 1969-73, 1st v.p.; mem. women's bd. Columbus Symphony, 1965-73, chmn. youth council, 1965-68, pres. elect women's assn., 1973, pres., 1974-76; chmn. juried art competition Central Ohio Arts Festival, 1969, 70, chmn. fine and applied arts, 1971, gen. chmn. of festival, 1972; area chmn. United Appeals Franklin County, 1966-68, Heart drive, 1968-75; pres. Ohio State U. Soc. Friends Sch. Music, 1977-78. Area leader Republican party, 1966-68. Mem. Am. Guild Organists, Choristers Guild Am., Fedn. Am. Bapt. Musicians, Center Sci. and Industry, Ohio State Hist. Soc., Ohio Soc. N.Y., Ohio Orgn. Orchs. (treas.), Nat. Trust U.S.A., Grange, Tau Beta Sigma, Delta Omicron, Kappa Delta (Central Ohio Woman of Yr. 1970). Mem. Order Eastern Star. Clubs: Ohio State University Alumnae of Franklin County (pres. 1962-64, 71-72). Home: 3355 Somerford Rd Columbus OH 43221

ALLEN, MARION CARROLL, clergyman; b. Spartanburg, S.C., Dec. 12, 1914; s. Albert Mayfield and Caroline May (Rogers) A.; B.A., Furman U., 1937; M.Div., Yale, 1940; M.A., Kans. U., 1960; m. Eleanor Earl Burt, July 31, 1943; children—Marian, Burt, Robert, Louise. Ordained to ministry Am. Bapt. Conv., 1940, received into United Ch. of Christ; pastor Bapt. chs., Bristol, Conn., 1940-47, Beaufort, S.C., 1947-50, Clemson, S.C., 1950-56, Lawrence, Kans., 1956-76; pastor First Congregational Ch., Topeka, 1976, Central Congregational Ch., 1977—; instr. religion Clemson U., 1951-56, instr. homiletics Central Sem., Kansas City, Kans., 1959-61, English, Kans. U., 1958, 76—. Bd. dirs. YMCA, U. Kans., 1956-60; v.p. Lawrence Friends of Music, 1968-75; sec. adv. bd. Kans. Sch. Religion, 1970-76. Mem. Topeka Ministerial Alliance, Lawrence Ministerial Aliancce, Topeka Council Chs., Consultation of Cooperating Chs. Kans., Kans. Okla. Conf. United Ch. of Christ. Clubs: Masons. Author: A Voice Not Our Own, 1963. Editor: The Springs of Learning, 1969. Editor: Serving in the Armed Forces, monthly 1972-74. Home: 2906 Alabama St Lawrence KS 66044 Office: 1248 Buchanan St Topeka KS 66604

ALLEN, MARTHA CLISE, ins. co. exec., counselor; b. Cleve., Apr. 25, 1918; d. Floyd W. and Kathleen (Lincoln) Clise; student U. Mich., 1936-38, 41, Wayne State U., 1938-40; m. Edwin C. Allen, Apr. 29, 1944; 1 son, Walter H. Editor and counselor Detroit Council for Youth Services, Detroit Bd. Edn., 1938-41; personnel adminstr. Detroit Ordnance Dist., U.S. Army, 1941-44; employment counselor Personnel Associates, Columbus, Ohio, 1961-67; personnel mgr. Midland Mutual Life Ins. Co., Columbus, Ohio, 1967—. Pres. PTA, Grand Island, N.Y., 1954; founder PTA, Levittown, Pa., 1956; tchr. Jr. Achievement Tng. Sessions for Officers, 1969, 71; mem. YWCA personnel com., Columbus, 1975; chairperson Nat. Found. for Infantile Paralysis, Grand Island, N.Y., 1954; pres. of churchwomen, St. Andrews Episcopal Ch., 1956-57; chairperson Altar Guild, St. John's Episcopal Ch., Worthington, Ohio, 1959-61. Mem. Personnel Soc. of Columbus (pres. 1975-76, dir. 1976-77), Am. Bus. Women's Assn. (pres. 1967-68, Woman of the Yr., Rose capital chpt. 1969), Am. Soc. for Personnel Adminstrn. (regional v.p. 1975-76, nat. sec. 1977), League of Women Voters (chairperson 1956-57), Adminstrv. Mgmt. Soc. (dir. Columbus chpt. 1969-72, v.p. 1973), Central Ohio Personnel Assn. (dir. 1973-75), Kappa Alpha Theta. Republican. Episcopalian. Office: 250 E Broad St Columbus OH 43215

ALLEN, MARTIN, educator; b. N.Y.C., Mar. 26, 1918; s. Isidor and Frances (Gudowitz) A.; A.B., Bklyn. Coll., 1938; M.S., U. Minn., 1941, Ph.D., 1944; m. Sophie Parker, June 13, 1942; children—Susan, Scott, Barbara, Robert. Instr. U. Minn., 1943-45; research asso. Allegany Ballistics Lab. Cumberland, Md., 1945; sr. tech. person B.F. Goodrich, Akron, Ohio, 1945-47; asso. prof. chemistry Butler U., Indpls., 1947-56; prof. Coll. St. Thomas, St. Paul, 1956—, chmn. dept. chemistry, 1975—, dir. div. scis. and math., 1977—; vis. prof. Hamline U., 1961-62; abstractor Chem. Abstracts Service, Columbus, 1957—. Fellow AAAS; mem. Am. Chem. Soc. (chmn. Minn. sect. 1968), Midwestern Assn. Chemistry Tchrs. in Liberal Arts Colls. (pres. 1964-65), Chem. Soc. London, AAUP, Fedn. Am. Scientists, Sigma Xi, Phi Lambda Upsilon. Home: 4620 Bassett Creek Ln Golden Valley MN 55422 Office: Dept Chemistry College St Thomas St Paul MN 55105

ALLEN, MILTON NICHOLAS, computer service co. exec.; b. N.Y.C., Apr. 15, 1927; s. Nicholas D. and Adele (Fortune) A.; student Princeton U.; B.S., U.S. Naval Acad., 1949; postgrad. Trinity Coll., 1955-56; m. Barbara Jane Scarlett, Feb. 21, 1954; children—Peter, Thomas, Jane. Commd. lt. USN, 1949, advanced through grades to lt., 1954, discharged, 1954; officer Conn. Gen. Life Ins. Co., Hartford, 1954-60; cons. Robert Heller & Assos., Cleve., 1960-64; asst. to pres. Sherwin Williams Co., Cleve., 1964-69; with Mandate Corp., cons. and computer services, Cleve., 1969—, pres., 1970—; dir. DeSantis Inc., Daro Industries, Day-Glo Color Corp., Burdox, Inc., Premier Electric Co. Pres. Goodrich Gannett Social Settlement, Cleve., 1972—; mem. vis. com. Case Western Res. U. Sch. Mgmt., Cleve., 1972—. Clubs: Cleve. Racquet, Union of Cleve. Home: 2879 Weybridge Rd Shaker Heights OH 44120 Office: 1717 E 9th St Cleveland OH 44114

ALLEN, PHYLLIS ADELLE GRISHAM (MRS. ROBERT MCCURDY ALLEN), charitable assn. exec.; b. Stockton, Calif., Aug. 11, 1927; d. Clarence William and Norma Grace (Collins) Grisham; student Long Beach City Coll., 1945-46, U. Oreg., 1957, Portland State U., 1967; m. Robert McCurdy Allen, Sept. 1968; children—Carole Hilles, Susan, Stephen, Thomas, Patricia. Women's dir., broadcaster KMED Radio and TV, Medford, Oreg., 1957-65; copywriter, account exec. Parma Advt., Portland, Oreg., 1965-66; sec.-treas., account exec. Williams Advt. and Pub. Relations, Portland, 1966-68; pub. relations dir. United Fund, Akron, Ohio, 1969-70; asso. pub. relations dir. Akron Gen. Med. Center, 1972-73; exec. dir. Akron Gen. Devel. Found., 1973—. Pres., Support, Inc., 1973-75. Recipient 1st Pl. Pillsbury invitational recipe contest Food Editors, 1964. Mem. Pub. Relations Soc. Am. (accredited mem.; sec. Akron chpt. 1973-74), Nat. Assn. Hosp. Devel., Ohio Hosp. Devel. Assn. (pres.), Akron Press Club, Women in Communications (sec. 1973-74). Home: 5740 West Blvd Canton OH 44718 Office: 400 Wabash Ave Akron OH 44307

ALLEN, RICHARD BLOSE, lawyer, editor; b. Aledo, Ill., May 10, 1919; s. James Albert and Claire (Smith) A.; B.S., U. Ill., 1941, J.D., 1947; m. Marion Treloar, Aug. 27, 1949; children—Penelope, Jennifer, Leslie Jean. Admitted to Ill. bar, 1947; staff editor Am. Bar Assn. Jour., 1947-48, 63-66, exec. editor, 1966-70, editor, 1970—; pvt. practice law, Aledo, 1949-57; gen. counsel Ill. State Bar Assn., 1957-63. Served from pvt. to maj. Q.M.C., AUS, 1941-46. Mem. Am., Ill. (mem. assembly 1972-74), Chgo. bar assns., Selden Soc., Scribes, Sigma Delta Chi, Kappa Tau Alpha, Phi Delta Phi, Alpha Tau Omega. Clubs: Tower (Chgo.); Mich. Shores (Wilmette). Home: 702 Illinois Rd Wilmette IL 60091 Office: 77 S Wacker Dr Chicago IL 60606

ALLEN, RICHARD HERBERT, orthopaedic surgeon; b. Janesville, Wis., Aug. 4, 1926; s. Herbert William and Helen Marie (Taylor) A.; student Dartmouth Coll., 1947; M.D., Harvard, 1950; m. Patricia LuAnne Warner, Oct. 23, 1955; children—Douglas C., Elizabeth S., David Herbert. Intern, Henry Ford Hosp., Detroit, 1950-51, mem. orthopaedic staff, 1951-56; pvt. practice medicine, specializing in orthopaedic surgery, Battle Creek, Mich., 1956—; mem. staff Leila Y. Post Montgomery Hosp., Community Hosps. (both in Battle Creek); cons. Albion (Mich.) Community Hosp., Southwestern Mich. Rehab. Center, Inc., Oaklawn Hosp., Marshall, Mich., 1958—; pres., dir. College St. Orthopaedics Profl. Corp. Served with USN, 1944-45, 52-54. Diplomate Am. Bd. Orthopedic Surgery, Nat. Bd. Med. Examiners. Fellow A.C.S.; mem. AMA, Mich., Calhoun County med. socs., Mich. Orthopaedic Soc., Detroit Acad. Orthopaedic Surgery, Am. Acad Orthopaedic Surgeons, Latin Am. Soc. Orthopaedics and Trauma. Club: Battle Creek Country. Home: 227 E Emmett St Battle Creek MI 49017 Office: 191 College St Battle Creek MI 49017

ALLEN, ROBERT DEAN, air force officer; b. Carroll, Iowa, Oct. 15, 1935; s. Arthur and Mary Elizabeth (Ferguson) A.; B.A., U. Wyo., 1958; grad. U.S. Air Force Squadron Officer's Sch., 1963; M.Ed., Coll. William and Mary, 1974; m. Sheryl Marie Conner, Apr. 20, 1957; children—Karen, Marcella, Steven, Christine. Commd. 2d lt. U.S. Air Force, 1958, advanced through grades to lt. col., 1974; chief of helicopter standardization, chief of instrument ground sch. Ellsworth (S.D.) AFB, 1964-66; spl. ops. helicopter pilot various SE Asia bases, 1966-67; instr. pilot helicopter combat crew Eglin (Fla.) AFB, 1968-69, plans officer Spl. Ops. Force, 1969-70; ops. officer, helicopter instr. Vietnamese Air Force, 1970; project officer testing equipment and aircraft Tactical Air Command, Langley (Va.) AFB, 1970-74; asso. prof. aerospace studies Iowa State U., Ames, 1974—. Decorated Silver Star, D.F.C., Air medal. Mem. Air Force Assn., Arnold Air Soc., Quiet Birdmen, Am. Personnel and Guidance Assn., U. Wyo., Coll. of William and Mary alumni assns. Republican. Methodist. Clubs: Iowa State U. Cyclone, Demolay, Masons. Home: 1710 Bel Air Dr Ames IA 50010 Office: 146 Armory Iowa State U Ames IA 50011

ALLEN, ROBERT SHAW, chem. engr.; b. Providence, Nov. 12, 1931; s. Ray Spencer and Madeline (Shaw) A.; B.S. in Chem. Engring., Worcester Poly. Inst., 1956; m. Norma Elaine Porter, Nov. 8, 1958; children—Trudi Lynn, Ronald Shaw. With Am. Cyanamid Co., 1956-59; with Dewey & Almy Chem. div. W.R. Grace Co., 1959-62, Monroe Mfg. Co., 1962-67; Neutron Produ- cts, Inc., 1967-68, Continental Oil Co., 1968-72, Allen-Herzog Asso., Framingham, Mass., 1972-73, World-Wide Constrn. Services, Inc., Wichita, Kans., 1973-76; prin. Allen Assos., engrs. and consultants, Wichita, 1976—. Chmn. Sedgwick County Republican Central Com., 1977—. Served with U.S. Army, 1953-55. Mem. Am. Inst. Chem. Engrs., Instrument Soc. Am., Wichita Area C. of C. Clubs: Wichita World Trade, Rolling Hills Country. Home: 229 N Westfield St Wichita KS 67212 Office: 9505 W Central Ave Suite 101 Wichita KS 67212

ALLEN, RONALD ROYCE, educator; b. Horicon, Wis., Dec. 8, 1930; s. Clayton Francis and Hazel Ann (Whipple) A.; B.S., Wis. State Coll., 1952; M.A., U. Wis., 1957, Ph.D., 1960; m. JoAnne Elizabeth Kuehl, Feb. 2, 1957; children—John Jeffery, David Jennings. Mem. faculty Amherst Coll. (Mass.), 1960-63; mem. faculty U. Wis., Madison, 1963—, prof. communication arts, curriculum and instruction, 1970—. Prin. investigator Wis. Research and Devel. Center for Cognitive Learning, 1964-69; del. White House Conf. on Children, 1971. Served to lt. USNR, 1952-56. Mem. Wis. Speech Assn. (pres. 1968-70), Speech Communication Assn. (ednl. policies bd. 1970-74, 2d v.p. 1977). Author: (with S. Anderson, Jere Hough) Speech in American Society, 1968; (with W. A. Linkugel, R. L. Johannesen) Contemporary American Speeches, 1965, rev. edit., 1972; (with Clay Willmington) Speech Communication in the Secondary School, 1972; (with S. Parish and C. David Mortensen) Communication: Interacting Through Speech, 1974; (with P. Judson Newcombe) New Horizons for Teacher Education in Speech Communication, 1974; (with Kenneth Brown) Developing Communication Competence in Children, 1976; (with Ray E. McKerrow) The Pragmatics of Public Communication, 1977. Home: 1809 Peacock Ct Sun Prairie WI 53590

ALLEN, SPENCER TURNER, ins. co. exec.; b. Milton, Fla., Feb. 1, 1924; s. Stephen Grover and Martha Ellen (Harter) A.; student Graceland Coll., Lamoni, Iowa, 1942-43, 46-47, Northwestern U., 1943-44, U. Calif., 1947-49; m. Dorothy B. Deal, June 7, 1947; children—Stephanie, Dawn, David, Paul. Supt. agencies Union Central Life Ins. Co., Cin., 1954-66; pres., chief exec. officer Farmers & Bankers Life Ins. Co., Wichita, Kans., 1967-68; pres., chmn. bd., chief exec. officer Midwest Life Ins. Co. of Lincoln (Nebr.), 1969-; dir. Nat. Bank of Commerce. Dir. S.E. Nebr. Health Planning Council; bd. trustees Graceland Coll.; treas., pres. Midwest Holding Corp., City of Hope, 1976-77; gen. campaign chmn. United Fund; exec. com. Cornhusker council Boy Scouts Am. Served to lt. comdr. USNR, World War II and Korea. C.L.U. Mem. Life Office Mgmt. Assn., Nat. Assn. Life Underwriters, Lincoln C. of C. Mem. Reorganized Ch. of Jesus Christ of Latter-day Saints. Clubs: Lincoln Country, Nebr., Univ. Home: 3000 Woodsdale Blvd Lincoln NE 68502 Office: 500 S 16th St Lincoln NE 68508

ALLEN, THOMAS ERNEST, lawyer; b. Salt Lake City, Sept. 30, 1939; s. Kenneth L. and Joyce Catherine (Thompson) A.; A.B., Dartmouth Coll., 1961; J.D., U. Mich., 1967; m. Elizabeth Harker Curtis, June 26, 1965; children—Kenneth, Susan, Gregory. Admitted to Minn. bar, 1967, Mo. bar, 1976, others; asso. mem. firm Peterson, Peterson & Allen, Albert Lea, Minn., 1967-76, partner, 1970-76; asso. mem. firm Biggs, Curtis, Casserly & Barnes, St. Louis, 1976-77; partner Curtis, Crossen, Hensley & Allen, Clayton, Mo., 1977—. Served with M.I., U.S. Army, 1962-64. Mem. Am., Minn., Mo., St. Louis Met. bar assns., Phi Kappa Psi. Republican. Episcopalian. Clubs: Lions, Mo. Athletic, Masons. Home: 423 Miriam St Kirkwood MO 63122 Office: 7912 Bonhomme St Suite 304 Clayton MO 63102

ALLEN, VERNON EUGENE, mktg. exec.; b. Cleve., Dec. 24, 1919; s. Vernon L. and Beatrice (Figgins) A.; student pub. schs., Cleve.; m. Florence Wilma Stanard, Mar. 5, 1942; children—Vernon William, Carol Jean Allen Holmes, Gregory, Holly L. Allen May. Machine operator, Tinnerman Products Inc., Cleve., 1938-42; devel. engr. Eaton Corp., Cleve., 1946-47, sales supr., 1947-70, sales mgr., 1970-72, div. marketing mgr., 1972—; mem. advisory bd. Investors Heritage Life Ins. Co., 1964-78. Capt. of Ohio Hwy. Patrol Aux., 1968-70. Served with C.E., U.S. Army, 1940-46; PTO, ETO. Decorated Bronze star. Mem. Home Appliance Mfrs. Assn., Sales Marketing Execs., Soc. of Automotvie Engrs., Cleve. Growth Assn., Am. Legion, VFW. Republican. Club: Wedgewood Country. Home: 14181 Cherokee Trail Middleburg Heights OH 44130 Office: PO Box 6688 Cleveland OH 44101

ALLEN, WILLIAM LEON, univ. dean; b. Landgraff, W.Va., Jan. 9, 1943; s. Bryant and Mattie Kate (Allen) B.; B.Ed., Bluefield State Coll., 1964; M.Ed., Ohio U., 1969, Ph.D., 1977; m. Brenda Marie Martin, Oct. 23, 1966; children—William Leon, Sabrina Yvette, Janette Nicole. Tchr. McDowell County Sch. System, Welch, 1964-68; asst. to dean Ohio U., 1969-75, asst. dean Univ. Coll., 1975—. Community center recreation dir. Council So. Mountains, Welch, W.Va., 1966-67. Mem. Nat. Assn. Student Personnel Adminstrs., NAACP, Am. Personnel and Guidance Assn., Am. Coll. Personnel Assn. Democrat. Baptist. Home: 141 Franklin Ave Athens OH 45701 Office: 140 Chubb Hall Athens OH 45701

ALLENDER, TERRANCE CALVIN, pharm. co. exec.; b. Davenport, Iowa, June 11, 1948; s. Bert Emerson and Susan Bea (Hornbuckle) A.; B.S., St. Ambrose Coll., 1972; M.S., U. Iowa, 1975; m. Jean Susan Hall, Aug. 24, 1974. Asst. horticulturist dept. botany U. Iowa, Iowa City, 1974-75; sales rep. Burroughs Wellcome Co., Research Triangle Park, N.C., 1976—; research asst. U. Iowa, 1974. Mem. Am. Soc. Plant Physiologists, Am. Hort. Soc., Nat. Wildlife Fedn., Iowa Acad. Sci., U. Iowa Alumni Assn. Clubs: Greater Green Bay Kiwanis, Masons, Shriners. Home and Office: 205-J Huth St Green Bay WI 54302

ALLEY, LOUIS EDWARD, educator; b. Drexel, Mo., Dec. 9, 1914; B.S. in Edn., Central Mo. State Tchrs. Coll., 1935; M.S., U. Wis., 1941; Ph.D., State U. Iowa, 1949; m. Mary Lee Brinegar, Nov. 26, 1936; children—Rebecca Ann, Louis William. Tchr. schs., Mo., Iowa, and Kans., 1935-43, 45-46; mem. faculty Univ. High Sch., State U. Iowa, 1946-54, asso. prof., head dept. phys. edn., 1953-54, vis. prof. under Fulbright program, Burma, 1949-50, mem. faculty State U. Iowa, 1953-60, prof., adminstrv. asst. phys. edn., 1959-60, prof. phys. edn., head dept. phys. edn. men, 1960—; adv. com. Athletic Inst., 1967-72; adviser Ednl. Policies Commn., 1965-68. Served to lt. USNR, 1943-45. Mem. Am. (pres. 1971-72), Central Dist. (pres. 1964-65), Iowa (pres. 1957-58) assns. health, phys. edn. and recreation, Nat. Coll. Phys. Assn. Men (pres. 1966-67), Am. Coll. Sports Medicine, Am. Acad. Phys. Edn. (pres. 1977-78), Nat. Assn. Standard Med. Vocabulary, Phi Sigma Epislon, Phi Kappa Phi, Phi Delta Kappa, Phi Epsilon Kappa. Clubs: Triangle (pres. 1957) (U. Iowa); Iowa City Kiwanis (past dir.). Contbr. profl. jours. Home: 1204 Ashley Dr Iowa City IA 52240 Office: Dept Physical Edn Univ Iowa Iowa City IA 52242

ALLEY, WILLIAM JACK, ins. co. exec.; b. Vernon, Tex., Dec. 27, 1929; s. W.H. and Opal M. (Cater) A.; A.A., Northeastern A. and M. Coll., 1949; B.B.A., U. Okla., 1951, J.D., 1954; m. Marilyn Walter, June 6, 1952; children—Susan Jane, Pamela Jean, Patricia Ann, Sarah Elizabeth. Atty., State Ins. Bd. Okla., 1956-57; asst. v.p. Pioneer Am. Ins. Co., 1957-59, v.p., 1959-60, v.p., agy. dir., 1960-66, dir., 1961-67, sr. v.p. marketing, 1966-67; v.p. Franklin Life Ins. Co., Springfield, Ill., 1967-69, sr. v.p., agy. dir., 1969-74, exec. v.p., 1974-75, pres., chief exec. officer, 1976—, chmn. bd., 1977—; pres., chmn. bd. Franklin United Life Ins. Co., 1976—; dir. First Nat. Bank, Nat. Ben Franklin Ins. Co. Ill.; dir. Franklin United Life Ins. Co., Central Ill. Pub. Service Corp. Bd. dirs. Meml. Hosps.; trustee Ill. Coll. Served with Judge Adv. Gen.'s Dept., USAF, 1954-56. C.L.U. Mem. Okla. Bar Assn., Life Office Mgmt. Assn. (asso.), Springfield Assn. Life Underwriters, Delta Sigma Pi, Phi Kappa Sigma, Phi Alpha Delta. Mason (32 deg., Shriner). Clubs: Tavern (Chgo.); Illini Country, Sangamo, Springfield Racquet (dir.) (Springfield, Ill.). Home: 2014 Illini Rd Springfield IL 62704 Office: 1 Franklin Square Springfield IL 62705

ALLINGTON, JAMES RICHARD, ins. co. exec.; b. Chillicothe, Ill., Apr. 4, 1933; s. Charles Fredrich and Jessie (Topping) A.; B.S. in Accounting, U. Ill., Urbana, 1959; m. Marilyn Louise Balke, Dec. 26, 1960; 1 dau., Diane Louise. Cost accountant Nat. Lock Co., Rockford, Ill., 1959-60; chief accountant, office mgr. Goss Co., Rockford, 1960-64; office mgr. mechanics div. Borg-Warner Corp., Rockford, 1964-67; controller Ill. Hosp. and Health Service, Inc., Rockford, 1967-71, exec. v.p., 1972—. Treas. No. Ill. chpt. Multiple Sclerosis Soc.; fin. adviser Jr. Achievement; bd. dirs. Winnebago County chpt. Am. Heart Assn. Served with USAF, 1951-55. Mem. Adminstrv. Mgmt. Soc. (past v.p., dir.). Home: 2143 Bellwort Dr Rockford IL 61108 Office: 227 N Wyman St Rockford IL 61101

ALLINGTON, ROBERT WILLIAM, precision instrument co. exec.; b. Madison, Wis., Sept. 18, 1935; s. William B. and Norma Evelyn (Peterson) A.; B.S., U. Nebr., 1959, M.S., 1961; m. Marilyn Kaylor. With Instrumentation Specialties Co., Lincoln, Nebr., 1961—, pres., 1961—. Bd. dirs. Lancaster County chpt. Nat. Found., March of Dimes; mem. Nebr. Crippled Children's Com., 1973—, chmn., 1975—; v.p. Community Health Care Assn., 1974—. Mem. Lincoln City-Lancaster County Planning Commn., 1967—, chmn., 1977—. NSF fellow, 1959-61. Registered profl. engr., Neb. Fellow Am. Inst. Chemists; mem. IEEE, Illuminating Engring. Soc., Nat. Soc. Profl. Engrs., Profl. Engrs. Nebr., Instrument Soc. Am., Nat. Rifle Assn. Kiwanian. U.S., fgn. patents in field. Home: 1551 Ridgeway Rd Lincoln NE 68506 Office: 4700 Superior Ave Lincoln NE 68504

ALLISON, RICHARD BRUCE, author, publisher; b. San Diego, May 10, 1949; s. Harry B. and Dorothy S. (Buick) A.; B.A., Brown U., 1971; postgrad. (grantee) Rhinelander Sch. Arts, 1977. Owner, publisher Sol Press, Madison, Wis., 1971—; owner Allison Tree Care Co., Madison, 1974—; Mem. Wis. Arborist Assn., Wis. Regional, Madison Area (dir.) writers assns., Internat. Soc. Arbor Writers. Author: Democrats in Exile, 1974; editor: Toward A Human Future, 1972; Humanizing Our Future, 1974. Office: 107 Minneola St Hinsdale IL 60521

ALLOWAY, R. BROOKE, lawyer; b. Columbus, Ohio, July 2, 1916; s. James William and Ninnette (McKinley) A.; B.A., Ohio State U., 1936; J.D., Harvard U., 1939; m. Jane Denman Reason, Sept. 3, 1938; children—Jeremy Reason, Andrea Jane. Admitted to Ohio bar, 1939; law clk. Judge Edward C. Turner, Columbus, 1939-40; practiced in Columbus, 1941-42, 49—; mem. firm Topper, Alloway, Goodman, DeLeone & Duffey, 1949—; spl. agt. FBI, Okla., Ill., Ind., 1942-44; contract termination atty. Studebaker Corp., South Bend, Ind., 1944-46; asst. atty. gen. state of Ohio, Columbus, 1946-49; spl. counsel Atty. Gen. of Ohio, 1949—. Mem. adv. bd. Ohio State U. Alumni, 1964-72; mem. centennial commn. Ohio State U. Vice chmn. Franklin County Republican Finance Com., 1963-65; mem., counsel Ohio Rep. Finance Com., 1965—. Recipient Centennial award for alumni Ohio State U., 1970. Mem. Ohio State U. Assn. (1st v.p. 1961-62), Am., Ohio State, Columbus bar assns., Ohio State U. Faculty Club. Clubs: Scioto Country, Columbus, University. Home: 1300 La Rochelle Dr Columbus OH 43221 Office: 17 S High St Columbus OH 43215

ALLYN, RICHARD, physician; b. Waverly, Ill., Oct. 16, 1913; s. Paul Richard and Lena (Turner) A.; A.B. with high honors, U. Ill., 1935; M.D., Columbia, 1939; m. Ruth Lefferts, Sept. 20, 1941; children—Thomas Richard, Barbara Loraine, Paul Lefferts, David Edwin. Intern St. Luke's Hosp., N.Y.C., 1939-40, resident in internal medicine, 1940-41; spl. fellow in internal medicine Mayo Found., Rochester, Minn., 1941-42; practice medicine specializing in internal medicine, cardiology, Springfield, Ill., 1946—; attending staff Meml. Hosp. Springfield, 1946—, pres. med. staff, 1950, sr. attending staff,

1966—, chmn. dept. medicine, 1951, 53; active staff St. John's Hosp., Springfield, 1946—, pres. med. staff, 1969, chmn. dept. medicine, 1957-58, 65-66, 70-75; clin. asso. So. Ill. U. Sch. Medicine, 1971-73, clin. prof. medicine, 1973—. Mem. adv. planning com. So. Ill. U. Sch. Medicine, 1969-72. Mem. ofcl. bd. 1st United Meth. Ch., Springfield, 1950—, mem. bldg. planning com., 1961—, trustee, 1962—, mem. bishop's lay adv. com. Ill. Area, Meth. Ch., 1965—; active Boy Scouts Am., 1958-59; med. adviser local bd. SSS, 1950—; mem. local med. group Ill. Adv. Com. for Med., Dental, Vet. and Allied Specialists 1950—; mem. adv. com. on terminology Commn. Profl. and Hosp. Activities, Ann Arbor Mich., 1971—; mem. med. adv. com. BiState Regional Med. Program, St. Louis, 1970-73; mem. task force cardiovascular rehab. Nat. Heart and Lung Inst., 1973-75; mem. proficiency evaluation program com. Coll. Am. Pathologists, 1973—. Trustee MacMurray Coll., Jacksonville, Ill., 1962—, treas. bd. trustees, mem. exec. com., 1971—; mem. Found. Med. Care Central Ill. Served to capt. M.C., AUS, 1942-46; ETO. Decorated Bronze Star. Recipient Bronze tablet U. Ill., 1935; Distinguished Eagle Scout award Boy Scouts Am., 1971; Alexander Cochran Bowen scholar N.Y. Acad. Medicine, 1941-42. Diplomate, also recertified Am. Bd. Internal Medicine. Regent, Am. Coll. of Physicians, 1977—; fellow A.C.P. (gov. Downstate Ill. 1970—, mem. com. on med. services 1969-70, chmn. com. on hosps. 1969-73, mem. exec. com. of bd. govs. 1972—, vice-chmn. bd. govs. 1975-76, chmn. med. practice com. 1973—, steering com. 1975-76), Am. Coll. Chest Physicians, Am. Coll. Cardiology; mem. A.M.A., Ill. (council on legislation and pub. affairs, 1967-71, chmn. sect. on medicine 1960-61, 77, also other branches), Sangamon County (spl. com. on grad. med. edn. 1965-69, mem. peer review com. 1970-73, chmn. 1974) med. socs., Am. (mem. profl. interrelationships com. 1969-71), Ill. (pres. 1960-62, mem. council 1958—) socs. internal medicine, Am. Cancer Soc. (past chmn. Sangamon County chpt.) Springfield Med. Club (past pres.), Ill. Heart Assn. (pres. 1969-70, chmn. sch. sci. edn. com. 1966-68, dir. 1965—, chmn. long-range planning com. 1970-71, chmn. task force cardiopulmonary resuscitation 1973—), Am. (fellow council clin. cardiology 1972, mem. assembly planning com. 1971-74), Sangamon County heart assns., Linnean Soc. N.Y., A.A.A.S., Am. Ornithologists Union, Wilson Ornithol. Club, Nat. Audubon Soc., Springfield Audubon Soc., Soc. Mayflower Descs. in State of Ill. (life), Mayo Alumni Assn., Am. Birding Assn., Phi Beta Kappa, Sigma Xi, Phi Kappa Phi, Phi Eta Sigma, Alpha Kappa Lambda. Clubs: Illini Country, Sangamo (Springfield). Mason, Rotarian. Author: Library for Internists, 1973, Library for Internists II, 1976. Home: 2020 Willemoore Av Springfield IL 62704 Office: Myers Bldg Springfield IL 62701

ALMBLAD, CARL WILLIAM, city planner; b. Chgo., Aug. 16, 1924; s. William Anders and Elsie (Buddenbaum) A.; student Ill. Inst. Tech., 1942-43; B.S. in Architecture, U. Ill., 1950; M. Urban Planning, Wayne State U., 1965; m. Sarah Martha Turner, Sept. 8, 1951; children—Lori, Jonathan, and Jill. City planner Chgo. Planning Commn., 1950-53; city planner Detroit City Plan Commn., 1953-74, planning head Community and Econ. Devel. dept., 1974—. Bd. dirs. Hanover-Grove Non-Profit Housing Corp. Served with AUS, 1943-46. Mem. Am. Soc. Planning Ofcls., Am. Inst. Planners (sec. Mich. chpt.). Registered architect, Ill. Home: 14200 Archdale St Detroit MI 48227 Office: 150 W Michigan Ave Detroit MI 48226

ALMOND, CARL HERMAN, physician, educator; b. Latour, Mo., Apr. 1, 1926; s. Hugh Herman and Sylvia (Morrison) A.; B.A., Washington U., St. Louis, 1949, M.D., 1953; m. Nancy Ginn, June 18, 1964; children—Carrie, Callie, Carl, Christopher. Rotating intern Los Angeles County Gen. Hosp., 1953-54; resident surgery U. Mich., Ann Arbor, 1954-56, jr. clin. instr. surgery, 1956-57, sr. clin. instr., 1957-58; fellow surg. pathology Barnes Hosp.-Washington, St. Louis, 1956; sr. surg. resident in urology Baylor U. Affiliated Hosps., 1958-59; resident thoracic surgery U. So. Calif., Los Angeles, 1959, fellow thoracic surgery, 1963; fellow thoracic surgery Brompton Hosp., London, Eng., 1962; asst. prof. surgery U. Mo. Sch. Medicine, Columbia, 1959-64, asso. prof. surgery, 1964-69, prof. surgery, chief thoracic and cardiovascular surgery, 1969—; vis. prof. U. Geneva (Switzerland), 1972-73. Served with USNR, 1944-46. Diplomate Am. Bd. Surgery, Am. Bd. Thoracic Surgery. Fellow A.C.S.: mem. AMA, Boon County Med. Soc., Frederick H. Coller Surg. Soc., St. Louis Surg. Soc., Am. Coll. Cardiology, Am., Mo. heart assns., Am. Soc. Artificial Internal Organs, Soc. Med. Cons. to Armed Forces, Am. Coll. Chest Physicians, So. Thoracic Surg. Assn., Central Surg. Soc., Am. Assn. Thoracic Surgery, Chest Club, Internat. Cardiovascular Soc., Soc. Thoracic Surgeons, Sigma Xi, Nu Sigma Nu, Sigma Chi. Contbr. articles to profl. jours. Home: 213 West Boulevard S Columbia MO 65201

ALMOND, GEORGE LEE, educator; b. Stoddard County, Mo., Dec. 30, 1914; s. Samuel Alexander and Diena (Brennecke) A.; B.A., Ohio State U., 1951, M.A., 1955, Ph.D., 1963; m. Jessie Angela Gnezda, Oct. 25, 1952; children—Diena Brennecke, Bernard Lee. With U.S. Engrs., 1943-46, AEC, 1947-48; instr. Mich. State U., East Lansing, 1957-58; asst. prof. U. Rochester (N.Y.), 1958-59, U. Cin., 1959-63; asso. prof. U. Maine, Orono, 1964-65, prof., 1966-70; prof. mktg. Youngstown (Ohio) State U., 1970—. Served with AUS, 1942-43. Home: 481 Francisca Ave Youngstown OH 44504

ALMQUIST, NEVIN ARTHUR, phys. therapist; b. Osage, Iowa, May 18, 1941; s. Delmar E. and Irma J. (Pacey) A.; B.S., U. No. Iowa, 1963; M.S., Ind. U., 1966; phys. therapy certificate U. Ia., 1967; m. Verla Jeannette Dick, Feb. 7, 1970. Biology tchr., athletic trainer Amarillo (Tex.) Pub. Schs., 1963-65; grad. asst. Ind. U., Bloomington, 1965-66; with Bothwell Hosp., Sedalia, Mo., 1967—, dir. phys. therapy, 1967—. Cons. therpist Virginia Flower Child Devel. and Rehab. Center, Sedalia, 1967—, Golden Valley Hosp., Clinton, Mo., 1972-74, Fairview Nursing Home, 1969—, State Fair Community Coll., Sedalia, 1971—; clin. instr. U. Mo., Columbia, 1969-71, Central Mo. State U., Warrensburg, 1970—; dir. Bothwell Hosp. Employees Credit Union, 1976-78, pres., 1977; instr. pulmonary rehab. State Fair Community Coll. Sch. Respiratory Therapy. Pres. Pettis County Heart Assn., 1970-72. Mem. Am. Pub. Health Assn., Am., Mo. phys. therapy assns., Am. Registry Rehab. Medicine, Iowa Phys. Therapy Alumni Assn., Sedalia (dir. 1968-69, 1st v.p. 1969-70), Mo. (regional v.p. 1970-71) jr. chambers commerce, Phi Sigma Epsilon. Home: 2502 Wing St Sedalia MO 65301 Office: 644 E 13th St Sedalia MO 65301

ALPER, ALBERT, cons. engr.; b. St. Louis, Oct. 12, 1912; s. Nathan W. and Anna (Schoenfeld) A.; B.S. in Civil Engring., Mo. Sch. Mines and Metallurgy, 1936; m. Sylvia Lasky, Nov. 26, 1937; children—Cynthia Merle (Mrs. Alan B. Raymond), Patricia Ann (Mrs. Norman Gold), Marc Howard. Various engring. positions, 1936-46; structural engr. J. Gordon Turnbull, Inc., Engrs.-Architects, St. Louis, 1946-49; design engr. Metz and Eason, Structural Engrs., St. Louis, 1949-51; self-employed cons. structural engr., Creve Coeur, Mo., 1951-70; pres., chmn. bd. Alper Assos., Inc., 1970—. Fellow ASCE; mem. Am. Concrete Inst., Am. Soc. Testing and Materials, Nat. Soc. Profl. Engrs., Cons. Engr. Council Mo. (dir. 1967-69, sec. 1977-78), Internat. Assn. Bridge and Structural Engrs. Jewish religion. Structural engring. projects include St. Louis Planetarium, Loretto Hilton Theatre Performing Arts, Park Tower Apts. Home: 17 Sherwyn Ln Creve Coeur MO 63141 Office: 1023 Executive Pkwy Dr St Louis MO 63141

ALPER, ZALMAN YAKOV, architect; b. Chgo., Mar. 18, 1928; s. Max and Pessie (Slutsky) A.; B.S., Ill. Inst. Tech., 1948; postgrad. Art Inst. Chgo., 1945-46; m. Miriam Brainin, June 9, 1949; children—Jonathan, Judith, Joshua. Partner Alper & Alper Architects, Chgo., 1950-69; dir. environ. design Urban Investment and Devel. Co., subsidiary Aetna Life & Casualty Co., Chgo., 1969-71; pres. The Planning Group subs. Urban Investment & Devel. Co., Chgo., 1971-73; pres. Alper & Alper Assos., Chgo., 1973—; chmn. bd. Internat. Bldg. and Devel. Corp. Chmn. housing and planning com. City Club, Chgo., 1964-67; mem. exec. com. Com. on Chgo's. Parks, 1967-69. Recipient awards for excellence of design AIA, 1963, 66. Mem. Am. Soc. Technion (dir. 1974-76), AIA, Ill. Soc. Architects, Assn. Engrs. and Architects in Israel, Met. Housing and Planning Council, Internat. Tech. Coop. Center, Bldg. Ofcls. Conf. Am. Clubs: Arts; Cliff Dwellers. Contbr. articles to profl. jours. Home: 2923 W Catalpa St Chicago IL 60625 Office: 444 N Michigan Ave Chicago IL 60611

ALSDORF, MARILYNN BRUDER (MRS. JAMES W. ALSDORF), civic worker, export co. exec.; b. Evanston, Ill., Apr. 5, 1926; d. Edward J. and Coramae (Young) Bruder; student Northwestern U. Sch. Journalism; m. James W. Alsdorf, Oct. 3, 1952; children—Gregg, Lynne, Jeffrey, James. Model, John Powers, N.Y.C., 1948, Patricia Stevens, Chgo., 1949-51. Vice pres. A.J. Alsdorf Corp. Exporters, Chgo. Mem. benefit com. Juvenile Protective Assn., Chgo., 1958-60; chmn. art library and exhbn. com. North Shore Country Day Sch., Winnetka, 1960-61; chmn. Benton House Meml. Garden Chgo. 1960-61; publicity com. Winnetka Garden Club, 1961, projects chmn., 1963-64, v.p., 1967; mem. exec. com. World Flower and Garden Show, 1963-64; mem., judge Garden Club Am.; mem. reception com. Arts Club, Chgo., 1961; bd. dirs. Alsdorf Found., Chgo.; governing life mem., vice-chmn. Oriental com., benefactor, pres. women's bd., hon. mem., trustee Art Inst. Chgo., also vice-chmn. classical com.; benefactor John Herron Art Assn., Indpls.; interior design cons. The Goodman Theatre. Trustee Museum of Contemporary Art, Chgo., Ravinia Festival Assn.; mem. woman's bd. U. Chgo.; mem. exec. com. of women's bd. Field Museum, Chgo.; mem. art adv. bd. U. Notre Dame, Martin D'Arcy Gallery Loyola U.; trustee Chgo. Hort. Soc.; community adviser Chgo. Jr. League; dir. Floral Arts Gallery. Recipient horticulture award World Flower Show, 1961; Distinguished Modern award Wedgwood Soc.; Camellia award Loyola U., 1977. Mem. Antiquarians of Art Inst. Chgo., Oriental Ceramic Soc., The Orientals, Sarah Siddons Soc., Compagnons de Beaujolais-Lyons, France, Guild Chgo. Hist. Soc. Gamma Phi Beta. Conglist. Clubs: Sunset Ridge Country (Northfield, Ill.); Bel Aire (Cal.) Country; Post and Paddock (Arlington, Ill.); Art's, Casino, Woman's Athletic (dir.) (Chgo.). Home: 301 Woodley Rd Winnetka IL 60093 Office: 3200 W Peterson Chicago IL 60645

ALSOP, DONALD DOUGLAS, judge; b. Duluth, Minn., Aug. 28, 1927; s. Robert Alvin and Mathilda (Aaseng) A.; B.S., U. Minn., 1950, LL.B., 1952; m. Jean Lois Tweeten, Aug. 17, 1952; children—David, Marcia, Robert. Admitted to Minn. bar, 1952, since practiced in New Ulm; mem. firm Gislason, Alsop, Dosland & Hunter, 1954-75; judge U.S. Dist. Ct. dist. Minn., 1975—. Instr. Am. Inst. Banking, 1956-60. Chmn. Brown County chpt. A.R.C., 1968-74. Chmn. Brown County Republican Com., 1960-64; chmn. 2d Congl. Dist. Rep. Com., 1968-72. Served with AUS, 1945-46. Mem. Am., Minn. bar assns., New Ulm C. of C. (pres. 1974-75), Order of the Coif. Home: 10 Lost Rock Lane North Oaks St Paul MN 55110

ALSPAUGH, LILYAN MAE, lectr., writer, educator; b. Chgo.; d. Frank R. and Sarah E. (Saunders) Haas; Ph.B., U. Chgo., 1927; M.A., Ohio State U., 1932; Ph.D., Mich. State U., 1969; m. Ralph B. Alspaugh, Nov. 28, 1928. Dir. community relations WKRC radio-TV, Cin., 1955-59; now profl. lectr. throughout U.S.; prof. marketing mgmt. and communications Sch. Bus. Adminstrn. Central Mich. Univ., Mt. Pleasant, 1964-77. Vice pres. pub. relations Albros, Inc., mgmt. engrs., 1957—. Guest W. German Govt., 1953; observer NATO Conf., Copenhagen, Denmark, 1953; interviewed ofcls. SHAPE and NATO, Paris, 1956, 63, 71. Alt. del. from A.A.U.W. to Bedford Coll., U. London, 1953. Named honored alumna Ohio State U., 1947; recipient Centennial achievement award Phi Mu, 1952; Achievement award A.A.U.W., 1952; citation award U. Chgo., 1952. Internat. study grantee Ohio div. A.A.U.W., 1953, fellowship Mich. div., 1965. Mem. A.A.U.W. (pres. Cin. 1944-46, Ohio pres. 1947-49, nat. v.p. 1949-53, dir. Mich. div. 1963-66), Pub. Relations Soc. Am., AIM, Am. Bus. Communication Assn., Am. Women Radio and TV, Speech Communication Assn. Am., Am. Marketing Assn., Am. Mgmt. Assn., Am. Acad. Polit. and Social Sci., Am. Acad. Religion, Am. Acad. Advt., Phi Beta Kappa, Delta Kappa Gamma (hon. life mem.), Sigma Iota Epsilon. Clubs: College (Cin.); Peninsular (Grand Rapids). Contbr. articles to ednl. and profl. jours. Home: 810 Pleasant Ave Mount Pleasant MI 48858

ALTAN, TAYLAN, mech. engr.; b. Trabzon, Turkey, Feb. 12, 1938; s. Seref and Sadife (Baysal) A.; came to U.S., 1963, naturalized, 1970; diploma in mfg. engring. Tech. U. Hannover (W.Ger.), 1962; M.S. in Mech. Engring., U. Calif., Berkeley, 1964, Ph.D., 1966; m. Susan Borah, July 18, 1964; children—Peri, Aylin. Research asst. U. Calif., Berkeley, 1963-66; research scientist DuPont de Nemours Co., Wilmington, Del., 1966-68; sr. research scientist Battelle Inst., Columbus, Ohio, 1968-73, research leader Battelle Columbus Labs., 1973—; adj. prof. indsl. engring. Ohio State U.; cons. in field to U.S. and fgn. cos. Mem. ASME (chmn. div. prodn. engring. 1977), Am. Soc. Metals, Soc. Mfg. Engrs., Internat. Prodn. Engring. Research Instn. Author: (with F.W. Boulger and J.R. Becker) Forging Equipment, Materials and Practices, 1973; contbr. numerous articles to nat., internat. tech. jours.; asso. editor Jour. Mech. Working Tech., 1976. Home: 1380 Sherbrooke Pl Columbus OH 43209 Office: Battelle Labs 505 King Ave Columbus OH 43201

ALTENHOFF, NORMAN RICHARD, bank holding co. exec.; b. Chgo., May 30, 1934; s. Alexander and Beulah P. (Potts) A.; student Georgetown U., 1952-56; B.S. in Bus. Adminstrn., Roosevelt U., 1970, M.S., 1973; m. Janet Barbara Saad, June 12, 1960; children—Alexander, Allison. System engr. IBM, Chgo., 1964-67; div. comptroller First Nat. Bank of Chgo., 1967-73; mgmt. cons. Lester B. Knight & Assos., Inc., Chgo., 1973-76; v.p. Citizens Bancorp., Sheboygan, Wis., 1976—; instr. Grad. Sch. Bus., De Paul U., Chgo., 1975. Bd. dirs. Trinity Luther Sch., Sheboygan. Served in USNR, 1956-58. Certified data processor Data Processing Mgmt. Assn. Mem. Am. Mktg. Assn., Bank Marketing Assn., Am. Bankers Assn., Nat. Assn. Accountants, Data Processing Mgmt. Assn., C. of C. Sheboygan Area. Clubs: Pine Hills Country, River Forest Tennis. Home: 434 Erie Ave Sheboygan WI 53081 Office: 636 Wisconsin Ave Sheboygan WI 53081

ALTER, FORREST HENRICI, JR., librarian; b. Pitts., July 15, 1915; s. Forrest Henrici and Agnes (Scott) A.; A.B., U. Pitts., 1936; B.S. in L.S., Columbia U., 1947. Asst. Detroit Pub. Library, 1947-50, 1st asst., 1951-53; librarian Film Council of Am., Evanston, Ill., 1953-55; liaison rep. Adult Edn. Assn. U.S. to Nat. Inst. Adult Edn., London, 1955-57; head, art music drama dept. Flint (Mich.) Pub. Library, 1958—. Bd. dirs. Internat. Inst. Flint, 1962-68; bd. dirs. Flint Community Concerts, Inc., 1969-72; adv. com. Genesee Community Coll. Community Services, 1969-71; music com. Mich. Council for the Arts, 1963—. Served to 1st lt. AUS, 1942-46. Mem. Nat. Inst. Adult Edn. (hon. life mem.), Am., Music, Flint Area (pres. 1962-63, Librarian of Yr. 1971), Mich. (chmn. adult edn. sect. 1959-60) library assns., Spl. Libraries Assn. (chmn. adv. council 1971-72, chpt. pres. 1966-67, 69-70), Flint Pub. Library Staff Assn. (pres. 1972), Adult Edn. Assn. Mich. (dir. 1962-66), Greater Flint Arts Council (treas. 1968-71, 72-75, v.p. 1975-76), Flint Inst. Music (trustee 1971—, chmn. library com. 1972-73, exec. com. 1974—, chmn. planning and policies com. 1974-75, sec. 1975-77, 2d v.p. 1977—), Flint Community Music Assn. (dir. 1959-68), Beta Phi Mu. Home: 1522 Cromwell St Flint MI 48503 Office: Flint Public Library 1026 E Kearsley St Flint MI 48502

ALTER, JOSEPH DINSMORE, physician; b. Lawrence, Kans., Apr. 19, 1923; s. David Emmet and Martha (Payne) A.; M.D., Hahnemann Med. Coll., 1950; M.P.H., U. Calif., Berkeley, 1961; m. Marian Elizabeth Wengert, May 31, 1946; children—Robert Emmet, Janet Lynn. Intern, Huntington Meml. Hosp., Pasadena, Calif., 1950-51; mem. med. staff Group Health Coop. Puget Sound (Wash.), 1951-60, chmn. family practice dept., 1956-57; field dir. Houses for Korea, Coordinated Community Devel. Project, 1953-54; lectr. med. care adminstrn. Sch. Pub. Health, U. Calif., Berkeley, 1961-62; lectr. Sch. Hygiene and Pub. Health, Johns Hopkins U., Balt., 1962-65, asst. prof., 1965-67, dep. dir. rural health research projects, dept. internat. health Sch. Hygiene and Pub. Health, Narangwal Village, Punjab, India, 1962-67, asst. prof. dept. internat. health Sch. Hygiene and Pub. Health, Balt., 1967-68; asso. prof., field prof. community medicine, dept. community medicine Coll. Medicine, U. Ky. Med. Center, 1968-70; med. dir. Pilot City Health Center, Cin., 1970-73, HealthCare of Louisville, 1973-75; chief domiciliary med. service VA Center, Dayton, Ohio, 1975-77, asso. chief staff for extended care, 1977; prof., chmn. dept. community medicine Wright State U. Sch. Medicine, 1977—. Chmn. Dayton regional exec. com., mem. nat. bd. Am. Friends Service Com.; trustee Quaker Heights, Waynesville, Ohio. Recipient Physician's Recognition award AMA, 1976. Diplomate Am. Bd. Preventive Medicine. Mem. Am. Pub. Health Assn., Am. Acad. Family Physicians, Am. Coll. Preventive Medicine, Ohio, Montgomery County med. assns. Quaker. Author: Narrowing Our Medical Care Gap, 1972; (with others) The Health Center Doctor in India, 1967, Doctors for the Villages, 1976. Contbr. articles in field to profl. jours. Home: 732 Avon Fields Ln Cincinnati OH 45229 Office: Dept Community Medicine Wright State U Sch Medicine Box 927 Dayton OH 45401

ALTERMAN, ROLLAND AUGUST, educator; b. Pittsburg, Kans., Mar. 8, 1919; s. August Herman and Amanda Louise (Albers) A.; B.S., Kans. State Tchrs. Coll., 1942, M.S., 1946; Ed.D., U. Pa., 1950; m. Mabel Jane Nash, June 11, 1943; children—Rolland August, Gregory Nash. Dir. phys. edn. Coll. High Sch., Pittsburg, 1938-41, 45-46; head dept. indsl. edn. Oswego (Kans.) High Sch., 1946-47, also dir. phys. edn., 1946-47; asst. prof. edn. and psychology Kans. State Tchrs. Coll., Emporia, 1949-50, supt. lab. schs., dir. supervised teaching, 1950-54, head dept. secondary edn., 1954-55, dir. audio-visual services, 1955-60, prof. edn. and library sci., 1955-60; asst. dir. tchr. edn. project Central Mich. U., Mt. Pleasant, 1960-64, prof. edn., 1964—. Cons. Liberal Arts Colls. and Univs. Conf., Harrisburg, Pa., 1967; mem. evaluation team Nat. Council for Accreditation of Tchr. Edn., 1962—. Served with USCG, 1942-45. Mem. NEA, Mich. Edn. Assn., Am. Ednl. Research Assn., Mich. State Tchrs. Assn., Nat. Council of Measurements, Central Mich. U. Faculty Assn., Kans. State Alumni Assn., Audio-Visual Instrn. Assn. (pres. 1956-57), Kans. State Assn. for Student Tchrs. (pres. 1953-54), Sigma Phi Epsilon, Phi Delta Kappa. Lutheran. Author: Social, Mental and Emotional Development of Children, 1950; A New Approach to Teacher Education, 1966. Home: 1344 North Dr Mt Pleasant MI 48858

ALTHAUSER, ROBERT PIERCE, sociologist; b. Cin., Dec. 8, 1939; s. Lester William and Helen Katherine (Pierce) A.; B.A., Carleton Coll., 1961; M.A. (NDEA fellow), Duke U., 1964; Ph.D. (NIMH fellow), U. N.C., Chapel Hill, 1967. Asst. prof. sociology Princeton U., 1967-73; asso. prof. Ind. U., 1973—; cons. in field. Mem. Am. Sociol. Assn. Author: (with Sydney S. Spivack) The Unequal Elites, 1975; contbr. articles on social research methodology to profl. jours. Home: 522 S Mitchell St Bloomington IN 47401 Office: Ballantine Hall 776 Sociology Dept Ind U Bloomington IN 47401

ALTHOLZ, HERBERT CARL, paper co. exec.; b. Chgo., Mar. 23, 1922; s. Leo S. and Adelaide Altholz; B.A., Northwestern U., 1943; postgrad. Grad. Sch. Internat. Studies, Geneva, Switzerland, 1961; m. Roxann Jacobs, Sept. 7, 1946; children—Walter, Charles, Thomas, John. With Inlander Steindler Paper Co., Elk Grove Village, Ill., 1946—, pres., 1953-70, chmn. bd., 1970—. Bd. dirs. YMCA, 1960-70, Nat. Jewish Hosp., 1960-70; trustee Wayland Acad., 1959-69. Served with AUS, 1941-46. Mem. Nat. Paper Trade Assn. (pres. 1973). Home: 1865 Dale St Highland Park IL 60035 Office: 2100 Devon St Elk Grove Village IL 60007

ALTIERI, RICHARD NUNZIO, chiropractor; b. Chgo., Jan. 7, 1947; s. Rocco C. and Marie Clarice (Pintozzi) A.; D.C., Nat. Coll. Chiropractic, 1969; m. Therese Marie Stolfa, June 1, 1968. Lab. asst. supt. Luth. Gen. Hosp., Park Ridge, Ill., 1969-74; practice chiropractic, Schaumburg, Ill., 1972—. Diplomate Nat. Bd. Chiropractic Examiners, 1969. Mem. Ill. Chiropractic Soc., Ky., Am. chiropractic assns., Sigma Phi Kappa (chancellor 1968). Office: 18 N Roselle Rd Schaumburg IL 60172

ALTMAN, JULES, dermatologist; b. Bklyn., June 5, 1931; s. Samuel and Bella (Sherak) A.; M.D., U. Mich., 1958; m. Deborah Levine, Aug. 29, 1956; children—Suzanne, David, Karen. Intern, Univ. Hosp., Ann Arbor, Mich., 1958-59; resident Mayo Clinic, Rochester, Minn., 1959-62; practice medicine specializing in dermatology; mem. staffs Detroit Gen. Hosp., Detroit Meml. Hosp.; clin. asso. prof. dermatology and syphilogy, Wayne State U. Active United Jewish Appeal, Detroit; mem. bd. dirs. Hillel Day Sch., Detroit. Mem. AMA, Mich. State, Macomb County med. socs., Am. Acad. Dermatology, Soc. Investigative Dermatology, Mich. Dermatological Soc., Am. Soc. Dermopathology. Jewish. Club: Wabeek Country. Contbr. articles to med. jours. and texts. Home: 1950 Westlake Ct Bloomfield Hills MI 48013 Office: 11012 E 13 Mile Rd Warren MI 48093

ALTMAN, MILTON HUBERT, lawyer; b. Mpls., July 18, 1917; s. Harry Edmund and Lee (Cohen) A.; B.S., U. Minn., 1938, LL.B., 1947; m. Helen Horwitz, May 21, 1942; children—Neil, Robert, James. Admitted to Minn. bar, 1947; partner Altman, Weiss & Bearmon, St. Paul, 1947—. Mem. gov's adv. com. on Constl. Revision, 1950, on Gift and Inheritance Tax Regulations, 1961-65; chmn. atty. gen.'s adv. com. on Consumer Protection, 1961-65. Spl. atty. for Minn. Bd. Med. Examiners, 1963-75; spl. atty. for U. Minn., 1963—. Lectr. U. Minn., 1966—; dir. SPH Hotel Co. Mem. nat. emergency com. Nat. Council on Crime and Delinquency, 1967—; mem. Minn.-Wis. small bus. adv. council SBA, 1968-70; mem., v.p. Citizens Council on Delinquency and Crime, 1968-76; bd. dirs. Correctional Service Minn., 1968-76; mem. Lawyers Com. for Civil Rights Under Law, 1965—. Chmn. Minn. Lawyers for Johnson and Humphrey, 1968. Bd. dirs. St. Paul Jewish Fund and Council, 1966-69, Minn. Soc. Crippled Children and Adults. Mem. Am., Minn. (chmn. tax sect.

1960-62), Ramsey County (exec. council 1968-71) bar assns., Am. Arbitration Assn., Fgn. Policy Assn. (nat. council 1969), U. Minn. Law Sch. Alumni Assn. (dir. 1967-70), UN Assn. (nat. legacies com. 1967), Am. Law Inst. Clubs: Minn. (dir. 1975—), Hillcrest Country; St. Paul Athletic. Home: 1921 Pinehurst Ave St Paul MN 55116 Office: Degree of Honor Bldg St Paul MN 55101

ALTNER, PETER CHRISTIAN, orthopedic surgeon, med. educator; b. Starnberg, Germany, Apr. 19, 1932; s. Bruno Robert and Gisela (Bruch) A.; came to U.S., 1961, naturalized, 1970; M.D., U. Kiel (Germany), 1957; m. Louise Ruth Bonney, Feb. 7, 1958; children—Linda Louise, Peter Eric, Karen Christine. Intern, Muhlenberg Hosp., Plainfield, N.J., 1952-59; resident orthopedics U. Chgo., 1962-64; asst. prof. U. Ill., Chgo., 1967-71; asso. prof., chief div. orthopedic surgery Chgo. Med. Sch. and Mt. Sinai Hosp. Med. Center, Chgo., 1971-73; prof. surgery U. Health Scis. Chgo. Med. Sch., also dir. amputee clinic Cook County Hosp., Chgo., 1967—. Chmn. Village of Northbrook (Ill.) Youth Commn. Recipient Raymond B. Allen Instructorship award U. Ill., 1968; Outstanding New Citizenship award of Met. Chgo., Citizenship Council Met. Chgo., 1970. Mem. Am. Acad. Orthopedic Surgeons, Ill., Chgo. orthopedic socs., A.C.S., AMA, Ill., Chgo. med. socs., Assn. Orthopedic Chairmen. Home: 290 Lee Rd Northbrook IL 60062 Office: North Chicago VA Hosp North Chicago IL 60064

ALTON, RALPH TAYLOR, bishop; b. Deerfield, Ohio, Aug. 10, 1908; s. John Taylor and Roberta Hazel (Schwartz) A.; A.B., Ohio Wesleyan U., 1928, D.D. (hon.), 1951; S.T.B., Boston U., 1932; m. Marian Bannon Black, July 23, 1931; children—Phyllis Ann (Mrs. Harold Thor Hansen), Bruce Taylor. Ordained to ministry Methodist Ch., 1932, pastor in Mass., Ohio and Wis., 1932-60; bishop Wis. area, 1960-72, Ind. area, 1972—. Sec. Council of Bishops, United Meth. Ch., 1972-76; mem. Gen. Conf. Meth. Ch., 1956, 60; res. mem. Meth. Jud. Council, 1956-60; pres. Bd. Higher Edn. and Ministry. Trustee Lawrence U., DePauw U., Ind. Central Coll., U. Evansville, Meth. Hosp. Ind. mem. World Council Chs. (mem. central com.). Home: 2241 Rome Dr Indianapolis IN 46208 Office: 1100 W 42d St Indianapolis IN 46208

AL-UGDAH, WILLIAM MUJAHID, social worker; b. Cin., Oct. 29, 1953; s. William Henry and Helen (Guerrant) J.; student Bowling Green State U., 1971-73, Xavier U., 1974—; m. Deborah Russell, Oct. 30, 1976. Staff, Cin. Enquirer Youth Jour., 1968-69, Bowling Green State U. Recruiter, 1971-72; counselor Upward Bound program U. Cin., 1972; counselor student devel. Bowling Green State U., 1972-73; social worker Hamilton County Welfare Dept., Cin., 1974—; founder, owner, exec. v.p. Sanitation Inc., Cin., 1975—. Rep. World Community Al'Islam in West for Martin Luther King Meml. Day Service, 1978. Muslim. Home: 1575 Dixmont Ave Cincinnati OH 45207 Office: 628 Sycamore St Cincinnati OH 45202

ALVARES, KENNETH MICHAEL, psychologist; b. Redding, Calif., July 31, 1944; s. George M. and Laurene F. (Hans) A.; B.A., Ind. U., 1966; M.A., U. Ill., 1970, Ph.D., 1970; m. Linda S. Cane, Aug. 31, 1968; children—Mary Kathryn, Christianne. With Aviation Research Lab., Champaign, Ill., 1969-70; with psychology dept. U. Ill., Urbana, 1970-71; psychologist personnel devel. Bowling Green (Ohio) State U., 1971—. Cons. to John F. Lawhon Furniture Co., Toledo Police Dept., Chgo. Police Dept., Pub. Service Ind., Fin. Computer Service Ohio. Home: 1320 S Orleans St Bowling Green OH 43402

ALVAREZ, ALBERT RICHARD, editor; b. N.Y.C., May 28, 1929; s. John B. and Anna (Martinez) A.; B.A., Wichita U., 1953; m. Claziena Beugelsdyk, Aug. 29, 1959; children—Debra Ann, Richard Alan, Steven Michael, Kenneth Brian. With Wall St. Jour., N.Y.C., 1948-49; sports writer Wichita (Kans.) Beacon, 1952-54, Wichita Eagle, 1954-63, 69-70; editor Cessna Cessquire, 1959-60; police reporter Wichita Eagle, 1960-61, sports desk editor, 1961-63; with Cessna Aircraft Co., Wichita, 1954-60, composition dir. avionics manuals, engring. publs., 1965—; editor Nat. Baseball Congress Ann., Wichita, 1964-70, 75, Wichita Petroleum Club Gusher, 1970—; spl. corr. Golf World, 1960—, Topeka Capital-Jour., 1964—, UPI, 1976—; sports editor The New Newspaper, weekly, 1973. Active various community drives. Mem. Golf Writers Assn. Am. Address: 1319 Del Mar St Wichita KS 67216

ALVINE, RAYMOND GUIDO, cons. engr.; b. Burlington, Iowa, Aug. 22, 1926; s. Clark B. and Marcelle (Guerbinot) A.; B.S., Iowa State U., 1949; m. Dorothy Ann Lux, Sept. 1, 1947; children—Mary (Mrs. Jonathan St. Clair), Michael, Joan (Mrs. Albert Pallone), Cynthia, Patricia, Douglas, Suzanne, Steven, Judith, Christine. With Fairmont Foods, Columbus, Ohio, 1949-50, Carl A. Goth, profl. engr., Omaha, 1950-51, Silas Mason Co., Burlington, Iowa, 1951-53; asso. Leo A. Daly Co., Omaha, 1953-61; pres. Raymond G. Alvine & Assos., Inc., mech. and elec. cons. engrs., Omaha, 1961—. Chmn. Omaha Bldg. Bd. Rev., 1973—, Omaha Steamfitters Bd. Examiners, 1970—, City of Omaha High Rise Bldg. Ordinance, 1973—. Bd. dirs. Mill Creek Corp., 1973—, Overland Hills Devel. Corp., 1975—. Registered profl. engr., Iowa, Nebr., S.D., Nev., V.I., Ariz., Kans., Calif. Mem. Am. Cons. Engrs. Council, ASME, Am. Soc. Heating, Refrigerating and Air Conditioning Engrs., Soc. Am. Mil. Engrs., Nebr. Cons. Engrs. Assn. (pres. 1969), Nebr. Cons. Engrs. Assn. (charter mem., pres. 1972), Automated Procedures for Engring. Cons. (charter mem., nat. pres. 1974-76), Pi Tau Sigma. K.C. Clubs: Toastmasters (pres. 1963), Exchange, Field; Press (Omaha). Home: 1910 S 32d Ave Omaha NE 68105 Office: 254 Aquila Ct Omaha NE 68102

ALVORD, JAMES C., JR., newspaper editor; b. Milw., July 10, 1944; s. James C. and Evelyn A.; B.S. in Journalism, U. Wis., 1966; m. Valerie J. Bonge, Mar. 30, 1976. Asst. editor World Book Ency., Chgo., 1966-68; asso. editor Nat. Retail Furniture Assn., Chgo., 1968-69; exec. editor Panax Pub. Co., Lansing, Ill., 1969—, also dir. Mem. Ill. (recognition for column 1970, 72, 75, 76), No. Ill., Hoosier press assns., Suburban Newspapers Am. (recognition for column 1973, 75, 76), Internat. Soc. Weekly Editors (Golden Quill award for column 1975). Home: 1220 Douglass Ave Flossmoor IL 60422 Office: 18127 William St Lansing IL 60438

ALWIN, LEROY VINCENT, JR., mech. engr.; b. Mpls., Sept. 23, 1931; s. LeRoy Vincent and Norma Constance (Hartmuth) A.; B.M.E., U. Minn., 1958; m. Barbara June Hecker, Sept. 23, 1972; children—Elizabeth Ann, Anthony Jay; stepchildren—Pamela Jeanne Bohach, Joel Edward Bohach. Engring. designer, asst. "Linac Project", Dept. Physics, U. Minn., Mpls., 1953-58; weather observer, forecaster, USN, Coco Solo, Canal Zone, 1954-56; design mech. engr. Temperature Control Div., Honeywell, Inc., Mpls., 1958-71; cons. mech. engr., v.p. Park Engring., Mpls., 1971—; proprietor Sugar Wood Farm, Mound, Minn., 1959—. Chmn., N. Am. Maple Syrup Council, 1975-77; chmn. Mound, Minn. Park Commn., 1968-71. Served with USNR, 1954-56. Registered profl. engr., Minn., Wis., Iowa, S.D., Mich. Mem. ASME, Am. Meteorol. Soc. Republican. Club: Engrs. Patentee in field; contbr. articles in field to profl. jours. Home: Robin Ln Mound MN 55364 Office: 5700 W 36th St Minneapolis MN 55416

AMADOR, LUIS V., surgeon; b. 1920; M.D., Northwestern U., 1944. Intern, U. Ill., 1944-45, resident in neurology and neurosurgery, 1945-46, 48-50, Rockefeller Found., 1951-52, Guggenheim fellow, 1954, neurosurgeon Children's Meml. Hosp., St. Joseph Hosp., Chgo., Luth. Gen. Hosp., Park Ridge, Ill.; clin. prof. neurol. surgery U. Ill. Coll. Medicine, Chgo. Bd. dirs. Spastic Paralysis Research Found. Served to capt. M.C., AUS, 1946-48. Diplomate Am. Bd. Neurosurgeons. Fellow A.C.S., Royal Soc. Medicine; mem. AMA, Congress Neurol. Surgeons, Am. Assn. Neurol. Surgeons, Central Neurosurg. Soc. (pres.), Internat. Soc. Pediatric Neurosurgery, Interurban Neurol. Soc. (dir.), Research Soc. Stereo encephalotomy, AAAS, Sigma Xi. Contbr. articles to books and profl. jours. Office: 700 N Michigan Ave Chicago IL 60611

AMANN, PETER HENRY, historian, educator; b. Vienna, Austria, May 31, 1927; s. Paul and Dora Iranyi; B.A., Oberlin Coll., 1947; M.A., U. Chgo., 1953, Ph.D., 1958; m. Enne Niemi, June 19, 1947; children—Paula, Sandra, David. Instr., European history Bowdoin Coll., Brunswick, Maine, 1956-59; asst. prof. history Oakland U., Rochester, Mich., 1959-64, asso. prof., 1964-65; asso. prof. history State U. N.Y., Binghamton, 1965-68; prof. history U. Mich., Dearborn, 1968—. Recipient Sr. Distinguished Teaching award U. Mich., Dearborn, 1975; Guggenheim fellow, 1963-64; Sr. Fulbright research fellow, 1963-64. Author: Revolution and Mass Democracy: The Paris Club Movement in 1848, 1976; editorial bd. French Hist. Studies, 1972-75; manuscript reader Cornell, Princeton, Yale univ. presses. Home: 2472 Grant Dr Ann Arbor MI 48104 Office: 4901 Evergreen St Dearborn MI 48124

AMAR, WESLEY FRANCIS, educator; b. Chattanooga, Mar. 10, 1913; s. Marion Benedict and Josephine (McGuinness) A.; tchrs. certificate, Chgo. Normal Coll., 1934; Ph.B., Loyola U., Chgo., 1936, M.A., 1941, Ed.D., 1958; Ed.M., Chgo. Tchrs. Coll., 1943; m. Yvonne Adele Van Lent, Aug. 7, 1943; children—Mubarak A., Yvonne (Mrs. Charles Frey). Tchr., Chgo. Pub. Schs., 1934-51; prin. Graham Elementary Sch., Chgo., 1951-60, Kelvyn Park High Sch., Chgo., 1960-66, Waller High Sch., Chgo., 1966-69; asso. prof. dept. secondary edn. No. Ill. U., DeKalb, 1969-77, prof. ednl. adminstrn., 1977—; participant North Central Assn. Schs. Evaluation Com., 1952—; lectr. in field. Lay asst. St. Procopius Benedictine Roman Catholic Monastery, 1973—. John Hay fellow U. Oreg., 1964. Mem. AAUP, Aquin Club, Chgo. Prins. Assn. (asso.), Phi Delta Kappa. Author: Inner City School Problems: An Educational Wasteland (cassettes). Contbr. articles to profl. jours. Home: 500 61st St Lisle IL 60532 Office: Northern Ill University Gabel Hall DeKalb IL 60115

AMARO, JOHN ANTHONY, chiropractor; b. Kansas City, Mo., Apr. 1, 1947; s. Carl and Virginia (Belmonte) A.; D. Chiropractic, Cleve. Chiropractic Coll., 1970; D. Phys. Therapy, Van Norman U., 1974; m. Emily Jo Ragusa, Nov. 3, 1973. Pvt. practice chiropractic N.E. Chiropractic Center, Kansas City, Mo., 1971-75, Metcalf Chiropractic Offices, Overland Park, Kans., 1975—. Served with 135th Hosp. Corps, AUS, 1970-73. Mem. Acupuncture Soc. Am. (v.p. 1974—), Mo. Acupuncture Soc. (pres. 1975—), Am., Kans., Mo., Ky. chiropractic assns. Home: 10715 W 101st Terr Overland Park KS 66214 Office: 7203 Metcalf Ave Overland Park KS 66204

AMAROSE, ANTHONY PHILIP, educator; b. Oneonta, N.Y., Mar. 17, 1932; s. Andrew and Rose (Minerosa) A.; B.S., Fordham Coll., 1953, M.S., 1957, Ph.D. in Cytology, 1959. Resident research asso. Argonne Nat. Lab., 1959-61; gen. pathology fellow Med. Sch., Harvard, Boston, 1961; research asso. Cancer Research Inst., New Eng. Deaconess Hosp., Boston, 1961-62; asst. prof. dept. obstetrics, gynecology, lectr. pathology Albany (N.Y.) Med. Coll., Union U., 1963-67, research asso. prof., 1966-67; asst. prof. Pritzker Sch. Medicine, U. Chgo., 1967-71, asso. prof., 1971—, dir. cytogenetic core lab. Biol. Scis. Div. Center Population Research, 1972-77, dir. cytogenetic lab. dept. obstetrics gynecology, 1975—. Cons. cytogenetics field. Trustee Charles Berger Scholarship Fund, Fordham U., 1966—. Served with AUS, 1953-55. Fellow Royal Microscopical Soc. (Gt. Britain); mem. N.Y. Acad. Scis., Am. Inst. Biol. Scis., Am. Soc. Cell Biology, AAAS, Environmental Mutagen Soc., Am. Soc. Human Genetics, Inst. Society, Ethics and Life Scis., Soc. Gynecologic Investigation, Am. Soc. Law and Medicine, AAUP, Sigma Xi. Contbr. profl. jours. Mem. internat. editorial bd. Excerpta Medica. Home: 5532 S Shore Dr Chicago IL 60637 Office: Box 446 5841 S Maryland Ave Chicago IL 60637

AMARY, ISSAM BAHJAT, adminstrv. recreation therapist; b. Jerusalem, July 11, 1942; s. Bahjat Kamel and Essaf (El-Khiami) El-Amary; came to U.S., 1962, naturalized, 1972; B.S., Mo. Valley Coll., 1968; M.S., Central Mo. State U., 1974; m. Wilma Jeanne Blinn, Aug. 20, 1967; children—Jason Issam, Jarred Jamal, Dax Tallal. Recreation therapist, dir. activity therapy Marshall (Mo.) State Sch. Hosp., 1969-75, unit dir., 1975—; exec. dir. Mo. Spl. Olympics, 1970-72, chmn. bd. dirs., 1970-73; founding mem. Betterment of Youth Program. Recipient Viki award in dramatic arts. Mem. Nat. Park and Recreation Assn., Nat. Therapeutic Recreation Soc. Clubs: Optimist (dir.), Masons. Author: Creative Recreation for the Mentally Retarded, 1974; A Taste of Lebanon, 1975. Home: 711 Plaza Dr Marshall MO 65340 Office: Marshall State School Hospital E Slater St Marshall MO 65340

AMATO, JOSEPH A., historian; b. Detroit, Aug. 31, 1938; s. Joseph and Ethel May (Linsdau) A.; B.A., U. Mich.; M.A., U. Laval, 1963; Ph.D., U. Rochester, 1970; married, Dec. 19, 1940; children—Felice, Anthony, Adam, Ethel. Instr. history N.Y. U., 1965-66, U. Calif., Riverside, 1966-68; mem. faculty dept. history SW State U., Marshall, Minn., 1969—, asso. prof., 1973—. Author: Emmanuel Mounier and Jacques Maritain: A French Catholic Understanding of the Modern World, 1975. Office: Dept History Southwestern Minn State Coll Marshall MN 56258

AMELING, NORMAN JOHN, constrn. co. exec.; b. East St. Louis, Ill., Dec. 11, 1923; s. Fred William and Elizabeth (Pottsel) A.; B.S. in Civil Engring., Washington U., St. Louis, 1947; m. Lorraine B. Mueller, Sept. 18, 1948; children—Kathleen, Barbara, Lois, David. Pres., treas. Woermann Constrn. Co., St. Louis, 1947—; tchr. Washington U., St. Louis, evenings 1956-64. Served with AUS, 1943-46; ETO. Registered profl. engr., Mo. Mem. ASCE, Engrs.' Club of St. Louis, Asso. Gen. Contractors St. Louis (treas. 1971-72 v.p. 1973-75, pres. 1976). Home: 8720 Del Vista St Louis MO 63126 Office: 7120 Manchester St St Louis MO 63143

AMENT, F. THOMAS, supr. lfilwaukee County (Wis.); b. Milw., Nov. 17, 1937; s. Frank G. and Hildegarde D. (Neubauer) A.; B.S. in Accounting, lfarquette U., 1959, LL.B., 1962; m. Jeanne M. Denys, Aug. 22, 1964; children—Christopher T., Peter J., Jennifer L. Admitted to Wis. bar, 1962; practiced in Milw., 1963—; supr. Milwaukee County Bd., 1968—, chmn., 1976—. Chmn. Milwaukee County Annuity and Pension Bd., 1972-76. Served with USAF, 1962. Mem. Am., Wis., Milw. bar assns., Amvets, Am. Legion, Cooperation West Side. Democrat. Roman Catholic. Home: 9023 W Hawthorne Ave Milwaukee WI 53226 Office: 901 N 9th St Milwaukee WI 53233

AMERINE, IVAN ROBERT, sales engr.; b. Galloway, Ohio, Aug. 6, 1930; s. Ivan Robert and Bernice (Fish) A.; B.S., Ohio State U., 1948-51; m. Alice Fulton, July 29, 1949; children—Stephen, David, Brian, Hal. Vice-pres., also dir. Capitol City Mfg. Co., Columbus, Ohio, 1951-56; pres., gen. mgr. Apco Fabricating Co., Columbus, 1956-66; pres., chmn. Columbus Form Tool Co., 1966-70; pres. Isco Inc., Worthington, Ohio, 1970—. Vestry, finance chmn. St. John's Episcopal Ch., Worthington, 1973-76. Mem. Soc. Mfg. Engrs. (sr.). Republican. Clubs: Brookside Golf and Country, Columbus Maennerchor, Elks, Masons, Shriners. Home: 2137 Castlecrest Dr Worthington OH 43085 Office: 893 High St Worthington OH 43085

AMERSLAV, ANDREW FICAJ, mech. design engr.; b. Jeannette, Pa., Oct. 20, 1918; s. Wasil Fedorow and Maria (Petechuk) Ficaj; student U. Wis., 1945-46, U. Minn., 1946-47, Mpls. Sch. Art, 1947-49, Donwoody Tech. Inst., Mpls., 1949-52; m. Marchenko, June 24, 1951; children—Mary Ann, Alexander. Draftsman, Elec. Machinery Co., Mpls., 1952-55; designer, layout Cornelious Co., Mpls., 1955-60; with Gen. Electronic Control, Mpls., 1960-62; design engr. Pako Corp., Mpls., 1960-65; FMC Corp. No. Ordnance Div., Mpls., 1965-70; cons., mech. design engr., solar and domestic heat conservation projects, Fridley, Minn., 1970—; tchr. Hennepin County (Minn.) Vocat. Tech. Schs.; designer solar hot water heater. Founder, chmn. bd. dirs. Seminarian Scholarship Fund., 1974—. Author publs. in field. Home and office: 870 W Moore Lake Dr Fridley MN 55432

AMES, EDWARD JAMES, mech. engr., lab. equipment mfg. co. exec.; b. Chgo., Mar. 22, 1934; s. Paul and Edna J. (Smith) A.; B.S.M.E., U. Ill., 1957; m. Patricia Rae Lemaster, May, 1958; children—Edward, Jeffrey, Christopher, Kevin, Sara. Lab. supr. Modine Mfg. Co., Racine, Wis., 1957-64, project engr., 1964-67; engring. mgr. Rheem Mfg. Co., Greenville, Ala., 1968-74; dir. engring. Labconoco, Kansas City, Mo., 1974—. Committeeman, Boy Scouts Am., 1965-66, cubmaster, 1972-73. Served with USN, 1960. Registered profl. engr., Wis., Mich. Mem. Am. Soc. Heating, Refrigeration, Air Conditioning Engrs., ASTM. Republican. Lutheran. Inventor in field. Home: 3212 W 97th Pl Leawood KS 66206 Office: Labconco Corp 8811 Prospect St Kansas City MO 64132

AMES, PETER LESLEY, ecologist; b. St. Paul, May 2, 1931; s. Theodore Gordon and Barbara (Holt) A.; grad. Phillips Acad., 1949; A.B., Harvard, 1958; M.S., Yale, 1962, Ph.D., 1965; m. Nancy Julia Pankratz, Sept. 13, 1958; children—Elizabeth, Charles Gordon. Asst. prof. zoology, asst. curator U. Calif. at Berkeley, 1965-68; asso. editor life scis. Ency. Brit., Chgo., 1968-72; resource ecologist, head dept. environ. scis. Harza Engring. Co., Chgo., 1973—. Bd. dir. Chgo. Audubon Soc., 1971—, v.p., 1971-75. Served with USAF, 1952-56. Contbr. articles in field to profl. jours. Home: 2713 Walnut Ave Evanston IL 60201 Office: 150 S Wacker Dr Chicago IL 60606

AMES, (POLLY) SCRIBNER, artist; b. Chgo., Feb. 16, 1908; d. Edward Scribner and Mabel (Van Meter) Ames; Ph.B., U. Chgo., 1928; student Art Inst. Chgo., 1929; pupil Hans Schwegerle, Munich, Germany, 1932, Jose de Creeft, N.Y.C., 1933, Hans Hofmann, N.Y.C., 1934-36. Tchr., City and Country Sch., N.Y.C., 1939-41; one-man shows Culture Center, Curacao, 1947, Cercle Universitaire, Aix-en-Provence, France, 1950, Esher-Surry Gallery, The Hague, Netherlands, 1949, Chardin Gallery, Paris, France, 1950, including 1020 Art Center, Chgo., Gilman Gallery, Chgo. Pub. Library. exhibited paintings in maj. U.S. cities, including Renaissance Soc., Arts Club Chgo.; executed wood carving U. Chgo. Lab. Sch.; appeared prodns. TV Sta. WTTW. Active, Recs. for Blind, Chgo., 1958—. Recipient Purchase award State Mus. Springfield, Ill., 1963. Mem. Archeol. Inst., Smithsonian Instn., Arts Club of Chgo. (dir.). Club: Quadrangle (U. Chgo.). Paintings include Impression of Geraldine Page in Sweet Bird of Youth; portraits of Povla Frijish, in Town Hall, N.Y.C., Bernadotte E. Schmitt, Marion Morehouse (Mrs. E.E. Cummings), Maureen Ting-Klein; wood carving Lab. Sch., U. Chgo., Seabird, Quadrangle Club. Author, illustrator: Marsden Hartley in Maine, 1972. Home: 5843 S Stony Island Ave Chicago IL 60637

AMFAHR, DONALD FRANCIS, food co. exec.; b. Jesup, Iowa, June 13, 1929; s. Conrad William and Margaret (Schuler) A.; grad. bus. adminstrn. Northwestern U., 1972; m. Patricia Jean Dolmseth, Dec. 5, 1947; children—Michael, Deborah, David, Jeffrey, Lori. Asst. mgr. Friedlander & Sons Jewelry, Bremerton, Wash., 1948-53; sales mgr. Continental Baking Co., 1954-65; with Salerno-Megowen Biscuit Co., Chgo., 1965—, dir. sales, 1968-70, v.p. sales, 1970—. Served with USNR, 1946-48, 51-52. Mem. Grocery Mfrs. Sales Execs. (pres. 1975-77), Merchandising Execs. Club (pres. 1974-76). Home: 1585 Riverview Dr Des Plaines IL 60018 Office: 7777 Caldwell St Chicago IL 60648

AMIDON, PAUL CHARLES, pub. co. exec.; b. St. Paul, July 23, 1932; s. Paul Samuel and Eleanor Ruth (Simons) A.; B.A., U. Minn., 1954; m. Patricia Jean Winjum, May 7, 1960; children—Karen, Michael, Susan. Bus. mgr. Paul S. Amidon & Assos., Inc., Mpls., 1956-66, pres., 1966—. Served with AUS, 1954-56. Home: 1582 Hillcrest Ave St Paul MN 55116 Office: 1966 Benson Ave St Paul MN 55116

AMIOT, GERALD JOSEPH, county ofcl.; b. Gentilly, Minn., Oct. 24, 1941; s. Patrick Joseph and Alice Dorothy (Noel) A.; grad. Vocational Tng. Corp., 1962. Clk. J.C. Penney Co., Crookston, Minn., 1963-65; asst. mgr., 1965-67; bookkeeper Polk County Hwy. Dept., Crookston, 1967-69; clk.-accountant Polk County Auditor's Office, Crookston, 1969-71, dep. auditor, 1971—. Treas. Pioneer Days Assn., Crookston, 1970-74, parade chmn., 1969—, pres., 1974; co-chmn. Crookston Bicentennial Celebration, 1975-76, sec., 1977—. Recipient J.C.I. Senatorship award Jaycees Internat., 1973, certificate merit Crookston C. of C., 1976. Mem. Minn. (chaplain 1966-67, v.p. 1970-71, sec. 1976-77, program mgr. 1977-78, U.S. dir. 1971-72; Outstanding State Dir. award 1970; chmn. first timers program 1975-76), Crookston (2nd v.p. 1968-69, state dir. 1967-68, 70-71; Man of Year award 1970, knight Royal Order Ox Cart 1971) Jaycees, Am. Fedn. State, County and Municipal Employees (sec.-treas. Crookston local). Roman Catholic (chmn. parish council finance com. 1973). K.C. (chancellor 1972), Eagle, Elk. Home: 204 1/2 N Minnesota St Crookston MN 56716 Office: Polk County Courthouse Crookston MN 56716

AMMER, WILLIAM, common pleas judge; b. Circleville, Ohio, May 21, 1919; s. Moses S. and Mary (Schallas) A.; B.S. in Bus. Adminstrn., Ohio State U., 1941, J.D., 1946. Admitted to Ohio bar, 1947; atty., examiner Ohio Indsl. Commn. Columbus, 1947-51; asst. atty. gen. State of Ohio, Columbus, 1951-52; practiced in Circleville, 1953-57, pros. atty. Pickaway County, Circleville, 1953-57, common pleas judge, 1957—; asst. city solicitor Circleville, 1955-57. Past pres. Pickaway County ARC, Am. Cancer Soc. Served with inf., AUS, 1942-46. Mem. Am., Ohio (chmn. criminal law com. 1964-67), Pickaway County (pres. 1955-56) bar assns., Ohio Common Pleas Judges Assn. (pres. 1968). Methodist. Mason (K.T., Shriner), Kiwanian (Ohio dist. chmn., past lt. gov.). Home: 141 Pleasant St Circleville OH 43113 Office: Courthouse Circleville OH 43113

AMMERMAN, JAY NEIL, bar assn. exec.; b. Richmond, Ind., Aug. 21, 1945; s. Francis Andrew and Pollyanna (Kitchel) A.; B.S. in Mathematics, U. Chgo., 1967, M.B.A. in Fin., 1977; M.S. in Mathematics (NSF fellow), Northwestern U., 1968; m. Paula Jean Lorig, Dec. 19, 1969; 1 son, Jason Lorig. Sr. programmer Vapor Corp., Chgo., 1969, systems analyst, 1970, sr. systems analyst, 1970-72, asst. mgr. systems and programming, 1972-75; mgr. systems and programming Am. Bar Assn., Chgo., 1975-77, asst. dir. data processing, 1977—. Bd. dirs. Hyde Park Co-op Credit Union, 5227 S. Blackstone Corp. Mem. GUIDE, (assn. for large scale IBM computer users), Sigma Xi, Beta Gamma Sigma. Home: 5222 S Blackstone St Chicago IL 60615 Office: 1155 E 60th St Chicago IL 60637

AMNEUS, PAYTON WILLIAM, metallurgist; b. Glendale, Calif., May 1, 1941; s. John Sigfrid and Carolyn Ann (Weaver) A.; B.S. in Chemistry, Wayne State U., 1971; m. Christine Carolyn Mozola, Dec. 12, 1964; 1 son, Erik Payton. Contact engr. Chrysler Corp., Hamtramck, Mich., 1963-67, test and devel. engr., Detroit, 1967, plant metallurgist, Indpls., 1967-73, prodn. supr., Indpls., 1973-74; chief metallurgist Dayton-Walther Corp., Portsmouth, Ohio, 1974—. Mem. YMCA. Mem. Am. Foundrymen's Soc., Theta Xi. Home: 653 Herms Hill Wheelersburg OH 45694 Office: 2400 E Charles St Portsmouth OH 45662

AMOS, DAVID ESPEJO, physician; b. San Marcelino, Zamboles, Mar. 20, 1942; s. Casimerol Aglibut and Esmerenciano (Espejo) A.; M.D., Far Eastern U., 1970; m. Lourdes Rosario Beltran, Dec. 20, 1969; children—David Ian B., Louella Marie B. Resident in family practice St. Michael's Hosp., Milw., 1971-74; gen. practice family medicine, Milw., 1974—. Diplomate Am. Bd. Family Practice. Fellow Am. Acad. Family Practice; mem. AMA, Wis., Milw. med. assns. Home: 8362 N 49th St Brown Deer WI 53223

AMOS, EVERETT R., dentist; b. Kirklin, Ind., Nov. 9, 1901; s. John Henry and Iva Belle (Stephenson) A.; B.A. magna cum laude et cum honore, St. John's Coll., 1929; student Indpls. Sch. Stenotypy; D.D.S. with honors, Ind. U., 1950; m. Martha J. Tilson, Apr. 1, 1944. Served with U.S. Mcht. Marine, 1929-34; tchr. English, typing, until 1942; mem. staff Ind. U. Sch. Dentistry, 1952-57, asst. prof. oral diagnosis, 1954-57; pvt. practice dentistry, Knox, Ind., 1957—; dental cons. Hogar de Ninos de Ejercicio Salvaje, Guadalajara, Mexico, 1970—. Served with USAAF, 1942-45; CBI. Mem. Soc. Ind. Pioneers, Am. Soc. Guadalajara, Guadalajara Soc. Prevention Cruelty to Animals, Omicron Kappa Upsilon, Psi Omega. Democrat. Methodist (chmn. bd. 1967-68). Kiwanian. Winner Am. Med. Joggers Assn. contigent to Boston Marathon in category of over 70 years of age, 1977. Home: 309 S Main St Knox IN 46534 also Veracruz Sur 28 No 4 Guadalajara Jalisco Mexico Office: 309 S Main St Knox IN 46534

AMOS, ROBERT WOODROW, newspaper exec.; b. Cambridge, O., Mar. 25, 1913; s. Harry Waller and Elizabeth Rose (Davies) A.; B.A., Denison U., 1935; m. Hannah Margaret Hutchison, Sept. 18, 1938; children—Margaret Ann (Mrs. Michael Riordan), Elizabeth (Mrs. Steven Ball). Reporter, Daily Jeffersonian, Cambridge, 1935-40, sports editor, 1940-43, city editor, 1943-47, editor, 1947-67, pres., editor, 1967-75, publisher, editor, 1975—, also dir.; dir. 1st Nat. Bank, Cambridge. Mem. City Forest Com., 1962—, Ohio Forestry Adv. Council, 1969-72; mem. advisory council SBA, 1967-69, nat. council, 1968-69; mem. Ohio Reclamation Bd. Rev., 1964-68, chmn., 1967-68; mem. Guernsey County Health Planning Council, 1971—; Trustee Guernsey County Pub. Library, 1942-68; trustee Denison U. Research Found., 1965-71; bd. dirs. Guernsey County Children Services, 1970-72, Guernsey County Hist. Soc.; trustee, bd. dirs. Ohio Arts and Crafts Found., pres., 1969; bd. dirs. Cambridge Area Met. YMCA, 1969-72, Guernsey County Humane Soc., 1972—; mem. advisory bd. Salvation Army, 1964-68, chmn., 1967. Mem. Ohio U.P.I. Editors Assn. (pres. 1971), Cambridge Area C. of C. (pres. 1975), Sigma Chi, Sigma Delta Chi. Democrat. Baptist. Clubs: Rotary (dir. 1969-71, 78—), Cambridge Country. Home: 1405 N 10th St Cambridge OH 43725 Office: 821 Wheeling Av Cambridge OH 43725

AMROLIA, DINYAR HOMI, physician; b. Bombay, India, July 29, 1937; s. Homi Edulji and Gool Homi (Contractor) A.; M.B. B.S., Ghandhi Med. Coll., Bhopal, India, 1961; m. Persis Shiavax Bhesania, Nov. 21, 1971; children—Ferzhin, Roxanne. Surg. registrar Gen. Infirmary, Pontefract, Yorkshire, Eng., 1966-67, City Hosp., Nottingham, Eng., 1967-69; orthopaedic registrar Derbyshire Royal Infirmary, Derby, Eng., 1969-71; practice medicine specializing in orthopedic surgery, Thompson and Gillam, Man., Can., 1971—; mem. staff Thompson Gen. Hosp., pres. staff, 1975—, also head dept. surgery; chief staff Gillam Hosp., 1972-75. Fellow Royal Coll. Surgeons (Eng.); mem. Brit., Canadian, Man. med. assns., Internat. Meditation Soc. Lion. Home: 119 Sauger Crescent Thompson MB Canada Office: Profl Bldg Thompson R8N 0K5 MB Canada

AMSTUTZ, HUBERT MENNO, physician; b. Pandora, Ohio, Dec. 9, 1901; s. Menno and Isadora (Copeland) A.; A.B., B.S., Ohio State U., 1921, M.A., 1927, M.D., 1934; m. Pearl Brechbill, June 14, 1925; 1 son, Hubert Nelson. Tchr. high sch., Bluffton, Ohio, 1921-24, Columbus, Ohio, 1924-29; instr. anatomy Ohio State U., Columbus, 1929-35; intern, Ohio State U. Hosp., 1934-35; gen. practice medicine, Lancaster, Ohio, 1935-42, specializing in otolaryngology, Lancaster, 1946—; resident 97th Evacuation Hosp., 1942-45; spl. tng. in plastic-maxillofacial surgery U. Pa., 1943; mem. staffs Lancaster-Fairfield County Hosp., pres. staff, 1962, bd. govs., 1955-59. Trustee, Lancaster-Fairfield County United Appeal, 1965-68. Served to lt. col. AUS, 1942-46. Diplomate Am. Bd. Otolaryngology. Fellow Am. Acad. Ophthalmology and Otolaryngology; mem. Fairfield County Med. Soc. (pres. 1949), Sigma Xi, Phi Delta Kappa, Alpha Omega Alpha, Phi Rho Sigma. Republican. Methodist (trustee 1940-47, mem. ofcl. bd. 1939-47). Mason, Kiwanian (pres. 1957). Club: Symposiarchs (pres. 1954) (Lancaster). Home: 132 N High St Lancaster OH 43130 Office: 227 E Main St Lancaster OH 43130

AMUNDSON, DOUGLAS GEORGE, retail exec.; b. Eau Claire, Wis., Apr. 6, 1947; s. Orval George and Freda Alvina (Borden) A.; student Aberdeen Sch. Commerce, 1965-66; m. Geraldine Faye Haaseth, Sept. 27, 1969. Mgr. shoe dept. S & L Dept. Store, Aberdeen, S.D., 1966-67; station agt. North Central Airlines, Chgo., 1967-68; inventory control accountant, Met. Steel, Chgo., 1968-72, domestic buyer, 1972-74; partner Carpetland Environmets, Brookings, S.D., 1974—. Mem. Brookings Jr. C. of C. (dir. 1976-77), Ambassadors Brookings C. of C. Club: Elks. Home: 1329 2d St Brookings SD 57006 Office: 312 5th St Brookings SD 57006

AMUNDSON, NANCY ELLEN ANDERSON, occupational therapist; b. Monroe, Wis., Oct. 10, 1936; d. Wallace Lowell and Martha Elizabeth (Burmaster) Anderson; student Kalamazoo Coll., 1954-55; B.S., U. Minn., 1958, postgrad., 1973—; m. Elmo Erickson, May 12, 1957 (dec. 1976); children—Jeffrey Alan, Darcy Lynn; m. 2d, Loren Amundson, 1971 (div. 1974). Therapist out-patient rehab. Mpls. Curative Workshop, 1960, outpatient therapy supr., 1961-62, 67-69; cons. Mpls. Nursing Homes, 1965-66; therapist Met. Med. Center, Mpls., 1970; cons. retarded children Didlake Sch., Manassas, Va., 1970-71; propr. Hand Some Things, Mpls., 1974-75; research coordinator Impact Inc., 1975-76; vol. learning disabilities Mpls. Sch. System, 1972—; vol. Vols. Am., 1972-73; leader 4-H, 1973-74; active Boy Scouts Am. Mem. Am., Minn. occupational therapy assns., Minn. Civil Liberties Union, Children's Home Soc. Minn., Delta Zeta. Democrat. Presbyterian. Home: Lake George MN 56458 Office: Easterwoods Box 1592 Lake George MN 56458

AMYX, MATTHEW CLAY, mfg. co. exec.; b. Gainesville, Mo., May 11, 1896; s. Sidney F. and Edgie (Patterson) A.; D.D.S., Kan. City U., 1925; m. Inda Mabel Sims, Oct. 7, 1915; children—Launa Edgie (Mrs. James Eiseman), Orin M. Pvt. practice dentistry, West Plains, Mo., 1925-64; founder West Plains Garment Co., 1927-43; founder, pres. Amyx Mfg. Co., West Plains, 1944—, Amyx Industries, Inc., West Plains, 1962—; founder Rainbow Trout & Game Ranch, Rock Bridge, Mo., 1954—; developer, founder, pres. Amyx Spring Valley Resort, Hammond, Mo., 1972—. Mayor, City of West Plains, 1944-52. Named Citizen of Year, Kiwanis, 1968. Mem. Mo. Bd. Dental Examiners, C. of C. Mem. Christian Ch. (dir.). Mason (Shriner), Rotarian. Club: West Plains Country. Home: Rural Route 3 West Plains MO 65775 Office: 648 Missouri Ave West Plains MO 65775

ANAGNOST, CATHERINE COOK, lawyer, accountant; b. Tegea, Greece, Feb. 10, 1919; d. Peter and Athena (Reppas) C.; Diploma, Northwestern U., 1942; m. Themis Anagnost, Aug. 15, 1942; children—Maria Athena, Alexander Themis, James Anthony. C.P.A., 1943; admitted to Ill. bar, 1948, U.S. Supreme Ct. bar, 1960; practiced law in Chgo., 1948—; partner Anagnost & Anagnost. Candidate for judge municipal court Chgo., 1960, 62, judge Circuit Ct., 1964, 74-76. Mem. Nat. Fedn. Republican Women, Chmn. Founders Day program Northwestern U., 1966. Bd. dirs. Chgo. chpt. Girl Scouts Am.; bd. dirs., v.p. Beverly Farm Found.; mem. bd. Women's Adv. Council N.Y. World's Fair. Recipient Merit award Northwestern U., 1964. Mem. Am. (ho. dels. 1965-67), Ill., Chgo., West Suburban (past pres.) bar assns., Women's Bar Assn. Ill., Hellenic Bar Assn. Chgo. (past pres., treas.), Internat., Nat. (pres. 1963-64) assns. women lawyers, Northwestern U. Alumni Assn., Am. Trial Lawyers Assn., Nat. fedns. bus. and profl. women's clubs, Assn. Plaintiffs Lawyers Ill., Internat. Fedn. Women Lawyers, Am. Assn. Atty.-C.P.A.'s. Republican. Clubs: Execs. (Chgo.); Order Eastern Star, White Shrine Jerusalem. Home: 2345 N Oak Park Ave Chicago IL 60635 Office: 11 S LaSalle St Chicago IL 60603

ANAGNOSTOPOULOS, CONSTANTINE EMMANUEL, chem. co. exec.; b. Athens, Greece, Nov. 1, 1922; s. Emmanuel Constantine and Helene (Michaelides) A.; B.S., Brown U., 1949; M.S., Harvard, 1950, Ph.D. (Univ. fellow), 1952; grad. Advanced Mgmt. Program, Columbia, 1964; m. Maria Tsagarakis, July 10, 1949; 1 son, Paul Constantine. Teaching fellow Harvard, 1951-52; research chemist Monsanto Co., St. Louis, 1952-56, research scientist, 1957-60, asst. dir. research, 1960-61, dir. research and devel., 1962-67, dir. rubber chems. organic div., 1968-69, dir. tire bus. group, 1970-71, gen. mgr. new enterprise div., 1971-75, gen. mgr. rubber chems. div., 1975—. Mem. Nat. Inventors Council, 1964-74, Presdl. Panel on Prizes for Innovation, 1972; mem. task force on patent system Nat. Acad. Engring., 1971. Served to capt. Brit. and Greek Army, 1941-46. Recipient teaching prize Harvard U., 1950, 51, 52. Mem. Am. Chem. Soc., Research Soc. Am. (v.p. 1959), Assn. Harvard Chemists, Soc. Chem. Industry, Sigma Chi. Clubs: Bellerive Country (St. Louis). Patentee in field. Home: 12101 Point Oak Rd St Louis MO 63131 Office: 800 N Lindbergh Blvd St Louis MO 63166

ANAS, GEORGE SAM, accountant; b. St. Catharines, Ont., Can., June 26, 1942; s. Sam G. and Helen (Katsikas) A.; student U. Western Ont., 1960-62; Chartered Accountant, Queen's U., Kingston, Ont., 1968; m. Reta Wammes, Oct. 11, 1975. With Clarkson, Gordon & Co., London, Ont., 1962-76, audit mgr., 1971-76; partner Anas, Neil & Co., chartered accountants, 1976—. Sec., treas. Greek Orthodox Ch., 1968—; treas. Greek Orthodox Diocese of Can., 1975—. Mem. Canadian, Ont., Western Ont. insts. chartered accountants, London C. of C., Am.-Hellenic Ednl. Progressive Assn. Liberal. Home: 11 Daleview Crescent London ON Canada Office: 201 Queens Ave London ON N6A 1J1 Canada

ANDAL, JERRY RAY, engr.; b. Viborg, S.D., Jan. 5, 1947; s. James Odell and Jean Roseline (Newmark) A.; B.S., S.D. State U., 1969; m. Linda Ann Ebbesen, Aug. 9, 1969; children—Neil, Shelly. Design engr. Crane and Excavator div. FMC Corp., Cedar Rapids, Iowa, 1969-74; project engr. TCI Power Products, Inc., Yankton, S.D., 1974-76; mgr. systems engring. Tri-County Irrigation, Chamberlain, S.D., 1976-77; chief engr. Kolman div. Athey Products Corp., Sioux Falls, S.D., 1977—. Mem. Am. Soc. Agrl. Engrs. (asso.), Soc. Automotive Engrs., S.D. State U. Alumni Assn. Baptist (deacon 1972-74). Home: Rural Route 2 Box 24 Centerville SD 57014 Office: PO Box 806 Sioux Falls SD 57101

ANDERL, STEPHEN, clergyman; b. Chippewa Falls, Wis., July 13, 1910; s. Henry A. and Katherine (Schneider) A.; B.A. magna cum laude St. John's U., 1932, M.Div., 1974; postgrad. Catholic U. Am., 1940. Ordained priest Roman Catholic Ch., 1936; curate in Wisconsin Rapids, Wis., 1936-37; pastor in Spring Valley, Wis., 1949-52, Hewitt, Wis., 1952-53, Assumption Parish, Durand, Wis., 1953—; tchr., guidance counselor, vice prin. Aquinas High Sch., La Crosse, Wis., 1937-49. Censor books, clergy examiner, vicar for religious Diocese of La Crosse, 1951—; vicar forane Durand Deanery, 1953—; diocesan chaplain Boy Scouts Am., Girl Scouts U.S.A., 1936-49; chaplain XII World Jamboree Boy Scouts, 1967, Nat. Jamboree Boy Scouts Am., 1969, 73; mem. Diocesan Clergy Personnel Bd., 1970-74; exec. sec. Cath. Youth Orgn., Diocese of La Crosse, 1938-49; diocesan dir. Sodality, 1938-49; cons. Central Commn. of Diocese of LaCrosse for Implementation of Vatican Council. Mem. exec. com. Chippewa Valley council Boy Scouts Am., mem. Nat. Cath. Com. Scouting, 1974-76; housing commr., La Crosse, 1948-49; mem. Gov.'s Com. on Children and Youth, 1957-63; adviser Wis. Youth Com., 1960—; mem. State Comprehensive Mental Health and Retardation Planning Com., Durand Community Council; dir. West Central Wis. Community Action Agy., OEO. Bd. dirs. La Crosse Diocesan Bd. Edn., La Crosse Diocesan Cath. Social Agy., Inc. Created domestic prelate with title of right reverend msgr. by Pope John XXIII, 1962; recipient Silver Beaver award Boy Scouts Am., 1968; St. George award, 1969. K.C. (4 deg., Chaplain). Author: Technique of the Catholic Action Cell, 1942; Papal Teaching on Catholic Action, 1946; The Religious and Catholic Action, 1947; Catholic Action, a Responsibility of the School, 1948; Parish of the Assumption, Life and Times of the Mystical Christ in Durand, 1960. Contbr. articles to religious mags. and jours. Address: 911 W Prospect St Durand WI 54736

ANDERS, LESLIE, educator; b. Admire, Kans., Jan. 22, 1922; s. Ray Leslie and Bertie Mae (Hasson) A.; A.B., Coll. Emporia, 1949; A.M. (Allen Cook White, Jr. fellow), U. Mo., 1950, Ph.D., 1954; m. Mardellya Mary Soles, Oct. 17, 1942; children—Geraldine (Mrs. Robert C. Hunt), Charlotte (Mrs. Alexander Wilson). Historian, Office of Chief of Engrs., Dept. Army, Balt., 1951-55; faculty history Central Mo. State U., Warrensburg, 1955—, prof., 1963—. Hon. commr. Mo. Am. Revolutionary Bicentennial Commn., 1974. Served with AUS, 1940-45. Mem. Am. Mil. Inst., State Hist. Soc. Mo., Mo. Hist. Soc., Sons of Union Vets. of Civil War, Scabbard and Blade, Phi Kappa Phi. Republican. Presbyn. Author: The Ledo Road, 1965; The Eighteenth Missouri, 1968; Education for Service, 1971; The Twenty-First Missouri, 1975. Home: 213 W South St Warrensburg MO 64093

ANDERSCH, CAROLYN ELIZABETH, psychologist; b. Montgomery, Ala., Jan. 22, 1942; d. Wayland H. and Carolyn Elizabeth (Shepherd) Price; student Huntingdon Coll., 1961-63; B.A., Auburn U., 1965, M.S., 1969; m. Marc A. Andersch, Mar. 23, 1973; children—Kenneth, Terri, Keith, Tania. Psychologist, Bryce State Hosp., Tuscaloosa, Ala., 1968-71; psychologist N.Central Mental Health and Retardation Center, Minot, N.D., 1972-75, inpatient unit Sekan Comprehensive Mental Health Services, Pittsburg, Kans., 1975—; instr. Chapman Coll., Minot Air Force Sta. Project dir. Crawford County humanities project Kans. Com. for Humanities. Mem. Am. Psychol. Assn. asso.). Home: 600 W Leighton St Frontenac KS 66762 Office: Sekan Inpatient Unit Mt Carmel Hospital Centennial and Rouse Sts Pittsburgh KS 66762

ANDERSEN, HAROLD WAYNE, newspaper exec.; b. Omaha, July 30, 1923; s. Andrew B. and Grace (Russell) A.; B.S. in Edn., U. Nebr., 1945, L.H.D. (hon.), 1975; m. Marian L. Battey, Apr. 19, 1952; children—David, Nancy. Reporter Lincoln (Neb.) Star, 1945-46; with Omaha World-Herald, Lincoln and Omaha, 1946—, v.p., bus. mgr., Omaha, 1964-66, pres., Omaha, 1966—; chmn. Fed. Res. Bank Kansas City; dir. Peter Kiewit Sons', Inc. Pres. Downtown Omaha, Inc.; dir. A.P., Raleigh News & Observer Pub. Co. (N.C.). Trustee U. Neb. Found., Freedom of Information Found.; bd. dirs. Newspaper Advt. Bur.; bd. dirs. Jr. Achievement Omaha, pres., 1964-65. Mem. Am. Newspaper Pubs. Assn. (dir. 1968—, past chmn.), Internat. Fedn. Newspaper Pubs. (v.p.), Omaha C. of C. (dir.), Phi Beta Kappa, Phi Gamma Delta. Republican. Presbyterian. Home: 6545 Prairie Ave Omaha NE 68132 Office: World-Herald Sq Omaha NE 68102

ANDERSEN, HARRY EDWARD, oil equipment co. exec.; b. Omaha, Apr. 25, 1906; s. John Anton and Caroline (Ebbensgaard) A.; student pub. schs. and spl. courses, including Ohio State U., 1957, U. Okla., 1959; Ph.D. in Bus. Adminstrn. (hon.), Colo. State Christian Coll., 1972; m. Alma Theora Vawter, June 12, 1931; children—Jeanenne Dee (Mrs. Gaylord Fernstrom) and Maureen Lee (Mrs. Roger Podany) (twins), John Harry. Founder N.W. Service Sta. Equipment Co., Mpls., 1934, pres., treas., 1956—; v.p., treas. Edgewater Inn Corp., Mpls.; dir. Franklin Nat. Bank, Mpls. Spl. dep. sheriff Hennepin County, 1951—; hon. fire chief of Mpls., 1951—; pres. Washington Lake Improvement Assn., 1955. Mem. Shrine Directors Assn. (N.W. gov.), Nat. Assn. Oil Equipment Jobbers (pres. 1957-58, dir. 1954-56), C. of C., Upper Midwest Oil Mans Club. Lutheran. Mason (32deg., K.T., Shriner), Jester. Clubs: Viking (pres.), Engineers, Toastmasters, Minneapolis Athletic, Golden Valley Golf, Le Mirador Country (Lake Geneva, Switzerland). Home: 2766 W River Pkwy Minneapolis MN 55406 Office: 2520 Nicollet Ave Minneapolis MN 55404

ANDERSEN, JAMES LOUIS, human relations cons.; b. Portland, Oreg., Dec. 7, 1935; s. Andrew Peter and Nina (Hjelm) A.; B.S., Dana Coll., 1958; M.S., Drake U., 1963; Ph.D., Fielding Inst., 1977; children from previous marriage—Kathleen, Rebecca, John. Tchr., Franklin Twp., Cooper, Iowa, 1958-59; counselor United Community Schs., Boone, Iowa, 1959-63; dir. counseling Algona (Iowa) Community Sch., 1963-76; pvt. practice program and staff devel. cons., Algona, 1975-77. Pres., Am. Field Service, Algona, 1965-69. Mem. Am., Iowa (pres. 1971-72, exec. dir. 1972-77) personnel and guidance assns., Am., Iowa sch. counselor assns., Iowa Human Resource Assn., Am. Assn. Specialists in Group Work. Home: 2824 Grand Ave Des Moines IA 50312

ANDERSEN, KENNETH ELDON, educator; b. Harlan, Iowa, Dec. 28, 1933; s. Edward and Anna Christina (Christiansen) A.; B.A., U. No. Iowa, 1954, M.A., 1955; Ph.D. (Merchant scholar 1958-59, Knapp fellow 1960-61), U. Wis., 1961; m. Mary Ann Klaaren, Aug. 20, 1964; 1 son, Erik LaMont. Instr. U. Colo., Boulder, 1955-56; instr. U. Mich., Ann Arbor, 1961-63, asst. prof., 1963-67, asso. prof., 1967-70; asso. prof. U. Ill., Urbana, 1970-73, prof. speech communication, 1973—, asso. head Dept. Speech Communication, 1971—; vis. prof. U. Ill. at Chgo. Circle Campus, 1966, U. So. Calif., Los Angeles, 1968. Served with AUS, 1956-58. Mem. Speech Communication Assn. (fin. bd., adminstrv. com. 1974-76), Central States Speech Assn. (Outstanding Young Tchrs. Speech award 1962, exec. sec., conv. mgr. 1969-72, editorial bd. 1967-70, pres. 1974-75), Am. Forensic Assn., Ill. Speech and Theatre Assn., AAUP, Am. Assn. Pub. Opinion Research, Internat. Communication Assn., Delta Sigma Rho-Tau Kappa Alpha. Author textbooks. Editor Jour. Am. Forensic Assn., 1968-71, editorial bd., 1964-68; editor Speaker and Gavel, 1975—. Contbr. articles to profl. jours. Home: 2002 Galen Dr Champaign IL 61820 Office: Dept Speech Communication 244 Lincoln Hall Univ Ill Urbana IL 61801

ANDERSEN, RICHARD R., city ofcl.; b. Omaha, Jan. 17, 1924; s. Alfred C. and Mary A.; B.S., U. Neb., also M.P.A.; m. Donna Andersen, Dec. 7, 1951. Chief of police, Omaha. Home: 601 S 67th St Omaha NE 68106 Office: Office of the Chief of Police Omaha NE 68102

ANDERSON, AMOS R., devel. co. exec.; b. Delavan, Wis., Feb. 11, 1920; s. Oscar Albert and Bertha (Ives) A.; B.S., Adrian Coll., 1942, D.Sc., 1965; postgrad. Ohio State U., 1942-43; m. Charlotte Bourland, Nov. 4, 1945; children—Dabney Jo, Mark V. Pres., Anderson Chem. Co., to 1958, Tex. Alkyls, Inc., 1958-65; gen. mgr. Anderson Chem. div. Stauffer Chem. Co., 1958-65, Silicone div., Adrian, Mich., 1964-66, v.p. parent co., 1958-66; pres., dir. Indsl. Accessories, Inc., 1964-66; pres. Valjo Corp., 1966—; organizer, pres. Anderson Devel. Co., Adrian, 1966—; pres. Am. Dynamics Internat., 1972-73, Interam. Zinc, Inc., 1974—; v.p., dir. Fabridyne, Inc., 1974-75, Kemerica, Inc., 1974-75; dir. Comml. Savs. Bank, Adrian. Trustee Adrian Coll. Mem. Am. Chem. Soc. Clubs: Lenawee Country (Adrian), Elks. Contbr. articles to chem. publs., including Ency. Polymer Sci. and Tech., Ency. Chem. Tech. Patentee in field. Home: 11 Lakeridge Dr Adrian MI 49221 Office: 1415 E Michigan St Adrian MI 49221

ANDERSON, ANNA WILDA, sec., artist; b. Pleasant Valley, W.Va., Apr. 5, 1902; d. Halbert Leroy and Lillie Coral (Hartley) Jones; grad. Elliott Bus. Coll., Wheeling, W.Va., 1921; postgrad. art W.Va. Wesleyan Coll., 1938; m. G. Elwood Anderson, Nov. 29, 1923; 1 dau., Dolores Anne. Secretary, Pennsboro (W. Va.) Meth. Ch., 1929-31, Sabra Meth. Ch., Morgantown, W.Va., 1939-41, Riverview Meth. Ch., Huntington, W.Va., 1942-43, Jackson Heights Meth. Ch., West Point, Ind., 1947-49, Rossville (Ind.) Meth. Ch., 1949-50, First Meth. Ch., Covington, Ind., 1952-59, Frankfort (Ind.) Tabernacle, 1960-61, Star City (Ind.) Meth. Ch., 1965-67; pvt. sec. to warden W.Va. Penitentiary, Moundsville, 1921-23; paintings include: Victory (honoring Winston Churchill), 1955; artist: Peace (velvet hangings with oil paintings), 1950. Hon. christener: S.S. Betty Zane, 1942. Home: 226 Wickersham Dr W Kokomo IN 46901

ANDERSON, AUSTIN GOTHARD, univ. adminstr.; b. Calumet, Minn., June 30, 1931; s. Hugo Gothard and Turna Marie (Johnson) A.; B.A., U. Minn., 1954, J.D., 1958; m. Catherine Antoinette

Spellacy, Jan. 2, 1954; children—Todd, Susan, Timothy, Linda, Mark. Admitted to Minn. bar, 1958, Ill. bar, 1962, Mich. bar, 1974; mem. firm Spellacy, Spellacy, Lano & Anderson, Marble, Minn., 1958-62; dir. Ill. Inst. Continuing Legal Edn., Springfield, 1962-64; dir. dept. continuing legal edn. U. Minn., Mpls., 1964-70, asso. dean gen. extension div., 1969-70; mem. firm Dorsey, Marquart, Windhorst, West & Halladay, Mpls., 1970-73; asso. dir. Nat. Center for State Cts., St. Paul, 1972-73; dir. inst. continuing legal edn., U. Mich., Ann Arbor, 1973—; adj. faculty U. Minn., 1974, Wayne State U., 1974-75, William Mitchell Coll. Law, 1973-74; project dir. Select Com. on Judiciary State of Minn., 1974-76; chmn. City of Bloomington (Minn.) Park and Recreation Adv. Commn., 1970-72; pres. bd. King Sch. Parent-Tchr. Orgn., 1977—; adv. coms. Ferris State, Madonna, Washtenaw Community colls. Served with USN, 1950-51. Mem. Assn. Legal Adminstrs. (pres. 1969-70), Am., Hennepin County, Ill., Minn., Washtenaw County bar assns., Am. Mgmt. Assn., Assn. Continuing Legal Edn. Adminstrs., State Bar Mich. Co-editor, contbg. author: Lawyer's Handbook, 1975. Home: 3617 Larchmont Dr Ann Arbor MI 48105 Office: 432 Hutchins Hall Ann Arbor MI 48109

ANDERSON, BENTON REES, cons.; b. East Dubuque, Iowa, Nov. 6, 1889; s. Franklin Pierce and Mary Elizabeth (Rees) A.; B.S., Cornell Coll., 1911; M.S., Wooster U., 1913; m. Wilma Lorraine Walker, May 28, 1917; children—Betty (Mrs. Gunnar W. Carlson), Barbara (Mrs. James C. Bradley). City engr., Marion, Iowa, 1914, West Liberty, Iowa, 1915-16; drainage engr. Clinton County, Iowa, 1917-19; field engr. Iowa Hwy. Commn., Clinton, 1920-21; city engr., Clinton, 1922-33, 36-62; engr. WPA, Dubuque, Iowa, 1934; engr. Clinton County, 1935; pvt. cons., Clinton, 1936-62; cons. City of Comanche, 1962-73, Clinton Airport Commn., 1962-73, Clinton Pub. Library, 1962-73. Recipient Samuel A. Greeley award Am. Pub. Service Assn., 1953; Man of Year award Clinton C. of C. and Sta. KROS, 1961. Registered profl. engr. Mem. Nat. Soc. Profl. Engrs., ASCE, Iowa Engring. Soc., Am. Pub. Works Assn. Republican. Presbyn. (elder 1940-50). Mason. Club: Clinton Engineers. Contbr. articles to profl. jours. Home and office: 1110 Pershing Blvd Clinton IA 52732

ANDERSON, BETTY LOU, banker; b. Morenci, Mich., Apr. 30, 1929; d. William John and Vera Fern (Parliament) Hall; student Delta Coll., 1970; m. Oct. 23, 1947 (div. June 1972); children—Jeffrey, Jerry Wynne, Lisa Marie. With Ogemaw Telephone Co., 1942-46, Mich. Bell Telephone Co., 1946-51, Hasty Clinic, 1952-55; with Farmers and Mchts. Bank, Rose City, Mich., 1959—, mgr., 1972-77, a v.p., mgr., 1977—. Mem. Nat. Assn. Bank Women, Mich. Bankers Assn., Rose City C. of C. (dir.). Home: 215 Campbell St Hale MI 48739 Office: 102 Main St W Rose City MI 48654

ANDERSON, BROR ERNEST, indsl. marking co. exec.; b. Mazeppa, Minn., Nov. 24, 1914; s. Ernest Bror and Huldah (Celine) A.; Ph.D., U. Minn., 1940; m. Ruth Vruwink, June 14, 1941; children—Erik, Bonnie, Kent. Research mgr. A.B. Dick Co., paper and fiber, Chgo., 1946-55, research mgr. mimeograph supplies, 1955-58; tech. dir. Wyomissing Corp., Reading, Pa., 1958-65; v.p., tech. dir. Weber Marking Systems, Arlington Heights, Ill., 1965—. Mem. TAPPI, Am. Chem. Soc. Patentee in field. Contbr. to profl. publs. in field. Office: 711 W Algonquin Rd Arlington Heights IL 60005

ANDERSON, CHARLES RALPH SEIBOLD, utility co. exec.; b. Des Moines, Jan. 12, 1927; s. Charles Ralph Samuel and Della Hope (Seibold) A.; student Iowa State U., 1944-45, 46; B.A., State U. Iowa, 1948, LL.B., 1950; m. Elmerine Lue Krohn, June 26, 1949; children—Melissa, Luanne, Samuel. Admitted to Iowa bar, 1950, practice in Danbury, 1950-56; with Iowa So. Utility Co., Centerville, 1956—, gen. counsel, 1968-73, sec., gen. counsel, 1973—. Dir. Farmers Savs. Bank, Danbury, 1951-56, asst. cashier, 1952-56; dir., sec. So. Iowa Mfg. Co., 1971. Mayor, City of Danbury, 1954; Republican twp. and precinct committeeman, Danbury and Centerville, 1950, 64-68; mem. Woodbury County Bd. Edn., Sioux City, 1953-56; mem. Centerville (Iowa) Community Sch. Dist. Bd. Edn., 1960-72. Served with USNR, 1945. Mem. Iowa, Fed. Power bar assns., Phi Delta Phi, Alpha Tau Omega. Methodist (trustee 1965-68). Mason, Elk. Club: Appanoose Country (Centerville). Home: 606 W Wall Centerville IA 52544 Office: 300 Sheridan Ave Centerville IA 52544

ANDERSON, CHARLOTTE LOUISE, ret. mfg. co. exec.; b. Kellerton, Ia., Jan. 20, 1921; d. Arthur Leroy and Atha Ina (Kuder) Lawhorn; student Augustana Coll., 1937-38, 50-52, U. Rochester, 1943-44, Marycrest Coll., 1956-58; m. Dale G. Anderson, Aug. 29, 1947; 1 dau., Christine D. Petty. Exec. sec. Deere & Co., Moline, Ill., 1944-58, mgr. library services, 1958-73, corporate historian, 1973-75, mgmt. devel. lectr., 1971-73; lectr., Am. Mgmt. Assn., 1966, 70; mem. steering com. Nat. Com. Concerned with Lit. of Hwy. Safety, 1971-72; mem. planning com. Quad-City Library Council, 1970-71; adv. council U. Ill. Grad. Sch. Library Sci., Ill. State Library, 1967-70; participant Fed. Info. Resources Council, 1971; mem. Bus. History Conf. Moline Bicentennial Commn. Pres., Augustana Coll. Parents Assn., 1972; bd. dirs. Council on Services for Aging, Rock Island County, 1976—, treas., 1976—; precinct committeeman Republican party, 1977—. Mem. Spl. Libraries Assn. (chmn. bus. and finance div. 1970-71), Soc. Am. Archivists, Am. Soc. State and Local History, Rock Island County Hist. Soc. (dir., mem. library com.). Republican. Presbyterian (life elder, Christian edn. com.). Home: 1402 1st St Moline IL 61265

ANDERSON, CHARTERS HARRY, actor, theatre dir., educator; b. Mpls., Dec. 29, 1942; s. Charters Wirth and Verna Eldora (Tollefsrud) A.; B.A. (Theater maj. scholar) U. Minn., 1965, B.S., 1975; postgrad. No. Ill. U., 1966; M.A., Mankato State Coll., 1970. Club solo singer throughout U.S., S. Am., 1964-65; tchr. high sch. Rochelle, Ill., 1966-68, tchr., freelance dir. Mpls. and Hopkins, Minn., 1968-69; dir. theater dept. Ill. Coll., Jacksonville, 1969-70; dir., tchr. Performing Arts Learning Center St. Paul Pub. Schs., 1970—; dir. prodns. The King and I, Jesus Christ Superstar, A Raisin in the Sun, The Crucible; tchr. pvt. acting students, dir. community and profl. theaters. Bd. dirs. Variety Hall Theatre, 1972-73. Mem. Am. Theatre Assn. Playwright: As I See It, You See It, We See It, 1973. Tesal (Teaching English as a Second Lang.) instr.; specializes in tng. Black Ams. for stage and film work. Home and office: 490 Summit Ave St Paul MN 55102

ANDERSON, CLARENCE AXEL FREDERICK, mech. engr.; b. Muskegon, Mich., Dec. 14, 1909; s. Axel Robert and Anna Victoria (Wikman) A.; student Muskegon Jr. Coll., 1929, Internat. Corr. Schs., 1934; m. Frances K. Swem, Apr. 9, 1934; children—Robert Curtis, Clarelyn Christine Anderson Schmelling, Stanley Herbert. With Shaw-Walker Co., Muskegon, Mich., 1928—, mech. engr., 1940-65, project engr., 1965-70, chief engr., 1970—. Mem. Christian edn. bd. Evangel. Covenant Ch., 1959-61, 67-73. Club: Holland (Mich.) Beagle (pres. 1966-68, 70-73, 75—). Home: 5757 E Sternberg Rd Fruitport MI 49415 Office: Shaw Walker Co Corner Western St and Division St Muskegon MI 49443

ANDERSON, DALE WALTER, ret. utility co. exec.; b. Cuba City, Wis., May 21, 1907; s. Walter Ray and Lula (Bunt) A.; B.S. in Elec. Engring., U. Mich., 1930; m. Helen Lucile Hemingway, June 24, 1933; children—Thomas D., William R. With No. Ind. Pub. Service Co., Hammond, 1930-77, elec. engr., 1930-49, supr. substa. engring., 1949-53, mgr. elec. engring., 1953-59, mgr. div. ops., 1959-67, v.p. div. ops., 1967-77; dir. Bank of Ind. Mem. exec. bd. Lake County Crippled Children Soc., Gary, Ind., 1967—, pres., 1967-68; mem. exec. bd. Trade Winds Rehab. Center, Gary, 1967—, pres., 1967-68; mem. exec. bd. Calumet Goodwill Industries, Hammond, 1966—, pres., 1977—; bd. dirs. Lake Area United Way, 1974-77. Registered profl. engr., Ind. Mem. IEEE (life), Ind. Gas Assn. (pres. 1969-70), Ind. Elec. Assn. (chmn. bd. 1974-75), Newcomen Soc. N.Am. Mason (32 deg., Shriner), Rotarian (pres. Hammond 1966-67). Home: 9324 Walnut Dr Munster IN 46321

ANDERSON, DAVID CLEM, city ofcl.; b. Schell City, Mo., Aug. 2, 1925; s. David C. and Maggie (Dunn) A.; grad. high sch.; m. Betty J. Lobdell, Aug. 15, 1947; children—Michael Lee, Cynthia Lynn. Civil engr. Kansas, Mo., 1946-61; supt. Jackson County (Mo.) Water Dist. No. 2, 1961; city engr., water, sewer supt., Gladstone, Mo., 1962—. Mem. men's com. Boy Scouts Am., 1955, counselor, 1961. Served with USAAF, 1943-46. Registered profl. engr., Mo. Mem. ASCE, Nat. Soc. Profl. Engrs., Am. Water Works Assn., Exec. Assos., Mo. Water Pollution Control Assn. Home: 606 E 67th Pl N Gladstone MO 64118 Office: 7010 N Holmes St Gladstone MO 64118

ANDERSON, DAVID DANIEL, educator; b. Lorain, Ohio; s. David and Nora Marie (Foster) A.; B.S., Bowling Green State U., 1951, M.A., 1952; Ph.D., Mich. State U., 1960; m. Patricia Ann Rittenhour, Feb. 1, 1953. From instr. to prof. dept. Am. thought and lang. Mich. State U., 1957—, editor U. Coll. Quar., 1971—; Fulbright prof. U. Karachi (Pakistan), 1963-64. Am. del. Internat. Fedn. Modern Langs. and Lit., 1969-75, Internat. Congress Orientalists, 1971-76. Served with USN, 1942-45, AUS, 1952-53. Decorated Silver Star; recipient Distinguished Alumnus award Bowling Green State U., 1976, Distinguished Faculty award Mich. State U., 1974. Mem. AAUP, Popular Culture Assn., Modern Lang. Assn., Soc. Study Midwestern Lit. (founder, exec. sec.), Assn. Gen. and Liberal Edn. Author: Sherwood Anderson, 1968 (Book Manuscript award 1961); Louis Bromfield, 1964; Critical Studies in American Literature, 1964; Sherwood Anderson's Winesburg, Ohio, 1967; Brand Whitlock, 1968; Abraham Lincoln, 1970; Suggestions for the Instructor, 1971; Robert Ingersoll, 1972; Woodrow Wilson, 1975. Editor: The Black Experience, 1969; The Literary Works of Abraham Lincoln, 1970; Sunshine and Smoke: American Writers and the American Environment, 1971; (with others) The Dark and Tangled Path, 1971; MidAmerica I, 1974; MidAmerica II, 1975; MidAmerica III, 1976; Sherwood Anderson: Dimensions of his Literary Art, 1976; Mid America IV, 1977; editor Univ. Coll. Quar. Home: 6555 Lansdown Dr Dimondale MI 48821 Office: Dept Am Thought and Lang Mich State U East Lansing MI 48824

ANDERSON, DAVID PRESLEY, fiberglass mfg. co. exec.; b. Newark, Ohio, Oct. 16, 1924; s. Roland and Emma Almira (Reynard) A.; B.S., Kent State U., 1949, M.Ed., 1953; m. Helen June Mason, Sept. 14, 1946; Children—Carol (Mrs. Dean Carlson), Barbara (Mrs. Victor A. Joyner), David, Beverly (Mrs. Jan K. Michalek), Kent, Kelly. Tchr., adminstr. in Ohio schs., 1949-56; with Owens-Corning Fiberglass Corp., 1956—, quality control engr., Barrington, N.J., 1962-66, mgr. prodn. planning, Kansas City, 1959-62, mgr. quality control, Toledo, 1966-68, quality control engr., mgr. process and quality control, Newark, 1968—. Served with USNR, 1943-46. Mem. Am. Soc. Quality Control, Am. Legion. Republican. Presbyn. Mason. Home: 1593 Krebs Court Newark OH 43055 Office: Case Ave Newark OH 43055

ANDERSON, DORRINE ANN PETERSEN (MRS. HAROLD EDWARD ANDERSON), librarian; b. Ishpeming, Mich., Feb. 24, 1923; d. Herbert Nathaniel and Dorothy (Eman) Petersen; B.S. with distinction, No. Mich. U., 1944; postgrad. Northwestern U., summer 1945, U. Wash., summer 1967, U. Mich. Extension, 1958-65, Western Mich. U., 1968; M.S.L., Western Mich. U., 1970; m. Harold Edward Anderson, Aug. 23, 1947; children—Brian Peter, Kent Harold, Bruce Herbert, Timothy Jon. Tchr. English jr. high sch., Eaton Rapids, Mich., 1944-45; tchr. English, speech Arlington Heights (Ill.) High Sch., 1945-48; tchr. English high sch., Nahma, Mich., 1948-49, 54-61, Gladstone, Mich., 1961-62; librarian Gladstone Sch. and Pub. Library, 1962—; acting dir. Mid-Peninsula Library Fedn., 1965-66; dir. media services Gladstone Area Pub. Schs., 1970—. Mem. Escanaba League Woman Voters, 1966—; pres. League Women Voters Delta County, 1970-72; mem. human resources subcom. Upper Peninsula Com. for Area Progress, 1964—, mem. human resources council, 1970—; mem. com. for library devel. Upper Peninsula, chmn. Delta County Library Bd., 1967-77; chmn. adv. com. Region 21 Ednl. Media Center, 1970—; chmn. Upper Peninsula Centralized Purchasing and Equipment Evaluation Com., 1973-76; mem. planning com. Upper Peninsula Reading Conf., 1973, 75, 78; mem. region 17, Polit. Action Team, 1968—; mem. Delta County Bicentennial Com., 1975, 76. County del. Delta County Democratic Party, 1968—. Named Tchr. of Yr., Region 17, 1969. Mem. Am., Mich. library assns., Mich. Assn. Sch. Librarians, Mich. Assn. Sch. Library Suprs., Am. Assn. Univ. Women, Mich. Assn. for Media in Edn., Assn. Ednl. Communications and Technology, Kappa Delta Pi, Delta Kappa Gamma, Phi Epsilon, Beta Phi Mu. Home: 1723 Montana Ave Gladstone MI 49837 Office: Gladstone Area Sch and Pub Library Gladstone MI 49837

ANDERSON, EDWARD EUGENE, child welfare adminstr.; b. Ft. Wayne, Ind., July 18, 1933; s. Howard John and Eileen Eleanor (Wager) A.; B.Th., Judson Coll., 1956; M.A., Ball State U., 1958; B.D., No. Baptist Theol. Sem., 1959; M.S.W., Washington U., St. Louis, 1969; m. Violet Marie Aldrich, Aug. 7, 1954; children—David, Amy. Ordained minister Am. Bapt. Ch. U.S.A., 1959; minister edn. 1st. Bapt. Ch., Muncie, Ind., 1957-58, Canton, Ill., 1959-63; asso. prof. sociology John Brown U., Siloam Springs, Ark., 1963-67; dir. social services Hudelson Bapt. Children's Home, Centralia, Ill., 1967-74, exec. dir., 1974—. Pres. Marion County Community Mental Health Tax Bd. Taxation, 1969—; bd. edn. Centralia City Schs., 1977—. Mem. Nat. Assn. Social Workers, Nat. Conf. Social Welfare, Ill. Welfare Assn., Child Care Assn. Ill., Ministers Council Am. Bapt. Chs. U.S.A., S. Central Community Concert Assn. (founder, pres. 1972-75), Am. Guild Organists (founder, dean Little Egypt chpt. 1973-74). Democrat. Club: Lions (pres. Centralia 1976-77). Home: 226 S Cherry St Centralia IL 62801 Office: PO Box 548 1400 E 2d St Centralia IL 62801

ANDERSON, EDWARD EVERETT, mech. engr.; b. Algona, Iowa, Jan. 9, 1941; s. Everett Joseph and Juen Arlene (Rasmussen) A.; B.S.M.E., Iowa State U., 1964, M.S.M.E., 1966; Ph.D., Purdue U., 1972; m. Sharon Ann Sanders, Apr. 13, 1963; children—David Edward, Julie Ann, Jill Leigh. Design engr. Lozier Corp., Omaha, 1959-61; instr. mech. engring. Iowa State U., 1966-68, vis. asst. prof. mech. engring., 1971; asst. prof. U. Southwestern La., 1972-74; asst. prof. S.D. Sch. Mines and Tech., 1974-76; asso. prof. U. Nebr., Lincoln, 1977—; cons. in field. Active Boy Scouts Am. Recipient Ralph R. Teetor award, Soc. Automotive Engrs., 1974; David Ross fellow, 1969; registered profl. engr., Iowa. Mem. ASME Pi Tau Sigma. Lutheran. Contbr. articles to profl. jours.; research in heat transfer, solar energy, wind energy. Home: 5208 Cameron Ct Lincoln NE 68512 Office: Dept Mech Engring U Nebr Lincoln NE 68588

ANDERSON, FRANCES SWEM (MRS. CLARENCE A.F. ANDERSON), nuclear med. technologist; b. Grand Rapids, Mich., Nov. 27, 1913; d. Frank Oscar and Carrie (Strang) Swem; student Muskegon Sch. Bus., 1959-60; certificate Muskegon Community Coll., 1964; m. Clarence A.F. Anderson, Apr. 9, 1934; children—Robert Curtis, Clarelyn Christine (Mrs. Roger L. Schmelling), Stanley Herbert. X-ray file clk., film librarian Hackley Hosp., Muskegon, Mich., 1957-59; student refresher course in nuclear med. tech. Chgo. Soc. Nuclear Med. Techs., 1966; radioisotope technologist and sec. Hackley Hosp., 1959-65; nuclear med. technologist Butler Meml. Hosp., Muskegon Heights, Mich., 1966-70, Mercy Hosp., Muskegon, 1970—. Mem. Muskegon Civic A Capella choir, 1932-39; mem. Mother-Tch. Singers, PTA, Muskegon, 1941-48, treas. 1944-48; with Muskegon Civic Opera Assn., 1950-51. Mem. Am. Soc. Radiologic Techs., Soc. Nuclear Medicine, Am. Registry Radiologic Technologists, Internat. Platform Assn. Mem. Evang. Covenant Ch. (mem. choir 1953—, choir sec. 1963-69, Sunday sch. tchr. 1954—, supt. Sunday Sch. 1975—). Home: 5757 E Sternberg Rd Fruitport MI 49415 Office: 1500 E Sherman Blvd Muskegon MI 49443

ANDERSON, GAYLORD ARTHUR, educator; b. Council Bluffs, Iowa, July 25, 1928; s. Arthur C. and Winifred (Streeter) A.; B.S., Iowa State U., 1951, postgrad., 1966; M.S., Omaha U., 1958; m. Bonnie Louise Christopher, Aug. 13, 1949; children—Susan, Sally, Sheri, Amy, Kristi. Dir. phys. edn. Edison Jr. High Sch., Council Bluffs, 1953-55; tchr. Abraham Lincoln High Sch., Council Bluffs, 1955-56; dir. phys. edn. Longfellow Jr. High Sch., Council Bluffs, 1956-58; prin. Petersen Sch., Council Bluffs, 1958-60; prin. Rue Sch., Council Bluffs, 1960-61, Edison Sch., Council Bluffs, 1961-64, Wilson Jr. High Sch., Council Bluffs, 1964-69, Thomas Jefferson High Sch., Council Bluffs, Iowa, 1969—. Mem. Pottawattamie County Mental Health Bd., 1967-72, vice pres., 1969, pres., 1970; vol. worker United Fund, 1958—; counselor Hawkeye Boys State 1958-60; asst. dist. commr. Trailblazer dist. Boy Scouts Am., 1970-74. Mem. adv. bd. Salvation Army, 1964—; pres. bd. dirs. Pottawattamie County Soc. Crippled Children, 1975. Served with USAF, 1951-52. Recipient Service Key award Ia. State U. Alumni, 1972. Mem. Council Bluffs C. of C., Nat. Assn. Secondary Sch. Prins., Iowa High Sch. Athletic Assn., Phi Delta Kappa. Republican. Methodist. Rotarian. Home: Route 4 Box 68 Council Bluffs IA 51501

ANDERSON, GEORGE REX, II, importer, wholesale co. exec.; b. Indpls., Aug. 10, 1944; s. George R. and Lucy J. (Walters) A.; B.S. in Accounting, Ind. U., 1975; m. Julie Ellen Sanders, Oct. 23, 1965; children—George Rex III, Christopher Linn. Pres., G.R. Anderson & Assos., Indpls., 1969-73; pres., chmn. bd. G.R. Anderson & Assos., Inc., Indpls., 1973—. Bd. dirs. World Trade Center, Indpls. Served to 1st lt. U.S. Army, 1964-67. Clubs: World Trade Club of Ind., Ind. U. Alumni, Sertoma; Rackets Four (Indpls.). Office: PO Box 41797 Indianapolis IN 46241

ANDERSON, GERALD DWIGHT, historian; b. Hitterdal, Minn., Nov. 18, 1944; s. Wilferd Dean and Violet Caria Maria (Heigg) A.; B.A., Concordia Coll., Moorhead, Minn., 1965; M.A., N.D. State U., Fargo, 1966; Ph.D., U. Iowa, 1973; 1 dau., Carmen Nell. Asst. prof. history Waldorf Coll., Forest City, Iowa, 1966-70, Drake U., Des Moines, 1973, Iowa Wesleyan Coll., Mt. Pleasant, 1974; instr. history Austin (Minn.) Community Coll., 1975; asso. dir. NW Minn. regional history center Moorhead State U., 1976—; com. staff Minn. State Senate, St. Paul, 1977—. Chmn. Highland Grove (Minn.) precinct Democratic-Farmer-Labor party, 1976—. Recipient faculty growth award Am. Luth. Ch., 1970; Concordia Coll. merit scholar, 1963-65, Washington semester scholar, 1964-65; U. Iowa history scholar, 1971-73. Mem. Am. Hist. Assn., Pi Gamma Mu (pres. Iota chpt. 1964-65). Lutheran. Author: Public Order and Civil Liberties in Britain, 1931-37, 1973. Office: NW Minn History Center Moorhead State U Moorhead MN 56560

ANDERSON, HARLEY ERIC, obstetrician, gynecologist, educator; b. Omaha, May 7, 1900; s. Charles Hjalmar and Theresa Anna (Ericksson) A.; B.Sc., U. Nebr., 1923, M.D., 1925; m. Jean Louise Hampton, Sept. 20, 1967; children,—John Harley, Georgiana Warburton Anderson Collins, Bruce Franklin. Practice medicine specializing in gynecology, Omaha, 1926—; asst. in bacteriology pathology U. Nebr., Omaha, 1926-31, instr. obstetrics gynecology, 1938-43, asst. prof., 1943-52, asso. prof., 1952-66, sr. cons., 1966—; clin. prof. Creighton U. Med. Sch., Omaha, 1970-74; mem. active staff Nebr. Meth. Hosp., Clarkson Hosp., Immanuel Hosp., U. Nebr. Hosps. Pres. dist. sch. bd., 1948. Diplomate Am. Bd. Obstetrics and Gynecology. Fellow A.C.S., Am. Coll. Obstetricians and Gynecologists, N.Y. Acad. Scis.; mem. Am. Cancer Soc. (pres. Nebr. div. 1962-63, bd. dirs. 1962-74), Am. Fertility Soc. (v.p. 1970), AMA, Omaha-Douglas County Med. Soc. (pres. 1959-60), Alpha Omega Alpha, Phi Delta Theta, Phi Rho Sigma. Republican. Episcoplaian. Contbr. articles to med. specialty jours. Office: 8601 W Dodge Rd #120 Omaha NE 68114

ANDERSON, HAROLD COULSTON, engr.; b. Cheshire, Conn., May 2, 1910; s. Elisha Coulston and Mary Louisa (Butler) A.; m. Grayce R. Bushey, Sept. 15, 1943; 1 son, Russel C. B.S., Oreg. State U., 1936; postgrad. Harvard, Mass. Inst. Tech., 1942-43; U. Md., 1956-58. Registered profl. engr., Oreg., Minn. Engr. engring. dept., office opinions and review, FCC, Washington, 1940-56; fellow engr. advanced devel. subdiv. Westinghouse Electric Corp., Balt., 1956-58; sr. staff engr. Litton Industries, Mpls., 1958—; delegate Internat. Electro-tech. Commn., 1974—; mem. tech. study group Canadian Standards Assn., 1970—; mem. com. Am. Nat. Standards Inst. Mem. IEEE, Am. Physical Soc., Nat. Soc. Profl. Engrs., Tau Beta Pi, Eta Kappa Nu, Pi Mu Epsilon. Holder numerous patents; contbr. articles to profl. jours. Home: 737 Forest Dale Rd New Brighton MN 55112 Office:

ANDERSON, HAROLD EDWARD, dermatologist; b. Battle Creek, Mich., Dec. 1, 1913; s. Olaf Andrew and Ethel Margaret (Stephen) Andersen; B.S., Battle Creek Coll., 1937; M.D., Loma Linda (Calif.) U., 1940; M.S., Wayne State U., Detroit, 1943; m. Mary Vivian Spomer, June 12, 1939; children—Robert, Nancy, Kent. Intern Henry Ford Hosp., Detroit, 1939-40; resident in dermatology Wayne State U., Detroit, 1940-43; practice medicine specializing in dermatology, Long Beach, Calif., 1943-50, Battle Creek, 1950—; mem. staff Leila Y. Post Montgomery Hosp., Community Hosp., Battle Creek Sanitarium Hosp.; cons. VA Hosp., Battle Creek; instr. Loma Linda U. Med. Sch., 1943-50. Diplomate Am. Bd. Dermatology. Mem. Am. Acad. Dermatology, AMA, Mich., Calhoun County med. socs., Mich., Central states dermatol. socs. Contbr. med. jours. Home: 951 Riverside Dr Battle Creek MI 49015 Office: 131 E Columbia Ave Battle Creek MI 49015

ANDERSON, HOWARD DOUGLAS, health agy. adminstr.; b. Lumpkin, Ga., Feb. 28, 1936; s. James M. and Lila M. (Glenn) A.; B.A., Morehouse Coll., 1968; m. Louise Clapp, Sept. 13, 1958; 1 son, Howard D.; m. 2d, Susan Benson, Oct. 10, 1975; stepchildren—Deborah, Robert Taylor. Postal clk., 1958-66; sales rep.

Merck Sharp & Dohme, Chgo., 1969-70; staff writer U. Chgo. Office Pub. Info., 1970-72; exec. dir. Midwest Assn. Sickle Cell Anemia, Chgo., 1972—. Bd. dirs. Chgo. Regional Blood Program; mem. citizens adv. council U. Chgo. Sickle Cell Center, U. Ill. Sickle Cell Center. Served with U.S. Army, 1958-60. Mem. Nat. Assn. Sickle Cell Disease (founder). Home: 2231 E 67th St Chicago IL 60649 Office: 202 S State St Suite 700 Chicago IL 60604

ANDERSON, JACK GARRETT, accountant; b. Tuscola, Ill., July 22, 1929; s. Clausie J. and Helen (Garrett) A.; B.S. in Accounting, U. Ill., 1947-52; postgrad. U. Chgo., 1965-67; m. Virginia Ruth Schrock, June 11, 1950; children—Kent Allen, Cynthia Rae, Brad Douglas, Clayton Garrett. Mem. audit staff Ernst & Ernst, C.P.A's, Chgo., 1952-59; asst. treas., controller Butler Co., Chgo., 1959-63; controller, dir. Butler Paper Co., Chgo., 1963-64; controller terminals div. Gen. Am. Transp. Corp., Chgo., 1964-70, mgr. profit planning and forecasting parent co., 1970-71; asst. comptroller GATX Corp., 1971—. Mem. Ill. Soc. C.P.A.'s, Am. Inst. C.P.A.'s. Baptist. Home: 1421 S Main St Wheaton IL 60187 Office: 120 S Riverside Plaza Chicago IL 60606

ANDERSON, JAMES HARRY, utility engr.; b. Mpls., Aug. 30, 1927; s. Harry Aden and Leilah Betty (Anderson) A.; B. Civil Engring., U. Minn., 1952; m. Marilyn Louise Graaf, Sept. 7, 1951; children—Christine, Richard, Mark, Susan. Cadet engr. Mpls. Gas Co., 1952-54, engr., 1954-56, coordinator suburban div. main and service, 1956-58, asst. chief engr., 1958-68, chief design engr., 1968-72; chief design engr. Minn. Gas Co., Mpls., 1972-76, chief engr., 1977—; mem. utility com. Nat. Transp. Research Bd.; lectr. in field. Chmn. Mpls.-St. Paul Met. Utilities Coordinating Com., 1973-75; planning commr. City of Bloomington, 1962-68, city councilman, 1971-75. Chmn. bd. dirs. South Hennepin County Human Service Council. Served with AUS, 1945-47; PTO. Registered profl. engr., Minn. Mem. Minn. Pub. Works Assn. (dir. 1966-72), Am. (chmn. com. distbn. design 1968-69, mem. com. system protection, gas industry rep. to Am. Pub. Works Assn., operating sect. award of merit 1964), Midwest gas assns., Nat., Minn. socs. profl. engrs., Mpls. Engrs. Club (pres. 1966, Engr. of Year award 1976), Am. Right-of-Way Assn. (internat. liaison com.), Bloomington (Minn.) C. of C., Am. Civil Engrs. Assn. Contbr. articles to trade mags. Home: 1400 E 100th St Bloomington MN 55420 Office: Minn Gas Co 733 Marquette Ave Minneapolis MN 55402

ANDERSON, JOHN BAYARD, congressman; b. Rockford, Ill., Feb. 15, 1922; s. E. Albin and Mabel Edna (Ring) A.; A.B., U. Ill., 1942, J.D., 1946; LL.M., Harvard U., 1949; m. Keke Machakos, Jan. 4, 1953; children—Eleanora, John Bayard, Diane, Karen, Susan Kimberly. Admitted to Ill. bar, 1946; practice, Rockford, 1946-48, 50-52, 55-56; with U.S. Fgn. Service, 1952-55, assigned West Berlin, Germany, 1952-55; states atty. Winnebago County, Ill., 1956-60; mem. 87th-95th Congresses from 16th Dist. Ill., chmn. House Rep. Conf., 1969—, mem. Rules Com., Joint Com. Atomic Energy; instr. Northeastern U. Law Sch., 1948-49. Bd. dirs. Youth for Christ; trustee Trinity Coll., Deerfield, Ill. Served with F.A., AUS, World War II. Mem. Winnebago County Bar Assn., Phi Beta Kappa. Republican. Mem. Evang. Free Ch. (past trustee). Author: Between Two Worlds: A Congressman's Choice, 1970; Vision and Betrayal in America, 1975. Editor Congress and Conscience, 1970. Home: 2711 Highcrest Rd Rockford IL 61107 also 2720 35th Pl NW Washington DC 20007 Office: 1101 Longworth House Office Bldg Washington DC 20515

ANDERSON, JOHN ERIC, mfg. co. exec.; b. Milw., June 27, 1927; s. Carl Gunnar and Anita Techla (Paff) A.; B.S. in Metall. Engring., 1951; m. Joanne Louise Olsen, June 21, 1952; children—Martha Ellen, Amy Lynita, Eric Gordon, Tobin Karl. Metall. engr. Gen. Electric, various locations, 1951-56; project prin. Parker Pen Co., Janesville, Wis., 1956-63, gen. mgr. Sintered Spltys. div., 1963-66; v.p. Panoramic Corp., subsidiary Parker Pen, 1966—; partner Coin Wash Laundry & Dry Cleaners, Janesville, 1968-70. Committeeman Boy Scouts Am., Janesville, 1969; committeeman YMCA, 1968-72. Served with AUS, 1945-46. Recipient scholarship Am. Smelting and Refining, 1949. Mem. Am. Powder Metallurgy Inst. (chmn. local sect. 1967-68), Am. Soc. Metals, Am. Inst. Mining, Metall. and Petroleum Engrs., Powder Metallurgy Parts Assn. (bd. dirs. 1969-72), Tau Beta Pi. Mem. Ch. Christ (ch. bd. 1969-72). Home: 2510 Ruger Ave Janesville WI 53545 Office: 1405 Riverside St Janesville WI 53545

ANDERSON, JOHN ROBERT, educator; b. Stromsburg, Nebr., Aug. 1, 1928; s. Norris Merton and Violet Charlotte (Stromberg) A.; student Midland Coll., 1945-46; A.A., Luther Jr. Coll., 1949; B.S., U. Nebr., Lincoln, 1951, M.A. in Mathematics, 1954; Ph.D., Purdue U., 1970; m. Bertha Margery Nore, Aug. 27, 1950; children—Eric Jon, Mary Lynn. Tchr. mathematics and coach, Bloomfield (Nebr.) High Sch., 1951-52; control systems analyst, Allison Div. Gen. Motors Corp., Indpls., 1954-60; prof. mathematics Depauw U., Greencastle, Ind., 1960, asst. dean, dir. grad. studies, 1973-76, dir. grad. studies, 1976—, res. dir. W. European Studies Program, W. Ger., France; dir. NSF Coop. Coll. Sch. Sci. Inst., 1969-70, instr. NSF summer inst., 1972; bd. dirs. Law Focused Edn., Indpls., 1975—, Ind. Regional Mathematics Consortium, 1977—. Bd. dirs. Br. No. 8115 Lutheran Brotherhood. Served with U.S. Army, 1946-48. U. Nebr. regents scholar, 1945-46; Danforth Teacher fellow, 1963-64; NSF sci. faculty fellow, 1964-65; Lilly Found. edn. grantee, summers 1961, 62, 63. Mem. Math. Assn. Am., Nat. Council Teachers of Mathematics, Sigma Xi, Pi Mu Epsilon, Beta Sigma Psi. Club: Rotary Internat. (sec., 1976-77., v.p. 1977-78). Home: 1560 Bloomington St Greencastle IN 46135

ANDERSON, JUDITH MARGO, counselor; b. Wisconsin Rapids, Wis., Oct. 3, 1953; d. George William and Jean Alice (Abel) Schmidt; B.S., U. Wis., 1975, M.S. in Rehab. Counseling, 1976; m. James Francis Anderson, Jr., Oct. 2, 1976. Practicum, diagnostic and treatment unit Waisman Center Mental Retardation and Human Devel., U. Wis., Madison, 1974, Madison Gen. Hosp., 1975, Madison Opportunity Center, 1975; intern Waisman Center, U. Wis., Madison, 1976; with Peoria (Ill.) Area Mental Health Center, Inc., 1976—, vocat. rehab. counselor, clin. therapist, 1976—; cons. in field. Mem. Am. Personnel and Guidance Assn., Am. Rehab. Counseling Assn., Nat., Ill. rehab. assns., Mortar Bd., Sigma Epsilon Sigma. Address: 4717 N Knoxville St Apt 701 Peoria IL 61614

ANDERSON, KARL PAUL, chemist; b. Fergus Falls, Minn., Jan. 10, 1934; s. Paul R. and Irma I. Anderson; B.Sc., Ohio State U., 1958; postgrad. (scholar) U. Gottingen (W.Ger.), 1956; m. Ruby M. Porter, Sept. 7, 1958; children—Ronald Richard, Karen Lynn. Devel. chemist Hanna Chem. Coatings Co., Columbus, Ohio, 1959-65, group leader metal deco. dept., 1965-67, coil coating dept, 1967-69, dir. coil coating div., 1971—; group leader coil coating lab. Lilly Indsl. Coatings, Indpls., 1969-70; v.p. Karencraft, Inc., Columbus, 1975—; dir. Corboard, Inc. Asst. scoutmaster Central Ohio council Boy Scouts Am., Columbus, 1969—; head coach N. Columbus Girls Baseball, 1977—, Univ. Boys Assn., Boys Basketball, 1974-75. Recipient Order of Arrow, Boy Scouts Am., 1976. Mem. Nat. Coil Coaters Assn., Cin. Dayton Indpls. Columbus Soc., Fedn. Socs. Coatings Tech., Nat. Flyers Assn., Scioto Model A Ford Club, North Columbus Ski Club, Buckeye Glider Club, Flying Farmers, Sigma Pi (sec., trustee), Phi Eta Sigma (treas.). Methodist. Club: Masons. Contbr. articles to profl. jours. Home: 612 E Como Ave Columbus OH 43202 Office: PO Box 147 Columbus OH 43216

ANDERSON, KARL STEPHEN, newspaper exec.; b. Chgo., Nov. 10, 1933; s. Karl William and Eleanore (Grell) A.; B.S. in Editorial Journalism, U. Ill., 1955; m. Saralee Hegland, Nov. 5, 1977; children by previous marriage—Matthew, Douglas, Eric. Successively advt. mgr., asst. to pub., plant mgr. Pioneer Press, Oak Park and St. Charles, Ill., 1955-71; asst. to pub., then pub. Crescent Newspapers, Downers Grove, Ill., 1971-73; asso. pub. and editor Chronicle Pub. Co., St. Charles, 1973—. Treas. St. Charles Softball Assn.; mem. St. Charles Econ. Devel. Commn.; dir. St. Charles Community Chest. Recipient C.V. Amenoff award Dept. Journalism, No. Ill. U., 1976. Mem. Ill. Press Assn. (Will Loomis award 1977, dir. and legis. chmn. 1978), Nat., No. Ill. (treas. 1978) newspaper assns., Suburban Newspapers Am., St. Charles C. of C. (pres. 1978), Sigma Delta Chi, Chi Psi. Clubs: Palisades Park Country, Rotary. Home: 520 S 12th St Saint Charles IL 60174 Office: 2601 E Main St Saint Charles IL 60174

ANDERSON, KENNETH OSCAR, film co. exec.; b. Rembrandt, Ia., Dec. 23, 1917; s. Oscar Frank and Ethel Mae (Anderson) A.; student Wheaton Coll., 1936-37, 45-51, Northwestern U., 1947-48; m. Doris Ilene Jones, Nov. 16, 1938; children—Naoma (Mrs. Larry Clark), Margaret (Mrs. T. Landon Mauzy), Donn, Lane, Max, Keno, Melody. Editor, Campus Life Mag., Wheaton, Ill., 1945-51; with Gospel Films, Muskegon, Mich., 1949-61, exec. producer, 1949-61; pres. Ken Anderson Films, Winona Lake, Ind., 1963—; dir. Master Investments Corp., Warsaw, Ind.; dir. Internat. Films, London, Eng., 1969-72, now dir. Editorial cons. Word Books, Waco, Tex., 1965—; vis. instr. Haggai Inst., Singapore, 1974—. Mem. pres.'s com. Grace Coll., Winona Lake, 1972—; adv. com. League for the Handicapped, Walworth, Wis., 1965—; bd. dirs. Youth Haven Ranch, Rives Junction, Mich., Crusade Evangelism, London, Ont., Can. Named Evang. Press Assn. Writer of Year, 1962; Nat. Evang. Film Found. award as Dir. of Year, 1970. Mem. Gidions Internat. Presbyterian (elder 1963—). Author: Himalyan Heartbeat, 1966; Stains on Glass Windows, 1969; Adjustable Halo, 1969; Satan's Angels, 1975; (with Tony Mockus) I'm Learning from Protestants How to be a Better Catholic, 1975; How to Be a Success Without Becoming a Failure, 1976; producer, dir. film of book Pilgrim's Progress, 1977. Home: 720 North Lake St Warsaw IN 46580 Office: PO Box 618 Winona Lake IN 46590

ANDERSON, LAVERNE ERIC, lawyer; b. Rockford, Ill., Feb. 24, 1922; s. Eric J. and Alma M. (Johnson) A.; LL.B., U. Ill., 1944, J.D., 1946; m. Lucille Hardy, Feb. 14, 1954. Admitted to Ill. bar, 1947, admitted to practice U.S. Treasury Dept., Fed. Ct.; individual practice law, Rockford, 1947-64; partner firm Nordquist and Anderson, 1965—; city atty., Rockford, 1947-53, corp. counsel, 1953-57. Mem. Ill., Winnebago County bar assns., Broadway Bus. Assn., Phi Eta Sigma, Phi Beta Kappa, Phi Kappa Phi. Lutheran. Clubs: Mason, Shriners (rep. Imperial Council, dir., El Hajj Caravanserai No. 4, potentate Tebala Shrine Temple, 1977). Office: 724 Broadway Rockford IL 61108

ANDERSON, LAWRENCE SVENTE, clergyman; b. Valparaiso, Ind., June 18, 1918; s. Lawrence Svente and Olga Regena (Wallin) A.; A.B., Valparaiso U., 1950; postgrad. Augustana Sem., 1950-53, Garrett Sem. Northwestern U., 1962, Mich. State U., 1969-71; m. Jennie Louise Nicholson, Dec. 5, 1943; children—Richard Lawrence, Paul Raymond, Philip Douglas, Mary Louise. Foreman, U.S. Steel, Gary, Ind., 1936-42; owner Anderson Heating & Electric, Chesterton, Ind., 1948-50; ordained to ministry Luth. Ch. Am., 1953; pastor Stratford (Iowa) Luth. Ch., 1953-60, 1st Luth. Ch., Prophetstown, Ill., 1960—. Mem. curriculum com. Northwestern Ill. Community Coll., 1964-65; mem. advisory bd. Prophets Riverview Center, 1965—. Chmn. civic div. Prophetstown Indsl. and Devel. Commn., 1962-66; chmn. publicity, fund drive, Prophetstown Riverview Center Nursing Home, 1965-66, 71-76. Bd. dirs. Evang. Luth. Good Samaritan Soc., Sioux Falls, S.D., sec. bd., 1972-76; bd. dirs. Winning Wheels, Prophetstown, 1968—; Whiteside County assn. for Retarded, Iowa Christian Rural Fellowship, Iowa State U., 1957-60. Served with USAAF, 1942-46. Lion. Club: Boosters. Home: 321 W 2d St Prophetstown IL 62177 Office: 300 W 3d St Prophetstown IL 61277

ANDERSON, LEROY HARVEY, engr., mktg. exec.; b. Thief River Falls, Minn., Aug. 24, 1940; s. Harley Lee and Thelma (Eeg) A.; B.S., U. Minn., 1963, M.S., 1965, Ph.D., 1969; m. Carol Gay DeGrote, Aug. 31, 1963; children—Michele, Renee, Matthew. Pres. Compace, Mpls., 1968-70, Comstar, Edina, Minn., 1970-74; marketing mgr. Warner & Swasey, Solon, Ohio, 1974-76; prin. LHA Assos., Chagrin Falls, Ohio, 1976-77; dir., gen. mgr. Realistic Control Corp., Davenport, Iowa, 1977—. Mem. automation com. Purdue U., 1975. Mem. Microcumputer Inst. of Nat. Electronic Conf., IEEE, IEEE Computer Soc. (pres. Cleve. chpt.), Sons of Norway, Eta Kappa Nu. Club: Tanglewood Country. Contbr. articles to profl. jours. Home: 1729 E 43d St Davenport IA 52807 Office: 404 W 35th St Davenport IA 52806

ANDERSON, LOIS DOROTHY, ret. nurse, ednl. psychologist; b. Alexandria, Minn., Jan. 7, 1925; d. Victor and Selma Eugenia (Johnson) Anderson; diploma in nursing Mounds-Midway Sch. Nursing, 1946; B.S., U. Minn., 1949, M.A., 1954, Ph.D., 1961. Asst. instr. Mound-Midway Sch. Nursing, St. Paul, 1946-47; instr. nursing U. Minn., Mpls., 1950-55; ednl. coordinator Sch. Nursing, Hamline U., St. Paul, 1955-58; coordinator video nursing edn. KTCA-TV and KTCI-TV, St. Paul, 1962-68; coordinator VA nursing research in nursing edn. VA Hosp., St. Cloud, Minn., 1969-71; coordinator nursing research in nursing edn., dir. nursing multimedia project, VA Hosp., Mpls., 1971-73, chief devel. edn. resource sect. Office of Asso. Chief Staff Edn., 1973-75, chief learning resources, 1975-77; cons. in field, lectr. Kirbach-Dahlby scholar, 1946-48; Student Project for Amity Among Nations scholar, 1952; NIH spl. nursing research fellow, 1958-60. Fellow Am. Acad. Nursing; mem. Am. Nurses Assn., Nat. League Nursing, AAAS, Health Scis. Communications Assn., Nat. Assn. Ednl. Broadcasters, Assn. Ednl. Communications and Tech., Sigma Theta Tau, Pi Lambda Theta, Psi Chi. Baptist. Home: 812 Hawthorne St Alexandria MN 56308

ANDERSON, LOIS MARILYN, psychologist; b. Cambridge, Minn., Mar. 19, 1934; d. Oliver Ferdinand and Marjorie Constance (Strait) Ledin; m. Malcolm Charles Anderson, July 9, 1960; 1 son, Andrew. B.S., Gustavus Adolphus Coll., 1956; Ph.D., U. Minn., 1969. Intern counseling Student Counseling Bur., U. Hosps. dept. of phys. medicine and rehab. U. Minn., 1959-60; research psychologist InterStudy, Mpls., 1969-73; coordinator state program mgmt. Minn. Dept. Adminstrn., St. Paul, 1973-77, asst. dir. Mgmt. Services div., 1977—. Governing mem. YMCA of Met. Mpls., 1971—; bd. mgmt. Northwest (Mpls.) YMCA, 1970-76; lectr. U. Minn. Grad. Schs. of Pub. Affairs and Social Work, 1975, 76; mem. Twin City Met. Council Advisory com. on Waste Mgmt. and Water Quality, 1976—. Mem. Am., Minn. psychol. assns., Am. Pub. Welfare Assn., Psi Chi, Pi Lamdba Theta. Recipient Annual Research award, Am. Rehab. Counseling Assn., 1965. Author: (with others) AFDC Employment and Referral Guidelines, 1973; Impact of Welfare Reform on the Elderly Poor, 1973; Medicaid Cost Containment and Long Term Care, 1976. Home: 4400 Victory Ave Minneapolis MN 55412 Office: 114 State Administration Bldg Saint Paul MN 55155

ANDERSON, LOWELL JOHN, pharmacist; b. Hoodsport, Wash., Feb. 14, 1939; s. Waldemar Raymond and Hannah (Ryberg) A.; student Gogebic Jr. Coll., 1957-58; B.S., U. Minn., 1962. Asst. mgr. Walgreen Drug Co., St. Paul, 1962; asst. chief pharmacist Northwestern Hosp., Mpls., 1963-65; with dept. adminstrn., div. procurement State Minn., 1965; v.p. Falcon Heights Pharmacy, St. Paul, 1966—. Mem. Minn. Bd. Pharmacy, 1969-73, pres., 1973; mem. allied health credentialling adv. com. Minn. Bd. Health, 1974-76. Vice chmn. Ramsey County Republican Com., 1971-73; mem. state exec. com. Minn. Young Rep. League, 1969-70; mem. Rep. State Central Com. Minn., 1970-74. Bd. dirs. Nat. Assn. Bds. Pharmacy Found., 1974; bd. dirs., v.p. Urban Concerns Workshops, 1977-78. Served with Intelligence Corps, AUS, 1963-69. Mem. Am. (vice chmn. Minn. policy com. profl. affairs 1977-78), Minn. (dir., speaker ho. dels. 1975-76, pres. 1978) pharm. assns., Nat. Assn. Bds. Pharmacy (chmn. internship com. 1973), Am. Council on Pharm. Edn. (dir.), U. Minn. Alumni Assn. (pres. Coll. of Pharmacy div. 1973-74), North Suburban St. Paul C. of C. (dir. 1974—), Falcon Heights Businessmens Assn. (v.p. 1973-74), Kappa Psi. Editorial advisory bd. Jour. Am. Pharm. Assn., 1975-77. Home: 1455 Arden View Dr Arden Hills MN 55112 Office: 1707 N Snell Ave St Paul MN 55113

ANDERSON, LOWELL VERNET, research photographer; b. Grafton, N.D., Jan. 10, 1942; s. Loren Wesley and Irene Eunice (Larson) A.; student Concordia Coll., 1960-61, U. N.D., 1965-66; grad. Brooks Inst. Photography, 1969; m. Mary Louise Dietrich, Sept. 3, 1966; children—Paul Lowell, Gretchen Louise. Indsl. photographer Control Data Corp., Mpls., 1969-70; contractor, indsl. photographer Pan Am. Airlines, 1973; owner Anderson Photography, gen. photography and infrared photography research, Grand Forks, N.D., 1969—. Served with 3d Armored Div., AUS, 1961-64. Mem. Profl. Photographers Am., Research on potato disease detection using aerial infrared photographs. Address: Route 1 Grafton ND 58237

ANDERSON, LUTHER ADOLPH, writer; b. Ironwood, Mich., Oct. 4, 1898; s. Peter Edward and Carolina (Gustafson) A.; B.C.S., DePaul Coll. Commerce, Chgo., 1924; Ph.B., U. Chgo., 1927; m. Ethel Marie Martin, Aug. 1, 1938. Pub. accountant Haskins & Sells, Chgo., 1928-30, Price Waterhouse, Milw., 1931-32; accountant Armour & Co., Ironwood, Mich., 1932-62; writer for hunting, fishing, camping publs., including Field & Stream, Outdoor Life, Sports Afield, Fur-Fish-Game, Ironwood, 1930—. Treas., Bethany Covenant Ch., Ironwood, 1937—, also choir dir.; bd. dirs. Salvation Army, Ironwood, 1961—. Author: Hunting, Fishing and Camping, 1945; Hunting the American Game Field, 1949; Hunting Deer and Small Game, 1959; Guide to Canoe Camping, 1969; How to Hunt American Small Game, 1969; How to Hunt Whitetail Deer, 1968; Hunting the Uplands with Shotgun and Rifle, 1977. Home: 139 S Curry St Ironwood MI 49938

ANDERSON, LYLE ARTHUR, bus. exec.; b. Jewell, Kan., Dec. 29, 1931; s. Arvid Herman and Clara Vera (Herman) A.; B.S., U. Kan., 1953; M.S., Butler U., 1961; m. Harriet Virginia Robson, June 12, 1953; children—Brian, Karen, Eric. Mgmt. trainee, internal auditor RCA, Camden, N.J. and Indpls., 1955-59; auditor Ernst & Ernst, C.P.A.'s, Kansas City, Mo., 1959-63; v.p. finance and adminstrn., treas., dir. Affiliated Hosp. Products, Inc., St. Louis, 1963-71; sr. v.p. finance and adminstrn. Kitchens of Sara Lee div. Consol. Foods Corp., Deerfield, Ill., 1971-74, exec. v.p., dir. parent co., Chgo., 1974-75; pres., chief exec. officer Autotrol Corp., Crystal Lake, Ill., 1976—. Served with AUS, 1953-55. C.P.A., Mo., Kan. Mem. Am. Inst. C.P.A.'s, Nat. Assn. Accountants, Omicron Delta Kappa. Republican. Presbyn. Home: 6709 Connecticut Trail Crystal Lake IL 60014 Office: 6200 Three Oaks Rd Crystal Lake IL 60014

ANDERSON, MICHAEL WAYNE, lawyer; b. Alton, Ill., Nov. 23, 1949; s. Laudwick Lloyd and Wilma Kathryn (Francis) A.; student Ill. Coll., 1967-70; B.S., Western Ill. U., 1972; J.D., John Marshall Law Sch., 1976. Regional dir. Ill. Region 12 Law and Justice Commn., Pontiac, 1972-73; admitted to Ill. bar, 1976; asso. firm Moore & Goetten, Jerseyville, Ill., 1976—. Mem. Ill. Bar Assn., Jerseyville Jaycees, Sigma Pi. Republican. Baptist. Home: Rural Route 3 Jerseyville IL 62052 Office: 116 W Pearl St Jerseyville IL 62052

ANDERSON, MILTON HENRY, psychiatrist, hosp. adminstr.; b. Omaha, July 31, 1919; s. Milton Henry and Emma Fay (Anderson) A.; student Northwestern U., 1937-38; A.B., Omaha U., 1941; M.D., U. Nebr., 1943; m. M. Margaret Cushing, July 24, 1943 (dec. 1960); children—Gregory Cushing, Milton Henry III, Herbert Clark, Eric Austin; m. 2d, J. Sue Roberts, Sept. 12, 1966. Intern Long Island Coll. Medicine, 1943-44; resident Lenox Hill Hosp., N.Y.C., 1944-45; clin. dir. Hastings (Nebr.) State Hosp., 1948-51; med. supt. Osawatomie (Kan.) State Hosp., 1951-53, Evansville State Hosp., 1953-69; dir. psychiat. unit Welborn Hosp., Evansville, 1969—. Cons. Deaconess, St. Mary's hosps., regional VA hosps., states Ill. and Ind.; bd. dirs. Evansville Child Guidance Clinic, 1953-62, Southwestern Ind. Mental Health Clinic, 1964-75. Served to capt. M.C., AUS, 1945-47. Bishop Clarkson resident physician, 1947-48; fellow Bennett Found., 1947-48. Diplomate Am. Bd. Psychiatry and Neurology. Fellow Am. Psychiat. Assn., Am. Orthopsychiat. Assn., AAAS, Am. Geriatric Soc.; mem. Central Neuropsychiat. Assn., Am. Med., Western electroencephalographic socs., Am. Epilepsy Soc., Am. Group Psychotherapy Assn., Assn. Research Nervous and Mental Diseases, Sigma Chi, Phi Rho Sigma. Mason (Shriner), Rotarian (pres. 1968-69). Clubs: Indpls. Athletic; Evansville Country; Santa Claus Country. Home: 800 Plaza Dr Evansville IN 47715 Office: 3700 Bellemeade St Evansville IN 47715

ANDERSON, NORVAL EUGENE, cons. engr.; b. Anna, Ill., Sept. 14, 1897; s. Frank Vestal and Lulu (Barr) A.; student Colo. Coll., 1916-18; B.S., U. Ill., 1920, C.E., 1934; student U. Chgo.; m. Lilla Turner, June 17, 1918 (dec. Feb. 1966); m. 2d, Ruth Rowena Barr Ferguson, Aug. 15, 1967. Advanced from jr. engr. through engr. of treatment plant design to chief engr., Chgo. San. Dist., 1920-64; now cons. engr.; mem. tech. com. Great Lakes-Ill. River Basins Study, USPHS; mem. tech. adv. com. Northeastern Ill. Met. Area Planning Commn. Received Ill. Award from Ill. Soc. Engrs., 1937. Radabaugh Award, Central States Sewage and Indsl. Wastes Assn., 1950. Diplomate Am. Acad. Environmental Engrs. Fellow ASCE; mem. Am. Water Works Assn., Inter-am Assn. San. Engrs., Water Pollution Control Fedn., Nat., Ill. socs. profl. engrs., Am. Water Resources Assn., Am. Legion, Masters of Foxhounds Assn., Sigma Tau. Clubs: Oak Brook Polo, Oak Brook Hounds; American Foxhound. Author papers in field. Active in design, constrn. water pollution control facilities, Chgo. Home: 618 S Catherine Ave La Grange IL 60525 Office: 200 E Ontario St Chicago IL 60611 Died Nov. 27, 1977.

ANDERSON, PAUL W., distbg. co. exec.; b. Chgo., June 17, 1940; s. Raymond C. and Julia A. (Greczula) A.; B.A., Loyola U., Chgo., 1966; M.B.A., Wayne State U., 1969; m. Barbara Fayne Nawrocki, Dec. 15, 1962. Sales corr. Midwest Steel Co., Portage, Ind., 1963-66; asst. mgr. leasing and rental ops. Ford Motor Co., Dearborn, Mich., 1966-69; pres. Anderson Distbg. Inc., Chgo., 1969—, Portion Systems, Chgo., 1976—; cons. food service and equipment. Roman Catholic. Clubs: Elks, YMCA. Invented electronic portion control system, 1976. Home: 721 Roppolo St Elk Grove IL 60007 Office: 5119 W Cermak Rd Chicago IL 60650

ANDERSON, PAUL WILLIAM, agrl. engr.; b. Prophetstown, Ill., Apr. 12, 1938; s. Harold Clifford and Arvilla Margarite (Swanson) A.; B.S., U. Ill., 1961; M.B.A., U. Wis., 1977; m. Lenda Lea Labertew, Mar. 5, 1961; children—Marcia, Roger, Cheryl, Lisa. Civil engr. Ill. Div. Hwys., Dixon, 1961-63; test engr. J.I. Case Co., Racine, Wis., 1963-64, supr. Ariz. Proving Grounds, Litchfield Park, 1964-70, project engr. hydraulics, Rock Island, Ill., 1970-71, quality control mgr. Rock Island plant, 1971-72, mgr. field service and product performance Agr. div., Racine, 1972-74, sr. project engr., 1975-77, store mgr., Janesville, Wis., 1977—. Mem. Nat. Soc. Profl. Engrs., Am. Soc. Agrl. Engrs. (sect. chmn. 1969), Soc. Automotive Engrs. Home: 743 Suffolk Dr Janesville WI 53545 Office: 1110 Hwy 14 East Janesville WI 53545

ANDERSON, PHILIP CARLTON, feed co. exec.; b. Lincoln, Nebr., Dec. 12, 1918; s. Carl Louis and Harriet (Barnett) A.; student U. Nebr., 1936-38; m. Norma Gene France, Nov. 4, 1940; children—Mark, Kent, Dale, Sara, Jane, Paul. Pres., founder Feed Service Corp., Crete, Nebr., 1951-76; pres. Tricarbon Corp., Crete, 1976—. Chmn. Saline County (Nebr.) Republican Com., 1964—; del. Rep. Nat. Conv., 1964; Rep. candidate for lt. gov., Nebr., 1966. Mem. Am. Assn. Acads. Sci., Nebr. Acad. Sci., Soc. Applied Spectroscopy, Internat. Platform Assn., SAR. Author: Spectral Energy Value System of Molecular Structures. Patentee chem. and mech. devices, animal feeding devices. Home: 1225 Jasmine Rd Crete NE 68333 Office: PO Box 242 Crete NE 68333

ANDERSON, RAY CARL, physician, educator; b. Duluth, Minn., Sept. 24, 1917; s. Anton and Marie Elizabeth (Nelson) A.; B.A., Gustavus Adolphus Coll., 1939; M.A., U. Minn., 1941, Ph.D., 1943, M.D., 1946; m. Hattie Beatrice Hobert, Feb. 8, 1941; children—David, Kathleen (Mrs. Michael Wirtanen). Intern, Univ. Hosp., Ann Arbor, Mich., 1946-47; resident U. Minn. Hosp., 1949-51; mem. faculty U. Minn., Mpls., 1949—, prof. pediatrics, 1970—; mem. staff U. Minn. Hosp., 1951—. Served to capt. AUS, 1947-49. Recipient award Gustavus Adolphus Coll., 1961. Diplomate in pediatric cardiology Am. Bd. Pediatrics. Mem. Am. Coll. Cardiology, Am. Acad. Pediatrics (chmn. sect. cardiology 1966-67), Soc. Pediatric Research, Sigma Xi, Alpha Omega Alpha. Contbr. to profl. publs. in field. Home: 5306 Hampshire Dr Minneapolis MN 55419 Office: Box 94 University Hosp Minneapolis MN 55455

ANDERSON, ROBERT ALFRED, diversified industry exec.; b. Wadena, Minn., Jan. 16, 1932; s. Alfred Emmanuel and Francis Agnes (Hassler) A.; B.B.A., U. Miami (Fla.), 1959; m. Janet Lynn Hemquist, Aug. 3, 1967. Various positions Viking-Land USA, Inc., Battle Lake, Minn., 1967-68, pres., 1968-71, dir., 1967—; various positions Explorers Highroad Found. Inc., Battle Lake, 1969-78, pres., 1971-73, dir., 1969—. Mem. Minn. Ho. of Reps., 1976—. Served with U.S. Army, 1952-54. Hon. citizen City of Winnipeg (Man., Can.), 1972. Clubs: Bal Moral Country, Ottertail Rod and Gun, Knob Hill Sportsmen's, Masons, Shriners, Elks, Am. Legion, VFW, Ducks Unlimited. Home: Route 1 Box 275 Richville MN 56576 Office: Box 28 Ottertail MN 56571

ANDERSON, ROBERT ARTHUR, author, educator; b. Worcester, Mass., Feb. 27, 1927; s. Louis Fredolph and Ethel Mae (Lowe) A.; A.B., Upsala Coll., 1951; M.A., U. No. Colo., 1953; m. Faye Ella Kroeger, Sept. 15, 1951; children—Jill Anderson, Ned. Tchr., Brighton (Colo.) Jr. High Sch., 1954-59, Duxbury (Mass.) High Sch., 1959-67, Daytona Beach (Fla.) Community Coll., 1967-73, Rich Central High Sch., Olympia Fields, Ill., 1974-77, Rich East High Sch., Park Forest, Ill., 1977—. Mem. City Council South Daytona. Served with USN, 1945-46. Mem. Ill. Edn. Assn., NEA, Nat. Council Tchrs. English. Author: Writers Rhetoric, 1971; A Lexicon of Literary Terms, 1977; Handbook of Theatrical Terms, 1977; also plays, articles in profl. writing mags. Home: 285 Fir St Park Forest IL 60466 Office: Sauk Trail & Westwood Sts Park Forest IL 60466

ANDERSON, ROBERT LOUIS, lawyer; b. Aberdeen, S.D., Oct. 13, 1938; s. Louis Roland and Charlotte Maude (Valle) A.; B.S., S.D. State U., 1960; J.D., U. Colo., 1966; m. Rosanne Jane Fritsche, Aug. 23, 1959; children—Erik Robert, Lars Robert. Admitted to Nebr. bar, 1966, since practiced in Lincoln; asso. Mason, Knudsen, Berkheimer & Endacott, 1966-70, partner, 1970-71; mem. firm Knudsen, Berkheimer, Endacott & Beam, 1971—. Served with USNR, 1960-63; now comdr. Res. Mem. Am., Nebr., Lincoln bar assns., Nat. Assn. R.R. Trial Counsel, Am. Trial Lawyers Assn., Fedn. Ins. Counsel, Naval Res. Assn. Lutheran. Home: 3136 Calvert Lincoln NE 68502 Office: 1000 NBC Center Lincoln NE 68508

ANDERSON, ROGER E., banker; b. Chgo., 1921; B.S., Northwestern U., 1942; m. Marilyn Spence. With Continental Ill. Nat. Bank & Trust Co., Chgo., 1946—, exec. v.p., 1968-73, chmn. bd., 1973—; chmn. bd. Continental Ill. Corp., 1973—, also dir.; dir. Continental Bank Internat., Continental Internat. Finance Corp., Banco Atlantico, Barcelona, Spain, Banque Americano-Franco-Suisse Pour le Maroc, Casablanca, Morocco., Armsted Industries, Internat. Harvester Co., S.C. Johnson & Son, Inc. Served with USNR, 1942-46. Home: 2423 Bennett Ave Evanston IL 60201 Office: 231 S LaSalle St Chicago IL 60693

ANDERSON, ROGER GORDON, clergyman; b. Milw., Feb. 1, 1937; s. Arthur Gordon and Dorothy Katherine (Junger) A.; B.A. in Bibl. Lit., Grace Bible Coll., 1958; postgrad. Purdue U., 1958-59; m. Marjorie Virginia Burleson, June 7, 1959; children—Jonathan P., Nancy L., Leslie Joan, Kristi Ann. Ordained minister Grace Gospel Fellowship, 1960; minister Grace Bible Ch., Lafayette, Ind., 1958-60, Preakness Bible Ch., Wayne, N.J., 1960-69, Bethesda Free Ch., Mpls., 1969—. Chmn. Evang. Ministers Fellowship Mpls., 1974-75; chmn. spiritual life com. Greater Mpls. Assn. Evangelicals, 1972-74. Bd. dirs. Grace Mission Inc., 1963—, Goodwill Home and Rescue Mission, Newark, 1961-69. Police chaplain Mpls., 1971—. Recipient distinguished service award Mpls., 1973, 77. Mem. St. Paul Highland PTA, Am. Sci. Affiliation, Grace Gospel Fellowship, Nat. Geog. Soc., Evangel Ministers Fellowship Mpls., Nat. Assn. Evangelicals. Contbr. articles to profl. publs.; radio appearances, 1976—. Home: 1406 S Cleveland St St Paul MN 55116 Office: 2600 E 38th St Minneapolis MN 55406

ANDERSON, ROGER LYLE, civil engr.; b. Rice Lake, Wis., May 12, 1952; s. Lyle Gordon and Mavis K. Anderson; B.S., U. Wis., 1974; m. Sandra J. Werner, May 18, 1974. Civil, structural engr. Procon, Inc. subs. Universal Oil Products, Des Plaines, Ill., 1975—. Recipient Am. Legion Certificate Sch. Achievement, 1970; certified engr.-in-tng., Wis., 1974. Mem. ASCE (asso.), Nat. Soc. Profl. Engrs., Chi Epsilon, Kappa Mu Epsilon. Home: 17W730 Butterfield Rd Apt 217 Oakbrook Terr IL 60181 Office: 30 UOP Plaza Des Plaines IL 60016

ANDERSON, ROGER SCOTT, mech. engr.; b. Chgo., Sept. 21, 1948; s. Dana and Patricia Jean (Randall) A.; B.S.M.E., U. Ill., 1972, M.S., 1973; m. Lydia Ann Estrella, Oct. 2, 1976; 1 dau., Randallyn Jean. Faculty, U. Ill., Urbana, 1972-73; mech. designer P & W Engrs., Chgo., 1974-75; mech. engr. St. James Hosp., Chicago Heights, Ill., 1975—; faculty Triton Coll., River Grove, Ill., 1974—. Mem. Am. Soc. Heating, Refrigerating and Air Conditioning Engrs. Contbr. articles to profl. jours. Home: 22426 York Ct Apt 1A Richton Park IL 60471 Office: 1423 Chicago Rd Chicago Heights IL 60411

ANDERSON, RONALD DEAN, social worker; b. Buffalo, Minn., May 7, 1934; s. Roy William and Esther Irene (Heyer) A.; student St. Cloud State Coll., 1957-59; B.A., U. Minn., 1962; M.S.W., U. Utah, 1964; m. Barbara Gilstad, June 24, 1961; children—Brent, Steven, Keith. Caseworker, Atkin County Welfare Dept., Atkin, Minn., 1964-66; asst. dir. Northwood Children's Home, Duluth, Minn., 1966-70; dir. Woodland Hills, adolescent treatment center, Duluth, 1970—. Precinct capt. Democratic Farm-Labor party, Duluth, 1968—, del. state conv., 1972. Served with USAF, 1954-57. Mem. Nat. Assn. Social Workers, Minn. Social Service Assn. Kiwanian. Home: Route 4 Box 469P Duluth MN 55803 Office: 4321 Allendale St Duluth MN 55812

ANDERSON, ROY LEONARD, health facility adminstr.; b. Duluth, Minn., Oct. 2, 1923; s. Edward and Mary (Dalseg) A.; B.A., U. Minn., 1949; M.S., N.D. State U., 1956; m. Evelyn Marion Anderson, June 19, 1943; children—David Roy, Jenalda Lynn. With N.W. Paper Co., Cloquet, Minn., 1945-49; social worker Carlton County (Minn.) Welfare Dept., 1949-50; with Lakeland Mental Health Center, Inc., Fergus Falls, Minn., 1950—, program dir., 1957—. Cons. Fergus Falls Sch. System, 1956-62, Pelican Rapids Sch. System, 1956-62, also various nursing homes. Mem. Fergus Falls City Health Bd., 1968-73; mem. Fergus Falls Adv. Com., 1973—; pres. Madison Elementary Sch. PTA, 1954, Roosevelt Park Sr. High Sch. PTA, Fergus Falls, 1963, Fergus Falls Joint PTA Council, 1962; mem. Minn. Adv. Com. on Deaf and Blind, 1969—. Bd. dirs. Minn. Congress Parents and Tchrs., 1958-66, chmn. mental health unit, 1958-66. Served with USMCR, 1942-43; with AUS, 1944-45. Recipient Minn. Alumni Recognition award Minn. 4-H. Mem. Minn. Welfare Assn., Minn. Assn. for Retarded Children, Mental Health Assn. Minn., Assn. of Out-Patient Clinics Am., Sons of Norway, Fergus Falls C. of C., Gamma Theta Upsilon, Kappa Omicron, Phi Alpha Theta. Lutheran (deacon, council). Kiwanian. Home: 821 S Sheridan St Fergus Falls MN 56537 Office: 126 E Alcott St Fergus Falls MN 56537

ANDERSON, SIDNEY ELMER, agrl. engr.; b. Vermillion, S.D., Aug. 26, 1915; s. John Alfred and Selma Elizabeth (Hoyer) A.; B.S., U. S.D., 1937; m. Edis Juel Orr, June 12, 1949; children—Lucinda Juel, Susan Elizabeth, Sidney Edison, Shawn David. Farmer, nr. Vermillion, 1937-40; with G.M. Allison Plant, Indpls., 1940-41; instr. U. S.D., Vermillion, 1947-51; product engr. John Deere Co., East Moline, Ill., 1951—. Served with USAAF, 1941-46; lt. col. Res., 1946-59. Mem. Am. Soc. Agrl. Engrs. Republican. Methodist. Home: Rural Route 3 Geneseo IL 61254 Office: 1100 13th Ave East Moline IL 61244

ANDERSON, THOMAS MILBURN, JR., lawyer; b. Ottawa, Ill., Dec. 25, 1934; s. Thomas Milburn and Bessie Mae (Olson) A.; student Am. U., 1955; B.A., Beloit Coll., 1956; J.D., U. Ill., 1959; children—Thomas Milburn III, John D., Mark E. Admitted to Ill. bar, 1959; asst. state's atty., LaSalle County, Ill., 1960-61; magistrate Circuit Ct. LaSalle County, 1963-64; partner firm Anderson & Anderson, Earlville, Ill., 1964—; spl. asst. atty. gen. State of Ill., 1969—. Mem. Ill. Agrl. Export Adv. Commn., 1968-71; zone chmn. Ill. Gov.'s Task Force Mental Health, 1972; mem. Ill. Gov.'s Adv. Council, 1969-72; U.S. rep. European N.Am. Conf. Young Polit. Leaders, Rome, Italy, 1970. Republican candidate for state's atty. of LaSalle County, 1964; mem. LaSalle County Rep. Finance Com., 1965-70, chmn. LaSalle County Rep. Central Com., 1974-76; precinct committeeman, 1969-76; regional campaign mgr. Ralph T. Smith for senator campaign, 1970; vice-chmn. Young Rep. Nat. Fedn., 1969-71, co-chmn. conv., 1969; Ill. 15th Congl. Dist. Rep. State Central committeeman, 1974—. Recipient Outstanding Young Rep. of Ill. award, 1969. Elk, Lion. Office: 201 S Ottawa St Earlville IL 60518

ANDERSON, VERLYN DEAN, librarian; b. Fergus Falls, Minn., Oct. 23, 1933; s. Arthur Ole and Cora Arvetta (Hovland) A.; B.A., Concordia Coll., 1956; M.A. in English Edn., U. Minn., 1962, M.A. in Library Sci., 1965, Ph.D. in Am. Studies, 1972; m. Evonne Oretta Beastrom, June 7, 1958; children—Kristi LuAnn, Karen Linnae, Randi Jo. Music librarian Nels Vogel Music Co., Moorhead, Minn., 1956-57; tchr. English, librarian Hawley (Minn.) Pub. Schs., 1957-58; tchr. English, Latin, Waconia (Minn.) Pub. Schs., 1958-62; asst. librarian acquisitions dept. Carl B. Ylvisaker Library, Concordia Coll., Moorhead, 1962-66, chief librarian, asso. prof. library sci., 1967—. Faculty Study scholar Concordia Coll., also Lutheran Brotherhood Faculty Growth grantee, 1966-67. Mem. Am., Minn. library assns., Am. Studies Assn., Norwegian-Am. Inst. Club: C-400 (Moorhead, Minn.). Home: 904 8th Ave S Moorhead MN 56560 Office: Carl B Ylvisaker Library Concordia Coll Moorhead MN 56560

ANDERSON, WALTER RAYMOND, veterinarian; b. Worthington, Minn., Mar. 1, 1902; s. Erick and Axa Natalia (Carlson) A.; D.V.M., Iowa State U., 1930; m. Irene Lucille Glade, June 21, 1957. Veterinarian, Bur. Animal Industry, U.S. Dept. Agr., 1933-35; prof. vet. medicine Iowa State U., Ames, 1935-39; veterinarian Farmers Hybrid Cos., Inc., Hampton, Iowa, 1948-61; practice of vet. medicine, McCook, Nebr., 1930-33, Slater, Iowa, 1939-41, Hampton, 1961—. Served to col. AUS, 1941-47. Mem. Am., Iowa vet. med. assns., Res. Officers Assn., Phi Kappa Phi, Phi Zeta, Gamma Sigma Delta. Republican. Lutheran. Address: 614 7th Ave NE Hampton IA 50441

ANDERSON, WENDELL RICHARD, senator Minn.; b. St. Paul, Feb. 1, 1933; s. Theodore M. and Glady (Nord) A.; B.A., U. Minn., 1954, J.D., 1960; m. Mary C. McKee, Aug. 11, 1963; children—Amy, Elizabeth, Brett. Admitted to Minn. bar, 1960, individual practice law, St. Paul; mem. Minn. Ho. of Reps., 1959-63, Minn. Senate, 1963-71, gov., 1971-76; chmn. Dem. Govs. Conf., 1974-75; chmn. platform com. Dem. Nat. Conv., 1976; appointed U.S. senate, 1976. Mem. U.S. Olympic hockey team, 1956, U.S. Nat. hockey team, 1955, 57. Served with AUS, 1959-63. Mem. Minn. Bar Assn., U.S. Olympians. Home: 1006 Summit Av St Paul MN 55105 Office: Office of Governor State Capitol Bldg St Paul MN 55155

ANDERSON, WILLIAM DAVID, coll. adminstr., pastor; b. Duluth, Minn., June 14, 1920; s. William David and Ella Elizabeth (Lane) A.; B.A., U. Minn., Duluth, 1950; M.Div., U. Dubuque Theol. Sem., 1953; m. Virginia Mae Graves, July 24, 1941; children—David Eugene, Debra Jo. Ordained to ministry United Presbyn. Ch., 1953; pastor 1st Presbyn. chs., Franklin Grove and Ashton, Ill., 1953-57, Canton, Ill., 1957-68; asso. prof. philosophy and religion John F. Kennedy Coll., Wahoo, Nebr., 1968-75, dean of men, chaplain, 1968-72, dean of coll., 1972-75; pastor 1st Congl. Ch., Wahoo, 1969-75; asso. prof. philosophy, dean of students Jamestown (N.D.) Coll., 1975—. Moderator, Rock River Presbytery, Synod of Ill., 1957, Peoria Presbytery, Synod of Ill., 1964. Served with cav. AUS, 1942-45. Decorated Bronze Star medal. Mem. Omaha Presbytery Synod of Lakes and Prairies, Sigma Phi Omega. Home: Jamestown Coll Jamestown ND 58401

ANDERSON, WILLIAM SUMMERS, bus. machines co. exec.; b. Hankow, China, Mar. 29, 1919; s. William G. and Mabel (Johnston) A.; came to U.S., 1972; Brit. citizen; m. Janice Elizabeth Robb, Oct. 8, 1947; children—Stephanie Gay, Irene Mabel, Hope Marian; student pub. schs. and Thomas Hanbury Sch., Shanghai, China. Internal auditor Hong Kong & Shanghai Hotels, Ltd., 1938-39; auditor Linstead & Davis, 1940-41; with Nat. Cash Register Co.'s Brit. Orgn., 1945; mgr. NCR Hong Kong, 1946-59; v.p. Far East, chmn. NCR Japan, 1959-72; pres., dir. NCR Corp., Dayton, Ohio, 1972, chief exec. officer, 1973, pres., chmn. bd., 1974-76, chmn. bd., 1976—; dir. R.J. Reynolds Corp.; vice chmn. Adv. Council on Japan-U.S. Econ. Relations; trustee Com. for Econ. Devel.; mem. internat. council Morgan Guaranty Trust Co.; dir. Nat. Council for U.S.-China Trade. Active, Sister Cities Internat. Conf. Bd.; chmn. Nat. Bd. of Smithsonian Assos.; adv. Council, Stanford Research Inst. Council; active United Negro Coll. Fund; bd. dirs. Far East-Am. Council Commerce and Industry, Inc., Internat. Exec. Service Corps, Japan Soc., Inc.; trustee Dayton Performing Arts Fund, Eisenhower Exchange Fellowships, Inc., Hundred Club. Mem. Assn. Internat. Accountants, Australian Soc. Accountants, Fgn. Policy Assn., Nat. Planning Assn. Clubs: Carmel (Calif.) Valley Golf and Country, Hong Kong Am., Hong Kong, Hong Kong Jockey; Links Club (N.Y.C.), Met. (Chgo.); Dayton Racquet, Moraine Country (Dayton); 300 Golf Club (Japan); Tokyo Am. Tokyo. Home: 895 W Rahn Rd Dayton OH 45429 Office: NCR Corp World Hdqrs Dayton OH 45429

ANDES, JOHN WILBUR, med. assn. exec.; b. Knoxville, Tenn., July 18, 1928; s. John Wilbur and Irene Dawkins (Garrett) A.; A.B., Princeton, 1948; m. Patricia Jane Guy, Nov. 20, 1954; children—Alan Patrick, Jane Alison. Claims mgr. Blue Cross-Blue Shield of Fla., Jacksonville, 1948-50, dir. profl. relations, 1952-57; asst. exec. sec. Am. Soc. Anesthesiologists, Park Ridge, Ill., 1957-58, exec. sec., 1958—. Served with USNR, 1950-52. Mem. Am. Assn. Med. Soc. Execs., Am. Soc. Assn. Execs., Profl. Conv. Mgmt. Assn., Park Ridge C. of C. Club: Princeton (Chgo.). Home: 1810 Walnut St Park Ridge IL 60068 Office: 515 Busse Hwy Park Ridge IL 60068

ANDONIAN, DAVID AARON, architect; b. Akron, Ohio, Aug. 19, 1924; s. Khoran Haig and Violet Mildred (Koonce) A.; B.Arch., U. Notre Dame, 1950; m. Lucille Bedrosian, Aug. 11, 1946; children—Charise Anita, Laura Leah, Karen Lee. Architect, Outcalt-Guenther Architects, Cleveland, 1950-51; asso. mem. Ward & Conrad, Cleve., 1951-60; partner Andonian & Ruzsa, architects, Cleve., 1960-69; prin. Andonian & Assos., architects, Cleve., 1969-76, David A. Andonian Architects, Inc., 1976—. Treas., mem. exec. com. A.G.B.U. Inc. of Am. Served with USNR, 1943-46. Mem. AIA, Guild for Religious Architecture, Nat. Council Archtl. Registration Bds. Republican. Mem. Armenian Apostolic Ch. Club: Cleveland Athletic. Prin. works include Div. Luth. Ch., Parma Heights, Armenian Apostolic Ch., Richmond Heights, Ohio, United Artist Broadcasting TV Studio, Parma, Ohio, La Place Shopping Bazaar, Beachwood, Ohio, main office Park View Fed. Savs. and Loan. Co., Cleve., Normandy III Sr. Citizens Apts., Rocky River, Ohio, Beach House Condominiums, Rock River, Mak Office Bldg., Brooklyn, Ohio. Home: 3326 Glencairn Rd Shaker Heights OH 44122 Office: Suite 4A Park Centre W 1701 E 12th St Cleveland OH 44114

ANDORFER, DONALD EDWIN, advt. co. artist; b. Clinton, Ia., Jan. 1, 1912; s. Arthur and Mildred Susan (Cram) A.; student Wis. State Coll., 1930-32, Art Inst. Chgo., 1946-47; m. Loretta Adeline Kuhnke, Dec. 24, 1935; children—Donald, Sylvia (Mrs. Gerry Schwindt), Joseph, Virginia (dec.). Free lance artist, Grand Rapids, Mich., 1936-50; artist So. States Coop., Richmond, Va., 1950-60; free lance artist, illustrator, South Bend, Ind., 1960-63; artist Fletcher & Assos., Advt. Inc., St. Joseph, Mo., 1963—; artist in residence North Mo. area Mo. State Council of Arts; represented in permanent collection at Mo. State Hist. Soc.; pvt. instr. in art; propr. Sundance Art Gallery, Denver. Mem. Grand Central Galleries, N.Y.C., Rural Am. Art Gallery, St. Joseph, Mo. Bd. dirs. Albrecht Gallery, 1966-69. Recipient numerous ribbons and trophies in art exhbns. Mem. Am. Artist Profl. League of N.Y., Soc. N. Am. Artists, Greater Kansas City Art Assn., Clinton (Mo.) Art Assn. Methodist (ofcl. bd. 1964-67). Clubs: Art Directors (Chgo.); Art Directors (Kansas City, Mo.). Illustrator: Nation of Might, 1942. Home: Rural Route 3 St Joseph MO 64505

ANDREAS, BRUCE FREDERICK, pathologist; b. Cleve., May 10, 1925; s. Frederick William and Edna Louise (Buehler) A.; A.B., Heidelberg Coll., 1949; M.D., Ohio State U., 1953; m. Jean Bobbitt, Aug. 28, 1954; children—Karen, Frederick, Patricia, Jonathan; m. 2d, Marie Greder Nimietz, July 4, 1976. Intern, Miami Valley Hosp., Dayton, Ohio, 1953-54, resident in pathology, 1954-58; pathologist, dir. lab., Geauga Community Hosp., Chardon, Ohio, 1959—, chief of staff, 1969-70; pres. Geauga Lab. Services, Inc.; regional dir. Ohio Peer Rev. Orgn., Inc. Charter mem., advisory com. Met. Health Planning Corp. N.E. Ohio, 1967—, trustee, 1967-76; del. Am. Cancer Soc., 1966-68; v.p. Geauga County Bd. Health, 1966-69. Served with U.S. Army, 1943-46. Decorated Bronze Star with two oak leaf clusters. Diplomate Am. Bd. Pathology. Fellow Coll. Am. Pathologists, Am. Soc. Clin. Pathologists; mem. AMA, Ohio Soc. Pathologists, Ohio State Med. Assn. (del.), Geauga County Med. Soc., Cleve. Acad. Medicine. Home: 11296 Brookside Rd Chardon OH 44060 Office: Geauga Community Hosp Box 249 Chardon OH 44024

ANDREAS, JOHN CARLTON, elec. products co. exec.; b. Bisbee, Ariz., Feb. 6, 1918; s. Sylvester G. and Jessie (Armstrong) A.; B.S., U. Ariz., 1940; postgrad. U. Pitts., 1941, Marquette U., 1950; m. Ruth E. Freeman, Oct. 2, 1938; children—Paula (Mrs. Thomas Kiske), John O. Engr., Westinghouse Co., Pitts., 1940-42; sr. engr. U.S. Navy Dept., Washington, 1942-45; chief elec. engr. Louis Allis Co., Milw., 1945-59; dir. engring., Curtiss-Wright-Utica div. Detroit, 1960-62; v.p. engring. Century Electric div. Gould, Inc., St. Louis, 1962—, also dir. Mem. industry sector adv. com. U.S. Dept. Commerce/U.S. Nat. Com. Internat. Standards. Registered profl. engr., Wis. Mem. Nat. Elec. Mfgrs. Assn. (bd. govs., chmn. indsl. equipment div., bd. dirs. Water Systems Council), IEEE, ASTM. Mason (32 deg. Shriner, K.T.). Home: 2036 Firethorn Dr St Louis MO 63131 Office: 1831 Chestnut St St Louis MO 63166

ANDREASEN, GEORGE FREDRICK, dentist, educator; b. Fremont, Nebr., Feb. 16, 1934; s. George T. and Laura Mae (Hynek) A.; B.S. (Regents scholar), U. Nebr., 1959, D.D.S., 1959, M.S. (NIH fellow), 1963; m. Nancy Coover, June 13, 1959; children—Susan, Robin. Research fellow Worcester Coll., Oxford, Eng., 1960-61; asst. prof. orthodontics U. Iowa Coll. Dentistry, Iowa City, 1963-67, asso. prof., acting head dept. orthodontics, 1967, asso. prof., head dept., 1968, prof., head dept. orthodontics, 1968—; practice dentistry, Iowa City, 1963—. Cons. to various dental corps. on dental materials. Named hon. adm. Nebr. Navy, 1972; U. Nebr. Alumnus Master, 1974. Fellow Am. Coll. Dentists, Royal Soc. Health (Eng.); mem. Am. Assn. Orthodontists (chmn. sci. com. 1971-72, nat. com. on research 1976-79), Iowa Orthodontic Soc. (pres. 1972-73), Am., Iowa dental assns., Univ. Dist. Dental Assn., Iowa Alumni Assn. (life), U. Iowa Med. Center (life), Am. Oxonion, Phalanx Blue Print Key, Sigma Xi, Pi Tau Sigma. Omicron Kappa Upsilon, Delta Tau Delta, Xi Psi Phi. Club: Athletic (Iowa City). Contbr. articles to profl. jours. Patentee in field. Home: 5 Lakeview Dr Rural Route 6 Iowa City IA 52240

ANDRES, LEO EDWARD, veterinarian; b. Guilford, Ind., Aug. 28, 1908; s. John A. and Cecilia L. (Merkl) A.; D.V.M., Ohio State U., 1932; m. Rita Cotter, Aug. 3, 1942 (dec. 1963); m. 2d, Bernice C. Hagan Troup, Nov. 13, 1965; 1 son, Richard; step-children—Phillis Knochel, Patricia Alberts. Practice vet. medicine, Tipton, Ind., 1932-33, Remington, Ind., 1934—, Kentland, Ind., 1965—. Mem. Am., Ind. (dir.), Northwest Ind. (past sec., past pres.) vet. med. assns., Kentland C. of C., Remington Service Club, Alpha Psi. Roman Catholic. Order of Foresters. Address: Box 291 Remington IN 47977

ANDRESS, SAMUEL COE, lawyer; b. Hayesville, Ohio, June 27, 1906; s. Upton Samuel and Millicent Alma (Coe) A.; A.B., Wittenberg U., 1925; LL.B., U. Cin., 1928. Admitted to Ohio bar, 1928, since practiced in Akron; sr. partner firm Roetzel & Andress. Dir. Akron Equipment Co., Jay-Em Corp., Hardware & Supply Co., Mac Allied Tools Corp. Trustee Akron Beacon Jour. Charity Fund, Akron Community Trusts, Children's Zoo. Served to lt. USNR, 1942-45. Mem. Am., Ohio, Akron bar assns., Akron C. of C. (past pres.), Order of Coif, Lambda Chi Alpha, Delta Sigma Rho, Phi Alpha Delta. Episcopalian. Rotarian. Clubs: City (pres. 1969), University, Portage, Sharon. Home: 161 E Fairlawn Blvd Akron OH 44313 Office: 1 Cascade Plaza Akron OH 44308

ANDREWS, CLARENCE ADELBERT, educator; b. Waterloo, Iowa, Oct. 24, 1912; s. Harry Leon and June Jennie (Jones) A.; student Sheldon Jr. Coll.; B.A., U. Iowa, 1954, M.A., 1960, Ph.D., 1963; m. Ollie Mae Easley, June 12, 1937; children—Linda (Mrs. Richard Thompson), Terry (Mrs. Leonardo Lasansky), Steven Randall. Mem. War Price and Rationing Bd., Sheldon, Iowa, 1941-42; exec. sec. Sheldon C. of C., 1941-42; owner House of Andrews, Sheldon, 1942-49; asst. prof. Colo. State U., Fort Collins, Colo., 1960-61; instr. U. Iowa, Iowa City, 1961-63, asst. prof., 1963-66, asso. prof., 1967-69, vis. prof. journalism, 1976—; prof. lang., lit. Mich. Tech. U., Houghton, 1971-75; adj. prof. Am. thought and lang. Mich. State U., East Lansing, 1975—. Vis. prof. Naval Ordnance Test Sta., China Lake, Calif., 1959; cons. Measurement Research Center, 1960. Mem. Mich. Council for Humanities, 1974-76. Bd. dirs. N.W. Iowa Def. Bonds Sales, 1942. Served with USAAF, 1944-46. Grantee, NDEA, 1968, NSF, 1964, 66, Ednl. Profl. Devel. Act, 1969, Mich. Tech. U., 1973. Mem. Soc. for Study Midwest Lit., Nat. Council Tchrs. English, Coll. Conf. Composition and Communications, Am. Bus. Communicators, Midwest Modern Lang. Assn., Phi Beta Kappa, Kappa Tau Alpha. Author: Technical and Scientific Writing, 1964; Writing, 1972; A Literary History of Iowa, 1972; Technical and Business Writing, 1974; Growing Up in Iowa, 1977. Editor Personnel Adminstr., 1960-61. Home: 108 Pearl St Iowa City IA 52240

ANDREWS, ERNEST EUGENE, psychotherapist; b. Holland, Mich., July 12, 1932; s. Clair Bernon and Helen Marie (Nemeth) A.; A.B., U. Mich., 1954, M.S.W., 1956; m. Janet Ruth Grover, June 18, 1955; children—Kathryn Mary, David Edward. Asst. dir. Child Guidance Clinic, Saginaw Mich., 1960-65; asst. prof. child devel. and family life Purdue U., Lafayette, Ind., 1965-70; pvt. practice psychotherapy, Lafayette, 1965-70; asso. prof. social work Ohio State U., Columbus, 1970-71, vis. asso. prof., 1971—; founder, dir. Family Inst., Cin., 1971—; founder Midwest Family Found., Cin., 1977—; adj. asst. clin. prof. psychology and psychiatry U. Cin., 1972—; cons. in field. Served with USPHS, 1956-58. Fellow Am. Group Psychotherapy Assn. (certificate of merit 1973), Am. Orthopsychiat. Assn.; mem. Royal Soc. Medicine (affiliate) (London). Author: The Emotionally Disturbed Family, 1974. Contbr. articles to profl. publs. Office: Family Inst 2600 Euclid Ave Cincinnati OH 45219

ANDREWS, HARRY LUBOMIR, mktg. analyst; b. Bklyn., Apr. 29, 1924; s. Harry and Natalia (Seniw) A.; B.Diplomacy, Latin Am. Inst., 1949; mortuary sci., Wayne State U., 1959; m. Eleanor J. Royal, Sept. 17, 1950; children—Michael T., Natalie A., Anne R., Steven E. Market research analyst Esso div. Standard Oil Co., N.Y.C., 1946-47, market research analyst Clark Equipment Co., Battle Creek, 1950-57; funeral dir. Royal Funeral Home, Battle Creek, Mich., 1957-64; with Marathon Electric Co., Wausau, Wis., 1964-67; market research analyst Drott Mfg. Co., Wausau, 1967—. Pres., Home Owners Assn., Battle Creek, 1955-57. Served with USNR, 1943-46. Mem. Am. Mktg. Soc. Republican. Mason (Shriner). Home: 1002 Stark Wausau WI 54401 Office: PO Box 1087 Wausau WI 54401

ANDREWS, JACK ROBERT, data processing co. exec.; b. Berwyn, Ill., Jan. 18, 1950; s. Jack Andrew and Margaret (DeLise) A.; student pub. schs. West Chicago, Ill.; m. Dianne Mary Rogers, June 7, 1969; children—Jacqui Lynette, Craig Robert. Mgr. data processing Aurora Metal Co. (Ill.), 1969-70, AAR Corp., Elk Grove, Ill., 1970-72; mgr. systems and programming George Ball Co., West Chicago, 1972-74; mgr. tech. services DuPage County, Wheaton, Ill., 1974-76; partner, exec. v.p. Data Systems Specialists, Inc., Elgin, Ill., 1976—, also dir.; pres., dir. Data Systems Ideas, 1977—; instr. Elgin Community Coll., Coll. DuPage, Glen Ellyn. Mem. DuPage County Republican Precinct Com. Mem. Nat. Assn. System 3 Users (past pres.), Data Processing Mgmt. Assn. (past dir.). Roman Catholic. Home: 2N551 Bernice Ave Glen Ellyn IL 60137 Office: 1078 Larkin Ave Elgin IL 60120

ANDREWS, JAMES LEWIS, educator, oral surgeon; b. Canton, Ohio, June 7, 1929; s. Lloyd F. and Gertrude (Griggs) A.; D.D.S. cum laude, Ohio State U., 1953; postgrad. Northwestern U., 1961-62; m. Joanne Mary Jenkins, Aug. 2, 1952; children—Susan L., Ellen J., David L. Intern oral surgery Univ. Hosps., Columbus, Ohio, 1953-54; commd. 1st lt. U.S. Army, 1954, advanced through grades to col. 1971; stationed Ft. Knox, Ky., 1954-57; oral surgeon U.S. Army Hosp., Berlin, Germany, 1958-61; resident oral surgeon Letterman Gen. Hosp., San Francisco, 1962-64, asst. chief oral surgery, 1965-66, chief oral surgery, 1966-68; chief dental services 106th Gen. Hosp., 1968-70; chief clinician dental clinic Camp Zama, Japan, 1970-71; oral surgeon Darnall Army Hosp., Ft. Hood, Tex., 1971-74, ret.; prof., chmn. dept. oral surgery U. Mo. Sch. Dentistry, 1974—. Diplomate Am. Bd. Oral Surgery. Fellow Am. Coll. Dentists; mem. Am. Soc. Oral Surgeons, Am. Acad. Oral Pathology, Am. Dental Assn., Omicron Kappa Upsilon. Mason. Contbr. articles to profl. jours. Address: UMKC Sch Dentistry 650 E 25th St Kansas City MO 64108

ANDREWS, LARRY HOWARD, data processing co. exec.; b. St. Peter, Minn., Mar. 28, 1942; s. Howard L. and Anna Mae (Bartak) A.; B.A., Doane Coll., 1965; m. Virginia Faye Rannie, Aug. 4, 1962; children—Kurt, Mark. Instr. math. Dist. 66 Schs., Omaha, 1965-66; computer systems analyst and programmer Western Electric Co., Omaha, 1966-69; data processing mgr. UNICO, Bellevue, Nebr., 1969-70; pres. ALR Computer Services, Omaha, 1970—; treas., dir. K-Kal Products Inc., 1976—. Mem. Assn. Computer Machinery, Data Processing Mgrs. Assn. Republican. Methodist. Clubs: Jaycees, Sertoma. Home: 8611 C St Omaha NE 68124 Office: 10701 Mockingbird Dr Omaha NE 68127

ANDREWS, MARK, farmer, congressman; b. Fargo, N.D., May 19, 1926; s. Mark and Lillian (Hoyler) A.; B.S., N.D. State U., 1949; m. Mary Willming, June 28, 1949; children—Mark III, Sarah Jane, Karen Louise. Farmer, Mapleton, N.D., 1949—; exec. com. Garrison Diversion Conservancy Dist., adminstrn. irrigation from Garrison Dam, 1955—; mem. 88th-92d Congresses from 1st. Dist. N.D., 93d-95th Congresses, at-large N.D.; mem. Congl. Environ. Study Conf.; ofcl. del. FAO Conf., Rome, 1975; founding mem. Congl. Rural Caucus. Mem. Rep. Nat. Com. for N.D.; Rep. nominee for gov. N.D., 1962. Dir. Cass County chpt. ARC. Named hon. Am. farmer Future Farmers Am., 1976. Mem. Rep. Nat. Farm Council, Young Rep. Nat. Fedn. (past vice chmn.), N.D. Young Republicans (past chmn.), Nat. Reclamation Assn. (chmn. land limitations com.), Farm Bur., Am. Legion, N.D. Stockmen's Assn., N.D. Crop Improvement Assn. (pres.) Greater N.D. Assn., Northwest Farm Mgrs., N.D. Water Users Assn. Episcopalian. Home: Mapleton ND 58059 Office: House Office Bldg Washington DC 20515

ANDREWS, MITCHEL MARTIN, JR., hosp. exec.; b. Detroit, Mar. 14, 1940; s. Mitchel Martin and Irene Louise (Purser) A.; B.A., Adrian Coll., 1962; postgrad. Mich. State U., 1966; m. Mary Louise Simpson, Aug. 23, 1969; children—Robert Mitchell, Brian Edward, Michelle Lynne. Tchr., Mackinaw City (Mich.) High Sch., 1962-63; v.p. No. Orchards Co., Cheboygan, Mich., 1964-74; dir. adminstrv. services Community Meml. Hosp., Cheboygan, 1975—; dir. Cheboygan State Bank, 1971—. Chmn. Cheboygan County Easter Seals Campaign, 1975. Bd. dirs. Community Meml. Hosp., Cheboygan, Mich., 1971-73, treas., 1973—. Served with AUS, 1963-64. Mem. Cheboygan Jr. C. of C. (sec. 1968), Alpha Tau Omega. Kiwanian (dir. 1972—, v.p. 1974-75, pres. 1976-77). Home: 603 Bay View Dr Cheboygan MI 49721 Office: 748 S Main St Cheboygan MI 49721

ANDREWS, MYRON FLOYD, veterinarian, educator; b. Huron, S.D., Dec. 8, 1924; s. Myron Thompson and Elsie Adeline (Dobratz) A.; student Utah State Agrl. Coll., 1946-48; A.B. in Biol. Scis., Stanford, 1950; D.V.M., U. Calif. at Davis, 1958; m. Avon Anderson, Sept. 15, 1948; children—Laurie, Rebecca. Fishery research biologist U.S. Fish and Wildlife Service, Annapolis, Md., 1950-51; sr. technician dept. surgery U. Calif. at Los Angeles Sch. Medicine, 1951-54; asst. prof. dept. vet. sci., N.D. State U., Fargo, 1958-60, 61-64, prof., chmn. dept. vet. sci., 1964—; dir. large animal clin. research sect. Norwich (N.Y.) Pharmacal Co., 1960-61, research cons., 1961, 62; research cons. Diamond Labs., Des Moines, 1963. Served with USNR, 1943-46. Mem. Am. Vet. Med. Assn., Am. Assn. Vet. Parasitologists, Wildlife Disease Assn., Sigma Xi. Mormon (pres. Dakota dist. 1965-70). Home: 2914 Edgemont St Fargo ND 58102

ANDREWS, ROGER DAVIS, judge; b. Lima, Ohio, Sept. 21, 1914; s. Clarence M. and Helen (Davis) A.; student Bluffton Coll., 1939-41; J.D., Ohio No. U., 1949; m. Josephine A. McKinnon, Dec. 31, 1960; children—David M., Karen Sue. Admitted to Ohio bar, 1949; practiced in Lima, 1949-61; law dir. City Lima, 1953-57, 58-61; judge Lima Municipal Ct., 1962-77, presiding judge, 1977—. Served to capt. AUS, 1941-45, 51-53. Decorated Bronze Star medal; recipient Traffic Ct. award Am. Bar Assn., 1967. Mem. Am., Ohio State bar assns., Ohio Municipal Attys. Assn. (pres. 1960), Ohio Municipal Judges Assn. (v.p. 1971), Am. Legion, V.F.W., S.A.R. Methodist. Kiwanian (local pres. 1960), Elk, Eagle. Home: 2200 High St Lima OH 45805 Office: PO Box 1093 Lima OH 45802

ANDREWS, THEODORE FRANCIS, ednl. adminstr.; b. Atchison, Kans., Aug. 17, 1917; s. Andrew M. and Mary E. (Ennis) A.; A.B., Emporia (Kans.) State Coll., 1940; M.S., U. Ia., 1942; Ph.D., Ohio State U., 1948; m. Mae Bryant, June 25, 1936 (div. Apr. 1969); children—Kenneth J., Glen K., Dwight B., Dwayne D.; m. 2d, Betty Jeanette Schaffer, Sept. 13, 1969. Asst. prof. biology Emporia State Coll., 1948-51, asso. prof., 1952-55, prof., 1956-57, prof., head dept. biology, 1957-63; cons. tchr. preparation Biol. Scis. Curriculum Study, Boulder, Colo., 1964-65; Am. Petroleum Inst. fellow F.T. Stone Inst. Hydrobiology, Ohio State U., 1946-48; asso. dir. Com. Undergrad. Edn. Biol. Sci., Washington, 1965-66; prof. biology George Washington U., 1965-66; dir. sci. Ednl. Research Council Am., Cleve., 1966-69; adj. prof. biology Ohio State U., 1966-69; dean Coll. Environmental and Applied Scis., Govs. State U., Park Forest South, Ill., 1969—, acting v.p. acad. affairs, 1976-77. Dir. NSF Academic Year In-Service and Summer Insts., 1958-64, dir. research participation programs for high sch. tchrs. and summer sci. tng. programs for high sch. students, 1956-64; cons. Harvard U. Nigerian Project, 1964, NSF, AID India Conf., 1966; numerous cons. and leadership positions; field reader Bur. Research, U.S. Office Edn., 1966-72. Served with USNR, 1943-46. Mem. Kans. Acad. Sci. (pres. 1958-60), Kans. Ornithological Soc. (pres. 1961), Nat. Assn. Biology Tchrs. (pres. 1964), Nat. Assn. Sci. Tchrs., NEA, Southwestern Assn. Naturalists (pres. 1962), AAAS, Am. Inst. Biol. Scis. (chmn. edn. com. 1975—), Ecological Soc. Am., Am. Assn. U. Adminstrs., Am. Assn. Colls. and Univs. (center asso. Center Planned Change 1976—), Alpha Kappa Lambda (pres. 1951-60), others. Contbr. to profl. publs. in field. Home: 809 Pin Oak Lane Park Forest South IL 60466

ANDREWS, THOMAS BROWN, V, utility exec.; b. Evanston, Ill., Sept. 21, 1933; s. Thomas and Elsie (Palmer) A.; B.F.A., Ohio U., 1955; postgrad. Ind. U., 1955-56; children—Thomas Brown VI, Ann Elizabeth. Pres. Andrews, Inc., Dayton, Ohio; dir. Western Savs. Assn., Dayton; partner Security Investments, Dayton, 1975—. Mem. Dayton City Commn., 1969-74; pres. Miami Valley Regional Transit Authority, 1971-75. Chmn. Dayton Pastoral Counseling Center, 1965-67. Served to lt. USNR, 1957-59. Named Young Man of Year, Dayton Jaycees, 1967. Episcopalian (vestryman 1969-71). Home: 436 Acorn Dr Dayton OH 45419 Office: 5 Troy St Dayton OH 45404

ANGELINE, JOHN FREDERICK, food co. exec.; b. Somerville, Mass., Sept. 29, 1929; s. Jack L. and Edith (Ciavatti) A.; B.S., Northeastern U., 1952, M.B.A., 1963; m. Doris Helen L'Heureux, Nov. 9, 1957; children—Karen E., Rachel A., Andrea M. Mgmt. cons. Arthur D. Little Inc., Cambridge, Mass., 1952-77; v.p. research and devel. grocery products Quaker Oats Co., Barrington, Ill. Mem. various town coms. and commns. Topsfield, Mass., 1963-76. Served with U.S. Army, 1954-62. Mem. Internat. Inst. Food Technologists, Phi Tau Sigma. Republican. Patentee prodn. odorless carbon. Contbr. articles to profl. jours. Home: 496 Thomas Dr North Barrington IL 60010 Office: 617 Main St W Barrington IL 60010

ANGERMAN, ROBERT BRYON, dentist; b. Gary, Ind., Jan. 18, 1938; s. Robert Ora and Lauretta Illa (Meyer) A.; D.D.S., Ind. U., 1968; m. Sarah Elizabeth Ingram, Sept. 11, 1965; children—Robert Bryon, Devin Elizabeth. Individual practice dentistry, Merrillville, Ind., 1969—; owner, pres. Angerman Dental Corp., 1968—; lectr., Pitts. Dental Sch., 1972; cons. Implants Internat., N.Y.C., 1971—; lectr. throughout U.S., Africa, S.Am. Served with USNR, 1957-61. Recipient numerous profl. awards. Mem. Am. Dental Assn., Am. Acad. Gen. Dentistry (chpt. pres. 1972), Psi Omega. Contbr. articles to profl. publs. Home: 13921 80th Pl Dyer IN 46311 Office: 1000 E 80th St Merrillville IN 46410

ANGINO, ERNEST EDWARD, educator; b. Winsted, Conn., Feb. 16, 1932; s. Alfred and Filomena Mabel (Serluco) A.; B.S., Lehigh U., 1954; M.S., U. Kan., 1958, Ph.D., 1961; m. Margaret Lachat, June 26, 1954; children—Cheryl Ann, Kimberly Ann. Geophysicist Western Geophys. Co., 1954; instr. U. Kans., 1961-62; asst. prof. dept. oceanography Tex. A. and M. U., College Station, 1962-65; with State Geol. Survey Kans., 1965-72; chief geochemistry sect., 1965-70, asso. dir., 1970-72; prof., chmn. dept. geology U. Kans., Lawrence, 1972—. Cons. Dow Chem. Co., Bur. Comml. Fisheries, Envicon, AEC, Midwest Research Inst., 1972—; dir. Oceanography Internat. Corp., 1969-72; mem. U.S. Nat. Com. Geochemistry, 1971-77. Served with AUS, 1955-57. Angino Buttress, Antarctica, named in his honor; recipient Antarctic Service medal Dept. Def., 1969. NSF summer fellow Oak Ridge Nat. Lab., 1963. Mem. Am. Chem. Soc., Am. Assn. Petroleum Geologists, Geol. Soc. Am., Kans. Geol. Soc., Geochem. Soc. (sec. 1970-76), Am. Profl. Geologists Assn., Soc. Econ. Paleontology and Mineralogy, Soc. Environ. Geochemistry and Health (councilor 1972-75). Author: (with G.K. Billings) Atomic Absorption Spectrometry in Geology, 1967, 2d edit., 1972. Editor: (with G.K. Billings) Geochemistry of Subsurface Brines, 1969; (with R. Hardy) Proceedings Third Forum Geology of Industrial Minerals, 1967. Home: 1215 W 27th St Lawrence KS 66044

ANGLE, CAROL REMMER, physician, educator; b. West Sayville, N.Y., Dec. 20, 1927; d. Henry J. and Anna Sophia (Hinck) Remmer; B.A., Wellesley Coll., 1947; M.D., Cornell U., 1951; m. William Dodge Angle, July 19, 1952; children—Marcia, John, Monica. Intern, N.Y. Hosp., N.Y.C., 1951-52, resident in pediatrics, 1952-53; resident in pediatrics U. Nebr. Hosp., 1953-54, instr. pediatrics U. Nebr., Omaha, 1954-67, asst. prof., 1967-68, asso. prof., 1968-71, prof., 1971—; dir. med. edn. Children's Meml. Hosp., Omaha, 1954-67; asst. prof. pediatrics Creighton U., Omaha, 1957-67; dir. Nat. Founds. Birth Defects Treatment Center, Omaha, 1974—; dir. pediatric renal clinic U. Nebr. Med. Center, 1966—; mem. Nebr. Renal Disease Commn., 1972—; mem. tech. advisory com. on over-the-counter drugs FDA, 1973—. Mem. Am. Assn. Poison Control Centers (pres. 1975-76, exec. com. 1976-78), Am. Fedn. Clin. Research, Midwest Soc. Pediatric Research, Am. Acad. Pediatrics, Soc. Pediatric Nephrology, Am. Pediatric Soc. Asso. editor Clin. Toxicology, 1969—; contbr. articles in field to profl. jours. Office: Univ Nebraska Medical School 42d and Dewey Aves Omaha NE 68105

ANGLE, CHESLEY WARD, nuclear power engr.; b. Miles City, Mont., July 1, 1929; s. Christopher Jacob and Eleanor (Broadus) A.; B.S., U. Wyo., 1961, M.S., 1963; m. Mary Jane Richards, Nov. 25, 1957; children—Diana Lynn, Kristie Kay, Darlene Jennifer, Bradley Ward, Karen Ann. Instr. engring. U. Wyo., Laramie, 1961-63; devel. engr. Gen. Electric Co., Richland, Wash., 1963-65; sr. devel. engr. Battelle NorthWest Labs., Richland, Wash., 1965-70; mgr. and process engr., nucler fuel procurement project Dairyland Power Co., LaCrosse, Wis., 1970—. Bd. dirs. Coulee Regional Festival Arts, 1972, 73, 75, 76. Served with USAF, 1951-55. Recipient Excellence award Battelle NW Labs., 1967. Registered profl. engr., Wis. Mem. ASME (sec. chpt. 1974, chmn. 1976-77, regional exec. com.), Am. Nuclear Soc., Nat. Soc. Profl. Engrs., ASTM. Republican. Congregationalist. Clubs: Shriners, Masons, Kiwanis (dir. 1973-77; pres. elect 1977). Contbr. articles to profl. jours. Home: 2839 Brook Ct LaCrosse WI 54601 Office: LaCrosse Boiling Water Reactor Genoa WI 54632

ANGST, JOHN EDWARD, transp. co. exec.; b. Buhl, Minn., Feb. 21, 1919; s. Robert A. and Virginia (de Haas) A.; A.B., Princeton, 1940; grad. Advanced Mgmt. Program, Harvard, 1956; m. Louise Woodruff, Aug. 14, 1945; children—Robert Woodruff, Carlton Clough, Louise. With Oglebay, Norton & Co., Cleve., 1940-41; v.p. Am. Car & Foundry div. ACF Industries, Inc., Chgo., 1945-61; gen. mgr. freight car div. Gen. Am. Transp. Corp., Chgo., 1961-63, v.p., 1963-64, group v.p., dir., 1964-68; v.p. Mo. Pacific R.R. Co., St. Louis, 1968—; chmn. bd. Am. Refrigeration Transit Co., Mo. Improvement Co.; dir. Trailer Train Co., Am. Rail Box Car Co., M-I R.R. Co., Fruit Growers Express Co., A.R.T. Equipment Corp. Trustee Lake Forest Acad., 1953. Served to maj. F.A., AUS, 1941-45. Mem. Newcomen Soc., ASME. Clubs: Union League, Glen View, Chicago (Chgo.); Cloud (N.Y.C.); Bohemian (San Francisco); St. Louis, Old Warson Country, Noonday, Wings St. Albans (St. Louis). Home: 1 Bridle Creek Rd St Louis MO 63124 Office: 210 N 13th St St Louis MO 63103

ANGUS, ROBERT DALE, govt. ofcl.; b. American Falls, Idaho, Oct. 2, 1930; s. Stephen Robert and Afton (Parker) A.; B.S., U. Calif. at Davis, 1954, D.V.M., 1956; M.P.H., U. Minn., 1967, postgrad., 1967-70; m. Vivien June Wheeler, May 10, 1961; children—Stephen Wade, Jyll, Scot Alan, Ryan Dee. Instr. clinics, surgery Colo. State U., Fort Collins, 1956-57; practice vet. medicine, Orland, Calif., 1957; engaged in state-fed. animal disease control activities, 1957-65; vet. med. officer U.S. Dept. Agr., Boise, Ida., also, St. Paul, 1965-70; vet. med. officer Vet. Services Lab., Nat. Animal Disease Center, Ames, Iowa, 1970—. Mem. Phi Zeta. Mem. Ch. of Jesus Christ of Latter-day Saints (various priesthood positions 1950—). Home: 3108 Northwood Dr Ames IA 50010 Office: Vet Services Lab APHIS Box 70 Ames IA 50010

ANHALT, LEONARD P., cons. engr.; b. Sheboygan, Wis., Feb. 21, 1927; s. Leonard F. and Anna M. (Schnettler) A.; B.S., Marquette U., 1951; m. Jane Page, Sept. 20, 1952; children—David, Kathy, Sarah, Tony. With Graef, Anhalt & Schloemer & Assos., Inc., Milw., 1961—, pres., 1968—. Served with AUS, 1945-46. Mem. Nat. Soc. Profl. Engrs., ASCE, Am. Concrete Inst., Wis. Soc. Profl. Engrs. Home: N76 W 22194 Chestnut Hill Rd Sussex WI 53089 Office: 6415 W Capitol Dr Milwaukee WI 53216

ANICHINI, MARIO, painter; b. Lucca, Italy, Sept. 26, 1941; s. Tarcisio Socrate and Clementina (Paladini) A.; came to U.S., 1955, naturalized, 1963; student pub. schs., Chgo.; m. Mary Dolores Bernardini, Nov. 26, 1961; children—Mary Ellen, Mario Peter. One-man show: Kenosha (Wis.) Pub. Mus., 1975; represented in permanent collections: Kenosha Pub. Museum, Salem (Wis.) Consol. Grade Sch., 1st Nat. Bank of Antioch (Ill.); numerous pvt. collections; paintings include: The Stone Age, 1973, Evolution, 1973, Flowering Pear Tree, 1975, Dimensional Illusion, 1972, Agony and Ecstasy, 1976, Life, 1977, Deep in the Valley, 1977, Spirit of St. Louis, 1978, also portraits. Mem. Smithsonian Inst., Chgo. Art Inst. Address: Route 4 PO Box 393C Antioch IL 60002

ANJARD, RONALD PAUL, materials specialist; b. Chgo., July 31, 1935; s. Auguste L. and Florence M. (Byrne) A.; B.S., Carnegie Mellon U., 1957; M.S., Purdue U., 1968; Asso. Sci., Ind. U., 1973; postgrad. Butler U., 1962-63, Ind. U. Law Sch., 1968-69, Purdue U., 1970-74, U. Wis., 1974—, Ivy Tech., 1975, La. State U., 1977-78; D.D. (hon.), Crown of Life Fellowship, 1973; Ph.R.D., P.A.D. (hon.), Christian Community Coll., 1974; children—Ronald P., Michael P., Michele M., John R. Engr., U.S. Steel Corp., Braddock, Pa., 1956-57; metall. engr. Crucible Steel Co., Pitts., 1957-58; process engr. Raytheon Mfg. Co., Newton, Mass., 1958-59; sr. engr. Delco Electronics, Kokomo, Ind., 1959—; instr. Ball State U., 1970-71, 75—, Kokomo Apprentice Program, 1971--; importer Anjard Imports, 1970—; free-lance writer, 1973—. Am., instl. rep., treas. Cub Pack, program chmn. Scout-A-Rama, chmn. Capital Fund Drive, 1966-70; discussion leader Mayor's Human Rights Com., 1965; chmn. Ho. of Laity, Greater Kokomo Assn. Chs., 1971, pres., 1972-75; ecumenical chmn. Diocese Lafayette (Ind.), mem. Diocesan Pastoral Council, 1972—, diocesan impact coordinator, 1972—; mem. Ind. Council Chs., 1971—; co-founder, pres. Devon Woods-Mayfield Homeowners Assn., 1970, v.p., 1971, sec., 1972, treas., 1972—; editor newspaper, v.p. Indian Heights Community Assn., 1963-67; chmn. for small bus. United Fund, 1970; pres. Howard County Heart Assn., 1973; capt.

Kokomo Community Concerts, 1969; judge Howard County Sci. Fair, 1970-73; chmn. Clay Twp. Bicentennial Com., 1974—; mem. exec. com. Kokomo Bicentennial Com., 1974—; govt. agys. chmn. Howard County Bicentennial Com., 1974—; capt. capital fund drive Sangralea Valley Boys Home Campaign, 1968; mem. Ind. Citizens Council Addictions, 1974-78, Ind. Adv. Com. Med. Assistance, 1973-75, Ind. Citizens' Adv. Council Alcoholism, 1973-75. Trustee Clay Twp., Ind., 1970-75; dir. 5th Dist., Ind. Twp. Trustees Assn., 1970-75; del. Republican State Conv., 1970, 74, dep. registration officer, 1970, 72, 74; mem. Rep. Nat. Com., 1970-75; resolutions chmn. Young Republicans Conv., 1969, state minority chmn., dir. Howard County Young Republicans, regional dir. No. Leadership Tng. Sch., chmn. 5th Dist. Young Reps., state vice chmn., exec. mem., candidate state treas., 1970, candidate for chmn. Ind. Young Reps., 1971; bd. dirs. Drug Abuse Council, Howard County; bd. dirs., membership chmn. Mental Health Assn. Howard County. Served to capt., Ordnance Corps, U.S. Army, 1957-66. Recipient Nat. Young Rep. Hard Charger award, 1970, Gen. Motors Community Service award, 1970, Jaycee Distinguished Service award, 1970, Distinguished Service award Ind. Young Reps., 1971, Layman of Year award K.C., 1971, Ind. Mental Health award, 1971-72, Heart Fund award, 1973, commendation Ind. Vols., 1975, award Greater Kokomo Council of Chs., 1975, named Outstanding Ind. Young Rep., 1970. Fellow Harry S. Truman Library, 1974—. Mem. Internat. Soc. for Hybrid Microelectronics (Midwest regional dir., state pres., treas., v.p., publicity chmn., program chmn. 1970—), Semicondr. Materials Soc., Am. Soc. Quality Control, Am. Soc. Metals, Am. Soc. Testing Materials (chmn. subcoms. 1963-68), Am. Inst. Mining and Metall. Engrs., Am. Ceramics Soc., Kokomo Engring. Soc. (mem. phenomena of man project), Internat. Platform Assn., Am. Indian Assn., Ind. Chess Assn., Ind., Howard County hist. socs., Kokomo Fine Arts Assn., Nat. Wilderness Soc., Nat. Trust Historic Preservation, Whitewater Valley R.R. Assn., Kokomo Mgmt. Club (auditor 1970), Am. Hort. Soc., Nat. Greentown Glass Assn., Sigma Xi. Lion. Home: 906 Bellevue Pl Kokomo IN 46901

ANKENBRAND, RALPH JAMES, coll. counselor; b. Mt. Carmel, Ill., Mar. 22, 1939; s. William H. and Lorene (Wahler) A.; B.S., Eastern Ill. U., 1960, M.S., 1963; Ph.D., St. Louis U., 1971; m. Susan Poe Syndergaard, Nov. 23, 1963; children—Mark, Christopher, Todd. Tchr., coach Jefferson Jr. High Sch., Charleston, Ill., 1960-65; counselor St. Louis Community Coll. at Florissant Valley, Ferguson, Mo., 1966—. Pres. Vogt Sch. PTA, 1976; adviser Catholic Youth Council. Mem. Am. Personnel and Guidance Assn. Democrat. Roman Catholic. Home: 711 Darst Rd Ferguson MO 63135 Office: 3400 Pershall Rd Ferguson MO 63135

ANKLAN, DEANE RICHARD, civil engr.; b. St. Paul, Feb. 7, 1926; s. Ben Henry and Marie Jeanette (Cherney) A.; student, U. Minn., 1943, 46-48, 52-65; B.A., Minn. Met. State Coll., 1975; m. Mary Arlyne Sullivan, Oct. 8, 1949; children—Karen Mary, James Richard, Denise Joan, Gregg Robert. Engring. tech. Minn. Hwy. Dept., St. Paul, 1947-50, civil engr., 1950-54; asst. maint. engr. Ramsey County Hwy. Dept., St. Paul, 1955-57, sr. engr., 1957-60, chief engr., 1960—. Pres. Lake Owasso Shores, Inc., St. Paul, 1964—; planning staff, faculty U. Minn. Continuation Study Center, Mpls., 1965—. Chmn. greater St. Paul/St. Croix Valley chpt. March of Dimes Nat. Found., 1968-69, exec. bd., 1970—; adv. group Nat. Research Council, Nat. Acad. Scis., i974—. Served with USAAF, 1944-45. Mem. Minn. County Hwy. Engrs. Assn. (pres. 1970), Minn. Soc. Profl. Engrs. (chpt. pres. 1972-73, dir. 1974), Nat. Soc. Profl. Engrs., Nat. Assn. County Engrs. (pres. 1971-72, research dir. 1974—), Minn. Local Rds. Research Bd. (chmn. 1974). Roman Catholic (trustee 1960-64). Home: 3153 Sandy Hook Dr Roseville MN 55113 Office: 502 Courthouse Saint Paul MN 55102

ANNEBERG, ADRIAN REAS, physician; b. Templeton, Iowa, Nov. 11, 1907; s. August R. and Bertha Anna (Kivits) A.; B.S., U. Iowa, 1930, M.D., 1932; m. Mary E. Parker, Mar. 24, 1932; children—Adriann, Bertha, Martha. Intern, Cin. Gen. Hosp., 1932-33; resident Barnes Hosp., St. Louis, 1933-36; pvt. practice medicine specializing in otolaryngology, Carroll, Iowa, 1936-48; physician Carrol Med. Center, Carroll, Iowa, 1948—; Served as capt. MC, U.S. Army, 1942-45. Mem. Iowa, Carroll County med. socs., AMA, Iowa (pres. 1970), Am. acads. ophthalmology and otolaryngology, Am. Assn. Physicians and Surgeons, Am. Council Otolaryngology, Iowa Assn. Retarded Children (pres. 1954), Carroll C. of C. (pres. 1939), Alpha Omega Alpha, Sigma Xi. Republican. Presbyterian. Club: Rotary (pres., 1949). Home: 413 Lynn St Apt 104 Carroll IA 51401 Office: 502 N Court St Carroll IA 51401

ANNETT, THOMAS, musician, educator; b. Galena, Ill., Jan. 25, 1892; s. Thomas and Martha (Anguin) A.; B Mus., Northwestern U., 1924; B.S., N.W. Mo. State Coll., 1926, A.M., 1932; Ed.D., U. Cin., 1938; m. Margaret Linfield, July 28, 1934. Instr., U. Oreg., 1916-19; pvt. studio, Omaha, 1919-21; head of piano N.W. Mo. State Coll. 1921-27; instr. Long Beach (Calif.) Jr. Coll., 1927-28; chmn. music dept. U. Wis., La Crosse, 1928-61, prof., 1956-62, prof. emeritus, 1962—; pvt. music studio, LaCrosse, 1962—; summer teacher No. Ia. U., 1928, Cin. Conservatory of Music, 1936, 37. U. Cin., 1938-42, 45; concert pianist, U.S. and abroad. Music adviser Nat. U.S.O., 1943-44. Served with A.E.F., 1917-19. Certified Nat. Assn. Piano Tchrs. Life fellow Inst. Arts and Letters Switzerland; mem. Music Tchrs. Nat. Assn., Music Educators Nat. Conf. (chmn. rural sch. music 1952-54). Nat. Guild Piano Tchrs. (bd. adjudicators), Wis. Music Tchrs. Assn. (bd. certification 1970-74, dir.), Am. Legion, Delta Upsilon, Phi Delta Kappa. Methodist. Kiwanian. Author: Music in the Rural Sch., 1938: Music for Recreation; also articles in mus. jours. Home: 123 N 14th St La Crosse WI 54601

ANNIS, SPERO, govt. ofcl.; b. Hamilton, Ont., Can., Nov. 2, 1915; s. George and Vasilo (Smerneos) A.; student pub. schs., Tilbury, Ont.; m. Sylvia Jean Jeffrey, Oct. 22, 1943; children—John George, Laurie Jane Annis McQuaig. Asst. mgr. Tilbury (Ont.) Liquor Control Bd., 1943-57, auditor, Windsor and Peterborough, 1957-75, dist. supr., Kitchener-Waterloo, 1975—. Exec. mem. Western Counties Baseball Assn., 1949-54, sec.-treas., bus. mgr., 1954-61; sec.-treas. Ont. Baseball Assn., 1962-76, exec. mem., 1949-62; sec.-treas. Eastern Ont. Baseball Assn., 1964-67; exec. mem. Canadian Fedn. Amateur Baseball, 1967-73, sec.-treas., 1973-75. Recipient Plaque and medal Western Counties Baseball Assn., 1961, Achievement award Govt. Ont., 1969, Plaque, Ont. Baseball Assn., 1976. Anglican. Clubs: Masons (past master), Order Eastern Star (past patron), Liquor Control Bd. Ont., Quarter Centry.

ANNO, JAMES NELSON, scientist, educator; b. Niles, Ohio, Feb. 6, 1934; s. James Nelson and Opal Mae (Gentry) A.; m. Janet Winkel, June 12, 1955; children—James David, Sara Jennifer, Jefferson Nelson. B.S., Ohio State U., 1955, M.S., 1961, Ph.D., 1965. Technician, Battelle Meml. Inst., Columbus, Ohio, 1953-55, supr. research reactor, 1955-60, asst. chief applied nuclear physics div., 1960-65, asst. chief lubrication mechanics div., 1965-67, chief lubrication mechanics div., 1967-70; asso. prof. nuclear engring. U. Cin., 1970-73, prof., 1973—. Mem. Am. Phys. Soc., Am. Nuclear Soc., Am. Soc. Engring. Edn., Newtown Acad. Scis. (pres.), Masons, Sigma Xi, Phi Beta Kappa, Sigma Pi Sigma. Recipient Civic award Columbus Jr. C. of C., 1961; honored by Sat. Evening Post, 1961. Author: Encyclopedia of Draw Poker, 1973; (with J.A. Walowit) Modern Development in Lubrication Mechanics, 1975; Wave Mech anics for Engineers, 1976; Mechanics of Liquid Jets, 1977; contbr. articles to profl. jours. Home: 5882 Ropes Dr Cincinnati OH 45244 Office: 509 Old Chemistry Bldg Cincinnati OH 45221

ANNUNZIO, FRANK, congressman; b. Chgo., Jan. 12, 1915; B.S., M.Ed., DePaul U.; m. Angeline Alesia, Dec. 28, 1935; children—Jacqueline (Mrs. Sal Lato), Linda (Mrs. William O'Donnell), Susan (Mrs. Kevin Tynan). Asst. supr. Nat. Defense Tng. Program Austin Eve. Sch., Chgo.; legislative, ednl. dir. United Steelworkers of Am., Chgo.: mem. 89th-95th congresses from 11th Dist. Ill. Dir. Ill. Dept. Labor; chmn. War Ration Bd. 40-20; mem. adv. com. on Unemployment Compensation; mem. adv. com. to Ill. Indsl. Commn. on Health, Safety; mem. adv. bd. Cook County (Ill.) Health and Survey; chmn. Community Services Com.; mem. Chgo. Commn. on Human Relations. Gen. chmn. Villa Scalabrini Devel. Fund; v.p., lay adv. bd. Villa Scalabrini Italian Old People's Home. Mem. Catholic Youth Orgn. K.C. (4 Deg.). Club: City (Chgo.). Office: Rayburn Bldg Washington DC 20515

ANSARI, MOHAMMED RAFIULLAH, surgeon; b. Gokaram, India, Oct. 10, 1935; s. Mohammed Mahboob and Abbas (Bibi) Ali; came to U.S., 1967, naturalized, 1977; B.Sc., M.B.B.S., Osmania U., Hyderabad, India, 1962; m. Raoof Yasmin, June 1, 1962; 1 dau., Farrah. Intern, Osmania Gen. Hosp., India, 1962-63, St. Lukes Hosp., St. Paul, 1967-68; Henry Ford Hosp., Detroit, 1968-72, resident surgeon, fellow in vascular surgery 1972-73; asst. surgeon Dist. Hosps., Warangal, India, 1963-67; staff surgeon Henry Ford Hosp., Detroit, 1973—; clin. instr. in surgery U. Mich., 1976—. Diplomate Am. Bd. Surgery. Fellow A.C.S., Am. Coll. Angiology; mem. AMA, Mich. Med. Soc., Detroit Surg. Soc., Detroit Surg. Assn., Acad. Surgery Detroit. Developer kidney cooling jacket for use during kidney transplantation. Home: 1481 Lila Dr Troy MI 48098 Office: 2799 W Grand Blvd Detroit MI 48202

ANSCHUTZ, GLENN WILLIAM, civil engr.; b. Wilson, Kans., Oct. 17, 1925; s. William Frederick and Hedwig Johanna (Schepmann) A.; B.S., Kans. U., 1950, postgrad., 1953; postgrad. Kans. State U., 1965-66; m. Margaret Helen Gartner, Sept. 6, 1953; children—Kent David, Mark Douglas. Road designer Kans. Hwy. Commn., Topeka, 1950-51, bridge designer, squad leader, 1951-58, engr. photogrammetry, 1958-62, engr. photronics, 1962-68, engr. design, 1968—; instr. U. Kans., Lawrence, 1953, Washburne U., Topeka, 1959-62. Mem. Transp. Research Bd. Scoutmaster, spl. awards chmn. Boy Scouts Am., Topeka, 1969—; dir., judging chmn., treas. Topeka Regional Sci. Fair, 1968—. Served with AUS, 1944-46, 50-51. Decorated Bronze Star. Fellow ASCE; mem. Am. Soc. Photogrammetry, Kans. Engring. Soc. (Engr. of Year award 1970), V.F.W., Nat. Soc. Profl. Engrs. (nat. dir.), Am. Inst. Traffic Engrs., Am. Assn. State Hwys. and Transp. Ofcls., Tau Beta Pi, Sigma Tau, Omicron Delta Kappa, Chi Epsilon. Contbr. articles to profl. jours. Home: 2600 W 9th St Topeka KS 66606 Office: State Office Bldg Topeka KS 66612

ANSHUTZ, WILLIAM MAURICE, radiologist; b. Somerton, Ohio, Sept. 16, 1917; s. Harvey and Atrella (Tomlinson) A.; A.B., Ohio State U., 1942; M.D., 1948; m. Betty Millisor, Sept. 10, 1944; children—Wendy Lee, Cathy Jo. Intern Lima (Ohio) Meml. Hosp., 1949; resident in radiology Henry Ford Hosp., Detroit, 1956-59; gen. practice medicine, Ohio, 1953-56; practice medicine specializing in radiology, Ind., 1959—; mem. staffs St. Francis Hosp., Beech Grove, Ind., 1959-61; radiologist; Meth. Hosp., Indpls., 1961-69; Witham Meml. Hosp., Lebanon, Ind., 1959-61, 70; Clinton County Hosp., Frankfort, Ind., 1969—. Served with U.S. Army, 1942-44; USAF, 1951-53. Decorated Bronze Star. Mem. AMA, Radiol. Soc. N.Am., Am. Coll. Radiology, Ind. Roentgen Soc. Republican. Methodist. Home and Office: 6340 Breamore Rd Indianapolis IN 46220

ANSON, JACK LEE, frat. conf. exec.; b. Andrews, Ind., Aug. 3, 1924; s. John C. and Ferol L. (Noble) A.; A.B., Colgate U., 1948. Sports editor Huntington (Ind.) Herald Press, 1942-43; with Phi Kappa Tau, 1948-70, field sec., 1948-50, asst. sec., 1950-60, adminstrv. sec., 1960-61, nat. editor, 1955-67, nat. sec., nat. treas., 1961-70; exec. dir. Nat. Interfrat. Conf., Inc., Indpls., 1971—. Served with AUS, 1943-46, 50-51. Mem. Coll. Frat. Secs. Assn. (past pres.), Coll. Frat. Editors Assn. (past pres.) Staffordshire Terrier Club Am., Midwest Staffordshire Terrier. Republican. Methodist. Clubs: Cin. Kennel; Cincinnati. Author: The Phi Kappa Tau Fraternity History, 1956. Editor N.I.C. Report; Campus Commentary. Contbr. articles to profl. jours. Home: 3812 Woodall Dr Indianapolis IN 46268 Office: 3901 W 86th St Indianapolis IN 46268

ANTHIS, BILL CLINTON, supt. schs.; b. Patoka, Ind., Oct. 4, 1926; s. George W. and Frona (Morrison) A.; B.S., Ind. State U., 1948, M.S., 1950; Ed.D., Ind. U., 1962; m. Patricia Weaver, May 23, 1952; 1 son, Clinton Weaver. Tchr. high schs., Rockville, Ind., 1948-51, Orleans, Ind., 1951-52; guidance and athletic dir. Princeton (Ind.) High Sch., 1952-57; guidance dir. North Side High Sch., Ft. Wayne, Ind., 1957-63, prin., 1963-73; asst. supt. Ft. Wayne Community Schs., 1973—. Instr. edn. Ind. U., part time, 1957-62; instr. psychology Purdue U., part time 1962-63; instr. guidance St. Francis Coll., Ft. Wayne, part time 1963—; Cons. Ind. U. Student Leadership Workshops, 1965-68; Charter mem. internat. schs. adv. council Experiment in Internat. Living. Mem. youth planning com. local chpt. A.R.C., 1967-68; v.p. exploring Anthony Wayne Area council Boy Scouts Am.; mem. citizens' com. Leadership Prayer Breakfast; chmn. edn. com. Bicentennial Commn. Ft. Wayne. Bd. dirs. Neighbors, Inc., 1962-67, v.p., 1964; bd. dirs. Mental Health Center, 1967—, v.p., 1968; bd. advisers Ind. U.-Purdue U. at Ft. Wayne; bd. dirs. Better Bus. Bur., United Community Services, Ind. Multiple Sclerosis Assn., YMCA, Channel 39 TV, Citizens Council for Program Devel. of Citizens Cable TV Co., Fort Wayne. Served USNR, 1945-46. Recipient Distinguished Alumni award Ind. State U., 1977. Mem. Nat. Assn. Secondary Sch. Prins. (participant study mission to E. Europe 1967), Am. Assn. Sch. Adminstrs. (life), Internat. Reading Assn., Assn. Childhood Edn. Internat., Ft. Wayne C. of C., Ind. PTA (life), Am. Legion, Phi Delta Kappa (pres. Fort Wayne chpt. 1976-77), Pi Gamma Mu, Kappa Delta Pi. Methodist. Mason (Shriner, 33 deg.), Rotarian (pres. Fort Wayne Club 1971-72, dir.). Contbr. articles to profl. jours. Home: 3939 Evergreen Ln Fort Wayne IN 46805 Office: 1230 S Clinton St Fort Wayne IN 46802

ANTHIS, PATRICIA WEAVER (MRS. BILL CLINTON ANTHIS), psychologist; b. Rockville, Ind., Dec. 22, 1930; d. Paul Commons and Ruth Mayme (Goddard) Weaver; R.N., Ind. State U., 1952, B.S., 1965; M.S., St. Francis Coll., 1966; m. Bill Clinton Anthis, May 23, 1952; 1 son, Clinton Weaver. Nurse, R.N. Gibson Gen. Hosp., Princeton, Ind., 1952-58; instr. St. Joseph's Hosp. Sch. Nursing, Ft. Wayne, Ind., 1959-66; sch. psychometrist Ft. Wayne Community Schs., 1966—; pvt. practice psychology, Ft. Wayne, 1966—. Instr. St. Francis (Ind.) Coll., part-time 1966-72. Bd. dirs. League for Blind, Ft. Wayne, 1959-65, sec., 1964-65. Mem. Laubach Soc., Assn. for Childhood Edn., Ft. Wayne Adminstrv. Assn., Internat. Reading Assn (pres. 1976-77), NEA, Nat. Assn. Sch. Psychologists, Ft. Wayne Psychologists Assn., Tri Kappa (sec. 1957-58), Delta Kappa Gamma (sec. 1972-73) (pres. 1976-78), Phi Delta Gamma. Mem. Order Eastern Star. Home: 3939 Evergreen Lane Fort Wayne IN 46815 Office: 1230 S Clinton St Fort Wayne IN 46802

ANTHONY, SAMUEL CARL, city ofcl.; b. Salt Lake City, Oct. 15, 1945; s. Walter Carl and Mary Victoria (Klisiewicz) A.; student Loyola U., U. Ill., S.W. Jr. Coll.; m. Janice Marie Kozicki, Sept. 16, 1967; children—Dawn Marie, Todd Carl. Cadet, Chgo. Police Dept., 1963-66, patrolman, 1966-68, patrolman/instr. safety edn. sect., traffic div., 1968—. Interpreter, Circuit Ct. Cook County, 1973—; instr. sign lang. Moraine Valley Community Coll., 1974—; coordinator Traffic Safety Bur., Ill. Assn. Deaf, 1974—; past instr. Central States Inst. Addiction; security Beverly Bank, Chgo., 1969-75. Past bd. dirs. Midwest Area Alcohol Edn. and Tng. Program. Mem. Nat. Assn. Deaf, Nat., Ill. (dir.) registries interpreters for deaf, Ill. Assn. Deaf. Home: 6828 W 64th Pl Chicago IL 60638 Office: 54 W Hubbard St Chicago IL 60610

ANTON, ANASTASIA, ret. librarian; b. Ft. Dodge, Ia., Apr. 20, 1928; d. Gust N. and Maria (Brotsos) Pappas; B.A., State U. Ia., 1950; M.A., U. Minn., 1957; m. George T. Anton, Sept. 16, 1961; children—Tom G., Blair. With Ft. Dodge (Ia.) Library, 1951-57; adminstr. library Robbinsdale (Minn.) High Sch., 1957-61; reference librarian Evanston (Ill.) Pub. Library, 1962; with Winnetka (Ill.) Pub. Library, 1969-76, reference and acquisitions librarian, 1974-76, now cons. Mem. Ill. Library Assn. Club: Winnetka (Ill.) Women's (mem. finance bd. 1971-74). Reviewer, Babbling Bookworm Newsletter, 1972—. Home: 290 Poplar St Winnetka IL 60093

ANTON, DONALD CHRIST, lawyer; b. St. Louis, Mar. 26, 1931; s. Christ J. and Ann L. (Thiel) A.; student Southwest Mo. State U., 1949-50, Kan. State U., 1950-51; B.S. in Bus. Adminstrn., Washington U., 1953, J.D., 1956; m. Aurora Ida Viglino, June 13, 1959; children—Donald K., Linda Ann. Gen. accountant Union Electric Co., St. Louis, 1952-53; admitted to Mo. bar, 1955, Fed. bar, 1955, U.S. Supreme Ct. bar, 1961; practiced in St. Louis, Hillsboro, Mo., Jefferson City, Mo., also Washington; mem. firm Evans and Dixon, St. Louis, 1954-55; atty. St. Louis Dist. Engrs., 1957-58; mem. firm Forgey and Sindel, St. Louis, 1958-59; probate and trust officer Mercantile Trust Co., St. Louis, 1959-60; mem. firm Hall, Reaban, Seigel and Scheele, St. Louis, 1960-63; partner firm Anton, Raleigh and Wynne, St. Louis, 1969—. Pres. Holiday Ins. Agy., St. Louis, 1960-63, Dory Realtors, St. Louis, 1959-69; sec. Pine Ford Land Co., St. Louis, 1962—; co-propr. Henny Penny Chicken Restaurant, St. Louis, 1966-69; pres. Diversified Cons., Inc., St. Louis, 1969—. Counsel SBA, St. Louis and Washington, 1962-65; spl. asst. to Atty. Gen. of Mo., 1967; asst. pros. atty. for Jefferson County (Mo.), 1968; counsel for Mo. Senate, 75th Gen. Assembly, Legis. Session, 1969; legal counsel Moline, Wellston, Pattonville-Bridgeton Terrace Fire Protection Dists., St. Louis County. Mem. Econ. Adv. Counsel, State of Mo., 1968-72; mem. PTA, St. Louis, 1967-72. Del. to Democratic Nat. Conv., 1964; del. to Mo. State Conv., 1968; chmn. Dem. Com., St. Louis County (Mo.), 1972—; Dem. committeeman Concord Twp., St. Louis County, 1968—; Dem. nominee St. Louis County Supr., 1974. Served to 1st. lt. AUS, 1955-58. Mem. Am. (banking and bus. law coms. 1961—, mem. taxation com. 1968—, uniform comml. code com. 1965-70), Fed. (sec. 1965-66), Mo. (mem. bus. orgns. com. 1964—) bar assns., Am. Judicature Soc., Jr. C. of C., Am. Turners, D.A.V., Delta Sigma Pi, Phi Delta Phi, Sigma Nu. Roman Catholic. Kiwanian, Lion. Club: Optimists. Home: 130 Sappington Ave Acres Dr St Louis MO 63126 Office: 50 Crestwood Executive Center St Louis MO 63126

ANTON, JOHN JAMES, food products mfg. co. exec.; b. St. Louis, June 27, 1942; s. John J. and Ruth Ann (Savage) A.; B.S. in Chemistry, U. Notre Dame, 1964; m. Carlin Louise Smith, Sept. 30, 1967; 1 son, John James. Mgr. of production and sales, poultry processing operation Ralston Purina Co., Waterville, Mass., 1964-66, asst. to gen. mgr. protein div., 1969-70, mgr. market devel. protein div. 1970-73, dir. of mktg., 1973-77, v.p. mktg. protein and dairy food systems div., St. Louis, 1977—, also dir. sci. services div., 1977—. Bd. dirs. Wis. Alumni Research Found. Inst., 1977—. Served to lt., inf., U.S. Army, 1966-69. Decorated Bronze Star. Mem. Inst. Food Technologists, Am. Meat Inst., Assn. of Cereal Chemists, Food Protein Council (chmn. 1977—). Republican. Roman Catholic. Club: Tennis and Golf. Home: 13419 Conway Rd St Louis MO 63141 Office: Checkerboard Sq 13T St Louis MO 63188

ANTONIC, JAMES PAUL, mktg. cons.; b. Milw., Mar. 29, 1943; s. George Paul and Betti Ware (Littler) A.; student U. Wis., 1960-64, Boston U., 1975-76; m. Irene Robson, Dec. 26, 1970. Owner JPA Supply and Warehouse Co., Milw., 1966-68; product mgr., market mgr. Delta Oil Products, Milw., 1968-74; v.p. internat. ops., Brussels, 1974-76; pres. Internat. Market Devel. Group, Milw., 1976—. Served with U.S. Army, 1964-66. Mem. Licensing Execs. Soc., Am. Mktg. Assn., World Trade Assn. Milw. Episcopalian. Home: 5259 N Santa Monica Blvd Milwaukee WI 53217 Office: 10500 N Port Washington Rd Mequon WI 53092

ANUNDSEN, BRYNJOLF BJORKHOLT, newspaper publisher; b. Decorah, Iowa, June 16, 1902; s. Brynjild and Helma (Hegg) A.; L.S., U. Wis., 1925; m. Ellen Killen, Sept. 4, 1925; children—John, Jane (Mrs. James Bullard). Treas., dir. Anundsen Pub. Co., Decorah News Co., 1947—. Vice consul of Norway for State of Iowa, 1952-74. Decorated knight 1st class Royal Order of St. Olav (Norway). Home: 709 E Main St Decorah IA 52101 Office: 108 Washington St Decorah IA 52101

ANUNDSEN, JOHN KILLEN, pub. co. exec.; b. Decorah, Iowa, Jan. 31, 1929; s. B.B. and Ellen D. (Killen) A.; B.S. in Commerce, U. Iowa, 1951; m. Mary Eleanor Glick, Sept. 10, 1952; children—Mark Steven, Erik Arthur. With the Anundsen Pub. Co., Decorah, Ia., 1952—, pres., 1954—; pres. Decorah News Co., 1954—; pres. Cobie Office Supply, 1970—, Graphics, Inc., Calmar, 1973—. Bd. dirs. Norwegian-Am. Mus., 1964—; chmn. Decorah Park Commn., 1973—. Served with USAF, 1951-53. Mem. C. of C. (pres. 1959-60), Decorah Ski Assn. (pres. 1963-64), Am. Legion, Decorah Jaycees (pres. 1957). Republican. Lutheran. Elk. Club: Oneota Golf and Country (pres. 1964-65) (Decorah). Home: 903 Park Decorah IA 52101 Office: 108 Washington St Decorah IA 52101

ANUNDSON, JOHN KENNETH, accounting service exec.; b. Volga, S.D., Aug. 26, 1923; s. John and Dagmar (Christensen) A.; student pub. schs., Volga; m. Joyce Naylor, Dec. 31, 1955; children—Steffanie, John. Sec. corp. Wander, Inc., Worthington, Ohio, 1958-74; pres., prin. Classic Computer Service, Inc., Columbus, Ohio, 1974—. Served with USN, 1943-46. Mem. Data Processing Mgmt. Assn., Ohio Contractors Assn. Office: 1166E Steelwood Rd Columbus OH 43212

ANURAS, SINN, gastroenterologist; b. Bangkok, Thailand, Apr. 6, 1941; s. Tiang and Ratana (Suppipat) A.; came to U.S., 1967; M.D., Chulalongkorn U., Thailand, 1966; m. Jitra Suppamongkol, Aug. 8, 1969; 1 dau., Piyawan. Intern, Resurrection Hosp., Chgo., 1967; resident in internal medicine VA Hosp., Long Beach, Calif., 1968-70; asst. prof. medicine U. Iowa, Iowa City, 1974—. Diplomate Am. Bd. Internal Medicine. Fellow A.C.P.; mem. Am. Gastroenterol. Assn. Buddhist. Research on intestinal motility, clin. liver disease. Home: 55

Arbury Dr Iowa City IA 52240 Office: University of Iowa Iowa City IA 52242

ANUTA, ALBERT EDWARD, JR., educator; b. Milw., Jan. 30, 1930; s. Albert Edward and Alice Evelyn (Hundt) A.; B.S. in Mech. Engring., Purdue U., 1955, M.S. in Mech. Engring., 1958. Engr., Gen. Electric Co., 1955-56; asst. prof. N.Mex. State U., 1963-66; asso. prof. U. N.D., 1966—. Served with USAF, 1948-52. Registered profl. engr., N.D. Mem. Soc. Profl. Engrs., Soc. Exptl. Stress Analysis, Sigma Xi, Sigma Tau, Tau Beta Pi, Pi Tau Sigma. Home: Box 8037 Grand Forks ND 58202 Office: Mech Engring Dept U ND Grand Forks ND 58201

ANZUR, STEPHEN DAVID, univ. adminstr.; b. Detroit, Jan. 26, 1947; s. Joseph and Susan A.; B.B.A., Western Mich. U., 1969; m. Sandra Lee Davis, June 1, 1968; children—Amy, Jennifer, Scott. Staff trainee Campus Crusade for Christ, U. Colo., 1969-70, dir. Colo. State U., 1970-72; asst. to dean students Spring Arbor (Mich.) Coll., 1972-75, dean students, 1975—, coach varsity wrestling, 1973-75, asst. coach, track, 1972-73. Bd. dirs. ARC, Spring Arbor, 1976-77. Mem. Am. Personnel and Guidance Assn., Am., Mich. coll. personnel assns., Assn. Christian Deans and Advisors of Men. Home: 129 Cottage Spring St Arbor MI 49283 Office: College Ave Spring Arbor MI 49283

APELQUIST, RONALD WILLIAM, ret. educator; b. Tracy, Minn., Apr. 1, 1909; s. John Carlton and Andreen (Howe) A.; student mech. engring. U. Wis., 1928-29; B.E., Wis. State U., 1932; M.A., U. Minn., 1940; grad. Command and Gen. Staff Sch., 1945; m. G. Irene Randklev, Mar. 30, 1942. Tchr., prin. pub. schs., Wis., 1932-39; tchr. pub. schs., Florence, Wis., 1939-41, Bemidji, Minn., 1941-42, St. Paul, 1956; salesman, sr. safety engr., mgr. loss prevention, ins., various locations, 1946-54; safety dir., oil refinery, Pine Bend, Minn., 1956; tchr. math. South Sr. High Sch., Mpls., 1957-74. Instr. extension div. Inst. Tech., U. Minn., 1957-64; mem. faculty Minn. Met. State Coll., St. Paul, 1970—. Sec. bd. trustees Grace Presbyterian Ch., Mpls., 1976—, pres., 1977—. Served with AUS, 1941-46. Mem. Am. Soc. Safety Engrs. (emeritus, Plaque award 1971), Mensa, Vets of Safety Internat. (pres. N.W. chpt. 1968-69, regional v.p. 1969-73, dir.-at-large 1973-76), Minn. Safety Council (dir. 1968-69), Am. Assn. Ret. Persons (pres. chpt. 1976-77), Phi Delta Kappa. Clubs: Masons, Shriners. Home: 5212 Washburn Ave S Minneapolis MN 55410

APFELBACHER, STEVEN FREDERICK, city ofcl.; b. St. Paul, Oct. 22, 1949; s. Fred and Shirley Marie (Choate) A.; B.S. in Econs., U. Minn., 1971; postgrad. (Taft Inst. on Govt. scholar) Macalester Coll., 1975; m. Nancy Jane Tome, Oct. 22, 1971. Tchr., St. Paul schs., 1971-76; exec. dir. community devel. City South Saint Paul (Minn.), 1976—; exec. dir. Housing and Redevel. Authority, South St. Paul, 1976—, Econ. Devel. Authority, South St. Paul, 1976—. Mem. South St. Paul City Council, 1971-75; acting mayor City of South St. Paul, 1975-76. Mem. Council on Urban Econ. Devel., Nat. League of Cities, Nat. Assn. Housing and Redevel. Ofcls., Nat. Community Assn. Presbyterian. Home: 212 4th Ave S South Saint Paul MN 55075

APILADO, MYRON, univ. adminstr.; b. Chgo., May 18, 1933; s. Inosencio Tadina and Ruth Moselle (Mays) A.; B.A., U. Md., 1971; M.A., Ball State U., 1973; Ed.D., U. S.D., 1976; m. Sherri Ann Mitchell, Oct. 21, 1972; children—Mariano, Kea, Kelli, Anthony, Adam. Mem. exec. com. Community Counseling Program, Torrejon, Spain, 1972; chmn. Ednl. Grad. Orgn. U. S.D., 1974, instr., 1975, asst. prof., 1976; dean for student devel. Peru (Nebr.) State Coll., 1976—; asso. editor AIM Mag., 1975—. Served with USAF, 1953-73. Decorated Bronze Star. Certified sch. psychologist, Iowa. Mem. Am. Psychol. Assn., Am. Personnel and Guidance Assn., Phi Delta Kappa. Home: 601 Nebraska Ave Peru NE 68421 Office: Peru State Coll Peru NE 68421

APP, PALMER, ins. co. exec.; b. Chgo., Jan. 4, 1916; s. Charles Max and Stella (Palmer) A.; B.A. magna cum laude, Brown U., 1937; m. Mary Pearl Williams, May 24, 1941; 1 son, Palmer. With Lumbermens Mut. Casualty Co., Chgo., 1937—, v.p., 1965—; with Am. Motorists Ins. Co., Chgo., 1937—, v.p., 1965—; with Am. Mfrs. Mut. Ins. Co., 1937—, v.p., 1965—; mgr. central div. Kemper Ins., Chgo., 1963-76, pres. central div., 1976—; dir. Am. Underwriting Corp., Chgo., Nat. Eastern Corp., Chgo., Atlantic Consumer Discount Corp., Chgo. Served to lt. (j.g.) USNR, 1943-45. Mem. Chgo. Assn. Commerce, Nat., Ill. assns. mut. ins. agts., Phi Beta Kappa, Theta Delta Chi. Clubs: Tower, Executives (Chgo.). Home: 3015 Payne St Evanston IL 60201 Office: Kemper Center Long Grove IL 60049

APPEL, WILLIAM CECIL, opera dir., educator; b. Somerset, Pa., Mar. 30, 1933; s. William C. and Dorothy (Wiley) A.; B.S., Ind. State Tchrs. Coll., 1954; M. Mus. cum laude, Ind. U., 1958; m. M. Jean Carter, Dec. 22, 1954; children—Carol, Nancy, James. Voice tchr., opera dir. U. Colo., 1958-61; profl. tenor singer opera, musical comedy, 1961-65; opera dir. voice tchr., choral condr. Western Mich. U., Kalamazoo, 1965—; prof. opera stage dir. Turnau Opera, Opera Assn. of Western Mich., 1968—. Served to lt. AUS, 1954-56. Home: 129 Cherry Hill Dr Kalamazoo MI 49007

APPLEBY, LESLIE VERE, architect; b. Wichita, Kans., Feb. 17, 1931; s. Vere Griffith and Marie Margaret (McCoy) A.; student Wichita State U., 1949-50; B.Arch., Kans. State U., 1958; m. Joyce Kimmel, July 3, 1952 (div.); children—Vickie Lee Appleby Cohen, Bryan Kent; m. 2d, Louise A. Gierscha, June 25, 1976. Architect William R. Brown, Ponca City, Okla., 1958-63; architect, mng. partner Shaver & Co., Salina, Kans., 1963-71; architect, sr. partner Appleby & Marsh, Wichita and Salina, 1971—; pres. Lamco Co., Salina, 1972—, 215 Group, Salina, 1974—. Pres. Okla. Jr. Miss Inc., Ponca City, 1961-63. Registered architect Kans., Okla., Mo., Iowa, S.D., Nebr., Tex., Tenn., Nat. Council Archtl. Registration Bds. Mem. AIA (Corp.), Kans. State U. Alumni Assn., Salina C. of C. Episcopalian. Elk. Club: Salina Country. Home: 647 Rockview Rd Salina KS 67401 Office: 2103 S Ohio St Salina KS 67401 also 200 E 1st St Wichita KS 67202

APPLEGATE, DOUGLAS, Congressman; b. Steubenville, Ohio, Mar. 27, 1928; grad. high sch.; m. Betty Jean Engstrom, 1950; children—Kirk, David. Engaged in real estate bus.; mem. Ohio Ho. of Reps., 1961-69, Ohio Senate, 1969-77; mem. 95th Congress from 18th Ohio Dist. Mem. Steubenville Community Club, Catholic Community Center, Polish Nat. Alliance. Democrat. Presbyterian. Clubs: Elks, Eagles, Polish Athletic. Office: Room 1330 Longworth House Office Bldg Washington DC 20515

APPLEGATE, KENNETH LEWIS, microbiologist; b. S.I., N.Y., Jan. 4, 1936; s. Henry Lewis and Blanche Augusta (Cockran) A.; student Rockland Community Coll., Suffern, N.Y., 1962-63; B.S., Central State U., Wilberforce, Ohio, 1966; M.S., Ohio State U., 1968, Ph.D., 1973; m. Dorothy L. Applegate; 1 dau., Karla. Mem. staff phys. edn. Rockland (N.Y.) State Hosp., 1955-57; teaching asst. microbiology Central State U., 1964-66; bacteriologist Ohio Dept. Health, Bur. Labs., Columbus, 1968-69; research asst. Ohio Agrl. Research and Devel. Center, Ohio State U., Columbus, 1969-70, research asso., 1970-72, research, 1973—; dir. water quality Ohio Environ. Protection Agy., Columbus, 1972—; cons. in field. Served with USAF, 1957-61. Registered Nat. Registry Microbiologists. Mem. Internat. Socs. Human and Animal Mycology, Mycol. Soc. Am., Soc. Applied Bacteriology, Creation Research Soc., Am. Inst. Biol. Sci., Am. Soc. Bacteriology, Am. Soc. Microbiology, Am. Acad. Microbiology (registered), Sigma Xi, Phi Tau Sigma. Contbr. articles to profl. pubis. Home: 7060 Worthington Rd Westerville OH 43081 Office: Ohio Environ Protection Agy Columbus OH 43215

APRIL, EDWIN, radiologist; b. Chgo., Jan. 23, 1940; s. Jack and Rachel L. (Putterman) A.; M.D., U. Ill., 1964; m. Merle Ann Hochberger, July 1, 1962; children—Ilene, Pamela, Jonathan. Intern, Cook County Hosp., Chgo., 1964-65; resident in radiology U. Chgo. Hosps., 1967-70; radiologist Passavant Hosp., Chgo., 1971-72, Ravenswood Hosp. Med. Center, Chgo., 1972—; mem. faculty U. Chgo. Sch. Medicine, 1970-71, Northwestern U. Sch. Medicine, 1971-72, U. Ill. Sch. Medicine, 1975—. Served with USAF, 1965-67. Diplomate Am. Bd. Nuclear Medicine, Am. Bd. Radiology. Mem. AMA, Ill. State, Chgo. med. socs., Am. Coll. Radiology, Chgo. Radiol. Soc., Radiol. Soc. N.Am., Soc. Nuclear Medicine.

ARABIA, PAUL, lawyer; b. Pittsburg, Kans., Mar. 28, 1938; s. John K. and Melva A. (Jones) A.; B.A. in Speech, Kans. State Coll., 1962; J.D. (fellow) with honors, Washburn U., 1966. Admitted to Kans. bar, 1966; partner firm Arabia & Wells, law office and bus. investments, Wichita, Kans., 1966—. Mem. Wichita Traffic Commn., 1966-71, chmn., 1968-69. Mem. Kans., Wichita, Sedgwick County bar assns., Phi Sigma Epsilon (dir. 1962-72), Phi Alpha Delta. Home: 1323 Denene Wichita KS 67212 Office: 120 S Market St Suite 518 Wichita KS 67202

ARAI, HAROLD YUTAKA, orthodontist; b. Los Angeles, Feb. 1, 1936; s. Akira B. and Joan Fusako (Fujisawa) A.; B.A., Ohio Wesleyan U., 1957; D.D.S., Loyola U., 1961, M.S., 1966; m. Irene Shigihara, Aug. 27, 1961; children—David Andrew, Shaunna Lynn. Pvt. practice orthodontics, Park Ridge, Ill., 1967—; Lectr. Loyola U., 1966-73, 77, Ind. U., 1975, Emory U., 1975, La. State U., 1977. Pres., U. Chgo. Jarabak Orthodontic Found., 1975-76; v.p. Denver Orthodontic Summer Seminar, 1974, pres., 1975-76; lectr. Fox River Valley Dental Soc. meeting. Served to capt. USAF, 1961-63. Mem. ADA (orthodontic chmn. sci. sessions 1974—), Japanese Civic Assn., Am. Assn. Orthodontics (clinician), Japanese Citizens League, Blue Key, Alpha Sigma Phi, Omicron Delta Kappa, Omicron Kappa Upsilon, Delta Sigma Delta. Author: Welcome to the World of Orthodontics, 1973. Home: 2146 Adams St Rolling Meadows IL 60008 Office: 101 S Washington Park Ridge IL 60068

ARAKAWA, KASUMI, physician, educator; b. Toyohashi, Japan, Feb. 19, 1926; s. Masumi and Fayuko (Hattori) A.; M.D., Tokyo Med. Coll., 1953; m. June Hope Takahara, Aug. 27, 1956; children—Jane Riet, Kenneth Luke, Amy Kathryn. Came to U.S., 1954, naturalized, 1963. Intern Iowa Methodist Hosp., Des Moines, 1954-56; resident U. Kans. Med. Center, Kansas City, 1956-58; practice medicine specializing in anesthesiology; Kansas City, Kans., 1958—; instr. anesthesiology U. Kans. Med. Center, Kansas City, 1961-64, asst. prof., 1964-71, asso. prof., 1971-77, prof., 1977—, chmn. dept. anesthesiology, 1977—; clin. asso. prof. U. Mo.-Kansas City Sch. Dentistry, 1973—. Fulbright scholar, 1954. Recipient Outstanding Faculty award Student AMA, 1970. Diplomate Am. Bd. Anesthesiology. Fellow Am. Coll. Anesthesiology; mem. Asso. Univ. Anesthesiologists (sec.-treas. 1969—), Acad. Anesthesiology, Japan-Am. Soc. Midwest (v.p. 1965, 71). Home: 7917 El Monte St Shawnee Mission KS 66208 Office: Univ Med Center 39 Rainbow St Kansas City KS 66103

ARBAUGH, ROBERT BRUCE, data processing exec.; b. Charleston, W.Va., Dec. 31, 1948; a. William Harry and Peggy Jane (Pitts) A.; B.S. in Elec. Engring., Milw. Sch. Engring., 1971; postgrad. (Asso. Western Univs. fellow) U. Ariz., 1971-73. With PolySystems, Inc., Chgo., 1973—, dir. data center, 1974—. Mem. IEEE, Am. Nuclear Soc. Episcopalian. Club: Lake Shore (Chgo.). Office: 400 55 E Jackson Blvd Chicago IL 60604

ARBEEN, LYNN ANDREW, architect; b. Chgo., Aug. 13, 1930; s. Linne Bernard and Anne Cecilia (Opdahl) A.; student Roosevelt U., 1947-48; B.Arch., U. Ill., 1956; m. Maria Louise Thys, Feb. 16, 1957;children—Jo Anne, Kurt Michael, Mark Francis. Designer-draftsman Perkins & Will, Architects, Chgo., 1956-58, Cone & Dornbusch, Architects, Chgo., 1958-59; projects coordinator Chgo. Bd. Edn., 1959—. Served with USN, 1948-52. Recipient honorable mention Beaux Arts Inst. Design, 1955. Mem. AIA (corporate). Republican. Episcopalian. Mason (Shriner). Patentee in hardware field. Home: 719 Clinton Pl River Forest IL 60305 Office: 228 N La Salle St Chicago IL 60601

ARBUCKLE, DOROTHY FRY (MRS. LLOYD ARBUCKLE), business exec., librarian; b. Eldred, Ill., Jan. 23, 1910; d. William George and Sylvia (Mitchell) Fry; student Northwestern U., 1927-28, U. Ill., 1928-30; m. Lloyd Arbuckle, May 13, 1933 (dec. May 1960); children—Kathryn Diane, William Franklin. Freelance reporter, Ind., Ill., 1931; librarian Lake Village Ind. Meml. Twp. Library, 1946—; petroleum jobber, distbr. Lake Village Shell Oil Co., 1960—; pres. Arbuckle Oil Co., Inc.; mem. Key Oil Man's Com., 1976—; rep. Internat. Oil Seminar, Monte Carlo, 1977. Pres. Lake Village Sch. Corp., 1962—; twp. chmn. Multiple Sclerosis, Newton County, Ind., 1962-65; active George Ade Hosp. Aux. Nat. industry chmn. Laymen's Nat. Bible Assn., 1970, 71. Bd. dirs. Newton County Hist. Soc. Corp., Newton County Mental Health, Newton County Comprehensive Health, Newton County Exec. Com. on Dr. Recruitment, Lake View Retirement Home; chmn. Lake Twp. Bi-Centennial Com., 1975-76; mem. com. Newton County Bicentennial Project, 1976—; mem. Arrowhead Country Fish and Wildlife Commn., 1976—. Recipient of George award Lafayette-Courier-Jour., 1964. Mem. Ind., Small library assns., Ill. Woman's Press Assn., Nat. Fedn. Press Women, Midland Authors, Children's Reading Roundtable, D.A.R., ASCAP, Ind., Ill., Newton County (vice pres., program chmn. 1966—) hist. socs., Am. Women Composers Inc., Laymen's Nat. Bible Soc. (industry assn. chmn. 1972), Ind. Oil Marketers Assn., Internat. Platform Assn., Grange. Presbyn. (elder 1973—). Mem. Order Eastern Star. Author: The After-Harvest Festival (Distinguished Lit. award Ind. U. 1956), 1955; Andy's Dan'l Boone Rifle (cited by Ind. U. 1967), 1965; (anthem, words and music) The Church Wherein I Worship, 1955; The Hour Will Come, 1962; (ballad) I Never Knew, 1960. Recorded song By the Kankakee River, 1973. Home: Lake Village IN 46349

ARCHAMBAULT, BENNETT, mfg. co. exec.; b. Oakland, Calif.; s. Albert Joseph and May (Smales) A.; m. Margaret Henrietta Morgan; children—Suzanne Morgan, Michele Lorraine, Steven Bennett; student Ga. Inst. Tech.; B.S., Mass. Inst. Tech. Vice pres., gen. mgr. M.W. Kellogg Co., N.Y.C., 1946-54; pres. Stewart-Warner Corp., Chgo., 1954—, chmn. bd., 1959—; pres., dir., chmn. bd. Stewart-Warner Corp. of Can., Ltd.; pres., dir. Stewart-Warner Datafax Corp., Thor Power Tool Co., Herramientas Thor de Mexico S.A. de D.V.; dir., chmn. bd. Thor-Fiap, S.p.A.; dir., pres., dir. gen. Stewart-Warner France, S.A.; dir., chmn. dirs. trust com. Harris Trust & Savs. Bank; dir., mem. exec. com. Kemper Corp., Lumbermens Mut. Casualty Co., Am. Motorists Ins. Co., Fed. Kemper Ins. Co., Am. Mfrs. Mut. Ins. Co.; dir., mem. audit, compensation and stock option coms. Trans Union Corp.; dir. Stewart-Warner, Ltd., Stewart-Warner Internat. Sales Corp., Harris Bankcorp, Inc.; mem. bd. adminstrn. Stewart-Warner, Alemite GmbH. Mem. Mayor's Com. for Econ. and Cultural Devel., Chgo.; mem. Republican Nat. Finance Com.; bd. govs. United Rep. Found. of Ill.; v.p., bd. dirs. Protestant Found. Greater Chgo.; trustee Better Govt. Assn., Ill. Inst. Tech. Research Inst.; trustee, mem. exec. com., chmn. nominating com. Ill. Inst. Tech.; trustee, mem. exec. com., chmn. nominating com. Mus. Sci. and Industry; mem. corp. devel. com. Mass. Inst. Tech.; mem. adv. council Northwestern U. Grad. Sch. Mgmt. Recipient medal of merit U.S.; His Majesty's medal for service in cause of freedom (U.K.). Mem. U.S. C. of C., Employers Assn. Greater Chgo., Ill. Mfrs. Assn., NAM, Soc. Automotive Engrs., Research Soc. Am., Newcomen Soc. N.Am. Clubs: Chicago, Commercial, Metropolitan, Racquet, Saddle and Cycle, Westmoreland Country, Executives, Economics, Mass. Inst. Tech. Home: 3240 Lake Shore Dr Chicago IL 60657 Office: 1826 Diversey Pkwy Chicago IL 60614

ARCHAMBAULT, RENE FRANCIS, surgeon, educator; b. Barre, Vt., Oct. 31, 1911; s. Francois Xavier and Antonia (Pauze) A.; B.A., U. Montreal, 1930; M.D., Creighton U., 1936; M.S., U. Pa., 1940; m. Marilyn Miehls, Oct. 13, 1950; children—George, Susan, Rene, Mary Ann. Intern, Mercy Hosp., Council Bluffs, Iowa, 1936-37; resident Sacred Heart Hosp., Allentown, Pa., 1938-40; practice medicine specializing in surgery, Barre, 1940-41, Wayne, Mich., 1951—; adminstr. Nankin Hosp., Wayne, 1951—; adj. asso. prof. anatomy Wayne State U., Detroit, 1957—. Del., Mich. Republican Conv., 1968. Served to maj. AUS, 1941-46. Diplomate Am. Bd. Surgery. Mem. Pan Am. Med. Assn., Am. Acad. Med. Adminstrs. (regional v.p. 1967). Contbr. articles to profl. jours. Home: 3429 Sophia St Wayne MI 48184 Office: 35550 Michigan St Wayne MI 48184

ARCHBOLD, THOMAS JOHN, trust farm ofcl.; b. Fargo, N.D., July 10, 1947; s. Francis John and Eileen Mary (Fridgen) A.; B.S., N.D. State U., 1969, M.S., 1972; m. Sharon Joan Daub, June 22, 1968; children—Jason Thomas, Kristin Leigh, Kerry Lynn. Research asst. N.D. State U., Fargo, 1969-72; asst. Burleigh County agt. Extension Service, U.S. Dept. Agr., Bismarck, N.D., 1972-73, Ransom County extension agt., Lisbon, 1973-75; farm mgr. 1st Bank of N.D., N.A., Fargo, 1975—. Sec., Ransom County Crop and Livestock Improvement Assn., 1973-75; dir. Extension Staff Devel. Adv. Com., 1974-75; sec. Ransom County Soil Conservation Dist., 1973-75, Ransom County Twp. Officers Assn., 1973-75; bd. dirs. Ransom County Fair Bd., 1973-75. Named Man of Year, Lisbon Jr. C. of C., 1974. Mem. Am., N.D. socs. farm mgrs. and rural appraisers, N.W. Farm Mgrs., N.D. Acad. Sci., Lisbon Jr. C. of C. (dir. 1975), Sigma Chi. Roman Catholic. Clubs: Agassiz, Fargo Elks, K.C. Home: 93 23d Ave N Fargo ND 58102 Office: Mchts Nat Bank & Trust Co Fargo ND 58102

ARCHER, BERNARD THOMAS, radiologist; b. Rock Island, Ill., Dec. 8, 1935; s. Marcus Matthew and Janet Christita (Rank) A.; student St. Ambrose Coll., 1953-56; M.D., U. Iowa, 1960; m. Doreen Mary Smith, Aug. 26, 1961; children—Martha, Amy, Christopher, Stephen, Megan, Matthew. Intern, Milw. County Gen. Hosp., 1960-61; resident Univ. Hosps. Cleve., 1963-66, fellow in radiology, 1966-67; practice medicine specializing in radiology, 1967—; pres. Huron Rd. Radiologists, Cleve., 1970—; dir. dept. radiology Huron Hd. Hosp., East Cleveland, Ohio, 1968—; clin. asst. prof. Case Western Res. U., 1977—. Served with USAF, 1961-63. Certified Am. Bd. Radiology. Mem. Am., Ohio State, Can-Am. med. assns., Acad. Medicine Cleve., Radiol. Soc. N. Am., Am. Col. Radiology, Ohio State, Cleve. Radiol. Socs. Roman Catholic. Home: 945 Eastlawn Dr Cleveland OH 44143 Office: 13951 Terrace Rd Cleveland OH 44112

ARCHER, JOSEPH PAIGE, cold storage and ice co. exec.; b. Toledo, Aug. 2, 1910; s. Joseph Paige and Leone Ione (Kimling) A.; student U. Mo., 1954-57; m. Rose Josephine Conrey, Nov. 4, 1935; children—Michael Paige, Mary Josephine (Mrs. Robert J. Bregenzer). With Artificial Ice Co., Kansas City, Mo., 1935-42; with Ice Service Co., 1942-44; field rep. United Air Craft, 1944-45; mgr. Ice Service Co., Kansas City, Mo., 1945-58; with Empire Cold Storage and Ice Co., Kansas City, Mo., 1958—, v.p., 1964—. Recipient Navy award for outstanding civilian contbn. for work done at United Aircraft, 1945. Roman Catholic. Home: 5566 Crestwood Dr Kansas City MO 64110 Office: 2722 Guinotte St Kansas City MO 64120

ARCHER, LAWRENCE HARRY, coll. dean; b. Shelby, Ohio, Aug. 24, 1923; s. Vercia Dale and Queen Victoria (Coffey) A.; B.S. in Civil Engring. with high distinction, Ohio No. U., 1947, B.S. in Edn. with high distinction, 1949; M.S., Bowling Green State U., 1950; postgrad. Ohio State U., 1963-64; m. Betty Bernadine Holloway, Oct. 21, 1942; children—Gretchen (Mrs. David Cadegan), Bonnie (Mrs. Carl Wilkerson), Dan, David, Eric, Laurie, Rod. Instr. civil engring. Ohio No. U., Ada, 1945-47, prof., 1947—, chmn. dept. civil engring., 1951-57, dean coll. engring., 1951—. Engring cons., 1951—; engring. examiner Ohio Bd. Registration Profl. Engrs., 1949—; NSF panelist, 1963—. Mem. Ada. Bd. Edn., 1968-71; chmn. Ohio Hwy. Users Conf., 1953-56, Ohio Hwy Legislative Study Com., 1953-55; active PTA, Boy Scouts Am.; chmn. Hardin County Hosp. Commn., 1962-71. Mayor, Ada, 1960-62. Served with USAAF, 1942-44. Decorated Air medal. Recipient Silver Beaver award Boy Scouts Am., 1959. Registered profl. engr. and surveyor, Ohio. Mem. Am. Legion, Am. Soc. Engring. Edn. (chmn. Ohio sect. 1960-61), Am. Bowling Congress, Ada Bowling Assn. (pres. 1975—), Alumni N-Men's Assn. (pres. 1976—), Am. Rifle Assn., Phi Kappa Phi, Tau Beta Pi, Omicron Delta Kappa, Kappa Mu Epsilon, Phi Eta Sigma. Methodist (chmn. ofcl. bd. 1956-63, Sunday Sch. tchr.). Clubs: 700; Order of Engr. (gov. Ohio bd. 1976—, mem. nat. bd. 1976—), Masons (32 deg.). Home: 251 W Buckeye Ave Ada OH 45810

ARCHER, WESLEY LEA, chemist; b. Marietta, Ohio, Feb. 20, 1927; s. Daniel Wesley and Thelma A. (Marsh) A.; B.A., Kalamazoo Coll., 1950; Ph.D., Ind. U., 1953; m. Mary Susan Walker, May 29, 1971; 1 son, James Wesley. Research chemist Irwin Neisler Co., Decatur, Ill., 1953-56; sr. research specialist Dow Chem. Co., Midland, Mich., 1956—. Served with USNR, 1945-46. Patentee in field. Home: 4101 Swede Rd Midland MI 48640 Office: Dow Center 2020 Midland MI 48640

ARCHER, WILLIAM HARLEY, state ofcl.; b. Milw., Apr. 30, 1934; s. Joseph W. and Mary (Marolf) A.; B.A. in Polit. Sci., Mich. State U., 1957; m. Cleo F. Mitchell, Aug. 6, 1960 (dec. Mar. 1972); children—William A., Lisa A., John J.; m. 2d, Kathryn A. Millner, Sept. 8, 1973; 1 dau., Patricia L.; 1 stepdau., Tamara J. Carlson. Lease exec. property mgmt. div. Mich. Dept. Mgmt. and Budget, Lansing, 1961-62, asst. chief mgmt. div., 1968-74; budget analyst Exec. Office of Gov., 1962-66; dep. dir. Mich. Dept. Licensing and Regulation, Lansing, 1966-68; dir. energy office Mich. Pub. Service Commn., 1974-76; dir. materials mgmt. Mich. Liquor Control Commn., 1976—. Adviser, Gov.'s Task Forces on Reorgn. State Govt., 1964-66; sec. Civil Service Pay Hearing Bd., 1972; vice chmn. Citizens Adv. Com. on Fiscal Reform, Lansing, 1966-67; fed. apptd. receiver Bear Mt. Recreation Area, 1973-74. Mem. Am. Records Mgmt. Assn. (chpt. pres. 1961), Mich. Energy Resources and Research Assn. (asso.).

Home: 3544 Josephine Lane Mason MI 48854 Office: State Secondary Complex Bilwood Hwy Lansing MI 48913

ARCHIBALD, GEORGE WILLIAM, found. exec.; b. New Glasgow, N.S., Can., July 13, 1946; s. Donald Edison and Lettie (MacLoed) A.; B.S., Dalhousie U., Halifax, N.S., 1968; Ph.D., Cornell U. Co-founder, co-dir. Internat. Crane Found., Baraboo, Wis., 1973—. Recipient research grants N.Y. Zool. Soc., World Wildlife Fund, Nat. Audubon Soc., Iran Dept. Environment. Mem. Nat. Audubon Soc., World Wildlife Fund, Frankfurt Zool. Soc., Korean Council Crane Preservation, Japan Wild Bird Soc., N.Y. Zool. Soc. Contbr. articles to profl. jours. Home and Office: Internat Crane Foundation City View Rd Baraboo WI 53913

ARCHIBALD, ROBERT DAVISON, lawyer; b. Girard, Ohio, Jan. 11, 1931; s. Kenneth Day and Margaret (Davison) A.; student Youngstown U., 1951; B.A., Coll. Wooster, 1953; LL.B., Western Reserve U., 1956, J.D., 1969; m. Mary Elliott, Aug. 20, 1955; children—Matthew, Timothy, Anne. Admitted to Ohio bar, 1956; asso. McNeal Schick & Archibald, Cleve., 1956-68, partner, 1968-70, sr. partner, 1970—. Mem. Counsel Human Relations, Cleve., 1960-65; mem. Cleveland Heights Counsel Human Affairs, 1960-70. Pres. The Corporation, Cleve., 1971-72; bd. trustees YMCA, Cleveland Heights, Ohio, 1972-75. Mem. Cleve. Bar (asso. chmn. judicial selection com. 1972-74, chmn. 1974-75), Am. (asso. chmn. arbitration com., editor Forum), Ohio bar assns., Ohio, Cleve. def. assns., Internat. Assn. Ins. Counsel, Def. Research Inst., Cleve.-Wooster Alumni Assn. (pres. 1965-66), Phi Delta Phi, Phi Delta Sigma. Home: 2225 Coventry Rd Cleveland Heights OH 44118 Office: 520 Williamson Bldg Cleveland OH 44114

ARCHIE, DAVID ESDEN, editor; b. Creston, Iowa, Sept 12, 1925; s. Willard David and Estelle (Esden) A.; A.B., Princeton, 1950; m. Joyce McDonnell, Apr. 18, 1964; children—David Thaddeus, Jeanette Marie. Asso. editor Look Mag., N.Y.C., 1950-52; editor Iowan mag., Shenandoah, Iowa, 1952—; pres. Mid-America Publishing Corp., Des Moines, 1963—. Mem. Gov's Com. Social and Econs. Trends, 1956, Gov.'s Fine Arts Com., 1961-62, Iowa Arts Council, 1966-75; exec. com. United Fund Iowa, 1956-60. Bd. dirs. Iowa Coll. Found., 1957-67, Child Guidance Center, 1972-74; bd dirs. Friends U. Iowa Library, 1965-67, chmn., 1966-67; mem. Des Moines adv. com. on excellence in urban design, 1970—. Served with USNR, 1944-46. Recipient Bent Cane award Des Moines Press and Radio Club, 1954. Presbyn. Home: 1 Lincoln Pl Dr Des Moines IA 50312 Office: 214 Ninth St Des Moines IA 50309

ARDAIOLO, FRANK PALMA, coll. adminstr.; b. Bklyn., Oct. 21, 1948; s. Salvatore P. and Helen (De Chiccio) A.; B.A., Assumption Coll., 1970; M.S., Ind. U., 1974, Ed.D., 1978. Asst. coordinator Ind. U., 1971-74; asso. dean students, dir. residence life, dir. coll. union, lectr. polit. sci. Belmont Abbey Coll., 1974-76; resident fellow, research asst. Ind. U. at Bloomington, 1976—, conf. coordinator The Law and Coll. Student Personnel, 1977—. Recipient Assumption Coll. Academic scholarship, 1966-70; Ind. U. Nat. Def. Fgn. Lang. and Area Study fellowship, 1970-71. Mem. Am. Coll. Personnel Assn., Am. Personnel and Guidance Assn., Nat. Assn. Student Personnel Adminstrs. Democrat. Roman Catholic. Home: 238 N Smith Rd Apt 34 Bloomington IN 47401 Office: Sch Edn 226 Ind U Bloomington IN 47401

ARDUSSI, WALLACE PHILIP, sales exec.; b. Detroit, Feb. 28, 1934; s. Wallace F. and Faith (Farmer) A.; B.S., U. Mich., 1958; m. Ann Covell, July 26, 1958; children—Suzanne, John, Elizabeth, Deborah. Sales engr. Variety Stamping Corp., Cleve., 1961-62, sales mgr., 1962-64, corporate sec., dir., 1964-69; prodn. mgr. The Auer Register Co., Cleve., 1964-65, mktg. mgr., 1965-66, corporate sec., 1964-69, dir., 1966—; br. mgr. Transport Pool, 1969-70, br. mgr. Rentco div. Fruehauf Corp., 1970-72, nat. accounts mgr., 1973—. Served to 1st lt. USAF, 1958-61; now capt. Res. Mem. Cleve. Engring. Soc., Soc. Mfg. Engrs., Am. Mgmt. Assn., Chi Phi. Presbyterian (deacon 1968-71, elder). Rotarian (dir. 1967-70, 75—, asst. sec. 1970-72, treas. 1975-76, sec. 1976-77, v.p. 1977-78). Home: 794 Pemberton Rd Grosse Pointe Park MI 48230 Office: 11143 Harper Ave Detroit MI 48232

ARENBERG, IRVING KAUFMAN, otologist; b. E. Chicago, Ind., Jan. 10, 1941; s. George Isador and Ada Yetta (Field) A.; B.A. in Zoology, U. Mich., 1963, M.D., 1967; m. Carol Ann Rakita, May 31, 1964; children—Daniel Kaufman, Michael Harrison, Julie Gayle. Intern in surgery Wesley Meml. Hosp., Chgo., 1967-68; asst. resident in surgery St. Luke's Hosp., St. Louis, 1968-69; NIH fellow Washington U. Sch. Medicine, St. Louis, 1969-70; resident in otolaryngology Barnes Hosp., St. Louis, 1970-74, NIH clin. fellow neuro-otology, 1974-75; vis. scientist Swedish Med. Research Council, 1975-76; asst. prof. U. Wis. Med. Sch. and Hosps., 1976—; chief, otolargyngology service VA Hosp., Madison, 1976—; dir. Internat. Meniere's Disease Study Center U. Wis. Hosps., 1972—; dir. neuro-otology lab. U. Wis. Hosps.; cons. Denver Surg. Developments, Inc. Served to lt. comdr. M.C., USNR, 1963-74. NINDS spl. tchr. investigator awardee, 1971-76. Diplomate Am. Bd. Otolargyngology. Fellow Am. Acad. Ophthalmology and Otolaryngology (research award 1969-70, 72, 74, 75); mem. AMA (Physician's Recognition award 1971, 74), AAAS, Electron Microscopy Soc. Am., Am. Assn. Anatomists, Am. Soc. Cell Biology, N.Y. Acad. Scis., Assn. Research Otolaryngology. Jewish. Asso. editor AMA Archives Otolaryngology, 1968—; contbr. med. jours. Home: 6209 S Highlands Ave Madison WI 53705 Office: 1300 University Ave Madison WI 53706

ARENDS, ROBERT EUGENE, microbiologist; b. Marvin, S.D., July 19, 1931; s. Alvin and Anne (Ramsey) A.; B.S., S.D. State U., 1959; m. Pauline Wyla Neilan, Aug. 2, 1959; 1 dau., Kayleen Ann. With Pet Inc., Greenville, Ill., 1959—, sr. research microbiologist, 1969-74, mgr. microbiology, 1975-77, mgr. Food sci. Contech Labs., 1977—. Mem. Greenville Planning Commn., 1961-65, Greenville City Council, 1966-70. Served with USAF, 1951-55. Mem. Am. Soc. Microbiology. Republican. Baptist. Home: 740 N Elm St Greenville IL 62246 Office: Louis Latzer Dr Greenville IL 62246

AREY, LEO BETRAM, clin. psychologist; b. Richfield, N.C., June 19, 1913; s. Nathan Green and Nina (Trexler) A.; m. Jennie Lind Mitchell, Dec. 31, 1941; A.B., Lenoir Rhyne Coll., 1935; Ph.D., U. Chgo., 1952. Registered psychologist, Ill., 1964; diplomate Am. Bd. Profl. Psychology. Psychology intern VA Hosp., Hines, Ill., 1947-51, staff clin. psychologist, 1952-61, research psychologist, 1962-66, asst. chief, psychology service, supervisory psychologist, psychiatry service, 1966—. Mem. Am., Midwest, Ill. psychol. assns., Ill. Group Psychotherapy Soc., Assn. Psychophysiol. Study Sleep, Am. Acad. Psychotherapists, Assn. Advancement Psychology, Sigma Xi. Contbr. to psychol. jours. and book. Home: 5532 South Shore Dr Chicago IL 60637 Office: Veterans Administration Hospital Psychology Service Hines IL 60141

ARGANBRIGHT, FRANK CLARENCE, journalist; b. Gosport, Ind., Oct. 10, 1919; s. Edward Dekker and Grace (Neal) A.; A.B. in Journalism, Ind. U., 1949. Reporter, Jour. and Courier, Lafayette, Ind., 1949-66, record columnist, feature writer, 1952-72, asst. city editor, 1963-66, city editor, 1966-71, mag. editor, 1971-72; sr. editor student affairs Purdue U. Office Pub. Info., West Lafayette, 1972—. Publicity chmn. United Fund, Lafayette, 1955; pub. relations chmn. Red Cross, 1974-77; bd. dirs. Lafayette Symphony, Inc., 1972—; adviser Delta Upsilon Fraternity chpt. Served with AUS, 1941-45, ETO. Decorated Bronze Star medal. Mem. Beta Alpha Chi. Home: 1805 Whitcomb Ave Lafayette IN 47904 Office: South Campus Courts Purdue U West Lafayette IN 47907

ARGENTO, DOMINICK, composer; b. York, Pa., Oct. 27, 1927; s. Michael and Nicolina (Amato) A.; B.Mus., Peabody Conservatory, 1951; Fulbright fellow, Conservatorio Cherubini, Florence, 1951-52; Ph.D., Eastman Sch. Music, 1957; m. Carolyn Bailey, Sept. 6, 1954. Prof. music U. Minn., Mpls., 1958—. Co-founder Center Opera, Mpls., Hilltop Opera, Balt. Served with AUS, 1945-47. Guggenheim grantee, 1957-58, 64-65. Recipient Pulitzer prize, 1975. Mem. A.S.C.A.P. Composer numerous operas, song cycles, choral and orchestral works. Home: 1919 Mt Curve Minneapolis MN 55403

ARGERSINGER, WILLIAM JOHN, JR., educator; b. Chittenango, N.Y., Apr. 14, 1918; s. William John and Elsie M. (Hosley) A.; A.B., Cornell U., 1938, Ph.D., 1942; m. Marjorie R. Hayes, Sept. 12, 1942; children—William John III, Peter Hayes, Ann Elizabeth II. Instr. chemistry Cornell U., 1942-44; chemist, research chemist, group leader Monsanto Chem. Co., 1944-46; with U. Kans., 1946—, asst. to asso. prof. chemistry, 1946-56, prof., 1956—, asso. dean Grad Sch., 1956-63, asso. dean Faculties, 1963-70, dean research adminstrn., 1970-72, vice chancellor for research and grad. studies, 1972—. Fellow AAAS, Am. Inst. Chemists; mem. Soc. Engring. Sci., Am. Chem. Soc., AAUP, Kans., N.Y. acads. sci., Phi Beta Kappa, Sigma Xi, Phi Kappa Phi, Phi Lambda Upsilon, Alpha Chi Sigma. Author textbook in advanced inorganic chemistry; articles on thermodynamics of electrolytes, physical chemistry. Home: 325 Park Hill Terrace Lawrence KS 66044

ARIAS, BELISARIO ANTONIO, neurol. surgeon; b. Santiago del Estero, Argentina, Jan. 7, 1929; came to U.S., 1958, naturalized, 1968; M.D., Cordoba U., Argentina, 1954; m. Noris Lorenzon, Oct. 8, 1955; children—Edward, Christina, Jessica. Med. resident, Army Hosp., Buenos Aires, Argentina, 1954-58; fellow in neurosurgery Lahey Clinic, Boston, 1958-59; resident in neurol. surgery Cook County Hosp., Chgo., 1959-60, U. Ill., Chgo., 1962-64; practice medicine specializing in neurol. surgery, Chgo. area, 1964—; clin. asso. prof. neurol. surgery Loyola U. Sch. Medicine, Chgo.; clin. asso. prof. neurol. surgery Abraham Lincoln Sch. Medicine U. Ill., Chgo., 1972—. Diplomate Am. Bd. Neurol. Surgeons. Fellow Am. Coll. Surgeons, Internat. Coll. Surgeons. Contbr. articles to med. jours. Office: 7310 W North Ave Elmwood Park IL 60635

ARIEFF, ALEX JOSEPH, neurologist; b. Bluffton, Ind., May 8, 1908; B.S., Northwestern U., 1929, M.B., 1932, M.D., 1933. Intern, East Moline Hosp., Moline, Ill., 1932; intern Cook County Hosp., Chgo., 1933, resident in pathology, 1934; asso. dept. neurology and psychiatry Med. Sch., Northwestern U., Chgo., 1935-38; practice medicine specializing in neurology, Chgo.; neurologist Passavant Meml. Hosp., VA Hosp., Hines, Ill.; prof. neurology and psychiatry Med. Sch., Northwestern U., 1973—; cons. neurology Chgo. Bd. Edn.; cons. Rehab. Inst. of Chgo. Diplomate Am. Bd. Psychiatry and Neurology. Mem. Am. Acad. Neurology, AAAS, Am. EEG Soc., AMA, Am. Neurol. Assn., Am. Psychiat. Assn., Central EEG Soc., Central Neuropsychiat. Assn., Chgo. Med. Soc., Chgo. Neurol. Soc. (pres. 1949), Ill. Epilepsy Soc. (chmn. med. adv. bd.), Ill. Med. Soc., Ill. Psychiat. Soc. (v.p.), Ill. Soc. Mental Hygiene, Internat. League Against Epilepsy, Sigma Xi. Contbr. articles in field to profl. jours. Home: 707 N Fairbanks Ct Chicago IL 60611

ARKEMA, KATHERINE KEMP, radiologist; b. Birmingham, Ala., Dec. 8, 1940; d. Karlton Hubert and Flora Mildred (Steel) Kemp; B.A. cum laude, Vanderbilt U., 1962; M.D., Baylor U., 1966; m. Edward L.S. Arkema, Jr., Aug. 21, 1971 (dec. 1974); children—Dawn Elizabeth, Kirsten Katherine, Elise Louisa Sue. Intern, Chgo. Wesley Meml. Hosp., 1966-67; resident Presbyn.-St. Luke's Hosp., Chgo., 1967-70, adj. in radiology, 1970-71; adj. in radiology Oak Park (Ill.) Hosp., 1971-72; attending radiologist Northwestern Meml. Hosp., Chgo., 1972—; asso. in radiology Northwestern U. Med. Sch., Chgo., 1972—. Diplomate Am. Bd. Radiology. Mem. AMA, Am. Coll. Radiology, Radiology Soc. N.Am., Gamma Phi Beta. Home: 2127 Hudson St Chicago IL 60614 Office: Northwestern Meml Hosp Chicago IL 60611

ARLINGHAUS, EDWARD JAMES, educator; b. Cin., Jan. 6, 1925; s. Edward A. and Irene (Custer) A.; B.B.A., U. Cin., 1948; M.B.A., Xavier U., 1958, M.Ed., 1971, M.S., 1973; m. Ilse Denninger, Aug. 10, 1974; 1 dau., Toni Gail. Dir. personnel tng. Mabley & Carew Co., Cin., 1948-51; sales researcher John Shillito Co., Cin., 1951-53; personnel devel. specialist Gen. Elec. Co., Cin., 1953-57; dir. personnel, pub. relations and security Jewish Hosp. of Cin., 1957-66; dir. grad. program in hosp. and health adminstrn. Xavier U., Cin., 1966—; bd. trustees Providence Hosp.; mem. health care sect. Cath. Conf. Ohio; sec. bd. trustees St. Francis Hosp., 1968-75; chmn. health manpower com. CORVA, Cin., 1970-75; sec. bd. trustees St. Mary's Hosp., Cin., 1968-72; mem. Ohio Bd. Examiners Nursing Home Adminstrs., 1974-76. Served with AUS, 1943-45; col. Res. Fellow Royal Soc. Health; mem. Am. Coll. Hosp. Adminstrs., Assn. Mental Health Adminstrs., Cath. Hosp. Assn., Scarbard and Blade, Phi Delta Kappa. Home: 7568 Trailwind Dr Montgomery OH 45242 Office: Xavier University Cincinnati OH 45207

ARLOOK, THEODORE DAVID, dermatologist; b. Boston, Mar. 12, 1910; s. Louis and Rebecca (Sakansky) A.; B.S., U. Ind. Sch. Medicine, 1932, M.D., 1934; postgrad. dermatology U. So. Calif., 1946-47. Intern, Luth. Meml. Hosp., Chgo., 1934-35; resident in dermatology Indpls. Gen. Hosp., 1947-49; practice medicine specializing in dermatology, Elkhart, Ind., 1950—; mem. staff Elkhart Gen. Hosp.; asso. mem. dermatology dept. Wishard Meml. Hosp., Indpls. Pres., Temple Israel, Elkhart, 1963-64; pres. B'nai B'rith, 1955. Served to capt. M.C. AUS, 1941-46; PTO. Diplomate Am. Bd. Dermatology. Mem. AMA, Am. Acad. Dermatology, Elkhart County Med. Soc. (pres. 1967). Contbr. articles to med. jours. Office: 912 W Franklin St Elkhart IN 46514

ARMACOST, JAMES OWEN, physician; b. Dayton, Ohio, Nov. 5, 1938; s. James Howard and Norma (Owens) A.; B.S., U. Dayton, 1964; student Ohio State U., 1958, 60; D.O., Kirksville Coll. Osteopathy, 1968; m. Sunnye Lea Lanham, Feb. 18, 1967; children—E. Ann, J. Eric, Andrew H. Intern, Flint Gen. Hosp., 1968-69, Naval Aerospace Med. Inst., 1969; flight surgeon, Adak, Alaska, 1970-71; resident in family practice, Phila. Naval Hosp., 1971, Camp Pendleton (Calif.) Naval Hosp., 1971-73; chief aviation, Whidbey Island, Wash., 1973-74; practice medicine specializing in family practice, Versailles, Ohio, 1974-75, Greenville, Ohio, 1976—; med. dir. Cade's Nursing Home. Mem. bldg. com. YMCA. Served with USN, 1969-74. Diplomate Am. Bd. Family Physicians; mem. Assn. Mil. Surgeons, Ohio Acad. Family Physicians, AMA, Ohio Med. Assn., Ohio Osteopathic Assn., Dayton Dist. Acad., Darke County Med. Assn. (v.p.). Club: Lions. Home: 2578 Greenville Nashville Rd Greenville OH 45331 Office: 414 Walnut St Greenville OH 45331

ARMANTROUT, MARY LYNN, TV producer; b. Milw., July 28, 1952; d. Richard Thomas and Lois Marion (Hale) Armantrout; B.A. in Social Work and Radio-TV, U. Wis., 1974. Producer programs on health, sports and women Sta. WHA-TV, Madison, Wis., 1973—. Mem. Nat. Assn. Ednl. Broadcasters (com. student affairs 1974-75). Home: 444 Jean St Madison WI 53706 Office: Station WHA-TV 821 University Ave Madison WI 53706

ARMENT, REX DALE, accountant; b. Quincy, Ill., Aug. 6, 1941; s. George Martin and Nora Marie (Gragg) A.; grad. Gem City Bus. Coll., 1961. Bookkeeper, Burdman Auto Parts, Inc., Kirksville, Mo., 1961-63; accountant N.E. Mo. Coop., Edina, 1963-65; owner Knox County Bookkeeping & Tax Service, Edina, 1965—. Part-time mgr. Knox County C. of C., 1967-70. Chmn., Edina Park Bd., 1974—; treas. City of Edina, 1970—. Mem. Nat. Soc. Pub. Accountants, Knox County C. of C. Mem. Christian Ch. Office: Box 233 Edina MO 63537

ARMOCK, FRANK LEROY, bus. counselor; b. Petoskey, Mich., Oct. 10, 1946; s. Amos B. and Mildred V. (Allerding) A.; Asso. Commerce, N. Central Mich. Coll., 1967; B.B.A., U. Mich., 1969; m. Diane K. Temple, Aug. 27, 1966; children—Christy Ann, Kimberly Kay. Accountant, Ford Motor Co., Detroit, 1967-69; supervising constrn. foreman Mich. Bell Telephone Co., Jackson, 1969-72; bus. counselor Gen. Bus. Services, Petoskey, Mich., 1973—; lectr. in field. Chmn. Littlefield Twp. Planning and Zoning Commn., 1975-76, vice-chmn., 1976—. Mem. Nat. Small Bus. Assn., Am. Soc. Bus. Cons.'s. Home: 4652 Moore Rd Oden MI 49764 Office: PO Box 156 Oden MI 49764

ARMSTRONG, A. JAMES, bishop; b. Marion, Ind., Sept. 17, 1924; s. Arthur J. and Frances (Green) A.; A.B., Fla. So. Coll., 1948, D.D., 1960; B.D., Candler Sch. Theology, 1952; D.D., DePauw U., 1965, Westmar Coll., 1971; L.H.D., Ill. Wesleyan U., 1970, Dakota Wesleyan U., 1970; m. Phyllis Jeanne Shaeffer, Feb. 26, 1942; children—James, Teresa (Mrs. John Etchison), John, Rebecca (Mrs. Ed Putens), Leslye. Ordained minister Methodist Ch., 1948; minister, Fla., 1945-58; sr. minister Broadway Methodist Ch., Indpls., 1958-68; bishop Dakotas area, Aberdeen, S.D., 1968—; instr. Christian Theol. Sem., Indpls., 1961-68. Del. Fourth Gen. Assembly World Council Chs.; del., mem. dept. internat. affairs Nat. Council Chs.; pres. ch. and soc. United Methodist Ch., 1972-76, v.p. Commn. Religion and Race, 1976—. Vice chmn. Hoosiers for Peace, 1968; mem. Nat. Coalition for a Responsible Congress, 1970. Mem. Ind. Democratic State Platform Com., 1968; co-chmn. Religious Leaders for McGovern, 1972. Trustee Dakota Wesleyan U., Methodist Hosp. (both Mitchell, S.D.). Served with USNR, 1942. Recipient Distinguished Service award Indpls. Jr. C. of C., 1959. Author: The Journey That Men Make, 1969; The Urgent Now, 1970; Mission: Middle America, 1971; The United Methodist Primer, 1973, 77; Wilderness Voices, 1974; The Nation Yet To Be, 1975; Truth-Telling: The Foolishness of Preaching in a Real World, 1977; (with others) War Crimes and the American Conscience, 1970; (with others) The Pulpit Speaks on Race, 1966; (with others) Rethinking Evangelism, 1971; (with others) What's a Nice Church Like You Doing In a Place Like This?, 1971. Home: 1419 N Main Aberdeen SD 57401 Office: Berkshire Plaza 405 NW 8th Ave Aberdeen SD 57401

ARMSTRONG, CHARLES WILLIS, constrn. co. exec.; b. Lansing, Mich., Sept. 25, 1929; s. John Richard and Mae (Crawford) A.; grad. high sch.; m. Patricia Kay Stoddard, Jan. 27, 1955; children—Jacqueline Joy, Rebecca Raye. Carpenter, Rekstad Builders, Inc., Downers Grove, Ill., 1962, 65-66; foreman, supt. Anton Sikich Builder, Naperville, Ill., 1962-65; supt. Don A. Tosi Builder, Naperville, Ill., 1966—. Architect, builder various inst. bldgs. Juneau Ice Field, Alaska, 1968. Mem. Earth Sci. Club No. Ill., Nat. Wildlife Fedn., Juneau Ice Field Research Assn., Assn. Mountaineering (charter mem., leader expdns.). Clubs: Sierra, Chicago Mountaineering, Iowa Mountaineers. Author: Trilobites of the Chicago Region, 1962. Home: 535 S Washington St Naperville IL 60540 Office: 804 Riva Rd Naperville IL 60540

ARMSTRONG, HART REID, religious orgn. exec.; b. St. Louis, May 11, 1912; s. Hart Champlin and Zora Lillian (Reid) A.; student Life Bible Coll., 1931; A.B., Christian Temples U., 1936; Litt.D., Geneva Theol. Coll. Wis., 1967; D.D., Central Sch. Religion, Surrey, Eng.; Th.D., Evang. Sem.; m. Iona Rhoda Mehl, Feb. 21, 1932; 1 son, Hart Reed III. Ordained to ministry Assembly of God Ch., 1932; pastor, 1932-34; dean Bible Standard Coll., Eugene, Oreg., 1935-40; missionary to Indonesia, 1941-42; editor Open Bible Publishers Des Moines, 1944-46, Gospel pub. House, Springfield, Mo., 1947-53, Gospel Light Publs., Glendale, Calif., 1954; crusade adminstr. Oral Roberts Assn., Tulsa, 1955-62; exec. dir. Assembly Homes, Inc., Glenwood, Minn., 1963-66; pres. Defenders of Christian Faith, Kansas City, Mo., 1967—, also editor nat. religious mag. The Defender, 1967—. Dir. and operator Evang. Press Service, 1950-54. Fellow Royal Soc. Arts; mem. Nat. Sunday Sch. Assn., Pope County Hist. Soc., Sigma Delta Chi. Rotarian (past charter pres. Glenwood, Minn.). Author: To Those Who Are Left, 1950; You Should Know, 1951; The Rebel, 1967; The Beast, 1967; How Do I Pray?, 1968; All Things for Life, 1969; What Will Happen to the United States?, 1969; Primer of Prophecy, 1970. World tour guide. Home: PO Box 11431 Kansas City MO 64112 Office: 155 N Market St Wichita KS 67202

ARMSTRONG, JOHN ROBERTS, editor; b. Springfield, Ill., Aug. 14, 1942; s. James E. and Violet O. (Roberts) A.; student U. Ill., 1961-62, Brooks Inst. Photography, 1965, Lincoln Land Coll., 1969; B.A., Sangamon State U., 1971, M.A., 1973; m. Cheryl Anne Keran, July 18, 1964; children—Anne Keran, John Roberts II. Editor, Herald-News Community Newspapers, Pawnee/Rochester, Ill., 1967; editor-in-chief Sports Spotlight newspaper, Springfield, 1968; pub. information specialist City Springfield Dept. Sts. and Pub. Improvements, 1964-69; founder Spectrum newspaper, Springfield, 1970; pub. Spectrum and Springfield Herald Spectrum newspaper, 1970—; editor Ill. Dept. Agr. AgScene mag., Springfield, 1973-77; pres. Armstrong Press, Springfield, 1977—; v.p., dir. Univ. Pubs., Inc., Springfield, 1974—. Radio operator Sangamon County Civil Def., 1959—; lobbyist, regional coordinator Ill. State Motorcycle Assn., 1967; mem. univ. assembly Sangamon State U., 1970, 71. Sec., Sangamon County Young Republicans, 1966-67. Recipient Service award Lincoln Land Coll., 1970. Mem. Am. Agrl. Editors Assn., Communications Officers State Depts. Agr., Central Electric Railfans Assn. Elk. Night photo editor Daily Illini, 1961; editor Source, 1972. Home: 1825 S Pasfield St Springfield IL 62704 Office: 2628 S Pasfield Springfield IL 62704

ARMSTRONG, NAOMI YOUNG, educator; b. Dermott, Ark., Oct. 17, 1918; d. Allen Wesley and Sarah Elizabeth (Fluker) Young; B.S., Northwestern U., 1961; L.H.D., U. Libre, Karachi, Pakistan, 1974; m. Joe Leslie Armstrong, July 17, 1938; 1 dau., Betty-Jo Armstrong Dunbar. Actress, Skyloft Players, also Center Aisle Players, Chgo., 1945-59; silk dress operator Rue-Ann Originals, Chgo., 1947-55; clk. Bur. Pub. Debt, 1955-56, IRS, 1956-59; caseworker Cook County Dept. Pub. Aid, Chgo., 1956-59; tchr. Chgo. pub. schs., 1962—, creative writing instr., 1975-77, instr. Social Center, 1965-67;

dramatic instr. Crerar Meml. Presbyn. Ch., Chgo., 1972. Mem. exec. bd., membership chmn. Northwestern U. Young Alumni Council, 1971-72; trustee World U., 1973-74. Recipient Hon. Gold diploma, spl. award 3d World Congress Poets, 1976; named Internat. Woman of 1975, United Poets Laureate Internat. others. Mem. United Poets Laureate Internat. (exec. bd.), Internat. Platform Assn. (life; bd. govs.; 3d Preview winner 1976), World Poets Resource Center, Poetry Soc. London, Centro Studi E. Scambi Internat., World Poetry Soc., Sigma Gamma Rho. Author: A Child's Easter, 1971; Expression I, 1973; Expression III, 1976. Address: 9257 S Burnside Ave Chicago IL 60619

ARMSTRONG, NEIL A., educator, former astronaut; b. Wapakoneta, Ohio, Aug. 5, 1930; s. Stephen Armstrong; B.S. in Aero. Engring., Purdue U., 1955; M.S. in Aerospace Engring., U. So. Cal.; m. Janet Shearon; children—Eric, Mark. With Lewis Flight Propulsion Lab., NACA, 1955; then aero. research pilot for NACA, later NASA, High Speed Flight Sta., Edwards, Cal.; astronaut Manned Spacecraft Center, NASA, Houston, Texas, back-up command pilot Gemini 5; command pilot Gemini 8, March 1966; backup command pilot Gemini 11; backup comdr. Apollo VIII; spacecraft comdr. Apollo XI, July 1969, 1st man to walk on moon; prof. aerospace engring. U. Cin., 1971—. Served as aviator USNR, 1949-52; Korea. Recipient numerous awards including Octave Chanute award Inst. Aero. Scis., 1962; John J. Montgomery award, 1962; AIAA Astronautics award, 1966; NASA Exceptional Service medal; Presdl. Medal for Freedom, 1969. Fellow Soc. Exptl. Test Astronautics, Am. Astron. Soc.; mem. Soaring Soc. Am. Office: Dept Aerospace Engineering U Cincinnati Cincinnati OH 45221

ARMSTRONG, PATRICIA KAY (MRS. CHARLES W. ARMSTRONG), ecologist, educator; b. Highland Park, Mich., Dec. 18, 1936; d. El M. and Vivian (Thompson) Stoddard; B.A. cum laude, N. Central Coll., Ill., 1958; postgrad. (Robert Ridgeway fellow) U. Chgo., 1967-68, M.S., 1968; m. Charles W. Armstrong, Jan. 27, 1955; children—Jacqueline Joy, Rebecca Raye. Sci. tchr. Washington Jr. High Sch., Naperville, Ill., 1960-69, head sci. dept., 1963-67; staff Inst. Glaciological and Arctic Scis., 1968; study botany, Juneau Ice Field, Alaska, 1966, 68; tchr. rock climbing, mountaineering, leader expdns., 1964—; asst. research specialist Morton Arboretum, Lisle, 1969—. Mem. Ill. Edn. Assn., Nat. Sci. Tchrs. Assn., Ecol. Soc. Am., Am. Mus. Nat. History, Arctic Inst. Am., Brit. Lichen Soc., Am. Bryological Soc., Wis. Regional Writers Assn., Sigma Xi, Tri Beta. Baptist. Clubs: Ia. Mountaineering; Chicago Mountaineering, Sierra (Chgo.). Author: Trilobites of the Chicago Region, 1962. Contbr. articles and photographs to nat. mags. Leader expdn. on E. face route to top of Longs Peak, Colo. Home: 535 S Washington St Naperville IL 60540 Office: Morton Arboretum Lisle IL 60532

ARMSTRONG, THEODORE MORELOCK, corporate exec.; b. St. Louis, July 22, 1939; s. Theodore Roosevelt and Vassar Fambrough (Morelock) A.; B.A., Yale, 1961; LL.B., Duke, 1964; m. Carol Mercer Robert, Sept. 7, 1963; children—Evelyn Anne, Robert Theodore. Admitted to Mo. bar, 1964; with Mo. Pacific Corp. and subsidiaries, St. Louis, 1964—, corporate sec., 1971-75; corporate sec. River Cement Co., 1968-75; asst. v.p. Mississippi River Transmission Corp., 1974-75; v.p. Gas Supply, 1975—. Mem. Am., Met. St. Louis bar assns., Mo. Bar, So. Gas Assn., Phi Alpha Delta. Republican. Presbyterian (deacon). Clubs: Clayton, Yale (St. Louis); Yale (N.Y.C.). Home: 307 Woodside Dr St Louis MO 63122 Office: 9900 Clayton Rd St Louis MO 63124

ARMSTRONG, WALLACE JACKSON, zoo exec.; b. Washington, May 14, 1928; s. Wallace Jackson and Rachel Grace (Dutton) A.; m. Janet Elaine McBurney, July 5, 1968; student U. Md., 1952-68. With Washington Nat. Zoo, 1945-46, 52-68, zoo policeman to sr. cat keeper, 1952-68; asst. dir. Kansas City (Mo.) Zoo, 1968-71, dir., 1971—. Mem. Am. Assn. Zool. Parks and Aquarians, Optimist Club. Writer columns for Wednesday mag. and F.O.Z. News. Home and office: Kansas City Zoo Kansas City MO 64132

ARNDT, ELIZABETH DELANO MOORE (MRS. JOSEPH MANNING ARNDT, JR.), civic worker; b. Newburyport, Mass., Aug. 25, 1920; d. Frederick Arnold and Miriam Chelis (Delano) Moore; Registered Nurse, Boston City Hosp. Sch. Nursing, 1941; m. Joseph Manning Arndt, Jr., May 11, 1946; children—Margaret Anne (Mrs. Jerry Shinn), Martha Howard (Mrs. Sam Maggard), Joseph lManning III, Marilyn Delano. Asst. head nurse outpatient dept. Boston City Hosp., 1941-42. Pres., Heart of Mo. council Girl Scouts U.S.A., 1967-71, council communicator region V, 1973, day camp dir., 1966-72; chmn. Centralia (Mo.) United Fund, 1967; sec. E. Central Mo. Mental Health Council, 1971-72; co-organizer Centralia Mental Health Council, 1972—. Pres., Centralia Federated Republican Women's Club, 1960-62; treas. 8th Dist. Republican Woman's Club, 1962; pres. Mo. Federated Rep. Woman's Club, 1969-71; del. Rep. Nat. Conv., 1962, 76; committeeman Rep. party, Centralia, 1966-74; chmn. youth involvement Nat. Federated Rep. Women, 1972-73; mem. Mo. State Rep. Com., 1970—. Served with Nurses Corps, AUS, 1942-46; ETO. Mem. Am. Legion, P.E.O. Mem. Christian Ch. (deaconess 1963-66). Club: Sorosis Federated Women's (pres. 1954-56), Bridge (Centralia). Home: 5 Sunrise Circle Centralia MO 65240

ARNDT, JOSEPH MANNING, elec. equipment co. exec.; b. Detroit, Mar. 3, 1919; s. Joseph Manning and Ella Mae (Howard) A.; B.S., U. Ill., 1941; m. Elizabeth Delano Moore, May 11, 1946; children—Margaret (Mrs. Jerry F. Shinn), Martha H. (Mrs. Samuel P. Maggard), Joseph Manning III, Marilyn D. Editor, Owens Ill. Glass, Alton, Ill., 1941-47; pub. editor A.B. Chance Co., Centralia Mo., 1947-50, employee mgr., 1950-55, dir. indsl. and pub. relations, 1955-60, v.p. indsl. and pub. relations, 1960—, dir., 1964—. Mem. Centralia (Mo.) Sch. Bd., 1959-62; mem. Boone County Sch. Bd., 1964-65. Trustee, The Chance Found., 1955—. Served to capt., AUS, 1942-46. Mem. Mo. C. of C. (dir. 1967-73), Am. Legion. Republican. Mem. Christian Ch. Kiwanian. Clubs: Centralia Country; Bella Vista (Ark.) Country. Home: 5 Sunrise Circle Centralia MO 65240 Office: 210 N Allen St Centralia MO 65240

ARNELL, PAULA ANN YOUNGBERG (MRS. RICHARD ANTHONY ARNELL), pathologist; b. Moline, Ill., Nov. 25, 1938; d. Paul Phillip and Mabel Eleanor (Arnell) Youngberg; B.A. summa cum laude, Augustana Coll., 1960; M.D., U. Iowa, 1964; m. Richard Anthony Arnell, June 28, 1964; children—Carla Ann, Paula Marie, Paul Anthony. Intern, St. Lukes-Mercy Hosp., Cedar Rapids, Iowa, 1964-65; resident pathology U. Iowa, Iowa City, 1965-68; chief resident State U. Iowa Hosp., Iowa City, 1968-69; pathologist, dir. labs. Luth. Hosp., Moline, Ill., 1969—; mem. staffs Moline Pub. Hosp., Franciscan Hosp., Rock Island, Ill. Sec., Rock Island County Blood Bank, 1972-73, v.p., 1973-74; cons. Rock Island Tb Center, 1970-72; profl. del. Am. Cancer Soc., 1971-73; tchr. Luth. Hosp. Sch. Inhalation Therapy, Sch. Nursing, 1970—; med. dir. Royal Neighbors of Am. Ins. Co., Rock Island; co-dir. Met. Med. Lab., Moline. Pres. Rock Island County Cancer Soc., 1970—; mem. alumni bd. dirs. Augustana Coll., Rock Island, 1972-75, chmn., 1977—; sec. med. sect. Nat. Fraternal Congress, 1976—; bd. dirs. Mississippi Valley Regional Blood Bank, 1973—. Fellow Am. Coll. Pathologists, Am. Soc. Clin. Pathologists; mem. Internat. Acad. Pathologists, Am. Assn. Cytologists, Am. Assn. Blood Banks, Am. Assn. Clin. Scientists, Am. Womans Med. Assn., AMA, Iowa Ill. med. socs., Phi Beta Kappa. Beta Beta Beta. Home: 3904 7th Ave Rock Island IL 61201 Office: Luth Hosp 501 10th Ave Moline IL 61265

ARNELL, RICHARD ANTHONY, radiologist, nuclear medicine physician; b. Chgo., Aug. 21, 1938; s. Tony Frank and Mary Martha (Oberman) Yaki; B.A. (Younker Achievement scholar), Grinnell Coll., 1960; M.D., U. Iowa, 1964; m. Paula Ann Youngberg, June 28, 1964; children—Carla Ann, Paula Marie, Paul Anthony. Intern, Mercy and St. Luke's hosps., Cedar Rapids, Iowa, 1964-65; resident in radiology and nuclear medicine U. Iowa Hosps., 1965-68; practice medicine specializing in radiology and nuclear medicine, Moline, Ill., 1968—; mem. Moline Radiology Assos., 1968—, v.p., 1970-77; mem. staffs Luth. Hosp., Moline Pub. Hosp.; trustee Midstate Found. for Med. Care, 1975-77, exec. com., 1976-77. Supt. Sunday Ch. Sch. St. John's Luth. Ch., Rock Island, Ill., 1974-77, mem. ch. cabinet, 1975-76; del. Chs. United of Scott and Rock Island counties, Ill., 1977; mem. nat. exec. com. Augustana Coll., Rock Island, Ill., 1977; bd. dirs. Luth. Hosp., Moline, 1977—. Recipient David Theophillus trophy for outstanding athlete Grinnell Coll., 1960; diplomate Am. Bd. Radiology, Am. Bd. Nuclear Medicine. Mem. Am. Coll. Radiology, Ill. Radiol. Soc., Am. Coll. Nuclear Medicine, Soc. Nuclear Medicine, AMA, Ill. (ho. of dels. 1974-77), Rock Island County (exec. com. 1974-77, peer-rev. com. 1975-77), Iowa-Ill. Central (pres. elect 1977) med. socs., Central Ill. Med. Assn. (v.p. 1977), Tri-City Med. Jour. Club (sec.-treas. 1972-77). Club: Short Hills Country. Home: 3904 7th Ave Rock Island IL 61201 Office: 1505 7th St Moline IL 61265

ARNESON, RICHARD ARLEN, food co. exec.; b. S. St. Paul, Minn., Dec. 18, 1933; s. Henry O. and Norma E. (Forieph) A.; student pub. schs., S. St. Paul; m. Marlene J. Samuelson, Nov. 18, 1967; children—Greg, Deborah, Craig, Mark, Mary, James. Supr., mgr. Applebaum Foods, St. Paul, 1951-67; div. mgr., asst. v.p. St. Louis Target Foods, Mo., 1968-74; unit mgr. Schnucks-Walgreens, Cape Girardeau, Mo., 1976—, dir. store ops., St. Louis, 1977—. Lutheran. Club: Optimists. Home: 2725 Tanglewood St Cape Girardeau MO 63701 Office: 19 S Kingshighway Cape Girardeau MO 63701

ARNETT, RICHARD HAYES, chiropractor; b. Columbus, Ohio, Aug. 6, 1922; s. George Walter and Vera Venone (Hayes) A.; student Bliss Coll., Columbus, 1942; D. Chiropractic, Lincoln Chiropractic Coll., Indpls., 1950; postgrad. Nat. Coll. Chiropractic, Lombard, Ill., 1971; m. Claire Frances Colwell, Nov. 20, 1948; children—Richard C., Mary Anne, Gregory, David, Catherine (Mrs. David Miller), John, Mark. Pvt. practice chiropractic Carey, Ohio, 1950-55, Linden, Ohio, 1955-60, Reynoldsburg, Ohio, 1961—; cons. in field. Mem. med. adv. com. Ohio Dept. Pub. Welfare, 1974-75. Mem. reelection com. Municipal Judge Leo Stark, 1973. Bd. dirs. United Cerebral Palsy Franklin County, 1956-58. Served with Q.M.C., AUS, 1943-46. Mem. Central Ohio (pres. 1975-76), Am., Ohio State (dir. Dist. 9 1975-76) chiropractic assns., Am. Legion, Fraternal Order Police Assos., D.A.V., Sigma Phi Lambda (a founder, 1st. sec. Indpls. 1948). Republican. Roman Catholic. K.C. (4 deg.), Kiwanian (v.p. Reynoldsburg 1973-74). Office: 7382 E Main St Reynoldsburg OH 43068

ARNETT, ROY LEE, constrn. co. exec.; b. Hutchinson, Kans., Dec. 27, 1932; s. Henry Austin and Doyn Virginia (Smith) A.; student Hutchinson Jr. Coll., 1954-55; m. Naomi Vadine Herrington, June 24, 1950 (dec. Feb. 1977); children—Vicki Lei, Claire Anne. With L.R. Foy Constrn. Co., Inc., Hutchinson, 1950-74, job supt., 1962-69, mgr. steel bldg. systems div., 1969-74; pres. Continental Structures Inc., Wichita, 1974—; mem. dealer council Star Mfg. Co., Oklahoma City, 1970, 71, 72; pres. Metal Bldg. Dealer Assn., Wichita, 1976. Named Hon. Okie by Okla. Gov., 1972. Author workbook and tng. films in field. Home: 1112 Peterson St Wichita KS 67212 Office: 805 S Main St Wichita KS 67213

ARNOLD, ARTHUR, neurosurgeon; b. N.Y.C., Sept. 21, 1921; A.B., U. Ala., 1942; M.D., Harvard U., 1946; m. Gladys Blakney, May 16, 1942; children—Richard Arthur, Donna Louise. Surg. intern Boston City Hosp., 1946-47; resident neurol. surgery St. Luke's, U. Ill. hosps., Chgo., 1949-52; individual practice, Hinsdale, Ill., 1952—, asst. prof. to asso. prof. neurol. surgery U. Ill. Coll. Medicine, 1952—; research prof. neurol. surgery Pritzker Sch. Med., U. Chgo., 1973—; cons. neurol. surgery Ill. Central, Hinsdale, LaGrange, Macneal (Berwyn) hosps.; cons. neurosurgeon Ill. Psychiat. Inst. Served to lt. (j.g.) M.C., USNR, 1947-49. Fellow Internat. Coll. Angiology, Harvey Cushing Soc., Am. Geriatric Soc.; mem. Am. Acad. Neurology, Radiation Research Soc., N.Y. Acad. Medicine, Chgo. Neurol. Soc., AMA, Am. Assn. Ry. Surgeons, Congress Neurol. Surgeons. Home: 735 McKinley St Hinsdale IL 60521 Office: 40 S Clay St Hinsdale IL 60521

ARNOLD, FRANK COPELAND, psychologist; b. Hillsboro, Ohio, Oct. 31, 1918; s. Samuel and Anna (Copeland) A.; B.S., Ohio State U., 1942, M.A., 1945; Ph.D., U. Syracuse, 19S1; m. Jane Wise, Oct. 6, 1945; children—Linda Arnold Glaviano, John, Barbara. Tchr., Lake Township, Millbury, Ohio, 1942-43; asst. psychologist Boys' Indsl. Sch., Lancaster, Ohio, 1943-45; spl. tchr. Syracuse (N.Y.) Detention Home, 1945-46; psychometrist for handicapped Psychol. Services Center, Syracuse U., 1947; instr., supr. mental hygiene Parent-Child Clinic 1947-48; asst. prof. psychology Bowling Green (Ohio) U., 1948-54, asso. prof., 1954-62, prof., 1962—, dir. guidance tng. program, 1948-66, dir. sch. psychology tng. program, 1955-69, dir. coll. student personnel tng. programs, 1965-69, dir. counseling center, 1955-76, counseling psychologist, 1976—. Active United Meth. Ch., 1948—. Recipient Service award Bowling Green U., 1974, Ohio State Testing Service Advisory Bd., 1974; licensed psychologist, Ohio. Mem. Am., Ohio (dir.) psychol. assns., Sigma Xi., Phi Delta Kappa. Contbr. articles to profl. jours. Home: 229 Crim St Bowling Green OH 43402 Office: Counseling Center Bowling Green State Univ Bowling Green OH 43403

ARNOLD, FRED ENGLISH, lawyer; b. Mexico, Mo., May 10, 1938; s. Charles P. and Mary Ellen (Blackman) A.; A.B., Harvard, 1960, LL.B., 1963; m. Dorothy Patricia Offutt, Dec. 31, 1966; children—Jane Ellen, Charles Pleasant III, Susan Joan. Admitted to Mo. bar, 1963; partner Thompson & Mitchell, attys., St. Louis, 1964—; dir. Artronix, Inc., St. Louis. Sec., St. Louis Children's Hosp. Devel. Bd., 1974-75. Served with AUS, 1963. Mem. Am. Bar Assn., Mo. Bar, Bar Assn. Met. St. Louis. Clubs: Harvard (sec. 1974-76, v.p. 1976—), Noonday. Home: 6369 Wydown Blvd Clayton MO 63105 Office: One Mercantile Center Suite 3400 St Louis MO 63101

ARNOLD, LEONARD CHARLES, physician, lawyer; b. Chgo., Aug. 26, 1921; s. Charles L. and Bessie (Schmigelsky) A.; B.S., Northwestern U., 1943, M.B., Chgo. Med. Sch., 1946, M.D., 1947; LL.B., John Marshall Law Sch., 1965, J.D., 1970; m. Janet Lorraine Bloom, Apr. 11, 1943 (div. Dec. 1961); children—Larry I. and Gary R. (twins), Bruce R., Leslie M.; m. 2d, Jeannette G. Zini, Nov. 14, 1962 (dec. July 1971); m. 3d, Dawn J. Cheskes, Apr. 13, 1973; children—Bradley Todd, Chad Douglas. Intern Edgewater Hosp., Chgo., 1946-47; gen. practice medicine, Chgo., 1947—; mem. attending staff Edgewater Hosp.; admitted to Ill. bar, 1965; practice law, Chgo., 1968—; instr. medico-legal seminar DePaul U. Coll. of Law; lectr. medico-legal subjects John Marshall Coll. Law, Chgo. Med. Sch. Served to capt. M.C., AUS, 1952-54. Fellow Am. Coll. Legal Medicine, Am. Acad. Family Practice (charter); mem. AMA, Chgo. Med. Soc., Chgo. Acad. Law and Medicine (co-founder), Acad. Psychosomatic Medicine, Ill., Chgo. bar assns., Am. Acad. Forsensic Sci., Tau Delta Phi. Co-editor: Med. Trial Technique Quarterly. Home: 1055 Starr Rd Winnetka IL 60093 Med office: 1700 W Lawrence Ave Chicago IL 60640 Legal office: 111 W Washington St Chicago IL 60602

ARNOLD, LYNN ELLIS, engring. mgr.; b. Cin., Nov. 17, 1934; s. Leslie Lee and Emma R. (Betscher) A.; Metall. Engr., U. Cin., 1957; M.S. in Mech. Engring., U. Ill., 1959. Grad. asst. U. Ill., Urbana, 1957-59; with Xtek, Inc., Cin., 1959—, tech. mgr., 1976—. Served with USAF, 1958-59. Registered profl. engr., Ohio. Fellow Am. Soc. Metals, AAAS; mem. Nat. (chmn. elect indsl. div.), Ohio (past pres. Cin. chpt., Young Engr. award 1965) socs. profl. engrs., ASME (past pres. Cin. sect., pres. Ohio council), Cin. Tech. and Sci. Socs. Council (past pres.), Engring. Soc. Cin. (past pres.), Am. Mgmt. Assn. (v.p.), Cin. Editors Assn. (past pres.), Tool Steel Mgmt. Club (past pres.), U. Cin. Engring. Alumni Assn. (v.p.), S.A.R. (past pres. Cin. chpt.), Audubon Soc. Ohio (past pres.), Ohio Audubon Council (past pres.), Tau Beta Pi, Alpha Sigma Mu, Alpha Phi Omega, Pi Delta Epsilon, Alpha Chi Sigma. Republican. Methodist. Author articles in field. Home: 5154 Montgomery Rd Cincinnati OH 45212 Office: 211 Township Ave Cincinnati OH 45216

ARNOLD, ORVILLE EDWARD, cons. engr.; b. Sparta, Wis., Sept. 30, 1933; s. Donald E. and Lenice (Reilly) A.; B.S., U. Wis., 1955; m. Mary Rose Gallagher, Nov. 30, 1957 (div. Jan. 1977); children—Donald E., David C., Beth A., Sandra M. Jr. engr. Inland Steel Co., East Chicago, Ind., 1955-56; structural engr. John J. Flad & Asso., architects and engrs., 1956-59, chief structural engr., 1959-63; partner, pres. Arnold & O'Sheridan, cons. engrs., Madison, Wis., 1964—. Mem. Middleton Pub. Works Com.; mem. Middleton Lake Problems Com.; mem., chmn. Wis. Structural Code Rev. Com.; mem. Wis. Exam. Bd. Architects, Engrs., Land Surveyors and Designers, 1974—. Pres., Mendota—Monona Lake Property Owners Assn., 1974. Registered profl. engr., Wis. Mem. ASCE (v.p. Wis. sect. 1969, pres. Wis. sect. 1970), Am. Concrete Inst., Nat. Soc. Profl. Engrs. K.C. Club: Gyro. Home: 3610 Lake Mendota Dr Madison WI 53705 Office: 815 Forward Dr Madison WI 53711

ARNOLD, ROBERT WILLIAM, lawyer; b. nr. Elkhorn, Wis., Sept. 29, 1930; s. Lyman Kent and Gertrude Emma (Nuoffer) A.; student Beloit Coll., 1948-49; LL.B., U. Wis., 1952; m. Barbara Jeanne Hoyt, Oct. 9, 1954; children—Bruce, John, Lynn. Admitted to Wis. bar, 1954; practiced in Elkhorn, 1956—. Commr., Walworth County Family Court, 1960—. Chmn., Elkhorn Community Chest Drive, 1957. Served to 1st lt. AUS, 1954-56. Mem. Wis., Walworth County (pres. 1974) bar assns., Family Court Commrs. Assn., Nat. Rifle Assn. (life), Wis. Rifle and Pistol Assn. (dir. 1972—), Pi Kappa Alpha, Delta Theta Phi. Republican. Mason. Club: Elkhorn Pistol. Home: Route 2 Elkhorn WI 53121 Office: 9 W Walworth St Elkhorn WI 53121

ARNOLDT, ROBERT PATRICK, internat. banking analyst; b. Chgo., Oct. 16, 1944; s. Frederick Werner and Margaret (O'Callaghan) A.; A.A., Chgo. City Coll., 1970; B.A. in History, Elmhurst (Ill.) Coll., 1973; postgrad. Northeastern Ill. U., 1974—; m. Patricia Ellen Ruh, Dec. 27, 1970; children—Robert Kevin Patrick, James Matthew Patrick, Kathleen Patricia Maureen. Dist. exec. Boy Scouts Am., Oak Park, Ill., 1970-71; supr. trust dept. Continental Ill. Nat. Bank, Chgo., 1972-77, analyst internat. banking dept., 1977—. Served with U.S. Army, 1965-68. Decorated Bronze Star medal, Air medal, Combat Infantryman's badge. Home: 1134 S Scoville Ave Oak Park IL 60304 Office: 231 S LaSalle St Chicago IL 60693

ARQUILLA, GEORGE, JR., gen. contractor; b. Chgo., Nov. 19, 1921; s. George and Emelia (Pechacek) A.; B.A., U. Chgo., 1945, M.B.A., 1946; m. Cherie Gist, Jan. 3, 1947; children—George III, Thomas Gist, Amy Ann. Supt., Burnside Constrn. Co., Glenwood, Ill., 1946-50, v.p., 1950-74, pres., 1974—; dir., chmn. bd. Heritage/Olympia Bank, Chicago Heights, Ill.; dir. Heritage/Pullman Bank, Chgo., Heritage Bancorp. Pres. Homebuilders Assn. Chicagoland, 1966-67. Mem. Nat. Assn. Home Builders (life dir.), Home Builders Assn. Greater Chgo., Phi Kappa Psi. Club: Olympia Fields Country. Home: 2232 Carroll Pkwy Flossmoor IL 60422 Office: 18400 S Halsted St Glenwood IL 60425

ARRASMITH, JEAN LEONORE, educator; b. Ames, Iowa, Apr. 22, 1923; d. Lyman Charles and Emma Lenora (Gildersleeve) Arrasmith; B.A. with honors, Iowa State Tchrs. Coll., 1945; M.A., U. Minn., 1952; Ph.D., U. Oreg., 1967. Tchr. pub. schs., Decorah, Iowa, 1945-47; instr. Macalester Coll., St. Paul, 1947-52, Iowa State Coll., Ames, 1952, 53-54; tchr., supr. pub. schs., Ames, 1953; instr., asst. prof. Purdue U., Lafayette, Ind., 1954-64; asso. prof., dir. women's phys. edn. U. Denver, 1964-73; prof. phys. edn. Ball State U., Muncie, Ind., 1973—, head women's phys. edn., 1973—. Dir. children's swimming and playground Ames Recreation Com., 1942-43; dir. waterfront, head counselor, program dir. Camp Tapawingo, Harrison, Maine, summers 1944-62; water safety instr. ARC, 1941-75, instr.-trainer, 1954-75; mem. exec. bd. Women's Nat. Aquatic Forum, 1956-62, nat. chmn., 1961-62, research chmn., 1963-66, mem. research com., 1969-72. Recipient 29-Year Service award ARC, 1970, Honor award Aquatioc Council, 1971, Colo. Assn. for Health, Phys. Edn. and Recreation, 1973. Mem. AAHPER (asso. jour. editor 1967-71, v.p., dir. 1972-73), also numerous other orgns. Contbr. articles to profl. jours. Home: 602 Sisk Rd Yorktown IN 47396 Office: Dept Women's Physical Edn Ball State University Muncie IN 47306

ARRIOLA, ALFREDO BORBON, surgeon; b. Dagupan, Philippines, Aug. 9, 1934; s. Ramon Rivera and Victoria Amistad (Borbon) A.; M.D., U. Santo Tomas, Manila, Philippines, 1961; m. Ofelia Layao Herrera, July 2, 1970; children—Jennifer Anne, Grace Angelica. Intern, N. Gen. Hosp., Manila, 1960-61, Luth. Hosp., Cleve., 1964-65; resident in surgery Swedish Hosp., Mpls., 1965-68, St. Lukes Hosp., Fargo, N.D., 1968-69; resident in surgery Evang. Deaconess Hosp., Detroit, 1969-70, sec. med. staff, 1975-76, vice chief staff, med. staff, 1977—; practice medicine specializing in surgery, Detroit, 1970—; dir. A.B. Arriola, M.D., P.C., Detroit, 1973—; sec. med. staff Lakeside Gen. Hosp., 1974. Nat. treas. Movement for Free Philippines, 1973-77. Named Outstanding Resident of Yr., Evang. Deaconess Hosp., 1969-70; diplomate Am. Bd. Surgery. Fellow Am. Soc. Abdominal Surgeons; mem. AMA (Physicians Recognition award), Philippine Med. Assn. Mich. (pres. 1975-76). Roman Catholic. Home: 1241 Hollywood St Grosse Pointe Woods MI 48236

ARROWSMITH, WALLACE GOLDIE, ret. city mgr.; b. Goffstown, N.H., Nov. 2, 1912; s. Wallace B. and Emily C. (Baldwin) Goldie; adopted son of Ernest Arrowsmith; student Wayne U., 1930-31, 43-44, Mich. State Normal Coll., 1931-32, U. Mich., nights 1945; also spl. courses in municipal adminstrn., certificate in mgmt., 1958; m. Mildred Ellen Bower, Sept. 27, 1935; children—Owen G., Brian G. Cost accountant Ford Motor Co., Dearborn, Mich., 1935-38; dist. mgr. Household Paper Products Co., Flint, Mich., and Detroit, 1938-43; project accountant, asst. housing mgr. Fed. Pub. Housing

Authority, 1943-47: partner Arrowsmith Bldg. and Constrn. Co.; co-owner Arrowsmith Sales Camp Craft, 1972—. Treas. Nankin Twp., Mich., 1947-49; village mgr., Wayne, Mich., 1949-60, city mgr., Wayne, 1960-73; interim city mgr., Garden City, Mich., 1975-76; chmn. Central Wayne Council sect. Detroit Met. Planning Commn., 1951-54; City of Wayne del. Gen. Assembly of Southeast Council of Govts., 1967-70; chmn. Central Wayne County Sanitation Authority, 1953-56, sec., 1957-67, vice chmn., 1967-68, 72-73, 76-77, chmn., 1968-69, 73-74, 77—, sec., 1970-72, dir., 1974-76; mem. Gov's conf. study com. on Mich. water, sewer and drainage needs, 1955-56. Mem. Wayne sect. United Community Services, 1969-75, chmn. crime and juvenile delinquency com., 1971-73, mem. sub-budget com., 1969-73, del., 1970-74; mem. adv. com. United Found. Western Wayne County; participant Menninger Found. Seminar, 1971. Trustee Mich. Municipal League, 1952-55, chmn. tng. com. mem. Detroit Area Nat. Task Force Labor Relations. Recipient 1st Gov.'s award for outstanding pub. ofcl. State of Mich., 1969. Mem. Internat. City Mgrs. Assn. (pres. Mich. chpt. 1961-62, instr. Inst. for Tng. in Municipal Adminstrn. 1963-72, chmn. spl. com. automatic data processing Mich. chpt. 1966-70, life), Am. Soc. Pub. Adminstrn., Jr. C. of C. (past pres.), Mich. Soc. Planning Ofcls. (dir. 1954-55, legislative com. mem. 1957-61), Mich. Municipal League (mem. urban devel. com. 1960-67, mem. urban affairs com. 1967-73, Wayne County legislative contact man 1961-73, con-con com., recipient spl. award merit 1960), Am. Water Works Assn., Am. Pub. Works Assn., ASME, Internat. City Mgmt. Assn. (chmn. Detroit area nat. task force race relations), Family Motor Coach Assn., Outdoor Resorts Am., Wayne C. of C. (treas. 1973-74, dir. 1974-75). Clubs: Rotary (v.p. 1965-66), Good Sam. Contbr. articles to profl. jours. Home: 4900 S Wayne Rd Wayne MI 48184 Office: 4900 S Wayne Rd Wayne MI 48184

ARSENEAULT, EDMOND JOHN, banker; b. Albany, N.Y., Oct. 27, 1927; s. John L. and Theodora (Layton) A.; Asso. of Sci., Hillyer Coll., 1949; certificate Am. Inst. Banking, 1959; m. Dorothy Szymanowski, July 2, 1949; children—Deborah, Patrice, Brett, Heidi, Brian. Adjuster, Comml. Credit Corp., Hartford, Conn., 1949-50, mgr., 1950-54; mgr. Phoenix State Bank and Trust Co., Hartford, 1954; time sales rep. Conn. Bank and Trust Co., Hartford, 1954-59; pres. Soy Capital Bank and Trust Co., Decatur, Ill., 1959—. Instr. various courses Am. Inst. Banking. Pres., Catholic Charities, Decatur, 1966-70; mem. lay bd. St. Teresa High Sch., Decatur, 1971—; pres. Am. Cancer Soc., Decatur, 1970-71. mem. City Council, Decatur, Ill., 1964-66. Mem. adv. com. U. Ill., 1970—. Served with USNR, 1945-46. Mem. Am. Bankers Assn., Am. Inst. Banking, Decatur C. of C. (pres. 1977). Democrat. Roman Catholic. Clubs: Country, Decatur. Home: 220 Michael St Decatur IL 62526 Office: 1501 E Eldorado St Decatur IL 62525

ART, ROBERT LEO, state ofcl.; b. Celina, Ohio, Oct. 12, 1932; s. Henry Francis and Lucina Ann (Rammel) A.; B.S., Ohio State U., 1959; m. Mary Jo Fetters, Oct. 27, 1956; children—Daniel Lee, David Robert, Andrew Jay, Ann Marie. Researcher, Ohio Dept. Transp., Columbus, 1960-65, right of way research supr., 1965-70, asst. adminstr. bur. appraisals, 1970-73, adminstr. bur. utilities and properties, 1973—. Served with AUS, 1953-55. Mem. Am. Right of Way Assn. (pres. Buckeye chpt. 1974, vice chmn. Region V 1976-77, chmn. 1977-78; named chpt. and regional Right of Way Man of Yr. 1972). Home: 65 Westwood Rd Columbus OH 43214 Office: 25 S Front St Columbus OH 43216

ARTHUR, ALAN JOHN, veterinarian; b. Hamilton, Ont., Can., Nov. 15, 1921; s. Thomas Edward and Jean Josephine (Tracey) A.; came to U.S., 1949; D.V.M., U. Toronto, 1949; m. Phyllis Evelyn Garson, Sept. 1, 1945; children—Alan, Susan, Kelly, Kevin. Mem. staff U.S. Bur. Animal Industry, 1949; asso. Blue Cross Animal Hosp., Cleve., 1949-51; owner, head Brooklyn Animal Hosp., Cleve., 1951—. Served with Royal Canadian Naval Res., 1940-45. Mem. Am., Ohio vet. med. assns., Cleve. Acad. Vet. Medicine. Roman Catholic. Club: Exchange. Home: 9695 Green Briar Dr Parma Heights OH 44130 Office: 4261 Pearl Rd Cleveland OH 44109

ARTHUR, LINDSAY GRIER, judge; b. Mpls., July 30, 1917; s. Hugh and Alice (Grier) A.; A.B., Princeton U., 1939; postgrad. Harvard U., 1939-40; LL.B., U. Minn., 1946, J.D., 1966; m. Jean Lorraine Johansen, Sept. 19, 1940; children—Lindsay Grier, Mollie Kristin, Julie Anne. Admitted to Minn. bar, 1946; practiced in Mpls., 1946-54; partner Nieman, Bosard & Arthur, 1949-54; judge Municipal Ct., 1954-61; judge juvenile div. Dist. Ct., Mpls., 1961—; mem. Chief Justice's Bicentennial Conf. on Dissatisfactions with Judiciary, 1976; del. Internat. Conf. Juvenile Ct. Judges, Paris, 1973, Oxford, 1974. Chmn., Clara Barton PTA, 1951-52, Park Bd. Millage Campaign, 1957, Downtown YMCA, 1956-57, Lower Loop Relocation Com., 1957-58, Bus.-Labor Tax Study, 1959-60; alderman, Mpls., 1951-54; forum instr. White House Conf. on Children, 1970; bd. dirs. Health and Welfare Council, 1963-65, Children's Hosp., 1949-50, 68—, Curriculum Coordinating Council, 1949-50, Community Fund, 1962-65, Bar None Ranch, Northrup Sch., 1967-70, Mpls. Capital Long-Range Improvements Com., 1954-74, Boys' Club, 1963-77, Urban Coalition, 1968-73, Nat. Center for State Cts., 1973-76; mem. Corrections Advisory Bd., 1977—. Served with USNR, 1942-45. Mem. Hennepin County Bar Assn. (exec. com. 1971-72), Jr. Bar Assn. (chmn. 1951-52), Nat. Council Juvenile Ct. Judges (pres. 1972-73). Lutheran. Author numerous books and articles. Home: 1735 Black Oaks Ln Wayzata MN 55391 Office: 328 Old Courthouse Minneapolis MN 55415

ARVESEN, NORMAN DEAN, lawyer; b. Montevideo, Minn., Nov. 8, 1913; s. Clarence E. and Eva Luella (Danielson) A.; student Luther Coll., 1930-32; B.A., St. Olaf Coll., 1932-34; LL.B., U. Minn., 1940; m. Iola Louise Garnaas, Sept. 28, 1940; children—Richard Norman, Susan Louise. High sch. tchr., Oberon, N.D., 1934-35; reporter Faribault (Minn.) Daily News, 1935-36; teller First Bank Stock Corp., Luverne, Minn., 1936-37; admitted to Minn. bar, 1940, practiced in Fergus Falls, 1940-42, 46—; mem. firm Arvesen, Donoho, Lundeen, Hoff & Svingen, 1946—; village atty. Battle Lake, Minn., 1963-75; city atty. Fergus Falls, 1946-48; counsel Otter Tail Lake Property Owners Assn. Dir. Otisco State Bank (Minn.). Mem. State Bd. Profl. Responsibility. Chmn. Otter Tail County Republican Com.; former mem. Minn. Rep. Com. Served with USAAF, 1942-46; PTO. Recipient War Service award Kiwanis, 1946. Mem. Internat. Acad. Trial Lawyers, Internat. Assn. Ins. Counsel, Def. Research Inst., Minn. Def. Lawyers Assn., Am. Legion, Delta Theta Phi. Mason, Elk. Home: Rural Route 2 Battle Lake MN 56515 Office: 125 S Mill St Fergus Falls MN 56537

ARVIN, CHARLES STANFORD, librarian; b. Loogootee, Ind., Apr. 17, 1931; s. Leland Stanford and Mary Hope (Armstrong) A.; A.B., Wayne State U., 1953, postgrad., 1956-57; M.A. in Library Sci., U. Mich. 1960. Asst. divisional Librarian U. Mich. Natural Sci. Library, 1960-62; head reference Genesee County Library, Flint, Mich., 1962-67, head central services, 1967—. Served with AUS, 1953-56. Mem. ALA, Mich. Library Assn., Mich., Ind., Genesee County hist. socs., ACLU. Club: Flint Library. Home: 702 W Oliver St Owosso MI 48867 Office: 4195 W Pasadena St Flint MI 48504

ASBJORNSON, HELEN E. (LONGSTRETH), real estate investment co. exec.; b. N.Y.C., Dec. 8, 1935; d. Clyde Marion and Elizabeth (Rudolph) Longstreth; B.A., State U. Iowa, 1957, J.D., 1959, postgrad., 1960; M.Ed., Mont. State Coll., 1961; postgrad. U. Minn., 1961-62; m. Norman H. Asbjornson, March 1963; children—Elizabeth Erica, Scott Marion. Mem. bus. adminstrn. staff Northwestern Bell Telephone Co., Omaha, 1959-60; bus. adminstrn. mgr. Diversified Equities, Mpls., 1961—. Vol. worker Children's Hosp.; active Omaha Symphony Guild, Women's Assn. of Joslyn Art Mus., Omaha Civic Music Assn. Mem. Am. Council Christian Ch., Amvets Aux., C. of C., Am. Legion Aux., State U. Iowa Alumni Assn., AAUW, Soc. Liberal Arts, Nat. Vocat. Guidance Assn., Am. Personnel and Guidance Assn., Inc., Nat. socs. profl. engrs. auxs., Omaha Montessori Soc., Nebr. Hist. Soc., Airplane Owners' and Pilots' Assns., Am. Citizens' Forum, Psi Chi, Kappa Beta Pi (pres. chpt. 1957-58, del. Province conv. 1958). Republican. Baptist. Home: 6442 Margaret's Ln Edina MN 55435

ASCHER, JAMES JOHN, pharm. co. exec.; b. Kansas City, Mo., Oct. 2, 1928; s. Bordner Fredrick and Helen (Barron) A.; student Bergen Jr. Coll., 1947-48, U. Kan., 1946-47, 49-51; m. Mary Ellen Robitsch, Feb. 27, 1954; children—Jill Denise, James John, Christopher Bordner. Rep., B. F. Ascher & Co., Inc., Memphis, 1954-55, asst. to pres., Kansas City, Mo., 1956-57, v.p., 1958-64, pres., 1965—. Bd. dirs. Childrens Cardiac Center, 1964—, pres., 1968-70; mem. central governing bd. Children's Mercy Hosp.; bd. dirs. Jr. Achievement of Middle Am., 1973-76; edn. chmn. Young Presidents' Orgn. 6th Internat. Univ. for Presidents, Athens. Served to 1st. lt. AUS, 1951-53. Decorated Bronze Star. Mem. Pharm. Mfrs. Assn., Drug, Chem. and Allied Trades Assn., Midwest Pharm. Advt. Club, Sales and Advt. Execs. Club, Am. Mgmt. Assn. (pres.'s assn.), V.F.W. (dir.), Young Presidents Orgn., Delta Chi. Rotarian. Clubs: Kansas City; Indian Hills Country (Prairie Village, Kan.). Home: 6706 Glenwood Shawnee Mission KS 66204 Office: 5100 E 59th St Kansas City MO 64130

ASGAR, KAMAL, educator; b. Tabriz, Iran, Aug. 28, 1922; s. Salman and Rogiyeh (Ordoubadi) Asghar Zadeh; came to U.S., 1946, naturalized, 1955; A.B. in Chemistry, Tech. Coll. of Iran, Tehran, 1945; B.S. in Chemistry, U. Mich., 1949, B.S. in Chem. Engring., 1951, Ph.D. in Dental Materials and Metallurgy, 1959; m. Safieh Seyedi, Sept. 4, 1948; children—Alexander Robert, Andrew A. Asst. lab. U. Mich., Ann Arbor, 1949-50, research asst., 1950-56, instr., 1956-59, asst. prof., research asso., 1959-62, asso. prof., 1962-66, prof. dental materials, 1966—. Pres. Cerebral Palsy Assn. Washtenaw County, Mich., 1968-70, bd. dirs., 1973—; bd. dirs. Mich. Cerebral Palsy Assn., 1970-73. Recipient Best Tchr. award U. Mich. Sch. Dentistry, 1963; Paul Gibbons award, 1971. Mem. Internat. Assn. for Dental Research (sec. Ann Arbor sect. 1954-57, pres. 1958-60; sec. dental materials group 1963-67, pres. 1968-69; Souder award 1970). Contbr. articles to tech. lit. Patentee in field. Home: 2240 Belmont St Ann Arbor MI 48104

ASH, CHARLES JOSEPH, orthopaedic surgeon; b. Denver, July 27, 1930; s. Joseph A. and Edna (Harter) A.; student Regis Coll., 1948-51; M.D., St. Louis U., 1955; m. Patricia Corcoran, June 9, 1955; children—Carol, Michael, Cynthia. Intern, Boston City Hosp., 1955-56; resident orthopaedics St. Louis U. Hosp. Group, 1956-60; practice medicine specializing in orthopaedic surgery, Springfield, 1960—; mem. staff St. John's Hosp., Cox Med. Center, Springfield. Bd. dirs. United Cerebral Palsy, Springfield. Fellow A.C.S. (chpt. sec.-treas. 1970—); mem. Am. Acad. Orthopaedic Surgery, Mid-Central States Orthopaedic Assn. Roman Catholic (mem. ch. council 1968—). Home: 743 Riverside St Springfield MO 65807 Office: Cox Med Tower Springfield MO 65802

ASH, JAMES BOYD, mktg. cons.; b. Ardmore Park, Pa., Feb. 10, 1927; s. Harrison Boyd and Wilda Jane (North) A.; B.S., U. Pa., 1949; M.S., Northwestern U., 1951; m. Iris Gaillard Pond, Mar. 14, 1953; children—Margaret Susan, Jeffrey Boyd. Mag., newspaper editor, Phila., Lancaster, Coatesville, Pa., 1949-52; asst. mgr. pub. relations Lukens Steel Co., Coatesville, 1952-59; mgr. pub. relations. advt. Borg-Warner Corp., Chgo., 1959-66; dir. pub. info. Perkins & Will Partnership, Chgo., 1966-68; v.p. Crown Center subs. Hallmark Cards, Kansas City, Mo., 1968-69; owner, operator James B. Ash Mktg. Counsel and Service, Shawnee Mission, Kans., 1969—; cons., lectr. in field. Chmn. indsl. div. Cancer Crusade, 1964, Chgo.; chmn. pub. relations United Fund Coatesville, Pa., 1958. Served with inf. and Transp. Corps, U.S. Army, 1945-47; PTO. Mem. Sigma Delta Chi. Methodist. Author: The Community Junior College: Why A Master Plan?, 1966. Contbr. articles to profl. archtl., engring., bus. publs., 1969—. Home: 3916 W 58th St Shawnee Mission KS 66205

ASH, PHILIP, educator; b. N.Y.C., Feb. 2, 1917; s. Samuel Kieval and Estella (Feldstein) A.; B.S.S., City Coll. N.Y., 1938; M.A., Am. U., 1949; Ph.D., Pa. State U., 1949; m. Ruth Clyde, Sept. 16, 1945 (div. dec. 1972); children—Peter, Sharon; m. 2d, Judith N. Cates, June 6, 1973. Analyst to unit chief, occupational research U.S. Dept. Labor, 1940-47; asst. to v.p. indsl. relations Inland Steel, 1952-68; cons. Manplan Cons., Chgo., 1968-75; prof. psychology, U. Ill. at Chgo. Circle, 1968—; dir. research John E. Reid & Assos., 1972—; dir. Ash, Blackstone & Cates, 1974—; bd. dirs. Vernon Psychol. Labs. Research fellow to asso. prof. Pa. State U., 1947-52; vis. prof. sociology U. Witwatersrand, Johannesburg, South Africa, 1975. Mem. pub. adv. com. Chgo. Commn. on Human Relations, 1957—; retirement com. Chgo. Commn. for Sr. Citizens, 1960—; chmn. State Ill. Psychologist Exam. Com., 1963-72. Tremaine scholarship. Diplomate indsl. psychology Am. Bd. Profl. Psychology. Fellow Am. Psychol. Assn. (pres. div. indsl. psychol. 1967-68), AAAS, Internat. Acad. Forensic Psychol.; mem. Chgo. Psychol. Assn. (pres. 1968-69), Ill. Psychol. Assn. (pres. 1964-65), Internat. Gerontological Assn., Midwest Psychol. Assn., Am. Personnel and Guidance Assn., Am. Psychology-Law Soc., Indsl. Relations Research Assn., Phi Beta Kappa, Sigma Xi, Psi Chi. Contributor numerous articles to profl. jours. Home: 4950 S Chicago Beach Dr Chicago IL 60615 Office: University of Illinois Box 4348 Chicago IL 60680

ASHBACH, DAVID LAURENCE, internist, nephrologist; b. Chgo., Nov. 17, 1942; s. Sol Henry and Lila Mae A.; A.B., Knox Coll., 1964; M.S., Case Western Reserve U., 1969, M.D., 1970; m. Arlene Rosenthal Nov. 28, 1963; children—Barbara, Deborah, Robert. Intern, Presbyterian-St. Luke's Hosp., Chgo., 1970-71, resident, 1971-73, fellow in nephrology, 1973-75; practice medicine specializing in nephrology, Homewood, Ill., 1975—; mem. staffs St. Margaret's Hosp., Hammond, Ind., Presbyterian-St. Luke's Hosp.; instr. Rush Med. Coll. Diplomate Am. Bds. Internal Medicine and Nephrology. Mem. A.C.P., Am. Internat. socs. nephrology. Jewish. Home: 20457 Ithica St Olympia Fields IL 60461 Office: 18656 Dixie Hwy Homewood IL 60430

ASHBRIDGE, G. HARRY, engring. exec.; b. Chincoteague, Va., Dec. 22, 1929; s. G. Harry and Laura (Thornton) A.; student Lehigh U., 1948-49; B.S. in Elec. Engring., Ill. Inst. Tech., 1953; m. Donna D. Thornburg, Mar. 14, 1975; children—Stephen Dale, Susan Lynn, Brian Lee, J. Casey Franklin. Devel. engr. Burroughs Corp., Paoli, Pa., 1955-58; product planning mgr. Bryant Computer Products div. Ex-Cel-O Corp., 1958-62; product mgr. tape memories Ampex Computer Products Co., 1962-63, sect. mgr. product planning, 1963-67, mgr. long range planning, 1967-68; mgr. product planning Gen. Electric Co., 1968-69; v.p. mktg. and product planning Telex Computer Products Corp., 1969-72, v.p. business and marketing opportunities, 1972-73; v.p. planning Control Data Peripheral Products Co., Mpls., 1973-75, v.p. new bus. planning, 1975—; dir. Micro-Bit Corp., Lexington, Mass.; mem. utilities bd. Control Data Corp.; sec. Peripheral Products Co.; audio cons. Hi-Fidelity Systems, Inc., Roslyn, Pa., 1955-58. Treas., Christian Lit. Evangelism, Inc. Served with USNR, 1949-53; with AUS, 1953-55. Mem. Research Soc. Am., IEEE, Tulsa C. of C., Nat. Assn. Evangelicals, Triangle. Democrat. Author and lectr. Patentee in field. Home: 12 Garden Dr Burnsville MN 55337 Office: Control Data Box O Minneapolis MN 55440

ASHBROOK, JOHN MILAN, congressman; b. Johnstown, Ohio, Sept. 21, 1928; A.B. with honors, Harvard U., 1952; J.D., Ohio State U., 1955; LL.D., Ashland Coll., 1963; m. Jean Spencer; children—Barbara, Laura, Madeline. Admitted to Ohio bar, 1955, practiced in Johnstown; pub. Johnstown Ind. weekly, 1953—; mem. 87th-95th congresses 17th Dist. Ohio. Mem. 102d-103d Ohio Gen. Assemblies; past chmn. Young Republican Nat. Fedn. Served with USN. Home: 8513 Hempstead Ave Bethesda MD 20034 Office: House Office Bldg Washington DC 20515

ASHBY, CHARLES FERG, physician; b. Fairmont, Nebr., Feb. 9, 1920; s. Albert A. and Gertrude (Ferg) A.; A.B., U. Nebr., 1942, B.S., 1940, M.D., 1942; m. Jean Fricke, Nov. 9, 1943; children—Sarah, James Richard. Intern, Wesley Meml. Hosp., Chgo., 1942-43; practice medicine, specializing in gen. practice, Geneva, Nebr., 1947—; mem. staff Fillmore County Hosp., Geneva, Thayer County Hosp., Hebron, Nebr., Warren Meml. Hosp., Friend, Nebr.; physician City of Geneva, 1948—; examiner F.F.A.; med. adv. local draft bd., 1969—; clin. asso. U. Nebr. Coll. Medicine; bd. dirs. Nebr. Med. Service. Chief, Geneva Vol. Fireman, 1948—; bd. dirs. Fillmore County Fair Bd., 1949—. Chmn. Republican County Com., 1962-66. Served with USN, 1941-47. mem. Am., Nebr. med. assns., Am., Nebr. (pres. 1965) assns. gen. practice, Nebr. Obstetrics Gynecology Assn. (pres. 1970), Am. Assn. Railroad Surgeons, Aerospace Med. Soc., Am. Legion, VFW, Delta Upsilon, Phi Rho Sigma. Mason (32 deg. Shriner), Odd Fellow, Elk, Lion (pres. 1958-59). Home: 723 N 11th St Geneva NE 68361 Office: 140 N 9th St Geneva NE 68361

ASHBY, DAVID WARD, health care mgmt. cons.; b. Des Moines, Feb. 5, 1946; s. Gerald Joseph and Elizabeth Elaine (Reese) A.; B.A., Willamette U., 1968; M.S., U. Ariz., 1971; M.B.A., Stanford U., 1973, M.S., Med. Sch., 1974; m. Susan Alice McGeehon, Dec. 28, 1968. Asst. to asst. v.p. med. affairs Stanford (Calif.) Med. Sch., 1973; mgmt. cons. KMB Health Systems, Sunnyvale, Calif., 1974; health med. div. Booz, Allen & Hamilton, San Francisco, 1974-76; dir. health care mgmt. services Arthur Young & Co., Columbus, Ohio, 1976—. Office: Arthur Young Co 100 E Broad St Columbus OH 43215

ASHBY, ROBERT NEWTON, radiologist, educator; b. Evansville, Ind., Sept. 10, 1935; s. Carl Toliver and Jonnie Fay (Todd) A.; A.B., Ind. U., 1957, M.D., 1960; m. Patricia Ann Gaskey, Aug. 16, 1958; 1 son, John Carl. Intern, Wesley Meml. Hosp., Chgo., 1960-61, resident in radiology, 1961-64; practice medicine specializing in radiology, Grand Rapids, Mich., 1966—; radiologist Kent Radiologic Inst., Grand Rapids, 1974—; cons. radiologist St. Mary's Hosp., Grand Rapids; asso. clin. prof. Mich. State U. Served to capt. USAF, 1964-66. Mem. AMA, Mich. State, Kent County (del. to state assn. 1972—) med. socs., Am. Coll. Radiology. Episcopalian. Home: 1034 Monterey St SE East Grand Rapids MI 49506 Office: 216 Med Arts Bldg 26 Sheldon St SE Grand Rapids MI 49502

ASHCRAFT, LAURIE CRAGG, mktg. exec.; b. Washington, May 28, 1945; d. Richard Edwards and Dorothy (Shawhan) Cragg; B.A., Northwestern U., 1967; m. C. Brian Pendleton, May 20, 1972 (div.); m. 2d, W. Dale Ashcraft, Sept. 3, 1977. Psychol. research analyst Allstate Ins. Co., Northbrook, Ill., 1968-70; project supr. Marsteller, Inc., Chgo., 1970-74; mktg. research mgr. corporate mktg. research dept. Internat. Harvester, Chgo., after 1974; now asso dir. mktg. research Libby, McNeill & Libby. Guest lectr. market research various univs. and assns. Mem. Am. Mktg. Assn. (chmn. career conf. 1975—, dir. chpt.), Jr. League Chgo., Nat. Orgn. Women, Alliance Francaise, Chgo. Council on Fgn. Relations. Alpha Delta Pi. Club: Woman's Athletic. Home: 333 Hollow Creek Racine WI 53402 Office: Libby McNeill & Libby 200 S Michigan Ave Chicago IL 60604

ASHE, A. J., rubber co. exec.; b. Kenton, Tenn., Nov. 20, 1924; s. Walter Dee and Audelle (Keathley) A.; B.S., U. Tenn., 1948; M.S., Cornell U., 1949, Ph.D., 1951; m. Robbie Jean Nixon, Sept. 5, 1946; children—John Allen, Robert Edwin, David Nixon. Marketing specialist U.S. Dept. Agr., Cornell U., Ithaca, N.Y., 1951-52; commodity analyst Armour & Co., Chgo., 1952-57; sales and econ. forecaster Butler Mfg. Co., Kansas City, 1957-60; mgr. econ. research, dir. bus. research, asso. dir. corp. planning dir. bus. research and planning The B. F. Goodrich Co., Akron, Ohio, 1960-70, v.p. econs. and planning, 1970-72, v.p. planning and devel., 1972-76, sr. v.p., 1976—; dir. Akron Nat. Bank. Mem. bus. research adv. council to Commr. of Labor Statistics, 1965-68; mem. balance of payments adv. tech. com. to Sec. Commerce, 1965-68; adviser UN Conf. on Trade and Devel., 1969, 76; econ. adv. bd. to Sec. Commerce, 1968-70, 75-76; mem. tech. cons. to Bus. Council, 1965-70, 72-77. Mem. planning and priorities com. United Community Council Akron, 1963-64; mem. citizens panel Econ. Growth of Akron Area, 1962; mem. discussion group indsl. economists Harvard Bus. Sch., 1965—; mem. com. on ch. and econ. life Nat. Council Chs., 1967-69; mem. City of Akron Human Relations Commn., 1970-73; fin. adv. com. Mayor of Akron, 1976-77. Bd. dirs. Akron U., 1967-70; trustee Akron Gen. Med. Center, 1972—, United Way of Summit County, 1975—, Stan Hywet Hall Found., 1970. Served with USNR, 1943-45. Mem. Am. Mgmt. Assn., Conf. Bus. Economists (chmn. 1972-73), Nat. Soc. Corporate Planning, Rubber Mfrs. Assn. (mem. econ. and statis. coms. 1961-76), Am. Mktg. Assn., Nat. Assn. Bus. Economists, Am. Econ. Assn., U.S. C. of C. (mem. banking, monetary and fiscal affairs com. 1971—), Internat. Rubber Study Group (adviser U.S. Dept. State 1969, mem. com. of experts on rubber 1972-73), Internat. Rd. Fedn. (dir. 1977), Phi Kappa Phi, Alpha Zeta. Baptist. Home: 2319 Chatham Rd Akron OH 44313 Office: 500 S Main St Akron OH 44318

ASHHURST, ANNA WAYNE, educator; b. Phila., Jan. 5, 1933; d. Astley Paston Cooper and Anne Pauline (Campbell) Ashhurst; A.B., Vassar Coll., 1954; M.A., Middlebury Coll., 1956; Ph.D., U. Pitts., 1967. English tchr. Internat. Inst. Spain, Madrid, 1954-56; asst. prof. Juniata Coll., Huntingdon, Pa., 1961-63; asst. prof. Spanish dept. Franklin and Marshall Coll., Lancaster, Pa., 1968-74, acting chmn. Spanish dept., 1972, convenor, fgn. lang. council, 1972-74; asso. prof. dept. modern fgn. langs. U. Mo., St. Louis, 1974—. Mem. Welcome Wagon Wagon of Lancaster, Pa., 1968-70, 71-74. Fulbright-Hays grantee, Colombia, S.Am., summer 1963; Ford Humanities fellow, summer 1970; Mellon fellow, 1970-71. Mem. Internat. Inst. in Spain, Instituto Internacional de Literatura Iberoamericana, AAUP, Modern Lang. Assn., Midwest Modern Lang. Assn., Am. Assn. Tchrs. Spanish and Portuguese, Women's Equity Action League (pres. Mo. div. 1975-76). Home: 328 Chez Paree Hazelwood MO 63042

ASHLEY, NOVA TRIMBLE, author; b. Selden, Kans., July 10, 1911; d. Rufus William and Margaret Gilliland (Lipton) Trimble; continuing edn. student Wichita State U., part-time 1967-71; m. James Ercle Ashley, Aug. 20, 1929; children—Keith, Kenneth, James (dec.), Joyce (Mrs. Donald C. Olson). Ins. supr. Wesley Med. Center, Wichita, Kans., 1952-70; creative writing tchr. Twentieth Century Club, Wichita, 1966-70; condr. numerous workshops. Named Kans.

Poet of Year, Chaparral Poets, 1969, 71, 73. Mem. Internat. Platform Assn., Nat. Fed. Press Women, Nat. League Am. Pen Women (pres. Wichita br. 1973—), Kans., Wichita press women, Kans. Authors Club (Poetry Achievement award 1977), Wichita Line Women, Midwest Chaparrals (bd. mem. Kans. chpt.), Kans. Press Women. Author: Through Ocean of Gold, 1963; Coffee with Nova, 1966; Loquacious Mood, 1970; Haps and Mishaps, 1973; Chin Up, Dad, 1976; Hang in There, Mom, 1976. Contbr. poetry and articles to profl. jours., mags. including McCall's, Good Housekeeping, Wall St. Jour., Ladies Home Jour., others; regular contbr. to Kans. Quar., The Humanist, others. Home: 2101 S Glendale St Wichita KS 67218

ASHLEY, THOMAS WILLIAM LUDLOW, Congressman; b. Toledo, Jan 11, 1923; s. William Meredith and Mary Alida (Ludlow) A.; student Kent (Conn.) Sch., 1939-42; A.B., Yale, 1948; LL.B., Ohio State U., 1951; m. Kathleen Lucey, Aug. 26, 1967; children—William Meredith Ludlow, Mark Michael. With Toledo Publicity and Efficiency Commn., 1948-51; admitted to Ohio Bar, 1951, practiced Whitehouse, Ohio and Toledo, 1951-52; counsel Formed Steel Products, 1951-52; co-dir. press sect., asst. dir. spl. projects Radio Free Europe Committee, 1952-54; mem. 84th to 95th Congresses, 9th Dist. Ohio, mem. com. on banking and currency, budget and mcht. marine and fisheries, chmn. subcom. on housing and community devel.; chmn. ad hoc com. on energy, 1974—. Served with Armed Forces, World War II; PTO. Democrat. Office: Rayburn Bldg Washington DC 20515 also Federal Bldg Toledo OH 43604

ASHMORE, RICHARD WALTER, state ofcl.; b. St. Paul, Aug. 1, 1923; s. Raymond Gerald and Caroline (Schwartz) A.; B.B.A. (honors) U. Wis., 1949; m. Elaine June Weary, Apr. 22, 1944; children—Steven M., Susan G. Field auditor Wis. Dept. State Audit, 1949-64; asst. supr. mun. audits Bur. Mun. Audit, Madison, Wis., 1964-70, chief mun. auditing Sect., 1970—. Served with AUS, 1943-45. Decorated Bronze Star with one oak leaf cluster, Purple Heart with one oak leaf cluster. C.P.A., Wis. Home: 1705 National Ave Madison WI 53716 Office: 201 E Washington Ave Madison WI 53702

ASHTON, EDWARD LOWELL, cons. engr.; b. Clinton, Iowa, Jan. 30, 1903; s. George Sterling and Blanche (Crapser) A.; B.S., State U. Iowa, 1925, M.S., 1926; m. Gladys Mae Brooker, June 8, 1928; children—Joye Annette (Mrs. S. Jack Davis), Ruth Beverly (Mrs. Ronald H. Johnson), Jane Blanche (Mrs. Sherman A. Nelson). Cons. engr., 1926-75, own firm in pvt. practice, 1936-75; asst. resident engr. Harrington, Howard & Ash, cons. engr., Kansas City, Mo., 1928-29; asso. engr. James A. Hook, cons. engr., St. Louis, 1929-33; asst. engr., div. dams U.S. Bur. Reclamation, Dept. Interior, Denver, 1933-35; chief designer, asso. engr. Howard, Needles, Tammen & Bergendoff, cons. engrs., Kansas City, Mo., 1935-42; asst. prof. civil engring. State U. Iowa, Iowa City, 1943-46, asso. prof., 1947-52, prof., 1952-55; chief structural engr. Douglas Air Cargo Okla. Aircraft Assembly plant Austin Co., Oklahoma City, 1942-43; researcher Office Naval Research, Washington, 1955-61; research cons. USAF Cambridge Research Center, Bedford, Mass., 1960-64; cons. bridge engr., designer, various Iowa cities, 1962-74. Mem. Iowa Athletic Bd., 1950-51. Registered profl. engr., Iowa, Mo. Mem. N.Y. Acad. Sci., ASCE, Am. Welding Soc. (chmn. Kansas City sect. 1937-38), Soc. Am. Mil. Engrs., Ia. Engring. Soc., AAUP, Am. Concrete Inst., Am. Soc. for Metals, Nat. Soc. Profl. Engrs., Sigma Xi, Tau Beta Pi, Chi Upsilon, Theta Tau (chpt. regent 1924-25), Dolphin (pres. 1924-25, nat. v.p. 1924-25), Iowa City C. of C. Rotarian. Clubs: Engineers (pres. 1956-57), Quarterback (Iowa City). Address: 820 Park Ave Iowa City IA 52240

ASHWOOD, LOREN FRISK, mgmt. cons.; b. Moline, Ill., Feb 27, 1917; s. Paul E. and Myrtle (Frisk) A.; B.S., U. Ill., 1939; m. Helen E. Passmore, Dec. 28, 1943; children—Ann F., Lorry B., Amy L., Andrew M. Tool designer Deere & Co., Moline, Ill., 1939-42; tool engr. Goodyear Aircraft Corp., Akron, Ohio, 1942-43, Phoenix, 1943-45; adminstrv. control engr. Ft. Wayne Corrugated Paper Co., Hartford City, Ind., 1945-55; plant mgr. Downing Box Co., Milw., 1955-69; regional sales mgr. Ward Machinery Co., Balt., 1969-73; product mgr., 1973-77; mgmt. cons., 1977—. Mem. Bd. Edn., Brookfield, Wis., 1960-62, clk., 1962-63; trustee village Elm Grove, Wis., 1966-69; mem. Bldg. Bd., Elm Grove, 1966-67, Bd. Appeals, 1968-69. Trustee Downing Box Employees Retirement Fund, 1959-69; mem. Longview Fibre Employees Retirement Bd., 1960-69. Mem. TAPPI (prodn. com. chmn. 1961-62, corrugated div. sec. 1963-64, vice chmn. 1965, chmn. 1967-68), Am. Radio Relay League, Zeta Psi. Methodist (elder, deacon, trustee). Home and Office: 1255 Lakeside Dr Elm Grove WI 53122

ASPEGREN, OLIVER RICHARD, JR., ins. exec.; b. Evanston, Ill., Nov. 16, 1913; s. Oliver and Lilian (Anderson) A.; student Northwestern U., 1931-34; B.A., U. Chgo., 1935; m. Ida Marie Kaufmann, Dec. 25, 1950;children—Adolph, Oliver Richard, III, Mary Nell. Asst. mgr. Northwestern Nat. Life Ins. Co., 1935-41; gen. agent Gen. Am. Life Ins. Co., Chgo., 1941-42; asst. dir. agencies Commonwealth Life Ins. Co., Louisville, Ky., 1946-47; Chgo. gen. agent Ohio Nat. Life Ins. Co., 1947—, chmn. field bd., 1955-56; pres. Aspegren Fin. Corp., Chgo., 1968—; also subsidiaries Aspegren Securities Corp. (now consol. into Aspegren Fin. Corp.), 1968-74, Aspegren Agy., Inc., Chgo., 1956—; dir. N.Am. Life & Casualty Co., Mpls., 1968-73. Served from ensign to lt. comdr., USNR, 1942-46. Mem. Nat. (vice chmn. com. on fed. law and legislation; mem. Million Dollar Round Table, 1956—), Chgo. (pres. 1960-61) assns. life underwriters, Ill. Life Underwriters Assn. (pres. 1965-66), Am. Soc. Chartered Life Underwriters (pres. Chgo. 1954-55), Phi Gamma Delta (past pres. Northwestern U. chpt. alumni assn.). Republican. Methodist (past mem. ofcl. bd.). Clubs: Lake Shore, Economic (Chgo.); Evanston Young Republicans (past pres.). Home: Route 2 Box 85 Mundelein IL 60060 Office: 222 S Riverside Plaza Chicago IL 60606

ASPELMEIER, KENNETH ALAN, lawyer; b. Burlington, Iowa, Mar. 21, 1935; s. Herbert Herman and Celia Ione (Cowger) A.; B.A. (Hubert E. Howard scholar), Parsons Coll., 1957; LL.B. (Root-Tilden scholar), N.Y. U., 1960; m. Shirley Jeanne Anderson, June 5, 1965; children—Lynne Ann, David Wayne. Admitted to Iowa bar, 1960, since practiced in Burlington; mem. firm Pryor, Riley, Jones, Walsh, 1961—; v.p., dir. Mediapolis Savs. Bank (Iowa). Bd. dirs. Mediapolis Community Schs., 1971—. Served with AUS, 1960-61, 62. Mem. Des Moines County Bar Assn. (pres. 1972-73). Rotarian. Home: Mediapolis IA 52637 Office: 321 N 3d St Burlington IA 52601

ASPER, BERNICE VICTORIA, newspaper editor; b. Luck, Wis., Apr. 1, 1920; d. Harry Lars and Christine Marie (Hilseth) Johansen; student Mpls. Bus. Coll., 1939; m. Verdie S. Asper, Dec. 23, 1942 (dec.); 1 dau., Vickie Sharon. Bookkeeper, news editor, proofreader Enterprise-Herald, Luck, Wis., 1943-44; cashier, sec. Thorp Fin. Corp., Frederic, Wis., 1948-53; editor Inter-County Leader, Frederic, 1963—, also columnist Midweek Musings, As Per Bernice, also editorial writer. Sec., Frederic Citizens Adv. Com., 1970—; bd. dirs. Western Wis. Health Systems Agy., 1976—; supt. St. Peters Lutheran Sunday Sch., 1947-77. Author: 75 Years in Frederic, 1976. Home: 501 W Linden St Frederic WI 54837 Office: 303 N Wisconsin Ave Frederic WI 54837

ASPIN, LESLIE, congressman; b. Milw., July 21, 1938; B.A. summa cum laude, Yale, 1960; M.A., Oxford U. (Eng.), 1962; Ph.D. in Econs., Mass. Inst. Tech., 1965; m. Maureen Shea, 1969. Asst. prof. econs. Marquette U., Milw., 1969-70; mem. 92d-95th Congresses from 1st Dist. Wis. Served from 2d lt. to capt. AUS, 1966-68. Mem. Phi Beta Kappa. Home: 205 15th St Racine WI 53403 Office: House Office Bldg Washington DC 20515

ASTRIN, MARVIN H., broadcasting co. exec.; b. Chgo., Feb. 10, 1925; s. Abe and Lena (Mandel) A.; student DePaul U., 1945-48, Roosevelt U., 1948-49, Northwestern U., 1949-50; m. Angie Brown, Mar. 15, 1977. Account exec. Batten, Barton, Durstine & Osborn, 1945-53, Weiss & Geller Advt., 1953-54, Tatham-Laird Advt., 1954-57; with WGN Radio, Chgo., 1957—, account exec. sales staff, 1957-61, western div. sales mgr. 1961, gen. sales mgr., 1961-65 v.p. radio sales WGN Continental Broadcasting Co., Chgo., 1965-74, acting asst. gen. mgr., 1974, v.p., mgr. sales, 1974—, also dir.; gen. mgr. WGN Radio, 1970-73, exec. v.p., gen. mgr., 1972-74; pres. WGN Continental Sales Co. Served with AUS, 1943-45. Mem. Radio Advt. Bur. (dir.). Mem. B'nai B'rith. Club: Broadcasting Advertising of Chgo. (pres.). Home: 6415 N Kilbourn St Lincolnwood IL 60646 Office: 2501 W Bradley Pl Chicago IL 60618

ATALLAH, YOUSEF HANNA, toxicologist; b. Shebin-El-Kom, Egypt, May 27, 1936; came to U.S., 1961; s. Hanna and Helen (Mansour) A.; m. Mary Ibrahim, May 30, 1968; children—Jacqueline, Hany. B.S., Ain Shams U., Cairo, Egypt, 1956, M.S., 1959; Ph.D., La. State U., 1966; sr. postdoctoral fellow U. Ky. Lexington, 1973. Lectr. biology and chemistry High Inst. Agr., Shebin-El-Kom, Egypt, 1959-61; asso. prof., toxicologist Nat. Research Center, Cairo, 1966-71; prof. U. Algiers, Algeria, 1971-73; group ldr. residue analysis Velsicol Chem. Corp., Chgo., 1974-75, mgr. environ. studies, 1975—. Mem. Am. Chem. Soc., Entomological Soc. Am., AAAS. Contbr. articles to profl. jours. Home: 1406 S Robert Dr Mt Prospect IL 60056 Office: 341 E Ohio St Chicago IL 60611

ATKIN, ROBERT BYRON, supt. schs.; b. Olean, Mo., Dec. 12, 1931; s. John Hayden and Mayme (Scott) A.; B.S. in Commerce, Southwest Mo. State Coll., 1952; postgrad., Central Mo. State Coll., 1955; M.Ed., U. Mo., 1958, Ed.D., 1970; m. Sylva Ann Knox, Sept. 19, 1954; children—John Richard, Steven Paul, DiAnne. Bookkeeper Ben Franklin Stores, 1947-52, mgr., 1952-53; bookkeeper Snodgrass Men's Wear, 1947-68; partowner A & B Accounting Service, 1951-52; accountant Hallmark Cards, 1953; bus. tchr., coach Oak Grove (Mo.) High Sch., 1953-55, prin., 1955-58; adminstrv. asst. Rolla (Mo.) Pub. Schs., 1958-63, prin. sr. high sch., 1963-64, supt. schs., 1964-69; asst. supt. North Kansas City (Mo.) Pub. Schs., 1969-73; supt. Raytown (Mo.) Pub. Schs., 1973—; chmn. Met. Sch. Study Group, 1976-77. Bd. dirs. Jr. Achievement, Kansas City; mem. Gov.'s Conf. on Edn., 1966, 76. Served with USNR, 1950-58. Mem. Am. (mem. study mission to Russia 1975, mem. ethics com. 1977—), Mid-Am., Mo. assns. sch. adminstrs. (mem. exec. com. 1969-71), S. Central Dist. Adminstrs. Assn. (pres. 1965-67), U. Mo. Alumni Assn. (dir. 1964-70), Southwest Mo. State Alumni Letterman's Assn., U. Mo.-Columbia Coll. Edn. Alumni (pres. 1968-70), Am. Assn. Sch. Personnel Adminstrs. (resolutions, constitution and by-laws com.), Mo. Valley Personnel Adminstrs. (chmn. 1971), Kappa Delta Pi, Phi Delta Kappa. Mem. Christian Ch. (elder). Mason (Shriner), Kiwanian (dir. 1975—). Home: 7043 Lakeshore Dr Raytown MO 64133 Office: Raytown C-2 Pub Schs 10500 E 60th Terrace Raytown MO 64133

ATKINS, BOBBIE JEAN JOHNSON, educator; b. Bastrop, La., July 8, 1944; d. Horace and Ida Mary (Chapman) Johnson; B.A., So. U., Baton Rouge, La., 1966; M.S., U. Wis., Madison, 1968, postgrad., 1970, 71, 76—; m. Marvin Atkins, May 10, 1969. Playground dir. Topeka Recreation Commn., 1965; tutor, counselor Upward Bound, U. Iowa, Iowa City, 1966; counselor, recreation specialist Lakeside Children's Center, Milw., 1968; counselor, tour coordinator Wis. Employment Service, Milw., 1968-71; instr., lectr., field coordinator U. Wis., Milw., 1972—. Certified rehab. counselor. Mem. Nat., Wis. rehab. assns., Nat. Assn. Non-White Rehab. Workers, Am. Personnel and Guidance Assn., Am. Rehab. Counseling Assn. (state div. chmn. 1972—, mem. exec. council 1975—), Nat. Council Rehab. Educators, Black Educators Council Human Services, Delta Sigma Theta. Baptist. Home: 5879 N 37th St Milwaukee WI 53209 Office: 745 Enders Hall U Wis Milwaukee WI 53201

ATKINS, JAMES ALBERT, food services adminstr.; b. Washington, Apr. 24, 1945; s. James Earl and Dorothy (Mix) A.; A.A. in Applied Sci., Ferris State Coll., 1966; m. Joan Marie Pierce, Nov. 7, 1976; 1 son, James Norman. Food service mgr., Fred Harvey Restaurants, Chgo., 1966-69; food and beverage mgr. Quality Motels, Jackson, Mich., 1969-70, St. Louis, 1970; food service mgr. Venture Stores, St. Ann, Mo., 1971; asst. dir. food services St. Francis Hosp., Evanston, Ill., 1971-72; gen. mgr. Food Mgmt. Assos., Glen Ellyn, Ill., 1973; asso. dir. of food services St. Annes Hosp., Chgo., 1973—, St. Elizabeth's Hosp., Chgo., 1973—; instr. (part-time) in food service curriculum Coll. of Du Page, Glen Ellyn, Ill., 1976—; chmn. food service com. Ancilla Domini Health Services, 1977—; cons. food services, 1975—; pres. J. Atkins & Assos., 1976—. Served with USN, 1967-68; Vietnam. Recipient Certificate of Recognition, Evanston Sch. System, 1973. Mem. Internat. Food Service Execs. Assn., Am. Soc. for Hosp. Food Service Adminstrs., Am. Hosp. Assn. Methodist. Club: Lion. Home: 6115 Knoll Wood Rd Clarendon Hills IL 60514 Office: 49S0 W Thomas Chicago IL 60651

ATKINS, ROBERT FRANKLIN, real estate cons.; b. Chgo., July 2, 1919; s. Ira L. and Blanche (Schwass) A.; grad. student Sch. Sales Mgmt. and Mktg., Rutgers State U., 1953-54; m. Violet Olson, June 23, 1945; children—Barbara Lynn, Robert Franklin. With W.H. Barber Oil Co., Chgo., 1946-67, v.p., gen. mgr., 1958-67; pres. Bargeway Systems, Inc., Glen Ellyn, Ill., 1967-73; comml.-indsl. real estate cons. Comml. Investment div. Rich Port Realtors, Oakbrook, Ill., 1974—. Served to lt. USAAF, 1941-45. Decorated Air medal with 3 oak leaf clusters, Purple Heart. Baptist. Home: 1234 Carriage Ln La Grange IL 60525 Office: Rich Port Realtors Oakbrook IL 60521

ATKINS, RUSSELL KELLY, poet, composer; b. Cleve., Feb. 25, 1926; s. Perry and Mamie (Harris) A.; student Cleve. Sch. Art, 1943-44, Cleve. Music Sch. Settlement, 1941-42, Cleve. Inst. Music, 1944-45; pvt. music study, 1950-54; hon. doctorate Cleve. State U., 1976. Founder, editor Free Lance Mag., 1950-51; lectr., reader Fenn Coll., Cleve. State U., John Carroll U., Lake Erie Coll., U. Oswego, Cooper Sch. Art, Ohio Poetry Soc. and Confs., Findlay Coll., schs., civic orgns., and others, 1963—; mem. staff Sutphen Music Sch., Cleve., 1957-60. Mem. Ohio Poets' Assn. Poets-in-the-Schs. program; mem. adv. panel Ohio Arts Council. Author: Phenomena 1961, Objects, 1963, Heretofore, 1968, Malificium, 1971, Here in the, 1976, also articles; composer The Burial for piano, 1956, Objects for Piano and Violin, 1955, Object-Forms for Piano and Cello, 1963, also other music for piano. Home: 6005 Grand Ave Cleveland OH 44104

ATKINS, STANLEY HAMILTON, bishop; b. Newcastle, Eng., Mar. 8, 1912; s. George Thomas and Ethel (Williams) A.; AKCL, King's Coll., London, 1938; D.D., Nashotah House, Wis., 1969; m. Mildred Maureen March, May 5, 1942; children—Frances Mary (Mrs. Del J. Johnson), Paul, Elizabeth. Ordained to ministry Episcopal Ch., 1938; served Diocese of Durham, Eng., 1938-49, Rupert's Land, Can., 1949-55, St. Paul's, Hudson, Wis., also St. Thomas Ch., New Richmond, Wis., 1955-62; archdeacon of Milw., 1962-69; coadjutor bishop of Eau Claire, Wis., 1969-70, bishop, 1970—. Trustee Nashotah House Sem., 1969—. Served as chaplain, lt. col. Brit. Army, 1941-46. Rotarian. Home: 145 Marston Ave Eau Claire WI 54701 Office: 510 S Farwell St Eau Claire WI 54701

ATKINSON, ARTHUR JOHN, JR., clin. pharmacologist, educator; b. Chgo., Mar. 22, 1938; s. Arthur John and Inez (Hill) A.; A.B. in Chemistry, Harvard U., 1959; M.D., Cornell U., 1963. Intern and asst. resident in medicine Mass. Gen. Hosp., Boston, 1963-65, chief resident and Howard Carroll fellow in medicine Passavant Meml. Hosp., Chgo., instr. in medicine Northwestern U., Chgo., 1967-68; fellow in clin. pharmacology U. Cin., 1968-69, asst. prof. pharmacology, 1969; vis. scientist dept. toxicology Karolinska Inst., Stockholm, Sweden, 1970; asst. prof. medicine and pharmacology Northwestern U., Chgo., 1970-73, asso. prof., 1973-76, prof., 1976—. Served with NIH, USPHS, 1965-67. Recipient Faculty Devel. award in clin. pharmacology Pharm. Mfrs. Assn., 1970-72; Burroughs Wellcome scholar in clin. pharmacology, 1972-77. Fellow A.C.P.; mem. Am. Fedn. Clin. Research, Am. Soc. for Clin. Investigation, Am. Soc. Pharmacology and Exptl. Therapeutics, Chgo. Soc. Internal Medicine, Alpha Omega Alpha. Club: Chgo. Yacht. Mem. editorial bd. jours. Rational Drug Therapy, 1972—, Clin. Pharmacology and Therapeutics, 1973—. Home: 54 E Division St Chicago IL 60610 Office: 303 E Superior St Chicago IL 60611

ATKINSON, JON GAROLD, paper mfg. co. info. systems exec.; b. Marion, Ind., June 10, 1948; s. Gail M. and Dorothy M. (Dudley) A.; student Electronic Computer Programming Inst., 1968, mgmt. devel. program Assn. Systems Mgmt., 1976; m. Marilyn June Ferguson, Nov. 2, 1967; children—Jon Joseph, Jason Michael, Gina Renae. With SCM Allied Paper Co., Marion, 1969—, sr. programmer/analyst, 1975-77, supr. programming and operations, 1977—. Bd. dirs. Oborn Midwest Fed. Credit Union, Marion, 1972—, pres., 1975, v.p., 1976. Mem. Assn. Systems Mgmt., Am. Mgmt. Assn., Amoco Motor Club, Worldwide Sportsmen's Club. Republican. Roman Catholic. Club: Shady Hills Golf. Home: 601 N 8th St Gas City IN 46933 Office: 2409 W 2d St Marion IN 46952

ATKINSON, TRACY, museum dir.; b. Middletown, Ohio, Aug. 10, 1928; s. Charles Taylor and Anne (Tracy) A.; B.F.A., summa cum laude, Ohio State U., 1950; M.A., U. Pa., 1951; postgrad. Bryn Mawr Coll., 1953, Mexico City Coll., 1950; children—Adrienne, Aimee, Ethan. Curatorial asst. Albright Art Gallery, Buffalo, 1956-59; asst. dir. Columbus (Ohio) Gallery Fine Arts, 1959-61, acting dir., 1961-62; dir. Milw. Art Center, 1962—. Mem. Milw. Landmarks Commn. (2d v.p. 1972-73), Midwest Museums Conf. (pres. 1971-72), Art Mus. Dirs. Assn., Am. Assn. Museums. Club: University (Milw.). Contbr. articles to profl. jours. Home: 1328 N Jefferson St Milwaukee WI 53202 Office: 750 N Lincoln Memorial Dr Milwaukee WI 53202

ATLEE, JOHN LIGHT, III, anesthesiologist, educator; b. Lancaster, Pa., Feb. 22, 1941; s. John Light and Ann (Stevens) A.; B.A., Franklin and Marshall Coll., 1963; M.D., Temple U., 1967, M.S. in Pharmacology, 1971; m. Barbara Jean Sanford, Feb. 3, 1968; 1 dau., Sarah Sanford. Intern, Germantown Dispensary Hosp., Phila., 1967-68; resident in anesthesiology Temple U. Hosp., Phila., 1968-70; asst. prof. anesthesiology U. Wis., Madison, 1973—. Served with USN, 1971-73. N.J. Heart Assn. grantee, 1970-71; Wis. Heart Assn. grantee, 1975-76; H.G. Barsumian, M.D., Meml. Fund grantee, 1975-77; diplomate Nat. Bd. Med. Examiners, Am. Bd. Anesthesiology. Fellow Am. Coll. Anesthesiologists; mem. AMA, Am., Wis. socs. anesthesiologists. Republican. Episcopalian. Contbr. articles in field to profl. jours. Home: 3873 State Hwy 19 Route 1 DeForest WI 53532 Office: 705 Center St U Wis Hosps Madison WI 53706

ATLEE, JUDITH DEHAVEN, univ. ofcl.; b. Lewisburg, Pa., July 29, 1945; d. Hugh Stewart and Dorothy Mae (Armstrong) Atlee; A.B. magna cum laude, Waynesburg (Pa.) Coll., 1967; M.A., U. Minn., 1971, Ph.D., 1975; m. Carl Leslie Harstad, Aug. 28, 1973. Counselor, then sr. adviser Pre-Health Scis. Office, U. Minn., Mpls., 1971-73, sr. adviser Health scis. Student Personnel Office, 1973-75, coordinator, 1975—, also instr. Mem. Am. Personnel and Guidance Assn., Central Assn. Advisers for Health Professions (exec. council), Sierra Club. Author, editor Health Careers in Minnesota, 1974—. Home: 1520 E Minnehaha Pkwy Minneapolis MN 55417 Office: 175 Frontier Bldg 701 Fulton St SE Univ Minn Minneapolis MN 55455

ATWELL, HAROLD EDWIN, aircraft co. exec.; b. St. Louis, Jan. 25, 1931; s. Theodore Archie and Minnie Emaline (Hodge) A.; B.S. in E.E., U. Mo., Rolla, 1956; m. Elsie Louise Lewis, Sept. 21, 1951; children—Cynthia, Gary, Theodore, Linda. Sr. engr. McDonnell Aircraft Corp., St. Louis, 1956-68; group engr. ECI Corp., St. Petersburg, Fla., 1968-71; pres. BCI Corp., Rolla, 1971—. Served with USAF, 1948-52. Mem. Component Mfrs. Council (exec. com.).Club: Rolla Lions. Home and office: PO Box 935 Rolla MO 65401

ATWOOD, BURTON HOMER, cons. ecologist; b. Chgo., Sept. 17, 1904; s. Burton and Mary (Stevenson)A.; B.S., Northwestern U., 1942—; m. Cleo Martin, Oct. 3, 1936; children—Katherine (Mrs. Charles Fritsch), Burton Homer III, Mary (Mrs. William Querhammer). Various sales and pub. relations positions Commonwealth Edison Co., Northbrook, Ill., 1925-60; staff asst. Crystal Lake dist., 1960-69; field rep. for the sec. U.S. Dept. Interior, Des Plaines, Ill., 1969-73; cons. ecologist, 1973—. Adv. council Ill. Water Pollution, 1951-56; gen. chmn. Cook County Clean Streams Com., 1954-60; adviser Great Lakes Fishery Commn., Ann Arbor, Mich., 1960—; mem. tech. com. USPHS, Great Lakes Project, 1962-65; mem. Ill. Commn. on State Parks, 1954-60; mem. Gov's. Adv. Council, Ill., 1969-73; commr. Great Lakes Basin Commn., 1969-73; sec.-treas. Izaak Walton League of Am. Endowment, 1955-69, hon. pres., 1970-73; sec. Crystal Lake Hosp. Assn., 1967—; trustee McHenry County (Ill.) Conservation dist., 1974—, pres., 1977—. Recipient nat. conservation award Am. Motors, 1962; conservation award Izaak Walton League, 1963; named to Conservation Hall of Fame Izaak Walton League, 1968; distinguished service award Crystal Lake Rotary Club, 1965. Registered profl. engr., Ill. Mem. Alaska Conservation Soc., Audubon Soc., Nat. Wildlife Fedn., Izaak Walton League Am. (life mem., nat. sec. 1955-61, nat. treas. 1961-66). Rotarian. Contbr. articles to profl. pubs. Home: 368 Cumberland Ln Crystal Lake IL 60014

ATWOOD, ROBERT ELMER, vision care co. exec.; b. LeMars, Iowa, Mar. 25, 1930; s. Elmer H. and Clara Marie (McCrory) A.; B.A., Westmar Coll., 1956; postgrad. Loyola U., 1970; postgrad. Ind. U., 1969; M.B.A., So. Ill. U., 1976; m. Elsie E. Barnes, Dec. 22, 1952; 1 dau., Michelle (Mrs. Joseph DeFano). Dep. adminstr. Nat. Easter Seal Soc., field service div., Chgo., 1969-71; exec. dir. Vision Inst. Am., St. Louis, 1972—; chief exec. operating officer Nat. Prepaid Health Plan, St. Louis, 1972—. Cons. group vision care, 1972—. Served to lt. col. USAF, 1951-55. Mem. Am. Assn. Assn. Execs., Res. Officers Assn. Club: Cherry Hills Country. Home: 834 Guenevere St Manchester MO 63011 Office: 7711 Carondelet St Louis MO 63105

ATZBERGER, FRANK JOHN, indsl. mfg. co. exec.; b. Cleve., Nov. 10, 1937; s. Frank Aloysius and Helen Catherine (Boufford) A.; B.S., U. Detroit, 1959; m. Maureen Frances McCarthy, Nov. 30, 1963; children—John, Mark, Craig, Kristin Elizabeth. Accountant, Pickands Mather & Co., Cleve., 1959-62; corporate planner Hanna Mining Co., Cleve., 1962-69; acquisitions cons. Peat Marwick Mitchell & Co., Cleve., 1969-70; controller Am. Koyo Corp., Cleve., 1972-73, treas., 1974-75, mgr. mktg., 1975; pres. Corplan, Inc., Rocky

River, Ohio, 1976—. Mem. Cuyahoga County Rep. Finance Com., 1962-70. Mem. U. Detroit Alumni Assn., Blue Key, Delta Sigma Pi. Rotarian. Clubs: Lakewood Country; Exec. West (Rocky River, Ohio). Home: 4583 Angela Dr Fairview Park OH 44126 Office: 518 Westgate Plaza 20325 Center Ridge Rd Rocky River OH 44116

AUCAR, ALFREDO, otorhinolaryngologist; b. Rancho Veloz, Cuba, Oct. 14, 1923; s. Santiago and America (Pedro) A.; B.S., U. Havana, 1944, M.D., 1953; m. Esther E. Cura, Apr. 18, 1953; children—Alfred S., Maria, John. Came to U.S., 1962, naturalized, 1969. Intern, Union Hosp., Fall River, Mass., 1953-54; resident ear, nose, throat, Boston City Hosp., 1954-56, Univ. Hosp., Havana, Cuba, 1956-59; practice medicine specializing in otorhinolaryngology, Havana, 1959-62, Kans. State Hosp., Larned and Winfield, 1963-69, Arkansas City, Kan., 1969—; mem. staff St. Francis Hosp., Wichita, Kans.; staff Meml. Hosp., Arkansas City, pres., 1973—; pres. Mauh Cauh Bldg. Corp., Arkansas City. Mem. AMA, Kans., Cowley County med. socs., Cuban Otolar Soc. (in exile), Am. Soc. Ophthalmology and Otolaryngology Allergy, Arkansas City C. of C. K.C., Kiwanian. Home: 2526 Valley View Dr Arkansas City KS 67005 Office: 2508 Edgemont St Arkansas City KS 57005

AUER, DELMAR LAVERNE, realtor; b. Whitley County, Ind., Dec. 10, 1929; s. John E. and Frances M. (Flaugher) A.; Asso. B.S., Internat. Coll., 1950; m. Marilyn J. Hoover, June 25, 1966; children—Richard, Sheila (Mrs. Michael Henderson), Lindy, Cindy. Realtor, Del Auer & Assos., Columbia City, Ind., 1969—. Mem. Whitley County Council, 1970-74, Ind. Ho. of Reps., 1974-76. Bd. dirs. Whitley County United Way. Mem. Nat. Assn. Auctioneers, Nat. Assn. Realtors. Home: Rural Route 9 Columbia City IN 46725 Office: 117 W Market St PO Box 526 Columbia City IN 46725

AUER, JOSEPH CURTIUS, farmer; b. Slater, Mo., Feb. 17, 1924; s. Joseph Henry and Nellie Eddie (Curtius) A.; grad. high sch.; m. Oma Ailene Awbrey, Mar. 1, 1952; children—Gale (Mrs. Thomas D. Coleman), Joseph Awbrey. Examiner, Mo. Hwy. Patrol, 1955; owner Auer Acres, Blackburn, Mo., 1956—, Auer Supply Co. Mem. Blackburn Town Bd., 1955-57, Sch. Bd., 1961-62. Mem. Blackburn PTA, 1960; pres. Blackburn Civic Club, 1953; mem. Crime Alert Club, 1972, Mo. Peace Officers Assn., 1955; leader 4-H Club, 1967-72. Served with AUS, 1948-49, 51. Baptist. Mason (32 deg.). Clubs: Blackburn Fishing (pres. 1955—), Lafayette County Citizens Radio, Marshall Radio. Address: RD 1 Box 2 Blackburn MO 65321

AUERBACH, MARSHALL JAY, lawyer; b. Chgo., Sept. 5, 1932; s. Samuel M. and Sadie (Miller) A.; student U. Ill.; J.D., John Marshall Law Sch., 1955; m. Carole Landsberg, July 3, 1960; children—Keith Alan, Michael Ward. Admitted to Ill. bar, 1955; pvt. practice law, Evanston, Ill., 1955-72; partner in charge matrimonial law sect., law firm Jenner & Block, Chgo., 1972—. Faculty, Ill. Inst. for Continuing Legal Edn. Fellow Am. Acad. Matrimonial Lawyers; mem. Ill. State (chmn. family law sect. 1971-72), Am. (vice-chmn. family law sect. com. for liaison with tax sect. 1974—) bar assns. Rotarian. Club: Executive (Chgo.). Author Ill. Marriage and Dissolution of Marriage Act, 1977. Home: 2314 Orrington Ave Evanston IL 60201 Office: 1 IBM Plaza Chicago IL 60611

AUFDENKAMP, JO ANN, librarian; b. Springfield, Ill., Mar. 22, 1926; d. Erwin C. and Johanna (Ostermeier) Aufdenkamp; B.A., MacMurray Coll. for Women, 1945; B.L.S., U. Ill., 1946; postgrad. U. Chgo., 1964-66; J.D., John Marshall Law Sch., Chgo., 1976. Asst. librarian, commerce library U. Ill., 1946-48; librarian Fed. Reserve Bank of Chgo., 1948—. Library cons. Office Nat. Planning, Liberia, 1963. Mem. Spl. Libraries Assn. Republican. Lutheran. Office: Box 834 Chicago IL 60690

AUGUSTIN, CARROLL DARWIN, ednl. adminstr.; b. Lorain, Ohio, June 6, 1933; s. Arthur Conrad and Edith (Rollason) A.; B.S. in Edn., Miami U., Oxford, Ohio, 1956, M.Ed., 1958; m. Penelope Gifford Tiedjens, Sept. 17, 1955; children—Leslie Gifford, Tracy Carroll, Lindsay Victoria. Tchr., Roosevelt Jr. High Sch., Hamilton, Ohio, 1956-59, Garfield High Sch., Hamilton, 1959-63; dir. adult and vocat. edn., supr. indsl. arts Hamilton Bd. Edn., 1963-66; supr. Miami U. Acad. Center, Hamilton, 1963-67; coordinator fed. study on drop-outs Greater Miami Conf. Schs., 1967; dir. vocat. edn. Butler County (Ohio) Schs., Hamilton, 1968—. Bd. dirs. Am. Cancer Soc., Hamilton, 1963-65, chmn. edn. com., 1964—; chmn. membership com. Hamilton YMCA, 1966, div. chmn. fund drive, 1970, chmn. gen. fund drive, 1971; bd. mgmt. Hamilton West YMCA, 1971—, chmn., 1974-75. Nat. Def. grad. fellow, 1966-67; recipient Outstanding Layman award YMCA, 1971. Mem. Hamilton Classroom Tchrs. Assn. (pres. 1962-63), Hamilton Assn. trade and industry (chmn. com. 1964), Miami-Hamilton Alumni Assn. (mem. control bd. 1963), Sigma Phi Epsilon, Epsilon Pi Tau, Kappa Phi Kappa, Phi Delta Kappa. Presbyterian. Kiwanian (pres. 1971). Home: 1538 Sunset Dr Hamilton OH 45013 Office: D Russel Lee Vocat Sch 3603 Hamilton-Middletown Rd Hamilton OH 45011

AUGUSTINE, GERALD HERMAN, agrl. co. exec.; b. Geddes, S.D., June 5, 1931; s. Joseph William and Alvina Juliana (Schilmoeller) A.; grad. high sch.; m. Kay Marie Parks, Nov. 11, 1961; children—Diane, James, Mary, Beth, Nancy, Kenneth. With Farmers Coop. Co., Remsen, Iowa, 1955-65, asst. mgr., 1956-65; pres., mgr. Remsen Roller Mill, Inc., 1965—. Mem. town council, Remsen, 1969-70, 71-75. Pres. St. Marys-St. Catherines Grade Sch. Bd., Remsen, 1970-73. Served with AUS, 1952-54. Roman Catholic. Home: 321 E 3d St Remsen IA 51050 Office: 108 W Nothem St Remsen IA 51050

AUGUSTINE, JACK H., coll. dean; b. Meadville, Pa., Mar. 6, 1933; s. Percy H. and Astrid (Holmquist) A.; A.B., Taylor U., 1955; B.D., Gordon Divinity Sch., 1959; M.A., Mich. State U., 1964; M.S., U. R.I., 1972; m. Ramona Ferguson, June 23, 1956; children—Robert Jack, Sheril Lynne, Steven Mark. Dir. athletics, coach basketball/baseball, asso. prof. Beskhire Christian Coll., Lenox, Mass., 1957-62; dir. athletics, head phys. edn. dept., dean students, asso. prof. phys. edn. Barrington (R.I.) Coll., 1962-74; dean students, coach basketball, asso. prof. Aurora (Ill.) Coll., 1974—. Cons., coach Nationalist Chinese Basketball Team, Taiwan, 1968. Mem. Barrington Bd. Recreation, 1971-74; bd. mgrs. YMCA, 1970-74. Mem. Am., Ill. personnel and guidance assns., AAHPER, Nat. Basketball Coaches Assn. Baptist. Club: Lions. Home: 1348 Park Manor Aurora IL 60506 Office: 347 Gladstone Ave S Aurora IL 60507

AUGUSTUS, WILLIAM EDGAR, supt. schs.; b. Urbana, Ill., Mar. 27, 1925; s. Ralph Edgar and Catherine Thorpe (Keegan) A.; B.S., Ill. State U., 1949; M.Ed., U. Colo., 1951; advanced certificate U. Ill., 1963; m. Annette M. Keeley, Aug. 18, 1956; children—Jeffrey Alan, Amy Louise. Elementary tchr., Aurora, Ill., 1950-53, jr. high sch. boys' counselor, 1953-56, jr. high sch. prin., 1956-63; prin. Bradford High Sch., Kenosha, Wis., 1963-64, Tremper High Sch., 1964-65, Thornridge High Sch., Dolton, Ill., 1965-68; supt. schs. Thornton Twp. High Schs., Harvey, Ill., 1968—. Bd. dirs Council of Govts. of Cook County, Ill., v.p., 1968—; bd. dirs. United Fund, Harvey, United Way of Suburban Chgo.; bd. govs. Glenwood (Ill.) Sch. for Boys. Served with USAAF, 1943-45. Mem. Am., Ill. assns., sch. adminstrs., Nat., Ill. assns. secondary sch. prins., NEA, Assn. Suburban Confs. (dir. 1968—, sec.-treas. 1971—), South Suburban Assn. Commerce and Industry (dir. 1968—), Phi Delta Kappa. Republican. Roman Catholic. Home: 18854 Juhlin Dr Homewood IL 60430 Office: 151 and Broadway Sts Harvey IL 60426

AULD, FRANK, psychologist; b. Denver, Aug. 9, 1923; s. Benjamin Franklin and Marion Leland (Evans) A.; m. Elinor James, June 29, 1946; children—Mary, Robert, Margaret. A.B., Drew U., 1946; M.A., Yale, 1948, Ph.D., 1950. Certified psychologist Mich., Conn., Ontario. Instr. psychology Yale, 1950-52, asst. prof., 1952-59; asso. prof. Wayne State U., 1959-61, dir. clin. psychology training program, 1960-66, prof. psychology, 1961-67; prof. U. Detroit, 1967-70, dir. psychol. clinic, 1967-69; prof. psychology U. Windsor, Ontario, Canada, 1970—. Chmn. Dearborn (Mich.) Community Council, 1962; mem. advisory com. on college work Episcopal Diocese Mich., 1962-71; cons. in field. Fellow Am. Psychol. Assn. (mem. com. on evaluation 1961-66); mem. Can., Mich. psychol. assns. Can. Assn. Univ. Tchrs., Soc. for Psychotherapy Research, Ont. Psychol. Assn. (mem. Edn. and tng. bd. 1976—), Scientific Research Soc. Am., Conn. State Psychol. Soc., (pres. 1958), Sigma Xi. Recipient Alumni Achievement award, Drew U., 1965. Author: Steps in Psychotherapy, 1953; Scoring Human Motives, 1969; contbr. articles to profl. jours. Home: 1340 Pierce St Birmingham MI 48009 Office: Dept Psychology U Windsor Windsor ON N9B 3P4 Canada

AULIE, RICHARD PAUL, educator; b. Chgo., May 17, 1926; s. Henry Martin and Thora Willa (Doderlein) A.; B.S., Wheaton Coll., 1948; M.S., U. Minn., 1953; Ph.D., Yale, 1968. Tchr. biology Northwestern Coll., Mpls., 1949-52; tchr. biology, chemistry Habibia Coll., Kabul, Afghanistan, 1953; tchr. biology Am. U., Cairo, Egypt, 1954-55; tchr. biology, gen. sci. Bloom Twp. High Sch., Chicago Heights, Ill., Evanston Twp. High Sch., 1955-62; biology expert UNESCO, U. Liberia, Monrovia, 1962-64; tchr. biology Chgo. State Coll., 1968-71; editor, writer sci. and math. biographies Ency. Britannica, 1971-72; lectr. natural sci. Loyola U., Chgo., 1972—. Served with USNR, 1943-45. USPHS trainee, 1964-68. Mem. History Sci. Soc., Nat. Assn. Biology Tchrs. (program chmn. conv. 1971), Agrl. History Soc., Nat. Sci. Tchrs. Assn. Presbyn. Contbr. articles on history of sci. to profl. jours. Home: 6806 S Jeffery Blvd Apt 2G Chicago IL 60649

AULT, ADDISON, educator; b. Boston, July 3, 1933; s. Warren Ortman and Myrtle Lavina (Wilcock) A.; B.A., Amherst Coll., 1955; Ph.D., Harvard, 1960; m. Janet Ruth Meade, Aug. 23, 1958; children—Margaret Ruth, Warren James, Addison David, Peter Harwell, Emily Elizabeth. Asst. prof. Grinnell Coll. (Ia.), 1959-61; research asso. Argonne (Ill.) Nat. Lab., 1961-62; prof. chemistry Cornell Coll., Mt. Vernon, Iowa, 1962—. NSF Sci. Faculty fellow, 1967. Mem. Am. Chem. Soc., Chem. Soc. London, AAAS, AAUP, Sigma Xi, Phi Beta Kappa. Author: Problems in Organic Structure Determination, 1967; Techniques and Experiments for Organic Chemistry, 1973, 2d edit., 1976; (with G.O. Dudek) NMR: An Introduction to Proton Nuclear Magnetic Resonance Spectroscopy, 1976. Home: 519 N 2d St W Mount Vernon IA 52314 Office: Cornell Coll Mount Vernon IA 52314

AULT, PHILLIP H., editor; b. Maywood, Ill., Apr. 26, 1914; s. Frank W. and Bernda (Halliday) A.; A.B., DePauw U., 1935; m. Karoline Byberg, June 5, 1943; children—Frank, Ingrid, Bruce. Reporter LaGrange (Ill.) Citizen, 1935-37; corr. editor U.P.I., Chgo., N.Y.C., Iceland, North Africa, London, Eng., 1938-48, bur. chief, London, 1944-45; asst. mng. editor, dir. editorial page Times-Mirror Co., Los Angeles, 1948; editorial page editor Los Angeles Mirror-News, 1948-57; exec. editor Asso. Desert Newspapers, 1958-67; asso. editor South Bend (Ind.) Tribune, 1968—. Mem. Am. Soc. Newspaper Editors, Western Writers Am., Sigma Nu. Author: This Is The Desert, News Around the Clock; How to Live in California, Home Book of Western Humor; Wonders of the Mosquito World; These Are the Great Lakes, Wires West, All Aboard! Co-author: Springboard to Berlin, 1943: Reporting the News; Introduction to Mass Communications. Home: 3025 Woodridge Av South Bend IN 46615 Office: South Bend Tribune South Bend IN 46626

AULVIN, JOHN LEWIS, lawyer; b. Albion, Ill., Feb. 22, 1934; s. George H. and Mary Claudine (Walsh) A.; B.A., U. Mo., 1959; J.D., Vanderbilt U., 1962; m. Rebecca Ann McAlister, Dec. 21, 1961; children—Valerie Ann, Brooksie Kay, Natalie Nicole. Admitted to Ill. bar, 1963; practiced in Mt. Carmel, Ill., 1963—; states atty. Wabash County, Ill., 1964-68. Asst. Sec.-treas. Columbian Fed. Savs. & Loan, Mt. Carmel, 1969-74; owner, dir. Landowners Abstracts & Titles, Ltd., Mt. Carmel. Served with USNR, 1959-60. Mem. Am., Ill., Southeastern Ill., Wabash County bar assns., Am. Judicature Soc., Ind. Oil Producers-TriState. Mason (32 deg., Shriner), Elk. Club: Petroleum (Evansville, Ind.). Home: 322 Park Rd Mount Carmel IL 62863 Office: 120 E 4th St Mount Carmel IL 62863

AUSDAL, ROBERT BURNS, investment co. exec.; b. Marshalltown, Iowa, Aug. 25, 1926; s. Peter and Gertrude Celina (Stackhouse) A.; B.A. with high distinction, U. Iowa, 1950; m. June Clark, June 3, 1952; children—Claudia June, Laura Krista, Robert Burns. Vice pres. Quail & Co., Davenport, Iowa, 1950-67, Dain, Kalman & Quail, Inc., Mpls., 1967-74; exec. v.p. Beyer-Ausdal Co., Davenport, 1974—. Served with USNR, 1944-46. Mem. Assn. Investment Brokers, Phi Beta Kappa, Alpha Kappa Psi. Clubs: Davenport Outing, Davenport. Home: 3306 33d Ave Ct Rock Island IL 61201 Office: 617 Davenport Bank Bldg Davenport IA 52801

AUSTIN, DONALD CASTLE, neurosurgeon; b. Indpls., Dec. 2, 1933; s. Rayburn Castle and Esther Marjorie (Rensberger) A.; A.B., Ind. U., 1955, M.D., 1958; m. Rudale Wallace, Dec. 1, 1965; children—Donald Castle, Sheryl, April, Jeffrey. Intern, Meth. Hosp., Indpls., 1958-59; resident Henry Ford Hosp., Detroit, 1959-63; practice medicine specializing in neurosurgery, Detroit, 1963—; vice chief dept. neurosurgery Harper-Weber Hosp.; chief sect. Hutzel Hosp., Detroit; clin. asst. prof. neurosurgery Wayne State Med. Sch., Detroit, 1972—. Research fellow Inst. Psychiat. Research, Ind. U. Med. Center, 1958. Mem. Congress Neurosurgeons, Am., Mich. assns. neurosurgeons, Detroit Surg. Soc. (pres. elect 1978), Detroit Med. Club (sec.-treas. 1972-73), Am., Mich., Wayne County med. assns., Detroit Acad. Surgery, Detroit Acad. Neurosurgery, Phi Chi. Home: 39 Hampton Rd Grosse Pointe Shores MI 48236 Office: 4727 St Antoine St Suite 406 Detroit MI 48201

AUSTIN, GARY FRANCIS, educator; b. Julesburg, Colo., Feb. 19, 1939; s. Leland Levik and Bertha Fern (Alderman) A.; A.A., McCook Coll., 1965; B.A., U. No. Colo., 1966, M.A., Ed.S. (Rehab. Services Adminstrn. fellow), 1968; Ph.D. (U.S. Office Edn. fellow), Northwestern U., 1973; m. Peggy Ann Tatum, June 11, 1961; children—Kenneth Duane, Shelly Jo. Dir. residential program for speech and hearing impaired young adults No. Ill. U., DeKalb, 1968—, asst. prof., 1972-74, asso. prof. communication disorders, 1974—. Cons. Ill. Div. Vocat. Rehab. in area of deafness, 1972-74, Ill. Dept. Children and Family Services, 1972-74, Tech. Edn. Research Assos., 1972-73, Waubonsee Community Coll., 1971-72, William Rainer Harper Community Coll., 1971—, Hinsdale (Ill.) S. High Sch., 1969-72. Served with USMCR, 1957-59. Mem. Nat., Ill. (pres.) rehab. assns., Profl. Rehab. Workers with Adult Deaf, Acad. Rehabilitative Audiology, Registry Interpreters of Deaf. Republican. Presbyterian (deacon 1973-76). Author: Bibliography: Deafness by G.F. Austin, 1973. Home: 811 W Fairview Dr DeKalb IL 60115

AUSTIN, JOHN ATWOOD, JR., psychologist; b. Detroit, Apr. 4, 1941; s. John Atwood and Mary R. (McEvoy) A.; B.S., U. Calif., Berkeley, 1963, M.S., 1968, Ph.D., 1972; divorced; children—John Atwood, III, Larissa. Staff psychologist Colo. State U., 1971-72, Hiawatha Valley Mental Health Center, Winona, Minn., 1974—; dir. counseling St. Mary's Coll., Winona, 1972—. Served with AUS, 1963-65. Mem. Am. Psychol. Assn., Am. Personnel and Guidance Assn., Am. Coll. Personnel Assn. Episcopalian. Home: 1406 W 4th St Winona MN 55987 Office: St Mary's Coll Winona MN 55987

AUSTIN, JOSEPH ALLEN, ry. exec.; b. Junction City, Ark., June 18, 1919; s. Eugene Joseph and Marjorie (Allen) A.; grad. Harvard U. Advanced Mgmt. Program, 1964; m. Martha E. Erwin, Dec. 21, 1940; children—Martha K. (Mrs. Robert Adam Rosen), Eugene J. With M.P. R.R., 1938—, asst. supt., 1952-54, supt., 1954-57, asst. chief personnel officer, 1957-58, gen. supt. transp., 1958-65, v.p. gulf region, Houston, 1965-67, asst. v.p. traffic, 1967-69, v.p. traffic, St. Louis, 1969-77, sr. v.p. traffic, 1977—. Mem. Am. Soc. Traffic and Transp., Nat. Freight Traffic Assn., Western R.R. Traffic Assn. (exec. com.), Delta Nu Alpha. Presbyterian. Mason (Shriner). Clubs: Mo. Athletic, Bellerive Country, St. Louis Traffic (St. Louis); Traffic, Union League (Chgo.); New York Traffic. Home: 15 Outer Ladue Dr Frontenac MO 63131 Office: 210 N 13th St St Louis MO 63103

AUSTIN, MICHAEL HERSCHEL, lawyer; b. nr. Water Valley, Miss., Nov. 7, 1896; s. Michael Green and Willie C. (Roberson) A.; student U. Miss., 1915-18, LL.B., 1922; postgrad. Akron U., 1919; postgrad. Ohio State U., 1919-21, J.D., 1923; m. Esther Catherine Seebach. Nov. 26, 1920 (dec.); m. 2d, Mary Inez Harpst. Tchr. pub. elementary sch., Miss., 1914-15; admitted to Miss. bar 1922, Ohio bar, 1924, since practiced in Columbus, O.; partner firm Pfeiffer and Austin, 1927-30. Franklin County atty. Farmers Home Adminstrn., 1963-70. Past mem. Chmn.'s Council Franklin County Democratic party; mem. Ohio Dem. party. Fellow of Harry Truman Library; honary fellow Truman Library Inst. Served with U.S. Army World War I, Recipient Cross of Honor, U.D.C., 1944, award for service to Am. Legion and vets. Am. Legion, Lancaster, Ohio, 1969; Golden Circle Certificate Ohio State U. Assn.; named mem. Exec. and Profl. Hall of Fame. Mem. Internat. Platform Assn., Am. Bar Assn. (estate gift tax sect.), Ohio, Columbus (mem. probate ct. com.) bar assns., Am. Judicature Soc., Columbus Real Estate Bd. (asso.). Ohio State U. Alumni Assn., Columbus Area C. of C., Am. Legion (post comdr. 1944-45, county comdr. 1953-54, dist. comdr. 1955-56, state treas. 1958-59, Big Four Vets. Council 1956-57, pres. Past Comdrs. Club 1960-61, judge adv. 12th dist. Ohio, 1967, 68, 69, 75-76, named 12th. dist. Outstanding Legionnaire). Phi Alpha Delta. Democrat. Mason. Clubs: Columbus Lawyers (past sec.), Franklin County Democratic. Home: 47 Richards Rd Columbus OH 43214 Office: 85 E Gay St Columbus OH 43215

AUSTINSON, CARLYLE PALMER, banker, city ofcl.; b. Fillmore, N.D., Oct. 10, 1914; s. Austin K. and Louise (Sterry) A.; student State Sch. Sci., Wahpeton, N.D., 1940; m. Helen Sylvia Rauk, 1941; children—Sharon Sylvia, Kent Carlyle. Asst. cashier First Internat. Bank, Esmond, N.D., 1941-43; cashier Farmers State Bank, Leeds, N.D., 1945-50; cashier Northwood State Bank (N.D.), 1950—, v.p., 1970-75, exec. v.p., 1975—, dir. 1958—, chief exec. officer, 1977—. Alderman, City of Northwood, 1952-56, mayor, 1958—. Bd. dirs. Northwood Deaconess Hosp. and Home Assn., pres., 1961—. Mem. nat. advisory council Nat. Fedn. Ind. Bus. Mem. Corp. United Hosp., Grand Forks, N.D. Served from pvt. to sgt., U.S. Army, 1943-45. Mem. N.D. Bankers Assn. (pres. N.E. dist. 1955, chmn. bank mgmt. com. 1957, chmn. Northeast dist. Centennial Commn. 1963, chmn. pub. relations 1964, mem. legis. com. 1972, 1st v.p. 1975, pres. 1976), League N.D. Municipalities (regional v.p. 1958, pres. 1961), Am. Legion (comdr. post 92 1967). Republican. Lutheran. Elk, Mason. Office: Northwood State Bank Northwood ND 58267

AUTHIER, RICHARD LAWRENCE, optometrist; b. Sioux City, Iowa, Nov. 5, 1937; s. Noe Vincent and Mary Louise (Menard) A.; student Central Mo. State Coll., 1956-58, Morningside Coll., 1958-59, U. Kan., 1959-60; D.Optometry, So. Coll. Optometry, 1963; m. Sandra Jean Day, Dec. 27, 1964; children—Christa Suzanne, Brian Jonathon, Adam Richard. Pvt. practice optometry, Beatrice, Nebr., 1964-67, Norfolk, Nebr., 1967—. Pres. !Bébaselo! Ltd. Mem. Am., Nebr. optometric assns., N.E. Nebr. Optometric Soc. (pres.), C. of C. (med. affairs com.), Norfolk Arts Council, Omega Delta. Rotarian. Home: 405 Ridgeway Dr Norfolk NE 68701 Office: 417 Norfolk Ave Norfolk NE 68701

AUTRY, CHARLES FRANKLIN, realty co. exec.; b. Pine Hill, Ala., Apr. 9, 1912; s. Noah Frank and Rosa (Marchand) A.; ed. high sch., Pine Hill; m. Betty Jane Bellfry, Oct. 25, 1975; children—William Franklin, Sandra Autry Ignatonis, Jean Autry Eubanks. With Birmingham Slag Co., (Ala.)., 1936-38; dam constrn. Kershaw Butler Constrn. Co., Sardis, Miss., at Norfolk (Va.) Naval Operating Base and Huntsville (Ala.) Arsenal, 1938-44; gen. supr. Kimbrough Constrn. Co., Mobile, Ala., 1945-50; project mgr. Shelby Constrn. Co., New Orleans, bldg. in Fla., Ohio, and Ind., 1951-54; v.p., mgr. bldg. ops. A.B.C. Constrn. Co., Indpls., 1955-61; v.p., J & L Realty Inc., Indpls., also mgr., developer Colony Woods Co., Indpls., 1962—. Republican. Methodist. Home: 2140D Boston Ct Indianapolis IN 46208 Office: 3901 W 30th St Indianapolis IN 46222

AUWAERTER, JOHN FRANCIS, mfg. co. exec.; b. Chgo., Aug. 24, 1925; s. Albert Frederick and Frances (Bennington) A.; B.S. in Elec. Engring., Northwestern U., 1948; J.D., DePaul U., 1956; m. Irene McElwain (div. Apr. 1977); 1 dau., Mary Reese. Sales engr., product devel. engr., dir. product devel., v.p. sales and fin. Teletype Corp., Skokie, Ill., 1952-71, v.p. sales and service, 1975—; dir. mfg. Western Electric Co., Indpls., 1971-7S. Address: 44 Park Ln Apt 223 Park Ridge IL 60068

AVECILLA, CONSTANTE SIMON, surgeon; b. Manila, Philippines, Nov. 24, 1936; s. Mariano and Ursula (Simon) A.; came to U.S., 1963; B.S. in Zoology, U. Philippines, 1957; M.D., U. of East, Philippines, 1962; m. Amelia G. Javier, Oct. 24, 1964; children—Michelle, Jean, Constance. Intern, St. Barnabas Med. Center, Livingston, N.J., 1962-63, resident in surgery, 1963-65, 66-67; resident in oncology Meml. Hosp. for Cancer and Allied Diseases, N.Y.C., 1965-66; resident in colorectal surgery Presbyn. Hosp., Dallas, 1967-69; staff surgeon VA Center, Hampton, Va., 1971-73; colorectal surgeon Marshfield (Wis.) Clinic, 1973—. Diplomate Am. Bd. Surgery, Am. Bd. Colorectal Surgery. Fellow A.C.S., Internat. Acad. Proctology, Am. Soc. Colon and Rectal Surgeons (asso.); mem. AMA, Wis. Surg. Soc., Wood County Med. Soc. Contbr. articles to profl. jours. Home: 1121 W Blodgett St Marshfield WI 54449 Office: Marshfield Clinic Marshfield WI 54449

AVEDISIAN, ARMEN GEORGE, bus. exec.; b. Chgo., Oct. 28, 1926; s. Karekin Der and Kardovil (Ignatius) A.; B.S., U. Ill., 1949; m. Dorothy D. Donian, Nov. 22, 1952; children—Guy A., Vann A., Donna A. Civil engr. Standard Paving Co., Chgo., 1949; constrn. supt. Gallagher Asphalt Corp., Thornton, Ill., 1950-55; v.p., dir. Am. Asphalt Paving Co., Chgo., 1956-64; chmn. bd., pres. Lincoln Stone Quarry, Inc., Joliet, Ill., 1964—, Avedisian Industries, Inc., Hillside, Ill., 1964—; chmn. bd. Delta Constrn. Corp., Joliet, 1968—, Swenson, Inc., Joliet, 1970—, Midstate Stone Corp., Gillespie, Ill., 1970—; chmn. bd., chief exec. officer Hillside (Ill.) Stone Corp., 1969—. Mem. pres.'s com., guarantor Lyric Opera, Chgo., 1968—; gov. life mem. Men's Council, Art Inst. Chgo., 1961—. Trustee Avery Coonley Sch. Served with AUS, 1944-45. Mem. Nat. Limestone Inst. (chmn. bd. 1971—), Midwest Crushed Limestone Inst. (pres. 1966-67), Nat. Crushed Stone Inst. (gov. 1972), Ill. Rd. Builders Assn. (dir., treas. 1963), Am., Western socs. civil engrs., Ill. Assn. Aggregae Producers (dir., pres. 1968). Sigma Nu. Clubs: Chicago Athletic, Chicago Yacht, Racquet (Chgo); Butterfield Country (Hinsdale, Ill.); Dunham Woods Riding (Wayne, Ill.); Lake Geneva (Wis.) Country. Home: 701 Taft Rd Hinsdale IL 60521 Office: Eisenhower Expressway and Mannheim Rd PO Box 669 Hillside IL 60162

AVEDON, BRUCE, ins. and securities exec.; b. Atlantic City, Dec. 31, 1928; s. N. Jay and Rosalie Ann (Sholtz) A.; B.S., Yale U., 1950; m. Shirlee Florence Young, May 29, 1951; children—Linda Michele, Bruce Frederick. Vice pres. Sholtz Ins. Agy., Inc., Miami, Fla., 1950-51; various positions to dir. planning State Mut. Life Assurance Co. Am., Worcester, Mass., 1953-69, also sec. Am. Variable Annuity Life Assurance Co., Worcester, 1967-69; v.p. equity products Ohio Nat. Life Ins. Co., Cin., 1969—, also pres. dir. O.N. Equity Sales Co., Cin, 1973—; pres., dir. O.N. Fund, Inc. Served to lt. AUS, 1951-53; maj. Finance Corps Res. ret. Mem. Am. Council Life Ins. (variable contracts com.), Investment Co. Inst. (pension com.), Life Office Mgmt. Assn. (ops. and procedures council), Nat. Assn. Securities Dealers (variable contracts com.), Res. Officers Assn., Mil. Order World Wars. Republican. Methodist. Clubs: Yale (Cin.), Masons, Order Eastern Star. Home: 6601 Hitching Post Ln Cincinnati OH 45230 Office: 237 William Howard Taft Rd Cincinnati OH 45219

AVERITT, GEORGE ROBERT, newspaper exec.; b. Peru, Ind., Aug. 5, 1931; s. Robert Chancellor and Cleo A. (Hite) A.; A.B., Ind. U., 1953, postgrad. 1954; postgrad. Mich. State U., 1956-59; m. Elizabeth Irene McDonnell, Nov. 26, 1955; children—Russell Cary, Heather Beth, Erica Irene. Econs. instr. Carnegie Inst. Tech., Pitts., 1959-60, Purdue U. North Central Campus, Michigan City, Ind., 1961—; dir. advt. promotion News-Dispatch, Michigan City, 1960-67, bus. mgr., 1967-73, gen. mgr., 1973-74, asso. pub., 1974—. Pres., Michigan City United Fund, 1967, Michigan City YMCA, 1975. Served to 1st lt., inf. AUS, 1954-56. Named Outstanding Young Man of Yr. Michigan City, Jr. C. of C., 1965. Mem. Am. Econ. Assn., Michigan City Area C. of C. (pres. 1971-72), Inst. Newspaper Controllers and Finance Officers, Sigma Delta Chi, Alpha Kappa Psi, Tau Kappa Epsilon. Unitarian. Elk, Rotarian. Home: 2918 Roslyn Trail LB Michigan City IN 46360 Office: 121 W Michigan Blvd Michigan City IN 46360

AVERY, BARBARA JEAN, guidance counselor; b. Bismarck, N.D., Dec. 29, 1950; d. Charles F. and Betty M. (Alpers) Keenan; L.P.N., St. Francis Sch. Nursing, 1969; B.A., Coll. St. Benedict, 1973; M.S., U. Wis., Madison, 1976; m. Stephen L. Avery, Dec. 20, 1975. L.P.N., Santa Barbara (Calif.) Gen. Hosp., 1969-70, Sauk Centre (Minn.) Gen. Hosp., 1970-71; camp nurse Easter Seal Camp for Disabled Children, Wis. Dells., Wis., 1972-73; tchr. Monona Grove Pub. Schs., Monona, Wis., 1973-75; devel. guidance counselor, City of Pulaski, Wis., 1977—. Mem. Am. Personnel and Guidance Assn. Home: 239 S St Augustine St Pulaski WI 54162

AVERY, DOUGLAS NORMAN, trade assn. exec.; b. Norwalk, Ohio, Mar. 15, 1925; s. Edwin A. and Fanny (Thayer) A.; student Ohio Wesleyan U., 1943-45; B.S., Bowling Green State U., 1948, M.A., 1953; m. Doris Jean Meek, Aug. 17, 1947; children—Gail, Joy, Edwin. Tchr., Findlay (Ohio) High Sch., 1948-55, Ohio State U., 1955-57, Ohio U., 1957-58; with Ohio Assn. Ins. Agts., Inc., Columbus, 1958—, exec. sec., 1958-71, exec. v.p., 1971—. Trustee Griffith Meml. Found., Ohio State U., bd. electors Ins. Hall Fame. Served with USNR, 1943-46. Mem. Ohio Trade Execs. Assn., Am. Soc. Trade Execs., Sigma Chi, Phi Delta Kappa. Mason (Shriner). Clubs: Columbus Athletic, University (Columbus). Home: 5386 Dunniker Park Dr Dublin OH 43017 Office: 1330 Dublin Rd Columbus OH 43215

AVILA, TERESITA DEDIOS, obstetrician, gynecologist; b. Danao City, Philippines, Apr. 22, 1943; d. Restituto Ramos and Teresa (DeDios) Avila; M.D., Cebu Inst. Medicine, Philippines, 1965; m. Francisco D. Varona, Oct. 12, 1974; children—Tessa Marie, Anna Marie. Asst. instr. Cebu Inst. Tech., Cebu Inst. Medicine, Philippines, 1965-66; intern W. Penn Hosp., Pitts., 1966-67; resident in obstetrics gynecology Trumbull Meml. Hosp., Warren, Ohio, 1967-70; Ford Found. fellow in reproductive endocrinology Michael Reese Hosp., Chgo., 1970-72; practice medicine specializing in obstetrics gynecology, Maywood, Ill., 1972—; asst. prof. obstetrics gynecology Loyola U. Stritch Sch. Medicine, Maywood, Ill., 1972—; cons. obstetrics gynecology Northlake (Ill.) Community Hosp., 1974—. Diplomate Am. Bd. Obstetrics Gynecology. Fellow Am. Coll. Obstetrics Gynecology. Roman Catholic. Office: 2160 S 1st Ave Maywood IL 60153

AVNY, WARREN YORAM, endodontist; b. Haifa, Israel, Nov. 29, 1941; s. Earl and Pnina (Dresner) A.; came to U.S., 1945, naturalized, 1952; student Roosevelt U., 1962; D.D.S., Loyola U., Chgo., 1966, M.S. (Grad. fellow), 1970; m. Marilyn Jean Seidel, Nov. 21, 1962; children—Michelle Lisa, Jeffrey Alan. Pvt. practice endodontics, Mt. Prospect, Glenview, Ill., 1969—; endodontic staff cons. St. Francis, Lutheran Gen. hosps., 1971—; asst. prof. endodontic dept. Loyola U. Dental Sch., 1970—. Served to capt. USAF, 1966-68. Fellow Am. Coll. Stomatologic Surgeons; mem. Am. Assn. Endodontists, Am. Dental Assn., Ill. State, Chgo., Israeli dental socs., Coolidge Endodontic Study Club. Mason (Shriner); mem. B'nai B'rith. Home: 336 Crescent Dr Glenview IL 60025 Office: 411 Walnut St Mount Prospect IL 60056 also 1775 Glenview Rd Glenview IL 60025

AWAIS, GEORGE MUSA, obstetrician, gynecologist; b. Ajloun, Jordan, Dec. 15, 1929; s. Musa and Meha (Koury) A.; A.B., Hope Coll., 1955; M.D., U. Toronto, 1960; m. Nabila Rizk, June 24, 1970. Intern, U. Toronto Hosps., Ont., Can., 1960-61, resident in obstetrics and gynecology, 1961-64, chief resident, 1965; chief resident Harlem Hosp., Columbia U., N.Y.C., 1966; asst. obstetrician and gynecologist, Cleve. Met. Gen. Hosp., 1967, asso., 1969; instr. obstetrics and gynecology Case Western Res. U., Cleve., 1967-70, asst. obstetrician and gynecologist MacDonald House, 1970, asst. prof., 1970, asst. clin. prof. dept. reproductive biology, 1971, asst. obstetrician and gynecologist Univ. Hosps., 1971; staff dept. gynecology, Cleve. Clinic Found., 1971—; chmn. dept. obstetrics and gynecology King Faisal Specialist Hosp. and Research Center, Riyadh, 1975-76; cons. panel mem. Internat. Corr. Soc. Obstetricians and Gynecologists, 1971. Diplomate Am. Bd. Obstetrics and Gynecology. Fellow A.C.S., Am. Coll. Obstetricians and Gynecologists, Royal Coll. Surgeons Can.; mem. AMA, AAAS, Acad. Medicine of Cleve., Am. Infertility Soc. Contbr. articles to publs. in field, papers, reports to confs., TV appearances, Saudi Arabia. Office: Dept Gynecology Cleveland Clinic Cleveland OH 44106

AXELROD, JACK MARTIN, foundry exec.; b. St. Louis, July 16, 1936; s. Sol and Marie Louise (Longo) A.; B.S., Washington U., St. Louis, 1958; postgrad. St. Louis U., 1960; m. Carol Adele Sugerman, June 16, 1957; children—Gary Paul, David Robert, Michael Howard. Ops. mgr. Klines-Franklin-Simon, St. Louis, 1957-60; group leader, fin. analyst McDonnell Aircraft Corp., St. Louis, 1960-64; prin. J. Axelrod, Accountant, St. Louis, 1964—; corporate comptroller, v.p. M.P.I., 1975—. Mem. Nat. Assn. Pub. Accountants, Indsl. Accounting Soc. Mo., Mo. Assn. Tax Practitioners. Jewish. Club: Rotary. Contbr. chpts. to Prentice-Hall Portfolio of Accounting. Home: 13000 Ferncrest Ct Creve Coeur MO 63141 Office: 102 N Cool Springs Dr O'Fallon MO

AXELROOD, HELEN BLAU, counselor, educator; b. Chgo., Feb. 13; d. Morris and Goldie (Bookstien) Blau; B.A., Roosevelt U., 1951, M.A., 1977; postgrad. guidance and counseling Marquette U., Wis.; m. Jack Axelrood, June 27, 1948; children—Lisa, Barney, Larry, Michael. TV and stage actress, 1951-74; actress-writer N.B.C. series Bible Time, 1960, series The Artist Speaks, 1970; actress Second City, Chgo., 1951-53; tchr. Chgo. Bd. Edn., 1958-62; art dir. Temple Emanuel, Chgo., 1957-58; primary supr. Temple Bethel, Chgo., 1965-66; vocat. guidance counselor, Evanston, 1976-77; guest on TV programs. Active Temple Beth El, Chgo. Recipient award for Dedicated Service Temple Beth Emet, 1960, Outstanding Service award, 1970. Mem. Am. Personnel, Guidance Assn., Assn. Specialists in Group Work, YMCA, Chgo. Art Inst. Research on sch. integration. Home and Office: 2022 Hawthorne Ln Evanston IL 60201

AXELSON, JOHN ANTON, educator; b. Lorain, Ohio, May 11, 1929; s. John August and Mildred Irene (Wolfrom) A.; B.S., Bowling Green U., 1951; M.A., U. Mich., 1956, Ph.D., 1965; m. Ernestine Delventhal, Aug. 10, 1957; children—Thomas, Jon, Kristin. Counselor, Lee M. Thurston High Sch., Redford Twp., Mich., 1955-65; prof., counseling lab. dir. No. Ill. U., DeKalb, 1965—; vis. prof. Kans. U., Lawrence, 1965, U. Mich., Ann Arbor, 1969. Mem. Citizens Adv. Com. to Schs., DeKalb, 1976-77; exec. bd. Luth. Campus Ministry, DeKalb, 1977; mem. com. Ill. Humanities Council, 1977. Served with U.S. Army, 1951-53. Recipient United Fund Campaign award, 1966, 67; registered psychologist, Ill., Ariz. Mem. Am. Personnel and Guidance Assn., Ill. Psychol. Assn. Lutheran. Author: Counselor Self-Evaluation Scale, 1975; Guiding Youth Who Are Disadvantaged, 1968. Home: 223 Ridge Dr DeKalb IL 60115 Office: No Ill Univ DeKalb IL 60115

AXELSON, JOSEPH ALLEN, profl. athletic corp. exec.; b. Peoria, Ill., Dec. 25, 1927; s. Joseph Victor and Florence Ealen (Massey) A.; m. Malcolm Rae Smith, Oct. 7, 1950; children—David Allen, Mark Stephen, Linda Rae; B.S. in Journalism, Northwestern U., 1949. Sports info. dir. Ga. So. Coll., 1954-55, pub. relations dir., 1957-60; sports info. dir. Furman U., 1956; pub. relations dir. Nat. Assn. Intercollegiate Athletics, Kansas City, Mo., 1961-62, asst. exec. sec., 1965-68; pub. relations dir. Bowling Proprs. Assn. Am., Park Ridge, Ill., 1963-64; exec. v.p., gen. mgr. Cin. Royals Profl. Basketball Team, 1969-72; mgr. Cin. Gardens, 1970-72; pres., gen. mgr. Kansas City Kings Profl. Basketball Team, 1972—; chmn. competition and rules coms. Nat. Basketball Assn., 1975—; dir. Kings Profl. Basketball Club, Inc., Perry Broadcasting Co., Lake Charles, La. Bd. dirs. Boys Clubs of Kansas City. Mem. Am. Philatelic Soc., Phi Kappa Psi. Club: Rotary. Named NBA Exec. of Year, The Sporting News, 1973. Home: 7344 Booth Ave Prairie Village KS 66208 Office: 1800 Genessee St Kansas City MO 64102

AXLEY, RALPH EMERSON, lawyer; b. Seymour, Wis., Jan. 12, 1902; s. Frederick William and Jennie C. (Gallagher) A.; B.A., U. Wis., 1923, LL.B., 1926; m. Katharine Nella Hartman, Sept. 10, 1928 (dec. Mar. 1967); children—Hartman, Francesca Jane; m. 2d, Elizabeth Kauffman Hahn, Jan. 21, 1968. Admitted to Wis. bar, 1925; practiced law with Axley Brynelson, Herrick & Gehl and predecessor firms, Madison, 1925—; v.p., dir. W T. Rogers Co. Mem. Am. (mem. council public utilities sect. 1953-57, chmn. standing com. 1952-53), Wis., Dane County bar assns., Am. Judicature Soc., Selden Soc., Delta Sigma Rho, Phi Delta Phi. Republican. Congregationalist. Mason (33 deg., Shriner). Clubs: Madison, Maple Bluff Country, Optimist. Contbr. symposium, also articles to Wisconsin Law Review, Labor Law Journal. Home: 3515 Sunset Dr Shorewood Hills Madison WI 53705 Office: 122 W Washington Ave PO Box 1767 Madison WI 53703

AXSOM, DOROTHY SKIRVIN, publicist; b. Bloomington, Ind., June 6, 1911; d. Obel E. and Goldie (Shields) Skirvin; grad. Bloomington Bus. Coll., 1942, postgrad., 1943; student Ind. U. various times; summer study DePaul U., 1944; m. Hezzie Axsom, Dec. 31, 1931. Secretarial, personnel, supervisory positions, industry and edn., 1941-56; Ind. exec. sec. Muscular Dystrophy Assns. of Am., Inc., 1956-58; exec. dir. United Cerebral Palsy of Ill., Inc., 1958-61; free lance writer, pub. relations, 1961—; dir. community relations Indpls. area ARC, 1962; dir. pub. relations Indpls. Diabetes Assn., 1962-69, Severin Hotel, 1964-66; pub., editor Handy-Cap Horizons, also pres.; assn. for community relations Westinghouse Mgmt. Services, Inc., 1966-68. Del., 7th Dist. Federated Clubs Ind.; del. Indpls. Council Women; mem. Greater Indpls. Arthritis Found. Named Hon. Citizen Tenn., Hon. Citizen Nashville, aide de camp Gov. Dunn, Tenn. Certified profl. sec. Nat. Secs. Assn. (past pres.). Mem. Christian Church (former supt. jr. high Sunday sch. dept.). Clubs: Doers; Greater Southside of Indianapolis. Contbr. articles to ch. and nat. mags. Author: Favorite Dishes of Famous People. Vol. planner, condr. cross-country tours for handicapped. Home and office: 3250 E Loretta Dr Indianapolis IN 46227

AYERS, LEONA WESTON, pathologist, physician, educator; b. Garner, N.C., Jan. 14, 1940; d. William Albert and Ida Bertha (Bell) Weston; B.S., Duke, 1962, M.D., 1967; m. James Cordon Ayers, Aug. 1, 1965; children—Ashley Albert, Alan Andrew. Intern, Duke U. Med. Center, Durham, N.C., 1967-68, resident in pathology, 1968-69; resident in pathology Univ. Hosps., Columbus, Ohio, 1969-71; individual practice medicine, specializing in pathology Columbus, Ohio, 1970—; dir. div. clin. microbiology Univ. Hosp., Columbus, 1970—; attending staff, 1971—; asst. prof. allied health professions Ohio State U., Columbus, 1974—, pathology, 1971-77. asso. prof. pathology, 1977—; cons. in field. Diplomate Am. Bd. Pathology. Mem. AAUP, Am. Med. Women's Assn., Am. Soc. Microbiology, S. Central Assn. Clin. Microbiology. Fellow Am. Soc. Clin. Pathologists. Contbr. articles to profl. publs. Home: 3402 Shattuck Ave Columbus OH 43221 Office: 410 W 10th Ave Columbus OH 43210

AYERS, RICHARD WAYNE, elec. mfg. co. exec.; b. Atlanta, Aug. 23, 1945; s. Harold Richard and Martha Elizabeth (Vaughan) A.; B.B.A., Ga. State Coll., 1967; M.B.A., Ind. U., 1969; m. Nancy Katherine Martin, Aug. 9, 1969. Specialist mktg. communications Gen. Electric Co., Schenectady, 1969-70, copywriter Lamp div., Cleve., 1970-73, supr., distbr. advt. and sales promotion, 1973-75, supr. comml. and indsl. promotional programs Gen. Electric Lamp Bus. Group, 1975—; lectr. in field. Recipient Best Indsl. Promotion award Advt. Age, 1974, Premium Showcase award Nat. Premium Sales Execs., 1975, 76, Gold Key award Nat. Premium Mfrs. Reps., 1976, 77, Golden Key Communicators award Factory mag., 1976. Dir.-at-large Ga. Young Reps., 1966-67. Mem. Blue Key, Delta Sigma Pi, Beta Gamma Sigma. Lutheran. Home: 23951 Lake Shore Blvd Apt 1213B Euclid OH 44123 Office: Nela Park Bldg 308 Cleveland OH 44112

AYERS, THOMAS G., utility exec.; b. Detroit, Feb. 16, 1915; s. Jule C. and Camilla (Chalmers) A.; A.B., U. Mich., 1937; LL.D., Elmhurst Coll., 1966; L.H.D. (hon.), De Paul U., 1977; m. Mary Andrew, Nov. 25, 1938; children—Catherine Mary (Mrs. James W. Allen), Thomas G., William Charles, Richard James, John Steven. With Pub. Service Co. No. Ill., 1938-52, mgr. indsl. relations, 1948-52; asst. v.p. Commonwealth Edison Co., Chgo., 1952, v.p., 1953-62, exec. v.p., 1962-64, pres., 1964-73, chmn., chief exec. officer, pres., 1973—, also dir.; dir. 1st Nat. Bank Chgo., N.W. Industries Inc., Zenith Radio Corp., Sears, Roebuck & Co., Tribune Co., G.D. Searle & Co.; chmn. Breeder Reactor Corp., Dearborn Park Corp. Chmn. Met. Crusade of Mercy, Chgo., 1969, Leadership Council Met. Open Communities; chmn. bd. trustees Northwestern U.; bd. dirs. Chgo. Symphony Orch. Mem. Chgo. Assn. Commerce and Industry (dir., past pres.). Clubs: Chicago, Economic, Mid-Day, Tavern, Metropolitan, Commercial, Commonwealth (Chgo.); Glen Oak Country. Home: 199 Montclair Ave Glen Ellyn IL 60137 Office: PO Box 767 One First Nat Plaza Chicago IL 60690

AYLIN, FLOYD EDWIN, wire mfg. co. exec.; b. Oakland, Calif., Oct. 4, 1940; B.S., San Jose State Coll., 1962, M.B.A., 1965. Spl. mgmt. cons. U.S. State Dept., Saigon, Vietnam, 1966-70; mgr. fin. analysis Am. Can Co., Printing div., Chgo., 1970-73, Tiger Leasing Group, Chgo., 1973-75; controller Columbia Tool div. TRW, River Grove, Ill., 1975-77; controller wire div. Bekaert Steel Wire Corp., Niles, Ill., 1977—. Vietnam cons. Ill. div. Nixon campaign com., 1972. Recipient Vietnam Service Medal, U.S. Dept. State, 1970. Mem. Fin. Mgmt. Assn. Republican. Lion. Home: 1560 N Sandburg Terr Apt 2005 Chicago IL 60610 Office: 6022 Touhy Ave Chicago IL 60648

AYRES, ROBERT FRANKLIN, supt. schs.; b. nr. Warren, Ind., Apr. 29, 1925; s. James Madison and Dora Evelyn (Lucas) A.; B.S., Butler U., 1949, M.S., 1952; postgrad. Purdue U., 1958-62; m. Helen Denton, Mar. 7, 1947; children—James Michael, Robert William, John David, Christopher Allen, Carolyn Ann. Tchr., dean of boys Frankfort High Sch. (Ind.), 1950-59, prin., 1959-65; asst. supt. schs. Huntington County, Ind., 1965-70; supt. schs. Rensselaer Sch. System, 1970-75; supt. Community Schs. Frankfort, 1975—. Instr., Huntington Coll., 1967-70. Exec. bd. Anthony Wayne council Boy Scouts Am.; bd. dirs. Huntington Coll. Found., Rensselaer chpt. Red Cross, Big Bros. Am., Retarded Children's Assn.; mem. Clinton County Area Plan Commn., 1976-77. Served to lt. AUS, 1943-46. Nat. Defense Edn. Act fellow, 1960; St. Joseph's Coll. fellow, 1974. Mem. Ind. Assn. Pub. Sch. Supts., N.E.A., Am. Legion, V.F.W., Ind. Schoomen's Club, Am. Assn. Sch. Adminstrs., Phi Delta Kappa, Lambda Chi Alpha, Tau Kappa Alpha, Alpha Phi Omega. Methodist. Optimist (pres. 1970), Rotarian, Lion. Home: 709 Williams Rd Frankfort IN 46041 Office: 50 S Maish Rd Frankfort IN 46041

AYRES, WALTER DAVID, JR., mfrs. rep.; b. Chgo., Jan. 25, 1936; s. Walter David and Helena Alexandria (Petraitis) A.; student Mech. Engring. (Armour Research Found. Scholar), Ill. Inst. Tech.; m. Catherine Ann Cooney, Oct. 20, 1956; children—Janet, Walter David, Joanne. Sales engr. Sciaky Bros., Inc., Chgo., 1971-73; cons. engr. Barnes & Reinecke Inc., Elk Grove Village, Ill., 1973-74; pres., chief tech. officer Redco, Inc., Chgo., 1974-75; sales mgr. Instrument Assos., Alsip, Ill., 1975—; pres. Zip Mfg. Co., Chgo. Mem. ASME, Instrument Soc. Am. (sr.), Western Soc. Engrs. Republican. Roman Catholic. Club: Elks. Patentee machine design, automation. Home: 7752 S Lawler Ave Burbank IL 60459 Office: 4833 W 128th Place Alsip IL 60658

BAAHLMANN, RALPH HENRY, dentist; b. Aviston, Ill., Sept. 26, 1924; s. Henry H. and Frances C. (Renschen) B.; R.N., Alexian Bros. Hosp. Sch. Nursing, 1942-45; student St. Louis U., 1945-48, D.D.S., 1952; m. Virginia O. Gangloff, June 14, 1952; children—Ralph Henry, Mark, Barbara, Matthew, Nancy, John. Instr. crown and bridge St. Louis U. Sch. Dentistry, 1952-53; pvt. practice dentistry, Alton, Ill., 1957—; pres. dental staff St. Joseph's Hosp., 1970-73. Pres. Ill. Dental Service Corp., 1972-74; sec. Ill. Dental Examining Com., 1972-75. Pres. Southwestern Ill. Easter Seal Soc., 1962-70; pres. Te Deum Internat., 1962-64. Served as lt., Dental Corps, USNR, 1954-56. Recipient Easter Seal Soc. award, 1970. Fellow Am., Internat. colls. dentists; mem. Am. Dental Assn., Ill., Chgo., St. Louis, Madison Dist. (pres. 1967-68) dental socs., St. Louis Dental Research Group, Delta Sigma Delta. Republican. Roman Catholic. K.C., Elk. Club: Lockhaven Country (dir. 1969-72) (Alton). Home: 5102 Jerome Dr Godfrey IL 62035 Office: 1114 Milton Rd Alton IL 62002

BAALMANN, RICHARD FENTON, retail hardware chain exec.; b. St. Louis, Oct. 30, 1935; s. Roderick Oliver and Melba (Bertholdt) B.; student St. Louis U., 1953-57; m. Kathleen Felke, June 12, 1957; children—Richard Fenton, Mary Kathleen, Margaret Grace, Anne Patricia. Vice pres. Mars Enders, Inc., retail hardware, St. Louis, 1956-68, pres., 1968—; pres. Hardware Center, Inc., retail hardware, St. Louis, 1956—; pres. Markat, Inc., St. Louis, 1970—. Vol. worker United Fund, 1960; sec. Nat. Cystic Fibrosis Research Found., 1973; chmn. St. Louis chpt. Jesuit Program for Living and Learning. Served as 1st lt. USAF, 1958-59. Mem. Brentwood C. of C. (pres. 1966), Young Pres.' Orgn., St. Louis Regional Commerce and Growth Assn., Advt. Club St. Louis, Delta Sigma Pi. Club: Rotary (pres. 1972). Home: 458 Bambury Way Saint Louis MO 63131 Office: 12834 Gravois St Saint Louis MO 63127

BAAR, LILLIAN MARY, bus. exec.; b. Chgo.; d. James and Frances (Stanek) Shuss; student evening sch. J. Sterling Morton Jr. Coll., 1934-36; m. William D. Baar, July 25, 1942; 1 dau., Judith Barbara (Mrs. Joseph L. Topinka). Sec. to pres. of Thordarson Mfg. Co., Chgo., 1935-37; sec. to ofcls. of Sears, Roebuck & Co., Chgo., 1937-43; real estate sales, Berwyn, Ill., 1943-44; now engaged as realtor and ins. broker with own firm The Baar Realty Co., Berwyn, 1944-69, cons., 1969—; ins. broker Lillian Baar Ins. Agy., 1969—; real estate cons., 1969-76; owner, operator Baar Baar Realtors, 1976—; local chmn. placement-survey Gov.'s Council Employment of Handicapped, 1965-73; v.p. Berwyn Community Chest, 1968-70, chmn., 1971-72, bd. dirs., 1970—; mem. MacNeal Meml. Hosp. Assn., Berwyn, Ladies Aid for Bohemian Home for Aged, Ladies Aux. Bohemian Charitable Assn. Chgo.; dir. DIALOGUE rec. service for blind, 1969-70, 1st v.p., 1971-73, pres., 1972-74. Recipient Rotary Internat. Citizen of Year award Berwyn Rotary, 1975-76. Mem. Cermak Rd. Bus. Assn. (pres. 1962-64, dir. 1965—), West Towns Bd. Realtors (pres. 1965), Nat. (mem. Nat. Inst. Real Estate Bds. 1968—, mem. Women's council), Ill., assns. real estate bds., Women in Real Estate, Ill. C. of C., Berwyn Business and Profl. Woman's Club (1st v.p. 1972, pres. 1973-75). Clubs: Mothers of Alpha Gamma Delta, Ladies Aux. The Bohemian of Ceska Beseda. Home: Riverside IL 60546 Office: 6335 W Cermak Rd Berwyn IL 60402

BAASCH, FRANK LEROY, dental lab. co. exec.; b. Des Plaines, Ill., Apr. 8, 1926; s. Oscar F. and Hilma M. (Wirkula) B.; ed. high sch.; m. Jocelyn Wilhelmina Loane, Oct. 7, 1950; children—Jody Baasch Springer, Thomas W. Apprentice dental technician Schroeder Dental Lab., Letarte Dental Lab., and Walter C. Vance Dental Lab., to 1949; dental technician, tech. instr. Northwestern U. Dental Sch., Chgo., 1949-57, guest lectr., 1974—; pres. Baasch Dental Lab. Inc., Lincolnshire, Ill., 1957—; cons. in field, lectr. Mem. panel on rev. dental devices FDA, HEW, 1975—; mem. Dental Lab. Conf., 1976—; dir. First Nat. Bank Lincolnshire. Served with U.S. Army, 1944. Certified dental technician. Mem. Ill. Dental Lab. Assn. (pres. 1976), Nat. Assn. Dental Labs. (del. 1976-77), Am. Dental Assn. (cons.), Dental Technicians Soc. Chgo. (pres.) Half Day-Lincolnshire C. of C., G.V. Black Soc. Northwestern U. Presbyterian. Clubs: Thorngate Country (Deerfield, Ill.), Rotary (pres. Deerfield-Lincolnshire Dist. 644 1976-77), Tennacqua Swim and Tennis, Bannockburn Tennis. Editorial bds. Dental Lab. Rev., Quintessence Internat. Dentaire. Home: 45 Oxford Dr Lincolnshire IL 60015 Office: 107 Schelter Rd Prairie View IL 60069

BABB, RAYMOND CHARLES, psychologist; b. Watertown, Wis., Aug. 29, 1941; s. John Fay and Irene Loraine (Ferguson) B.; B.A., Westmar Coll., 1963; M.S., Va. State Coll., 1966; Ed.D., U. S.D., 1968; postgrad. U. Minn., 1964, U. So. Ill., 1966, Winona State Coll., 1967, U. Wis.-La Crosse, 1968, U. Iowa, 1969; m. Linda Kae Liebing, Sept. 2, 1961; children—Robin Ray, Toby Don, Heidi Sue. Tchr. pub. schs., Wallace, Idaho, 1963, New London, Wis., 1964, Caledonia, Minn., 1966-68, asst. prof. Briarcliff Coll., 1968-69, U. Wis., Eau Claire, 1970-72; asso. prof. Lewis U., 1972-74; clin. psychologist, Soldiers Grove, Wis., 1974—; Licensed real estate broker. Mem. Am. Psychol. Assn., Am. Assn. Suicidologists, Am. Personnel Guidance Assn., ACLU, Phi Delta Kappa. Author book on suicide; discovered specie of fish blood parasite. Unitarian. Home and Office: Rural Route 1 Soldiers Grove WI 54655

BABCOCK, DANIEL LAWRENCE, engr., educator; b. Phila., Nov. 25, 1930; B.S., Pa. State U., 1952; M.S., Mass. Inst. Tech., 1953; Ph.D. (N.Am. Rockwell Corp. fellow), U. Calif., Los Angeles, 1970. Chemist, tech. writer Dow Corning Corp., Midland, Mich., 1956-59; tech. editor Chem. Propulsion Info. Agy., Johns Hopkins U., 1959-62; supr., project engr., sr. specialist in chem. rocket propulsion Space div. Rockwell Internat. Corp., Downey, Calif., 1963-69; fellow NASA-ASEE summer program in engring. systems design Langley Research Center, Va., 1971; asso. prof. dept. engring. mgmt. U. Mo.-Rolla, 1970—, mem. acad. council, 1971-73, 77—. Registered profl. engr., Mo. Asso. fellow Am. Inst. Aeros. and Astronautics; mem. Am. Soc. Engring. Edn. (past chmn. engring. mgmt. div.), Am. Soc. Quality Control (certified quality engr.), Joint Engring. Mgmt. Conf. (mem. sponsors com.), Project Mgmt. Inst., Soc. Am. Mil. Engrs., Tau Beta Pi, Phi Kappa Phi, Phi Lambda Upsilon. Contbr. articles to profl. jours. Office: U Mo-Rolla Dept Engring Mgmt Rolla MO 65401

BABCOCK, DENNIS ARTHUR, theatre exec.; b. Berkeley, Calif., June 16, 1948; s. Frederick and Dorothy Marie (Vogt) B.; B.S., Iowa State U., 1970; M.A. (Oscar T. Firkins fellow), U. Minn., 1972, Ph.D., 1975; m. Lorene Kay Evenson, Mar. 7, 1970; 1 dau., Bri Nicole. Dir. theater Urbandale High Sch., Des Moines, 1970-72; dir. publs. Guthrie Theater, Mpls., 1973—; v.p. DB2 Prodns., Inc., pres. Lorden Interiors, Inc. Mem. Internat. Assn. Bus. Communicators. Democrat. Lutheran. Author: Careers in the Theater, 1975. Home: 3218 Lee Ave N Minneapolis MN 55422 Office: Vineland Pl Minneapolis MN 55403

BABCOCK, WILLIS, engr.; b. Waukesha, Wis., May 31, 1922; s. Barney and Helen (Reuter) B.; student Northland Coll., 1941-42, Mass. Inst. Tech., 1945-48, Cornell U., 1948; m. Elizabeth Anne Zimmerman, Sept. 26, 1947; children—Rudolph, Kathryn, Willis W., Gregory, Janet, Deborah. Chief engr. Domestic Engine and Pump Co., Shippensburg, Pa., 1948-53; chief engr. research and devel. Aurora Pump Co. (Ill.), 1953-59; v.p. engring., exec. v.p., gen. mgr. Carver Pump Co., Muscatine, Iowa, 1959-63, cons., 1963-64; chief engr. Mission Valve & Pump Co., Houston, 1964-66; dir. research and devel. Mech. Equipment Co., New Orleans, 1966-68; program mgr. N.W. Labs., Richland, Wash., 1968-70; sr. project engr. Emco Wheaton Inc., Conneant, Ohio, 1971-72; chief engr. Starite Ind., Inc., Delavan, Wis., 1972-77; chief hydraulic engr. Wayne Home Equipment Co., Ft. Wayne, Ind., 1977—. Served with AUS, 1942-45. Mem. ASME, Nat. Soc. Profl. Engrs. Baptist. Home: 4919 Wheatridge Rd Fort Wayne IN 46815 Office: 801 Glasgow Ave Fort Wayne IN 46815

BABICH, ROBERT JOSEPH, assn. exec.; b. Virginia, Minn., Dec. 17, 1926; s. John A. and Anne (Pavlicevic) B.; student Mesaba State Jr. Coll., 1947-49; B.S., U. No. Colo., 1951; children—Craig Robert, Michelle Anne, John Robert. Tchr., coach Brookston (Minn.) High Sch., 1952-54; dir. bus. mgr. Virginia (Minn.) Pub. Schs., 1954-56; owner, pres. Mesaba Mech. Engring. Contractors, Virginia, 1956-66; dir. Econ. Devel. Adminstrn., U.S. Dept. Commerce, No. Central States, Duluth, Minn., 1965-68; exec. v.p. Northeastern Minn. Devel. Assn., Duluth, 1976—; chmn. bd. dirs. No. State Bank, Virginia, 1974-77. Pres. Duluth Seaway Port Authority; mem. City Council, Virginia, 1962-63. Bd. dirs. Our Lady of Lourdes Cath. Sch., Virginia. Served with USAAF, 1944-46. Mem. Nat. Assn. Mech. Contractors, Am., Minn. indsl. devel. councils, V.F.W., Am. Legion, C. of C. Democrat. Roman Catholic (dir.) K.C. Moose, Elk. Club: Duluth Athletic. Home: 15 Merritt Dr Virginia MN 55792 Office: Alworth Bldg Duluth MN 55802

BABLER, JAMES HAROLD, educator; b. Evanston, Ill., June 14, 1944; s. Bernard Joseph and Berenice A. (Brunk) B.; B.S. magna cum laude, Loyola U. Chgo., 1966; Ph.D. (NIH fellow), Northwestern U., 1971. Asso. prof. chemistry Loyola U. Chgo., 1970—. Mem. Am. Chem. Soc., AAAS, Internat. Platform Assn., Sigma Xi. Patentee in field. Home: 125 Callan Ave Evanston IL 60202 Office: 6525 N Sheridan Rd Chicago IL 60626

BABRIS, PETER JOE, educator; b. Atasiene, Latvia, Jan. 31, 1917; s. Dominik and Katrina (Pastors) B.; came to U.S., 1950, naturalized, 1955; B.A., U. Latvia, 1940-44; M.A., U. S.D., 1952; Ph.D., Walden U., 1972; m. Janina Birins, Dec. 31, 1951. Tchr., prin., Latvia, 1939-44; tchr. Displaced Persons Camps, Oldenburg, Germany, 1945-50, Kewanee (Ill.) High Sch., 1955-56, Milw. U. Sch., 1956-57, Arlington (Ill.) High Sch., 1958—. Served with Latvian Army, 1938-40. Mem. Nat., Ill. edn. assns., Classical Assn., German Assn., Latvian Academition Assn. Author: Baltic Youth Under Communism, 1967. Research ch. of silence, genocide in the Soviet Union; Siberia - land of punishment. Home: 108 S Patton St Arlington Heights IL 60005 Office: Euclid at Walnut Sts Arlington Heights IL 60004

BACCI, GUY JOSEPH, II, heavy equipment mfg. co. exec.; b. Chgo., Dec. 18, 1925; s. Guy Joseph and Lydia M. (Bagnatori) B.; B.S., Ill. Inst. Tech., 1961; M.B.A., U. Chgo., 1970; m. Angeline Fiorda, Oct. 26, 1946; children—Guy Joseph III, Geoffrey J. Indsl. engr. Internat. Harvester, Melrose Park, Ill., 1946-53, supr. wage and salary, 1953-59, chief indsl. engr., 1960-61, corporate indsl. engr. mfg. research, 1962-66, gen. supr. indsl. engring. mfg. services, 1967-72, corporate mgr., 1972—; instr., Ill. Inst. Tech., 1967—. Adviser, Jr. Achievement, 1958-60, judge nat. awards, 1965-65; mem. bus. adv. council Loyola U. Sch. Bus. Adminstrn., 1972—. Served with USNR, 1944-46. Registered profl. engr., Calif. Recipient Outstanding Alumnus award Ill. Inst. Tech., 1973. Mem. Indsl. Engring. (nat. adv. council), Methods, Time, Measurement Assn. (dir.), Am. Inst. Indsl. Engrs. (award 1965). Club: Glenview Men's Golf. Home: 1039 Meadowlark Ln Glenview IL 60025 Office: 401 N Michigan Ave Chicago IL 60611

BACH, IRA J., govt. ofcl., regional planner; b. Chgo., May 19, 1906; s. Jacob Lester and Rachel (Rose) B.; student U. Ill., 1926-27, Harvard, 1929-30; B.S., Mass. Inst. Tech., 1932; m. Ruth Lackritz, May 22, 1934 (dec. 1961); children—John Lawrence, Caroline Ruth (Mrs. Dennis P. Marandos); m. 2d, Muriel Dunkleman Wolfson, Apr. 14, 1963; 1 step-daughter, Susan Wolfson. Partner archtl. firm Lichtmann and Bach, Chgo., 1935-42; project planner Wash. Terr. Housing Project, Ogden, Utah, 1942-44; dir. Tri-County Regional Planning Commn., Denver, 1944-45; dir. planning Chgo. Housing Authority, 1946-47; exec. dir. Cook County Housing Authority, 1947-48; exec. dir. Chgo. Land Clearance Commn., 1948-57; commr. planning Dept. City Planning, Chgo., 1957-67; exec. dir. Chgo. Dwelling Assn., 1965-69; pres. Urban Assos. of Chgo., Inc., 1969-75; adminstr. Ill.-Ind. Bi-State Commn., 1975—; vis. lectr. Yale, 1960—; lectr. in field. Sec. Commn. Chgo. Hist. and Archtl. Landmarks; mem. Northeastern Ill. Met. Area Local Govt. Services Commn., 1958-62; pres. Northeastern Ill. Met. Area Planning Commn., Chgo., 1968-75; co-chmn. Interstate Planning Commn., 1972-75; cons. renovation Chgo. Pub. Library Cultural Center, Dearborn R.R. Sta. Named Chgo. Man of Year in Architecture and Engring. Chgo. Jr. C. of C., 1960; recipient City Planning award Municipal Art League Chgo., 1960, Honor award Citizens Greater Chicago. Mem. Am. Inst. Planners (past pres. Chgo. chpt.), AIA, Am. Soc. Planning Ofcls., Nat. Assn. Housing and Redevel. Ofcls., Chgo. Assn. Commerce and Industry (Ind. devel. com.), Lambda Alpha (pres. Ely chpt. 1953-57), Sigma Alpha Mu. Clubs: Tavern, Arts. Author: Uniform Building Code of Colorado, 1945; Uniform Sub-Division Regulation of Colorado, 1945; Chicago on Foot, 1969; also papers and articles on housing. Contbr. to Am. Peoples Ency. Arts, Architecture mag. Author 3d edit. Chgo. on Foot series of archtl. walks. Home: 748 Buena Ave Chicago IL 60613 Office: Ill-Ind Bi-State Commn 33 N LaSalle St Chicago IL 60602

BACH, MURIEL DUNKLEMAN (MRS. IRA J. BACH), author, actress; b. Chgo., May 14, 1918; d. Gabriel and Deborah (Warshauer) Dunkleman; student Carleton Coll., 1935-37; B.S. in the Arts, Northwestern U., 1939; m. Joseph Wolfson, June 16, 1940 (div. Apr. 1962); 1 dau., Susan; m. 2d, Ira J. Bach, Apr. 14, 1963; stepchildren—Caroline (Mrs. Dennis Paul Marandos), John Lawrence. Researcher original manuscripts for One-Woman Theatre, also costume designer, writer, set designer; actress TV commis., indsl. films, radio commls.; photographic model; co-dir. Chappell-Bach Assos. Active sr. citizens groups, youth groups. Recipient Career Achievement award Chgo. Area Profl. Pan Hellenic Assn., 1971. Mem. Screen Actors Guild, AFTRA, Zeta Phi Eta. Clubs: Arts, Tavern (Chgo.). Author: (plays) Two Lives, 1958; ... because of Her!, 1963; Madame, Your Influence is Showing, 1969; MS ... Haven't We Met Before?, 1973; Lady, You're Rocking the Boat!, 1976; also author vignettes for theater. Address: 748 Buena Ave Chicago IL 60613

BACH, STEVE CRAWFORD, judge; b. Jackson, Ky., Jan. 31, 1921; s. Bruce Grannis and Evelyn (Crawford) B.; A.B., Ind. U., 1943, J.D., 1948; postgrad. Eastern studies U. Mich., 1944, U. Nev. Trial Judges Coll., 1966, U. Minn. Juvenile Inst., 1967; m. Rosemary Husted, Sept. 6, 1947; children—John Crittenden, Greta Christine. Admitted to Ky., Ind. bars, 1948; atty. Bach & Bach, Jackson, 1948-51; investigator U.S. CSC, Indpls., 1951-54; individual practice law, Mt. Vernon, Ind., 1954-65; judge 11th. Jud. Circuit, Mt. Vernon, 1965—. Mem. planning com., seminar moderator Ind. Conf. Crime and Delinquency, Indpls., 1968; tchr. seminar on juvenile delinquency Ind. Trial Judges Assn., 1969, del. Internat. Youth Magistrates Conf., Geneva, Switzerland, 1970, Oxford, Eng., 1974; faculty adviser Criminal Law Inst., Nat. Trial Judges Coll., 1973; v.p. Ind. Council Juvenile Ct. Judges, 1975. Pres., Greater Mt. Vernon Assn., 1958-59. Bd. dirs. Regional Mental Health Planning Commn., Criminal Justice Planning Commn. 8th Region Ind., Evansville, Ind.; mem. Juvenile Justice div. Ind. Jud. Study Commn.; mem. Ind. Gov.'s Juvenile Delinquency Prevention Adv. Bd., 1976-77. Served with intelligence Signal Corps, AUS, 1943-46. Mem. Nat. Council Juvenile Ct. Judges, Am. Legion, Ind. Soc. Chgo., Ind. State Bar Assn. (del.), Ind. Judges Assn. (bd. mgrs. 1966-71), Sigma Delta Kappa, Delta Tau Delta. Democrat. Methodist. Mason (Shriner), Kiwanian, Elk. Initiated changes juvenile ct. procedures including work program for boys on welfare or ct. probation, presentation plaques to schs. without juvenile delinquency, suspension drivers license of youths committing juvenile offenses, weekends in jail for lesser offenders. Home: 512 Walnut St Mount Vernon IN 47620 Office: Courthouse Mount Vernon IN 47620

BACHARACH, JOHN ALBERT, pub. health ofcl.; b. nr. Frankfurt, Germany, Mar. 25, 1926; s. Max and Sofie (Simon) B.; B.S., Syracuse U., 1950; M.P.H., U. Minn., 1956; m. Hilde Guth, Feb. 29, 1952; children—John Michael, David William. Came to U.S., 1927, naturalized, 1932. Part-time sanitarian Miami U., 1951-52; dist. sanitarian Delta Menomonie Health Dept., Mich., 1952-55; pub. health educator Pa. Dept. Health, 1956-58, regional pub. health edn., 1958-60; dir. city county health dept. Eau Claire (Wis.) Bd. Health, 1960—; mem. faculty Eau Claire State U. Bd. dirs. Eau Claire County Guidance Clinic, 1961—, pres., 1976; bd. dirs. Eau Claire Coordinating Council, 1963—, Alcohol Council, 1976; mem. Gov's Comprehensive Health Planning Adv. Council, 1968; mem. meat inspection council Wis. Dept. Agr., 1972—; mem. joint com. on edn. Wis. Assn. Milk and Food Sanitarians and Wis. Environ. Health Assn. Bd. dirs. Group Health Coop. Eau Claire. Fellow Am. Pub. Health Assn.; mem. Wis. Pub. Health Assn., Royal Soc. Promotion Health, Wis. Full Time Health Officers Assn. (sec. 1972), Nat. Assn. County Health Ofcls. (bd. dirs. 1976—), Am. Acad. Health Adminstrs., Retardation Assn. Club: Lake Wissota Yacht (commodore 1971). Contbr. articles to profl. jours. Home: 104 E Truman Ave Eau Claire WI 54701 Office: Bd Health City-County Health Dept Eau Claire WI 54701

BACHEM, WOLFGANG ALBERT, elec. engr.; b. Chgo., June 20, 1929; s. Albert Joseph and Erica Yvonne (Pietsch) B.; B.S. in Elec. Engring., U. Ill., 1951; m. Carole M. Zohm, Apr. 10, 1953; children—Byron, Steven, Mark, Erica Lee, Paul. Tachometer engr. Sun Electric Co., Chgo., 1952-53; contract adminstr. Boeing Co., Seattle, 1961-63; engr. estimator various contractors Chgo., Seattle, 1953-61, contract adminstr., 1963-69; elec. engr., contract adminstr. Village of Arlington Heights, Ill., 1969—; chmn. Roadway Lighting Forum, Chgo., 1976-77. Pres., Apple Valley Civic Assn., 1967-68. Village trustee Village of Third Lake, Ill., 1971-75, mayor, 1977—. Mem. Am. Pub. Works Assn., Am. Water Works Assn., Inst. Traffic Engrs., Illuminating Engring. Soc., Internat. Municipal Signalmen's Assn., IEEE, Tech. Soc. Chgo. (pres. 1967-68). Elk. Home: 41 N Lake 3d Lake Lake Villa IL 60046 Office: 33 S Arlington Heights Rd Arlington Heights IL 60005

BACHHUBER, EDWARD AUGUST, surgeon, educator; b. Mayville, Wis., Mar. 13, 1912; s. Alphons E. and Marie (Bach) B.; B.S., U. Wis., 1935; M.D., Harvard U., 1937; postgrad. U. Pa., 1940-41; m. Romana J. Ryan, Oct. 18, 1941; children—Patricia, Edward M., Timothy T., Stephen R., Daniel F., Elizabeth Ann, Mary, Thomas M. Intern Milw. County Gen. Hosp., 1937-38, resident in surgery, 1938-40, chief res., 1945-46; practice memicine specializing in surgery, 1946—; mem. staffs VA Hosp., Milw. County Gen. Hosp., St. Joseph's Deaconess and Columbia hosps. Milw., instr. anatomy Marquette U., 1946-48, asso. in anatomy, 1948-70, instr. in surgery, 1948-51, asso. in surgery, 1951-52, asst. prof., 1952-55, asso. prof., 1955-70, prof. surgery and anatomy, 1970—, asst. dean sch. medicine, 1949-55, asso. dean 1956-65, asst. chmn. div. surgery, 1953-58, chmn. adminstrv. com. 1963-64. Pres. Wis. Lung Assn., 1969-70; med. chmn. fund dr. Milw. div. Am. Cancer Soc.; trustee Alverno Coll., 1969-71. Served to lt. col. U.S. Army, 1941-46. Decorated Bronze Star; recipient Distinguished Service award Med. Coll. Wis., 1977; certified A.C.S. (fellow) Mem. Am., Wis. heart assns., AMA, Milw. Acad. Medicine (pres. 1968), Milw. Acad. Surgery (pres. 1977), Wis. State, Milw. County med. socs., Milw. Research Club, Wis., Milw. surg. socs., Wis. Thoracic Soc., Alpha Omega Alpha. Contbr. articles to med. jours. Home: 607 River Dr Mayville WI 53050 Office: 8700 W Wisconsin Ave Milwaukee WI 53226

BACHHUBER, THOMAS DUANE, coll. adminstr.; b. Neenah, Wis., Oct. 25, 1948; s. John Martin and Helen Ann (Jordahl) B.; B.A., Ripon Coll., 1971; M.Ed., U. Va., 1973, Ed.D., 1975; m. Leslie Ann Smith, May 22, 1971; children—Elizabeth Helen, Emily Louise. Dir., Acad. & Career Planning, Coe Coll., Cedar Rapids, Ia., 1975—, dir. career counseling and placement, 1974-75. Mem. Am. Coll. Personnel Assn. (mem. directorate, 1976—), Coll. Placement Council, Am. Personnel and Guidance Assn., Nat. Assn. Student Personnel Assns. Author: (with Dr. Richard Harwood) Directions: A Guide to Career Planning, 1977. Contbr. articles in field to profl. jours. Home: 3217 14th Ave SE Cedar Rapids IA 52403 Office: Acad and Career Planning Coe Coll Cedar Rapids IA 52402

BACHMAN, DAVID CHRISTIAN, orthopaedic surgeon; b. Peoria, Ill., Apr. 11, 1934; s. Leland Alvin and Elsie May (Springer) B.; B.A., Goshen Coll., 1958; M.D., Northwestern U., 1962; m. Betty June Foster, Sept. 9, 1956; children—Lynne Allison, Laura Ailene. Intern Cook County Hosp., Chgo., 1962-63; resident orthopaedic surgery Northwestern U. Med. Sch., 1963-67; practice medicine specializing in orthopaedic surgery, Chgo., 1967—; mem. staffs Northwestern Meml. Hosp., Chgo., Childrens Meml. Hosp., Chgo., Grant Hosp., Chgo.; dir. Center for Sports Medicine, Northwestern U. Med. Sch.; team physician Chgo. Bulls, Nat. Basketball Assn., 1967—; asst. prof. dept. orthopaedic surgery Northwestern U. Med. Sch., 1967—. Mem. Ill., Chgo. med. socs., AMA, Am. Coll. Sports Medicine, Am. Acad. Orthopaedic Surgery, A.C.S., Am. Orthopedic Soc. for Sports Medicine, Phi Rho Sigma. Presbyterian (elder 1965—). Address: 233 E Erie St Chicago IL 60611

BACHMAN, ERNEST, found. exec.; b. Moundridge, Kans., Mar. 25, 1895; s. Peter and Katharena (Mueller) B.; student Wichita Bus. Coll., 1913; m. Prisca G. Krehbiel, June 18, 1919; children—Dale V., Florene (Mrs. W.K. Wiens), Elaine (Mrs. Irvin Goertzen), Kathryn (Mrs. Don Penner), Donovan. With Schowalter Found., Inc., Newton, Kans., 1953—, v.p., 1956—, farm mgr., 1956—. Pub. relations dir. Bethel Coll., North Newton, Kans., 1952-60; pres. Newton Council Retarded Children, 1958-61; with ch. extension service Mennonite Gen. Conf., 1961-63; bldg. fund raiser Prairie View Hosp., Newton, 1967-68; state dir. Christian Rural Overseas Program, 1947-72; pres. Mennonite Aid Union Kans., 1960-71, dist. sec., 1971—. Home: 309 Allison St Newton KS 67114 Office: 726 Main St Newton KS 67114

BACHMAN, GEORGE CRAIG, banker; b. Marion, Kans., June 4, 1923; s. George Fredrick and Mary Ann (Rathbone) B.; student Kans. State Coll., 1941-43, Wichita U., 1945, Kans. State Coll., 1945-47; m. Katherine Johanna Lohmuller, June 14, 1947; children—Bruce Lohmuller, Melissa Mathew, Johanna. Bookkeeper-teller 1st Nat. Bank, Centralia (Kans.), 1947-48, asst. cashier, 1948-51, v.p., 1951-66, pres., 1966—, also dir.; v.p., treas. Lohmuller-Bachman, Inc.; dir. Fed. Res. Bank Kansas City (Mo.); former mayor of Centralia. Former mem. exec. bd. Jayhawk area council Boy Scouts of Am., 1956-70; former mem. Kans. Econ. Research Adv. Com.; former mem. conf. council Kans.-Okla. Conf., United Ch. of Christ. Former chmn. Nemaha County Republican Central Com. Trustee Kans. State U. Endowment Assn. Served 1st lt. USAAF, 1942-45. Decorated Air medal (Army). Mem. Am. Legion, Kans. Bankers Assn. (fed. legis. commn., statewide advt. commn.), Am. Bankers Assn. (past fed. legis. adv. com.), Kans. State U. Alumni Assn. (dir.). Mason, Lion (past pres., dir.) Address: Centralia KS 66415

BACHMAN, JERALD GRAYBILL, research psychologist; b. Harrisburg, Pa., Oct. 20, 1936; s. Jacob Clarence and Harriet Ann (Mathias) B.; A.B., Lebanon Valley Coll., 1958; M.A. (NSF fellow), U. Pa., 1961, Ph.D. (NSF fellow), 1962; m. Virginia Arlene Ludy, Nov. 28, 1957; children—Terri Lynne, Steven J., Jon Andrew. Asst. instr. psychology U. Pa., 1959-62; lectr. in psychology U. Mich., 1963—, study dir. Survey Research Center, Inst. for Social Research, 1962-67, sr. study dir., 1967-72, program dir., research scientist, 1972—; field reader Office Edn.; cons. in field; mem. advisory panel Nat. Center Ednl. Statistics study; mem. advisory bd. Evaluation and Tng. Inst. Precinct del. Democratic Party, 1976-77; v.p., dir. Loch Erin Property Owners Assn., Ann Arbor, Mich., 1977-78. Nat. Inst. Drug Abuse grantee, 1975-79, Nat. Inst. Edn. grantee, 1973-76, Office Naval Research grantee, 1972-74, Army Research Inst. grantee, 1974-75, others. Mem. Soc. Psychol. Study Social Issues, Inter Univ. Seminar on Armed Forces, Soc., Am. Psychol. Assn., AAAS, Sigma Xi. Author or co-author 5 books in Youth in Transition series, 1968-78; author Youth Look at National Problems, 1971; The All-Volunteer Force: A Study of Ideology in the Military, 1977; contbr. articles to profl. publs. Home: 2124 Stephen Terr Ann Arbor MI 48103 Office: Survey Research Center Inst for Social Research U of Mich Box 1248 Ann Arbor MI 48106

BACHMANN, BRUCE RALPH, mortgage banker; b. Chgo., Aug. 15, 1934; s. Louis A. and Goldie (Polk) B.; B.S., U. Wis., 1956; m. Ann Cohen, June 26, 1957; children—Stephen, Cathy, Besty, Andrew. Merchandise mgr. Polk Bros., Chgo., 1958-68; exec. v.p. Heitman Mortgage Co., Chgo., 1969-73; pres. Philipsborn Equities, Inc., Chgo., 1973—. Bd. dirs. Young Men's Jewish Council, Chgo. Served with U.S. Army, 1956-58. Registered real estate broker, Ill. Mem. Chgo. Mortgage Banker Assn., Urban Land Inst. Democrat. Clubs: Econs., Exec. of Chgo. Home: 888 Elm Pl Glencoe IL 60022 Office: 111 E Wacker St Chicago IL 60601

BACHMANN, CARL ANTHONY, union ofcl.; b. Dayton, Ohio, June 14, 1917; s. Adolph and Anna J. (Geyer) B.; student labor courses Roosevelt Coll., 1953, Cornell U., 1953, U. Wis., 1958; m. Rita E. Clark, July 22, 1950; 1 son, Joseph Carl. Served as enlisted man U.S. Navy, 1939-47; air conditioning mechanic Monsanto Research Corp., Miamisburg, Ohio, 1948-53; steward local union 7-4200 Oil Chem. and Atomic Workers, Dayton, Ohio, 1948-50, rec. sec., 1949-51, pres., 1951-53; internat. rep. Oil, Chem. and Atomic

Workers Internat. Union, 1953—. Trustee Cath. Social Services, Dayton, 1969-75. Dayton Democratic ward leader, 1968-74; mem. Montgomery County Dem. Exec. Com., 1969—. Roman Catholic. Home: 1415 Westbrook Rd Dayton OH 45415

BACHMANN, ROGER WERNER, educator; b. Ann Arbor, Mich., Dec. 11, 1934; s. Werner Emanuel and Marie (Kanphurst) B.; B.S., U. Mich., 1956, Ph.D. (NSF fellow), 1962; M.S., U. Idaho, 1958; postgrad. Woods Hole Oceonographic Inst., 1961-62; m. Marilyn Dorthy Davidson, Mar. 26, 1960; children—David Werner, Carol Elizabeth. Research zoologist U. Calif. at Davis, 1962-63; asst. prof. zoology and entomology Iowa State U., Ames, 1963-67, asso. prof., 1967-71, prof., 1971—, acting chmn. dept. animal ecology, 1975-76. Mem. AAAS, Am. Inst. Biol. Scis., Am. Soc. Limnology and Oceanography, Iowa Acad. Sci., Sigma Xi, Phi Kappa Phi. Contbr. articles on limnology to profl. jours. Home: Route 4 Ames IA 50010

BACHNER, DONALD JOSEPH, mfg. co. exec.; b. Chgo., Aug. 17, 1930; s. Louis Henry and Catherine Patricia (O'Connell) B.; B. Social Sci. cum laude, St. Mary's Coll., 1952; C.P.A., U. Ill., 1958; m. Marie K. Boucher, Mar. 16, 1974; children—(by previous marriage) Charles, Margaret; Timothy, Patricia. With Capitol Food Industries, Inc., Chgo., 1957-67, v.p. Eversweet Foods, Inc. subsidiary, 1958-61, treas., 1961-62, pres. Bowey's, Inc. subsidiary, Chgo., 1965-67, v.p. parent co., 1962-67; mgr. corporate planning Ill. Tool Works, Inc., Chgo., 1967, v.p. European operations, 1968, group v.p. internat., 1969-72, pres. internat. group, 1972—. Served with AUS, 1952-54. Office: 8501 W Higgins Rd Chicago IL 60631

BACHOCHIN, FRANK THOMAS, mktg. research exec.; b. Oak Park, Ill., Sept. 28, 1946; s. Frank Andrew and Dorothy Ann (Domeraski) B.; student St. Mary's Coll., 1964-66; B.S., U. Detroit, 1968; M.B.A., U. Cin., 1970; 1 son, Matthew. Account exec. Burke Mktg. Research, Cin. and Glen Ellyn, Ill., 1968-75; research supr. Needham, Harper & Steers Advt., Chgo., 1976; field research mgr. McDonald's Corp., Oak Brook, Ill., 1977—. Active community youth orgn. Burke Mktg. Research fellow, 1968-69. Mem. Am. Mktg. Assn., Pi Delta Epsilon. Home: 1551 Beverly Circle W Hanover Park IL 60103 Office: McDonald's Plaza Oak Brook IL 60521

BACINO, TED J., fin. co. exec.; b. Rockford, Ill., Nov. 13, 1933; s. Joseph A. and Mary M. (Spinello) B.; B.S., No. Ill. U., 1956, M.S., 1965; m. Janis B. Marinelli, Nov. 18, 1961; children—Geoffrey Stuart, Michelle Suzanne, Lara Marie. Tchr., coach St. Thomas High Sch., Rockford, 1958-61; tchr., coach Boylan High Sch., Rockford, 1961-64, dean students, 1964-69, asst. prin., 1969-71; dir. coll. relations and publs. Rock Valley Coll., Rockford, 1971-75; exec. asst. to Ill. Sec. of State, Springfield, 1975-77; v.p. mktg. United Fin. Services Corp., Rockford, 1977—. Dir. Starlight Theatre, summers 1970-75; dir. Cabaret Dinner Theatre, Clock Tower Inn, Henrici's, Rockford; drama critic WRRR Radio, WREX-TV, Rockford, 1973-75; mem. Winnebago County Bi-Centennial Commn., 1973-75; bd. dirs. Rockford Symphony Orch. Assn., New Am. Theatre, Rockford, Rockford Arts Council. Served with AUS, 1956-58. Mem. Pub. Relations Soc. Am. (asso.), Am. Coll. Pub. Relations Assn. Home: 707 Reynolds St Rockford IL 61103 Office: One United Financial Center Rockford IL 61101

BACKER, HORST HELMUT, pub. relations cons.; b. Duesseldorf, Germany, Jan. 6, 1921; s. Paul Clemens and Luise (Weinberg) B.; came to U.S., 1936, naturalized; M.S., Ind. U., 1946; Ph.D., U. Chgo., 1949; m. Susan J. Busch, Jan. 15, 1962; children—Patricia, Chali J. Backer Lane. Free-lance radio actor, Chgo., 1938-41; faculty Ind. U., 1945-47; pub. relations cons. in entertainment, hotel and trade assn. fields, 1947—; pres. H.H. Backer Assos., Inc., trade show prodn., multiple trade assn. mgmt., Chgo., 1947—; pub. Pet Age mag., 1971—; free-lance writer consumer and trade publs.; cons. U.S. Dept. Commerce, 1947-76. Bd. dirs. Lake Shore Found. for Animals, N.S.D.A. Ins. Trust Fund. Served as maj. U.S. Army, 1940-45, Mem. U.S. C. of C., Am. Soc. Assn. Execs., Chgo. Exec. Forum, Art Inst. Chgo., Mid-North Assn. Club: Chicago Press. Contbr. articles to consumer and trade publs. Office: H H Backer Assos Inc 2561 N Clark St Chicago IL 60614

BACKS, ALTON JOSEPH, radiologist; b. Minster, Ohio, Dec. 23, 1925; s. Leo Henry and Olga Mary (Harlett) B.; B.S., U. Dayton, 1948; M.D., Loyola U., Chgo., 1952; m. Alice Louise Heuel, Sept. 20, 1952; children—Steven, Thomas, Christine, James, Barbara, Peter. Intern, St. Joseph's Hosp., South Bend, Ind., 1952-53; gen. practice medicine, South Bend, 1953-66; mem. staff St. Joseph's Hosp., 1953-66, dir. med. edn., 1960-65; resident in radiology Rush-Presbyterian St. Luke's Hosp., Chgo., 1966-69; attending radiologist St. Joseph's Hosp., South Bend and Mishawaka, Ind., 1969—; instr. radiology U. Ill., 1966-69. Served with USN, 1944-46. Diplomate Am. Bd. Radiology. Mem. AMA, Am. Coll. Radiology, Ind. State, St. Joseph County med. socs., Am. Soc. Therapeutic Radiologists, Am. Acad. Family Practice. Roman Catholic. Home: 1831 N Kessler Blvd South Bend IN 46616 Office: 919 E Jefferson Blvd South Bend IN 46622

BACON, DONALD ELLIOT, printing co. exec.; b. Charleston, Ill., July 9, 1909; s. Richard O. and Millie (Walton) H.; grad. Universal Sch. Commerce, Kansas City, Mo., 1932; grad. Internat. Accountants Chgo., 1938; m. Thelma J. Dennis, Mar. 2, 1935; children—Janice Rae (Mrs. Jack A. Malik), Donald Dennis, William Blair, Barbara Jane. Accountant, R.R. Donnelley & Sons Co., Chgo., 1934-48, budget dir., 1948-57, cost accountant, 1957-59, div. controller, 1959-63, distbn. mgr., 1963-71, corporate traffic mgr., 1971-74; pres. Theldon, Inc., 1974—. Chmn., Mag. and Mail Order Pubs. and Printers Traffic Com., 1971-74. Drainage commr., Momence-Pembroke, Ill., 1973—. Bd. dirs. South Suburban Council Handicapped Children, 1957-60; pres. Kankakee Assn. Mentally Retarded, 1972—. Recipient Neil Denen award, Planning Execs. Inst., 1965. Mem. Planning Execs. Inst. (pres. Chgo. chpt. 1954-57, pres. Calumet region 1958-59, nat. treas. 1955-56, dir. 1956-60, pres. 1961-62, life emeritus award 1976). Lutheran. Home: Route 3 Box 41 Momence IL 60954 Office: 189 E Court St Kankakee IL 60901

BACON, FRANK RIDER, chemist; b. Wilton Junction, Iowa, Apr. 28, 1914; s. Frank R. and Grace Gwendolyn (Woodhouse) B.; B.S., Iowa State U., 1935; M.S., Washington U., St. Louis, 1937; m. Eleanor Jane Bennett, June 25, 1938; children—John B., George W., Katherine (Mrs. John M. Endersbe). With Owens-Ill., Inc., Toledo, 1937—, chief surface chemistry, 1958—. Fellow Am. Ceramic Soc. (chmn. Northwestern Ohio sect. 1956, chmn. glass div. 1959); mem. Am. Chem. Soc. (sect. chmn. 1950), ASTM (chmn. subcom. chem. properties of glass 1962—), Sigma Xi, Tau Beta Pi. Presbyterian (elder 1957—). Home: 3153 Darlington Rd Toledo OH 43606 Office: PO Box 1035 Toledo OH 43666

BACON, ROBERT, industrial co. exec.; b. Detroit, June 27, 1923; s. H. Raymond and Marjorie K. (Baumgartner) B.; m. Joanne Plante, Dec. 18, 1944; children—Diane M., R. Drew, Cynthia M., Char E., Bruce R. Founder, pres. Applied Handling Inc., Dearborn, Mich., 1952—. Served with USAF, 1943-46. Clubs: Detroit Athletic, The Recess. Home: 20 Lakecrest Ln Grosse Pointe Farms MI 48236

BACON, WILLIAM CORNELIUS, carferry co. exec.; b. Manistee, Mich., July 8, 1928; s. Glenn Dennis and Lillian Maxine (Reed) B.; student Mich. State U., 1946; masters license USCG, 1958; m. Mary Mildred Graves, Dec. 25, 1950 (div. June 1973); children—Kim Cornelius, Beth Ellen, Lori Kay; m. 2d, Olive Jane Brandt, Oct. 19, 1974. Ordinary seaman Ann Arbor R.R. Car ferries, 1948-49, able seaman, 1949-53, mate, capt., 1953-63, port capt., Elberta, Mich., 1963—; dir. Ann Arbor Employees Fed. Credit Union, 1965-67, pres., 1967—. Chmn. Marine Exhibits Mus., 1969—; bd. visitors Great Lakes Maritime Acad., 1970—. Served with AUS, 1950-52. Mem. Benzie Area (bd. dirs. 1970—, pres. 1972-75), Great Lakes hist. socs., Great Lakes Maritime Inst., Frankfort C. of C. (dir. 1970-72). Lutheran. Mason (32 deg. Shriner, past master), Rotarian (pres.). Home: 1160 Martin Dr Frankfort MI 49635 Office: 1224 Furnace Ave Elberta MI 49628

BACON, WILLIAM THOMPSON, JR., investment co. exec.; b. Chgo., Feb. 6, 1923; s. William Thompson and Martha (Smith) B.; B.A., Yale, 1945; m. Margaret Hoyt, Apr. 18, 1942; children—William Thompson III, Catherine Bacon Von Stroh, Hoyt Wells, J. Knight, Christopher S. Asst. cashier First Nat. Bank of Chgo., 1946-55; partner Bacon, Whipple & Co., Chgo., 1956—; dir. Sageguard Services, Inc., Walbro Corp., C.S.C., Inc. Trustee Hadley Sch. for Blind, Wilmette, Ill., Fountain Valley Sch., Colorado Springs, Colo. Served with AUS, 1943-44. Mem. Delta Kappa Epsilon. Republican. Episcopalian. Clubs: Yale (pres. 1962-63), Chgo., Univ. (Chgo.); Onwentsia (Lake Forest, Ill.); Shoreacres (Lake Bluff, Ill.); Old Elm (Ft. Sheridan, Ill.); Indian Hill (Winnetka, Ill.); Yale (N.Y.C.). Home: 1300 N Waukegan Rd Lake Forest IL 60045 Office: 135 S LaSalle St Chicago IL 60603

BACZKOWSKI, RICHARD BODGAN, automotive engr.; b. Luck, Poland, Apr. 13, 1933; s. Feliks Stefan and Maria Helena (Kwiatkowski) B.; came to U.S., 1958, naturalized, 1963; B.S. in Engring., So. Ill. U., 1967; m. Jeorjett Moawad, Jan. 23, 1971; children—Victor, Margaret. Designer, then test engr. Internat. Harvester Co., Libertyville, Ill., 1958-70; prin. engr. AM Gen. Corp., Chgo., 1970-74, mgr. engring., Wayne, Mich., 1974—. Served with AUS, 1958. Mem. Soc. Automotive Engrs., Am. Def. Preparedness Assn. Republican. Roman Catholic. Home: 2731 Newport Rd Ann Arbor MI 48103

BADE, JAMES CARL, assn. exec.; b. Evanston, Ill., May 2, 1932; s. Carl John and Esther (Winkleman) B.; B.S., Northwestern U., 1954; m. Yvonne Auffant, June 17, 1956; children—Wendy Lynn, Lisa Carol, Susan Lee. News editor Des Plaines (Ill.) Journal, 1956-58, Des Plaines (Ill.) Suburban Times, 1958-59; night editor, feature mag. editor Waukegan (Ill.) News-Sun, 1959-64; pub. relations dir. Chgo. Heart Assn., 1964-66; pub. relations exec., Field Enterprises, Chgo., 1966-68; pub. relations dir. Kendall Coll., Evanston, Ill., 1968-71; dir. communications Evanston C. of C., 1971-72; exec. dir. State St. Council, Chgo., 1972—; pub. relations cons., 1964—; sec., dir. Taurus Corp., 1960-68. Mem. Fremont (Ill.) grade sch. bd., 1963-70. Served with AUS, 1954-56. Mem. Am. C. of C. Execs., Internat. Downtown Execs. Assn. Home: 130 N Sylvan Dr Mundelein IL 60060 Office: 36 S State St Chicago IL 60603

BADEER, HENRY SARKIS, educator; b. Mersine, Turkey, Jan. 31, 1915; s. Sarkis and Persape Hagop (Koundakjian) B.; M.D., Am. U. Beirut, Lebanon, 1938; m. Mariam Mihran Kassarjian, July 12, 1948; children—Gilbert H., Daniel H. Came to U.S., 1965, naturalized, 1971. Gen. practice medicine, Beirut, 1940-51; asst. instr. Am. U. Beirut Sch. Medicine, 1938-45, adj. prof., 1945-51, asso. prof., 1951-62, prof. physiology, 1962-65, acting chmn. dept., 1951-56, chmn. dept., 1956-65; research fellow Harvard Med. Sch., 1948-49; prof. physiology Creighton U. Med. Sch., Omaha, 1967—, acting chmn. dept., 1971-72. Vis. prof. physiology U. Ia., Iowa City, 1957-58, Downstate Med. Center, Bklyn., 1965-67; mem. med. com. Azounieh Sanatorium, Beirut, Lebanon, 1961-65; mem. research com. Nebr. Heart Assn., 1967-70. Rockefeller fellow, 1948-49; grantee Med. Research Com., Am. U. Beirut, 1956-65; Golden Apple award Student AMA, 1975. Mem. AAAS, Internat. Soc. for Heart Research, Am. Physiol. Soc., N.Y. Acad. Scis., Sigma Xi, Alpha Omega Alpha. Contbr. articles to profl. jours. Home: 2808 S 99th Ave Omaha NE 68124 Office: 2500 California St Omaha NE 68178

BADENHOOP, HERMAN JOHN, financial services co. exec.; b. Elmira, N.Y., Aug. 28, 1918; s. Herman, Jr. and Rose H. (Hofmeister) B.; B.S., U. Md., 1940; m. Martha Elizabeth Carter, July 5, 1941; children—John C., Suzanne B., W. Carter. Spl. agt. U.S. Fidelity & Guaranty Co., 1946-54; with St. Paul Cos., Inc., 1954—, sec., 1965-67, asst. v.p., 1967-68, v.p., 1968—, also dir.; dir. St. Paul Leasing Co., Postal Finance Co., St. Paul Fire & Marine Ins. Co.; pres. St. Paul Land Resources, Inc. Bd. dirs. Minn. Opera Co. Served from 2d lt. to lt. col. AUS, 1940-45; ETO. Decorated Bronze Star medal. Episcopalian. Clubs: Gyro Internat. (v.p.), Minn. (St. Paul); Apostle Islands Yacht (commodore) (Bayfield, Wis.). Home: 500 Salem Church Rd Sunfish Lake Village St Paul MN 55118 also Madeline Island La Pointe WI 54850 Office: 385 Washington St Saint Paul MN 55102

BADER, DONALD JAMES, lawyer; b. Mendota, Ill., Oct. 5, 1939; s. Donald Larkin and Mary Lucille (Hanley) B.; B.S. in Gen. Engring. with honors, U. Ill., 1962, LL.B., 1964; m. Katherine Marie Rader, June 10, 1961; children—Robin Lyn, Edward Charles, Michael Louis. Admitted to D.C. bar, 1965, Ill. bar, 1966, Patent bar, 1966; patent examiner U.S. Patent Office, Washington, 1964-66; patent atty. IIT Research Inst., Chgo., 1966-68, Anderson, Luedeka, Fitch, Even & Tabin, Chgo., 1968-70, Panduit Corp., Tinley Park, Ill., 1970-72; partner Bader and Roth, Olympia Fields, Ill., 1972—; officer, dir. Lincolnway Mgmt., Inc., Matteson, Ill., 1977—. Lectr. on prins. U.S. Patent System, Midwest Coll. Engring., Lombard, Ill., 1968. Mem. Zoning Bd. Appeals, Park Forest, Ill., 1968; mem. Plan Commn., Park Forest, 1968-70, chmn., 1969; trustee Village of Park Forest, Ill., 1970-72; chmn. Park Forest Constn. Com., 1971-72, Park Forest Recreation Bd., 1972-75; publicity chmn. South Suburban Citizens Com. Ill. Constn., 1970. Mem. Ill., Chgo. bar assn., Patent Law Assn. Chgo. (chmn. com. 1971), Park Forest C. of C. (dir.). Republican. Roman Catholic. Club: Rotary (sec. 1977-78). Home: 321 Herndon St Park Forest IL 60466

BADER, KENNETH LEROY, assn. exec.; b. Carroll, Ohio, May 4, 1934; s. Troy Ora and Clara Louise (Walter) B.; B.Sc., Ohio State U., 1956, M.Sc., 1957, Ph.D., 1960; m. Linda Mary Silbaugh, Sept. 17, 1955; children—Bradley, Brent. Instr. agronomy Ohio State U., Columbus, 1957-60, counselor Coll. Agronomy, 1957-60, asst. prof. agronomy, 1960-63, asso. prof., 1963-67, asst. dean Coll. Agr., 1964-67, prof., dean of students, 1968-72; vice chancellor, prof. agronomy U. Nebr., Lincoln, 1972-76; chief exec. officer Am. Soybean Assn., 1976—. Mem. Regional Planning Com., Crime Commn., 1972, exec. com. Columbus Conv. Bur., 1965-71. Bd. dirs. YMCA, chmn., 1969-71. Am. Council on Edn. fellow, 1967-68. Mem. AAAS, Am. Soc. Agronomy, Am. Assn. Higher Edn., Nat. Assn. Student Personnel Adminstrn., Sigma Xi, Alpha Zeta. Lutheran (treas. 1964-67). Contbr. articles on agronomy to sci. publs. Home: 1204 Oak Park Blvd Cedar Falls IA 50613

BADGER, JAMES GOLVIN, JR., banker; b. Kiln, Miss., Apr. 19, 1920; s. James Golvin and Charlotte (Blodgett) B.; B.S., Northwestern U., 1941; m. Margaret E. King, Oct. ll, 1941; children—James K., Mary Ellen. With First Nat. Bank Chgo., 1941-69, v.p., 1961-69; pres. Met. Bank and Trust Co., Chgo., 1969-71; sr. v.p. Amalgamated Trust & Savs. Bank, Chgo., 1969-71; vice-chmn. Nat. Security Bank of Chgo., 1971-72, chmn., 1972—. Served to lt. USNR, 1943-46. Mem. Navy League, Delta Tau Delta. Republican. Clubs: Westmoreland Country (Wilmette); Metropolitan (Chgo.). Home: 922 Cherokee Rd Wilmette IL 60091 Office: 1030 W Chicago Ave Chicago IL 60622

BAEBLER, ARTHUR GEORGE, assn. exec.; b. St. Louis, Mar. 5, 1932; s. Arthur Philip and Clara (Henke) B.; B.S., Mo. Sch. Mines, 1955; M.B.A., St. Louis U., 1960; m. Iva Lea C. Modde, Nov. 17, 1956; children—Matthew G., Andrew C. Sales engr. Union Electric Co., St. Louis, 1956-60, indsl. devel. engr., 1960-64, mgr. indsl. devel. div., 1964-68, mgr. area devel. dept., 1968-74; gen. mgr. Regional Commerce and Growth Assn., St. Louis, 1974—; sec. 1st Mo. Corp. Commr. St. Louis Municipal Devel. Commn., 1967—, St. Louis County Bus. Devel. Commn., 1969—; chmn. East St. Louis Indsl. Devel. Commn. Served to capt. AUS, 1956. Mem. St. Louis C. of C. (chmn. econ. devel. com.), Soc. Indsl. Realtors, Tau Beta Pi, Pi Tau Sigma, Phi Kappa Phi. Republican. Roman Catholic. Clubs: University; Engineers of St. Louis. Home: 20 Fox Meadows Sunset Hills MO 63127 Office: 10 Broadway St Louis MO 63102

BAER, AUSTIN ROBERT, mfg. co. exec.; b. N.Y.C., May 19, 1929; s. Julius W. and Ida E. (Simel) B.; student Ga. Inst. Tech., 1947-49; B.S. in Mech. Engring., Mass. Inst. Tech., 1949-52; m. Claire E. Ross, Oct. 24, 1954; children—Indy Sue, David Clayton, Kerry Ann, Julie W. Instr. creative engring. lab. Mass. Inst. Tech., 1952-55; cons. new product devel., N.Y.C., 1955-58; head dept. product design N.C. State Coll., Raleigh, 1958-62; pres., Roton Corp., Coral Gables, Fla., 1962-68; pres., Roton div. Allied Products Corp., Chgo., 1968—. Co-founder Research Triangle New Product Devel. Com., Raleigh, N.C., 1961; co-founder Med. Engring. Council, N.C. State Coll., 1967; chmn. Entrepreneurship Workshop Mass. Inst. Tech., 1971. Bd. dirs. Raleigh Chamber Music Soc., 1962. Recipient Grand Prize, Hess Bros. versatility in design competition, 1956, 1st prize, Design U.S.A., Dept. Commerce, 1965, Best Component award Internat. Extrusion Design Competition, 1972. Mem. Indsl. Design Edn. Assn. (v.p. 1962), Mass. Inst. Tech. Alumni Club (sec. 1972), Phi Epsilon Pi. Jewish religion. Contbr. articles to profl. jours. Patentee in field. Home: 430 E Kolberg Ct Villa Park IL 60181 Office: 5401 W Roosevelt Rd Chicago IL 60650

BAER, DAVID, JR., lawyer; b. Belleville, Ill., Sept. 24, 1905; s. David and Sunshine (Lieber) B.; LL.B., Washington U., 1928; m. Mary Lynne Cockrell Sweet, Apr. 18, 1938. Partner firm Barnard and Baer, lawyers, St. Louis; dir. Lindell Trust Co.; former pres., dir. Mo.-Lincoln Trust Co.; former dir. Scullin Steel Co., St. Louis. Mem. St. Louis Boy Scout Endowment Fund Com. Served as sgt. AUS, 1943-45. Mem. Estate Planning Council St. Louis (pres. dir.), Am., Mo., St. Louis (past chmn. group ins. com.) bar assns., Washington U. Law Alumni Assn., Jr. (life), Ill. Jr. (past pres.), U.S. Jr. (senator) chambers commerce. Mason, De Molay (past master councilor, sr. mem.; mem. Legion of Honor). Club: Mo. Athletic. Home: 725 S Skinker Blvd St Louis MO 63105 Office: 818 Olive St St Louis MO 63101

BAER, JOHN RICHARD FREDERICK, lawyer; b. Melrose Park, Ill., Jan. 9, 1941; s. John Richard and Zena Edith (Ostreyko) B.; B.A. (Ill. State scholar), U. Ill., 1963, J.D., 1966; m. Linda Gail Chapman, Aug. 31, 1963; children—Brett Scott, Deborah Jill. Admitted to Ill. bar, 1966, U.S. Supreme Ct., 1969, D.C. Ct. Appeals, 1975; asso. firm Keck, Cushman, Mahin & Cate, Chgo., 1966-74, partner, 1974—; instr. Advanced Mgmt. Inst., Lake Forest (Ill.) Coll., 1975-76; speaker before profl. groups. Mem. Deerfield (Ill.) Home Rule Study Commn., 1974-75, Deerfield Plan Commn., 1976—. Mem. Am., Fed., Ill. bar assns., Phi Delta Phi. Democrat. Asst. editor U. Ill. Law Forum, 1965-66. Home: 700 Appletree Lane Deerfield IL 60015 Office: 8300 Sears Tower 233 S Wacker Dr Chicago IL 60606

BAER, ROGER KERN, educator; b. Boston, Nov. 8, 1928; s. Jacob and Bessie Lee (Cohen) B.; B.S., Am. U., 1951; M.A., Cath. U. Am., 1956; Ph.D., U. Chgo., 1970; m. Hillevi Karin Piekkola, June 23, 1963; children—Elizabeth Maria, Jacob William. Statistician, demographer population div. U.S. Bur. Census, Suitland, Md., 1964-66, U.S. Bur. Labor Statistics, Washington, 1966-68; asst. prof. Roosevelt U. Coll. Bus. Adminstrn., Chgo., 1968-72; asso. prof. dept. sociology/anthropology St. Cloud (Minn.) State Coll., 1972—. Served with AUS, 1951-53. Mem. Population Assn. Am., Am. Sociol. Assn. Editorial cons. Demography, 1973-76. Home: 1710 13th Ave SE St Cloud MN 56301

BAETZHOLD, HOWARD GEORGE, educator; b. Buffalo, Jan. 1, 1923; s. Howard Kuster and Harriet Laura (Hofheins) B.; student Brown U., 1940-43, Mass. Inst. Tech., 1943-44; A.B. magna cum laude, Brown U., 1944, M.A., 1948; Ph.D., U. Wis., 1953; m. Nancy Millard Cheesman, Aug. 5, 1950; children—Howard King, Barbara Millard. Asst. dir. Veterans Coll., Brown U., Providence, 1947-48, dir., 1948-49, admissions officer, 1948-50; teaching asst. U. Wis.-Madison, 1950-51, asst. to asso. dean Coll. Letters and Sci., 1951-53; asst. prof. Butler U., Indpls., 1953-57, asso. prof., 1957-67, prof. English, 1967—; vis. prof. U. Del., summer 1963. Mem. Indpls. Com. Internat. Visitors, 1965—. Served to 1st lt. AC, AUS, 1943-46. Butler U. faculty fellow, 1957-58, 69-70; Am. Philos. Soc. grantee, 1958; Am. Council Learned Socs. grantee, 1967. Mem. AAUP (v.p. state conf. 1955), Modern Lang. Assn., Am. Studies Assn. (nat. council 1974-76), Midwest Modern Lang. Assn., Ohio-Ind. Am. Studies Assn. (pres. 1967-68), Indpls. Urban League, Art Assn. Indpls., Kessler-Riverview Neighborhood Assn., Butler U. Odd Topics Soc., Delta Upsilon. Author: Mark Twain and John Bull: The British Connection, 1970. Contbr. articles to profl. publs. Home: 6723 Riverview Dr Indianapolis IN 46220

BAFFES, CHRIS GUS, surgeon; b. New Orleans, May 23, 1931; s. Gus and Tina (Bores) B.; B.S., Tulane U., 1953, M.D., 1955; m. Kathy Reitenbach, Apr. 7, 1967; children—Cyndie, Laura, Karen, Greg, Glen, Sharon, Tina. Intern, Charity Hosp., New Orleans, 1955-56, resident gen. and thoracic surgery, 1956-61; practice medicine specializing in surgery, Chgo., 1953—; mem. staff Swedish Covenant Hosp., Chgo.; asst. prof. surgery Rush Med. Coll., Chgo., 1974—. Served to capt. AUS, 1961-63. Fellow A.C.S., Am. Coll. Chest Physicians, Am. Coll. Angiology; mem. N.Y. Acad. Sci. Contbr. articles to profl. jours. Home: 418 Huber Ln Glenview IL 60025 Office: 6305 N Milwaukee Ave Chicago IL 60645

BAGBY, MARVIN ORVILLE, chemist; b. Macomb, Ill., Sept. 27, 1932; s. Byron Orville and Geneva Floriene (Filbert) B.; B.S., Western Ill. U., 1957, M.S., 1957; m. Mary Jean Jennings, Aug. 31, 1957; children—Gary Lee, Gordon Eugene. With No. Regional Research Center, U.S. Dept. Agr., Peoria, Ill., 1957—, research leader, 1974—. Served with AUS, 1953-55. Mem. Am. Chem. Soc., AAAS, TAPPI. Methodist. Contbr. articles in field to profl. jours. Home: 209 S Louisiana St Morton IL 61550 Office: 1815 N University St Peoria IL 61604

BAGLEY, JAMES EDWARD, hosp. adminstr.; b. Waterloo, Iowa, Sept. 21, 1930; s. William Franklin and Margaret (Craig) B.; grad. pub. schs.; B.Pub. Adminstrn., Upper Iowa U., 1975; credentials advanced hosp. and health care adminstrn. U. Minn., 1976; M. Hosp. Adminstrn., U. Minn., 1977; m. Kathie Rebecca Smith, Nov. 29, 1968; children—Cheryl, Kathleen, Debra, Vicki, Sharri, Lauri. Psychiat. aide U.S. VA Hosp., Knoxville, Iowa, 1952-56; sr. patrolman State Iowa Dept. Pub. Safety, Iowa Falls, 1956-63; adminstr. Ellsworth Municipal Hosp., Iowa Falls, 1963-68; adminstr. Greene County Med. Center, Jefferson, Iowa, 1968—. Chmn. Iowa Hosp. Purchasing Council. Served with USN, 1948-52. Licensed nursing home adminstr., Iowa; licensed hosp. adminstr. State Minn. Fellow Am. Acad. Med. Adminstrs. (v.p. region VII; Newcomer award Med. Adminstr. of Year 1977); mem. Am., Iowa (chmn. SW region 1971, chmn. div. plant ops. 1969-70, chmn. div. long term care 1974-75, chmn. div. long term care statistics 1975-76, trustee, treas. 1977-78), hosp. assns., Iowa Assn. Homes for Aging (dir. 1975-76). Methodist (chmn. bd. trustees 1971). Lion, Elk. Home: 507 Rushview Dr Jefferson IA 50129 Office: 1000 W Lincolnway Jefferson IA 50129

BAHADUR, CHANCE, fin. exec.; b. Agra, India, Nov. 22, 1942; s. Krishna and Rajeshwari (Mathur) B.; Sc.B., Agra U., 1959; S.B., Kans. State U., 1962; M.B.A., U. Chgo., 1969; m. Donna Narolewski, Jan. 6, 1963; children—Mark, Miles. Came to U.S., 1959, naturalized, 1967. Mktg. and devel. positions in chem. and processing industries, 1962-67; marketing coordinator Ill. Inst. Tech. Research Inst., Chgo., 1967-69; regional mgr. Virtual Computer Services, Inc., Chgo., 1969-70; asst. to pres. Monsanto Enviro-Chem Systems, Inc., Chgo., 1970-73; corporate banking loan officer First Nat. Bank Chgo., 1973-76; dir. treasury ops. Esmark, Inc., 1976-77, asst. treas., 1977—. C.P.A., Ill. Mem. Am. Inst. Chem. Engrs. (chmn. Chgo. sect. 1972-73), Am. Inst. C.P.A.'s, Ill. C.P.A. Soc., Chgo. Council Fgn. Relations (mem. com. fgn. affairs), Beta Gamma Sigma. Clubs: Admiral's (N.Y.C.); Cabaret (London, Eng.); Stonehenge Golf, Biltmore Country (Barrington, Ill.); Monroe (Chgo.). Contbr. articles on mktg., finance and orgn. to profl. media. Home: 93 Flint Dr Barrington IL 60010 Office: 55 E Monroe Chicago IL 60603

BAIA, ARLENE VIVIAN SKJEVELAND, nursing educator; b. Duluth, Minn., Aug. 15, 1922; d. Theodore Owen and Pearl Ruby (Thompson) Skjeveland; B.S. in Nursing Edn., U. Minn., 1945; M.S. in Edn., Iowa State U., 1973; children—Barbara Baia Thompson, Gloria Bonnie (dec.). Instr., U. Minn. Sch. Nursing, Mpls., 1945-46; asso. dir. edn. Naeve Hosp. Sch. Nursing, Albert Lea, Minn., 1954-60; instr. St. Joseph Sch. Nursing, Mason City, Iowa, 1960-62, Meth. Kahler Sch. Nursing, Rochester, Minn., 1962-68; instr. nursing North Iowa Area Community Coll., Mason City, 1968—. Recipient certificate for distinguished teaching in nursing Rochester C. of C., 1964. Mem. Am. (council advanced practitioners in med.-surg. nursing), Iowa (chmn. rev. panel for continuing edn. 1972-76) nurses assns., P.E.O. Republican. Congregationalist. Club: Order Eastern Star. Home: 417 S Tennessee Pl Apt 6 Mason City IA 50401 Office: 500 College Dr Mason City IA 50401

BAIER, MARTIN, ins. co. exec.; b. Kansas City, Mo., Dec. 7, 1922; s. Harry and Yetta (Stein) B.; B.A., B.S. U. Mo., 1943, M.A., 1970; m. Dorothy Fay Rathbun, Mar. 7, 1948; 1 dau., Donna Denys. Advt. prodn. mgr. Box Office Mag., Kansas City, Mo., 1937-42; advt. mgr. Tension Envelope Corp., Kansas City, 1946-54; v.p., gen. mgr. M.P. Brown, Inc., Burlington, Ia., 1954-60; with Old Am. Ins. Co., Kansas City, Mo., 1960—, v.p. mktg., 1967—, also dir.; v.p., dir. R-X Mktg. Inc., Kansas City, Mo., 1971—; lectr. U. Mo., 1969—. Bd. dirs. Univ. Assos. of U. Mo., Kansas City, pres., 1970-71, adv. council Sch. Adminstrn.; bd. dirs. Inst. Community Studies, Kansas City, Mo., Friends Library U. Mo. at Kansas City. Served to lt. USNR, 1942-46. Recipient Outstanding Service award Kansas City Advt. Club, 1952; Alumni Achievement award U. Mo., 1970, Alumni service award, 1977; Mktg. Man of Year Sales and Mktg. Execs. Kansas City, 1974. Mem. Direct Mail Mktg. Assn. (Best of Industry award 1950). Am. Econ. Assn., Sales and Mktg. Execs. Kansas City (pres. 1967-68), Navy League (dir. Greater Kansas City), U. Mo.-Kansas City Alumni Assn. (bd. dirs.). Clubs: Rockhill Tennis, Masons, Omicron Delta Epsilon. Contbr. articles to profl. jours. Home: 5410 Sunset Dr Kansas City MO 64112 Office: 4900 Oak St Kansas City MO 64141

BAIER, WILLIAM HERBERT, scientific co. exec.; b. Chgo., Oct. 1, 1922; s. Henry and Anna (Friedl) B.; m. Patricia Ann Ward, Sept. 13, 1958; B.S. in Mech. Engring., Ill. Inst. Tech., 1944, B.S. in Elec. Engring., 1949, M.S. in Mech. Engring., 1950, Ph.D., 1958. Instr., Ill. Inst. Tech., 1947-50; designer Hannifin Corp., Chgo., 1951-53; sr. research engr. Armour Research Found., 1953-63; mgr. aerospace mechanisms Emerson Electric Co., St. Louis, 1964-65; mgr. research Thor Power Tool Co., Aurora, Ill., 1966-69; v.p. research and engring. Central Sci. Co., Chgo., 1968—. Pres., bd. dirs. DuPage Inst. for Research and Edn., Downers Grove, Ill., 1968—. Mem. ASME (sec. B40 com. 1969—), Am. Vacuum Soc., Am. Phys. Soc., Sigma Xi, Tau Beta Pi, Pi Tau Sigma. Contbr. articles in applied math. and design engring. to profl. jours.; patentee in field. Home: 3624 Creekwood Ct Downers Grove IL 60515 Office: 2600 S Kostner Ave Chicago IL 60623

BAILEY, EARL GLENN, JR., veterinarian; b. Maywood, Mo., Aug. 1, 1920; s. Earl Glenn and Lessie Alma (Pittman) B.; student Culver-Stockton Coll., 1949; Asso. in Sci., John Tarleton Agrl. Coll., 1940; D.V.M., Texas A. and M. Coll., 1943; m. Barbara Louise Shelby, Dec. 31, 1969; children—Larry Stephen, Carolyn Sue, Barbara (Mrs. James Hendley); 1 stepdau., Sheri. Owner, Stoddard Animal Clinic, Dexter, Mo., 1946—. Pres., Stoddard County Fair, 1967—, Dexter Municipal Airport Bd., 1970—. Served as maj., Vet. Corp., AUS, 1943-46; PTO. Mem. AMVA, Mo. (exec. bd. 1954-59, pres. 1960-61, mem. numerous com., Mo. Vet. of Year award 1972), S.E. Mo. (pres. 1949-51) vet. med. assns., Am. Assn. Equine Practitioners, Mo. Quarter Horse Assn. (dir. 1955-60), Dexter C. of C., Am. Legion, Nat., Ark.-Mo. cutting horse assns. Democrat. Mem. Christian Ch. (deacon 1966-70). Mason, Lion. Club: Bootheel Saddle (Dexter). Address: Route 4 Dexter MO 63841

BAILEY, EUGENE CARY, cons. engring. co. exec.; b. Chgo., Apr. 7, 1910; s. Alexander Davidson and Alice (Cary) B.; B.S. in M.E., Purdue U., 1932, M.S. in M.E., 1933; m. Marie F. Kerker, Apr. 21, 1931 (dec.); M. 2d Janet L. Sampson, Jan. 24, 1938; children—Willard N., Robert E., Alice (dec.). With Commonwealth Edison Co., Chgo., 1933-75, system mech. and bldg. engr., 1954-62, adminstv. engr. for v.p., 1962-75; v.p. bus. devel. John Dolio & Assos. (now Dolio and Metz Ltd.), Chgo., 1975—; cons., resource recovery and nuclear and fossil power engring. Trustee Lyons Twp. High Sch. Dist. 204, 1956-69; trustee Coll. of Du Page (Ill.), 1970-77. Served from 1st lt. to capt. U.S. Army, 1942-45. Registered profl. engr., Ill. Fellow Am. Soc. Mech. Engrs.; mem. Western Soc. Engrs., Am. Welding Soc., Am. Nuclear Soc., Ill. Soc. Profl. Engrs. Republican. Congregationalist. Clubs: Union League Chgo., Antique Auto Am. Home: 81 S 6th Ave LaGrange IL 60525 Office: 208 S LaSalle St Chicago IL 60604

BAILEY, GWENDOLYN LEE MANNING, educator; b. Dayton, O., Sept. 1, 1930; d. Edgar William and Thelma Evelyn (Doughman) Vahle; B.S. in Edn., U. Dayton, 1963, M.S. in Edn., 1969; m. Charles Sydney Bailey, Aug. 3, 1949; 1 son, Bruce Eugene. Tchr., Northridge Morrison Elementary Sch., Dayton, 1960-63; tchr. Beavercreek Fairbrook Elementary Sch., Xenia, Ohio, 1963-70, counselor Beavercreek High Sch., 1970—. Co-chmn. United Appeal. Mem. Am., Ohio, Miami Valley personnel and guidance assns., NEA, Ohio, Western Ohio edn. assns., Ohio High Sch. Drill Team Assn. (v.p., state dir.), Half-Time U.S.A., Ohio Sch. Counselors Assn., Beavercreek Classroom Tchrs. Assn. Home: 4218 Walbridge Trail Dayton OH 45430 Office: 2940 Dayton-Xenia Rd Xenia OH 45385

BAILEY, HOWARD LOWDEN, ednl. cons. co. exec.; b. Dayton, Ohio, Dec. 20, 1927; s. Harry Joseph and Ruth Marion (Lowden) B.; B.S., Central Mich. U., 1952; M.A., U. Mich., 1961; m. Cosette Arlene Quillen, Mar. 25, 1948; children—Shannon Sue, Kevin Howard, Bridget Kathleen. Tchr., Chula Vista (Calif.) High Sch., 1959-61; regional mgr. EDL/McGraw Hill, Huntington, N.Y., 1961-67; pres. Learning Consultants, Inc., Medina, Ohio, Detroit and San Diego, 1968—; pres. Handles, Inc.; cons. to various sch. systems. Served with USN, 1945-47. Mem. Nat. Audio-Visual Assn., Internat. Reading Assn., Medina C. of C. Clubs: Westfield Country (Medina); Cuymaca (San Diego). Home: Box 152 Westfield Center OH 44251 also 1760 Avenida del Mundo Coronado CA 92118 Office: 690 Lafayette Rd Medina OH 44156

BAILEY, JAMES SPENCER, counseling psychologist; b. Milw., Aug. 2, 1932; s. James Spencer and Ruth Marcella (McLaughlin) B., Sr.; B.A., St. John's Coll., 1958; M.S. in Counseling, U. Wis. at Oshkosh, 1971; Ed.D., Okla. State U. at Stillwater, 1973; m. Charlene Therese Sitkowski, June 13, 1968; children—Karen Ruthann, Kevin Walter. Ordained priest Roman Catholic, 1958; installment loan officer Crocker Bank, San Jose, Calif., 1968-69; counselor high sch., Two Rivers, Wis., 1969-71; counseling psychologist, counselor educator NE. Mo. State U., Kirksville, 1973—; cons. mental health assns.; teaching group procedures, seminars. Advisor Planned Parenthood, Parents without Partners; Newman advisor, 1975—; chmn. parish council, 1973-75. Mem. Am. Psychol. Assn., Am. Personnel and Guidance Assn., Phi Delta Kappa. Democrat. Contbr. articles to profl. jours. Home: Rt 3 Box 165C Orrick Mine Rd Kirksville MO 63501 Office: NE MO State U Kirksville MO 63501

BAILEY, MELANIE ANNE, counselor; b. Pitts., Feb. 19, 1948; d. John J. and Kathryn M. (Dickson) Bailey; B.S., U. Kans., 1969; M.Ed., Howard U., 1973. Tchr., Lincoln Jr. High Sch., Kansas City, Mo., 1969-73; supervising instr. Adult Edn. Program, Kansas City, Mo., 1971; counselor Metropolitan Community Coll., Kansas City, Mo., 1973—; human relations facilitator Black Motivation Tng. Center, Kansas City, Mo., 1973-74. Bd. dir. Greater Kansas City YWCA. Mem. Am., Mo. personnel and guidance assns., Nat., Mo. vocat. assns., Alpha Kappa Alpha (v.p. Mu Omega chpt.). Home: 640 E Meyer Blvd Kansas City MO 64131 Office: 560 Westport Rd Kansas City MO 64111

BAILEY, MERRITT ELTON, JR., publishing co. exec.; b. Denver, Feb. 24, 1921; s. Merritt Elton and Edwina Louise (Cox) B.; B.S., Iowa State U., 1949, M.S., 1951; m. Grace Alberta Crabtree, Mar. 30, 1940; 1 dau., Shirley Louise (Mrs. Jonathan Ruhe). Asso. editor Iowa State U. Press, Ames, 1949-51, sales mgr., 1951-63, dir., 1963—. Pres. Story County Tb and Health Assn., 1954-56, Meeker Sch. PTA, Ames, 1952-54; chmn. Citizens' Com. for Adequate Schs., Ames, 1958-59; mem. Gov.'s Council on Edn., 1959-60; chmn. troop Tall Corn council Boy Scouts Am., 1952-53; v.p. Ames Library Bd., 1977—. Served with USAF, 1942-45. Mem. Ames Jaycees (dir. 1950-53), Assn. Am. U. Presses (dir. 1971), Actors Inc. (dir. 1964-67), Sigma Delta Chi. Mem. Christian Ch. (dir. 1960-65). Elk, Moose. Home: 1716 Maxwell St Ames IA 50010

BAILEY, MICHAEL ALAN, educator; b. Akron, Ohio, Feb. 5, 1951; s. Frank Augustus and Mable (Pryor) B.; B.S. in Edn., Kent State U., 1974, Ed.M., 1977; m. Rosa Lee Williams, Mar. 27, 1970. Clothing salesman Phillip's Men's & Boy's Store, Akron, 1967-69; pressman Karman Rubber Co., Akron, 1972; tchr. Cleve. Bd. Edn., 1973-77; indsl. arts tchr. Children's Aid Soc., Cleve., 1974—; track coach Wilbur Wright Jr. High Sch., Cleve., 1975-77; jr. Olympic coach, Cleve., 1977. Mem. Am. Personnel and Guidance Assn., North-Eastern Ohio Indsl. Arts Assn., Indsl. Edn. Club of Cleve., Greater Cleve. Track Coaches Assn., Kent State U. Alumni Assn., Cleve. Tchrs. Union. Home: 4804 Walford Rd Warrensville Heights OH 44128

BAILEY, NEAL JAMES, optometrist, educator; b. Gardenville, N.Y., Nov. 6, 1917; s. Frank William and Dorothy Roseanna (Frankenstein) B.; B.S. in Optometry, Ohio State U., 1947, Ph.D. in Physiol. Optics, 1954; m. Florence Evelyn Hansen, Feb. 15, 1941; children—Nancy (Mrs. Richard Brigleb), Anita. Practice optometry, Escanaba, Mich., 1947-50, Columbus, O., 1958—; asso. optometry Ohio State U., Columbus, 1950-54; asst. prof. optometry Ind. U., Bloomington, 1954-57, asso. prof., 1958; asst. prof. optometry Ohio State U., 1960-70, clin. prof. optometry, 1970—. Cons. Dept. Pub. Welfare, Columbus, 1969-72; investigator, Bausch & Lomb Soflens, Rochester, N.Y., 1968—, Dow-Corning Silcon Lens Chgo., 1970—, Warner-Lambert Griffin Lens, Buffalo, 1971—, Calcon Labs. Gelflex Lens, El Monte, Cal., 1972—, Frontier Hydro-Marc Lens, Jacksonville, Fla., 1974—. Mem. Nat. Eye Research Found., 1950—. Am. Optometric Found. fellow, 1954-58. Diplomate Am. Acad. Optometry. Mem. Am., Ohio optometric assns., Am. Acad. Optometry, AAUP, Sigma Xi. Editor: Contact Lens Forum. Home and office: 32 E 15th Av Columbus OH 43201

BAILEY, RAY VERNON, patent lawyer, property mgr.; b. Royal, Iowa, Dec. 14, 1913; s. George Lewis and Marie (Albers) B.; B.A. cum laude, State U. Iowa, 1935, J.D. cum laude, 1937; m. Velda Maxine Sheldon, June 18, 1938; children—Theron Sheldon, George Bryan. Admitted to Ia. bar, 1937, Ill. bar, 1938; research patent counsel U.S. Gypsum Co., Chgo., 1937-39; asso. Home State Bank, Royal, 1940; partner Dick, Bailey & Fletcher, also Dick and Bailey, Des Moines, 1941-42; investigator U.S. Civil Service Commn., 1942-43; patent adviser Rock Island (Ill.) Arsenal, 1943-45; property mgmt., legal and patent work, Clarion, Ia., 1945-74, Millers Bay, Milford, Iowa, 1974—; v.p., dir. Okoboji Protective Assn.; owner Century Farm. Past mem. Iowa Ho. Reps., past mem. ethics com., departmental rules review com., banking laws revision com. Mem. exec. bd. Prairie Gold council Boy Scouts Am.; mem. Iowa Bd. Regents, 1969—, chmn. banking com.; mem. Iowa Higher Edn. Facilities Commn., 1971—; past mem. alumni council U. Ia.; past chmn. pub. affairs com. Wright County Extension Council, past pres. Clarion Devel. Commn. Bd. dirs. U. Ia. Research Found. Recipient Silver Beaver award Boy Scouts Am. Mem. Am. (patent laws revision com.), Iowa, Wright County, Dickinson County bar assns., State U. Iowa Alumni Assn. (past pres. Clarion chpt.), Iowa Patent Law Assn., U. Iowa Parents Assn. (past pres.). Lion. Address: Millers Bay Milford IA 51351

BAILEY, RICHARD PAUL, coll. pres.; b. Stockton, Ill., Oct. 9, 1922; s. Parke O. and Nellie Mae (Lauer) B.; B.A., N. Central Coll., 1943; M.A., U. Wis., 1949, Ph.D., 1959; m. Olive Jean Hughes, Dec. 21, 1943; children—Susan, Jo Ellen, Dan, Carla, Anne. Tchr. high schs., Belleville and Mansfield, Ohio, 1946-48; instr. English, Wis. State U., 1949-53; research asst. Bd. of Regents State Colls., Madison, Wis., 1953-59; pres. Yakima (Wash.) Valley Coll., 1959-62, Northland Coll., Wis., 1962-68, Hamline U., St. Paul, 1968-75; dean Gen. Coll., U. Minn., 1975—. Columnist, Wis. Jour. Edn., 1962-68, Mpls. Star, 1972—; pres. Minn. Pvt. Coll. Council, 1971-72. Trustee James Jerome Hill Reference Library, 1971—. Served to lt. USNR, 1943-46. Mem. Wis. Assn. Ind. Colls. and Univs. (past pres.), Minn. Assn. Post-Secondary Edn. (pres. 1975-76). Mem. United Ch. of Christ. Home: 2169 Fulham St St Paul MN 55113

BAILEY, ROBERT HOWARD, architect; b. Mattoon, Ill., July 4, 1929; s. Howard Mitchel and Mary (Trotter) B.; B.S, in Archtl. Engring., U. Ill., 1952. Architect, pres. B.A.S.E. Architects, Inc., Indpls., 1955—. Served with AUS, 1952-54. Fed. registered fall-out shelter analyst. Mem. AIA, Nat. Council Archtl. Registration Bds., Constrn. Specification Inst., Ind. Farm Bur., Am. Concrete Inst., U.S. Auto Club, U. Ill, Alumni Assn. Republican. Methodist. Elk. Structural design for over 300 bldgs. including Southport, Shelbyville and Greencastle High Sch. fieldhouses, Butler U. Carillon. Home: 4029 N Arlington Ave Indianapolis IN 46226 Office: 10 E 106th St Indianapolis IN 46280

BAILEY, THOMAS CORWIN, II, assn. exec.; b. York Center, Ohio, June 6, 1910; s. Coy D. and Clara May (Knox) B.; B.S., Ohio No. U., 1939; M.A., Ohio State U., 1946; m. Rayda A. Converse, May 29, 1936; children—Thomas Corwin III, Gary Lee, Joyce Ann. Supt. schs., Westville, Ohio, 1941-46, Haysville, 1946-51, Canton South, Canton, 1951-54, Geneva, 1954-62, Auglaize County, Wapakoneta, 1962-72; sec. Auglaize County Agrl. Soc., Wapakoneta, 1973—. Ednl. cons., lectr. Mem. Am., Buckeye assns. sch. adminstrs., Ohio County Supts. Assn. Mason (32 deg.), Rotarian. Address: 604 W Auglaize St Wapakoneta OH 45895

BAILEY, V. MAXINE SHELDON (MRS. RAY V. BAILEY), civic worker; b. Rowan, Iowa, Feb. 20, 1915; d. Guy R. and Edna (Schroeder) Sheldon; B.A., State U. Iowa, 1937; m. Ray V. Bailey, June 18, 1938; children—Theron Sheldon, G. Bryan. Tchr. high schs., Thor, Iowa, 1937-38, Moline, Ill., 1944-45. Mem. Clarion (Iowa) Planning and Zoning Commn., 1961-74. Mem. Nat. Com. for Support Pub. Schs.; mem. curriculum and programming com. Iowa State Edn. TV. Mem. AAUW (Clarion br. pres. 1945-55, mass media chmn. Iowa div. 1958-62, 1st v.p., program chmn. 1962-64, div. pres. 1964-66, mem. conv. program com. 1967, 69, regional v.p., mem. nat. bd. 1971-75, bd. dirs. ednl. found.), Iowa Legis. Ladies League, U. Iowa Alumni Council. Democrat. Methodist (past chmn. edn. commn.). Home: Millers Bay Milford IA 51351

BAILEY, WANITA MAE, psychotherapist; b. Worthington, Ind., June 24, 1907; d. James Monroe and Icis May (Harrel) Burris; B.M., Butler U., 1940; M.Ed., Ind. U., 1955, Ed.S., 1963, Ed.D., 1966; postgrad. Harvard U., 1968; m. James Gordon Bailey, May 18, 1936. Music supr. Wright Twp. (Ind.) Schs., 1939-44; personnel dir. James G. Bailey Co., Worthington, 1944-46, St. Louis, 1946-54; counselor Orlando, Fla., 1956-58; vocat. counselor YWCA, 1958; dir. pupil personnel services Hobart (Ind.) Twp. Schs., 1960-66; dir. Camp Fire Girls, Whiting, Ind., 1967; vis. prof. Wis. State U., Platteville, summer 1967; dir. placement Vincennes (Ind.) U., 1967-72; licensed psychologist, personnel cons., Washington, Ind., 1967—; personnel cons. to Lake County (Ind.) heavy industry, social agys., labor unions, 1963-67, Daviess County Hosp., 1976—, Prairie Village Nursing Home, 1976. Membership chmn. Ind. Hosp. Aux., 1954; pres. House of Episcopal Women, Vincennes, 1976-77. Recipient civilian merit award AF, 1964, award of year Ind. Restaurant Assn., 1964; recipient grant NDEA, 1964; participant Ford Found. and Ind. Higher Edn. Council, 1962-64, Honor Inst., Harvard U., 1968. Mem. Am., Ind. psychol. assns., Am. Personnel and Guidance Assn., Nat. Vocat. Guidance Assn., Nat. Council Health Providers in Psychology, AAUW, Phi Lambda Theta. Clubs: Bus. and Profl. Women's (pres. 1943-45), Gen. Federated, Eastern Star. Composer: Phi Sigma Mu Nat. Prayer Song, 1939. Author: Vocation-Placement for Mentally Retarded Adolescent, 1960. Home: 613 N 4th St Vincennes IN 47591 Office: 511 E Main St Washington IN 47501

BAILEY, WELTMAN DAWES, dentist; b. Harvill, Mo., Jan. 26, 1927; s. Henry Andrew and Lula Beatrice (Simms) B.; B.S., U. Wis., 1950; D.D.S., Meharry Med. Coll., 1956; M.Health Service Adminstrn., U. Mo. at Kansas City, 1972; m. Margaret D. Barber, Sept. 22, 1952; children—Sandra, Weltman Dawes, Peter, Robert. With Pabst Brewing Co., summers 1947-50, Gt. No. Ry., 1953-55; intern Portsmouth (Va.) City Dental Clinic, 1956-57; practice dentistry, Norfolk, Va., 1958-66, Kansas City, Mo., 1967—; gen. dentist Wayne Minor Neighborhood Health Center, Kansas City, 1968—; chief of staff dental surgery Norfolk Community Hosp., 1965-66; mem. staffs St. Joseph Hosp., Martin Luther King Hosp., Kansas City. Mem. Regional Health and Welfare Council, 1969-70; vis. prof. Kansas City Met. Jr. Coll., 1970; med. adv. com. Mo. Div. Family Services. Bd. dirs. Mid-Am. Comprehensive Health Planning Agy., 1970-71, Rehab. Inst.; bd. govs. Citizens Assn. Kansas City, Mo. Served with AUS, 1945-47. Fellow Royal Soc. Health; mem. Am. Soc. for Pub. Adminstrn., Am., Mo. pub. health assns., Nat. Rehab. Assn., Am. Assn. Hosp. Dentists, Am. Dental Assn. and affiliates, Nat. Dental Assn. and affiliates, NAACP, Urban League, YMCA, Alpha Phi Alpha. Baptist (ch. trustee 1967—). Contbr. articles in field to profl. jours. Home: 10433 Grand St Kansas City MO 64114 Office: 4301 The Pased Kansas City MO 64110

BAILEY, WILSON PEASE, pediatrician; b. Waverly, N.Y., Sept. 1, 1929; s. Percival Dee and Ella Marie (Wilson) B.; B.A., Alfred U., 1952; Dr. Osteopathy, Kirksville (Mo.) Coll. Osteo. Medicine, 1959; M.D. (Mead Johnson fellow), Calif. Coll. Medicine, 1962; m. Barbara Ann Miller, Apr. 5, 1958; children—Wilson Pease, John, Valerie, Bruce. Intern, Kirksville Osteo. Hosp., 1959-60, resident, 1960-62, chmn. dept. pediatrics Kirksville Coll. Medicine and Surgery, 1962-68, med. dir. children and youth program, 1966-68, asso. prof., 1965—; practice medicine specializing in pediatrics, Kirksville, 1968—; mem. staff attending pediatric Grim Smith Hosp., Kirksville, chief of staff, 1970-73; cons. OEO programs, rural pediatrics; lectr. N.E. Mo. U., 1962-72. Mem. Sch. Bd. Dist. III, 1972-73, pres., 1972-75; chmn. Head Start Bd., 1966-70. Served to maj. M.C., AUS, 1952-55. Diplomate Coll. Osteo. Pediatricians. Mem. Mo. Assn. Osteo. Physicians, Am. Coll. Osteo. Pediatricians, N.E. Mo. Osteo. Physicians, Am. Osteo. Assn. Mason. Club: Kirksville Country. Contbr. articles to profl. jours. Home: RD 3 Kirksville MO 63501 Office: 2905 N Baltimore St Kirksville MO 63501

BAILLON, AUSTIN JOHN, real estate exec.; b. Duluth, Minn., June 22, 1927; s. Autin L. and Marie M. (McDonald) B.; B.A., U. Minn., 1950; B.S., St. Paul Coll. Law, 1952, LL.B., 1954; J.D., William Mitchell Coll. Law, 1969; m. Caroline Myers, Aug. 16, 1968; children—Caroline M., Paul A., Peter M., Catherine G., Alexander R., Frances E. Claims examiner Minn. Mut. Life Ins. Co., St. Paul, 1950-52, claims mgr., 1952-54, atty. legal dept., 1954-55; sales mgr., appraiser F. M. and E. V. Dolan, Realtors and Appraisers, St. Paul, 1955-56; pres. Baillon Co., Realtors, Real Estate Brokerage and Investment, St. Paul, 1956—; founder, pres. St. Paul Title Ins. Co. subs. St. Paul Cos., Inc., 1963-67; founder Baillon Mortgage Corp., 1964, Bailon Agy., Inc., 1963. Bd. dirs. Minn. Landmarks, 1971-74. Served with USCG, 1945-46, U.S. Army, 1951-54. Mem. Soc. Real

Estate Appraisers (past sec.-treas., dir.), Am., Minn. State, Ramsey County bar assns., St. Paul Bd. Realtors (past treas., dir.), St. Paul Bldg. Owners and Mgrs. Assn., Chi Psi, Delta Theta Phi. Clubs: Minn. (dir. 1970-73), Athletic (St. Paul); K.C.; Somerset Country; Biltmore Hunting. Office: Saint Paul Bldg Saint Paul MN 55102

BAIN, RALPH LEE, educator; b. Los Angeles, May 8, 1933; s. Edwin Vance and Josephine Louise (Matrisciano) B.; B.S. in chemistry, U. Ill., 1956; Ph.D., Oreg. State U., 1964; 1 dau., Tuvana Louise. Asst. prof. U. Sask. (Can.), 1964-66; mem. faculty So. Ill. U., Edwardsville, 1966—, prof. chemistry, 1976—, chmn. dept., 1970-73, 76—. Mem. Ill. Com. on Water Resources, 1976—. Served with AUS, 1956-58. Univ. Coll. London hon. research fellow, 1973-74; recipient grants NSF, 1969-70, NIH, 1976-78, Ill. Office Edn., 1973, Ill. Dept. Mental Health, 1976. Mem. Canadian Inst. Chemistry, Am. Chem. Soc., Chem. Soc. London, Ill. Acad. Sci. Contbr. articles to profl. jours. Home: 88 Eastmoor Rd Rt 1 East Alton IL 62024 Office: Box 65 Edwardsville IL 62026

BAIR, BRUCE B., lawyer; b. St. Paul, May 26, 1928; s. Bruce B. and Emma (Stone) B.; B.S., U. N.D., 1950, J.D. 1952; m. Jane Lawler, July 19, 1952; children—Mary Jane, Thomas Bruce, Susan Kay, Barbara Ann, Patricia Louise, James William, Joan Marie, Bruce Blythe, III, Jeffrey Mark. Admitted to N.D. bar, 1952; pvt. practice law, Mandan, N.D., 1955—; partner firm Bair, Brown & Kautzmann and predecessor firm, Mandan, 1957—; dir. Bank of Tioga (N.D.), 1959—. Spl. asst. atty. gen., N.D., 1967—; exec. com. Internat. Assn. Milk Control Agys., 1970—. Pres. Sch. Bd. St. Joseph's Catholic Ch., Mandan, N.D., 1967-68; mem. sch. bd. Mandan Pub. Schs., Dist. 1, 1971-77. Chmn. Morton County Republican Party, 1958-62; mem. Rep. State Central Com., Morton County, 1962-67; Rep. precinct committeeman, 1956-70. Served to 1st lt. USAF, 1952-55. Mem. Mandan C. of C. (pres. 1962), N.D. State, Am., Morton County bar assns., Assn. Trial Lawyers Am., Am. Legion. Roman Catholic. Rotarian, Elks. Home: Box 100 Mandan ND 58554 Office: 210 1st Ave NW Mandan ND 58554

BAIR, MEDFORD DANIEL, optometrist; b. Findlay, Ohio, July 28, 1918; s. Fred Ensor and Ora Diveta (Waltimire) B.; student Ohio State U., 1937-38, Eastern Oreg. Coll. Edn., 1944; D. Optometry, Ill. Coll. Optometry, 1948; m. Virginia Donna Reber, June 1, 1947; children—Judy Louise, Gary Lee. Individual practice optometry, Findlay, 1948—; optometrist Findlay Optometry Clinic Inc., Findlay, 1970—, pres., 1970—; lectr. optometric clin. hypnosis. Pres. Marinewood Enterprises, Inc., Port Clinton, Ohio, 1964-66, dir., 1963—; lectr. in field. Pres. Vision League of Ohio, 1968-69. Bd. dirs. Northwest Ohio Lions Eye Bank. Served to 2d lt., USAAF, 1942-45; PTO. Mem. Am. (mem. Speaker's Bur.), Ohio optometric assns., Am. Soc. for Optometric Clin. Hypnosis. Mason, Lion (pres. 1959-60), Elk. Editor: Ophthalmic Hypnotherapy Quar., 1971—. Home: 215 6th St Findlay OH 45840 Office: 123 W Sandusky St Findlay OH 45840

BAIR, RICHARD MCKINNON, constrn. co. exec.; b. St. Paul, June 4, 1915; s. Homer and Grace Ethel (Hall) B.; student Mich. State Coll., 1933-36; m. Evelyn Louise Sadler, July 3, 1936; children—Janet (Mrs. Paul Carey Murdock), James Lee. Project supr. O.W. Burke Constrn. Co., 1936-61; pres. Bair Constrn. Inc., 1961-64; v.p. A.J. Etkin Constrn. Co., Oak Park, Mich., 1964-75; v.p. Midco Drilling Co., Jedah, Saudi Arabia, 1975-77; estimator Minoru Yamasaki and Assos., 1977—. Mem. Engring. Soc. Detroit. Mason. Home: 1258 Priscilla Ln Rochester MI 48063

BAIRD, CLYDE RAY, coll. vice pres.; b. Attica, Kans., Jan. 31, 1921; s. Clyde and Elva (Copeland) B.; A.B., Southwestern Coll., Winfield, Kans., 1942; M.A., Columbia, 1947; Ed.D., U. Okla., 1956; m. Ann Anderson, Oct. 4, 1944; 1 dau., Catherine Ann. Asst. prof. edn., counselor guidance bur. Kans. State Coll., Pittsburg (now Pittsburg State U.), 1947-53, dir. admissions, registrar, 1953-66, asso. prof. edn., 1957-58, prof., 1958—, registrar, 1966-68, exec. v.p., 1968—; cons. examiner N. Central Assn., 1971—. Served with USAF, World War II. Mem. Am. Psychol. Assn., Am. Personnel Guidance Assn., Am. Assn. Coll. Registrars, Kans. Guidance Assn. Methodist. Home: Rural Route 4 Pittsburg KS 66742 Office: Pittsburg State U Pittsburg KS 66762

BAIRD, GEORGE WALTER, computer programming mgr.; b. Pitts., Dec. 22, 1931; s. Victor William and Ellen Elizabeth (Murphy) B.; B.A. in Math., Dartmouth, 1953; postgrad. San Diego State Coll., 1959-61, U. So. Calif., 1964-65, U. Calif. at Los Angeles, 1966-67, U. Minn., 1970; m. Catherine Alfreda Komoroski, May 29, 1954; children—Linda Rose, Grace Lorraine. Systems analyst Computer Scis. Corp., Los Angeles, 1961-65; project leader Digitek Corp., Los Angeles, 1965, sr. staff analyst Programmatics, Inc., Los Angeles, 1966-67; computer programming mgr. West Pub. Co., St. Paul, 1967—. Served as lt. USNR, 1953-61. Mem. Assn. for Computer Machinery (v.p. membership 1972-73), Sigma Alpha Epsilon. Episcopalian. Home: 5483 Woodlawn Circle Prior Lake MN 55372

BAIRD, JAMES KENNETH, lawyer, telephone co. exec.; b. Egypt, Jan. 10, 1917 (parents Am. citizens); s. James Wallace and Maude (Edgerton) B.; A.B., Monmouth Coll., 1937; M.B.A., Northwestern U., 1938, J.D., 1941; m. Sally Maenza, Feb. 2, 1957; children—Robert, Joan, D'arcy, Bruce, Stacey. Admitted to Ill. bar, 1941, D.C. bar, 1946, Wis. bar, 1968, Fla. bar, 1975, U.S. Supreme Ct. bar, 1948; atty. solicitor's office, U.S. Dept. Labor, Washington, 1941-42; atty. Tax Ct. U.S., Washington, 1942-43; pvt. practice law, Chgo., 1946-51; mem. firm Baird & Lundquist, Zion, Ill., 1958-67; sr. v.p., gen. counsel Universal Telephone, Inc., Milw., 1967—, also dir. Bd. dirs., pres. Kenneth Baird Found., 1968—. Served to lt. USNR, 1943-46, to lt. comdr., 1951-53. Mem. Ill., Wis., Fla., Chgo. bar assns. Republican. Presbyterian. Home: 4617 N Wilshire Rd Whitefish Bay WI 53211 Office: 231 W Wisconsin Ave Milwaukee WI 53203

BAIRD, JAMES NICHOLSON, JR., obstetrician-gynecologist; b. N.Y.C., Feb. 29, 1940; s. James Nicholson and Jean (Sanford) B.; B.S., Ohio State U., 1962, M.D. cum laude (Dean's award), 1966; m. Veronica De Prisco, Aug. 25, 1962; children—Lisa Nicholson, James Nicholson III. Intern, Riverside Methodist Hosp., Columbus, Ohio, 1966-67, resident in obstetrics and gynecology, 1968-71; practice medicine specializing in obstetrics and gynecology, Columbus, 1971—; mem. staff Riverside Meth. Hosp., Ohio State U. Hosp.; mem. faculty Ohio State U. Coll. Medicine. Diplomate Am. Bd. Obstetrics and Gynecology. Mem. AMA, Am. Coll. Obstetrics and Gynecology, Columbus Gynecol. and Obstetric Soc. (treas. 1975, sec. 1976, pres. elect 1977), Internat. Soc. Aquatic Medicine, Acad. Medicine of Franklin County, Ohio State Med. Assn., Alpha Omega Alpha, Phi Gamma Delta (pres. bd. dirs. 1971-73). Republican. Roman Catholic. Clubs: City, Columbus, Scioto Country, Pres.'s of Ohio State U. Home: 4700 Old Ravine Ct Columbus OH 43220 Office: 3545 Olentangy River Rd Columbus OH 43214

BAIRD, MARIE LOUISE (MRS. HUGH ALEXANDER BAIRD), ret. librarian; b. St. Paul, Feb. 28, 1910; d. Adolph and Etta Eunice (Kannary) Larson; B.A., Carleton Coll., 1932; M.A., Columbia, 1937; postgrad. Mankato State Coll., summers 1958-60; m. Hugh Alexander Baird, June 19, 1937; children—Gwen (Mrs. Donald Hagen), Helen (Mrs. James Philip Sundquist), Macaran. Tchr. pub. sch., Ellendale, Minn., 1932-34; tchr. English, librarian, drama coach, Dodge Center (Minn.) Pub. Sch., 1934-36, 1956-68, librarian, drama coach, 1968-74. Organizer, Dodge County Mental Health Assn., 1955. Bd. dirs. Dodge Center Library. Mem. ALA, Phi Beta Kappa. Republican. Conglist. Home: 303 Central Ave N Dodge Center MN 55927

BAIRD, OREN KENNETH, realtor; b. Charlestown, Ind., Jan. 25, 1919; s. Orva J. and Mary C. (Crum) B.; grad. Central Normal Coll., 1939; B.S., Centerbury Coll., 1947; attended sales and bus. mgmt. course Internat. Harvester Central Sch., Chgo., 1953, Ind. Sch. Real Estate, Indpls., 1961, Dale Carnegie Sales Course, 1967; m. Phyllis Stoller, Aug. 22, 1947; children—Chrisa, David, Dwight, Beth, Mark, Bruce. Tchr., Charlestown, Ind., 1939-41; owner, mgr. Kenny's Restaurant, Charlestown, Ind., 1940-41; sales trainee Internat. Harvester Co., Indpls., 1947, retail truck salesman, Indpls., 1951-52; owner, mgr. O.K.'s City Restaurant, Danville, Ind., 1947-50; post info. and edn. officer Camp Atterbury, Ind., 1950-51; pres., mgr. in charge of sales Internat. Harvester Dealer Acton, Ind., 1952-60; tchr. Franklin (Ind.) Twp. Schs., 1960-64; ins. agent, 1960—; real estate sales, 1961—; real estate broker, pres. Baird Co., Realtors, Indpls., 1968—. Chmn. Hendricks County (Ind.) Crusade for Freedom, 1951-52; chmn. Danville (Ind.) Boy Scout Fund, 1952, institutional rep. Boy Scouts Am., 1954-58. Pres. Acton (Ind.) Community Council, 1955; dir. of civilian defense, Hendricks County (Ind.), 1950; mem. Marion County (Ind.) Plan Commn., 1954-57; pres. Franklin Central High Sch. Bldg. Corp., 1958—. Trustee, Franklin Twp., 1967—. Served to 1st lt. 83rd Inf. Div., AUS, 1941-46. Decorated Purple Heart, Bronze Star medal. Named Man of the Year, Suburban Multl-list Exchange (SMILE), 1972. Mem. Indpls., Hancock County bds. of realtors, Nat. Inst. Farm and Land Brokers (pres. Ind. chpt. 1974-75), Nat. Inst. Real Estate Brokers, Nat. Assn. Home Bldrs. (asso. mem.), Suburban Multl-list Exchange (pres. 1972), Hot-Line Ltd. Inc. Realtors (E. rep. 1971—), Am. Legion, D.A.V., Wanamaker Bus. Mens Assn., '40 and 8', Canterbury Coll. Alumni Assn. (pres. 1950-51), Zeta Sigma Nu. Presbyterian (elder 1972—). Mason (Shriner). Home: 9960 Southeastern Ave Indianapolis IN 46239 Office: The Baird Co Realtors 1821 S Post Rd Indianapolis IN 46239

BAIRD, ROBERT DAHLEN, religions scholar, educator; b. Phila., June 29, 1933; s. Jesse Dahlen and Clara (Sonntag) B.; B.A., Houghton Coll., 1954; B.D., Fuller Theol. Sem., 1957; S.T.M., So. Meth. U., 1959; Ph.D., U. Iowa, 1964; m. Patty Jo Lutz, Dec. 18, 1954; children—Linda Sue, Stephen Robert, David Bryan, Janna Ann. Instr. philosophy and religion U. Omaha, 1962-65; fellow Asian religions Soc. for Religion in Higher Edn., 1965-66; asst. prof. religion U. Iowa, Iowa City, 1966-69, asso. prof., 1969-74, prof., 1974—; faculty fellow Am. Inst. Asian Studies, India, 1972. Mem. Am. Acad. Religion, Assn. Asian Studies. Democrat. Presbyterian. Contbr. articles in field to profl. jours.; author: Category Formation and the History of Religions, 1971; (with W. Richard Comstock, et al) Religion and Man: An Introduction, 1971; Indian and Far Eastern Religious Traditions, 1972; editor and contbr. Methodological Issues in Religious Studies, 1975. Home: Route 1 Box 67 Iowa City IA 52240 Office: School of Religion University of Iowa Iowa City IA 52242

BAISCH, STEPHEN JAMES, cons. engr.; b. Ironwood, Mich., Oct. 28, 1917; s. Michael Carl and Mary A. B.; B.M.E., U. Wis., Madison, 1942; m. Edith Anna Mary Moore, June 6, 1942; children—Michael, James, Timothy. With Thilmany Pulp & Paper Co., Kaukauna, Wis., 1945-58, chief engr., to 1958; pres. S.J. Baisch Assos., Inc., Kaukauna, 1958—; dir. Potsdam Paper Co. (N.Y.). Mem. sch. bd., 1960-63. Served from 2d lt. to maj. U.S. Army, 1942-45. Registered profl. engr., Wis. Mem. ASME, Soc. Profls., TAPPI, Nat., Wis. socs. profl. engrs., C. of C., Scabbard and Blade, Pi Mu Epsilon. Republican. Roman Catholic. Clubs: Butte Des Morts Country, Rotary, Lions, K.C., Elks. Patentee in field. Home: 111 Idlewild St Kaukauna WI 54130 Office: 809 Hyland Ave Kaukauna WI 54130

BAJEK, WALTER ADAM, mech. engr.; b. Chgo., Dec. 24, 1928; s. Walter J. and Clara (Haiden) B.; B.S., Ill. Inst. Tech., 1952, M.S., 1963; m. Rosemary F. Hackworth, Aug. 7, 1955; children—Amanda Carolyn, Elizabeth Rosemary. Instrument engr. Universal Oil Products Co., Des Plaines, Ill., 1949-67, sr. instrument engr., process div., 1967-69, asst. mgr. instrument devel. dept., 1970-75, mgr. Monirex Systems, 1975—; instr. basic instrumentation course Lewis Coll. Pres., Lombard PTA Council. Served with Chem. Corps, AUS, 1953-55. Decorated Army Commendation medal. Registered profl. engr., Ill. Fellow Instrument Soc. Am. (pres. Chgo. sect.; dir. chem. and petroleum div. 1966-68, v.p. Dist. VI, recipient award 1970, pres. 1975-76; chmn. honors and awards com. 1977), AAAS, Nat. Soc. Profl. Engrs.; mem. Ill. Soc. Profl. Engr., Chgo. Tech. Soc. Council (pres. 1970-72), USCG Aux. Lion (pres. 1973-74), K.C. (4 deg.). Contbr. papers to tech. lit. Home: 43 W Potomac St Lombard IL 60148 Office: 20 Uop Plaza Mount Prospect and Algonquin Rds Des Plaines IL 60016

BAJUS, BEVERLY ANN BROUGHTON (MRS. DONALD A. BAJUS), food co. exec.; b. Biggar, Sask., Can., Apr. 12, 1938; d. Roy S. and Helen T. (Fowler) Broughton; came to U.S., 1959; B.Sc., U. Man. (Can.), 1959; m. Donald A. Bajus, Aug. 9, 1958. Home economist in consumer kitchens Internat. Multifoods Corp. (formerly Internat. Milling Co., Inc.), Mpls., 1960-63, dir. kitchens, 1963-70, dir. new product devel., consumer products div., 1970-76, product mgr. Kretschmer Cereals, 1976—. Corporate rep. Downtown Council Mpls., 1972—, dir., 1974—. Bd. dirs., v.p. Cricket Theatre, 1974—, Greater Mpls. Arts Commn., 1977—; mem. career adv. panel St. Olaf Coll., Northfield, Minn., 1975—. Mem. Am. (hostess state chmn. 59th ann. meeting 1968), Minn. (adv. bd. 1966-67) home econs. assns., Home Economists in Bus. (nat. chmn. bylaws com. 1968-69), Twin Cities Home Economists in Bus. (chmn. 1965-66), Grocery Mfrs. Am. (consumer services com. forum chmn. 1969), U. Man. Alumni Assn. (pres. Minn. br. 1970-75), Kappa Kappa Gamma (v.p. 1965-66). Club: Zonta Internat. (bd. dirs., editor newsletter 1968-69) (Mpls.). Co-developer CoolRise method yeast baking. Home: 3414 Zenith Ave S Minneapolis MN 55416 Office: 1200 Multifoods Bldg Minneapolis MN 55402

BAKEN, ROBERT EDWARD, elec. engr.; b. Oak Park, Ill., Feb. 2, 1930; s. Edward Albert and Katherine C. (Schlegal) B.; student DePaul U., 1947-49; B.S., Ill. Inst. Tech., 1958; m. Barbara Marie Marik, Aug. 2, 1975. Draftsman Chgo. Park Dist., 1950-51, Commonwealth Edison, Chgo., 1953-55; with Dept. Pub. Works, City of Chgo., 1955-68, civil engr., 1958-68; with Dept. Water and Sewers, City of Chgo., 1968—, asst. engr. water distbn., 1975—. Served with U.S. Army, 1951-53. Mem. ASCE (del. to Ill. Engring. Council), Western Soc. Engrs. (chmn. community affairs div.), Am. Water Works Assn. Roman Catholic. Clubs: Elmhurst Country, Chgo. Dist. Golf Assn. Home: 4624 N Commons Dr Apt 410E Chicago IL 60656 Office: 1000 E Ohio St Chicago IL 60611

BAKER, BARNET, civil engr.; b. Boston, Oct. 7, 1898; s. Joseph and Sarah (Bloch) B.; B.S. in Civil Engring., Case Inst. Tech., 1922; m. Florence Kleinman, July 25, 1923; children—Saul Phillip, Melvin. Plant engr. Columbia Chem. Co., Barberton, Ohio, 1922-23; asst. civil engr. City of East Liverpool (Ohio), 1923-24; mem. engring. staff City Cleve., 1924-69, asst. civil engr., sr. asst. civil engr., civil engr., 1924-63, chief civil engr., 1963-69. Mem. social agy. com. Jewish Welfare Fedn. Cleve., 1948-57. Bd. dirs. Ind. Montefiore Shelter Home, pres., 1952-54. Zone warden, Cuyahoga County, Ohio, World War II. Registered profl. engr., Ohio. Fellow ASCE (life); mem. Cleve. (charter, life), Ohio, Nat. socs. profl. engrs., Am. Pub. Works Assn. (life). Mason (Shriner, 32 deg., pres. Sr. Shriners Club 1974-75). Home: 3263 DeSota Ave Cleveland Heights OH 44118

BAKER, BETTY LOUISE, mathematician, educator; b. Chgo., Oct. 17, 1937; d. Russell James and Lucille Juanita (Timmons) B.: B.E., Chgo. State U., 1961, M.A., 1964; Ph.D., Northwestern U., 1971. Tchr. math. Harper High Sch., Chgo., 1961-70; tchr. math. Hubbard High Sch., Chgo., 1970—, also chmn. dept. Cultural arts chmn. Hubbard Parents-Tchrs.-Student Assn., 1974-76, 1st v.p., 1977—; organist Hope Lutheran Ch., 1963—. Univ. fellow, 1969-70; certified tchr. math., elementary grades, Ill. Mem. Nat., Ill. councils tchrs. of math., Math. Assn. Am., Chgo. Tchrs. Union, Nat. Council Parents and Tchrs. (life), Kappa Delta Pi, Pi Lambda Theta, Sch. Sci. and Math. Assn., Luth. Collegiate Assn., Kappa Mu Epsilon, Rho Sigma Tau, Mu Alpha Theta (sponsor). Club: Walther League Hiking. Contbr. articles to profl. jours. Home: 3214 W 85th St Chicago IL 60652 Office: 6200 S Hamlin St Chicago IL 60629

BAKER, BRUCE NELSON, educator; b. St. Louis, Dec. 9, 1930; s. Roland Sears and Elvera Anne (Bergmeier) B.; A.B., Princeton, 1953; M.B.A., Stanford, 1955, postgrad., 1957; D.Pub. Adminstrn. with distinction, George Washington U., 1971; m. Mary Kathryn Shaw, Feb. 27, 1965; children—Sara Susan, Ashlee Anne, Andrea Lynne, Melanie Marie, James Winslow. Sr. mfg. engr., ops. planning analyst Lockheed Aircraft Corp., Sunnyvale, Cal., 1957-61; mgmt. systems supr. Philco-Ford Corp., Palo Alto, Calif., 1961-62; sr. cons. Mgmt. Systems Corp., Newport Beach, Calif., 1962-64; lectr. U. Calif. Extension at Berkeley, 1964-65; lectr., prof. U. So. Calif., Los Angeles, 1965-69; lectr. George Washington U., 1969-71; asso. prof. Boston Coll., Chestnut Hill, Mass., 1971-73; prof. mgmt. U. Wis., Oshkosh, 1973—. Pres., InterSystems, Inc., mgmt. cons., 1973—. Dir. long range planning task force Fox River area council Girl Scouts U.S.A., 1973-75. Served with USNR, 1956-57. NASA grantee, 1972-74. Mem. Am. Soc. Pub. Adminstrn., Acad. Mgmt., Project Mgmt. Inst., World Future Soc. (v.p. Boston-Cambridge chpt. 1971-73), Gen. Soc. Mayflower Descs. Author: An Introduction to PERT-CPM, 1964. Editorial bd. Project Mgmt. Quar., 1973—. Home: 1215 Spruce St Oshkosh WI 54901

BAKER, CARLYLE, oil co. exec.; b. Somerville, Ohio, May 25, 1917; s. I.C. and Ruth (Muff) B.; B.S., Ohio State U., 1938; student Princeton, 1943, Harvard, 1943-44, N.Y. U., 1965; m. Lillian Callaway, May 11, 1940; children—Carole, Constance. Chmn. bd., chief exec. officer Certified Oil Co., Columbus, Ohio, 1939—, now chief exec. officer; pres. Midwest Distbg. Co., Xtra Oil Co., Columbus. Served to lt. USNR 1943-46. Mem. Columbus Petroleum Club (pres.), Am. Petroleum Inst., Ohio Petroleum Marketers Assn., Independent Gasoline Marketers Council, Independent Oil Marketers Ind. Clubs: Rotarian. Scioto Country, Columbus, Columbus Athletic, Young Businessmen's, Columbus, Gyro; Ocean Reef (Key Largo, Fla.). Home: 1981 Cambridge Blvd Columbus OH 43221 Office: 303 S Front St Columbus OH 43215

BAKER, CLARENCE ALBERT, SR., structural steel constrn. co. exec.; b. Kansas City, Kans., July 2, 1919; s. Earl Retting and Nancy Jefferson (Price) B.; student Kans. U., 1939-40, Finley Engring. Coll., 1937-39, Ohio State U., 1967, 69; m. Marjorie Ellen Yoakum, Mar. 19, 1959; children—Clarence Albert, Jorgeann (Mrs. Harry L. Hiebert); stepchildren—Robert Beale, Barbara Anne Stegner (Mrs. Robert T. Kenney II). With Kansas City (Kan.) Structural Steel Co., 1937—, shop supt., 1959-68, v.p., plant mgr., 1968-73, v.p. plant ops., 1973-77, v.p. engring., 1977—, also dir.; dir. All Points Van Lines. Curriculum adv. Kansas City (Mo.) Met. Jr. Coll., 1971-72, Kansas City Vocat. Tech. Sch., 1973—. Committeeman, Republican Party, 1970-72; chmn. City of Mission (Kans.) Rep. Party, 1970-72; councilman, City of Merriam, Kans., 1957-59. Adv. bd. Wentworth Mil. Acad. Served with USNR, 1944-46. Mem. Am. Welding Soc. (pres. 1970-71, chmn. 1970), Kans. Engring. Soc., Kansas City C. of C. Mason. Home: 6635 Milhaven Dr Mission KS 66202 Office: 21st and Metropolitan Sts Kansas City KS 66106

BAKER, CLIFTON EARL, engring. and constrn. co. exec.; b. Harriettsville, Ohio, May 11, 1923; s. Lewis Raymond and Freda Edith (Parks) B.; B.S., Ohio U., 1943; M.S., Ohio State U., 1947; m. Louise Hodgson, Aug. 20, 1947; children—Peggy Lee, Terrie Sue. Jr. structural designer Goodyear Aircraft Co., Akron, Ohio, 1943-44, Austin Co., Cleve., 1945-46; structural designer Design Service Co., 1947; sr. structural designer H. K. Ferguson Co., Cleve., 1947-51, structural group leader, Ft. Detrick, Md., 1951, structural div. chief, project engr., Frederick, Md., 1951-53, staff engr., Cleve., 1953-54, asst. dist. chief engr., Los Angeles, 1954-55, San Francisco, 1955-57, dist. chief engr., Cleve., 1957-59, dir. indsl. bldgs. div., 1959-61, dir. missile div., Los Angeles, 1961-63, v.p., dir., Cleve., 1963-74, pres., 1974—; pres. H.K. Ferguson Engring. Co., 1961—; chmn. bd. Hale & Kulgren, 1974—. Served with AUS, 1944-45. Decorated 2 Bronze star medals. Registered profl. engr., Ala., Alaska, Ariz., Ark., Calif., Colo., Conn., Del., Fla., Ga., Idaho, Iowa, Ky., La., Maine, Md., Mass., Mich., Minn., Miss., Mo., Mont., Nebr., Nev., N.H., N.J., N.Mex., N.Y., Ohio, Okla., Oreg., Pa., S.C., S.D., Tenn., Tex., Utah, Va., Vt., Wash., W.Va., Wis., Wyo. Mem. Council on Engring. Laws, The Beavers, Moles, Am. Ordnance Assn., Am. Ry. Engring. Assn., ASTM, ASCE, Nat., Cleve., Ohio socs. profl. engrs. Mason. Clubs: Westwood Country (Rocky River, Ohio), Clev. Athletic. Home: 21565 Avalon Dr Rocky River OH 44116 Office: 1 Erieview Plaza Cleveland OH 44114

BAKER, DONALD EUGENE, librarian; b. Winamac, Ind., Oct. 8, 1945; s. Willard Jared and Beulah Belle (Taylor) B.; A.B., Ind. U., 1966, A.M., 1968, M.Library Sci., 1976; Asst. editor Indiana Mag. of History, Bloomington, 1972-74; head librarian Willard Library of Evansville (Ind.), 1976—. Served with USAF, 1968-72. Mem. Tri State Genealogical Soc. (dir. ex officio), Four Rivers Area Library Services Authority (dir.), Ind. U. Grad. Library Sch. Alumni Assn. (dir.), Soc. Indiana Archivists, Midwest Archives Conf., Ind. Library Assn., ALA, Adminstrs. Large Pub. Libraries in Ind. Episcopalian. Club: Kiwanis. Home: 874 Sunset Tower Evansville IN 47713 Office: Willard Library 21 1st Ave Evansville IN 47710

BAKER, DONALD ROBERT, indsl. engr.; b. Kansas City, Mo., Sept. 5, 1903; s. Leonard Hassell and Roma Lillian (Horn) B.; B.S., Mo. Sch. Mines, 1925; m. Vera Christensen, June 30, 1928; children—Jean Elizabeth (Mrs. John L. Morrissey), Robert Christensen. Mining engr. Oglebay, Norton & Co., Montreal, Wis., 1925; mine supt. Comml. Metals Mining Co., Joplin, Mo., 1926; chief-of-party, mine examiner Poillon and Poirier, Nfld., 1926; v.p., gen. mgr. Ralph-Baker Corp., Borger, Tex., 1926-29; petroleum engr. Indian Ter., Ill. Oil Co., Oklahoma City, 1930-33; cons., air conditioning contractor, Kansas City, Mo., 1933-42; engr., mgr. research Marley Co., Kansas City, Mo., 1942-63; engring. cons., Blue Springs, Mo., 1963—. Pres. Sni A Bar Twp. Republican Club, 1958; dir., mem. exec. com. Jackson County Rep. Club, 1962—. Registered profl. engr., Mo. Mem. Am. Inst. Mining Engrs., ASME, Am. Soc. Heating, Refrigeration and Air Conditioning Engrs., Am. Wood Preservers Assn., Am. Scandinavian Found., Jackson County Hist. Soc. Friends of Art, People to People, Native Sons Kansas City, Pi Kappa Alpha (nat. officer 1947-51), Theta Tau, Tau Beta Pi. Methodist. Mason. Clubs: Blue Springs Golf and Country, Scandinavian of Kansas City. Patentee in field. Contbr. articles to profl. jours. Home: 1800 Smith St Blue Springs MO 64015

BAKER, DONALD WHITELAW, educator; b. Boston, Jan. 30, 1923; s. Merrill Ellsworth and Isa Margaret (Dempsey) B.; A.B., Brown U., 1947, A.M., 1949, Ph.D., 1955; postgrad. Harvard, summer 1950, 51; m. Natalie Jane Krentz, May 2, 1945; children—Pamela Jane, Alison Jean. Asst. English, Brown U., 1947-48, instr. English, 1948-52; asst. prof. English, Wabash Coll., 1953-58, dir. drama, 1954-60, asso. prof., 1958-67, prof., 1967—, poet in residence, 1965—, Milligan prof. English lit., 1976—; dir. Gt. Lakes Colls. Assn. New Writers Awards, 1976—. Pres. Montgomery County (Ind.) Democratic Men's Club, 1968—; pub. relations coordinator West Central Ind. Citizens for McCarthy, 1968; mem. New Dem. Coalition, Lafayette, Ind., 1968—. Served to 1st lt. USAAF, 1942-46. Recipient McLain-McTurnan award Wabash Coll., 1967. Fellow writing fiction Nat. Endowment for Arts, 1974-75. Mem. A.A.U.P., Nat. Council Tchrs. English (adv. bd. for achievement awards 1968-71), Modern Lang. Assn., Phi Beta Kappa. Author: Twelve Hawks and Other Poems, 1974. Contbr. to periodicals and anthologies. Address: 16 Harry Freedman Pl Crawfordsville IN 47933

BAKER, EDWIN ROSS, nuclear engr.; b. Washington, Mo., Nov. 22, 1951; s. Ross Jessie and Edith Verline (Smith) B.; B.S. in Nuclear Engring. (Curators scholar), U. Mo., 1973. Field engr., nuclear power stas., Gen. Electric Co., Conn., Ill., Nebr., Minn., Japan, 1973—. Mem. Am. Nuclear Soc. Baptist. Office: General Electric Co 814 Commerce Ave Oak Brook IL 60521

BAKER, FRANK MYERS, advt. agy. exec.; b. Reading, Mich., Nov. 15, 1908; s. Frank E. and Florence (Myers) B.; student Ohio Wesleyan U., 1930; m. Dorothea G. Belton, June 14, 1931; children—David J., Florence (Mrs. Ronald Fluty). Radio announcer CBS, Chgo., 1935-36; writer NBC, Chgo., 1936; chmn. Grant, Wright & Baker Inc., Chgo., 1953—; pres., chmn. bd. Cor-Com Inc., Chgo., 1972—. Bd. mgrs. Chgo. Met. YMCA, 1963-76; bd. dirs. Off-the-Street Club, 1964-76. Served as 1st. lt., USMCR, 1944-46. Mem. Chgo. Federated Advt. Club (pres. 1959-61), Advt. Fedn. Am. (dir. 1961). Club: Chgo. Yacht. Home: Bloomingdale MI 49026 Office: 520 N Michigan Ave Chicago IL 60611

BAKER, JAMES DAVID, univ. adminstr.; b. St. Louis, Jan. 8, 1946; s. James Matthews and Margaret Ellen (Brewer) B.; B.S., U. Mo.-Columbia, 1969, M.Ed., 1970; m. Elizabeth Stuart McMullen, Dec. 22, 1966; children—Patrick Lyman, John Matthews. Instr. psychology, supr. student teaching in behavioral sci. U. Mo., Columbia, 1968-70; guidance counselor Columbia Pub. Schs., 1970-77; asso. dir. admissions, aids and awards Columbia Coll., 1977—. Mem. Columbia City Council Youth Commn., 1976—; treas. Columbia Police Res., 1975—, dir., 1978—; asst. dist. commr. Boy Scouts Am., 1976—; bd. dirs. Front Door Youth Counseling Agy., 1977—. Mem. Mo. Tchrs. Assn., Mo. Guidance Assn., Am. Personnel and Guidance Assn. (profl.), Pub. Offender Counselors Assn., Phi Delta Kappa. Presbyterian. Home: 1208 Subella St Columbia MO 65201 Office: Columbia Coll 10th and Rogers Sts Columbia MO 65201

BAKER, JAMES EDWARD SPROUL, lawyer; b. Evanston, Ill., May 23, 1912; s. John Clark and Hester (Sproul) B.; A.B., Northwestern U., 1933, J.D., 1936; m. Eleanor Lee Dodgson, Oct. 2, 1937 (dec. Sept. 1972); children—John Lee, Edward Graham. Admitted to Ill. bar, 1936, to practice U.S. Supreme Ct., 1957; practiced in Chgo., 1936—; asso. firms Cutting, Moore & Sidley, 1936. Sidley. McPherson, Austin and Burgess, 1937-41, 46-47, partner Sidley, Austin, Burgess & Harper, 1948-49, partner firm Sidley, Austin, Burgess & Smith, 1949-67; partner firm Sidley & Austin, Chgo., 1967—. Lectr., Northwestern U. Sch. Law, Chgo., 1951-52. Nat. chmn. Stanford Parents Com., 1970-75. Served to comdr. USNR, 1941-46. Fellow Am. Coll. Trial Lawyers (regent 1974—, sec. 1977—); mem. Am., Ill., Chgo. bar assns., Bar Assn. 7th Fed. Circuit, Order of Coif, Phi Lambda Upsilon, Sigma Nu. Republican. Methodist. Clubs: University, Midday, Legal, Law (Chgo.); Westmoreland Country (Wilmette, Ill.). Home: 1300 N Lake Shore Dr Chicago IL 60610 Office: 1 First Nat Plaza Chicago IL 60603

BAKER, JERRY WAYNE, library adminstr.; b. Hamilton, Ohio, Aug. 25, 1933; s. Broadus and Lucille (Hall) B.; A.B., Murray State U., 1957; M.A., Ind. U., 1966; m. Beverley Anne Leeper, July 9, 1955; children—Carol Elizabeth, Bradley Wayne, Scott David. Tchr. various schs., 1958-63; dir. Owensboro-Daviess County (Ky.) Pub. Library, 1963-65; asst. dir. U. Evansville (Ind.) library, 1965-66, asso. dir., 1966-67; dir. Ohio No. U. Ada, 1967—. Active Boy Scouts Am., 1962-63, 68-70. Served to 1st lt. AUS, 1957, 58. Mem. Ohio Library Assn. (chmn. coll. and univ. roundtable 1971-72, chmn. awards and honors com. 1977-78), Ohio Coll. Assn. (pres. librarian's sect. 1972-73), Acad. Library Assn. Ohio. Home: 224 Grandview Blvd Ada OH 45810 Office: Heterick Meml Library Ohio Northern U 525 S Main St Ada OH 45810

BAKER, JOHN BRADEN, neurologist; b. Brockville, Ont., Can., Jan. 3, 1929; s. Elmore Bruce and Nelda Beatrice (Jackson) B.; A.B., Syracuse U., 1951; M.D., U. Buffalo, 1955; m. Juanita Evelyn King, Aug. 13, 1960; children—Laura Beth, John Bruce. Intern, Boston City Hosp., 1955-56; resident in neurology Boston City Hosp., 1957-59; instr. neurology Marguette U.-Med. Coll. Wis., Milw., 1961-62, asst. prof., 1962-67, asso. prof., 1967-70, asso. clin. prof., 1970—, chmn. dept. neurology, 1965-67; individual practice medicine, specializing in neurology Waukesha, Wis., 1970—; chief medicine Elmbrook Meml. Hosp., Milw., 1975—; chief neurology, EEG labs. Waukesha Meml. Hosp. and Elmbrook Meml. Hosp., 1970—. Served with USNR, 1959-61. Mem. AMA, Wis., Waukesha County med. socs., Am. EEG Soc., Am. Acad. Neurology, Assn. Research Nervous and Mental Diseases. Methodist. Researcher multiple sclerosis, 1964—, Parkinsonism, 1969—; cons. in field. Home: 830 Janacek Dr Waukesha WI 53186 Office: 1111 Delafield St Waukesha WI 53186

BAKER, JOHN STEVENSON (MICHAEL DYREGROV), author, collector, donor; b. Mpls., June 18, 1931; s. Everette Barrette and Ione May (Kadletz) B.; B.A. cum laude, Pomona Coll., Claremont Colls., 1953; M.D., U. Calif. at Berkeley and San Francisco, 1957. Writer, 1958—; book cataloger Walker Art Center, Mpls., 1958-59; editor, writer neurol. research articles L.E. Phillips Psychobiol. Research Fund, Mpls., 1960-61. Recipient Distinguished Service award Minn. State Hort. Soc., 1976. Mem. Nu Sigma Nu. Contbr. articles and poetry to various publs. Donor numerous varieties of plants to Minn. Landscape Arboretum and Nat. Arboretum, papers of LeRoi Jones and Hart Crane to Yale U., Brahms recs. to Bennington Coll., many others. Office: PO Box 16007 Minneapolis MN 55416

BAKER, LEE WENDELL, pub. relations counsel; b. Bowen, Ill., Dec. 27, 1919; s. Samuel Albert and Ethel May (Nash) B.; B.S., Bradley U., 1942; m. George Ann McGreevy, June 9, 1945 (dec.); m. 2d, Jean Hammond Otto, Nov. 23, 1973. Editor, writer UPI, St. Louis, Indpls., Chgo. and Milw., 1942-45; successively pub. relations asst., mgr. information services, mgr. information and community services Allis-Chalmers Corp., Milw., 1945-65; v.p. Owen King Assos., Milw., 1966-67; pres., owner Lee Baker Assos., Milw., 1967—; instr. pub. relations U. Wis. Extension, 1954-56. Bd. dirs. Family Service of Milw., 1958-72, Greater Milw. chpt. A.R.C., 1968-70, Milw. Mental Health Assn., 1964-77, pres., 1974-76; bd. dirs. Ballet Found. Milw., 1970—. Recipient appreciation and pub. service awards A.R.C., Milw. Mental Health Assn. Mem. Pub. Relations Soc. Am. (accredited, bd. dirs. Wis. chpt. 1962-65, pres. 1964-65), West Allis C. of C. (bd. dirs. 1960-65). Club: Milw. Press (past gov., v.p.). Contbr. articles profl. mags., trade jours. Home: 1033 E Ogden Ave Milwaukee WI 53202 Office: 1442 N Farwell Ave Milwaukee WI 53202

BAKER, LUELLA AUSTELIA, archives aid; b. Kansas City, Mo., Nov. 15, 1943; d. Harold Elijah and Elizabeth (Henry) B.; student pub. schs., Los Angeles. Clerk, IRS, Los Angeles, Calif., 1963-68; file clerk VA, W. Los Angeles, Calif., 1969-72; archives aid Fed. Archives and Record Center, GSA, Laguna Niguel, Calif., from 1974. Mem. Nat. Trust for Historic Preservation. Mem. Peace and Freedom Party. Seventh-day Adventist. Address: PO Box 19893 Kansas City MO 64108

BAKER, MARIAN GRAY CHAMBERS, occupational therapist; b. Youngstown, Ohio, Feb. 5, 1931; d. James Edward and Josie Bell (Alston) Chambers; B.S., Washington U., St. Louis, 1958; M.A. in Vocat. Rehab. Counseling, Wayne State U., 1977; m. James Baker, Aug. 2, 1958. Staff therapist Deaconess Hosp., St. Louis, 1958-63; dir. occupational and recreational therapy Kenny-Mich. Rehab. Found., Pontiac (Mich.) Gen. Hosp., 1963—. Cons. occupational therapy Grovecrest Convalescent Center, Pontiac, 1970—. Vol. case aide worker Oakland County Juvenile Ct., 1969—. Mem. World Fedn. Occupational Therapists, Am., Mich. occupational therapy assns., Negro Bus. and Profl. Women. Elk. Home: 163 Green St Pontiac MI 48053 Office: Pontiac Gen Hosp Seminole at W Huron Pontiac MI 48053

BAKER, MARVIN GLENN, educator; b. Kokomo, Ind., Oct. 23, 1925; s. Leonard Glenn and Iva (Mahres) B.; B.Ed., Marion Coll., 1949; M.A., Ball State Tchrs. Coll., 1953, Ed.D., 1964; m. Lois Evelyn Jackson, Aug. 11, 1946; children—Evangeline Ruth, Verna Jean, Della Jane. Tchr., Andrews (Ind.) High Sch., 1949-50; instr. George Fox Coll., Newberg, Oreg., 1950-52; tchr. Willamina (Oreg.) Elem. Schs., 1952-54, Marion (Ind.) Pub. Schs., 1954-61; asst. prof. edn. Ind. Central Coll., Indpls., 1962-64, prof. edn., chmn. dept. edn., 1964-67; prof., chmn. div. Marion (Ind.) Coll., 1967-70; resource tchr. Marion Community Schs., 1970—; ednl. cons. Creative Ednl. Services, Inc., 1967—; mem. summer faculty Ball State Tchrs. Coll., 1962. Bd. dirs. Marion (Ind.) Urban League, 1960-62; founder, dir. T-Cay-O, College Age Youth Outreach, 1968, Singing Travelers, 1969—. NDEA fellow, 1961-62. Mem. NEA, Ind. State Tchrs. Assn. (past pres. elem. sect. eastern div.), Nat. Council Tchrs. English (mem. com. on creativity and children's writing), Phi Delta Kappa. Author: Motivation for the Release of Creativity Through Creative Writing, 1963; Land of the Mighty Miami, 1964; Phonetic Discrimination Inventory, 1965; Meet Albert Lee, 1965; (book of songs) Creatively His, 1973; My Home Town, 1973; Peter Marshall: Messenger for the Chief, 1975. Home: 4420 S Selby St Marion IN 46952

BAKER, MARY EVELYN SHOEMAKER (MRS. RICHARD HEINLEY BAKER), ret. librarian; b. Columbus, Ohio, May 8, 1912; d. Abram Jackson and Martha Maria (Dailey) Shoemaker; B.A., Ohio State U., 1934; M.S. in Library Sci., Western Res. U., 1935; m. Richard Heinley Baker, Sept. 18, 1937; children—Richard Shoemaker, David Guy. Mem. staff library Ohio State U. at Columbus, 1935-37, 38-44, 55-74, part-time, 1955-66, adminstrv. asst., 1958, serial cataloger, 1958-67, asst. reviser, sr. cataloger, 1967-68, head serial div. catalog dept., 1968-71, head catalog dept., 1971-74. Den mother Cub Scouts Am., Columbus, 1953-58. Mem. Am. (sec. serials sect. resources and tech. div. 1970-73), Ohio, Ohioana (chmn. various coms.) library assns., Ohio Valley Group Tech. Service Librarians, PEO, Phi Mu. Congregationalist (library com. 1950—, chmn. 1962-64, 76—, co-chmn. 1974-76). Clubs: University's Women (past pres.), Agricultural Circle (past pres.), (Columbus). Home: 2444 Arlington Ave Columbus OH 43221

BAKER, RAY MITCHELL, motor express co. exec.; b. Washington, Ind., June 20, 1917; s. Earl Ray and Effie May (Conolty) B.; student pub. schs.; m. Mary Elizabeth Stone, Jan. 27, 1940; children—Paul M., Mary Rae, Beverly Ann, Emily Jane. Salesman classified advt. Washington Daily Times, 1950-52, circulation, 1952-54, small feature writer, 1954-55, city editor, 1955-56, news editor, 1956-64; one of founders, mng. editor Valley Advance, Vincennes, Ind., 1964-67; mem. faculty Vincennes U., 1964-67, now guest lectr.; gen. mgr. Klemeyer Lumber Co., Inc., 1967-68; dir. public relations and advt. I & S-McDaniel, Inc., Vincennes, 1968-74, dir. corporate relations, 1974-76; sales rep. Briggs Transp. Co., 1977—. Active rehab. of alcoholics; permanent committeeman Red Cross Blood Bank Program, 1971. Bd. mem. Bus., Industry and Small Community Resource Service, 1972; dir. Daviess County United Fund, 1958-59. Mem. Washington City Plan Commn., 1957-64, v.p., 1958-59; mem. Washington Zoning Bd. Appeals, 1961-64. Served from pvt. to master sgt., AUS, 1943-46. Recipient Byliner award Vincennes U., 1970. Mem. Am. Legion (vice comdr. 1953-54), Washington C. of C. (founding com.). Democrat. Clubs: Elks, Rotary. Home: 424 N 4th St Vincennes IN 47591

BAKER, ROBERT CLIFFORD, lawyer; b. Madison, S.D., May 21, 1924; s. Charles William and Alice E. (Fods) B.; B.A., U. Minn., 1948; J.D., George Washington U., 1952; m., Aug. 20, 1955; children—Charles, William, Emily, Beverly; m. 2d, Elvera Sellin, Oct. 22, 1977. Admitted to D.C. bar, 1952, Minn. bar, 1955, U.S. Patent and Trademark office, 1952; patent searcher law dept. Swift & Co., Washington, 1948-50; inventions analyst Office of Naval Research, Dept. Navy, Washington, 1951-52; asso. firm Abbott, Coulter & Kinney, St. Paul, 1954-64, partner, 1965-67; individual practice law St. Paul, 1967—. Mem. Mental Health Study Com. St. Paul, 1967-68; del. Minn. State Republican Conv., 1972; mem. worship and music com. Gloria Dei Luth. Ch., 1977. Served with USAAF, 1943-45, U.S. Army, 1952-53. Mem. Am., Minn., Ramsey County bar assns., Am. Patent Law Assn., Minn. Patent and Trademark Law Assn. (chmn. Internat. indsl. property legislation com. 1977). Clubs: Lost Spur Country, Shriner, Masorn, Toastmasters Internat. (gov. Area 12 St. Paul 1975-76). Home: 80 Birnamwood Dr Burnsville MN 55337 Office: 1395 Northwestern National Bank Bldg St Paul MN 55101

BAKER, ROBERT EUGENE, orthodontist; b. St. Paul, Mar. 31, 1923; s. Joseph O. and Eleanor (Morrison) B.; D.D.S., U. Minn., 1945; m. Marillyn June Harris, Sept. 6, 1945; children—Lynn Sandra, Charles Robert, James Harris. Practice dentistry specializing in orthodontics, St. Paul, 1947—; pres. Dr. Robert E. Baker Ltd., 1970—. Mem. City Council Dellwood (Minn.), 1974-76. Served with USN, 1945-47. Fellow Am. Coll. Dentists; mem. ADA, Minn. Dental Assn., St. Paul Dist. Dental Soc., m. Assn. Orthodontists, Midwestern, Minn. socs. orthodontists, Central Assn. Dentists and Physician, Charles H. Tweed Found. for Orthodontic Research, Upper Midwest Orthodontic Study Club # 1, Xi Psi Phi, Sigma Alpha Epsilon. Episcopalian. Club: Rotary. Home: 11 Dellwood Ave White Bear Lake MN 55110 Office: 1044 Lowry Medical Arts Bldg St Paul MN 55102

BAKER, ROBERT HAROLD, dentist; b. nr. Castlewood, S.D., Sept. 25, 1901; s. Charles Frederick and Marie Ann (Krause) B.; D.D.S., U. Minn., 1924; m. Janice Amelia Moore, Apr. 13, 1930; children—Sherry Ann (Mrs. Clayton Shoemaker), Nancy Lou (Mrs. Harlan Teskey). Practice dentistry, Blue Earth, Minn., 1924—. Mem. Blue Earth Bd. Pub. Works, 1947-71, Blue Earth Cemetery Bd., 1956—, Blue Earth Charter Commn. Served to lt. comdr., Dental Corps, USNR, World War II. Mem. So. Minn. Dental Soc. (pres.) Am., Minn. (trustee 1952-58, v.p. 1963-64) dental assns., Am. Legion (comdr. 1949), C. of C. of Blue Earth (past pres.), Delta Sigma Delta. Republican. Episcopalian. Mason (Shriner), Kiwanian (past pres.). Clubs: Riverside Golf (Blue Earth); Century (U. Minn.). Address: 1234 S Galbraith St Blue Earth MN 56013

BAKER, SAUL PHILLIP, physician; b. Cleve., Dec. 7, 1924; s. Barnet and Florence (Kleinman) B.; B.S. in Physics, Case Inst. Tech., 1945; postgrad. Western Res. U., 1946-47; M.Sc. in Physiology, Ohio State U., 1949, M.D., 1953, Ph D. in Physiology 1957. Intern Cleve. Met. Gen. Hosp., 1953-54; sr. asst. surgeon gerontology br. Nat. Heart Inst., NIH, Balt. City Hosps. and Johns Hopkins Hosp., Balt., 1954-56; sr. asst. resident in internal medicine U. Chgo. Hosps., 1956-57; asst. prof. internal medicine Chgo. Med. Sch., 1957-62; asso. prof. internal medicine Cook County Grad. Sch. Medicine, Chgo., 1958-62; practice medicine specializing in geriatrics, cardiology, internal medicine, Cleve., 1962-70, 72—; head dept. geriatrics St. Vincent Charity Hosp., Cleve. 1964-67; now with Gerontology Research Center Nat. Inst. Aging NIH; mem. staff Hillcrest Hosp.; cons. internal medicine and cardiology Bur. Disability Determination, Old-Age and Survivors Ins., Social Security Adminstrn., 1963—; cons. internal medicine City of Cleve., 1964—; medicare med. cons. Gen. Am. Life Ins. Co., St. Louis, 1970-71; cons. internal medicine and cardiology Ohio Bur. Workmen's Compensation, 1964—; cons. cardiovascular disease FAA, 1973—; cons. internal medicine and cardiology State of Ohio, 1974—. Mem. sci. council Am. Heart Assn. Northeastern Ohio affiliate; adv. com. Sr. Adult div. Jewish Community Center Cleve.; mem. com. older people Fedn. Community Planning Cleve. Fellow Am. Coll. Cardiology, AAAS, Gerontol. Soc. (regent for Ohio), Am. Geriatrics Soc., Cleve. Med. Library Assn.; mem. Am. Physiol. Soc., Am., Ohio med. assns., N.Y. Acad. Scis., Chgo. Soc. Internal Medicine, Am. Fedn. Clin. Research, Soc. Exptl. Biology and Medicine, Diabetes Assn. Greater Cleveland (profl. sect.), Am. Heart Assn. (fellow council arteriosclerosis), Nat. Assn. Disability Examiners, Nat. Rehab. Assn., Am. Pub. Health Assn., Assn. Am. Med. Coll., Acad. Medicine Cleve. (council epidemiology and prevention), Internat. Soc. Cardiology, Sigma Xi, Phi Delta Epsilon, Sigma Alpha Mu (past pres. Cleve. alumni). Mason (32 deg. Shriner). Club: Cleveland Clinical (past sec.). Contbr. articles to profl. sci. jours. Home: 200 Chatham Way Mayfield Heights OH 44124 Office: 6803 Mayfield Rd Mayfield Heights OH 44124

BAKER, WADE FRANKLIN, lawyer; b. nr. Carbondale, Ill., Dec. 30, 1919; s. Robert David and Lillian May (Damron) B.; B.E., So. Ill. U., 1941; LL.B., Lincoln Coll. of Law, 1950; m. Mary Eleanor LaClair, June 29, 1947; 1 dau., Denise Ann. Asst. sec., counsel Ill. Bar Assn., 1946-57; admitted to Ill. bar, 1950, Mo. bar, 1957; exec. dir., editor jour. Mo. Bar, Jefferson City, 1957—. Bd. dirs. YMCA, 1969-70, Meml. Hosp., Jefferson City, 1970—, pres., 1971-72. Served to maj., arty. AUS, 1942-46, 51-52. Decorated Bronze Star. Mem. Mo. Bar, Am., Cole County bar assns., Am. Judicature Soc., Nat. Assn. Bar Execs., Phi Alpha Delta, Kappa Phi Kappa. Methodist (dir., trustee, 1958-72). Mason. Clubs: Jefferson City Country, Rotary (pres. Jefferson City 1966-67). Author: (with E. A. Richter) Public Attitudes Survey of Legal Profession in Missouri, 1963. Home: 2505 Orchard Ln Jefferson City MO 65101 Office: 326 Monroe St Jefferson City MO 65101

BAKER, WAYNE, ednl. service co. exec.; b. Taylor, Mich., May 14, 1942; s. Clarence and Louise (O'Guin) B.; A.A., Mich. Christian Jr. Coll., 1962; B.A., David Lipscomb Coll., 1964; postgrad. Pepperdine Coll., 1969-70; m. Darlene J.L. Pobur, July 28, 1962; children—Terry, Jodi, Gwendolyn, Brent, Elizabeth. Admissions counselor Mich. Christian Jr. Coll., 1965-68; asso. dir. admissions Pepperdine U., Malibu, Calif., 1968-70; exec. v.p. Youth Outreach Found., Memphis and editor Teenage Christian Mag., Memphis, 1969-71; v.p. mktg. Coll. Service Corp., Southfield, Mich., 1975—. Recipient European Study grant Youth Outreach Found., 1970. Mem. Am. Assn. Admissions Counselors, Am. Assn. Collegiate Admissions Counselors and Registrars, Mich. Fin. Aid Assn. Contbr. articles to ch. related jours. Home: 760 Center St Northville MI 48167 Office: 29200 Southfield Rd Southfield MI 48076

BAKER, WESLEY CARREL, agrl. products co. exec.; b. Leon, Iowa, July 20, 1919; s. Vernon Lee and Esther May (Norman) B.; B.S., Iowa State U., 1952; m. Clarine G. Morrison, Nov. 11, 1939; children—Ronald C., Sheryl Lynn (Mrs. John Diedenhoffen). Salesman, Colonial Baking Co., Des Moines, 1946-48, Omar Baking Co., Des Moines, 1948-50; with Internat. Multifoods, Inc., Mpls., 1953—, corporate v.p., gen. mgr. agrl. products div., 1969—. Served with USNR, 1944-46. Mem. Am. Feed Mfrs. Assn. (exec. council 1973-74, dir. 1972-75, chmn. bd. dirs. 1974-75), Sales and Mktg. Execs. Assn. Methodist (dir.). Mason, Rotarian. Home: 5401 W 60th St Edina MN 55436 Office: 1200 Multifoods Bldg Minneapolis MN 55402

BAKEWELL, STANLEY ELLSWORTH, personnel cons.; b. Eagle Bend, Minn., Apr. 10, 1920; s. Benjamin Levis and Eva Mary (Macaulay) B.; B.S. in Fgn. Service, Georgetown U., 1947-49; B.S. in Edn. and Animal Industry, U. Minn., 1943. Econ. asst., vice consul U.S. Fgn. Service, Am. embassy, Mexico City, Mexico, 1949-52; sr. market analyst Kimberly Clark Corp., Neenah, Wis., 1952-60; mgr. market research Forest Products div. Owens-Ill. Glass Co., Toledo, 1960-64; project dir. indsl. research Elrick & Lavidge, Chgo., 1964-66; pres., gen. mgr. Bryant & Bakewell Marketing Personnel div. Bryant Assos., Chgo., 1967—. Trustee Bakewell Investment Trust. Served to lt. (j.g.) USNR, 1944-46. Mem. Chgo. Symphony Soc., Am. Mktg. Assn., Am. Iris Soc., Chgo. Council Fgn. Relations, Alpha Gamma Rho. Republican. Episcopalian. Clubs: Chgo. Athletic Assn., Whitehall, Georgetown (Chgo.). Home: 411 Hickory St Joliet IL 60435 Office: Bryant Assos John Hancock Center 875 N Michigan Ave Chicago IL 60611

BAKKE, GILBERT BENJAMIN, constrn. co. exec., mech. engr.; b. Milw., Sept. 13, 1937; s. Martin A. and Lydia Mary (Wittenberger) B.; B.S. in Mech. Engring., U. Wis., 1961; m. Lorraine Frenz, Aug. 11, 1961; children—Lila, Laura, James, Rebekah. Chief engr., Alby Mfg. Co., Waterford, Wis., 1961-63; design engr. Nomad Equipment, Milw., 1963; design engr. Rex Chainbelt, Milw., 1963-68; mgr. Bakke Electric Co., Waterford, 1968-73, propr., pres., 1973—; propr., pres. Aber Cutters Co., Waterford, 1976—. Chmn. Waterford Fire and

Police Commn., 1976—; mem. Waterford Sch. Bd., 1972—. Registered profl. engr., Wis. Mem. Am. Soc. for Metals. Lutheran. Club: Lions (pres. 1976—). Home: 646 E Main St Waterford WI 53185 Office: 513 Aber Dr Waterford WI 53185

BAKSH, KARIM, dentist; b. Whim, Corentyne, Guyana, S.Am., Mar. 20, 1938; s. Kadir and Mooneran (Lall) B.; came to U.S., 1958, naturalized, 1971; student Mankato State Coll., 1960; D.D.S., Northwestern U., 1964; m. Judith H. Kittleson, Aug. 28, 1964; children—E. Karima, M. Rehannah. Practice dentistry, Chgo., 1967—; instr. Sch. Dentistry, Northwestern U., Chgo., 1964-67, teaching asso., 1967—. Home: 180 E Pearson St Chicago IL 60611 Office: 720 N Michigan Ave Chicago IL 60611

BALACEK, THOMAS VINCENT, corp. exec., engr.; b. N.Y.C., Sept. 24, 1937; s. Theodore Vincent and Margaret Alice (Tuohy) B.; student Acad. Aeros., 1956-60; m. Joyce Eldeene Iden, Nov. 19, 1960; children—Thomas Vincent, Valerie Anne, William Theodore, Paul Frederick. Started as engr. Executone, Inc., N,Y.C., 1958-60, U.S. Testing Co., Inc., Hoboken, N.J., 1961; sales engr. Nuclear-Chgo. subsidiary G.D. Searle, Des Plaines, Ill., 1961-65, regional mgr., 1966-67, sales mgr., 1968, advt. mgr., 1969; v.p. sales and marketing Telemed Corp., Hoffman Estates, Ill., 1969-76; pres. Cardiassist Corp., Hoffman Estates, Ill., 1976—. Home: 506 N River Rd Fox River Grove IL 60021 Office: 2119 Stonington Ave Hoffman Estates IL 60195

BALAGOT, REUBEN CASTILLO, anesthesiologist; b. Manila, Philippines, July 28, 1920; s. Pedro G. and Ambrosia (Castillo) B.; B.S., U. Philippines, 1941, M.D., 1944; came to U.S., 1949, naturalized, 1955; m. Lourdes Ramirez, July 10, 1946; children—Joseph, Edgar, Victoria (Mrs. Peter Hermann), Ophelia. Intern, Philippine Gen. Hosp., Manila, 1943-44; resident U. Ill., Chgo., 1949-50, research fellow, 1951, clin. instr., 1952-54, asst. prof., 1954-56, asso. prof., 1956-60, prof., 1960—, chmn. dept., 1969-71; chmn. Chgo. Med. Sch., Downey, Ill., 1971—; asst. head div. anesthesiology Grant Hosp., 1957, Ill. Masonic Hosp., 1966-67; pres. St. Lukes Hosp., 1967-71, Hines (Ill.) VA Hosp., 1971-75. Served with AUS, 1944-46. Named Distinguished Physician of Year, Philippine Med. Assn., 1968. Diplomate Am. Bd. Anesthesiology. Fellow Am. Fedn. Clin. Research; mem. AMA, A.C.S., AAUP, AAAS, N.Y. Acad. Sci., Ill., Chgo. med. socs., Am. Soc. Anesthesiologists, Ill. Soc. for Med. Research, Am. Writers Research, Am. Assn. for Med. Instrumentation, Sigma Xi. Contbr. articles to profl. jours. Home: 4246 Hazel St Chicago IL 60613 Office: 4332 Oakton St Skokie IL 60076

BALAZS, BILL (BELA) ANTAL, mech. engr.; b. Miercurea-Ciuc, Romania, June 13, 1933; s. Andras and Emilia (Sallo) B.; came to U.S., 1957, naturalized, 1962; B.S., U. Budapest (Hungary), 1955; diploma tool die engring. Acme Tech. Inst., Cleve., 1963; A.P.M., John Carroll U., 1976; m. Vivienne Miskey, Apr. 1, 1960; 1 dau., Corrinne. Instr. tool die engring., machine design, indsl. electronics, Acme Tech. Inst., 1960-65; design engr., heating, ventilating, Morrison Product Inc., Cleve., 1963-65; project engr. Reuter-Stokes, Inc., Cleve., 1965-70, engring. project mgr., 1970-73, engring. mgr., chief engr., 1973—. Pres., Transylvania Hungarian League, 1960—. Registered profl. engr., Calif. Mem. Am. Inst. Indsl. Engrs., Instrument Soc. Am., Soc. Mfg. Engrs., ASME, Am. Nuclear Soc., Nat., Ohio socs. profl. engrs. Designer nuclear radiation detectors and multi-sensor environ. radiation monitoring systems. Home: 7500 Woodlake Dr Walton Hills OH 44146 Office: 18530 S Miles Pkwy Cleveland OH 44128

BALBACH, DANIEL ROSSWELL, orthodontist; b. Grand Rapids, Mich., Jan. 17, 1938; s. William Rosswell and Clarice J. (Lybart) B.; A.S., Grand Rapids Jr. Coll., Grand Rapids, 1957; D.D.S., U. Mich., Ann Arbor, 1961, M.S. in Orthodontia, 1965; m. Barbara Jean Sands, June 21, 1968; children—Jane Anne, John Daniel. Clin. instr. U. Mich., 1961-62, asst. prof., 1965-69; research asso. Center Human Growth and Devel., U. Mich., 1969-71; spl. lectr. Case Western Res. U., Cleve., 1972-75; lectr. U. Western Ont., 1973—, also pvt. practice specializing in orthodontia, Ann Arbor, 1965—; mem. human subject review com. U. Mich. Sch. Dentistry; mem. research team Found. Orthodontic Research. Sect. leader United Fund, St. Joseph Hosp. Bldg. Fund. Mem. Am., Mich. dental assns., Washtenaw Dist. Dental Soc. (past pres.), Mich. Orthodontic Alumni (sec.-treas.), Am. Soc. Dentistry for Children, Am. Assn. Orthodontics, Great Lakes Soc. Orthodontics, Mich. Soc. Orthodontists, Phi Kappa Phi, Omicron Kappa Upsilon. Republican. Baptist. Clubs: Ann Arbor Rotary, Barton Boat. Home: 3989 Penberton St Ann Arbor MI 48105 Office: 1303 Packard St Ann Arbor MI 48104

BALCH, DURWARD EARL, lawyer; b. Quinn, S.D., Aug. 19, 1909; s. Oscar Earl and Jane Elizabeth (Duck) B.; student Dickinson State Coll., 1927-29; LL.B., U. N.D., 1932; m. Borghild Marie Mork, Dec. 30, 1958. Admitted to N.D. bar, 1932, Minn. bar, 1944, U.S. Supreme Ct., 1940; partner firm Cain & Balch, Dickinson, N.D., 1932-35; spl. agent, administrv. asst. to dir. FBI, 1935-39; spl. asst. to U.S. Atty. Gen. Criminal div. U.S. Dept. Justice, 1939-44; counsel Gen. Mills, Inc., Mpls., 1944-51, v.p. personnel adminstrn., 1951-60; prin. D.E. Balch mgmt. counsel, 1960-72; mgmt. counsel Balch & Watson, Inc., Mpls., 1972—. Trustee The Menninger Found., Topeka, Kans., Hennepin Ave United Methodist Ch., Mpls., Hennepin Ave United Methodist Ch. Found. Served with USNR, 1938-41. Clubs: Mpls., Mpls. Athletic, Lafayette Country. Home: 4350 Brookside Ct Minneapolis MN 55436 Office: Suite 352 Shelard Plaza Minneapolis MN 55426

BALDOCK, ROBERT LEMORE, food technologist; b. Summer Shade, Ky., Sept. 4, 1915; s. Marcus Logan and Myrtie (Smith) B.; student Western Ky. U., 1935-36, Purdue U., 1942, U. Minn., m. Ona Williams, Apr. 10, 1938; children—Robert, James, Martha. Quality control technician Libby, McNeill & Libby, Blue Island, Ill., 1941-47; quality control supr., Eureka, Ill., 1947-53, research technologist mfg. research, Blue Island, 1953-58, quality control. supr., Rochester, Minn. Mem. Bd. Edn., Metcalfe County, Ky., 1940-41; adv. bd. mem. Rochester Area Vocat. Sch., 1970—. Mem. Inst. Food Technologists, Nat. Rifle Assn. Home: 311 Highland Ct SW Rochester MN 55901 Office: 1217 SE Third Ave Rochester MN 55901

BALDONI, LOUIS PAUL, physician; b. Trenton, Mich., Dec. 10, 1929; s. Romolo and Dosolina Maria (Moretti) B.; student U. Detroit, 1947-48; B.S., Mich. State U., 1951; M.D., U. Mich., 1955; m. Martha A. Watt, Aug. 25, 1951; children—John M., Kathleen M., Mary M., Paula E. Intern, St. Vincent's Hosp., Toledo, 1955-56, asst. resident, 1958-59; practice medicine, specializing in family practice, Perrysburg, Ohio, 1959—; mem. staffs Mercy Hosp., Toledo, St. Luke Hosp., Maumee, Ohio; clin. asso. Med. Coll. Ohio at Toledo, 1970. Mem. Wood County Bd. Health, 1961—. Served to capt. M.C., AUS, 1956-58. Diplomate Am. Bd. Family Practice. Mem. AMA, Ohio, Wood County (pres. 1963-65) med. socs., Am. Acad. Family Practice, NAACP (life mem.). Home: 731 Hickory St Perrysburg OH 43551 Office: 195 E Boundary St Perrysburg OH 43551

BALDUS, ALVIN JAMES, congressman; b. Hancock County, Iowa, Apr. 27, 1926; s. Leo and Mildred (Corbin) B.; A.A., Austin (Minn.) Jr. Coll., 1948; m. A. Lorayne Reiten, Sept. 26, 1959; children—Deborah, Bruce, Rebecca, John, Daniel. Mfrs. agt. Viking Mfg. Co., farm machinery mfrs., 1950-51, Allis Chalmers Mfg. Co., 1953-62; investment broker Investors Diversified Sers., 1963-74; mem. Wis. Ho. of Reps. from 69th Dist., 1966-74, asst. majority floor leader, 1973-74; mem. 94th-95th Congresses from 3d dist. Wis.; mem. agr. com., com. on small bus. Chmn., Caddie Woodlawn Meml. Com., 1970; pres. Dunn County unit Am. Cancer Soc., 1972. Served with U.S. Mcht. Marine, 1944-46, U.S. Army, 1951-53; PTO. Decorated Bronze Star, Combat Inf. badge. Mem. Am. Legion, D.A.V. Democrat. Club: Toastmasters (pres. Menomonie, area gov. 1968). Address: 1901 S Broadway Box 41 Menomonie WI 54751

BALDWIN, GORDON BREWSTER, educator; b. Binghamton, N.Y., Sept. 3, 1929; s. Schuyler Forbes and Doris Ambeline (Hawkins) B.; LL.B., Cornell U., 1953; B.A., Haverford Coll., 1950; m. Helen Louise Hochgraf, Feb. 1, 1958; children—Schuyler, Mary Page. Admitted to N.Y. bar, 1953; practiced in Rochester, Rome, N.Y., 1953, 57; prof. law U. Wis. Law Sch., Madison, 1957—, asso. dean law, 1968-70, dir. officer edn., 1972—. Chair of internat. law U.S. Naval War Coll., 1963-64; Fulbright prof., Cairo, Egypt, 1966-67, Tehran, Iran, 1970-71; lectr. State Dept., Cyprus, 1967, 69, 71; counselor on internat. law Dept. of State, 1975-76, cons., 1976-77; cons. U.S. Naval War Coll., 1961-65; chmn. screening com. on law Fulbright Program, 1974. Mem. Mayor of Madison's Com. on Merger of City and County, 1970-71. Served to capt. AUS, 1953-57. Ford Found. fellow, 1962-63. Mem. Wis. State Bar (vice-chmn. sect. on individual rights 1973-75), Order of Coif, Phi Beta Kappa. Rotarian. Office: Law Sch U Wis Madison WI 53706

BALDWIN, LANNES WEAVER, JR., psychologist; b. Okla. City, June 20, 1932; s. Lannes Weaver and Alice Jane (Davis) B.; B.A., Bethany Nazarene Coll., 1962; M.Ed., Okla. U., 1967, Ph.D., 1972; m. Betty Gwendolyn Hicks, Nov. 5, 1953; children—Deborah, Mark, Cynthia, Michelle. Tchr. pub. schs., Okla. City, 1963-68; vocational rehabilitation counselor Central State Mental Health Center, Norman, Okla., 1968-72; asst. prof. psychology Evangel Coll., Springfield, Mo., 1972-74; psychologist VA Hosp., Battle Creek, Mich., 1974—; bd. dirs. Samaritan Counseling Center, Battle Creek, 1976—. Mem. Am., Mich. psychol. assns. Democrat. Mem. Assemblies of God Ch. Home: 525 Woods End Kalamazoo MI 49001 Office: VA Hosp Battle Creek MI 49016

BALDWIN, LLOYD DEANS, computer co. exec.; b. Logan, Utah, Feb. 15, 1936; s. Kelvin Alma and Helen Ann (Deans) B.; student pub. schs., Bountiful, Utah; m. Arlene Ruth Simonis, Oct. 17, 1960; children—Rebecca Ann, Danna Lynn, David Alma, Stefanie Janine, Karina Louise, Emaline Sarah, Carl Nathaniel. Engr., Sperry Engring Co., 1958; missionary Ch. of Jesus Christ Latter-day Saints, 1959-60; engr. IBM, 1960, tech. and mgmt. positions, San Jose, Calif., 1961-69, regional mgr., 1968-69; asst. to v.p. mktg. Info. Storage Systems, Cupertino, Calif., 1969-71; dir. ops. Cincom Systems, Cin., 1971-75; pres. Lloyd Baldwin & Assos., Cin., 1975-76; v.p. Pansophic Systems Inc., Oak Brook, Ill., 1976—. Trustee Deaconess Hosp., Cin., 1974. Served with USN, 1954-58. Mem. Software Industry Assn. (dir. 1970-77, pres. 1975-76), Computer Industry Assn. Club: Rotary. Home: 4495 Swartz St Lisle IL 60532 Office: 709 Enterprise Dr Oakbrook IL 60521

BALES, JERALD KEITH, lawyer, ins. co. exec.; b. Newton, Iowa, July 13, 1926; s. Merl A. and Margaret E. (McVicker) B.; A.B., Kans. U., 1950, LL.B., 1951; m. Irma Lou Rick, Dec. 28, 1949; children—Rick Walker, Anne Eleanor, Scott McVicker. Admitted to Mo. bar, 1951; practice law, mem. firm Langworthy, Matz & Linde, Kansas City, Mo., 1951-55; trust officer Union Nat. Bank, Kansas City, 1955-60; v.p., gen. counsel Business Men's Assurance Co. Am., Kansas City, 1972-77, exec. v.p., gen. counsel, 1977—, dir. 1970—; v.p. BMA Corp., Kansas City, 1967-77, sec., 1974-77, dir., 1968-77. City councilman, Mission, Kans., 1955-58; police judge, Mission, 1958-61. Served with AUS, 1945-46. Mem. Am., Mo. bar assns., Assn. Life Ins. Counsel, Lawyers Assn. Kansas City, Am. Life Ins. Assn. (state v.p. 1965-67, 77—, joint legis. com. 1969-73), Delta Upsilon. Clubs: Mission Hills (Kans.) Country; University (Lawrence, Kans.). Office: 1 Penn Valley Park Kansas City MO 64141

BALESTER, RAYMOND J., psychologist; b. Albion, N.Y., Dec. 9, 1917; s. Joseph and Mary (Carlo) B.; m. Vivian Shelton Standerfer, 1956; children—Walter, Carla, Mark. B.S. in Edn., State U. N.Y., Brockport, 1942; M.L., U. Pitts., 1947; Ph.D., Vanderbilt U., 1956. Dep. commr. Tenn. Dept. Mental Health, Nashville, 1957-60; chief experimental and pilot tng. programs, NIMH, HEW, Bethesda, Md., 1960-63; acting chief Div. Manpower and Tng. Programs. NIMH, Chevy Chase, 1963-67, dep. asst. dir. Extramural Programs, NIMH, Chevy Chase, 1967-69; vice provest Social and Behavior Sci., Case Western Res. U., Cleve., 1969-74; supt. Cleve. Psychiat. Inst., 1974—; mem. Mayor's Commn. on Aging, Cleve.; trustee Beech Brook, Rape Crises Center, Cleve., Suicide Prevention Center, Cleve.; v.p. Cleve. Area Arts Council. Licensed psychologist, Tenn., Ohio. Mem. Am. Psychol. Assn., AAAS, Sigma Xi. Recipient Career Tchr. award USPHS, 1957. Home: 2460 Edgehill Rd Cleveland Heights OH 44106 Office: 1708 Aiken Ave Cleveland OH 44109

BALFOUR, HENRY HALLOWELL, JR., pediatrician, virologist, educator; b. Jersey City, Feb. 9, 1940; s. Henry Hallowell and Dorothy Kathryn Dietze B.; A.B. with honors, Princeton, 1962; M.D., Columbia, 1966; m. Carol Lenore Pries, Sept. 23, 1967; children—Henry Hallowell III, Anne Lenore. Intern, U. Minn. Hosps., Mpls., 1966-67; resident pediatrics Babies Hosp., Columbia-Presbyn. Med. Center, N.Y.C., 1967-68; asst. prof. lab. medicine, pathology, pediatrics U. Minn., 1972-75, asso. prof., 1975—, dir. sect. virology, 1972—, dir. div. clin. microbiology, 1974—; cons. clin. virology VA Hosp., Mpls., 1973—. Served to capt. M.C., USAF, 1968-70. NIH grantee, 1974—. Diplomate Am. Acad. Pediatrics. Mem. Am. Fedn. Clin. Research, Am. Soc. Microbiology, Am. Soc. Tropical Medicine and Hygiene, Soc. Exptl. Biology and Medicine, Northwestern Pediatric Soc., Soc. Pediatric Research, Central Soc. Clin. Research, Acad. Clin. Lab. Physicians and Scientists. Contbg. author: Current Therapy, (by Howard F. Conn), 1976. Contbr. clin. and research articles to med. jours. Home: 6820 Harold Ave N Minneapolis MN 55427 Office: Box 437 Mayo U Minn Hosps Minneapolis MN 55455

BALK, HARLAN GEORGE, nursing home adminstr.; b. Clinton, Iowa, Dec. 6, 1933; s. George P. and Martha Ione (Rush) B.; student Western Ill. U., 1952-53; m. Virgilee Ann Cochran, Dec. 30, 1956; children—Mark, Raena Lee, Shera Lin, Dell Ann. Supr. A.C. Nielsen, Clinton, 1956-59; owner, mgr. restaurant, Fulton, Ill., 1959-61; adminstr., pres. Grandview Manor, Camp Point, Ill., 1962—; pres. Montebello Manor Corp., Hamilton Ill., Harmace Corp., Clearwater, Fla., Harlan G. Ball Enterprises, Inc., Security Services Fla., Inc. Served with AUS, 1954-56. Mem. Ill. Health Care Assn. (formerly Ill. Nursing Home Assn.) (dist. pres. 1970-71), Adams County Nursing Home Assn. (pres. 1967-69), Am. Health Care Assn., Am. Coll. Nursing Home Adminstrs. Club: Spring Lake Country. Home: Route 2 Camp Point IL 62320 Office: 205 Spring Camp Point IL 62320

BALL, CHESTER EDWIN, editor; b. Seth, W.Va., Aug. 19, 1921; s. Roman Harry and Hattie (White) B.; A.B., Marshall U., 1942; M.A., Ohio State U., 1947; m. Betty June Hively, Dec. 29, 1945; children—Beth Elaine (Mrs. John Michael Watkins), Harry Stuart, Chester Edwin. Stringer, Charleston (W.Va.) Daily Mail, 1936-40; reporter, copy editor Huntington (W.Va.) Pub. Co., 1945, 47-48; asso. pub. Wolf Pub. Co., Cin., 1953-55; instr. journalism Marshall Coll., Huntington, W.Va., 1947-51; asst. prof. journalism Ohio State U., Columbus, 1951-56, publs. editor Engring. Expt. Sta., 1956-63; tech. editor, editorial and printing dept. head Ohio State U. Research Found., Columbus, 1963—. Mem. Hilliard (Ohio) Charter Commn., 1958-63, vice-chmn., 1958, sec., 1960-61, 62-63; treas. Hilliard chpt. Am. Field Service, 1974-76, pres., 1976-77; mem. Scioto Darby Bd. Edn., Hilliard, 1962—; bd. dirs. Franklin County Epilepsy Assn., 1976—. Served with AUS, 1942-45. Decorated Silver Star, Bronze Star medal with one oak leaf cluster, Purple Heart with two oak leaf clusters. Mem. Soc. Tech. Communication (chpt. chmn. 1968-69), In-Plant Printing Mgmt. Assn. (pres. 1971), Reserve Officers Assn. (sec.-treas., pres. Huntington, W.Va. 1948-50), Sigma Delta Chi. Republican. Methodist (mem. bd. ushers 1956—). Kiwanian. Home: 6174 Sunny Vale Dr Columbus OH 43228 Office: 1314 Kinnear Rd Columbus OH 43212

BALL, KENNETH LEON, printing co. exec.; b. N.Y.C., Aug. 11, 1932; s. Oscar and Elvira B.; A.B., Antioch Coll., 1954; Ph.D., Washington U., St. Louis, 1959; m. Patricia Ann Whitley, June 23, 1957; children—David B., Dana K. Indsl. psychologist Orchard Paper Co., St. Louis, 1957-59; gen. mgr. Orchard Pacific Paper Co., Los Angeles, 1960-62; v.p. human relations Orchard Paper Co., St. Louis, 1963-65; v.p., sec., dir. Orchard Corp. Am., St. Louis, 1966-74, exec. v.p., dir., 1975—; guest lectr. indsl. psychology Washington U. Dir. Jewish Vocational and Ednl. Service, 1975—; adv. com. chmn. Family and Children Service, Clayton, Mo., 1973-75; advisor Metroplex, 1973-75. Mem. Am., Mo. (certified), St. Louis psychol. assns., AAAS. Contbg. author to Humanining Organizational Behavior (Meltzer and Wickert, ed.), 1976. Home: 9875 Northbridge St Saint Louis MO 63124 Office: 1154 Reco St Saint Louis MO 63126

BALL, LLOYD RICHARD, lawyer; b. Hawarden, Iowa, Feb. 12, 1931; s. Lloyd Ross and Helen (Wells) B.; B.A., State U. Iowa, 1953; LL.B., U. Nebr., 1956. Admitted to Iowa bar, 1956; since practiced in Hawarden. Mayor City of Hawarden, 1960-62, city atty., 1968-70. Served to 1st lt. JAG, USAF, 1956-58. Mem. Am., Iowa Sioux County bar assns., Am. Judicature Soc., Am. Legion, Internat. Platform Assn., Delta Tau Delta, Delta Theta Phi. Congregationalist (deacon). Clubs: Masons (master 1965), Rotary (past pres. Hawarden), Capitol Hill (Washington). Home: 1025 Ave M Hawarden IA 51023 Office: 817 Central Ave Hawarden IA 51023

BALL, LOUIS ALVIN, ins. co. exec.; b. Kansas City, Mo., Oct. 25, 1921; s. George Rhodom and Frances Mariam (Beals) B.; B.A. in Bus. Adminstrn., Kans. State U., 1947; m. Norma Jane Laudenberger, Jan. 17, 1947. Asst. purchasing agt. Kansas City (Mo.) br. Found Motor Co., 1942-46; with Farm Bur. Mut. Ins. Co., Inc., Manhattan, Kans., 1947—, claims underwriting mgr., 1956-61, systems and procedures mgr., 1961—, asst. sec., 1977—. Mem. Nat. Assn. Ind. Insurers, Conf. Casualty Cos., Assn. Systems Mgmt. (Internat. Merit award 1971, Kansas City chpt. Merit award 1970, Kansas City chpt. Diamond Merit award 1977). Club: Manhattan Country. Home: 1101 Pioneer Ln Manhattan KS 66502 Office: 2321 Anderson Ave Manhattan KS 66502

BALL, WILLIAM BATTEN, govt. ofcl.; b. San Antonio, Aug. 28, 1928; s. William Henry and Lillian Edna (Young) B.; student Wilson Jr. Coll., 1944-45; B.Sc. in Accounting, Roosevelt U., 1955, M.B.A. in Accounting, 1960; J.D., Chgo. Kent Coll. Law, 1968; m. Charlie Mae Cooper, Nov. 9, 1956; children—Jeffrey C., Kathleen L., William E. Revenue officer IRS, Chgo., 1955-57, revenue agt., 1959-67, appellate appeals officer, 1967—; accountant, jr. exec. Supreme Life Ins. Co., 1957-59; auditor Ill. State Dept. Labor, 1959. Troop committeeman, instl. rep. Chgo. Area council Boy Scouts Am., 1968—; mem. of prin., dist. supt. selection Amelia D. Hookway Elementary Sch. Council, Dist. 16 Sch. Council, 1968-72. Served with AUS, 1951-53. Mem. Am., Nat., Ill., Cook County bar assns., Chgo. Assembly, Kappa Alpha Psi (keeper of exchequer 1976—). Methodist (chmn. adminstrv. bd. 1973—). Clubs: St. Ignatius Coll. Prep. Fathers; Duces Athletic, Social and Civic (sec. fin. 1970-76). Home: 8355 S Perry Ave Chicago IL 60620 Office: IRS 219 S Dearborn St Chicago IL 60604

BALL, WILLIAM JAMES, physician; b. Charleston, S.C., Apr. 16, 1910; s. Elias and Mary (Cain) B.; B.S., U. of South, 1930; M.D., Med. Coll. S.C., 1934; m. Doris Hallowell Mason, July 9, 1938. Intern, Roper Hosp., Charleston, 1934-35; resident dept. pediatrics U. Chgo. Clinics, 1935-37; instr. pediatrics Med. Coll. S.C., 1938-42; practice medicine specializing in pediatrics, Charleston, 1938-42, Aurora, Ill., 1951-70; physician student Health Service No. Ill. U., 1970-72; cons. Mooseheart, Ill.; mem. staff Copley Meml., St. Joseph Mercy hosps.; pediatrician N.W. Clinic, Minot, N.D., 1946-51; asso. prof. Sch. Nursing, No. Ill. U., 1971-72. Mem. Bd. Health, Aurora, Ill., 1958-62; pediatrician, div. services for crippled children U. Ill., 1952—; pediatric cons. sch. dists. 129 and 131, Aurora, also DeKalb County Spl. Edn. Assn., 1972—, also Northwestern Ill. Assn. Handicapped Children. Served to capt. M.C., AUS, 1942-46; col. Res., ret. Diplomate Am. Bd. Pediatrics. Fellow Royal Soc. Health, Am. Acad. Pediatrics; mem. AMA, Kane County Med. Soc. (pres. 1962), Am. Heart Assn., Am. Sch. Health Assn., Am. Cancer Soc., Easter Seal Soc., Phi Beta Kappa, Phi Chi, Pi Kappa Phi. Republican. Rotarian. Club: Union League (Aurora). Address: 433 S Commonwealth Ave Aurora IL 60506

BALLANCE, L(EWIS) CHARLES, financial planner; b. Paw Paw, Mich., Dec. 30, 1915; s. Lee Charles and Sarah Eleanor (Sheldon) B.; A.B., U. Mich., 1937; m. Mildred L. Herkner, June 19, 1940; children—Lee, Stephen, Ann, Robert. Supr., Nat. Youth Adminstrn., Lansing, Mich., 1937-42; estimator sub contract work J.A. Ross & Co., Chgo., 1946-50; buyer J.W. Milliken, Inc., Traverse City, Mich., 1950-57; agt. Union Central Life Ins. Co., 1957-61; cons. Met. Life Ins. Co., 1961-66; account rep. financial adv. clinic Western Mich., Inc., 1967—. Bd. dirs. Grand Traverse Bay YMCA, 1967-74, pres., 1970-72; bd. dirs. Mich. State YMCA. Served to lt. USNR, 1942-46. C.L.U. Mem. Northwestern Mich. Assn. Life Underwriters (pres. 1962-63). Kiwanian (pres. 1968-69). Home: 1206 Peninsula Ct Traverse City MI 49634 Office: PO Box 202 Traverse City MI 49684

BALLANTINE, WHITNEY WILLIAM, lawyer; b. Detroit, July 21, 1910; s. Samuel Emerson and Lottie Andrew (Voorhees) B.; student Wayne U., 1928-30; LL.B., Detroit Coll. Law, 1934; m. Dorothy Edith Wilkinson, Mar. 9, 1940; children—Whitney William, Katherine Johnston, Barbara Katz. Admitted to Mich. bar, 1934, practiced in Detroit until 1942, in Wayne, Mich., 1946—; spl. agt. FBI, 1942-44. Promoter, part owner Fellows Creek Golf Club, Inc., Wayne, 1961—. Justice of Peace, Wayne, 1947-57; mem. Wayne Community Sch. Bd., 1947-57, Wayne Village Council, 1958-60, Wayne Charter Commn., 1959-60, Wayne City Council, 1960-64. Served with USMCR, 1944-46. Rotarian (pres. 1958-59). Clubs: Fellows Creek Golf (pres. 1961—), Washtenaw Country. Home: 3255

Williams St Wayne MI 48184 Office: 36046 Michigan St Wayne MI 48184

BALLARD, JOHN STUART, mayor; b. Akron, Ohio, Sept. 30, 1922; s. Irby S. and Sarah (McCormick) B.; A.B., U. Akron, 1943; LL.B., U. Mich., 1948; m. Ruth Frances Holden, Oct. 22, 1949; children—Susan, Karen, John H., Mark, Ward. Admitted to Mich. bar, 1948, Ohio bar, 1949; spl. agt. FBI, 1949-52; practice law, Akron, 1952-56; pros. atty. Summit County, Ohio, 1957-64; practice law, Akron, 1964-65; mayor of Akron, 1966—. Mem. Summit County Republican Exec. Com., 1956—; candidate for U.S. Senator from Ohio, 1962. Served with inf. AUS, 1943-46. Recipient Distinguished Service award Akron Jaycees, 1957. Mem. Akron Bar Assn. Episcopalian. Home: 107 Kenilworth Dr Akron OH 44313 Office: Municipal Bldg High St Akron OH 44308

BALLARD, LESTER ARTHUR, JR., gynecologist; b. Columbus, Ohio, Aug. 31, 1929; s. Lester Arthur and Mildred (McCullour) B.; B.A., Ohio State U., 1951, M.D., 1955; children by previous marriage—Brent, Julie. Intern, resident obstetrics and gynecology Western Res. U., Cleve., 1956-60; asst. prof. obstetrics and gynecology Case Western Res. U., Cleve., 1962-66, asst. clin. prof., 1966—; mem. staff Cleve. Clinic, 1966-74, head dept. gynecology, 1974—. Diplomate Am. Bd. Obstetrics and Gynecology. Mem. Am. Coll. Obstetrics and Gynecology (chmn. Ohio sect. 1975—), AMA, Central Assn. Obstetrics and Gynecology, Continental Gynecology Soc., Humane Soc., Cleve. Obstetrics and Gynecology Soc. (pres. 1975-76), A.C.S., Am. Soc. Cytology, Am. Fertility Soc., Central Travel Club. Home: 36000 Fairmount St Chagrin Falls OH 44022 Office: 9500 Euclid Av Cleveland OH 44106

BALLINGER, LEONARD DANIEL, ednl. adminstr.; b. Charleston, Mo., May 17, 1933; s. Leonard Daniel and Maegerie Kathryn (Baker) B.; B.S., U. Mo., 1955; M.S., So. Ill. U., 1964; postgrad. St. Louis U., 1967-68; m. Shirley Ann Swank, Jan. 31, 1953; 1 son, Stephen Daniel. Clin. coordinator, lectr. rehab. Mo. Dept. Edn., St. Louis, 1958-65; specialist in counseling testing, job devel. and placement, dir. mgmt. analysis Human Devel. Corp., N.Y.C., 1965-68; supr. State Schs. Trainable Mentally Retarded, St. Louis, Mo., 1968—. Instr. psychology Thomas Dunn Memls. adult Edn. Program, St. Louis, 1965—; cons. Job Corps Tng. Center, St. Louis, 1965-66. Mem. adv. com. Day Activity Center, St. Louis, 1969-70; mem. adv. com. St. Louis Assn. Retarded Children, 1973-74. Served to capt. USAF, 1955-58. Recipient Counselor of Year award Mo. div. Vocat. Rehab., 1962. Mem. Mo. Tchrs. Assn. Mem. Ch. of Nazarene (Christian edn. dir. 1966-71, missionary pres. 1965-68, youth pres., 1959-63, youth dir. 1960-61). Contbr. articles to profl. publs. Home: 491 Electra Dr Arnold MO 63010 Office: 5707 Wilson St St Louis MO 63110

BALLMER, RAY WAYNE, mining co. exec.; b. Santa Rita, N.Mex., May 6, 1926; s. Gerald Jacob and Martha Clara (Wilhelmson) B.; student U. N.Mex., 1943-44, U. Calif. at Los Angeles, 1944-45; B.S., N.Mex. Inst. Mining and Tech., 1949; M.S. in Indsl. Mgmt., (Sloan fellow) Mass. Inst. Tech., 1960; m. Doris J. Greer, July 8, 1945; children—Geraldine Lee, Ray James. With Kennecott Copper Corp., Ariz. and Utah, 1949-69; mng. dir. Bougainville Copper Ltd., Papua, New Guinea, 1969-75; pres. Amoco Minerals Co., Chgo., 1975—. Served with USN, 1943-46. Mem. Am. Inst. Mining, Metall. and Petroleum Engrs., Mining and Metall. Soc. Am., Australasian Inst. Mining and Metallurgy, Am. Mgmt. Assn. Lutheran. Clubs: Westmoreland, Mid-Am.; Athenaeum (Melbourne, Australia). Address: Amoco Minerals Co Box 5910A-5406A Chicago IL 60680

BALLUFF, EDWARD LOUIS, architect; b. Oak Park, Ill., Oct. 26, 1930; s. Louis Nicholas and Marie (Lamar) B.; B.S., U. Ill., 1956; m. Roseanne O'Laughlin, Nov. 21, 1953; children—Vincent, Louise, John. With Louis N. Balluff & Assos., architects and engrs., Chgo., 1956-60; partner Balluff & Balluff, Elmhurst, Ill., 1960—; pres. Mgrs. for Constrn., Inc.; instr. architecture Triton Jr. Coll., River Grove, Ill., 1967-68. Mem. Elmhurst Archtl. Commn., 1962—; chmn. High Sch. Caucus, 1967-68; chmn. Elmhurst Total Community Devel., 1968-70. Served with AUS, 1951-53. Mem. Western Communities Architects Assn. (v.p. 1970-72, pres. 1973-75), C. of C. (dir. 1966-69). Rotarian (pres. 1969-70). Prin. archtl. works include St. Francis Xavier Cabrini Hosp., Chgo., 1961, Stanley Field, Jr. High Sch., Northfield, Ill., 1964, Edgewood Elementary Sch., Woodridge, Ill., 1967, Longwood Elementary Sch., Naperville, Ill., 1970, Romeoville (Ill.) High Sch., 1973, Bolingbrook (Ill.) High Sch., 1974. Home: 231 N Washington St Hinsdale IL 60521 Office: 194 W Lake St Elmhurst IL 60126

BALMA, MICHAEL JAMES, JR., drug mfg. co. exec.; b. Joliet, Ill., Sept. 9, 1930; s. Michael James and Martha (Harris) B.; m. Janice T. Brethorst, June 10, 1951; children—Melinda, Michael James, Martha. B.S., Purdue U., 1951, M.S., 1952, Ph.D. in Indsl. Psychology, 1954. With flight propulsion div. Gen. Electric, Cin., 1954-63; with Abbott Labs., Chgo., 1963—, v.p. personnel, 1966—. Bd. dirs., v.p. Clara Abbott Found., 1971—; bd. dirs. Lake County Urban League, 1965-71, pres., 1967-69; dir. United Community Services of Lake County, 1967-70. Mem. Am. Psychol. Assn., C. of C. (dir. 1967-70), Pharm. Mfrs. Assn. (past chmn.) personnel sect.), Soc. Personnel Adminstrs., Inst. Medicine Chgo., Chgo. Yacht, Lake Forest-Lake Bluff Bath and Tennis. Chmn. Lake Bluff Police Commn., 1974—. Co-author: (with C.H. Lawshe) Principles of Personnel Testing, 1966. Contbr. articles to profl. jours. Home: 241 W Blodgett St Lake Bluff IL 60044 Office: Abbott Park North Chicago IL 60064

BALOFF, NICHOLAS, univ. adminstr.; b. San Francisco, Aug. 9, 1937; s. Nicholas Boris and Emily (Ersunoff) B.; B.S. with Highest Honors, U. Calif., Berkeley, 1959; S.M., Mass. Inst. Tech., 1960; Ph.D., Stanford, 1963; m. Alice Bea Garcia, Dec. 23, 1955; children—Steven Nicholas, Katherine Louise. Asst. prof. bus. adminstrn. U. Chgo., 1963-67; prof. U. Del Valle, Colombia, 1965; asso. prof., div. dir. Stanford (Calif.) U., 1967-72; prof., dean Coll. Bus. Adminstrn. U. Okla., Norman, 1972-76; prof., dean Sch. Bus. and Pub. Adminstrn. Washington U., St. Louis, 1976—; cons. McKinsey & Co., 1962-66, Ford Found., 1965-67; dir. ANTA Corp., Oklahoma City. Bd. dirs. U. Hosp., Oklahoma City, 1972-75, Kerr Found., Oklahoma City, 1972-76. Registered profl. engr., Okla., Calif. Mem. Inst. Mgmt. Scis., AAAS, Inst. Decision Scis., Am. Econ. Assn., Sigma Xi, Beta Gamma Sigma, Tau Beta Pi, Alpha Pi Mu. Contbr. articles to profl. jours. Address: Washington Univ St Louis MO 63130

BALOGH, JOSEPH DAVID, credit agy. exec.; b. Detroit, Mar. 12, 1930; s. Joseph and Mary Ann (Koska) B.; grad. Coll. Advanced Traffic, Detroit, 1954; student Henry Ford Community Coll., 1957-62, Washtenaw Community Coll., 1975; m. Mary Caroline Ladd, Dec. 16, 1949; children—Celeste Jeanine, Constance Denice. Traffic supr. Ford Motor Co., Dearborn, Mich., 1959-68; gen. mgr. Fleak Carloading Co., Chgo., 1968; traffic rep. Ford Motor Co., Fin. and Ins. Subs.'s, Dearborn, 1969—. Chmn. food services Chelsea (Mich.) Community Fair, 1973; instr. med. self-help course Office CD, Wyandotte, Mich., 1963; mem. Chelsea Village Planning Commn., 1974-77. Served with USMCR, 1947-50. Mem. Motor City Traffic Club, Coll. Advanced Traffic Detroit Alumni Assn. Methodist (treas. 1963). Clubs: Moose, Rod and Gun (Chelsea). Home: 236 E Middle St Chelsea MI 48118 Office: Ford Motor Credit Co PO Box 1732 Dearborn MI 48121

BALSLEY, LAWRENCE EDWARD, fan engr.; b. Chgo., Dec. 10, 1945; s. Lorne Neal and Marie (Bernds) B.; student Millikan U., 1964-66; B.M.E., U. Ill., 1973. Design engr., Crane Packing Co., Morton Grove, Ill., 1973-74; design engr. ILG Industries div. Carrier Corp., Chgo., 1974—. Served with AUS, 1968-71. Mem. ASME, Soc. Automotive Engrs. Republican. Presbyterian. Club: Schusser's Ski. Home: 7522 N Hoyne Ave Chicago IL 60625 Office: 2856 N Pulaski Rd Chicago IL 60641

BALTAZZI, EVAN SERGE, bus. cons.; b. Izmir, Turkey, Apr. 11, 1921; s. Phocion G. and Agnes (Varda) B.; Dr. es Sciences Physiques, Sorbonne, 1949; Ph.D., Oxford U., 1954; m. Nellie D. Biorlaro, July 17, 1945; children—Angie S., James P., Marie I. Came to U.S., 1959, naturalized, 1964. In charge research French Nat. Research Center, Paris, 1947-59; group leader organic chemistry research Nalco Chem. Co., Chgo., 1959-61; mgr. organic chemistry sect. Ill. Inst. Tech. Research Inst., Chgo., 1961-63; dir. research graphic research and devel. center Addressograph-Multigraph Corp., Warrensville Heights, Ohio, 1963-77; bus. cons., 1977—; chmn. bd., pres. Am. Self Protection Assn. Inc. Chmn. Internat. Symposium Photocondr. Image Tech., 1974; chmn. Gordon Research Conf. Chemistry and Physics of Photocondrs. Instr. judo West Suburban YMCA, Chgo., 1959-71, nat. YMCA rep. for judo, 1965—. pres. sports and phys. edn. methods research confs.; mem. U.S. Olympic Com. for Judo, Amateur Athletic Union nat. com. for judo, 1965-71. Fellow Am. Inst. Chemists (vice chmn. Chgo. sect. 1969-71); mem. Am. Chem. Soc. (com. manpower policy 1974), Soc. Photog. Scientists and Engrs. (dir. 1974—), N.Y. Acad. Scis. Mason (Shriner). Contbr. articles to profl. publs. Inventor chem. shorthand, new self-def. "A.S.P." (Am. Self-Protection). Patentee in field. Home: 825 Greengate Oval Northfield OH 44067 Office: 19701 South Miles Pkwy Warrensville Heights OH 44128

BALTZELL, JAMES HENRY, educator; b. Sumner, Ill., May 12, 1922; s. George Alvin and Elsie Kelsey (Palmer) B.; A.B., U. Ill., 1944; M.A., Ind. U., 1949, Ph.D., 1952; postgrad. Laval U., summer 1950 (Fulbright-Hayes award) Sorbonne, 1952-53; m. Permsuk Injun, July 3, 1969; children—Lorena Kay, James Henry II. Instr. U. Ill., Urbana, 1951-52; tchr. John Burroughs Sch., Clayton, Mo., 1953-54; asst. prof. Coll. William and Mary, Williamsburg, Va., 1954-56; asst. prof. So. Methodist U., Dallas, 1956-58; prof. Calif. State Coll. at Long Beach, 1958-71; prof. French lang. and lit. So. Ill. U. at Edwardsville, 1971—. Dir., Inst. French, NDEA, summer 1966. Served with AUS, 1943-45. Decorated chevalier Ordre des Palmes Academiques. Mem. Am. Assn. Tchrs. French, Modern Lang. Assn., Phi Beta Kappa, Phi Kappa Phi, Eta Sigma Phi, Pi Delta Phi. Author: The Octosyllabic Vie de Saint Denis, 1953; Les Meilleures Nouvelles de Marcel Ayme, 1964. Contbr. numerous articles to profl. publs. Home: 536 Sunset Dr Edwardsville IL 62025

BALUNAS, LEONARD CHARLES, psychologist; b. N.Y.C., May 22, 1941; s. Leonard Charles and Dorothy Veronica (Opperman) B.; m. Rosemary Burbridge, Aug. 14, 1965; children—Mary. B.A., Manhattan Coll., 1963; M.S., State U. N.Y., Buffalo, 1966, Ph.D., 1971. Certified consulting psychologist, Mich. Intern, Niagara County Mental Health Clinic, 1969-70; clin. psychologist Niagara County Mental Health Dept., Niagara Falls, N.Y., 1970-73, supervising clin. psychologist, 1973-74; chief clin. psychologist Beth Moser Mental Health Clinic, Jackson, Mich., 1974—; pvt. practice psychology, Jackson, 1976—. Bd. dirs. Goodwill Industries of Central Mich., 1976—. Mem. Am., Mich. psychol. assns., Am., Mich. socs. clin. hypnosis. Home: 1103 S Bowen St Jackson MI 49203 Office: 2424 Spring Arbor Rd Jackson MI 49203

BAMBENEK, GREGORY PETER, physician; b. Rochester, Minn., Dec. 24, 1947; s. Hubert James and Evelyn June (Peterson) B.; B.A., Beloit Coll., 1970; M.D., U. Minn., 1974. Research asst. psychiatry Mayo Clinic, Rochester, Minn., 1968-69; researcher WHO, Taiwan, South Viet Nam, India, Mid-East, 1969, Chippewa Indian Alcoholics, NIMH, 1972; resident psychiatry U. Minn., Mpls., 1974-77; psychiat. cons. Crisis Intervention Center, Hennepin County Med. Center, Mpls., Hennepin County Adult Corrections Facility. Bd. dirs. Winona County Progress and Preservation Assn., Inc., Winona, Minn., Help Encourage Landmark Preservation, Richmond, Va. Mem. Minn. Psychiat. Residents Assn., Phi Beta Pi, Tau Kappa Epsilon. Home: 509 Harriet St Winona MN 55987 Office: Dept Psychiatry U Minn Minneapolis MN 55455

BAMBRICK, JAMES JOSEPH, labor relations exec.; b. N.Y.C., Apr. 26, 1917; s. James Joseph and Mae (Murphy) B.; B.S., N.Y. U., 1940, M.B.A., 1942; B.S., U.S. Merchant Marine Acad., 1946; m. Margaret Mary Donlan, June 26, 1948; children—Patricia Bambrick Benek, Thomas G., Mary Bambrick Schneider, Kathleen, James Joseph. Union organizer Service Employees Internat. Union, N.Y.C., 1938-40; exec. dir. The Labor Bur., N.Y.C., 1940-42; personnel dir. All Am. Aviation, Inc., Wilmington, Del., 1942-44; labor editor Prentice-Hall, Inc., N.Y.C., 1946-47; mgr. labor relations research The Conf. Bd., N.Y.C., 1947-58; labor economist The Standard Oil Co. of Ohio, Cleve., 1957—. Instr. N.Y. U., 1946-53, John Carroll U., Cleve., 1968-71; lectr. Cleve. State U., 1963-68; mem. U.S. Bur. Labor Statistics Bus. Research Adv. Council, 1971-76, mem. com. on -consumer and wholesale prices, 1972-76, com. wages and indsl. realtions, 1960-76. Ohio Rep. finance committeeman, Cuyahoga-Lake Div., 1963—, chmn., 1965-69. Adv. council admissions N.Y. U. Alumni, 1963—. Served with USNR, 1944-46. Named Hibernian Man of the Year, 1974. Fellow Soc. for Advancement Mgmt.; mem. Nat. Panel Arbitrators, Am. Arbitration Assn., Am. Econ. Assn. Roman Catholic. K.C. Club: City (Cleve.). Author: Handbook of Modern Personnel Adminstrn., 1972. Contbr. articles to profl. jours. Home: 2704 Berkshire Rd Cleveland Heights OH 44106 Office: 1511 Midland Bldg Cleveland OH 44115

BAMFORD, JACQUELINE LOU, psychologist; b. Detroit, Feb. 12, 1931; d. James Frank and Lula Lolita (Parr) Bamford; B.S., Abilene Christian U., 1953; M.A., Wayne State U., 1961. Psychophysiol. research technician Lafayette Clinic, Detroit, 1958-65, research psychologist, 1965-70; psychologist Traverse City (Mich.) State Hosp., 1970—; counselor, N.W. Counseling Service, Detroit, 1963-70. Mem. Soc. for Psychophysiol. Research, Biofeedback Soc. of Am., Biofeedback Soc. of Mich., Am., Mich. psychol. assns. Mem. Ch. of Christ. Clubs: Zonta Club of Traverse City. Contbr. articles in field to profl. jours. Home: 806 W 7th St Traverse City MI 49684 Office: Box C Traverse City MI 49684

BAMMANN, DERWOOD EUGENE, dentist; b. Pontiac, Ill., Apr. 10, 1929; s. John Henry and Edna Marie (Brown) B.; student Ill. State U. at Normal, 1947-49; B.S. cum laude, U. Ill., 1951, M.S., 1955, D.D.S., 1962; m. Bernice L. Maurer, Feb. 5, 1950; children—Angela (Mrs. Robert Matthey), Cynthia, Eloise, Francie. Tchr. high sch., Newman, Ill., 1951-54, Beecher, Ill., 1954-58; practice dentistry, Beecher, 1962-68, Crete, Ill., 1968—; adj. faculty U. Ill. Coll. Dentistry, 1976—; cons. Ill. Dental Service Corp., Chgo., 1972—. Bd. dirs. Comprehensive Health Planning Council Will, Grundy and Kankakee counties, v.p., 1974-75, pres., 1976. Mem. Am. Endodontic Soc., Will County Dental Soc. (pres. 1969-70), ADA, Acad. Gen. Dentistry, Crete C. of C. (v.p., dir. 1976—), Psi Omega. Lutheran. Club: Lions. Home: 48 Woodland Glen Park Forest IL 60466 Office: 1397 Main St Crete IL 60417

BANACH, ART JOHN, graphic art exec.; b. Chgo., May 22, 1931; s. Vincent and Anna (Zajac) B.; grad. Art. Inst. of Chgo., 1955; pupil painting studies Mrs. Melin, Chgo.; m. Loretta A. Nolan, Oct. 15, 1966; children—Heather Anne, Lynnea Joan. Owner, dir. Art J. Banach Studios, 1949—, cartoon syndicate for newspapers, house organs and advt. functions, 1954—, owned and operated advt. agy., 1954-56, feature news and picture syndicate, distbn. U.S. and fgn. countries. Dir. Speculators S Fund. Recipient award 1st Easter Seal contest Ill. Assn. Crippled, Inc., 1949. Chgo. Pub. Sch. Art Soc. Scholar. Mem. Artist's Guild Chgo., Am Mgmt. Assn., Chgo. Assn. of Commerce and Industry, Chgo. Federated Advt. Club, Am. Mktg. Assn., Internat. Platform Assn., Chgo. Advt. Club, Chgo. Soc. Communicating Arts. Clubs: Columbia Yacht, Advertising Executives; Art Directors (Chgo.). Address: 1076 Leahy Circle E Des Plaines IL 60016

BANAS, EMIL MIKE, physicist, educator; b. East Chicago, Ind., Dec. 5, 1921; s. John J. and Rose M. (Valcicak) B.; ed. Ill. Benedictine Coll., 1940-43; B.A. (U.S. Rubber fellow), U. Notre Dame, 1954, Ph.D., 1955; m. Margaret Fagyas, Oct. 9, 1948; children—Mary K., Barbara A. Instr. math. and physics Ill. Benedictine Coll., Lisle, 1946-48, asso. faculty mem., 1971—, trustee, 1959-61; with Civil Service, State of Ind. Hammond, 1948-50; lectr. physics Purdue U., Hammond, 1955-60; research physicist Standard Oil Co., Hammond, 1955—. Served with USNR, 1943-46. Certified state tchr., Ill., Ind. Mem. Ill. Benedictine Coll. Alumni Assn. (dir. hon., named alumnus of yr., 1965, pres. 1959-60), Sigma Pi Sigma. Roman Catholic. Clubs: Soc. of Procopians. Contbr. articles to sci. jours. Home: 8 Huntington Circle W Naperville IL 60540 Office: AMOCO Research Center Naperville IL 60540

BANAS, THOMAS PAUL, pub. affairs exec.; b. Detroit, Apr. 15, 1937; s. Ted J. and Pearl (Danielowicz) B.; Ph.B., U. of Detroit, 1958; M.B.A., Wayne State U., 1964; m. Carolyn Ann Burch, May 23, 1958; children—Scott, Amy, Polly. Gen. tech. aide City of Detroit, 1958-60; market research asst. Micromatic Hone Corp., Detroit, 1960; copywriter Ruben Advt., Detroit, 1960-61; promotion writer The Detroit News, 1961-63; publicity mgr. Sta. WWJ AM-FM-TV, 1963-67; sr. writer G. & D Communications Inc., Detroit, 1967; asst. promotion mgr., Sta. WWJ AM-FM-TV, 1967-73, community relations dir., 1973-76; sr. v.p., P/R Asso., Inc., Detroit, 1976-78; exec. dir. Am. Lung Assn. S.E. Mich., Detroit, 1978—. Instr. Highland Park Coll., 1968-70, U. of Detroit, 1970. Bd. dir. Royal Oak Boy's Club, 1974—; bd. exec. com. Southeastern Mich. Chpt. ARC, 1973—; bd. dirs. S.E. Mich. Travel and Tourist Assn., 1973—, Regional Citizens, Inc., 1976—; mem. communications arts adv. panel Mich. Council for the Arts, 1975—, Comprehensive Health Planning Council S.E. Mich., 1973-76, Oakland County Mental Health Bd., 1976—, Pleasant Ridge City Commn., 1973-77; del. S.E. Mich. Council Govts., 1973-77; coordinator Internat. Freedom Festival, 1977. Recipient Mich. Vol. Leadership award, 1972, Spl. Tribute Mich. Ho. Reps., 1973. Mem. Pub. Relations Soc. of Am. Clubs: Detroit Press, Adcraft (Detroit). Home: 9 Wellesley Ave Pleasant Ridge MI 48069 Office: 28 W Adams St Detroit MI 48226

BANCROFT, THEODORE ALFONSO, educator, statistician; b. Columbus, Miss., Jan. 2, 1907; s. Frank Hammond and Laura Louise (Cox) B.; B.A., U. Fla., 1927; M.A., U. Mich., 1934; Ph.D., Iowa State U., 1943; m. Lenore Springer, Dec. 1, 1933; children—Alice Muriel, Lenore Louise. Teaching asst. math. Vanderbilt U., 1937-38; head math. dept. Mercer U., 1938-41; asso. prof. math. U. Ga., 1946-47; dir. statis. lab. Auburn U., 1947-49; asso. prof. Iowa State U., 1949, dir., head statis. lab., dept. statistics, 1950-72, prof. statis. lab. and dept. statistics, 1972-77, prof. emeritus, 1977—. UN assignment Middle East, India, 1954, Mexico, 1955, Univ. tng. command Italy, 1945; vis. prof. Japan Soc. Promotion of Sci., U. Philippines, 1973, Cath. U. Chile, 1975. Recipient A. Wilton Park award, Eng., 1976. Fellow Am. Statis. Assn. (pres. 1970), AAAS, Inst. Math. Statistics; mem. Biometric Soc. (mem. council and past pres. Eastern N.Am. region), NRC, Sigma Xi, Phi Kappa Phi, Mu Sigma Rho (dir.). Home: 3515 Woodland Ave Ames IA 50010

BAND, JORDAN CLIFFORD, lawyer; b. Cleve., Aug. 15, 1923; s. Samuel Melville and Helen Rita (Krause) B.; student U. Ala., 1943-44; B.B.A., Western Res. U., 1947, LL.B., 1948; m. Alice Jean Glickson, Apr. 27, 1946; children—Terril, Stefanie, Claudia. Admitted to Ohio bar, 1948; since practiced in Cleve., 1948—; mem. firm Ulmer, Berne, Laronge, Glickman & Curtis, Cleve., 1948—; sec., dir. Burdox, Inc., Midwestern Land Devel. Corp., Robert Levin Carpet Co., Hodgson Houses Inc. Nat. chmn. Nat. Jewish Community Relations Adv. Council, 1967-70, exec. bd., 1970—; nat. treas. Nat. Conf. Soviet Jewry, 1973-76; chmn. Greater Cleve. Conf. on Religion and Race, 1966; chmn. Cleve. Jewish Community Fedn. Del. Assembly, 1962-65; steering com. Nat. Urban Coalition, 1967-70; nat. bd. govs. Am. Jewish Com., 1970-73; exec. com. Jewish Community Fedn. of Cleve., 1967—; mem. Community Relations Bd., City of Cleve., 1970—; trustee Bur. for Careers in Jewish Service, 1970-73; trustee American-Israel Pub. Affairs Com., 1967-75; nat. chmn. Nat. Commn. on Equal Opportunities, 1964-67. Served with AUS, 1943-46. Recipient Kane leadership award Jewish Community Fedn. Cleve., 1961. Mem. Am., Ohio, Cleve. bar assns., Order of Coif. Club: Oakwood (Cleveland Heights). Home: 18483 Parkland Dr Shaker Heights OH 44122 Office: 1100 Keith Bldg Cleveland OH 44115

BANDA, ARPAD FREDERIC, educator; b. N.Y.C., June 16, 1928; s. John and Terecia (Varga) B.; B.S. in Social Scis., City Coll. N.Y., 1950; M.B.A., N.Y. U., 1956, Ph.D., 1964, C.F.A., 1977. Instr. econs. Milw.-Downer Coll., 1959-61, Upsala Coll., 1961-62; asst. prof. econs., fin. U. Hartford (Conn.), 1963-66, asso. prof., 1966-68, chmn. dept., 1966-67; asso. prof. fin. U. Akron (O.), 1968-71, prof., 1971—, head dept., 1970-73, 77—. Elder, Hungarian Reformed Ch. Akron; pres. Hungarian Found., Inc.; v.p. Lorantffy Care Center, Inc.; bd. dirs. Am. Hungarian Fedn., 1977—. Mem. Fin. Mgmt. Assn. (coordinating editor jour. 1970-75), Am., Ohio (pres. 1972-73), Eastern (dir. 1975—) fin. assns. Home: 2299 Winter Pkwy Cuyahoga Falls OH 44221 Office: 302 E Buchtel Ave Akron OH 44325

BANDIOLA, BENJAMIN ESCANER, educator; b. Valladolid, Negros Occidental Philippines, Oct. 11, 1926; s. Ambrocio Kanja and Hortencia Cruz (Escaner) B.; came to U.S., 1967, naturalized, 1974; B.S., Philippine Union Coll., 1953, M.A., 1959; Ph.D. (Grad. Coll. fellow), U. Ia., 1961; m. Anita Cuenca Javellana, Apr. 8, 1952; children—Vivien Ann (Mrs. Gerald Wilton Koh), Rene Arthur, John Alden, Lillian Ruth, Ivan Oliver. Tchr. Magallon (Philippines) Pub. Schs., 1948-49, elementary supr., 1949-53, elementary prin., 1953-55, chmn. dept. elementary edn., 1955-57; instr. edn. and psychology Philippine Union Coll., 1957-59; Fulbright scholar, research asst. U. Iowa, 1959-61; dean Sch. Edn. Philippine Union Coll., 1962-64, Sch. Grad. Studies, 1964-67; prof. edn. and psychology Union Coll., Lincoln, Nebr., 1969—. Research cons. Philippine Women's U., Manila; lectr. U. of East Grad. Sch. Edn., Manila; lectr. Philippine Normal Coll., Manila. Recipient Philippine Union Coll. Golden Jubilee certificate of Appreciation, 1967, Outstanding Alumnus in Edn. award, 1976; Nebr. Humanities and Social Scis. Devel. Program research grantee, 1971. Mem. Philippine Assn. for Grad. Edn., Philippine Fulbright Scholars Assn., Am. Ednl. Research Assn.,

AAUP, Assn. for Supervision and Curriculum Devel., Nebr. Council Tchr. Edn., Phi Delta Kappa. Home: 3910 La Salle Lincoln NE 68516

BANDO, HIRO WALTER, accountant; b. San Francisco, May 28, 1912; s. Tokujiro Walter and Kazuko (Akeda) B.; A.B., Leland Stanford U., 1933; M.B.A., Wayne State U., 1953; m. Fumi Patricia Takemoto, Oct. 20, 1945; children—Patricia Alice, Hiro Walter. Partner firm Bando Bros., San Mateo, Calif., 1933-41; adminstrv. asst. War Relocation Authority, Topaz, Utah, 1942-45; accountant Bloomingdale Bros., N.Y.C., 1945; traffic clk. Garwood Industries, Detroit, Wayne, Mich., 1946-50; C.P.A. firm Touche, Ross, Bailey & Smart, Detroit, 1951-62; partner firm Bando & Young, C.P.A.'s, Detroit, 1963—; pres. H. Walter Bando, C.P.A., P.C. Trustee Center for Health Edn. (formerly the McGregor Center), Detroit. C.P.A., Mich. Mem. Am. Inst. C.P.A.'s, Mich. Assn. C.P.A.'s Episcopalian. Home: 24031 Norwood St Oak Park MI 48237 Office: 23100 Providence Dr Southfield MI 48075

BANDY, IRENE GESA, state ofcl.; b. Montgomery, W.Va., Aug. 30, 1940; d. Ernest and Gesa (Koehne) Wolff; B.S.Ed., Ohio U., 1962; M.A., Eastern Ky. U., 1967; postgrad Ohio State U.; 1 son, Nicholas. Tchr., pub. schs., Gainesville, Fla., 1962-64, Cin., 1964-65; guidance supr. Eastern Ky. U., Richmond, 1967-68; counselor, jr. high sch., Napoleon, Ohio, 1968-73; cons. Ohio Div. Guidance and Testing, Columbus, 1973-76, asst. dir., 1977—. Mem. Am. (chmn. Midwest region 1977-78), Ohio personnel and guidance assns., Assn. Counselor Educators and Suprs. (co editor Newsletter 1976-77), Am. Sch. Counselors Assn., Nat. Vocational Guidance Assn., Ohio Sch. Counselors Assn., Ohio Assn. Counselor Educators and Supervisors, Phi Delta Kappa. Home: 1922 Queensbridge Dr Worthington OH 43085 Office: 65 Front St S Rm 1005 Columbus OH 43215

BANERJEE, SAMARENDRANATH, orthopaedic surgeon; b. Calcutta, India, July 12, 1932; s. Haridhone and Nihar Bala (Mukherjee) B.; M.B. B.S., R.G. Kar Med. Coll., Calcutta, 1957; postgrad. U. Edinburgh, 1965-66; m. Hima Ganguly, Mar. 1977. Intern R.G. Kar Med. Coll., 1956-58; resident in surgery Bklyn. Jewish Hosp. Med. Center, 1958-60, Brookdale Med. Center, Bklyn., 1960-61, Jersey City Med. Center, 1961-63; research fellow Hosp. for Sick Children, U. Toronto (Ont., Can.), 1968-69; practice medicine specializing in orthopedics, Sault Ste. Marie, Ont.; past pres. med. staff, chmn. exec. com. Gen. Hosp., Sault Ste. Marie; cons. orthopaedic surgeon Gen. Hosp., Plummer Meml. Hosp., Crippled Children Center, Ministry Nat. Health and Welfare, Dept. Vets. Adminstrn.; civilian orthopaedic surgeon to 44th Div. Armed Forces Base Hosp., Kaduna, Nigeria, 1969. Trustee Gen. Hosp., Sault Ste. Marie, 1975. Miss Betsy Burton Meml. fellow, 1963-64. Fellow Royal Coll. Surgeons Can., A.C.S., Royal Coll. Surgeons Edinburgh; mem. Canadian Orthopaedic Assn., Canadian Med. Assn. Home: 271 McGregor Ave Sault Ste Marie ON P6A 3X1 Canada Office: 125-955 Queen St East Sault Ste Marie ON Canada

BANERJEE, TARIT KUMAR, oncologist and internist; b. Calcutta, India, May 3, 1939; s. Sailendra Nath and Leelaboti (Mukherjee) B.; student Coll. Arts and Sci., Jadavpur, India, 1957; M.B. B.S., Calcutta Nat. Med. Coll., 1963; m. Suvra Mukherjee, Oct. 12, 1971; 1 dau., Sumana. Came to U.S., 1964, naturalized, 1972. Intern, Irwin Hosp., New Delhi, India, 1963-64; intern Lutheran Hosp., Cleve., 1964-65, resident, 1965-67; resident Roswell Park Meml. Inst., Buffalo, 1967-68, cancer research fellow, 1968-69; clin. asst. U. Alta. (Can.) Hosp., Edmonton, 1969-71; mem. staff Marshfield (Wis.) Clinic, 1972—; sr. investigator Eastern Coop. Oncology Group. Diplomate Am. Bd. Internal Medicine, Am. Bd. Med. Oncology. Fellow Royal Coll. Physicians Can.; mem. Am. Soc. Clin. Oncology, A.C.P., AMA, Wood County Med. Soc. Research in leukocyte mobilization in normal man, acute leukemia and chronic myelocytic leukemia. Office: Marshfield Clinic Marshfield WI 54449

BANET, ODELL JOSEPH, banker; b. Floyds Knobs, Ind., Dec. 17, 1919; s. Joseph and Eva (Zimmerman) B.; student pub. schs. New Albany, Ind.; m. Berniece E. Schmidt, May 17, 1947; children—Michael, Stephen, Paul, Ralph, Thersa, Joan. Bookkeeper, Floyd County Bank, New Albany, 1940-73, v.p., 1973—, cashier, 1974—. Mem. Floyd County Council, 1966-76. Served with USAAF, 1942-45. Mem. VFW. Roman Catholic. Home: Rt 1 Box 40 Scottsville Rd Floyds Knobs IN 47119 Office: PO Box 320 New Albany IN 47150

BANFIELD, THOMAS VINCENT, II, nuclear engr.; b. Gettysburg, Pa., Mar. 13, 1933; s. Thomas Vincent and Nellie Ray (Van Metre) B.; B.S., U.S. Naval Acad., 1954; M.B.A., U. Chgo., 1975; m. Jacqueline Pommier, Dec. 21, 1957; children—Eric-Charles, Nathalie. Commd. ensign U.S. Navy, 1954, advanced through grades to comdr., 1968, active duty, 1954-63, res., 1963—; nuclear engr., research reactor operations Argonne (Ill.) Nat. Lab., 1963-74, div. mgr., 1971-74, mgr. materiel services, 1974-77, controller, 1977—. Mem. Am. Nuclear Soc., Sigma Xi (pres. Argonne chpt. 1973-74). Home: 1091 Candlewood Dr Downers Grove IL 60515 Office: Argonne National Lab Argonne IL 60439

BANGHART, JOHN THOMAS, agr. exec.; b. Chgo., May 18, 1936; s. Thomas C. and Madelon B.; B.A., Wabash Coll., 1958; M.B.A., U. Chgo., 1970; m. Lynn Katherine Bennett, Jan. 29, 1972. Pres., Harvard Sod Nursery, Chgo., 1961-73; pres. John T. Banghart Co. farm properties, Chgo. area, Skokie, Ill., 1971—; dir. 1st Nat. Bank Skokie. Pres., Harborside Condonimium I, 1977; trustee Village of Skokie, 1965-68. Recipient Distinguished Service award Jr. C. of C. Mem. Ill. Farm Bur. Republican. Christian Scientist. Home: One the Court of Harborside Northbrook IL 60062 Office: Box 547 Skokie IL 60076

BANICH, FRANCIS EDWARD, surgeon; b. Chgo., Aug. 30, 1932; s. Frank M. and Mary (Grill) B.; B.S., Loyola U., 1953, M.D., 1957; m. Gloria Joan Shegenda, June 15, 1957; children—Carolyn, Francis, James. Intern, Cook County Hosp., Chgo., 1957-58, resident 1958-63; practice medicine specializing in surgery, Chgo., 1965—; attending surgeon St. Anne's Hosp., Chgo., St. Joseph Hosp., Chgo., Fost McGaw Hosp. of Loyols U., Maywood, Ill., 1965-77, Presbyn. St. Luke's, 1977—; cons. gen. surgery U.S. Naval Hosp., Great Lakes, Ill.; asso. prof. dept. surgery Cook County Postgrad. Sch. Medicine, 1965—; asst. clin. prof. dept. surgery Stritch Sch. Medicine, Loyola U., 1969-77, Rush Presbyn. St. Luke Med. Coll., 1977—; adviser Colostomy Club, Am. Cancer Soc., Ileostomy Club of Chgo.; chmn. mastectomy-ostomy rehab. com. Am. Cancer Soc. Served to lt. comdr. MC USNR, 1963-65. Diplomate Am. Bd. Surgery. Mem. A.C.S., Am. Proctological Soc., Ill., Chgo. surg. socs., Inst. Medicine Chgo., Internat. Acad. Proctology, Royal Soc. of Medicine, Am. Soc. Colon and Rectal Surgeons. Club: Oak Park Country (River Grove, Ill.). Patentee ligator. Home: 1842 N 77th Ave Elmwood Park IL 60635 Office: 6710 W North Ave Chicago IL 60635

BANISTER, OLIVE KENNEDY, rehab. adminstr.; b. Cleve., July 31, 1910; d. William James and Sarah Ann (Scull) Kennedy; B.A., Ohio State U., 1932; postgrad (Fellow) Western Res. U., 1932-34; M.A., Tchrs. Coll. Columbia U., 1942; Dr. Humane Letters, Ursuline Coll., 1975; m. Harold F. Banister, Aug. 18, 1934; 1 son, William Kennedy. Social worker, Cleve. Social Service Agencies, 1932-37, founder vocational counseling service, 1939, 1st dir. Vocational Guidance Bur., 1949-56, exec. dir. Vocational Guidance and Rehab. Services, 1956-75; rehab. project dir. Cancer Center, Inc., Cleve., 1975—. U.S. rep. Rehab. Intenat. Commn. on Vocational Rehab., 1972—; internat. and U.S. cons. HEW. Recipient Distinguished Service award United Torch Services Cleve., 1975. Mem. Nat. (trustee, Pres.'s award 1972, Mary E. Switzer award 1975), Ohio rehab. assns., Am. Personnel and Guidnce Assn. (life), Nat. Vocational Guidance Assn., Fedn. Community Planning Cleve. (past trustee), Assn. Rehab. Facilities (past dir., com. chmn.), Pi Lambda Theta, Kappa Delta Pi. Home: 2235 Overlook Rd Cleveland OH 44106 Office: 11001 Cedar Ave Cleveland OH 44106

BANKER, JOHN DAVIS, banker; b. Plattsburg, N.Y., Nov. 4, 1922; s. Carl John and Ethel Caroline (Davis) B.; B.A. in Econs., Williams Coll., 1943; grad. Midwest Banking Inst., U. Minn., 1969; m. Elizabeth Claire Hubbard, Apr. 10, 1943; children—John Davis, Mark Hubbard (dec.), Susan Catherine, Deborah Ellen. Lab. engr. Sprague Electric Co., North Adams, Mass., 1943-45; teller Union Nat. Bank, Minot, N.D., 1945-47; asst. cashier Mchts. & Farmers Bank, Cavalier, N.D., 1947-49, First State Bank, Park River, N.D., 1949-53; pres., dir. Citizens State Bank, Mohall, N.D., 1953—, Mohall Motel, 1971—; dir. Anderson Mfg., Southey, Sask., Can., Anderson Industries. Mayor Mohall, N.D., 1972—; commr. Mohall Municipal Airport Authority, 1970-72. Bd. dirs., past pres. Community Chest; past county dir. Greater N.D. Assn.; formerly active Boy Scouts Am. Mem. State Central com., N.D. Rep. party, 1958-70, precinct committeeman, 1958-70; mem. Mohall City Council, 1962-66. Bd. dirs. North Central Mental Health and Retardation Center, chmn., 1969-70; bd. dirs. Renville-Bottineau Sr. Citizens Home, Renville-Bottineau Meml. Hosp., North Central Nursing Home, Mohall. Mem. Mohall (dir. 1962—), Lake Metigoshe (pres. 1963-64) improvement assns., N.W. N.D. (pres. 1962-63), N.D. (exec. com. 1962-66) bankers assns., Aircraft Owners and Pilots Assn., Internat. Flying Bankers Assn., Ind. Bankers Assn. Am., Ind. Bankers N.D. (charter, pres. 1969-70), Internat., N.D. (dir. 1972—, pres. 1973-74) flying farmers. Methodist (trustee). Mason (Shriner), Elk, Eagle. Clubs: Minneapolis Athletic; Park River Commercial (pres. 1951); Minot Country; Mohall Country, Mohall Community (pres. 1966-68). Home: 502 2d St SE Mohall ND 58761 Office: 101 Main St W Mohall ND 58761

BANKHEAD, LOWELL CAREY, JR., banker; b. Hannibal, Mo., Oct. 14, 1947; s. Lowell Carey and Erma Lee (Green) B.; student U. Md., 1971-72, Central Meth. Coll., 1968-73; A.B., Moberly Jr. Coll., 1968; m. Charla Marie Rockett, Sept. 15, 1968; children—Lowell Carey, Chanda Rose Lee. Examiner for various counties, Mo. State Auditor's office, 1967-68; exec. v.p., Higbee (Mo.) Savs. Bank, 1973—; agt. Bankhead Ins. Agency, 1973—. Mayor of Higbee, 1974—; mem. Higbee bd. aldermen, 1973-74; vice chmn. Mark Twain regional advisory commn., 1974—; active in Democratic campaigns, 1962—. Served with USAF, 1968-73. Hon. fellow Harry S. Truman Library Inst.; mem. Am., Mo. (Agrl.-Rural Affairs Com., 1976—) Bankers Assns. Mem. Christian Ch. (Disciples of Christ). Clubs: Monticello Assn., Lions, Am. Legion, Masons, Knights Templar. Office: PO Box 38 Higbee MO 65257

BANKOFF, MILTON LEWIS, physician; b. N.Y.C., Dec. 20, 1918; s. Jacob and Sarah (Rashkin) B.; B.S., L.I.U., 1938; M.S., N.Y.U., 1939, M.D., 1943; m. Sylvia Rosner, June 16, 1940; children—Barbara, David, Peter, Nancy. Intern. U.S. Marine Hosp., Stapleton, S.I., N.Y., 1943-44; pvt. practice medicine Michigan City, Ind., 1944—;dir. Clinic Hosp., 1951-52, Doctors Hosp., 1952, chief of staff, 1953-54, 56-57. past pres.; pres. Clinic Assos., 1955-66; chief office of group practice devel. Dept. Health, Edn. and Welfare, Washington, 1967-69. Pres. Michigan City Bd. Health, 1967, Laporte County (Ind.) Bd. Health, 1975—. Chmn. Jewish Welfare Bd., Michigan City, 1956-57, Sinai Lecture Forum, 1954—; bd. dirs. YMCA, Tb Assn., Doctors Hosp. Found. Served as ensign USN, 1940-44. Fellow Am. Acad. Family Practice; mem. Am., Ind., Laporte County med. assns., Am., Ind. socs. anesthesiologists, Laporte County Med. Soc. (pres. 1960). Jewish religion (pres. Temple 1958). Clubs: Pottawattomie Country, Rotary (dir.). Home: 307 Kenwood Pl Michigan City IN 46360 Office: 1225 E Coolspring Ave Michigan City IN 46360

BANKS, STEWART WILLARD, realtor; b. Waterbury, Conn., May 3, 1937; s. Leon Wesley and Myrtle Emma (Platt) B.; student U. Conn., 1954-56, Ohio U., 1962-64; children—David, Susan, Julie. Sales and mgmt. positions J.P. Banks Real Estate, Bethlehem, Conn., 1952-59; salesman, mgr. M.A. Gire & Co. Realtors, Reynoldsburg, O., 1964-73; owner Stew Banks & Co. Realtors, 1973—. Treas., City of Reynoldsburg, 1969—. Served with USAF, 1959-64. Named Outstanding Young Man of Reynoldsburg, Reynoldsburg Jaycees, 1970; named to Million Dollar Sales Clubs, Ohio and Columbus bds. realtors. Mem. Nat., Ohio, Columbus real estate bds., Jaycees (pres. Reynoldsburg 1968-69, v.p. Ohio 1969-71). Club: Masons (32 deg.). Home: 1779 Kaiser Dr Reynoldsburg OH 43068 Office: 6500 E Main St Reynoldsburg OH 43068

BANMEN, JOHN, Canadian provincial ofcl.; b. Rosthern, Sask., Can., June 3, 1935; B.Ed., U. B.C., 1962, B.A., 1964, M.Ed., 1967; Ph.D., U. Wyo., 1970; m. Anne Iris Pawson, June 28, 1958; children—Chris, Stephen, Jason. Supr. guidance and counseling services Man. Dept. Edn., Winnipeg, 1965-70, supr. Student Personnel Services, 1970-72, dir. profl. devel. br., 1972-75; asst. dep. minister Man. Dept. Health and Social Devel., 1975-76; asso. dep. minister Man. Ministry Corrective and Rehab. Services, 1976-77, dep. minister, 1977—. Family therapist Red River Family and Marriage Counseling Assos., part-time 1970—; staff U. Man., Winnipeg, part-time 1970-72. Bd. dirs. Canadian Mental Health Assn., 1974-76; bd. govs. Alcoholism Found. Man., 1974—. Mem. Canadian Guidance and Counseling Assn. (sec.-treas. 1967-71, pres. 1973-75), Am., Canadian psychol. assns. Contbr. articles to profl. jours. Home: 74 Lonsdale Dr Winnipeg MB R2Y 0N2 Canada Office: 313 Legislative Bldg Broadway Winnipeg MB R3C 0V8 Canada

BANNES, LORENZ THEODORE, constrn. co. exec.; b. St. Louis, Oct. 24, 1935; s. Lawrence Anthony and Louise Clair (Vollet) B.; B.S. in Civil Engring., St. Louis U., 1957; m. Janet Ann Bruening, Aug. 10, 1957; children—Stephen W., Michael F., Timothy L. From project engr. to exec. v.p. Gamble Constrn. Co. Inc., St. Louis, 1960-69, pres., 1969-72; founder, pres. Bannes-Shaughnessy, Inc., St. Louis, 1972—; dir., v.p. St. Louis Constrn. Manpower Corp., 1977—. Tchr. civil engring. dept. St. Louis U., 1969—; tchr. contracting and concrete methods U. Mo. Extension Center, 1970—; tchr. constrn. mgmt. Grad. Engring. Center, U. Mo., St. Louis, 1968—, Sch. Architecture, Washington U., St. Louis, 1974—. Mem. adv. com. in civil engring. Florissant Valley Community Coll.; mem. adv. com. constrn. tech. Jefferson Coll. Chmn. trustees Aspenhof, 1973; adv. bd. Little Sisters of Poor, 1975—; nat. bd. Living and Learning, Jesuit ednl. program for disadvantaged. Served with USAF, 1957-60. Recipient Alumni Merit award St. Louis U., 1972. Mem. Nat. Soc. Profl. Engrs. (recipient Young Engr. of Year award 1971), Mo. Soc. Profl. Engrs. (chmn. Y.E. com.), Concrete Council of St. Louis (pres. 1972-73, Distinguished Service award 1973), Asso. Gen. Contractors Am. (Nat. Build/Am. award 1973), St. Louis (Chmn. of Year 1973), ASCE (nat. com. constrn. research 1973-74), Young Presidents Orgn., Engrs. Club St. Louis (dir. 1975), Nat. Assn. Women in Constrn. (hon., Distinguished service award 1974). Home: 724 Paschal Dr St Louis MO 63125 Office: 6780 Southwest Ave St Louis MO 63143

BANNISTER, MARGARET ALICE TRIMBLE, ednl. adminstr.; b. Oklahoma City, Dec. 15, 1924; d. Clyde Waldrop and Mary Melissa (Murray) Trimble; B.A. in Journalism, U. Okla., 1945; teaching certificate U. Mo., St. Louis, 1969, postgrad. extension, 1970-71; postgrad. U. Wash., 1973; m. Lawrence R. Bannister, Jan. 18, 1947 (div. 1968); children—Karen, Barbara Jean, Sally Ann. Reporter, Alva (Okla.) Review-Courier, 1945-46, Clinton (Okla.) Daily News, 1946-47; pub. relations asst. U. Okla., Norman, 1947-51; editorial asst. Consol.-Vultee Aircraft Corp., Ft. Worth, 1951-53; coordinator community relations Berkeley (Mo.) Sch. Dist. (merged with and name changed to Ferguson Sch. Dist. R-2 1975), 1968-72, dir. community relations, 1973—. Mem. Women in Communications, St. Louis Press Club, Nat. Sch. Pub. Relations Assn. (officer Greater St. Louis chpt. 1969-71, 73-74), YWCA, Soroptimists Internat. (charter mem. N. St. Louis County chpt.). Methodist (past mem. bd. stewards, youth council). Home: 2040 Argo Dr Florissant MO 63031 Office: 655 January Ave Ferguson MO 63135

BANSER, ROBERT FRANK, JR., journalist; b. Chgo., Aug. 20, 1946; s. Robert Frank and Alice Rita (Proctor) B.; student Chgo. City Coll., 1965-67; B.S., No. Ill. U., 1969; M.A., 1972; m. Lucille Ann Collins, Nov. 7, 1976. News reporter Paddock Publs., Arlington Heights, Ill., 1968; adminstrv. intern, City of Elgin, Ill., 1969-71; gen. assignment news reporter Star-Tribune, Publs., Chicago Heights, Ill., 1971-76, asso. editor, 1976—. Mem. Internat. City Mgmt. Assn., Soc. Profl. Journalists, Chgo. Headline Club, Sigma Delta Chi, No. Ill. U. Alumni Club. Roman Catholic. Home: 1346 Campbell Ave Chicago Heights IL 60411 Office: 1526 Otto Blvd Chicago Heights IL 60411

BANTON, JAMES FOWLER, ops. research exec.; b. Chgo., May 29, 1937; s. Fowler Boyton and Margaret (Gilruth) B.; student U. Wis., 1955-57; B.S., U. Ill., 1959; M.S., Ill. Inst. Tech,, 1963; m. Susan Abendroth, Sept. 1, 1966; children—James Andrew, Pembrook Collin and Bridget Gilruth (twins). Began as mgr. project control Gen. Telephone & Electronics, Chgo., 1961-63; program dir., ops. analysis Rexnord, Milw., 1964-68, cons. mgr., 1968—; lectr. U. Wis., 1967—. Mem. Gov.'s Commn. Higher Edn. Mem. Brookfield Park and Recreation Commn., 1975—, chmn., 1977—; pres. Willaura West, 1977—. Mem. Ops. Research Soc. Am. (gen. chmn. 43d nat. meeting, mem. publs. com. 1967-73, chmn. nat. meetings com. 1973—), Inst. Mgmt. Sci. (chpt. chmn. 1966-67, v.p. meetings 1977, chmn. combined nat. meetings com. with Ops. Research Soc. Am. 1975—). Roman Catholic. Home: 15875 Ridgefield Ct Brookfield WI 53005 Office: 333 Bishops Way Brookfield WI 53005

BANZHAF, CAROL ROTTIER, civic worker; b. Beaver Dam, Mich., Sept. 16, 1923; d. John A. and Marguerite (Mueller) Rottier; student Calvin Coll., 1942-43; A.B., Kalamazoo Coll., 1946; postgrad. Long Beach State Coll., 1954; M.A., Stetson U., 1959; m. Roger A. Goodspeed, 1946; children—Linn Marie, Carol Rottier; m. 2d, Henry F. Banzhaf, Aug. 6, 1965. Service rep. Mich. Bell Telephone Co., Grand Rapids, 1946; receptionist Littles' Studio, Palm Beach, Fla., 1947; tchr. kindergarten Cosa Mesa Union Schs., Calif., 1953-55; directress St. James' Day Sch., Ormond Beach, Fla., 1955-60; dean of girls, tchr. English, Milw. U. Sch., 1960-65; tchr. adult edn. Milw. Area Tech. Coll., 1973-75. Bd. dirs. Vol. Services of Greater Milw., 1963-66, Episcopal Campus Rectory, Milw., 1964-72, Women of St. Mark's Episcopal Ch., 1967-73, St. John's Home, Milw., 1976—; bd. dirs. Women of St. Simon the Fisherman, Port Washington, Wis., 1973—, chmn., 1974-76; vol. Lit. Services Wis. Mem. Nat. Women Deans and Counselors, Am. Personnel and Guidance Assn. Episcopalian. Home: Rural Route 1 5236 Sandy Beach S Belgium WI 53004

BANZHAF, CLAYTON HARRIS, fin. exec.; b. Buffalo, Dec. 24, 1917; s. Joeseph Maximilian and Elizabeth (Harris) B.; M.B.A., U. Chgo., 1954; m. Dolores Gavins, Dec. 30, 1962; children (by former marriage)—Barbara A. (Mrs. Thomas T. Grimmett), Debra R. (Mrs. Stephen T. York), William Clay. With Sears, Roebuck and Co., 1936—, trainee, Buffalo, 1936, retail auditor, Phila., 1939-41, Washington, retail controller, Washington, 1946-48, retail controller, Pitts., 1949-50, wage and salary adminstr., nat. personnel dept., Chgo., 1950-58, asst. treas., 1958-60, sr. asst. treas., 1961-75, treas., 1975-76, v.p., treas., 1976—; pres., Sears Roebuck Acceptance Corp., Wilmington, Del., 1963-72, dir., 1972—; mng. dir. Sears Overseas Finance N.V. Curacao, N.A., 1973—; treas. Sears Internat. Finance Co., Sears Roebuck Overseas, Inc., Lifetime Foam Products Inc., Terminal Freight Handling Co., Sears Roebuck de P.R., Tower Ventures Inc.; asst. treas. Sears Roebuck S/A, Banco de Credito Internacional S/A, Western Forge Co.; dir. Am. Credit Corp., Charlotte, N.C., Homart Devel. Corp., Bancode Credito Internacional S/A, Lake Shore Land Assn., Inc., Chgo., Sears Overseas Finance N.V., Curacao, Western Forge Corp., Colorado Springs, Colo. Mem. exec. bd. Chgo. area council Boy Scouts Am., 1963-68, adv. bd., 1969—; bd. dirs. United Way Met. Chgo., 1975—; active Am. Cancer Soc., 1958-60. Served from pvt. to maj., AUS, 1941-45. Mem. Chgo. Fin. Execs. Inst. (pres. Chgo. chpt. 1972-73, nat. dir. 1975—, v.p. Midwest Area 1977—), Stock Transfer Assn., Art Inst. Chgo., A.I.M. (pres.'s council 1966-69, fellow 1967-69), Internat. Platform Assn., Chgo. Assn. Commerce and Industry, Newcomen Soc., U. Chgo. Alumni Assn. (alumni council Grad. Sch. Bus. 1969—, pres. 1972-75), C. of C. U.S. (com. banking and monetary policy 1967-72, mem. banking monetary and fiscal affairs com. 1972—). Clubs: Executive, Union League, (chmn. house com. 1969-71, dir. 1969-72, 2d v.p. 1977—), Economic, Arts, Medinah Country, Metropolitan, Saddle and Cycle, Chicago (Chgo.). Republican. Presbyterian. Mason. Home: 1130 N Lake Shore Dr Chicago IL 60611 Office: Sears Tower Chicago IL 60684

BARAN, WILLIAM LEE, food scientist; b. Chgo., Mar. 8, 1943; s. William John and Dorothy Pearl (Silverthorne) B.; A.A., Wright City Coll., Chgo., 1963; B.S., Ia. State U., 1966, M.S., 1968; Ph.D., Mich. State U., 1973; m. Lesley Ann Mentch, Nov. 22, 1975. Grad. asst. Ia. State U., Ames, 1966-68; regional milk and food cons. HEW-USPHS-FDA, Atlanta, 1968-70; research asst. food sci. and human nutrition Mich. State U., East Lansing, 1970-73; food scientist Quaker Oats Co., Barrington, Ill., 1973—. Alumni bd. rep. Coll. Agr. and Natural Resources, Mich. State U., 1975—. Asst. canine trainer Seeing Eye Inc., Morristown, N.J., 1964; asst. scoutmaster Chgo. council Boy Scouts Am., 1961-63. Served to lt. (s.g.), USPHS, 1968-70. Iverson Hon. Dairy Industry scholar, 1964-65. Mem. Inst. Food Technologists, Commd. Officers Assn. USPHS, Am. Soc. Microbiology, Sigma Xi, Gamma Sigma Delta. Mason (32 deg.). Contbr. articles to profl. jours. Home: 421 Krenz Ave Cary IL 60013 Office: 617 W Main St Barrington IL 60010

BARANKO, EMIL WAYNE, rancher; b. Belfield, N.D., Feb. 25, 1935; s. Steve and Olga (Evoniuk) B.; student Dickinson State Coll., 1953-54; m. Marcia Jane Ryberg, June 16, 1962; children—Gregg Alan, Gail Ann, Glenn Anthony. Surveyor N.D. Hwy. Dept., 1954-55; heavy equipment operator Schulz & Lindsey Constrn. Co., 1955-57; rancher, Fairfield, N.D., 1959—; dir. N.D. Farmers Union

Mutual Ins. Co., N.D. Farmers Union, N.D. Farmers Union Service Assn.; pres. Billings County Farmers Union, 1968-72, 74-76. Mem. Billings County Sch. Bd., Medora, N.D., 1966-70, pres., 1970-74; chmn. SW N.D. Ad Hoc Com. on Water Resources, 1976—; bd. dirs. Billings County Water Mgmt. Dist., 1976—. Served with AUS, 1957-59. Recipient Agriculturist award N.D. State U., 1974. Mem. Medora Grazing Assn. (dir. 1972—). Democrat. Ukrainian Catholic (chmn. social com. 1967-68). Eagle, Elk. Home: Fairfield ND 58627

BARANOWSKI, EDWARD ALFRED, credit union exec.; b. Milw., Apr. 8, 1938; s. Edward and Rose Victoria (Schweda) B.; B.Ed., Wis. State U., 1959; M.S., U. Wis., 1969; m. Marlowe Rae Zoberski, June 11, 1960; children—Michael, Debra. Tchr. Wausau (Wis.) Pub. Schs., 1959-65; field rep. Wis. Credit Union League, Madison, 1965, gen. mgr. Univ. Faculty Credit Union, Madison, Wis., 1965-76, pres. U. Wis. Credit Union, 1976—; dir. Park Bank Madison; pres. Topics Unlimited, Madison, 1971—; lectr. in field. Bd. dirs. Four Lakes Council, Boy Scouts Am., 1966—. Named mgr. of yr. Soc. Advancement Mgmt., 1975. Mem. Credit Union Exec. Soc., Soc. Certified Consumer Credit Execs., Internat. Platform Speakers Assn., Phi Delta Kappa. Rotary. Home: 1222 Meadowlark Dr Madison WI 53716 Office: 1433 Monroe St Madison WI 53711

BARB, MARGARET ELLEN, educator; b. Elkins, W.Va., Nov. 7, 1931: d. Harold Edward and Viva (Hart) Barb; B.S., W.Va. Wesleyan Coll., 1953; M.S. in Home Econs. Edn., W.Va. U., 1960; postgrad. Kent State U., 1960-64. Home econs. tchr. Harbor High Sch., Ashtabula, Ohio, 1953-56; tchr. home econs. J.R. Williams Jr. High Sch., Painesville, Ohio, 1956-61, 68-70, sch. counselor, 1961-68, 70—. Mem. W.Va. U. Home Econs. Alumnae Assn., Am. Personnel and Guidance Assn., Nat. Vocat. Guidance Assn., Am., Ohio sch. counselors assns., Alpha Gamma Delta, Delta Kappa Gamma. Presbyn. Home: 368 Rockwood Dr Painesville OH 44077

BARBEE, JAMES MAX, veterinarian; b. Sutton, Nebr., Nov. 3, 1923; s. James Sheldon and Opal Pauline (Foster) B.; student Doane Coll., 1941-42; D.V.M., Kans. State U., 1945; m. Betty Lavonne Gustafson, Apr. 17, 1949; children—James Carl, Steven George, Thomas David. Gen. practice veterinary medicine Barbee Veterinary Clinic, Sutton, Nebr., 1945—; v.p. Sutton Ready Mix, Inc., 1961-65; pres. Barbee, Inc., 1963—, Barbee Ponderosa, Inc., 1963—; sec. Sutton Lumber and True Value, 1963—. Pres. Sutton Community Council, 1952-54; pres. Sutton Sch. Bd. Edn., 1954-63; state conf. moderator United Ch. Christ, 1974; lay del. United Ch. Christ Nat. Synod, 1971, 73, 75; dir. exec. com. Interchurch Ministries of Nebr., Inc., 1973-75, sec., 1976. Served with U.S. Army, 1943-44. Mem. Am., Nebr. veterinary med. assns., Am. Assn. Bovine Practitioners, Am. Assn. Swine Practitioners. Clubs: Am. Legion, Sutton Comml., Lions Internat., Blue River Flying, Sutton Golf. Home: 555 Way Ave Sutton NE 68979 Office: 388 Saunders Ave Sutton NE 68979

BARBER, ANDREW BOLLONS, banker; b. Joliet, Ill., Apr. 8, 1909; s. Charles and Pauline Inez (Bollons) B.; student U. Ill., 1929-31; B.S., Northwestern U., 1939; m. Bette Jo Johnson, May 1, 1963; children—Suzanne (Mrs. Terrence J. Ryan), Nancy, Mary Jane (Mrs. Robert Holt). With Union Nat. Bank, Joliet, Ill., 1940—, pres., 1972-73, chmn. bd., 1974—; dir. Citizens Nat. Bank, Waukegan, Ill., Nat. Bank North Chicago (Ill.), Streator (Ill.) Nat. Bank. Chmn. Will County Savings Bond Program, 1946-74; chmn. Will County Land Clearance Commn., 1968-72; mem. Joliet (Ill.) Parking Commn., 1950-70. Bd. dirs. Credit Bur. Will County, Midwest region Boys Club Am.; trustee Lewis U., Lockport, Ill. Mem. C. of C., Nat. Boys Club (N.Y.C.) (asso.). Kiwanian. Clubs: Country (Joliet, Ill.); Three Rivers Yacht (Wilmington, Ill.); Chgo. Yacht. Home: 415 Western Ave Joliet IL 60435 Office: 50 W Jefferson St Joliet IL 60431

BARBER, FRANK ALVA, accountant; b. Central City, Iowa, Nov. 22, 1915; s. Clare Charles and Letha Jane (Lockwood) B.; B.A., Coe Coll., 1937; m. Marion Sinora Hansen, Sept. 16, 1939; children—Kenneth Frank, James George. Asst. credit mgr. Cities Service Oil Co., St. Paul, 1937-42; head disbursement sect. U.S. Rubber Co., Des Moines, 1942-45; office and credit mgr. Firestone Tire & Rubber Co., Waterloo, Iowa, 1945-47; owner accounting and tax service, Waterloo and Cedar Falls, Iowa, 1947—. Vol., Big Bros. Am., Waterloo, 1961-73. Bd. dirs., treas. Girl Scouts Am., Waterloo, 1953-57. Mem. Nat. Soc. Pub. Accountants, Accountants Assn. Ia. Conglist. Club: Exchange (Waterloo). Address: 4223 Hillside Dr Cedar Falls IA 50613

BARBER, KENT GRAVES, state ofcl.; b. Skidmore, Mo., Oct. 26, 1915; s. Alonzo A. and Hattie (Graves) B.; B.S., N.W. Mo. State Coll., 1947; M.A., U. Mo., 1950; m. Ilda Blanche Simmons, Mar. 18, 1938; children—Gary Kent, Terry Lynn. Tchr. elementary sch. Nodaway County, Mo., 1936-39; flight engr. N.Am. Aviation, Kansas City, Mo., 1942-43; supt. schs. Holt County R-I, Maitland, Mo., 1947-53, Gentry County R-D, Stanberry, Mo., 1953-60, Clinton County R-III, Plattsburg, Mo., 1960-66; dir. sch. laws State Dept. Edn., Jefferson City, Mo., 1966—. Served with AUS, 1944-45. Mem. Am., Mo. assns. sch. adminstrs., Mo. Tchrs. Assn., Phi Delta Kappa. Methodist. Mason. Home: 303 Norris Dr Jefferson City MO 65101 Office: Jefferson Bldg Jefferson City MO 65101

BARBERIO, ANTHONY BEN, assn. exec.; b. Des Moines, Nov. 22, 1938; s. Joseph H. and Mary Ann (Gentile) B.; B.A., Drake U., 1963, M.B.A., 1971; m. Sandra Wayne, Mar. 9, 1963; children—Michael, Michelle. Product mgr. Aloe, div. Brunswick, St. Louis, 1968-69; research coordinator Monsanto Chem. Co., St. Louis, 1969-70; research program dir. Iowa State Edn. Assn., Des Moines, 1971—. Bd. dirs. Des Moines Talented and Gifted Assn., 1976. Served with USMC, 1956-58. Mem. NEA, Nat., Profl. staff orgns. Home: 1330 62d St Des Moines IA 50311 Office: 4025 Tonawanda Dr Des Moines IA 50312

BARBIERI, JAMES CHARLES, newspaperman; b. Park Ridge, Ill., Dec. 20, 1928; s. Joseph Francis and Vera (Gillick) B.; B.A. magna cum laude, DePauw U., 1950; m. Barbara Carolyn Forsell, Apr. 28, 1951; children—Charles Edward, Cynthia Jean. Advt. staff mem., reporter Bluffton Evening News-Banner, Bluffton, Ind., 1950, advt. mgr., circulation mgr., 1950—, bus. mgr., 1957-75, gen. mgr., 1975—; sec., dir. Bluffton News Banner Corp., 1975—. Active Boy Scouts Am. Publicity and advt. chmn. Wells County Republican com., 1964—. Served with AUS, 1951-53. Mem. Ind. Newspaper Advt. Execs. Assn., Central States Circulation Mgrs. Assn., Bluffton C. of C. (past dir.), Inland Daily Press Assn., Am. Legion. Presbyterian. Kiwanian. Home: 621 S Williams St Bluffton IN 46714 Office: 125 N Johnson St Bluffton IN 46714

BARBOLINI, ROBERT R., chem. engr.; b. N.Y.C., May 30, 1938; s. Renato J. and Dorothy L. (Curry) B.; B.S., Mass. Inst. Tech., 1959; M.Engring., Yale U., 1962; M.B.A., U. Chgo., 1973; m. Betty M. Halford, Sept. 11, 1976. Chem. engr. Union Carbide Corp., Tonawanda, N.Y., 1959-60; project mgr. Process Plants Corp., N.Y.C., 1961-68; asst. chief engr. Met. San. Dist. Greater Chgo., 1968—; dir., pres. 201 E Chestnut Condominium Assn. Registered profl. engr., Conn., Ill., N.Y. Mem. Water Pollution Control Fedn., Air Pollution Control Assn., Am. Pub. Works Assn. Home: 2500 Lakeview Ave Chicago IL 60614 Office: 100 E Erie St Chicago IL 60611

BARBORIAK, JOSEPH JAN, pharmacologist; b. Kremnica, Slovakia, Feb. 19, 1923; s. Joseph M. and Amalie (Kostial) B.; B.S., Slovak Inst. Tech., 1946; Sc.D., Swiss Fed. Inst. Tech., 1953; m. Gertrude M. Zmarzlak, Sept. 15, 1956; children—Peter N., Daniel P., Eric M. Came to U.S., 1953, naturalized, 1959. Research asso. Swiss Inst. Tech., Zurich, 1947-53, Yale Sch. Medicine, New Haven, 1954-59; group leader Mead Johnson & Co., Evansville, Ind., 1959-61; chief biochemistry sect. VA Center, Wood, Wis., 1961—; asst. prof. pharmacology Marquette U. Sch. Medicine (now Med. Coll. Wis.), Milw., 1962-66, asso. prof. 1966-71, prof. pharmacology, 1971—. Mem. Am. Inst. Nutrition, Soc. for Exptl. Biology and Medicine, Societe de Chimie Biologique (Paris), Am. Acad. Allergy, Internat. Soc. Biochem. Pharmacology, Am. Soc. Pharmacology and Exptl. Therapeutics, Sigma Xi. Contbr. numerous articles to profl. publs. Address: VA Center Wood WI 53193

BARBOUR, FLEMING ARNOLD, physician; b. Elkhart, Ind., July 28, 1909; s. Harry A. and Hartie (Hixon) B.; B.S., Mich. State U., 1932; M.D., U. Mich., 1936, M.S. in Ophthalmology, 1940; m. Marian Elizabeth Patch, June 21, 1936; children—David, Philip, Elizabeth (Mrs. Patrick H. Stine). Intern, Hurley Hosp., Flint, Mich., 1936-37; resident, instr. ophthalmology Med. Sch., U. Mich., Ann Arbor, 1937-40; practice medicine, specializing in ophthalmology, Flint, 1940—; mem. staff McLaren, St. Joseph, Genesee Meml. hosps. (all Flint); dir. 1st Fed. Savs. & Loan Assn., Flint, U.S. Sugar Co. Pres., Flint Com. on Alcoholism, 1959, Greater Flint Council Chs., 1963, Flint chpt. Red Feather Fund, 1962; trustee Flint Inst. Music, 1968—, pres., 1971-73; bd. dirs. YMCA, Flint, 1956-70, res., 1960-62, Mich. world service chmn., 1965-68; chmn. bd. trustees Mott Childrens Health Center, Flint, 1968—; bd. dirs. coordinating council U. Mich., Flint, 1970, mem. devel. council, 1972, mem. Flint. citizens adv. com., 1975—, mem. exec. com. Presidents Club, 1974—; bd. dirs. Internat. Inst., 1970-72. Served to lt. comdr. M.C., USNR, 1943-46. Recipient Liberty Bell award City of Flint, 1965, Service award Flint Interfaith Council, 1974, Distinguished Alumni Service award U. Mich., 1975. Diplomate Am. Bd. Ophthalmology. Fellow A.C.S.; mem. Genesee County (past pres.), Mich. (chmn. ophthalmol. sect. 1959; certificate of commendation 1968) med. socs., Flint Acad. Surgery (pres. 1959), Clubs: Flint City (pres. 1970—), Flint Golf (dir. 1958-60), U. Mich. (pres. 1949) (Flint). Home: 2015 Lincoln Dr Flint MI 48503 Office: 606 Mott Bldg Flint MI 48502

BARBU, ROBERT CORNELL, ednl. adminstr.; b. Cleve., Apr. 11, 1937; s. Cornelius Alexander and Flora Jane (Siegler) B.; B.S., Ohio State U., 1959; M.Ed., Kent State U., 1972; m. Janice Marilyn Jacobs, Nov. 28, 1960; children—Scott, Terrance, Troy. Engring. drawing instr. West Tech. High Sch., Cleve., 1960-65; instr. electronics Westlake (Ohio) High Sch., 1965-70; AV-ITV dir. Westlake City Schs., 1970—; v.p. Profl. Computer Services, Inc., Avon Lake, Ohio, 1971, Guidelines, Inc., Fairview Park, Ohio, 1975. Chmn. audio-visual com. Greater Cleve. Sch. Supts. Group Purchasing Council, 1976-77; recreation dir. City of Avon Lake, 1974-75. Mem. Assn. Ednl. Communication Tech., Ohio Ednl. Library Media Assn. (dist. dir. 1978—), Nat., Ohio edn. assns., Northeastern Ohio Tchrs. Assn., Ohio Indsl. Arts Assn., Westlake Tchrs. Assn., Nat. Ski Patrol System, Boy Scouts Am. Writer, producter, host instrnl. TV series Choose It, 1974. Home: 32699 Carriage Ln Avon Lake OH 44012 Office: 27830 Hilliard Rd Westlake OH 44145

BARCLAY, ALLAN GENE, psychologist, educator; b. Masonville, Iowa, Dec. 22, 1930; s. Otho R. and Marian (Lee) B.; student U. Louisville, 1949-50; A.B. cum laude, U. Tulsa, 1955; postgrad. U. Iowa, 1955-56; Ph.D., Washington U., St. Louis, 1960; m. Betty J. Harrison, Sept. 13, 1952; children—Lisa, Allan. Clin. psychologist Mental Hygiene Clinic, VA Regional Office, St. Louis, 1959-60; faculty St. Louis U., 1960—, prof. psychology, 1965—, asso. univ. research adminstr., 1968-72, dir. program in developmental psychology, 1965—, dir. Sch. Medicine Child Devel. Clinic, 1972—; chief psychologist dept. pediatrics Cardinal Glennon Meml. Hosp. for Children, St. Louis, 1960—. Cons. to hosps., govt. agys.; spl. adviser Pres.'s Com. on Mental Retardation; councilor Joint Commn. on Hosps., Accreditation Council on Facilities for Mentally Retarded. Bd. dirs., mem. adv. com. New Hope Found. St. Louis, 1977—; bd. dirs., mem. profl. adv. com. Youth Emergency Services. Served with AUS, 1948-52. Grantee USPHS, 1961, 62, U.S. Children's Bur., 1960-68, Joseph P. Kennedy, Jr. Found., 1965, Children's Research Found., 1965, Office Econ. Opportunity, 1965-68, Social Rehab. Service, 1972—; pres. New Hope Found. Diplomate Am. Bd. Examiners in Profl. Psychology; mem. Nat. Register Health Service Providers in Psychology. Fellow Am. Orthopsychiat. Assn.; Soc. for Rorschach Research and Projective Techniques, Mo. Psychol. Assn., Internat. Council Psychologists; mem. Am. (fellow div. clin. psychology, fellow div. developmental psychology, mem. bd. profl. affairs, sec.-treas. div. clin. psychology, also div. mental retardation), Midwestern (asso. conv. mgr.), Southwestern psychol. assns., AAAS, AAUP, Am. Assn. Mental Deficiency, So. Soc. Philosophy and Psychology, Soc. Research in Child Devel. Inter-Am. Soc. Psychology, Internat. Council Psychologists (treas.), Am. Pub. Health Assn., AMA, Sword and Key, Sigma Xi, Pi Gamma Mu, Psi Chi (nat. pres.), Phi Gamma Kappa. Editor: Jour. Profl. Psychology; contbr. articles to publs. Home: 6939 Washington St St Louis MO 63130

BARCUS, ROBERT GENE, assn. exec.; b. Monticello, Ind., Oct. 22, 1937; s. Harold Eugene and Marjorie Irene (Dilling) B.; B.P.E. (Alumni scholar 1957), Purdue U., 1959; M.A., Ball State U., 1963; postgrad. Ind. U., summer 1966; supts. license Butler U., 1967; m. Mary Evelyn Shull, Aug. 9, 1959; children—Jennifer Sue, Debra Lynn. Tchr., coach Wabash (Ind.) Jr. High Sch., 1959-63; tchr. Wabash High Sch., 1963-64; tchr., coach North Central High Sch., Indpls., 1964-65; salary cons. Ind. State Tchrs. Assn., Indpls., 1965-67, asst. dir. research, 1967-68, dir. spl. services, 1968-70, exec. asst., 1971-72, adminstrv. asst., 1972-73, asst. exec. dir. spl. services, 1973—. Mem. NEA, Am. Assn. Sch. Adminstrs., Wabash City (past pres.), Washington Twp. (past pres.) tchrs. assns., Kappa Delta Pi, Pi Delta Kappa. Mem. Ch. of the Brethren (clk. 1966-74). Clubs: Indpls. Press, Columbia, Indiana Schoolmen's. Home: 8127 Hoover Ln Indianapolis IN 46260 Office: 150 W Market St Indianapolis IN 46204

BARD, GORDON NEAL, food co. exec.; b. Auburn, Ind., May 4, 1938; s. Howard Orville and Wilma (Becker) B.; B.S. (Expressways scholar), Tri-State U., 1960; M.B.A., Mich. State U., 1962; m. Dorothy K. Shore, Dec. 31, 1960; children—Deborah Dawn, Denise Rene. Mgmt. trainer Transam. Freight Lines, Chgo., 1960-61; distbn. trainee, coordinator Dow Chem. Co., Midland, Mich., also Chgo., 1962, 64-65; distbn. analyst Miles Labs., Elkhart, Ind., 1965-70; mgr. distbn. and traffic frozen foods div. and gen. mgr. Freeze Point Systems div. Stokely Van Camp, Indpls., 1970—. Served with AUS, 1962-64. Mem. Nat. Council Phys. Distbn. Mgmt. (chmn., founder Indpls. Roundtable), Am. Frozen Food Distbn. Com. (chm. productivity 1974—, statis. coms. 1974-75), Internat. Frozen Food Assn. (distbn. com. 1974-75), Indpls. Traffic Club, Alpha Beta Alpha. Methodist (usher 1972-75, adminstrv. bd. 1974-75). Lion. Contbr. article to profl. jour. Home: 1929 Hamilton Ln Carmel IN 46032 Office: 941 N Meridian St Indianapolis IN 46206

BARDEEN, JOHN, physicist, educator; b. Madison, Wis., May 23, 1908; s. Charles Russell and Althea (Harmer) B.; B.S., U. Wis., 1928, M.S., 1929; Ph.D., Princeton, 1936; D.Sc. (hon.), Union Coll., 1955, U. Wis., 1960; m. Jane Maxwell, July 18, 1938; children—James Maxwell, William Allen, Elizabeth Ann (Mrs. Greytak). Geophysicist Gulf Research & Devel. Corp., Pitts., 1930-33; asst. prof. physics U. Minn., 1938-41; with Naval Ordnance Lab., Washington, 1941-45; research physicist Bell Telephone Labs., Murray Hill, N.J., 1945-51; prof. physics and elec. engring. U. Ill., Urbana, 1951-75, emeritus, 1975—. Mem. Pres.'s Sci. Adv. Com., 1959-62. Recipient Ballantine medal Franklin Inst., 1952; John Scott medal, Phila., 1955; Fritz London award, 1962; Vincent Bendix award, 1964; Nat. Medal Sci., 1966; Michelson-Morley award Case Western Res. U., 1968; co-recipient Nobel prize in physics, 1956, 72; Presdl. Medal of Freedom, 1977. Fellow Am. Phys. Soc. (pres. 1968-69, Buckley prize 1954); mem. Am. Acad. Arts and Sci., Am. Philos. Soc., Nat. Acad. Sci. Nat. Acad. Eng. Home: 55 Greencroft Champaign IL 61820

BARDIS, PANOS DEMETRIOS, sociologist, author, editor; b. Lefcohorion, Arcadia, Greece; m. Donna Jean; children—Byron Galen, Jason Dante; B.A. magna cum laude, Bethany (W.Va.) Coll., 1950; M.A., Notre Dame U., 1953; Ph.D., Purdue U., 1955. Prof. sociology, editor Social Sci., U. Toledo, 1959—; cons. Nat. Assn. Standard Med. Vocabulary, 1963—; Am. rep. Internat. Congress Social Scis., Barcelona, Spain, 1965, 66, 71; participant Conf. International de Sociologie de la Religion, Rome, 1969, Strasbourg, 1977, Internat. Sci. Congress, Athens, Greece, 1973, 77, Internat. Conf. on Love and Attraction, Swansea, Wales, 1977, Nat. Council on Family Relations, Toronto, Can., 1973, Ohio Acad. Scis., 1975. Sec.-treas. World Student Relief, Athens, 1947-48; chmn. crime reduction com. Commn. for Community Devel., Toledo, 1967-68; trustee Marriage Mus., N.Y.C. Fellow AAAS, Am. Sociol. Assn., Institut Internat. de Sociologie (chmn. membership com. 1970—, coordinator for U.S.A. 1974—, participants confs. Rome 1969, Montreal, 1972, Caracas, 1972), Internat. Inst. Arts and Letters (life), World Acad. Scholars; mem. AAUP, Am. Soc. Neo-Hellenic Studies (bd. advisers), Democritos, Group for Study Sociolinguistics, Inst. for Mediterranean Affairs (adv. council), Internat. Sci. Commn. on Family, Internat. (Am. rep., Evian, France 1966, Rome 1969, Varna, Bulgaria 1970, Algiers 1972, Toronto 1974), N.Central sociol. assns., Modern Greek Soc., Nat. Acad. Econs. and Polit. Sci. (dir.), Nat., Ohio councils on family relations, Nat. Soc. Lit. and Arts, Nat. Writers Club, N.Y. Acad. Scis., Nat. Soc. Published Poets, Alpha Kappa Delta, Phi Kappa Phi, Pi Gamma Mu, Kappa Delta Pi. Recipient award for outstanding achievement in edn. Bethany Coll., 1975, Outstanding Teaching award Toledo U., 1975; Author: Studies in Marriage and the Family, 1975; History of the Family, 1975; The Family in Changing Civilizations, 1969; Ivan and Artemis (novel), 1957; The Future of the Greek Language in the United States, 1976; Encyclopedia of Campus Unrest, 1971; also articles in profl. jours. Editor, asso. editor or book rev. editor 20 nat. and internat. jours. Composer songs for mandolin: Byron Ballad, 1972; Carnival Dance, 1972; The Gypsy Dreamer, 1973; Jeu de Jason, 1973; Lamentation, 1973; Merlin's Magic, 1973; Minerva Melody, 1973; The Nereid of the North, 1973; Threnody, 1974; Verlaine's Chanson d'Automne, 1974; The Pines of Olympia, 1975; Echoes of Arcadia, 1975; The Dance of the Neutrino, 1975; Multis cum Lacrimis, 1976. Office: U Toledo Toledo OH 43606

BARDWELL, ARTHUR GLENN, JR., mktg. exec.; b. El Paso, Tex., July 11, 1921; s. Arthur Glenn and Esther Valina (Crow) B.; B.S., N.Mex. State U., 1941; m. Helen Elizabeth Field, Oct. 3, 1942; children—Arthur Glenn IV, Marcia Ellen. Instr. mech. engring. dept. Tex. A. and M. U., 1941-42; with Stanley Cons., engrs., architects, planners, mgmt. cons., Muscatine, Ia., 1946—, project mgr., 1952-73, indsl. marketing coordinator, 1969—, also dir. mktg. Dist. chmn. Buffalo Bill council Boy Scouts Am., 1960-62, bd. dirs., 1958-64. Served with USAAF, 1942-46. Recipient Silver Beaver award Boy Scouts Am., 1969. Mem. Nat. Soc. Profl. Engrs., Am. Inst. Steel Engrs., Iowa Engring. Soc. Home: 1010 Robin Rd Muscatine IA 52761 Office: Stanley Bldg Muscatine IA 52761

BARDWELL, MAUREEN ANN, educator; b. Pittsfield, Mass., Feb. 6, 1952; d. Harry Pitts and Mary Katherine (Lenihan) B.; B.S. (Coll. scholar, Edith Scott Magna scholar), Am. Internat. Coll., 1973; M.A., Bowling Green State U., 1975, postgrad. (Univ. fellow), 1975—. Teaching asst. computer programming Bowling Green (Ohio) State U., 1973-74, teaching asst. math., 1974-75, teaching fellow, 1975—. Recipient award Mass. Soc. C.P.A., 1972. Mem. Assn. Computing Machinery, Am. Math. Soc., Alpha Chi, Omicron Delta Epsilon. Democrat. Roman Catholic. Office: Dept Math Bowling Green State U Bowling Green OH 43403

BARE, MARK RICHARD, orthodontist; b. Princeton, Ill., Dec. 15, 1943; s. Keith A. and Margaret (Matthews) B.; D.D.S., U. Ill., 1967; M.S., Northwestern U., 1972; m. Varla Jane Bergholt, Sept. 10, 1966; children—Aaron, Christopher. Practice dentistry specializing in orthodontics, Rock Island, Ill., 1972—. Bd. dirs. Illowa Health Systems Agy. Served with U.S. Army, 1967-70. Mem. Am. Orthodontic Assn. (recipient research award 1973), ADA. Clubs: Rotary, Izaak Walton League. Office: 2334 31st Ave Rock Island IL 61201

BAREFIELD, IVOR MAE, psychologist; b. Richland Hill, La., Oct. 10, 1919; d. Charles Herman and Amelia (Scott) Rogers; B.Ed., Chgo. State U., 1957, M.Ed., 1964; postgrad. Ill. Inst. Tech., 1966-69; diploma Okolona Jr. Coll., 1940; m. Curtis G. Barefield, Apr. 29, 1950; children—Ernest G., Curtis G., Sandra (Mrs. John S. Ross), Diane Renée (Mrs. Milton L. Wilburn). Tchr., Parkman Elementary Sch., Chgo., 1957-67; instr. Summer Social Center Program, Chgo., 1960-64; homebound tchr. Family Living Center 2, Chgo., 1967-68; sch. psychologist, Bur. Child Study, Chgo., 1968—. State evaluator, pupil personnel services Office Supt. Pub. Schs., 1971-73. Bd. dirs. Chgo. State U., 1974-76. Mem. Chgo. Tchrs. Union, Am., Ill. psychol. assns., Am. Assn. Social Psychiatry, Chgo. Area Assn. Sch. Psychologists, Chgo. State U. Alumni Assn. (pres. 1977-78), Kappa Delta Pi. Baptist. Home: 822 E 76th St Chicago IL 60619

BARENBERG, ERNEST JOHN, educator; b. nr. Herndon, Kan., Apr. 9, 1929; s. John Joseph and Helena (Geerdes) B.; student Wichita State U., 1948-50; B.S., Kan. State U., 1953; M.S., U. Kan., 1958; Ph.D., U. Ill., 1965; m. Virgie Katherine Rawline, Sept. 5, 1953; children—Katherine, Janet, Rita, Michael, Gena, Myra. Aircraft designer Cessna Aircraft Co., Wichita, Kan., 1953; instr. civil engring. U. Kan., Lawrence, 1955-58, asst. prof., 1958-60; research asst. U. Ill. at Urbana, 1960-63, prof., 1971—; br. chief U.S. Army C.E., 1971-73, cons., 1958—; lectr. Ill. Dept. Transp., 1970—; cons. FAA, 1973; participant fed. workshops, seminars on transp. Active Little League, YMCA. Served to 1st lt. AUS, 1953-55. Recipient Everitt award for teaching excellence, 1971. Mem. ASCE, Nat. Soc. Profl. Engrs., Am. Soc. for Engring. Edn., Am. Soc. Testing and Materials, Nat. Acad. Sci., Am. Road Builders Assn., Sigma Xi, Theta Xi, Tau Beta Pi. Republican. Contbr. articles to profl. publs. Home: 617 W Church St Champaign IL 61820 Office: 111 Talbot Lab Univ Ill Urbana IL 61801

BARG, WILLIAM HENRY, mapping co. exec.; b. Geneva, Ill., June 23, 1930; s. William F. and Theodora H. (Peterson) B.; B.S. in Math., Bradley U., 1954; postgrad. U. Ill., U. Mich., No. Ill. U.; m. Irene Adele Bradshaw, Oct. 11, 1952; children—Scot, Renee, Steven, Michele, Timothy. Mapping maintenance specialist Sidwell Co., West Chicago, Ill., 1950-56, project liaison and coordinator, 1956-59, sales mgr., 1959-64, v.p., mktg. dir., 1964—. Served with USMC, 1950-52. Mem. Am. Soc. Photogrammetry, Am. Congress Surveying and Mapping, Internat. Assn. Assessing Officers, Ill. Assessment Inst., Soc. for Mktg. Profl. Services. Presbyterian. Club: Masons. Contbr. articles in field to profl. jours. Home: 537 W Evergreen Wheaton IL 60187 Office: 28W240 North Ave West Chicago IL 60185

BARGER, CECIL EDWIN, advt. agy. exec.; b. Marshall, Mo., June 19, 1917; s. James Edwin and Jessie (Witcher) B.; B.S. in Agrl. Journalism, U. Mo., 1938; postgrad. Columbia, evenings 1946-47, Northwestern U., evenings 1955-56. Asso. editor. Topeka, 1939-42; copywriter Wildrick & Miller Advt. Agy., N.Y.C., 1945-48, account exec., 1952-54; account exec. promotion dept. Aubrey, Finlay, Marley & Hodgson Advt. Agy., Chgo., 1948-51, creative dir. farm plans bd., 1954-59; v.p. Compton Advt., Inc., Chgo., 1959-65; v.p. Sander Allen Advt., Inc., Chgo., 1966—. Breeder angus cattle, Arrow Rock, Mo., 1956—. Mem. Nat. Agri-Mktg. Assn. (charter, v.p.), Alpha Gamma Rho. Mem. Christian Ch. Clubs: Chicago Advertising (dir., treas.), Chicago Farmers. Home: 900 Lake Shore Dr Chicago IL 60611 Office: 101 E Ontario St Chicago IL 60611

BARGER, CHARLES WILLIAM, engring. co. exec.; b. Chgo., Dec. 21, 1938; s. Leslie Donald and Adeline Esther (Schaade) B.; student U. So. Calif., 1957-58; m. Marilyn Ann Brown, Feb. 7, 1959; children—Karen, Angela, Michael. Rodman to v.p. R.W. Petrie & Assos. Inc., Benton Harbor, Mich., 1959-69; pres., owner Barger Engring. Inc., St. Joseph, Mich., 1969—. Chmn. St. Joseph Cath. Parish Council, 1975-77. Registered profl. engr. Mich., Ind. Mem. Mich. (pres. 1975-76), Nat. profl. engrs. in pvt. practice, Mich., Nat. socs. profl. engrs., Am. Cons. Engrs. Council, Twin Cities Area C. of C. Home: 4066 Woodland Ln St Joseph MI 49085 Office: 612 Main St St Joseph MI 49085

BARGER, JOHN WALTER, educator; b. Huntsville, Mo., Feb. 24, 1918; s. Walter Wade and Grace (Summerfield) B.; grad. Moberly Jr. Coll., 1938, Albion State Normal Coll., 1939; B.S., U. Mo., 1948, Ph.D., 1951; m. Lois May Creed, May 26, 1939; children—Valda M. Barger Pancoast, C. Renee Barger Goddijn, A. Elizabeth Barger Holquist. Research chemist E.I. DuPont de Nemours & Co., Waynesboro, Va., 1951-56; asst. dir. chemistry div. Midwest Research Inst., Kansas City, Mo., 1956-68; mem. faculty S.W. Bapt. Coll., Bolivar, Mo., 1968-72, chmn. chemistry dept., 1968-72; chmn. math and sci. dept. McDonald County High Sch., Anderson, Mo. 1972—. Served with USNR, 1944-45. DuPont Co. fellow, 1950. Mem. Am. Chem. Soc. (sect. treas. 1955-56), Mo. Tchrs. Assn. Baptist (trustee 1969—). Odd fellow. Patentee in field. Contbr. to profl. publs. in field. Home: Box 33 Anderson MO 64831 Office: McDonald High Sch Anderson MO 64831

BARGER, MELVIN DEAN, pub. relations exec.; b. Norfolk, Nebr., Sept. 9, 1925; s. Learner Addison and Bertha Evelyn (Swisher) B.; A.A., Jackson Community Coll., 1970; B.A. in Communications cum laude, U. Toledo, 1975; m. Loraine Schroeder, Sept. 3, 1960; children—Wayne, Craig, Dean, Lynne. Material control supr. Aeroquip Corp. (co. became subs. Libbey-Owens-Ford Co. 1968), Jackson, Mich., 1952-56, editor co. mag., asst. advt. mgr. in charge pub. relations, 1956-63, mgr. pub. relations, 1964-72; editorial writer Wall Street Jour., N.Y.C., 1963-64; dir. corporate communications Libbey-Owens-Ford Co., Toledo, 1972—. Publicity dir. Jackson County United Fund; publicity chmn. Midwest Space Fair, Jackson; pub. relations adviser Com. orn Med. Opportunities in Jackson; mem. pub. relations adv. group Nat. Council Better Bus. Burs.; vice chmn. pub. relations United Fund; bd. dirs. Goodwill Industries Toledo, Toledo Opera Assn. Served with USN, 1943-46; PTO. Recipient George Washington Honor medal Freedoms Found., Valley Forge, Pa., 1967; Outstanding Health Service award Mich. Med. Soc., 1969. Mem. Pub. Relations Soc. Am. (accredited). Republican. Sunday columnist Jackson Citizen Patriot, 1969-72; contbr. articles to various publs.; many TV news commentaries. Home: 4800 Turnbridge Circle Toledo OH 43623 Office: 811 Madison Ave Toledo OH 43695

BARGER, ROBERT NEWTON, III, educator; b. Peoria, Ill., Oct. 29, 1938; s. Robert Newton and Catherine Marie (O'Brien) B.; B.A., St. Paul Sem., 1961, M.A., 1966, M.Div., 1975; M.A., Coll. St. Thomas, 1966; Ph.D. in Am. Ednl. History (Fred S. Bailey scholar), U. Ill., 1976; m. Josephine Disser, Aug. 6, 1976. Ordained priest Roman Catholic Ch., 1965; asst. pastor, tchr. St. Paul Parish and Sch., Danville, Ill., 1965-69; tchr. Schlarman High Sch., Danville, 1965-69; lectr. in religion, adminstr. inter-foundational acad. program, campus minister for Newman Found., U. Ill., Urbana-Champaign, 1969-75, counselor office student services, 1975-76, vis. instr. dept. ednl. policy studies, 1976-77; asst. prof. philosophy and history of edn. Eastern Ill. U., 1977—; participant Internat. Geophys. Year, Antarctica, 1956-57; observer aboard 1st USAF flight over South Pole, Oct. 26, 1956; campus minister Parkland (Community) Coll., 1974-75; pres. Religious Workers Assn. at U. Ill., 1973-74, Com. for a Healing Repatriation, Inc., 1974—; vis. chaplain U.S. Ho. of Reps., 1974; mem. atty. tribunal, mem. bd. consultors Diocese of Peoria, 1974-76. Mem. U.S., Midwest history of edn. socs., Midwest Philosophy of Edn. Soc. Author: A History of the Catholic Cemeteries of the City of Peoria, 1673-1945, 1965; Amnesty: What Does It Really Mean?, 1974; John Lancaster Spalding: Catholic Educator and Social Emissary, 1977; contbr. articles and revs. to profl. publs. Home: 1208 Douglas Dr Charleston IL 61920 Office: 213 Buzzard Edn Bldg Eastern Ill U Charleston IL 61920

BARISAS, BERNARD GEORGE, JR., biochemist; b. Shreveport, La., July 16, 1945; s. Bernard George and Edith (Bailey) B.; B.A., U. Kans., 1965; B.A. (Woodrow Wilson fellow, Rhodes scholar), Oxford U., 1967; M.Ph., Yale U., 1967, Ph.D., 1971; m. Judith Kathleen O'Rear, May 29, 1973. NIH postdoctoral trainee Yale U., 1971-72, research asso., 1972; NIH postdoctoral fellow U. Colo., Boulder, 1973-75, lectr. chemistry, 1975; asst. prof. biochemistry St. Louis U. Sch. Medicine, 1976—. Sec. Mo. Rhodes Scholarship Selection Com., 1976-77. Mem. Am. Assn. Immunologists, Am. Alpine Club, Biophys. Soc., Am. Chem. Soc., AAAS, AAUP, N.Y. Acad. Scis., Sigma XI, Phi Beta Kappa, Omicron Delta Kappa, Phi Lambda Upsilon, Pi Mu Epsilon, Delta Phi Alpha. Episcopalian. Contbr. articles to profl. jours. Home: 10257 Meadowood Overland MO 63114 Office: Dept Biochemistry St Louis U Sch of Medicine 1402 S Grand St Louis MO 63104

BARKER, DAVID ALLEN, ins. co. exec.; b. Charleston, W.Va., Oct. 29, 1940; s. Jesse Sebert and Eleanor Emma (Baber) B.; B.A., Morris Harvey Coll., 1971; postgrad Marshall U., 1972; m. Phyllis M. Walker, July 31, 1964; children—Pamela Dawn, Andrew David, Rebecca Lynn. Sales rep. Met. Life Ins. Co., Charleston, 1973-76, sales mgr., Columbus, Ohio, 1976. Pres. Marmet (W.Va.) City Planning Commn., 1973-74; pres. Marmet Civic Welfare Council, 1972-75. Served with USNR, 1958-61. Mem. Nat. Assn. Life Underwriters, Poca River Hunting and Fishing Club. Mem. Ch. Nazarene. Office: 370 S 5th St Columbus OH 43215

BARKER, ELIZABETH BELL, psychiatrist; b. Knoxville, Tenn., Mar. 17, 1930; d. Robert Monroe and Myrtle L. (Derkle) Bell; B.A., Johnson (Tenn.) Bible Coll., 1950; B.A., U. Tenn., 1952, M.D., 1955; m. Othello Dale Smith, Feb. 26, 1971; children—Jennifer, Susan. Resident in psychiatry Gailor Meml. Hosp., Memphis, Tenn., 1957-60; pvt. practice medicine, specializing in psychiatry, Tripoli, Libya, 1960-63, Memphis 1964-65, Prairie Village, Kans., 1965—; cons. Memphis Pub. Schs., 1964-65, City of Shawnee Mission (Kans.), 1965—; co-founder Gestalt Found. Kans., 1975; faculty Center for Sexual Enrichment, U. Kans. Med. Center, Kansas City, 1975—; cons. Johnson County (Kans.) Family Ct., 1977—, Johnson County Mental Health Assn., 1972. Mem. Am. Psychiat. Assn., AMA, Kans., Johnson County med. socs., Transaction Analysis Assn. Internat. Methodist. Contbr. articles to profl. and legal jours. Office: 4121 W 83d St Prairie Village KS 66208

BARKER, GREGSON LEARD, business forms printing co. exec.; b. Chgo., Jan. 19, 1918; s. Walter R. and Margaret (Gregson) B.; children (by previous marriage)—Margaret Louise (Mrs. George Thompson), John Leard, Eric Walter, William Jordan; m. 2d, Betty McPherson King, Apr. 27, 1968 (div.). With UARCO Inc., designers, printers bus. forms, Barrington, Ill., 1937—, v.p., 1949-51, exec. v.p., 1951-55, pres., 1955—; dir. LaSalle Nat. Bank, Chgo., Chgo. Profl. Basketball Corp., Hammond Corp., 1st Nat. Bank, Barrington. Mem. citizens bd. U. Chgo.; bd. dirs., v.p. Jr. Achievement, Chgo.; bd. dirs. Infant Welfare Soc. Chgo., Chgo. Crime Commn. Mem. Ill. Mfrs. Assn. (pres., dir.), Chgo. Assn. Commerce and Industry (v.p., dir.), Employers Assn. Chgo. (dir. 1956-59), Chgo. Presidents Orgn., Northwestern U. Assos. Republican. Episcopalian. Clubs: Economic, Executives, Chicago Commonwealth, Chicago, Mid America, Commercial, Racquet (Chgo.); Barrington Hills Country; Meadow, Lyford Cay (New Providence, Bahamas). Home: 81 Meadow Hill Rd Barrington IL 60010 Office: UARCO Inc W County Line Rd Barrington IL 60010

BARKER, KEITH RENE, investment banker; b. Elkhart, Ind., July 28, 1928; s. Clifford C. and Edith (Hausmna) B.; A.B., Wabash Coll, 1950; M.B.A., Ind. U., 1952; children (by previous marriage)—Bruce C., Lynn K.; m. 2d, Elizabeth S. Arrington, Nov. 24, 1965; 1 dau., Jennifer Scott. Sales rep. Fulton, Reid & Co., Inc., Ft. Wayne, Ind., 1951-55, office, 1955-59, asst. v.p., 1960, v.p., 1960, dir., 1961, asst. sales mgr., 1963, sales mgr., 1964, dir. Ind. ops.; sr. v.p. Fulton, Reid & Co., 1966-75; pres., chief exec. officer Fulton, Reid & Staples, Inc., 1975—; exec. com. Cascade Industries, Inc.; bd. dirs. Fulton, Reid & Staples, Inc., Nobility Homes, Inc. Pres. Historic Ft. Wayne, Inc.; mem. Smithsonian Assos. Bd. dirs. Ft. Wayne YMCA, 1963-64. Served to lt. USNR, 1952-55. Recipient Achievement certificate Inst. Investment Banking, U. Pa., 1959. Mem. Ft. Wayne Hist. Soc. (v.p.), Alliance Francaise, V.F.W. (past comdr.), Co. Mil. Historians, Phi Beta Kappa. Episcopalian. Mason. Clubs: Ft. Wayne Country, Cleveland Yachting, Beaver Creek Hunt, Cleve. Athletic. Home: 351 Cranston Dr Berea OH 44017 Office: 800 Penton Plaza Cleveland OH 44114

BARKER, KENT PURCELL, internat. fin. cons.; b. Virginia, Minn., Sept. 17, 1933; s. Purcell Edgar and Ruth Parmalee (Butler) B.; B.A., U. Minn., 1958; m. Patricia Louise McMahon, Sept. 6, 1958; children—Kent Purcell, Kathryn Anne, Kristine Louise, Kate Parmalee. Group sales rep. Hartford Ins. Group, Mpls., 1955-62, Denver, 1962-65; employee benefit analyst 3M Co., St. Paul, 1965-68; mgr. employee benefits Control Data Corp., Mpls., 1968-74, exec. cons. corporate compensation, 1974—; pres. Swiss Internat. Services, Inc., 1975—; lectr. on employee benefits U. Minn., 1972-75. Chmn. benefit design com. Twin City Health Maintenance Orgn., 1972-75; chmn. benefits com. Gov's. Commn. on Handicapped, 1973-74; chmn., Citizens League, 1968; rep. Western Area Fire Tng. Bd., 1974—; vice-chmn. spl. finance com. for Eden Prairie (Minn.) Schs., 1972. Chmn. exec. com. Republican party, Eden Prairie, 1966-67. Bd. dirs. Mpls. War Meml. Blood Bank. Mem. Am. Soc. Ins. Mgmt., Council Employee Benefits (chmn. internat. meeting 1973), Minn. Assn. Commerce and Industry (unemployment compensation legislative adv. com. 1968-74). Episcopalian (sr. warden 1971-72). Mason (Shriner), Lion. Contbr. articles to profl. jours. Home: 15801 Cedar Ridge Rd Eden Prairie MN 55343 Office: 7900 Xertes Ave S Suite 818 Minneapolis MN 55431

BARKER, WALTER LEE, thoracic surgeon; b. Chgo., Sept. 9, 1928; s. Samuel Robert, M.D., and Esther (Meyerovitz) B.; A.B. cum laude, Harvard U., 1949, M.D., 1953; m. Betty Ruth Wood, Apr. 4, 1967. Intern, resident in gen. and thoracic surgery Cook County Hosp. and Presbyn. St. Luke's Med. Center and affiliated hosps., Chgo., 1953-62; practice medicine specializing in thoracic surgery, Chgo., 1962—; asso. clin. prof. surgery U. Ill.; head sect. thoracic surgery Cook County Hosp. Served with M.C., USNR, 1955-57. Diplomate Am. Bd. Surgery, Am. Bd. Thoracic Surgery. Fellow Am. Coll. Chest Physicians, A.C.S.; mem. Am. Assn. Thoracic Surgery, AMA, Boylston, Chgo., Ill. med. socs., Chest Club, Chgo., Ill., Central surg. socs., Inst. Medicine, Soc. Thoracic Surgeons (founding mem.), Sigma Xi. Author: The Post Operative Chest, 1977. Contbr. articles profl. jours. Research on tuberculosis, pleural infections, lung cancer. Home: 2912 N Commonwealth Ave Chicago IL 60657 Office: 2913 N Commonwealth Ave Chicago IL 60657

BARKET, ALEXANDER JOHN, banker, bldg. exec.; b. St. Louis, June 9, 1916; s. Joseph Thomas and Bertha (Jacob) B.; B.S. in Accounting and Finance, St. Louis U., 1940; m. Mary Kathleen Clark, Dec. 7, 1941; children—Thomas Preston, Mary Kay, Alexander John, Susan Ann, Linda Josephine, Loretta Alice. Asst, comptroller Tower Grove Bank, St. Louis, 1933-36; sr. accountant Boyd Cronk & Co., C.P.A.'s, St. Louis, 1937-42; comptroller MacDonald, Tarlton & Patti Constrn. Co., Kansas City, Mo., 1943-52; pres. Met. Constrn. Co., Kansas City, Mo., 1952—; chmn. bd. Civic Plaza Nat. Bank, 1963—, Met. Constrn. Co, Postal Leasing Corp., Civic Plaza Mortgage Investment Co., all Kansas City, Mo. Chmn., Kansas City Municipal Indsl. Devel. Commn., 1962-64; mem. Mo. State Bd. Accountancy, 1940—; chmn. Nat. Housing Commn., 1958-60; former mem. Pres. Johnson's Adv. Bd. Sr. Citizen Housing, former mem. Adv. Bd. on Air Pollution; trustee Downtown Hosp., Kansas City. Recipient Archtl. award for Civic Plaza Nat. Bank Bldg., Kansas City Downtown Com., 1962; named Man of Year, K.C. chpt., Rockne Club, U. Notre Dame, 1961. Mem. Am.'s Indsl. Devel. Council, Bldg. Owners Mgrs. Assn., Tau Kappa Epsilon. Democrat. Roman Catholic. Clubs: Kansas City; Blue Hills Country. Home: 108 W 125th Terrace Kansas City MO 64145 Office: 6000 E 60th St Kansas City MO 64130

BARKLEY, JOHN RICHARD, newspaper editor; b. Charlotte, N.C., July 12, 1932; s. Henry Brock and Maurine (Dutt) B.; student U. N.C., 1950-51, 55-56; m. Robbie Nell Taylor, June 27, 1959; children—Susan Maurine, John Richard. News editor Laurens (S.C.) Advertiser, 1957-60; bur. chief Anderson (S.C.) Ind., 1960-63; area editor Sandusky (Ohio) Register, 1963-64; editorial page editor Savannah (Ga.) Morning News, 1964-66; mng. editor Augusta (Ga.) Herald, 1966-68; mng. editor Kokomo (Ind.) Tribune, 1968-70, editor, 1970—. Trustee region V Ind. Vocat. Tech. Coll., 1972—. Served with AUS, 1952-55. Named Man of Year, 1959. Methodist. Mason, Kiwanian. Office: 300 Union St Kokomo IN 46901

BARKLEY, MARK ERNEST, computer co. exec.; b. Alpine, Ala., Oct. 2, 1932; s. Simon and Ruby Goodgame (Bledsoe) B.; B.S., Ala. State U., 1957; postgrad. Ohio State U., 1960, Washington U., St. Louis, 1967—; M.S., Atlanta U., 1963; m. Arrie Ann Morton, Oct. 4, 1959. Tchr. math. pub. schs., Prattville, Ala., 1957-60, Tuscaloosa (Ala.) pub. schs., 1960-61; cartographer Aero. Chart & Info. Center, St. Louis, 1962-64, mathematician, 1964-69; mathematician U.S. Army Aviation Systems Command, St. Louis, 1969-70, ops. research analyst, 1970-73, supervisory ops. research analyst, 1973-74, ops. research analyst, 1974-77, supervisory ops. research analyst, Black Hawk project mgr. U.S. Army Materiel and Readiness Command, St. Louis, 1977—; pres. Program Innovators, Inc., St. Louis, 1970-71, v.p., 1973—, chmn. bd. dirs., 1972—. Dir., Mart Credit Union, St. Louis, 1972—. Served with AUS, 1953-55. Recipient certificate of Achievement, U.S. Army, 1973, Sustained Superior Performance award, 1974. NSF grantee. Mem. Ops. Research Soc. Am., Assn. for Computing Machinery, Soc. Logistics Engrs., Army Aviation Assn. Am., Ala. State U. Alumni Assn. (pres. chpt. 1974), Beta Kappa Chi. Baptist (deacon 1970—). Club: Masons. Home: 4106 Dressel Ave Saint Louis MO 63120 Office: 3515 Belaire Pl Saint Louis MO 63121

BARKLEY, OWEN HERBERT, indsl. photographer; b. Muskegon Heights, Mich., Aug. 9, 1922; s. Kirk Delmont and Mabel Eva (Fowler) B.; student U.S. Navy Photo Sch., 1943, Nat. Camera Repair Sch., 1968; m. Karen Ann Gray, Nov. 13, 1965; children—Matthew Scott, Russell Dean, Jeffrey Wade. Served to chief photographer, USN, 1943-64; mem. photog. sales-service dept. Crescent Camera & Lithography Supply Corp., Kalamazoo, 1965-66; indsl. photographer Clark Equipment Co., Battle Creek, Mich., 1966—; co-owner K & D Photography Studio; works exhibited nat. conv. Profl. Photographers Am., 1975, featured in mag. article, 1976. Pres. Village of Climax, Mich., 1976-78. Mem. Profl. Photographers Am., Soc. Photog. Technologists. Mason (pres. temple bd. assn. 1974); mem. Order Eastern Star (past patron). Home: 126 N Main St Climax MI 49034 Office: 24th St Battle Creek MI 49016

BARKS, HORACE BUSHNELL, editor, publisher; b. St. Louis, July 13, 1921; s. Horace B. and Cordie (Sherrow) B.; A.B., Westminster Coll., 1942; M.S.J., Northwestern U., 1947; m. Elsie Dickson, June 14, 1947; children—Elizabeth (Mrs. Jeremy Van Ness), Jean (Mrs. Leonard Freed), Joseph, Barbara, William. Editor, pub. Grocer's Digest, Chgo., 1948-51, St. Louis, 1951-54; pres. Barks Publs., St. Louis, 1951-66; editor, pub. Elec. Apparatus mag., 1964—; editor, pub. Mining Equipment News, 1966-69; editor, pub. Electric Heat mag., 1971—; v.p. Mulville-Barks Pubs., Inc., Chgo., 1966-70; pres. Barks Publs., Inc., 1970—. Faculty, Washington U., 1962-66. Bd. dirs. Am. Bus. Press, 1973-76. Served with USNR, 1942-46; ETO. Mem. Sigma Delta Chi. Episcopalian. Home: 202 E Walton Pl Chicago IL 60611 Office: 400 N Michigan Ave Chicago IL 60611

BARKS, HOWARD WILLIAM, clergyman; b. Chgo., July 25, 1920; s. Howard William and Ruth Ellen (Jefferson) B.; B.S., U. Toledo, 1943; postgrad. Northwestern Law Sch., 1947-48; B.D., Seabury Western Theol. Sem., 1951, M.Div., 1971. Tchr. high sch., Quincy, Ill., 1946-47; ordained to ministry Protestant Episcopal Ch., 1951; vicar All Soul's Mission, Waukegan, Ill., 1951-52; rector St. Margaret's Ch., Chgo., 1952-62, Ch. of St. John the Evangelist, Flossmoor, Ill., 1962—. Chmn. Diocesan Com. on Legislation, 1967—; diocesan rep. Episc. Charismatic Fellowship. Mem. Flossmoor Community Relations Commn., 1964-72. Treas., bd. dirs. Episcopal Coop. of Chgo. Past pres. South Suburban Inter-Faith Clergy Council; past pres. South Suburban Humane Soc. Served to 1st lt. USMCR, 1942-46. Mem. Am. Soc. Ch. Architecture, Homewood-Flossmoor Ministerial Assn. (past pres.), Sigma Phi Epsilon. Clubs: University (Chgo.); Bedlington Terrier of Am. (v.p., dir.). Home: 2638 Park Dr Flossmoor IL 60422 Office: Park Dr and Leavitt Ave Flossmoor IL 60422

BARKSDALE, A. BEVERLY, museum mgr.; b. Greenville, S.C., Nov. 21, 1913; s. Alfred D.L. and Susan (McGee) B.; A.B magna cum laude, Furman U., 1935; Mus.B., La. State U., 1938, Mus. M., 1939; m. Mildred E. King, May 31, 1937; children—Alfred D., Daniel M. Instr. music Coll. Emporia (Kans.), 1939-40; instr. music Toledo Mus. Art, 1940-41, supr. music, 1941-57, organized, wrote catalogues for several exhbns. of mus. materials; mgr. Cleve. Orch., 1957-65, gen. mgr., 1965-70; gen. mgr. Cleve. Mus. Art, 1970—. Mem. music adv. panel Nat. Endowment for Arts, 1970-73; chmn. music adv. panel Ohio Arts Council, 1976—; v.p. Midwest Mus. Conf., 1977—; mem. adv. bd. Riemenschneider Bach Inst. Trustee Cleve. Inst. Music, Cleve. Music Sch. Settlement. Recipient award of merit Nat. Assn. Am. Composers and Condrs., 1952. Mem. Delta Sigma Phi, Pi Gamma Mu, Phi Mu Alpha Sinfonia. Clubs: Rowfant. Home: 2608 Lee Rd Cleveland Heights OH 44118 Office: Cleve Mus Art 11150 East Blvd Cleveland OH 44106

BARKSDALE, CLARENCE MARTIN, lawyer; b. St. Louis, Dec. 10, 1899; s. Richard C. and Louise (Babington) B.; J.D., Washington U., St. Louis, 1923; m. Elizabeth Caulfield, Sept. 18, 1926; children—Henry Caulfield, Clarence Caulfield. Admitted to Mo. bar, 1923, since practiced in St. Louis; partner firm Barksdale, Adams, Chorlins & Young. Mem. Mo. Human Rights Commn., 1964-66. Bd. dirs. Jefferson Nat. Meml.; bd. dirs. Family and Children's Service, 1948-59, chmn. bd., 1951-52; trustee Washington U., 1954-56, St. Louis Country Day Sch., 1947; bd. dirs. St. Louis Coll. Pharmacy, 1967-70, Girls' Home, 1966-72. Served pfc. USMC, World War I. Mem. Am., Mo., St. Louis (exec. com. 1944-46, v.p., 1947) bar assns., Washington U. Law Alumni Assn. (past pres.), Kappa Alpha, Delta Theta Phi, Omicron Delta Kappa. Congregationalist. Clubs: John Marshall Lawyers (pres. 1944); University, Clayton. Home: 11 Whitehall Ct St Louis MO 63144 Office: 11 S Meramac St St Louis Mo 63105

BARKSDALE, RICHARD KENNETH, educator, univ. adminstr.; b. Winchester, Mass., Oct. 31, 1915; s. Simon Daniel and Sarah Irene (Brooks) B.; A.B., Bowdoin Coll., 1937; A.M., Syracuse U., 1938; Ph.D., Harvard U., 1951; L.H.D., Bowdoin Coll., 1972; m. Mildred A. White, Apr. 15, 1960; children—Maxine, James, Richard, Calvin. Instr. English So. U., 1938-39; chmn. dept. English Tougaloo Coll., 1939-42; prof. N.C. Central U., 1949-53, dean Grad. Sch., 1953-58; prof., chmn. dept. Morehouse Coll., 1958-62; prof. Atlanta U., 1962-67, dean Grad. Sch., 1967-71; prof. English U. Ill., 1971—, acting head dept., 1974, asso. dean Grad. Coll., 1975—. Mem. bd. overseers Bowdoin Coll., 1974—; mem. adminstrv. bd. Nat. Fellowships Fund for Black Americans; cons. Ford Found., Office of Edn. Mem. Nat. Council Tchrs. English (bd. dirs. 1972-74), Coll. Lang. Assn. (pres. 1973-75), Phi Beta Kappa. Author: Langston Hughes: Poet and His Critics; co-editor Black Writers of America. Contbr. articles to profl. jours. Home: 2207 Wyld Dr Urbana IL 61801 Office: 330 Adminstrn Bldg Grad Coll U Ill Urbana IL 61801

BARLOW, F(RANK) JOHN, mech. contracting co. exec.; b. Milw., July 12, 1914; s. Ernest A. and Alice E. (Norton) B.; B.S. in Mech. Engring., U. Wis., 1937; m. Dorothy M. Marx, Oct. 13, 1935; children—Joyce D., Bonnie M., Joan C., Grace M., Jacqueline S.,

Wendy J., Terri L., Alice M. Engr., Buffalo Forge Co., 1937-40, sales engr., Chgo., 1940-42: plant engr. A.O. Smith Corp., Milw., 1942-44; chief mech. engr. Western Condensing Co., Appleton, Wis., 1944-46. prodn. mgr., 1946-53; owner Azco, Inc., Appleton, 1953—, pres., 1959—, pres. Sanco, Inc., Appleton, 1959—. Baldwin Barlow Corp., Appleton, 1965—, Tippy Taco House, 1968—, The Downey Co., Milw.; treas. Winagamie Corp., 1965—; dir. First Nat. Bank Appleton. County chmn. March of Dimes, 1957—, state co-chmn., 1958, industry chmn. com. fund dr., 1968-69. Bd. dirs., exec. com. Air Wis.; bd. dirs. Nat. Certified Pipe Welding Bur.; trustee Azco Employees Profit Sharing Trust. Recipient Industry award Wis. Soc. Profl. Engrs., 1967. Mem. Mech. Contractors Assn. Am. (nat. dir., pres. 1974-75), Mech. Contractors Assn. Wis. (pres.), Wis. Soc. Profl. Engrs. (chpt. pres. 1968—), Am. Soc. Heating, Refrigerations and Airconditioning Engrs., Appleton C. of C., ASCE, Flying Engrs., Civil Air Patrol, Nat. Soc. Profl. Engrs. Club: Butte Des Morts Golf (dir., pres. 1961, 62). Mason (Shriner). Rotarian, Elk (past exalted ruler). Home: 178 River Dr Appleton WI 54911 Office: PO Box 228 Appleton WI 54911

BARNARD, KATHLEEN RAINWATER, educator; b. Wayne City, Ill., Dec. 28, 1927; d. Roy and Nina (Edmison) Rainwater; B.S., So. Ill. U., 1949, M.S., 1953; postgrad. Ind. U., 1953; Ph.D., U. Tex., 1959; m. Donald L. Barnard, Aug. 17, 1947 (div. Mar. 1973); children—Kimberly, Jill. Tchr. pub. high sch., Wayne City, Ill., 1946-51; faculty asst., lectr. Vocat. Tech. Inst., So. Ill. U., Carbondale, 1951-53; lectr. bus. edn. Northwestern U., Chgo., 1953-55; chmn. dept. bus. adminstrn. San Antonio Coll., 1955-60; chmn. dept. bus. edn. DePaul U., Chgo., 1960-62, adj. prof., fall 1976; chmn. dept. bus. City Colls. Chgo., 1962-67, prof., 1968—, exec. sec., bd. dirs. credit union, 1975—; cons., evaluator Ill. Program for Gifted Children, State Demonstrator Center, Oak Park (Ill.) Pub. Schs.; cons. First Nat. Bank Chgo., 1974; ednl. cons. Ency. Brit., 1969. Cons. edn. and tng. div. Continental Ill. Nat. Bank & Trust Co., Chgo., 1967, Victor Corp., 1965—; cons. IBM, Inc., summer 1968. Mem. Chgo. Assn. Commerce and Industry (edn. com.), North Central Bus. Edn. Assn., Adminstrv. Mgmt. Soc., Delta Kappa Gamma, Pi Omega Pi, Alpha Delta Pi (sponsor), Sigma Phi (sponsor), Delta Pi Epsilon (pres. Alpha Theta chpt. 1958). Club: Zonta (Chgo.). Contbg. author: College Typewriting, 1960; Business Correspondence, 1962. Home: 920 Courtland Ave Park Ridge IL 60068 Office: 64 E Lake St Chicago IL 60601

BARNARD, ROBERT DANE, educator; b. Chgo., Mar. 17, 1929; s. Robert Dane and Kathleen Ann (Drake) B.; B.E.E., Bklyn. Poly. Inst., 1952, M.E.E., 1955; Ph.D., Case Western Res. U., 1959; m. Jean Ruth McMahan, July 23, 1949; children—Christine (Mrs. Gerald Andres), Laura (Mrs. Keith Carlson), Timothy, Janet (Mrs. David Peitz). Mem. tech. staff Bell Telephone Labs., Murray Hill, N.J., 1959-65; prof. elec. engring. Wayne State U., Detroit, 1965—. Served with USNR, 1946-48, 52-53. Mem. Am. Math. Soc., Soc. Indsl. and Applied Math., Indsl. Math. Soc. (editorial bd. 1968—), IEEE, Sigma Xi, Eta Kappa Nu, Tau Beta Pi. Contbr. articles to profl. jours. Home: 1363 Seville Rd Rochester MI 48063 Office: Wayne State U Detroit MI 48202

BARNARD, WILLIAM CLARK, journalist; b. Cleve., Jan. 2, 1938; s. William E. and Mary (Zeek) B.; student John Carroll U., 1957-59, Case-Western Res. U., 1960; m. Mildred Barnard, June 24, 1961; children—Mary Elizabeth, Geoffrey, Ann Genevieve. Mem. staff Cleve. Plain Dealer, 1957—, successively police reporter, rewriteman, criminal cts. reporter, 1957-65, city hall reporter, 1964-69, polit. editor, 1969-71, chief editorial writer, 1971—. Mem. Council on the Future of the Growth Assn. Served with AUS. Recipient Press Club award, 1967; Enterprise award A.P. Mem. Nat. Conf. Editorial Writers, Am. Soc. Newspaper Editors, Am. (chmn. Nat. conv. 1968), Cleve. (exec. bd. 1963-70, chmn. Plain Dealer unit 1964) newspaper guilds, Sigma Delta Chi (dir. 1971). Home: 3084 E Overlook Rd Cleveland Heights OH 44118 Office: 1801 Superior Ave Cleveland OH 44114

BARNES, BILL LLOYD, clergyman, sem. ofcl.; b. Kansas City, Mo., July 16, 1926; s. William Lloyd and Augusta (Moore) B.; B.A., Drake U., 1948; M.Div., Christian Theol. Sem., 1952; M.S., Butler U., 1957; m. Shirley Nadine Malone, Oct. 9, 1945; children—Judith Diane (Mrs. Robert Stall), Janis Caryl (Mrs. Kent Barnard). Student minister in Kellogg, Iowa, 1946-48, Indpls., 1948-52; ordained to ministry Disciples of Christ Ch., 1947; minister in St. Louis, 1952-60; dir. devel. Christian Theol. Sem., Indpls., 1960-67, v.p. devel., 1967—. Mem. home and state missions planning council Disciples of Christ 1956-60; sec. Mo. Disciples State Conv., 1954; evangelism rep. St. Louis Met. Ch. Fedn., 1956; pres. St. Louis Ministers, 1957, Disciple Ministers, 1959; substitute tchr. TV program Lessons for Living, Sta. WTTV, Indpls., 1962-65; ministerial enlistment chmn. St. Louis Counseling Center, 1959; mem. Ch. Fedn. New Direction Com., 1973, 74. Mem. bd. higher edn. Disciples of Christ, 1961—, chmn. Ind. inter agy. com., 1971-75, chmn. askings commn., 1972-73; chmn. time place com. Indiana Christian Church Conv., 1964-66. Community relations representative YMCA, St. Louis, 1955; institutional rep. Boy Scouts Am., St, Louis, 1955-60; mem. Indpls. Urban Forum Series Com., 1969-70. Served with USAAF, 1945. A Seminarian of Year Sermon contest winner Pulpit mag., 1951, 52; recipient Distinguished Alumnus award Christian Theol. Sem., 1975. Mem. Sem. Mgmt. Assn. (pres. 1972-74), Hoosier Power Squadron (chaplain 1971—), Theta Phi. Kiwanian. Clubs: Riviera, Indpls. Athletic. Contbr. articles and Sunday Sch. lessons to religious publs. Home: 411 Braeside South Dr Indianapolis IN 46260 Office: 1000 W 42d St Indianapolis IN 46208

BARNES, BRUCE FRANCIS, cons. engr.; b. Evanston, Ill., Nov. 18, 1926; s. Bruce Francis and Ruth Evelyn (Achuff) B.; B.M.E., Washington U., St. Louis, 1949; m. Gwendolyn Lou Gnaegy, Feb. 17, 1951; children—Sharon Anne Barnes Koch, Steven Bruce. With Fairbanks Morse Engine div. Colt Industries, Beloit, Wis., 1949-68, area sales mgr. St. Louis, 1960-68; asso. Warren & Van Praag, Inc., St. Louis, 1969-72; pres., gen. mgr. Barnes, Henry, Meisenheimer & Gende, Inc., St. Louis, 1972—. Mem. adminstrv. bd. Webster Hills United Meth. Ch., 1968—. Served with USAF, 1944-45. Recipient Order of the Arrow, Boy Scouts Am., 1967. Mem. Nat., Mo. socs. profl. engrs., ASME, Engrs. Club St. Louis. Clubs: Pachyderm, Mo. Athletic. Home: 1503 Azalea Dr Webster Groves MO 63119 Office: 4658 Gravois Ave Saint Louis MO 63116

BARNES, DANIEL FRANCIS, clin. psychologist; b. Chgo., May 9, 1945; s. John James and Stella Agnes (Lukasik) B.; B.S. (William S. Cook scholar, Loyola Journalism scholar), Loyola U., Chgo., 1967; M.A. (USPHS fellow, Haggin scholar), U. Ky., 1969, Ph.D., 1972; m. Noel Carol Smoron, Aug. 1, 1970; children—Robyn Joy, Amanda Joy. NIMH predoctoral psychology intern Worcester (Mass.) State Hosp., 1971-72; staff psychologist, student counseling services Loyola U., Chgo., 1972-74, acting dir., 1974-75, dir., 1975—; clin. psychologist CMBY Clinic, Elmhurst, Ill., 1973—; pvt. practice clin. psychology, 1973—. Mem. Am., Midwest, Ill. psychol. assns., Chgo. Psychol. Club, Nat. Registry Health Service Providers, (div. psychotherapy, div. clin. psychology), Blue Key. Home: 9413 Lincolnwood Dr Evanston IL 60203

BARNES, ELMA O., author, civic worker; b. Wilmington, Ill., May 1, 1908; d. James L. and Dorothea (Koehler) Barnes; certificate in dramatic art Conservatory of Music, Joliet, Ill., 1923-27; student Gallagher Bus. Sch., Kankakee, Ill., 1927-28; diploma Marquette Inst., 1932. Feature writer Wilmington Adv., 1955-77, publicity, 1968—; sec. Wilmington C. of C., 1955-74, exec. v.p., sec., 1964-70; commentator news program radio sta. WCSJ, Morris, Ill., 1964-66; police reporter City of Wilmington, 1966-68, 71-74; publicity Recreation Civic Center, 1969-76; reporter Wilmington Fire Dept., 1968-77. Recipient certificate of appreciation Malcolm Mayo Post VFW, 1963; Meritorious Service award Lester Smith Am. Legion Post, 1964, Pub. Recognition citation, 1969, citation for services to aux. in communications and publicity, 1970; Pub. Service award Fedn. of Police, 1972; Pub. Service award Trailways council Girl Scouts U.S.A., 1975; certificate of appreciation Rotary Club, 1975. Mem. 1st Christian Ch. Author: Letters to a Convalescent, 1958; (children's books) Peb and His Animal Kingdom, 1960, Let's Go to the Country, 1976; (pageant) Highlights of Yesteryear for 125th Anniversary of Wilmington, 1961; Journey to Eternal Life, 1971; A Sinner's Dilemma, 1971; compiler histories for Wilmington Fire Dept., 1968, Lester Smith Am. Legion Post, 1963, 1st Nat. Bank, 1968. Writer poems. Home: 815 Jackson St Wilmington IL 60481

BARNES, FRANCIS MERRIMAN, JR., physician; b. Middletown, N.Y., Aug. 20, 1881; s. Francis M. and Mary (Reynolds) B.; A.B., Hamilton Coll., 1903, A.M., 1906; M.D., Johns Hopkins, 1907; m. Carleta Kimlin, Aug. 15, 1918; 1 son, Francis Merriman III. Asst. physician, dir. clin. lab. Sheppard & Enoch Pratt Hosp., Towson, Md., 1907-09; clin. dir. St. Elizabeth Hosp., Washington, 1910-15; instr. psychiatry George Washington U., Washington, 1911-13; asst. prof. nervous and mental diseases St. Louis U., 1913, asso. prof., 1920-23; asso. prof. psychiatry Washington U. Med. Sch., St. Louis, 1914-50; lectr. psychiatry and vocation edn. postgrad. Harvard Sch. Medicine, 1921; psychiatrist St. Mary Hosp., St. Louis, 1913-70, Barnes Hosp., St. Louis, 1914-50, St. John's Hosp., 1914, St. Louis City Sanitarium, 1950; neuro-psychiatrist U.S. Vets. Bur., 1919-23. Served with AUS, World War I. Fellow Am. Psychiat. Assn. Contbr. articles to profl. jours. Address: Sunridge Tower Rd Route 2 Hillsboro MO 63050

BARNES, JOCELYN THOMAS, plastic mfg. co. exec.; b. Highland Park, Mich., Feb. 11, 1928; s. Thomas F. and Elizabeth (Bennetts) B.; student U. Mich., 1945-48; B.S., Lawrence Inst. Tech., 1951; m. Jo Ann Barbara Barnes; children—Suzanne, Thomas F. II, Shari, Greg, Valerie. Sales engr. Spaulding Fibre Co., Detroit, 1953-56; mfrs. rep., Detroit, 1956-62; v.p., gen. mgr. Lexalite Corp., Charlevoix, Mich., 1962-72; pres. Lexalife Internat. Corp., 1973—. Served to 1st lt. AUS, 1951-53. Registered profl. engr., Mich. Mem. Illuminating Engring. Soc., Soc. Plastics Engrs. Home: Indian Trails Route 3 Charlevoix MI 49720 Office: Lexalite Corp US 31 N Charlevoix MI 49720

BARNES, ROBERT ALLAN, univ. adminstr.; b. Cleve., May 3, 1927; s. Ernest and Ethel (Lanham) Y.; B.S., Miami U., Oxford, Ohio, 1949; M.A., Columbia, 1952; Ph.D., Ohio State U., 1962; m. Betty Ammerman, June 24, 1950; children—Paul, Carolyn. Chmn. dept. music N.C. State U., Raleigh, 1956-62; asst. to pres. Ohio State U., Columbus, 1962-65, dir. Newark campus, 1965—; pres. Central Ohio Tech. Coll. Served with USNR, World War II. Author: Fundamentals of Music, 1964. Home: 659 Canterbury Ct Newark OH 43055

BARNES, ROBERT WILLIAM, JR., artist, educator; b. Westfield, Mass., Apr. 30, 1933; s. Robert William and Nellie Dorothy (Bannish) B.; student Applied Art Acad., Akron, Ohio, 1956-60; m. Andrea Lorraine Ehlert, Aug. 9, 1974; children—Robert William, Natalie Lorraine; children from previous marriage—Vickie Lynn, Sheila Kay, Deborah Gay, Mary Ann, Robin Michele. With Timken Roller Bearing, Canton, Ohio, 1952; car insp. Nickle Plate R.R., Brewster, Ohio, 1952-57; welder Maycomber Structural Steel, Canton, 1957-58; artist, art editor Roadway Express, Inc., Akron, Ohio, 1958-60; instr. Applied Art Acad., Akron, 1959; graphic design artist Packaging Corp. Am., Rittman, Ohio, 1960-66; asso. art dir. Folding Carton div. St. Regis Paper Co., Cleve., 1972-77; art dir. Menasha Corp., Neenah, Wis., 1977—; editorial cartoonist News Banner, Wadsworth, Ohio; freelance artist, tchr. art; exhibited in one-man show, N.Y.C., 1964; exhibited in numerous group shows; represented collections at Conover Gallery, Edgartown, Mass., others; tchr. Baycrafters, Inc., Bay Village, Ohio. Served with AUS, 1953-55. Recipient nat. award Ann. Nat. Newspaper Contest, Toronto, Ont., Can., 1974. Mem. Akron Soc. Artists, Cuyahoga Valley Art Center (pres.). Home: 711 John St Menasha WI 54952

BARNES, RONALD LEIGH, electronic research and devel. co. exec., elec. engr.; b. Winfield, Kans., June 8, 1940; s. Kirby Paul and Mary (Doramus) B.; B.S. in Physics, Wichita State U., 1963, M.E.E., 1968, M.S. in Physics; m. Geraldine Caruer, Mar. 21, 1958; children—Kim, Mike, Cherie. Elec. design engr. Beech Research & Devel. Co., Boulder, Colo., 1963-64; asso. engr. The Boeing Co., Wichita, Kans., 1964-65; dir. research and devel. Albright Neucleonics, Inc., Wichita, 1965-66; sr. electronic system engr. Beech Aircraft Corp., Wichita, 1966-69, data engr., 1969-70, value engr., 1970-72; founder Barnes Devel. Co., Wichita, 1969, pres., 1969-77; electro-optics staff engr. The Boeing Co., Wichita, 1975-76. Chmn. Wichita Water Festival, 1969. Registered profl. engr., Kans. Mem. IEEE, Am. Phys. Soc. Democrat. Methodist. Address: 1350 Fieldcrest Wichita KS 67209

BARNETT, ARTHUR MALCOLM, physician; b. Rumuruti, Kenya, E. Africa, Dec. 3, 1910; s. Albert Edwin and Elma (Nicher) B.; came to U.S., 1924, naturalized, 1933; B.S., U. of S.C., 1933; M.D., Columbia U., 1937; postgrad. N.Y. Polyclinic Med. Sch. and Hosp., 1946, Hackensack Gen. Hosp., 1951, 1957-58; diplome de medicin colonial, Inst. de Medicine Tropicale, Prince Leopold, Antwerp, Belgium, 1953; m. Elizabeth Margaret Stevenson, Jan. 4, 1941; children—William A., Mary E. Barnett Starr, A. Steven Barnett. Intern, Hackensack (N.J.) Gen. Hosp., 1937-39, resident in surgery, 1940; supt. leprosarium and hosp., Kolo Ndoto, Tanganyika, Africa, 1947-51; supt. gen. hosp., Rethi, Congo Belge, Africa (Zaire), 1953-57, Kijabe Med. Center, Kijabe, Kenya, Africa, 1959-63; exec. staff mem. Central Du Page Hosp., Winfield, Ill., 1965—, Geneva (Ill.) Community Hosp., 1965—, Marionjoy Rehab. Hosp., Wheaton, Ill., 1974—, v.p., 1976; pvt. practice medicine specializing in family medicine, Wheaton, Ill., 1964—; med. dir. Du Page County Convalescent Home, Wheaton, 1976—. Served to maj. USAAF, 1942-46. Diplomate Am. Bd. Family Medicine. Mem. AMA (continued edn. awards yearly), DuPage County, Ill. med. assns., Christian Med. Soc., Phi Beta Kappa. Baptist. Home: 2 S 025 Yvonne Ln Wheaton IL 60187 Office: 214 N Hale St Wheaton IL 60187

BARNETT, CARL AMOS, JR., accountant; b. Gallipolis, Ohio, Jan. 2, 1948; s. Carl Amos and Helen Mae (Mercer) B.; Asso. in Bus., Portsmouth Interstate Bus. Coll., 1966-68. Accountant, Albert E. Brakenbury, Jr., Jackson, O., 1967-71; accountant Jimmie L. Moore, pub. accountant, Jackson, 1972-73, Ron's Previously Owned Autos, Jackson, 1973-74, Reasor Equipment, Jackson, Ohio, 1974—. Mem. Fraternal Order Police Assos. (sec.-treas. 1971—). Home: 67 Parkview Ave Jackson OH 45640 Office: 1 E Broadway Jackson OH 45640

BARNETT, D. EARL, advt. exec.; b. Trenton, Tenn., Nov. 9, 1917; s. D. Earl and Maude (Patrick) B.; grad. Cleve. Sch. Art, 1939; m. Laura E. Parkhurst, May 30, 1951; children—James T., Susan, Jeanie M., David C., John R. Asst. display dir. Bry-Block Corp., Memphis, 1939-40; asst. display dir. Old King Cole, Canton, Ohio, 1940-41; supr. merchandising div. W.L. Stensgaard, Chgo., 1946-48; display designer/illustrator Kling Studios, Chgo., 1948-57; v.p. J.M. Callan Co., Chgo., 1957-62; creative dir. Peter A. Conway & Assos., Chgo., 1962-74; merchandising mgr. Nat. Creative Merchandising, Arlington Heights, Ill., 1974—. Served with Q.M.C., AUS, 1942-46. Mem. Cooperstown Art Assn. Home: 2221 Prairie St Glenview IL 60025 Office: 3000 Malmo Dr Arlington Heights IL 60005

BARNETT, JAMES BRIAN, steel co. exec.; b. St. Louis, Mo., June 20, 1946; s. Alvin Lester and Dorothy B. (Hamburg) B.; B.S., Defiance Coll., 1968; m. Holly Jayne Spayd, Apr. 30, 1977. Sales exec. Barsteel div. U.S. Industries, Detroit, 1968—; exec. v.p. Lawndale Steel Co. Inc., Detroit, 1971-76; pres., Hancock Steel Processing Co. Inc., Detroit, 1976—; chmn. Barnett Telephone and Telegraph Co., Detroit, 1976—. Charter mem., past spl. project chmn. Troy Optimist Club. Mem. Steel Service Center Inst., Assn. of Steel Distrs. Office: 4086 Michigan Ave Detroit MI 48210

BARNETT, JOHN VINCENT, assn. exec.; b. Lapel, Ind., July 23, 1912; s. Harley E. and Vayne (Castor) B.; student Ind. U., 1930-33; m. Jane Callane, Feb. 10, 1940; children—Bonnie (Mrs. Larry Burdick), John. Statistician, Ind. Dept. Pub. Welfare, 1934-42; asst. research dir. Ind. C. of C., Indpls., 1942-52, dir. taxation dept., 1952-61, dir. research, 1962, exec. v.p., 1962—. Past pres. Council of State Chambers Commerce; mem. adv. council Ind. Dept. Commerce; mem. adv. com. polit. edn. Ind. State U. Mem. Ohio River Basin Com. chmn. Ind. Vocat. Tech. Coll.; bd. dirs. Ivy Tech. Found. Mem. C. of C. of U.S., Ind. Commerce Execs. Assn. (past pres.), Ind. Soc. of Chgo., Ind. U. Alumni Assn. (pres.), Ind. Partners Ams. Republican. Presbyterian. Mason, Elk. Clubs: Columbia, Press, Meridian Hills Country (Indpls.); Ulen Country (Lebanon). Home: 8750 Washington Blvd W Dr Indianapolis IN 46240 Office: 143 N Meridian St Indianapolis IN 46204

BARNETT, JOSEPH H., lawyer, state legislator; b. Sioux Falls, S.D., Nov. 3, 1931; s. William H. and Julia (Gurtel) B.; student Augustana Coll., 1950-51; B.A. magna cum laude, Coll. St. Thomas, St. Paul, 1953; LL.B., U. S.D., 1957; m. Kathleen D. Bolger, Feb. 23, 1954; children—Joseph P., John D., Paul T., Sheila Ann, Rita M., Theresa J., William M., James R., Patricia A. Admitted to S.D. bar, 1957; law clk. U.S. Dist. Ct. for S.D., 1957-58; practice law, Aberdeen, S.D., 1958—; partner firm Siegel, Barnett, Schutz, O'Keefe & Ogborn, 1963—; mem. S.D. Ho. of Reps., 1967—, speaker pro tem, 1971-72, minority leader, 1973-74, speaker, 1975-76. Mem. S.D. Bd. Bar Examiners, 1963-71. Served with Signal Corps, AUS, 1953-55. Named Most Outstanding Young Republican Legislator, S.D. Rep. legislators, 1967. Mem. Am., Brown County (pres. 1966-67) bar assns., State Bar Assn. S.D., Internat. Soc. Barristers, Am. Bd. Trial Advocates. K.C., Elk, Kiwanian. Home: 1411 N 4th St Aberdeen SD 57401 Office: Capitol Bldg Aberdeen SD 57401

BARNETT, RALPH LIPSEY, mech. engr.; b. Chgo., July 15, 1933; B.C.E., Ill. Inst. Tech., 1955, M.S. in Mechanics, 1958; married; 2 children. Asso. research engr. structural mechanics Armour Research Found., Chgo., 1955-60; evening instr. civil engring. Ill. Inst. Tech.; structural research engr. research and devel. dept. Stanray Corp., Chgo., 1960-62; sr. research engr., group leader Ill. Inst. Tech. Research Inst., Chgo., 1962-68; evening instr. mech. and aerospace engring. Ill. Inst. Tech., 1967-69, mem. faculty full time, 1969—, prof. mech. and aerospace engring., 1969—; dir. research and devel., dir. rubber lab., dir. indsl. chemistry lab. Felt Products Mfg. Co., Skokie, Ill., 1968-69; v.p. Triodyne, Inc., cons. engr., Skokie, 1972—. CECO Steel Co. scholar, 1953; Armour Research Found. research fellow, 1955. Mem. Am. Acad. Mechanics, ASCE (Collingwood prize 1960, Prize paper Chgo. sect. 1962), ASME, Am. Concrete Inst., Am. Soc. Safety Engrs., Nat. Safety Council, Graphic Arts Tech. Found., Am. Soc. Metals, Am. Nat. Standards Inst., Am. Soc. Engring. Edn., AAUP, Sigma Xi, Chi Epsilon, Pi Tau Sigma, Tau Beta Pi. Author papers, chpts. in books. Address: 2721 Alison Ln Wilmette IL 60091

BARNETT, RICHARD GENE, exec. adminstr.; b. Rock Island, Ill., Oct. 9, 1919; s. Frederick Henry and Hanna Annette (Grippe) B.; student schs., Rock Island; student labor relations U. Iowa; m. Bette Jane Mattson, Oct. 14, 1944; 1 dau., Mary Jane Barnett Flaherty. Program analysis officer, Rock Island (Ill.) Arsenal, 1961-72, civilian exec. asst., managerial asst. to comdg. officer, 1972—. Budget com., combined fed. campaign, 1968-69; bd. dirs. First United Methodist Ch., 1952-60. Served with U.S. Army, 1944-46. Decorated Bronze Star, Purple Heart; recipient decoration for meritorious civilian service Dept. Army, 1976. Mem. Nat. Rifle Assn., Am. Def. Preparedness Assn. Club: Masons. Home: 3127 29th Ave Rock Island IL 61201 Office: Rock Island Arsenal Rock Island IL 61201

BARNETT, ROBERT EUGENE, veterinarian; b. Kirksville, Mo., Aug. 18, 1947; s. Cleo Barnett and Ruby Barnett Lindquist; D.V.M., U. Mo., 1971; m. Doris Irene Mauck, Aug. 19, 1967; 1 dau., Martha Jane. Gen. practice veterinary medicine, Fulton, Mo., 1971—, specializing in equine medicine, surgery, Fulton, 1971—; lectr., mem. staff William Woods Coll., Fulton, 1973—. Chmn. Legis. Com. Fulton, 1977—. Mark Morris fellow, 1968; W. Central V.M.A. Leadership award, 1968; Groth Research award, 1970. Mem. AVMA, Am. Animal Hosp. Assn., Am. Assn. Equine Practitioners, Veterinary Med. Assn., Soc. Theriogenology, Assn. Veterinary Anesthesiologists, Am. Assn. Animal Welfare Veterinarians, Veterinary Med. Assn. E. Mo., Mo. C. of C., dir. 1977). Club: Fulton Morning Optimist. Home and Office: Highway 54 S Fulton MO 65251

BARNETT, ROBERT FULTON, JR., radiologist; b. Pitts., Feb. 7, 1929; s. Robert Fulton and Mary Elizabeth (Henry) B.; A.B., Princeton U., 1946-50; M.D., U. Pa., 1954; m. Elizabeth Sherwood McConnel, June 21, 1952; children—Katherine, Robert, William, James. Intern, Henry Ford Hoso., Detroit, 1954-55; communicable disease officer Los Angeles County (Calif.) Health Dept., 1957-58; resident in radiology U. Mich., Ann Arbor, 1958-61; practice medicine specializing in radiology, Grayling, Mich., 1961-69, Cadillac, Mich., 1961—; clin. instr. radiology, U. Mich., 1960-61; cons. in field; dir. radiology, nuclear medicine Mercy Hosp., Cadillac; cons. med. arts. group, Cadillac; dir. 1st Nat. Bank of Evart (Mich.). Served with M.C., USN, 1955-57. Diplomate Am. Bd. Radiology. Mem. AMA, Mich. State, Wexford-Missaukee County (sec. 1963-64, pres. 1964-65) med. secs., W. Mich., Mich. radiol. secs., Am. Coll. Radiology, F.J. Hodges Radiology Soc., Phi Beta Kappa. Republican. Presbyterian. Home: 1000 Stimson St Cadillac MI 49601 Office: Mercy Hosp Cadillac MI 49601

BARNETT, WILLIAM A., lawyer; b. Chgo., Oct. 13, 1916; s. Leo James and Anita (Olsen) B.; LL.B., Loyola U., Chgo., 1941; m. Evelyn Yates, June 23, 1945; children—William, Mary Leone (Mrs. John J. Fahey), Therese, Kathleen (Mrs. William D. Norwood). Admitted to Ill. bar, 1941; with U.S. IRS, 1948-54, atty. chief counsel's office, Chgo., 1948-52, dist. counsel penal div., Detroit, 1952-54; chief tax atty. U.S. Atty's Office, Chgo., 1955-60; practitioner before the 6th Circuit Court of Appeals, since 1954, 7th Circuit Ct. Appeals, since 1955, U.S. Supreme Ct., since 1959. Mem. Am., Fed., Ill. and 7th Circuit bar assns., Am. Judicature Soc., Nat. Assn. Criminal Def. Lawyers. Home: 1448 Norwood St Chicago IL 60660 Office: 135 S LaSalle St Chicago IL 60603

BARNETTE, EMMA CHRISTINE HANSEN (MRS. FOSTER I. BARNETTE), bottling co. cons.; b. Omaha; d. Jens Nielsen and Laurentine C. (Larsen) Hansen; student pub. schs.; m. Foster I. Barnette, Aug. 23, 1930. Dress designer M.E. Smith Co., Omaha, 1917-20, Ely Walker Dry Goods, St. Louis, 1920-33, Carson Pirie Scott Co., Chgo., 1933-35, Lee Garment Co., Chgo., 1935-40; v.p., treas. Pepsi-Cola Bottling Co., Rockford, Ill., 1945-73, cons., 1973—. Presbyterian. Club: Quota. Home: 23 Country Club Beach Rockford IL 61103 Office: 4622 Hydraulic St Rockford IL 61108

BARNEY, FREDERICK ALBERT, camp owner, adminstr., educator; b. Meadville, Pa., June 13, 1922; s. Glenn Edward and Cecelia Genevieve (Kebort) B.; B.S., U. Eastern Mich., 1948; M.A., U. Mich., 1950; m. Marilyn Mellon, May 6, 1944; 1 dau., Ann Cecelia. Coach, Kinde (Mich.) High Sch., 1950-51, Mt. Morris (Mich.) High Sch., 1951-53; prin. Montrose (Mich.) High Sch., 1953-57; tchr., intramural dir. New Trier High Sch., Winnetka, Ill., 1957—; pres., dir. Vernon Oaks Country Day Sch., Deerfield, Ill., 1963; lectr. in field. Served with AUS, 1942-45; ETO. Decorated Combat Inf. Badge. Mem. Nat. Intermural Assn., Ill., Nat. edn. assns., AAHPER, Am. Camping Assn. Rotarian. Home: 1480 Chippewa St Deerfield IL 60015 Office: Vernon Oaks Country Day Sch 3140 Riverwoods Rd Deerfield IL 60015

BARNEY, JAMES ARTHUR, SR., credit union exec.; b. Evansville, Ind., May 8, 1916; s. Charles W. and Mary Magelen (Hufnagel) B.; student pub. schs., Ind., FBI Police Schs., 1040-65; m. Eleanor P. Mominee, July 6, 1934; children—James A., Helen Ann. With Evansville Police Dept., 1940-65, detective lt., 1956-65, retired, 1965; treas. Evansville Orthopedics Co., Inc., 1969—; mgr., treas. Evansville Police Fed. Credit Union, 1965—; pres. dir. Ind. Credit Union League. Cadidate for Mayor, primary, 1972. Mem. Credit Union Nat. Assn. (nat. dir.), Credit Union Exec. Soc. (past pres. Ind. Hoosier's). Roman Catholic. Clubs: Civitan, Central Turners, Eagles, Fraternal Order of Police. Home: 1201 S Weinbach Ave Evansville IN 47714 Office: Civic Center-Police Hdqrs Evansville IN 47708

BARNEY, LEROY, educator; b. Blackfoot, Idaho, Apr. 17, 1930; s. Bryan Lee and Lillian Gertrude (Dixon) B.; B.S. in Elementary Edn. (Scholarship "A"), Utah State U., 1956, M.S. in Sch. Adminstrn., 1959; Ed.D. in English (Ford fellow), U. No. Colo., 1965; m. Arla Marie Worlton, June 5, 1953; children—Vicki, Sharyn, Kevin, Ronald, Paula, Daryl. Tchr., Portland, Oreg., 1956-57, Logan, Utah, 1957-64; faculty No. Ill. U., DeKalb, 1965—, prof. edn., 1972—. Cons. to over 197 sch. dists., 1977; instr. radiol. defense monitor, Utah, Colo., Ill., 1964—. Served with USAF, 1948-53. Mem. Nat. Edn. Assn., Nat. Council of Tchrs. English, Internat. Reading Assn., Phi Kappa Phi, Phi Delta Kappa. Republican. Mem. Ch. of Jesus Christ of Latter-day Saints. Author: Building Reading Power, 1969; The Teaching Act Applied to Science, 1969; Phonics, The First Approach to Reading, 1977. Contbr. articles to field to profl. jours. and mags. Home: 240 Tilton Park Dr DeKalb IL 60115

BARNEY, MICHAEL CHARLES, microbiologist; b. Celina, Ohio, Sept. 27, 1946; s. Fredrick Charles and Dorothy Elizabeth (Shafer) B.; student U. Ill., 1964-65, Parsons Coll., 1966-67; B.S., U. Wis., 1970, M.S., 1972; postgrad. Med. Coll. Wis., 1974. Tchr. biology and microbiology U. Wis., Oshkosh, 1970-72; sr. research microbiologist Miller Brewing Co., Milw., 1973—. Mem. Nat. Mgmt. Assn., Am. Soc. Microbiology, Am. Soc. Cereal Chemists, Soc. Indsl. Microbiology, Am. Soc. Brewing Chemists (chmn. subcom. microbiol. controls, Phi Sigma Epsilon. Contbr. articles to profl. jours. Home: 2325 N 83d St Wauwatosa WI 53213 Office: 4000 W State St Milwaukee WI 53201

BARNHART, GENE, lawyer; b. Pineville, W. Va., Dec. 22, 1928; s. Forrest H. and Margaret (Harshman) B.; student W.Va. U., 1946-48; student Coll. Steubenville, 1949-50; J.D., U. Cin., 1953; m. Shirley L. Dunn, Jan. 28, 1952; children—Sheryl Lynne (Mrs. Dickey), Deborah Lee, Taffie Elise, Pamela Carole, Margaret Melanie. Admitted to Ohio bar, 1953; counsel clothing br. Armed Services Procurement Agy., Washington, Phila., 1953-55; asso. firm Black, McCuskey, Souers & Arbaugh, Canton, Ohio, 1955-60, partner, 1961—; lectr. Ohio Legal Center Inst., Ohio Bar Assn., Am. Inst. Banking. Mem. Jackson Local Bd. Edn., 1966-74, pres., 1970; mem. Jackson Twp. Bd. Zoning Appeals, 1964—; publicity co-chmn. Jackson Citizens Com., 1961-73; vice-chmn. Jackson Zoning Ordinance Revision Com.; mem. community planning com. United Way of Central Stark County; past pres. Council of Chs. of Central Stark County; pres. Family Counseling Services Central Stark County. Trustee Jackson Civic Assn., Info. and Referral Com., Interfaith Campus Ministry Kent State-Stark Regional Campus, Cancer Edn. and Research Found. Served with USNR, 1948-49. Mem. Stark County (exec. com.), Ohio State (legal edn. com., com. legal specialization), Am. bar assns., Order of Coif; Phi Alpha Delta. Mem. Calvary Chapel (choir). Home: 2805 Coventry Ln NW Canton OH 44708 Office: 1200 Harter Bank Bldg Canton OH 44702

BARNHART, RICHARD EDWIN, ednl. adminstr.; b. Indpls., Apr. 3, 1922; s. Wilbur S. and Mabel (Stutsman) B.; B.A., Manchester Coll., 1947; M.S., Ind. U., 1949, Ed.D., 1952; m. Fern Rohrer, Oct. 9, 1943; children—Donald Lee, Barbara June. Tchr. pub. sch., Westfield, Ind., 1947-49; dir. guidance Columbus (Ind.) High Sch., 1952-53; dir. adminstrv. services Terre Haute (Ind.) pub. schs., 1953-55; asst. supt. Cedar Rapids (Ia.) pub. schs., 1955-59; supt. Grand Forks (N.D.) pub. schs., 1959-65, Bloom Twp. High Sch., Chicago Heights, Ill., 1965-69; dir. Curriculum div. Mich. State Dept. Edn., Lansing, 1969—. Bd. dirs. Mental Health Assn., Mental Health Center, St. James Hosp., Chicago Heights, Ill. Served with AUS, 1943-46. Mem. Am. Assn. Sch. Adminstrs., Am. Psychol. Assn., Phi Delta Kappa. Presbyterian. Rotarian. Contbr. articles in field to profl. jours. Home: 2958 Crestwood Dr East Lansing MI 48823 Office: Box 420 Mich Dept Edn Lansing MI 48911

BARNHILL, HELEN IPHIGENIA, mgmt. cons. co. exec.; b. Ponce de Leon, Fla., Nov. 10, 1937; d. Willie David and Faustanna (Campbell) Ponds; B.A. in Sociology, Marquette U., 1966; Ph.D. (hon.), Lakeland Coll., 1975; children—Carmen A., Jerdie L., Althea Y., Stanley M., Hillary L., Kelli M., Dana M. Caseworker, Milw. Urban League, 1962-65; coordinator housing and pub. accomodations State of Wis., Milw., 1965-70; dir. Project Equality of Wis., Milw., 1970-73; pres. Barnhill, Hayes & Crosby, Inc., Mgmt. Cons.. Milw., 1973—; instr. mgmt. cons. U. Wis. Extension, 1976-77. Trustee Fellowship Community United Ch. Christ; bd. dirs. Lakeland Coll., 1976—; chmn. exec. council United Ch. Christ, 1975-77; mem. Gov.'s Manpower Planning Council, 1971-77; bd. dirs. Better Bus. Bur. Milw., 1977—. Recipient award for Community Service, B'nai B'rith, 1969; Freedom of Residence award, 1966; award for Bus. Achievement, Wis. Women's Polit. Caucus, 1976; Bus. Leader award YWCA, 1977. Mem. Am. Soc. Tng. and Devel., Adminstrv. Mgmt. Soc., Personnel-Indsl. Relations Assn., Tempo. Office: 633 W Wisconsin Ave Suite 310 Milwaukee WI 53203

BARNHILL, ROBERT LESTER, JR., salesman; b. Jacksonville, Fla., Dec. 8, 1922; s. Robert Lester and Lellia Dean (Shelley) B.; B.S., U. Wis., 1952; postgrad. Drake U., 1956, George Williams Coll., 1957; m. Doris Harlene Verchio, Mar. 24, 1951; children—David, Laurel, Robert III. Active youth worker YMCA, Milw., Des Moines, Ft. Dodge, Iowa, St. Joseph, Mo., 1941-63; tchr. Ind. Sch. Dist., Denver, 1964-67; dir. camping and recreation Easter Seal Soc. Iowa, Des Moines, 1967-76; mgr. Des Moines chpt. Izaak Walton League, 1976-77; salesman Sears Roebuck & Co., 1977—. Adminstrv. adviser Am. Indian Culture Center, Des Moines, 1969-72; adult adviser, leader Makowaian Indian Lore Club, 1952—. Served with C.E., AUS, 1943-46. Mem. Am. Camping Assn. (section v.p. 1970-71), Izaak Walton League (chpt. dir. 1971-73). Rotarian, Optimist. Address: 6873 NW 5th Ct Des Moines IA 50313

BARNSTORFF, HENRY DRESES, chem. co. chemist; b. Cin., July 26, 1925; s. Hermann and Johanna Elizabeth (Kahr) B.; A.B., Missouri Valley Coll., 1946; B.S., U. Mo., 1948, M.A., 1949; Ph.D. (Am. Cyanamid Co. fellow), U. Colo., 1953; m. Josephine Ann Sylvester, Sept. 2, 1950; children—Margaret J., Katherine A., John K. Staff mem. Spencer Chem. Co., Pittsburg, Kans., 1953-56; research chemist Monsanto Co., St. Louis, 1953-56, sr. research chemist, 1956-63, research specialist, 1963-65, mgr. profl. employment, 1965-67, research staff mgr., 1967-71, sr. research specialist, 1971—. Served with USNR, 1943-45. Mem. Am. Chem. Soc. (chmn. St. Louis sect. 1966), Mo. Acad. Sci., Sigma Xi, Phi Lambda Upsilon, Beta Beta Beta. Patentee in field. Contbr. articles to profl. jours. Home: 1003 Glenmoor Lane Glendale MO 63122 Office: 800 N Lindbergh Blvd Creve Coeur MO 63166

BARON, RAYMOND CHARLES, dentist; b. Mpls., Nov. 9, 1928; s. Raymond Frank and Rosalia Mary (Rutten) B.; student St. John's U., 1946-49; B.S., D.D.S., U. Minn., 1953; m. Frances Mary Hynan, Nov. 16, 1957; children—Constance Anne, John Charles. Practice dentistry, Mpls., 1955-59, Wayzata, Minn., 1959—. Pres. Perident Inc., Wayzata, 1972—, Quadent Studios Inc., Wayzata, 1972-76; past dental cons. Angles Home, Minnetonka, Minn., 1960-62. Pres. Home and Sch. Assn. of St. Margaret Mary Sch., 1968-70, mem. sch. bd., 1970-72. Trustee Rosalia M. Baron Trust. Served with Dental Corps, USAF, 1953-55. Recipient certificates of appreciation Wayzata Lions Club, 1969, Golden Valley Hockey Ass., 1971. Mem. North Side, Mpls., Minnetonka (pres. 1965-66) dental assns., Acad. for Study Dental Occlusion (program chmn. 1972-73). Republican. Roman Catholic. K.C. (4 deg.), Kiwanian. Home: 5111 Thotland Rd Minneapolis MN 55422 Office: 250 North Central Wayzata MN 55391

BARONE, JAMES VINCENT, dentist; b. Detroit, Sept. 19, 1925; s. Joseph J. and Jennie (Petix) B.; B.A., Wayne State U., 1946; D.D.S., U. Detroit, 1949; m. Kathleen Louise Dailey, June 17, 1950; children—James V., Kathleen L. (Mrs. Michael Pegg), Mark J., Linda M., Mary Beth, Patrick T. Practice dentistry, Detroit, 1949-72, Birmingham, Mich., 1972—; mem. staff Childrens Hosp. Mich., 1949-55; clin. asso. prof. dept. prosthetics U. Detroit Dental Center, 1960—. Served to capt., Dental Corps, AUS, 1955-57. Fellow Internat., Am. coll. dentists, Acad. Gen. Dentistry; mem. Oakland County Dental Soc. (liaison trustee 1972—), Am. (del. 1972-77), Mich. (chmn. com. dental practice 1970-71, trustee 1972-76, pres. elect 1977-78) dental assns., Acad. Dental Medicine, Am. Equilibration Soc., Detroit Dental Clinic Club (complete denture sect.), Pierre Fauchard Acad., Am. Prosthodontic Soc., U. Detroit Dental Alumni (pres. 1965), U. Detroit Dental Century Club (founder, pres. 1965), Detroit Dist. (v.p. 1967, pres. 1969), Central (pres. 1960) dental socs., Delta Sigma Delta, Omicron Kappa Upsilon, Phi Sigma Epsilon. Republican. Roman Catholic. K.C. Contbr. articles to Jour. Prosthetic Dentistry. Home 4697 Wendrick Dr West Bloomfield MI 48033 Office: 31001 Lahser Rd Birmingham MI 48010

BARR, DONALD WESLEY, fin. co. exec.; b. Ashland, Ohio, Jan. 1, 1914; s. Burton H. and Eva May (Hout) B.; student Dickinson Bus. Coll., Princeton U., 1940-41; m. Jeanne Isabel, Oct. 13, 1950; children—Donna Jean, Melanie Cheryl, Cynthia Sue. Founder, Don Barr Associates, Inc., Mansfield, Ohio, 1949, pres., 1949—; founder Don Barr, Inc., Mansfield, Ohio, 1957, pres., 1957—; founder Don Barr Investment Co., Mansfield, Ohio, 1966, pres., 1966—; mem. advisory bd. Richland Bank, 1960-77. Pres. Jr. Achievement Mansfield, 1962-63. Served with U.S. Army, World War II. Mem. Nat. Bus. Forms Assn. Club: Rotary. Home: 2100 Lexington Ave Mansfield OH 44907 Office: PO Box 1328 Mansfield OH 44901

BARR, JOAN HARRIS, career counselor; b. N.Y.C., July 30, 1926; d. William Eber and Rachel Augusta (Sheffield) Harris; B.A., Ohio Wesleyan U., 1947; M.Ed., Kent State U., 1975, postgrad., 1976—; m. Wayne Arthur Barr, 1949 (div. 1969); children—Jacqueline and Jeffrey (twins). Sec. to v.p. Internat. B.F. Goodrich, 1949-54; sec. to headmaster Old Trail Sch., Bath, Ohio, 1969-73; sec. to v.p. pub. affairs Kent State U., 1973-74; aftercare counselor Portage Family Counseling and Mental Health Services, Ravenna, Ohio, 1976-77; asso. Cons.'s for Orgnl. and Personal Effectiveness, Inc., Kent, 1976—; pvt. practice career counseling; psychiat. social worker Western Res. Psychiat. Habilitation Center, 1977—. Mem. Am., Ohio personnel and guidance assns., Assn. Specialists in Group Work, Nat. Employment Counselors Assn., Nat., Ohio vocat. guidance assns., Assn. Humanistic Edn. and Devel., Am. Rehab. Counseling Assn., Ohio Assn. Counselor Edn. and Supervision, Kappa Kappa Gamma, Gertrude Sandford Doll Club. Home and Office: 3575 Darrow Rd Stow OH 44224

BARR, JOHN MONTE, lawyer; b. Mt. Clemens, Mich., Jan. 1, 1935; s. Merle James and Wilhelmina Marie (Monte) B.; student Mexico City Coll., 1955; B.A., Mich. State U., 1956; J.D., U. Mich., 1959; m. Marlene Joy Bielenberg, Dec. 17, 1954; children—John Monte, Karl Alexander, Elizabeth Marie. Admitted to Mich. bar, 1959, since practiced in Ypsilanti; mem. firm Ellis B. Freatman, Jr., 1959-61; partner, chief trial atty. Freatman, Barr, Anhut & Moir and predecessor firm, 1961—. Lectr. bus. law Eastern Mich. U., 1968-70. Pres. Ypsilanti Family Service, 1967; mem. Ypsilanti Y Com., 1971; sr. adviser Explorer law post Portage Trail council Boy Scouts Am., 1969-71, commr. Potawatomi dist., 1973-74, commr. Washtenong dist., 1974-75. Served with AUS, 1959-60. Mem. State Bar Mich. (grievance bd. 1969—, state rep. assembly 1977), Am., Ypsilanti, Washtenaw County (pres. 1975-76) bar assns., Am., Mich. trial lawyers assns., U.S. (instr. piloting, seamanship, sail), Ann Arbor (comdr. 1972-73) power squadrons. Lutheran. Clubs: Ypsilanti Breakfast Optimist (v.p. 1965), Washtenaw County, Washtenaw Sportsman's (Ypsilanti); Great Lakes Cruising (Chgo.). Contbr. articles to boating mags. Home: 1200 Whittier Rd Ypsilanti MI 48197 Office: 105 Pearl St Ypsilanti MI 48197

BARR, KENNETH JOHN, petroleum co. exec.; b. Birmingham, Ala., Aug. 25, 1926; s. Archie and Mable Leona (Griffith) B.; B.S. in Chem. Engring., Auburn U., 1947; postgrad. Inst. Mgmt. Northwestern U., 1964; m. Jeanne Bonner, Jan. 22, 1951; children—Marsha Jeanne, Kenneth John, Darren Clint. With Amoco Prodn. Co., 1948-1973, jr. petroleum engr., Hobbs, N.Mex., 1948-49, chief engr., 1962-65, v.p. and div. mgr., New Orleans, 1970-73, mgr. prodn. and v.p. prodn. Amoco Can. Petroleum Co. (subs.), Calgary, Alta., Can., 1965-70; gen. mgr. supply and coordination dept. Standard Oil Co. Ind., Chgo., 1973-75; exec. v.p. Amoco Internat. Oil Co., Chgo., 1975, Amoco Prodn. Co., 1975—. Served with USAAF, 1945. Mem. Soc. Petroleum Engrs. Clubs: Tchefuncta Country, Mid-Am. Office: 200 E Randolph Dr Chicago IL 60601

BARR, RAYMOND ALLEN, sch. adminstr.; b. Stoutland, Mo., Sept. 7, 1922; s. Keller R. and Maggie (Jacobs) B.; B.S., S.W. Mo. State Coll., 1947; M.E., Kans. State Tchrs. Coll. at Pittsburg, 1953; postgrad. U. Mo., 1949; m. Edith Wilma Harvey, Sept. 9, 1949; children—Patrick, Dea Anne. Athletic coach, tchr. Willard (Mo.) High Sch., 1947-48, Liberal (Mo.) High Sch., 1948-52; prin. Liberal High Sch., 1952-55, Marshfield (Mo.) High Sch., 1955-60; supt. schs. Marshfield Reorganized Sch. Dist., 1960—. Served with USAAF, 1942-45. Decorated Air Medal with 3 oak leaf clusters, D.F.C. Mem. Am., Mo. assns. sch. adminstrs., S.W. Mo. Adminstrs. (pres. 1966-67), Mo. Tchrs. Assn., NEA, Am. Legion. Baptist. Lion (pres. 1962-63). Home: 1319 W Washington Marshfield MO 65706 Office: Box B Marshfield MO 65706

BARR, RODERICK WOOD, communications exec.; b. Oak Park, Ill., Jan. 2, 1931; s. Charles Lee and Aileen (Wood) B.; B.A., Northwestern U., 1952; m. Barbara Bates, July 12, 1952; children—Carolee, Daniel, Diane, Roderick. Sales rep. U.S. Gypsum Co., Chgo., 1955-59, Union Carbide Corp., Chgo., 1959-68; founder, pres. Applied Facsimile Communications Inc., Cin., 1968-74, Fleetline Permit Service Inc., Cin., 1974-76, Tel-Graphic Products Inc., Cin., 1976—; dir. Am. Facsimile Systems Inc. Served with U.S. Army, 1952-54. Roman Catholic. Clubs: Union League (Chgo.); Univ. (Cin.). Home: 7260 Drake Rd Cincinnati OH 45243

BARR, ROY RASSMANN, lawyer; b. Chgo., Sept. 28, 1901; s. Alfred Eugene and Pauline (Rassmann) B.; student Northwestern U., 1918-20; Ph.B., U. Chgo., 1923; J.D., John Marshall Law Sch., Chgo., 1924; m. Katharine Roberts, Sept. 9, 1924; children—Robert Roy (dec.), Barbara Ann (Mrs. Robert E. Newlin), Alfred Eugene II. Admitted to Ill. bar, 1924; in law office of father, 1924, practiced law as Barr & Barr, 1924-26, then Barr, Barr & Corcoran; now individual practice, Chgo. Mem. Am., Ill. State (sr. counselor), Chgo., West Suburban bar assns., Am. Judicature Soc., Phi Sigma Soc., Delta Sigma Phi. Congregationalist. Mason. Clubs: Pierce Arrow Society; Veteran Car Club of Great Britain; Antique Automobile Club of Am.; Horseless Carriage; Classic Car of Am.; Interfraternity Chgo. Home: 423 Lenox St Oak Park IL 60302 Office: 10 S La Salle St Chicago IL 60603

BARRANGER, JOHN PAUL, electronics engr.; b. Worcester, Mass., July 26, 1930; s. Paul M. and Martha (Hubert) B.; B.S. in Engring., George Washington U., 1957, M.S. in Elec. Engring., Purdue U., 1960; Ph.D. in Elec. Engring., Case Western Res. U., 1969; m. Elizabeth Sheehy, Aug. 11, 1956; children—Gregory, Christopher, Melissa, Mary, Theresa, Linda, Ann, Paul. Design engr., ITT Fed., Ft. Wayne, Ind., 1957-60; devel. engr. Gen. Motors Electronics, Milw., 1960-63; research engr. NASA Lewis Research Center, Cleve., 1963—; cons. in electronics and instrumentation to various govt. agys., 1970—. Served with USN, 1951-55. Mem. Ohio Soc. Profl. Engrs., IEEE, Am. Brit. socs. nondestructive testing. Contbr. numerous articles on electronics and instrumentation to profl. jours. Home: 22324 Sharon Ln Fairview Park OH 44126 Office: NASA Lewis Research Center Cleveland OH 44135

BARRE, HENRY JOHN, educator; b. Tampa, Kans., Apr. 11, 1905; s. Fred D. and Adeline (Indorf) B.; B.S. in Agrl. Engring., Kans. State U., 1930; M.S., Iowa State U., 1933, Ph.D., 1938; m. Gertrude Ann Mesha, Aug. 31, 1935; children—James F., Mary Adeline, Jeanne Ann. Asst. and asst. prof. Iowa State U., 1930-38; agt. in charge grain storage investigations USDA Ames, Iowa, 1938-43; prof., head dept. agrl. engring. Purdue U., 1943-52; cons. agrl. engr., Columbus, Ohio, 1953-62; prof. agrl. engring. Ohio State U., Columbus, 1962-73, prof. emeritus, 1973—. Cons. CCC, USDA, 1939-52, Ford Found., Punjab Agrl. U., Ludhiana, India, 1966, 67, 70, Internat. Rice Research Inst., Sri Lanka, 1974; mem. agrl. bd. NRC. Recipient citation for research achievement USDA, 1946; Golden Plate award Am. Acad. Achievement, 1972; Distinguished Engring. Service award Kans. State U., 1974. Mem. Am. Soc. Agrl. Engrs. (v.p. 1956-58; Cyrus Hall McCormick Medal 1971). Am. Soc. Engring. Edn. (council) 1949-52), AAAS, Nat. Soc. Profl. Engrs. Author: (with L.L. Sammett) Farm Structures, 1950. Home: 305 W New England Ave Worthington OH 43085 Office: 2073 Neil Ave Columbus OH 43210

BARRELL, ROBERT POINDEXTER, psychologist; b. Buckingham, Va., Jan. 27, 1919; s. Charles Martin and Fannie Stuart (Hall) B.; B.A., Hampden-Sydney Coll., 1940; M.A., Ohio State U., 1941; Ph.D., U. Mich., 1951; m. Lorna K. Mill, June 9, 1957. Clin. psychologist VA Hosp., New Orleans, 1951-54, North Chicago, Ill., 1954—. Served with U.S. Army, 1942-46. Mem. AAAS, Gerontological Soc., Am., Midwestern, Ill. (pres. 1976-77) psychol. assns., N.Y. Acad. Scis. Home: 344 Tiffany Dr Waukegan IL 60085

BARRETT, EDWARD DUANE, dentist, microbiologist; b. Detroit, July 1, 1925; s. Thomas Joseph and Thelma Louise (Johnson) B.; student Marquette U., 1944-45; B.S., U. Detroit, 1947, M.S., 1949, D.D.S., 1954; postgrad. Wayne State U., 1949-50; m. Evelyn Thelma Trammell, Sept. 2, 1950; children—Heather, Mary Patricia, Theresa, Edward D., Margaret. Microbiologist, Wayne State U., Detroit, 1948-50; practice dentistry, Auburn Heights, Mich., 1955—; mem. microbiology faculty U. Detroit Dental Sch., 1950-57, grad. div., 1965-70, dir. continuing edn., 1977—. Pres. Auburn Heights Boys Club, 1960-66; Active Pontiac (Mich.) United Fund, 1963-65. Bd. mgrs. Rochester (Mich.) YMCA, 1971-77, chmn., 1973-75. Served with USNR, 1944-46. Mem. Am. Acad. Oral Medicine, Am. Acad. Gen. Dentistry (pres. Mich. 1976—), U. Detroit Dental Alumni Assn., Oakland County Dental Soc. (pres. 1969-70), Am., Mich. dental assns., Am. Legion, Alpha Sigma Nu, Psi Omega. Roman Catholic. K.C., Elk. Club: Auburn Heights Lions (pres. 1960-61). Author: (with Mattman, Barrett) Laboratory Experiments in Nursing Microbiology, 1952; (with Mattman, Barrett) Laboratory Experiments in Medical Microbiology, 1956; (with Mattman, Barrett, Rossmore) Exercises in Introductory Microbiology, 1958. Contbr. articles to sci. and profl. jours. Home: 220 Rochdale St Rochester MI 48063 Office: 3926 Auburn Rd Auburn Heights MI 48057

BARRETT, RICHARD HAMILTON, property mgmt. co. exec.; b. Columbus, Ohio, Oct. 30, 1916; s. Starling Heston and Bertha (Aid) B.; B.S., Ohio State U., 1938; m. Jeanne M. Webb, Sept. 9, 1939; children—Phillip H., Patricia L., Deborah A. Accountant, Price, Waterhouse & Co., Detroit, 1938-43, sr. accountant, 1946-47; sr. accountant Keller, Kirschner, Martin and Clinger, Columbus, 1947-48; treas., dir. Gen. Maintenance & Engring. Co., Columbus, 1948-68, sec., 1948-66, exec. v.p., 1966-68; dir., sec.-treas. Werner Constrn. Co., 1960-68, Interstate Maintenance & Engring. Co., 1948-68, Imeco Constrn. Co., Springfield, Ohio, Buckeye Cattle Co., 1962-68; pres., dir. Barrett Corp., Columbus, 1968-70; gen. mgr. Precision/Del. Corp., Delaware, Ohio, 1970-71; nat. exec. v.p.

Klingbell Mgmt. Co., Columbus, 1971-74; v.p., gen. mgr. Indiana Mgmt. Co., Indpls., 1974—. Served with AUS, 1943-45; ETO. Decorated Bronze Star, Purple Heart. Mem. Apt. Assn. Ind. (pres. 1977), Ohio State U. Alumni Assn., Sigma Chi. Club: University (Columbus). Home: 4612 Somerset Way S Carmel IN 46032 Office: 3380 Founders Rd Indianapolis IN 46268

BARRETT, ROBERT ALLEN, state ofcl.; b. South Bend, Ind., Sept. 19, 1941; s. David L. and Maxine (Shulte) B.; diploma in data processing Bus. Service Assos., 1960; student Ind. U., 1959-63, B.S. in Bus. Mgmt., 1977; m. Pamela Sue Rerick, Oct. 30, 1959; 1 son, Robert Randall. Systems analyst Univac div. Sperry Rand, Ft. Wayne, 1964-66, McCray Corp., refrigeration mfg., Ft. Wayne, 1966-67, REA Magnet Wire Co., Ft. Wayne, 1967-68; customer service data processing Peoples Trust Bank, 1968-69; data processing mgr. Fort Wayne Drug Co. (Ind.), 1969-72; exec. dir. Inter-Agy. Drug Abuse Council, Fort Wayne, 1972-74; dir. Region II Ind. Criminal Justice Planning Agy., 1974—. Mem. curriculum com. Ind. U. Div. Tech. Studies, 1972—; chmn. adv. com. County Data Processing Bd., 1972-74. Bd. dirs. Fort Wayne Soap Box Derby Inc., 1969-70. Mem. Jaycees (pres. Fort Wayne 1969-70, nat. dir. 1970-71, v.p. Ind. 1971-72, met. officer 1972-73; named Outstanding Local Pres. Ind. 1970), C. of C. (dir. Fort Wayne 1969-70), Sigma Chi. Home: 2710 Garden Park Dr Fort Wayne IN 46825 Office: 1025 Anthony Wayne Bank Bldg Fort Wayne IN 46802

BARRETT, WILLIAM CARROLL, supt. schs.; b. Hibbing, Minn., Sept. 4, 1920; s. Clinton Lewis and Olive Anna (Donovan) B.; A.B. Western Mich. U., 1943, M.A., 1953; postgrad. U. Detroit Law Sch., 1946-48, Mich. State U., 1953-56; grad U.S. Army War Coll., 1973; m. Jennifer Hynd, Oct. 25, 1975. Tchr. pub. schs., Grand Ledge, Mich., 1953-55; supt. schs. Hubbardston, 1956-59, Fowler, 1959-62, Coloma, 1962—. Served with AUS, 1942-45, 50-51; ETO; now col. Res., comdt. 5033 USAR Sch. Mem. Am., Mich. assns. sch. adminstrs., Res. Officers Assn., Am. Legion, Alpha Kappa Delta, Gamma Eta Gamma. K.C. Home: 6026 N US 33 Coloma MI 49038 Office: PO Box 218 Coloma MI 49038

BARRETTE, PATRICK EMILE, engineer; b. St. Paul, Mar. 4, 1949; s. Rene L. and Judith (Smolik) B.; student U. Wis., 1967-69, U. Minn., 1974-76. Field engr. LeSueur (Minn.) Foundry, 1977, Schlumberger Well Services, Pleasanton, Tex., 1977—. Served with USAF, 1969-74. Mem. Am. Foundrymen' Assn., Am. Def. Preparedness Assn. Home: PO Box 396 Maiden Rock WI 54750 Office: PO Box 1846 CH Laredo TX 78040

BARRICK, LOUISE GRIDER (MRS. HARRY THOMAS BARRICK), ret. librarian; b. Brazil, Ind., Apr. 19, 1912; d. John Ernest and Dean (O'Connor) Grider; B.S., Ind. State U., 1933, library certificate, 1967; m. Harry Thomas Barrick, Dec. 26, 1938; children—Judith (Mrs. Robert Stull), Thomas Gordon. Adult edn. bus. tchr. Cannelton (Ind.), 1933-34; bus. tchr. Staunton (Ind.) High Sch., 1934-39; sec. econs. dept. Ind U., Bloomington, 1939-41; operator pvt. typing sch., Terre Haute, Ind., 1959-64; adult edn. bus. tchr. Vigo County Sch. Corp., Terre Haute, 1964-65; asst. librarian Meadows br. Vigo County Pub. Library, Terre Haute, 1965-66, librarian South br. library, 1966-77. Pres. PTA, Terre Haute, 1954-56, Crittenton Bd., Terre Haute, 1955-57. Bd. dirs. Adult and Child Guidance Clinic, 1964-66. Mem. Staff Assn. Vigo Pub. Library (pres. 1970-71), Am., Ind. library assns., P.E.O., Sigma Kappa. Methodist (sec. ofcl. bd. 1960-64). Club: Woman's Department (v.p. 1964-65) (Terre Haute). Home: 340 S 22d St Terre Haute IN 47803 Office: Southland Shopping Center Terre Haute IN 47802

BARRINGTON, BRUCE DAVID, hosp. data processing exec.; b. Chgo., Apr. 9, 1942; s. Arthur Richard and Lorene Cora (Powell) B.; B.S. in Math., Bradley U., 1964; m. Gayle Ann Wilcoxen, June, 1970; 1 son, Arthur Richard, II. Systems analyst Caterpillar Tractor Co., Peoria, Ill., 1965-67; mgr. hosp. systems devel. McDonnell Douglas Automation Co., Peoria, 196/-73; founder, exec. v.p. HBO & Co., Peoria, 1973—; mem. Peoria Data Processing Commn. Mem. Assn. Systems Mgmt. (founder local chpt. 1969, pres. 1971-72). Mem. First Federated Ch. of Peoria. Club: Country of Peoria. Developer hosp. computing systems. Office: 4700 N Sterling Ave Peoria IL 61614

BARRON, ALEXANDER FRASER, sales cons.; b. Ord, Nebr., Apr. 21, 1891; s. John Fraser and Adelaide L. (McCarthy) B.; B.S. in Mech. Engring., U. Ill., 1915; m. Esther E. Anderson, Feb. 6, 1937 (dec. July 29, 1952). Draftsman, Am. Smelting & Refining Co., Perth Amboy, N.J., 1915-16; draftsman Rodman Virginian Ry. Co., Princeton, W.Va., 1917; draftsman U.S. Smelting, Refining & Mining Co., East Chicago, Ind., 1918; sales engr. Maher Eng. Co., Chgo., 1919-23; propr. A. F. Barron 1923—: originator Universal Automatic Engine Controller. Served as corporal, Company F., 305th Engrs., 1918-19; sgt. Intelligence Sect., 80th Div. Hdqrs., 1919; overseas 12 months. Registered Profl. Engr., Ill. Mem. 80th Div. Vet Assn. Nat. Soc. Profl. Engrs., Instrument Soc. Am., Am. Waterworks Assn., Nat. Fire Protection Assn., Mfrs. Agts. Nat. Assn., Tau Beta Pi, Pi Tau Sigma. Club: Columbia (Indpls.). Home: C-3A Camden Ct 11551 S Western Ave Chicago IL 60643 Office: 53 W Jackson Blvd Chicago IL 60604

BARRON, ARTHUR WILLIAM, hosp. exec.; b. Ottawa, Ill., Oct. 30, 1920; s. Arthur William and Elizabeth (Pleskovitch) B.; B.S., U. Ill., 1943; M.B.A., U. Chgo., 1962; m. Mary M. Freeman, May 22, 1948; children—Paula, Margaret, Mary. Tax accountant Kimberly-Clark Corp., Neenah, Wis., 1946-51; comptroller Franciscan Sisters of Sacred Heart, Mokena, Ill., 1951-59, financial cons., 1959-60, adminstrv. asst., 1960-76, exec. asst. to pres., 1976—, also dir., cons. Pres. bd. edn. Diocese of Joliet, 1970-74. Served with USNR, 1943-46. Mem. Hosp. Financial Mgmt. Assn. (chpt. pres. 1954-55, dir. 1956-57, hosp. adv. bd. 1959—), Am. (ho. of dels.), Ill. (trustee) hosp. assns., Am. Inst. C.P.A.'s, Cath. Hosp. Assn. Republican. Roman Catholic. K.C. Clubs: University of Chicago Executive Program; Joliet Country, Joliet Tennis. Home: 1310 W Acres Rd Joliet IL 60435 Office: Route 1 Mokena IL 60448

BARRON, HOWARD ROBERT, lawyer; b. Chgo., Feb. 17, 1930; s. Irving P. and Ada (Astrahan) B.; Ph.B., U. Chgo., 1948; B.A., Stanford U., 1950; LL.B., Yale, 1953; m. Marjorie Ruth Shapira, Aug. 12, 1953; children—Ellen Jean, Laurie Ann. Admitted to Ill. bar, 1953; associate of firm of Jenner & Block and predecessor firms, Chgo., 1957-64, partner, 1964—. Regional rep. Ill., exec. com. Yale Law Sch. Assn., 1971-77; chmn. Chgo. maj. gifts com. Yale Law Sch. Sesquicentennial Campaign. Mem. bd. edn. Lake County Sch. Dist. 107, Highland Park, Ill., 1964-71, pres., 1969-71; chmn. com. on interdistrict cooperation Lake County Sch. Dists. 106-113, 1967-68; pres. Lake County Sch. Bd. Assn., 1970-71; mem. Bd. Edn. Lake County High Sch. Dist. 113, 1973-77. Served to lt. (j.g.) USNR, 1953-57. Mem. Chgo. (grievance com. 1965-73), Ill. (chmn. antitrust sect. 1968-69), Am. bar assns. Clubs: Yale Law Sch. Assn. Ill. (pres. 1966), Legal of Chicago, Law of Chicago, Cliff Dwellers, Standard. Contbr. articles to profl. jours. Home: 433 Ravine Dr Highland Park IL 60035 Office: One IBM Plaza Chicago IL 60611

BARROW, ROBERT RUFFIN, life ins. co. exec.; b. Ft. Meyers, Fla., July 31, 1945; s. David Woolfolk and Marion Thorp (Little) B.; B.B.A., U. Wis.-Milw., 1974; M.B.A., Harvard U., 1976; m. Barbara Mary Ann Carol King-Ginnasi, Dec. 21, 1970; children—Annibale Ruffin (dec.), Caroline Constance Ruffin, Elizabeth Parham Ruffin. Exec. asst. to pres. Internat. Gen. Ins. Corp., Milw., 1969-73, pres., 1977—; pres. Tex. Internat. Life Ins. Co., Austin, 1973-76, Internat. Inc., Milw., 1976—; dir. Nationwide Equities Corp., 1973—. Trustee Brown Deer Library, 1971-73; nat. vice-chmn. Nat. Fedn. Young Republicans, 1973-75; trustee Barrow Med. Found., 1973—. Served with U.S. Army, 1966-67. Republican. Episcopalian. Club: Milwaukee Country. Home: 8303 N Greenvale St Milwaukee WI 53217 Office: PO Box 17667 Milwaukee WI 53217

BARRY, HILARY DONAVAN, constrn. co. exec.; b. Underwood, Minn., July 22, 1934; s. Bernard Daniel and Fern (Donely) B.; grad. U. Minn., Morris, 1952; m. Cheryl Louise Teske, Aug. 22, 1952; children—Mark, Scott, Cynthia, Carla, Tamara, Teresa, Bruce, Amy, Patrick, Kimberly. Laborer with various constrn. cos., 1952-56; owner, mgr. Barry Constrn. Co., Lake Wilson, Minn., 1956—; pres., dir. Valhalla Devel., Slayton, Minn., 1968—, Valhalla Recreation, 1968—; pres. Barry Co. of Minn., 1969-77, Tour Airways, Inc., comml. helicopter operation, Rapid City, S.D., 1970-71. Mem. Gov.'s Adv. Commn. Dept. Econ. Devel., 1972-77. County chmn. Democratic Farmers Labor Party, 1962-68, mem. exec., central coms., 2d dist., 1962-68, del. state conv., 1962, 64, 66, 68, 70, del. nat. conv., 1968. Mem. Asso. Gen. Contractors Minn., Southwestern Minn. Contractors Assn. (pres. 1960-68, dir. 1957—), Helicopter Assn. Am. Roman Catholic. K.C., Address: Lake Wilson MN 56151

BARRY, JAMES P(OTVIN), writer, editor, assn. exec.; b. Alton, Ill., Oct. 23, 1918; s. Paul Augustine and Elder (Potvin) B.; m. Anne Elizabeth Jackson, Apr. 16, 1966; B.A. cum laude, with distinction Ohio State U., 1940. Commd. 2d. lt. Arty., U.S. Army, 1940, advanced through grades to col., 1953; served ETO, 1944-46; adviser to Turkish Army, 1951-53; detailed Army Gen. Staff, Washington, 1953-56; ret., 1966; adminstr. Capital U., Columbus, Ohio, 1967-71; freelance writer, editor, Columbus, 1971-77; dir. Ohioana Library Assn., 1977—; editor Ohioana Quar., 1977—; photographer, exhbn. and book illustrator, 1968—. Recipient award Am. Soc. State and Local History, 1974. Mem. Gt. Lakes, Marine, Ohio hist. socs., World Ship Soc., Phi Beta Kappa. Clubs: Royal Can. Yacht; Columbus Country. Author: Georgian Bay: The Sixth Great Lake, 1968; The Battle of Lake Erie, 1970; Bloody Kansas, 1972; The Noble Experiment, 1972; The Fate of the Lakes, 1972; The Louisiana Purchase, 1973; Henry Ford and Mass Production, 1973; Ships of the Great Lakes, 1973; The Berlin Olympics, 1975; The Great Lakes: A First Book, 1976; Old Forts of the Great Lakes, 1978. Home: 353 Fairway Blvd Columbus OH 43213 also Thunder Beach PO Penetanguishene ON Canada Office: 1105 Ohio Depts Bldg 65 S Front St Columbus OH 43215

BARRY, THOMAS HUBERT, pub. co. exec.; b. Phillips, Wis., Mar. 18, 1918; s. John Sumner and Helen (Maloney) B.; student U. Notre Dame, 1936-38; B.A., Marquette U., 1941; m. Rosemary Klein, July 8, 1944; children—Kathleen (Mrs. J. Douglas Ingram), Patricia (Mrs. Thomas Turriff), Mary Beth (Mrs. William O'Donnell), Julie (Mrs. David Carden). Western mgr., welding engr. McGraw Hill Pub. Co., Chgo., 1947-53; Western mgr. Iron Age, Chilton Co., Chgo., 1953-66; Western mgr. Control Engring., Dun-Donnelley Pub. Co., Chgo., 1966-69, sales mgr., N.Y.C., 1969-72, asso. pub., Chgo., 1972—. Served with USMCR, 1941-47. Decorated Bronze Star medal, Purple Heart medal. Mem. Nat. Indsl. Advertisers Assn., Assn. Indsl. Advertisers (dir. Chgo. chpt. 1963-65), Bus.-Profl. Advtg. Assn., Indsl. Mktg. Club St. Louis, Rockford Advtg. Club, Reserve Officers Assn., K.C. Roman Catholic. Clubs: Notre Dame Club of Chgo., Marquette U. Club Chgo., Holy Name Soc. Home: 628 Carriage Hill Dr Glenview IL 60025 Office: 222 S Riverside Plaza Chicago IL 60606

BARSAMIAN, ARTHUR, indsl. photographer; b. Nortonville, N.D., Jan. 25, 1925; s. Shnork Charles and Angeline (Raphaelian) B.; student Lawrence Coll., 1944-45, Marquette U., 1945, Layton Sch. Art, 1946-47, Antonelli Sch. Photography, 1947; M.Photographer, Profl. Photographers Am., 1973; m. Agnes Perzigian, June 11, 1949; children—Arthur Alan, Jeffrey David. Indsl. photographer Ladish Co., Cudahy, Wis., 1948-57; supr. photography AC Spark Plug div. Gen. Motors Corp., Milw., 1957-72, motion picture cameraman GM Photo, Detroit, 1973-74, supr. photography AC Spark Plug div. Flint, Mich., 1974—. Served with USNR, 1943-46. Mem. Wis. Indsl. Photographers Assn. (charter mem., pres. 1964), Profl. Photographers Am. (indsl. councilman State Wis. nat. council 1964-72). Mem. Armenian Chs. N.Am. (diocesan del. 1966-70, chmn. parish council 1970-71). Home: 1055 Arden Ln Birmingham MI 48009 Office: 1300 N Dort Hwy Flint MI 48556

BARSI, LOUIS MICHAEL, univ. adminstr.; b. Port Reading, N.J., Aug. 26, 1941; s. Louis Joseph and Mary Alice B.; B.A., U. Okla., 1963; M.A., Central Mich. U., 1966; M.A., U. No. Iowa, 1971. Tchr. Searing Sch., N.Y.C., 1963-64; Annunciation High Sch., Detroit, 1964-65; instr. history, pol. sci., Muskegon (Mich.) Community Coll., 1966-68; dean students Mount St. Clare Coll., Clinton, Iowa, 1969-76; coordinator fin. aids U. Wis., Waukesha, 1977—. Group leader Student Personnel Conf., U. No. Iowa. Bd. dirs. H.A.N.D.S., Clinton, Iowa, 1970-71. Teaching assistantship, Central Mich. U., 1965-66; research assistantship, U. No. Iowa, 1968-69; assistantship U. Wis., Stout, 1976-77. Mem. Am. Personnel And Guidance Assn., Am., Wis. coll. personnell assns., Wis. Vocational Guidance Assn., Phi Delta Kappa, Phi Alpht Theta. Home: 197 Hill Ct Hartland WI 53029 Office: Univ Wis Waukesha WI 53186

BARSKY, DAVID, ophthalmologist; b. Regina, Sask., Can., Jan. 13, 1929; B.S., U. Sask., 1947; M.D., C.M., Queen's U., Kingston, Ont., 1953; came to U.S., 1953, naturalized, 1958. Rotating intern D.C. Gen. Hosp., Washington, 1953-54; resident in ophthalmology Henry Ford Hosp., Detroit, 1954-57, Kresge Eye Inst., Detroit, 1954-55; practice medicine specializing in ophthalmology, Wyandotte, Mich., 1958—; staff ophthalmologist Henry Ford Hosp., 1957-58; chief surgery Wyandotte Gen. Hosp., 1963, chief staff, 1967, mem.-at-large exec. com., 1973-74, sr. attending ophthalmology, 1960—; courtesy staff Oakwood Hosp., Dearborn, Mich., 1958-60, Harper Hosp., Detroit, 1974; attending Detroit Gen. Hosp., 1967; dir. Detroit Inst. Ophthalmology, 1973—; cons. USPHS Hosp., Grosse Point, Mich., 1965; chief pathology Kresge Eye Inst., 1974-76; clin. asso. prof. Wayne State U. Med. Sch. Diplomate Am. Bd. Ophthalmology. Fellow Am. Acad. Ophthalmology and Otolaryngology. Mem. AMA, Mich., Wayne County med. socs., Mich. (sec. 1970-72), Detroit ophthalmolical socs., Assn. Research Ophthalmology, Pan-Am. Assn. Ophthalmology, Georgiana Dvorak Theobald Ophthalmic Pathology Soc., N.Y. Acad. Scis., Kresge Eye Inst. Alumni Assn. (pres. 1966—). Contbr. med. jours. Home: 1701 Camelot Dr Trenton MI 48183 Office: 100 Oak St Wyandotte MI 48192

BARSKY, SIDNEY, dermatologist, educator; b. Chgo., July 3, 1918; s. Arthur and Gussie (Zeinfeld) B.; B.S., U. Ill., 1941, M.D., 1943; children—Gary Jay, Bonnie Lynn; m. Ruth J. Rizman, Mar. 15, 1977; stepchildren—Edna, Simona. Intern, Cook County Hosp., Chgo., 1944; resident, 1947-50; attending dermatologist Cook County Hosp., Chgo., 1953—; clin. instr. dermatology, U. Ill. Sch. of Medicine, Chgo., 1951-58; clin. asst. prof., 1958-62, clin. asso. prof., 1962-75, clin. prof., 1975—; chmn. div. of dermatology Cook County Hosp., 1967—; practice medicine specializing in dermatology, Oak Brook, Ill., 1950—. Served to capt. M.C., U.S. Army, 1944-46. Diplomate Am. Bd. Dermatology, Am. Bd. Dermatopathology. Mem. AMA, Ill. State, Chgo. med. socs., Am. Acad. of Dermatology, Soc. for Investigative Dermatology, Am. Soc. of Dermatopathology. Jewish. Clubs: Bnai Brith. Home: 519 Atwood Ct Elmhurst IL 60126 Office: 120 Oakbrook Center Mall Oak Brook IL 60521

BART, WILLIAM MARVIN, psychologist; b. Chgo., Nov. 29, 1943; s. Joseph Marvin and Madelynne Joanne (Stroik) B.; B.S., Loyola U., Chgo., 1965; A.M., U. Chgo., 1967, Ph.D., 1969. Asst. prof. ednl. psychology U. Minn., Mpls., 1969-72, asso. prof. ednl. psychology, 1972—. Mem. Am. Psychol. Assn., Am. Ednl. Research Assn., Soc. Research in Child Devel., Jean Piaget Soc. Recipient Fulbright-Hays Research scholar, W.Ger., 1974-75; contbr. articles to Jour. Math. Psychology, Jour. Ednl. Psychology. Home: 609 Jefferson St NE Minneapolis MN 55413 Office: 330 Burton Hall U Minn Minneapolis MN 55455

BARTA, GERALD THOMAS, elec. engr.; b. Milw., May 15, 1921; s. John George and Theresa Anna (Klien) B.; student Marquette U., 1940-43; B.E.E. cum laude, Notre Dame U., 1947; m. Sylvia Helen Wegner, July 13, 1946; children—Kathleen Jean, Patricia Ann, Mary Ellen, Thomas Joseph. Sales engr. Ind. Steel Products Co., Valparaiso, 1947-48, design engr., 1948-52, chief insp., 1952-54; mgr. quality control Ind. Gen. Corp., Valparaiso, 1954-56, sr. devel. engr., 1956-61; v.p. plant mgr. B.L. Downey Co., Chgo., 1961-62; chief product devel. engr. Ind. Gen. Corp., 1962-64, chief engr., 1964-65, mgr. engring., 1965-76, mgr. quality assurance and standards, 1976-77, mgr. customer service, 1977—. Served with USMCR, 1943-46. Mem. IEEE, C. of C., Pi Mu Epsilon. Roman Catholic. Patentee in field. Home: 2257 Montdale Rd Box 128 Valparaiso IN 46383 Office: 405 Elm St Valparaiso IN 46383

BARTELS, CARL FREDERICK, civil engr., land surveyor; b. Dubuque, Iowa, Oct. 3, 1904; s. Edward C. and Bertha (Rusch) B.; B.S. in Civil Engring., Iowa State U., 1925; m. Mildred Edith Azeltine, Nov. 25, 1926; children—Beverly Ann, Nancy Jane, Sara Suzanne, Carole Mildred. Field and office engr. City of Lakeland (Fla.), 1925-28, J.B. Owens Constrn. Co., Chattanooga, 1928-29; bldg. commr. City of Dubuque, 1929-37; cons. civil engring., land surveying, Dubuque, 1937—, with Bartels Lemay Haas & Fay; engr. Dubuque Bd. Dock Commrs., 1935-60. Recipient Community Service award Iowa State Alumni Assn. Mem. ASCE, Dubuque Shooting Soc. Presbyterian. Clubs: Masons, Shriners. Home: 1550 Alta Pl Dubuque IA 52001 Office: 1166 Main St Dubuque IA 52001

BARTHELMAS, NED KELTON, stock broker; b. Circleville, Ohio, Oct. 22, 1927; s. Arthur and Mary Bernice (Riffel) B.; B.S. in Bus. Adminstrn., Ohio State U., 1950; m. Marjorie Jane Livezey, May 23, 1953; children—Brooke Ann, Richard Thomas. Stock broker Ohio Co., Columbus, 1953-58; pres. First Columbus Securities Corp., stock brokers and investment bankers, 1958—; pres. dir. Ohio Fin. Corp., Columbus, 1960—, United Capital Corp; dir. Republic-Franklin Life Ins. Co., Nat. Foods, Franklin Nat. Corp., Lancaster Colony Corp., 1st Nat. Equity Corp., Midwest Equity Corp., Court Realty Co., Medex Inc., Liebert Corp.; chmn., trustee Am. Guardian Fin.; trustee Republic Fin. Trust. Served with Adj. Gen.'s Dept., AUS, 1945-47. Mem. Nat. Assn. Securities Dealers, Nat. Stock Traders Assn., Securities Industry Assn., Nat. Investment Bankers Assn. (pres. 1973), Ohio Investment Dealers (pres. 1973), Columbus Jr. C. of C. (pres. 1956), Ohio Jr. C. of C. (trustee 1957-58), Columbus Area C. of C. (dir. 1956; named an outstanding young man of Columbus, 1962), Am. Mgmt. Assn. (pres.'s council), Young Pres. Orgn. (pres. 1971), Newcomen Soc., Phi Delta Theta. Clubs: Executives, Stock and Bond, Columbus Athletic, Columbus, Scioto Country (Columbus); Crystal Downs Country (Frankfort, Mich.). Home: 1998 Cambridge Blvd Columbus OH 46221 Office: 42 E Gay St Columbus OH 43215

BARTHOLOMAY, HENRY, III, ins. agy. exec.; b. Chgo., Nov. 26, 1923; s. Henry Conrad and Virginia (Graves) B.; student Harvard Coll., 1941-42; m. Julia Louise Adams, May 12, 1944; children—Henry A., Charles A., Lucy C., Julia L., Marian M. Ins. broker, Chgo., 1946-55; partner Bartholomay Bros., Chgo., 1955-62; partner Bartholomay & Clarkson, Chgo., 1963; v.p., dir. Alexander & Alexander, Inc., Chgo., 1963-73, sr. v.p., dir., 1973—; dir. Zenith United Corp., 1962—. Chmn. Winnetka Citizens com., 1958; chmn. Cook County March Dimes Campaign, 1961. Bd. dirs., pres. Grant Hosp., Chgo.; bd. dirs., treas. Cook County chpt. Nat. Found.; trustee Francis W. Parker Sch., 1958-69. Served to 1st lt. USAAF, 1942-46. Decorated Air medal with two oak leaf clusters, D.F.C. Mem. Transp. Assn. Am. (dir. 1972—), Nat. Assn. Metric Edn. (dir.), Western Golf Assn. (dir.). Republican. Episcopalian. Clubs: University, Chgo., Racquet, Glenview; Riomar Country; Johns Island. Home: 745 Locust St Winnetka IL 60093 Office: 2 N Riverside Plaza Chicago IL 60606

BARTHOLOMAY, WILLIAM CONRAD, ins. exec.; b. Evanston, Ill., Aug. 11, 1928; s. Henry C. and Virginia (Graves) B.; student Oberlin Coll., 1946-49, Northwestern U., 1949-1950; B.A., Lake Forest Coll., 1950; m. Gail Dillingham, May 25, 1968; 1 dau., Karen; children (by previous marriage)—Virginia, William T., Jamie, Elizabeth, Sara. Asso. Bartholomay & Clarkson, Chgo., 1950-63, v.p. Bartholomay & Clarkson div. Alexander & Alexander, 1963-65; pres., dir. Surprise, Inc., 1954-77; pres., dir. Olson & Bartholomay, 1965-69; chief exec. officer Frank B. Hall & Co. of Ill.; vice-chmn., dir. Frank B. Hall & Co., Inc., mgr. central div.; chief exec. officer Frank B. Hall & Co. Services Co.; v.p., dir. Atlanta LaSalle Corp.; dir. Seeburg Corp. Chmn. Atlanta Braves, Inc.; dir. Turner Communications Corp., Nat. Security Bank Chgo., NW Fin. Corp., A/L Sports, Inc., Eastman & Beaudine, Inc. Bd. dirs. Chgo. Maternity Center, 1955—; bd. govs. Sarah Siddons Soc.; former trustee Lake Forest Coll., Ogelthorpe Coll. Served as non-commd. officer USNR, 1951-54. Mem. Million Dollar Round Table (life), Young Presidents Orgn. Delta Kappa Epsilon. Episcopalian. Clubs: Racquet (dir. 1957—), University, Economic, Chicago, Saddle and Cycle, Executives, Commonwealth (Chgo.); Shoreacres (Lake Bluff, Inc.); Peachtree, Piedmont Driving, Commerce, Atlanta Country (Atlanta); Onwentsia (Lake Forest, Ill.); Lake Geneva Country (Wis.); Deep Dale, Links, Economic (N.Y.C.). Home: 209 E Lake Shore Dr Chicago IL 60611

BARTHOLOMEW, FRED IRV, realtor; b. Grafton, N.D., July 23, 1939; s. Byron Fred and Frances Ethel (Misialek) B.; B.S., U. N.D., 1961; m. Barbara Ann Richardson, Feb. 23, 1963; children—Lisa Lynn, Cynthia Carole, Michelle Marie. Tchr., Bur. Indian Affairs, Mandaree, N.D., 1963-65, Grand Forks (N.D.) Pub. Schs., 1965-68; salesman, Red River Realty, Grand Forks, 1965-67; pres., gen. mgr. Belmont Builders, Inc., Grand Forks, 1967-74, now dir.; pres., gen. mgr. Belmont Devel., Inc. div. Belmont Gallery Homes, 1974—. Served with AUS, 1961-63. Named Realtor of Year, Grand Forks Bd. Realtors, 1971. Mem. Nat., N.D. (pres. 1976) assns. realtors, Nat. Assn. Home Builders (dir. 1969), Am. Legion, D.A.V., Grand Forks Bd. Realtors (pres. 1971), Grand Forks Multiple Listing Service (pres. 1971), Grand Forks Jr. C. of C. (dir. 1966), Sigma Nu. Lutheran (councilman 1969). Elk. Club: Sertoma (dir. 1971) (Grand Forks).

Home: 3519 Chestnut St Grand Forks ND 58201 Office: 2903-B Knight Dr Grand Forks ND 58201

BARTIMUS, WESLEY, ret. supt. schs.; b. Brownstown, Ill., Dec. 12, 1911; s. Jesse Monroe and Amanda (Warner) B.; B.S. in Edn., So. Ill. U., 1950, M.S., 1954; m. Ethel Rose Loveless, Oct. 26, 1935; children—Derald Wesley, Joanne Ellen (Mrs. James Carrol Sills). Rural sch. tchr., Fayette County, Ill., 1934-42; supt. Brownstown City Schs., 1946-48: asst. supt. Brownstown Community Unit, 1948-54, supt., high sch. prin., 1954-64; asst. supt. schs. Nashville (Ill.) Community Consol. Sch. Dist., 1964-65, supt. schs., 1965-74. Twp. supr., Wheatland. 1940-44. Served with USNR, 1943-46. Mem. Fayette County Ret. Tchrs. Assn., Am. Legion, Phi Delta Kappa. Mem. 1st Christian Ch. Clubs: Masons, Shrine, Lions (club treas., pres., dist. gov. 1963-64, chmn. dist. nominating com. 1964-65, chmn. dist. conv. 1965-66, chmn. dist. care com. 1966-69, chmn. dist. redistricting com. 1968-69, chmn. dist. youth com. 1969-72, dist. chmn. Leo Clubs 1970-73, 2d v.p., dist. rep. Camp Lions 1963-74, dist. chmn. constn. and by laws com. 1976—). Home: 321 W Grandview Dr Vandalia IL 62471

BARTKIW, NYKOLA, clin. psychologist; b. Fishbach, Germany, Oct. 4, 1945; s. John and Maria (Misik) B.; came to U.S., 1954, naturalized, 1960; B.A. in Psychology, U. Mich., 1969; M.A. in Clin. Psychology, Oakland U., Rochester, Mich., 1973; Ph.D. in Clin. Psychology, Heed U., 1977; m. Pearl Eve Pytlowanyj, May 1, 1976; 1 dau., Olena Maria. Alcoholism therapist Hurley Hosp., Flint, Mich., 1969-71; dir. alcoholism tng. therapy Pontiac (Mich.) Osteopathic Hosp., 1971; clin. psychologist, coordinator out-reach clinic Pontiac Gen. Hosp. Mental Health Clinic, 1972-77; clin. supr. Genesee County (Mich.) Community Mental Health, Flint, 1977—; cons. Family and Children Services of Oakland County Alcoholism Program., Rapp, Inc. Drug Abuse Treatment Clinic, Rochester Area Youth Guidance. Licensed psychol. examiner, Mich. Mem. Am. Psychol. Assn. Home: 3390 Thomas Rd Oxford MI 48051

BARTLETT, BUD (BYRON ALLAN), TV exec.; b. Las Vegas, Nev., Feb. 14, 1940; s. Byron Edwin and Yvonne (Lodwick) B.; B.A. in Radio-TV, Ariz. State U., 1963; M.A. in Radio-TV-Film, U. Denver, 1967. Producer Sta. KAET-TV, Phoenix, 1963-65; producer, instr. So. Ill. U. Broadcasting Service, Carbondale, 1966-71; instructional TV specialist TV sect. Ill. Office Edn., Springfield, 1971—; pres. Springfield Ednl. Communications Assn., 1977—. Served with U.S. Army, 1963. Mem. Nat. Assn. Ednl. Broadcasters. Author: By Wave and Wire, 1974. Home: Springfield IL 62701 Office: 100 N 1st St Springfield IL 62777

BARTLETT, EDWIN BALL, JR., musician, conductor; b. Milw., Jan. 24, 1917; s. Edwin Ball and Julia Resor (Foster) B.; student Eastman Sch. of Music, 1935-38; B.S., U. Wis., 1941; m. Marian Manhardt, Feb. 22, 1942 (div.); children—Edwin B., Barbara, Cynthia, Marian. With Milw. Stampng Co., 1941-44, O'Neil Duro Co., 1944-46; with Best Block Co., Milw., 1946-61, sec.-treas., 1948-61; with Universal Battery Co., 1962; mgr. S.F. Bartlett and Assos., Chgo., 1962-63; owner, operator Wis. Clock Co., Milw.. 1963-69; conductor, Crown Opera Co., Ill. State Opera Co., Gt. Lakes Opera Co., Little Opera Co. Highwood, Am. Opera Co., Chgo. area, 1966-73; musical dir., conductor Juneautown Opera Co., Milw., 1973—; bd. dirs. Florentine Opera Co., 1956-77. Home and Office: 705 W Bradley Rd Milwaukee WI 53217

BARTLETT, PETER GREENOUGH, engring. co. exec.; b. Manchester, N.H., Apr. 22, 1930; s. Richard Cilley and Dorothy (Pillsburg) B.; Ph.B., Northwestern U., 1955; m. Jeanne Eddes, July 8, 1954; children—Peter G., Marta, Lauren, Karla, Richard E. Engr., Westinghouse Electric Co., Balt., 1955-58; mgr. mil. communications Motorola, Inc., Chgo., 1958-60; pres. Bartlett Labs., Inc., Indpls., 1960-63; asso. prof. elec. engring. U. S.C., Columbia, 1963-64; dir. research Eagle Signal Co., Davenport, Iowa, 1964-67; div. mgr. Struthers-Dunn, Inc., Bettendorf, Iowa, 1967-74; pres. Automation Systems, Inc., Eldridge, Iowa, 1974, also dir. Active Boys Scouts Am.; pres. bd. dirs. Save, Inc., 1965-67. Mem. IEEE. Republican. Presbyterian. Patentee in field. Home: 2336 E 11th St Davenport IA 52803 Office: Lancer Park Eldridge IA 52748

BARTLETT, SYLVIA ROSETTE, chiropractic physician; b. nr. Lennox, S.D., July 20, 1906; d. Iver Johannesen and Ingeborg Selina (Engebretson) Lukken; student Canton Lutheran Normal, 1924; D. of Chiropractic, Tex. Chiropractic Coll., 1928; m. Norman Brace Bartlett, July 15, 1929; children—Norman, Beverly (Mrs. J.B. Miles, Sylvan, Diana (Mrs. E.E. Staton). Practice chiropractic medicine, Brownwood, Tex., 1928, Pineridge Indian Reservation, Martin, S.D., 1930-39, Lennox, 1939-46, Sioux Falls, S.D., 1946-48, St. Louis, 1948-56, Vida, Mo., 1956—. Mem. health com. Extension div. U. Mo., 1975—. Mem. Am., Mo. State (Pioneer award 1967), S.D. State chiropractic assns., Am. Council on Physiotherapy, Council of Women Chiropractors, Nat. Health Fedn., Sacro-Occital Research Soc. Internat., Tri-State Cranial Research Soc. Founder, developer bi-polar therapy. Address: Star Route PO Box 26 Vida MO 65581

BARTLETT, WILLIAM MCGILLIVRAY, hosp. supply co. exec.; b. Rockford, Ill., Sept. 17, 1932; s. Leonard Brown and Elizabeth (McGillivray) B.; B.S., C.E., Duke, 1954; postgrad. mgmt. Northwestern U., 1971; m. Janice L. Wessinger, Aug. 10, 1954; children—Steven M., R. Scott, Eliz Lynn. With J.L. Clark Mfg. Co., Rockford, Ill. and Chgo., 1958-68, mgr. housewares div., Chgo., 1966-68, mgr. plastics div., Chgo., 1968; v.p., pres. surg. instrument div. Am. Hosp. Supply Corp., Chgo., 1968-74; pres. Atlantic Internat. div. Am. Hosp. Supply Corp., 1975—. Asso. prof. mil. sci. Notre Dame U., South Bend, Ind., 1956-58. Served to lt. USNR, 1954-58; China, Korea. Clubs: Skokie Country (Glencoe, Ill.); Winnetka (Ill.) Yacht. Home: 503 Orchard Ln Winnetka IL 60093 Office: 2020 Ridge Ave Evanston IL 60091

BARTLETTE, DONALD LLOYD, social worker, cons.; b. Walhalla, N.D., Dec. 17, 1939; s. Abraham Bruno and Lily Alice (Houle) B.; Ph.B., U. N.D., 1962; M.A., N.D. State U., 1966; m. Julie Gay Poer, Feb. 1, 1969; children—Lisa Maaca, Joanna Leigh, Andrea Gay, Marisa Anne, Laura Bethany. Program dir. Camp Grassick, N.D., 1959-62; Unit supr., counselor Cambridge State Sch. and Hosp., 1963-64; group worker Children's Village, Fargo, N.D., 1964-65; supr. Meth. Children's Village, Detroit, 1966-68; program dir. Mich. Children's Inst., Ann Arbor, 1968-70; exec., program dir. Madison County Assn. for Retarded, 1970-71; dir. program and social work services Outreach Community Center, Mpls., 1972-73; exec. dir. Minn. Epilepsy League, St. Paul, 1974-75; cons. in retardation, 1972-75; coordinator spl. services, adviser Human Rights Commn. City of Bloomington, 1975—. Field work instr. Sch. Social Work, U. Minn., Augsburg Coll., Mpls., 1972-73; off-campus tchr. in retardation and social work Anderson Coll., 1970-71; adj. faculty Univ. Without Walls, U. Minn., 1972-73. Founder Bartlette Scholarship award U. N.D., 1971-75; pres. Nat. Minority Affairs Coalition, 1977-78, sec., 1976-77; mem. Met. Developmental Disabilities Task Force, 1975; chmn. Pub. Info. Coalition Project on Developmental Disabilities, 1974-75; vol. mem. Pres.'s, Minn. Gov.'s coms. on employment handicapped; task force minority affairs Pres.'s Com. Mental Retardation. Bd. dirs. N.W. Hennepin Human Services Council, 1975-76; bd. dirs., chmn. poverty com. Anoka County Assn. for Retarded, 1974—; Fellow Acad. Ednl. Disciplines; mem. Am. Acad. Mental Retardation, Nat. Assn. Social Workers, Nat. Assn. Retarded Children (dir., chmn. com. on poverty and mental retardation 1973-74), Am. Assn. Mental Deficiency, Nat. Congress Am. Indians, Soc. for Protection Unborn through Nutrition (asso.). Baptist (house ch. pastor). Author: Macaroni at Midnight. Home: 7909 Noid Dr Brooklyn Park MN 55428

BARTLEY, EDWARD ROSS, franchising co. exec.; b. Washington, Oct. 25, 1920; s. Edward Ross and Pearl (Meyers) B.; B.S., Ind. U., 1942; m. Mary Schmitz, Jan. 22, 1977; children from previous marriage—Deborah Hilburn, Edward Ross III. Dir. mktg. research B.F. Goodrich Co., Akron, 1960-63; dir. planning Armour & Co., Chgo., 1963-70; v.p. mktg. Armour Food Co., Phoenix, 1970-73; v.p. mktg. Swiss Colony Stores, Monroe, Wis., 1973—. Bd. dirs. Monroe United Fund, 1976—; pres. Inverness (Ill.) Homeowners Assn., 1972-73. Served with USCG, 1942-45. Mem. Am. Mktg. Assn. (past v.p. dir.). Republican. Presbyterian. Clubs: Monroe Country, Alpine Curling. Home: 2708 22d Ave Monroe WI 53566 Office: 1 Alpine Ln Monroe WI 53566

BARTLEY, ROGER ARTHUR, funeral home exec.; b. Canton, Ohio, Apr. 3, 1950; s. Leroy Gilbert and Marilyn Rose (Jackson) B.; B.S., Mount Union Coll., 1972; m. Sherry Lynn Catlett, Apr. 7, 1973; children—Todd Douglas, Corey Andrew. Sports editor, advt. mgr. Minerva (Ohio) Leader, 1973-74; funeral dir. Bartley Funeral Home, Minerva, 1974—. First aid instr. and trainer Minerva chpt. ARC; mem. Minerva Bicentennial Commn., 1975-77. Served with AUS, 1972-73. Mem. Ohio Funeral Dirs. Assn., Ohio Assn. Emergency Med. Services. Republican. Methodist. Editor: Living Out Our Heritage, bicentennial history book, 1976. Home: 203 W Lincolnway Minerva OH 44657 Office: 205 W Lincolnway Minerva OH 44657

BARTLEY, VERNON HERBERT, surgeon; b. Meerut, India, Nov. 15, 1925; s. Alfred Herbert and Agnes (McDonald) B.; certificate Oxford (Eng.) U., 1942; M.B., B.S., Guy's Hosp. Med. Sch., London, 1954; came to U.S., 1957, naturalized, 1963; m. Audrey Jane Helmer, Sept. 30, 1969; children—Janet, Heather, Karen, Andrea. Practice medicine specializing in surgery and traumatology, Cin., 1957-61; surgeon Eagle River (Wis.) Meml. Hosp., 1961-65, Gen. Hosp. Stambaugh, Mich., 1961-65, St. Mary Nazareth Hosp., Chgo., 1966-67, Meml. Hosp. DuPage Counnty (Ill.), Elmhurst, 1967—; co-founder, med. dir. DuPage County EMT-A Program, 1969—; bd. dirs., sec.-treas. Emergency Service Physicians Ltd., Elmhurst, Ill. Served to capt., British Armed Forces, 1943-47. Diplomate Am. Bd. Surgery. Fellow Royal Coll. Surgeons (Can.), Am. Coll. Surgeons. Republican. Office: 223 N York St Elmhurst IL 60126

BARTLING, CHARLES EDWIN, communications co. exec.; b. Deland, Fla., Aug. 25, 1938; s. Edwin Phillip and Mabel Emma (Brooks) B.; B.A., Edn., U. Fla., 1959; M.S. in Journalism, Northwestern U., 1962; m. Ann Louise Sisinger, Sept. 2, 1967; children—Hugh, Allison. Midwestern bur. chief Am. Banker Newspaper, Chgo., 1964-68; dir. communications Bank Mkgt. Assn., Chgo., 1968-70; v.p. Teach'em, Inc., Chgo., 1970-73; pres. CEBAR Communications, Inc., Evanston, Ill., 1973—; served with U.S. Army, 1956. Mem. Am. Soc. Bus. Press Editors (exec. v.p., 1973—). Chgo. Conv. and Tourism Bur. Home: 2923 Lincoln St Evanston IL 60201 Office: 2735 Central St Evanston IL 60201

BARTOLETTI, CAROL JANE, coll. adminstr.; b. Bklyn., Aug. 11, 1942; d. Otto David and Jane Mary (Sincavage) Vergari; B.A., Trenton State Coll., 1964; M.Ed., Pa. State U., 1967. Dir. planning, Warren Trumbull Council Econ. Opportunity, Warren, Ohio, 1971-72; coordintor admissions and counseling Kent State Trumbull Campus, Warren, Ohio, 1972-73, dir. student services, 1973-77; dir. admissions Mpls. Coll. Art and Design, 1977—. Mem. Am. Assn. Higher Edn., Am. Personnel and Guidance Assn., Am. Coll. Personnel Assn., Nat. Vocational Guidance Assn., Nat. Council Student Devel. Home: 3150 Lake Calhoun Pkwy W Minneapolis MN 55416 Office: 200 25th St E Minneapolis MN 55404

BARTOLETTO, AVELLINO JOSEPH, steel co. exec.; b. Woonsocket, R.I., Oct. 18, 1927; s. Joseph and Pasqualina (Ventre) B.; B.S. in Elect. Engring., Norwich U., 1952; M.B.A., Villanova U., 1962; m. Anne Marie Jette, June 9, 1952; 4 daus., Lisa Anne, Laurie Jane, Nancy Ellen, Donna Marie. With Gen. Electric Co., 1952-65, Lamp Div., 1952-54, power transformer dept., 1954-55, appliance motor dept., 1955-59, project mgr. Missile and Space Div., 1959-65; quality assurance mgr., major appliance divs., Westinghouse Electric, Columbus, Ohio, 1965-68; product integrity dir., Massey Ferguson, Toronto, Ont., 1968-70; v.p., gen. mgr. Temperform, Novi, Mich., 1970-72, pres., 1972—. Served with U.S. Army, 1946-47. Mem. Am. Soc. Quality Control (sr.), Am. Soc. Metals, Am. Foundryman's Soc. Roman Catholic. Club: Fairlane. Home: 2503 Wickfield Rd Orchard Lake MI 48033 Office: 25460 Novi Rd Novi MI 48050

BARTOLOME, FRANCISCO MABALAY, food technologist; b. Manila, P.I., Nov. 6, 1939; s. Fruto Feliciano and Emiliana (Mabalay) B.; came to U.S., 1965; B.S. in Chem. Engring., U. Philippines, 1962; M.S., Purdue U., 1968, Ph.D., 1971; m. Dr. Linda Gutierrez, Sept. 3, 1966. Product devel. mgr., packaging engr. Procter & Gamble, Manila, 1962-65; group leader product devel. Hunt-Wesson Foods, Inc., Fullerton, Calif., 1971-75; dir. research and devel. Golden Dipt Co., Millstadt, Ill., 1975-77; mgr. tech. devel. Pillsbury Co., Mpls., 1977—; instr. chem. engring. Manuel L. Quezon U., Manila, 1965-65; research asst. Purdue U., 1966-71. Recipient Dee Chuan grant, 1962. Mem. Inst. Food Technologists, Am. Assn. Cereal Chemists, Phi Tau Sigma. Home: 6214 Patchin Circle Saint Louis MO 63128 Office: 425 Main St SE Minneapolis MN 55414

BARTON, CONSTANCE ELISABETH CORNICK, hosp. adminstr.; b. Quincy, Ill., Oct. 8, 1932; d. Lester Theodore and Wilma Martha (Lohr) Cornick; B.J., U. Mo., 1954; postgrad. U. Toledo, 1963-64; children—Leslie Jane Barton, Todd Cornick Barton. Gen. assignment reporter Pekin (Ill.) Daily Times, 1954-55; Lawton (Okla.) Constitution Press, 1955-56; soc. editor Quincy Herald Whig, 1956-58; gen. assignment reporter Findlay (Ohio) Republican Courier, 1958-61; editor, sales promotion Air Way Corp., Toledo, 1961; dist. dir. Toledo Girl Scout Council, 1961-64; press rep. United Fund Greater St. Louis, 1964-65; dir. pub. relations Barnes Hosp., St. Louis, 1965—; staff dir. Task Force on Communications, NIH, Bethesda, Md., 1977—; cons. in field; chmn. pub. relations program com. Midwest Health Congress, 1971; chmn. Am. Mgmt. Assn. Seminars on Employee communications, 1970—. Bd. dirs. Leukemia Soc. Am., 1975—. Recipient First in Ohio award Ohio Women's Newspaper Assn., 1961; 1st place Total Pub. Relations Programs, 1973; 1st place, citation employee communications Midwest Health Congress, 1973; MacEachern award of Merit, 1974. Mem. Acad. Hosp. Pub. Relations, Pub. Relations Soc. Am., Met. St. Louis Hosp. Assn., Indsl. Press Assn., Nat. Press Club, Theta Sigma Phi. Presbyterian. Edit. supr. From the NIH column. for Jour. AMA, 1977—. Home: 441 W Jackson Saint Louis MO 63119 also 1 Lorraine Ct Rockville MD 20852 Office: 9000 Rockville Pike Bldg 31 Room 4B-63 NIH Bethesda MD 20014

BARTON, EDWARD READ, lawyer; b. Kalamazoo, May 10, 1938; s. Clare A. and Caroline (Read) B.; B.S., Mich. State U., 1960; J.D., Cornell U., 1964, M.Pub. Adminstrn., 1964. Admitted to Mich. bar, 1965, since practiced in Allegan. Commr., Allegan County Circuit Ct., 1966-68; Allegan County, 1969-72. Mem. Allegan County (sec.-treas. 1967-73), Am. bar assns., State Bar Mich., Am. Trial Lawyers, Am. Judicature Soc., Jaycees, FarmHouse Frat., Phi Alpha Delta. Home: 920 Miller Rd Plainwell MI 49080 Office: 312-B Trowbridge St Allegan MI 49010

BARTON, ROBERT JAMES, city ofcl.; b. Springfield, Ohio, Nov. 11, 1932; s. Robert C. and Alice (Moomaw) B.; B.J., U. Mo., 1954; m. Constance Cornick, Dec. 11, 1954; children—Leslie Jane, Todd Cornick. Reporter, Quincy (Ill.) Herald-Whig, 1956-58; pub. relations rep. Marathon Oil Co., Findlay, Ohio, 1958-61; pub. relations mgr. AP Parts Corp., Toledo, Ohio, 1961-64; dir. pub. relations St. Louis (Mo.) Police Dept., 1964—; lectr. univs. and colls., FBI Acad., Ft. Gordon, Ga.; cons. police depts. Pub. relations com. mem. C. of C.; mem. Mayors Council on Auto Theft, dir. Aunts and Uncles; active Boy Scouts of Am. Served with U.S. Army, 1954-56. Mem. Pub. Relations Soc. of Am., Nat. Assn. of Police Community Relations Officers (pres.), Indsl. Press Assn., Press Club, Sigma Delta Chi. Republican. Presbyterian. Contbr. articles in field to auto mags. and law enforcement jours. Home: 441 W Jackson Rd Webster Groves MO 63119 Office: 1200 Clark St St Louis MO 63103

BARTON, ROBERT KENNETH, obstetrician, gynecologist, former naval officer, educator; b. Fountain City, Ind., Feb. 23, 1922; s. Kenneth Merle and Ethel Alta (Alexander) B.; B.S., Ball State U., 1943; postgrad. Cornell U., 1943-44; M.D., U. Cin., 1948; m. Mary Catherine Core, June 14, 1954; children—Mary Catherine, Molly Caroline. Commd. lt. j.g. U.S. Navy, 1948, advanced through grades to capt., 1974; intern Bethesda (Md.) Naval Hosp., 1948-49, resident in obstetrics gynecology, 1949-50; resident in obstetrics gynecology Chelsea (Mass.) Naval Hosp., 1952-53, San Diego Naval Hosp., 1953-57; staff Naval Hosp. Camp Lejeune, N.C., 1957-59; sr. med. officer Naval Support Activities, London, 1959-62; chief obstetrics gynecology, Quantico, Va., 1962-64, Naval Hosp., Boston, 1964-68; dep. comdg. surgeon, Vietnam, 1968-69; dir. profl. div. Bur. Medicine, Washington, 1969-73; spl. asst. comdg. officer Nat. Naval Med. Center, Bethesda, Md., 1973-74; ret., 1974; asso. clin. prof. Boston U. Med. Sch., 1964-68; clin. instr. Tufts U. Sch. Medicine, 1964-68; asso. prof. obstetrics gynecology Mich. State U., E. Lansing, 1974—; dir. obstetrics gynecology Saginaw (Mich.) Coop. Hosps., 1974—. Diplomate Am. Bd. Obstetrics Gynecology. Fellow Am. Coll. Obstetricians Gynecologists, A.C.S., Royal Soc. Medicine, Am. Fertility Soc., Assn. Mil. Surgeons, AMA. Republican. Episcopalian. Home: 20 Corral Dr Saginay MI 48603

BARTON, TERRY ALAN, psychotherapist; b. Gary, Ind., Sept. 9, 1947; s. Frank and Eleanor Helen (Dobis) B.; B.A., U. Chgo., 1970; M.S., George Williams Coll., 1975; m. Amy Laura Wilson, July 18, 1970; children—Rachel Elizabeth, Sarah Blair. Caseworker Cook County Dept. Pub. Aid, Chgo., 1970-71; emergency social worker Ill. Dept. Children and Family Services, Chgo., 1971-74; psychotherapist Grant Hosp. mental health clinic, Chgo., 1974-77; pvt. practice psychotherapy, Chgo., 1975—. Bd. Elders St. Pauls United Ch. of Christ. Tutition scholar U. Chgo. Mem. Assn. Humanistic Psychology, Assn. Rehab. Counseling, Am. Personnel and Guidance Assn. Democrat. Home: 3522 N Bosworth St Chicago IL 60657

BARTONE, FRANCIS FREDERICK, physician, educator; b. Phila., Dec. 11, 1931; s. Joseph and Mary (Della Corte) B.; A.B., U. Pa., 1953; M.D., Jefferson Med. Coll., 1957; m. Jerelen Adams Huskey, July 9, 1966; stepsons—Robert, David (Huskey). Intern, Jefferson Med. Coll. Hosp., Phila., 1957-58, resident, 1961-63; resident in urology N.Y. Hosp., 1960-61, in surgery U. Kans. Med. Center, 1963-65; practice medicine specializing in urology, Omaha, 1967—; instr. urology U. Okla. Med. Center, 1965-67; faculty U. Nebr. Med. Center, Omaha, 1968—, chmn. dept. urology, 1970—, prof. urology, 1971—, asso. prof. pediatrics, 1976—; chief urology Omaha VA Hosp., 1970—; sr. research fellow in pediatric urology U. Liverpool, Eng., 1974; mem. med. adv. bd. Omaha Ostomy Assn. Exec. com. Omaha Chamber Music Com., 1974—. Fellow A.C.S., Am. Acad. Pediatrics (affiliate); mem. AMA, Nebr. Med. Assn., Omaha-Douglas County Med. Soc., Am. Urol. Assn., N.Y. Acad. Scis., Soc. U. Urologists., Assn. Am. Med. Colls., Mid-West Clin. Soc., Pediatric Urologic Soc. Council on Urology, Nat. Kidney Found., Internat. Affairs Soc. Roman Catholic. Club: Rotary. Contbr. articles to profl. jours. Home: 5909 Blondo St Omaha NE 68104 Office: 42d St and Dewey Ave Omaha NE 68105

BARTRON, G. ROBERT, physician; b. Watertown, S.D., Nov. 12, 1920; s. Harry J. and Mary (Harigan) B.; B.S., Northwestern U., Chgo., 1942, M.D., 1944; m. Jean Marie Potticary, June 15, 1942; children—Lynn (Mrs. Roger Fox), Stephanie J. (Mrs. Scott Miscione), Robert Gregory. Intern, resident Cook County Hosp., Chgo., 1943-46, resident asso. Bartron Hosp. & Clinic, Watertown, 1946-52; dir. Bartron Hosp. and Clinic, 1955-57; dir. Bartron Clinic, 1958—; clin. preceptor for the U. S.D. Med. Sch., 1957-72, Clin. asst. prof. surgery, 1972—; coroner Codington County 1957—. Dir. med. div. area disaster planning and civil def., 1958—. Vice pres., med. dir. Midland Nat. Life Ins. Co., Watertown; dir. Farmers and Mchts. Bank of Watertown. Mem. S.D. Senate, 1964-70, pres. pro tem, 1968-70. Served with USAAF, 1953-55. Diplomate Am. Bd. Abdominal Surgery. Mem. Internat. Coll. Surgeons, Internat. Acad. Proctology, S.D. Med. Assn. (past pres.), AMA. Home: Hidden Valley Watertown SD 57201 Office: 320 7th Ave SE Watertown SD 57201

BARTZ, RICHARD OTTO, lawyer; b. Milw., May 29, 1929; s. Otto Richard and Ella Rose (Miske) B.; B.S. in Agrl. Engring., U. Wis., 1951, B.S. in Mech. Engring., 1955; J.D., Am. U., 1961; m. Mary Anna Hemp, Dec. 25, 1955; children—Christina, R. John, Steven, Paul and James and Thomas (triplets). Admitted to Va. bar, 1961, Ia. bar, 1962, Minn. bar, 1965, U.S. Dist. Ct. bar, 1965, So. Dist. Ct. Ia. bar, 1963, U.S. Supreme Ct. bar, 1972, U.S. Patent Office bar, 1961; patent examiner U.S. Patent Office, Washington, 1956-61; asso. atty. firm Oldham & Oldham, Akron, O., 1961-62, R.L. Lowell, Des Moines, 1962-64, Moore, White & Burd, Mpls., 1964-66; partner firm Burd, Braddock & Bartz, Mpls., 1966—; pres. Innovative Tech., Inc., Mpls., 1971—; sec. Geurts, Inc., Mpls., 1971—, Jack Mack Inc., 1973—, North Star Patents Inc., 1974—, Bolduc Enterprises, Inc., 1975—. Served with USMC, 1951-53. Mem. Am., Va., Minn., Hennepin County bar assns., Minn. Patent Law Assn. Patentee fluid collection and storage, earth working tools, constrn. toys. Home: 7017 Mark Terr Dr Edina MN 55435 Office: 1300 Foshay Tower Minneapolis MN 55402

BARUT, CLARA JEAN, counselor, educator; b. Toledo, July 6, 1945; d. Albin and Henrietta Theodosia (Marshall) Barut; B.S., Mary Manse Coll., 1967; M.A., Bowling Green State U., 1971; postgrad. U. Toledo, 1974-78. Research technician Med. Coll. Ohio, Toledo, 1974-75, ednl. coordinator, cons. regional comprehensive childrens services, dept. pediatrics, 1975-76; health planning adminstr., bur. crippled childrens services, div. maternal and child health Ohio Dept. Health, Toledo, 1977—. Mem. Am. Personnel and Guidance Assn., Am., Midwest psychol. assns., Ohio Assn. Counselor Edn. and

Supervision, Ohio Pub. Health Assn., Mary Manse, Bowling Green State U. alumni assns. Home: 556 Mettler St Toledo OH 43608 Office: PO Box 1603 Columbus OH 43216

BARUTH, CARROLL LEE, psychologist; b. Wagner, S.D., May 22, 1941; s. George L. and Helen F. (Crilly) B.; B.A., St. Marys Coll., 1963; Ph.D., U. N.M., 1971; m. Kathleen M. Kuethe, Apr. 15, 1968; 1 dau., Lisa Ann. Dir. Edu-Cultural Service Center, Mankato (Minn.) State U., 1972-73; supt. Brewster (Minn.) Pub. Schs., 1973-75; research dir. Ednl. Cooperative Service Unit, Rochester, Minn., 1975-76; pvt. practice psychologist, Rochester, Minn., 1977—. Mem. Am., Minn. psychol. assns., Am. Personnel and Guidance Assn., Minn. Sch. Psychologists Assns., Minn. Sch. Bds. Assn., Phi Kappa Phi. Home: 802 22d St NW Austin MN 55912 Office: 1551 9th Ave SE Rochester MN 55901

BARZAN, LEONARD ANGELO, food co. exec.; b. Chgo., Jan. 4, 1922; s. Angelo Roger and Rose Susan (Arrighi) B.; B.S., U. Ill., 1943; m. Jeanne Hilbert, Dec. 17, 1949; children—Virginia, Donald. Audit staff firm Haskins & Sells, Chgo., 1946-51; div. controller City Products Corp., Chgo., 1951-61; financial vice-corp. sec., also dir. John R. Thompson Co., Chgo., 1961-72; v.p. fin. Green Giant Co., Le Sueur, Minn., 1973—. Mem. Restaurant Sch. Adv. Bd. Triton Jr. Coll., 1972-73; mem. adv. com. Canners Exchange Subscribers, 1976. Served with USNR, 1943-45. C.P.A., Ill., Minn., D.C. Mem. Am. Inst. C.P.A.'s. Home: 16601 Blenheim Way Minnetonka MN 55343 Office: Hazeltine Gates Chaska MN 55318

BASCUNANA, JOSE LUIS, mech. engr.; b. Paris, France, Feb. 10, 1927; s. Luis and Isabel (Merino) B.; came to U.S., 1958, naturalized, 1970; B.S., Inst. Cath. Arts and Industry, Madrid, Spain, 1947; M.S. in Mech. Engring., U. Rochester, 1961, Ph.D., 1968; m. Irene Farina, Mar. 11, 1957; children—Xavier, Alicia, William, Irene, Henry. Engine design engr. Central Study Tech. Automotive, Madrid, Spain, 1947-56, head automobile sect., 1956-58; sr. project engr. Barreiros Diesel, S.A., Madrid, Spain, 1961-63; sr. research engr. emissions sect. Ford Motor Co., Dearborn, Mich., 1967-70; project mgr., div. emission control tech. EPA, Ann Arbor, Mich., 1970—. Served with Spanish Air Force, 1947-48. Broderson fellow, 1964-67. Mem. Soc. Automotive Engrs., ASME, Air Pollution Control Assn., Combustion Inst., Nat. Soc. Profl. Engrs., Coordinating Research Council, Sigma Xi. Roman Catholic. Home: 3391 Bluet Dr Ann Arbor MI 48105 Office: 2565 Plymouth Rd Ann Arbor MI 48105

BASEL, ARTHUR RICHARD, psychiatrist; b. Hawks, Mich., June 24, 1923; s. Albert E. and Dora E. (Noffze) B.; B.A., U. Mich., 1950, M.D., 1954; m. Marie E. Zittel, June 10, 1955; children—Dean, Mark. Intern, Munson Hosp., Traverse City, Mich., 1954-55; resident in adult psychiatry Northville (Mich.) State Hosp., 1960-63; resident in child psychiatry Lafayette Clinic, Detroit, 1965-67; dir. Northville Children's Hosp., 1963-65; practice medicine specializing in psychiatry, Bay City, Mich., 1967-68, Auburn, Mich., 1968—; mem. staff St. Luke's, Midland hosps., Bay Med. Center; instr. St. Luke's Family Practice Center; cons. psychiatrist Child and Family Services of Bay, Saginaw and Midland counties, Clare and Tuscola sch. dists., Bay City and Saginaw Catholic Family Services. Served with U.S. Army, 1955-57. Diplomate Am. Bd. Psychiatry and Neurology. Mem. AMA, Am. Psychiat. Assn., Mich. State Med. Soc., Mich. Acad. Child Psychiatry. Home: 1895 Hotchkiss Rd Freeland MI 48623 Office: 4804 Garfield Rd Auburn MI 48611

BASHAW, WAYNE ERNEST, trade co. exec.; b. Elizabeth, Ill., Aug. 16, 1917; s. Ernest L. and Bertha L. (Fanst) B.; B.S., U. Ill., 1941; M.B.A., N.Mex. State U., 1972; m. Dorothy T. Sare, Feb. 5, 1944; children—Dianne, Carole, John, Catherine, Robert. Personnel mgr. Horder's div. Boise-Cascade Co., Chgo., 1947-48, indsl. sales mgr., 1948-49; pres. Bedford Supply Co. (Ind.), 1949-52; v.p., gen. mgr. Pounsford Stationery Co., Cin., 1952-54; pres. Office Supply Co., Las Cruces, 1952—. Vice-chmn. City of Las Cruces Minority Housing Com., 1967—; mem. N.Mex. State Vocat. Com., 1971—; bd. dirs. Planned Parenthood Las Cruces. Served with USNR, 1941-45. Chmn. bus. adv. com. N.Mex. State U. Vocat. Sch., Las Cruces, 1974—. Mem. Kappa Tau Alpha. Republican. Clubs: Kiwanis, Toastmasters, Elks. Home: Route 1 Elizabeth IL 61028 Office: Office Supply Co Las Cruces NM 88001

BASHE, WINSLOW JEROME, JR., physician; b. Chgo., Mar. 10, 1920; s. Winslow Jerome and Elizabeth (Souhrada) B.; B.S., Seton Hall Coll., 1942; M.D., Loyola U., Chgo., 1945; M.P.H., Columbia, 1959; m. Carol Louise Griffin, Sept. 10, 1952; children—Mary Elizabeth, Winslow Jerome III, Paula Irene. Intern, Gorgas Hosp., Ancon, C.Z., 1945-46; resident Sea View Hosp., S.I., N.Y., 1948-50, Childrens Hosp., 1950; research fellow Children's Hosp., Phila., 1951-53; practice medicine specializing in pediatrics, Trenton, N.J., 1953-57; instr. pediatrics U. Pa., Phila, 1951-53, Ohio State U., Columbus, 1957-63, asst. prof. preventive medicine, 1959-62; epidemiologist Ohio Dept. Health, Columbus, 1957-63, tng. coordinator, 1960-63, dir. maternal and child health, 1970-72, now cons.; asso. prof. preventive medicine U. Cin., 1963-70, asso. prof. pediatrics, 1967-70; asso. prof. preventive medicine and pediatrics Ohio State U., Columbus, 1971—. Cons. Pub. Health Service, health planning, 1968-72. Served to Capt. M.C., AUS, 1946-48. Diplomate Am. Bd. Pediatrics. Mem. A.A.U.P., Ohio Med. Assn., Clark County Med. Soc., Sigma Xi. Contbr. articles to profl. jours. Home: 500 Zeller Dr Springfield OH 45503 Office: Ohio State U Columbus OH 43210

BASHSHUR, RASHID LUTFALLAH, educator; b. Safita, Syria, May 8, 1933; s. Lutfallah M. and Yamna (Day'a) B.; came to U.S., 1956, naturalized, 1968; B.A., Am. U. Beirut (Lebanon), 1954, M.A., 1956; Ph.D., U. Mich., 1962; m. Naziha W. Sima'an, Sept. 10, 1957; children—Ramona, Noura. Instr. sociology Am. U. Beirut, 1954-56; lectr. sociology Eastern Mich. U., Ypsilanti, 1958-60; asso. prof. med. care orgn. U. Mich., Ann Arbor, 1962—; staff asso. in charge med. care orgn. Nat. Acad. Scis., 1970-72. Cons. various agys., research orgns. USPHS grantee, 1963-69; HEW grantee, 1969-70; NSF grantee, 1973-75. Mem. Am. Pub. Health Assn., Am. Sociol. Assn., Arab Am. Orgn. Ann Arbor (pres. 1970), Arab Am. U. Grads. (v.p. 1967-68, sec. 1975). Author: Telemedicine, 1975. Contbr. articles to profl. jours. Home: 1383 Esch Ct Ann Arbor MI 48104

BASILE, ABIGAIL JULIA ELLEN HERRON (MRS. JOSEPH BASILE), employment counselor, state ofcl.; b. St. Louis, June 15, 1915; d. Charles Arthur and Abigail (Edwards) Herron; student Kansas City Jr. Coll., 1948-50, U. Kans., 1959; B.S. in Bus. Adminstrn., Rockhurst Coll., 1965; M. Ed., U. Mo., 1967; m. Joseph Basile, Aug. 15, 1939. Employment security dep. Mo. Div. Employment Security, Kansas City, 1945-59, youth coordinator, employment counselor, 1959-65; counselor-supr. Youth Opportunity Center, 1965-66; supr. spl. applicant services Mo. Employment Service. Kansas City, 1966-67, supr. counseling, 1967—. Sec., Inter-Agy. Com. Rehab., 1967-69. Mem. Mo. Assn. Social Welfare. Mem. Am. Personnel and Guidance Assn., Nat. Vocat. Assn., Internat. Assn. Personnel in Employment Security (Mo. pres. 1966-67, internat. sec. 1968), Nat. Rehab. Assn., Am. Legion Aux. Democrat. Episcopalian. Home: 5221 N Wayne St Kansas City MO 64118 Office: 1411 Main St Kansas City MO 64105

BASILE, RUTH LEBARON RUTLEDGE, civic worker; b. Chgo., Nov. 25, 1912; d. William Askins and Bess (LeBaron) Rutledge; R.N., Evanston Hosp., 1934; A.B., Northwestern U., 1934; m. William B. Basile, July 25, 1935; children—Bette Claire (Mrs. William Eugene Kattmann), William Basil, Ralph Rutledge. Active infant welfare, 1958—. Publicity work D.A.R., 1960-61, 65—, Women's Soc. Christian Service, North Shore Meth. Ch., 1960—, ch. sch. sec. Glencoe, 1962—. Mem. Cultural Devel. Program, 1964. Mem. D.A.R., Evanston Hosp., Northwestern alumnae assns., P.E.O. (chpt. treas. 1967—). Club: Women's Library (Glencoe). Home: 501 Monroe Ave Glencoe IL 60022

BASILE, WILLIAM BASIL, mfg. exec.; b. Chgo., Mar 17, 1911; s. Ralph and Carmelia (D'Urso) B.; Ph.B., U. Chgo., 1931, J.D., 1933; research asso. Northwestern U. Law Sch., 1933-34; m. Ruth Rutledge, July 25, 1935; children—Bette Claire, William Basil, Ralph Rutledge. Admitted to Ill. bar, 1933, practiced in Chgo., 1934-43; v.p., dir. indsl. relations Richardson Co., 1943-52, dir. 1944—, exec. v.p., 1952-53, pres. 1953-74, chmn., 1974—, atty. price adjustment bd. AAF. 1943. Mem. Am., Ill. bar assns., Chgo. Mus. Natural History, Art Inst. Chgo., Phi Alpha Delta, Alpha Sigma Phi. Clubs: Skokie Country (Glencoe); Columbia (Indpls.); University, Economic (Chgo.). Home: 501 Monroe Ave Glencoe IL 60022 Office: Richardson Co 2400 E Devon Ave Des Plaines IL 60018

BASKIN, JOHN ROLAND, lawyer; b. Cleve., Dec. 23, 1916; s. Roland A. and Frances M. (Schwoerer) B.; A.B. magna cum laude, Western Res. U., 1938, LL.B., 1940; m. Madeline Stricker, Feb. 26, 1949 (dec. 1965); d., Barbara Anne; m. 2d, Betty Anne Meyer, May 12, 1967. Admitted to Ohio bar, 1940, FCC, 1949, U.S. Supreme Ct., 1955; practiced in Cleve., 1940—, asso. mem. firm Baker, Hostetler & Patterson, 1941-54, partner, 1954—. Spl. agt. AUS CIC, U.S. Atomic Bomb project, 1942-46, CIC officer, Armed Forces Spl. Weapons project, 1951-52. Mem. Am., Ohio, Cleve. bar assns., Order of the Coif, Phi Beta Kappa, Delta Tau Delta, Delta Theta Phi, Court of Nisi Prius. Republican. Episcopalian. Clubs: Union, Mayfield Country (Cleve.); University (Washington). Home: 2679 Ashley Rd Shaker Heights OH 44122 also Buttonwood Bay Key Largo FL 33037 Office: Union Commerce Bldg Cleveland OH 44115

BASS, EDWARD LELAND, furniture co. exec.; b. Russia, Dec. 25, 1900; s. Philip and Bertha (Shenkarov) B.; came to U.S., 1904, naturalized, 1915; B.A., Northwestern U., 1919; LL.B., Chgo. Kent Coll. Law, 1923, LL.M., 1928, J.D., 1969; m. Maraly Weinstein, June 13, 1943; 1 child. Pres., chmn. Bass Bros. Furniture Co., Chgo., 1922—; organizer, dir. Park Nat. Bank of Chgo., 1950—; admitted to Ill. bar, 1926. Mem. Selective Service Bd., 1942-46; pres. Republican orgn. 36th ward Chgo., 1928-32. Recipient award ARC, 1959. Mem. Nat. Homefurnishings Assn. (All Am. Mcht. award 1959), Chgo. Homefurnishings Assn. (pres., dir. 1939-40, Furniture Man of Year 1956), Am. Bar Assn., Chgo.-Kent Alumni Assn. Jewish. Home: 100 Bellvue Pl Chicago IL 60611 Office: 2945 Milwaukee Ave Chicago IL 60618

BASS, LARRY JUNIOR, clin. psychologist, educator; b. Granby, Mo., Aug. 2, 1944; s. Harold Virgil and Mildred Lucille (Charlton) B.; B.S., U. Mo., 1966, M.S. (NDEA fellow), 1967; Ph.D., Washington U., St. Louis, 1972; m. Meredith Aenone Copeland, Aug. 17, 1968; children—Mark, Darren, Adam. Research asst. Washington U., 1967-68, staff psychologist Child Guidance Clinic, 1970; intern Mt. Zion Med. Center, San Francisco, 1968-69; clin. psychologist Jewish Hosp., St. Louis, 1971-75; asst. prof. Evangel Coll., Springfield, Mo., 1975—; pvt. practice clin. psychology, Springfield, 1975—. Mem. Am., Mo. psychol. assns., Phi Delta Kappa. Home: 1009 E Meadowlark St Springfield MO 65807 Office: 1443 N Robberson St Suite 506 Springfield MO 65802

BASS, NATHAN WINTHROP, mfg. exec.; b. N.Y.C., Apr. 14, 1917; s. Harry W. and Cady B.; B.S., Cornell U., 1941; m. Audrey DeJong, Apr. 30, 1943; children—Barbara DeJong, Andrew Freeman, Thomas Alden. Soil surveyor Soil Conservation Service, Washington, 1941-42; chief Be Ta Electronics units WPB, Washington, 1942-45; with Brush Wellman, Inc. and predecessor, Cleve., 1945—, v.p., 1951—. Mem. Am. Ceramic Soc., Am. Power Metallurgy Inst., Am. Soc. Metals, Am. Nuclear Soc., Am. Inst. Aeros. and Astronautics, Armed Forces Communications Electronics Assn., Soc. Aerospace and Material Process Engrs., Soc. Automotive Engrs., Am. Def. Preparedness Assn., Am. Soc. Testing and Materials. Clubs: Copper (N.Y.C.); Cleveland Skating. Contbr. to The Role of Beryllium in Industry, 1955. Home: 13703 Ardoon Rd Cleveland OH 44120 Office: Brush Wellman Inc 17876 Saint Clair Ave Cleveland OH 44110

BASSETT, JOSEPH SAMUEL, surgeon; b. Blissfield, Mich., Feb. 25, 1932; s. Samuel J. and Flora (Abourezk) B.; student Adrian Coll., 1954-55, U. Mich., 1955-57; M.D., Wayne State U., 1961; m. Anna Mancini, Apr. 3, 1971. Intern, St. Joseph Mercy Hosp., Ann Arbor, Mich., 1961-62; resident Wayne State U. Affiliated Hosps., Detroit, 1962-68; practice medicine, specializing in cardiac surgery, Detroit and Southfield, Mich., 1968—; mem. staff Mt. Carmel Mercy Hosp. and Med. Center, Harper Hosp., Grace Hosp., Sinai Hosp., Providence Hosp., Detroit Gen. Hosp., Children's Hosp. of Mich.; clin. instr. dept. surgery Wayne State U. Sch. Medicine, Detroit, 1968-72, clin. asst. prof., 1972—; clin. asst. prof. dept. thoracic sur surgery Mercy Coll., Detroit, 1973—. Diplomate Am. Bd. Surgery, Am. Bd. Thoracic Surgery. Fellow A.C.S., Am. Coll. Cardiology; mem. Soc. Thoracic Surgeons, AMA, Midwest, Detroit surg. assns., Mich. State, Wayne County, Oakland County med. socs., Mich. Thoracic Soc., Detroit Acad. Surgery. Club: Oakland Hills Country. Home: 16253 Mayfair Dr Southfield MI 48075 Office: Suite 1416 N Park Plaza 17117 W Nine Mile Rd Southfield MI 48075

BASSETT, SHELDON JOE, coach, educator; b. Des Moines, July 6, 1938; s. Theodore W. and Mabel E. (McDonald) B.; B.S., Taylor U., 1962; M.S., Ind. U., 1967, postgrad., 1968-69. Tchr.-coach Lansing (Ill.) Jr. High Sch., 1962-66, New Trier High Sch., Winnetka, Ill., 1967-68, Niles E. High Sch., Skokie, Ill., 1969-70; freshman basketball coach Ind. U., Bloomington, 1968-69; asst. basketball, tennis coach, asst. prof., chmn. dept. phys. edn., athletic dir., intramural dir. Taylor U., Upland, Ind., 1970—, coordinator, dean of boys basketball camp, 1962—; mem. U.S. Collegiate Sports Council, 1976—. Athletic dir. Word of Life Camp, Schroon Lake, N.Y., 1957-61. Named Hoosier Buckeye Conf. Tennis Coach of Year, 1972-77. Mem. NEA, AAHPER, Nat. Assn. Basketball Coaches, Am. Camping Assn., Fellowship of Christian Athletes, Taylor U. Alumni Assn. (pres. Chgo. 1969-70), Taylor U. Trojan Club (exec. dir. 1970—), Nat. Assn. Intercollegiate Athletics Tennis Coaches (Coach of Year, Dist. 21 1971-78, Regional Coach of Year 1977, sec. 1974—, v.p. 1975, pres. 1977). Author: Circuit Training for Tennis, 1976; Simulated Circuit Training for Tennis Team, 1976; Basketball Camp Manual for Camp Directors, 1976-77; Tips on Tennis, 1976-78. Home: 210 N 8th St Upland IN 46989

BASSIOUNI, M. CHERIF, educator; b. Cairo, Egypt, Dec. 19, 1937; s. Ibrahim and Amina (Khatab) B.; A.B., Coll. Holy Family, Cairo, 1955; postgrad. Dijon U. Sch. Law, France, 1955-57, U. Geneva (Switzerland), 1957; LL.B., U. Cairo (Egypt), 1961; J.D., Ind. U., 1964; LL.M., John Marshall Lawyers Inst., 1966; S.J.D., George Washington U., 1973; m. Rossana Cesari, Dec. 17, 1962. Came to U.S., 1961, naturalized, 1966. Admitted to Ill, D.C. bars, 1967; practiced in Chgo., 1967—; prof. law DePaul U., 1964—. Fulbright-Hays vis. prof. internat. criminal law U. Freiburg (Germany), 1970; vis. prof. law N.Y.U. Sch. Law, 1971; guest scholar Woodrow Wilson Internat. Center for Scholars, Washington, 1972; cons. Chgo. Bd. Edn., 1965-69, chmn. adv. bd. law in Am. soc. project, 1973-75; lectr. in field; spl. cons. Fifth UN Congress Crime Prevention, 1975. Bd. dirs., dean Internat. Inst. Advanced Criminal Scis. (Italy); bd. dirs. sec.-gen. Internat. Assn. Penal Law, 1974—. Decorated Order Merit (Egypt); commendatore Order Merit Italy, also grande ufficiale; recipient Outstanding Citizen of Year award Citizenship Council Met. Chgo., 1967. Mem. World Peace Through Law, Am. Soc. Internat. Law, Am. (chmn. com. internat. legal edn. 1974—), Ill. (chmn. sect. on internat. law 1972-73, sect. council 1970-77), Chgo. (chmn. com. on criminal legislation 1967-69) bar assns., MidAm. Arab. C. of C. (chmn. 1973-74, 76-77, sec. gen. counsel 1974-76, pres. 1976—), Assn. Arab-Am. U. Grads. (bd. dirs. 1967-74, pres. 1969-70), Phi Alpha Delta. Author: Criminal Law and Its Processes, 1969; The Law of Dissent and Riots, 1971; (with V.P. Nanda) International Criminal Law, 2 Vols., 1973; (with Eugene Fisher) Storm Over The Arab World, 1972; International Extradition and World Public Order, 1974; International Terrorism and Political Crimes, 1975. Editor: Issues in the Mediterranean, 1976; Citizens Arrest: The Law of Arrest, Search and Seizure, 1977; Substantive Criminal Law, 1978. Co-editor-in-chief Revue Internat. de Droit Penal, 1973—; editor The Globe, 1970—, Am. Jour. Comparative Law, 1972—. Home: 1130 N Lake Shore Dr Chicago IL 60611 Office: 25 E Jackson St Chicago IL 60604

BASU, ASIT PRAKAS, statistician; b. Jessore, India (now Bangladesh), Mar. 17, 1937; B.Sc., Calcutta U., 1956, M.Sc., 1958; Ph.D., U. Minn., 1966. Asst. prof. statistics U. Wis., Madison, 1966-68; mem. research staff IBM Research Center, Yorktown Heights, N.Y., 1968-70; asst. prof. indsl. engring. and mgmt. sci. Northwestern U., Evanston, Ill., 1970-71; asso. prof. math. U. Pitts., 1971-74; prof. statistics U. Mo., Columbia, 1974—. Fellow Royal Statis. Soc., mem. Am. Statis. Assn., Inst. Math. Statistics, Calcutta Statis. Assn., Sigma Xi. Contbr. articles to profl. jours. Home: 3709 W Rollins Rd Columbia MO 65201 Office: Dept Statistics Univ Mo Columbia MO 65201

BASU, PRODYOT KUMAR, coll. adminstr.; b. Lucknow, India, Nov. 15, 1939; s. Krishna Kamal and Usha Rani B.; came to U.S., 1974, naturalized, 1974; B.S., Lucknow U., 1957; B.C.E., Jadavpur U., 1961; M.Engring., Calcutta U., 1963; D.S., Washington U., St. Louis, 1977; m. Liliya Bhattacharya, Jan. 24, 1966; 1 son. Sr. fellow Govt. India, 1961-64; lectr. civil engring. Bengal Engring. Coll., 1964-72; asst. prof., 1972-74; faculty Univ. Coll. Washington U., 1974-76, research engr., 1976-77, sr. research engr., 1977—, asso. dir. Center for Computational Machines, 1977—. Recipient Sir Arthur Cotton Meml. Gold medal, Instn. Engrs., India, 1970-71. Mem. ASCE, Instn. Engrs., Indian Geotech. Soc., Indian Soc. Tech. Edn., Sigma Xi. Contbr. articles in field to profl. jours. Home: 2003 A Laclede Station Rd Saint Louis MO 63143 Office: Box 1130 Saint Louis MO 63130

BASU, SHANKAR, mfg. co. exec.; b. Calcutta, India, May 17, 1947; s. Sephalendu and Roma (Roychowdury) B.; came to U.S., 1970, naturalized, 1974; B.S. in Metall. Engring., Indian Inst. Tech., 1970; M.S. (grantee 1971, scholarship 1972), U. Minn., 1973, M.B.A., 1976. With Am. Hoist & Derrick Co., St. Paul, 1972—, mgr. mktg. analysis, 1977—. Mem. Soc. Metall. Engrs. (chpt. pres. 1970), N.Am. Soc. Corporate Planners, Am. Mktg. Assn. Clubs: Am. Ski, Am. Hoist Golf League. Address: 1455 E Upper 55th St Inver Grove Heights MN 55075

BASU, SUBHASH CHANDRA, biochemist, educator; b. Calcutta, India, May 28, 1938; s. Sunil Chandra and Kamala (Paul) B.; came to U.S., 1961, naturalized, 1975; B.S., Calcutta U., 1958, M.S. (Jubilee Postgrad. scholar), 1960, D.Sc., 1976; Ph.D., U. Mich., 1966; m. Manju Dutta, Nov. 25, 1966; children—Sanmit Kumar, Radit Kumar. Lectr. in chemistry Vidyasagar Coll. Calcutta U., 1960-61; teaching and research fellow U. Mich., 1961-65; Helen Hay Whitney research fellow Johns Hopkins U., 1967-70; asst. prof. chemistry, biochem. biophys. program U. Notre Dame, 1970-76, asso. prof., 1976—; cons. Miles Labs., Elkhart, Ind. Pres. Indian Students Assn., U. Mich., 1963-65. Recipient Univ. Gold medal Calcutta U., 1958, 60; NIH grantee, 1971—; Nat. Cancer Inst., grantee, 1975—. Mem. Am. Soc. Biol. Chemists, Internat. Soc. Neurochemistry, Soc. Complex Carbohydrate, N.Y. Acad. Scis., Soc. Cryobiology. Hindu. Research on glycosphingolipids, DNA synthesis. Home: 17784 Darden Rd South Bend IN 46635 Office: Dept Chemistry U of Notre Dame Notre Dame IN 46556

BATCH, JOHN MARTIN, research adminstr.; b. Helena, Mont., Nov. 16, 1925; s. Otto Carl and Leah (Hartman) B.; B.S., Mont. State U., 1944, M.S., 1950; Ph.D. (Shell Oil fellow), Purdue U., 1955; m. Donna Rae Ogden, Jan. 11, 1973; children—Laura, James, Dana, Michelle. Research mgr. Gen. Electric Co., Richland, Wash., 1958-65; mgr. engring. dept. Battelle-Northwest, Richland, 1965-70, sr. staff engr., 1970-71, asso. lab. dir., 1971-73; lab. dir. Battelle-Columbus Div., Columbus, Ohio, 1973—; v.p. Battelle Meml. Inst., Columbus, 1976—; dir. Olentangy Mgmt. Co. Mem. adv. com. to mech. engring. dept. Ohio State U., Columbus; trustee Columbus Gallery Fine Arts; trustee, chmn. fin. com. Columbus Coll. Art and Design. Served with USNR, 1943-46. Registered profl. engr., Wash. Mem. Am. Nuclear Soc., ASME, Columbus Area C. of C. (dir.), Sigma Xi, Sigma Pi Sigma. Episcopalian. Clubs: Ohio State U. Golf (Columbus), Elks. Contbr. articles in field to profl. jours. Home: 2370 Wimbledon Rd Columbus OH 43220 Office: 550 King Ave Columbus OH 43201

BATCHELDER, ANNE STUART (MRS. CLIFTON BROOKS BATCHELDER), former publisher, polit. party ofcl.; b. Lake Forest, Ill., Jan. 11, 1920; d. Robert Douglas and Harriet (McClure) Stuart; student Lake Forest Coll., 1941-43; m. Clifton Brooks Batchelder, May 26, 1945; children—Edward, Anne Stuart, Mary Clifton, Lucia Brooks. Clubmobile driver A.R.C., Eng., Belgium, France, Holland and Germany, 1943-45; pub., editor Douglas County Gazette, 1970-75; dir. Waterloo State Bank; mem. U.S. Checkbook Com. Mem. Republican Central Com. Nebr., 1955-62, 70—, vice chmn. Central Com., 1959-64, now chmn., mem. finance com., 1957-64; chmn. women's sect. Douglas County Rep. Finance Com., 1955, vice chmn. com., 1958-60; v.p. Omaha Woman's Rep. Club, 1957-58, pres., 1959-60; alternate del. Nat. Conv., 1956, 72; mem. Rep. Nat. Com. for Nebr., 1964-70; asst. chmn. Douglas County Rep. Central Com., 1971—; 1st v.p. Nebr. Fedn. Rep. Women, 1971-72, pres., 1972-74; chmn. Nebr. Rep. Com., 1975—; Rep. candidate for lt. gov., 1974. Sr. v.p. Nebr. Founders Day, 1958; past trustee Brownell Hall, Vis. Nurse Assn. Mem. Mayflower Soc., Colonial Dames, P.E.O., Nat. League Pen Women, Zonta. Presbyterian (elder). Clubs: Omaha Country, Omaha. Home: 6875 State St Omaha NE 68152

BATCHELOR, WILBUR COMMODORE, consultant; b. Canajoharie, N.Y., May 6, 1890; s. August Conrad and Catherine (Foeller) Stumpfel; B.Phys. Edn., Springfield Coll., 1913, M. Phys.

Edn. (hon.), 1931; M.A., (fellow), Clark U., 1919; Ed.D., U. Pitts., 1936; m. Mary Elizabeth Stowell, July 28, 1914; children—Kenyon Stowell, Bruce Bingham, Richard Lanckton. Boys phys. dir. Bridgeport (Conn.) YMCA, 1908-09; youth dir. Olivet Congl. Ch., Springfield, Mass., 1909-11; asst. phys. dir. Springfield high schs., 1911-13; phys. dir. Westinghouse Air Brake YMCA, 1913-15; prof. phys. edn. and hygiene Rensselaer Poly. Inst., 1915-20; supt. pub. recreation, Utica, N.Y., 1920-23, dir. Ft. Worth Dept. Pub. Recreation, 1923-25; supt. Pitts. Bur. Recreation, also dir. dept. recreation Pitts. Bd. Edn., 1925-35; prof. social group work, youth leadership and recreation adminstrn. Ohio State U., 1935-60, now prof. emeritus; exec. dir. Neighborhood House, 1942-45; cons. in youth services and recreation, 1930-70; lectr., pub. speaker. Mem. curriculum com. profl. tng. White House Conf. Child Health and Protection, 1929-32; vice chmn. Columbus Recreation Commn., 1941-46; mem. Columbus City Planning Commn., 1964-68, Columbus Devel. Commn., 1968-72; Franklin County Regional Planning Commn., 1965-69, Mid Ohio Regional Planning Commn., 1969-73; mem. Columbus YMCA Helping Hand Bd., 1969-73, Columbus Sr. Citizen Adv. Council, 1970-77. Field commr. Boy Scouts, Utica, 1920-23, Ft. Worth, 1923-25, Pitts., 1925-35, Columbus, 1935-41. Bd. dirs. Gladden Community House, 1943-46, Central Community House, 1944-47, Neighborhood House, 1945—. Recipient Tarbell Medallion award, Springfield Coll., 1936. Mem. Am. Recreation Soc., Am. Youth Hostels, Inc. (founder; chmn. Central Ohio council 1942-44, nat. council 1961-67), Nat. Assn. Social Workers (charter), Nat. Recreation Park Assn. (Meritorious Service award 1971), Social Workers Club Columbus and Franklin County (pres. 1941-42), Ohio Parks and Recreation Assn. (hon. life mem.; pres. 1936-39. Meritorious Service award 1963), Am. Camping Assn. (Ohio chpt. service award 1973), Assn. Indian Affairs. Acad. Certified Social Workers (charter), Alpha Phi Omega, Alpha Kappa Alpha. Conglist. (bd. deacons 1966-70). Contbr. articles to profl. jours. Condr., dir. community surveys of youth services, pub. recreation and parks in Detroit, Wayne County, Reading, Berks County, Pitts., Allegheny County, Omaha, Huntington, W.Va., Norfolk and Portsmouth. Va., Racine, Wis., Columbus, Toledo, Cuyahoga Falls, Massillon and Elyria, Ohio, others. Home: 198 Acton Rd Columbus OH 43214

BATE, CHARLES THOMAS, lawyer; b. Muncie, Ind., Nov. 14, 1932; s. Thomas Elwood and Vina Florence (Jackson) B.; A.B., Butler U., 1955, postgrad., 1955-56; student Christian Theol. Sem., Indpls., 1956-57; J.D., Ind. U., 1962; m. Barbara Kay Dailey, June 17, 1955; children—Charles Thomas, Gregory Andrew, Jeffrey Scott. Admitted to Ind. bar, 1962; staff adjuster State Automobile Ins. Assn., Indpls., 1953-57, claim supr., 1958-59, office mgr., 1960-61, casualty claim mgr., 1961-62, atty., 1962-63; mem. firm Smith & Yarling, Indpls., 1963-67; partner Soshnick & Bate, Shelbyville, Ind., 1967—. Dir., v.p., gen. counsel Discovery Life Ins. Co., Indpls., 1966-70. Bd. dirs. Nat. Pensions Bd. of Ch. of God; trustee Warner Pacific Coll., Portland, Oreg., 1977—. Recipient Merit award Ind. Jud. Council, 1962, Outstanding Student award Ind. U. Law Week, 1962; name Profl. Man of Day radio sta. WIFE, 1971, 72. Mem. Am., Ind., Indpls., Shelby County bar assns., Am. Judicature Soc., Am. Arbitration Assn. (panel arbitrators), Am., Ind. trial lawyers assns., Am. Platform Assn. Republican. Mem. Ch. of God (dir. Glendale Ch. of God Inc. 1958—, lay speaker 1962—, sec. nat. by-laws com. 1968—). Clubs: Shelbyville Elks; Columbia (Indpls.). Home: Box 26 Shelbyville IN 46176 Office: 24 W Broadway Shelbyville IN 46176

BATES, CHARLES JOHNSON, food co. exec.; b. Dayton, Ohio, May 4, 1930; s. Philip Knight and Eleanor (Johnson) B.; B.S., Calif. Inst. Tech., 1951; Ph.D., Mass. Inst. Tech., 1957; m. Nancy Trebler Lindbeck, June 27, 1953; children—Charles Johnson, Richard L., Priscilla P. With Procter & Gamble Co., Cin., 1957-72, mgr. indsl. food tech. service, 1964-67, mgr. sanitation products sales, 1967-72; v.p. tech. Am. Maize Products Co., Hammond, Ind., 1972—. Scoutmaster Dan Beard council Boy Scouts Am., 1969-72, bd. dirs. Calumet council, 1975—. Mem. Inst. Food Technologists, Am. Assn. Cereal Chemists, Sigma Xi, Phi Tau Sigma, Phi Lambda Upsilon. Republican. Mason. Home: 760 Williams Dr Crown Point IN 46307 Office: 113th St Hammond IN 46326

BATES, GEORGE EDWARD, JR., historian; b. Omaha, June 6, 1939; s. George Edward and Audrey (Potts) B.; A.B., U. Nebr., 1960; A.M., U. Mich., 1967; Ph.D., U. Ill., 1970; children—George Edward III, Thomas Wagner. Asst. prof. history Winona (Minn.) State U., 1970-72, asso. prof., 1973—; dir. Southeast Minn. Hist. Center; officer, Minn. Commn. United Ministries to Higher Edn., 1974—. Officer, 1st Congls. Ch., Winona, 1973-75; pres. United Campus Ministry Bd., Winona, 1974; officer Winona County Hist. Soc., 1976—. Served to lt. USN, 1960-65. Fellow Newberry Library, Chgo.; fellow U. Ill., 1970; recipient grants Winona State U., 1973, 75, Minn. Hist. Soc. research grants, 1977. Mem. Am. Hist. Assn., Orgn. Am. Historians, Minn., Winona County hist. socs., Am. Soc. 18th Century Studies, Minn. Assn. Collecting Agencies, Beta Theta Pi. Office: Dept History Winona State Univ Winona MN 55987

BATES, HENRY ELMER, JR., librarian; b. Quincy, Mass., Dec. 2, 1932; student Bentley Coll. Accounting and Fin., 1950-52; A.B., Boston U., 1960; M.L.S., Simmons Coll., 1962. Accountant, Bethlehem Steel Co., Quincy; with Thomas Crane Pub. Library, Quincy, 1952-67, reference librarian, 1962, asst. librarian, 1962-64, head librarian, 1964-67; head librarian Newton (Mass.) Free Library, 1967; asso. dir. Pub. Library D.C.; asst. chief librarian Chgo. Pub. Library, 1970; now dir. Milw. Pub. Library. Served in U.S. Army, 1953-56. Mem. ALA, Wis. Library Assn. Office: 814 W Wisconsin Ave Milwaukee WI 53233

BATES, MARK WELDON, fund adminstr.; b. Bloomington, Ill., Aug. 14, 1934; s. Ralph Elbert and Margaret (Weldon) B.; student U. Ill., 1952-54; B.S. in Journalism, Northwestern U., 1956; m. Janet Alice Fjellberg, Jan. 5, 1957; children—Michael John, Scott Weldon, Anne Elizabeth. Personnel asst. Washington Nat. Ins. Co., Evanston, Ill. 1957-58; asst. dir. devel. Northwestern U., Evanston. 1958-61; dir. devel. Ill. Inst. Tech., Chgo., 1961-67, v.p. instl. devel., 1968-72, v.p. planning and devel., 1975—; exec. v.p. Am. Fund for Dental Health, Chgo., 1973-75. Served with AUS, 1957. Mem. Nat. Soc. Fund Raisers, Chgo. Soc. for Fund Raising Execs. (pres. 1972-73), Union League Club. Clubs: Economic, Chicago Press; Michigan Shores; Wilmette. Home: 2345 Ashland Ave Evanston IL 60201 Office: 10 W 33d St Chicago IL 60616

BATES, MARY JOYCE, pub. relations exec.; b. New Albany, Ind., Apr. 19, 1919; d. Raymond William and Mary Joyce (Austin)-Renn; B.B.A., U. Cinn., 1942; m. Carl L. Bates, Apr. 28, 1956 (dec.). Pub. relations account exec. Bob Long Assos., Indpsl., 1961-63; pub. relations dir. Indpls. Symphony Orchestra, 1963-65; program adminstr. Avco Broadcasting Corp., 1955-60, mgr. and v.p. pub. relations, 1965-71, v.p. communications, 1971-74; gen. pub. relations and advt. mgr. Cin. Bell, Inc., 1974—. Mem. community bd. Sta. WGUC, Cin.; bd. trustees Unity Center of Cin.; mem. pub. relations com. Xavier U., Cin. Recipient Nat. Headliner award, Women in Communications, Inc., 1972. Mem. Pub. Relations Soc. Am., Women in Communications, Inc. Home: 1617 E McMillan Cincinnati OH 45206 Office: 307 E 4th St Cincinnati OH 45202

BATES, ROBERT L., heavy equipment co. exec.; b. Senecaville, Ohio, Jan. 27, 1924; s. Leroy E. and E. Ruth (McLaughlin) B.; B.S., Ohio State U., 1948; Chem. Engr., U. Dayton, 1958, M.B.A., 1967; m. Betty E. Bartels, June 9, 1945; children—Stephen, Linda Bates Puthoff, Catherine Bates Brown, Elizabeth. Chem. engr. Monsanto Chem. Co., Miamisburg, Ohio, 1948-51; chief engr. Process Equipment div. Internat. Engring. Co., Dayton, Ohio, 1951-53; v.p. Chemineer, Inc., Dayton, 1953-62, pres., 1962—, dir., 1953—; dir. Allied Tech., Inc., Dayton; adj. asso. prof. chem. engring. Ohio State U., 1957—, mem. adv. council Coll. Adminstrv. Scis., 1974—, mem. joint policy com. Exec. Devel. Com., 1976—. Chmn., City of Oakwood (Ohio) Youth Commn., 1970-74; mem. Mayor's Council on Econ. Devel., 1977—; pres. bd. trustees Dayton Art Inst.; trustee Newfields Community Authority; mem. adv. council spl. edn. Antioch Coll., 1967-69. Fellow Am. Inst. Chem. Engrs., Am. Inst. Chemists; mem. Am. Chem. Soc., Am. Mgmt. Assn., AAAS, Dayton Engrs. Club (Outstanding Achievement award 1970), C. of C. (chmn. design rev. com., river corridor com. 1973), Ohio State Pres.'s Club (Columbus), Dayton Racquet Club, Moraine Country Club. Recipient Texnikoi Outstanding award, 1966, Outstanding Alumnus award, 1972, both from Ohio State U.; contbr. articles to profl. jours.; patentee in field. Home: 20 Walnut Ln Dayton OH 45419 Office: 1801 E 1st St Dayton OH 45401

BATIE, HARLEY WALTER, dentist; b. Overton, Nebr., Sept. 15, 1925; s. Ellis Henry and Hilda Marie (Nelson) B.; B.Sc., U. Nebr., 1950; D.D.S., 1952; m. Mary Helen Mitchell, June 6, 1948; children—Kim Mitchell, Ann Jeannette. Gen. practice dentistry, Lexington, Nebr., 1952—; clin. asso. U. Nebr. Dental Coll., 1969—. Mem. Nebr. Bd. Dental Examiners, Central Regional Dental Testing Service Bd. Pres. Community Concert Assn., 1972-76; mem. Library Bd., 1955-70. Bd. dirs. U. Nebr. Found.; mem. adv. council Coll. Dentistry, U. Nebr. Served with AUS, 1944-46. Fellow Internat. Coll. Dentists (pres. chpt. 1977-78); mem. NW Dist. Dental Soc. (pres. 1959), Neb. Dental Study Club (organizer, pres. 1952-59), Lexington C. of C. (dir. 1966-67), Delta Sigma Delta. Methodist. Mason (Shriner). Home: 1812 N Hoover St Lexington NE 68850 Office: 617 N Grant St Lexington NE 68850

BATINICH, MARY ELLEN (MRS. ALEX BATINICH), educator; b. Eveleth, Minn., Apr. 20, 1923; d. James Vincent and Mary (Noldin) Mancina; A.S., Eveleth Jr. Coll., 1943; M.A., Northwestern U., 1958, Ph.D., 1963; m. Alex Batinich, Apr. 20, 1946. Substitute tchr. various Chgo. Pub. Schs., 1949-51; master tchr. Elihu Yale Sch., Chgo., 1959, tchr., 1951-63; instr. Chgo. Tchrs. Coll., 1961-62, 68-69; prin. John A. Walsh Elementary Sch., Chgo., 1963-65, Carver Evening High Sch., 1966-68, Sbarbaro Sch., 1967-70, Schmid Sch., 1970-72; coordinator research and evaluation Chgo. Pub. Schs., 1972—; lectr. Chgo. State Coll., 1963-65, 68-69. Del. White House Conf. on Children and Youth, 1970. Recipient numerous citations and awards. Mem. Internat. Reading Assn., Nat. Soc. for Study Edn., Chgo. Area Reading Assn. (pres. 1968-69, dir.), Ill. Reading Council (pres. 1970-71), Italian Library-Mus. (dir. 1970—), Gregorian Educators' Soc. (pres. 1965-67), Arrigo Vets. Ladies Aux. (pres. 1974-75). Author, illustrator: Minnesota Souvenir Coloring Book; Invest in the Future: A College Education, 1969; Italian Ethnic Studies Guide, 1970. Contbr. articles to profl. publs. Office: 228 N LaSalle St Chicago IL 60611

BATMAN, HOWARD TAYLOR, lawyer; b. Marengo, Ind., Dec. 17, 1906; s. Emery Everett and Vada Florence (Taylor) B.; A.B., Ind. U., 1929; children—Barbara (Mrs. James L. MaGirl), Geraldine (Mrs. Jack Booth). Admitted to Ind. bar, 1933; atty., gen. mgr., counsel John F. Lynch, Inc., Terre Haute, Ind., 1948—; gen. mgr., counsel Lynch Coal Operators Reciprocal Assn., Terre Haute, 1948—; dir. Morris Plan Bank, Terre Haute, Ohio Valley Gas Corp., Cameron Gas Co., Moore-Langen Printing & Pub. Co., Distbrs. Terminal Corp., Am. Baking Power Co. Pub. counselor Pub. Service Commn. Ind., 1941-43. Mem. Ind. Gen. Assembly, 1939-41. Bd. dirs. Boys Club, Terre Haute, 1969—. Served with USNR, 1943-45. Mason, Elk. Clubs: Columbia (Indpls.); Indpls. Athletic; Country (Terre Haute); Federal City (Washington). Home: 25 Hamilton Dr Terre Haute IN 47803 Office: 710 Ohio St Terre Haute In 47808

BATSAKIS, JOHN GEORGE, pathologist; b. Petoskey, Mich., Aug. 14, 1929; s. George John and Stella (Vlahakis) B.; B.S., Va. Mil. Inst., 1950; student Albion Coll., 1947-50; M.D., U. Mich., 1954; m. Mary Janet Savage, Dec. 28, 1957; children—Laura, Sharon, George. Intern George Washington U. Hosp., Washington, 1954-55; resident U. Mich. Med. Center, Ann Arbor, 1955-59, asst. prof. pathology, 1962-64, prof., 1968—, co-dir. Clin. Labs., 1973—. Cons. pathology programs AUS. Served to capt. M.C., AUS, 1959-61. Diplomate Am. Bd. Pathology. Fellow Coll. Am. Pathology, A.C.P., Am. Soc. Clin. Pathologists; mem. Royal Coll. Medicine, Assn. Clin. Scientists, Assn. Clin. Biochemists U.K., Am. Thyroid Assn., Am. Ordnance Assn., Am. Assn. Mil. Surgeons. Author: Interpretive Enzymology, 1967; Diagnostic Enzymology, 1970; Microscopic Pathology, 1964; Tumors of the Head and Neck, 1974. Contbr. articles to profl. jours. Home: 2114 Delaware Dr Ann Arbor MI 48103 Office: Dept Pathology Medical Center Univ Michigan Ann Arbor MI 48104

BATT, CATHERINE JEAN, pub. relations exec.; b. Cleve., Aug. 8, 19S2; d. John J. and Edith M. (DeFrench) Corrado; B.A. in Journalism, U. Toledo, 1974; m. Nick D. Batt, Sept. 7, 1974. Cons. writer Doehler-Jarvis div. N.L. Industries, Toledo, 1974; asst. pub. relations dir. Toledo Area C. of C., 1974-75; pub. and employee info. specialist The Andersons, Maumee, Ohio, 1975—. Advisor, Jr. Achievement of N.W. Ohio, 1971-73; campaign mgr. Nick Batt for State Rep. Com., 1976. Mem. Press Club Toledo, Women in Communications (v.p. Toledo chpt.), Pub. Relations Soc. Am. (treas. N.W. Ohio chpt.). Democrat. Roman Catholic. Clubs: Toledo Bar Aux., U. Toledo Alumni Assn. Home: 4957 San Joaquin Dr Toledo OH 43615 Office: PO Box 119 Maumee OH 43537

BATTIS, THOMAS JEROME, lawyer; b. St. Paul, Nov. 8, 1926; s. Nicholas Joseph and Margaret (Riley) B.; B.S.L., U. Minn., 1947, J.D., 1949; m. Alice Marie Brand, Apr. 15, 1950; children—Timothy J., David E., Kathleen M., Cynthia A., Jeffrey P., Jerome T., Steven M. Admitted to Minn. bar, 1949, since practiced in St. Paul; partner Murnane, Murnane, Battis & Conlin, St. Paul, 1951-75; mem. firm Richard D. Allen, Ltd., Mpls., 1975—; prof. William Mitchell Coll. Law, 1958-59; pres., dir. Prior Lake Area Devel. Corp., 1970—. Mem. Sch. Dist. 719 Bd., 1964-68, treas., 1964, pres., 1968. Served with USAAF, 1945. Mem. Am., Minn., Ramsey County bar assns., Am. Judicature Soc., Nat. Rifle Assn., Nat. Wild Life Assn., Ramsey County Hist. Soc., Phi Delta Phi. Republican. Roman Catholic. Club: Serra. Home: Route 1 Shakopee MN 55379 Office: North Federal Bldg St Paul MN 55101

BATTISON, JOHN HENRY, broadcasting exec.; b. Wembley, Eng., Sept. 11, 1915; s. John Charles and Emily Florence (Butler) B.; B.S., U. London; Sc.D., FSCC, 1973; m. Cicely Church, 1942 (div. 1954); children—Diana Penelope, John Christopher; m. 2d, Nancy H. Mackenzie, 1954 (div. 1971); children—Florence Victoria, Jonathon, Mark Battison; m. 3d, Sara Bennett, 1971. Research engr. EKCO Radio Co., 1934-37; mem. tech. div. Brit. Air Ministry, 1937-39; tech. dir. Midland Broadcasting Co., 1945-47; asst. chief allocations engr. ABC, 1947-49; asso. editor Tele-Tech. Mag., 1949-52; faculty mem. N.Y.U., 1949-52; dir. TV Comml. prodn. Dancer Fitzgerald Sample, Inc., 1951; dir. TV Nat. Council Chs., 1951-52; dir. Nat. Radio Inst., Washington, 1952-54; asso. prof. Am. U., 1952-54; gen. mgr., dir. engring. CHCT-TV, Calgary, Alta., Can., 1954-55; broadcast cons. engr., Washington, 1955; pres., gen. mgr., dir. engring., KAVE and KAVE-TV in name of Voice of the Caverns, Inc., Carlsbad, N.M.; tech. controller programs A-R Ltd., Eng., 1958-59; pres., dir. Engring. Internat. Telecommunication Cons., Inc., 1959-63; v.p., dir. engring. Nat. Roadar, Inc., 1966—; head Frequency Allocation Group IIT Research Inst., 1963-68, also cons. engr.; mgr. communications, electronics div. Chesapeake Instrument Corp., 1968-70, chief engr. Saudi Arabian TV; cons. engr. Smith Electronics Inc., 1970-72; dir. engring. WINW, Canton, Ohio, 1972-74, Ohio Communications, Inc., Cleve., 1973-75; pres. Batcom Internat. Communications, Inc., 1975—. Former trustee Annapolis Jr. High Sch. Served as Squadron Leader, R.A.F., 1939-45. Registered profl. engr., Washington; splty. broadcast and film engring. Sr. mem. Inst. Radio Engrs.; mem. Brit. Inst. Radio Engrs., Soc. Motion Picture and TV Engrs., Nat. TV Film Council, Soc. Broadcast Engrs. (past pres.), Nat. Press Club Anglican. Rotarian. Clubs: Radio and TV Executives (N.Y.C.); Broadcasters (Washington); Riverside Country (Carlsbad); Annapolis Yacht; Link; Internat. Sporting, RAF (London). Episcopalian (lay reader). Author 15 books on broadcasting, tv, films, tech. matters; also author numerous articles tech. jours. Home: 10073 Echo Hills Dr Brecksville OH 44141 also St Charles Apts Beirut Lebanon Office: Batcom Bldg PO Box 8 Cleveland OH 44141

BATTISTI, FRANK JOSEPH, fed. judge; b. Youngstown, Ohio, Oct. 4, 1922; s. Eugene and Jennie (Dalesandro) B.; B.A., Ohio U., 1947; LL.B., Harvard U., 1950. Admitted to Ohio bar, 1950; asst. atty gen. Ohio, 1950; atty. Admitted to Ohio bar, 1950; asst. atty gen. Ohio, 1950; atty. adviser C.E., U.S. Army, 1951-52; 1st asst. dir. law, Youngstown, 1954-59; judge Common Pleas Ct., Mahoning County, Ohio, 1959-61; U.S. judge No. Dist. Ohio, Cleve., 1961-69, chief judge, 1969—. Served with C.E., U.S. Army, 1943-45; ETO. Mem. Am., Mahoning County, Cleve. bar assns., Am. Judicature Soc. Roman Catholic. Office: 302 US Courthouse Cleveland OH 44114

BATTON, CALVERT VORWERK, appliance co. exec.; b. Cuyahoga Falls, Ohio, June 29, 1926; s. Ramsey T. and Mildred B. (Vorwerk) B.; student Bowling Green U., 1946; B.S. in Bus. Adminstrn., Kent State U., 1950, postgrad. Grad. Bus. Sch., 1960-63; m. Edith Sayre Jones, May 18, 1957; children—Susan, Sally, Pamela. With Hoover Co., Canton, Ohio, 1951—, auditor, 1951-53, mgr. br. office, 1953-56, mgr. field accounting, 1956-58, gen. office mgr., 1958-61, asst. budget mgr., 1961-62, mgr. adminstrv. services, 1962-64, asst. v.p., 1964-65, adminstrv. v.p., 1965—; adv. bd. dirs. Diebold Research, Inc. Bd. dirs. United Way, Canton. Served with AUS, 1944-45. Mem. Adminstrv. Mgmt. Soc., Nat. Assn. Accountants, Am. Mgmt. Assn., Conf. Bd., Kent U. Alumni Assn. (dir.), Sigma Delta Epsilon. Republican. Presbyn. Home: 245 21st St NW Canton OH 44709 Office: Box 2200 North Canton OH 44720

BATZA, EUGENE MANN, audiologist-speech pathologist; b. Canton, Ohio, Mar. 22, 1917; s. George and Vera (Mann) B.; B.A., Coll. Wooster, 1937; M.A., Northwestern U., 1951, Ph.D., 1956; m. Anne Marie Phillips, Apr. 18, 1946; children—Valerie, Nancy. Lectr., Northwestern U., Evanston, Ill., 1951-54; asst. prof. Bowling Green (Ohio) State U., 1954-57; asso. prof. Vanderbilt U. Sch. Medicine and George Peabody Coll., Nashville, 1957-63; chief coordinator speech pathology services Bill Wilkerson Hearing and Speech Center, Nashville, 1957-62, dir. tng. and research, 1962-63; vis. prof. North Tex. State U., Denton, 1963-64; mem. profl. staff Cleve. Clinic, 1964—, also faculty mem. Cleve. Clinic Ednl. Found. Cons. cerebral palsy program Nashville Pub. Schs., 1957-62, Nashville Mental Health Center, 1957-62; adj. prof. Cleve. State U., 1973—; Mem. med. profl. adv. com. United Cerebral Palsy Tenn., 1963. Served with AUS, 1942-46; ETO. Grantee, Nat. Soc. Crippled Children and Adults, 1957, Office Vocational Rehab., 1959, NIH, 1962. Mem. Am. Speech and Hearing Assn. (regional legis. cons. 1971-73), Am. Cleft Palate Assn., Council Exceptional Children, Am. Acad. Ophthalmology and Otolaryngology, MENSA, Am. Congress Rehab. Medicine, Internat. Assn. Logopedics and Phoniatrics. Home: 14975 Hill Dr Novelty OH 44072 Office: 9500 Euclid Ave Cleveland OH 44106

BAUCH, NORBERT GEORGE, physician; b. Milw., Feb. 12, 1921; s. Walter Herman and Amanda Louise (Butter) B.; student Milw. State Tchrs. Coll., 1938-40; B.S., Marquette U., 1942, M.D., 1945; m. Geraldine Bernice Lingen, Mar. 23, 1946; children—Thomas Walter, Nancy Gay, Robert John, William Lauren (dec.), Barbara Joan. Intern, Milwaukee County Gen. Hosp., Wauwatosa, Wis., 1945-46; resident St. Michael Hosp., Milw., 1948-49; gen. practice medicine, Milw., 1949—; mem. staff St. Michael Hosp., Milw., 1948—, chmn. resident-intern com., 1955-71, dir. family practice specialty residency training program, 1971—; clin. instr. internal medicine Med. Coll. Wis., 1971-75, asso. clin. prof. family practice, 1975—; dir. Model Family Practice Unit, Milw., 1971—, dir. med. edn., 1974—. Alienist Milwaukee County Probate Ct., 1949—. Mem. troop com. Boy Scouts Am., Milw., 1957—. Served to lt. (j.g.) USNR, 1946-47. Diplomate Am. Bd. Family Practice. Mem. Am., Wis. (pres. 1968), Milw. (pres. 1961) acads. gen. practice, AMA, Wis. Med. Soc., Med. Soc. Milwaukee County, Soc. Tchrs. Family Medicine, Phi Chi. Episcopalian. Home: 2525 N 88th St Wauwatosa WI 53226 Office: 2400 W Villard Ave Milwaukee WI 53209

BAUCOM, WILLIAM ERNEST, advt. display co. exec.; b. Richmond, Va., Jan. 25, 1925; s. Ivey William and Ella (Bradshaw) B.; student U. Ala., 1943; B.M.E., Va. Poly. Inst., 1949; M.B.A., Harvard U., 1952; m. Joyce Nadine Evans, Dec. 30, 1949; children—Dee Evan, Sandra Barbee, Ann Willison. With Gen. Electric Corp., Lynn, Mass., 1949-50; pres., founder Evans-Baucom & Assos., Inc., Massillon, Ohio, 1952—, also dir.; dir. Polygraphic Inc. Served with U.S. Army, 1943-46. Mem. Point of Purchases Inst., Wire Mfrs. Assn. Republican. Clubs: Shady Hollow Country (pres. 1975-77), Massillon. Home: 1923 Coventry Rd NE Massillon OH 44646 Office: 2037 Wales Rd NE Massillon OH 44646

BAUDER, GARY LEE, accounting co. exec.; b. Sturgis, Mich., Nov. 28, 1949; s. Ray Orlo, Jr. and Grace Marguerite (Haney) B.; A.A., Glen Oaks Community Coll., 1970; certificate in jr. accounting, State Tech. Inst. and Rehab. Center, 1974. Supervisory trainee Arch Workshop, Inc., Sturgis, 1969-71; mgr. B & F Tax & Accounting Service Corp., Sturgis, 1974-76, pres., dir., 1976—; dir., instr. income tax div. B & F Tax Tng. Inst.; instr. personal income taxes Sturgis Pub. Sch. Sec.-treas. Glen Oaks Community Coll. Circle K, 1968-70; notary pub. Mich.; treas. St. Joseph County (Mich.) Young Democrats, 1968-70; precinct del. St. Joseph County Dem. Party, 1970. Mem. Distributive Edn. Clubs Am., Glen Oaks Community Coll. alumni assns., Sturgis C. of C., Am. Mgmt. Assn., Nat. Small Bus. Assn., St. Joseph County Wheelchair Sports Boosters Assn. Recipient Outstanding Service awards Mich. Assn. Distributive Edn. Clubs Am., 1970, Glen Oaks Community Coll. Boosters, 1970; named Officer of Year, Distributive Edn. Clubs Am., 1970-71. Office: 221 Susan St Sturgis MI 49091

BAUER, FLORENCE MARVYNE (MRS. W. W. BAUER), artist, author; b. Elgin, Ill.; d. John Charles and Mary (Williams) Chetwynd-Marvyne; grad. Ch. Sch. Art, Chgo., 1916; postgrad. Art Inst. Chgo., Layton Sch. Art, Milw.; m. W.W. Bauer, Feb. 8, 1920; children—William Waldo (dec.), John Robert, Ann Bauer Wetzel, Charles Marvyne. Author: Behold Your King, 1945; Abram Son of Terah, 1948; Daughter of Nazareth, 1955; Lady Besieged, 1960; (with W.W. Bauer) Way to Womanhood 1965, To Enjoy Marriage, 1967; also mag. articles, radio scripts, one-act plays. Recipient award Friends of Lit. for Behold Your King, 1947. Mem. Soc. Midland Authors, Nat. League Am. Pen Women. Address: 406 Laurel Ave Wilmette IL 60091

BAUER, FRANK CHARLES, biostatistician; b. Milw., Sept. 28, 1910; s. Charles C. and Frieda (Herbst) B.; A.B., Beloit Coll., 1933; m. Margaret Elizabeth Rider, May 7, 1935; children—Barbara (Mrs. Gordon E. Fornell), F. Charles, Cynthia (Mrs. Emil Ludwig), William. Statistician, Works Project Adminstrn., Washington, Atlanta, 1934-36; chief results statistician US PHS, 1936-39; chief prodn. statistician Dept. of Justice, 1940-42; tech. adviser Census Bur., 1942-47; chief biostatistician Chgo. Bd. Health, 1948-68; analyst Bur. Labor Statistics, 1968-75; owner All Suburban Travel Agy., Western Springs. Mem. standing com. Nat. Office Vital Statistics. Pres. adult bd. dirs. Lyons Twp. Youth Orgn., 1958—; pres. LaGrange Park Recreation Assn.; del., assembly, coordinating com. Forest Road PTA; chmn. bd. LaGrange Park Little League; pres., del. assembly Dist. 102 Sch. Bd.; pres. Pony League Baseball, LaGrange Park, Ill.; v.p. Am. Legion Baseball, LaGrange Park; pres. Brookfield Sr. Babe Ruth Baseball. Fellow Am. Pub. Health Assn.; mem. Middle States, Ill. pub. health assns., Assn. State and Territorial Dirs. Research, Nat. Assn. Cost Accountants. Am. Statis. Assn., Am. Soc. Quality Control, Tau Kappa Epsilon. Mason (32 deg., Shriner). Author: Progress in the Prevention of Needless Neonatal Deaths, 1952. Contbr. numerous medico-statis. articles to sci. jours. Home: Route 2 Box B-84 Waupaca WI 54981 also 2008 Roma Way Boynton Beach FL 33435

BAUER, FREDERICK CHARLES, pathologist, educator; b. Champaign, Ill., Jan. 19, 1918; s. Frederick Charles and Louise Wallace (Garrett) B.; B.S., U. Ill., 1939; M.D., Harvard U., 1943; Ph.D., U. Chgo., 1949; m. Margaret Jane Vaniman, June 21, 1941; children—Richard Charles, Peter Frederick. Intern, St. Luke's Hosp., Chgo., 1943-44, resident in pathology. 1944-45, 47-49; asst. attending and attending pathologist St. Luke's Hosp. and Presbyn.-St. Luke's Hosp., Chgo., 1950-60; dir. dept. pathology Silver Cross Hosp., Joliet, Ill., 1960—, chief of staff, 1968-69; clin. asso. prof. pathology U. Ill. Bd. trustees Coll. of St. Francis. Served with M.C., U.S. Army, World War II. Seymour Coman fellow in pathology U. Chgo., 1947-49; diplomate Am. Bd. Pathology. Fellow A.C.P.; mem. Coll. Am. Pathologists, Am. Soc. Clin. Pathologists, Ill. Soc. Pathologists (pres.), Am. Assn. Pathologists, Internat. Acad. Pathology. Presbyn. Clubs: Rotary, Chgo. Yacht. Contbr. articles in pathology to med. jours. Office: Silver Cross Hosp 1200 Maple Rd Joliet IL 60432

BAUER, GRAYDON MILFORD, engring. cons.; b. Galien, Mich., July 4, 1921; s. William Fredrick and Venus (Hanover) B.; B.S. in Elec. Engring., Am. Tech. Inst., Chgo., 1941; postgrad. Acme Sch. Engring., 1948-49, Ind. U., 1957-58; m. Jean A. Ackerman, June 14, 1951; children—Archie A., Kevin L. Project engr. Clark Equipment Co., Buchanan, Mich., 1947; gen. mgr. Berrien Concrete Products Co., Galien, 1954-62: mfg. mgr., corporate engr. Walkden Concrete & Assos. Cos. (merger Berrien Concrete Products Co. and Walkden Cos.), 1956-63; ind. practice as constrn. engring. cons., 1963—; elec. cons. United Indsl. Engring Corp., Madison Heights, Mich., 1964-66; mfg. engr. Dodge Truck div. Chrysler Corp., Detroit, 1966-73, plant environ. control adminstr. Warren Truck Assembly Plants, 1973-75, mfg. facilities engr., 1975—; sec.-treas. Berrie Concrete Products Co., 1954; sec. Towne & Country Pools, Inc., 1962-65. Served with AUS, 1942-46. Mem. Welding Engrs. Soc., IEEE. Lion. Contbg. author: Electrical Standards, 1975. Home: 5895 Burnham Rd Bloomfield Hills MI 48013

BAUER, GREGORY ANTHONY, mfg. co. exec.; b. Chgo., Jan. 17, 1928; s. Joseph and Helen (Syms) B.; B.S., Ill. Inst. Tech., 1951; postgrad. Indsl. Mgmt. Inst., Lake Forest Coll., 1965-69; m. Dorothy Elizabeth Petrusky, May 8, 1965; 1 dau., Martha. Prodn. supr. Merck & Co., Danville, Pa., 1951-53; devel. engr. Abbott Lab., Waukegan, Ill., 1953-55, pilot plant group leader, 1955-59, sect. head devel., 1960-67, mgr. devel., 1967-69, mgr. operation prodn., 1969—. Chmn. Planning Commn., Wadsworth, Ill., 1963—, Zoning Bd. Appeals, 1963—. Served with AUS, 1947-48. Mem. Am. Inst. Chem. Engrs. Recipient Abbott Sci. Achievement award, 1964. Patentee in bulk pharms. Home: 3958 Elm Lane Waukegan IL 60085 Office: Abbott Labs North Chicago IL 60064

BAUER, HARLAN JOHN, publishing co. exec.; b. Cin., Dec. 11, 1916; s. Elmer John and Ione (Koehne) B.; student Case Inst., 1946-48; B.B.A., U. Cin., 1950; m. Carol Caliendo, Nov. 15, 1958; children—Harlan John, Betsy, Susan. With Peat, Marwick, Mitchell & Co., C.P.A.'s, Cin., 1950-53; div. controller Baldwin-Lima-Hamilton Corp., Waltham, Mass., 1953-60; dir. accounting Cummins Engine Co., Columbus, Ind., 1963-67; v.p., treas. Hitchcock Pub. Co., Wheaton, Ill., 1967—. Bd. dirs. So. States Indsl. Council, 1971—; treas. Town of Wheaton, 1976—. Served with USAAC, 1941-44. C.P.A., Ohio. Mem. Beta Gamma Sigma. Home: 1789 Gone Away Lane Wheaton IL 60187 Office: Hitchcock Publishing Co Hitchcock Bldg Wheaton IL 60187

BAUER, JOSEPH LEO, orthodontist; b. Springfield, Mo., Apr. 8, 1920; s. George L. and Mary Ann (White) B.; student S.W. Mo. State Coll., 1939-41; D.D.S., St. Louis U., 1945; M.S., U. Iowa, 1948; m. Olive Fern Egan, Oct. 26, 1946; children—Mary Therese (Mrs. Gary Kielhofner), Rebecca Diane, Joseph Leo II, Lauren Ann, Cynthia Louise, Peter Jeffrey. Practice orthodontics, Springfield, 1948—; vis. lectr. St. Louis U., 1950, asso. clin. prof., 1976—; mem. Mo. Splty. Bd., 1967—, chmn., 1972-76. Served with USNR, 1943-47. Fellow Am., Internat. colls. dentists; mem. Am., Mo., Springfield Dist. dental assns., Am., Mo. orthodontics assns., Charles Tweed Found. Orthodontic Research, C. of C. K.C. (grand knight 1955). Home: 2530 S Wallis Smith Ave Springfield MO 65804 Office: 1736 E Sunshine Blvd Plaza Towers Springfield MO 65804

BAUER, NANCY MCNAMARA, TV and radio network exec.; b. Madison, Wis., Mar. 17, 1929; d. Richard Hughes and Lucy Jane (Whitaker) Marshall; B.A., U. Wis., 1950, M.S., 1963; m. J.B. McNamara, Dec. 29, 1952 (div. Mar. 1962); children—Margaret Ann, William Patrick; m. 2d, Helmut Robert Bauer, Mar. 10, 1974. Elementary tchr., Madison, 1963-66; specialist ednl. communications U. Wis., Madison, 1966-71, asst. prof., 1971-72; dir. educative services Ednl. Communications Bd., Wis. Ednl. TV and Radio Networks, Madison, 1972—; dir. Central Ednl. Network, 1973—, exec. com., 1973-74, chmn. Instructional TV Council, 1977—; adv. bd. Instructional TV Co-op., 1972—, exec. com., 1976-77. Ford Found. scholar, 1961-63; recipient Ohio State award, 1975, Am. Bar Assn. Gavel award, 1975, Am. Legion Golden Mike award, 1976. Mem. Nat. Assn. Ednl. Broadcasters. Producer, writer numerous instructional series, as nationally distributed Patterns in Arithmetic and Looking Out Is In, TV, 1967, Inquiry: The Justice Thing, radio, 1973. Home: 127 Kensington Dr Madison WI 53704 Office: 732 N Midvale Blvd Madison WI 53705

BAUER, NORMAN WILLIAM, computer systems exec.; b. Bay City, Mich., Jan. 16, 1927; s. William John and Emma Margaret (Eichinger) B.; student Ga. Mil. Acad., 1944, Northeastern Sch. Commerce, Bay City, 1947-49; m. Arline Anita Bork, Sept. 9, 1950; children—Kathleen, David, Eric, Dan. Clk., C.D. Wood, Gulf Oil Co. distbr., Bay City, 1949-50; expediter Dow Chem. Co., Midland, Mich., 1951-57, sr. systems developer, 1958—. Served with U.S. Army, 1945-47, 50-51. Certified data processor. Mem. Am. Topical Assn., Luth. Laymen's League. Lutheran (mem. Aid Assn. for Lutherans). Home: 5434 Hilltop Dr Bay City MI 48706 Office: Dow Chemical 690 Bldg Midland MI 48640

BAUER, ROBERT OSCAR, univ. adminstr.; b. Pitts., Apr. 27, 1922; s. Oscar L. and Henrietta (Mohr) B.; B.S., Wichita State U., 1948; M.Litt., U. Pitts., 1949; postgrad. U. Ill., 1959-62; m. Florence Elizabeth Bunyar, July 9, 1943. Sales, Lever Bros. Co., 1940-42; mgr. Montgomery Ward & Co., 1949-52; buyer Hellums Furniture Co., Wichita, Kans., 1952-55, A.W. Hinkel, Wichita, 1955-57; asst. prof. Wichita State U., 1957-59; instr. U. Ill., 1959-62; adminstrv. asst., exec. v.p. Profl. Photographers Am., Milw.. 1962-65; asso. dir. adminstrv. service Univ. Extension, U. Wis., Milw., 1965—. Cons. to bus., mgmt., marketing. Served with USMCR, 1942-45, 51-52. Mem. Nat. Council Small Bus. Mgmt. Devel. (pres. 1973-74), Civitan Internat. (pres. 1958); Alpha Kappa Psi, Phi Mu Alpha. Baptist. Mason (Shriner). Editorial advisory bd. Jour. Small Bus. Mgmt., 1972—. Home: 5008 N Shoreland Ave Whitefish Bay WI 53217 Office: 929 N 6th St Milwaukee WI 53203

BAUER, RODNEY EDWARD, packaging co. exec.; b. Chgo., July 14, 1927; s. Adolph Edward and Lydia Bertha (Karp) B.; student Mass. Inst. Tech., 1945-46, 47-48; B.S. summa cum laude in Bus. Adminstrn., Northwestern U., 1949; m. Jane Randolph King, June 14, 1952; children—Wanda Louise, Pamela Randolph. With Kalamazoo Vegetable Parchment Co., paper and packaging, 1949-59, nat. accounts exec., 1956-59; Eastern sales mgr. Daubert Chem. Co., Chgo., 1959-63; Eastern sales mgr. Minerva Wax Paper Co. div. Alco Standard, Minerva, Ohio, 1963-68, v.p. mktg., 1968-71, pres., 1971—; dir. Minerva br. 1st Nat. Bank Canton (Ohio). Chmn. Bd. Edn. Gloria Dei Luth. Sch., Teaneck, N.J., 1957-59; chmn. Rotary-Minerva Exchange Student program, 1970-72. Served with AUS, 1946-47, 50-51. Mem. Northwestern U. Alumni Assn., Am. Forestry Assn., Nat. Rifle Assn., Beta Gamma Sigma, Kappa Sigma. Lutheran (v.p. congregation 1970-72). Clubs: New York Athletic; Canton; Atwood Yacht (Dellroy, O.). Home: 4165 Surrey Dr Minerva OH 44657 Office: Minerva Wax Paper Co 310 Grant Blvd Minerva OH 44657

BAUER, WILLIAM JOSEPH, judge; b. Chgo., Sept. 15, 1926; s. William Francis and Lucille (Gleason) B.; A.B., Elmhurst Coll., 1949; J.D., De Paul U., 1952; m. Mary Nicol, Jan. 28, 1950; children—Patricia, Linda. Admitted to Ill. bar, 1951; partner firm Erlenborn, Bauer & Hotte, Elmhurst, 1953-64; asst. state's atty., Du Page County, Ill., 1952-56, 1st asst. state's atty., 1956-58, state's atty., 1959-64; judge Jud. Circuit Ct., 1964-70; U.S. atty., 1970-71; judge U.S. Dist. Ct., 1971-75, U.S. Ct. Appeals, 1975—. Instr. bus. law Elmhurst Coll., 1952-59. Trustee Meml. Hosp. Du Page; bd. dirs. Elmhurst Coll. Pres. Elmhurst Young Republicans, 1958-59. Served with AUS, 1945-47. Mem. Am., Ill., Du Page County bar assns., Ill. State's Attys. Assn. (dir.). Roman Catholic. Clubs: Glen Oak Country (Glen Ellyn, Ill.); Union League (Chgo.). Home: 213 Grace St Elmhurst IL 60126 Office: 219 S Dearborn St Chicago IL 60604

BAUERMEISTER, HERMAN OTTO, lawyer; b. St. Louis, Jan. 18, 1914; s. Herman Kristian and Anne (Hohl) B.; B.S., Armour Inst. Tech., 1937; M.S., Ill. Inst. Tech., 1941; J.D., DePaul U., 1946; m. Caroline Jespersen, Aug. 5, 1939; m. 2d, Patty S. Slocombe, Mar. 26, 1971. Admitted to Mo., Ill., Ohio D.C. bars; chem. engr. Commonwealth Edison Co., Chgo., 1937-40; patent examiner U.S. Patent Office, Washington, 1940-42; research engr. Sinclair Refining Co., East Chicago, Ind., 1942-46; patent atty. Monsanto Co., St. Louis, 1946—. Mem. Am. Bar Assn., Am. Patent Law Assn., Am. Chem. Soc., Am. Photog. Soc. Home: 617 Candleberry Dr St Louis MO 63122 Office: 800 N Lindbergh Blvd St Louis MO 63166

BAUGHN, MICHAEL LYNN, educator; b. Colby, Kans., Apr. 30, 1948; s. James Leslie and Wilma Jean (Burkhead) B.; A.B., Asbury Coll., 1970; M.S., Ft. Hays Kans. State Coll., 1976; Tchr., Brewster (Kans.) Unified Sch. Dist., 1970-76, instr. secondary social studies, 1970—, prin., 1976—; curator Butterfield Trail Mus., 1966-73, elementary supr., 1973-76. Dep. sheriff Thomas County, 1970—, Logan County, 1970—, dir. Brewster Civil Def., 1971—; city marshal, Brewster, 1970-74; mem. Brewster City Council, 1974—; pres., Butterfield Trail Assn., 1974—; chmn. Hi-Plains History Commn., 1971-73, dir. pub. relations, 1973—; vol. rural fireman, 1975—; precinct committeeman Republican party, 1974—; justice of peace, 1972-74. Mem. Northwestern Plains Am. Revolution Bicentennial Park Assn. (pres. 1974—), Western Plains Arts Council (sec. 1973-74). Clubs: Masons (past master), Shriners, Lions (pres. 1975). Home: PO Box 216 Brewster KS 67732 Office: Unified Sch Dist No 314 Brewster KS 67732

BAUM, MICHAEL HARVEY, urban mgmt. analyst; b. Massillon, Ohio, Aug. 16, 1949; s. Harvey and Agnes Joyce (Bowles) B.; A.A., U. Cin., 1969, B.S. in Secondary Edn., 1972; M. Pub. Adminstrn., Kent State U., 1975; m. Mary Ann Kennedy, Mar. 16, 1972. Substitute tchr. Cin. and Canton (Ohio) schs., 1972-75; with pub. service City of Canton, 1975—, cons. to mayor, 1976, now coordinator environ. affairs; cons. Model Cities Program of Cin., 1972. Mem. steering com. Citizens Council to NEFCO, Northeastern Ohio 4-County Planning Orgn.; mem. ICMA Proj. Solid Waste Mgmt. Transfer Team. Bd. dirs. Canton Ecology Center; coordinator student programs Cin. YMCA, 1968-72; mem. Cin. Human Relations Commn., 1970-72. Mem. Am. Soc. for Pub. Adminstrn., Internat. City Mgmt. Assn., Govt. Refuse Collection and Disposal Assn., Am. Pub. Works Assn., Inst. Solid Waste, Inst. Equipment Services, Street Maintenance and Sanitation Ofcls. of Ohio (participant Ann. Conf. 1976), Am. Pub. Works Hist. Soc., Ohio Acad. Sci. (sect. ecol. and adminstrv. sci.), Jaycees, Greater Canton C. of C., Beta Gamma Sigma, Pi Alpha Alpha. Republican. Roman Catholic. Club: Toastmasters. Home: 811 Bennington Ave NE Massillon OH 44646 Office: Canton City Hall 6th Floor 218 Cleveland Ave SW Canton OH 44702

BAUM, WERNER A., univ. chancellor; b. Giessen, Germany, Apr. 10, 1923; s. Theodor and Beatrice (Klee) B.; m. Shirley Bowman, Jan. 20, 1945; children—Janice Michelle, Sandra Roslyn; came to U.S., 1933, naturalized, 1934; B.S., U. Chgo., 1943, M.S., 1944, Ph.D., 1948; D.Sc., Mt. St. Joseph Coll., 1971; D.P.A., Husson Coll., 1972; D.Sc., U. R.I., 1974. Teaching asst. U. Chgo., 1943, instr., 1943-44, 47, research asst., 1946; research asso., asst. prof. U. Md., 1947-49; asso. prof., head dept. meteorology Fla. State U., 1949-51, prof., head dept., 1951-58, dir. univ. research, 1957-58, dean Grad. Sch., dir. research, 1958-60, dean faculties, 1960-63; v.p. acad. affairs, prof. meteorology U. Miami, 1963-65; v.p. sci. affairs, prof. meteorology N.Y. U., 1965-67; dep. adminstr. Enviro. Sci. Services Adminstrn., 1967-68; pres., prof. geography and physics U. R.I., Kingston, 1968-73; chancellor U. Wis., Milw., 1973—; mem. sci. adv. council Tex. Christian U. Research Found., 1967-73, 74—; trustee Univ. Corp. for Atmospheric Research, 1959-63, 65-67, corp. sec., 1963-67, chmn. joint evaluation com., 1972; U.S. rep., panel experts on meteorol. edn. and tng. World Meteorol. Organ., UN, 1971—; mem. Nat. Adv. Com. on Oceans and Atmosphere, 1971-73, 76-77, Nat. Sea Grant Program Adv. Panel, 1974—. Mem. Greater Milw. Com. for Community Devel., 1975—; bd. dirs. Milw. Symphony Orch., 1974, Greater Milw. Survey Social Welfare and Health Services, Inc., 1974—; hon. dir. Goethe House, Milw., 1973; treas., mem. exec. com. Com. Urban Program Univs., 1976—; life-time trustee U. R.I. Fellow Am. Meteorol. Soc. (Spl. citation 1962, Charles Franklin Brooks award 1975, pres. 1977—), Am. Geophys. Union, AAAS; mem. Phi Beta Kappa, Sigma Xi, Phi Kappa Phi, Beta Gamma Sigma, Chi Epsilon Pi, Sigma Pi Sigma. Clubs: Cosmos (Washington); Univ. (Milw.). Recipient Honors medal Fla. Acad. Scis., 1964; Author: Russian-English Dictionary of Meteorological Terms and Expressions, 1950; contbr. articles to sci. jours. Home: 4430 N Lake Dr Milwaukee WI 53211 Office: U Wis PO Box 413 Milwaukee WI 53201

BAUMAN, GEORGE DUNCAN, publisher; b. Humboldt, Iowa, Apr. 12, 1912; s. Peter William and Mae (Duncan) B.; student Loyola U., Chgo., 1930-35; J.D., Washington U., St. Louis, 1948; Litt.D. (hon.), Central Methodist Coll.; m. Nora Kathleen Kelly, May 21, 1938. Reporter, Chgo. Herald Examiner, 1931-39; archtl. rep. Pratt & Lambert, Inc., Chgo. and St. Louis, 1939-43; with St. Louis Globe-Democrat, 1943—, personnel mgr., 1951-59, bus. mgr., 1959-67, publisher, 1967—; dir. City Bank St. Louis. Bd. dirs. Boys Clubs Am., 1969—, St. Louis YMCA, 1967-72, St. Louis City Welfare Commn., 1967-70, Better Bus. Bur., 1968-72, St. Louis Municipal Theatre Assn., 1968—, St. Louis Symphony Soc., 1968—, Arts and Edn. Council, 1972—; mem. lay adv. bd. St. Vincent's Hosp., 1952—, pres. 1957-58; mem. voting membership bd. Blue Shield, 1968-77; mem. nat. citizen's adv. com. Assn. Am. Med. Colls., 1975—; mem. lay adv. bd. DePaul Community Health Center, 1975—; adv. bd. St. Louis Med. Soc., 1976—; mem. exec. bd. St. Louis council Boy Scouts Am., 1967—, mem. Pres.'s council St. Louis U., 1968—; bd. visitors Mo. Mil. Acad., 1970—; mem. adv. bd. Newman Chapel, 1964—, pres., 1968—; bd. dirs. Policemen and Firemen Fund St. Louis, 1959—, sec., 1963-69, pres., 1969-70; bd. dirs. Herbert Hoover Boys Club, St. Louis, 1966—, pres., 1968, 76; bd. dirs. United Way Greater St. Louis, 1964—, mem. exec. com., 1964— v.p., 1968-71; chmn. exec. com. and regional adv. com. Bi-State Regional Med. Program, 1968-75; bd. dirs. Health and Welfare Council Met. St. Louis, 1960-70, pres., 1965-67; bd. dirs. Sec. Bd. Election Commns., St. Louis, 1957-61; bd. dirs. Catholic Charities, 1967—, pres., 1969-70; bd. dirs. Child Center Our Lady of Grace, 1965, pres., 1965-68; bd. dirs. Jr. Achievement Mississippi Valley, 1953-74, v.p., 1968; mem. Conv. and Visitors Bur. of Greater St. Louis, 1968-77, v.p., 1974, pres., 1975-76; bd. dirs. Dismas House, 1964-73, pres., 1968; bd. dirs. Human Life Found., 1973—, Downtown St. Louis, Inc., 1977—; trustee Mo. Baptist Hosp., 1970—, exec. com., 1974—, treas., 1977—; trustee Jefferson Nat. Expansion Meml. Assn., 1968—, Mo. Pub. Expenditure Survey, 1968—, Freedoms Found. at Valley Forge, 1968-75, David Ranken Jr. Tech. Inst., 1969—, Nat. Jewish Hosp. and Research Center, 1970—, Govtl. Research Inst., 1968—. Decorated Knight of Malta; recipient Distinguished Alumnus citation Washington U., 1972, Bus. Leader of Year award Religious Heritage Am., 1973, citation Loyola U. Alumni Assn., 1973; named to Loyola U. Athletic Hall of Fame, 1976. Mem. Am. Newspaper Pubs. Assn., Am. Soc. Newspaper Editors, Newspaper Personnel Relations Assn. (past pres.), Mo. (dir. 1969-74), St. Louis (exec. com. 1969-73, dir. 1969-73) chambers commerce, Mo. Acad. Squires, Bar Assn. St. Louis, Am., Mo. bar assns., Advt. Club of St. Louis (gov. 1972-75). Club: Media (dir. 1968—) (St. Louis). Home: 6233 Northwood Ave St Louis MO 63105 Office: St Louis Globe-Democrat 12th Blvd at Convention Plaza St Louis MO 63101

BAUMAN, ROBERT EDWARD, aero. engr.; b. St. Charles, Mo., July 15, 1937; s. Roman and Dorthea (Fisher) B.; B.S. in Aero. Engring., St. Louis U., 1958, M.S., 1966; children—Michael, Cynthia, Stephanie. With Emerson Electric Co., St. Louis, 1958—, sr. engr. aeromechanics group, 1972-74, group. engr. airborne and rocket systems group, 1975—. Mem. Am. Inst. Aeros. and Astronautics, Emerson Engrs. Club. Patentee in field. Home: 3012 Ridgeview Saint Charles MO 63301 Office: Emerson Electric Co 8100 Florissant Saint Louis MO 63136

BAUMEISTER, CARL F., physician; b. Dolliver, Iowa, May 15, 1907; s. Charles F. and Lida Bard (Moore) B.; B.S.; Chicago U., 1930; M.D., Iowa U., 1933; m. Eleanor Hoskins, Apr. 19, 1930; children—Richard. Physician. internal med., Ind. U. Hosps., 1933-36, Louisville U. Hosps., 1936-37, Council Bluffs Clinic, 1937-43, Berwyn (Ill.) Surburban Med. Center, since 1943; mem. staff MacNeal Meml. Hosp., Berwyn; instr. internal medicine U. Ill., 1943-50, clin. asst. prof., 1950-71, 73—; clin. asst. prof. medicine Stritch Sch. Medicine Loyola U., Maywood, Ill., 1971-73; med. staff Loyola U. Hosp., 1971-73. Fellow Inst. of Medicine Chgo.; member AMA, Am. Heart Assn., Assn. Am. Med. Colls., Am. Med. Writers Assn., Am. Diabetes Assn., S.A.R., N.Y. Acad. Sci. Mason. Contbr. articles to med. jours. Abstract editor on med. education Excerpta Medica of Amsterdam. Author: Computer Diagnosis of the Acute Surgical Abdomen. Research diagnosis and treatment new type vascular headache. Home: 120 S Delaplaine Rd Riverside IL 60546 Office: 3340 S Oak Park Ave Berwyn IL 60402

BAUMEISTER, ELEANOR H. (MRS. CARL F. BAUMEISTER), club woman; b. Lake Linden, Mich., Oct. 2, 1909; d. Thomas and Sarah (Madigan) Hoskins; B.; Music Edn., U. Minn., 1930; m. Carl Frederick Baumeister, Apr. 19, 1930; 1 son, Richard. Co-founder, advt. mgr. The Corn Belt Livestock Feeder trade mag., 1948-51. Publicity dir. Patron's Council, Riverside-Brookfield High Sch., 1951-53; pres. MacNeal Meml. Hosp. Women's Auxiliary, 1956, mem. adv. bd., 1957. Bd. dirs. Riverside Pub. Library, 1961-71, pres., 1967-71; dir. Ill. P.E.O. Home, Knoxville, 1956-58, fin. adviser, 1958-63; vice chmn. bd. dirs. Southwest Suburban chpt. Am. Cancer Soc., 1968-69, chmn. bd. dirs. Central Suburban unit, 1969-71, sec.-treas. Central Suburban unit, 1972—; sec. Dist. 208 Caucus; mem. citizens adv. bd. Morton Coll. Sch. Nursing, 1972—. Mem. Gen. Fedn. Women's Clubs, P.E.O. (pres. Riverside 1955-56, 60-61, Ill. corr. sec., 1956-57, rec. sec. 1957-58). Republican. Presbyterian. Clubs: Chgo. Farmers, Riverside Woman's (pres. 1954-56, chmn. auditing com. 1963). Home: 120 S Delaplaine Rd Riverside IL 60546

BAUMHART, RAYMOND CHARLES, univ. pres.; b. Chgo., Dec. 22, 1923; s. Emil and Florence (Weidner) B.; B.S., Northwestern U., 1945; Ph.L., Loyola U., 1952, S.T.L., 1958; M.B.A., Harvard, 1953, D.B.A., 1963. Ordained priest Roman Catholic Ch., 1957; asst. prof. mgmt. Loyola U., Chgo., 1962-64, dean Sch. Bus. Adminstrn., 1964-66, exec. v.p., acting v.p. Med. Center, 1968-70, pres., 1970—; research fellow Cambridge Center for Social Studies, 1966-68; dir. Continental Ill. Corp. Jewel Cos., Inc. Trustee Boston Coll., St. Louis U. Served to lt. (j.g.) USNR, 1944-46. John W. Hill fellow Harvard, 1961-62. Mem. Assn. Jesuit Colls. and Univs. (dir.), Nat. Council Better Bus. Burs. (dir.), Fedn. Ind. Ill. Colls. and Univs. (dir.). Clubs:

Commercial, Mid-America (Chgo.). Author: An Honest Profit, 1968; (with Thomas Garrett) Cases in Business Ethics, 1968; (with Thomas McMahon) The Brewer-Wholesaler Relationship, 1969. Corr. editor: America, 1965-70. Home: 6525 N Sheridan Rd Chicago IL 60626

BAUMHOEFNER, ARLEN HENRY, mfg. exec.; b. Watawon County, Minn., Nov. 28, 1945; s. Oscar Otto and Lillain Emma (Kahler) B.; B.A., Concordia Coll., 1967; postgrad. U. Tenn., 1973; grad. Coll. Advanced Traffic and Transp., 1971. Mgmt. trainee N.W. Bell Telephone Co., Fargo, N.D., 1967-68; asst. traffic mgr. Wilson-Sinclair, Albert Lea, Minn., 1968-71; distbn. mgr. Sharpe Mfg. Co., Mpls., 1971-73; gen. mgr. Trend Devel. Corp., Mpls., 1973-76; pres., owner ABI Corp., Mpls., 1976—. Named Jaycee of month, 1970. Mem. Nat. Council Phys. Distbn. and Mgmt., Am. Soc. Traffic and Transp., Delta Nu Alpha. Republican. Lutheran. Home and office: 429 S Oliver Ave Minneapolis MN 55405

BAUTISTA, RENATO GO, educator; b. Manila, Philippines, Mar. 27, 1934; s. Teodulo and Felicidad (Tiongko-Go) B.; B.S. in Chem. Engring., U. Santo Tomas, Philippines, 1955; S.M., Mass. Inst. Tech., 1957; Ph.D., U. Wis., 1961. Asst. assayer Philex Mining Corp., Philippines, 1955; research metallurgist Allis Chalmers Mfg. Co., Milw., 1957-58, A. Soriano Corp., Manila, Philippines, 1963-67; research asso., U. Wis., Madison, 1961-63, Rice U., Houston, 1967-69; asso. prof. chem. engring. Iowa State U., Ames, 1969-75, 76—; vis. scientist Warren Spring Lab., Stevenage, U.K., 1975-76; vis. prof. dept. material sci. and metallurgy Imperial Coll., London, 1976. Mem. Am. Inst. Chem. Engrs., Am. Inst. Mining, Metall. and Petroleum Engrs., Am. Chem. Soc., Sigma Xi, Phi Lambda Upsilon. Contbr. articles to profl. jours. Patentee in field. Home: 3404 Buchanan Ct Ames IA 50010

BAXTER, CHARLES MORLEY, educator, poet; b. Mpls., May 13, 1947; s. John Thomas and Mary Barber (Eaton) B.; B.A., Macalester Coll., 1969; Ph.D., State U. N.Y. at Buffalo, 1974; m. Martha Ann Hauser, July 12, 1976. Asst. prof. dept. English, Wayne State U., Detroit, 1974—. Wallace fellow, 1967. Mem. Phi Beta Kappa. Asso. editor The Minn. Rev., 1968-69; editor Audit/Poetry, 1973-74; asst. editor Criticism, 1976—; author: (poetry) The South Dakota Guidebook, 1974, Chameleon, 1970; also articles, short stories. Home: 1585 Woodland Dr Ann Arbor MI 48103 Office: Dept English Wayne State U Detroit MI 48202

BAXTER, JOSEPH DIEDRICH, dentist; b. New Albany, Ind., Sept. 11, 1937; s. James William, Jr. and Beatrice (Diedrich) B.; A.B., Ind. U., 1959, D.M.D., U. Louisville, 1969; m. Carroll Jane Bell, Dec. 23, 1972. Practice dentistry, New Albany, 1969—. Bd. dirs. Floyd County (Ind.) Econ. Opportunity Corp., 1971-76. Served with AUS, 1960-61. Mem. Floyd County Dental Soc. (pres. 1972-74), Am. Dental Assn., Phi Gamma Delta. Republican. Methodist. Home: 36 Bellewood Dr New Albany IN 47150 Office: Professional Arts Bldg New Albany IN 47150

BAXTER, LORAN FRANCIS, mfg. co. exec.; b. Omaha, Mar. 30, 1926; s. Harold Cameron and Valerie Muriel (Ganow) B.; B.A., U. Nebr., 1948; M.A., So. Methodist U., 1950; Ph.D., U. Colo., 1957; m. Margaret Lehfeldt, June 6, 1948; children—Loran Francis, Judith. Cons. psychologist J.R. Martin Assos., N.Y.C., 1957-60; with Babcock & Wilcox, Barberton, Ohio, 1960—, mgr. market sales, 1968-70, gen. mgr., 1970—. Mem. adv. bd. Barberton Tech. Sch., 1960-62, chmn. adv. com. County 4H, 1971-73, Children and Family Service Soc., 1960-68. Served with USNR, 1943-46, AUS, 1950-53. USPHS fellow, 1953-55; VA psychology tng. grantee, 1956-57. Mem. Barberton C. of C. Republican. Methodist. Home: 4000 Shaw Rd Akron OH 44313 Office: 1501 Raff Rd SW Canton OH 44710

BAXTER, MARILYNN RUTH, educator; b. Chgo.; d. George Byron and Ruth Quinn (Hurd) Baxter; B.A., State U. Ia., 1958; postgrad. U. Edinburgh, 1960, Sch. Actor's Co., N.Y.C., 1963; M.A., U. Wis., 1965, Ph.D., 1973; postgrad. Lee Strasberg Dir.-Actor Workshop, 1968, Shakespeare Summer Sch., U. Birmingham (Eng.), 1973. Spl. events coordinator Marshall Field & Co., Chgo., 1958-60; with Barter Theatre, Abingdon, Va., 1962; instr., supr. dept. curriculum and instruction U. Wis., 1964-67; mem. communications faculty, dir. Parkside Players, U. Wis. at Parkside, Kenosha, 1967-74; asst. prof. speech communication and theatre U. Wis.-Whitewater, 1975—. Mem. U. Wis. Arts Council, 1969-70, Greater Kenosha Arts Council, 1969-78; mem. Kenosha County Am. Revolution Bicentennial Commn. Ford Found. fellow, 1967. Mem. Am. Theatre Assn., Speech Assn. Am., Central States Speech Assn., D.A.R. (regent chpt. 1974-77, Wis. chaplain 1977—), AAUW, Soc. Mayflower Descs., Nat. Soc. Magna Charta Dames, Plantagenet Soc., Wis. Theatre Assn., U. Wis. Alumni Assn., Kappa Alpha Theta (pres. chpt. 1957-58, mem. adv. bd. chpt. 1965-67). Home: 4627 Spring Brook Rd Rockford IL 61111 Office: University of Wis Whitewater WI 53190

BAXTER, REGINALD ROBERT, plant food co. exec.; b. Cushman, Ark., May 14, 1925; s. Remmel and Mary (Wilson) B.; B.S. in Chem. Engring., U. Ark., 1948; M.S., Iowa State U., 1949; m. Jameson Adkins, Jan., 1976; 1 son, Sean Lee. With Pan-Am. So. Refineries, Standard Oil Co. of Ind., New Orleans, 1949-56; with Standard Oil of N.J., Cartegena, Colombia, 1956-63; Esso Research & Engring., N.J., 1963-65, First Nitrogen Corp., Donaldsonville, La., 1965-67; v.p.-mfg. CF Industries, Inc., Long Grove, Ill., 1967-69, exec. v.p.-mfg., 1969-71, pres., 1971—; pres. Energy Coop., Inc., Long Grove, Ill., 1976-77; pres. Agri-Trans; dir. LVO Internat. Co-chmn. Nat. Com. on Locks and Dam 26, 1976-77. Mem. Intternat. Phosphate Industry Assn. (exec. com. 1975-76), Nat. Council Farmer Coops. (dir. 1971—). Office: CF Industries Inc Salem Lake Dr Long Grove IL 60515

BAYER, HARMON SYMOND, mgmt. cons. co. exec.; b. Boston, Sept. 11, 1919; s. Abraham Henry and Miriam (Opp) B.; B.S., U. Mich., 1941; m. Adele Anne Allen, Dec. 20, 1941; children—Edward A., Charles S., Gerald E., Irene S. San. engr. USPHS, Washington, 1941-43; research and devel. engr. Peninsular Grinding Wheel Co., Detroit, 1946-49; head staff quality control engring. Ford div. Ford Motor Co., Dearborn, Mich., 1949-52; pres. Bayer & McElrath, Inc., Mgmt. Cons., Orchard Lake, Mich., 1952-77; pres. Harmon S. Bayer & Assos., W. Bloomfield, Mich., 1978—; vis. lectr. U. Mich., Ann Arbor, 1955-70, Wayne State U., Detroit, 1949-52, Mich. State U., E. Lansing, 1952-55, Marquette U., Milw., 1952-55. Served to capt., San. Corps, AUS, 1943-46. Registered profl. engr., Calif. Fellow Am. Soc. Quality Control, AAAS; mem. Am. Mgmt. Assn. Contbr. articles to profl. jours. Home: 6873 E Knollwood Circle West Bloomfield MI 48033 Office: 6668 Orchard Lake Rd Suite 203 West Bloomfield MI 48033

BAYH, BIRCH E., JR., senator; b., 1928; s. Birch E. Bayh; grad. Purdue U. Sch. Agr., Ind. U. Law Sch.; m. Marvella; 1 son, Evan. Mem. Ind. legislature, 8 years, speaker Ind. Ho. of Reps., 1959, minority leader, 1957, 61; mem. U.S. Senate from Ind., 1963—, chmn. Transp. Appropriations Com. Owner farm nr. Terre Haute, Ind. Named one of Am.'s Ten Outstanding Young Men, U.S. Jr. C. of C., 1963. Democrat. Home: Rural Route 2 West Terre Haute IN 47808 Office: Room 363 Russell Senate Office Bldg Washington DC 20510

BAYLY, MELVYN ARTHUR, obstetrician and gynecologist; b. Jarrow, Alta., Can., Oct. 16, 1919; s. Milton Dawson and Myrtle Ivy (Waite) B.; came to U.S., 1920, naturalized, 1925; A.B., DePauw U., 1940; M.D., Northwestern U., 1943, postgrad., 1944, 46, 48-49; postgrad. Harvard U., 1946-47; m. Lila Ann Seneff, June 12, 1942; children—Melvyn Arthur, Marsha (Mrs. Robert Brown Schoene), Ronald Dawson, Philip Scott. Intern, Wesley Meml. Hosp., Chgo., 1943-44, resident, 1944, 48, 49; resident Boston Lying-In Hosp., 1946-47; practice medicine specializing in obstetrics and gynecology, Chgo., 1949—; mem. courtesy staff Wesley Meml. Hosp., 1949-52, asst. attending, 1952-55, asso. attending, 1955-58, sr. attending, 1958—; attending physician Northwestern Meml. Hosp., 1973—, chief staff, 1970-71; attending physician Chgo. Maternity Center, 1949-68, chmn. dept. obstetrics and gynecology, 1970-73; chief obstetrics and gynecology Wesley Pavilion, Northwestern Meml. Hosp., 1973—; mem. med. staff Women's Hosp., 1972—, chief of gynecology, 1974—; chmn. med. adv. com. McGaw Med. Center, 1974—; instr. Northwestern Med. Sch., 1952-54, asso. prof., 1954-58, asst. prof., 1958, asso. prof., 1968-71, prof., 1971—. Mem. exec. com. Ill. Sch. Dist. 202, 1965-66; committeeman, Boy Scouts Am., 1954-70. Bd. dirs. Chgo. Wesley Meml. Hosp., 1970-73. Served with M.C., AUS, 1945-47; ETO. Diplomate Am. Bd. Obstetrics and Gynecology. Fellow A.C.S., Am. Coll. Obstetricians and Gynecologists, Central Assn. Obstetricians and Gynecologists, Chgo. Inst. Medicine; mem. AMA, Ill., Chgo. med. socs., Chgo. Gynecol. Soc., Sigma Nu, Nu Sigma Nu. Clubs: Glen View, Klinger Lake. Contbr. chpts. to books, articles to profl. jours. Home: 1215 Forest Ave Evanston IL 60202 Office: 333 E Superior St Chicago IL 60611

BAZARKO, VOLODYMYR OREST, lawyer; b. Myciw, Ukraine, June 14, 1940; s. Ivan and Natalia (Saykewych) B.; came to U.S., 1949, naturalized, 1958; B.S. with honors, Pratt Inst., 1962; M.S., John Carroll U., 1966; J.D. cum laude, Cleve. State U., 1970; m. Lydia Z. Chylak, Aug. 24, 1963; children—Andrew, George. Research engr. NASA, Lewis Research Center, 1962-63, aerospace research engr., 1965-69; v.p. Mural & Son, Inc., 1969-71; admitted to Ohio bar, 1970; partner firm Bazarko, Futey and Oryshkewych, Cleve., 1971—; tchr. real estate law John Carroll U., 1973—. Served with C.E., U.S. Army, 1963-65. Mem. Am., Cleve., Cuyahoga County bar assns., Ukrainian Nat. Republican Fedn. (treas.), Shevchenko Sci. Soc. (bd. dirs.). Contbr. articles to profl. jours. Home: 8400 Oak Knoll Ct North Royalton OH 44133 Office: 5691 State Rd Parma OH 44134

BEACH, HARRY ADAM, judge; b. Bloomingdale, Mich., July 8, 1938; s. Harry William and Cecile Mildred (Emmons) B.; B.A., Western Mich. U., 1960; LL.B., Wayne State U., 1963; m. Donna Marie Longjohn, June 12, 1964; children—Adam, Marcy, Matthew. Admitted to Mich. bar, 1963; mem. firm Wickett, Erickson & Beach, Plainwell, Mich., 1963-76; dist. judge 57th Dist. Ct., Allegan, Mich., 1976—. Commr., Allegan County Bd., 1968-72; chmn. Allegan Dept. Pub. Works, 1969-76. Bd. dirs. Plainwell Sr. Citizens Home. Mem. Allegan County (pres. 1976), Kalamazoo County bar assns., Plainwell Jr. C. of C. (dir.). Mason, Elk, Rotarian, Kiwanian. Home: 1197 103d Ave Plainwell MI 49080 Office: Dist Ct Offices Allegan County Bldg Allegan MI 49010

BEACH, LESLIE ROBERT, educator, psychologist; b. Crystal Valley, Mich., Aug. 29, 1926; s. Harry Romaine and Eva May (Wightman) B.; B.A., Houghton Coll., 1949; M.Ed., Wayne State U., 1954; Ph.D., U. Mich., 1957; m. Carla Mae Cannon, Dec. 6, 1963; children—Randall, Lisa, Michael. Instr. psychology Gen. Motors Inst., Flint, Mich., 1949-57; asso. prof. Whitworth Coll., 1957-63; asso. prof. edn. Bowling Green State U., 1963-64; prof. psychology Hope Coll., 1964—, chmn. dept., 1968-71, 74—; adj. prof. U. Mich. Extension, 1968—. Cons. Ottawa County (Mich.) Community Mental Health Services. Served with USNR, 1944-46, 51-52. Kettering Found. grantee, 1961-63, NIMH grantee, 1964-65; U.S. Office Edn. grantee, 1966-68; certified cons. psychologist, Mich. Mem. Am., Midwestern psychol. assns., Assn. Humanistic Psychology. Presbyn. (elder). Author: Psychology in Business, 1957; also articles. Home: 221 W 12th St Holland MI 49423 Office: Hope Coll Holland MI 49423

BEACHLER, KENNETH CLARKE, univ. adminstr.; b. Battle Creek, Mich., Oct. 11, 1935; s. Hubert Waldo and Nina Kathryn (Eitelbuss) B.; B.A. with high honors, Mich. State U., 1963. Profl. actor and singer, Chgo., 1955-57; radio announcer WKAR-AM/FM, East Lansing, Mich., 1959-62, WSWM-FM, East Lansing, 1962-64; music program dir. WKAR-FM, East Lansing, 1964-70; dir. lecture concert series Mich. State U., East Lansing, 1971—. Host weekly radio program Arts Billboard, 1972—. Mem. media relations com. Ingham County United Community Chest, 1969-70; chmn. pub. relations Met. Lansing Arts Council, 1970-72. Bd. dirs. Lansing Symphony Orch., 1971-73, Okemos Barn Theatre, 1970-71. Served with AUS, 1957-59. Named Best Actor Okemos Barn Theatre, 1974. Mich. State U. Bd. Trustees tuition scholar, 1960, Hinman Broadcasting scholar, 1961-63. Mem. Internat. Soc. Performing Arts Adminstrs. (dir. 1974—), Assn. Coll., Univ. and Community Arts Adminstrs. Mem. United Ch. of Christ. Rotarian. Home: 1450 Hitching Post Rd East Lansing MI 48823 Office: Mich State U East Lansing MI 48824

BEADLE, GEORGE WELLS, biologist, educator; b. Wahoo, Nebr., Oct. 22, 1903; s. Chauncey Elmer and Hattie (Albro) B.; B.S., U. Nebr., 1926, M.S., 1927, D.Sc. (hon.), 1949; Ph.D., Cornell U., 1931; M.A., Oxford U., 1958, D.Sc. (hon.), 1959; D.Sc. (hon.), Yale U., 1947, Northwestern U., 1952, Rutgers U., 1954, Kenyon Coll., 1955, Wesleyan U., 1956, U. Birmingham, 1959, Pomona Coll., 1961, Lake Forest Coll., 1962, U. Rochester, 1963, U. Ill., 1963, Brown U., 1964, Kans. State U., 1964, U. Pa., 1964, Wabash Coll., 1966, Syracuse U., 1967, Loyola U., Chgo., 1970, Hanover Coll., 1971, Eureka Coll., 1972, Butler U., 1973, Gustavus Adolphus, 1975, Ind. State U., 1976; LL.D. (hon.), U. Calif., Los Angeles, 1962, Miami U., 1963, Brandeis U., 1963, Johns Hopkins U., 1966, Beloit Coll., 1966, U. Mich., 1969; D.H.L., Jewish Theol. Sem. Am., 1966, DePaul U., 1969, U. Chgo., 1969, Canisius Coll., 1969, Knox Coll., 1969, Roosevelt U., 1971, Carroll Coll., 1971; D.Pub. Service (hon.), Ohio No. U., 1970; m. Marion Cecile Hill, Aug. 22, 1928 (div. 1953); 1 son, David; m. 2d, Muriel Barnett, Aug. 12, 1953; 1 stepson, Redmond James Barnett. Teaching asst. Cornell U., 1926-27, experimentalist, 1927-31; NRC fellow Calif. Inst. Tech., 1931-33, instr., 1933-35, prof. biology, chmn. div. biology, 1946-60, acting deal faculty, 1960-61; guest investigator Institut de Biologie Physicochimique, Paris, 1935; asst. prof. genetics Harvard U., 1936-37; prof. biology Stanford U., 1937-46; Eastman vis. prof. Oxford U., 1958-59; pres., trustee, prof. biology U. Chgo., 1961-68, pres. emeritus, William E. Wrather Distinguished Service prof. emeritus, hon. trustee, 1969—; mem. Pres.'s Sci. Adv. Com., 1960. Pres., Chgo. Hort. Soc., 1968-71; bd. dirs. Inst. Biomed. Research, AMA, 1968-70; trustee Mus. Sci. and Industry, Chgo., 1967-68, Nutrition Found., 1969-73, Pomona Coll., 1958-61, Calif. Inst. Tech., 1969-75; mem. sci. adv. bd. Robert A. Welch Found., 1971—. Mem. Nat. Acad. Sci. (council 1969-72), Am. Philos. Soc., Royal Soc., Danish Royal Acad. Sci., Japan Acad. (hon.), Instituto Lombardi di Scienze e Lettre (Milan), AAAS (pres. 1946), Am. Acad. Arts and Scis., Genetics Soc. Am. (pres. 1955), Genetic Soc. (Gt. Britain), Indian Soc. Genetics and Plant Breeding, Indian Nat. Sci. Acad. (hon.), Twelfth Internat. Congress Genetics (hon. pres. 1968), Phi Beta Kappa, Sigma Xi. Clubs: Tavern, Chgo. (Chgo.). Decorated Order St. Olaf; recipient Lasker award, 1950, Dyer award, 1951, Emil Christian Hansen prize (Denmark), 1953, Albert Einstein Commemorative award in sci., 1958, Nobel prize in physiology and medicine, 1958, Am. Cancer Soc. award, 1959, Kimber Genetics award, 1960, Priestley Meml. award, 1967, Edison award for best sci. book for youth, 1967, Donald Jones medal, 1972. Author: (with A.H. Sturtevant) An Introduction to Genetics, 1939; Genetics and Modern Biology, 1963; (with Muriel B. Beadle) The Language of Life, 1966. Home: 5533 S Dorchester Ave Chicago IL 60637 Office: Dept Biology U Chgo Chicago IL 60637

BEADLE, MURIEL MCCLURE BARNETT, civic worker, writer; b. Alhambra, Calif., Sept. 14, 1915; d. Richard and Eunice L. (Bothwell) McClure; B.A., Pomona Coll., 1936, LL.D., 1973; D.H.L., Mundelein Coll., 1966; m. Joseph Y. Barnett, July 3, 1941 (dec. Feb. 1951); 1 son, Redmond James; m. 2d, George Wells Beadle, Aug. 12, 1953. Advt. copywriter Carson Pirie Scott & Co., Chgo., 1936-40, Bullock's Pasadena (Calif.), 1945-48; fashion editor, women's editor Los Angeles Mirror-News, 1948-58; free-lance writer newspapers and mags., 1958—. Lectr. on edn. and social welfare, cons. various educator groups, 1957—; v.p. Pasadena Com. on Pub. Edn., 1957-60; mem. Pasadena Library Bd., 1959-61; chmn. Harper Ct. Found., Chgo., 1962-72. Recipient citation City of Pasadena, 1960, citation for service to pub. edn. Pasadena Edn. Assn., 1959, award Chgo. Friends of Lit., 1962, Thomas Alva Edison Found., 1967, Delta Kappa Gamma, 1971. Mem. Phi Beta Kappa, Delta Kappa Gamma. Democrat. Club: Fortnightly, Friday (Chgo.). Author: These Ruins Are Inhabited, 1961; (with husband) The Language of Life, 1966; A Child's Mind, 1970; Where Has All the Ivy Gone?, 1972; The Fortnightly of Chicago: The City and Its Women, 1873-1973, 1973; A Nice Neat Operation, 1975; The Cat, 1977. Address: 5533 Dorchester Ave Chicago IL 60637

BEAHM, EDGAR HIRAM, physician; b. Bison, Kans., Dec. 10, 1913; s. Frederich and Emma Marie (Stang) B.; A.B., U. Kans., 1937, M.A., 1939, M.D., 1944; m. Dorothy Beatrice Stillions, Sept. 7, 1938; children—Barbara Jean, Dorothy Catherine (Mrs. Kenneth R. Alvar), Edgar Eugene, Thomas Marion, Franklin David. Instr. bacteriology, Creighton U., 1939-41; intern Trinity Luth. Hosp., Kansas City, Mo., 1944; practice medicine, specializing in family practice, Independence, Kans., 1947—; chief staff Mercy Hosp, Independence, 1960, 66; dir. Montgomery County Health Dept., Independence, 1967—; med. adviser Montgomery County Draft Bd., 1949—. Active Boy Scouts of Am. Served as maj., M.C., AUS, 1944-46. Recipient award, Boy Scouts of Am., 1961. Fellow Am. Acad. Family Physicians (charter); mem. AMA (recognition award 1969, 72, 75), Kans., Southeast Kans. med. socs., Kans. State, Independence chambers commerce. Presbyterian (elder 1950—). Clubs: Elks, Masons (32 deg.), Shriners, Rotary. Home: 2600 N Penn Ave Independence KS 67301 Office: Profl Bldg Independence KS 67301

BEAL, BERT LEONARD, JR., elec. engr.; b. Birmingham, Ala., June 19, 1911; s. Bert Leonard and Catherine (Marks) B.; B.S., Washington U., St. Louis, 1934; m. Josephine Watkins, Feb. 24, 1943; 1 son, Albert G. Asst. mine mgr. So. Coal, Coke & Mining, Belleville, Ill., 1935-36; engr. Carrier Corp., Newark, 1936-37; asst. foreman, foreman tng. supr., engr., asst. gen. mech. supt. St. Joe Minerals Corp., Bonne Terre, Mo. 1937-54. gen. mech. supt., 1954-66, dir. engring., 1966-75; pres. Beal Enterprises, engring. cons. and agribus., 1975—; dir. Lead Belt Water Company. Active in civic affairs. Trustee Presbyterian Children's Home, bd. chmn., 1973. Served from lt. to lt. col. AUS, 1941-46. Registered profl. engr. Mem. Soc. Mining Engrs., Rivermines Engrs. Club (sec. 1951, v.p. 1952, pres. 1953), St. Francis County Hist. Soc. (pres. 1964), Am. Legion. Presbyterian (deacon, elder). Rotarian (sec. 1955, dir. 1972). Home and Office: 615 W Columbia St Farmington MO 63640

BEAL, JACK LEWIS, educator; b. Harper, Kans., July 7, 1923; s. Ellis E. and Kathryn (Domnick) B.; B.S., U. Kans., 1948, M.S., 1950; Ph.D., Ohio State U., 1952; m. Earlene M. Maninger, Aug. 22, 1948; children—Linda Sue, Michael L., Karen Ann. Teaching asst. U. Kans., 1947-48, instr., 1948-50; asst. prof. pharmacognosy Ohio State U., 1952-57, asso. prof., 1958-62, prof., 1963—; vis. scientist U. Baghdad, 1961. Mem. U.S. Pharmocopeia Revision Com., 1975—. Served with AUS, 1943-46. Recipient Lehn-Fink award, U. Kans., 1948, Edwin L. Newcomb meml. award in pharmacognosy Am. Found. Pharm. Edn., 1958; NSF faculty fellow, 1958-59. Fellow Acad. Pharm. Scis.; mem. Am. Soc. Pharmacognosy (past pres.), Acad. Pharm. Scis. (past chmn. pharmacognosy and natural products sect.), Sigma Xi, Rho Chi, Phi Lambda Upsilon, Kappa Psi, Rho Pi Phi. Mem. Christian Ch. Editor: Lloydia-Jour. Natural Products. Contbr. articles profl. jours. Home: 5544 Rockwood Rd Columbus OH 43229

BEAL, MYRON CLARENCE, osteo. physician; b. N.Y.C., Dec. 4, 1920; s. Clarence Joseph Weber and Birdice Elvira (Flint) B.; A.B., U. Rochester, 1942; D.O., Chgo. Coll. Osteo. Medicine, 1945; M.S. in Physiology, U. Chgo., 1949; m. Esther Naomi DeLong, Sept. 11, 1948; children—Rebecca (Mrs. Keith Johnson), Myron Flint, Shelley (Mrs. Peter Reese), Julie, Christina. Asst. dir. clinics Chgo. Coll. Osteo. Medicine, 1946-49; instr. London (Eng.) Coll. Osteopathy, 1949-51; pvt. practice osteo. medicine, Rochester, N.Y., 1951-74; prof. biomechanics Coll. Osteopathic Medicine, Mich. State U., East Lansing, 1974—, acting chmn. biomechanics, 1975—. Mem. Nat. Bd. Examiners for Osteo. Physicians and Surgeons, 1960—; mem. N.Y. State Bd. Medicine, 1961-73. Trustee Chgo. Coll. Osteo. Medicine. Fellow Am. Acad. Osteopathy; mem. Am. Osteo. Assn., N.Y. State Osteo. Soc., Mich. Assn. Osteo. Physicians and Surgeons. Presbyterian (elder). Office: East Fee Hall Coll Osteopathic Medicine Mich State U East Lansing MI 48824

BEAL, WANDA ELNORA RADER (MRS. HOWARD WILLIAM BEAL), artist; b. Flint, Mich.; d. Glen and Nettie (Capron) Rader; student U. Oreg., 1946-47, Denver U., 1953, U. Colo., 1964-66; pvt. study art 1962-64; B.A. in Art Edn., S.W. State U., 1977; M.S. in Art Therapy, Emporia State U., 1978; m. Howard William Beal, June 22, 1947; children—Wesley William, Patrice Annette, Cynthia Joan. Woman's page editor Limon (Colo.) Leader, 1953-54; writer Colo. Dept. Edn., 1961; columnist Week End, Colorado Springs, Colo., 1956; stringer Denver Post, 1956—; contbr. articles to Empire Mag., 1956—; clothing designer, 1969—; one man shows Cooper Theatre, Denver, 1st Nat. Bank, Sterling, Colo., Colo. State U., Ft. Collins, Western Fed. Bldg., Colorado Springs, Denver (all 1967); exhibited in group shows Sterling, Colo., 1st Nat. Bank, Ft. Morgan, Nat. League Am. Pen Women, Durango and Colorado Springs, Denver Co., Traveling Show (all 1967); represented in permanent collections, banks and individuals. Tchr. ceramics, recreation art, oil painting 1960—; interior designer Trail Inn, Limon, Colo., 1969. Mem. Colo. Fedn. Womans Club, 1950—, pres., 1959, historian, 1966-67; dist. chmn. Make It Yourself With Wool, 1952-53. Bd. dirs. ARC. Charles E. Tuttle Co. Nonfiction fellow 1964; First place State Lecture Contest Nat. League Am. Pen Women, 1967, 1st place mixed media, State meet, 1969. Mem. Nat. League Am. Pen Women (state art chmn., 1964-65, state pres. 1968—), Fashion Group. Methodist. Home: 729 Lake Ave Worthington MN 56187

BEALL, CHARLES WILLIAM, veterinarian; b. Clarksburg, Ind., Aug. 21, 1930; s. Frank Churchill and Sarah Edna (Rose) B.; D.V.M., Ohio State U., 1958; B.S. in Agr., Purdue, 1952; m. Sibyl Janet Dethloff, Sept. 9, 1956; children—Sarah Elizabeth, Janet Stanley. Veterinarian, Princeton, Ind., 1958-59; area veterinarian U.S. Dept. Agr. Regulatory Service, New Albany, Ind., 1959-60, veterinarian-in-charge hog cholera eradication Lowndes County, Ga., 1962-64, research vet., project leader atrophic rhinitis Nat. Animal Disease Lab., Ames, Iowa, 1964-65, asst. animal supply officer, 1965—; research asso. U. Fla., Gainesville, 1960-62. Served to 1st lt. AUS, 1952-54. Mem. Am. Vet. Medicine Assn., Am. Assn. Lab Animal Sci. (dir. Iowa br. 1971—), Am. Soc. Animal Sci., Am. Soc. Lab. Animal Practitioners, Farm House, Ceres, Scabbard and Blade, Omega Tau Sigma, Phi Zeta, Alpha Zeta. Presbyterian (elder 1966-69). Home: 1201 Iowa Ave Ames IA 50010 Office: PO Box 70 Ames IA 50010

BEALL, GLENN LEE, engr.; b. Henry County, Ill., Aug. 13, 1933; s. William Allen and Lillie Lucille (Lee) B.; student Monmouth Coll., 1952-55; B.S., Bradley U., 1957; m. Patsy Jo Wheeler, Aug. 29, 1953. Facilities design engr. Gen. Electric Co., Bloomington, Ill., 1957-58; sect. head plastic product research and devel. Abbott Labs., N. Chgo., Ill., 1958-68; pres. Glenn Beall Engring., Inc., Gurnee, Ill., 1968—, pres. Glenn Beall Industries, Gurnee, 1975—. Served with USN, 1958. Recipient Sci. Achievement award Abbott Labs., 1965. Mem. Soc. Plastic Engrs. (pres. Chgo. sect., 1967-68, certificate of merit, 1970), ASME, Soc. Plastics Industry (dir.; recipient Midwest sect. Founders award 1977), Packaging Inst. Club: Triton Skin and Scuba Diving (Triton of Year 1973). Contbr. papers to seminars; patentee in field of plastics. Home: 885 S Riverside Dr Gurnee IL 60031 Office: 887 S Riverside Dr Gurnee IL 60031

BEAM, JAMES ALFRED, business exec.; b. Mt. Vernon, Ohio, May 14, 1908; s. Frank L. and Anna L. (Bogardus) B.; student Rensselaer Poly. Inst., 1927, Mass. Inst. Tech., 1928, Ohio State U., 1929-32; m. Margaret A. Rudin, Feb. 16, 1938; children—Frank L., John Dann. Pres., Kokosing Realty Corp., Mt. Vernon, Ohio, 1952—; v.p., 1st Fed. Savs. & Loan, Mt. Vernon, 1949—; owner Millstone Cabinet Shop, Mt. Vernon, 1949—. Mem. City Council, Mt. Vernon, 1947; trustee Am. Humanicas Found., Beta Theta Pi, Ohio State U.; curator Old Tool Crib Mus., Mt. Vernon. Served with USNR, 1944-45. Recipient Silver Beaver, Boy Scouts Am., 1955, Silver Antelope, 1949; named Man of Hour, Mt. Vernon News. Mem. Mt. Vernon C. of C. (past pres.), Symposiarchs (past nat. pres.). Republican. Presbyn. Kiwanian (pres., lt. gov. 1949), Mason (32 deg.,). Home: 120 E Chestnut St Mount Vernon OH 43050 Office: Newark Rd Route 4 Mount Vernon OH 43050

BEAMS, GLEN JAMES, lawyer; b. Spencerville, Ind., Dec. 1, 1914; s. Robert Glen and Lillian Berdein (James) B.; A.B., Ind. U., 1938, LL.B., 1939; m. Ruth Pletcher, Oct. 18, 1941; children—Mary (Mrs. David L. Phillips), John M. Admitted to Ind. bar, 1939; since practiced in Fort Wayne; partner Helmke, Philips & Beams, 1945-71, Helmke, Beams, Boyer & Wagner and predecessors, 1972—. Chmn., Allen County Election Bd., 1945, 50; chief dep. prosecutor Allen County, 1951-54, pros. atty., 1955-58. Bd. dirs. Parkview Meml. Hosp., Fort Wayne, Ind., pres., 1975—. Served with USAAF, 1942-45. Mem. Delta Chi. Republican. Methodist (trustee N. Ind. conf. 1969-76). Clubs: Masons, Kiwanis. Home: 6821 Forest Glen Ct Fort Wayne IN 46805 Office: 309 Standard Bldg Fort Wayne IN 46802

BEAN, MARVIN DAY, clergyman; b. Tampa, Fla., Sept. 8, 1921; s. Marvin Day and Lillian (Howell) B.; A.B., Fla. So. Coll., 1946, M.S. in Social Work, Vanderbilt U., 1948; postgrad. Ohio State U., 1951-52, Northwestern U., 1950; B.D., Garrett Theol. Sem., 1950; children—Bethany Louise, Thomas Holmes, Carol Sue. Ordained to ministry Methodist Ch., 1950; pastor, Lena Vista, Fla., 1946; asso. pastor San Marcos Meth. Ch., Tampa, 1947; pastor Cedar Lake (Ind.) Meth. Ch., 1948-50, Shepard Meth. Ch., Columbus, Ohio, 1951-68, Stonybrook Meth. Ch., Gahanna, Ohio, 1960-65, Obetz (Ohio) Meth. Ch., 1968-73, Neil Ave. Ch., Columbus, 1973—. Asst. to exec. sec. Meth. Union in Ch. Extension, Columbus, 1965-74; v.p. com. info. and pub. relations Ohio Conf. Meth. Ch., 1964-68, vice chmn. health and welfare ministries, 1968-72, chmn. urban life com. Bd. Missions, 1968-70, asso. sec. Bd. Missions, 1968-72, chmn. Services to Children and Youth, 1962-72; chmn. research Ohio Area Study on Aging, Ohio area Meth. Ch., 1959-64; sec. Columbus dist. conf. Meth. Ch., 1960-68; chmn. sch. religion Columbus area Council Chs., 1953; mem. exec. com., trustee Meth. Retirement Center Central Ohio, Columbus; trustee United Meth. Children's Home, Worthington, Ohio, 1973-74; chmn. bd. trustees Neil Ave. Found. Served with AUS, 1943-46. Recipient Wolfley Found. recognition award for inner city work, 1961. Fellow Religious Research Assn.; mem. Columbus Meth. Ministerial Assn. (pres. 1960-61), Ohio Council Chs. (rep. com. strategy and planning 1965-68). Nat. Assn. Social Workers, Acad. Certified Social Workers. Author: A Guide to United Methodist Building, 1973; You Are on the District Board, 1974. Contbr. articles to profl. jours. Home: 148 E Cooke Rd Columbus OH 43214 Office: 1033 High St Worthington OH 43085

BEAN, STEPHEN MICHAEL, foundry exec.; b. Detroit, Aug. 9, 1940; s. Jack and Ruth (Lederer) B.; B.A., Mich. State U., 1963; M.A., Western Mich. U., 1965; m. Bette Diane Corn, May 2, 1964; children—Eric, Lisa. With Bay City Foundry Co., Southfield, Mich., 1966—, v.p. sales, 1969—. Bd. dirs. West Bloomfield United Fund, 1970—. Mem. Sales and Mktg. Execs. Internat., Assn. Iron and Steel Engrs., Am. Foundrymens Soc. Contbr. articles profl. jours. Home: 3160 Parkland Dr West Bloomfield MI 48033 Office: PO Box 643 Franklin MI 48025

BEANEY, WILLIAM DEWEY, educator; b. Rochester, N.Y., July 21, 1930; s. William C. and Eva Viola (Bear) B.; B.S., State U. N.Y., 1952, M.S., 1953; postgrad. Pa. State U., 1961, U. Ill., 1963-70; m. Mary Louise Ridall, July 2, 1954; children—Carol Lynn, John Archie. Tchr. sci. Hilton Central Sch. (N.Y.), 1953; tchr., audio-visual dir. Conawago Twp. Sch., Hanover, Pa., 1958-61; chmn. dept. biol. scis. Olivet Nazarene Coll., Kankakee, Ill., 1961—. Comml. photographer N.Y. State, 1951-54. Pres., Park Villa, Arrowhead Hills and Mel Ray Improvement Assn., 1974—. Served with USAF, 1954-58. Mem. Am. Inst. Biol. Scis., Nat. Assn. Biology Tchrs., Nat. Sci. Tchrs. Assn., Phycol. Soc. Am., Bot. Soc. Am., Ill. State Acad. Sci., Kappa Delta Pi. Home: Route 2 Bourbonnais IL 60914 Office: Olivet Nazarene Coll Kankakee IL 60901

BEARCE, JAMES RICHARD, hotel exec.; b. Canandaigua, N.Y., July 4, 1928; s. Richard Leslie and Lillian Elizabeth (Whitter) B.; student Sch. Hotel Adminstrn., Cornell U., 1952; m. Dorothy Pearson, Aug. 30, 1964; children—Leslie, Stephen, Howard, Michael, James Richard. Dir. sales Southeastern Alsonett Resort Hotels, St. Petersburg, Fla., 1955-59; asst. gen. mgr., dir. sales Key Biscayne Hotel and Villas (Fla.), 1959-67; gen. mgr. Holiday Inn De, San Juan, P.R., 1967-68; v.p., gen. mgr. Emerald Beach Hotel, Nassau, Bahamas, 1969-70; sr. v.p. Robert F. Warner, Inc., N.Y.C., 1970-72; v.p. resort ops. Innisbrook, Tarpon Springs, Fla., 1971-74; v.p. Bahamas, Princess Hotels Internat., Hamilton, Bermuda, 1974-75; gen. mgr. Sandpiper Bay, Port St. Lucie, Fla., 1975-77; dist. dir. hospitality div. Hemsley-Spear, N.Y.C., 1977—. Served in 82d Airborne Div., U.S. Army, 1946-48. Mem. Hotel Sales Mgmt. Assn. Internat. (past pres., certified hotel sales exec., elected to Hall of Fame), Am. Hotel and Motor Hotel Assn., Chevalier des Chaines des Rotisseurs, Cornell Soc. Hotelmen. Republican. Episcopalian. Clubs: Skal (past pres. Miami, Fla.); Masons, Shriners (Tampa, Fla.). Contbr. articles to profl. jours. Home and office: 7th and Adams St Springfield IL 62701

BEARD, MARION L. PATTERSON (MRS. F.E. BEARD), artist, educator, lectr.; b. Vincennes, Ind.; d. George M. and Mattie (Purcell) Patterson; B.S., Ind. State U.; M.F.A., U. Syracuse; m. Francis E. Beard, Dec. 22, 1963. Art supr. in Knox County, Ind. since 1930; art supr. Vincennes City Schs. since 1936; faculty mem. adult edn. art dept. Ind. U., Vincennes U., 1951-53; prof. oil painting Vincennes Univ. Ednl. Center; supt. art edn. Vincennes City Schs., 1955—; art critic tchr. Ind. State Tchrs. Coll., 1957—, Ind. U., 1961-62. Exhibited water colors: Am. Water Color Soc., N.Y. Water Color Club, 1941; Hoosier Salon, yearly since 1942; Ind. Artist-John Herron Art Museum, 1942-44; Nat. Assn. Women Artists, 1943-49; Wabash Valley Artists, Swope Art Gallery, 1947-49; Ind. Artists, Inc., 1948; 2 paintings in 34th Nat. Exhbn. at Ogunquit (Maine) Art Center, 1954; one man show H. Lieber Gallery, Indpls., 1967. Mem. adv. board So. Ind. Regional Scholastic Art Exhibitions, 1955-56. Recipient of Margaret George Bridwell Memorial Prize; First award Hoosier Salon, 1942; Hon. Mention Ind. Artists, 1942; first award, William E. Block Prize, Hoosier Salon, 1948, 2d award Wabash Valley Artists, 1948, 1st in water color, 1950. Fellow Intercontinental Biog. Assn. Eng.; mem. Western Arts Assn. (state membership chmn. 1952-53), Nat. (state membership chmn. 1953-54), Ind. art edn. assns., Ind. Artists' Club, Inc., Art Assn. Indpls., Nat. Assn. Woman Artists, NEA, Ind. Teachers Assn., Vincennes Tchrs. Assn., Indpls. Mus. Art, AAUW, Internat. Platform Assn., M.B.L.S. (adv. mem.), Psi Iota Xi. Presbyterian. Home: Route 1 Vincennes IN 47591

BEARD, MARTIN LUTHER, surgeon; b. Forrest County, Miss., July 15, 1926; s. Luke and Gertie (Johnson) B.; B.S., Tougaloo Coll., 1953; M.D., Meharry Med. Coll., 1960; m. Delores Ratliff, Aug. 23, 1952; children—Myrna, Martin. Intern, Kate B. Reynolds Meml. Hosp., Winston-Salem, N.C., 1960-61, resident, 1961-64; surg. fellow Mpls. VA Hosp., 1964-67; practice medicine specializing in surgery, Flint, Mich., 1967—; asst. clin. prof. surgery Mich. State U.; part-time plant physician Fisher Body #1, Flint. Diplomate Am. Bd. Surgery. Fellow A.C.S.; mem. Omega Psi Phi. Baptist. Club: Optimists. Home: 1109 Barrington Dr Flint MI 48503 Office: 4250 N Saginaw St Flint MI 48505

BEARD, WARD POWERS, assn. exec.; b. Brookings, N.D., Oct. 4, 1920; s. Ward P. and Marion Elizabeth (Miller) B.; B.S., George Washington U., 1943; m. Lucy Palmer Meade, July 18, 1942; children—Mary, Bill, Russell, James, Tom. Personnel mgr. of sales tng. Mich. Assn. Blue Cross Plans, Detroit, 1946-64; cons. Nat. Assn. Blue Cross Plans, N.Y.C., 1960; cons. Florez Inc., Detroit, 1965; dir. of edn. and research Florists Transworld Delivery Assn., Southfield, Mich., 1966—. Served with Signal Corps, U.S. Army, 1943-46; PTO. Recipient Nat. Research and Edn. award Mich. State Florists Assn., 1977. Mem. Am. Soc. Tng. and Devel., Mich. Soc. Instructional Tech. Unitarian. Home: 1685 Allard Grosse Pointe MI 48236 Office: 29200 Northwestern Hwy Southfield MI 48037

BEARDEN, DAVID LEONARD, family service counselor; b. Paterson, N.J., Oct. 28, 1939; s. Leonard Landis and Gwendolyn Leah (Kimble) B.; B.A. in Chemistry, Blackburn Coll., 1961; B.D., Garrett Evang. Sem., 1965; M.S. in Edn., Kearney State Coll., 1972; m. Carolyn Sue McCullough, Apr. 13, 1965; children—Elaine Anne, Bradley David. Clergyman, United Ministries in Higher Edn., Kearney (Nebr.) State Coll., 1965-74; counselor Family Service, Hancock County (Ohio), 1975—; Parent Effectiveness Tng. instr.; team tchr. marriage and family living; advisor Internat. Student Assn. Kearney State Coll., 1970-74; advisor Parents Without Partners, Kearney, 1973-75. Mem. Am. Personnel and Guidance Assn., Am. Assn. Marriage and Family Counselors (asso.-in-tng.), Am. Assn. Sex Educators, Counselors and Therapists, Ohio Council Family Relations. Democrat. Methodist. Home: 737 Lincolnshire Ln Findlay OH 45840 Office: 426 W Sandusky St Findlay OH 45840

BEARDSLEY, JOHN DEIGHTON, lawyer; b. Sioux City, Iowa, Feb. 24, 1904; s. Isaac Franklin and Ella Jean (Tyrer) B.; LL.B., U. Iowa, 1928; m. Marie K. Raber, Oct. 5, 1929; children—Joyce (Mrs. R. G. Zeitler), Nancy (Mrs. T. H. Danaher), John T. Admitted to Iowa bar, 1928, practiced in Sioux City, 1928-42, Onawa, Iowa, 1942—; city atty. Sioux City, 1934-38, Onawa, 1942—. Pres. Onawa Devel. Corp., 1964—; dir., sec., treas. Langen Grain Co., Grain Storage, Inc., Onawa. chmn., Monona County (Iowa) unit Nat. Found. Infantile Paralysis, 1944-64. Chmn. Monona County Rep. Com., 1948-60. Mem. Monona County, Iowa, Am. bar assns., Phi Delta Phi, Omicron Delta Kappa, Theta Xi. Republican. Methodist. Kiwanian. Home: 1314 Diamond St Onawa IA 51040 Office: 1019 9th St Onawa IA 51040

BEART, ROBERT WOODWARD, lawyer; b. Chgo., Nov. 13, 1917; s. Ralph Woodward and Florence (Olson) B.; A.B., Augustana Coll., 1939; J.D., Chgo. Kent Coll., 1948; M.P.L., John Marshall Law Sch., 1950; grad. Advanced Mgmt. Program, Harvard, 1958; m. Helen Wamsley, Oct. 25, 1942; children—Robert Woodward, Beth Joanne. Admitted to Ill. bar, 1947; practiced in Chgo.; jr. mem. firm Olson & Trexler, 1946-48; patent atty., sr. v.p. Ill. Tool Works (co. name now Ill. Tool Works Inc.), Chgo., 1948-70, now patent legal counsel, sr. v.p., also dir.; dir. Luth. Mut. Life Ins. Co. Trustee Ill. Inst. Tech., Inst. Gas Tech., Luth. Gen. Hosp., Park Ridge, Ill., NW Suburban council Boy Scouts Am. Served to maj. USAAF, 1942-46. Decorated Bronze Star medal. Mem. NAM, Am., Chgo. (legis. com.) patent law assns., Ill. Mfrs. Assn. (pres., mem. patent com.). Lutheran. Club: Economic (Chgo.). Home: 20680 W Exeter Rd Kildeer IL 60047 Office: 8501 W Higgins Rd Chicago IL 60631

BEATON, IAN WILSON, advt. agy. exec.; b. Sydney, N.S., Can., Mar. 10, 1924; s. William Murray and Margaret (MacKenzie) B.; came to U.S., 1924, naturalized, 1945; B.S., Northwestern U., 1950; m. Carol Jean Lindner, Dec. 30, 1950; children—Lynda (Mrs. Charles Ainsworth, Jr.), Scot. Merchandising mgr. AC Spark Plug Div., Gen. Motors Corp., 1950-56; copywriter Leo Burnett Co. Mich. Inc. (formerly D. P. Brother & Co.), 1956-58, account exec., 1958-61, v.p., gen. account exec., 1961-66, v.p., adminstrn., personnel, 1966-70, v.p., account supr., 1970-74; v.p., sr. account supr. Campbell-Ewald Co., Detroit, 1975—. Served with AUS, 1943-45; PTO. Mem. Detroit Advt. Assn., Pi Kappa Alpha. Presbyterian. Clubs: Detroit Adcraft, Great Oaks Country, Recess. Home: 1200 Oakwood Ct Rochester MI 48063 Office: Gen Motors Bldg Detroit MI 48202

BEATTIE, STANLEY EDWARD, lawyer; b. Detroit, Feb. 8, 1905; s. Stanley Andrew and Mary Rose (Lane) B.; A.B., U. Detroit, 1927, LL.B., Harvard U., 1930; LL.D. (hon.), Thomas M. Cooley Law Sch., 1976; m. Marion Moore, Oct. 30, 1934; children—Mary Ann (dec.), Stanley Andrew, Kevin Moore, Robert Brian, Martha Rose Beattie Graham. Admitted to Mich. bar, 1930, since practiced in Detroit; mem. firm Bellanca and Beattie; lectr. U. Detroit Sch. Law, 1934-59; mem. Mich. Bd. Law Examiners, 1948-73. Mem. Am., Mich. Detroit bar assns. Republican. Roman Catholic. Clubs: Detroit Athletic, Detroit Yacht, Harvard of Eastern Mich. Cons., adviser West Pub. Co. on Michigan Law and Practice Ency. Home: 729 Pemberton Rd Grosse Point Park MI 48236 Office: 20480 Vernier Rd Harper Woods MI 48225

BEATTIE, WILLIAM JOHN, III, foundry exec.; b. St. Louis, Nov. 18, 1933; s. William John and Mary Ellen (Chipley) B.; student Washington U., St. Louis, 1951-54, Tex. Christian U., 1958-61; m. Rebecca Sue Czeschin, July 11, 1970; children—William, Ann, Todd, Chad, David. Engring. supr. Emerson Electric Co., St. Louis, 1966-69; asst. mktg. mgr. Meyer Labs. Inc., Maryland Heights, Mo., 1969-70; v.p., gen. mgr. Forecast, Inc., Kirkwood, Mo., 1970-74; pres. St. Charles Aluminum Casting Co. (Mo.), 1974—. Planning and zoning commr. City of St. Charles, 1976—; bd. dirs. Boys Club St. Charles. Served with USAF, 1954-56; Korea. Mem. Am. Foundrymen's Soc. Republican. Presbyterian. Home: 2916 Thrush Dr Saint Charles MO 63301 Office: 1868 Scherer Pkwy Saint Charles MO 63301

BEATTY, DANIEL DAVIS, ednl. adminstr.; b. Elrod, S.D., Sept. 19, 1918; s. Francis Garfield and Edith Nettie (Braga) B.; B.A., Hope Coll., 1947; M.B.A., U. Mich., 1949; postgrad. U. Kan., 1952-53; m. Harriet Cornelia Grote, Oct. 23, 1944; children—Edith Ellen, Rebecca Marie, Margaret Grace. Asso. prof. William Jewell Coll., Liberty, Mo., 1949-52; instr. U. Kan., 1952-53; asst. exec. sec. Kans. Citizens Comn. on Assessment Equalization, Topeka, 1953-54; budget analyst dept. adminstrn., asst. to chmn. Kans. Senate Com. of Ways and Means, 1954-56; prof., bus. mgr. Kans. State U., 1956-72, v.p. bus. affairs, prof., 1972—. Dir. 1st Nat. Bank, Manhattan, Kans. Commr., City of Manhattan, 1963-65. Trustee Riley County Meml. Hosp., 1961-63. Served with USNR, 1940-46; ret. comdr. Res. Mem. Manhattan C. of C. (past dir.), Central Assn. Coll. and Univ. Bus. Officers. Coll. and Univ. Personnel Assn., Naval Res. Assn. Methodist. Mason, Rotarian (pres. 1967-68), Elk. Club: Manhattan Country. Home: 817 Vattier Manhattan KS 66502 Office: Kan State U Manhattan KS 66506

BEATTY, FRANK STEWART, psychologist; b. Denver, May 29, 1930; s. Eugene Carl and Gertrude Anna (Gruenler) B.; B.A., U. Denver, 1954, M.A., 1957; m. Jeanne Marie Aich, Aug. 20, 1954; 1 son, Bradley Alan. Intern, N.H. State Hosp., Concord, 1958-59; research asst. Sonoma (Calif.) State Hosp., 1959-60; counselor Colo. State Dept. Rehab., Denver, 1962-63; psychologist Mental Health Center No. Iowa, Mason City, 1963—. Served with USAF, 1950-52. Certified, licensed psychologist, Iowa. Mem. Am., Iowa psychol. assns., Council for the Nat. Register of Health Service Providers in Psychology, Acad. Psychologists in Family and Marriage Counseling. Contbr. articles to Jour. Psychology. Home: 1119 2nd St SW Mason City IA 50401 Office: Box 1463 Mason City IA 50401

BEATTY, LOWELL CRAWFORD, ret. machine tool co. exec.; b. Pitts., Aug. 19, 1910; s. William Robert and Jesse Catherine (Bitner) B.; B.S., Purdue U., 1931; m. Virginia Prohl, Oct. 10, 1932; children—Phyllis Ann (Mrs. Tom Henkelmann), William Crawford. With Beatty Machine & Mfg. Co., Hammond, Ind., 1933-76, pres. 1943-76. Clubs: Masons, Shriners, Woodmar Country (Hammond). Home: 1826 Camellia Dr Munster IN 46321

BEATTY, NORMAN JACKSON, assn. exec.; b. Indpls., June 17, 1925; s. Norman Madrid and Edith Gail (Jackson) B.; B.S., Ind. U., 1947, LL.B., 1948, J.D., 1967; m. Patricia Mae Jowitt, Feb. 6, 1948; children—Stephen E., Norman R. Admitted to Ind. bar, 1949, Ill. bar, 1963; mem. staff atty. gen. Ind., 1948-53, dep. atty. gen., 1950-53; gen. counsel Ind. Dept. Revenue, 1953-56; mgr. tax and legis. dept. Ind. Mfrs. Assn., Indpls., 1956-62; mgr. tax dept. Ill. C. of C., Chgo., 1962-70; exec. v.p. Civic Fedn., Chgo., 1971—. Adviser, Commn. on State Tax and Financing Policy Ind., 1959-62; sec. Ill. Joint Com. on Revenue Articles, 1963-71; sec. Ill. Citizens Com. for New Revenue Article, 1965-66; mem. Ill. Gov.'s Revenue Study Com., 1968-69; mem. task force on finance Ill. Gov.'s Commn. on Schs., 1972; chmn. com. on state income and bus. taxation Nat. Tax Assn., 1972-74; mem. Cook County Home Rule Commn., 1973. Served with USNR, 1943-46. Mem. Am., Ill., Chgo. bar assns., Nat. Tax Assn., Chgo. Tax Club, Delta Upsilon, Sigma Delta Kappa. Episcopalian. Home: 5555 N Sheridan Rd Chicago IL 60640 Office: 29 E Madison St Chicago IL 60602

BEATTY, ROBERT ALFRED, surgeon; b. Colchester, Vt., May 7, 1936; s. George Lewis and Leila Margaret (Ebright) B.; B.A., U. Oreg., 1959, B.S., 1960, M.D., 1961; m. Frances Calomeni, Aug. 24, 1963; children—Bradford, Roxanna. Intern, U. Ill. Research and Edn. Hosp., Chgo., 1961-62; resident neurosurgery U. Ill., 1962-66; practice neurosurgery, Hinsdale, Ill., 1967—; mem. staff Hinsdale San., Community Meml. Hosp., LaGrange, Ill., Meml. Hosp., Elmhurst, Ill., Edward Hosp., Naperville, Ill., Central DuPage Hosp., Winfield, Ill., U. Ill. Hosp., Chgo.; clin. asso. prof. neurosurgery U. Ill., 1967—; adviser Marion Joy Rehab. Center, Wheaton, Ill., 1969-72. Served to capt. M.C., AUS, 1968. Research fellow St. George's Med. Sch., London, 1966-67. Diplomate Am. Bd. Neurol. Surgery. Mem. AMA, Ill. Med. Soc., Dupage County Med. Soc., Am. Assn. Neurol. Surgeons, A.C.S., Congress Neurol. Surgeons, SAR, Phi Beta Kappa, Phi Beta Pi, Phi Kappa Psi. Republican. Club: Oak Brook Bath and Tennis. Contbr. profl. jours. Research on intracranial aneurysms, lumbar discs. Office: 40 S Clay St Hinsdale IL 60521

BEATY, MARJORIE HECKEL (MRS. DONALD WILLIAM BEATY), mathematician; b. Buffalo, Jan. 21, 1906; d. Henry George and Josephine Mary (Fisher) Heckel; A.B., U. Rochester, 1928, M.A., 1929; postgrad. Brown U., 1929-31; Ph.D. (fellow), U. Colo., 1939; m. Donald William Beaty, Mar. 30, 1933; children—Debra (Mrs. Albert Baity Blanton II), Mary (Mrs. Joseph Ruey Edelen, Jr.). Grad. asst. Brown U., 1929-31, U. Colo., Boulder, 1935-38; instr. U. S.D., Vermillion, 1931-35, asst. prof. math., 1938-41, 56-58, acting dean of women, 1941, asso. prof. math., 1958-61, prof. math., 1961-76, prof. emeritus, 1976—, coll. lectr., 1965. Sec. Clay County Republican Central Com., 1950-76; treas. ad hoc com. Modernization S.D. Cts., 1972-75. Mem. S.D. Acad. Sci., Am. Math. Soc., S.D. Acad. Sci., AAUW, P.E.O., Mortar Bd., Phi Beta Kappa, Sigma Xi, Pi Mu Epsilon, Delta Kappa Gamma, Omicron Delta Kappa, Alpha Lambda Delta, Chi Omega. Congregationalist. Club: Order of Eastern Star. Home: 314 Canby St Vermillion SD 57069 Office: Dept Math U SD Vermillion SD 57069

BEAUCH, ROBERT NIMMO, constrn. co. exec.; b. Saginaw, Mich., Jan. 1, 1929; s. James and Isabelle Muir (Reid) Nimmo; B.S. in Chem. Engring., U. Toledo, 1950, postgrad. Law Sch., 1955-56; m. Jean Alta Zimmerman, Dec. 6, 1952; children—Timothy Allan, Carol Jean, Robert Todd, Paul Douglas, Mary Sue. Engr., Toledo Engring. Co., Inc., 1953-54, project engr., 1954-58, asst. chief engr., 1958-64, contract mgr., 1964-70, sec., 1970—; sec. Tecoglass, Inc., 1975—. Served with AUS, 1950-52. Registered profl. engr., Ohio; licensed gen. engring. contractor, Cal. Mem. Nat. Soc. Profl. Engrs., Ohio, Toledo soc. profl. engrs., Am. Ceramic Soc. (chmn. N.W. Ohio sect. 1966), Tech. Soc. Toledo, Lutheran (synod rep. 1972-75, pres. ch. council 1973-74). Home: 3141 Rocksberry St Toledo OH 43614 Office: 3001 Sylvania Av Toledo OH 43614

BEAUDOIN, GREGORY DAVID, retailer; b. Cadillac, Mich., Feb. 14, 1947; s. William Francis and Flora Jeanette (Sawin) B.; student Northwestern Mich. Coll., 1965-66, No. Mich. U., 1966-67; B.S., Central Mich. U., 1967-69; m. Patricia Agnes Sivak, May 10, 1969; children—Anne-Terese Renee, David Gregory, Daniel Stephen. Tchr. sci. Fowler (Mich.) Pub. Schs., 1969-70; mgr. Bill's Motor Sales, Cadillac, 1971—. Chmn. Wexford County Republican Party, 1977—; mem. Wexford County Rep. Exec. Com., 1976; dir. Wexford County Juvenile Ct. Vols., 1974—; mem. Haring Twp. Bd. Appeals, 1976—; chmn. Haring Twp. Bldg. Com., 1976—; vol. United Way of Wexford County, 1975, 76; bd. trustees Haring Twp. Bd. Suprs., 1976—. Served with U.S. Army, 1970-71. Republican. Roman Catholic. Home: 1907 6th St Cadillac MI 49601 Office: 1129 N Mitchell St Cadillac MI 49601

BEAUMIER, JOHN HENRY, orthopaedic surgeon; b. Escanaba, Mich., Aug. 29, 1931; s. Henry Joseph and Lillian Helen (Belanger) B.; B.A., No. Mich. U., 1953; M.D., Marquette U., 1957; grad. Mayo Grad. Sch. Orthopaedic Surgery, 1966; m. Mary Jane McKenna, July 2, 1958; children—Jack, Anne, Patrick, Michael, Matthew, Casey, Colin, Mary Kathleen. Intern, U.S. Naval Hosp., Great Lakes, Ill., 1957-58; resident Grad. Sch., Mayo Clinic, 1962-66; practice medicine, specializing in orthopaedic surgery, Marshfield (Wis.) Clinic, 1966-68, The Orthopaedic Clinic, Grand Forks, N.D., 1968—; part-time tchr. U. N.D. Sch. Physiotherapy; part-time team physician U. N.D. Mem. Right to Life Com., N.D., 1971—; mem. N.D. Cath. Conf., 1970—. Served with USNR, 1957-62. Mem. AMA, N.D. Med. Soc., Am. Acad. Orthopaedic Surgery, Holy Name Soc. Home: 1510 Belmont Rd Grand Forks ND 58201 Office: Columbia Rd Grand Forks ND 58201

BEAUMONT, GEORGE HAYDON, drug mfg. co. exec.; b. Kansas City, Mo., July 3, 1930; s. Taney Justice and Helen (Haydon) B.; student St. Joseph Jr. Coll., 1948-50; B.S., U. Mo., Columbia, 1952; m. Carolea Ann Sawyers, Mar. 7, 1953; children—Jill Ann, Marsee Pem, Julie Haydon. Mgr. sales promotion S.C. Johnson & Son, Racine, Wis., 1954-61; pres. Leewood Products Inc., St. Joseph, Mo., 1961-65; account supr. S.C.I. div. Interpublic Inc., N.Y.C., 1965-67; dir. chain store sales Ambassador div. Hallmark Cards Inc., Kansas City, Mo., 1967-69; v.p. mktg. Rexall Drug Co., St. Louis, 1969—. Served with USNR, 1952-54. Presbyterian. Clubs: Sales Promotion Exec., St. Louis Advt., St. Louis Sales Exec., Elks, Masons, Shriners. Home: 316 San Angelo St Chesterfield MO 63017 Office: 3901 N Kingshighway Blvd Saint Louis MO 63115

BEAVER, WILLIAM LEE, JR., electric co. exec.; b. Kuttawa, Ky., June 16, 1917; s. William Lee and Ida (Perryman) B.; grad. St. Louis U., 1939; m. Mary Eva Rodgers, June 18, 1940; children—Douglas Alden, Betsy Lee. C.P.A., Price-Waterhouse & Co., St. Louis, 1936-42; treas., dir Artophone Corp., St. Louis, 1946-62; fin. v.p., treas., dir. Sachs Electric Co., St. Louis, Mo., 1962—; v.p., treas., dir. Sachs Properties, Inc., 1968—; exec. v.p., treas., dir. Sachs Holdings, Inc., 1973—; dir. Chesterfield Bank, Chesterfield Village, Mo. Dist. chmn. Boy Scouts Am., 1963; area chmn. ARC, 1955-56; chmn. Health and Hosp. Panel, 1966—; cabinet mem. United Fund, 1962—. Mem. exec. com., chmn. fin. com., 1st v.p. Mo. Bapt. Hosp. Served with USAAF, 1942-45. Mem. Financial Exec. Inst. (chpt. pres. 1966—, nat. dir. 1973—, Midwest area v.p. 1976-77), Nat. Assn. Accountants, Am. Inst. C.P.A.'s, Fin. Analyst Soc. Baptist (deacon, trustee). Clubs: Media, Noonday, Castle Oak, Norwood Hills Country. Home: 27 Bellerive Acres St Louis MO 63121 Office: 16300 Justus Post Rd Chesterfield Village MO 63017

BEAVERS, ADDISON MORTON, former judge; b. nr. Mt. Summit, Ind., May 29, 1910; s. William Addison and Mabel (Morton) B.; A.B., Butler U., 1935; J.D., Ind. U., 1934; m. Marjoria Roth, Aug. 8, 1934; 1 dau., Nancy (Mrs. John Steed). Admitted to Ind. bar, 1934, practiced in Boonville, 1934-51; judge Warrick Circuit Ct., Boonville, 1951-76; v.p., dir. Warrick Loan & Savs. Assn., Boonville, 1949—; dir. Warrick Nat. Bank, Boonville. Chmn. Ind. Civil Code Study Commn., Ind. Jud. Study Commn. Past pres. Ind. Soc. for Crippled Children and Adults; 1st chmn. Regional Mental Health Planning Commn., 1963-66; past moderator permanent jud. commn. U.P. Ch., U.S.A. Pros. atty., Warrick County, Ind., 1937-39, county atty., 1934-36, 39-41; dep. Atty. Gen. of Ind., 1941-43; mem. Ind. Ho. of Reps., 1951. Bd. dirs. Ind. Inter-Ch. Center, Indpls., Synod of Ind. U.P. Ch. Served to lt. USNR, 1944-46. Mem. Am., Ind. (past chmn. ho. of dels.) bar assns., Am. Judicature Soc., Ind. Judges Assn. (pres. 1956-57), Nat. Council Juvenile Ct. Judges, Ind. Conf. Social Work. Clubs: Masons (32 deg., Shriner), Elks. Home: 121 Hargrave St Boonville IN 47601 Office: Courthouse Boonville IN 47601

BECERRA, LAWRENCE, elec. and mech. components and systems mfg. co. exec.; b. N.Y.C., Sept. 22, 1926; s. Rosendo and Adeline (Diaz) B.; student Acad. Aeros., 1948; B.S. in Aero. Engring., U. Paris, 1952; LL.B., Atlanta Law Sch., 1959; postgrad. exec. program U. Chgo., 1968; M.B.A., M.B.M., Sussex (Eng.) Coll. Tech., 1975; m. Virginia Warren Pierce, Aug. 2, 1975; children—Linda Ruberto, Laureen Demma, Larry M., Carla, Dawn, Lisa, Maria. Internat. mgr. Sprague Electric Co., North Adams, Mass., 1961-64; dir. for Latin Am., P.R. Mallory Co., Mexico, 1965-70; internat. dir. Golconda Corp., Chgo., 1970-71; v.p. internat. Rockwell Internat., Detroit, 1971-74; v.p. internat. ops. Essex Internat., Detroit, 1974—; dir. Essex Electrica, Mexico City. Served with U.S. Army, 1943-44. Mem. Soc. Internat. Execs., Licensing Execs. Soc. Sigma Delta Kappa. Clubs: Rolls Royce Owners, Jaguar. Home: 2685 Amberly Rd Birmingham MI 48010 Office: 6233 Concord Ave Detroit MI 48211

BECHERER, CARL VICTOR, dentist; b. Belleville, Ill., Aug. 6, 1925; s. Paul William and Eleanore Lena (Heafner) B.; student Marquette U., 1943-44, D.D.S., 1948; m. Helen Patricia Hoffman, Jan. 13, 1945; children—Patricia (Mrs. Ivo Spalatin), Jeff C., William C., Marybeth, John C., Daniel J. Pvt. practice dentistry, Wauwatosa, Wis., 1948—; asst. clin. prof. Marquette U. Sch. of Dentistry, Milw., 1949-55, 72—. Treas. parents assn. Divine Saviour High Sch., Wauwatosa, Wis., 1963-64; mem. North Ave. Advancement Assn., Wauwatosa, Lakeland Environ. Protective Assn., Lac du Flambeau, Fence Lake Advancement Assn., Lac du Flambeau; mem. Wauwatosa Rep. Club, 1971-72. Served with USN, 1944-45; 1st lt. Dental Corps, AUS, 1951-53. Recipient Distinguished Alumnus award Psi Omega Alumni Assn., 1972. Fellow Internat. Coll. Dentists, Acad. Gen. Dentistry; mem. ADA, Wis. (ho. of dels. 1964-75), Greater Milw. (dir. 1967-72) dental assns., Wis. Gnathological Soc., Assn. Am. Dentists, Acad. Operative Dentistry, Am. Soc. Dentistry for Children, Fedn. Dentaire Internationale, Chgo. Dental Soc., Milw. Dental Forum (sec.-treas. 1972-74, v.p. 1974-75, pres. 1975-76), Wis. Wildlife Assn., Marquette U. Alumni Assn. (dir. 1970-76), Marquette U. Dental Alumni Assn. (dir. 1964-69, pres. 1969-70), Wauwatosa C. of C., Psi Omega, Omicron Kappa Upsilon. K.C. Clubs: St. Pius X Men's, Marquette Minutemen, Marquette Warriors. Home: 2578 N 67th St Wauwatosa WI 53213 also Box 151 Route 2 Lac du Flambeau WI 54538 Office: 7013 W North Ave Wauwatosa WI 53213

BECHT, SUE CAROL, farm equipment exec., farmer; b. Shelbyville, Ind., Sept. 13, 1934; d. Carl Edwin and Capitola (Southard) Murrell; ed. Terhune Bus. Coll., Franklin Coll., spl. courses; m. Charles William Becht, Feb. 14, 1954; children—Fred, Todd. Asst. mgr. 150 cow dairy farm, 1960-62; mgr. grocery store, Moscow, Ind., 1963-64; owner, mgr. Becht Sales & Service, Milroy, Ind., 1964—, also mgr. farm. Trustee, Milroy Methodist Ch., 1971-74; den mother Cub Scouts, 1970-75; chmn. Anderson Twp. United Fund. Named Dealer of Year, Badger Northland, 1969; recipient Silver Sales award Beard Industries, 1971, Best Speech award Dale Carnegie, 1976. Mem. Bus. and Profl. Women, Rush County C. of C., Ind. Implement Dealers Assn., Psi Iota Xi (Girl of Year 1975). Office: RR 1 Milroy IN 46156

BECHTEL, DONALD LEON, educator; b. LaCrosse, Wis., Feb. 7, 1941; s. Leon Joseph and Helen (Lehmann) B.; B.S., U. Wis. at LaCrosse, 1963; M.A., U. S.D., 1964; Ed.D., U. S.D., 1968. Instr. Kohler (Wis.) High Sch., 1964-66; asso. prof. history edn. U. Wis. at Rice Lake, 1966—. Curriculum and research grantee U. Wis. Mem. Ham Radio Club, Phi Delta Kappa, Kappa Delta Pi, Phi Alpha Theta. Contbr. articles to profl. jours. Home: 815 S 8th St LaCrosse WI 54601 Office: Dept History Univ Wis Rice Lake WI 54868

BECHTHOLD, GEORGE WALTER, mgmt. cons.; b. Waterloo, Iowa, July 20, 1941; s. Gilbert Fredrick and Calista Ada (Biles) B.; B.S. in Bus. Adminstrn., Northwestern U., 1963; M.B.A. with honors, U. Mich., 1970; m. Margaret June Habicht, Sept. 14, 1963; children—Mary Lee, Jeffrey Todd. Interviewer, Market Facts, Inc., Chgo., 1961-63; transp. analyst, Ford Motor Co., Dearborn, Mich., 1967-70; prin. A.T. Kearney, Inc., Cleve., 1970-74, Los Angeles, 1975-76; pres. The MCS Group, Kansas City, Mo., 1976—; spl. advisor to M.B.A. program U. So. Calif., 1974-76. Pack com. chmn. Heart of Am. council Boy Scouts Am., 1976—; mem. Village Church, Prairie Village, Kans. Served with USN, 1963-67. Mem. Nat. Council Phys. Distbn. Mgmt., N.Am. Soc. Corp. Planning. Club: Homestead Country (Prairie Village). Editor, contbr. regular monthly article to Mgmt. Perspectives, Warehouse Distbr. News, 1973—. Home: 3317 W 68th St Mission Hills KS 66208 Office: 633 E 63d St Kansas City MO 64110

BECICH, RAYMOND BRICE, hosp. adminstr.; b. Chgo., Jan. 9, 1945; s. Nicholas Gabriel and Rose Christine (Spillar) B.; A.B., Ind. U., 1966; M.S. (USPHS fellow) Columbia, 1968. Adminstrv. officer USPHS Hosp., Harlem, Mont., 1968-69, dir., 1969-72; dir. USPHS Hosp., Rapid City, S.D., 1972—. Fellow Am. Coll. Hosp. Adminstrs.; mem. Am. Hosp. Assn., Am. Pub. Health Assn. Kiwanian. Address: 4106 Jackson Blvd Rapid City SD 57701

BECK, CARL FREDERICK, lawyer; b. Mason City, Iowa, Mar. 9, 1913; s. Allan F. and Clara Erma (Strahan) B.; B.A., State U. Iowa, 1933, J.D., 1935; m. Hester Wehrle, June 15, 1936; children—John A., Jane (Mrs. Philip N. Moss). Admitted to Iowa bar, 1935, since practiced in Mason City; partner firm Smith & Beck, 1939-60, Beck, Butler & Pappajohn, 1960-73, Beck, Pappajohn & Shriver, 1973—; pres. Higley Cold Storage, Inc., 1954—; sec., dir., gen. counsel Iowa Terminal Railroad Co.; sec., dir. Metalcraft, Inc., Klipto Printing Co., all Mason City; dir. Central Nat. Bank & Trust Co., Des Moines, Central Nat. Bancshares, Inc., Des Moines, United Home Bank and Trust Co., Mason City. Bd. dirs. Iowa chpt. Arthritis Found., 1962—; vice chmn. bd. dirs. Iowa chpt. ARC, 1957-58. Served with AUS, 1943-45. Mem. Am., Iowa, 3d Dist. (pres. 1958-59) bar assns., Am. Judicature Soc. Mason, Elk. Home: 2001 Northshore Dr Clear Lake IA 50428 Office: 800 Brick & Tile Bldg Mason City IA 50401

BECK, CLIFFORD CARL, pharm. co. exec.; b. Racine, Wis., May 15, 1927; s. Niels Kristian and Anna Louise (Nielsen) B.; B.S., Mich. State Coll., 1953; D.V.M., Mich. State U., 1954, M.S., 1959; m. Joyce Louise Cathey, June 10, 1955; 1 son, Bruce James. Practice vet. medicine, Manchester, Mich., 1954-55; ambulatory clinician Mich. State U., East Lansing, 1955-63, extension veterinarian, 1963-69; asso. dir. clin. investigation Parke, Davis & Co. Research Labs., Ann Arbor, 1969-71, dir. animal health therapeutics, 1971-73, dir. animal health dept., 1973—. Vet. cons. Shepherd Mag., 1962—. Served with USNR, 1945-48. Mem. Am., Mich. vet. med. assns., Indsl. Vets. Assn., U.S. Animal Health Assn., Am. Assn. Bovine Practice, Am. Assn. Equine Practice, Am. Assn. Sheep and Goat Practice (pres. 1973-74, 74-75), Am. Assn. Zoo Veteranarians, Phi Zeta. Contbr. articles to pubs. Home: 10800 Noggles Rd Manchester MI 48158 Office: 2800 Plymouth Rd Ann Arbor MI 48106

BECK, ERNEST WILLIAM, med. illustrator; b. Salzderhelden, Germany, Jan. 2, 1923; s. Fred August and Marie (Kuker) B.; came to U.S., 1925; B.S., Northwestern U., 1946; student Art Inst. Chgo., 1946-47; certificate U. Ill. Coll. Medicine, 1948; m. Joan Shirley Wagner, Sept. 9, 1945; children—Christopher, Melinda. Exec. mng. editor Jour. A.M.A. and ten specialty jours., 1972-73. Mem. Assn. Med. Illustrators (pres. 1965-66, recipient outstanding service award 1968, treas., gov.), Am. Med. Writers Assn., Midwest Pharm. Advt. Club, Beta Theta Pi. Methodist. Club: Lake Forest. Author, illustrator: The Canine, 1967; The Feline, 1969; The Horse, 1971; Pregnancy in Anatomical Transparencies, 1962; Upper Respiratory Tract Transparencies, 1966; New Era Health Charts, 1965. Illustrator: The Esophagus and Pharynx in Action, 1949; Operative Technique, 1949; Thinking About God's World—Knowing God's World, 1957; Christopher's Textbook of Surgery, 1956; Health for Life, 1961; Nechtow and Reich's Gynecology, 1961; Pediatric Orthopedics, 1972; Textbook of Anatomy and Physiology, 9th edit., 1975; Textbook of Physiology, 17th edit., 1971; O.R. Nursing: Preoperative Care and Draping Technique. Artist contbr. to Compton's Ency., Ency. Americana, World Book, Collier's Ency. Home: 905 Castlegate Ct Lake Forest IL 60045

BECK, FRANCES JOSEPHINE MOTTEY (MRS. JOHN MATTHEW BECK), educator; b. Eleanora, Pa., July 12, 1918; d. George F. and Mary (Wisnieski) Mottey; B.S., Ind. State Tchrs. Coll., 1939; M.A., U. Chgo., 1955; m. John Matthew Beck, Aug. 23, 1941. Jr. visitor Pa. Dept. Pub. Assistance, 1940-41; asst. to the sec. dept. edn. U. Chgo., 1952-58, asst. sec., 1958, asst. dean of students Grad. Sch. Edn., 1958-75; asst. to dean Sch. Edn., De Paul U., Chgo., 1975—; reading instr. Central YMCA, Chgo., 1958-61. Mem. Nat., Ill. assns. women deans and counselors, Internat. Reading Assn., Delta Kappa Gamma. Pi Lambda Theta (nat. v.p. 1966-70, 1st v.p. 1971-74), Sigma Sigma Sigma. Co-author: Extending Reading Skills, 1976; author articles in field. Office: 2323 N Seminary Chicago IL 60614

BECK, JOAN WAGNER, journalist; b. Clinton, Iowa, Sept. 5, 1923; d. Roscoe Charles and Mildred (Noel) Wagner; B.S. in Journalism cum laude, Northwestern U., 1945, M.S. in Journalism, 1947; m. Ernest William Beck, Sept. 9, 1945; children—Christopher, Melinda. Radio script writer O.W.I., Voice of Am., 1945-46; copy writer Marshall Field & Co., 1947-50; feature writer Chgo. Tribune, 1950—, writer syndicated column about young people, 1956-61, syndicated column about children, 1961-72, daily features editor, 1972-76, mem. editorial bd., editorial page columnist, 1976—. Hon. chmn. Mother's March of Met. Chgo. chpt. Nat. Found. March of Dimes, 1970-75. Helen Baker Cody award Chgo. Welfare Pub. Relations Bd., 1955; Trans-World Airlines Travel Feature award, 1954; Portal House award Chgo. Com. on Alcoholism, 1955; Asso. Press award for best newspaper feature series award, Ill., 1964, best feature, 1966; Alumni Merit award Northwestern U., 1965, Alumnae award, 1977; nat. award of achievement Alpha Chi Omega, 1966; 1st place award Penney-U. Mo., 1973. Mem. Theta Sigma Phi, Alpha Chi Omega. Methodist. Clubs: Chicago Press; Lake Forest. Author: How to Raise a Brighter Child, 1967; (with Dr. Virginia Apgar) Is My Baby All Right?, 1973; Effective Parenting, 1976. Home: 905 Castlegate Ct Lake Forest IL 60045 Office: Chgo Tribune 435 N Michigan Ave Chicago IL 60611

BECK, JOHN ALLAN, real estate exec.; b. Kansas City, Mo., Aug. 29, 1941; s. Carl Frederick and Hester (Wehrle) B.; student Cornell Coll., 1959-61; B.B.A., State U. Iowa, 1963; m. Elizabeth B. Cole, Feb. 29, 1964 (div. Dec. 1971); children—Christopher A., Allan J.; m. 2d, Eileen A. Heeren, Nov. 22, 1974. Salesman, Dow Chem. Co., Midland, Mich., Chgo., Dallas, 1963-67; v.p. Beck Bros. Co., Realtors, Mason City, Iowa, 1967-73, pres., owner, 1972; pres. N.Am. Motorsport Corp., Mason City, 1968-75, chmn. bd., 1975-76; pres. Winnebago Builders Corp., Mason City, 1971—; v.p. Mason City Investment Co., Higley Cold Storage Co. Pres., South Side Library and Garden, 1972-73; chmn. Mason City Devel. Com., 1973; mem. Mason City City Council, 1969-74; exec. dir. N. Iowa Fair Assn., 1971-75. Bd. dirs. Mason City Civic Center Found., North Iowa Area Community Center Found., Iowa Arthritis and Rheumatism Found., 1971-76. Mem. Nat. Assn. Realtors, Exec. Officers Council, Mason City C. of C. (dir. 1975—), Mason City Bd. Realtors (pres. 1974-76). Club: Masons. Home: 10 26th St SW Mason City IA 50401 Office: 633 15th St SE Mason City IA 50401

BECK, JOHN MATTHEW, educator; b. Rogoznig, Austria, Apr. 10, 1913; s. Matthias and Antoinette (Bukowski) B.; came to U.S., 1914, naturalized, 1942; B.S., Ind. State Coll. (Pa.), 1936; M.A., U. Chgo., 1947, Ph.D., 1953; m. Frances Josephine Mottey, Aug. 23, 1941. Tchr., Clymer (Pa.) High Sch., 1937-41; instr. history and philosophy of edn. De Paul U., 1948-53; instr. Chgo. State College, 1953-56, chmn. dept. edn., 1959-60, asst. dean, prof. edn., 1960-66, dean coll., 1966-67; dir. Chgo. Tchr. Corps, 1967—; exec. dir. Chgo. Consortium Colls. and Univs., 1968—; prof. urban tchr. edn. Govs. State U., 1972—; cons. U.S. Office of Edn., 1968—. Mem. Ill. State Advisory Com. on Guidance, 1963—, Citizens Schs. Com., Chgo., 1953—; chmn. curriculum adv. com. Ednl. Facilities Center, Chgo., 1971—; exec. bd. Cook County OEO, 1971—; adv. com. interstate interinstnl. cooperation Ill. Bd. Higher Edn., 1972—; mem. Chgo. Mayor's Adv. Commn. Sch. Bd. Nominations, 1975. Bd. govs. Chgo. City Club, 1961—, v.p., 1962-63, 64-65. Served with AUS, 1941-46. Decorated Bronze Star. Recipient W. Germany grant, 1972. Fellow AAAS, Philosophy of Edn. Soc.; mem. Am. Hist. Assn., Am. Edn. Research Assn., Ill. Edn. Assn. (pres. Chgo. div. 1960-62). Co-author: Extending Reading Skills, 1976. Editor: Chgo. Sch. Jour., 1964-65; co-editor: Teaching the Culturally Disadvantaged Child, 1966; contbr. articles to profl. jours. and encys. Home: 5832 Stony Island Ave Chicago IL 60637 Office: 2235 N Sheffield Ave Chicago IL 60614

BECK, JOHN ROLAND, biol. services co. exec.; b. Las Vegas, N.Mex., Feb. 26, 1929; s. Roland Lycurgus and Betty Lind (Shrock) B.; B.S., Okla. A. and M. Coll., 1950; postgrad. U. Tex., 1954; M.S., Okla. State U., 1957; postgrad. George Washington U., 1965; m. Doris Aliene Olson, Feb. 9, 1951; children—Elizabeth Joan, Thomas Roland, Patricia Lind, John William. Biologist, King Ranch, Tex., 1950-51; wildlife mgmt. fellow Okla. A. and M. Coll., 1951, asst. instr., 1952-53; instr. physiology U. Tenn., 1954-55; control agt. U.S. Fish and Wildlife Service, N.D., 1953-54, research biologist, Idaho, 1955-57, control biologist, Ohio, 1957-65, Va., 1967-69; dir. Job Corps Center, U.S. Dept. Interior, Okla., 1965-67; v.p. Bio-Serv Corp., Troy, Mich., 1969—; lectr. preventive medicine Ohio Coll. Vet. Medicine, 1957-65; lectr. econ. biology Bowling Green State U., 1958-77; grain sanitation cons. Ohio Grain and Feed Dealers Assn., 1958-65; mem. Interagy. Bd.-U.S. Civil Service Examiners, Dallas, 1965-67; mem. Ohio Gov.'s Com. on Pesticides, 1961-63; chmn. adv. bd. pesticide tech. Ferris State Coll., 1972-77. Bd. dirs. Braes of Bloomfield, 1970-72, pres., 1971; bd. dirs. Birmingham YMCA. Fellow Royal Soc. Health (London, Eng.); mem. Mich. Pest Control Operators Assn. (pres. 1970-72, dir., 1973—), Nat. Pest Control Assn. (dir. 1972-75, award 1970, 75), ASTM (chmn. com. on vertebrate pesticides 1973—), Nat. Environ. Health Assn., Wildlife Soc., Entomol. Soc. Am., Pi Chi Omega (dir. 1972-76, pres. 1977). Republican. Baptist (deacon 1957-75). Mason, Rotarian (chmn. youth support com. Detroit 1972-73). Contbr. articles to profl. publs. Home: 6100 Idlewyle St Birmingham MI 48010 Office: Bio Service Corp 1130 Livernois St Troy MI 48084

BECK, JOSEPH GEORGE, musician; b. Youngstown, Ohio, Feb. 19, 1935; s. George B. and Anna (Eveland) B.; student Youngstown U., 1953-56; Mus.B., Westminster Choir Coll., 1956-59; M.A., Kent State U., 1966, postgrad. in music edn., 1969—; m. Sara Louise Ramser, Nov. 17, 1962. Mem., soloist Westminster Choir, Princeton, N.J., 1958-59; pvt. vocal tchr., Youngstown, 1959-62; minister of music, Lowell Ch., Canton, Ohio, 1962-64; instr. music, dir. glee clubs Kent State U., 1964-69; minister music, Main St. Meth. Ch., Akron, 1966-69; vocal dir. Kent State Summer Theater, Kent, Ohio, 1966-68; vocal cons. Kent State U. Theater and Speech Therapy depts.; vis. instr. music dir. chapel choir, voice instr. Mt. Union Coll., Alliance, Ohio, 1968-69; asst. prof., dir. choral activities Webster Coll., St. Louis, 1969-72; mus. dir., cons. dept. theater arts, 1970-72; mus. dir. Repertory Theatre, 1969-70; asst. prof., dir. choral and vocal activities St. Louis U., 1973—, musical dir. theater dept., 1974-76. Master class student John Finley Williamson, choral and voice, 1954-63, Roger Wagner, choral, 1970, Robert Shaw, choral, 1972. Served with AUS, 1960-61. Mem. Am. Choral Dirs. Assn. (chmn. local arrangements com. for nat. conv. 1975), AAUP, Assn. Choral Condrs., Nat. Assn. Tchrs. Singing, Music Educators Nat. Conf. Phi Mu Alpha Sinfonia, Alpha Psi Omega. Democrat. Book reviewer, choral reviewer for Am. Music Teacher mag., 1966-72; contbr. to The Choral Jour., 1976—. Home: 520 Edgar Ct St Louis MO 63119

BECK, LOUIS GEORGE, med. supply co. exec.; b. Bklyn., May 31, 1946; s. Louis and Carmen Mildren (De Rosa) B.; A.A., Temple U., 1969; B.S. in Med. Tech., Cleve. State U., 1971; m. Mary Catherine Manley, Aug. 10, 1974; 1 dau., Kelly Ann. Med. technician Episcopal Hosp., Phila., 1967-69; dir. purchasing Healthco-Schuemann-Jones Co., Cleve., 1969-72; mfrs. rep. Christiansen & Barber Assoc., Chgo., 1972-76; pres. Corpsman Med. Supply Co., Lodi, Ohio, 1976—. Served with USN, 1964-67; Vietnam. Decorated Air medal with 3 oak leaf clusters, Purple Heart with 2 oak leaf clusters, Bronze Star, Navy Commendation medal, Vietnamese Cross of Gallantry, Vietnamese Army Service medal; certified med. lab. technologist, blood bank technologist, notary public. Mem. Am. Legion, VFW, DAV. Republican. Roman Catholic. Club: Medina Kiwanis. Home: 8721 Chippewa Rd Chatham OH 44254 Office: PO Box 276 Lodi OH 44254

BECK, ROBERT KNOWLTON, newspaper pub.; b. Centerville, Iowa, July 17, 1915; s. Jesse McFall and Edna (Needham) B.; B.A., Iowa Wesleyan Coll., 1937, LL.D. (hon.), 1977; m. Charlotte V. Allen, June 24, 1939; children—Thomas Allen, Barbara (Mrs. Phil Climie), Martha (Mrs. Roger Bryant). Editor-pub. Daily Iowegian and Citizen, Centerville, Iowa, 1943—; asso. pub. Weekly Corydon Times-Republican, 1967—; partner Daily Blade-Tribune, Oceanside, Calif., 1943-54, asso. pub. semi-weekly newspaper Glendora, Charter Oak, Azusa, 1958-65; chmn. bd. dirs. Centerville Nat. Bank, 1968-76; pres. Centerville Broadcasting Co., 1948-54. Mem. Iowa Ho. of Reps.,

1953-54; mem. Iowa Hwy. Commn., 1955-59; commr. Iowa Devel. Commn., 1969—. Bd. trustees Iowa Wesleyan Coll., 1962—; trustee Hoover Library Assn., 1975—. Recipient 1st place in Iowa for editorial writing excellence, 1954; newspaper classed 1st in Ia. cities 12000 population or less, 1951, 53, 60, 2d place, 55, 57, 58; recipient Des Moines Press and Radio Bent Cane award, 1960; Ia. Master-Editor Pub. award, 1963, Iowa Daily Press Community Service award, 1963. Mem. Iowa Daily Press Assn. (dir.), Iowa Press Assn. (past pres.), C. of C. (past pres.), Iowa Good Roads Assn. (pres. 1963-65, chmn. bd. 1966-74), Am. Legion, Sigma Delta Chi. Methodist (del. jurisdictional conf. 1952 and 1964). Mason, Elk, Lion (past pres.). Clubs: Centerville Country (past pres.); Rathbun Lake Assn. (pres.). Home: 707 Drake Ave Centerville IA 52544 Office: 105-7 N Main St Centerville IA 52544

BECK, SALLY BELL, psychologist, educator; b. Indpls., May 16, 1931; d. Godfrey and Else (Zorn) Bell; m. Richard J. Beck, June 14, 1953. A.B., Butler U., 1953; M.A., U. Ill., 1956, Ph.D., 1960. Certified psychologist, Ind. Asst. prof. psychology Purdue U., 1962-64; asso. prof. Butler U., 1964-68, prof., 1968—; pvt. practice psychology, Indpls., 1963—. Mem. Am., Midwestern, Ind. (past sec.) psychol. assns., Marion County Muscular Dystrophy Assn. (past pres.), AAAS, Sigma Xi, Phi Kappa Phi, Psi Chi, Kappa Alpha Theta. Recipient Sta. WIFE ward for Community Service, 1968. Contbr. articles in field to profl. jours. including Jour. Experimental Psychology, Jour. of Personality and Social Psychology and others. Home: 4801 E 65th St Indianapolis IN 46220 Office: Department of Psychology Butler University Indianapolis IN 46206

BECKEN, RUSSELL WARREN, utility exec.; b. Theif River Falls, Dec. 20, 1912; s. Peter and Minnie (Habedank) B.; Elec. Technician, Dunwoody Inst., 1932; m. Marjorie A. Whitney, June 30, 1941; children—Carol, Peder. Electrician, Pato Gold Mining Inc., Colombia, S. Am., 1934-36; elec. serviceman and local mgr. Interstate Power Co., Bemidji and Cass Lake, Minn., 1936-44; dispatcher Otter Tail Power Co., Fergus Falls, Minn., 1944-50, div. engr., Jamestown, N.D., 1950-54, constrn. supt., Fergus Falls, 1954-58, supt., 1958-74, mgr. transmission and distbn., 1974—. Dist. chmn. Boy Scouts Am., 1962, recipient Dist. Merit award, 1976. Mem. IEEE (sr. mem., chmn., dir. Red River Valley sect. 1960-78), Fergus Falls C. of C. Republican. Lutheran. Club: Elks. Home: 1320 Linwood Ct Fergus Falls MN 56537 Office: 215 S Cascade St Fergus Falls MN 56537

BECKER, BENJAMIN MAX, lawyer; b. Chgo., Feb. 3, 1909; s. Max and Etta (Molschansky) B.; J.D., DePaul U., 1933; m. Jean Merin, Dec. 25, 1930; children—David M., Merle Lynn. Admitted to Ill. bar, 1935; since practiced in Chgo.; partner firm Warden & Becker, 1935-42; asso. mem. firm Levinson Becker Peebles & Swiren, 1942-47; sr. partner firm Becker & Savin, 1947-72; counsel firm Antonow & Fink, Chgo., 1973—. Dir. DePaul Inst. Fed. Taxation, 1952, 53. Chmn. bd., gen. counsel Am. Growth Industries, Inc., Am. Growth Devel. Corp., Burr Ridge Club Co., Oak Brook Club Co., all Oak Brook, Ill.; dir. Traffic Service Corp., Washington, John E. Staren & Co., Chgo.; chmn. bd., gen. counsel Hausske-Harlen Furniture Mfg. Co., Peru, Ind. Mem. Chgo. City Council, 1947-55. Bd. dirs. Chgo. chpt. UN Assn.; trustee Julian Research Found. Recipient distinguished service award Chgo. Life Ins. Underwriters Assn., 1970, several civic awards. Mem. Am., Ill., Chgo. bar assns., Internat. Soc. Law, Decalogue Soc. Clubs: Covenant of Ill. (dir.), City (Chgo.). Author: (with Edward Warden) Illinois Lawyer's Manual (2 vols.) 1939, (with Bernard Savin and David M. Becker), ann. supplements, 1948—; (with David M. Becker) Simplified Estate Planning, 1965; (with Bernard Savin and David M. Becker) Legal Checklists (2 vols.), 1966, ann. supplements, 1967; Is the United Nations Dead, 1969; (with Fred A. Tillman) The Family Owned Business, 1975. Contbr. numerous articles to profl. jours. Home: 342 Charal Ln Highland Park IL 60035 Office: 111 E Wacker Dr Chicago IL 60601

BECKER, DAVID NORBERT, ins. co. exec.; b. St. Louis, July 18, 1945; s. William Paul and Estelle Katherine (Meyer) B.; B.S. cum laude, St. Louis U., 1967, Ph.D. (fellow), 1973; M.A. (fellow) Washington U. St. Louis, 1969, A.S.A., 1977; m. JoAnn Elizabeth Clark, June 7, 1969. Instr. John Burroughs Sch., Ladue, Mo., 1969-70; instr. math. St. Louis U., 1970-73; asst. prof. math St. Francis Coll., Fort Wayne, Ind., 1973-75; mem. controllers dept. Lincoln Nat. Life Ins. Co., Fort Wayne, 1975—. Asso. fellow Soc. Actuaries; mem. Am. Math. Soc., Math. Assn. Am., Pi Mu Epsilon. Home: 7102 Woodhue Ln Fort Wayne IN 46804 Office: 1401 S Harrison St Fort Wayne IN 46801

BECKER, EDWARD BROOKS, govt. ofcl.; b. Emporia, Kans., Aug. 12, 1931; s. Earl N. and Ethel (Brooks) B.; B.A., Kans. State Tchrs. Coll., 1953; Ph.D. in Chemistry, U. Kans., 1959; m. Mary Helen Clark, June 20, 1959; children—Susan, Donna, John. Sr. research chemist PPG Industries, Barberton, Ohio, 1960-61; project mgr. Am. Machine & Foundry Co., Alexandria, Va., 1961-64; research chemist Gulf Oil Co., Overland Park, Kans., 1964-67, Pitts., 1967-70; dir. air pollution control and solid waste mgmt. Wis. Dept. Natural Resources, Madison, 1970—. Chmn. State and Territorial Air Pollution Program Adminstrs., 1974. Pres. Allegheny County council Camp Fire Girls, Pitts., 1968-70. Served with AUS, 1953-55. Mem. Am. Chem. Soc., Am. Inst. Chemists, A.A.A.S., Wis. Acad. Scis., Arts and Letters, Philos. Soc. Washington, Am. Pub. Works Assn., Air Pollution Control Assn. Home: 1132 University Bay Dr Madison WI 53705 Office: PO Box 7921 Madison WI 53707

BECKER, JASON C., diversified food mfg. co. exec.; b. Boston, May 28, 1929; s. David I. and Anna (Auerbuch) B.; A.B., Brown U., 1950; postgrad. U. Rochester, 1950-51; M.B.A. with honors, Harvard U., 1958; m. Carol Burtanger, July 28, 1955; 4 daus. Staff accountant Kendall Co., Walpole, Mass., 1955-56; account exec. Benton and Bowles, N.Y.C., 1958-62; various positions Gen. Foods Corp., White Plains, N.Y., 1962-69, asst. to pres., dir. corporate devel., mktg. mgr., 1965; pres., chief exec. officer, dir. Am. Consumer Products, Greenwich, Conn., 1969-74; v.p. Gen. Mills, Inc., Mpls., 1974—, v.p., gen. mgr. Northstar div., 1976—; dir. Saluto Foods Corp. Bd. dirs. Food Protein Council, Minn. Soc. for Crippled Children and Adults. Served with USNR, 1951-55. Clubs: Harvard Bus. Sch. Minn., Brown Univ. of Minn. Home: 3145 North Shore Dr Wayzata MN 55391 Office: PO Box 1113 Minneapolis MN 55440

BECKER, MAURICE EDWIN, virologist, state ofcl.; b. Prattsville, N.Y., Sept. 5, 1921; s. Gordon Earl and Harriet Isabel (Warner) B.; B.S., Cornell U., 1947, M.S., 1949; Ph.D. (research fellow), Purdue U., 1954; m. Eugenia Wilkin, Sept. 20, 1947; children—Sylvia (Mrs. Terry Pow), Stanley, Gary, Sheryl. Asst. microbiology N.Y. State Agr. Expt. Sta., Geneva, 1947-49; instr. microbiology Fla. State U. at Tallahassee, 1949-51; chief virology div. Md. Dept. Pub. Health, Balt., 1954-60, Mich. Dept. Pub. Health, Lansing, 1960—. Served with Inf., F.A., AUS, 1943-46. Decorated Purple Heart; recipient Meritorious Research award Purdue U., 1954. Mem. Am. Soc. Microbiology, Am. Med. Writers Assn., Am. Tissue Culture Assn., Mich. Bot. Soc., Sigma Xi. Contbr. articles profl. jours. Pioneer in invention of apparatus which permits persons with leg paralysis to play Hammond electric organ, 1973. Home: 1750 Nemoke Trail 4 Haslett MI 48840 Office: Mich Dept Pub Health 3500 N Logan St Lansing MI 48914

BECKER, MILLIE ANNA, educator; b. Centralia, Ill.; d. Louis and Elizabeth (Mueller) Becker; student summers So. Ill. U., Eastern Ill. U.; grad. Chgo. Tchrs. Coll.; Ph.B., U. Chgo., 1936, postgrad., 1936-41. Tchr., Centralia Area Schs., then Andrew Jackson Sch., Chgo., A.O. Sexton Sch., Chgo., Horace Mann Sch., Chgo. Mem. Nat. Soc. for Study Edn., Internat. Reading Assn., NEA, Ill. Edn. Assn., UN Assn. U.S.A., Nat. Congress Parents and Tchrs., Chgo. Kindergarten Primary Assn., Chgo. Tchrs. Union, U. Chgo. Alumni Assn., Phi Beta Kappa. Mem. United Ch. Christ. Address: 7637 S Loomis Blvd Chicago IL 60620

BECKER, NORMAN OTTO, surgeon; b. Fond du Lac, Wis., Jan. 16, 1918; s. John H. and Otillia A. (Graf) B.; B.A., U. Wis., 1940, M.D., 1943; m. Mildred Murdoch, June 20, 1943; children—Mary Gail, James Murdoch, Julia Brown, Constance Marjorie. Intern, resident, chief resident in surgery Cleve. Met. Hosp., 1943-49; surgeon Asso. Physicians, Fond du Lac, 1949—; asst. clin. prof. surgery U. Wis. Bd. dirs. Med. Coll. Wis.; dir. 1st Wis. Nat. Bank, Fond du Lac. Bd. dirs., exec com. U. Wis. Found.; pres. Citizens Council of U. Wis. Center. Served with USNR, 1944-46; PTO. Diplomate Am. Bd. Surgery. Fellow A.C.S. (bd. govs.); mem. Wis., Fond du Lac County med. socs., AMA, U. Wis. Alumni Assn. (past pres., Distinguished Service award 1976), Wis. Surg. Soc. (past pres.). Lutheran. Club: Fond du Lac Rotary (past pres.). Home: 1022 Mary Hill Park Fond du Lac WI 54935 Office: 505 E Division St Fond du Lac WI 54935

BECKER, ROLFE ALLEN, ophthalmologist, educator; b. Seattle, Aug. 27, 1930; s. Solomon and Josephine (Eichenwald) B.; B.A., U. Wash., 1952, M.D., 1957; m. Sylvia Schwarz, May 15, 1960; children—Bryan, Erica. Intern, Mpls. Gen. Hosp., 1957-58; resident in ophthalmology U. Minn. Hosps., including Mayo Clinic, Mpls. and Rochester, Minn., 1958-61; practice medicine specializing in ophthalmology, Kansas City, Mo., 1961—; instr. medicine U. Mo., Kansas City, 1972—; mem. staffs Menorah Med. Center, 1961—, bd. dirs., 1974—; mem. staff Bapt. Meml. Hosp.; mem. courtesy staff St. Luke's Hosp.; asso. clin. prof. ophthalmology Kans. U. Med. Center; asso. mem. examining bd. Am. Bd. Ophthalmology. Diplomate Am. Bd. Ophthalmology. Fellow A.C.S.; mem. AMA, Mo., Jackson County (Mo.) med. socs., Am. Acad. Ophthalmology (certificate of award for distinguished service 1976), Mo. Ophthalmology Soc., Kansas City Soc. Ophthalmology and Otolaryngology (pres. 1975). Club: Masons. Home: 6501 Wenonga Rd Shawnee Mission KS 66208 Office: 601 E 63d St Kansas City MO 64110

BECKER, SALLY ELECTA NORRIS (MRS. ALFRED D. BECKER), chem. cons.; b. Penn Yan, N.Y., Dec. 7, 1923; d. Ralph Thomas and Mary Leah (Post) Norris; A.B., Smith Coll., 1945; M.B.A., Northwestern U., 1964; m. Alfred D. Becker, Oct. 19, 1944; children—Stephen, Howard, Ralph. Owner, mgr. Chem. Bus. Consultants, Wilmette, Ill., 1964-69, Studio Research Assos., 1972—. Home: 348 Sterling Rd Kenilworth IL 60043

BECKER, SAMUEL LEO, communications scientist; b. Quincy, Ill., Jan. 5, 1923; s. Nathan and Rose (Dicker) B.; B.A., U. Iowa, 1947, M.A., 1949; Ph.D., 1953; postgrad. Columbia U., 1958-59; m. Ruth Henrietta Salzmann, June 14, 1953; children—Judith Ann, Harold Craig, Anne Louise. Broadcaster WTAD, Quincy, Ill., 1942, WTMV, St. Louis, 1947-48; instr. communications U. Wyo., Laramie, 1949-50; instr. speech, dramatic art U. Iowa, Iowa City, 1950-55, asst. prof., 1955-57, asso. prof., 1957-61, prof., 1961—, chmn. dept., 1968—; vis. prof. communications U. Wis., 1956; Fulbright prof. U. Nottingham (U.K.), 1963-64. Bd. dirs. Goodwill Industries SE Iowa, 1965-76. Served with inf., U.S. Army, 1942-45. Decorated Bronze Star. Fund for Adult Edn. mass media fellow, 1958-59. Mem. Speech Communication Assn. (pres. 1974), Nat. Assn. Ednl. Broadcasters (dir. 1958-60), Internat. Communcation Assn., Internat. Assn. Mass Communication Research, AAAS, Central States Speech Assn., AAUP, ACLU. Jewish. Author: (with Clay Harshbarger) Television, 1958; (with O. Brockett and D. Bryant) A Bibliographical Guide to Research in Speech and Dramatic Art, 1963; (with C. Baird and F. Knower) General Speech Communication, 1971; Essentials of General Speech Communication, 1973. Editor Speech Monographs, 1969-71. Contbg. author books, contbr. articles to profl. publs. Home: 521 W Park Rd Iowa City IA 52240

BECKER, STEPHEN SCOTT, food co. exec.; b. Milw., Dec. 20, 1945; s. Clarence and Pearl (Robbin) B.; student Tufts U., 1964-65; B.B.A., U. Wis., 1968; M.B.A., Marquette U., 1972; m. Barbara Usinger, Feb. 6, 1969; 1 son, Andrew David. With Becker Food Co., Inc., Milw., 1968—, v.p., 1974—, also dir. Bd. dirs. U. Sch. of Milw. Alumni Assn., 1974—. Served to staff sgt. USAR, 1968-74. Mem. Nat. (dir. 1976—), Milw. (pres. 1975-77) assns. of meat purveyors, Wis. Livestock and Meat Bd. (dir.), Am. Mktg. Assn., Internat. Foodservice Execs. Assn., Wis. Restaurant Assn. Clubs: Rotary, Milw. Athletic, Brynwood Country, Civil War Round Table of Milw. Mem. mktg. abstracts editorial staff Jour. of Mktg., 1976—. Home: 8016 N Poplar Dr Milwaukee WI 53217 Office: 4160 N Port Washington Rd Milwaukee WI 53212

BECKER, WILLIAM DENNIS, health adminstr.; b. St. Louis County, Mo., Oct. 23, 1931; s. Robert James and Virginia Hazel (Windmoeller) B.; B.S., U. Mo., 1953; postgrad. So. Ill. U., Edwardsville, 1974—; m. Mary Ann Hanson, Sept. 27, 1952; one dau., Katherine Ann; one son, William David. Mdse. mgr., asst. mgr. sales Brown Shoe Co., St. Louis, 1953-68; mgr. contract service A.S. Aloe Co., St. Louis, 1968-69; adminstrv. officer health planning Alliance for Regional Community Health, Inc., St. Louis, 1969-73, dep. dir., 1973-76; exec. dir. Mo. Area V Health Systems Agency, Poplar Bluff, 1976—. Pres. Clayton (Mo.) Brownbilt Credit Union, 1964-68; active YMCA. Served as officer USAF, 1953-55; Korea. Mem. Am. Assn. Comprehensive Health Planners, Mo. Pub. Health Assn. Mem. United Ch. Christ. Lion. Home: 2132 Autumn Rd Poplar Bluff MO 63901 Office: 211 S Broadway St Poplar Bluff MO 63901

BECKER, WILLIAM HENRY, fed. judge; b. Brookhaven, Miss., Aug. 26, 1909; s. William Henry and Verna (Lilly) B.; m. Geneva Moreton, June 9, 1932; children—Frances (Mrs. Robert A. Mills), Patricia (Mrs. Richard H. Hawkins), Nancy (Mrs. G. Lemuel Hewes), Geneva (Mrs. Edwin H. Jacks), William Henry, III; student La. State U., 1927-28; LL.B., U. Mo., 1932. Admitted to Miss. bar, 1930, Mo. bar, 1932, U.S. Supreme Ct. bar, 1937. Asso. firm Clark & Becker, Columbia, Mo., 1932-36; mem. firm, 1936-44, 46-61; spl. counsel Mo. Ins. Dept., 1936-44; spl. asst. to dir. Econ. Stablzn., Washington, 1945-46; chmn. Mo. Supreme Ct. Com. to draft Mo. Rules of Civil Procedure, 1952-59, spl. commr. Mo. Supreme Ct., 1954-58; judge U.S. Dist. Ct., Western Dist. Mo., Kansas City, 1961—, chief judge, 1965-77; mem. com. on operation jury system U.S. Jud. Conf., 1966-68, chmn. sub-com. to draft Jury Selection and Service Act of 1968, 1966-67, mem. coordinating com. for multiple litigation, 1962-68, vice chmn., 1967-68; mem. U.S. Jud. Panel on Multi-dist. Litigation, 1968-77; faculty Fed. Jud. Center Seminars and Workshops for U.S. Dist. Judges, 1968—. Served as lt. (j.g.) USN, 1944-45. Fellow Am. Bar Found., Am. Coll. Trial Lawyers, Am. Coll. Probate Counsel; mem. Am. Judicature Soc., Lawyers Assn. Kansas City, Am., Fed., Mo., Kansas City bar assns., Order of Coif. Bd. editors: Manual for Complex Litigation, 1968—. Home: 1026 W 63d St Kansas City MO 64113 Office: 741 US Courthouse 811 Grand Ave Kansas City MO 64106

BECKER, WILLIAM KOHL, engr.; b. St. Louis, June 13, 1927; s. William C. and Bessie (Kohl) B.; m. Lois Matthews, Feb. 4, 1951; 1 dau., Joan. B.S., Washington U., 1949; M.S., U. Ill., 1951. Registered profl. engr., Iowa, Mo., Minn., Nebr., Ohio, Pa., Tex., and others. Structural engr. Convair Aircraft Inc., Ft. Worth, 1953-55, William C. E. Becker, St. Louis, 1955-70; pres. Becker, Becker and Pannell, Inc., St. Louis, 1970—. Bd. govs. Washington U., 1975—, chmn. alumni annual giving fund Sch. of Engring. and Applied Sci., 1975—. Mem. Am. Soc. Civil Engrs., Am. Concrete Inst., Nat., Mo. socs. profl. engrs., Am. Consulting Engrs. Council, Mo. Athletic Club, Rotary, William Greenleaf Eliot Soc., Theta Xi, Sigma Xi, Sierra Club. Office: 411 N 7th St Saint Louis MO 63101

BECKETT, GRACE, educator; b. Smithfield, Ohio, Oct. 7, 1912; d. Roy M. and Mary (Hammond) Beckett; A.B., Oberlin Coll., 1934, A.M., 1935; Ph.D., Ohio State U., 1939. Music supr. Pub. Schs., Kelleys Island, Ohio, 1935-36; grad asst. econs. Ohio State U., 1936-39; asso. prof. econs. and music Ind. Central Coll., 1939-41: with U. Ill., 1941—, asst. prof. econs., 1945-51, asso. prof. econs., 1951-73, asso. prof. emerita, 1973—. Mem. Am., Midwest econ. assns., Music Educators Nat. Conf., Ill. Music Educators Assn., Econ. History Assn., Am. Finance Assn., Am. Hist. Assn., AAAS, N.Y. Acad. Scis., Ohio Acad. History, Hist. Soc. Pa., Ohio, Md. hist. socs., Ohio, Md. geneal. socs., Ill. Music Tchrs. Assn., Music Tchrs. Nat Assn., Interlochen Alumni Assn., Oberlin Friends of Art, Nat. Sch. Orch. Assn., Alpha Lambda Delta (hon.), Phi Beta Kappa, Pi Lambda Theta, Phi Chi Theta (hon.). Methodist. Club: University of Ill. Women's. Author: Reciprocal Trade Agreements Program, 1941, 72; contbr. profl. pubs. Address: PO Box 386 Urbana IL 61801

BECKETT, JAMES MARION, contrn. co. exec.; b. Wichita, Kans., Jan. 1, 1913; s. Loren Franklin and Mary Magdolene (Tolley) B.; ed. high sch.; m. Margaret M. Newell, Mar. 9, 1940. Owner, operator Beckett Erection Co., pre-engineered bldgs., Shawnee Mission, Kans., 1933—; erection supr. Butler Mfg. Co., Shawnee Mission, 1941-45. Mem. Metal Bldg. Dealers Assn. Republican. Mem. Christian Ch.-Disciples. Clubs: Exchange (pres. Kansas City 1960, Shawnee Mission 1955-56, nat. pres. 1965-66). Home and office: 5252 W 65th Pl Shawnee Mission KS 66202

BECKLEY, KENNETH F., data processing co. exec.; b. Hartford, Conn., Dec. 29, 1934; s. Kenneth F. and Mary (Brigham) B.; B.S., U. Me., 1957; postgrad. U. Wis., 1967; m. Gloria Skolasinski, 1974; children by previous marriage—Michael S., Patricia A., Richard K., Matthew H.; adopted children—Teri J., Kellie L. System analyst, EAM foreman, programming supr., control supr. Allis Chalmers Mfg. Co., Milw., 1957-67; data center mgr. Travenol Labs., Deerfield Ill., 1967-70, mgr. systems planning, 1970-72, mgr. data center, 1972-76, mgr. corporate hardware and communications planning, 1976—. Instr. data processing ops. Milw. Inst. Tech., evenings 1964. Served with AUS, 1958-60. Mem. Data Processing Mgmt. Assn. Home: 1007 Main St Antioch IL 60002 Office: Deerfield IL 60015

BECKMANN, HEINO ALBERT PAUL, polit. scientist, educator; b. Celle, Germany, June 24, 1940; s. Wilhelm Heinrich and Erika Anna (Stecher) B.; came to U.S., 1965; student Freie Universitat Berlin, 1963-65; M.A., U. Pa., 1967, Ph.D., 1975; m. Waltraud Nolte, July 30, 1965; 1 son, Andreas Stecher. Research asst. Fgn. Policy Research Inst., Phila., 1966-70; mem. editorial research bd. Orbis, Jour. World Affairs, 1968-70; lectr. polit. sci. PMC Colls., Chester, Pa., 1968-70; asso. prof. Coll. St. Teresa, Winona, Minn., 1970—, chmn. dept. social scis., 1970-73, 77—; dep. dir., lectr. seminar civil affairs units. U.S. Army Res., 1969. Trustee Coll. St. Teresa, 1977—. Served to maj. German Fed. Armed Forces, 1960-63. Fulbright grantee, 1965-69, U. Pa. Free U. Berlin exchange scholar, 1965-66, H.B. Earhart fellow, 1969-70, NSF grantee, 1971; recipient Distinguished Service medal German Fed. Armed Forces, 1976. Mem. Am., Midwest polit. sci. assns., Acad. Polit. Sci., Conf. Group German Politics, Nat. Geog. Soc. Home: Purzi Route 3 Winona MN 55987

BECRAFT, JOHN RICHARD, petroleum cos. exec.; b. Rushville, Ind., Mar. 21, 1919; s. Frank W. and Pearl (Casey) B.; student Advanced Mgmt. Program Harvard, 1958; m. Esther Irene Moore, Feb. 24, 1943; children—Frank Joseph, Sue Ann. Maintenance supr. Great Lakes Pipeline Co., Sioux Falls, S.D., 1951-56, mgr. engring. constrn., Kansas City, Mo., 1956-63; pres. No. Gas Products Co., Omaha, UPG, Inc., Omaha, Hydrocarbon Transp. Inc., Omaha, No. Helex, Omaha, 1963-76, also dir.; pres., presiding chmn. No. Liquid Fuels Cos., Omaha, 1976, also dir.; dir., exec. operating com. NNG, dir. Peoples Natural Gas div., No. Petrochem. Co. Mem. task group transp. and storage Emergency Adv. Com. for Natural Gas, 1973. Pres. Omaha chpt. Arthritis Found., 1974; bd. dirs. Nebr. Arthritis Found. Served with AC, AUS, 1941-45. Mem. Assn. Oil Pipe Lines, Pipeliners Club, Nat. Rifle Assn., Omaha Press Club, Petroleum Clubs of Tulsa, Great Bend (Kans.), Midland (Tex.). Methodist. Office: 2223 Dodge St Omaha NE 68102

BECVAR, STEPHEN LEE, plastic mfg. co. owner; b. Omaha, June 24, 1939; s. Joseph Louis and Stacia Elizabeth (Janecek) B.; B.S. in M.E., S.D. State Coll., 1956-60; postgrad. Mankato State Coll., 1969; m. Bettie Lou Cooke, Jan. 25, 1962; children—James, Louis, Myra Marie, Theresa Michele, William Lee. Engr., asst. prodn. mgr. Cantex Industries, Inc., Mineral Wells, Tex., 1964-65; prodn. mgr., plant engr. Western Plastics, Hastings, Nebr., 1966-68; project engr. Nat. Poly Products, Mankato, Minn., 1968-71; owner, mgr., sec-treas. Century Plastics, Inc., Hayfield, Minn., 1971—. Asst. sec. Hayfield Firemen, 1973—; mem. Hayfield City Council, 1973-76. Served with U.S. Army, 1961-64. Named Outstanding Jaycee of the Year, Hastings Jr. C. of C., 1967. Mem. Am. Soc. Agrl. Engrs., Minn. Land Improvement Contractors Assn., Mankato Jr. C. of C. (dir. 1969-70). K.C. Clubs: Toastmasters (sgt. at arms 1969-70) (Mankato); Commercial (dir. 1972) (Hayfield). Home and Office: Box 51 Hayfield MN 55940

BEDARD, GEORGE RUDOLPH, realtor; b. near Dayton, Minn., Sept. 28, 1909; s. John Baptiste and Clara Louise (Trombley) B.; grad. high sch., Mpls.; m. Ruth Elizabeth DuBeau, Aug. 5, 1935; children—Robert, Dennis, John, James, Thomas, Jeanne Marie. Typist, acctg. clk. No. State Power Co., Mpls., 1927-45; partner DeLuxe Oil Co., Osakis, Minn., 1945-46; partner Colliers Barbecue Restaurant, Hibbing, Minn., 1946; owner-cook George's Barbecue Restaurant, Brainerd, Minn., 1947-57; real estate broker-owner George Bedard Real Estate, Brainerd, 1956—. Mayor Brainerd, 1970-74; 1st chmn. Brainerd United Fund, 1969; chmn. St. Joseph's Hosp. Expansion Fund, 1970; chmn. Save Historic Water Tower Com., 1968-73; pres. Crow Wing State Park Chapel Restoration Com., 1973-74. Mem. Brainerd Area Bd. Realtors (pres. 1965), Minn. Assn. Realtors (pres. 1971, dir. 1970—), Nat. Assn. Realtors (dir. 1975—), Brainerd C. of C. (pres. 1963), Nat. Inst. Real Estate Brokers. Republican. Roman Catholic. Clubs: K.C. (4th degree, grand knight 1969), Elks, Eagles, Moose, Exchange. Home: 710 N 4th St Brainerd MN 56401 Office: 1123 S 6th St Brainerd MN 56401

BEDARD, JAMES HARRY, realtor; b. Hibbing, Minn., Oct. 4, 1946; s. George R. and Ruth E. (DuBeau) B.; B.A. in Polit. Sci., St. Mary's Coll., Minn., 1968; grad. Realtors Inst., 1971; m. Caren M. Crowther, Nov. 25, 1972. Salesman George Bedard Real Estate Co., Brainerd, Minn., 1968—, gen. office mgr., 1972—; lectr. home mgmt. course at Brainerd Community Coll., 1971-73. Mem. Brainerd City Planning Commn., 1969—; capt. United Fund Drive, Brainerd, 1969-70; div. capt. St. Joseph's Hosp. Fund Drive, Brainerd, 1969—. Mem. Winona County (Minn.) Republican Exec. Bd., 1966-68; Rep. chmn. City of Brainerd, 1969-71; Rep. chmn. Crow Wing County (Minn.), 1973-75; Minn. State del. to Rep. Conv., 1969-75; mem. advisory bd. Salvation Army, 1977. Named Outstanding Young Man of Brainerd, Jaycees, 1970. Mem. Crow Wing County Hist. Soc., Brainerd Bd. Realtors (pres. 1975), Brainerd Jaycees (dir. 1969-70, pres. 1971-72). Roman Catholic. Elk, Moose, Rotarian (dir.). Home: 513 E St Brainerd MN 56401 Office: 119-23 S 6th St Brainerd MN 56401

BEDELL, BERKLEY, congressman. Mem. 94th-95th Congresses from 6th Iowa Dist. Office: US House of Representatives Washington DC 20515

BEDNARCZYK, WALTER WILLIAM, labor relations exec.; b. Mpls., Apr. 3, 1944; s. Walter A. and Vera G. (Haraburda) B.; B.A., St. Thomas Coll., 1966; M.A., U. Minn., 1969; m. Colette M. Berdan, Mar. 22, 1975. Personnel adminstr. Control Data Corp., Mpls., 1968; instr. gen. bus. Mainland Coll., Texas City, 1969-70; employee relations rep. Union Carbide Corp., Texas City, 1969-70; indsl. relations dir. Cornelius Engring. Center, Mpls., 1971-73; pres. Employee Relations Associates, Mpls., 1973-76; dir. labor relations Toro Inc., Mpls., 1977—; instr. mgmt. St. Thomas Coll., St. Paul, Minn., 1976; cons. employee relations Alpha Associates, Inc., Mpls., 1976—. Mem. Mpls. Park and Recreation Commn., 1971-74, city treas., 1974-76. Accredited Personnel Diplomate. Mem. Am. Soc. Personnel Adminstrs. Roman Catholic. Home: 5117 Richmond Dr Edina MN 55436 Office: 8111 Lyndale Ave S Minneapolis MN 55420

BEDWELL, HORACE WADE, clergyman, psychologist, pub. schs. adminstr.; b. Washington, Jan. 26, 1936; s. Horace V. and Wilda W. (Jenkins) B.; B.A., Harding Coll., 1959; M.Ed., U. Mo., 1964; Ed.S., SE Mo. State U., 1974; Ph.D., So. Ill. U., 1977; m. Emma F. Jarrell, June 25, 1955; children—Michael, Jonathan. Ordained to ministry Ch. of Christ, 1954; tchr. Scott County (Mo.), 1960-62, prin. elementary sch., 1962-65, dir. elementary edn., 1965-67; psychol. cons. Mo. Div. Mental Health, Sikeston (Mo.) Regional Diagnostic Clinic, 1967-74; dir. spl. services Sikeston Pub. Schs., 1968-69, dir. Child Study Center, 1969—, adminstr., 1969—; instr. edn. and psychology SE Mo. State U., 1974—; bd. dirs. Sikeston Community Sheltered Workshop. Certified elementary tchr., prin., schs. supt., sch. psychol. examiner, Mo. Mem. Mo. Tchrs. Assn., SE Mo. Dist. Prins. Assn., Am. Psychol. Assn., Am. Assn. Mental Deficiency, Phi Delta Kappa. Home: 501 N Ingram St Sikeston MO 63801 Office: Lee Hunter Sch Sikeston MO 63801

BEDWELL, TOMMY JOE, mech. engr.; b. Linton, Ind., June 17, 1939; s. Harry Clifford and Mary Teressa (White) B.; B.M.E., Rose Poly. Inst., 1961; m. Freda Faye Speedy, June 16, 1961; 1 dau., Cathy Lynne. Engr., Ind. Pub. Service Co., summer 1960; test engr. truck div. Internat. Harvester, Ft. Wayne, Ind., 1961-64, rotational trainee, 1964-65, devel. engr. research div., 1965-68, sr. devel. engr., 1968-75; staff engr. piston design and devel. Bohn Aluminum and Brass Co. div. Gulf and Western Industries, Inc., South Haven, Mich., 1975—. Registered profl. engr., Ind. Mem. Soc. Automotive Engrs., Am. Soc. for Metals. Republican. Mem. Christian Ch. Club: Masons. Home: 1194 Euna Vista Dr Holland MI 49423 Office: Bohn Aluminum and Brass Co Aylworth and Indiana Sts South Haven MI 49090

BEECH, ROBERT PAUL, psychologist; b. Denver, Dec. 31, 1940; s. Kenneth Albert and Ruth Elvie (Paulson) B.; m. Mary Jane Higdon, June 12, 1962; children—Robert D., Richard A. B.A. cum laude Colo. U., 1962, M.A., 1964; Ph.D., Mich. State U., 1967. Research fellow Am. Inst. Indian Studies, 1967-68; asst. prof. ednl. psychology N.Y. U., 1968-73, project dir. Evaluation of Computer Assisted Instruction Program, Center for Field Research and Social Services, 1969-70; mem. consulting faculty Center Continuing Edn. Ill. State Psychiatric Inst., 1976—. Scoutmaster Thatcher Woods Area council Boy Scouts Am., 1977; precinct capt. All Am. Village Party, Oak Park, Ill., 1977; coordinator research, tng. and evaluation Subregion 8 Ill. Dept. Mental Health and Devel. Disabilities. Certified psychologist, Mich. Mem. Am., Midwestern psychol. assns., Acad. Psychologists in Marital and Family Therapy, Soc. Psychol. Study of Social Issues, Internat. Council of Psychologists, Psi Chi, Phi Kappa Phi. NIMH fellow, 1964-67. Author: Evaluation of the Dial-a-Drill Program, 1969-70; Evaluation of NYC High School Auxiliary Program, 1973. Editor: (with J. Ramsey) Psychological Foundations of Education, 1969; (with M.J. Beech) Bengal: Change and Continuity, 1971. Contbr. articles in field to profl. jours. Home: 1134 S Gunderson St Oak Park IL 60304 Office: 4200 N Oak Park Ave Chicago IL 60634

BEECHEM, HENRY ALBERT, chem. co. owner; b. Claridge, Pa., Apr. 30, 1906; s. Joseph and Victoria (Jankowska) B.; student Mich. State U., 1927-29, U. Chgo., 1930; B.S., Mich. State U., 1932; m. Mabel Crandell, Dec. 24, 1937; children—Katherine Ruhlman, Janie Atkinson, Michael. Chemist, Mich. Dept. Health, Lansing, 1932-36; chemist Standard Brands, Chgo., 1936-40; owner Beechem Labs., St. Johns, Mich., 1940—; ret. research chemist Stetson U., Deland, Fla., 1961—. Chem. cons. Jergens, Inc., Cleve., 1962—. Fellow AAAS. Contbg. editor Graphic Arts Monthly, 1940-59. Contbr. articles to profl. jours. Patentee in field. Home: 64 Dover St Pentwater MI 49449 also 435 S Stone St Deland FL 32720 Office: 1100 W State St St Johns MI 48879

BEECHER, LEE HEWITT, psychiatrist; b. Mpls., Feb. 18, 1939; s. James Morrison and Ruth Eleanor (Borgendale) B.; B.A., Carleton Coll., 1961; B.S., U. Minn., 1965, M.D., 1965; children—James Arthur, Lynn Ruth. Intern, Hennepin County Gen. Hosp., Mpls., 1965-66; resident psychiatry U. Chgo., 1966-69; psychiatrist Mpls. Clinic Psychiatry and Neurology, 1972-73; pvt. practice psychiatry, St. Louis Park, Minn., 1973—; mem. staff Met. Med. Center, Meth. Hosp.; clin. asst. prof. dept. psychiatry and family practice U. Minn., 1973—. Served with USNR, 1969-72. Diplomate in psychiatry Am. Bd. Psychiatry and Neurology. Mem. AMA, Am. Psychiat. Assn. Home: 7574 Mariner Point Maple Grove MN 55369 Office: 6490 Excelsior Blvd St Louis Park MN 55426

BEECHER, REXINE ELLEN, civic worker; b. Eldora, Iowa, Aug. 16, 1915; d. Vernon Richard and Gladys Metha (Bateson) Wardman; student U. No. Iowa, 1936-37; B.A., State U. of Iowa, 1939; m. Loyd Giff Beecher, June 15, 1939; 1 dau., Ellen Beth Beecher Feldick. Legal sec. Bateson & Ryan, attys., Eldora, Iowa, 1932, 33-35; asst. bus. mgr. College Eye Newspaper, Cedar Falls, Iowa, 1936-37; sec. econs. dept. Iowa State U., Ames, 1961-62; tchr. English, Union (Iowa) Sch., 1962-63; librarian Union Pub. Library, 1967-69. Mem. D.A.R. (state registrar 1976—), Farm Bur. Republican. Home: Rural Route 1 Union IA 50258

BEECHY, ATLEE, educator; b. Berlin, Ohio, Oct. 27, 1914; s. George Warren and Katie (Beechy) B.; B.S., Goshen Coll., 1935; Ph.D., Ohio State U., 1958, M.A., 1940; m. Winifred Irene Nelson, May 24, 1941; children—Karen (Mrs. Gerald L. Kreider), Judith (Mrs. Gordon Dyck), Susan (Mrs. John Enz). Tchr. elementary sch., Homes County, Ohio, 1932-37; tchr. elementary and jr. high sch., Inner City, Columbus, 1937-43; dean of men Goshen Coll. (Ind.), 1949-55, dean students, 1956-66, dir. office experimentation, 1967-70, prof. psychology, 1959—, coordinator counseling services, 1971—. Vis. prof. Ohio State U., summers 1959-60; Fulbright lectr. Allahabad U., India, 1960-61; cons. in personnel and human relations, India, 1968, 70, 72, 74, Indonesia, 1971. Mem. Elkhart County Mental Health Assn., 1966—; dir. Vietnam Christian Service, Vietnam, 1966. Mem. Internat. Peace Acad., Phi Delta Kappa. Mem. Mennonite Ch. (exec. com. central com. 1961—, chmn. relief and service com. 1961-75, dir. European central com. 1946-49, ch. world service com. 1975—). Author: (with Winifred Beechy) Vietnam: Who Cares?, 1968; (with W. Beechy and R. Keim) The Church: The Reconciling Community 1970; After High School, What?, 1969; Space Theory of Personality: A Psychosocial Approach, 1973. Home: 1916 Woodward Place Goshen IN 46526

BEEKHUIS, GERARDUS JAN, surgeon; b. Benoni, South Africa, Apr. 24, 1931; s. Gerardus and Mynsje (Pleysier) B.; student Christian Bros. Coll., South Africa, 1942-46; M.D., Pretoria (South Africa) U., 1952; children—Vicki, Fritha, Jan. Came to U.S., 1953, naturalized, 1962. Intern, Pretoria Gen. Hosp. and Henry Ford Hosp., Detroit, 1953-54; resident Detroit Gen. Hosp., 1954-56, Washington U., 1956-57; practice medicine specializing in cosmetic facial surgery, Detroit, 1957—; mem. staff Harper, Sinai hosps., Detroit; prof. dept. otolaryngology Wayne State U. Sch. Medicine, 1963-72. Fellow Am. Acad. Facial Plastic and Reconstructive Surgery (pres. 1973-74), Am. Acad. Ophthalmology and Otolaryngology, Am. Soc. Head and Neck Surgery, A.C.S., Am. Assn. Cosmetic Surgeons; mem. Triologic Soc., Physician's Wine Appreciation Soc. Greater Detroit (pres. 1971-73). Contbr. chpts. to books, articles to profl. jours. Home: 475 Goodhue Ct Bloomfield Hills MI 48013 Office: 573 Fisher Bldg Detroit MI 48202

BEEKS, JOHN CHARLES, educator; b. Eagleville, Mo., July 7, 1924; s. Jesse William and Gladys (Leeper) B.; B.S., U. Mo., 1948, M.A., 1955, Ed.D., 1964; m. Eula Arlene Trullinger, July 29, 1944; children—Beverly Kay (Mrs. Eric Ronald Johansen), Patricia Ann (Mrs. Richard M. Dowden). Vocational agr. instr. Galt (Mo.) Consol. Schs., 1948-51; vocational agr. instr. Stanberry (Mo.) R-II Sch., 1951-57; prof., chmn. dept. agr. and scis. N.W. Mo. State U., Maryville, 1958—, dir. coll. farms, coll. pres.'s adv. com. Pres. Mo. Community Betterment, Maryville, 1968—. Served with AUS, 1944-46; ETO. Decorated Bronze Star with oak leaf cluster. Mem. Nat. Assn. Coll. Tchrs. Agr. (pres.), Am. Soc. Agronomy, Crop Sci. Soc. Am., Soil Sci. Soc. Am., Gamma Sigma Delta, Phi Delta Kappa. Methodist. Mason (Shriner), Lion. Contbr. articles to profl. jours. Home: 309 Clayton Ave Maryville MO 64468

BEELMAN, GARY SCOTT, dentist; b. Columbus, Ohio, Feb. 4, 1935; s. Floyd C. and Alice H. (McCormick) B.; B.S., Washburn U., Topeka, 1960; D.D.S., U. Mo., Kansas City, 1964; m. Bonnie Becker, Jan. 31, 1960; children—Gregory Scott, Bradly Kent, Brit Allen. Dental health officer Topeka Shawnee County, 1964-65; pvt. practice dentistry, Topeka, 1965—; chief dental cons. Kans. Neurol. Inst., 1966—. Mem. City-County Adv. Bd. Health, Disaster Adv. Council. Served with U.S. Army, 1954-56. Recipient Research grant from U.S. Govt. through U. Mo., 1963-64, award of merit clinic presentation Mo.-Kans. Dental Meeting, 1964. Mem. Am., Kans., Shawnee County dental assns., Fedn. Dental Internat., Xi Psi Phi. Republican. Episcopalian. Club: Topeka Country. Home: 1216 W 29th St Topeka KS 66611 Office: 1319 Huntoon St Topeka KS 66604

BEEM, JOHN KELLY, mathematician; educator; b. Detroit, Jan. 24, 1942; s. William Richard and June Ellen (Kelly) B.; A.B. in Math., U. So. Calif., 1963, M.A. in Math. (NSF fellow), 1965, Ph.D. in Math. (NSF fellow), 1968; m. Eloise Masako Yamamoto, Mar. 24, 1964; 1 son, Thomas Kelly. Asst. prof. math. U. Mo., Columbia, 1968-71, asso. prof. math., 1971—. Mem. Math. Assn. Am., Am. Math. Soc., Phi Beta Kappa. Home: 1106 Pannell St Columbia MO 65201

BEERMAN, BURTON, musician; b. Atlanta, June 12, 1943; s. Mannie Robert and Ida (Minsk) B.; B.M., Fla. State U., 1966; M.M., U. Mich., 1968, D.M.A., 1971; m. Stella Celeste Hataszti, Aug. 3, 1962; 1 son, Raymond Brent. Asso. prof. music composition and history Bowling Green (Ohio) State U., 1970—; vis. lectr. U. Utah, 1975; composer; works include: Mixtures for Voices, Instruments, Tape and Theatre, Frame for Six Flutes, Sensations for Clarinet and Tape. Compositions selected for internat. competition and performance Gaudeamus Internat. Festival, Netherlands, 1969, 76; recipient 1st prize Pitts. Flute Club, 1970, 2d prize Louisville Brass Quintet, 1975. Mem. Am. Composers Alliance, Broadcast Music, Inc., Am. Soc. Univ. Composers, Ohio Theory-Composition Tchrs. Home: 1628 Juniper Dr Apt 92 Bowling Green OH 43402 Office: College of Musical Arts Bowling Green State University Bowling Green OH 42403

BEERMANN, ALLEN JAY, state ofcl.; b. Sioux City, Iowa, Jan. 14, 1940; s. Albert and Amanda (Schoenrock) B.; B.A., Midland Luth. Coll., 1962; J.D., Creighton U., 1965; m. Linda Dierking, May 23, 1971. Radio announcer KHUB, Fremont, Nebr., 1960-62; admitted to Nebr. bar, 1965; adminstrv. asst. to sec. state Nebr., 1965-67, dep. sec. state, legal counsel Lincoln, 1967-71, sec. state, 1971—. Mem. exec. bd. Lancaster County (Nebr.) Cancer Soc., 1968—, Cornhusker council Boy Scouts Am., 1969—, Tabitha Devel. Corp., Lincoln. Bd. dirs. Nebraskaland Found., Immanual Med. Center. Capt. Nebr. N.G. Recipient Distinguished Service plaque Omaha Legal Aid Soc., 1965, Outstanding Young Man award Nebr. Jaycees. Mem. Am., Nebr. bar assns., Nebr. Press Assn., Nat. Assn. Secs. State (pres.), Internat. Platform Assn., Am. Judicature Soc., Am. Interprofl. Inst., Nat. Honor Soc., Am. Legion, Pi Kappa Delta, Phi Alpha Delta. Lutheran. Elk. Contbg. editor Neb. State Govt., 1966—. Home: 4730 A St Lincoln NE 68510 Office: Dept of State Capitol Bldg Lincoln NE 68509

BEERS, THELMA SNEED (MRS. RUSSELL JAMES BEERS), microbiologist, educator; b. Newport, Ky., June 6, 1913; d. Mayce Cannon and Edna (Dyer) Sneed; B.A. cum laude, U. Minn., 1934, M.A., 1936, B.S. in Edn., 1939, Ph.D. in Bacteriology, 1949; m. Russell James Beers, Dec. 27, 1950 (dec. July 1967); children—Barbara Lee, Shirley Kay. Tchr. biology Robbinsdale (Minn.) High Sch., 1939-45; research, teaching asst. U. Minn., 1945-48; bacteriologist Am. Crystal Sugar Co., St. Paul, 1948-49; instr. bacteriology Kans. State U., Manhattan, 1949-51; research asst. U. Ill., 1951-53; microbiologist Viobin Corp., Monticello, Ill., 1953-54; research in bacteriology Iowa State U., Ames, 1958-69; tchr. Edina (Minn.) Pub. Schs., 1969-70; research U. Minn., 1970—. Mem. Am. Soc. for Microbiology, AAAS, AAUW, D.A.R., Amateur Fencing League Am., Sigma Xi, Sigma Delta Epsilon, Iota Sigma Pi. Clubs: Ames Woman's (pres. 1968-69), Iowa State University Faculty Women's; Women's Color Photo (Mpls.) (pres. 1947-48; U. Minn. Faculty Women's. Home: 11609 Bren Rd Minnetonka MN 55343

BEERS, THOMAS WESLEY, educator; b. Greensburg, Pa., Oct. 23, 1930; s. Walter Leon and Margaret Ellen (Murtland) B.; B.S. in Forestry, Pa. State U., 1955, M.S. in Forest Mgmt. (St. Regis Paper Co. grantee), 1956; Ph.D. in Forest Mgmt., Purdue U., 1960; m. Florence Carolyn Miller, Jan. 31, 1953; children—Thomas P., Timothy C., Todd G., Theodore W. Instr. Purdue U., West Lafayette, Ind., 1956-60, asst. prof., 1960-65, asso. prof., 1965-69, prof. forestry, 1969—. Dir. Foresters, Inc. Served as sgt. AUS, 1950-52. Mem. Sigma Xi, Phi Kappa Phi, Xi Sigma Pi, Gamma Sigma Delta. Author: (with Husch and Miller) Forest Mensuration, 1972; (with Miller) Manual of Forest Mensuration, 1973. Home: 201 N 350 W West Lafayette IN 47906

BEERS, VICTOR GILBERT, editor; b. Sidell, Ill., May 6, 1928; s. Ernest S. and Jean H. (Bloomer) B.; A.B., Wheaton (Ill.) Coll., 1950; M.R.E., No. Bapt. Sem., 1953, M.Div., 1954, Th.M., 1955, Th.D., 1960; Ph.D., Northwestern U., 1963; m. Arlisle Felten, Aug. 26, 1950; children—Kathleen, Douglas, Ronald, Janice, Cynthia. Prof. No. Bapt. Sem., Chgo., 1954-57; editor Sr. High Publications, David C. Cook Pub. Co., Elgin, Ill., 1957-59, exec. editor, 1959-61, editorial dir., 1961-67; pres. Creative Designs, Elgin, Ill., 1967—. Dir. Wheaton (Ill.) Youth Symphony, 1961-63, pres., 1962-63; trustee David C. Cook Found., Elgin, 1965-67, Wheaton Coll., 1975—; bd. dirs. Christian Camps, Inc., N.Y.C., 1972—. Baptist. Author: A Child's Treasury of Bible Stories, 4 vols., 1970; Family Bible Library, 10 vols., 1971, others. Address: Route 1 Box 321 Elgin IL 60120

BEERS, WILLIAM O., food co. exec.; b. Lena, Ill., May 26, 1914; s. Ernest and Rosa (Binz) B.; student U. Wis., 1933-37, LL.D., 1970; m. Mary Elizabeth Holmes (dec.); m. 2d, Frances Lemaux Miller, Feb. 17, 1954; children—Marila M. Beers Beatty, Barbara Ann Beers Guzzardo, Mary Elizabeth, Richard W., Duncan R. Miller. With Kraft, Inc., 1937—, pres., 1968-73, chmn., 1973—, pres. Kraft Foods Div., 1965-68, also dir.; dir. A.O. Smith Corp., Am. Airlines, Mfrs. Hanover Trust Co., Mfrs. Hanover Corp., Sears, Roebuck & Co., U.S. Steel Corp. Chmn. exec. com. Food and Drug Law Inst.; mem. Bus. Council and Bus. Roundtable; trustee Com. for Econ. Devel., Consumer Research Inst.; bd. dirs. Evanston (Ill.) Hosp., U. Wis. Found. Mem. NAM (dir.), Chgo. Council Fgn. Relations (dir.), Grocery Mfrs. Assn. (chmn.), Conf. Bd. (vice chmn.). Clubs: Econ. (N.Y.C., Chgo.); Union League, Links (N.Y.C.); Chgo., Old Elm (Chgo.); Blind Brook (Portchester, N.Y.); Indian Hill (Winnetka, Ill.). Office: Kraft Inc Kraft Ct Glenview IL 60025

BEESTMAN, GEORGE BERNARD, chemist; b. Hammond, Wis., July 17, 1939; s. Herman Anton and Mary (Ter Beest) B.; B.S., Wis. State U., 1961; M.S., U. Wis., 1967, Ph.D., 1969; m. Donna J. McDowell, July 10, 1965; children—Joan Ardith, Scott McDowell. Sr. research chemist herbicide formulation Monsanto Agrl. Products Co., St. Louis, 1968-73, research specialist herbicide formulation, 1973—. Bd. dirs. Greeley Community Center; chmn. research and devel. subcom. Presbyn. Commn. Community, Aging, Service and Healing. Mem. Am. Soc. Agronomy, Weed Sci. Soc. Am. (chmn. soil aspects sect. 1977), Soil Sci. Soc. Am., Council Agrl. Sci. and Tech., pres. Monsanto Sci. Club br. 1973—), Sci. Research Soc. Am. (sec. Monsanto Sci. Club br. 1971, pres. 1973—), AAAS. Presbyterian. Contbr. articles to profl. jours. Home: 13124 Old Farm Rd St Louis MO 63142 Office: 800 N Lindbergh Blvd St Louis MO 63166

BEETS, F. LEE, ins. co. exec.; b. Paola, Kans., Apr. 2, 1922; s. William Francis and Nellie (Bryan) B.; B.B.A., Tulane U., 1945; postgrad. Harvard U., 1945, evening sch. U. Kansas City, Rockhurst Coll.; m. Dorothy Loraine Shelton, June 20, 1945; children—Randall Lee, Pamela Lee. Sr. accountant Lunsford Barnes & Co., Kansas City, Mo., 1946-49; v.p., gen. mgr. Viking Refrigerators, 1949-53; v.p., sec.-treas. Equipment Finance Co., 1949-53; exec. v.p., treas., gen. mgr. T.H. Mastin & Co., Consol. Underwriters, Mo. Gen. Ins. Co., Plan-O-Pay, Inc., Mid-Am. Data Co., B O L Assos., Inc., 1953-69; now chmn. bd. chief exec. officer Fin. Guardian Group, Inc., Fin. Guardian Ins. Agy., Inc., Fin. Compensation Cons., Inc., Worldsurance, Inc., Risk Adminstrn. Services, Inc., Financial Guardian Internat. B.V. Served with USNR, 1942-45. C.P.A., Mo. Mem. Mo. Soc. C.P.A.'s, Am. Inst. C.P.A.'s, Soc. C.P.C.U.'s, Pi Kappa Alpha, Sigma Tau Gamma, Phi Mu Alpha Sinfonia. Club: Masons. Home: 7901 Bristol Ct Prairie Village KS 66208 Office: 3100 Broadway Kansas City MO 64111

BEGO, GENE LELAND, business exec.; b. Indpls., May 1, 1924; s. Carey Joseph and Agnes (Goins) B.; B.S., Purdue U., 1949; m. Elaine Lillian Rea, Apr. 22, 1950 (dec. June 1966), children—Carol Gene, Robert Rea. With Cummins Engine Co., Inc., Columbus, Ind., 1951-61, dir. mktg. services, 1959-61, v.p., bd. dirs. Cummins Diesel Sales, 1959-61; with B. F. Goodrich Indsl. Products Co., 1961-67, v.p. mktg. 1963-67; v.p. mktg. B. F. Goodrich Tire Co., Akron, Ohio, 1967-70, exec. v.p., 1970-72; pres. Robert Bosch Corp., Broadview, Ill., 1973—. Mem. Old Portage dist. orgn. and extension com. Boy Scouts Am., Akron, 1964, dist. chmn., 1966-67. Bd. dirs. Akron Goodwill Industries, 1967—; mem. bd. Akron YMCA, 1967—, chmn. West Akron br., 1965—; trustee Yankton (S.D.) Coll. Served to 1st lt. USAAF, 1943-45. Decorated D.F.C. Mem. Am. Mktg. Assn., Am. Mgmt. Assn. (mktg. planning council 1966—), Am. Supply and Machinery Mfrs. Assn. (vice chmn. 1963-64), Rubber Mfrs. Assn. (exec. com. indsl. products div. 1965-66), Akron Jr. C. of C., Lambda Chi Alpha. Presbyterian (deacon). Mason, Elk. Clubs: Fairlawn Country. Home: 3000 N Sheridan Rd Chicago IL 60657 Office: 2800 S 25th Ave Broadview IL 60153

BEHFOROOZ, ALI, educator; b. Qum, Iran, May 24, 1942; s. Assadollah and Batool (Poostforoosh) Poostchi; came to U.S., 1970, naturalized, 1976; B.S., M.S., Tehran U.; M.S., Mich. State U., 1972, M.S., 1973, Ph.D., 1975; m. Farideh Ari, July 1, 1971; 1 son, Amir. Instr. mathematics U. Tehran, 1965-70; research asst. Mich. State U., 1972-74; dir. instl. research Moorhead State U., 1974-76, asst. prof. computer sci., 1974-76, asso. prof., 1974—. Ednl. TV of Iran grantee. Mem. Assn. Computing Machinery. Contbr. articles in field to profl. jours. Home: 401 37th Ave S Moorhead MN 56560 Office: Moorhead State University Moorhead MN 56560

BEHLE, ROLAND CARL, assn. exec.; b. Rolling Prairie, Wis., May 31, 1912; s. Carl Paul and Clara (Stutz) B.; student Fountain City Bus. Coll., Fond du Lac, Wis., 1929; m. Margaret Werner, Nov. 26, 1936. Stock clk. J.C. Penny Co., Beaver Dam, Wis., 1931-33; asst. mgr. Jerrold's Inc., Beaver Dam, Wis., 1933-34; asst. mgr. Jerrold's Inc., Watertown, Wis., 1934-37; partner Behle Bros. Co., Juneau, Wis., 1937-45; ownership Behle Bros. Co., Juneau, Wis., 1945-64; exec. sec. Wis. Cheese Makers Assn., Madison, 1964—; mng. dir. Wis. Cheese Found., Madison, Wis., 1964—. Mem. dairy adv. council Wis. Dept. Agr.; adviser, dept. life sci. and industry U. Wis., 1972—; mem. adv. council, dairy div. Moraine Tech. Inst., 1975—. Bd. dirs. Luth. Hosp., Beaver Dam, Wis., 1956-68; bd. dirs., treas., 1964-68. Mem. Wis. Soc. Assn. Execs., Wis. Dairy Tech. Assn., Southeastern Wis. Cheese Assn. (past pres.). Lutheran. Home: 400 Kenyon Lane Beaver Dam WI 53916 Office: 115 W Main St Madison WI 53703

BEHLMANN, F. LEE, aerospace co. exec.; b. Florissant, Mo., Apr. 24, 1922; s. John H. and Mary A. (Gettemeier) B.; m. Eileen R. Healy, Dec. 31, 1944; 1 dau., Sheila. B.S., DePaul U., 1951. Engring adminstr. to mgr. McDonnell Aircraft Co., St. Louis, 1951-68; dir. engring adminstn. and chmn. performance measurement systems McDonnell Douglas Astronautics, St. Louis, 1968—; chmn., pres. Florissant Tire Center, 1963—; dir., v.p. Behlmann GMC Trucks, Florissant, 1971—; pres. Behlmann Investments, Florissant, 1970—; dir., v.p. Behlmann Gas Co., Florissant, 1972—, Hi-Way Car Wash, Florissant, 1961—. Mem. Am. Legion, Am. Mgmt. Assn., Am. Inst. Aeros. and Astronautics, Am. Inst. Indsl. Engrs., Air Force Assn. Home: 1410 Saint Louis St Florissant MO 63033 Office: PO Box 516 Saint Louis MO 63166

BEHNKE, DONALD JOHN, supt. schs.; b. Galva, Ill., Nov. 3, 1935; married. B.S. in Edn., Ill. State U., 1957; M.S. in Edn., State U. N.Y., 1964; Ed.D. in Edn., Columbia U., 1969. Adminstrn. intern Sarotoga County (N.Y.) Schs., Mechanicville, 1964-65, adminstrn. asst. Hewlett-Woodmere (N.Y.) Sch. Dist. #14, 1965-67, asst. supt., 1967-71; supt. schs. Villa Park (Ill.) Elementary Sch. Dist. # 45, 1971—. Mem. C. of C. (dir. 1971—), Ill., Am. assns. sch. adminstrs., Nat. Sch. Pub. Relations Assn., W. Suburban Supts. Assn., No. Ill. Supts. Roundtable, Citizens Edn. Council. Contbr. articles to profl. jours. Home: 553 Harmony Ln Lombard IL 60148 Office: 255 W Vermont St Villa Park IL 60181

BEHNKE, WALLACE BLANCHARD, JR., utility co. exec.; b. Evanston, Ill., Feb. 5, 1926; s. Wallace Blanchard and Dorothea (Bull) B.; B.S., Northwestern U., 1945, B.S. In Elec. Engring., 1947; m. Joan Fortune Murphy, Sept. 24, 1949; children—Susan Behnke Jones, Ann B., Thomas W. With Commonwealth Edison Co., Chgo., 1947—, div. v.p., 1962-66, asst. to pres., 1966-69, v.p., 1969-73, exec. v.p., 1973—; dir. Lake View Trust and Savs. Bank, Atomic Indsl. Forum. Dir. United Way Metro. Chgo., Met. Crusade of Mercy, Robert Crown Center for Health Edn., Northwestern Meml. Hosp. Served with USNR, 1943-46, 1950-52. Mem. Am. Nuclear Soc., Atomic Indsl. Forum, IEEE, Western Soc. Engrs. Episcopalian. Clubs: Chgo., Econ. of Chgo., Hinsdale Golf, Comml. Home: 311 S Oak St Hinsdale IL 60521 Office: Box 767 Chicago IL 60690

BEHREND, ELAINE, nursing home adminstr.; b. Cedar Rapids, Iowa, July 27, 1936; d. Jesse P. and Wanda C. (Williams) Baker; m. Jerrold A. Behrend, June 19, 1976; children from previous marriage—Jesse B., Sheila J. Green. Nursing home adminstr. Continental Care Inc., Cedar Falls, Iowa, 1972-75; nursing home adminstr. Winfield (Iowa) Health Care and Retirement Center Inc., 1975—. Mem. Am. Coll. Nursing Home Adminstrs., Iowa Health Care Assn. Baptist. Home: PO Box 22 Winfield IA 52659

BEHRENFELD, JAMES RAYMOND, mktg. cons.; b. Marshall, Minn., Aug. 3, 1932; s. Raymond George and Ann Marie (Carey) B.; ed. Pitts. Art Inst., Art Center Sch. of Los Angeles, Los Angeles City Coll., U. Calif. Los Angeles Extension, U. Calif. Extension; m. Cassandra Lipinski, Mar. 17, 1972; children—Eric, Kurt. Prodn. mgr. McCarty Advt., Los Angeles, 1957-59; sales mgr. Elgin Davis Studios, Inc., Los Angeles, 1961-64; nat. sales mgr. Dickens Design Group, Chgo., 1964-65; pres. Communications Internat., Inc., Chgo., 1965-72, CI Prodns., Inc., Chgo., 1972—; sales and mktg. cons. Served with USNR, 1951-55; ETO, PTO. Recipient numerous design and graphics awards. Mem. Los Angeles Sales/Mktg. Execs. (nominee top salesman awards 1961, 62), Field Mus. Chgo. Mem. Art Dirs. Club Los Angeles, Sales and Mktg. Execs. (Los Angeles, Chgo.), Exec. Club Chgo. Republican. Roman Catholic. Home: 1130 Inverrary Ln Deerfield IL 60015 Office: 6200 N Hiawatha Ave Chicago IL 60646

BEHRENS, DONALD EDWIN, advt. agy. exec.; b. Grand Rapids, Mich., Oct. 27, 1919; s. Douglas Fredrick and Vera Elizabeth (Gorham) B.; grad. high sch.; m. Lovela Jean McClellan, June 11, 1943; children—Kathleen (Mrs. John Curry), Carol (Mrs. Jerry Underwood), Donna (Mrs. John Linsey), Barbara (Mrs. Allan Dodds). Copywriter, Jaqua Co., Grand Rapids, Mich., 1945-52, v.p., creative dir., 1952-55, v.p., account exec., 1955-59, v.p., account supr., 1959-62, sr. v.p., group supr., 1965—, sec., 1976—. Vice-chmn. pub. relations United Fund, 1964; pub. relations chmn. United Community Services, 1964-66; mem. exec. bd. Mich. Synod Lutheran Ch., 1970—, sec., 1977—. Served with USNR, 1941-45. Mem. Grand Rapids Advt. Club (program chmn., pres. 1952-53), Indsl. Marketers of Western Mich. (sec. 1963-65), Grand Rapids C. of C. Home: 1740 Lockmere SE Grand Rapids MI 49508 Office: 101 Garden St SE Grand Rapids MI 49502

BEIDEMAN, RONALD PAUL, chiropractor; b. Norristown, Pa., Mar. 22, 1926; s. Jonas Paul and Bertha May (Cane) B.; student Temple U., 1948; D. Chiropractic, Nat. Coll. Chiropractic, Chgo., 1952; postgrad. Wheaton Coll.; B.A., Lewis U., 1976; m. Lorraine Marian Barrett, Aug. 19, 1950; children—Ronald Paul, J. Kirk. Dir. dept. diagnosis Nat. Coll. Chiropractic, Chgo., 1952-66, registrar, 1966—, dean admissions and records, 1973—; exam. physician Chgo. Gen. Health Service, 1954-65; lectr. in field; pvt. practice chiropractic Chgo., 1954—. Prof., Nat.-Lincoln Sch. Postgrad. Edn., 1964—. Served with USAAF, 1944-46. Mem. Nat. Coll. Chiropractic (corp. sec. 1972—), Nat. Bd. Chiropractic Examiners (chmn. test com. 1967-69), Ill., Chgo. chiropractic socs., Am. Chiropractic Assn., Am. Legion (post comdr. 1957-58), Am., Ill. assns. Collegiate Registrars and Admissions Officers, Ill. Assn. Student Financial Aid Adminstrs., Nat. Assn. Coll. Admissions Counselors, Sigma Phi Kappa, Lambda Phi Delta. Contbr. articles to profl. publs. Home: 411 Graham St Lombard IL 60148 Office: 200 E Roosevelt Rd Lombard IL 60148

BEIER, GARY JON, orthodontist; b. Milw., Apr. 7, 1941; s. Archie Carl and Evelyn Constance (Ellingsen) B.; D.D.S., Marquette U., 1965; certificate in orthodontics Ind. U., 1969; m. June Beatrice Vodicka, June 22, 1963; children—Charles, Linda. Practice dentistry specializing in orthodontics, Wausau, Wis., 1969—; mem. staff Wausau Hosp. North, 1970—. Mem. cooperative office edn. com. Wausau Dist. Sch., 1970-72; chmn. Bd. Appeals, Rothschild, Wis., 1972-75. Bd. dirs. United Way Marathon County, Wis., 1974-76; trustee Village of Rothschild (Wis.), 1975—. Served with Dental Corps, USNR, 1965-67. Mem. ADA, Am. Assn. Orthodontists, Marathon County Dental Soc., Wis. Soc. Orthodontists, Omicron Kappa Upsilon, Alpha Sigma Nu. Clubs: Snowmobile, Rothschild Urbanaires. Home: 604 Williams St Rothschild WI 54474 Office: 630 1st St Wausau WI 54401

BEILFUSS, BRUCE F., state chief justice; b. Withee, Wis., Jan. 8, 1915; s. Walter W. and Elsie C. (Dodte) B.; B.A., U. Wis., 1936, J.D., 1938; m. Helen Hendrickson; m. 2d, DeEtte Knowlton, Oct. 17, 1961; 1 son, Mark. Admitted to Wis. bar, 1938; dist. atty. Clark County, 1941-48; circuit judge 17th Jud. Circuit, 1948-63; justice Supreme Ct. Wis., 1964-76, chief justice, 1976—. Active Big Bros. Dane County. Served to lt. (j.g.) USNR, 1942-45. Mem. Am., Wis., Dane County bar assns., Am. Judicature Soc., Inst. Jud. Adminstrn., Am. Law Inst. Club: Rotary. Home: 4402 Fox Bluff Rd Middleton WI 53711 Office: Office of Chief Justice Supreme Ct State Capitol Madison WI 53702

BEIMDIEK, DONALD URBAN, lawyer; b. St. Louis County, Mo., Nov. 16, 1928; s. Urban E.A. and Minnie C. (Kamprad) B.; B.S., Northwestern U., 1951, J.D., 1954; m. Carolyn Anderson, June 7, 1958; children—Stephen Lee, Beverly Ann, Lynn Carolyn, Karen Elizabeth. Admitted to Mo. bar, 1954, Ill. bar, 1955; asso. Lashly & Neun, 1956-62; partner firm Armstrong, Teasdale, Kramer & Vaughan, St. Louis, 1963—; city atty. City of Richmond Heights (Mo.), 1963-72, city counselor, 1972-76; spl. counsel Mo. Bd. Pub. Bldgs., 1975—. Mem. St. Louis County Bd. Zoning Adjustment, 1962-77. Served with AUS, 1954-56; ETO. Mem. Am., Mo., Ill., St. Louis bar assns. Clubs: Masons, Mo. Athletic. Home: 33 Sussex Dr Brentwood MO 63144 Office: 611 Olive Saint Louis MO 63101

BEINEKE, LOWELL WAYNE, educator; b. Decatur, Ind., Nov. 20, 1939; s. Elmer Henry and Lillie Agnes (Snell) B.; B.S. (Bell Aircraft scholar 1957-58; Westinghouse scholar 1958-61), Purdue U., 1961; postgrad. Univ. Coll., London, Eng., 1962-63; M.A., U. Mich., 1962, Ph.D. (NSF fellow 1961-62, 63-65, teaching fellow 1964-65), 1965; m. Judith Rowena Wooldridge, Dec. 23, 1967; children—Jennifer Elaine, Philip Lennox. Research asso. U. Mich., Ann Arbor, 1966-67, prof. math. Inst. for Social Research, 1961-62; asst. prof. Purdue U., Fort Wayne, Ind., 1965-68, asso. prof., 1968-71, prof. math., 1971—; tutor Oxford (Eng.) U., 1973-74, Open U., summer 1974, 75. Mem. Common Cause, Am. Math. Soc., Math. Assn. Am., AAUP, Sigma Xi, Phi Kappa Phi, Phi Eta Sigma, Pi Mu Epsilon. Democrat. Mem. United Ch. of Christ. Editorial bd. Jour. Graph Theory, 1975—, asso. editor, 1977—. Home: 4529 Bradwood Terr Fort Wayne IN 46815 Office: Purdue U Fort Wayne IN 46815

BEINTKER, MARJORIE ROSE, ednl. adminstr.; b. St. Louis; d. Charles Edward and Ethel Emma (Bentmann) Beintker; B.A., Maryville Coll. of the Sacred Heart. Sec. and adminstrv. asst. to purchasing agt. Aloe sci. div. A.S. Aloe Co., St. Louis, until 1956; office mgr. Leander & Boardman, St. Louis, 1957-58; editor Ozark Air Lines, Lambert Field, St. Louis, 1958-65; dir. pub. info., pub. relations and placement Parks Coll. Aero. Tech. of St. Louis U., also editor Parks Coll. News and Aerospace Bull., from 1965; now pub. relations asst. Spl. Sch. Dist. St. Louis County; tutor history. Mem. Bona Vivants, 1958—. Mem. Airline Editors Assn. (chmn. 1964-65), Aviation Space Writers Assn., Midwest Coll. Placement Assn., Nat. Sch. Pub. Relations Assn. (Greater St. Louis, Show Me State chpts.), Press Club Met. St. Louis, AAUW. Home: 1056 Bittner St St Louis MO 63147 Office: Spl Sch Dist St Louis County 12110 Clayton Rd Town and Country MO 63131

BEISSWENGER, NORMAN FREDERICH, office service co. exec.; b. Cleve., Oct. 24, 1918; s. Carl and Emma (Stahl) B.; B.S. in Mech. Engring., Ohio State U., 1942; m. Eleanor Murray, Dec. 25, 1950. Research and devel. engr. Detroit Diesel Allison div. Gen. Motors Corp., Indpls., 1942-57; pres. Standby Office Service, Inc., Indpls., 1957—. Mem. Ind. Assn. Temp. Services (pres. 1976-77), Soc. for Advancement of Mgmt. (pres. 1960-61), Adminstrv. Mgmt. Soc. (pres. 1965-66), Nat. Assn. Accountants (pres. 1971-72), Nat. Assn. Temp. Services (past dir.), Ind. Office Service Inst. (treas.). Republican. Roman Catholic. Clubs: Indpls. Athletic, Columbia. Home: 3137 Melbourne Rd S Dr Indianapolis IN 46208 Office: 130 E Washington St Indianapolis IN 46204

BEITLER, ROGER T., supt. schs.; b. Berne, Ind., Dec. 19, 1929; s. Hugo R. and Gertrude (Hirschy) B.; B.S., Ball State U., 1952, M.A., 1953; postgrad. Miami U., Oxford, Ohio, 1953-54; Ed.D., Ind. U., 1958; postgrad. Kent State U., 1959, 61, 68-70; m. Esther Louise Clark, Apr. 11, 1954; children—Mark Alan, Ann Louise, Lyn Andrea. Tchr. social studies Beiger Sch., Mishawaka (Ind.) City Schs., 1955-57; dir., asst. prof. secondary edn. Ashtabula Center, Kent (Ohio) State U., 1958-63, asso. prof., asso. dir. secondary edn. div. academic centers, 1963-65; field specialist N.E. region Ohio Office of Opportunity, Kent, 1965; supt. schs. Ashtabula (Ohio) Area City Schs., 1965-71, North Ridgeville (Ohio) City Schs., 1971—; chmn. Lorain County (Ohio) Co-op. Ednl. Planning Com., 1974—; mem. program and planning com. Lorain County Sch. Ofcls. Forum, 1974-76. Bd. dirs. N.E. Ohio council Boy Scouts Am., 1965-71, chmn. Explorer scouting Firelands area council, 1974-76; mem. park and recreation adv. com. North Ridgeville, 1972-75, Citizens League of North Ridgeville, 1973—. Served to 1st. lt. USAF, 1952-55. Recipient Distinguished Service award Ashtabula Jr. C. of C., 1961, Silver Beaver award Boy Scouts Am., 1968, Distinguished Alumni Service award Ball State U. Alumni Assn., 1970, Scouter's Tng. award Boy Scouts Am., 1971, Educator of Year award Ohio PTA, 1977. Mem. Am. (adv. bd. nat. acad. for sch. execs. 1974-75), Buckeye (profl. rights and responsibilities com. 1973-75, legis. com. 1968-69) assns. sch. adminstrs., Greater Cleve. Sch. Supts. Assn. (social com. 1974—), Nat. Acad. Sch. Execs. (profl. devel. award 1974), NEA, Ohio Council Social Studies, Nat. Soc. Study of Edn., Nat. Orgn. Legal Problems of Edn. (program planning com. 1959-60), Northeastern Ohio Sch. Bds. Assn. (regional sec. 1963-65), Ohio, Northeastern Ohio assns. supervision and curriculum devel., Ind. Schoolmen's Club, Phi Delta Kappa (Distinguished Service award 1975, pres. N.E. Ohio chpt. 1967-69, pres. Golden Crescent Ohio chpt. 1974-75), Kappa Delta Pi. Methodist (lay speaker 1974). Clubs: Elks, Kiwanis (Distinguished Service award 1961, pres. 1973-74, lt. gov. Div. 13, 1976-77). Author: Technical Education and University Programs for Stark County Regional Campus, 1964; also weekly newspaper columns; contbr. articles on edn. to profl. publs. Home: 5031 Meadow Moss Ln North Ridgeville OH 44039 Office: 35895 Center Ridge Rd North Ridgeville OH 44039

BEITO, GEORGE ANTHONY, banker; b. Thief River Falls, Minn., Jan. 11, 1933; s. George A. and Anne J. (Strande) B.; B.A., St. Olaf Coll., Northfield, Minn., 1955; grad. Rural Banking Sch., 1968; m. Gretchen Urnes, June 29, 19S7; children—David A., Kathryn A., Laura E. Asst. cashier No. State Bank, Gonvick, Minn., 1958-60, v.p., Thief River Falls, 1960-65, pres., chmn. bd., 1965—; pres., chmn. bd. Security State Bank (Oklee, Minn.), No. State Bank (Gonvick), 1st Nat. Bank (McIntosh, Minn.). Treas. Northland Community Coll. Found.; pres. adv. council Northland Community Coll.; adv. com. Thief River Falls Area Vocational Tech. Inst.; treas. Jobs, Inc.; v.p. congregation Trinity Lutheran Ch. Served with USNR, 1955-58. Named outstanding young man of Thief River Falls, 1962. Mem. Minn. Bankers Assn. (mem. council 1970-73, pres. 1977-78), Thief River Falls C. of C. (pres. 1963). Clubs: Rotary, Elks, Eagles. Home: 2211 Nelson Dr Thief River Falls MN 56701 Office: 201 E 3d St Thief River Falls MN 56701

BEKKUM, OWEN D, utility co. exec.; b. Westby, Wis., Mar. 2, 1924; s. Alfred T. and Huldah (Storbakken) B.; B.B.A., U. Wis., 1950; postgrad. Northwestern U.; m. Dorothy A. Jobs, Aug. 26, 1950. Auditor, Arthur Andersen & Co., 1951-57; acquisition auditor Hertz Corp., 1957-60, asst. treas., 1960-62; with No. Ill. Gas Co., 1963—, mgr. tech. accounting, 1964-66, asst. comptroller, 1966-68, comptroller, 1968-70, adminstrv. v.p., 1970-73, exec. v.p., 1973-76, pres., 1976—, also dir.; exec. v.p., dir. NI-Gas Supply, Inc., 1971-76, pres., 1976—; exec. v.p., dir. NI-Gas Exploration, Inc., 1973-76, pres., 1976—; pres., dir. Mid-Continent Gas Storage Co., 1975—, Mid-Continent Gasification Co., 1976—; dir. NICOR Inc., NICOR Exploration Co., NICOR Resources Ltd., NICOR Transp. Co., NICOR Belize Inc., New Eng. Energy Co. Bd. dirs. Jr. Achievement Chgo., 1975—, Protestant Found. Greater Chgo., 1975—, Pace Inst., 1977—. Served with AUS, 1943-46. C.P.A., Wis., Ill. Mem. Am. Mgmt. Assn., Am. Inst. C.P.A.'s, Fin. Exec. Inst., Am. Gas Assn. Clubs: Execs., Mid-Day, Econ. (Chgo.). Home: 46 Royal Vale Dr Oak Brook IL 60521 Office: PO Box 190 Aurora IL 60507

BELCHER, MICHAEL JAY, psychologist; b. Bremerton, Wash., May 30, 1947; s. Tom and Ann (Brown) B.; m. Francine C. Hochman, Jan. 25, 1975; B.A., Pacific Luth. U., 1969, M.A., 1971; Ph.D., Ill. Inst. Tech., 1973. Hosp. attendant Western State Hosp., Tacoma, 1967-70; caseworker Wash. Dept. Pub. Welfare, Bremerton, 1970-71; co-dir., clin. dir. Moultrie County (Ill.) Mental Health Center, 1973-74; exec. dir. Green County (Ill.) Guidance Center, 1974-75; dir. depts. psychology, social services, activity therapy Children's Med. Center, Dayton, Ohio, 1975-76; pres. Miami Valley Psychol. Services, Inc., Dayton, 1976—; asst. prof. psychology Eastern Ill. U., Charleston, 1974; adj. asst. prof. Wright State U., Dayton, 1975. Registered psychologist, Ill.; lic. psychologist, Ohio. Mem. Am., Ill. psychol. assns., Am. Soc. Clin. Hypnosis. Home: 2651 Coppersmith Ave Dayton OH 45414 Office: 11 W Monument St Suite 211 Dayton OH 45402

BELDAVS, JAZEPS TEODOR, physician; b. Liel-Auce, Latvia, Jan. 20, 1914; s. Karl Voldemar and Maria (Bekman) B.; M.D., U. Latvia, 1940; diploma anesthesia McGill U., 1955; m. Alice Haltneris, Dec. 8, 1951; 1 son, Robert. Intern, Univ. Hosp., Riga, Latvia, 1940-41; resident Royal Victoria Hosp., 1952, Queen Elizabeth Hosp., 1953, Queen Mary Vets. Hosp., 1954 (all Montreal); practice medicine, specializing in surgery, Latvia, 1940-43; practice medicine, specializing in anesthesiology, Montreal, 1952-54; chief anesthetist Inst. Cardiology, Montreal, Que., Can., 1967-68, Windsor Western Hosp., Ont., 1968—. Fellow Royal Coll. Physicians Can.; mem. Internat. Anesthesia Research Soc., Canadian Med. Assn., N.Y. Acad. Scis. Home: 425 Granada W Windsor ON Canada Office: PO Box 1358 Windsor ON Canada also Windsor Western Hosp Centre-Prince Rd Windsor ON Canada

BELDER, EDNA MAE, bus. woman; b. Holland, Mich., Oct. 26, 1925; d. Melvin Ernest and Delia Elizabeth (Ratering) Cook; student pub. schs., Holland; m. Jason M. Belder, July 10, 1946; children—Mary Ann, Ruth Elaine, Gretchen Sue. Bookkeeper, Holland State Bank, 1943-46, Old State Bank, Fremont, Mich., 1946-49; sec. Reber & Reber, attys., Fremont, 1949-54; bookkeeper Cooks Star Hatchery, Inc., Fremont, 1954-63, sec., 1963-69, v.p., 1969—. Mem. Ch. of the Living Christ. Home: 5127 56th St Fremont MI 49412

BELEW, DAVID LEE, paper mfg. co. exec.; b. Falmouth, Ky., Aug. 26, 1931; s. Leland W. and Eleanor (Conrad) B.; A.B., Coll. William and Mary, 1953; m. Margery Bonner Beckett, July 3, 1953; children—Guy Beckett, Sally Conrad. Vice pres. Rowe & Wyman Advt. Agy., Cin., 1954-60; mgr. advt. and sales promotion Beckett Paper Co., Hamilton, Ohio, 1960-72, v.p. adminstrn., 1972-74, pres., 1974—; dir. West Side Fed. Savs. & Loan, Hamilton. Chmn. fund raising Children's Home Christmas Fund, Hamilton, 1964-71; chmn. Hamilton Area arts fund drive Cin. chpt. United Fund, 1971-72, active United Appeals, Hamilton, 1964-72; mem. steering com. Spiritual Forum, Hamilton, 1971-72. Mem. Parks and Recreation Commn., City of Hamilton, 1974—. Bd. dirs. Hamilton Symphony; bd. dirs. Hamilton Boys' Club, 1964-70, pres., 1969; bd. dirs. Hamilton Community Found., 1961—, pres., 1970-71; trustee Ohio Council on Econ. Edn., 1974—; mem. advisory council Miami U. Sch. Applied Scis.; trustee Greater Cin. Center Econ. Edn. Recipient Distinguished Service award Hamilton Jr. C. of C., 1964; named 1 of 5 Outstanding Young Men Ohio, Ohio Jr. C. of C., 1964; named Indsl. Citizen Year, Hamilton Indsl. Mgmt. Club, 1965. Mem. Cin. Advt. Club, Newcomen Soc. N.Am., Sales Assn. Paper Industry (nat. v.p.), Paper Makers Advt. Assn. (past pres.), Hamilton Assn. Trade and Industry, Hamilton Tennis Assn. (founder 1973). Episcopalian. Clubs: Hamilton City (trustee), Round Table, Kingsgate Racquet, New London Hills (Hamilton), Middletown (Ohio) Tennis; Bankers (Cin.). Home: 318 S D St Hamilton OH 45013 Office: 4th and Buckeye Sts Hamilton OH 45012

BELFOUR, ALBERT J., computer co. exec.; b. Bklyn., Feb. 11, 1927; s. Julius and Jennie (Zarkin) B.; student Northeastern U., 1943-44; m. Evelyn Jane Morrison, Mar. 17, 1970; children—Shelly, Billy; children by previous marriage—Conrad, Diane Belfour Hawkins. Weather specialist U.S. Weather Bur., Washington, 1946-47; micro-meteorologist AEC, Brookhaven, N.Y., 1947-51; lab. dir. Parsons Corp., Traverse City, Mich., 1952-59; owner, mgr. Belfour Stulen, Inc., Traverse City, 1959-71; mgr. Belfour Stulen div. Coll. Am. Pathologists, Traverse City, 1971-75, dir. Computer Center, 1975—. Vice pres. Suttons Bay (Mich.) Sch. Bd., 1962-70; bd. dirs. Leelanau Meml. Hosp., 1972—; chmn. bd. Traverse City Human Relations Commn., 1970, N.W. Mich. Child Guidance Clinic, 1970-71. Served with USNR, 1944-46. Mem. ASTM (fatigue of aircraft structures com. 1955-72). Club: Great Lakes Cruising (Chgo.). Contbr. articles to profl. jours. Home: Gills Pier Rd Northport MI 49670 Office: 13919 W Bay Shore Dr Traverse City MI 49684

BELIAN, GARABED, dentist; b. Jerusalem, Palestine; s. Sarkis and Haigouhi (Markarian) Behesnilian; student Coll. Des Freres, Jerusalem, 1948, Coll. Des Trois Docteurs, Beirut, Lebanon, 1949; Docteur en Chirugie Dentaire, Universite Saint Joseph, 1953; D.D.S., U. Detroit, 1960; B. Music, Detroit Inst. Musical Arts, 1968; M.A., Wayne State U., 1975; m. Isabelle G. Sapsezian, Nov. 30, 1969; children—Ara Garabed, Lisa S., Raffi Sarkis. Came to U.S., 1956, naturalized, 1962. Active profl. music groups, 1949-53; pvt. practice dentistry, Middle East, 1953-56; bio-chem. researcher Bauer & Black, Chgo., 1956-58; pvt. practice dentistry, Detroit, 1960—. Pres., Art Center Chamber Music Players, 1967-69. Mem. Am., Mich. dental assns., Detroit Dental Soc., Founders Soc. Detroit Inst. Arts and the Antiquaries Detroit Inst. Arts. Collector modern art and antiquities. Home: 7297 Kingswood Dr Birmingham MI 48010 Office: 4342 W Vernor St Detroit MI 48209

BELING, EARL HENRY, cons. engr.; b. Chgo., Dec. 24, 1901; s. Frederick W.C. and Alma (Brown) B.; B.S. in Mech. Engring. (with honors), U. Ill., 1923; m. Marian Armstrong (dec. Oct. 1970); m. 2d, Lucile B. Cobb, Mar. 6, 1971; children—Alice Beling Jenks, Eleanor Beling Lydick, Thomas E.; stepchildren—Stephen A. Cobb, William B. Cobb, Joanna Cobb Beirmann. Design engr. Warren, Webster & Co., Chgo., 1923-28; dir. research, salesman, sales mgr., dir. Herman Nelson Corp. div. Am. Air Filter, Moline, Ill., 1928-36; founder Beling Engring Cons., Moline, 1936, partner, chmn. bd., 1975—; co-founder, sec., treas. Ill. Bldg. Industry Alliance, 1958; pres. Moline Central Properties, Inc., 1974—. Pres. Moline Bd. Edn., 1941-47; vice chmn. Gov. Green's Revenue Commn., 1947-50; resource person Ill. Pre-White House Conf. Edn., 1955; affiliated with Boy Scouts Am.; co-founder Quad City Music Guild, 1949; pres. First Moline Neighborhood Redevel. Corp., 1971—; mem. com. Moline Centennial Celebration, 1972; bd. dirs. Alaska Meth. U.; del. Twelfth World Meth. Conf., Denver, 1971. Registered profl. engr., N.Y., Ill., Tex., Md., Wis., Ariz., Mich.; recipient Distinguished Alumni award Dept. Mech. and Indsl. Engring U. Ill., 1969; Engr. of the Year award Quint Cities Nat. Engrs. Week, 1977. Mem. Am. Soc. Heating Refrigeration and Air Conditioning Engrs., ASME, Nat., Ill. socs. profl. engrs., Profl. Engrs. Pvt. Practice, Nat. Fire Protection Assn., Nat. Water Well Assn., Ill. Assn. Sch. Bds. (dir.), Upper Rock Island

County C. of C., numerous others. Clubs: Rotary (Moline), Union League (Chgo.), Moline High Twelve. Lodges: Shriner, Mason, Elks (Moline), Doris (#319). Contbr. numerous articles to Ill. Sch. Bd. Jour. Home: 3601 7th St Moline IL 61265 Office: Beling Bldg 16th St at 10th Ave Moline IL 61265 Died Mar. 17, 1977.

BELJAN, JOHN RICHARD, physician, educator; b. Detroit, May 26, 1930; s. Joseph and Margaret Anne (Brozovich) B.; B.S., U. Mich., 1951, M.D., 1954; m. Bernadette Marie Marenda, Feb. 2, 1952; children—Ann Marie, John Richard, Paul Eric. Intern, Univ. Hosp., Ann Arbor, Mich., 1954-55, resident in surgery, 1955-59; dir. med. services Stuart Co., Pasadena, Calif., 1965-66; asst. to asso. prof. surgery U. Calif., Davis, 1966-74, asst. to asso. prof. engring., 1968-74, asst. to asso. dean Sch. Medicine, 1970-74; prof. surgery Wright State U. Med. Sch., Dayton, Ohio, 1974—, prof. biomed. engring., 1974—, dean Med. Sch., vice provost univ., 1974—. Mem. exec. council Miami Valley Health Systems Agy.; trustee Wright State U. Found., Drew Health Center. Served with USAF, 1955-65. NASA grantee, 1968—; NIH grantee, 1967—; diplomate Am. Bd. Surgery. Fellow A.C.S., Royal Soc. Medicine; mem. IEEE, Instrumentation Soc. Am., Biomed. Engring. Soc., AAAS, AAUP, Assn. Acad. Surgery, Civil Aviation Med. Soc., Dayton Surg. Soc., Société Internationale de Chirurgie, Montgomery County Med. Soc., Ohio Med. Assn., AMA, Flying Physicians Assn., Sigma Xi, Phi Beta Kappa, Phi Kappa Phi. Contbr. articles to profl. jours. Home: 1315 Glen Jean Ct Dayton OH 45459 Office: Sch Medicine Wright State U Dayton OH 45431

BELK, FRED RICHARD, historian; b. Kansas City, Mo., Mar. 13, 1937; s. Oliver W. and Crystal (Prock) B.; Ph.D., Okla. State U., 1973; m. Nadine K. Rochon, Nov. 22, 1961; children—Stephanie, Stephen, Christopher. Various positions YMCA, Kansas City, Ft. Worth and San Francisco, 1955-65; ordained minister Presbyn. Ch., 1966; minister Perry, Okla., 1966-69; faculty Sterling (Kans.) Coll., 1969—, asso. prof. history, 1969—, outstanding tchr., 1971—. Nat. Tchr. fellow, 1971-72. Mem. Kans., Am. hist. assns., Conf. Faith and History, Pi Gamma Mu, Phi Alpha Theta. Democrat. Author: The Great Trek, 1976. Contbr. articles to profl. publs. Home: 406 W Washington St Sterling KS 67579

BELKNAP, ELMER CLINTON, social worker; b. Gordon, Nebr., Dec. 24, 1905; s. Elmer Curtis and Kitty Luella (Moss) B.; B.A., Simpson Coll., 1929; M.A., U. Chgo., 1937; m. Mildred Pearl Breniman, May 23, 1932; children—Rowan Curtis, Dean Edward. Asso. boys' work sec. YMCA, Sioux City, Iowa, 1930-31; jr. boys clubs and handicraft dir. U. Chgo. Settlement House, 1932-33; sr. case worker Cook County Bur. Pub. Welfare, Chgo., 1933-34; dir. Hall County Emergency Relief and Pub. Assistance Adminstrn., Grand Island, Nebr., 1934-44; Nebr. field rep. Nat. Found. Infantile Paralysis, N.Y.C. and Lincoln, Nebr., 1944-65; with Nebr. State Dept. Pub. Welfare, Lincoln, 1965—, med. social work cons., 1969-76; mem. Nebr. Crippled Children Adv. Com., Lincoln, 1947-55, Nebr. Health Planning Com., 1947-52, Nebr. Comprehensive Health Planning Adv. Council, 1967-69. Bd. dirs. Lancaster County chpt. Nat. Found.-March of Dimes, 1965-69. Recipient Distinguished Service citation Nat. Found.-March of Dimes, N.Y.C., 1964. Mem. Am. (nat. bd. dirs. 1968-69), Nebr. (pres. 1937-38) pub. welfare assns., Nebr. Pub. Health Assn. (state sec. 1955-56), Nat. Rehab. Assn. (state dir. 1961-64), Nebr. State Hist. Soc., New Eng. Historic and Geneal. Soc., Pi Kappa Delta. Methodist (chmn. com. edn. 1955-56). Author: A Belknap Genealogy, 1974; A Moss Genealogy, 1977. Home: 2019 Harwood St Lincoln NE 68502 Office: 1526 K St 4th Floor Lincoln NE 68508

BELKNAP, WILLIAM WALKER, II, chiropractor; b. New Philadelphia, Ohio, Sept. 27, 1936; s. William Walker and Helen Eleanor (Stroud) B.; student Pa. Mil. Coll., 1954-55; D.C., Lincoln Chiropractic Coll., 1959; m. Joyce Carroll, Dec. 16, 1966; children—John William, Robert William, Anne Carroll. Intern, Spears Chiropractic Hosp., Denver, 1959-61; practice chiropractic, New Philadelphia, 1963—. Pres. Ohio Chiropractic Bd. Examiners, 1975—. Mem. Comprehensive Health Planning Com., Tuscarawas County, Ohio, 1974—. Bd. dirs. Tuscarawas County Automobile Assn. Am., 1973—. Served with M.C., AUS, 1961-63. Mem. Am., Ohio, Tuscarawas Valley (v.p. 1975—) chiropractic assns. Episcopalian (vestryman 1974—). Mason (32 deg.), Elk, Lion. Home: 965 N Broadway New Philadelphia OH 44663 Office: 238 N Broadway New Philadelphia OH 44663

BELL, ANTHONY MICHAEL, elec. engr.; b. Evergreen Park, Ill., Oct. 25, 1952; s. Anthony and Ann (Lombardo) B.; B.S., Bradley U., 1974; m. Ellen Edgeworth, July 20, 1974. Engr., Underwriters Labs., Inc., Chgo., 1974—, Mem. Soc. Automotive Engrs., IEEE. Roman Catholic. Contbr. articles in field to profl. jours. Home: 640 Riedy St Lisle IL 60532 Office: 207 Ohio St Chicago IL 60611

BELL, CHARLES EDWARD, psychologist; b. Galveston, Tex., Feb. 7, 1936; s. Ben Franklin and Johnnie Odet (Rush) B.; B.S., U. Houston, 1962, M.A., 1965; Ed.D., N. Tex. State U., 1977; m. Marvell Marie Mossom, Dec. 20, 1968; children—Charles Butler, Beverly Ann, Laurie Marvell. Asst. prof. Ouachita Bapt. U., Arkadelphia, Ark., 1967-69; staff psychologist Benton (Ark.) State Hosp., 1968-71; staff psychologist Vernon (Tex.) Project for Drug Dependent Youth, 1973-74; staff psychologist S.E. Kans. Mental Health Center, Humboldt, 1974—; vis. prof. Vernon Regional Jr. Coll., 1974, Henderson State Coll., 1967-68; teaching fellow U. Houston, 1963-67, N. Tex. State U., 1972-73. Chmn. bd. dirs. Circle B Boys Ranch, Inc. Mem. AAUP, Am., Southwestern psychol. assns., Phi Chi, Phi Delta Kappa. Democrat. Baptist. Clubs: Rotary, Kiwanis, Elks. Author: Transactional Analysis for Classroom Teachers, 1977. Home: 612 E 10th St Chanute KS 66720 Office: 201 S 9th St Humboldt KS 66748

BELL, CHARLES EUGENE, JR., indsl. engr.; b. N.Y.C., Dec. 13, 1932; s. Charles Edward and Constance Elizabeth (Verbelia) B.; B. Engring., Johns Hopkins U., 1954, M.S. in Engring., 1959; m. Doris R. Clifton, Jan. 14, 1967. Indsl. engr. Signode Corp., Balt., 1957-61, asst. to plant mgr., 1961-63, plant engr., 1963-64, div. indsl. engr., Glenview, Ill., 1964-69, asst. to div. mgr., 1969-76, engring. mgr., 1976—. Served with U.S. Army, 1955-57. Registered profl. engr., Calif. Mem. Am. Inst. Indsl. Engrs., Indsl. Mgmt. Club Central Md. (pres. 1964). Republican. Roman Catholic. Club: Winnetka-Northfield Social Group. Home: 288 Dickens St Northfield IL 60093 Office: 3650 W Lake Ave Glenview IL 60025

BELL, CHARLES NORMAN, food co. exec.; b. Brady, Tex., Dec. 17, 1926; s. Gardise Delma and Lula Mae (Black) B.; student U. Tex., 1943, 46, 47; m. Dorothy L. Tippett, Dec. 31, 1951; children—Timothy W., Belinda L., Suzanne N. Gen. mgr. Leach Hatcheries Inc., Memphis, Mo., 1955-56; pres. Bell & Crowley Hatcheries, Memphis, Mo., 1957-61; sales mgr. Arbor Acre Farms, Spring Dale, Ark., 1962-63; v.p. Tyson Foods, Springdale, 1964-67; pres. Bell Egg Farms Inc., Joplin, Mo., 1967—; pres. Mid Am. Foods, Humboldt, Iowa. Served with USN, 1944-46. Mem. United Egg Producers (Atlanta), Joplin C. of C. (recipient Pacesetter Award 1971), V.F.W. Republican. Clubs: Twin Hills Country. Home and office: Box 197 Rt 7 Joplin MO 64801

BELL, CHARLES ROBERT, JR., lawyer; b. Wichita, Kans., July 14, 1930; s. Charles Robert and Margie Frances (Wooddell) B.; A.B., Princeton U., 1952; LL.B., Harvard U., 1955; m. Janice Elizabeth Little, Dec. 8, 1951; children—Barbara Elizabeth, Charles Robert, Nancy Louise, Bradley Lamar, James Sidney. Admitted to Mass. bar, 1955, Kans. bar, 1959; asso. J. Watson Flett, Boston, 1955-56; atty. Amortibanc Investment Co., Wichita, 1958-60; mem. firm Morris, Laing, Evans, Brock & Kennedy, Wichita, 1960-74, Brick and Bell, 1974—; dir., gen. counsel ADCO Airlines, Wichita, 1966—, Floair, Inc., 1968—, Kurdian Internat. Transport, Inc., 1974—; pres., chmn. bd. Prepaid Legal Services Kan. Inc.; mem. panel arbitrators Am. Arbitration Assn., 1969—. Mem. Met. Area Planning Commn. Served with USNR, 1956-58. Mem. Am., Kans. bar assns. Republican. Presbyterian (deacon 1964—, ch. trustee 1968-71). Clubs: Rotary, Ninnescah Yacht (Wichita). Home: 216 N Terrace St Wichita KS 67208 Office: Brick and Bell Suite 790 Central Plaza Bldg Wichita KS 67202

BELL, CHARLES THOMAS, lawyer; b. Carthage, Ill. Dec. 20, 1915; s. Earl N. and Julia (Conley) B.; A.B., Carthage Coll., 1937; postgrad. U. Ill., 1937-38; privately tutored in law, 1938-41; m. Maxine Lucille Burling, Nov. 12, 1940; children—Charles T., Linda Lee. Admitted to Ill. bar, 1941, since practiced in Carthage; asst. atty. gen. State of Ill., 1957-61. Dir. 1st Nat. Bank of Carthage. Bd. dirs., treas. Coll. Ednl. Found., 1964-67; trustee, treas. Robert Morris Coll., 1965-68; adv. hosp. council Ill. Dept. Pub. Health, 1972—. Served as ensign USNR, 1943-45. Member Am., Ill. bar assns. Clubs: Masons; Ill. Athletic (Chgo.). Home: 744 E Wabash Ave Carthage IL 62321 Office: 416 Main Carthage IL 62321

BELL, DAVID ARTHUR, advt. co. exec.; b. Mpls., May 29, 1943; s. Arthur E. and Frances (Tripp) B.; B.S., Macalester Coll., 1965; m. Patricia O'Brien, June 22, 1968; children—Jenney L., Jennifer L., Jeffrey D. With Leo Burnett Co., Chgo., 1965-67; with Knox Reeves Advt., Mpls., 1967-75, pres., 1973-75; sr. v.p., gen. mgr. Bozell & Jacobs, Inc., Mpls., 1975—, also dir. Chmn. pub. relations St. Paul United Way, 1976, advt. coordinator United Way Am., 1977; chmn. sustaining memberships YMCA, 1977, chmn. camping program; trustee Macalester Coll. Served with Minn. Air N.G., 1965-71. Mem. N.W. Council Advt. Agys. (dir.), Am. Assn. Advt. Agys. (chmn. Twin City council 1976), Minn. Ad Fedn., Minn. Press Club. Presbyterian. Clubs: Mpls. Athletic, Mpls. Golf. Home: 1815 Humboldt Ave S Minneapolis MN 55404 Office: 100 6th St N Minneapolis MN 55401

BELL, EARL PENDLETON, JR., sch. adminstr.; b. Roanoke Rapids, N.C., Jan. 14, 1938; s. Earl Pendleton and Alice Leigh (Proctor) B.; B.A. in History, Wake Forest U., 1961; postgrad. Stanford U., 1967; m. Donna Jean Campbell, Aug. 27, 1960; children—Timothy Stuart, Karen Lynn. Tchr. Am. History Kecoughtan High Sch., Hampton, Va., 1962-66; tchr. Am. history Lab. Schs. U. Chgo., 1966—, pres. faculty assn., 1975—, chmn. social studies dept., 1975—, dir. debate, 1966—; mem. state debate com. Ill. High Sch. Assn., 1976-77. Home: 1105 Abbot St Park Forest South IL 60466 Office: 1362 E 59th St Chicago IL 60637

BELL, G(EORGE) WILBUR, farmer; b. Saidora, Ill., Sept. 2, 1912; s. Charles Raymond and Eva (Kramer) B.; student Bradley U., 1930-32, U. Ill., 1934; m. Alma Bernadene Malsbury, June 10, 1934. Farmer, Chandlerville, Ill., 1934—; grain dealer, 1940—; v.p., dir. Havana Nat. Bank (Ill.), 1956—. Mem. citizens com. U. Ill. Bd. dirs. K.T. Home for Aged and Infirm; exec. dir. K.T. Eye Found., 1973—. Mem. Mason County Farm Bur., Flying Farmers Prairie Farmer Land, Internat. Flying Farmers, Airplane Owners and Pilots Assn., Bradley U. Nat. Alumni Assn., Philalethes Soc., Acacia (hon.). Methodist. Mason (33 deg., Shriner, Jester, K.T., grand master grand encampment K.T. U.S.A.). Clubs: Union League (Chgo.); Sangamo (Springfield, Ill.). Home: Rural Route 2 Box 10 Chandlerville IL 62627 Office: PO Box 579 Springfield IL 62705

BELL, GLEN HUGH, lawyer; b. Sac City, Iowa, Aug. 1, 1902; s. Hugh Ross and Mary Elma (Hollway) B.; B.A., U. Wis., 1925, J.D., 1927; m. Frances Alice Lewis, May 10, 1930; children—Dorothy (Mrs. Robert J. Anderson), Hugh H. Admitted to Wis. bar, 1927; since practiced in Madison; mem. firm Bell, Metzner & Seibold, S.C., 1927—; gen. counsel Lake Superior Dist. Power Co., Ashland, Wis., 1949-73; gen. counsel, sec., dir. Wis. So. Gas Co., Inc., Lake Geneva, 1949—, North-West Telephone Co., Tomah, 1949—; gen. counsel Wis. Fuel & Light Co., Manitowoc, 1964—. Lectr. law U. Wis. Law Sch., 1939-51. Bd. dirs. University YMCA, 1956-65, United Givers Orgn., 1959-61. Mem. Am. Bar Assn., State Bar Wis., Fed. Power Bar Assn., Dane County Bar Assn. (pres. 1949), Am. Coll. Trial Lawyers, Phi Beta Kappa, Order of the Coif, Delta Sigma Rho. Club: Madison. Home: 3906 Cherokee Dr Madison WI 53711 Office: 222 W Washington Ave Madison WI 53703

BELL, HARRY MICHAEL, real estate exec.; b. Chgo., June 7, 1908; s. George R. and Margaret M. (Hogan) B.; student Chgo. Tchrs. Coll., 1929-32; J.D., Loyola U., Chgo., 1935; m. Grace Louise Simpson, Dec. 29, 1932; children—Barbara, David, Donald. Admitted to Ill. bar, 1935; pres. Bell & Hefter, Inc., real estate, Chgo., 1950—. Chmn., Real Estate Examining Bd. State of Ill., 1960-64. Employer trustee Health and Welfare Trust Local 399, Union Operating Engrs., Nat. Pension Trust Bldg. Service Employees Union, Pension Trust Local Firemen and Oilers Union 7. Mem. Nat. Assn. License Law Ofcls. (v.p. 1964-68), Bldg. Owners and Mgrs. Assn. (treas., dir.), Chgo. Bar Assn. Roman Catholic. Club: Ill. Athletic. Home: 2507 W 114th St Chicago IL 60655 Office: 111 N Wabash Ave Chicago IL 60602

BELL, JOHN LOUIS, surgeon; b. Aurora, Ill., Nov. 17, 1920; s. George Clawson and Loretta Marie (Frisbie) B.; student Duke U., 1938-41; B.S., Northwestern U., 1942, M.D., 1945, M.S., 1949; m. Ruth Dering, June 8, 1944 (dec. Apr. 1968); children—Robert, James, Barbara, Michael, John; m. 2d, Jane Siegel, Dec. 30, 1968; 1 child, Gale. Intern, Cook County Hosp., Chgo., 1944-45; resident Passavant Meml. Hosp., Chgo., 1947-50; practice medicine specializing in hand surgery, Chgo., 1951—; attending surgeon Passavant Meml. Hosp., Chgo., 1952—, VA Research Hosp., Chgo., 1954—; asso. attending surgeon Cook County (Ill.) Hosp., 1949-58; asso. prof. surgery Northwestern U. Sch. Med., 1964-74, prof. clin. surgery, 1974—. Served as lt. (j.g.), M.C., USNR, 1945-47. Diplomate Am. Bd. Surgery. Mem. AMA, Ill., Chgo. med. socs., Chgo. Surgical Soc., Central, Western surgical assns., Chgo. Inst. Medicine, Halsted Soc., Am. Assn. Surgery of Trauma, Am. Coll. Surgeons, Soc. Med. Cons. to Armed Forces, Am. Soc. Surgery of Hand (historian 1962-69, v.p. 1970, (pres. 1972), Groupe D'Etude de la Main, Flint Acad. Surgery (hon.), St. Paul Surg. Soc. (hon.), Sigma Xi. Clubs: Sunset Ridge Country (Northbrook, Ill.). Home: 3 Ct of Fox River Valley Lincolnshire IL 60015 Office: 707 N Fairbanks Ct Chicago IL 60611

BELL, JOHN RICHARD, dentist; b. Peoria, Ill., May 18, 1922; s. Ross G. and Frances A. (Seiler) B.; D.D.S., Washington U., St. Louis, 1946. Gen. practice dentistry, Peoria, Ill., 1946—; mem. hosp. staff St. Francis Hosp., Peoria, Ill. 1953—. Dental cons. Aetna Life & Casualty Co. Bd. dirs., treas. Peoria County chpt. Am. Cancer Soc. Served to lt. comdr. USNR, 1954-56. Mem. Am. Dental Assn., Ill., Peoria Dist. (treas. 1963-65, pres. 1965-66) dental socs., Peoria Assn. Commerce, Sigma Chi, Delta Sigma Delta. Republican. Roman Catholic. Home: 3522 N Bigelow St Peoria IL 61604 Office: 813-14 Jefferson Bldg Peoria IL 61602

BELL, JOHN STANLEY, steel sales co. exec.; b. Milw., May 29, 1918; s. Rae F. and Rose B. (Crelly) B.; A.B., Princeton, 1939; m. Eleanor Conners, Feb. 1942 (div.); children—John D., Rosemary, Anne Laura; m. 2d, Joan D. Kleinschmidt, Oct. 1967. With Inland Steel Co., Chgo., 1939-42; founder, pres. Bell Steel Sales, Inc., Milw., 1945—. Pres. Wis. chpt. Steel Service Center Inst. Vol. worker Milw. Community Chest, 1947-59. Bd. dirs. United Way, Milw. Repertory Theatre, Curative Workshop Milw. Served to lt. USNR. 1942-45. Clubs: Milwaukee Country, University (Milw.); University College (Princeton). Home: 2650 N Terrace Ave Milwaukee WI 53211 Office: 131st and Silver Spring Dr Butler WI 53007

BELL, JOHNSTON BARBER, gasket mfg. co. exec.; b. Lewisburg, W.Va., Oct. 7, 1928; s. Johnston Ewing and Berenice Wagar (Barber) B.; B.S. cum laude, Marshall U., 1950; M.B.A., Northwestern U., 1954; m. Lillian Antoinette Matuzas, Dec. 17, 1960; children—Joseph Lewis, David Edwin. Staff auditor Lybrand, Ross Bros. & Montgomery, C.P.A.'s, Chgo., 1954-58; internal auditor N.Am. Life Ins. Co., Chgo., 1958-59; staff accountant Montgomery Ward & Co., Chgo., 1959-60; asst. treas. Griffin Wheel Co., Chgo., 1961-65; asst. treas. F.D. Farnam Co., Necedah, Wis., 1966-67; treas., 1967—; dir. F.D. Farnam Co., Lyons, Ill. Co-chmn. fin. dr. Boy Scouts Am., Tomah, Wis., 1971; chmn. bd. Tomah Sch. of Childhood Inc., 1970-73. Served to lt. (j.g.) USNR, 1951-53; now comdr. Res. C.P.A., Ill. Mem. Ill. Soc. C.P.A.'s, Naval Res. Assn., Navy League U.S., Res. Officers Assn. (life), Beta Alpha Psi, Tau Kappa Epsilon. Congregationalist (deacon, chmn. bd. trustees). Clubs: Masons, Parkway Garden (pres. 1970-71) (Tomah). Home: 1216 Lincoln Ave Tomah WI 54660 Office: 8405 W 45th St Lyons IL 60534

BELL, NICHOLAS MONTGOMERY, II, pub. relations exec.; b. St. Louis, May 5, 1921; s. Richard E. and Marjorie Peper (Bell) Hinrichs; A.B., Knox Coll., 1941; postgrad. Northwestern U., 1941-42. Pub. relations and fund raising counsel, Chgo., 1947-51; pres. Nicholas M. Bell II & Assos. Chgo., 1952—. Served as officer AUS, 1942-46; ETO. Mem. Pub. Relations Soc. Am., Chgo. Assn. Commerce and Industry (govt. affairs com. 1968—, ednl. com. 1968—, pub. relations com. 1968—), VFW (comdr. 1953), Sigma Nu. Episcopalian. Clubs: Lions; Minn. (St. Paul). Office: PO Box 1427 Chicago IL 60690

BELL, ROBERT GENE, architect; b. Sterling, Ill., June 27, 1929; s. Milford Bundy and Irene Lavern (Bohnett) B.; B.S. in Archtl. Engring., Iowa State U., 1951; M.Arch., Cranbrook Acad. Art, 1955; m. Betty Louise Christian, Aug. 19, 1951; children—Barbara Ann, David Bundy, Steven Christian. Architect, Alden B. Dow & Assos., Midland, Mich., 1955-62; architect Graheck, Bell, Kline & Brown, Traverse City, Mich., 1962—, exec. v.p., 1968—; pres. RGB Corp., land devel., Traverse City, 1964—; gen. partner Bluff Village Cos., land acquisition, 1972—. Chmn., Peninsula Twp. Bd. Zoning Appeals, 1968—; mem. environ. arts com. Mich. Council for the Arts, 1966—; chmn. Mich. Gov.'s Spl. Commn. on Architecture, 1971—; chmn. Traverse Bay Regional Planning. Served as 1st lt. USAF, 1952-54. Mem. Mich. Soc. Architects (pres. No. Mich. chpt. 1964), Mich. Assn. Professions, Mich. Soc. Planning Ofcls. Home: 2494 E Carroll Rd Traverse City MI 49684 Office: 521 Randolph St Traverse City MI 49684

BELL, ROBERT MARK, lawyer; b. Oshkosh, Wis., Feb. 19, 1942; s. Frank H. and Marian W. (Thiessen) B.; B.S. in Econs., U. Wis., 1964, J.D., 1967; m. Jeanne L. Niotis, Dec. 8, 1962; children—Steven Andrew, Rodric James. Admitted to Wis. bar, 1967; practice law, mem. firm, Bell, Bell & Short, Fort Atkinson, Wis., 1967—; dist. atty. Jefferson County (Wis.), 1968-72; cons. Jefferson County Sheriff's Dept., 1969-72; town atty., Koshkonong, Wis., 1969—. Del. Wis. Republican Convs., 1968—; exec. com. Jefferson County Rep. Party, 1967—. Bd. dirs. Fort Atkinson Beautification Found., 1968—, v.p., 1974-76, pres., 1976-77; committeeman local council Boy Scouts Am., 1974—, asst. scoutmaster, 1977—. Mem. Am., Wis., Jefferson County (treas. 1971-72) bar assns., Am. Judicature Soc. (life), Wis. Dist. Attys. Assn. (2nd v.p. 1972-73), Jefferson County Realtors Assn. (asso.), Fort Atkinson Hist. Soc. (life), Wis. Alumni Assn. (life), Fort Atkinson Jaycees (v.p. 1971, dir. 1968-70), Wis. U.S. jaycees (asso.). Methodist (pres. 1972-73, pres. adminstrv. bd. 1973-76, trustee Wis. conf. 1974—, sec. investment policy com.). Home: Route 4 S Main Rd Fort Atkinson WI 53538 Office: 218 S Main St Fort Atkinson WI 53538

BELL, SAMUEL ALVIN, ret. steel co. exec.; b. Zanesville, Ohio, Dec. 25, 1910; s. Samuel Hamilton and Lulia Blanche (Crabtree) B.; B.S., Muskingum Coll., 1931; M.S., Mass. Inst. Tech., 1933; m. Mary Eleanor Peirce, Sept. 12, 1936; children—Susan Bell Williams, Samuel Peirce. With Armco Steel Corp., Middletown, Ohio, 1934-76, sr. research engr., 1945-51, sr. research engr., 1951-68, supr., 1968-72, mgr., 1972-76. Committeeman Boy Scouts Am., 1942-52; bd. govs. United Way, 1968—; mem. exec. com. Butler-Warren Area Health Planning Assn., 1969—; bd. dirs. Middletown Giant Step, Inc., 1976—, Salvation Army, 1977—. Registered profl. engr., Ohio. Mem. Am. Inst. Mining, Metall. and Petroleum Engrs., Am. Soc. Metals, Assn. Iron and Steel Engrs. Presbyterian. Clubs: Masons, Kiwanis. Patentee in field. Home: 4101 Manchester Rd Middletown OH 45042

BELL, SCOTT ALLEN, mktg. exec.; b. Independence, Mo., June 16, 1951; s. Robert Allen and Joan (White) B.; B.S. in Architecture, U. Ill., 1974; m. Karen Sue Dailey, Aug. 14, 1976. Adminstrv. dir., Assn. for Retarded Children, St. Louis, 1975-77; mktg. rep. IBM, St. Louis, 1977—; chmn. Ill. Guidance Center, U. Ill., Champaign, 1972; v.p. grad. bus. students Washington U., St. Louis, 1974-75. Active St. Louis Assn. for Retarded Children. Recipient Excellence in Mktg. award IBM, 1977. Mem. U. Ill. Alumni Assn. (life), Assn. of M.B.A. Execs. Methodist. Clubs: Ski, Scuba Diving. Home: 12562 Sunview Dr Creve Coeur MO 63141 Office: 788 Office Pkwy St Louis MO 63141

BELL, WILLIAM FLETCHER, state ofcl.; b. Lawrence, Kans., July 26, 1929; s. Maurice L. and Hazel (Chanay) B.; B.S., U. Kans., 1957; m. Mona Jean Slack, Aug. 13, 1950; children—Steven Michael, Nancy Diane. With ins. dept. State Kansas, Topeka, 1957—, policy examiner, 1958-61, accident and health supr., 1961, asst. commr. ins., 1961-71, commr. ins., 1971—; sec. Kans. Judges Retirement Bd., 1971-75; chmn. Kans. Com. on Surety Bonds and Ins., 1971—; mem. adv. com. Kans. Pub. Employees Deferred Compensation Plan, 1976—. Mem. Kans. Safety Council, 1971-76. Served with USAF, 1951-53. Mem. Nat. Assn. Ins. Commrs. (pres. 1973-74, chmn. or mem. numerous coms. and subcoms.), Am. Legion. Republican. Baptist. Clubs: Kiwanis; Lawrence Country, Univ. (Lawrence). Home: 843 W 22d St Lawrence KS 66044 Office: State Office Bldg Topeka KS 66612

BELL, WILSON TOWNSEND, banker; b. St. Louis, Feb. 24, 1934; s. Francis James and Dorothy May (Townsend) B.; B.A., Vanderbilt U., 1955; postgrad. Stonier Grad. Sch. Banking, Rutgers, 1968; m. Marilyn Joan Weber, June 29, 1957. Elec. sales Wagner Electric Corp., 1957-59; comml. loan officer Bank of St. Louis, 1959-67; v.p.

The Boatmen's Nat. Bank of St. Louis, 1967-72; pres. Big Bend Bank, St. Louis, 1972—. Chmn. Vanderbilt U. Living Endowment Fund Dr. of St. Louis, 1970; treas., mem. exec. bd. Loretto-Hilton Repertory Theatre, St. Louis. Served to 1st lt. AUS, 1955-57. Mem. Am. Inst. Banking (asso. dist. councilman 1970-75, chpt. pres. 1969-70), Robert Morris Assos. (chpt. pres. 1969-70, nat. com. on internat. lenders 1970-71), Friends of Scouting, Tenn. Soc. of St. Louis, Webster Groves C. of C. (pres. 1977), Sigma Nu. Clubs: Masons, Sunset Country, St. Louis Vanderbilt (treas. 1970, pres. 1972). Address: 8045 Big Bend Blvd St Louis MO 63119

BELLA, DANTINA CARMEN QUARTAROLI, psychologist; b. Providence, May 11, 1922; d. Bernardo and Jennie (Zinno) Quartaroli; M.A., Alfred U., 1952, M.S. in Adminstrn., U. Notre Dame, 1973; postgrad. U. Mich., 1977; m. Salvatore J. Bella, Dec. 30, 1946; children—Theresa, Joseph, Jennifer. Rehab. counselor R.I. Dept. Edn., 1942-46; admissions counselor Coll. Bus. Adminstrn., Boston U., 1946-49; asst. to dean Coll. of Ceramics, Alfred (N.Y.) U., 1949-53; dir. pupil personnel services, asst. prin. Marian High Sch., Mishawaka, Ind., 1968-74; registrar, admissions officer Ind. Vocat. Tech. Coll., South Bend, 1974-76; psychologist, resident counselor Forever Learning Inst., South Bend, 1977—; textbook cons. South Bend Community Sch. Corp., 1974-77; cons. teen-women career planning YWCA, 1974—; lectr., workshop coordinator, 1974—. Bd. dirs. Cath. Social Service Center, 1968—, Women Career Center, 1974; pres. South Bend Commn. on Status of Women, 1975—. Mem. Am. Personnel and Guidance Assn., Nat. Cath. Guidance Assn., AAUW, Beta Gamma Sigma. Democrat. Roman Catholic. Author: Sexism in Textbooks, 1975; The Portrayal of Women's Roles in Modern Textbooks, 1977; also asso. producer TV series Pub. Broadcasting System, Older Women and their Needs, 1976, 77. Home: 1029 Clermont Dr South Bend IN 46617 Office: 107 S Greenlawn Ave South Bend IN 46617

BELLES, FRANK EDWARD, combustion scientist; b. Cleve., Feb. 28, 1923; s. Frank E. and Olive I. (Hull) B.; B.S. in Chemistry, Western Res. U., 1947; M.S. in Phys. Chemistry, Case Inst. Tech., 1952; m. Jean M. Eighmey, Feb. 22, 1946; children—Richard H., Sarah E., John E. Aeronautical research scientist Nat. Adv. Com. for Aeronautics, Cleve., 1947-58; head gas dynamics and kinetics sects. NASA, Cleve., 1958-71, chief propulsion chemistry br., 1971-72, dir. Aerospace Safety Research and Data Inst., 1972-74; mgr. research and devel. Am. Gas Assn. Labs., 1974—. Served with USNR, 1943-46. Mem. Am. Chem. Soc., Combustion Inst., AAAS, Phi Beta Kappa, Sigma Xi. Office: 8501 E Pleasant Valley Rd Cleveland OH 44131

BELLI, ELMER FRED, orthodontist; b. Campbell, Ohio, Apr. 7, 1937; s. Domenic and Adeline (Fiorenzia) B.; D.D.S. cum laude, Ohio State U., 1961; M.S., U. Ill., 1966 Gen. practice dentistry, Youngstown, Ohio, 1964, practice dentistry, specializing in orthodontics, Warren, Ohio, 1966—. Chmn. Warren Citizens Com. for Flouridation 1968—. Served with Dental Corps, USAF, 1961-62, intern USAF Hosp., Lackland, 1962-64; Germany. Mem. Am. Assn. Orthodontists, Ohio, Corydon Palmer, Warren (past treas., pres. 1974-75) dental socs., Crippled Childrens Assn. Ohio, Cleve. Soc. Orthodontists, Delta Sigma Delta, Omicron Kappa Upsilon, Phi Eta Sigma. Contbr. articles to profl. jours. Home and Office: 1100 Elm Rd NE Warren OH 44483

BELLINGER, AMY LOU, pub. relations exec.; b. Alma, Mich., Aug. 8, 1954; d. Richard R. and Mary Alice (Sanderson) Bellinger; B.A., Central Mich. U., 1974; certificate Poly. of Central Lon. Sch. of Photography, London, Eng., 1972; m. Dennis L. Silverstein, July 2, 1976 (div. July 1977). Asst. spl. events coordinator Nat. Bank of Detroit, 1974-76; v.p. in charge pub. relations PR&D, St. Louis, 1976-77; pub. relations dir. Direct Mail Corp. Am., St. Louis, 1977—. Active worker various polit. campaigns. Mem. Internat. Assn. Bus. Communicators, Pub. Relations Soc. Am., Home Builders Assn. Greater St. Louis, ACLU. Liberal Democrat. Contbr. articles to various mags. and newspapers. Home: 4482 Lindell Blvd Saint Louis MO 63108 Office: 1533 Washington Saint Louis MO 63103

BELLIS, WARREN TARLETON, educator; b. Joplin, Mo., Apr. 1, 1923; s. Maurice Owen and Anna Viola (Golding) B.; student Joplin Jr. Coll., 1941-42; Mus.B., U. Mich., 1949, Mus.M., 1950; D.Mus. Arts, 1967; m. Lois Maxine Bailey, June 10, 1969; children—Lynda Kay, Gary, Lori Dee, Elizabeth Ann, William Alan. Instr. woodwinds Wis. State Coll., Milw., 1950-52; mem. Milw. Symphony Orch., 1951-52; prof. music U. Idaho, Moscow, 1952-66, dir. bands, 1952-66; prof. music and music edn. U. Mo., St. Louis, 1967—, dir. instrumental music and woodwinds, 1967—. Bd. dirs. Greater St. Louis Music Festivals, 1973—. Served with USAAC, 1943-45. Decorated Air medal (7), D.F.C. Mem. Mo. Music Educators Assn. (dir. coll. div. 1972-74), Coll. Band Dirs. Nat. Assn. (state chmn. 1960-64), Am. Bandmasters Assn., Coll. Band Dirs. Nat. Assn. (state chmn. 1975—), Nat. Assn. Coll. Wind and Percussion Instrs. (chmn. 1955-59), Music Educators Nat. Assn., Phi Kappa Phi, Phi Mu Alpha Sinfonia, Pi Kappa Lambda, Kappa Kappa Psi, Phi Beta Mu. Home: 2900 Ridgeview Dr St Louis MO 63121 Office: 8001 Natural Bridge Rd St Louis MO 63121

BELLOW, SAUL, writer; b. Lachine, Quebec, Can., June 10, 1915; s. Abraham and Liza (Gordon) B.; student U. Chgo., 1933-35; B.S., Northwestern U., 1937, Litt.D., 1962; hon. degrees Bard Coll., 1962, Harvard U., 1972, Yale U., 1972, McGill U., 1973, Brandeis U., 1974, Hebrew Union Coll.-Jewish Inst. Religion, 1976, Trinity Coll., Dublin, 1976; m. Anita Goshkin, Dec. 31, 1937; 1 son, Gregory; m. 2d, Alexandra Tschacbasov, Feb. 1, 1956; 1 son, Adam; m. 3d, Susan Glassman, Dec. 10, 1961; 1 son, Daniel. Tchr., Pestalozzi-Froebel Tchrs. Coll., Chgo., 1938-42; faculty Princeton U., N.Y.U., U. Minn.; faculty English dept. U. Chgo., 1963—, mem. Com. on Social Thought, 1963—, chmn., 1970-76, now Raymond W. and Martha Hilpert Gruner Distinguished Service prof. Decorated Croix de Chevalier des Arts et Lettres (France); recipient Nat. Inst. Arts and letters award, 1952; Nat. Book Award in Fiction for The Adventures of Augie March, 1954, Herzog, 1965, Mr. Sammler's Planet, 1970; Friends of Lit. Fiction award, 1960; Internat. Lit. prize, 1965; Communicator of Year award, U. Chgo., 1971; Soc. Midland Authors Fiction award, 1976; Nobel Prize for lit., 1976; Guggenheim fellow, 1955-56; Ford Found. grantee, 1959-61. Mem. Am. Acad. Arts and Scis. Author: Dangling Man, 1944; The Victim, 1947; Best Stories of 1950; The Adventures of Augie March, 1953; Seize The Day, 1956; Henderson The Rain King, 1959; Herzog, 1964; (Internat. Lit. prize 1965, James L. Dow award, 1964); Last Analysis (play), 1964; Mosby's Memoirs and Other Stories, 1968; Mr. Sammler's Planet, 1969; Humboldt's Gift, 1975 (Pulitzer Prize 1976); To Jerusalem and Back: A Personal Account, 1976. Contbr. fiction to nat. mags. and lit. quars. Address: Univ Chicago Chicago IL 60637

BELLOWS, GLEN LEE, cons. engr.; b. Spencer, Iowa, Jan. 9, 1937; s. Glen LeVern and Virginia Irene (Adams) B.; B.S. in M.E., U. Ill., 1959; m. Sylvia Ruth Dean, June 11, 1959; children—Alice, Ann (dec.), Kevin, Peter. Mech. engr. Brown, Manthei, Davis & Mullins, Champaign, Ill., 1959-65; prin., v.p., treas. Buchanan, Bellows & Assos., Ltd., Bloomington, Ill., 1966—; tchr. seminar Am. Mgmt. Assn., 1974. Bd. dirs. McLean County Occupational Devel. Center, 1969—, treas., 1972-73, 75—; vice chmn. Bloomington Bldg. Code Review Bd., 1972—; mem. Bloomington Heating and Cooling Bd., 1969—, Normal (Ill.) Heating and Cooling Bd., 1973—. Registered profl. engr., Ill., Iowa, S.C. Mem. Am. Soc. Heating, Air Conditioning and Refrigeration Engrs., Constrn. Specifications Inst., Nat., Ill. socs. profl. engrs., Ill. C. of C., Delta Sigma Omicron (Harold Sharper service award 1959). Republican. Mormon (ward bishop 1977—). Home: 210 Foster Dr Normal IL 61761 Office: 1509 N Clinton Blvd Bloomington IL 61701

BELLVILLE, THOMAS STANLEY, educator; b. Kimbolton, Ohio, Jan. 23, 1926; s. William Stanley and Louella May (Booth) B.; B.S. cum laude, Cedarville Coll., 1959; postgrad. Kent State U., 1958, 63; m. Lois Irene Cotterman, Oct. 27, 1947; children—Thomas Eugene, Cheryl Ann, Deborah Kay. Tchr., coach, Rushville Union, 1953, Baltic, O., 1954; chemist Sharp, Shurtz Lab., Lancaster, Ohio, 1955; prin. Baltic Local Sch., 1956-60, exec. head, 1961-64; tchr. New Philadelphia City Sch., Baltic, 1965—. Pres., Tri County Community Improvement Corp., Baltic, 1972—. Mem. Village Council, 1967-72, mayor, 1972-75. Served with USNR, 1944-46: PTO. Mem. Am. Legion. Methodist. Lion. Home: Box 164 Baltic OH 43804

BELMONTE, JOHN VIRGIL, surgeon; b. Chgo., Jan. 1, 1938; s. John Virgil and Anne (Izzo) B.; B.S., John Carroll U., 1956; M.S., U. Ill., 1967; student Loyola U. Med. Sch., 1963; m. Sherill K. Premo, Sept. 26, 1964; children—John, Kristen Ann, Braden, Pamela. Intern, Cook County Hosp., Chgo., 1963-64; resident in surgery Hines (Ill.) VA Hosp., 1964-68; practice medicine specializing in surgery, Oak Park, Ill., 1968—; mem. staff Gottlieb Hosp., Central DuPage Hosp., Oak Park Hosp. Served to maj. U.S. Army, 1968-70. Diplomate Am. Bd. Surgeons. Fellow A.C.S.; mem. Ill., Du Page County, Chgo. med. socs., AMA, Am. Trauma Soc., Pan-Pacific Surg. Soc. Roman Catholic. Home: 1319 Park Ave River Forest IL 60305 Office: 6429 W North Ave Suite 201 Oak Park IL 60302

BELOTE, DONALD ALLEN, auditor; b. Greenway, Ark., Mar. 3, 1946; s. Dewey E. and Geraldine A. (Lawrence) B.; student U. Md., 1967-68; B.A. magna cum laude, Western Mich. U., 1971; m. Cheryl Dawn Dafoe, Dec. 19, 1970. Sr. auditor Ernst & Ernst, Kalamazoo, Mich., 1972-74; sr. internal auditor Upjohn Co., Kalamazoo, 1974—. Active United Way. Served with USAF, 1965-68; Vietnam. C.P.A., Mich. Mem. Am., Mich. assns. C.P.A.'s, Am. Accounting Assn., Nat. Assn. Accountants. Elk. Home: 2230 Waverly St Kalamazoo MI 49007 Office: 7000 Portage Rd Kalamazoo MI 49001

BELSARE, JAYANT VISHNU, physician; b. Sinner, India, Dec. 19, 1938; s. Vishnu Govind and Triveni Vishnu (Khaladkar) B.; came to U.S., 1967; M.B., B.S., U. Poona, 1963; M.S., 1966; m. Vasanti Sakharam Kulkarni, Feb. 26, 1966; 1 dau., Shubhada. Intern, CPR Hosp., Kolhapur, India, 1962; resident in gen. surgery Sassoon Hosps., Poona, 1963-64, in anesthesia, 1964-65, in orthopedics, 1965; jr. lectr. B.J. Med. Coll., Poona, 1965-66; hon. surgeon Talegaon Gen. Hosp. (India), 1966-67; resident surgery Watts Hosp., Durham, N.C., 1967-69, Johnston Willis Hosp., Richmond, Va., 1969-71; preceptee surgery Surg. Asso., Mason City, Iowa, 1971-72; pvt. practice surgery, Clarinda, Iowa, 1972-73, Mt. Pleasant, Iowa, 1973—; mem. staff Henry County Health Center, Mt. Pleasant, Burlington (Iowa) Med. Center; med. adviser Henry County Cancer Soc. Diplomate Am. Bd. Surgery. Fellow Royal Coll. Surgeons Can., A.C.S., Am. Soc. Abdominal Surgeons, Iowa, Henry County med. socs., AMA. Home: 1107 Linden Ct Mount Pleasant IA 52641 Office: 114 E Monroe St Mount Pleasant IA 52641

BELSHAN, MILO LEO, county ofcl., farmer; b. Myrtle, Minn., Dec. 14, 1922; s. Louis A. and Josephine (Benesh) B.; grad. high sch.; m. Betty Jane Johnson, Sept. 5, 1948, children—Marilyn, Michael, Daniel. Farmer Haywood Twp., Minn., 1949—; mem. Freeborn County Bd. County Commrs., Albert Lea, Minn., 1959—. Mem. Freeborn County Welfare Bd., 1959—, chmn., 1963-64; bd. mem. So. Minn. Mental Health Center, 1963—; mem. Freeborn County Extension Com., 1960—, chmn., 1961-63; bd. govs. Power Plant Siting Task Force, 1972-73; mem. pub. relations com. Naeve Hosp., 1965—. Served with AUS, 1943-46; PTO. Mem. State Assn. County Ofcls. (mem. planning and recreation com. 1968—), Minn. Assn. Counties (chmn. planning and recreation com. 1971—), Farmers Union (chmn. 1954-59), V.F.W., Am. Legion, Western Bohemian Fraternal Assn. Democrat. Lutheran. Home: Rural Route 1 Glenville MN 56036 Office: Freeborn County Courthouse Albert Lea MN 56007

BELT, FOREST H., editor, author, photographer; b. St. Louis, July 4, 1932; s. Forest and Eula (Carnahan) B.; student colls. Crittenden County, Ky., 1946-50; children by former marriage—Eydie, Larry Allen, Pamela Sue. Editor PF Reporter, Broadcast Engring., Indpls., 1962-65, Radio Electronics, N.Y.C., 1966-67; author 50 books, 1967—; editor miscellaneous books and mags., 1967—; contbr. numerous articles to popular mags., 1960—; faculty Indpls. Art League, 1972—. Home: PO Box 68110 Indianapolis IN 46268 Office: PO Box 68120 Indianapolis IN 46268

BELTER, ROBERT FRANK, graphic arts supply co. exec.; b. Batesville, Ind., Sept. 2, 1935; s. Albert F. and Cora S. (Becker) B.; B.A., Hanover Coll., 1957; M.B.A., Ind. U., 1958; m. Carolyn Anne Byrkett, Dec. 21, 1956; children—Deborah, Jill Anne, Todd Robert. Successively asst. accounts payable mgr., br. store office mgr., asst. to gen. mdse. mgr., div. sales mgr. L.S. Ayres & Co., Indpls., 1958-66; controller Topics Newspapers, Inc., 1966-69; staff asst. to controller, accounts payable mgr. The May Co., Cleve., 1969-71; v.p., gen. mgr. Portage Newspaper Supply Co., Akron, Ohio, 1971—. Mem. Cuyahoga Valley Businessmen's Assn. (dir. 1976-77). Home: 2370 Yellow Creek Rd Akron OH 44313 Office: PO Box 5500 Akron OH 44313

BELTZ, CHARLES ROBERT, engr.; b. Pitts., Feb. 23, 1913; s. Charles Fred and Ester (Johnston) B.; student Greenbrier Mil. Sch., 1930-33; M.E., Cornell U., 1934; B.S. in Aero. Engring., U. Pitts., 1937; m. Amy Margaret Ferguson, Oct. 23, 1935; children—Charles R., A.M. Bonnie (Mrs. Hatch), Homer F., William T., Carol E. (Mrs. Marks), M. Joy (Mrs. O'Keefe). Engr. Crane Co., 1937-39; design engr. Stout Skycraft Corp., 1939-43; project engr. Cycle-Weld Labs., 1943-44; project engr., mgr. Fairchild E & A Corp., Roosevelt Field, 1944-46; corp. engr. Chrysler Corp., 1946-47; pres. Charles R. Beltz & Co., Detroit, 1947—, Beltz Engring. Labs., 1950—, Beltz Parts and Services, Inc., 1954—, Beltemp, Inc., 1969—. Mem. Nat. Aero. Assn. (pres.), Air Conditioning Inst. (pres.), Inst. Aero. Scis. (vice chmn.). Am. Heating, Refrigerating and Air Conditioning Engrs. (contbg. author), N.Y. Acad. Scis., Engring. Soc. Detroit, Detroit Mus. Art Founders Soc., Detroit Hist. Soc., Internat. Plastic Aircraft Soc., Air Force Assn., Detroit Bd. Commerce. Clubs: Aero (dir.), Economic, Curling (Detroit); Grosse Pointe Yacht; Lost Lake Woods. Author: Ice Skating; Skating Weather or Not: ABC's Air-conditioning; Roatable Aircraft. Home: 500 Lakeland Ave Grosse Pointe MI 48230 Office: 15001 Charlevoix Ave Grosse Pointe Park MI 48230

BELZER, JEFFREY A., lawyer; b. Mpls., Sept. 8, 1941; s. Meyer S. and Kathleen (Bardin) B.; B.A., St. Cloud State U., 1963; J.D., Drake U., 1968; m. Marguerite V. Walesch, Oct. 1, 1966; children—Steven, Michael, Anna. Admitted to Minn. bar, 1968, U.S. Dist. Ct. bar., 1969; mem. firm Henretta, Muirhead, McGinty, Ltd., Mpls., 1968-71; pres., sr. atty. Belzer & Brenner Ltd., Mpls., 1971—; pres., dir. Walesch Estates, Inc., Mpls., 1971—, Walesch Devel. Co., Mpls., 1969—. Mem. Am., Hennepin County, Minn. bar assns., Phi Alpha Delta. Club: Lions. Staff Drake Law Rev., 1966-67. Office: 7200 France Ave S #337 Minneapolis MN 55435

BELZILE, JOSEPH DANIEL, dentist, army officer; b. Van Buren, Maine, May 9, 1930; s. Joseph Paul and Anne Elizabeth (Cyr) B.; B.S., Coll. Holy Cross, Worcester, Mass., 1953; D.D.S., U. Pa., 1957; Ph.D., Georgetown U., 1965; m. Beverly Renee Bernier, Aug. 10, 1963; children—Joseph Daniel, Michael William, Mark Gregory. Commd. 2d lt. U.S. Army, 1956, advanced through ranks to col., 1972; intern Tripler U.S. Army Hosp., Honolulu, 1957-58; periodontist 25th Inf. div. Schofield Barracks, Hawaii, 1958-60; post dental surgeon U.S. Army Garrison, Fort Totten, N.Y., 1960-62; resident in pathology Armed Forces Inst. Pathology, Washington, 1965-66; researcher U.S. Army Inst. Dental Research, Washington, 1966-69; oral pathologist Ireland Army Hosp., Ft. Knox, Ky., 1969-73, Brooke Army Med. Center, San Antonio, 1973-77, Dental Activity, Med. Activity Dept., Fort Riley, Kans., 1977—; asst. prof. oral pathology Georgetown U., 1965-71; asso. prof. pathology U. Tex., San Antonio, 19777; cons. oral pathology 1st Army Dental Surgeon, Reynolds Army Hosp., Ft. Sill, Okla., U.S. Army Hosp., Ft. Campbell, Ky., U.S. Army Hosp., Ft. Jackson, S.C., Darnall U.S. Army Hosp., Ft. Hood, Tex. Diplomate Am. Bd. Oral Pathology, Am. Bd. Oral Medicine. Fellow Am. Acad. Oral Pathology, Am. Coll. Dentists; mem. ADA, Psi Omega. Roman Catholic. Home: 352 Ray Rd Fort Riley KS 66442 Office: Dental Activity Med Activity Dept Fort Riley KS 66442

BEMIS, EDWIN LEWIS, pathologist, lab. dir.; b. Fond du Lac, Wis., Oct. 11, 1923; s. Edwin Loren and Sophia Marie (Buechner) B.; M.D., Marquette U., Milw., 1950; m. Cecile Adelle Prudell, Aug. 1, 1942; children—Edwin Loren, Catherine Ann, Bridget Mary, William Robert, James Joseph, Peter John, Margaret Clare. Intern, Milw. County Gen. Hosp., Milw., 1950-51; resident in clin. and anatomic pathology VA Center Hosp., Wood, Wis., 1956-60; asst. dir. labs. St. Francis Hosp., Milw., 1960-61; dep. dir. labs. Deaconess Hosp., Milw., 1961—, vice chief med. staff, 1967—; asst. clin. prof. pathology Med. Coll. Wis., 1962—; instr. med. tech. Marquette U., 1962—; med. dir. sickle cell center Deaconess Hosp., Milw. Recipient awards for art, photography and sci. exhbts. Fellow Coll. Am. Pathology, Am. Soc. Clin. Pathology, Am. Phys. Art Assn. (life). Contbr. articles to med. jours. Home: 1540 N 119th St Wauwatosa WI 53226

BEMMANN, KATHRYN MARIE CHIZEK, physician; b. Manitowoc Wis., Oct. 29, 1931; d. Frank and Celia (Cigler) Chizek; B.S. in Medicine, Marquette U., 1953, M.D., 1956; m. Irving Stewart Bemmann, May 3, 1958. Intern St. Joseph Hosp., Milw., 1956-57; staff physician Milw. (Wis.) County Hosp. for Mental Disorders, 1957-58; resident Asso. Training Program in Psychiatry of Milw., 1958-61; staff psychiatrist Milw. Psychiat. Hosp., 1961-62; practice medicine specializing in psychiatry, Waukesha, 1962—; courtesy med. staff Waukesha Meml. Hosp., 1962—, med. dir. psychiat. unit, 1968-70; asso. psychiat. staff Milw. Psychiat. Hosp.; instr. psychiatry Marquette U., Milw., 1960-64, asst. clin. prof., 1964—, faculty moderator women med. students, 1964-69. Founding mem. Waukesha County Rape Crisis Counseling Service, 1975. Recipient CAROL award Wis. Jaycettes, 1961. Diplomate Am. Bd. Psychiatry. Fellow Am. Psychiat. Assn.; mem. AMA, Wis., Waukesha County med. socs., Wis. Psychiat. Assn. (pres.-elect chpt. 1976, chmn. com. on women 1976), Am. Med. Women's Assn. (coordinator dist. br. 1977), NOW (bd. dirs.), Gamma Pi Epsilon. Home: S 46 W 22338 Tansdale Rd Waukesha WI 53186 Office: 251 W Broadway St Waukesha WI 53186

BENDEL, RUTH THOMPSON (MRS. VICTOR D. BENDEL), artist, designer; b. Hinsdale, Ill., Jan. 6, 1910; d. George Anthony and Elsea (Sprinks) Thompson; student Grinnell Coll., 1927-28, Chgo. Sch. Art Inst., 1929-34; m. Oscar van Tellingen, June 10, 1936 (dec. Oct. 1946); children—Dirk Anthony, Frederic Goudy; m. 2d, Victor D Bendel, Apr. 16, 1948. Designer, Fisher-Price Toys Inc., East Aurora, N.Y., 1953-69; illustrator Ding Dong Sch. books, Rand McNally Co. Chgo., 1953-56; cover designs Jack and Jill books, others Curtis Pub. Co., Phila., 1956-69; designer Am. Decal Co., Chgo., 1943—; illustrator, writer Thai Diary, Bangkok World, Thailand, 1967-68. Mem. Children's Reading Round Table, Women's Nat. Book Assn., Bangkok Art Assn., Hinsdale Community Artists, Soc. Typog. Arts, Artists Guild Chgo., Alumni Assn. Sch. Art Inst. Chgo. Author: Bangkok: a Thai Diary, 1972. Home: 24 W Ogden Ave Hinsdale IL 60521

BENDEL, WILLIAM LOUIS, JR., physician; b. Monroe, La., Mar. 1, 1921; s. William Louis and Marie (Gariepy) B.; B.S., Tulane U., 1941, M.D., 1944; Ph.D. in microbiology, Baylor U., 1966; m. Margaret Rose Butler, Feb. 18, 1944 (dec. Jan. 1970); children—Susan Marie, Jan Ann; m. 2d, Kathleen Doris Mabley, Apr. 16, 1971. Intern, Charity Hosp., New Orleans, 1944, resident gen. surgery, 1949-52, resident thoracic surgery, 1952; resident gen. surgery Mt. Carmel Mercy Hosp., Detroit, 1947-48; surgery teaching fellow Tulane U., New Orleans, 1948-49; gen. practice medicine, Monroe, 1953-58; resident pathology Baylor U. Med. Center, Dallas, 1959-63; dir. labs. Unity Hosp., Mpls. Served from 1st lt. to capt., M.C., AUS, 1945-46. Diplomate in anatomic pathology and clin. pathology Am. Bd. Pathology, Am. Bd. Med. Microbiology. Mem. AMA, Minn., Hennepin County med. assns., Holy Name Soc., Alpha Kappa Kappa, Kappa Sigma. Republican. Roman Catholic. Club: K.C. (4 deg.). Contbr. numerous articles to med. jours. Home: 10022 E River Rd NW Coon Rapids MN 55433 Office: Unity Hosp Fridley MN 55432

BENDER, JOHN HENRY, JR. (JACK), editorial cartoonist; b. Waterloo, Ia., Mar. 28, 1931; s. John Henry and Wilma (Lowe) B.; B.A., U. Ia., 1953; M.A., U. Mo., 1962; postgrad. Art Inst. Chgo., Washington U., St. Louis; m. Jo Ann J. Packey, June 13, 1953; children—Thereza, John IV, Anthony. Art dir., asst. editor Commerce Pub. Co., St. Louis, 1953-58; editor Florissant Reporter, 1958-61; editorial cartoonist Waterloo Courier, 1962—, asso. editor, 1975—; sports cartoons Baseball Digest Mag., Athletic News, others. Served with USAF, 1954-56, now col. Res. Recipient Best Editorial award Mo. Press Assn., 1960; Grenville Clark Editorial Page award, 1968, Freedoms Found. award, 1969, 71, 75. Mem. Assn. Am. Editorial Cartoonists, Nat. Cartoonists Soc., Sigma Chi. Author: Pocket Guide to Judging Springboard Diving; (with Dick Smith) Inside Diving; (with Ed Gagnier) Inside Gymnastics. Home: 2904 Cottage Row Rd Cedar Falls IA 50613 Office: Box 540 Courier Waterloo IA 50704

BENDER, PAUL L., hosp. adminstr.; b. Bluffton, Ind., Mar. 5, 1918; s. Lawrence L. and Elizabeth A. (Reiff) B.; B.S., Purdue U., 1939; m. Maro L. Bradburn, Apr. 6, 1941; children—Paul L., Linda (Mrs. Carl M. Heuer). With Goodman Mfg. Co., indsl. machinery, Chgo., 1939-47; owner L.L. Bender Co., elec. equipment, Bluffton, Ind., 1947-70; exec. dir., adminstr. Wells Community Hosp., 1970—, pres. hosp. bd., 1953-70. Active Mental Health Assn., United Fund,

Cemetary assn., Agrl. Achievement Assn., and other civic groups. Sec., City Plan Commn., Bluffton, Ind., 1953. Mem. exec. bd. Anthony Wayne council Boy Scouts Am., 1962—. Recipient Silver Beaver award Boy Scouts Am., 1966, community service award Wells County, 1971. Mem. Am. Inst. Elec. and Electronic Engrs., Am. Acad. Med. Adminstrs., Hist. Soc. (pres. 1966-70), Bluffton C. of C. (pres. 1954). Methodist. (trustee 1956-58). Clubs: Elks, Lions (dir. 1948—). Home: 506 W Ohio St Bluffton IN 46714 Office: 1100 S Main St Bluffton IN 46714

BENDORF, RONALD LEE, psychiatrist; b. Omaha, Oct. 19, 1937; s. Matt Rasmussen and Irma Deloice (Savage) B.; student U. Omaha, 1955-58; B.S., M.D., U. Nebr., 1962; m. Judith Ann Macey, Jan. 12, 1958; children—Shelley, Sherry, Eric, David, Jodie, Jennifer, Adam. Resident in psychiatry Nebr. Psychiat. Inst., Omaha, 1969-72; dir. outpatient service Immanuel Community Mental Health Center, Omaha, 1972-73; practice medicine specializing in psychiatry, Council Bluffs, Iowa, 1973—; mem. vol. faculty, asso. prof. psychiatry U. Nebr., 1972-77. Served as flight surgeon USN, 1964-69; Vietnam. Diplomate Am. Bd. Psychiatry Neurology. Republican. Mormon. Office: Suite 501 1st Fed Savs Loan Bldg Council Bluffs IA 51501

BENDUHN, JAMES RICHARD, chem. and process equipment co. exec.; b. Cleve., Nov. 18, 1946; s. Raymond and Alice (Czarniak) B.; B.B.A., Ohio U., 1970; postgrad Kent State U., 1973-74; m. Joyce A. Rushiaczyk, Oct. 4, 1969; children—Stacey Lynn, Eric Raymond. Jr. draftsman Process Systems, Cleve., 1964, Laurenuk Design, Cleve., 1964; asst. buyer The Sherwin Williams Co., Cleve., 1968-73; salesman Dimlich-Radcliffe Co. (now Dar-Tech, Inc.), Cleve., 1973—, treas., 1975—. Served with USAR, 1968-74. Mem. Cleve. Soc. Coatings Technology, Cleve. Paint and Coatings Assn., Cleve. Chem. Assn. Home: 6250 Sharondale Dr Solon OH 44139 Office: 4900 Lakeside Ave Cleveland OH 44114

BENEDICT, JOHN ANTHONY, social worker; b. Pittsburg, Kans., June 27, 1943; s. Frances Loriene B.; B.A. in English Lit., St. Meinrad Coll., 1965; M.S. in Counselor Edn., Kans. State Coll., Pittsburg, 1975; m. Marcia Kathleen McCullough, Nov. 22, 1974; 1 stepdau., Amber Peterson. Family social service worker Parsons (Kans.) area office Kans. Social and Rehab. Services, 1965-66, social worker, family services, 1968-69, income maintenance worker, 1969-71, Work Incentive Program social service worker, 1971-77, social worker II, protective service work, youth, 1977—. Vice pres. Labette County Cancer Soc., 1969, 70, pres., 1971, 72; mem. Parsons Youth Council, 1969—; mem. community action bd. Labette County Mental Health, 1969, 73. Served in U.S. Army, 1966-68. Mem. Am., Kans. personnel and guidance assns., Nat. Vocational Guidance Assn., Pub. Offenders Counselors Assn., Nat. Com. Prevention of Child Abuse. Roman Catholic. Home: 1226 Kimball St Parsons KS 67357 Office: 109 S 22d St PO Box 914 Parsons KS 67357

BENEKE, MILDRED (MILLIE) STONG (MRS. ARNOLD W. BENEKE), civic worker; b. Prairie City, Iowa; d. Rueben Ira and Lillian (Garber) Stong; student Wash. U., 1942-43; off-campus student U. Minn., Mankato State Coll., 1945-67; m. Arnold W. Beneke, Aug. 10, 1939; children—Bruce Arnold, Paula Rae, Bradford Kent, Cynthia Jane (Mrs. Daniel Berger), Lisa Patrice. Exec. sec. chmn. Vol. Services, St. Paul, Am. Red Cross, 1940-41; v.p. Pi House, St. Paul, 1972—; founder, bd. dirs. chmn. Project Interaction Boutique, Minn. Correctional Instn. for Women, Shakopee, 1971—, supervising vol., 1970—. Chmn. McLeod County Diversion Program, 1974—; mem. Glencoe Community Bicentennial Commn., 1975-76. Republican chairwoman McLeod County (Minn.), 1969-73; mem. Rep. Minn. Platform com., 1970; McLeod County del. Rep. Minn. Central Com., 1969—; mem. Minn. Task Force Criminal Justice Commn., 1974—; mem. Rep. Feminist Caucus; alderman Glencoe City Council, 1974-77. Glencoe elderly housing named Millie Beneke Manor in her honor, 1977. Mem. Glencoe Bus. and Profl. Women (Woman of Year 1975), Ripon Soc. Lutheran. Columnist, Council Memos from Millie, Glencoe Enterprise. Home: Glenview Woods Glencoe MN 55336

BENES, CHARLES JAMES, banker; b. Cleve., May 22, 1904; s. James and Mary (Poskecil) B.; student Dyke Coll. Bus., 1919-20; m. Rose AnnaBelle Jankovsky, July 20, 1950; children—Charles J. Sec., treas. First Fed. Savs. & Loan Assn., Cleve., 1933—, also dir. Commr. zoning and planning City of Pepper Pike, Ohio, 1956-69. Mem. Am. Savs. and Loan Inst. (pres. Northeast Ohio chpt. 1951-52). Mason (Shriner, 32 deg.). Club: Mentor (Ohio) Yachting. Home: 29026 Gates Mills Blvd Pepper Pike OH 44124 Office: Park Centre 1255 Superior St Cleveland OH 44114

BENGTSON, LAWRENCE OSCAR, lawyer; b. Smolan, Kans., Dec. 10, 1922; s. G.E. and Augusta (Ohman) B.; A.B., Washburn U., 1948, LL.B., 1950; m. Marjorie Oborg, Feb. 22, 1953; children—Michael, David. Admitted to Kans. bar, 1950, since practiced in Salina; U.S. commr. for Kans., 1954-68; city atty., Salina, 1962—. Dir. Assaria State Bank (Kans.), chmn. bd. dirs., 1973—; dir. Swedish-Am. Ins. Co. Chmn. bd. trustees St. Johns Hosp. Served as pilot USAAC, 1943-46. Lutheran (exec. council Luth. Ch. in Am. 1966-70). Clubs: Masons, Shriners. Home: 2100 Edgehill Rd Salina KS 67401 Office: 114 E Iron Ave Salina KS 67401

BENINSON, JOSEPH, physician; b. Bklyn., Apr. 17, 1918; s. Isadore and Ida (Kopaloff) B.; B.S., Tex. A. and M. Coll., 1943, D.V.M., 1947; M.D., U. Tex., 1951; m. Evelyne M. Holschauer, July 17, 1977; children—Maureen, Ellen, Ilene, Fern. Intern, U. Tex. Sch. Medicine, Galveston 1951-52, resident, 1952-53; resident Henry Ford Hosp., Detroit, 1953-55; practice of medicine, specializing in dermatology, Detroit, 1955—; mem. staff Henry Ford Hosp., Detroit. Served with AUS, 1942-46. Fellow Am. Coll. Angiology (v.p. 1964—), Brazilian Coll. Angiology (hon.); mem. Am. Acad. Dermatology, Soc. Investigative Dermatology, Detroit Dermatol. Soc., AMA, Internat. Soc. Lymphology, Wayne County Med. Soc. Mem. editorial bd. Angiology, 1967—; contbr. articles to publs. Home: 4743 Burnley Dr Bloomfield Hills MI 48013 Office: Henry Ford Hosp 2799 W Grand Blvd Detroit MI 48202

BENJAMEN, LYSLE IRVING, mfg. exec.; b. Detroit, July 20, 1927; s. Lysle Christopher and Ruth (Boss) B.; B.S., U.S. Coast Guard Acad., 1950; M.S., Rensselaer Poly. Inst., 1955; Ph.D., Mich. State U., 1966 Prodn. engr. Eaton Mfg. Co., Battle Creek, Mich., 1955-57; asst. prof. fin. and mgmt. Ferris State Coll., Big Rapids, Mich., 1958-59; engr. mgr. Dearborn Marine Engines, Inc., Madison Heights, Mich., 1959-62; exec. v.p. Midwest Machine Co. of Indiana, Inc., Marysville, Mich., 1962-70; partner Benjamen & Maurer Co., Birmingham, 1970-75, Benjamen & Co., 1975—; dir. Media Tech. Corp., Unimart Internat. Ltd., Gowani Corp. Lectr. indsl. mgmt. U. Detroit. Served to lt. USCGR, 1945-54. Certified mfg. engr. Mem. Engring. Soc. Detroit, Am. Soc. Naval Engrs., Am. Arbitration Assn., Crisis Club, Phi Sigma Epsilon, Beta Gamma Sigma, Sigma Xi. Republican. Episcopalian. Elk. Mason (Shriner). Patentee in field. Home: 3860 Northdale Bloomfield Hills MI 48013 Office: 725 S Adams Rd Birmingham MI 48011

BENJAMIN, ADAM, JR., congressman; b. Gary, Ind., Aug. 6, 1935; s. Adam and Margaret (Marjanian) B.; B.S., U.S. Mil. Acad., 1958; J.D., Valparaiso U., 1966; m. Patricia Ann Sullivan, July 31, 1966; children—Adam III, Alison Louise, Arianne. Commd. 2d lt. U.S. Army, 1958, advanced through grades to 1st lt., 1959; resigned, 1961; zoning adminstr. City of Gary, 1963-65; exec. sec. to mayor Gary, 1965-66; admitted to Ind. bar, 1966, U.S. Supreme Ct. bar; atty. firm Benjamin, Greco & Gouveia, Gary, 1966—; mem. Ind. Ho. of Reps. from Lake County, 1966-70, Ind. Senate from 4th Dist., 1970-76; mem. 95th Congress from 1st Dist. Ind. Mem. Ind. Jud. Study Commn., State Budget Com. Bd. dirs. N.W. Ind. Med. Edn. Center. Served with USMCR, 1952-54. Named Outstanding Freshman Democrat Rep., mems. Ho. of Reps., 1967, Outstanding Am. of Assyrian Descent, Assyrian Am. Fedn., 1967; Mr. Young Dem., Lake County Young Dems., 1972; recipient Good Govt. award Gary Jr. C. of C., 1967, Outstanding Young Am. award East Gary Jr. C. of C., 1970, Citizens Action award Ind. Crime Commn., 1969. Mem. Am., Ind., Lake County bar assns., Am. Judicature Soc. Home: 2106 W 3d Pl Hobart IN 46342 Office: 3637 Grant St Gary IN 46408

BENJAMIN, HARRISON RUSSELL, electromech. engr.; b. Hastings, Minn., July 7, 1934; s. Harry Murtice and Florence Elizabeth (Severson) B.; m. Patti Cox, July 16, 1960; children—David, Lisa. B.S. in Engring. with distinction, U. Minn., 1956, postgrad., 1958. Instr., U. Minn. Inst. Tech., 1957-58; electromech. engr. Gen. Mills electronics div., Mpls., 1958-61; engr. mgr. Control Data Corp., Mpls., 1961-68, dir. engring., 1969-71, gen. mgr. terminal devel. div., 1972-75, gen. mgr. small computer devel. div., 1976, gen. mgr. data systems devel., 1977—. Bd. dirs. Elbit Inc., Haifa, Israel, 1975—; mem. Com. for Effective Crime Control. Recipient Honor Student award U. Minn. Mem. Territorial Pioneers Assn. Minn., Hort. Soc. (Minn.), Nat. Rifle Assn., Model T Collectors Assn., Aircraft Owners and Pilots Assn., Tau Beta Pi. Home: 4805 Eriks Blvd Eagan MN 55122 Office: 2401 N Fairview Ave Saint Paul MN 55113

BENJAMIN, IVY, pathologist, educator; b. Rajasthan, India, Mar. 25, 1932; d. Thomas and Annamma (Cherian) Thomas; came to U.S., 1966, naturalized, 1969; M.D., Christian Med. Coll., Vellore Madras (India) U., 1956; m. Philip Benjamin, Aug. 18, 1960; children—Ivan, Evan, Bevan, Cyril. Intern, Christian Med. Coll. Hosp., 1956-57, Montreal Children's Hosp., 1962-63, 64-65, Royal Victoria Hosp., 1965-66; resident Mc Gill U., Montreal, Que., Can., 1971-72; asst. pathologist Mt. Sinai Hosp., Cleve., 1972-76; instr. in pathology St. Louis U., 1972-76, asst. prof. pathology, 1976—; co-dir. Medi-Nuclear Inst., St. Louis. St. Louis U. grantee, 1975-76. Mem. St. Louis Soc. Pathologists. Research on human breast cancer heterotransplantation into new born rats. Home: 1418 Old Farm Dr Saint Louis MO 63141 Office: 1402 S Grand Blvd Saint Louis MO 63104

BENJAMIN, JAMES WILLIAM, lawyer; b. Kansas City, Mo., Apr. 14, 1926; s. Wm. S. and Nelle (Cottingham) B.; B.S., Northwestern U., 1946; J.D., U. Mo., Kansas City, 1949; m. Norma H. Carter, Dec. 26, 1965; children—Lynn Marie, Steven. Admitted to Mo. bar, 1949; practiced in Kansas City, 1949—; partner Rogers, Field, Gentry, Benjamin & Robertson, 1950—. Lectr., U. Mo., Kansas City, pres. Law Found. Served to lt. USNR, World War II, Korea. Recipient President's award, Mo. Bar Assn., 1970. Mem. Am. Judicature Soc., Am. Bar Assn., Kansas City Bar Assn. (past pres.), Internat. Assn. Ins. Counsel, U. Mo.-Kansas City Alumni Assn. (pres. 1959-60), Phi Delta Phi. Democrat. Mem. Christian Ch. (chmn. bd.). Mason (32 deg., Shriner), K.C. Club: Sertoma of Kansas City (officer). Home: 5701 N Jackson St Kansas City MO 64119 Office: 600 E 11th St Kansas City MO 64106

BENJAMIN, JOHN HOWARD, state ofcl.; b. Tampa, Fla., Mar. 6, 1914; s. John and Helen (Sullivan) B.; B.S., Roosevelt U., 1951; m. Roberta Ann Lockhart, Dec. 3, 1938. With Ill. Dept. Labor, Chgo., 1946—, dir. claims processing, adjudication and monetary determination, 1951—; owner, realtor Benjamin Real Estate Co., Chgo., 1951—. Vice pres. D'Puc Credit Union, Chgo. Served with AUS, 1943-46. Decorated Silver Star. Mem. Am. Legion (comdr. 1972-74), Omega Psi Phi. Office: 910 S Michigan Ave Chicago IL 60605

BENJAMIN, NEAL B. H., civil engr.; b. Santa Cruz, Calif., Oct. 24, 1934; s. Charles Hugh and Mildred Emily (Neal) B.; B.S., U.S. Coast Guard Acad., 1956; B.C.E., Renssalaer Poly. Inst., 1962; M.S.C.E., Stanford U., 1967, Ph.D., 1969; m. Mary Louise Schroeder, July 6, 1963; children—Charles Edward, Julia Anne, Kathryn Mary. Served in U.S. Coast Guard, 1956-66; research asst. Stanford U., 1966-69; asst. prof. civil engring. U. Mo., Columbia, 1969-72, asso. prof., 1972-75, prof., 1975—. Registered profl. engr., Mo. Mem. ASCE, Nat., Mo. socs. profl. engrs., Am. Assn. Cost Engrs., Project Mgr. Inst., NEA, Am. Arbitration Assn. Roman Catholic. Contbr. articles in constrn.-mgmt. to profl. jours. Home: 1108 S Glenwood Columbia MO 65201 Office: 1034C Engring Bldg U Mo Columbia MO 65201

BENJAMIN, PHILIP PALAMOOTTIL, dir. med. lab.; b. Eraviperur, India, Sept. 5, 1932; s. Philip and Annamma (Chacko) C.; B.S., Madras, India, 1952; M.Sc., St. Johns, India, 1955; Ph.D., McGill, 1964; m. Ivy Thomas, Aug. 18, 1960; children—Ivan, Evan, Bevan, Cyril. Asst. prof. radiochemistry/radiology Case Western Res. U., Cleve., 1966-71; asst. prof. Ewing Coll. Allahabad U., India., 1955-60, 65-66; cons., sr. research asso. Squibb, Abbott labs. and others, 1967-73; pres., dir. Medi-Nuclear Inst., Inc., St. Louis, 1973—. Grantee Am. Cancer Soc., Squibb Inst. Med. Research. Fellow Indian Chem. Soc., Am. Inst. Chemists; mem. Soc. Nuclear Medicine, Sigma Xi. Patentee in electrolyic complexations of proteins and radio isotopes and their clin. applications. Contbr. to profl. jours. Home: 1418 Old Farm Dr Creve Coeur St Louis MO 63141 Office: 6218 Clayton Ave St Louis MO 63139

BENJAMIN, ROBERT MORRIS, clergyman; b. Chgo., Apr. 2, 1939; s. Harry Lande and Esther (Hirsch) B.; B.A., U. Cin., 1961; B.H.L., Hebrew Union Coll., 1965, M.A. in Hebrew Letters, 1969; m. Annette Shields, Sept. 3, 1961; children—Rissa Ann, Suzanne, Jeffrey Abram. Rabbi, Temple Beth El, Fargo, N.D., 1966-68, Congregation Beth El, Windsor, Ont., 1968-70, United Hebrew Congregation, 1970-73, Temple Emanuel, Davenport, Iowa, 1973—; chaplain U.S. Penitentiary, 1970-73; mem. faculty Sch. Religion N.D. State U., 1966-68; adj. prof. humanities Ind. State U.; lectr. Jewish Chataqua Soc.; mem. faculty St. Ambrose Coll., Davenport, 1974—, Augustana Coll., Rock Island, Ill., 1977—. Cons. Health Edn. Council, Fargo Pub. Schs; pres. Vigo County Assn. Mental Health. Bd. overseers Sheldon Suope Art Gallery; bd. dirs. Community Mental Health Center Scott County, Marriage and Family Counseling Service; mem. Davenport Civil Rights Commn. Mem. Ind., Chgo. bds. rabbis, Midwest Assn. Reform Rabbis, Campus Pastors Council, Jewish Chautauqua Soc. (life), Central Conf. of Am. Rabbis. Rotarian. Author: The Jewish People in America, 1972. Home: 3127 Fernwood Davenport IA 52807 Office: 12th and Mississippi Davenport IA 52803

BENKERT, ARTHUR CHURCHILL, lawyer; b. Monroe, Wis., May 20, 1911; s. Arthur Patterson and Lottie (Churchill) B.; B.A., U. Wis., 1934, LL.B., 1936; m. Delphine S. Heston, Oct. 18, 1937; children—Carolyn Bishop, Ruth Ann Benkert Bailey, Roberta L. Benkert Bernet. Admitted to Wis. bar, 1936; partner firm Benkert, Speilman & Asmus, Monroe; dir. Comml. & Savs. Bank, Monroe. City atty., Monroe, 1939-59; chmn. Zoning Bd. Appeals Monroe, 1972—. Served with U.S. Army, 1945-46. Mem. Green County (past pres.), Am., Wis. bar assns., Phi Kappa Phi. Mem. United Ch. of Christ. Clubs: Monroe Country, Madison, Kiwanis (lt. gov. 1964), Mason. Home: 1403 17th Ave Monroe WI 53566 Office: PO Box 89 Monroe WI 53566

BENNETT, CHARLES LOUGHEED, nuclear physicist; b. Duluth, Minn., Dec. 27, 1949; s. Robert Lougheed and Shirley Mae (Peterson) B.; B.A. cum laude, U. Minn., 1972; M.A., U. Rochester, 1975, Ph.D., 1977. Research asst. U. Rochester (N.Y.), 1972-76, research asso., 1976—; programming cons. Centre de Recherches Nucléaires, Strasbourg, France, 1974. Res. del. Minn. Democratic Conv., 1972. Mem. Am. Math. Assn., AAAS, Am. Phys. Soc. Club: U. Rochester Folk Dance. Contbr. articles to profl. jours. Home: 829 4th Ave SW Grand Rapids MN 55744 Office: Nuclear Structure Research Lab U Rochester Rochester NY 14623

BENNETT, DOROTHY ROSEMARY KIRK (MRS. GAIL BENNETT), bus. exec.; b. Des Moines, July 22, 1901; d. Sherman and Rose (White) Kirk; B.A., Drake U., 1923; m. Gail Bennett, June 5, 1926; children—Gail Kirk, Patricia Jane (Mrs. P. Bennett Biram). Tchr. high sch., Baxter, Iowa and La Fayette, Ill., 1923-26; dir., sec., treas. Bennett Bros., Inc. Ill., Bennett Bros., Inc. N.Y., 1963—. Mem. sr. bd. Evanston Infant Welfare, 1963-71. Mem. Kappa Kappa Gamma. Republican. Presbyn. Home: 311 Woodley Rd Winnetka IL 60093 Office: 30 E Adams St Chicago IL 60603

BENNETT, ESTHER VORENA, naturalist; b. Columbia, S.C., July 2, 1921; d. Samuel R. and Amanda (Templeton) B.; B.A., U. N.C., 1942; certificate in mus. tng. Buffalo Mus. Sci., 1949; M.S., So. Ill. U., 1953; Ph.D., Cornell U., 1961. Jr. chemist Am. Enka Rayon Corp. (N.C.), 1942-44; asst. in biology U. N.C., Greensboro, 1944-48; asst. prof., curator edn. So. Ill. U. Mus., Carbondale, 1949-63; asst. prof. agronomy; asso. editor Wheat Abstracts, U. Nebr. at Lincoln, 1964; city naturalist, dir. Chet Ager Nature Center, Lincoln, 1966-76; adminstrv. supr. athletics, outdoor edn. and recreation Lincoln Parks and Recreation Dept., 1976—. Mem. Inland Bird Banding Assn., Wilson Ornithol. Soc., Am. Ornithol. Union, Nebr. Ornithologists Union (pres. 1976-77), Cornell Lab. Ornithology, Assn. Interpretive Naturalists, Nebr. Recreation and Park Assn., So. Ill. Audubon Soc. (hon.), Sigma Xi, Phi Kappa Phi, Sigma Delta Epsilon (pres. chpt. 1968-69). Episcopalian. Clubs: Altrusa Internat. (rec. sec. Lincoln 1970-71; dir. 1973-74, 74-75), Garden, Audubon Naturalists (v.p. 1965-66, pres. 1966-67), Diggers Garden (sec.-treas. 1975-76), Key (Lincoln). Home: 1641 Devoe Dr Lincoln NE 68506 Office: Park and Recreation Dept 2740 A St Lincoln NE 68502

BENNETT, GERALD ANTHONY, bank exec.; b. Chgo., Sept. 8, 1933; s. Anthony Andrew and Victoria Marie (Matoske) Behmetiuk; B.A., Loyola U., Chgo., 1955; diploma Ill. Bankers Sch., 1971, Am. Bankers Assn. Installment Sch., 1966, Am. Bankers Assn. Comml. Lending Sch., 1976; m. Alma Rita Skeczka, Nov. 22, 1958; children—Michael and Michelle (twins). Note teller South Chgo. Bank, Chgo., 1959-62; asst. cashier Calumet Nat. Bank, Hammond, Ind., 1962-65; asst. v.p. Olympia State Bank, Chicago Heights, Ill., 1965-70; v.p. North Bank, Chgo., 1970-73; v.p. Steel City Nat. Bank, Chgo., 1973—; faculty mem. Am. Inst. Banking, 1965—. Bd. dirs. Sch. Dist. #151, South Holland, Ill., 1968-71, sec., 1970-71. Served with U.S. Army, 1956-58. Named man of year South Chicago Kiwanis Club, 1976. Mem. Am., Ill. bankers assns. Address: 3030 E 92d St Chicago IL 60617

BENNETT, HUGH MERTON, business exec.; b. Arlington, S.D., June 19, 1913; s. Michael Aaron and Lillian Mae (Thomas) B.; student S.D. State Coll., 1928-29; m. Muriel June Dill, Sept. 3, 1940; children—Becky (Mrs. Loren Gene Converse), Bonnie (Mrs. James Jay Hvistendahl), Robert Leon. Owner Hugh M. Bennett Livestock Co., Arlington, S.D., 1938—; buyer John Morrell & Co., Sioux Falls, 1941—; dir. Citizens State Bank, Arlington. Mem. Arlington Pub. Sch. Bd., 1952-75, pres., 1954-74. Named Outstanding bd. mem. S.D. Sch. Bds., 1964. Methodist. Mason, Kiwanian. Home and Office: Box 334 Arlington SD 57212

BENNETT, IVAN FRANK, educator, psychiatrist; b. Hartford, Conn., Sept. 6, 1919; s. Frank and Iva (Bacon) B.; B.S., Trinity Coll., 1941; M.D., Thomas Jefferson U., 1944; m. Audrey Poley, Sept. 23, 1944; children—Ivan Stanley, Judith Anne. Intern, Jefferson Hosp., Phila., 1944-45, resident, 1945-46; asst. physician State Hosp., Harrisburg, 1948-50, asst. chief acute intensive treatment service, chief physiol. treatment sect. VA Hosp., Coatesville, Pa., 1950-56; chief psychiat. research, psychiatry and neurology service, dept. medicine and surgery VA, Washington, 1956-58; clin. investigator Lilly Lab. for Clin. Research, Eli Lilly & Co., Indpls., 1958-63, sr. physician, 1963-76, clin. investigator, 1976—; instr. psychiatry U. Pa. Sch. Medicine, 1954-56; clin. asst. prof. psychiatry Georgetown U. Sch. Medicine, 1956-58; asst. prof. psychiatry Ind. U. Sch. Medicine, 1958-62, asso. prof., 1962-72, prof., 1972—. Mem. pharmacology and therapeutic study sect., div. research grants NIH, 1956-58, mem. behavioral scis. study sect., 1956-58; mem. profl. adv. com. Ind. Mental Health Assn., 1958—; asso. staff physician dept. neuropsychiatry Marion County Gen. Hosp., Indpls., 1958—; dir. Lilly psychiat. clinic Marion County Gen. Hosp., Indpls., 1959—; mem. sci.-med. adv. bd. Manfred Sakel Inst., 1960-70; mem. adv. com. on alcoholism Ind. Dept. Mental Health, 1961-69, med. research com., 1962-68, mem. adv. com. div. drug abuse, 1971-74; bd. dirs. Marion County Assn. Mental Health, 1967-73, profl. adv. com., 1967—, exec. com., 1969-73; cons. drug abuse Gen. Bd. Christian Social Concerns of Meth. Ch., 1967—; mem. standing com. to study mental health laws of Ind., 1968-70; mem. Gov.'s Com. Study Mental Health Laws, 1970—; mem. adv. com. drug edn. Ind. State Health Commr., 1968-74; cons. Indpls. Family Service Assn., 1966—, personnel com., 1969—; mem. project com. drug abuse programs Ind. Dept. Pub. Instrn., 1970-71; mem. sci. adv. com. Nat. Coordinating Council Drug Edn., 1972-76; mem. controlled substances adv. com. State of Ind., 1973—; cons. dept. psychiatry Mayo Clinic, Rochester, Minn., 1976—. Bd. dirs., mem. exec. com. Community Addiction Services Agy., Indpls., 1971—; bd. dirs. U.P. Met. Center, 1974-76. Served with AUS, 1946-48. Diplomate Am. Bd. Neurology and Psychiatry. Fellow A.C.P., Am. Psychiat. Assn., Am. Coll. Neuropsychopharmacology (charter); mem. AMA, Ind., Marion County med. socs., Soc. Biol. Psychiatry, Eastern Psychiat. Research Assn., Ind. Psychiat. Soc. (pres. 1970-71), Sigma Xi. Contbr. articles to profl. jours. Home: 8452 Green Braes N Dr Indianapolis IN 46234 Office: 307 E McCarty St Indianapolis IN 46206

BENNETT, JAMES PAUL, radiologist; b. Chgo., Oct. 27, 1896; s. Svante and Hulda Eselia (Johnson) B.; B.S., U. Chgo., 1918, M.S. (Chemistry fellow), 1922; grad. evening sch. Moody Bible Inst., 1923; M.D., Rush Med. Coll., 1927. Intern, Swedish Covenant Hosp., also Cook County Hosp., Chgo., 1927-30; resident in specialties including pathology, internal medicine, radiology Cook County Hosp., Chgo., 1930-34, asso. roentgenologist, 1934-44, mem. teaching staff in X-ray, 1938-44, cons. in diagnostic X-ray, 1962—; radiologist Bethany Brethren Hosp., Chgo., 1941—, Meth. Hosp., Gary, Ind., 1944-62. Bd. dirs. Evang. Child and Family Welfare Agency, Pacific Garden

Mission, Door of Hope Rescue Mission. Recipient Outstanding Service award Cook County Hosp., 1967; diplomate Am. Bd. Radiology. Mem. Christian Med. Soc., AMA, Ill. State, Chgo. med. socs., Ill. Radiological Soc., Am. Coll. Radiology, Am. Roentgen Ray Soc., Radiol. Soc. N.Am., Pan Am. Med. Soc., Phi Beta Kappa, Sigma Xi. Contbr. articles in field to profl. jours. Home: 5130 N Albany Ave Chicago IL 60625 Office: 3821 W Washington St Chicago IL 60624

BENNETT, JEROME PATRICK, thermometer co. exec.; b. Crooksville, Ohio, Apr. 15, 1934; s. Frederick Anthony and Eululia Dorthey (Sherer) B.; B.S., Xavier U., 1957; m. Verna Eileen Wappner, June 25, 1960; children—Kathleen, Patrick, Michael, Daniel Joseph. Vice pres. sales Ohio Thermometer Co., Springfield, Ohio, 1970—, also dir.; pres., dir. Continental Travel Service, Springfield, 1970—; officer, dir. Cedar Ltd. Inc., 1973—; dir. Crooksville Bank, 1968—. Served with AUS, 1957-60. Mem. Springfield C. of C., Xavier U. Alumni Assn. (dir. 1959-61). Club: Springfield Advertising (dir. 1965-67). K.C. Home: 2716 Rebecca Dr Springfield OH 45503 Office: 33 Walnut St Springfield OH 45599

BENNETT, JOYCE MIGNON, counselor; b. Atlanta, Dec. 9, 1948; d. William Walter and Dorothy Mae (Sabb) B.; B.S., Spelman Coll., 1971; M.A., Atlanta U., 1973. Counselor, Wilberforce (Ohio) U., 1973—, coordinator counseling and testing, 1977—, fgn. student adviser, 1973-77, instr., 1973-77. Mem. Am. Personnel and Guidance Assn., Nat. Assn. Fgn. Student Affairs, Ohio Coll. Health Assn., Assn. Non-White Concerns, Am. Coll. Personnel Assn. Baptist. Address: PO Box 204 Wilberforce OH 45384

BENNETT, LAWRENCE A., psychologist, criminal justice research dir.; b. Selma, Calif., Jan. 4, 1923; s. Walter Allen and Eva Elenor (Hall) B.; A.B. in Psychology, Fresno State Coll., 1948; M.A. in Psychology, Claremont Grad. Sch. (Calif.), 1954, Ph.D. in Psychology, 1968; m. Beth J. Thompson, Aug. 14, 1948; children—Yvonne I., Glenn L. Psychologist, Fresno County (Calif.) Child Guidance Center, 1948; parole officer Calif. Dept. Corrections, Los Angeles, Glendale, 1952, psychologist Calif. Instn. Men, Chino, 1953, vocat. counselor, 1954, dept. supr. clin. psychology, Sacramento, 1960-67, chief of research, 1967-76; psychologist Deuel Vocat. Inst., Tracy, Calif., 1955-56; psychol. supr. Calif. Med. Facility, Vacaville, 1956-60; dir., asso. prof. Center for Study Crime Delinquency Corrections So. Ill. U., Carbondale, 1976—; pvt. practice clin. psychology, Davis/Sacramento, 1958-76; instr., U. Calif., Berkeley, Davis, Chapman, Sacramento State U., U. So. Calif., So. Campus; dir. Am. Justice Inst., Sacramento; dir. Calif. Crime Technol. Research Found.; mem. Yolo County (Calif.) Mental Health Advisory Bd., 1971-75, chmn., 1972; mem. Calif. Interdept. Research Coordinating Com., chmn., 1970. Served with U.S. Army, 1942-45, as psychologist, 1950-51. Contbr. articles to correctional jours. Home: 629 Surrey Ln Carbondale IL 62901

BENNETT, LERONE, JR., author, editor; b. Clarksdale, Miss., Oct. 17, 1928; s. Lerone and Alma (Reed) B.; B.A., Morehouse Coll., Atlanta, 1949, Litt.D., 1966; m. Gloria Sylvester, July 21, 1956; children—Alma Joy, Constance, Courtney, Lerone III. Reporter, Atlanta (Ga.) Daily World, 1949-52, city editor, 1953; asso. editor Jet Mag., Chgo; asso. editor Ebony mag., Chgo., 1954-62, sr. editor, 1962—. Bd. dirs. Morehouse Coll., Nat. Black United Fund. Recipient Patron Saints award Soc. Midland Authors, 1962. Author: Before the Mayflower: A History of the Negro in America, 1619-1964, 1962; The Black Mood, 1964; What Manner of Man: A Biography of Martin Luther King, Jr., 1964; Confrontation: Black and White, 1965; Pioneers in Protest, 1968, The Challenge of Blackness, 1972; The Shaping of Black America, 1975. Contbr. to publs. Home: 1308 E 89th St Chicago IL 60619 Office: Ebony Mag 820 S Michigan Ave Chicago IL 60616

BENNETT, MATTHEW COLE, surgeon; b. Basrah, Arabia, July 9, 1912; s. Arthur King and Christine (Iverson) B.; came to U.S., 1917; A.B., No. Mich. Coll., 1933; M.D., U. Mich., 1937; m. Claire McNaughton, Aug. 8, 1941; children—Christine, Matthew, Stuart, George. Intern, Pa. Gen. Hosp., Phila., 1937-40; resident surgery Detroit Receiving Hosp., also instr. surgery Wayne U., 1940-43; pvt. practice surgery, Marquette, Mich., 1945—; staff St. Luke's, St. Mary's hosps., Marquette, Francis Bell Meml. Hosp., Ishpeming; cons. surgery K.I. Sawyer Air Force Base. Dir. Union Nat. Bank, Marquette, Mich. Trustee No. Mich. U. Devel. Fund. Served with AUS, 1942-45. Diplomate Am. Bd. Surgery. Fellow A.C.S.; mem. AMA, Mich. Marquette-Alger County med. socs., Mich. Indsl. Med. Assn.. Nat. Rehab. Assn. Presbyn. Rotarian. Home: 11 Marquette Dr Marquette MI 49855 Office: Marquette Medical Center Marquette MI 49855

BENNETT, MILTON CHESTER, heavy machinery mfg. co. exec.; b. Brighton, Colo., Apr. 25, 1926; s. Leslie James and Ruth (Sayre) B.; B.S. in Mech. Engring., U. Wis., 1957, B.S. in Agr., 1957; m. Bernadette Agatha Dresen, Oct. 10, 1970; children—Diane, Michele. With J.I. Case Co., Racine, Wis., 1957-61, 62—, project engr., 1962-66, dept. engr. small tractor design Clausen Plant, 1966-68, dept. engr. hydraulic design Rock Island (Ill.) Plant, 1968—; with Modine Mfg. Co., Racine, 1961-62. Served with AUS, 1945-46, USNR, 1950-54; Korea. Decorated Air Medal. Mem. Soc. Automotive Engrs., Am. Soc. Agrl. Engrs., Aircraft Owners and Pilots Assn., Nat. Pilots Assn., Fluid Power Soc. Patentee in field. Home: 1611 27th St Moline IL 61265 Office: 625 3d Ave Rock Island IL 61201

BENNETT, OLGA, lawyer; b. Viroqua, Wis., May 5, 1908; d. John Henry and Olga (Omundson) Bennett; B.A., U. Wis., 1928, LL.B., 1935. Asst. cashier Farmers Bank, Viroqua, 1929-32; admitted to Wis. bar, 1935; practiced in Viroqua, 1941-70; law clk. to justice Wis. Supreme Ct., Madison, 1936-41; partner firm Bennett & Bennett, 1941-56; individual practice, 1956-70; city atty. City of Viroqua, 1946-48; county judge Vernon County, Viroqua, 1970-76; individual practice law, Viroqua, 1976—; mem. Lower West Central Criminal Justice Planning Council, 1972—, Vernon County Hwy. Safety Commn. Mem. Am., Vernon County bar assns., State Bar Wis., Am. Judicature Soc., Nat. Coll. State Judiciary, Vernon County Hist. Soc., Benchers, Kappa Beta Pi. Republican. Lutheran. Home: 322 N Dunlap Ave Viroqua WI 54665 Office: 210 N Main St Viroqua WI 54665

BENNETT, PAUL ALLEN, life ins. exec.; b. Brookline, Mass., Apr. 10, 1928; s. Carlton Elwood and Martha Alice (Briggs) B.; A.A., Boston U., 1951, B.S., 1953; M.A., Ball State U., 1977; m. Claire Elaine Richardson, Aug. 31, 1950; children—Pamela A., Sandra A., Debora A., Robert R. With Paul Revere Life Ins. Co., Worcester, Mass., 1953-58; with Jefferson Nat. Life Ins. Co., Indpls., 1958—, successively v.p. planning and pub. relations, v.p. personnel and pub. relations, v.p. pub. relations and sales promotion; nat. profl. adviser Pub. Relations Student Soc. Am. Served with U.S. Army, 1945-48. Mem. Pub. Relations Soc. Am., Indpls. Pub. Relations Soc., Life Advertisers Assn., Boston U. Alumni Council, Indpls. C. of C., Sigma Delta Chi. Republican. Unitarian. Clubs: Indpls. Athletic, East Chop Beach, East Chop Tennis, Indpls. Sailing, Masons, Shriners. Home: 5044 Laurel Hall Dr Indianapolis IN 46226 Office: One Virginia Ave Indianapolis IN 46204

BENNETT, RICHARD CHARLES, quality control exec.; b. Oshkosh, Wis., July 27, 1944; s. Ralph Eugene and Dorothy Mae (Manuel) B.; B.S., Wis. State U., 1968; M.S., U. Wis., 1975; m. Janice Beth Folk Firkus, Aug. 5, 1972; children—Jason Michael Firkus, Kristopher Brett. Grad. student asst. U. Wis., Oshkosh, 1973-74; live culture specialist and mgr. Mogul edn. div. Mogul Corp., Stillwater, Minn., 1975-76; quality control mgr. Stauffer and Sons, Inc., Blue Mounds, Wis., 1976—. Served to 1st lt. AUS, 1968-71. Mem. Am. Soc. Microbiology, Alpha Kappa Lambda. Home: 303 Durtschi Dr Mount Horeb WI 53572 Office: PO Box 68 Blue Mounds WI 53517

BENNETT, RICHARD LIVINGSTON, obstetrician, gynecologist, sex educator and therapist; b. Akron, Ohio, July 23, 1937; s. Howard Livingston and Annabell Lee (Sweeney) B.; A.B., Oberlin Coll., 1960; M.D., Jefferson Med. Coll., Phila., 1964; Ph.D., Inst. for Advanced Study of Human Sexuality, San Francisco, 1976; children—Richard, Robert, Ann Marie. Intern, Akron City Hosp., 1964-65, resident in obstetrics and gynecology, 1965-69; med. dir. Planned Parenthood of Summit County, 1969-76; practice medicine specializing in obstetrics and gynecology, Akron, 1969—; founder, pres., exec. dir. Akron Forum, Inc., for Study of Human Sexuality, 1972—; chairperson bd. dirs. faculty Inst. for Advanced Study of Human Sexuality, 1976—; med. dir. Akron Women's Clinic, 1976—; sr. staff Akron City Hosp.; courtesy staff Akron Gen. Med. Center, Children's Hosp. Akron; med. adv. bd. Childbirth Edn. Assn. Akron. Served with USNR, 1955-63. Diplomate Am. Bd. Obstetrics and Gynecology, Nat. Bd. Med. Examiners. Fellow Am. Coll. Obstetricians and Gynecologists, Am. Fertility Soc.; mem. Akron Obstet. and Gynecol. Soc. (v.p. 1977-78), Am. Assn. Planned Parenthood Physicians, Am. Assn. Sex Edn., Counselors and Therapists (regional bd.), AMA, Ohio Med. Assn., Sex Info. Council U.S., Soc. Sci. Study Sex, Summit County Med. Soc. Club: Cascade. Office: Suite 512 III Cascade Plaza Akron OH 44308

BENNETT, ROBERT LATHROP, mgmt. cons.; b. Manhattan, Kans., May 16, 1931; s. Richard Ross and Lillian (Lathrop) B.; B.S. in Mech. Engring., Kans. State U., 1962; m. Marian Parsons Walters, Dec. 25, 1975; children—Rebecca, R. Bradford, Deborah J., Bruce R. With plant engring. and mfg. dept. CPC Internat., North Kansas City, Mo., 1962-65; project engr. indsl. sales and corp. devel. Gen. Foods Corp., Kankakee, Ill. and White Plains, N.Y., 1965-74; with engring. and archtl. sales dept. Globe Engring. subs. Esmark, Chgo., 1974-75; pres. R.L. Bennett & Assos., Inc., mgmt. cons., Batavia, Ill., 1975—; guest lectr. Cornell Food Packaging. Mem. ASME, Inst. Food Technologists, Master Brewers Assn. Am., Bus. and Profl. Advt. Assn., Sigma Chi. Republican. Inventor in field. Home: 421 N Batavia Ave Batavia IL 60510 Office: PO Box 456 Batavia IL 60510

BENNETT, ROBERT THOMAS, lawyer, accountant; b. Columbus, Ohio, Feb. 8, 1939; s. Frank Edmund and Mary Catherine (Weiland) B.; B.S., Ohio State U., 1960; J.D., Cleve. Marshall Law Sch., 1967; m. Ruth Ann Dooley, May 30, 1959; children—Robert Thomas, Rose Marie. Admitted to Ohio bar, 1967; C.P.A., Ernst and Ernst, Cleve., 1960-63; with tax assessing dept. Cuyahoga County (Ohio) Auditor's Office, Cleve., 1963-70; mem. firm Bartunek, Bennett, Garofoli and Hill, Cleve., 1970—; mem. bd. Cuyahoga County Port Authority. Exec. vice chmn. Cuyahoga County Rep. orgn. Republican. Roman Catholic. Clubs: Cleve. Athletic, Citizens League, Edgewater Yacht, Fairview Park Rep., City Club Cleve. Contbr. article to profl. publs. Home: 4800 Mastick Rd Fairview Park OH 44126 Office: 1512 Euclid Ave Cleveland OH 44115

BENNETT, RUSSELL CHARLES, architect; b. Shirland, Ill., Apr. 3, 1927; s. Charles Frederick and Anna Sophia Margareta (Dahlgren) B.; B.S., U. Ill., 1952; m. Paula Mathilda Soetens, Sept. 12, 1959; children—Susan Maria, Jeffrey Russell. Structural designer Swift & Co., Chgo., 1952-55; architect Bradley & Bradley, Architects, Rockford, Ill., 1955-57; architect Gilbert A. Johnson, Rockford, 1957-64; asso. Gilbert A. Johnson, Kile, Seehausen & Assos., Rockford, 1964-72; architect Seigfreid, Johnson, Edwards, Rockford, 1973—. Scoutmaster local troop Sinnissippi council Boy Scouts Am., 1963—. Sec. Bd. Edn. Shirland Sch. Dist. 134, 1963-66; town clk., Shirland, 1969-77, supr., 1977—. Served with AUS, 1946-48. Recipient Silver Beaver award Boy Scouts, 1974, Arrowhead Dist. award, 1973; Shirland Area Community Service award Rotary, 1974. Mem. AIA, ASCE, U. Ill. Alumni Assn., Gargoyle, Sigma Tau. Home: 7093 Forest Preserve Rd Rockton IL 61072

BENNETT, W(ALTER) BURR, JR., structural engr.; b. Honesdale, Pa., Oct. 11, 1920; s. Walter Burr and Wilhelmina (Schoell) B.; student U. Buffalo, 1946-47; B.C.E. magna cum laude, Syracuse U., 1950; m. Marie P. Hollfelder, June 2, 1949; children—Gregory Burr, Susan Elizabeth. Dep. supt. hwys. Niagara County (N.Y.) Dept. of Hwys., 1950-54; plant engr. Frontier Dolomite Concrete Products, Lockport, N.Y., 1954-56; mgr. structural bur. Portland Cement Assn., Chgo., 1956-67, dir. engring. services dept., 1967-68; exec. v.p. Prestressed Concrete Inst., Chgo., 1968—. Mem. exec. com., v.p. U.S. br. Fedn. Internat Precontraint. Served with USAAF, 1941-45. Decorated D.F.C., Air medal. Fellow Am. Concrete Inst.; mem. ASCE, Prestressed Concrete Inst. (bd, dirs. 1966-67), Internat. Assn. Bridge and Structural Engrs., Tau Beta Pi, Sigma Pi Sigma. Home: 260 E Chestnut St Chicago IL 60611 Office: Prestressed Concrete Inst 20 W Wacker Dr Chicago IL 60606

BENNINGTON, DONALD LEE, guidance counselor; b. Akron, Ohio, Jan. 21, 1936; s. John Olden and Helen Amanda (Herrin) B.; B.A. in Edn., Ariz. State U., 1969; M.A., John Carroll U., 1976; children by previous marriage—Jeanne, Jesse, Jacques, Jonathan, John; m. 2d Judith Lynn Mahnke, Apr. 14, 1973. Clerk, U.S. Postal Service, Akron, Ohio, 1957; accounting clerk Statewide Contractors, Inc., Glendale, Ariz., 1960-64; cost accountant Meyer & Lundahl Mfg. Co., Phoenix, 1964-68; purchasing agent Standard Oil Co. (Ohio), Cleve., 1970—. Served with USN, 1953-57. Mem. Am. Personnel and Guidance Assn., Am. Coll. Personnel Assn., Nat. Vocational Guidance Assn., Purchasing Mgmt. Assn., Gamma Theta Upsilon. Home: 6376 Lear Nagle Rd North Ridgeville OH 44039

BENNIS, WARREN, author, cons.; b. N.Y.C., Mar. 8, 1925; s. Philip and Rachel (Landau) B.; A.B., Antioch Coll., 1951; hon. certificate econs., U. London (Eng.), 1952; Ph.D., Mass. Inst. Tech., 1955; LL.D., Xavier U., 1972; L.H.D., Hebrew Union Coll., Cin., 1974; m. Clurie Williams, Mar. 30, 1962; children—Katharine, John Leslie, Will Martin. Asst. prof. psychology Mass. Inst. Tech., 1953-56, prof., 1959-67, asst. prof. psychology and bus. Boston U., 1956-59; provost State U. N.Y. at Buffalo, 1967-68, v.p. for acad. devel., 1968-71; pres. U. Cin., 1971-77; vis. lectr. Harvard, 1958-59; vis. prof. U. Lausanne (Switzerland), 1961-62; cons. in field, 1955—. Mem. White House Task Force on Sci. Policy, 1969; adv. bd. Fed. Jud. Center, Fed. Exec. Center; mem. vis. com. in humanities Mass. Inst. Tech.; mem. Dept. Transp. Task Force to study FAA; chmn. Nat. Advisory Commn. Higher Edn. for Police Officers, 1976. Served to capt. AUS, World War II. Decorated Bronze Star, Purple Heart. Mem. Am. Mgmt. Assn (dir.), AAAS, Am. Psychol. Assn., Am. Sociol. Assn., U.S. C. of C. (adv. group scholars) Author: Planning of Change, 1961, 3d edit., 1976; Interpersonal Dynamics, 1963, 3d edit., 1973; The Temporary Society, 1968; Organizational Development: Its Nature, Origins, and Prospects, 1969; Management of Change and Conflict, 1972; The Leaning Ivory Tower, 1973; Beyond Bureaucracy, 1974; The Unconscious Conspiracy: Why Leaders Can't Lead, 1976. Address: U Cin Cincinnati OH 45221

BENNISON, CHARLES ELLSWORTH, bishop; b. Janesville, Wis., July 23, 1917; s. Floyd William and Cleo Leona (Wilson) B.; student Lawrence Coll., 1935-38; B.A., U. Minn., 1939; B.D., Seabury-Western Theol. Sem., 1942, D.D., 1960; m. Marjorie Elizabeth Haglun, June 16, 1942; children—Charles Ellsworth, Mary, John. Ordained priest Episcopal Ch., 1942; rector, Hastings, Minn., 1942-45, Joliet, Ill., 1945-52, St. Luke's Ch., Kalamazoo, 1952-60; bishop Diocese Western Mich., Kalamazoo, 1960—. Trustee Seabury-Western Theol. Sem. Mem. SAR, Beta Theta Pi. Clubs: Torch, Rotary, Park. Address: 3305 Lake Hill Dr Kalamazoo MI 49008 also 2600 Vincent Ave Kalamazoo MI 49008

BENNYHOFF, GARY CURTIS, pub. relations co. exec.; b. La Crosse, Wis., Dec. 4, 1931; s. Curtis Glenn and Dolores Adele (Moeglein) B.; B.A., U. Minn., 1957; m. Rose Mary Minchow, July 1, 1955; children—Eric G., Polly D. News editor KSUM radio sta., Fairmont, Minn., 1957, KSTP radio and TV sta., St. Paul, 1957-58, WCCO radio sta., Mpls., 1959-65; pub. info. dir. State of Minn., St. Paul, 1965-69; pub. relations mgr. Carlson Cos., Mpls., 1969-72; account exec. N.W. Ayer & Son Inc., Fargo, N.D., after 1972; columnist Jim Peterson's Outdoor News, Golden Valley, Minn., 1968—; lectr. N.D. State U., Fargo, 1975. Served with USAF, 1951-52. Mem. Pub. Relations Soc. Am., Minn. Press Club (charter mem., dir. 1971-72), Outdoor Writers Assn. Am., Assn. Gt. Lakes Outdoor Writers, Fargo-Moorhead Advt. Club (dir. 1972-75), Sigma Delta Chi. Home: 3276 N Knoll Blvd Wauwatosa WI 53222 Office: 2266 N Prospect Ave Milwaukee WI 53202

BENOIT, ROBERT EUGENE, glass and ceramic engr.; b. Detroit, Feb. 14, 1939; s. Alexis Eugene and Gladys Estelle (Snyder) B.; A.S. cum laude, Henry Ford Coll., 1974; m. Nancy Ann Kopp, Aug. 2, 1958; children—Robert, David. Research engr. Glass Tech. Center Ford Motor Co., Lincoln Park, Mich., 1967—, electron microscopist Sci. Labs., Dearborn, Mich., 1960-67, glass and ceramic engr. Glass div., Lincoln Park, 1967—. Mem. Electron Microscopy Soc. Am., Am. Ceramic Soc. (Ann. Micrographic Exhbn. 1st and 2d pl. awards 1971). Home: 29661 Buckingham St Livonia MI 48154 Office: Glass Tech Center 25500 W Outer Dr Lincoln Park MI 48146

BENSON, CLIFFORD DEMPSTER, surgeon; b. Iola, Wis., Oct. 23, 1902; s. Edwin Bernhardt and Emma Caroline (Olson) B.; B.S., U. Wis., 1926; M.D., Northwestern U., 1928; m. Mary Louise Cappleman, Jan. 24, 1931 (dec. 1975); 1 dau., Mary Katharine Benson Collins. Intern, Harper Hosp., Detroit, 1928-29, resident in gen. surgery, 1929-33; resident in thoracic surgery Herman Kiefer Hosp., Detroit, 1933-34; practice medicine specializing in surgery, Detroit, 1934-74, Grosse Pointe Farms, Mich., 1974—; mem. staff Children's Hosp. of Mich., Detroit, surgeon-in-chief, 1958-68; mem. cons. staff St. John's Hosp., Detroit, Bon Secours Hosp., Grosse Pointe, Detroit Gen. Hosp., Harper Hosp.; prof. clin. surgery Wayne State U.; Forschall lectr. U. Dublin, 1969. Served to comdr. M.C., USN, 1942-46. Recipient Gold medal Brit. Assn. Pediatric Surgery, 1969; diplomate Am. Bd. Surgery, Am. Bd. Thoracic Surgery. Fellow Am. Surg. Assn., A.C.S.; mem. Am. Assn. Thoracic Surgeons, Western, Central, Pan Pacific surg. assns., Am. Pediatric Surg. Assn., Soc. Internat. Surgery, Soc. Surgery Alimentary Tract, Am. Acad. Pediatrics, Detroit Acad. Surgery (pres. 1961), Detroit Acad. Medicine (pres. 1961). Republican. Presbyterian. Club: Country of Detroit. Editor: (with Mustard, Ravitch, Snyder and Welch) Pediatric Surgery, 2d edit., 1969. Contbr. articles to surg. jours. Home: 17609 Maumee Rd Grosse Point MI 48230

BENSON, DALE STANLEY, physician; b. Peoria, Ill., June 26, 1941; s. John Charles and Mary Charlotte (Welles) B.; B.A., Greenville Coll., 1963; M.D., Ind. U., 1967; m. Barbara Ruth Wilson, June 22, 1963; children—Christina Noel, Charles Thomas, David Paul. Intern, Meth. Hosp., Indpls., 1967-68, resident, 1968-69; med. dir. Neighborhood Health Centers, Meth. Hosp., Indpls., 1969—; faculty Meth. Hosp. Dept. Grad. Med. Edn., 1969—; asst. prof. dept. family practice Ind. U. Sch. Medicine. Bd. dirs. Met. Health Council, 1969-74, S.E. Health Center, Inc., 1969—, Central Ave. Community Health Council, 1970-73, Woodstock Children's Home, 1970-72. Recipient Distinguished Service awards Indpls. Jr. C. of C., 1973, Coll. Chaplains, Am. Protestant Hosp. Assn., 1973; Pres.'s Phys. Fitness award, 1973; Physician's Recognition award AMA. Diplomate Am. Bd. Family Practice. Mem. Am. Acad. Family Physicians, Free Meth. Med. Fellowship. Author: Nightcall, 1969; Problem Oriented Practice, 1976; Policies and Procedures for a Drug Abuse Treatment Center, 1977. Home: 3817 Dona Court Carmel IN 46032 Office: 1205 N Central Ave Indianapolis IN 46203

BENSON, DENNIS KEITH, social scientist; b. Dayton, Ohio, Dec. 20, 1946; s. Charles Prue and Virginia Elizabeth (Zindorf) B.; B.A., Miami U., 1969; M.A. (fellow), Ohio State U., 1972, Ph.D. (fellow), 1976; m. Rose Anne Fredericks, Aug. 30, 1969; 1 son, Kristopher Elliott. Simulation dir. behavioral scis. lab., Ohio State U., Columbus, 1969-73, survey research dir., 1972-73, dep. dir., 1971-73, project dir. Coll. Social Work, 1977; asso. dir. Benchmark program Acad. for Contemporary Problems, Columbus, 1973-74, dir., 1974-75; v.p., treas. C. C. DeJon, Ltd., Columbus, 1976—; project dir. Capital U., Columbus, 1977-78; cons. in field. Bd. trustees, corr. sec. N.W. Civic Assn., 1972-73; state issues coordinator Ohio Carter Campaign Staff, 1976; mem., chmn. com. Central Ohio Bicentennial Commn., 1975-76. Mem. Am. Assn. for Pub. Opinion Research, Am. Soc. for Pub. Adminstrn., World Future Soc., Ohio, U.S. Capital hist. socs., U.S. Olympic Soc., Victorian Village Soc., Nat. Space Inst. Democrat. Mem. Am. Bapt. Ch. Author: A Guide to Survey Research Terms, 1975. Contbg. author: Simulation and Games, 1972. Home and Office: 94 W Hubbard Ave Columbus OH 43215

BENSON, DOROTHY ANN DURICK (MRS. ROBERT BRONAUGH BENSON), psychologist, business exec.; b. Grand Forks, N.D.; d. William James and Grace (Johnson) Durick; B.S. with distinction, U. N.Mex., 1950; M.A. in Psychology, U. Minn., 1952; m. Robert Bronaugh Benson, May 8, 1954. Research asst. psychology dept., U. Minn., 1950-52; instr., counselor Student Counseling Service, Kans. State Coll., 1952-54; psychometrist, counselor Stephens Coll., 1957-58; exec. asst. Benson Bldg. Materials, Inc. and Benson Lumber & Supply Co., Columbia, Mo., 1958-61; partner of Koti Krafts from Finland. Active mem. League of Women Voters, Columbia, 1955—, bd. dirs., 1955-61, pres., 1958-59; mem. exec. bd. U. Mo. YWCA, 1962-64. Mem. Phi Kappa Phi, Psi Chi, Phi Sigma. Home: PO Box 3 Columbia MO 65201 Office: Benson Bldg Materials Inc 710 Business Loop 70 W PO Box 3 Columbia MO 65201

BENSON, EARL LEWIS, govt. ofcl.; b. Trenton, N.J., May 2, 1946; s. Arthur Earl and Isabelle (Carlson) B.; B.A., Trenton State Coll., 1970, M.A., 1972. Equal opportunity specialist in employment U.S. Equal Employment Opportunity Commn., Newark, 1971-74, Miami, Fla., 1974-75, Detroit, 1976—. Served with USNR, 1964-66. Mem. Assn. Am. Geographers, Nat., N.J. councils geog. edn. Home: 17250 Wildwood Ave Roseville MI 48066 Office: 231 W Lafayette St Room 461 Detroit MI 48226

BENSON, FRANKLIN DONOHUE, civil engr.; b. Grand Rapids, Mich., Nov. 15, 1940; s. Mons Herman and Ethel Louise (Donohue) B.; B.C.E., U. Idaho, 1963; m. Lois Fern McComber, Dec. 19, 1964; children—Laura Joanne, Mons Franklin. With FAA, 1967—, civil engr., Seattle, 1968-76, asst. airports dist. office mgr., Mpls., 1976—. Served to capt. USAF, 1963-67. Registered profl. engr., Idaho, Wash. Mem. ASCE (Outstanding Civil Engr. Student, Columbia sect. 1963), League Am. Wheelmen. Episcopalian. Clubs: Elks, Pilots. Home: 14318 Golf View Dr Eden Prairie MN 55343 Office: 6301 34th Ave S Minneapolis MN 55450

BENSON, JAMES DEWAYNE, coll. dean; b. Fairbury, Nebr., June 23, 1925; s. Earl William and Cleone Matilda (Wycoff) B.; B.S.C., Creighton U., 1949; M.A., U. Iowa, 1952, Ph.D., 1958; m. Maran Schueller, May 23, 1948; children—David, Barbara, Mary, Stephen. Instr. Gen. Motors Inst., Flint, Mich., 1950-52; asst. prof. mktg. Iowa State Coll., 1952-54, 55-57; asso. prof. So. Ill. U., Carbondale, 1957-62; asso. prof., dir. grad. studies in bus. U. Iowa, 1962-70; dean Coll. Bus. Adminstrn. No. Ariz. U., 1970-73; corp. dir. mktg. Motorola Inc., Chgo., 1973-75; dean Coll. Bus. No. Ill. U., 1975—; dir. BeeLine Transp. Co., Omaha, Motorola Teleprograms, Chgo. Served to 2d lt. USAAF, 1943-45. Nat. Assn. Purchasing Agts. faculty fellow, 1962; Ariz. Acad. fellow, 1971-76. Mem. Am., Quad-Cities (v.p. 1964-66) mktg. assns., Midwest Econs. Assn., Midwest Bus. Adminstrn. Assn., Am. Assembly Collegiate Schs. Bus., Midwestern Assn. Deans Colls. Bus. Republican. Roman Catholic. Clubs: Kiwanis, Kishwaukee Country, Elks. Author: Merchandising and Salesmanship for New and Used Cars, 1952. Home: 2 Golf View St DeKalb IL 60115 Office: 225 Wirtz Hall No Ill U DeKalb IL 60115

BENSON, JOSEPH, librarian; b. Chgo., Oct. 9, 1919; s. Charles Edward and Fae (Pritchett) B.; student Wright Jr. Coll., 1947-48; M.A., U. Chgo., 1955; m. Martha J. Kloo, May 24, 1968. Asst. librarian Nat. Soc. Crippled Children and Adults, Chgo., 1951, Wright Jr. Coll., 1951-56; librarian Municipal Reference Library, Chgo., 1956-67, Joint Reference Library of Pub. Adminstrn. Service, Chgo., 1967-74, Chgo. Transit Authority, 1974—; mem. Commn. on Chgo. Archtl. Landmarks, 1957—; mem. Nat. Adv. Council on Project Urbandoc, Ill. State Library Adv. Council on Library Devel.; v.p. bd. dirs. Ill. Regional Library Council, 1971-76; mem. Ill. steering com. Illinet Ohio Coll. Library Center. Mem. Am. Soc. Pub. Adminstrn. (pres. Chgo. chpt. 1960-61), Spl. Libraries Assn. (nat. chmn. social sci. div. 1961-62), Am. Assn. Law Libraries (past nat. treas., pres. Chgo. chpt.). Club: Arts. Author various articles pub. in profl. jours. Home: 1366 E Madison Park Chicago IL 60615 Office: Chgo Transit Authority Mdse Mart Chicago IL 60654

BENSON, LARRY WILLIAM (BILL), appliance mfg. co. exec.; b. Clinton, Iowa, Feb. 18, 1939; s. George Christian and Martha (Jansen) B.; B.A., Wartburg Coll., 1963; m. June E. Schindler, June 9, 1962; children—Scott, Monica, Kelly, Sonia. With Maytag Co., Newton Iowa, 1963-66, Grand Rapids, Mich., 1964-65, service supr., Westville, Ind., 1965-66, bus. mgr., Peoria, Ill., 1966—. Served with USN, 1959-61. Trustee, chmn. area young life com., tchr. Club: Kiwanis. Home: 4520 Hetherwood St Peoria IL 61614 Office: 4510 War Memorial Dr Peoria IL 61614

BENSON, PAUL, fed. judge; b. Verona, N.D., June 1, 1918; s. Edwin C. and Annie (Peterson) B.; B.S.C., U. N.D., 1942; LL.B., George Washington U., 1949; m. Dec. 29, 1942; children—Santal E. Manos, Polly Benson Diem, Amy, Laurel L., Peter. Admitted to N.D. bar; adminstrv. asst. to Senator Milton R. Young, 1946-49; asso. firm H.B. Spiller and Cavalier, 1949-50; mem. firm Shaft, Benson, Shaft and McConn, 1950-71; atty. gen. State of N.D., 1954-55; now chief judge U.S. Dist. Ct., Dist. N.D., Fargo. Tchr. U. N.D. Chmn. Grand Forks County chpt. ARC, 1954-55. Served with USNR, 1942-46. Mem. Am. Bar Assn., Am. Judicature Soc., State Bar Assn. N.D., Am. Legion, V.F.W. Lutheran (pres. congregation Grand Forks 1959). Clubs: Masons, Shriners, Elks. Home: 619 21st Ave South Fargo ND 58102 Office: 340 Federal Bldg PO Box 3164 US Courthouse Fargo ND 58102

BENSON, ROBERT BRONAUGH, retail lumber exec.; b. Pleasant Hill, Mo., May 16, 1923; s. Herbert Lowell and Sarah Amelia (Bronaugh) B.; student Kan. City U., 1942; B.A., Mo. U., 1951; m. Dorothy Ann Durick, May 8, 1954. Co-owner Benson Lumber Co., Columbia, Mo., 1958—; pres., treas., dir. Benson Lumber & Supply Co., Columbia, 1958—; v.p., dir. Benson Bldg. Materials, Inc., Columbia, 1958—; partner, Osage Bldg. Supply Co., 1958—; partner, Benson Bros., Columbia, 1952. Active Boy Scouts Am.; bd. dirs. Mid-Mo. Devel. Council, 1960-64. Served with AUS, 1943-46; ETO. Decorated Bronze Arrowhead. Mem. Mid-Am. (dir. 1974), Southwestern (dir. 1970-73) lumbermen's assns., Mo. Archaeol. Soc., Am. Forestry Assn., Forest History Soc., Nat. Trust Historic Preservation. Presbyterian. Club: Country Mo. (Columbia). Home: 1706 Green Meadow Rd Columbia MO 65201 Office: 710 Business Loop 70 W Columbia MO 65201

BENTLAGE, RICHARD AUGUST, youth adminstr.; b. Indpls., June 26, 1936; s. Kurt Fred and Marie (Rossi) B.; grad. summa cum laude Elkhart U., 1955; pre-med. student Ind. U., 1955-58; m. Geraldine R. Daley, Nov. 27, 1958; children—Mark R., David K., Paula A. Adminstrv. asst. disaster relief ARC, Indpls., 1955-56; X-ray technologist radiol./nuclear St. Vincent's Hosp., Indpls., 1956-57; med./X-ray technologist and dept. head Morgan Health Center, Indpls., 1957-58; med. research technologist, med./surg. staff VA Hosp., Indpls., 1958-61; med. technologist, med. staff White County Meml. Hosp., Monticello, Ind., 1961-64, lab. supr., dept. head, 1964-75; exec. dir. Youth Service Bur. White County, Monticello, 1975—; cons., lectr. in field. Treas., Yeoman PTA, 1974-76. Served in USNR, 1953-61. Mem. Am. Med. Technologists, Am., Ind. socs. med. technologists, Nat. Assn. Prevention Profls., Pub. Offender Councilors Assn., Assn. Specialists in Group Work, Am. Personnel and Guidance Assn., Ind. Youth Service Burs. Assn., Pi Rho Zeta (life). Roman Catholic. Home: 1242 Lookout Dr Monticello IN 47960 Office: PO Box 965 City Park Monticello IN 47960

BENTLEY, JAMES HERBERT, elec. engr.; b. Portland, Oreg., May 23, 1935; s. Robert Athy and Helen Louise (Niles) B.; B.S. in Elec. Engring., Mich. Tech. U., 1957; M.S. in Elec. Engring. (Hughes Fellow), U. So. Calif., 1959; m. Elizabeth Anne Willard, Aug. 19, 1958; children—Mary Katherine, John Robert. Elec. engr. Hughes Aircraft Co., Los Angeles, 1957-59, Philco Corp., Palo Alto, Calif., 1960-64, Bendix Corp., Washington, 1964-65, Univac, St. Paul, 1965-68, Honeywell, Inc., Mpls., 1968-76, 3M Co., St. Paul, 1976—; dir. Ecology Enterprises, Inc.; instr. refresher course in elec. engring., Mpls. Chmn., Edina Environ. Quality Commn., 1975-76; mem. exec. com. Dist. 39, Republican Party. Recipient Mayor's commendation award City of Edina, 1976; registered profl. engr., Minn. Mem. Nat., Minn. socs. profl. engrs., IEEE, Tau Beta Pi, Eta Kappa Nu. Presbyterian. Club: Minnesota Valley Country. Home: 5120 Grove St Edina MN 55436 Office: 3M Center Saint Paul MN 55101

BENTLEY, THOMAS HORTON, III, constrn. co. exec.; b. Milw., Aug. 3, 1946; s. Thomas Horton and Virginia M. (Zivney) B.; B.S. in Bus. Adminstrn., Bucknell U., 1969; m. Sally Lynne Ross, Oct. 9, 1971. Sec.-treas. Thomas H. Bentley & Son Inc., Milw., 1970-78, dir., 1970-78, export mgr., export boxing div., 1969-78; chmn. legis. com. Gen. Contractors Milw. chpt., 1972-78, Allied Constrn. Employers Assoc., 1974-78; chmn. Nat. A.G.C. Legis. Network, Wis., 1974-78; vice chmn. City of Milw. Bd. of Standards and Appeals; advisory mem. Law Related Ed. Project of Wis. Bar Found. Mem. Builders Exchange, Asso. Gen. Contractors, Allied Constrn. Employers Assn. Lutheran. Clubs: Town Tennis, Le (tennis), Wis. Sons of Bosses Internat. (v.p., Milw. chpt.), Milw. North Shore Racquet. Office: 3131 W Mill Rd Milwaukee WI 53209

BENTON, LEVEVIAN MCDANIEL, educator; b. Gary, Ind., Aug. 5, 1925; d. Lohney Lee and Geneva (Scott) McDaniel; A.B., Clark Coll., Atlanta, 1946; M.A., Atlanta U., 1957; m. Norman Charles Benton, Aug. 14, 1959. Camp counselor Karamu House, Cleve., 1946; tchr. Friendship Sch. for Mentally Retarded Children, Gary, 1947-49; elementary tchr. Dept. Interior, Ft. Totten, N.D., 1951-54, Indian Service, Macy, Nebr., 1954-55, Cheyenne Agy., S.D., 1955-56, Oglala Community Sch., Pine Ridge, S.D., 1956-66; tchr. educable Mentally handicapped Scottsbluff (Nebr.) Pub. Sch., 1966-77, tchr. intermediate reading, 1977—. Precinct committeeperson Republican Party, 1966-68. Mem. Nat., Nebr., Scottsbluff (welfare com. and negotiation team 1970-73, profl. growth com. 1973—), AAUW, NAACP (br. sec. 1966—), Bus. and Profl. Women's Clubs, Delta Kappa Gamma. Methodist (social concern chmn., treas. Wesleyan Service Guild). Home: 522 E 12th St Scottsbluff NE 69361

BENTON, ROBERT DEAN, state ednl. adminstr.; b. Guthrie Center, Iowa, July 22, 1929; s. John H. and Luella M. (Rawlings) B.; B.A., U. No. Iowa, 1951, M.A., 1956; Ed.D., Colo. State Coll., 1961; m. Rachel Swanson, July 29, 1951; children—Camille, John, Scott. Tchr., Ruthven, Iowa, 1953-56, Mason City, Iowa, 1956-58; dir. pub. info., coordinator secondary edn., Rapid City, S.D., 1958-61, asst. supt. in charge of instrn., 1961-66; supt. schs. Council Bluffs, Iowa, 1966-72; state supt. pub. instrn. State of Iowa, 1972—; part-time journalism tchr. summer sessions Colo. State Coll., 1959-61. Mem. Iowa Adv. Council for Vocat. Edn., 1970—. Hon. chmn., mem. founding com. Friends of Music Community Concert Series, 1967. Bd. dirs. Chanticleer Community Theater, 1968—, Christian Home, 1968—. Served with USMC, 1951-53. Named Boss of the Year, Jaycees, Council Bluffs, 1970; Outstanding Young Man of the Year, Jr. C. of C., Rapid City, 1965. Mem. NEA, C. of C., Phi Delta Kappa, Theta Alpha Phi. Methodist. Rotarian. Home: 2921 Kendallwood Circle Des Moines IA 50321 Office: Grimes Office Bldg Des Moines IA 50319

BENTON, ROBERT WILMER, coll. pres.; b. Guthrie Center, Iowa, Aug. 28, 1931; s. Howard Jasper and Nellie Mae (Gustin) B.; B.A., Northwestern Coll., 1955; Th.M., Dallas Theol. Sem., 1959; postgrad. Simpson Coll., 1963-64; Th.D., Grace Theol. Sem., 1968; postgrad. U. Nebr. at Lincoln, 1974—; m. Beryl Edna Anderson, Aug. 20, 1955; children—Gregory, Steven, Sharon, Linda. Ordained to minstry Conservative Bapt. Ch., 1959; pastor Martensdale Community Ch., 1959-64, Tippecanoe Community Ch., 1964-67; instr. O.T. Studies, Grace Coll. of the Bible, Omaha, 1967-71, pres., 1971—. County committeeman Republican party, 1962-64; mem. bd. reference Gospel Missionary Union, Smithville, Mo.; mem. adv. bd. World Impact, Omaha; mem. exec. com. Am. Assn. Bible Colls., Wheaton, Ill.; bd. dirs. Valley View Retirement Home, Des Moines. Home: 101 Jennings Route 5 Box 93 Council Bluffs IA 51501 Office: 1515 S 10th St Omaha NE 68108

BENTZEL, CHARLES HOWARD, mfg. co. exec.; b. Balt., July 30, 1926; s. Charles Howard and Mary William (Burton) B.; B.A. in Bus. Adminstrn., U. Balt., 1952, B.S. in Accounting, 1954; m. Wanda Lee Baer, July 26, 1947; children—Howard, Craig, Leslie. Comptroller, Industrias Kaiser Argentina, Buenos Aires, 1962-68; v.p. fin., treas. Roblin Industries, Inc., Buffalo, 1968-69; dir. fin., sr. treas. ITT-Standard Electrica, Rio de Janeiro, Brazil, 1969-71; dir. fin. controls, asst. comptroller ITT-Europe, Brussels, Belgium, 1971-75; v.p., comptroller ITT-Rayonier, N.Y.C., 1975-76; v.p. fin., treas. Trane Co., LaCrosse, Wis., 1976—; dir. First Nat. Bank of LaCrosse, Coldex Trane do Brasil, Kubota, Ltd. (Japan). Served to 1st lt. USMC, 1943-47. C.P.A., Md. Mem. Fin. Execs. Inst. (chmn. internat. planning com.), Am. Accounting Assn., Nat. Assn. Accountants, Brazilian Fin. Exec. Inst. (founding pres., hon. life mem.). Republican. Clubs: Masons; New York Athletic; Marco Polo; LaCrosse. Contbr. to Corporate Accountants Handbook, 1976. Home: 7262 Ridgeview Rd LaCrosse WI 54601 Office: 3600 Pammel Creek Rd LaCrosse WI 54601

BERBERIAN, RALPH HARRY, bus. exec.; b. Fresno, Calif., May 21, 1922; s. Harry Avak and Almas (Garabedian) B.; m. Donna Kniffen; children—Chere, Raffie, Sandy, Sheldon, Dawn, Barclay. Produce grower, packer, Calif., Ariz.. 1946-60; owner Horizon Land Corp., Tucson, 1960-63; account exec. Am. Inst. Mktg. Systems, 1963-71; gen. mgr. Gen. Duplicators, St. Louis, 1971—. Mem. Democratic Com., Reedley, Calif., 1948-50. Served with USAF, 1941-46. Home: 7 Grand Circle Dr St Ann MO 63074 Office: 1601 Washington St Louis MO 63103

BERCAW, JACK NOWEN, automobile co. exec.; b. Auburn, Ind., Nov. 7, 1946; s. Dick Charles and Lois Olivia (Buttermore) B.; A.A. in Accounting, Internat. Bus. Coll., 1970; m. Elaine Marie Sintros. Nov. 29, 1969; children—Kristin, Damon. Bus. mgr., treas. Maxton Motors, Inc., Butler, Ind., 1969—. Asst. scoutmaster Boy Scouts Am.; chmn. Butler United Fund, Butler Days Com. Served with Finance Corps, U.S. Army. Mem. Butler C. of C. (pres.), Butler Retail Merchants Assn. (treas.). Republican. Methodist. Clubs: Am. Legion, Eagles. Home: 320 N John St Butler IN 46721 Office: 114 W Main St Butler IN 46721

BERENS, JOHN SYLVESTER, educator; b. Appleton, Wis., June 26, 1935; s. Sylvester John and Sylvia Marie (Rabe) B.; A.B., Ripon Coll., 1957; M.B.A., Ind. U., 1958, D.B.A., 1969; m. LaRue Ann Waldkoetter, Aug. 6, 1960. With Shillitos Dept. Store, Cin., 1959-61; asst. prof. Ind. State U., Terre Haute, Ind., 1964-70, asso. prof.. 1971-76, prof. marketing, 1977—; vis. asso. prof. marketing Ind. U., Bloomington, summer 1976; coordinator Retail Employee Devel. Program, Sch. Bus., Ind. State U., 1974, 75. Mem. Central Bus. Dist. com., Terre Haute area C. of C., 1972-75. Served with USAR, 1957-65. Mem. Am. Marketing Assn., Midwest Bus. Adminstrn. Assn., Midwest Marketing Assn., Delta Sigma Pi, Phi Beta Kappa, Beta Gamma Sigma. Roman Catholic. Contbr. articles in field to profl. jours.; author: Contemporary Retailing: Cases from Todays Marketplace, 1977. Home: 681 Barbour Ave Terre Haute IN 47804 Office: Sch Bus Ind State U Terre Haute IN 47809

BERENS, LAWRENCE PENINGTON, hosp. adminstr.; b. N.Y.C., June 24, 1943; s. Conrad and Frances Penington (Cookman) B.; B.A., U. N.D., 1969; M.B.A., U. Chgo., 1971; m. Ann Benning Baxter, July 10, 1968; children—Hope Brockett, Amy Lawrence, Emily Wharton, Brooke Van Alstyne. Summer adminstr. Michael Reese Hosp. Med. Center, Chgo., 1970; adminstrv. asst. U. Chgo. Hosp. and Clinics, 1971-72; asst. adminstr. Christ Hosp., Oaklawn, Ill., 1972-75; adminstr. div. medicine Cleve. Clinic Found., Cleve., 1976—; cons. long range planning and health care mgmt.; mem. faculty Webster Coll. Grad. Level Health Facilities. Commodore No. Ohio sea scouts program Boy Scouts Am. Served with USAF, 1964-68. Ray Brown fellow, 1969-70. Mem. Am. Acad. Med. Adminstrs., Am. Coll. Hosp. Adminstrs., Am. Coll. Med. Group Adminstrs., Am. Hosp. Assn., Hosp. Financial Mgmt. Assn., Hosp., Mgmt. Systems Soc., Internat. Hosp. Fedn., Ill., Ohio hosp. assns., Pan Am. Health Orgn., Soc. for Computer Medicine, Health Care Adminstrs. Assn. N.E. Ohio. Club: Mentor Harbor Yachting. Home: Pennhouse Hill Creek Lane Gates Mills OH 44040 Office: Cleveland Clinic Found 9500 Euclid Ave Cleveland OH 44106

BERENZWEIG, JACK CHARLES, lawyer; b. N.Y.C., Sept. 29, 1942; s. Sidney A. and Anne R. (Dubowe) B.; B. Elec. Engring., Cornell U., 1964; J.D., Am. U., 1968; m. Susan J. Heberle, Aug. 8, 1968. Admitted to Va. bar, 1968, Ill. bar, 1969, 7th Fed. Circuit, 1971, U.S. Supreme Ct., 1972; patent examiner U.S. Patent Office, 1964-66; patent agt. U.S. Naval Air Systems Command, 1966-68; atty. with firm Hume, Clement, Brinks, Willian & Olds, Ltd., Chgo., 1968—. Mem. Am., Chgo. (defense of prisoners com. 1970—), Ill. bar assns., Va. State Bar, Bar Assn. of 7th Fed. Circuit, Delta Theta Phi, Tau Epsilon Phi. Club: Union League (Chgo.). Home: 1407 E Fleming Dr S Arlington Heights IL 60004 Office: 1 IBM Plaza Chicago IL 60611

BERETVAS, ANDREW FRANCIS, physicist; b. Los Angeles, Sept. 11, 1939; s. Andor and Helen M. (Sellei) B.; B.S., U. Chgo., 1960, M.S., 1962, Ph.D., 1968. Research asst. Fermi Inst., U. Chgo., 1963-67; asst. prof. physics State U. N.Y., Buffalo, 1968-74; computer cons. U. Chgo., 1974-75; research asso. high energy physics Northwestern U., Evanston, Ill., 1975-76, Argonne (Ill.) Nat. Lab., 1976—. Mem. Am. Phys. Soc., Am. Assn. Physics Tchrs. Address: 6101 N Sheridan Rd Chicago IL 60660

BERG, B(ENJAMIN) ROBERT, psychotherapist; b. Flushing, N.Y., Apr. 10, 1925; s. Joseph M. and Belle (Bennett) B.; B.A., U. Wis., 1947, M.S., 1949; m. Priscilla Arlene Mourning, June 1, 1963 (div. Apr. 1976); children—Lawrance A., David M., Mark, Paul, Lisa, Nancy. Psychiat. social worker Psychiat. Clinic, Children's Village, Dobbs Ferry, N.Y., 1949-51, Kings County Hosp., Bklyn., 1952; caseworker Community Casework Soc., unit dir. Treatment Camp, N.Y.C., 1952-54; supr. children's services Jewish Family & Children's Service, Mpls., 1954-61, dir. casework, 1961-62; pvt. practice psychotherapy, Mpls., 1962—; v.p., treas. Gross, Charnley, Berg, Inc., 1963—; sec.-treas. Rx Ranch Corp., 1959—, Burnt Chimneys of Minn., Inc., 1972—; cons. Am. Lung Assn. Camp Superkids. Bd. dirs. Oak Park Home, Mpls., 1962—, v.p., 1963-64; bd. govs. Mpls. YMCA. Served with USNR, 1944-46. Mem. Am. Group Psychotherapy Assn., Nat. Assn. Social Workers, Register Clin. Social Workers, Acad. Certified Social Workers, ACLU. Author: Psychology in Children's Camping, 1958. Contbr. numerous articles to profl. jours. Home: Route 2 Box 235A Prior Lake MN 55372 Office: 1427 Med Arts Bldg Minneapolis MN 55402

BERG, EVELYNNE MARIE, educator; b. Chgo.; d. Clarence Martin and Mildred (Strnad) B.; B.S. with honors, U. Ill., 1954; M.A., Northwestern U., 1959. Geography editor Am. Peoples Ency., Chgo., 1955-57; social studies tchr. Hammond (Ind.) Tech.-Vocat. High Sch., 1958-59; geography tchr. Carl Schurz High Sch., Chgo., 1960-66; faculty geography Morton Coll., Cicero, Ill., 1966—. Asst. leader Cicero council Girl Scouts U.S.A., 1951-53; mem. Greater Chgo. Citizenship Council. Fulbright scholar, Brazil, 1964; NSF scholar, 1963, 65, 71-72; NDEA fellow, 1968-69; recipient award Ill. Geog. Soc., 1977. Fellow Nat. Council Geog. Edn. (state coordinator 1973-74, exec. bd. 1973-77); mem. Nat., Ill. (sec.-treas. 1968-69, sec. 1969-70 v.p. 1970-71, pres. 1971-72), De Paul U., Chgo. geog. socs., Am. Overseas Educators (sec. 1974-76, v.p. 1977-78), AAUW (Chgo. br. rec. sec. 1963-65), Assn. Am. Geographers, Ill., Chgo. acads. sci., AAAS (scholarship 1973-74), Des Plaines Valley Geol. Soc., Nat. Assn. Geology Tchrs., AAUP, Nat., Ill. councils social studies, Geol. Soc. Am. Sigma Xi, Sierra Club. Clubs: Order Eastern Star, Bus. and Profl. Women's. Contbr. to profl. jours. Home: 3924 N Pioneer Ave Chicago IL 60634 Office: Morton Coll 3801 S Central Ave Cicero IL 60650

BERG, GARY ALLEN, educator; b. Powers Lake, N.D., Feb. 26, 1944; s. Odleif Chester and Bernice Annette (Thompson) B.; B.S. in Bus. Edn., Minot State Coll., 1962; M.S. in Bus. Edn., U. N.D., 1967; Ed.D. in Bus. Edn., U. Nebr., 1972; m. Mary Elizabeth Hill, June 11, 1967; children—Jason Allen, Justin Allen. Asst. prof. bus. edn. No. State Coll., Aberdeen, S.D., 1967-70; grad. asst. in secondary edn. U. Nebr., Lincoln, 1970-71; prof. bus. edn. No. State Coll., Aberdeen, 1971—; pres. Western Wear Corp., 1977—; dir. Office Career Cons.'s, Aberdeen, 1977—; cons. Singer Corp., S.D., 1970-73, Sharp Electronics, Inc., N.J., 1969-74. Mem. Am., S.D. vocat. assns., Nat., Mountain-Plains bus. edn. assns., S.D. Bus. and Office Edn. Assn., Pi Omega Pi, Delta Pi Epsilon, Phi Delta Kappa. Republican. Lutheran. Club: Elks. Author: Business Problems and Applications with Electronic Calculations, 1971; Business Electronic Calculator Text, 1978; contbr. numerous articles on bus. edn. to profl. jours. Home: PO Box 796 Melgaard Rd Aberdeen SD 57401 Office: PO Box 752 Jay St Aberdeen SD 57401

BERG, KENNETH EDWARD, newspaper editor; b. New Ulm, Minn., June 28, 1925; s. Edward John and Laura A. (Sturm) B.; B.S., Mankato (Minn.) State Coll., 1950; m. Marilyn A. Bresnan, Nov. 25, 1950; children—Julie, Steven, Kevin, Nancy. Sports editor Mankato Free Press, 1943, reporter, photographer, city editor, 1946-52, editor, 1966—; asso. editor Mason City (Iowa) Globe-Gazette, 1952-66. Indsl. promotion Minn. Gov.'s Citizens Council on Aging, 1968-71, Fine Arts, 1967—; active Boy Scouts Am. Bd. dirs. Guthrie Theater Found., Mpls., Minn. Valley Mental Health Center. Served with AUS, 1944-46. Mem. Nat. Assn. Editorial Writers, Iowa A.P. Telegraph Editors Assn. (past pres.), A.P. Mng. Editor Assn., Minn. A.P. Mng. Editors Assn. (past pres.), Mid-Am. Press Inst. (dir.), Minn. News Execs. Conf. (past pres.), Am. Soc. Newspaper Editors, 2d Dist Editorial Assn. (sec.-treas.), Pi Delta Epsilon. Home: 322 State St Mankato MN 56001 Office: 418 S 2d Mankato MN 56001

BERG, KENNETH ERIC, broadcasting co. exec.; b. Mpls., Dec. 10, 1935; s. Axel Olaf and Gladys Emilia (Ahlstrom) B.; grad. Dunwoody Inst., Mpls., 1955; grad. broadcasting Brown Broadcasting Sch., Mpls., 1959, grad. engring., 1960; m. Martha Lois Moore, Aug. 26, 1961; children—Scott, Kevin. Announcer, KXGN Radio and TV, Glendive, Mont., 1959-60, KJAY Radio, Topeka, 1961, KWOA Radio, Worthington, Minn., 1961-62; with KLMS Radio, Lincoln, Nebr., 1962-77, program dir., 1963-65, account exec., ops. mgr., 1965-71, sales mgr., 1971-77; account exec. Radio Sta. KAKE, Wichita, Kans., 1977—. Pres., Ruth Pyrtle PTA, 1974-75; mem. Downtown Lincoln Promotion Council, 1974—; mem. exec. com. Lancaster County Arthritis Found. Served with AUS, 1956-59. Mem. Lincoln C. of C. (pub. relations com. 1970-77), Nebr. Broadcasters Assn., Lincoln Advt. Club (dir.). Methodist. Office: PO Box 1240 Wichita KS 67001

BERG, KENNETH PAUL, cons. retirement mgmt.; b. Boone, Iowa, May 30, 1922; s. Elmer John and Irene Elma (McFee) B.; B.A., John Fletcher Coll., 1946; M.R.E., Southwestern Sem., 1948; Ph.D., State U. Iowa, 1952; D.Min., San Francisco, Theol. Sem., 1974; m. Jean Marie Johnson, Oct. 26, 1944; children—Kenneth Paul, Susan Jean.

Ordained to ministry, United Ch. of Christ, 1948; student pastor, Iowa, Tex., Calif., 1941-53; pastor United Ch. of Christ, Ottumwa, Iowa, 1953-59, Presbyn. Chs., Walnut Springs and Spruce, Mo., 1961-62, 1st Presbyn. Ch., Lee's Summit, Mo., 1962-70; interim pastor S.E. Presbyn. Ch., Kansas City, Mo., 1970-71, Barbee Meml. Presbyn. Ch., Excelsior Springs, Mo., 1973-74; pres., founder Christian Services, Inc., Lee's Summit, 1960—; pres. Christian Home Services, Inc., Lee's Summit, and Des Moines, 1971—; pres., exec. dir. John Knox Village, Lee's Summit, 1970-74; keynote speaker various nursing home and state convs. on aging. Speaker, resource person Interfaith Coalition on Aging, Lee's Summit, 1972-76. Founder, builder Internat. Ch. and Geriatrics Hosp. and Research Center, Lee's Summit, 1976. Mem. Lee's Summit C. of C. (named Outstanding Citizen of Lee's Summit 1972), Gerontological Soc., Better Bus. Bur. Rotarian, Lion. Author: One Man's Manner and Methods, 1971; Affordable Life-Care Retirement Living, 1972; Senior Power: New Life for the Church, 1974. Founder, exec. dir. Sr. Power mag., 1974. Home: 604 S Murray Rd Lee's Summit MO 64063 Office: PO Box 7 Lee's Summit MO 64063

BERG, LOY CARLETON, real estate broker; b. Campbell, Minn., Apr. 6, 1924; s. Carl O. and Grace (Loeks) B.; student Interstate Bus. Coll., 1948-49, N.D. State Sch. Sci., 1950-51; grad. Realtors Inst. (Minn.), 1972; m. Eline D. Bjornaas, Aug. 20, 1949; children—Pamela, Lon, Eric. Owner real estate, ins. agy., Campbell, 1948-52, Breckinridge, Minn., 1952—, State Farm Ins. Agy., 1948—; farmer, Wilkin County, Minn., 1953—; pres. Belman Inc., Campbell, 1961—, Shelberness Inc., Breckenridge, 1972—; dir. 1st. Nat. Bank Breckenridge, Comstock and Holy Cross Ins. Co. Bd. mem. Campbell Pub. Sch. Bd., 1970-72; adv. bd. Minn. Dakota Vocat. Career Center, 1973—. Served with U.S. Mcht. Marine, 1944-45, AUS, 1945-47. Mem. Farmers Co-op. Elevator Assn. (chmn. 1974—), Minn. Assn. Realtors, Lake Region Bd. Realtors, Nat. Inst. Farm and Land Brokers, Nat. Assn. Ind. Fee Appraisers. Republican. Mem. United Ch. Christ (state dir.). Mason (Shriner), Rotarian; mem. Order Easter Star. Address: Stratford Hotel Bldg Breckenridge MN 56520

BERG, MARIE HIRSCH (MRS. KURT N. BERG), educator; b. Mannheim, Germany, Mar. 20, 1909; d. Julius and Frieda (Simon) Hirsch; Ph.D., U. Heidelberg (Germany), 1934; postgrad. Northwestern U., 1941-47, U. Mich., 1948-52; m. Kurt N. Berg, Jan. 15, 1935 (dec. Nov. 1960); 1 son, Michael C. Came to U.S., 1940, naturalized, 1946. Research asso. Northwestern U. Dental Sch., 1941-47; research asso. dermatology U. Mich., 1948-51; research asso. Wayne County Gen. Hosp., 1951-52, U. Minn., 1952-57, 59-60, adj. faculty, 1976—; chief chemist St. Luke's Hosp., 1946-48; asst. prof. dept. chemistry and biology Hamline U., St. Paul, 1952-59; prof. sci., chmn. dept. natural sci. and math. Northwestern Coll., Mpls., 1960-70; lectr. sci. and fire protection Met. Community Coll., 1967-76. Named hon. fire chief, Mpls. Fellow AAAS (com. for encouraging women to enter sci. 1957-66), Am. Sci. Affiliation; mem. Am. Chem. Soc., Minn. Acad. Sci. (scholarship com. 1965-70, mem. editorial bd. 1965-68, Distinguished Service in Sci. Edn. award 1977), Minn. Coll. Chemistry Tchrs. (chmn. 1969), Nat. Assn. Fire Sci. and Adminstrn., Internat. Soc. Fire Service Instrs., AAUW, Sigma Xi, Iota Sigma Pi (coordinator nat. council 1963-72), Sigma Delta Epsilon (pres. 1969-70, nat. council 1967-71). Home: 4910 Circle Downs Minneapolis MN 55416

BERG, OBED JOHAN, orthodontist; b. Fairview, S.D., Oct. 10, 1916; s. Alfred Elias and Ausper (Uleberg) B.; student St. Olef Coll., 1935-37; student Augsburg Coll., 1937-38; B.A., St. Olaf Coll., 1939; D.D.S., U. Iowa, 1947. m. Marlys Hov Berg, Sept. 20, 1941; children—William Rolland, Gordon Alfred. Practice gen. dentistry, Decorah, Iowa, 1947-55, specializing in pedodontics, 1956-60, orthodontics, 1960—; instr. pedodontia U. Iowa, Iowa City, 1955-56. Mem. Decorah Sch. bd., 1958-60, Northeast Ia. Mental Health bd., 1964-66. Served to capt. USAF, 1951-53; Korea. Mem. Am., Ia., Chgo. dental assns., Am. Assn. of Orthodontists, Dubuque Dist. Dental Soc. (pres. 1961-62), V.F.W., Psi Omega, Smyra (pres. 1976-77). Lutheran. Rotarian (pres. 1972-73), Sons of Norway, Sierra Club. Clubs: Oneonta Golf and Country, Nordmanns Forbundet. Home: 308 Grove St Decorah IA 52101 Office: 308 Grove St Decorah IA 52101

BERG, ROGER JOEL, clothing mfg. co. exec.; b. Allegan County, Mich., Feb. 25, 1943; s. Arnold William and Eileen Linnea (Johnson) B.; A.A., Muskegon Bus. Coll., 1967; children from previous marriage—Christine Marie. Scott Alan, Julia Ann. Mgr. cost accounting Westran Corp., Muskegon, Mich., 1965-71; asst. treas. Glen of Michigan, Inc., Manistee, 1971—; treas. Patchwork Stores, Inc.; sec. treas. By-Lake Corp. Served with USN, 1963-65. Mem. Am. Legion. Republican. Roman Catholic. Clubs: St. Joseph Civic, Eagles. Elks. Home: 303 5th Ave Apt 1 Manistee MI 49660 Office: 77 Hancock St Manistee MI 49660

BERG, RUSSELL GEORGE, photo co. exec.; b. Oak Park, Ill., Feb. 23, 1925; s. Elmer William and Olga (Larson) B.; B.S., Northwestern U., 1949; m. Corinne Eleanor Campbell, Aug. 23, 1945; children—Jeffrey, Paul, William, Carolyn. Dir. budgets and profit planning Fairbanks Morse & Co., 1954-59; from exec. v.p. to pres. Crown Bremson Industries, 1961-64; pres., gen. mgr. Berkey Photo Service, Inc., Des Plaines, Ill., 1964—. Mem. spl. taxpayers com. on state budget, Wis., 1955. Served with USAF, 1943-46. Mem. Des Plaines C. of C. (bd. dirs. 1977—). Office: 220 Graceland St Des Plaines IL 60016

BERG, STANTON ONEAL, firearms and ballistics cons.; b. Barron, Wis., June 14, 1928; s. Thomas C. and Ellen Florence (Nedland) Silbaugh; student U. Wis., 1949-50; LL.B., LaSalle Extension U., 1951; postgrad. U. Minn., 1960-69; m. June K. Rolstad, Aug. 16, 1952; children—David M., Daniel L., Susan E., Julie L. Claim rep. State Farm Ins. Co., Mpls., Hibbing and Duluth, Minn., 1952-57, claim supt., 1957-66, divisional claim supt., 1966-70; firearms cons., Mpls., 1961—; regional mgr. State Farm Fire and Casualty Co., St. Paul, 1970—. Instr. home firearms safety, Mpls.; cons. to Sporting Arms and Ammunition Mfrs. Inst.; lectr. on forensic ballistics. Adv. bd. Milton Helpern Internat. Center for Forensic Scis., 1975—; mem. bd. cons. Inst. Applied Sci., Chgo.; cons. for re-exam. of ballistics evidence in Sirhan case Superior Ct. Los Angeles, 1975. Served with CIC, AUS, 1948-52. Fellow Am. Acad. Forensic Sci.; mem. Assn. of Firearm and Tool Mark Examiners (exec. council 1970-71, Distinguished Mem. and Key Man award 1972, spl. honors award 1976), Forensic Sci. Soc., Internat. Assn. for Identification (mem. firearms subcom. of sci. and practice com. 1961-74), Am. Ordnance Assn., Nat. Rifle Assn., Minn. Weapons, Internat. Cartridge collectors assns. Contbg. editor Am. Rifleman mag., 1973—. Contbr. numerous articles on firearms and forensic ballistics to profl. publs. Address: 6025 Gardena Ln NE Minneapolis MN 55432

BERG, WARREN GLENN, coll. adminstr.; b. Chgo., June 9, 1924; s. Sydney Olaf and Loraine Elizabeth (Schwank) B.; B.A., Luther Coll., Decorah, Iowa, 1948; M.A., U. Iowa, 1950, Ph.D., 1960; m. M. Janice Reid, Dec. 28, 1946; children—Paula Berg Hovde, Kristin Berg Gilbert, Kari Berg Barth, Jon, Erik. Faculty, Luther Coll., Decorah, 1948—, sports info. dir., 1950-65, prof. econs., 1961—, head dept. econs. and bus. adminstrn., 1955—, dean academic affairs, 1973-75. Sr. Fulbright-Hays prof. Royal U. Malta, 1966-67; dir. Inst. in Am. Studies for Scandinavian Educators, summers 1964—. Mem. pub. relations com. Nat. Collegiate Athletic Assn., 1958-65; bd. dirs. Minn. Pub. Radio, 1973—. Served to ensign USNR, 1942-46; PTO. Named Outstanding Young Man of Year, Decorah Jr. C. of C., 1957; recipient various scholarships, fellowships. Mem. Am. Econ. Assn., Am. Accounting Assn. (research com. 1965-66), Coll. Sports Info. Dirs. Am. (past pres.), Beta Alpha Psi, Omicron Delta Epsilon. Lutheran (ch. pres.). Club: Rotary (pres. Decorah 1962). Home: 626 Center St Decorah IA 52101

BERGAN, CAROLYN WIDENER, civic worker; b. Crawfordsville, Ind., Oct. 1, 1928; d. Leslie F. and Mary Donnis (Saidla) Widener; B.S., Purdue U., 1950; M.S., Butler U., 1953; m. John J. Bergan, Aug. 4, 1951; children—Elizabeth, Margaret, John. Chmn. Ill. Day Care Standards Commn., 1965—; v.p. Welfare Council Met. Chgo., 1968-69, pres., 1969-71; v.p. Chgo. Commons Assn., 1969-75, pres., 1975—; chmn. Chgo. Head Start, 1966-69; mem. Mayor's Commn. Sch. Bd. Nominations, 1969—; mem. vis. com. Sch. Social Service Adminstrn. U. Chgo., 1970—, mem. women's bd., 1970—; mem. Bd. of Edn., State of Ill., 1975—; bd. dirs. United Way Met. Chgo., 1976—; bd. dirs. Latino Inst.; hon. trustee Francis W. Parker Sch., 1976—. Named Chicagoan of Year in Welfare, Jr. C. of C., 1971; recipient Phoenix award for civic leadership DePaul U., 1970. Mem. Mortar Bd., Kappa Gamma. Home: 2305 N Commonwealth Ave Chicago IL 60614

BERGAN, JOHN, physician; b. Tampico, Mexico, 1927; M.D., U. Ind., 1954. Intern Ind. U. Med. Center Hosps., 1954-55; resident Chgo. Wesley Meml. Hosp., 1955-59, attending staff Northwestern Meml. Hospitals (formerly Wesley Meml. Hosp.); attending staff, cons. VA Research Hosp., USPHS Hosp.; from clin. asst. in surgery to prof. surgery Northwestern U. Sch. Medicine, Chgo., 1959—, chief transplantation div., 1973-75; dir. A.C.S.-NIH Organ Transplant Registry, 1973-76, chief div. vascular surgery, 1975—. Served with USNR, 1945-48. Diplomate Am. Bd. Surgery. Fellow A.C.S. (dir. Organ Transplant Registry); mem. Am. Surg. Assn., Soc. Univ. Surgeons, AMA. Office: 251 E Chicago Ave Chicago IL 60611

BERGE, EARL ORVILLE, supt. schs.; b. Bode, Iowa, Mar. 21, 1917; s. Thomas H. and Mollie M. (Enockson) B.; B.A., Luther Coll., 1938; M.S., Drake U., 1948; postgrad. Iowa State U., 1961-63; Ph.D., State U. Iowa, 1967; m. Irene Selma Heller, June 15, 1941; children—Sandra (Mrs. James Champion), Jerrie (Mrs. Denny Ellis), Bruce, Jeanne (Mrs. Nick Daniel), Jolene, Janene. Acting prin., coach, tchr., Frederika, Iowa, 1938-40, supt. schs., 1940-42, 46-47; supt. schs., Seymour, Iowa, 1947-57, Clear Lake, Iowa, 1957-67; supt. Fort Dodge (Iowa) Community Schs., 1967—. Dir. Ia. Pharmacy Service Corp. Bd. control Iowa High Sch. Athletic Assn., 1964-67; mem. Iowa High Sch. Ins. Co., 1964—; mem. Gov.'s Commn. on Children and Youth, 1968-71; mem. adv. com. State Fire Marshall, 1967—; research bd. Iowa Research Center, U. Iowa, Iowa City, 1967-74). Spl. agt. CIC, War Dept., 1942-46. Recipient Outstanding Service award Am. Inst. Commerce, 1962, golden plaque award, 1973. Mem. Am., Iowa (sec.-treas. 1957) assns. sch. adminstrs., Nat. Fedn. State High Sch. Assns. (pres., citation 1977), City Supts. Assn., Fort Dodge C. of C. (ambassador 1968—), Nat. CIC Assn., Phi Delta Kappa. Lutheran. Elk, Lion, Rotarian. Clubs: Walt Whitman, Century. Home: 2905 16th Ave N Fort Dodge IA 50501 Office: 330 1st Ave N Fort Dodge IA 50501

BERGE, KENNETH GEORGE, physician; b. Wahkon, Minn., Feb. 9, 1926; s. Henry Bertin and Edith Francis (Collin) B.; B.A. magna cum laude, U. Minn., 1948, B.S., 1949, M.B., 1951, M.D., 1952; M.S. in Medicine, Mayo Grad. Sch. Medicine, 1955; m. Aline H. Hoyt, Sept. 1, 1948; children—Elizabeth Ann (Mrs. Richard M. Devine), William Hoyt, Keith Hoyt. Intern, Boston City Hosp., 1951-52; resident in medicine Mayo Grad. Sch. Medicine, Rochester, Minn., 1952-55, instr., 1957-62, asst. prof., 1962-69, asso. prof. medicine, 1969-74, prof. medicine, 1974—, NW Area Found. prof. community medicine, 1977—; physician Kennecott Copper Corp., Ray, Ariz., 1952; asst. to staff Mayo Clinic, Rochester, 1955, staff physician, internist, 1955—, head sect. medicine, 1970—, pres. voting staff, 1976; bd. dirs., mem. exec. com. Rochester Meth. Hosp., 1970—, chmn. com. clin. pastoral care, 1970—. Mem. epidemiology, biometry adv. com. Nat. Heart and Lung Inst., NIH, 1970-72; mem. policy adv. bd. hypertension detection, follow-up program NIH, 1972—, vice-chmn. steering com. coronary drug project 1962—, mem. policy-data monitoring bd. aspirin myocardial infarction study, 1975—. Mem. Olmsted County Bd. Health, 1975—, vice chmn., 1976, chmn., 1977. Served with USNR, 1944-46. Recipient Outstanding Tchr. award Internal Medicine Residents Edn. com. Mayo Grad. Sch., 1970, 71, 74. Fellow A.C.P., mem. AMA (Billings Silver medal 1957), Am., Great Plains (chmn. profl. edn. com. 1972-74) heart assns., Sigma Xi, Alpha Omega Alpha, Phi Chi. Methodist (lay leader 1964-66). Bd. editors Minn. Medicine, 1972-74. Contbr. articles and chpts. to tech. jours. Clin. research in cardiovascular disease and diabetes. Home: 1451 Woodland Dr SW Rochester MN 55901 Office: 200 1st St SW Rochester MN 55901

BERGEN, THOMAS JOSEPH, lawyer; b. Prairie du Chien, Wis., Feb. 7, 1913; s. Thomas Joseph and Emma Marilla (Grelle) B.; student U. Wis., 1930-32; J.D., Marquette U., 1937, postgrad., 1937-38; m. Jean Loraine Bowler, May 29, 1941 (dec. Aug. 1972); children—Kathleen Bergen McElwee, Eileen Bergen Bednarz, Patricia Bergen Buss, Thomas Joseph, Patrick Joseph, John Joseph. Admitted to Wis. bar, 1937, U.S. Supreme Ct. bar, 1972; practiced in Milw., 1937—; exec. sec. Wis. Assn. Nursing Homes, 1957-71; legal counsel, exec. dir. Am. Coll. Nursing Home Adminstrs., Milw., 1967-68; treas., exec. dir. Nat. Geriatrics Soc., Milw., 1971-72; sec., dir. Bayside Nursing Home, Milw., 1967—; pres., dir. N.W. Med. Centers, Inc., also Northland Med. Centers, Inc. (both Milw.), 1968—; mem. program planning com. Nat. Conf. on Aging, also del. to conf., 1974; panel speaker Nat. Justice Found. conv., 1974. Bd. dirs., treas. Nat. Geriatrics Ednl. Soc., 1971—; bd. dirs., pres. Wis. Justice Found., 1971—. Served with AUS, 1943, 44. Recipient Merit award Wis. Assn. Nursing Homes, 1962, Outstanding Leadership award Nat. Geriatrics Soc., 1976. Mem. Am., Wis., Milw. bar assns., Real Estate Profls. Assn. (pres. 1974—), Am. Med. Writers Assn., Delta Theta Phi, Delta Sigma Rho. Roman Catholic. Editor: Silver Threads, Wis. Assn. Nursing Homes publ., 1963-71, News Letter, Am. Coll. Nursing Home Adminstrs., 1967-68, Views and News, Nat. Geriatrics Soc., 1971—; contbr. articles to nursing home publs. Home: 10324 W Vienna Ave Wauwatosa WI 53222 Office: 212 W Wisconsin Ave Milwaukee WI 53203

BERGER, ALAN I., lawyer; b. St. Louis, Aug. 23, 1933; s. Sam and Evelyn Ruth (Wittner) B.; A.B., Washington U., 1954, J.D., 1959; m. Harriette Sue Ofstein, Feb. 19, 1961; children—Rochelle Lynn, Rachel Lea. Admitted to Mo. bar, 1959, since practiced in St. Louis; asso. firm Guffey and McMahon, 1959-60, John R. Stockham, 1960-61; mem. firm McMahon and Berger, 1961—; instr. in labor law St. Louis U., 1961-66. Served to 1st lt., AUS, 1954-56. Mem. Am., Mo. bar assns., Bar Assn. of Met. St. Louis (chmn. labor law sect. 1970), Washington U. Club, Phi Delta Phi. Clubs: Media, Racquet. Home 27 Westwood Country Club St Louis MO 63131 Office: 7701 Forsyth Blvd Clayton MO 63105

BERGER, ARTHUR ESER, pharmacology-managerial cons.; b. Bronx, N.Y., Sept. 18, 1942; s. Morris and Frances (Pollman) B.; B.A. in Zoology, Kans. U., 1964; m. Margaret W. Gagne, Oct. 11, 1976. Supr., Malaria Research, Kansas City, Mo., 1964-66, Harry Truman Research Lab., Kansas City, Mo., 1967-72; asso. dir. Quincy Research Center, Kansas City, Mo., 1973-76; managerial cons. Berger-Boyer Assos., Kansas City, Mo., 1977—. Served with USAF, 1966-72. Mem. AAAS. Jewish. Home and office: 221 W Dartmouth St Kansas City MO 64113

BERGER, CHARLES JAMES, gynecologist; b. Cleve., Apr. 19, 1922; s. Louis Joseph and Catherine Eleanor (Slemer) B.; B.S., U. Detroit, 1943; M.D., Wayne State U., 1945; M.P.H., U. Mich., 1969. Intern Mount Carmel Mercy Hosp., Detroit, 1945-46, resident, 1946-49; pvt. practice specializing in gynecology and obstetrics, Royal Oak, Mich., 1949-60, Southfield, Mich., 1960-68; chief div. maternal health Mich. Dept. Pub. Health, Lansing, 1969—. Cons. Mt. Carmel Mercy Hosp., Detroit. Exec. bd. Southeastern Mich. Family Planning Project, Detroit, 1972-75; lectr. pub. health Mich. State U., East Lansing, 1971-75, asst. clin. prof. obstetrics, gynecology and reproductive biology, 1975—. Bd. dirs. Mich. Population Council, 1970-75. Diplomate Am. Bd. Obstetrics and Gynecology. Fellow Am. Coll. Obstetrics and Gynecology (founding), A.C.S., Royal Soc. Health (London); mem. Am. Coll. Preventive Medicine, N.Y. Acad. Scis., Royal Soc. Medicine, Am. Pub. Health Assn., AMA, Pan Pacific Surg. Assn., Am. Fertility Soc., Pan Am., World med. assns., Delta Omega, Phi Kappa Phi. WHO grantee, 1971; USPHS fellow, 1968-69. Roman Catholic. Elk, K.C. Club: Detroit Yacht. Home: 450 Burgandy Sq East Lansing MI 48823 Office: 3423 N Logan St Lansing MI 48906

BERGER, EMIL JOSEPH, ednl. adminstr.; b. St. Cloud, Minn., Dec. 30, 1917; s. Peter George and Mathilda Regina (Ruhland) B.; B.E., St. Cloud State Coll., 1939; M.A., No. Colo. U., 1947; Ph.D., U. Minn., 1962; m. Lorraine Cecelia Corrigan, Apr. 19, 1944; children—Mary (dec.), Margaret (Mrs. William Prugh), Carol (Mrs. Mark Stehly), Jean (Mrs. Michael Gugisberg), James, Peter. Tchr. Kimball High Sch., 1939-41; prin. Remer (Minn.) High Sch., 1941-42; tchr. Dowling Coll. High Sch., Des Moines, 1942-43, Atwater High Sch., 1946, Monroe High Sch., St. Paul, 1946-60; coordinator math. St. Paul Pub. Schs., 1960-72, adminstr. instructional research and evaluation, 1972—; asso. prof. mathematics Coll. St. Catherine, 1947-70; vis. prof. Columbia U., summer 1968; cons. Nat. Assessment Ednl. Progress, 1967-72. Mem. Sch. Mathematics Study Group Writing Team; del. Internat. Congress Math., Moscow, USSR, 1966. Scoutmaster Boy Scouts Am., Remer, 1941-42. Served with AUS, 1943-45. Mem. Nat. Council Tchrs. Math. (past dir.), Math. Assn. Am., AAAS, Soc. Indsl. and Applied Math., Minn. Council Tchrs. Math. (past pres.), Nat. Council Measurement in Edn., AAAS, Central Assn. Sci. and Math. Tchrs., Am. Math. Soc., Minn. Acad. Sci., Am. Ednl. Research Assn., Nat. Consortium Options in Pub. Edn., Phi Delta Kappa. Club: Midway Speed Skating (past v.p.). Author: (with others) Seeing Through Mathematics, Books One, Two, Three; Fundamental Mathematical Structures: Algebra, 1966; Mathematics Concepts Applications, First Course and Second Course, 1969; Practice Tablet for Mathematics Concepts Applications First and Second Course, 1970. Editor: Instructional Aids in Mathematics Yearbook, 1973; dept. editor for Devices for the Math. Classroom in Mathematics Tchr., 1950-56. Home: 771 W Hoyt Ave St Paul MN 55117 Office: 360 Colborne St St Paul MN 55102

BERGER, JOHN EDWARD, real estate exec.; b. Chgo., Feb. 18, 1929; s. Edward and Marie Dorothy (Mahoney) B.; B.S., Loyola U., 1952; m. Mary Rose Lennon, Nov. 17, 1956; children—John Edward, Michael G., William F., Mary Therese, Joan M., Nancy M. Owner, real estate broker John E. Berger & Co., Chgo., 1954-73 (merger McKey & Paogue, Inc., 1973), v.p., 1973—, dir., 1974—. Vice pres. S.E. Community Orgn., Chgo., 1962-64. Served to lt. USMC, 1951-53. Mem. Chgo. Real Estate Bd. (v.p. 1970—, dir. 1968-70, gov. brokers div. 1967-68), South Side Real Estate Bd. (pres. 1973—, dir. 1968-70), Beverly Suburban Real Estate Bd. (treas. 1976, dir. 1977), Chgo. Property Mgrs. Assn., Loyola U. Alumni Assn., Ill. Assn. Real Estate Bds. (dist. v.p. 1969-70), Chgo. Athletic Assn. Club: Flossmoor Country. Home: 2832 Bob-O-Link Rd Flossmoor IL 60422 Office: 10540 S Western Chicago IL 60643

BERGER, KENNETH WALTER, audiologist; b. Evansville, Ind., Mar. 22, 1924; s. Walter P. and Ida (Block) B.; B.A., U. Evansville, 1948; M.A., Ind. State U., 1949; Ph.D., So. Ill. U., Carbondale, 1962; m. Barbara Jane Steadman, Aug. 31, 1946; children—Robert W., Kenna J., Laura M., Karen S. Speech and hearing therapist pub. schs., Carmi, Ill., 1955-61; dir. audiology Kent State U., (Ohio), 1962—, prof., 1967—. Served to capt. U.S. Army, 1943-46, USAF, 1951-55. Fellow Am. Speech and Hearing Assn., Am. Audiology Soc., Acoustical Soc. Am. Author: Speechreading: Principles and Methods, 1971; The Hearing Aid: Its Operation and Development, 1974. Home: 647 Longmere Dr Kent OH 44240 Office: Speech and Hearing Clinic Kent State Univ Kent OH 44242

BERGER, MILES LEE, land economist; b. Chgo., Aug. 9, 1930; s. Albert E. and Dorothy (Ginsberg) B.; student Brown U., 1948-50; m. Sally Eileen Diamond, Aug. 27, 1955; children—Albert E., Elizabeth Ann. Engaged in real estate appraisal, research and devel., econs. fields, 1950—; mng. chmn. Berger Co., Mpls. and Chgo., 1950—; chmn. bd. Mid-Am. Appraisal & Research Corp., Chgo., 1959—) also dir.; chmn. bd. Real Estate Services Corp., 1969—; vice chmn. bd. Heitman Group, 1970—; prin. econ. cons. Columbia Nat. Bank, Chgo., 1965—; dir. Evans, Inc., Canadian Mortgage Investors; trustee Heitman Mortgage Investors. Commr., vice chmn. Chgo. Plan Commn., 1967—; cons. city Chgo. on Ill. Central Air Rights, 1967—; trustee Latin Sch. Chgo., 1967-73, treas., 1953-55, bd. dirs. Latin Sch. Found.; bd. dirs. Albert E. Berger Found. Mem. Am. Inst. Real Estate Appraisers, Soc. Real Estate Appraisers, Soc. Real Estate Counselors, Am. Right-of-Way Assn., Nat. Assn. Housing and Redevel. Ofcls., Nat. Tax Assn., Internat. Assn. Assessing Officers, Lambda Alpha. Jewish (trustee synagogue). Home: 1325 N Astor St Chicago IL 60610 Office: 180 N LaSalle St Chicago IL 606O1

BERGER, PAUL HAROLD, adminstrv. and loan assn. exec.; b. Cleve., Oct. 14, 1924; s. Ted. Ross and Helen (Hirsh) B.; student Tex. A and M. Coll., 1942-43; So. Methodist U., 1946-47, U. Chgo., 1947-51; M.A. in Social Scis., U. Chgo., 1956; m. Phillis Ottem, July 31, 1954; children—Jessica E., Avery Ross. Adminstrv. asst. to Alderman Robert E. Merriam, 1949-51; sales rep. Mich. Steel Supply, Chgo., 1951-53, Abbot Screw & Bolt Co., Chgo., 1953-54; campaign staff Merriam for Mayor Com., 1954-55; ins. broker, Chgo., 1955—; chmn. bd., pres Hyde Park Fed. Savs. & Loan Assn., Chgo., 1961—. Dist. chmn. Boy Scouts Am., 1968-69; treas. Mid South Side Health Planning Orgn., 1969-72, Gateway Houses Found., Inc., 1969-74; bd. dirs. SE Chgo. Commn., 1963—, Woodlawn Hosp., Hyde Park-Kenwood Community Conf., 1964-67; bd. dirs., treas. First Unitarian Soc. Chgo., treas., 1963-64; bd. dirs. Mary McDowell Settlement, 1957-64, v.p., 1960-61; bd. dirs. Chgo. Renewal Efforts Service Corp., 1973—, chmn., 1976—; bd. dirs., pres. Hyde Park-Kenwood Devel. Corp., 1974—; bd. dirs. Met. Fair and Expn. Authority, 1975—, Community Services and Research Corp., 1975—. Served with AUS, 1943-46. Life mem. Million Dollar Round Table.

Clubs: Economic, Quadrangle (Chgo.). Home: 5816 S Blackstone Ave Chicago IL 60637 Office: 5250 S Lake Park Ave Chicago IL 60615

BERGERON, ALLEN LLOYD, computer systems ofcl.; b. Kimberly, Wis., June 1, 1951; s. James Bernard and Julietta Ann (Lenz) B.; B.A. in Bus. Adminstrn., U. Wis., Superior, 1973. Sales rep. Burroughs Corp., 1973-74, ty. mgr., Duluth, Minn., 1974—. House father Courage House Group Home, 1974-75. Named Man of Year Alpha Xi Delta, 1973, Sigma Tau Gamma, 1972; recipient Legion of Honor, Burroughs Corp., 1975. Mem. U. Wis. Alumni Assn., Sigma Tau Gamma. Clubs: Toastmasters, Icarus Skydiving. Home: PO Box 16 Brainerd MN 56401 Office: 1118 E Superior St Duluth MN 55802

BERGERON, JULIEN ETIENNE, govt. ofcl.: b. Iroquois Falls, Ont., Can., July 3, 1930; s. Joseph Philippe and Emilia (Seguin) B.; grad. high sch.; m. Mona Page, June 13, 1953; children—Denis, Claude, Robert, Jo-Anne. Clk., treas. Twp. Mountjoy, Ont., 1951-57; mem. adminstrv. staff City Timmins, Ont., 1957—, clk.-adminstr., 1963-73, city adminstr., 1973—. Mem. Ont. Municipal Adminstrs. Assn., Internat. Inst. Municipal Clks. (certified municipal clk.), Assn. Municipalities Ont. (past exec. v.p., dir.), Internat. City Mgmt. Assn. Club: Hollinger Golf (Timmins). Home: 568 Hemlock St Timmins ON Canada Office: 220 Algonquin Blvd E Timmins ON P4N 1B3 Canada

BERGGREN, KARL FRANCIS, banker; b. Lindstrom, Minn., Aug. 14, 1918; s. Frans Elof and Jennie Matilda (Quarn) B.; student Northwestern U., 1965, 66, U. Colo., 1969, 71; m. Eleanor M. Mattson, Mar. 21, 1945; 1 son, Jay F. Salesman, Pillsbury Mills, Inc., Mpls., 1946-49; loan officer Security Loan & Thrift, Brainerd, Minn., 1949-56; with Farmers & Mchts. Bank & Trust, Watertown, S.D., 1956—, v.p., 1963—, trust officer, 1964—. Bd. mem. City Recreation Dept., Watertown, 1965-70; pres. bd. Watertown United Fund, 1965-71; bd. mem. Codington County Crippled Children, Easter Seal of Codington County; adv. bd. Aviation Mechanics Sch., Watertown, 1968—, Lake Area Vocat. Sch., Watertown, 1968—. Served with USAAF, 1941-45. Mem. Nat. Assn. Real Estate Bds., Life Underwriters Assn., S.D. Bankers Assn. (bd. mem. state trust com. 1968—), Am. Legion (post comdr. 1953). Mason (Shriner), Elk. Club: Watertown Country. Home: 1126 N Park St Watertown SD 57201 Office: 35 1st Ave NE Watertown SD 57201

BERGGREN, RONALD BERNARD, physician; b. Staten Island, N.Y., June 13, 1931; s. Bernard and Florence (Schmidt) B.; B.A., Johns Hopkins U., 1953; M.D., U. Pa., 1957; m. Mary Beth Griffith, Nov. 25, 1954; children—Karen Ann, Eric Griffith. Intern U. Pa. hosp., Phila., 1957-58, resident in surgery, plastic surgery, 19S8-63, 63-65; fellow in surgery U. Pa., 1954-65; asst. prof. surgery Ohio State U., 1965-68, asso. prof., 1968-73, prof., 1973—, dir. div. plastic surgery, 1965; dir. div. plastic surgery Children's Hosp., 1967; practice medicine specializing in plastic surgery Columbus; mem. staff Ohio State U. hosps., Children's Hosp., Columbus. Diplomate Am. Bd. Surgery, Am. Bd. Plastic Surgery. Fellow A.C.S.; mem. Central and Columbus Surg. Soc., Am. Soc. Plastic and Reconstructive Surgeons, Ohio Valley Plastic Surg. Soc., Am. Cleft Palate Assn., AMA, Am. Assn. Plastic Surgeons, Franklin County Med. Soc., Soc. Cryosurgery, Surgery of Trauma Assn., Plastic Surg. Research Council, Soc. Cryobiology, N.Y. Acad. Scis., Assn. Acad. Surgeons. Am. Burn Assn., Am. Trauma Soc., Am. Soc. Aesthetic Plastic Surgery, Am. Soc. Maxillofacial Surgeons, Phi Kappa Psi, Alpha Kappa Kappa, Sigma Xi. Home: 1960 Hampshire St Columbus OH 43221 Office: 410 10th Ave W Columbus OH 43210

BERGHOEFER, LEONARD ANTON, farm mgr.; b. Hampton, Iowa, Mar. 10, 1934; s. Edward Albert and Emma Louise (Reinking) B.; B.S., Colo. State U., 1961. Partner, Berghoefer Livestock & Grain Co., Hampton, Iowa. 1962—, mgr., 1962—; founder, pres., chmn. bd. Franklin County Land Co. Inc., 1964—. Mem. Farm Bur., County Beef Producers, Iowa Cattleman's Assn. Lutheran. Home: Rt 4 Box 48 Hampton IA 50441 Office: Rt 3 Hampton IA 50441

BERGHUIS, MELVIN EARL, educator; b. Clara City, Minn., Oct. 19, 1915; s. Jacob Peter and Johanna Elizabeth (Nieuwenhuis) B.; student Northwestern Jr. Coll., 1932-33; A.B., Calvin Coll., 1936; M.A., U. Mich., 1949; Ph.D., Mich. State U., 1964; m. Barbara Jane Heetderks, Sept. 20, 1940; children—Robert Earl, Jane Berghuis Hull, David Melvin. Tchr., prin. Allendale (Mich.) Christian Schs., 1937-39; tchr. Baxter (Mich.) Christian Jr. High Sch., 1939-41, Chgo. Christian High Sch., 1941-45, Grand Rapids (Mich.) Christian High Sch., 1946-48; asst. prof. speech Calvin Coll., Grand Rapids, 1948-57, registrar, 1958-61, dir. student acad. services; 1961-64, v.p. for student affairs, 1964-71, prof. speech, 1971—, chmn. dept. speech, 1952-69, instr. Mich. State U., East Lansing, 1957-58. Pres. met. Grand Rapids Adult Edn. Council, 1959; mem. adv. com. Mich. Scholarship Program, 1964-71; mem. scholarship com. Grand Rapids Found., 1967-71. Served with USN, 1945-46. Mem. Speech Communication Assn., Central States, Mich. speech assns., Mich. Intercoll. Speech League (treas. 1950-54, pres. 1960-61), Mich. Assn. Coll. Registrars and Admissions Officers (v.p. 1966-69), Nat. Union Christian Schs. Mem. Christian Ref. Ch. (elder 1952-54, 61, 64-67). Home: 1718 Radcliff Ave SE Grand Rapids MI 49506

BERGIA, ROGER MERLE, ednl. adminstr.; b. Peoria, Ill., Nov. 26, 1937; s. Merle Frederick and Doris Ann (Markham) B.; B.A., Eureka Coll., 1960; M.A., Bradley U., 1967, postgrad., 1968—; m. Valerie Jean Lane, Oct. 16, 1960; children—Lori, Amy, Beth. Tchr., coach Jr. High Sch., Peoria Heights Sch., 1960-65; prin., Kelly Ave. Grade Sch., Peoria Heights, Ill., 1965-74; supt. Peoria Heights Schs., 1974—. Mem. exec. com. W.D. Boyce council Boy Scouts Am. Mem. Phi Delta Kappa, Lambda Chi Alpha. Republican. Presbyterian. Home: 6723 N Gem Ct Peoria IL 61614 Office: 1316 E Kelly Ave Peoria Heights IL 61614

BERGLAND, BOB SELMER, sec. agr.; b. Roseau, Minn.. July 22, 1928; s. Selmer Bennett and Mabel (Evans) B.; Sears Roebuck scholar U. Minn., 1946-48; m. Helen Elaine Grohn, June 24, 1950; children—Dianne, Linda, Stevan, Jon, Allan, Billy, Franklyn. Field rep. Minn. Farmers Union, 1948-50; farmer, 1950—; mem. 93d-94th Congresses from 7th Dist. Minn.; sec. agr., 1977—. Sec. Roseau County Democratic Farmer-Labor Party, Minn., 1951-52, chmn., 1953-54; chmn. Minn. Agr. Stblzn. and Conservation Service Com., Dept. Agr., 1961-62; dir. Midwest Area Agr. Stblzn. and Conservation Service, 1963-68; candidate U.S. Ho. of Reps., 1968. Recipient Gold Letter award U. Minn. Mem. Minn. Farmers Union, Nat. Farmers Orgn. Lutheran. Mason, Lion, Eagle. Address: Route 3 Roseau MN 56751

BERGMAN, ALBERT SOLOMON, watchmaker, musician; b. Chgo., Aug. 7, 1920; s. Marcus and Eva (Bzura) B.; student Chgo. Sch. Watchmaking, 1949; m. Janet Louise Marx, June 15, 1947; children—Shelley, Gary, Dana. Watchmaker Waltham Watch Co., Chgo., 1952—. Violinist Chgo. Civic Orch., 1941—, Nat. Youth Adminstrn. Orch., 1941-42, New Orleans Symphony, 1946-47. Served with AUS, 1942-45. Mem. Chgo. Fedn. Musicians, Am. Radio Relay League. Home: 1817 GW Hood Ave Chicago IL 60660 Office: Waltham Watch Co 400 S Jefferson St Chicago IL 60606

BERGMAN, ROBERT SCRIBNER, toy co. exec.; b. Aurora, Ill., Nov. 23, 1934; s. Ross M. and Mary O. (Ochsenschlager) B.; B.S., Ill. Inst. Tech., 1956; postgrad., Stanford U., 1956-58; m. Patricia LeBaron, June 10, 1956; children—David C., Lynne M., Joseph R. With Hughes Aircraft Co., Culver City, Calif., 1956, Gen. Electric Co., Palo Alto, Calif., 1957, Sylvania, Mountain View, Calif., 1958-61; with Processed Plastics, Montgomery, Ill., 1961—, pres., 1969—; pres. Bergman Mfg. & Trading, Montgomery, 1962—; v.p. Moldrite Plastic and Engrng., Montgomery, 1962—, Moldrite Tool and Die, Addison, Ill., 1965—; treas. Intertoy, Montgomery, 1977—, Graphic Label Co., Oswego, Ill., 1977—; dir. David Lipman Ltd., Leeds, Yorkshire, Eng., 1977—. Mem. Am. Phys. Soc., Toy Mfrs. Am. Republican. Ch. of Christ. Club: Elks. Home: 1330 Monoa Ave Aurora IL 60506 Office: 1001 Aucutt Rd Montgomery IL 60538

BERGMAN, ROY THOMAS, surgeon; b. Cassopolis, Mich., Dec. 20, 1935; s. Roy Edwin and Lois (Townsend) B.; B.S. with high honors, Mich. State U., 1957, D.V.M. with high honors, 1959; M.D., Northwestern U., 1964; m. Sally Jo Proshwitz, June 28, 1958; children—Roy T., Amy Lynn, Samara Edlyn. Rotating intern Evanston (Ill.) Hosp. Assn., 1964-65, resident in gen. surgery, 1967-71; Am. Cancer Soc. clin. fellow in oncological surgery Northwestern U., Chgo., 1970-71; practice medicine specializing in gen. surgery and oncology, Escanaba, Mich., 1972; mem. staff St. Francis Hosp., Escanaba, 1972—, chmn. tumor bd., 1972—, also chief of staff; instr. surgery U. So. Calif. Med. Center, Los Angeles, 1972-73; asst. prof. surgery Mich. State U. Coll. Human Medicine, East Lansing, 1974—, also surg. coordinator Upper Peninsula med. edn. program. Served to capt. M.C., U.S. Army, 1965-67. Diplomate Am. Bd. Surgery. Fellow A.C.S. (local chmn. com. trauma), Alpha Omega Alpha. Office: Doctors Park Escanaba MI 49829

BERGMANN, WINOGENE LOUISE, library adminstr.; b. Milw.; d. William and Helen (Buck) Bergmann; B.A., Milw.-Downer Coll., 1931; certificate in econs. Univ. Coll., Exeter, Eng., 1931; M.S. in Library Sci., Columbia U., 1952; postgrad. U. Wis., Milw., 1956—. Sch. librarian Juneau High Sch., Milw., 1932-56; coordinator library services Milw. Pub. Schs., 1956—. Pres. Inter-Group Council, Milw., 1965-66; mem. Mayor's Beautification Com., Milw., 1966—, vice chmn., 1970. Mem. ALA, AAUW, Wis. Library Assn., Library Council Met. Milw. (pres. 1975—), Assn. Supervision and Curriculum Devel., Internat. Platform Assn., Wis. Audio-Visual Assn., Assn. for Ednl. Communications and Tech., Nat. Assn. Female Execs., Wis. Assn. Suprs. and Curriculum Devel., Delta Kappa Gamma. Club: Zonta. Contbr. articles to publs. Home: 709 E Juneau Ave Milwaukee WI 53202 Office: 5225 W Vliet St Milwaukee WI 53208

BERGQUIST, RICHARD ROBERT, plant pathologist; b. Turtle Lake, N.D., July 31, 1939; s. Ernest Oscar and Florence Josephine (Backman) B.; B.S., N.D. State U., 1961, M.S., 1966; Ph.D., Cornell U., 1970; m. Patricia Ann Cassidy, Aug. 8, 1964; children—Mara Lyn, Shawn Michael, Kami Mari, Ian Paul, Ty Richard, Inga Ann. Plant pathologist Hawaii Agrl. Expt. Sta., U. Hawaii, Honolulu, 1970-74; plant pathologist Pfister Hybrid Corn Co., El Paso, Ill., 1974—. Agrl. cons. on tropical diseases of corn and sorghum. Served with AUS, 1964-66. Mem. Mycol. Soc. Am., Crop Sci. Soc. Am., Phytopath. Soc. Am. Sigma Xi, Alpha Gamma Rho, Blue Key. Contbr. articles to profl. jours. Home: 401 E 6th St El Paso IL 61738 Office: Pfister Hybrid Corn Co El Paso IL 61738

BERGREN, ORVILLE VERNON, assn. exec.; b. Mpls., Nov. 5, 1918; s. Axel Martin and Norah Marie (Lager) B.; B.S.C., U. N.D., 1940; J.D., George Washington U., 1949; m. Caroline Regina Braun, Aug. 14, 1943; children—Stephen B., Scott O., Susan C. Commd. 2d lt. USMC, 1940, advanced through grades to col., 1957; inf. command and legal assignments; Congl. liaison for Sec. of Def., 1957-60; ret., 1960; asst. to exec. v.p. A.O. Smith Corp., Milw., 1960-62; v.p. ops. A.O. Smith Harvestore Products Inc., Arlington Heights, Ill., 1962-65; sec. Ill. Mfrs. Assn., Chgo., 1965-72, exec. v.p., 1972-74, pres., 1974—. Chmn. Conf. of State Mfrs. Assns., 1974-75. Decorated Legion of Merit, Bronze Star. Mem. Order Coif, Alpha Tau Omega. Methodist. Clubs: Chicago, Economic, Union League, Executives, Biltmore Country. Home: 251 Woodland Dr Barrington IL 60010 Office: 135 S LaSalle St Chicago IL 60603

BERGSMA, RALPH THOMAS, architect, real estate devel. co. exec.; b. Detroit, June 3, 1931; s. Ralph Robert and Edna Faye (Lowery) B.; B.S., Mich. State U., 1953; B.A. in Architecture, U. Mich., 1959; m. Lynda Jane Leaver, Jan. 30, 1954; children—Kirk Randall, Brian Keith, Eric Ross. Project dir. Smith, Hinchman & Grylls Assos., Detroit, 1958-64; partner Johnson, Johnson & Roy, Inc., Ann Arbor, Mich., 1964-69; pres. Property Devel. Group, Inc., Ann Arbor, 1969—. Asst. prof. dept. landscape architecture U. Mich., 1964-67. Served to 1st lt. USAF, 1953-55. Registered architect, landscape architect. Mem. AIA, Mich. Soc. Architects (treas. 1968-69), C. of C., Soc. Coll. and Univ. Planning (charter mem.), Nat. Council Archtl. Registration Bds., U.S. Power Squadron. Home: 622 Washington St Traverse City MI 49684 Office: PO Box 1266 Traverse City MI 49684

BERGSMA, THOMAS ROBERT, marketing exec.; b. Des Moines, Apr. 27, 1945; s. Robert Thomas and Dolores Emma (Fischer) B.; B.S. in Bus. Adminstrn., Drake U., 1970; M.B.A., Loyola U., Chgo., 1977; m. Dixie Ann Overton, May 20, 1967; children—Brenda Kristine, Lisa Cathleen. Programmer analyst, asst. sec. to nat. subcom. Electronic Funds Transfer System, Fed. Res. Bank Chgo., 1970-72; sr. marketing rep. Honeywell, Inc., Des Moines, 1972-74; marketing dir. IMPACT Services div. Pioneer Hibred Internat., Inc., Des Moines, 1974—; owner Midwest Computer Store. Former deacon, now trustee auditor Highland Park Lutheran Ch. Served with USNR, 1966-68; Vietnam. Mem. Data Processing Mgmt. Assn. Democrat. Home: 115 NW 7th Pl Grimes IA 50111 Office: 7200 NW 62d Ave Des Moines IA 50322

BERGSTEIN, STANLEY FRANCIS, harness racing exec.; b. Pottsville, Pa., June 19, 1924; s. Milton I. and Esther (Rosenzweig) B.; student Northwestern U., 1941-42, Medill Sch. Journalism, 1946-47; m. June Carol Hanna, June 4, 1950; children—Alfred, Lisa. Account exec. Jame S. Kearns Assos. publicity, Chgo., 1946-48; columnist Daily Racing Form, 1948-49; announcer Harlem Globetrotters basketball, 1948-54; race announcer Chicago, Detroit and Boston harness tracks, 1949-60; pub. Chgo. Trotter, 1954-57; writer, CBS-TV, Chgo., 1957; racing sec. Sportsman's Park, Chgo., 1958-61; exec. sec. Harness Tracks of Am., Chgo., 1961—; exec. dir. Harness Racing Inst., 1961—; v.p., publicity pub. relations U.S. Trotting Assn., 1968-75; chmn. editorial bd., exec. editor Hoofbeats mag., 1968-75; mem. Am. Horse Council Racing Advisory Com. TV and radio sports announcing Chgo., Los Angeles, N.Y.C. and Detroit, 1950—; pres. Am. Horse Pubs., 1971-72. Bd. dirs. Grayson Found. Served with AUS, 1942-45. Decorated Bronze Star. Mem. U.S. Harness Writers Assn., AFTRA, Sigma Delta Chi. Club: Chicago Press. Home: 727 Cleveland Rd Hinsdale IL 60521 Office: 333 N Michigan Ave Chicago IL 60601

BERGSTROM, RICHARD NORMAN, civil engr.; b. Chgo., Dec. 11, 1921; s. Carl William and Ellen Amanda Victoria (Anderson) B.; B.S. in C.E., Ill. Inst. Tech.. 1942, M.S., 1952; m. Patricia Ann Chessman, Apr. 19, 1947; children—George Norman, James Donald. Laura Ann, Martha Jean. Design engr. Carnegie Ill. Steel Corp.. Gary. Ind., 1942; structural engr. Sargent & Lundy, Engrs.. Chgo., 1946-56, asso.. 1956, partner, 1966—, mgr. tech. services dept., 1977—. Mem. nuclear standards mgmt. bd. Am. Nat. Standards Insf., 1975—. Stated clk. Presby. Ch. of Barrington (Ill.), 1975-76. Served to lt., USNR, 1942-46. Decorated Purple Heart. Registered profl. engr., Ark., Calif., Colo., Ill., Ind., Iowa, Ky., La., Mich., N.Y., Ohio, Okla., S.C., Tenn., Tex., Wis. Fellow Am. Soc. C.E., Am. Cons. Engrs. Council; mem. Am. Nuclear Soc., ASME, Am. Concrete Inst., Am. Inst. Steel Constrn., Western Soc. Engrs., Ill. Cons. Engrs. Council. Presbyn. Clubs: Union League, Barrington Hills Country, Desert Forest Golf, Monroe, Meadow, Poplar Creek Racquet. Contbr. articles in field to profl. jours. Home: 274 Leeds Dr Barrington Hills IL 60010 Office: 55 E Monroe St Chicago IL 60603

BERGWALL, WARREN LUND, physician; b. Jamestown, N.Y., Feb. 7, 1921; s. Anders Elof and Alice Hildergard (Lund) B.; A.B., Taylor U., 1947; M.D., Ind. U., 1951; m. Miriam June Pugh, June 3, 1944; children—Sue Ann, Scott Alan. Intern Indpls. Gen. Hosp., 1951-52; practice medicine, specializing in gen. practice, Denmark, Wis., 1953-55, Muncie, Ind., 1955—; mem. staff Ball Meml. Hosp., Muncie; indsl. physician Marhoefers Packing Co., Muncie, 1961—; coroner Delaware County, 1957-61. Bd. trustees Muncie Sch. Bd., 1964-68. Del. state Republican conv., 1956—. Served to 1st lt. USAAC, 1943-46. Diplomate Am. Bd. Family Practice (charter mem.). Mem. Am., Ind. med. assns., Delaware-Blackford County Med. Soc., Am., Ind. acads. gen. practice, Indsl. Med. Assn., Am. Acad. Psychosomatic Medicine. Kiwanian. Home: 2708 W Burnell Dr Muncie IN 47304 Office: 3111 W Jackson St Muncie IN 47303

BERHOW, JOHN LEWIS, hosp. adminstr.; b. Mason City, Iowa, July 22, 1935; s. Sophes Harold and Javerna Caroline (Kalsem) B.; student St. Olaf Coll., 1953-54, Drake U., 1954-55; certificate health care facilities adminstrn. U. Cal. at Santa Barbara, 1968-69; m. Lena Delores Howell, Oct. 26, 1955; children—John Lewis, Bruce Wayne. Bus. mgr. Mercy Hosp., Des Moines, 1965-67; asst. adminstr. Mary Greeley Meml. Hosp., Ames, Iowa, 1967-69; adminstr. Floyd County Meml. Hosp., Charles City, 1969-72, Community Gen. Hosp., Sterling, Ill., 1972-75; exec. dir. North Iowa Med. Center, Mason City, 1975—. Mem. Floyd County (Iowa) Rep. Central Com., 1969-72. Bd. dirs. Charles City (Iowa) YMCA, 1971. Served with AUS, 1956. Mem. Am. Acad. Med. Adminstrs. Elk, Rotarian (dir. 1969-72). Home: 2700 North Shore Dr Clear Lake IA 50428 Office: 102 N Washington St Mason City IA 50401

BERK, BURTON BENJAMIN, optometrist; b. Cleve., Jan. 31, 1930; s. Benjamin C. and Ruth S. (Hirsohn) B.; B.S. in Optometry, Ohio State U., 1953; m. Margery A. Rocco, June 17, 1951; children—Deborah L., Bruce C., Michael S., Lawrence R. Practice optometry, Columbus, O., 1953—. Instr. optometry Ohio State U., 1967—. Dir. Corporate Futures, Rochester, N.Y.; sec. Ohio Profl. Investment Corp., 1968—. Pres. Ohio State Bd. Optometry, 1972—. Mem. Nat. Eye Research Found., Optometric Extension Found., Inc., Ohio Vision Service, Better Vision Inst., Vision League of Ohio. Fellow Am. Acad. Optometry; mem. Central Ohio, Ohio, Am. optometric assns., Phi Sigma Delta. Republican. Mem. B'nai B'rith. Clubs: Whitehall Lions, Presidents of Ohio State U. Home: 2775 Brentwood Rd Columbus OH 43209 Office: 5180 E Main St Columbus OH 43213

BERK, JAMES EDWARD, appliance co. exec.; b. Queens, N.Y., Sept. 26, 1945; s. Francis A. and Florence (Jacques) B.; B.B.A., Baruch Coll., Coll. City N.Y., 1969; M.B.A., U. City N.Y., 1972; m. Mary Ann Kelley, Nov. 6, 1965; children—Kimberly Ann, James Joseph. Nat. product mgr. Garland div. Welbilt Corp., Maspeth, N.Y., 1964-71; mktg. mgr. Micro Electronic Products, Inc., Maspeth, 1971-73; v.p. Greenville Products Corp., subs. White Consol. Industries, Greenville, Mich., 1973—; educator, speaker in field. Recipient certificate of achievement N.Y.C.'s Mayor's Com., 1963. Mem. Am. Mktg. Assn., Nat. Mgmt. Assn., W. Mich. Health Systems Agency. Republican. Roman Catholic. Club: East Hills Tennis and Racquet. Home: 491 Prestwick St SE Grand Rapids MI 49506 Office: 635 W Charles St Greenville MI 48838

BERK, WILLIAM LEO, sanitary engr.; b. Dayton, Ohio, Nov. 30, 1923; s. Leo Edward and Gladys (Smith) Berk; m. Dorothy Ethel Turnbull, Oct. 21, 1950. B.C.E., U. Notre Dame, 1947; M.C.E., U. Minn., 1950. Design engr. Greeley & Hansen, Cons. Engrs., Chgo., 1947-49; san. engr. Am. Well Works, Aurora, Ill., 1952-55; asst. mgr. sewage treatment dept. Yeoman Bros., Melrose Park, Ill., 1955-61; v.p. Lakeside Equipment Corp., Bartlett, Ill., 1961—; partner Seeger & Berk, San. Consultants, Aurora, Ill., 1953-57. Sec., Aurora Y's Men's Club, 1953, pres., 1954, mem. bldg. com., 1955. Registered profl. engr.. Ill. Mem. Water Pollution Control Fedn., Am. Water Works Assn., Nat., Ill. socs. profl. engrs., Retired Officers Assn. Contbr. articles to tech. jours. Patentee in field. Home: 1204 W Lonnquist Blvd Mount Prospect IL 60056 Office: 1022 E Devon Ave Bartlett IL 60103

BERKBUEGLER, JOHN WILLIAM, med. record adminstr.; b. Apple Creek, Mo., Nov. 2, 1936; s. August W. and Ida Christine (Kirn) B.; student Maryhurst Normal, 1954-56; A.A., Donnelly Jr. Coll., 1964; B.S. in Med. Records Adminstrn., Southwestern Okla. U., Weatherford, 1970; M.Ed., Central Mich. U.; 1 son, John William. Asst. dir. St. Mary's Hosp., Kansas City, Mo., 1959-60, Providence Hosp., Kansas City, Kans., 1960-61; dir. med. record services St. Margaret Hosp., Kansas City, Kans., 1961-64, St. Francis Hosp., Tulsa, 1964-68, St. Anthony Hosp., Oklahoma City, 1968-70; dir., asst. prof. med. records adminstrn. program Ill. State U., Normal, 1970-73, also mem. pres.'s task force on instructional media and tech. dir. med. records Galesburg (Ill.) Cottage Hosp., 1973-74, Columbus-Cuneo-Cabrini Med. Center, Chgo., 1974-76; dir., asst. prof. health data systems U. Wis.-Milw., 1976—; instr. med. terminology Avila Coll., Kansas City, Mo., 1962-63; cons. med. record adminstr. hosps., Mo., Kans., Okla., Ill., Iowa; cons. med. records acad. programs, Okla., Ala., Ill. Mem. bd. edn. St. Eugene Parish, Oklahoma City. Mem. Am., Okla. (past pres.), Ill. (past pres.) med. record assns., Okla. Soc. Tumor Registry Secs. (past pres.). Contbr. articles in field to profl. jours. Home: 4122 N Stowell Ave Shorewood WI 53211 Office: Sch Allied Health Professions U Wis-Milw Milwaukee WI 53201

BERKE, JOSEPH JEROLD, surgeon; b. Detroit, June 22, 1933; s. Sydney S. and Dorothy (Eskay) B.; B.S., U. Mich., 1953, M.D., 1957, M.S. in Anatomy, 1957, Ph.D. in Anatomy, 1958; m. Pauline Masse, Dec. 11, 1966; children—Richard, Rachel, Jason. Intern Phila. Gen. Hosp., 1958-59; Mayo Found. fellow, 1959-64; resident Mayo Clinic, Rochester, Minn., 1959-64; practice medicine specializing in neurosurgery, Rochester, 1959-64, Detroit, 1964—; chief dept. neurosurgery Evang. Deaconess Hosp., Detroit, 1967—; chief dept. neurosurgery N. Detroit Gen. Hosp., 1967—, dir. neurophysiology, 1974—; cons. to Alexander Blain Hosp., Doctors Hosp., Lakeside Gen. Hosp., Sinai Hosp. Diplomate Am. Bd. Neurol. Surgery, Am. Bd. Nuclear Medicine. Fellow A.C.S., Internat. Coll. Surgeons; mem. AMA, Mich., Wayne County med. socs., Am. Coll. Nuclear Medicine, Congress Neurol. Surgeons (registration com. 1970-73),

Am. EEG Soc., Detroit Surg. Soc., Mich. Acad. Sci. Arts and Letters. Home: 1535 Island Ln Bloomfield Hills MI 48013 Office: 3333 E Jefferson St Detroit MI 48207

BERKEBILE, DALE EUGENE, orthopedic surgeon; b. Chgo., Feb. 18, 1935; s. Dale Eugene and Elizabeth Jane (Cook) B.; A.B., DePauw U., 1957; M.S., U. Ind., 1958, M.D., 1962; m. Mary Carroll Jordan, Aug. 25, 1957; children—Charles Jordan, Mary Susan, Sarah Elizabeth. Intern, U. Wis. Hosps., Madison, 1962-63, resident in orthopedic surgery, 1964-66, 68-69; resident in gen. surgery St. Joseph Hosp., Marshfield, Wis., 1963-64; practice medicine specializing in orthopedic surgery, Rapid City, S.D., 1969—; orthopedic surgeon staff Rapid City Regional Hosps., Ft. Meade (S.D.) VA Hosp., 1969—. Served with M.C., U.S. Army, 1966-68. Diplomate Am. Bd. Orthopedic Surgeons. Fellow A.C.S., Am. Acad. Orthopedic Surgeons (bd. councilors). Methodist. Home: 1717 West Blvd Rapid City SD 57701 Office: 725 Meade St Rapid City SD 57701

BERKLEY, ELIOT S., council exec.; b. Kansas City, Mo., Oct. 12, 1924; s. Walter J. and Erni (Stulz) Berkowitz; B.A., Harvard U., 1947; M.A., Princeton U., 1949, Ph.D., 1952; m. Marcia Russell, June 28, 1958; children—Emily, Eliot A. Lectr. in history and govt. U. Kansas City, 1952-59; asst. to dir. Greater Kansas City Adult Edn. Assn., 1954; admissions counsellor U. Kansas City, 1954; exec. dir. Internat. Relations Council, Kansas City, 1955-60; instr. social sci. Kansas City Art Inst. and Sch. Design, 1956-59, dean adminstrn., 1959-60, v.p. devel., 1960-61, coll. dean, 1961-65; asst. to dir., cons. Fulbright Orientation Center, U. Minn., 1967; exec. dir. Internat. Relations Council, 1965—; dir. Kansas City Assembly on U.S. and Eastern Europe, 1968, on Uses of Seas, 1969; lectr. Baker U.-So. Meth. U., 1976; advisory bd. Kansas City Regional Council Higher Edn., 1977—; mem. Am. Council Germany. Hon. bd. dirs. Rockhurst Coll.; chmn. Kansas City chpt. Am. Jewish Com., 1966-68; bd. dirs. Jewish Vocat. Service Kansas City, 1964-73, 76—; chmn. Mayor's UN Day Com., 1968; bd. dirs. Nat. Council Community World Affairs Orgn.; chmn. faculty devel. grants com. Kansas City Regional Council Higher Edn., 1963-65; mem. Mid-continent adv. bd. of Speaker Services for UN; mem. exec. com., bd. trustees Conservatory Music Kansas City, 1958-59; bd. dirs. Urban League Kansas City, 1956-59, People to People Council Greater Kansas City, 1961-64, Kansas City Civil Liberties Union, 1961-73, Westport Coop. Mission, Planned Parenthood Western Mo.-Kans., 1974-76; chmn. Com. Internat. Visitors and Students Greater Kansas City, 1966-69; regional vice-chairman U.S. Com. UN, 1962-64; citizens adv. com. Met. Jr. Coll. Kansas City, 1967-69; mem. Chancellor's advisory council Met. Community Colls., Kansas City, Mo., 1977—; sec. Tension Envelope Found. Served with AUS, 1943-46. Named Kansas City World Citizen of Year, 1975. Mem. Midwest Polit. Sci. Assn., Internat. Studies Assn., Friends of Art, Acad. Polit. Sci., Am. Soc. Internat. Law, Am., Mo. polit. sci. assns., Mo. Assn. Social Welfare (2d vice chmn. Kansas City sect. 1974-76), Am. Fgn. Service Assn., Soc. Citizens Edn. World Affairs. Clubs: Harvard, Princeton (Kansas City). Home: 1014 W 63d St Kansas City MO 64113 Office: Internat Relations Council 210 Westport Rd Kansas City MO 64111

BERKO, MARTIN JOSEPH, psychologist; b. Cleve., Nov. 29, 1925; s. Arthur Eugene and Alice (Gelberger) B.; B.S., Case Western Res. U., 1948; M.A., Wichita State U., 1951; Ph.D., Cornell U., 1965. Psychologist, Inst. Logopedics, Wichita, Kans., 1949-62; USPHS research fellow Cornell U., 1963-65, sr. research asso., 1966-73; dir. Berko Cons. Services, Kettering, Ohio, 1974—. Advisor to tech. assistance program City of Kettering; bd. dirs. Dayton Vocat. Services Inst. Recipient grants United Cerebral Palsy Assn., Office Naval Research; Pioneer Service award United Cerebral Palsy, 1968. Mem. Am. Psychol. Assn., AAAS (resource adv. group, project on handicapped in sci.), Internat. Soc. Cybernetic Medicine, Profl. Workers in Rehab., N.Y. Acad. Scis., Sigma Xi, Phi Kappa Phi, Delta Epsilon. Author: Speech Therapy in Cerebral Palsy, 1960; Communication Training in Childhood Brain Damage, 1966; Management of Brain Damaged Children, 1970. Contbr. articles to profl. jours. Home and Office: 501 Moss Oak Dr Kettering OH 45429

BERKOWITZ, HERBERT M., retail trade cons.; b. Omaha, Oct. 27, 1913; s. Jacob and Rose (Schonberger) B.; student Creighton U., 1932-35; m. Nicole Allard, 1972. With Hinky Dinky Supermarkets, 1931-70, v.p., sales mgr., 1962-68, pres. Leased Dept. div., 1968-70, co. acquired by J.C. Penney Co., 1970; sr. v.p. Supermarkets Interstate div. J.C. Penney Co., Omaha, 1970-77; cons. retail merchandising, 1977—. Served with AUS, 1942-45. Decorated Bronze Star, Silver Star. Mem. Am. Legion, Supermarket Inst., Topco Assos., Omaha C. of C. Mem. B'nai B'rith. Club: Field (Omaha). Home: 8405 Indian Hills Dr Omaha NE 68114 Office: 8990 W Dodge Rd Suite 211 Omaha NE 68114

BERLACHER, FRANZ JOSEPH, physician; b. Toledo, Dec. 18, 1928; s. Franz Joseph and Theresa Marie (Domalski) B.; student Notre Dame, 1945-47; B.S., U. Chgo., 1949, M.D., 1951; m. Audrey Elizabeth Boicey, Jan. 6, 1951; children—Paul, Deborah, Robert, Laura, Mark, Gregory, Gretchen. Intern, Henry Ford Hosp., Detroit, 1951-52, resident, 1952-54, fellow in cardiology, 1956-57; practice medicine specializing in cardiology and internal medicine, Sylvania, Ohio, 1958—; dir. cardiology Mercy Hosp., 1965—; chief coronary care unit, 1967—; asst. clin. prof. medicine Med. Coll. Ohio, 1975—. Served with U.S. Army, 1955-56. Diplomate Am. Bd. Internal Medicine (cardiovascular subsplty.). Fellow Am. Coll. Cardiology, A.C.P., Am. Soc. Internal Medicine. Roman Catholic. Club: Toledo Athletic. Home: 29 Meadow Ln Toledo OH 43623 Office: 5600 Monroe St Sylvania OH 43560

BERLAND, THEODORE, author; b. Chgo., Mar. 26, 1929; s. Samuel and Lena (Siegel) B.; B.S. in Journalism, U. Ill., 1950; A.M. in Sociology, U. Chgo., 1972; m. Cynthia Rich, Dec. 23, 1956; children—Leslie Myra, Elizabeth Ann, David Rueben. Gen. assignment reporter, wire editor Champaign-Urbana (Ill.) Courier, 1950-51; sci. writer Michael Reese Hosp., Chgo., 1955-56, 66—; sci. writer, editor Research Reports, U. Chgo. pub. relations office, 1956-59; free lance writer, Chgo., 1959—; partner Pub. Relations Group, 1975—; fgn. corr. Chgo.'s American, Algiers, 1962, Chgo. Daily News, Antarctica, 1963, AMA News, Rotarian Mag., Caribbean, 1965; cons. EPA, 1971—; instr. sci. writing Medill Sch. Journalism, Northwestern U., 1973, 75; instr. nutrition Columbia Coll., 1977. Pres. North Town Community Council, 1970-73, also Citizens Against Noise; pres. dist. 2 edn. council Chgo. Bd. Edn., 1972-73; dir. Camp Chi; v.p. Bernard Horwich Jewish Community Center, 1970-75, pres., 1975-77; pres. Jewish Community Council West Rogers Park, 1975-76; bd. dirs. Ind. Voters Ill., 1974-75, Citizens Schs. Com., 1974-75. Recipient Journalism award Am. Osteo. Assn., 1963; certificate of Recognition med. journalism awards contests AMA, 1964, 66; 8th prize U.S. sect. Internat. Honeywell/Asahi Pentax Photo Contest, 1965; Med. Journalism award Ill. Med. Soc., 1967; Sci. Writers award ADA, 1968, 69; Distinguished Service in Journalism award Am. Optometric Assn., 1973; Distinguished Achievement in Med. Writing award Chgo. chpt. Am. Med. Writers Assn., 1973; Beth Fonda award for excellence in Med. feature writing, 1975. Fellow Am. Med. Writers Assn. (chmn. freelance directory 1974-77); mem. Headline Club Chgo. (treas. 1972-73), Overseas Press Club, Chgo. Press Club, Authors Guild, Nat. Assn. Sci. Writers (chmn. freelance com.), Am. Soc. Authors and Journalists, Soc. Midland Authors (pres. 1975—), Women in Communication, Soc. Profl. Journalists, Chgo. Nutrition Soc. Author: The Scientific Life, 1962; (with Alfred E. Seyler) Your Children's Teeth, 1968; The Fight for Quiet, 1970; (with Mitchell Spellberg) Living with Your Ulcer, 1971; (with Robert Addison) Living with Your Bad Back, 1972; (with Gordon Snider) Living with Your Bronchitis and Emphysema, 1972; (with Richard Perritt) Living with Your Eye Operation, 1973; Rating the Diets, 1974, rev. edits. 1975, 76, 77, 78; (with Leslie Sandlow and Richard Shapiro) Living with Your Colitis and Hemorrhoids and Related Disorders, 1976; (with Frank Z. Warren) Acupuncture Diet, 1976; contbg. author: Stimulus, 1960; Perspectives on Living, 1962; Compact Handbook of College Composition (Maynard J. Brennan), 1964; A Treasury of Tips for Writers, 1965; Great Ideas Today, 1966; World Book Year Book, 1970; Crisis of Survival, 1970; Writing the Magazine Article, 1971; Readings in Health, 1972; The Endangered Environment (Ashley Montagu), 1974; Current Thinking and Writing, 1976; Together, 1977; contbr. over 200 articles to major mags. including Parade, Better Homes and Gardens, Saturday Evening Post, TV Guide, Woman's Day, Family Circle, Today's Health, Family Health, Reader's Digest, Redbook, Humanitas, New Eng. Jour. Medicine, others; author column The Thin Man, Chgo. Daily News, also numerous newspapers through United Feature Syndicate and Enterprise Sci. Service; author documentary movies. Home: PO Box 59170 Chicago IL 60659

BERLIN, RAYMOND, dentist; b. Birmingham, Ala., July 28, 1931; s. Max S. and Minnie (Summers) B.; B.S., U. Ala., 1952, D.M.D., 1956; certificate prosthodontics Loyola U., 1976; m. Silvia Pulin, June 30, 1957; children—Gerald, Donna, Marcia, Alan. Intern, USPHS Hosp., Chgo., 1956-57; sr. asst. dental surgeon USPHS Hosp., Chgo., 1957-59; practice dentistry Tinley Park, Ill., 1959-67, Park Forest, Ill., 1967-77, Olympia Fields, Ill., 1977—; clin. asst. prof. Loyola Sch. Dentistry, Maywood, Ill., 1964—. Mem. Chgo. Dental Soc. (pres. South Suburban br. 1971-72), Internat. Acad. Gnathology, Am. Equilibration Soc., Acad. Gen. Dentistry, Northeastern Gnathological Soc. Phi Beta Kappa, Omicron Kappa Upsilon, Omicron Delta Kappa. Home: 3014 Polly Ln Flossmoor IL 60422 Office: 5 Plaza St Park Forest IL 60466

BERMAN, HERBERT MARTIN, lawyer; b. Louisville, Mar. 22, 1936; s. Robert J. and Freda (Baer) B.; B.A., Ind. U., 1958; LL.B., U. Louisville, 1961; m. Sondra Ann Ignatow, Dec. 21, 1958; children—Michael, Frances, Jennifer. Admitted to Ky. bar, 1961, Ill. bar, 1971; asso. firm Shaikun & Helmann, Louisville, 1961-62; field atty. NLRB, Cin., 1962-63; asst. gen. counsel Internat. Brewery Workers Union, Cin., 1963-68; labor relations counselor Brunswick Corp., Chgo., 1968-70; asso. firm Lederer, Fox & Grove, Chgo., 1970-73; partner firm Arnold & Kadjan, Chgo., 1973-76; pres., partner firm Berman & Landrum Ltd., Chgo., 1976—. Mem. Am. Arbitration Assn. (panel), Am. Bar Assn., Soc. Profls. in Dispute Resolution. Home: 244 Willow Ave Deerfield IL 60015 Office: 180 N LaSalle St Chicago IL 60601

BERMAN, REUBEN, physician; b. Mpls., Feb. 8, 1908; s. Alexander M. and Sarah R. (Cohen) B.; B.A. summa cum laude, U. Minn.. 1929, M.B., 1932, M.D., 1933; m. Isabel Rosenstein, July 26, 1931; children—David, Elizabeth, Samuel, Ruth, Theodore, Jean. Intern, Mpls. Gen. Hosp., 1932-33, resident in cardiology, 1934-37; practice medicine specializing in cardiology, Mpls., 1937—; mem. med. staff Mt. Sinai Hosp., 1951—, dir. med. edn., 1974-77; faculty U. Minn., 1933—, clin. prof. medicine emeritus, 1976—. Served with M.C., U.S. Army, 1940-45; ETO. Decorated Bronze Star medal; Croix de Guerre; recipient Harold S. Diehl award U. Minn. 1975, Bolles Rogers Bowl award Hennepin County Med. Soc., 1977. Fellow A.C.P., Am. Coll. Cardiology; mem. Am. Heart Assn. (past pres. Minn. affiliate), Mpls. Soc. Internal Medicine, Minn. Med. Assn. (Pres.'s award 1974). Jewish. Editor: Minn. Medicine, 1971-74. Home: 5620 Edgewater Blvd Minneapolis MN 55417 Office: Med Arts Bldg Minneapolis MN 55402

BERNABUCCI, JOHN ROGER, JR., bottling co. exec.; b. Jamestown, N.D., Aug. 9, 1930; s. John Roger and Mary (Schwader) B.; B.S., U. N.D., 1952; m. Geraldine Desjardins, Nov. 8, 1952; children—Mary Theresa, Paul Anthony. With Coca-Cola Bottling Co., Jamestown, N.D., 1952—, corporate sec., 1954-64, pres., gen. mgr., 1964—, also dir.; pres., dir. Coca-Cola Bottling Co., LaCrosse, Wis., No. Plains Investment Co., Jamestown; chmn. bd. dirs. Stutsman County State Bank Jamestown, 1972—. Vice pres. Jamestown Indsl. Devel. Corp. Chmn. Stutsman County Republican Com., 1960-66; state finance chmn. N.D. Rep. Party; mem. N.D. Ho. of Reps., 1966-70. Bd. dirs. Jamestown Urban Renewal Agy., 1972—, Jamestown Hosp., 1972—. Mem. Nat. Soft Drink Assn. (dir. 1971—), Jamestown C. of C. (pres. 1972-74). Lutheran. Mason (Shriner), Elk, Lion. Home: 1712 Elmwood Pl Jamestown ND 58401 Office: 1016 10th St SE Jamestown ND 58401

BERNARD, BURTON CHARLES, lawyer; b. St. Louis, Oct. 19, 1926; s. Adolph and Anne (Koplovitz) B.; A.B., Washington U., 1947; LL.B., Harvard U., 1950. Staff mem. Ill. Commerce Commn., Chgo., 1950-51; practice in Granite City, Ill., also Edwardsville, Ill., also St. Louis, 1951—; asst. states atty. Madison County, Ill., 1957-66. Pres. Jewish Fedn. So. Ill., 1970-72; trustee, mem. exec. com. Jefferson Nat. Meml. Assn.; mem. Tri-City Regional Port Dist., 1975—. Served from pvt. to sgt., AUS, 1945-46. Mem. Madison County Bar Assn. (chmn. judiciary com. 1963-64), Madison County Hist. Soc. (dir., past pres.), Am. Legion, Am., Ill., Mo., St. Louis, Tri-City, Chgo. bar assns., Ill. Hist. Soc. (bd. dirs. 1960-63), Am. Jewish Hist. Soc. (exec. council 1970-73), Phi Beta Kappa. Democrat. Contbr. articles to legal jours. Home: 2446 State St Granite City IL 62040 Office: Bernard and Davidson State Loan Bldg Granite City IL also National Bank Bldg Edwardsville IL 62025 also Boatsmen's Bank Bldg St Louis MO

BERNARDIN, JOSEPH LOUIS, archbishop; b. Columbia, S.C., Apr. 2, 1928; s. Joseph and Maria M. (Simon) B.; A.B. in Philosophy, St. Mary's Sem., 1948; M.A. in Edn., Cath. U. Am., 1952. Ordained priest Roman Catholic Ch., 1952; asst. pastor Diocese Charleston, S.C., 1952-54, vice chancellor, 1954-56, chancellor, 1956-66, vicar gen., 1962-66, diocesan consultor, 1962-66, adminstr., 1964-65; aux. bishop Atlanta, 1966-68; sec., mem. exec. com. Nat. Conf. Cath. Bishops- U.S. Cath. Conf., gen. sec., 1968-72, pres., 1974-77; archbishop Cin., 1972—. Mem. Sacred Congregation for Bishops, 1973—; del. World Synod of Bishops, 1974, 77, mem. Permanent Council, 1974—; mem. Pontifical Commn. Social Communications, Rome, 1970-72. Mem. Am. Revolution Bicentennial Advisory Council, 1975; mem. Pres.'s Advisory Com. Refugees, 1975. Address: 29 E 8th St Cincinnati OH 45202

BERNAT, LEO ALLEN, social ins. cons.; b. St. Paul, Apr. 13, 1923; s. Maier and Bertha (Weisz) B.; B.S. in Chemistry, U. Minn., 1944, Ph.D. in Bus. Adminstrn., 1967; m. Emilia Kaczor, Dec. 26, 1970. Research asst. agronomy U. Minn. 1948-68, statistician in home econs., 1948, research asst. indsl. relations, 1957-58; legis. research supr., econ. research supr., supr. employment statistics Minn. Dept. Employment Security, 1949-56, 59-60; cons. social ins. Minn. Research Assos., St. Paul, 1956—, proprietor, 1958—; research cons. Minn. Dept. Edn., 1971—; instr. statistics U. Minn., Mpls., 1961-67. Mem. Am. Fedn. Sch. Adminstrs. AFL-CIO, 1973—. Mem. Bd. Commrs. Mpls. Housing and Redevel. Authority, 1974-77. Trustee Minn. Glaziers and Allied Trades Retirement Plan, 1970-75. Mem. Indsl. Relations Research Assn., Am. Edn. Finance Assn., Nat. Planning Assn., Am. Statis. Assn., Casualty Actuarial Soc. (asso. actuary), Biometrics Soc., Internat. Actuarial Assn. Home: 401 5th St SE Minneapolis MN 55414 Office: 204 Franklin Ave W Minneapolis MN 55404 also Capitol Square Bldg St Paul MN 55101

BERNETT, THEODORE BYRON, mgmt. cons.; b. Chgo., Aug. 30, 1924; s. Joseph and Julia (Gorski) B.; B.S. in M.E., U. Ill., 1950; student bus. adminstrn., U. Wis., Milw., 1953-54; m. Helen Brower, Apr. 23, 1949; children—Richard, Michael, James. Julie, Amy. Engring. draftsman Abbott Labs., 1950-53; sr. project engr. AC Spark Plug div. Gen. Motors Corp., 1957-64; head process engring. dept. Anaconda Wire & Cable Co., 1964-66; founder T.B. Bernett & Assos. Mgmt. Cons., developers of mgmt. technique to manufacture at minimal cost, Kenosha, Wis., 1975—. Served with USNR, 1943-46. Mem. ASME. Developed technique to satisfy all theoretical sterility considerations that must be met to process plastic pouches in a retort, also mechanism to generate mathematically correct involute teeth on any size ellipse. Home: 6622 59th Ave Kenosha WI 53142

BERNHARD, JOHN TORBEN, univ. pres.; b. N.Y.C., June 24, 1920; s. Torben Martin and Mary (Nielsen) B.; B.S., Utah State U., 1941; M.A., U. Cal. at Los Angeles, 1949, Ph.D., 1951; LL.D., Quincy Coll., 1970; m. Ramona Bailey, June 2, 1941; children—John Gary, Scott Martin, Randall Lee, Julie Ann. Prof. polit. sci. Brigham Young U., 1959-68, dean humanities and social scis., 1962-68; pres., prof. polit. sci. Western Ill. U., Macomb, 1968-74, Western Mich. U., Kalamazoo, 1974—. Served to lt. (j.g.) USCGR. Mem. Am. Assn. Higher Edn., Am. Polit. Sci. Assn., Pi Sigma Alpha, Pi Gamma Mu, Xi Sigma Pi, Sigma Nu, Sigma Iota Epsilon, Phi Delta Kappa, Phi Kappa Phi, Pi Delta Epsilon. Mem. Ch. of Jesus Christ of Latter-day Saints. Home: 1201 Short Rd Kalamazoo MI 49008 Office: Western Mich U Kalamazoo MI 49008

BERNHARDT, CARL FRED, savs. and loan exec.; b. Evansville, Ind., Sept. 8, 1918; s. Henry Fred and Rose Barbara (Haaga) B.; B.B.A., Lockyears Bus. Coll., 1938; m. Ann Meeks, Aug. 30, 1941; children—Carl Fred, Wayne A. With Home Fed. Savs. and Loan Assn., Evansville, Ind., 1938—, pres., 1964—. Mem. North Side Bus. Mens Assn. (pres. 1969). Eagle, Moose, Kiwanian, Mason (Shriner). Mem. Evangelical Ch. Home: 3316 Kern Rd Evansville IN 47712 Office: 120 N Main St Evansville IN 47711

BERNICK, EMIL LEE, polit. scientist; b. Hammond, Ind., May 26, 1947; s. Leslie M. and Harriet Ann (Kraus) B.; B.A., U. Okla., 1968, M.A., 1972, Ph.D., 1976; m. Joanne Gail Cristol, Oct. 11, 1969; children—Ethan Michael, Joshua Allen. Tchr. Sch. Dist. 151, South Holland, Ill., 1968-70; spl. instr., spl. program for gifted Thornton Twp., Harvey, Ill., 1969; research asst. Bur. Govt. Research, U. Okla., Norman, 1972-74, spl. instr. human relations, 1974; vis. instr. Iowa State U., Ames, 1974-75, instr. polit. sci., 1975-76, asst. prof., 1976—, asst. dir. pub. adminstrn. programs, 1975—; program analyst HUD, 1977-78. NSF grantee, 1974-76; NASPAA fellow, 1977. Mem. Am., Midwest, So. polit. sci. assns., Am. Soc. Pub. Adminstrn., Southwestern Social Sci. Assn., Alpha Epsilon Pi, Pi Sigma Alpha. Home: 516 Lynn St Ames IA 50010

BERNS, CHARLES, physician; b. Lomza, Poland, Mar. 13, 1902; s. Kalman and Cecelia Berns; came to U.S., 1906, naturalized, 1917; A.B., Western Res. U., 1923; M.D., Ind. U., 1927; m. Delnet Cohn, June 15, 1937; children—Kenneth Ira, Karen (Mrs. Norton Newborn). Intern, resident, St. Vincent's Charity Hosp., Cleve., 1927-29; practice medicine specializing in opthalmology and otolaryngology, Cleve., 1929-34; mem. staff Cleve. VA Hosp. and regional office, 1946—, chief eye, ear, nose and throat outpatient clinic, 1963—; asst. supr. health Cleve. pub. schs., 1930-40; dir. med. br. U.S. Army Res. Sch., Cleve., 1952-60. Active YMCA. Served to col. M.C., AUS, 1942-46. Diplomate Am. Bd. Otolaryngology. Fellow A.C.S., Acad. Ophthalmology and Otolaryngology; mem. Pan Am. Assn. Oto-Rhino-Laryngology and Broncho-Esophagology, Mil. Order World Wars, AMA, Cleve. Acad. Medicine, Ohio Med. Assn., Cleve. Otolaryngology Club, U.S. Ret. Officers Assn., Am. Legion, Alpha Omega Alpha. Club: Cleveland Business Men's. Home: 3319 Avalon Rd Shaker Heights OH 44120 Office: 10701 East Blvd Cleveland OH 44106

BERNS, HENRY DONALD, automotive engr.; b. Bladen, Nebr., Dec. 31, 1938; s. Henry P. F. and Blanche M. (Kaufman) B.; B.S. with distinction, U. Nebr., 1961, M.S., 1963; Ph.D., Kans. State U., 1969; m. Marilyn Joyce Kuhn, Jan. 27, 1960; children—Daniel, Beth. Instr., research asst. Kans. State U., 1963-68; sr. engr. Deere & Co., Moline, Ill., 1969-72, mgr. applied mechanics, 1972—. Regents scholar U. Nebr., 1956, NDEA fellow Kans. State U., 1963-66. Mem. Soc. Automotive Engrs. (com. mem. 1970—), Am. Soc. Agrl. Engrs., Soc. Exptl. Stress Analysis (chmn. local sect. 1971-72), Pi Tau Sigma, Sigma Tau, Pi Mu Epsilon. Methodist (chmn. council ministries 1977—). Home: 1885 25th Ave Ct Moline IL 61265 Office: John Deere Rd Moline IL 61265

BERNSTEIN, ARTHUR, physician; b. Chgo., Aug. 21, 1908; s. Philip and Sarah (Goldstein) B.; B.S., U. Ill., 1931, M.D., 1934; m. Juanita Steman, May 19, 1936; children—Sidney, Henry, Louis. Intern, Cook County Hosp., Chgo., 1933-34, resident in internal medicine, 1935-37; practice medicine specializing in internal medicine, Chgo., 1937—; staff Cook County Hosp., 1937—, asst. med. supt., 1946-69; clin. asso. prof. medicine U. Ill., 1936—; attending physician dept. medicine Columbus-Cuneo-Cabrini Med. Center, 1950—; prof. medicine Cook County Hosp. Grad. Sch. Medicine, 1946—. Served to lt. comdr. M.C., USNR, 1944-46. Fellow A.C.P.; mem. AMA, Chgo. Soc. Internal Medicine, Inst. Medicine Chgo., Am. Diabetes Assn., Am. Heart Assn., Soc. Med. History Chgo., Am. Assn. for History of Medicine. Jewish. Club: Standard of Chgo. Contbr. articles to profl. jours. Editor: Interns Manual, 1954-71. Home: 860 Lake Shore Dr Chicago IL 60611 Office: Suite 1929 25 E Washington St Chicago IL 60602

BERNSTEIN, BENJAMIN TOBIAS, machine co. exec.; b. Bklyn., Apr. 4, 1934; s. Harry and Sarah (Greenberg) B.; B.S., Bklyn. Coll., 1956; Ph.D., Iowa State U., 1959; m. Claire Lampert, Dec. 25, 1956; children—Louis David, Elizabeth Rebecca. AEC research fellow Ames (Iowa) Labs., AEC, 1956-59, postdoctoral research asso., 1959-60; mem. staff Union Carbide Research Inst., Tarrytown, N.Y., 1960-62; mgr. physics, electronics Am. Standard, N.Y.C., 1962-66; dir. engring. Singer Indsl. Products, N.J., 1966-70; v.p. Union Spl. Corp., Chgo., 1970—. Mem. exec. bd. Clara Barton Sch., Edison, N.J., 1965-70. Fellow Am. Inst. Chemists; mem. Am. Inst. Physics. Contbr. numerous articles to profl. jours. Patentee in field. Home: 1428 Sheridan Rd Highland Park IL 60035 Office: Union Spl Corp 400 N Franklin St Chicago IL 60610

BERNSTEIN, CHARLES BERNARD, lawyer; b. Chgo., June 24, 1941; s. Norman and Adele (Shore) B.; A.B., U. Chgo., 1962; J.D., DePaul U., 1965; m. Roberta Luba Lesner, Aug. 7, 1968; children—Edward Charles, Louis Charles. Admitted to Ill. bar, 1965,

U.S. Supreme Ct. bar, 1972; asso. firm Axelrod, Goodman & Steiner, Chgo., 1966-67, firm Max & Herman Chill, Chgo., 1967-74; mem. firm Bellows & Assos., Chgo., 1974—; basketball press dir. U. Chgo., 1967-74. Recipient Am. Jurisprudence award, 1963; citation meritorious service Dist. Grand Lodge 6 B'nai B'rith, 1969; My Brothers Keeper award Am. Jewish Congress, 1977. Mem. Chgo., Ill. State bar assns., Chgo. Jewish Hist. Soc. (treas., dir. 1977—), Chgo. Pops Orch. Assn. (treas., exec. com. 1975—), Am. Jewish Hist. Soc., Art Inst. of Chgo., Chgo. Hist. Soc., Jewish Geneal. Soc. (dir. 1977—), Nu Beta Epsilon. Club: B'nai B'rith. Contbr. articles to profl. jours. and mags. Home: 5457 S Hyde Park Blvd Chicago IL 60615 Office: 100 N LaSalle St Chicago IL 60602

BERNSTEIN, MALCOLM ALBERT, ins. agt.; b. Cin., Feb. 18, 1933; s. Herbert B. and Mildred (Abrohams) B.; B.S., U. Pa., 1954; m. Ann Maxine Berkman, Nov. 24, 1960; children—Sarah Elizabeth, Alexander Isaac Joshua. With Isaacs & Bernstein Inc., Cin., 1954-69; v.p. Frederick Rauh & Co., Cin., 1969—; publisher Music & Matter mag., 1958-59; pres. Dimension Cincinnati mag., 1963-65. Bd. dirs. Cin. Jewish Community Relations Center, 1958—, Jewish Family Service, 1965—, Assn. Home Care Agencies, 1976—, Easy Riders, 1975—. CPCU. Mem. Queen City Assn. (dir. 1968-69), Soc. CPCU. Jewish. Club: Losantiville Country. Home: 59 Oliver Rd Cincinnati OH 45215 Office: 3300 Central Pkwy Cincinnati OH 45225

BERNSTEIN, SHELDON, food and feed industry co. exec.; b. Milw., Mar. 23, 1927; s. Jacob Louis and Tillie (Lewis) B.; B.S., U. Wis., 1949, Ph.D. (NIH Research fellow), 1952; m. Estelle Lou Katz, June 27, 1948; children—Bradley, Richard, Jodi. Teaching asst. physiol. chemistry U. Wis., 1950-52; asso. biochemist Upjohn Co., Kalamazoo, 1952-53; dir. research and devel. Amber Labs. & Milbrew, Inc., Milw., 1954-57, v.p. research and devel., 1957-65, pres., 1965—. Mem. food products adv. com. U. Wis., 1975—. Served with USNR, 1944-46. Fellow Am. Inst. Chemists, A.A.A.S., mem. Inst. Food Tech., Wis. Acad. Sci., Am. Chem. Soc. (counselor div. microbe chemistry, tech. 1972—), Master Brewers Assn. Am., Am. Soc. Microbiology, Am. Feed Mfrs. Assn. (nutrition council 1968—), Animal Nutritions Research Council, Sigma Xi, Phi Beta Kappa. Jewish (pres. synagogue, Milw. synagogue council). Home: 201 W Bradley Rd Milwaukee WI 53217 Office: 330 S Mill St Juneau WI 53039

BERNTSON, STANLEY MARSHALL, banker; b. Chgo., Aug. 5, 1907; s. Bernard E. and Margurite (Nelson) B.; student at the Northwestern U., 1925-27; m. Lillian Adelaine Johnson, Oct. 14, 1933; children—Gail Lynda, Grant Morgan. Accountant George Reinberg Co., Chgo., 1929-35, George May & Co., 1935-36; exec. sec. Derby Laundry, 1936-40; pres. Fidelity Fed. Savs. & Loan Assn., 1940—; v.p. Mars Realty Co., 1945—; exec. sec. Samuel Olson Mfg. Co., 1943-56. Dir. Elmhurst YMCA; chmn. bd. Home of Onesiphorus; bd. dirs. Lydia Children's Home; trustee Trinity Seminary. Mem. Chgo. Area Council Savs. Assns. (past pres.), Chgo. Better Govt. Assn., Nat. League Insured Assns. (legislation com.), Ill. Savs. and Loan League (director), United States Savs. and Loan League (mem. legislation com.), Chamber of Commerce (dir.). Mem. Evang. Free Ch. Kiwanian (dir.). Home: 211 Winthrop Ave Elmhurst IL 60126 Office: 5455 W Belmont Ave Chicago IL 60641

BEROUNSKY, JOSEPH FRANK, electronics engr.; b. Omaha, Mar. 2, 1930; s. Joseph John and Mary (Kracl) B.; m. Mary Francis Taylor, Apr. 8, 1947; children—Joseph John, Mary Catherne (Mrs. John Whitney), Chris Alan. Radio technician Gen. Communications Co., Inc., Omaha, 1961-66, service mgr., 1966-73, systems engr., 1973—. Mem. Ak Sar Ben Radio Club (v.p., pres. 1962-63), Eagles. Home: 9010 Valley St Omaha NE 68124 Office: 827 S 20th St Omaha NE 68108

BERREAU, ALFRED JAMES, architect; b. Brewster, Minn., Aug. 25, 1932; s. Rudolph Vincent and Margaret (Schrieber) B.; student Worthington Jr. Coll., 1956-57; B.Arch. with distinction, U. Minn., 1961; m. Rosemary Elizabeth Forrette, Sept. 1, 1956; children—Linda Marie, Shaun Forrette, Nicholas Forrette, Alfred Justin. Asso. Graffunder-Nagle & Assos., Mpls., 1961-65; architect, v.p. Graffunder-Berreau & Assos., Inc., Mpls., 1965-71; pres. A.J. Berreau & Assos., Inc., Mpls., 1971—, Environ. Process, Inc., Mpls., 1972—. Cons. Mpls. Housing Authority, 1967—. Pres. Golden Valley (Minn.) Fine Arts, 1969. Served with AUS, 1953-55. Mem. AIA, Minn. Soc. Architects, Minn. Sch. Facilities Council. Roman Catholic. Prin. works include U. Minn. Sci. Bldg., Morris, Housing for Elderly, Mpls., Lyndale Sch., Mpls., Land O'Lakes Plant, Spencer, Wis., Kroger Co.-Pace Dairy Foods Plant, Rochester, Minn., Nobles County Govt. Complex, Worthington, Minn., Land O'Lakes Cheese Plant, Perham, Minn., DoBoy Industries Milk Replacer Plant, New Richmond, Wis., Consol. Co-op. Office and Warehouse Bldg., Worthington, Minn., 1st Dist. Assn. Cheese Plant, Litchfield, Minn. Home: 204 Meander Rd Golden Valley MN 55422 Office: 1220 Glenwood Ave Minneapolis MN 55405

BERREY, ROBERT WILSON, III, lawyer, judge; b. Kansas City, Mo., Dec. 6, 1929; s. Robert Wilson and Elizabeth (Hudson) B.; A.B., William Jewell Coll., 1950; M.A., U. S.D., 1952; LL.B., Kansas City U., 1955; LL.M., U. Mo. at Kansas City, 1972; grad. Trial Judges Coll., U. Nev., 1972; m. Katharine Rollins Wilcoxson, Sept. 5, 1950; children—Robert Wilson IV, Mary Jane, John Lind. Admitted to Mo. bar, 1955, Kans. bar, 1955, since practiced in Kansas City; asso. mem. firm Shugert and Thomson, 1955-56, Clark, Krings & Bredehoft, 1957-61, Terry and Welton, 1961-62; judge 4th Dist. Magistrate Ct., Jackson County, Mo., 1962—; mem. Supreme Ct. Com. to Draft Rules and Procedures for Mo.'s Small Claims Ct., 1976, 77. Vol. Legal cons. Psychiat. Receiving Center. Del. Atlantic Council Young Polit. Leaders, Oxford, Eng., 1965; Kansas City rep. to President's National Conference on Crime Control; del.-at-large White House Conf. Aging, 1972; pack chmn. Cub Scouts Am.; counselor, com. mem. Boy Scouts Am.: vice chmn. water fowl com. Mo. Conservation Fedn., 1968-69, chmn. water fowl com., 1971-73; v.p. Cook PTA, 1967-68; mem. cts. and judiciary com. Mo. bar, 1969-73; mem. Midwest region adv. com. Nat. Park Service, 1973—, chmn., 1973-77; mem. Mo. State Judicial Planning Commn., 1977; bd. dirs., founder Kansas City Open Space Found., 1976. Regional dir. Young Rep. Nat. Fedn., 1957-59, gen. counsel, 1959-61, nat. vice-chmn.; chmn. Mo. Young Rep. Fedn., 1960, nat. committeeman, 1959-60, 61-64; Mo. alternate at large Republican Nat. Conv., 1960, asst. gen. counsel, 1964, del. state and dist. convs., 1960, 64, 68. Bd. dirs. Naturalization Council, Kansas City, pres., 1973—; trustee Kansas City Mus., 1972-73. Recipient Distinguished Service award Mo. bar, 1973. Mem. Kansas City Bar Assn., Urban League (mem. bd.), S.A.R., Kansas City Mus. Natural Sci. Soc. (charter), Delta Theta Phi, Pi Gamma Mu, Tau Kappa Epsilon. Mem. Christian Ch. Mason, mem. DeMolay Legion Honor. Clubs: Ward Parkway Country (mem. bd.); Kansas City; Waldo Optimist (v.p. 1967-68); Capitol Hill (Washington). Home: 1235 W 58th St Kansas City MO 64113 also summer Route 2 Battle Lake MN Office: Jackson County Ct House Kansas City MO 64106

BERRY, BREWTON, writer, editor, educator; b. Orangeburg, S.C., Aug. 9, 1901; s. Joseph A. and Frances Deborah (Pike) B.; A.B., Wofford Coll., 1922; B.D., Yale, 1925; Ph.D., U. Edinburgh, 1930; m. Margaret Woods. Sept. 11, 1926; children—Margaret Berry Curtin, Deborah Berry Houser. Asst. prof. sociology and anthropology U. Mo., 1931-37, prof., 1945; prof., head dept. sociology and anthropology, U. R.I., 1945-46; prof. sociology and anthropology Ohio State U., Columbus, 1946-64, mem. editorial bd. univ. press, 1964—; dir. Archaeological Survey Mo., 1933-45; curator Anthrop. Mus., U. Mo., 1931-45. Mem. Ohio Gov.'s Advisory Com. on Refugees, 1955-60; chmn. refugee com. Episcopal Diocese So. Ohio, 1953-56. Fellow Am. Anthrop. Assn., mem. Am. Sociol. Assn., Mo. Archeol. Soc. (hon. life). Phi Beta Kappa (pres. Ohio State U. chpt. 1964), Sigma Xi. Episcopalian. Clubs: Scioto Country, Torch (past pres.), Faculty, Book and Bond (Yale). Author: You and Your Superstitions, 1940, 2d edition, 1974; Race Relations, 1951; Race and Ethnic Relations, 1958, revised editions, 1965, 77; Fundamentals of Sociology, 1950; Almost White, 1963, revised edition, 1969; The Education of American Indians, 1967, 68, 73, The Blending of Races, 1972; Editor: The Missouri Archaeologist: The First Ten Years, 1975. Editor The Mo. Archaeologist, 1934-45, The Ohio Valley Sociologist, 1947-50; asso. editor Am. Sociol. Review, 1953-56. Home: 2221 Brixton Rd Columbus OH 43221 Office: 1775 S College Rd Columbus OH 43210

BERRY, CLYDE MARVIN, educator; b. Posey, Ill., June 18, 1913; s. James Frederick and Mary Caroline (Crocker) B.; B.S., McKendree Coll., 1933; M.S., U. Ill., 1936; M.S., U. Iowa, 1940, Ph.D., 1941; m. Jean Wilson, June 9, 1940; children—David Kent, Phyllis Ann, Alicia Lynn. With USPHS, 1941-48, chief indsl. hygiene engr., 1946-48; chief indsl. hygienist Esso Standard Oil Co., 1948-55; prof. Coll. Medicine U. Iowa, Oakdale Campus, 1955—; asso. dir. Inst. Agrl. Medicine, 1955—. Mem. Sigma Xi, Alpha Chi Sigma, Sigma Zeta, Phi Lambda Upsilon. Unitarian. Mason, Rotarian. Home: 906 S Lucas St Iowa City IA 52240 Office: Oakdale Campus University of Iowa Oakdale IA 52319

BERRY, DON VICTOR, accountant; b. Chgo., Feb. 1, 1934; s. Eugene T. and Marion M. (Messenger) B.; A.B., Wheaton Coll., 1956; M.B.A., Northwestern U., 1959; m. Gracia Peterson, Sept. 5, 1959; children—Pamela, Jefferson. Brand mgr. Pillsbury Co., Mpls., 1959-65; v.p. fin. Blue Seal/REMI Foods, Chgo., 1965-71, Richard Allan Med. Industries, Evanston, Ill., 1972-76; asst. comptroller Itofca, Inc., Clarendon Hills, Ill., 1976—. Mem. Ill. C.P.A. Soc., Am. Marketing Assn. Presbyn. Home: 20W636 22nd St Lombard IL 60148 Office: 2 S Walker St Clarendon Hills IL 60514

BERRY, EDWIN C., co. exec., TV moderator, civic leader; LL.D., Western Mich. U., 1973; L.H.D., Chgo. State U., 1973; LL.D., Northwestern U., 1975; m. Betsy Gordon Bell; 1 son, Joseph; foster children—Myron Wahls, Charles Carter. With Nat. Urban League in Pitts., Portland, Chgo. for 33 yrs.; spl. asst. to pres., urban affairs officer, corp. cons. personnel programs Johnson Products Co., Chgo., 1970—; treas., adminstrv. officer George E. Johnson Found., George E. Johnson Ednl. Fund. Moderator People to People program WGN-TV, Chgo. Mem. fund raising com. Chgo. Urban League, Chgo. Community Fund, Leadership Council for Met. Open Communities, Woodlawn Devel. Corp., Chgo. United, Chgo. Alliance Businessmen, Nat. Com. against Discrimination in Housing. Recipient John F. Kennedy award Catholic Interracial Council; Citation of Honor Stateway Mother's Soc.; Citation for outstanding service and leadership in black community The Woodlawn Orgn.; Golden Oil Can award Chgo. Econ. Devel. Corp.; named Chicagoan of the Year Chgo. Jr. Assn. Commerce and Industry; Man of Year Ada S. McKinley House; Laureate Lincoln Acad. Mem. UN Assn. of U.S.A. (chmn. Ralph Bunche awards panel). Mem. editorial bd. The Chicago Reporter. Office: Johnson's Products Co 8522 S Lafayette Ave Chicago IL 60620

BERRY, JAMES WILLIAM, lawyer; b. Moline, Ill., June 14, 1947; s. James Thomas and Betty (Spires) B.; B.S., U. Iowa, 1969, J.D., 1973; m. Jill Reed, Sept. 7, 1968. Admitted to Iowa bar, 1973; asso. firm Dircks & Saylor, Davenport, Iowa, 1973-75; individual practice law, Davenport, 1975—. Served with U.S. Army, 1969-70. Mem. Am., Iowa State, Ill. State, Scott County bar assns. Home: 4843 Gaines Davenport IA 52806 Office: 1414 W Locust St Davenport IA 52804

BERRY, LLOYD EASON, educator; b. Houston, Aug. 1, 1935; s. Joel Halbert and Fay (Eason) B.; B.A., U. N.C., 1957, M.A. (Carnegie Found. grantee), 1958; Ph.D. (Marshall scholar), Magdalene Coll., Cambridge U., 1960; m. Elizabeth Moncrief Perry, Dec. 28, 1955 (div. 1971); children—Susan Antoinette, Lloyd Eason, Sharon Louise; m. 2d, Deborah J. Goss, Apr. 9, 1977. Asst. prof. English, U. Ill., 1960-63, faculty fellow, 1962, asso. prof., 1963-66, prof., 1966-72, asso. Center for Advanced Study, 1968-69, asst. to chancellor, 1969-70, asst. chancellor, 1970-72; prof. English, dean Grad. Sch., U. Mo. at Columbia, 1972—, dir. research, 1972—; mem. Marshall Scholarship Commn., 1970-75, chmn., 1972-75. Bd. dirs. Nat. Acad. Arts, Univ. YMCA; trustee Carle Hosp. Found. Am. Philos. Soc. grantee, 1963, 65; Henry H. Huntington Library fellow, 1965; Folger Shakespeare Library fellow, 1965; Guggenheim fellow, 1966-67. Mem. Modern Lang. Assn., Modern Humanities Research Assn., Milton Soc. (exec. com. 1964-72), Renaissance Soc. Am. (adv. com.), Renaissance English Text Soc. (returning officer and exec. com. 1965-72), Malone Soc., Bibliog. Soc., Cambridge Bibliog. Soc. (sec. for U.S. and Can. 1960—), Marshall Scholars (permanent sec., exec. com. 1967-75), Assn. Grad. Schs. (policy com. 1974—), Central Renaissance Conf. (pres. 1969-70, exec. com. 1973—), Phi Beta Kappa, Phi Kappa Phi, Sigma Tau Delta, Pi Gamma Mu, Alpha Chi, Kappa Tau Alpha. Baptist. Clubs: Rotary, Oxford-Cambridge Boat Race Dining of Ill. Author: A Bibliography of Studies in Metaphysical Poetry, 1939-60, 1964; The English Works of Giles Fletcher, the Elder, 1964; John Stubb's Gaping Gulf with Letters and Other Relevant Documents, 1968; Rude and Barbarous Kingdom; Russia in the Accounts of Sixteenth Century English Voyagers, 1968; The Dramatic Works of George Chapman, 1969; The Geneva Bible: A Facsimile of the 1560 Edition, 1969; contbr. articles to profl. jours. Home: 613 Randy Ln Columbia MO 65201 Died Dec. 20, 1977.

BERRY, LOREN MURPHY, business exec.; b. Wabash, Ind., July 24, 1888; s. Charles D. and Elizabeth (Murphy) B.; student Northwestern U., 1909-10; LL.D., Rio Grande (Ohio) Coll.; m. Lucile Kneipple, June 9, 1909 (dec.); children—Loren Murphy, Martha Sue Fralm, John William, Elizabeth Anne Gray; m. 2d, Helen Anderson Henry, Aug. 28, 1938 (dec.); 1 son, Leland; m. 3d, Ruth Heston. Newspaper reporter, Wabash, Ind., Joliet, Ill., Chgo.; sold telephone directory advt., Marion, Ind., 1910, St. Louis, Louisville, Indpls., which developed into nat. sales orgn. of L. M. Berry & Co., main office, Dayton, Ohio, now vice chmn. bd.; dir. emeritus United Telecommunications, Inc., Kansas City, Mo., 3d Nat. Bank & Trust, Dayton; dir. Super Food Services, Inc., Dayton, Laughter Corp., Dayton, Hulman Realty Co., Dayton. Mem. Republican Nat. Fin. Com., Washington. Bd. dirs. Jr. Achievement, Dayton; trustee Rio Grande Coll. Mem. U.S. Ind. Telephone Pioneers (pres. 1938-39), Bell Telephone Pioneers Assn. (v.p. N.C. Kingsbury chpt. 1939-40). Republican. Episcopalian. Mason (32 deg., Shriner). Clubs: Dayton City, Engineers, Kiwanis, Dayton Country, Moraine Country, Bicycle (Dayton); Surf (gov.), Committee of 100, Indian Creek, Bath (Miami Beach, Fla.); Bohemian (San Francisco); Capitol Hill (Washington). Home: 1155 Ridgeway Rd Dayton OH 45419 also Surf Club Apts 9133 Collins Ave Miami Beach FL 33154 Office: 3170 Kettering Blvd PO Box 6000 Dayton OH 45401 also 5050 W Lemon St PO Box 23987 Tampa FL 33622

BERRY, LUCILLE MARIE, coll. adminstr.; b. Nameoki, Ill., June 2, 1936; d. P. Louis and Frieda Catherine (Feltman) Berry; B.S., St. Louis U., 1958, M.S. in Commerce, 1963. Supr. cashiers St. Louis U., 1958-64, supr. grants and contracts, 1964-66, chief funds accountant, 1966-71; fin. asst. to provincial treas. Religious of the Sacred Heart, 1971-74, provincial treas., 1974-75; controller Maryville Coll., St. Louis, 1975-76, dir. bus. and fin., 1976—, adj. instr., 1972-76, adj. asst. prof., 1976—. Mem. Am. Soc. Women Accountants, Am. Assn. Accountants, Mo. Assn. Accounting Educators, Midwest Bus. Adminstrs. Assn., Pi Lambda Theta. Home: 9626 Old Bonhomme St Louis MO 63132 Office: 13550 Conway Rd St Louis MO 63141

BERRY, PAUL DESHON, chem. co. exec.; b. Garrett, Ill., Jan. 15, 1921; s. Jacob Claude and Helen Ruth (DeShon) B.; A.B., Baker U., 1942; M.A., U. Nebr., 1948; m. Margaret Kester, Aug. 16, 1945; children—Michael, Thomas, JoAnn. With Union Carbide Co., S. Charleston, W.Va., 1948-70, group leader, 1958-68, market mgr., 1968-70; market devel. mgr. Houdaille Industries, Huntington, W.Va., 1970-72; product mgr. Textile Rubber & Chem. Corp., Dalton, Ga., 1972-73; gen. mgr. Gen. Latex & Chem. Corp. Ohio, Ashland, 1973—. Served to lt. comdr. USN, 1942-48. Mem. Soc. Plastics Engrs., Sigma Xi. Club: Country of Ashland, Elks. Home: 1123 Jackson Dr Ashland OH 44805 Office: PO Box 498 Ashland OH 44805

BERRY, ROBERT NEIL, tool co. exec.; b. Iowa City, Iowa, Mar. 21, 1933; s. Harlen Neil and Lila Ann (Dow) B.; student Allied Inst. Tech., 1955-57; m. Brenda V. Harberts, June 14, 1969; children—Tracy, Neil; children by previous marriage—Renee, Randy, Robert, Rhonda, Richard. Apprentice tool maker Progressive Tool Co., Waterloo, Iowa, 1950-55, shop foreman, 1955-60; founder Berry Tool & Die Co., Cedar Falls, Iowa, 1960, pres., chmn. bd., 1965—; founder Berry Notching Systems, Inc., 1970, chmn. bd., pres., 1970—; owner Art Bronze Co., Waterloo, 1977—; pres. Berry Industries, Inc., 1977—. Mem. adv. bd. Hawkeye Inst. Tech., Waterloo, 1967—. Served with AUS, 1954-55; Korea. Mem. Soc. Mfg. Engrs. (sr.), Cedar Falls C. of C. (chmn. mfg. bur. 1964-66), N.E. Iowa Bus. Club (pres. 1968-69), Iowa Mfrs. Assn., Nat. Fedn. Small Business. Methodist (bd. dirs. 1968-71, fin. bd. 1977—). Club: Rotary. Patentee in field. Home: 4214 Newland Dr Cedar Falls IA 50613 Office: 1906 State St Cedar Falls IA 50613

BERRY-CABAN, CRISTOBAL SANTIAGO, historian; b. Aguadilla, P.R., Jan. 9, 1953; s. Charles William and Maria de Lourdes (Caban) B.; B.A., Coll. Sacred Heart, 1974; M.A., Marquette U., 1976. Tchr. high sch., Liceo Interam. Castro. Rio Piedras, P.R., 1974; curriculum writer Midwest Materials Devel. Center, Milw. Pub. Schs., 1975-76; project specialist U. Wis., Milw., 1977—. Mem. Am. Hist. Assn., Ateneo Puertorriqueno, Midwest Inst. Puerto Rican Studies and Culture, Soc. Historians of Am. Fgn. Relations. Roman Catholic. Author: Aromaliris, 1974. Asso. editor La Guardia, 1974—, Jour. Contemporary Puerto Rican Thought, 1976—. Home: 836 14th St N #404 Milwaukee WI 53233 Office: 805 5th St S Milwaukee WI 53204

BERRYMAN, ALICE DAVIS (MRS. CECIL WELLS BERRYMAN), concert pianist, composer, educator; b. North Platte, Nebr.; d. George Warren and Alice (Clark) Davis; studied piano with August Borglum, Omaha, Wager Swayne, Paris, Rudolph Ganz, Switzerland, Me., Denver, N.Y.; mus. analysis Cecil Berryman; theory, harmony, composition and orchestration with Emile Schvartz, Paris Conservatoire; student music course New Coll. Oxford (Eng.) U., 1969; m. Cecil Wells Berryman; children—Edward Davis, Warren Leigh, Rudolph Barton. Concert pianist, numerous concerts alone and in joint with husband and three sons, Paris, N.Y. and Midwest, 1912—; debut Princess Theatre, N.Y., 1915; accredited tchr. piano Berryman Piano Conservatory, 1916—, U. Omaha, 1930-57; work shop tchrs. and players courses Presbyn. U., 1929; nat. judge of piano, Tex., Iowa, Ohio, Va., Tenn., Wis., Alaska, Mo., 1939—; judge internat. record contests, 1954-68. Named to Piano Guild U.S.A. Hall of Fame, 1968. Mem. Am. Coll. Musicians (nat. membership com., accredited tchr.), Nat. (certification 1969), Nebr. (exec. com., recipient certificate of profl. advancement, exam. chmn. bd. certification), Omaha (pres. 1977-78) music tchrs. assns., Nat. Soc. Lit. and Arts, Nat. Guild Piano Tchrs. (faculty; chmn. bd. certification State of Nebr.). P.E.O. Presbyterian. Numerous compositions published. Home: 5018 Izard St Omaha NE 68132

BERRYMAN, ROBERT ARMINE, hosp. adminstr.; b. Caruthersville, Mo., Nov. 27, 1925; s. Ralph Armine and Mildred (Elliott) B.; student Hendrix Coll., 1946-47, Gradwhol Coll., 1947-48, Columbia U., 1952-53; m. Glenda Rae Akin, July 10, 1965; children—David Eugene, Michael Robert, Regan Ann, Lindsey Rae. Chief lab. and X-Ray technician, acting adminstr. Mo. Delta Community Hosp., Sikeston, 1948-51; chief lab. and x-ray technician, asst. adminstr. Dunklin County Meml. Hosp., Kennett, 1952-54; adminstr. Randolph County Meml. Hosp., Pocahontas, Ark., 1955-62; dist. coordinator guest houses, nursing homes Crawford Corp., Baton Rouge, 1963-64; adminstr. Wycoff Heights Hosp., Bklyn. and Queens, N.Y., 1964-70; adminstr. Murphy Med. Center, Warsaw, Ind., 1970—. Cons. archtl. design and furnishing Lawrence County Meml. Hosp., Walnut Ridge, Ark., 1960-62, Stuttgart Meml. Hosp., (Ark.), 1958-59; Forrest Meml. Hosp., Forrest City, Ark., 1959; cons. lectr. Columbia U., 1964-66. Bd. dirs. Blue Cross of Ark., 1959-61, Fedn. Am. Hosps., 1974—. Served with USNR, 1942-46; PTO. Mem. Am. Coll. Hosp. Adminstrs., Ind. Hosp. Assn. Democrat. Methodist. Mason, Rotarian (pres. 1960-61). Contbr. to profl. pubs. in field. Home: 1101 Rd 15 S Warsaw IN 46580 Office: PO Box 89 Warsaw IN 46580

BERSCHE, JOSEPH EDWIN, constrn. co. exec.; b. Fairmont, W.Va., Oct. 17, 1931; s. G. Joseph and Jessie Naomi (Darling) B.; student Mich. State Normal Sch., 1949-50, Nyack Coll., 1950-51, U.S. Navy Engring. Sch., 1952; m. Barbara Carol Stegmaier, June 9, 1956; children—Craig, Chris, Kimberly Jo, Curt, Barbi Jo. Pres., Bersche Constrn. Co., Pontiac, Mich., 1956-66; exec. v.p., dir. Hannan Co., Cleve., 1967-77; pres. Inland Constrn., Inc., Chgo., 1977—. Trustee Nyack (N.Y.) Coll., Stow Alliance Fellowship. Served with USN, 1951-55. Club: Hudson Country. Office: 845 N Michigan Ave Chicago IL 60611

BERTZ, EDWARD JOSEPH, profl. assn. exec.; b. Loyal, Wis., Aug. 4, 1926; s. Edward Clemens and Florence Genevieve (Hannan) B.; B.Sc., St. Norbert Coll., 1949; postgrad. Okla. A. and M., 1944-45, St. Francis Sem., 1953-55; m. Marie Agnes Gray, Dec. 24, 1968; children—Edward O'Neill, Neil Hannan. Tchr. maths. Holy Cross Sem., LaCrosse, Wis., 1955-58; asst. editor Times-Review, 1958-64, editor, 1964-68; dir. El Centro de Opportunidad, Chicago Heights, Ill., 1968-69; asst. dir. div. plant ops. Am. Hosp. Assn., Chgo., 1969-70, dir., 1970-75, mgr. dept. health facilities and standards, 1975—. Dir. tech. mission program Cath. Diocese of LaCrosse, to Latin Am., 1960-68. Pres., Hosp. Adminstrs. Council, LaCrosse, Wis., 1966-68; mem. LaCrosse Diocesan Central Commn., 1965-68. Served with USNR, 1944-46. Home: 125 Westwood Dr Park Forest IL 60466 Office: 840 N Lake Shore Dr Chicago IL 60611

BESANCON, ROBERT MARTIN, physicist, editor; b. Missoula, Mont., July 29, 1910; s. Albert and Selma Alvida (Peterson) B.; B.A. in Physics, U. Mont., 1931; postgrad. U. Chgo., 1937-38; M.A., U. Ill., 1933; m. Leigh Martin, Dec. 24, 1947. Instr. physics and math. No. Mont. Coll., Havre, 1936-37; from instr. to asso. prof. physics U. Ill. Med. Center, Chgo., 1938-55; sr. physicist, phys. scis. adminstr. USAF, Wright-Patterson AFB, Ohio, 1955-75; compiler, editor Ency. Physics, Van Nostrand, Reinhold, Dayton, Ohio, 1964—. Served with USAF, 1942-46. Fellow AAAS; mem. Am. Phys. Soc., Am. Assn. Physics Tchrs., Air Force Assn., Dayton Area C. of C. (mem. world trade com. 1966—), Sigma Pi Sigma, Pi Mu Epsilon, Psi Chi, Rho Chi. Author: Experiments in General Physics, 2d edit., 1958; (with Leonard D. Powers) Laboratory Manual in General Physics, 1939. Home and Office: 515 Grand Ave Dayton OH 45405

BESCHLOSS, MORRIS RICHARD, valve mfg. co. exec.; b. Berlin, Mar. 7, 1929; s. Otto and Manya (Levine) B.; B.S., U. Ill., 1952; m. Ruth Greenwald, Nov. 13, 1954; children—Michael, Steven. Advt. mgr. Hammond Valve Corp. (Ind.), 1956-58, asst. sales mgr., 1958-61, field sales mgr., 1961-62, v.p. sales, 1962-63, pres., 1963-68, chmn. bd., 1968—, also dir.; pres. Conval Corp., 1968—; v.p., dir. Condec Corp.; pres. Plumbing-Heating-Cooling Info. Bur., 1971-72, chmn. bd., 1973—. Pres. Flossmoor-Homewood (Ill.) Area Sch. Bd., 1969-73. Served from 2d lt. to capt. AUS, 1952-54. Recipient Distinguished Eagle award Boy Scouts Am., 1974. Mem. Young Pres.'s Orgn., Valve Mfrs. Assn. (dir., pres. 1971-73), Assn. Industry Mfrs. (charter pres.), Tau Delta Phi, Sigma Delta Chi, Alpha Phi Omega. Home: Chicago IL 60611 Office: 875 N Michigan Ave Chicago IL 60611

BESHEARS, JAMES KEITH, railroad ofcl.; b. Springfield, Mo., Mar. 9, 1914; s. James Robert and Maude (Granthom) B.; student pub. schs.; student exec. development program U. Ga., 1953, exec. program bus. adminstrn., Columbia, 1956, advanced mgmt. program, U. Hawaii, 1960; m. Mildred Fern Thomas, June 1, 1936; children—Jeri, Judy. With St. L.-S.F. R.R., 1936—, successively brakeman, condr., safety supr., terminal trainmaster, asst. supt., supt. terminals, div. supt., 1953-55, dir. labor relations, 1955-57, v.p. personnel, Springfield, 1957-74, v.p. labor relations, Springfield, 1975-76, v.p. labor relations and personnel, 1976—; dir. FTC. Mem. exec. com., bd. trustees Frisco Employees Hosp. Assn. Mem. nat. council YMCA's. Mem. Nat. Def. Transp. Assn. (life; continental membership com. transp. dept.), Am. Mgmt. Assn., Springfield C. of C., Exec. Assn. Grad. Sch. Bus. of Columbia, Presbyn. Mason. Club: Hickory Hills Country. Home: Route 12 Box 343-A Arlington Dr Springfield MO 65804 Office: 3253 E Trafficway Springfield MO 65802

BESORE, GEORGE RALEIGH, JR., ins. exec.; b. Zanesville, Ohio, June 26, 1924; s. George Raleigh and Helen L. (Reidhaar) B.; B.A., Muskingum Coll., 1948; postgrad. Stanford U., 1948-49; m. Mary Emma Beryl Taylor, Nov. 26, 1946; children—Mary Louise, Elizabeth Nora, Marjorie Ann, Mark Harford. Cost accountant subs. Blum's Candy Co., San Francisco, 1949-52; group pension rep. Conn. Gen., 1952-55; account exec. Marsh & McLennan, San Francisco, 1955-58; staff benefits analyst H.J. Kaiser & Co., Oakland, Cal., 1958-62; mgr. life, group and pension dept. W.H. Markham & Co., St. Louis, 1963-68; regional group mgr. ITT Hamilton Life Ins. Co., Denver, 1968-69; supt. mass merchandising Nat.-Ben Franklin Life Ins. Co., Chgo., 1969-70; with Conn. Mut. Life Ins. Co., Chgo., 1970—. moderator Life Underwriter Tng. Council, 1972-75. Served with AUS, World War II. C.L.U. Fellow Life Mgmt. Inst.; mem. Nat., Ill., Chgo. assns. life underwriters, Chgo. Employee Benefits Assn. Clubs: Commonwealth (Calif.); Life Executives. Home: 424 Oak St Glen Ellyn IL 60137 Office: 180 N LaSalle St Suite 1700 Chicago IL 60601

BEST, JAMES REYNOLDS, mktg. exec.; b. Chgo., Feb. 20, 1934; s. James McLeod and Mary Leone (Burns) B.; B.S. in Physics, Washington and Lee U., 1956; M.S. in Bus. Adminstrn., Wayne State U., 1966; m. Linda Louise Richmer, Aug. 8, 1959. Project mgr. Research Center, Owens-Corning Fiberglass Corp., Grandville, O., 1956-59; mfrs. rep., incorporator Stark & Sons Assos., Inc., Detroit, 1959-63; owner, mgr. Glass Hawk Engring. Co., Livonia, Mich., 1960-63; sales engr. Cimastra div. Cin. Milling Machine Co., Pleasant Ridge, Mich., 1963-66; mktg. mgr. Owens-Corning Fiberglass Corp., Toledo, 1966-74, industry mgr., 1974—. Mem. Am. Phys. Soc., Soc. Plastics Engrs., Sigma Chi. Patentee fiberglass field. Designer reinforced plastics estimator slide rule. Home: 3238 Hargo Rd Toledo OH 43606 Office: Owens-Corning Fiberglas Corp Toledo OH 43604

BEST, LINDA LOUISE RICHMER, psychologist; b. Newark, Ohio, Apr. 12, 1934; d. William Raymond and Mary (Price) Richmer; B.S., Ohio U., 1959; M.S., U. Mich., 1963; Ph.D., U. Toledo, 1975; m. James R. Best, Aug. 8, 1959. Tchr., Miamisburg, Ohio, 1955-56, Newark, 1956-59, Inkster, Mich., 1959-60, Livonia, Mich., 1960-62, psychologist Dearborn (Mich.) pub. schs., 1964-66, Mason Consol. Schs., Erie, Mich., 1966-71, U. Toledo, 1971-73, Monroe County (Mich.) Intermediate Sch. dist., 1973-75; pvt. practice as psychologist, Toledo, 1975—. Vol. Toledo Hosp., 1972-73. Mem. Am. Psychol. Assn., NW Ohio Rehab. Assn. (bd. 1977-79), Kappa Delta Pi. Home: 3238 Hargo Rd Toledo OH 43606 Office: Suite 209E 5151 Monroe St Toledo OH 43623

BEST, ROBERT ELLIS, newspaper publisher; b. Jefferson City, Mo., July 25, 1931; s. Ellis John and Nellie Carol (Murphy) B.; B.S. in Agr., U. Mo., 1953, postgrad. journalism, 1956; m. Marion Elizabeth Denny, Dec. 28, 1954; children—Kathleen Leigh, Robert Reed. Editor, Lancaster Farming, Quarryville, Pa., 1956-59; dir. info. Pa. Dept. Agr., Harrisburg, 1959-61; publisher Moultrie County News, Sullivan, Ill., 1961—, Bethany (Ill.) Echo, 1973—; dir. publicity Pa. Farm Show, 1959-61; instr. Lake Land Community Coll., Mattoon, Ill., 1970—. Chmn., Moultrie County Regional Planning Commn., 1962-75. Mem. Ill. Press Assn. (pres.), So. Ill. Editorial Assn. (dir.). Home: 1017 E Jackson St Sullivan IL 61951 Office: PO Box A Sullivan IL 61951

BETTER, EDWARD FRANCIS, III, steel fabricating co. exec.; b. Watertown, Mass., Sept. 18, 1927; s. Edward Francis and Elizabeth (Glancy) B.; B.S., Am. Internat. Coll., 1953; m. Julia Alice Kerr, Dec. 6, 1958; children—Susan Elizabeth, William Edward. Time study engr. Rex Chainbelt Co., Milw., 1953-55, student engr., 1955-56, sales engr., 1956-60; mgr. operations Ohio Corrugating Co., Warren, 1960-63, v.p. operations and engring., 1963-69, former sr. v.p., sec., now pres., treas., chief exec. officer, also dir.; dir. Bostwick Steel Lath Co., Niles Bank Co., both Niles, Ohio. Rep., mem. body council U.S.A. Standards Inst., 1967-69. Vice pres. adv. bd. Trumbull br. Kent State U.; bd. dirs. ARC Trumbull County (Ohio); pres. bd. trustees Trumbull Meml. Hosp. Found., Warren. Served to capt. USAF, 1949-55. Mem. Am. Iron and Steel Inst., Am. Iron and Steel Engrs., Am. Soc. for Metals, Steel Shipping Container Inst. Warren Area C. of C. Club: Youngstown (Ohio); Buckeye, Trumbull Country (Warren). Home: 219 Country Club Dr Warren OH 44484 Office: Warren OH 44481

BETTERTON, RONALD MORTON, civil engr.; b. Knoxville, Iowa, Apr. 8, 1942; s. Merle Edwin and Dorothy Lee (Thomas) B.; student Iowa State U., 1960-62, Drake U., 1962-64; m. Molly June Stittsworth, Dec. 22, 1962; children—Gregory Alan, Joel Scott, Cynthia Hope. Mem. staff C.E., U.S. Army, Rock Island, Ill., 1962-69; engr., office mgr. K.S. Kramme Inc., bridge contractors, Des Moines, 1969-71; county engr. Greene County, Jefferson, Iowa, 1971—. Mem. Iowa Engring. Soc., Nat. Assn. County Engrs., Ia. County Engrs. Assn., Am. Road Builder Assn. Republican. Mem. Christian Ch. Mason. Researcher fibrous concrete overlay for concrete pavement, 1973. Office: County Ct House Jefferson IA 50129

BETTIS, ZACK FRANKLIN, utility co. exec.; b. Blanket, Tex., Apr. 2, 1927; s. Harry Moody and Elizabeth (Dabney) B.; B.J., U. Mo., 1949; m. Kathryn Lee, July 2, 1949; children—Zack Franklin, Gail, Elizabeth, Kathryn. Dir. continuity WFFA-Radio, Dallas, 1949-52; with Southwestern Bell Telephone Co., 1952—, dir. labor relations, St. Louis, 1977—. Pres. Parkway Sch. Dist., St. Louis County, 1971—; chmn. St. Louis Conf. on Edn., 1972-75, St. Louis U. Pub. Relations Council, 1971—; mem. Mo. Bd. Edn., 1973—, v.p., 1974-75, pres., 1975-76; trustee Blue Cross Assn. St. Louis; mem. adv. council U. Mo., St. Louis, 1977. Served with USCGR, 1945-46. Mem. Pub. Relations Soc. Am., Nat. Assn. State Bds. Edn. (dir.). Methodist. Club: Forest Hills Country. Home: 25 Brookwood St Saint Louis MO 63131 Office: 1010 Pine St Saint Louis MO 63101

BETTS, HENRY BROGNARD, physician; b. New Rochelle, N.Y., May 25, 1928; s. Henry Brognard and Marguerite Meredith (Denise) B.; A.B., Princeton U., 1950; M.D., U. Va., 1954; m. Monika Christine Paul, Apr. 25, 1970; 1 dau., Amanda. Intern, Cin. Gen. Hosp., 1954-55; resident, teaching fellow N.Y. U. Med. Center Inst. Rehab. Medicine, N.Y.C., 1958-63; practice medicine, specializing in phys. medicine and rehab., Chgo., 1963—; staff physiatrist Rehab. Inst. Chgo., 1963-64, asso. med. dir., 1964-65, med. dir., 1965-69, v.p., med. dir., 1969—; Paul B. Magnuson prof., also chmn. dept. rehab. medicine Northwestern U., 1967—, prof., 1968—; chmn. phys. medicine and rehab. Northwestern Meml. Hosp.; cons. Chgo. Wesley Meml. Hosp., Passavant Meml. Hosp., Chgo.; mem. United Cerebral Palsy Steering Com., 1967—; mem. med. adv. com., pres. Am. Congress Rehab. Medicine, 1975—; chmn. taskforce on rehab. Ill. Cancer Council; chmn. Gov.s Com. for Employment of Handicapped. Served with USNR, 1956-58. Named Physician of Year, Ill. Gov.'s Com., 1964; recipient commendation Ill. Gen. Assembly, 1967, citation for meritorious service Pres.'s Com. on Employment of Handicapped, 1965. Diplomate Am. Bd. Phys. Medicine and Rehab. Mem. Ill. Med. Soc. (chmn. com. on rehab. services), Assn. Academic Physiatrists (pres. 1968-69). Contbr. articles to profl. jours. Home: 1727 N Orleans St Chicago IL 60614 Office: 345 E Superior St Chicago IL 60611

BETZ, GARY ARLIN, dentist; b. Minerva, Ohio, Nov. 13, 1938; s. Donald Arlin and Twylah B. (Kibler) B.; D.D.S. cum laude, Ohio State U., 1963; m. Kathryn F. Doty, Dec. 22, 1961; children—Cynthia, Deborah, Gary Arlin. Pvt. practice dentistry, Westerville, Ohio, 1965—; faculty Ohio State U. Dental Sch., 1965-77. Mem. Jaycee speaking com. for Sch. Bd., 1973—. Served as capt. Dental Corps, USAF, 1963-65. Mem. ADA, Columbus, Ohio dental assns., Westerville Dental Study Club (v.p. 1974-75, pres. 1975—), Council Columbus Dental Vets., Columbus Figure Skating Club (chmn. Tri-State Figure Skating Championships 1975, chmn. Summer Figure Skating Competition 1976), Buckeye Figure Skating Club (pres. 1976-78), Psi Omega, Omicron Kappa Upsilon. Republican. Club: Masons. Home: 161 Walnut Ridge Ln Westerville OH 43081 Office: 509 S Otterbein Ave Westerville OH 43081

BETZER, JOSEPH GEORGE, film producer; b. Buffalo, Aug. 13, 1917; s. Anthony John and Bernadine M. (Carroll) B.; student St. Joseph's Collegiate Inst., Buffalo, 1930-34, Buffalo State Tchrs. Coll., 1934-38; m. Ruth Julia Steffan, Dec. 28, 1940. Publicity dir. WEBR-WBEN, Buffalo, 1938-39; radio editor Buffalo Evening News, 1940-41; scenario writer Army Signal Corps Tng. Film Prodn. Lab., Wright Field, Ohio, 1942-43; dir. creative services Sarra, Inc., Chgo., 1944-55; account exec. Vogue Wright Studios, Chgo., 19S5-56; v.p. Cal Dunn Studios, Chgo., 1957-67; pres. Betzer Prodns., Inc., Chgo., 1967—; owner mail order service Geneva House, Chgo. Mem. Chgo. Audio-Visual Producers Assn. (dir.), Nat. Acad. TV Arts and Scis., Chgo. Unlimited, Am. Assn. Film Producers (founding mem. 1947, sec. 1947-54). Republican. Home: 8912 Harms Rd Morton Grove IL 60053 Office: 450 E Ohio St Chicago IL 60611

BEUC, RUDOLPH, JR., architect, real estate broker; b. St. Louis, Nov. 7, 1931; s. Rudolph M. and Lillian Ann (Rethemeyer) B.; B.Arch., Washington U., St. Louis, 1955; m. Mildred Hild, Jan. 25, 1968; children—Rudolph III, Ralph M. Archtl. draftsman Bank Bldg. & Equipment Corp. Am., St. Louis, 1950, Hammond & Gorlock, architects, St. Louis, 1957-58; designer Schwarz & Van Hoefen, architects, St. Louis, 1958; architect George E. Berg Architects, St. Louis, 1958-60; architect R. Beuc, Architects, Inc., St. Louis, 1960—, pres., 1960—, also dir.; pres., dir. Hilterdevco, Inc., St. Louis, 1964—, Keokuk Investment Inc.; dir. Rethemeyer Coffee Co., Inc., St. Louis. Bldg. commr., Peerless Park, 1967—. Served with AUS, 1955-57. Mem. AIA, Soc. Am. Registered Architects, Mo. Assn. Registered Architects, Mo. Assn. Bldg. Ofcls. and Inspectors, Webster Groves C. of C., Am. Legion, St. Louis Ambassadors. Mason, Lion; mem. Order Eastern Star, DeMolay. Clubs: High Twelve (past state pres.), Scottish Rite, Washington University, Westborough Country. Home: 138 W Glendale Rd St Louis MO 63119 Office: 142 W Glendale Rd St Louis MO 63119

BEUM, ROBERT LAWRENCE, editor; b. Mt. Vernon, Ohio, Aug. 20, 1929; s. Robert Francis and Florence Catherine (Draper) B.; B.A., Ohio State U., 1952, M.A., 1958; m. Phyllis Ann Fisher, July 10, 1954; children—Valerie Ann, Elaine Frances, Paul Vernon. Instr. English, U. Nebr., 1958-61; asst. prof. English, Creighton U., Omaha, 1962-65; asst. prof. English, Nebr. Wesleyan U., Lincoln, 1965-68; asso. prof. English, St. Dunstan's U., Charlottetown, P.E.I., Can., 1968-69, U. Lethbridge (Alta.), 1970-71, U. P.E.I., Charlottetown, 1971-74; asso. prof. N.D. State U., Fargo, 1974-75; sr. editor U. Mid-Am., Lincoln, Nebr., 1976—. Mem. Royal Stuart Soc., Milton Soc. Am. Episcopalian. Author: Poems and Epigrams, 1964; (with Karl Shapiro) A Prosody Handbook, 1965; Spenser's 'Epithalamion, 1968; The Poetic Art of William Butler Yeats, 1969; (with James W. Sire) Paper on Literature: Models and Methods, 1970; Ten for the Light (poems), 1971; contbr. to mags. and newspapers throughout U.S., Can., Europe, Australia. Home: 3103 S 16th St Lincoln NE 68502 Office: 1600 N 33d St Lincoln NE 68503

BEUSE, DONALD LEE, foundry exec.; b. Davenport, Iowa, July 2, 1933; s. William Alfred and Helen (Hartog) B.; grad. high sch.; m. Beverly June Burkamper, Dec. 21, 1956. Apprentice pattern maker Blackhawk Foundry, 1950-53, Iowa Pattern Works, 1955-67; owner, pres. Buese's Pattern Works, LeClaire, Iowa, 1967—. Vol. tchr. Quad Cities Pattern Makers Apprentice Program, 1964-67, pres. com., 1968-70; vol. LeClaire Fire Dept., 1968—, pres. 1970; mem. citizens' adv. com. Black Hawk Coll., 1974—. Democratic committeeman, 1958-60. Served with AUS, 1953-55. Mem. Am. Foundrymens Assn., LeClaire Bus. Mens Assn., Am. Legion (vice comdr. 1962), Aircraft Owners and Pilots Assn. Mason (Shriner), Moose. Club: Clinton Engineers. Home: RR 1 Box 336 LeClaire IA 52753 Office: 304 S Cody Rd LeClaire IA 52753

BEUTLER, FREDERICK JOSEPH, educator; b. Berlin, Germany, Oct. 3, 1926; s. Alfred David and Kaethe (Italiener) B.; came to U.S., 1936, naturalized, 1943; B.S., Mass. Inst. Tech., 1949, M.S., 1951; Ph.D., Calif. Inst. Tech., 1957; m. Suzanne Armstrong, Jan. 6, 1969; children—Arthur David, Kathryn Ruth, Michael Ernest. Mem. faculty U. Mich. at Ann Arbor, 1957—, prof. info. and control engring., 1963—, chmn. computer info. and control engring. program, 1970, 77—; vis. prof. Calif. Inst. Tech., 1967-68; vis. scholar U. Calif. at Berkeley, 1964-65; various cons. appointments at various times; dir. Wine Importers, Inc. Bd. dirs. Ann Arbor Civic Theatre, 1976—. Served with AUS, 1945-46. Club: Economic (Detroit); Barton Boat (sec. 1972-74) (Ann Arbor). Mem. Soc. Indsl. and Applied Math. (council 1969-74), Am. Math. Soc., Inst. Math. Statistics, AAUP, Am. Soc. Engring. Edn., IEEE, Am. Arbitration Assn., Sigma Xi. Editorial cons. Math. Revs., 1962-64, 75—; mng. editor SIAM Jour. on Applied Math., 1970-75; editor SIAM Rev., 1967-70. Contbr. articles to profl. jours., chpts. in books. Home: 1717 Shadford Rd Ann Arbor MI 48104

BEUTNER, GRANT CHARLES, chem. corp. exec.; b. Mpls., Nov. 5, 1922; s. Charles Theodore and Louise Alida (Hasselton) B.; B.S., U. Chgo., 1949; M.S., Marquette U., 1958; m. Rosemary Ann McLaughlin, June 21, 1952; children—Jeffrey, Nancy, Andrea. Research chemist, Graphic Arts Tech. Found.. Chgo., 1949-50; research dir., Western Pub. Corp., Racine, Wis., 1950-54; pres., bd. chmn., RBP Chem. Corp., Milw., 1954—, Automated Systems Inc., Brookfield, Wis., 1968—; dir. Brandt Corp., Howard Co. Served with USAAF, 1943-46. Mem. Am. Chem. Soc., AAAS, Printing Industries Am., Nat. Assn. Photo-Lithographers, Graphic Arts Tech. Found. Club: Masons. Contbr. articles to publs.; patentee in field of chemistry. Home: Route 1 Dousman WI 53118 Office: 150 S 118th St Milwaukee WI 53214

BEVERLEY, JOHN LOUIS, JR., photographer; b. Phila., July 6, 1930; s. John Louis and Venela Mae (Chapman) B.; B.S. in Elec. Engring., Rutgers U., 1962; M.S., Drexel Inst. Tech., 1964; Ph.D., Oxford U., 1975. Enlisted U.S. Navy, 1947, commd. Warrant Officer, 1967, advanced through grades to lt., 1973; served in U.S.S. Missouri, 1948-49, Korea, 1950-51; assigned U.S. Naval Air Sta., Pensacola, Fla., 1952-53, Am. embassy, Amman, Jordan, 1960, Saigon, Vietnam, 1967, London, Eng., 1973-75, ret., 1975; owner, operator photography store Chgo., 1976—. Decorated Silver Star, Purple Heart with 3 clusters, Air Medal, D.S.C.; Rhodes scholar, 1963; Pres.'s fellow, 1968. Mem. Naval Inst., Ret. Officers Assn., Profl. Photographers Am., Nat. Press Photographers Assn., IEEE, VFW, Am. Legion. Democrat. Baptist. Club: Elks. Home and office: 6030 N Sheridan Rd Chicago IL 60660

BEVERLY, EVE MARIE DE SAVIEU, primary sch. tchr.; b. Chgo., Dec. 23, 1928; d. Charles Adrian and Lubertha (Peters) De Savieu; B.S. in Edn., Lincoln U., Jefferson City, Mo., 1952; M.A., Roosevelt U., 1975; Ph.D., Union Grad. Sch., 1977; m. Sherman Beverly, Jr., June 25, 1960; children—Shereen LuKathy, Lisa Marie, Tajma Lazette. Tchr. primary grades Chgo. pub. schs., 1952-67, also adult edn., Head Start, day camp; tchr. primary grades Dist. 108, Highland Park, Ill., 1967—; lectr. Coll. Lake County, Grayslake, Ill., 1977—; real estate broker, 1955—; pres. Highland Park Edn. Assn., 1973-74; cons. workshops. Bd. dirs. N. Shore Mental Health Assn., 1967-68, Irene Josselyn Clinic, Northfield, Ill., 1967-68; mem. Deerfield (Ill.) Human Relations Com., 1967—. Mem. Nat., Ill. edn. assns., Ill. Personnel and Guidance Assn., Am. Coll. Personnel Assn., Ill. Assn. Non-White Concerns in Personnel and Guidance, Assn. Black Psychologists, Internat. Transactional Analysis Assn., Jack and Jill Am., Delta Sigma Theta. Lutheran. Address: 1327 Central Ave Deerfield IL 60015

BEVERSDORF, SAMUEL THOMAS, composer, educator; b. Yoakum, Tex., Aug. 8, 1924; s. Samuel T. and Estelle M. (Hamblen) B.; Mus.B. (Hoblitzel fellow) cum laude, U. Tex., 1945; Mus.M., Eastman Sch. of Music, U. Rochester, N.Y., 1946, Dr. Mus. Arts (Danforth fellow), 1959; m. Norma Iris Beeson, June 26, 1945; children—Anne Elizabeth, Paula Lynne Gabbard, Sarah Katherine, Samuel Thomas III, David Quentin. First trombonist Houston Symphony Orch., 1946-48, resident composer, 1946-48; instr. music composition U. Houston, 1946-48; bass trombonist Pitts. Symphony Orch., 1948-49; faculty Sch. of Music, Ind. U., Bloomington, 1951—, prof. music composition, 1964—; composer-in-residence, guest prof. Bucknell U., Lewisburg, Pa., 1970-71; guest condr. Indpls. Symphony Orch., 1951, Houston Symphony Orch., 1953, Eastman-Rochester Summer Symphony Orch., 1957. World premieres include Christmas Sonata for horn and piano, Eastman Sch. of Music, 1946, Symphony No. 1, Eastman-Rochester Symphony Orch., N.Y., 1946, Reflections for small orch., Houston Symphonette, 1950, Suite on Baroque Themes for clarinet, violincello and piano, U. Houston, 1948, Mexican Portrait, Houston Symphony, 1948, Concerto Grosso, Pitts. Symphony, 1951, Quartet No. 1, Berkshire Quartet, Bloomington, Ind., 1952, Symphony for Winds and Percussion, Ind. U. Wind Ensemble, 1954, Quartet No. 2, Berkshire Quartet, Bloomington, 1956, Symphony No. 3 for Orch., Ind. U. Philharmonic Orch., 1958, Serenade for small orch., U. Tex., 1956, Sonata for Tuba and Piano, Ore. U., 1956, Serenade for Winds and Percussion, Eastman Wind Ensemble, Rochester, 1958, The Rock (Oratorio), Bloomington, 1958, Concerto for Violin and Orch., Eastman-Rochester Symphony, 1957, Symphony No. 4, Ind. U. Philharmonic Orch., 1960, Variations for Piano, Can. Broadcasting Co., 1959, Sonata for Trumpet and Piano, Ind. U., 1962, Variations for Orch., Ind. U. Orch., 1963, Sonata for Violin and Piano, Festival of Am. Music, Rochester, N.Y., 1964, Sonata for Flute and Piano, Pan Am. Festival of Contemporary Music, 1965, Generation with the Torch, Bayreuth, Germany, 1965, Divertimento da Camera for Flute, Oboe, Double Bass, Harpsichord, Hanover Coll., 1968, Sonata for Violoncello and Piano, San Francisco Jewish Community Center, 1970, and others; works commd. by Houston Symphony Orch., 1953, Ind. U., 1967, Cin. Symphony, 1953, Teltschik duo Pianists, 1951, Variations for Piano, B. Borzormenyí-Nagy, 1959, Houston Youth Orch., 1964, Bucknell U., 1970, Concerto for Tuba, Harvey Phillips, 1975, Sonata for Violin and Harp, Jacques Israelievitch, 1975. Served with USAAF World War II. Recipient Distinguished Service to Music award Tex. Fedn. of Music Clubs, 1970. Mem. ASCAP (Spl. award 1965-77), Am. Fedn. of Musicians, AAUP, Phi Mu Alpha Sinfonia, Pi Kappa Lambda. Mason. Author-librettist The Rock, 1956; (operas) The Hooligan, 1964, The Metamorphosis, 1968. Transcribed various 18th. Century mus. compositions for trombone and piano. Home: 4950 E Cedar Crest Bloomington IN 47401 Office: MA 307 Indiana Univ School of Music Bloomington IN 47401

BEVIRT, JOSEPH LLOYD, mgmt. cons.; b. St. Louis, June 22, 1931; s. William John and Jennie Laura (Roehm) B.; B.S., U. Mo.. 1953. M.S. in Biolytical Chemistry, 1956; m. Wilma Leah Evans, Aug. 2, 1953; children—Renee Patrice, Josette Laura, Bruce Joseph. Chemistry instr. U. Mo., 1955-56; chemist Dow Chem. Co., Midland, Mich., 1956-61, market analyst, 1962-66, dir. mktg. research Pacific div., Hong Kong, 1967-70, tech. products mktg. mgr., 1971-72; sales and project dir. Nat. Mktg. Surveys, Midland, 1973-74, sr. mktg. analyst, 1975—; cons. to White House; instr. mktg. Saginaw Valley Coll., 1976—; bus. advisor Chinese U. Hong Kong, 1969-72. Vice pres. Lake Huron Area council Boy Scouts Am., 1973—; bd. dirs. Midland County Cancer Soc., 1976—, Trout Unltd., 1976—; chmn. Mackinac Trail Commn., 1958-67, 76—. Served with U.S. Army, 1953-55. Recipient Mich. Congress Parents Parents and Teachers Distinguished Service award, 1967; Silver Beaver award Boy Scouts Am., 1977. Mem. Am. Chem. Soc.. Chem. Mktg. Research Assn., Am. Mktg. Assn., Market Research Soc. Hong Kong, Sci. Research Soc. Am., MPC Couples Club, Alpha Chi Sigma. Presbyterian. Clubs: Sugar Springs Country, Hong Kong Country, Luzerne. Author: The Determination of Lindane Residues, 1956; contbr. articles, chpts. to tech. jours., texts. Home: 1211 Kingsbury Ct Midland MI 48640 Office: Dow Chemical USA 2020 Dow Center Midland MI 48640

BEXTEN, DONALD GENE, drapery co. exec.; b. Monroe County, Mich., SePt. 2, 1936; s. Lawrence Arnold and Geraldine (Brewster) B.; educated Mich. State U., 1959; m. Marcia Lee Pilkerd, Sept. 17, 1961; children—Tamara Sue, Jill Annette. Newscaster WSPD-TV, Toledo, 1960-64; v.p. Flournoy & Gibbs, Inc. Toledo, 1964-73; owner, exec. Elden Draperies, Inc., Sylvania, Ohio, 1973—; lectr. in field. Republican. Clubs: Toledo Exchange (past dir., v.p.), Toledo Sales & Mktg. (past dir., v.p.), Advt. (past dir., v.p.), Sylvania Reps. Home: 5824 Tantallon Circle Sylvania OH 43560 Office: 3416 Silica Rd Sylvania OH 43560

BEYER, DONALD JAMES, ins. co. exec.; b. Fond du Lac, Wis., Apr. 25, 1922; s. Orwin F. and Delia E. (Chassee) B.; student Wis. State U., Oshkosh, 1943; LL.B., U. Wis., 1948; m. Joan C. Gratton, Nov. 11, 1950; children—Karen, Linda, Anne. Sec.-treas. Fond du Lac County Abstract Co., Fond du Lac, Wis., 1948-50; trust officer Bank of Madison (Wis.), 1950-53; asst. sec. Wisconsin Life Ins. Co., Madison, 1953-59, exec. v.p., 1964-68, pres., 1968—; dir. Hilldale State Bank, Mid-Am. Assos., Inc., Wis. Life Fund, Inc., Wis. Life Corp., Inc., Wis. Life Iowa, Inc., Affiliated Bank Corp. Served with USAAF, 1943-45. Mem. Wis., Dane County bar assns., Sierra Club, Optimist Internat., Gamma Eta Gamma. Roman Catholic. Home: 3106 Pelham Rd Madison WI 53713 Office: Wisconsin Life Insurance Co PO Box 5099 Madison WI 53713

BEYER, STEPHEN LUCIAN, lawyer; b. Shawano, Wis., Feb. 13, 1940; s. Kenneth Earl and Nancy Margaret (Davis) B.; student U. Wis. at Madison, 1961; LL.B., Marquette U., 1964; m. Bridget Alice Brenzel, June 16, 1962; children—Bradford John, Andrew William, Susan Nancy, Karl George. Admitted to Wis. bar, 1964; practiced in Shawano, 1964-65, New London, Wis., 1965—; mem. firm Winter & Beyer & Lindgren, 1964-65, partner, 1965—; sec., chmn. bd., dir. Curtis Corp., New London, 1972—; pres., dir. Sylvan Devel. Corp., 1970—; sec., dir. F & B Inc., 1971—; v.p., dir. David L. Rusch Enterprises, Inc., New London, 1974—. Mem. Waupaca County Republican Exec. Com., 1971—; del. Wis. Rep. Conv., 1972, 73, 74. Pres. bd. dirs. New London Community Hosp.; v.p., dir. St. Joseph Residence Inc. Mem. Am., Wis., Waupaca County (pres.) bar assns., Marquette Law Alumni Assn., Delta Theta Phi, Sigma Chi. Republican. Episcopalian. Rotarian. Asso. editor Marquette Law Rev., 1962-64. Home: 1909 Mayflower Ct New London WI 54961 Office: 308 St John's Pl New London WI 54961

BEZANE, NORMAN GILBERT, publs. mgr.; b. Oak Pk., Ill., Feb. 1, 1938; s. Gilbert John and Mildred Margaret (Vanderslice) B.; B.S. in Communications, U. Ill., 1960; m. Sara Kay Foley, June 21, 1969; 1 dau., Foley. Asst. editor Chgo. bur. Bus. Week, 1962-66; press relations mgr. SRA subs. IBM, Chgo., 1966-68; v.p. B.E. Ury Assos., Chgo., 1968-72; publs. mgr. FMC Corp., Chgo., 1972—. Recipient Volunteer Services award, Chgo. Economic Devel. Corp., 1970; award from Soc. of Pubs. Designers, 1976. Mem. Pub. Relations Soc. of Am., Internat. Assn. Bus. Communicators (Merit award 1977), Publicity Club of Chgo. (dir., Golden Trumpet award 1977), Sigma Delta Chi. Editor: FMC Progress, 1972—. Home: 1836 N Mohawk St Chicago IL 60614 Office: 200 E Randolph St Chicago IL 60601

BHAKTHAVATHSALAN, AMRUTHA, physician; b. Mysore State, India, Mar. 1, 1933; d. K. and Uma (Devi) Marilingappa; came to U.S., 1966; B.S., Maharani's Coll. for Women, Bangalore, Mysore State, India, 1950; B. Medicine, B. Surgery, Univ. Med. Coll., Mysore, India, 1955. House surgeon, rotating intern Meml. Hosp., Niagara Falls, N.Y., 1966-67; resident obstetrics gynecology, pathology St. Thomas Hosp., Akron, O., 1967; resident obstetrics/gynecology Med. Coll. Ohio at Toledo and Asso. Hosps. Program, Toledo Hosp., 1968, Maumee Valley Hosp., 1969, St. Vincent Hosp., 1969, Toledo Hosp., 1970; chief resident obstetrics/gynecology Maumee Valley Hosp., 1970-71; instr. dept. obstetrics and gynecology Med. Coll. Ohio, Toledo, 1971-73; fellow perinatology Nassau County Med. Center, East Meadow, N.Y., 1973-74; research asso., 1974-75; asst. prof. dept. obstetrics/gynecology State U. N.Y., Stonybrook, 1975-76; physician-in-charge div. obstetrics, dept. obstetrics and gynecology Queens Hosp. Center Affiliation L.I. Jewish-Hillside Med. Center, Jamaica, N.Y., 1975-76; perinatologist N.W. Ohio Regional Perinatal Center, Toledo Hosp., 1976—; clin. asst. prof. dept. obstetrics/gynecology Med. Coll. Ohio, Toledo, 1976-77, clin. asso. prof., 1977—. Diplomate Am. Bd. Obstetrics and Gynecology. Fellow Am. Coll. Obstetricians and Gynecologists; mem. Am. Med. Women's Assn., Inc., Ohio State Med. Assn., Toledo Soc. Obstetrics/Gynecology, Toledo Acad. Medicine. Contbr. articles to profl. jours. Office: NW Ohio Regional Perinatal Center Toledo Hosp 2142 N Cove Blvd Toledo OH 43606

BHATIA, SHYAM S(UNDER), geographer, educator; b. Rawalpindi, Pakistan, July 7, 1924; s. Nanak Chand and Lajya (Wati) B.; m. Sushil Bhatia, June 9, 1950; children—Niru, Veena; came to U.S., 1966, naturalized, 1972; M.A., U. Panjab, Lahore, 1947; Ph.D. (Fulbright scholar), U. Kans., 1959. Asso. prof. U. Delhi, 1959-66, chmn. dept. geography, 1959-62; asso. prof., prof. U. Wis., Oshkosh, 1966—; vis. asso. prof. Sch. Internat. Studies, New Delhi, 1960-64; vis. prof. San Diego State U., 1975-76; program chmn. Conf. on S.Asia, 1974. Fellow Am. Geog. Soc.; mem. Assn. Am. Geographers, Assn. Asian Studies, Population Assn. Am., Alan Gutmacher Inst., Sigma Xi, Candle Light Club. Author: Age and Sex Structure of Wisconsin Population, 1960-70; Age and Sex Structure of Wisconsin Villages, 1970; Age and Sex Structure of Wisconsin Cities, 1970; contbr. to Ency. Brit., 1960-73. Office: Dept Geography U Wis Oshkosh WI 54901

BHATT, ASHOK GAJANAN, mech. engr.; b. Baroda, India, May 23, 1941; s. Gajanan Shankerlal and Shantaben (Gajanan) B.; came to U.S., 1967, naturalized, 1971; M.S., U. India, 1958-63, B.S. in Mech. Engring., 1969; M.A. in Bus. Adminstrn., 1978; m. Sudha Keshavdeo Trivedi, Apr. 13, 1974; 1 son, Sandeep. Mech. engr. Mellish & Murray Co., Chgo., 1970-72; design engr. Schmidt, Garden and Erickson, Chgo., 1972-74; with K & W Design and Constrn., Markham, Ill., 1974-75; sr. designer Perkins and Will, Engrs., Chgo., 1975; research engr. Capital Devel. Bd., State of Ill., Springfield, 1975—. Mem. thermal and lighting efficiency standards adv. com. Ill. Energy Resources Commn., 1976-77, solar energy tech. adv. com. on legislation, 1976-77; mem. Inter-Agy. Task Force on State of Ill. Energy Reorgn. plan, 1976-77; pres. India Assn. Met. Chgo., 1972. Mem. Am. Soc. Heating, Refrigerating and Air Conditioning Engrs., ASME, Internat. Solar Energy Soc. Hindu. Author: Comprehensive Study of P.S.S.C. Physics, 1967, 2d edit., 1971. Home: 243 S Durkain Dr Springfield IL 62704 Office: 401 S Spring St Springfield IL 62706

BHATTACHARYA, AMAR NATH, educator; b. Calcutta, India, Oct. 1, 1934; s. Ramesh Chandra and Hiron Moyee (Ghosal) B.; B. in Vet. Sci., D.V.M., Bengal Vet. Coll., 1957; M.S. in Pharmacology, Ohio State U., 1963, Ph.D. in Pharmacology (NIH Pre-doctoral fellow 1965-67), 1967; m. Minati Bhattacharya, Aug. 19, 1966; 1 dau., Sandra Sarbori. Came to U.S., 1961, naturalized, 1969. State veterinarian Govt. of West Bengal, India, 1957-59; instr. clin. vet. medicine and pharmacology Bengal Vet. Coll., 1959-61; research asst. pharmacology Coll. Medicine, Ohio State U., Columbus, 1962-67; research asso. in pharmacology and medicine, 1968; Ford Found. research fellow in physiology Sch. Medicine, U. Pitts., 1968-70; mem. faculty Ohio No. U., Ada, 1970—, asst. prof. pharmacology, 1970-74, acting chmn., 1972-74, asso. prof., 1974—. Social and program chmn. India Assn., Pitts., 1969-70. Mem. Soc. for Study Reproduction, Ohio Veterinary Med. Assn., Rho Chi, Kappa Psi. Home: 335 Grandview Blvd Ada OH 45810

BHATTAD, SITARAM MANIKALAL, microbiologist; b. Ambada, India, June 23, 1941; s. Manikalal J. and Kashi B.; B.S., Nat. Dairy Research Inst., India, 1967; M.S. in Food Sci., U. Sask. (Can.), 1970; postgrad. Ohio State U., 1970-72; m. Chanda A. Dammani, May 1, 1968; children—Vijay, Jay; Research asso. Ohio State U., 1970-72; quality control supr. Shasta Beverages div. Consol. Foods Corp., Columbus, Ohio, 1972-73; food technologist, project coordinator Kitchens of Sara Lee div., Deerfield, Ill., 1973-74; microbiologist in charge lab. services canned meat div. Libby McNeill & Libby div. Nestle Enterprises, Inc., Chgo., 1974—; founder C & S Importers and Exporters, Northbrook, Ill., 1976—; dir. food and agrl. U.S. Tech. Inc., Livonia, Mich., 1975—; founder-editor Dairy Science Mag., 1967—. Mem. Inst. Food Technologists, Am. Soc. for Quality Control, Toastmasters Internat. (v.p. Northshore chpt. 1976, pres. 1977, ednl. lt. gov. area 3, 1977, Outstanding Toastmaster Year award, 1976). Contbr. articles to profl. jours. Home: 1814 Kiest Ave Northbrook IL 60062 Office: 1700 W 119th St Chicago IL 60643

BIAL, ANDRE JOSEPH, diversified industry exec.; b. Lakewood, O., Sept. 27, 1937; s. Joseph John and Sophia (Hlavko) B.; A.B., U. Mich., 1960, M.B.A., 1961; m. Kay Louise Krahnke, Aug. 12, 1960; children—Robert J., Andrea K. Adminstrv. asst. comml. loans Central Nat. Bank, Cleve., 1961-65; v.p. nat. div. Bank of Commonwealth, Detroit, 1965-69; v.p., treas. MSP (Mich. Screw Products) Industries Corp., diversified industry, Center Line, Mich., 1969-77; v.p. finance DeVlieg Machine Co., Royal Oak, Mich., 1977—; dir. Ventrola Mfg. Co., Mills Products Corp. Served with AUS, 1960. Mem. Greater Detroit C. of C., Center Line C. of C., N. Am. Soc. Corporate Planning (dir.), U. Mich. Alumni Assn., Kappa Sigma. Republican. Episcopalian. Club: Birmingham (Mich.) Athletic. Home: 205 Lake Park Birmingham MI 48009 Office: Fair St Royal Oak MI 46068

BIBBO, MARLUCE, physician, educator; b. Sao Paulo, Brazil, July 14, 1939; d. Domingos and Yolanda (Ranciaro) Bibbo; M.D., U. Sao Paulo, 1963, Sc.D., 1968. Intern, Hosps. das Clinicas, U. Sao Paulo, 1963, resident in obstetrics and gynecology, 1964-66; instr. dept. morphology and obstetrics and gynecology U. Sao Paulo, 1966-68, asst. prof., 1968-69; asst. prof. sect. cytology dept. obstetrics and gynecology U. Chgo., 1969-73, asso. prof., 1973—, asso. prof., 1973—, asso. prof. pathology, 1974—; asso. dir. Cytology Lab., Approved Sch. Cytotech. and Cytocybernetics, AMA-Am. Soc. Clin. Pathologists, 1970—. Fellow Internat. Acad. Cytology; mem. Am. Soc. Cytology (chmn. com. new mems. 1972—). Contbr. numerous articles to profl. jours. Home: 400 E Randolph St Apt 2009 Chicago IL 60601 Office: 5841 S Maryland Ave Chicago IL 60637

BIBER, JAKUB JAN, physician; b. Chyrow, Poland, Sept. 12, 1900; s. Marek and Regine (Lowenthal) B.; M.D., U. Vienna, 1924; M.D., U. Cracow, 1925; postgrad. U. Hosp. Vienna, 1925-27; m. Felicja Maria Hausen, Mar. 15, 1926. Chief ear, nose, throat dept. Gen. Hosp. Przemysl, Poland, 1928-41; chief asst. Met. Ear, Nose & Throat Hosp., London, England, 1949-52, Battersea Gen. Hosp., 1949-52; practice medicine specializing in ear, nose, throat, plastic surgery, Delaware, O., 1956—; mem. staff Meml. Grady Hosp., Delaware, Ohio. Served with British Army, 1941-49. Fellow Royal Soc. Medicine, Am. Acad. Ophthalmology and Otolaryngology, Internat. Acad. Cosmetic Surgery, Am. Acad. Facial Plastic and Reconstructive Surgery; hon. fellow Hellenic Oto-neuro-opthalmolog. Soc. Greece. Contbr. to profl. publs. in field. Address: 98 W Winter St Delaware OH 43015

BIBERSTINE, ROMANEL RUTH, real estate broker; b. Muncie, Ind., Feb. 8, 1925; d. Chauncey Kenneth and Cleeda Emily (Schafer) Reid; student Purdue U., 1943, 64; grad. Ind. Realtor's Inst., Ind. U., 1971; m. Joegene Biberstine, June 18, 1944; children—Elaine (Mrs. Lawrence J. Schiel), Brenda, William Reid. Real estate broker, owner Biberstine Real Estate, LaPorte, Ind., 1965—. Bd. dirs. Family Service Assn. LaPorte County (Ind.), 1967-74, Fairview Youth Residential Treatment Center, LaPorte, Ind., treas., 1973—. Mem. LaPorte Bd. Realtors Inc. (sec.-treas. 1972-73, v.p. 1974, pres. 1975-76), Tri Kappa. Methodist (mem. bd. trustees 1972-74, sec. bd. 1973). Home: 609 Waverly Rd LaPorte IN 46350

BICKEL, ERMALINDA, real estate broker; b. Casole Bruzio Provincia di Cosenza, Italy, Nov. 8, 1919; d. Saverio and Emilia (Fortino) Fortino; came to U.S., 1927, naturalized, 1927; student pub. schs. Italy, Elkhart, Ind.; m. William E. Bickel, Aug. 10, 1946; 1 dau., Patricia Ann Heiser. Office clk. Gen. Telephone, Elkhart, Ind., 1939-41; sec. to pres. of Ames Co. div. Miles Labs., Inc., Elkhart, 1941-52, tech. sec. pharmacy research dept., 1962—; free lance legal sec., 1956-61; owner, founder Blue Chip Realty, Inc., Elkhart, Ind., 1968—. Mem. Nat., Ind., Elkhart real estate bds., Delta Theta Tau, Zonta, Elkhart C. of C. Roman Catholic. Office: 26258 Cottage Ave Elkhart IN 46514

BICKLEY, JOHN HOWARD, JR., lawyer; b. Chgo., May 12, 1929; s. John H. and Letta (McGraw) B.; student Evanston Twp. Community Coll., 1948; J.D., Chgo. Kent Coll. Law, 1951; m. Joan Marino Bickley, June 19, 1976; children by previous marriage—John H. III, Lisa F., Kathryn M. Admitted to Ill. bar, 1952; partner Peterson, Bogucki & Bickley, Attys., Chgo., 1957-67, individual practice, Chgo., 1968—; mem. firm Bickley & Stern; spl. asst. atty. gen., Ill., 1968-69; chief, environmental control div. Atty. Gen.'s Office, State of Ill., 1970-71; asst. U.S. atty. Dept. Justice, No. Dist. Ill., 1955-57; trial atty. Forest Preserve Dist. Cook County. Spl. prosecutor Chgo. Police Burglar Scandal, 1961; mem. lecture forum Mid-West U.S. Atty. Conf., 1963; mem. dist. council SBA, 1971-72; legal cons. Ill. State Bd. Elections. Trustee, Village of Mount Prospect (Ill.), 1961-63, 1st v.p. Regular Republican Orgn., Elk Grove Twp., 1961-62; candidate for states atty. Cook County, 1964. Served with USMCR, now lt. colonel (ret.). Named one of Chgo.'s 10 Outstanding Young Men, Chgo. Jaycees, 1964; One of Outstanding Young Men U.S., 1965. Mem. Internat. Acad. Law and Sci., Ill., Chgo., Fed. (pres. Chgo. chpt. 1972-73) bar assns., Am. Arbitration Assn. (nat. panel arbitrators), Am., Ill. (pres. 1971-72), trial lawyers' assns., Trial Lawyers' Club Chgo., soc. Trial Lawyers, Law Club Chgo., Legal Club of Chgo., Globe and Anchor Soc. Ill. (past pres.), Am. Legion. Episcopalian. Mason (32 deg., Shriner). Secured conviction of syndicate crime leader Paul (The Waiter) Ricca, 1957. Club: Tavern (Chgo.). Home: 6 Ct of Bucks County Lincolnshire IL 60015 Office: 77 W Washington St Chicago IL 60602

BICKMORE, JOHN TILGHMAN, physician; b. Cin., Jan. 30, 1920; s. Harley Lester and Mary Eleanor (Tilghman) B.; B.Sc., U. Cin., 1942, M.D., 1944; m. Emilie Duccilli, Aug. 3, 1945; children—Carol (Mrs. Richard DeOrzio), John Timothy. Intern, Cin. Gen. Hosp., 1944-45; resident St. Louis U. Grad. Sch. Medicine, 1946-48; practice medicine, specializing in otolaryngology and allergy, Dayton, Ohio, 1948—; asso. clin. prof. otolaryngology Wright State U.; asst. clin. prof. dept. otolaryngology U. Cin.; sr. attending staff Miami Valley Hosp., Dayton, Children's Med. Center, Dayton, Kettering (Ohio) Med. Center, mem. staff Cin. Gen. Hosp. Mem. at large Kettering-Steyr (Austria) Sister City Com., 1972-74. Served to lt. (j.g.) USNR, 1945-46; lt. USNR, 1952-54. Fellow Am. Coll. Allergy (asso.); mem. Am. Laryngol., Rhinol. and Otolaryn. Soc., Am. Soc. Facial Plastic & Reconstructive Surgery, Am. Acad. Opthalmology and Otolaryngology, Am. Soc. Ophthalmologic and Otolaryngol. Allergy (past v.p.), Beta Theta Pi. Republican. Roman Catholic. Contbr. articles to profl. jours. Home: 3241 Ridgeview Ave Kettering OH 45409 Office: 300 IBM Bldg Dayton OH 45402

BICKNELL, JAMES LEE, missile co. exec.; b. Benton Harbor, Mich., Oct. 28, 1928; s. Delosse Emerson and Mary Lee (Bare) B.; B.S., Mich. State U., 1950; postgrad. Def. Lang. Inst., 1951-52; m. Jeanne Frances Labadie, Sept. 3, 1955; children—John Charles, Patricia Lee. With Aerospace div. Bendix Corp. Mishawaka, Ind., 1954—, head material analysis lab., 1963—. Served with Security Agy., AUS, 1951-54. Recipient Colwell award Soc. Automotive Engrs., 1968. Mem. Soc. Applied Spectroscopy, Am. Soc. Testing and Materials, Alpha Chi Sigma. Lion (dir. Cassopolis, Mich.). Home: RD 5 Box 352 Cassopolis MI 49031 Office: Bendix Corp 400 S Beiger St Mishawaka IN 46544

BICKSLER, JAMES LAZAROFF, ednl. adminstr.; b. Belvidere, Ill., July 11, 1937; s. John L. and Katherine (Lazaroff) B.; B.A., Beloit Coll., 1959; M.B.A., N.Y. U., 1960, Ph.D., 1967; m. Conchita Gentolia, Sept. 1, 1974. Financial economist Stanford Research Inst., 1965-67; asst. prof. U. Hawaii, 1968-69; asso. prof. Rutgers U. Grad. Sch. Bus., 1970—, dir. research, 1974—; econ. cons. Iowa State Commerce Commn., 1973—. Adv. dir. Fed. U. of Rio de Janeiro (Brazil). Mem. Am. Econ. Assn., Am. Finance Assn. Author: Methodology in Finance, 1972; Investment Portfolio Decision Making, 1974. Contbr. numerous articles to finance jours. Home: 920 Maple Av Belvidere IL 61008 Office: Rutgers U 92 New St Newark NJ 07102

BIDDINGER, JOHN WESLEY, financial exec.; b. Indpls., May 5, 1940; s. Noble L. and Eleanor Jane (Lynch) B.; B.S., Ind. U., 1963; m. Margaret Jo Hunt, Sept. 1, 1962; children—Karen Elizabeth, Katherine Jane. With City Securities Corp., Indpls., 1963—, salesman, 1963-67, v.p., 1967-69, exec. v.p., dir.. 1969—; dir. Anacomp Inc., Noble Romans Inc.; registered prin., mem. Chgo. Bd. Options Exchange; mem. arbitration com. Chgo. Bd. Options. Bd. dirs. Starlight Musicals. Hon. Ky. col., col. a.d.c. Tenn. Mem. Confrerie des Chevaliers du Tastevin, Les Amis du Vin, Nat. Assn. Securities Dealers, Indpls. Bond Club, Nat. (nominating com., affiliate liaison com.), Indpls. (inaugural pres.) security traders assns., Indpls. Jaycees, Well House Soc., Indpls. Mus. Art, Cousteau Soc., Oceanic Soc., Ind. U. Sch. Bus. Alumni Assn., Ind. U. Alumni Assn. (chmn. nominating com., mem. dues, ins. and outdoor edn. coms.), Dean's Assos. Ind. U. Bus. Sch., Ind. U. Varsity Club, Ind. U. Hoosier 100, Sigma Chi. Clubs: Masons, Pointe Golf and Tennis, Meridian Hills Country, Univ., Columbia, Manor House, Andre's. Home: 9121 Spring Hollow Dr Indianapolis IN 46260 Office: 400 Circle Tower Indianapolis IN 46204

BIDWELL, THOMAS LEROY, controls mfg. co. exec.; b. Greenville, O., July 27, 1932; s. Kenneth Renzie and Catherine Odine (Wilt) B.; grad. high sch.; m. Mary Grace Turicchi, Aug. 30, 1950; children—Paula Maria (Mrs. Wright), Thomas Christopher. Engr., Stamco Inc., New Bremen, Ohio, 1953-56; with Crown Controls Corp., New Bremen, 1956—, gen. mgr., 1961-72, v.p., 1971—; v.p. Crown Controls Internat., Crown Controls Australia Pty. Ltd.; dir. Industrias Montarcargas S.A. de Mexico. Bd. dirs. Material Handling Inst., Indsl. Truck Assn. Home: 811 N Buckeye St Celina OH 45822 Office: 40 S Washington St New Bremen OH 45869

BIDWILL, WILLIAM V., football exec. Mng. gen. partner St. Louis Cardinals Football Team. Office: Saint Louis Cardinals 200 Stadium Plaza Saint Louis MO 63102*

BIEBER, ELIZA DAVIS (MRS. ROBERT R. BIEBER), librarian; b. Stickney, Mo., Oct. 2, 1916; d. John Thomas and Emma (Berry) Davis; A. Library Sci., Community Coll. (Chgo.), 1966; student Chgo. Tchrs. Coll., 1966-67; B.A., Trinity Christian Coll., 1973; m. John Lewis Wyss, Sept. 21, 1940 (div. May 1969); 1 dau., Konda Eliza Wyss Pulley; m. 2d. Robert Richard Bieber, Dec. 5, 1970. Librarian Bedford Park Library, Argo, Ill., 1964-65; head librarian Acorn Pub. Library, Oak Forest, Ill., 1967-72, South Stickney Pub. Library, Burbank, Ill., 1972—. Pres. P.T.A., Bedford Park, 1962. Mem. ALA, Ill. Library Assn., Library Administrs. No. Ill., So. Suburban Librarians Assn. (chmn. comn. on edn., sec. 1973-75). Home: 16621 Gaynelle Rd Tinley Park IL 60477

BIEBERLY, FRANK GEARHART, ret. agronomist; b. Spearville, Kans., Feb. 29, 1912; s. Alois R. and Marie (Budig) B.; B.S. in Agronomy, 1938, M.S. in Agronomy, 1949; m. Genevieve Lillian Scheffer, Dec. 27, 1939; children—Jeanne (Mrs. Dean Hannebaum), Janet (Mrs. Raymond Wilkerson), Frank Gearheart, John, Jerilyn (Mrs. Shannon Broussard), Joseph, Julie. Tchr., Paxico (Kans.) High Sch., 1938-41; asst. county agt. Morris County Council Grove, Kans., 1941-42; county agt. Hamilton County, Syracuse, Kans., 1942-46; extension agronomist Kans. State U., Manhattan, 1946—, sect. leader extension agronomy, 1961-77. Recipient Edn. Service award Kans. Fertilizer and Chem. Inst., 1969. Mem. Am. Soc. Agronomy, Gamma Sigma Delta, Epsilon Sigma Phi (certificate recognition 1972). Roman Catholic. Home: 1021 Houston St Manhattan KS 66502 Office: Waters Hall Kans State U Manhattan KS 66506

BIEDERMAN, CHARLES JOSEPH, artist; b. Cleve., Aug. 23, 1906; s. Joseph and Josephine (Kostinec) B.; student Art Inst. Chgo., 1926-29; D.F.A. (hon.) Mpls. Coll. Art and Design, 1973; m. Mary Katherine Moore, Dec. 25, 1941; 1 dau., Anna. Exhibited at one man shows Matisse Gallery, N.Y.C., 1936, Arts Club, Chgo., 1941, Katherine Kub Gallery, Chgo., 1941, St. Paul Gallery of Art, 1954, Columbia U. Sch. Arch., 1963, Ga. Inst. Tech., Atlanta, 1963, Walker Art Center, Mpls., retrospective, 1965, Hayward Gallery, London, Eng., retrospective, 1969, Mpls. Inst. Arts, retrospective, 1976, also Rochester (Minn.) Art Center, 1967, Gallery 12, Mpls., 1971; exhibited group shows Albright Art Gallery, Buffalo, 1936, Reinhardt Gallery, N.Y.C., 1936, Galerie Pierre, Paris, 1936, Mayor Gallery, London, 1936, Stedelijk Museum, Amsterdam, 1962,

Kunstgewerbemuseum, Zurich, 1962, Marlborough Gerson Gallery, N.Y.C., 1964, Carnegie Internat., Pitts., 1964, Whitney Ann. Exhbn. Sculpture, N.Y.C., 1964, 66; Walker Biennial Walker Art Center, Mpls., 1964, 66, Denver Mus., 1965, Marlborough Gallery Fine Arts, London, 1966, Museum of Contemporary Art, Chgo., Ill., 1968, Akron (Ohio) Art Inst., 1971, Zabriskie Gallery, N.Y.C., 1972, Dallas Mus. Fine Arts, 1972, Annely Juda Fine Art, London, Univ. Mus., Austin, Tex., 1973, Sheldon Art Mus., Lincoln, Nebr., 1974, Mich. Artrain, 1975; represented in permanent collections Mus. Modern Art, N.Y.C., Phila. Mus. Art, U. Sask. Art Gallery, Saskatoon, Can., Walker Art Center, Tate Gallery, London, Eng., Kroller-Muller Museum, Otterlo, Holland, Des Moines Art Center, Art Inst. Chgo., U. East Anglia, Eng., Mpls. Inst. Art, McCrory Found., N.Y.C. Recipient Sikkens award, Stedelijk Museum, Amsterdam, 1963, Ford Found. award, 1964, Walker Biennial Donor's award, 1966, Nat. Council on the Arts award, 1966, award Minn. State Arts Council, 1969, Nat. Found. for Arts award, 1971, Fine Arts award Minn. br. AIA, 1971; Nat. Endowment for Arts award, 1973. Author: Art as the Evolution of Visual Knowledge, 1948; Letters on the New Art, 1951; The New Cezanne, 1958. Contbr. articles to art jours. Address: Route 2 Red Wing MN 55066

BIEDERMAN, EARL DONALD, explosive powder mfg. co. exec.; b. Cleve., May 28, 1935; s. Hy and Sally Ann (Simon) B.; B.S., Miami U., 1957; M.S., Purdue U., 1959; m. Marianne Miller, June 13, 1959; children—Scott. Asst. football, basketball, baseball coach Wabash Coll., 1957-58; head football coach, dept. head social studies Toronto (Ohio) Bd. Edn., 1958-60, Mentor (Ohio) Bd. Edn., 1960-63; sales rep. Texaco, Inc., Cleve., 1963-65, dist. sales supr., 1965-70; sales coordinator Ammonium Nitrate sales, West Coast regional mgr. Seismic and Pipeline Explosives div. Austin Powder Co., Cleve., 1970—; area scout Cin. Bengals, 1967—. Recreation commnr., Solon, Ohio, 1972-74; bd. dirs. Grantwood Municipal Golf Course, Solon, 1972-75. Mem. Am. Inst. Mining Metall. and Petroleum Engrs., Soc. Exploration Geophysicists, Permian Basin Geophys. Soc., Geophys. Soc. Alaska, N.Mex. Mining Assn., Colo. Mining Assn., Casper Geophys. Soc., Delta Kappa Epsilon. Home: 408 Mill Pond Rd Aurora OH 44202 Office: 3735 Green Rd Beachwood OH 44122

BIEDERMAN, LINDA BARI, sch. psychologist; b. Cin., Nov. 18, 1947; d. Joseph and Virginia (Bogdan) Biederman; B.A. in Psychology with honors, U. Cin., 1969, certificate in sch. psychology, 1977; M.A. in Clin. Psychology, Xavier U., Cin., 1971. Intern psychologist Longview State Hosp., Cin., 1969-70; psychology trainee Children's Hosp., Cin.. 1976; intern sch. psychologist Hailton County Bd. Edn., Cin., 1976-77; cons. sch. psychologist Children's Hosp., Cin.. 1977—. Mem. Am. (asso.), Ohio (asso.). psychol. assns., Ohio, Southwestern Ohio sch. psychologists assns., Psi Chi.

BIEHL, ELAINE HARNER, lawyer; b. Wilmington, Ohio, Apr. 22, 1950; d. Orville David and Anna Louise (Mathews) Harner; B.A., Ohio State U., 1972; J.D., Loyola U., Los Angeles, 1975; m. Tom Biehl, June 13, 1971. Admitted to Ohio bar, 1975; individual practice law, 1975-76; staff atty. Geene Clinton Pub. Defender Program, Wilmington, 1976, sr. staff atty., 1976-77, pub. defender, 1978—. Mem. Ohio Pub. Defenders Assn. (bd. dirs.), Am., Ohio, Clinton County bar assns, Phi Alpha Delta, Alpha Chi Omega. Quaker. Home: 207 N Lincoln St Wilmington OH 45177 Office: 3d Floor Court House Wilmington OH 45177

BIELAWSKI, WALTER LEONARD, editor, publisher; b. Harvey, Ill., Nov. 6, 1926; s. Joseph and Caroline (Smaga) B.; student Thornton Jr. Coll., 1944-47, Roosevelt U., 1948; B.S., Loyola U., Chgo., 1950, M.B.A., 1971. Reporter, Harvey News-Bee, 1950, asst. editor, 1952-53, editor-in-chief, 1953-57, editor, pub., 1957-71, emeritus, 1971—, pres. Harvey News-Bee, Inc., 1957-66; dir. Pub. Info. and Edn., Harvey, 1959-62; pres. Bielawski Enterprises, Inc., Marion County, Ark.; co-owner Harvey Motel (Ill.). Chmn. Harvey Armory Com., 1961-63. Served with USNR, 1944-46, 50-51. Mem. Am. Legion, Polish Legion Am. Veterans, Am. Vets. Fgn. Wars, C. of C. Mountain Home (Ark.), Harvey Assn. Commerce and Industry (chmn. indsl. devel. com. 1966), Harvey Hist. Soc. (trustee), Internat. Platform Assn., Loyola U., Grad. Sch. Bus. alumni assns., Phi Mu Chi. Clubs: Polish Social (Baker County, Ark.), K.C., Moose. Address: 253 E 159th St Harvey IL 60426

BIESTER, JOHN LOUIS, educator, ednl. adminstr.; b. Aurora, Ill., Aug. 29, 1918; s. Fred Leslie and Mary (Lintner) B.; B.A., Beloit Coll., 1941; M.S., Syracuse U., 1943, Ph.D. (Bristol Labs. fellow), 1959; m. Harriett Ruth Mackey, June 7, 1947; children—Mary, John. Research chemist Standard Oil Co. Ind., Whiting, 1943; asst. prof. chemistry Beloit (Wis.) Coll., 1948-58, asso. prof. chemistry, 1958—, dir. three NSF insts., 1961-64, asso. dir. field placement, 1964-69, dir. field placement, 1969—, dir. career planning, 1975—; Asso. program dir. acad. and inservice insts. NSF, Washington, 1961-62; cons. NSF/Columbia U. Sci. Insts., Poona, India, 1964; cons. insts. sect. NSF, 1962-68; cons. coop. edn. various colls. Mem. Citizens Adv. Commn., Beloit, 1968-71, chmn., 1970-71; bd. dirs. Stateline Welfare Planning Council, Beloit, 1972—, mem. exec. com., 1975—. Served to sgt. Q.M.C., AUS, 1944-46. Fellow Am. Inst. Chemists; mem. AAAS, Coop. Edn. Assn., Midwest Coll. Placement Assn., Phi Beta Kappa, Sigma Xi. Contbr. articles in field to Jour. Am. Chem. Soc., 1959, Cooperative Edn. Jour., 1969, 72, 74. Home: 2525 Clifcorn Dr Beloit WI 53511

BIETER, JEROME THOMAS, hosp. cons.; b. Faribault, Minn., Feb. 1, 1922; s. Nicholas Charles and Anna Rose (Dobner) B.; B.B.A., U. Minn., 1943, M.H.A., 1949; m. Anne L. Sheary, July 14, 1951; children—Kimberly Ann, Margaret Susan. Adminstrv. asst. R.I. Hosp., Providence, 1949-51, asst. dir., 1951-53; adminstr. Uniontown (Pa.) Hosp., 1953-56; sr. cons. James A. Hamilton Assos., Inc., Mpls., 1956-74, prin., pres., dir. programming and spl. studies div., 1974—; dir. Wilhite Instrument Co., Mpls.; asst. prof. program in hosp. and health care adminstrn. U. Minn., Mpls., 1956—. Served with AUS, 1943-45. Fellow Am. Coll. Hosp. Adminstrs. (chmn. task force prins. appointment and tenure exec. officers 1973—); mem. Am. Assn. Hosp. Cons. (pres. 1975—), Am. Assn. Hosp. Planning, Am., Minn. hosp. assns., Beta Gamma Sigma. Home: 4628 Bruce Ave Edina MN 55424 Office: 2331 University Ave SE Minneapolis MN 55414

BIETI, FREDERICK GEORGE, elec. engr.; b. Highland Park, Mich., Feb. 28, 1940; s. Fernando Richard and Gladys Pauline B.; B.S. in Elec. Engring., Mich. Tech. U., 1964; m. Betty Mae Aho, June 17, 1961; children—Richard, Martin. Elec. engr. Chevrolet Motor Div., Gen. Motors Corp., Warren, Mich., 1964-67; project engr. Systems Control Corp., Iron Mountain, Mich., 1967-72; owner F.G. Bieti & Assos., Iron Mountain, 1972—; owner Z & R Elec. Service, Inc., Iron Mountain, 1976—; cons. in field. Chmn. Breitung Twp. Water and Sewer Bd., 1975—; com. mem. Dickinson County Taxpayers Assn., 1977—. Registered profl. engr. Mich., Wis. Mem. Mich. Registered Profl. Engrs. (pres. Douglas Houghton chpt. 1974—), IEEE, Solar Engring. Inst., Nat. Soc. Profl. Engrs. Clubs: Pine Grove Country, Elks. Home: Star Route 3 Box 3132 Iron Mountain MI 49801 Office: PO Box 242 Iron Mountain MI 49801

BIETZ, ALAN DEE, zoo dir.; b. Lincoln, Nebr., Feb. 14, 1946; s. Albert D. and Rose D. (Harr) B.; teaching degree in Biology, Union Coll., 1968, B.S. in Phys. Edn., 1968; m. Melody Caroon, July 10, 1968; children—Judd Alan, Allison Deanna. Tchr. pub. schs. Houston, 1968-70, Newbery Pauk Acad., Thousand Oaks, Calif., 1970-71, Sheyenne River Acad. Harvey, N.D., 1971-73; dir. Lincoln (Nebr.) Children's Zoo, 1973—. Profl. fellow Am. Assn. Zool. Parks and Aquariums, Am. Assn. Zoo Veterinarians, Am. Assn. Zoo Keepers. Republican. Clubs: Kiwanis, Jaycees. Office: Lincoln Children's Zoo 2800 A St Lincoln NE 68502

BIGELOW, WHEELOCK, JR., chem. co. exec.; b. N.Y.C., May 31, 1921; s. Wheelock and Arlene (Keeler) B.; m. Barbara D. Hammett, Oct. 21, 1950; children—Charles, William, Barbara. Sales mgr. Liquid Carbonic Corp., N.Y.C., Phila. and Chgo., 1946-57; sales mgr., regional gen. mgr. Cardon Dioxide div. Chemetron Corp., Cleve. and Chgo., 1957-70, v.p. div., 1971—. Served to capt. USMC, 1942-46. Clubs: Rotary, Harvard (Chgo.); Chikaming Country (Lakeside, Mich.). Home: 253 E Delaware Pl Chicago IL 60611 Office: 111 E Wacker Dr 19th Floor Chicago IL 60601

BIGGAR, EDWARD SAMUEL, lawyer; b. Kansas City, Mo., Nov. 19, 1917; s. Frank Wilson and Katharine (Rea) B.; A.B., U. Mich., 1938, J.D., 1940; m. Susan Bagby, July 9, 1955; children—John Edward, Julie Anne, Nancy Rea, William Bagby, Martha Susan. Admitted to Mo. bar, 1940; asso. firm Stinson Mag, Thomson, McEvers and Fizzell, attys., Kansas City, Mo., 1948-50, partner, 1950—; sec., dir. Russell Stover Candies, Inc., Kansas City, Mo., 1960—; v.p., dir. Ward Paper Box Co., Kansas City, Mo., 1955—; dir. Western Chem. Co., Kansas City, Rothchild's, Inc., Kansas City, Cereal Food Processors, Inc., Kansas City. Chmn. Citizens Assn. Kansas City, Mo., 1959-60; bd. dirs., v.p. Greater Kansas City YMCA, 1965—; chmn. Transp. Planning Commn. Greater Kansas City, 1964-65; mem. Met. Planning Commn., Kansas City Region, 1966-67; pres. Kansas City (Mo.) unit Am. Cancer Soc., 1956-58. Trustee Sunset Hill Sch., Kansas City, Mo., 1971—. Served to 1st lt., USAAF, 1942-45. Mem. Lawyers Assn. Kansas City (pres. 1966-67), Mo. Bar, Am., Kansas City bar assns., Am. Judicature Soc., Order of Coif. Phi Beta Kappa, Phi Delta Phi, Phi Delta Theta. Rep. Presbyn. Home: 1221 Stratford Rd Kansas City MO 64113 Office: 2100 Ten Main Center Kansas City MO 64105

BIGGERS, DARLENE FAY, univ. adminstr.; b. Chgo.. June 8, 1946; d. Charles Carpenter Biggers and Ruby May (Ernst) Jacobs; B.A., U. No. Iowa, 1968; M.A., U. No. Colo., 1975. Tchr. English, Jefferson High Sch., Cedar Rapids, Iowa, 1968-75; dean women Upper Iowa U., Fayette, 1975—; lectr. women's issues. Active AAUW, NOW, Iowa Women's Polit. Caucus. Mem. NEA (life), Am. Personnel and Guidance Assn., Am. Coll. Personnel Assn., Nat. Assn. Women Deans, Adminstrs. and Counselors, Delta Kappa Gamma. Democrat. Home: Box 513 Fayette IA 52142

BIGGERT, ELIZABETH COLETTE, librarian; b. Columbus, Ohio, Sept. 23, 1915; d. E. Faber and Mary (Cotter) Biggert; B.A., summa cum laude, St. Mary of Springs (now Ohio Dominican) Coll., 1937; B.S. in L.S., Western Res. U., 1938. Cataloger, Toledo Pub. Library, 1939-40; reference librarian Ohio Hist. Soc., Columbus, 1940-43, manuscripts librarian, 1946-53; reference librarian Columbus Pub. Library, 1953-56; librarian econs. library Battelle Meml. Inst., Columbus, 1956—. Chmn. bus. and prof. unit Columbus Symphony Orch., 1963-64, bd. trustees, 1965-67. USNR, 1943-46. Mem. Spl. Libraries Assn. (chpt. sec. 1972-73, pres. 1976-77), Res. Officers Assn. (chpt. 1957-58, Ohio historian 1958-61, pres. Columbus Naval Services chpt. 1966-67), Ohio Dominican Coll. Alumni Assn. (pres. 1951-52, mem. bd. 1969-72), Kappa Gamma Pi. Republican. Roman Catholic. Author: Guide to the Manuscripts in the Library of the Ohio State Archaeological and Historical Society, 1953. Home: 2851 Bexley Park Rd Columbus OH 43209 Office: Battelle Memorial Inst 505 King Ave Columbus OH 43201

BIGHAM, DARREL EUGENE, historian; b. Harrisburg, Pa., Aug. 12, 1942; s. Paul D. and Ethel B.; B.A., Messiah Coll., 1964; postgrad. Harvard Divinity Sch., 1964-65; Ph.D., U. Kans., 1970; m. Mary Elizabeth Hitchcock, Sept. 23, 1965; children—Matthew, Elizabeth. Asst. prof. history Ind. State U., Evansville, 1970-75, asso. prof., 1975—. Exec. dir. Leadership Evansville, 1976—; dir. archives div. Conrad Baker Found., 1971—; chmn. Evansville Bicentennial Council, 1974-77; bd. dirs. Evansville Museum, 1972—, sec., 1977—; trustee Evansville Vanderburgh County Pub. Library, 1971—; bd. dirs. Freedom Festival, 1976-77, Conrad Baker Found., 1971—. Rockefeller Brothers Theol. fellow, 1964-65; NDEA fellow, 1965-68. Mem. Soc. Indiana Archivists (dir. 1972-75, pres. 1977-78), Am. Hist. Assn., Orgn. Am. Historians, Southern Hist. Assn. Episcopalian. Clubs: Rotary, Petroleum, Oak Meadow Country. Home: Rt 4 Box 155 Evansville IN 47712 Office: Dept History Ind State Univ Evansville IN 47712

BIGLER, W(ILLIAM) PAUL, corp. exec.; b. nr. Franklin, Pa., Oct. 5, 1904; s. William and Carolin (Gilmore) B.; grad. Perkiomen Sch., 1923; m. Sarah Tate, Dec. 21, 1940; 1 dau., Nancy Ann Bigler Kersey. Mgr. repair parts sales service Joy Mfg. Co., 1926-34, dir. purchases, 1934-37; indsl. purchasing agt. Semet Solvay Engring. Corp., 1937-38; div. mgr. editorial research McGraw-Hill Pub. Co., 1938-40; sales mgr. Mining Machine Parts, Inc., Cleve., 1940-43, gen. mgr., 1943-48, pres., chmn. bd., 1948-67; pres. L. W. Kelley Co., Inc., 1958-67, Compass Equipment Co., Wichita, Kans., 1957-67; pres. Bigler Investment Corp.; v.p. Circle Oil Co., Sage Drilling Co., 1957-67. Mem. Am. Inst. Mining, Metall. and Petroleum Engrs., Am. Mining Congress, Rocky Mountain, W.Va., Ill. mining insts. Clubs: Country; Cleve. Skating; Franklin; United Hunts; Met. (N.Y.C.). Home: 828 Greengate Oval Greenwood Village Northfield OH 44067 also San Remo Club Boca Raton FL 33431

BIGLEY, JAMES PHILIP, telephone co. exec.; b. Viroqua, Wis., July 28, 1912; s. Lawrence A. and Ellen (McCall) B.; m. Dorothy Bent, Aug. 28, 1948. Officer, dir. State Bank of LaCrosse (Wis.), 1930-47, State Bank of Viroqua, 1947-55, 70—; dir. Viroqua Telephone Co., 1948—, sec., treas., mgr., 1954-62, pres., mgr., 1962—; pres. Viroqua Bldg. Corp., 1965—; dir. Capital TransAm. Corp., Capital Indemnity Corp. Chmn. Viroqua Housing Authority, 1969—. Exec. sec. Rep. Party of Wis., 1955-57. Served from pvt. to 1st lt., 32d Div., AUS, 1942-46. Mem. LaCrosse Jr. C. of C. (pres. 1939), 32d Div. Vets. Assn. (nat. pres. 1957-58), Am. Legion, Vets. Fgn. Wars, Wis. Telephone Assn. (pres. 1962), U.S. Ind. Telephone Assn. (dir., v.p. 1974—). Elk, Eagle (Wis. pres. 1952-53, internat. pres. 1959-60, financial adviser 1962-69, 75—). Home: 3 S Washington Heights Viroqua WI 54665 Office: 114 E Court St Virogua WI 54665

BIGLEY, THOMAS CREVISTON, JR., lawyer; b. Indpls., Aug. 4, 1939; s. Thomas Creviston and Rebecca Elizabeth (Sharpnack) B.; student Stanford U., 1956-58; A.B., Ind. U., 1960, J.D., 1963; m. Carol Lynn Holmes, June 4, 1960; children—David Randolph, Susan Elaine. Admitted to Ind. bar, 1963; mem. firm Sharpnack, Bigley, David & Rumple, Columbus, Ind., 1966—. Instr. negotiable instruments Am. Inst. Banking, 1967. Atty., Bartholomew County Library Bd., 1967—. Served with AUS, 1963-66. Mem. Am., Ind., Bartholomew County bar assns., Columbus C. of C., Phi Delta Phi, Phi Kappa Psi. Methodist. (supt. ch. sch. 1969-70, mem. adminstrv. bd. 1967—, chmn. 1974—). Clubs: Kiwanian (bd. dirs. 1972—, pres. 1977-78), Toastmaster (pres. 1972—, area gov. 1973). Home: 3445 Riverside Dr Columbus IN 47201 Office: PO Box 310 Columbus IN 47201

BIHLER, FREDERICK HENRY, JR., elec. products mfg. co. exec.; b. N.Y.C., Sept. 8, 1926; s. Frederick H. and Isabelle A. (Ziegler) B.; B.E.E., N.Y. U. 1950; m. Ruth H. Hinck, Sept. 18, 1948 (dec. June 1973); children—Barbara A., Douglas M., Carol R., Susan L.; m. 2d, Nancy E. Woodruff, Feb. 22, 1975. With Ribble Engring. Co., Hackensack, N.J., 1950-54, Regent Controls, Inc., Stamford, Conn., 1954-62, Furnas Electric Co., Batavia, Ill., 1962-69, Norbatrol Electronics Corp., Murrysville, Pa., 1969-70; v.p. C.P. Clare & Co., elec. products, Chgo., 1970-77, Fujissu Am. Inc., CS div. Electronic Components, Lake Forest, Ill., 1977—. Served with USNR, 1943-46. Mem. IEEE, Petroleum Electric Supply Assn., Nat. Soc. Profl. Engrs., Am. Mktg. Assn., Newcomen Soc., Stamford Engring. Soc. (dir. 1960-62). Patentee automatic control system. Home: 435 E Illinois Rd Lake Forest IL 60045 Office: PO Box 694 Lake Forest IL 60045

BIHR, EDWIN DURRETT, shoe co. exec.; b. Columbia, Mo., Oct. 4, 1917; s. Frank and Lula (Durrett) B.; student U. Mo., 1935-38; m. Jacqueline Ann Chrane, Dec. 27, 1938; 1 son, Robert Edwin. With C.B. Miller Shoe Co., Columbia, 1930-38, v.p., 1945-52, owner, pres., 1952—; mgr. Taylor Shoe Co., Fulton, Mo., 1938; owner Bihr Shoe Co., Marshall, Mo., 1938-45; owner shoe dept. Parks Parkade Plaza; Pres. Columbia Sch. Bd., 1953—; mem. planning com. Governor's Conf. on Edn., 1966, chmn. conf., 1968; v.p. Mo. Council on Edn., 1967-69, pres., 1969—. Bd. dirs. Central Midwest Regional Ednl. Lab., St. Louis, Mid-Continent Regional Ednl. Lab., Kansas City; trustee Mo. State Tchrs. Retirement System, 1970—. Served with Signal Corps, AUS, 1943-45. Recipient Layman of Year award Mo. chpt. Phi Delta Kappa, 1966; citation for distinguished service to edn. Coll. Edn. U. Mo., Columbia, 1967. Mem. Nat. Shoe Retailers Assn., V.F.W., Am. Legion, Nat. (nat. dir.), Mo. (past pres., dir.) sch. bds. assns., C. of C. (past pres.). Democrat. Mem. Christian Ch. (deacon). Home: 900 W Broadway Columbia MO 65201 Office: 800 E Broadway Columbia MO 65201

BILANDIC, MICHAEL A., city ofcl.; b. Chgo., Feb. 13, 1923; s. Matthew and Domenica (Lebedina) B.; B.S., St. Mary's Coll., Winona, Minn., 1941-43, 46; postgrad. U. Notre Dame; J.D., DePaul U., 1948; m. Heather Morgan, July 15, 1977. Admitted to Ill. bar, 1949; partner firm Anixter, Bilandic & Pigott, and predecessors, Chgo., 1963-77; master in chancery Circuit Court of Cook County (Ill.), 1964-67; spl. asst. to Atty. Gen., 1965-68; acting mayor City of Chgo., 1977, mayor, 1977—. Democratic alderman Chgo. City Council, 1969-77, chmn. com. on environ. control, 1970-74, chmn. fin. com., 1974-77. Served to 1st lt. USMC, 1943-46. Mem. Am., Ill., Chgo. bar assns., Catholic Lawyers Guild. Roman Catholic. Office: Office of the Mayor City Hall 121 N LaSalle St Chicago IL 60602*

BILBREY, WALTER GREEN, JR., planning service co. exec.; b. Lima, Ohio, June 17, 1926; s. Walter Green and Cecile lHannah (Bowers) B.; B.S., Manchester Coll., 1949; m. Helen Jane Peterson, Dec. 24, 1964; children—Mark William, Scott Ashley. Cons., Life Ins. Marketing Research Assn., Hartford, Conn., 1960-64; v.p. marketing Provident Life Ins. Co., Bismarck, N.D., 1964-71; pres., dir. Planning Services Internat., Inc., Bismarck, 1971—. Served with USNR, 1944-46; comdr. Res. ret. Mem. Am. Coll. Life Underwriters, Nat. Assn. Life Underwriters, Nat. Pilots Assn., Nat. Rifle Assn. Republican. Mormon. Club: Elks. Home: 917 N Washington St Bismarck ND 58501 Office: Dakota Northwestern Bldg Suite 510 400 Broadway Bismarck ND 58501

BILEYDI, SUMER MEHMET, advt. agy. exec.; b. Antalya, Turkey, Feb. 7, 1936; s. Abdurrahman M. and Neriman (Akman) B.; B.A., Mich. State U., 1961, M.A., 1962; m. Lois Elloine Goode, Dec. 30. 1961; children—Can M., Sera N. Mktg. cons., export, Promotion Center, Ankara. Turkey, 1962; planner Gardner Advt. agy., St. Louis, 1963-65; planning supr. Batten, Barton, Durstine & Osborn, N.Y.C., 1965-69; asso. dir. Ketchum, Macleod & Grove, Pitts., 1969-73; v.p., dir. Carmichael Lynch, Inc., Mpls., 1973—. Pres., Turkish Am. Assn., 1974-75. Mem. Am. Mktg. Assn., Advt. Research Found., Advt. fedn. Minn. Islam. Club: Minn. Turkish Am. Contbr. articles to profl. jours. Home: 16670 Baywood Terr Eden Prairie MN 55344 Office: 100 22d St E Minneapolis MN 55404

BILGER, RAYMOND PAUL, chain store exec.; b. Chgo., Oct. 26, 1915; s. Luke Anthony and Esther Louise (Wilson) B.; B.A., U. Ill., 1937, J.D., 1939; m. Evelyn Mildred Halvorsen, Dec. 4, 1943; children—Judith Evelyn (Mrs. Martin McLean), Laura Jean (Mrs. Robert Stephenson). With Sears, Roebuck and Co., 1939—, mgr. fed. taxes, 1958-71, dir. fed. taxes, 1971-73, gen. mgr. tax dept., 1973-74, v.p. taxes, 1974—. Lectr. in taxation U. Chgo. Bus. Sch., 1951-54. Mem. Lombard (Ill.) Sch. Bd., 1954-60, pres., 1957-60; mem. Plum Meml. Library Bd., Lombard, 1963-73, pres., 1971-73. Mem. Am., Chgo. bar assns., Tax Execs. Inst. (pres. Chgo. chpt.), Zeta Psi. Methodist. Republican. Club: River Forest Country (dir. 1974-75) (Elmhurst, Ill.); Metropolitan, Attic (Chgo.). Home: 6 Oak Brook Club Dr Oak Brook IL 60521 Office: Sears Tower Chicago IL 60684

BILLINGS, JANE KELLY, librarian; b. Watertown, Wis., June 10, 1916; d. William Edward and Elizabeth (Knaak) Kelly; student Northwestern Coll., 1934-36; B.A., U. Wis., 1938, B.L.S., 1939, M.A., 1962; m. Robert E. Billings, Oct. 12, 1941. Asst. librarian Watertown (Wis.) Pub. Library, 1933-38; librarian Pub. Library, Clintonville, Wis., 1939-49; dist. coordinator library/media services Clintonville, 1949—; mem. faculty U. Wis. Library Sch., summers 1963-71, chmn. adv. council, 1965-67. Chmn. Gov.'s Council on Library Devel. Mem. Am., Wis. (dir. 1960-63, past pres., Librarian of Yr. 1963) library assns., Nat., Wis. edn. assns., Central Wis. Edn. Assn. (pres. 1973-74), Clintonville Edn. Assn. (pres. 1962-63), AAUW, Wis. Hist. Soc., U. Wis. Alumni Assn., U. Wis. Library Sch. Alumni Assn., Delta Kappa Gamma (pres. 1966-68). Republican. Conglist. Mem. Order of Eastern Star (past matron). Editor: Library Curriculum Guide, 1967-69. Contbr. to English Jour., Wis. Library Bull., Wis. Jour. Edn. Home: 158 N Clinton Ave Clintonville WI 54929 Office: 255 N Main St Clintonville WI 54929

BILLINGS, THOMAS MICHAEL, physician; b. Spearville, Kans., Dec. 31, 1939; s. Wayne Gordon and Lillian Rebecca (Horning) B.; B.A., Sterling Coll., 1962; M.D., U. Kans., 1966; m. Nancy McCreery, Aug. 2, 1963; children—Brian Michael, David Allen, John Todd. Intern, Kans. City Gen. Hosp. & Med. Center, 1966-67; USPHS fellow Indian Service, Eagle Butte, S.D., 1967-69; med. missionary, Evanelical Covenant Ch., Karawa, Zarie (Congo), Africa, 1969-71; practice medicine specializing in family practice, McPherson, Kans., 1971—. Served with USPHS, 1967-69. Diplomate Am. Bd. Family Practice. Baptist. Home: 704 Somerset St McPherson KS 67460 Office: 400 W 4th St McPherson KS 67460

BILLINGSLEY, JOHN SMITH, radiologist; b. Newton, Iowa, Jan. 16, 1929; s. John William and Mary Mable (Smith) B.; B.A., Simpson Coll., 1951; M.D., Western Res. U., 1955; m. Cleo Eloise Jones, Aug.

25, 1952; children—John Elliott, James William, Joseph Crane. Intern, Iowa Meth. Hosp., Des Moines, 1955-56; fellow in radiology Mayo Clinic, Rochester, Minn., 1956-59; practice medicine specializing in radiology, Ft. Wayne, Ind., 1961—; asso. Duemling Clinic; staff Luth. Hosp.; asso. faculty Ind. Sch. Medicine, Ft. Wayne Center Med. Edn. Served to capt. M.C., AUS, 1959-61. Mem. Am. Coll. Radiology, AMA, Ind. Med. Assn., Ind., Iowa hist. socs., Am. Def. Preparedness Assn., Nat. Rifle Assn. Club: Ft. Wayne Country. Home: 4720 Crestwood Dr Fort Wayne IN 46807 Office: 2828 Fairfield Ave Fort Wayne IN 46807

BILLMIRE, FRANK GILLAM, machine tool distbr.; b. Rochelle, Ill., Mar. 31, 1908; s. Frank and Pearl (Knapp) B.; student Bradley U., 1926-30; m. Helen Marie Hill, May 20, 1927; children—Frank William, Elizabeth Joan Mayer. Purchasing agt., Russell Burdsall & Ward, Rock Falls, Ill., 1930-44; div. sales engr. Pratt & Whitney Co., Chgo., 1944-51; sales mgr. Gagefix Mfg. Co., Chgo., 1951-52; gen. west sales mgr. Taft Peirce Mfg. Co., Woonsocket, R.I., Chgo., 1952-63; sales engr. Select Machine Sales Inc., East Moline, Ill., 1963—; also dir., pres., chmn., bd. Mem. East Moline C. of C. (dir. 1974-76), Soc. Mfg. Engrs., Nat. Machine Tool Distbrs. Assn. Republican. Episcopalian. Clubs: Short Hills Country, Execs. of Chgo., Mason, Shriners, Elks. Home: 622 29th Ave East Moline IL 61244 Office: 918 15th Ave East Moline IL 61244

BILODEAU, RICHARD GERARD, radiologist; b. Lewiston, Maine, June 12, 1938; s. Gerard Philemon and Blandine Yvette (Goulet) B.; B.S. cum laude, U. Notre Dame, 1960; M.; M.D., Georgetown U., 1964; m. Mary Gertrude Kuntz, June 17, 1961; 1 dau., Laura Lynn. Intern, Albany (N.Y.) Med. Center, 1964-65, resident in internal medicine, 1965-66; gen. practice medicine, Cambridge, Md., 1966-69; resident in diagnostic radiology Ind. U. Med. Center, Indpls., 1969-72; practice medicine specializing in radiology, Noblesville, Tipton, and Elwood (all Ind.), 1972—; chief radiologist Tipton County Hosp.; staff radiologist Riverview Hosp., Noblesville, Mercy Hosp., Elwood. Diplomate Am. Bd. Radiology. Mem. Am. Coll. Radiology, Ind. Roentgen Soc., AMA, Hamilton County Med. Soc. Republican. Roman Cath. Clubs: Columbia, (Indpls.). Home: Rural Route 6 Box 400 Noblesville IN 46060 Office: Riverview Hosp Noblesville IN 46060

BINCER, ADAM MARIAN, educator; b. Krakow, Poland, Apr. 25, 1930; s. Henryk and Renata (Landau) B.; came to U.S., 1949, naturalized, 1953; B.S., Mass. Inst. Tech., 1953, Ph.D., 1956; m. Wanda Lawendel, Apr. 2, 1972; children—Yvonne, Brian, Michael; children by previous marriage—Andrea, Ronnie. Research physicist Brookhaven Nat. Lab., Upton, N.Y., 1956-58; research physicist U. Calif. at Berkeley, 1958-60; asst. prof. theoretical physics U. Wis., Madison, 1960-62, asso. prof., 1962-67, prof., 1968—. Mem. Am. Phys. Soc. Contbr. articles to profl. jours. Office: Dept Physics U Wis Madison WI 53706

BINDLEY, JOE HOOVER, educator; b. Marion, Ohio, Aug. 15, 1922; s. Calvin Bennett and Harriet Esther (Hoover) B.; B.A., Coll. Wooster, 1947; M.A., U. Calif. at Los Angeles, 1957; Ph.D., U. Pitts., 1959; m. Norma Gertrude Shawl, Sept. 18, 1973. Instr., acting chmn. dept. polit. sci. Coll. Wooster, 1950-57; asso. dir. Citizenship Clearing House Western Pa., U. Pitts., 1957-58; asso. prof., dir. research local govt. and politics Knox Coll., 1958-66; asso. prof. U. Mo., St. Louis, 1966-68; prof., chmn. dept. polit. sci. Wittenberg U., Springfield, Ohio, 1968—. Cons. polit. edn., Chgo., 1959-60; cons. various Ill. polit. campaigns, 1960-62; city charter rev. cons., Ohio, 1972-73; mem. Knox County (Ill.) Bd. Suprs., 1962-66; vice-chmn. Republican central com., Clark County, Ohio 1976—; trustee Clark Tech. Coll., 1977-79. Served with AUS, 1943-46. Falk Found. grantee, 1952, 55, 58, 62; Ford Found. grantee, 1963; Luth. Ch. Am. grantee, 1971. Mem. Am., Midwest (exec. council 1972-76) polit. sci. assns., Ohio Assn. Economists and Polit. Scientists. Rotarian. Club: University. Contbr. articles, book revs. to profl. jours. Home: 2564 Erter Dr Springfield OH 45503

BINGHAM, ROBERT SEMLER, ednl. adminstr.; b. Gustavus, Ohio, July 18, 1930; s. Glenn A. and Cora (Semler) B.; B.S., Ashland Coll., 1953; M.Ed., Kent State U., 1961; m. Kathryn Smith, July 11, 1954; children—Michael Patrick, Douglas Lee, Becky Ann. Tchr. Green Local Schs., Smithville, Ohio, 1953, Gustavus Local Schs., 1953-55; Ashland City Schs., 1957-59; bus. mgr. Ashland City Schs., 1959-66; coordinator pupil transp., Ohio State Dept. Edn., 1966; v.p. bus. affairs Ashland Coll., 1966—. Dir. Ashland Bank and Savs. Mem. Community Improvement Corp. Bd. dirs. YMCA, Ashland Hosp. Assn. Served with M.C., AUS, 1955-57. Mem. Am. Assn. Sch. Adminstrs., Assn. Sch. Bus. Ofcls. U.S. and Can., C. of C. (past pres.), Nat. Assn. Ednl. Buyers, Nat., Central assns. coll. and univ. bus. officers, Coll. and U. Personnel Officers. Presbyn. (elder). Kiwanian (past lt. gov.). Home: 1112 Cooper Dr Ashland OH 44805 Office: 401 College Ave Ashland OH 44805

BINNER, ELMER ARTHUR, fund-raising co. exec.; b. Cleve., May 28, 1919; s. Douglas Arthur and Eleanor Ann (Meyer) B.; B.A., Fenn Coll., 1952; postgrad. Oberlin Coll., 1952-54, Ind. U., 1962-63; m. Elma Caroline Sadler, June 1, 1940; children—Wesley Calvert, Carolyn Ruth. Asst. forman Indsl. Rayon Corp., 1938-46; gen. foreman Lansing Mfg. Co., 1946-47; program dir. Lake County YMCA, Painesville, Ohio, 1947-52, gen. exec. dir., 1952-61; asso. gen. exec. dir. Greater Indpls. YMCA, 1960-71, gen. exec. dir., 1970-71; dir. fin. devel. New Hope Found., 1972; prin. Jerold Panas & Partners, Chgo., 1973—. Republican. Methodist. Kiwanian. Home: 8107 Bromley Pl Indianapolis IN 46219 Office: 500 N Michigan Ave Suite 620 Chicago IL 60611

BINNEY, PAUL AUSTIN, psychologist, mental health adminstr.; b. Madison, Wis., Aug. 8, 1927; s. William Roland and Ernestine (Roth) B.; B.A. with honors, U. Wis., Madison, 1949, M.A., 19S1; Ph.D. in Psychology, State U. Iowa, Iowa City, 1965; m. Ruth Elaine Marsh, Oct. 24, 1953; children—Dane, Craig. Instr. high sch., Spring Green, Wis., 1949-50; asst. youth counselor Wis. Child Center, Sparta, 1951; coordinator sr. citizens program Madison Community Center, 1951; supr. recreation No. Colony and Tng. Sch., Chippewa Falls, Wis., 1956-57, tchr., 1954-56, dir. vocat. rehab., 1956-57; dir. tng. Woodward (Iowa) State Hosp. Sch., 1957-58; dir. summer workshops for spl. educators State U. Iowa, Iowa City, 1957-58; dir. spl. edn. Iowa Dept. Pub. Instrn., Bremer, Blackhawk, Butler counties, 1958-63; asst. dir. mental retardation, mental health zone, Ill. Dept. Mental Health, Peoria, 1965-66, asst. mental health supt. Peoria State Hosp., 1966-73, asst. mental health supt. Galesburg (Ill.) Mental Health Center, 1974-77; pvt. practice clin. psychology, Warren, Ohio, 1977—; asso. clin. prof. psychology Bradley U., Peoria, 1965-66, 66-67; pvt. practice psychology, 1966—; NIMH grantee lectr. psychology Knox Coll., Galesburg, Ill., 1967; asso. prof. psychology Western Ill. U., Macomb, Ill., 1967-68, 68-69, 69-70, 70-71; clin. asso., psychiatry, psychology, Peoria Sch. Medicine, 1973—. Certified profl. psychologist, Ill., Iowa, Wis., Ohio. Mem. Am., Ohio psychol. assns., Assn. Mental Health Adminstrs. Home: 412 Warren Ave SE Vienna OH 44473

BINNING, ROBERT CHRISTIE, chem. research co. exec.; b. Baton Rouge, Feb. 11, 1921; s. Francis Henry and Mary Lillian (Romero) B.; B.S., La. State U., 1948, M.S., 1950, Ph.D., 1952; m. Lucille Annette Giese, May 27, 1944; children—Robert, Janet (Mrs. Donald Breidenbach), John, Adele. Research chemist Am. Oil Co., Texas City, Tex., 1952-55, group leader, 1955-58; group leader Monsanto Co., Dayton, Ohio, St. Louis, 1958-60, sr. group leader, 1960-61, project mgr., 1961-64; research mgr. Monsanto Research Corp., Dayton, 1964-65, asst. dir., 1965-75, dir. environ. research and devel., 1975—. Chmn. camping and activities com. Mainland dist. Bay Area council Boy Scouts Am., 1956-57; v.p. Dad's Assn., Butler U., 1972-73, pres. 1973-74. Served with USAAF, 1940-45. Decorated D.F.C., Air medal with two oak leaf clusters. Fellow Am. Inst. Chem. Engrs., Am. Inst. Chemists; mem. Am. Chem. Soc. (chmn. examination subcom. com. high sch. chem. edn. Southeastern Tex. sect. 1955-56), Am. Def. Preparedness Assn., Internat. Soc. Tech. Assessment, World Future Soc., Alpha Chi Sigma. Methodist (chmn. commn. edn., bd. stewards 1957-58). Contbr. articles to profl. publs. Patentee in field. Home: 3473 Tall Timber Trail Dayton OH 45409 Office: 1515 Nicholas Rd Dayton OH 45407

BINOTTI, DAVID ALLEN, orthodontist; b. Chgo., Apr. 8, 1943; s. Evo Joseph and Anne (DiVita) B.; D.D.S., Loyola U. (Chgo.), 1967, M.S. in Oral Biology, 1969, Certificate Specialty Orthodontics, 1969; m. Barbara J. Rizzo, June 24, 1967; children—Eric David, Nicholas Allen. Practice orthodontics, Oak Lawn, Ill., 1969—, Lombard, Ill., 1971—; asso. with Dr. Ernest Panos, Chgo., 1969-74; clin. instr. dept. orthodontics Sch. Dentistry, Loyola U., 1969-72. Mem. ADA, Chgo. Dental Soc., Am. Assn. Orthodontists, Ill. Soc. Orthodontists. Roman Catholic. Office: 5208 W 95th St Oak Lawn IL 60453 also 805 S Main St Suite 2 Lombard IL 60148

BIPES, ROGER LUELLYEN, mech. engr.; b. Brownton, Minn., Dec. 12, 1936; s. Leullyen L. and Elda M. (Reiter) B.; B.S. in Mech. Engring., Ind. Inst. Tech., 1958; m. Janice M. Doctor, June 14, 1958; children—Timothy, Thomas, Trisha. Test engr. Ind. and Mich. Electric Co., Lawrenceburg, Ind., 1957-61; sr. indsl. hygienist Nat. Lead Co. of Ohio, Fernald, 1961-66; chief engr. MC & R Mfg. Chemists, Norwood, O., 1966—. Mem. Am. Soc. Safety Engrs., So. Ohio Fire Protection Assn. Republican. Lutheran. Home: 547 Hayes St Lawrenceburg IN 47025 Office: 2909 Highland St Norwood OH 45212 -

BIRCH, JOHN EDWARD, home builder, realtor; b. Chgo., Oct. 3, 1917; s. John Edward and Veronica (Motyka) B.; B.A. in Edn., B.A. in Banking and Finance, U. Ill., 1940; M.B.A., Northwestern U., 1942; Ph.D. in Bus. Adminstrn., Colo. State Coll.; children—John Edward, Christopher J., Terrie J., Laurence P. Pres., John Birch & Co., also Cherrywood Homes, Alert Carpentry Corp., Durable Masonry Corp., Lombard, Ill., 1955—, Country Club Hills, Lombard, 1956—; pres. Terrie Birch & Co. Mem. Planning Commn. DuPage County, Ill. Bldg. Authority, 1977—. Mem. adv. bd. Lyons Township Republican Party. Trustee Mid-Am. Hearing Found. of Wesley Meml. Hosp. Served from pvt. to col., USAAF, 1942-46. Ky. Col. Mem. Home Builders Assn. Chicagoland (life dir.), Nat. Assn. Homebuilders, Nat., Ill. assns. real estate bds., DuPage Bd. Realtors, U.S. C. of C., Chgo. Assn. Commerce and Industry (com. mem.), Am. Legion, Art Inst. Chgo., U. Ill. Alumni Assn. (life). Clubs: Moose, Glen Oaks Country, Village (Western Springs, Ill.); Rotary (Oakbrook, Ill.); Torch; Oakbrook Polo. Home: 3331 S Oak Park Ave Berwyn IL 60402 Mailing address: PO Box 247 Lombard IL 60148

BIRD, DON-MICHAEL, stock brokerage exec.; b. West Palm Beach, Fla., Mar. 9, 1930; s. F. Donald and Marion E. (White) B.; B.S. in Commerce, U. Va., 1952; postgrad., 1952-54; m. Audrey Lawrence, Sept. 5, 1953; children—Meri-Beth, Michael, Lawrie. Vice pres. White Constrn. Co., Ill., La., Wis., 1956-58; stock broker Blunt, Ellis & Simmons, Inc., Chgo., 1958—. Lectr. N.Y. Inst. Finance. U. Chgo. Republican precinct capt., 1968—, chmn. nominating com. caucus, 1967—. Served to lt. AUS, 1954-56. Clubs: Indian Hill, University, Mid-Day, Farmington Country. Home: 160 Birch St Winnetka IL 60093 Office: 111 W Monroe St Chicago IL 60603

BIRD, HARRIE WALDO, JR., psychiatrist, educator; b. Detroit, Sept. 21, 1917; s. Harrie Waldo and Ann Josephine (Tossy) B.; A.B., Yale, 1939; postgrad. U. Mich. Med. Sch., 1939-41; M.D., Harvard, 1943; m. Della Mae Clemmer, Jan. 4, 1943; children—Harrie Waldo, Kathleen Delame, Deborah (Mrs. Michael A. Hall), Mark Henry, Mathew, Liza. Intern, Phila. Gen. Hosp., 1943-44; resident Menninger Sch. Psychiatry, Topeka, Kan., 1946-48; chief infirmary sect. Winter VA Hosp., Topeka, 1946; psychiatrist Adult Psychiat. Clinic, Detroit, 1949, acting dir., 1950; psychiat. cons. Mich. Epilepsy Center, Detroit, 1950-55; asso. prof. psychiatry U. Chgo., 1955-56; asso. prof. psychiatry U. Mich. 1956-63, asst. dean Med. Sch., 1959-61; prof. psychiatry, asso. dean St. Louis U. Sch. Medicine, 1965-68, clin. prof. psychiatry, 1970—; dir. Family Psychicenter, Inc., St. Louis, 1972—; clin. instr. psychiatry Wayne State U., Detroit, 1952-55; seminar dir. Mental Health Inst. St. John's U., 1954-73; vis. lectr. Ypsilanti (Mich.) State Hosp., 1962-65; asso. grad. faculty U. Tex., El Paso, 1969-70. Cons. psychiatrist VA Hosp., Ann Arbor, Mich., 1956-64, John Cochran VA Hosp., St. Louis, 1965-68, St. Louis VA Hosp., 1971—; panel cons. USIA, 1959—; cons. to surgeon gen. U.S. Army, 1968-70. Bd. dirs. Mich. Epilepsy Center, 1956-63, Cranbrook Sch., 1961-63. Served with M.C., AUS, 1944-46. Recipient St. John's U. Mental Health Inst. award. Fellow Am. Psychiat. Assn.; mem. AMA, Group for Advancement Psychiatry, Am. Psychosomatic Soc., Am. Psychopath. Assn., Mo. State, St. Louis med. socs., Eastern Mo. Psychiat. Soc., Wayne County Soc. Mental Health (dir. 1956-63), Mich. Epilepsy Assn. (dir. 1956-63), El Paso Mental Health Assn. (dir. 1969-70), Phi Beta Kappa. Home: 62 Conway Ln St Louis MO 63124 Office: 10287 Clayton Rd St Louis MO 62124

BIRD, MILFORD GILBERT, mech. engr.; b. Algona, Iowa, Jan. 21, 1917; s. Henry Francis and Verona May (Gilbert) B.; student Chgo. Tech. Coll., 1938-41, U. Minn., 1949-53; m. Bernice Laura Stoeckel, Sept. 9, 1944; children—Ronald Gilbert, Bonnie Laura. With CCC, Grand Rapids, Minn., 1934; asst. to ednl. adviser Roberts-Hamilton Co., Mpls., 1933-38; draftsman Tri-City Roofing & Sheet Metal Works, Whiting Ind, 1938-41; office mgr. Honeywell, Inc., Mpls., 1944-45; field research engr. Reese Assos., Mpls., 1945-49; pres. Bird, Bird & Assos., Mpls., 1949-73; mech. engr. U.S. Postal Service, St. Paul, 1973—. Served with U.S. Army, 1941-44. Mem. Minn. Assn. Cons. Engrs. (pres. 1966-67), Am. Cons. Engrs. Council (nat. dir. 1970-72), Nat., Minn. socs. profl. engrs., Profl. Engrs. In Govt. Republican. Lutheran. Home: 3200 46th Ave N Robbinsdale MN 55422 Office: 180 E Kellogg Blvd St Paul MN 55169

BIRD, RICHARD MAYWOOD, educator; b. Lansing, Mich., May 22, 1934; s. John Wendell and Dorothy (Maywood) B.; A.A. cum laude, Lansing Community Coll., 1964; B.A. with high honors, No. Mich. U., 1965, M.A. in English, 1969; children—Christopher John, Kathy Ann. Adminstrv. asst., writer Upper Peninsula Com. for Area Progress, Escanaba, Mich., 1965-66; instr. English, No. Mich. U., Marquette, 1968-72; instr. English and humanities Lansing Community Coll., 1972—. Cons. inservice lang. arts writing workshops Emerson Sch., Ionia, Mich., 1974—, Twin Lakes Sch., Muir, Mich., 1975—. Served with USMC, 1952-55. Recipient Creative Writing Contest Citation of Honor award Story Col.l., 1968, Gilbert Brown Meml. award No. Mich. U., 1965. Mem. Tchrs. of English to Speakers of Other Langs., Mich. Coll. English Assn., AAUP, Nat. Council Tchrs. English, Alpha Phi Gamma. Address: 232 East Owen Hall Mich State U East Lansing MI 48823

BIRDCELL, GAIL ELAINE, librarian; b. Akron, Ohio, Jan. 12, 1943; d. Herbert Marvin and Florence May (Strickland) Tabbut; B.A., Pa. State U., 1965; M. Librarianship, U. Wash., 1969; m. John James Birdcell, Feb. 23, 1973 (div.). Lit. searcher Pa. Tech. Assistance Program, University Park, Pa., 1967-68; field intern Nat. Lending Library for Sci. and Tech., Boston SPA, Great Britain, 1969; dir. libraries and learning resources devel. Ind. Vocational Tech. Coll., Indpls., 1970-73; dir. library and information services Am. States Ins. Cos., Indpls., 1973-74; head br. Lake County Pub. Library, Hobart, Ind., 1974; chief adminstrv. officer Northwest Ind. Area Library Services Authority, Chesterton, 1975—; mem. librarians com. Consortium for Urban Edn., Indpls., 1972—. Mem. Am., Ind., Spl. library assns., Midwest Multi-type Library Coordinators Group. Home: 1716 E 33rd Pl Hobart IN 46342 Office: 200 W Indiana Ave PO Box 948 Chesterton IN 46304

BIRENBAUM, WILLIAM M., coll. pres.; b. Macomb, Ill., July 18, 1923; s. Joseph and Rose (Whiteman) B.; student Iowa State Tchrs. Coll., 1943; J.D., U. Chgo., 1949; L.H.D., Columbia Coll., Chgo., 1970; m. Helen Bloch, Mar. 8, 1951; children—Susan, Lauren Amy, Charles. Dir. student affairs U. Chgo., 1949-54, mem. faculty social scis. coll. of univ., 1950-54, dean students Univ. Coll., 1955-57; dir. research. conf. bd. Asso. Research Councils, Ford Found. project study post-doctoral internat. ednl. exchanges, 19S4-55; asst. v.p. Wayne State U., 1957-61; dean New Sch. Social Research, N.Y.C., 1961-64; v.p., provost Bklyn. Center, L.I. U., 1964-67; pres. Edn. Affiliate. Bedford-Stuyvesant Devel. & Services Corp., Bklyn., 1967-68; pres. S.I. Community Coll., 1968-76, pres. Antioch Coll., 1976—, also leader study mission to People's Republic China, 1973; mem. faculty N.Y. U. Grad. Sch. Edn., 1969-70. Cons., Austrian Ministry Edn., Vienna, 1969; higher edn. adviser Republic of Zambia, 1972; cons. U. Zambia, 1972; guest lectr. 4th Internat. Congress, for Sci. Edn., Sorbonne, Paris, France, 1973; vis. prof. U. Mass., Amherst, 1974-75. Founder, Nat. Student Assn., 1946-48, chmn. nat. faculty bd., 1950-54; pres. Assn. Community Councils Met. Chgo., 1955-57; chmn. Mich. Cultural Commn.. 1960-61; founder, original dir. Detroit Adventure, vol. assn. cultural instns., 1958-61; mem. Bd. Edn., dists. 21-22, N.Y.C., 1962-64; bd. dirs. Bklyn. chpt. Am. Civil Liberties Union, 1967—, chmn. acad. freedom com., 1967—; chmn. edn. com. Met. council Am. Jewish Congress, 1967—, chmn. acad. freedom com., 1967—; trustee Little Red Schoolhouse on Bleecker St. N.Y.C., 1963—; bd. adv. Bklyn. Acad. Music, 1965—, Bklyn. Inst. Arts and Scis. mem. mass media program com. Religion in Am. Life, 1969—; mem. adv. council Korean Student Assn., N.Y., 1969—; adv. bd. ERIC Clearinghouse for Jr. Coll., Los Angeles, 1970—; mem. commn. on curriculum Am. Assn. Jr. Colls., 1970—; mem. nat. adv. council Eastern Va. Med. Sch., 1971—; bd. govs. Rochdale Inst., 1972—; bd. dirs. Brotherhood-in-Action, 1972—, Regional Plan Assn., 1972—. Trustee Friends World Coll., Westbury, N.Y. Mem. Chgo. Bar Assn., Delta Sigma. Author: Overlive: Power, Poverty and the University, 1968; Something for Everybody is Not Enough: An Educator's Search for His Education, 1971. Contbg. author: Student Personnel Work in Urban Colleges. Office: Antioch College Yellow Springs OH 45387

BIRK, ROBERT EUGENE, physician; b. Buffalo, Jan. 7, 1926; s. Reginald H. and Florence (Diebolt) B.; A.B., Colgate U., 1948; M.D., U. Rochester, 1952; m. Janet L. Davidson, June 24, 1950; children—David Eugene, James Michael, Patricia Jean, Thomas Spencer, Susan Margaret. Intern, resident Henry Ford Hosp., Detroit, 1952-57, chief 2d med. div., 1961-66, asst. to chmn. dept. medicine, 1965-66; practice medicine, specializing in internal medicine, Grosse Pointe, Mich., 1966—; sr. active staff St. John Hosp., 1966—, chief dept. medicine, 1967-70, dir. health edn., dir. grad. med. edn., 1975—; asst. prof. medicine Wayne State U., 1969—. Mem. trustee's council U. Rochester, 1973-75, Med. Center alumni council, 1974-75; corporate mem. bd. Boys Clubs Met. Detroit, 1973—. Served with Army of U.S., 1943-46. Diplomate Am. Bd. Internal Medicine. Fellow A.C.P.; mem. Am. Soc. Internal Medicine, AMA, Assn. Hosp. Med. Edn., Alpha Tau Omega. Republican. Episcopalian. Clubs: Grosse Pointe, Renaissance. Contbr. articles in field to profl. jours. Home: 10 Stratford Pl Grosse Pointe MI 48230 Office: 17894 Mack Ave Grosse Pointe MI 48224

BIRKELAND, CHARLES JOHN, horticulturist, educator; b. Warwick, N.D., Apr. 16, 1916; s. John and Harriett Agnes (Watts) B.; B.S., Mich. State Coll., 1939; M.S., Kans. State Coll., 1941; Ph.D., U. Ill., 1947; m. Wilma Florine Evans, Dec. 25, 1941; children—Charles Evans, Janis Lynn, John Richard. Grad. asst. Kans. State Coll., 1939-41, asst. horticulturist, 1941-46; grad. asst. U. Ill., Urbana, 1946-47, asst. prof. dept. horticulture, 1947-49, prof. and head dept., 1949—. Served to lt. USNR, 1942-46. Fellow AAAS; mem. Bot. Soc. Am., Ill. Hort. Soc., Ill. Vegetable Assn., Ill. Florists Assn., Ill. Nursery Men's Assn., Am. Inst. Biol. Scis., Am. Soc. Hort. Sci., Am. Pomol. Soc., Vegetable Growers Assn. Am., Am. Genetics Assn., Bot. Soc. Am., Ill. Acad., Naval Res. Officers Assn., Sigma Xi (research award), Phi Alpha Xi, Alpha Zeta, Phi Kappa Phi, Gamma Sigma Delta, Phi Sigma, Alpha Gamma Rho. Republican. Unitarian. Rotarian. Clubs: Lincoln Debate, University, Urbana Golf and Country. Contbr. bulls. and articles in sci. and hort. jours. Home: 2111 Zuppke Dr Urbana IL 61801

BIRR, DONALD JAMES, univ. adminstr.; b. Kankakee, Ill., June 8, 1921; s. Herman Frederick and Anna (Falkenhan) B.; B.S., U. Ill., 1950, Ed.M., 1952; postgrad. Ill. State U., 1957-61; Ed.D., Mich. State U., 1969; m. Doris Mae Hertz, Oct. 10, 1942; children—Judith (Mrs. Lee Williams), Cheryl (Mrs. Russell Dierking), Beverly (Mrs. Jeffrey Larson), Randall. Tchr. math. John Deere Jr. High Sch., Moline, Ill., 1950-55; jr. high sch. prin. Charleston, Ill., 1956-58, Kewanee, Ill., 1958-60, Wheaton, Ill., 1960-66; full prof. edn., jr. high sch. coordinator U. Wis.-Eau Claire, 1966—. Cons. individualized math. program Rice Lake Middle Sch. (Wis.). Served with USNR, 1942-45; PTO. Grantee Wis. Improvement Program, U. Wis. Found., 1972-73. Mem. NEA (life, Ill. del. 1962), Nat. Assn. Secondary Sch. Prins. (adv. com. 1957-63), Ill. Jr. High Sch. Prins. Assn. (dir. 1956-62, pres. 1962-63), Wis. Assn. Jr. High Sch. Prins. (chmn. tchr. edn. com. 1969-70), Phi Delta Kappa. Club: Bus. and Profl. Couples (Eau Claire). Home: 222 McKinley Ave Eau Claire WI 54701

BISARYA, ARVIND KUMAR, structural engr.; b. Indore, India, Oct. 27, 1942; s. Radhey Behari and Savitri Devi (Saxena) Lall; came to U.S., 1969, naturalized, 1976; B.S. in Civil Engring., U. Indore, 1966; diploma in structural engring. U. Dundee, Scotland, 1969; M.S. in Structures and Construction Mgmt., U. Mo., Columbia, 1977; postgrad. N.D. State U., 1969-70; m. Pushpa Verma, Mar. 24, 1974; 1 son, Amit Kumar. Jr. engr. Pub. Works Dept.. Govt. of India, Bhopal, 1967-68; structural designer Taliaferro & Browne Cons. Engrs., Kansas City, Kans., 1970-74; project designer Butler Mfg. Co., Kansas City, Mo., 1974-75; project design engr. Black and Veatch Cons. Engrs., Kansas City, Mo., 1975—. Mem. ASCE. Home: 9500

Drury St #203 Kansas City MO 64137 Office: 1500 Meadowlake Pkwy Kansas City MO 64114

BISCHOF, MILTON, JR., architect, county ofcl.; b. St. Louis, Aug. 17, 1929; s. Milton J. and Catherine M. (Kersting) B.; B.Arch., Washington U., St. Louis, 1952; m. Evelyn Bright, June 28, 1952; children—Deborah Ann, Lauri Ann, Mark. Architect Bernard Bloom, St. Louis, 1954-58; partner Manske-Dieckmann & Partners, architects, St. Louis, 1958-71; project architect Hellmuth, Obata & Kassabaum, Inc., St. Louis, 1971—. Adv. bd. Spanish Lake Bank & Trust Co. Mem. adv. com. U.S. Dept. Transp., 1968—; mem. Missouri River Bridge Com., Open Space Council; regional rep. Architects in Govt. Chmn. Lewis and Clark Dist. council Boy Scouts Am., 1969-72; mem. Lewis and Clark Trail Commn.; hon. commr. Mo. Bicentennial Commn.; vice chmn. United Fund; past pres. council North County Improvement Assn.; co-chmn. St. Louis Spirit of '76. Chmn. St. Louis County Planning Commn., 1967; councilman St. Louis County, 1968-76, chmn., 1972; past pres. Spanish Lake Republican Club; Rep. candidate for congress from 9th Mo. Dist., 1974. Mem. legislative com. Nat. Paraplegia Found., St. Louis; v.p. Christian Hosp. N.W. St. Louis County. Pres. Spanish Lake Improvement Assn., Mo. U. Extension Service. Served with AUS, 1952-54. Mem. A.I.A., Mo. Assn. Registered Architects (past dir.), St. Louis County League Municipalities (dir.), Mo. Assn. Counties (dir.), Florissant Valley C. of C., Kappa Sigma. Republican. Roman Catholic (mem. ch. council). Kiwanian (pres. local club 1964, 66). Clubs: Bellefontaine Country (pres. 1963), Jamestown Racquet, Media, St. Louis Ambassadors, Advt. Greater St. Louis, Pachyderm (2d v.p.). Home: 6 Elmcrest Acres St Louis County MO 63138 Office: 315 N 9th St St Louis MO 63101

BISH, MILAN DAVID, land devel. co. exec.; b. Harvard, Nebr., July 1, 1929; s. Charles and Mabel Etta (Williams) B.; B.A., Hastings Coll., 1951; m. Allene R. Miller, Mar. 17, 1951; children—Cynthia, Linda, Charles. Pres., Bish Machinery Co., Grand Island, Nebr., 1965-73, Mid-Continent Enterprises, 1974—; dir. Comml. Nat. Bank, Grand Island. State chmn. Nebr. Republican party, 1971-72; mem. Rep. Nat. Com., 1971-72; mem. Rep. Exec. Com. Nebr., 1972-74; Nebr. chmn. Citizens for Reagan, 1976; chmn. Nebr. del. Rep. Nat. Conv., 1976; mem. steering com. Citizens for the Republic. Named Ambassador of Nebr. Mem. C. of C. (pres. 1977). Mason (32 deg., Shriner), Elk, Eagle, Rotarian (dist. gov. 1970-71). Clubs: Riverside Golf, Liederkranz, Platt Deutsch. Home: 2012 W Louise St Grand Island NE 68801 Office: PO Box 1365 Grand Island NE 68801

BISHARA, SAMIR EDWARD, orthodontist; b. Cairo, Egypt, Oct. 31, 1935; s. Edward Constantin and Georgette Ibrahim (Kelela) B.; came to U.S., 1968. naturalized, 1976; B. in Dental Surgery, Alexandria U., Egypt, 1957, diploma in Orthodontics, 1967; M.S., U. Iowa. 1970, certificate in Orthodontics, 1970, D.D.S., 1972; m. Cynthia Jane McLaughlin, July 3, 1975; 1 dau., Dina Marie. Practice gen. dentistry, Alexandria, Egypt, 1957-66, specializing in orthodontics, Iowa City, Iowa, 1970—; fellow in clin. pedodontics Guggenheim Dental Clinic, N.Y.C., 1959-60; resident in oral surgery Moassat Hosp., Alexandria, Egypt, 1960-61, mem. staff, 1961-68; asst. prof. Coll. Dentistry, U. Iowa, Iowa City, 1970-73, asso. prof., 1973-76, prof., 1976—, investigator Cleft Palate Research Program, 1970—; vis. prof. Alexandria U., 1974-75. Bd. dirs. Am. Cleft Palate Ednl. Found., mem. lay edn. com., 1975-76. Recipient Best Prof. award Dept. Orthodontics, U. Iowa, 1974. Mem. Am., Egyptian, Iowa dental assns., Midwestern Soc. Orthodontists, Am. Assn. Orthodontics, Internat. Dental Fedn., Iowa Orthodontic Soc., AAAS, Internat. Assn. for Dental Research, Am. Cleft Palate Assn., Johnson County, U. Dist. dental socs., Assn. of Egyptian Am. Scholars, Omicron Kappa Upsilon, Sigma Xi. Mem. Christian Orthodox Ch. Contbr. articles on orthodontics to profl. jours. and book chpts. Home: 1014 Penkridge Dr Iowa City IA 52240 Office: Orthodontic Dept College of Dentistry Iowa City IA 52242

BISHEA, PAUL MAURICE, pub. relations exec.; b. Elnora, Ind., Dec. 27, 1931; s. Albert M. and Doris (Rodenbeck) B.; B.S. in Agrl. Mgmt., Purdue U., 1955; m. Nancy J. Van Voorhis, Dec. 26, 1955; children—Douglas M., Ann E., Jana E. Pub. relations rep. Nat. City Bank of Evansville (Ind.), 1959-61; mgr. pub. info. Mead Johnson & Co., Evansville, 1961-65; pub. relations account exec. Barkin-Herman & Assos., Milw., 1965-69; v.p. pub. relations McDonald Davis & Assoc., Milw., 1969-74; partner Williams Bishea & Assocs., Inc., 1974-75; pres. Bishea, Meili & Assos., Inc.. Milw., 1975—; instr. pub. relations U. Wis., 1976—. Mem. communications com. United Fund, 1973; bd. dirs. Voluntary Action Center Greater Milw., 1976—. Served with USCG, 1955-59. Mem. Pub. Relations Soc. Am. (pres. Wis. chpt. 1974). Conglist. Home: 5687 N Bay Ridge Ave Whitefish Bay WI 53217 Office: 312 E Wisconsin Ave Milwaukee WI 53202

BISHOP, ALLEN JOHN, savs. and loan assn. exec.; b. Berwyn, Ill., Feb. 17, 1948; s. John Edward and Mildred Alice (Chovancek) B.; B.S., Eastern Ill. U., 1971, M.B.A., 1972; m. Christine Ann Orbeck, June 8, 1974. With Clyde Savs. and Loan Assn., North Riverside, Ill., 1973—, dir. mktg., 1975-76, asst. v.p., dir. mktg., 1976—; instr. Inst. Fin. Edn., Morton Coll., 1973-74. Mem. Savs. Assn. Council (dir.), Savs. Instns. Soc. Am. (dir. chpt. 1; Mktg. award 1976), Eastern Ill. U. Alumni Assn. Chgo. Fin. Advertisers, Delta Chi, Delta Mu Delta. Roman Catholic. Home: 9645 W 57th St Countryside IL 60525 Office: 7222 W Cermak Rd North Riverside IL 60546

BISHOP, DOLLOFF FREDERICK, JR., research chem. engr.; b. Everett, Mass., May 26, 1935; s. Dolloff Frederick and Lillian Avernia (Veinot) B.; B.S. in Chem. Engring., U. Mass., 1956; M.S., U. Cin., 1966; m. Catherine Ann Foglia, June 11, 1959; children—Dolloff Frederick III, Bianca Lisa. Commd. officer USPHS, Cin., 1962-66; chem. engr. R.A. Taft San. Engring. Center, Cin., 1962-66; chief D.C. Pilot Plant field sta. Nat. Environmental Research Center, U.S. EPA, Washington, 1966-74, chief tech. devel. support br. Municipal Environ. Research Lab., Cin., 1974—. Tchr. Evening Coll., U. Cin., 1962-66, George Washington U., 1972; cons. U.S. AEC, 1968. Mem. bd. of rev. Israel Water Resources Devel. and Utilization Program, 1972. Mem. bldg. program Henson Valley Montessori Sch., Prince Georges County, Md., 1972-74, program coordinator, 1972-74. Recipient Capitol Engrs. of Yr. award, 1969, certificate of merit Am. Chem. Soc., Bronze medal EPA, Hatfield award Water Pollution Control Fedn., 1975. Mem. Am. Inst. Chem. Engrs., Water Pollution Control Fedn., Tau Beta Pi. Republican. Presbyterian. Patentee in water pollution control. Home: 6995 Goldengate Dr Cincinnati OH 45244 Office: Environmental Research Center US Environmental Protection Agy Cincinnati OH 45268

BISHOP, DONALD E., state senator; b. Almont, Mich., Feb. 27, 1933; s. G.C. and Jane (Wise) B.; B.A. in Polit. Sci., Oberlin Coll., 1955; J.D., Detroit Coll. Law, 1966; m. Nancy Michael, Aug. 6, 1955; children—Rebecca, Susan, Judy, Martha, Michael. Admitted to Mich. bar, 1967; atty. Martin & Bishop, Rochester, Mich., 1967—; mem. Mich. Ho. of Reps., 1966-70; mem. Mich. Senate, 1970—, mem. com. on corps. and econ. devel., mem. judiciary com., mem. commerce com.; dir. Nat. Bank of Rochester; incorporator Rochester Retirement Homes, Inc. Mem. Mich. Law Revision Commn., 1975—; mem. Uniform State Law Commn. Served with AUS, 1955-57. Home: 2332 W Avon Rd Rochester MI 48063 Office: 103 E 4th St Rochester MI 48063

BISHOP, EARL DEAN, civil engr.; b. McGehee, Ark., Aug. 9, 1932; s. Earl E. and Margaret Ervine (Lee) B.; m. Bonita Massey, Feb. 12, 1955; children—Keith, Sharon, Lynn, Kent. B.S. in Civil Engring., La. Poly. U., 1958. Project engr. firm Howard, Needles, Tammen & Bergendoff, Kansas City, Mo., 1958-67; partner firm Boyd, Bishop & Brown, Kansas City, 1967-69; pres. Bishops Engrs., Inc., Kansas City, 1969—. Mem. vol. staff Heart of Am. dist. Boy Scouts Am., 1975-76. Registered profl. engr., Ark., Nebr., Kans., Iowa, Mo., Ohio. Mem. ASCE, Nat. Mo. socs. profl. engrs., Am. Pub. Works Assn. Recipient award Midwest Concrete Industries Bd., 1974. Contbr. articles to profl. jours. Home: 407 Ponca Dr Independence MO 64056 Office: 5100 Main St Kansas City MO 64112

BISHOP, GILBERT CLARE, surgeon; b. Leonard, Mich., Sept. 30, 1899; s. Frank Leo and Genevieve (Thomas) B.; student Oberlin Coll., 1919-21, U. Mich., 1918-23; M.D., U. Chgo. (Rush), 1926; postgrad. U. Pa., 1944-45; m. Jane Lucile Wise, Sept. 22, 1925; children—Robert, Dean, Barbara, Donald, Malcolm, David. Intern, Henry Ford Hosp., Detroit, 1925-26; student surgery Elizabeth Hosp., Vienna, Austria, 1927-28, Allgemeines Krankenhaus, Vienna, 1930-31; founder, adminstr. Bishop Hosp., Almont, Mich., 1935-59; resident in surgery Guthrie clinic, Sayre, Pa., 1945-46; surgeon-in-chief Community Hosp., Almont, 1959-70; semi-retired, 1973—. Diplomate Am. Bd. Surgery. Fellow A.C.S.; mem. AMA, Mich. Med. Soc., Detroit, Flint acads. surgery, Republican. Congregationalist. Office: 409 E St Clair St Almont MI 48003

BISHOP, JACK LAWSON, JR., diversified products mfg. co. exec.; b. Rockville Centre, N.Y., Dec. 3, 1939; s. Jack Lawson and Elizabeth Janet (Blee) B.; B.S. in Chem. Engring., U. Colo., 1961; Ph.D., U. Ill., 1972; m. Donna Norine Leavens, June 24, 1962; children—Elizabeth Anona, Jack Lawson III, Kathleen Anne, Caroline Donna Van Alstine. Product devel. engr., mgmt. scis. specialist Dow Corning Corp., Midland, Mich., 1961-72; instr. Central Mich. U., Mt. Pleasant, 1969-70; mgr. mgmt. scis. Ky. Fried Chicken, Louisville, 1972-73; mgr. econ. and gen. research May Dept. Stores Inc., St. Louis, 1973-76; mgr. operational studies Brunswick Corp., Chgo., 1976—. Mem. Opns. Research Soc. Am., Chgo. Council Fgn. Relations, Inst. Mgmt. Sci.. Econometric Soc., Am. Econ. Assn., Am. Statis. Assn., Nat. Assn. Bus. Economists. Author: Insect, Disease and Weed Control, 1972; Practical Emulsions, 1968. Home: 916 Maple Ave Evanston IL 60202 Office: 1 Brunswick Plaza Skokie IL 60076

BISHOP, JOYCE ANN ARMENTROUT, counselor, educator; b. West Mansfield, Ohio, June 16, 1935; d. Frederic J. and Marjorie Vere (Stephens) Armentrout; A.B., Albion Coll., 1956; B.A., Western Mich. U., 1969; children—Belinda Lee, Thomas James. Tchr. phys. edn. Walled Lake (Mich.) Jr. High Sch., 1956-58; tchr. adult edn. pub. sch., Milw., 1959-65, Lakeview Schs., Battle Creek, Mich., 1966—; dir. student activities, Olivet (Mich.) Coll., 1969-71, also asst. prof., counselor; counselor Kellogg Community Coll., Battle Creek, 1971—. Sec. adult bd. Teens Inc., 1965-68. Mem. Com. to Rev. Articulation Matters (charter), Mich. Assn. Coll. Registrars and Admissions Officers, AAUW, Am., Mich. personnel and guidance assns., Am. Sch. Counselors Assn., Am. Coll. Personnel Assn., Mich. Assn. Coll. Registrars and Admissions Officers (com. on coll. articulation), Beta Beta Beta, Alpha Chi Omega. Lutheran. Home: 721 Eastfield Dr Battle Creek MI 49015 Office: 450 North Ave Battle Creek MI 49016

BISHOP, LAWRENCE RAY, lawyer; b. Douglas, Wyo., May 10, 1934; s. Cecil Lawrence and Mable (Spracklin) B.; student U. Wyo., 1952-53; B.S., U. Utah, 1956; postgrad. Duke, 1956-57; J.D., U. Mich., 1963; m. Sharleen Jo Bowe, June 9, 1956. Admitted to Mich. bar, 1963; asst. prosecutor Washtenaw County, Ann Arbor, Mich., 1964-66; partner firm Thompson, Bishop, Tryand & Thompson and predecessor firms, Ann Arbor, 1966-73; partner firm Forsythe, Campbell, Vandenberg, Clevenger & Bishop, Ann Arbor, 1973—. Dir. Central Title Services, Inc., Ann Arbor; v.p. House of Suren, Inc. Chmn. Ann Arbor chpt. Cancer Crusade, 1966—, Ann Arbor Mich. Week, 1967; mem. Mich. Mental Health Advisory Bd. Treas. Washtenaw Republican Com., 1967-73; mgr. several polit. campaigns. Served with USN, 1957-60. Mem. Washtenaw County (past pres.), Am. (chmn. legal asst. com., econs. sect.), Mich. (counsel grievance com., mem. state rep. assembly) bar assns., Am. Trial Lawyers Assn., Ann Arbor Police Officer Assn. (hon.), Scabbard and Blade, Sigma Chi, Tau Epsilon Rho, Mensa. Mason (Shriner). Club: Barton Hills. Author books and articles. Asst. editor Mich. Law Rev., 1962-63. Home: 2759 Colony Rd Ann Arbor MI 48104 Office: 111 S Main St Ann Arbor MI 48108

BISHOP, LESTER J., hosp. service co. exec.; b. Huntington, N.Y., Dec. 28, 1919; s. Louis Conklin and Margaret (Bosch) B.; B.S., U. Mass., 1942; m. Helen Stigall, Mar. 2, 1946; children—Stuart Allan, Robert Louis. Sr. navigator Pan Am. World Airways, 1945; with Wyeth Labs. pharm. mfr. div. Am. Home Products Corp., 1945-66, dist. mgr. Columbus, Ohio, 1950-63, div. mgr., 1963-66; v.p. Cortez F. Enloe, Inc., N.Y.C., 1966; v.p., Partner Bell & Bishop, Inc., N.Y.C., 1966-68; group v.p. The Mogul Corp., Cleve., 1968-72; founder, pres. Pharmacy Systems, Inc., Columbus, 1972—; Bishop Enterprises, Inc., 1977—. Pres. Peddie Sch. Father's Assn., 1965-66, com., 1964-65. Served to 1st lt. USAAF, 1942-45; ETO. Decorated D.F.C. with 2 oak leaf clusters, Air medal with 5 oak leaf clusters. Mem. Newcomen Soc. N.Am. Pharm. Advt. Club N.Y., Aircraft Owners and Pilots Assn., Am. Pharm. Assn., Am. Soc. Hosp. Pharmacists, Kappa Sigma. Mem. Community Ch. Clubs: Presidents (Ohio State U.); Scioto Country (Columbus); Century of U. Mass.; Wequetonsing Club and Association (Wequetonsing, Mich.); Muirfield Village Golf (Dublin, Ohio); Mayfield Country (Lyndhurst, Ohio). Home: 3070 Oakridge Rd Columbus OH 43221 also summer 36 4th Ave Wequetonsing MI 49740 Office: Pharmacy Systems Inc Columbus OH

BISHOP, LOIS CARLSON, lawyer; b. Chgo., July 22, 1933; d. Emery Leroy and Edna Marguerite (Anderson) Carlson; B.A., U. Chgo., 1952; J.D. cum laude, Northwestern U., 1976; m. Roger Bruce Bishop, Feb. 3, 1961. Underwriter, Chgo. Title and Trust Co., Chgo., 1952-59; escrow officer, 1959-73; admitted to Ill. bar, 1976, Fla. bar, 1977; individual practice law, Lincolnshire, Ill., 1976—. Environ. chmn., mem. exec. bd. Rainbow Neighbors, 1968-73; mem. governing council Clean Air Co-Ordinating Com., 1969-73; legis. chmn. N. Shore Bus. and Profl. Women's Clubs, 1977—; mem. steering com. Stop Airport in Lake, 1970. Mem. Am., Ill., Chgo. bar assns., Fla. Bar, ACLU (mem. women's rights com. 1969-71). Home: 1290 Scott Ave Winnetka IL 60093 Office: 430 Milwaukee Ave Lincolnshire IL 60069

BISHOP, MARS PAUL, textile brokerage co. exec.; b. Chgo., Feb. 12, 1899; s. Adamniram Judson and Frederica Paulina (Wittenberg) B.; B.S., Brown U., 1921; m. Madrice Zimmerman, Feb. 12, 1933 (dec.); m. 2d, Marian Keitel, Mar. 31, 1951; 1 dau., Norma Bishop O'Keefe. Pres., Tillinghast-Stiles Co., Providence, 1945—. Served with U.S. Army, 1918. Republican. Methodist. Clubs: Jonathan, Union League, Westmoreland Country, Mason, Sons of Am. Revolution. Home: 2746 Broadway Evanston IL 60201 Office: 327 S LaSalle St Chicago IL 60604

BISHOP, MYRON CHARLES, educator; b. Camden, Ohio, Nov. 24, 1906; s. Orval E. and Edna (Charles) B.; B.S., Miami U., Oxford, Ohio, 1930; M.S., Ohio State U., 1938; postgrad. U. Pitts., 1934-35, Cleve. Art Sch., 1935-36, Ind. U., 1947-48; m. Elizabeth L. Fischer, Nov. 9, 1968; children—Henry Lee, Sanchen Ann (Mrs. Thomas Barnum). Tchr., cons. engring. graphics Findlay (Ohio) Coll., 1930-34; faculty Ohio No. U., Ada, 1932-34, Bowling Green (Ohio) U., 1933-34, Bluffton (Ohio) Coll., 1937-38; tchr. indsl. arts Lakewood Schs., Cleve., 1940-42; asso. prof. engring. Evansville (Ind.) U., 1943-47; indsl. real estate cons., realtor, tool design cons. Columbus, Ohio, 1948-58; faculty So. Ill. U., Edwardsville, 1958—, now emeritus asso. prof. Bd. dirs. YMCA, Edwardsville, 1963-75. Mem. Phi Kappa Tau. Presbyterian (deacon 1964-65). Mason (Shriner, 32 deg.). Home: 316 Thomas Terr Edwardsville IL 62025

BISHOP, ROBERT DEANE, nuclear engr.; b. Emporia, Kans., June 23, 1946; s. Clarence Dwight and Cora Frances (Foley) B.; m. Sheila Roberts, Dec. 18, 1976. B.S., Kans. State U., 1969; M.B.A., U. Chgo., 1977. Engr. in tng. State of Kans., 1969; nuclear engr. Commonwealth Edison Co., Dresden sta., 1971-75, tech. staff supr. LaSalle County sta., 1975—. Served to 1st lt., inf. U.S. Army, 1970-71. Decorated Bronze Star medal; licensed nuclear reactor operator. Mem. Am. Nuclear Soc. Home: 113 Prairie Dr Minooka IL 60447 Office: LaSalle County Station Box 240 Marseilles IL 61341

BISHOP, WELKER HENRY, JR., educator, univ. adminstr.; b. Ashland, Ohio, Nov. 15, 1926; s. Welker Henry and Mildred Elizabeth (Craven) B.; student Ashland Coll., 1944-45, Yale, 1945-46; B.Ed., Ashland Coll., 1950; M.Ed., U. Wyo., 1961, Ed.D., 1964; m. Mary Louise Mitchell, May 26, 1962; children—Clifford Mitchell, Kris Janese. Tchr., Grand Rapids (Ohio) Schs., 1950-51, Savannah (Ohio) Schs., 1951-57; prin. Savannah High Sch., 1957-60; grad. asst. U. Wyo., 1960-62; dir. Crane-Hill Halls, U. Wyo., 1962-63, asst. dean men, 1963-64; dir. housing, asst. dean for housing, prof. higher edn. Ball State U., Muncie, Ind., 1964—. Cons. univ. housing. Bd. dirs. Ball State Fed. Credit Union; trust officer Ball State Fed. Credit Union. Mem. Am. Personnel and Guidance Assn., Am. Coll. Personnel Assn., Assn. Counselor Educators and Suprs., Nat. Assn. Student Personnel Adminstrs., Assn. Coll. and Univ. Housing Officers (pres.), Phi Delta Kappa, Psi Chi. Lion. Home: 4605 Gishler Dr Muncie IN 47304

BISKIS, EDWARD GEORGE, indsl. energy co. exec.; b. Coaldale, Pa., Apr. 2, 1935; s. Edward Raymond and Alice Marie (Witcofsky) B.; B.S. cum laude, Pa. State U., 1957; M.S., Cornell U., 1959; Ph.D., Northwestern U., 1963; m. Sandra Marie Welter, Feb. 10, 1962; children—Edward John, Patricia Ann, Suzanne Marie. Asst. research scientist Martin Marietta Corp., Denver, 1961-63; project mgr. comml. devel. Air Products & Chemicals, Inc., Allentown, Pa., 1963-68; dir. chem. diversification No. Natural Gas Co., Omaha, 1968-72; pres. BTU Contracts, Inc., indsl. energy, Lincolnwood, Ill., 1973—, also dir. Research cons. Northwestern U., 1961. Group leader Republican Workshop Ill., 1959-61. Mem. Am. Inst. Chem. Engrs., Am. Chem. Soc., Cryogenic Soc. Am., Am. Welding Soc., N.Y. Acad. Scis., Sigma Xi, Tau Beta Pi, Phi Eta Sigma, Sigma Tau, Phi Lambda Upsilon, Patentee in field. Home: 235 Laurel Ave Wilmette IL 60091 Office: 6432 Ridgeway Ave Lincolnwood IL 60659

BISKUP, GEORGE J(OSEPH), clergyman; b. Cedar Rapids, Iowa, Aug. 23, 1911; s. Frank L. and Julia (Kuda) K.; A.B., Loras Coll., 1933; student Gregorian U., Rome, 1933-37. Ordained priest Roman Cath. Ch., 1937; curate St. Raphael's Cathedral, Dubuque, Iowa, 1937-39; mem. faculty Loras Acad. and Loras Coll., 1939-48; head art dept. Loras Coll., 1941-48; minutante sacred congregation Oriental Ch., Vatican City, 1948-51; chancellor of Archdiocese of Dubuque, 1951-52, vicar gen., 1952-65, aux. bishop, 1957-65; bishop of Des Moines, 1965-67; co-adjutor archbishop of Indpls., 1967—; pastor St. Joseph's Ch., 1951-52; chaplain Mt. Loretta Convent, Dubuque, 1952-58; archdiocesan dir. Cath. Cemeteries, 1953-58, pastor Ch. of the Nativity, 1958-65. Vice-pres. Archdiocese of Dubuque, Inc., 1952-65. Papal chamberlain, 1949, domestic prelate, 1951. Address: 1350 N Pennsylvania St Indianapolis IN 46202

BISSELL, ROBERT KENYON, lawyer; b. Cambridge, Mass., Apr. 13, 1927; s. Howard Seymour and Marcia Geneve (Kenyon) B.; student Hiram Coll., 1945, Bowdoin Coll., 1948; A.B., Swarthmore Coll., 1949; J.D., Harvard, 1952; m. Martha Larsen, June 30, 1970; children—Whit, Brooke; children by previous marriage—Alice Seymour, Edward Holmes. Admitted to Ohio bar, 1952; asso. Frederick W. Dorn, Esq., Cleve., 1952-62; partner Schneider, Smeltz, Huston & Bissell, 1962—; sec., dir., gen. counsel Brown Fintube Co., Elyria, Ohio, 1962-67; sec., dir., gen. counsel Neal Moving & Storage Co., Cleve., 1962—. Law dir. Village of Gates Mills, Ohio, 1962—, Village Hunting Valley, 1968—. Trustee Hiram Coll., 1969—, sec., 1971—. Served with USNR, 1945-46. Mem. Am., Ohio, Cleve. bar assns., Cuyahoga County Law Dirs. Assn. (pres. 1972-73), Am. Judicature Soc., Garfield Soc. Hiram Coll. Clubs: Harvard (Cleve.), Cleve. Skating, Cleve. Playhouse. Home: 3018 Edgewood Rd Pepper Pike OH 44124 Office: 1525 National City Bank Bldg Cleveland OH 44114

BISSELL, STEVEN LEWIS, entertainment agy. exec.; b. Iowa City, Iowa, Jan. 30, 1949; s. Lewis Austin and Berniece Margaret (Helmer) B.; student U. Iowa, 1968. Owner Bissell Talent Agency, Iowa City, 1965—; owner, operator Plastic Fantastic, light show, Iowa City, 1969-71; owner New World Entertainment Agy., New World Prodns., Iowa City, 1972—. Chmn. Jerry Lewis Labor Day telethon com. Iowa City Muscular Dystrophy Assn., 1977. Recipient Spoke award U.S. Jaycees, 1977. Mem. Student Producers Assn. (co-chmn., founder 1974—). Democrat. Home: 712 Dearborn Iowa City IA 52240 Office: Room 317G Zoology Annex U Iowa Iowa City IA 52242

BISSELL, WALTER HENRY, financial cons.; b. Wausau, Wis., Jan. 11, 1932; s. Walter Henry and Mary H. (Dingee) B.; B.A., Lawrence U., 1954; M.B.A., Harvard U., 1958; m. Jane W. Doherty, May 31, 1958; children—Jeffrey W., Nancy J., Katherine E. Investment analyst Harris Trust Savs. Bank, Chgo., 1958-64, asst. cashier comml. banking dept., 1964-66; investment analyst Duff & Phelps, Chgo., 1966-68, v.p., 1968—. Served with USAF, 1954-56. Certified Financial Analyst, Ill. Mem. Investment Analysts Soc. Chgo., Beta Theta Pi. Republican. Episcopalian. Club: Univ. (Chgo.). Home: 338 Fairview Ave Winnetka IL 60093 Office: 55 E Monroe St Chicago IL 60603

BISSEY, WILLIAM KARL, bank exec.; b. Columbus, Ind., Aug. 18, 1940; s. Harry Carl and Mary M. (Fleming) B.; B.S. (Ford fellow, 1960-63), Ind. U., 1962, M.B.A., 1964. Purchasing agt. Arvin Industries, Inc., Columbus, 1964-68; instr. Ohio No. U., Ada, 1968-73; credit analyst Mchts. Nat. Bank, Indpls., 1974—. Served with U.S. Army, 1963-64. Mem. Am. Philatelic Soc., Fin. Mgmt. Assn., Alpha Kappa Psi, Delta Sigma Phi, Beta Gamma Sigma, Omicron Delta Epsilon. Presbyterian. Home: 8305 Sobax Dr Indianapolis IN 46268 Office: 11 S Meridian St Indianapolis IN 46204

BITONTE, DOMINIC ANTHONY, dentist; b. Youngstown, O., July 20, 1924; s. Anthony Frank and Gemma (LaGuardia) B.; D.D.S., Ohio State U., 1947, postgrad. 1955-62; postgrad. Temple U., 1958, 61, Western Res. U., 1960, 62; m. Helen M. Furr, Feb. 8, 1946; children—A. Gary, David A., Dianne M. Intern, St. Vincent Hosp., Cleve., 1947; pvt. practice dentistry, Youngstown, Ohio, 1947—. Mem. Ohio Dental Bd. Examiners, 1962-63. Mem. adv. bd. Mahoning Nat. Bank, 1970-76, now dir. Mem. Mahoning County Planning Commn. Bd. dirs. Youngstown Symphony Soc., 1956-66, Latin Culture Found. Served with AUS, 1943-44, USNR, 1952-54. Fellow Internat. Coll. Dentists; mem. Am., Ohio dental assns., Am. Assn. Dental Examiners, Corydon Palmer Dental Soc. (pres. 1966-67), Ohio State U. Alumni Assn. (county pres. 1969-71). Roman Catholic. Club: Youngstown. Home: 1347 St Albans Dr Youngstown OH 44511 Office: 26 Market St Youngstown OH 44503

BITTENBENDER, RICHARD CHASE, container mfg. co. exec.; b. Ames, Iowa, Jan. 2, 1918; s. Harry Artley and Bess Abbott (Chase) B.; A.B., Wittenberg U., 1940; M.B.A., Harvard U., 1947; m. Imogene Knost, Apr. 5, 1945; children—Richard Chase, Elizabeth (Mrs. Richard O. Perry), Thomas T. With Container Corp. Am., 1947—, gen. mgr. carton div., Solon, Ohio, 1965-66, dir. personnel, Chgo., 1966—, v.p., 1967-73, sr. v.p., dir., 1973—, dir. equal employment opportunity activities, 1972-74, sr. v.p. employee relations and corporate communication, 1974-77, exec. v.p. human resources, 1977—. Trustee Wittenberg (Ohio) U. Served to capt. USMCR, 1942-46. Clubs: Economic, Executives, University (Chgo.). Home: 1670 Mission Hills Rd E Northbrook IL 60062 Office: One First National Plaza Chicago IL 60670

BITTING, PHYLLIS DIANE, real estate broker; b. Kosciusko County, Ind., Oct. 11, 1935; d. Earl Vance and Edna Ruth (Powers) Davis; student Ind. U., 1971, 75-77; m. James Duane Bitting, June 26, 1953; 1 son, Andrew Vance. Real estate broker Center Realty, Warsaw, Ind., 1973—; sec., treas. Koscuisko Bd. Realtors, Warsaw, 1975-76, v.p., 1977-78, pres., 1978—; state sec. by law com. Ind. Assn. Realtors, Indpls., 1977—. Trustee, Walnut Creek United Methodist Ch., Warsaw, 1977—. Mem. Nat. Bd. Realtors, D.A.R. (regent Anthony Vigo chpt. 1974-75). Home: Route 2 Box 456 Warsaw IN 46580 Office: 2304 E Center St Warsaw IN 46580

BITTINGER, EUGENE PRESTON, architect; b. Dayton, Pa., Mar. 3, 1924; s. Samuel Preston and Lena Marie (Milliren) B.; B. Arch., Carnegie-Mellon U., 1951; M.B.A., Baldwin-Wallace Coll., 1976; m. Mary Elizabeth Butler, Sept. 8, 1951; children—Jon Scott, Linda Jill, Marc Bret, Erik Eugene. Designer J. Kenneth Myers, AIA, Pitts., 1946-51; site planner Richard Hawley Cutting & Assos., AIA, Cleve., 1951-53; chief designer George S. Voinovich & Assos., AIA, 1953-67; planner Eugene Preston Bittinger, AIA, Berea, Ohio, 1967-72; prin. Hubbell & Benes & Hoff, Inc., architects and engrs., Cleve., 1972-73; v.p., dir. archtl. dept., prin. Trygve Hoff & Assos., architects and engrs., Cleve., 1973-75; v.p. architecture Trygve Hoff-Roy F. Weston, Cleve., 1975-76; pres. Bittinger Architects, AIA, Berea, 1977—. Mem. Carnegie-Mellon Admissions Council, 1963-76. Mem. charter review commn., Berea, 1966; mem. estimating bd., Berea, 1965—; mem. Architects Rev. Urban Renewal, Berea, 1972, Bd. Zoning and Bldg. Code Appeals, Berea, 1972—; chmn. Town Center Landscaping Com., Berea, 1972-73. Vice-chmn. bd. mgrs. Eleanor B. Rainey Meml. Inst., 1960—. Served with USMCR, 1942-46. Registered profl. architect, Ohio, Pa., Tenn., Fla. Registered fall-out shelter analyst, U.S. Dept. Def., 1969-79. Recipient Founders scholar award Carnegie Mellon U., 1950, award for excellence AIA, 1951. Mem. AIA, Architects Soc. Ohio, Beaux Arts Soc., Carnegie-Mellon Alumni Cleve. (pres. 1977), Tau Sigma Delta, Phi Kappa Phi. Methodist (adminstrv. bd. 1955-72, trustee 1973-76). Club: Sports Car Am. (Cleve.). Prin. archtl. works include West Lake Masonic Temple, 1968; Olin Chem. Plant & Offices, 1969; R.T. Plastics Plant and Offices, 1970; Nationwide Communications Radio Facility, 1971; E.C. Kitzel & Sons, Inc. mgf. plant and offices, 1972; Service Core Facility, Deaconess Hosp. of Cleve., 1975; Abele Davis Corp. facility, 1977. Home: 280 Rowan Dr Berea OH 44017 Office: 48 Front St Berea OH 44017

BITZEGAIO, HAROLD JAMES, judge; b. Coalmont, Ind., Jan. 29, 1921; s. Gilbert and Dora (Burns) B.; B.S., Ind. State U., 1948; J.D., Ind. U., 1953; m. Betty Jean Law, Apr. 15, 1950; children—Judith L. (Mrs. Kenneth R. Wallin), Gail Ann, Susan Rae (Mrs. Paul Gregory Denyer), James Robert, Jane Ellen. Admitted to Ind. bar, 1953; pvt. practice law Terre Haute, Ind., 1953-58; chief judge Superior Ct., Vigo County, Ind., 1959—. Mem. Ind. adv. com. U.S. Com. on Civil Rights, 1961-70; chmn. Mayor's Com. on Human Relations, 1967-68. Bd. dirs. Wabash Valley council Boy Scouts Am., 1960—; bd. advisers Ind. Jud. Center. Served to lt. comdr., USNR, 1941-46. Decorated D.F.C. with gold star, Air Medal with 2 gold stars (Navy), Purple Heart (U.S.). Mem. Am., Ind., Terre Haute bar assns., Ind. Judges' Assn. (pres.), Am. Judicature Soc., Nat. Rifle Assn. (life mem.), Ind. U. Law Alumni Assn. (past pres.), Ducks Unltd. (nat. trustee). Democrat. Clubs: Elks, Country (Terre Haute, Ind.). Home: 1710 Ohio St Terre Haute IN 47807 Office: Court House Terre Haute IN 47801

BITZES, JOHN GEORGE, historian, educator; b. Omaha, Dec. 9, 1926; s. George John and Yasseme (Gillas) B.; B.A. cum laude, U. Nebr., 1954, Ph.D., 1976; m. Helen Loras, Aug. 18, 1963; children—James George, Mark John. Tchr., Am. history, Creston (Iowa) Pub. Sch. System, 1959-61; tchr. social studies Omaha Pub. Sch. System, 1961—; lectr. modern European history U. Nebr., Omaha, 1966—; Vice pres. Built-Rite Corp., Dallas. Recipient James L. Sellers Meml. award, 1971; Maude Hammond Fling dissertation travel fellow, Eng., 1974. Mem. Phi Beta Kappa, Phi Alpha Theta. Republican. Greek Orthodox. Home: 13575 Walnut St Omaha NE 68144

BIVANS, JACK, broadcasting exec.; b. Evanston, Ill., Aug. 30, 1925; s. Walter J. and Edna Mae (Cooney) B.; student DePaul U., 1943-44, Northwestern U., 1946-49; m. Geraldine J. Johnson, July 28, 1962; children—Kirby, Scott, Kathy, Marcia, Kim, Donald, Paul. Freelance radio actor, various Chgo. and network broadcasts, 1938-56; sales rep. Medusa Portland Cement Co., Chgo., 1956-59; Adam Young Inc., Chgo., 1959-61; with CBS-WBBM Chgo., 1961-68, gen. sales mgr., 1964-68; gen. sales mgr. WFLD-TV, Chgo., 1968-72, v.p., gen. sales mgr., 1972-74; v.p. Field Communications Corp., Chgo., 1972-74; v.p., gen. mgr. Magic City Communications Corp., WCRT/WQEZ, Birmingham, Ala., 1974-76; nat. sales mgr. Century Broadcasting Corp. W-100/FM 100 Chgo., 1976—. Served with USAAF, 1944-46. Decorated Air medal. Mem. Broadcast Advt. Club, Chgo. Advt. Club, Grocery Mfrs. Sales Execs., Broadcast Pioneers, Nat. Acad. TV Arts and Scis., Sigma Alpha Epsilon. Club: Mdse. Execs. Home: 313 Burlington St Western Springs IL 60558 Office: 875 N Michigan Ave Chicago IL 60611

BIWERSI, GARY LEE, steel broker; b. Milw., Feb. 3, 1944; s. Leland Henry and Ludmila Mary B.; student Suomi Coll., 1962-63, Marquette U., 1963-71; m. Deanna Mary LaDuke, July 27, 1973; stepchildren—Julie, Melissa, Beth, Michael. Sales rep. Bethlehem Steel Corp., Milw., 1964-71; territorial mgr. Nat. Steel Service div., Fox River Valley area, 1971-72; sales mgr. Bailey Bohrman Steel Corp., Milw., 1973-74; pres. Biwersi & Assos., Inc., Milw., 1974—. Republican. Lutheran. Clubs: Milw. Racketball, B'nai B'rith, Masons, Shriners. Home: Rt 4 Box 408 Mukwonago WI 53149 Office: W303S10236 Oconee Dr Mukwonago WI 53149

BIXBY, DON WILLARD, device mfg. co. exec.; b. Roanoke, Va., Apr. 15, 1940; s. Willard and Helen (Bogan) B.; student U. Ill., 1958-59, So. Ill. U., 1959-61; m. Nancy Jane Way, Nov. 15, 1968; children—Don Allen, David Andrew. With Am. Device Mfg. Co., Inc., Steeleville, Ill., 1961—, v.p. sales, 1966-70, pres., 1970—, also dir.; dir. Diamond West Corp., Scotco Data Communications Inc., N.Y.C. Mem. Nat. Indsl. Conf. Bd., 1964—. Bd. dirs. Sparta Community Hosp. Served with AUS, 1962. Mem. Mail Receptacle Mfrs. Assn. (chmn. 1972-74), Builders Hardware Mfrs. Assn. (exec. com. 1972-74), N.A.M., So. Ill. Golf Assn., N.G. Assn. U.S. Methodist. Elk. Clubs: Chester Country; Sparta Country (Ill.); Glen Echo Country, Missouri Athletic, Admirals (St. Louis). Home: Rural Route 2 Sparta IL 62286 Office: 1003 W Broadway Steeleville IL 62288

BIXBY, GLENN ALLEN, educator; b. Holden, Mo., Aug. 2, 1923; s. Alva and Katherine (Dickerson) B.; A.A., Graceland Coll., 1947; B.S. in Edn., Central Mo. State U., 1953, Specialist Edn., 1973; M.A. in Music Edn., Drake U., 1956; m. Bonnie Lee Stuck, Aug. 25, 1945; children—Sylvia Ann (Mrs. Charles Basford), Steven, John, Linda, James. Tchr. elementary sch., jr. high sch., high sch. vocal music, Lamoni, Ia., 1953-65; faculty music edn. Central Mo. State U., Warrensburg, Mo., 1965—. Tenor soloist; mem. Warrensburg Community Chorus. Committeeman, Boy Scouts Am., Lamoni, 1954-60. Served with USNR, World War II; South Pacific. Recipient Distinguished Music Alumnus award Central Mo. State U., 1970. Mem. Mo. State Tchrs. Assn., Music Educators Nat. Conf., Mo. Music Educators Assn., Phi Delta Kappa, Pi Kappa Lambda. Mem. com. to revise book, "Music for the Elementary Schools of Missouri," Mo. State Dept. Edn., 1969. Office: Central Mo State U Edn Bldg Warrensburg MO 64093

BIXBY, JOHN NELSON, food co. exec.; b. Appleton, Wis., Dec. 25, 1914; s. Phil Taylor and Alice (Nelson) B.; B.S. in Bio-chemistry, U. Wis., 1937, M.S., Ph.D. in Biochemistry and Food Sci., 1954; m. Gloria Ann Hulit, Sept. 16, 1938; children—John Nelson, Howard H., Robert W. Biochemist, Ovaltine Food Products Co., Villa Park, Ill., 1937-51, research supr., 1954-63; teaching asst. U. Wis., Madison, 1951-54; dir. research H.C. Christians Co., Chgo., 1963-70; sr. scientist Land O'Lakes, Inc., 1970—. Mem. Am. Chem. Soc., Inst. Food Technologists, Am. Dairy Sci. Assn., AAAS, Sigma Xi, Phi Kappa Phi, Phi Lambda Upsilon, Phi Sigma, Alpha Zeta, Phi Eta Sigma, Alpha Gamma Rho. Research on nutritional value of milk to humans and animals. Home: 530 Webster St Red Wing MN 55066 Office: 614 McKinley Pl Minneapolis MN 55413

BIXBY, WILLIAM HERBERT, elec. engr.; b. Indpls., Dec. 28, 1906; s. George Linder and Carrie (Tilton) B.; B.S.E., U. Mich., 1930, M.S., 1931, Ph.D., 1933; M.M.E., Chrysler Inst. Engring., 1935; m. Dorothy Bancroft Tibbits, Jan. 17, 1963. Spl. problems engr. Chrysler Corp., Detroit, 1933-36; instr. to prof. elec. engring. Wayne U., 1936-57; v.p. for applied research Power Equipment Co., 1957-61, v.p. research Power Equipment div. North Electric Co., Galion, Ohio, 1961—; cons. engr. Power Equipment Co., Detroit, 1937-56. Fellow AAAS, IEEE; mem. Engring. Soc. Detroit, Sigma Xi. Home: 5274 Riverside Dr Columbus OH 43220 Office: 1090 W Henderson Rd PO Box 14316 Beechwold Sta Columbus OH 43214

BJORK, EDWARD M., JR., real estate exec.; b. Minot, N.D., Jan. 17, 1928; s. Edward M. and Amanda A. (Knutson) B.; student U. N.D., 1949-50, Minot Bus. Coll., 1950-51; grad. Revac Inst. Investment Counseling, 1973; student U. Mont., 1974; m. Jacqueline R. Peterson, Aug. 20, 1950; children—Kevin, Vicki, David. Sales mgr. Voeller Furniture Co., Minot, 1951-67; salesman Fisher Motor Co., Minot, 1967-70; investment counselor, sales mgr. Minot Realty Inc., 1970—. Tchr. investment real estate to adult edn. classes; instr. Minot State Coll. Active Community Chest. Served with AC, USNR, 1946-48. Certified bus. councilor. Mem. Minot Jr. C. of C., Minot High Booster Club (pres. 1973-75), Exchange Club (pres. 1959-60), Minot, Nat. (Cadillac Top Salesman award 1968-69, Top 400 Buick Salesman in Nation 1969) bds. realtors, N.D. Adult Edn. Assn., Am. Legion, Million Dollar Club. Lutheran (deacon). Elk, Eagle. Club: Minot Country. Home: 217 25th St NW Minot ND 58701 Office: 219 S Main St Minot ND 58701

BJORKLUND, RICHARD CARL, newspaper editor; b. Chgo., Sept. 25, 1930; s. Carl Egon and Anna Mae (Smith) B.; B.A., Roosevelt U., 1953; postgrad. Chgo. Kent Coll. Law, 1955-56; m. Joan Diane Kraeft, June 30, 1956; children—Steven, Christopher. Reporter, Lerner Newspapers, Chgo., 1955-57, exec. editor, 1973—; reporter, mng. editor Skokie (Ill.) News, 1957-59; asso. editor Publishers Aux., Chgo., 1959-60; staff writer editor Jour. Am. Ins., Chgo., 1960-67; mng. editor Bus. Ins., Chgo., 1967, editor, to 1973; v.p. Myers Pub. Co. Dir., past pres. Ravenswood Lake View (Chgo.) Hist. Assn.; mem. citizens council Center for Physically Developmentally Handicapped, City Colls. Chgo.; mem. Chgo. Com. Urban Opportunity; dir. Sulzer Family Found., Chgo. Author: R.S. Solinsky: Dean of the Can Industry, 1968; Ravenswood Manor: Indian Prairie to Urban Pride, 1964. Home: 2959 Wilson Ave Chicago IL 60625 Office: 7519 N Ashland Ave Chicago IL 60626

BJORNNES, NORMAN PETER, dentist; b. Duluth, Minn., Feb. 20, 1916; s. Carl Johann and Olga Elene (Anderson) B.; B.A., St. Olaf Coll., 1938; postgrad. Stanford, 1941-42, Ohio State U., 1954; D.D.S., U. Minn., 1947; m. Clara Mae Rasmussen, Feb. 10, 1945; children—Jon David, Karolin Elene Carter, Norman Peter. Practice of dentistry, Mpls., 1947—. Active Viking council Boy Scouts Am., 1954-63, PTA, Mpls., 1952-70. Served with USAF, 1942-43, AUS, 1951-52. Fellow Am. Coll. Dentists; mem. World Brotherhood Exchange Dentists (sec. 1961), Am. Dental Assn., Minn., Mpls. Dist. dental socs., Optimist Club, Norwegian Torske Klubben, G.V. Black Club, Sons of Norway. Lutheran (pres. congregation 1968-69). Contbr. articles to profl. pubs. Lectr. Home: 5628 Chowen Ave S Edina MN 55410 Office: Downtown Profl Bldg 822 Marquette Ave #200 Minneapolis MN 55402

BJUGSTAD, ARDELL JEROME, biologist; b. Sheldon, N.D., Apr. 28, 1933; s. Carl and Anne (Schultz) B.; Asso. Sci., N.D. Sch. Forestry, 1957; B.S. with honors, N.D. Agrl. Coll., 1959; Ph.D., N.D. State U., 1965; m. Jeanette Maye Bussman, June 14, 1959; children—Roberta DiAnn, Rochelle Arnett. With wildlife habitat and range research program Forest Service, U.S. Dept. Agr., Columbia, Mo., 1963-71, Washington, 1971-74, project leader, 1968-71, asst. chief program, 1971-74, program leader, Rapid City, S.D., 1974—. Served with AUS, 1951-52. Mem. Am. Inst. Biol. Sci., Soc. Range Mgmt., Nat. Wildlife Fedn., Sigma Xi, Xi Sigma Pi, Phi Kappa Phi, Alpha Zeta. Home: Box 617 Suburban Route Rapid City SD 57701 Office: Forest Service SD Tech Rapid City SD 57701

BLABOLIL, CHARLES JOSEPH, mktg. services co. exec.; b. Cleve., Jan. 18, 1933; s. Charles and Rose (Jirik) B.; student Mich. State U., 1950-52; B.B.A. in Mktg. and Econs., Western Res. U., 1954; m. Lois Mae Stanek, June 13, 1953; children—Sherry Lois, Richard Allen. Mem. mktg. staff Am. Steel and Wire div. U.S. Steel Corp., Cleve., 1954-60; dir. merchandising 3M Co., St. Paul, 1960-62; account exec., regional v.p. Maritz, Inc., Fenton, Mo., 1962-70, corporate officer, 1970-72; pres. Maritz Travel Co. div. Maritz, Inc., Fenton, 1972-76, also pres. subs.'s, Eng., Spain, Mex., Hawaii, Jamaica, France, Italy; pres. Internat. Discoveries div. ITA, Inc., St. Louis, also exec. v.p. parent co., West Des Moines, Iowa. Bd. dirs. YMCA, Boy Scouts Am. Mem. Sales Promotion Execs. Assn., Am. Soc. Travel Agts., Navy League, Lafayette Athletic Assn. (pres. 1972-73). Clubs: Forest Hills Country, Bay Hill Country. Home: 2909 Orchard Dr West Des Moines IA 50265

BLACK, ANITA, journalist; b. Manitowoc, Wis.; d. Walter Herman and Else Henrietta Johanna (Kaems) Biesemeyer; B.A., U. Wis. Sch. Journalism; m. Russell Paul Gamble, June 8, 1971. Women's news editor Daily Progress, Charlottesville, Va., 1949-62; fashion editor, asst. women's editor Times-Dispatch, Richmond, Va., 1962-63, women's news editor, 1963-65; men's fashion editor, women's news reporter Milw. Sentinel, 1965—. Recipient Lulu awards Men's Fashion Assn. Am., 1965, 66, 67, 69, 70, 71; Caswell-Massey men's fashion reporting award, 1968. Mem. Nat. Fedn. Press Women (charter v.p. Va. affiliate 1958-65), Women in Communications, Sigma Delta Chi, Milw. Press Club. Office: Milw Sentinel Milwaukee WI 53201

BLACK, ASA CALVIN, JR., anatomist, educator; b. Clarksville, Tenn., Jan. 2, 1943; s. Asa C. and Josephine Elizabeth Black; m. Cynthia Woods, Apr. 3, 1971. B.A., Vanderbilt U., 1965, Ph.D. in Anatomy (NIH predoctoral fellow), 1974. Asso., U. Iowa, Iowa City, 1973-74, NIH postdoctoral fellow Coll. Medicine, 1974-75, asst. prof. dept. anatomy Coll. Medicine, 1975—; instr. anatomy Vanderbilt U., Nashville, 1972-73. Mem. AAAS, Am. Assn. Anatomists, Am. Chem. Soc., Am. Inst. Biol. Scis., Am. Soc. Neurochemistry, Brit. Brain Research Assn., European Brain Behavior Soc., Internat. Soc. Neurochemistry, Sigma Xi. Contbr. chpts. to books, articles to biol. jours. Home: 801 Woodside Dr Iowa City IA 52240 Office: U Iowa Coll Medicine 1-402 Basic Science Bldg Dept Anatomy Iowa City IA 52242

BLACK, CARL DEAN, newspaper editor; b. Lapeer, Mich., Sept. 2, 1929; s. Gardner A. and Hazel (Avis) B.; student Albion Coll., 1947-49, Fort Huron Jr. Coll., 1955-56; m. Carlene M. Sasinowski, Apr. 26, 1958; children—Lisa Marie, Karen Sue, Susan Lynn, Michael Carl. Advt. mgr. Sanilac Jeffersonian, 1955-60, editor, 1960—, pres. Sanilac Jeffersonian, Inc., 1970—; pres., mgr. Thumb Print, Inc., 1974—; pres. Sandusky Pub. Inc., 1974—; co-pub. Sandusky (Mich.) Republican-Tribune, 1974—; dir. Mich. Press Service, Inc. Sec., Croswell Indsl. Devel. Corp., 1960—; mem. Croswell Hosp. Holding Corp. Served with USAF, 1951-55. Mem. Mich. Press Assn. (past pres.), Delta Sigma Phi. Home: Wells St Croswell MI 48422

BLACK, CHARLES EDWARD, obstetrician-gynecologist; b. Schneider, Ind., Mar. 24, 1922; s. Louie Alexander and Erma May Bell (Allison) B.; B.S., Ind. U., 1948, M.D., 1951; m. Judith M. Brawner, 1951; children—Theo Warren, Timothy Eaton, Beverly Susan, Patricia Ellen, Daniel Arthur, Jennifer Marilyn. Intern, Ind. U. Med. Center, Indpls., 1951-52; staff physician Oak Ridge Nat. Lab., 1952; gen. practice medicine, Hammond, Ind., 1953-55; resident in obstetrics and gynecology U. Ill. Research and Ednl. Hosps. and Clinics, Chgo., 1955-58; practice medicine specializing in obstetrics and gynecology, Gary, Ind., 1958-59, Monroe, Mich., 1963—; mem. staff Toledo Clinic, 1959-63; mem. staff Mercy Meml. Hosp.; asst., dept. obstetrics and gynecology U. Ill. Coll. Medicine, 1955-57, instr., 1957-58, clin. instr., 1958-59. Mem. Monroe Bd. Edn., 1970—, v.p., 1975—; mem. Monroe County Tax Allocation Bd., 1975—. Served with U.S. Army, 1940-45. Decorated Europe and African campaign medal with 5 battle stars; diplomate Am. Bd. Obstetrics and Gynecology. Mem. AMA, Am. Coll. Obstetricians and Gynecologists, Mich. State, Monroe County med. socs., Mich., Toledo obstetrical and gynecol. socs., Am. Assn. Sch. Bds. Republican. Methodist. Club: Masons. Office: 721 N Macomb St Monroe MI 48161

BLACK, ELLIOTT MICHAEL, mfg. co. exec.; b. Balt., Apr. 2, 1940; s. Samuel and Dorothy (Nathanson) B.; B.S. in E.E., Drexel U., 1961; M.A. in Adminstrn., George Washington U., 1968; m. Gilda Ann Appel, Sept. 2, 1974. Sr. Product mgr. Black and Decker Mfg. Co., Towson, Md., 1957-68; dir. operations and gen. mgr. Cosco Appliances, Inc., 1969-71; dir. product mgmt. Skil Corp., Chgo., 1972-76; v.p. mktg. Dumore Co., Racine, Wis., 1976—; dir. Indsl. Dynamics Corp. Vice-pres. Md. Diabetic Assn., 1967-69; bd. dirs. Racine Symphony, 1977—. Mem. Am. Supply and Machinery Mfrs. Assn., Am. Mktg. Assn., Small Motor Mfrs. Assn., Sales and Mktg. Execs. Assn. of Chgo. (bd. dirs.), Sales and Mktg. Execs. of Racine/Kenosha, Internat. Brotherhood of Magicians, Soc. of Am. Magicians, Magic Circle (London). Home: 111 Eleventh St Racine WI 53403 Office: 1300 17th St Racine WI 53403

BLACK, FERNE MAY BEEBE, librarian; b. Cleve., May 16, 1920; d. Harry Jay and Dorothy (Schmidt) Beebe; student Ohio U., 1938-40; A.B., Calif. State U., 1959; M.L.S. cum laude, U. So. Calif., 1961. Research librarian Aeronutronic div. Ford Motor Co., Newport Beach, Calif., 1961-65; info. specialist Battelle Meml. Inst., Columbus, Ohio, 1965-66; supr. library acquisitions group Aerospace Corp., Los Angeles, 1966-67; librarian Cleve.-Seven Counties Land Use/Transp. Study, 1967-69; asst. librarian Parma Heights (Ohio) Pub. Library, 1969-70; head acquisitions Cuyahoga Community Coll., Cleve., 1970-75, mgr. tech. processing div., 1975—, asst. prof. library-media tech., 1974—, mem. adv. council, 1975—; mem. survey team Survey of Sci.-Info. Manpower in Engring. and the Natural Scis., NSF, 1966. Mem. Spl. Libraries Assn. (pres. Cleve. chpt. 1972-73), Am. Inst. Aeros. and Astronautics, Library Council Greater Cleve. (com. on library resources), AAUP, Beta Phi Mu, Zonta (sec. 1977-78, dir. 1974—). Home: 12040 Lake Ave Apt 102 Lakewood OH 44107 Office: 2900 Community Coll Ave Cleveland OH 44115

BLACK, HARRY GEORGE, author; b. Hammond, Ind.. Jan. 31, 1933; s. Harry Howard and Therese (Greb) B.; student U. Ind., 1955-57; B.A. in Sociology, Roosevelt U., 1959; m. Marilyn Gaye Gibbons, June 24, 1961; children—Gaye Jean, Robin, James. Interviewer counselor Ind. Employment Service, 1959-64; substitute tchr. Hammond (Ind.) Pub. Schs., 1964-74; writer editor Our Humble Opinion, 1968-69; author, speaker, Midwest U.S., 1974—; author: The Lost Dutchman Mine, A Short Story of a Tall Tale, 1975; Survival in the Wilds, 1977; contbr. articles and stories to mags. and newspapers. Home and office: 7406 Monroe Ave Hammond IN 46324

BLACK, JAMES DENNIS, dentist; b. Chgo., Sept. 19, 1940; s. Milton J. and Gladys E. (Hagel) B.; student Ind. U., 1958-61; D.M.D., U. Louisville, 1965; m. Carol Sandra Chupp, Sept. 1, 1964; children—Brian Jennings, Kristy Anne. Dental intern USPHS Hosp., New Orleans, La., 1965-66; staff dental officer U.S. Penitentiary, Terre Haute, Ind., 1966-68; pvt. practice gen. dentistry, Tell City, Ind., 1968—; dir. Black Equipment Co., Evansville. Mem. Perry County Health Plan Council; chmn. Environmental Health Task Force. Bd. dirs. Student Scholarship Loan Found., 1968-71, chmn.,

1969. Served with USPHS, 1965-68. Recipient distinguished service award Tell City Jr. C. of C. Mem. Am., Ind. (council dental care problems 1975-77) dental assns., First Dist. Dental Soc., Tell City Jr. C. of C. (external v.p., bd. dirs. 1969-70), Delta Sigma Delta, Phi Delta, Beta Delta, Phi Kappa Phi, Omicron Kappa Upsilon. Methodist. Home: 2120 Franklin St Tell City IN 47586 Office: 1045 12th St Tell City IN 47586

BLACK, JOHN BUNYAN, civil engr.; b. Kansas City, Mo., Dec. 25, 1927; s. Ernest Bateman and Faye Irene (Bunyan) B.; B.S., U. Kans., 1949; m. Marilyn McConnell, Feb. 2, 1957; children—Katherine Faye, Helen Winslow, Robert Winslow II. Asst. resident engr. Black & Veatch, cons. engrs., Los Alamos, 1949-50; engr. Alvord, Burdick & Howson, engrs., Chgo., 1953-65; project mgr. Greeley & Hansen, engrs., 1966-67, asso., 1968-74; owner John B. Black Cons. Engrs., 1975—. Served with AUS, 1951-52. Registered profl. engr., Calif., Iowa, Ill., Mich., Mo., Man., N.Y., Ind., Wis., Va. Fellow ASCE (com. water laws 1977—; dir. Ill. sect. 1977—); mem. Am. Water Works Assn., Central States Water Pollution Control Assn., Man. Assn. Profl. Engrs., Sigma Alpha Epsilon. Republican. Episcopalian. Club: Colo. Mountain (Boulder). Home: 595 Washington Ave Glencoe IL 60022 Office: 2 N Riverside Plaza Chicago IL 60606

BLACK, KENNETH WALLACE, lawyer; b. Peoria, Ill., Dec. 10, 1912; s. Wallace J. and Margaret (Robinson) B.; B.S., Bradley U., 1934; J.D., U. Chgo., 1937; m. Edith Adele Lowry, Aug. 10, 1938; children—Barbara (Mrs. Robert Walker Brown), Kenneth L., Bruce W. Admitted to Ill. bar, 1937, since practiced in Peoria and Washington, Ill.; partner, Black, Black & Borden, 1940—; also partner Black & Black, 1976—; city atty., Washington, 1941-53, 57—. Sec., dir. 1st Nat. Bank, Washington, Ill. Pres. Washington Twp. Library Bd., 1951-72. Vice chmn. Tazwell County Republican Central Com., 1956—; alt. del. Rep. Nat. Conv., 1968. Trustee Bradley U., 1942—, chmn. bd. trustees, 1971—; past pres. Ill. Valley Library System Bd. Mem. Am., Ill., Peoria County, Tazwell County (past pres.) bar assns., Am. Judicature Soc., S.A.R., Phi Alpha Delta, Sigma Chi. Lutheran. Mason (Shriner). Clubs: Country, Creve Coeur (Peoria, Ill.). Home: 501 S Main St Washington IL 61571 Office: 115 Washington Sq Washington IL 61571 also 832 First Nat Bank Bldg Peoria IL 61602

BLACK, MICHAEL SHERMAN, research structural engr.; b. Terre Haute, Ind., Apr. 1, 1949; s. Orman Leslie and Evelyn Clara (Enyart) B.; B.S.C.E., Rose Poly. Inst., 1971; M.S.C.E., Purdue U., 1977. Engr., Bur. Planning Ill. Dept. Transp., Springfield, 1971; structural engr. Pub. Service Co. of Ind., Plainfield, 1974-76; structural engr. Purdue U. Grad. Sch., 1976—. Served with C.E. U.S. Army, 1971-73. Purdue U. research grantee, 1976-77; registered profl. engr., Ind. Mem. ASCE, Soc. Am. Mil. Engrs., Smithsonian Assos. Mem. United Church of Christ. Home: 7017 Wabash Ave Terre Haute IN 47803 Office: Purdue U Civil Engring Bldg 430 West Lafayette IN 47906

BLACK, ROBERT LOUNSBURY, JR., judge; b. Cin., Dec. 11, 1917; s. Robert Lounsbury and Anna (Smith) B.; A.B., Yale, 1939; LL.B., Harvard, 1942; m. Helen Huntington Chatfield, July 27, 1946; children—William Chatfield, Stephen Lounsbury, Luther Fletcher. Admitted to Ohio bar, 1946, practiced in Cin., mem. firm Graydon, Head & Ritchey, 1953-72; judge Common Pleas Ct., Cin., 1973-77, Ct. Appeals, Cin., 1977—. Chmn. Cin. Human Relations Commn., 1967-70. Mayor Village of Indian Hill, 1959-65. Served from 2d lt. to captain, AUS, 1942-45, Decorated Bronze Star medal. Mem. Phi Beta Kappa. Clubs: Commonwealth, Queen City, Camargo (Cin.). Episcopalian. Home: 5900 Drake Rd Cincinnati OH 45243 Office: Hamilton County Ct House Cincinnati OH 45202

BLACK, THOMAS ALEXANDER, JR., dentist; b. Pitts., Jan. 10, 1943; s. Thomas Alexander and Griselda (Best) B.; B.S., Purdue U., 1965; D.M.D., Washington U., St. Louis, 1975, M.B.A., 1975; m. Sandra Jean Gredys, May 10, 1969. Prodn. supr. Proctor & Gamble, St. Louis, 1968-69; with Mallinckrodt Chem. Works, St. Louis, 1969-71; gen. practice dentistry, Marlborough, Mo., 1976—; clin. instr. dentistry Wash. U., St. Louis, 1976—; staff dentist Bethesda Dilworth Meml. Home. Deacon, mem. choir Webster Groves (Mo.) Presbyn. Ch. Served to capt. C.E., AUS, 1965-68. Mem. Am., Mo. dental assns., Greater St. Louis Dental Soc., Acad. Gen. Dentistry, Soc. Am. Mil. Engrs., Xi Psi Phi, Alpha Phi Omega. Club: Rotary. Home: 445 Cannonbury Dr Webster Groves MO 63119 Office: 8460 Watson Rd Suite 112 Marlborough MO 63119

BLACK, THOMAS CLAIBORNE, JR., ophthalmologist; b. Norton, Kans., Dec. 11, 1938; s. Thomas Claiborne and Susan Pauline (Terbush) B.; student Duke U., 1955-58; M.D., La. State U., 1962; m. Patricia Louise Cover, Apr. 21, 1969. Intern, Madigan Gen. Hosp., Tacoma, 1962-63; resident U. Kan. Med. Center, Kansas City, 1965-68; practice medicine, specializing in ophthalmology, Kansas City, Mo., 1968—; asso. Kan. U. Med. Center, Kansas City, Kans., 1968—; mem. staff St. Lukes, Bapt. hosps., Kansas City, Mo. Served with AUS, 1962-65. Decorated Air medal with 3 oak leaf clusters. Mem. A.C.S., Am. Acad. Ophthalmology and Otolaryngology, AMA, Jackson County Med. Soc., Sigma Nu. Home: 6411 Belinder Shawnee Mission KS 66208 Office: 601 E 63d St Kansas City MO 64110

BLACK, WALTER KERRIGAN, lawyer; b. Birmingham, Ala., Jan. 27, 1915; s. Timuel Dixon and Mattie (McConner) B.; A.B., U. Ill., 1939; LL.B., John Marshall Law Sch., 1952; m. Dorothy E. Wickliffe, July 2, 1950. Admitted to Ill. bar, 1952; partner firm McCoy & Black, Chgo., 1952-59; partner firm McCoy Ming & Leighton, Chgo., 1959-64; partner firm McCoy, Ming & Black, Chgo., 1965-77; prin. firm Mitchell Hall Jones & Black, Chgo., 1977—; village atty. Robbins (Ill.), 1952-69, East Chicago Heights (Ill.), 1954-69, 77—; hearing examiner Ill. Fair Practices Commn.; arbitrator Am. Arbitration Assn., 1971—. Mem. governing bd. Cook County Legal Assistance Found., Inc. Served with AUS, 1942-46. Mem. Ill., Chgo., Cook County bar assns., Kappa Alpha Psi. Mem. A.M.E. Ch. (atty., trustee) Home: 2231 E 67th St Chicago IL 60649 Office: 134 S LaSalle St Chicago IL 60603

BLACK, WARREN MORRIS, marine hardware co. exec.; b. Cleve., Apr. 8, 1933; s. Herman and Julia (Warren) B.; student Cornell U., 1950-51, Case Inst. Tech., 1951-53; B.B.A., Western Res. U., 1960; m. Marion Osborn Black, Apr. 25, 1964; children—Rachel Walton (one dau.). Dir. marketing Rotor Tool Co., Cleve., 1961-67; mgr. marketing Fluid Controls Inc., Mentor, Ohio, 1968-69; v.p., treas. Merriman Holbrook Inc., Grand River, Ohio, 1969-71, pres., 1971—, chmn., 1973—; dir. A.F. Brock Co. Served with USN, 1953-57. Licensed marine engr. Mem. Nat. Assn. Engine and Boat Mfrs., Assn. Mgmt. Excellence, Cleve. Engring. Soc., Mentor Harbor Yachting Club: Am. Legion. Home: Fairmount Rd Newbury OH 44065 Office: 301 Olive St Grand River OH 44045

BLACKARD, CLYDE ERHARDT, urologist; b. Indpls., Nov. 28, 1932; s. Clyde Wesley and Ruth Alvina (Erhardt) B.; B.S., Butler U., 1953; M.D., Ind. U., 1957; m. Louise Genge, Feb. 16, 1957; children—Brian Lee, Scott Wesley, Lenore Ruth. Intern, U. Nebr. Hosp., Omaha, 1957-58; resident gen. surgery Creighton U. Hosp., Omaha, 1958-59; resident urology U. Louisville Hosps., 1959-62; asst. chief urology Mpls. VA Hosp., 1962-69, chief urology, 1969-75; mem. faculty U. Minn. Health Scis. Center, Mpls., 1962—, prof. urologic surgery, 1974—; exec. mem. VA Coop. Urol. Research Group, 1967-75. Nat. Cancer Inst. grantee, 1967-75. Diplomate Am. Bd. Urology. Mem. AMA, A.C.S., Am. Urol. Assn., Internat. Soc. Urology, Alpha Omega Alpha. Mem. editorial bd. Minn. Medicine, 1972—. Contbr. articles to med. jours. and textbooks. Home: 4808 Kingsdale Dr Bloomington MN 55437 Office: St Louis Park Med Center 5000 W 39th St St Louis Park MN 55416

BLACKBOURN, JAMES WILLIAM, educator; b. Kenosha, Wis., Mar. 27, 1949; s. Archie William and Thelma La Vonne (Henry) B.; B.A. in Chemistry, U. Wis., 1971, postgrad. in physiology, also in elec. and computer engring.; m. Barbara Lee Davis, June 12, 1970; 1 son, James William II. Asst. gamma ray spectroscopist dept. chemistry U. Wis., Madison, 1967-71, teaching asst. dept. chemistry, 1971-72, organic chemist sch. pharmacy, 1972-73, NMR spetroscopist, 1973—. Home: 462 Jean St Madison WI 53703 Office: 1302 Pharmacy Bldg Univ Wis Madison WI 53706

BLACKBURN, GEORGE KANADA, income tax service exec.; b. Hillisburg, Ind., Feb. 1, 1902; s. Benjamin Theodore Riggs and Rosetta Bell (Reed) B.; m. Edith Faustine McCartney, Oct. 23, 1922; children—George Kanada, Betty, Janet, Arvine, Marilyn; student pub. schs., Indpls. Night supr. Diamond Chain Co., Indpls., 1922-32; supr. P.R. Mallory, 1932-40; with Allison div. Gen. Motors Corp., 1940-51; self employed ins. agt. and income tax service, 1948-67, income tax service, 1967—. Instr., Indpls. Area chpt. ARC, 1960-74; pres., v.p., sec.-treas., lt., capt. Wayne Twp. Vol. Fire Dept., 1942-72, certificate of appreciation, life mem., 1972. Recipient certificates of award Ind. Trauma Com. A.C.S., 1967, H. & R. Block Income Tax Tng.. 1966. Mem. Am. Def. Preparedness Assn., Ind. Firefighters Assn., Ind. Vol. Firemens Assn., Am. Assn. Ret. Persons. Clubs: Masons, Shriners, Old Timers or Founders Club Wayne Twp. Fire Dept. Home and Office: 5133 W Naomi St Indianapolis IN 46241

BLACKBURN, HENRY WEBSTER, JR., physician; b. Miami, Fla., Mar. 22, 1925; s. Henry Webster and Mary Frances (Smith) B.; student Fla. So. Coll., Lakeland, Fla., 1942-43; B.S., U. Miami, 1947; M.D., Tulane U., 1948; M.S., U. Minn., 1957; m. Nelly Paula Trocme, Jan. 10, 1951; children—John Keith, Katherine Ann, Heidi Elizabeth, Intern, Chgo. Wesley Meml. Hosp., 1948-49; resident staff Am. Hosp. of Paris, France, 1949-50; med. officer in charge USPHS, Salzburg, Austria, and Munich, Germany, 1950-53; med. fellow U. Minn., 1953-56; research asso. Lab. Physiol. Hygiene, U. Minn. and asso. med. dir. Mut. Service Ins. Co., St. Paul, 1956-58; asst. prof. physiol. hygiene U. Minn., Mpls., 1958-61, asso. prof., 1961-68, prof., 1968—, lectr. medicine, 1956—, dir. lab. physiol. hygiene Sch. Pub. Health, prof. medicine Sch. Medicine, 1972—; vis. prof. U. Geneva, 1970. Chief med. cons. underwriting Mut. Service Ins. Cos., 1972—; cons. USPHS, 1960—, WHO, 1965—, NASA, 1968—. Mem. adv. bd. Life Ins. Md. Research Fund, 1960-63; bd. mgrs., med. sect. Am. Life Conv.; bd. dirs. Minn. Jazz Sponsors, Inc. Served to lt. (j.g.) USNR, 1942-50, asst. surgeon to med. dir. USPHS Res., 1950-68. Fellow Am. Coll. Cardiology, Am. Epidemiol Soc., Am. Pub. Health Assn.; mem. A.M.A., Ramsey County Med. Assn., Am. Heart Assn. (chmn. council on epidemiology; dir. 1971—), Internat. Soc. Cardiology (mem. council epidemiology), Internat. Epidemiol. Soc., Am. Life Ins. Assn. (bd. mgrs.), Alpha Omega Alpha. Author: Cardiovascular Survey Methods, also articles. Asso. editor Circulation, 1968-70. Home: 2108 Oliver Ave S Minneapolis MN 55405

BLACKBURN, MARSH HANLY, food co. exec.; b. Ft. Thomas, Ky., Nov. 13, 1929; s. Hanly R. and Lois E. (Marsh) B.; student Wabash Coll., 1947-48; B.S., Ind. U., 1952; m. Mary Klimek; children—Steven, Kevin, Marsha. Retail sales mgr. Hoosier Brokerage Co., Indpls., 1953-58, pres., 1958-66; with Sales Force Cos., Inc. (name formerly Seavey & Flarsheim Brokerage Co.), O'Hare, Ill., 1966—, pres. 1973—; dir. Franklin Nat. Life Ins. Co., Ft. Wayne, Ind., 1961—, Gen. Grain, Indpls., 1971—, Tidewater Grain, Phila., 1971—, Early & Daniel, Cin., 1971—. Bd. dirs. Ind. U. Bus. Sch. Council. Served with AUS, 1952-53. Decorated Bronze Star. Mem. Nat. Food Brokers Assn., Food Distbn. Research Council (charter), Young Presidents' Orgn., Presidents Assn., Newcomen Soc. N.Am., Merchandising Execs. Chgo. Club, Beta Theta Pi. Clubs: Chicago Yacht; Ocean Reef; Metropolitan; Distinguished Alumni (Ind. U. Sch. Bus.). Home: 400 E Randolph St Chicago IL 60601 Office: 4333 Transworld Ave Schiller Park IL 60176

BLACKBURN, RICHARD SHAW, chem. mfg. co. exec.; b. Cleve., Apr. 17, 1930; s. Harry Chester and Ethel May (Shaw) B.; B.S., Ohio State U., 1956; m. Joan Delores Samaha, Nov. 12, 1952; children—Kathleen, Elizabeth, Margaret. Sr. accountant Frank, Seringer & Chaney, C.P.A.'s, Norwalk, O., 1957-61, supr., 1962-64; treas. Milan Steel & Constrn. Co., also Milan Steel, Inc. (companies merged as Milan Stee Industries, Inc.), Akron, 1964-73, also dir.; owner Edwards Lab., Norwalk, 1973—. Chmn. March of Dimes drive, 1959-60. Mem. council City of Norwalk, 1960-65; mem. Huron County Democratic Central Com., 1970-71. Bd. dirs. Fisher-Titus Hosp. Assn., pres., 1976-77; trustee, treas. Milan Hist. Mus., 1974. Mem. Am. Inst. C.P.A.'s, Ohio Soc. C.P.A.'s (taxation com. 1969), U.S., Ohio N.G. assns., Nat. Assn. Accountants (dir. 1968), V.F.W., Ohio State U. Alumni Assn., Sigma Pi, Beta Alpha Psi. Clubs: Masons, Elks. Home: RD 1 Old State Rd Milan OH 44846 Office: 202 Milan Ave Norwalk OH 44857

BLACKMAN, NATHANIEL, JR., ednl. adminstr.; b. Chgo., July 20, 1930; s. Nathaniel and Mamie (Griffin) B.; B.A., De Paul U., Chgo., 1951, M. Ed., 1956; children—Belinda, Nathaniel III; m. Virginia Ely, Dec. 23, 1973; 1 stepson, Jeffrey. Tchr., Chgo. Pub. Schs., 1951-60, asst. prin., 1960-66, asst. to dist. supt., 1966-68, elementary sch. prin., 1968-70, prin. Metro High Sch., 1970—; lectr., Nova (Fla.) U., 1974; cons. Alternative Edn. St. Louis, St. Paul, U. Hawaii, Dependents Overseas Sch.; lectr., cons. Internat. Consortium for Options in Options in Pub. Edn.-Ind. U. Mem. Chgo. River City Commn., 1974-76. Bd. dirs. Center for New Schs. Served with AUS, 1954-56. Mem. Nat. Assn. Secondary Sch. Prins., Sch. Mgmt. Group, Chgo. Prins. Assn., De Paul Alumni Assn. (dir.), Phi Delta Kappa. Roman Catholic. Home: 8237 St Lawrence St Chicago IL 60619

BLACKMAN, ROBERT CHESTER, plant engring. adminstr.; b. Cleve., Dec. 26, 1914; s. Roy Chester and Norma Matilda (Fruechtel) B.; B.S. in Mech. Engring., Case Inst. Tech., 1936; B.S. in Elec. Engring., Va. Poly. Inst., 1937, M.S. (fellow) in Power Engring., 1938; m. Gertrude Joan Scheutzow, June 25, 1939 (dec. 1942); 1 dau., Judith Ann Blackman Yeager; m. 2d, Helen Miriam Lybrook, Oct. 9, 1943; 1 dau., Helen Jane Blackman Lossing. Instr., Antioch Coll., Yellow Springs, Ohio, 1938-40, supr. of power plant, 1938-40; powerhouse engr. Allison Div., Gen. Motors Corp., Indpls., 1940-42, supt. of powerhouse of all plants, 1945-47, plant engr. transmission ops., 1959-64, divisional plant engr., 1964-67, mfg. mgr. transmission ops., 1967-74, dir. of plant engring., Indpls. ops., 1974—, supr. of maintenance, utilities, environmental lab., bldg. construction, transmission and aircraft ops., 1974—; Detroit Diesel Allison Div. adviser to Jr. Achievement companies, 1971-73; chmn. of plant engrs. of Gen. Motors Corp., 1951-54. Chmn. of Mfg. Solicitation for United Fund, Indpls., 1966-68; chmn. Gen. Motors Energy conservation com., 1971-74; mem. Greater Indpls. Progress Com., 1968-71, Waterways Task Force of Greater Indpls., 1970-74; chmn. fin. com. of Marion County council Girl Scouts U.S., 1954-55; precinct fin. chmn. Republican Party, 1966-68; chmn. exec. bd. Crestview Christian Ch., 1961-64; bd. dirs. Am. Lung Assn. of Central Ind., pres., 1976-77; bd. dirs. PTA, Indpls., 1952-54. Recipient Recognition Award Md. v. Med. Center, 1978. Registered profl. engr. Ind. Mem. Am. Inst. of Plant Engrs., Am. Inst. Power Engrs. (hon., continuing edn. com.), ASME, Am. Inst. Elec. Engrs., Am. Soc. Heating and Air Conditioning Engrs. (pres. central Ind. sect. 1951-52), Indpls. C. of C., Indpls. Mus. of Art, Sigma Xi, Theta Tau, Republican. Clubs: Masons, Scottish Rite, Torch (pres. Indpls. chpt. 1973-74), Riviera. Home: 4162 Kessler Blvd N Dr Indianapolis IN 46208 Office: 4700 W 10th St Speedway IN 46206

BLACKWELL, HENRY BARLOW, II, lawyer; b. Salem, Ill., Feb. 15, 1928; s. Carl G. and Goldie Blanche (Hill) B.; B.S., U. Ill., 1952; J.D., Ind. U., 1956; m. Nancy Neckers, June 21, 1952; children—Nancy Anne, James Stokely, Thomas Barlow. Admitted to Ind. bar, 1956, U.S. Supreme Ct. bar, 1961; asst. auditor Mchts. Nat. Bank, Indpls., 1952-53; indsl. engr., personnel rep., atty. Eli Lilly & Co., 1953-62; atty., asst. sec., Eli Lilly Internat. Corp., 1962-70, sec., asst. gen. counsel, 1970-77, sec., gen. counsel, 1977—; dir. Indpls. Indians, Inc., baseball team, 1967—, chmn. bd., 1971-75. Mem. pres.'s council and exec. com. Brebeuf Preparatory Sch., Indpls., 1972—. Bd. dirs. Happy Hollow Children's Camp, 1964—, pres., 1968-71; bd. dirs., mem. exec. com. Indpls. chpt. ARC, 1975—. Served with USNR, 1946-48. Mem. Am., Ind., Indpls. bar assns., Indpls Legal Aid Soc., English Speaking Union, Ind. State Mus. Soc., Indpls. Zool. Soc., Indpls. Children's Mus., Ind. State Symphony Soc., U. Ill. Alumni Assn. (pres. 1977, dir.), U.S. Trotting Assn., Phi Delta Phi, Phi Sigma Kappa. Clubs: Meridian Hills Country; Econ. of Indpls.; Lawyers; Columbia. Home: 7240 N Pennsylvania St Indianapolis IN 46240 Office: 307 E McCarty St Indianapolis IN 46206

BLAGBROUGH, ELIZABETH M. (MRS. HARRY PUTNAM BLAGBROUGH), fine art appraiser; b. Orlando, Fla., Sept. 8, 1926; d. Calvin Burr and Maud Alice (Wagner) McCaughen; B.A., Washington U., 1948; m. Harry Putnam Blagbrough, June 30, 1951; children—Helen Blagbrough Henderson, Harry Putnam, Alicia. Apprentice appraiser McCaughen & Burr, Inc., Fine Arts, St. Louis, 1948-70, appraiser, v.p., dir., 1970—. Pvt. appraisals by referral, 1970—; lectr. fine arts, art history; co-founder Valuers Consortium, Houston, 1972, vice chmn., bd. dirs., 1974—, pres., 1975. Vice pres. bd. trustees Cupples House, St. Louis. Mem. Internat. Platform Assn., P.E.O., Am. Soc. Appraisers (sr., internat. bd. examiners, sec. St. Louis chpt., chpt. treas. 1974-75, 1st v.p. 1976-77, pres. St. Louis chpt. 1977-78, del. internat. conf., preparator lectr. presentations, chmn. internat. bd. publs.), Appraisers Assn. Am. (sr. mem.; mem. internat. publs. bd.; co-chmn. personal property fine arts, internat. bd. examiners; 1st v.p. St. Louis chpt. 1976-77). Methodist. Home and Office: 340 S Elm Saint Louis MO 63119

BLAIN, ALEXANDER, III, surgeon; b. Detroit, Mar. 9, 1918; s. Alexander William and Ruby (Johnson) B.; student Washington and Lee U., 1935-37; B.A., Wayne U., 1940, M.D., 1943; M.S. in Surgery, U. Mich., 1948; m. Josephine Woodbury Bowen, May 3, 1941; children—Helen Bowen, Alexander IV, Bruce Scott Murray, Josephine Johnson; m. 2d, Mary E. Mains, 1968. House officer, Halsted fellow in surgery Johns Hopkins, 1943-46; resident surgeon U. Hosp., Ann Arbor, Mich., 1946-50; instr. surgery U. Mich., 1950-57; clin. asst. prof. surgery Wayne State U., 1962—; also surgeon-in-chief Alexander Blain Hosp., Detroit, 1953—; consultant surgeon Highland Park Gen. Hosp., St. Joseph's Hosp.; asso. surgeon Detroit Gen. Hosp, Pres., Met. Detroit Family Service Assn., 1962-63, Detroit Museum Soc., 1961-62; staff Harper Hosp., Detroit, Crittenton Hosp., Rochester, Mich., Detroit Deaconess Hosp. Mem. Detroit Zool. Park Commn., 1974—. Trustee Alexander Blain Meml. Hosp., 1942-67, Ostego Meml. Hosp. Found., Gaylord, Mich., 1976—. bd. dirs. Detroit Zool. Soc., 1972-75. Served as lt. M.C., AUS, 1942-44, maj., 1955-57. Diplomate Am. Bd. Surgery. Fellow A.C.S., N.Y. Acad. Scis.; mem. Internat. Cardiovascular Soc., F.A. Coller Surg. Soc., Am. Fedn. for Clin. Research, Cranbrook Inst. Sci. Soc. Vascular Surgery, Am. Thyroid Assn., Societie Internationale de Chirurgie, Mich. Med. Soc. (chmn. surgical section 1963), Assn. Clin. Surgery, Pan-Pacific Surg. Assn., Nu Sigma Nu, Phi Gamma Delta. Clubs: Grosse Pointe Otsego, Prismatic (pres. 1967), Detroit, Detroit Racquet (pres. 1977-78), Cardio-Vascular Surgeons (pres. 1961-62). Author: (with F. A. Coller) Indications For and Results of Splenectomy, 1950; Prismatic Papers and an Ode, 1968; Prismatic Haiku Poems (Remembered Voices), 1973; also numerous articles surg. jours. Editorial bd. Review Surgery, 1959—. Home: 8 Stratford Pl Grosse Pointe MI 48230 Office: Blain Clinic 2141 E Jefferson Hosp Detroit MI 48207

BLAIN, CHARLOTTE MARIE, physician; b. Meadeville, Pa., July 18, 1941; d. Frank Andrew and Valerie Marie (Serafin) B.; student Coll. St. Francis, 1958-60, DePaul U., 1960-61; M.D., U. Ill., 1965; m. John G. Hamby, June 12, 1971 (dec. May 1976); 1 son, Charles J. Hamby. Intern, U. Ill. Hosps., Chgo., resident, 1967-70; practice medicine specializing in internal medicine, Elmhurst, Ill., 1969—; instr. medicine U. Ill. Hosp., 1969-70; asst. prof. medicine Loyola U., 1970-71; mem. staff Elmhurst Meml. Hosp., 1970—. U. Ill. fellow in infectious diseases, 1968-69. Mem. AMA, Am. Med. Women's Assn., Am. Soc. Internal Medicine, A.C.P., Am. Fedn. Clin. Research, Nat. Soc. Residents and Interns, Am. Acad. Family Practice, Am. Profl. Practice Assn., AAAS, Am. Soc. Contemporary Medicine and Surgery. Roman Catholic. Club: Univ. (Chgo.). Contbr. articles and chpts. to med. jours. and texts. Home: 320 Cottage Hill Elmhurst IL 60126 Office: 135 Cottage Hill Elmhurst IL 60126

BLAIN, DONALD GRAY, physician; b. Detroit, Feb. 27, 1924; s. Alexander and Ruby (Johnson) B.; ed. Princeton, 1946; M.D., Wayne State U., 1950; m. Grace Carpenter, June, 1954; children—Elizabeth, Ian, Patricia. Intern, Union Meml. Hosp., Balt., 1950-51; gen. surg. resident Ch. Home Hosp., Balt., 1953-55, Henry Ford Hosp., Detroit, 1955-56, Alexander Blain Hosp., Detroit, 1956-58; staff Blain Hosp.; resident urology N.C. Bapt. Hosp., Winston-Salem, 1962-65; instr. urology Bowman Gray Sch. Medicine, Winston-Salem, 1962-65; pvt. practice urology, Mount Clemens, Mich., 1965—. Mem. Gov.'s Conf. on Health Manpower, 1973. Served to capt. USAF, 1951-53. Diplomate Am. Bd. Urology. Fellow A.C.S.; mem. Macomb County Med. Soc. (past pres.), Am. Assn. Clin. Urologists, Am. Urologic Assn., St. Andrews Soc. Republican. Presbyterian. Clubs: Country of Detroit, Metamora Hunt, Ridgefield Hunt, Sedgefield Hunt. Home: 34136 E Jefferson St Clair Shores MI 48082 Office: 198 S Gratiot St Mount Clemens MI 48043

BLAIR, ALLAN EDWARD, oral surgeon; b. Cleve., June 4, 1929; s. Samuel Charles and Rose (Weiss) B.; B.A., Ohio State U., 1951, D.D.S., 1955, M.Sc., 1960; m. Judith Ann Hare, June 11, 1971; children by previous marriage—Bradley, Brian, Scott; stepchildren—Joel, Beth. Intern Ohio State Univ. Hosp., Columbus, 1957-58, resident oral and maxillofacial surgery, 1958-60; practice dentistry specializing in oral and maxillofacial surgery, Columbus, Ohio, 1960—; asst. prof. physiology Ohio State U., Columbus, 1960—, asst. prof. oral surgery, 1967—; mem. staff University, Childrens, St. Anthony, Mt. Carmel hosps. Recipient Outstanding Faculty Mem. award Ohio State U., 1975. Diplomate Am. Bd. Oral

Surgery. Fellow Am. Dental Soc. Anesthesiology, Internat. Assn. Oral Surgeons; mem. Am., Ohio (pres. 1976-77), Great Lakes socs. oral surgeons, ADA, Alpha Omega, Sigma Alpha Mu. Club: Hoover Yacht. Contbr. articles in field to profl. jours. Home: 2526 Stafford Pl Columbus OH 43209 Office: 3242 E Main St Columbus OH 43213

BLAIR, DOUGLAS PETER, ednl. assn. exec.; b. Corning, N.Y., June 10, 1934; s. George Elmer and Alice B. (Salls) B.; B.S., Ill. State U., 1961, M.S., 1964; postgrad. 1965—; m. Martha Ann Glisson, Nov. 22, 1956; children—Roger, John, Steven. Prin., Downs Grade Sch., Downs, Ill., 1957-63; prin. Tri Valley Jr. High Sch., Ellsworth, 1963-65; supt. schs., Atlanta, 1965-67; asst. supt. schs., Olympia Schs., Minier, Ill., 1967-69, supt. schs., 1969-76; dir. field service Ill. Assn. Sch. Bds., 1976—. Mayor, Village of Downs, Ill., 1965, trustee, 1961-65. Served with USAF, 1953-55. Mem. Am., Ill. (dir., state legis. chmn. 1975-76, pres. elect 1976-77) assns. sch. adminstrs., Nat., Ill. (legis. chmn. corn belt div. 1972-75) assns. secondary sch. adminstrs., McLean County Sch. Masters (pres. 1962-63). Methodist (treas. 1961-64). Rotarian (bd. dirs. 1966-71). Home: 602 S Mary St Atlanta IL 61723 Office: Ill Assn Sch Bds 330 Iles Park Pl Springfield IL 62718

BLAIR, EUGENE SCHLEGEL, orthodontist; b. Akron, O., Jan. 25, 1924; s. Samuel Clarence and Faith (Schlegel) B.; student U. Akron, 1941-43, U. Mich., 1943, Roosevelt Coll., 1946; D.D.S., U. Ill., 1950, M.S., 1952; m. Pauline Gucker, Dec. 28, 1946; children—Carol L., Robert E., Richard C., Thomas D. Pvt. practice orthodontics, Elgin, Ill., 1952—. Pres. Fox Valley Mental Health Assn., bd. edn. Ill. Sch. Dist. Served as 1st lt. U.S. Army, 1943-46. Mem. Am. Assn. Orthodontists, ADA, Ill., Fox Valley (pres. 19S7) dental socs., Midwestern (pres. 1977), Ill. (pres. 1965) socs. orthodontists, Chgo. Assn. Orthodontists (pres. 1964-65). Presbyterian. Club: Kiwanis (pres. 1961) (Elgin). Home: 1103 Florimond Dr Elgin IL 60120 Office: 3 S Crescent St Elgin IL 60120

BLAIR, JOSEPH SKILES, JR., educator; b. Niles, Ohio, Dec. 16, 1919; s. Joseph Skiles and Elizabeth Leo (Higgins) B.; B.S., Kent State U., 1942; M.A., Columbia U., 1948; Ph. D., (Danforth Found. fellow), Ohio State U., 1962; m. Marjorie Ella Jacot, June 15, 1946; children—Brenda Ruth, Lawrence Paul. Exec. dir. City Coll. N.Y. YM-YWCA and N.Y. U. Med. Students Club, 1948-52; coll. exec. Ohio-W.Va. area YMCA, 1952-59; ednl. services mgr. Nationwide Ins. Co., 1962-68; prof. Franklin U., Columbus, Ohio, 1968—; owner, mgr. Brookside Conf. Center; pres. Vicinia, Inc. Moderator, Univ. Bapt. Ch. Mem. Speech Communication Assn., Am. Mgmt. Assn., Assn. Ednl. Communications and Tech. Home: 254 E Torrence Rd Columbus OH 43214 Office: 201 S Grant Ave Columbus OH 43215

BLAIR, MARVIN SMITH, engr.; b. Killeen, Tex., June 8, 1924; s. Thomas Earle and Margaret Elizabeth (Beaumier) B.; B.B.A., U). Hawaii, 1968; M.A., U. Nebr., 1973; m. Baylor Doris Hale, Feb. 5. 1944; children—Marvin S., Jr., Margaret Baylor. Commd. ensign U.S. Navy, 1942, advanced through grades to capt., 1966; comdr. of Tunny, Daniel Webster, fleet submarine tng. facility, Hawaii, 1957-68; served on 6 submarines and 2 maj. staffs, 1944-73; ret., 1973; nuclear tech. specialist in charge quality assurance Omaha Pub. Power Dist., 1973-74, div. mgr. environ. and regulatory affairs, 1974-77; sr. project engr. Gibbs & Hill, Inc., Omaha, 1977—. Decorated Legion of Merit. Mem. Naval Inst., ASME, Navy League, Subvets World War II. Republican. Baptist. Clubs: Plaza, Fontenelle Hills Country, Masons. Home: 414 Greenbriar Ct Bellevue NE 68005 Office: 8420 W Dodge Rd Omaha NE 68114

BLAIR, MARY AGNES, cons. spl. edn.; b. Richmond, Mo., Jan. 14, 1909; d. Andrew and Lydia (Ward) Blair; B.S., Eastern Mich. U., 1940, Ed.D. (hon.), 1955; M.Ed., Wayne State U., 1946. Tchr., supr. elementary sch. Mich. Sch. Deaf, Flint, 1927-28; tchr., dir. spl. edn. Dearborn (Mich.) Pub. Sch., 1940-46; cons. spl. edn. Mich. Dept. Edn., Lansing, 1946-76; univ. summer prof. spl. edn. numerous univs. U.S., Can., 1946-76. Bd. dirs., Mich. Easter Seal Soc., 1946-75, and Lansing chpt.; bd. dirs. Bay Cliff Camp for Handicapped Children, summer 1947. Recipient Eastern Mich. Distinguished Alumni award, 1977, Beekman award, 1977, Mich. State Dept. Edn. award, 1977, award Mich. Suprs. Pub. Sch. Programs for Hearing Impaired, 1977, others. Mem. Eastern Mich. Alumni Assn. (pres. 1962) United Cerebral Palsy Assn (profl. bd. 1949-77), Mich. (award 1976), Am. speech and hearing assns., Council Exceptional Children, Mich. Parents and Tchrs. Hearing Impaired (state cons. spl. edn. 1946-77) Wayne State U. Alumni Assn. Presbyterian. Home: 1108 W Ionia St Lansing MI 48915

BLAIR, TERRENCE LEE, fin. and data processing cons.; b. LaPorte, Ind., Nov. 23, 1946; s. Stanley F. and Edna (Bluhm) B.; B.B.A., Loyola at Chgo., 1969; M.B.A., U. Notre Dame, 1971; m. Judy Leigh Johnson, June 20, 1969; children—Tiffany, Holly, Emily. Fin. planning asso. Assos. Fin. Planning and Control Co., South Bend, Ind., 1970-71; fin. planning specialist Charles F. Kettering Found., Dayton, 1972—; cons. T.L. Blair & Assos., Dayton, 1974—. Mem. Soc. Computer Simulation. Roman Catholic. Home: 10280 Grand Vista Dr Dayton OH 45459 Office: 5335 Far Hills Ave Dayton OH 45429

BLAISDELL, FRED WILLIAM, govt. engr.; b. Goffstown, N.H., July 21, 1911; s. William Edwin and Flora Margaret (Lucas) B.; B.S., U. N.H., 1933, C.E., 1950; M.S., Mass. Inst. Tech., 1934; m. Harriet M. Anderson, Apr. 19, 1935; children—Nancy (Mrs. Alveres M. Trelstad), Jean (Mrs. Vernon D. Warmbo), Fred S. Tech. asst. Mass. Inst. Tech., Cambridge, 1934-35; hydraulic engr. U.S. Dept. Agr. Bur. Standards, Washington, 1936-40, St. Anthony Falls Hydraulic Lab., Mpls., 1940—, project supr., 1943-68, research leader, 1968—, location leader, 1972—, tech. adviser, 1974—. Recipient Rickey medal ASCE, 1949, J.C. Stevens award, 1969; Superior Service award U.S. Dept. Agr., 1950; Outstanding Achievement award U. N.H. Coll. Tech., 1971, Certificate of Merit U.S. Dept. Agr., 1972; named Fed. Civil Service Employee of the Year, 1964. Registered profl. engr., Minn. Fellow ASCE, Am. Soc. Agrl. Engrs.; mem. Internat. Assn. Hydraulic Research, Soil Conservation Soc. Am., Sigma Xi. Contbr. chpts. to books. Home: 4540-30 Ave South Minneapolis MN 55406 Office: St Anthony Falls Hydraulic Lab 3d Ave SE at Mississippi River Minneapolis MN 55414

BLAKE, FRANK BURGAY, med. record librarian; b. N.Y.C., Feb. 10, 1924; s. Francis Gilman and Marguerite (Burgay) B.; B.S., U. Minn., 1947; M.S., N.Y. U., 1951; diploma Air U., 1960; m. Filomena Yolanda Ciaccio, Dec. 15, 1962; children—Anthony Francis, Robert Burgay. Staff U.S. Army Hosp., Ft. Ord, Calif., 1964-65; med. record librarian County of Tulare, Visalia, Calif., 1966-69, Winnebago (Wis.) Mental Health Inst., 1970—; exec. dir. Medica, Inc., Tulare, Calif., 1968-70. Cons. Brown County Mental Health Center, Green Bay, Wis., 1971-76; cons. Med. record program evaluation Herzing Insts., Inc., Milw., 1971—, mem. bd. advisers med. stenographer program, 1971-72; bd. advisers med. record technician program Moraine Park Tech. Inst., Fond du Lac, Wis., 1974—. Mem. Northeastern Assn. Med. Record Librarians (v.p. 1970-71). Contbr. articles to profl. jours. Home: 1103 E Irving Ave Oshkosh WI 54901 Office: Winnebago Mental Health Inst Winnebago WI 54985

BLAKE, MARTIN IRVING, educator; b. Paterson, N.J., Oct. 20, 1923; s. Jacob and Rose (Leen) B.; B.S., L.I. U., 1947; M.S., Rutgers U., 1950; Ph.D., Ohio State U., 1952; m. Sylvia Coonin, Nov. 25, 1948; children—Rhonda, David, Kenneth, Harriet. Asst. prof. pharmacy Duquesne U., Pitts., 1952-55; prof. pharmacy N.D. State U., Fargo, 1955-59; resident research asso. Argonne (Ill.) Nat. Lab., 1959-60; faculty U. Ill., Chgo., 1960—, prof. pharmacy, head dept., 1961—, asst. dean, 1977—. Cons. Argonne Nat. Lab., 1960—, Hines (Ill.) VA Hosp., 1966—. Mem. Ill. Bd. Pharmacy, 1975—, chmn., 1977; mem. Nat. Formulary Bd., 1965-75; mem. U.S. Pharmacopoeia Revision Com., 1970-80. Served with inf. AUS, 1943-46; ETO. Mem. Am. Chem. Soc., AAAS, Am. (com. on profl. affairs 1976-77), Ill. (chpt. pres. 1972-73) pharm. assns., AAUP, U.S. Pharmacopeial Conv., Nat. Assn. Bds. Pharmacy (mem. blue ribbon com. 1969—), Sigma Xi (chpt. pres. 1965-66). Author: Systematic Organic Chemistry, 1957. Contbr. articles in field to profl. jours. Home: 9023 Kenton St Skokie IL 60076 Office: University Illinois 833 S Wood Chicago IL 60612

BLAKE, PAUL ROBERT (BOB), broadcasting exec.; b. Raleigh, N.C., Nov. 11. 1943; s. John Claude and Delia Irene (Smith) B.; B.S., East Carolina U., 1966; M.Ed., Temple U., 1971. Dir. TV and radio ops. U. Del.. Newark, 1966-70, founder radio sta., 1968; dir. audience promotion stas. WFIL-TV-FM and WPVI-TV, Phila., 1970; gen. mgr. Sta. WGLS-FM, Glassboro (N.J.) Sfate Coll.. 1970-74; sta. mgr. Sta. WEKU-FM, Eastern Ky. U., Richmond, 1974-75; founder sta. WDCB-FM, Coll. of DuPage, Glen Ellyn, Ill., 1975, sta. mgr., 1975—; property master East Carolina Summer Theatre, Greenville, N.C., 1964-65; sec. radio adv. com. N.J. Pub. Broadcasting Authority, 1972-74; promotion, bus. and house mgr. Glassboro Summer Theatre, 1972-74. Mem. Nat. Assn. Ednl. Broadcasters, Internat. Radio, TV Soc., Assn. Ednl. Communications, Tech. Editor children's musicals The Fabulous Fable Factory, Mr. Herman and the Cave Company, The Princess, the Poet and the Little Gray Man, 1976-78. Home: Apt 2B 474 Raintree Ct Glen Ellyn IL 60137 Office: Sta WDCB-FM Learning Resources Center Coll DuPage Glen Ellyn IL 60137

BLAKE, THOMAS CLINTON, steel co. exec.; b. Bushton, Ill., July 19, 1927; s. Emmette Lee and Maude Ellen (Craft) B.; student U. Tenn., 1946; B.S., U. Cin., 1949; m. Gwyn M. Adams, July 20, 1946; children—Terri Lynn (Mrs. Roscoe A. Ronto), Lisa Ann. Profl. football player, 1949-51; gen. mgr. Warren Steel Corp., Middletown, Ohio, 1951-54; exec. v.p. Fed. Steel Corp., Dayton, Ohio, 1954-64; pres. Blake Steel Service, Inc., Middletown, 1964—, chmn. bd., 1964—; dir. 1st Nat. Bank, Middletown, Mid-Am. Properties, Inc., Middletown Area Devel. Co., B.S.S. Realty. Chmn. Middletown City Commn., 1969—; mem. Park Bd. 1969—, Library Bd., Middletown Golf Commn., 1970—; pres. Jr. Achievement, 1972—, Big Bros.; pres. YMCA, 1972-74; pres. Preble-Shawnee Sch. Bd., 1962-68. Bd. dirs. ARC. Fellow Am. Mgmt. Assn.; mem. Mensa, Newcomen Soc., Middletown C. of C., Sigma Sigma. Lion. Clubs: Forest Hills Country, Brown's Run Country, Wildwood (Middletown); Agonis (Dayton); Cincinnati, Bankers (Cin.). Home: 2017 Tullis Dr Middletown OH 45042 Office: 1211 Hook Dr Box 446 Middletown OH 45042

BLAKE, THOMAS GAYNOR, chemist; b. Nashville, Sept. 24, 1917; s. Robert Edwin and Dorothy (Gaynor) B.; student Princeton U., 1935-38; B.A., Central Meth. Coll., Fayette, Mo., 1940; postgrad. Washington U., St. Louis, 1942-44; m. Jane Elizabeth Spore. May 2, 1942; children—Dorothy Gaynor, Thomas Gaynor. Project engr. Explosives div. Olin Mathieson Chem. Corp., East Alton, Ill., 1941-48, head explosives chem. sect., 1948-54, dir. research and devel. explosives div., 1954-56; asst. dir. research and devel. armament div., Universal Match Corp., Ferguson, Mo., 1956-58; pres., dir. research Hanley Industries Inc.. St. Louis, 1958—; lectr. cons. in field. Mem. Am. Def. Preparedness Assn. (life), Am. Soc. Indsl. Security, Mo. Athletic Club, Engrs. Club St. Louis. Congregationalist. Patentee in field. Home: 16430 Old Jamestown Rd Florissant MO 63034 Office: 4575 Goodfellow Blvd St Louis MO 63120

BLAKELY, ROBERT FRASER, educator, geophysicist; b. Newark, Apr. 1, 1921; s. Richard Mathew and Maude Estelle (Fraser) B.; A.B., Miami U., Ohio, 1946; M.A., 1948; Ph.D., Ind. U., 1974; m. Rosanna Lieurance, Jan. 31, 1943; children—Robert Louis, Linda Ann. Spectrographer Ind. Geol. Survey, Bloomington, 1949-52, geophysicist, 1952—; asso. prof. geology Ind. U., 1970—. Served with USAAF, 1943-46. Mem. Soc. Exploration Geophysicist. Am. Geophys. Union, Am. Meteorol. Soc.. Assn. Computing Machinery, AAAS, Seismol. Soc. Am., Ind. Acad. Sci. Presbyn. Contbr. articles to profl. jours. Home: 116 S Meadowbrook Ave Bloomington IN 47401 Office: 611 N Walnut Grove Bloomington IN 47401

BLAKEMORE, WILLIAM STEPHEN, surgeon, educator; b. Stockdale, Pa., June 22, 1920; s. Issac Thompson and Mary Jane (Crockette) B.; B.S., Washington Jefferson Coll., 1942; M.D., U. Pa., 1945; postgrad. George Washington U., 1946-47; m. Elaine Claire Hooven, Apr. 2, 1949; children—William Stephen, Holly, Karin, Stephenie, Mary Jane, Laurel. Intern Hosp. of U. Pa., 1945-46, asst. resident in surgery, 1946, 48-51, resident in surgery, 1951-52; asst. resident in pediatric surgery Children's Hosp. of Phila., 1949; practice medicine specializing in gen. and thoracic surgery, Phila., 1952-73, Toledo, Ohio, 1973—; asst. instr. in surgery U. Pa., Phila., 1949-51, Damon Runyon clin. fellow, 1950, instr. in surgery, 1951-52, asso. in surgery, 1952-54, asst. prof. surgery, 1954-60, J. William White asst. prof. surg. research, 1956-61, asso. prof. surgery, 1960-62, asso. dir. Harrison dept. surg. research, 1961-73, prof. surgery, 1962-72, chmn. dept. surgery, 1962-72; attending physician in thoracic surgery Phila. Gen. Hosp., 1952-73; asso. surgeon Hosp. of U. Pa., 1952-73, asst. chief of surg. clinic, 1955-62, surgeon-in-chief, 1962-73; vis. fellow Karolinska Hosp., Stockholm, Sweden, 1953-54; chief of surgery Emergency Am. Med. Team to Algeria, 1962; cons. in surgery U.S. VA Hosp., Wilmington, Del., 1962-66; dir. surgery Med. Coll. Hosp., Toledo, 1973—; prof. surgery Med. Coll. of Ohio, Toledo, 1973—, chmn. dept. surgery, 1973—; mem. study sect. surgery NIH, 1965-69; mem. NRC Com. on Blood and Transfusion Problems, 1962-66. Served to lt. (j.g.), M.C., USNR, 1946-48. I.S. Ravdin Traveling fellow, 1953-54; recipient Nat. Humanitarian award Order of Ahepa, 1962, Medal of St. Paul, Greek Orthodox Ch., 1973; diplomate Am. Bd. Surgery, Am. Bd. Thoracic Surgery. Mem. A.C.S., Am. Surg. Assn., Am. Coll. Chest Physicians, Am. Coll. Cardiology, Am. Assn. for Cancer Research, Internat. Cardiovascular Soc. (sec. N.Am. chpt. 1973-77, pres. elect 1977—), Am. Heart Assn. (mem. council 1972—), Pa. Assn. for Thoracic Surgery, Soc. U. Surgeons, Soc. Vascular Surgery, AAAS, Halsted Soc. (pres. 1975), Soc. Surgery Alimentary Tract, Am. Physiol. Assn., N.Y. Acad. Scis.. Soc. Med. Consultants Armed Forces, Coll. of Physicians of Phila., Am. Trauma Soc., AAUP, Collegium Internat. Chirurgiae Digestivae, Internat. Soc. Surgery, Soc. Nuclear Medicine, Tacoma Surg. Club (hon.), Soc. of Surg. Chairmen, Phila. Acad. Surgery (recorder 1967-72), Alpha Omega Alpha, Alpha Kappa Kappa. Author: (with I.S. Ravdin) Current Perspecfives in Surgery, Current Perspectives in Cancer Therapy, 1966; (with L.K. Ferguson) Current Perspectives in Surgery, Current Perspectives in Gastroenterology, 1967; (with W.T. Fitts. Jr.) Current Perspectives in Surgery, Current Perspectives in Management of the Injured Patient, 1969; contbr. numerous articles in cardiovascular physiology and surgery to med. jours.; editorial cons. Surgery, 1957—, Jour. of Trauma, 1967—, Archives of Surgery, 1975. Home: 3230 Strayer St Maumee OH 43537 Office: CS #10008 Toledo OH 43699

BLAKEY, LILLIAN LUELLA, educator; b. Lake City, Iowa, Feb. 17, 1909; d. Axel M. and Nellie (De Burgh) Halvorsen; Two Year certificate, Buena Vista Coll., (Storm Lake, Iowa), 1949; B.S. in Edn., Drake U., 1952. M.A., 1957, postgrad., summers 1959-68, 70; m. Paul Blakey, Sept. 19, 1942. Tchr. pub. schs., Lytton. Iowa, 1936-46; mgr., councilor children's books C.K. Wilson Book Store, Quincy, Ill., 1946-47; tchr. pub. schs., Vinton, Iowa, 1947-49, Glick Sch., 1949—. Math. adviser Iowa Council Tchrs. Math., 1970-72, mem. program com., 1974. Rep. Am. Assn. Childhood Edn. and Alpha Delta Kappa to Gov.'s Conf. on Traffic Safety. 1966, rep. Marshalltown Bus. and Profl. Women, 1967. Mem. Iowa Fedn. Republican Women, 1965—, Marshalltown Area Community Hosp. Aux. Named Marshalltown Elementary Tchr. Year, 1967; recipient Fisher Ednl. award Fisher Found., Fisher Gov. Co., 1967, Willard J. Combs Aerospace award Aerospace Edn. Council Ia., 1970. Mem. N.E.A. (life), Iowa Edn. Assn., Am. Assn. Childhood Edn., Nat. Archives. Iowa Ornithologists Assn. (charter mem.), Iowa Math. Council, Iowa Women's Traffic Safety Council, Marshalltown Area Community Hosp. Assn., Nat. Trust for Historic Preservation, Smithsonian Instn., Alpha Delta Kappa (life mem.; internat. regional grand v.p. 1965-67. chmn. internat. credential com. 1971—, chmn. internat. balloting com. 1969, mem. internat. bldg. expansion com., rep. North Central region 1973-74, state by-laws chmn. 1976-78). Home: 301 S 9th St Marshalltown IA 50158 Office: 301 S 9th St Marshalltown IA 50158

BLAMEY, RICHARD LYLE, accountant; b. Fond du Lac, Wis., Dec. 13, 1941; s. Lyle Donald and Lucille Hazel (Immel) B.; B.B.A., U. Wis., 1965; m. Ann-Elizabeth McCallum, Aug. 14, 1977; 1 son, Richard Scott. Staff accountant Ronald Mattox & Assos., Madison Wis., 1965-71, audit mgr., Fond du Lac, 1971-74, partner, 1974-75; partner Alexander Grant & Co., Fond du Lac, 1975—; v.p., treas. Ledgeview Devel. Corp., Fond du Lac, 1971-77, pres., 1977—. Mem. Fond du Lac Civic Center Com., 1972—; adviser Jr. Achievement, 1974-75; chmn. accountants div. Dane County United Fund drive, 1970-71; first reader First Ch. of Christ Scientist, Fond du Lac, 1975-78; bd. dirs., treas. Student Center Found., Madison, 1969-71. Mem. Nat. Assn. Accountants (pres. chpt.), Am., Wis. (chmn. practice mgmt. com. and seminar 1972) insts. C.P.A.'s, Fond du Lac Jaycees (v.p. 1974-75), U. Wis. Alumni Assn. (pres. 1977-78). Republican. Clubs: South Hills Country, Elks, Wis. Region Classic Car, Antique Auto Club Am., Rotary, Sailing (Fond du Lac). Home: 247 Bayberry Ln Fond du Lac WI 54935 Office: 20 Forest Ave Fond du Lac WI 54935

BLANCHARD, B(IRDSALL) EVERARD, ednl. cons.; b. Chgo., Oct. 19, 1909; s. Birdsall Everard and Mary Alice (Vandervest) B.; B.S., Western Mich. U., 1931; M.S., State U. Iowa, 1932; M.A., U. Chgo., 1946, Ph.D., 1957; m. Ann Quaglia, Oct. 25, 1949; children—Sharon Reyn, David Everard. Ordained to ministry United Meth. Ch., 1936; minister Meth. chs. in Ill., Fla., Va., Nfld., 1936-51; dir. health and phys. edn. jr. high sch., Villa Park, Ill., 1932-36; dir. athletics and phys. edn. McKendree Coll., Lebanon, Ill., 1936-38; asst. supr. adult and vocat. edn. State of Ill., Glen Ellyn, 1938-41; dir. health and phys. edn. jr. high sch., Ft. Myers, Fla., 1941-42; prin. high sch., Cross City, Fla., 1943-46; supt. pub. schs., Minden City, Mich., 1946-47; prof. edn. Elmhurst (Ill.) Coll., 1947-48; prof. edn., dir. tchr. edn. Erskine Coll., Due West, S.C., 1948-49; dean grad. and undergrad. studies Overseas div. U. Md., 1949-51; prof. edn., dir. student teaching Plymouth (N.H.) State Coll., 1951-55; vis. prof. edn. Nat. Coll. Edn., Evanston, Ill., 1961-62; prof. edn. DePaul U., Chgo., 1962-75, dir. Ednl. Field Service, 1962-74, dir. Opinion Poll Survey Center, 1963-69, coordinator grad. programs office, 1966-75; vis. prof. edn. Defiance Coll., 1955-56; pres. Villa Ednl. Research Assos., Villa Park, 1975—; supt. Mil. Dependent Schs., 1949-51; mem. exec. com. Assn. for Field Service in Tchr. Edn., 1963-69. Recipient citation Princeton U., 1973; named hon. Ky. col. Mem. Internat. Assn. for Advancement Ednl. Research, NEA (life mem., citation 1960), Phi Delta Kappa, Kappa Delta Pi, Sigma Theta Gamma. Author: Destination Teaching, 1960; Introductory Statistics for Student of Education, 1963; A Survey of Illinois Catholic Secondary Schools, 1966; Illinois Index for Selecting Textbooks, 1968; A Profile of Behavioral Characteristics Peculiar to Articulation in American Educational Programs, 1972; contbr. articles to ednl. jours. Home and Office: 303 Astor Ct Villa Park IL 60181

BLANCHARD, JAMES J., Congressman; b. Detroit, Aug. 8, 1942; B.A., M.B.A., Mich. State U., Lansing; J.D., U. Minn.; m. Paula Parker; 1 son, Jay. Admitted to Mich. bar, 1968; legal aide Mich. sec. of state, 1968-69; adminstrv. asst. to atty. gen. State of Mich., 1970-71, asst. dep. atty. gen., 1971-72, asst. atty. gen., 1969-74; mem. 94th-95th congresses from 18th Mich. Dist. Mem. Assn. Asst. Attys. Gen., State Bar Mich., Am. Bar Assn. Democrat. Club: Jaycees (Ferndale, Mich.). Office: 330 Cannon House Office Bldg Washington DC 20515

BLANCO-GONZALEZ, MANUEL, educator, writer; b. Cadiz, Spain, Sept. 2, 1932; s. Bernardo and Elena (Goldberg) B.-G.; Bachiller, Colegio Nacional Manuel Belgrano, Buenos Aires, Argentina, 1951; postgrad. Universidad de La Paz (Bolivia), 1952-56; M.A., U. Chgo., 1959; m. Elfriede Stuerzebecher, July 18, 1964; children—Bernardo, Ricardo. Instr., U. Ill. at Navy Pier, Chgo., 1959-60; instr. Loyola U., Chgo., 1960-62; instr. U. Calif. at Riverside, 1962-63; lectr. U. Chgo., 1963-64; instr. U. Ill. at Circle Campus, Chgo., 1964-69, asso. prof. Spanish, 1970—. Mem. Modern Langs. Assn., Am. Assn. Tchrs. Spanish and Portuguese, AAUP, U. Chgo. Alumni Assn. Author: Los Cantos de Cain, 1955, Las Trompetas del Juicio Final, 1957, La Luna en Lluvia, 1960, Un Amor Para Electra, 1961, Tu Mundo Propio, 1962, J.L. Borges, el Tiempo en su Obra, 1963, Fenix, 1963, Cancion Desnuda, 1964, Ya no es la Primavera Pasada, 1967, Memoria y Tiempo, 1970, Gente, 1971, Ritos de Pasaje, 1977. Co-editor: Velazquez Spanish-English, English-Spanish Dictionary, rev. edit., 1964. Contbr. articles in field to profl. jours. (Bolivia, Argentina, Spain, Chile, U.S.). Office: Spanish Dept U Ill Circle Campus Chicago IL 60680

BLAND, ROBERT DANIEL, educator; b. Terre Haute, Ind., Aug. 23, 1937; s. William Frank and Pearl Averil (Morgan) B.; B.S., Ball State U., 1960, M.S., 1964; Ph.D., U. Minn., 1971; m. Mary Ellen Anderson, July 28, 1968; children—Cynthia, Stephanie. Coordinator gen. biol. program U. Minn., Mpls., 1970-74; chmn. dept. biology Coll. St. Thomas, St. Paul, 1974—. Mem. Minn. Acad. Sci., Am. Inst. Biol. Scis., AAUP, Phycological Soc. Am. Author: General Biology Laboratory Guide, 1973; Freshwater Biology, 1974; Dissertation Abstracts, 1971; contbr. articles to profl. jours. Home: 1639 Ridgewood Ln St Paul MN 55113 Office: Dept Biology Coll of St Thomas St Paul MN 55105

BLANK, JOHN L., accountant; b. Chgo., May 27, 1926; s. John L. and Josephine H. (Busker) B.; B.B.A., U. Mich., 1946; M.B.A., Ind. U., 1950; m. Jacqueline Richards, May 22, 1954; children—John L., Janice. Accountant, Peat, Marwick Mitchell, Chgo., 1947-49; accountant Arthur Andersen & Co., Chgo., 1950-54, mgr., 1956-64; merger officer, chmn. mgmt. com. United Wallpaper Co., Aurora, Ill.,

1954-56; corporate controller Chgo. Bridge & Iron Co., Oak Brook, Ill., 1964-69; exec. v.p., treas. Satelite 3-in-1 Corp., Atlanta, 1969-70; pvt. practice accounting, Hebron, Ind., 1970—. Served with USNR, 1944-47. C.P.A. Home and Office: 422 S 600 W Hebron IN 46341

BLANK, ROLF ALLAN, pub. relations exec.; b. Appleton, Minn., Dec. 17, 1937; s. Taalkeus Alfred and Anita Louraine (Houltzhouser) B.; student Northwestern U., 1959; B.Sc. in Speech, Am. U., 1963; m. Rachel Hampton, Aug. 20, 1960; children—Elizabeth, Mark. Supr. produce publicity Armstrong Cork Co., Lancaster, Pa., 1963-66; supr. pub. relations Young & Rubicam, Inc., Chgo., 1966-73; owner Rolf Blank Pub. Relations, Chgo., 1973—. Vice pres. bd. deacons Winnetka (Ill.) Congregational Ch., 1973, chmn. fund drive, 1975; bd. govs. Winnetka Community House, 1976—. Served to lt. (j.g.), USNR, 1960-63. Mem. Pub. Relations Soc. Am. (accredited), Winnetka Community Theatre. Republican. Club: Chgo. Publicity. Home: 577 Oak St Winnetka IL 60093 Office: 520 N Michigan Ave Chicago IL 60611

BLANKENBAKER, RONALD GAIL, physician; b. Rensselaer, Ind., Dec. 1, 1941; s. Lloyd L. and Lovina (Anderson) B.; B.S. in Biology, Purdue U., 1963; M.D., Ind. U., 1968, M.S. in Pharmacology, 1970. Intern, Meth. Hosp. Grad. Med. Center, Indpls., 1968-69, resident in family practice, 1969-71; med. dir. Indpls. Home for Aged, 1971—, Am. Mid-Town Nursing Center, Indpls., 1974—; asst. prof. family practice Ind. U., Indpls., 1973—; dir. family practice edn. Meth. Hosp. Grad. Med. Center, 1971—; family practice editor Reference and Index Services, Inc., Indpls., 1976—; legis. lobbyist Ind. Acad. Family Physicians, 1973—; med. advisor New Hope Found. of Am., Inc., 1974—. Bd. dirs. Meals on Wheels, Inc., Peoples Health Center Indpls., Marion County Cancer Soc. Served to maj. USAF, 1971. Recipient Service to Mankind award Sertoma Club, 1976, Outstanding Alumnus award Mt. Ayr (Ind.) High Sch., 1976; diplomate Am. Bd. Family Practice. Fellow Am. Acad. Family Physicians, Soc. Prospective Medicine (v.p., dir.); mem. AMA, Ind. Acad. Family Physicians, Ind. Allied Health Assn. (pres. 1973-74), Soc. Tchrs. Family Medicine, Ind. Arthritis Found. (dir.), Ind. Lung Assn. (dir.). Republican. Home: 5207 Washington Blvd Indianapolis IN 46220 Office: 1604 N Capitol Ave Indianapolis IN 46202

BLANKENSHIP, EARL, JR., wholesale co. pres.; b. Marion, Ill., June 14, 1923; s. Earl and Helen Wilson (McKinney) B.; B.S., So. Ill. U., 1949; m. Dolly Mae Palmer, Mar. 12, 1949; children—Earl III, Neil, Mona. With Blankenship Auto Parts Co., Marion, pres., 1969—; sec., treas. E. Blankenship & Co., Marion, 1972—. Served with USAAF, 1943-46. Home: 2202 W Main St Marion IL 62959 Office: 704 W Main St Marion IL 62959

BLANKENSHIP, MARSHALL LEE, dermatologist; b. Ramsey, Ill., Dec. 10, 1933; s. Merrill F. and Helen G. (Sloan) B.; B.S., U. Ill., 1956, M.D., 1958; m. Barbara K. Kanchier, June 21, 1958; children—Kathryn H., Marshall L., Jr. Intern, Ill. Central Hosp., Chgo., 1958-59; resident Northwestern U., Chgo., 1961-64; asso. in dermatology, 1963-71; practice medicine specializing in dermatology, Oak Lawn, Ill., 1964—; asst. prof. dermatology Rush Med. Coll., 1971-77; prof. dermatology Cook County Grad. Sch., 1966-77. Served with U.S. Army, 1959-61. Mem. Chgo. (treas. 1970-73, sec. 1973-76, pres. 1976), Ill. (sec. 1974-77, pres.-elect 1977) dermatol. socs., Chgo., Ill. State med. socs., AMA, Am. Acad. Dermatology (chmn. adv. bd. council 1977-79), Noah Worchester Dermatol. Soc. Home: 1333 Hillview Rd Homewood IL 60430 Office: 4647 W 103d St Oak Lawn IL 60453

BLANKENSHIP, RAYFORD T., lawyer; b. Lawrenceburg, Tenn., Apr. 20, 1941; s. Troy M. and Eula (Marks) B.; B.A., U. Louisville, 1963, LL.B., 1965; m. Linda K. Burton, Nov. 22, 1969; children—Pamala, James. Mem. firm T. Williams, John C. Wolfe, Indpls., also asso. Max Chilcote, Atty., 1965—. Arbitrator, Ind. Labor Dept., Midwest Intergovtl. Tng. Com. Labor Relations div. Am. Arbitration Assn., 1970—; comml. pilot. Served with USAF, 1959-63. Mem. Practicing Law Inst. Mason. Home: RD 4 Box 501B Greenwood IN 46142 Office: PO Box 782 Indianapolis IN 46206

BLANKENSHIP, RICHARD ROLAND, restaurant chain exec.; b. Peoria, Ill., Apr. 3, 1934; s. Roland Oscar and Frieda Irene (Hills) B.; B.S., Bradley U., 1956; m. Constance JoAnn Palmisano, June 21, 1970; children—Brenda, Melanie, Suzanne, Richard. Vice-pres. Dog n Suds Inc., Champaign, Ill., 1960-68, also dir.; partner Cal's Inc., West Dundee, Ill., 1969—, also dir.; partner B & G Devel. Co., West Dundee, 1969—; pres. Archie's Food Systems, Joliet, 1972-74; partner Landings Inc., Huntley, Ill., 1972-74, also dir.; partner Monarch Devel. Co., Champaign, 1967-70, also dir. Air Force div. chmn. United Fund Jacksonville, Fla., 1968. Served to capt. USAF, 1970. Mem. Alpha Kappa Psi. Home: Box 59 Route 1 Huntley IL 60142 Office: Box 264 Route 31 West Dundee IL 60118

BLASCO, ALFRED JOSEPH, bus. and fin. cons., bank exec.; b. Kansas City, Mo., Oct. 9, 1904; s. Joseph and Mary (Bevacqua) B.; student Kansas City Sch. Accountancy, 1921-25, Am. Inst. Banking, 1926-30; Ph.D. (hon.), Avila Coll., 1969; m. Kathryn Oleno, June 28, 1926; children—Barbara (Mrs. Charles F. Mehrer III), Phyllis (Mrs. Michael R. O'Connor). From office boy to asst. controller Commerce Trust Co., Kansas City, Mo., 1921-35; controller Interstate Securities Co., Kansas City, 1935-45, v.p., 1945-53, pres., 1953—, chmn. bd., 1961-68; sr. v.p. ISC Fin. Corp., 1968-69, hon. chmn. bd., 1970—; chmn. bd. Red Bridge Bank, 1966-72; chmn. bd. Mark Plaza State Bank, Overland Park, Kans., 1973—; vice-chmn. bd. Old Security Ins. Cos., 1952—; spl. lectr. consumer credit Columbia, N.Y.C., 1956, U. Kans., Lawrence, 1963-64. Mem. Fair Pub. Accomodations Com., Kansas City, Mo., 1964-68; pres. Catholic Community Library, 1955-56. Ward Committeeman, Kansas City, Mo., 1972-76. Pres. hon. bd. dirs. Baptist Meml. Hosp., 1970-74; chmn. bd. dirs. St. Anthony's Home, 1965-69; chmn. bd. trustees Avila Coll., 1969—. Decorated papal knight Equestrian Order Holy Sepulchre of Jerusalem, 1957, knight comdr., 1964, knight grand cross, 1966, lt. No. Lieutenancy U.S., 1970—; named Bus. Man of the Year, State of Mo., 1957; named Man of the Year, City of Hope, 1973; recipient Community Service award Rockne Club of Notre Dame, 1959. Mem. Soc. St. Vincent de Paul (pres. 1959-67), Am. Indsl. Bankers Assn. (nat. pres. 1956-57), Am. Inst. Banking (pres. Kansas City chpt. 1932-33), Bank Auditors and Controllers Assn., Fin. Execs. Inst. Am. (pres. Kansas City chpt. 1928-29), Nat. Assn. Accountants, Kansas City C. of C. Rotarian. Clubs: Kansas City, Hillcrest Country, Serra (pres. 1959-60). Contbr. articles to profl. jours. Home: 11705 Central St Kansas City MO 64114 Office: 3430 Broadway St Kansas City MO 64141

BLASK, WILLIAM ROBERT, ednl. cons.; b. Racine, Wis., Aug. 5, 1936; s. William Carl and LaVerne Pauline (Ernst) B.; B.A., Lawrence U., Appleton, Wis., 1961; teaching certificate DePaul U., 1961; m. Gail Annette Jones, Aug. 4, 1962; children—Bradley John, Christopher Ernst. Instr. tchrs. Stockton (Calif.) Unified Sch. Dist., 1965-66; tchr. El Paso pub. schs., 1966-68; tchr. data processing So. Colo. State Coll., Pueblo, 1968; systems engrs. IBM Corp., 1968-72; mgr. research and devel. DE-CO Services div. D.H. Baldwin Co., Denver, 1972-73; ednl. data processing edn. coordinator, adminstr. Colo. Blue Cross/Blue Shield, Denver, 1973-77; ednl. cons. Deltak, Oak Brook, Ill., 1977—; tchr. Met. State Coll., Denver, 1974-77, mem. bus. student advisory council; co-founder Info. Services Trainers; cons. in field. Active local Boy Scouts Am. Recipient Dist. Mgrs. award IBM Corp., 1970. Mem. Am. Soc. Tng. and Devel., Soaring Soc. Am., Gamma Delta (internat. field sec., internat. alumnus-at-large). Democrat. Lutheran. Editor: Luth. Alumnus, 1962-63. Home: 336 E York St West Chicago IL 60185 Office: 1221 Kensington Oak Brook IL

BLATT, MORTON BERNARD, med. illustrator; b. Chgo., Jan. 9, 1923: s. Arthur E. and Hazel B.; student Central YMCA Coll., 1940-42, U. Ill., 1944-45. Tchr., Ray-Vogue Art Schs., Chgo., 1946-51; med. illustrator VA Center, Wood, Wis., 1951-57, Swedish Covenant Hosp., Chgo., 1957-76. Med. illustrator Laidlaw Bros., Pubs., River Forest, Ill., 1956-59, cons., artist health textbooks, 1956-59; illustrator health and body charts Standard Edn. Soc., Chgo., 1960; art editor Covenant Home Altar. Served with USAAF, 1943-44. Mem. Art Inst. Chgo., Am.-Scandinavian Found., Asso. Ch. Press, Evangelical Press Assn. Mem. Evang. Covenant Ch. Clubs: Chicago Press, Saugatuck Yacht. Illustrator: Atlas and Demonstration Technique of the Central Nervous System, 1961, also numerous med. jours.; illustrator, designer numerous books, record jackets and covenant Hymnal. Art editor Covenant Companion, 1958—. Address: Box 714 100 Park St Tanglewood Saugatuck MI 49453

BLATT, SIDNEY ISRAEL, chem. co., container co. exec.; b. Columbus, Ohio, June 5, 1921; s. Rudolph S. and Clara (Mattlin) B.; student Ohio State U., 1941-43, B.S. in Bus. Adminstrn., 1946; m. Selma Mae Kantor, July 11, 1943; children—Gail (Mrs. Peter C. Taub), Cynthia (Mrs. Jeffrey Paine), Laura Jo (Mrs. Edward Paul). Vice pres. Columbus Barrel Cooperage Co., 1947-50, pres., 1950-55; pres. Columbus Steel Drum Co. div. Franklin Steel Co., Columbus, 1955—; pres. Surface Research Corp., Columbus, 1959—. Bd. dirs. Columbus Jewish Fedn., 1966—, v.p., 1968-74, pres., 1974-76, mem. exec. com., 1966—; chmn. Jewish Community Relations Com., 1969-73. Bd. dirs. Big Bro. Assn., 1967-70, Heritage House, Jewish Center; v.p. Temple Israel Found., 1970-72. Served with inf. AUS, 1943-45. Decorated 5 Battle Stars; named Ohio Small Bus. Man of Yr., 1970; recipient Plaque for outstanding leadership State Israel Bonds, State of Israel, 1968. Mem. Nat. Barrel and Drum Assn. (dir., treas., mem. exec. com.), Pres. Assn. Jewish (pres. temple 1977—). Club: Winding Hollow Country (pres. (Columbus). Home: 330 Stanbery Columbus OH 43209 Office: 1385 Blatt Blvd Blacklick OH 43004

BLAUSTEIN, HOWARD YALE, ins. co. exec., painter; b. Hazelton, Pa., May 29, 1930; s. Alan Jacob and Ethel (Gauz) B.; student Syracuse U., 1951; m. Joyce Ellen Dean. Jan. 27, 1969; children from previous marriage—William, Jill Ellen, Joyce Nancy, Brian. Life ins. agt. Conn. Mut., Utica, N.Y., 1955-59; dist. mgr. Mass. Mut., Utica, 1959-65; gen. agt. Variable Life Ins. Co., lMiami, Fla., 1965-67; v.p., also dir. of sales Variable Annuity Mktg. Co., Chgo., 1967—; pres. Intangible Marketing, Inc., Unity Plan, Inc.; gen. partner Pub. Employees Adminstrn. and Computer Enterprises; one-man shows paintings, 1974, 75. Chmn. United Jewish Appeal, 1964. Served with U.S. Army, 1952-55. Recipient Mass. Mut. Man of the Year award, 1961-64, Variable Annuity Life Ins. Co. Glen Holden Mgmt. award. 1968. Mem. Million Dollar Round Table (life), Chgo. Life Underwriters Assn., Nat. Assn. of Securities Dealers, Chgo. Assn. of Commerce and Industry. Democrat. Jewish (dir. temple). Clubs: Masons, K.P., B'nai B'rith, Covenant; Ravinia Country, Lacosta Country. Home: 280 Woodview Rd Barrington IL 60601 Office: 180 N LaSalle St Chicago IL 60601

BLAZER, SONDRA KAY GORDON, free lance journalist, writer; b. Middletown, Ohio, June 2, 1937; d. John Charles and Ora Lillie (Stewart) Gordon; A.A. magna cum laude, U. Cin., 1975; m. Ralph J. Bays, Feb. 17, 1956 (dec. 1969); children—Sherry Kay, Cynthia Rae, Robert Jay. Reporter, ch. editor Middletown Jour., 1955-56; mng. editor Warren County Reporter, Lebanon, Ohio, 1966-72; corr. Franklin (Ohio) Chronicle, 1974—; free lance journalist, 1973—. Mem. Ohio Gov.'s Traffic Safety Com., 1972—; mem. Warren County Bd. Mental Health and Retardation, 1972—, now chmn.; mem. citizen's adv. com. Lebanon Correctional Instn., Lebanon, 1971—; sec. Warren County Safety Council, 1972—; bd. dirs. Warren County com. Ohio Easter Seal Soc. for Crippled Children and Adults, 1967—; mem. Warren County Bd. Elections, 1974—, Warren Profl. Health Adv. Com.; bd. dirs. Warren United Appeal; sec. Warren County Disaster Services Orgn.; sec., Warren County Democratic Women's Club, 1963-67, Warren County Dem. Central and Exec. Com., 1965—; precinct committeeman Dem. party, 1964—; mem. Ohio Dem. Century Club; mem. land use subcom. Ohio-Ky.-Ind. Council Govts., 1975—. Winner 1st pl. Beta Sigma Phi internat. short story contest, 1964, Ohio Dept. Hwy. Safety Media contest, 1970. Mem. Ohio Corrections and Ct. Assn., Am. Police and Fire Reporters Assn., Nat. Council Crime and Delinquency, Internat. Platform Assn., Phi Kappa Epsilon, Alpha Sigma Lambda. Methodist (Sunday sch. tchr. 1963-72, sec. worship commn. 1972-75). Address: 3730 Beatrice Dr Franklin OH 45005

BLAZEY, LAWRENCE EDWIN, artist, indsl. designer; b. Cleve., Apr. 6, 1902; s. John and Anna (Cook) B.; grad. Cleve. Inst. Art, 1921-24; postgrad. U. London, 1925, Cranbrook Acad., 1952; m. Mildred M. Schlect, Oct. 6, 1934; 1 dau.. Beverly. Artist comml. advt. Manning Studios, Cleve., 1926-32; co-founder, v.p. Designers for Industry Inc., Cleve., 1934-52; product devel. engr. Ohio Tool Co., Cleve., 1941-43; co-founder, v.p. Terra Industries, Cleve., 1956-60; v.p.. chief engr. Tapco Products Inc., Detroit, 1963-69; pvt. practice as cons. indsl. designer, product devel. engr., archtl. designer Bay Village, Ohio, 1952—; exhibited in numerous 1-man, group shows throughout U.S., 1932—. Mem. Fine Arts Com. Cleve. City Plan. Com.. 1944-60; chmn. rev. bd. City of Bay Village, 1973—. Mem. Indsl. Designers Soc. Am., Ohio Designer Craftsmen's Soc., Artists Coop., Cleve. Soc. Artists, Baycrafters, Mensa, Ancient Astronauts Soc., Cleve. UFO Soc., Internat. Platform Soc. Mem. Eckankar Ch. Mason (32 deg.). Home: 537 Juneway Dr Bay Village OH 44140

BLEKFELD, GLEN MEROLD, accounting, data processing co. exec.; b. Chicago Heights, Ill., May 18 1939; s. Chester G. and Avanelle F. (Durham) B.; student Thornton Jr. Coll., 1959-61; m. Joann Marie Haddock, Feb. 9, 1968; children—(from a previous marriage) Laurel D., Kathleen M.; 1 stepson Jon K. Sutherland. Payroll clerk, data process operator Sinclair Refining Co., Harvey, Ill., 1959-60; computer specialist Nat. Cash Register Co., Chgo., 1960-61; dir. data processing R.J. Kearns & Co., Montgomery, 1961—. Bd. dirs. data processing edn. Waubonsee Community Coll. Served with AUS, 1956-59. Home: Route 1 Box 585 Oswego IL 60543 Office: 39 Montgomery Rd Montgomery IL 60538

BLESKACEK, GERALD EDWARD, bus. developer; b. Chippewa Falls, Wis., Sept. 29, 1931; s. Edward and Loretta (Samens) B.; B.S., Stout State U., 1962; m. Joan Berg, Aug. 21, 1952; children—Debra, Terri. Owner. mgr. Jerry Bleskacek Constrn. Co., Bloomer, Wis.. 1958-61; pres., gen. mgr. Pecha & Bleskacek Contrn., Bloomer, 1961-67, Tri City Contractors, Inc., 1967-74, P & B Enterprises Inc., 1974—; dir. A-1 Redi Mix Inc., A-1 Aggregates, Bloomer; sec. Service Devel. Corp., Barron, Wis. Served with AUS, 1952-54. Mem. Bloomer C. of C., Bloomer Indsl. Devel. Soc., Bloomer Hist. Soc., Am. Legion, VFW. Republican. Roman Catholic. Club: Moose. Home and office: PO Box 206 Bloomer WI 54724

BLESSING, CHARLES ALEXANDER, city planner; b. Montrose, Colo., May 23, 1912; s. Albert N. and Harriet N. (Brevoort) B.; B.S. in Archtl. Engring., U. Colo., 1934; B.Arch., Mass. Inst. Tech., 1937, M. City Planning, 1939; m. Elizabeth C. Long, Aug. 18, 1940; children—Bayard W., Curtis B. Planning engr. N.H. Planning and Devel. Com., 1940-41; city planner Chgo. Plan Commn., 1942; asso. archtl. engr. U.S. Army Engrs. Office, 1943; with mil. govt. program USNR, Princeton, 1944; dir. urban research U.S. Navy Mil. Govt. Program, Princeton, 1944-45, U.S. Navy Mil. Govt. Center, Monterey, Cal., 1945; city planning officer Hdqrs. SCAP, Tokyo, Japan, 1945-46; regional planning engr. Greater Boston Devel. Com., 1946-48; dir. planning Chgo. Plan Commn., 1948-53; dir. city planning Detroit City Plan Commn., 1953-74; dir. city planning community and econ. devel. dept. City of Detroit, 1974—. Adj. asso. prof. city planning Wayne State U. Mem. demonstration grant com. HHFA, 1954-59; chmn. S.E. Region Citizens Adv. Com. on Sch. Needs, Detroit, 1957-58; pres. Detroit Met. Area Regional Planning Commn., 1958-59; mem. Mich. Cultural Commn., 1961-62; cons. planning com. on housing Nat. Adv. Com. on Housing for White House Conf. on Aging, 1959; mem. housing census adv. com. U.S. Bur. of Census, 1960; mem. Nat. Indsl. Zoning Com., 1949-53; mem. vis. com. Dept. City and Regional Planning, Mass. Inst. Tech., 1960; vice chmn. Detroit Com. on Neighborhood Conservation and Improved Housing, 1955-60; mem. adv. com. Community Facilities Adminstrn. Design Honor Awards Program, 1964; mem. Met. planning com. Hwy. Research Bd., 1964-67: mem. archtl. and engring. adv. com. Fed. Reconstrn. and Devel. Planning Commn. Alaska, 1964; chmn. adv. commn. Platte River Valley Reconstrn. Denver, 1965; mem. adv. com. to Urbandoc Com. Housing and Home Finance Agy. U. City N.Y., 1965-67; mem. nat. adv. council Urban Am., 1966-67; mem. adv. design com. HUD Region IV, Chgo., 1966-67; cons. to adv. com. Centennial World Conf., Toronto, 1967; mem. Adv. Com. on Environmental Quality, Nat. Found. Arts, 1971; mem. exec. com. NSF Hwy. Research Bd., 1969-71; mem. Mich. Bd. Registration Profl. Community Planners, 1968—, chmn., 1974-75; mem. environmental arts adv. panel Mich. Council of Arts, 1973-75; mem. bd. planning consultants City of Sao Paulo (Brazil), 1968-69; mem. cons. bd. regional plan for Grand Coulee Dam region U.S. Bur. Reclamation, 1968; mem. bd. model Neighborhood Housing Corp., Detroit, 1973—; mem. design jury for Colo. Supreme Ct. Bldg., Colo. Heritage Center, 1974; mem. various other coms. Mem. citizens adv. planning and devel. com. Wayne County Community Coll., 1971—. Served to lt. USNR, 1943-46, Recipient Citation for Excellence in Community Architecture, AIA, 1965; 4th Biennial Design Excellence award HUD, 1970; Urban Design award Progressive Architecture, 1971; Distinguished Engring. Alumnus award U. Colo., 1972. Registered architect, Ill. Fellow AIA (chmn. urban design com. 1962-63, citation for excellence in community arch. 1965, gold medal Detroit chpt. 1972, medal Cities in Perspective 1976); mem. Am. Inst. Planners (nat. pres. 1958-60, chmn. nat. com. profl. registration planners 1970-71), ASCE (chmn. exec. com. city planning div. 1958), Western Soc. Engrs. (chmn. edn. com. 1951-52), World Soc. Ekistics, U.S. Jr. C. of C. (chmn. profl. adv. com. comml. devel.), Mich. Acad. Arts and Scis., Tau Beta Pi, Sigma Tau, Chi Epsilon, Lambda Alpha. Clubs: University, Witenegemot, Prismatic (Detroit). Author: The Form of Cities in Perspective, 1973; (with T. McCroskey and J. Ross McKeever) Surging Cities, 1948. Contbr. numerous articles to profl. jours. Home: 2532 Seminole Ave Detroit MI 48214 Office: 350 E Congress St Detroit MI 48226

BLESSING, LARRY RICHARD, accountant; b. Kansas City, Kans., Nov. 4, 1943; s. Ernest Anthony and Frances Elizabeth (Stock) B.; B.B.A., U. Mo. at Kansas City, 1964; m. Jane Erickson, July 4, 1971. Accountant, Leon A. Carter Ltd., Mission, Kans., 1961—. Mem. Pub. Accountants Assn. Kans. (dir.), Nat. Soc. Pub. Accountants. Lutheran. Home: 4809 W 61st Terr Mission KS 66205 Office: 5800 Foxridge Dr Mission KS 66202

BLETZACKER, RICHARD WELCH, civil engr.; b. Lancaster, Ohio, Jan. 24, 1926; s. Clarence A. and Frances K. (Welch) B.; student Central Mich. Coll., 1944-45, U. Mich., 1945-46; B. Civil Engring., Ohio State U., 1949, M.Sc., 1961; m. Maxine T. Schorr, June 30, 1949; children—Karl R., Joan M. Civil engr. Ohio Dept. Hwys., Columbus and Marietta, 1949-52; sales engr. J.T. Edwards Co., Columbus, Ohio, 1954-57; research asso. Ohio State U., Columbus, 1957-61, asst. prof., 1961-64, asso. prof. civil engring., 1964—, dir. bldg. research lab., 1958—; cons. engr. for indsl. firms, trade assns. and govt. agencies. Exec. com. mem. Columbus and Franklin County Civil Defense, 1964—. Served with USNR, 1944-46, 52-54. Mem. ASCE (Simpson award 1951), Am. Concrete Inst., ASTM (merit award 1977), Nat. Fire Protection Assn., Sigma Xi. Contbr. research articles to profl. jours. Home: 4160 Waddington Rd Upper Arlington OH 43220 Office: 2070 Neil Ave Columbus OH 43210

BLEVINS, WILLIAM EDWARD, banker; b. Pocahontas, Va., Oct. 18, 1927; s. Howard M. and Elsie Jane (Wire) B.; A.B., Marshall U., 1951; M. Pub. Adminstrn., City U. N.Y., 1960; m. Mary Hester Jenkins, Aug. 25, 1951; children—Jeffrey Alexander, Jennifer Lynn, Bradley Edward. Mgr. personnel Equitable Life Assurance Soc., N.Y.C., 1951-66; dir. manpower planning and mgmt. devel. Nat. Bank of Detroit, 1967-68, v.p., dir. personnel, 1969-74, sr. v.p., 1974—; mem. nat. employer com. U.S. Dept. Labor Manpower Adminstrn., 1973-75; mem. Mich. Manpower Commn., 1969-71. Mem. personnel adv. com. Mich. State U. Sch. Labor and Indsl. Relations, 1968—; bd. dirs. Mich. Soc. Mental Health, 1970-74, chmn. indsl. mental health com., 1970-74; bd. dirs. Mich. Diabetes Assn., 1974-76; trustee, sec. Bon Secours Hosp., 1973—. Served with USAAF, 1946-47. Recipient Outstanding Alumnus award Marshall U., 1976. Mem. Am. Inst. Bankers (bd. regents Detroit chpt. 1972—), Employers Assn. Detroit (treas., dir.), Am. Mgmt. Assn. (personnel planning council 1972-75), Am. (chmn. personnel div. 1975-76, govt. relations council 1974-77, dir. 1975-76), Mich. (chmn. personnel com. 1975-76) bankers assns., Detroit Personnel Dirs. Group, Lambda Chi Alpha, Omicron Delta Kappa. Republican. Congregationalist. Clubs: Detroit Athletic, Econ. Detroit; Grosse Pointe (Mich.) Yacht. Office: 611 Woodward Ave Detroit MI 48226

BLIETZ, DUANE LESLIE, city ofcl.; b. Chgo., July 29, 1927; s. Arthur W. and Catherine (Taylor) B.; student Wright Jr. Coll., 1948-50, LaSalle U., 1956-60; B.S. in Bus. Adminstrn., Roosevelt U.; m. Ruth Gilke, Sept. 22, 1956; children—Howard, Leslie, David. Comptroller City of Des Plaines (Ill.). Treas. Des Plaines Park Dist., 1964-75. C.P.A., Ill. Mem. Municipal Finance Officers assns. U.S. and Can., Ill. Municipal Finance Officers Assn. (pres. 1973—), Chgo. Met. Finance Officers Assn. (pres. 1971-72), Am. Inst. C.P.A.'s. Elk. Home: 494 Amherst Ave Des Plaines IL 60016 Office: 1420 Miner St Des Plaines IL 60016

BLIKRE, CLAIR TALMER, ednl. adminstr.; b. Powers Lake, N.D., Nov. 23, 1924; s. Theodore C. and Clara (Jacobson) B.; B.A., U. N.D., 1948, Ed.D., 1960; M.A., Colo. State U., 1953; m. LaVonne Ardis Nygaard, Aug. 20, 1950; 1 dau., Cindy Lou. Prin. pub. sch., Tioga, N.D., 1948-50; supt. Butte, N.D., 1950-52; sales rep. Balfour Jewelry,

Mont., 1952-53; supt. schs., Alexander, N.D., 1953-55, Rolla, 1955-58, Stanley, 1958-62, Yankton, S.D., 1962-65; dean So. State Coll., S.D., 1965-66; pres. N.D. State Sch. of Sci., Wahpeton, 1966—; cons. pub. sch., vocat. edn. Commr. North Central Assn. Secondary Schs. and Colls., 1974—. Trustee N.D. Masonic Found., 1973—. Served with USAAF, 1943-46. Recipient John Hays fellowship, 1965; Nat. Outstanding Leadership and Service award Am. Legion, 1970, 71, Outstanding Boss of Yr. award, 1973. Mem. NEA, N.D. Ednl. Assn., Am. Tech. Edn. Assn., Am. Assn. Sch. Adminstrs., Am., N.D. (exec. sec. 1957-62) assns. sch. adminstrs., Am. Legion (dir. edn. scholarship program in N.D., 1968-73), C. of C. Lutheran. Mason (32 deg., Shriner, state gen. purposes and policy com. 1969-73, jr. grand steward N.D.), Elk, Rotarian (pres. local club 1975-76). Home: 1029 Valley St Wahpeton ND 58075

BLINCOE, RICHARD ALOYSIUS, mech. engr.; b. Dayton, Ohio, Nov. 28, 1934; s. Richard A. and Rose Gertrude (Joyce) B.; B.S. in Mech. Engring., U. Dayton, 1956; m. Peggie E. Millikin, Sept. 3, 1955; children—Richard, Kathleen, Karen, Thomas, David, Gregory. Design engr. aeroproducts operation Gen. Motors Corp., 1956-60; mech. engr. aero. equipment U.S. Air Force, Wright-Patterson AFB, Ohio, 1960-65; sect. chief devel. engring. Nat. Water Lift Co., Kalamazoo, 1965-69, engring. mgr., 1969-77, dir. engring., 1977—. Com. chmn. Cub Scouts Am., 1972-74; coach Little League, Kalamazoo, 1976. Registered profl. engr., Ohio, Mich. Mem. Am. Helicopter Soc., Am. Def. Preparedness Assn. Patentee linear hydraulic servo motor. Office: 2220 Palmer St Kalamazoo MI 49001

BLINKS, JOHN ROGERS, physician; b. N.Y.C., Mar. 21, 1931; s. Lawrence Rogers and Anne Catherine (Hof) B.; A.B., Stanford U., 1951; M.D., Harvard U., 1955; m. Doris Marie Chambers, Dec. 28, 1953; children—Susan Mayo, Sarah Russell, Elizabeth Rogers. Med. house officer Peter Bent Brigham Hosp., Boston, 1955-56; research asso. Nat. Heart Inst., Bethesda, Md., 1956-58; faculty Harvard Med. Sch., Boston, 1958-68, instr., 1958-61, asso., 1961-64, asst. prof. pharmacology, 1964-68, John and Mary R. Markle Found. scholar, 1961-66; head dept. pharmacology Mayo Found., Rochester, Minn., 1968—; asso. prof. pharmacology Mayo Grad. Sch. Medicine, 1968-72, prof., chmn. dept. pharmacology Mayo Med. Sch., 1973—; hon. research asst. dept. physiology Univ. Coll., London, 1962-63; vis. lectr. dept. physiology U. Auckland (N.Z.), 1974; established investigator Am. Heart Assn., 1965-70, mem. research com., 1975—; mem. program projects com. Nat. Heart and Lung Inst., 1968-72, mem. cardiology adv. com., 1976—; chmn. Gordon Research Conf. on Heart Muscle, 1970; mem. external adv. bd. Pa. Muscle Inst., 1975-77. Served with USPHS, 1956-58. Mem. AAAS, Am. Soc. Pharmacology and Exptl. Therapeutics, Am. Physiol. Soc., Biophys. Soc., Cardiac Muscle Soc., Soc. Gen. Physiologists. Field editor cellular pharmacology Jour. Pharmacology Exptl. Therapeutics, 1969-71, mem. editorial bd., 1965-77; mem. editorial bd. Circulation Research, 1970-74. Home: 2715 Salem Rd SW Rochester MN 55901 Office: Dept Pharmacology Mayo Found Rochester MN 55901

BLINN, ROBERT DANFORTH, mfg. co. exec.; b. Glens Falls, N.Y., July 14, 1933; s. Morse C. and Elizabeth C. B.; B.S. in Accounting and Finance, Bryant Coll., 1958; m. Patricia J. Cleland, Apr. 1, 1956; children—Jonathan, Timothy, Julie. With Owens-Corning Fiberglas Co., Toledo, 1957—, systems and programming mgr., 1969-73, corp. systems mgr., 1973-77, project dir., 1977—. Active Toledo Area Council Boy Scouts Am., 1971—; coach Little League, Toledo, 1967-77. Served with U.S. Army, 1953-55; ETO. Mem. Data Processing Mgmt. Assn. Democrat. Roman Catholic. Clubs: Bavarian Sports, Keyser Sch. Boosters. Home: 820 Whitehorse Ct Perrysburg OH 43551 Office: Owens-Corning Fiberglas Co One Levis Square Toledo OH 43659

BLISS, DWIGHT LEWIS, automotive engr.; b. Wellsboro, Pa., Dec. 18, 1946; s. Hugh Dwight and Mary A. (Erway) B.; student Mansfield State Coll., 1965-66; B.M.E., Gen. Motors Inst., 1970. With Chevrolet Motor div. Gen. Motors Corp., Warren, Mich., 1970—, design engr., 1974-76, product planner, 1976—. Served with USAF, 1971. Mem. Soc. Automotive Engrs. Republican. Baptist. Clubs: Racquet, Ski, Cross Country Motorcycle, Environ. Protection. Author: Emission Test Procedure, 1970. Home: 26805 Newport St Warren MI 48089 Office: 30003 Van Dyke St Warren MI 48092

BLISS, GEORGE WILLIAM, newspaperman; b. Denver, July 21, 1918; s. William Lane and Marie (Bresnan) B.; student Northwestern U., 1938; m. Helen Jeanne Groble, June 29, 1940 (dec. June 1959); children—William R., George L., Dennis M., Marianne, Carol, Helen Jeanne; m. 2d, Therese O'Keefe, Aug. 11, 1960; 1 son, Terrence. With Chgo. Evening Am., 1937-42; with Chgo. Tribune, 1942-68, 71—, labor editor, 1953-68, dir. investigative task force, 1971—; chief investigator Better Govt. Assn., 1968-71, also acting exec. dir. Chgo. Tribune Task Force, 1971. Served with USNR, World War II. Recipient Edward Scott Beck award Chgo. Tribune, 1954. 58, 73; Spot News Reporting award Chgo. Newspaper Guild, 1957, A.P., 19S8, 59; Pulitzer prize for local reporting, 1962, 73, 76; Jacob Scher award, 1973; News Writing award A.P. Ill., 1972, 74, A.P. Editors Assn., 1974; Inland Daily Press Assn. award, 1974; News award U.P.I., 1974. Mem. Chgo. Newspaper Reporters Assn. Clubs: Press, Ill. Athletic Assn. (Chgo.). Home: 9605 S Lawndale Ave Evergreen Park IL 60642 Office: 435 N Michigan Ave Chicago IL 60611

BLISS, RICHARD LAWRENCE, architect; b. Grand Rapids, Mich., Oct. 30, 1918; s. John Lawrence and Lilian Irma (Rombauer) B.; B.Arch., Washington U., St. Louis, 1940, M.Arch., 1941; postgrad. Mass. Inst. Tech., 1941-42; m. Nancy Jane Hamilton, Oct. 1, 1948; children—Mark Hamilton, Emily Forester. Draftsman, Labeaume, Abbot & Unland, Architects, St. Louis, 1945-46; draftsman Joseph D. Murphy, Architect, St. Louis, 1946-48; project architect Wedemeyer & Hecker, Architects, St. Louis, 1950-51; project architect P. John Hoener & Assos., Architects, St. Louis, 1956-69; project architect Wedemeyer, Cernik, Corrubia, Inc., St. Louis, 1969—. Instr. history of architecture Univ. Coll., Washington U., St. Louis, 1971—. Recipient various fellowships. Fellow AIA (corporate); mem. Constrn. Specification Inst., St. Louis Landmarks, Inc., Heritage Club St. Louis, Mo. Heritage Trust Inc. Contbr. photographs to Father of Skyscrapers (Mervyn Kaufman), 1969; contbr. articles to profl. jours. Home: 1034 Forest Ave Kirkwood MO 63122 Office: Railway Exchange Bldg 611 Olive St Suite 1770 St Louis MO 63101

BLISS, RONALD GENE, writer. broadcasting system adminstr.; b. Atwood, Kans., Aug. 12, 1942; s. Wilbur Cyril and Mary Lucille (Makings) B.; student Fort Hays State U., 1960-62; B.A., Kans. State U., 1964; M.A., U. Mo.. 1969; m. Margaret Jane Keeler. July 25, 1965; children—Eric Dean, Kirk Ronald. City hall reporter, Findlay (Ohio) Republican-Courier, 1964; news editor Free Press Tribune. Colby. Kans., 1965-66; writer of TV news features and documentaries U. Mo.. Columbia, 1966-69; TV investigative reporter Kans. State Network, Sta. KARD-TV, Wichita, 1969-76, dir. pub. affairs. 1976—; author: Indian Softball Summer or Kackapoos Never Say Good-Bye. 1974; contbr. articles to various mags.; guest lectr. Fort Hays Kans. State U., 1974. Recipient Merit award Ch. World Services, 1972; Citation for Best TV Documentary, Kans. Assn. of Broadcasters, 1972. Mem. Nat. Assn. of Ednl. Broadcasters, Nat. Broadcast Assn. for Community Affairs, Nat. Acad. TV Arts Scis. Mem. Ch. of God. Home: 620 James St Maize KS 67101 Office: 833 N Main St Wichita KS 67201

BLIXT, ALBERT BERNARD, JR., lawyer, photographer; b. Detroit, Jan. 25, 1945; s. Albert Bernard and Ella Nora (Erlandson) B.; B.A., U. Mich., 1967, J.D., 1973; m. Jill Elaine Atkinson, May 10, 1969; 1 son, David Alexander. Owner, Photography by Al Blixt, Ann Arbor, Mich., 1969-73; founder, pres. Photo-Graphics, Ltd., Ann Arbor, 1973—; admitted to Mich. bar, 1974, since practiced law, Ann Arbor; asst. pros. atty., Washtenau County, Mich., 1975—. Instr. photography Washtenaw Community Coll., 1974; instr. bus. law Eastern Mich. U., 1977. Mem. profl. photographers Am., Mich., Ann Arbor, State Bar Mich. Photo editor Ann Arbor Scene, 1970—. Contbr. photography to profl. jours. and mags. Home: 1324 Forest Ct Ann Arbor MI 48104 Office: 219 Nickels Arcade Ann Arbor MI 48104

BLIXT, ROBERT EDMUND, investment adminstr., state ofcl.; b. Worthington, Minn., July 9, 1927; s. Edmund Loren and Evelyn (Liljegren) B.; A.A., Worthington Jr. Coll., 1947; B.A. magna cum laude, St. Olaf Coll., 1949, M.S., U. Colo., 1951, J.D., 1953; m. Mary Ellen Cooke, Aug. 3, 1951 (div. Mar. 1976); children—Jerold Robert, Loren Henry, Kathy Ellen (dec.), Kristin Mary, Lisa Jean. Admitted to Minn. bar, 1955; instr. U. Colo., 1950-53; securities analyst, Northwestern Nat. Bank, Mpls., 1953-56; investment counsel, bd. regents U. Minn., 1957-60; exec. sec., Minn. Bd. of Investment, St. Paul, 1960—. Trustee, treas. Baptist Hosp. Fund. Mem. Twin Cities Soc. Security Analysts (pres. 1968-69), Inst. Chartered Fin. Analysts (v.p. 1974-75, pres. 1975-76, trustee 1972—), Financial Analysts Fedn. (dir. 1970-72, 75-76). Home: 535 W Sandhurst Dr Apt #320 St Paul MN 55113 Office: MEA Bldg 55 Sherburne Ave St Paul MN 55155

BLOCH, HENRY WOLLMAN, tax preparation co. exec.; b. Kansas City, July 30, 1922; s. Leon Edwin and Hortence (Bienenstok) B.; B.S., U. Mich., 1943; m. Marion Ruth Helzberg, June 16, 1951; children—Robert, Thomas, Mary Jo, Elizabeth Ann. Pres., Chief exec. officer H. & R Block, Inc., Kansas City, 1955—; dir. Commerce Bank, The Vendo Co., Nat. Fidelity Life Ins. Co., Employers Reins. Corp. Mem. council of fellows Nelson Gallery Found.; past dir., v.p. Civic Council of Greater Kansas City; past dir., mem. exec. bd. Heart of Am. council Boy Scouts Am.; active Heart of Am. United Way. Vice chmn. bd. dirs. Kansas City Art Inst.; v.p., bd. dirs. Menorah Med. Center; pres., bd. dirs. H & R Bloch Found.; pres., bd. dirs. Jewish Fedn. and Council of Greater Kansas City, U. Mo., Kansas City, Midwest Research Inst., Am. Jewish Com., Kansas City Museum, Assn. Trusts and Founds., Indian Hills Homes Assn., Harry S Truman Good Neighbor Award Found.; past pres. bd. dirs. Memorah Med. Center Found., Found. for a Greater Kansas City; trustee Clearinghouse for Midcontinent Founds.; bd. regents Rockhurst Coll.; mem. Prime Time Com.; met. chmn. Nat. Alliance Businessmen; bd. govs. Am. Royal Assn. Served with USAAF, 1943-45. Decorated Air medal with 3 oak leaf clusters. Mem. Kansas City C. of C. (past pres.). Jewish. Clubs: Rotary, Oakwood Country, Kansas City Racquet, Carriage. Home: 6400 Wenonga Terr Shawnee Mission KS 66208 Office: 4410 Main St Kansas City MO 64111

BLOCH, IVAN SOL, realtor; b. Detroit, Nov. 16, 1940; s. Howard and Pauline Betty (Davis) B.; student U. Miami (Fla.), 1958-59, Oakland Community Coll., 1966-68; m. Linda Ehrlich, Oct. 14, 1963; children—Brian, Amy. Partner, Bloch Bros. Corp., land devel., Waterford, Mich., 1962-66; pres. Brian Realty, Birmingham, Mich., 1966—, Waterford Mortgage Co., Birmingham, 1968—, Uniprop/Mich. Mgmt. Co., Birmingham, 1969—. Co-chmn. finance Levin for Gov., 1970, 74, Kelly for Senate, 1972; mem. central finance com. Mich. Democratic party, 1973—; mem. Dem. Nat. Finance Com.; mem. Dem. 500 Club. Hon. mem. Boys Town. Mem. Nat. Assn. Real Estate Brokers, Real Estate Security and Syndication Inst. Mem. B'nai B'rith (nat. humanitarian award com. 1971-72). Home: 1440 Old Salem Ct Birmingham MI 48009 Office: 480 Pierce St Birmingham MI 48011

BLOCK, JEROME EDWARD, physician; b. Phila., Feb. 3, 1938; s. Charles and Eleanor Helen (Deutsch) B.; B.S., Muhlenberg Coll., 1960; M.D., N.J. Coll. Medicine, 1964; m. Lynne JoAnn Heckinger, Oct. 8, 1958; children—Vici Janis, Michael Alan, Debra Jill, Steven Jeffery. Intern in medicine Los Angeles County Gen. Hosp., Los Angeles, 1964-65. resident in internal medicine. 1965-67; resident in internal medicine Harbor Gen. Hosp., Torrance, Calif., 1967-68; gen. practice medicine, Monterey Park, Calif., 1965-67, practice medicine specializing in internal medicine, Sedalia, Mo., 1969—; mem. staffs Bothwell Meml. Hosp., Fitzgibbon Meml. Hosp., Marshall, Mo.; instr. in medicine, U. Calif. at Los Angeles, Torrance, 1968-69; asst. clin. prof. medicine, U. Mo., Columbia, 1969-73, asso. clin. prof., 1973—; med. dir. respiratory technician program State Fair Community Coll., Sedalia, 1975—. Served to maj. Army N.G., 1965-72. Recipient Tchr. of Year award Harbor Gen. Hosp., 1969; diplomate Am. Bd. Internal Medicine. Fellow A.C.P.; mem. Am., Mo. (del. 1973—) med. assns., Am. Soc. Internal Medicine, Pettis County (Mo.) Med. Soc. (pres. 1971-73), Royal Soc. Medicine. Contbr. articles to profl. jours. Home: Rural Route 2 Sedalia MO 65301 Office: 1718 S Ingram St Sedalia MO 65301

BLOCK, PAUL, JR., newspaper publisher, chemist; b. N.Y.C., May 11, 1911; s. Paul and Dina (Wallach) B.; grad. Hotchkiss Sch., Lakeville, Conn., 1929; A.B., Yale U., 1933; student Columbia U., 1933-34, Harvard U., 1934-35; Ph.D., Columbia U., 1943; m. Eleana Barnes Conley, 1940 (div. 1947); 1 son, Cyrus P.; m. 2d, Marjorie McNab Main, May 26th, 1948 (dec. Sept. 1960); children—Allan James, John Robinson; m. 3d, Mary Gall Petok, 1965; 3 children by previous marriage. Reporter Toledo Blade, 1935, became polit. writer, 1938, asst. editor, 1941, co-pub., 1942, now chmn. bd.; co-pub. Pitts. Post Gazette, 1944—; fellow Mellon Inst. Indsl. Research, Pitts., 1943-44, hon. fellow, dept. pharmacology, Yale U., 1948-49. Chmn. bd. trustees Med. Coll. Ohio, Toledo, 1964-70; chmn. Toledo Devel. Com., 1975—. Mem. Am. Chem. Soc. N.Y. Acad. Scis., Am. Soc. Newspaper Editors, Internat. Press Inst. (chmn. Am. Com. 1958-61), Sigma Xi. Home: 4059 River Rd Toledo OH 43614 Office: Toledo Blade Co 541 Superior St Toledo OH 43660

BLODGETT, GARY BURL, orthodontist; b. Pleasantville, Iowa, Oct. 17, 1937; s. Burl William and Ethel Ann (Taylor) B.; D.D.S., U. Iowa, 1962, M.S., 1967; m. Sandra Jean Hodgson, June 29, 1956; children—Todd, Troy, Suzette. Chief dental officer Fed. Correctional Instn., LaTuna, Tex., 1963-65; practice dentistry specializing in orthodontics, Mason City, Ia., 1967—. Dental div. chmn. United Fund, Mason City, 1969; membership com. YMCA, 1968-72. Served with USPHS, 1962-65. Mem. North Central Dist. Dental Soc. (pres. 1971-72), Am., Iowa dental assns., Iowa Orthodontic Soc. (pres. 1974), Am. Assn. Orthodontists, Midwestern Soc. Orthodontists. Republican. Methodist. Mason. Home: 1050 Meadow Lake Dr Mason City IA 50401 Office: 307 Brick and Tile Bldg Mason City IA 50401

BLODGETT, GEOFFREY THOMAS, educator; b. Hanover, N.H., Oct. 13, 1931; s. Harold William and Dorothy Briggs B.; A.B., Oberlin Coll., 1953; A.M., Harvard U., 1956, Ph.D., 1961; m. Jane McCall Taggart, Dec. 22, 1954; children—Lauren Elizabeth, Barbara Jane. Sally McCall. Instr. history Oberlin Coll., 1960-62, asst. prof., 1962-66, asso. prof., 1966-68, prof., 1968—, chmn. dept. history, 1969-73; columnist Oberlin News-Tribune, 1972—. Mem. Oberlin City Planning Commn.. 1970-73; chmn. Oberlin Hist. Preservation Commn., 1974—. Served with U.S. Navy, 1953-55. Social Sci. Research Council fellow, 1959-60; Am. Council of Learned Socs. fellow, 1973-74; Charles Warren Center fellow, 1973-74. Mem. Am. Hist. Assn., Orgn. Am. Historians. Democrat. Author: The Gentle Reformers: Massachusetts Democrats in the Cleveland Era, 1966; contbr. essays to The Gilded Age, 1970; Victorian America. 1976. Home: 273 Oak St Oberlin OH 44074 Office: Department History Oberlin College Oberlin OH 44074

BLODGETT, JOHN WOOD, former lumber exec.; b. Grand Rapids, Mich., May 24, 1901; s. John Wood and Minnie (Cumnock) B.; A.B., Harvard, 1923; m. Sarah Reed Gallagher, Sept. 28, 1939 (div. Dec. 1963); children—Julia Reed (Mrs. John R. Curtis, Jr.), Katherine Blodgett Winter, Sarah Wood (Mrs. Prescott Nelson Dunbar); m. 2d, Edith Irwin Ferris, June 21, 1967. Dir. U.S. Nat. Bank, 1929-52; chmn. Blodgett Co., Ltd., 1932-37; pres. Mich.-Cal. Lumber Co., Camino, Calif., 1936-65; pres. Consolidated Timber Co., Portland, Oreg., 1934-49; chmn. Wright-Blodgett Co., Ltd., Grand Rapids, Mich., 1936-47; pres. Western Mgmt. Co., Grand Rapids, 1937-55; sec., mem. bd. mgrs. Hill-Davis Lumber Co., Arcata, Calif., 1937-58; dir. Arcata Redwood Co., 1947-67, sec., 1959-66; dir. Arcata Nat. Corp., 1967-68; dir. Booth-Kelly Lumber Co., 1941-59. Trustee Blodgett Meml. Hosp., Grand Rapids, 1941—; mem. overseer com. to visit Harvard Library, 1972—, to visit Harvard dept. athletics, 1973—; adv. com. Harvard Fund Council, 1952-55; mem. overseers com. to visit Harvard Forest, 1949-62. Mem. U.S. Naval Inst., USN League, Am. Ordnance Assn., S.A.R. Mason. Clubs: River, Harvard (N.Y.C.); Bohemian (San Francisco); Chicago, Racquet (Chgo.); Kent Country, University, Peninsular (Grand Rapids); University (Portland, Ore.). Home: 250 Plymouth Rd SE Grand Rapids MI 49506 Office: Peoples Bldg Grand Rapids MI 49503

BLODGETT, VIRGINIA JUNE BALLARD (MRS. RALPH WESLEY BLODGETT), ednl. adminstr.; b. Detroit; d. William King and Marie (Crossley) Ballard; A.B., Asbury Coll., 1935; M.S., Butler U., 1967; postgrad. U. Louisville, Ind. State U., Ball State U., Ohio State U., San Francisco State U., Ph.D. (hon.), Colo. State Christian Coll.; m. Ralph Wesley Blodgett, Sept. 25, 1935; children—Vivian Sue (Mrs. William E. Shields), Rebecca June (Mrs. Ron Downing), Judith Elaine (Mrs. David Purvis). Tchr. Dependent Schs., Europe, 1951-54, English various high schs., Ind., Va., Fla., 1942—, chmn. English dept. Woodview Sch., Indpls., 1961—, dean girls, 1964—; instr. evening div. Ind. Central Coll., Indpls., 1964-69, adult counselor, 1965—. Active various community drives. Gen. Electric Co. fellow, 1967. Mem. Am., Ind. (sec. 1969) assns. women deans and counselors, Ind. State Tchrs. Assn., Warren Twp. Classroom Tchrs., Central Ind. Personnel and Guidance Assn., Alpha Delta Kappa. Methodist (tchr. ch. schs. 1935—). Home: PO Box 21 Willow Branch IN 46187 Office: 901 N Post Rd Indianapolis IN 46219

BLOEMKER, GERALD WILLIAM, concrete co. sales exec.; b. Independence, Mo., Jan. 9, 1936; s. August Ernest and Ethel Rose (Bennet) B.; student Kansas City Jr. Coll., 1955, 56; m. Mary Janice Markland, Dec. 19, 1958; 1 son, Michael Douglas. Clk. mail room Standard Oil Co. Ind., Kansas City, Mo., 1954-55, asst. supt. mail ops., 1955-57, clk. bulk sta. and truck ins., 1957-59; sales desk W.S. Dickey Clay Co., Kansas City, Mo., 1959-61, gen. rep. sales, 1961-62, terr. rep. sales, 1962-65, mgr. Kansas City sales and ops., 1965-76, sales rep. Barbour Concrete Co., Inc., Independence, 1976—. Bd. dirs. Stanley C. Palmer Meml. Scholarship Fund. Mem. Independence (Mo.), Kansas City (Mo.) C. of C., Am. Pub. Works Assn. (pres. chpt. 1973), Nat. Am. Pub. Works Assn. (mem. ho. of dels. 1974), Soc. Am. Mil. Engrs., Internat. Assn. Plumbing and Mech. Ofcls., Internat. Conf. Bldg. Ofcls., Mid-West Concrete Industry Bd., Kansas City City Engrs. Club, Heavy Constrn. Assn. Kansas City, Nat. Rifle Assn. (instr. hunter safety 1969-75). Home: 12310 E 41st Terr Independence MO 64055 Office: 21521 Truman Rd Independence MO 64056

BLOM, ERIC DAVIS, speech pathologist; b. Hamburg, N.Y., Sept. 24, 1943; s. Knut A. and Kitty (Davis) B.; B.S., Miami U., Oxford, Ohio, 1966; M.A., Ball State U., 1967; Ph.D., U. Md., 1972; m. Sally Morrison, June 9, 1968. Instr. speech pathology U. Md., College Park, 1967-70; trainee audiology, speech pathology VA Hosp., Washington, 1970-72, chief audiology, speech pathology service, VA Hosp., Indpls., 1972—; adj. asso. prof. speech pathology Purdue U., West Lafayette, Ind., 1974—, Ball State U., Muncie, Ind., 1974—; lectr. in field. Vice-pres. bd. dirs. Marion County unit Ind. div. Am. Cancer Soc., 1976—, state service com., 1975—. Va. Edn. and Tng. grantee, 1975—. Mem. Am. (certificate clin. competence), Ind. speech and hearing assns. Republican. Lutheran. Researcher assessment surg., prosthetic methods of voice restoration after surg. removal of larynx. Office: 1481 W 10th St Indianapolis IN 46202

BLOMGREN, DONALD M., hosp. adminstr.; b. Berwyn, Ill., July 9, 1934; s. Maurice A. and Alice E. (Billings) B.; B.A., Augustana Coll., Rock Island, Ill., 1956; m. Harriett C. Johnson, Aug. 2, 1958; children—Susan, William. Asst. adminstr. MacNeal Meml. Hosp., Berwyn, 1956-69; adminstr. Lawrence County Meml. Hosp., Lawrenceville, Ill., 1969—. Chmn. Lawrence County Home Health Adv. Com., 1970—. Mem. Am., Ill. hosp. assns. Presbyterian. Clubs: Elks, Kiwanis (past pres.). Home: 1005 Judd St Lawrenceville IL 62439 Office: W State St Lawrenceville IL 62439

BLOMGREN, HOLTON EUGENE, assn. exec.; b. Mpls., Mar. 22, 1916; s. Henning Alfred and Jean (Holton) B.; B.A., U. Minn., 1938; M.B.A., Harvard U., 1940; M.A., George Washington U., 1965; grad. Army Command and Gen. Staff Coll., 1956, Army War Coll., 1963; m. Elouise Breckenridge, Nov. 14, 1942; children—Peter Frederick, Donna Lynne (Mrs. Aubrey S. Garrison), Philip Michael, Diane Elizabeth. Joined U.S. Army, 1941, advanced through grades to col., 1971; faculty Adj. Gen. Sch., 1942-47; gen. staff Hdqrs. Europe, 1948-51; faculty Army Finance Sch., 1952-55, comdt., 1967-71; gen. staff Army Hdqrs., Washington, 1956-60, 63-65, Vietnam, 1965-66; ret., 1971; chief exec. Ind. Manufactured Housing Assn., Indpls., 1971—. Financial adviser Minister Def. Thailand, 1960-62; zoning cons. County Plan Commns. State Ind.; registered lobbyist Ind. Gen. Assembly; govtl. affairs rep. manufactured housing industry. Decorated Legion Merit with oak leaf cluster, Air medal, Bronze Star medal. Named Sagamore of Wabash; Legion of Hoosier Heroes. Mem. Ret. Officers Assn., Harvard Alumni Assn., Chi Psi. Club: Columbia. Home: 6909 Crickelwood Rd Indianapolis IN 46220 Office: 3210 Rand Rd Indianapolis IN 46241

BLOMGREN, OSCAR CLARENCE, JR., mfg. co. exec.; b. Winnetka, Ill., Apr. 16, 1929; s. Oscar Clarence and Carrie Elizabeth (Williamson) B.; A.B., Dartmouth, 1951; m. Priscilla Anne Perry, Feb. 16, 1952 (div. 1975); children—Oscar Clarence III, Teri Lynn; m. Beryl Anderson Houdzk, 1975. With Tuxco Corp., North Chicago, Ill., 1952—, v.p., 1958-67, pres., 1967—, also dir.; exec. v.p., dir. Inter-Probe, Inc., 1969—; dir. Von Toll Designs, Inc. Dir. Lake County Republican Fedn., 1962-68; chmn. No. Ill. Citizens for

Goldwater, 1963-64; chmn. Greisheimer Campaign Com., 1972—. Recipient Design Excellence award Design News, 1969, Entrepreneur of Year award, 1973. Mem. Electrostatic Soc. Am., Navy League (pres. Lake County council 1975-76), Gamma Delta Chi. Club: Exchange (pres. 1954-58) (Evanston). Patentee in field. Home: 1230 North Western Ave Lake Forest IL 60045 Office: 1539 Morrow St North Chicago IL 60064

BLOMQUIST, ROGER VINCENT, environ. engring. co. exec.; b. Iron Mountain, Mich., Feb. 11, 1944; s. William Thure and Ellen Dagmar (Johnson) B.; B.S. with honors, Mich. State U., 1966; Ph.D., U. Wis., 1971; exec. devel. program Cornell U., 1976; m. Patricia Ann Beaty, Sept. 6, 1969; children—Jason, Matthew. Agronomist, Internat. Minerals and Chem. Co., Libertyville, Ill., 1966; research asso. U. Wis., Madison, 1966-70; postdoctoral research fellow U. Guelph, Ont., Can., 1971; v.p., treas., dir. Nat. Biocentric Inc., St. Paul, 1971—; mem. adv. com. Rice Creek Watershed Dist.; mem. Ramsey County Engring. and Environ. Adv. Com. Precinct vice chmn. Democratic Farm Labor party, 1976-78, del., dist. conv., 1972, 74, 76, del. county conv., 1972. Bush Found. fellow, 1976; Wis. Alumni Research Found. fellow, 1967-70; Louis Ware scholar, 1966; 4-H scholar, 1962-66. Mem. Nat., Minn. assns. environ. profls., Water Pollution Control Fedn., Air Pollution Control Assn., Izaak Walton League, Am. Soc. Agronomy, Sales and Mktg. Execs., New Brighton Jaycees (v.p. 1973), Sigma Xi, Alpha Zeta. Lutheran. Home: 2023 Pleasant View Dr New Brighton MN 55112 Office: 2233 Hamline Ave N Saint Paul MN 55113

BLOMSTER, GALEN GRANT, banker; b. Rush City, Minn., Sept. 29, 1942; s. Grant Kenneth and Frances (Norling) B.; B.S., U. Minn., 1964; M.S., Purdue U., 1966, Ph.D., 1969; m. Judith Irene Englof, June 27, 1964; children—Robert Dean, Mark Andrew, David Grant. With Nat. Cash Register Co., Dayton, Ohio, 1968-74, operations research cons. retail systems devel., 1970-74; corp. economist, dir. corp. bus. planning systems devel. Magnavox Co., Ft. Wayne, Ind., 1974-75; corporate economist N.Am. Phillips Co., Fort 1975-77; sr. economist Northwestern Nat. Bank, Mpls., 1977—; 1975—; founder, part-owner Agrl. Market Research Inc., Des Moines, 1967—. Dairy and Food Industry Supply Assn. fellow, 1964-65; U.S. Dept. Agr. grantee, 1966-67. Mem. Am. Marketing Assn., N. Am. Soc. Corporate Planners, Inst. Mgmt. Scis., Am. Agrl. Econ. Assn., Alpha Zeta. Lutheran (treas. ch. council 1969-76). Home: 16935 21st Ave N Wayzata MN 55391 Office: Northwestern Nat Bank 7th and Marquette Minneapolis MN 55480

BLONSKY, EUGENE RICHARD, neurologist; b. Chgo., Dec. 28, 1934; s. Louis J. and Winnifred Frieda (Weinberg) B.; A.B. cum laude, Harvard, 1955; M.D., Northwestern U., 1959; m. Susan Lynne Schmidt, Nov. 23, 1974; children—Peter Miller, Susan Beth, Adam Neil, Stephen Richard. Intern, Cook County Hosp., Chgo., 1959-60; resident neurology Northwestern U. Med. Center, 1960-63; practice medicine, specializing in neurology, 1963—; attending staff Northwestern Meml. Hosp.; cons. neurology Highland Park Hosp.; faculty Northwestern U. Med. Sch., Chgo., 1963—, asst. prof. neurology, 1967—; faculty Cook County Grad. Sch. Medicine, Chgo., 1971—. Mem. med. adv. bd. United Parkinson Found., 1968—. Diplomate Am. Bd. Psychiatry and Neurology. Mem. Am. Acad. Neurology, AMA, AAAS, Am. Psychiat. Assn., Am. Geriatric Soc., Chgo. Neurol. Soc. (pres. 1975-76), Sigma Xi, Phi Delta Epsilon. Home: 990 N Lake Shore Dr Chicago IL 60611 Office: 251 E Chicago Ave Chicago IL 60611

BLOOD, ROBERT O., marriage counselor; b. Concord, N.H., Aug. 15, 1921; s. Robert Oscar and Pauline (Shepard) B.; m. Margaret Cheek, Aug. 26, 1944; children—Peter, Alan, Lawrence, Jonathan. A.B., Dartmouth Coll., 1942; B.D., Yale Div. Sch., 1945; M.A., U. Minn., 1950; Ph.D., U. N.C., 1952. Mem. faculty William Penn Coll., 1946-49, Merrill-Palmer Inst., 1951-52; mem. faculty sociology U. Mich., 1952-67, Internat. Christian U. (Japan), 1967-69; mem. faculty Pendle Hill, Wallingford, Pa., 1969-73; pvt. practice marriage counseling, exptl. workshops, Ann Arbor, Mich., 1973—. Fellow Am. Assn. Marriage and Family Counselors; mem. Nat. Council Family Relations, Assn. Humanistic Psychology, Phi Beta Kappa. Fulbright Found. grantee, 1958-59. Author: (with D. M. Wolfe) Husbands and Wives, 1960; Love Match and Arranged Marriage, 1967; The Family, 1972; (with Margaret C. Blood) Marriage, 1978. Address: 2005 Penncraft Ct Ann Arbor MI 48103

BLOODGOOD, DOUGLAS COTTON, banker; b. Grand Rapids, Mich., Oct. 9, 1938; s. Thomas Clinton and Rose Aileen (Cotton) B.; B.A., Mich. State U., 1964; m. Kathryn Ann Cross, Oct. 7, 1967; children—Amy Aileen, Patrick Douglas. Comml. loan officer Mich. Nat. Bank, Grand Rapids, 1964-69, v.p. internat., 1969—. Adv. com. marketing dept. Ferris State Coll., bus. sch. Grand Rapids Jr. Coll. Served with USNR, 1957-60. Mem. World Affairs Council Western Mich. Mich. Internat. Council. Congregationalist. Clubs: Lions, W. Mich. World Trade. Home: 1040 Oakleigh RD NW Grand Rapids MI 49504 Office: 65 Monroe Ave NW Grand Rapids MI 49501

BLOOM, BARBARA IRENE, labor relations specialist; b. Chgo., Jan. 16, 1933; d. Max S. and Carolyn Barbara (Gumbiner) B.; B.A., Oberlin Coll., 1954; M.S. in Indsl. Relations, Loyola U., Chgo., 1976. Asst. buyer, Sterling Lindner Davis, Cleve., 1954-55; asst. Midwest editor Mademoiselle mag., Chgo., 1955-59; asst. buyer Bramson, Inc., Chgo., 1959-60; editor Am. Savs. & Loan Inst., Chgo., 1960-62; pub. relations writer, mag. editor Traffice Inst. Northwestern U., Evanston, 1962-65; staff specialist manpower and labor relations, sec. Council on Manpower and Edn. Am. Hosp. Assn., Chgo., 1965—; mem. health manpower adv. com. Nat. Health Council; chmn. adv. com. health careers guidebook HEW Labor Dept. Recipient Cynthia Warren award Health and Manpower, 1974; Merit certificate Indsl. Editors Assn. Chgo.. 1965. Mem. Am. Personnel and Guidance Assn., Execs. Club Chgo., Chgo. Area Oberlin Alumni Club (exec. com.). Home: 2416 Greenleaf Ave W Chicago IL 60645 Office: 840 N Lake Shore Dr Chicago IL 60611

BLOOM, MAX S., tobacco distbr.; b. Chgo., Aug. 2, 1907; s. Samuel and Mary (Becker) B.; B.A., U. Chgo., 1928; m. Mary F. Bernstein, Apr. 11, 1967; children—Donald, Barbara, Stephen. With S. Bloom, Inc., Chgo., 1928—, pres., now chmn. Mem. Nat., Ill. assns. tobacco distbrs., Nat. Confectionary Wholesalers Assn. Club: Rotary. Home: 2933 Sheridan Rd Chicago IL 60657 Office: 5401 S Dansher Rd Country Side IL 60625

BLOOM, SAM OLIVER, farmer, state legislator; b. nr. Penock, Minn., June 18, 1915; s. Lars O. and Malene (Blom) B.; student pub. schs. of N.D.; m. Thora P. Slaaen, Oct. 24, 1936; children—Don O., Roger D., Marjorie Ann. Farmer, Alkabo, N.D., 1936—; owner, mgr. gen. store, 1939-58; mem. N.D. Ho. of Reps., 1958—, chmn. edn. com., 1965. Dir. Alkabo Farmers Elevator. Local chmn., bd. dirs. March of Dimes, 1948-55; chmn., bd. dirs. Cancer Dr., 1945-52; vice chmn. adv. com. Williston center U. N.D., mem. adv. com. vocat. edn., 1969—, pres., 1973-75. Mem. Sch. Bd. Alkabo, 1944-59, pres. bd., 1945-59, bd. mem. Divide County reorganized sch. dist., 1962-64, 71-76, pres., 1974-76; Ivy County Sch. Officer, 1975-77; supr., Westby Twp. Bd., 1944-47, chmn., 1945-47; mem. Divide County Redistricting Bd., 1953-59. Mem. Nat. Farm Orgn. (mem. Divide county grain bd. 1968—, chmn. 1968-69), Divide County Hist. Soc. (dir. 1970—), Divide County Sch. Officers Orgn. (pres. 1957-59). Lutheran (deacon). Club: Toastmasters (pres. 1976—). Address: Grenora ND 58845

BLOOM, STEPHEN JOEL, distbn. vending co. exec.; b. Chgo., Feb. 27, 1936; s. Max Samuel and Carolyn (Gumbiner) B.; B.B.A., U. Mich., 1958; m. Nancy Lee Gillan, Aug. 24, 1957; children—Anne, Bradley, Thomas, Carolyn. Salesman. then gen. mgr. Cigarette Service Co., Countryside, Ill., 1957-65, pres., chief exec. officer, i965—; pres., dir. Inter-Continental Cons. Corp., Balt. Bd. dirs. Clarendon Hills (Ill.) United Fund, 1975—; finance chmn. DuPage County Republican Com., 1976. Named Man of Year, Chgo. Tobacco Table, 1972. Mem. Nat. Automatic Mdsg. Assn. (Minuteman award 1974), Nat. (Young Exec. of Year award 1973), Ill. assns. tobacco distbrs. Club: Chgo. Rotary. Home: 3 Hamill Ln Clarendon Hills IL 60514 Office: 5401 S Dansher Rd Countryside IL 60525

BLOOMQUIST, ARNOLD ROBERT, sheet metal mfg. co. exec.; b. Mpls., Feb. 16, 1927; s. Eric and Esther (Johnson) B.; B.M.E., U. Minn., 1950; B.S., William Mitchell Coll., 1968; m. Norma Loberg, May 24, 1952; children—Mark, Michael, Steven. Mgr. die casting Char-Lynn Co., Mpls.. 1950-67; v.p., Milw. Die Cast Co., 1967-69, Hartzell Mfg. Co., St. Paul, 1970-73; pres. H.J. Shotwell Co., Mpls., 1974—. Served with USAAF, 1945-46. Mem. Metal Fabricators Assn. Republican. Lutheran. Rotary. Home: 6720 Point Dr Edina MN 55435 Office: 5721 W 36th St Minneapolis MN 55416

BLOOR, THOMAS HAROLD, med. supply co. exec.; b. Mansfield, Ohio, Mar. 31, 1930; s. J. William and Miriam V. (Rife) B.; B.A., Amherst Coll., 19S1; m. Mary Claparols. Sept. 15, 19S6 (div.); children—William M., Joseph T. Salesman, Caldwell & Bloor Co., Warren, Ohio, 1954-56, gen. mgr., Mansfield, Ohio, 1957-62, pres., Mansfield. 1962—; dir. Richland Trust Co., Mansfield Bldg. & Loan, Lumberman's Mut. Ins. Co. Finance chmn. Richland County Republicans, 1964-70. Served to sgt., USMC, 1951-53. Mem. Am. Surg. Trade Assn. (v.p.). Methodist. Home: 714 Cloverleaf Ct Mansfield OH 44904

BLOSSER, HENRY GABRIEL, educator; b. Harrisonburg, Va., Mar. 16, 1928; s. Emanuel and Leona (Branum) B.; B.S., U. Va., 1951, M.S., 1952, Ph.D., 1954; m. Priscilla May Beard, June 30, 1951 (div. Oct. 1972); children—William Henry, Stephan Emanuel, Gabe Fawley, Mary Margaret; m. 2d, Mary Margaret Gray, Mar. 16, 1973. Physicist, Oak Ridge Nat. Lab., 1954-56, group leader, 1956-68; asso. prof. Mich. State U., East Lansing, 1958-61, prof., dir. Cyclotron Lab., 1961—; cons. Oak Ridge Nat. Lab., 1958-62, 72—, U. Mich., 1960-61, Washington U., St. Louis, 1961-62, Lawrence Radiation Lab., 1962, U. Md., 1962-65; Princeton, 1965—. Bd. dirs. Midwestern Univs. Research Assos., 1960-63. Served with USNR, 1946-48. NSF predoctoral fellow, 1953-54; NSF sr. postdoctoral fellow, 1966-67; Guggenheim fellow, 1973-74. Recipient Mich. State U. Distinguished Faculty award, 1972. Mem. Phi Beta Kappa, Sigma Xi, Kappa Alpha Order. Home: 609 Beech St East Lansing MI 48823

BLOTCKY, ALAN JAY, nuclear physicist; b. Omaha, July 5, 1930; s. Paul and Evalyn Sylvia (Meyer) B.; B.S., Carnegie Inst. Tech., 1952; M.S., Creighton U., 1971; m. Wanda June Richmond, Jan. 20, 1953; children—Steven, Beth. Sect. head, mass spectrometer maintenance sect. Goodyear Atomic Corp., Portsmouth, Ohio, 1953-55; cons. physicist, mfrs. rep. A.J. Blotcky & Assos., Omaha, 1955-57; reactor supr. VA Hosp., Omaha, 1957—, research physicist, 1957—, radiation safety officer, 1957—; instr. Creighton U. Coll Medicine, 1958—. Service chief Omaha/Douglas County Civil Def., 1962—; pres. Operation Bridge, Inc., 1972, 77—, Swanson Community Club, 1966-67, Omaha Awareness and Action, 1976—. Recipient Chief Med. Dirs. Pub. Service award VA, 1970. Mem. Am. Nuclear Soc., Soc. Nuclear Medicine, Am. Soc. Testing Materials, Health Physics Soc., Am. Assn. Physicists in Medicine, Instrument Soc. Am.. Am. Phys. Soc. Jewish. Club: Rotary (pres. West Omaha 1973-74). Contbr. articles in field to profl. jours. Home: 306 N 92d St Omaha NE 68114 Office: VA Hosp 4101 Woolworth Ave Omaha NE 68105

BLOUIN, MICHAEL T., Congressman. Mem. 94th-95th Congresses from 2d Iowa dist. Office: Room 213 Cannon House Office Bldg Washington DC 20515

BLOUNT, WILBUR CLANTON, physician; b. Columbus, Ohio, Feb. 5, 1929; s. Percy Hammond and Bayetta (Dent) B.; B.Sc. in Bacteriology. Ohio State U., 1951, postgrad., 1951-52, M.D., 1959; m. Elsie M. Paradis, Mar. 20, 1976; children—Angela Diane, Wilbur Salee. Intern U. Ill. Research and Exptl. Hosps., Chgo., 1959-60; practice gen. medicine, Williamson, W. Va., 1960-62; resident dept. ophthalmology Coll. Medicine, Ohio State U., 1964-67; spl. NIH fellow retinal surgery U. Minn., 1967-71; practice medicine specializing in ophthalmology, Oberlin, Ohio, 1969-71; mem. staff U. Ky. Med. Center, Good Samaritan Hosp., Lexington, Ky.; instr. ophthalmology Coll. Medicine, Ohio State U., Columbus, 1970-71; asst. prof. surgery, dept. ophthalmology U. Ky. Med. Center, Lexington, 1971-77. Served to 1st lt. USAF, 1954-56. Fellow Aerospace Med. Assn. (asso.) A.C.S.; mem. AMA, Ohio, Lorain County med. assns., Soc. U.S. Air Force Flight Surgeons, Soc. Mil. Ophthalmologists. Club: Rotary. Home: 837 Sheridan Ave Columbus OH 43209 Office: 340 E Town St Columbus OH 43215

BLUE, JANET L. ROBERTS (MRS. SHERWOOD BLUE), lawyer; b. Hamilton, Ohio, June 21, 1933; d. Sam G. and Jessie (Weybright) Roberts; A.B., Ind. U., 1954, J.D., LL.B., 1957; m. Sherwood Blue, Apr. 9, 1961. Admitted to Ind. bar, 1957; practiced in Indpls., 1957—; mem. firm Sherwood Blue, 1957-63; partner firm Blue & Roberts, 1964—; mem. staff Ct. Appeals Ind., 1967—, commr.-adminstr., 1970—. Mem. Meth. Hosp. Vols. Corps, 1963—, Indpls. Symphonic Choir, Indpls. Matinee Musicale. Meth. Hosp. Found. fellow, 1971—. Mem. Internat., Am., Ind., Indpls. bar assns., Indpls. Legal Aid Soc., Indpls. Lawyers Assn., Am. Judicature Soc., Art Assn. Indpls., Meth. Hosp. White Cross Guild, Ind. U. Sch. Law Alumni Assn. Republican. Methodist. Clubs: Indianapolis Athletic, Athenaeum Turners, Riviera, Indianapolis Press. Home: 1460 E 77th St Indianapolis IN 46240 Office: Ill Bldg Indianapolis IN 46204

BLUEMLE, PAUL EDWARD, ednl. adminstr.; b. Springfield, Ohio, Sept. 9, 1926; s. Carl Henry and Mary Ann (Wolbert) B.; B.B.A. magna cum laude, Xavier U. (Ohio), 1951; M.A., U. Oreg., 1953; postgrad. (All-Univ. grantee) Mich. State U., 1957-63; m. Helen Jean Smain, Sept. 13, 1958; children—Joy, Christine, Jude, Laura, Peter. Reporter, Springfield (Ohio) Daily News, 1943-51; exec. sec. Young Christian Students, Chgo., 1952-54; dir. pub. relations Thomas More Coll., Covington, Ky., 1954-55; bus. mgr. Today mag., Chgo., 1955-56; instr. Mich. State U., E. Lansing, 1956-59; editor univ. publs. Bowling Green State U., Ohio, 1959-60; asst. prof., asso. prof., exec. sec., asst. dean Monteith Coll., Wayne State U., Detroit, 1960-76; admissions dir., asst. to v.p. for academic affairs, asst. dean U. Detroit, 1976—; bd. dirs. Chgo. Research Group Corp., 1956-73. Pres. sch. bd. St. Mary's Parish, Royal Oak, Mich., 1966; mem. Citizens Adv. Commn., Ferndale (Mich.) Sch. Dist., 1972; chmn. com. on community Archdiocese of Detroit, 1972-74. Served with U.S. Army, 1945-46. Mem. Nat. Assn. Coll. Admissions Counselors, Soc. Profl. Journalists, Am. Newspaper Guild (v.p. Springfield 1945), AAUP (sec. Wayne State U. chpt. 1971-72), Kappa Tau Alpha. Roman Catholic. Home: 16 Hanover Rd Pleasant Ridge MI 48069 Office: 4001 W McNichols Rd Detroit MI 48221

BLUESTEIN, JUDITH ANN, diversified industry exec., educator; b. Cin., Apr. 2, 1948; d. Paul Harold and Joan Ruth (Straus) Bluestein; B.A., U. Pa., 1969; postgrad. Am. Sch. Classical Studies, Athens, Greece, 1968, Vergilian Soc., Italy, 1970, 75, Hebrew Union Coll. Jewish Inst. Religion, Jerusalem, 1971; M.A. in Religion (university fellow), Case Western Res. U., 1973, M.A. in Latin, 1973; postgrad. Am. Acad., Rome, 1975. Sec., Paul H. Bluestein & Co., Cin., 1964—; v.p. Panel Machine Co., 1966—, Blujay Corp., 1966—, Ermet Products Corp., 1966—; partner Companhia Engenheiros Industrial Bluestein do Brasil, Cin., 1971—; tchr. Cin. Pub. Schs., 1973—. Mem. Archeological Inst. Am., Classical Assn. Middle West and South (v.p. Ohio 1976—), Am. Classical League, Ohio Classical Conf. (council 1976—), Vergilian Soc., Soc. Bibl. Lit., Am. Philological Assn., Philol. Inst., Cin. Assn. Tchrs. Classics (pres. 1977-78), N.Am. Patristics Soc., Cin. Tchrs. Assn., Ohio Edn. Assn., NEA. Address: 3420 Section Rd Cincinnati OH 45237

BLUESTEIN, PAUL HAROLD, mgmt. engr.; b. Cin., June 14, 1923; s. Norman and Eunice D. (Schullman) B.; B.S., Carnegie Inst. Tech., 1946, B. Engring. in Mgmt. Engring., 1946; M.B.A., Xavier U., 1973; m. Joan Ruth Straus, May 17, 1943; children—Alice Sue (Mrs. Greenbaum), and Judith Ann. Time study engr. Lodge & Shipley Co., 1946-47; adminstrv. engr. Randall Co., 1947-52; partner Paul H. Bluestein & Co., mgmt. cons., 1952—, Seinsheimer-Bluestein Mgmt. Services, 1964—, Companhia Engenheiros Industrial Bluestein do Brasil, 1970—; gen. mgr. Baker Refrigeration Co., 1953-56; pres., dir. Tabor Mfg. Co. 1953-54, Blujay Corp., 1954—, Blatt & Ludwig Corp., 1954-57, Jason Industries, Inc., 1954-57, Hamilton-York Corp., 1954-57, Earle Hardware Mfg. Co., 1955-57, Hermas Machine Co., 1956—, Panel Machine Co., Ermet Products Corp. 1957—, Tyco Labs., Inc., 1968-69, All-Tech Industries, 1969, Del. Tisco Corp., 1970-71; gen. mgr. Hafleigh & Co., 1959-60; sr. v.p., gen. mgr., McCauley Ind. Corp., 1959-60; v.p., gen. mgr. Farmco Machine div. Worden-Allen Co., 1974-75; gen. mgr. Am. Art Works div. Rapid-Am. Corp., 1960-63; sec.-treas., dir. Liberty Baking Co., 1964-65; pres. Duguesne Baking Co., 1964-65, Goddard Bakers, Inc., 1964-65; pub. Merger and Acquisition Digest, 1962—; exec. v.p. Peck, Stow & Wilcox Co., 1976-77; dir. Norameo, Inc., 1964-67. Served from pvt. to tech. sgt. AUS, 1943-46. Registered profl. engr., Ohio. Mem. ASME, Soc. Internat. Devel., Am. Inst. Indsl. Engrs., Joint Engring. Mgmt. Conf. Mem. B'nai B'rith. Home: 3420 Section Rd Amberley Village Cincinnati OH 45237 Office: 3420 Section Rd Cincinnati OH 45237

BLUHM, MAURICE JOSEPH, realtor; b. Chgo., Apr. 7, 1916; s. Joseph V. and Rose (Bailey) B.; B.B.A., Northwestern U., 1938; m. Ethel Mary Meyer, July 4, 1940; children—Mark Alan, Barbara Ann. Auditor, Gen. Operating Co., Chgo., 1934-36, supr., 1936-37, gen. mgr., 1937-41; founder Midwest Operating Co., Kansas City, Mo., 1944, now pres.; pres. Maurice J. Bluhm & Co., Realtors, Kansas City, 1945—, Mo., 1962—, Bluhm Investment Co., Inc., Kansas City, 1966—; pres. Plaza Inn Co., Kansas City, Plaza Motor Inn, Inc., Plaza Inn Internat., Inc.; dir., mem. exec. com. Starlight Theatre, Kan. City. Pres. Mayor's Corps of Progress for Greater Kansas City, 1973-76, vice chmn. bd. dirs., 1976—; commr. Greater Kansas City Sports Commn. Bd. dirs., mem. exec. com. Conv. and Visitors Bur.; trustee Kansas City Philharmonic Orch.; bd. dirs. Nat. Council on Alcoholism, Country Club Plaza Assn.; bd. govs. Am. Royal Assn. Served with USAAF, 1941-44. Decorated Purple Heart, Air medal with silver oak leaf cluster; named Man of Yr., Mo. Hotel and Motel Assn., 1972; named Man of Year Fleet Res. Assn., 1972, ann. Humanitarian award, 1976. Mem. Hotel and Motel Greeters Assn. Internat., gov.), Nat. Assn. Real Estate Bds., Nat. Inst. Real Estate Brokers, Ark.-Mo.-Kans.-Okla. Lodging Assn. (pres. 1971-72), Mo. (v.p. 1966-73, pres. 1973-74), Kansas City (pres. 1969-72, chmn. bd. 1972-75) hotel and motel assns., Mo., Kansas City real estate assns., Nat., Mo. restaurant assns., Am. Legion, Kansas City C. of C., Mo. C. of C. Mason (Shriner, 32 deg.). Clubs: Meadowbrooke Golf and Country (Prairie Village, Kan.); Blue Springs (Mo.) Golf and Country; Question (Independence, Mo.); Mo. Yacht (Lake Lotawana, Mo.). Home: F-3 Route 4 Lake Lotawana Lees Summit MO 64063 Office: 45th and Main Sts care Hilton Plaza Inn Kansas City MO 64111

BLUM, ALBERT ELMER, veterinarian; b. nr. Hopewell, Mo., June 8, 1923; s. Edward Robert and Mollie Laura (Roux) B.; B.S., U. Mo., 1949, M.S., 1953, D.V.M., 1954; m. Martha Ava Reid, Sept. 23, 1950; 1 son, Karl Edward. Practice vet. medicine, Crystal City, Mo., 1954—; owner, mgr. Blum Animal Hosp., Festus-Crystal City, 1954—. Bd. dirs. Mo. Vet. Supply Co., Inc.; pres. Twin City Grocery, Inc., 1969—. Trustee, v.p. Jefferson County Health Dept., 1959—. Trustee Jefferson Coll., 1965—; bd. mgrs. Mo. Baptist Children's Home, 1962-68; county rep. Coll. Agr. Found., 1968. Served with USNR, 1943-46. Recipient Coll. Agr. Centennial award U. Mo., 1971; named Mo. Veterinarian of Yr., 1969. Mem. Mo., Am. vet. med. assns., Mo. Vet. Med. Alumni Assn. (pres. 1964), Festus-Crystal City C. of C. Mason (32 deg., Shriner); mem. Order Eastern Star. Baptist (chmn. bd. dirs. 1964). Home: Box 170 Crystal City MO 63019 Office: Box 170 Crystal City MO 63019

BLUM, ANDRE, city ofcl.; b. Hungary, Aug. 6, 1931; s. Nicholas and Rose (Fried) B.; brought to U.S., 1938, naturalized, 1945; B.S., U. Calif. at Los Angeles, 1956; M.A., U. Wis., 1969; m. Anna M. Sved, Aug. 30, 1961; children—Ronald E., Leah M. Sr. accountant Touche, Ross & Co., C.P.A.'s, N.Y.C., 1956-60; chief of audits County of Orange, Santa Ana, Calif., 1960-66; dir. finance City of Madison, Wis., 1966-73, dir. adminstrn., 1973—. Mem. Orange County (Calif.) Democratic Central Com., 1966. Served with USAF, 1951-53. C.P.A., N.Y., Cal., Wis. Mem. Wis. Municipal Finance Officers Assn. (state chmn. 1969—, chpt. pres. 1970), Am. Soc. Pub. Adminstrs. (chpt. pres. 1970), Inst. Internal Auditors (chpt. pres. 1966), Municipal Finance Officers Assn. U.S. and Can. (exec. bd. 1974-76). Home: 2634 Park Place Madison WI 53705 Office: City-County Bldg Madison WI 53709

BLUM, JOHN FRANCIS, realtor; b. Kansas City, Mo., Jan. 14, 1933; s. John Francis and Frances Clara (Geisendorf) B.; grad. high sch. Salesman, Rex Andrews Realtors, Kansas City, Mo., 1969-71; owner Blum Real Estate Co., Kansas City, Mo., 1971—. Mem. Longfellow Community Assn., 1972—, Longfellow Steering Com., 1973—. Mem. Mo. Assn. Realtors. Address: 2518 Charlotte St Kansas City MO 64108

BLUM, RICHARD CARL, musician, educator; b. Oak Park, Ill., Jan. 3, 1929; s. Carl William and Grace (Frohlich) B.; Mus.B., Eastman Sch. Music, 1950; m. Martha J. Francis, May 29, 1954; children—Carol, George. Prin. viola San Antonio Symphony, 1950-51, 53-56, Dallas Symphony, 1956-57, St. Louis Sinfonetta, 1953-57, Grant Park Symphony of Chgo., 1954-58; viola Pro Arte Quartet, U. Wis., 1957—; asso. prof. music U. Wis., Madison. Served with AUS, 1951-53. Home: 6501 Olympic Dr Madison WI 53705

BLUMBERG, BURTON STUART, health care exec.; b. Balt., Dec. 23, 1946; s. Harry and Jane Hoffman (Schwartz) B.; B.S., U. Md., 1968; M.B.A. in Health Care Adminstrn., George Washington U., 1970; m. Ana Delia Guerrero, Aug. 18, 1972; children—Johanna Patricia, Roland Tadeo. Cons., Venezuelan Dept. Health, Caracas, 1971-73; adminstrv. dir. Coromoto Hosp., Maracaibo, Venezuela, 1973-74; planning dir. Albert Einstein Coll. Medicine, Bronx, N.Y., 1974-76; pres. Gold Internat., N.Y.C., 1976; v.p. Hanover Publs., N.Y.C., 1976—; exec. dir. Migrant Health Service, Moorhead, Minn., 1976—; adj. prof. Moorhead State U., 1977. Recipient W. Glen Ebersole Merit Award, 1970. Mem. Am., Minn. pub. health assns., Nat., MW assns. community health centers, MW Migrant Health Consortium. Jewish. Home: 928 24th Ave S #15 Moorhead MN 56560 Office: Box 63 Moorhead State Univ Moorhead MN 56560

BLUME, HERBERT EDWARD, accountant; b. Tripoli, Ia., Sept. 20, 1917; s. William C. and Hulda D. (Hagenow) B.; student LaSalle Extension U., 1943-44; m. Elvera E. Kelling, Sept. 25, 1938; children—Carol (Mrs. Merlin H. Franzen), Marjorie (Mrs. Arthur F. Maynard), Marilyn (Mrs. Robert F. Seefeld). Farmer, nr. Tripoli, 1938-40; pvt. tax practice, Tripoli, 1944—; pvt. practice accounting, 1945—; treas. Tripoli Devel. Corp., 1959—; pres. Aids for Handicaps, Inc., 1958—; pub. Farm Record. Sec. Bremer County Zoning Commn., 1963—; pres. Accountants Assn. Iowa, 1970-71. Accounting practitioner, 1975—. Mem. Nat. Soc. Pub. Accountants (accredited), Assn. of Enrolled Agts., Luth. Laymen's League, Farm Bur. Republican. Lutheran (sec. finance Iowa dist. east Luth. Ch.-Mo. Synod, 1960-66). Patentee stairwalking crutches, 1945. Address: Tripoli IA 50676

BLUMENTALS, EDITE, advt. agy exec.; b. Riga, Latvia, Feb. 28, 1928; d. Rolands and Monica (Boka) B.; B.A., U. Minn., 1955. Came to U.S., 1950, naturalized, 1955. Adminstrv. asst. to dir. Minn. Alumni Assn., U. Minn., Mpls., 1957-61; asst. to field mgr. Mendota Research Group, Englewood, N.J., 1960-61; research supr. Campbell-Mithun, Inc., Mpls., Chgo., 1961—. Mem. Am. Mktg. Assn., Minn. Alumni Assn., Imeria. Home: 6007 N Sheridan Rd Chicago IL 60660 Office: 111 E Wacker Dr Chicago IL 60601

BLUMENTHAL, HERMAN THEODORE, educator; b. N.Y.C., Apr. 8, 1913; s. Samuel and Jennie (Price) B.; B.S., Rutgers U., 1934; M.S., U. Pa., 1936; Ph.D., Washington U., St. Louis, 1938, M.D., 1942; m. Eleonore Gottlieb, Aug. 18, 1940 (dec. 1972); children—Daniels S., Frederic A.; m. 2d, Margaret B. Phillips, May 29, 1974; 1 son, Edward P. Resident in pathology jewish Hosp., St. Louis, 1942-43; dir. labs. of various hosps., 1945-65; asso. prof. pathology St. Louis U., 1947-52; faculty Washington U., 1965—, research prof. gerontology, 1965—, dir. Midwest Med. Lab., 1965—. Served to maj. M.C., AUS, 1942-45. Mem. Soc. Exptl. Biology and Medicine, Am. Heart Assn., Am. Diabetes Assn., Am. Assn. for Cancer Research, Soc. Pathologists and Bacteriologists, Am. Soc. Exptl. Pathology, Gerontological Soc., AAUP, Sigma Xi. Author: (with J.G. Probstein) Pancreatitis-A Clinical-Pathological Correlation, 1954. Editor: Cowdry's Arteriosclerosis-A Survey of the Problem, 2d edit., 1967; Medical Aspects of Gerontology, 1962; Interdisciplinary Topics in Gerontology, Vols. 1-8, 1968-71. Contbr. articles on aging, transplantation, endocrinology, cancer, pathology to profl. jours. Home: 1940 N Geyer Rd St Louis MO 63131

BLUNT, STANHOPE E., JR., advt. agy. exec.; b. LaJunta, Colo., Mar. 4, 1922; s. Stanhope E. and Jane (Thompson) B.; B.B.A., U. Minn., 1946; m. Barbara Douglass, Apr. 2, 1949; children—Douglass, Brian, Melissa. Dist. sales mgr. Western Airlines, Minn., 1948-57; with Campbell-Mithun, Inc., Mpls., 1957—, account exec., 1957-63, v.p., gen. mgr. Denver office, 1963-69, pres., 1970-72, chmn. bd., 1972—. Mem. Minn. Advt. Rev. Bd. Sect. chmn. major firms div. United Way Mpls. Bd. dirs. Mpls. Better Bus. Bur.; mem. adv. council U. Minn. Sch. Journalism. Served to 1st lt. USAAF, World War II; ETO. Mem. Northwest Advt. Golfers Assn. Clubs: Advt. of Minn., Minneapolis, The Tower (gov.), Interlachen Country, Northwest Tennis. Home: 4 Merilane St Edina MN 55436 Office: Northstar Center Minneapolis MN 55402

BLYTHE, JAMES DAVID, II, lawyer; b. Indpls., Oct. 20, 1940; s. James David and Marjorie (Horne) B.; B.S., Butler U., 1962; J.D., Ind. U., 1966; m. Sara Sue Frantz, Nov. 21, 1974. Admitted to Ind. bar 1966; individual practice law, Indpls., 1966—; staff asst. U.S. Ho. of Reps., 1965-69; asst. majority atty. Ind. Ho. of Reps., Indpls., 1967, 69; dep. prosecutor Marion County, 1966, 68; travel agt. Skyline Travel, Inc., Indpls., 1972—; host Ask a Lawyer TV series. Co-chmn. membership Friends of Channel 20 Pub. TV, 1975-76. Bd. dirs. Am. Cancer Soc. Marion County, 1972-77, crusade chmn., 1973-75, pres., 1975-76, state crusade com., 1974-76; bd. dirs. Crossroads of Am. council Boy Scouts Am., 1970—, v.p., 1977-78; bd. dirs. Salvation Army, 1976-77. Recipient Richard E. Rowland award Indpls. Jr. C. of C., 1971-72, Outstanding Service award, 1972-73, Lacy Meml. award, 1974, Distinguished Service award Indpls. Jaycees, 1976, Jaycee senator, 1977; named Man of Year, Am. Cancer Soc. Marion County, 1974, Outstanding Young Hoosier Ind. Jaycees, 1976; recipient Scroll of Friendship, Jamaica, 1971. Mem. Ind. Jr. C. of C. (ambassador of goodwill W.I. 1971), Ind., Indpls. (grievance chmn. 1974-76, asst. county coordinator grievance com. 1977-78) bar assns., Kappa Sigma, Phi Delta Phi. Home: 11028 Lakeshore Dr E Carmel IN 46032 Office: 156 E Market St Indianapolis IN 46204

BOAND, CHARLES W., lawyer; b. Bates County, Mo., Aug. 19, 1908; s. Albert and Edith Nadine (Pipes) B.; A.A., Jr. Coll. Kansas City, U. Mo. at Kansas City; M.B.A. and LL.B. cum laude, U. Chgo.; children—Bard, Barbara. Admitted to Ill., Mo., D.C., U.S. Supreme Ct. bars; asso. firm Moore and Fitch, St. Louis, 1933; atty. Gen. Counsel's Office, U.S. Treasury Dept., 1933-36; asso. Wilson & McIlvaine, Chgo., 1937-42, partner, 1945—. Mem. citizens bd. U. Chgo., 1963—; mem. cabinet U. Chgo. Alumni, 72—, v.p., 1973-75, pres., 1975—; mem. council on Grad. Sch. Bus., U. Chgo., 1961-68; mem. alumni bd. U. Chgo. Law Sch., 1940-70, pres., 1967-69; trustee Muskingum Coll., 1968—. Served active duty USNR, 1942-45, now lt. comdr., ret. Mem. Am., Ill. (chmn. sect. corp. and securities law 1954-56), Chgo. (past chmn. corp. law com.), Fed., 7th Circuit bar assns., Nat. Conf. Lawyers and C.P.A.'s, Newcomen Soc. N.Am., Order of Coif, Beta Gamma Sigma, Sigma Chi, Phi Alpha Delta. Presbyterian (stated clk. Barrington 1962-65). Clubs: Carlton, Chgo., Mid-Am., Met., Law, Legal, Chgo. Execs., Barrington Hills Country (dir. 1948-55); Nat. Lawyers (Washington). Editor U. Chgo. Law Rev., 1932-33. Home: Route 1 Cuba Rd Barrington IL 60010 Office: 135 S LaSalle St Chicago IL 60603

BOATRIGHT, DAVID JOEL, actuary; b. Nashville, Sept. 9, 1941; s. Otis Hugh and Mary Ilen (Staples) B.; B.A., Fisk U., 1961; postgrad Northeastern U., 1965-66, Roosevelt U., 1974-75; m. Leila Kathryn Hickson, Aug. 26, 1962; children—David, Faye, Kathryn, Karen. Actuarial asst., Blair Follis Allen & Walker, Nashville, 1961-64; acutarial asso. John Hancock Life Ins. Co., Boston, 1964-70; chief actuary Mass. Gen. Life Ins. Co., Boston, 1970-72; actuary Allstate Ins. Companies, Chgo., 1972-74; pres. Personal Med. Services Inc., Chgo., 1974—, also chmn. Mem. West Suburban Boston council Boy Scouts Am., 1972; chmn. Ill. Community Health Action Program, 1974; mem. Ill. Health Systems Area for Kane, Lake and McHenry counties. Mem. Soc. Actuaries, Am. Acad. Actuaries, Ill. Health Ins. Council, Chgo. C. of C., Group Health Assn. Am., Beta Kappa Chi. Republican. Mem. Ch. of Christ. Home: 1 Yorkshire Dr Lincolnshire IL 60015 Office: 327 LaSalle St S Chicago IL 60604

BOAZ, HAROLD CHAMBERLAIN, JR., ednl. adminstr.; b. Pana, Ill., May 20, 1934; s. Harold C. and Evelyn E. (Morrison) B.; B.A., U. Evansville, 1959; M.A., Ball State U., 1963; postgrad. U. Wash., 1966, Kans. State U., 1967; Ph.D., Northwestern U., 1977; m. E. Joanne Miner, Mar. 24, 1956; children—Jill, Nathan. Tchr., Lafayette Central Sch., Roanoke, Ind., 1960-63; tchr., asst. prin. Fort Wayne (Ind.) Pub. Schs., 1963-68; prin. Todd Sch., Lincolnwood, Ill., 1968—. Mem. del. assembly Crusade Mercy, Fort Wayne, Ind., 1967-68; mem. Winnetka (Ill.) Community Caucus, 1973-74; instr. first aid Fort Wayne chpt. ARC, 1967-68. Served with USMCR, 1952-55. Fellow NDEA, 1967, NSF, 1966. Mem. NEA, Ill. Prins. Assn., Ill. Elementary Prins. Assn., Nat. Assn. Elementary Prins., Niles Township Prins. Assn. (pres.), Field Mus. Natural History. Methodist. Contbr. to profl. publs. in field. Home: 1508 Forest Ave Wilmette IL 60091 Office: 3925 Lunt St Lincolnwood IL 60045

BOBERG, JOHN THEODORE, priest, educator; b. Covington, Ky., Mar. 27, 1934; s. John Theodore and Mildred (Fagedes) B.; B.A., Divine Word Sem., Techny, Ill., 1961; D. Missiology, Gregorian U., Rome, 1967. Ordained priest Roman Catholic Ch., 1961; editor, dir. Divine Word News Service, Rome, 1963-66; prof. missions Divine Word Sem., Techny, Ill., 1967-69; prof. missions Cath. Theol. Union, Chgo., 1969—. Mem. Divine Word Missionaries, Am. Soc. Missiology (v.p. 1976-78), Assn. Profs. Missions (sec.-treas. 1970-76). Editor religious pamphlets and papers. Home and Office: 5401 S Cornell Chicago IL 60615

BOBLAK, FRANK JOSEPH, realtor; b. Chgo., Aug. 11, 1920; s. Frank and Wanda (Pedzimaz) B.; B.S. with honors, Bradley U., 1950; grad. Realtors Inst., Peoria, Ill., 1972; m. Joan M. Page, Apr. 25, 1946 (div. May 1971); children—James S., Kenneth F. (dec.), Marilyn J., Gregory J. Real estate broker, Oak Lawn, Ill., 1961—; owner Frank Boblak & Assos., Realtors, 1964—. Organizer, chmn. troop Chicago area council Boy Scouts Am., 1967; finance chmn. Oak Lawn Baseball for Boys; mem. Oak Lawn Bicentennial Commn. Served as 1st lt. AUS, 1942-48. Named Realtor of the Year, S.W. Suburban Bd. Realtors, 1971. Mem. Nat., Ill. (dir.) assns. realtors, S.W. Suburban Bd. Realtors (pres. 1971—), S.W. Suburban Multiple Listing Corp. (pres. 1969), V.F.W., Oak Lawn C. of C. (pres. 1974, dir. 1976, advisory bd. 1977). Rotarian (dir. 1968-71), K.C. Office: 9632 S Cicero Ave Oak Lawn IL 60453

BOBO, MERTON ARTHUR, trust co. exec.; b. Greenfield, Mass., Feb. 10, 1926; s. Earl Alexander and Evelyn May (Poole) B.; student Suffolk U., 1948; J.D., New Eng. Sch. Law, 1951; m. Janet Adelaide Newsom, June 21, 1952; children—James C., Amanda J., Suzanne J. Admitted to Mass. bar, 1953; with Ins. Co. N.Am., Phila., 1951-53; individual practice law, Greenfield, Mass., 1953-55; claims rep. Hartford Accident & Indemnity Co., Hartford, Conn., 19S5-57; asst. trust officer First Nat. Bank & Trust Co., Greenfield, Mass., 1957-62; asso. trust officer Safe Deposit Bank & Trust Co., Springfield, Mass., 1962-67; v.p., trust officer First Nat. Bank & Trust Co.. Fargo, N.D., 1967-77; pres. First Northwestern Trust Co. N.D., 1978—; instr. in comml. law, negotiable instruments, advanced estate planning. V.P., gen. chmn. Fargo-Moorhead United Way, 1971; active Ind. Coll. Fund, 1974; trustee Holyoke Pub. Library, 1963-67; pres. Franklin County Mental Health Assn., 1959. Served with USN, 1943-47. Decorated D.F.C., Air medal. Mem. Mass., N.D. bar assns., Red River Valley (pres. 1975), Pioneer Valley (pres. 1959), Hampden County (pres. 1963) estate planning councils. Clubs: Fargo Country, Southgate Racquet, Eagles, Elks. Home: 602 24th Ave S Fargo ND 58102 Office: 15 Broadway St Fargo ND 58102

BOBSIN, ROBERTA JANETTE, sch. counselor; b. Chgo., Aug. 1, 1927; d. William Henry and Lois Leota (Law) Bobsin; B.S., U. Ill.. 1949; M.A., No. Ill. U., 1959, diploma as guidance specialist, 1969. Phys. edn. tchr. suburban area pub. schs., Chgo., 1947-68; dir. Camps Girl Scouts U.S., summers, 1949-60; sch. counselor pub. schs. Belvidere, Ill., 1969-77; active parent group leadership, Belvidere, 1970. Mem. NEA (life), Ill. Edn. Assn., Am. Sch. Counselor Assn., Am., Ill. personnel and guidance assns., Jr. High Belvidere Tchrs. Assn. (membership chmn. 1972-73). Alpha Delta Kappa. Mem. United Ch. Christ. Home: 4153 Eastridge Dr Rockford IL 61107 Office: Belvedere Jr High Sch Belvedere IL 61008

BOBULSKI, EDWARD M., graphic arts co. exec., artist; b. Peoria. Ill., Apr. 7, 1939; s. Stephen Jerome and Maureen Alice (O'Grady) B.; B.A., U. Ill.. Champaign-Urbana, 1959; M.B.A., Loyola U., Chgo., 1961; m. Angela Marie Steffano, June 11, 1960; 1 son, Andre. Comml. artist Terra Arts, Inc., Chgo., 1961-63, creative dir., 1963-66, v.p. production, 1966-71; owner, pres. Dezign, Ltd., 1971—; instr. graphic design Northwestern Evening Div.. Chgo., 1966—; exhibited in numerous one man and group shows. Democratic precinct capt., 1970—; bd. dirs. D.A. Smythe Found., 1970—. Mem. Am. Assn. Graphic Artists. Democrat. Roman Catholic. Clubs: K.C., Rotary, Kiwanis, Ill. Athletic. Author: Graphic Design for the Novice, 1972. Home: 6121 N Sheridan Rd Chicago IL 60660

BOCK, ALLAN CLARENCE, aerial survey exec.; b. Elbow, Sask., Can., Mar. 22, 1912; s. Clarence and Alice Ethelwyn (Dodge) B.; came to U.S., 1919, naturalized, 1950; student U. Ill., 1934, U. Minn., 1937-38, Curtiss Wright Aeronautical U., 1932-33; children—Sunny, Vally, Darrel, Carson; m. Joanne L. Johnson, Apr. 30, 1977; stepchildren—David, Brian, Lisa and Holly Johnson. With Mark Hurd Aerial Surveys, Inc., Golden Valley, Minn., 1937—, pres., 1945—, dir., 1945—, chmn. bd. 1968—; chmn. bd., dir. Pan Am. Aerial Surveys, 1953—; pres., chmn. bd. Ram Inc., 1953—, Hurd Mapping Corp., 1956—. Served with USAAF, 1935-37. Mem. Am. Soc. Photogrammetry (dir. 1956-59), Legis. Council Photogrammetry (pres. 1964-65). Club: Wayzata (Minn.) Country. Home: 12 Loring Rd Hopkins MN 55343 Office: 345 Pennsylvania Ave S Golden Valley MN 55426

BOCK, LEO LOUIS, elec. engr.; b. Poole, Nebr., Jan. 7, 1927; s. Louis Alex and Mary (Heerman) B.; B.S.E.E., U. Nebr., 1951; m. Verona Velma Hafner, Dec. 18, 1951; children—Diane, Gerald, Karen, Michael, Lawrence. Elec. engr. Sperry Univac, 1951-55, engring. mgr., 1955-61, product planning mgr., 1961-65; sr. engr. IBM Corp., Oswego, N.Y., 1965-68; product planning mgr. Mohawk Data Scis., Herkimer, N.Y., 1968-69; coordinator for product Planning Sperry Univac, St. Paul, 1969-70, mktg. mgr., 1970-77, navy systems market planning mgr., 1977—. Served with USAF, 1945-46. Mem. IEEE. Republican. Lutheran. Home: 10824 York Ave S Bloomington MN 55431 Office: Univac Park St Paul MN 55165

BOCKELMAN, J(OHN) RICHARD, lawyer; b. Chgo., Aug. 8, 1925; s. Carl August and Mary (Ritchie) B.; student U. Wis., 1943-44, Northwestern U., 1944-45, Harvard U., 1945, U. Hawaii, 1946; B.S. in Bus. Adminstrn., Northwestern U., 1946; M.A. in Econs., U. Chgo., 1949, J.D., 1951. Admitted to Ill. bar, 1951; atty.-adviser Chgo. ops. office U.S. AEC, 1951-52; asso. firm Schradzke, Gould & Ratner, Chgo., 1952-57, Brown, Dashow & Langeluttig, Chgo., 1957-59, firm Antonow & Weissbourd, Chgo., 1959-61; partner firm Burton, Isaacs, Bockelman & Miller, Chgo., 1961-69; practiced in Chgo., 1970—. Prof. bus. law Ill. Inst. Tech., Chgo., 1950—, lectr. econs. De Paul U., Chgo., 1952-53; dir., v.p., sec. Secretaries, Inc., Chgo., Beale Travel Service, Inc., Chgo.; dir., sec. Mid-West Dynamometer & Engring. Co., River Grove, Ill.; dir., v.p. Universal Distbrs., Inc., Chgo. Served with USNR, 1943-46. Mem. Am., Ill. Chgo. bar assns., Catholic Lawyers Guild Chgo., Phi Delta Theta. Clubs: Chicago Athletic Assn., Boyar, Ltd., Barclay Ltd., Whitehall, Internat. (Chgo.); Anvil (East Dundee, Ill.). Home: 1212 Lake Shore Dr Chicago IL 60610 Office: 69 W Washington St Chicago IL 60602

BOCKSERMAN, ROBERT JULIAN, mfg. co. exec.; b. St. Louis, Dec. 20, 1929; s. Max Louis and Bertha Anna (Kremen) B.; B.S., U. Mo., 1952, M.S., 1955; m. Clarice Kreisman, June 9, 1958; children—Michael, Joyce, Carol. Chemist, Sealtest Corp., Peoria, Ill., 1955-56; prodn. mgr. Allan Drug Co., St. Louis, 1957-58; research chemist Monsanto Co., St. Louis, 1958-67, purchasing agt., East St. Louis, Ill., 1968; pres. Pharma-Tech Industries, Inc.. Union, Mo., 1969—; v.p., dir. Sentinel Pharmacal Corp. Commr. Boy Scouts Am.; bd. dirs. Dielman Sch., Olivette, Mo., 1968-73. Served with U.S. Army, 1952-54; Korea. Mem. Am. Chem. Soc., Packaging Inst., AAAS, Indsl. Pharmacisfs Assn. St. Louis, St. Louis Pharmacists Assn., Sigma Alpha Mu. Phi Delta Chi. Club: Masons. Home: 54 Morwood Lane Creve Coeur MO 63141 Office: Route 3 Box S21A Union MO 63084

BODE, SANDRA JEAN, ednl. adminstr.; b. Warren, Ohio, Apr. 20, 1941; d. Gilbert Vernon and Clara Helen (Mount) Reed; student Kent (Ohio) State U., 1959-62; B.S. in Edn., Youngstown (Ohio) State U., 1964; postgrad. Purdue U., 1969-70; M.S. in Edn., No. Ill. U., 1977; m. Glen Harold Bode, June 6, 1964. Tchr. elementary sch., Mineral Ridge, Ohio, 1962-66, Kent pub. schs., 1966-68, Duneland Sch. Corp., Chesterton, Ind., 1969-70, Overseas Dependent Schs., Germany, 1971-73; coordinator career edn. Thornton Area Pub. Sch. Corp., 1973-76; dir. DuPage Elementary Career Edn. Center, Wheaton, Ill., 1976—; mem. teaching staff Nat. Coll. Edn., Evanston, Ill.; cons. to Cook and DuPage Counties. Home: 726 S Adams St Hinsdale IL 60521 Office: 421 N County Farm Rd Wheaton IL 60187

BODEN, ROBERT FRANCIS, lawyer, educator; b. Milw., June 4, 1928; s. Francis X. and Edith A. (Ebert) B.; Ph.B., Marquette U., 1950, J.D., 1952; LL.D., Carthage Coll., 1975; m. Patricia M. Gill, July 10, 1954. Admitted to Wis. bar, 1952; asso. Quarles, Spence & Quarles, Milw., 1952-56; gen. practice Milw., 1956-63; lectr. Marquette U. Law Sch., 1959-63, asst. prof., 1963-65, asso. prof., 1965-71, prof., 1971—, acting dean, 1965-66, dean, 1966—; editor Wis. Continuing Legal Edn. Jour., 1964-70. Chmn. adminstrn. of justice com. State Bar Wis., 1970—, research reporter creditor-debtor law revision project, 1971—; pres. Law Projects, Inc., 1970—; mem. Gov.'s Spl. Com. on Jud. Orgn., 1971—. Mem. Wis. Judicial Council, 1961-71, chmn., 1963-65; mem. Milw. Police Edn. Study Com., 1967-69; chmn. Wis. Garnishment Law Revision Com., 1968-69; chmn. Wis. Supreme Ct. Chief Judge Study Com., 1974-75. Bd. dirs. Milw. Legal Aid Soc., 1969-74. Fellow Am. Bar Found.; mem. Am. (mem. council on legal edn. and bar admission, spl. com. on legal assts. 1974—), Wis., Milw. bar assns., Am. Law Inst., Am. Judicature Soc., Delta Theta Phi, Alpha Sigma Nu. Author: Bankruptcy Practice in Wisconsin, 1966; Wisconsin Creditor-Debtor Law, 1971; Basic Bankruptcy Law, 1973; also contbr. articles in field to profl. jours. Home: 1404 Lynne Dr Waukesha WI 53186 Office: 1103 W Wisconsin Ave Milwaukee WI 53233

BODEN, WORTHEY CARL, physician; b. Iowa, June 9, 1912; s. George and Mary (Neil) B.; B.S., U. Iowa, 1935, M.D., 1935; m. Lois Elizabeth Clark, Aug. 21, 1936; children—Carla (Mrs. H. Ely Britton), Nancy (Mrs. Carl Bylin), Emily (Mrs. William Whittemore III), Charles. Intern, Recieving Hosp., Detroit; resident U. Iowa Hosp., Iowa City, 1936-40, Presbyn. Hosp., Chgo., 1945-46; practice medicine specializing in ophthalmology and otolaryngology, Knoxville, Iowa, 1946-49, Sioux City, Iowa, 1949—; mem. staffs St. Lukes Hosp., St. Vincent's Hosp., St. Joseph Mercy Hosp., all Sioux City. Served with USAAF, 1940-45. Mem. Am. Acad. Ophthalmology and Otolaryngology, Internat. Coll. Surgeons, A.C.S., Iowa State Med. Soc. Republican. Methodist. Mason, Lion. Home: 3924 Hamilton Blvd Sioux City IA 51104 Office: 622 4th St Sioux City IA 51101

BODENE, JACK ALLEN, electronic designer; b. Chgo., July 31, 1908; s. Samuel and Tillie (Baumstark) Bodenstein; student Rochester Inst. Tech., 1943—; m. Virginia Ringgold, June 3, 1933 (div. June 1942). Tchr. art Fed. Sch. Art, 1930-32; profl. photographer Ins-Don Alford, Chgo.; with Beltone Electronics Co., Chgo., 1966; artist-in-residence Truman Coll., Chgo.; numerous one-man shows in art and photography. Served with Armed Forces, 1942-45. Decorated Bronze Star medal, Purple Heart. Democrat. Jewish. Home: 3616 Pine Grove St Chicago IL 60613 Office: 4201 Victoria St Chicago IL 60646

BODENSTEINER, ROBERT THEODORE, trucking industry exec.; b. Decorah, Iowa, May 14, 1933; s. Cyril Mathew and Acquin Marie (Kilcoin) B.; B.S., Iowa State U., 1955; postgrad. Iowa U., 1957; postgrad. N.Y. City Coll., 1958; m. Amalia Frances Valenti, Nov. 28, 1959; children—Theodore Girard, David Neil, Susan Frances. Internal auditor N.Y. Life Ins. Co., N.Y.C., 1957-59; adminstrv. asst. Ft. Dodge (Iowa) By-Products Co., 1960-63; spl sales agent Lincoln Nat. Life Ins. Co., Ft. Dodge, 1963-67; stock and commodity broker Lamson Bros. and Co., Ft. Dodge, 1967-73, pres., gen. mgr. Center Line, Inc., Ft. Dodge, 1973—; bd. dirs. Ft. Dodge By-Products Co., Webster Rendering Co., Hot Line, Inc., Bowlerama, Inc., Air Lanes, Inc., Center Line, Inc. Pres., Sertoma Club of Ft. Dodge, 1967, gov. W. Iowa dist. Sertoma Internat., 1970-72. Served to lt. j.g. USN, 1955-57. Recipient various sales awards, Lincoln Nat. Life Ins. Co. and Lamson Bros. & Co. Mem. Ft. Dodge C. of C., Nat. C. of C. Republican. Roman Catholic. Clubs: Barbershoppers. Home: 2209 N 22d St Fort Dodge IA 50501 Office: Box 1275 Fort Dodge IA 50501

BODER, CLARETTA KELSO, ednl. adminstr., psychologist, counselor; b. McDonald, Pa., Nov. 19, 1920; d. William Wallace and Prudence Ann Jane (McEwen) Kelso; B.B.A., Westminster Coll., 1942; postgrad. Washington and Jefferson Coll., summer 1950; M.A., Ohio State U., 1964, Ph.D. in Guidance and Counseling, 1976; m. William Dunbar Boder, Jan. 3, 1942; children—Susan Ann Boder White, Richard Dale, Linda Lee Boder Walters. Tchr., Cecil Twp. Sch. Dist.. McDonald, 1943-50; supr. bus. office Beverly Heights United Presbyn. Ch., Mt. Lebanon, Pa., 1951-52; tchr. Claysville (Pa.) Sch. Dist., 1954-55, Southwestern City Sch. Dist., Columbus, Ohio, 1955-61; tchr. and guidance counselor Grandview Heights (Ohio) City Sch. Dist., 1961-69; vocat. guidance coordinator Eastland Joint Vocat. Sch. Dist., Groveport, Ohio, 1969—; instr. psychology Franklin U., Columbus, 1976-77; instr. Ohio State U., 1974; cons. Ohio State U., 1971, Kent State U., 1975; guest lectr. Ohio State U., 1970-75; chmn. in-service programs Eastland Joint Vocat. Sch., 1970-77; counseling psychologist, 1977—; mem. planning com. All Ohio Guidance Conf., 1968-69. Elder, Blvd. United Presbyn. Ch., 1964-67, deacon, 1961-63. Recipient Dwight Arnold Outstanding Counselor award, 1970. Mem. NEA, Ohio Ednl. Assn., Am., Ohio (Distinguished Service award 1975, pres. guidance div. 1974-75) vocat. assns.. Ohio Sch. Counselors Assn. (co-editor newsletter 1966), Am. Personnel and Guidance Assn., Phi Delta Kappa, Delta Kappa Gamma (v.p. 1974-76), Beta Sigma Omicron. Republican. Club: Order Eastern Star. Contbr. articles on guidance and counseling to profl. jours. Home: 1921 Elmwood Ave Columbus OH 43212 Office: 4465 S Hamilton Rd Groveport OH 43125

BOECK, LAVERNE DWAINE, adminstrv. microbiologist; b. Johnson, Nebr., May 16, 1930; s. Otto Bernhard and Alma Marie (Stutheit) B.; student U. Nebr., 1947-49, Wartburg Coll., 1949-50; B.S. in Biology, Butler U., 1958, M.S. in Microbiology, 1963; m. Fredia Mae Jarrett, Oct. 25, 1953; children—Deborah, Kirk, Bruce, Eric, Gregg, Craig. Clerical engring. analyst, Allison Div. Gen. Motors Corp., Indpls., 1953-57; asso. microbiologist, Eli Lilly & Co., Indpls., 1958-63, microbiologist, 1963-65, asst. sr. microbiologist, 1965-67, asso. sr. microbiologist, 1967-72, sr. microbiologist, 1972—. Served to lt. Antiaircraft Arty. U.S. Army, 1951-53. Mem. Am. Soc. Microbiology, Soc. Indsl. Microbiology, Am. Chem. Soc., Sigma Xi. Republican. Lutheran. Contbr. articles in field to profl. jours.; patentee in field. Home: 741 Chapel Hill West Dr Indianapolis IN 46224 Office: Eli Lilly Research Labs Indianapolis IN 46206

BOECKLIN, PEG PITMAN (MRS. ROLAND BOECKLIN), ret. univ. adminstr.; b. Bisbee, Ariz., Dec. 11, 1910; d. Laurence Minot and Elise Maude (Aztle) Pitman; B.A., Smith Coll., 1933; m. Roland Boecklin, June 16, 1941 (dec.); 1 son, Arnold Pitman. Mng. editor Intercollegiate Daily News, 1933-34; personnel dir. Jordan Marsh Co., Boston, 1935-36; circulation cons. Pubs. Service, Inc., 1937-40; placement dir., instr. Fisher Bus. Schs., Boston, 1940-41; vocational cons. Ohio Wesleyan U., Delaware, 1949-50, placement dir., 19S0-68, dir. career planning and placement center. 1968-76, emeritus, 1976—; cons. to various univs. on placement and career planning of liberal arts grads., 1976—. Mem. Am. Soc. Personnel Adminstrn., Internat. Assn. Personnel Women, Am. Inst. Mgmt., Midwest Coll. Placement Assn., Assn. Sch. Coll. and Univ. Staffing (pres. Ohio sect. 1968-69), Am. Assn. Univ. Adminstrs. Contbr. articles to mags. Home: 52 Westgate Dr Delaware OH 43015

BOEHLKE, WILLIAM FREDERICK, JR., truck leasing co. exec.; b. Chgo., Dec. 16, 1946; s. William Frederick and Cynthia Charlotte (Blackmore) B.; B.S., Wharton Sch. U. Pa., 1969; m. Christine Ann Chervenak, July 19, 1969. Financial analyst Three L Corp., Chgo., 1971-73; sec., controller INE Inc., Elkhart, Ind., 1973-75, v.p. mktg., 1975—, also dir.; merger and acquisitions cons., 1970—. Mem. Northern Ind. Motor Carriers, Elkhart C. of C., Elkhart Traffic Club. Club: South Bend Press. Home: 2012 Bridgeview Trail South Bend IN 46637 Office: 2220 Toledo Rd Elkhart IN 46514

BOEHM, FRITZ RUDOLPH, chiropractic orthopedist; b. Chgo., Feb. 6, 1944; s. Fritz Franz and Erna Ida (Boettcher) B.; D.C., Nat. Coll. Chiropractic, 1968, postgrad. in Orthopedics, 1970-72; m. Jean Ann Stevens, Dec. 18, 1976; children—Jennifer Lynn, Betty Lynn. Practice chiropractic, Manistee, Mich., 1968—, specializing in chiropractic orthopedics, 1972—. Mem. Commn. for Chiropractic Comprehensive Health Plan in Mich., 1974—. Served with USNR, 1962-64. Recipient Highest Achievement as Undergrad. in Chiropractic Profession award Chi Rho Sigma, 1968. Mem. Am., Mich. State chiropractic assns., Mich. Soc. Chiropractic Orthopedists, Am. Council Chiropractic Orthopedics, Manistee Jaycees, Chi Rho Sigma (pres. chpt. 1967). Rotarian, Eagle. Home: 714 Elm St Manistee MI 49660 Office: 388 1st St Manistee MI 49660

BOEHM, RICHARD THEODORE, lawyer; b. Columbus, Ohio, Sept. 11, 1914; s. Carl Henry and Louise Catherine (Knoderer) B.; A.B., Capital U., 1935; J.D., Ohio State U., 1938, B.S. in Bus. Adminstrn., 1948; m. Charlotte Ann Drake, Apr. 25, 1941; children—Anne Elizabeth (Mrs. Michael M. Wilson), Barbara Drake. Admitted to Ohio bar, 1938, also U.S. Supreme Ct., Tax Ct. bars; practiced law in Bowling Green, Ohio, 1938-40, Columbus, 1941-42, 46-51, 53—; spl. counsel to tax commr. of Ohio, also Buckeye Fed. Savs. & Loan Assn. Dir. various corps. Lectr. Ohio Legal Center Insts., 1968-71; lectr. Coll. Law, Ohio State U., 1956-63, Coll. Law, U. Cin., 1959—, Cleve. Midwest Tax Conf., 1959, practicing law insts. Ohio State Bar Assn., 1956—, Ohio Continuing Legal Edn.; witness on broadening tax base Ways and Means Com. 85th Congress; life mem. Judicial Conf., Sixth Circuit Ct.; arbitrator labor cases and Am. Arbitration Assn.; hearing examiner Ohio Civil Rights Commn.; master commr., referee, ct. of common pleas. Fellow Ohio Bar Found.; mem. Am. Legion Band, Columbus. Dem. candidate Franklin County common pleas judge, 1968. Trustee Magnetic Springs Hosp. Found.; mem. Ohio State U. Alumni Band; gen. counsel Candlewood Lake Assn., Harrison Twp. Property Owners Assn. Served from ensign to lt. comdr. USNR, 1942-46, 51-52. C.P.A., Ohio. Mem. Am., Ohio, Columbus (past chmn. centennial events com., past chmn. legal insts. com. past chmn. fed. courts coms.), Fed. bar assns., Ohio Soc. C.P.A.'s (lectr. 1969—), Columbus Fedn. Musicians., Soc. Preservation and Encouragement Barbershop Quartet Singing Am., Scribes. Clubs: Vaudvillities, Saturday Evening (past pres.), Columbus Maennerchor, Hauscappelle, Torch (past pres. 1973), Ohio State University Faculty, TBDBITL. Episcopalian (past vestryman, past sr. warden). Author: Professional Corporations, 1962; Taxes on Politics, 1970; Political Contributions, 1970; also numerous tech. articles; contbg. author: Ohio History, 1974, 75; German Village Society pamphlets, 1969-71. Home: 2435 Kensington Dr Columbus OH 43221 Office: 1200 W 5th Ave Columbus OH 43212

BOEHME, WERNER RICHARD, research co. exec.; b. Englewood, N.J., Jan. 15, 1920; s. Richard and Olga (Reineking) B.; B.S., Poly. Inst. Bklyn., 1942; Ph.D. (Frederick Gardner Cottrell Research fellow 1946-47, NIH Research fellow 1947-48), U. Md., 1948; M.B.A., U. Chgo., 1971; m. Jean Hayden, May 17, 1946; children—Christine (Mrs. Henry Bevilacqua), Arthur. Asst. chemist Gen. Dyestuff Corp., N.Y.C., 1937-41; research chemist Winthrop Chem. Co., Rensselaer, N.Y., 1942-44; research chemist Nat. Drug Co., Phila., 1948-52; mgr. dept. chemistry Ethicon, Inc., Somerville, N.J., 1952-61; dir. central research Shulton, Inc., Clifton, N.J., 1961-62; pres., gen. mgr. A.M. Arnold Labs., Inc., Somerville, N.J., 1962-67; mgr. chem. ops., dir. research and devel. Dawes Labs., Inc., Chgo., 1967-73; tech. dir. Fats & Proteins Research Found., Inc., Des Plaines, Ill., 1973—. Served with USNR, 1944-46. Fellow Am. Inst. Chemists; mem. Am. Chem. Soc., N.Y. Acad. Scis., AAAS, Am. Oil Chemists Soc., Inst. Food Technologists, Sigma Xi, Alpha Chi Sigma. Contbr. articles in field to profl. jours.; patentee in field. Home: 2 S 403 Oaklawn Dr Glen Ellyn IL 60137 Office: 2720 Des Plaines Av Des Plaines IL 60018

BOEHMER, GERALD LEO, real estate broker; b. Flint Hill, Mo., May 7, 1944; s. Urban Joseph and Martha Marie (Feldewerth) B.; B.S., St. Louis U., 1966; M.S., So. Ill. U., 1971; children—Tracy Ann, Eric Lee. Profl. baseball player Chgo. White Sox, 1966-68; tchr. high sch., O'Fallon, Mo., 1967-69, 71-73; with Cleo Poore Brockman Inc., Wentzville, Mo., 1971-73; owner, operator Gerald L. Boehmer Realty Co., Wentzville, 1973—; sec. Dawn Investment Co. Roman Catholic. Winner awards in athletics. Home: 808 Parr St Wentzville MO 63385 Office: Route 2 Wentzville MO 63385

BOELTER, ROBERT IRVIN, advt. agy. exec.; b. Eau Claire, Wis., Nov. 21, 1940; s. Robert H. and La Vyne M. (Sherman) B.; B.S., U. Wis., Madison, 1965; m. Sept. 4, 1965; 1 son, Christopher. Art dir. Waldbilling & Besteman, Inc., Madison, 1966-67; creative dir. Stephan & Brady, Inc., Madison, 1967-70; art dir. Hoffman, York, Baker & Johnson, Chgo., 1970-71. Milw., 1971-73; pres. Boelter Co., Madison and Milw., 1973—; tchr. Madison Area Tech. Coll., 1966-67, mem. comml. art adv. bd., 1976-77. Recipient numerous awards for advt. creative work, including those from Madison Advt. Club, 1967-70, 74-77, Milw. Advt. Club, 1977, Milw. Art Dirs. Club, 1966-71, Milw. Soc. Communicating Arts, 1972-76, Am. Advt. Fedn., 1975-76, Am. Bus. Press Assn., 1972. Mem. Am. Mktg. Assn., Milw. Soc. Communicating Arts, Madison Advt. Club, North Central Briarders (founding pres. 1976-77), Briard Club Am. (v.p.), Nat. Dog Breed Club, Nat. Model Railroaders Assn. Home: 4383 Windsor Rd Windsor WI 53598 Office: 110 E Main St Madison WI 53703

BOEMI, A. ANDREW, banker; b. N.Y.C., Mar. 3, 1915; s. S. and Marietta (Boemi) B.; B.C.E., Coll. City N.Y., 1936, M.C.E., 1938; m. Flora Dorothy DeMuro, Apr. 26, 1941; children—Andrew A., Marcia Rosamond Buchanan. Engr., Gibb & Hill, Cons. Engrs., N.Y.C., 1937; city planner N.Y. Planning Comm., 1938-41; cons. U.S. Bur. Budget, Exec. Office of President, Washington, 1942; asst. loan officer, planning cons., asst. v.p., v.p. First Fed. Savs. & Loan, Chgo., 1946-57; chmn. bd., pres. Madison Bank & Trust Co., Chgo., 1957—; pres., chmn. bd. Madison Financial Corp., Chgo., 1974—; chmn. bd. Madison Nat. Bank of Niles (Ill.), 1976—. Mem. exec. com. Archdiocesan Commn. Human Relations and Ecumenism; mem. Mayor's Commn. Landmarks Preservation Council. Bd. dirs. Met. Housing and Planning Council, 1950—, pres., 1975-76; mem. Elementary Sch. Bd., Park Ridge, Ill., 1953-59, pres., 1956-59; citizens bd. Loyola U., Chgo.; chmn. Joint Action Com. Civic Assns. for location Chgo. campus U. Ill., 1960-61; chmn. Gateway Com., Chgo., 1958-63; bd. dirs. Duncan YMCA. Served from ensign to lt. comdr. USNR, 1942-46. Recipient commendation from sec. navy, World War II. Mem. Am. Bankers Assn., Assn. for Modern Banking in Ill. (v.p. 1974-75, dir.), Am. Soc. C.E., Am. Inst. Planners, Assn. Commerce and Industry (chmn. comml. devel. com.), Navy League U.S., Newcomen Soc. N. Am., Am. Legion, Lambda Alpha, Alpha Beta Gamma. Republican. Roman Catholic. Clubs: Economic, Bankers, Metropolitan, University (Chgo.); Park Ridge Country. Home: 1110 N Lake Shore Dr Apt 7-S Chicago IL 60611 Office: 400 W Madison St Chicago IL 60606

BOER, ROGER WILLIAM, lawyer; b. Holland, Mich., July 2, 1934; s. William Henry and Frances (Hulst) B.; A.B., Calvin Coll., 1956; J.D., Wayne State U., 1960; m. Judith L. Jaqua, June 21, 1958; children—William, James, Charles, Martha, Karen. Admitted to Mich. bar, 1960; since practiced in Grand Rapids; partner firm McKee & Boer, 1961-63, Rhoades, Garlington, McKee & Boer, 1963-65, Rhoades, McKee & Boer, 1965—; dep. pros. atty. Kent County, Mich., 1963-64; dir. B.B.G. Corp., Wilwin Dunes Ltd., Hillhope, Inc., Grand Rapids. Spl. counsel Mich. House and Senate Investigating coms. Workmen's Compensation, 1965-66. Trustee Pine Rest Christian Hosp., Grand Rapids, Pine Rest Rehab. Services Corp.; bd. dirs. Wedgewood Acres Home for Boys, Grand Rapids. Mem. Mich. Bar Assn., Am. Trial Lawyers Assn., Best Recommended Ins. Attys. Home: 961 Gladstone St East Grand Rapids MI 49506 Office: Suite D Waters Bldg Grand Rapids MI 49502

BOERGER, WILLIAM GEORGE, oral surgeon; b. St. Cloud, Minn., May 30, 1941; s. Milton Carl and Geneva Marie (Spaniol) B.; student Crosier Sem., Onamia, Minn., 1959-61, St. Cloud State Coll., 1961-63; B.S., U. Minn., 1965, D.D.S., 1967; m. Hiroko Hamada, Nov. 16, 1968 (separated Feb. 1977); 1 son, Jeffrey. Resident in oral surgery U. Minn., Mpls., 1969-72; practice oral surgery, Wayzata, Minn., 1972—, also Edina, Minn.; mem. staffs Methodist Hosp., St. Louis Park, Minn., Fairview Southdale Hosp., Edina, also Children's Health Center, Mpls. Served with USNR, 1967-69. Fellow Am. Dental Soc. Anesthesiology; mem. Am. Dental Assn., Minn., Mpls. Dist. dental socs., Am., Mpls., Minn. socs. oral surgeons, Minnetonka, Bloomington dental study clubs, Southdale Dental Soc., Omicron Kappa Upsilon. Office: 250 N Central Ave Wayzata MN 55391

BOERS, RICHARD WILLIAM, city ofcl.; b. Rochester, N.Y., Apr. 21, 1941; s. Harvey William and Sarah Elizabeth (Jones) B.; B.S., Cornell U., 1963; postgrad. U. Mich., 1963-64, U. Toledo, 1964-65. With div. of parks City of Toledo, 1964-66, commr. of forestry, 1966-73, commr. forestry and open space planning, 1973—. Liaison officer Arts Commn. of Greater Toledo, 1972-76, Toledo Bicentennial Commn., 1974—, Internat. Park Bd., 1976—. Exec. sec. George P. Crosby Gardens Bd., 1972—; coordinator Mid-Mgmt. Steering Com. City of Toledo; ex-officio bd. mem. Spectrum, Friends of Fine Arts; bd. dirs. Neighborhood Improvement Found. of Toledo, 1970—, Internat. Inst. of Toledo, 1973—; bd. control Neighborhood Housing Services; mem. Greenbelt Pkwy. Mgmt. Team; trustee Oldwest End Assn., 1973-75; mem. advisory bd. Grad. Sch. Pub. Adminstrn. U. Toledo. Named one of top ten young men of year Toledo Jaycees, 1973. Mem. Am. Soc. Landscape Architects (chmn. Maumee Valley chpt. 1971-72), Soc. Municipal Arborists (pres. 1974-76), Sigma Phi Epsilon. Mason. Clubs: Netherlands; Toledo Artists (trustee 1970—), Tile, Cornell (Toledo). Home: 2016 Scottwood Toledo OH 43620 Office: 2201 Ottawa Pkwy Toledo OH 43606

BOERSMA, WILLIAM CARTER, banker; b. Zeeland, Mich., May 10, 1946; s. William Theodore and Harriet Rose (Pyle) B.; B.A., Hope Coll., 1968; m. Cheryl Ann Phillips June 28, 1968; children—Jeffrey William, Jeanne Marie. Investment officer Mich. Nat. Bank, Grand Rapids, Mich., 1968-73; trust officer, investment officer bank portfolio First Nat. Bank & Trust Co., Sturgis, Mich., 1973—. Dir. United Fund, Sturgis; mem. bd. review, Sturgis; chmn. 1977 Mich. Week, Sturgis; pres. First Presbyterian Ch., 1975, treas., 1976—. Mem. Mich. Bankers Assn. (trust div.). Republican. Clubs: Rotary (sec. 1976—). Home: 1006 Galyn St Sturgis MI 49091 Office: 207 E Chicago Rd Sturgis MI 49091

BOESCH, HENRY JOHN, JR., civil engr.; b. Evanston, Ill., Nov. 28, 1927; s. Henry John and Bess (Brownlee) B.; B.S. in Civil Engring., Northwestern Tech. Inst., 1950; m. Geraldine F. Mawicke, Nov. 17, 1949; children—Geraldine, Teresa, Christine, David, Kathleen. Engr. various municipalities and contractors, 1950-63; resident engr. Ill. Div. Hwys., Elgin, 1963-68; v.p. Advance Cons. Engrs., Inc., Hinsdale, Ill., 1968-76; pres. Boesch Cons. Engrs., Inc., Bolingbrook, Ill., 1976—. Mem. ASCE, Nat., Ill. socs. profl. engrs., Am. Inst. Planners, Am. Ry. Engring. Assn., Am. Concrete Inst., Inst. Traffic Engrs., Am. Forestry Assn., Am. Cons. Engrs. Council, Cons. Engrs. Council Ill., Pi Kappa Alpha. Home and office: 213 Tomahawk Ct Bolingbrook IL 60439

BOESE, GILBERT KARYLE, zoo adminstr.; b. Chgo., June 24, 1937; s. Carl Henry and Winifred (Mack) B.; B.A., Carthage Coll., 1959; M.S., No. Ill. U., 1965; Ph.D. (NIMH trainee), Johns Hopkins, 1972; m. Wilma Lou Blenz, Dec. 19, 1959; children—Ann Carroll, Peter Austin. Tchr., Hinsdale, Ill., 1960-62, Addison, Ill., 1962-65; instr. biology Thornton Jr. Coll., Harvey, Ill., 1965-67; asst. prof. Elmhurst (Ill.) Coll., 1967-69, vis. lectr., 1971—; curator Chgo. Zool. Park, Brookfield, Ill., 1971-72, asso. dir., 1972—; mem. Balt. Zool. Park Primate Adv. Com., 1970; v.p. Chgo. Zool. Soc., 1976—. Mem. Sci. Curriculum Com. DuPage County, 1965-67. Grantee, Elmhurst Coll., 1968, Chgo. Zool. Soc. for African study, 1971, 74, Johns Hopkins, 1971. Mem. Animal Behavior Soc., Am. Assn. Zool. Parks and Aquariums, Nat. Mustang Soc., Phi Sigma. Club: Adventurers. Home: 618 S Grace St Lombard IL 60148 Office: Chgo Zool Park 8400 W 31st St Brookfield IL 60513

BOESE, ROBERT ALAN, forensic chemist; b. Chgo., Mar. 30, 1934; s. Fred W. and Adeline B. (Kondrad) B.; A.A. in Chemistry, Wright Jr. Coll., 1960; B.S. in Chemistry, Ill. Inst. Tech., 1969, M. Pub. Adminstrn., 1974; m. June C. Franke, Dec. 10, 1955; children—Mark A., Brian A. Patrolman, Chgo. Police Dept., 1956-58, investigator crime lab., 1958-60, firearms examiner, 1960-63, sr. firearms examiner, 1963-65, chemist, crime lab., 1965-71, chief chemist, 1971-74, tech. coordinator, 1974—; pres. B and W Cons. Forensic Chemists, Inc.; part time faculty St. Xavier Coll.; lectr. Northwestern U., Ill. Inst. Tech., U. Notre Dame, Loyola U., Chgo. Police Acad.; state instr. in use of breathalyzer; mem. Task Force for Evaluation of Ill. Crime Lab System, 1974-75. Fellow Am. Acad. Forensic Scis. (criminalistics sect.); mem. Am. Chem. Soc., Midwestern Assn. Forensic Scientists (founder, pres. 1976-77), Am. Firearms and Tool Marks Examiners (charter), Chgo. Gas Chromatography Discussion Group, Am. Soc. Pub. Adminstrn. Clubs: Masons, Shriners. Expert witness in firearms identification and forensic chemistry municipal, county, fed. cts.; contbr. articles to profl. jours. Home: 5657 S Mason Ave Chicago IL 60638 Office: Chicago Police Dept 1121 S State St Chicago IL 60605

BOESE, VIRGINIA ELLEN, curator; b. Troy, Ohio, July 16, 1907; d. William Harry and Virginia Grace (Meeker) Gilbert; student Western Coll. for Women, Oxford, O., 1924-26; B.A., Ohio Wesleyan U., Delaware, 1928; m. Carl Wimmler Boese, Aug. 5, 1929. Tchr. Latin and English, Concord Twp. Sch., Miami County. Ohio, 1928-29; legal sec. to William Harry Gilbert, Troy, 1931-45; dir. Troy Hist. Soc., 1965—, archivist-librarian, genealogist, 1966—, dir. hist. room, 1966—; dir., curator Overfield Log Tavern Mus., 1966-75; asst. curator, 1975—. Pres., violinist Troy Music Club, 1932-33; pres. Troy Altrurian Club, 1933-34; pres. Current Events Club. 1954-55. Co-recipient, with husband, Community Service award Troy Jr. C. of C., 1972. Mem. DAR, Colonial Dames XVII Century, LWV, Daus. of Founders and Patriots Am., Phi Mu, Kappa Delta Pi. Republican. Presbyn. (deacon). Author: Overfield Genealogy Research Notes, 1968, rev., 1970; Revolutionary Soldiers of Miami County, Ohio, 1976; Meeker Genealogy, 1975. Compiler, Index to Beers 1880 History, 1973. Home: 106 S Plum St Troy OH 45373 Office: 201 E Water St Troy OH 45373

BOESEL, MILTON CHARLES, JR., lawyer, bus. exec.; b. Toledo, July 12, 1928; s. Milton C. and Florence (Fitzgerald) B.; B.A., Yale U., 1950; LL.B., Harvard U., 1953; m. Lucy Laughlin Mather, Mar. 25, 1961; children—Elizabeth Parks, Charles Mather, Andrew Fitzgerald. Admitted to Ohio bar, 1953, Mich. bar, 1953; partner firm Ritter, Boesel, Robinson & Marsh, Toledo, 1956—; dir. First Nat. Bank Toledo. Served to lt., USNR, 1953-56. Episcopalian. Mason. Clubs: Toledo, Toledo Country (Toledo); Leland (Mich.) Country. Home: 2268 Innisbrook Rd Toledo OH 43606 Office: 240 Huron St Toledo OH 43604

BOGDANSKY, JOHN, engring. co. exec.; b. Chgo., Dec. 21, 1926; s. John and Violet (Stevens) B.; student Mich. State U.; m. Jean Gaetke, Feb. 13. 1951. Owner, operator Blue Lake Resort, Fountain, Mich., 1962-66; individual practice ins., real estate salesman Fountain, 1962-66; engring. draftsman, designer Harlo Corp., Grandville, Mich., 1966-70; sec.-treas., mgr. Alpha-Tran Engring. Co., Walker, Mich., 1970—, also dir. Served with inf., U.S. Army, 1945-46; PTO. Elk. Home: 7033 Goldenrod Dr Rockford MI 49341 Office: 3303 Remembrance Rd Walker MI 49504

BOGERT, JOHN ALDEN, dentist; b. Oelwein, Iowa, July 25, 1933; s. Alden F. and Helen B. (Baker) B.; D.D.S., State U. Iowa, 1958; M.S.D., U. Mo., 1960; m. Virginia Lea Johnston; children—John Alden III, David C., Anne C. Practice dentistry specializing in pediatric dentistry, Kansas City, Mo., 1960—. Chmn. U.S. Olympic Swimming Com., 1968-76, mgr. U.S. Olympic Swim Team, 1972, 76. Comdr. USNR. Diplomate Am. Bd. of Pedodontics. Fellow Am. Acad. Pedodontics; mem. Greater Kansas City Dental Soc. (pres. 1971), Mo. Dental Assn. (bd. govs. 1972—), Amateur Athletic Union of U.S. (swimming chmn. 1968-72). Office: 4240 Blue Ridge Blvd Kansas City MO 64133

BOGG, RICHARD ALLAN, educator; b. Grosse Pointe, Mich., May 31, 1934; s. Sydney Elmer and Dorothy Marie B.; B.B.A., U. Mich., 1956, Ph.D., 1971; postgrad. U. Exeter (Eng.), 1957-58; M.H.A., Washington U., St. Louis, 1960. Asst. adminstr. Port Huron (Mich.) Hosp., 1960-62; research asso. U. Mich. Sch. Pub. Health, 1965-69; asso. prof. dept. community medicine Faculty Medicine, U. Alta., Edmonton, Can., 1969-72; asst. prof. dept. sociology Ball State U., Muncie, Ind., 1972—. Bd. dirs. Planned Parenthood of Delaware County, 1973-75. USPHS trainee, 1962-65; HEW Childrens Bur. research grantee, 1966-68, Mich. Ho. of Reps. spl. research grantee, 1968. Mem. Am. Sociol. Assn., ACLU. Contbr. articles to profl. jours. Home: Rural Route 2 Daleville IN 47334 Office: Dept Sociology Ball State U Muncie IN 47306

BOGGESS, THOMAS PHILLIP, III, graphics arts co. exec.; b. Greenville, Ky., Jan. 22, 1921; s. William C. and Gertrude Lucille (Lumpkins) B.; grad. high sch.; m. Ann Marie Mossner, Sept. 1, 1942; children—Thomas Phillip IV, Nancy L. Vice-pres. Alfred Mossner Co., Chgo., 1945-70, pres., 1970—, also dir.; dir. Blue Printers Supply Corp., Chgo. Chmn. zoning bd. of appeals, Village of River Forest, Ill., 1950—. Served with USNR, 1942-45. Decorated Purple Heart. Mem. Blue Print Club of Chgo. (pres. 1957-62). Club: Oak Park Country. Home: 335 Gale Ave River Forest IL 60305 Office: 108 W Lake St Chicago IL 60601

BOGGS, GARY PATRICK, metallurgist; b. Blackey, Ky., Mar. 25, 1946; s. Earl and Mabel (Dixon) B.; student U. Ky., 1964-67, Franklin U., 1976-77; m. Carol Ann Hamb, Sept. 16, 1967; children—Angela Suzanne, Gary Patrick. Chem. technician N.Am. Rockwell, Winchester, Ky., 1968-72; plant metallurgist Rockwell Internat., Marysville, Ohio, 1972—. Bd. dirs. Union County YMCA, 1976-77; bd. dirs. Union County Council on Alcoholism, 1976-77. Mem. Electroplaters Soc., Am. Soc. Metals. Democrat. Baptist. Home: 307 Elwood Ave Marysville OH 43040 Office: PO Box 178 Marysville OH 43040

BOGGS, JOSEPH DODRIDGE, pediatric pathologist; b. Bellefontaine, Ohio, Dec. 31, 1921; s. Walter C. and Birdella Z. (Coons) B.; A.B., Ohio U., 1941, Litt.D., 1966; M.D., Jefferson Med. Coll., 1945; m. Donna Lee Shoemaker, June 12, 1964; 1 son, Joseph Dodridge. Intern, Jefferson Med. Coll. Hosp., Phila., 1945-46; resident Peter Bent Brigham Hosp., Boston, 1946-48, asso. pathologist 1947-51; instr. pathology Harvard Med. Sch., Boston, 1948-51; with Childrens Meml. Hosp., Chgo., 1951—, dir. labs. 1951—; prof. pathology Northwestern U., Chgo., 1952—; dir. BSP Ins. Co., Phoenix. Mem. med. adv. bd. Ill. Dept. Corrections, Springfield,

1971-77. Bd. dirs. Blood Services, Phoenix, 1972, Community Hosp., Evanston, 1958-61, Lorreto Hosp., Chgo., 1971-72. Served to capt., M.C., AUS, 1948-51. Mem. Am. Soc. for Study of Liver Disease, N.Y. Acad. Scis., Midwest Soc. Pediatric Research, Inst. Medicine, Ill. Soc. Pathologists (pres. 1965), Ill. Assn. Blood Banks (pres. 1969-70). Contbr. articles to profl. jours. Home: 1448 N Lake Shore Dr Chicago IL 60610 Office: Childrens Memorial Hospital 2300 Childrens Plaza Chicago IL 60614

BOGUE, GRANT, sociologist; b. Kansas City, Mo., Aug. 28, 1928; s. Granvol Hurst and LaVerna M. (Harris) B.; B.A., Mich. State U., 1950, M.A., 1954; Ph.D., Wayne State U., 1963; m. Patricia L. Prosser, June 3, 1953; children—Lynn, Ross, Ann. Staff, acting exec. dir. Detroit Commn. on Children and Youth, 1954-59; instr. sociology and anthropology Allegheny Coll., 1959-63; asst. prof. sociology and anthropology U. Ark., 1963-66, Tex. A. and M. U., 1966-67; prof. sociology and anthropology Western Ill. U., Macomb, 1967—, chmn., 1967-71. Served with USAF, 1951-53. Mem. Am. Sociol. Assn., Population Assn. Am., Western Ill. U. Fedn. Profs. (pres. 1970-71), Macomb Area Flyers Assn. (pres. 1970-71). Contbr. articles to profl. jours. Address: Dept of Sociology Western Ill U Macomb IL 61455

BOHLEY, PAUL BRANCH, pump products mfg. co. exec.; b. Medina, Ohio, Dec. 14, 1923; s. Christian Gotleib and Bessie Louise (Dickerman) B.; student Ohio State U. Coll. Agr., 1941-43, 46-47; m. Dorothy Louise Persons, May 26, 1944; children—Donna Allyn (Mrs. Larry Alan Davis), Keith Persons. Owner-operator Crestview Farms, producers hybrid corn and certified small grain, Medina, 1945-62; gen. sales mgr. O-Y-O Seed Assos., Inc., Marysville, Ohio, 1962-65; sales mgr. agrl. products Gorman Rupp Co., mfr. pumps and associated products, Mansfield, Ohio, 1965—. Mem. Buckeye Consol. Sch. Bd., 1952-64, pres., 1952-53, 61-62. Served with USAAF, 1942-45; lt. col. Res. (ret.). Decorated D.F.C., Air medal with 5 oak leaf clusters. Mem. Nat. Fertilizer Solutions Assn. (dir. 1972, nat. v.p. 1970-73), Sprinkler Irrigation Assn. (chmn. membership com. 1972, chmn. Waste Water resources com. 1973-74, dir. 1974-75, pres. elect 1977), Ohio Flying Farmers Assn. (dir. 1947-48, 74-76, sec. 1948, pres. 1978), Am. Legion, V.F.W., Medina C. of C., Air Force Assn., Ohio Future Farmers Assn. (hon.), Nat. Security Council, Alpha Zeta. Republican. Methodist (lay minister 1955-60). Lion (sec. 1948-52). Contbr. to profl. publs. in field. Home: 5986 Branch Rd Medina OH 44256 Office: 305 Bowman St Mansfield OH 44902

BOHLIM, RICHARD CHARLES, civil engr.; b. Michigan City, Ind., Sept. 5, 1952; s. George A. and Margaret (Elias) B.; B.S.C.E., Ind. Inst. Tech., 1974. Service engr. Combustion Engring., Martins Creek, Pa., 1974, Boston, 1974-75, St. Louis, 1975-76, lead service engr. for combustion engring., Lawrence, Kans., 1976—. Mem. ASCE (citation award 1974), Alpha Sigma Phi. Roman Catholic. Club: Moose. Home: 202 Raven Dr Michigan City IN 46360 Office: PO Box 522 Lawrence KS 66044

BOHLMANN, PAUL FRANK, home furnishings co. exec.; b. Watertown, Wis., Dec. 31, 1925; s. Frank and Mary (Heist) B.; student Rockford Sch. Bus., 1949-51; m. Dorothy M. Fendt, Aug. 7, 1948; children—Jeffrey, John, Michael, Martin. With Brandt Automatic Cashier, Watertown, 1947-49; accountant Sealtest Ice Cream, Rockford, Ill., 1951-55, John Knobel & Son, Rockford, 1955-63; with Weiman Co., Inc., Chgo., 1963—, sec., 1970—, sec.-treas., 1977—. Served with USNR, 1943-47. Roman Catholic. Elk. Home: 420 Pebble Creek Rd Palatine IL 60067 Office: 4801 W Peterson Ave Chicago IL 60646

BOHON, ELLIS G(RAY), pub. accountant, mgmt. cons., computer programmer, tax cons.; b. LaBelle, Mo., Sept. 1, 1902; s. Frank W. and Lee (Ellis) B.; student Westminster Coll., Fulton, Mo., 1920-21; B.S. cum laude, Knox Coll., Galesburg, Ill., 1924; postgrad. Walton Sch. Commerce, 1927-29, Northwestern U., 1930-33, 1935, 1965-66, YMCA Community Coll., 1963-71, Chgo. Bd. Trade Grain Inst., 1955, 56 (all Chgo.); C.P.A., U. Ill., 1935; m. Joyce L. Finlayson, Apr. 15, 1939; children—Walter Duncan, Ellis Gray, II (dec.). Staff accountant Ernst & Ernst, C.P.A.'s, Chgo., 1927-30; partner R. L. Pearce & Co., C.P.A.s', 1930-36; propr. E. G. Bohon & Co., C.P.A.'s, 1936—; former lectr. Am. Inst. Banking, Walton Sch. Commerce, Ill. Inst. Tech., Chgo., Lake Forest (Ill.) Coll. Former advisor, treas. Lakes chpt. Order DeMolay, bus. men's adv. council Jones Comml. High Sch. (Chgo.). Enrolled as atty. Tax Ct. U.S.A.; C.P.A., Ill., Ky., Iowa, Mo., Ind. Member Am. Inst. C.P.A.'s, Am. Accounting Assn., Ill. (past chmn. tech. com.), Ia. socs. C.P.A.'s, Nat. Assn. Accountants, Am. Arbitration Assn., Accounting Research Assn., SCORE, ACTION, Am. Inst. Laundering, Ky. Hist. Soc., Midwest Bus. Adminstrn. Assn., Phi Delta Theta. Presbyterian. Mason (Shriner, treas. club). Clubs: Monroe, Union League, Plaza, Swedish Glee. Author papers. Home: 523 E North Ave Lake Bluff IL 60044 Office: 140 S Dearborn St Chicago IL 60603

BOHROFEN, ELDON LA VERN, banker; b. Dallas Center, Iowa, July 14, 1941; s. Kenneth John and Lucille (Hawbaker) B.; B.S., Drake U., 1963, J.D., 1966; grad. Nat. Trust Sch., Northwestern U., 1972; m. Judith Beth Storey, Apr. 2, 1966; children—Heather Marie, Peter Charles. Admitted to Iowa bar, 1966, Wis. bar, 1974; mem. faculty bus. adminstrn. dept. Wis. State U., Whitewater, 1966-68; trust officer First Nat. Bank, Sioux City, Iowa, 1968-69; v.p., trust officer Union Bank & Trust Co., Ottumwa, 1969-74; v.p., sr. trust officer Citizens Bank of Sheboygan (Wis.), 1974—; instr. comml. law Am. Inst. Banking, Sioux City, 1969, Ottumwa Heights Coll., 1970-74; Bd. dirs. Sheboygan Sr. Citizens; chmn. found. div. Sheboygan United Way; mem. adv. com. Lakeland Coll. Endowment Fund; mem. trust fund devel. com., exec. bd. Bay Lake council Boy Scouts Am.; trustee Sheboygan YMCA Endowment Trust; sec., bd. dirs. Sheboygan Rotary Found. Nat. Merit scholar, 1959-60. Mem. Am., Iowa, Wis., Sheboygan County bar assns., Sheboygan County Life Underwriters, Sheboygan C. of C., Wis. Trustees Assn., Sheboygan County YMCA, Phi Delta Theta. Lutheran (fin. com.). Clubs: Rotary, Pine Hill Country. Home: 423 Timberlake Rd Sheboygan WI 53081

BOIKAN, WILLIAM SCLAIR, physician; b. Odessa, Russia, Apr. 8, 1904; s. Morris and Fanny (Dorfman) B.; B.S., U. Ill., 1926, M.S., 1928, M.D., 1928; m. Ila Sclair, Aug. 3, 1929; children—Sergus, Sandra; came to U.S., 1908, naturalized, 1925. Intern, Cook County Hosp., Chgo., resident, 1929-30; resident U. Vienna (Austria), 1930-31; practice medicine specializing in cardiology, Chgo.; chief, heart clinics Cook County Hosp.; asst. prof. medicine U. Ill., Chgo., 1935-63; attending cardiologist St. Joseph Hosp., Chgo., 1963—, mem. teaching and cons. staff, 1963—. Billings and Fenger fellow, 1930-31. Fellow ACP, Am. Coll. Cardiology, Am. Heart Assn.; mem. AMA, Ill., Chgo. med. socs., Inst. Medicine, Chgo. Soc. Internal Medicine, Sigma Xi. Contbr. articles to profl. jours. Home: 3800 Lake Shore Dr Chicago IL 60613 Office: 25 E Washington St Chicago IL 60602

BOILORE, ALLAN EARL, profl. bus. cons.; b. Alpena, Mich., Aug. 10, 1941; s. Earl Louis and Rosalie (Homant) B.; B.A., Mich. State U., 1963; m. Sally Ann Lixie, Sept. 28, 1963; children—Karen, Bradley, David, Jeff. With Kent Moore Orgn., Inc., Jackson, Mich., 1963-64; account exec. Profl. Mgmt., Inc., Lansing, Mich., 1964-69; pres., Profl. Med. Systems, Lansing, 1972—. Mem. Nat. Soc. Profl. Bus. Consultants (chmn. pub. relations com., 1974—, dir., 1974—). Kiwanian. Certified profl. bus. cons. Home: 327 W South Mason MI 48854 Office: 531 N Clippert St Lansing MI 48912

BOLDUC, OLIVER JOSEPH, cons. engr.; b. Chgo., July 19, 1924; s. Oliver Joseph and Margaret (Schartle) B.; B.S. in Chem. Engring., U. Ill., 1950; m. Barbara Ann, June 19, 1948; children—Robert, Wendy, Brian, Gail (Michael Powers), Carol, Christine. Chem. engr. fats and oils Armour & Co., Chgo., 1950-54; chief chemist Keystone Aniline & Chem. Co., Chgo., 1954-55; project engr. plant design Blaw-Knox Co., Pitts., 1955-58; chief process engr. chem. plant design Davidson-Kennedy Assos., Chicago Heights, Ill., 1958-61; asst. div. mgr. Austin Co., Cleve., process div. Des Plaines Ill., 1961-71; v.p., engring. mgr. chem. and indsl. plant design Mid-Am. Engrs., cons. engrs., Chgo., 1971-77; v.p. Midwest region Jacobs Engring. Co., 1977—. Served as 1st. lt., A.C., AUS, 1942-45. Decorated Air Medal, D.F.C. Registered profl. engr. numerous states. Mem. Am. Inst. Chem. Engrs., Am. Assn. Cost Engrs. Home: 719 N Douglas Ave Arlington Heights IL 60004 Office: Mid-Am Engrs 1 N Wacker Dr Chicago IL 60606

BOLEN, DOUGLAS LYNN, educator; b. Lima, Ohio, Nov. 25, 1945; s. Ira Harold and Nellie Mae (Jones) B.; A.A. in Bus. Adminstrn., Northwestern Sch. Commerce, 1966; B.A. in Bus. Adminstrn., Ohio No. U., 1968; M.B.A., U. Dayton, 1974; Ed.S., U. Toledo, 1976; m. Julia Kathryn Martin, Aug. 9, 1974. Instr. bus. edn. Wapakoneta (O.) Sr. High Sch., 1968-71; instr. bus. edn., also wrestling and baseball coach Lima Shawnee Sr. High Sch., 1971-72; asst. prof. bus. technologies Lima Tech. Coll., Ohio State U., 1974-76, also chmn. div., asst. dir. for instl. planning; dean instrn. Marion (Ohio) Tech. Coll., 1976—. Owner Douglas L. Bolen, Pub. Accountant, Marion, 1973—. C.P.A., Ohio. Mem. Am. Accounting Assn., Nat. Assn. Accountants, Nat. Soc. Pub. Accountants, Am. Inst. Decision Scis., Am. Mgmt. Assn., Am. Soc. Tng. and Devel., Soc. Data Educators, AAUP, Ohio Assn. Two-Year Colls., Assn. M.B.A. Execs., Smithsonian Assos., Am. Tech. Edn. Assn., Inst. Certified Profl. Mgrs. Democrat. Methodist. Elk. Home: 1790-1 Summerset Dr Marion OH 43302

BOLEN, WALDO EMERSON, JR., vending machine and steel stamping co. exec.; b. Chgo., Oct. 15, 1931; s. Waldo Emerson and Ellen (Keating) B.; student Lake Forest Acad., 1948-50, U. Mich., 1950-52, Colo. Coll., summer 1951, Grinnell Coll., 1952-54; A.B., U. Ariz., 1955; m. Chatka A. Busck, Aug. 14, 1954 (div. Dec. 1968); children—Emerson A., Clifford K., Lawrence B.; m. 2d, Virginia R. Robinson, Sept. 9, 1972. Asst. sales mgr. Northwestern Corp., Morris, Ill., 1957-59, asst. to pres., 1959-60, pres., 1960—; pres. Fielden Electronics, 1969—; dir. Grundy County Nat. Bank. Mem. sch. bd. Morris High Sch., 1963-66, Morris Grade Sch., 1969-71. Served with AUS, 1955-57. Republican. Episcopalian. Club: Morris Country (dir. 1967-70). Home: 725 W Jackson St Morris IL 60450 Office: 900 E Armstrong St Morris IL 60450

BOLES, HOBART PAUL, entomologist; b. Brandsville, Mo., Jan. 16, 1918; s. Walter Edwin and Ivy (Nations) B.; A.B., Southwestern Coll., Winfield, Kans., 1939; M.S., Kans. State U., 1947, Ph.D., 1967; m. Donis Juanita Hutchinson, June 18, 1944; 1 dau., Catherine Sue. Asso. prof. Huron (S.D.) Coll., 1947-52; grad. teaching asst. Kans. State U., Manhattan, 1952-54, adj. asst. prof., 1975; asst. prof. entomology U. Ark., Fayetteville, 1954-56; research entomologist Stored Rice Insects Lab., U.S. Dept. Agr., Houston, 1956-59, Stored Products Insects Lab., Savannah, Ga., 1959-65, U.S. Grain Mktg. Research Center, Manhattan, Kans., 1965—. Served with AUS, 1942-46. Mem. Am. Registry Profl. Entomologists, Kans. Entomol. Soc., Entomol. Soc. Am., Sigma Xi, Pi Gamma Mu, Gamma Sigma Delta. Contbg. author: Insect Colonization and Mass Production, 1966. Contbr. articles to profl. jours. and govt. publs. Home: 3020 Payne Dr Manhattan KS 66502 Office: 1515 College Ave Manhattan KS 66502

BOLICK, DAVID DEAN, fertilizer co. exec.; b. Bloomfield, Iowa, June 1, 1932; s. David Henry and Hazel LaFern (Parker) B.; student North East Mo. State U., 1951-53; B.S.C.E., U. Iowa, 1955; m. Elizabeth Ann Morgan, Nov. 25, 1955; children—Sandra, Carolyn, Barbara. Mgmt. trainee Morgan Oil Co., Wyaconda, Mo., 1957-67; dist. sales rep. Hawkeye Chem. Co., Clinton, Iowa, 1967-69; pres., gen. mgr. Morgan Oil Co. Inc., fertilizers, Wyaconda, Mo., 1969—. Sec., mem. Wyaconda C-1 Sch. Bd., 1964-67. Served with U.S. Army, 1955-57. Mem. Fertilizer Inst., Nat. Fertilizer Solutions Assn., Mo. Agr. Industries Council (dir.), Mo. Liquid Plant Food Assn. Republican. Methodist. Clubs: Shriners, Masons. Home: 504 Market St N Memphis MO 63555 Office: Main St Wyaconda MO 63474

BOLIN, RUSSELL LEROY, constrn. co. exec.; b. Edgewood, Ill., Apr. 6, 1918; s. Fred Oscar and Lulu Margaret (Culley) B.; student Ill. Coll., 1936-38; B.S., Ind. State U., 1947; M.S., U. Ill., 1953; m. Anne May Mooney, Nov. 1, 1944; 1 dau., Diane Gege. Coach, Westville (Ill.) High Sch., 1947-51; with R.H. Bishop Co., Champaign, Ill., 1955—, sec., 1963—, v.p., 1970—. Served to maj. USAAF, 1941-46, USAF, 1951-53. Decorated Air medal, D.F.C. Named Basketball Coach of the Year, Vermilion County (Ill.) Coaches, 1951; recipient YMCA award for service to youth, 1968. Mem. Plumbing, Heating and Cooling Assn. Central Ill. (pres. 1962-66, state dir. to Ill. Plumbing and Heating Assn. 1975, 76), Am. Legion, V.F.W., Gamma Nu. Club: Moose. Home: Rural Route 1 Box 179 Fairmount IL 61841 Office: 3506 N Mattis Av Champaign IL 61820

BOLING, PAUL RICHARD, truck trailer distbg. co. exec.; b. Indpls., July 21, 1927; s. Allen Ray and Alta Reed (Kellams) B.; student Purdue U., 1952-54; m. Shirley Ann Barnard, Jan. 12, 1946; children—Pamela Ann, Janiel. Foreman Peerless Pump div. F.M.C., 1947-54; precision insp. Ind. Gear Works Co., Indpls., 1954-56; salesman, sales mgr., dist. sales mgr. Combined Ins. Co. Am., 1956-58; salesman Gen. Trailer Co. Inc., Indpls., 1958-65, sales mgr., 1965-70, exec. v.p., gen. mgr., 1970—, also dir.; pres. Wilson Trailer Co. Distbr. Council, 1977-78. Mem. Ravens Metal Products Distbr. Adv. Council, 1976—. Served with USNR, 1945-47. Mem. Ind. Motor Truck Assn., Indpls. Motor Truck Assn., Indpls. Traffic Club. Baptist. Clubs: Antelope, Masons. Home: 2229 Hogan Dr Indianapolis IN 46229 Office: 546 W Wilkins St Indianapolis IN 46225

BOLINGER, GEORGE NOEL, metal goods mfg. co. exec.; b. Shelbyville, Ill., Feb. 27, 1903; s. George C. and Grace (Odenbaugh) B.; B.S., U. Ill., 1925; m. Virginia Dove, Sept. 8, 1927 (dec. Oct. 1973); children—George F., Virginia J. Bolinger Craig, Robert N. Asst. sec. Sta-Rite Hair Pin Co., Shelbyville, 1928-29, dir., 1929-30, v.p., dir. 1930-38, pres., treas., 1938-39; pres., dir. Sta. Rite Ginnie Lou, Inc., mfrs. bobby pins, metal goods and spltys., Shelbyville, 1939—; dir. Shelby County State Bank. Mem. Beta Gamma Sigma. Author: Keys of Fortune, 1942. Inventor hairdressing accessories, draftless fireplace, automatic ice cream dipper, flashlights. Home: 515 N Morgan St Shelbyville IL 62565 Office: 143 E Main St Shelbyville IL 62565

BOLINSKE, ROBERT EDWARD, allergist; b. Kaukauna, Wis., Oct. 6, 1924; s. Edward J. and Hyacinth A. (Krautkramer) B.; M.D., Marquette U., Milw., 1948; m. Anne Kramolowsky, Oct. 20, 1957; children—Mary Jane, Kathryn, Janet, Ellen, Robert. Practice medicine specializing in allergy, St. Louis, 1958—; asst. clin. prof. St. Louis U. Med. Sch., 1960—. Served with M.C. USAF, 1954-56. Fellow Am. Acad. Allergy, Am. Coll. Allergists, Am. Assn. Clin. Allergy Immunology; mem. Mo. Allergy Assn. (pres. 1976-77). Roman Catholic. Home: 56 Portland Dr Frontenac MO 63131

BOLLER, JOHN CHARLES, realtor; b. Kansas City, Mo., Oct. 13, 1923; s. Robert Otto and Ina Dorothy (Dickerson) B.; B.S. in Agr. with honors, Kan. State U., 1947; m. Betty Ruth Stamp, Aug. 18, 1944; children—Rebecca (Mrs. Robert Dale England), Lisa Kay. On farm tng. instr. VA, Urbana and Wheatland, Mo., 1947-51; fieldman, field services Mo. Farm Bur. Fedn., Jefferson City, 1951-58, dir. field services, 1958-63; owner, operator Boller Realtors & Hickory County Insurors, Inc., Hermitage, Mo., 1963—. Vice pres. Boller-Freeman Devel. Co., 1966—; owner Boller Appraisal Co., 1963—; pres. Hickory Co. Insurors, Inc., 1966—, Hermitage Telephone Co., 1955; dir. Bank of Hermitage. Organizer, scout camporee Lakeland Dist. council Boy Scouts Am., 1966; mem. Gov.'s Com. Missourians for Progress, 1961; pres. Pomme de Terre Lake League, 1966; Hickory County rep. S.W. Mo. Research Center, 1966. Served to 1st lt. AUS, 1943-46. Mem. Ozark Bd. Realtors (pres., legis. dir. 1975). Mem. Christian Ch. Lion, Mason (Shriner); mem. Order Eastern Star. Address: RD 1 Box 25 Hermitage MO 65668

BOLLING, GLENN LOYD, constrn. co. exec.; b. Ft. Scott, Kans., May 2, 1923; s. Ira Melvin and Oma Alice (Isebrandt) B.; grad. high sch.; m. Ila Louise Gaines, Aug. 10, 1946; children—Marilyn (Mrs. Larry Lewis), Debra Lee, Mark Loyd. Pres., B. and H Homes, Inc., 1948—; chmn. bd. Superior Modular Homes, 1970—. Advance Systems Homes, 1972—; dir. North Hills Bank, Mem. Mem. Gov.'s Bldg. Code Com., 1972-73; mem. Kansas City Bd. Appeals, 1966—. Served with AUS, 1942-45. Decorated Air medal with five oak leaf clusters, D.F.C. Mem. Home Builders Assn. (dir. 1966—), Citizens Assn. Clubs: Blue Hills Country, Leawood South Country. Home: 11401 Madison St Kansas City MO 64114 Office: 4949 Woody Creek Rd Parkville MO 64152

BOLLING, RICHARD (WALKER), congressman; b. N.Y.C., May 17, 1916; s. Richard Walker and Florence (Easton) B.; A.B., U. South, Sewanee, Tenn., 1937, A.M., 1939; postgrad. Vanderbilt U., 1939-40; D.C.L. (hon.), U. of South; LL.D., Rockhurst Coll.; m. Jim Grant, Jan. 13, 1964; 3 children. Dir. student activities, vets. affairs U. Kansas City, 1946-47; nat. vice-chmn. Am. Vets. Com., 1947-48; mem. 81st-95th congresses from 5th Mo. Dist., mem. house rules com., chmn. joint econ. com.; mem. steering and policy com. Democratic Caucus. Served to lt. col. AUS, 1941-46; PTO. Recipient Congl. Distinguished Service award Am. Polit. Sci. Assn. Democrat. Episcopalian. Author: House Out of Order, 1965; Power in the House, 1968, rev. edit., 1974. Home: 722 Walnut St Kansas City MO 64106 Office: US Courthouse 811 Grand Kansas City MO 64106 also Rayburn House Office Bldg Washington DC 20515

BOLSINGER, DON CLARK, lawyer; b. Cin., Jan. 21, 1931; s. Hiram Conrad and Opal Wintona (Ballard) B.; A.B., U. Cin., 1952, LL.B., 1954; m. Suzanne Ebersole, Aug. 21, 1954; children—Gregg David, Holly Susan, Brad Jeffrey. Admitted to Ohio bar, 1954, since practiced in Cin.; mem. firm Bolsinger & Bolsinger, 1954-64, Eiselein & Bolsinger, 1964-76; individual practice, 1976—. Lectr. legal seminars U. Cin., Cin. schs., adult edn. classes; referee Hamilton County Domestic Relations Ct., 1961-65. Co-chmn. bldg. fund drive Blue Ash (Ohio) YMCA, 1968—. Councilman, City of Madeira, 1965-69. Bd. dirs. Citizens United for Good Schs., 1968, Hamilton County Child Welfare Com., 1969. Served with AUS, 1955-56. Recipient Hon. Citizenship award City of Madeira, 1969. Mem. Ohio (family law com. 1966—, sec. 1973—, lectr. 1973, 74, 75, 77), Cin. (chmn. membership com. 1969, chmn. domestic relations com. 1970-72, lectr. 1964, 65, 76, 77) bar assns., United Presbyn. Men (trustee 1972-76, pres. 1974). Presbyterian (ch. trustee 1965-67, session 1969-71, 76—). Kiwanian (pres. 1967). Home: 7205 Sycamore Hill St Madeira OH 45243 Office: Don C Bolsinger 706 First National Bank Bldg 4th and Walnut Sts Cincinnati OH 45202

BOLT, ORREN ANTHONY, endodontist; b. Grand Rapids, Mich., Dec. 24, 1915; s. Rhine and Jennie (De Pree) B.; student Calvin Coll., 1933-35; D.D.S., U. Mich., 1940; m. Helen Mae Hoogsteen, Apr. 12, 1941; children—Norma Jean (Mrs. Lewis Van Kuiken), Marcia Ruth (Mrs. Paul Walters), Edward Rhine. Practiced gen. dentistry, Grand Rapids, 1940-60; practice dentistry specializing in endodontics, Grand Rapids, 1960—. Instr. Grand Rapids Jr. Coll., 1970—; chmn. Mich. Com. Dental Edn., 1962-68; mem. adv. com. dental edn. Ferris State Coll., Grand Rapids Jr. Coll.; lectr., clinician in dental edn. Mem. Mich. Gov.'s Adv. Com. Comprehensive Health Planning, 1969-70. Bd. dirs. Kent County chpt. Am. Heart Assn., Grand Rapids Symphony Orch. Served with USNR, 1941-45. Fellow Am. Coll. Dentists; mem. Am., Chgo., Mich. (chmn. various coms.) dental assns., Mich. Endodontic Assn. (pres. 1970), Am. Assn. Endodontists (dir. 1969-72), Fedn. Dentaire Internationale, Brit. Endodontic Soc. Mem. Christian Ref. Ch. (former deacon, trustee). Contbr. articles to dental jours. Home: 1043 Santa Barbara Dr SE Grand Rapids MI 49506 Office: 500 Cherry St SE Grand Rapids MI 49503

BOLTE, CARL EUGENE, JR., realtor; b. Kansas City, Mo., Feb. 4, 1929; s. Carl Eugene and Muriel Denslow (Eastman) B.; B.S., U. Mo. at Columbia, 1951, A.B., 1955. Asst. to pres. Paul Hamilton Co. realtors, Kansas City, Mo., 1956-60, exec. v.p., 1960—; v.p. Hamilton Bolte Ins. Agy., Inc., 1970—; mng. partner Bolte & Bolte Farms, Lawson and Slater, Mo., 1973—; dir. State Bank Slater; lectr. in field. Mem. Kansas City adv. com. U.S. Bicentennial, 1974—; chmn. bd. Goodwill Industries, 1975-76; mem. steering com. Salvation Army Christmas drive, 1957—; mem. exec. com. Crippled Children/Easter Seals, 1970-76; mem. adv. bd. Salvation Army, 1975—. Bd. govs. Citizens Non-Partisan Assn. Kansas City, 1960—; sec. Starlight Theatre, Kansas City. Served to lt. (j.g.) USNR, 1951-54; capt. Res. Mem. Naval Res. Assn., Mil. Order World Wars, Res. Officers Assn., ASCAP. Christian Disciples of Christ (deacon). Hon. fellow Harry S. Truman Library. Club: Rotary (pres. elect). Author: (plays) Give 'em Hell, Harry, 1971; ann. Kansas City Bar Assn. shows, 1962-70; ann. Univ. Club Show, 1957-74; Double Double, 1964; Full House, 1966; A Royal Welcome, 1972. Composer numerous songs including Marilyn—the Most, 1962; A Royal Welcome, 1972; part of scores of mus. comedies. Home: 3548 Wyoming St Kansas City MO 64111 Office: 4333 Madison Ave Kansas City MO 64111

BOLTON, DAN WILSON, III, chiropractor, acupuncturist; b. Topeka, Oct. 6, 1947; s. Dan Wilson and Betty Jean (Crews) B.; D.C., Palmer Coll. Chiropractic, 1970; B.A., Kans. Newman Coll., 1975; postgrad. in Acupuncture Columbia Inst., N.Y.C., 1974; m. Suzanne M. Hopkins, June 29, 1969; children—Dan Wilson IV, Christine Ellen. Practice chiropractic, Wichita, Kans., 1970—, practice acupuncture, 1974—; dir. Wichita Chiropractic Center, also acupuncturist clinic for med. hopeless children, 1974-76. Served with USAR, 1967-73. Recipient Blue Medallion Club award Clinic Masters Inc., 1975. Mem. Research for Acupuncture Soc. Kans. (dir.), acupuncture socs. Am., Kans., Kans., Am. chiropractic assns. Optimist. Home: 1751 S Seneca St Wichita KS 67213 Office: 1728 S Seneca St Wichita KS 67213

BOLZ, HAROLD AUGUST, engring. coll. dean emeritus; b. Cleve., May 27, 1911; s. William and Amelia A. (Waechter) B.; B.M.E., Case Inst. Tech., Cleve., 1933, M.M.E., 1935; Dr. Engring. (hon.), Purdue U., 1964, Tri-State Coll., 1973; m. Harriett Seymour Hallock, Aug. 7, 1937; children—William Scott, Everett Arthur, Eric Harold. Devel. engr. Weatherhead Co., Cleve., 1935-38; instr. machine design Purdue U., 1938-40, asst. prof. mech. engring., 1940-42, asso. prof., 1942-46, head dept. gen. engring., prof. indsl. engring., 1946-54; asso. dean Coll. Engring. Ohio State U., Columbus, 1954-58, dean, 1958-76, dean emeritus, 1976—. Trustee Goodwill Industries of Central Ohio. Registered profl. engr., Ind., Ohio. Fellow AAAS, ASME; mem. Am. Soc. Engring. Edn. (v.p. 1964-66, pres. 1971-72), Nat., Ohio socs. profl. engrs., Sigma Xi, Sigma Pi, Tau Beta Pi, Pi Tau Sigma, Theta Tau. Contbr. articles on machine design, engring. and personnel relations to tech. pubs.; editor Materials Handling Handbook. Home: 3097 Herrick Rd Upper Arlington Columbus OH 43221

BOLZ, HARRIETT (MRS. HAROLD A. BOLZ), musician; b. Cleve.; d. Roscoe Scott and Anna (Griffith) Hallock; B.A., Western Res. U., 1933; M.A., Ohio State U., 1958; m. Harold A. Bolz, Aug. 7, 1937; children—William Scott, Everett Arthur, Eric Harold. Composer, pianist numerous compositions; songs with piano, with string accompaniments, religious anthems, sonata for cello and piano, sonata for string and woodwind septet, contata for chorus and orch., sonatina for clarinet and piano; pub. Four Christmas Songs, Carol of the Flowers, 1967; Duo Scherzando, 1968; Two Madrigals for Christmas, 1968; That I May Sing, 1970; Sweet Jesus; Polychrome Patterns for Clarinet and Piano performed Lincoln Center, N.Y.C., 1971. Performances Chgo., Cleve., Indpls., Lafayette, Kokomo, Ind., Columbus, Ohio, Toledo, Miami Beach, Fla., Salt Lake City, Mpls., Cin. Mem. Arlington-Grandview unit Columbus Symphony Orchestra. Recipient 1st prize for piano composition Nat. Fedn. Music Clubs Adult Contest, 1965; 1st prize religious anthem Nat. League Am. Pen Women, 1970. Mem. Nat. League Am. Pen Women (1st prize, Spl. Bicentennial Music award 1976), Women's Aux. ASME, Women's Music Club Columbus (dir.), Nat. Assn. Am. Composers and Condrs., Ohio Fedn. Music Club: (dir.), Theta Lambda Phi, Phi Beta (Pi Nu chpt., Rose award). Club: Ohio State University Women's. Composer: Duo Scherzando for trumpet in B-flat and piano, Pageant for Woodwind Quintet. Home: 3097 Herrick Rd Columbus OH 43221

BOMGARDNER, STEPHEN RALPH, nursing dir.; b. Hays, Kans., Nov. 1, 1950; s. Hugh R. and Lois Irene (Sleichter) B.; student Ft. Hays (Kans.) State Coll., 1968-70; B.S.N., Wichita (Kans.) State U., 1973; m. Judith Katherine Roberts, May 15, 1971; 1 son, Jeremy Jacob. Staff nurse St. Joseph Med. Center, Wichita, 1973; staff nurse, gen. duty, Plainville (Kans.) Rural Hosp., 1973-74, coordinator inservice edn., staff nurse, 1975-76, dir. nursing, 1977—; supr. intensive care-coronary care unit Lincoln County Hosp., Fayetteville, Tenn., 1974-75; disaster nurse, nursing dir. ARC, Rooks County, Kans.; pub. lectr. coronary care nursing; instr. basic human sexuality jr. and sr. high schs.; mem. region 1 council Kans. Emergency Med. Services. Mem. Am., Kans. nurses assns., Kans. Assn. Hosp. Edn. Coordinators, Kans. Soc. Nursing Service Dirs. Home: Plainville KS 67663 Office: Plainville Rural Hospital 304 S Colorado St Plainville KS 67663

BOMZER, HERBERT WALLACE, univ. exec.; b. Bklyn., Sept. 23, 1925; B.A., Bklyn. Coll., 1948; M.A. (fellow), U. Del., 1950; postgrad. Columbia, 1950-53, Bklyn. Poly. Inst., 1953-58; Ph.D., U. Ill., 1974; m. Estie Ann Lipman, Nov. 21, 1951; children—Charles Alan, Sue Merle, David Jay. Instr. math. U. Del., 1948-50, Erasmus Hall High Sch., 1950-51; asst. prof. math. C.W. Post Coll., 1960-63; lectr. Gen. Precision, Inc., mem. faculty math. dept. Fairleigh Dickenson U., 1965-68; asso. prof. bus. adminstrn. Ill. State U., 1974-77; prof. bus. adminstrn., chmn. info. systems and analysis dept. Central Mich. U., 1977—; statistician Aberdeen Proving Grounds, 1948-50; engr., project supr. Ford Instrument Co., 1951-57; asst. to v.p., dir. ops. Autometric Corp., N.Y.C., 1957-63; program mgr. advanced systems, dept. head-analysis Kearfott Systems div. Gen. Precision, Inc., Wayne, N.J., 1963-68; dir. systems mgmt. Magnavox Co., Urbana, Ill., 1968-69; asst. dir. data processing U. Ill., Champaign, 1970-78. Chmn. reconnaissance and surveillance Mil. Ops. Research Soc., 1966-68; mem. computer com. Jerusalem Econ. Conf., 1972—; cons. UN ILO, 1976. Pres., U. Ill. Hillel Found.; v.p., bd. dirs. Shelter Rock Community Center, 1958; chmn. bd. dirs. Jr. League Infants Home, Bklyn., 1942-43; bd. dirs. Fed. Charities, 1969—; mem. Herricks Sch. Adv. Council, 1958-63, North Caldwell Adv. Bd., 1965-68, Eagle Rock council Boy Scouts Am., 1965-68 Champaign Sch. Adv. Com., 1972—. State of N.Y. scholar, 1953-58. Mem. IEEE, Am. Statis. Assn., Nat. Mgmt. Assn., Pi Mu Epsilon. Contbr. articles to profl. jours. Patentee in field. Address: 1334 Center Dr Mount Pleasant MI 48858

BONACKER, DONALD EDWARD, lawyer; b. Eureka, Mo., Sept. 21, 1932; s. Kenneth Edward and Matilda Anna (Ficken) B.; A.B., Washington U., St. Louis, 1957, J.D., 1959; m. Joyce Sybil McGee, Dec. 26, 1953; children—Scott Edward, Lisa Ann. Admitted to Mo. bar, 1959, since practiced in Springfield; asst. pros. atty. Greene County (Mo.), 1961-62; instr. adult edn. program in polit. sci., constl. decisions and bus. law Drury Coll., 1962-67; instr. legal seminars. Mem. Alumni Council Washington U., 1972—. Trustee Springfield-Greene County Library, pres., 1975. Served with AUS, 1954-56. Mem. Am., Mo., Greene County bar assns., Am. Trial Lawyers Assn., Mo. Library Assn. Republican. Mem. United Ch. of Christ. Club: Kiwanis. Bd. editors Washington U. Law Quar., 1958-59. Home: 802 Maplewood St Springfield MO 65804 Office: 406 McDaniel Bldg Springfield MO 65806

BONACKER, JOYCE SYBIL, painter, art gallery exec.; b. Jerseyville, Ill., Feb. 9, 1932; d. Benjamin Franklin and Minnie Iona (Willis) McGee; student Southwest Mo. State U., 1969, Drury Coll., 1972, Art Mus. Sch. Art, 1962-72, So. Mo. Coll., 1971; m. Donald Edward Bonacker, Dec. 26, 1953; children—Scott Edward, Lisa Ann. Two-person shows: William Woods Coll., Fulton, Mo., 1976, Cottey Coll., Nevada, Mo., 1976; three-person shows: Sch. of Ozarks, Point Lookout, Mo., 1975, Robert Johnson Art Center, Springfield, Mo., 1975; also group and juried nat., internat. shows; represented in permanent collections: Springfield (Mo.) Art Mus., Sch. of Ozarks, Springfield Community Center, Women's Center, Springfield; owner, mgr. Bonacker-Parlato Art Studio, Springfield, Mo., 1970-71; chmn., co-founder Park Central Art Gallery, Springfield, 1972—, instr. art workshops, 1972, 77; instr. Art Mus. Sch. Art, Springfield, 1975—. Recipient awards Southwest Mo. Mus. Assos., 1970, Sch. of Ozarks, 1971, Am. Watercolor Soc., 1971, Arts Council, Tulsa, 1971, Mo. Women in Arts, 1974. Mem. Internat. Soc. Artists, So., Midwest watercolor socs., Southwest Mo. Mus. Assos.. Watercolor Soc. Ala. Home: 802 Maplewood St Springfield MO 65807 Office: 324 1/2 South Ave Springfield MO 65806

BOND, CHRISTOPHER SAMUEL, former gov. of Mo.; b. St. Louis, Mar. 6, 1939; s. Arthur D. and Elizabeth G. (Green) B.; B.A. with honors, Princeton, 1960; LL.B., U. Va., 1963; LL.D., Westminster Coll., Fulton, Mo., 1973, William Jewell Coll., 1973, Drury Coll., 1976; m. Carolyn Reid, May 13, 1967. Admitted to Mo. bar, 1963, U.S. Supreme Ct. bar, 1967; law clk. to chief judge U.S. Ct. of Appeals, 5th Dist., Atlanta, 1963-64; asso. firm Covington & Burling, Washington, 1965-67; pvt. practice law, Mexico, Mo., 1968; asst. atty. gen., chief counsel consumer protection div. State of Mo., 1969-70; auditor State of Mo., 1971-72, gov., 1973-77; pres. Gt. Plains Legal Found., Kansas City, Mo., 1977—. Mem. Republican Govs. Assn. (chmn. 1974-75), Nat. Govs. Conf. (exec. com. 1974-76), Jaycees (one of 10 outstanding young men in Am. 1974). Presbyterian. Clubs: Optimists, Rotary. Home: 14 S Jefferson Rd Mexico MO 65265

BOND, DOROTHY ANN, cartoonist, lectr.; b. Chgo.; d. William George and Helga (Hansen) Peterson; student Chgo. Acad. Fine Arts; m. John Delmar Bond (divorced); children—John Delmar, Raleigh V. Civilian sec. in USN, 1940-44; syndicated cartoonist, 1945—; artist Northwest Hosp., 1970—; portrait artist, 1971—. Sponsor of The Easter Seal Soc. Hon. mem. Nat. Socs. Assn., Toastmistress Club, Chgo. Boys' Clubs, numerous other nat. and local orgns. Author cartoon books: Government Gertie, 1944, Navy Nora, 1945, Office Daze, 1945, The Second Baby, 1946, Life With the Boss, 1947, Mama, The Unsung Heroine, 1948; Meet Me in The Ladies Room, 1948; All Men Are Dogs, 1950; Let's Have a Baby, 1950; Your First or Second Baby?, 1956; Life with The Doctor n' Nurse, 1960; With Love Bobbi Borcherdt, 1961; Bobbi Borcherdt Presents, 1962; Heartwarmers, 1963; Bobbi Borcherdt's 100th Anniversary Booklet, 1968. Creator Dietsticker Cards, 1965; ReaLemon advt. series, 1968; newspaper feature Delightful Dietips, 1966. Address: 2450 N Washtenaw Ave Chicago IL 60647

BOND, ORIEL EDMUND, artist; b. Altus, Okla., July 18, 1911; s. Bert Galen and Bertha Ellen (Hughes) B.; student Rockford Coll., 1930-37; m. Dorothy Olive Swanson, Sept. 5, 1936; children—Bruce Edmund, Judy Kay (Mrs. Jay McCartney Hanson). Comml. artist J.L. Clark Mfg. Co., Rockford, Ill., after 1946; v.p., dir. J.L. Clark Assos., 1948—; one-man shows Burpee Art Gallery, 1956, 59, Belle Keith Gallery, 1967, 72, Rock River Savs. & Loan Co., 1969 (all Rockford), Geneseo (Ill.) Woman's Club, 1970, 71; exhibited in group shows at Burpee Art Gallery, 1937, 38, 56, 58, 60, 68, Wright Art Center, Beloit (Wis.) Coll., 1956, 57, 59, 60, 62, 63, Ill. State Fair, Springfield, 1959, 60, Am. Artists Profl. League, N.Y.C., 1971, 72, Profl. Artists and Designers Guild, Rockford, 1960, 61, 62, Winston-Salem (N.C.) Conv. Center, 1970, Hilton Inn, Williamsburg, Va., 1970, Downtown Gallery, Beloit, 1969, Colonial Village Mall, Rockford, 1962-76, Home Savs. & Loan Co., Rockford, 1962-74, Rockton (Ill.) Art Fair, 1971, 72, 73, 75, Wilhelm Tell Art Fair, New Glarus, Wis., 1972, 73, 75, Sterling (Ill.) Art Fair, 1972, Rock River Savs. & Loan Co., 1966, Greenwich Village Fair, Rockford, 1955-63, 71, 72, 73, 75, Beloit and Vicinity Art Fair, 1963, Janesville (Wis.) Art Fair, 1973, Belle Keith Art Gallery, Rockford, 1959; Precinct committeeman Rockford Republican Com., 1956-58, 60. Recipient 1st popular award Rockford Art Assn., 1956, 58, 60, Ill. State Fair, 1959, Colonial Village Mall, 1972, Sterling Art Fair, 1972; 1st, 2d and 3d awards Rockton Art Fair, 1971, 72, 75, 2d place award Wilhelm Tell Art Fair, 1972; 2d and 3d place popular award Wright Art Center, 1959, 1st popular award, 1962. Mem. Profl. Artists and Designers Guild (sec. 1959-60, v.p. 1961, 1st and 2d popular awards 1961, 62), Am. Artists Profl. League, Nat. Soc. Lit. and Arts. Home: 7816 Bond Dr Roscoe IL 61073

BOND, RICHARD JORDAN, banker; b. Oaktown, Ind., June 12, 1933; s. Starner and Margaret (Jordan) B.; student Purdue U., 1951-54; m. Janet Arline Knotts, June 27, 1954; children—Connie L., Richard J., Mary Kay. Exec. v.p. Midwest Homes, Inc., Oaktown, Ind., 1958-62, dir., 1958-66; branch mgr. Security Bank & Trust Co., Oaktown, 1962-67, exec. v.p., Vincennes, 1967-69, pres., 1969—, dir., 1963—; dir. Modern Facilities, Inc., Oaktown Lumber, Inc., H.J.B. Corp., D.B.S., Inc., Farmersburg Industries, Inc. Bd. dirs. Knox County Hosp. Assn., 1963—, Gov.'s Council for Private Action, Ind., 1970—, Vincennes U. Found. Bd., Inc. Mem. Wabash Valley Assn., Harmony Soc., Alpha Gamma Rho. Republican. Mem. Christian Ch. Mason, Elk. Home: Oaktown IN 47561 Office: 20 N 3d St Vincennes IN 47591

BONDA, ALVA TED, car rental and service industry exec., profl. baseball exec.; b. Cleve., June 1, 1917; s. Jacob Nathan and Nettie (Wasserman) B.; student pub. schs.; m. Marie C. Ermisch, Oct. 27, 1940; children—Penny (Mrs. Merrill Solomon), Joel, Thomas. Owner, operator car rental bus., 1945-49; pres. Airport Parking Co., 1949-68; pres. Cleve. Indians Baseball, Inc.; chmn. bd. Penril Corp.; dir. Avis Rent a Car, Cleve. Cavaliers Corp., MCI Communications Corp. Active NCCJ, Jewish Community Fedn., Jewish Welfare Fund, Glenville YMCA, Cleve. Police Athletic League; pres. Greater Cleve. Growth Corp., Cuyahoga unit Am. Cancer Soc.; trustee, chmn. bd. fellows Brandeis U. Served with AUS, 1941-45. Clubs: City, Oakwood Country (Cleve.); Palm Beach Country (Fla.). Home: 2 Bratenahl Pl Cleveland OH 44108 Office: 1700 Investment Plaza Cleveland OH 44114 also Cleve Indians Cleveland Stadium Cleveland OH 44114

BONDAR, ANDREW ARTHUR, dentist; b. Manchester, N.H., Oct. 23, 1914; s. Arthur George and Anna (Greneshen) B.; student U. N.H., 1932-34; D.M.D., Tufts U., 1938; diploma U.S. Army Med. Field Service Sch., 1969; certificate Command and Gen. Staff Coll., 1972; m. Ellen Ferguson Stewart, July 24, 1953; 1 dau., Billie Arlene. Pvt. practice dentistry, Manchester, 1939-42, 46-49; dentist VA Hosp., Battle Creek, Mich., 1949—. Lectr., clinician dist. and local dental socs. in N.H., N.Y., Que., Can. Asst. coach Jr. Am. Legion Baseball Team, Manchester, 1947-49; nat. chmn. Nat. German Prisoner of War Meml. Service, Ft. Custer, Mich., 1973-75. Served to capt. AUS, 1942-46, now col. Res. ret. Mem. Am., New Eng. dental assns., Northeastern Dental Soc., Am. Assn. Hosp. Dentists, Assn. U.S. Army, Tufts Coll., U. N.H. alumni assns., Res. Officers Assn. U.S. (sec.-treas. Battle Creek chpt., dental surgeon Mich. dept. 1973-77), Assn. Mil. Surgeons U.S., Am. Soc. Geriatric Dentistry (nat. treas.), Am. Acad. Gen. Dentistry, Fedn. Am. Scientists, AAAS, Fedn. Dentaire Internationale, Midwest Acad. Prosthodontics, Am. Legion, VFW, 40 and 8. Club: Elks. Home: 519 Alvena Ave Battle Creek MI 49017

BONDOC, ATILANO DIAZ, civil engr.; b. Philippines, Apr. 9, 1936; s. Lourdes Diaz; came to U.S., 1967, naturalized, 1975; B.S. in Civil and Sanitary Engring., Mapua Inst. Tech., 1960; m. Carmelita, Apr. 20, 1968; children—Norman, Alexandria, Ellen. Civil engr. U.S. Steel Co., Chgo., 1968-69, Dept. of Transp., State of Ill., Chgo., 1969-73, Bechtel Power Corp., Norwalk, Calif., 1973-75, EPA, Chgo., 1976—. Registered profl. engr., Ill., Calif. Mem. ASCE, Philippine Engrs. and Scientists Orgn. (press relations officer). Club: Toastmaster Internat. Home: 6430 N Damen Ave Chicago IL 60645 Office: 230 S Dearborn St Chicago IL 60604

BONE, VIDA MARIE, employment cons. co. exec.; b. Vero Beach, Fla., Feb. 14, 1926; d. Raymond Lee and Emma Evangeline (DeFoe) Gore; student schs. Vero Beach; m. Charles Northington Bone, Oct. 11, 1944; children—Charles Raymond, Leonard Olin. With Winn Dixie Grocery Co., Miami, Fla., 1948-59; pvt. practice as beautician, 1960-66; supr. Servomation of Chgo., 1966-67; employment counselor Hallmark Personnel, Chgo., 1967-69; pres., owner, operator Employment Consultants Inc., Lansing, Ill., 1970—. Mem. Nat. (certified), Ill. employment assns. Republican. Lutheran. Club: Lansing Sportsman. Home: 17034 Oakwood St Lansing IL 60438 Office: 2325 177th St Lansing IL 60438

BONEMEYER, MAURICE H., dentist; b. Fargo, N.D., Dec. 23, 1924; s. Henry G. and Irene Ida (Aust) B.; student Sacremento Jr. Coll., 1943; Baylor U., 1943-44; D.D.S., Marquette U., 1951; m. Mary Jean D'Orazio, Nov. 23, 1950; children—M. Dana, Mary, Peter, David, Gina. Practice dentistry, Gackle, N.D., 1951-53, Fargo, N.D., 1953—. Dir. N.D. Dental Service Corp; adv. bd. Zirc Corp. Pres. N.D. State Bd. Dental Examiners, 1972—; chmn. N.D. Dental Ins. Com., 1958—. Served with AUS, 1943-45. Decorated Purple Heart with oak leaf cluster. Mem. N.D., Am. dental assns., S.E. Dental Dist. Soc. (pres. 1959-60), Chgo. Dental Soc., Am. Assn. Dental Examiners, Am. Coll. Dentists, Am. Legion, D.A.V., N.D. Retriever Club, Psi Omega. Elk. Club: Fargo Country. Home: 618 19th Ave S Fargo ND 58102 Office: 601 Black Bldg Fargo ND 58102

BONESS, ROBERT WILLIAM, elec. engr.; b. Hinsdale, Ill., Sept. 11, 1940; s. Edward Louis and Catherine Marie (Becker) B.; B.S. in Elec. Engring., Ill. Inst. of Tech., 1977; m. Vicki Ann Vespa, June 24, 1967; children—Andrea Evlyn, Steven Edward. Designer, McDonald Engring. Co., Chgo., 1966-68; design group leader, elec. engr. Fluor Pioneer Inc., Chgo., 1968—. Served with U.S. Army, 1964-66. Registered profl. engr., Ill. Roman Catholic. Home: 1608 Herbert St Downers Grove IL 60515 Office: 200 W Monroe St Chicago IL 60606

BONFIELD, GENEVIEVE KRIESEL, securities broker; b. Michigan City, Ind., Dec. 23, 1913; d. Gustav Herman and Clara Mae (Brodersen) Kriesel; B.A., Eastern Mich. U., 1934; postgrad. Ind. U., 1938, Ariz. State U., 1955, Purdue U., 1962; m. Charles Edward Bonfield, Jan. 26, 1941 (dec.); children—Claire (Mrs. William G. Baldry, Jr.), Phyllis (Mrs. Phillip Keidaish), Charles Edward (dec.). Tchr. English, Elston Sr. and Jr. High Schs., Michigan City, 1934-41, 60-69; editor, pub. Shorelines, Michigan City, 1939-40; owner, operator Bonfield Speakers Agy., Michigan City, 1942-54; pres. Bonfield Motor Co. and Bonfield Farm Implement Corp., Michigan City, also La Porte, Ind., 1964-68; sec., broker Investors Diversified Services, Michigan City, 1969-73. Bd. dirs. LaPorte County Mental Health Assn., 1965—, Ind. Mental Health Assn., 1974—; charter pres. Michigan City Recycling Group, 1974-76; deaconess 1st Presbyterian Ch., 1974-77; mem. pub. policy com. Nat. Mental Health Assn., 1975—. Recipient Dist. Service award Ind. Mental Health Assn., 1971-74, Outstanding Service award Ind. Fedn. Bus. and Profl. Women's Clubs, 1971. Mem. Ind. Congress Parents and Tchrs. (life mem.), Ind. Fedn. Bus. and Profl. Women's Clubs (dir. 1969-71, 72-73), AAUW (dir. Ind. div. 1941-43, 71-75, charter pres. Beverly Shores br. 1972-74), LWV (area pres. 1970-72) Internat. Platform Assn., Internat. Biog. Assn., Kappa Delta Pi (hon.). Presbyn. (pres. Women's Assn. 1952-54). World Traveler. Home: 2005 Lake Shore Dr Long Beach Michigan City IN 46360

BONGERS, LEO VINCENT, dentist; b. Des Moines, July 19, 1922; s. Leo Vincent and Kathryn Ann (Keeler) B.; B.Sc., Creighton U., 1943, D.D.S., 1948; m. Margaret M. Stanosheck, June 17, 1943; children—Barry, Dennis, Mary Margaret, James, Teresa, Patricia. Gen. practice dentistry, Hanover, Kans., 1948—, Marysville, Kans., 1966—. Pres. Kan. Dental Bd., 1969-72. Mem. president's council Marymount Coll., Salina, Kans., 1967-71. Pres. Hanover City Council, 1953. Bd. dirs. Lakemary Center for Exceptional Children, Paola, Kans., 1968-77; pres. adv. bd. Creighton U. Dental Coll., 1977—. Served with AUS, 1944-46: PTO. Recipient Kans. State Service award U.S.O., 1966-68; by mayoral proclamation June 2, 1968 Dr. L. Bongers family day. Fellow Internat. Coll. Dentists; mem. Am. Assn. Dental Examiners (v.p. 1975), Kans. Dental Assn. (pres. 1972-73), Am. Dental Assn. (del. 1972), Am. Soc. Dentistry for Children, Hanover C. of C. (pres. 1956), Am. Legion, Pierre Fauchard Acad. (trustee 1975—), Kans. Pub. Health Assn., Omicron Kappa Upsilon, Alpha Sigma Nu. K.C. (state dep. 1966-68). Office: Profl Bldg Hanover KS 66945

BONGIORNO, JOHN ANTHONY, sales rep.; b. Chgo., Sept. 29, 1951; s. John Anthony and Stephanie Marie (DiTusa) B.; A.S. in Accounting and Bus. Adminstrn., Triton Coll., 1971; student in Mktg. U. Ill., Chgo. Circle, 1969-73; m. Sharon Louise Bernath, July 12, 1975. Sales rep. electronic data processing Reynolds & Reynolds Co., Chgo. office, Elk Grove Village, 1973-75, sales rep. automotive forms, 1975—. Named to 300 Club Reynolds and Reynolds Co., for sales excellence, 1975-77. Mem. Am., Chgo. mktg. assns. Roman Catholic. Clubs: Forest Grove Swim and Racquet, Hawthorne Racquetball. Home: 150 Midway Ln Vernon Hills IL 60061 Office: 2001 Landmeier Rd Elk Grove Village IL 60007

BONGIOVANNI, CHARLES ANTHONY, optometrist; b. Toledo, Aug. 8, 1937; s. Frank Joseph and Rose Theresa (Cicero) B.; B.S. in Chemistry, U. Detroit, 1959; B.S. in Optometry, Ohio State U., 1963; m. Carmen Magdalena Rodriguez, Dec. 18, 1965. Asso., Donald H. Lakin, East Detroit, 1963-66; practice optometry specializing in children and young adults, Southfield, Mich., 1965—. Cons. spl. edn. vision problems Farmington and Madison Heights sch. dists., 1965—. Home: 20905 Laurelwood St Farmington MI 48024 Office: 20180 W 12-Mile Rd Southfield MI 48076

BONIOR, DAVID EDWARD, congressman; b. Detroit, June 6, 1945; s. Edward John and Irene (Gaverluk) B.; m. Sybil Louise Rader, Nov. 25, 1967; children—Julie, Andrew; B.A., U. Iowa, 1967; M.A., Chapman Coll., 1972. Mem. Mich. Ho. of Reps., 1973-76; mem. 95th Congress from 12th Mich. Dist. Home: 23500 Denton Bldg R Apt 203 Mount Clemens MI 48043 Office: 1123 Longworth House Office Bldg Washington DC 20515

BONKALO, ALEXANDER, psychiatrist, clin. adminstr.; b. Hungary, Jan. 24, 1912; s. Alexander and Edith (Kalman) B.; M.D., Med. Sch. Budapest, 1937; postgrad., Budapest, Hungary, Berlin, Stockholm; m. Judith Hampel, 1927; children—Annemarie, Judy. Intern, Univ. Hosps., Budapest, 1935-36, resident in neurology Neuropsychiat. Hosp. U. Budapest, 1937-41, resident in psychiatry, 1941-44; resident Kaiser Wilhelm Inst., Berlin, 1938-39; asst. prof. Neuropsychiatric Hosp. U. Budapest, 1938-47; chief of service Toronto (Ont., Can.) Psychiat. Hosp. and Survey Place Central, 1953—; mem. faculty U. Toronto, 1954—, prof. psychiatry, 1974—; pvt. practice psychiatry. Fellow Royal Coll. Medicine Canada; mem. Canadian, Ont. psychiat. assns. Contbr. articles to med. periodicals. Home: 12 Fidelia Ave Toronto ON M4N 3E8 Canada Office: 600 Sherbourne Ave Toronto ON M4X 1W4 Canada

BONSALL, HARRY WALTER, realtor; b. Canton, Ohio; s. John Walter and Strausie Mary (Goshorn) B.; student Canton Bus. Coll., 1934-35, Kent State U., 1935-37. With Bonsall Agy., Canton, broker, 1945—. Bd. dirs. Canton Meals on Wheels, 1972-76. Mem. adminstrv. bd. Westbrook United Methodist Ch. Served with AUS, World War II. Mem. Humane Soc., Stark County Hist. Soc., YMCA, Canton Art Inst. Mem. Canton Bd. Realtors (past treas., sec., dir. 1955, 65), Am. Legion. Mason (Shriner).

BONSTEDT, THEODOR, psychiatrist; b. Russia, Feb. 4, 1924; s. Richard and Natalie (Zybulewska) B.; came to U.S., 1950, naturalized, 1955; M.D., U. Munich (Germany), 1950; M.S. in Psychiatry, U.

Mich., 1958; m. Dorothy M. Becker, May 3, 1952; children—Theodore, Stephen, Angelina. Intern, St. Francis Hosp., Peoria, 1951; resident U. Mich. Hosp., Ann Arbor, 1953-55, 57-58; dir. Marion (Ohio) County Mental Health Clinic, 1958-60; dir. outpatient clinic Rollman Psychiat. Inst., Cin., 1960-68, dir. day hosp., 1970-72, coordinator tng., 1972-75; dir. psychiatry Health Maintenance Plan, Cin., 1975—; Asso. clin. prof. psychiatry U. Cin. Coll. Medicine, 1974—. Bd. dirs. Cin. Council on Alcoholism, 1962-68. Served to capt. M.C., USAF, 1955-57. Diplomate Am. Bd. Neurology and Psychiatry. Fellow Am. Psychiat. Assn.; mem. Ohio Assn. Psychiat. Clinic Dirs. (pres. 1971), Ohio Community Mental Health Forum (pres. 1972), Hamilton County Acad. Medicine. Home: 991 Hollytree Dr Cincinnati OH 45231 Office: 2915 Clifton Ave Cincinnati OH 45220

BONUS, HAROLD WILLIAM, dentist; b. Chgo., Jan. 26, 1941; s. Vincent Leo and Virginia (Barys) B.; student Providence Coll., 1958-60; B.S., U. Ill., 1962, D.D.S., 1964, M.S. in Pedodontics, 1966; m. Carol Lynne Vavrina, June 19, 1965; children—Maria, Kurt. Practice dentistry specializing in pedodontics, Glen Ellyn, Ill., 1968—. Faculty dept. pediatric dentistry U. Ill. Coll. Dentistry, Chgo., 1969—, asso. prof., 1973—; cons. Central DuPage Hosp., Winfield, Ill., 1968—, U. Ill. Hosp., Chgo., 1976—; lectr. in field. Mem. vocat. guidance com. Glenbard High Sch., Glen Ellyn, 1970—; counselor Tri County Dental Asst. Soc., 1971-72. Served to capt. AUS, 1966-68. United Cerebral Palsy Found. clin. fellow, 1965. Fellow Am. Acad. Pedodontics, Ill. Acad. Pedodontics; mem. Glen Ellyn C. of C., Am. Soc. Dentistry Children (treas. Ill. 1970-73, sec. 1973-74, v.p. 1974-75, pres. 1976-77), Am. Dental Assn., Chgo., Ill. dental socs., Am. Assn. Dental Educators, Am. Soc. Preventive Dentistry, Glen Ellyn Hist. Soc. Author: Handbook of Clinical and Laboratory Pedodontics, 1972; Clinical and Laboratory Handbook for Pediatric Dentistry, 1977. Contbr. articles to jour. Dental office featured in pamphlets of ADA, also mags. Home: 111 Brandon Ave Glen Ellyn IL 60137 Office: 493 Duane St Glen Ellyn IL 60137

BOOE, JAMES MARVIN, chem. exec.; b. Austin, Ind., Nov. 12, 1906; s. James Ross and Grace (Hesler) B.; B.S., Butler U., 1928; m. Dortha Maud Weaver, July 30, 1938; children—James Marvin, Ann Marie, John Weaver. Chemist, Indpls. Plating Co., 1929; chief chemist P. R. Mallory & Co., 1929-45, dir. electrochem. research, 1945-51, exec. chem. engr., 1951-53, dir. chem. and metall. research corp. labs., 1953-63; dir. chem. labs. Mallory Capacitor Co., Indpls., 1963-72, cons., 1972—. Advisory bd. Am. Security Council. Accredited profl. chemist Am. Inst. Chemists. Recipient Army-Navy E civilian award, Naval Ordnance Devel. award. Fellow Am. Inst. Chemists; mem. Am. Chem. Soc., Electrochem. Soc., Irvington Hist. Soc., Am. Def. Preparedness Assn., Smithsonian Instn. (asso.), Indpls. Mus. Art, Goodwill Industries, Benton House Assn., Ransburg YMCA, Presbyterian (elder). Kiwanian. Patentee in field. Research on electrolytic capacitors, batteries, resistors, semiconductors. Home: 548 N Audubon Rd Indianapolis IN 46219 Office: 3029 E Washington St Indianapolis IN 46201

BOOK, IMOGENE IRIS CLARK (MRS. WILTZ ALONZO BOOK), librarian; b. Mt. Vernon, Ill., Dec. 12, 1924; d. Keith and Mona (Hawkins) Clark; B.S., So. Ill. U., 1946, postgrad., 1955, summer 1956; M.S., U. Ill., 1960, certificate of advanced study in librarianship, 1966; m. Wiltz Alonzo Book, Aug. 18, 1946; children—Douglas Keith, Karen Lynn. Tchr. secondary schs., Bellmont, Ill., 1946-47, Marissa, Ill., 1947-48, Bluford, Ill., 1955-56; tchr. Mt. Vernon Twp. High Sch., 1954-55, 56-57, librarian, 1958-62; librarian Mt. Vernon Community Coll., 1956-67, mem. adv. council, 1961-69; librarian Rend Lake Coll., Mt. Vernon, 1967-70, dir., 1970—. Cons., Student Ill. Edn. Assn., 1966-69; adviser Rend Lake Coll. Student Edn. Assn., 1956—; mem. adv. council U. Ill. Grad. Sch. Library Sci., 1962-64; mem. Ill. Commn. Tchr. Edn. and Profl. Standards, 1966-69. Mem. Ill. (legis. devel. com. 1965-70), Jefferson County (sec. 1964-65, pres. 1965-66), Mt. Vernon (pres. 1959-60) edn. assns., NEA, ALA, Ill., Mt. Vernon (sec. 1962-63, v.p. 1963-64, pres. 1964-65) library assns., Ill. Audiovisual Assn., Ill. Assn. Sch. Librarians (sec. 1958-59), Ill. Assn. Coll. and Research Librarians (vice chmn. 1974-75, chmn. 1975-76), Delta Kappa Gamma (chpt. v.p. 1964-66, rec. sec. 1966-68, pres. 1968-70). Home: 912 S 21st St Mount Vernon IL 62864 Office: Rend Lake Coll Route 1 Ina IL 62846

BOOK, KENNETH MERTEN, instl. equipment mfg. co. exec.; b. Lorain, Ohio, July 25, 1938; s. Harvey J. and Katherine (Merten) B.; B.S., Kent State U., 1960, M.Ed., 1963; Ph.D., U. Ariz., 1965; m. Terrel J. Dawson, June 17, 1961; children—Lorraine A., Rene R. Asst. supt. bus. affairs Pub. Schs., New Castle Ind., 1967-69; v.p. mktg. Peabody Seating Co. and Mutschler Brothers Co. div. Am. Standard, North Manchester, Ind., 1969-74; v.p. ednl. sales Am. Seating Co., Grand Rapids, Mich., 1975-76, v.p., gen. mgr. E.H. Sheldon & Co. subs., Muskegon, 1976-77, v.p. adminstr. parent co., Grand Rapids, 1977—. Mem. adv. bd. Jr. Achievement, engring. and tech. programs adv. council Western Mich. U., adv. bd. Internat. Mgmt. Council. Mem. Nat. Sch. Supply and Equipment Assn. (chmn. mfgs. council; dir.), Am. Mgmt. Assn., Am. Mktg. Assn., Assn. Sch. Bus. Ofcls., Phi Delta Kappa. Club: Athletic. Home: 7156 Oran St SE Grand Rapids MI 49506 Office: 901 Bradway Ave NW Grand Rapids MI 49504

BOON, DONALD JACKSON, pediatrician; b. Chgo., May 9, 1937; s. Clifton Udonna and Lila Jean (Jackson) B.; B.S., Purdue U., 1959; M.S., U. Ill., 1963, M.D., 1963; m. Mary Alice Stanley, June 8, 1963; children—Diana Jean, Sharon Marie. Intern, Hennepin County Gen. Hosp., Mpls., 1963-64; gen. practice medicine, Aurora, Ill., 1964; resident in pediatrics Univ. Okla., 1968-70; pediatric gastroenterology fellow, 1970-71; practice medicine specializing in pediatrics, Springfield, Ill., 1971—; mem. staff St. John's Hosp., Meml. Med. Center, Springfield Community Hosp.; cons. Ill. Div. Vocat. Rehab., Fed. Disability Program, 1973—, Goodwill Industries, 1976—, McFarland Mental Health Center, 1976; clin. asso. Southern Ill. Univ. Sch. Medicine, 1971—, U. Okla. Children's Meml. Hosp., 1970-71; chmn. task force Devel. of Curriculum in Gastrointestinal System, 1973; lectr. in Dominican Republic, 1971-74. Pediatrician for Community Action Agency, 1974-76; vis. physician for Sangamon County Jail, 1976-77. Served to capt. U.S. Army Med. Corps, 1964-67. Licensed physician, Ill., U.S. Pub. Health Service research fellow. Diplomate Nat. Bd. Med. Examiners, Am. Bd. Pediatrics. Fellow Am. Acad. Pediatrics; mem. AMA, AAAS, Sangamon County, Ill. State, Christian Med. Socs., N.Am. Soc. Pediatric Gastroenterology, Am. Acad. Allergy, Sociedad Dominicana de Pediatria (hon. mem.), PTA, Am. Physicians Poetry Assn. Republican. Methodist. Clubs: Springfield Pediatric, Fellowship of the Upper Room, Springfield Municipal Choir. Contbr. articles in field to med. jours. Author numerous articles, poems, letters, devotions. Home and office: 2 Leeds Dr Springfield IL 62702

BOONE, HAROLD CLETUS, educator; b. Dugger, Ind., Aug. 14, 1924; s. Charles F. and Mary Ethel (Eaves) B.; B.S., Ind. State U., 1951, M.S., 1953; postgrad. Ind. U., 1965-66, 68; m. Virginia Ruth Brenton, Oct. 15, 1949; children—Lisa (Mrs. R. Whybrew), Kathy (Mrs. Tom Jones), Karen, Charles, Douglas. Tchr., Indpls. Pub Schs., 1952-63; state supr. indsl. arts Ind. Dept. Pub. Instrn., Indpls., 1963-65, state dir. div. schoolhouse planning, 1965-67; ednl. cons. Louis C. Kingscott Assos., architects, engrs., Indpls., 1967-70; supt. schs. South Putnam Community Sch. Corp., Putnamville, Ind., 1970-75; asst. prof. tech. Ind. State U., 1975—. Mem. Selective Service Bd. Putnam County, 1972-75; dir. state dept. edn. div. United Fund campaign, Indpls., 1964-65. Campaign mgr. for Democratic candidate state supt. pub. instrn., Indpls., 1968. Served with inf. AUS, 1943-45; ETO. Decorated Bronze Star medal (2). Mem. Ind. Indsl. Edn. Assn. (dist. chmn. 1961-62), State Indsl. Arts Assn. (adv. bd. 1965-67), Ind. Sch. Bds. Assn., Ind. Assn. Pub. Sch. Supts., Future Farmers Am., Am. Legion (vice comdr. 1949), Epsilon Pi Tau, Tau Kappa Epsilon. Mason (Shriner), Lion. Contbr. articles to profl. publs. Home: Route 2 PO Box 111 Farmersburg IN 47850

BOONKHAM, CHOTCHAI, internist; b. Cheingrai, Thailand, May 29, 1943; s. Boonsing and Homhuon (Yantadilok) B.; came to U.S., 1969; M.D., Siriraj Med. Sch. and Hosp., Bangkok, Thailand, 1968; m. Sumalee Ratanagorn, May 1, 1972; children—Surachade, Monica. Intern, N.Y. Poly-clinic Hosp., N.Y.C., 1969-70; resident in internal medicine Shadyside Hosp., Pitts., 1970-71, St. Mary's Health Center, St. Louis, 1971-73; practice medicine specializing in internal medicine, Overland, Mo., 1973-76, Bridgeton, Mo., 1976—. Diplomate Am. Bd. Internal Medicine. Mem. A.C.P., AMA, Mo., St. Louis med. assns., Am. Soc. Geriatrics, Am., Mo. socs. internal medicine. Buddhist. Home: 15424 Highcroft Dr Chesterfield MO 63017 Office: Suite 220 3466 Bridgeland Dr Bridgeton MO 63044

BOOR, MYRON VERNON, psychologist, educator; b. Wadena, Minn., Dec. 21, 1942; s. Vernon LeRoy and Rosella Katharine (Eckhoff) B.; B.S., U. Iowa, 1965; M.A. (USPHS fellow), So. Ill. U., 1967, Ph.D., 1970; Clin. psychology intern Galesburg (Ill.) State Research Hosp., 1968-69; research psychologist Milwaukee County Mental Health Center, 1970-72; asst. prof., clin. psychologist Ft. Hays State U., Hays, Kans., 1972-76, asso. prof., clin. psychologist, 1976—. Certified psychologist, Kans. Mem. AAUP, Am. Psychol. Assn., Assn. Advancement Psychology, AAAS. Contbr. articles to refereed psychology jours. Home: 2505 Custer Rd Hays KS 67601 Office: Ft Hays State U Hays KS 67601

BOOS, ROBERT WALTER, supt. schs.; b. Dixon, Ill., July 22, 1931; s. Walter Edward and Helen Frances (Curran) B.; B.S., No. Ill. U., 1952; M.A., U. Ill., 1961; Ph.D., U. Ottawa, 1968; children—Robert Walter III, Craig A. Tchr. Glenview (Ill.) Jr. High Sch., 1955-61; prin. Pleasant Ridge Sch., Glenview, 1961-63, Clyde L. Lyon Sch., 1963-69; asst. supt. Arlington Heights Pub. Schs., 1969-71; supt. schs. McHenry Pub. Schs., 1971—. Lectr. North Park Coll., Chgo., Chgo. Consortium, Queen's U. Kinston, Ont., Can.; cons. Continental Bank, Chgo. Mem. Arlington Heights Cultural Commn., 1969-72; mem. ednl. adv. com. Northwest Edn. Coop., 1969-72. Served with AUS, 1952-54. Mem. NEA, Ill. Edn. Assn., Am., Ill. assns. sch. adminstrs., Am. Ednl. Research Assn., Kappa Delta Pi, Phi Delta Kappa. Contbr. to profl. publs. in field. Home: 1515 W Brandon Rd Glenview IL 60025 Office: 3926 W Main St McHenry IL 60050

BOOSALIS, ELSIE, real estate mgmt. exec.; b. Cedar Rapids, Iowa, Dec. 1, 1913; adopted dau. of Peter and Rose (Halleck) Boosalis; student, Phoenix Bus. Coll., 1943-44, Northwestern U., 1952-53, U. Minn. Property mgr. Peter Boosalis Bldg. Trust, Mpls., 1953—, trustee, 1960—. Dir. Greater Lake St. Council. Mem. Mpls. Soc. Fine Arts, Minn., Hennepin County hist. socs., Mpls. C. of C., Minn. Orchestral Assn., Am. Swedish Inst. Home: 4551 Dupont Ave S Minneapolis MN 55409 Office: 806 E Lake St Minneapolis MN 55407

BOOTH, ANDREW DONALD, univ. pres.; b. East Molesey, Surrey, Eng., Feb. 11, 1918; s. Sidney Joseph and Katherine Jane (Pugh) B.; B.Sc., U. London, 1941, D.Sc., 1951; Ph.D., U. Birmingham (Eng.), 1944; m. Kathleen Hylda Valerie Britten, Aug. 31, 1950; children—Ian, Amanda. Came to Can., 1962. Nuffield fellow U. London, 1946-52, lectr., 1952-54, reader, 1954-57, prof., 1957-62, also head dept. computer sci., 1957-62; head dept. elec. engring. U. Sask. (Can.), Saskatoon, 1962-63, dean coll. engring., 1963-72; pres. Lakehead U., Thunder Bay, Ont., Can., 1972—. Chmn. Wharf Engring. Labs., Banbury, Eng., 1955-62; mem. NRC Can., 1975—. Chmn. TV Adv. Council, Thunder Bay, 1972—; chmn. Univs. sector Metric Commn. Can., 1975—. Bd. dirs. Thunder Bay Symphony. Recipient Centennial medal Can., 1967; hon. fellow Inst. Linguistics, 1960. Fellow Inst. Physics, IEEE, Royal Soc. Arts; mem. Assn. Colls. and Univs. of Lakeside (chmn. 1974-75), Royal Canadian Mil. Inst. Clubs: Athenaeum (London), University of Toronto (hon.). Author: Fourier Technique, 1948; (with K.H.V. Booth) Automatic Digital Calculators, 1953, 56, 65; Numerical Methods, 1956, 58, 66; Automation and Computers, 1959, 66; Mechanical Resolution of Linguistic Problems, 1958; Digital Computers, 1965; others. Contbr. articles to sci. jours. Patentee in field of electronics. Home: 701 Confederation Dr Thunder Bay ON Canada Office: Office of the President Lakehead University Thunder Bay ON Canada

BOOTH, CAMERON, artist; b. Erie, Pa., Mar. 11, 1892; s. George Buchan and Ada (Brown) B.; student Art Inst. Chgo., 1912-17, traveling scholarship, 1917; student Hans Hoffmann Mahler Schs., Munich, Germany, 1927-28; H.H.D., Hamline U., 1949; m. Pearle M. Miller, Dec. 9, 1923. Instr. Art Students League, N.Y.C., 1944-48; lectr. art U. Minn., 1950-60, emeritus, 1960—; guest prof. painting U. Calif. at Berkeley, 1957-58; one-man shows Denver Art Mus., 1936, Art Inst. Chgo., 1942, Walker Art Center, 1953, Mpls. Inst. Art, 1958, Bertha Schaefer Gallery, N.Y.C., 1945, 50, 53, 55, 57, 59, 60, Howard Wise Gallery, N.Y.C., 1964, De Young Meml. Mus, San Francisco, 1961, Ford Found. Retrospective Exhbn., 1961-63; exhibited group shows Carnegie Inst., 1923, 24, 28, 30, 43, 44, 46, 64, Art Inst. Chgo., 1923, 24, 31, 34-37, 40, 42, 44, 46, Pa. Acad. Fine Art, 1924, 25, 43, 46; represented in pub. collections including Pa. Acad. Fine Art, Newark Mus., Denver Art Mus., San Francisco Mus. Art, Mus. Modern Art, N.Y.C., Guggenheim Mus., N.Y.C., Art Inst. Chgo., Art Students League N.Y., N.Y. Met. Mus. Art, Mpls. Inst. Arts, Phillips Collection, Washington, U. Calif. at Berkeley, U. Minn., Walker Art Center, Mpls., Butler Art Inst., Youngstown, O. John Simon Guggenheim Meml. Found. fellow in painting, 1942. Address: 3408 Park Terr Minneapolis MN 55406

BORCHAK, ROBERT GEORGE, surgeon; b. Cairnbrook, Pa., July 9, 1926; s. Michael and Mary (Dubosh) B.; B.S., U. Detroit, 1950; M.D., Wayne U., 1954; m. Agnes Therese Lesmeister, June 16, 1951; children—Robert M., Deborah, Paul, Michael, Denise, James. Intern, St. Joseph Mercy Hosp., Detroit, 1954-55, resident gen. surgery, 1955-57, chief resident, 1958-59, mem. teaching staff, 1960—; fellow in surgery Detroit Receiving Hosp., 1957-58; asst. surgeon UMW Miner's Hosp., Va., 1959-60; chief of surgery Holy Cross Hosp.; sr. surgeon Detroit Meml., S. Macomb hosps.; practice gen. surgery, Detroit, 1960-65, Harper Woods, Mich., 1965—; pres. M.D. Profl. Corp., Emergencycare Profl. Corp. Served with USNR, 1944-46. Diplomate Am. Bd. Surgery. Fellow A.C.S. (chmn. Macomb County com. trauma); mem. Detroit Surg. Soc., Midwest, Detroit surg. assns., Wayne County, Mich. State med. socs., AMA, Pan Am. Med. Assn., Am. Trauma Soc., Detroit Acad. Surgery, Nat. Assn. Underwater Instrs., Wayne U. Alumni Assn., U.S. (lt.), Grosse Pointe power squadrons, Phi Rho Sigma. Clubs: Lochmoor Country, Grosse Point Crisis. Home: 31 Renaud Rd Grosse Pointe Shores MI 48236 Office: Eastland Profl Bldg Harper Woods MI 48236

BORCHERT, PHILIP, drilling co. exec.; b. Cleve., Jan. 12, 1951; s. Ben Paul and Amme Marie (Babic) B.; B.S. in Accounting, U. Dayton, 1973; m. Annamarie C. Hague, Oct. 12, 1974. Field supr. Borchert Fence Co., Cleve., 1973-74, v.p., 1975—; pres. Cleve. Drilling and Earth-boring Co., 1977—. Roman Catholic. Clubs: Cleve. Athletic, Cleve. Jaycees, Bratenahl Adult Boosters, U. Dayton Alumni. Home: 10109 Burton Ave Bratenahl OH 44108 Office: 2751 E 55th St Cleveland OH 44104

BORDEN, GLEN LAFON, lawyer; b. Edison, Nebr., Jan. 8, 1911; s. Harvey Elwood and Grace Isabel (McCoy) B.; A.B., Kearney State Tchrs. Coll., 1935; M.A., U. Iowa, 1940; postgrad. Stanford U., 1937; J.D., U. Ill., 1958; m. Constance Isabel Borden, June 21, 1941; children—Scott W., Stuart P. Tchr. pub. schs., Waco, Nebr., Logan, Iowa, Grinnell, Iowa; prin., Waco, 1935-38; departmental tchr. Logan, 1938-39, Grinnell, 1939-40; admitted to Ill. bar, 1942; mem. firm Black, Black & Borden, Peoria, Ill., 1945—, Liggett Borden & Borden, Wyoming, Ill., 1960—. Dir. Wyoming Bank & Trust Co. Bd. dirs. Peoria Pub. Library, 1950-62, pres., 1954—; mem. Wyoming Library Bd., 1963-72. Served to 1st lt. AUS, 1942-45. Decorated Purple Heart. Mem. Am., Ill., Stark County (pres. 1963-77) bar assns., Am. Legion (post comdr. 1950), Phi Alpha Delta. Clubs: Creve Coeur (Peoria); Midland Country (Kewanee, Ill.). Home: 400 W Olive St Wyoming IL 61491 Office: 832 First Nat Bank Bldg Peoria IL 61602 also Williams St Wyoming IL

BORENSTINE, ALVIN JEROME, search co. exec.; b. Kansas City, Mo., Dec. 14, 1933; s. Samuel and Ella C. (Berman) B.; m. Roula Alakiotou, Dec. 31, 1976; B.S. in Econs., U. Kans., 1956; M.B.A., U. Pa., 1960. Analyst, Johnson & Johnson, New Brunswick, N.J., 1961-62; systems mgr. Levitt & Sons, Levittown, N.J., 1962-66; dir. mgmt. info. services Warren Brothers Co., Cambridge, Mass., 1966-71; mgr. fin. and adminstrv. systems Esmark, Inc., Chgo., 1971-72; pres. Synergistics Assos., Chgo., 1972—; cons. Blue Cross Assn. Mem. Assn. for Systems Mgmt. (pres. Boston chpt. 1969, Distinguished Service award 1970), EDP Auditors Assn., Am. Mgmt. Assn., B'nai B'rith. Systems and Procedures Assn. research fellow, 1959-60; Eddie Jacobson Found. scholar, 1958-60. Home: 6033 N Sheridan Chicago IL 60660 Office: 875 N Michigan Ave Suite 3722 Chicago IL 60611

BORG, LARRY ARTHUR, veterinarian; b. Kewanee, Ill., July 16, 1941; s. Arthur Edwin and Virginia Mertice (Cooper) B.; D.V.M., U. Ill., 1967; m. Barbara Kay Drescher, Aug. 8, 1964; children—Kara Marie, Matthew David. Veterinarian, Rooker Vet. Hosp., Davison, Mich., 1967-70; owner, operator, pres. State Rd. Vet. Clinic, Davison, 1971—. Active 4-H. Mem. Am., Mich. vet. med. assns., Am. Assn. Equine Practitioners. Lutheran. Home: 2174 Winding Way Dr Davison MI 48423 Office: 5363 N State Rd Davison MI 48423

BORK, KENNETH CALVIN, dentist; b. Mt. Prospect, Ill., Sept. 23, 1931; s. Frank L. and Anna M. (Kloske) B.; student U. Ill., 1948-50, Ill. Coll., 1950-51; D.D.S., Northwestern U., 1955, postgrad., 1977; postgrad. Loyola U., 1970, U. Detroit, 1971, Inst. Myo-Functional Therapy, 1975, U. Ala., Birmingham, 1976; m. Florence T. Masewski, Aug. 1, 1953; children—David, Douglas, Karen, Thomas, Kristine, Debra. Pvt. practice dentistry, Elgin, Ill., 1957—; sec., dental staff Sherman Hosp., Elgin, Ill., 1967-68, pres., 1968-69. Bd. dirs. Kane County Heart Assn., 1970-73. Served with USAF, 1955-57. Mem. Am. Dental Assn., Ill., Fox Valley, Elgin (pres. 1966-67) dental socs. Roman Catholic (pres. parish council 1970). Home: 259 River Bluff Rd Elgin IL 60120 Office: 1795 Grandstand Pl Elgin IL 60120

BORKHOLDER, FREEMON, bldg. co. exec.; b. Bremen, Ind., Oct. 11, 1932; s. Daniel J. and Emma (Coblentz) B.; student pub. schs.; m. Margaret Hershberger, Apr. 25, 1956; children—Lorene Kay, Suetta, Dwayne Allan, Jonathan Jay, Cheryl Elaine. With Coppes Inc., Nappanee, Ind., 1955-62; owner, pres. F.D. Burkholder Co., Nappanee, 1960—; v.p. Borkholder Bldgs., Nunica, Mich., 1967—, Newmar Industries, Nappanee, 1968—. Bd. dirs. Hope Rescue Mission, South Bend, Ind. Mem. Nat. Frame Builders Assn. (pres. 1971-72, dir.), Internat. Platform Assn. Mennonite. Home: RD 1 Bremen IN 46506 Office: PO Box 32 Nappanee IN 46550

BORMAN, LEONARD DAVID, anthropologist; b. Toledo, May 24, 1927; s. William and Gertrude (Glass) B.; student U. Toledo, 1946-48; M.A., U. Chgo., 1952; Ph.D., U. Chgo., 1965; m. Marcia Ann Sweet, Dec. 18, 1960; children—Deborah Lee, Curtis Scott. Field worker Penobscot Indians, Oldtown, Maine, 1951, Kalmuk Buddhist Mongols, Phila., N.J., 1952-56; program dir. Friends Neighborhood Guild, Phila., 1954-56; chief anthropology service VA Hosp., Downey, Ill., 1958-65; asso. dir. planning and devel. mental health div. Chgo. Bd. Health, 1965-66, cons. mental health div., 1966-67; dir. program devel. Stone-Brandel Center, Chgo., 1966-70; program dir. W. Clement and Jessie V. Stone Found., Chgo., 1970-74; research asso., dir. Self-Help Inst., Center Urban Affairs Northwestern U., 1974—; research asso. dept. behavioral sci. U. Chgo., 1976—; pres. Self-Help Devel. Inst., Evanston, 1975—; cons. VA Hosp., 1966-69; research asso. U. Chgo., 1966-67; lectr. Harverford Coll., 1955-56, Northwestern U., 1961-62, 66-68, Ill. State Psychiat. Inst., 61-62; lectr., cons. Ill. State Psychiat. Inst., 1965-68; asso. dept. neurology and psychiatry Northwestern U. Med. Sch., Chgo., 1968—; clin. asst. prof. Chgo. Med. Sch., U. Health Scis., Chgo., 1968-74; mem. vis. scientist program NSF-Am. Anthrop. Assn., 1969-75; scholar in residence St. Xavier's Coll., Chgo., 1972; cons. Workgroup Task Force Manpower NIMH, 1977; cons. community support systems panel Pres.'s Commn. on Mental Health, 1977; chmn. planning and devel. com. Michigan Ave. Hosp., Chgo., 1965; pub. mem. Ill. Mental Health Fund Adv. Com., 1967-69; mem. editorial bd. Action People Ednl. TV Series, Chgo., 1968-69; cons. gen. chpt. meeting Sisters of St. Scholastica, 1968-69; cons. Religious Soc. Sacred Heart, 1969-72. Bd. dirs. Am. Indian Center, Chgo., 1956-68, chmn. grand council, 1968-70; profl. adviser, bd. dirs. The Lambs, Chgo., 1967-70; cons. N. Am. Indian Found., 1974—; mem. adv. bd. Nat. Self-Help Clearinghouse, N.Y.; bd. dirs. Council for Study of Mankind, 1977. Served with USNR, 1945-46. Ford Found. grantee, 1952-54; Spencer Found. grantee, 1974-75; Stone Found. grantee, 1974-75; Joyce Found. grantee, 1976-77; NIMH grantee, 1977-79. Fellow Soc. Applied Anthropology, Am. Anthrop. Assn., Royal Anthrop. Inst. Gt. Britain and Ireland; asso. Current Anthropology; mem. Acad. Certified Social Workers, Nat. Assn. Social Workers, Council on Anthropology and Edn., Council on Med. Anthropology, Evanston Mental Health Soc., Sigma Xi. Research in anthropology. Home: 2405 Lawndale Evanston IL 60201 Office: Center Urban Affairs 2040 Sheridan Rd Evanston IL 60201

BORMES, ROBERT EDWARD, surgeon; b. Beardsley, Minn., June 7, 1927; s. Alfred H. and Kathryn J. (Atkinson) B.; student St. Thomas Coll., 1947; M.D., Loyla U., Chgo., 1951; m. Patricia A. Mullen, Sept. 6, 1950;children—Robert A., David M., Thomas P., Peter D., James X, Gregory W., Rebecca A. Intern, St. Francis Hosp., Evanston, Ill., 1951-52; resident in gen. surgery, surg. splty. tng. VA Hosp., Wood, Wis., also Marquette U., Milw., 1952-53, 55-58; instr. in surgery Marquette U., asst. chief surgery Wood VA Hosp., 1958-59; pvt. practice surgery Aberdeen, S.D., 1959—; mem. staff Dakota Midland Hosp., Aberdeen; pres. Profl. Group, Inc., Aberdeen, 1961-68, Bormes Profl. Assn., Aberdeen, 1962—, Berkshire Investment Co.,

1964—, Berkshire Capital, Inc., 1966—. Pres. bd. trustees Dakota Midland Hosp., Aberdeen, 1965-75. Served to lt. USNR, 1953-55. Diplomate Am. Bd. Surgery. Fellow A.C.S. (S.D. pres.). Roman Catholic. Home: 12 Lilac Ln Aberdeen SD 57401 Office: Berkshire Plaza Aberdeen SD 57401

BORNEMEIER, DWIGHT DANIEL, mfg. co. exec.; b. Limon, Colo., Oct. 29, 1934; s. Daniel Simon and Martha Elizebeth (Ohs) B.; A.B., North Central Coll., 1956; M.S., Kans. State U., 1960, Ph.D., 1964; m. Betty Lou Skiles, May 11, 1963; 1 son, Dwight Daniel. Physicist, U.S. Naval Weapons Center, China Lake, Calif., 1956-58; engr. Autonetics, Inc., Downey, Calif., 1960-61; asso. research physicist U. Mich., 1965-69, asst. prof., 1969-70; v.p., dir. Sensors, Inc., Ann Arbor, Mich., 1972—. Mem. Am. Phys. Soc., Optical Soc. Am., IEEE, Mich. Energy and Resources Research Assn. (dir. tech. programs), Sigma Xi. Presbyterian (elder). Patentee in field. Home: 1218 Van Dusen Dr Ann Arbor MI 48103 Office: 11607 Woodbine St Detroit MI 48239

BORNMANN, JOHN ARTHUR, educator; b. Pitts., May 1, 1930; s. John Arthur and Iona Ann (Flanegin) B.; B.S., Carnegie-Mellon U., 1952; postgrad. (Fulbright fellow) Technische Hochschule, Stuttgart, Germany, 1956-57; Ph.D., Ind. U., 1958; m. Sandra Lee Reel, June 12, 1954; children—Patricia Lee, Carol Ann. Research chemist E.I. du Pont de Nemours Co., Parlin, N.J., 1958-60; research asso. Princeton, 1960-61; asst. prof. chemistry No. Ill. U., DeKalb, 1961-65; prof. chemistry Lindenwood Colls., St. Charles, Mo., 1965—, chmn. dept., 1965—. Research participant Oak Ridge Nat. Lab., 1967, 68; faculty fellow Manned Spacecraft Center, Houston, 1970, 71; resident asso. Argonne Nat. Lab., 1973. Drug analyst for law enforcement agys., St. Charles, 1974—. Fellow Am. Inst. Chemists; mem. Am. Chem. Soc. Lutheran (elder, chmn. bd. stewardship 1973-74, chmn. bd. edn. 1971-72, chmn. bd. elders 1976-77). Contbr. articles to profl. jours. Home: 3 Briarwood Ln St Charles MO 63301

BORSCH, REUBEN A., lawyer; b. Collinsville, Ill., Mar. 7, 1903; s. Frederick C. and Sarah (Wrigley) B.; A.B., Ill. Wesleyan U., 1925; B.A. in Jurisprudence, Oxford (Eng.) U., 1927, B.C.L., 1928; m. Pearl Irene Houk, May 3, 1930; children—Barbara (Mrs. James Osborn Kaull), Frederick Houk, Jane Robbins Carter. Admitted to Ill. bar, 1929; partner Winston & Strawn, Chgo., 1944—; dir., sec. Fahralloy Co., Harvey, Ill.; dir. Sommer & Maca Industries, Inc., Cicero, Ill.; counsel Ingalls Meml. Hosp., Harvey, Ill. Bd. dirs. Youth Guidance, Chgo.; trustee Episcopal Diocese Chgo. Endowment Fund, Ill. Wesleyan U. Mem. Am., Ill., Chgo. bar assns., Tau Kappa Epsilon. Episcopalian. Republican. Clubs: Law (sec.-treas. 1960-62), Mid-day, Executives (pres. 1955-56) (Chgo.); Hinsdale Golf. Home: 133 E Walnut St Hinsdale IL 60521 Office: One First Nat Plaza Chicago IL 60603

BORUFF, JOHN DAVID, govt. ofcl.; b. Lakewood, Ohio, July 8, 1930; s. Glenn Tourner and Edith (Weybright) B.; A.B., Ind. U., 1953, M.S., 1965; m. Martha Lois Myers, June 12, 1953; children—Martha Yvonne, Audrey Elaine, David Paul, Kenneth Edward. Sanitarian, Ind. State Bd. of Health, 1957-60; tng. officer Div. of Food and Drugs, Ind. State Bd. of Health, 1960-63; health edn. cons. Div. of Health Edn., 1963-65; health-housing coordinator Associated Migrant Opportunity Services, Inc., Indpls., 1965-66; extension health edn. specialist Purdue U., 1966-69; mem. staff div. pub. health records, coordinator health data unit pub. health statistics Ind. Bd. Health, 1969—. Former sec. mem. bd. dirs. Ind. Assn. of Sanitarians, Inc. former editor The Hoosier Sanitarian. Active Boy Scouts Am.; prin. clarinetist Montgomery County Civic Band, Ind. Nat. Guard Res. Band. Served with USCGR, 1953-57; sr. asst. sanitarian USPHS Res. Mem. USPHS Commd. Officers Assn., Theta Xi, Kappa Kappa Psi. Presbyterian (elder, past stated clk.). Mason. Home: RR 1 Box 182 Roachdale IN 46172 Office: 1330 W Michigan St Indianapolis IN 46206

BOSS, BERTRAM JOAB, med. group adminstr.; b. Marcus, Iowa, Oct. 1, 1917; s. Joab Bertram and Sarah (Gurley) B.; student Nat. Bus. Coll., Sioux City, Iowa, 1937-38; m. Agnes E. Gronlund, Apr. 17, 1949; children—Beverly Ann, Susanne Marie, David Alan. With Fairmont Foods Co., 1938-63, br. controller, 1948-63; adminstr. Neuropsychiat. Clinics, Fargo, N.D., 1963-70; controller Dakota Clinic, Fargo, N.D., 1970-72; adminstr. Albert Lea (Minn.) Clinic, 1972—. Mgmt. cons., dir. computer center exec. com. Blue Shield-Blue Cross, 1967—. Fellow Am. Coll. Med. Group Adminstrs.; mem. Med. Group Mgmt. Assn., N.D. Clinic Mgrs. Assn. (chmn. Blue Shield liaison com. 1968—), Fargo (com. chmn. 1967—), Moorhead (com. chmn. 1967—) chambers commerce, Minn. Clinic Mgrs. Assn., S.C.V., S.A.R. (sec.-treas. 1966-72). Kiwanian (Moorhead, dir., chmn. finance 1964-68, 69, pres. 1971-72, dir. Albert Lea 1976—). Author: Tall Are The Hills, 1972. Home: 1201 W Richway Dr Albert Lea MN 56007 Office: 1602 Fountain St Albert Lea MN 56007

BOSS, EDWARD HERMAN, JR., economist; b. Oak Park, Ill., Mar. 12, 1938; s. Edward Herman and Lorraine (Hoffman) B.; B.A., Albion Coll., 1960; M.B.A., Columbia, 1962; spl. student Grad. Sch. Bus., U. Chgo., 1968. Econ. analyst Continental Ill. Nat. Bank & Trust Co., Chgo., 1962-67, asst. economist, 1967-69, asso. economist, 1969-73, v.p., 1973—. Lectr. Roosevelt U. Bus. Sch. Served with USAF, 1963. Mem. Nat. Assn. Bus. Economist (chpt. sec.-treas. 1969-70, pres. 1970-71, council 1974-77), Am. Fin. Assn., Alumni Assn. Grad. Sch. Bus. Columbia U. Editor weekly bank newsletter, 1967—; cons. economist Bankers Monthly mag., 1975—. Home: 1310 Ritchie Ct Chicago IL 60610 Office: 231 S La Salle St Chicago IL 60693

BOSS, RICHARD DALE, ednl. adminstr.; b. Delphos, Kans., Nov. 2, 1922; s. Burton Wesley and Una Levona (Treadwell) B.; B.Ed., Colo. State U., 1953; M.Ed., Oreg. State U., 1958, Ed.D., 1968; m. Alice Mae Nelson, July 4, 1944; children—William, Rosemary. Dir. adult and vocat. edn., Astoria, Oreg., 1958-62; pres. Clatsop Community Coll., Astoria, 1962-66; dir. Portland (Oreg.) Vocat. Village and Residential Manpower Center, 1968-72; research asso. U. Wis. at Madison, 1973-75; now with So. Ill. U., Carbondale. Research specialist, center vocat. and tech. edn. Ohio State U., 1972-73. Crusade chmn. Am. Cancer Soc., 1959. Served with AUS, 1943-46; ETO. Mem. Am. Assn. Jr. Colls., NEA, Am. Vocat. Assn., Am. Legion, Phi Delta Kappa, Epsilon Pi Tau. Episcopalian (vestryman, chmn. bldg. com.). Kiwanian (lt. gov. N.W. dist. 1965), Elk. Author: Accreditation: Its Purposes, Aims and Goals, 1965; The Community/Junior College—A Bibliography, 1967. Home: 116 N Lark Ln Carbondale IL 62901

BOSSERT, EDWARD FRANCIS, engring. co. exec.; b. Kansas City, Mo., Jan. 5, 1934; s. Leonard Francis and Anna Margaret (Murphy) B.; B.S. in Mech. Engring., U. Mo. at Columbia, 1957; m. Catherine Eloise Reynolds, Oct. 20, 1974; children by previous marriage—Daniel F., David E., Douglas L. Resident engr. Black & Veatch, Engrs., Kansas City, Mo., 1957-64; utilities supr. Monsanto Nylon Mfg. div., Pensacola, Fla., 1964-66; project engr. R.W. Beck & Assos., Engrs., Denver, 1966-67; mgr. bulk handling systems Black Sivalls & Bryson, Kansas City, 1967-69; mgr. prodn., plant engr. Smith & Loveless, Lenexa, Kans., 1969-70; regional v.p. L. Robert Kimball & Asso. Engrs. and Architects, St. Joseph, Mo., 1970-75; regional cons. Williams & Works, engrs., Grand Rapids, Mich., 1975—; guest lectr. Mo. Western State Coll., 1973-74. Mem. ASME, Am. Pub. Works Assn., Mo. Soc. Profl. Engrs. (pres. N.W. chpt. 1973), Rural Northland Devel. Assn. (pres. 1973), Phi Kappa Theta. Mem. Christian Ch. Elk. Club: East Hills Sertoma. Home: 546 Greenwood SE East Grand Rapids MI 49506 Office: 611 Cascade West Pkwy Grand Rapids MI 49506

BOSSERT, EDWARD OLIVER, city ofcl.; b. Reddick, Ill., July 11, 1915; s. Oliver James and Nellie (Unz) B.; B.A., N. Central Coll., Naperville, Ill., 1938; M.A., U. Chgo., 1947; m. Margaret Bower, Aug. 12, 1950; children—Joan, Janet. Supt., Lemont (Ill.) Dist. 210 Schs., 1950-75; mem. Lemont Plan Commn., 1968—, chmn., 1970—. Served to lt. col. AUS, 1940-46. Decorated Croix de Guerre (France); recipient Outstanding Citizen award Lemont Jaycees, 1972, Lemont C. of C., 1974. Mem. Am. Assn. Sch. Adminstrs., Am. Legion, Phi Delta Kappa. Lion. Home: 863 McCarthy St Lemont IL 60439 Office: 800 Porter St Lemont IL 60439

BOSSHARD, JOHN, lawyer, bus. exec.; b. LaCrosse, Wis., Sept. 28, 1920; s. John and Effie (Kremmer) B.; Ph.B., U. Wis., 1942, LL.B., 1947; M.B.A. with distinction, Harvard, 1947; m. Rylla J. Hattan, June 15, 1944; children—John III, Sabina, William, Kurt. Admitted to Wis. bar, 1947, since practiced in LaCrosse; dist. atty. LaCrosse County, 1950-54; judge LaCrosse County Small Claims Ct., 1954-60; pres. 1st Nat. Bank Bangor (Wis.), 1962—; exec. v.p. LaFarge State Bank (Wis.), 1969—; pres. Farmers State Bank Hillsboro (Wis.), 1970—, Bosshard Bauco Ltd.; pres. Bangor Area Devel. Corp., 1962—, pres. LaCrosse Area Econ. and Devel. Corp., Inc., 1971-73; chmn. bd. Bank of Mauston, Grand Marsh State Bank; dir. 9th Dist. Fed. Res. Bank Mpls., Twin City Ready Mix, Inc., Bosshard Enterprises, Inc., Mpls., Sparta Warehouse, Inc., LaCrosse, Bank of Mauston (Wis.); guest lectr. U. Wis. Law Sch., 1972-73. Clk., Bangor Area Schs., 1949-73. Mem. Wis. Coordinating Council for Higher Edn., 1968-70; chmn. Minn.-Wis. Boundary Area Commn., 1965-69; pres. St. Francis Found.; pres. St. Francis Hosp. Bd. Served as 1st lt. AUS, 1944-47. Mem. Am., LaCrosse County (pres. 1969-70) bar assns., LaCrosse County Hist. Soc. (sec. 1950-52), LaCrosse County Bankers Assn. (pres. 1971). Home: Bangor WI 54614 Office: Schneider Bldg LaCrosse WI 54601

BOSTIC, JAMES REGAN, mktg. exec.; b. Pipetone, Minn., May 18, 1940; s. Alva A. and May Ellen (Regan) B.; B.A., U. Minn., 1963; M.S.J., Northwestern U., 1964; D.B.A., Pacific Western U., 1976; m. Helen Wentz, Jan. 22, 1966. Research and teaching asst. in consumer motivation Northwestern U., 1963-64; advt. and sales promotion planner Ford Motor Co., 1965-66; asst. mktg. research mgr. General Mills, Inc., 1966-67; advt. account exec. Campbell-Mithun, 1967-68; dir. mktg. Jeep vehicles, dir. advt. and merchandising, dir. mktg., planning Am. Motors, 1968-71; v.p. marketing Starcraft Corp., 1971-73; dir. mktg. Oldsmobile div., Gen. Motors, Lansing, Mich., 1974—; dir. evening div. advt. program, also lectr. U. Minn., 1966-68. Served to lt. AUS, 1954. Mem. Am. Mktg. Assn. Club: Detroit Ad Craft, Detroit Economic. Composer of Willmar Community College Song, 1964. Home: 4729 Clydesdale Rd Lansing MI 48906 Office: 920 Townsend St Lansing MI 48921

BOSTLEMAN, FREDERICK WILLIAM, constrn. co. exec.; b. Toledo, June 25, 1921; s. Frederick Henry and Alice Wilhelmina (Marquardt) B.; student Toledo U., 1940; m. Mary Kathleen Shaner, July 11, 1942; children—Richard L., Bonnie, Mark. Founder Bostleman Corp., Toledo, 1946, inc., 1957, pres., owner, 1957—, chmn. bd., 1975—; owner, pres. Merriweather Realty Co., Toledo, 1958—; governing dir. Bostleman Internat. Ltd., Montserrat, British West Indies, 1968—. Trustee Toledo Area Constrn. Workers, Health, Welfare Fund, 1960-74. Chmn., trustee Sylvania Township, 1956-74; chmn. Sylvania Township Zoning Appeals Bd., 1956-64; chmn. Sylvania City, Township Republican Com., 1967-69; mem. exec. com. Lucas County Rep. Com., 1974. Bd. dirs. Luth. Orphans and Old Folks Soc. Toledo, YMCA Camp Storer. Served with USAAF, 1942-46. Mem. Toledo Home Builders Assn. (pres. 1957), Asso. Gen. Contractors (pres. chpt. 1960-61, sec. Ohio council, 1961-62), Toledo Bldg. Congress (pres. 1962-63), Toledo Small Bus. Assn., (bd. dirs. 1962), Am. Arbitration Assn., Toledo C. of C. (trustee 1962). Lutheran (Ch. council 1968—). Mason (Shriner, Jester). Clubs: Inverness Country; Toledo; Montserrat Golf Montserrat Yacht (Montserrat, B.W.I.); Montserrat (Plymouth, B.W.I.). Home: 4106 Merriweather Toledo OH 43607 Office: 410 Ryder Rd Toledo OH 43607

BOSTON, LEONA, orgn. exec.; b. Joliet, Ill., Aug. 4, 1914; d. Dorie Philip and Margaret (Mitchell) Boston; student LaSalle Extension U., 1936-37, 1946, U. Chgo., 1944-45. Tchr., Nat. Stenotype Sch., Chgo., 1937; stenotypist Rotary Internat., Evanston, Ill., 1937-44, sec. to comptroller, 1944-50, head personnel dept., 1950-65, exec. asst. to gen. sec., 1965-76. Bd. dirs. YWCA, Evanston, 1961-63. Mem. Bus. Profl. Women's Club Evanston. Evang. (fin. sec. 1965-68). Club: Zonta (v.p., chmn. program com. 1969-70, pres. 1970-71, chmn. membership com. 1976-78) (Evanston, Ill.). Home: 500 Lake St Evanston IL 60201

BOSWELL, JAMES EDWARD, diversified co. exec.; b. Winona, Mo., Aug. 31, 1910; s. Thomas Walton and Ethel B. (Jamieson) B.; B.S. in Civil Engring., Ga. Sch. Tech., 1933; m. Lois D. Kamerer, June 7, 1936; children—James Edward, Susan Elizabeth, John Joseph. Founder, owner Ind. Stave Co., Inc., Lebanon, Mo., 1934—; pres. Harrison Furniture Mfg. Co.; dir. Mo. Bank. Bd. dirs. Lebanon Community Center. Mem. Mo. (v.p. 1971—), Lebanon chambers commerce, Mo. Forest Products Assn. (dir. 1972—), Asso. Cooperage Industries Am., So. States Indsl. Council (dir.). Kiwanian. Clubs: Media, LOYA. Home: 960 S Jefferson St Lebanon MO 65536 Office: 1078 S Jefferson St Lebanon MO 65536

BOSWELL, JERRY DON, ednl. adminstr.; b. Cape Girardeau, Mo., Jan. 5, 1935; s. Clyde Russell and Mamie Ann (Steeg) B.; B.B.A., Wash. U., 1962, M.B.A., 1964; D.B.A., Ind. U., 1969; m. Elizabeth Ann Mohns; children—Laura, Victoria, Eric. Accountant, Liberty Loan Corp., St. Louis, 1962-63; prof., adminstr. Ind. U. at Ft. Wayne, 1966-72; chmn. Bd. Pub. Works, City of Ft. Wayne, Ind., 1972-76; prof. bus. adminstrn., chmn. dept. St. Francis Coll., Ft. Wayne, 1977—; cons. Summit Assos., Ft. Wayne, 1976—. Cons. Chmn. Three Rivers Coordinating Council, 1973-74; chmn. Urban Trans. Adv. Bd., 1974-76; mem. Ft. Wayne City Plan Commn., 1972-76. Mem. Chancellor's Adv. Council, Ind. U.-Purdue U. at Ft. Wayne. Mem. Midwest Intergovtl. Personnel Council, Ft. Wayne C. of C., Downtown Ft. Wayne Assn. (hon. dir.), Beta Gamma Sigma, Alpha Kappa Psi. Home: 2821 Devon Dr Fort Wayne IN 46815 Office: 2701 Spring St Fort Wayne IN 46808

BOSWELL, NATHALIE SPENCE, speech pathologist; b. Cleve., May 9, 1924; d. Harrison Morton and Nathalie Muriel (Clem) Spence; student Skidmore Coll, 1941-42; Mus.B. in Edn., Northwestern U., 1945; M.A., Western Res. U., 1961; m. June 15, 1946; children—Louis Keith, Donna Spence, Deborah Anne Boswell Hill. Speech therapist Highland View Hosp., Cleve., 1961-64; speech pathologist Cleve. VA Hosp., 1964—; chmn. Equal Employment Opportunity Counselors, 1969-74, Fed. Women Speakers Bur., 1968—, Fed. Career Info. Program, 1970—, Fed. Coll. Relations Council, 1970—, Fed. Exec. Bd., 1972-73. Mem. Cleve. Orch. Chorus, 1969—; patron Police Athletic League. Recipient Performance award Equal Employment Opportunities, 1973; licensed speech pathologist, Ohio. Mem. Am. (certificate of clin. competence), Ohio speech and hearing assns., Aphasiology Assn. Ohio, Chi Omega Alumni Assn., Musical Arts Assn., Western Res. Hist. Soc., Cleve. Mus. Natural History, Cleve. Mus. Art, Smithsonian Assos., Nat. Wildlife Fedn., Nat. Trust Hist. Preservation, Am. Heritage Soc. Episcopalian. Home: 2946 Berkshire Rd Cleveland Heights OH 44118 Office: 10701 East Blvd Cleveland OH 44106

BOSWELL, ROBERT BOWEN, automobile co. exec.; b. Washington, Feb. 14, 1920; s. Roscoe Conkling and Ida Blanche (Fowler) B.; B.S. in Metall. Engring., U. Mich., 1942; m. Ruth Ione Capron, Aug. 16, 1942; children—Robert Capron, James Russell, John Richard. Research metallurgist Chrysler Corp., Highland Park, Mich., 1946-50, chief metallurgist Tank Engine div., New Orleans, 1951-54, chief engr. Forge and Foundry div., Highland Park, 1955-60, mgr. product engring. various mfg. divs., Detroit, 1961-75, mgr. material cost and value analysis, Highland Park, 1975—; evening sch. instr. Wayne State U., 1948-51. Served to lt. Ordnance, USNR, 1942-45. Mem. Am. Soc. Metals (chmn. Detroit chpt. 1961-62), Soc. Automotive Engrs. (governing bd. Detroit sect. 1964-66). Republican. Presbyterian. Club: C.I.T. (Detroit) Contbr. articles trade jours. Patentee in field. Home: 4332 MacQueen Dr Orchard Lake MI 48033 Office: Chrysler Corp Box 1919 Detroit MI 48288

BOSWORTH, CYRUS MILBURN, chem. engr.; b. Cleve., Oct. 15, 1917; s. Cyrus Milburn and Abigail Rose (Berger) B.; B.S., Antioch Coll., 1941; M.S., Syracuse U., 1962; children—William, Sarah (Mrs. Laurent Gerome), Theodore; m. 2d, Janet Jackson, Oct. 22, 1972. Plant chemist Kollsman Instrument Co., Elmhurst, N.Y., 1941-45; materials engr. Carrier Corp., Syracuse, N.Y., 1945-50, research engr., 1950-62, sr. cons., 1962-72; environmental control engr. Tee-Pak, Inc., Danville, Ill., 1972—. Chmn. Clean Air Com., Omondaga County, 1965-67. Fellow Am. Soc. Heating, Air Conditioning and Refrigerating Engrs. (recipient Wolverine Diamond Key 1965); mem. Am. Chem. Soc., Am. Inst. Chem. Engrs. (chmn. Syracuse sect. 1959-60, Central Ill. sect. 1976), Air Pollution Control Assn. Contbr. articles to profl. jours. Patentee in field. Home: 374 Cedarwood N Danville IL 61832 Office: Tee-Pak Inc 915 N Michigan Danville IL 61832

BOSWORTH, DOUGLAS LEROY, farm implement mfg. co. exec.; b. Goldfield, Iowa, Oct. 15, 1939; s. Clifford LeRoy and Clara (Lonning) B.; B.S. in Agrl. Engring., Iowa State U., 1962; M.S. in Agrl. Engring., U. Ill., 1964; m. Patricia Lee Knock, May 28, 1961; children—Douglas, Dawn. With John Deere Harvester Works, East Moline, Ill., 1959—, reliability mgr., 1967-71, div. engr. disk harrows, 1971-75, mgr. mfg. engring., 1976—. Mem. Am. Soc. Agrl. Engrs. (chmn. Ill.-Wis. 1973-74, dir. 1974-76; Engring. Achievement Young Designer award 1973), Soc. Exptl. Stress Analysis (vice chmn. 1967-68), Soc. Automotive Engrs., Soc. Mfg. Engrs., Soc. Indsl. Engrs., Sigma Xi, Alpha Epsilon, Gamma Sigma Delta. Lutheran. Home: 4432 37th Ave Rock Island IL 61201 Office: 1100 13th Ave East Moline IL 61244

BOTCH, RAYMOND PAUL, mgmt. cons.; b. Wibaux, Mont., Feb. 23, 1911; s. Louis Dominic and Ann Sophia (Katcheroski) B.; Ph.B., Carroll Coll., Helena, Mont., 1933; M.B.A., Northwestern U., 1936; m. Laura Chipman, Feb. 7, 1942; children—Raymond Paul, Dennis C., Ruthann, Beatrice H., Laurie K. With Griffenhagen & Assos., govt. cons., Chgo., 1936-42; dir. Waterbury (Conn.) Taxpayers' Assn., 1942-46; bus. mgr. Carroll Coll., Helena, Mont., 1947-50; cons. Internat. City Mgmt. Assn., Chgo., 1947-48; city mgr. Pendleton, Oreg., 1950-55, Elgin, Ill., 1955-61, Rock Island, Ill., 1961-77; govt. mgmt. cons. Beling Cons., Moline, Ill., 1977—. Served as chief warrant officer Ordnance Corps, AUS, 1943-47. Named Rock Island Boss of Year, Jaycees, 1966. Mem. N.W. (pres. 1952-53), Ill. (pres. 1968) city mgrs. assns. K.C., Moose, Elk. Editor: Municipal Finance Administration, 1947. Home and Office: 8130 Ridgewood Rd Rock Island IL 61201 Office: 1528 3d Ave Rock Island IL 61201

BOTHFELD, ROBERT, automotive engr.; b. Sherborn, Mass., Sept. 26, 1920; s. Theodore and Viola May (Clark) B.; B.S.M.E., Tufts Coll., 1943; M.S. Engring. in Mech. Engring., U. Mich., 1947; m. Helen Audrey Marsh, Apr. 21, 1946; children—Robert, Bronwyn Lee, Holly Marsh. With Gen. Motors Co., 1947—, buyer, methods supr., developmental engr. truck and coach dept., Pontiac, Mich., 1950-5S, prodn. engr. gen. offices Fisher Body div., Warren, Mich., 195S—, supr. prodn. engring., 1972—. Active Boy Scouts Am., 1949-57. Served with USN, 1943-46. Registered profl. engr., Ohio. Mem. Soc. Automotive Engrs., Engring. Soc. Detroit, Nat. Soc. Profl. Engrs. Republican. Presbyterian. Club: Otsego-Hidden Valley Ski. Home: 1448 Maryland Blvd Birmingham MI 48009 Office: 30001 Van Dyke Rd Warren MI 48090

BOTHWELL, WILBER CLARENCE, educator; b. Kansas City, Mo., May 15, 1910; s. Clarence Harvey and Maud (Wetherby) B.; B.A., Drury Coll., 1931; M.A., Washington U., St. Louis, 1933, Ph.D., 1941; m. Marcella Lester, July 4, 1948; children—Alfred, William, Brent Susan, Marcella Roper. Instr. econs. Washington U., 1935-41; sr. staff mem. Govtl. Research Inst., St. Louis, 1941-42; prof. econs., polit. sci. Drury Coll., Springfield, Mo., 1946-58, dir. Breech Sch. Bus. Adminstrn., 1958-61, 65-67, prof. econs. and bus. adminstrn., Ford Found. curriculum study liberal arts program in bus. adminstrn., 1959-60. Mem. panel arbitrators Fed. Mediation and Conciliation Service and Am. Arbitration Assn.; permanent arbitrator Dayco Corp. and United Rubber Workers, Internat. Paper Co. and United Paperworkers Internat. Union. Served from 2d lt. to maj., USAAF, 1942-46; lt. col. res. Mem. Am. Econ. Assn., Nat. Acad. Arbitrators, Phi Beta Kappa. Rotarian. Contbr. articles to profl. jours. Home: 1307 E Meadowmere Springfield MO 65804

BOTSFORD, LLOYD ARLEN, realty co. exec.; b. Grand Rapids, Mich., Sept. 19, 1930; s. Lloyd D. and Beulah Alice (Raak) B.; student U. Mich. extension, 1955-63; certificate Grad. Realtors Inst.; m. Carol Joy Wirt, Aug. 15, 1952; children—Richard, Linda, Larry. Salesman, Albert Realtors, Grand Rapids, Mich., 1955-65; mgr. new homes dept. Westdale Realtors, Grand Rapids, 1965-66, mgr. Grandville br. office, 1966-67, gen. sales mgr. 14 offices, 1967—, pres., gen. sales mgr. Grand Rapids ops. Westdale Co., 1967—; v.p. Westdale Investment, Grand Rapids, 1968—. Mem. Grand Rapids Real Estate Bd., 1955—. Trustee Westdale Retirement Employee's Trust. Served with Submarine Service, USNR, 1949-50. Recipient Grand Rapids Sales and Marketing award Sales and Mktg. Execs. Club, 1968, Salesmaster's Inc. award, 1969. Mem. Am. Bus. Club (pres. 1967), Grand Rapids Real Estate Bd. Million Dollar Producer Club (life), Sr. Sales Award Group (life). Home: 8160 Wilderness Lake Trail Ada MI 49301 Office: 3435 Lake Eastbrook St SE Grand Rapids MI 49506

BOTTGER, LORNA CONLEY (MRS. RICHARD EDWARD BOTTGER), educator; b. nr. Paris, Mo., Dec. 18, 1910; d. Wilber Samuel and Eva Pearl (Byars) Conley; B.S. in Edn., N.E. Mo. State U., 1937, M.A. in Adminstrn., 1968; postgrad. So. Ill. U., 1967-68; m. Richard Edward Bottger, Nov. 29, 1941. Tchr., Monroe County (Mo.) rural schs., 1928-37, Hancock Pl. elementary schs., St. Louis,

1937-43, Paris (Mo.) pub. schs., 1943-58; tchr. social studies Hazelwood Jr. High Sch., St. Louis, 1958-73; bookkeeper, saleswoman, County Gas & Electric Co., Paris, Mo., 1945-63, co-owner, 1964-65. Mo. del. Meth. Young People's Conf., Memphis, 1935; counselor Meth. Youth Conf., Central Coll., Fayette, Mo., 1936; pres. Meth. Youth Orgn., 1932-37, dist. dir., 1934-37, pres. Mo. conf. Fayette sub-dist., 1933; tchr., counselor Goodwill Summer Camp, St. Louis, 1940; del. Mo. Gov.'s Conf. on Edn., 1966, 68; mem. Monroe County Young Democratic Club, 1940—, Women's Dem. Club, 1944—, Mo. State Dem. Club, 1952—; Dem. State committeewoman, 1957-62; mem. platform com. Dem. Nat. Conv., 1960, del., 1960; del. Dem. State Conv., 1956, 60, 68; Ann. Lorna Bottger MNEA-PAC award established in her honor by polit. action com. Mo. Nat. Edn. Assn., 1975. Mem. NEA (life), Mo. (del. 1964-65), St. Louis Suburban (del. 1964-65, mem. polit. action com. on edn. 1970—), Hazelwood Community (legis. chmn. 1958-60, chmn. welfare com. 1965-66) tchrs. assns., Mo. Hist. Soc. (life mem.), Mo. Assn. Tchrs. Social Studies, Nat., Greater St. Louis councils for social studies, N.E. Mo. State U. Alumni Assn. (charter life), Kappa Kappa Iota. Methodist. Club: Mark Twain Country (charter mem.) (Paris). Home: 131 Payne St Paris MO 65275

BOUGHTON, SPENCER DALE, banker; b. Clinton, Mo., May 4, 1927; s. Charles Frank and Garnet Matilda (Spencer) B.; student Central Mo. State Coll., 1949-51, U. Mo., 1957-60; m. Evelyn Ann Diemler, Oct. 30, 1965; children—Charles, Jayne. Asst. office mgr. Comml. Credit Corp., Kansas City, Mo., 1951-53; credit supr. Vendo Co., Kansas City, Mo., 1953-59; supervisory loan officer SBA, Kansas City, Mo., 1959-69; with Commerce Bank of University City (Mo.), 1969-74, pres., 1971-74, also dir.; pres. Plaza Bank West Port, St. Louis, 1974—. Mem. University City Devel. Commn., 1971—. Served with USNR, 1944-46, AUS, 1949-50, USAF, 1950-51. Mem. Mo. C. of C., University City C. of C. (pres. 1970). Democrat. Roman Catholic. Home: 1834 Walnutway Dr Saint Louis MO 63141 Office: 12011 Marine Ave Saint Louis MO 63141

BOULA, JAMES ALBERT, instructional materials co. exec.; b. Chgo., Sept. 11, 1913; s. Joseph and Matilda (Bilek) B.; A.A. in Architecture, Crane Jr. Coll., 1933; B.S. in Edn., Meth., U. Ill., 1937; M.A. in L.S., U. Chgo., 1949, Certificate of Advanced Study in Curriculum, 1970; m. Lillian H. Yunger, May 8, 1943; 1 son, James Edward. Coach, tchr. math. Fort Hays (Kans.) pub. schs., 1937-39; tchr. math. Chgo. area pub. schs., 1939-41; tchr. math. Chgo. pub. schs., 1946-49; asst. dir. instructional materials Joliet (Ill.) High Sch. and Joliet Jr. Coll., 1949-59; dir. Instructional Materials for Ill., Springfield, 1959-71; pres. Instructional Materials Service, Allegan, Mich., 1971—. Cons. for elementary and secondary schs., North Central Assn. Colls. and Secondary Schs., U.S. Office Edn. Bd. dirs. Ill. Reading Service, 1959-71. Served with AUS, 1941-46; Col. Res. ret. Decorated Purple Heart. Mem. Ill. Audio Visual Assn. (dir. 1959-71), Am., Ill. (dir. 1959-71) assns. sch. librarians, N.E.A., ALA, Ill. Library Assn., Am. Assn. Sch. Adminstrs., Mich. Assn. for Media in Edn., Am. Assn. Ednl. Communication and Tech., Ill. Assn. for Supervision and Curriculum Devel., Alpha Kappa Pi (treas. 1937). Mem. Czech Fraternal Lodge. Editor, Ill. Jour. Edn., 1963, 64, 66, Ill. Instructional Materials Bull., 1960. Contbr. articles to profl. jours. Home: 1749 Tom Nolan Rd Route 3 Allegan MI 49010 Office: Box 81 Allegan MI 49010

BOULLION, JAMES DONALD, pub. relations co. exec.; b. Eau Claire, Wis., Apr. 10, 1933; s. Gerald and Bernadette Elizabeth (Kaufman) B.; B.S. in English, U. Wis. at Eau Claire, 1960; m. Janet Gayle Johnson, Feb. 1, 1958; children—James Alan, Deborah, Bridgette, Barbara. Reporter/editor, Eau Claire Leader-Telegram, 1956-62; exec. dir. Wis. Mental Health Adv. Com., Madison, 1963-67; editor of pub. CUNA Mut. Ins. Soc., Madison, 1967-68; owner/pres. James Boullion Asso., Madison, 1968—. Cons. Wis. Credit Union League, Wis. Assn. Nursing Homes, Wis. Acad. Trial Lawyers, Wis. Podiatry Soc., Tavern Hosts of Wis. Bd. dirs. Big Bros. of Dane County, Wis. Spl. Olympics, Madison Opportunity Center; trustee Wm. S. Hobbins Found. Served with AUS, 1952-55. Mem. Madison Press Club, Madison Advt. Club, Madison Sales and Mktg. Execs. Club: Madison. Home: 6410 Olympic Dr Madison WI 53705 Office: 30-on-the-Square Suite 801 Madison WI 53703

BOULOS, BADI MANSOUR, pharmacologist, physician, educator; b. Alexandria, Egypt, July 3, 1930; s. Nakhla and Olga (Matta) B.; came to U.S., 1960, naturalized, 1972; M.D., U. Alexandria, 1953, diploma in Pharmacology, 1958, diploma in Tropical Medicine, 1960; M.S. with honors in Radiation Research, U. Iowa, 1962; Ph.D. in Med. Pharmacology, U. Mo., 1965; m. Gerda Dorothy Bergen, July 6, 1964; children—Badi Emil, Thomas N., Daniel N., Matthew Henry. Intern, U. Alexandria Hosp., 1953-54; resident Coptic Hosp., Alexandria, 1954-55; practice medicine specializing in Obstetrics and gynecology, Alexandria, 1956-60, occupational medicine U. Ill. Med. Center, Chgo., 1972—; med. officer UN Relief and Welfare Agy., Gaza Strip, 1954-56; instr. pharmacology U. Alexandria, 1958-60, asst. prof. pharmacology, 1965-66; asst. scientist Cancer Research Center, Columbia, Mo., 1966-68; asst. prof. pharmacology U. Mo., Columbia, 1968-70; asso. prof. occupational medicine and environ. medicine U. Ill., Chgo., 1972—; cons. in toxicology to Ill Crime Commn., 1974—, FDA, 1974—, Ill. Inst. of Environ. Quality, 1972—, Nat. Inst. Occupational Safety and Health, U.S. Dept Labor, numerous others; mem. Task Force Toxic Chem. Substances Am. Chem. Assn., 1974—, pres. Ill. Cancer Council, 1974—. USPHS fellow, 1970-72; NIH grantee, 1971-72, 74-75; Fulbright scholar, 1960-64. Mem. Am. Pub. Health Assn., Am. Soc. Pharmacology and Exptl. Therapeutics, Am. Soc. Toxicology, Am. Cancer Soc., N.Y. Acad. Sci., AMA. Episcopalian. Contbr. articles on pharm. research to sci. jours. Home: 812 Heritage Dr Addison IL 60101 Office: School of Public Health Univ of Illinois PO Box 6880 Chicago IL 60680

BOULWARE, ROLIN TRAVIS, lawyer; b. Canton, Mo., May 20, 1927; s. Morris Travis and Velma Lydia (Womack) B.; B.A., Culver-Stockton Coll., 1949; J.D., U. Mo., 1952; m. Twila Mae Ayers, June 6, 1948; children—Beverly Joan, William Travis, Robert James. Admitted to Mo. bar, 1952; practiced in Hannibal, 1952-54, Shelbina, 1954—; dir. Shelbina Mercantile Bank. City atty., Shelbina, 1971-74; pros. atty. Shelby County, 1956-62. Trustee Hannibal LaGrange Coll., Hannibal, 1973—. Mem. Am., Shelby County bar assns., Am. Judicature Soc., Shelbina C. of C. Democrat. Baptist (deacon 1966—). Mason (K.T.). Home: 623 S Center St Shelbina MO 63468 Office: 115 E Walnut St Shelbina MO 63468

BOUMA, DONALD HERBERT, educator, sociologist; b. Grand Rapids, Mich., Feb. 9, 1918; s. Fred D. and Anna (Breen) B.; B.A., Calvin Coll., 1940; M.A., U. Mich., 1943; Ph.D., Mich. State U., 1952; children by previous marriage—Gary, Margene (Mrs. Philip Burnett), Jack; m. 2d, Ruby Warner, Sept. 14, 1974. Asst. prof. sociology Calvin Coll., Grand Rapids, 1946-60, prof., 1953-60, head dept., 1950-60; prof. sociology Western Mich. U., Kalamazoo, 1960—; lectr. sociology U. Mich., Ann Arbor, 1948-68; vis. prof. sociology Mich. State U., East Lansing, 1964, 66, 68; cons. juvenile cts., sch. systems, urban poverty programs. Chmn., Gov.'s Com. Fulbright Scholarships, 1950-73; pres. Kent Council Social Agys., 1954-60; adviser U.S. Civil Rights Commn., 1968-74. Served with USNR, 1944-46. Recipient Acad. award for teaching, research Mich. Acad. Sci., Arts, Letters, 1965; Teaching Excellence award Western Mich. U., 1970. Mem. Am., Mich. (pres. 1963), N. Central sociol. assns., Am. Soc. Criminology. Author: Dynamics of School Integration: Problems in the North, 1968; Kids and Cops-Mutual Hostility, 1969; contbr. articles to profl. jours. Home: 78 Lake Doster Dr Plainwell MI 49080 Office: Western Mich U Kalamazoo MI 49019

BOUSFIELD, ALDRIDGE KNIGHT, educator; b. Boston, Apr. 5, 1941; s. Weston Ashmore and Thelma (Knight) B.; S.B., Mass. Inst. Tech., 1963, Ph.D., 1966; m. Marie Vastersavendts, June 8, 1968. Lectr., Brandeis U., Waltham, Mass., 1966-67, asst. prof., 1967-72; asso. prof. U. Ill. Chicago Circle, 1972-76, prof. math., 1976—; Office of Naval Research research asso., 1966-67. NSF research grantee, 1967—. Mem. Am. Math. Soc., Math. Assn. Am., Sigma Xi. Author: (with D. Kan) Homotopy Limits Completions and Localizations, 1972; contbr. articles to profl. jours. Home: 400 E Randolph St Chicago IL 60601 Office: Math Dept U Ill at Chicago Circle Chicago IL 60680

BOUSLOG, NYE FULTON, banker; b. Paris, Ill., June 27, 1920; s. Charles R. and Noma Belle (Fulton) B.; B.S., U. Ill., 1943; grad. Sch. Banking, U. Wis., 1968; m. Mildred Joan Curl, July 19, 1945; children—Carol Ann, Stephen Nye, Lynn Marie, John Michael. Farm adviser McDonough County, Ill., 1946-54; with Union Nat. Bank, Macomb, Ill., 1954—, loan officer, sr. v.p., farm service mgr., 1960—. Mem. Macomb Community Sch. Dist. Sch. Bd., 1962-71, pres. 1970-71; treas. YMCA, Macomb, 1967-71; bd. dirs. Western Ill. U. Found. Served to 1st lt., AUS, 1943-46. Recipient Achievement award 4-H Club, Macomb, 1960; named hon. chpt. farmer Future Farmers Am., 1970; recipient Sears Roebuck Found. scholarship, 1940-43; award of merit, citation for service to agr. U. Ill. Coll. Agr., 1977. Mem. Am., Ill. socs. profl. farm mgrs. and rural appraisers, Am. Legion, V.F.W., Gamma Sigma Delta. Roman Catholic (parish organizer, mem. parish council 1967-70). Clubs: K.C., Elks, Rotary (pres. 1976-77). Mem. Money Maker panel Prairie Farmer magazine, 1966-77. Home: 804 Madelyn Ave Macomb IL 61455 Office: Union National Bank Macomb IL 61455

BOUTROS, AZMY, physician; b. Cairo, Egypt, June 28, 1927; s. Ragheb and Alice (Barsoum) B.; M.B., Ch. B., Cairo U., 1950; m. Ida Winnifred Phillips, Dec. 9, 1960; children—Diana, Philip. Came to U.S., 1963, naturalized, 1968. Intern, resident in anesthesiology Cairo U. Hosps., 1951-54; resident in anesthesiology Birmingham, Eng., 1955-57, McGill U., 1958-60; asst. prof. U. Sask., 1960-63; asst. prof. anesthesiology U. Iowa, Iowa City, 1963-66, asso. prof., 1966-70, prof., 1970-77; dir. intensive care unit U. Iowa Hosps.; chmn. div. anesthesiology Cleve. Clinic Found., 1977—. Diplomate Am. Bd. Anesthesiology. Fellow Faculty Anaesthetists of Royal Coll. Surgeons (Eng.), Royal Coll. Physicians (Can.); mem. A.M.A., Canadian, Iowa med. assns., Am. Soc. Anesthesiologists, Canadian Anaesthetists Soc., Soc. Critical Medicine, IEEE, N.Y. Acad Scis., Assn. Univ. Anesthetists. Home: 7 Daisy Ln Pepper Pike OH 44124 Office: Cleveland Clinic Found Cleveland OH

BOUZEK, ROBERT EDWARD, pub. relations counselor; b. Prairie du Chien, Wis., Sept. 24, 1933; s. Edward James and Emma Regina (White) B.; student Marquette U., 1951-52; B.S.J., U. Wis.-Madison, 1962; m. Mary Elizabeth Scott, Dec. 20, 1960; children—Michaelle (Mrs. Arnold Rothenbaum), Elizabeth Mary, Lisa Diane, Jane Ann. Editor, Courier-Press, Prairie du Chien, 1957-58; govtl./bus. reporter Waukesha (Wis.) Freeman, 1958-59; reporter, copy editor Wis. State Jour., Madison, 1959-63; copy editor supr. Milw. Jour., 1963-67; pub. relations specialist Am. Mut. Ins. Alliance, Chgo., 1967-68; pub. relations counsel Carl Byoir & Assos. Inc., Chgo., 1968-70; account supr. Harshe-Rotman & Druck Inc., Chgo., 1970-77, v.p., 1977—. Vestryman St. Paul's Episcopal Ch., Riverside, Ill., 1977—. Served with USAF, 1953-57. Recipient Golden Trumpet award Publicity Club Chgo., 1976. Mem. Pub. Relations Soc. Am. (accredited). Poetry included in anthology The Singing Winds, 1959. Home: 69 E Quincy St Riverside IL 60546 Office: 444 N Michigan Ave Chicago IL 60611

BOVICH, EDWARD HUGH, cement co. exec.; b. N.Y.C., Sept. 20, 1924; s. Edward Francis and Beatrice Catherine (Gilmartin) B.; student Cathedral Coll., N.Y.C., 1942-44, U.S. Mcht. Marine Acad., Kings Point, N.Y., 1944-45; A.B., St. Basil's Coll. and Sem., Stamford, Conn., 1949; postgrad. Fordham U., 1950-51, DePaul U., 1954; m. Michele Marie Denaro, June 6, 1953; children—Mary Beatrice, Patricia Marie, Edward Philip, John Patrick. Instr., Fordham U., 1951; spl. agt. FBI, various locations, 1951-57; dist. dir. Nat. Safety Council, Pitts., 1957-59; exec. dir. Bd. Commerce, Wyandotte, Mich., 1959-62; dir. marketing Wyandotte Chems. Corp., 1962-65, gen. mgr. cement div., 1966-70; pres., chmn. bd. Wyandotte Cement, Inc., 1971—; dir. Wyandotte Stone Co.; adv. bd. Am. Mut. Ins. Co.; v.p. Old Harbor Marina, Clinton, Conn., 1974-76; pres. Material Transfer Corp., Deaborn, Mich., 1975—. Spl. rep. Pa., President's Com. for Traffic Safety, 1958; pres. Sacred Heart Sch. Bd., Dearborn, Mich., 1967-68, Sacred Heart Council, 1969-70; chmn. Chem. Industry United Found., 1969-72. Bd. mgmt. YMCA Detroit Met. Area, 1967-68; bd. dirs. Mt. Kelly Cemetery, Dearborn. Served with USNR, 1945-46. Named Outstanding Young Man of Year, Wyandotte, 1961. Mem. Soc. Former FBI Agts. (past chmn. Mich. chpt.), Portland Cement Assn. Chgo. (dir.), Sales and Mktg. Execs. Detroit (past chmn. Speakers Bur.), Assn. Execs. Met. Detroit, Buffalo, Detroit, Rochester chambers commerce. Clubs: Buffalo; Dearborn Country. Author: CBS Radio Show, Your FBI, Chgo., 1957. Home: 752 Wagner Ct Dearborn MI 48124 Office: Box 420 Wyandotte MI 48192

BOWDEN, JOSEPH VERNAL, microbiologist; b. Lewiston, Utah, Dec. 21, 1943; s. Clifford Stokes and Brelia Orella (Orchard) B.; B.S., Brigham Young U., 1971; m. Robinette Evangeline Perry, July 24, 1967; children—Brelan, Josie, Corey, Jeanette. Supr. microbiology Miles Labs., Elkhart, Ind., 1971-75; sr. tech. product specialist Ames Co., Elkhart, Ind., 1975—. Served with U.S. Army, 1965-67. Mem. Am. Soc. Clin. Pathology, Am. Soc. Microbiology, South Central Assn. Clin. Microbiology. Mormon. Club: Toastmasters. Home: 55604 Byrd St Osceola IN 46561 Office: 1127 Myrtle St Elkhart IN 46514

BOWDEN, OTIS HEARNE, II, mgmt. cons. firm exec.; b. Stuttgart, Ark., Jan. 2, 1928; s. Otis Hearne and Donna (Trice) B.; B.S. in Bus. Adminstrn., Washington U., 1950, M.B.A., 1953; m. Helen Carol Lamar, June 25, 1949. Financial analyst St. Louis Union Trust Co., St. Louis, 1950-53; dist. mgr. TRW, Inc., Cleve., 1953-63; dir. Mass Transit Center, B.F. Goodrich Co., Akron, Ohio, 1963-67; v.p. E.A. Butler Assos., Inc., Cleve., 1967-71; pres. Bowden & Co., Inc., Cleve., 1972—; guest lectr. Akron U., 1972—. Nat. promotion dir. Laymen's Hour Radio Broadcast, 1959-63; chmn. commerce and industry div. United Fund of Greater Cleve., 1962; pres. Am. Baptist Men of Ohio, 1962-63. Trustee Alderson-Broaddus Coll., Philippi, W.Va.; alumni bd. govs. Washington U., St. Louis; bd. dirs. Am. Bapt. Fgn. Mission Soc., 1962-71; regional dir. Project Winsome Internationale. Served with USMCR, 1951. Mem. Am. Mgmt. Assn., Am. Mktg. Assn. Club: Rotary (trustee 1975—). Home: 1816 Brookshire Rd Akron OH 44313 Office: Terminal Tower Cleveland OH 44113

BOWDLE, FREDERICK CHARLES, obstetrician, gynecologist; b. Napoleon, Ohio, Mar. 31, 1934; s. Charles P. and Reta Belle (Stuempel) B.; student U. Mich., 1952-55, M.D., 1959; m. Sandra Kay Lowe, June 22, 1963; children—Brian Frederick, Julie Rochelle. Intern, St. Vincent Hosp. and Med. Center, Toledo, 1959-60, resident, 1962-65, now mem. staff, chmn. dept. obstetrics and gynecology, 1971-75, practice medicine specializing in obstetrics and gynecology, Toledo, 1965—; mem. staffs Toledo Hosp., Med. Coll. Ohio; clin. asst. prof. obstetrics and gynecology Med. Coll. Ohio, Toledo, 1972—; mem. profl. edn. com. Lucas County (Ohio) unit Am. Cancer Soc., 1971. Served as capt. M.C. USAF, 1960-62. Diplomate Am. Bd. Obstetrics and Gynecology. Fellow Am. Coll. Obstetrics and Gynecology, A.C.S.; mem. Acad. Medicine of Toledo and Lucas County, Toledo, Mich. socs. obstetrics-gynecology, Central Assn. Obstetrics-Gynecology, AMA, U. Mich. Alumni Assn., Ohio State Alumni Assn. Republican. Methodist. Clubs: Royal Order Jesters, Masons, Shriners. Home: 4629 Beaconsfield Ct Toledo OH 43623 Office: 706 Madison Ave Toledo OH 43624

BOWDLER, ANTHONY JOHN, physician, educator; b. London, Eng., Oct. 16, 1928; s. Edward Thomas and Clara McBean (Anthony) B.; B.Sc., U. Coll., London, 1949, M.B., B.S., 1952, M.D. (Bilton Pollard fellow), 1963, Ph.D., 1967; postgrad. (Buswell Sr. fellow), U. Rochester, 1962-64; m. Eleanor Madeleine Sladen, July 30, 1955; children—Noelle Clare, Jonathan Francis. Came to U.S., 1967. Intern, University College Hosp., London, 1952, Hammersmith Hosp., London, 1953, Brompton Hosp., London, 1956, Dorking Hosp., Surrey, Eng., 1957; registrar and research fellow U. Coll. Hosp., London, 1958-62; sr. instr. U. Rochester (N.Y.), 1962-64; sr. lectr. U. Coll. Hosp. Med. Sch., London, 1964-67; asso. prof. medicine, Mich. State U., E. Lansing, 1967-70, prof. medicine, 1971—. Served as surgeon lt., Royal Navy, 1953-55. Fellow Royal Coll. Physicians; mem. Am. Fedn. Clin. Research, Central Soc. Clin. Research, Am. Soc. Hematology, Am. Assn. Blood Banks, Med. Research Soc. London, Brit. Med. Assn., Royal Soc. Medicine (London). Researcher in internal medicine. Home: 1939 Oneida Dr Okemos MI 48864 Office: Michigan State University East Lansing MI 48824

BOWEN, CHARLES H., materials analysis co. exec.; b. Chgo., Sept. 11, 1928; s. Charles Henry and Dorothy Marion (DeRogue) B.; B.S. in Radio Engring., Chgo. Tech. Coll., 1951; m. Susan M. Moore, Aug. 20, 1960; children—Beth Anne, Amy Jane. Supr. electronics shop, 1953-60; electronics engr. Hallicrafters Corp., 1960-62; electronics engr. A.B. Dick Co., 1962-66; project engr. Automatic Electric Labs., Northlake, Ill., 1966-68; mgr. data processing, electronics engr. Walter C. McCrone Assos., Chgo., 1968—. Served with Signal Corps, U.S. Army, 1951-53. Mem. IEEE, Am. Radio Relay League. Club: Masons. Home: 128 Clara Pl Elmhurst IL 60126 Office: 2820 S Michigan Blvd Chicago IL 60616

BOWEN, GLEN LOWELL, mech. engr.; b. Lincoln Twp., Mich., Dec. 14, 1912; s. Roy David and Margaret (Bell) B.; grad. Automotive Engr., Gen. Motors Inst., 1937, B.M.E., 1958; m. Emily Savickas, Feb. 18, 1939; children—Thomas, Suzanne, Patrice. With research div. Gen. Motors Corp., 1935-42, 43-45, designer Detroit Transmission div., 1943-45; drafting room supr. Lee Engring. Co., Detroit, 1942-43; chief engr. Henderson Engring. Co., Detroit, 1945-48; chief engr., v.p. engring. Jered Industries, Hazel Park, Mich., 1948-61; pres., chmn. bd. G.L. Bowen & Co., Warren, Mich., 1961-72; mgr. design engring. gen. products div. Teledyne Continental Motors Co., Muskegon, Mich., 1973—. Registered profl. engr., Mich. Recipient Design News award for article, 1968. Mem. Nat. Mgmt. Assn., Assn. U.S. Army, Am. Def. Preparedness Assn., Phi Sigma Phi. Republican. Roman Catholic. Author, patentee in field. Home: 2449 Mulberry St Bloomfield Hills MI 48013 Office: 76 Getty St Muskegon MI 49442

BOWEN, KEVIN FRANCIS, food co. exec.; b. Providence, Sept. 1, 1948; s. Francis A. and Katherine (O'Connor) B.; B.A., Brown U., 1970; M.A., Calif. State U., Los Angeles, 1971; Ph.D. (Research fellow), Dartmouth Coll., 1976; m. Marianne E. Klinkenberg, Dec. 16, 1972. Sr. research analyst Quaker Oats Co., Chgo., 1976-77, research supr., 1977—. Mem. Am. Mktg. Assn., Advt. Research Found. Home: 345 Fullerton Pkwy Chicago IL 60614 Office: Quaker Oats Co Merchandise Mart Plaza Chicago IL 60654

BOWEN, MARCIA ANN, assn. exec.; b. Hammond, Ind., June 14, 1943; d. Carl and Elvera Louella (Toepfer) Adams; student Calif. State U., 1961-62, Cerritos Coll., 1971-72; m. Terrence Edwin Bowen, Mar. 21, 1971; 1 dau., Melinda Suzanne Goodwin. Office mgr. Hartfield Zodys, Inc., Los Angeles, 1967-70; asst. to the accounting mgr. Maxon Industries, Inc., Huntington Park, Calif., 1971-72; bookkeeping supr. Disposable Research Industries, Inc., City of Industry, Calif., 1972-73; mgr. accounting dept. Air Resources, Inc., Palatine, Ill., 1973-75; dir. fin. and adminstrn. Profl. Photographers of Am., Inc., Des Plaines, Ill., 1975—. Mem. Chgo. Soc. of Assn. Execs. Home: 311 Amherst Court Vernon Hills IL 60061 Office: 1090 Executive Way Des Plaines IL 60018

BOWEN, OTIS RAY, physician, gov. Ind.; b. nr. Rochester, Ind., Feb. 26, 1918; s. Vernie and Pearl (Wright) B.; A.B. in Chemistry, Ind. U., 1939, M.D., 1942; hon. LL.D., Valparaiso, 1973, Vincennes, Butler U., Anderson Coll., Ind. U., Tri-State Coll., Calumet Coll., U. Evansville, Ind. State U., Rose-Hulman Inst.; m. Elizabeth A. Steinmann, Feb. 25, 1939; children—Richard H., Judith I. McGrew, Timothy R., Robert O. Intern, Meml. Hosp., S. Bend, Ind., 1942-43; gen. practice medicine, Bremen, Ind., 1946-72; past. mem. staff Bremen Community Hosp., Parkview Hosp., Plymouth, Ind., Meml., St. Joseph's hosps., South Bend, St. Joseph Hosp., Mishawaka, Ind.; gov. Ind., 1973—; clin. prof. Ind. U. Sch. Medicine, 1976—. Coroner Marshall County, Ind., 1952-56; dir. health services Marshall County Civil Defense, 1959-62; mem. Ind. State Com. for Eradication Tb; mem. Pres.'s Com. Fed. Paperwork, 1975—, Pres.'s Com. Sci. and Tech., 1976—; mem. Edn. Commn. States, 1973—, chmn. elect, 1976-77; mem. exec. com. Council State Govts. Mem. Tri Valley council Boy Scouts Am.; past mem. Ind. Recreation Council; adv. com. on curricula Vincennes U.; advisory bd. Indpls. chpt. Fellowship Christian Athletes. Mem. Ind. Ho. of Reps., 1956-58, 60-72, minority leader house of reps., 1965-67, speaker house, 1967-72, chmn. legis. council Ind. Gen. Assembly, 1967-68, 70, 72; mem. intergovtl. relations com. Nat. Legis. Council. Trustee Ancilla Coll. Served from 1st lt. to capt., M.C., AUS, 1943-46. Recipient Alumni of Yr. award Ind. U. Med. Sch., 1971, merit award Ind. Pub. Health Assn., 1971, Benjamin Rush award pub. service AMA, 1973, Distinguished Service award Future Farmers Am., 1976. Mem. Am., Ind. (mem. legislative commn. 1958—, 13th Dist. councilor 1965-67), 13th Dist. (past pres.), Marshall County (past pres.), 13th Dist. (past pres.) med. assns., Ind. Mental Health Assn., Am., Ind. gen. practice assns., Trudeau Society, Farm Bureau, Marshall County Tb Soc. (v.p.), Bremen C. of C., Am. Legion, V.F.W., Alpha Omega Alpha, Phi Beta Pi, Delta Chi. Lutheran (past v.p. congregation; past chmn. sch. bd.; past chmn. bd. finance). Kiwanian (past pres., past dir.). Contbr. articles to med. jours. Home: 304 N Center Bremen IN 46506 Office: Office of Gov Room 206 State House Indianapolis IN 46204

BOWEN, RICHARD LEE, architect; b. Canton, Ohio, Nov. 1, 1935; s. Ray Leed and Lillian (White) B.; B.Arch., Case-Western Res. U., 1959; m. Robin Straley Herrington, Dec. 17, 1955; children—Laurel Ann, Richard Lee, David H., Sean Andrew, Scott Edward. Propr. Richard L. Bowen and Assos., architects, engrs. and planners, Cleve., 1960—; partner Com-Del Devel. Co.; pres. Chagrin Valley Constrn. Co., Richard L. Bowen & Assos. Inc. of Fla., Richard L. Bowen AIA & Assos. Inc. of Ohio; dir. Thermal King Sales and Service Cleve., Thermal King Sales and Services Columbus, Ohio, Thermal King Sales and Services Akron, Ohio, Refrigerated Leasing, Inc., Am. Nat. Bank, Parma, Ohio. Mem. archtl. adv. bd. region 5 Gen. Services Adminstrn. Mem. exec. com. Cuyahoga County Republican Party. Mem. A.I.A., Royal Archtl. Inst. Can., Royal Inst. Brit. Architects, Soc. Archtl. Historians, Nat. Council Archtl. Registration Bds., Ch. Archtl. Guild, Architects Soc. Ohio, Soc. Ch. Architects, Phi Gamma Delta. Mem. Disciples of Christ Ch. Clubs: Clevelander, Cleve. Athletic, Skating, Playhouse, Chagrin Valley Country, Mentor Harbor Yachting (Cleve.); Lauderdale Yacht (Ft. Lauderdale, Fla.); Jockey (Fla.). Office: 13124 Shaker Square Cleveland OH 44120

BOWEN, STEPHEN FRANCIS, JR., ophthalmic surgeon; b. Worcester, Mass., Jan. 6, 1932; s. Stephen Francis and Margaret Helen (O'Brien) B.; A.B. cum laude, Holy Cross Coll., 1952; M.D., Tufts U., 1956; M.Sc., U. Minn., 1962; m. Ann Marie Nooney, July 5, 1958; children—Mary Beth, Alisa, Stephen, Margo. Intern, U. Minn., Hosp., 1956-57; fellow in ophthalmology Mayo Clinic, Rochester, Minn., 1959-62; practice medicine specializing in ophthalmology, St. Louis, 1962—; faculty St. Louis U. Med. Sch., 1962—, clin. prof. ophthalmology, 1972—, dir. sect. neuroophthalmology, 1962—. Cons. question and answer sect. Jour. AMA, 1968—. Served to lt. comdr. M.C., USNR, 1957-59. Mem. Mo. Ophthalmologic Soc. (pres. 1968-69), Nat. Mayo Eye Alumni Assn. (pres. 1971-72, dir. 1965-68, 70-73), Mayo Alumni Assn. (dir. 1973—), Sigma Xi. Roman Catholic. Contbr. articles to tech. jours. Home: 50 Portland Dr Frontenac MO 63131 Office: 16 Hampton Village Plaza St Louis MO 63109

BOWEN, STEPHEN NEWBURY, diversified industry exec.; b. Norwalk, Ohio, Aug. 9, 1935; s. Harold Stephen and Mary Elizabeth (Prechtel) B.; m. Marilyn Ann Sennett, Jan. 17, 1956; children—Barbara, Harold, Susan, Charles, Christopher, David, Geoffrey. Writer, E. Ohio Gas Co., Cleve., 1958-59; mgr. communications Lubrizol Corp., Cleve., 1959-67; asst. dir. pub. relations Watts, Lee & Kenyon, advt., Cleve., 1968-69; regional dir. corp. relations TRW, Los Angeles, 1969-72, dir. pub. relations, Cleve., 1972—, dir. corporate advt. and identity, 1977—. cons. in field. Trustee Hiram House, Cleve. Mem. Pub. Relations Soc. Am. (accredited), Assn. Nat. Advertisers, Greater Cleve. Growth Assn. Home: 8055 Monterey St Chesterland OH 44026 Office: TRW 23555 Euclid Ave Cleveland OH 44117

BOWER, JAY ROSS, realtor; b. Quincy, Ill., July 8, 1936; s. J. Ross and Edna (Blentinger) B.; B.S., Culver-Stockton Coll., 1967; m. Shirley Day, Aug. 5, 1956; 1 dau., Lisa Lynne. Partner, Bower & Son Realtor, Quincy, Camp Point and Mt. Sterling, 1958—; owner Prescription Shop, Camp Point, Ill., 1960-63, Fluffy Fluff Laundromat, Camp Point, 1959-68, Bower Gallery of Homes, 1972, Shirlyn Acres Farm, 1967—; co-owner Towne & Country Abstract & Title Co., Quincy, 1963—, Bower & Son Ins., Quincy, 1964-73; pres. Home & Farm, Inc., Quincy, Prestige Homes, Inc., 1975—; regional councilman Ill. Gallery of Homes, 1974—; dir. Lincoln Loan Co., Quincy. County chmn. Community Chest, 1959; asso. mem. Adams County Family Service Agy., 1963—. Bd. dirs. Culver-Stockton Coll. Alumni. Served with AUS, 1957-58. Recipient Good Citizenship award Adams County Community Chest, 1959, named Community Leader of Am., 1969, among Outstanding Young Men of Am., 1967. Mem. Nat. Assn. Realtors, Nat. Inst. Farm and Land Brokers (mem. ednl. com., pres. Ill. chpt. 1974—; accredited), Sales and Mktg. Execs. of Quincy, Quincy C. of C., Camp Point Businessmen's Assn., Ill. (mem. legislative com. 1973), Quincy bds. realtors, Nat. Mktg. Inst. Realtors (certified residential broker), Mu Theta Nu, Tau Kappa Epsilon. Democrat. Mem. Christian Ch. Lion. Home: 104 N 5th St Quincy IL 62301 Office: 5th and Maine Sts Quincy IL 62301

BOWES, ARTHUR STUTZ, JR., bus. exec.; b. Chgo., Apr. 7, 1932; s. Arthur Stutz and Jane (Mattison) B.; student Purdue U., 1950-51; B.S., Northwestern U., 1958, M.B.A., 1959; m. Barbara Ann Hoops, Jan. 24, 1953; children—Linda Jane, Karen Ann. Investment analyst, research dir. H.M. Byllesby & Co., Chgo., 1960-64; v.p. and dir. Advance Ross Corp., Chgo., 1964-66; v.p. Utah Shale Land Corp., Chgo., 1964-66; pres. Lab Tronics, Inc., Chgo., 1965-66; pres. Wolf Ridge Minerals Corp., Denver, Colo., 1966-72; pres., dir. Am. Butternut Co., Columbia City, Ind., 1966-75; chmn., dir. Indsl. Resources, Inc., Chgo.; chmn., dir. Advance Ross Corp., Chgo.; dir. Holmes & Co., Columbia City, Ind., Organic Nutrients, Inc., Sacramento, Utah Shale Land & Minerals Corp., Chgo. Vice pres., sec. Bowes Found., Chgo., 1960—. Served with AUS, 1952-55. Mem. Investment Analysts Soc., Phi Gamma Delta, Beta Gamma Sigma. Republican. Club: Mid-Day (Chgo.). Home: 815 Windsor Rd Glenview IL 60025 Office: 135 S LaSalle St Room 600 Chicago IL 60603

BOWIE, EDWARD JOHN WALTER, hematologist; b. Church Stretton, Eng., Mar. 10, 1925; s. Edgar Ormond and Ann Brown (Lorrimer) B.; M.A., Wadham Coll. Oxford U., 1949, B.M., B.Ch., 1952; M.S., U. Minn., 1961; m. Trudi Ulrich, Dec. 22, 1948; children—Katherine, Christopher, John, James. Came to U.S., 1957, naturalized, 1963. Cons. in hematology Mayo Clinic, Rochester, Minn., 1960-70, head. sect. hematology research, 1971—; prof. medicine and lab. medicine Mayo Med. Sch., Rochester, 1974—. Served with Royal Naval Vol. Reserve, 1943-46. Fellow A.C.P. Author: (with others) The Diagnosis of Bleeding Disorders, 1969, 2d edit., 1975; The Mayo Clinic Laboratory Manual of Hemostasis, 1971. Home: 2221 Lenwood Dr SW Rochester MN 55901 Office: Mayo Clinic Rochester MN 55901

BOWLING, DAVID SAMUEL, geophysicist; b. Bennett, Ky., July 10, 1929; s. Reece Madison and Nancy Elizabeth (Knipp) B.; B.A., Berea Coll., 1956; m. Anna Louise Ogle, Dec. 22, 1955; children—Marla Lucille, Theresa Anne, David Reece, John Anthony. Computer trainee Geophys. Service Inc., Dallas, 1956-56, 2d computer, 1956-57, 1st computer, 1957-59, seismologist, 1959-60, party chief, 1960-62; cons. geophysicist Bowling, Roberson and Ward Seismic Assos., Norman, Okla., 1962-63; area supr. explosives product group Monsanto Co., St. Louis, 1963-68; project engr. G.W. Murphy Industries Inc., Houston, 1968-70, ops. mgr., 1970; partner White Engring. Assos. Inc., Joplin, Mo., 1970—, pres., 1972—. Served to sgt., U.S. Army, 1948-52. Registered geophysicist, Calif.; certified geologist Maine; certified profl. geol. scientist Assn. Profl. Geol. Scientists. Mem. Soc. Exploration Geophysicists, AAAS, ASTM, Soc. Am. Mil. Engrs., Seismol. Soc. Am., Am. Assn. Petroleum Geologists (asso.). Methodist. Clubs: Masons, K.T. Home: Route 7 Box 145 Joplin MO 64801 Office: PO Box 1256 Joplin MO 64801

BOWLING, WILLIAM GLASGOW, educator; b. St. Louis, May 7, 1902; s. William Walter and Mary Susan (Glasgow) B.; A.B., Washington U., St. Louis, 1924, A.M., 1925; student Harvard U., 1930-31; m. Violet Whelen, Aug. 3, 1933; 1 son, Townsend Whelen. Instr., asst. prof., asso. prof. English, Washington U., 1925-70, prof. emeritus, 1970—, asst. to dean, acting dean, dean Univ. Coll., 1925-42; dean Coll. Liberal Arts, 1942-46; dean men, 1942-44; civilian adminstr. Pre-professional Unit of Army Specialized Tng. Program, Washington U., St. Louis, 1943-44, dean admissions, 1946-65, univ. historian, 1965—, univ. grand marshal, 1960-68. Part time drama critic, St. Louis Times, 1929-30; pioneer at Washington U. in radio in edn., alumni insts. and ednl. motion pictures; exec. sec. Washington U. Assn. Lecture Series, 1940-47. Pres. local PTA, Clayton, Mo., 1946-47. Recipient Washington U. Alumni award, 1960. Mem. Greater St. Louis Council Tchrs. of English (pres. 1936-39; exec. sec., 1939-41), Am. Assn. Collegiate Registrars and Admissions Officers (hon.; book rev. editor quarterly jour., College and University 1955-66), St. Louis Audubon Soc. (pres. 1950-52, mem. bd. dir., 1944—), Phi Delta Theta, Omicron Delta Kappa, Phi Delta Kappa. Republican. Episcopalian. Club: University (St. Louis). Contbr. to jours. Address: 7408 Washington Ave St Louis MO 63130

BOWMAN, ARNOLD PAUL, food products co. exec.; b. Sikeston, Mo., Sept. 5, 1920; s. A. Paul and Margaret Emily (Dover) B.; student SE Mo. State Coll., 1938-41; B.S. in Chemistry, U. Wis., 1949; m. Jean Welke, Mar. 7, 1941; children—Melissa Hamilton (Mrs. Lee C. Brumley), Mary Linville. With Scott County Milling Co., Sikeston, 1932-37; lab. technician Reiss Dairy Sale, Sikeston, 1937-39; with Oscar Mayer and Co., Madison, Wis., 1948—, group v.p., 1971—, also dir.; dir. Anchor Savs. and Loan, Prima Meats Ltd., Tokyo, Japan, Oscar Mayer, S.A., Valencia, Spain, Venezolona Empocadova C.A., Caracas, Venezuela; chmn. bd. Sci. Protein Labs., Waunahee, Wis., Quality Control Spice, Madison, Clausens, Woodstock, Ill. Pres. United Community Chest, 1968, gen. chmn., 1965. Chmn. Dane County Republican Finance Com., 1962-63. Bd. dirs. Big Bros. Dane County, 1967, Jr. Achievement, 1963-67. Served to capt. USAF, 1941-47. Mem. Madison C. of C. (pres. 1970, dir. 1969-71), Inst. Food Technologists, Am. Soc. Quality Control, Am. Chem. Soc., Wis. Alumni Assn., Inst. Mgmt. Sci. Baptist. (trustee 1963). Kiwanian (dir. 1963). Home: 1101 Farwell Dr Madison WI 53704 Office: PO Box 1409 Madison WI 53701

BOWMAN, DOUGLAS CLYDE, educator; b. St. Louis, Oct. 20, 1925; s. Douglas Clyde and Evelyn Frances (Matthews) B.: B.S., Puget Sound U., 1948, B.E., 1949; M.S., U. Wash., 1957, Ph.D., 1958; m. Evelynne Jean Hanson, Aug. 15, 1955; children—Pamela Dawn, Douglas Craig, Cynthia Sue. Instr., U. Wash., 1958; instr., asst. prof. Northwestern U. Dental Sch., 1959-64; asst. prof., asso. prof. physiology Loyola U. of Chgo. Sch. Dentistry, Maywood, Ill., 1965—, coordinator conjoint teaching, 1969—. Mem. AAAS, N.Y. Acad. Scis., Chgo. Inst. Medicine, Sigma Xi, Phi Sigma, Omicron Kappa Upsilon. Contbr. articles to profl. jours. Home: 152 S Milton St Glen Ellyn IL 60137 Office: 2160 S 1st Ave Maywood IL 60153

BOWMAN, JAMES DALE, indsl. engr.; b. Emporium, Pa., Mar. 25, 1929; s. Andrew D. and Margaret (Narby) B.; B.S., Pa. State U., 1958, M.S., 1964; m. Irene Mary Magagnotti, Aug. 20, 1951. Apprentice, Gen. Electric Co., Erie, Pa., 1947-51, project engr., 1953-54; instr., asst. prof. indsl. engring., 1958-67, head Automation Lab., 1958-67; tng. and product mgr. Bellows Valvair, Akron, Ohio, 1967-70, dir. tng., 1970-73, mgr. systems engring., Zanesville, Ohio, 1973-74, mktg., sales mgr., 1974-75, dir. tng. Bellows Internat., Akron, 1976, group engring. mgr., 1977—. Served with AUS, 1951-52. Mem. Soc. Mfg. Engrs., Soc. Advancement Mgmt. (dir. 1959-66), Alpha Pi Mu. Home: 557 Schocalog Rd Akron OH 44320 Office: 200 W Exchange St Akron OH 44309

BOWMAN, MARK DOUGLAS, structural engr.; b. Logansport, Ind., Aug. 9, 1952; s. John Robert and Mable Louise (Nelson) B.; B.S.C.E. (Elks Scholarship award), Purdue U., 1974, M.S.C.E. (Nellie Munson award), 1975; postgrad. U. Ill., 1977—; m. Barbara Baerwald, Aug. 6, 1977. Civil engr. Chgo. Bridge & Iron Co., Oakbrook, Ill., summer 1974; teaching and lab. asst. Purdue Univ., W. Lafayette, Ind., 1974-75; structural design engr. Precast/Schokbeton Inc., Kalamazoo, Mich., 1975-77. Mem. ASCE, Am. Concrete Inst., Prestressed Concrete Inst., Nat., Mich. soc. of profl. engrs., Nat. Geog. Soc., Phi Kappa Phi, Chi Epsilon, Tau Beta Pi. Methodist. Clubs: Triangle Fraternity. Asst. editor Mich. Civil Engr., 1976-77. Home: 301 E White St Apt 6 Champaign IL 61820 Office: Civil Engring Bldg U Ill Urbana IL 61801

BOWMAN, MONROE BENGT, architect; b. Chgo., Aug. 28, 1901; s. Henry William and Ellen Mercedes (Bjork) B.; m. Louise Kohnmann, Nov. 1944; 1 son, Kenneth Monroe; B.Arch., Ill. Inst. Tech., 1924. Registered architect, Ill., Wis., Ind., Ohio, Colo. Asso., Benjamin H. Marshall, Chgo., 1926; exhibited models and photographs of Bowman Bros. comtemporary designs at Mus. Modern Art, N.Y.C., 1931; pvt. practice architecture, Chgo., 1941-44; asso. Monroe Bowman Assos., Chgo., 1945—; cons. Chgo. Dept. City Planning, City of Sparta (Wis.), Alfred Shaw, Architect. Mem. Navy League U.S. Important works include Boeing Aircraft bldgs., Wichita, Kans., Emerson Electric bldgs., St. Louis, Maytag Co., Newton, Iowa, Douglas Aircraft bldgs., Park Ridge, Ill., Shwayder Bros. bldgs., Denver, Clark Equipment Co., Buchannon, Mich., Radio-TV Sta. WHO, Des Moines, Foote, Cone & Belding offices, Chgo., Burridge Devel., Hinsdale, Ill., Yacht Club and recreational facilities, Lake Bemiji, Minn., United Airlines offices downtown Chgo., Automatic Sprinkler Corp., Chgo., King Machine Tool div. Am. Steel Foundries, Cin., Marine Terr. Apts., Chgo., Dorchester Park Apts., Chgo., Manteno (Ill.) State Hosp., No. Ill. Gas Co. bldgs., LaGrange, Joliet, Streator and Morris, 1340 Astor St. Apt. Bldg., Burnham Center, Chgo., NSF, Green Bank, W.Va., Naval Radio Research Sta., Sugar Grove, W.Va., Columbus Boy Choir Sch., Princeton, N.J. Home: 1566 Oak Ave Evanston IL 60201

BOWMAN, PHILIP LOREN, lawyer; b. Hutchinson, Kans., June 18, 1936; s. Hugh Dell and Lael (Griffeth) B.; A.A., Hutchinson Jr. Coll., 1956; B.Bus. Adminstrn., U. Kans., 1958, J.D., 1961; m. Barbara Louise Erickson, Aug. 17, 1957; children—Marc Erickson, Brenda Louise, Andrew Philip. Admitted to Kans. bar, 1961; v.p. Bushton State Bank (Kans.), 1961-62; mem. firm Adams, Jones, Robinson & Malone, 1962—; city atty. Andover, Kans., 1965—; dir. Insured Titles, Inc. Active Cub and Boy Scouts Am. Trustee Watkins Found., 1973—. Mem. Am., Kans., Wichita bar assns., Kans. U. Law Soc. Contbr. articles in field to profl. jours. Home: 20 Cypress Dr Wichita KS 67206 Office: 201 N Main St Wichita KS 67201

BOWMAN, WILLIAM WALTER, III, real estate exec.; b. Topeka, Kans., Sept. 26, 1926; s. William Walter and Ethel Lee (Hawk) B.; B.A., William Jewell Coll., 1951: m. Barbara Ballard, July 21, 1956; children—William Walter IV, Robert Vern, Blair Mathew, Brenda Elizabeth. Asst. dir. admissions Northwestern U., Evanston, Ill., 1952-54; real estate salesman Thompson-Brown Co., Farmington, Mich., 1954-60, v.p., 1960-63, exec. v.p., 1963—. Chmn. Indsl. Devel. Com., Farmington, Mich., 1960-69. Pres., Farmington Indsl. Devel. Corp., 1963-69; v.p., bd. dirs., exec. com. YMCA, 1967-69; dir. New Horizons for Retarded Young Adults, 1968-69. Served with USMC, 1944-46. Mem. Detroit Real Estate Bd., Soc. Indsl. Realtors, Western Wayne Oakland County Bd. Realtors, United Northwestern Realtors Assn. (dir. 1969-75, pres. 1973, Mich. Realtor of Year 1973), Farmington C. of C. (past pres.), Bd. of Commerce (dir. 1964-69). Club: Exchange (dir., past pres.). Home: 21430 Haggerty Rd Northville MI 48167 Office: 32823 W 12 Mile Rd Farmington MI 48024

BOWNE, JAMES DEHART, museum exec.; b. Phila., Mar. 5, 1940; s. Ira Ervin and Mary Bradway (Powell) B.; student George Washington U. and Corcoran Sch. of Art, 1962, 63, 66, 67; A.A., Sandhills Community Coll., 1968; A.B. (Delta Phi Delta Alumni scholar), East Carolina U., Greenville, N.C., 1970; M.A., U. N.C., Chapel Hill, 1972; m. Cheryl Jean Thompson, June 15, 1974; 1 dau., Heather Leigh. Grad. asst. U. N.C., 1971, research fellow, 1972; curatorial asst. Ackland Art Center, Chapel Hill, N.C., 1971; dir.-curator Lauren Rogers Library and Mus. of Art, Laurel, Miss., 1972-75; dir. Sheldon Swope Art Gallery, Terre Haute, Ind., 1975—. Instr. painting and drawing; art judge; artist; pres. Laurel Arts Council, 1973-75; bd. dirs. Terre Haute Symphony, 1976—. Served with AUS, 1958-61. Mem. Am. Assn. Museums, Coll. Art Assn., Smithsonian Instn. Nat. Assn., Assn. Councils of Arts, Miss. Art Assn., Nat. Soc. Lit., Arts, Ind. Arts Commn., Midwest Mus. Conf., Assn. Ind. Museums, Midwest Art History Soc., Nat. Exchange Club, Phi Sigma Pi, Delta Phi Delta. Republican. Rotarian. Contbr. articles to A Medieval Treasury From Southeastern Collections, and numerous articles on art to newspapers. Home: 63 S 20th St Terre Haute IN 47803 Office: 25 S 7th St Terre Haute IN 47807

BOXWELL, LLOYD LEE, veterinarian; b. Martelle, Iowa, June 11, 1917; s. William Lee and Leureta Amy (Eldred) B.; student Lenox Jr. Coll., 1936; D.V.M., Iowa State U., 1940; m. Margaret K. Slater, May 11, 1941; children—Roberta Lee, Sandra Catheryn, Donald Arthur. Gen. practice veterinary medicine, Princeton, Ill., 1940, Nashua, Iowa, 1940-42, Cedar Falls, Iowa, 1942—. Mem. Am., Iowa, Eastern Iowa, Cedar Valley vet. med. assns., C. of C. Presbyterian. Clubs: Lions, Masons. Office: 315 State St Cedar Falls IA 50613

BOYAJIAN, JAMES ARAM, cons. engr.; b. Sivas, Turkey, Mar., 1905; s. John O. and Anna H. (Kosharian) B.; came to U.S., 1907, naturalized, 1928; B.S.E., Northwestern U., 1933, E.E., 1934, M.S. in Physics, 1940; m. Eleanor L. Astenius, Aug. 2, 1930; children—James Aram, Phyllis Elaine Boyajian Murphy, John Wayne. Cons. plastics engr., electromech. engring., chief research and devel. engr. Gen. Household Utilities Corp., 1934-38; J.P. Seeburg Corp., Chgo., 1938-42; chief engr. Gen. Radio and TV Corp., Chgo., 1942-43; chief engr. Metal Specialties Mfg. Co., Chgo., 1943-44; owner, operator Triumph Mfg. Co., Chgo., 1943-60, Product Mfg. and Engring. Co., Chgo., 1944-55, Production Tool Co., Schiller Park, Ill., 1940-60; instr. plastics engring., Northwestern U., Evanston, Ill., 1945—; cons., prin. James A. Boyajian and Assos., Morton Grove, Ill., 1942—. Registered profl. engr., stationery engr.; licensed real estate broker. Mem. IEEE, Soc. Plastics Industry, ASME, Soc. Plastics Engrs., AAAS, Physics Club of Chgo. Clubs: Masons, Shrine. Address: 5707 Crain St Morton Grove IL 60053

BOYD, DONALD HEGLAND, accountant; b. Roland, Iowa, Dec. 20, 1919; s. Otis S. and Olive E. (Hegland) B.; student Waldorf Coll., 1937-38; B.S., Dubuque U., 1941; certificate of voice Tampa U., 1945, Iowa State U., 1948; m. Marie G. Rossa, Apr. 9, 1944; children—Kathryn Boyd Zipf, William K., Paula M. (dec.), Beverly Noel Frandson. With Interstates Power Co., Dubuque, Iowa, 1941; accountant Epperson & Co., Tampa, Fla., 1946-47; prin. Boyd Ins. Agy., Don H. Boyd, Accounting Practioner, Roland, Iowa, 1947—; pres. BDS Co., Roland, 1972-75, County Mut. Systems, Inc., Roland, 1974—. Faculty voice Tampa U., 1946-47; dir. Story County Women's Chorus, Roland Men's Chorus, 1950-60. Pres., Roland Community Club, 1951-52; mem. town council Roland, 1962-64. Served with AUS, 1941-46; PTO. Recipient award Nat. Soc. Accountants, 1974; Dist. Dir. of Year award Iowa Accountants, 1969. Mem. Am. Legion (finance officer 1952-53), Accountant's Assn. Iowa, Nat. Soc. Pub. Accountants. Lutheran. Elk, Kiwanian. Inventor computer system. Home: 405 Martha St Box 289 Roland IA 50236 Office: 517 Main St Roland IA 50236

BOYD, JOHN ADDISON, JR., civil engr.; b. Kansas City, Mo., Dec. 20, 1930; s. John Addison and Sarah Frances (Burger) B.; B.S., U. Kans., 1952, M.S. in Civil Engring., 1960; m. Rosemary Kennedy, Jan. 31, 1953; children—Mary A., John K., Thomas K., Christopher K., William K. Constrn. engr. T.F. Marbut, Emporia, Kans., 1956-58; instr. civil engring. U. Kans., Lawrence, 1958-60, lectr. structural engring., 1958-75; engr. Howard, Needles, Tammeh & Bergendoff, Kansas City, Mo., 1960-66; partner Boyd, Brown & Stude, Kansas City, 1966—; lectr. U. Mo. Served with USNR, 1953-57. Recipient Young Engr. award Mo. Soc. Profl. Engrs., 1964, Nat. Design award Transworld Airlines Overhaul Complex Kansas City Internat. Airport, 1973. Am. Inst. Steel Constrn. research grantee, 1960. Mem. Naval Res. Assn. (pres. Santa Fe Trail chpt. 1973-74), Soc. Am. Mil. Engrs. (pres. 1972), Mo. Profl. Engrs. in Pvt. Practice (pres. 1973), Midwest Concrete Industry Bd. (pres. 1974), Constrn. Industry Affairs Council, ASCE, Sigma Tau, Phi Delta Theta. Home: 8101 El Monte St Prairie Village KS 66208 Office: 4635 Wyandotte St Kansas City MO 64112

BOYD, JOHN HARVEY, JR., journalist, educator; b. Martinsville, Ind., Sept. 4, 1922; s. John Harvey and Virginia (Wadsworth) B.; B.S., Ind. U., 1948; M.A., 1955; m. Marie Helen Potter, Nov. 14, 1947; children—John Harvey III, Matthew Wadsworth. Picture editor Acme Newspictures and NEA Service, Chgo. bur., 1947; instr. journalism U. Ala., Tuscaloosa, 1950-53; news editor Pensacola (Fla.) Jour. and Sunday News-Journal, 1953-54; tri-state editor Evansville (Ind.) Press, 1954-61; asst. prof. journalism U. Evansville, 1961-65; asst. prof. Sch. Journalism, Mich. State U., East Lansing, Mich., 1965-68; asso. prof. journalism Sch. Journalism, U. Mo., 1968-71; city editor Columbia Missourian, 1968-71; asso. prof. journalism Ind. State U., Terre Haute, 1971—, adviser to Ind. Statesman, 1971—, dir. journalism, 1974—. Served with A.C., AUS, 1943-46. Mem. Assn. for Edn. in Journalism, Sigma Delta Chi, Pi Delta Epsilon, Lambda Chi Alpha. Home: 4414 N Scenic Dr Bloomington IN 47401 Office: The Statesman Ind State U Terre Haute IN 47809

BOYD, JOHN KENT, advt. exec.; b. Portsmouth, Ohio, Oct. 17, 1910; s. Lambert Thomas and Faery Ann (Ritter) B.; student Tulane U., New Orleans, 1927-29; m. Jeanne Marie Dunlap, Dec. 26, 1935; children—John Kent, Barbara Ann. In advt. dept. Am. Rolling Mill Co., Middletown, Ohio, 1929-31; advt. mgr. Pittsburgh and Midway Coal Mining Co., Kansas City, Mo., 1932-35; v.p. Ferry-Hanly Co., 1935-44; partner Bruce B. Brewer & Co., Kansas City and Mpls., 1944-66; pres., chief exec. officer Bruce B. Brewer Co., Inc., 1967-72, chmn. bd., chief exec. officer, 1972-75; dir. Marco Mfg. Co., past pres., dir. Quivira, Inc.; pres. Kaybee, Inc. Co-chmn. United Funds publicity com., 1953; dir. United Cerebral Palsy Assn. of Kansas City; active Boy Scouts Am.; bd. govs. Starlight Theatre Assn., YMCA, Quiet Birdmen; bd. dirs. Kansas City Crime Commn. Control adv. com. FAA Kanas City Air Traffic. Named Man of Yr. in Gen. Aviation, 1969; recipient silver medal Am. Advt. Fedn., 1972. Mem. A.I.M., Nat. Aero. Assn., Am. Legion, Kansas City Sr. Golf Assn., Kansas

City Promotion Com., Airplane Owners and Pilots Assn. (nat.). Am. Marketing Assn. (dir. Kansas City chpt.), Am. Royal Assn. (gov.), C. of C., Snipe Class Internat. Racing Assn., Nat. Pilots' Assn. (dir.) Am. Bonanza Soc., Air Force Assn., Silver Wings Fraternity, Wisdom Soc. Clubs: Kansas City, Advertising, Sales Executives, Quivira Country, Mission Hills Country, Aero of Kansas City, OX5 of America; Capital Hill (Washington); Quivira Sailing (past commodore); Diamondhead Yacht and Country. Author: Jerry Dalrymple, 1931. Home: Lake Quivira Kansas City KS 66106 Office: 3 Crown Center 2440 Pershing Rd Kansas City MO 64108

BOYD, ROZELLE, ednl. adminstr., city ofcl.; b. Indpls., Apr. 24, 1934; d. William Calvin and Ardelia Louise (Leavell) Boyd; B.A., Butler U., 1957; M.A., Ind. U., 1964. Social worker Marion County (Ind.) Dept. Pub. Welfare, Indpls., 1957; tchr. Indpls. Pub. Schs., 1957-68, adult edn. counselor, 1963-67; lectr. history Ind. U., Bloomington, 1967—, asst. dean Univ. div., 1968-76, asso. dean, 1976—. Mem. Marion County Council, 1965-69; mem. Indpls. City Council, 1970—; mem. Dem. Nat. Com., 1972—; pres. Mid-Am. Assn. Ednl. Opportunity Program Personnel, 1976. Lilly fellow in U.S. history, 1963; recipient teaching award Valley Forge Freedoms Found., 1967. Mem. Alpha Phi Alpha (man of year 1966). Presbyterian (elder). Home: 2527 E 35th St Indianapolis IN 46218 Office: Maxwell Hall Ind U Bloomington IN 47401

BOYD, WILLARD LEE, JR., univ. pres.; b. St. Paul, Mar. 29, 1927; s. Willard Lee and Frances L. (Collins) B.; B.S.L., U. Minn., 1949, LL.B., 1951; LL.M. (William W. Cook fellow 1951-52), U. Mich., 1952, S.J.D., 1962; LL.D., Buena Vista Coll., 1969, Coe Coll., 1969, Marycrest Coll., 1974, U. Fla., 1974; L.H.D., Cornell (Iowa) Coll., 1974; Litt.D., Simpson Coll., 1976; m. Susan Kuehn, Aug. 28, 1954; children—Elizabeth Kuehn, Willard Lee III, Thomas Henry. Admitted to Minn. bar, 1951, Iowa bar, 1958; asso. firm Dorsey, Owen, Marquart, Windhorst & West, Mpls., 1952-54; mem. faculty U. Iowa Coll. law, 1954—, prof., 1961—, asso. dean Coll. Law, 1964, v.p. academic affairs, dean faculties at univ., 1964-69, pres., 1969—. Vice pres., trustee Iowa Measurement Research Corp.; U.S. del. to Spl. Commn. on Succession of The Hague Conf. Pvt. Internat. Law, 1970-72; mem. commn. on fed. relations Am. Council Edn., 1971-74; chmn. Iowa Gov.'s Com. for Assemblies on Future of Iowa, 1972-74; chmn. Iowa 2000 Com., 1975—; mem. Nat. Council on Arts, 1976—; mem. Iowa Coordinating Council for Post High Sch. Edn., 1968—, chmn., 1976; mem. U.S. Senate Commn. on Operation of the Senate, 1975-76. Bd. dirs. Center for Research Libraries, 1965-68, chmn. 1968; bd. commrs. Nat. Commn. on Accrediting, 1970-74, pres., 1974; bd. dirs. Harry S. Truman Library Inst., 1969—, Council Post-secondary Accreditation, 1977. Served with USNR, 1945-46. Recipient Outstanding Achievement award U. Minn., 1972. Mem. Am. (past chmn. com. social, labor and indsl. legislation sect. internat. and comparative law, chmn. ednl. policy com. legal edn. sect. 1975), Iowa bar assns., Am. Assn. UN, Nat. Assn. State Univs. and Land Grant Colls. (commn. arts and scis. 1969-73, adv. com. Office Advancement Pub. Negro Colls. 1972—), Order of Coif. Congregationalist. Contbr. articles to profl. jours. Home: 102 Church St Iowa City IA 52240 Office: 101 Jessup Hall Iowa City IA 52242

BOYER, DWIGHT, journalist, author; b. Elyria, Ohio, Nov. 18, 1912; s. Lawrence H. and Susan (Mortimer) B.; grad. high sch.; m. Virginia Stokes, July 22, 1937; 1 son, Lawrence Herbert. Staff photographer, feature writer Toledo Blade, 1944-54; feature writer Sunday mag. Cleve. Plain Dealer, 1954—. Mem. Marine Hist. Soc. Detroit, Gt. Lakes Hist. Soc., Ohioana Soc., Press Club Cleve., Fairport Harbor Hist. Soc. (trustee), Burroughs Nature Club, Holden Arboretum, Gt. Lakes Found., Sigma Delta Chi. Author: Great Stories of the Great Lakes, 1966, Ghost Ships of the Great Lakes, 1968; True Tales of the Great Lakes, 1971; Strange Adventures of the Great Lakes, 1974; Ships and Men of The Great Lakes, 1977. Home: 7188 Maple St Mentor OH 44060 Office: 1801 Superior Ave Cleveland OH 44114

BOYER, FRANK HENRY, lawyer; b. Chatham, Ont., Dec. 16, 1913; s. Alphy J. and Mary Louise (Crump) B.; A.B., Kenyon Coll., 1938; LL.B., U. Mich., 1948; m. Dorothy McDonald, Sept. 14, 1940 (dec. Dec. 1954); children—Thomas H., Frank H. Admitted to Mich. bar, 1948; asso. John C. Evans, 1948-53, partner Evans, Boyer, 1953-54, sr. partner Evans, Boyer, Luptak & Briggs, Detroit, 1954-71, Boyer & Briggs, 1971-74; resident partner Oakland County office Butzel, Long, Gust, Klein & Van Zile, 1974—; dir. F.J. Boutell Driveway Co., Inc., J.C. Goss Co., Mich. Tent & Awning Co., John Johnson Co., Detroit Cover Co. Trustee Elsie L. McReynolds Charitable Trust; co-trustee Joseph H. Dancy Trust, M.E. Boutell Trust. Served to 1st lt. AUS, 1943-45. Mem. Am., Mich., Detroit bar assns. Episcopalian. Clubs: Detroit Athletic, Bloomfield Hills Country. Home: 1508 Hidden Valley Ln Rochester MI 48063 Office: Bloomfield Hills MI 48013

BOYER, JEANE STANLEY, farmer; b. Tipton County, Ind., Sept. 3, 1927; s. Roy D. and Murta Mae (Hunter) B.; student Purdue U., 1945-46; m. Billa A. Cunningham, June 20, 1948; 1 dau., Annette G. (Mrs. B.D. Justice). Farmer Tipton County, 1948—. Mem. adv. bd. Jefferson Twp., Tipton County, 1962-66, trustee, 1966-74; mem. Welfare Bd. Tipton County, 1971—; mem. Farm Bur. Tipton County. Served with AUS, 1946-47. Republican. Mem. Christian Ch. (sec. 1971-73). Elk, Moose, Odd Fellow, Mason, Lion (pres. 1969-70, treas. 1969-73, dir. 1969—). Address: Rural Route 1 Kempton IN 46049

BOYER, RALPH L., ret. mech. engr.; b. Botkins, Ohio, Aug. 4, 1901; s. Calvin O. and Ethel (Lucas) B.; B.M.E., Ohio State U., 1924, M.E., 1930; m. Doris Dormire, June 7, 1924; 1 dau., Jean Boyer Marshall. Diesel engr. Elmer A. Sperry Co., Bklyn., 1922-26; diesel engr. Cooper Bessemer Corp., Mt. Vernon, Ohio, 1926-29, asst. chief engr., 1929-38, chief engr., 1938-50, v.p., chief engr., 1950-56, v.p., dir. engring., 1956-65. Pres. Community Concerts, Mt. Vernon, 1947-58; mem. Mt. Vernon Bd. Edn., 1944-47; trustee Martin Meml. Hosp., chmn. bd., 1959-66; mem. nat. staff ARC, 1963-66. Recipient Lamme Gold medal award Ohio State U. Fellow ASME; mem. Sigma Xi. Republican. Methodist. Clubs: Masons, Pres.'s Ohio State U. Author: Time Capsules, 1976; contbr. numerous articles on thermodynamics and mech. engring. to profl. jours.; developer of high compression gas engine and originator jet gas turbine. Address: 1011 New Gambier Rd Mount Vernon OH 43050

BOYER, RAY DAVID, lawyer; b. Marion, Ind., Oct. 31, 1938; s. John Walter and Grace M. (Beshgetoor) B.; A.B. cum laude, Taylor U., 1961; J.D. cum laude, U. Pa., 1964; m. Joan Sue Graffis, June 3, 1962; children—Katherine Joan, R. David, Sarah Elizabeth, Stephen Thomas. Admitted to Ind. bar, 1964; law clk. Ind. Supreme Ct., 1964-65; asso. Helmke, Philips, & Beams, law firm, Fort Wayne, Ind., 1965-70, partner firm Helmke, Beams & Boyer, 1970—; dep. pros. atty., Allen County, Ind., 1965-70. Mem. Interfaith Commn., Allen County, 1970—, treas., 1973; chmn. YMCA Camp County br., Fort Wayne. Precinct committeeman Allen County Republican Central Com., 1971—. Bd. dirs. Met. YMCA, Fort Wayne Rescue Mission; bd. dirs. Child Care of Allen County, 1969—, pres., 1973. Mem. Am., Ind., Allen County (treas. 1970-71) bar assns., Am. Judicature Soc., Chi Alpha Omega. Mennonite (sec. 1971—). Kiwanian. Home: 5334 Bluffside St Fort Wayne IN 46815 Office: 309 Standard Bldg Fort Wayne IN 46802

BOYER, SELWYN LEWIS, family and marriage therapist; b. Chgo., Oct. 7, 1928; s. Irving and Jean B.; student Coll. City N.Y.-City U. N.Y., 1946-48; B.A., U. Wis., Milw., 1952; M.S.W., U. Wis., Madison, 1955; postgrad. U. Chgo., 1965-66; m. Gwen E. Bersch, June 30, 1957; children—Andrew, Leslie, Rebecca. Caseworker, Family Service Milw., 1955-57; casework specialist Family Service Los Angeles, 1958; sr. psychiat. social worker Mental Health Center, Waukesha, Wis., 1958-60; exec. dir. Family Service, Winona, Minn., 1960-62, Family Service, Aurora, Ill., 1962-65; adminstrv. dir. Outpatient Services Mercyville Inst. Mental Health, Aurora, 1966-68; pvt. practice marriage and family therapy, Glen Ellyn, Ill.; mem. staff Mercyville Inst. Mental Health, Aurora, 1965-77; family therapy cons. Kane County (Ill.) Diagnostic Center, 1973—. Mem. bd. health City of Aurora. Democratic nominee U.S. rep. 15th Congl. Dist., 1966; chmn. Kane County (Ill.) Citizens Com. for Humphrey, 1968; candidate Ill. State Central Committeeman, 1970. Served with AUS, 1952-54. Nat. Inst. Mental Health grantee, 1965-66. Mem. Am. Assn. Marriage and Family Counselors (approved supr.), Acad. Certified Social Workers, Nat. Assn. Social Workers, Nat. Conf. Social Welfare, Alpha Delta. Home: 816 Palace St Aurora IL 60506 Office: 420 Pennsylvania Ave Glen Ellyn IL 60137

BOYKE, BRUCE CARL, contractor, concrete and masonry; b. Chgo., May 12, 1930; s. Carl and Elsie Marie (La Ffin) B.; student public schs., Zion, Ill.; m. Kathleen J. McManaman, Sept. 16, 1950;children—Laura, Karen, Bruce, Blair, Kerry. Founder, pres. Bruce Concrete Constrn., Inc., Skokie, Ill., 1959—; formed Bruce Boyke Masonry Corp., Skokie, 1963—. Bruce Boyke Imperial Manor, Waukegan, 1964 (pres.); founder Bruce Boyke's Imperial Towers, Waukegan, 1968—. Spl. mem. Boy Scouts America. Republican committeeman Waukegan, 1951-53. Served with AUS, 1947-51. Mem. Chgo. Assn. Commerce and Industry (indsl. devel. com.), Lake County Contractors Assn., Zion Benton C. of C., Waukegan-North Chicago C. of C. Home: 1450 N St Mary's Rd Libertyville IL 60048 Office: 805 Baldwin Waukegan IL 60085

BOYKIN, OTIS FRANK, electronic research cons.; b. Dallas Tex., Aug. 29, 1920; s. Walter Benjamin and Sarah (Cox) B.; student Fisk U., 1938-41, Ill. Inst. Tech., 1947-49; m. Pearlie Mae Kimble, Sept. 30, 1940. Foreman, Majestic Radio & TV Corp., Chgo., 1941-44; research engr. P.J. Nilsen Research Labs., Oak Park, Ill., 1944-49; pres. Boykin-Fruth, Inc., Chgo., 1949-52; chief chemist on ceramics and plastics Radio Industries, Chgo., 1952-55; sr. project engr. C.T.S. Corp., Elkhart, Ind., 1957-64; research cons. on electronic components, 1964—. Adviser on sci. projects Dunbar High Sch., Chgo., 1974-77. Recipient Cultural Sci. Achievement award Old Pros Unlimited Club. Mem. AAAS, Internat. Soc. for Hybrid Micro-electronics, Physics Club of Chgo. Roman Catholic. Inventor numerous electronic components; patentee in field; instrumental in developing resistance control unit for first heart pace makers. Address: 8215 S Maryland Ave Chicago IL 60619

BOYKIN, WILLIAM GENE, assn. exec.; b. Apperson, Okla., Nov. 10, 1925; s. Jesse Spencer and Mary Jane (Patton) B.; B.A., Okla. State U., 1950; m. Rebecca Louise Burke, Sept. 7, 1974; children by previous marriage—Vicki Lynn, William David, Sherri Lea, Mark Shawn. Publisher, Van Buren County (Ark.) Dem., 1950-51; editor Park Cities (Tex.) News, 1951-53, Capitol Hill (Okla.) Beacon, 1953-55; asst. mgr. Okla. Press Assn., 1955-57; exec. Atkinson Enterprises, Oklahoma City, 1957-63; asso. editor Oklahoma City Jour., 1963-66; exec. dir. Allied Daily Newspapers, Seattle, 1966-69, Fla. Press Assn.; 1970-71, Tex. Press Assn., 1971-74, Inland Daily Press Assn., Chgo., 1974—. Served with USNR, 1944-46. Certified assn. exec. Mem. Newspaper Assn. Mgrs., Inc. (pres. 1975-76), Am. Soc. Assn. Execs., Chgo. Soc. Assn. Execs., Sigma Delta Chi. Methodist. Club: Chgo. Press. Office: 100 W Monroe St Chicago IL 60603

BOYLAN, HUNTER REED, coll. adminstr.; b. Cleve., Apr. 3, 1945; s. Chester Reed and Dorothy Virginia (Hunter) B.; B.A., Miami U., Oxford, Ohio, 1967; M.Ed., Temple U., 1970; Ph.D. (NEA fellow), Bowling Green U., 1977; m. Gwendolyn Anne Workman, Aug. 17, 1968; 1 dau., Heather Marie. Asst. dir. residence, adviser to fraternities Temple U., 1967-69; hall dir., research asst. Bowling Green State U., 1969-71, acad. adviser, 1971-72, asst. dir. for acad. services and research, student devel. program, 1972-73, acting dir. modular achievement center, 1973, coordinator acad. devel. and instruction, 1973—; cons. instructional devel. Served with USAF, 1967. Recipient Outstanding adviser award Temple U., 1969, Outstanding Hall Dir. award Bowling Green State U., 1971; Office Edn. grantee, 1975; Bowling Green State U. grantee, 1976. Mem. Nat. Assn. Student Personnel Adminstrs., Am. Personnel, Guidance Assn. (dir. Commn. XVI), Am. Coll. Personnel Assn., Ohi Developmental Edn. Assn., Sigma Nu. Presbyterian. Contbr. articles on instructional devel. and individualized learning systems to profl. jours.; editor Am. Coll. Personnel Assn. Commn. Newsletter, 1977—. Home: 606 Orleans Ave Bowling Green OH 43402 Office: DEP204 Library Bowling Green U Bowling Green OH 43403

BOYLE, JOHN ELBRIDGE, dentist; b. Kalamazoo, Dec. 25, 1921; s. Frank James and Edna Henrietta (Schultz) B.; student Kalamazoo Coll., 1940-41; B.A., Western Mich. Coll., 1943; D.D.S., Northwestern U., 1946; m. Annette Kleinman, May 31, 1947; children—Teresa Ann, Susan Jeanne, Wendy Jane, John Michael. Practice dentistry, Winnetka, Ill., 1948—; sec. Hubbard Woods Med.-Dental Bldg., 1970—. Bd. dirs. Ann. Mid-West Seminar Dental Medicine. Served to capt. AUS, 1948. Fellow Am. Coll. Dentists; mem. Chgo. Dental Soc. (chmn. 1948—), Mid-Century Combine (pres. 1968), Northwestern U. Alumni Assn. (pres. 1974-75), Componenent Dental Soc. (chmn. 1948-72), Am. Dental Assn., Ill. State, Dental Soc., Odontographic Soc. Chgo. Roman Catholic. Rotarian (treas. 1971-72, pres. 1975-76). Clubs: Progressive (sec. 1972-73, pres. 1976-78) (Chgo.); North Shore Country (Glenview, Ill.); Michigan Shore (Wilmette); Berrien Hills Country (Benton Harbor, Mich.); Serra (Evanston). Home: 373 Glendale Ave Winnetka IL 60093 Office: 840 Green Bay Rd Winnetka IL 60093

BOYNTON, VERN MELVIN, pipeline testing co. exec.; b. Benton Harbor, Mich., May 8, 1925; s. Lester Earl and Ida Mardell (Cowell) B.; student Engrs. Sch., Ft. Belvoir. Va., 1944; m. Vera Lynn Cox, Nov. 3, 1946; children—Douglas William, Karen Lynn. Asst. to city engr., Benton Harbor, Mich., 1946-47; field engr. Consoer Townsend Assocs., Benton Harbor, 1947-48, Ford Bacon & Davis Inc., N.Y.C., 1948-50, Brown & Root Co., Houston, 1951-52; pipeline engr. Mich. Wis. Pipe Line Co., Detroit, 1950-51; office engr. Ford Bacon & Davis Constrn. Corp., Monroe, La., 1952-54, chief field engr., 1952-56; project mgr. Fish Engring. Corp., Houston, 1956-59; projects engr. Somerville Constrn. Co., Grand Rapids, Mich., 1959-67; v.p., gen. mgr. Universal Hydro-Test Corp., Ann Arbor, Mich., 1967—. Served with C.E., U.S. Army, 1943-46. Republican. Methodist. Clubs: Masons, Shriners. Home: 1191 Bandera Dr Ann Arbor MI 48103 Office: 7700 Jackson Rd Ann Arbor MI 48103

BOYSAW, HAROLD EDWARD, former pub. welfare adminstr.; b. Joliet, Ill., Oct. 28, 1912; s. John and Julia (Fleming) B.; B.A., Ill. Wesleyan U., 1938, L.H.D., 1965; M.A., U. Chgo., 1952; m. Lucille Williams, Aug. 10, 1941. Caseworker, City Chgo. Relief Adminstrn., 1938-41; with Cook County Dept. Pub. Aid, Chgo., 1941—, supervising caseworker, 1948-52, asst. office supr., 1952-60, office supr., 1960-62, adminstrv. field supr., 1962-69, dep. dir. adminstrv. services, 1969-74, asst. to dir. community services, 1974-75. Mem. Citizens Com. Juvenile Ct. Bd. dirs. Chgo. chpt. Am. Cancer Soc., Big Bros. Met. Chgo., Tb Inst. Chgo. and Cook County; trustee Ill. Children's Home and Aid Soc. Served with U.S. Army, 1943-45. Mem. Nat. Assn. Social Workers, Acad. Certified Social Workers, Am. Pub. Welfare Assn., Am. Sociol. Assn., Ill. Welfare Assn., Chgo. Urban League, NAACP, Nat. Conf. Social Welfare, Alpha Phi Alpha. Club: City (gov.) (Chgo.). Home: 11360 S Aberdeen St Chicago IL 60643 Office: 624 S Michigan Ave Chicago IL 60605

BOYSEN, A. J., farm mgr.; b. Morning Sun, Iowa, Nov. 1, 1925; s. Boyd August and Margaretha Elizabeth (Dohrman) B.; student Iowa State U., 1946-48, exec. devel. program Iowa Wesleyan Coll., 1964-65; m. Dorothy Ellen Wright, Oct. 17, 1948; children—Robert Boyd, Karen Elaine. Farm owner, operator, Louisa County, Iowa, 1949—; farm mgr., Louisa and Des Moines County, Iowa, 1968—; appraiser Louisa County, 1971—; pres., mgr. Stoney Brook Farms, Inc.; leader, 4-H camp trustee, Iowa; mem. Louisa County extension com. Farm Bur.; leader youth tour People to People Internat. Active United Fund. Served to cpl. USAAF, 1944-46. Recipient 4-H awards. Mem. Iowa Soc. Farm Mgrs. and Rural Appraisers, Louisa County Soy Bean Assn. (charter pres.), Louisa County Beef Producers (dir.), Am. Angus Soc., Pro-Farmers Am. Republican. Methodist. Home and office: 720 S 5th St Wapello IA 52653

BOZORGI, SIAVOSH, thoracic and cardiovascular surgeon; b. Khoramabad, Iran, Apr. 8, 1938; s. Asadollah and Behjat (Foroughi) B.; student Tehran (Iran) U. Med. Sch., 1962; M.D., U. Pa., 1966; m. Bonnie Hughes, Nov. 5, 1966; children—Darius, Susan. Intern, Norwalk (Conn.) Hosp., 1963, Cleve. Met. Gen. Hosp., 1963-64; resident surgery Grad. Hosp., U. Pa. at Phila., 1964-67, also asst. instr. surgery in med. sch., 1964-66, instr. surgery, 1967-67; chief resident surgery St. Luke's Hosp., Bethlehem, Pa., 1967-68; chief resident thoracic and cardiovascular surgery Albert Einstein Coll. Medicine, Yeshiva U., N.Y.C., 1968-70, also asst. instr. thoracic surgery; clin. research fellow thoracic and cardiac surgery Mt. Auburn Hosp., Boston, 1970-71, Peter Bent Brigham Hosp., Boston, Harvard Med. Sch.; practice medicine, specializing in thoracic and cardiovascular surgery, Dayton, Ohio, 1971—; mem. staff Good Samaritan Hosp., St. Elizabeth Hosp., Children's Med. Center, Kettering Hosp., Miami Valley Hosp.; asst. clin. prof. surgery Wright State U. Med. Sch., Dayton. Diplomate Am. Bd. Surgery. Fellow A.C.S., Am. Coll. Angiology, Soc. Thoracic Surgeons; mem. Am. Thoracic Soc., Am., Ohio State med. assns., Am. Coll. Chest Physicians, Am. Coll. Cardiology, Montgomery County (O.) Med. Soc., Am. Heart Assn., Dayton Surg. Soc. Contbr. articles to profl. jours. Home: 324 Thelma St Dayton OH 45415 Office: Grant-Deneau Tower Room 1810 4th and Ludlow Sts Dayton OH 45402

BRACHMAN, MEROM, chem. co. exec.; b. Ft. Worth, Oct. 6, 1936; s. Abraham J. and Sarah (Ruby) B.; A.B. magna cum laude, Harvard, 1958, A.M. in History, 1961; m. Judith Yenkin, Dec. 19, 1957; children—Lavea, Sarai, Shael. Adminstrv. asst. to Senator J.S. Cooper of Ky., Washington, 1963-68; with Yenkin Majestic Paint Corp., Columbus, Ohio, 1968—, dir. mfg. and purchasing, 1969—, v.p., sec., 1970—, gen. mgr. Ohio Polychem. Co. div., 1974—, exec. v.p., 1975—, also dir.; dir. affiliated cos. Majestic Paint Centers, Yenkin Majestic Paint Corp.; pres. Woodland Corp., Columbus; mng. partner Wye Co. Ltd., Columbus, Yakima, Wash., 1971—. Chmn. regional adv. council Small Bus. Adminstrn., 1971-74; vice chmn., bd. dirs. Am. Way Found., Columbus, 1971—; mem. Franklin County Bd. SSS, 1971-75. Republican mem. bipartisan Ohio Ethics Commn., 1975—, chmn., 1976—. Trustee Columbus Sch. Girls, 1974—; mem. nat. com. Harvard Center Jewish Studies, 1975—. Mem. exec. com. White House Conf. Children and Youth, 1970-71; mem. exec. com. United Community Council Columbus, 1969-74; mem. City of Columbus Campaign Finance and Ethics Commn., 1974—. Served with USAF, 1961-62. Recipient Congl. Staff award Am. Polit. Sci. Assn., 1967. Jewish. Club: Crichton (trustee 1976—). Home: 115 S Drexel Ave Columbus OH 43209 Office: 1920 Leonard Ave Columbus OH 43219

BRACKBILL, EUGENE ARTHUR, environ. cons.; b. Lancaster, Pa., Dec. 17, 1947; s. Arthur Harlan and Elaine May (Charlton) B.; B.S. in Mech. Engring., Rose Poly. Inst., 1969; M.S. in Environ. Engring., U. Cin., 1978; postgrad. Pa. State U., Middletown, 1973-74. Fluid systems engr. Armstrong Cork Co., Lancaster, 1969-70, project engr., 1971-74; specialty process equipment engr. Fluor Engrs. and Constructors, Anaheim, Calif., 1974-75; dir. ops. Pollution Control Sci., Inc., Miamisburg, Ohio, 1975—. Served to 1st lt. U.S. Army, 1970-71; Vietnam. Decorated Bronze Star; registered profl. engr., Ohio. Mem. ASTM, Air Pollution Control Assn., Source Evaluation Soc., ASME, Nat., Ohio socs. profl. engrs. Episcopalian. Home: 1112-B Eagle Feathers Circle West Carrollton OH 45449 Office: 6015 Manning Rd Miamisburg OH 45347

BRACKETT, EDWARD BOONE, III, surgeon; b. Fort Worth, Jan. 5, 1936; s. Edward Boone and Bessie Lee (Hudgins) B.; student Tex. Tech. Coll., 1957; M.D., Baylor U., 1961; m. Jean Elliott, July 11, 1959; children—Bessie, Geoffrey, Elliot Mencken, Edward Boone IV, Anneke Gail. Intern, Cook County Hosp., Chgo., 1961-62; resident Northwestern U., Chgo., 1962-66; practice medicine specializing in orthopedic surgery, Oak Park, Ill., 1966—, Westgate Orthopaedics Ltd., Oak Park, 1969—; mem. staff Loyola U., West Suburban Hosp., Oak Park Hosp., Loretto Hosp. Chmn. bd. Chgo. Loop Mediclinic, 1973-75; cons. orthopedic surgery City Service Oil Co., 1970. Guarantor Lyric Opera Chgo., 1971-75. Served as lt. comdr. USNR, 1967-69; Vietnam. Diplomate Am. Orthopedic Bd. Surgery. Fellow A.C.S., Am. Acad. Orthopedic Surgeons; mem. Am. Trauma Soc. (founder), Royal Soc. Medicine, A.M.A., Sigma Alpha Epsilon, Phi Eta Sigma, Phi Chi, Alpha Epsilon Delta. Cons. orthopedic editor Jour. Indsl. Medicine, 1966-67. Home: 318 N Linden St Oak Park IL 60302 Office: 1145 Westgate St Oak Park IL 60301

BRACY, ARNOLD LEE, minister; b. Charlotte, Mich., Jan. 13, 1938; s. Ellis Elwood and Ardis Zella (Rice) B.; grad. Grand Rapids Sch. Bible and Music, 1958; m. Darlene Humbarger, Sept. 20, 1957; children—Arnold Lee, Carl, David, Diane. Ordained to ministry Ind. Fundamental Chs. Am., 1964; pastor Lake Odessa (Mich.) Bible Ch., 1958-60, Pilgrim Congl. Ch. of Metamora (Mich.), 1960-64, Calvary Bible Ch., Lapeer, Mich., 1964—; mgr. WMPC radio, Lapeer, 1965—; chaplain Lapeer State Home and Tng. Sch., 1964-66; pres. S.E. sect. Ind. Fundamental Chs. Am., v.p. Mich. region, 1974-77. Mem. Lapeer County Bd. Social Services, 1967-69, Lapeer County Bd. Commrs., 1970-74; exec. com. Lapeer County Republican party, 1970-77. Named Young Man of Year, Jr. C. of C., 1973. Home: 941 S Main St Lapeer MI 48446 Office: 923 S Main St Lapeer MI 48446

BRADBURN, NORMAN M., educator; b. Lincoln, Ill., July 21, 1933; s. Hubert Benjamin and Mary Celeste (Marshall) B.; B.A., U. Chgo., 1952; B.A., Oxford U. (Eng.), 1955; M.A., Harvard, 1958,

Ph.D. in Social Psychology, 1960; m. Wendy McAneny, Dec. 15, 1956; children—Isabel Stuart, Andrew Marshall, Laura Humphreys. Asst. prof. behavioral sci. U. Chgo., 1960-65, asso. prof., 1965-67, prof., 1967—, chmn., dept. of behavioral sci., 1973—, Tiffany and Margaret Blake Distinguished Service prof., 1977—; sr. study dir. Nat. Opinion Research Center, Chgo., 1961—, dir., 1967-71. Alexander von Humboldt scholar U. Cologne (Germany), 1970-71. Fellow Am. Sociol. Assn.; mem. Am. Statis. Assn. Author: (with D. Caplovitz) Reports on Happiness, 1967; The Structure of Psychological Well-Being, 1970; (with S. Sudman, G. Gockel) Side by Side: A Study of Integrated Neighborhoods, 1971; (with S. Sudman) Response Effects in Surveys, 1974. Home: 5326 S University Ave Chicago IL 60615

BRADBURY, MARION LESLIE, JR., lawyer; b. Salem, Ill., Nov. 13, 1917; s. Marion Leslie and Gladys Marie (Evans) B.; A.B., U. Mich., 1939, LL.B., 1942; m. Elizabeth Shipman, Sept. 19, 1942; children—Gregory E., Ann S. Admitted to Mich. bar, 1942; since practiced in Muskegon; partner Landman, Hathaway, Latimer, Clink & Robb, 1969—; dir. Lakeshore Machinery & Supply Co., Steel Fabricating Co., Lakeway Chems., Inc., Cole Bakeries, Inc.; sec., dir. Muskegon Tool Industries, Inc., Swedish Wire Corp., others. Pres. North Muskegon (Mich.) Bd. Edn., 1950-59; bd. dirs. Muskegon Progress and Devel. Fund, Inc., Western Mich. Center Handicapped Children. Served with USAAF, 1942-46. Mem. Am., Muskegon County (pres. 1955-56) bar assns., State Bar Mich., Muskegon Area C. of C. (dir.), Am. Bus. Clubs, Theta Delta Chi. Clubs: Rotary, Century, Country (Muskegon). Home: 429 E Circle Dr North Muskegon MI 49445 Office: 500 Hackley Bank Muskegon MI 49440

BRADEMAS, JOHN, congressman; b. Mishawaka, Ind., Mar. 2, 1927; s. Stephen J. and Beatrice Cenci (Goble) B.; B.A. magna cum laude (Vets. nat. scholar) Harvard U., 1949; D. Phil. (Rhodes scholar), Oxford U., Eng., 1954; hon. fellow Brasenose Coll., Oxford U.; L.H.D. (hon.), U. Evansville, Mt. St. Mary's Coll., Newburg, N.Y., Brandeis U.; LL.D. (hon.), U. Notre Dame St. Mary's Coll., Notre Dame, Ind., Middlebury Coll., Tufts U., Columbia Coll., Chgo., Ball State U., Marian Coll.; m. Mary Ellen Briggs, July 9, 1977. Legis. asst. to U.S. Senator Pat McNamara, 1955, adminstrv. asst. U.S. Rep. Thomas L. Ashley, 1955; exec. asst. to presdl. nominee Stevenson, 1955-56; asst. prof. polit. sci. St. Mary's Coll., Notre Dame, Ind. 1957-58; mem. 86th-95th Congresses from 3d Dist. Ind. now majority whip. Mem. coms. edn. and labor, House adminstrn. Mem. overseers com. to visit Grad. Sch. Edn. Harvard U.; mem. adv. council Coll. Arts and Letters, U. Notre Dame; mem. Hist. Publs. and Records Commn.; mem. Nat. Commn. Financing Post secondary Edn., 1972-73; mem. central com. World Council Chs. Recipient office of Secretariat of Order of St. Andrew, Patriarch Athenagoras I. Served with USNR, 1945-46. Fellow Am. Acad. Arts and Scis.; mem. Phi Beta Kappa. Methodist. Mason, Ahepa. Home: 750 Leland Ave South Bend IN 46616 Office: Longworth House Office Bldg Washington DC 20515

BRADEN, BERWYN BARTOW, lawyer; b. Pana, Ill., Jan. 10, 1928; s. George Clark and Florence Lucille (Bartow) B.; student Carthage Coll., 1946-48; student U. Wis., 1948-49, J.D., 1959; m. Barbara Carol Brellenthin, Oct. 15, 1949; children—Scott, Mark, Mathew, Sue, Ralph, Ladd, Brad. Admitted to Wis. bar, 1959, U.S. Supreme Ct. bar, 1965; partner firm Genoar & Braden, Lake Geneva, Wis., 1959-63; individual practice law, Lake Geneva, 1963-68, 72-74; partner firm Braden & English, Lake Geneva, 1968-72, Braden & Olson, Lake Geneva, 1974—; counsel Citizens Nat. Bank, 1959—, also dir.; city atty. Lake Geneva, 1962-64, tchr. Law Sch. U. Wis., 1977. Bd. dirs. Lake Geneva YMCA. Served with USMCR, 1945-46. Mem. Walworth County (pres. 1962-63), Am., Chgo. bar assns., State Bar Wis., Bar Assn. 7th Fed. Circuit, Wis. Acad. Trial Lawyers (sec. 1975, treas. 1976, dir. 1977), Assn. Trial Lawyers, Phi Alpha Delta. Home: 851-A Lakeshore Dr Lake Geneva WI 53147 Office: 401 Broad St Lake Geneva WI 53147

BRADEN, ROSETTA AEDOTER BALKO (MRS. RALPH R. BRADEN), real estate broker; b. Detroit; d. Michael D. and Mary Ann (Shubrak) Balko; student Wayne U., 1942-45; certificate in real estate U. Mich., 1960, grad. Monrow Bus. U.; m. Ralph R. Braden. With Monsanto Chem. Co., Trenton, Mich., 1950-57; owner Rosetta A. Braden Real Estate Co., Grosse Ile, Mich., 1957—, pres., 1966—. Mem. Nat. Assn. Real Estate Bds., Nat. Inst. Real Estate Brokers, Internat. Real Estate Fedn., Internat. Traders Club, Mich. Real Estate Assn., Down River Bd. Realtors, Detroit Real Estate Bd., Soc. Exchange Counselors, Nat. Secs. Assn. (pres. chpt.), Women's Bus. and Profl. Club, Founder Soc. Detroit Inst. Arts. Internat. Platform Assn. Clubs: Grosse Ile Golf and Country, Grosse Ile Yacht, Grosse Ile Garden, Fairlane Athletic. Home: 27532 East River Rd Grosse Ile MI 48138 Office: 8990 Macomb St Grosse Ile MI 48138

BRADFORD, GLENN EDWIN, lawyer; b. Granite City, Ill., Jan. 31, 1947; s. Marcus Clay and Edith Melvina (Rose) B.; student U. South Fla., 1965-68; B.S. in Gen. Bus. Adminstrn., So. Ill. U., Edwardsville, 1971; J.D., Emory U., 1974; m. Melida Rosa Pereira, Sept. 2, 1967. Stock broker McCourtney Breckenridge & Co., St. Louis, 1968-70; admitted to Ill. bar, 1974; partner firm Pratt, Pierce & Bradford, Ltd., East Alton, Ill., 1974—; dir. Taco Bandit, Inc.; dir., exec. v.p. Advance Capital Corp. Mem. Ill. State, Am. bar assns., Ill., Am. trial lawyers' assns., Emory U., So. Ill. U.-Edwardsville (charter) alumni assns., Emory U. Moot Ct. Soc., Delta Sigma Pi, Phi Delta Phi. Democrat. Home: 37 Saint Rose Dr Collinsville IL 62234 Office: PO Box 179 Hwy 111 at Airline Dr East Alton IL 62024

BRADFORD, KIMERLEE JAY, mech. engr.; b. Putnam, Conn., Mar. 22, 1932; s. H. Jay and Dorothy Gertrude (Martin) B.; B.S., U. N.H., 1965; postgrad. U. Ariz., 1970-73; m. Shigeko Shikuma, June 18, 1955; children—Jon Chandler, Karyl Ann, William Jay, Charles Martin. Enlisted USAF, 1950, advanced through grades to maj., 1965; missile opns. officer, N. Mex., West Germany, 1957-60; missile maintenance officer, West Germany, 1960-62; program mgmt. specialist, Los Angeles, 1965-70; ret., 1970; reliability engr. Control Data Corp., St. Paul, 1973—. Committeeman Boy Scouts Am., 1972-73. Recipient Tech. Excellence award Control Data Corp., 1977. Mem. Am. Soc. Mech. Engrs., Retired Officers Assn. Home: 310 107th St W Bloomington MN 55420 Office: 4201 Lexington Ave St Paul MN 55112

BRADFORD, WILLIAM STEPHEN, orthodontist; b. Boston, July 23, 1912; s. Joseph S. and Anna (Hogarty) B.; B.S., Harvard U., 1934, postgrad. Engring. Sch., 1935-36; D.D.S., Northwestern U., 1944; M.S., U. Kansas City Dental Sch., 1948; m. Barbara Ann Kennedy, May 30, 1942; children—Martha Ann, William Stephen. Researcher, neurologic unit Harvard Med. Sch., 1935-36; researcher New Eng. Lime Co., Canaan, Conn., 1936-38; chem. rep., New Eng., Ohio Chem. Co., 1938-41; practice dentistry specializing in orthodontics, Highland Park, Ill., 1948—; asst. prof. orthodontics Loyola U., Chgo., 1969—. Vice pres. Suburban Arts Center; mem. Zoning Bd. Appeals Highland Park. Mem. Harvard Assn. Chemists, Harvard Graduates Soc., Field Museum Natural History, Am. Assn. Orthodontists, Am. Dental Assn., Highland Park C. of C. (dir., pres.), Ill. Doberman Pinscher Club (pres.). Club: Rotary (dir., pres.). Home: 3001 Ridge Rd Highland Park IL 60035 Office: 1964 Sheridan Rd Highland Park IL 60035

BRADFORD, WILLIAM TRUE, geophysicist; b. Los Angeles, Nov. 18, 1941; s. Charles Monroe and Martha Lena (Trueblood) B.; B.S., Calif. State Coll. at Long Beach, 1964; M.S., U. So. Calif., 1967; m. Sheila M. Donatelli, June 26, 1965; children—Dale W., Sara M. Geophysicist, Humble Oil & Refining Co., Los Angeles, 1966-69; sr. geophysicist Skelly Oil Can., Calgary, Alta., 1969-74; staff geophysicist Amoco Internat. Oil Co., Chgo., 1974—. Research and tng. fellow U. So. Calif., 1964-67; N.S.F grantee, 1966. Mem. Soc. Exploration Geophysicists, Can. Soc. Exploration Geophysicists, Pacific Assn. Petroleum Geologists. Republican. Lutheran. Club: Berkeley Racquet. Office: 200 E Randolph Dr Chicago IL 60680

BRADLEY, JAMES RICHARD, savs. and loan exec.; b. Madison, Wis., Oct. 17, 1925; s. Louis Frederick and Floretta Genevieve (Viele) B.; B.S., U. Wis., 1950; grad. degree U. Ind. Savs. and Loan Grad. Sch., 1966; m. Arlene F. Parman, Jan. 26, 1952; children—James Richard, Thomas J., Timothy W., Robert A. Office mgr. Comml. Credit Corp., 1951-56; mgr. Home Savs. and Loan Assn., Madison, Wis., 1956—, also dir.; pres., dir. Devel. Services, Inc., 1971—, Gen. Investment Services, Inc., 1977—. treas., dir. Madison Savs. and Loan Housing Corp., 1973—. Chmn. Mayor's Adv. Com. on Govtl. Econs., 1969-71; pres. Nakoma Sch. PTA, 1967-68; adviser Madison Area Tech. Coll., 1973—. Bd. dirs. Madison Asso. Credit Bur., 1973—, United Cerebral Palsy Dane County, 1977—, Boy Scout Drum & Bugle Corps Found., 1977—. Served with USAAF, 1944-46; USAF, 1950-51. Recipient key man award Madison Jr. C. of C., 1960. Mem. U.S. (advt. com. 1970-71), Wis. (dir. 1969-70, chmn. advt. and pub. relations com. 1974-75, legis. com. 1977—) savs. and loan leagues, Wis. Savs. and Loan Inst. (chpt. pres. 1961-62), U.S. League Savs. Assns. (environment and land use com., consumers affairs com. 1977-78). Madison C. of C. (low income housing com. 1969-70). Mason (32 deg., Shriner), Elk, Optimist (dir. Madison 1965—). Home: 4110 Mandan Crescent St Madison WI 53711 Office: 2 S Carroll St Madison WI 53703

BRADLEY, MILTON RICHARD, radio exec.; b. Kansas City, Mo., Nov. 16, 1927; s. Milton Russell and Geraldine (Westenberger) B.; B.S., S.W. Mo. State U., 1950; m. Celeste Ferree, Aug. 12, 1951 (dec. Mar. 1971); children—Chris, Tim, Lacey, Heather, Donnie; m. 2d, Dee Herda, Mar. 17, 1973. Salesman, KICK Radio, Springfield, Mo., 1950-51, sales mgr., 1951-54; founder, pres. Magic Circle Radio Network, Springfield, 1954—, also broadcaster football and basketball games S.W. Mo. State U.; Part owner KTGR KTGR-FM radio, Columbia, 1967—. Mem. St. Louis Media Club, Kansas City Ad Club, Mo. Broadcasters Assn., S.W. Mo. State U. Allumni (dir. 1965-69), Alpha Psi Omega. Clubs: Springfield Tip Off, Quarterback, Springfield Swim. Home: 2230 Inglewood St Springfield MO 65804 Office: 1525 S Glenstone St Springfield MO 65804

BRADLEY, SISTER RITAMARY, educator; b. Stuart, Iowa, Jan. 30, 1916; d. James Francis and Alice (Muldoon) Bradley; Ph.B., Marygrove Coll., 1938, M.A., 1945; Ph.D., St. Louis U., 1953; LL.D., (hon.), Marquette U., D.H.L., Fordham U., 1960. Asst. prof. dept. English, Marycrest Coll., 1940-56; instr., novitiate, juniorate Sisters of Humility of Mary, Ottumwa, Iowa, 1957-61; asst. exec. sec. Sister Formation Conf., Nat. Cath. Ednl. Assn., Washington, 1961-64; hon. fellow, dept. English, U. Minn., 1964-65; prof. English St. Ambrose Coll., Davenport, Iowa, 1965—, Black Hawk Coll., 1971—. Dir. Seminars in Philosophy, Cath. U. Am., 1963, 64; asst. dir. Workshop for Sisters, Marquette U., 1964. Mem. Modern Lang. Assn., Religious Edn. Assn. Contbr. articles profl. jours., chpt. to book. Editor Sister Formation Bull., 1954-64, 14th-Century English Mystics Newsletter, 1974—. Address: 2317 Western Ave Davenport IA 52803 also 518 W Locust Davenport IA 52803

BRADLEY, WARREN QUENTIN, radiologist; b. Willisville, Ill., Dec. 18, 1921; s. E.J. and Lela A. (Gwin) B.; A.B., So. Ill. U., 1948; M.D., U. Ill., 1952; m. Joan L. Kimber. Aug. 20, 1950 (dec. 1972); children—Janet K., Diane L. Intern, Ill. Central Hosp., 1952-53; resident in radiology U. Ill. Hosps., Chgo., 1953-56; practice medicine specializing in radiology, Lincoln, Nebr., 1956—; clin. instr. radiology U. Nebr. Served with USNR, 1942-46. Diplomate Am. Bd. Radiology. Fellow Am. Coll. Radiology. Office: 206 S 13th St Lincoln NE 68508

BRADLEY, WILLIAM ARTHUR, educator; b. Lansing, Mich., Nov. 11, 1921; s. Arthur and Amy F. (Barringer) B.; B.S. in Civil Engring., Mich. State U., 1943; M.S., U. Ill., 1947; Ph.D., U. Mich., 1956; m. Elizabeth G. Ewing, June 29, 1949; children—David, Nancy, Susan. Engr., Douglas Aircraft, El Segundo, Cal., 1943-44; engr. G.M. Foster, Bridge Cons., Lansing, 1945-46; mem. faculty Mich. State U., East Lansing, 1947—, prof. mechanics and civil engring., 1961—; cons., Dow Chem. Corp., 1959-61. Mem. Lansing Orgn. for Schs. Bd. dirs. West Side Neighborhood Assn. Recipient Distinguished Faculty award Mich. State U., 1963; Western Electric Fund award, 1966. Mem. ASCE, Am. Concrete Inst., Internat. Assn. for Bridge and Structural Engrs., Am. Soc. for Engring. Edn., Sigma Xi, Phi Kappa Phi, Tau Beta Pi, Chi Epsilon. Home: 1919 W Kalamazoo St Lansing MI 48915 Office: Coll Engring Mich State U East Lansing MI 48824

BRADLEY, WILLIAM FERDIE, veterinarian; b. Topeka, Feb. 16, 1926; s. Aubrey J. and Bernice (Davis) B.; B.S., Kans. State U., 1953, D.V.M., 1953; m. Beverly Ann Torrens, Aug. 23, 1953; children—William Ferdie, Roger A., Philip B., John S., Kent R. Mem. profl. staff Mexico (Mo.) Animal Hosp., 1953-55; owner, chief of staff Bradley Vet. Hosp., Lawrence, Kans., 1957—. Chmn. 4-H County Fund dr., community leader, 1975—, also project dir.; active Boy Scouts Am. Mem. Lawrence Sch. Bd., 1963-74, 75—, pres., 1971-75; pres. Local Govt. Research Corp. of Kans., 1970. Chmn. alumni athletic bd. Kans. State U., 1970, 71, 72. Bd. dirs. Kan. State U. Endowment Assn., 1974, Boys Clubs; bd. dirs. United Ministries in Higher Edn. Kans. U., 1975—, chmn., 1977-78; trustee Wakarusa Twp., Kans., 1975—. Served with USAF, 1955-57. Recipient Nat. award for hosp. design Vet. Econs. Jour., 1966, Kiwanis Family Builders award, 1975, Sertoma Service to Mankind award, 1974, named Boss of Year, Jr. C. of C., 1970. Mem. Am. Animal Hosp. Assn., Am., Kans. (dir. N.E. dist. 1966-69), Douglas County (pres. 1976) vet. med. assns., Lawrence C. of C. (dir. 1970), Kans. Sch. Bd. Assn. (v.p. 1973-74), Kans. State U. Alumni Assn. (dir. 1967-70). Republican. Presbyn. (ruling elder, chmn. fellowship div.). Mason (Shriner), Lion (pres. Lawrence 1960; zone chmn., dep. dist. gov. 1975). Club: Knife and Fork (pres. 1969) (Lawrence). Home: Route 2 Box 107 Lawrence KS 66044 Office: 935 E 23d St Lawrence KS 66044

BRADSHAW, CARL JOHN, diversified corp. exec.; b. Oelwein, Iowa, Nov. 1, 1930; s. Carl John and Lorraine Lillian (Thiele) B.; B.S., U. Minn., 1952, J.D., 1957; LL.M., U. Mich., 1958; M.Jur., Keio U. (Tokyo), 1961; m. Katsuko Anno, Nov. 5, 1954; children—Carla Kozette, Arthur Herbert, Vincent Marcus. Admitted to Minn. bar, Okinawa bar; atty. Graham, James & Rolph, San Francisco and Tokyo, Japan, 1959-63; asso. prof. law U. Wash., Seattle, 1963-65; asst. to pres. Oak Industries, Inc., Crystal Lake, Ill., 1964-66, v.p., dir. fgn. ops., 1967-70, v.p. corporate devel., 1970-72, pres. CATV div., 1972-73, group v.p. Communications Group, 1973-76, sr. v.p., 1976—, also corporate dir. Served with USNR, 1952-55. Mem. Minn. Bar Assn., Am. Soc. Internat. Law, Japan Am. Soc. Chgo., Internat. Fiscal Assn. Home: 535 Elm Rd Barrington Hills IL 60010 Office: South Main St Crystal Lake IL 60014

BRADSHAW, WILLIAM DAVID, physician; b. Barnett, Mo., Jan. 23, 1928; s. Ivor E. and Pearl Susan (Tipton) B.; B.S., Central Mo. State Coll., 1950; B.S., U. Mo., 1952; M.D., U. Kans., 1954; m. Dorothy Weir, Aug. 21, 1951; children—Deborah, Jane. Intern, U. Kans., Kansas City, 1954-55; gen. practice medicine, Clinton, Mo., 1955—; mem. staff Golden Valley Meml. Hosp., until 1975, Sac Osage Hosp., until 1975; preceptor Mo. U. Med. Sch., Clinton; dir. continuing med. edn. U. Mo., Columbia, 1976—, asso. prof. dept. family and community medicine, 1976—. Examiner FAA, 1960—; mem. Mo. Bd. of Health, 1969—, vice chmn., 1972-73, chmn., 1973-74. Mayor, Clinton, 1960-64; coroner Henry County (Mo.), 1955-59; chmn. Comprehensive Health Planning Commn., Kaysinger Basin, 1971-73. Bd. dirs. Kansas City area Boy Scouts Am., 1967—, Fellowship Christian Athletes, Clinton, 1968-75. Diplomate Am. Bd. Family Practice (charter mem.). Mem. Mo. Med. Assn. (dist. counselor 1968-76), Mo. U. Med. Alumni (gov. 1970-76), Mo. Planners Assn. (orgn. chmn. 1964). Baptist. Rotarian (pres. 1970, dist. gov. 1971-72). Home: 3410 Woodtrail Terr Columbia MO 65201 Office: U Mo Med Center 807 Stadium Dr Columbia MO 65201

BRADSTRUM, ROY ELMER, JR., pub. relations exec.; b. Highland Park, Mich., Nov. 23, 1925; s. Roy E. and Bernice (Bayley) B.; A.B. U. Mich., 1948; m. Mary Jacqueline Larson, Oct. 1, 1950; children—Julie Ann, Roy Todd. Advt. supr. AT & T, 1959-62; with Ill. Bell Telephone Co., Chgo., 1948-59, 62—, advt. mgr. 1964-68, pub. relations mgr., 1968-70, pub. relations mgr. community relations, 1970—; pres., chmn. bd. The Fisherman's Co. Mem. Bishop's Com., Clarendon Hills, 1957-59; pres. Clarendon Hills Community Fund, 1957; mem. adv. council Night Pastor, Chgo., 1964-67. Mem. planning bd. Council on Population and Environment, 1973, now bd. dirs.; sec. T.R.U.S.T. Served with AUS, 1943-45. Decorated Purple Heart. Recipient Keyman award Chgo. Jr. C. of C. Mem. Ill. C. of C., Art Inst., Theta Delta Chi. Episcopalian. Home: 448 Raintree Ct Glen Ellyn IL 60137 Office: 225 W Randolph St Chicago IL 60606

BRADT, ACKEN GORDON, ret. banker, educator; b. Wichita, Kan., Sept. 22, 1896; s. Charles Edwin and Nellie (Acken) B.; A.B., Northwestern U., 1920, M.B.A., 1941; m. Aliff Bosier, June 18, 1918; children—Elizabeth Margaret (Mrs. Leonard S. Parsons), Virginia Helen Fullerton, Gordon Edwin. Asst. sec. Bd. Fgn. Missions, Presbyn. Ch. U.S.A., 1920-28; with Continental Ill. Nat. Bank and Trust Co., Chgo., 1928-62, 2d v.p., 1943-59, v.p., 1959-62; mgmt. cons; lectr. mgmt., mem. faculty Northwestern U., 1944—, past mem. adminstrv. com. chmn. bd. mgrs. of Fin. Pub. Relations; sect. leader, lectr. Sch. Banking, U. Wis., Pacific Coast Sch. Banking, U. Wash., Sch. Pub. Relations, Northwestern U.; lectr. Bank Pub. Relations Sch., Princeton, Sch. Banking, South La. State U., Grad. Sch. Banking, So. Meth. U. Chmn., Evanston (Ill.) Mayor's New Generations Service Bd. Mem. council exec. devel. program U. Ill.; past chmn. bus. edn. adv. council Bd. Edn. Chgo. Pub. Sch. com. on policy and curriculum Ill. Bankers Sch. Former sec., mem. exec. com., dir. McCormick Theol. Sem., Chgo.; past mem. exec. com. Evanston Council Chs.; past v.p., dir. Evanston YMCA; former vice chmn. Chgo. Community Fund-Red Cross Joint Appeal; vice chmn. budget com. Chgo. Community Fund. Pres. United Community Services of Evanston, Inc.; trustee, dir. Evanston Pub. Library. Mem. Am. Bankers Assn. (com. banker edn. programs), Am. Inst. Banking (former chmn. and mem. bd. regents Chgo. chpt.), Financial Pub. Relations Assn. (past treas.), Ill. Bankers Assn. (chmn. com. on edn., mem. pub. relations div.), Ill., Evanston (dir.), chambers commerce, Evanston Hist. Soc., Chgo. Assn. Commerce and Industry, Sigma Alpha Epsilon (life mem.). Presbyterian (ruling elder). Clubs: Kickers, Kiwanis, University (Evanston). Author: How to Triple Your Talents and Multiply Your Earning Power, 1963: The Secrets of Getting Results Through People, 1968; Five Keys to Productivity and Profits, 1973; also articles in mgmt. field. Home and Office: 606 Michigan Ave Evanston IL 60202

BRADT, DONA MARY, librarian; b. Hastings, Minn., Oct. 17, 1930; d. Edwin Gervase and Maude Marie (Hatten) Sontag; B.A. in Bus. Adminstrn., Met. State U., 1975; children—Michael Edwin, Robert Dana, Jeffery Arnold, Peter Mathew. Legal sec. firm Langevin & Langlais, Newport, Minn., 1964-65; librarian Economics Lab., Inc., St. Paul, 1965—. Mem. ALA, Minn. Library Assn., Am. Soc. for Info. Sci., Spl. Libraries Assn., AAAS. Roman Catholic. Home: 7981 115th St South Cottage Grove MN 55016 Office: Economics Laboratory Inc Osborn Bldg St Paul MN 55102

BRADTKE, PHILIP JOSEPH, architect; b. Chgo., Aug. 13, 1934; s. Felix Anthony and Frances Agnes (Mach) B.; B.Arch. cum laude, U. Notre Dame, 1957; m. Diane Gloria Westol, Oct. 19, 1963; children—Michael Thomas, Christine Ann. With Belli & Belli, architects, engrs., 1957-64, project architect, 1960-64; with A.M. Kinney Assos., Inc., Skokie, Ill., 1964—, project mgr., 1967-74, v.p., 1974—. Guest lectr. architecture Notre Dame U., 1974. Recipient design awards Beaux-Arts Inst. Design, 1955, Indpls. Home Shows, 1956, 59, Ch. Property and Adminstrn. Mag. Archtl. Competition, 1956. Mem. A.I.A. (chpt. housing com. mem. 1968—, chmn. honor awards program 1973, treas. Chgo. chpt. 1975-76). Club: Notre Dame (Chgo.). Home: 1040 Queens Ln Glenview IL 60025 Office: 4747 Dempster St Skokie IL 60076

BRADY, BARBARA ROSEWATER (MRS. WILLIAM WEBB BRADY), civic worker, writer; b. Omaha, Feb. 27, 1918; d. Stanley M. and Barbara (McAlvay) Rosewater; A.B., U. Neb., 1939; m. William Webb Brady, Sept. 28, 1940; children—Barbara Leslie (Mrs. Richard K. Karchmer), Nancy Webb (Mrs. Scott W. Shafer), Katherine Anne, Margaret Louise. Fashion editor Chgo. Daily News, 1941-43; reporter Omaha World-Herald, 1944. Commentator Meet the Chs. program Sta. WRMN, Elgin, Ill., 1950-51. Mem. Elgin Jr. Service Bd., 1947-52; mem. exec. bd. Friends of Judson Coll., 1963-66, 70—, pres., 1967-68, v.p., 1972—, mem. coll. faculty, 1969-70; bd. dirs. YWCA, Elgin, Ill., 1951-52. Named Elgin Woman of the Year, 1968; recipient Golden Eagle award Judson Coll. Mem. League Woman Voters (dir. Elgin 1962-63), Mortar Board, Theta Sigma Phi. Republican. Baptist. Author: Come See Where Jesus Lived. 1954. Contbr. articles to Read, Woman's Day, Sunday Digest, Mother's Mag., Christian Mother, New Century Leader, Sunday Pix. Address: 332 Vincent Pl Elgin IL 60120 also 121 Lake Shore Dr Lake Geneva WI 53147

BRADY, EDWARD GEORGE, advt./pub. relations exec.; b. Canton, Ohio, Dec. 26, 1949; s. Joseph W. and Agnes C. (Bogovich) B.; B.S., Kent State U., 1971; m. Lois F. Lazor, Oct. 9, 1971; children—Bridget C., Blaise J. Announcer, WKNT Radio, Kent, Ohio, 1969-71, WBNR/WSPK Radio, Poughkeepsie, N.Y., 1971-72; promotion mgr. advt./pub. relations exec., announcer KAKE-TV and Radio, Wichita, Kans., 1972-75, promotion mgr. KAKE-TV, 1975-76; program dir., talk show moderator Radio Sta. WSUM, Cleve., 1976-77; announcer WMGC/WDOK, Cleve., 1977; prodn. dir., announcer Radio Sta. WSLR, Akron, Ohio, 1977—. Recipient Addy award Wichita Ad Club, 1974. Mem. Greater Cleve. Radio-TV Council, Broadcasters Promotion Assn. Home: 5570 Treetop Ct Parma OH 44134 Office: 369 S Portage Path Akron OH 44320

BRADY, HARLAN JOHN, guidance counselor; b. N.Y.C., June 6, 1933; s. Matthew John and Loretta M. (Mulligan) B.; B.S. in Med. Biology, St. Peters Coll., 1954; M.S. in Counseling and Guidance, Troy State U., 1975; m. 2d. B. Marie Habben, May 12, 1976; children by previous marriage—Mary Kathleen, James Matthew, Harlan Joseph, Erin Alyse. Commd. officer U.S. Army, 1954; advanced through grades to maj., ret., 1976; chief chem. research facility, Vietnam, 1964-66, div. chief, Office of Chief of Info., 1966-69; pub. affairs, press officer for Lt. Gen. McLaughlin, 1969-74; dir. counseling, Carthage, Ill., 1976—; cons. in field; dir. Hopewell (Va.) Drug Abuse Program, 1969-74. Active Boy Scouts, Am.. 1969-73; Girl Scouts U.S.A., 1966-69; Little League, 1966-69; sec. Tri-city Community Adv. Council, 1969-74. Decorated Bronze Star, Honor medal with 3 oak leaf clusters (Viet-Nam). Mem. Am. Personnel and Guidance Assn., Am. Rehab. Assn., Publicity Club N.Y.C., VFW. Roman Catholic. Club: Masons. Contbr. articles to profl. jours. Home: 146 Main St Carthage IL 62321

BRADY, JAMES FERREL, JR.. engrng. co. planning exec.; b. Frankfort. Ky., Nov. 9, 1920; s. James Ferrel B.; B.M.E., U. Louisville, 1943; m. Rosa Lee Mettling, Jan. 21, 1944; children—Patricia Lee. Cynthia Lee, James Ferrel, III. Design engr. Douglas Aircraft Co., Los Angeles, 1943-48, engrng. mgr., 1948-50; with Gen. Dynamics Corp., 1950-66, 71—, dir. program devel. div., San Diego, 1971-72, dir. corp. advanced planning Hdqrs., St. Louis, 1972—; with Gen. Electric, 1966-71. Registered profl. engr., Calif. Fellow Am. Inst. Aeros. and Astronautics (asso.); mem. Coll. of Cardinals. Club: Toastmasters (pres. local club 1952-53). Contbr. articles on nuclear-powered aircraft, manned air breathing aerospace systems and rocket reuseable transport systems to profl. jours. Home: 1162 Appleseed Ln Saint Louis MO 63132 Office: General Dynamics Room 1505 7733 Forsyth Blvd Saint Louis MO 63105

BRADY, JAMES NIEL, state ofcl.; b. Vandalia, Ill., July 22, 1925; s. John and Annetta (Owen) B.; B.S., U. Ill., 1950; m. Dorothy Jean Trexler, Aug. 8, 1948; 1 dau. Pamela (Mrs. Mark E. Massie). Geologist, Ashland Oil and Refinery Co., Ashland, Ky., 1950-66; cons. geologist, Mt. Gilead, Ohio, 1966-67; draftsman County Engr.'s Office, Mt. Gilead, 1967-69; geologist, engr. Western Exploration, Inc., Cardington, Ohio, 1969-72; oil and gas insp. State of Ohio, 1972—. Served with USAAF, 1944-46; PTO. Mem. Am. Assn. Petroleum Geologists. Home and office: 446 Catalpa Ln Mount Gilead OH 43338

BRADY, WILLIAM ARTHUR, speech pathologist; b. Titusville, Pa., May 13, 1942; s. Walter Robert and Alma Cecelia B.; B.S. in Speech and Speech Correction, Clarion State Coll., 1966; M.Ed. in Speech Pathology (Office Edn. fellow), Pa. State U., 1967; postgrad. in Speech Pathology Kent State U. Speech therapist Lawrence County (Pa.) Pub. Schs., 1966-68, Titusville (Pa.) Area Schs., summer 1966, Ellwood City (Pa.) Area Schs., 1968; instr. speech pathology dept. Edinbor State Coll., summer 1968, Clarion State Coll., 1968-69, Ill. State U., 1969-70, Allegheny Coll., 1970-71; teaching fellow in speech pathology Kent State U., 1971-74, adj. asso. prof. speech pathology, 1976-77; dir. speech pathology St. Elizabeth Hosp. Med. Center, Youngstown, Ohio, 1974—. Mem. Am. (certified in clin. comptence in speech pathology), Ohio (chmn. com. clin. and hosp. affairs 1976-77), Mahoning Valley (v.p. 1976-77) speech, hearing assns., Aphasiology Assn. of Ohio. Contbr. articles to profl. jours. Home: 4521 Washington Sq Apt 2 Youngstown OH 44515 Office: PO Box 1790 Youngstown OH 44501

BRADY, WILLIAM HAMPTON, bishop; b. Aquasco, Md., Sept. 7, 1912; s. Henry Bernard and Maude Catherine (Gibbons) B.; student Charlotte Hall Mil. Acad., 1924-28; A.B., U. Md. 1935; student Gen. Theol. Sem. 1938, S.T.D., 1954: D.D., Nashotah Sem., 1953; m. Margaret Lodge Brady, June 4, 1944; children—Mary Margaret, Anne Louise, William Hampton, Bernard Lodge. Ordained deacon, priest, Episcopal Ch., 1938; asst. rector Ch. of Resurrection, N.Y.C., 1938-40; rector St. Paul's Ch., Savannah, Ga., 1940-48, Alton, Ill., 1948-53: bishop-coadjutor Diocese of Fond du Lac, Wis., 1953-56, bishop, 1956—. Home: 75 W Division St Fond du Lac WI 54935 Office: 39 N Sophia St Fond du Lac WI 54935

BRADY, WILLIAM WEBB, lawyer; b. Elgin, Ill., Nov. 9, 1914; s. William Henry and Helen L. (Webb) B.; student U. Ariz., 1932-35: B.S., Northwestern U., 1936. J.D., 1940; m. Barbara M. Rosewater, Sept. 28, 1940; children—Barbara Leslie Brady Karchmer, Nancy Webb Brady Shafer, Katherine Anne, Margaret Louise. Pub. accountant Arthur Andersen & Co., Chgo., 1936-37; admitted to Ill. bar. 1940; asso. Mayer. Meyer, Austrian & Platt, Chgo., 1940-42; trial atty. Office Contract Settlement, Washington, 1945; practice law, Elgin, 1946—, partner firm Brady, McQueen, Martin, Callahan & Collins; v.p. Larkin Bank, Elgin, 1970-77, now dir.; dir. First Nat. Bank, Elgin; mem. faculty Northwestern U., 1938—. Trustee Judson Coll., Elgin, 1963-70, chmn., 1963-68; trustee No. Bapt. Theol. Sem., Oakbrook, Ill., 1962—, Bapt. Theol. Union, Chgo., 1975—; pres. adv. bd. St. Joseph Hosp., Elgin, 1972—. C.P.A., Ill. Mem. Am., Ill., Chgo., Kane County, Elgin bar assns. Baptist. Clubs: Union League (Chgo.); Elgin Country. Contbr. to legal books, jours. Home: 332 Vincent Pl Elgin IL 60120 Office: 80 Fountain Sq Plaza Elgin IL 60120

BRAHE, NEIL BENTON, dentist; b. Appleton, Wis., June 21, 1926; s. Ralph Bertrand and Mary Jesse (O'Brien) B.; student Ripon Coll., 1946-49; D.D.S., Loyola Coll., Chgo., 1953; m. Grace Jensen, Oct. 23, 1948; children—Alison Ann, David Carlton, Bruce Benton. Mem. faculty Marquette U., Milw., 1961—, asst. prof. dental practice adminstrn., 1961-65; gen. practice dentistry, Appleton, 1953—; founder, pres. Project D, Appleton, 1961—. Mem. Am. Greater Milw. dental assns., Wis. State, Chgo. (asso.) dental socs., Outagamie Dental Soc., A.V. Purinton Acad., Am. Legion, Appleton C. of C. Clubs: Rotary, Northside Bus., Appleton Yacht, Oshkosh Power Boat, Elks, Masons. Author: Dental Assistants' Self Training Program, 1967; Executive Dynamics in Dental Practice, 1969; We Like These Ideas, 1970, Wonderful World of Modern Dentistry, 1971, Great Ideas for Dental Practice, 1972; (with Alison A. Brugger) Dental Letter Book, 1975. Office: 335 E Wisconsin St Appleton WI 54911

BRAINARD, EDITH MAE, ret. librarian; b. Guthrie County, Iowa; d. Charles W. and Henrietta (Martin) Brainard; B.A., U. Iowa, 1927, M.A., 1928; B.S., U. Minn., 1932; U. Chgo. Library Sch., 1944-45. High sch. and jr. coll. tchr., St. Johns, Ariz., Waukon, Iowa, 1928-31; librarian Eldora (Ia.) Pub. Library, 1933-36, Southwestern Coll., 1936-42, Itasca Jr. Coll., 1942-43, Gustavus Adolphus Coll., 1943-44, Ill. Wesleyan U., 1945-47, James Millikin U., 1947-51; asst. librarian Portland (Ore.) State Extension Center, 1951-52; head circulation and reference John McIntire Library, Zanesville, Ohio, 1952-53; head librarian McKinley Meml. Library, Niles, Ohio, 1953-69; lectr. U. Minn. Library Sch., summers 1937-42. Mem. Mayor's Com. on Comic Books. Member Niles Girl Scout Council, 1964-65. Mem. Am., Ohio, Kans., (past pres.) Ia., Ill. library assns., Bus. and Profl. Women's Club (past pres. Eldora, pres. Niles 1959-60). Author articles profl. and ednl. jours. Home: 333 W Park Ave Niles OH 44446

BRAKER, WILLIAM PAUL, aquarium exec.; b. Chgo., Nov. 3, 1926; s. William Paul and Minnie (Wassermann) B.; m. Patricia Reese, Sept. 2, 1950; children—Helen Elizabeth, William Paul, III, Nancy Carol, Gretchen Patricia; B.S., Northwestern U., 1950; M.S., George Washington U., 1953; postgrad. U. Chgo., 1954-58. Aquarist, John G. Shedd Aquarium, Chgo., 1950, asst. curator, 1953-60, asst. dir., 1960-64, dir., 1964—; tissue culture research Nat. Cancer Inst., Bethesda, Md., 1952; cons. Nat. Fisheries Center and Aquarium, Dept. Interior, Aquarium and Marine Stadium sects. Pardisan, Tehran, Iran; aquarium cons. for proposed Marine Park in State of Singapore. Auditor, Rich Twp. Govt., 1975—; trustee Prairie State Coll., 1970-74. Mem. Shedd Aquarium Soc. (trustee, sec.), Am. Assn. Zool. Parks and Aquariums (past pres., chmn. legis. com.), Internat. Union of Dirs. Zool. Gardens, Am. Soc. Ichthyologists and Herpatologists, Com. on Traffic of Noxious Animals, Am. Fisheries Soc., Kennicott Club (past pres.). Author: How to Keep Saltwater Fishes; Marine Tropicals; Enjoy a Saltwater Aquarium; Exploring and Understanding Fish; editorial adviser The Sea and Its Wonderful Creatures; editor column The Aquarium mag.; contbr. articles to Ency. Brit., Ency. Americana. Home: RFD 1 Sunset Rd Matteson IL 60443 Office: 1200 S Lake Shore Dr Chicago IL 60605

BRAMAN, DONALD WILLIAM, pub. relations exec.; b. Mpls., June 19, 1917; s. Maurice I. an Ida (Garber) B.; B.A. cum laude, U. Minn., 1937; m. Sally Davidson, June 16, 1946 children—Stuart, Sandra, Richard. Mem. editorial staff Mpls. Star, 1937-41; account exec. Manson-Gold Advt. Agy., Mpls., 1946-47; pub. relations staff Toni Co., St. Paul, 1947-50; asso. dir. pub. relations Olmsted & Foley Advt. Agy., Mpls., 1950-58; owner, pub. relations counsel Don Braman & Assos. (merged with Doremus & Co.), Mpls., 1958-67. pres. corp., 1967-77; v.p., regional mgr. Doremus & Co., 1977—. Guest Lectr. pub. relations U. Minn. Chmn. Mpls. Symphony Orch. Guaranty Fund Campaign, 1966. Dir. Hennepin County chpt. Nat. Found. for Infantile Paralysis, 1951-56; bd. dirs. Friends of Mpls. Pub. Library. Served with USMC, 1941-45. Mem. Nat. Investors Relations Inst. (v.p., dir. Minn. chpt. 1976-77, pres. 1977-78), Pub. Relations Soc. Am. (chpt. pres. 1963, mem. exec. com. counselor's sect. 1969-70), Minn. Press Club (sec. 1966-67), C. of C., Journalism and Mass Communications Alumni Assn. U. Minn. (dir., pres. 1975-76), Sigma Delta Chi (dir. 1970), Phi Epsilon Pi, Delta Phi Lambda. Mason (32 deg., Shriner). Club: Minneapolis Athletic. Home: 19 S 1st St Minneapolis MN 55401 Office: 650 Baker Bldg Minneapolis MN 55402

BRAMHALL, ROBERT RICHARD, cons.; b. Ft. Smith, Ark., Oct. 30, 1927; s. Richard Marion and Ima Lucille (Stovall) B.: A.B., Harvard U., 1951, M.B.A., 1960; m. Mary Margaret Bundy, Aug. 10, 1957; children—Robert Richard, Laura Louise. With mktg. adminstrn. Gen. Electric Co., N.Y.C., 1954-66, Philco-Ford subs. Ford Motor Co., Phila., 1966-68, Warwick Electronics subs. Whirlpool Corp., Niles, Ill., 1968-70; exec. chmn. Robert R. Bramhall and Assos., Lake Forest, Ill., 1970—; cons. to Rockwell Internat., Bunker-Ramo Corp., Dan River Inc., TRW, Memorex, J.P. Stevens, G.D. Searle, Molex. Pres. Chgo. Tennis Patrons, Inc., 1974-75. Served with U.S. Army, 1946-48. Republican. Baptist. Clubs: Bath and Tennis (Lake Forest); Harvard Bus. Sch. of Chgo. Home: 855 Buena Rd Lake Forest IL 60045 Office: 222 Wisconsin St Lake Forest IL 60045

BRANAGHAN, RICHARD LEROY, SR., health agy. exec.; b. Providence, Feb. 10, 1923; s. Roy and Agnes (Bush) B.; ed. Kent State U.; m. Catherine R. McMahon, May 4, 1946; children—James R., Paula J. Branaghan Suveges, Patricia H. Branaghan Wise, Virginia M., Richard Leroy, Russell J. On-the-job trainer passenger service United Air Lines, Cleve. Hopkins Airport, 1957-65; exec. dir. Nat. Hemophilia Found., No. Ohio chpt., 1965-69, regional dir., 1969-71, dr. field services, asst. exec. dir., N.Y.C., 1971-73; exec. dir. Nat. Commn. to Combat Huntington's Disease, N.Y.C., 1973-75; dir. devel. Child Guidance Center, Cleve., 1975—; exec. v.p. Nat. Huntingtons Disease Assn., Cleve., 1975—. Dir. vets. affairs, vol. asst. to mayor Pawtucket (R.I.), 1948-53; spl. asst. to U.S. Senator J. Howard McGrath, R.I. office, 1946-48. Served with U.S. Army, 1943-45; ETO. Recipient Vol. awards United Air Lines, 1966, Nat. Hemophilia Found., 1970. Mem. Nat. Soc. Fund Raisers, Ohio Council Fund Raising Execs., Am. Vets. (past state dept. vice comdr. R.I.). Democrat. Roman Catholic. Club: Roadrunner's (exec. sec. 1969-70) (Cleve.). Home: 1545 Elmwood Ave Lakewood OH 44107 Office: Lakewood Center N Bldg Sta 431 14600 Detroit Ave Lakewood OH 44107

BRANAHL, ERWIN FRED, aero. engr.; b. St. Louis, Mar. 8, 1922; s. Erwin Edward and Mildred (Kelle) B.; B.S., Washington U., St. Louis, 1943, M.S., 1951; m. Adeline Elizabeth Sweeney, Apr. 15, 1944; children—Sandra Beatrice, James Erwin. Stress analyst Curtiss-Wright Corp., 1943-44; with McDonnell Douglas Co., 1946—, v.p., gen. mgr. Astronautics Co., St. Louis, 1974—. Served to lt. (j.g.) USNR, 1944-46. Registered profl. engr., Mo. Fellow Am. Inst. Aeros. and Astronautics (asso.); mem. Am. Ordnance Assn. Lutheran (ch. pres. 1966-71). Home: 14 Lake Pembroke St Louis MO 63135 Office: PO Box 516 St Louis MO 63166

BRANCH, CHARLES BENSON, chem. mfg. exec.; b. Omaha, May 23, 1915; s. Karl Stonem and Olava Christina (Larsen) B.; A.B., Western Res. U., 1937; m. Shirley Marie Dasher, Aug. 26, 1939 (div.); children—Jaquith L. Wright, Pamela J. Bendall, Kristi Marie Moore, Gretchen Kit Romano, Andrea Denise, Derek, Timotha Victoria; m. 2d, Anita M. Iasenzaniro, May 1976. With Dow Chem. Co., Midland, Mich., 1937—, beginning as trainee, successively staff cellulose products, plastics sales, styrene prodn. supt., coatings sales, mgr. tech. service and devel., mgr. plastics dept., 1937-59, dir., 1958—, exec. v.p., mem. exec. com. 1962-71, pres., chief exec. officer, chmn. exec. com., 1971-76, chmn. bd., mem. exec. com., 1976—; pres. Dow Chem. Internat., A.G., 1959-62; vice-chmn. Dow Chem. Iberica S.A.; dir. Asahi-Dow, Ltd., First Midland Bank & Trust, Midland, BankAm. Corp.; chmn. Dow Banking Corp. Mem. plastics adv. com. Princeton U., 1956-59. Mem. Mfg. Chemists Assn. (chmn. plastics com. 1954-56), Soc. Plastics Industry (dir. 1956-59), Am. Chem. Soc., Phi Beta Kappa, Lambda Chi Alpha. Office: 2030 Bldg Dow Center Midland MI 48640

BRANCH, MARJORIE BEATRICE, ednl. adminstr.; b. Chgo., Mar. 31, 1927; d. Foster Raymond and Josephine Beatrice (Statum) Branch; B.A. in Christian Edn., Wheaton Coll., 1955; M.A. in Edn., U. Chgo., 1959; student Northwestern U., 1946-48; postgrad. Chgo. Tchrs. Coll., 1959-61. Instr., Carver Bible Inst., 1955-57; tchr. Chgo. Bd. Edn., 1957-66, adminstr. dept. human relations, 1966-72, adminstr. dept. govt. funded programs, 1972-73, prin. Leif Ericson Elementary Sch., 1973—. Instr. community organizing and citizenship tng., 1966-71. Adv. council Met. Comprehensive Health Care Orgn., 1970-71. Bd. dirs. LWV Citizen Info. Service, 1966-72, Tri-Community Day Care Center. Chgo.. 1973—. Mem. Assn. Adminstrv. Women (dir. Met. Chgo. chpt.), Chgo. Prins. Assn. Mem. Christian Ch. (dir. religious edn. 1969-72), Phi Delta Kappa. Home: 3021 S Michigan Ave Chicago IL 60616 Office: 3600 W 5th Ave Chicago IL 60624

BRAND, MILTON IRVING, marketing cons. firm exec.; b. Hartford, Conn., Mar. 1, 1925; s. Louis and Esther (Karshen) B.; B.S., Trinity Coll., Conn., 1948; postgrad. U. Conn., 1949-51, Boston U., 1952, Northeastern U., 1953; m. Caroline M. Grobard, Oct. 31, 1945; children—Esta Lynne, David Allan, Naomi Faith, Jonathan Elihu. With Pratt & Whitney Aircraft Corp., East Hartford, Conn., 1948-52; mem. research staff Mass. Inst. Tech., Cambridge, Mass., 1952-54; cons. Nowland Co., Greenwich, Conn., 1954-57; dir. product planning services Burroughs Corp., Detroit, 1957-60; pres. Brand, Gruber & Co., Southfield, Mich., 1960—. Served with USNR, 1943-46. Mem. Am. Marketing Assn. (pres. Detroit chpt. 1972-73), Am. Mgmt. Assn. Contbg. author: The Professionals Look at New Products, 1968. Home: 30985 Pointe of Woods Dr Farmington Hills MI 48018 Office: 17117 W Nine Mile Rd Suite 1020 Southfield MI 48075

BRANDABUR, JAMES FRANCIS, lawyer; b. Cleve., June 9, 1934; s. John Joseph and Genevieve Mary (O'Hara) B.; A.B. in Polit. Sci., Xavier U., 1956; postgrad. Georgetown U., 1956-57; LL.B., U. Cin., 1959; m. Sara Marion White, June 8, 1957; children—John Joseph III, Michael S., James C., Patrick F., Mary Beth, Amy M. Admitted to Ohio bar, 1959; with Gen. Motors Corp., 1959-61; partner firm Brandabur, Campbell, Finlay, Johnson, McCormick & Weckstein, Xenia, Ohio, 1976—; dir. Xenia Nat. Bank. Mem. Xenia City Bd. Zoning Appeals, 1967-68; pres. YMCA of Xenia and Greene County, Ohio; park commr. Greene County Park Dist., 1963—. Mem. Greene County Law Library Assn. (trustee 1965), Greene County (pres. 1965), Ohio bar assns., Greene County Fish and Game Assn., Phi Delta Phi. Roman Catholic. Optimist (pres. 1962). Home: 490 N King St Xenia OH 45385 Office: Suite One 260 N Detroit St Xenia OH 45385

BRANDEL, PAUL WILLIAM, lawyer, business exec.; b. Chgo., Oct. 7, 1911; s. Carl P. and Christine (Johnson) B.; grad. North Park Acad., Chgo., 1928; grad. North Park Coll. 1930, LL.D., 1972; J.D., Chgo. Kent Coll. Law, 1933; LL.D., Trinity Coll., 1968, Ill. Benedictine Coll., 1973; m. Bernice Peterson Stege, Jan. 3, 1976; 1 dau., Carola Ruth (Mrs. Loren Anderson). Admitted to Ill. bar, 1933, since practiced in Chgo.; partner Brandel, Olson, Johnson & Erickson; chmn. bd. Barrington State Bank, Schaumburg State Bank; pres. Paul W. Brandel Enterprises, Inc. Chmn. bd. Stone-Brandel Center; bd. dirs. Am. Found. of Religion and Psychiatry, Youth for Christ Internat., Religious Heritage Am., Paul Carlson Found., Ill. Inst. Tech.; adv. bd. Salvation Army, Goodwill Industries. Mem. Am., Ill., Chgo. bar assns., Gideons. Mem. Evang. Covenant Ch. Am. (chmn. bd., trustee). Kiwanian. Clubs: Union League, Michigan Shores, Svithoid, Nordic Law, Chicago Athletic Assn., Swedish (Chgo.); Lauderdale Yacht; Everglades (Palm Beach, Fla.). Home: 2515 Mayapple Ct Northbrook IL 60062 Office: 111 W Washington St Chicago IL 60602

BRANDEL, VALERIE JANE, counselor; b. Jefferson, Wis., Jan. 26, 19S3; d. Jacob William Brandel; B.S. in Edn. Art, U. Wis., Whitewater, 1975, M.S., 1976. Grad. asst. U. Wis., Whitewater, 1975-76; art tchr. Northlake (Wis.) Elementary Sch., 1975-76; guidance counselor Palmyra (Wis.) Elementary Sch., 1975—, art tchr., 1975—. Mem. Am. Personnel and Guidance Assn., Nat., Wis. Edn. Assn., Nat., Wis. Art Edn. Assns. Republican. Lutheran. Club: Meadow Springs Country (Jefferson, Wis.). Home: 404 S Whitewater Ave Jefferson WI 53549

BRANDER, MERLE EDWARD, civil engr.; b. Menominee, Mich., Nov. 5, 1939; s. GustaAdolph and Margaret Lillian (Johnson) B.; B.S. with honors, Mich. Coll. Mining and Tech., 1962; m. Shirley Louise Peterson, Jan. 2, 1965; children—Clayton Merle, Kent Edward. Engr. Underwriters Lab., Northbrook, Ill., 1967-68; cons. engr. constrn. materials Wiss, Janney, Elstner & Assos., Northbrook, 1968-74; dir. constrn. services Soil Testing Services of Wis., Inc., Green Bay, 1974—. Served to capt. USMC, 1962-67. Registered profl. engr. Ill., Wis., Mich., Kans. Mem. Am. Concrete Inst., Nat. Soc. Profl. Engrs. Soc. Fire Protection Engrs., ASCE, Prestressed Concrete Inst., VFW. Baptist. Author: Introduction to Celestial Navagation and Piloting, 1966. Home: 2527 Oakwood Dr Green Bay WI 54303 Office: 504 Lambeau St Green Bay WI 54303

BRANDES, ANNETTE THERRIEN, educator; b. Cokato, Minn., Nov. 6, 1940; d. Frederick George and Geneva Orcella (Therrien) Brandes; B.S., U. Minn., 1962, M.A., 1967; postgrad. Ariz. State U., 1969; Ph.D., U. Chgo., 1978. Tchr. phys. edn. Meml. High Sch., Eau Claire, Wis., 1962-64; phys. edn. specialist Stillwater (Minn.) Schs., 1964-66; counselor Centennial High Sch., Circle Pines, Minn., 1966-68, St. Louis Park (Minn.) Schs., 1968-69; dir. counseling Rhein-Main Am. Schs., Frankfurt, West Germany, 1969-71; asst. dean students (dean of women) Westminster Coll., Salt Lake City, 1971-72; head counselor, instr. dept. psychology St. Scholastica Coll., Duluth, Minn., 1972-74. Cons. edn. and human relations, Duluth. Leader, Girl Scouts U.S.A., Duluth, 1972-74. Laverne Noyes Found. scholar, 1974-75. Recipient Arrowhead Leadership award U. Minn., Duluth, 1961. Mem. Am. Ednl. Research Assn., Pi Lambda Theta. Club: Zonta International (Duluth). Author novels under pseudonym. Home: 1S-278 Wenmoth Batavia IL 60510

BRANDES, NORMAN SCOTT, psychiatrist; b. N.Y.C., Dec. 19, 1923; s. Frederick Emile and Claire (Grodin) B.; B.A., N.Y. U., 1947; M.D., U. Tenn., 1950; m. Pat Ruth Greenwood, Dec. 16, 1950; children—Roger Neil, Fred Emile, Deborah Ann. Intern, N.Y. Polyclinic Postgrad. Med. Sch. and Hosp., N.Y.C., 1950-51; resident Brooke Army Hosp., San Antonio, 1952-53, Ft. Campbell (Ky.) Hosp., 1953-54, Bridgeport (Conn.) Gen. Hosp., 1954-55, Ohio State U. Hosp., 1955-57; practice medicine specializing in psychiatry, Columbus, Ohio, 1957—; cons. Starling-Loving Mental Health Clinic, Ohio State U., Columbus, 1957-60; asst. dir. Columbus Children's Psychiat. Hosp., 1957-58, dir., 1958-60; cons. adolescent psychiatry Columbus State Hosp., 1961-66; asst. clin. prof. psychiatry Ohio State U., Columbus, 1966-69, asso. clin. prof., 1969—; sr. faculty Columbus Inst. for Tng. in Group Psychotherapy, 1968-72; mem. staff Riverside Meth. Hosp., 1958—, Children's Hosp., Ohio State U. Hosp., 1958—. Served to capt., M.C., AUS, 1951-58. Diplomate Am. Bd. Psychiatry and Neurology; certified in psychoanalysis Nat. Accreditation Assn. for Psychoanalysis. Fellow Am. Psychiat. Assn., Am. Assn. of Psychoanalytic Physicians, Am. Group Psychotherapy Assn. (dir. 1970-75, chmn. fellowship com. 1970-72, editor newsletter 1973-77, teaching award 1971); mem. A.M.A. (physician's recognition award 1969), Columbus Acad. of Medicine, Tri-State Group Psychotherapy Assn. (pres. 1966-67, recognition plaque award 1972), Ohio Psychiat. Assn., Soc. for Adolescent Psychiatry, Greater Columbus Tennis Assn. (dir.). Clubs: Athletic of Columbus, Columbus Indoor Tennis, Swim and Racquet. Editor, chief contbg. author: Group Therapy for the Adolescent, 1973; (audio tape) Para-analytic Treatment Approaches to Adolescent Group Psychotherapy, 1974; author, producer: (audio tape cassette book) From The Therapy Bag of An Adolescent Group Therapist, 1976. Contbr. articles on psychotherapy to newspapers, profl. jours. Home: PO Box 14049 Columbus OH 43214 Office: 6230 Busch Blvd #310 Columbus OH 43229

BRANDIN, DONALD NELSON, bank holding co. exec.; b. N.Y.C., Dec. 28, 1921; s. Nils F. and Dorothy May (Mead) B.; A.B., Princeton U., 1944; m. Yvonne V. Tetrault, Apr. 13, 1946; children—Robert N., Patricia A., Douglas M. With Bankers Trust Co., N.Y.C., 1946-56; v.p. Boatmen's Nat. Bank, St. Louis, 1956-67, sr. v.p., 1967-68, chmn. exec. com., 1968-70, pres., chief operating officer, 1971-72, chmn. bd., pres., chief exec. officer, 1973—; exec. v.p. Boatmen's Bancshares,

Inc., St. Louis, 1969-72, chmn. bd., chief exec. officer, 1973—; dir. Boatmen's Bank & Trust Co. (Kansas City, Mo.), Boatmen's Union Nat. Bank (Springfield, Mo.), Boatmen's Life Ins. Co. (Phoenix), Mo. Mortgage & Investment Co., Petrolite Corp., William S. Barnickel & Co., Civic Center Redevel. Corp., Fed. Res. Bank of St. Louis, Laclede Ave. Real Estate, Inc. Bd. dirs. St. Louis Regional Commerce and Growth Assn., United Way of Greater St. Louis, St. Louis Symphony Soc. Served to capt. U.S. Army, 1943-46. Mem. Assn. Bank Holding Cos. (dir.), Assn. Res. City Bankers, Am., Mo. bankers assns., Bank Adminstrn. Inst., Robert Morris Assos., Fin. Execs. Inst. Clubs: Old Warson Country, St. Louis Stadium, Met. (Chgo.), Kansas City. Home: 3 Coach N Four Ln Frontenac MO 63131 Office: 100 N Broadway PO Box 236 Saint Louis MO 63166

BRANDIS, ROLF WERNER, film writer-dir.; b. Unsleben, Germany, Apr. 6, 1930; s. Adolf and Ruth Ellen (Rosenbaum) B.; brought to U.S., 1938, naturalized, 1940; Ph.B., U. Chgo., 1950; m. Marlene M. Antler, May 2, 1954; children—Alan, Marion, Judith. Writer, TV dir. Edward H. Weiss and Co., advt. agy., Chgo., 1954-65; v.p., writer, dir. documentary and fictional films Fred A. Niles Communications Centers, Inc., Chgo., 1965—. Tchr. film seminars at various schs.; founder, dir. Film Acting Workshop, Chgo., 1970, acting coach, 1971—. Recipient award Atlanta Film Festival, 1969, N.Y. Internat. Film Festival, 1970, 73, 74, Hemisfilm Festival, 1970. Author: TV or not TV, 1953. Writer-dir. (film) A Fable, 1968. Home: 1022 Sheridan Rd Evanston IL 60202

BRANDT, LLOYD LOUIS, bank exec.; b. Garnavillo, Iowa, July 4, 1920; s. Louis Henry and Amanda Helen (Matt) B.; B.S., Iowa State U., 1949; m. Lois Mae Parkin, Sept. 9, 1950; children—Lynn Lorraine, Mark Curtis. S.E. div. mgr. McNary Farm Mgmt. Co., Rochester, Minn., 1950-54; dir. markets State of Minn., St. Paul, 1954-55; with Mpls. C. of C., 1955-72, legis. mgr., 1960-72; v.p. First Bank System, Mpls., 1972—. Pres. Arrow Estates, Inc., Mpls., 1970—. Mem. Met. Council Zool. Adv. Com., Mpls., 1971; mem. Minn. Amendments Com., 1973-74; pres. Voyageurs Nat. Park Assn., 1974—. Bd. dirs. Met. Citizens League, 1974—, treas., 1974-75; bd. dirs. Childrens Home Soc., 1974—, Inter-Varsity Christian Fellowship, 1973—. Served with M.C., AUS, 1942-46. Mem. Mpls. C. of C. (vice chmn. taxation com. 1975—). Club: Mpls. Athletic. Home: 141 Oakwood Dr New Brighton MN 55112 Office: 1300 First Nat Bank Bldg Minneapolis MN 55480

BRANDT, ROBERT BARRY, retail exec.; b. Lebanon, Pa., Nov. 13, 1948; s. Marlin Jay and Arlene Hilda (Bowman) B.; B.A., Lebanon Valley Coll., 1971; postgrad United Theol. Sem., 1971-73; m. Ruth Ann Peterson, June 6, 1970; 1 son, Matthew Scot. Licensed United Methodist Ch., 1968, Ordained to ministry, 1972; minister Enders Powells Valley, Pa., 1968-69; asst. minister Lebanon Covenant, Pa., 1969-71, Christ Ch., Kettering, Ohio, 1971-73; computer operator Rike's Dept. Store of Federated Dept. Stores, Inc., Dayton, 1973-74, computer opns. mgr., 1974-77, computer systems analyst, 1977--. Democrat. Home: 4801 Far Hills Ave Apt A-1 Dayton OH 45429 Office: 107 Main St N Dayton OH 45401

BRANDT, ROBERT FRED, mgmt. cons.; b. Bklyn., Mar. 1, 1917; s. Fred Louis and Adele (Hoeft) B.; B.S. cum laude, N.Y. U., 1944, M.B.A., 1948; postgrad. George Washington U., 1952-56; m. Irva A. Tarnstrom, June 24, 1945; children—Ruth A., Robert M. Pub. accountant Scouvell Wellintgon & Co., N.Y.C., 1944; disbursing officer Time, Inc., N.Y.C., 1945; with U.S. Gen. Accounting Office, Washington, 1946-61, chief of planning, 1953-56, dir. Far East br., European br., 1956-61; staff cons. Com. on Fgn. Affairs, U.S. Ho. of Reps., Latin Am. and Africa, 1961-68; mgmt. cons. Peat, Marwick, Mitchell & Co., Kansas City, Mo., 1969; sec. of adminstrn. State of Kans., 1970-73; exec. sec. Kansas, Paraguay Partnership, Inc.; mgmt. cons. Elmer Fox & Co., Washington, 1973; investments, 1975—. C.P.A., D.C., Kans. Mem. Gov.'s Com. Exec. Reorgn., Intergovtl. Adv. Com., 1970-73. Mem. Am. Inst C.P.A.'s, Fed. Govt. Accountants Assn. (chpt. pres.), Am. Soc. Pub. Adminstrs. (com. chmn.), Order Demolay, Beta Gamma Sigma. Lutheran (trustee). Home: 601 N 3d St Lindsborg KS 67456

BRANDT, WARREN WILLIAM, chemist, univ. pres.; b. Lansing, Mich., July 11, 1923; s. Warren Fisher and Esther Antell (Mortimer) B.; B.S., Mich. State U., 1944, postgrad., 1946; Ph.D., U. Ill., 1949; m. Esther Mae Cass, Mar. 18, 1944; children—Richard Warren, Sherry Ann. Teaching asst. Mich. State U., 1943-44, 46-47; teaching asst. U. Ill., 1947-48, univ. fellow, 1948-49; instr. Purdue U., 1949-50, asst. prof., 1950-55, asso. prof., 1955-61; head dept. chemistry Kans. State U., Manhattan, 1961-63, asso. dean Coll. Arts and Scis., 1962-63; dean Grad. Sch., Va. Poly. Inst., Blacksburg, 1963-65, v.p., 1963-68, exec. v.p., 1968-69; pres. Va. Commonwealth U., Richmond, 1969-74, So. Ill. U. at Carbondale, 1974—. Guggenheim fellow Oxford U., 1958. Mem. Am. Chem. Soc. (past sec.-treas.. chmn. div. analytical chemistry), A.A.A.S., Phi Lambda Upsilon (nat. treas.), Alpha Chi Sigma, Phi Kappa Phi, Omicron Delta Kappa. Home: University House So Ill U Carbondale IL 62901

BRANHAM, JERRY JUNIOR, educator; b. Grain Valley, Mo., Apr. 18, 1921; s. John Anderson and Meda Almira (Stroud) B.; student Knox Coll., 1966, U. Cin., 1964; B.S., Eastern Ill. U., 1962; m. Barbara Jeanette Wilson, Jan. 1, 1942. Graphics technician Abercrombie-Harrison Oil Co., Old Ocean, Tex., 1943-44, Shell Oil Co., Roxana, Ill., 1944-58; tchr., Cumberland High Sch., Toledo, Ill., 1962-67; cognicator of systems approach Lake Land Coll., Mattoon, Ill., 1967—. Originator, cognicator systems approach Shiloh Area Bicentennial Anniversary Found., 1974-75; active Lincoln heritage in Coles County, Ill. Served with USNR, 1942-43. Named Tchr. of Year, Cumberland High Sch., 1964, Outstanding Educator of Am., Lake Land Coll., 1972, Edn. award Central Ill. Constrn. Specification Inst., 1976. Mem. Constrn. Specifications Inst., Am. Soc. Engring. Edn., NEA, Nat. Micrographics Assn., Profl. Photographers Am., Phi Delta Kappa, Epsilon Pi Tau. Presbyterian (elder). Mason. Club: Golf and Country (Mattoon). Home: 400 S 11th St Mattoon IL 61938

BRANIGIN, ROBERT MARDIS, lawyer; b. Louisville, Feb. 4, 1934; s. Roger Douglas and Josephine Ruth (Mardis) B.; B.A. cum laude, Amherst Coll., 1956; J.D., U. Mich., 1959; m. Linda Seaton, Nov. 24, 1961; children—Susan Rachel, Anne Mardis, Kathleen Seaton, Robert Douglas. Admitted to Ind. bar, 1960; asso. Stuart, Branigin, Ricks & Schilling, Lafayette, Ind., 1960-65; partner Branigin, DeMoss and Jones, Franklin, Ind., 1966-70, Branigin and Demoss, Franklin, 1971—. Dir. The Edinburg State Bank (Ind.), United Fund chmn., Johnson County, 1967-68; treas. Johnson County Mental Health Assn., 1967; mem. pres.'s adv. council Franklin Coll., 1970—. Served with AUS, 1959-65. Mem. Am., Ind. State (bd. mgrs. 1968-70), Johnson County bar assns., Ind., Johnson County hist. socs., Am. Judicature Soc., Franklin C. of C. (v.p. 1970), Phi Gamma Delta, Alpha Chi, Phi Delta Phi. Baptist (deacon 1977—). Mason (32 deg.), Elk. Club: 50 of Johnson County (Ind.) (pres. 1977); Hillview Country (pres. 1971) (Franklin, Ind.); Sagamore of the Wabash. Home: 1205 E Jefferson St Franklin IN 46131 Office: 103 E Monroe St Franklin IN 46131

BRANN, EDWARD R(OMMEL), journalist; b. Rostock, Mecklenburg, Germany, May 20, 1920; s. Guenther O.R. and Lilli (Appel) B.; came to U.S., 1938, naturalized, 1966; B.A., Berea Coll., 1945; M.A., U. Chgo., 1946; postgrad. U. Wis., 1948-56; m. Helen Louise Sweet, Dec. 9, 1948; children—Johannes Weidler, Paul George. Asst. membership sec. central YMCA, Chgo., 1946-48; asst. editor Credit Union Mag., Madison, Wis., 1955-65; dir. hist. projects, asst. dir. publs. CUNA Internat., Inc., Madison, 1965-70, staff historian, 1958-65; asst. dir. publs. Credit Union Nat. Assn., Inc., Madison, 1970-72, asst. dir. communications, 1973—, sr. editor Credit Union mag., 1973—; dir. hist. projects World Council of Credit Unions, Inc., 1970—, dir. European relations, 1972—. Active ARC, bd. dirs. Dane County chpt. Recipient Christo et Ecclesiae award Concordia Coll., Milw., 1968, Distinguished Alumnus award Berea Coll., 1977; named Ky. col. Mem. Am. Hist. Assn., Am. Polit.Sci. Assn., NEA, Assn. for Higher Edn., Coop. Editorial Assn., Luth. Laymen's League, Internat. Polit. Sci. Assn., Wis. Hist. Soc., Internat. Raiffeisen Union, Delta Phi Alpha, Pi Gamma Mu. Lutheran. Clubs: Madison Press, Chicago Press. Contbr. articles to profl. jours. Home: PO Box 383 Madison WI 53701 Office: PO Box 431 Madison WI 53701

BRANN, LESTER WILLIAM, JR., assn. exec.; b. Madison, Wis., Mar. 24, 1925; s. Lester William and Esther (Jacobsen) B.; student Los Angeles City Coll., 1944; J.D., U. Wis., 1950; m. Lois Winter, Sept. 4, 1948; children—Lester William III, Thomas Edwin. Admitted to Wis. bar, 1950, practiced law in Racine, 1950-57; mgr. legislation div., Milw. Assn. Commerce, 1957, adminstrv. asst., 1957-59, sec., 1959-60, exec. v.p., dir., 1960-67; dir. Am. C. of C. Execs., 1967-71, vice chmn., 1971-73, chmn. elect, 1973-74, chmn., 1974-75; exec. v.p. Ill. C. of C., 1967-70, pres., 1970—; exec. v.p., dir. Credit Bur. Milw., Inc., 1960-67. Alderman, Racine, 1953-55. Vice pres., dir. Wis. Indsl. Research Council, 1964-67. Dir. Ill. Council Econ. Edn. Served inf., AUS, 1943-46. Decorated Purple Heart. Mem. Am., Wis. bar assns., Ill. C. of C. execs., Wis. Alumni Assn., Wis. Law Alumni Assn., Kappa Sigma, Phi Alpha Delta. Clubs: Economic, Union League, Executives, Tower (Chgo.). Home: 337 Forest Rd Hinsdale IL 60521 Office: 20 N Wacker Dr Chicago IL 60606

BRANNON, VICTOR DEWITT, research inst. exec.; b. Des Moines, Aug. 26, 1909; s. Ralph William and Carrie Pearl (Hamblin) B.; A.B., U. Ariz., 1931, A.M., 1932; student U. Wis., 1935-36; Ph.D., U. Mo., 1938; m. Dorothy Ellen Webb, Aug. 20, 1933; children—Vicki Rae, Richard Carlyle. Instr. polit. sci. U. of Ariz., summers 1931, 33; tchr. social scis. San Simon High Sch., 1933-34; research asst. N.Y. Bd. of Regents Inquiry into the cost and character of pub. edn., 1936-37; researcher and statistician Mo. State Highway Dept. and Mo. State Planning Bd., 1938-39; asst. dir. St. Louis Govtl. Research Inst., 1939-46, dir., 1947—; research cons. St. Louis, St. Louis County Bd. Freeholders, 1954, bd. trustees Met. St. Louis Sewer Dist., 1955, St. Louis Charter Bd. Freeholders, 1956-57; research cons. St. Louis Police Dept., 1947-49, 1957-65; sec. Constl. Revision Study Com., 1962; research cons. Com. on Municipalities and Services in St. Louis County, 1958. Adv. council U. Mo. Sch. Bus. and Pub. Adminstrn., 1965-66. Mem. Govtl. Research Assn. (trustee 1950, 51, pres. 1961-62), Mo. Hist. Soc., Phi Kappa Phi, Phi Delta Kappa. Author articles on polit. sci. Home: 7 Hillard Rd Glendale MO 63122 Office: 915 Olive R 908 St Louis MO 63101

BRANOVACKY, EUGENE M., orthopaedic surgeon; b. Skoplje, Yugoslavia, May 31, 1928; s. Mileta and Maria (Pelech) B.; came to U.S., 1967; M.D., U. Belgrade, 1954; m. Bozenna Kawiecka, Nov. 29, 1972; 1 son, George. Tchr., researcher basic sci. U. Bern, Basel, Lausanne, Switzerland, 1957-60; intern Ottawa (Can.) Gen. Hosp., 1960-62; resident orthopaedic surgery French U., Montreal, Que., Can., 1962-66; practice medicine specializing in orthopaedic surgery, Chgo., 1967—; clin. asso. dept. orthopaedics U. Ill. Med. Sch., 1972—; head orthopaedic sect. Ravenswood Hosp., Chgo., 1972. Diplomate Am. Bd. Orthopaedic Surgery. Fellow A.C.S., Am. Acad. Orthopaedic Surgeons. Home: 2905 W North Shore Chicago IL 60645 Office: 4921 N Western Ave Chicago IL 60625

BRANOVAN, LEO, educator; b. Kishinev, Roumania, Apr. 17, 1895; s. Itzik and Sophia (Swartz) B.; B.S. in Elec. Engring., U. Wis., 1924; M.S. in Applied Math., U. Chgo., 1927; postgrad. in applied math. While involved as cons. mathematician Columbia, 1935-38; m. Pearl Lhevine, July 7, 1933; 1 dau., Rosalind (Mrs. Gerald Turner). Engr., Gen. Electric, Fort Wayne, Ind., 1924-26; instr. math. U. Minn., 1927-31; cons. mathematician J.P. Goode Co., Chgo., 1932-34; cons. mathematician to engrs., N.Y.C., 1935-38; instr. math. Bklyn. Poly. Inst., 1939-44; instr. Marquette U., 1944-49, asst. prof., 1949-54, asso. prof. math., 1955-70, prof. emeritus, 1970—. Mem. Am. Math. Soc., Am. Soc. Engring. Edn., AAAS, AAUP, Wis. Acad. Arts, Letters and Sci., Société Mathematique de Belgique, Unione Matematica Italiana, Wiskundig Genootschap te Amsterdam, Dansk Matematsk Forening, Österreichische Mathematische Gesellschaft, Svenska Matematikersamfundet, Pi Mu Epsilon. Clubs: Wis. Alumni, Easter Seal Soc. (Milw.); Quarter Century, Loyalty (Marquette U.); Quarter Century, Professional, Partner of Youth (Milw. Central YMCA). Research umbilics in hyperspace, application of differential equations to engring. problems. Home: 3201 N 48th St Milwaukee WI 53216

BRANSBY, ERIC JAMES, muralist, educator; b. Auburn, N.Y., Oct. 25. 1916; s. Charles Carson and Lillian Holland (Dowsett) B.; profl. certificate Kans. City Art Inst., 1938-42; B.A., Colo. Coll., 1947, M.A., 1949; M.F.A., Yale U., 1952; m. Mary Antoinette Hemmie, Nov. 23, 1941; 1 dau., Fredericka Jo. One-man shows include: Okla. Art Center, Oklahoma City, 1973, U. Mo., Kansas City, 1971, 77, Denver U., 1966, Mulvane Art Center, Topeka, Kans., 1975, Kans. State U., Pittsburg, 1977; several group shows; locations of murals include: Mech. Engring. Bldg., U. Ill., 1953; planetarium USAF Acad., Colorado Springs, 1961-70; U. Mo., Kansas City, 1973-75; Municipal Bldg., Sedalia, Mo., 1977; represented in permanent collections; instr. U. Ill., Urbana, 1950-52; asst. prof. art Western Ill. U., Macomb, 1963-65; asso. prof. art U. Mo., Kansas City, 1965-70, prof., 1970—. Served with inf. AUS, 1942-45. Recipient Veatch award U. Mo., 1977; Edwin Austin Abbey Found. mural painting fellow, 1952. Mem. Nat. Soc. Mural Painters, AAUP, Coll. Art Assn., Phi Kappa Phi. Home: 401 E 54th St Kansas City MO 64110 Office: Dept Art University Missouri Kansas City MO 64110

BRANSCOMB, MARJORIE BERRY STAFFORD (MRS. LEWIS CAPERS BRANSCOMB, JR.), accountant, mfg. co. exec.; b. Birmingham, Ala., Jan. 13, 1915; d. George T. and Margaret (Berry) Stafford; B.S., U. Ala., 1936; M.S., U. Ill., 1947; postgrad. Ohio State U., 1964; m. Lewis Capers Branscomb, Jr. Jan. 15, 1938; children—Lewis Capers, III, Ralph Stafford, Carol Jean, Lawrence McGehee. Statis. clk. Gen. Motors Acceptance Corp., Birmingham, 1936-38; asst. regional supr. Bur. Labor Statistics, Atlanta, 1939-41; v.p., dir. Birmingham Mfg. Co., 1955—; treas. Birmingham Totem-All Inc., 1965—; cons. taxes, accounting problems. Mem. Columbus Gallery Fine Arts, 1956—. Mem. Franklin County Democratic Com., precinct capt. Upper Arlington, Ohio, 1973—. Mem. UN Assn. (treas. 1965-66, mem. finance com. 1963-66), Common Cause (activator 1972-75), ACLU, Friends of Ohio State U. Libraries, Alpha Omicron Pi. Episcopalian. Clubs: Crichton (Columbus, Ohio); Ohio State University Women's (pres. 1970-71). Author: A Decade of Improvement in Public Finance Reporting, 1947. Home: 3790 Overdale Dr Columbus OH 43220

BRANSDORFER, STEPHEN CHRISTIE, lawyer; b. Lansing, Mich., Sept. 18, 1929; s. Henry and Sadie (Kohane) B.; A.B., Mich. State U., 1951; J.D., U. Mich., 1956; LL.M., Georgetown U., 1958; m. Peggy Ruth Deisig, May 24, 1952; children—Mark, David, Amy, Jill. Admitted to Mich. bar, 1956, U.S. Ct. of Appeals for D.C., 1959, U.S. Supreme Ct. bar, 1959; trial atty. U.S. Dept. Justice, Washington, 1956-58; spl. asst. U.S. atty., D.C., 1958-59, also atty-editor U.S. Dept. Justice, Washington; asso. Miller, Johnson, Snell & Cummiskey Grand Rapids, Mich., 1959-63, partner, 1963—. Vis. instr. Mich. State U., 1973—; lectr. Inst. Continuing Legal Edn., 1973—. Mem. Mich. Supreme Ct. com. on standard jury instructions 1963-72, com. on rules of evidence, 1975—; mem. Mich. Civil Service Commn., 1975—, chmn., 1977—. Pres. Grand Rapids Child Guidance Clinic. Served with AUS, 1951-53. Fellow Am. Bar Found.; mem. Am., Grand Rapids (trustee) bar assns., State Bar of Mich. (commr. 1968—, pres. 1974-75), Bar Assn. D.C., Phi Alpha Delta, Delta Chi. Presbyterian (elder). Home: 7250 Bradfield Rd Ada MI 49301 Office: 465 Old Kent Bldg No 1 Vandenberg Center Grand Rapids MI 49503

BRANSFIELD, JAMES JOSEPH, surgeon; b. Chgo., Nov. 8, 1932; s. James J. and Beatrice C. (Greene) B.; B.S. in Biochemistry, Loyola U., Chgo., 1955, M.D., 1957; m. Virginia Kay Paully, Dec. 17, 1967; 1 dau., Helena. Intern Cook County (Ill.) Hosp., Chgo., 1957-58, resident in surgery, 1958-60, 62-65; practice medicine specializing in surgery, Chgo., 1966—; asst. dir. surg. edn. Columbus-Cuneo-Cabrini Med. Center, Chgo., 1967—, sr. attending surgeon, 1968, chief of surgery Cabrini Hosp., 1973—; attending surgeon Augustana Hosp., Chgo., 1971-77; police surgeon Chgo. Police Dept., 1967—; asso. in surgery Northwestern U. Med. Sch., Chgo., 1968—. Mem. Chgo. Com. on Trauma, 1968—. Served to lt. comdr., M.C., USNR, 1960-62. Diplomate Am. Bd. Surgery. Mem. Chgo. Med. Soc., A.C.S., Chgo. Surg. Soc., Pan Pacific Surg. Assn., Univ. Assn. for Emergency Med. Services, Aerospace Med. Assn., Phi Chi. Club: Lake Shore Athletic. Contbr. articles to profl. jours. Home and Office: 6200 N Knox Chicago IL 60646

BRANSON, BYRON MONROE, research physicist; b. Greensboro, N.C., June 24, 1929; s. Byron Russell and Bessie Gilmore (Phipps) B.; B.S. in Physics, Guilford Coll., 1951; m. Wilhelmina Braddock, Sept. 7, 1957; children—Sara Carolyn, Hannah Bess, Christopher Byron. Tchr. public schs., Guilford, N.C., 1952-53; exec. sec. Homewood Friends Meeting (Quakers), Balt., 1953-56; physicist, chief radiometrics Robert A. Taft San. Engring. Center, USPHS, Cin., 1957-66; research physicist, chief radiation protection Nuclear Medicine Lab., Bureau Radiol. Health, FDA, Cin., 1966—; lectr. Dept. Radiology, U. Cin. Coll. Medicine, 1969—. Active Religious Soc. Friends, 1947—; mem. exec. com. Ohio Valley Yearly Meeting, 1966—; trustee Friends Home, Inc., 1966—, v.p., 1972-76, pres., 1976—; block chmn. N. Avondale Neighborhood Assn., chmn. Pupil Enrrichment Program, 1973-75. Recipient Superior Work Performance award USPHS, HEW, 1958; High Quality Performance, Quality Increase award FDA, USPHS, HEW, 1971. Mem. Soc. Nuclear Medicine, Health Physics, Soc., Am. Assn. Physicists in Medicine of Am. Inst. Physics, Internat. Radiation Protection Assn., Sci. Research Soc. N. Am., Sigma Xi. Clubs: Mason. Contbr. articles in field to sci. jours. Home: 3923 Leyman Dr Cincinnati OH 45229 Office: Nuclear Medicine Lab FDA Cincinnati Gen Hosp Cincinnati OH 45267

BRANT, JEROLD OWEN, ins. co. exec.; b. Carroll County, Ind., Oct. 22, 1937; s. Ruthford F. and Mary Louise (Hillis) B.; degree bus. adminstrn. Ind. Central U., 1969; m. Billie Janis Arnold, May 26, 1962; children—Lisa Kay, Owen Keith. With Ind. Blue Cross and Blue Shield, Indpls., 1961—, dir. data processing, 1976—. Served with USNR, 1959-61. Mem. Data Processing Mgmt. Assn. (pres. Central Ind. chpt. 1973). Republican. Lutheran. Clubs: Masons, Shriner. Home: 801 Knollwood Dr Greenwood IN 46142 Office: 120 W Market St Indianapolis IN 46204

BRANTLEY, ROBERT LOUIS, mgmt. cons. co. exec.; b. Alton, Ill., Jan. 24, 1946; s. James and Frank (Broylds) B.; B.S., Ill. Coll., 1968; M.B.A., Northwestern U., 1970; m. Astra Paullette Williams, Jan. 30, 1967; 1 son, Damon Wiley. Internat. program developer YMCA Center Internat. Mgmt. Studies, N.Y.C., 1972-73; sr. dir. Office World Devel., Internat. Div., Nat. Council YMCA, N.Y.C., 1973-74; dir. student affairs Northeastern Ill. U. Center Inner-City Studies, Chgo., 1974-76; pres., exec. dir. Afro-Youth Community, Inc., Chgo., 1975—; pres., chmn. bd. dirs. Diversified Assos. Mgmt. and Organizational Negotiations, Inc., Detroit, 1977—. Mem. Am. Personnel and Guidance Assn., Am. Mgmt. Assn. Home: 1424 E 49th St Chicago IL 60615 Office: 417 E 47th St Chicago IL 60653

BRANTON, DONALD LEE, food co. exec.; b. Westboro, Wis., Jan. 21, 1933; s. James Ernest and Agnes Violet (Nelson) B.; B.S. in Agr., U. Wis., 1958, B.S. in M.E., 1959; m. Carol Jeanene Schwebke, Sept. 18, 1971; children—John Patrick, James Alan, Jason Donald. Farm adviser Wis. Pub. Service Corp., Green Bay, 1959-61; farm mgr. Paragon Elec. Co., mfr. automatic timing devices, Two Rivers, Wis., 1961-65; engring. mgr. dairy and food equipment div. Sta-Rite Industries, Inc., Delavan, Wis., 1965-74; pres. Systems Design Ltd., Delavan, 1974—. Dist. tng. chmn. Big Foot council Boy Scouts Am., 1970-71, com. mem., 1966-69. Served with AUS, 1955-57. Registered profl. engr., Wis. Mem. Nat. Soc. Profl. Engrs., Am. Soc. Agrl. Engrs. (sec. sect. 1968). Republican. Methodist (chmn. adminstrv. bd. 1971-74). Mason. Patentee in field. Home: Box 43 Route 4 Delavan WI 53115 Office: Route 4 Delavan WI 53115

BRANZ, KENNETH WESLEY, investment mgmt. exec.; b. Pontiac, Ill., Aug. 22, 1922; s. Henry J. and Myrtle (Tronc) B.; student Ill. Wesleyan U., 1941-43, 46-47, U. Pa. Wharton Sch., 1967-69; m. Marian J. Anderson, Apr. 6, 1947; children—Kay, Susan, Barbara, Patricia, Nancy, Eric. With Paul H. Davis & Co., Chgo., 1950-51; office mgr. Jean A. McCoy & Sons, Pontiac, 1952-56; asst. mgr. Tabor & Co., Decatur, Ill., 1956-61; regional v.p. Eaton & Howard, Inc., Chgo., 1961-76; owner, operator Addison Graphics (Ill.), 1977—. Served with USNR, 1942-46. Mem. Sigma Chi. Clubs: Union League, Bond (all Chgo.). Home: 276 Arlington St Elmhurst IL 60126 Office: 607 S Addison Rd Addison IL 60101

BRAR, AMARJIT SINGH, scientist; b. Srinagar, India, Mar. 24, 1934; s. Jasbir Singh and Baldev (Kaur) B.; came to U.S., 1957; naturalized, 1966; B.S., Punjab U., India, 1953; diploma Mech. Engring., Victoria Jubilee Tech. Inst., Bombay, India, 1957; postgrad. U. Minn., 1960-63; M.S. in Metall. Engring., U. Mont., 1966; m. Bimla Chadha, Feb. 29, 1964; children—Jess, Kim. Tool designer Am. Hoist & Derrick Co., St. Paul, 1957-60; research asst. U. Minn., 1960-63; metallurgist Twin City Testing & Engring. Lab., St. Paul, 1962-64; metallurgist Gould, Inc., Mpls., 1966-69; sr. material scientist Control Data Corp., Mpls., 1969-76, Magnetic Peripherals, Inc., 1976—. Mem. Am. Soc. for Metals, St. Paul Camera Club, Sikh Study Circle (pres. 1973—), Internat. Inst., Indo Am. Club (sec. 1958-60, treas. 1961-62). Contbr. articles to profl. jours. Home: 7205 Heatherton Circle Edina MN 55435 Office: 7801 Computer Ave Minneapolis MN 55435

BRASHEAR, WILLIAM RONALD, lawyer; b. Royal Oak, Mich., Oct. 8, 1932; s. William Wilson and Theresa Elizabeth (Briggi) B.; A.B., U. Mich., 1953, M.A., 1956, J.D., 1956; M.A., Princeton, 1958, Ph.D., 1959; postgrad. Oxford U., 1955; m. Lydia Mary Rothman, Jan. 14, 1961; children—Ruth Margot, Lydia Louise. Admitted to Mich. bar, 1957; asso. firm Brashear, Conley & Tangora, Livonia, Mich., 1958-61, partner, 1961—; adj. prof. English lit. Wayne State U., 1959-71. Bd. dirs. Cranbrook Music Guild, Inc., pres., 1968-70; bd. dirs. Livonia Rotary Youth Found., Inc., 1964-67, pres., 1965-66. Mem. Am., Mich., Detroit, Livonia bar assns., Modern Lang. Assn., Tennyson Soc., Phi Beta Kappa, Phi Kappa Phi, Phi Eta Sigma. Author: The Living Will, 1969; The Gorgon's Head, 1976. Contbr. to profl. publs. in field. Home: 3665 Lakecrest Dr Bloomfield Hills MI 48013 Office: 32900 5 Mile Rd Livonia MI 48154

BRASTED, DAVID HUMPHREY, savs. and loan exec.; s. Kenneth Parker and Lulu (Humphrey) B.; B.A., Beloit Coll., 1960; m. Sarah Ann Taleen, Dec. 31, 1960; children—Elizabeth Taleen, Barbara Humphrey. With Mid Kans. Fed. Savs. & Loan Assn. of Wichita, 1960—, asst. sec., 1961-62, sec., 1962-65, v.p., sec., 1965-72, sr. v.p., 1972-77, exec. v.p., 1977—; pres. Amarado Investment Co., Inc., 1973. Budget com. United Fund, Wichita, 1969—. Bd. dirs. Wichita Assn. Homebuilders, 1963—, Wichita Council Community Devel., 1963-65, Greater Downtown Wichita, Inc., 1969—, Family Consultation Service, Wichita Symphony Soc., 1970—, Historic Wichita, 1971; trustee Wichita Art Mus. Found., 1970-74. Mem. Wichita Bd. Realtors, Phi Kappa Psi. Republican. Congregationalist. Club: Rotary. Home: 401 N Roosevelt Wichita KS 67208 Office: 230 S Market St Wichita KS 67202

BRATTAIN, WAYNE KEITH, bacteriologist; b. Anderson, Ind., Apr. 28, 1948; s. V. Keith and Esther Louise (Jenkins) B.; B.S., Ball State U., 1970, M.A., 1973; postgrad. Ind.-Purdue U., 1974-75; m. Sally A. Brown, Feb. 12, 1971. Tchr. biology, chemistry Lapel (Ind.) Schs., 1970-72; bacteriology instr. Ind. Central U., Indpls., 1972-73; bacteriologist, Ind. State Bd. Health, Indpls., 1973—. Guest lectr. Ind. U. Med. Center, 1975. Mem. Am. Soc. Microbiology. Author: Procedure Manual for Water Bacteriologists, 1974. Home: 5533 Antonelli Ln Indianapolis IN 46227 Office: 1330 W Michigan St Indianapolis IN 46204

BRAUDE, ADELE COVY (MRS. JACOB M. BRAUDE), designer; b. Cin.; d. Tobias and Martha (Rosenberg) Covy; student U. Cin. Coll. Music; m. S. Henry Englander, Feb. 10, 1927 (dec. Aug. 1944); children—Ann Englander, Jane E. (Mrs. Berkson); m. 2d, Jacob M. Braude, Feb. 22, 1946 (dec. Dec. 24, 1970). Sec.-treas. The Nordell Co., 1931-44, pres., 1944-47; dir. The Gidding Co., 1946-58. Pres., Cin. chpt. Los Angeles Sanitorium, 1935; v.p. Jr. Council Jewish Women, Cin., 1936; pres. nat. women's com. Greater Chgo. chpt. Brandeis U., 1956; mem. Com. Restoration of Hull House; bd. dirs. Chgo. Women's Aid, Deborah Women's Club; active fund drives A.R.C., Community Fund. Designer, builder miniature rooms done to scale, reprodns. of ancient, period and historic rooms and bldgs. Address: 1000 Lake Shore Plaza Chicago IL 60611

BRAUER, DONALD GEORGE, urban planning cons.; b. Clinton, Iowa, Nov. 24, 1929; s. Alvin P. and Mildred Rose (King) B.; A.A., Clinton Jr. Coll., 1949; B.S. in Civil Engring., Iowa State U., 1951; M.A. in Pub. Adminstrn., U. Minn., 1956; m. Borghild Gudrun Erickson, June 16, 1956; children—Mark, Sonja, Susan. Engr., Pitts.-Des Moines Steel Co., Des Moines, 1952-54; adminstrv. asst. to mgr. Village of Edina, Minn. 1956-59; chief engr. Harrison, Brauer-Ruppel, Edina, 1960-63; pres. Brauer & Assos., Inc., Edina, 1964—; v.p., dir. Brauer & Assos., Rocky Mountain Inc., Denver, 1967—. Vis. lectr. Tex. A. and M. U., 1970, U. Minn., 1968, 70, 72, U. Wis. at Eau Clair, 1969, Utah State U., 1971, U. Ga., 1974. Served with USAF, 1951-53. Research fellow U. Minn., 1955-56. Fellow ASCE; mem. Am. Camping Assn. (sect. dir. nat. standards com.), Minn. Zool. Soc. (citizens' com. zoo selection), Nat. Soc. Profl. Engrs. Rotarian. Club: Decathelon Athletic (Bloomington, Minn.). Designer, St. Croix Wild River Plan, 1971, Honeywell Employee Recreation Area, Mpls., 1964, Braemar Golf Course, Edina, 1964, Wood Lake Nature Interpretive Area, 1970, Thunder Bay (Ont., Can.) Open Space Plan, 1972, Ft. Snelling Nat. Cemetery Master Plan, 1974, the Ridges Master Plan, 1974. Home: 6116 Parnell Ave S Edina MN 55424 Office: 6440 Flying Cloud Dr Eden Prairie MN 55343

BRAUER, ERICH FREDERICK, minister, educator; b. Crete, Ill., Apr. 12, 1911; s. Fred Ernest and Anna Emily (Meyer) B.; diploma Concordia Theol. Sem. St. Louis, 1935; M.A., Marquette U., 1957; m. Esther Grotheer, May 8, 1937; children—Emily (Mrs. Clyde R. Billings), Priscilla (Mrs. F. William Boelter). Ordained to ministry Luth. Ch.-Mo. Synod, 1937; pastor Grace Luth. Ch., Little Rock, 1937-44, St. Paul Luth. Ch., St. Joseph, Mo., 1944-49, Immanuel Luth. Ch., Temple, Tex., 1949-53; adminstr. asst. edn. and youth ministries S. Wis. dist. Luth. Ch.-Mo. Synod, Milw., 1953-75; asso. pastor Sherman Park Luth. Ch., Milw., 1975—. Mem. Gov.'s Commn. on Home and Family, 1970—, Milw. Commn. on Helping Handicapped, 1971—. Recipient Distinguished Service award for pub. relations Valparaiso U., 1952. Author: Christian Parenthood, 1960. Home: 2920 N 70th St Milwaukee WI 53210 Office: 2703 N Sherman Blvd Milwaukee WI 53210

BRAUER, LINDA ANNETTE LEWIS, dentist; b. Olympia, Wash., June 7, 1949; d. William Dell and Yvonne Mae (Cline) Lewis; student Sweet Briar Coll., 1967-69; B.A., U. Kans., 1971; D.D.S., U. Mo.-Kansas City, 1975; m. Warren Allen Brauer, Sept. 6, 1975; children—Erich Lewis and Scott Warren (twins). Dentist, Winnebago County Health Dept., Rockford, Ill., 1975—. Mem. advisory bd. dental assts. program Rock Valley Coll., 1975-77; mem. youth advisory com. Our Saviors Lutheran Ch., Rockford, Ill., 1976-77. Mem. Phi Kappa Phi, Omicron Kappa Upsilon, Pi Beta Phi, Xi Psi Phi. Club: Order of Eastern Star. Home: 234 Evelyn Ave Apt 3 Loves Park IL 61111

BRAUN, ROBERT ALEXANDER, psychiatrist; b. Chemnitz, Germany, Dec. 14, 1910; s. Leo and Bertha (Eisenschiml) B.; came to U.S., 1939, naturalized, 1946; M.D., U. Vienna (Austria), 1937; m. Gertrud E. Mittler, Jan. 6, 1946; children—Eleanor, Ronald. Intern, William McKinley Meml. Hosp., Trenton, N.J., 1940-41; resident in psychiatry Rochester (Minn.) State Hosp., 1950-51, staff psychiatrist, 1951-56; resident in psychiatry Lafayette Clinic, Detroit, 1956-58, staff psychiatrist, 1958-60; clin. dir. Clinton Valley Center (formerly Pontiac State Hosp.), Pontiac, Mich., 1960-63, dir. Oakland Div., 1963—; clin. asso. prof. dept. psychiatry Mich. State U., 1969—. Diplomate Am. Bd. Psychiatry Neurology; fellow Am. Psychiat. Assn.; mem. Royal Soc. Medicine (Eng.). Home and office: 18610 Hartwell Ave Detroit MI 48235

BRAUN, ROBERT CLARE, assn. exec.; b. Indpls., July 18, 1928; s. Ewald Elsworth and Lila (Inman) B.; B.S. in Journalism-Advt., Butler U., 1950; postgrad. Ind. U., 1957, 66. Reporter, Northside Topics Newspaper, Indpls., 1949, advt. mgr., 1950; asst. mgr. Clarence E. Crippen Printing Co., Indpls., 1951; corp. sec. Auto-Imports, Ltd., Indpls., 1952-53; pres. O. R. Brown Paper Co., Indpls., 1953-69; Robert C. Braun Advt. Agy., 1959-70, Zimmer Engraving Inc., Indpls., 1964-69; former chmn. bd. O. R. Brown Paper Co., Zimmer Engraving, Inc.; advt. cons. Rolls-Royce Motor Cars, 1957-59; exec. dir., chief exec. officer Historic Landmarks Found., Ind., 1969-73; exec. v.p., purchasing Mgmt. Assn. Indpls., 1974—; gen. mgr. Midwest Indsl. Show, 1974—, Midwest Office Systems and Equipment Show, 1974—, Grand Valley Indsl. Show, 1974—. Chmn. Citizens' Adv. Com. to Marion County Met. Planning Dept., 1963; pres. museum com. Indpls. Fire Dept., 1966—; mem. Mayor's Contract Compliance Adv. Bd., 1977—; mem. adv. com. Historic Preservation Commn. Marion County, 1967-73; mem. Met. Mus. Art, Indpls. Mus. Art. Bd. dirs. Historic Landmarks Found. Ind., 1960-69; dir., sec. Ind. Arthritis and Rheumatism Found., 1960-67, pres., 1969, dir., 1970—, dir. Asso. Patient Services, 1976—; pres. Amanda Wasson Meml. Found., 1961-72, Huggler-Ault Meml. Trust, 1961-72. Recipient Meritorious Service award St. Jude's Police League, 1961, citation for meritorious service Am. Legion Police Post 56, 1962. Mem. Marion County Hist. Soc. (dir. 1964—, pres. 1965-69, 74-76), Am. Guild Organists (mem. Indpls. chpt., charter mem. Franklin Coll. br.), Ind. Museum Soc. (treas., dir. 1967-74), Internat. Fire Buff Assos., Indpls. Second Alarm Fire Buffs (sec.-treas. 1967, pres. 1969), Ind. Hist. Soc., Nat. Hist. Soc., Nat. Trust Historic Preservation, Smithsonian Assn., Soc. Archtl. Historians, Am. Heritage Soc., N.A.P.M. Editors Group, Am. Assn. State and Local History, Decorative Arts Soc. Indpls., Ind. Soc. Assn. Execs., Nat. Assn. Purchasing Mgmt., Purchasing Mgmt. Assn. Indpls. (dir. 1974—), Victorian Soc. Am. (nat. sec. 1971-74), Lambda Chi Alpha, Alpha Delta Sigma, Sigma Delta Chi, Tau Kappa Alpha. Club: Indpls. Press, Rolls-Royce Owners. Editor Historic Landmarks News, 1969-74; Hoosier Purchasor mag., 1974—. Home: 1415 W 52d St Indianapolis IN 46208 Office: 527 Glendale Bldg 6100 N Keystone Ave Indianapolis IN 46220

BRAUNSCHNEIDER, GEORGE EDWARD, physician; b. Grand Rapids, Mich., Sept. 16, 1920; s. George Frank and Bernice Isabel (Brechting) B.; student Aquinas Coll., 1937-39; B.S., Mich. State U., 1941, M.S., 1947; M.D., Marquette U., 1953; m. Dolores Lucille Bouwens, Aug. 18, 1942; children—David E., Kristine A., J. Michael, Kathleen M., Jeanine D. Instr. natural sci. Mich. State U., 1946-49; intern St. Mary's Hosp., Grand Rapids, Mich., 1953-54; practice medicine, Grand Rapids, 1954—; mem. staffs St. Mary's Hosp., Grand Rapids, Butterworth Hosp., Grand Rapids; med. dir. West Cath. High Sch., Grand Rapids, 1963-74, Villa Maria Sch. for Girls, Grand Rapids, 1954-74; part owner Alpine Med. Center, Grand Rapids, 1966—. Med. coordinator disaster program Greater Grand Rapids Hosp. Council, 1972—. Served with AUS, 1943-46; col. M.C. Res., 1972—, comdr. 317th Convalescent Center, Kalamazoo, 1976. Diplomate Am. Bd. Family Practice. Mem. W. Mich. Acad. Family Physicians (sec.-treas. 1965-72), Kent County Med. Soc. (chmn. disaster com. 1971-76), Sigma Xi, Alpha Omega Alpha. K.C. Office: Alpine Med Center 2410 Gaynor Ave NW Grand Rapids MI 49504

BRAUNWARTH, JOHN BERNARD, chem. co. exec.; b. Prentice, Wis., July 14, 1929; s. Isadore Henry and Florence (Keenan) B.; B.S., Milton Coll., 1951; postgrad. Marquette U., 1951-52; Research chemist Pure Oil Co., Union Oil Co., Crystal Lake, Ill., 1952, 54-61, sr. research chemist, 1961-65; mgr. research Varney Chem. Co. div. No. Petrochem. Co., Janesville, Wis., 1965-72; v.p. tech. devel. Armstrong Chem. Co. Inc., Janesville, 1972—, also dir. Owner, operator thoroughbred race horse nursery, stable, Janesville, 1966—. Served with AUS, 1952-54. Mem. Am. Chem. Soc., A.A.A.S., Am. Soc. Quality Control, Am. Med. Technologists Assn., Horsemen's Benevolent and Protective Assn., Serra Internat. Roman Catholic. Patentee in field. Home: Rural Route 4 Janesville WI 53545 Office: 1530 S Jackson St Janesville WI 53545

BRAUTIGAM, FRANK ADOLPH, florist; b. Chgo., Dec. 8, 1915; s. Frank and Lillian Victoria (Rentzsch) B.; student pub. schs., Chgo. Owner Frank Brautigam Landscaping, 1935-39; owner, adminstr. Brautigam Florist, Chgo., 1940—, Brautigam Florist-Gifts, Brautigam Internat., Brautigam MiniMarket. Served with AUS, 1943-45. Mem. Allied Florists Assn. Ill. (past dir., pres.), Ill. State Florists Assn. (dir., past pres.), Florists Transworld Delivery (dir., past pres.), Ill. Retail Merchants Assn., Chgo. Assn. Commerce and Industry, Portage Park C. of C. (past pres.), Mich., Ind. state florists assns., Interflora (past world pres.). Clubs: Lions (past pres.). Home: 4026 N Central Ave Chicago IL 60634 Office: 4020 N Central Ave Chicago IL 60634

BRAY, PIERCE, telephone co. exec.; b. Chgo., Jan. 16, 1924; s. Harold A. and Margaret (Maclennan) B.; B.A., U. Chgo., 1948, M.B.A., 1949; m. Maud Dorothy Minto, May 14, 1955; children—Margaret Dorothy, William Harold, Andrew Pierce. Fin. analyst Ford Motor Co., Dearborn, Mich., 1949-55; cons. Booz, Allen & Hamilton, Chgo., Manila, P.I., 1955-58; mgr. pricing Cummins Engine Co., Columbus, Ind., 1958-61, controller, 1961-66; v.p. finance Weatherhead Co., Cleve., 1966-67; v.p., treas. Mid-Continent Telephone Corp., Hudson, Ohio, 1967-70, v.p. finance, treas., 1970—, dir., 1976—; dir. Cardinal Fund; instr. finance and econs. U. Detroit, 1952-54. Mem. alumni council U. Chgo. Sch. Bus. Trustee Pepper Pike Civic League; trustee, v.p. finance Beech Brook (treatment center for emotionally disturbed children). Served with AUS, 1943-46; PTO. Mem. Fin. Execs. Inst., U.S. Ind. Telephone Assn. (chmn. investor relations com.), Cleve. Treasurers Club, Delta Upsilon. Presbyterian (elder). Clubs: Downtown Athletic (N.Y.C.); Midday (Cleve.). Home: 31173 Northwood Dr Pepper Pike OH 44124 Office: 100 Executive Pkwy Hudson OH 44236

BRAY, WILLIAM GILMER, former congressman; b. Mooresville, Ind., June 17, 1903; s. Gilmer and Dorcas M. (Mitchell) B.; LL.B., Ind. U., 1927; LL.D., Vincennes U., Butler U., Marian Coll.; m. Esther F. Debra, Aug. 16, 1930; 1 son, Richard D. Admitted to Ind. bar 1927; pros. atty. 15th Ind. Jud. Dist., Martinsville, 1926-30; pvt. law practice Martinsville, 1930-41, 46-51; mem. 82d-93d Congresses from 6th-7th Ind. Dists. Served as capt. to col. U.S. Army, 1941-46; tank officer, P.T.O., 1941-45; dep. property custodian Am. Mil. Govt. in Korea, 1945-46. Decorated Silver Star. Mem. Vets. Fgn. Wars, Am. Legion, Tau Kappa Alpha, Acacia. Republican. Mason (33 deg., Shriner). Moose, Elk, Eagle. Clubs: Kiwanis, Capitol Hill, Columbia. Author: Russian Frontiers-from Muscovy to Khrushchev. Home: 489 N Jefferson St Martinsville IN 46151 Office: 210 E Morgan St Martinsville IN 46151

BREED, STERLING LARUE, educator; b. Paw Paw, Mich., Oct. 9, 1928; s. LaRue H. and Eda Lord (Ayars) B.; B.S., Western Mich. U., 1955, M.A., 1958; postgrad. Mich. State U., 1960-65, U. Mich., 1973-75; m. Betty Hansen, June 17, 1953; 1 son, Thomas Sterling. With Mich. State Police, Traverse City, 1950-53; jr. high sch. tchr., Paw Paw, 1955-56; asst. dean men Western Mich. U., Kalamazoo, 1956-60, counselor, 1960-68, asso. prof. counseling, coordinator acad. counseling, 1968-73, dir. Counseling Center, 1973-76, prof., 1977—. Bd. dirs. Mich. League for Nursing, 1974-77, pres. elect, 1977-78. Served with AUS, 1946-48; ETO. Recipient citation for meritorious service Mich. State Police, 1952. Mem. Mich. Coll. Personnel Assn. (pres. 1971-72), Am. Coll. Personnel Assn. (Mich. membership chmn. 1964-77), Mich. Personnel and Guidance Assn. (exec. bd.), Am. Assn. Humanistic Edn., Am. Assn. Higher Edn., Nat. League Nursing, AAUP, Nat. Vocat. Guidance Assn., Am. Mgmt. Assn., Sigma Tau Gamma (nat. pres. 1964-66), Phi Delta Kappa. Home: 867 Dobbin Dr Kalamazoo MI 49007

BREEDEN, REX EARL, real estate exec.; b. French Lick, Ind., Oct. 19, 1920; s. Charles H. and Ella (Lashbrooks) B.; B.S., Ind. State U., 1942; m. Joy R. Conley, Apr. 19, 1941 (div.); children—Rebecca (Mrs. Robert Cseszko), Jeanne K. (Mrs. James Matson), Diane; m. 2d, Barbara Horst Ruggles, Aug. 4, 1965. High sch. tchr., 1942-43; designer Gulf Shipbldg. Corp., 1943; pres., founder Brex Corp., 1946; founder, pres. Breeden, Inc., Columbus, Ind., 1951—; pres., founder Parkside Investment Corp., Columbus, 1960—, various other real estate devel. and investment firms; founder, dir. Columbus Bank & Trust Co., Columbus, Ind. Real estate commr. State of Ind., 1958—. Bd. dirs. William Laws Negro Scholarship Found.; trustee Ind. State U. Served to lt. (j.g.) USNR, 1943-46; PTO. Mem. Soc. Indsl. Realtors, Theta Chi. Presbyterian. Clubs: Harrison Lake Country (Columbus); Columbia (Indpls.); Ocean Reef; Key Largo. Home: Indian Hills Columbus IN 47201 Office: 1427 Washington St Columbus IN 47201

BREEN, KATHERINE ANNE, speech and lang. pathologist; b. Chgo., Oct. 31, 1948; d. Robert Stephen and Gertrude Catherine (Bader) Breen; B.S., Northwestern U., 1970; M.A. (U.S. Rehab. Services trainee), U. Mo., Columbia, 1971. Speech/lang. pathologist Fulton (Mo.) pub. schs., 1971-73; co-dir. Easter Seal Speech Clinic, Jefferson City, Mo., summers 1972, 73; speech/lang. pathologist Shawnee Mission (Kans.) pub. schs., 1973—; pvt. practice speech therapy; cons. E. Central Mo. Mental Health Center; guest lectr. Fontbonne Coll., St. Louis. Clin. certification in speech pathology. Mem. Am., Kans. speech and hearing assns., NEA, Mo. State Tchrs. Assn., Kansas City Alumni Assn. of Northwestern U. (mem. alumni admissions council), Friends of Art Nelson/Atkins Art Gallery and Museum (vol.), Zeta Phi Eta. Methodist. Home: 8-17 1100 County Line Rd Kansas City KS 66103 Office: 5005 W 95th St Shawnee Mission KS 66207

BREGSTONE, CLIFFORD EARL, bus. forms co. exec.; b. Chgo., Jan. 19, 1939; s. Philip P. and Beatrice S. (Sisken) B.; B.A., Miami U. (Ohio), 1960; m. Joan Kottler, Sept. 30, 1944; children—Debby, Pam, Greg. Salesman, Royal McBee Corp., Chgo., 1961-62; founder, pres. CBI Bus. Forms Co., Chgo., 1962—. Mem. Nat. Bus. Forms Assn. (Mem. of Year 1972). Club: Optimists. Home: 1180 Valley Rd Bannockburn IL 60015 Office: 3322 W Peterson St Chicago IL 60659

BREHER, WILLIAM RUSSELL, ins. servicing assn. exec.; b. Battle Creek, Mich., Nov. 10, 1922; s. Aaron Leonard and Lucille Clara (Hager) B.; B.A., Mich. State U., 1948; M.S., U. Wis., 1949; m. Thomasine Irene Neering, July 25, 1959; children—Joseph, Nathan, Kate, David. With U.S. Labor Dept. Washington, 1950-52; with Ford Motor Co., 1953-71, dir. employe benefits and services, Sao Raulo, Brazil, 1968-70, spl. assignment indsl. relations, Dearborn, Mich., 1970-71; exec. dir. Mich. Edn. Spl. Services Assn., East Lansing, 1971—; bus. adviser Mich. Dept. Commerce. Bd. dirs. Big Brothers Wayne County, 1956-60. Served with U.S. Army, 1943-46. Decorated Combat Infantryman. Mem. Nat. Spl. Services Assn. (exec. com.), MEA (asst. exec. dir.), Internat. Found. Employee Benefit Plans, Group Health Assn. Am., Mich. State U. Alumni Club. Roman Catholic. Clubs: Moose, Walnut Hills Country. Home: 1001 Cowley St East Lansing MI 48823 Office: 1480 Kendale Blvd East Lansing MI 48823

BREHM, THEODORE LOUIS, pub. accountant; b. Richmond, Ind., Feb. 17, 1925; s. Kenneth Louis and Bess (Moore) B.; student St. Johns U., 1943. Ball State U., 1945: A.A., George Washington U., 1948, B.A., 1948; m. Marilyn Joan Wiggins, May 6, 1950 (dec. Jan. 1971); children—Timothy Lee, Pamela Sue, Warren Daniel; m. 2d, Armonella Rose Walter, June 24, 1971; 1 adopted dau., Kelly LuAnne. Jr. accountant R.G. Rankin & Co., Washington, 1948; sr. accountant Bernard & Huffer, C.P.A.'s, Muncie, Ind., 1948-50; sr. accountant G. F. Detmer & Co., C.P.A.'s. Fort Wayne Ind. 1950-51; cost accountant controller tres. Asbestos Mfg. Co. Huntington Ind. 1951-57; sr. accountant Koeneman Borger Krouse & Dinius C.P.A.'s Fort Wayne 1957-58; exec. v.p. gen. mgr. Shuttleworth Inc. Warren Ind. 1958-59; sr. accountant Cooper, Brandt, and Brunner C.P.A.'s Fort Wayne 1959-61; principle T. L. Brehm & Co. C.P.A.'s Fort Wayne 1961—; pres. Arlington Investment Corp. Fort Wayne, 1963—; trustee, treas. Investors Trust 1965—; dir. pres. Arlington Mortgage Co. Inc.; dir. sec. Arlington Mortgage Co. Inc.; dir. sec. Arlington Utilities Inc.; dir. French Constrn., Inc., Fort Wayne, Manchester Tool & Die, Inc., North Manchester, Ind. Treas., v.p., nat. rep., dir. Anthony Wayne Council, Boy Scouts of Am., 1961—; v.p., dir. Youth for Christ, Ft. Wayne area. Served with AUS, 1944-45. Mem. Am. Inst. C.P.A.'s, Ind. Assn. C.P.A.'s, Fort Wayne Home Builders Assn. (dir.), Fort Wayne C. of C., Huntington C. of C. (v.p. 1957), Sigma Chi. Methodist (trustee). Kiwanian Clubs: Summitt, Sertoma, Olympia. Home: 4543 Shenandoah Circle Fort Wayne IN 46805 Office: 4635 Arlington Park Blvd Fort Wayne IN 46805

BREIBACH, THOMAS BRAUN, mfg. co. exec.; b. Columbus, Ohio, May 28, 1930; s. Henry Peter and Hilda G. (Braun) B.; B.C.S., Bliss Coll., Columbus, 1961; postgrad. in Mgmt., Ohio State U., 1961-65, Ind. No. U., 1969-71; m. Mabel June Neff, Dec. 15, 1951; children—James Thomas, Julie Ann. Sales research auditor C.E.C.O. Mktg., Cons. and Research Inc., San Francisco, 1964-66; mgr. sales analysis Ross Labs., Inc., Columbus, 1966-68; purchasing agt., mgr. city sales Ohio Furnace Co., Columbus, 1968-70; with Lennox Industries, Inc., Columbus, 1970—, mktg. adminstr., 1970—. Mem. Hilliard (Ohio) Planning and Zoning Commn., 1967—, Hilliard Park and Recreation Commn., 1976—; vice chmn. Hilliard Soc. Arts, 1977—. Served in USN, 1947-50, in USAF, 1950-54. Mem. Nat. Mktg. Assn. (Man of Year 1974), Internat. Soc. Mktg. Adminstrs. (dir.), Am. Mktg. Assn. Democrat. Methodist. Club: Masons. Home: 5117 Grandon Dr Hilliard OH 43026 Office: 1711 Olentangy River Rd Columbus OH 43212

BREIHAN, EDNA MARIA THIES (MRS. ARMIN HENRY BREIHAN), ret. educator; b. Flossmoor, Ill., Jan. 22, 1911; d. Henry Frederick and Anna (Cohrs) Thies; student Valparaiso U., 1928-30; A.B., Coll. of St. Francis, 1953; M.Ed., De Paul U., 1957; certificate advanced study in reading U. Chgo., 1966; m. Armin Henry Breihan, June 26, 1937; children—Joanne, James. Tchr., Lutheran Parochial Schs., Detroit, Chgo., 1930-37; pvt. tchr. remedial reading, Homewood, Ill., Flossmoor, 1945-51; tchr. Culbertson Sch., Joliet, Ill., 1953-57, Central Sch., Lockport, Ill., 1955-58; reading cons. Lockport Twp. High Sch. 1958-66; reading coordinator Lockport Twp. Sch. Dist. 205, 1966-71, chmn. reading dept., 1971-75. Mem. Lockport Woman's Club (hon.), NEA, Nat. Soc. for Study Edn., Internat. Reading Assn. (past pres. Will County council), Ill. Edn. Assn., Internat. Platform Assn., Lockport Bus. and Profl. Women's Assn., Assn. Supervision and Curriculum Devel., Am. Inst. Mgmt., AAUW, Delta Kappa Gamma, Chi Sigma Xi. Lutheran. Club: Joliet Country. Home: 1512 Briggs St Lockport IL 60441

BREITMEYER, RUDOLF GUSTAV, hosp. adminstr.; b. Hildesheim, Germany, Aug. 9, 1941; s. Gustav and Julia (Stasiaczek) B.; came to U.S., 1957, naturalized, 1962; B.A., Lewis Coll., 1963; Ph.D., U. Ill., 1968. Psychologist, Adler Center, Champaign, Ill., 1968-70; dir. pace sociolization pgram Adolf Meyer Center, Decatur, Ill., 1970-72, dir. Pace Evaluation and Tng., 1972-73, asst. supt. prof. and clin. support services, 1973—; adj. asst. prof. clin. psychology U.

Ill., Urbana-Champaign, 1971-72; cons. New Castle (Ind.) State Hosp., 1974—. Mem. Am. Psychol. Assn. Home: 576 W Ash St Decatur IL 62526 Office: Adolf Meyer Center Decatur IL 62526

BREKKEN, PHILIP MICHAEL, counselor; b. Crookston, Minn., Jan. 22, 1952; s. Albert Jerome and Wanda Irene (Pester) B.; B.A., Denver U., 1974; B.A. in Psychology and Social Work, St. Cloud State U., 1975, M.S. in Counseling and Guidance, 1975; m. Terri Ann Boucher, Nov. 26, 1976. Guidance counselor Drug Abuse Program Red Lake (Minn.) Band Chippewa Indians, 1976—; facilitator, auditor Drug Info. Service, Minn. Behavorial Inst., Anoka, 1976—. Mem. chem. dependency adv. bd. Upper Miss. Mental Health Center, Bemidji, Am. Indian Drug Coalition. Mem. Am. Personnel and Guidance Assn., Assn. Non-White Concerns in Personnel and Guidance, Minn. Chem. Dependency Assn., Amateur Hockey Assn. U.S. Home: Rural Route #6 Box 374 Bemidji MN 56601 Office: PO Box 50 Red Lake MN 56671 MBI 431 1/2 E Main St Anoka MN 55303

BRELSFORD, WILLIAM H., II, mathematician, educator; b. Dayton, Ohio, July 15, 1939; s. William H. Brelsford and Martha Beverly (Bunger) Brelsford Rose; B.S. in Edn., Ashland (Ohio) Coll., 1961; postgrad. Xavier U., 1965; M.A.T. (NSF grantee), Southeastern (Okla.) State Coll., 1966; postgrad. (NSF grantee) U. Kans., 1967, (NSF grantee) Oberlin Coll., 1968, Kent (Ohio) State U., 1973; m. Joanne Rosalie Winfield, July 25, 1959; children—Gregg Lee, Mark Allen, Joel Lance. Tchr. math., athletic coach, Madison Twp. Schs., Dayton, Ohio, 1961-67; asst. prof. math., football coach, Ashland Coll., 1967—. Mem. Nat. Council Tchrs. Math., Math. Assn. Am. Mem. Brethren Ch. Home: 1651 Co Rd 995 RD 6 Ashland OH 44805 Office: Ashland Coll Ashland OH 44805

BRENEMAN, JAMES CHESTER, physician; b. Sherburn, Minn., Mar. 20, 1922; s. Henry Ellis and Clara S. (Larson) B.; B.A., Gustavus Adolphus Coll., 1942; B.S., U. Minn., 1945, M.D., 1946; m. Marylou Joyce Helmerson, Oct. 4, 1946; children—Craig J., Lisa Jill. Intern, San Francisco Hosp., 1945-46; resident Swedish Hosp., Mpls., 1946: practice medicine specializing in allergy, Galesburg, Mich., 1948—; clin. instr. Borgess Hosp., 1950-66; pres. Galesburg Clinic, Inc. 1964—, Nursing Homes Corp., 1969-77, Kalamazoo Med. Profl. Corp., 1968—; v.p. Burgess Internat. Corp., 1968-76. Pres., Enuresis Found., 1963-66, Allergy-Immunology Internat., 1965—. Served to capt., M.C., AUS. 1946-48. Recipient Ross award for outstanding contbn. to med. lit., 1959; award for excellence Internat. Coll. Angiology, 1964; Honors Achievement award Angiology Research Found., 1964-65. Diplomate Am. Bd. Allergy and Immunology. Mem. AMA, Mich. Med. Soc., Am. Coll. Allergists (chmn. food allergy com. 1971—, bd. regents 1975—), Kalamazoo Acad. Medicine, N.Y. Acad. Scis., Mich. Allergy Soc., Kalamazoo C. of C. (past pres. Galesburg div.), Lambda Sigma. Author: Help Your Bedwetting Child, 1962; Basics of Food Allergy, 1977; contbr. articles to med. jours. Patentee med. and surg. instruments. Home: 9880 E Michigan Ave Galesburg MI 49053 Office: Box 177 Galesburg MI 49053

BRENNAN, CONSTANCE LOUISE, gerontol. counselor; b. Keokuk, Iowa, May 30, 1952; d. Lowell Dixon and Doris Josephine (McCollister) B.; B.S., Central Mo. State U., 1974; M.S., U. Nebr., Omaha, 1977. Nurse aid Prairie View Nursing Home, Lewiston, Mo., 1969-70; resident asst. Central Mo. State U., Warrensburg, 1971-72; nurse aid Pleasant View Nursing Home, Warrensburg, 1973-74; resident adviser Excelsior Springs (Mo.) Job Corps. Center for Women, 1974-75; nurse aid Med. Personnel Pool, Omaha, 1975-77; asst. gerontology U. Nebr. at Omaha, 1977—, also research asst. U. Nebr. Med. Center. Profl. and Bus. Women's Club scholar, 1970. Mem. Am., Nebr. personnel and guidance assns., Gerontol. Soc.. Western Gerontol. Soc., Nat. Council Aging, U. Nebr. Gerontol. Assn. (pres. 1976-78), Counseling and Guidance Student Assn., Psi Chi. Club: Central Mo. State U. Psychology (pres. 1972-74). Home: 139 N 32d Ave Apt 3 Omaha NE 68131

BRENNAN, DAVID LEO, lawyer; b. Akron, Ohio, July 5, 1931; s. Daniel Clarke and Josephine Agnes (Winum) B.; B.Sc., Ohio State U., 1953; J.D., Western Res. U., 1957; m. Ann Elizabeth Amer, July 6, 1957; children—Elizabeth, John, Kathleen, Nancy. Admitted to Ohio bar, 1957; practice law, Akron, 1957—; pres. firm Amer, Cunningham & Brennan, 1963—; chmn. bd. Hamlin Steel Products, Inc., SW Wheel & Mfg. Co., Dallas, LEC Electric, Dallas, Brenlin Corp., Las Vegas; dir., officer Neilson Wheel Co., Milw., Hamlin Constrn. Co., Akron, Ohio, City Machine and Wheel Co., Akron; trustee Delnor Neptune Properties, 1973—. Trustee Akron Bar Assn. Found., St. Sebastian Parish Found. Mem. Akron (sec. 1970-72, officer 1972—), Am., Ohio bar assns. Home: 1200 Sunset View Dr Akron OH 44313 Office: First Nat Tower Akron OH 44308

BRENNAN, GALE PATRICK, publisher, author; b. Manitowoc, Wis., Mar. 12, 1927; s. Harold and Irene (Cavanough) B.; Ph.B. in Journalism, Marquette U., 1951; m. Mary Elizabeth Casey, Jan. 31, 1953; children—Katherine (Mrs. Tom Dillig), Bridget Gale, John Patrick, Brian Daniel, Peter Thomas (dec.), Patrick Cavanaugh, Maura Casey, Margaret Mary, Shiela Marie, Therese Elizabeth, Joel Thomas, Sarah Mauve. Writer, Milw. Cath. Charities, 1951; editor Miller Brewing Co., Milw., 1951-55; writer, editor Robin Press Pubs., Milw., 1955-58; pres. Communications Inc. & Gale Brennan & Assos. writing, advt., pub. relations, Milw., 1958—; pres. Brennan Books, Inc., Milw., 1972—, also author, editor. Served with AUS, 1945-47. Clubs: Milwaukee Press, Oconomowoc Golf, Wauwatosa Curling. Author: Elihu the Elephant, 1970; Gloomy Gus the Hippotomus, 1970; Dugan the Duck, 1976. Editor: Emil the Eagle, 1971; Freddie the Frog, 1972; Ulysses S. Ant and Robert E. Flea, 1976. Home: 18660 Bonnie Ln Brookfield WI 53005 Office: 2120 W Clybourn St Milwaukee WI 53233

BRENNAN, ROBERT WALTER, assn. exec.; b. Chgo., Mar. 12, 1934; s. Walter R. and Grace A. (Mason) B.; B.S., U. Wis., Madison, 1957; m. Mary J. Engler, June 15, 1962; children—Barbara, Susan (twins). Tchr., coach Waukesha (Wis.) High Sch., 1960-63; track coach U. Wis., Madison, 1963-71; exec. asst. to mayor City of Madison, 1971-73; pres. C. of C., Madison, 1973—; dir. Cherokee Park, Inc. Chmn. bd. dirs. Clyde Dupin Reachout Ministries, 1974—; mem. bd. dirs. Bill Glass Evangelistic Assn., 1972—. Named Madison Favorite Son, 1971. Mem. Wis. C. of C. (dir.), Downtown Rotary, Madison Urban League, U. Wis., Alumni Assn., Nat. W Club, Wis. Urban League, C. of C. Execs., Wis. Hist. Soc., Fellowship Christian Athletes, Theta Delta Chi, Phi Epsilon Kappa. Midwest correspondent Track & Field News, 1963-71; spl. events cons. Letterman Mag., 1971. Home: 5514 Comanche Way Madison WI 53704 Office: PO Box 71 Madison WI 53701

BRENNEMAN, RALPH FRANCIS, mfg. co. exec.; b. Cedar Rapids, Iowa, Feb. 6, 1932; s. Ernest E. and Mary N. (Webster) Brenneman; m. Sandra Lee Matthews, Dec. 10, 1955; children—Brad, Lisa, Scott, Erin, R. David. Buyer, Collins Radio Co., 1954-59; asst. mgr. Deeco Inc., 1959-63; purchasing mgr. Collins Radio Co., 1963-73; founded Brenneman & Asso. Inc., 1973—. Mem. Chs. United, Cedar Rapids/Marion, Iowa; past mem. exec. com. Lutheran Interparish Ministry, chmn. joint purchasing com.; chmn. tast force for aux. funding Luth. Family Service; benevolence rep. Iowa Synod, Luth. Ch. in Am. Mem. Elks, Am. Assn. Small Businessmen, IEEE. Home: 1915 McGowan Blvd Marion IA 52302 Office: 225 35th St Marion IA 52302

BRENNER, HOWARD JOSEPH, banker; b. Tell City, Ind., Sept. 16, 1919; s. Fred N. and Ida G. (Lanman) B.; grad. high sch.; courses Am. Inst. Banking; m. Florence M. Hollahan, June 4, 1947; children—Ann, Howard J. Clk., asst. cashier Tell City Nat. Bank, 1937-42; asst. nat. bank examiner 8th Fed. Res. Dist., 1942-46; auditor, asst. cashier, corr. bank rep. First Nat. Bank, Memphis, Tenn., 1946-50; exec. v.p., dir. City Bank and Trust Co., Natchez, Miss., 1950-59; pres., dir. Tell City (Ind.) Nat. Bank, 1959—; dir. Louisville br. Fed. Res. Bank. Mem. Sch. Reorgn. Com., Tell City. Bd. dirs. Perry County Meml. Hosp. Found.; sec.-treas. Tell City Nat. Found., Inc.; v.p. Hemophilia of Ind., Inc. Mem. Ind. Bankers Assn. (treas., dir.), Independent Bankers Assn. Ind. (dir.), C. of C. (pres. 1963-64). Clubs: K.C., Kiwanis (pres. 1969-70), Moose, Hoosier Heights Country (Tell City). Home: 548 25th St Tell City IN 47586 Office: 601 Main St Tell City IN 47586

BRENNER, ROSAMOND DROOKER, musician; b. Cambridge, Mass., Mar. 23, 1931; d. Abraham Lazarus and Mary (Jacobs) Drooker; A.B., Radcliffe Coll., 1953, A.M. in Teaching, 1954; postgrad. (Fulbright grantee) Vienna (Austria) Acad. Music, 1954-56; profl. certificate in organ Geneva Conservatory Music, 1959; Ph.D. (Univ. scholar), Brandeis U., 1968; m. Alfred E. Brenner, June 28, 19S8; children—Tamara, Kendra, Lyle. Teaching fellow in music Brandeis U., 1964-66; prof. music history, form. analysis, Boston Conservatory Music, 1967-70; prof. musicology Am. Conservatory Music, Chgo., 1971-75; mem. faculty Columbia Coll., Chgo., 1972-74; organist, choir dir. Phillips Congl. Ch., Mass., 1969-70, Trinity Episcopal Ch., Wheaton, Ill., 1971—; pvt. tchr. organ, piano. Radcliffe scholar, 1953-54. Mem. Am. Guild Organists (asso.), Coll. Music Soc., Ill. State Music Tchrs. Assn., Am. Musicological Soc., Glen Ellyn (Ill.) Musicians' Club. Bahai. Musical compositions include: The Choice, cantata, 1975; The Trumpet-Pen, oratorio, 1977. Home: 726 N Park Blvd Glen Ellyn IL 60137

BRENNY, DENNIS HAROLD, dentist; b. St. Cloud, Minn., Oct. 24, 1939; s. Edward Matthew and Regina Marie (Bolduc) B.; student St. Cloud State Coll., 1957-58; D.D.S., Creighton U., 1964; m. Mary Elizabeth McCollum, Dec. 28, 1963; children—Gregory Paul, Christine Therese, Troy Anthony. Dentist, Payne Ave. Med. Clinic, St. Paul, 1966-67; practice dentistry, Crystal, Minn., 1967-69, Mpls., 1969—; tchr. dental health Osseo and Mpls. Pub. Sch. Systems, 1968—. Pres., Christian Family Movement, 1970-71; mem. head music coordination St. Gerards Liturgy Commn., 1971-72, chmn., 1973-74; area rep. St. Gerard's Parish Council, 1974-76, family center coordinating couple, 1974-75; pre marriage instr. Catholic Youth Center, 1968-70; active Community Action, 1970; asst. Webelos leader Boy Scouts Am., 1976-77. Served to capt. M.C., USAF, 1964-66. Mem. Mpls. Dist., Northside dental socs. Clubs: Creighton University Alumni (sec.-treas. 1968-69, v.p. 1970-71), Creighton (pres. 1972-73) (both Omaha, Neb.). Home: 8530 Riverview Ln N Minneapolis MN 55444 Office: 4050 Colfax Ave N Minneapolis MN 55412

BRENTON, WILLIAM HENRY, banker; b. Dallas Center, Iowa, June 30, 1924; s. Woodward Harold and Etta (Spurgeon) B.; B.S. in Commerce, U. Iowa, 1949; grad. Advanced Mgmt. Program Harvard, 1971; m. Natalie Graham, June 15, 1948; children—Woodward Graham, Natalie, William Henry. Cashier, v.p. Northwest Des Moines Nat. Bank, 1950-55; v.p. Nat. Bank of Des Moines, 1955-58, pres., chmn., 1958—, dir., 1955—; treas. Brenton Banks, Inc., 1955-64, pres., 1964-69, chmn. bd., 1969—; chmn. bd. Benton Co. Bank & Trust Co., Vinton, Iowa, Brenton Bank & Trust Co., Cedar Rapids, Iowa, First Nat. Bank Perry (Iowa), Jefferson (Iowa) State Bank, Palo Alto Co. State Bank, Emmetsburg; dir. South Des Moines Nat. Bank, Brenton Bank & Trust Co., Clarion, Brenton Bank & Trust Co., Urbandale, Brenton State Bank, Dallas Center, Brenton State Bank, Eagle Grove, Dallas County State Bank, Fidelity Brenton Bank & Trust Co., Marshalltown, First Nat. Bank, Davenport, Iowa, NW Brenton Nat. Bank, Des Moines, Employers Mut. Co., Des Moines, Warren County Bank & Trust Co., Indianola; pres., treas. Brenco Automation Center, Inc.; chmn. Brenton Bros., Inc. Bd. dirs. Des Moines Art Center, pres., 1970-72; trustee Coffin Fine Arts Trust; bd. dirs. Iowa Methodist Hosp., Des Moines, Greater Des Moines Com.; trustee, mem. exec. com. Drake U., Des Moines; trustee Iowa Coll. Found. Served with USAAF, 1943-46. Mem. Beta Gamma Sigma, Delta Tau Delta. Republican. Presbyterian. Clubs: Wakonda, Des Moines (Des Moines); University (Chgo.); Tryall (Jamaica). Office: 2840 Ingersoll Ave Des Moines IA 50312

BRESLIN, JOHN BERNARD, hosp. food service adminstr.; b. Altoona, Pa., Sept. 2, 1930; s. Cornelius Aloysius and Marcella Edna (McGraw) B.; Asso. in Accounting, Zeth Bus. Coll., 1948; m. Katherine Ann Stefanic, Sept. 8, 1956; children—Neal, Maureen, Stephanie, Marcella. Agt., Union News Co., Greensburg, Pa., 1948-49; storeroom mgr. Northwest Airlines, Washington, 1949, St. Paul, 1950-51, Detroit, 1951-56; asst. gen. mgr. Willowrun Airport, Ypsilanti, Mich., 1961-65; gen. mgr. Profit Foods Co., Chgo., 1965-67, Machus Red Fox Inc., Birmingham, Mich., 1967-69; asst. to pres. Hosp. Dietary Inc., Detroit, 1969-70; dir. food services St. Joseph Hosp., Mt. Clemens, Mich., 1970—; instr. culinary arts dept. Macomb County Community Coll., 1972-78; cons. to food and beverage industry, 1967—. Served in U.S. Army, 1951-52; Korea. Recipient Instns. Mag. Design award for Total Design, 1968, Plaque award Mich. Hosp. Assn., 1973. Mem. Am. Soc. Hosp. Food Service Adminstrs., Am. Hosp. Assn., Food Service Execs. Assn., Mich., Nat. (Gold medal menu award 1966, 67, 68, 71, 76) restaurant assns. Roman Catholic. Home: 35335 Alta Vista Sterling Heights MI 48077 Office: 215 North Ave Mount Clements MI 48043

BRESNAHAN, RICHARD ANTHONY, army officer; b. Fitchburg, Mass., Nov. 14, 1924; s. James Anthony and Eva Ora (Gagnon) B.; m. Rachel A. DeLisle, Dec. 30, 1946; children—Mark Kevin, Kenneth Michael; student Colgate U., 1943; B.S., U.S. Mil. Acad., 1946; postgrad. Command and Gen. Staff Coll., 1958, Army War Coll., 1966, U. Pitts, 1969. Commd. 2d lt. U.S. Army, 1946, advanced through grades to maj. gen., 1973; instr. phys. edn. U.S. Mil. Acad., 1954-57; mem. staff and faculty Command and Gen. Staff Coll., Ft. Leavenworth, Kans., 1958-61; served with 7th U.S. Army, Germany, 1961-63; comdr. 1st Bn., 13th Inf., 8th Inf. Div., Germany, 1963-64; served with Hdqrs. Central Army Group, Germany, 1964-65, Tng. Div., Office Dep. Chief of Staff, Personnel, Washington, 1966-67, Office Army Chief of Staff, Washington, 1967-68; chief Force Devel. Div., Hdqrs. U.S. Army, Vietnam, 1968-69; comdr. 1st Brigade, 101st Airborne Div., Vietnam, 1969; dir. mil. studies Far East, dept. mil. planning Army War Coll., Carlisle Barracks, Pa., 1969-70, chief of staff, sec., 1970-71; chief Strategic Plans/Policy Div., Office Joint Chiefs of Staff, Washington, 1971-73; chief of staff Fifth U.S. Army, Ft. Sam Houston, Tex., 1974-75; comdr. U.S. Army Readiness Region V, Ft. Sheridan, Ill., 1975—. Mem. exec. council, bd. dirs. Chgo. USO, 1976—. Mem. Assn. U.S. Army. Decorated Silver Star medal, Legion of Merit with 3 oak leaf clusters, Bronze Star medal, Air medal with 13 oak leaf clusters, Army Commendation medal with 2 oak leaf clusters, Combat Inf. badge with star, Republic of Vietnam Gallantry Cross with palm and oak leaf cluster, Parachutist badge. Home: 111 Logan Loop Fort Sheridan IL 60037 Office: Hdqrs US Army Readiness Region V Fort Sheridan IL 60037

BRESSLER, (MAYBELLE) JEAN, educator; b. Oakland, Nebr.; d. Daniel Arthur and Maybelle Blanche (Guss) Bressler; B.A., U. Nebr., 1950, M.A 1958, Ph.D., 1965. Tchr. English, Pacific Beach Jr. High Sch., San Diego, 1950-52; tchr. English, Spanish, South High Sch., Omaha, 1952-59; teaching asst. English, U. Nebr., 1959-61; tchr. English, Spanish, South High Sch., Omaha, 1961-63, chmn. English and fgn. lang. dept., 1963-66; instr. English, U. Nebr., 1964, asst. prof. English edn., 1966-69, asso. prof., 1969—. Pilot tchr. Project English, Omaha Pub. Schs., 1962-66; co-dir. Workshop in English for Tchrs. in Dist. 66 Schs., 1967; mem. North Central Assn. Evaluation Team, 1969—; co-dir. workshop in mem. ad hoc com. certification English and lang. arts linguistics, 1970-71; dir. workshop in humanities; adviser Nebr. chpt., Nat. Assn. for Humanities Edn., Nebr. Alliance for Arts. Chmn. Henry Doorly Zoo Docents. Mem. NEA, Nat. Council Tchrs. English, Tchrs. English to Speakers of Other Langs., Nebr. Theatre Assn., Internat. Reading Assn., Am. Dialect Soc., Assn. Supervision and Curriculum Devel., Neb. Council Tchrs. English, Conf. English Edn., Conf. Coll. Composition and Communication, Internat. Fund Animals, Fund for Animals (dir.), Nat. Mustang Assn., Omaha Zool. Soc. (dir.), Animal Protection Inst. (dir.), Nat. Cat Protection Soc., Pet Pride, Joslyn Art Mus., Kappa Delta Pi, Republican. Episcopalian. Contbr. articles to profl. jours. Home: 12724 Arbor St Omaha NE 68144

BRETT, RICHARD JOHN, speech pathologist; b. Chgo., Sept. 5, 1921; s. Richard J. and Emily (Salter) B.; B.Ed., No. Ill. State Tchrs. Coll., 1943; M.S., U. Ill., 1947; student U. Amsterdam (Holland), 1949, U. Chgo., 1948-49, 62, 66-67, Northwestern U., 1967. Speech supr. Summer Residential Clinic, U. Ill., Urbana, 1948, 50, 52; speech pathologist Waukegan (Ill.) High Schs., 1946—; chmn. Chgo. Regional Interviewing Com. for Exchange of Tchrs., U.S. Office Edn., 1962—; del. to Internat. Fedn. of Free Tchr. Unions, Switzerland. 1949. Founder, Pub. Sch. Caucus, Chgo., 1973, chmn., 1973-76. Served with U.S. Army, 1943-45. Mem. Am. (membership com. 1975-77, conv. program com. 1974, 77), Ill. (chmn. legis. com. 1964-65, treas. 1977—) speech hearing assns., Internat. Council Exceptional Children (pres. Chgo. suburban chpt. 1949-50), Am. (co-chmn. internat. relations com. 1952-63), Ill. (chmn. profl. standards com. 1952-57), Lake County (pres. 1949-51, 64-67) fedns. tchrs., UN Assn., Mus. Contemporary Art, ACLU, Common Cause. Clubs: National Travel, Travelers Century. Compiler: World Study and Travel for Teachers, 1952—; editor Five-O-Format, 1951-56, 66-69. Home: 616 4th St Waukegan IL 60085 Office: Waukegan East High School 1011 Washington St Waukegan IL 60085

BREWER, DONALD EDWARD, advt. agy. exec.; b. Indpls., Mar. 8, 1921; s. Donald Edward and Virginia Ann (Pickens) B.; B.S. in Elec. Engring., Purdue U., 1943; m. Annie Elizabeth Muller, Aug. 12, 1943; children—Donald, Richard, David. Asst. sales mgr. Esterling-Angus Co., Indpls., 1946-48; acct. exec. C.M. Gray Advt., Detroit, 1948-52; sales mgr. Radioactive Products Inc., Detroit, 1952-54; founder, pres. Brewer Assos. Inc., Dearborn, Mich., 1954—; dir. First Fed. Savs. Dearborn. Bd. dirs. Dearborn YMCA, Met. Detroit council Girl Scouts U.S.A. Served to lt., USNR, 1944-46. Mem. Assn. Indsl. Advertisers. Dearborn C. of C. (dir. 1971—), Sigma Delta Chi, Beta Theta Pi. Home and Office: 806 Oakwood Blvd Dearborn MI 48124

BREWER, GEORGE EUGENE FRANCIS, chem. cons.; b. Vienna, Austria, Jan. 23, 1909; s. Ernest and Sophia (Segalla) B.; A.B., State Coll. Vienna, 1928; M.Sc., U. Vienna, 1930, Ph.D. in Chemistry, 1932; m. Frances Joan Werner, June 29, 1933 (dec. Nov. 1965); m. Maxine R. Levin, Mar. 4, 1967. Came to U.S., 1940, naturalized, 1945. Asst. lectr. U. Vienna (Austria), 1933-36; tech. mgr. S. Wolf & Co. Textile Refining Mill, Erlach, Austria, 1936-38; lectr. Inst. de l'Industrie Textile de Brabant, Bruxelles, Belgium, 1939; prof. Rosary Coll., River Forest, Ill., 1940-43; bio-chemist NRC project, Elgin (Ill.) State Hosp., 1943-44; prof. chemistry, head dept. Marygrove Coll., Detroit, 1944-67; cons. Ford Motor Co., Detroit, 1957-67, staff scientist Mfg. Devel. Center, Dearborn, Mich., 1968-72; now coating cons. Matiello Meml. lectr. Fedn. of Socs. Paint Tech., 1973. Mem. NRC Com. on Ciphers, Codes and Punched Card Techniques, Washington, 1957-59; abstractor Chem. Abstracts, 1948-63. Recipient Midgley medal Detroit sect. Am. Chem. Soc., 1969, Doolittle award, div. organic coatings and plastics chemistry, 1969. Fellow Am. Inst. Chemists (chmn. Mich. inst. 1969, pres. 1977); mem. Am. Chem. Soc. (councillor, 1951—; chmn. Detroit sect., 1960, sec. div. organic coatings and plastics chemistry 1971, chmn. 1974), AAAS, Met. Detroit Sci. Club (dir. 1948), N.Y. Acad. Sci., Nat. Sci. Tchrs. Assn., Catholic Austrian Confraternity, Chem. Coaters Assn. (program chmn. 1971-73, dir. 1974—, pres. 1976), Assn. Analytical Chemists (pres. 1959), Mich. Coll. Chem. Tchrs. Assn. (pres. 1954), Engring. Soc. Detroit, Assn. Cons. Chemists and Chem. Engrs. Contbr. articles to profl. jours. Patentee electrophoretic deposition organic coatings. Home: 11065 E Grand River Rd Brighton MI 48116 Office: care Coating Cons 11065 E Grand River Rd Brighton MI 48116

BREWER, JAMES ASHLEY, automobile mfg. co. exec.; grad. So. Meth. U.; postgrad. Rice Inst. Div. mgr. Ford Motor Co. Mem. Alpha Tau Omega. Clubs: Masons, Shriners. Home: 25910 Kilreigh Dr Farmington Hills MI 49025

BREWER, JOSEPH EVERETT, psychologist; b. Joplin, Mo., May 31, 1914; s. Icem Elva and Maude (McCool) B.; student Parsons Jr. Coll., 1932-34; B.A., U. Kan., 1936, M.A., 1937; Ph.D., U. Ill., 1940; m. Helen Margaret Davidson, Sept. 11, 1936; children—Margaret Antoinette, David Everett. Research asso. U. Ill., Urbana, 1940-41; clin. psychologist Louisville Mental Hygiene Clinic, 1941-46; insr. U. Louisville, 1942-46; asst. dir. Wichita (Kan.) Guidance Center, 1946-49, dir., 1949—. Chmn. adv. commn. Instl. Mgmt. and Community Mental Health Programs, State of Kan., 1968-72. Fellow Am., Kan. psychol. assns.; mem. Wichita Psychol. Assn. (pres. 1966-67), Assn. Dirs. Community Mental Health Centers of Kan. (pres. 1963-68). Home: 2531 N Roosevelt St Wichita KS 67220 Office: 415 N Poplar St Wichita KS 67214

BREWER, MAXINE REGINA ROSENTHAL (MRS. GEORGE E.F. BREWER), artist; b. Toledo, Aug. 31, 1909; d. Edwin M. and Ester (Loeb) Rosenthal; student Wicker Art Sch., Detroit, 1922-27, Andre L'Hote Atelier, Paris, France, 1930-31, Art Sch. Soc. Arts and Crafts, Detroit, 1945-47; m. Hoke Levin, Sept. 14, 1933 (dec. 1960); children—Barbara (Mrs. Reuben Bergman), Frances (Mrs. Koerner), Margaret (Mrs. John Larcade); m. 2d, George E.F. Brewer, Mar. 4, 1967. Dir., Newman Devel. Co., Detroit, 1935-45, Hadley of Worcester, Mass., 1960-63, Hadley of Springfield, Mass., 1960-63; one man show at Detroit Artists Market, 1933; exhibited in group shows at Mich. Artists Annual Exhbn., Am. Painting and Sculpture, Chgo., Pa. Acad. Fine Arts, South Bend Art Assn., Mich. Regional, Mich. Watercolor Soc., Toledo Area Artists, Scarab Club Watercolor Exhbn.; represented in permanent collections at Northwood Inst., Midland, Mich. Pres., Balmoral Found., Detroit, 1956-58, Hoke and Maxine Levin Found., Detroit, 1958-76; 1st pres. Detroit City

Theater, 1967-68, bd. dirs., 1969—; sec. bd. trustees Art Sch. Soc. Arts and Crafts, Detroit, 1957-69, v.p., 1970—; mem. bd. advisers Wayne State U. Press. Recipient 1st prize oils Detroit Soc. Women Painters and Sculptors, 1956, 58, 59, 60. Mem. Detroit Symphony Soc., Founders Soc. Detroit Inst. Arts, Archives Am. Art, Council Jewish Women, Friends Detroit Pub. Library, Livingston County Art Assn., Detroit Soc. Women Painters and Sculptors, Mich. Acad. Sci., Arts, and Letters. Office: 11065 E Grand River Rd Brighton MI 48116

BREWER, ROBERT JAMES, accountant; b. Racine, Wis., Sept. 27, 1941; s. Burton Roy and Henrietta Carrie (Christenson) B.; grad. high sch.; m. Susan Estelle Degarmo, May 26, 1962; children—James and John (twins), Deborah, Jeffrey. Jr. accountant, Raymond P. Myer & Co. C.P.A.'s, Racine, 1959-63; office mgr., accountant Horner Farms, Union Grove, Wis., 1963-69; pvt. practice pub. accounting, Union Grove, Wis., 1969—. Sec., dir. Horner's Farms, Inc., 1973—, Horners, Inc., 1973—. Active Boy Scouts; adviser Jr. Achievement; mgr. Mt. Pleasant Recreation Softball League, 1974-75; active fund drive for Meml. Pool, 1972—. Accredited Accreditation Council for Accountancy. Served with USAR, 1961-67. Mem. Nat. Soc. Pub. Accountants, Nat. Assn. Accountants, Wis. Assn. Accountants. Methodist. Lion. Home and Office: 408 S Fancher Rd Racine WI 53406

BREWER, RUTH RUSSELL (MRS. JOHN I. BREWER), civic worker; b. Great Bend, Kan., June 21, 1904; d. Francis Vernon and Jettie (McBride) Russell; B.A., U. Wis., 1921; M.A., Columbia, 1923; m. John I. Brewer, June 2, 1928; 1 son, John V. Instr., Bradley U., Peoria, Ill., 1923-26; service rep. Trift Inc., Oak Park, Ill., 1927. Head surg. dressing unit ARC, Denver, 1943-44; chmn. women's div. Joint Appeal, Chgo., 1957; mem. woman's planning bd. Crusade of Mercy, 1957-69; treas. Kenwood Social Service Club, Chgo., 1953, 1st v.p., 1954, pres., 1955; treas. women's bd. Women's Aux. of Goodwill Industries, 1962-63. Bd. dirs., corr. sec., 1st v.p. woman's aux. Infant Welfare Soc., Chgo., 1960-63, pres., 1965-66, bd. advisers woman's aux., 1967-69, bd. dirs., 1968-71. Mem. Woman's bd. YWCA-Met. Chgo., 1968—. Mem. Kappa Alpha Theta. Club: Woman's Athletic (Chgo.). Home: 860 Lake Shore Dr Chicago IL 60611

BREY, JUDITH MARGRAVE, counselor; b. Saginaw, Mich., Feb. 14, 1937; d. Charles Vincent and Dorothy Margaret (Robarge) Margrave; B.A., Aquinas Coll., 1959; M.A., Western Mich. U., 1971; children—Harold Dean, Jr., Jarl Joseph. Dir. alumni relations Aquinas Coll., 1969-72, counselor Human Devel. Center, 1969-72; counselor Forest Hills Central High Sch., Grand Rapids, Mich., 1972—; pvt. practice counseling, Grand Rapids, Mich., 1976—. Pres. St. Marys Hosp. Guild, Grand Rapids. Mem. Mich. (pres.), Am., W. Mich. personnel guidance assns., Mich. Assn. Measurement and Evaluation in Guidance. Club: Women's City (Grand Rapids). Home: 1681 Radcliff St SE Grand Rapids MI 49506 Office: 2300 Raybrook St SE Suite 305 Grand Rapids MI 49506 and 5901 Hall St SE Grand Rapids MI 49506

BREZILL, THOMAS CHRISTOPHER, JR., counselor, educator; b. Chgo., Mar. 15, 1946; s. Thomas C. and Willie Margaret (Schooley) B.; student Loop Jr. Coll., 1965-66, Nev. So. U., 1968; B.A., Western Ill. U., 1972; M.S., 1973; postgrad. U. N.C., 1974, U. Ill., 1976, George Williams Coll., 1977; m. Kassandra Irene Rainge, Apr. 24. 1976. Computer operator Sears Roebuck & Co., Chgo., 1968-71; resident hall asst. Western Ill. U., 1970-71; student tchr. Farragut High Sch., Chgo., 1972; intern Chgo. City Colls., 1972; instr. psychology N.C. A. and T. State U., Greensboro, 1973-75, dir.-coordinator student activities, 1973-75; tchr. B.O.A.S.T. Program, Chgo. Bd. Edn., 1975-76; counselor Olive Harvey Coll., Chgo., 1975-77, Malcolm X Coll., Chgo., 1977—; organizer Student Leadership Conf., 1970, 71; co-founder Prairie Courts Tutoring Center, 1966. Recipient Humanitarian award Western Ill. U.; EDPA-HEW fellow, 1972. Mem. Nat. Assn. Student Personnel Adminstrs., Ill. Guidance and Personnel Assn., Nat. Entertainment Conf., Am. Coll. Personnel Assn., Am. Personnel and Guidance Assn., Assn. Non-White Concerns, Am., Ill. fedns. tchrs., Cook County Tchrs. Union, Phi Alpha Theta; Alpha Phi Alpha. Democrat. Roman Catholic. Clubs: Esquire, Inc., Mahja Rahja, Inc. Home: 221 W 90th Pl Chicago IL 60620 Office: 1900 W Van Buren St Chicago IL 60612

BRICK, SIDNEY J., lawyer; b. Wichita, Kans., Feb. 21, 1909; s. Herman and Rose (Ringel) B.; student U. Wichita, 1927-30; LL.B., U. Kans., 1933, J.D., 1933; m. Clarice Ann Dugan, Nov. 28, 1943; 1 son, Daniel G. Admitted to Mo. bar, 1933, Kans. bar, 1934; asso. Miller, Gumbiner & Sheffrey, Kansas City, Mo., 1933-34, Long, Depew & Stanley, 1934-40, partner, 1940-46; pvt. practice, Wichita, Kans., 1947-54, 73-74; partner, Brick & Beaty, 1954-60, Brick, Beaty & Bonwell, 1960-67, Coombs & Brick, 1967-73, Brick & Bell, 1974—; dir. Fruhauf Uniforms, Inc., Wichita. Pres., Wichita Community Chest, 1952. Bd. dirs. Wesley Med. Center, 1969—; bd. regents U. Wichita, 1958-64, chmn., 1963; bd. dirs. Kansas region NCCJ, 1948-56, co-chmn., 1950. Served with USAAF, 1942-46. Recipient distinguished service award Wichita State U. Mem. Am., Kans., Wichita (gov. 1949) bar assns., Sigma Alpha Mu. Republican. Jewish. Mem. B'nai B'rith; Elk, Kiwanian (pres. 1970). Clubs: Wichita, Wichita State Univ. Century and Shocker. Home: 6615 Rockwood Rd Wichita KS 67206 Office: Suite 790 Century Plaza Bldg 111 W Douglas St Wichita KS 67202

BRICKER, DALE EUGENE, state ofcl., polit. worker; b. Dover, Ohio, Jan. 29, 1925; s. Frank Benjamin and Beatrice Mae (Rodd) B.; student aviation Furman U., 1944; 1 son, Barry Owen. With Westinghouse Corp., Mansfield, Ohio, 1946-49; sales and promotion Welsh News Agy., 1949-52; inspection and cataloging technician Shelby Air Force Depot (Ohio), 1952-58; clk. of council City of Mansfield, 1958-63; office mgr., dir. of elections Richland County (Ohio) Bd. Elections, 1964—. Vice pres., asst. treas., dir. Shelby Fed. Employees Fed. Credit Union, 1954-58; sec. exec. com. Richland County Rep. Central and Exec. Coms., 1958-76, vice chmn., coordinator of activities, 1976—; mem. county central com., 1958—; pres. Young Rep. Club. 1959, Outstanding Young Rep. of Year, 1959; sec. Rep. Central Com., 1961-62; life mem., parliamentarian, program dir. Rep. Club of Richland County, 1964-68, pres., 1968-76, bd. dirs., 1976—, editor Party Line; mem. Ohio State Rep. Central and Exec. Com., 1972—, chmn. election legis. com., 1973—, mem. state conv. com., del. to state convs.; corr. sec. Mansfield Citizens Scholarship Chpt., 1961-62; counselor Mansfield dist. Boy Scouts Am. Served with AUS, 1943-46. Mem. Ohio Assn. Election Ofcls. (trustee, mem. legis. com., pres. 1973, life), Am. Legion, Fraternal Order Police Assn. (2d v.p.), Sons of Italy, Liederkranz, Roseland Grange. Mem. Christian Ch. Clubs: Lions (charter), Masons, Mansfield Stamp and Coin (pres. 1956-58, gov., 1959-62, 64-66, life), Toastmaster (pres. Mansfield 1962, 69-70, ednl. v.p. 1970-72, dir., 1972—, Toastmaster of Year 1962, Distinguished Service award 1963, editor T.M. Tidings, dir. 1972—). Office: Richland County Adminstrn Bldg 7 S Diamond St Mansfield OH 44902

BRICKHOUSE, JOHN B. (JACK), radio, TV sports mgr.; b. Peoria, Ill., Jan. 24, 1916; s. John William and Daisy (James) B.; student Bradley U., Peoria; m. Nelda Teach, Aug. 7, 1939; 1 dau., Jean. Comml., sports announcer Sta. WMBD, Peoria, 1934-40; with WGN, Chgo., 1940-43, 44—, v.p., mgr. sports WGN and WGN TV, 1948—; v.p., mgr. sports WGN Continental Broadcasting Co., 1970—; free lance, comml. announcer, Chgo., 1945; sports announcer, 1947, N.Y. Giants baseball announcer, N.Y.C., 1946. Broadcaster radio and/or TV play-by-play World Series, All Star Baseball Game, All Star Football game, Rose Bowl, Sugar Bowl, Am. Bowl, Orange bowl, Chgo. Cubs, Chgo. White Sox games, Golden Gloves, Louis-Charles and Walcott-Charles fight, Rep. and Dem. nat. convs., Roosevelt Inauguration (1945), Chicago Bears football games, Chgo. Bulls basketball games, Inaugural Ball, Papal audience. Bd. dirs. Chgo. Boys Clubs, City of Hope, Chgo. Wesley Meml. Hosp.; trustee St. Procopius Coll., Bradley U., Peoria, Ill. Served as pvt. USMCR, 1943-44. Recipient numerous Emmy awards, bronze medallions for World Series coverage Look mag., 1954, 59; Man of Year award City of Hope, 1966; Communications award Lincoln Acad., 1968; named Best Sports Announcer, Am. Coll. Radio Arts and Scis.; Nat. Sportscasters and Sportswriters award as outstanding sportscaster of year in Ill. (5 times), Acor award Am. Coll. Radio Arts, Nat. Sportswriters and Broadcasters awards, many others. Mem. Western Golf Assn. (dir.), Acad. Television Arts and Scis. (past pres., gov. Chgo. chpt.). Writer for Chgo. Today, Chgo. Tribune, Ency. Brit. Yearbook, others; pub. Jack Brickhouse's Major League Baseball Record Book, 21 edits. Home: 1100 Locust Rd Wilmette IL 60091 Office: WGN Continental Broadcasting Co 2501 W Bradley Pl Chicago IL 60618

BRICKLEY, JAMES H., univ. pres.; b. Flint, Mich., Nov. 15, 1928; s. J. Harry and Marie E. (Fischer) B.; Ph.B., U. Detroit, 1951, LL.B., 1954; LL.M., N.Y.U., 1958; m. Marianne E. Doyle, June 16, 1950; children—Janice Marie, James T., William J., Brian J., Kathleen Mary, Kelle Ann. Spl. agt. FBI, 1954-58; admitted to Mich. bar, 1959; chief asst. pros. atty. Wayne County, 1967-70; lt. gov. of Mich., 1971-74; pres. Eastern Mich. U., Ypsilanti, 1975—; lectr. in govt. U. Detroit, 1959—. Mem. Detroit Common Council, 1962-65, pres. pro tem, 1966-67; bd. dirs. Met. Fund, Detroit, 1976—; mem. exec. com. SE Mich. Council Govt., 1976—; mem. Nat. Council Fin. Aid to Students. Mem. Am., Mich. bar assns., Former Spl. Agts. of FBI, Soc. Delta Theta Phi. Roman Catholic. Office: Eastern Mich U Ypsilanti MI 48197

BRICKMAN, ROBERT OTTO, landscape co. exec.; b. Chgo., Jan. 22, 1938; s. Theodore William and Amy Edith (Kitzelman) B.; B.A. in Bus. Adminstrn., Lake Forest Coll., 1960; m. Gail Field Walkemeyer, Aug. 29, 1959; children—Jill, Barbara, Cynthia. Sales rep. UARCO, Inc., Chgo., 1960-61; landscape supr. Theodore Brickman Co., Long Grove, Ill., 1961-63, sales mgr., 1964-67, v.p., sec., 1967—. Mem. exec. bd. N.W. Council Boy Scouts Am., 1976-77; trustee Immanuel Ch. New Jerusalem, Glenview, 1971—. Recipient distinguished service award Countryside Center Handicapped. Mem. Associated Landscape Contractors Am. Republican. Club: Rotary (sec. 1963-65, pres. 1973-74, dist. gov.'s rep. 1974-77). Home: 1015 Gladish Lane Glenview IL 60025 Office: Long Grove Rd Long Grove IL 60047

BRIDEWELL, DAVID ALEXANDER, lawyer; b. Forrest City, Ark., Dec. 8, 1909; s. Alexander Carver and Martha Elizabeth (Hatcher) B.; A.B., U. of South, 1930; M.A., Princeton, 1932; J.D., George Washington U., 1938; m. Mary Frances Badger, May 21, 1949; children—Jonathan, Alexander. Admitted to Ark. bar, 1933, D.C. bar, 1938, Ill. bar, 1939; legal asst. to gen. counsel Fed. Home Loan Bank Bd., Fed. Savs. and Loan Ins. Corp., also Home Owners' Loan Corp., 1935-38; practice law, Forrest City and Jonesboro, Ark., 1933-34, Chgo., 1939—; mem. firm Russell, Bridewell, Sembower & Cook, 1940—, mng. partner, 1945—; dir. Winnetka Bank (Ill.), First Bank & Trust Co., Palatine, Ill., Elmhurst Fed. Savs. & Loan Assn. (Ill.), Kankakee Fed. Savs. & Loan Assn. (Ill.), First Fed. Savs. & Loan, Crystal Lake, Ill., Barrett Paint Co., No. Ark. Telephone Co.; lectr. bus. law Northwestern U., 1940-60. Bd. dirs. Chgo. Hearing Soc., Malcolm Henning Found., Henry C. Wood Found. Served to capt. AUS, 1944-45; ETO. So. Social Sci. Research fellow, 1930-32. Mem. Am. (mem. council sect. corp., banking and bus. law 1959-63), Ill. (mem. council comml. banking and bankruptcy law sect. 1966-72), Chgo. bar assns., Kappa Sigma. Episcopalian. Club: University of Chicago; Old Willow (Northbrook, Ill.). Author: Bailment, Liens and Pledges, 1941; Credit Unions, 1941, Selected Illinois Statues, 1941. Home: 789 Burr Ave Winnetka IL 60093 Office: 1 First Nat Plaza Chicago IL 60603

BRIDGES, AFTON C., ednl. adminstr.; b. Ozark, Mo., Oct. 4, 1918; s. Charles O. and Josie B. Bilyeu B.; B.S., S.W. Mo. State Coll., 1939; M.A., U. Mo., 1940, postgrad. 1941, 65-66; B.S. in Bus. Adminstrn. Drury Coll., 1954; m. Marian A. Marzetti, Sept. 14, 1944; children—Barbara (Mrs. Gerald J. Reynaud), Robert. Prin., Conway (Mo.) Consol. Schs., 1941-42; staff counseling and guidance dept. Harvard, 1946-47; exec. G.D. Milligan Dry Goods Co., Springfield, Mo., 1948-64; cons. psychologist Chinburg Psychiat. Clinic, Springfield, 1954-58; coordinator spl. edn. Springfield Pub. Schs., 1964—; lectr. in field. Mem. Mo. Adv. Council Vocat. Edn., 1968—; mem. various adv. coms. Mo. Dept. Edn. Bd. dirs. Springfield Sheltered Workshop Inc., chmn. budget and personnel com., 1966-68; pres. bd. Springfield Speech and Hearing Clinic, 1968-69. Served with JAG Dept., AUS, 1942-46. Mem. Springfield Edn. Assn., Mo. Tchrs. Assn., Mo. Assn. Retarded Children (dir. 1968-70), Council Exceptional Children (pres. Mo. fedn. 1972-73), Nat. Council Adminstrs. Spl. Edn. (pres. Mo. 1974-75), Mo., S.W., Am. psychol. assns., Greene County Mental Health Assn., Mo. Crippled Children's Soc. (adviser to bd. dirs. 1966-68), Kappa Alpha. Methodist (dir.). Kiwanian (chmn. underprivileged com. 1975—). Club: Hickory Hills Country. Home: 1205 S Delaware St Springfield MO 65804 Office: 940 N Jefferson St Springfield MO 65802

BRIDGES, ALVIN LEROY, physician; b. Dayton, Ohio, June 6, 1925; s. John Cornelius and Essie May (Leigh) B.; B.S., U. Dayton, 1948; M.D., Meharry Med. Coll., 1952; m. Lois Belle Blinks, Dec. 23, 1951; children—Alvin Leroy, Keith, Lori, Cornelius. Intern, Kansas City Gen. Hosp., 1952-53; resident in internal medicine Vets. Hosp., Dayton, 1953-54; practice medicine specializing in internal medicine, Anderson, Ind., 1954—. Served with AUS, 1943-46. Diplomate Am. Bd. Family Practice. Fellow Am. Acad. Family Physicians; mem. Internat. Soc. Internal Medicine, Nat., Ind. med. assns. Methodist. Home: Rural Route 10 Box 268 Anderson IN 46011 Office: 1302 Madison Ave Anderson IN 46011

BRIDGES, CHARLES HENRY, food co. exec.; b. Fairport, N.Y., Jan. 23, 1913; s. Charles Sampey and Jessie Anna (Talman) B.; B.S. in Chemistry, Cornell U., 1934, M.S., 1936, Ph.D., 1938; m. Henrietta Bull, Dec. 31, 1940 (dec. Jan. 1963); children—Sally, Julie (Mrs. Robert Seiter), Charles Henry; m. 2d, Florence Allen, May 26, 1964. Chem. engr. Kellogg Co., Battle Creek, Mich., 1938-39, process engr., 1947-52, asst. plant mgr., 1952-59, mgr. packaging devel., 1959-75, v.p. packaging devel., 1975—; chem. engr. Sharples Chems., Inc., Wyandotte, Mich., 1940-42; staff chem. engr. Eastman Kodak Co., Rochester, N.Y., 1942-47. City commr. City of Battle Creek, 1974—; bd. dirs. Gravure Research Inst., 1976—. Registered profl. engr., N.Y. Mem. Am. Inst. Chem. Engrs., Soc. Printing House Craftsmen, Sigma Xi, Tau Beta Pi. Presbyterian. Kiwanian. Home: 40 Clinton Dr Battle Creek MI 49017 Office: Kellogg Co Battle Creek MI 49016

BRIDGES, CHARLEY DAY, profl. services co. exec.; b. Wentworth, Mo., July 22, 1929; s. Walter Robert and Beulah (Higgins) B.; Asso. Sci. in Engring., Mo. So. Coll., 1960; postgrad. Kans. State Coll., 1961-62; m. Edith June McClinton, 1948; children—Harold David, Lee Allen, Glen Wayne. Sr. mathematician Rocketdyne div. N.Am. Rockwell Corp., Neosho, Mo., 1958-62, test engr., 1962-66, quality control analyst, 1966-67; sr. programmer and analyst Rockwell Internat. Corp., Tulsa, 1967-68; mgr. systems and data processing Nat. Gypsum Co., Parsons, Kans., 1968-70; adminstrv. services mgr. Day & Zimmermann, Inc., Parsons, 1970-73, controller, 1973-75, dir. fin. and adminstrn., 1975—. Leader of 4-H Club, Neosho, 1964-73; mem. bd. edn. Sch. Dist. 113, Sarcoxie, Mo., 1956-58, Diamond Sch. Dist., 1966-68; mem. Newton County Soil and Water Conservation Dist., 1972—; chmn. Young Republicans, Joplin Jr. Coll., 1957; ch. sch. tchr. Diamond (Mo.) United Meth. Ch., 1960—; bd. dirs. Freedom Community Assn., 1960-65. Recipient Top 10 awards N.Am. Rockwell, 1965-66, Leadership award Mo. Extension Service, 1964-73. Mem. Nat. Mgmt. Assn. (Silver Knight of Mgmt. award 1977, Outstanding Service award 1973, 77; chmn. mgmt. devel. com., dir.), Mo. Farmers Assn. Clubs: Masons, Red Cross Gallon. Home: Rural Route 1 Sarcoxie MO 64862 Office: Kansas Army Ammunition Plant Parsons KS 64757

BRIDGES, EDWARD TRENT, educator; b. Rainelle, W.Va., Dec. 1, 1942; s. Samuel Trent and Jessie Rae (Lusher) B.; A.B., Berea Coll., 1965; M.S., U. Ky., 1967, Ph.D. (Univ. fellow), 1970; m. Allene Alice Fitzwater, June 7, 1965; children—Stacy Lynn, Brian Trent. Prof. chemistry Shawnee Coll., Ullin, Ill., 1970—. Mem. Entomol. Soc. Am., Jaycees, Grad. Students Entomology U. Ky. (pres. 1968-69), Sigma Xi. Presbyterian. Club: Civitan (pres. 1973-74). Home: Box 64 Hilanoa Metropolis IL 62960 Office: Shawnee Coll Ullin IL 62992

BRIDGWATER, DONALD DEAN, zoo ofcl.; b. Dodge City, Kans., Oct. 9, 1938; s. Vernon Edgar and Veva Francis (Cook) B.; m. Gloria Elaine Johnson, Apr. 24, 1968; children—Jeffrey, Shelly, Kelly, Johnson; B.S., Bethany (Okla.) Nazarene Coll., 1961; M.S., Okla. State U., 1964; postgrad. U. Okla., 1965-67. Asst. prof. biology Bethany Nazarene Coll., 1962-66; sci. curator Oklahoma City Zoo, 1966-68; gen. curator Nat. Zool. Park, Smithsonian Instn., 1968-70; asst. dir. Minn. Zool. Garden, St. Paul, 1970-71, gen. dir., 1971—; chmn. Internat. Species Inventory System, Captive Species Populations Specialist Group, Survival Service Commn., mem. Internat. Union for Conservation of Nature. Fellow, Am. Assn. Zool. Parks and Aquarians (Outstanding Service award); mem. Am. Soc. Mammalogists, Sigma Xi, Phi Sigma, Phi Kappa Phi. NSF fellow, 1961-62; NSF research grantee, 1963-64; Editor: Saving the Lion Marmoset, 1972; Contbr. articles on animal behavior, mg- mt. and captive propagation to profl. jours. Office: 12101 Johnny Cake Ridge Rd Apple Valley MN 55124

BRIDWELL, RICHARD EDSEL, lawyer; b. Zanesville, Ohio, Mar. 16, 1926; s. Grover Cleveland and Lenora Ruth (Swingle) B.; B.S. in Bus. Adminstrn., Ohio State U., 1949, J.D., 1951. Admitted to Ohio bar, 1951, Fla. bar, 1971. practice law, Zanesville, O., 1951—; asst. pros. atty. Muskingum County, Ohio, 1953-61, pros. atty., 1961—; officer, dir. Kane Devel. Corp., Zanesville, 1962—, Maria Adornetto Restaurant, Inc., Zanesville, 1968—. Chmn. Muskingum County chpt. ARC, 1960-63; pres. Muskingum County chpt. United Fund, 1963. Bd. dirs. Muskingum Valley Improvement Assn., 1963—, legal counsel, 1963—. Served with AUS, 1944-46. Decorated Bronze Star medal. Named outstanding young man Ohio, Ohio Jaycees, 1960. Mem. Fla., Ohio, Muskingum County (pres. 1963) bar assns., Nat. Dist. Attys. Assn., Ohio Pros. Attys. Assn., Am., Ohio trial lawyers assns., V.F.W., Am. Legion, D.A.V., Delta Theta Phi. Republican. Presbyterian. Elk, Lion, Eagle. Club: LeClub Internat. (Ft. Lauderdale, Fla.). Home: 3590 Riverside Airport Rd Zanesville OH 43701 Office: Suite 201 28 N 4th St Zanesville OH 43701

BRIEDE, ROBERT PAUL, elec. contracting co. exec.; b. Ft. Wayne, Ind., May 8, 1923; s. Paul Herman and Mathilda Marie (Berling) B.; student U. Detroit, 1941-43; B.S. in Mech. Engring., Purdue U., 1945; postgrad U. Chgo., 1946-47; m. Betty Marie Cavitt, Aug. 21, 1946. Estimator, Dooley-St. Arnaud Elec. Constrn. Co., Chgo., 1946-48; estimator Elec. Constrn. and Machinery Co., Kalamazoo, 1948-50; owner, pres. Motor Shop Elec. Constrn. Co., Battle Creek, Mich., 1950—; trustee City of Battle Creek Elec. Bd. Div. chmn. United Fund, Battle Creek. Served with U.S. Navy, 1945-46. Mem. ASME, Nat. Assn. Elec. Contractors, Mich., Battle Creek Engring. socs., Purdue Alumni Assn. Republican. Roman Catholic. Clubs: Rotary, Country (Battle Creek); Minges Creek Racquet, West Hills Racquet, K.C. Home: 249 Honey Ln Battle Creek MI 49015 Office: 40 Bartlett St Battle Creek MI 49016

BRIERS, JAMES LAURENCE, pub. utility exec.; b. N.Y.C., Sept. 24, 1923; s. Larry Tennyson and Evelyn (Groeble) B.; student Oberlin Coll., 1941-43; B.S., Ohio State U., (summa cum laude), 1948; M.B.A., Western Res. U., 1965; student Goethe U. (Frankfurt, Germany), 1951-52; m. Evalena Caton, Oct. 7, 1950; 1 dau., Cynthia Katherine. With Ohio Bell Telephone Co., Cleve., 1949—, successively asst. comml. mgr., 1953, comml. mgr., 1954-58, sales mgr., 1959, exec. asst. bus. research, revenue requirements, 1960-62, dist. comml. mgr., 1962-64, named comml. supr. wages and working conditions, 1965, now comml. supr. personnel; undergrad. asst. Ohio State U., 1948. Cons. ednl. TV, WWIZ; vice chmn. polit. adv. com. 7 County Transp. and Land Use Study; transp. cons. Cleve. Growth Bd.; lectr. Cleve. State U., 1964. Vice chmn. United Appeals, Columbus, Ohio, 1958; pub. relations com. Council Social Agys., 1958; chmn. Bay Village Planning Commn., Cleve., 1963—, Indsl. Devel. Commn., 1963—; v.p. Regional Planning Commn. Co-Founder Columbus Youth Found., 1956; dir. Pilot Dogs, 1958-59; bd. dirs. Cleve. West Shore YMCA, 1965—. Served with USAAF, 1942-46; served to capt. USAF, 1950-52. Mem. Acad. Mgmt. Am. Econ. Assn., Am. Polit. Sci. Assn., Ohio State U. Alumni Assn., Oberlin Coll. Alumni Assn., Urban League, Midwest Orgn. Devel. Network, Beta Gamma Sigma. Republican. Home: 26601 Normandy Rd Bay Village OH 44140 Office: 100 Erieview Plaza Cleveland OH 44114

BRIESACHER, FRED EDWARD, JR., retail store owner; b. St. Louis, Feb. 4, 1926; s. Fred Edward and Julia Ann (Layton) B.; E.E., Hadley Tech. Sch.; m. Edna Louis Baumgartner, Dec. 30, 1944; children—Carol (Mrs. Gene Gassner), Linda (Mrs. Steven Johnson), Nancy (Mrs. Dennis Bays). Owner, TV-Appliance Store, Waynesville, Mo., 1952—; owner, mgr. KFBD Radio, AM-FM, Waynesville, 1964—. Served with USAAF, 1944-45. Mason (Shriner). Address: Route 2 Box 2B Waynesville MO 65583

BRIESE, ERWIN ELLIOTT, steel fabricating co. exec.; b. Rochester, Minn., July 3, 1924; s. Erwin Leo and Louise (Elliott) B.; student Georgetown U., 1943; Ph.B., U. Chgo., 1947; B. Agrl. Engring., U. Minn., 1950; m. Margaret Marie Imlay, Sept. 14, 1946; children—Patrick V., Stephen E., Jan T. Briese Grundhauser, Margo M. Briese Wilson, Mary Elizabeth, John I., Diane M. With Briese Steel Co., Dodge Center, Minn., 1950-76, constrn. supr., engr., 1950-60, sec., 1960-69, pres., 1969-76; pres. Briese Iron Works, Inc., Rochester, 1974—. Mem. curriculum adv. bd. for engring. tech. Rochester State Jr. Coll., 1970—; mem. welding adv. com. Rochester

Area Vocat. Sch., 1968-74; mem. Rochester Catholic Bd. Edn., 1971-77, pres., 1973. Served with AUS, 1942-45. Mem. Am. Soc. Agrl. Engrs., Am. Concrete Inst., Nat. Assn. Archtl. Metal Mfrs. Roman Catholic (pres. parish council 1967, lay minister of the eucharist 1974—). Clubs: Rotary, K.C., Rochester Serra. Home: 2765 Riverside Ln NE Rochester MN 55901 Office: PO Box 6346 Rochester MN 55901

BRIGDEN, ROBERT CAMPBELL, investment broker; b. Cleve., May 19, 1942; s. James H. and A. Margaret (Campbell) B.; B.S. in Indsl. Tech., Ohio U., 1967; m. Nancy Romain Schwarzmann, Feb. 24, 1973. Asst. sales engr. Westinghouse Elec. Co., Columbus, Ohio, 1967-68; securities broker J.N. Russell Co., Cleve., 1969-74, Blyth Eastman Dillon, Cleve., 1974-75, CleveCorp Securities, Cleve., 1975—; developer, partner Manor Apts., Alexander Apts.; advisor Newark Wire Cloth Co., Verona Realty. Active Big Bros. Greater Cleve., 1973—; mem. adv. bd., past dir. Salvation Army, 1977—. Served as paratrooper AUS, 1962-64. Mem. Soc. for Advancement Mgmt. (mem. bd., recipient Spark, Community Improvement and Nat. awards), Theosophical Soc., Jr. C. of C. Presbyterian. Clubs: Cleve. Athletic, Jewish Community Center, Cleve. Rotary, Cleve. Bond. Home: 3455 Edison Rd Cleveland OH 44121 Office: 1010 Euclid Ave Cleveland OH 44115

BRIGGS, FRANK ROY, health care cons; b. South Elgin, Ill., Jan. 5, 1916; s. Frank Roy and Gertrude Louise (Burns) B.; A.B., Ind. State U., 1938, M.A., 1940; postgrad. in journalism, Northwestern U., 1940-41; m. Mary Elisabeth Burnett, Feb. 1, 1941; children—Ann, Mary, Frank Roy. Faculty, Ind. State U., 1947-49; adminstr. Union Hosp., Terre Haute, Ind., 1949-51, Abbott Hosp., Mpls., 1951-61; partner Herman Smith Assos., Cons., Hinsdale, Ill., 1962—. Served with USNR, 1942-47; PTO. Fellow Am. Coll. Hosp. Adminstrs.; mem. Am. Assn. Hosp. Consultants (pres. 1978), Internat. Hosp. Fedn. Home: 14 Kyle Ct Clarendon Hills IL 60514 Office: 120 E Ogden Ave Hinsdale IL 60521

BRIGGS, JOHN LAWRENCE, genealogist; b. Battle Creek, Mich., Oct. 6, 1905; s. Mark Roy and Mary Esther (Noyes) B.; m. Ida McCauley, Aug. 20, 1929; 1 son, Stanley John; m. 2d Glenna Wrate Todd. B.A.S., Chgo. YMCA Coll., 1929; M.A., Mich. State U., 1961; M.A., Western Mich. U., 1962. Certified rehab. counselor, 1972. Asst. exec. Boy Scouts Am., Beloit, Wis., 1929-30, exec. Mt. Clemens, Mich., 1931-37, Ft. Wayne, Ind., 1937-38; caseworker Kalamazoo (Mich.) Welfare Dept., 1939-41; placement specialist War Manpower Commn. and State Employment Service, Kalamazoo, 1942-47; rehab. counselor V.R.S., Kalamazoo, 1947-76; pvt. practice genealogy, Kalamazoo, 1976—. Mem. Nat., Am. rehab. assns., Nat., Mich. rehab. counciling assns., Nat. Vocat. Guidance Assn., Am., Mich., Kalamazoo County personnel and guidance assns., Mich. Psychol. Assn., Am., S.W. Mich. iris socs., Kalamazoo Valley Geneal. Soc., Am. Assn. Retired Persons, Mich. State Retired Employees Assn. Home and Office: 2316 March St Kalamazoo MI 49001

BRIGGS, JOHN MANCEL, III, lawyer; b. Muskegon, Mich., May 24, 1942; s. John Mancel, Jr. and Margaret Jane (Wren) B.; B.S., U. Mich., 1964; J.D., 1967; m. Janice R. Dykema, May 20, 1967; children—Jennifer, Jill. Admitted to Mich. bar, 1968; asso. Parmenter, Forsythe & Rude, Muskegon, 1967-70, partner, 1970—. Bd. dirs. Muskegon-Oceana County Legal Aid, 1970-73, pres., 1972-73; bd. dirs. Big Bros. of Greater Muskegon, 1970-75, sec., 1970-74; bd. dirs. Y Family Christian Assn., 1970—, chmn. membership com., 1972-76, 1st v.p., 1974-76, pres., 1976—; active Muskegon County United Appeal, 1968-75, co-chmn. attys. sect. profl. div., 1971. Served with AUS, 1967-68. Recipient Carl Gussin Meml. award U. Mich. Law Sch., 1967. Mem. Am., Muskegon County (sec. 1970-71, pres. 1975-76) bar assns., State Bar Mich., Muskegon County U. Mich. Alumni Assn. (dir. 1975—), Phi Kappa Tau. Clubs: Rotary (sgt.-at-arms 1975-76), Elks. Home: 2504 Hathaway Ct Muskegon MI 49441 Office: 500 Nat Lumberman's Bank Bldg Muskegon MI 49440

BRIGGS, PAUL WARREN, supt. schs.; b. Mayville, Mich., Nov. 23, 1912; s. Arthur Eugene and Lydia (Miller) B.; A.B., Western Mich. U., 1934; M.A., Mich. State U., 1943; postgrad. Columbia, 1956; Ed.D., Baldwin-Wallace Coll., 1964, Central State U., 1965, Cleve. State U., 1966; L.H.D., Case Inst. Tech., 1966; m. Arvilla Moran, June 18, 1933; children—Betty Ann (Mrs. Loren Smith), James A. Tchr., prin. Brown City (Mich.) High Sch., 1934-40; tchr. Bay City (Mich.) Central High Sch., 1940-42, vice prin., 1942-43, prin., 1943-53; supt. schs., Bay City, 1953-57, Parma Pub. Schs., 1957-64, Cleve. Pub. Schs., 1964—. Mem. summer sch. staff Mich. State U., 1947-50; lectr. edn. U. Mich., 1952, Columbia, 1965, Ohio State U., 1963; adj. prof. Cleve. State U. Bd. mgrs. Cleve. Met. YMCA, 1964—; mem. exec. bd. Greater Cleve. council Boy Scouts Am., 1960—; mem. exec. com. Nat. Urban Coalition; hon. life mem. Nat. PTA; mem. council gt. city schs. edn. commn. states; exec. com. Ohio Ednl. TV Network commn. Bd. dirs. Greater Cleve. Growth Assn. Recipient Ann. Brotherhood award NCCJ, 1974, Am. Vocat. Assn. award, 1974. Mem. Nat., Ohio (life) edn. assns.; Am., Ohio assns. schs. adminstrs., Mich. High Sch. Athletic Assn. (exec. com. 1949-53). Clubs: Rotary (past pres. Bay City), Masons (33 deg., Shriner). Home: 11625 Edgewater Dr Cleveland OH 44102 Office: 1380 E 6th St Cleveland OH 44114

BRIGGS, ROBERT ALFRED, civil engr.; b. Detroit, Aug. 22, 1913; s. Harry B. and Elsa (Neusesser) B.; B.S., Mich. State U., 1937; postgrad. U. Tenn., 1942-43, Lawrence Inst. Tech. Engr., 1945; m. Janet Wilson Bruce, Nov. 26, 1938; children—Harry Alfred, Christine Carole (Mrs. Gerald Campbell), Beryl Ann (Mrs. Timothy O. O'Farrell). Civil engr. Mich. Hwy. Dept., Lansing, 1937-40, TVA, Knoxville, 1941-42; engr. Square Tool & Die Co., Detroit, 1943-44, Monroe Auto Equipment Co. (Mich.), 1945, Mech. Handling System, Detroit, 1946; civil engr. Detroit Edison Co., 1947-64, dir. civil engring div., 1964-70; cons. engr., 1970-72, dir. archtl. civil engring. div., 1973—. Named Outstanding Civil Engr., Mich., 1972. Registered profl. engr. Mich. Fellow ASCE; mem. Am. Concrete Inst. (dir.), Soc. Am. Mil. Engrs. (dir.), Seismol. Soc. Am., Japanese Soc. Soil Mechanics and Found. Engring., Mich. Engring. Soc., Am. Arbitration Assn., Engring. Soc. Detroit, Internat. Soc. Soil Mechanics and Found. Engring., Internat. Platform Assn., Toastmasters Internat. Presbyn. Clubs: Rivers Edge Marina and Country; Grosse Ile Yacht. Home: 21425 Salisbury Grosse Ile MI 48138 Office: 2000 2d St Detroit MI 48226

BRIGGS, ROY FRANCIS, real estate broker; b. Akron, Mich., Feb. 24, 1911; s. Jacob John and Mary Jane (Graham) B.; student Ferris State Coll., 1929; m. Pauline Ahr Sandham, Oct. 5, 1935; children—John Sandham, Ransom Ahr. With Hubbard State Bank, Bad Axe, Mich., 1929-37; sales rep. Mich. Mut. Liability Co., Bad Axe and St. Johns, Mich., 1937-41; co-owner Community Frozen Food Lockers, St. Johns, 1940-56; pres., dir. The Briggs Co., real estate, St. Johns, 1941—; dir. Clinton Nat. Bank & Trust Co., St. Johns. Justice of peace, 1942-46; mem. Zoning Bd., City of St. Johns, 1942-62. Trustee, bd. dirs. Clinton County Meml. Hosp., 1962—; bd. dirs. Higgins Lake Property Owners Assn., 1970-73. Mem. C. of C. (pres. 1958). Republican. Methodist. Home: 511 S Mead St St Johns MI 48879 Office: 200 W State St St Johns MI 48879

BRIGGS, WILLIAM BENAJAH, aero. engr.; b. Okmulgee, Okla., Dec. 13, 1922; s. Eugene Stephen and Mary Betty (Gentry) B.; B.A. in Physics, Phillips U., 1943, D.Sc. (hon.), 1977; M.S. in Mech. Engring., Ga. Tech., 1947; m. Lorraine Hood, June 6, 1944; children—Eugene Stephen II, Cynthia Anne, Julia Louise, Spencer Gentry. Aero. scientist, Nat. Advisory Commn. for Aeros., Cleve., 1948-52; propulsion engr. Chance Vought Aircraft/LTV, Dallas, Tex., 1952-64; mgr. advanced planning McDonnell Douglas Co., St. Louis, 1964—; mem. NASA Planetary Quarantine Advisory Panel. Vice chmn. Bd. Christian Bd. Publ., St. Louis, 1974—; chmn. Disciples Council of Greater St. Louis, 1969-73. Served with USN, 1943-46; PTO. Mem. Am. Inst. Aeros. and Astronautics (dir. region 5 1974-77, v.p. mem. services 1978-79), Am. Nuclear Soc. Democrat. Mem. Disciples of Christ Ch. Club: Masons. Contbr. articles on aero. engring. to profl. jours. Patentee in field. Home: 1819 Bradburn Dr St Louis MO 63131 Office: PO Box 516 McDonnell Douglas Astronautics Co St Louis MO 63166

BRIGHAM, EDWARD MORRIS, III, assn. exec.; b. Battle Creek, Mich., Feb. 15, 1930; s. Edward Morris and Elmina Belle (Steffe) B.; A.B., Albion Coll., 1952; M.A., U. Mich., 1960; m. Judith Anne Bingham, Apr. 20, 1954; children—Jennifer Anne, Valerie Elaine, Mark Edward. Tchr. biology Flint (Mich.) Pub. Schs., 1956-68; N. Midwest rep. Nat. Audubon Soc., Red Wing, Minn., 1968-77, dir. div. regional activities, 1977—, dir. Audubon workshop, Sarona, Wis., 1971-76; organizer, dir. Seven Ponds Nature Center, Dryden, Mich., 1966-68, bd. sponsors, 1968—; mem. adv. bd. Northwoods Audubon Center (Minn.), 1976—. Dir. Flint Sci. Fair, 1964; mem. regional environ. edn. council, Minn., 1973-76; mem. endangered species recovery team for black-footed ferret, 1974—). Mem. Mich. Audubon Soc. (pres. 1968, editor Newsletter 1966-68), Beta Beta Beta, Delta Sigma Rho, Theta Alpha Phi, Omicron Delta Kappa, Tau Kappa Epsilon. Unitarian Universalist (ch. moderator 1966). Address: Route 4 Red Wing MN 55066

BRIGHAM, JAMES REMMERS, indsl. marking co. exec.; b. St. Louis, Apr. 25, 1922; s. James Watkins and Florence (Remmers) B.; B.S., Washington U., 1943; postgrad. Duke, 1944; m. Barbara Ramsay, Apr. 15, 1944; children—James Remmers, Barbara (Mrs. James Clutts), Sarah (Mrs. W. Charles Grace). Sales rep. IBM, 1945-48; prodn. mgr. Diagraph Bradley Industries, Inc., Herrin, Ill., 1949-50, plant mgr., 1950-52, sales mgr., 1952-58, exec. v.p., 1958-64, pres., 1964—; dir. Distribix, Air Ill., Hayes Fair Acres, Inc., Manchester Bank. Mem. export expansion council U.S. Dept. Commerce, 1968—. Mem. Bd. Edn. Carbondale, Ill., 1955-64. Trustee So. Ill. U. Found. Recipient Presdl. citation Employment of Handicapped, 1963. Mem. Ill. Mfg. Assn. (dir.). Elk. Clubs: Union League (Chgo.); University, Old Warson Country (St. Louis). Home: Route 4 Carbondale IL 62901 Office: Box 520 Herrin IL 62948

BRIGHT, JAMES OLIVER, mfg. co. pres.; b. Greensburg, Ind., June 9, 1930; s. Charles Raymond and Verna Lucille (Robbins) B.; grad. high sch.; m. Linda Lou Beaver, Aug. 8, 1975; children by previous marriage—Paula Raye (Mrs. B. Smith), Linda (Mrs. Web Hagadone), Timothy James, Daniel Leslie. With Allison div. Gen. Motors Corp., Indpls., 1952-55; tool and die maker, 1953-55; spl. machine builder Universal Match Corp., Lebanon, Ind., 1955-56; with Vibromatic Co. automation machine bldg., Noblesville, Ind., 1957—, gen. mgr., 1967—, pres., 1969—. Active United Fund. Bd. dirs. Noblesville Boys Club. Served with USNR, 1948-52. Recipient Bronze medallion Nat. Boys Club, 1974. Republican. Episcopalian. Clubs: Masons, Elks, Kiwanis. Home: 204 Amhurst Circle Noblesville IN 46060 Office: 1301 S 6th St Noblesville IN 46060

BRIGHTMAN, ALAN HARRY, II, veterinary ophthalmologist; b. Longbranch, N.J., Apr. 14, 1943; s. Alan H. and Gretchen A. (Van Sluyters) B.; B.A., Kans. U., 1967; B.S., Kans. State U., 1972, D.V.M., 1974; M.S., U. Ill., 1977. Intern, U. Calif. Coll. Veterinary Medicine, Davis, 1974-75; resident in ophthalmology U. Ill. Coll. Veterinary Medicine, Urbana, 1975-77, staff veterinary ophthalmology sect., dept. veterinary clin. medicine, 1977—, asst. prof. medicine, 1977—. Served to capt. AUS, 1967-69. Decorated Combat Infantryman Badge. HEW grantee, 1976-77. Mem. AVMA, Am. Animal Hosp. Assn., Am. Soc. Veterinary Ophthalmologists, Kans., Ill. veterinary med. assns., Kans. U., Kans. State U. alumni assns., Delta Chi, Phi Zeta, Gamma Sigma Delta. Republican. Episcopalian. Club: Scuba Diving Veterinarians. Contbr. articles to profl. jours. Office: Dept Clinical Veterinary Medicine Univ Ill Urbana IL 61801 -

BRILL, DAVID MARVIN, food service exec.; b. Chgo., Apr. 30, 1938; s. Marty and Frances (Feder) B.; student U. Ill., 1954-57; B.A., Lake Forest Coll., 1958, M.S. in Food Facilities Engring., Cornell U., 1960; M.B.A., U. Chgo., 1962; m. Carol Mills, Nov. 29, 1959; children—Melinda Sue, Jennifer-Lynn, Andrew Robert. Mem. advt. staff Grubb-Petersen Co., 1959-60; exec. v.p. M. L. Brill & Co., Chgo., 1964-68; asst. to pres. Nat. Tea Co., Chgo., 1968-71; food service exec. Holleb & Co., Bensenville, Ill., 1971—; food cons., 1960—; guest lectr. U. Ill., 1964, 66, 68; pres. Dacar Assos. Ltd., food service cons., Highland Park, Ill., 1965—. Head, Highland Park Jewish United Fund Dr., 1968; bd. dirs. Highland Park Hosp., 1961—. Served with USMCR, 1958-60. Recipient award Chgo. Jewish Appeal, 1966, Instns. award Instns. mag., 1966. Mem. Cornell Soc., Chefs du cuisine, Les Amis des Escoffier, Catering Execs. Club Am., Alpha Delta Sigma, Pi Lambda Phi. Club: Covenant (past pres.). Home: 914 Rolling Wood Rd Highland Park IL 60035 Office: PO Box 34 Highland Park IL 60035

BRILL, EVAN LUTHER, computer scientist; b. Ohio, Apr. 13, 1939; s. Paul Luther and Nellie Frances (Gregg) B.; B.S. in Physics, Ohio State U., 1964, M.S. in Computer Science, 1967; m. Nancy Ann Berner, June 17, 1961; children—Darcie Lynn, Craig Alan. Research asso. Ohio State U., Columbus, 1964-67; principal researcher Battelle-Columbus Labs., Columbus, 1967-74, asso. section mgr., 1974-77, project mgr., 1977—. Served with U.S. Army, 1957. Mem. Assn. Computing Machinery, Sigma Xi. Methodist. Developer computer systems for human services, marine safety, criminal justice info., and others. Home: 2132 Cheltenham Rd Columbus OH 43220 Office: 505 King Ave Columbus OH 43201

BRILLHART, DONALD DWIGHT, chem. engring. co. exec.; b. nr. Napoleon, Ohio, Jan. 25, 1918; s. Vernon Gale and Nora (Nelson) B.; B. Chem. Engring. Cleve. State U., 1948; m. Catherine C. Chant, Nov. 20, 1948; children—Dorothy Noreen, Barbara Gale. Chemist Aluminum Co. of Am., Cleve., 1941-42, Stevens Grease and Oil Co., Cleve., 1948-53; pres. Pro-Chem, Inc., Cleve., 1954—. Lectr. div. continuing edn. Cleve. State U., 1972—. Republican precinct committeeman, Maple Heights, Ohio, 1956-59. Served with USAF, 1943-47. Mem. Am. Chem. Soc., AAAS. Patentee in lubricants and corrosion inhibitors. Researcher on fatty acids and their relation to degenerative diseases. Home: 14713 Rockside Rd Cleveland OH 44137 Office: 16536 Broadway St Cleveland OH 44137

BRILLHART, MAXINE T., physician; b. Coffeyville, Kans., Nov. 11, 1915; d. Forest C. and Rena H. (Huffman) Thornton; M.D., U. Kan., 1950; m. Roy William Brillhart, Nov. 15, 1935; children—Robert Allen, Roy William. Intern Providence Hosp., Kansas City, Kans., 1950-51, now staff; pvt. practice medicine, Kansas City, 1951—; staff Bethany, St. Margaret, Providence hosps. Dir., sec. Allied Investors, Inc.; dir., v.p. sec. Med. Offices Lab. Mem. Kans. Commn. on Status of Women, 1966. Recipient Matrix award Theta Sigma Phi, 1969. Fellow Am. Acad. Family Physicians; mem. Am., Kans., Wyandotte County med. assns., Am., Kans., Wyandotte County (sec.-treas. 19S7-58) acads. gen. practice, World, Am. Women's med. socs., S.W. Clin. Soc., English-Speaking Union, Internat. Personnel Research Soc., Am. Biog. Inst., Internat. Platform Assn. Methodist. Clubs: Women's City, Soroptimist (pres. Kansas City 1965-66, Woman of Year 1962). Home: 4540 County Line Rd Kansas City KS 66106 Office: 1610 Washington Blvd Kansas City KS 66102

BRINDLE, ELWOOD HAROLD, editor; b. Kearny, N.J., Apr. 6, 1917; s. James and Emily (Hunt) B.; student Rutgers, 1938-39, Columbia, 1940-41; m. Dorothy Collins, Sept. 6, 1947; children—Paul William, Anne Frances, Ralph Collins. Corr., Prudential Ins. Co., 1934-42; copywriter Gamble-Skogmo, Inc., 1945-47, Batten, Barton, Durstine & Osborn, 1947-67; editor Govt. Product-News, Mpls., 1967-71; editor-in-chief Lakewood Publs., Inc., 1971-72; free-lance editor-writer, 1973—. Co-founder Webfooters Friends, Inc., 1973. Dir. Minn. Fellowship of Congregationalists, 1964-67. Served to 2d lt. USAAF, 1942-45. Decorated Air medal with 2 clusters. Mem. League to Uphold Congl. Principles, Minn. Mycological Soc. Co-author: America's Best Garden Flowers; Vegetable Gardening from the Ground Up. Address: 5405 Abbott Pl Edina MN 55410

BRINGARDNER, THOMAS ALBERT, savs. and loan exec.; b. Columbus, Ohio, July 21, 1925; s. Edwin W. and Dorothy (Bergin) B.; B.S., Ohio State U., 1949; m. Mary Louise Mulloney, May 19, 1951; children—Thomas Albert, Richard D., Daniel E., Jeffrey. With Dollar Savs. Assn., Columbus, 1948—, sec., 1951—, exec. v.p., 1966-76, pres., 1976—, also dir. Active United Community Council; mem. finance com. Diocesan Child Guidance, Columbus, 1962—. Served with USAAF, 1944-46. Mem. Sr. Real Estate Appraisers (sr. mem.), Columbus Savs. and Loan Inst. (pres. 1957-58), Nat. Cath. Community Service, St. Catherine Holy Name Soc. (v.p. 1960—), Sigma Alpha Epsilon Alumni Assn. (pres. 1953-54), Am. Legion (treas. 1953-54). Clubs: Catholic Men's Luncheon (treas. 1952-53), Rotary (pres. 1971-72). Columbus Country. Address: 2661 Bexley Park St Columbus OH 43209

BRINGHAM, WILLIAM TALBERT, JR., hotel exec.; b. Hinsdale, Ill., Dec. 13, 1953; s. William Talbert and Ruth Irene (Jaeger) B.; student Kendall Coll., Evanston, Ill., 1971-72; B.A., Albion (Mich.) Coll., 1975. Staff asst. Sigma Chi Fraternity, 1973-75, contbg. editor Sigma Chi mag., 1973—, pres. Albion Coll. chpt., 1974-75; desk mgr. Marriott Hotel Corp., Chgo., 1976-77, personnel mgr., 1977—; faculty Sigma Chi Leadership Sch., 1975—. Precinct capt. Republican Party. Mem. Sigma Chi (publs. bd. 1975—). Club: Westmoreland Country (Wilmette, Ill.). Editor: Northfield Twp. Republican Orgn. Newsletter, 1976-77; sr. staff writer Albion Coll. Pleiad, 1974. Home: 4020 Bunker Ln Wilmette IL 60091 Office: Marriott Hotel Corp W Higgens Rd Chicago IL 60631

BRINGHAM, WILLIAM TALBERT, SR., fraternity exec.; b. Normal, Ill., Dec. 16, 1924; s. Russell Wilson and Sarah E. (Talbert) B.; Ph.B., Illinois Wesleyan University, 1948; J.D., Vanderbilt University, 1951; grad. trust devel. school Northwestern U. Sch. Commerce, 1953; m. Ruth Irene Jaeger, Jan. 10, 1947; 1 son, William Talbert. Spl. agt. FBI, 1951-52; exec. sec. Sigma Chi Frat., 1954—; exec. dir. Sigma Chi Found., 1956—, also sec.; also sec. bd. grand trustee of Sigma Chi, exec. v.p., sec. exec. com., and sec. grand council Sigma Chi Fraternity (name later changed to Sigma Chi Corp.). Mem. corp. Kendall Coll.; del. Sch. Bd. Caucus. Del. Ill. Republican Conv., now Northfield Twp. Rep. committeeman, former trustee Wilmette, Ill. Former chmn. and Police Commn., Wilmette, Ill. Served with USNR, 1942-46. Named flying col. Delta Airlines, ambassador Trans World Airlines, admiral Am. Airlines; recipient Grand Consul's Citation, recipient Order of Constantine award. Mem. Am. Personnel and Guidance Assn., Am. Soc. Assn. Execs. (Key award 1973), Wilmette, Evanston hist. socs., Travelers Protective Assn., Am. Legion, Frat. Execs. Assn. (pres., exec. com.). Internat. Platform Assn., Evanston C. of C. (past dir.), S.A.R., Chgo. Soc. Assn. Execs., Phi Delta Phi. Mason (Shriner, 33 deg., K.T.) Kiwanian (past pres.), Royal Order Scotland. Clubs: University (pres.) (Evanston). Author booklet on alumni chpts. Sigma Chi. Chmn. com. that edited Visitation Manual for College Fraternities. Address: 4020 Bunker Ln Wilmette IL 60091

BRINK, KENNETH WAYNE, financial exec.; b. Holland, Mich., Nov. 4, 1938; s. Gerrit and Eleanor June (Drenten) B.; B.A., Hope Coll., 1960; M.B.A., U. Mich., 1961; m. Beverly Ann Nordyke, Aug. 26, 1961; children—Timothy Wayne, Sheila Lynn. Accountant, Ernst & Ernst, Grand Rapids, Mich., 1961-66; with Interstate Motor Freight System, Grand Rapids, 1966—, controller, 1969-72, controller, v.p., 1972-73, v.p. finance and adminstrn., 1973—, also dir. C.P.A., Mich. Mem. Nat. Assn. Accountants, Am. Inst. C.P.A.'s, Mich. Assn. C.P.A.'s, Tax Execs. Inst., Am. Trucking Assn. (nat. accounting and finance council), Financial Execs. Inst. Mem. Reformed Ch. Am. (treas. 1971). Clubs: Peninsular, Cascade Hills Country (Grand Rapids). Home: 3320 Fillmore St Jenison MI 49428 Office: 134 Grandville Ave Grand Rapids MI 49503

BRINK, LAWRENCE RAY, architect; b. Fremont, Mich., Sept. 14, 1937; s. Walter Ernest and Carolyn Jeannette (Brown) B.; student Alma Coll., 1957; studied with Frank Lloyd Wright, 1958-59; B.Arch., U. Mich., 1963; m. Susan Marie Michner, May 25, 1969; children—Gina Marie, Lawrence Todd. Individual archtl. practice, Ann Arbor, Mich., 1967—. Mem. AIA (chpt. dir.), Constrn. Specifications Inst., Ann Arbor C. of C. Designer Village Bell Restaurant, Ann Arbor; project architect, chief designer Ann Arbor Hilton Inn and Restaurant; architect Patrick Petroleum Home Office, Liberty Centre, Ann Arbor, Schaffer Lumber, Jackson, Mich., Jackson Profl. Plaza, North Territorial Family Med. Clinic, Dexter, Mich. Home: 3995 Pemberton Ann Arbor MI 48104 Office: 2378 E Stadium St Ann Arbor MI 48104

BRINK, WILLIAM RUDOLPH, mfg. co. exec.; b. Holland, Mich., Feb. 20, 1931; s. Rudolph and Helen (Takken) B.; B.A., Mich. State U., 1954; m. Carol Fredericks, July 14, 1956; children—Susan, Karen. With Arthur Andersen & Co., C.P.A.'s, Detroit, 1954-64; v.p., dir. Valeron Corp., Oak Park, Mich., 1964—. C.P.A., Mich. Home: 30511 Georgetown Dr Birmingham MI 48010 Office: 20800 Coolidge Rd Oak Park MI 48237

BRINKER, ELAINE ISABELLE, utility co. exec.; b. Washington, Mo., Apr. 15, 1950; d. Leander Peter and Hilda Anna (Voss) Brinker; B.S. in Edn., U. Mo., 1972, postgrad, 1974-76. Tchr. math. Warrenton (Mo.) High Sch., 1972-73, St. Francis Borgia High Sch., Washington, Mo., 1973-74; jr. analyst mgmt. systems U. Mo., 1974-76, tchrs. asst., 1975-76; sr. analyst Southwestern Bell, St. Louis, 1976—. Mem. Mo. State Tchrs. Assn., Computing Machinery (sec. student chpt. 1975-76). Democrat. Roman Catholic. Home: Apt 2C 6321 S Grand St Saint Louis MO 63111 Office: 14 S 4th St Saint Louis MO 63102

BRINKLEY, GEORGE ARNOLD, JR., educator; b. Wilmington, N.C., Apr. 20, 1931; s. George Arnold and Ida Bell (West) B.; A.B., Davidson Coll., 1953; M.A., Columbia U., 1955; Ph.D., 1964; m. Ann Mae Kreps, Aug. 9, 1959; 1 dau., Heidi Ann. Instr. govt. Columbia U., 1957-58; faculty U. Notre Dame, 1958—, prof., 1970—, chmn. dept. govt., 1969-77, dir. program Soviet and East European studies, 1969—, dir. Inst. Internat. Studies, 1975—. Ford Found. fellow, 1954-57; Inter-U. Com. Travel grantee to USSR, 1962-63; Council Fgn. Relations Internat. Affairs fellow, 1968-69. Mem. Council Fgn. Relations, Am. Assn. Advancement Slavic Studies, Am. Polit. Sci. Assn. Author: The Volunteer Army and Allied Intervention in South Russia, 1966. Office: Dept Govt U Notre Dame Notre Dame IN 46556

BRINKLEY, WILLIAM JOHN, educator; b. Shawneetown, Ill., Dec. 8, 1925; s. William Henry and Frances (Leath) B.; B.S., U. Ill., 1945. Tchr. high sch., McLeansboro, Ill., 1945—, high sch. coordinator vocations, 1968—. Mem. adv. bd. Ill. Edn. Council, 1967—; mem. Pres.'s Com. 100, 1968; mem. Hamilton County Bicentennial Com.; chmn. rehab. com. McCoy Meml. Library and Hamilton County Hist. Soc. Bldg.; mem. Hamilton County Republican Com., 1950-68. Recipient Tchr. of Year award U. Ill. Edn. Dept., 1963; Merit award Gov. Ill. 1964; Distinguished Service award Future Farmers Am., 1967; George Washington medal honor Freedoms Found. Am., 1966, 69. Mem. NEA, Ill. Edn. Assn., Hamilton County (pres. 1970), Gallatin County hist. socs., Nat., Ill. (Tchr. of Tchrs.) assns. vocat. agr. tchrs., Rend Lake Symphony Soc., Arts and Humanities Soc., SAR, Hereditary Register of U.S., Phi Beta Kappa, Delta Sigma Phi. Presbyn. Mason, Kiwanian, Elk, Lion. Home: 401 Washington St S McLeansboro IL 62859 Office: 200 S Pearl St McLeansboro IL 62859

BRINKMAN, DONALD RAYMOND, computer services co. exec.; b. Aurora, Ill., Jan. 20, 1941; s. Edward and Bernice (Sinoskey) B.; B.S. in Engring., U. Mich., 1963, M.B.A., 1965; m. Jean Ann Bush, Sept. 15, 1961; children—Michelle, Robert. Research engr. U. Mich., Ann Arbor, 1963-65; exec. trainee Lockheed Ga. Co., Marietta, Ga., 1965-66; dist. mgr. Am. Appraisal Co., Mpls., 1966-68, regional mgr., Chgo., 1968-71; pres., founder Am. Valution, Des Plaines, Ill., 1971-74; pres., founder Valuation Systems Corp., Rolling Meadows, Ill., 1974—; advisor SEC; guest lectr. U. Chgo., U. Wis., Northwestern U. Mem. Nat. Assn. Accountants (guest speaker). Contbg. author: Handbook of Modern Accounting; Handbook of Cost Accounting. Contbr. articles in field to profl. jours. Home: 608 Carlsbad Trail Roselle IL 60172 Office: 5005 Newport Dr Rolling Meadows IL 60008

BRINKMAN, RAMON MINOR, bus. exec.; b. Vicksburg, Mich., July 17, 1930; s. Ernest B. and Mary (Elsman) B.; B.A., U. Ill., 1952; M.B.A., U. Mich., 1957; m. Deanna Raarup, Sept. 17, 1965; children—Gunther Matthew, Derek Alexander. Financial analyst SEC, 1957-59; v.p. Bache & Co., Inc., 1959-70; v.p. Frank's Nursery Sales, Inc., Detroit, 1970—; also dir.; dir. Spencer Foods, Inc. Served with USNR, 1952-55. Club: Down Town. Home: 1100 Three Mile Dr Grosse Pointe Park MI 48230 Office: 6399 E Nevada St Detroit MI 48234

BRINKMANN, WALTRAUD AUGUSTA ROSALIE, educator, geographer; b. Berlin, Germany, Mar. 26, 1937; d. Wilhelm Friedrich and Maria (Kutzki) B.; B.Sc. with distinction, U. Calgary (Alta.), 1967, M.Sc., 1969; Ph.D., U. Colo., 1974. Office clk., bookkeeper, Germany, Can., 1956-64; asso. investigator U. Colo., 1972-74; asst. prof. dept. geography and Inst. Environ. Studies, U. Wis., 1974—. Mem. Am., Canadian meteorol. socs., Am., Canadian assns. geographers, Am. Quaternary Assn. Contbr. articles to profl. jours. Home: 6302 Mineral Point Madison WI 53705 Office: Dept Geography U Wis Madison WI 53706

BRINKMEYER, WILLIS ROBERT, farm corp. exec.; b. Beatrice, Nebr., Jan. 4, 1931; s. Henry and Amelia Marie (Helmke) B.; graduate Bus. Adminstrn., Lincoln (Nebr.) Sch. Commerce; m. Shirley Louis Mitchell, Jan. 1, 1961; children—Renee, Mae Marie. Pres. Brinkmeyer Farms, Inc., Cortland, Nebr., 1972—. Mem. 18th Dist. Jud. Nominating Commn., 1973—. Mem. Top Farmers of Am. Republican. Lutheran. Home: Route 1 Cortland NE 68331

BRISCOE, KEITH G., coll. pres.; b. Adams, Wis., Oct. 16, 1933; B.S., Wis. State U., La Crosse, 1960; M.Ed., U. N.H., 1968; postgrad. Case Western Res. U., Iowa State U., U. Wis., Okla. State U.; LL.B. (hon.), Coll. Idaho, 1978; m. Carmen Irene Schweinler, Aug. 15, 1956; 1 dau., Susan Ann. Asst. dir. Coll. Union, Wis. State U., Stevens Point, 1960-62, U. N.H., 1962-64; dir. Coll. Union, dir. student activities, asst. prof. student life Baldwin Wallace Coll., Berea, Ohio, 1964-70; v.p. Coll. Steubenville (Ohio), 1970-74; pres. Buena Vista Coll., Storm Lake, Iowa, 1974—; higher edn. cons. Cuyahoga Community Coll., Coll. Wooster; v.p., treas. Ednl. Task, Inc., Berea, 1967-69; mem. nat. adv. bd. Coll. Transition Program, Berea, 1967-69; bd. dirs., treas., mem. exec. com. Nat. Council Advancement Small Colls., 1977—; Active Boy Scouts Am.; bd. dirs. Iowa Coll. Found., Iowa Lung Assn., Served with AUS, 1956-58. Mem. Assn. Coll. and Univ. Concert Mgrs. (trustee) UN Assn., Iowa Assn. Pvt. Colls. and Univs. (treas., exec. com. 1977—). Phi Epsilon Kappa, Phi Delta Kappa. Republican. Methodist. Clubs: Masons, Des Moines, Order of the Arch, Rotary. Author: Directory of College Unions, 1963; An Annotated Bibliography of the College Union, 1967; Alternatives to Financing Higher Private Education, 1973. Contbr. articles to profl. jours. Address: Office of Pres of Buena Vista Coll Buena Vista Coll Storm Lake IA 50588

BRISKIN, GERALD, psychologist; b. N.Y.C., Sept. 11, 1929; s. Benjamin and Minni Frances (Hutt) B.; B.A., U. Mich., 1950, M.A., 1951, Ph.D., 1954; m. Gloria Gene Clark, Sept. 11, 1952; children—Brett, Casey Buff. Dir. Byron Harless & Assos., Psychol. Consultants, Miami, Fla., 1957-58; dir. clin. services Psychol. Services Inc., Detroit, 1958-60; pvt. practice psychology, Garden City, Mich., 1960—. Dir. dept. clin. psychology Wyandotte Gen. Hosp. (Mich.), 1970—. Adj. prof. psychology U. Detroit, 1974—; cons. VA, 1965—, Lutheran Soc. Services Mich., 1962—. Pres., Varsity Acres Inc. harness horse breeding and racing, 1962—; sr. partner Amerael Petroleum, Garden City, 1974—. Served with AUS, 1952-57. Mem. Am. Psychol. Assn., Mich. Soc. Cons. Psychologists (chmn. standards and ethics com. 1963-68), Nat. Rehab. Assn., Council Advancement Psychol. Professions and Scis. Author: The Clinical Use of the Revised Bender-Gestalt Test, 1960; Letters from Dean, 1975. Office: 29055 Ford Rd Garden City MI 48135

BRISSMAN, BERNARD GUSTAVE, ins. co. exec.; b. St. Paul, May 10, 1919; s. Gustave Erie and Emma Barbara (Beetsch) B.; student U. Minn., 1937-41, 45-47, Butler U., 1963-67; m. Frances Irene Shackleton, May 30, 1942; children—Gerald B., Jonathan C., Joan (Mrs. George Perkins), Roland A., William G. Spl. agt. Gen. Accident, Mpls., 1945-49; mgr. Fireman's Fund, Mpls., 1949-54; v.p. Am. States Cos., Indpls., 1954—; dir. Am. States Ins. Co., Am. States Ins. Co. Tex., Am. Economy Ins. Co., Am. States Life Ins. Co., Preferred Ins. Co., Am. Union Ins. Co., Am. States of Tex. Lloyds. Served to capt. AUS, 1941-45. Mem. Chartered Property and Casualty Underwriters (pres. Minn. chpt. 1953, pres. Ind. chpt. 1956), Underwriting Execs. Council (pres. 1968). Clubs: Indianapolis Athletic, Indianapolis Sailing. Home: 8062 Claridge Rd Indianapolis IN 46260 Office: 500 N Meridian Indianapolis IN 46204

BRISTER, FRANK RAYFIELD, ednl. media specialist, educator; b. Gloucester, Mass., May 8, 1928; s. Frank John and Gladys Mae (Reid) B.; B.A. in Humanities (Rotary scholar), U. Hartford (Conn.), 1965; M.S. in TV-Radio, Syracuse U., 1966, certificate advanced studies, 1969. Coordinator audiovisual services Univ. Coll., Syracuse (N.Y.) U., 1966-69; dir. audiovisual services Ferris State Coll., Big Rapids, Mich., 1969-74, asst. prof. Sch. Edn. Learning Resources, chief instr. media tech. program learning resources careers, 1974—; cons. media utilization workshop modules to improve classroom instruction; author ednl. and community service mediated programs. Home: 504 S Michigan Ave Big Rapids MI 49307

BRISTOW, EUGENE KERR, educator; b. Birmingham, Ala., Feb. 12, 1927; s. Eugene B. and Hope (Kerr) B.; A.B., Ind. U., 1950, M.A. 1952; Ph.D., U. Iowa, 1956; m. Norma L. Jones, June 17, 1950; children—Pamela Ruth, Michael Eugene, Carol Jean, Mary Katherine. Tchr. New Albany (Ind.) High Sch., 1950-51, Reitz High Sch., Evansville, Ind., 1952-54; asst. prof. MacMurray Coll., 1956-57; instr. Ind. U., 1957-60, asst. prof. speech and theatre, 1960-68, asso. prof., 1968-71, asso. prof. theatre drama, 1971—, grad. sch. fellow, 1951-52, asso. prof. theatre and drama Russian East European Inst., Ind. U., 1972—; research fellow State U. Iowa, 1955-56; vis. asso. prof. U. Calif., Santa Barbara, 1968-69. Served with USAAF, 1945-46. Recipient Citation for Outstanding Contbn. to Democratic Processes, Mayor of Bloomington, Ind., 1959; named Outstanding Young Speech Tchr., Central States Speech Assn., 1957. Mem. AAUP, Modern Lang. Assn., Speech Communication Assn., Am. Theatre Assn., Am. Assn. Advancement Slavic Studies, Internat. Fedn. for Theatre Research, Am. Soc. for Theatre Research, Theatre Library Assn. Author: Five Plays of Alexander Ostrovsky, 1969. Contbr. articles profl. jours. and author several pamphlets. News editor Ednl. Theatre Jour., 1960-63. Home: 604 Staats Dr Bloomington IN 47401

BRITT, JAMES THOMAS, lawyer; b. Kansas City, Mo., Feb. 27, 1904; s. Aylett T. and Katherine B. (Henderson) B.; LL.B., Washington U., St. Louis, 1926; m. Ruth E. Burgin, Sept. 18, 1930; children—Thomas Burgin, Robert McCammon. Admitted to Mo. bar, 1926, since practiced in Kansas City; sr. partner firm Spencer, Fane, Britt & Browne, 1951—; instr. Real Estate Bd. Inst., 1945-66. Mem. bd. visitors Jackson County, Mo., 1948-53; bar com. 16th Jud. Circuit Mo., 1942-49; legal adviser local SSS, 1939-75; sec., dir. Commonwealth Theatres, Inc., 1965-77. Chmn. recreation adv. com. Kansas City, Mo., 1955-62. Co-founder, bd. dirs. Nat. Council Alcoholism Kansas City area, pres., 1966-67, exec. v.p., 1967-68; chmn. citizens' advisory bd. City-County Office Aging, 1969-72; bd. dirs. Kansas City Social Health Soc., 1969-72; chmn. citizens adv. bd. City-County Office Aging, 1969-72; mem. Mo. Advisory Council on Alcoholism; bd. dirs., exec. com., v.p. Starlight Theatre Assn. Mem. Am., Mo., Kansas City bar assns., Lawyers Assn. Kansas City, Kappa Alpha, Phi Delta Phi. Rotarian. Club: Kansas City; River. Contbr. articles to legal jours. Home: 409 W 58th Terr Kansas City MO 64113 Office: Power & Light Bldg Kansas City MO 64105

BRITT, RONALD LEROY, mech. engr.; b. Abilene, Kans., Mar. 1, 1935; s. Elvin Elbert and Lona Helen (Conn) B.; B.S.M.E., Wichita State U., 1963; m. Judith Ann Salter, June 29, 1957; children—Brett Gavin, Mark Damon, Melissa. Product engr. to product planner Hotpoint div. Gen. Electric Co., Chgo., 1963-68; product planner Norge Co., Chgo., 1968; product mgr., asst. dir. engring. Leigh Products Inc., Coopersville, Mich., 1968-74; mgr. research and devel. Miami-Carey div. Jim Walter Corp., Monroe, Ohio, 1974—. Active, Boy Scouts Am., 1970-73, PTA, 1973—. Served with U.S. Army, 1958-60. Recipient Inventor's award Gen. Electric Co., 1967. Mem. ASME. Republican. Congregationalist. Clubs: Free Blown Glassblowing, Carnival and Art Glass Collectors. Patentee in field. Home: 2605 Central Ave Middletown OH 45042 Office: 203 Garver Rd Monroe OH 45050

BRITT, RUTH EVANGELINE BURGIN (MRS. JAMES T. BRITT), civic worker; b. Fayette, Mo., Mar. 15, 1907; d. Samuel Herschel and Lora (Miller) Burgin; student Wesleyan Woman's Coll., 1926-27; A.B., Tallahassee Woman's Coll., 1928; m. James T. Britt, Sept. 18, 1930; children—Thomas Burgin, Robert McCammon. Mem. Woman's City Club, Kansas City, Mo., 1931—, chmn. hosp. com., 1931-35; mem. Guild Friends Art at William Rockhill Nelson Gallery, 1961—, fireside com. Kansas City Art Inst., 1948-49, women's div. Kansas City Philharmonic Assn., 1966—, Kansas City Mus. Assn., 1966—; chmn. Christian-social relations Women's Soc. Christian Service, 1946-48, pres., 1937-38, chmn. missions, 1961-63; chmn. St. Francis Aux. of St. Francis Home for Boys, Salina and Ellsworth, Kans., 1946-48, supplies com. Community Chest Dr., 1951; vol. visitor for aged Mattie Rhodes Settlement House, 1948; Hosp. Gray Lady, 1948-50; mem. bd. George H. Nettleton Home for Aged Women, 1969-71. Pres., Young Women's Democratic Club, 1931-33. Mem. U.D.C., D.A.R. (regent 1942-43). Methodist (adminstrv. bd. 1970—). Address: 409 W 58th Terr Kansas City MO 64113

BRITT, STEUART-HENDERSON, mktg. cons.; b. Kingdom of Callaway; s. Dr. A.T. and Katherine (Henderson) B.; A.B., Washington U., St. Louis, 1931, M.A., 1932; Columbia U. Sch. of Law; Ph.D. in Psychology, Yale U., 1935; m. Marion M. Hansell, June 1, 1936. Admitted to bar and practiced law in Mo., 1929; admitted to bar N.Y., 1936, U.S. Supreme Court, 1936, U.S. Court of Appeals for D.C., 1937; fellow Washington U., 1931-32; fellow and asst. in psychology Inst. of Human Relations, Yale U., 1932-35; research asst. Inst. Ednl. Research, Columbia U., 1935-36; asst. prof. psychology George Washington U., Washington, 1936-42; sec. Emergency Com. in Psychology, 1941-42; exec. sec. National Resources Planning Bd.'s Com. on Wartime Requirements for Specialized Personnel, 1942; exec. dir. Office of Psychol. Personnel, Nat. Research Council, Washington, 1942-43, also sec. Emergency Com. in Psychology, 1942-43; cons. Nat. Resources Planning Bd. and War Manpower Commn., Washington, 1941-43; exec. McCann-Erickson, Inc., N.Y.C., 1945-51; v.p. Needham, Louis & Brorby, Inc., Chgo., 1951-56; adminstrv. v.p. Earle Ludgin & Co., Chgo., 1956-57; prof. mktg. and advt. Northwestern U., 1957-75; pres. Edn. Marketing & Mgmt. Found., 1950-71; pres. Britt and Frerichs, Inc., mktg. research firm, 1971-77, chmn., 1977—; cons. Westinghouse Ann. Sci. Talent Search, 1942-60; cons. editor McGraw-Hill series in advt. and mktg., 1951-64; editorial dir. Mktg. Sci. Inst., 1967-68; mktg. cons. Leo Burnett Co., 1957-68; producer Ann. Advt. Age Creative Workshop, 1958-70. Lectures and seminars countries of Europe and Asia, Australia, New Zealand. Served from lt. to lt. comdr., USNR, hdqrs. Comdr. in Chief U.S. Fleet, 1943-45. Recipient alumni citation Wash. U., 1959. Diplomate indsl. psychology Am. Bd. Examiners in Profl. Psychology; registered psychologist, Ill. Fellow Am. Psychol. Assn., Am. Sociol. Assn., Am. Acad. Advt.; mem. Am. Mktg. Assn., Philippine Mktg. Assn., ESOMAR. Clubs: Cosmos (Washington); Yale (N.Y.C.); University (Chgo.); Plaza (Chgo.); Canal Shores Golf (Evanston). Author and editor 16 books including: Social Psychology of Modern Life, 1941, rev. 1949; (with I. Gaeber) Jews in a Gentle World, 1942; Selected Readings in Social Psychology, 1950; (with D.B. Lucas) Advertising Psychology and Research, 1950; The Spenders, 1960 (transl. into Spanish); (with D.B. Lucas) Measuring Advertising Effectiveness (transl. into Dutch, German, Italian, Japanese) 1963; (with H. W. Boyd, Jr.) Marketing Management and Administrative Action, 1963, rev., 1968, 73, 77; Consumer Behavior and the Behavioral Sciences, 1966; Do Advertising Agencies Train Trainees?, 1968; Consumer Behavior in Theory and in Action, 1970; Psychological Experiments in Consumer Behavior, 1970; Marketing Manager's Handbook, 1973; Psychological Principles of Consumer Behavior, 1917; also over 200 articles; also editor 51 books in 3 book series. Editor: Jour. of Mktg., 1957-66. Home: 211 Greenleaf Ave Wilmette IL 60091 Office: 637 Library Pl Evanston IL 60201

BRITTAIN, RICHARD EDWARD, coll. pres.; b. Frankfort, Ind., May 14, 1917; s. Walter Grover and Mary (Dill) B.; B.Mus. Edn., VanderCook Coll. Music, 1941, M.Mus. Edn., 1955; m. Sophia Gorlach, May 13, 1942; children—Bonnie Jean, Robert Richard. With VanderCook Coll. Music, Chgo., 1936—, prof. music edn., 1946—, pres., 1975—. Pres., Westchester P.T.A., 1963-64. Exec. bd. dirs. Mid West Nat. Band and Orch. Clinic, 1974-75. Served to lt., 11th Airborne Div., AUS, 1941-45. Mem. Am. Bandmasters Assn., Coll. Band Dirs. Assn., Leblanc Music Educators (nat. adv. bd.), Kappa Kappa Psi. Episcopalian. Home: 1625 Hawthorne Ave Westchester IL 60153 Office: 3209 S Michigan Ave Chicago IL 60616

BRITTEN, WILLIAM HARRY, editor, pub.; b. Zearing, Iowa, Aug. 25, 1921; s. Harry William and Gertrude Alice (Lehman) B.; B.A., Western Union Coll., 1943; student Iowa State Coll., summer 1942; M.A., State U. Iowa, 1948. Reporter, Worcester (Mass.) Telegram, 1948-55; landscaper John F. Keenen, Leicester, Mass., 1956; sales dept. clk. Reed & Prince Mfg. Co., Worcester, 1957-63, inventory control clk., 1964, chief expeditor, 1965; state editor Marshalltown (Ia.) Times-Republican, 1965-66, staff writer, 1966-67; news editor Denison (Ia.) Bull. and Rev., 1967-68; city editor Boone News Republican, 1968; editor, pub., owner The Tri-County News, Zearing, 1968—; editor, pub. Hubbard (Iowa) Rev., 1969-72. Sec. Young Men's Republican Club, Worcester, 1957; corr. sec. Young People's Rep. Club, 1958; mem. Ward 8 Rep. Com., Worcester, 1960-65; Rep. candidate Mass. state legislature, 1960; ward chmn. to elect Edward W. Brooke atty. gen. Mass., 1962, 64; bd. dirs. Story County Cancer Soc., 1976—. Served with AUS, 1943-45. Mem. Iowa Press Assn., Nat. Newspaper Assn., Am. Fedn. Arts., Westmar Coll., U. Iowa alumni assns. Mem. Ch. of Christ. Home: Pearl St Zearing IA 50278 Office: Main St Zearing IA 50278

BRITTON, DONALD ROBISON, arts adminstr.; b. Phila., Oct. 8, 1937; s. Frank Robison and Gladys Rebecca (Hoff) B.; student Haverford Coll., 1955, Chgo. City Coll., 1973; m. Susan Marchant, Mar. 3, 1964; children—Eve Marchant, Christopher Robison. Actor, Columbia Pictures, also various Broadway shows, 1956-61; dist. mgr. Trans-Lux Theatres, N.Y.C., 1962-66; mng. dir. Meadow Brook Theatre, Detroit, 1966-70; founder, exec. dir. Upstage: Detroit, Inc., 1971-72; bus. mgr. Lyric Opera of Chgo., 1972—; v.p., treas. Opera Sch. Chgo., 1975—. Regional adjudicator Am. Coll. Theatre Festival, 1971-72; lectrs. various colls. and univs. Bd. dirs. Mich. Council on Arts, 1969-70. Served with AUS, 1961. Mem. Assn. Theatrical Press Agts. and Mgrs., Asso. Councils on Arts. Club: Arts, Saddle and Cycle (Chgo.). Home: 232 E Walton Pl Chicago IL 60611 Office: 20 N Wacker Dr Chicago IL 60606

BRITTON, RICHARD HARWOOD, optometrist; b. Lansing, Mich., Apr. 25, 1932; s. Oscar and Lilah (Stafford) B.; student U. Mich., 1950-51, Mich. State U., 1951-52; Dr. Optometry, Ohio State U., 1955; m. Marinell G. Bailey, May 20, 1956; children—Donna Jo, Richard Harwood II, Elizabeth Ann (dec.), Mark Eric, Jeffry Alan, Kevin Michael. Individual practice optometry, Howell, Mich., 1958—; founder Central Mich. Optometric Center, 1962, mem. bd., 1962-65; lectr.; partner, co-owner Britco Corp., 1962—; past pres. Howell Holding Corp. No. 2 (real estate). Mem. health manpower sect. regional med. program, 1968-72, also Mich. Comprehensive Health Care Planning Commn., 1968-72; mem. Mich. Gov.'s Health Adv. Bd., 1968-72; adv. bd. vision sect. Mich. Dept. Health, 1970-75. Bd. dirs. Coll. Optometry Ferris State Coll., 1974—, also adv. bd. optometric assistance program, 1972-75; mem. exec. bd. Wolverine council Boy Scouts Am., 1975—. Served with AUS, 1955-58. Recipient Key Man award Mich. Optometric Assn., 1968, Mich. Optometrist of Yr. award, 1971-72. Mem. Central Mich. Optometric Soc. (optometrist of Yr. 1968, 71), Am. (chmn. new acad. facilities 1968-70), Mich. (chmn. new acad. facilities 1966-74, chmn. practice mgmt. com. 1962-66, trustee 1967-72, pres. 1970-71) optometric assns., Mich. Assn. Professions (dir., exec. bd. 1970-73), Epsilon Psi Epsilon. Presbyterian. Mason, Elk. Inventor. Home: 3194 Golf Club Rd Howell MI 48843 Office: 1191 Bryon Rd Howell MI 48843

BRIXIUS, FRANK JOSEPH, lawyer; b. St. Cloud, Minn., May 23, 1938; s. Albert J. and Mary Kathryn (Thiesen) B.; B.S. (William scholar), U. Minn., 1961; J.D., William Mitchell Coll. Law, 1966; m. Suzanne DeLong, July 14, 1962; children—Elizabeth Ann, Mary Alanah, Frank Joseph. With First Nat. Bank Mpls., 1962-66; admitted to Minn. bar, 1966; asso. firm Hvass, Weisman & King, Mpls., 1966—, partner, 1969—. Mem. Greenwood (Minn.) City Council, 1970-71, 71—, chmn. adv. com., 1970, council rep. to Hennepin County League Municipalities and Met. League Municipalities, 1972—; mayor, Greenwood, 1973—; co-chmn. Hennepin County Criminal Justice Council, 1974-75. Dir. Suburban Rate Authority; dir., mem. exec. com. Suburban League Municipalities, 1974-75, also chmn. pub. safety dept. 1974-75. Trustee Alpha Nu Trust Fund, 1974—. Recipient West Publishing Outstanding Law Student award, 1965. Mem. Am., Minn., Hennepin County bar assns., Am., Minn. trial lawyers assns., Assn. Met. Municipalities (dir., exec. com. 1974-75), Am. Judicature Soc., Chi Psi. Home: 21720 Fairview Greenwood MN 55331 Office: 715 Cargill Bldg Minneapolis MN 55402

BROCHER, TOBIAS HEINZ, physician, educator; b. Danzig, Apr. 21, 1917; s. Albert B. and Clara M. (Stenzel) B.; came to U.S., 1968; B.A., Paulsen Coll. (Germany), 1935; M.D., U. Berlin (Germany), 1942; m. Dorothy Allen Barash, Dec. 26, 1974; children by previous marriage—Stefanie, Corinna (Mrs. von Cramon), Muni Michael Barash, Jeffry Andrew Barash, Ace Alan Barash. Intern, Charité Hosp., Berlin, 1942-43; resident Psychiat. State Hosp., Schussenried, Germany, 1945-46; practice medicine, specializing in psychiatry, Stuttgart, Germany, 1947-48, Frankfurt/Main, 1964-68, Pitts., 1968-70, Topeka, 1970—; dir. State Mental Hosp. Schussenried, 1947-53; dir. Inst. for Psychotherapy, Stuttgart, 1953-63; asso. dir. Sigmund Freud Inst., Frankfurt/Main, 1963-68; prof. psychiatry and psychoanalysis Justus Liebig U., Giessen, Germany, 1962-72; prof., dir. Center for Applied Behavioral Sci., Topeka, 1972—; Maurice Falk prof. U. Pitts., 1968-70; cons. to UN, 1956, UNESCO, 1964. Trustee U. Ulm, Donau, 1955—. Fellow European Inst. for Transnat. Research, Internat. P.E.N.; mem. Am., Internat., German psychoanalytic assns., Am. Psychiat. Assn., Am. Acad. Psychiatry and Law, AMA. Lion. Author: The Unknown Ego, 1969; Group Dynamics and Education, 1967; El Yo e Los Otros, 1968; Psicologia dell' Io, 1971; Aufstand Gegen Tradition, 1972; Difficulties of Loving, 1974; Stages of Life, 1976; others. Producer ednl. films, 1957-74. Office: PO Box 829 Menninger Found Topeka KS 66601

BROCK, THOMAS WALTER, glass co. exec.; b. Marion, Ind., Feb. 15, 1931; s. Richard Mark and Beulah Blanch (Gransinger) B.; B.S., Ball State Tchrs. Coll., 1953; M.S., U. Toledo, 1962; m. Lois Maxine Robinson, Feb. 19, 1951; children—Teresa Eileen, William Jeffrey. With Owens Illinois Inc., Toledo, 1953—, materials and process engr., 1966-74, contract adminstr., 1974—. Pres., Mt. Vernon PTA, 1963. Mem. Am. Ceramic Soc., Soc. Glass Tech., Nat. Contract Mgmt. Assn., Sigma Xi. Republican. Methodist. Patentee in glass-ceramic materials and products. Home: 2539 Orkney Dr Toledo OH 43606 Office: PO Box 1035 Toledo OH 43666

BROCK, THOMAS WAYNE, food mfg. co. exec.; b. Cin., Jan. 26, 1943; s. Gene Allen and Marcella Lucille B.; B.S., U. Cin., 1966; m. Carol Jean Klein, July 24, 1965; children—Marck, Kimberly, Deborah, Dwayne. With Gen. Foods Corp., various locations, 1966-71, region asst., White Plains, N.Y., 1970, sales devel. asst., 1970-71; dist. mgr. Purex Corp., Chgo., 1971; area mgr. Bristol Myers Co. Drackett div., Chgo., 1972-74; br. mgr. Unifax Inc., Macon, Ga., 1974-75; nat. sales mgr. Sunmark Cos., St. Louis, 1975-77; v.p. broker sales Borden Foods Co., Columbus, Ohio, 1977—. Mem. Youth Sports Council. Mem. Nat. Food Brokers Assn. Home: 4131 Lyon Dr Upper Arlington OH 43220 Office: 180 Broad St E Columbus OH 43215

BROCKHAUS, JOYCE PATRICIA, nurse; b. Tampa, Fla., May 21, 1946; d. John Paul and Lorraine Elizabeth (Zoll) Dees; degree in nursing Belleville (Ill.) Jr. Coll., 1966; B.S., Washington U., St. Louis, 1968; M.S.N., U. Mo.-Columbia, 1971; Ph.D., St. Louis U., 1976; m. Robert Herold, June 13, 1970; children—Cheryl Lynn, Robert Harold, Jr. Staff nurse Washington U. Health Service, St. Louis, 1966-68; head nurse St. Louis State Hosp.-Youth Center, 1968-70, coordinator in-service edn., 1971-72; v.p. Progressive Mgmt. Enterprises Ltd., St. Louis, 1971; instr. nursing U. Mo.-Columbia, 1972-73; clin. instr. nursing St. Louis U., 1973-76, asst. prof., 1977—; cons. in field. NIMH fellow, 1966-71. Fellow N. Am. Center on Adoption; mem. Am., Mo. nurses assns., Nat. Soc. Autistic Children, Open Door Soc. Mo., Mo. Foster Care Assn., Am. Psychol. Assn., Am. Personnel and Guidance Assn., Phi Theta Kappa, Sigma Theta Tau. Home: 10000 Hilltop Dr Saint Louis MO 63128 Office: 1504 S Grand St Saint Louis MO 63104

BROCKOPP, DANIEL CARL, clergyman, educator, assn. exec.; b. Park Falls, Wis., Sept. 7, 1934; s. William George and Martha Anna (Baumann) B.; student Concordia Coll., 1952-55; B.Th., Concordia Sem., 1961; S.T.M., Lutheran Sch. Theology, Chgo., 1966. Ordained to ministry Luth. Ch., 1962; instr. liturgy and ch. music Concordia Sem., Springfield, Ill., 1962-64; asst. prof. theology Valparaiso (Ind.) U., 1964—, precentor Chapel of the Resurrection, 1964—, asst. dean, 1975—; exec. sec. Luth. Soc. for Worship, Music and the Arts, Valparaiso, 1969—; editor Response in Worship, Music and the Arts, 1973; dir. Inst. Liturgical Studies, 1975—. Mem. Am. Soc. for Ch. Architecture, Art Inst. Chgo., Luth. Soc. Worship, Music and the Arts, N.Am. Acad. Liturgy.

BRODHEAD, JOHN, ins. co. exec.; b. Springfield, Ill., June 12, 1917; s. John and Dorothy (Farish) B.; A.B., Amherst Coll., 1940; postgrad. Washington U., St. Louis, 1949-50; m. Josephine Carr, Aug. 1, 1942; 1 dau., Josephine B. Brodhead Roberts. Partner, George D. Capen & Co., St. Louis, 1945-63; v.p. and mgr. Marsh & McLennan Inc., St. Louis, 1963-71, exec. v.p. and dir., 1969, div. mgr. so. div., 1969-73; head nat. sales New Bus. Devel., St. Louis, 1973—; dir. Marlennan Corp., N.Y.C. Active United Fund St. Louis, 1946—, Arts and Edn. Council, 1963—, St. Louis County Watchdog com., 1969, Municipal Opera Guarantee, 1967—, Backstoppers, 1965—, St. Louis Easter Seals, 1971—. Bd. dirs. St. Louis County Day Sch., Rehab. Center St. Louis, St. Louis Assn. Retarded Children. Child Guidance Clinic. Served to lt. comdr. USNR, 1940-45. Decorated Navy Cross medal with Gold Star medal. Mem. Mo. Hist. Soc. Clubs: St. Louis Country, Rolling Rock, Log Cabin, Deer Creek, Racquet, Twenty-Nine, Noonday. Home: 4 Town and Country Dr Saint Louis MO 63124 Office: 515 Olive St Saint Louis MO 63101

BRODHEAD, WILLIAM MCNULTY, congressman; b. Cleve., Sept. 12, 1941; s. William McNulty and Agnes (Franz) B.; A.B., Wayne State U., 1965; J.D., U. Mich., 1967; m. Kathleen Garlock, Jan. 16, 1965; children—Michael, Paul. Admitted to Mich. bar, 1968, practiced in Detroit, 1968-74; mem. Mich. Ho. of Reps., 1970-74; mem. 94th-95th Congresses from 17th Mich. dist. Home: 24261 Grand River Ave Detroit MI 48219 Office: 416 Cannon House Office Bldg Washington DC 20515

BRODKEY, ROBERT STANLEY, chem. engr.; b. Los Angeles, Sept. 14, 1928; s. Harold R. and Clara (Goldman) B.; m. Martha Mahr, Dec. 22, 1958 (div. Nov. 1971); 1 son, Philip Arthur; m. 2d, Carolyn Patch, Dec. 6, 1975; A.A., San Francisco City Coll., 1948; B.Chemistry, U. Calif. at Berkeley, 1950, M.S. in Chem. Enging., 1950; Ph.D. in Chem. Enging. (Gulf Oil fellow), U. Wis., 1952. Research chem. engr. Esso Research & Enging. Co., Linden, N.J., 1952-56, Esso Standard Oil Co., Bayway, N.J., 1956-57; asst. prof. chem. enging. Ohio State U., Columbus, 1957-60, asso. prof., 1960-64, prof., 1964—; cons. Union Carbide Chem. Co., Charleston, W.Va., 1964—. Expository lect. GAMM Conf., 1975. Fellow Am. Inst. Chemists; mem. Am. Inst. Chem. Engrs., Am. Chem. Soc., N.Y. Acad. Scis., Soc. Enging. Sci., Soc. Rheology, Sigma Xi, Phi Lambda Upsilon, Alpha Gamma Sigma. Recipient Outstanding Paper of Year award Canadian Jour. Chem. Enging., 1970; NATO sr. fellow in sci., 1972, Alexander Von Humboldt Found. sr. U.S. scientist award, 1975 (both at Max Planck Institut fur Stromungsforschung, Gottingen, West Germany). Author: Fluid Motion and Mixing, 1966; The Phenomena of Fluid Motions, 1967. Editor: Turbulence in Mixing Operations, 1975. Contbr. articles to profl. jours. Patentee in field. Home: 246 N Delta Dr Columbus OH 43214 Office: 140 W 19th Ave Columbus OH 43210

BRODLEY, JOSEPH FRANKLIN, educator; b. Washington, Sept. 22, 1926; s. Joseph and Francis Barbara (Gross) B.; B.A., U. Calif. at Los Angeles, 1946-49; LL.B., Yale, 1952; LL.M., Harvard, 1953; m. Angeli Bolwin, June 4, 1960; children—Barbara Joanna, Carla Elizabeth. Admitted to Calif. bar, 1953, N.Y. bar, 1956; asso. firm Dewey, Ballantine, Palmer & Wood, N.Y.C., 1956-61; partner Richards, Watson & Hemmerling, Los Angeles, 1961-68; prof. law Ind. U., Bloomington, 1968—. Lectr., U. So. Calif., 1964-68. Served with JAG Corps, USAF, 1953-56. Mem. Am. Assn. Law Schs. (chmn. antitrust and econ. regulation sect. 1974—), Am. Bar Assn. (chmn. antitrust law subcom. on exempt occupations 1970-74), Phi Beta Kappa. Bd. advisers Antitrust Bull., Jour. Reprints of Antitrust Law and Econs. Contbr. legal articles to publs. Home: 2300 Browncliff St Bloomington IN 47401 Office: Law Sch Ind U Bloomington IN 47401

BRODMAN, ESTELLE, librarian; b. N.Y.C., June 1, 1914; d. Henry and Nettie (Sameth) Brodman; A.B., Cornell U., 1935; B.S., Columbia U., 1936, M.S., 1943, Ph.D., 1953; D.Sc. (hon.), U. Ill., 1974. Asst. librarian N.Y. Hosp. Sch. Nursing, 1936-37; loan desk asst. to acting librarian med. library Columbia, 1937-49; chief reference div. and asst. librarian for reference services Nat. Library of Medicine, 1949-61; librarian, asso. prof. med. history, Washington U. Sch. Medicine, St. Louis, 1961-64, librarian, prof. med. history, 1964—; instr. Columbia Sch. Library Service, 1946-51; lectr. Cath. U. Dept. Library Sci., 1957; vis. prof. Japan Library Sch., Keio U., Tokyo, Japan, 1962, U. Mo., 1971, 73; expert in documentation Central Planning Inst., New Delhi, Institute, 1967-68, S.-E. Regional Office, WHO, New Delhi, 1970, UN Population div., Bangkok, Thailand, 1973, SE Asia, 1976, UN Fund Population Activities, 1976. Cons. NIMH. Mem. Pres.'s Nat. Adv. Commn. on Libraries; chmn. biomed. communications study sect. NIH, 1973-75. Mem. Am., Med. (pres. 1964-65, dir. 1961-64, editor bull. 1947-57, Noyes award 1971) library assns., Spl. Libraries Assn. (past dir.), Am. Assn. History Medicine, Bibliog. Soc. Am. Author: Development of Med. Bibliography, 1954. Home: 4464 W Pine Blvd St Louis MO 63108 Office: Washington U Sch Medicine St Louis MO 63110

BRODRICK, HERMON STEPHENS, architect; b. Greenville, Ohio, Jan. 31, 1917; s. Omar S. and Treva Mae (Stephens) B.; B. Arch., Miami U., Oxford, Ohio, 1938; m. Norma Virginia Stewart, Feb. 8, 1941; children—Margaret Elizabeth, Pauline Louise. Draftsman, Walker & Norwick, 1938-41; architect Walker, Norwick & Templin, 1946-51; partner Walker Norwick & Assos., 1951-59, Brodrick & Makarius, 1959-67, Brodrick, Makarius, Moulenbelt & Seifert, Dayton, Ohio, 1967-75; supt. bldg. inspection City of Kettering (Ohio), 1976—. Mem. Bd. Bldg. Code Standards of Montgomery County, 1963-73, Kettering Planning Commn, 1972-75. Served with USAF, 1943-45. Mem. AIA, Architects Soc. Ohio (pres. 1959). Mem. United Ch. of Christ (trustee Ohio conf. 1970-73; corp. bd. world ministeries 1970-73). Home: 272 Balmoral Dr Kettering OH 45429 Office: 2305 Farhills Ave Dayton OH 45419

BRODSKY, JACK DAVID, gynecologist; b. Boston, Oct. 26, 1922; s. Julius and Augusta (Rogers) B.; student Tufts, 1939-46, M.D., 1946; m. Lois E. Prince, Sept. 3, 1948; children—Larry S., Daniel P., Cheryl K., Marla R. Intern Michael Reese Hosp., Chgo., 1946-47, resident, 1950-53; practice medicine, specializing in obstetrics and gynecology Champaign, Ill., 1953—; mem. staff Burnham City Hosp., Mercy Hosp., McKinley Hosp., Gibson City Hosp. Served with USAF, 1947-49. Mem. Phi Beta Kappa, Phi Delta Epsilon, Alpha Epsilon Pi. Rotarian. Home: 710 Lasell St Champaign IL 61820 Office: 301 E Springfield St Champaign IL 61820

BROECKER, HOWARD WILLIAM, lawyer; b. Chgo., May 16, 1940; s. Wallace Charles and Edith May (Smith) B.; student N. Central Coll., Wheaton Coll., 1959-63; J.D., Ill. Inst. Tech., 1966; m. Candace Balfour, Aug. 19, 1961; children—Peter Jon, Christopher Curtis, Anne Llewellyn. Admitted to Ill. bar, 1966; asso. Ehrlich, Bundesen, Friedman & Ross, Chgo., 1966-67, Ehrlich, Bundesen & Cohn, 1967-70; partner Ehrlich, Bundesen, Broecker & Sproger, 1970—; lectr. Ill. Inst. Continuing Legal Edn., 1970—, Fox Valley Bd. Realtors, 1975—; instr. Am. Savs. and Loan Inst., 1971-72. Bd. dirs. Sunny Ridge Children's Home, 1975—. Mem. Am., Ill., Chgo. bar assns., Am. Acad. Matrimonial Lawyers (bd. mgrs. 1977—), Ill. Inst. Tech. Chgo. Kent Alumni Assn. (pres. 1975-77), Chgo. Council Lawyers. Baptist. Home: 5 N 074 Route 31 Saint Charles IL 60174 Office: 69 W Washington St Chicago IL 60602 also 115 Campbell St Geneva IL 60134

BROGAN, JOHN CLINTON, ins. co. exec.; b. Antioch, Ill., June 9, 1915; s. Hugh John and Margaret Ellen (Smith) B.; B.A., U. Ill., 1936; m. Eleanor Kirkland, July 14, 1950; 1 dau., Tracy; stepchildren—James S. Kemper, Linda Kemper Fair. With Zurich Ins. Co., Chgo., 1937-41, 46-49, Rollins Burdick Hunter Co., Chgo., 1949-56; Youngberg-Carlson Co., Chgo., 1956—, now chmn.; chmn. bd. Chgo. Helicopter Airways, 1962-66, Instnl. Ins. Co. of Am., 1960-67, Ford City Bank, 1965-68, J.H. Lea and Co., 1962—, Scarborough and Co., 1974—. Served to brig. gen. F.A. U.S. Army, 1936-37, 41-46. Decorated Legion of Merit, Bronze Star, Air medal, Croix de Guerre. Clubs: Mid Day (Chgo.), Glen View (Golf, Ill.), LaQuinta (Calif.) Country, Metropolitan Club of Chgo., Tavern Club of Chgo. Home: Two Elm Circle Golf IL 60029 Office: 222 N Dearborn St Chicago IL 60601

BROHEN, HARRY GENE, assn. exec.; b. Orange, N.J., Sept. 27, 1926; s. Harold William and Loretta Agnes (LaTourette) B.; A.B., Rutgers U., 1951; M.Ed., Xavier U., 1969; postgrad. No. Ill. U., 1973; m. Anne Chapola, Dec. 11, 1958; 1 dau., Brenda. Dir. pub. relations, Rutgers U., Newark, 1951-52; reporter Morristown (N.J.) Daily Record, 1952-53, Newark Evening News, 1953-57; pres. Harry Brohen Assos., Newark, 1957-58; dir. pub. relations and advt. United Fund Dade County, 1958-61; dir. community services ARC; asso. dir. advt. and pub. relations div. Cin. Area United Appeal, 1961-69; dir. promotion and pub. relations devel. United Community Funds and Councils of Am., N.Y.C., 1969-70; dir. pub. relations and advt. Met. Crusade Mercy/Community Fund Chgo., 1970-74; v.p. pub. relations and advt. Nat. Assn. Realtors, Chgo., 1974—. Vice pres. Superior Advt. Inc., Chgo., 1974—. Mem. nat. pub. relations adv. com. United Way Am., 1971-73. Served with USNR, 1943-46. Mem. Pub. Relations Soc. Am., Pub. Relations Clinic Chgo., Advt. Club Chgo., Nat. Assn. Real Estate Editors, Press Club Chgo., Am. Mgmt. Assn., Smithsonian Inst. Home: 1520 N Chippewa Dr Naperville IL 60540 Office: 155 E Superior St Chicago IL 60611

BROLANDER, GLEN EARL, ednl. adminstr.; b. Rockford, Ill., Dec. 14, 1929; s. Earl Raymond and Verona (Lindblom) B.; B.S., U. Ill., 1951; M.A., U. Ky., 1956; m. Lois Elaine Nestander, Nov. 7, 1959; children—Randall John, Sheryl Ann. Asst. comptroller Augustana Coll., Rock Island, Ill., 1953-59, comptroller, 1959-61, treas., comptroller, 1961-65; v.p. for financial affairs and treas., 1965—. Dir. Black Hawk Fed. Savs. and Loan Assn. Pres., Sac-Fox council Boy Scouts Am., 1964-65, Illowa council, 1968-70; pres. Rock Island Community Chest, 1964-65; v.p. United Appeal Rock Island County, 1965-66. Bd. dirs. Luth. Hosp., Moline, Ill., 1960-69, 72—, pres., 1965-68, 74-75. Served to 1st lt. AUS, 1951-53. Named Young Man of Year, Rock Island Jr. C. of C., 1959; recipient Silver Beaver award Boy Scouts Am.. 1959. Mem. Rock Island C. of C. (pres. 1973-74, dir. 1966-68, 70-75), Nat., Central assns. coll. and univ. bus. officers, Swedish Pioneer Hist. Soc. (dir. 1973—), Phi Gamma Delta, Alpha Phi Omega. Lutheran. Kiwanian. Home: 3231 29th Ave Ct Rock Island IL 61201 Office: 639 38th St Rock Island IL 61201

BRONSON, KENNETH, judge; b. Detroit, Feb. 3, 1934; s. Charles and Anne (Pearlman) B.; A.B., U. Mich., 1958; J.D., Wayne State U., 1957; m. Andrea M. Arrieta, Nov. 14, 1974; children—Keith, Andrew, Steve, Pandy, Bill, Bruce. Instr. English constl. history U. Mich., 1957-58; admitted to Mich. bar, 1957; practiced in Ann Arbor and Ypsilanti, Mich.; asso. firm Bonisteel & Bonisteel, 1957-59; atty. City of Ypsilanti, 1959-75; mem. firm Bronson & Egnor, 1969-75; judge, City of Saline (Mich.), 1965-68; spl. asst. pros. atty., 1959-65. Mem. Gov.'s Spl. Com. on Traffic Safety, 1964-68; mem. State Bar Assembly, 1972-76. Mem. Am. Judicature Soc., Am. Bar Assn. (editor State Bar Jour. 1973—). Clubs: Bayview Yacht (Detroit); Washtenaw Country (Ypsilanti). Home: 3520 E Huron River Dr Ann Arbor MI 48104 Office: Washtenaw County Service Center Washtenaw Ave Ann Arbor MI 48104

BROOKER, DONALD BROWN, educator; b. Troy Grove, Ill., Dec. 5, 1916; s. Claud and Lucy Whitner (Munro) B.; A.A., Iberia Jr. Coll., 1936; B.S., U. Mo., 1947, M.S., 1949; m. Thelma Georgia Vaughn, Sept. 12, 1936; children—Larry Brown, Nancy Jill. Auditor, Prodn. Mktg. Adminstrn., Columbia, Mo., 1938-42; instr. Purdue U., Lafayette, Ind., 1949-51; mem. faculty U. Mo., Columbia, 1951—, prof. agrl. engring., 1962—. Served with USAAC, 1942-45. Fellow Am. Soc. Agrl. Engrs.; mem. Nat., Mo. socs. profl. engrs., Am. Soc. Enging. Edn., Am. Soc. Agrl. Engrs. (chmn. mid-central region 1962, dir. 1976-78), Sigma Xi, Phi Kappa Phi, Tau Beta Pi, Pi Tau Sigma, Gamma Sigma Delta, Alpha Epsilon. Author: (with others) Drying Cereal Grains, 1974. Contbr. articles to profl. jours. Home: 2314 Ridgemont St Columbia MO 65201 Office: Dept Agricultural Engineering Univ Mo Columbia MO 65201

BROOKFIELD, DUTTON, clothing mfr., rancher; b. Kansas City, Mo., Dec. 31, 1917; s. Arthur D. and Elizabeth (Blish) B.; B.S., U. Mo., 1939; m. Betty Bell, Nov. 16, 1940; children—Karen Ann, Arthur Dutton II, Charles R., Betty Bell. Pres. Unitog Co., Kansas City, Mo., 1953—; dir. First Nat. Bank, Kansas City, First Nat. Charter Corp., Kansas City, Southwestern Bell Telephone Co., St. Louis, Am. Can Co., Kansas City Power & Light Co.; trustee Northwestern Mut. Life Ins. Co., Milw., 1968—, mem. exec. com., 1970—. Mem. Bd. Police Commrs., Kansas City, 1957-61. Bd. dirs. Civic Council Greater Kansas City, pres., 1970-71; bd. dirs. United Funds, Kansas City, Mo.; chmn. athletic council U. Mo., 1952-55; vice chmn. trustees U. Mo. at Kansas City, 1962; trustee Midwest Research Inst., 1955—; trustee Barstow Sch., pres. bd., 1958; nat. chmn. U. Mo. Devel. Fund. Served to 1st lt. AUS. Mem. N.A.M. (dir.), U. Mo. Gen. Alumni Assn. (pres. 1955-56), C. of C. of Greater Kansas City (pres. 1972-73). Republican. Presbyterian. Clubs: Kansas City, Kansas City Country, Rotary (pres. 1954-55) (Kansas City); River, Carriage. Home: 310 W 49th St Kansas City MO 64112 Office: 101 W 11th St Kansas City MO 64105

BROOKMAN, JOHN F., assn. pub. relations dir.; b. Chgo., July 31, 1919; s. Roy A. and Helen J. (Tobin) B.; B.A. in Bus., Wright Jr. Coll., 1939; B.S. in Speech, Northwestern U., 1948. Radio and TV writer, radio dir., TV producer NBC, Chgo., 1948-60; dir. communications United Dairy Industry Assn. and Am. Dairy Assn., Rosemont, Ill., 1960—. Served with USAAF, 1941-46. Decorated D.F.C. with 2 oak leaf clusters, Air Medal with 7 oak leaf clusters. Mem. Pub. Relations Soc. Am. (accredited), Am. Assn. Agrl. Editors, Agrl. Relations Council. Home: 486 Brookside Rd Barrington IL 60010 Office: 6300 N River Rd Rosemont IL 60018

BROOKS, CAROLINE VOGEL (MRS. KENNETH LEE BROOKS), pub. relations exec., journalist; b. Wichita Falls, Tex., June 10, 1938; d. Irvin John and Mary Caroline (Meredith) Vogel; student Midwestern U., 1956-58; B.J., U. Tex., 1960; m. Kenneth Lee Brooks, Mar. 31, 1961; children—Amelia Louise, Mary Caroline. Reporter Wichita Falls (Tex.) Times, 1960-61; editorial asst. U. Denver, 1961-62; dir. pub. relations William Jewell Coll., Liberty, Mo., 1962-65, 70-71; interim editor Liberty (Mo.) Tribune, 1969; instr. journalism Maple Woods Community Coll., Kansas City, Mo., 1971, asst. to pres. for info. services, 1971-77; free lance writer, 1969—; pub. relations exec. H&R Block, Inc., Kansas City, Mo., 1977—. Mem. adv. com. Park Hill Continuing Edn. Recipient 1st Place award Nat. Fedn. Press Women, 1971, 72, 1st Place award Mo. Press Women, 1970, 71, 72, 73. Mem. Women in Communications (v.p.), Nat. Fedn. Press Women, Mo. Press Women, Kansas City Pub. Relations Soc., Pub. Relations Soc. Am. Editor Progress Edit. Townsend Communications, 1971—. Home: 6107 NW Karen Rd Kansas City MO 64151 Office: 4410 Main St Kansas City MO 64111

BROOKS, CLARENCE RAE, psychologist; b. Springfield, Ill., Apr. 22, 1928; s. John Orville and Vivian Lenora (Redding) B.; A.A., Springfield Jr. Coll., 1962; B.S. in Edn., Ill. State U., 1964; M.A., Bradley U., 1966; Ed.S., U. Iowa, 1970; Ph.D., St. Louis U., 1973; m. Mildred May Bischoff, July 28, 1956; children—Diana, Stephanie (Mrs. Clyde Hook), Constance, Henry, James. Tchr., Peoria Psychiat. Hosp., 1964-66; psychologist Keokuk (Ia.) Pub. Schs., 1966-68; psychologist, area spl. edn. dist. Belleville, Ill., 1968—. Pvt. practice, Belleville, 1972—; cons. St. Johns Childrens Home, Belleville, 1969—. Served with USNR, 1945-49. Mem. Am., Ill. (sec. 1974-75) psychol. assns., Council Exceptional Children, N.E.A. (life). Contbr. profl. jours. Home: 16 St John Dr Belleville IL 62221 Office: 101 E B St Belleville IL 62221

BROOKS, DONALD, computer engr.; b. Lincoln, Nebr., Nov. 25, 1944; s. Frank Wendell and Donna Jean (Silvers) B.; student Central Mo. State U., 1969-70; m. Mary Margaret Dann, June 25, 1966; children—William Christopher, Brian Daniel, Rebecca Ann. With IBM, 1965—, asso. customer engr., Columbia, Mo., 1965-67, resident customer engr., Warrensburg, Mo., 1967-76, sr. resident customer engr., 1976—. Active Kansas City council Boy Scouts Am., 1956—, neighborhood commr., 1971-73. Served with USNR, 1962-65. Recipient Means Service award IBM, 1973, 75. Presbyterian (elder). Mason, Optimist (lt. gov. Mo. dist. 1975—). Home: 811 E Market St Warrensburg MO 64093 Office: 1200 E Baltimore Kansas City MO 64121

BROOKS, DONALD ARTHUR, research co. exec.; b. Providence, July 16, 1941; s. Howard Murray and Marion Eleanor (Cook) B.; B.S., Lowell Tech. Inst., 1962; M.S., Air Force Inst. Tech., 1964; M.B.A., U. Chgo., 1977; m. Margot Dean Burke, Aug. 12, 1962; children—Carrie Dean, Carla Lynne. With Walter C. McCrone Assos., Inc., ultramicro analytical services research cons. lab., Chgo., 1968—), exec. v.p., 1969-75, pres., 1975—, also dir. Served to capt. USAF, 1962-68. Mem. Am. Nuclear Soc., State Microscopy Soc. Ill. Home: 500 S Edgewood Ave La Grange IL 60525 Office: 2820 S Michigan Ave Chicago IL 60616

BROOKS, GLADYS SINCLAIR, exec.; b. Mpls., June 8, 1914; d. John Franklin and Gladys (Phillips) Sinclair; student U. Geneva, Switzerland, 1935; B.A., U. Minn., 1936; LL.D., Hamline U., 1966; m. Wright W. Brooks, Apr. 17, 1941; children—Diane (Mrs. Peter Tischendorf), John, Pamela (Mrs. Jean Marc Perraud). Dir. Farmer's and Mechanics Bank, 1973—; mem. Met. Council, 1974—. Lectr. world affairs, 1939—; mem. Mpls. City Council, 1967-73; mem. Met. Airports Commn., 1971-74; pres. World Affairs Center U. Minn., 1976—. lectr. on world tours as Am. specialist U.S. Dept. State; 1959-60; mem. Mpls. Charter Commn., 1948-51; pres. YWCA, 1953-57, mem. nat. bd., del. world meeting, Denmark; pres. Minn. Internat. Center, 1953-63; chmn. Minn. Women's Com. for Civil Rights, 1961-64; mem. U.S. Com. for UNICEF, 1959-68; mem. Gov.'s Adv. Com. Children and Youth, 1953-58, Minn. Adv. Com. Employment and Security, 1948-50; Midwest adv. com. Inst. Internat. Edn.; mem. nat. com. White House Conf. Children and Youth, 1960; chmn. Gov.'s Human Rights Commn., 1961-65; dir. Citizens Com. Delinquency and Crime. Del. Rep. Nat. Conv., 1952; state chmn. Citizens for Eisenhower, 1956; founder, pres. Rep. Workshop; co-chmn. Mpls. Bicentennial Commn., 1974-76. Pres. Internat. Center for Fgn. Students; dir. Minn. Alumni Assn.; trustee United Theol. Sem., YWCA, Hamline U. Recipient Centennial Women of Minn. award Hamline U., 1954; Woman of Distinction award AAUW, Mpls. 1956; Woman of Year award YWCA, 1973; Brotherhood award NCCJ, 1975; Service to Freedom award Minn. State Bar Assn., 1976. Mem. World Affairs Council (pres. 1942-44), Minn. League Women Voters (dir. 1940-45), Mpls. Council Ch.

Women (pres. 1946-48), Nat. (mem. gen. bd., v.p.), Minn. (1st woman pres., Christian service award 1967), Mpls. (v.p. 1946-48) councils chs., United Ch. Women (bd. mgrs.), Minn. UN Assn. (dir.), Nat. League Cities (human resources steering com. 1972-73), Am. Acad. Polit. Sci., AAUW, Women's Symphony Assn., Delta Sigma Rho. Presbyn. Clubs: Zonta, Women's (Mpls.). Home: 5056 Garfield Ave S Minneapolis MN 55419 Office: Metro Sq Bldg St Paul MN

BROOKS, LYNNDON ARDEN, agrl. engr.; b. Kaukauna, Wis., June 16, 1925; s. Henry F. and Hulda A. (Krueger) B.; student Western Mich. Coll., 1944, U. Notre Dame, 1944-45; B.S. Agr., U. Wis., 1948, B.S. in Civil Engring., 1949, M.S., 1958; m. Norma A. Sassen, Aug. 5, 1950; children—Gregory, Carol. Dist. engr. U.S. Soil Conservation Service, Waukesha, Wis., 1949-50; dir. Electric Research Farm, U. Wis., Madison, 1950-60, prof. agrl. engring., 1975—; sec.-mgr. Wis. Farm Progress Days Inc., 1976—; agrl. extension engr., 1960—. Sec.-treas. Wis. Farm Electric Council, 1963—; cons. Electricity on the Farm Mag., 1963. Mem. U. Wis. Found., 1955. Bd. dirs. Oakwood Luth. Homes Assn., 1969-75; pres. Oakwood Village Inc., 1974-75. Served with USNR, 1944-45. Recipient Blue Ribbon award Am. Soc. Agrl. Engrs., 1956. Registered profl. engr., Wis. Mem. Am. Soc. Agrl. Engrs. (chmn. electric power and processing div. 1967-68), Madison Tech. Club, Alpha Zeta, Phi Lambda Upsilon, Delta Theta Sigma (nat. sec. 1958-62). Lutheran (mem. future planning com. 1968—). Mason (Shriner), Elk. Home: 229 Carillon Dr Madison WI 53705

BROOKS, PATRICK WILLIAM, lawyer; b. Grinnell, Iowa, May 11, 1943; s. Mark Dana and Madge Ellen (Walker) B.; B.A., State Coll. Iowa, 1966; J.D., U. Iowa, 1971; m. Mary Jane Davey, Dec. 17, 1966; children—Carolyn Walker, Mark William. Classroom tchr. Waterloo (Iowa) Community Sch. Dist., 1966-68; admitted to Iowa bar, 1971, U.S. Dist. Ct., 1971, U.S. Supreme Ct. bar, 1974; atty. Donohue & Brooks, West Union, Iowa, 1971-72; partner Mowry, Irvine & Brooks, Marshalltown, Iowa, 1972—. Mem. Fayette County Republican Central Com., 1971-72; chmn. platform resolutions com. Fayette County Rep. party, 1972. Trustee Iowa Law Sch. Found., 1970-71. Mem. Am., Iowa (rep. to young lawyer's sect. 1971-72), Marshall County bar assns., Assn. Trial Lawyers Iowa, Iowa Def. Counsel Assn., Phi Alpha Delta. Home: 1319 W Church St Marshalltown IA 50158 Office: 25 N Center St Marshalltown IA 50158

BROOKS, RACHEL JEAN, univ. ofcl.; b. Chgo., Apr. 11, 1953; d. Marion Rudolph and Shirley (Young) B.; B.A. cum laude, Ill. Wesleyan U., 1975; M.S., Western Ill. U., 1977. Residence hall dir. Ball State U., Muncie, Ind., 1977—. Delta Theta Tau grantee, 1976-77. Mem. Am. Personnel and Guidance Assn., Assn. Counselor Edn. and Supervision, Am. Coll. Personnel Assn., Nat. Assn. Women Deans, Adminstrs. and Counselors. Home: 5 S 371 Radcliffe Rd Naperville IL 60540 Office: Knotts Hall Ball State U Muncie IN 47306

BROOKS, RANDY LYNN, civil engr.; b. Flint, Mich., Sept. 23, 1950; s. Jack Dee and Betty May (Fendt) B.; B.S. in Civil Engring., Mich. Tech. U., 1972; M.B.A., Eastern Mich. U.; m. Martha Louise Phelps, Aug. 28, 1971; children—Jason, Jack. Field engr. Genesee County Drain Commn., Flint, 1972; sales engr. Trane Co., Baton Rouge, La., 1973; project engr. Chris Nelson Constrn. Co., Royal Oak, Mich., 1974; engring. cons. Dundee (Mich.) Cement Co., 1974—. Mem. ASCE, Am. Concrete Inst., Nat. Ready-Mixed Concrete Assn., A.S.T.M., Sigma Phi Epsilon. Lutheran. Home: 8553 Windsor Ct Ypsilanti MI 48197 Office: PO Box 122 Dundee MI 48131

BROOMFIELD, WILLIAM S., Congressman; b. Royal Oak, Mich., Apr. 28, 1922; s. S. C. and Fern (Taylor) B.; student Mich. State U.; m. Jane Smith Thompson, 1951; children—Susan, Nancy, Barbara. Mem. Mich. Ho. of Reps., 1948, 50, 52, speaker pro tem, 1953; mem. Mich. Senate, 1954-56; mem. 85th-95th congresses from 19th Mich. Dist., ranking Republican on Com. Internat. Relations, mem. Small Bus. Com.; U.S. del. NATO Parliamentarians' Conf., Paris, 1960, NATO Conf., Denmark, 1975, U.S.-U.K. Parliamentary Conf., Bermuda, 1962, Can.-U.S. Interparliamentary Conf., 1961, 62, 63, 64, 67-69, 72, Mex.-U.S. Interparliamentary Group, 1969-74, 22d UN Gen. Assembly; congressional adviser Conf. of Com. on Disarmament, Geneva, 1970, 71, 72, 73, 74. Pres., Nat. Rep. Club of Capitol Hill, 1970-74; mem. Nat. Fgn. Relations Council of Am. Legion, 1974. Presbyterian. Clubs: Masons, Lions, Odd Fellows, Optimists. Home: Birmingham MI Office: Room 2435 Rayburn House Office Bldg Washington DC 20515*

BROPHY, GERALD ROBERT, purchasing exec.; b. Lamar, Nebr., Sept. 30, 1923; s. Michael John and Myrtle Ruth (Hogsett) B.; student Hastings Bus. Coll., 1941, Aerial Photo Sch., 1941-42, Kans. State Tchrs. Coll., 1943-44; m. Viola Hughes, Mar. 9, 1942; children—Vaunda Lee, Robert Clyde, Gerald Anthony (div. Oct. 1958); m. Loretta Mae Campbell, Mar. 23, 1960; children—Richard Lee, Kenneth Eugene, Cynthia Rogene. Constrn. foreman Guy F. Atkinson Constrn. Co., 1947-51; constrn. supt. Claussen, Olson & Brenner Constrn. Co., 1951-57; chief engr. Nebr. Atomic Power Plant, Korshoj Constrn. Co., 1958-59; field engr. Western Constrn. Missle Bases, 1959-60; sales engr. Columbia Steel Tank Mfg. Co., Kansas City, Mo., 1960-65; sales engr. Darby Corp., Kansas City, Kans., 1965-69, purchasing mgr., 1969-71; purchasing agt. Kitterman Corp., Kansas City, Mo., 1972—. A.d.c. Gt. Frontier dist. Heart of Am. council Boy Scouts Am., 1968—, hon. Mic-o-say. Served with USAAF, 1943-46; ETO. Mem. Mensa, Purchasing Mgrs. Assn. Roman Catholic. Clubs: Eagles; A-G Investment (pres. 1968-69) (Kansas City, Kans.). Home: 7813 NW Avalon St Parkville MO 64152 Office: 4100 Riverside St Kansas City MO 64150

BROPHY, JAMES THOMAS, investment banker; b. Toledo, Dec. 15, 1927; s. Vincent Luke and Adelaide Cable (Mettler) B.; B.S. with honors, U. Ill., 1950; m. June G. Habicht, June 30, 1951; children—Teresa, Jayne, Thomas. Accountant, Touche, Niven, Bailey & Smart, Chgo., 1950-54; with Lake Shore Nat. Bank, Chgo., 1954-56; investment banker Bacon, Whipple & Co., Chgo., 1956—; dir. Lawson Products, Inc., United Fire & Casualty Co. C.P.A. Mem. Investment Analysts Soc. Chgo. Clubs: Univ., Mid-Day, Econ. Home: 808 McKinley Ln Hinsdale IL 60521 Office: 135 S La Salle St Chicago IL 60603

BROSE, MERLE LEVERNE, physician; b. Cedar Falls, Iowa, Aug. 23, 1922; s. Robert Lisle and Amy Belle (Shedd) B.; B.S., U. Wis., 1943; M.D., 1946; m. Phyllis Marie Magill, Jan. 10, 1948; children—Linda, Cheryl (Mrs. Clark Kleinheinz), Pamela, Sandra (Mrs. Gerald Jackson), William. Intern, Columbia Hosp., Wilkinsburg, Pa., 1946-47, resident in surgery, 1947-48; gen. practice medicine, Irwin, Pa., 1950-63; med. dir. Nat. Union Ins. Co., Pitts., 1962-63; gen. practice medicine, Menomonee Falls, Wis., 1963-65; physician Health Service, U. Wis., Madison, 1965—; faculty U. Wis. Med. Sch., 1965—. Served to capt. USAF, 1948-50. Mem. U.S. Power Squadrons (Madison squadron sec. 1969, treas. 1970, adminstrv. officer 1971, exec. officer, 1972, dist. adminstrv. officer 1972, comdr. 1973, grade Navigator 1970, dist. exec. officer 1974, dist. comdr, 1975). Mason. Home: 4517 Gregg Rd Madison WI 53705 Office: 1552 University Av Madison WI 53706

BROST, EILEEN MARIE, guidance counselor; b. Medford, Wis., July 18, 1909; d. Peter and Pauline (Rudolph) Brost; B.A., Loyola U., 1939; M.A., St. Xavier U., 1954; M.Ed., Loyola U., 1970; postgrad. Alverno Coll., Milw. State Tchrs. Coll., DePaul U., Lewis U., Marquette U., Alfred Adler Inst., Chgo. Joined Sch. Sisters of St. Francis, Roman Catholic Ch., 1925; tchr. various locations, Ill., Oreg. and Wis., 1927-68; religious edn. coordinator St. Anne's Parish, Barrington, Ill., 1968-72; guidance counselor, various schs., Chgo. Pub. Sch. System and Chgo. Archdiocese, 1972—. Certified tchr., Wis.; Braille certificate. Mem. Chgo. Tchrs. Union, Am. Guidance and Personnel Assn., Assn. for Non-White Concerns, Am. Sch. Counselor Assn. Roman Catholic. Home: 1851 N Karlov Apt 2 Chicago IL 60639 Office: 4103 W Cortland Chicago IL 60639

BROTHERS, BUDD RITTER, business exec.; b. Youngstown, Ohio, Jan. 8, 1931; s. Bern Ritter and Esther Maureen (Newton) B.; B.S., Youngstown Coll., 1948; m. Patricia Susan Jones, Sept. 5, 1952; 1 dau., Bonnie Robin. Stock boy Boardman Roofing Supply, Youngstown, 1946-48, asst. mgr., clerk, 1948-52, gen. mgr., 1954-64; pres. 20th Century Paint Products, Youngstown, 1964-70, chmn. bd., 1971-72; chmn. bd. Century 21, Inc., Youngstown, 1972—. Mem. C.O.E. adv. bd., Mahoning County, Ohio; vice chmn. bd. zoning appeals, Austintown Twp., Mahoning County, 1965—, v.p. bd. edn., 1970-72, pres. bd. edn., 1972; vice chmn. exec. com. Republican Party, 1965-69. Served with AUS, 1952-54. Mem. Austintown Good Govt. League (pres. 1963-68), Ohio Sch. Bds. Assn., Nat. Decorating Products Assn., Alpha Phi Omega Alumni. Mason. Specialist in new paint products research, paint chem. product devel. Home: 3966 Avalon Ct Youngstown OH 44515 Office: 3711 Mahoning Ave Youngstown OH 44515

BROUILLETTE, DONALD GEORGE, grain merchandising exec.; b. Fowler, Ind., Nov. 7, 1930; s. Frederick George and Estella Theresa (Steinmetz) B.; student St. Joseph's Coll., 1948-49; m. Marilyn K. Strasburger, Aug. 11, 1956; children—Michelle, JoAnn, Michael, Timothy, Susan. Partner, Freeland Park Grain Co., Freeland Park, Ind., 1953-65; owner Dunn Grain Co. (Ind.), 1965-73; pres. Demeter, Inc., Fowler, Ind., 1973—; dir. C and S Mfg. Co.; pres. Brouillette Inc. Dir. Benton Community Sch. Corp., 1964-71, Ind. Sch. Bd. Assn., 1967-71; pres. Benton Community Mental Health Assn., 1968. Served with USAF, 1950-53. Mem. Nat. (dir.), Ind. (pres.), Ill. (dir.) Grain and Feed Assns. Office: Box 465 Fowler IN 47944

BROUWER, JEROME JOSEPH, elec. engr.; b. Fort Wayne, Ind., Jan. 27, 1939; s. Wayne John and Constance Mary (Johnson) B.; B.S. in Elec. Engring., Ind. Inst. Tech., 1962; m. Judith Ellen Freimuth, Sept. 6, 1958; children—Gregory, Christopher, Kevin, Kurt. Elec. technician ITT Fed., Fort Wayne, Ind., 1958-60; jr. engr. Magnavox, Fort Wayne, 1960-62; with Tex. Instruments, Dallas, 1962-71, Dayton, Ohio, 1971—, program mgr., 1967-71, mgr. mktg., 1971—. Mem. Nat. Aero. and Electronics Conf. (v.p.; Outstanding Service award 1976), Air Force Assn., Nat. Assn. Remotely Piloted Vehicles, Am. Inst. Aeros. and Astronautics, Air Force Assn. Patentee electronic resolved radar sweep generator. Home: 1600 Mapleton Dr Centerville OH 45459 Office: 4124 Linden Ave Dayton OH 45432

BROWN, ALMA ROSE, social worker; b. Memphis, Nov. 18, 1953; B.A. in Sociology, Ind. U., 1975, M.S. in Counseling and Guidance, 1976. Resident asst. Ind. U., 1973-76; caseworker, minority recruiter Big Sisters Greater Indpls., 1977; orientation adviser, instr. Ind. U., fall 1976; counselor Center Women, Ind. U.-Purdue U., Indpls., fall 1976, student activities officer, 1977—. Mem. Nat. Assn. Women Deans, Adminstrs. and Counselors, Am. Personnel and Guidance Assn., Pi Lambda Theta. Democrat. Baptist. Home: 4954 Brock St Indianapolis IN 46254 Office: 925 W Michigan St Indianapolis IN 46202

BROWN, ALVA LEE, data processing co. exec.; b. Kremmling, Colo., Oct. 17, 1924; s. Robert Allen and Minerva Elizabeth (Lee) B.; student pub. schs., Denver; m. Betty Jo Daughtry, Dec. 22, 1948; children—James Robert, Barbara Lee. With Bell Telephone Co., Los Angeles, 1950-68; state data communications coordinator Gov's. Office, State Wash., Olympia, 1968-69; pres., Data Documents Systems Corp., Merriam, Kans., 1969—; v.p., Data Documents, Inc., Omaha, 1969—; owner, Circle B Orchards, Paola, Kans., 1971—, Brown Land and Investments, Paola, 1969—; dir. Santa Fe Trail State Bank. Active ARC, United Fund. Mem. com. to elect Reagan Gov., Los Angeles, 1965-66. Served with USNR, 1944-45; PTO. Mem. Am. Legion. Methodist. Lion. Home: Rural Route 5 Paola KS 66071 Office: 5441 Merriam Dr Merriam KS 66203

BROWN, ARTHUR LINWOOD, II, surgeon; b. Winchester, Mass., Mar. 8, 1937; s. Linwood Foster and Carolyn (Williamson) B.; B.A., Princeton U., 1959; M.D., Columbia U., 1963; m. Judith Coburn, July 11, 1959; children—Jennifer, Arthur Linwood III. Intern Mpls. Gen. Hosp., 1963-64; resident in surgery Henry Ford Hosp., Detroit, 1966-70; pvt. practice medicine, Kalamazoo, 1970—; surgeon, treas. Kalamazoo Surgery, P.C.. 1973—; mem. staff Borgess Hosp., Bronson Meth. Hosp.; asst. clin. prof. Mich. State U., 1976—; adj. clin. instr. Western Mich. U., 1974—. Fund worker United Way, Kalamazoo County, 1975; patron Kalamazoo Symphony Orch., Kalamazoo Art Center. Served as capt. U.S. Army, 1964-66. Diplomate Am. Bd. Surgery. Fellow A.C.S.; mem. Kalamazoo Acad. Medicine, Mich. Med. Soc., SW Mich. Surg. Soc., Midwest Surg. Assn., AMA, Roy D. McClure Surg. Soc. Republican. Episcopalian. Clubs: West Hills Tennis, North Shore Tennis. Home: 4150 Lakeside Dr Kalamazoo MI 49008 Office: 504 Bronson Med Center 252 E Lovell St Kalamazoo MI 49006

BROWN, ARVILL BUELL, civil engr.; b. Wetonka, S.D., Aug. 5, 1923; s. Arvill Clay and Anna (Gunderson) B.; B.S., Tri-State Coll., Ind., 1946; certificate small homes council course U. Ill., 1954; m. June Strong, Oct. 13, 1944; children—Duane Arvill, LuReign Anne, Anita June. Asst. project engr. Ind. State Hwy. Dept., 1946-47; project engr. Tri-State Coll., Angola, Ind., 1947-48; field engr. James Stewart Corp., Chgo., 1948-50; chief engr., gen. field supt. and estimator Fisher-Stoune, Inc., Decatur, Ill., 1950-60; chief engr. aluminum bldg. products div. Maco Corp., Huntington, Ind., 1960-64; partner B & K Engring. Company, Huntington, 1963-64, v.p., 1964-65, pres. B & K Engring., Inc., Kendallville, Ind., 1966-77, also dir.; pres. Brown Cons. Engrs., Inc., Kendallville, 1977—; owner Arvill B. Brown, profl. engr., Kendallville, 1971—; constrn. mgr., engr. Great Lakes Bible Coll., Lansing, 1971-76; pres. Noble County (Ind.) Plan Commn., 1967-71; hwy. engr. Noble County, 1965-71, surveyor, 1967-71; mem. Noble County Drainage Bd., 1967-71. Active Boy Scouts, Cub Scouts; trustee, sec., forwarding agt. Christian Edn. Assn. of Orient, Inc., 1968—; mem. exec. com. New Chs. Christ Evangelism, 1965—; dir. Lake James Christian Assembly, Angola, Ind., 1970-75; nat. alumni dir. Tri-State Coll., Angola, Ind., 1971-75. Served with USNR, 1944-46. Registered profl. engr., Ill., Ind., Ohio, Mich., Ky., Minn., Wis., Ga.; profl. land surveyor, Ind.; certified fallout shelter analyst U.S. Dept. Def.; certificates on energy-comml. and residential bldgs., Wis. Mem. Nat., Ind. socs. profl. engrs., ASCE (v.p. N.E. Ind. sect. 1971), Ind. Soc. Profl. Land Surveyors, Decatur Contractors Assn. (past sec.-treas.). Mem. Ch. of Christ (elder). Patentee in field. Home: 357 N Main St Kendallville IN 46755 Office: 212 S Main St Kendallville IN 46755

BROWN, AUSTIN ERROL, mfg. co. exec.; b. Floyd County, Ga., Feb. 6, 1939; s. Willie Luther and Audrey Mae (Latimore) B.; B.F.A., Ohio U., 1961; m. Phyllis Jeanne Leahr, June 16, 1962; children—Jeffery Maurice, Michael William. Systems engr. IBM, Cin., 1968-70; EDP mgr. Am. Sign Co., Florence, Ky., 1970-74, Midland Ross Corp., Cin., 1975—; timesharing coordinator Cin. Electronics, 1974-75. Pres. Lexington Heights Civic Assn., 1970; mem. bd. at large Jane Hoop PTA, 1974-75; Webelos leader Boy Scouts Am., 1973-77. Served to capt. Signal Corps, U.S. Army, 1961-68. Decorated Army Commendation medal. Mem. Common IBM Users Group, Nat. Assn. IBM System 3 Users. Home: 9397 Sherborn Dr Cincinnati OH 45231 Office: 10605 Chester Rd Cincinnati OH 45215

BROWN, BAIRD, ret. ins. co. exec.; b. Chgo., Aug. 8, 1922; s. George Frederic and Irene (Larmon) B.; A.B., Washington and Lee U., 1949; student U. Chgo., 1946-48. Vice pres. Geo. F. Brown & Sons, Inc. Chgo., 1948-52, dir., sec., 1952-70, v.p., 1957-70; exec. v.p., dir. Interstate Nat. Corp., 1970-74; v.p. Interstate Fire & Casulty Co., Chicago Ins. Co. Pres. Internat. Visitors Center, 1964-65, Lyric Opera Guild, 1958-59; mem. Ill. Arts Council, 1966-67; mem. Joseph Jefferson Awards Com., 1971—. Served with USAAF, 1943-45. Mem. UN Assn. (dir. Chgo. br. 1967-73), Sigma Chi. Club: Arts. Home: 2440 N Lakeview Ave Chicago IL 60614

BROWN, BENJAMIN DAVID, comml. artist; b. Chgo., Dec. 18, 1920; s. Israel and Rose (Greenberg) B.; student Ray Sch. Art, 1939-40, Am. Acad. Art, 1940-42, Art Inst. Chgo., 1943-44, DePaul U., 1944-45; m. Goldie Roman, Oct. 14, 1945; children—Barbara Lynn, Gary Allen. Founder AAA Advertisers, Chgo., 1945-46; partner A.B. Showcard Studio, Chgo., 1946-66, pres. A.B. Showcard Studio, Inc., 1966—. Pres. Bar Gar Found., Inc., 1960—. Mem. Artist Guild Chgo., Jewish Religion (trustee congregation). Mem. B'nai B'rith. (past lodge pres.). Exhibited painting Chgo. Art Inst., 1950, 64, McCormick Place Gallery, 1964. Home: 1555 Astor St Chicago IL 60610 Office: 63 E Adams St Chicago IL 60603

BROWN, CHARLES ASA, lawyer; b. Woodsfield, Ohio, Oct. 17, 1912; s. Charles A. and Anna Miriam (Hayes) B.; A.B. Va. Mil. Inst., 1931-35; student U. Mich., 1937; LL.B., Western Reserve U., 1938 children—Charles A. III, Ridgley. Admitted to Ohio bar, 1938, pvt. practice Portsmouth, 1938—; asst. atty. gen. State of Ohio, 1963; owner Raven Rock Farm and Feurt Farm, Scioto River Farm Tract, Winters Farm. Lectr. Indian lore. Active Boy Scouts Am., 1946—, serving as merit badge counselor, exec. bds. Scioto Area council, Portsmouth dist. commr., scout master troop 12, 1966—, developer, adviser Indian dance team Portsmouth dist., 1964—, v.p. Scioto Area council, 1967-68, nat. rep. Nat. council, 1967-68; advisory council Girl Scouts of Am., 1947-48; advisory chief Indian Tribes, 1961-63; councilman Western Black Elk Keetowah, Cherokee Nation, 1964—; mem. Cedar River Tulsa Muskogee Band. Bd. dirs. Portsmouth Little League Baseball Assn., 1957-58, Scioto County unit Am. Cancer Soc., 1973—; advisory bd. Practical Nurses Assn., 1960-61; lay reader Anglican Orthodox Ch. 1st lt. to capt. U.S. Army, 1941-46; lt. col. Res. (ret.). Decorated Bronze Star with oak leaf cluster, Purple Heart, Am. Defense medal, Victory medal, three battle stars, Occupational medal, European theatre ribbon. Named Ky. Col.; recipient Silver Beaver award Boy Scouts Am., 1968, Vigil Order of Arrow, 1971. Mem. Am. Indian, Ohio, Portsmouth (trustee 1966—) bar assns., Am. Legion, VFW, DAV, Nat. Rifle Assn., Ohio Farm Bur., various Am. Indian orgns. Episcopalian (lay reader, sr. warden, medal of merit 1961). Odd Fellow, Redman, Mason (32 deg., master of lodge 1965, Shriner, K.T.; past comdr.; trustee lodge 1966-71; excellent high priest chpt. 1976-77, K.P. (grand tribune Ohio 1961, past chancellor comdr.), Elk, Eagle, Fraternal Order of Police. Mem. Order Eastern Star (patron 1966, trustee 1967-70). Designer flood wall, Portsmouth, Ohio, 1936. Office: 721 Washington St Portsmouth OH 45662

BROWN, CHARLES HENRY, investment banker; b. Chgo., Aug. 5, 1888; s. Charles Christian and Amelia (Kane) B.; A.B., Amherst Coll., 1916; m. Bertha Alling, June 6, 1931; children—Alling Christian, Charles Henry. With Brown Mfg. Co., Chgo., 1916-26; investment banker Spencer Trask & Co., Chgo., 1926-32, Fairman, Harris & Co., Inc., Chgo., 1932-56, Bache & Co., 1956-67; oil producer Okla. and Ill., 1932—; lectr. Dir. Forward Movement; v.p. Druce Lake Camp Assn.; chmn. bd. trustees, Lord Jeff Scholarship Fund. Mem. English Speaking Union (dir.), Alpha Delta Phi (dir. Western assn.). Republican. Presbyterian (elder, commr. to Gen. Assembly 1952, past pres. Ch. Extension Bd.). Clubs: Amherst of Chgo. (past pres.); Onwentsia, University, Winter Sports Car of Am., Antique Automobile of Am., Executives. Home: 410 Washington Rd Lake Forest IL 60045

BROWN, CHARLES HOWARD, physician; b. Bklyn., Apr. 4, 1913; s. Charles Harvey and Julia (Heath) B.; A.B. with distinction and high honors, Wesleyan U., 1934; postgrad. Yale, 1933-34; M.S. in Psychology, U. Chgo., 1936, M.D., 1938; m. Dorothy Mary Boros; children—Christopher Heath, Judith Harvey (Mrs. Williams), Donald Howard, Norene L. McCormac, Candace L. (Mrs. Morris), Lisbeth P. McCormac. Instr. psychology U. Chgo., 1935-36; intern Henry Ford Hosp., Detroit, 1938-39, resident in medicine, 1939-40, 45-48; staff Cleve. Clinic Found. and Cleve. Clinic Hosp., 1948—, head dept. gastroenterology, 1959-72, sr. cons. gastroenterology, 1972-75, cons. emeritus, 1975—; asso. prof. Cleveland Clinic Ednl. Found., 1948-59, prof. gastroenterology, 1959-75. Bd. govs. Cleve. Clinic, 1964-69, trustee, 1967-69. Served from first lt. to maj., flight surgeon, AUS, 1941-46. Recipient Sports' Illustrated 25th anniversary All American award, 1958, distinguished alumnus award Wesleyan U., 1959. Diplomate Am. Bd. Internal Medicine, Am. Bd. Gastroenterology. Hon. fellow Am. Coll. Gastroenterology 1961; Fellow A.C.P. (life); mem. AMA (cons. pharmacy and chemistry 1955-58), Am. Fedn. Clin. Research, Am. Gastroent. Assn., Am. Soc. for Gastrointestinal Endoscopy (pres. 1967), Acad. Psychosomatic Medicine, Am. Therapeutic Soc., Am. Assn. for Study of Liver, Cleve. Gastroent. Club (pres. 1964-66), Phi Beta Kappa, Phi Nu Theta, Nu Sigma Nu, Alpha Omega Alpha. Author: Diagnostic Procedures in Gastroenterology, 1967. Contbr. numerous articles to med. jours. Producer ednl. movies on gastroent. subjects. Home: 14856 Hook Hollow Novelty OH 44072 Office: 2020 E 93d St Cleveland OH 44106

BROWN, CHARLES ROLAND, educator; b. Beaver City, Nebr., May 26, 1915; s. Delbert L. and Anna (straube) B.; B.A., Kearney State Coll., 1936; M.A., Colo. State Coll., 1946; m. I. Lavonne Query, July 26, 1939; children—Tommy Lee (dec.), Lonnie Dean. Tchr. Hendley (Neb.) Pub. Schs., 1936-37; tchr., prin. Wilsonville (Nebr.) High Sch., 1937-40; prin. Orleans (Nebr.) High Sch., 1940-44; supt. schs., Orleans, 1944-47, North Bend, Nebr., 1947-59, Maple Valley Community Sch., Mapleton, Iowa 1959—. Mem. Am., Iowa assns. sch. adminstrs., Iowa High Sch. Speech Assn. (exec. com. 1962—, pres. 1976-77), Phi Delta Kappa. Methodist. Rotarian (pres. 1966-67). Home: 109 N 8th St Mapleton IA 51034

BROWN, CLARENCE J., congressman; b. Columbus, Ohio, June 18, 1927; s. Clarence J. and Ethel (McKinney) B.; B.A. in Econs., Duke U., 1947; M.B.A., Harvard U., 1949; m. Joyce Eldridge, June 11, 1955; children—Elizabeth Ellen (dec. Mar. 1964), Clarence J., Catherine McKinney, Roy E. Editor, Blanchester (Ohio) Star Republican, 1949-53; editor, pub. Franklin (Ohio) Chronicle, 1953-57; editor Urbana (Ohio) Daily Citizen, 1957-65, pub., 1959-67; established, mgr. Sta. WCOM-FM, Urbana, 1963-65; pres. Brown Pub. Co., 1965-77, chmn. bd., 1977—; mem. 89th to 95th Congresses, 7th Ohio Dist., mem. govt. ops., interstate and fgn. commerce, joint econ., ad hoc energy coms. Past pres. Urbana and Franklin chpts. ARC; past pres. Champaign County Young Republican Club; asst. sgt.-at-arms Rep. Nat. Convs., 1944-64, del., 1972, 76; mem. Champaign County Rep. exec. com., 1963—. Served to lt. (j.g.) USNR, 1951-53; Korea. Mem. Nat. Newspaper Assn., Farm Bur., Blanchester, Franklin, Urbana chambers commerce, Sigma Delta Chi (past pres. Central Ohio chpt.). Presbyterian (trustee). Clubs: Lions, Rotary, Masons (33 deg.), Shriners. Home: 430 Scioto Urbana OH 43078 also 5817 Marbury Rd Bethesda MD 20034 Office: 2242 Rayburn House Office Bldg Washington DC 20515

BROWN, CLARENCE JOSEPH, traffic ofcl., union exec.; b. Topeka, Sept. 16, 1920; s. Joe and Salome (Brundgardt) B.; student Wichita Bus. Coll., 1948-49; m. Pearl Marie Rollings, July 15, 1946; children—Beverly Danley, Patricia Wemmer, Vicky McFadden. Rate tariff analysis traffic dept. Santa Fe Trailways Transp., Wichita, Kans., 1946—. Mem. Wichita Human Relations Commn., 1959-65; bd. dirs. Cath. Social Service, 1962-65, Sedgwick County chpt. A.R.C., 1961—; mem. Community Planning Council, 1961—, pres., 1969-70; pres. Wichita Area Community Action Program, 1968-70; v.p. Coalition Planning Council, 1970-73; mem. Sedgwick County North Area Mental Health Adv. Bd., 1972—, pres., 1973—. Served with U.S. Army, 1942-46; PTO. Mem. Brotherhood Ry. and Steamship Clks., Freight Handlers, Express and Sta. Employees (div. chmn. 1951-76, 78—), Wichita Labor Fedn. AFL-CIO (recording sec.), Brotherhood Ry. Airlines Clks. (chmn. bd. trustees), VFW. Democrat. Roman Catholic. Clubs: K.C., Moose. Home: 1522 N Sheridan St Wichita KS 67213

BROWN, DAVID LAWRENCE, pub. relations exec.; b. Columbia, Mo., Nov. 22, 1940; s. Harry Eugene and Jessie (Shaw) B.; B.J., U. Mo., 1961; m. Patricia Kay Houk, Aug. 31, 1962. Reporter Columbia (Mo.) Daily Tribune, 1961-62; field editor Mo. Farmer mag., Columbia, 1962-64; publs. editor Internat. Harvester Co., Chgo., 1964-66; dir. publs. Nat. Easter Seal Soc., Chgo., 1966-68; free-lance writer, photojournalist, Chgo., 1968-70; founder Dave Brown and Assos., pub. relations firm, Oak Brook, Ill., 1970—. Mem. Pub. Relations Soc. Am. (accredited), Am. Soc. Mag. Photographers, Nat. Agrl. Advt. and Mktg. Assn., Am. Agrl. Editors Assn., Agrl. Relations Council, Sigma Delta Chi. Clubs: Chicago Headline, Chicago Publicity. Home: 329 Bedford Dr Bolingbrook IL 60439 Office: 900 Jorie Blvd Suite 70 Oak Brook IL 60521

BROWN, DONALD DURAND, dentist; b. South Bend, Ind., Apr. 24, 1925; s. Coyle Augustus and Barbara M. (Marzuki) B.; student U. Notre Dame, 1946-48; D.D.S., Loyola U., 1952; m. Ada Lee Winat, Aug. 15, 1952; children—Sandra Lee, Paula Ann, Carole Ann. Fellow in orthodontics, Loyola U., Chgo., 1952-53; instr. U. Ill. Coll. Dentistry, Chgo., 1953-55; practice dentistry, Marion, Ind., 1955—; coordinator dental edn. Marion Community Schs. Charter mem. bd. dirs. Marion Devel. Com. Served with AUS, 1943-46; PTO. Mem. Pierre Fauchard Acad., Am., Ind. dental assns., Grant County (pres. 1960-61), Wabash Valley (v.p. 1961-62, pres. 1962-63) dental socs., Delta Sigma Delta. Presbyn. Rotarian (pres. 1972-73), Elk. Home: 1607 N Denver Dr Marion IN 46952 Office: Marion Nat Bank Bldg Marion IN 46952

BROWN, DOROTHEA NELL WILLIAMS (MRS. IRA H. BROWN), ednl. adminstr.; b. Kansas City, Kans., Dec. 23, 1918; d. Van Wilford and Ethel Lee (Connor) Williams, Sr.; student Prairie View Coll., 1936-37; B.S., Huston-Tillotson Coll., 1939; postgrad. Fenn Coll., 1952-54; M.A., John Carroll U., 1959; postgrad. Ohio State U., 1960, Western Res. U., 1967, U. Akron, 1973—; m. Ira H. Brown, Aug. 28; 1 dau., Michele. Tchr., Trinity (Tex.) Ind. Schs., 1939-41, Austin (Tex.) Pub. Schs., 1941-43; asst. mgr. Youngstown Met. Housing Authority, 1947-51; with Cleve. Pub. Schs., 1951-71, asst. prin. Harry E. Davis Jr. High Sch., 1962-64, Charles W. Eliot Jr. High Sch., 1964-71; coordinator tchr.-leader program Martha Holden Jennings Found., Pace Assn., Cleve., 1969-71; coordinator open univ. program Ohio U., 1971-72; program officer Coll. Edn., Kent (Ohio) State U., from 1972; dir., dean Office Instructional Personnel Devel., Cuyahoga Community Coll., Cleve., 1976—. Coll. counselor Glenville High Sch., 1969-71; in-service tchr. human relations Cleve. Bd. Edn., 1966-70; resource person to Ind. Schs. Talent Search Program, Boston, 1964—; edn. cons. Cleve. Commn. on Higher Edn., 1971—. Mem. Action Grown Up, Businessmen's Interracial Com., Found. Center, Cleve. Bd. dirs. Lake Erie council Girl Scouts U.S.A., mem. nat. vol. tng.; past trustee Harvard Community Services Center, Cleve., Goodrich Social Settlement; bd. dirs. Cleve. Internat. Program. Mem. Nat., Ohio assns. women deans and counselors, Am. Personnel and Guidance Assn., Ohio Sch. Counselors Assn., Northeastern Assn. Women Deans Adminstrs. and Counselors, Human Relations Council (sec. 1966-71, trustee), Women's Civic League Cleve., Jack and Jill Inc., NAACP, Links, Urban League, United Negro Coll. Fund, Alpha Kappa Alpha (chpt. pres. 1957-60), Phi Delta Kappa. Episcopalian. Club: Women's City (Cleve.). Contbg. editor New Lady Mag., Hayward, Cal., 1967—. Home: 3061 Albion Rd Cleveland OH 44120 Office: Cuyahoga Community Coll Dist Office 700 Carnegie Ave Cleveland OH 44115

BROWN, EDWARD HERRIOT, JR., fishery research biologist; b. Dover, N.J., Jan. 2, 1926; s. Edward Herriot and Helen Augusta (Danielson) B.; student Rutgers U., 1946-48; B.S., Mich. State U., 1950; M.S., Ohio State U., 1961; postgrad. U. Mich., 1963-65; m. Shirley Marie Klopp, Oct. 11, 1952; children—Lista, Cynthia, Jennifer, Lesley. Asst. leader, project leader fishery research projects Ohio div. Wildlife, Xenia, 1952-58, Delaware, 1958-62; leader fishery research projects Gt. Lakes Fishery Lab., U.S. Fish and Wildlife Service, Ann Arbor, Mich., 1962—. Active P.T.A. Ann Arbor. Served to cpl. USAAF, 1944-46; PTO. Recipient award Wildlife Soc., 1972; Outstanding achievement award Ohio Wildlife Mgmt. Assn., 1961. Mem. Am. Fisheries Soc., Am. Inst. Fishery Research Biologists (dir. dist. 1974—), Internat. Assn. Gt. Lakes Research, Phi Kappa Phi. Roman Catholic. Home: 2552 Old Boston Ct Ann Arbor MI 48104 Office: 1451 Green Rd Ann Arbor MI 48105

BROWN, EDWIN LEWIS, JR., lawyer; b. Parker, S.D., Mar. 15, 1903; s. Edwin Lewis and Lucy Elizabeth (Lowenberg) B.; J.D., U. Nebr., 1926; m. Faye Hulbert, May 8, 1926; children—Betty Lou (Mrs. Philip Trainer), Lewis Charles. Admitted to Nebr. bar, 1926, Ill. bar, 1933, U.S. Supreme Ct., 1960; practice in Chgo., 1933—; partner firm Brown, Stine & Cook, (now Brown, Stine, Cook & Hanson), 1950—. Mem. wills and bequests com. Shriners Crippled Childrens Hosp., Chgo. Bd. dirs. Comml. Law Found. Mem. Am., Ill., Chgo. bar assns., Am. Judicature Soc., Comml. Law League Am. (pres. 1963-64), Phi Alpha Delta. Republican. Presbyterian. Mason (32 deg., K.T., Shriner). Clubs: Union League, Monroe (Chgo.); Westmoreland Country (Wilmette, Ill.). Home: 2617 Hurd Ave Evanston IL 60201 Office: 135 S La Salle St Chicago IL 60603

BROWN, ERIC VAN DYKE, JR., lawyer; b. Grand Rapids, Mich., Feb. 11, 1940; s. Eric V. and Margaret Ann (Davis) B.; B.A. in Econs., U. Mich., 1962, LL.B., 1965; m. Linda B. Bird, June 23, 1965; children—Scott Eric, Julie Lyn, Mathew Charles. Admitted to Mich. bar, 1965; with Brown, Colman & DeMent, Kalamazoo, 1965—, partner, owner, 1967—; sec. to bd., dir. Indsl. State Bank & Trust Co., Kalamazoo, 1971—, ISB Fin. Corp., 1971—. Del., Kalamazoo County Republican Conv., 1972. Sec., bd. dirs. Kalamazoo Consultation Center; bd. dirs. Jr. Achievement Kalamazoo. Named one of Outstanding Young Men of Am., 1971. Mem. Am., Mich. (mem. council for young lawyers sect. 1966-72), Kalamazoo County bar assns. Club: Rotary. Author: Law for the Clergy, 1970. Home: 6742 Angling Rd Kalamazoo MI 49003 Office: 125 W Walnut St Kalamazoo MI 49007

BROWN, ERNEST RAY, constrn. co. exec.; b. Merna, Nebr., Dec. 18, 1921; s. Ernest Chloe and Jennie Rae (Sickler) B.; student pub. schs.; m. Dorothy Anne Dinwiddie, Nov. 6, 1938; children—Nedra (Mrs. Nedra Auch Moedy), Sabra (Mrs. Dwaine Lauer), Doran Ray. Constrn. worker, 1936-43; founder, pres. Brown & Denesia Constrn. Co., Broken Bow, Nebr., 1946—; founder, pres. Nursing Home Bldg., Inc., 1964—; dir. Phillips Homes, Inc., Southview Manor; pres. Med. Facilities, Cash and Carry Lumber Co. Served with USNR, 1943-46. Named Nebr. diplomat. Mem. Internat. Platform Assn., Am. Legion (comdr. 1947). Republican. Elk. Home: 152 SE St Broken Bow NE 68822 Office: E Broadway Broken Bow NE 68822

BROWN, FORREST HARRY, environ. engr., home inspection cons.; b. Sedalia, Colo., May 27, 1921; s. Harry Bradford and Katie May (Lange) B.; B.S. in Aero. Engring., U. Colo., 1953; B.D., Lincoln U., 1957; m. Muriel Elizabeth Judd, Nov. 4, 1955. Missionary project engr. U.S. Presbyterian Ch., San Sebastian, P.R., 1957-60; test engr. Beech Aircraft Co., Boulder, Colo., 1961-63, Brown Engring. Co., Huntsville, Ala.. 1963-68, Spaco Co., Huntsville, Ala., 1968-71; environ. engr. Met. San. Dist. of Greater Chgo., 1972-74, L.B. Knight Co., Chgo., 1974-76; home inspection cons., Ala., 1969-72, River Forest, Ill., 1976—. Mem. Huntsville Community Chorus Bd., 1965-72, treas., 1967-72; mem. Bldg. Bd. of Appeals and Water Coms., Village of River Forest, 1977—. Served with USAAF, 1943-46; PTO. Registered profl. engr., Ala., Ill., Ind. Mem. Nat., Ill. socs. of profl. engrs. Republican. Presbyterian. Address: 7214 Quick Ave River Forest IL 60305

BROWN, FRANCIS ROBERT, educator; b. Fairbury, Ill., Dec. 19, 1914; s. Edwin Henry and Annie L. (Besgrove) B.; B.E., Ill. State U., 1937; M.A., Columbia, 1940; Ed.D., U. Ill., 1954; m. Helen Elizabeth Tucker, Aug. 27, 1940; children—Robert Alan, David Lee, Bruce William, Mark Leslie. Tchr., head dept. math. Centennial Jr. High Sch., Decatur, Ill., 1937-41; tchr. Decatur High Sch., 1941-42; civilian instr., adminstr. USAAF, Chanute Field, Ill., 1943-44; asst. prof. math. Millikin U., Decatur, 1946-49; prof. math. Ill. State U., Normal, 1949—, dir. div. univ. extension and field services, 1958-73, asst. dir. summer session, 1968-77, dir. div. continuing edn. and pub. service, 1973-77. State math cons. Office of Supt. of Pub. Instrn., Springfield, Ill., 1960-63; cons. Homer Consol. Sch. System, Lockport, Ill., 1971-72. Mem. Ill. Law Enforcement Commn., 1970—, chmn., 1977-78; cons., chmn. Citizens Study Com. for Developing Bldg. Codes, Normal, 1973-74. Served with USAAF, 1944-46. Recipient Max Beberman award Ill. Council Tchrs. Math., 1974. Mem. Nat. Council Tchrs. Math. (coordinator Onarga community devel. 1966-69), Mathematical Assn. Am., Nat. Univ. Extension Assn., Assn. Field Services for Tchr. Edn. (pres. 1964-65), Asso. Orgns. Tchr. Edn. (chmn. 1969-70), Am. Assn. Colls. for Tchr. Edn. (exec. bd. 1969-70), NEA, Ill. Council Tchrs. Math. (pres. 1961-62), Ill. Adult Edn. Assn. (pres. 1962-63), Adult Edn. Assn. U.S.A. (dir. 1963-66), Phi Delta Kappa, Kappa Phi Kappa, Phi Kappa Phi, Kappa Mu Epsilon, Kappa Delta Pi. Mem. Christian Ch. (elder 1943—). Kiwanian (dir. 1973-75). Author: Numbers and Operations, 1963; New Dimensions in Mathematics-Grades 1-6, 1970; Mathematics Course/Grade 7, 1973; Mathematics Course 2, Grade 8, 1973. Mem. editorial com. Ill. Quar., 1965-77; mem. editorial rev. com. Math. Tchr.-Nat. Council for Tchrs. Math., 1964—. Home: 601 Normal Ave Normal IL 61761

BROWN, GARRY ELDRIDGE, congressman; b. Schoolcraft, Mich., Aug. 12, 1923; s. E. Lakin and Blanche (Jackson) B.; B.A., Kalamazoo Coll., 1951; J.D., George Washington U., 1954; L.H.D. (hon.), Lawrence Inst. Tech., 1964; children—Frances E., Mollie E., Amelia L., Abigail V. Admitted to Mich. bar, 1954; partner Ford, Kriekard, Brown and Staton, Kalamazoo, 1954-67; commr. So. div. U.S. Dist. Ct. Western Dist. Mich., 1957-62; mem. Mich. Senate, 1962-66; mem. 90th-95th Congress 3d Dist. Mich. Del. Mich. Constl. Conv., 1961-62. Served to 2d lt., inf. AUS, 1946-47. PTO. Mem. Am., Mich., Kalamazoo County, D.C. bar assns., Schoolcraft Jr. C. of C. (chmn. bd.). Am. Legion. Republican. Elk. Home: 321 W Eliza St Schoolcraft MI 49087 Office: 2446 Rayburn House Office Bldg Washington DC 20515

BROWN, GEORGE EDWARD, rehab. counselor; b. St. Joseph, Mo., Dec. 1, 1942; s. Ivor Frank and Dora (Trimble) B.; A.A., St. Joseph Jr. Coll., 1963; B.S., NW Mo. U., 1967; M.Ed., Lincoln U., 1972; m. Elaine Lyle, Jan. 20, 1966; children—Susan Jane, David Marvin. Parole officer Mo. Bd. Probation and Parole, Jefferson City, 1967-70, supr., 1970-72; treatment coordinator Reality House, Inc., Columbia, Mo., 1972-73, dir., 1973—; cons. to Mo. Inst. Reality Therapy. Mem. Mid-Mo. Council Criminal Justice (mem. correction com.), Am. Personnel and Guidance Assn., Assn. Specialists in Group Work, Mo. Halfway House Assn. (v.p.). Home: 1348 S Victoria Ave Columbia MO 65201 Office: 1409 Rosemary Ln Columbia MO 65201

BROWN, GERHARD JULIAN, diversified cos. exec.; b. Garretson, S.D., Mar. 14, 1918; s. John and Carrie Christina (Berdahl) B.; grad. Garretson pub. schs.; m. Arleen I. Ustrud, Oct. 9, 1941; children—Galen, Clarence, Lois, Charles, Larry, Bruce, Judy, Linda; m. 2d, Evelyn D. Wiggins, May 6, 1966. With Montgomery Ward, Sioux Falls, S.D., 1947-57, dept. head, 1951-57; owner Brown's Dept. Store, 1957-64; real estate broker, Dell Rapids, S.D., 1964—; adminstr. Terrace Manor, Dell Rapids, 1970—, exec. sec. Dell Rapids (S.D.) Nursing Home, Inc., 1970—; pres. Dells Terrace, Inc., 1970—. Chmn., Dell Rapids Planning and Zoning Com., 1976-78; mem. S.D. Peer Review Com. S.D. Nursing Home Assn., 1976-77. Served with U.S. Army, 1941-45. Mem. Am. Coll. Nursing Home Adminstrs., Nat. Nursing Home Assn., Am. Legion. Republican. Lutheran. Clubs: Masons. Home: 1208 N Clark St Dell Rapids SD 57022 Office: 1400 Thresher Dr Dell Rapids SD 57022

BROWN, HERBERT SHANKLIN, judge; b. Trenton, Mo., Oct. 3, 1915; s. Herbert Everly and Blanche (Shanklin) B.; A.A., Trenton Jr. Coll., 1935; LL.B., U. Mo., 1938; postgrad. U. Wis., 1937; m. Dorothy Mae French, July 18, 1942; children—Linda L., Cynthia Diane, Brian H. Admitted to Mo. bar, 1938; since practiced in Trenton, Mo.; spl. agt. FBI, 1941-43; dir. Peoples State Bank, Spickard, Mo.; judge probate and magistrate cts. Grundy County (Mo.), 1975—. Pros. atty. Grundy County, 1939-40, 1946-50. Served with AUS, 1943-46. Mem. Am., Mo., Grundy County bar assns. Republican. Mem. Christian Ch. (pres. ofcl. bd. 1953-54). Mason (Shriner), Elk. Home: 600 Town and Country Ln Trenton MO 64683 Office: Grundy County Courthouse Trenton MO 64683

BROWN, HUBERT LESLIE, lay ch. worker; b. Norristown, Pa., Nov. 27, 1945; s. Albert and Leslie (Forbes) B.; A.A., United Weyleyan Coll., 1966; B.A., Goshen Coll., 1971; M.Ed., Ind. U., 1975; m. Helen A. Reichel, Sept. 14, 1968; children—Donald, Leslie. Pastor, Bethel Mennonite Ch., Norristown, 1966-69; phys. dir. YMCA, Norristown, 1968-69; exec. dir. Elkhart (Ind.) Urban League, 1971-73; counselor Ind. U., South Bend, 1973-74; exec. sec. student services Mennonite Bd. Missions, Elkhart, 1974—; vice chmn., then chmn. Mennonite Minority Ministries Council; chmn. Mennonite Nat. Home Missions Com.; mem. bd. Mennonite Ch. Hist. Com.; chmn. Ministries to Blacks in Higher Edn. Bd. dirs., chmn. program com. Elkhart Urban League; bd. dirs. Sickle Cell Anemia Found.; spl. cons. H.O.M.E. Inc. Recipient certificate of appreciation Ind. Dept. Pub. Instrn., 1972; Community Service award Elkhart Community Schs. Human Relations Program, 1976; Service Appreciation plaque Ind. U. Spl. Services Program, 1974. Mem. NAACP, Am. Personnel and Guidance Assn., Assn. Coordination Univ. Religious Affairs, Nat. Campus Ministry Assn., Mid-Am. Assn. Ednl. Opportunity Program Personnel. Author: Black and Mennonite, 1976. Home: PO Box 771 Elkhart IN 46515

BROWN, JOAN LEE, nurse clinician; b. Jackson, Mich., Oct. 13, 1945; d. Jack Winton and Alma Florence (Gibbard) Brown; B.S. in Nursing, Spalding Coll., Louisville, 1968; M.S. in Nursing, U. N.C., 1972; m. Thomas H. Shultz, Dec. 22, 1975. Nurse intensive-care units various instns.; instr. med. surg. nursing U. N.C., Chapel Hill, 1972-73; evening supr. Addison (Mich.) Community Hosp., 1973-74; clin. specialist in psychiatry Chelsea (Mich.) Community Hosp., 1976—; psycho-therapist group and individual therapy; lectr. in field. Mem. Am. Assn. Critical Care Nurses, U. N.C. Alumni Assn., Spalding Coll. Alumni Assn., Nat. Intravenous Therapy Assn., Am. Personnel and Guidance Assn. Sigma Theta Tau. Methodist. Home: PO Box 326 Somerset Center MI 49282 Office: 775 S Main St Chelsea MI 48118

BROWN, JOAN PHILLIPS, human relations cons., civic worker; b. Chgo.; d. Rufus and Lueola (Reed) Phillips; B.A., Roosevelt U., 1954; M.A., U. Chgo., 1963; m. Diego Milan Brown, May 8, 1955 (div. Dec. 1957). Teenage program dir. YWCA Met. Chgo., 1957-61, dir. westside area, 1963-65, dir. human relations, 1965—. Coordinator, Women Mobilized for Change, Chgo., 1966—; actress, mgr. Drama, Inc., Chgo., 1955-61; talent coordinator Ebony Talent Assos., Inc., Chgo., 1969—; convenor Pressure Group of Catalysts, Chgo., 1968—; mem. women's bd. Chgo. Urban League, 1968—; adminstrv. dir. Ebony Talent Creative Arts Found., Chgo.; regional coordinator, mem. U.S.A. zonal bd. 2d World Festival Black and Afrikan Art and Culture, Lagos, Nigeria; bd. dirs. First World Found., co-ordinator First World, internat. jour. Black thought. Co-editor Psalms of Protest, 1965. Home: 7637 S Bennett St Chicago IL 60649 Office: 37 S Wabash Chicago IL 60649

BROWN, KEITH, educator, musician; b. Colorado Springs, Colo., Oct. 21, 1933; s. Kenneth Vernon and Audrey Lucille (Nelson) B.; B.Mus., U. So. Calif., 1957; M.Mus., Manhattan Sch. Music, 1964; m. Leslee Joanne Scullin, June 13, 19S4; children—Robert Vernon, Lise Joanne, Kristin Patricia. Trombonist, N.Y. Brass Quintet, 1958-59; asso. 1st trombonist Phila. Orch., 1959-62; 1st trombonist Met. Opera Orch., 1962-65; dir. instrumental activities, prof. music, conductor univ. orch. Temple U., Phila., 1965-71; prof. music, conductor Univ. Orchs. and contemporary chamber ensemble, Ind. U., Bloomington, Ind., 1971—; mem. faculty, solo trombonist Aspen Festival, 1957-69; participant Marlboro Festival, 1970—; prin. trombonist Casals Festival, San Juan, P.R., 1958—; conductor, music dir. Bloomington Symphony Orch., 1975—. Served with U.S. Army, 1953-56. Mem. Music Educators Nat. Conf., Internat. Trombone Assn., Ind. U. Friends of Music, Pi Kappa Lambda. Methodist. Club: Rotary. Home: 2114 Georgetown Rd Bloomington IN 47401 Office: Sch Music Indiana U Bloomington IN 47401

BROWN, MABEL ESTLE (MRS. ROBERT G. BROWN), co-owner lapidary; b. nr. Letts, Iowa, Oct. 6, 1907; d. Chester Miller and Mayme (Bell) Estle; B.A., U. Iowa, 1929; M.S., Ia. State U., 1953; m. Robert G. Brown, Dec. 30, 1931; children—Patricia Jane (Mrs. Lester Hoback) Linnaeus E. Tchr., Conesville (Iowa) High Sch., 1930-32, 42-48, Nichols (Ia.) High Sch., 1949-50; grad. asst. journalism Iowa State U., Ames, 1950-53; tchr. English, Lone Tree (Iowa) High Sch., 1953-60, dir. guidance, 1960-70, ret.; partner Orono Lapidary, Conesville, Iowa, 1970—. Treas., Muscatine County (Iowa) Farm Bus. Womens Chorus, 1933-39; chmn. Carrie Stanley Scholarship com. Lone Tree Schs., 1962-70. Mem. Iowa Acad. Sci., AAAS, NEA, Am., Iowa personnel and guidance assns., Nat. Council Tchrs. English, Internat. Reading Assn., Iowa, Lone Tree (sec. 1965-70) edn. assns., Future Tchrs. Am. (advisor Lone Tree chpt.), Theta Sigma Phi. Republican. Home: Route 1 Conesville IA 52739 Office: Orono Lapidary Conesville IA 52739

BROWN, MABEL WELTON, lawyer; b. Geneseo, Ill., Dec. 7, 1916; d. Harry E. and Mabel (Welton) Brown; B.A., Oberlin Coll., 1938; J.D., U. Chgo., 1941. Partnership with father, Harry E. Brown, atty., 1941-44, sole owner, 1944—; atty. for Green River Spl. Drainage dist., Henry and Bureau counties, Ill. Chmn. Geneseo Planning Commn., 1961-68. Mem. Am., Ill., Henry County (sec.-treas. 1971-73, pres. 1974-75) bar assns., Am. Judicature Soc., Kappa Beta Phi. Republican. Methodist. Home: 115 E North St Geneseo IL 61254 Office: 115 N State St Geneseo IL 61254

BROWN, MARVIN, advt. agy. exec.; b. Boston, Mar. 17, 1926; s. Frank A. and Frances (Caplan) B.; student Cornell U., 1943-44, U. Mo., 1946-49; B.J., N.Y. U., 1955; m. Constance Ruth Kaminsky, Sept. 5, 1948; children—Valerie Kay, Mark Kenneth, Randall Craig. Reporter, asst. city editor Shreveport (La.) Times, 1949-53; pub. relations mgr. Glenn Mason Advt., Shreveport, 1953-54; advt. and pub. relations dir. Radio-TV Tng. Assn., N.Y.C., 1954-57; creative services mgr. Nationwide Ins. Cos., Columbus, Ohio, 1957-64; pub. Key Mag., Columbus, 1959—; pres. Marbro Advt., Inc., Columbus, 1965—; dir. Key Mags., Inc., Detroit; guest lectr. Franklin U., Columbus, 1974—. Pres. Columbus Quincentennial Expn., 1970—; v.p. Columbus Jewish Center, 1976—. Served with U.S. Army, 1944-46. Mem. Columbus Advt. Fedn. (pres. 1972-73), Columbus Area C. of C. (dir. 1972-73). Club: Columbus Athletic. Home: 1774 Kenwick Rd Columbus OH 43209 Office: 71 E State St Columbus OH 43215

BROWN, MERLE J., surgeon; b. Colo, Iowa, Jan. 16, 1905; s. Jesse J. and Emma (Dolph) B.; B.A., U. Iowa, 1927, M.D., 1933; C.M., U. Pa., 1938; m. Lisette Edith Brooke, June 22, 1933; children—Phullis Jean Brown Frank, Carolyn Mary Brown Samuels. Instr. sci. Lincoln High Sch., Vinton, Ia., 1927-29; intern City Hosp. of Akron (Ohio), 1933-34; resident Guthrie Clinic and Robert Packer Hosp., Sayre, Pa., 1936-38; fellow in gen. surgery, 1936-38; practice medicine specializing in surgery, Davenport, Iowa, 1938-42, 46—; pres. med. staff St. Luke's Hosp., Davenport, 1940-41, instr. surgery Sch. of

Nursing, 1941-42, 46-56, now mem. staff; asst. chief of surgery Mercy Hosp., Davenport, 1947-48, now mem. staff. Dir. Jim Samuels Equipment Co., Inc., Denver, 1971-75, Profl. Arts Bldg., Ltd., Davenport, v.p., 1973—. Chmn. awards and gift com., quad-city Sci. Fair, 1955-57. Served to lt. col., M.C., AUS, 1942-46. Diplomate Am. Bd. Surgery. Fellow A.C.S. (gov. 1962-73); mem. Iowa Acad. Surgery (founder 1953), AMA, Pan Am. Med. Assn., Iowa, Scott County (sec. and program chmn. 1948-56) med. socs., Assn. of Mil. Surgeons (life), Collegium Internat. Chirurgie Digestivae, Central Surg. Assn., Soc. Surgery Alimentary Tract, Pan-Pacific Surg. Assn., Internat. Soc. Surgery, Ia. Clin. Surg. Soc., Alpha Kappa Kappa, U. Iowa Alumni Assn. Clubs: Davenport, Rock Island Arsenal Golf, Quarterback, Outing. Contbr. articles on surgery to profl. jours. Home: 2247 Fairhaven Rd Davenport IA 52803 Office: 121 W Locust St 307 Professional Arts Bldg Davenport IA 52803

BROWN, MEYER, safety profl.; b. Bklyn., Aug. 18, 1913; s. Nathan and Rebecca (Mendelovitz) B.; B.S. in Commerce, Roosevelt U., 1946; postgrad No. Ill. U., 1969-72; m. Adele Yanow, Sept. 6, 1942; children—Howard, Brent, Phillip. Safety supt. U.S. Post Office, Chgo., 1957-68; regional safety mgr. Def. Contract Adminstrn. Service, Def. Logistics Agy., Chgo., 1968-73; safety dir. Dept. Pub. Works, City of Chgo., 1973-74; mgr. safety IIT Research Inst., Chgo., 1974-75; safety dir., coordinator Ill. Tollway, Oak Brook, 1976—. Certified safety profl., hazard control mgr. Mem. Am. Soc. Safety Engrs., Constrn. Safety Assn. Am. (v.p. 1972-74), Fed. Safety and Fire Council (chmn. Chgo. 1970-74), Vets. of Safety, Am. Indsl. Hygienists Assn., Am. Conf. Govt. Hygienists, Nat. Safety Council (mem. exec. bd. pub. employee div. 1977—), Campus Safety Assn. Recipient U.S. Post Office Superior Accomplishment award, 1959, 68; Def. Supply Agency Outstanding Performance award, 1969. Home: 9617 N Tripp Ave Skokie IL 60076

BROWN, MICHAEL JAMES, psychologist; b. Phila., Mar. 14, 1947; s. Richard Lynn and Gertrude May (McTamany) B.; B.A., Mich. State U., 1969, M.A., 1971, Ph.D., 1974; m. Susan Brady, Dec. 30, 1967; children—Jennifer, Emily. Mich. Certified Psychol. Examiner, 1971; Mich. Certified Psychologist, 1975. Counselor, Lansing (Mich.) Boys Tng. Sch., 1968-71; psychologist Ingham Community Mental Health Center, Lansing, 1971-73; dir. tng. Tri-County Drug Treatment Programs, Lansing, 1973-74; dir. tng. Huron Valley Inst., Ann Arbor, Mich., 1974—; adj. prof. Sch. Community Medicine, Mich. State U., 1972-73; lectr. Oakland U., Rochester, Mich., 1973-74; lectr. social work Mich. State U., 1974-75. Mem. Am. Rehab. Counselors Assn. (mem. research com. 1972-73), Internat. Transactional Analysis Assn. (mem. sch. com. 1974-76, mem. tng. standards com. 1976—), Am. Psychol. Assn., Phi Beta Kappa, Phi Eta Sigma. Author: Psychodiagnosis in Brief, 1977; co-author (with Stanley Woollams and Kristyn Huige) Transactional Analysis in Brief, 1974; (with Taibi Kahler) NoTAtions: A Guide to Transactional Analysis Literature, 1977. Contbr. to Transactional Analysis jour. Home: 2305 Yorktown St Ann Arbor MI 48105 Office: Huron Valley Inst 6869 Marshall Rd Dexter MI 48130

BROWN, MICHAEL WAYNE, lawyer; b. Ryan, Okla., Jan. 13, 1940; s. Lawrence Julian and Nadine A. (Roberts) B.; B.S., U. Nebr., 1962, J.D., 1965; children—Michael Sean, Susan Paige. Admitted to Nebr. bar, 1965; mem. firm Beynon, Hecht & Fahrnbruch, Lincoln, 1965-68, Healey, Healey, Brown, Wieland & Glynn, 1968—, partner, 1968—. Tchr. seminars trial advocacy excellence U. Nebr., 1970—. Active ecol. affairs. Recipient first prize ASCAP, 1965. Mem. Am., Nebr., Lincoln bar assns., Am. Trial Lawyers Assn., Nebr. Assn. Trial Attys., Barristers Club, Kappa Sigma. Republican. Unitarian. Elk. Club: University. Home: Box 83104 Lincoln NE 68528 Office: 1141 H St Lincoln NE 68508

BROWN, MRS. MILTON, clubwoman; b. Portsmouth, Ohio, Aug. 23, 1919; d. Enos and Mary (Garrett) Hampton; student pub. schs.; m. Milton H. Brown, July 24, 1947; 1 son, Larry. Bookkeeper, sec. Jos. Brown Inc., 1973-77. Pres. Mercy Hosp. Guild, 1962—; treas. Mercy Guild Twigg; chmn. Polio Drive, 1959-60, Cancer Drive, 1961; chmn. Girl Scout Cookie Drive, 1960-66, bd. mem. council; gen. chmn. dist. 8, Federated Fall Conf.; Ohio Federated dist. 8 chmn. Leadership Devel., 1966-68; health and welfare chmn. So. Ohio, 1964-68; dist. sec. Federated Clubs, 1963-65; pres. New Century Club, 1965-67, sec., 1971-72, asst. sec., 1972-73; pres. Junior Women's City Club, 1960—. Home: 1245 Rosemount Rd Portsmouth OH 45662

BROWN, MILTON DOUGLAS, educator; b. Glennie, Mich., Oct. 24, 1916; s. Courtland Simeral and Erba Mae (Sedley) B.; B.S., Central Mich. U., 1941; M.B.A., U. Denver, 1952; Ph.D. (Kellogg fellow), U. Mich., 1964; m. Maria Teressa Herrmann, July 24, 1971; 1 son, Michael Burke Shay. Bus. tchr. T.L. Handy High Sch., Bay City, Mich., 1948-52; advt. mfr.'s rep. Grand Rapids, Mich. for Alexander Film Co., Colorado Springs, Colo., 1952-60; dir. higher edn. Mich. Edn. Assn., East Lansing, 1964-67; asso. prof. higher edn. Iowa State U., Ames, 1967—. Exec. sec. Mich. Assn. Higher Edn., 1964-67; cons. community colls. Mich., Ohio, Iowa, 1964—. Mem. Mich. Gov.'s Commn. on Home and Family Living, 1965-67. Served with USAAF, 1941-45. Mem. Am. Assn. Higher Edn., Am. Assn. Jr. Community Colls., N. Central Council on Jr. Community Colls. Moose. Clubs: Y's Men (Bay City, Mich.); Ames (Iowa) Golf and Country. Author: The Extent of the Detroit Teacher Shortage, 1966. Home: 2619 Ferndale St Ames IA 50010

BROWN, MONICA V., health orgn. exec.; b. Auckland, New Zealand; student Auckland U., U. Cin. Exec. dir. Health Careers Assn. Greater Cin., 1963-70; project dir. Health Careers of Ohio-Operation MEDIHC Project, Coll. Medicine, Ohio State U., Columbus, 1970—; mem. adv. com., past adj. instr. Community Health Program, Coll. Community Services, U. Cin., 1970—; mem. adv. com., dept. health tech. Cin. Tech. Coll., 1973—; sec. bd. trustees Health Careers of Ohio, Inc., 1970—; mem. steering com., project dir. Invitational Conf., Health Careers of Ohio and Health Resources Adminstrn., HEW, Columbus, 1973-74, mem. adv. com. Health Manpower Linkage System Project, Ohio Dept. Health, 1974-76; mem. Urbana (Ohio) Coll. Social Service Adv. Council, 1976—; cons. various health orgns. Mem. Gov.'s Task Force Jobs for Vets., 1971-76. Mem. Pub. Relations Soc. Am. (asso.), Am., Ohio pub. health assns., Am. Soc. for Allied Health Professions (sec. council individual mems., trustee 1975—), Am. Assn. for Comprehensive Health Planning, Am. Soc. for Health Manpower Edn. and Tng. (dir. Ohio chpt. 1976—), Nat., Ohio (dir. 1971-74) leagues for nursing, Central Assn. Advisers to Health Professions, Am. Council on Health Manpower (dir. 1976—). Contbr. articles on health to profl. jours. Home: 1000 Urlin Ave Apt 521 Columbus OH 43212 Office: PO Box 5574 Columbus OH 43221

BROWN, NORMAN ALLEN, ednl. adminstr.; b. Temperance, Mich., Oct. 18, 1938; s. Wilfred B. and Vivian Ione (Allen) B.; B.S., Mich. State U., 1960, M.A., 1965, Ph.D., 1970; m. Bernice J. Treadway, Jan. 2, 1960; children—Barry, Judith, Rebecca, Douglas. Rural youth specialist U.S. Dept. State, Far East, 1959-60; vocat. agr. instr. Bath (Mich.) Schs., 1960-63; extension 4-H Youth Agt., Ann Arbor, Mich., 1964-65; coordinator student programs Mich. State U., East Lansing, 1965-70, asst. dir. resident instrn., 1970-72, state dir. 4-H youth programs, 1972—, also prof. Cons. to Minister Edn., Algeria, 1971, Partners of the Ams., 1974—; dir. Peace Corps Intern Program, P.I., 1970-72. Chmn., Community Chest Drive, 1971-72; nat. sec. Future Farmers Am., 1958-59; sec. Mich. 4-H Found.; trustee Nat. 4-H Council; chmn. 4-H in Century III com.; bd. dirs., v.p. Mich. Partners of Ams.; mem. Bd. Edn., Bath. Mem. Mich. Assn. Tchrs. Vocat. Agr. (sec.-treas. 1962), Farm House (dir. 1969-71), Alpha Zeta, Phi Kappa Phi. Baptist. (chmn. bd. 1970- 71). Contbr. to profl. publs. in field. Home: 7409 Clark Rd Bath MI 48808 Office: 175 S Anthony East Lansing MI 48823

BROWN, NORMAN STEPHEN, artist; b. Chgo., June 21, 1912; s. Norman Charles and Anna (Kirchner) B.; student Art Inst. Chgo., Comml. Art Inst., Chgo., DePaul U.; m. Helen M. Schilf, May 4, 1938 (dec.); children—Mary Ellen, Norman Stephen, Michael, Mark, Edward. Portraits include: Pope Pius XII, Samuel Cardinal Stritch, George Cardinal Meyer, Gov. Dan Walker Ill. Served with AUS, 1943-46. Recipient medal U.S. Flag Assn. Mem. Artists Guild Chgo., Palette & Chisel Acad., Chgo. Municipal Art League. Home: 1163 Elmwood Ave Deerfield IL 60015 Studio: 1012 Dearborn St N Chicago IL 60610

BROWN, ORIL IRENE, psychologist; b. Maumee, Ohio, Sept. 16, 1908; d. Edwin J. and L. Irene (Remelsbecker) Brown; student U. Toledo, 1926-28; B.S. cum laude, Northwestern U., 1930; M.A., George Washington U., 1951, Ph.D., 1965. Asst., Medill Sch. Journalism, Northwestern U., 1930-36; copyreader European edit. N.Y. Herald-Tribune, Paris, France, 1936-37; editorial work, free-lance writing, Chgo., 1930-36, 37-42; asst. editor Fgn. Broadcast Intelligence Service, Washington, 1942-51; research asst. Human Resources Research Office, Washington, 1952-53; pub. sch. psychologist, Portsmouth, Va., 1953-54; staff psychologist N.D. State Hosp., Jamestown, 1955-57; instr. psychiatry Med. Coll. of Va., 1957-60; staff psychologist Danville (Pa.) State Hosp., 1960-64; staff psychologist Mental Hygiene Clinic, Toledo, 1964, acting chief psychologist, 1965-68, psychologist dir. I, 1968-70, psychologist dir. II, 1970—. Mem. League Women Voters (dir. 1966-67), Am., Ohio, Midwestern, Southeastern psychol. assns., Internat. Council Psychologists, AAUW (dir. 1973-75), Maumee Valley Hist. Soc., Sigma Xi. Republican. Episcopalian. Contbr. articles to profl. jours. Home; 2270 Townley Rd Toledo OH 43614 Office: Suite 106 3450 W Central Ave Toledo OH 43606

BROWN, PATRICIA LYNN, info. scientist, lab. exec.; b. Lafayette, La., Oct. 1, 1928; d. William Madison and Maude Juanita (Thomas) Brown; B.S. in Chem. Engring., U. Southwestern La., 1947; M.A. in Chemistry, U. Tex., 1949. Instr. analytical chemistry Smith Coll., Northampton, Mass., 1949-50; chemist R&M Labs., Peabody, Mass., 1950; research asso. indsl. toxicology Albany (N.Y.) Med. Coll., 1950-51; mem. info. services staff Ethyl Corp., Ferndale, Mich., 1951-55; sr. tech. writer, editor, staff engr. Westinghouse Atomic Power Div., Pitts., 1955-57; supr., then mgr. info. services, tech. info. cons. Tex. Instruments, Dallas, 1957-66; sr. info. scientist, sr. researcher Battelle Columbus (Ohio) Labs., 1966-76; mgr. sci. services Travenol Labs., Morton Grove, Ill., 1976—. Loaned exec. United Way Campaign, 1972, 73. Bd. dirs. Engring. Socs. Library, 1961-63, 66-71. Mem. Soc. Women Engrs. (pres. 1961-63), Am. Chem. Soc., Spl. Libraries Assn., Soc. Applied Learning Tech., Am. Soc. Info. Sci., Soc. Tech. Communication. Author publs. in field. Home: 1109 Skylark Dr Palatine IL 60067 Office: 6301 Lincoln Ave Morton Grove IL 60053

BROWN, RAE HAEFEL (MRS. JOHN ANTHONY BROWN), real estate co. exec.; b. Chgo., Apr. 19, 1921; d. Albert and Rose (Kunz) Haefel; student Rosary Coll., 1939-41; B.A., Mundelein Coll., 1943: m. John Anthony Brown, Nov. 23, 1946; children—John Albert, Christopher Paul. Reporter, New World Newspaper, Chgo., 1943-44; asso. editor Modern Beauty Shop mag., Chgo., 1944-54; free-lance writer, 1954-64; pub. relations dir., asst. v.p. Baird & Warner, Inc., real estate, Chgo., 1964-73, v.p., 1973—. Vice pres. Palos Twp. Regular Republican Orgn., 1965. Mem. Chgo. Real Estate Bd., Palos Twp. Rep. Women's Orgn., Nat. Real Estate Referral Orgn. Contbr. articles to profl. jours. Home: 1549 Wedgefield Circle Naperville IL 60540 Office: 115 S LaSalle St Chicago IL 60603

BROWN, RICHARD OSBORNE, physician; b. Detroit, May 20, 1930; s. Richard Wells and Flossie Eva (Osborne) B.; B.A., Wayne State U., 1953; M.D., Howard U., 1959; m. Dolores Debro, Jan. 23, 1954; children—Richard Debro, Kevin Michael; m. 2d, Martha Evelyn McGregor, Oct. 6, 1973. Intern Wayne County Gen. Hosp., 1959-60; resident ophthalmology Homer G. Phillips Hosp., St. Louis, 1962-65; staff ophthalmologist CHA-Met. Hosp., Detroit, 1965-67; practice medicine specializing in ophthalmology, Detroit, 1967—; chief med. staff Kirwood Gen. Hosp., 1974-76, now trustee. Cons., Met., SW Detroit, Lakeside, Kirwood hosps. Mem. Draft Bd., 1971-76. Served with AUS, 1953-55. Mem. Am. Assn. Ophthalmology, AMA, Wayne County, Detroit (treas. 1972—), Mich. State med. socs., Detroit C. of C., Am. Profl. Practice Assn., Council Med. Staffs Mich. (dir. 1971—). Episcopalian. Home: 9000 E Jefferson Apt 2610 Detroit MI 48214 Office: 3800 Woodward St Detroit MI 48201

BROWN, RICHARD PEABODY, lawyer, publisher; b. Kansas City, Mo., Apr. 11, 1927; s. Alpha Nelson and Margerie (Peabody) B.; A.B., U. Mo., 1949, LL.B., 1952; m. Bette J. Allen, June 17, 1955; children—Laurie Ann, Richard P. Admitted to Mo. bar, 1952; individual practice law, Kansas City, 1952-54; atty. Bendix Corp., Kansas City, 1954-72; pub. The Wednesday Mag., Kansas City, 1972—; dir. Peoples Bank of Kansas City; pres. Brookside Merchants Assn., 1976, 77; bd. dirs. Waldo Bus. Assn. Past pres. Kansas City chpt. Sons of Revolution, also past pres. Mo. Soc. Served with USN, 1944. Mem. Mo. Press Assn. Home: 5513 W 86 Terr Overland Park KS 66207 Office: 6314 Brookside Plaza Kansas City MO 64113

BROWN, ROBERT BAXTER, JR., tool mfg. co. exec.; b. St. Louis, Mar. 5, 1931; s. Robert Baxter and Helen Marie (Costello) B.; B.S., Mass. Inst. Tech., 1952; m. Shriley Mae Knupp, June 9, 1956; children—Lucy Claire, Robert Baxter III. Supr. customer services Monsanto Co., St. Louis, 1956-59; sales engr. Hydro Aire div. Crane Co., St. Louis, 1959-61; area sales mgr. Parker Aircraft div. Parker Hannifin, St. Louis, 1961-67; pres. Alliance Tool Co., St. Louis, 1967—, also dir. Served with USN, 1952-56. Mem. Nat. Fedn. Ind. Bus., Nat. Tool & Die Assn., Soc. Mfg. Engrs. Roman Catholic. Home: 7 Trails End Ln St Louis MO 63124 Office: 9494 Watson Industrial Park St Louis MO 63126

BROWN, ROBERT ORDWAY, food products co. exec.; b. Tyler, Minn., July 31, 1917; s. Peter J. and Ella M. (Hansen) B.; B.Chem. Engring., U. Minn., 1939; m. Margrethe Frederiksen, June 12, 1943; children—Rolf, Linnea (Mrs. Lauren Berg), Karla, Paul, Grete. Sect. head. Pillsbury Mills, Mpls., 1939-56; cons. engr. Robert O. Brown Co., Mpls., 1956—. Mem. Am. Inst. Chem. Engrs., AAAS, Am. Assn. Cereal Chemists, N.Y. Acad. Scis., Inst. Food Technologists, Am. Soc. Heating, Refrigerating and Air Conditioning Engrs. Home: 4500 Morningside Rd Minneapolis MN 55416 Office: 4200 Cedar Ave Minneapolis MN 55407

BROWN, ROGER TRUMAN, veterinarian; b. Slater, Iowa, Sept. 2, 1938; s. Truman Mark and Ruth Theressa (Olson) B.; D.V.M., Iowa State U., 1963; m. Nancy Lee Dunham, Dec. 29, 1961. Gen. practice veterinary medicine, Bethesda, Md., 1965-70, Omaha, Nebr., 1970—; owner Bel Air Animal Clinic, Omaha, 1970—; chmn. bd. dirs., veterinary practice cons. Ancom, Inc.; chmn. bd. dirs. Ornamental Fish Industries, Cartel, Inc. Served with Veterinary Corps, U.S. Army, 1963-65. Mem. Am., Nebr. veterinary med. assns., Am. Animal Hosp. Assn., Nebr. Acad. Veterinary Medicine, Am. Maltese Assn., Nebr. Kennel Club, Kappa Sigma. Republican. Lutheran. Co-author monthly syndicated maltese column Popular Dogs mag., 1973-75, also audio-visual client edn. filmstrips. Home: 1417 S 136th St Omaha NE 68144 Office: 12100 West Center Rd Omaha NE 68144

BROWN, SCOTT ROBERT, JR., steel products co. exec.; b. Lincoln, Nebr., Nov. 15, 1932; s. Scott Robert and Marie Josephine (Deardorff) B.; B.S. in Bus. Adminstrn., U. Nebr., 1955; m. Clarice LaVern Freye, Aug. 2, 1953; children—Rick Robert, Janene LaVern Brown Schneider. Agt., Farmers Ins. Group, Lincoln, Nebr., 1955-56; constrn. foreman B & M Drywall, Des Moines, Iowa, 1956-57; with Brownie Mfg. Co., Waverly, Nebr., 1957—, v.p., gen. mgr., 1961—, exec. v.p. bd. dirs., 1961—. Active Boy Scouts Am., 1963-74; vol. fireman, Waverly, 1960-75. Mem. Nat. Fedn. Ind. Businessmen, Nat., Waverly (past sec.) chambers of commerce. Republican. Methodist. Clubs: Mason, Shriner. Home: 1855 18th Ave Waverly NE 68462 Office: 1777 Hwy 6 Waverly NE 68462

BROWN, SEYMOUR, anesthesiologist; b. St. Louis, Aug. 26, 1915; s. Adolph S. and Rose (Carson) B.; B.S., Washington U., St. Louis, 1936, M.D., 1940; m. Rose Ann Tropp, Dec. 25, 1941; children—Alvin Richard, Donald Elliott. Intern in pathology Barnes Hosp., St. Louis, 1940; rotating intern Ill. Research Edn. Hosp. U. Ill., Chgo., 1941; fellow in anesthesiology Lahey Clinic, Boston, 1943; sr. asst. prof. anesthesiology St. Louis U., 1952—; practice medicine specializing in anesthesiology, Creve Coeur, Mo.; dir. anesthesiology St. John's Hosp. and St. John's Mercy Med. Center, 1946-75; chief anesthesiology St. Louis County Hosp., 1946-72; cons. in field; mem. exec. bd. St. John's Hosp., St. Louis, St. Louis County Hosp. Bd. dirs. Shaare Emeth Temple, St. Louis. Served from lt. j.g. to lt. comdr. M.C., USNR, 1941-46. Recipient Mercy award St. John's Mercy Hosp., 1970; diplomate Am. Bd. Anesthesiology. Fellow Am. Coll. Anesthesiology; mem. AMA, Am., St. Louis and Mo. socs. anesthesiologists, Internat. Anesthesiology Research Soc., World Fedn. Anesthesiologists, St. Louis Med. Soc., St. Louis Surg. Soc., N.Y. Acad. Scis., Mo. Soc. Medicine, Sigma Xi, Alpha Omega Alpha. Republican. Club: Ambassadors. Contbr. articles to med. jours.; anesthesiology editor Clin. Medicine, 1953-65. Home: 2421 Baxton Way Chesterfield MO 63017 Office: 621 S Ballas Rd Creve Coeur MO 63141

BROWN, SEYMOUR R., lawyer; b. Cleve., Oct. 24, 1924; s. Leonard and Ella (Rubinstein) B.; B.A., Case-Western Res. U., 1948; J.D., Cleve. State U., 1953; m. Madeline Kusevich, July 8, 1956; children—Frederic M., Thomas R., Barbara L.N. Admitted to Ohio bar, 1953; practice law, Cleve., 1953-57; sec. Warren Family Bank; partner Danaceau, Brown & Hausler, Cleve., 1957—; pres. Carnegie Financial Corp., Cleve., 1961—; dir. numerous small Ohio cos.; spl. counsel to atty. gen. State of Ohio, 1963-70. Mem. exec. com. Cuyahoga County Republican Orgn., 1966—. Served with AUS, 1943-45. Decorated Purple Heart, Bronze Star. Mem. Am., Ohio, Greater Cleve. bar assns., Am. Arbitration Assn., Zeta Beta Tau (nat. v.p., nat. bd. dirs. 1970—). Clubs: City of Cleve. (pub. affairs com.), Masons. Editor, pub. Gt. Lakes Architecture, 1955-59. Home: 3718 Meadowbrook Blvd University Heights OH 44118 Office: 1501 Euclid Ave Cleveland OH 44115

BROWN, SPENCER DEAN, assn. exec.; b. Cape Girardeau, Mo., Mar. 5, 1940; s. Riley Elwood and Rubye (Spencer) B.; B.S., SE Mo. State U., 1960; M.S., So. Ill. U., 1972; m. Jean Ashley, Dec. 14, 1974; children—Tara Lynn, Christine Denise. Tchr. Farmington (Mo.) Sr. High Sch., 1960-62; program mgr. Radio Sta. KDEX Radio, Dexter, Mo., 1963-64; tchr. Hazelwood (Mo.) Jr. High Sch., 1964-69; UniServ dir. St. Louis Suburban Tchrs. Assn., 1969-72; UniServ exec. dir. Indpls. Edn. Assn., 1972—; dir. Nat. Staff Orgn., 1973—. Treas. polit. action coms., Mo., 1970-71, Ind., 1973-76; pres. United Parents Indpls., 1976. Recipient Spoke award Farmington Jr. C. of C., 1962, Indpls. Edn. Assn. achievement award, 1973, Ind. Tchrs. Assn. editorial award 1977. Mem. NEA, Phi Delta Kappa, Kappa Delta Pi. Club: Indpls. Press. Home: 7757 Redcoach Dr Indianapolis IN 46250 Office: 4002 Meadows Dr Suite 308 Indianapolis IN 46205

BROWN, SPENCER HUNTER, historian; b. Knoxville, Tenn., June 10, 1928; s. John Orville and Edith Frances (Hunter) B.; B.A. in Teaching Social Studies magna cum laude, U. Ill., 1954, M.A. in History (Fellow), 1955; Ph.D. in History (African studies fellow), Northwestern U., 1964; m. Doris Lucille Craig, Aug. 4, 1951; 1 dau., Rebecca Lee. Tchr., then tchr./chmn. social scis. dept. Carl Sandburg High Sch., Orland Park, Ill., 1955-59; mem. faculty Western Ill. U., Macomb, 1962—. prof. history, 1971—, chmn. dept., 1976—. Served with USNR, 1945-47. Ford Found. fellow, 1961-62. Mem. African Studies Assn., Am. Hist. Assn., AAUP, Phi Beta Kappa, Phi Eta Sigma. Gen. editor Jour. Developing Areas, 1965-76. Home: Box 47 Tennessee IL 62374 Office: Dept History Western Ill Univ Macomb IL 61455

BROWN, STELLA CHANEY, advt. agy. exec.; b. East St. Louis, Ill., Apr. 1, 1924; d. James Oscar and Lela Elizabeth (Hartill) Chaney; student Northwestern U., 1941-42, Jefferson Coll., 1942-45; m. A. Harvey Brown, Nov. 1, 1946 (div. Nov. 1960); children—Wendy Alexandra, Deborah Elisabeth. Advt. mgr. Sonnenfelds, St. Louis, 1943; dir. men's wear advt. Stix, Baer & Fuller, St. Louis, 1944; account exec., copy writer Hillman Shane Breyer Agy., Los Angeles, 1945; copy dir. Harry Serwer Agy., N.Y.C., 1945-46; advt. mgr. Libson Shops, St. Louis, 1946-47; asst. advt. dir. Edison Bros. Stores, Inc., 1947-53; copy dir., account exec. Hirsch-Tamm & Ullman Agy., 1957-58; pres. Stella Chaney Brown Advt., Inc., Clayton, Mo., 1959—; dir. St. Louis Broadcasting Co., Inc.; fashion editor Prom Mag., 1946—. Mem. Am. Fedn. Astrologers. Editor: Wheelspin, 1953-58, Parents Without Partners Newsletter. Address: 9180 Ladue Rd St Louis MO 63124

BROWN, TERRY KENNEDY, hosp. supply co. exec.; b. Grand Rapids, Mich., May 3, 1936; s. Roy Everett and Maxine Barnard (Kennedy) B.; B.A., Kalamazoo Coll., 1959; postgrad. Wayne State U., 1965-67; m. Mary Sansalone, Aug. 17, 1973; children—Serena Ilse, Kelly Marie. Sales rep., product mgr., sales mgr. Parke, Davis & Co., Detroit, 1961-75; sales mgr. Ipco Hosp. Supply Co., Livonia, Mich., 1976—. Mem. Sigma Rho Sigma. Republican. Presbyterian. Home: 2571 Fox Chase Troy MI 48098 Office: 35255 Glendale Livonia MI 48150

BROWN, THOMAS ACRES, lawyer, county ofcl.; b. Watseka, Ill., Apr. 26, 1931; s. George L. and Ethel (Acres) B.; B.S., Ind. U., 1954; J.D., Emory U., 1960; m. Ann B. Bohdan, Feb. 5, 1955; children—Megan Sue, Thomas R. Admitted to Ind. bar, 1960; dep. atty. gen. (Ind.), 1960-64; pros. atty. Hartford City, Ind., 1967—; mem. Ind. Mental Health Study Commn., 1960—, vice chmn. legis.

com., 1969—; mem. Ind. Criminal Code Commn., 1973—. Bd. dirs. Blackford County Mental Health Assn., pres., 1971; bd. dirs. Blackford County Tb. Assn. Served with AUS, 1954-56. Mem. Am., Blackford County bar assns., Nat. Dist. Attys. Assn., Ind. Pros. Attys. Assn. (pres. elect 1977-78), Fraternal Order Police, Am. Legion, Phi Delta Phi, Sigma Pi. Mason, Elk, Rotarian (pres. 1971-72). Home: 1412 N Jefferson St Hartford City IN 47348 Office: 117 N High St Hartford City IN 47348

BROWN, THOMAS CARTWRIGHT, bus. cons.; b. Warren, Ind., Jan. 18, 1913; s. Ervin Byron and Edith (Cartwright) B.; B.S. in pub. adminstrn., U. Mo., 1934; M.A., Ball State U., 1972, postgrad. fellow, 1975—; postgrad. Instituto Tecnológico y de Estudios Superiores de Monterrey (Mexico), summer 1972; m. Martha Helen O'Brien, Nov. 22, 1947; children—Beverly Sue, Martha Melinda. Research and prodn. control Sheller Mfg. Corp., Portland, Ind., 1935-37, chief chemist, 1937-43, dir. research and process engring., 1946-57; consulting Ransburg Electro-Coating Corp., Indpls., 1957-60, in charge of mg. operations, 1958-60; partner Mid-America Internat., Indpls., 1960-64; pres., chmn., owner Intercor, Inc., Pennville, Ind., 1964—; cons. Fire-Trol Corp., 1964—; dir. Capitol Oil, Inc. First v.p. Region VI Planning and Devel. Commn., State of Ind., 1973, pres., 1974, mem., 1975; Region VI rep. to Ind. Assn. Regional Councils, 1975. Trustee, Middle dist. Town Bd., Pennville, 1971—. Served as lt. (s.g.), USNR, 1943-46. Recipient 8 battle stars on PTO Ribbon. Mem. ASTM, Am. Hist. Assn., Conf. Latin Americanist Geographers, Am. Chem. Soc. (rubber div.), Res. Officers Assn., Am. Legion, U.S. Naval Inst., Internat. Platform Assn., C. of C., Delta Upsilon, Gamma Theta Upsilon, Alpha Kappa Psi, Phi Alpha Theta. Presbyterian. Mason (32 deg., Shriner, K.T.), Elk. Address: 145 S Union St Pennville IN 47369

BROWN, VERNAL CARROL, farmer, civic worker; b. McDonough County, Ill., Aug. 4, 1920; s. Clayton Lamb and Mary Ellen (Lawyer) B.; grad. high sch.; m. Mildred Marie Miller, Apr. 27, 1943; children—Reginald Mace, Joyce Elaine. Farmer nr. Vermont, Ill., 1945—. Dir. Ill. Agrl. Assn., 1958-73. Mem. adv. prodn. policy panel to Pres. of U.S. and Council Econ. Advisers, 1973. Bd. dirs. Country Capital Investment Fund., 1969—; trustee Vermont Fire Protection Dist., 1956—. Served with USNR, 1942-45. Mem. Interstate Producers Livestock Assn. (dir. 1962-73). Mem. Christian Ch. (trustee 1972—, elder 1956—). Home: Rural Route 1 Vermont IL 61484

BROWN, WAYNE LAWRENCE, accountant; b. Woodstock, Ill., Mar. 21, 1936; s. Lawrence Raymond and Marian Elizabeth (Collen) B.; B.B.A., U. Minn., 1958; m. Madeline Bonny, Apr. 30, 1959; children—Rita, Phillip, Steven, Patrick, Loren. Auditor, Peat, Marwick, Mitchell & Co., C.P.A.'s, Mpls., 1958-61, James G. Condon & Co., C.P.A.'s, Woodstock, Ill., 1961-63; owner Wayne L. Brown & Co., Accountants and Auditors, Woodstock, Ill., 1963—; pres. Brown's Data Processing, Woodstock, Ill., 1970—; dir. State Bank Woodstock, Am. Litho Arts, Inc., Donahue Furniture Co., J.V. Doehren Co., D. C. Warehouse, Inc. Trustee, Seneca Twp., 1971—; treas., dir. Meml. Hosp. McHenry County. Mem. Nat. Soc. Pub. Accountants. Clubs: Elks, K.C. Home: 3711 Franklinville Rd Woodstock IL 60098 Office: 1700 S Eastwood Dr PO Box 728 Woodstock IL 60098

BROWN, WESLEY ERNEST, U.S. judge; b. Hutchinson, Kans., June 22, 1907; s. Morrison H.H. and Julia (Wesley) B.; student Kans. U., 1925-28; LL.B., Kansas City Law Sch., 1933; m. Mary A. Miller, Nov. 30, 1934; children—Wesley Miller, Mary Loy (Mrs. John K. Wiley). Admitted to Kans., Mo. bars, 1933; pvt. practice, Hutchinson, Kans., 1933-58; county atty. Reno County, Kans., 1935-39; referee in bankruptcy U.S. Dist. Ct. Kans., 1958-62; judge U.S. Dist. Ct. Kans., 1962—, now chief justice. Dir. Nat. Assn. Referees in Bankruptcy, 1959-62; mem. jud. conf. U.S. Bankruptcy Adminstrn., 1963—. Served with USNR, 1944-46. Mem. Am., Kans. State (exec. council 1950-65, pres. 1964-65), Reno County (pres. 1947), Wichita bar assns., Southwest Bar Kans., Delta Theta Phi. Home: 1401 W River Blvd Wichita KS 67203 Office: US Dist Ct PO Box 28 Wichita KS 67201

BROWN, WILLIAM DARREL, nuclear engr.; b. Portland, Oreg., June 2, 1939; s. Charles Frank Lafollette and Mildred Caroline (Bredenbeck) B.; B.S. in M.E., Oreg. State U., 1961; M.S., U. Wash., 1970; m. Sharon Lee Hawley, July 14, 1961; children—Shannon, Ross, Robby. Project engr., Esco Inc., Portland, Oreg., 1961-62; prin. engr. Silver Eagle Co., Portland, 1963-64; design engr. Omark Industries Inc., Portland, 1965-66; mech. engr. Sandwell Intrnat., Inc., Portland, 1967-68; mech. engr. Pacific Rim Inc., Tacoma, Wash., part time 1968-70; mech. engr. Sargent & Lundy, Chgo., 1970-73; sr. nuclear engr. Fluor Pioneer Inc., Chgo., 1973—. Cons. Inst. Cultural Affairs. Mem. Village of Oak Park Econ. Devel. Com., 1973; co-founder Beye Neighborhood Council, Oak Park, 1973—; mem. Townmeeting Task Force 1975-76. Mem. Am. Nuclear Soc. Democrat. Mem. Ch. Disciples of Christ. Home: 546 N Humphrey St Oak Park IL 60302 Office: 200 W Monroe St Chicago IL 60606

BROWN, WILLIAM EVERETT, chem. engr.; b. Auburn, N.Y., Nov. 9, 1927; s. Everett Lawton and Helen May (Rasmussen) Brown; m. Natalie Smith, Oct. 3, 1953; children—Matthew, Kevin, Paul, Lorraine, Rebecca. B.S., Syracuse U., 1951; with Dow Chem. Co., Midland, Mich., 1951—, head testing sect., 1956-62, head performance and design, 1962-66, sr. sect. head automotive sect., 1967, new applications devel., 1967-70, tech. mgr. new ventures research and devel., 1970-74, research mgr. Saran and Converted Products research, 1974—. Chmn. Planning Com., Bay-Midland OEO, 1970-72. Mem. Am. Soc. Testing and Materials, Sci. Research Soc. Am., Sigma Xi. Contbr. articles to profl. jours. Editor: Testing of Polymers, book series, 1965-70. Home: 505 Rodd St Midland MI 48640 Office: Dow Chem USA Saran and Converted Products Research Midland MI 48640

BROWN, WILLIAM JOSEPH, state ofcl.; b. Youngstown, Ohio, July 12, 1940; s. Joseph and Margaret (O'Neil) B.; B.A., Duquesne U.; J.D., Ohio No. U.; m. Cheryl Pocock, May 11, 1974. Former atty. OEO, Youngstown; now atty. gen. Ohio. Chmn. Humphrey for Pres. Com. Columbiana County, Ohio, 1968; mem. jud. council Democratic Nat. Com. Served with AUS. Mem. Mahoning County, Columbiana County bar assns., Nat. Assn. Attys. Gen. (mem. exec. com., chmn. consumer protection com.). Roman Catholic. Address: State Office Tower Columbus OH 43215

BROWN, WILLIAM LACY, agrl. products co. exec.; b. Arbovale, W.Va., July 16, 1913; s. Tilden L. and Mamie Hudson (Orndoff) B.; B.A., Bridgewater (Va.) Coll., 1936; postgrad. Tex. A. and M. Coll., 1936-37; M.S., Washington U., St. Louis, 1940, Ph.D., 1942; m. Alice Hevener Hannah, Aug. 17, 1941; children—Alicia Anne, William Tilden. Tchr. biology Middlebrook (Va.) High Sch., 1936; tech. asst. Agr. Expt. Sta., Tex. A. and M. Coll., 1936-37; research fellow Mo. Bot. Gardens, St. Louis, 1937-41; geneticist U.S. Dept. Agr. and U.S. Golf Assn., Greens sect., Washington, 1941-42; geneticist in charge corn breeding Rogers Seed Co., Olivia, Minn., 1943-45; geneticist dept. plant (name change to Pioneer Hi-Bred Internat., Inc. 1971), Johnston, Iowa, 1945-58, asst. dir. research, 1958-65, dir. co., Des Moines, 1962—, v.p., dir. research, 1965—, exec. v.p. 1973-75, pres., 1975—; extra-mural prof. botany Washington U., St. Louis, 1957—. Mem. sub-panel Pres.'s Sci. Adv. Com. on World Food Supply, Washington, 1966-68; adviser Joint U.S. Dept. Agr.-State Agrl. Experiment Sta. Task Force on Corn and Grain Sorghum, Washington, 1968-74; Mem. Bd. Edn., Johnston Consol. Sch. Dist., 1958-64, pres., 1961-62. Chmn. regional bd. Am. Friends Service Com.; trustee, Accokeek (Md.) Found.; trustee Bridgewater Coll.; bd. regents Nat. Colonial Farm. Fulbright research fellow Imperial Coll. Tropical Agr., Trinidad, W.I., 1952-53; Univ. fellow Drake U., Des Moines, 1970—. Fellow Am. Soc. Agronomy; mem. AAAS, Am. Inst. Biol. Scis., Bot. Soc. Am., Genetics Soc. Am., Genetics Soc. Can., Nat. (governing bd. Agrl. Research Inst. 1967-69), Iowa acads. sci., Soc. Plant Taxonomists, Soc. for Econ. Botany, Am. Seed Trade Assn., Sigma Xi. Quaker. Clubs: Hyperion Field, Prairie, Des Moines (Des Moines). Author: (with Henry A. Wallace) Corn and Its Early Fathers, 1956. Contbr. articles to profl. jours. Home: 6980 NW Beaver Dr Johnston IA 50131 Office: 1206 Mulberry St Des Moines IA 50308

BROWN, WILLIAM TERRENCE, accountant; b. Kansas City, Mo., Dec. 6, 1941; s. William Francis and Ninalee (Timmons) B.; m. Kathleen Rae Ball, May 28, 1966; children—Stephen M., Christopher M.; B.S., Rockhurst Coll., 1963; J.D., U. Mo., Kansas City, 1969. Admitted to U.S. Tax Ct. bar, 1972; with Sernes, Chandler, Schupp & Conneally, C.P.A.'s, Kansas City, 1962-64; mng. partner Brown & Co., C.P.A.'s, Kansas City, Mo., 1964—. Lay mem. mediation bd. Jackson County Med. Soc., 1975; treas., bd. dirs., mem. exec. com. Legal Aid and Defender Soc. Kansas City; bd. dirs. Pre-Trial Diversion Services, Inc., 1975—, Estate Planning Assn. Kansas City, 1966-68; mem. exec. council to Mike White, Jackson County Exec. Mem. Am. Inst. C.P.A.'s. Home: 1807 E 97th Terr Kansas City MO 64131 Office: 8080 Ward Pkwy Suite 440 Kansas City MO 64131

BROWN, WILLIS WINSTON, former govt. ofcl., utility exec., civil engr.; b. Haviland, Kans., Dec. 3, 1912; s. Meredith O. and Nan O. (Baer) B.; student Ft. Hays State Coll., 1932-35, Mo. Sch. of Mines, 1946-47; m. Viva Anna Mulch, Nov. 21, 1937; children—Charles Wayne, Karen Kay, Ronald Rex, Dwane Dee. Project engr. Taylor & Brown Co., Salina, Kans., 1947-48; salesman Salina Tractor Co., 1948-50; propr. Brown Constrn. Co., Downs, Kans., 1950-53; sec. treas. Downs Constrn. Co., Inc., 1951-58; appraiser FHA, Topeka, 1958-60, chief of ops., 1960-66, asst. dir., 1966-71, dep. dir., 1971-75, ret. 1976; right-of-way agt. So. Bell Telephone Co., 1977—. Surveyor, Osborne Co., 1947-53. Served to capt. USAAF, 1942-43, to capt. AUS, 1943-45. Decorated Silver Star medal with oak leaf cluster, Purple Heart, Bronze Star medal; Croix de Guerre (France). Mem. ASCE, Am. Legion, VFW, Am. Theatre Orgn. Soc., Phi Kappa Phi, Phi Mu Alpha, Optimist Club. Methodist (trustee 1973—). Rotarian. Home: 3600 Jewell St Topeka KS 66611

BROWNE, ALDIS JEROME, JR., real estate broker; b. Chgo., Mar. 21, 1912; s. Aldis J. and Elizabeth (Cunningham) B.; B.A., Yale U., 1935; m. Bertha Erminger, Oct. 22, 1938; children—Aldis J. III, Howell E., John Kenneth. Vice pres., dir. Browne & Storch Inc., and predecessors, Chgo., 1935—, dir., 1961—; dir. English Speaking Union, Civic Fedn., Mil. Order World Wars; chmn. Bldg. Review Bd. Lake Forest (certificate appreciation). Vestryman, St. James Episcopalian Ch., 1947-60. Trustee Old Peoples Home, Chgo. Served to capt. USNR. Mem. Chgo. (dir.), Ill., N. Side Chgo. real estate bds., Nat. Realtors Assn., Order Founders and Patriots (gov. Ill. chpt.), Soc. Colonial Wars, Chgo. Art Inst. (life), Navy League (past dir.). Republican. Clubs: Chgo., Tavern, Army Navy Washington, Masons. Home: 921 N Church Rd Lake Forest IL 60045 Office: 100 E Ohio St Chicago IL 60611

BROWNE, JANE COTTON, family planning specialist; b. St. Paul, Nov. 19, 1912; d. Donald Reed and Grace (Gillette) Cotton; student Wells Coll., 1930-32; m. Harry C. Browne, May 17, 1941 (div. May 1954); 1 son, Marshall Gillette. Adminstrv. asst. Cargill, Inc., Mpls., 1944-45; office mgr., dir. spl. gifts Am. City Bur., Portland, 1947-48; dir., field cons. Planned Parenthood N.Y. (Eastern League), Chgo., 1958-69; chmn. exec. dirs. council Planned Parenthood-World Population, 1965-68; mem. steering com. N. Cook County OEO, 1966-69; gov. bd. Cook County OEO, 1966-69; mem. health com., welfare com., Evanston Anti-Poverty Council, 1967-69; mem. Population Assn. Am., Inc., Am. Pub. Health Assn., 1962—, Am. Pub. Welfare Assn., 1962—, Nat. Conf. Social Welfare, 1951—; founder, mem. Family Planning Coordinating Council Met. Chgo., 1967-71; mem. Gov.'s state-wide adv. council Ill. div. Health Planning and Resource Devel., Com. on Health Care Facilities, 1968; mem. profl. adv. panel Welfare Council Met. Chgo., 1969-70; mem. adv. council Comprehensive Health Planning, Met. Chgo., 1969-71; mem. Planned Parenthood adv. com. for Evanston and N. Shore Health Dept., 1969; project dir. OEO Family Planning Grant, Ark., 1970-71; research asso., family planning cons. Center for Population Studies U. Minn., 1970—; family planning cons. Interfacia, HEW, Great Lakes Region, Chgo., 1972-73. Cons. to USAID, fall 1968; spl. cons. family planning OEO, Washington, 1970-73; family planning cons. Model Cities, HUD, 1971-72, Boone-Young Assos., N.Y.C., 1973, Roy Littlejohn, Region V, Chgo., 1973-74; real estate sales Fredrick Herfurth Real Estate Co., Mpls.; travel cons. Omni Travel, St. Paul. Mem. budget allocations com. United Way, Mpls., 1973-76; bd. dirs. Opportunity Workshop, Mpls., 1973—, Met. YMCA, Mpls., 1977—. Sr. fellow Adlai Stevenson Inst. Internat. Affairs, 1969-70. Republican. Episcopalian. Address: 205 S Barry Ave Apt 302 Wayzata MN 55391

BROWNE, PHILIP JOHN, mgmt. cons.; b. Newark, Jan. 25, 1937; s. A. Philip and Mildred (Smith) B.; B.S., U. Conn., 1959; M.S., San Jose State U., 1963; Ph.D., U. Oreg., 1971; m. Gloria Jean Jackson, Sept. 21, 1963; children—Christopher J., Todd P. Tchr., East Hartford (Conn.) High Sch., 1959-60; buyer trainee Kaman Aircraft Corp., 1960-61; adminstrv. asst. Lockheed Missiles and Space Co., 1962-64; instr. bus. adminstrn. Eastern. Wash. State Coll., 1964-66; orgn. devel. intern Weyerhaeuser Co., 1969; mgr. mgmt. edn. Allstate Ins. Co., Northbrook, Ill., 1972-75; orgn. devel. cons. Harbridge House, Inc., internat. mgmt. cons. firm, Northbrook, 1975—. Mem. Am. Psychol. Assn., Am. Soc. Tng. and Devel., Acad. of Mgmt., Gestalt Inst. of Cleve. Contbr. articles to profl. jours. Home: 191 Pleasant Rd Lake Zurich IL 60047 Office: 2875 Milwaukee Ave Northbrook IL 60062

BROWNELL, FREDERICK GWYN, pub. relations counsel; b. Yonkers, N.Y., Jan. 1, 1901; s. Andrew Simmons and Matilda (Gwyn) B.; m. Florence Marshall Kerr, June 30, 1925 (dec.); 1 son, Graham Marshall; m. 2d, Catherine Van Horn, May 24, 1950; B.S., N.Y. U., 1923. Asst. alumni sec. N.Y. U., 1923-25; advt. sales rep. A.W. Shaw Co., 1925-27; asst. advt. mgr. Aetna Life Ins. Co., 1927-28; asst. account exec. Moss-Chase Co., 1928-30; editor Trend, 1930-33; polit. writer Buffalo Times, 1933-35; asst. news and editorial dir. Gannett Newspapers, 1935-42; asso. editor American mag., 1942-51; pub. relations cons., Detroit, 1951-57; gen. mgr. Detroit div. Philip Lesly Co., 1957-63; pres. Editorial Assos., Detroit, 1963-71; chmn., chief adminstrv. officer Kenneth Drake Assos., Inc., Detroit, 1971-74; prin. Brownell & Staff, Detroit, 1974—. Bd. dirs. Well-Being Service for Aging, 1968-74; trustee Vis. Nurse Assn. Met. Detroit. Mem. Pub. Relations Soc. Am., Nat. Investor Relations Inst., Am. Soc. Journalists and Authors, Garden Writers Assn. Am., Detroit Press Club, Savoyard Club. Home: 709 Harcourt Rd Grosse Pointe Park MI 48230 Office: 406 City Nat Bank Bldg Detroit MI 48226

BROWNING, D. DEAN, banker; b. Christopher, Ill., July 24, 1951; s. Frank S. and Lucille D. (Sileven) B.; student in Accounting, John A. Logan Coll., 1971; grad. Ill. Bankers Sch., 1976; m. Vicki Lee Lance, Mar. 13, 1971; children—Kristi Lynn, Kyle Lance. Bookkeeper, note teller Bank of Benton, Ill., 1972-74; teller to asst. v.p., cashier to exec. v.p. Johnston City (Ill.) State Bank, 1974—. Baptist. Clubs: Lions (sec. 1975-76, 76-77, sec. treas. 1977-78), Dist. I-CS (cabinet sec. treas. 1976-77). Home: Route 1 Johnston City IL 62951 Office: 100 West Broadway Johnston City IL 62951

BROYHILL, ROY FRANKLIN, agrl., indsl. equipment mfg. exec.; b. Sioux City, Ia., June 20, 1919; s. George Franklin and Effie (Motes) B.; B.B.A., U. Neb., 1940; m. Arline W. Stewart, January 30th, 1943; children—Craig, Kent, Bryce. Trainee mgr. Montgomery Ward Co., 1940; U.S. Army, 1940-41; semi-sr. accountant L. H. Keightley, 1941-42; chief accountant Army Exchange Service, Sioux City, Iowa, 1942-46; chmn. bd., pres. Broyhill Inc., 1946—; pres. Star Printing & Pub. Co., South Sioux City, since 1949; treas. The Broyhill Corp., 1953—; dir. Great West Ins. Co., South Sioux City, Nebr., 1st Nat. Bank, Sioux City, Iowa Mayor, Dakota City, Nebr., 1951-53. Mem. Small Bus. Adv. Council, Omaha; exec. bd. Atokad Horse Racing Assn. Former Rep. State Central Com. Trustee U. Nebr. Found. Served with U.S. Army, 1940-41. Mem. Nat. Fertilizer Solutions Assn. (dir. 1956—), U.S. (mfg. com. 1961), So. Sioux City chambers commerce, Nebr. Assn. Commerce and Industry (dir. 1972—), Farm Equipment Mfrs. Assn. (dir. 1966-74, pres. 1972), Anhydrous Ammonia Inst., Am. Legion, U. Nebr. Alumni Assn. (dir. 1961—), Beta Theta Pi, Alpha Kappa Psi. Mason (Shriner), Kiwanian. Home: 1610 Broadway Dakota City NE 68731

BRUBAKER, LEONARD HATHAWAY, physician; b. Macon, Ga., July 14, 1934; s. Leonard Hathaway and Martha Frances (Bush) B.; A.B. in Chemistry, Duke U., 1956; M.S. in Biochemistry, Emory U., 1964, M.D., 1964; m. Margaret Rowland Miles, June 22, 1957; children—Martha Susan, Alice Elizabeth, Lenna Carol. Intern, Atlanta VA, Emory U. Hosps., 1964-65, asst. resident, 1965-66; clin. asso. leukemia service medicine branch Nat. Cancer Inst., Bethesda, Md., 1966-68; fellow hematology and med. oncology Ohio State U. Hosp., Columbus, 1968; asst. prof. medicine U. Mo., Columbia, 1969-73, asso. prof., 1973—. Served with USN, 1956-59; USPHS, 1966-68. Diplomate Am. Bd. Internal Medicine. Fellow Am. Coll. Physicians; mem. Am. Soc. Hematology, Am. Fedn. for Clin. Research. Methodist. Contbr. articles to med. jours. Home: 2322 Meadow Lark Ln Columbia MO 65201 Office: Dept Medicine 807 Stadium Rd Columbia MO 65201

BRUBAKER, RICHARD FRETWELL, ophthalmologist; b. Macon, Ga., Feb. 13, 1937; s. Leonard Hathaway and Martha Frances (Bush) B.; B.S., Davidson Coll., 1959; M.A., Harvard U., 1963, M.D., 1963; m. Nancy Moore Ogle, Aug. 14, 1965; children—Jill Hathaway, Richard Bartlett, Heather Elizabeth. Intern in gen. surgery Mass. Gen. Hosp., 1963-64; resident in ophthalmology Mass. Eye and Ear Infirmary, 1964-68; cons. ophthalmology Mayo Clinic, Rochester, Minn., 1970—; asst. prof. ophthalmology, Mayo Grad. Sch., 1971-75, asso. prof., 1975—; mem. vision research program com. Nat. Eye Inst., 1975-78; chmn. ophthalmology research com. Ophthalmology Dept. Mayo Clinic, 1970—. NIH grantee, 1970—. Diplomate Am. Bd. Ophthalmology. Mem. Am. Assn. Ophthalmology; AM., Minn. med. assns., Am. Acad. Ophthalmology and Otolaryngology, Zumbro Valley Med. Soc., Biophys. soc. Home: 601 Memorial Pkwy Rochester MN 55901 Office: 200 1st St SW Rochester MN 55901

BRUCK, JOHN ALBERT, co. exec.; b. Indpls., July 10, 1921; s. Louis William and Olma (Steeg) B.; B.S., Purdue U., 1946; m. Marilyn Demaree, May 20, 1945; children—Louis William III, John Mark, Katherine Demaree (Mrs. Thomas Walsh), Kristine Steeg (Mrs. Paul Jerome Honerlaw). Chem. engr. product devel. dept. package soap and detergent div. Procter & Gamble Co., Cin., 1946-70, group leader, 1949-57, sect. head, 1957-62, asso. dir., 1962-70, asso. dir. paper products div., 1970-74, asso. dir. profl. and regulatory services internat. div., 1974—. Pres., Ridgewood Civic Assn., 1960-61. Served with AUS, 1942-45. Mem. Am. Inst. Chem. Engrs., Nat. Wildlife Fedn., N.Y. Acad. Scis., Cin. Engring. Soc. Republican. Mason. Club: Wyoming (Ohio) Golf. Home: 325 Whitthorne Dr Wyoming OH 45215 Office: Ivorydale Technical Center Cincinnati OH 45219

BRUCKNER, CLARENCE AUGUST, real estate exec.; b. Chgo., Aug. 7, 1931; s. Clarence R. and Elizabeth K. (McCarl) B.; student U. Ill., 1949-51; children—Linda, Lisbeth, Paul, Curt. Vice pres. Donald F. Moore, Inc., 1955-67; pres. C.A. Bruckner & Assos., Inc., Oak Brook, Ill., 1967—, Bruckner, Fitts & Assos., Inc. 1977—; sec. Woodsmyth Corp., 1977—; gen. partner Commerce Sq., 1975—. Served with USAF, 1951-52. Mem. Soc. Real Estate Appraisers (past pres. Chgo. chpt.), Am. Inst. Real Estate Appraisers, Jr. Real Estate Bd. Chgo. (past pres.). Methodist. Club: Masons. Home: 2200 S Stewart St Lombard IL 60148 Office: 903 Commerce Dr Oak Brook IL 60521

BRUEGGEMANN, WALTER GEORGE, ophthalmologist; b. Ft. Wayne, Ind., July 21, 1930; s. Walter C. and Loraine M. (Goeglein) G.; B.S., Purdue U., 1952; M.D., Ind. U., 1967; m. Marguerite J. Hamman, Oct. 27, 1957; children—Stephen, Gregory, Jane, Thomas. Pharmacist drug store, New Haven, Ind., 1954-62; intern Meth. Hosp., Indpls., 1967-68, resident in ophthalmology, 1968-71; practice medicine specializing in ophthalmology, Columbus, Ind., 1971—; courtesy staff Ind. U. Med. Center; active staff Bartholomew County (Ind.) Hosp. Served with U.S. Army, 1952-54. Mem. AMA, Ind. State, Bartholomew, Brown County Med. Assns., Am. Acad. Ophthalmology and Otolaryngology, Am. Assn. Ophthalmology, Ind., Indpls. Ophthalmology and Otolaryngology Socs. Republican. Lutheran. Club: Lions (pres., 1954, zone chmn., 1960, dep. gov., 1961). Home: Box 92 Route #9 Columbus IN 47201 Office: 411 Plaza Dr Columbus IN 47201

BRUENING, WILLIAM PAUL, controls co. exec.; b. St. Louis, Mar, 8, 1935; s. Francis Joseph and Crystal Verda (Baumgartner) B.; B.E.E., U. Dayton, 1957. Sales engr. Cutler-Hammer Inc., St. Louis, 1957-63, O'Brien Equipment Co., St. Louis, 1963-69; v.p., sec. Central Controls Co., Inc., St. Louis, 1969-76; pres. Process Controls Co., Inc., St. Louis, 1976—; dir. Bannes-Sheughnessy Inc. Served with U.S. Army, 1957-63. Mem. Instrument Soc. Am., Confrerie des Chevaliers du Tastevin (sr.), Commanderie de Bordeaux. Republican. Roman Catholic. Clubs: St. Louis, Mo. Athletic, Rolls-Royce Owners. Home: 6813 Aliceton Ave Saint Louis MO 63123 Office: 20 American Industrial Dr Maryland Heights MO 63043

BRUESCHKE, ERICH EDWARD, physician, researcher, educator; b. near Eagle Butte, S.D., July 17, 1933; s. Erich Herman and Eva Johanna (Joens) B.; B.S. in Elec. Engring., S.D. Sch. Mines and Tech., 1956; postgrad. U. So. Calif., 1960-61; M.D., Temple U., 1965; m. Frances Marie Bryan, Mar. 25, 1967; children—Erich Raymond, Jason Douglas, Tina Marie, Patricia Frances, Susan Eva. Intern, Germantown Dispensary and Hosp., Phila., 1965-66; mem. tech. staff Hughes Research & Devel. Labs., Culver City, Calif., 1956-61;

practiced gen. medicine in Fullerton, Calif., 1968-69; dir. research Ill. Inst. Tech. Research Inst., Chgo., 1969-76. Research asst. prof. Temple U. Sch. Medicine, Phila., 1965-69; mem. staff Mercy Hosp. and Med. Center, Chgo., 1970-76; vis. prof. Rush Med. Coll., Chgo., 1974-76, prof., chmn. dept. family practice, 1976—. Bd. dirs. Comprehensive Health Planning Met. Chgo., 1971-74. Served with USAF, 1966-68. Diplomate Am. Bd. Family Practice, Nat. Bd. Med. Examiners. Fellow, Am. Acad. Family Physicians; mem. IEEE (chmn. Chgo. sect. Engring. in Medicine and Biology group 1974-75), Am. Soc. Artificial Internal Organs, Soc. for Study of Reproduction, Am. Fertility Soc., Am. Occupational Med. Assn. (recipient Physician's Recognition award 1969, 72, 75), Chgo. Med. Soc., Am. Heart Assn., Assn. for Advancement Med. Instrumentation, N.Y. Acad. Scis., Sigma Xi, Phi Rho Sigma, Eta Kappa Nu. Contbr. numerous articles to profl. jours. Home: 314 N Lincoln St Hinsdale IL 60521 Office: Rush-Presbyn-St Luke's Med Center West Congress Pkwy Chicago IL 60612

BRUESKE, FRANK(LIN) HAROLD, assn. exec.; b. Plainview, Minn., Nov. 11, 1936; s. Ray C. and Mary (Yarolimek) B.; B.A., Winona (Minn.) State U., 1958; m. Rose Marie Warner, July 29, 1958; children—John, Christine, Anne. Dir. communications Watkins Products, Inc., Winona, 1965-71; dir. pub. relations Coll. St. Theresa, Winona, Minn., 1971-72; nat. membership dir. Nat. Conf. Cath. Charities, Washington, 1972-74; dir. communications Data Processing Mgmt. Assn., Park Ridge, Ill., 1974-77; mgr. pub. relations and communications div. Lions Internat., Oak Brook, Ill., 1977—. Active 4-H. Mem. Chgo. Soc. Assn. Execs. Editor Data Mgmt. Mag., 1974—. Home: 12821 60th St Bristol WI 53104 Office: 300 22d St Oak Brook IL 60570

BRUGLER, RICHARD KENNETH, steel and iron mfg. co. exec.; b. Warren, Ohio, Oct. 28, 1928; s. Herman Kenneth and Mildred Marrietta (Fell) B.; B.S. in Mech. Engring., Case Inst. Tech., 1952, B.S. in Elec. Engring., 1954; m. Jean Elizabeth Brooks, Dec. 22, 1951; children—David Kenneth, Diane Jean, Eric Paul, Kurt Ernst. Draftsman, Perfection Stove Co., Cleve., 1951-52; lab. machinist Thompson Products Co., Cleve., 1952-54; with Heltzel Co., Warren, 1954—, chief engr., 1962-65, v.p. engring., 1965—; chmn. Concrete Plant Mfrs. Bur., 1975-78. Served with USNR, 1946-48. Mem. Nat. Readymix Assn. (dir.), Nat., Trumbull County (sec. 1976-78) socs. profl. engrs., IEEE (sr.), Nat. Scalemens Assn., Antique Wireless Assn., Palatine Soc. Methodist. Club: Masons. Patentee in field. Home: 1359 Beechcrest St Warren OH 44485 Office: 1750 Thomas Rd Warren OH 44481

BRUINS, ELTON JOHN, educator, minister; b. Fairwater, Wis., July 29, 1927; s. Clarence Raymond and Angeline Theodora (Kemink) B.; B.A., Hope Coll., 1950; B.D., Western Theol. Sem., 1953; S.T.M., Union Theol. Sem., N.Y., 1957; Ph.D., N.Y. U., 1962; m. Elaine Ann Redeker, June 24, 1954; children—Mary Elaine, David Lewis. Ordained to ministry Ref. Ch., 1954; pastor ch., Elmsford, N.Y., 1955-61, Flushing, N.Y., 1961-66; asst. prof. religion Hope Coll., 1966-70, asso. prof., 1970-73, prof., 1973—, chmn. religion dept., 1977—. Archivist, Netherlands Mus., Holland, Mich., 1968—, Western Theol. Sem., Holland, 1967-71, 74—. Served with USNR, 1945-46. Mem. Am. Soc. Ch. History, Soc. Am. Archivists, Wis. State Hist. Soc., Mich. Hist. Soc. Author: The Americanization of a Congregation, 1970; also archive guides. Address: Hope Coll Holland MI 49423

BRULC, DENNIS JOSEPH, artist; b. Milw., Aug. 30, 1946; s. Albin and Caroline (Mazza) B.; B.F.A., U. Wis., 1969. Exhibited one man shows Milw. Art Center, Dean Gallery, Mpls., Bresler Galleries, Milw.; exhibited group shows Walker Art Center, Mpls., Cal. State U., Sacramento, 20 American Printmakers, State U. N.Y.; represented in permanent collections Milw. Art Center, Winston Collection, Detroit, Johnson Collection, Racine, Wis.; developer Vapour Dye Process, 1967; artist Pneumatic Matrice sculpture, Milw. Art Center, 1969; graphic designer, artist-in-residence U. Wis., Oshkosh, 1973. Albrecht Durer grantee, Germany, 1972; Better Films scholar, 1966. Mem. Artists for Peace, Arts Tech. Found. (pres. 1968-71), Artsupports (pres. 1975—), Nat. Soc. Lit. and Arts. Author: 4,000 Years at the Rodeo, 1974; Lunch Boxes I've Opened, 1975; Drive Inns I've Known, 1975. Home: 4038 S 75th St Milwaukee WI 53220 Office: 152 W Wisconsin Ave Milwaukee WI 53203

BRULL, HANS FRANK, social worker; b. Berlin, Germany, May 17, 1921; s. Victor and Ellen (Berendsen) B.; came to U.S., 1933, naturalized, 1943; B.A., City Coll. N.Y., 1949; M.S.W., U. Pa., 1951; postgrad. U. Chgo., 1962; m. Rose Weiss, May 3, 1953 (div.); children—Ellen Sandra, Steven Victor; m. 2d, Olive Rue, Dec. 20, 1969. Caseworker Childrens Ct. Clinic, Melbourne, Australia, 1951, Jewish Family and Childrens Service, Mpls., 1951-53, Jewish Children's Bur., Chgo., 1953-56; head sch. social work dept. New Trier High Sch.-W., Northfield, 1963—; clin. asst. prof. Sch. Social Work, Smith Coll., Northampton, Mass., 1975. Pvt. practice as psychiat. social worker, Winnetka. Mem. citizens adv. com. Youth Employment Service, 1965—; pres. Glenview Human Relations Com., 1963-64; mem. bd. Gates House Inc., 1970-73. Served with M.I., AUS, 1943-46. Fellow Ill. Soc. Clin. Social Work; mem. Nat. Assn. Social Workers (mem. state bd. 1976-77, del. nat. assembly 1977). Contbr. articles to profl. publs. Home: 1416 Edgewood Ln Winnetka IL 60093 Office: 525 Winnetka Ave Winnetka IL 60093

BRUMBACK, DAVID LADOYT, bank exec.; b. Van Wert, Ohio, Dec. 27, 1893; s. David LaDoyt and Elizabeth (Pinkerton) B.; student Wooster U., 1911-13, U. Cin., 1913-16; m. Gladys Gilliland, Apr. 15, 1922; children—David LaDoyt III, Nancy Ellen (Mrs. Mark M. Kruvand). Asst. cashier Van Wert Nat. Bank, 1922-25, v.p.-cashier, 1925-28, pres., 1928-61, chmn. bd., 1961—; dir. Kennedy Mfg. Co., Alpha Cellulose Corp. Mem. Van Wert City Council, 1924-32; chmn. Van Wert County U.S. Savings Bond Com., 1925; treas. Van Wert Asso. Charities, Trustee Van Wert County Found. Served to lt. AUS, 1915-19. Mem. Nat. Wildlife Assn., Wilderness Soc., Archeology Assn., Ohio Van Wert County hist. socs., Am. Legion, VFW, YMCA, Sigma Chi, Republican. Presbyterian. Clubs: Sierra, Summit, Shawnee Country, Masons (32 deg.). Home: 1005 S Walnut St Van Wert OH 45891 Office: 102 E Main St Van Wert OH 45891

BRUNDT, OLE, art dir., advt. designer; b. Copenhagen, Denmark, June 30, 1924; s. Johan and Helene (Andersen) B.; came to U.S., 1948, naturalized, 1953; student Acad. Merc. Art, 1940-44, Royal Danish Acad. Fine Art, 1942-44, Bus. Coll. Kobmandsskolen, 1945-48, U. Chgo., 1960-62; diploma in advt. copywriting, Chgo. YMCA Coll., 1970; m. Margaret Simko, Sept. 11, 1954; 1 son, Jeffrey Johan. Staff artist Berlingske Tidende Newspaper, Copenhagen, 1946-47; art dir. Krieger & Ragsdale, Evansville, Ind., 1949-50, Match Corp. of Am., Chgo., 1950-51, Fairbank Morse Co., Chgo., 1951-52, Standard Pub. Co., Cin., 1952-53, Sorenson Studios, Chgo., 1953-54; free lance art dir., Chgo., 1954-59; exec. art dir. Gardner, Stein & Frank, Inc., Chgo., 1959-74; art dir., cons., designer Ole Brundt Art Direction/Design, Barrington, Ill., 1974—; design cons. Chgo. Boys Club, Chgo. Foundlings Home; cartoonist Chgo. Settlement House. Mem. Danish Nat. Soc. Recipient awards Comml. Art mag. Nat. Litho Assn., 1954, Art Direction mag. Am. Hotel/Motel Assn., 1959, Graphic Arts Council Chgo., 1960, Deans Milk exhibit Chgo. Foundlings Home, 1970. Home and office: 12 Oak Ridge Ln Barrington IL 60010

BRUNELLE, THOMAS EUGENE, econ. lab. exec.; b. Crookston, Minn., Feb. 12, 1935; s. Hormidas Joseph and Eraine Marie (Crompe) B.; B.S., Coll. St. Thomas, St. Paul, 1957; M.S., U. Minn., 1962, Ph.D., 1968; m. Sheila Ann Hedding, July 19, 1958; children—Suzanne Renee, Kathleen Ann, Elizabeth Ann. With Econs. Lab., Inc., St. Paul, 1957—, asst. mgr. organic biol. research, 1967-69, mgr. corporate research and devel., 1969-72, asst. v.p. research and devel., 1972-75, v.p. corporate sci. and tech., 1975—. Served with USNR, 1959-67. Mem. AAAS, Am. Chem. Soc., Am. Oil Chemists Soc.

BRUNER, EDWARD M., educator; b. N.Y.C., Sept. 28, 1924; s. Milton J. and Bessie (Hinds) B.; B.A., Ohio State U., 1948, M.A., 1950; Ph.D., U. Chgo., 1954; m. Elaine C. Hauptman, Mar. 21, 1948; children—Jane R., Dan M. Instr. dept. anthropology U. Chgo., 1953-54; asst. prof. dept. anthropology Yale, 1954-60; asso. prof. dept. anthropology U. Ill., Urbana, 1961-65, prof., 1965—, head dept. anthropology, 1966-70, dir. Doris Duke Am. Indian Oral History Project, 1967-73, also mem. faculty coms. Cons. Ford Found., Nat. Assessment Edn. in Indonesia, 1969-70; chmn. test com. in anthropology Ednl. Testing Service, Princeton, 1967-69; cons. cultural anthropology rev. com. NIMH, 1966; mem. grants com. Social Sci. Research Council, N.Y.C., 1966. Center for Advanced Study in Behavioral Sci. fellow, 1960-61; sr. scholar East West Center, Inst. Advanced Projects, Honolulu, 1963; research grantee NIMH, NSF, Wenner Gren Found., Ford Found., Social Sci. Research Council. Fellow Am. Anthrop. Assn.; mem. Royal Anthrop. Soc., Am. Ethnol. Soc., Soc. Applied Anthropology, Assn. for Asian Studies (mem. Indonesian studies com. 1973—, chmn. 1976-78). Contbr. articles to profl. jours. Field research Am. Indians, Indonesia. Home: 2022 Cureton Dr Urbana IL 61801

BRUNER, PHILIP LANE, lawyer; b. Chgo., Sept. 26, 1939; s. Henry Pfeiffer and Marjorie (Williamson) B.; A.B., Princeton U., 1961; J.D., U. Mich., 1964; M.B.A., Syracuse U., 1967; m. Ellen Carole Germann, Mar. 21, 1964; children—Philip Richard, Stephen Reed, Carolyn Anne. Admitted to Wis. bar, 1964, Minn. bar, 1968; mem. firm Briggs and Morgan, St. Paul, 1967—; instr. William Mitchell Coll. Law, St. Paul, 1970—; lectr. law seminars U. Minn., 1969—, U. Wis., 1975—, So. Methodist U., 1977—, U. Denver, 1975—. Bd. dirs., sec. Minn. Protestant Found., 1975—. Served to capt. USAF, 1964-67. Recipient Distinguished Service award St. Paul Jaycees, 1974. Mem. Am., Fed., Minn., Wis., Ramsey bar assns. Club: St. Paul Athletic. Contbr. articles to profl. jours. Home: 8432 80th St N Stillwater MN 55082 Office: 2200 1st National Bank Bldg Saint Paul MN 55101

BRUNER, WALLY, writer, producer, director, performer; b. Woodbury County, Iowa, Mar. 4, 1931; s. Wallace Albert and Audrey Grace (Scott) B.; student Ind. U., 1951-52; 8 children by previous marriage; m. 2d., Natalie Martin, Aug. 3, 1968; children—Wallace, Natalie. White House correspondent ABC-TV, Washington, 1964-66; commentator UPI, MetroMedia Corp., 1966-68; emcee What's My Line, 1968-72; co-host Wally's Workshop, 1972—; pres. Pan MEdia Products, Inc., Indpls., 1972—; pres. MediCine Corp., Indpls., 1974-76, also dir.; Owner, gen. partner Walnat Co., Indpls., 1972—; cons. Hardware Wholesalers, Inc., Fort Wayne, Ind., 1974. Candidate for U.S. Ho. of Reps., 7th Dist., Ind., 1960; campaign mgr. U.S. Senate, 1968; dir. Salvation Army, Indpls., 1972-73; state chmn. Am. Cancer Soc., Ind., 19—; chmn. Ind. Easter Seal Campaign, 19—. Democrat. Author: 27 books on home repair; creator Wally's Workshop TV Series, 19—. Office: 3430 N Illinois Indianapolis IN 46208

BRUNETTE, BRUCE JONATHAN, electronics co. exec.; b. Superior, Wis., Aug. 13, 1946; s. William Alexander and Veronica G. (Herrick) B.; B.M.E., U. Wis., Madison, 1969; M.B.A., U. Minn., 1973; m. Carol Jane Cziok, Oct. 17, 1970; 1 son, David. Assembly prodn. engr. Honeywell, Mpls., 1969-71; new venture analyst Medtronic, Mpls., 1973-76, corporate product mktg. mgr., 1976-78, corporate strategic planning mgr., 1978—. Democratic precinct del., 1970—; alt. del. Minn. Dem. state central com., 1975—, Minn. Dem. Conv., 1972; mem. citizens adv. com. to Mpls. City Council, 1973-75; tutor St. Joseph's Home for emotionally disturbed children, Superior, Wis., 1965. Mem. Am. Mktg. Assn., Wisconsin Alumni Assn., Lambda Chi Alpha, Pi Tau Sigma, Beta Gamma Sigma. Home: 12833 Polk St NE Minneapolis MN 55434 Office: 3055 Old Hwy 8 Minneapolis MN 55418

BRUNING, JOHN CLAYTON, JR., educator; b. Toledo, Jan. 14, 1943; s. John Clayton and Charlotte (McQuillen) B.; m. Christine M. Cripe, June 20, 1964; children—Tracy, Craig, Emily; B.B.A., U. Toledo, 1966; M.Ed., Bowling Green State U., 1972. Clk., Kroger Co., Toledo, 1959-66; salesman Procter & Gamble Co., Cin., 1966-68; instr. Owens Tech. Coll., Toledo, 1968-73, asst. prof. mktg., 1973-76, asso. prof., 1976—, pres. Faculty Council, 1974-75, chmn. community affairs com., 1974-75; owner, operator part-time resume writing bus. Basketball coach St. Clements CYO, 1974-75; coach grade sch. girls' softball teams; active Little Flower Ch. Festival and Diocese Devel. Fund, Little Flower Mens Club, 1976—, Jr. Achievement, 1972-73, Channel 30 Buy-In, 1974-75, U. Toledo Alumni Telethon, 1974, Sigma Phi Epsilon Alumni Housing Bd., 1972, Distributive Edn. Clubs Am., 1969—, Am. Cancer Soc., 1972—, South Toledo YMCA Indian Guides, 1976—, Ballet Arts Guild, 1973—, Toledo Zool. Soc., 1976—; mem. pride adv. com. Toledo Bd. Edn., 1976. Mem. Am. (collegiate relations dir. 1977—), Owens mktg. assns., Nat., Ohio edn. assns., Ohio Assn. Two Year Colls., Ohio Assn. Mktg. Mgmt. Educators, Advt. Club Toledo, U. Toledo, Bowling Green State U., St. Francis de Sales High Sch. (ofcl. rep. Class 1961) alumni assns., Old Newsboys Goodfellow Assn., Delta Pi Epsilon. Home: 2274 Rosehill St Toledo OH 43615 Office: Owens Coll Toledo OH 43699

BRUNNER, JULES TERRENCE, lawyer, assn. exec.; B.S., J.D., U. Wis. at Madison. Exec. dir. Better Govt. Assn., Chgo. Office: 230 N Michigan Ave Better Govt Assn Chicago IL 60601

BRUNOW, EDWIN EDWARD, metall. cons.; b. Milw., July 28, 1912; s. John Johann and Anna Henrietta (Radmann) B.; student U. Wis., Milw., 1931-38, Marquette U., 1933-36; m. Grace Gladys Alma De Sham, June 27, 1942; children—Barry W., Nancy G. Brunow Hornsby. Plant metallurgist Sivyer Steel Co., Milw., 1938-59, metall. engr., 1959-63, tech. dir., 1963-69; metall. engr. Ervin Industries, Adrian, Mich., 1969-74, tech. dir., 1974-77; metall. cons., 1977—. Vice-chmn. Potawatomi council Boy Scouts Am.; mem. local sch. bds., 1953-58. Mem. Am. Foundrymen's Soc., Am. Soc. Metals, ASTM, Steel Founders Soc. Am. Research included cast armor plate, early warning system, minuteman silos, nuclear reactors. Home: 1343 Feeman Ct Adrian MI 49221

BRUNS, BILLY LEE, cons. elec. engr.; b. St. Louis, Nov. 21, 1925; s. Henry Lee and Violet Jean (Williams) B.; B.A., Washington U., St. Louis, 1949, postgrad. Sch. Engring., 1959-62; m. Lillian Colleen Mobley, Sept. 6, 1947; children—Holly Rene, Kerry Alan, Barry Lee, Terrence William. Supt., engr., estimator Schneider Electric Co., St. Louis, 1950-54, Ledbetter Electric Co., 1954-57; tchr. indsl. electricity St. Louis Bd. Edn., 1957-71; pres. B.L. Bruns & Assos., cons. engrs., St. Louis, 1963-72; v.p., chief engr. Hosp. Bldg. & Equipment Co., St. Louis, 1972-76; pres., prin. B.L. Bruns & Assos. cons. engrs., St. Louis, 1976—; tchr. elec. engring. U. Mo. St. Louis extension, 1975-76. Mem. Mo. Adv. Council on Vocat. Edn., 1969-76, chmn., 1975-76; leader Explorer post Boy Scouts Am., 1950-57. Served with AUS, 1944-46: PTO, Okinawa. Decorated Purple Heart. Registered profl. engr., Mo., Ill., Wash., Fla. Mem. Nat., Mo. socs. profl. engrs., Profl. Engrs. in Pvt. Practice, Am. Soc. Heating, Refrigeration and Air Conditioning Engrs., Illuminating Engrs. Soc., Am. Mgmt. Assn. Baptist. Club: Masons. Tech. editor The National Electrical Code and Blueprint Reading, Am. Tech. Soc., 1959-65. Home: 1243 Hobson Dr Ferguson MO 63135 Office: 6500 N Broadway St Louis MO 63147

BRUNTON, DELBERT BRAMMELL, dentist; b. Wenatchee, Wash., June 27, 1922; s. Walter Clive and Cora Etta (Brammell) B.; student McPherson Coll., 1940-42, U. Oreg., 1942-43; B.S., S.E. Mo. State U., 1944; D.D.S., U. Detroit Sch. Dentistry, 1947; m. Mary Helen Steimle, June 24, 1944; children—Judith Karen (Mrs. James R. Carter), Janet M. (Mrs. Patrick R. Ruopp), Jill Beth. Dentist, Cape Girardeau, Mo., 1953—; mem. staff S.E. Mo. Hosp., St. Francis Hosp. Treas., County Heart Fund, 1956-71; mem. spl. citizens com. Bd. Edn., 1958; mem. nominating com. Girl Scouts, 1965-67, mem. exec. com., 1965-67. Served with USNR, 1943-46, 1951-53. Mem. Mo. Dental Assn. (gov. 1977—), S.E. Mo. Dental Soc. (pres. 1966-67), Acad. Gen. Dentistry, Jr. C. of C., Delta Sigma Delta (life). Baptist (deacon 1949, chmn. bd. 1962, trustee 1971—). Club: Optimist (pres. 1960-61) (Cape Girardeau). Home: 3217 Kage Hills Dr Cape Girardeau MO 63701 Office: 1822 Broadway Cape Girardeau MO 63701

BRUSH, BROCK EDWIN, physician; b. Amherstburg, Ont., Can., July 4, 1911; s. Frank and Ida (Bratt) B.; came to U.S., 1936, naturalized, 1941; A.B., M.D., U. Western Ont., 1936; M.Sc., Wayne U., 1938; m. Mary Ellen Burnett, Aug. 1, 1940; 1 dau., Cynthia B. Intern Providence Hosp., Detroit, 1936-37; resident gen. surgery Henry Ford Hosp., Detroit, 1938-43. Instr. physiology Wayne U., 1937; surgeon-in-chief 1st surg. div. Henry Ford Hosp., 1946—; past pres., chmn. med. and sci. com. Mich. Cancer Found. Chmn. bd. dirs. Trustee Boys Clubs Met. Detroit, Met. Detroit Com. Fellow ACS; mem. Am., Central, Western, Pan Pacific, Detroit surg. assns., Royal Soc. Medicine, Am. Thyroid Assn., Acad. Surgery (past pres.), Detroit Acad. Medicine (past pres.), Mich. (pres.), Wayne County (past pres.) med. socs., Am. Geriatric Soc. (past pres.), Canadian Physiol. Soc., Detroit Hist. Soc., Alpha Omega Alpha, Alpha Kappa Alpha, Masons, Economic Club Detroit, Dearborn Country Club. Asso. editor Detroit Med. News. Home: 22313 Cherryhill Dr Dearborn MI 48124 Office: Henry Ford Hosp Detroit MI 48202

BRUSH, RICHARD WALTER, psychiatrist; b. Youngstown, Ohio, May 22, 1933; s. Walter Louis and Evelyn May (Williams) B.; B.S., Youngstown (Ohio) U., 1954; M.D., Ohio State U., 1958; m. Ruth Evelyn McCall, Aug. 15, 1954; children—Mark Walter, Keith Alwyne. Intern, White Cross Hosp., Columbus, Ohio, 1958-59; resident in psychiatry, U. Hosps. Columbus, 1959-62; practice medicine specializing in psychiatry, Columbus, 1964-68, Cin., 1968—; cons. Franklin County Child Welfare Bd., Columbus State Hosp., 1964-68, Rollman Psychiatric Inst., Cin., 1968—; asst. clin. prof. psychiatry, Ohio State U., 1966-68; asso. attending staff mem., Mt. Carmel Hosp., Columbus, 1964-68; courtesy staff, U. Hosp., Columbus, 1966-68; exec. dir., div. mental health, Cin. Bd. Health, 1968-70; med. dir., Municipal Ct. Psychiatric Clinic, Cin., 1968-70; asst. attending staff, Good Samaritan Hosp., Cin., 1968-74, courtesy staff, 1974—; asst. clin. prof. psychiatry, U. Cin., 1968; bd. dirs. Pastoral Counselling Services Greater Cin., 1968-74; bd. dirs. Cin. Free Clinic, 1969-74; attending psychiatrist, staff, Cin. Gen. Hosp., 1969—; clinician in psychiatry Out-Patient Dept., Cin. Gen. Hosp., 1969—; candidate in tng., Chgo. Inst. Psychoanalysis, 1968-73, Cin. Psychoanalytic Inst., 1973—. Served as capt., U.S. Army, 1962-64. Diplomate Am. Bd. Psychiatry and Neurology. Fellow Am. Psychiatric Assn.; mem. Am. Psychoanalytic Assn., Ohio Psychiatric Assn., Ohio Med. Assn., Cin. Acad. Medicine, Cin. Psychiatric Assn. Democrat. Methodist. Contbr. articles in field. Home: 2692 Cyclorama Dr Cincinnati OH 45211 Office: 2600 Euclid Ave Cincinnati OH 45219

BRUSKE, GEORGE WILLIAM, farm supplies co. exec.; b. Pitts., May 22, 1927; s. Norbert and Marjorie (Glass) B.; B.A., U. Mich., 1951; m. Irene Ann Mooney, June 12, 1946; children—Regina Crosby, George Robert. With Standard Oil Co. Ind., various locations, 1951-67, mktg. dir. Amoco Australia, Sydney, 1961-66; v.p. mktg. Southwest Grease & Oil Co., Inc., Wichita, Kans., 1967-73; dir. advt. and sales promotion Farmland Industries, Inc., Kansas City, Mo., 1973—. Mem. advt. com. Universal Coop. Vice pres. mktg. March of Dimes, Wichita, 1971-72; capt. Wesley Hosp. Fund Drive, Wichita, 1970; active United Fund, Wichita, 1971-72. Bd. dirs. New Mark Community Christian Concern. Served with USAAF, 1945-46. Mem. Am. Petroleum Inst., Soc. Automotive Engrs., Am. Soc. Lubrication Engrs., Advt. and Sales Execs. Club, Nat. Agri-Mktg. Assn. (chpt. v.p.), Theta Delta Chi, Sigma Delta Chi. Home: 6109 NW Webb Circle Kansas City MO 64151 Office: 3315 N Oak Trafficway Kansas City MO 64116

BRYAN, A(LONZO) J(AY), service club ofcl.; b. Washington, N.J., Sept. 17, 1917; s. Alonzo J. and Anna Belle (Babcock) B.; student pub. schs.; m. Elizabeth Elfreida Koehler, June 25, 1941 (div. 1961); children—Donna Elizabeth, Alonzo Jay, Nadine; m. 2d, Janet Dorothy Onstad, Mar. 15, 1962; children—Brenda Joyce, Marlowe Francis, Marilyn Janet. Engaged as retail florist, Washington, N.J., 1941-64; now dir. field service Kiwanis Internat., Chgo. Fund drive chmn. ARC, 1952; bd. dirs. Washington YMCA, 1945-55, N.J. Taxpayers Assn., 1947-52; mem. Washington Bd. Edn., 1948-55. Mem. Washington Grange, Sons and Daus. of Liberty, Soc. Am. Florists, Nat. Fedn. Ind. Businessmen, Florists Telegraph Delivery Assn., C. of C. Presbyterian (elder). Clubs: Masons, Tall Cedars of Lebanon, Jr. Order United Am. Mechanics, Kiwanis (pres. Washington (N.J.) 1952, lt. gov. internat. 1953-54, gov. N.J. dist. 1955, sec. N.J. dist. 1957-64, sec. S.E. area Chgo. 1965-74; editor The Jersey Kiwanian 1958-64). Home: River Plaza Apt 2512 405 N Wabash Ave Chicago IL 60611 Office: Kiwanis Internat 101 E Erie St Chicago IL 60611

BRYAN, ARTHUR ELDRIDGE, JR., lawyer; b. Webster City, Iowa, July 28, 1924; s. Arthur Eldridge and Grace Lillian (Glassburner) B.; student U. Mo., 1943-44; B.A., State U. Iowa, 1949, J.D., 1951; m. Elizabeth Ann Stubbings, Oct. 18, 1958; children—Elizabeth Grace, Arthur Eldridge, John Milner, Daniel Franklin. With U.P. R.R. Co., Omaha, 1942-54; partner McDermott, Will & Emery, Chgo., 1954—. Dir., sec. Burdett Mfg. Co., Chgo., 1966—, Gits Bros. Mfg., Chgo., 1967-68; dir., v.p., sec. Yuma Mesa Devel. Co., Yuma, Ariz., 1967—; chmn. bd. dirs., chief exec. officer Lake Arrowhead Devel. Co. (Calif.), 1971—. Lectr. taxation U. Chgo., Marquette U., No. Ill. U. Mem. com. on legis. action New Trier (Ill.) High Sch., 1974—; active Boy Scouts Am., Glencoe, Ill., 1968-74; mem. adv. bd. United Settlement Appeal, Chgo., 1962. Bd. dirs., treas., pres. exec. com. Erie Neighborhood House, Chgo.,

1958—; trustee N. Central Coll., Naperville, Ill.; sec., chmn. bd. trustees, sec. prudential bd. Glencoe Union Ch., 1969—. Served with inf. AUS, 1942-46; ETO, PTO. Decorated Combat Inf. badge. Mem. Am. (chmn., spl. adviser sect. taxation com. on comml. banks and financials 1966—), Ill., Ia., Chgo. bar assns., Ill. C. of C. (chmn. fed. tech. tax com.), Chgo. Assn. Commerce and Industry (fed. appropriations and expenditures com. 1968—). Clubs: Chgo., Mid-Day, Monroe, Executive (Chgo.); Skokie Country; Des Moines. Contbr. articles to profl. jours. Home: 565 Washington St Glencoe IL 60022 Office: 111 W Monroe St Chicago IL 60603

BRYAN, HENRY C(LARK), JR., lawyer; b. St. Louis, Dec. 8, 1930; s. Henry Clark and Faith (Young) B.; A.B., Washington U., St. Louis, 1952, LL.B., 1956; m. Sarah Ann McCarthy, July 28, 1956; children—Mark Pendleton, Thomas Clark, Sarah Christy. Admitted to Mo. bar, 1956; law clk. to fed. judge, 1956; asso. McDonald & Wright, St. Louis, 1956-60; partner, McDonald, Bernard, Wright & Timm, St. Louis, 1961-64, partner McDonald, Wright & Bryan, 1964—; v.p., dir. Harbor Point Boat & Dock Co., St. Charles, Mo., 1966—, Merrell Ins. Agy., 1966—. Served to 1st lt. AUS, 1952-54. Mem. Am., Mo., St. Louis (past chmn. probate and trust sect., marriage and divorce law com.) bar assns., Kappa Sigma, Phi Delta Phi. Republican. Episcopalian. Elk. Home: 41 Ladue Terr Ladue MO 63124 Office: 11 S Meramec St Louis MO 63105

BRYAN, LESLIE A(ULLS), transp. economist; b. Bath, N.Y., Feb. 23, 1900; s. D(aniel) Beach and Anna (Aulls) B.; B.S., Syracuse U., 1923, M.S., 1924, J.D., 1939; Ph.D., Am. U., Washington 1930; Sc.D. (hon.), Southwestern Coll., 1972; m. Gertrude Catherine Gelder, Aug. 22, 1931; children—Leslie A., George G. Prof. bus. adminstrn. Southwestern Coll., Winfield, Kans., 1924-25; asst. coach track Syracuse U., 1925-42, dir. athletics, 1934-37, also instr., 1925-28, asst. prof. transp., 1928-31, asso. prof., 1931-39, prof., 1939-45, Franklin prof. transp., 1945-46; pres. Seneca Flying Sch., Syracuse, N.Y., 1943-46; dir. Inst. Aviation and prof. mgmt. U. Ill., 1946-68, emeritus, 1968—; staff lectr. Air U., 1956-59. Dir. U. Fed. Savs. & Loan Assn., 1960-71. Cons. FAA, 1959-61; mem. Pres. Kennedy's Task Force on Nat. Aviation Goals, 1961; mem. Ill. Aerospace Edn. Com., 1961-72, chmn., 1963-64; adv. bd. ATC, 1964, 67-69, cons., 1965-69; acting dir. athletics U. Ill., 1965-66; faculty rep. Intercollegiate Conf. (Big Ten), 1959-68. Pres., Arrowhead council Boy Scouts Am., 1954-60, mem. regional exec. com., 1959-71, nat. council, 1960-71; past mem. aviation adv. bd. Norwich U. Served as lt., inf. and A.C., U.S. Army, 1917-19; ret. col. USAFR. col. CAP. Chmn. Pres. Eisenhower's Aviation Planning Group, 1957-58; adv. com. Dulles Internat. Airport, 1958-62; dir. aviation N.Y. State 1945; mem. Ill. Bd. Aero. Advisors, 1949-68; transp. cons. Nat. Resources Planning Bd., 1942-44. Pres. Eastern Intercollegiate Boxing Assn., 1936-38; N.Y. State Aviation Council, 1944-46. Recipient Brewer Trophy award, 1953, Distinguished Service medal CAP, 1954, Sigma Delta Chi award, 1954; Arents Medal, 1955; Air Power award, 1956; Silver Beaver, Boy Scouts Am., 1957; Silver Antelope award, Boy Scouts Am., 1959; Tissandier diploma Fedn. Aeronautique International, 1958; Continental Air Command certificate of recognition, 1960; A.R.C. award, 1946; award of merit Air Tng. Command, 1965; Elder Statesman of Aviation, 1966; Distinguished Pub. Service award FAA, 1965; Patriots medal S.A.R., 1968, Distinguished Alumni award Am. U., 1969; Letterman of Distinction, Syracuse U., 1969); citation Air Force Assn., 1976. Fellow U. Aviation Assn. (pres. 1948-49); mem. Nat. Aero. Assn. (v.p. 1953-56, 60, 61, 65, 66, bd. dirs. 1950-52, 57-59, 62-64), Nat. Aerospace Edn. Council (pres. 1952-53, 64-65, dir. 1959-71), Am. Soc. Traffic and Transp. (mem. bd. examiners 1948-61), Am. Assn. Airport Execs. (pres. 1955-56, President's award 1959), Aerospace Writers Assn., Nat. Air Council, Am. Inst. Aeros. and Astronautics, Newcomen Soc. N.Am., Geneal. Soc. Ill. (pres. 1972-73, Distinguished Service award 1974), Nat. Huguenot Soc. (pres. Ill. 1971-73, pres. gen. 1977—, Nat. Distinguished Service award 1976), S.A.R. (pres. Ill. 1974-76, genealogist gen. 1973-75, trustee 1975-76, v.p. gen. 1976-77, Minute Man award 1976, Gold Good Citizen award 1976), Am. U. Alumni Assn. (chmn. bd. govs. 1970), Soc. of Cincinnati, Zeta Psi, Phi Delta Phi, Phi Kappa Phi, Phi Kappa Alpha, Alpha Kappa Psi, Alpha Phi Omega, Kappa Phi Kappa, Alpha Delta Sigma, Delta Nu Alpha, Pi Gamma Mu, Alpha Eta Rho, Sigma Alpha Tau, Tau Omega, Beta Gamma Sigma, Scabbard and Blade, Arnold Air Soc., Pershing Rifles. Clubs: University (Urbana); Rotary, Dial; Army and Navy (Washington); Champaign Country. Author: Aerial Transportation, 1925; Industrial Traffic Management, 1929; Principles of Water Transportation, 1939; Air Transportation (with G.L. Wilson), 1949; Aviation Study Manual (with others), 1949; Traffic Management in Industry, 1953; (with others) Fundamentals of Aviation and Space Technology, 1959, rev. edit. 1968; The Aulls Genealogy, 1974; also monographs, articles. Contbr. Compton's Ency., World Book Ency., Ency. of Sci. and Tech., Am. Educator Ency., Universal Standard Ency., Our Wonderful World Ency. Adviser, cons. various publs. Address: 34 Fields E Champaign IL 61820

BRYAN, MARTIN, educator; b. St. Joseph, Mo., Aug. 10, 1908; s. Frank and Maggie Edith B.; M.A., Iowa State U., 1943; Ph.D., Northwestern U., 1953; m. Mary Ann Stoffregen, June 4, 1955; 1 dau., Pamela Ann. Taft fellow U. Cin., 1952, asso. prof. speech, 1958-66, prof. speech, 1968-75, prof. communication, 1975—; Fulbright appointee Seoul Nat. U., Seoul Korea, 1962-63; exec. sec. Council for Internat. Edn. and Programs, U. Cin., 1971-73. Mem. Ohio Coll. Assn. (exec. com. internat. div.), AAUP, Speech Communication Assn. (mem. Commn. for Internat. and Intercultural Communication), Communication Assn. Pacific (bd. emeritus advisers). Presbyterian. Author: Dynamic Speaking, 1962; contbr. articles to profl. publs. Home: 2822 Stratford St Cincinnati OH 45220 Office: 637 B Pharmacy U of Cin Cincinnati OH

BRYAN, MONK, bishop; b. Blomming Grove, Tex., July 25, 1914; s. Gid. J. and Era (Monk) B.; B.A., Baylor U., 1935; M.Th., So. Meth. U., 1938; D.D., Central Meth. Coll., Fayette, Mo., 1958; m. Corneille Downer, July 22, 1941; children—Lucy (Mrs. Samuel S. Barlow, Jr.), James J., Robert M. Ordained to ministry United Meth. Ch., 1939; consecrated bishop, 1976; minister Boyce Circuit, Waxahachie Dist., Central Tex. Conf., 1939-40, St. Lukes Meth. Ch., St. Louis, 1940-47, Centenary Meth. Ch., Bonne Terre, Mo., 1947-49, Meth. Ch., Maryville, Mo., 1949-57, Mo. United Meth. Ch., Columbia, 1957-76; bishop S.Central Jurisdictional Conf., Lincoln, Nebr., 1976—; mem. World Meth. Council, 1953—, participant Confs., Lake Junaluska, N.C., 1956, Oslo, Norway, 1961, London, 1966, Denver, 1971, Dublin, Ireland, 1976, exchange minister in Eng., 1953; pres. Mo. Conf. Bd. Edn., 1956-64, Mo. Council Chs., 1966-68; chmn. Mo. East Conf. Bd. Christian Social Concerns, 1968-72; mem. Meth. Gen. Bd. Christian Social Concerns, 1964-72; vice chmn. finance com., mem. divs. ecumenical and inter-religious concerns and health and welfare Meth. Gen. Bd. Global Ministries, 1972-76. Bd. dirs. Wesley Found., Columbia, 1957-76, Columbia United Fund, 1964-70; trustee So. Meth. U., 1952-68, 76—, St. Paul Sch. Theology, Kansas City, 1968-72, 76—, Mo. Sch. Religion, Columbia, 1957-76, Philander Smith Coll., Little Rock, 1976—, Lydia Patterson Inst., El Paso, 1976—, Mt. Sequoyah Assembly, Fayetteville, Ark., 1976—, Nebr. Wesleyan U., 1976—, Omaha Meth. Hosp., 1976—, Bryan Meml. Hosp., 1976—, Western Nebr. Gen. Hosp., 1976—; mem. adv. council Gt. Rivers council Boy Scouts Am., 1960-76. Clubs: Masons (K.T., 33 deg.), Rotary. Recipient Silver Beaver award Boy Scouts Am., 1972. Home: 3080 Stratford Ave Lincoln NE 68502 Office: 2641 N 49th St Lincoln NE 68504

BRYAN, WILLIAM ALONZO, univ. dean; b. Valdosta, Ga., July 16, 1938; s. William E. and Lottie Mae (Dees) B.; B.S., Fla. State U., 1960; M.S., Ind. U., 1961; Ed.D., U. Wyo., 1970; m. Marian Eleanor Cooper, Aug. 4, 1963; children—Paige Ellen, Erin Dees, William Ross. Asst. dean men U. Wyo., Laramie, 1968-69, hall dir., 1967-68, dir. student services Coll. Nursing, 1969-71; asso. dean admissions, student personnel, dir. student services Med. Center, U. Ky., Lexington, 1971-73, asso. dean students U. Tex., Austin, 1973-76; dean student devel. U. N.D., Grand Forks, 1976—. Mem. Am. Coll. Personnel Assn., Am. Personnel Guidance Assn., Nat. Assn. student Personnel Adminstrs., Am. Assn. Higher Edn., Wyo. Personnel Guidance Assn., N.D. Personnel Deans, Phi Delta Kappa. Presbyn. Home: 3615 10th Ave N Grand Forks ND 58201 Office: Office Student Development Box 8191 Grand Forks ND 58202

BRYANT, ANTUSA SANTOS, educator; b. Camiling, Tarlac, Philippines, Aug. 22, 1934; d. Andres Corpuz and Mercedes (Perez) Santos; E.T.C., Philippine Normal Coll., 1952, B.S., 1954; M.A., Ball State Tchrs. Coll., 1957; Ed.D., Ind. U., 1959; m. Benjamin F. Bryant. Came to U.S., 1956. Psychology intern Laurelton (Pa.) State Sch. and Hosp., 1963; psychologist Faribault (Minn.) State Sch. and Hosp., 1963-65; prof. spl. edn. Mankato (Minn.) State Coll., 1965—. Cons. St. Peter Security Hosp., Owatonna State Sch. Continuing Adult Edn. Program. St. Paul; v.p. Edu Con Diversified, Inc., St. Paul, Internat. Peace scholar P.E.O., 1956-58; Altrusa Internat. scholar for women, 1957-59; Fulbright scholar, 1956-59. Mem. NEA, Minn. Edn. Assn., Council for Exceptional Children, Adult Edn. Assn. U.S., Am. Assn. Mental Deficiency, Am. Ednl. Research Assn., Minn. State Colls. Inter-faculty Orgn., Pi Lambda Theta. Home: 230 N Ash St Belle Plaine MN 56011

BRYANT, DONALD LOYD, JR., ins. agency exec.; b. Mt. Vernon, Ill., June 30, 1942; s. Donald Loyd and A. Eileen (Galloway) B.; B.A., Denison U., 1964; J.D., Washington U.. 1967; m. Doris Hughes, Sept. 3, 1966; 1 son, Derek Lawrence. Admitted to Mo. bar, 1967; agt. Equitable Life Assurance Soc. U.S., St. Louis, 1968—; pres. Donald L. Bryant & Assos., 1969-74, Bryant Fin. Planning, Inc., St. Louis, 1974—. Bd. dirs. St. Louis Area council Boy Scouts Am., 1974—; bd. dirs. United Way, St. Louis; trustee Ladue Chapel, 1973-75. Served with U.S. Navy, 1967. Mem. Am., Mo. bar assns., Assn. Advanced Life Underwriting, St. Louis Estate Planning Council. Republican. Presbyterian. Clubs: Bellerive Country, St. Louis, Mo. Athletic. Home: 3 Picardy Ln Saint Louis MO 63124 Office: Suite 1770 100 N Broadway Saint Louis MO 63102

BRYANT, TERRY LYNN, counselor; b. Parsons, Kans., Mar. 26, 1952; d. Earl Morris and Neva L. (Sissel) B.; A.A., Labette Com. Jr. Coll., 1972; B.S., Kans. State Coll., 1974, M.S., 1975. Counselor, Kans. State Dept. Human Resources, Pittsburg, 1976—. Mem. Am. Personnel and Guidance Assn., Kans. Assn. Battered Women, Assn. Specialists in Group Work, Internat. Assn. Personnel in Employment Security. Baptist. Home: 203 E Monroe St Pittsburg KS 66762 Office: 1st and Pine Sts Pittsburg KS 66762

BRYANT, WADE, air force officer; b. Aiken, S.C., Aug. 18, 1948; s. Melvin and Matilda (Smith) B.; B.A., Benedict Coll., 1971; M.Ed., U. S.C., 1974; Ph.D., So. Ill. U., 1977; m. Odessa Hill, Aug. 16, 1975. Youth counselor Dept. Juvenile Correction, Columbia, S.C., 1971-72; adminstrv. lab. technician asst. Savannah River plant AEC, Aiken, S.C., 1972-73; adminstrv. asst., dept. minority affairs U. S.C., Columbia, 1973-74; dir. student resident life Benedict Coll., Columbia, 1974-75; adminstrv. asst., med. prep. program So. Ill. U., Carbondale, 1976-77; commd. 2d lt. U.S. Air Force, 1977; adminstrv. exec. support officer Scott AFB, Belleville, Ill., 1977—. Mem. Am. Personnel and Guidance Assn., Nat. Assn. Student Personnel Adminstrs., Am. Assn. Higher Edn., AAUP, Air Force Assn., Am. Def. Preparedness Assn., Phi Delta Pi, Pi Lambda Theta, Phi Delta Kappa. Democrat. Baptist. Club: Masons. Home: Rural Route 1 Box 133 O'Fallon IL 62269 Office: Scott AFB Belleville IL 62225

BRYDGES, LOUIS WORTHINGTON, lawyer; b. Fox Lake, Ill., June 24, 1932; s. Louis W. and Edith (Stanley) B.; student Beloit Coll., 1950-54; J.D., Washington U., 1958; m. Sandra Eustice; 1 son, Louis Worthington. Claims rep. State Farm Mut. Ins. Co., St. Louis, 1957-58; admitted to Ill. bar, 1958, Mo. bar, 1958, U.S. Supreme Ct., 1963, U.S. Ct. Appeals bar, 1974, U.S. Ct. Claims bar, 1975; asso. Diver, Diver & Ridge, 1959-62; mng. partner Diver, Ridge, Brydges & Bollman, 1962-76, Diver, Brydges, Bollman, Grach and Riseborough, 1976—; dir. Trans-Air Corp. Atty. Bd. of Edn., Fox Lake Grade Sch., 1962, Fox Lake Village atty., 1963-65. Vice pres. Oak Plaines Council Boy Scouts Am., 1970-71. Bd. dirs. YMCA. Mem. Fed., Am., Ill., Lake County (bd. govs. 1960—) bar assns., Mo. Bar Assn., Am. Judicature Soc., Soc. Trial Lawyers, Lawyer-Pilots Bar Assn., Assn. Ins. Attys., Internat. Assn. Ins. Council, Lake County Trial Lawyers Assn. (dir. 1975—), Ill. Def. Counsel, Am. Arbitration Assn., Sigma Alpha Epsilon, Delta Theta Phi. Home: 262 Harding Ave Waukegan IL 60085 Office: 111 N County St Waukegan IL 60085

BRYER, HARRY MORTON, optometrist; b. Chgo., June 29, 1921; s. Irving and Rose (Hammerstein) B.; student Central YMCA Coll. (Chgo.), 1939, Pasadena Jr. Coll., 1942; O.D., Ill. Coll. Optometry, 1948; m. Bernice Seratan, June 27, 1948; children—Andrea Sue, Lawrence William, Wendy Anne. Practice optometry, Bridgeview, Ill., 1963—. Co.-chmn. local Optometric Extension Program, 1969—. Served with AUS, 1939-45; ETO. Mem. West Suburban Optometric Assn. (v.p.), Ill. Coll. Optometry Alumni Assn. Century Club. Club: Ravinia Green Country (Deerfield, Ill.). Home: 563 Sumac Rd Highland Park IL 60035 Office: 8745 S Harlem Ave Bridgeview IL 60455

BRZEZINSKI, EDWIN BRONISLAW, lawyer; b. St. Louis, May 26, 1931; s. Bronislaw and Helen (Bratkowski) B.; A.B., Washington U., St. Louis, 1953, J.D., 1958; m. Eleanor R. Twardzik, May 22, 1955; children—Edwin Bronislaw, Ellen Susan, Elaine Victoria. Admitted to Mo. bar, 1958; mem. firm Forgey & Sindel, St. Louis, 1959-62; atty. Mo. Hwy. Commn., St. Louis, 1962-74, charge dist. legal div., 1967-74; asst. U.S. atty., St. Louis, chief lands div., 1974—. Vice pres. Girls div. Khoury League, 1973-75; treas. Long Sch. PTA, 1967-68; coach Girls Softball, 1971—; cubmaster Boy Scouts Am., 1965-67; mem. exec. com. Lindberg Booster Club, 1972-73; trustee Polish Nat. Catholic Ch.; mem. Zoning Bd. Crestwood (Mo.), 1972—. Served to 1st lt. AUS, 1953-55; Korea. Mem. Kosciuszko Found., Mo., Met. St. Louis bar assns., Am. Legion, Delta Theta Phi. Clubs: Masons, Shriners. Home: 9148 Pardee Spur Crestwood MO 63126 Office: 1114 Market St Saint Louis MO 63101

BRZEZINSKI, IGNATIUS FRANK, dentist; b. Chgo., Nov. 15, 1919; s. Frank Anthony and Mary (Orlowski) B.; D.D.S., Loyola U. (Chgo.), 1944; m. Therese Victoria Istok, Nov. 23, 1950; children—Paul Frank, Daniel Steven, Carol Ann. Practice gen. dentistry, Chgo., 1947—; asst. clin. prof. operative dentistry Sch. Dentistry Loyola U., 1970—. Served to lt. Dental Corps, USNR, 1944-46. Fellow Internat. Coll. Dentists; mem. Chgo. Dental Soc. (past pres. N.W. br.), Dental Arts Club Chgo., Am. Prosthodontic Soc., Pierre Fauchard Acad., Acad. Gen. Dentistry. Clubs: Polish Am. Comml., Toastmasters. Home: 5440 N Panama St Chicago IL 60656 Office: 5301 W Fullerton St Chicago IL 60639

BUBIN, THOMAS FRANK, advt. agy. exec.; b. Flint, Mich., Sept. 2, 1922; s. Frank Theodore and Catherine Ann (Marzonie) B.; student Flint Jr. Coll., 1940-42, U. Mich., 1946-47; B.A., Western Mich. U., 1949; m. Deloris Zada Walther, May 17, 1947; children—Bethany Ann, Thomas Eric, Polly Elaine, Bruce Bennet, Rebecca Eileen. Asst. advt. mgr. Shakespeare Co., Kalamazoo, 1949-55, mgr. advt. and pub. relations, 1955-63; pres., gen. mgr., chmn. bd. Tom Bubin & Assos. (name changed to Bubin, Brewer, Begg & Williams Advt.), Kalamazoo, 1963—. Pres. St. Augustine Sch. Bd., 1969-70. Bd. dirs. St. Agnes Foundling Home, pub. relations adviser, 1963-69. Served with AUS, 1942-46. Decorated Bronze Star, Purple Heart. Mem. Outdoor Writers Assn. Am., Kalamazoo Valley Club Printing House Craftsmen (dir. 1967-71, pres. 1969-70, named craftsman of Yr. 1970), C. of C. K.C., Elk. Home: 2331 Althea St Kalamazoo MI 49007 Office: 1825 Ravine Rd Kalamazoo MI 49007

BUCCINO, RAY JOSEPH, biochemist; b. Bridgeport, Conn., Aug. 10, 1933; s. Ray Joseph and Minnie Veronica (Adiletta) B.; B.S.S., Fairfield U., 1955; B.S., U. Conn., 1958, Ph.D., 1968 (NIH fellow), 1968; m. Gayla Mae Harper, July 2, 1960; children—Linda Marie, Amy Elizabeth. Research asso. pharmacology Baylor Coll. Medicine, Houston, 1968-69; asst. prof. Defiance (Ohio) Coll., 1969-72; clin. biochemist Defiance Hosp., 1972—. Am. Cancer Soc. postdoctoral fellow, 1968-69. Mem. Am. Assn. for Clin. Chemistry, AAAS, Am. Chem. Soc., Am. Soc. Hosp. Pharmacists, Sigma Xi, Phi Lambda Upsilon, Rho Chi. Home: 1598 Woodhurst Dr Defiance OH 43512 Office: 1206 E 2d St Defiance OH 43512

BUCHAN, ROBERT WESLEY, museum ofcl.; b. Gordon, Nebr., Dec. 15, 1933; s. Cecil Glenn and Blanche Irene (Goslin) B.; A.B. in History, Williams Coll., 1972; student U. N.Mex., 1951-52, U. Neb., 1954, Chadron State Coll., 1960—; m. Bertha L. Clark, May 20, 1952; children—Robert Wesley, Willard, Burton, Barbara, Byron. Curator, Sheridan County Hist. Soc. Inc., Rushville, Nebr., 1965—; pres. Dept. of Platte (Nebr.), 1974—. Mem. Democratic Central Com. Sheridan County, 1965-69. HEW grantee, 1969. Elk. Home: 409 Main St Gordon NE 69343 Office: PO Box 86 Rushville NE 69360

BUCHANAN, GERALD SNYDER, physician; b. Albert Lea, Minn., Jan. 28, 1920; s. Frank Merton and Verian Almeda (Snyder) B.; B.S., Union Coll., 1949; M.D., Loma Linda U., 1949; m. Laura Mae Martin, Sept. 9, 1945; children—Gerald Duane, Douglas Lee, Randall Stuart. intern Hurley Hosp., Flint, Mich., 1949-50; practice gen. medicine, Fenton, Mich., 1950-51, Deer River, Minn., 1951-54, Ithaca, Mich., 1956-57, Holly, Mich., 1957—; mem. staff Hurley, McLaren, St. Joseph, Genesee Meml. hosps. (all Flint). Pres. North Oakland unit Mich. Cancer Found., 1968-70. Served to capt. USMC, 1954-56. Home: 15318 Riviera Shores Dr Holly MI 48442 Office: 3741 Grange Hall Rd Holly MI 48442

BUCHANAN, ROBERT ALEXANDER, physician, pharm. research exec.; b. Detroit, Sept. 8, 1932; s. Alexander Duncan and Genevieve (Hodgson) B.; m. Jeannine Duffell, Jan. 6, 1962; children—Lawrence, Elizabeth, Gregory; M.D., U. Mich., 1957; intern Phila. Gen. Hosp., 1957-58; pediatric resident U. Mich., 1960-62. Diplomate Am. Bd. Pediatrics. Flight surgeon USAF, 1958-60; pvt. practice medicine, specializing in pediatrics, Ann Arbor, Mich., 1962-66; med. investigator, dept. clin. investigation Parke, Davis & Co., Ann Arbor, 1966-67, asst. dir., 1967-68, asso. dir., 1969-76, dir. clin. research dept., 1974—; dir. Guthrie Clin. Research Found., 1968—; mem. courtesy staff St. Joseph Mercy Hosp., Ann Arbor; sr. examiner FAA, Washtenaw County; clin. asso. prof. pediatrics U. Mich. Med. Center. Bd. ushers 1st Presbyn. Ch., 1964—; pres. Bader Sch. Parent-Tchr. Orgn., 1977—; council mem. Wolverine council Boy Scouts Am., 1970—. Fellow Am. Acad. Pediatrics; mem. AMA, Mich., Washtenaw County med. socs., Am. Therapeutic Soc., Biomedical Engring. Soc., Racquet Club of Ann Arbor, Barton Boat Club (commodore 1967), Huron Valley Tennis Club. Editor: (with others) Antiepileptic Drugs, 1972, Adenine Arabinoside: An Antiviral Agent, 1975; contbr. articles to profl. jours. Home: 3045 Foxcroft St Ann Arbor MI 48104 Office: 2800 Plymouth Rd Ann Arbor MI 48106

BUCHER, HENRY HALE, JR., educator; b. Hainan Island, China, Mar. 7, 1936; s. Henry Hale and Louise Catron (Scott) B. (parents Am. citizens); student Davidson Coll., 1954-56; B.A., Am. U. of Beirut, 1958; postgrad. Univ. Coll., Legon, Ghana, 1960-61, Sorbonne U. Paris, 1962-63; M.Div., Princeton Theol. Sem., 1962; M.A. (Ford fellow), U. Wis., Madison, 1971, Ph.D., 1977; m. Emily Orr Clifford, June 22, 1969; 1 son, Clifford Hale. Ordained to ministry United Presbyterian Ch., U.S.A., 1962; intern service and study project in Gabon, under World Student Christian Fedn. of Geneva, 1962-65; mem. staff dept. higher edn. Nat. Council of Chs., N.Y.C., 1965-68; program dir. Ams. for Middle East Understanding, N.Y.C., 1969; curriculum specialist African studies program U. Wis., Madison, 1977—; lectr. on So. Africa; mem. Madison Area Com. on So. Africa, 1969—, Madison Friends of Internat. Students, 1975—; Fulbright/Hays Doctoral Dissertation Research Abroad fellow, Gabon, Senegal, France, 1973-74. Mem. Am. Hist. Assn., African Studies Assn., Societe des Africanistes, Societe Francaise d'Histoire d'Outre-Mer, Soc. Intercultural Edn., Tng. and Research, Wis. Council Social Studies. Author: The Third World: Middle East, 1973; contbr. articles on Africa, Middle East to profl. publs. Home: 3157 Buena Vista Madison WI 53704 Office: 1454 Van Hise Hall 1220 Linden Dr Madison WI 53706

BUCHMAN, MARSHALL HARDING, physician; b. Fort Wayne, Ind., July 22, 1924; s. Ross Alfred and Dessie Virginia (Harding) B.; B.S., Purdue U., 1950, M.S., 1952; M.D., U. Louisville, 1959; m. Winifred Eloise Geddes, June 5, 1954; 1 son, Joseph. Tchr. jr. high sch., New Albany, Ind., 1950-54; intern St. Joseph Infirmary, Louisville, 1959-60; practice medicine, New Albany, Ind., 1960—; staff Floyd Meml. Hosp., New Albany, chief staff, 1969; staff Silvercrest Hosp., New Albany. Mem. Floyd County Bd. Health, 1964—, chmn., 1970, 77. Served with AUS, 1943-46; ETO, PTO. Mem. AMA, Ind. (del. 1968, 69, 70), Floyd County (pres. 1971-72) med. assns., Delta Rho Kappa, Kappa Delta Pi, Alpha Epsilon Delta, Alpha Kappa Kappa. Methodist. Home: 1824 State St New Albany IN 47150

BUCHMAN, RANDALL LOREN, educator; b. Oak Harbor, Ohio, May 12, 1929; s. Charles and Cora (Scholt) B.; A.B., Heidelberg Coll., 1952; M.A., Ohio State U., 1958; postgrad. Kent State U., 1963-64, Ball State U., 1967—; m. Marilyn Alyce Patterson, Aug. 16, 1952; children—Deborah, Randall, Kevin. Historian, librarian Ohio Hist. Soc., Columbus, 1953-55; tchr./coach West Jefferson (Ohio) Schs., 1955-58, Ravenna (Ohio) City Schs., 1958-64; asso. prof. history and historic archaeology Defiance (Ohio) Coll., 1964—, exec. dir. devel. pub. affairs, 1976—; lectr. Ball State U., 1968. Cons. Ohio State Dept. Edn., 1970, Heidelberg Coll., 1974-75, Ohio State U., 1975. Mem. Defiance Planning Commn., 1971—, Ohio Am. Revolution Bicentennial Adv. Commn. Committeeman, Defiance County Rep.

Party, 1972—. Active Boys' Clubs, YMCA, Boy Scouts Am. Mem. Soc. Historic Archaeologists, Am. Assn. State and Local History, Soc. Am. Archaeologists, Am. Assn. Mus., Ohio Valley Archaeol. Conf., Nat. Council Social Studies, Phi Alpha Theta, Lambda Alpha, Pi Gamma Mu. Mem. United Ch. of Christ (moderator 1971-72, trustee Ohio conf. 1974-76). Contbr. articles to profl. jours. Editor: Field Reports in Archaeology, 1968—; Wood's Jour. of the Northwestern Campaign of 1812-1813, 1975; The Historic Indian of Ohio, 1976. Home: 730 E High St Defiance OH 43512 Office: N Clinton St Defiance OH 43512

BUCHSIEB, WALTER CHARLES, orthodontist; b. Columbus, Ohio, Aug. 30, 1929; s. Walter William and Emma Marie (Held) B.; B.A., Ohio State U., 1951, D.D.S., 1955, M.S., 1960; m. Betty Lou Risch, June 19, 1955; children—Walter Charles II, Christine Ann. Pvt. practice dentistry specializing in orthodontics, Dayton, Ohio, 1959—; cons. orthodontist Miami Valley Hosp., Childrens Med. Center, Dayton. Mem. fin. and program com. United Health Found., 1971-73; mem. dean's adv. com. Ohio State U. Coll. Dentistry; bd. dirs. Hearing and Speech Center, 1968—, 2d v.p., 1976—. Served to capt. AUS, 1955-58. Mem. Am. (alt. del. 1968—), Ohio (sec. council legislation 1969—) dental assns., Am. Coll. Dentists, Dayton Dental Soc. (pres. 1970-71), Great Lakes Soc. Orthodontists (sec.-treas. 1972-75, pres. 1977-78), Internat. Coll. Dentists, Am. Assn. Orthodontists (chmn. council legislation 1976), Pierre Fauchard Acad., Ohio State U. Alumni Assn., Delta Upsilon, Psi Omega. Republican. Lutheran (elder 1965-68, v.p. 1974). Clubs: Masons, Rotary (pres. 1973-74). Home: 1101 Viewpoint Dr Dayton OH 45459 Office: 5335 Far Hills Ave Dayton OH 45429

BUCK, BERNESTINE BRADFORD, ednl. counselor; b. Altheimer, Ark., July 25, 1926; d. Henry Walker and Dora Lois (Sims) Bradford; B.A., Stowe Tchrs. Coll., 1950; M.S., U. Mo., 1973; m. Joseph Wellington Buck, Oct. 1, 1950; children—Stanley W., Linda Carol, Debra Lois. Tchr. pub. schs., St. Louis, 1950-73, sch. counselor, 1973—. Mem. U. Mo. scholarship com., 1954-77. Mem. NEA, St. Louis Tchrs. Assn., Am., Mo. personnel and guidance assns., St. Louis Guidance Assn. Baptist.

BUCK, ROBERT ANTHONY, plant engr.; b. Toledo, Dec. 27, 1915; s. Harvey Adam and Ruth Ann (Riopelle) B.; student Curtis Wright Tech. Inst., 1942; m. Jean Elizabeth Blanchong; children—Carol Ann, James Robert, Ronald Edward, Donna Marie, Kenneth Alan, Marilyn Jean. With E.W. Bliss Co., Toledo and Chgo., 1936-63, service engr., Chgo., 1960, sales engr., 1961-63; plant engr. HandyButton Machine Co., Chgo., 1963—. Served with U.S. Army, 1942-45. Roman Catholic. Clubs: Midway Flyers, Ind. Order Foresters. Home: 733 Grove Ave S Oak Park IL 60304 Office: 2255 Rockwell St S Chicago IL 60608

BUCK, ROBERT MALEY, veterinarian; b. Roswell, S.D., Oct. 28, 1907; s. Eugene Clarence and Violet (Maley) B.; D.V.M., Iowa State U., 1930; m. Lucille Florence Beschta, June 6, 1935; children—Robert, Rosemary, Suzanne and LeAnne (twins). Pvt. practice veterinary medicine specializing in sheep diseases, Howard, S.D., 1930-33, Belle Fourche, S.D., 1933-65, 67—; mem. S.D. Livestock Sanitary Bd., Pierre, 1965-67. Mem. Belle Fourche (S.D.) City Council, 1942-47. Mem. S.D., Am. veterinary med. assns., K.C. Republican. Roman Catholic. Home: 1049 Kingsbury St Belle Fourche SD 57717 Office: PO Box 399 W Hwy 212 Belle Fourche SD 57717

BUCKELLEW, WILLIAM FRANKLIN, educator; b. Georgetown, Ill., June 10, 1928; s. Frank and Verla Buckellew; B.S., N.D. State U., 1953; M.S., U. Ill., 1954; Ed.D., U. Ark., 1968; postgrad. Quincy Coll., No. Ill. U., Ind. State U., Ind. U.; m. Lois Ann Soliah, Apr. 9, 1952; children—Michael, Mark, Jon. Tchr., coach Kankakee (Ill.) Pub. Schs., 1954-56; chmn. phys. edn. and athletic dept. Lake Park High Sch., Medinah, Ill., 1956-62; asst. prof., dir. lab. sch. phys. edn. Eastern Ill. U., Charleston, 1962-67, asso. prof. statistics and research, 1968-70, prof., chmn. dept. phys. edn., 1970-73, chmn. combined men and women phys. edn. dept., 1974-77, also mem. council on acad. affairs, council on tchr. edn. Mem. evaluation team Nat. Council for Accreditation Tchr. Edn., 1971—; mem. psychomotor assessment com. Ill. Office Edn., 1974-75. Mem. Community Swimming Pool Com., 1970-74. Served with USAAF, 1946-49. Mem. Nat. (life), Ill. edn. assns., Am. (sec. measurement, evaluation sect.), Ill. (chmn. research com. 1969-71, pres. S. E. dist. 1965-66) assns. health, phys. edn. and recreation, Ill. Assn. for Higher Edn., Nat. Coll. Phys. Edn. Assn. for Men, Ill. Assn. for Profl. Preparation in Health, Phys. Edn. and Recreation (pres. elect 1977—), Ill. Assn. Higher Edn., N.Am. Soc. for Psychology Sport and Phys. Activity, Phi Epsilon Kappa (faculty adviser), Sigma Alpha Epsilon, Phi Delta Kappa. Methodist. Mason, Rotarian. Contbr. AAHPER Ency. Phys. Edn., 1977, also articles to profl. jours. Home: 1602 Shaffer Pl Charleston IL 61920

BUCKINGHAM, RICHARD ALBERT, otologist; b. Chgo., Dec. 27, 1922; s. Brice Albert and Mary Eugenia (Ahern) B.; student Loyola U., Chgo., 1941-43; M.D., U. Ill., 1946, postgrad., 1949-50; m. Mary Grace Carney, Dec. 28, 1946; children—Rosamond, Richard, John, Marita, Barbara, Lawrence, Roberta, Donald, Celeste, Elisabeth. Intern, Cook County Hosp., Chgo., 1946-47, resident, 1949, 50-52; practice medicine specializing in otolaryngology, Chgo., 1952—; mem. staff Resurrection, Presbyn. St. Luke's, Hines VA hosps. Served to lt. (j.g.) USNR, 1947-49. Decorated comdr. Order del Condor de los Andes (Bolivia). Diplomate Am. Bd. Otolaryngology. Mem. Am., Pan. Am. med. assns., Am. Acad. Ophthalmology and Otology, Am. Triological Soc., Chgo. Med. Soc., Chgo. Laryngol. and Otological Soc., Ill. Med. Soc., Am. Otological Soc., Deutsche Gesellschaft für Hals-Nasen-Ohren-Heilkunde und Kopf-und Hals-Chirurgie (hon.), Sigma Xi. Author: (with others) Atlas of Otorhinolaryngology and Brochoesophagology, 1969; (with Galdino E. Valvassori) Tomographs and Cross Sections of the Ear, 1975. Home: 434 Willow Rd Winnetka IL 60093 Office: 145 S Northwest Hwy Park Ridge IL 60068

BUCKINGHAM, WILLIAM BRICE, physician; b. Chgo., July 25, 1924; s. Brice Albert and Mary (Ahern) B.; m. Margery L. Cross, Sept. 15, 1950; children—Cathlin, Megan, Gillian, William Brice, Peter, Michael, John, Maura, Mark, David, Diedre; student John Carroll U., Cleve., 1942-44; M.D., U. Ill., 1947, B.S., 1956; intern Cook County Hosp., Chgo., 1947-49, resident, 1950-52; fellow Northwestern U., 19S1-52. Diplomate Am. Bd. Internal Medicine. Practice medicine, specializing in internal medicine, Chgo., 1952—; attending physician Oak Park Hosp., 1952—, Augustana Hosp., Chgo., 1954-66; staff physician Oak Forest Tb. Hosp., 1952-55; asso. attending pulmonary disease sect. Cook County Hosp., 1952-56, attending physician, 1956-64, chief pulmonary sect., 1963-64, attending physician dept. medicine, 1964-66; cons. DeKalb County Tb. Hosp. and Clinic, 1954-60; attending physician St. Elizabeths Hosp., Chgo., 1954-65, St. Josephs Hosp., Chgo., 1964-68; attending physician VA Research Hosp., Chgo., 1960-70, cons. pulmonary diseases, 1970; attending physician Northwestern Meml. Hosp., 1966—, dir. pulmonary lab., 1968-75; clin. asst. Northwestern U. Med. Sch., 1952-56, instr., 1956-59, asso. in medicine, 1959-68, asst. prof., 1968-70, asso. prof., 1970—, chief, sect. gen. medicine, 1975—; mem. sci. adv. com. Municipal Tb. Sanitarium, 1968-72; cons. in tb. Ill. Dept. Pub. Health, 1973—; tb. control officer Chgo. Bd. Health, 1974—; vis. prof. medicine Universidad Autonoma de Guadalajara Med. Sch., 1975; cons. med. editor Quality Rev. Bull., Joint Commn. on Accreditation of Hosps., 1975. Fellow A.C.P. (pres. Ill. chpt. 1966-67, gen. chmn. First Fall Sci. Assembly, Chgo. 1969), Inst. of Medicine Chgo.; mem. AMA, Am., Ill. (exec. council 1965—, pres. 1973-75), Chgo. socs. internal medicine, Am. Thoracic Soc., Ill., Chgo. med. socs., Chgo. Tb. Inst. (dir.), Am. Assn. Inhaalation Therapists (bd. med. advisers 1969-72), Riverside Golf Club. Contbr. articles to profl. jours. Home: 319 Linden St Oak Park IL 60302 Office: 222 E Superior St Chicago IL 60611

BUCKINGHAM, WILLIAM THOMAS, ednl. co. exec.; b. Lancaster, Ohio, Dec. 21, 1921; s. Carl William and Hazel Leola (Stebleton) B.; B.A., Otterbein Coll., 1945, B.Sc., 1966; postgrad U. Notre Dame, 1960, Ohio U., 1977; m. Dorothy Ruth Coleman, Mar. 25, 1955; children—Michael, Pamela, Julie. Prin. chemist Battelle Meml. Inst., Columbus, Ohio, 1941-46, 54-56; asst. prof., chief chemist Ohio State U., Columbus, 1947-54; spl. projects officer, mgr. labs. Foseco, Inc., Cleve., 1956-68; asso. sponsor Dale Carnegie Courses, Sunbury, Ohio, 1969—; pres. Buckingham Orchards, Sunbury, 1959—. Mem. Am. Chem. Soc. (sr.), Ohio Hort. Soc. Republican. Methodist. Patentee fields electronics, chemistry, metallurgy. Home and Office: 8803 Cheshire Rd Sunbury OH 43074

BUCKLEY, CHESTER FRANCIS, mfg. co. exec.; b. Taunton, Mass., Jan. 9, 1903; s. John Joseph and Nora Anna (Brosnan) B.; Sc.B. in Elec. Engring., Mass. Inst. Tech., 1926; m. Julia Dorothy Troy, June 30, 1934; children—Barbara (Mrs. Gerald R. Holdridge), Paul, Robert, Kevin. Engring. asst. Bklyn. Edison Co., N.Y.C., 1926-27; asst. mgr. and gen. mgr. Taunton (Mass.) Elec. Co., 1927-47; works mgr. Nat. Silver Co., Taunton, 1947-53; engring. cons., Boston, 1953-57; pres. Standard Transformer Co., Warren, Ohio, 1957-62; pres. Am. Gage & Machine Co., Chgo., 1962-70, chmn. bd., 1970—. Chmn. Internat. Metals & Machines Co., 1970—, Ludlow Industries, Des Plaines, Ill., 1972—; dir. Katy Industries, 1970, Drovers Nat. Bank, 1972. Chmn. Community Council, Taunton, 1943-46. Trustee Morton Hosp., 1948-53. Mem. Nat. Machine Tool Builders, Nat. Elec. Mfrs., Phi Kappa Theta. Roman Catholic. Clubs: Mass. Inst. Tech. of Chgo., S.W. Fla., Chgo., Oak Park Country, Buckeye, Trumbull Country, Sara-Bay Country, Bird Key Yacht. Home: 1100 Imperial Dr Sarasota FL 33580 Office: 2200 O'Hare Lake Plaza Des Plaines IL 60018

BUCKLEY, HERMAN G., merchandising exec.; b. Denver, Sept. 29, 1902; s. Joseph and Rose B.; student U. Colo., 1919-22; m. Lillian E. Johnson, Oct. 11, 1949 (dec.); children—E. Michael, Joy Ann, J. Glen, H. Scot; m. 2d, Gertrude Libowitz, Jan. 7, 1977. With Goldblatt's Dept. Store, Chgo., 1923—, v.p. and dir. stores. 1955-63, v.p. and dir. merchandising, 1963-69, also dir., v.p., gen. mgr., 1969—; dir. merchandising div. Nat. Merchants Assn., 1968—. Served to 1st lt. AUS, 1943-45. Mem. Field Mus. Natural History. Mem. B'nai B'rith. Home: 1000 Lake Shore Plaza Chicago IL 60611 Office: 333 S State St Chicago IL 60604

BUCKLEY, ROBERT MICHAEL, clin. psychologist; b. Chgo., Oct. 20, 1927; s. Michael Francis and Lillian Ruth (Johnson) B.; B.S., Ill. Inst. Tech., 1960, M.S., 1963, Ph.D., 1970; m. Alice Kay Hanson, Oct. 17, 1959; children—Michelle, Tamara, Shawn. Chemist, metallurgist, Nalco, Chgo., 1952-56; psychologist, Chgo. Bur. Child Study, 1964-66, Speed Ednl. Coop., Chicago Heights, Ill., 1966-77; clin. psychologist, pres. Buckley-Long Assos. Ltd., Homewood, Ill., 1974-77. Active Citizens for Congressman Berwinski. Served with USN, 1945-47. Mem. Am., Midwest, Ill. psychol. assns., Biofeedback Socs. Am., Ill. (chmn. instrumentation com). Club: VFW. Contbr. research reports on biofeedback to confs. Home: 4732 W 176th St Country Club Hills IL 60477 Office: 18019 Dixie Hwy Homewood IL 60430

BUCKMAN, CHARLES EDWARD, JR., telephone co. exec.; b. Kansas City, Mo., Sept. 27, 1943; s. Charles Edward and Geraldine Clara (Herold) B.; student Ill. State U., 1961-64; B.S., Quincy Coll., 1966; postgrad. U. Ill., 1967-68; m. Judith Brosi, Nov. 19, 1966; children—Christine Elaine, Erin Noel, Brian Charles. Juvenile parole agent Ill. Youth Commn., 1966-67, regional supr., Springfield, 1967-68; account salesman Ill. Bell Telephone, Moline, 1967-70, communications cons., 1970-72, data communications specialist, 1972-74, account mgr., 1974-76, mgr. data tech. support, Chgo., 1976-77, product mgr., 1977—. Treas. Christian Family Movement, 1975-76; mem. religious edn. bd. Sacred Heart Ch., Moline, 1975-76; mem. curriculum adv. com. Black Hawk Coll., Moline, 1973-76. Mem. Data Processing Mgmt. Assn. Roman Catholic. Home: 1081 Challdon Ct Naperville IL 60540 Office: 225 W Randolphd HQ 26D Chicago IL 60606

BUCKMAN, CLARENCE BENNETT, state ofcl.; b. Little Falls, Minn., July 7, 1914; s. Mark and Grace (Schroeder) B.; B.S. in Forestry, U. Minn., 1940; m. Virginia Hall, July 19, 1941; 1 dau., Barbara Ann. With J.C. Campbell Forest Products Co., Duluth, Minn., 1941; foreman U.S. Bur. Entomology and Plant Quarantine, Duluth, 1941; bookkeeper Robertson Lumber Co., St. Cloud, Minn., 1942; dist. ranger Minn. Div. of Forestry, Dept. Conservation, Natural Resources, Littlefork, 1946, timber appraiser, 1946-50, forest mgr., 1950-51, sr. timber appraiser, 1951-56, supr. state timber sales, St. Paul, 1956-61, chief state land mgmt., 1961-67, dir. div. lands and forestry, 1967-69, dep. commr. dept. natural resources, 1969-77; lectr., U. Minn. Coll. Forestry, vis. prof., 1977—; lectr. Minn. rep. Pub. Land Law Rev. Commn., 1969. Active Boy Scouts Am. Served to 1st lt. AUS, 1942-46. Mem. Am. Legion, Soc. Am. Foresters, Am. Forestry Assn., Nat. Assn. State Foresters. Mason. Contbr. articles to profl. jours. Home: 2169 Wellesley Ave St Paul MN 55105 Office: 658 Cedar St St Paul MN 55101

BUCKMAN, JEFFREY, physician; b. Chgo., Sept. 22, 1942; s. Morris and Ethel (Warter) B.; B.A., Northwestern U., 1964; M.S., Syracuse U., 1965; M.D., Chgo. Med. Sch., 1969; m. Myrna Saltzman, May 29, 1968; children—Ari Daniel, Lori Sue, Tami Michele. Intern, Cleve. Clinic, 1969, resident in medicine, 1970-72, fellow in nephrology, 1972-73; gen. practice internal medicine, Niles, Ill., 1973—; attending physician Luth. Gen. Hosp., Park Ridge, Ill., 1973—, chmn. med. audit com. div. medicine, 1974—; clin. asst. prof. medicine Abraham Lincoln Sch. Medicine, 1975—. Trustee, Maine Twp. Jewish Congregation, Des Plaines, Ill. Office: 9101 N Greenwood Ave Niles IL 60648

BUCKNELL, DONALD HOWARD, guidance counselor; b. Hardy, Nebr., Apr. 17, 1928; s. Howard Nelson and Bernice Marie (Farnham) B.; B.S., U. Nebr., 1950; M.A., U. No. Colo., 1962. Tchr. Rosalie (Nebr.) High Sch., 1953-54, Pawnee City (Nebr.) Sch., 1954-61, Wahoo (Nebr.) Sch., 1962-71; admissions counselor Midland Luth. Coll., Fremont, Nebr., 1972-73; counselor Ednl. Service Unit 2, Fremont, Nebr., 1973-75, Adams Central Sch., Hastings, Nebr., 1975—. Pres. Hastings Hist. Soc., 1976—. Served with U.S. Army, 1950-52. Mem. Am., Nebr. personnel and guidance assns., Am. Sch. Counselors Assn., Nat. Vocat. Guidance Assn., Cornhusker Counselor Assn., Phi Delta Kappa. Democrat. Clubs: Kiwanis (pres. Hastings 1975—), Am. Legion, V.F.W., Masons, Shriners. Home: 143 E A St Hastings NE 68901 Office: Box 1088 Hastings NE 68901

BUCUR, NICHOLAS ANTHONY, III, data processing exec.; b. Managua, Nicaragua, Oct. 11, 1950 (parents Am. citizens); s. Nicholas A. and Jacoba (Galo) B.; student Cuyahoga Community Coll., 1969-71. Propr., Infinity Co., pub., Cleve., 1968—, data processing cons., 1973—; editorialist WZAK Radio, Cleve., 1969-73, dir. pub. affairs, 1975—, moderator, announcer People's Voice program, 1973—; pub. Cleve. Feminist mag., 1973; systems mgr. Systems Info. Services, Cleve., 1976—; instr. data processing Cuyahoga Community Coll. Vice pres. Greater Cleve. Young Republican Club, 1971; mem. human relations com. Fedn. for Community Planning, 1973. Mem. Mensa. Club: Cleve. City. Home: 10206 Clifton St Cleveland OH 44102 Office: 19201 Villaview St Cleveland OH 44119

BUDETTI, JOSEPH ANTHONY, otorhinolaryngologist; b. N.Y.C., Mar. 12, 1911; s. Paul Emil and Lucrezia (Contini) B.; B.S., Fordham U, 1932; M.D., N.Y. Med. Coll., 1936; postgrad Washington U., 1938-39; children—Marie Therese (Mrs. Charles Norris), Joseph Bart, Peter Paul, Dorothy Rose. Intern, New Rochelle (N.Y.) Hosp., 1936-37, resident, 1937-38; resident Washington U. Med. Barnes Hosp., 1938-39; practice medicine specializing in ear, nose and throat, N.Y.C., 1939-42, New Rochelle, N.Y., 1946-48, Wichita, Kans., 1953—; with Wichita Ear, Nose & Throat Assos., P.A., 1971—; mem. staffs Wesley Med. Center, St. Francis Hosp., (both Wichita); instr. otolaryngology N.Y. Med. Coll., 1939-48; cons. otologist Inst. Logopedics, Wichita. Served to lt. col. AUS, 1942-46, 48-53. Fellow Japan Otolaryngology Soc., Mid Am. Hearing Research Found., Am. Acad. Ophthalmology and Otolaryngology, Am. Soc. Ophthalmology and Otolaryngology Allergy, Am. Otorhinologic Soc. Plastic Surgery, Centurion Club of Deafness Research; mem. Am. Council Otolaryngology, Indsl. Med. Assn., AMA, Kans. Med. Soc., Pan Am. Congress Otorhinolaryngology, 38th Parallel Med. Soc. Korea. Rotarian. Contbr. numerous articles to med. jours. Home: 427 N Hillside Wichita KS 67214 Office: 427 N Hillside St Wichita KS 67214

BUDNY, JOHN ARNOLD, toxicologist; b. Chgo., Apr. 9, 1943; s. Walter J. and Rosella B. (Robinson) B.; m. Mary Catherine Madonich, Aug. 3, 1968; children—Matthew John, Hallie Catherine. B.S., Lewis U., 1965; Ph.D., Ohio State U., 1970. Toxicologist, research dept. Procter & Gamble Co., Cin., 1970-75; toxicologist Diamond Shamrock Corp., Painesville, Ohio, 1975, asso. dir. toxicology, 1976, chief toxicology, 1977—. Mem. Am. Chem. Soc., AAAS, Soc. Toxicology, N.Y. Acad. Sci., Cleve. Med. Library Assn. Contbr. articles to sci. jours. Home: 3349 Elsmere Rd Shaker Heights OH 44120 Office: Diamond Shamrock Corp PO Box 348 Painesville OH 44077

BUDREAN, GEORGE VIRGIL, pub. relations exec.; b. East Chicago, Ind., Apr. 15, 1935; s. John and Anna (Rau) B.; B.S., Purdue U., 1959; m. Janice Arlene Blackburn, Apr. 24, 1965; children—Paul Christian, Jonathan Thomas, Kathleen Mary. Reporter, Chgo. Tribune, 1959-60; publicity rep. Internat. Harvester, Chgo., 1960-62; asst. dir. pub. info. Am. Dental Assn., Chgo., 1963-64; asso., Gardner, Jones & Cowell Pub. Relations, Chgo., 1964-65; communications specialist Xerox Corp., Rochester, N.Y., 1965-68; nat. project dir. Millers Nat. Fedn., Chgo., 1971-72; dir. pub. info. Nat. Safety Council, Chgo., 1972—. Served with USMCR, 1954-56. Mem. Pub. Relations Soc. Am., Publicity Club Chgo., Chgo. Press Club. Home: 18817 Royal Rd Homewood IL 60430 Office: 425 N Michigan Ave Chicago IL 60611

BUDRYS, STANLEY, physician; b. Vilkija, Lithuania, July 14, 1916; s. Juozas and Sofia (Kazukaitis) B.; M.D., U. Vytautas The Great, Kaunas, Lithuania, 1940; m. Milda Kurshas, Oct. 19, 1941; 1 dau., Grazina (Mrs. Hubert S De Santis). Came to U.S., 1947, naturalized, 1949. Intern Holy Cross Hosp., Chgo.; practicing physician, Kaunas, Lithuania, 1941-44; med. officer UNRRA, Stuttgart, Germany, 1946-47; gen. practice medicine, Chgo., 1949—; mem. staff Central Community Hosp., Holy Cross Hosp., Chmn. bd. Boy Scout Camp Rakas, Custer, Mich. Mem. Ill. Lithuanian Med. Soc. (pres. 1957), AMA, Ill. Med. Soc., Am. Acad. Family Physicians. Lithuanian Am. Med. Assn. (pres. 1965), Fraternitas Lithuanica (pres. 1968—). Editor, pub.: Inaugural Medical Dissertation on Kidney and Bladder Stone, 1965. Editor: Lithuanian Am. Med. Jour., 1960-65. Home: 990 N Lake Shore Dr Apt 10B Chicago IL 60611 Office: 2751 W 51st St Chicago IL 60632

BUDZAK, KATHRYN SUE (MRS. ARTHUR BUDZAK), physician; b. Racine, Wis., May 6, 1940; d. Raymond Philip and Emma Kathryn (Sorensen) Myer; student Stephens Coll., 1957-58, Luther Coll., 1958-59; B.S. with honors, U. Wis. at Milw., 1962; M.D., U. Wis., 1969; m. Arthur Budzak, Dec. 21, 1961; children—Ann Elizabeth, Lynn Marie. Intern, Madison (Wis.) Gen. Hosp., 1969-70; emergency physician, emergency suite St. Mary's Hosp., Madison, 1971-75; urgent care screening physician Dean Clinic, Madison, 1975—. Mem. Am. Coll. Emergency Physicians, AMA, Am., Wis. acads. family practice, Wis., Dane County med. socs., Am. Med. Women's Assn., Wis. Med. Alumni Assn., Sigma Sigma Sigma. Presbyterian. Mem. editorial bd. Wis. Med. Alumni Quar. Home: 6110 Davenport Dr Madison WI 53711 Office: 1313 Fish Hatchery Rd Madison WI 53715

BUEHL, ISABELLE ANN, pathologist; b. Ramsey, Ind., Sept. 2, 1934; d. Joseph Hubert and Daisy Leoma (Thevenot) Davis; A.B., Ind. U., 1956, M.D., 1959; m. Robert Theodore Buehl, Sept. 14, 1957. Intern, Meth. Hosp., Indpls., 1959-60; resident in pathology U. Ind. Med. Center, Indpls., asst. prof. Ind. U. Sch. Medicine, 1964—; partner med. lab., Indpls., 1966—; dir. lab. Hancock County Meml. Hosp., Greenfield, Ind.; bd. dirs. Central Ind. Regional Blood Bank, Kenderick Meml. Hosp. Mem. Coll. Am. Pathologists, Am. Soc. Clin. Pathologists, AMA, Ind. Assn. Pathologists, Ind., Marion County med. socs. Contbr. med. jours. Home: Rural Route 3 Box 229 Greenwood IN 46142 Office: 301 E 38th St Indianapolis IN 46205

BUEHNER, DONALD FRANCIS, physician; b. Mt. Vernon, Ind., Sept. 11, 1918; s. Sylvester Henry and Anna (Engelhart) B.; A.B., Wabash Coll., 1941; M.D., St. Louis U., 1950; m. Lucille Margaret Kollker, Dec. 31, 1941 (dec.); children—Dr. Donald C., Timothy K., Rebecca Ann, Lucinda Jane, Nicholas J.; m. 2d, Jeanne McPherson Knight, Nov. 12, 1976. Intern Protestant Deaconess Hosp., Evansville, Ind., 1950-51; practice medicine, specializing in family practice, Evansville, Ind., 1951—; mem. staff St. Mary's Hosp., pres. 1959—; past pres. Evansville Med. Arts Bldg., Inc. Served with AUS, 1942-45. Diplomate Am. Bd. Family Practice. Fellow Am. Acad. Family Practice (dist. pres. 1968); mem. AMA (Physician Recognition award 1970-77), Assn. Am. Physicians and Surgeons, Am. Coll. Clin. Pharmacology, Pan Am. Med. Assn., Beta Theta Pi. Roman Catholic. Club: Rolling Hills Country (Newburgh, Ind.). Home: 1200 Bonnie View Evansville IN 47715 Office: Medical Arts Bldg Evansville IN 47715

BUELL, RICHARD HERMAN, paper co. exec.; b. St. Louis, Dec. 27, 1915; s. Adolph Arthur and Aimee (Herman) B.; A.B., U. Mo., 1938; m. Jane Abraham, Oct. 16, 1951; children—Dorothy Jean, Nina Jane, Richard Herman. With Ropak Corp. (formerly Rosenthal Paper Products Co.), St. Louis, 1938—, v.p. 1954—, also dir., exec. v.p., dir. Foam Fabricators Ltd., Ropak of Tex. Vice pres. United Fund, 1966-67; co-chmn. div. Jewish Fedn., 1966-67. Served to capt. USAAF, 1941-46. Mem. Zeta Beta Tau. Republican. Jewish (trustee temple 1966-67). Mason; mem. B'nai B'rith. Clubs: Westwood Country (Ladue, Mo.); University (dir.), Rotary (pres. 1967-68) (St. Louis). Home: 6 Wendover Dr Ladue MO 63124 Office: 200 Lynch St St Louis MO 63118

BUER, HOWARD HENRY, coll. adminstr.; b. Milw., Jan. 14, 1922; s. Henry William and Hertha Martha (Hinz) B.; B.C.E., M.C.E., U. Wis.; m. Raymir Behrens, Feb. 23, 1946; children—Karen Diane, Scott Howard. Instr. civil engring. U. Wis., Madison, 1948-51; analyst Chance Vought Aircraft Co., Dallas, 1951-52; asst. prof. civil engring. U. Del., Newark, 1952-54; instr. engring. mechanics U. Wis., Madison, 1954-55; asst. to chief structural engr. Mead & Hunt, cons. engrs., Madison, 1955-64; sci. programmer U. Wis. Phys. Scis. Lab., Stoughton, 1964-67; dir. adminstrv. data processing The Principia, St. Louis, 1968—; structural engr. mem. City of Madison Bd. Bldg. Examiners and Appeals, 1963-64. Served with C.E., U.S. Army, 1942-46. Registered profl. engr., Wis.; registered bus. programmer, certified data processor. Mem. Assn. Computer Machinery, Assn. Systems Mgmt., Data Processing Mgmt. Assn., Soc. Preservation and Encouragement of Barber Shop Quartet Singing in Am., Chi Epsilon, Tau Beta Pi. Republican. Christian Scientist. Club: Masons. Home: 920 Dutch Mill Dr Ballwin MO 63011 Office: 13201 Clayton Rd Saint Louis MO 63131

BUERK, HANS GUENTHER, wholesale trade co. exec.; b. Rottweil, Germany, Nov. 23, 1924; s. Christian and Johanna Anna (Martin) B.; M.B.A., U. Tuebingen, 1949; m. Utta Santo-Passo, Aug. 4, 1961; 1 dau., Joan Cristina. Came to U.S., 1961, naturalized, 1967. With Dr. Treude Assn., Stuttgart, West Germany, 1950-54; controller A.G. Messerschmitt, Munich, West Germany, 1955-57; jr. partner Koeck, Baden-Baden, West Germany, 1958-61; cost accountant Harris Trust & Savs. Bank, Chgo., 1962-63; auditor Chemetron Corp., Chgo., 1963-66; with Robert Bosch Corp., Broadview, Ill., 1966—, v.p. finance, 1971—, also dir.; dir. Robert Bosch Ltd., Can., Robert Bosch Packaging Machine Corp. Served with German Army, 1942-45. Mem. Am. Mgmt. Assn. (presidents council 1973—). Home: 3400 N Lake Shore Dr Chicago IL 60657 Office: 2800 S 25th Ave Broadview IL 60153

BUERKI, LYNN HERMAN, farmer; b. Wichita, Kans., Feb. 19, 1933; s. Herman Joseph and Lynda H. (Brunkau) B.; grad. high sch.; m. Shirley Ann Parry, July 30, 1954; children—Daniel Joseph, Pamela Lynn, Patricia Ann. Self-employed as farmer, Wichita, Kan., 1950—. Supr. Sedgwick County Conservation Dist., 1956—, chmn., 1965—; spl. dep. assessor, twp. trustee, Sedgwick County, Kans., 1962-72; spl. cons. to Sedgwick County Assessor, 1967—; instr. Wichita-Eagle Young Hunters Safety Clinic, 1970—, sta. dir., 1973—; mem. Sedgwick County Environ. Task Force, 1970-74; mem. Sedgwick County Community Health Planning Bd., 1971—; mem. Regional Health Planning Bd., 1971—; mem. Sedgwick County Sand Pit and Gravel Com., 1974—; Mem. Profl. Farmers Am., Top Farmers Am., Nat. (mem. soil stewardship com. 1974—), Kans. (dir. 1968—, pres. 1974) assns. conservation dists. Nazarene. Republican. Address: Route 8 14707 W Pawnee St Wichita KS 67235

BUERKLE, JOSEPH TERRY, lawyer; b. Cape Girardeau, Mo., July 26, 1943; s. Robert McEndree and Julia (Bohnsack) B.; B.S. in Bus. Banking and Finance, U. Mo., 1965, J.D., 1968; m. Judith H. Gausnell, Dec. 6, 1975; children by previous marriage—Darcy Catherine, Christian Alexander, Jason McEndree. Admitted to Mo. bar, 1968; mem. firm Buerkle, Buerkle & Lowes and predecessor firm, Jackson, Mo., 1968-71, partner, 1971—; asst. pros. atty. Cape Girardeau County, 1969-72, asst. city atty., Jackson, 1968-69; v.p. Computer Network Ltd., Ste. Genevieve, Mo., Gazebo Ltd., Cape Girardeau. Mem. Am. Cancer Soc., S.E. Mo. Hosp. Assn., 1971—, Mo. Coordinating Bd. Higher Edn., 1974—, Friends St. Francis Hosp., 1975—; v.p. Cape County Young Republicans Club, 1970-71; chmn. Cape County sect. Bond-for-Gov. campaign com., 1972. Mem. Am., Mo. (former mem. young lawyers council; mem. pub. info. com. 1968-75, ins. programs com. 1970-76), St. Louis Met., Cape County bar assns., Nat. Assn. Dist. Attys., Assn. Trial Lawyers Am., Mo. Assn. Trial Lawyers, Am. Judicature Soc., U. Mo. Alumni Assn. (chmn. Cape Girardeau chpt. 1968-75), Cape Girardeau Hist. Soc., Sigma Rho Sigma, Phi Delta Phi, Sigma Alpha Epsilon. Rep. Roman Catholic. Club: Cape Girardeau Country. Home: 2532 Timber Ln Cape Girardeau MO 63701 Office: 709 E Main St Jackson MO 63755

BUERLING, SIEGFRIED FRIEDEL, hist. village ofcl.; b. Essen, Germany, Jan. 29, 1932; s. Friedrich and Bertha Wilhelmiene (Wackermann) B.; came to U.S., 1959, naturalized, 1968; grad. trade sch.; m. Heidi Elisabeth Heid, Aug. 31, 1957; children—Peter Johannes, Bruce Thomas, Curt Tracy. With Buerling Cabinet Shop, Essen, 1945-56; furniture restorer Canadiana Antiques, Montreal, Que., Can., 1956-59; preparator Western Reserve Hist. Soc., Cleve., 1959-62, supr. ops., 1962-66, mgr. ops., 1966-70, mgr. properties, 1970-74, dir. Hale Farm and Village, Bath, Ohio, 1975—, dir. dept. properties and preservation, 1977—; v.p. ops. Cuyahoga Valley Preservation and Scenic R.R. Assn.; restoration cons. Bd. dirs. Hower House Found., Akron, Ohio, 1974—; trustee Northeastern Ohio Inter Museums Council. Recipient Woodrow Wilson award Woodlawn Conf., Nat. Trust for Historic Preservation, 1971; Outstanding Citizen award Nationality Services Center Greater Cleve., 1975. Mem. Internat. Council Crafts and Interpretation. Rotarian (dir. 1975—). Home: 2743 Oak Hill Rd Bath OH 44210 Office: 2686 Oak Hill Rd Bath OH 44210

BUESCHEL, RICHARD MARTIN, advt. exec.; b. Chgo., Dec. 26, 1926; s. Martin William and Helen Gloria (Kernacs) B.; B.A., Ill. Coll., 1951; Asso. in Sci., Wright Jr. Coll., 1949; m. Helen Marian Snyder, Nov. 24, 1951; children—Stacey Brooks, Megan Conley. With Wallace-Ferry-Hanly Advt., Chgo., 1952-55; jr. account exec. Erwin Wasey & Co., advt., 1955-57; account exec. Erwin, Wasey, Ruthrauff & Ryan, advt., 1957-59; pres. Waldie and Briggs, Inc., advt., 1959-75; sr. v.p., creative dir. Ladd/Wells/Presba Inc., advt., 1975—; instr. Master's program Roosevelt U.; cons. Am. Heritage, 20th Century Fox Film Studios. Bd. dirs. N.W. Suburban YMCA, Des Plaines, Ill., 1965—. Served with USAAF, 1945-46. Mem. Bus. and Profl. Advt. Assn. (nat. dir. 1969—, chpt. pres. 1968-69), Am. Assn. Advt. Agys. (gov. Chgo. council 1971-75), Author's Guild, Inc., Authors League Am., Inc., Am. Aviation Hist. Soc., Field Mus. of Natural History, Soc. Indsl. Archeology, Smithsonian, Chgo. Advt. Club (dir. 1971-73). Author: Communist Chinese Airpower, 1968; Aircam Fighters Series, 8 vols., 1970-71; Aircam Bombers Series, 4 vols., 1972-73; Attack from the Air-Pearl Harbor, 1971; Lemons, Cherries and Bell Fruit Gum, 1977; Classic Slot Machines, 1977. Editor: Copy Chicago, 1966-68, Air Progress, 1965-68, Air Combat, 1968-73, The Coin Slot, 1975—. Home: 414 N Prospect Manor Mount Prospect IL 60056 Office: 55 W Wacker Dr Chicago IL 60601

BUESS, CHARLES MERLYN, chemist, educator; b. Forest, Ohio, Apr. 22, 1922; s. Charles Amos and Jessie Katherine (Benning) B.; B.S., Ohio State U, 1942; M.S., Western Res. U., 1946; Ph.D., U. So. Calif., 1950; postgrad. Northwestern U., 1949-51; m. Anita Durand, June 7, 1953; children—Alice Katherine Buess Fisher, Charles Louis, Ann Lynn Buess Livingston, Zoe Bell. Chemist, NACA, Cleve., 1943-46; asst. prof. U. Ga., Athens, 1951-56; asso. prof. U. Ky., Lexington, 1956-57; asso. prof. U. So. Calif., Los Angeles, 1957-61; prof. chemistry Wichita (Kans.) State U., 1961—. Vis. sr. scientist Jet Propulsion Lab., Pasadena, Calif., 1966. Fellow AAAS, Am. Inst. Chemists; mem. Am. Chem. Soc., Chem. Soc. (London), Kans. Acad. Sci., Phi Beta Kappa, Sigma Xi, Phi Kappa Phi, Phi Lambda Upsilon. Contbr. articles to profl. jours. Home: Rural Route 1 Box 81A Benton KS 67017 Office: Dept Chemistry Wichita State Univ Wichita KS 67208

BUESSER, ANTHONY CARPENTER, lawyer; b. Detroit, Oct. 15, 1929; s. Frederick Gustavis and Lela (Carpenter) B.; B.A. in English with honors, U. Mich., 1952, J.D., 1960; m. Carolyn Sue Pickle, Mar. 13, 1954 (div. Feb. 1973); children—Kent Anderson, Anthony Carpenter, Andrew Clayton; m. 2d, Bettina Rieveschl. Admitted to Mich. bar, 1961; asso firm Chase, Goodenough & Buesser, Detroit, 1961-66; partner firm Buesser, Buesser, Snyder & Blank, Detroit, also Bloomfield Hills, 1966—. Trustee, chmn. bd. Detroit Country Day Sch., Birmingham, Mich., 1970—. Served with AUS, 1953-55. Recipient Avery Hopwood award major fiction U. Mich., 1953. Mem. Am., Mich., Detroit (pres. 1976-77), Oakland County bar assns., Am. Judicature Soc., Am. Arbitration Assn. (arbitrator), Alpha Delta Phi, Phi Delta Phi. Club: Thomas M. Cooley, Detroit, Detroit Athletic (Detroit). Home: 1508 Sodon Lake Rd Bloomfield Hills MI 48013 Office: 4100 Penobscot Bldg Detroit MI 48226

BUETHE, FRANK ALAN, utility line clearance co. exec.; b. Salem, Mass., Sept. 25, 1938; s. Walter Carl and Harriett Hart (Bartlett) B.; B.A., Dartmouth Coll., 1961; M.B.A., U. Pa., 1967; m. Pamela Barbara Dabe, Oct. 14, 1972; children—Paige Harrill, Julie Anna, Neil Bartlett. Business intern Mead, Johnson Inc., Evansville, Ind., 1968-69; asst. v.p. J.B. Ivey & Co., Charlotte, N.C., 1969-76; pres. Acme Tree Surgery Co., Inc., DePere, Wis., 1976—. Served with USMC, 1961-65. Decorated 5 Air Medals. Mem. Nat. Arborists Assn., Internat. Brotherhood Magicians, Soc. Am. Magicians, Optimist Internat., Beta Gamma Sigma. Episcopalian. Home: 505 Hilltop Dr Green Bay WI 54301 Office: PO Box 7 Hwy G DePere WI 54115

BUFFARDI, LOUIS JOSEPH, candy mfg. co. exec.; b. Chgo., Mar. 27, 1914; s. Salvatore J. and Carmella (Pagano) B.; student Northwestern U., 1932-35; LL.B., Kent Law Sch., 1938; m. Dorothy Ann Parrillo, Jan. 6, 1940; children—James S., Louis P., Carmellyn R., Donna T. Admitted to Ill. bar, 1938; practiced in Chgo., 1938-40; treas., atty. Ferrara Candy Co., Chgo., 1940-42, treas., atty., 1946—; electronic analyst Motorola, Inc., Chgo., 1942-44; bacteriological chemist Meadowmor Dairy, Chgo., 1944-46. Chgo. area candy industry sect. leader Community Fund, A.R.C., 1942-52. Bd. dirs. Villa Scalabrini, old peoples home. Recipient 10 year service award Red Feather, 1953. Mem. Ill. Bar Assn., Nat. Confectioner's Assn., NAM, Nat Small Bus. Men's Assn., Catholic Lawyer's Guild, Chgo. Justinian Soc. Lawyers. Ill. C. of C., Chgo. Mus. Natural History, Lyric Opera Guild of Chgo., Northwestern U. Alumni Assn. Moose. Clubs: Chicago Candy Technology, Chicago Candy Production. Home: 121 Briarwood Loop Oak Brook IL 60521 Office: 7301 W Harrison St Forest Park IL 60130

BUFFINGTON, RICHARD DEAN, ins. co. exec.; b. Cedar Rapids, Iowa, July 15, 1926; s. Lloyd Raymond and Gladys Mae (Wabel) B.; B.A., Coe Coll., 1949; m. Suzanne Louise Stuckey, Nov. 21, 1953; children—Mary, Mark, Ann, John, Jean, Diana, David, Lynn. Tchr. math. and sci. Sigourney (Iowa) Ind. Sch., 1949; payroll auditor Iowa Nat. Mut. Ins. Co., Omaha, Kansas City, Mo., 1949-54, spl. agt., Atlantic, Iowa, 1955-59; casualty underwriter Universal Surety Co., Lincoln, Nebr., 1959-61; office mgr. Walt Sweeney-Eiche Ins. Agy., 1962-65; underwriting mgr. Tri-State Ins. Co. Minn., Luverne, 1965—. Ins. instr. adult distributive edn. Lincoln Pub. Schs., 1964-65. Chmn., Mo. Valley Conf., 1968, planning com., 1973; fund chmn. Red Arrow Community Fund, Luverne, 1968-69, bd. dirs., 1968-77, budget com., 1971-76, gen. chmn., 1977; bd. dirs. Health Systems Agency Six; active Little League, 1971-73; pres. hosp. bd., Luverne Community Hosp., 1974; active Cub and Boy Scouts Am. Served to 2d lt. AUS, 1944-47. Mem. C.P.C.U. Soc. (instr. courses 1967-77, chpt. pres. 1970; nat. committeeman 1973-75, 77), S.D. Underwriters Assn., VFW, Am. Legion. Clubs: Elks, Lions (sec.-treas. 1971), Rotary, Luverne Country. Home: 517 N Freeman St Luverne MN 56156 Office: 1 Roundwind Rd Luverne MN 56156

BUHROW, WILLIAM LLOYD, surgeon; b. Waverly, Iowa, June 10, 1935; s. Lloyd Frederick and Florence Eleanor (Babcock) B.; B.A., State U. Iowa, 1960, M.D., 1964; m. Terry Joan McKean, June 2, 1963; children—Matthew W., Lisa D., Adam S. Intern, Letterman Gen. Hosp., San Francisco, 1964-65; resident gen. surgery Walter Reed Gen. Hosp., Washington, 1965-69; pvt. practice medicine Clinton, Iowa, 1972—; med. dir. inhalation therapy Clinton Community Jr. Coll., 1975—. Bd. dirs. Clinton ARC, 1974—. Served with AUS, 1963-72. Fellow A.C.S.; mem. Alpha Omega Alpha. Home: 715 Orchard Ln Clinton IA 52732 Office: Bluff Med Center 240 N Bluff Blvd Clinton IA 52732

BUIST, RICHARD JAMES, physicist; b. Grand Rapids, Mich., Oct. 14, 1937; s. George Robert and Thelma Gertrude (Archer) B.; B.Sc., Ohio State U., 1961, M.Sc., 1968; m. Linda Kay Ashley, Aug. 11, 1961; children—Pamela Sue, Julie Lynne, Laura Ann, Cathy Ellen, Richard James. Physicist solid state materials research group Battelle Meml. Inst., Columbus, Ohio, 1961-67; materials research physicist Roy C. Ingersoll Research Center of Borg-Warner Corp., Des Plaines, Ill., 1967-72; engring. mgr. Borg-Warner Thermoelectrics, Des Plaines, 1972—; instr. short course thermoelectrics U. Tex., Arlington, 1972—. Nation chief YMCA Indian Princess Father/Dau. Program. Mem. Am. Phys. Soc., Sigma Xi. Developer unique thermoelectric design capability and improved system performance. Home: 341 Winston Dr Palatine IL 60067 Office: Wolf and Algonquin Rds Des Plaines IL 60018

BULEN, L. KEITH, lawyer; b. Pendleton, Ind., Dec. 31, 1926; s. Lawrence and Ople (Benefiel) B.; A.B., Ind. U., 1949. J.D., 1952; children—Leslie, Lisa, Kassee, Kellee; m. 2d, N. Carole Guillot. Admitted to bar, 1952; sr. partner firm Bulen, Castor & Robinette. U.S. del. Econ. and Social Council, Geneva, Switzerland, 1970, 73; U.S. observer Nat. Resources Conf., Nairobi, Kenya, Africa, 1972. Chmn. Marion County (Ind.) Republican Orgn., 1966-72, 11th Dist. Rep. Orgn., 1966-74; mem. exec. com. Ind. Rep. Com., 1968-74; mem. Rep. Nat. Com. for Ind., 1968-74, exec. com., 1968-74; del. Rep. Nat. Conv., 1968, 72, 76—; mem. Ind. Ho. Reps., 1960-64. Served to sgt. USAAF, 1945-46. Recipient Good Govt. award Indpls. Jaycees, 1973. Mem. Am., Ind., Indpls. bar assns., Ind. U. Alumni, 500 Festival Assn., Sigma Nu, Phi Delta Phi. Mem. Christian Ch. Mason (Shriner), Antelope (Man of Year 1966). Clubs: Caravan, Columbia, Englewood Lodge, Capitol Hill. Home: 8323 Rahke Rd Indianapolis IN 46217 Office: 1 Indiana Sq Indianapolis IN 46204

BULGRIN, WALTER WILLIAM, mech. engr.; b. Akron, Dec. 27, 1907; s. William Charles and Minnie (Damerow) B.; student Akron U., nights, 1926-29; m. Marilyn Mae Shreve Ritter, Apr. 4, 1964; children—Grace Joan Bulgrin Gilbertson, Kathleen Susan Bulgrin Shelton, Rebecca Allane Ritter Vigdor, Pamela Sue Ritter. With Firestone Steel Products Co., Akron, 1925-73, chief engr., 1949-73, ret., now engring. cons., Wadsworth, Ohio, 1973—. Mem. Soc. Auto. Engrs. (recipient 25 Year Active Member award 1974), Am. Assn. Retired Persons. Republican. Lutheran. Clubs: Firestone Country, Rawiga Country. Patentee in automotive rims and wheels, beverage containers. Home and Office: 543 Woodland Ave Wadsworth OH 44281

BULKELEY, PETER ZANE, univ. dean; b. San Francisco, Mar. 17, 1934; s. Milton and Mary Franklin (Zane) B.; B.A., Bowdoin Coll., 1956; B.S., Mass. Inst. Tech., 1956, M.S., 1957; Ph.D., Stanford, 1962; m. Karen Knueppel Hazen, July 31, 1976; children—Thomas Zane, Charles Philip; 1 stepson, Jeffrey Brewster Hazen. Dir. design div. mech. engring. Stanford, 1963-69, dean students, 1969-70, asso. chmn. dept. mech. engring., asso. prof., 1965-72; dean Coll. Engring. and Tech., Bradley U., Peoria, Ill., 1972—. Cons. editor Brooks-Cole Pub. Co. Bd. dirs. Inter-Am. Improvement Assn., 1971-72; adv. bd. dirs. Inst. for Mobility Aids. Mem. Am. Soc. Engring. Edn., Am. Soc. M.E., N.Y. Acad. Scis., Sigma Xi. Republican. Episcopalian. Rotarian. Contbr. articles to profl. jours. Home: 2708 W Winterberry Ln Peoria IL 61604 Office: Jobst Hall College of Engineering Bradley University Peoria IL 61625

BULKLEY, BETTY LOU COMPTON (MRS. ROY LYMAN BULKLEY), occupational therapist; b. Lawrence, Kan., July 24, 1926; d. James Howard and Florence Mildred (Lemon) Compton; B.S. in Occupational Therapy, U. Kans., 1950, M.A. in Speech Communication, 1975; m. Roy Lyman Bulkley, Oct. 22, 1949; 1 son, Timothy Howard. Occupational therapist Topeka State Hosp., 1949-52, chief occupational therapy, 1961-69, dir. activity therapy dept., 1969—; cons. Topeka Presbyn. Manor, 1970—; lectr. U. Kan. Occupational Therapy Evaluation Techniques, Lawrence, 1973. Sec., Shawnee County Republican Central Com., 1968. Mem. Am., Kan. (v.p. 1964, pres.-elect) occupational therapy assns. Home: 3929 Dixie Ct Topeka KS 66614 Office: 2700 W 6th St Topeka KS 66606

BULL, LAWRENCE MYLES, engr.; b. Aliquippa, Pa., Feb. 20, 1931; s. Thomas Leslie and Gertrude Margaret (Miller) B.; B.E.E., Ind. Inst. Tech., 1955; m. Emily Jane Antal, June 7, 1958; children—L. Michael, Louis A., Laura A., James C. Transmission corrosion engr. Manufactures Light & Heat Co., Pitts., 1955-64; corrosion engr. Columbia Gas System-Pitts. Group Co., Pitts., 1964-68; project engr. Columbia Gas Systems Service Corp., Marble Cliff, Ohio, 1968-73; mgr. Columbia Gas Distbn. Co., Columbus, Ohio, 1973—. Served with U.S. Navy, 1948-52. Mem. ASME, ASTM, Nat. Assn. Corrosion Engrs., Nat., Ohio socs. profl. engrs. Republican. Roman Catholic. Clubs: Brookside Civic Assn., Northington Athletic Assn. Home: 6666 McVey Blvd Worthington OH 43085 Office: 99 N Front St Columbus OH 43215

BULL, SHEELAGH GRAHAM, psychologist; b. Oliver, B.C., Can., Jan. 14, 1943; d. John Ibbotson and Stella Adair (Gilmer) Hope; came to U.S., 1968; B.A., U. B.C., 1965; M.A., U. Oreg., 1968, Ph.D., 1971; m. Christopher Neil Bull, Sept. 12, 1964; children—Catriona Hulley, Hillary Alexis. Sch. counsellor Burnaby, B.C., 1967-68; vis. asst. prof. psychology U. Ind., summer 1971; intern in child clin. psychology Kansas Univ. Med. Center, 1972-73; pvt. practice child psychology, Kansas City, Mo., 1973—. Certified psychologist, Kans., sch. psychologist, Mo. Mem. Am., Kans., Mo. psychol. assns., Soc. Pediatric Psychologists. Home: 438 Greenway Terr Kansas City MO 64113 Office: Suite 300 6314 Brookside Blvd Kansas City MO 64113

BULLARD, THOMAS ROBERT, retail book exec.; b. Chgo., May 6, 1944; s. Henry M. and Ethel (Munday) B.; B.S., Ill. Inst. Tech., 1966; M.A., Northwestern U., 1968; Ph.D., U. Ill. at Chgo. Circle, 1973. Teaching asst. history U. Ill. at Chgo. Circle, 1969-73; head nautical dept. Owen Davies, bookseller, Chgo., 1973—; instr. history Sch. Art Inst. Chgo., 1975-77; cons. in field. Nat. Merit scholar, 1961-62, Hon. Ill. State scholar, 1962. Mem. Am. Hist. Assn., Orgn. Am. Historians, U.S. Naval Inst., Internat. Naval Research Orgn., Navy Records Soc. (U.K.), Central Electric Railfans Assn., Electric Railroaders Assn., Chgo., Aurora & Elgin Electric Ry. Hist. Soc. Mem. United Ch. Christ. Home: 228 N Lombard Ave Oak Park IL 60302 Office: Owen Davies Bookseller 1214 N LaSalle St Chicago IL 60610

BULLARD, WADE ARTHUR, JR., corp. exec.; b. Wilmington, N.C., Jan. 23, 1931; s. Wade Arthur and Mildred (Anderson) B.; student Columbus U. (Washington), 1949-51; B.B.A., U. Mich., 1957; children—Linda Kay, Cynthia Ann. Pres. gen. mgr. Patterson's, Sturgis, Mich., 1957—, also dir.; v.p., dir. Clark Plastic Engring. Co., Sturgis, 1967-73; pres. dir. Plastek Co., 1968—, Colonial Motor Inn., Inc., 1964-76, Wade Bullard, Inc. chmn. bd. Aronco Plastics, Inc., 1974-75. (all Sturgis), 1969—; Mem. Sturgis Bd. Zoning Appeals, 1967—; Sturgis city commr., 1975—; dir. Bd. Pub. Works, St. Joseph County, 1976—; pres. Klinger Lake Assn., Sturgis, 1969-71; pres., mem. bd. dirs. Sturgis Improvement Assn., 1966—. Served with CIC, AUS, 1951-54; Korea. Decorated Bronze Star medal, UN Service medal, Nat. Def. Service medal. Episcopalian. Elk. Club: Klinger Lake Country (Sturgis). Home: Klinger Lake Sturgis MI 49091 Office: 1106 W Chicago St Sturgis MI 49091

BULLER, WESLEY DALE, sch. prin.; b. Goessel, Kans., Oct. 6, 1928; s. David D. and Lydia (Schmidt) B.; B.A., Southwestern Coll., 1951; M.S., Kans. State Coll., 1960; certificate adminstrn. Wichita State U., 1972; m. Joyce A. Lachenmaier, Aug. 7, 1952; children—Sandra Kaye, Debra Denise, Gregory Keith. Tchr., athletic coach Byers (Kans.) High Sch., 1954-55, Erie (Kans.) High Sch., 1955-60, Bethel Coll., North Newton, Kans., 1960-65; football coach, admissions counselor Friends U., Wichita, Kans., 1965-69, Southwestern Coll., Winfield, Kans., 1969-72; prin. Woodson County Sch. Dist. 366, Yates Center, Kans., 1972-76, Decatur Community Jr. High Sch., Dist. 294, Oberlin, Kans., 1976—. Pee Wee baseball coach Yates Center, 1974. Served with AUS, 1951-53. Mem. Fellowship Christian Athletes (pres. 1971), Kans., Nat. assns. elementary sch. prins., Nat., Kans. edn. assns., Nat. Assn. Inter-Collegiate Athletics. Rotarian (pres. 1974—). Home: PO Box 311 Oberlin KS 67749 Office: 605 E Commercial St Oberlin KS 67749

BULLIS, HAROLD OWEN, lawyer; b. Robinson, N.D., Oct. 2, 1923; s. Harold Edward and Clara (Hedahl) B.; student N.D. State Sch. Sci., 1941-42, Mo. Sch. Mines, 1943-44; A.B., Jamestown Coll., 1948; J.D., U. N.D., 1954; m. Dolores Jean Fuhrman, Sept. 7, 1952; children—Rebecca, John, James, Mark. Prin., coach Litchville (N.D.) High Sch., 1948-50; admitted to N.D. bar, 1954; law clk. U.S. Ct. of Appeals judge, Fargo, N.D., 1954; exec. sec. U.S. Senator from N.D., 1954-59; pvt. practice law, Wahpeton, N.D., 1959-69; U.S. atty. Dist. of N.D., Fargo, 1969—. States atty. Richland County, N.D., 1963-67; mem. N.D. Ho. of Reps., 1967-69. Chmn. Wahpeton United Fund, 1962; chmn. Richland County Republican Orgn., 1967; mem. Jamestown Coll. Alumni Bd. Served with AUS, 1943-45. Decorated Purple Heart with cluster. Mem. Order of Coif. Methodist. Mason,

Elk, Eagle, Kiwanian (pres. Wahpeton club 1967). Editor in chief N.D. Law Rev., 1954. Home: 909 Southwood Dr Fargo ND 58102 Office: US Fed Bldg and Court House Fargo ND 58102

BULLOCH, JAMES, assn. exec.; b. Highland Park, Mich., June 3, 1933; s. Andrew James and Margaret Napier (Hodge) B.; B.B.A., U. Mich., Ann Arbor, 1955, M.B.A., 1957; Ph.D. (Herman Miller scholar), Ohio State U., 1961; m. Davette Mary Britton, Sept. 4, 1954; children—Sandra Lea, Ann Elizabeth, Robert Alan. Staff accountant Gregg Velker & St. John, Ann Arbor, 1954-57; instr. accounting Ohio State U., Columbus, 1957-60; lectr. accounting U. Mich., 1960, asst. prof., 1961-65, asso. prof., 1965-71, prof., 1972, adj. prof., 1974—; dir. Inst. Mgmt. Accounting of Nat. Assn. Accountants, Ann Arbor, 1972—. Treas. council Huron Valley Girl Scouts U.S.A., 1963-69. C.P.A., Mich. Mem. Nat. Assn. Accountants, Am. Inst. C.P.A.'s, Am. Accounting Assn., Mich. Assn. C.P.A.'s. Author: Defense Contract Costing: State of the Art, 1972. Asso. editor Mgmt. Accounting, 1977—. Home: 2006 Mershon St Ann Arbor MI 48103 Office: 570 City Center Bldg Ann Arbor MI 48104

BULLOCK, JOSEPH DANIEL, pediatric allergist; b. Cin., Jan. 23, 1942; s. Joseph Craven and Emilie (Woide) B.; B.A., Wittenberg U., 1963; M.D., Ohio State U., 1967; m. Martha Ann Foss, June 20, 1964; children—Jennifer Zane, Sarah Harrison. Intern, Ohio State U. Hosp., Columbus, 1967-68, resident in pediatrics, 1968-69; fellow in pediatric allergy immunology U. Calif., San Francisco, 1969-71; practice medicine specializing in pediatric allergy immunology, Columbus, Ohio, 1971—; clin. asst. prof. pediatrics Ohio State U., Columbus, 1971—. Recipient Clemens von Pirquet award, 1968, 69, 70, 71; Allergy Found. Am. scholar, 1966; Mead Johnson scholar, 1968. Mem. Am. Acad. Allergy, Am. Acad. Pediatrics. Republican. Lutheran. Contbr. papers on allergy to med. jours. Office: 85 E Wilson Bridge Worthington OH 43085

BULTEMA, JOHN HENRY, corp. exec.; b. Muskegon, Mich., June 19, 1923; s. Harry and Dena (Kuiper) B.; ed. Muskegon pub. schs.; m. Elizabeth Jane Rosema, Mar. 1, 1944; children—Mary Beth Bultema Lobbezoo, Barbara Bultema Pennell, John Henry II, Ann Bultema Jackson, Carol J. Bultema Millman, Thomas J., Elizabeth, James, Paul. Pres., dir. Bultema Dock & Dredge Co., Muskegon, from 1947; chmn. Manisteel, Inc., from 1954, B.I.C. Corp., 1960-75; dir. Manistee Bank & Trust Co. (Mich.), Muskegon Bank & Trust Co., Farms of Mich., By-Lake Corp., Moonlite Motel Corp. Mem. Inst. Creation research expdn. to Turkey, 1972. Dir. Grace Bible Coll., 1968—, Grace Youth Camp, 1960—. Served with USNR, World War II. Mem. Manistee C. of C. (pres. 1957-58). Republican. Mem. Berean Ch. Rotarian (pres. 1956-57). Patentee underwater pipeline constrn. Home: 625 Seminole St Muskegon MI 49441 Office: 1060 Judson St Spring Lake MI 49456 also 1920 Lakeshore Dr Muskegon MI 49441

BULTHUIS, JAMES HOWARD, real estate appraiser; b. Chgo., Oct. 16, 1939; s. Henry and Gertrude (Sterenberg) B.; student Calvin Coll., Grand Rapids, Mich., 1957-59, Elmhurst (Ill.) Coll., 1960; m. Claudia Blair, June 1, 1968; children—Matthew Reese, Allen Barton. Salesman, Warren Realty, Hillside, Ill., 1965-67; real estate appraiser, mgr. spl. properties dept. appraisal div. St. Paul Fed. Savs. & Loan Assn., Chgo., 1967-74; sr. appraiser Harris Bank, Chgo., 1974—; dir. Hillside Disposal Service Inc. Served with AUS, 1962-64. Mem. Am. Inst. Real Estate Appraisers (sr. real property appraiser), Soc. Real Estate Appraisers (dir. Ill. chpt. 6, 1977—). Republican. Mem. Christian Reformed Ch. Home: 526 N Catherine St LaGrange Park IL 60525 Office: 111 W Monroe St Chicago IL 60640

BUMGARDNER, BEVERLY MARANEY, sch. counselor; b. Uniontown, Pa., Oct. 10, 1932; d. Nicholas Vincent and Isobel Marie (Bearzi) Maraney; B.S. in Edn., W. Va. U., 1954; M.Ed., Cleve. State U., 1977; m. James I. Bumgardner, June 23, 1956; children—Daniel James, Richard Alan. Tchr. elementary sch., Lakewood, Ohio, 1954-56, Willoughby, Ohio, 1959-61, Perry, Ohio, 1964-67, Painesville, Ohio, 1969-75; counselor elementary sch., Painesville Bd. of Edn., 1975—. Active Fair Housing Bd. of Painesville, 1971-76. Mem. Am., Ohio personnel and guidance assns., Ohio Sch. Counselors Assn. Republican. Roman Catholic. Clubs: AAUW. Home: 254 Cumings Rd Painesville OH 44077 Office: 200 W Walnut St Painesville OH 44077

BUMP, MILO SHANNON, packing co. exec.; b. Topeka, Kans., Oct. 26, 1922; s. Wilson Raymond and Pearle Julia (Pickering) B.; m. Reba Mae McCaleb, July 19, 1974; 1 son, Shannon Kevin. Parts and material handler Boeing Airplane Co., Wichita, Kans., 1942-47, expediter, 1947-52, sr. supr., exptl. prodn. control, 1952-55, programmer, analyst, 1955-60; systems analyst Martin-Marietta Co., Denver, 1960-62; mgr. engring. systems Gen. Electric Co., Huntsville, Ala., 1962-66, internal cons. systems, Phoenix, 1967-69; sr. cons. Computer Scis. Corp., St. Louis, Chgo. and London, 1969-71; mgr. data processing Du Quoin Packing Co. (Ill.), 1971—. Served with USAAF, 1942-45; ETO. Mem. St. Louis Honeywell Users Group (past treas.). Home: 207 S 3d St Elkville IL 62932 Office: PO Box 186 Du Quoin IL 62832

BUMP, WILBUR NEIL, lawyer; b. Peoria, Ill., July 12, 1929; s. Wilbur Earl and Mae (Nelson) B.; B.S., State U. Iowa, 1951, J.D., 1958; m. Elaine Bonneval, Nov. 24, 1951; children—William Earl, Jeffrey Neil, Steven Bonneval. Admitted to Iowa bar, 1958; asst. corp. counsel Meredith Pub. Co., Des Moines, 1958-59; asst. city atty. City of Des Moines Legal Dept., 1959-61; solicitor gen. Iowa Atty. Gen. Office, Des Moines, 1961-64; practiced in Des Moines, 1964—. Mem. bd. advisers Salvation Army. Served with USAF, 1951-54. Mem. Am., Iowa (bd. govs. 1976—), Polk County (pres. 1976-77) bar assns. Club: Kiwanis (pres. 1974-75). Presbyterian (elder). Home: Route 2 Winterset IA 50273 Office: 712 Financial Center Des Moines IA 50309

BUMPUS, F(RANCIS) MERLIN, biochemist; b. Rome, Ky., Dec. 6, 1922; s. Francis Xavier and Bertha G. (Robertson) B.; B.S., Purdue U., 1944; M.S., U. Wis., 1947, Ph.D., 1949; m. Hazel Smith, June 21, 1947; children—Peter B., Roger N. Staff research div. Cleve. Clinic Found., 1949-61, asst. dir. research div., 1961-66, sci. dir. cardiovascular research program, 1966-67, chmn., sci. dir. research div., 1968-71, chmn. research div., 1971—; mem. study sect. NIH; adj. prof. Cleve. State U. Recipient Purdue Frederick award 1967, Stouffer award, 1968. Mem. Am. Chem. Soc., AAAS, Am. Soc. Biol. Chemists, Swiss Chem. Soc., Am. Heart Assn. (council high blood pressure research), Am. Soc. Nephrology, Soc. Exptl. Biology and Medicine. Editor: (with I.H. Page) Handbook of Experimental Pharmacology, Vol. 37, 1973. Home: 75 Winterberry Ln Chagrin Falls OH 44022 Office: 9500 Euclid Ave Cleveland OH 44106

BUNGE, ROBERT PIERCE, educator; b. Oak Park, Ill., Sept. 24, 1930; s. George Herbert and Caroline Elizabeth (Pierce) B.; Ph.M., Roosevelt U., 1973; Ph.D., DePaul U., 1975; m. Muriel Perlman, Mar. 17, 1956; step-children—Harmon Berns, Hilary Berns. Tchr. adult evening sch. Maine Twp., Park Ridge, Ill., 1962-74; with Bunge Movers, Evanston, Ill., 1968-72; lectr. Roosevelt U., Chgo., 1971, 73, DePaul U., Chgo., 1974—. Lectr., women's groups, bus. groups; commencement speaker N. Shore Country Day Sch., Winnetka, Ill., 1974. Served with AUS, 1952-54; PTO. Mem. Internat. Platform Assn., Am. Philos. Assn., Theosophical Soc. Author: Sioux Language Phrase Book, 1976. Contbr. articles to profl. jours. Home: 215C Dodge St Evanston IL 60202 Office: Philosophy Dept DePaul U 2323 N Seminary Ave Chicago IL 60614

BUNGER, DARWIN LEE, lawyer; b. New Hampton, Iowa, Nov. 5, 1940; s. William Herman and Vera (Straw) B.; student Wartburg Coll., 1958-61; B.A., U. No. Iowa, 1963; J.D., U. Ia., 1966; m. Judith Kay Ward, Aug. 18, 1963; children—Chad William, Michele Ann, Jason Ward. Admitted to Iowa bar, 1966; asso. firm Wunschel & Schechtman, Carroll, Iowa, 1966-69; sole practice, Carroll, 1969-70; partner firm Kurth & Bunger, Carroll, 1970—. Mem. 3d Precinct Republican Com., 1968—; city councilman, 1974—. Mem. Am. (mem. Am. citizenship com. 1969-72), Iowa (chmn. bridge-the-gap com. 1973-74, mem. exec. com. young lawyers sect. 1974—, chmn. law related edn. com. 1976—), Carroll County (sec. treas. 1967-72) bar assns., Am. Trial Lawyers Assn., Iowa Assn. Trial Lawyers. Lutheran. Atty. for plaintiff in Bunger vs. IHSAA land mark case, 1972. Home: 629 Hidden Valley Rd Carroll IA 51401 Office: 225 E 7th St Carroll IA 51401

BUNN, STUART EASTHAM, mech. equipment mfg. co. exec.; b. Atchison, Kans., May 26, 1919; s. George Peter and Helen (Eastham) B.; student Coll. of Wooster, 1937-38; B.S., Kans. U., 1942; m. Jeanne Frances Brock, Feb. 19, 1944; children—James S., Steven E., Jennifer Lynn. Design engr. J.F. Pritchard & Co., Kansas City, Mo., 1946-51; mfg. rep. S.E. Bunn Co., Prairie Village, Kans., 1951-60; pres. Ball Valve Co., Shawnee Mission, Kans., 1960—, also chmn. bd.; dir. RBBKT&H Investors, Inc., Tulsa. Served to 1st lt. USAAF, 1943-46. Mem. ASME, Refrigeration Engrs. and Technicians Assn. (dir. 1972), Beta Theta Pi. Republican. Presbyterian. Clubs: Brookridge Country (Overland Park, Kans.); Engineers (past pres.) (Kansas City). Patentee in field. Home: 9124 Delmar St Prairie Village KS 66207 Office: PO Box 388 Shawnee Mission KS 66201

BUNTE, FREDERICK JOSEPH, educator; b. Columbus, Ohio, Dec. 19, 1937; s. Fred Joseph and Margaret Louise (Murday) B.; m. Judith Schueneman, June 27, 1964; children—Susan, Rebecca. B.S., Ohio State U., 1959, M.A., 1964, Ph.D., 1972; A.S.B.A., Franklin U., 1974. Chmn., tchr. social studies Upper Arlington St. High Sch., Columbus, Ohio, 1959-65; instr. sociology Franklin U., Columbus, 1965-72, prof., chmn. div. social and behavioral sci., 1972-74, dean Gen. Coll., 1974—, dean academic affairs, 1975—. Edn. chmn. Clintonville-Beechwold (Ohio) Human Relations Council, 1972-73. Mem. Am. Sociol. Assn., Am. Assn. for Higher Edn., Nat. Council for Social Studies. Clubs: Kiwanis, Met. (Columbus). Home: 287 Frontenac Pl Worthington OH 43085 Office: 201 S Grant Ave Columbus OH 43215

BUNTING, THOMAS GEORGE, chemist; b. Wheeling, W.Va., Nov. 2, 1941; s. Thomas B. and Elsie Elizabeth (Koler) B.; B.S., Wheeling Coll., 1963; Ph.D. (NDEA fellow), Kans. State U., 1966; m. Janet Mary Setler, Aug. 29, 1964; children—Christine Marie, Karen Elizabeth, Kimberly Maureen. Chemist, Esso Research & Engring. Co., Linden, N.J., 1966-68; staff scientist Chase Brass & Copper Co., Cleve., 1968-72; sect. head analytical research dept. Ross Labs., Columbus, Ohio, 1972—. Mem. Am. Chem. Soc., Am. Conservative Union, Citizens for Republic, Young Ams. for Freedom, Phi Lambda Upsilon. Patentee in field. Home: 4624 Northtowne Blvd Columbus OH 43229 Office: 625 Cleveland Ave Columbus OH 43216

BUOY, HAROLD JOSEPH, trade union ofcl.; b. Sadorus, Ill., July 30, 1921; s. Charles Andrew and Orpha Helena B.; grad. high sch.; student trade union program, Harvard; m. Mary Eileen Rairden, Oct. 1, 1943. Pres., gen. chmn. dist. 24 Internat. Brotherhood of Boilermakers, Iron Shipbuilders, Blacksmiths, Forgers & Helpers, AFL-CIO, 1949, dist. rep., Washington, 1950-53, Internat. Hdqrs., Kansas City, Kan., 1953-56, Washington, 1956, internat. rep., 1959, del. to Japan, 1960, legis. asst. to internat. pres., 1962, mem. nat. legis. council AFL-CIO, 1963, rep. of Internat. Brotherhood to Internat. Metal Workers Fedn., 1963, acting internat. pres., 1970, internat. pres., 1970—, elected pres., 1973—; chmn. bd. dirs. Brotherhood State Bank. Served with AUS, World War II. Decorated Bronze Star medal. Mem. Am. Royal Assn. (bd. govs.). Home: 7827 Walker Kansas City KS 66112 Office: 570 NB Bldg 8th Ave at State Kansas City KS 66101

BURACK, SAMUEL, psychiatrist; b. Chgo., Jan. 14, 1912; s. Hyman and Ida (Glasser) B.; B.S., U. Ill., 1934, M.D., 1936; m. Hynda S. Busch, Nov. 24, 1940; children—Robert C., Robyn H. Intern, Cook County Hosp., Chgo., 1937-38; resident Ill. Psychiatry and Neurology Inst., Chgo., 1940-41, 46; resident State Hosp., Kankakee, 1938-41; trainee Chgo. Inst. for Psychoanalysis, 1953-59; practice psychiatry, Chgo., 1946—; acting supt. Chgo. Community Clinic, 1946-50; asst. to chief med. officer Ill. Dept. Pub. Welfare, Chgo., 1951-52; asst. to dep. dir. Mental Health Service, Chgo., 1952-53; attending physician psychiatry West Side VA Hosp., Chgo.; clin. asso. prof. psychiatry Chgo. Med. Sch., 1953-69, U. Ill. Med. Sch., Chgo., 1969—. Served to capt. AUS, 1941-45. Diplomate Am. Bd. Psychiatry and Neurology. Fellow Am. Psychiat. Assn. Home: 5828 N St Louis Ave Chicago IL 60659 Office: 166 E Superior St Chicago IL 60611

BURBRIDGE, G(EORGE) WINSTON, assn. exec.; b. Grand Rapids, Apr. 7, 1918; s. Harry C. and Grace M. (OHearn) B.; student Grand Rapids Jr. Coll., 1936-37; B.A., U. Mich., 1940; m. Florence R. Garrett, July 11, 1942; children—Gary Wynn, Patricia Jane. Cost accountant Wolverine Brass Co., Grand Rapids, 1940-42; sales rep. Universal Atlas Cement Co., Mich. territory, 1944-55; exec. v.p. Builders Exchange of Grand Rapids and Western Mich., 1955—; exec. dir. Greater Mich. Home and Garden Show, 1955—. Mem. Citizens Adv. Council for Civic Improvement, Grand Rapids. Bd. dirs. John Ball Zool. Soc., local chpt. ARC; past pres. The Bridge; mem. planning bd., budget com. United Fund and Community Services. Served with AUS, 1942-44. Mem. Am. Soc. Assn. Execs., Mich. Assn. Execs., Grand Rapids Safety Council (bd. mem.), Internat. Builders Exchange Execs. (past pres.), Nat. Assn. Pub. Expn. Mgrs. (past pres.). Rotarian. Clubs: Blythfield Country. Contbr. articles to profl. jours. Home: 2042 Parade Dr NW Grand Rapids MI 49505 Office: 4461 Cascade Rd SE Box 2031 Grand Rapids MI 49501

BURBRIDGE, ROGER JAMES, guidance counselor; b. Manchester, Iowa, Mar. 11, 1944; s. Will F. and Helen C. (McMahon) B.; B.S., Upper Iowa Coll., 1965; M.A., U. No. Iowa, 1970; m. Diane Marie Gordon, Aug. 10, 1974; children—James Christopher, Kevin William. Tchr., coach Garwin (Iowa) Community Schs., 1965-71; counselor, coach Alburnett (Iowa) Community Schs., 1971—. Dir., Alburnett Basketball camp, 1976; bd. dirs. Garwin Community Club, 1967. Recipient Community Service to Youth plaque, Garwin Community Club, 1971. Mem. Alburnett Edn. Assn., Garwin Edn. Assn., NEA, Ia. Edn. Assn., Ia. Personnel and Guidance Assn., Am. Personnel and Guidance Assn. Roman Catholic. Address: Route 1 Alburnett IA 52202

BURCH, JOHN ELLIS, obstetrician, gynecologist; b. Jackson, Ga., Dec. 12, 1915; s. John W. and Kathryn H. B.; B.S., U. Mich., 1937, M.D., 1941; m. Helen R. Stultz, Sept. 1, 1937. Intern, Wayne U. Med. Sch., Detroit, and Detroit Receiving Hosps., 1941-42, resident in obstetrics gynecology, 1941-45; practice medicine specializing in obstetrics gynecology, Joplin, Mo., 1947-77; chief of staff, head of dept. Freman Hosp., 1953, 67-68, mem. ednl. com., 1977—; chief of staff, head of dept. St. Johns Hosp., 1952—; mem. Am. Com. Maternal Welfare. Served to capt. M.C. AUS, World War II. Diplomate Am. Bd. Obstetrics Gynecology. Mem. Jasper County (Mo.) Med. Soc. Methodist. Office: 200 Medical Arts Bldg Joplin MO 64801

BURCHARD, MAX NORMAN, sociologist; b. Seward County, Kans., May 27, 1925; s. Charlie and Jenny Grace (Swink) Burchard; m. June Larsen, Sept. 11, 1948; children—Denise, Clyde, Marti, Norman, Melissa, Brett, Tracey. A.B., San Jose State Coll., 1949; A.M. (Alice Howard Frost scholar), U. Nebr., 1951, Ph.D. (Alice Howard Frost scholar in sociology), 1955. Instr., U. Omaha, 1952-54, Chico State Coll., 1954-55; asst. prof., dept. chmn. Marietta Coll., 1955-60; asst. prof. U. N.D., 1960-62, asso. prof. and dept. chmn., 1962-64; asso. prof. and dept. chmn. Moorhead (Minn.) State Coll., 1964-68; prof., dept. chmn. sociology Iowa Wesleyan Coll., Mt. Pleasant, 1968-75, asst. dean, 1969-70, chmn. dept. behavioral scis., 1975—. Bd. trustees First Unitarian Ch., Marietta, Ohio, 1958-60; pres., Planned Parenthood of Henry County, Iowa, 1971-76; sec., Planned Parenthood of S.E. Iowa, 1974-75, treas., 1975—; bd. dirs. Henry County Izaak Walton League. Mem. Am., Iowa (sec.-treas. 1976—) sociol. assns., Midwest Sociol. Soc. (bd. dirs. 1963-64), AAUP (Iowa Wesleyan chpt. pres. 1972-73), Soc. Study Social Problems. Author: Sociology, 1967. Home: 307 Poplar St Mt Pleasant IA 52641 Office: Iowa Wesleyan College Mt Pleasant IA 52641

BURCHFIELD, JOHN CLARENCE, anesthesiologist, educator; b. Holland, Ohio, May 28, 1935; s. Clarence Donovan and Anna Evelyn (Farnsworth) B.; B.S., Mich. State U., 19S7; M.D., Ohio State U., 1965; m. Janice L. Schad, July 29, 1958; children—John, Brenda. Intern, Toledo (Ohio) Hosp., 1965-66, resident in anesthesiology, 1966-68, mem. attending staff dept. anesthesia, 1968-69; mem. staff dept. anesthesia Ohio State U. Hosps., Columbus, 1969—, asst. prof. dept. anesthesia Ohio State U., 1969—, asst. prof. Sch. Allied Med. Professions, 1969—. Diplomate Am. Bd. Anesthesiologists. Fellow Am. Coll. Anesthesiologists; mem. Columbus Soc. Anesthesiologists (pres.), Ohio State U. Med. Soc. Republican. Mem. Ch. of Christ. Home: 5812 Rocky Rill Rd Worthington OH 43085

BURCHINAL, ALBERT WILLIAM, social work dir.; b. Connellsville, Pa., Oct. 6, 1920; s. John Henry and Anna Eliza (Gaster) B.; B.S. in Econs., Thiel Coll., 1952; M.S.W., U. Pitts., 1954, M.P.H., 1961; m. Katharina Berta Lutz, Nov. 10, 1948; children—John Robert, James Albert, Charles Stephen, William Leighton, David Lutz. Dir. family service dept. Luth. Community Services, Springfield, Ohio, 1954-60; med. social work research asso., birth defects clin. study center Children's Hosp., Columbus, Ohio, 1961-63; instr. Ohio State U. Sch. Social Work, Columbus, 1963-64; research dir. United Community Council, Columbus, 1964-68; project dir. div. adminstrn. on aging Ohio Dept. Mental Hygiene and Corrections, Columbus, 1968-69; coordinator mental retardation services Richland County Mental Health and Mental Retardation Bd., Mansfield, Ohio, 1969-70; dir. social services Mt. Vernon (Ohio) State Inst., 1970—; mem. central humanization com. Ohio Dept. Mental Health and Mental Retardation, 1973-75. Mem. tech. advisory com. Franklin County Regional Planning Commn., 1965-69; bd. dirs. Mid-Ohio Health Planning Council 1971—; mem. Columbus Met. Census Tract Com., 1964-69, Knox County Health Planning Council, 1971—, Knox County Mental Health Assn., 1971—, Knox County Assn. for Retarded Citizens, 1971—; mem. program and facilities coms. Columbus Met. Area Community Action Orgn., 1965-66; active Boy Scouts Am.; mem. Clark County com. Gov.'s Commn. on Aging, 1960; mem. Citizens' Advisory Com. Knox County Regional Planning Commn., 1973—, vice chmn., 1976—. Trustee Clark County Mental Health Assn., Planned Parenthood Clinic, Springfield. Served with U.S. Army, 1945-47. Mem. Nat. Assn. Social Workers (state com. Ohio chpt., exec. com., charter, chpt. chmn. med. and health services council 1963—, chpt. treas. 1968-69), Am. Assn. Social workers, Am. Assn. Med. Social Workers, Acad. Certified Social Workers, Am. Assn. Sex Educators, Counselors and Therapists, Luth. Welfare League Cent. Ohio (mem. family service advisory com. 1967-70), Luth. Conf. Social Concern, Nat. Conf. Social Welfare (life), Am. Assn. for Mental Deficiency, Ohio Assn. for Retarded Children, Mt. Vernon Area C. of C. Am. Pub. Health Assn., Ohio Welfare Conf., Alpha Phi Omega, Am. Legion. Rotarian. Lutheran (mem. Ohio dist. social service com. 1965-68). Home: 346 Illinois Ave Westerville OH 43081 Mailing Address: PO Box 622 Mt Vernon OH 43050

BURCKEL, NICHOLAS CLARE, archives dir., univ. adminstr.; b. Evansville, Ind., Aug. 15, 1943; s. Arthur Joseph and Anna Irene (Dorsey) B.; A.B., Georgetown U., 1965; M.A., U. Wis., Madison, 1967, Ph.D. (Ford Found. fellow), 1971; m. Lenore Mary Herriges, June 21, 1969. Asst. archivist U. Wis., Madison, 1971-72, dir. archives and area research center, Parkside, 1972—, exec. asst. to chancellor, Parkside, 1975—, chairperson U. Wis. system archives council, 1976—; v.p. Midwest Archives Conf., 1976-78. Mem. Soc. Am. Archivists (chairperson coll. univ. archives com.). Abstractor, Wis. Mag. History for Am.: History and Life, 1972—; book rev. editor Midwestern Archivist, 1973—. Home: 2422 West Lawn Ave Racine WI 53405 Office: Univ Wisconsin Parkside Kenosha WI 53141

BURD, LEO PAUL, patent lawyer; b. Dubuque, Iowa, Nov. 11, 1920; s. Leo Joseph and Helen (Tench) B.; student S.D. State Coll., 1939-40; A.B., U. S.D., 1943; J.D., Georgetown U., 1950; m. June Elaine Madsen, Dec. 28, 1954; children—Margareth Ann, Victoria Jennifer. Examiner, U.S. Patent Office, Washington, 1946-51; admitted to Minn. bar, 1954; patent lawyer Continental Oil Co., Ponca City, Okla., 1952-53; practiced in Mpls., 1953—; mem. firm Paul, Moore and Dugger, 1953-56, Moore, White and Burd, 1956-65, Braddock and Burd, 1965-66, Burd, MacEachron, Braddock, Bartz & Schwartz, 1967-68, Burd, Braddock & Bartz, 1968—. Dir. Kenwood Isles Area Assn., 1969-71. Mem. Mpls. Soc. Fine Arts, Walker Art Center, Friends of Pub. Library, Mpls. Symphony Assos. Served with USNR, 1943-46. Fellow AAAS; mem. Am., Minn., Hennepin County bar assns., Am., Minn. (gov. 1963-65, v.p. 1967-68, pres. 1968-69) patent law assns., Am. Judicature Soc., Minn. Meml. Soc. (dir. 1968—, v.p. 1970-73, pres. 1973-77), Patent Office Soc., Trademark Soc., Am. Chem. Soc., Minn. Acad. Sci. (dir. 1971-74), Am. First Day Cover Soc. (regional v.p. 1975—). Roman Catholic. Home: 2225 E Lake of the Isles Pkwy Minneapolis MN 55405 Office: Foshay Tower 821 Marquette Ave Minneapolis MN 55402

BURDEN, EARL, JR., city ofcl.; b. Clinton County, Ohio, May 25, 1927; s. Earl and Mary Elizabeth (Sturgeon) B.; grad. Bliss Bus. Coll.; student Traffic Inst., Northwestern U.; m. Jean Evelyn Burke, Apr. 26, 1947; children—Regina Lynn (Mrs. Edgar Swanson), Eric Jay. Mem. Columbus Police Dept., 1952—, now chief police. Served with USNR, 1945-46. Recipient award merit Columbus Bar Assn. Mem. Internat. (exec. com.), Ohio (chmn. legis. com.) assns. chiefs police, Fraternal Order Police. Methodist (adminstrv. bd. 1973—). Club: Kiwanis (Distinguished Service award Columbus), Mason. Home: 3676 Eisenhower Rd Columbus OH 43224 Office: 120 W Gay St Columbus OH 43215

BURDICK, BRUCE MEREDITH, psychiatrist, clinic adminstr.; b. Lansing, Mich., Dec. 27, 1925; s. Austin Frederick and Jessie Vena (Stabler) B.; B.A., Andrew's U., 1948; M.D., Loma Linda U., 1953; m. Jeanne Helen Hutchison, Sept. 14, 1947; children—Paul Meredith, Karl Douglas. Gen. rotating intern Los Angeles County Gen. Hosp., 1952-53; gen. practice medicine, Lynwood, Calif., 1953-54; physician, surgeon So. Calif. Edison Co., Los Angeles, 1954-57; fellow Menninger Sch. Psychiatry, resident psychiatry VA Hosp., Topeka, 1957-60; staff psychiatrist Kans. Neurol. Inst., Topeka, 1960-62; fellow psychiatry, delinquency and criminology Menninger Found., Topeka, 1962-64; staff psychiatrist Kans. State Reception and Diagnostic Center, Topeka, 1964-72; adminstrv. and clin. dir. Manhattan (Kans.) Psychiat. Clinic, 1972—; psychiat. cons. Riley County Juvenile Ct., Manhattan, 1972—; pres. med. staff Meml. Hosp., Manhattan, 1976; vice-chmn. Kans. Adult Authority, 1977—. Pres., Potwin Elementary Sch. PTA, 1969-70; explorer adviser Boy Scouts Am., 1969-74. Bd. dirs. Riley County Mental Health Assn. Served with USNR, 1945-46. Rotarian. Home: 611 Houston St Manhattan KS 66502 also 429 Greenwood Ave Topeka KS 66601 Office: 426 Houston St Manhattan KS 66502

BURDICK, QUENTIN NORTHROP, U.S. senator; b. Munich, N.D., June 19, 1908; s. Usher Lloyd and Emma (Robertson) B.; B.A., U. Minn., 1931, LL.B., 1932. Admitted to N.D. bar, 1932, practiced in Fargo, 1932-58; mem. 86th Congress, N.D. at large; member U.S. Senate from N.D., 1960—. Democrat. Home: 1110 S 9th St Fargo ND 58102 Office: Old Senate Office Bldg Washington DC 20510

BURDON, WILLIAM FONTAINE, advt. agy. exec.; b. Ware, Mass., Dec. 21, 1926; s. Paul P. and Dorothy S. (Schaninger) B.; Asso. B.A., Curry Coll., Boston, 1951; m. Leonora Foronda, Sept. 10, 1954; children—Susan Lee, Linda Marie. With NBC, 1952-54; exec. v.p., creative dir. Marvin Hult & Assos., advt., Peoria, Ill., 1955-61; pres. Burdon Advt., Inc., Peoria, 1962—. Mem. adv. bd. YWCA; bd. dirs. Central Ill. Landmark Found. Interactive Cable for Handicapped. Served with U.S. Army, 1945-47. Author published poetry. Home: 1827 W Sunnyview Dr Peoria IL 61614 Office: 207 Main St Bldg Peoria IL 61602

BURESH, ERNEST JOSEPH, banker; b. nr. Cedar Rapids, Iowa, Oct. 28, 1926; s. Joe and Emma Ann (Stanek) B.; B.S., Iowa State U., 1948; LL.B., State U. Iowa, 1957; m. Joanne Paulsen, Nov. 24, 1949; children—Wendy Sue, Sandra Jane. Admitted to Iowa bar, 1957; trust officer Mchts. Nat. Bank, Cedar Rapids, 1957-63; pres., dir. Citizens Savs. Bank, Anamosa, Iowa, 1963—; pres. City Nat. Bank, Cedar Rapids, 1967—, dir., 1966—; dir. Farmers Savs. Bank, Martelle, Iowa, Farmers Savs. Bank, Victor; pres., dir. Exchange State Bank, Springville, Iowa, Onslow Savs. Bank. Pres. Swisher (Iowa) Independent Sch. Dist., 1950-53; mayor Swisher, 1950-54. Bd. dirs., exec. com. Hall Found., Cedar Rapids; bd. dirs. U. Iowa Found.; pres., dir. Anamosa Devel. Corp.; bd. dirs., sec.-treas. Anamosa Community Hosp., Inc.; trustee, mem. exec. com., fin. com. Cornell Coll., Mount Vernon. Mem. gov.'s advisory commn. on Corrections Relief, 1976-77. Served to capt. AUS 1944-46. Mem. Iowa Bar Assn., Am. Legion. Republican. Presbyterian. Mason (32 deg. Shriner). Clubs: Fawn Creek Country (Anamosa); Cedar Rapids Country. Home: 311 N Ford St Anamosa IA 52205 Office: 215 E Main St Anamosa IA 52205

BURG, LAWRENCE EDWARD, stock broker; b. LaPorte, Ind., Apr. 2, 1913; s. Clifford Ash and Hazel D. (Russell) B.; student bus. coll., spl. courses Northwestern U., 1946-47; m. Mary Ewing Glickauf, Jan. 10, 1942; children—Kenneth, Bruce, Louise, Mary. Salesman, Commonwealth Edison Co., Chgo., 1931-32, dist. rep., 1937-51; salesman Burg. Typewriter Service, 1933, Williams & Meyer Co., 1934-35, Standard Oil Co. (Ind.), 1935-36; owner Minit-Fry Potato Co., 1951-54, pres., 1954-61; mgr. research dept., asst. sec. Wm. M. Tegtmeyer Co., 1961-65; registered rep., research cons., mut. funds specialist Woolard & Co., Chgo., 1965—; owner Minit Calculator; former partner St. Lawrence Chem. Products Co. Registered rep. Nat. Assn. Security Dealers. Served with AUS, 1941-45. Mem. Am. Security Council (nat. adv. bd.), Am. Contract Bridge League, Internat. Platform Assn., Am. Legion, U.S. Chess Fedn., Aerial Phenomena Orgn. Research, Nat. Investigation Com. on Aerial Phenomena, Toastmasters Internat. Christian Scientist (1st reader 1959-62, asst. com. on publ. for Ill. 1962—). Clubs: Homewood-Flossmoor Chess, Beverly Social. Home: 17752 Dixie Hwy Homewood IL 60430 Office: 135 S LaSalle St Chicago IL 60603

BURG, MACLYN PHILIP, historian; b. Hoquiam, Wash., Jan. 30, 1927; s. LeRoy Peter and Beatrice Norma (McKay) B.; B.A., U. Wash., 1951, M.A. (NSF fellow), 1967, Ph.D., 1971; m. Patricia Ann Kelsey, Aug. 26, 1950; children—Jacquelyn, Kerry, Alan, Scott. Tchr., Longview (Wash.) pub. schs., 1951-65; instr. U. Wash., Seattle, 1966-70; oral historian, Dwight D. Eisenhower Library, Abilene, Kans., 1970—; lectr. Am. sect. Inst. of Gen. History, Acad. of Scis. of USSR, 1973; asst. dir. NDEA Summer Inst., U. Wash., 1966, 68. Served with U.S. Army, 1945-46. Mem. Orgn. of Am. Historians, Am., So. hist. assns., Kans. State Hist. Soc., Orders and Medals Soc. of Am., Royal Norfolk Regiment Assn. (hon. mem.), Phi Alpha Theta. Contbr. articles and revs. on history to scholarly jours.; editorial bd. Oral History Rev., 1974—. Home: 514 NW 3rd St Abilene KS 67410 Office: Dwight D Eisenhower Presidential Library Abilene KS 67410

BURGER, GEORGE VANDERKARR, wildlife biologist; b. Woodstock, Ill., Jan. 22, 1927; s. Irwin Louis and Nettie Anna (Vanderkarr) B.; B.S., Beloit Coll., 1950; M.S., U. Calif., 1952; Ph.D., U. Wis., 1958; m. Jeannine Ingram Willis, June 23, 1949; children—Suzanne Linda, Christine Melissa, Nancy Willis. Tchg. asst., biology, U. Calif., Berkeley, 1950-52; instr. life sci., Contra Costa Jr. Coll., Richmond, Calif., 1952-54; fellow Wisc. Alumni Research Found., U. Wisc., Madison, 1954-58; field rep. Sportsmen's Service Bureau, LaCrosse, Wisc., 1958-62; mgr. wildlife Remington Arms Co., Chestertown, Md., 1962-66; gen. mgr. Max McGraw Wildlife Found., Dundee, Ill., 1966—. Mem. Kane County (Ill.) Regional Planning Commn., 1975—. Served with U.S. Army, 1945-46. Recipient Nature Conservancy award, 1954; Green Trees award Milw. Green Trees Club, 1958. Mem. Wildlife Soc., Am. Fisheries Soc., Izaak Walton League of Am., Nat. Wildlife Fed., Assn. Great Lakes Outdoor Writers, Outdoor Writers Assn. Am., Sigma Xi. Congregationalist. Club: Kiwanis Internat. Author: Practical Wildlife Mgmt., 1973; editor Wildlife Soc. Bulletin, 1972-75; asso. editor Shooting Times Magazine, 1968—. Home: 1766 Country Knolls Ln Elgin IL 60120 Office: PO Box 194 Dundee IL 60118

BURGER, HENRY G., anthropologist; b. N.Y.C., June 27, 1923; s. B. William and Terese R. (Felleman) B.; B.A. with honors (Pulitzer scholar), Columbia U., 1947, M.A., 1965, Ph.D. in Anthropology (State doctoral fellow), 1967. Indsl. engr. with various firms, 1947-51; mfrs. rep., 1952-55; social sci. cons., N.Y.C., 1956-67; lectr. innovational strategy City Coll., City U. N.Y., 1957-65; anthropologist Southwestern Co-op. Ednl. Lab., Albuquerque, 1967-69; adj. prof. U. N.Mex., Albuquerque, 1969; asso. prof. anthropology and edn. U. Mo., Kansas City, 1969-73, prof., 1973—, founding mem. univ.-wide doctoral faculty, 1974—; anthrop. cons. VA, Kansas City, Mo., 1971-72. Served to capt. AUS, 1943-46. NSF research grantee, 1970. Fellow Am. Anthrop. Assn. (life), Council on Anthropology and Edn., Soc. Applied Anthropology, Current Anthropology, AAAS, Internat. Union Anthrop. and Ethnol. Scis., World Acad. Art and Sci., Royal Anthrop. Inst. Gt. Britain and Ireland (life); mem. Soc. Med. Anthropology, Semiotic Soc. Am., Soc. Profl. Anthropologists, Am. Ethnol. Soc., Internat. Founds. of Edn. Soc., AAUP, Central States Anthrop. Soc., Assn. Internationale pour la Recherche. . .des Methodes. . .Structuro-Globales, Soc. for Gen. Systems Research (chpt. pres. 1963-64, dir. 1964-68), Phi Beta Kappa. Author: Ethno-Pedagogy, 1st, 2d edits., 1968; contbr. articles to profl. publs., also manuscript referee; adv. editor Anthropology and Edn. Quar., 1975—. Home: 7306 Brittany Shawnee Mission KS 66203 Office: U Mo Kansas City MO 64110

BURGER, RICHARD ALLEN, photographer; b. Milw., Oct. 26, 1941; s. James George and Catherine (Schwandt) B.; Asso. in Applied Sci. Photography, Milw. Tech. Coll., 1961; m. Mary Elizabeth Kane, June 22, 1968; children—Kathleen Mary, Matthew James. Free-lance photographer, Milw., 1965—. Served with USAF, 1961-65. Recipient 100 Best award Milw. Soc. Communicating Arts, 1973. Mem. Wis. Indsl. Photographers, Profl. Photographers Am., Illustrators and Designers Mils. Eagle. Address: 2127 S 102d St West Allis WI 53227

BURGERT, ALFRED LELAND, banker; b. Lawrence, Kans., Mar. 14, 1924; s. Alfred Leander and Myrtle Alma (Atkinson) B.; student Sterling Coll., 1942, Muskingum Coll., 1943; B.S., U. Kans., 1948, J.D., 1950; diploma Stonier Grad. Sch. Banking of Rutgers U., 1964; m. Betty Jane Koontz, Aug. 21, 1946; children—Maretta Kay, Alfred Lee, Philip Lynn. With 1st State Bank & Trust Co., Pittsburg, Kans., 1950—, exec. v.p., chief exec. officer, 1972-73, pres., chief exec. officer, 1973—, trust officer, dir., 1967—. Trustee Pittsburg YMCA, also past pres.; bd. dirs. Mid-Am., YMCA, treas. Mt. Carmel Hosp. Planning Com.; mem. Pittsburg Pub. Library Bd.; pres. Kans. State Coll. of Pittsburg Endowment Assn., 1975-77. Served with AUS, 1943-46. Mem. Kans. Bankers Assn. (past pres. trust div., past exec. com.), Pittsburg C. of C. (pres. 1971-72), Kans., Crawford County bar assns., Phi Alpha Delta. Republican. Presbyterian (elder). Clubs: Lions (pres. Pittsburg 1965-66), Crestwood Country. Home: 1406 S Catalpa St Pittsburg KS 66762 Office: 417 N Broadway Pittsburg KS 66762

BURGERT, ERAN OMER, JR., pediatrician, hematologist, oncologist;b. Glasgow, Mo., Aug. 22, 1924; s. Eran Omer and Dessie Fern (Beeler) B.; M.D., U. Okla., 1947; M.S., U. Minn., 1953; m. Helen Louise Eifert, Sept. 5, 1948; children—Mark, Stephen, Carolyn. Intern, St. Luke's Hosp., Chgo., 1947-48; resident in pediatrics Mayo Grad. Sch., U. Minn., 1948-50, 52-53; asst. prof. Creighton U., 1953-57; mem. staff Mayo Clinic, Rochester, Minn., 1957—, prof. pediatrics Mayo Med. Sch.; Mem. Minn. adv. com. to Dept. Pub. Welfare, 1969—; advisor on childhood cancer Am. Cancer Soc., 1977. Served with USNR, 1950-52. Mem. AMA, Am. Acad. Pediatrics, Am. Soc. Hematology, Am. Soc. Clin. Oncology, Am. Assn. Cancer Research, N.W. Pediatric Soc., N.Y. Acad. Scis., Sigma Xi. Presbyterian. Contbr. articles profl. jours., chpts. in books. Research on protocol monitoring for acute leukemia treatment. Home: 2109 Lenwood Dr SW Rochester MN 55901 Office: Mayo Clinic Rochester MN 55901

BURGESS, HAROLD DEMPSTER, lawyer; b. Dundee, Ill., July 10, 1895; s. John W. and Sadie E. (Dempster) B.; ed. pub. schs., Beatrice, Neb.; student U. Colo., 1913-14, U. Neb., 1914-17, A.B., in Absentia, 1920; student U. Chgo., 1920-21; m. Mary Ellen Evans, Sept. 16, 1964. Admitted to Ill. bar, 1921, and since practiced in Chgo.; of counsel firm Spray, Price, Cushman, Keck, Mahin & Cate, 1934—. Mem. Am., Ill. State, Chgo., 7th Dist. bar assns., Legal Club Chgo., The Law Club. Republican. Episcopalian. Clubs: Metropolitan; Edgewood Valley Country (La Grange). Home: 300 E Claymoor Hinsdale IL 60521 Office: 134 S LaSalle St Chicago IL 60603

BURGESS, HERBERT EARL, JR., bldg. products, mfg. co. exec.; b. Orono, Me., Apr. 21, 1926; s. Herbert Earl and Edwidge May (Buribye) B.; grad. Windsor (Ont., Can.) Training and Reestablishment Inst., 1946; student Queens U., 1948, George Washington U., 1950-51; m. Loretta Marie Hebert, Oct. 3, 1948; children—Gary, Jill, Neil. Buyer, Acme White Lead & Color Works, Detroit, 1947; with Fenestra, Inc., 1947-62, clk., Detroit, 1948-49, office mgr., Washington, 1949-51, salesman, Cin., 1951-53, br. mgr., Louisville, 1953-57, regional mgr., Atlanta, 1957-62, div. mgr., Detroit, also Erie, Pa., 1962-65; v.p., gen. mgr. Berry Door Co., Ltd., Toronto, Ont., Can., 1965-69; v.p., gen. mgr. Stanley-Berry Ltd., Toronto, 1969-75; gen. mgr. Stanley Door Systems div. Stanley Works, Birmingham, Mich., 1969—, pres., 1975—; pres. Stanley Door Systems, Toronto, Ont., Can., 1969—; pres. Stanley Taymouth, Ltd., 1969—; v.p. The Stanley Works, New Britain, Conn., 1972—. Bd. dirs. Birmingham Community House Assn., 1974—, pres., 1976-77. Served with Royal Can. Elec. and Mech. Engrs., 1943-46. Mem. Door Operator and Remote Controls Mfrs. Assn. (dir. 1969-72), Insulated Steel Door Systems Inst. (dir. 1975, v.p. 1977), Birmingham Bloomfield C. of C. (pres. 1973, bd. dirs. 1970-73), Greater Detroit C. of C. Mason. Home: 3905 Oakland Dr Birmingham MI 48010 Office: 2400 E Lincoln Rd Birmingham MI 48012

BURGETTE, JAMES MILTON, dentist; b. Toledo, Aug. 18, 1937; s. James Martin and Louise (Milton) B.; A.B., Lincoln U., 1959; D.D.S., Howard U., 1964; m. Carolyn Harris, Aug. 24, 1963; children—Stephanie, James, Ngina. Practice dentistry, Detroit, 1967—. Dir. Morrison & Assos., Detroit. Sec. Wolverine Polit. Action Com., Detroit, 1971—. Mem. Detroit Pub. Sch. Health Council. Bd. dirs. Comprehensive Neighborhood Health Services; mem. coordinating council Black Christian Nationalist Ch.; mem. deacon bd. Shrine of Black Madonna; trustee Comprehensive Health Planning Council Southeastern Mich. Served to lt. Dental Corps, USNR, 1964-67. Mem. Nat. Dental Assn. (mem. ho. of dels., parliamentarian 1977), Wolverine Dental Soc. Mich. (editor news jour. 1971; recipient meritorious service award 1972, pres. 1976), Acad. Gen. Dentistry, Am. Profl. Practice Com., Howard Alumni Assn. (sec. 1969-70), Chi Delta Mu, Omega Psi Phi. Club: Masons. Home: 1660 Lincolnshire Dr Detroit MI 48203 Office: 5050 Joy Rd Detroit MI 48204

BURGFECHTEL, ROBERT FRANCIS, physician; b. Marshalltown, Iowa, Feb. 1, 1942; s. Francis L. and Lorraine R. Burgfechtel; student U. Notre Dame, 1960-63; M.D., U. Iowa, 1967; m. Bette Jo Tomhave, Aug. 14, 1965; children—Jeff, John. Intern, Hurley Hosp., Flint, Mich., 1967-68; practice family medicine, Red Cedar Clinic, Menomonie, Wis., 1970—; coroner Dunn County, 1975-76. Served in USAF M.C., 1968-70. Diplomate Am. Bd. Family Practice. Mem. AMA, Wis. Med. Soc., Am. Acad. Family Practice, Menomonie C. of C. (pres. 1978). Republican. Roman Catholic. Club: K.S. Home; 1015 River Heights Rd Menomonie WI 54751 Office: 2211 Stout Rd Menomonie WI 54751

BURGHER, LOUIS WILLIAM, physician, educator; b. Centerville, Iowa, Oct. 31, 1944; s. Wendell and Dorothy (Probasco) B.; B.S., U. Nebr., 1966, M.D. with honors, 1970, M.Med. Sci., 1972; m. Kathy Lynne Dworak, June 4, 1966; children—Tanya Jo, Tara Lynn, Lucas William. Intern U. Nebr. Coll. Medicine, 1970-71, resident in internal medicine, 1971-72; practice medicine, specializing in pulmonary medicine, Omaha, 1974—; NIH fellow in pulmonary diseases Mayo Grad. Sch. of Medicine, Rochester, Minn., 1972-74, asst. prof., 1974—; clin. research asso. in pulmonary disease U. Nebr. Coll. of Medicine, 1969-72; med. dir. of pulmonary medicine Bishop Clarkson Meml. Hosp., Omaha, 1974—; Tb cons. to Nebr. Dept. Health, 1972—. Med. dir. Nebr. Opportunity for Vols. in ACTION, 1971-72. Recipient Upjohn award Nebr. coll. Medicine, 1970. Diplomate Am. Bd. Internal Medicine, subsplty. bd. pulmonary medicine. Fellow Am. Coll. Chest Physicians; mem. AMA (council on med. edn. 1973-78), Nebr. Med. Assn. (com. on med. edn. 1971-72), Am. Thoracic Soc., Zumbro Valley Med. Soc. (exec. com. 1973-74), Univ. Med. Center House Officers Assn. (pres. 1971-72), Mayo Fellows Assn. (pres. 1973-74), Nat. Acad. Scis. (mem. task force study Inst. Medicine, mem. liaison com. on med. edn. 1974—). Contbr. articles on pulmonary disease to profl. jours. Home: 1014 5111 Plaza Omaha NE 68154 Office: Bishop Clarkson Meml Hosp Dewey Ave and 44th St PO Box 3328 Omaha NE 68103

BURGIN, LEONARD A., physician; b. Cin., Feb. 7, 1927; s. Samuel and Sylvia (Doll) B.; B.S., U. Cin., 1947, M.D., 1950; m. June Burgin, May 31, 1953; children—Lester Jay, Lynn Gail, Cynthia Rosa, Seth Louis. Intern, Kings County Hosp., 1950-51; jr. resident in medicine Cin. Gen. Hosp., 1951-52, jr. resident in pathology, 1952-53; sr. resident in medicine Boston City Hosp., 1953-54; fellow in medicine (hematology), instr. medicine Duke U. Sch. Medicine, 1954-55; fellow in hematology, blood research lab. New Eng. Center Hosp., Boston, 1955; practice medicine specializing in internal medicine and hematology, Cin., 1958—; mem. staff Holmes, Jewish, Bethesda, Deaconess, and Christ hosps.; asso. med. dir. Drake Meml. Hosp., 1977—; asso. clin. prof. medicine U. Cin. Served to capt. U.S. Army, 1955-57. Mem. A.C.P., Am. Soc. Hematology, AMA, Ohio Med. Assn., Acad. Medicine Cin., Cin. Soc. Internal Medicine, Phi Beta Kappa, Alpha Omega Alpha. Home: 6696 Fair Oaks Dr Cincinnati OH 45237 Office: 400 Melish Ave Cincinnati OH 45229

BURK, KEITH EUGENE, mgmt. cons.; b. Albion, Mich., May 31, 1941; s. Wilson Eugene and Ruth Elizabeth (Chamberlain) B.; B.S., Western Mich. U., 1969; m. Darlene Carole Nelson, Feb. 2, 1963; children—Linnea Ruth, Eric Eugene. Lab. technician U.S. Plywood (name now Champion Internat.), 1965-67, mgr. tech. engring., 1967-69, tech. service mgr., 1969-70; engring. mgr. Dover Corp., Portage, Mich., 1970-71; engr. A.B. Cassedy & Assos., Ridgefield, Conn., 1971-73, group engr., 1973-74, asst. chief, 1974-76, chief, 1976—. Mem. Kalamazoo Civic Theater, 1973—. Served with U.S. Army, 1961-63. Mem. Am. Mgmt. Assn., Am. Inst. Aeros. and Astronautics. Republican. Christian Scientist. Club: Coterie Dance. Patentee in field.

BURK, NORMAN, dentist; b. Dallas, Sept. 28, 1937; s. Rubin and Lena (Shodnisky) B.; B.S., Okla. U., 1959; D.D.S., U. Mo., 1952, grad. degree oral surgery, 1965; m. Beverly Rae Hyken, Aug. 27, 1961; children—Ronald, Steven. Practice dentistry specializing in oral surgery, Kansas City Mo., 1965—; chief oral surgery depts. Bapt. Meml. Hosp., Menorah Med. Center, 1972-73. Clin. asso. prof. oral surgery U. Mo. Sch. Dentistry, part time, 1969—; vol. oral surgeon Kansas City Golden Gloves; volunteer campaign worker Jewish Fedn., 1971—. Bd. dirs. Kehilath Israel Syngogue. Diplomate Am. Bd. Oral Surgery. Mem. Am., Dental Assn., Am., Midwestern, Kansas City (pres. 1974) socs. oral surgeons, Nat. Geographic Soc., Univ. Dental Study Club (pres. 1968-69), Alpha Epsilon Delta, Omicron Kappa Upsilon. Mem. B'nai B'rith. Home: 8400 Delmar Prairie Village KS 66207 Office: 701 E 63d St Kansas City MO 64110

BURK, WILLIAM CHARLES, railroad pub. relations rep.; b. Beaumont, Tex., Aug. 19, 1921; s. John Leonard and Dona (Robinson) B.; student Central State Coll., Edmund, Okla., 1939-42, Inst. Bus. Econs., U. So. Cal., 1955; m. Mary Irene Meyer, Aug. 19, 1945; children—John Paul, Donald William, Mary Catherine. Newspaper work in Okla. before World War II; system photographer A., T.S.F. Ry., Los Angeles, 1946-47, spl. rep. in Chgo., 1947-53, spl. rep. pub. relations, Topeka, Kans., 1953-61; mgr. pub. relations Santa Fe Ry. System, Chgo., 1961-73, v.p. pub. relations, 1973—. Trustee William Allen White Found. Mem. R.R. Pub. Relations Assn., Pub. Relations Soc. Am. (mem. seminar Cornell U., 1962), Pub. Relation Clinic, Soc. Am. Travel Writers, Am. Agrl. Editors Assn., Soc. Profl. Journalists, Sigma Delta Chi, Alpha Tau Omega. Republican. Episcopalian. Mason (Shriner). Clubs: Athletic, Press (Chgo.); Press, Kansas City (Kansas City, Mo.); Michigan Shores (Wilmette); Nat. Press (Washington). Home: 923 Cornell St Wilmette IL 60091 Office: 80 E Jackson Blvd Chicago IL 60604

BURKART, ARNOLD EMIL, educator; b. Medicine Hat, Alta., Can., Dec. 23, 1927; s. John and Marie (Dressler) B.; A.B., Fresno State U., 1954, M.A., 1958; Ed.D., Ind. U., 1973; m. Dorothy Lucille Conn, Aug. 13, 1950; children—Connie Arleen, Bradley Kevin. Tchr. music pub. schs. Fresno County, Calif., 1948-61; music supr. Madera, San Benito, Tulare counties, Calif., 1961-67; state music cons., Ind., 1971-72; prof. music edn. Ball State U., Muncie, Ind., 1967—. Vis. prof. San Francisco State U., 1967, Ind. U., 1970, Valdosta (Ga.) State Coll., 1969, Alverno (Wis.) Coll., 1968, Fla. Atlantic U., 1974. Pres., San Benito County Concert Assn., 1963; commr. Madera (Calif.) People to People Program, 1966-67. Bd. dirs. Tulare County Symphony Assn., 1961-62. Served with USAF, 1951-53. Mem. Orff-Schulwerk Assn. (pres. 1968-70, exec. sec. 1970-74), Music Educators Nat. Conf., Ind. Elementary Music Educators Assn. (pres. 1975-76). Editor, pub. Keeping Up with Music Education, 1973—. Contbg. author Growing with Music series, 1970. Home: 1220 Ridge Rd Muncie IN 47304

BURKE, BETSEY JANE, zool. adminstr.; b. S. Weymouth, Mass., Mar. 24, 1945; d. Harrison Lester and Helen (Langhorst) B.; B.S. in Animal Sci., U. Maine, 1967. Research asst. Jackson Lab., Bar Harbor, Maine, 1967-69; zoo attendant Kansas City Zoo, Mo., 1970-72, zoo attendant II, 1972-73, zool. curator, 1973—. Mem. Am. Assn. Zool. Parks and Aquariums, Am. Assn. Zoo Keepers. Home: 7401 E 79th St Kansas City MO 64138 Office: Kansas City Zoo Kansas City MO 64132

BURKE, ELDON RAY, educator; b. Walkerton, Ind., June 14, 1898; s. Albert Frederick and Lucy May (Freed) B.; A.B. Manchester Coll., 1922; M.A., U. Chgo., 1926, Ph.D., 1936; Litt.D., Manchester Coll., 1977, St. Francis Coll., 1975; m. Cecil Lula Davis, Sept. 18, 1924; 1 dau., Alice Virginia Burke Wend. Tchr., Marshall County (Ind.) pub. schs., 1916-18, 22-24; tchr. Ohio No. U., 1927-31, Shimer Coll., 1932-37, Ball State U., 1937-41; relief worker, dir. Brethren Service Commn., Europe, 1941-46; field rep., dir. CRALOG, Germany, 1946-51; field sec. Iraq Internat. Vol. Services, Inc., 1954-56; field sec. Manchester Coll., 1956-68; prof., chmn. dept. history St. Francis Coll., 1969—. Asia Soc. and Ind. U. grantee, 1960-64. Mem. Assn. Asian Studies, Am., Ind. hist. socs., Ind. Social Sci. Acad. Mem. Ch. of Brethren. Contbr. articles in field to profl. jours. Home: 402 N Mill St North Manchester IN 46962

BURKE, EMMETT CHARLES, educator; b. Montgomery, Ala., Jan. 30, 1920; s. William J. and Ethel (Scott) B.; A.B., B.S., Roosevelt U., 1945; M.A., Loyola U., 1953; M.Ed., DePaul U., 1954; O.D., Ill. Coll. Optometry, 1947; m. Sarah Scott, Aug. 14, 1949. Sr. caseworker

Ill. Pub. Aid Commn., Chgo., 1948-56; asst. prin. Wm. Carter Pub. Sch., Chgo., 1957—; asst. prof. Nat. Coll. of Edn., Chgo., 1969—; dir. Washington Pk. YMCA, Afro-Am. Family and Community Services. Active Nat. Urban League, NAACP. Served with USAAF, 1942-45. Certified social worker, Ill. Mem. Nat. Assn. of Black Profs. (dir.), Chgo. African-Am. Tchrs. Assn. (dir.), Chgo. Asst. Prins. Assn. (dir.), Chgo. Council for Exceptional Children (dir.), AAUP, NEA, Phi Delta Kappa. Clubs: Alpha Phi Alpha. Home: 601 E 32nd St Chicago IL 60616 Office: 5740 S Michigan Ave Chicago IL 60637

BURKE, ERWIN FREDERICK, audio-visual exec.; b. Knowlton, Wis., Oct. 27, 1916; s. Max E. and Tillie (Hartman) B.; grad. high sch.; m. Helen G. Toth, July 18, 1939; children—Allan Frederick, James Edwin. Owner, Burke's Motion Picture Co., South Bend, Ind., 1936-46; audio-visual dir. South Bend Sch. City, 1941-46; owner Burke's Audio-Visual Center, 1946-70, now pres. Burke's Audio-Visual Center, Inc. Audio-visual cons. for many sch. systems. Mem. South Bend Civic Planning Assn.; active Boy Scouts Am. Served with USNR, 1945-46. Mem. C. of C., NEA, Am. Soc. for Tng. and Devel., Nat. Audio-Visual Assn. (treas.), Gravel Lake Assn. (pres.). Presbyterian. Mason, Elk, Kiwanian (past pres.). Home: 3516 Woodmont Dr South Bend IN 46614 Office: 2207 S Michigan St PO Box 2799 South Bend IN 46680

BURKE, J(OHN) BRUCE, educator; b. Akron, Ohio, Sept. 23, 1933; s. Charles Mayhew and Esther (Plum) B.; A.B., Colgate U., 1955; M.Th., Union Theol. Sem., 1958; Ph.D. (Woodrow Wilson fellow), Syracuse U., 1963; m. Nancy Dobson, July 30, 1955 (div. Oct. 1974); children—Anne, Abigail, Sarah; m. 2d, Colleen J. Kahler, May 24, 1975. Instr., Syracuse (N.Y.) U., 1959-64; asst. prof. Mich. State U., East Lansing, 1964—, asso. prof. edn., 1967-69, prof., 1969—. Partner, Kagan/Burke Inc., 1974—. Cons. U.S. Office Edn., 1969-74, Ill. Office Supt. Pub. Instrn., 1973—. Rep., area United Way, 1973-75. Fulbright Hays fellow, 1965. Mem. AAUP, Nat. Assn. Humanities Edn. Presbyn. Author: Foundations of Christianity, 1970; Curriculum Designs for Competency Based Education, 1973; Influencing Human Interaction in Public Schools, 1976. Home: 430 W Jefferson St Grand Ledge MI 48837 Office: Coll Edn Mich State U East Lansing MI 48824

BURKE, MARGARET ROSE HOGLUND, educator; b. Chgo., Jan. 28, 1927; d. Gregory S. and Alice A. (O'Donnell) Hoglund; B.Ed., Chgo. Tchr.'s Coll., 1948; M.S., Chgo. State U., 1976; div.; children—Thomas, George, Jeanne, Donna. Tchr., Chgo. City Schs., 1948—, adjustment tchr., 1974—. Recipient Outstanding Educator award Mexican Community Comm., 1977. Mem. Am. Personnel and Guidance Assn. Roman Catholic. Home: 820 Elder Rd Apt C311 Homewood IL 60430 Office: 8255 S Houston St Chicago IL 60617

BURKE, MARIANNE, lawyer; b. Chgo., May 29, 1940; d. Walter James and Irene Georgia (Johnson) Burke; B.A., U. Ill., 1962; J.D., De Paul U., 1967; m. Harry Gerdy, Sept. 13, 1970. Admitted to Ill. bar, 1967; atty. Legal Aid Bur., Chgo., 1967-71; asst. pub. defender of Cook County, Chgo., 1971—, now supr. trial div. Mem. Chgo. Bar Assn., Lex Legio Soc. Democrat. Home: 5901 N Sheridan Rd Chicago IL 60660 Office: 2600 S California St Chicago IL 60608

BURKE, MICHAEL AUSTIN, ednl. adminstr.; b. Chgo., Oct. 14, 1937; s. Walter and Mary (Jennings) B.; B.A. in Philosophy, Kilroe Coll., 1960; S.T.L., Cath. U., 1965, M.A. in Mediaeval History, 1966. Ordained priest Roman Cath. Ch., 1963; treas., prof. preaching Sacred Heart Monastery, Hales Corners, Wis., 1965-71; dir. St. Joseph's Indian Sch., Chamberlain, S.D., 1971—; office mgr. Christian Preaching Conf., 1971-72, bd. dirs., 1970-74. Mem. Am., Cath. hist. assns., Acad. Polit. Sci. K.C. (4 deg.) (chaplain Bishop Henni Assembly 1967-69). Home: St Joseph's Indian Sch Chamberlain SD 57325 Office: St Joseph's Indian Sch Chamberlain SD 57325

BURKE, PAUL STANLEY, JR., ins. co. exec.; b. St. Paul, Aug. 5, 1926; s. Paul Stanley and Loretta Josephine (Bertrang) B.; B.B.A., U. Minn., 1956; m. Irene Marie Wagner, Apr. 22, 1950; children—John, Steven, Nancy, Lawrence, Linda, James, Thomas. Regional mgr. Minn. Mutual Life Ins. Co., Los Angeles, 1950-61; pres. Paul Burke & Assos., Inc., ins. consultants and adminstrs., Mpls., 1961-73, Trust Life Ins. Co. Am., Scottsdale, Ariz., 1968-73, Purchase & Discount Buying Service Corp., 1977—; dir. Lindbom & Assos., Inc., St. Paul. Pres., Boys Clubs of Mpls., 1974-76. Served with USAAF, 1944-47. Mem. Pilots Internat. Assn. (pres. 1966-73). Republican. Roman Catholic. Club: Mpls. Athletic. Home: 27 Circle W Edina MN 55436

BURKE, ROBERT DON, state ofcl.; b. Lansing, Mich., July 21, 1923; s. Frank and Minnie Emma (Paasch) B.; student Mich. State U., 1941-43, 46-48; m. Ione Elizabeth Murphy, Mar. 12, 1949; children—Robert D., Frank D., Patrick M. Auditor, Mich. Office Auditor Gen., Lansing, 1949-53; chief accountant Mich. Conservation Dept., Lansing, 1953-65, chief adminstrv. services div., 1965-73, chief mgmt. services, 1973—. Pres., Genesee Sch. PTA, 1964, 65; mem. Lansing Citizen's Adv. Com. on Ednl. Opportunity, 1965-66. Served with USAAF, 1943-46. Mem. Govtl. Accountants Assn., Conservation Bus. Mgmt. Assn. (pres. 1959), Mich. State Employees Assn. (sec. 1952), Mich. State U. Central Mich. Alumni Club. Lutheran (pres. 1950, 55, elder 1972-74). Home: 1700 Tecumseh River Dr Lansing MI 48915 Office: Dept Natural Resources Mason Bldg Lansing MI 48926

BURKE, ROBERT HARTLEY, credit card co. exec.; b. Englewood, N.J., Feb. 25, 1939; s. August and Helen (Hartley) B.; B.S. in Marketing, St. Peter's Coll., 1960; m. Cathleen A. Smyth, Apr. 4, 1964; children—Christine, Michael. Marketing rep. 3 M Co., St. Paul and N.Y.C., 1962-68; pension adminstr. Conn. Gen. Life, Bloomfield, 1968-69; marketing mgr. Banc Systems Assn., Cleve.,1969-70, dir. marketing, 1970-71, v.p., 1971—, sec., 1976—. Served to 1st lt. AUS, 1960-62. Mem. Am. Mgmt. Assn., Am. Inst. Banking, Am. Mktg. Assn., Bank Mktg. Assn. Office: 20325 Center Ridge Rd Rocky River OH 44116

BURKE, THOMAS STEPHEN, sch. adminstr.; b. Chgo., Dec. 13, 1922; s. Patrick Joseph and Bridget Josephine (Murphy) B.; B.Ed., Chgo. Tchrs. Coll., 1945; M.Ed., Loyola U., Chgo., 1955; m. Ruth Ellen Wendt, Aug. 23, 1947; children—Thomas Patrick, James William, John Joseph. Tchr., St. Rita High Sch., Chgo., 1945-47; tchr. Chgo. Pub. Schs., 1947-58, asst. prin. Beale Sch., 1951-61, prin., Deneen Sch., 1961-69, Englewood Evening Sch., 1966-68, Hubbard Evening Sch., 1968-71; pres. Chgo. Prins. Assn., Am. Fedn. Sch. Adminstrs., AFL-CIO, 1969-73; prin. Morgan Park High Sch., Chgo., 1973—. Sec. sch. adminstrs. and suprs. organizing com. AFL-CIO, 1971-76. Mem. Am. Assn. Sch. Adminstrs., Chgo. Prins. Assn., Ill. Prins. Assn., Nat. Assn. Elementary Sch. Prins., Nat. Assn. Secondary Sch. Prins., NEA, Am. Fedn. Sch. Adminstrs. (v.p. 1976—), Nat. Soc. for Study of Edn., Am. Inst. Parliamentarians (chpt. treas. 1977—), Chgo. State U. Alumni Assn. (pres. 1976-77), St. Thomas More Holy Name Soc., Phi Delta Kappa. Democrat. Roman Catholic. Clubs: Kiwanis, K.C., Elks (Chgo.). Home: 3171 W 83d Pl Chicago IL 60652 Office: 1744 W Pryor Ave Chicago IL 60643

BURKEMPER, JAMES JOSEPH, real estate exec.; b. St. Louis, Sept. 25, 1931; s. Joseph Francis and Agnes Virginia (Seymour) B.; student U. Chgo., 1955-56; B.A. (HEW scholar), Washington U., St. Louis, 1959; m. Jane Elizabeth Berry, May 28, 1960; children—Ira, Paul, Bruce, Hilary, Caroline. With N.Y., Chgo. & St. Louis R.R., St. Louis, 1950-51; with Ira E. Berry, Inc., real estate, St. Louis, 1959—, exec. v.p., 1970—. Bd. dirs. United Cerebral Palsy Assn. Greater St. Louis, Loretto-Hilton Repertory Theatre, St. Louis, Little Symphony Concerts Assn., St. Louis. Served with USNR, 1951-55. Mem. Internat. Real Estate Fedn., Real Estate Bd. Met. St. Louis. Club: St. Louis, University, Algonquin Country (St. Louis). Home: 26 Brentmoor Park Clayton MO 63105 Office: 7701 Clayton Rd St Louis MO 63117

BURKET, GAIL BROOK, author; b. Stronghurst, Ill., Nov. 1, 1905; d. John Cecil and Maud (Simonson) Brook; A.B., U. Ill., 1926; M.A. in English Lit., Northwestern U., 1929; m. Walter Cleveland Burket, June 22, 1929; children—Elaine (Mrs. William L. Harwood), Anne, Margaret (Mrs. James Boyce). Pres. woman's aux. Internat. Coll. Surgeons, 1950-54, now bd. dirs. Mus.; nat. vice chmn. Am. Heritage of DAR, 1971-74; pres. Northwestern U. Guild, 1976—, sec. Evanston women's bd. Univ. Settlement, 1976—. Recipient Robert Ferguson Meml. award Friends of Lit., 1973. Mem. Nat. League Am. Pen Women (Ill. state pres. 1952-54, nat. v.p. 1958-60), Soc. Midland Authors, Poetry Soc. Am., Women in Communications, AAUW (pres. N. Shore br. 1961-63), Daus. Am. Colonists (state v.p. 1973-76), Colonial Dames Am. (chpt. regent 1974—), Zonta, Phi Beta Kappa, Delta Zeta. Author: Courage Beloved, 1949; Manners Please, 1949; Blueprint for Peace, 1951; Let's Be Popular, 1951; You Can Write a Poem, 1954; Far Meadows, 1955; This is My Country, 1960; From the Prairies, 1968. Contbr. articles, poems to lit. publs. Address: 1020 Lake Shore Dr Evanston IL 60202

BURKEY, LEE MELVILLE, lawyer; b. Beach, N.D., Mar. 21, 1914; s. L. M. and Mina (Horner) B.; B.A., U. Ill., 1936. M.A., 1938; J.D. with honors, John Marshall Law Sch., 1943; m. Lorraine Burghardt, June 11, 1938; 1son, Lee Melville III. Tchr., Princeton, Ill., 1937-38. Harvey, 1938-43; admitted to Ill. bar, 1944; atty. Office of Solicitor. U.S. Dept. Labor, 1944-51; lectr. bus. law Roosevelt Coll., 1949-52; partner law firm Asher, Greenfield, Goodstein, Pavolon and Segall, and predecessor firms, 1952—. Mem. Northeastern Ill. Planning Commn., 1969-73, pres., 1970—; mem. Employment Security Adv. Bd., 1970-73. Trustee, Village of LaGrange, 1962-68, mayor, 1968-73, village atty., 1973—. Recipient Distinguished Alumnus award John Marshall Law Sch., 1973. Mem. Am., Ill., Chgo., bar assns., Order of John Marshall, S.A.R. Congregationalist. Mason. Club: LaGrange Country. Author numerous articles on lie detector evidence. Home: 926 S Catherine St LaGrange IL 60525 Office: 228 N LaSalle St Chicago IL 60601

BURKHALTER, LAMBERT CHARLES, assn. exec.; b. Belnap, Iowa, July 25, 1921; s. Charles Faye and Lucia Halfa (Moss) B.; grad. high sch.; m. Venetta Maxine Ellis, June 10, 1946; children—Robert Dwight Wilbanks, Gerald Lee. Engineman, Burlington No., Inc., Ottumwa, Iowa, 1941-72; state legis. dir. United Transp. Union, Des Moines, 1972—. Mem. U. Iowa Center for Labor Mgmt., 1960, Gov.'s Task Force on Energy Policy, 1974, Manpower Services Council, 1974—; legis. rep., chmn. Iowa Fraternal Congress, 1971—. Mem. Am. Legion, Burlington Vets. Assn. (pres. 1968). Mason; mem. Order Eastern Star. Mem. Christian Ch. Clubs: East Des Moines, Bohemian. Home: 8712 Carole Circle Des Moines IA 50322 Office: Capital City Bank Bldg Des Moines IA 50309

BURLISON, BILL D., congressman; b. Wardell, Mo.; s. John I. and Lilly (Marler) B.; B.A., B.S. in Edn., M.Ed.; LL.B., U. Mo.; m. Barbara Ann Humphreys; children—James David, Laura Ann, Andrew Jefferson. Pros. atty. Cape Girardeau County, Mo., 3 terms; former asst. atty. gen. Mo.; mem. 91st-95th Congresses from 10th Dist. Mo.; mem. Com. Appropriations, subcom. agr., def., Com. Intelligence; chmn. subcom program and budget; zone 13 whip. Past pres. Cape Girardeau County Sch. Bd.; mem. exec. com. Democratic Congl. Campaign Com. Served with USMCR, 3 1/2 years. Home: 740 Watkin St Cape Girardeau MO 63701 Office: Longworth House Office Bldg Washington DC 20515

BURMAN, MARSHALL LYLE, lawyer; b. Chgo., July 22, 1929; s. Henry L. and Florence (Rosin) B.; B.S., Northwestern U., 1951; LL.B., Yale, 1954; m. Marian Sondheimer, June, 1953 (div. 1966); children—Julie Anne, Jamie Alison. Admitted to Ill. bar, 1954; practiced in Chgo., 1957—; asso. Arvey, Hodes, Costello & Burman, and predecessor, 1957-60, mem. firm, 1961—. Dir. Heitman Mortgage Investors, TCI, Inc. Mem. financial investment adv. panel Amtrak, 1970-75. Pres. Young Mens Jewish Council, 1965; chmn. Bus. Assistance Program, 1966-67. Served with AUS, 1954-56. Recipient medallion Boys Clubs Am., 1966. Mem. Ill., Chgo. bar assns., Phi Alpha Delta, Phi Epsilon Pi. Clubs: Yale, Standard (Chgo.); Harmonie (N.Y.C.). Home: 180 E Pearson St Chicago IL 60611 Office: 180 N LaSalle St Chicago IL 60601

BURMAN, SHELDON OSCAR, surgeon, educator; b. Syracuse, N.Y., Dec. 15, 1926; s. Aaron and Augusta K. (Kaplan) B.; B.A., Syracuse U., 1947; M.D., State U. N.Y. Upstate Med. Center, 1951; m. Diane B. Berger, June 24, 1961; children—Allison Beth, Jocelyn Holly, Harrison Emory Guy. Intern, Univ. Hosps. Cleve., Western Res. U., 1951-52, resident, 1952-53; spl. surg. fellow Postgrad. Med. Sch. of London, 1953-55, also asso. in research Med. Research Council Gt. Britain; asst. prof. surgery N.Y. Med. Coll., N.Y.C., 1961-66, asso. prof., 1967-68; asso. attending surgeon Flower and Fifth Ave. Hosp., N.Y.C., 1961-68; asso. vis. surgeon Met. Hosp., N.Y.C., 1961-68; prof., chmn. dept. thoracic and cardiovascular surgery U. Sherbrooke Med. Center Hosp., Sherbrooke, Que., Can., 1968-70; prof. surgery Abraham Lincoln Sch. Medicine, U. Ill., 1970-75; prof., dir. div. thoracic and cardiovascular surgery U. Health Scis. Chgo. Med. Sch., 1975—; chief thoracic and cardiovascular surgery N. Chicago VA Hosp., Edgewater Hosp., Chgo.; attending surgeon St. Mary of Nazareth Hosp., Chgo.; cons. St. Therese Hosp., Waukegan; vis. faculty Great Lakes Naval Regional Med. Center. Served with USAF, 1955-56, USN 1945-46. Diplomate Am. Bd. Surgery, Am. Bd. Thoracic Surgery. Fellow Royal Soc. Medicine (Eng.), N.Y. Acad. Medicine, N.Y. Soc. Thoracic Surgery, A.C.S., Am. Coll. Chest Physicians, Inst. Medicine Chgo., Internat. Soc. Surgery, Internat. Cardiovascular Soc., Am. Coll. Cardiology, Midwest Surg. Assn., Sigma Xi; mem. Nathan A. Womack Surg. Soc., Warren H. Cole Soc., Can. Soc. Clin. Investigation, Cardiac Soc. Montreal, Can. Cardiovascular Soc., Chgo. Surg. Soc., Ill., Lake County med. socs., AMA. Author publs. in field. Home: 247 Prospect Ave Highland Park IL 60035 Office: VA Hosp North Chicago IL 60064

BURMEISTER, FLORENCE ESTELLE, librarian, educator; b. Cleve., Apr. 17, 1929; d. William Frederick and Josephine (Kostal) Burmeister; A.B., Western Res. U., 1956, M.S. in L.S., 1958. Library aide Cleve. Pub. Library, 1948-55, asst. childrens librarian E. 131st St. br., 1956-57, childrens librarian Miles Park br., 1958-60, Fleet br., 1960-61; children's books reviewer Booklist and Subscription Books Bull., A.L.A., Chgo., 1962-63; head young peoples and childrens dept. Skokie (Ill.) Pub. Library, 1963—; chmn. children's library services workshop for Bur Oak Library System Joliet, 1968-70; vis. lectr. dept. library sci. Rosary Coll., River Forest, Ill., 1967—. Instr. U.S. Office Edn. Inst. on Library Services for Gifted Children Tex. Woman's U., Denton, summer 1970; asst. prof. pub. library services for children, extension div. U. Ill., spring 1971. Mem. Am. (past com. chmn.; mem., publicity chmn. Newbery Caldecott awards com. 1969-70, chmn. Charles Scribner's Sons awards com. 1971-72, chmn. children's services div. arrangements com. 1972), Ill. (mem. exec. bd., past sect. chmn., del. Ill. Commn. on Children, recipient Davis Cup, Children's Librarians Sect. 1972) library assns., Library Adminstrs. Council No. Ill. (past sect. pres.; chmn. children's reference services workshop 1969), Chgo. Library Club, Childrens Reading Round Table Chgo. (award com. 1968, 74), Case Western Res. U. Sch. Library Sci., Flora Stone Mather Coll. alumni assn., Beta Phi Mu. Unitarian. Home: 201 E Walton St Chicago IL 60611 Office: 5215 Oakton St Skokie IL 60076

BURNER, DAVID MILTON, JR., lawyer; b. Decatur, Ill., Jan. 17, 1931; s. David Milton and Mary Virginia (Baldwin) B.; A.B. (Econ.), Dartmouth Coll., 1953; J.D., Northwestern U., 1959; m. Barbara Hunt, Nov. 24, 1956; children—Mary V., Deborah H., Clark D., Sarah A. Admitted to Ill. bar, 1960; asso. firm Murphy, Pearson and O'Connor, Chgo., 1959-60; asst. trust counsel, Harris Trust and Savs. Bank, Chgo., 1960-69; asso. firm Kirkland and Ellis, Chgo., 1969-76, firm Chadwell, Kayser, Ruggles, McGee and Hastings, Chgo., 1976—; instr. John Marshall Law Sch., Am. Inst. Banking. Mem. Gov's. advisory counsel, 1969-73; bd. zoning appeals, Western Springs, Ill., 1967—, chmn., 1971—: treas., vestryman, All Saints Episcopal Ch. Served with U.S. Army, 1953-56, 61-62. Mem. Am., Ill. (lectr.), Chgo. (chmn. trust law com., 1970-71) Bar Assns., Res. Officers Assn., Mil. Order of the World Wars. Clubs: Village (Western Springs), LaGrange Country. Home: 4101 Clausen Ave Western Springs IL 60558 Office: 8500 Sears Tower 233 S Wacker Dr Chicago IL 60606

BURNETT, DONALD EWING, librarian; b. Anna, Ill., Feb. 2, 1938; s. William Ewing and Ottie May (Cotter) B.; B.S. in Social Sci., Murray State U., 1963, M.A. in Edn., 1968; M.L.A., George Peabody Coll., 1970; m. Carol Jane Fee, Sept. 2, 1967; children—Andrea Lynn, Laura Susan. Librarian, Peoria (Ill.) Pub. Schs., 1963-66; dir. libraries Anna Community Dist. 37, 1966—; dir. gen. and edn. libraries Anna State Hosp., 1969—; region 5 library cons. Ill. Dept. Mental Health. Trustee Ill. Library Bd.; mem. Stinson Meml. Library Bd. Served with U.S. Army Reserve, 1960-66. Mem. Young Democrats, Nat., Ill. (del. 1966-70), Union County (legal chmn. 1966-70) edn. assns., A.L.A., Phi Delta Kappa, Beta Phi Mu, Tau Kappa Epsilon. Democrat. Presbyn. (deacon 1968-72, mem., clk. session 1973—). Elk. Club: Internat. Relations. Home: Box 471 Anna IL 62906 Office: 1000 N Main Anna IL 62906

BURNETT, FRANCES (MRS. HINTON J. BAKER), concert pianist, educator; b. Centralia, Ill.; d. Bernard J. and Olive (Burnett) Baumhueter; B.M., Cin. Conservatory of Music, 1941, M.Mus., 1942; m. Hinton J. Baker, June 24, 1943, (div. Mar. 1956); children—Eve Elizabeth, Marie Celeste. Concert pianist, chamber and solo performances with orch. and in recitals including: Town Hall, N.Y., Phillips Gallery, Washington, Music Hall, Cin., Harvard U., Boston U., U. N.H., Durham, Jordan Hall, Boston, Gardner Mus., Boston, Nat. Gallery Orch., Washington, also TV and radio; concert tours, Europe, 1967, 68, 70, U.S., 1971, 72, (with cellist Gordon Epperson) Ariz., Ohio, D.C., 1974; rec. artist BBC, London, Eng., 1970; instr. The Knox Sch. for Girls, Cooperstown, N.Y., 1946-47, Trinity U., San Antonio, Tex., 1948-49, Longy Sch. of Music, Cambridge, Mass., 1956-64; prof. Bowling Green U., 1964—, master classes, 1972—, head keyboard dept. Trustee Creative Arts Community, Toledo. Recipient research grants Bowling Green State U. Mem. Nat. Music Tchrs. Assn., Nat. Piano Guild, Pi Kappa Lambda, Phi Beta. Has performed world premieres of Am. composers' works; recorded Golden Crest Records. Home: 23 Georgetown Dr Bowling Green OH 43402

BURNETT, JAMES PAUL, JR., molecular biologist; b. McCormick, S.C., Sept. 15, 1935; s. James Paul and Mary Edith (Sturkey) B.; B.S., U. S.C., 1955; Ph.D., Ind. U., 1960; m. Delores Diane Wilson, Aug. 9, 1957; children—James Walter, Charles Neal. NIH postdoctoral fellow Harvard, 1960-61; sr. biochemist Eli Lilly & Co., Indpls., 1962-69, research biochemist, 1970-74, research asso., 1975—, head cell biology research, 1977—; asso. prof. microbiology Ind. U., Indpls., 1974—. Mem. Am. Soc. Microbiology, Sigma Xi, Phi Lambda Upsilon, Phi Beta Kappa. Contbg. author books; contbr. articles to profl. publs. molecular biology of tumor viruses. Home: 7641 Brookview Ln Indianapolis IN 46250 Office: 307 E McCarty St Indianapolis IN 46202

BURNETT, JEAN BULLARD (MRS. JAMES R. BURNETT), biochemist; b. Flint, Mich., Feb. 19, 1924; d. Chester M. and Katheryn (Krasser) Bullard; B.S., Mich. State U., 1944, M.S., 1945, Ph.D. (Council fellow), 1952; m. James R. Burnett, June 8, 1947. Research asso. dept. zoology Mich. State U., East Lansing, 1954-59, dept. biochemistry, 1959-61, acting dir. research biochem. genetics, dept. biochemistry, 1961-62, asso. prof., asst. chmn. dept. biomechanics, 1973—; asso. biochemist Mass. Gen. Hosp., Boston, 1964-73; prin. research asso. dermatology Harvard, 1962-73, faculty medicine, 1964-73, also spl. lectr., cons., tutor Med. Sch. USPHS, NIH grantee, 1965-68; Gen. Research Support grantee Mass. Gen. Hosp., 1968-72; Ford Found. travel grantee, 1973: Am. Cancer Soc. grantee, 1971-73; recipient Med. Found. award, 1970. Mem. AAAS, Am. Chem. Soc., Am. Inst. Biol. Sci., Genetics Soc. Am., Soc. Investigative Dermatology, Sigma Xi (Research award 1971), Pi Kappa Delta, Kappa Delta Pi, Pi Mu Epsilon, Sigma Delta Epsilon. Home: PO Box 308 Okemos MI 48864 Office: Dept Biomechanics East Fee Hall Mich State U East Lansing MI 48824

BURNETT, JOSEPH GEDDES, architect; b. Indpls., Oct. 26, 1923; s. Leo and Naomi (Geddes) B.; B.S., U.S. Mcht. Marine Acad., 1944; postgrad. U. Mich., 1946-48; B.S., Ill. Inst. Tech., 1952; m. Sara Vail Loutrel, Aug. 17, 1968; children—Laurie, Lynn, John, James. Research asst. Ill. Inst. Tech., Chgo., 1952-54; with Mies Van der Rohe architect, Chgo., 1954-59, Bertrand Goldberg Assos., 1959-64, C.F. Murphy Assos., 1964-70; prin. Joseph Burnett, Chgo., 1970—. Served with U.S. Mcht. Marine, 1942-46. Mem. Mayor Daley's Adv. Com. on Bldg. Code Amendments, 1970—. Mem. AIA, Mem. Council Archtl. Registration Bds. Recipient 1st prize lamp design Mus. Modern Art, 1952, Chgo. Dwelling Assn. and AIA low cost housing competition, 1969. Architect Thornwood House, Park Forest South, Ill., 1974. Home: 1646 N Sedgwick St Chicago IL 60614 Office: 154 E Erie St Chicago IL 60611

BURNETT, MARIE MIRANTI, psychologist; b. Bklyn., Oct. 12, 1932; d. James Paul and Katherine Lorraine (Caprio) Miranti; B.A., Bates Coll., 1955; M.A., Wetern Res. U., 1967, Ph.D., 1969; m. Allison L. Burnett, June 12, 1955 (div. 1972); children—Gene Paul, Allison James, Carla Marie. Staff psychologist, adult and child guidance center St. Francis Hosp., Evanston, Ill., 1970-74, chief psychologist, 1974—, dir. alcohol treatment program, 1975—; pvt. practice psychology, 1971—. Mem. Am., Midwestern, Ill. psychol. assns., Assn. Labor Mgmt. Adminstrs. and Cons. on Alcoholism, Acad. Psychologists in Marital and Family Therapy, Ill. Alcoholism and Drug Dependence Assn. Home: 207 Lake St Evanston IL 60201 Office: 1609 Sherman St Evanston IL 60201

BURNETT, PATRICIA HILL, artist, polit. orgn. ofcl., lectr.; b. Bklyn., Sept. 5, 1920; d. William Burr and Mimi (Uline) Hill; student U. Toledo, 1937-38, Goucher Coll., 1939-40; student Master's program Inst. D'Allende, Mexico, 1967, Wayne State U., 1972; student of John Carroll, Detroit, 1941-44, Sarkis Sarkisian, Detroit, 1956-60, Wallace Bassford, Provincetown, Mass., 1968-72, Walter Midener, Detroit, 1960-63; m. Harry Albert Burnett, Oct. 9, 1948; children—William Hill Lange, Harry Burnett III, Terrill Hill, Hillary Hill. Actress, Lone Ranger program Radio Blue Network, 1941-45; tchr. of painting and sculpture U. Mich. Extension, Ann Arbor, 1965—; lectr. N.Y. Speakers Bur., 1971—; propr. Burnett Studios, Detroit, 1962—, mgr., 1962—. Numerous one-woman shows of paintings and sculpture include: Scarab Club, Detroit, 1971, Midland (Mich.) Art Center, Wayne State U., Detroit, The Gallery, Ft. Lauderdale, Fla., Agra Gallery, Washington, Salon des Artes, Paris; numerous group shows including: Palazzo Pruili Gallery, Venice, Italy, 1971, Detroit Inst. of Arts, 1967, Butler Mus., N.Cleve., 1972, Windsor (Ont., Can.) Art Center, 1973, Weisbaden (Germany) Gallery, 1976; represented in permanent collections: Detroit Inst. of Arts, Wayne State U., Detroit, Wooster (Ohio) Coll., Ford Motor Co., Detroit, Bloomfield Art Assn., Bloomfield Hills, Mich., also private collections; numerous portrait paintings including portraits of Indira Ghandi, Benson Ford, Joyce Carol Oates, Mrs. Edsel Ford, Betty Ford, Roman Gribbs, Princess Olga Mrivani, Lord John Mackintosh, Marlo Thomas, Congresswoman Martha Griffiths. Chairwoman of Mich. Women's Commn., 1972—; pres. Detroit House of Correction Commn., 1975—; treas. Republican Dist. 1 of Mich., 1973—; mem. Issues Com., Republican State Central Com., 1975-76; sec. Republican State Ways and Means Com., 1975—; mem. Mich. State Advisory Council Vocat. Edn. Recipient Silver Salute award Mich. State U., 1976, Most Popular award San Diego Sculpture Show, 1971, First prize award Cape Cod Artists Show, 1968; named Distinguished Woman of Mich., Bus. and Profl. Women's Orgn., 1974, Distinguished Woman Northwood Inst., 1977. Mem. Detroit Inst. Arts (dir. membership com. 1958—), Nat. Assn. of Commns. for Women (sec., dir. 1976-78), Mich. Acad. of the Arts, Detroit Soc. of Women Painters and Sculptors, Women in the Arts, Scarab Club (dir. 1962-63), Ibex Club (pres. 1951), Nat. Orgn. for Women (nat. bd. 1971-75, del. UN conf., Mex., 1975), Women's Econ. Club, Alpha Phi. Episcopalian. Club: Zonta Internat. Contbr. articles to art jours. Home: 18261 Hamilton Rd Detroit MI 48203 Office: 217 Farnsworth Detroit MI 48202

BURNS, BETTY JANE, pianist, acad. dir.; b. St. Louis, Sept. 16, 1926; d. James Arnest and Elizabeth Livina (Allen) Delvas: student Washington U., St. Louis, 1950-51, Sherwood Coll., 1959-60: m. Douglas Corzine Burns, Sept. 8, 1945; children—Cynthia Burns La Fata, Stephen, Clark, Nathan. Piano tchr., St. Louis, 1944—; clinician Nat. Piano Found., St. Louis, 1962-73: dir. New Music Acad., St. Louis, Florissant, Mo., 1968—; chmn. piano proficiency dept., Webster Coll., 1969-73; adjudicator, cons. in field: condr. workshops for music tchrs. Mem. Nat. Music Tchrs. Assn., St. Louis Piano Tchrs. Forum. Club: Soroptimists. Author: You Do It, vols. 1-3, 1972, vols. 4-6, 1973, vol. 7, 1976. Home: 118 S Clay St Saint Louis MO 63135

BURNS, C(HARLES) PATRICK, hematologist; b. Kansas City, Mo., Oct. 8, 1937; s. Charles Edgar and Ruth (Eastham) B.; B.A., U. Kans., 1959, M.D., 1963; m. Janet Sue Walsh, June 15, 1968; children—Charles Geoffrey, Scott Patrick. Intern, Cleve. Met. Gen. Hosp., 1963-64; asst. resident in internal medicine, Univ. Hosps., Cleve., 1966-68, sr. resident in hematology, 1968-69: instr. medicine Case Western Res. U., 1970-71; asst. chief hematology Cleve. VA Hosp., 1970-71; asst. prof. medicine U. Iowa Hosps., Iowa City, 1971-75, asso. prof. medicine, 1975—; cons. U.S. VA Hosp. Served to capt. M.C., AUS, 1964-66. Am. Cancer Soc. fellow in hematology-oncology, 1968-69; USPHS fellow in medicine, 1969-70. Diplomate Am. Bd. Internal Medicine, subsplty. bds. hematology, med. oncology. Fellow A.C.P.; mem. Am. Soc. Hematology, Am. Assn. Cancer Research, Internat. Soc. Hematology, Central Soc. Clin. Research, Am. Soc. Clin. Oncology, Soc. Exptl. Biology and Medicine, Am. Fedn. Clin. Research, Lambda Chi Alpha, Phi Beta Pi, Alpha Omega Alpha. Research and publs. on leukocyte biochemistry, leukemia and hematology. Home: 2046 Rochester Ct Iowa City IA 52240 Office: Dept Medicine University Iowa Hospitals Iowa City IA 52242

BURNS, DAVID FRANKLIN, mgmt. cons.; b. Nashville, Tenn., Nov. 25, 1938; s. Herman Franklin and Robbye Lucile (Hall) B.; B. Mech. Engring., Vanderbilt U., 1960; M.B.A., Harvard U., 1965; m. Kyungja Lee, Aug. 24, 1974. Dept. mgr. Gulton Industries, Metuchen, N.J., 1965-66, asst. mfg. mgr. electron components div., 1966-67, marketing mgr. EMI Devices, 1967-68; gen. mgr. Gudeman Co., Chgo., 1968-69; partner Stone Mgmt. Corp., Chgo., 1970—; lectr. Northwestern U. Grad. Sch. Mgmt., 1975-76, Keller Grad. Sch. Mgmt., 1977—. Served with USN 1960-63. Mem. Nat. Council Small Bus. Mgmt. Devel., Am. Prodn. and Inventory Control Soc., Nat. Council Physical Distribution Mgmt. Baptist. Clubs: Harvard Bus. Sch. (Chgo.), Harvard (Chgo.), Vanderbilt (Chgo.), Chgo. Council Fgn. Relations. Author: Computer Time Sharing, 1966. Office: 208 S LaSalle St Chicago IL 60604

BURNS, JOHN TOLMAN, elec. products mfg. co. exec.; b. Montgomery, Ala., May 16, 1922; s. Loren Julius and Harriett Janett (McFerran) B.; B.S., U. Louisville, 1943; m. Patricia Ellen Jacques, Sept. 25, 1954; children—Scott F., Kent T. With Sperry Rand Corp., 1956—, v.p. GM Vickers internat. div., 1964-68, pres. Sperry Vickers div., Troy, Mich., 1968—. Served to lt. (j.g.) USNR, 1944-46. Home: 4423 Ardmore Dr Bloomfield Hills MI 48013 Office: 1401 Crooks Rd Troy MI 48084

BURNS, MICHAEL JOHN, lawyer, banker; b. Galesburg, Ill., Dec. 16, 1946; s. John H. and Louise (Little) B.: B.A., Knox Coll., 1969; J.D., U. Denver, 1971; LL.M., U. Mo., 1972; m. Rebecca Harman, June 3, 1972; children—Patrick John, Michael John. Admitted to Colo. bar, 1971, Mo. bar, 1972, Ill. bar, 1973; individual practice law, Kansas City, Mo., 1971-72, Denver, 1972-73: v.p. Bank of Galesburg (Ill.), 1972-73, Nat. Bank Joliet (Ill.), 1973—; v.p., dir. Midwest Ins. Co.; dir. Midwest Bankshares. Republican candidate for Jackson County (Mo.) pros. atty., 1972. Mem. Am., Ill., Mo., Colo. bar assns., Am. Bankers Assn. Roman Catholic. Home: 1153 Glenwood St Joliet IL 60435 Office: 121 N Chicago St Joliet IL 60431

BURNS, MICHAEL PAUL, auditor; b. Highland Park, Mich., Dec. 2, 1935; s. Gerald Dennis and Stella Marie Stanislaw B.; A.A. cum laude, Chgo. City Coll., 1961; B.S. in Bus. Adminstrn., cum laude, Roosevelt U., 1962; m. Rosemarie Klem, Aug. 25, 1962; children—Dennis Anthony, Michael Paul, Mary Therese. Mem. staff Peat Marwick Mitchell & Co., C.P.A.'s, Chgo., 1962-65, Pullman Bank & Trust Co., Chgo., 1965-68, Scot Lad Foods Inc., Chgo., 1968-72; with I.C. Industries Inc., Chgo., 1972—. Trustee Village of Thornton (Ill.), 1970-72, treas., 1972-77. Served with AUS, 1954-57. Mem. Am. Inst. C.P.A.'s, Ill. State C.P.A.'s, Nat. Accounting Assn., Ill. Municipal Treas.'s Assn. Home: 16730 Clyde Ave South Holland IL 60473 Office: 1 Illinois Center 111 E Wacker Dr Chicago IL 60601

BURNS, NEAL MURRAY, marketing exec.; b. Chgo., July 16, 1933; s. Jack Arnold and Esther (Dinitz) B.; student U. Chgo., 1949-51; B.S., U. Ill., 1955; M.S., McGill U., 1957, Ph.D., 1959; m. Phyllis Syrene Hirsch, Mar. 25, 1974; children—Marc, Scott. Head psychopharmacology dept. Parke-Davis Inc., Detroit, 1958; chief environ. stress br. Air Crew Equipment Lab., USN, Phila., 1959-61; dir. life scis. div. Decker Corp., Bala Cynwyd, Pa., 1961-62; dir. mktg. Systems and Research Center, Honeywell, Inc., Mpls., 1962-72; asso. exec. dir Higher Edn. Coordinating Bd., Minn., 1972-76; pres. Marketec, Inc., Mpls., 1976—; mktg. cons., 1973-76; pres. Valle D'Or Home Owners Assn., 1975-77. USPHS grantee, 1955-58. Mem. Am. Mgmt. Assn., Am. Psychol. Assn., IEEE, Am. Assn. Consultants. Editor: Unusual Environments and Human Behavior (R. Chambers and E. Hendler), 1963. Home: 7603 Harold St Golden Valley MN 55426 Office: Marketec Inc 227 Shelard Plaza Minneapolis MN 55427

BURNS, RICHARD DON, orthodontist; b. Leon, Iowa, Nov. 29, 1939; s. Leslie Warren and Ethel (Shafer) B.; D.D.S. summa cum laude, State U. Iowa, 1963; M.S.D. in Dentistry, Ind. U., 1966. Practice orthodontics, Elkhart, Ind., 1967—; founder, pres., treas., dir. OrthoTek, Inc., Elkhart, 1968—, Westwood Realty Elkhart, Inc., 1968—, Lancer Advt. Agy. Inc., Elkhart, 1971—; founding pres. Richard D. Burns Orthodontics, Inc., 1970—; mem. adv. bd. John Wesleyn Ins. Co., Indpls., 1971—. Trustee Richard D. Burns Orthodontics Profit Sharing and Pension Trusts, OrthoTek Profit Sharing and Pension Trust. Served with USPHS, 1963-64, USAF, 1966-67. Mem. Am., Ind. dental assns., Elkhart County Dental Soc. (past pres.), Am. Assn. Orthodontists, Ind. Soc. Orthodontists (pres., past sec.), Great Lakes Soc. Orthodontists, Am. Soc. Dentistry for Children, Omicron Kappa Upsilon, Psi Omega, Sigma Phi Epsilon. Methodist. Kiwanian. Inventor dental appliance; designer orthodontic pub. relations products. Home: 2413 Greenleaf Blvd Elkhart IN 46514 Office: 1750 Kilbourn St Elkhart IN 46514

BURNS, RICHARD HOWARD, food preparation equipment mfg. co. exec.; b. Ridgewood, N.J., Sept. 26, 1930; s. Robert Orr and Opal May (Shirreffs) B.; B. Applied Art, Auburn U., 1952; m. Beverly Duncan Ritchie, Sept. 9, 1953; children—Richard Howard, Laura Elizabeth. Designer, Hobart Corp., Troy, Ohio, 1955-57, project engr., 1957-66, mgr. indsl. design, 1966—; owner, pres. Richard H. Burns's Assos., indsl. design and engring. cons. Mem. Troy Beautification Com., 1972—, chmn., 1977; mem. Troy City Council, 1978—. Served with U.S. Army, 1953-55. Mem. Troy C. of C., Am. Def. Preparedness Assn. Republican. Presbyterian. Kiwanian. Patentee in field. Home: 662 Clarendon Rd Troy OH 45373 Office: World Hdqrs Ave Troy OH 45373

BURNS, RICHARD PRICE, chemist, educator; b. Bartlesville, Okla., Sept. 19, 1932; s. Harvey Leroy and Hazel Fern (Price) B.; B.A., Okla. Baptist U., 1954; Ph.D., U. Chgo., 1965; m. Dora Jeanette Riley, Sept. 1, 1969; children—Steven Anthony, Jonathan Eric. Jr. chemist summers Phillips Petroleum Co. Bartlesville, Okla., 1954-56, Lawrence Livermore Lab. U. Calif., 1956-59; asst. prof. chemistry U. Ill. Circle, Chgo., 1965-71; asso. prof., 1971—; cons. in field. NSF grantee. Mem. Am. Chem. Soc. Democrat. Baptist. Office: Univ Ill Circle Campus PO Box 8198 Chicago IL 60680

BURNS, ROBERT LEROY, periodontist; b. Leon, Iowa, Apr. 29, 1937; s. Leslie Warren and Ethel Irene (Shaffer) B.; B.A., U. Iowa, 1959, D.D.S., 1962; M.S.D., U. Ala., 1968; m. Olivia Marie Heiple, Sept. 15, 1961; children—Robert LeRoy, Jon, Teresa, Natalie. Intern, Houston VA Hosp., 1962-63; intern, resident U. Ala. Med. Center, 1965-67; asst. dentist U. Ky., 1967-69; practice dentistry, specializing in periodontics, Des Moines, 1969—. Pres. Dynamic Dental Systems, Inc., West Des Moines, Iowa; founder Healthline Preventive Health Care Affiliates, Health Horizons; founder, dir. Centers for Health & Life, Inc., Preventive Oral Health Care Affiliates, Naturo-Nutrio-Bionics. Served with USAF, 1963-65. Fellow Internat. Coll. Applied Nutrition, Internat. Acad. Preventive Medicine; mem. Am. Acad. Periodontology (Orban prize in periodontics 1968, Community Service award 1974), Am., Iowa dental assns., Des Moines Dist. Dental Soc., AMA, Am. Osteo. Assn., Student Osteo. Med. Assn., Am., Iowa diabetes assns., Iowa Soc. Periodontology, Am. Soc. Preventive Dentistry, Soc. Prospective Medicine, Am. Acad. Psychosomatic Medicine. Home: 1218 24th St West Des Moines IA 50265 Office: 2600 Harding Rd Des Moines IA 50310

BURNS, RUSSELL EUGENE, lawyer, banker; b. Sandwich, Ill., Apr. 26, 1941; s. Harry Harold and Gladys Lucille (Rasmusson) B.; B.B.A., U. Tex., 1963, J.D., 1965; m. Lola June King, Dec. 28, 1963; children—Natalie, Bradley. Admitted to Tex. bar, 1965, Ill. bar, 1966; asst. atty. City of Houston, 1965-66, De Kalb, Ill., 1966-69; practice in De Kalb, 1966—; pres. Leland Nat. Bank (Ill.), 1975-77, chmn. bd., 1977—. Committeeman, De Kalb Republican Com., 1972-74. Mem. Am., Ill., Tex., De Kalb County bar assns., Delta Theta Phi. Republican. Methodist (trustee 1971-74). Elk. Home: Route 2 De Kalb IL 60115 Office: 363 E Lincoln Hwy De Kalb IL 60115

BURNS, WILLIAM JOSEPH, psychologist; b. Sioux Falls, S.D., Aug. 29, 1936; s. William James and Murriel Alvira (Pollard) B.; M.Ed., S.D. State U., 1966; M.S., Va. Commonwealth U., 1972; Ph.D., U. N.D., 1974; m. Kayreen Ann Jurica, Dec. 20, 1968; children—William John, Tonia Ann. Intern, Dede Wallace Mental Health Center, Nashville, 1973; fellow U. Colo. Med. Center, Denver, 1974; child psychologist Children's Meml. Hosp., Chgo., 1975—; asso. in psychiatry and pediatrics Northwestern U., 1977—. Certified psychologist, Ill. Mem. Am., Midwestern, Ill. psychol. assns., Internat., Am. socs. clin. hypnosis, Psi Chi. Roman Catholic. Home: 2001 Keeney St Evanston IL 60202 Office: 2300 Children's Plaza Chicago IL 60614

BURNS, WILLIAM OLIVER, ins. co. exec.; b. Monticello, Ill., June 24, 1930; s. Guy O. and Nellie (McWhorter) B.; B.S., U. Ill., 1954; m. Marilyn Cannon, Aug. 10, 1962; children—Lindsay Clodfelter, Michael Clodfelter. With State Farm Life Ins. Co., Bloomington, Ill., 1959—, controller, 1961-64, v.p., controller, 1964-67, v.p., 1967-76, v.p., treas., dir., 1976—. Mem. adv. bd. St. Josephs Hosp. Served with AUS, 1951-53. Fellow Soc. Actuaries, Life Office Mgmt. Inst.; mem. Am. Coll. Life Underwriters, Financial Execs. Inst. Club: Bloomington Country. Home: Rural Route 7 Bloomington IL 61701 Office: #1 State Farm Plaza Bloomington IL 61701

BURNSIDE, BRADLEY ALLEN, cons.; b. Chgo., Dec. 13, 1921; s. Harry Boland and Gladys (Allen) B.; B.A., Knox Coll., 1946, B.S., 1946; postgrad. Northwestern U., 1943, Purdue U., 1944; m. Nancy Woolger, Feb. 23, 1952; children—Barbara, Bradley, With Time, Inc., Chgo., 1952-62, regional mgr. House & Home mag., 1952-58, mgr., 1958-62; exec. v.p. W.H. Long Marketing Co., Greensboro, N.C., 1962-64; mgr. Chgo. area Am. Builder Mag., 1964-68; exec. dir. Water Conditioning Found., Northfield, Ill., 1968-74; industry cons. Kitchen and Bath Mag., Palm Springs, Calif., 1971-74; now fin. and mktg. cons. Jades, S.A., Antigua, Guatemala; sr. cons. Career Mgmt., Inc. Exec. dir. Water Conditioning Found. Inst., Northfield, 1968-74. Trustee Bus. Inst., Coll. of Desert, Palm Desert, Calif. Served with USMCR, 1944-45. Recipient service award Water Conditioning Found., 1966, Turtle award, 1971. Mem. Water Quality Research Council, Am. Mil. Engrs. Assn., Am. Wood Preservers Assn., ASTM, Iowa Water Conditioning Assn. (life), Tau Kappa Epsilon. Club: Chgo. Knox. Home: 1628 Blackthorn Dr Glenview IL 66025

BURNSIDE, RONALD LEE, educator; b. Piqua, Ohio, Dec. 19, 1940; s. Donald R. and Virginia (Thompson) B.; B.A., Miami U., Oxford, Ohio, 1966; M.A., Purdue U., 1970; m. Patricia S. Campbell, June 13, 1964; children—Julie, Melisa, Tommy, Beth Anne. Asst. program dir. Piqua YMCA, 1963-64; asso. program dir. Hamilton (Ohio) YMCA, 1964-68; program dir. Logansport (Ind.) YMCA, 1968-70; juvenile probation officer, Indpls., 1970-71, Dayton, Ohio, 1971-72; faculty dept. philosophy Sinclair Community Coll., Dayton, 1972—, asst. prof., 1975—. Served with USMCR, 1958-61. Mem. Am. Philos. Assn., Ohio Valley Philosophy Edn. Soc. Methodist (dir.). Home: 304 Eller Ave Englewood OH 45322

BURNSTEIN, HAROLD ROBERT, lawyer; b. Chgo., May 28, 1919; s. Samuel and Fay (Fine) B.; B.S.C., Northwestern U., 1940; J.D., DePaul U., 1950; m. Harriet Kahn, May 25, 1946; children—Clifford Nolan, Joan Ellen. Pub. accountant Katz, Wagner & Co., Chgo., 1940-41; tax accountant Consol. Vultee Aircraft Corp., San Diego, 1941-45; tax accountant Hughes and Hughes, Chgo., 1946-50, now counsel; admitted to Ill. bar, 1950, since practiced in Chgo. Past chmn. Highland Park Voters Assn.; mem. Dist. 108 Sch. Bd., Highland Park, 1967-73, pres., 1972-73; mem. Highland Park Library Bd., 1974—; bd. dirs. North Suburban Library System, 1976—. Mem. Am., Chgo. (com. fed. taxation, chmn.) bar assns., Ill. Soc. C.P.A.'s, Am. Inst. C.P.A.'s, Am. Acad. Polit. and Social Sci., DePaul Bd. Assos., Chgo. Council on Fgn. Relations, Beta Alpha Psi. Jewish. Clubs: Birchwood (past pres.) (Highland Park); Standard, Economic (Chgo.). Contbr. articles on fed. taxation to profl. jours. Home: 510 Ravine Dr Highland Park IL 60035 Office: 135 S LaSalle St Chicago IL 60603

BURRITT, JOHN KERNS, librarian; b. Tomahawk, Wis., May 28, 1923; s. Harry and Mary (Robertson) B.; student U. Wis., 1941-42; B.A., Wartburg Coll., 1949; M.A., U. Ill., 1963; grad. Wartburg Sem., 1952. Ordained to ministry Luth. Ch., 1952; pastor 1st Luth. Ch., Ohio, Ill., 1952-58, St. John's Luth. Ch., Princeton, Ill., 1952-58; librarian Wartburg Sem., Dubuque, Iowa, 1958—. Active ARC. Mem. AAUP, Am. Theol. Library Assn. Home: 2217 Woodland Dubuque IA 52001 Office: 333 Wartburg Pl Dubuque IA 52001

BURT, JASPER NATHANIEL, lawyer; b. Balt., Dec. 15, 1940; s. Jasper Farmar and Dorothy (Wise) B.; B.A., Muskingum Coll., 1962; J.D., Ohio No. Law Sch., 1965; m. Judith Ann Dickson, June 28, 1963; children—Christopher Alan, David Dickson. Admitted to Ohio bar, 1966; asso. firm Frericks & Howard, Marion, Ohio, 1966-71, partner firm Parsell & Burt Marion, 1971—. Dir. Don Hall, Inc., Twin Oaks Mobile Home Park, Inc., Stan Day Enterprises, Inc.; pres., dir. Sky Tours, Inc.; Travelair Taxi, Inc. Trustee Goodwill Industries Marion, Marion County Soc. Crippled Children and Adults. Mem. Am., Ohio, Marion County bar assns., Marion County Law Library Assn. (sec. treas.). Presbyn. (elder). Mason, Kiwanian. Club: Marion Country. Home: 1070 Cambridge Ave Marion OH 43302 Office: Marion County Bank Bldg Marion OH 43302

BURT, JOHN HARRIS, bishop; b. Marquette, Mich., Apr. 11, 1918; s. Bates G. and Emily May (Bailey) B.; B.A., Amherst Coll., 1940, D.D. (hon.), 1960; B.A., Va. Theol. Sem., 1943, D.D. (hon.), 1967; D.D. (hon.), Youngstown U., 1958, Kenyon Coll., 1967; m. Martha M. Miller, Feb. 16, 1946; children—Susan, Emily, Sarah, Mary. Boys worker Christodora House, N.Y.C., 1940-41; ordained to ministry Episcopal Ch., 1943; canon Christ Ch. Cathedral, rector St. Paul's Ch., St. Louis, 1943-44; chaplain to Episcopal students U. Mich., 1946-50; rector St. John's Ch., Youngstown, Ohio, 1950-57, All Saints Ch., Pasadena, Calif., 1957-67; bishop coadjutor Ohio, 1967-68; Episcopal bishop of Ohio, 1968—. Pres. So. Calif. Council Chs., 1962-65; mem. bd. Ch. Soc. Coll. Work, 1964-71; chmn. clergy deployment bd. Episcopal Ch., 1971-73; mem. governing bd. Nat. Council Chs., 1969—; chmn. com. theology Episcopal Ch. House of Bishops, 1973—; chmn. Standing Commn. Ecumenical Relations, Episcopal Ch., 1973—; chmn. faith and order com. Ohio Council Chs., 1970-74; vice chmn. Urban Bishops' Coalition Episcopal Ch., 1977—. Pres. Youngstown Coordinating Council, 1954-56, Pasadena Community Council, 1964-66. Trustee Pomona Coll., 1963-66, Va. Theol. Sem., 1967-72, Kenyon Coll., 1967—, Colgate-Rochester Div. Sch., 1968—; bd. dirs. United Way Los Angeles, 1964-67, Inst. Am. Democracy, 1967—, Ams. for Energy Independence, 1975—. Served as chaplain USNR, 1943-46. Recipient Arvona Lynch Human Relations award Youngstown, 1956; Rissica Human Relations award Jewish War Vets., 1966; Pasadena Community Relations award, 1967; Cleve.'s Simon Boliver award, 1972. Mem. Phi Gamma Delta. Co-author: World Religions and World Peace, 1969. Home: 18200 Shelburne Rd Shaker Heights OH 44118 Office: 2230 Euclid Ave Cleveland OH 44115

BURT, MICHAEL PATRICK, mech. engr.; b. Fort Riley, Kans., Jan. 20, 1950; s. James Derek and Wanda Jane (Eaton) B.; B.M.E., Gen. Motors Inst., 1973; M.B.A. postgrad. Eastern Mich. U., 1975—; m. Susan Marie Oglesbee. Project engr. Detroit Diesel Allison div. Gen. Motors, Detroit, 1973—. Heritage chmn. Westland Bicentennial Com., 1974-76; adviser Jr. Achievement, 1977. Mem. Westland Jaycees (spoke of year 1975, adminstrv. v.p. 1976, dir. 1975), Redford Jaycees, Soc. Auto. Engrs. Presbyterian. Club: Masons. Home: 14016 Westgate Dr Redford MI 48239 Office: 13400 Outer Dr W Detroit MI 48228

BURT, WARREN THOMAS, JR., fund raiser; b. Detroit, Dec. 15, 1931: s. Warren Thomas and Medora Sharta (Harrison) B.; B.S., Mich. State U., 1953; m. Janet Marian Williams, Jan. 26, 1961; children—Pamela Margaret, Amy Susan. Asso. unit dir. United Found., Detroit, 1956-59, unit dir., 1959-68, asso. campaign dir., 1968-74, v.p.-campaign, 1974—; instr. Nat. Acad. Voluntarism, Alexandria, Va., 1974—. Served in U.S. Army, 1954-56. Mem. Sales/Mktg. Execs. Detroit, Mktg. Communication Execs. Internat., Am. Mktg. Assn. Presbyterian. Clubs: Recess, Farmington Country, Court House Tennis and Racquet. Office: 1528 Woodward Ave Detroit MI 48226

BURTCHAELL, JAMES TUNSTEAD, ednl. adminstr.; b. Portland, Oreg., Mar. 31, 1934; s. James Tunstead and Marion Margaret (Murphy) B.; A.B., U. Notre Dame, 1956; S.T.B., Pontificia Universita Gregoriana, Rome, 1958; S.T.L., Cath. U. Am., 1960; Ph.D., Cambridge U., 1966. Ordained priest Roman Catholic Ch., 1960; mem. Congregation Holy Cross, 1953; asst. prof. Bibl. studies U. Notre Dame (Ind.), 1966-68, asso. prof., 1969-75, prof., 1975—, chmn. dept. theology, 1968-70, provost, 1970—. Fellow, trustee U. Notre Dame. S.A. Cook Bye- Fellow Gonville and Caius Coll., Cambridge, 1965-66. Fellow Soc. for Religion Higher Edn.; mem. Am. Acad. Religion (pres. 1970-71), Soc. Bibl. Lit., Cath. Bib. Assn., Cath. Theol. Soc., Phi Beta Kappa. Author: Catholic Theories of Biblical Inspiration Since 1810; A Review and Critique, 1969; Philemon's Problem, 1973. Office: Office Provost U Notre Dame Notre Dame IN 46556

BURTON, CHARLES VICTOR, physician, surgeon; b. N.Y.C., Jan. 2, 1935; s. Norman Howard and Ruth Esther (Putziger) B.; m. Noel Michelle Kleid, Aug. 26, 1961; children—Matthew, Timothy, Andrew; student Johns Hopkins U., 1952-56; M.D., N.Y. Med. Coll., 1960; intern surgery Yale U. Med. Center, 1961-62; asst. resident neurol. surgery Johns Hopkins Hosp., Balt., 1962-66. chief resident, 1966-67. Diplomate Am. Bd. Neurol. Surgery, Nat. Bd. Med. Examiners. Research fellow Nat. Polio Found., 1956, HEW, 1958; neurosurg. fellow Johns Hopkins Hosp., 1960-61, 62-67, 69-70; asso. chief surgery, chief neurosurgery USPHS Hosp., Seattle, 1967-69; vis. research affiliate Primate Center, U. Wash., 1968-69; asst. prof. neurosurgery Temple U. Health Scis. Center, Phila., 1970-73, asso. prof., 1973-74, neurol. research coordinator, 1970-74; dir. dept. neuroaugmentive surgery Sister Kenny Inst., Mpls., 1974—; co-chmn. Joint Neurosurg. Com. on Materials and Devices, 1973—; chmn. Internat. Standards Orgn., 1974—, FDA adv. panel on neurologic devices, 1974—; mem. U.S. Biomed. Instrumentation Delegation to Soviet Union, 1974. Fellow A.C.S.; mem. Congress Neurol. Surgeons (chmn. com. on materials and devices 1972—), Am. Assn. Neurol. Surgeons, Minn. Neurosurg. Soc., Am. Congress Rehab. Medicine, AAAS, Assn. for Advancement Med. Instrumentation, ASTM (chmn. com. on materials 1973—), Internat. Soc. for Study of Lumbar Spine, Am. Nat. Standards Inst. (med. device tech. adv. bd. 1973—), Hennepin County Med. Soc., Minn. Med. Assn. (Gold medal award for best sci. presentation at 1975 Meeting), Cor et Manus Soc., Alpha Epsilon Delta. Home: 18409 Minnetonka Blvd Wayzata MN 55391 Office: Sister Kenny Inst 2545 Chicago Ave Minneapolis MN 55404

BURTON, DANIEL FREDERICK, educator; b. Chgo., Oct. 3, 1915; s. Clyde Daniel and Hazel Lucille (Henthorn) B.; A.A., U. Chgo., 1936, M.S., 1940, Ph.D., 1947; m. Verona Devine, July 22, 1950; 1 son, John Daniel. Instr. botany Miss. State Coll., 1945-48; asst. prof. biology Mankato (Minn.) State Coll., 1948-50, asso. prof., 1950-60, prof., 1960-75, asso. dir. campus planning, 1973-75; adminstrv. asst. to vice chancellor for mgmt. Minn. Community Coll. System, 1976—. Mem. Minn. State Bd. Edn., 1971—, pres., 1972. Served with AUS, 1942-46. Lion. Home: 512 Hickory St Mankato MN 56001

BURTON, GEORGE TREMBLE, JR., mech. engr.; b. Detroit, Jan. 14, 1924; s. George Tremble and Marie Elizabeth (Hess) B.; B.Mech.Engring., U. Detroit, 1950; m. Anna Margaret Spence, Oct. 4, 1952; children—Ellen, Thomas, Kathryn, Linda, Daniel. Project engr. Ford Sci. Lab., Dearborn, Mich., 1953-55; sr. research engr. Williams Research Corp., Walled Lake, Mich., 1955-59; with Bendix Research Labs., Southfield, Mich., 1959—, mgr. aerospace instrumentation dept., 1969-73, dir. automotive program mgmt. center, 1973—. Served with USNR, 1943-45. Mem. Soc. Automotive Engrs., Am. Mgmt. Assn., Tau Beta Pi, Pi Tau Sigma. Roman Catholic. Author, editor in field. Home: 29720 Aberdeen St Southfield MI 48076 Office: Bendix Research Labs Bendix Center Southfield MI 48076

BURTON, JAMES ARTHUR, mgmt. cons.; b. Columbus, Ohio, Nov. 29, 1938; s. Mutual and Ruth Naomi (Lawson) B.; student Franklin U., 1964-66, 68; m. Enilie Kirkling, Dec. 18, 1955; children—James Arthur, Joel A., Jack A., Jacqueline A. With Ranco, Inc., Columbus, 1957-68, inventory cost controller, 1964-66, buyer, 1966-68; dep. dir. finance and adminstrn. CMACAO, Columbus, 1968-70; dir. mktg., v.p. bus. ops. ECCO Devel. Corp., 1970-71, pres., 1971-72; exec. dir. Exec. Bus. Devel. Corp., Columbus, 1972—. Bd. dirs. Opportunity Products Inc.; scoutmaster Boy Scouts Am., 1962-65; pres. male chorus Macedonia Bapt. Ch., 1972-74, chancel choir, 1974-75. Mem. Columbus Regional Minority Purchasing Council (treas.), NAACP, Urban League. Clubs: Columbus Old Timers (pres.), Masons. Home: 2188 Oriole Pl Columbus OH 43219 Office: 595 Broad St E Columbus OH 43215

BURTON, MARY JOAN (MRS. ROBERT E. BURTON), ednl. adminstr.; b. Hamilton County, Ind., July 1, 1918; d. William Nelson and Sybil Anna (Inman) Smith; primary certificate Ball State Tchrs. Coll., Muncie, Ind., 1938; B.S. in Edn., Ind. U., 1942, M.S. in Edn., 1960; m. Robert Ermer Burton, May 26, 1940; children—Ann E. (Mrs. J. Stephen Grimes), John E., Nancy E. (Mrs. Luis A. Morales), William L., James A. Tchr., Union Twp. Schs., Howard County, Ind., 1938-39, Westfield (Ind.) Schs., 1939-40; tchr. grade sch. Broadview Sch., Bloomington, Ind., 1956-63, tchr. educable retarded, 1963-65; tchr. trainable retarded Headley Sch., Bloomington, 1965-68; dir. Stone Belt Center for Retarded Citizens, Bloomington, 1968—. Sec., Monroe County Health Planning Council, 1972-73, Owen-Monroe County Health Planning Council, 1973-76, Regional 10 Health Planning Council, 1973-76; mem. Region 2 Subarea Advisory Council S. Ind. Health Systems Agency, 1977—. Mem. Council for Exceptional Children (pres. S. Central Ind. 1966, 72-73), Am. Assn. Mental Deficiency, Delta Kappa Gamma (pres. Beta Lambda chpt. 1966, corr. sec. Alpha-Epsilon state 1969-71), Pi Lambda Theta (dir. Iota chpt. 1971). Methodist. Club: Altrusa (pres. 1977-78). Home: 501 S Swain Ave Bloomington IN 47401 Office: 2815 E 10th St Bloomington IN 47401

BURTON, RALPH ASHBY, mech. engr.; b. Shreveport, La., Oct. 31, 1925; s. Cleveland Cunningham and Sadie (King) B.; B.S., U. Ark., 1947; M.S., U. Tex., 1951, Ph.D., 1952; m. Nancy Gaines, Aug. 4, 1948; 1 son, Ralph G. Research instr., U. Ark., Fayetteville, 1947-49; teaching fellow U. Tex., Austin, 1949-52; asst. prof. Mass. Inst. Tech., Cambridge, 1952-54; asso. prof. U. Mo., Columbia, 1954-58; staff scientist, sect. mgr. SW Research Inst., San Antonio, 1958-67; liaison scientist U.S. Office Naval Research, London, 1967-69; prof. mech. engring. Northwestern U., Evanston, Ill., 1969—. Mem. ASME, Am. Soc. Elec. Engrs., Am. Soc. Indsl. Engrs., AAUP, Sigma Xi. Republican. Presbyterian. Author: Vibration and Impact, 1958. Home: 719 Central St Evanston IL 60201 Office: Dept Mech Engring Northwestern U Evanston IL 60201

BURTON, WALTER ERVIN, writer; b. McMechen, W.Va., Nov. 18, 1903; s. David William and Mary Lucinda (Yoho) B.; student U. Akron, 1922-23, Johns Hopkins, 1923-24, 27-28. Editorial staffs Evening Times, Times-Press, Herald Pub. Co., Akron, 1922-27. Mem. Nat. Assn. Home and Workshop Writers. Contbr. numerous articles to mags. including Popular Mechanics, Popular Sci., others. Author: Home-Built Photo Equipment, 1947; The Story of Tire Beads and Tires, 1954, others. Editor: Engineering with Rubber, 1949; Patentee in field. Address: 1032 Florida Ave Akron OH 44314

BURTSCHI, JOSEPHINE FRANCES, artist; b. Vandalia, Ill., July 4, 1909; d. Joseph Charles and Olivia Pauline (Yoos) B.; student Maryville Coll., St. Louis, 1927-29. Owner, curator Little Brick House, Vandalia, Ill., 1957—; artist, book illustrator, historian. Mem. Fayette County (Ill.) Sesquicentennial Commn., 1967-68, Fayette County Bicentennial Commn., 1974-76. Recipient medallion Ill. Sesquicentennial Commn., 1968; certificate Ill. Bicentennial Commn., 1976; plaque Jane Isbell, 1962. Mem. Fayette County Cultural and Arts Assn., Ill. Hist. Soc. (75th Jubilee com.), Vandalia Hist. Soc. (pres. 1972—). Illustrator: Vandalia: Wilderness Capital of Lincoln's Land, 1963; A Port Folio for James Hall, 1968; James Hall of Lincoln's Frontier World, 1977. Home: 307 N 6th St Vandalia IL 62471 Office: 621 Saint Clair St Vandalia IL 62471

BURTSCHI, MARY PAULINE, author historian, educator; b. Vandalia, Ill., Feb. 22, 1911; d. Joseph Charles and Olivia Pauline (Yoos) Burstchi; student St. Mary of Woods Coll., 1929-30; B.A., St. Louis U., 1933; M.A., U. Ill., 1954. Tchr. high sch., Carlyle, Ill., 1936-39, Effingham, Ill., 1939-70; cons. research historian Vandalia Hist. Soc.; mem. state history com. Ill. Sesquicentennial Commn., 1968; chmn. Fayette County Bicentennial Commn., 1974-76; chmn. Fayette County Bicentennial Council, 1976—; poetry cons., bd. dirs. Fayette County Cultural and Arts Assn., 1974—. Recipient bronze medallion for hist. research for Ill. Sesquicentennial, 1968, award for teaching in student teaching program Eastern Ill. U., Charleston, 1970, award Ill. Bicentennial Commn., 1975, plaque, 1976. Mem. Ill. (dir. 1965-68, v.p. 1968—, chmn. Diamond Jubilee com. 1973-74), Vandalia (pres. 1962-65, v.p., 1972—), Effingham Regional (dir. 1962-64) hist. socs., Coll. Edn. of U. Ill. Alumni Assn. (dir. 1970-72, sec.-treas. 1972—), Friends of Old Vandalia Statehouse, Delta Kappa Gamma. Roman Catholic (pres. Sir Thomas More Soc. 1971-72). Club: Vandalia Women's (v.p. 1974—). Author: Vandalia Wilderness Capital of Lincoln's Land (award Ill. State Hist. Soc. 1965), 1963; A Port Folio for James Hall, 1968; A Guide Book of Historic Vandalia, 1974; editor: Seven Stories, 1975. various hist. soc. publs. Home: 307 N 6th St Vandalia IL 62471

BURWELL, STANLEY WOODRUFF, surgeon; b. Detroit, Apr. 4, 1916; s. Stanley Burgess and Margaret (Hayward) B.; A.B., Columbia Coll., 1938; M.D., Columbia U., 1942; m. Louise McGregor, Sept. 2, 1941; children—Bruce McGregor, John Woodruff. Intern, U.S. Naval Hosp., Bremerton, Wash., 1942-43; resident Lynchburg (Va.) Gen. Hosp., 1948-49; fellow in surgery Lahey Clinic, Boston, 1949-50; practice medicine specializing in surgery, Muncie, Ind., 1951—; mem. staff Ball Meml. Hosp., Muncie; cons. to industry. Served in USN, 1942-47. Diplomate Am. Bd. Surgery. Fellow A.C.S.; mem. AMA, Ind., Delaware County med. socs., Muncie Acad. Medicine. Republican. Presbyterian. Clubs: Rotary (Muncie); Delaware Country. Home: 3204 W Gilbert St Muncie IN 47304 Office: 424 W Jackson St Muncie IN 47305

BURZYNSKI, PETER RAYMOND, psychologist, educator; b. Watertown, Wis., May 7, 1948; s. Eugene Edward and Helen Louise (Krieger) B.; B.A., Lawrence U., 1970; M.S., Ind. State U., 1971, Ed.S., 1972, Ph.D. (Univ. fellow), 1977. Sch. psychometrist LaPorte (Ind.) Community Sch. Corp., 1972-74; co-dir. Porter Evaluation Center, Terre Haute, Ind., 1974-75; asst. prof. psychology Vincennes (Ind.) U., 1976—; counselor Internat. Ranger Camps, Leysin, Switzerland, 1970, Fredricksvaerk, Denmark, 1973. Youth activities dir. YMCA, Appleton, Wis., 1968-70, LaPorte, 1972-73. Mem. Am., Ind. psychol. assns., Nat. Assn. Sch. Psychologists, AAUP, Phi Delta Kappa, Lambda Psi Sigma. Blumberg Spl. Edn. Edowment Fund grantee, 1976; Author: Archeus and I, 1970; (with K. Zucker) The Paired Hands Test-Adult, The Paired Hands Test-Secondary, 1976; Contbr. articles to profl. jours. Office: Psychology Dept Vincennes U Vincennes IN 47591

BUSBOOM, DEAN RAY, engring. co. exec.; b. Lincoln, Nebr., Mar. 19, 1946; s. Elmer Frederick and Claudine (Armstrong) B.; B.S. in Chem. Engring., Purdue U., 1968. Engr., Alexander Engring. Co., Gulfport, Miss., 1968-71; pres. partner Busboom & Jones Assos., Indpls., 1971—; dir., pres. Drake Industries, Constantine, Mich., 1973—, Mich. Casket Co. Inc., Detroit, 1976-78, Taylor & Gaskin Tank Co., Constantine, 1976—, Elrich Mfg. Co. Inc., Modoc, Ind., 1977-78, Sandage Fire Protection Co., San Diego, 1977—; lectr. Wayne State U., Detroit; chmn. bd. Expanso, Harrisonville, Mo., Jordan Aircraft, Kansas City, Mo. Sponsor Salvation Army. Mem. So. Ind. Operators Assn., Casket Mfrs. Assn., Am. Mgmt. Assn., U.S. C. of C. Lutheran. Clubs: Lions (sponsor handicapped olympics San Diego); Masons (Bloomington, Ind.). Home: Rural Route Box 174C Unionville IN 47468 Office: 7636 N Hilltop Dr Unionville IN 47468

BUSCH, MERRILL JOSEPH, editor, pub., author; b. Jordan, Minn., July 25, 1936; s. Albert Meinrad and Hildegarde (Bauer) B.; student St. Thomas Coll., St. Paul, 1954-57; B.A., U. Minn., 1958, postgrad., 1958-59; m. Mary Daphne Meteraud, Oct. 16, 1965; children—Christopher, Jennifer, Amy. Editor, pub. Upper Midwest Investor mag., 1960-62, Mid-Am. Investor mag., 1962-63; editor Minn. Alumni mag., 1963-64; mng. editor Cereal Sci. Today and Cereal Chemistry mag., 1965-72; editor Cereal Industry Newsletter, 1970-72; dir. publs. Am. Assn. Cereal Chemists, 1965-72, Am. Phytopathological Soc., 1968-72, also gen. mgr. both orgns., 1970-72; mng. editor Nematology mag., 1971-72, Phytopathology mag., 1968-72, Phytopathology News, 1968-72, Comml. West mag., 1972-76, Greater Mpls. mag., 1972—, The Gold Book, 1974—, 9th Fed. Directory Banks, and Nat. Fin. Marketplace, 1974-76; mng. editor mag. div., bus. and fin. editor Sun Newspapers, Inc., Edina, Minn., 1972—, dir. spl. publs., 1976—, dir. promotion, mktg., 1977—; dir. Cybx Corp., Mpls.; editor, pub. Cable TV Report, 1970-74, Foodservice Tng. Report, 1972-76; dir. Gaslight Sq. Properties. Served with AUS, 1959-60. Recipient Recognition award Mpls. C. of C., 1975; work included in tricentennial time capsule Minn. Bicentennial Commn., 1976. Mem. Am. Soc. Bus. Press Editors, Am. Mgmt. Assn., Fin. Communications Soc., Am. Council Biology Editors, Soc. Publ. Designers, Mediaeval Acad. Am., Am. Soc. Assn. Execs., Nat. Assn. Sci. Writers, Midwest Mail Mktg. Assn. (dir.), Antique and Classic Boat Soc. (dir.), Phi Beta Kappa. Republican. Roman Catholic. Clubs: Minn. Press; Mpls. Athletic. Author: Training Yourself Series, Six Keys Series, You're Important Series; My Career; Sanitation Series; writer-producer ednl. filmstrips, films, recs. Home: 2120 Girard Ave S Minneapolis MN 55405 also Route 1 Box 186 Shorewood Dr St Michael MN 55376 Office: 6601 W 78th St Edina MN 55435

BUSCH, THEODORE NORMAN, cons. shooting range design; b. Cleve., Dec. 29, 1919; s. Theodore S. and Norma B.; student pub. schs. Cleve.; m. 2d, Sené Rosene, June 30, 1961; 1 dau. from previous marriage—Kathy Clayton. Dir. tech. communications DoAll Co., Des Plaines, Ill., 1952-62; v.p. Shooting Equipment, Inc., Chgo., 1962-69; v.p. Caswell Equipment Co., Inc., Mpls., 1969—; v.p. Sente Co. Ind., Mpls., 1976—. Served with USAAF, World War II. Mem. Am. Soc. Quality Control, Soc. Mfg. Engrs., Internat. Assn. Chiefs of Police. Author: Fundamentals of Dimensional Metrology, 1963; Guidelines for Police Shooting Ranges, 1977. Contbr. articles to profl. jours. Patentee in field. Home: 400 Groveland St Minneapolis MN 55403 Office: 1221 Marshall St NE Minneapolis MN 55413

BUSCHBACH, THOMAS CHARLES, geologist; b. Cicero, Ill., May 12, 1923; s. Thomas Dominick and Vivian (Smiley) B.; B.S., U. Ill., 1950, M.S., 1951, Ph.D., 1959; m. Mildred Merle Fletcher, Nov. 26, 1947; children—Thomas Richard, Susan Kay (Mrs. Pete Elmer), Deborah Lynn (Mrs. Gary Baker). With Ill. Geol. Survey, 1951—, geologist lead and zinc mining, Galena, 1951-54, geologist for stratigraphy, Urbana, 1954—. Geologic cons. petroleum, nuclear reactor siting, motion pictures. Served to lt. comdr. USNR, 1942-47. Fellow Geol. Soc. Am.; mem. Am. Assn. Petroleum Geologists (chmn. stratigraphic correlations com. 1970-73), Soc. Petroleum Engrs., Assn. Engring. Geologists. Home: 604 Park Ln Champaign IL 61820 Office: 268 Natural Resources Bldg Urbana IL 61801

BUSEN, KARL MAX, physicist, radio-TV mfg. co. exec.; b. Bonn, Germany, Apr. 19, 1918; s. Heinrich Ferdinand and Hedwig Conradine (Frankowski) B.; B.S., U. Munich (Germany), 1949, Dr. rer. Nat., 1956, postgrad. (German Research Council scholar), 1955-56; m. Johanna Christine Berberich, Jan. 4, 1952. Patent agt. Siemens & Halske, Munich, 1956-58; sr. engr. Sprague Electric Co., North Adams, Mass., 1958-60, sect. head, 1960-63, dept. head, 1963-69; mgr. Zenith Radio Corp., Chgo., 1969—; vis. instr. optics and nuclear physics, Williams Coll., Williamstown, Mass., 1961-69. Mem. Electrochem. Soc., Am. Assn. Physics Tchrs. Contbr. articles to profl. jours. Home: 505 Kingston Terr Deerfield IL 60015

BUSH, ALEXANDER THEOPHILE, steel industry exec.; b. Dollar Bay, Mich., Nov. 4, 1896; s. E. Theophile and Belle (Moralee) B.; B.S. in Chemistry, U. Ill., 1918; M.B.A., U. Chgo., 1942; m. Bernice Wittman, Aug. 26, 1926 (dec. Feb. 1968). Salesman Johns-Manville Co., Chgo., 1928-36; sales mgr. Owens-Ill. Glass Co., Toledo, Ohio, 1936-38; with Acme Steel Co., Chgo. and Riverdale, Ill., 1940-60, dir. distbn. services, until 1960; owner, pres. Vulcania Inc., Manhattan, Ill., 1960—. Mem. grants-in-aid com. U. Ill. Found., 1968—; mem. dean's fund U. Chgo. Sch. Bus. Served with U.S. Navy, 1918. Mem. Am. Mktg. Assn. (past pres.), Am. Soc. Metals, Blast Furnace and Coke Plant Assn., Beta Gamma Sigma. Mason. Club: President's (U. Ill., Urbana). Home: 245 Trask St Manhattan IL 60442 Office: PO Box 93 Manhattan IL 60442

BUSH, BONNIE BETH, historian; b. N.Y.C., Aug. 4, 1938; d. Abe Milton and Estelle R. (Phillips) Schwartz; B.A., New Sch. Social Research, 1963; M.A., N.Y. U., 1964, Ph.D., 1976; m. Irving M. Bush, June 23, 1958; children—Alan Michael, Steven Douglas. Dir. sects. of history of medicine dept. urology Cook County Grad. Sch. Medicine, Hektoen Inst. Med. Research, Chgo., 1966-75; lectr. history of medicine Northwestern U. Sch. Medicine, 1968-69: adj. prof., vice chmn. dept. history and philosophy of medicine Chgo. Med. Sch., 1969-73, adj. asso. prof., 1974-76, asso. prof., vice chmn. dept., 1976-77, asso. prof., chmn. dept., 1977—; dir. Center for Study of Urinary Tract Infection, 1974—; pres. Med. Office Services, Inc. Mem. Am. Assn. History of Medicine, Soc. History of Medicine Chgo. (past pres.), AAAS, Am. Hist. Assn., Assn. Am. Med. Colls., Philosophy of Sci. Assn., Soc. History of Tech., Orgn. Am. Historians, Soc. Social History of Medicine. Jewish. Contbr. articles to profl. jours. Home: Honey Bush Farm Burlington IL 60109 Office: UHS Chgo Med Sch 2020 W Ogden Chicago IL 60612

BUSH, GORDON KENNER, JR., newspaper publisher; b. Athens, Ohio, July 30, 1934; s. Gordon K. and Izotta (Ackerman) B.; A.B., Colgate U., 1956; M.B.A., Harvard U., 1960; m. Margene Gilson, Aug. 2, 1958; children—Frederick Gordon, David Gilson. Nat. advt. sales Rochester (N.Y.) Times-Union and Democrat and Chronical, 1960-62; asst. pub. The Athens Messenger, 1962-65, pub., editor, 1965—; sec.-treas. The Messenger Pub. Co., 1965-72, pres.-treas., 1972—; dir. Athens Nat. Bank. Pres., Community Improvement Corp. Athens; civilian aide to sec. of army for So. Ohio, 1969-72; trustee Ohio U.; chmn. Hock-Hocking dist. Boy Scouts Am., 1977—. Served with AUS, 1956-58. Named Outstanding Young Man of Year, Athens Jaycees, 1966; recipient Community Service award Southeastern Ohio Regional Council, 1968; Distinguished Service award in journalism Ohio U., 1973. Mem. Athens (dir., pres. 1969-70), Ohio (dir., exec. com.) chambers commerce, Ohio Pub. Law Research Inst. (steering com.), SAR, Order of Symposiarch, Sigma Delta Chi, Beta Theta Pi. Club: Rotary. Home: 54 Utah Pl Athens OH 45701 Office: Route 33 North and Johnson Rd Athens OH 45701

BUSH, HAROLD, clin. psychologist; b. Chgo., Dec. 27, 1923; s. Herman and Rose Minnie (Weisman) B.; Ph.D., Ill. Inst. Tech., 1971. Part-time instr. Roosevelt U., Chgo., 1967-72; staff psychologist Southeast Mental Health Center, Chgo. Bd. Health, 1968-76; dept. cons. Patient and Family Counseling Center, Little Co. of Mary Hosp., Evergreen Park, Ill., 1974—; pvt. practice psychotherapy, psychol. testing and consultation, Chgo., 1969—. Served with AUS, 1943-46. Licensed psychologist, Ill., Calif. Mem. Ill., Calif., Am. psychol. assns., Nat. Register of Health Service Providers in Psychology. Jewish. Home: 201 E Chestnut St Apt 17B Chicago IL 60611 Office: 30 N Michigan Ave Suite 1714 Chicago IL 60602

BUSH, MARTIN HARRY, museum dir.; b. Amsterdam, N.Y., Jan. 24, 1930; s. Martin J. Bush; B.A., State U. N.Y., Albany, 1958, M.A., 1959; Ph.D., Syracuse (N.Y.) U., 1966; divorced; children—Lisa, Jennifer, Pamela. Acting sr. historian N.S. State Edn. Dept., 1961-62, cons., 1962-63; instr. history Syracuse U., 1963-65, asst. dean acad. resources, 1965-70; asso. prof. history Wichita State U., 1970—, dir. Edwin A. Ulrich Museum Art, 1974—, v.p. acad. resource devel., 1974—; vice chmn. Kans. Com. Humanities, 1971-74, Kans. Pub. TV Service, 1973—, Univ. Press Kans., 1972-73; bd. dirs. Wichita Festivals, Inc., 1971-74, Mid-Am. Art Alliance, 1973-76. Author: Ben Shahn: The Passion of Sacco and Vanzetti, 1968; Revolutionary Enigma, 1969; Doris Caesar, 1970; Goodnough, 1973; Forty Two Great Men of History, 1974; Duane Hanson, 1976; Ernest Trova, 1977; also catalogs, articles, brochures. Home: 202 N Rock Rd Wichita KS 67206 Office: Wichita State Univ Box 46 Wichita KS 67208

BUSH, WILLIAM SHIRLEY, educator; b. Plant City, Fla., July 21, 1929; s. William Shirley and Annie Vera (Crews) B.; B.A., John B. Stetson U., 1950; M.A., U.S.D., 1953; docteur, La Sorbonne, U. Paris, 1959; m. Muriel Mary Sutcliffe, Apr. 2, 1959; children—Anastasia, James, John, Andrew. Instr. Romance langs. Duke, 1959-62, asst. prof., 1962-65, asso. prof., 1965-66; asso. prof. French, U. Western Ont., London, 1966-67, prof., 1967—. Fulbright fellow, 1956-57; Fulbright prize award, 1957-58; Duke U. research council summer fellow, 1962, 65; Canada Council leave fellow, 1972-73. Mem. Canadian Assn. Univ. Tchrs., Association des Professeurs de Francais des Universites Canadiennes. Greek Orthodox. Author: Souffrance et Expiation dans la Pensee de Bernanos, 1962; L'Angoisse du Mystere: Essai sur Bernanos et M. Ouine, 1966; Bernanos, 1969. Editor: Regards sur Baudelaire, 1975. Home: 81 Wychwood Park London ON N6G 1R4 Canada Office: Dept French Univ Western Ont London ON Canada

BUSHELMAN, THEODORE JOSEPH, airport exec.; b. Lakeside Park, Ky., Jan. 30, 1936; s. Steve William and Irene (Egnor) B.; E.E., Ohio Mechanics Inst., 1956; B.S. in Radio and TV Production, Cin. Coll. Conservatory Music, 1959; B.S. in Edn., U. Cin., 1958; m. Gloria Jean Meissner, Apr. 10, 1975; children—Stephen, Geoffrey, Kimberly TeDene, Christopher, Ted J. Pr Producer, dir. WKRC-TV, Cin., 1956-60; v.p. engring. KIOO Radio Sta., Oklahoma City, 1960-63; gen. mgr. Sta. WKKY, Erlanger, Ky., 1963-67; dir. community relations Greater Cin. Airport, 1967—. Vice chmn. Transit Authority No. Ky., Newport, 1971—; chmn. No. Ky. United Appeal, Cin., 1972; chmn. Boone County (Ky.) Library Bd., 1973—; mem. advisory bd. Salvation Army, Covington, Ky., 1974—; dir. ARC, Cin., 1974—; dir. No. Ky. Conv. Visitors Bur., 1974—. Named Outstanding Jaycee of the Year, Boone County, 1965-66, Outstanding Young Man, No. Ky., 1968. Mem. Ky. State C. of C. (dir. 1970-72), No. Ky. C. of C. (pres. 1972), Cin. C. of C. (chmn. pub. relations com. 1976), Airport Operators Council Internat., Am. Assn. Airport Execs., Pub.

Relations Soc. Am. Home: 8 Gibbons Dr Florence KY 41042 Office: PO Box 75000 Cincinnati OH 45275

BUSS, DANIEL FRANK, environ. scientist; b. Milw., Jan. 13, 1943; s. Lynn Charles and Pearl Elizabeth (Ward) B.; B.S., Carroll Coll., 1965; M.S. in Biology, U. Wis., 1972, M.S. in Environ. Engring., 1977; m. Ann Makal, Jan. 22, 1977. Dir. limnological studies Aqua-Tech, Inc., Waukesha, Wis., 1969-72; project mgr. environ. studies Point Beach Nuclear Plant, Two Creeks, Wis., 1972-76; dir. aquatic studies environ. sci. div. Camp Dresser & McKee, Inc., Milw., 1977—; guest lectr. on nuclear power and the environment. Mem. Am. Nuclear Soc. (sec.-treas. Wis. sect.), Midwest Soc. Electron Microscopists, Internat. Soc. Theoretical and Applied Limnology and Oceanography, Internat. Assn. for Gt. Lakes Research, N.Am. Benthological Soc. Author: Seasonal Ultrastructural Variations in the Rostral Neurohypophysis of the Alewife in Lake Michigan, 1972; An Environmental Study of the Ecological Effects on Lake Michigan of the Thermal Discharge from the Point Beach Nuclear Plant, 1976. Home: 5543 N Shasta Dr Glendale WI 53209 Office: 6132 W Fond du Lac Ave Milwaukee WI 53218

BUSSABARGER, ROBERT FRANKLIN, artist; b. Corydon, Ind., Sept. 17, 1922; s. Russell and Alice Franklin (Schuck) B.; B.A., Wittenberg U., 1944; M.A. in Art, Mich. State U., 1947; postgrad. Ohio State U., 1949-51; m. Mary Louise Sterling, May 12, 1946; children—Wendi Jean, David Robin. Tchr. art Benton Harbor (Mich.) Pub. Schs., 1948-49; instr. art Mich. State U., 1947; asst. prof. art Stephen F. Austin State U., 1951-53; prof. art U. Mo., Columbia, 1953—, chmn. dept., 1970-73; sculptor, painter; works represented in: Mr. India Collection, Springfield Art Mus., Mo. Hist. Soc., U. Mo. Art Archtl. Mus.; bd. Maplewood Barn Theatre; adv. bd. Columbia Art League; chmn. Columbia Commn. on the Arts, 1975—. Served to lt. (j.g.), USNR, 1943-46; PTO. Fulbright exchange fellow, 1961-62; faculty fellow to India, 1968-69. Mem. Mo. Crafts Council, Nat. Council Edn. for Ceramic Arts, Columbia Art League, Danforth Assos. Democrat. Episcopalian. Home: 1914 Princeton St Columbia MO 65201 Office: A126 Fine Arts Bldg University Missouri Columbia MO 65201

BUSSARD, LAWRENCE A., govt. ofcl.; b. Bath County, Va., Aug. 24, 1924; s. Arnold Herron and Mary (Jones) B.; A.A., St. Mary's Sem. and U., 1946; A.B., Loras Coll., 1949; M.S. in Social Work, Va. Commonwealth U., 1954; m. Constance Locher, Nov. 19, 1960; children—Anthony L., Marie, Martha. Chief psychiat. social worker Lincoln (Ill.) State Sch., 1949-54; asst. dir. div. mental retardation services, Dept. Mental Health, Springfield, Ill., 1954-69, mental health supt. Warren G. Murray Children's Center, Centralia, Ill., 1969, Elisabeth Ludeman Mental Retardation Center, Park Forest, Ill., 1969-71, Lincoln State Sch., Ill., 1971-74, William Howe Devel. Center, Tinley Park, 1974; adminstr. state operated residential services, Springfield, 1974—; sr. health officer USPHS, 1956—. Mem. Adv. Study Com. on Mental Retardation, 1964—; mem. first White House Conf. on Mental Retardation, 1965; exec. sec. Gov. Commn. Mental Retardation, 1958; tech. advisor, del. Ill. White House Conf. Children and Youth, 1960, 70; del. 6th White House Conf. Children and Youth, Washington, 1960. Mem. Lincoln Meml. Garden, Springfield, Ill. Established Locher-Bussard Scholarship Fund, Clarke Coll., 1970. Mem. Nat. Assn. Social Workers, Am. Acad. Certified Social Workers, Am. Assn. on Mental Deficiency, Nat. Assn. Retarded, Ill., Bath County (Va.) hist. socs., Ill. State Mus. Soc., Clayville Arts and Crafts, Springfield Art Assn., Va. Mus. Fine Arts. Roman Catholic. Club: Elks. Home: 203 10th St Lincoln IL 62656 Office: 402 State Office Bldg Springfield IL 62706

BUSSE, ROBERT WILLIAM, JR., chiropractic physician, health services adminstr.; b. Detroit, Jan. 25, 1926; s. Robert William and Amelia Pauline (Daniel) B.; student Drake U., 1947-48; D. Chiropractic, Palmer Coll. Chiropractic, 1962; m. Marilyn Ann Gaynor, June 5, 1965; children—Kristen Lynn, Liesa Karen. Pvt. practice as chiropractic Internist, Utica, Mich., 1962-65; dir. Avon Med. Group, Utica, Sterling Heights, Mich., 1964—; pres., chmn. bd. Roblyn Enterprises; med. dir. Humanity House of Romeo, Alcoholic Rehab. Center, Romeo, Mich., 1974; dir. ALCCO Centers, Roseville, Mich. Cons. alcohol abuse problems Humanity House of Romeo, 1972-74, Nat. Council Alcoholism, 1972—. Served with USNR, 1943-45. Fellow Am. Coll. Chiropractic Internists; mem. Nat. Council on Alcoholism, Am. Council on Diagnosis and Internal Disorders, Am. (cons. 1960—), Mich. (chmn. com. on alcoholism 1974-75), chiropractic assns., Mich. Alcohol and Addiction Assn. Home: 11175 Gates Ave Romeo MI 48065 Office: 42700 Van Dyke St Sterling Heights MI 48078

BUSTA, MILAN G., banker; b. Cleve., Nov. 10, 1924; s. Charles and Mary (Krejci) B.; student John Carroll U., 1942-43; B.B.A., Ohio State U., 1946; postgrad. Ind. U., 1971; m. Jeanne Cervenka, Jan. 15, 1949; children—Michael J., William E., Paul T. Residential home builder, land investor, 1948-57; sr. accountant Basic Inc., Cleve., 1957-59; sec. treas. Tiger Brands Inc., Cleve., 1960-62; treas. Regulus Inc., Cleve., 1962-63; v.p., treas. Union Financial Corp., Cleve., 1963—; exec. v.p. Union Savs. Assn., Cleve., 1963-74, pres., mng. officer, 1974—, also dir.; pres., dir. Union Fin. Investment, Union Service Corp., Bayridge Estates; dir. Wellington Mortgage Co. Merit badge counselor Cleve. council Boy Scouts Am., 1950-65; mem. Brecksville (Ohio) Little Theatre; bd. dirs., treas. St. Augustine Manor, 1974—, Neighborhood Housing Service Cleve. Mem. Nat. Assn. Accountants, Delta Chi. Roman Catholic. Clubs: Cleveland Athletic, Treasurers, Westwood Country, Rotary. Home: 12550 Lake Ave Lakewood OH 44100 Office: 1 Terminal Tower Cleveland OH 44113

BUSTOW, SHELDON MARC, hosp. adminstr.; b. Cleve., Dec. 16, 1948; s. Jack and Elizabeth (Sopko) B.; B.A. in Sociology, Miami U., Oxford, Ohio, 1971; M.A. in Health Care Adminstrn., George Washington U., 1973; m. Debra Shatz, Aug. 29, 1971; 1 dau., Adena Sima. Adminstrv. resident Fairview State Hosp., Costa Mesa, Calif., 1972-73; planning officer Ohio Div. Mental Retardation, Columbus, 1973-75; asst. supt. Columbus (Ohio) State Inst., 1975—. Mem. Assn. Mental Health Adminstrs., Am. Hosp. Assn., Gerontol. Soc., Am. Assn. Mental Deficiency. Home: 64 N Cassady St Columbus OH 43209 Office: 1601 W Broad St Columbus OH 43223

BUTIN, JAMES WALKER, physician; b. Fredonia, Kans., July 13, 1923; s. James A. and Berenice Marie (Walker) B.; A.B., U. Kans., 1944, M.D., 1947; M.S. in Medicine, U. Minn., 1952; m. Betty Belle Launder, June 29, 1949; children—Richard Edward, Philip Walker, Lucy Elizabeth, John Murray. Intern, U. Kans. Med. Center, 1947-48; resident in pathology, 1948; fellow in internal medicine Mayo Found., 1949-52; practice medicine specializing in internal medicine and gastroenterology, Wichita, Kans., 1952—; mem. staff Wichita Clinic, St. Francis Hosp., Wesley Med. Center; asso. prof. Wichita Br., Kans. U. Sch. Medicine. Summerfield scholar, 1940-44. Diplomate Am. Bd. Internal Medicine (gastroenterology). Mem. A.C.P., AMA, Am. Gastroenterol. Assn., Am. Assn. History Medicine, Kans., Sedgwick County (past pres.) Christian med. socs., Wichita Med. Edn. Assn. (chmn. 1973-74), Mayo Alumni Assn., Wichita Audubon Soc. (past pres.), Kans. Ornithol. Soc. (past pres.), Phi Beta Kappa, Alpha Omega Alpha, Nu Sigma Nu, Beta Theta Pi. Republican. Episcopalian. Contbr. articles to med. jours. Home: 38 Mission Rd Wichita KS 67206 Office: 3244 E Douglas Ave Wichita KS 67208

BUTLER, BENJAMIN EDWARD, transp. co. exec.; b. Omaha, Mar. 28, 1930; s. Benjamin William and Evea V. (Still) B.; B.A., U. Nebr., 1952; m. Gloria Hunt, Nov. 7, 1953; children—Matt Lewis, John William. Prodn. mgr. KTVH, Hutchinson, Kans., 1952-53; program dir. KCKT-TV, Great Bend, Kans., 1954-55; mgr. Radio Sta. KIHO, Sioux Falls, S.D., 1956-57; pres. Hunt Transp., Inc., Omaha, 1957—; dir. Northwestern Nat. Bank, Omaha, Releasing Corp., Rock Island, Ill. Bd. dirs. YMCA, 1970-72. Mem. Am. Trucking Assn. (chmn. livestock div.), Livestock Conservation Assn. (pres.), Livestock Conservation, Inc. (nat. safety chmn.), Council Bus. Execs. Creighton U., Nebr. Motor Carriers Assn. (pres.). Home: 1617 S 109th St Omaha NE 68144

BUTLER, BROOKS ALLEN, surgeon; b. Mpls., Mar. 26, 1939; s. Melvin Edward and Grace C. (Mix) B.; B.S., U. Minn., 1962, M.D., 1964; m. Janice Yvonne Sandstrom, Aug. 5, 1961; children—Jennifer, Scott, Chad. Intern, Harbor Gen. Hosp., Torrance, Calif., 1964-65; surg. resident, U. Minn., Mpls., 1967-72; surgeon, Physicians Clinic, St. Paul, 1972—; chief of staff, Mounds Park Hosp., 1976; chief of surgery, Midway Hosp., 1976; clin. asst. prof. dept. surgery, U. Minn. Fellow A.C.S., Minn. Surg. Soc.; mem. St. Paul Surg. Soc. Home: 13506 Larkin Dr Minnetonka MN 55343 Office: 451 N Dunlap St Saint Paul MN 55104

BUTLER, GERALDINE HEISKELL (GERRI), designer, artist; b. Detroit, Sept. 6, 1930; d. Artist Kavassel and Geraldine Gentle (Heiskell) B.; student Wright Jr. Coll., 1946; B.E., Chgo. U., 1948; B.A. in Edn. (Delta Sigma Theta Scholar), Chgo. Art Inst., 1949, M.A. in Edn., 1950; postgrad. Harvard U., 1962-64. Tchr. pub. elementary schs., Chgo., 1949-52; tchr. art Chgo. pub. high schs., 1953-61; supr. art Chgo. Bd. Edn., 1962-75; graphic art and media coordinator, dept. instrn. Chgo. Bd. Edn., 1976-77; founder, prin. Gehebu-AK, design cons. services, Chgo., 1976—; founder, prin. Butler Studios, creative designer, Chgo., 1977—; one-man shows include: Saxon Gallery, Chgo., Roosevelt Hotel, N.Y.C., Henri IV Restaurant, Cambridge, Mass., Hilton Trinidad, B.W.I., Goldstein Gallery, Chgo.; group shows include: Triangle Gallery, Chgo., McCormick Pl., Chgo., Hyde Park Art Center, Chgo., Ill. State Fair, Peninsula Exhbts., Door County, Wis.; represented in permanent collections: rental gallery Art Inst. Chgo., Huntington Hartford Collection, N.Y.C.; judge numerous exhbts. and competitions; art cons. and designer. Mem. Ill. wing CAP, 1963—. Huntington Hartford fellow, 1956-58. Mem. Internat., Ill., Nat. art edn. assns., Western Arts Assn., Am. Craftsmen Assn., Alumni Chgo. Art Inst., Soc. Typog. Arts, Artists Guild Chgo., Chgo. Soc. Artists, N. Shore Art League, Hyde Park Art Center, Evanston Art Center, Triangle-Lincoln Park Art Center, Am. Youth Hostles, Delta Kappa Gamma, Delta Sigma Theta. Episcopalian. Office: PO Box 11360 Chicago IL 60611

BUTLER, JAMES THOMAS, broadcasting exec.; b. Peoria, Ill., May 30, 1921; s. Thomas A. and Estelle (Maloney) B.; grad. Bradley U., 1942; m. Jean Claire Eliel; children—Nancy (Mrs. Chester Davis Rudolf III), James T., Jeffrey, Cynthia. Exec. v.p. Hearst Radio, Inc., Milw., 1966—; v.p., gen. mgr. WISN div. Hearst Corp., Milw., 1959—; gen. mgr. Sta. WISN-TV, Milw., 1965—, v.p., 1959—. Bd. dirs. St. John's Home, Better Bus. Bur., Milw. Internat. Band; exec. dir. Milw. Summerfest, 1977—. Served with AUS, 1942-46. Mem. Broadcast Pioneers, Nat. Broadcasters Club, Milw. Assn. of Commerce. Clubs: North Hills Country, Milwaukee Press, Wisconsin (Milw.). Home: 12650 W Bluemound Rd Elm Grove WI 53122 Office: 120 N Harbor Dr Milwaukee WI 53202

BUTLER, KENNETH B., business exec.; b. Richland, Mich., Aug. 27, 1902; s. Ross S. and Jennie (Blain) B.; B.A., U. Wis., 1925; m. Wilma Steinberg, Nov. 5, 1925; 1 son, Roger Lee. Reporter, Madison (Wis.) Capital Times, 1923-25; editor Mendota (Ill.) Sun-Bull., 1925-27; pub. Constantine (Mich.) Advertiser Record, 1927-31; mgr. Conco Press, Mendota, 1931-41; pres. Wayside Press, 1941—; pres. Kenneth B. Butler and Assos., 1938—; founder Butler Typo-Design Research Center, 1951, Time-Was Village Mus., 1967; lectr. Medill Sch. Journalism, Northwestern U.; bus. mgr. P.E.O. Record, 1931—. Gen. chmn. Mendota Centennial Jubilee, 1953, Mendota Autorama, 1955, 57, 59, 61, Constantine (Mich.) Centennial, 1928; mem. Sweet Corn Festival Com., 1962; chmn. Nat. Glidden Tour., 1963. Bd. dirs. LaSalle County unit Am. Cancer Soc. Named Kiwanis Man of Year, 1953; recipient Community Service award C. of C., 1976. Mem. Mendota Athletic Booster Soc., Ill. State, Mendota (dir. 1947-53) chambers of commerce, Am. Bell Assn., Farm Bur., Ill. Mfrs. Assn., Mark Twain Soc., LaSalle County Hist. Soc., Sigma Delta Chi. Republican. Presbyterian (elder). Elk. Clubs: Horatio Alger (co-founder, pres. 1965-67); Antique Automobile Am. (dir. Ill. region, pres. 1960-61, treas. 1967-68, nat. bd. dirs., dir. activities Central region), Steam Car, Classic Car, Pierce Arrow Society, Rolls Royce Owners, Model T Ford, Horseless Carriage, Men's Garden Am. Author: Headline Design, 1949; Effective Illustration, 1952; 101 Layouts, 1954; Double Spreads, 1955; Back of the Book Makeup, 1957; Ken Butler's Layout Scrapbook, 1958; Display Type Faces, 1959; Back of the Book Makeup, 1960; Borders, Boxes and Ornamentation, 1961; How To Stage an Oldtime Auto Event, 1961. Co-author: Magnificent Whistlestop. Editor Sidelights. Contbr. articles to profl. pubs. Speaker and lectr. Home: 1325 W Burlington Rd Mendota IL 61342 Office: 1501 Washington Rd Mendota IL 61342

BUTLER, NOBLE LYNCH, family therapist; b. Dodge City, Kans., Apr. 5, 1934; s. Lester Henry and Flossie (Taylor) C.; B.A. cum laude, Baylor U., 1955; M. Div., Southwestern Sem., 1958; M.A., Ph.D. cum laude, Boston U., 1962; m. Sara Elizabeth Nevins, Aug. 6, 1956; children—Sara, Noble, Valerie. Pvt. practice marital and family psychotherapy, Wheaton, Ill., 1962-67; asso. prof. psychology No. Baptist Sem., Oak Brook, Ill., 1967-71; chief edn., asst. prof. clin. psychiatry Center for Family Studies, Inst. of Psychiatry, Northwestern U. Med. Sch., Chgo., 1971—; cons. Chgo. Pub. Schs., 1974-75, Catholic Social Services, Peoria, 1975-77, Milw. Psychiat. Services, 1975-77, Family Practice Center U. Ill., 1976-77, Lakeside VA, 1976-77. Mem. Sesquicentennial Commn., Ind., 1966. Danforth Found. fellow, Menninger Found., Topeka, Kans., 1962; recipient Jaycee Distinguished Service award, Man of the Yr., 1966. Mem. Am. Psychol. Assn., Am. Assn. of Marriage and Family Counselors, Am. Orthopsychiatric Assn., Soc. of Tchrs. of Family Medicine. Baptist. Clubs: Rotary, Chgo. Council on Foreign Affairs. Home: 21W143 Kensington St Lombard IL 60148 Office: 10 E Huron St Chicago IL 60611

BUTLER, WILFORD ARTHUR, JR., assn. exec.; b. Grand Rapids, Mich., Apr. 17, 1937; s. Wilford A. and Dorothy (French) B.; B.A., Western Mich. U., 1961; M.B.A., Fla. Atlantic U. Dir. pub. relations Preferred Ins. Co., Grand Rapids, 1961-62; asst. to chmn. Delta Upsilon fraternity, N.Y.C., 1962, exec. sec., Indpls., 1963-76, exec. dir., 1976—; advisor Mid-Am. Interfrat. Assn., 1965-77. Mem. Am. Coll. Frat. Bicentennial Commn. study, 1975-77. Recipient Salisbury-Scott award Tau Kappa Epsilon, 1975. Mem. Assn. Coll. Frats. (pres. 1974), Frat. Execs. Assn. (sec., editor 1974, pres. 1976-77), Commn. on Fraternity Research (treas. 1972-75), Am. Soc. Assn. Execs. (certified; mem. editors and pubs. sect. adv. bd.), Delta Upsilon (editor monthly Newstrends 1971—, quar. 1973—). Clubs: Indpls. Alumni of Delta Upsilon, Columbia (Indpls.). Author: Executive Compensation Trends. Editor, Our Record, 1963—, Provision of Leadership corp. officers guide. Office: PO Box 40108 Indianapolis IN 46240

BUTSON, WALLACE JAMES, veterinarian; b. Ghent, Minn., Sept. 18, 1918; s. John Thomas and Emma Moline (Ostul) B.; D.V.M., Iowa State U., 1944; m. Edna Winifred Knuths, Dec. 14, 1944; children—Pamela (Mrs. Michael Lund), John, James, Michael, Constance, Patrick. Vet. insp. Bur. Animal Industry, U.S. Dept. Agr., St. Paul and Mexico City, 1944-49; practice vet. medicine, LaPorte City, Iowa, 1949-51, Wells, Minn., 1951-72; owner, operator S.P.F. Lab. Wells, 1961—; dir. Wells Fed. Savs. & Loan. Pres. Nat. Specific Pathogen-Free Swine Accrediting Agy. Conrad, Ia., 1966-69, dir. 1963-66, 69-71. Vol. fireman, 1952-54. Bd. dirs. Wells-Easton Sch. Bd., 1955-70, treas. 1958-70. Served with AUS, 1943-44. Named honorary chpt. farmer Future Farmers Am., 1953. Mem. Am., Minn. (chmn. audit com. 1970—) vet. med. assns., Am. Assn. Lab. Animal Sci., Am. Assn. Swine Practicioners, Indsl. Vet. Assn., AAAS, Minn. Pork Producers Assn., South Central Minn. Vet. Assn., Minn. Specific Pathogen Free Assn. (sec. 1967-71), Am. Legion. Methodist (trustee). Mason. Home: 600 6th SW Wells MN 56097 Office: 470 3d St SE Wells MN 56097

BUTT, STANLEY JOHN, farm mgr.; b. Tarkio, Mo., Feb. 25, 1930; s. Otto Henry and Ella (Laumann) B.; student Tarkio Coll., 1949; B.S., N.W. Mo. State Coll., 1953; M.S., Ia. State U., 1956; m. Anna Mildred Maxon, June 10, 1955; children—Frederick Lynn, Lisa Ann. Gen. mgr. Midwest div. Norris Farms, Havana, Ill., 1957—; animal nutrition and feed cons. Norris Grain Co., Chgo., 1957—, Ill. and Norris Cattle Co., Ocala, Fla., 1957—. Chmn. Spoon River dist. Boy Scouts Am. Bd. dirs. Mason-Fulton Med. Found., Fulton County ARC. Served with AUS, 1953-55. Mem. Am. Soc. Animal Sci., Cornbelt Beef Council, Nat. Livestock Feeders Assn. (dir.), Hoof and Horn Nat. Block and Bridle (hon.), Internat. Platform Assn., Am. Nat. Cattlemen, Phi Sigma Epsilon. Republican. Lutheran. Optimist. Home: RR 1 Lewistown IL 61542 Office: Box 486 Havana IL 62644

BUTTREY, DONALD WAYNE, lawyer; b. Terre Haute, Ind., Feb. 6, 1935; s. William Edgar and Nellie Madaline (Vaughn) B.; B.S., Ind. State U., 1956; J.D., Ind. U., 1961; m. Judith Ann Miller, Feb. 2, 1957; children—Greg, Alan, Jason. Admitted to Ind. bar, 1961; law clk. to chief judge U.S. Dist. Ct. So. Dist. Ind., 1961-63; mem. firm McHale, Cook & Welch, Indpls., 1963—. Mem. adv. com. Little Red Door of Marion County Cancer Soc., Inc., 1972-74, Tabernacle Recreation Program, Indpls., 1972-74; chmn. Ind. Lawyers for Humphrey for Pres., 1972; precinct committeeman Indpls. Democratic Com., 1971-74; mem. Slating Conv. Rules Com., 1973, Greater Indpls. Dem. Fin. Com., 1972, 76—. Served with AUS, 1956-58. Mem. Am. (mem. coms. taxation sect.), Ind., Indpls. bar assns., Phi Delta Phi, Theta Chi. Methodist. Clubs: Indpls. Athletic, Univ., Highland Country. Editor Ind. Law Jour., 1960-61. Home: 38 E 52d St Indianapolis IN 46205 Office: 1122 Chamber of Commerce Bldg 320 N Meridian St Indianapolis IN 46204

BUTTS, ARDEN ELDRIDGE, childrens counselor; b. Ryder, N.D., May 15, 1933; s. Charles Henry and Agnes Emily (Houpt) B.: B.S., Minot State Coll., 1960; M.S., N.D. State U., 1967; postgrad. U. N.D., 1968-69; m. Carol June Baisch, Sept. 9, 1956; children—Carrie Lynn, Mark Charles. Tchr., coach Bottineau (N.D.) Schs., 1960-66; dir., counselor Upper Deslacs Guidance Project, Bowbells, N.D., 1967-70; dir. Early Identification Project, Minot, N.D., 1970-72, dir. Ward County Spl. Edn. Program, 1972-73; elementary counselor Minot Pub. Schs., 1973-77; instr. grad. extension courses N.D. State U., Fargo, 1972-77; cons. in field. Mem. Alumni Bd. Minot State Coll., 1973—; pres. Zion Luth. Ch., Minot, 1976. Served with U.S. Army, 1956-58. Mem. Nat. Edn. Assn., N.D. Edn. Assn., Am., N.D. Personnel and Guidance assns., Parent Teachers Assn., Am., N.D. sch. counselors assns., Minot State, N.D. State U. alumni assns., Am. Legion. Lutheran. Clubs: Elks, Eagles, Masons. Contbr. articles in field to profl. jours. Home: 617 16th Ave SW Minot ND 58701 Office: Dakota Elementary Minot Pub Schs Minot ND 58701

BUTTS, STANLEY VERNON, psychologist; b. Withamsville, Ohio, Apr. 2, 1938; s. Vernando and Florence Lenora (Ludlow) B.; B.A., U. Mich., 1960; M.A., U. Kans., 1962, Ph.D., 1967; m. Melinda Jan Bloodhart, Jan. 26, 1964; children—Jonathan, David. Pvt. practice psychology, Kansas City, Mo., 1967—; staff psychologist VA Hosp., Leavenworth, Kans., 1967-69; asst. prof. U. Kans. Med. Center, Kansas City, Kans., 1969-75; sr. scientist Midwest Research Inst., Kansas City, Mo., 1975-76; Mem. Am., Mo. psychol. assns., Assn. Advancement Psychology, Sigma Xi. Mem. Ch. of Christ. Rotarian. Contbr. articles in field to profl. jours. Home: 5124 Cody St Shawnee KS 66203 Office: 751 E 63d St Kansas City MO 64110

BUTYNSKI, WILLIAM, psychologist; b. Keene, N.H., May 11, 1944; s. William and Stella (Zavorotny) B.; B.A., Catholic U. Am., 1966; Ph.D., U. Vt., 1974; m. Benedetta Rizzi, June 11, 1966; children—Sonya Lynn, Sara Louise, William, Michael. Research asso. Aspects Behavioral and Environ. in Traffic Safety, U. Vt., Burlington, 1968-69; dir. Drug Rehab. Commn., State of Vt., Waterbury, 1969-72; dir. Vt. Alcohol and Drug Abuse Program, Montpelier, 1972-74; exec. dir. Midwestern Area Alcohol Edn. and Tng. Program, Inc., Chgo., 1974-77; project dir. sci. Mgmt. Corp. Decision Studies Group, Washington, 1977—; co-dir. New Eng. Sch. Alcohol Studies, 1973. NDEA fellow, 1966-69; Nat. Safety Council grantee, 1969-72. Mem. Am. Psychol. Assn., Alcohol and Drug Problems Assn. N.Am. (v.p. 1976-77, treas. 1975-76, bd. dirs. 1974-77), Nat. Assn. State Drug Abuse Program Coordinators (founding mem., bd. dirs. 1971-74), Nat. Rehab. Assn., Am. Pub. Health Assn. Roman Catholic. Home: 18341 Gladville Ave Homewood IL 60430 Office: 1730 K St NW Suite 1201 Washington DC 20006

BUXTON, LUELLA SKILBRED (MRS. WILLIAM C. BUXTON), author, genealogist; b. Berlin, Wis., July 13, 1934; d. Lawrence G. and Hattie (Becker) Skilbred; student Ripon Coll., 1952-54; 1952-54; B.S. in English and Edn., Marian Coll., 1956; B.S. in Journalism, Marquette U., 1958; m. William C. Buxton, May 8, 1964; 1 son, William Charles II. Asst. women's news editor Fond du Lac (Wis.) Commonwealth Reporter, 1958-59; women's news editor Oneonta (N.Y.) Daily Star, 1959-60, feature writer Oshkosh (Wis.) Northwestern, 1962-63; fashion copywriter Gimbel Bros., Milw., 1963-66; free lance writer periodicals and mags. Mem. Wis., Norwegian Am., Fon du Lac County (charter) geneal. socs., Theta Sigma Phi. Episcopalian. Author: The Old Testament for Beginners, 1960; We Love the Place, O God, 1961; The New Testament for Beginners, 1964; A Song of Saints, 1966; When the Church Was Young, 1966; Christian News-Herald, 1968; Letters to Young Christians, 1972; Anderson-Espeland-Skilbred Genealogy, 1976, other genealogies. Home: 122 E Forest Ave Neenah WI 54956

BUZZA, EDWARD JOHN, lawyer; b. Milw., June 4, 1945; s. Edward Joseph and Elizabeth Gertrude (Kress) B.; B.A., Marquette U., 1967, J.D., 1969; m. Mary Irene Herdina, Jan. 27, 1968; 1 dau., Lynn Beth. Admitted to Wis. bar, 1969; mem. firm Terwilliger,

Wakeen, Piehler, Conway & Klingberg, Stevens Point, Wis., 1976—; dir. Travel Shop, Inc., Stevens Point and Wisconsin Rapids, Wis., Midstate Distbrs. Corp. Bd. dirs. Portage County Civil Legal Aid Soc., 1974—, United Way of Portage County, 1976—, U. Wis. Stevens Point Found., 1976—. Mem. Am., Portage County (pres. 1974) bar assns., State Bar Wis., Central Wis. C. of C., Phi Alpha Delta. Elk (presiding justice 1972—, trustee 1975—), Kiwanian (trustee 1972-74). Home: 1808 April Lane Whiting Stevens Point WI 54481 Office: 1308 Main St Stevens Point WI 54481

BUZZOTTA, VICTOR RALPH, psychologist; b. St. Louis, Mar. 18, 1931; s. Joseph and Antonina (Morella) B.; A.B., Washington U., St. Louis, 1952, Ph.D., 1956; m. Merle Lee Brock, Aug. 29, 1953; children—Robert Joseph, Ann Nina. Psychologist, VA Hosps., 1956-58; cons. Ill. Dept. Mental Hygiene, 1958-61; dir. Psychol. Assos., Inc., St. Louis, 1958—; lectr. Washington U., 1956-61. Lic. psychologist, Ill.; certified psychology Mo. Psychol. Assn. Mem. Mo. Psychol. Assn. (treas. 1959-62), Am., Midwestern psychol. assns. Author: Effective Selling Through Psychology, 1973; Dimensional Management Strategies, 1971; Effective Motivation Thru Performance Appraisal, 1977; contbr. articles to profl. jours. Home: 9466 Bonhomme Woods St Louis MO 63132 Office: 8201 Maryland St St Louis MO 63105

BYARS, GEORGE GLEN, mfg. co. exec.; b. Kell, Ill., Jan. 8, 1921; s. William Duncan and Mildred Belle (Scott) B.; grad. high sch.; grad. Dale Carnegie Course, 1957; m. Alma Gladys Hawkins, May 3, 1942; children—Sharelle Kay (Mrs. David Barry Moranville), Beverly Suzanne, Catherine Ann. Tool and die maker, Bronson's, Blue Island, Ill., 1941-42; with Sola Basic Industries div. Dowzer Electric, Mt. Vernon, Ill., 1947—, plant supt., 1957-74, v.p. Sola Basic Industries div. ELE-Q, Carolina, P.R., 1974—, Dowzer Electric, 1977—. Mem. Bluford Sch. Bd. Edn., 1956-70; mem. Jefferson County Extension Council, U. Ill., 1965-69. Bd. dirs. Sandia Chico Christian Mission, 1970—. Served with USNR, 1942-45. Mem. Christian Ch. (deacon 1963-66, elder 1967-76). Home: Route 4 Mount Vernon IL 62864 Office: 510 S 1st St Mount Vernon IL 62864

BYE, BRUCE WILLIS, farm orgn. exec.; b. Portland, Ind., June 11, 1946; s. Herbert Clair and Alma Berniece (Stein) B.; B.S. in Agrl. Econs., Purdue U., 1968; M.S. in Agrl. Econs., Pa. State U., 1973; m. Ilze Erna Henkels, Aug. 31, 1968; children—Leanne Nora, Kent Andrew. Market analyst F S Services, Inc., Bloomington, Ill., 1973-74; market analyst Ind. Farm Bur. Coop. Assn., Inc., Indpls., 1974-75, mem. cabinet, 1976—; asst. mgr. Ind. Farm Bur. Coop., Indpls., 1975-76, mgr. econ. and market research dept., 1976—. Bd. dirs. Metro-Health Plan, Indpls., 1975—; mem. council Bethany Luth. Ch., Indpls. Served in U.S. Army, 1968-71; Vietnam. Decorated Bronze Star medal, Army Commendation medal with oak leaf cluster. Mem. Am. Marketing Assn. (pres. Central Ind. chpt. 1977-78), Am. Agrl. Econs. Assn., Gamma Sigma Delta, Omicron Delta Epsilon. Republican. Home: 1216 Alton St Beech Grove IN 46107 Office: 120 E Market St Indianapolis IN 46204

BYER, STEPHEN BARRY, mdse. cons. exec.; b. Chgo., Apr. 3, 1942; s. David Sidney and Blossom (Schiff) B.; student U. Ill., 1958-62, Northwestern U., 1960-61; m. Barbara Lynn Sokolec, Aug. 15, 1964; children—Matthew Ross, Joshua Ben, Benjamin Saul, Sarah Ann, Rebecca Anne. Traffic supr. Fuller & Smith & Ross, Inc., Chgo., 1959-60; media dir. Richard Newman Advt., Champaign, Ill., 1961-62; gen. mgr. contract services div. Cowles Communications, Inc., Des Moines, 1963-67; exec. v.p. Whitney-Forbes, Inc., Chgo., 1967-69; sr. v.p., corp. dir. mktg. Playboy Enterprises, 1969-70; pres. Byer/Intermark, Inc., 1970-73, chmn. bd., 1973—; pres. Kinetic Technologies, Inc., 1970—. Mem. Am. Mktg. Assn., Mail Advt. Club Chgo., Direct Mail Advt. Assn., Chgo. Assn. Commerce and Industry, Mchts. and Mfrs. Club. Clubs: Internat. (chmn.), Whitehall, Barclay (Chgo.); Des Moines. Author: Hefner's Gonna Kill Me When He Reads This, 1972. Address: 625 N Michigan 15th Floor Chicago IL 60611

BYERLY, DALE LEROY, mfg. co. exec.; b. Elkhart, Ind., Nov. 27, 1926; s. Raymond C. and Flossie Rebecca (Rigby) B.; B.S. in Mech. Engring., U. Toledo, 1951; m. Patricia Frances Wilburn, Jan. 27, 1951; children—Douglas Dean, Rebecca Ann. Detailer, Toledo Scale Co. (Ohio), 1951-53; asst. project engr. Elec. Auto Lite Co., Toledo, 1953-58; Project engr. Bridgeport Brass Co., Adrian, Mich., 19S8-59; asst. dir. production and mfg. engring. Champion Spark Plug Co., Toledo, 1959—. Treas. Cub Scouts, 1958-60; active Big Brothers, 1960-62, Jr. Achievement, 1963-64; precinct committeeman Republican Party, 1964-66. Served with USN, 1945-46. Mem. Soc. Mfg. Engrs. (vice chmn.), Toledo Mgmt. Assn. (dir. 1975-77). Roman Catholic. Club: Laurel Hills. Patentee in field. Home: 2138 Glen Arbor Toledo OH 43614 Office: 900 Upton Ave Toledo OH 43607

BYERS, RAYMOND HOWARD, supt. schs.; b. Ollie, Iowa, Dec. 1, 1911; s. Walter and Philora Matilda (VanOrsdall) B.; B.S., William Penn Coll., 1934; M.A., State U. Iowa, 1939; m. Evelyn Elizabeth Wonderlich, Aug. 9, 1939; children—Raymond Robert, Susan Elizabeth. Tchr. elementary sch., Hedrick, Iowa, 1930-31; tchr. jr. high sch., Ollie, 1931-33; prin. Competine (Iowa) Twp. High Sch., 1933-38, supt., 1938-49; supt. Fremont (Iowa) Community Schs., 1949—; dir. Fremont Leisure Living Inc., Fremont Devel. Corp. Council mem. Iowa Girls' High Sch. Athletic Union, 1939—, Jack North award, 1975. Pres. Keokuk County (Iowa) Young Democrat's Club, 1934-36. Gym named in his honor, 1975. Mem. Am., Iowa assns. sch. adminstrs., Iowa Edn. Assn., Iowa Farm Bur. Methodist. Mason, Lion. Home: Main St Fremont IA 52561 Office: Box 68 Fremont IA 52561

BYINGTON, RICHARD PRICE, surg. supply co. exec.; b. Grand Rapids, Mich., July 24, 1940; s. Stanley J. and Constance Y. (Des Noyer) B.; B.S. in Pharmacy, Ferris State Coll., 1962; m. Margaret Ellen Evert, Aug. 26, 1961; children—James, Michael, Connie. Pub. relations rep. Mich. State Pharm. Assn., Lansing, 1962; pharmacist White & White Pharmacy Inc., Grand Rapids, 1962-63; sales rep. White & White Surg. Supply Inc., Grand Rapids, 1963-67, sales mgr., 1967-70, exec. v.p., 1970-74, pres., 1974—; mem. Nursing Home Adminstrs. Licensure Bd., 1970—. Mem. Am. Surg. Trade Assn. (bd. dirs.), Am., Mich. State, Kent County pharm. assns. Roman Catholic. Clubs: Lions, Peninsular. Home: 3341 Ashton Rd SE Grand Rapids MI 49506 Office: 19 La Grave Ave SE Grand Rapids MI 49503

BYRD, MORRIS PHILLIP, TV producer; b. Texarkana, Ark., Oct. 30, 1946; s. Morris and Berniece Lucille (Black) B.; student U. Ark., 1964-66; B.A., U. Denver, 1968, M.A., 1969. Producer/dir. WSIU-TV, Carbondale, Ill., 1972-74, WETV-TV, Atlanta, 1974-75; sr. producer cultural programming WMVS and WMVT-TV, Milw., 1975—; lectr. dept. Radio-TV, So. Ill. U., Carbondale, 1972-74. Served in U.S. Army, 1969-72. Recipient Emmy award Nat. Acad. TV Arts and Scis., 1976. Mem. Nat. Assn. Ednl. Broadcasters, Soc. Motion Picture TV Engrs. Democrat. Methodist. Home: 3423 N 78th St Milwaukee WI 53222

BYRNE, DAVID FRANKLIN, ednl. adminstr.; b. Pontiac, Ill., Dec. 11, 1924; s. Ira Counsel and Vera Ruth (Rittenhouse) B.; student Ill. State Normal U., 1942-44; B.S., U. Ill., 1948, M.S. with highest honors, 1949, Ed.D. with highest honors, 1964; m. Elizabeth C. Gebhardt, Dec. 16, 1944; children—David, William, Paul. Vocational agr. instr., Altamont, Ill., 1949-54; supt. schs. Altamont Unit Dist. 10, 1954-58; prin. East Leyden High Sch., Franklin Park, Ill., 1958-65; supt. Leyden Community High Sch. Dist. 212, Franklin Park, 1965—. Chmn. Franklin Park Planning Commn., 1969-72. Served with USNR, 1943-46. Mem. Ill. Assn. Sch. Adminstrs. (pres. 1976). Lion, Mason. Home: 3310 Calwagner St Franklin Park IL 60131 Office: 3400 Rose St Franklin Park IL 60131

BYRNE, DONN ERWIN, psychologist, academic adminstr.; b. Austin, Tex., Dec. 19, 1931; s. Bernard Devine and Rebecca (Singleton) B.; B.A., Calif. State U., Fresno, 1953, M.A., 1956; Ph.D., Stanford U., 1958; m. Lois Ann Pugsley, Sept. 12, 1953; children—Keven Singleton, Robin Lynn. Instr. psychology Calif. State U., San Francisco, 1957-59; asst. prof., psychology, U. Tex., Austin, 1959-62, asso. prof., 1962-66, asst. chmn., 1964-66; vis. prof. psychology Stanford U., Palo Alto, Calif., 1966-67, U. Hawaii, Honolulu, 1968; prof. psychology U. Tex., 1966-69, dir. exptl. personality program, 1963-69; prof. psychology Purdue U., W. Lafayette, Ind., 1969—, chmn. social personality program, 1972—; panel mem. NSF grad. fellowship program NRC, 1972; NIH participant Inst. Sex Research Summer Program, 1974; invited participant numerous univ. colloquia; numerous presentations to various psychol. assns. convs.; recipient NSF, NIMH, U. Tex. Research Inst., USAF, and other grants. Author: (with H.C. Lindgren) Psychology: An Introduction to the Study of Human Behavior, 1st edition, 1961; (with P. Worchel) Personality Change, 1964: An Introduction to Personality: A Research Approach, 1966; (with M.L. Hamilton) Personality Research: A Book of Readings, 1966; The Attraction Paradigm, 1971; (with R.A. Baron and W. Griffitt) Social Psychology: Understanding Human Interaction, 1st edition, 1974; (with R.A. Baron and B. Kantowitz) Psychology: Understanding Behavior, 1977; (with L.A. Byrne) Exploring Human Sexuality, 1977; contbr. numerous articles to psychol. jours. and chpts. to anthologies. Home: 515 Hillcrest Rd West Lafayette IN 47906

BYRNE, FRANCES EDIE, med. soc. exec.; b. Cleve., Nov. 13, 1918; d. William N. and Ota Dale (Rinehart) Edie; grad. Findlay Bus. Coll., 1938; m. William Francis Byrne, Feb. 14, 1944; children—Belinda, Brenda. Sec., Ohio Fuel Gas Co., Findlay, 1937-43; legal sec. Office of Price Adminstrn., Savannah, Ga., 1944-47; sec. for physician, Findlay, 1951-53, Cooper Tire & Rubber Co., Findlay, 1953-56; dir. adminstrv. services Am. Cancer Soc., Indpls., 1958—. Mem. Adminstrv. Mgmt. Assn., Phi Beta Psi. Republican. Roman Catholic. Home: 1807 Christopher Ln Speedway IN 46224 Office: 2700 E 55th Place Indianapolis IN 46220

BYRNE, JAMES JOSEPH, archbishop; b. St. Paul, July 28, 1908; s. Philip J. and Mary (McMonigal) B.; student Nazareth Hall Prep. Sem., 1924-27, St. Paul Sem., 1927-33; S.T.B., Cath. U. Am., 1933; summer student U. Minn., 1933; S.T.D., U. Louvain (Belgium), 1937; S.T.D. degree. Ordained priest Roman Cath. Ch., 1933; prof. theology and philosophy St. Thomas Coll., St. Paul, 1937-45; part time prof. theology St. Catharine Coll., St. Paul, 1941-47; prof. theology St. Paul Sem., 1945-47; auxiliary bishop of St. Paul, 1947-56; bishop of Boise, Idaho, 1956-62; archbishop of Dubuque (Iowa), 1962—. Home: 1105 Locust St Dubuque IA 52001 Office: 1229 Mt Loretta Dubuque IA 52001

BYRNE, JOSEPH CYRIL, lawyer; b. Omaha, May 24, 1935; s. Cyril John Emmet and Wilma Esther Jueleen (Carter) B.; B.A., U. Nebr. at Omaha, 1957; J.D., Creighton U., 1960; m. Eleanor Joan Engle, July 20, 1957; children—Eric Joseph, Carey Eleanor. Admitted to Nebr. bar, 1960; individual practice law, Omaha, 1960—. Pres., chmn. bd. Northwest Baptist Home Soc., 1965-74; pres. Nebr. Baptist State Conv., 1972; dir. Omaha Met. Assn. Chs., 1968-72. Mem. Am., Nebr., Omaha bar assns. Republican. Club: Exchange (pres.). Home: 8030 Spaulding St Omaha NE 68134 Office: 10828 Old Mill Rd Suite 6 Omaha NE 68154

BYRNE, MICHAEL JOSEPH, bus. exec.; b. Chgo., Apr. 3, 1928; s. Michael Joseph and Edith (Lueken) B.; B.Sc. in Mktg., Loyola U., Chgo., 1952; m. Eileen Kelly, June 27, 1953; children—Michael Joseph, Nancy, James, Thomas, Patrick, Terrence. Sales engr. Emery Industries, Inc., Cin., 1952-59; with Pennsalt Chem. Corp., Phila., 1959-60; with Oakton Cleaners, Inc., Skokie, Ill., 1960-70, pres., 1960-70; pres. Datatax Inc., Skokie, 1970-74, Dataforms & Midwest Mktg. Assn., 1970—, Metro Tax Service Inc., 1975—. Served with Army Ordinance, 1946-48. Mem. VFW, Alpha Kappa Psi. Club: Toastmasters Internat. Home: 7350 Main St Niles IL 60648 Office: 8745 N Keeler Ave Skokie IL 60076

BYRON, BARRY MICHAEL, lawyer; b. Cleve., July 20, 1931; s. Carl J. and Elizabeth (Lewis) B.; student Union Coll., 1949-51; B.S., Georgetown U., 1954; J.D., Case Western Res. U., 1956; m. Judith Lytle, June 8, 1963; children—Barry Michael Jr., Stephen L., Matthew L. Admitted to Ohio bar, 1956; practiced in Painesville, Ohio, 1966—; law clk. U.S. Dist. Judge Charles J. McNamee, Cleve., 1958-60; 1st asst. pros. atty., Lake County, Ohio, 1961-66; mem. firm Baker, Byron & Hackenberg, Painesville, 1966—; gen. counsel Lake Met. Housing Authority, 1967—; law dir. city of Willoughby Hills 1968—, City of Willowick, O., 1973; acting judge Willoughby (Ohio) Municipal Ct., 1971-72. Instr. Ohio Peace Officers Tng. Program, 1968—; spl. counsel Lake County, Madison Twp., Grand River Village, Ohio, 1970—. Treas. Lake County exec. com., central com. Democratic Party, 1970—. Mem. Am. Arbitration Assn. (mem. panel 1967), Nat. Dist. Attys. Assn., Fed., Am., Ohio, Lake County (pres. 1973-74) bar assns., Ohio Municipal League, Phi Delta Phi. Home: 38033 Dodd's Hill Dr Willoughby Hills OH 44094 Office: Lakeshore Trust Bldg Painesville OH 44077

BYRON, WILLIAM DEVEREUX, brokerage and warehousing exec.; b. Hagerstown, Md., Jan. 18, 1925; s. William D. and Katherine (Edgar) B.; Phillips Exeter Acad., 1939-42, B.S., U. Md., 1951; m. Sibille Herrmann, June 4, 1966. Pres., treas., dir. W.H. Edgar & Sons, Inc., Detroit, 1959—; pres., treas., dir. Gt. Lakes Sugar & Warehousing, Inc.; dir. W.D. Byron & Sons, Inc., Lake Shore Sugar Co. Served with USNR, 1944-46. Mem. Am. Mgmt. Assn., Am. Warehouse Assn., Nat. Food Brokers Assn., Am. C. of C. in London, Nat. Council Phys. Distbn., Can. Assn. Phys. Distbn. Mgmt. (founder mem.), Mich., Detroit hist. socs., Mich., N.C. warehousemen's assns. Clubs: Detroit Economic, Country of Detroit; Grosse Pointe Country. Office: 1575 Lafayette St E Detroit MI 48207

BYRUM, JOHN CATRON, veterinarian; b. Kokomo, Ind., July 23, 1946; s. Richard Earl and Mary Kathryn (Catron) B.; student Manchester Coll., 1964-67; D.V.M., Purdue U., 1971; m. Gail Elaine Cordes, July 28, 1967; children—Roger Eric, Kathryn Elaine, Kristen Marie, Kara Renee. Owner Twelve Mile Vet. Clinic (Ind.), 1971—. 4-H Club sci. leader, 1972, 74, 76—; dir. local govt. housing project, 1976—. Mem. Am., Ind., Dist. (v.p. 1975, pres. 1976) vet. med. assns., Am. Assn. Swine Practitioners, Am. Assn. Bovine Practitioners. Mem. Ch. of Brethren (Sunday Sch. tchr.). Club: Lions (local v.p. 1975, pres. 1976). Home: Rural Route 1 Twelve Mile IN 46988

CABLE, ROBERT DOYLE, JR., psychologist; b. Oneonta, N.Y., Oct. 18, 1943; s. Robert Doyle and Mabel (Olmstead) C.; B.S., Mich. State U., 1966; M.A., Western Mich. U., 1969; m. Cheryl Bond, Nov. 17, 1972; children—Caryn, Kirsten. Staff psychologist Kalamazoo Child Guidance Clinic, 1969-71; dir. Hull Paulson Day Treatment Center, Kalamazoo, 1971-73; unit supt. Lakeside Residence for Boys and Girls, Kalamazoo, 1971—; mem. utilization and placement rev. com., dept. social services Mich. Fedn. Child Caring Agys. Lic. psychol. examiner, Mich. Mem. Am., Southwestern Mich. psychol. assns., Mich. Assn. Profl. Psychologists. Home: Rural Route 1 Flach Rd Mendon MI 49072 Office: 3921 Oakland Dr Kalamazoo MI 49008

CABLE, STEPHEN JAMES, ceramic tile mfr.; b. Canton, Ohio, May 7, 1924; s. Davis Arthur and Gail (Watson) C.; B.S., Case-Western Res. U., 1950; advanced mgmt. tng. Emory U., 1966-67; m. Jane Irwin Purdy, June 24, 1948; children—Nancy Jane, Davis James. Plant engr. Sparta Ceramic Co., 1950-54, plant mgr., 1954-56; successively mgr., sec., group v.p. Spartek, Inc. (formerly U.S. Ceramic Tile Co.), Canton, 1956—, also dir.; pres., dir. Polywood Corp., North Canton; v.p., dir. Joseph A. Locker Co., Canton. Trustee Canton YMCA. Served to 2d lt. Transp. Corps, AUS, 1943-46. Mem. Sigma Xi, Tau Beta Pi, Alpha Chi Sigma. Clubs: Canton (trustee), Congress Lake (Hartville, Ohio). Contbr. articles trade jours. Patentee in field. Home: 44 East Dr Congress Lake Hartville OH 44632 Office: 1375 Raff Rd Canton OH 44710

CABOT, JOSEPH, pedodontist; b. Detroit, Oct. 15, 1921; s. Benjamin and Ethel (Gutkovsky) C.; B.S., Wayne State U., 1942; D.D.S., U. Mich., 1945, M.S., 1947; m. Ruth Weiner, Aug. 19, 1945; children—Bonnie (Mrs. James Kaufman), Gary Michael, Elizabeth Ann, Jon Elliott. Mott fellow U. Mich., 1945-46; pedontic fellow Hurley Hosp., Flint, Mich., 1946-47; individual practice pedontics, Detroit, 1947-55, Lathrup Village, Mich., 1969—. Mem. bd. Delta Dental Plan Mich., 1959—, pres., 1963-66; pres., Detroit Dental Aid, 1952-55. Local bd. chmn. Selective Service, 1959-67, appeal bd. chmn., 1969—, dental adviser to state dir., 1968—; assemblyman United Community Services, 1971—. Served to maj. Dental Corps, AUS, 1955-57. Fellow Internat. Coll. Dentists, Am. Coll. Dentists, Am. Acad. Pedodontics; mem. Am. (ho. of dels. 1965-76, trustee 1977—), Mich. (pres. 1975-76) dental assns., Mich. Soc. Dentistry for Children (pres. 1953-54), Detroit Dist. Dental Soc. (Merit award 1964, pres. 1966-67), Kenneth A. Easlick Grad. Soc. (pres. 1973—), Omicron Kappa Upsilon, Alpha Omega. Lion. Home: 3159 Interlaken St Orchard Lake MI 48033 Office: 18239 W 12 Mile Rd Lathrup Village MI 48076

CABRERA, DONATO MARTIN, JR., surgeon; b. Philippines, Feb. 28, 1934; s. Donato and Angeles Sauco (Martin) C.; M.D., St. Thomas U., 1958; m. Mary Ora Smith, May 20, 1961; children—Alan, Cheryl, Jeffrey, Steven, Brian. Intern, Oak Park (Ill.) Hosp., 1959-60; resident Harper Hosp., Detroit, 1962-63, Alexander Blain Hosp., Detroit, 1963-65, Mt. Carmel Mercy Hosp., Detroit, 1965-66; practice medicine specializing in gen. surgery, Saginaw, Mich., 1969—; asso. clin. prof. surgery Mich. State U. Coll. Human Medicine, 1975—. Diplomate Am. Bd. Surgery. Fellow A.C.S. Home: 5296 Clydesdale St Saginaw MI 48603 Office: 1600 N Michigan St Saginaw MI 48602

CACCAMO, LEONARD PAUL, cardiologist; b. Youngstown, Ohio, Dec. 19, 1922; s. Domnick Paul and Louise (Massonie) C.; B.S. in Biology, Youngstown State U., 1944; M.D., Bowman Gray Sch. Medicine, 1947; m. Shirley Hyde, Aug. 13, 1949; children—David Paul, Barbara Ann, Deana Jo, Karen Louise. Intern, Rochester Gen. Hosp., 1948-49; resident in internal medicine St. Elizabeth Hosp. Med. Center, 1949-50, VA Hosp., Allen Park, Mich., 1950-52; clin. instr. Wayne State U., 1952-55; acting sect. chief cardiology VA Hosp., Allen Park, 1952-55; dir. med. edn. for internal medicine St. Elizabeth Hosp. Med. Center, Youngstown, 1959-62, dir. electrocardiography and coronary care unit, 1962—, dir. med. edn., 1970—. Chmn. Mahoning Shenango Area Health Edn. Network; trustee Northeastern Ohio Univs. Colls. of Medicine. Fellow Am. Coll. Cardiology (Ohio gov. 1965-68), A.C.P., Assn. Hosp. Med. Edn., AMA; mem. Am. Soc. Clin. Pharmacology and Therapeutics, Am., Ohio (pres. 1966-68) socs. internal medicine, Med. Educators Assn. Presbyterian (elder). Club: Masons, Shriners. Author: (with Kessler and Azneer) Diabetic Acidosis; Resuscitation. Home: 45 Redfern Dr Youngstown OH 44505 Office: 1044 Belmont St Youngstown OH 44505

CACERES, DOUGLAS, physician, educator; b. Bogota, Columbia, S.Am., Feb. 10, 1937; s. Cesar Felipe and Maria Elisa (Rosas) C.; came to U.S., 1963, naturalized, 1975; B.S., Colegio Nacional de San Bartolome, 1956; M.D., U. Nacional de Colombia, 1962; m. Ruth Angela Vega, June 9, 1966; children—Douglas F., Vivian Marcela, Michele Andrea, Andrew Allan. Intern, Meml. Hosp., Albany, N.Y., 1963-64; resident anesthesiology U. Pitts., 1964-66; staff anesthesiologist Hosp. Militar Central, Bogota, 1966-68; fellow in anesthesia Ind. U., 1968, 69, asst. prof., 1969—. Mem. Am., Ind. socs. anesthesia, Indpls. Soc. Anesthesiologists, Am. Coll. Anesthesiology, Anesthesia and Analgesia Research Soc.

CACIOPPO, ANTHONY JOSEPH, engring. psychologist; b. Akron, Ohio, Oct. 13, 1923; s. Carlo and Mary Julia (Almerico) C.; B.S., Kent State U., 1948; M.A., 1949; Ph.D., U. Iowa, 1954; m. Wilma Jean Love, Sept. 11, 1949; children—Diana Cacioppo Bockelman, Toni Cacioppo Tell, Gian. Process engr. Ravenna (Ohio) Ordnance Plant, 1952-53; head biomech. engring. Goodyear Aerospace Corp., Akron, 1953—, research mgr. life sci. dept., 1961-63, chief scientist fgn. tech. div. Wright Patterson AFB, 1963—. Served with USAAF, 1942-45. Fulbright scholar U. Rome, 1951-52. Mem. Sigma Xi, Psi Chi, Alpha Kappa Delta. Club: Masons. Home: 2871 Stauffer Dr Xenia OH 45385 Office: Fgn Tech Div Wright Patterson AFB OH 45433

CADIEUX, EUGENE ROGERS, ins. co. exec.; b. Detroit, Feb. 14, 1923; s. Harold S. and Nadia (Rogers) C.; student U. Detroit Coll. Commerce and Finance, 1941-42, Sch. Law, 1952; m. Leontine R. Keane, May 10, 1975. With bond dept. Standard Accident Ins. Co., Detroit, 1951-54; bond mgr. Am. Ins. Co., Detroit, 1954-65, Fireman's Fund, Cin., 1965-66, Md. Casualty Co., Detroit, 1966-75, Zervos Agency, Inc., 1975; cons. to contractors, 1957—. Asst. dir. boys work Internat Assn. Y's Mens Clubs, 1953; committeeman YMCA, Detroit; mem. citizens council Internat. Inst., 1977—; trustee Joint Meml. Day Assn. Served with AUS, World War II. Mem. Surety Assn. Mich. (sec. 1958), Am. Assn. State and Local History, Mich., Detroit (sec. 1970—, trustee), Cin. (com. on library and acquisitions) hist. socs., S.A.R. (pres. Mich. soc. 1961-62, bd. mgrs., nat. Americanism com.), Friends Pub. Library Cin., Friends Pub. Library Grosse Pointe (hist. com.), Delta Sigma Pi, Gamma Eta Gamma. Clubs: Players, Country (Detroit), Algonquin. Home: 208 Ridgemont Rd Grosse Pointe Farms MI 48236 Office: 24724 Farmbrook St Southfield MI 48034

CADIEUX, LEONTINE KEANE (MRS. EUGENE R. CADIEUX), ednl. adminstr.; b. Grosse Pointe, Mich., July 8, 1920; d. William Edward and Leontine Nathalie (D'Haene) Keane; B.A., Manhattanville Coll., 1941; M.A., U. Detroit, 1951; m. Eugene R. Cadieux. Supr. report writers Signal Corps Lab., Detroit, 1942-45;

instr. English U. Detroit, 1947-51; women's editor WJLB, 1951-53; broadcaster, writer, producer WDTR, 1953-55; asst. to exec. sec. WTVS, 1955-58; dir. radio-tv publicity Wayne State U., 1958-66, dir. information Coll. Lifelong Learning, 1966—, instr. Univ. Center for Adult Edn., 1963—, editor Wayne State U. Press, 1967-72. Mem. Tribute Fund United Community Services, 1966-73, mem. Pub. Relations Adv. Bd., United Found., 1974-76. Bd. dirs. Detroit City Theatre Assn., 1967—; bd. dirs. Southeastern Mich. chpt. ARC, 1962-72, also mem. pub. relations adv. com.; bd. dirs. Manhattanville Coll., 1956-59, League of Catholic Women, 1974—; mem. citizens council Internat. Inst., 1977—. Mem. Pub. Relations Soc. Am. (chpt. sec. 1971, v.p. 1972, treas. 1970, pres. 1973), Am. Women in Radio and TV (chpt. pres. 1961-63), Asso. Alumnae of Sacred Heart (corr. sec., 1969-71), Detroit Women Writers, Detroit Hist. Soc. (trustee 1971-77), Women in Communications (chpt. pres. 1968-70). Clubs: Manhattanville (Detroit), Detroit Press, Country Club (Detroit), Grosse Pointe Ski. Editor: Detroit Yiddish Theatre, 1967; Quotable Quotes on Education, 1968; Axiomatic Set Theory, 1969; The Challenge of German Literature, 1971. Home: 208 Ridgemont Rd Grosse Pointe MI 48256 Office: Coll Lifelong Learning Wayne State U Detroit MI 48202

CADLE, JOHN JOSEPH, educator; b. Sweet Springs, Mo., Apr. 21, 1939; s. James Michael and Mary Arabelle (Bailey) C.; B.S., Central Mo. State U., 1965, M.S., 1967; D.Ed. (fellow), U. So. Miss., 1970; m. Linda May Affolter, Oct. 27, 1962; children—Kimberly Lynne, David Jason. Tchr., Consol. Dist. 1, Hickman Mills, Mo., 1965-67; tchr., prin. pub. schs. Elkins, Ark., 1967-68; asso. prof., head dept. phys. edn. Upper Iowa U., Fayette, 1970—; coordinator dir. recreation program univ.-Fayette Community Sch.-Town of Fayette, 1974-76. Pres., Iowa Heart Assn., Fayette County, 1974-75. Served with USN, 1957-61. Recipient U.S. Presdl. Sports award in jogging, 1974, 76, Presdl. Letter of Commendation, Upper Iowa U., 1973. Mem. Am. Coll. Sports Medicine, Am. Alliance for Health, Phys. Edn. and Recreation, Nat. Assn. Intercollegiate Athletics, Phi Epsilon Chi, Alpha Chi Omega. Home: 607 Washington St Fayette IA 52142 Office: Dept Health Phys Edn and Recreation Fayette Upper Ia Univ Fayette IA 52142

CADMAN, WILSON KENNEDY, utility co. exec.; b. Wichita, Kans., Sept. 7, 1927; s. Wilson K. and Ethel Louise (Wheeler) C.; A.B. in Personnel Mgmt., Wichita State U., 1951; postgrad., 1953; postgrad. Okla. State U., 1965; m. Mary Roslyn Rowley, Nov. 22, 1950; children—Elizabeth Louise, Robert Wilson. With Kans. Gas & Electric Co., Wichita, 1951—, mgr. Wichita div., 1967-70, v.p., 1970—; dir. SW Fed. Savs. & Loan Assn., Wichita. Budget chmn. United Fund, Wichita; bd. dirs. Better Bus. Bur., Wichita; mem. exec. com. Wichita Area Devel., Inc.; pres. E.S. Edgerton Med. Research Found., Wichita. Served with USN, 1945-46. Mem. Mo. Valley Electric Assn. (chmn. gen. mgmt. com.), Edison Electric Inst. (mktg. exec. com.), Sales and Marketing Execs. Wichita (pres. 1965-66), Wichita Area C. of C. (vice chmn. mil. affairs com.), Phi Lambda Psi. Clubs: Wichita, Crestview Country, Topeka, Kiwanis. Home: 6512 Aberdeen St Wichita KS 67206 Office: 201 N Market St Wichita KS 67202

CADMUS, MARTIN CHARLES, research microbiologist; b. N.Y.C., Nov. 19, 1933; s. Charles Elmer and Anne (Donald) C.; B.S., U. Md., 1956; m. Karen Ann Conway, Mar. 20, 1965; children—David Alan, Kathleen Renee. Researcher microbial polysaccharides, related enzymes No. Regional Research Lab., Agrl. Research Service, U.S. Dept. Agr., Peoria, Ill., 1956—. Served with USNR, 1957. Recipient Superior Service award U.S. Dept. Agr., 1968. Mem. Am. Soc. Microbiology. Co-developer xanthan gum. Contbr. articles to profl. jours. Patentee in field. Home: 6728 N Parkwood Dr Peoria IL 61614 Office: Agrl Research Service No Regional Research Lab 1815 N University St Peoria IL 61604

CADMUS, ROBERT RANDALL, physician; b. Little Falls, N.J., June 16, 1914; s. Harold and Laura (Randall) C.; B.A., Coll. Wooster, 1936; M.D., Columbia, 1940; D.Sc. (hon.), N.J. Coll. Medicine and Dentistry, 1971; m. Lorna Peterkin, Sept. 8, 1941; children—Robert Randall, Lorna. Resident in surgery Columbia, Presbyn. Med. Center, N.Y.C., 1940-42, dir. Vanderbilt Clinic, adminstrv. asst. in charge profl. services to patients, 1946-48; asst. dir. U. Hosps., Cleve., 1948-50; dir. N.C. Meml. Hosp., 1950-62, cons. dir., 1962-66; prof. hosp. adminstrn. U. N.C., 1950-66, chmn. dept. hosp. adminstrn. Sch. Medicine, 1962-66; pres. N.J. Coll. Medicine and Dentistry, Newark, 1966-71; exec. dir. Med. Center Southeastern Wis., Milw., 1971-75; exec. med. dir. Found. Med. Care Evaluation Southeastern Wis., Milw., 1975—; prof. preventive medicine Med. Coll. Wis., Milw., 1971—; pres. N.C. Hosp. Edn. and Research Found., 1961-62, research dir., 1962-66; cons. USPHS Hosp., S.I., 1966-71, VA Hosp., East Orange, N.J., 1966-71. Mem. NIH Nat. Adv. Gen. Med. Scis. Council, 1970-74, Comprehensive Health Planning Council N.J., 1968-71; mem. Wis. Gov.'s Task Force on Health Policy and Planning, 1971-72; bd. dirs. Health Systems Agy., Milw., 1976—. Served to lt. col. USAAF, 1942-46. Decorated by govt. Tunisia for control Bubonic Plague, World War II. Mem. AMA, N.C. (pres. 1961-62, Distinguished Service award 1967), Wis. hosp. assns., Am. Coll. Hosp. Adminstrs. (chmn. bd. ednl. policy 1958-63), Am. Assn. Hosp. Consultants, NIH (mem. com. on Nat. Inst. Arthritis and Metabolic Diseases program grants 1960-64, com. on gen. clin. research center grants), Council Med. Adminstrs. (pres. 1959-60), Med. Adminstrs. Conf., Assn. Tchrs. Preventive Medicine, Assn. Am. Med. Colls., Assn. Acad. Health Centers, Med. Soc. Wis., Alpha Omega Alpha, Omicron Kappa Upsilon. Mem. editorial bd. So. Hosps. mag., 1960-65. Prin. investigator research grant hospital-physician relationships NIH, 1959-63, N.C. Ambulance Study, USPHS, 1961-66; Community Hosps. Study, 1963-66, Lab. Manpower, Dept. Labor, 1963-66. Home: 8851 N Tennyson Dr Milwaukee WI 53217 Office: 411 E Mason St Milwaukee WI 53202

CADWALLADER, THOMAS CHRISTY, psychologist; b. Pitts., June 30, 1932; s. Glenn Albert and Alice Clara (Christy) C.; A.B., Bucknell U., 1954; Ph.D., State U. N.Y. at Buffalo, 1959; m. Eva Hauel, Aug. 3, 1953; children—Mark Elliott, Lorraine Diane; m. 2d Joyce Vermeulen, Mar. 25, 1970. Asst. prof. Cornell Coll., Mt. Vernon, Iowa, 1964-66, asso. prof., 1966-73; prof. Indiana State U., Terre Haute, 1973—; research fellow dept. history sci. Harvard U., 1972-73. Served to Capt. U.S. Army, 1957-64. Mem. AAAS, Am. Assn. History Medicine, Am. Assn. Univ. Profs., Am. Eastern, Midwestern, Southeastern psychol. assns., Charles S. Peirce Soc., The Internat. Soc. for the History Behav. and Social Scis., History Sci. Soc., N.Y. Acad. Scis., Semiotic Soc. Am., Southern Soc. Philosophy and Psychology, Sigma Xi. Contbr. numerous articles in field to profl. jours. Home: 2231 N 12th St Terre Haute IN 47804 Office: Dept Psychology Indiana State Univ Terre Haute IN 47809

CADY, ELWYN LOOMIS, JR., medicolegal cons.; b. Ames, Ia., Feb. 21, 1926; s. Elwyn Loomis and Annabel (Lacey) C.; student Washington U., St. Louis, 1943-44, 46-48, U. Kansas City, 1949-50; J.D., Tulane U., 1951; B.S. in Medicine, U. Mo., 1955; m. Jane Carolyn Elliott, Jan. 27, 1964; children—James Anson, Kathryn Anne; stepchildren—Martin Norman Jensen III, Paul Elliott Jensen. Athletic coach Vermillion (Kan.) Rural High Sch., 1948-49; medicolegal cons., Kansas City, Mo., 1951—; dir. law-medicine program U. Kansas City, 1951-56; asst. dir. Law-Sci. Inst., asso. prof. law U. Tex., 1956-57; of counsel firm Koenig, Dietz, Hermann & Abels, St. Louis, 1959-74; gen. counsel Elliott Oil, Inc., Independence, Mo., 1966—, Raidorama, Inc., Kansas City, Mo., 1960—. Mem. com. mgmt. Eastern Jackson County Planned Parenthood Clinics, 1970—. Served with F.A., AUS, 1944-45; ETO. Recipient gold medal Law-Sci. Acad. Am., 1968. Mem. A.A.A.S., Nat. Geog. Soc., Am. Acad. Forensic Scis. (chmn. jurisprudence sect. 1954-55), Am., St. Louis, Kansas City, Eastern Jackson County bar assns., Mo. Bar, Mo. Writers' Guild (pres. 1967-68), Internat. Soc. Gen. Semantics, Am. Legion (post comdr. 1966-67, Mo. chmn. blood donor program 1968-69), Internat. Platform Assn., Phi Alpha Delta, Phi Beta Pi, Tau Kappa Epsilon. Author: Law and Contemporary Nursing, 1963. Home: 1919 Drumm Av Independence MO 64055 Office: 1919 Drumm Av Independence MO 64055

CAFFARELLI, ROBERT NICHOLAS, lawyer; b. Chgo. Heights, Ill., Mar. 20, 1933; s. Joseph and Emma (Bramanti) C.; B.S. magna cum laude, U. Notre Dame, 1955; J.D., DePaul U., 1958; m. Patricia Anne McNally, Feb. 17, 1962; children—Michael Robert, Mary Beth. Admitted to Ill. bar, 1958; practiced in Chgo., 1959—; asst. U.S. atty., 1959-62; asso. McDermott, Will & Emery, 1962-63; partner Walsh & Case, 1964-68, Caffarelli & Wiczer, Ltd., 1968-73, Boodell, Sears, Sugrue, Giambalto & Crowley, 1975—; dir. Nagle Pumps, Inc., Chicago Heights, Ill., 1972—, Vulcan Tube & Metals Co., Chicago Heights, 1965—. Mem. Ill. bar assn., Justinian Soc. Lawyers. Clubs: Lawyers, Chicago Athletic, Notre Dame (Chgo.); Olympia Fields (Ill.) Country. Editorial bd. DePaul Law Preview, 1957-58. Home: 41 Graymoor Ln Olympia Fields IL 60461 Office: One IBM Plaza Chicago IL 60611

CAFIERO, EUGENE ANTHONY, automobile co. exec.; b. N.Y.C., June 13, 1926; s. Anthony Eugene and Frances D. (Lauricella) C.; A.B., Dartmouth, 1946; postgrad. Rutgers U., 1947-48, Columbia, 1948-49, U. Mich., 1950-51; M.S. (Sloan fellow), Mass. Inst. Tech., 1959; m. Nancy Appleton Barnard, Jan. 23, 1960; children—Clayton, Anne, Sarah. With David Smith Steel Co., N.Y.C., 1947-49; with Ford Motor Co., Edgewater, N.J. and Dearborn, Mich., 1949-51; indsl. engr. Briggs Mfg. Co., Detroit, 1951-53; with Chrysler, Detroit, 1953—, v.p. Latin Am. ops., 1968-70, group v.p. U.S. and Can. automotive, 1970-72, group v.p. N.Am. ops., 1972-74, sr. exec. v.p., 1974-75, pres., 1975—. Served with USNR, 1946-47. Mem. Soc. Automotive Engrs., Engring. Soc. Detroit, Nat. Mgmt. Assn., Soc. Sloan Fellows. Presbyn. Clubs: Oakland Hills Country, Detroit Athletic. Home: 3753 Burning Tree Dr Bloomfield Hills MI 48013 Office: 1200 Lynn Townsend Dr Highland Park MI 48231

CAHILL, CHARLES ADAMS, III, psychiatrist; b. Milw., Mar. 2, 1930; s. Charles Adams and Beatrice C.; A.B., Harvard, 1951, M.D., 1955. Intern N.C. Meml. Hosp., Chapel Hill, 1955-56; resident Menninger Found., Topeka, Kan., 1956-58, Bellevue Psychiat. Hosp., N.Y.C., 1960-61; practice medicine specializing in psychiatry, Milw., since 1961; mem. staff Manitowoc (Wis.) County Hosp., 1971-74, Racine (Wis.) County Hosp., 1962-74; psychiat. cons. Milw. pub. schs., 1970-74; med. dir. Racine County (Wis.) Mental Health Clinic, 1962—; Manitowoc County Counseling Center, 1970—, Mental Health Center for Calumet County, Chilton, Wis., 1971—; psychiatrist Fond du Lac County Mental Health Center, 1973-75, 76—, Family Counseling Center Kenosha County, 1974-75, 76-77, Sheboygan County Mental Health Center, 1977—; psychiat. cons. Guidance Clinic of Lower Keys, Fla., 1975, Milw. County House of Corrections, 1969-73, 77—, Wis. Div. Corrections, Bur. Clin. Services, 1976—. Mem. mental health adv. com., Wis. Legis. Council, 1966-68. Served with M.C., USNR, 1958-60. Diplomate Am. Bd. Psychiatry and Neurology. Mem. AMA, Am., Wis. psychiat. assns. Contbr. articles to profl. publs. Address: 622 E Lake View Ave Milwaukee WI 53217

CAHILL, EDWARD THOMAS, grain co. exec.; b. Emington, Ill., June 21, 1922; s. Edward Michael and Catherine Agnes (Conroy) C.; grad. high sch.; m. Mary Darlene Kerwin, Sept. 2, 1950; children—Marianne, Marilyn, Marcia, Michael, Thomas. Mgr. Cahill Grain Co., Blackstone, Ill., 1946—, part owner, 1970—; owner Sunbury, Nevada Grain Co., Dwight, Ill., 1966—, Blackstone Grain Co., 1973—. Served with USAAF, 1943-46. Mem. Ill. Grain Dealers Assn. (legis. bd. 1973), Am. Legion. Clubs: Lions, Elks. Home: 110 N Lane St Ransom IL 60470 Office: Rural Route 1 Blackstone IL 61313

CAHILL, JAMES EDWARD, newspaper exec.; b. Chgo., July 8, 1925; s. Francis William and Jane (Howard) C.; student De Paul U., 1946-47; m. Helen R. Rossini, Aug. 16, 1952; children—Karen, James H., Janet, Catherine, Patricia. Copy boy Chgo. Daily Times, 1942-43; city desk asst., police reporter Chgo. Sun Times, 1946-50; with Chgo. Tribune, 1950—, mem. circulation dept., 1953-66, asst. country circulation mgr., 1966-71, mgr., 1971-75, mgr. circulation sales and promotion, 1975—. Served with USCGR, 1943-46. Roman Catholic. Home: 5216 W Patterson Chicago IL 60641 Office: 435 N Michigan Ave Chicago IL 60611

CAHILL, LAWRENCE PATRICK, coll. adminstr., clergyman; b. Middletown, Ohio, Jan. 20, 1922; s. Jones Martin and Florence Elizabeth (Smith) C.; student St. Mary Sem., 1942-47; M.A., John Carroll U., 1956; postgrad. Case Western Res. U., 1956-60. Ordained to ministry, Roman Cath. Ch., 1947; asst. pastor chs., Barberton, Ohio, 1947-53, Cleve., 1954; prof. history Borromeo Coll., Wickliffe, Ohio, 1954-60, vice rector, 1956-60, prof. history, 1971—, pres., 1975—; pres. St. John Coll. Ohio, Cleve., 1960-71. Mem. City of Cleve. Community Relations Bd., 1963—, vice chmn., 1970—; chmn. Ohio Found. Ind. Colls., 1969-70; trustee Cuyahoga Plan, 1974. Mem. Nat. Cath. Edn. Assn., Am. Hist. Assn., Am. Cath. Hist. Assn. Democrat. Home and office: 28700 Euclid Ave Wickliffe OH 44092

CAHILL, MARY FRAN, journalist; b. Milw.; d. Morgan Joseph and Claire Catherine (Warnimont) C.; B.A., M.A., Marquette U. Photojournalist Cedarburg (Wis.) News Graphic, 1965-67; photojournalist Milw. Jour., 1967-76, feature writer, 1976—, mem. unit holders council Jour. Co., 1977—. Hon. mem. Milw. Fire Dept. Recipient Distinguished Service award Milw. Fire Dept., 1972, 74, 75, 77; certificate of appreciation USCGR, 1975, 77. Mem. Nat. Press Photographers Assn., Wis. News Photographers Assn. (sec. 1973-75), Women in Communications, Milw. Press Club, Zool. Soc. Milwaukee County, Wis. Emergency Med. Technicians Assn. (Woman of Year award 1975), Sigma Delta Chi, Phi Mu, Phi Alpha Theta, Pi Gamma Mu. Roman Catholic. Club: Nordic Ski. Home: 3318 N 53d St Milwaukee WI 53216 Office: 333 W State St Milwaukee WI 53201

CAHOY, ROGER PAUL, research chemist; b. Colome, S.D., Feb. 19, 1927; s. Vincent F. and Edna A. (Rogers) C.; B.A., Dakota Wesleyan U., 1950; M.A., U. S.D., 1952; Ph.D. (NSF fellow), U. Nebr., 1956; m. Blanche L. Lang, Nov. 25, 1950; children—Michael, Daniel, Scott, Cheryl. Devel. chemist silicone products dept. Gen. Electric Co., 1956-60; research chemist Spencer Chem. Co., 1960-63; sr. research chemist Gulf Oil Chems. Co., Merriam, Kans., 1963-77, supr. product devel. sect., 1977—. Mem. Am. Chem. Soc. Contbr. articles to profl. jours. Patentee in field. Home: 8100 W 72d Terr Overland Park KS 66204 Office: Gulf Oil Chemicals Co Merriam KS 66202

CAIN, MARVIN JAMES, veterinarian; b. Dayton, Ohio, Aug. 1, 1931; s. Forrest H. and Loa (Wagaman) C.; D.V.M., Ohio State U., 1955; m. Coralie Lusk, Aug. 6, 1955; 1 dau., Catherine Brett. Asso. veterinarian Jensen Animal Hosp., Cleve., 1955-56, College Hill Animal Hosp., Cin., 1956, Park Hills, Walnut Hills hosps., also Cin. Zoo, 1957; owner, veterinarian Mt. Healthy Animal Hosp., Cin., 1957—; owner thoroughbred farm Liberty Hill Farm, Walton, Ky., 1968—. Mem. Am., Ohio, Cin. veterinary med. assns., Internat. Veterinary Acupuncture Soc., Thoroughbred Breeders Ky. Home: 7474 Greenfarms St Cincinnati OH 45224 Office: 9199 Pippin Rd Cincinnati OH 45239

CAIN, WARREN EUGENE, plastics co. exec.; b. Byesville, O., Aug. 12, 1923; s. Delmer Reed and Emma M. (Sealock) C.; B.S. in Elec. Engring., Ohio U., 1949; m. Patricia Ann Blount, Apr. 6, 1952; children—Susan, Timothy, Rebecca. Design engr. Meridian Plastic, 1950-56; chief engr. Yardley Plastics, 1956-61, Pittsburg Plastics, 1961-64, Como Plastics, 1966-69; gen. mgr. Ohio Plastics Co., Frazeysburg, 1970-75; pres., gen. mgr. Tact, Inc., Newark, Ohio, 1975—. Active, Licking County council Boy Scouts Am., 1974-75. Served with USAAF, 1942-45. Decorated Air Medal. Mem. Soc. Plastics Engrs., Am. Legion, Acacia Frat. Presbyn. (trustee). Mason, Lion (v.p.). Home: 1166 James Rd Newark OH 43055 Office: Ohio Plastics Co 2d St Frazeysburg OH 43822

CAIN, WILLIAM ALLEN, lawyer; b. Chgo., Nov. 9, 1924; s. Albert Paul and May (Gainer) C.; LL.B., DePaul U., 1946, J.D., 1971; m. Audrey Helene Rosin, Nov. 28, 1953; children—May Lydia, Jordan Scott. Admitted to Ill. bar, 1947, since practiced in Chgo.; partner law firm Cain & Cernek. Past mem. caucus com. Sch. Dist. 108, Highland Park, Ill.; counsel Skokie Police Patrolmen's Assn., North Suburban Police Patrolmen's Assn. Commnr. Sheriff Lake County Commn. Narcotics and Drug Abuse, 1972-73. Past pres. S.E. Clavey Homeowners Assn., Highland Park, Ill.; flotilla staff officer USCG Aux., 1974-75. Mem. bd. assos. DePaul U., 1972-73. Mem. Am. (com. criminal law, mem. speakers bur.), Ill. (Am. citizenship com., com. on fair trial-free press 1977—), Chgo. (past chmn. def. of prisoners com.; chmn. com. narcotics and drug abuse 1972) bar assns., Chgo. Trial Lawyers Club, Assn. Def. Lawyers, Internat. Platform Assn., Am. Guild Variety Artists (mem. Chgo. br. exec. com., chmn. 1968), Nat. Assn. Def. Lawyers in Criminal Cases (Ill. chmn. strike force 1976-77), Am. Judicature Soc., Assn. Trial Lawyers Am., Nat. Geog. Soc., Vol. Talent Pool Highland Park, Ill. Mem. B'nai B'rith (dir. Lincolnwood 1974-75). Club: Belmont Yacht (dir. 1977-78). Profl. hypnotist, lectr. Starred on Pantomine Party, WBKB-TV, Chgo., 1953. Office: 221 N LaSalle St Tower Suite 3316 Chicago IL 60601

CAIRNS, DENNIS ABBEY, mfg. co. exec.; b. Greenville, Mich., Nov. 14, 1941; s. Ronald Robert and Grace Helen (Abbey) C.; B.B.A., Western Mich. U., 1964; m. Linda Gaines Loughlin, Aug. 6, 1966; children—Benjamin, David. Account exec. Young & Rubicam, Detroit, Memphis, N.Y.C., P.R. and Atlanta, 1966-71; v.p. account services Aardvark Advt. Agy., Atlanta, 1971-72; dir. sales promotion Tom O'Ryan Advt. Co., Atlanta, 1972-73; mktg. mgr. Sea Pines Co., Atlanta, 1973-74; mgr. mkt. planning Muskegon (Mich) Piston Ring Co., 1974—; adj. faculty Grand Valley State Coll.; cons. advt. agys. Mem. Am. Mktg. Assn. (dir. Western Mich. chpt.). Home: 221 Barber Ct Spring Lake MI 49456 Office: 1839 6th St Muskegon MI 49443

CAIRNS, ELTON JAMES, chem. engr.; b. Chgo., Nov. 7, 1932; s. James Edward and Claire Angele (Larzelere) C.; B.S., Mich. Tech. U., 1955; Ph.D., U. Cal., 1959; m. Helen Garnett Burroughs, Feb. 28, 1959; 1 dau., Valerie Helen; m. 2d, Miriam Esther Citron, Dec. 26, 1974. Chemist U.S. Steel Co., 1953; soils research chemist U.S. Army Corps Engrs., 1954-55; chem. engr. Oak Ridge Nat. Lab., 1955; teaching asst. thermodynamics U. Calif., 1957-58; phys. chemist, electrochemist Gen. Electric Research Lab., 1959-66; phys. chemist, group leader Argonne Nat. Lab., 1966-69, sect. head, 1970-73; asst. dept. head electrochemistry Gen. Motors Research Lab., Warren, Mich., 1973—; cons. U.S. Dept. Interior and U.S. Dept. Def., 1969-71, 73—; mem. subpanel Panel Electrically Powered Vehicles of U.S. Dept. Commerce, 1967-68; cons. NASA, 1970-71; mem. subpanel com. motor vehicle emissions Nat. Acad. Sci., 1971-73; mem. steering com. Intersoc. Energy Conversion Engring. Conf., 1969—, chmn. steering com., 1974, gen. chmn., 1976. Mem. adv. bd. Advances in Electrochemistry and Electrochem. Engring., 1975—; mem. nat. battery advisory com. ERDA, 1977—. Recipient Francis Mills Turner award, Electrochem. Soc., 1963; Dow Chem. Co. fellow, 1955-56; Univ. fellow, 1956-57; Nat. Sci. Found. fellow, 1957-58. Fellow Am. Inst. Chemists; mem. Electrochem. Soc., A.A.A.S., Am. Chem. Soc., Am. Inst. Chem. Engrs., Internat. Soc. Electrochemistry. Author: (with H.A. Liebhafsky) Fuel Cells and Fuel Batteries, 1968. Battery div. editor of Jour. Electrochem. Soc., 1969—. Contbr. articles to profl. jours. Patentee fuel cells and high temperature batteries. Home: 30289 Spring River Dr Southfield MI 48076 Office: General Motors Research Laboratories 12 Mile Rd and Mound Rd Warren MI 48090

CALABRIA, ALFRED DAVID, steel corp. exec.; b. Hartford, Conn., Sept. 25, 1947; s. Vincent Joseph and Clementina (Daloe) C.; certificate (NSF scholar) U. Bridgeport, 1964; B.M.E., Drexel U., 1970; M.Adminstrv. Sci., Johns Hopkins U., 1974; m. Cynthia Jane Hooper, Sept. 10, 1971; children—Gina Lauren, Adam Michael. With Armco Steel Corp., 1966—, devel. engr., Balt., 1973-75, product specialist, Middletown, Ohio, 1975-76, sr. product specialist, 1976—; instr. Miami U., 1976; mem. program adv. and rev. com. M.Adminstrv. Sci. program Johns Hopkins U. Advisor Jr. Achievement, Balt., 1972; dir. Harford County (Md.) Young Republicans, 1974. Served with USAR, 1970-76. Fellow Am. Iron and Steel Inst.; mem. ASME. Roman Catholic. Club: Gourmet. Home: 5105 Phillip Ct Middletown OH 45042 Office: Armco Internat Div Armco Steel Corp Middletown OH 45042

CALANDRA, CARL WAYNE, metal products mfg. co. exec.; b. Altoona, Pa., Sept. 11, 1942; s. Carl A. and Leanore G. (Ferrari) C.; B.A., Ohio U., 1965; M.B.A., Case Western Res. U., 1969; m. Barbara J. Bell, June 12, 1965; children—Amy Lynn, Sarah Marie. Mgmt. cons. Robert Heller Assos., Cleve., 1967-70; dir. corporate planning and devel. U.S. Concrete Pipe Co., Cleve., 1970-73; dir. sales and mktg. Brook's Perkins, Inc., Livonia, Mich., 1973—. Mem. N.Am. Soc. Corporate Planning, Am. Mktg. Assn., Psi Chi, Delta Tau Delta. Presbyterian. Home: 110 Denbar Rd Bloomfield Hills MI 48013 Office: 12633 Inkster Rd Livonia MI 48150

CALANDRA, JOSEPH CARL, educator, physician; b. Chgo., Mar. 17, 1917; s. Domenic W. and Angela (Palma) C.; B.S., Lewis Inst., 1938; Ph.D., Northwestern U., 1942, M.D., 1950; m. Patricia Mader, Sept. 9, 1944; children—Carolyn P. (Mrs. Thomas Selsor), Susan J. (Mrs. Thomas Sylvester), Joseph D., David B. Intern Henrotin Hosp., Chgo., 1950-51; asst. prof. biochemistry Northwestern U., Chgo., 1942-50, asso. prof., 1950-53, prof., 1954—, prof. pathology Dental and Med. Sch., 1955—. Pres. Indsl. Bio-Test Labs., Northbrook, Ill., 1952—; dir. Nalco Chem. Co., Chgo. Bd. dirs. Skokie Valley Community Hosp. Diplomate Am. Bd. Clin. Chemists. Fellow Soc.

Clin. Pharmacology and Chemotherapy; mem. A.M.A., A.A.A.S., Am. Chem. Soc., Am. Indsl. Hygiene Assn., Am., European socs. toxicology, Sigma Xi, Phi Lambda Upsilon, Omicron Kappa Upsilon. Roman Catholic. Contbr. articles profl. jours. Home: 4630 Elm Terr Skokie IL 60076 Office: 1810 Frontage Rd Northbrook IL 60062

CALBERT, JERALD DAVID, lawyer; b. Indpls., Dec. 14, 1937; s. Hildon Robert and Mamie Etheline (Hunt) C.; A.B., Hanover Coll., 1960; J.D., Ind. U., 1966; m. Janet Lorene Hedrick, June 25, 1960; children—Lorilee Ann, Bradley Manson, Eric Hildon. Claims adjuster, claim mgr., ins. cos., 1961-66; admitted to Ind. bar, 1966; partner Houck & Calbert, Greencastle, Ind., 1966-74; now sr. v.p. firm Calbert & Bremer; dir. Greencastle Devels. Inc.; instr. bus. law DePauw U., 1970—. Bd. dirs. Coop. Office Edn. Program, Greencastle, 1970-71, Putnam County Health Careers Found., 1970—, West Central Econ. Devel. Commn., State Ind., 1975, Ind. U. Sch. Law Indpls. Alumni Assn. Served with USAF, 1961, 63. Recipient distinguished service award for community service, 1970; fellow Hanover Coll. Mem. Ind., Putnam County bar assns., Greencastle C. of C. (pres. 1971, dir. 1969-72), Internat. Platform Assn., Phi Delta Theta. Elk. Club: Windy Hill Country. Home: 309 Greenwood Av Greencastle IN 46135 Office: 11 1/2 S Indiana St Greencastle IN 46135

CALDARELLI, DAVID DONALD, otolaryngologist; b. Chgo., Nov. 7, 1941; s. David D. and Violet (Angus) C.; student U. Wis., 1961; M.D., U. Ill., 1965, M.S., 1965; m. Janna Sue Nowak, Apr. 1, 1967; children—Leslie Ann, Adam David. Intern, Presbyn. St. Luke's Hosp., Chgo., 1965-66, resident surgery, 1966-67; resident otolaryngology, U. Ill. Eye and Ear Infirmary and Research and Edn. Hosps., Chgo., 1967-70; practice medicine, specializing in otolaryngology, Chgo., 1974—; sr. attending physician, chmn. dept. otolaryngology and bronchoesophagology Rush Med. Coll., Rush-Presbyn.-St. Luke's Med. Center, Chgo., 1974—; attending otolaryngologist Univ. Ill. Research and Edn. Hosps., Chgo., 1970—, St. Francis Hosp., Evanston, Ill., 1974—; otolaryngologist Center for Craniofacial Anomalies, U. Ill., Chgo., 1970—; asst. otolaryngology Coll. Medicine, U. Ill., Chgo., 1967-70, instr. otolaryngology, 1970—; prof., chmn. dept. otolaryngology and bronchoesophagology, Rush Med. Coll., Chgo., 1974—; Cons. Otolaryngologist Chgo. Contagious Disease Hosp., 1975—. Recipient Bordan Found. Undergrad. Research award in medicine, 1965. Nat. Inst. Nervous Diseases and Blindness Research trainee, 1967-70; Ford Found. fellow, 1964; Nat. Inst. Health grantee, 1963, 65. Diplomate Am. Bd. Otolaryngology. Fellow A.C.S.; mem. AMA, Am. Acad. Ophthalmology and Otolaryngology, Am. Council Otolaryngology, Am. Cleft Palate Soc., Chgo. Laryngol. and Otol. Soc., Pan Am. Assn. Oto-Rhino-Laryngology and Broncho-Esophagology, Soc. Acad. Chmn. Otolaryngology, Soc. Univ. Otolaryngologists, Am. Broncho-Esophagological Assn., Triological Soc., Am. Cancer Soc. (unit dir. 1972-75), AAUP. Contbr. articles to profl. jours. and textbooks. Home: 101 Greenleaf Evanston IL 60202 Office: 1753 W Congress St Chicago IL 60612

CALDEIRA, JOSEPH LEONARD, real estate broker; b. Lowell, Mass., Sept. 7, 1944; s. Antonio Goncalves and Mary Suzanne (Sousa) C.; B.A., U. Mass., 1966; m. Chantel Zina Kolar, June 14, 1969; children—J. Leonard, Michael Jason. Real estate salesman Wm. A. White & Sons, N.Y.C., 1969-71; asst. v.p., real estate broker Cushman & Wakefield, Inc., Chgo., 1971-76; real estate broker LaSalle Partners, Inc., Chgo., 1976—. Served to capt. U.S. Army, 1966-68. Decorated Bronze Star. Mem. Chgo. Real Estate Bd., Nat., Ill. assns. realtors. Roman Catholic. Home: 4333 Johnson Ave Western Springs IL 60558 Office: 208 S LaSalle St Chicago IL 60604

CALDERWOOD, ROBERT GEDDES, oral and maxillofacial surgeon, anesthesiologist; b. Chgo., Feb. 14, 1936; s. Robert Geddes and Elizabeth Ann (Shaw) C.; B.S., Roosevelt U., 1957; D.D.S., Loyola U., Chgo., 1961; M.S., State U. Iowa, 1964; m. Suelen Gay, May 1, 1965; children—Robert Geddes III, Scott William. Resident oral surgery U. Iowa Hosp., 1961-64; resident anesthesiology Marion County Gen. Hosp., Indpls., 1964; asst. prof. surgery, chief oral surgery U. Chgo., 1964-68; pvt. practice oral and maxillofacial surgery, Peoria, Ill., 1968-70; pvt. practice oral and maxillofacial surgery, anesthesiology, Iron Mountain, Mich., 1970—; chmn. dept. anesthesiology, oral and maxillofacial surgery Dickinson County Meml. Hosp., Iron Mountain, 1970—; attending in anesthesiology, part-time in oral and maxillofacial surgery VA Hosp., Iron Mountain, 1970—; cons. maxillofacial surgery Hospital Generale, Managua, Nicaragua. Diplomate Am. Bd. Oral Surgery. Fellow Am. Coll. Oral and Maxillofacial Surgeons, Am. Dental Soc. Anesthesiology; mem. Am., Mich., Midwestern, Internat. socs. oral surgeons, Mich. Med. Soc., Mich. Dental Soc., Pan-Am. Med. Assn., Am. Dental Assn. Asso. editor Revista De La Federacion Odontololica De Centroamerica Y Panama. Research in use of polydimethly siloxane in reconstructive surgery. Home: Route 2 Box 765 Spread Eagle WI 54121 Office: Medical Park Iron Mountain MI 49801

CALDERWOOD, WILLIAM ARTHUR, physician; b. Wichita, Kans., Feb. 3, 1941; s. Ralph Bailey and Janet Denise (Lacey) C.; M.D., U. Kans., 1968; m. Kathleen Jane Bergen, Mar. 3, 1962; children—Lisa Beth, William Arthur. Intern, Wesley Med. Center, Wichita, 1968-69; gen. practice family medicine, Salina, Kans., 1972—; pres. staff St. Johns Hosp., Salina, 1976; dist. coroner, Salina, 1973—. Served to lt., M.C., USN, 1969-70. Diplomate Am. Bd. Family Practice. Fellow Am. Acad. Family Physicians. Home: 142 Seitz Dr Salina KS 67401 Office: 135 E Claflin St Salina KS 67401

CALDWELL, ALAN CLAYPOOL, ins. co. exec.; b. Tucumcari, N.Mex., Aug. 13, 1940; s. Robert Claypool and Della Wilhemina (Quelle) C.; B.S., U. Ill., 1963; M.S., So. Ill. U., 1971; m. Mary Lois Casey, June 8, 1968. With CNA Ins. Co., Chgo., 1966—, asst. dir. marketing information, 1967-71, mktg. planner, 1971-75, sr. planner, 1975-76, field mktg. cons., 1977—. Served with AUS, 1963-64. Mutual fund registered rep. Fellow Acad. Marketing Sci., mem. Am. Marketing Assn. Republican. Baptist. Home: 810 West Ln Geneva IL 60134 Office: CNA Ins CNA Plaza Chicago IL 60685

CALDWELL, A(RCHIE) LEE, savs. and loan co. exec.; b. Doniphan, Mo., Oct. 10, 1901; s. Archie Fred and Maude Mae (Lee) C.; Ph.G., Phila. Coll. Pharmacy and Sci., 1921, Ph.C., 1922; m. Dorothy Heebner Newman, Oct. 17, 1925; children—Archie Lee, Robert Newman. Instr., Phila. Coll. Pharmacy and Sci., 1923-25; staff pharm. research and devel. Eli Lilly & Co., Indpls., 1925-37, head nutrition and vitamin research, 1937-50, head product tech. service, 1950-66; v.p. Fletcher Ave. Savs. & Loan Assn., Indpls., 1966—, also dir.; v.p. Nor-Brook Civic League, 1947. Trustee Phila. Coll. Pharmacy and Sci. Fellow Am. Inst. Chemists; mem. Am. Chem. Soc., Am. Pharm. Assn., N.Y., Ind. acads. sci., AAAS, Upsilon Sigma Phi. Republican. Presbyterian. Mason (K.T., Scottish Rite), Elks. Clubs: Scientech (Indpls.); Country, Indpls. Aero (pres. 1949, 60). Patentee in field. Researcher barbituric acid compounds, antioxidants in pharms., oil-soluble vitamins, liver protein purification for nutritional uses. Home: 1049 W 141st St Carmel IN 46032 Office: 150 E Market St Indianapolis IN 46204

CALDWELL, F(RANCIS) EARL, city ofcl.; b. Nashville, Nov. 8, 1926; s. Hubert B. and Nancy (McQuiston) C.; student Detroit Coll. Applied Sci., 1952-53; m. Myrtle D. Pugh, June 14, 1947; children—Linda Sue, James Earl, Timothy Lee. Engring. specifications analyst Ford Motor Co., Dearborn, Mich., 1953—; planning commr. Dearborn Heights, Mich., 1961-67, city councilman, 1967—. Bd. dirs. D.A.V. Meml. Home, Dearborn. Served with AUS, 1944-45; ETO. Decorated Purple Heart. Mem. D.A.V. (comdr. Dearborn chpt. 1957), Nat. Order Trench Rats. Elk, Mason. Home: 4154 Vassar St Dearborn Heights MI 48125 Office: 6045 Fenton St Dearborn Heights MI 48127

CALDWELL, JACK LANDIS, bottled water co. exec.; b. Hastings, Nebr., July 25, 1923; s. Paul Bryon and Alice (Sheeley) C.; student Ohio Wesleyan U., 1941-42; B.B.A. with distinction, U. Minn., 1947, M.B.A., 1963; m. Claire Elaine Kent, Dec. 4, 1942; children—Vicki Lee (Mrs. Marc A. Jensen), Shari Lou (Mrs. Steven Parsley). With Glenwood-Inglewood Co., Mpls., 1947—, treas., 1953-64, exec. v.p., gen. mgr., 1964—; sec., dir. Affiliated Investors Inc., 1962—; dir. Pioneer Power Co., St. Paul. Lectr. Sch. Bus., U. Minn., 1965-77. Treas., Mpls. Mayor's Commn. on Human Relations, 1954-58. Bd. dirs. Mpls. Acquatennial Assn., 1955-56, Mpls. Council Civic Clubs, 1955-56, Mpls. chpt. ARC, 1955-56; bd. dirs. Mpls. War Meml. Blood Bank, 1957—, pres., 1969. Served with USAAF, 1942-45. Mem. Mpls. C. of C. (dir.), Am. Bottled Water Assn. (chmn. comptrollers com. 1957-77), Nat. Assn. Cost Accountants, UN Assn. (chmn. finance com., dir. Minn. chpt.), Sigma Chi. Club: Minneapolis Golf (Mpls.). Home: 7205 Harriet S Minneapolis MN 55423 Office: Glenwood Ave at Thomas Ave Minneapolis MN 55405

CALDWELL, JAMES HUDSON, physician; b. Bellaire, Ohio, Mar. 27, 1939; s. Robert Martin and Goldie LaFern (Jeffers) C.; B.Sc., Ohio State U., 1959, M.D., 1963; m. Patricia Audrey Boleman, May 12, 1973; children by previous marriage, Laura Jane, Jeffrey Aitken, Emily Karen, 1 son present marriage, Christopher James. Intern U. Chgo., 1963-64; resident in medicine, Ohio State U., 1964-65, 67-68, fellow in gastroenterology, 1968-70, asst. prof. medicine, 1970-76, asso. prof., 1976—, attending physician, 1970—; cons. VA and USAF hosps., 1970-76. Served with USAF, 1965-67. Diplomate Am. Bd. Internal Medicine. Fellow A.C.P.; mem. Am. Gastroenterological Assn., Am. Fedn. Clin. Research, AAAS. Clubs: Midwest Gut, Ohio State U. Pres.'s. Research in field. Contbr. articles to med. jours. Home: 1502 Cardiff Rd Upper Arlington OH 43221 Office: 410 W 10th Ave Columbus OH 43210

CALDWELL, JAMES MARSHALL, accountant; b. Chillicothe, Ohio, Aug. 1, 1939; s. Marshall and Emma (Gillette) C.; B.B.A., Ohio U., 1963; m. Pamela Lynne Marsh, June 13, 1963; children—Jennifer Lynne, James Patrick. Dep. auditor Ross County (Ohio), 1960-63, county commr., 1977—; tchr. Jackson (Ohio) City Schs., 1963-64; accountant Chillicothe, 1961—. City councilman, City of Chillicothe, 1968-74; pres. Ross County Young Republican Club, 1968-69. Bd. dirs. Ross County Community Improvement Corp.; trustee Mid-Ohio Health Planning Fedn. Mem. Pub. Accounting Soc. of Ohio (pres. So. Ohio chpt. 1974-75), Chillicothe-Ross C. of C. (dir. 1970-73, pres. 1973), Chillicothe Jaycees (Citizen of Year 1973). Methodist (mem. adminstrv. bd. 1971-74, chmn. council ministries 1975-76). Kiwanian, Elk. Home: 306 Fairway Av Chillicothe OH 45601 Office: PO Box 1640 Chillicothe OH 45601

CALDWELL, KENNETH SIMMS, mgmt. cons.; b. Mpls., Oct. 10, 1923; s. Kenneth Simms and Margaret Matilda (Peterson) C.; B.S. in Mech. and Indsl. Engring., U. Calif., 1947; m. Alice Elizabeth Featherstone, Apr. 12, 1952; children—Barbara Catherine, Margaret Elizabeth, Kenneth Simms. Cons., Ernst & Ernst, Los Angeles, 1947-50, 53-54, mgr. in charge mgmt. cons. services, San Francisco, 1954-61, Los Angeles, 1961-63, prin., Cleve., 1963-67, prin., nat. dir. govt. services, Cleve., 1967-76; prin. Nat. Mgmt. Cons. Services, Cleve., 1976—; lectr. Municipal Finance Officers Assn. Chmn. bd. dirs. Luth. Med. Center, Cleve.; trustee Luth. Med. Center Found.; vice-chmn. Greater Cleve. Growth Assn. for Downtown Devel., 1969-71, for Transp., 1971-73; trustee Cotillion Soc., 1971-73. Served as 1st lt. U.S. Army, 1950-53. Registered profl. engr., Calif. Mem. Nat., Ohio soc. profl. engrs., ASME, Am. Inst. of Indsl. Engrs., Cleve. Engring. Soc. (trustee 1969-73). Republican. Lutheran. Clubs: Mayfield Country, Cleve. Athletic, Rotary, Masons. Author: Budgeting for Small Governmental Units, 1976; contbr. articles to profl. jours. Home: 2719 Cranlyn Rd Shaker Heights OH 44122 Office: 1300 Union Commerce Bldg Cleveland OH 44115

CALDWELL, ROBERT HARLAN, constrn. and mfg. co. exec.; b. Jacksonville, Ill., Aug. 16, 1922; s. Harlan Lee and Vera (Kahl) C.; B.S., U. Ill., 1947; m. Joan Shade, July 7, 1951; children—Shelley Jo, Robert Norman, Patricia Ruth. Vice pres. Caldwell Engring. Co., contractors, Jacksonville, Ill., 1947-50, pres., 1950-64, chmn. bd., 1965-66; partner Caldwell Rhoads Co., cons. engrs., 1948-70, also dir.; v.p., sec. Calenco Equipment Co., 1959-66; pres., dir. Builders Ready Mix & Supply Co., 1961-70; chmn. bd. Key Life Ins. Co., also dir.; pres. dir. Grizzly Corp., Bob Caldwell Co., Jacksonville; sec.-treas. State Mech. Contractors, Inc., Jacksonville, 1973—; dir. Central United Life Ins. Co., Sioux City, Ia., Central United Corp. Chmn. Morgan County (Ill.) United Fund, 1957. Served with USNR, 1942-46. Named Ky. Col. Registered profl. engr., Ill. Mem. Nat., Ill. socs. profl. engrs., Asso. Gen. Contractors of Ill. (pres. 1966), Ill. (v.p.), Jacksonville (pres. 1972-74) chambers commerce, Am. Mil. Engrs., Sigma Alpha Epsilon. Conglist. Mason (Shriner), Elk, Rotarian (pres. 1954-55, gov. internat. orgn.). Home: 1042 W State St Jacksonville IL 62650 Office: PO Box 555 205 Kosciusko Jacksonville IL 62650 also 100 N Johnson St Jacksonville IL 62650

CALDWELL, WILLIAM IGNATIUS, JR., lawyer; b. Chgo., Sept. 10, 1942; s. William Ignatius and Margaret Ellen (Murphy) C.; B.A., Marquette, 1964; J.D., Loyola U., Chgo., 1967; m. Margaret Schalke, Aug. 20, 1966; children—Laura, Kathleen, Matthew, Christine. Admitted to Ill. bar, 1967; bus. cons. Technomic Research, Inc., Chgo., 1966-67; mem. firm McCarthy, Wytrie, Lyons & McCarthy, Chgo., 1967, Caldwell, Berner & Caldwell, Woodstock, Ill., 1967—. Tchr., McHenry County Jr. Coll., 1968; hearing officer Ill. Pollution Control Bd. Co-founder Woodstock Rescue Squad. Precinct committeeman Woodstock Democratic Com., 1967-71. Bd. dirs., sec., pres. Meml. Hosp. McHenry County (Ill.). Mem. Am., Ill., McHenry County bar assns., Ill. Trial Lawyers Assn., Ill. Def. Counsel, Loyola U. Dean's Club. Blue Key, Delta Theta Psi. Roman Catholic. K.C., Rotarian. Home: 3009 Red Barn Rd Crystal Lake IL 60014 Office: 100 1/2 Cass St Woodstock IL 60098

CALDWELL, WILLIAM LYMAN, radiotherapist, oncologist, educator; b. Honolulu, Nov. 12, 1929; s. William Butterfield and Alice Thomas (Strong) C.; B.A., Stanford U., 1951, M.D., 1955; married; children by previous marriage—Benjamin, Samuel, Alan, Megan, Erica, Bret. Intern, San Francisco Gen. Hosp., 1954-55; resident in radiology Stanford U. Hosps., San Francisco, 1956-59; Nat. Cancer Inst. spl. fellow Inst. Cancer Research, London, 1963-64; asst. prof. radiology Stanford U., 1964-66; asso. prof. Vanderbilt U., 1966-69, prof., 1969-71, dir. radiotherapy, radiation research, 1966-71; prof. radiology U. Wis., Madison, 1971—, prof. human oncology, 1975—, dir. radiotherapy center, 1971—; asso. dir. Wis. Clin. Cancer Center, 1973—; mem. com. on health care resources in VA NRC, 1973-77; mem. Cancer Research Center com. Nat. Cancer Inst. Clin. Sect., 1975—. Served to maj. U.S. Army, 1955-63. Diplomate Am. Bd. Radiology (guest examiner). Fellow Am. Coll. Radiology; mem. AMA, Am. Soc. Therapeutic Radiologists, Am. Radium Soc., Radiol. Soc. N.Am., AAAS, Radiol. Research, Alpha Omega Alpha. Democrat. Unitarian. Author: Cancer of the Urinary Bladder, 1970; Moments of Decision in Bladder Cancer, 1974; editor; Procs. of Conf. on Time-Dose Relationships in Clin. Therapy, 1975; contbr. numerous articles to med. jours. Home: 5316 Lake Mendota Dr Madison WI 53705 Office: 1300 University Ave Madison WI 53706

CALENDINE, RICHARD HARLEY, coll. adminstr.; b. Parkersburg, W.Va., Oct. 25, 1939; s. Harley William and Margaret Irene (Armstrong) C.; B.A., W.Va. Wesleyan Coll., 1962; M.A., Ohio State U., 1966; m. Georgeann Allard, Aug. 22, 1964; children—Caren Ferree, Michelle Louise. Terminal clk. Am. Bitumals and Asphalt Co., Marietta, Ohio, 1959-61; asst. dir. student financial aids Ohio State U., Columbus, 1964-67, counseling psychologist Counseling Center, 1967-74; financial aids officer Columbus Tech. Inst., 1974—. Individual practice psychology, Columbus, 1973—. Mem. Am., Ohio psychol. assns., Nat., Ohio assns. student financial aid adminstrs., Phi Delta Kappa, Omicron Delta Kappa, Psi Chi. Presbyn. (chmn. bd. deacons 1973). Mason. Author: College Majors as a Guide to Career Planning, 1972. Home: 111 Webster Park Columbus OH 43214

CALHOUN, HAZEL RANDOLPH, univ. adminstr.; b. Cin., Oct. 1; d. Solomon Elbert and Clara Hollins (Griffin) Randolph; B.S., Hampton (Va.) Inst., 1948; M.S.W. (Dean's fellow), Wayne State U., 1960. Caseworker, Family Service of Oakland County, Mich., 1960-62; psychiat. social worker Wayne County Gen. Hosp. and Consultation Center, Eloise, Mich., 1962-65; dir. social services State of Mich., 1965-72; ombudsperson, U. Mich. at Ann Arbor, 1972—. Tchr., Wayne County Community Coll. Mem. Hampton Nat. Centennial Com., 1967-68. Recipient Mayor's award for pub. service, Detroit, 1967, NIMH grantee, 1958. Mem. Chums, Inc. (co-founder Detroit chpt.), Am. Assn. Marriage and Family Counselors, Nat. Assn. Social Workers, Acad. Certified Social Workers, Conf. Advancement Pvt. Practice, Am. Personnel and Guidance Assn. in Higher Edn., Mich. Assn. Marriage Counselors, AAUW, Mich. Inter-Profl. Assn. Marriage, Family and Divorce, Mich. Assn. Psychoanalysis, Nat. Urban League, LWV, Nat. Council Negro Women, Wayne State U. Sch. Social Work (dir. 1960-65, sec. 1961-63, Nat. Hampton Inst. (Midwest regional v.p. 1964-67) alumni assns., Grace Episcopal Ch. Altar Guild, Delta Sigma Theta. Clubs: Zonta Internat., Faculty Women's U. Mich., Univ. Home: 1048 Greenhills Dr Ann Arbor MI 48105

CALHOUN, RAYMOND JOSEPH, stone co. exec.; b. Morrison County, Minn., May 9, 1920; s. George Edward and Clara Christine (Portz) C.; student St. John's U., 1938-39; m. Helen Edryce, July 30, 1941; children—Robert John, Carol Rae Bolduc, Timothy, Donald. Salesman, Little Falls Granite Works (Minn.), 1941-47, sales mgr., 1947-67, pres., 1967—; pres. subsidiary, St. Cloud Meml. Co. (Minn.), 1969—; pres. CNG Land Holding Co., Little Falls, 1964—; owner Calhoun Rentals Co., Little Falls, 1971—; pres. NW Monument Builders, Little Falls, 1970-74, also dir. Pres. St. Mary's Bd. Edn., 1966-70; mem. City of Little Falls City Council, 1969—, pres., 1973—; pres. Little Falls chpt. Am. Cancer Soc., 1962-64; active Boy Scouts Am. Served with USNR, 1942-45; PTO, ATO. Mem. Am. Legion, VFW, Republican. Roman Catholic. Clubs: Exchange (pres. Little Falls 1960—), K.C., Moose. Home: 1205 Riverview St Little Falls MN 56345 Office: S Hwy 10 Little Falls MN 56345

CALHOUN, WILLIAM KENNETH, II, retail co. exec.; b. Emporia, Kans., Sept. 4, 1944; s. William Gunn and Dorothy (Crain) C.; B.S., Kans. U., 1966; m. Judith Elaine Cartright, Oct. 17, 1964; children—Stephani Kay, Melissa Anne. Buyer, Target Stores, Mpls., 1966-67; sec.-treas. Newman's Inc., Emporia, Kans., 1967—; dir. Citizens Nat. Bank Emporia, 1976—. Bd. dirs., treas. Calhoun Found., 1967—; chmn. Project Pride, 1971-72; pres. bd. United Way Emporia, 1976-77. Mem. Emporia C. of C. (v.p. 1973-74). Clubs: Emporia Country (pres. 1975). Rotary. Office: Box B Emporia KS 66801

CALIAN, CARNEGIE SAMUEL, educator; b. N.Y.C., July 1, 1933; s. Frank and Zekieh (Halajian) C.; B.A., Occidental Coll., 1955; M. Div., Princeton Theological Seminary, 1958; D. Theol. magna cum laude, U. Basel, 1962; m. Doris S. Zobian, Sept. 12, 1959; children—Lois, Philip, Sara. Student asst. First Presbyn. Ch., Haddonfield, N.J., 1956-58; ordained to ministry Presbyn. Ch., 1958; asst. pastor, Calvary Presbyn. Ch., Hawthorne, Calif., 1958-60; with U. Dubuque Theol. Sem., 1963—, vis. prof. theology, 1963-67, asso. prof. theology, 1967-72, prof. theology, 1972—; J. Omar Good vis. distinguished prof. evang. Christianity Juniata Coll., 1975-77. Cons., trustee, United Presbyn. Ch. Commn. on Ecumenical Mission and Relations, cons. Nat. Council Churches. Among Outstanding Young Men Am., 1967; among Outstanding Tchrs. Am., 1971, 73; recipient prof. fellowship in industry, 1968; Patriarchal medal of honor from Rumania, 1970; Sealantic fellowship, 1970. Fellow Case-Study Inst., Harvard Grad. Sch. Bus., Soc. Human Values in Higher Edn.; mem. Am. Theol. Soc., Am. Acad. Religion, Soc. Sci. Study religion, AAUP, Cath. Theol. Soc., Am. Soc. Christian Ethics, Soc. Health and Human Values, N. Am. Acad. Ecumenists, Eastern Orthodox-Reformed Dialogue, World Alliance Reformed Churches. Rotarian (internat. chmn. Dubuque 1967-69). Author: The Significance of Eschatology in the Thoughts of Nicolas Berdyaev, 1965; Icon and Pulpit, 1968; Berdyaev's Philosophy of Hope, 1968; Grace, Guts and Goods, 1971; The Gospel According to the Wall Street Journal, 1975; Today's Pastor in Tomorrow's World, 1977; contbg. author The New Man: An Orthodox and Reformed Dialogue, 1973; The Byzantine Fellowship Lectures, 1974; contbr. to Ency. Brit., 15th edit., 1974. Home: 1925 Marion St Dubuque IA 52001 Office: 2570 Asbury Rd Dubuque IA 52001

CALIM, FREDERICK THOMAS, tool and die co. exec.; b. Dayton, Ohio, Oct. 14, 1938; s. Thomas Aman and Mary Ann (Matta) C.; student Columbus Bus. U., 1958, U. Dayton, 1959; m. Betty Jean Packer, June 14, 1958; children—Deanna E., Scott Alan, Randy Wayne. Partner, Master Swaging, Inc., Jackson Center, Ohio, 1960-70, pres., chief exec. officer, dir., 1970-76; pres., dir. chief exec. officer Gen. Tool & Die, Columbia, S.C., 1976—; dir. Argus Inc., Palisade Park, N.J., Galion Metallic Co., Wapakoneta, Ohio, Interphoto Corp., Palisades Park, Seaport Corp., Oakland, Calif. Pres. Civic Assn. Jackson Center, 1969-70, trustee, 1969—. Moose. Patentee in field. Home: PO Box 158 Jackson Center OH 45334 Office: Master Swaging Co Jackson Center OH 45334

CALIRI, JOSEPH LOUIS, lawyer, corp. exec.; b. Rochester, N.Y., Mar. 16, 1916; s. Salvatore and Maria Teresa (Bottazzi) C.; A.B., U. Rochester, 1938; LL.B., Cornell, 1941; m. Dorothy Ann McGrath, Aug. 19, 1944; children—Robert Redmond, Barbara Jane. Admitted to N.Y. bar, 1941, Ill. bar, 1974; law dept. Kraft, Inc. (formerly Nat. Dairy Products Corp.), N.Y.C., 1941-51, asst. sec., 1951-52, sec., 1952-71, v.p., 1971—. Mem. Chgo. Bd. of Trade; mem. Citrus Assos. N.Y. Cotton Exchange, Inc. Past pres. Bd. Edn., Union Free Sch. Dist. No. 9, West Islip, L.I. Mem. Am. Judicature Soc., Am. Soc. Corp. Secs., Am., Ill., Chgo. bar assns., Cornell Law Assn., Phi Beta Kappa,

Alpha Phi Delta. Clubs: Magoun Landing Yacht (West Islip, N.Y.); Cornell (N.Y.); Mich. Shores, Westmoreland Country (Wilmette, Ill.); Union League, Executives (Chgo.). Home: 1500 Sheridan Rd Wilmette IL 60091 Office: Kraft Ct Glenview IL 60025

CALISOFF, CHARLES IRA, lawyer; b. Chgo., Mar. 19, 1934; s. Abraham M. and Jeanne S. (Abbell) C.; B.A. with high honors, U. Ill., 1955; J.D., Yale U., 1958; m. Sherry Herman, Mar. 11, 1962; children—Joy, Adam. Admitted to Ill. bar, 1959, U.S. Dist. Ct. No. Dist. Ill., U.S. Ct. Appeals 7th Circuit bars, 1960, U.S. Ct. Claims bar, 1962, U.S. Supreme Ct. bar, 1963; examiner Northwestern U. Sch. Bus. Law, 1960-70; asst. to Ill. bar examiners, 1966—; govt. appeal agt., 1967-68; hearing officer Ill. Pollution Control Bd., 1971—. Mem. Ill. Local Draft Bd. 17, 1968—. Served with Ill. N.G., 1959. Recipient C. LaRue Munson award Yale, 1956. Mem. Am. Acad. Matrimonial Lawyers (counsel 1973-77, v.p. 1977—). Mason, Moose. Club: Standard (Chgo.). Home: 2711 Crabtree Ln Northbrook IL 60062 Office: 72 W Adams St Chicago IL 60603

CALKINS, MYRON DONALD, city ofcl.; b. Tacoma, Oct. 1, 1919; s. Donald James and Mabel (Adams) C.; B.S. in Civil Engring. with honors, Wash. State U., 1942; Mgmt. Engr., U. Mo. at Rolla, 1975; m. Nettie Alice Overman, June 21, 1942; children—Susan Jean, Ronald James, Donald Cyrus. Hydraulic engr. U.S. Geol. Survey, Portland, Ore., 1942-44, 46-47; bridge design engr. Wash. Hwy. Dept., Olympia, 1947-48; project engr. City of Tacoma, 1948-55, city engr., 1955-64; dir. pub. works, Kansas City, Mo., 1964—. Mem. Tacoma City Planning Commn., 1955-64. Served with USNR, 1944-46. Recipient Certificate of Recognition, Wash. State U. chpt. Am. Rd. Builders Assn., 1962, Outstanding Service award Nat. Soc. Profl. Engrs., 1964, Meritorious Service award Wash. chpt. Am. Pub. Works Assn., 1965; certificate merit for leadership Am. City mag., 1968, 71, 73; Top Ten Pub. Works Man of Year award Am. Pub. Works Assn., 1973. Registered profl. engr., Mo., Wash. Diplomate Am. Acad. Environ. Engrs. Fellow ASCE (chpt. pres. 1962); mem. Am. Pub. Works Assn. (nat. dir. 1965-69, nat. v.p. 1969-70, nat. pres. 1970-71, pres. Wash. chpt. 1960-61, pres. Kansas City Met. chpt. 1967-68, trustee edn. found. 1965-70, 73—, chmn. 1976—, dir. hist. soc. 1976—), Nat. Soc. Profl. Engrs. (pres. Western Mo. chpt. 1968-69), Am. Rd. Builders Assn. (v.p. central dist. municipal and airport div. 1975—), Soc. Am. Mil. Engrs. (chpt. dir. 1975—), Midwest Concrete Industries Bd., Hwy. Engrs. Assn. Mo., Tau Beta Pi, Sigma Tau, Sigma Alpha Epsilon. Episcopalian. Club: Kansas City Engineers (pres. 1969-70). Home: 3918 Indianola Dr Kansas City MO 64116 Office: Dir Pub Works 20th Floor City Hall 414 E 12th St Kansas City MO 64106

CALKINS, RICHARD M., lawyer; b. Washington, Oct. 1, 1931; s. Frederick T. and Alice (Wirth) C.; B.S., Dartmouth, 1953; J.D., Northwestern U., 1959; m. Anita Rojeanne Adcock, Mar. 16, 1963; children—Christine, Frederick, Kathryn. Admitted to Ill. bar, 1959; asso., partner firm Chadwell, Keck, Kayser, Ruggles and McLaren, Chgo., 1960-69; partner firm Burditt and Calkins, Chgo., 1969—. Prof. John Marshall Law Sch., Chgo., 1969—. Mem. Am., Ill., Chgo. bar assns., Order of Coif. Contbr. articles to profl. publs. Home: 1725 Central Ave Wilmette IL 60091 Office: 135 S LaSalle St Chicago IL 60603

CALL, CLIFFORD WOODROW, coffee co. exec.; b. St. James, Minn., Feb. 13, 1919; s. Theodore John and Caroline Olivia (Nelson) C.; B.B.A., U. Minn., 1949; m. Fern Margaret Lesch, May 26, 1946; children—Christopher, Curtis. With McGarvey Coffee Inc., Mpls., 1949—, accounting office mgr., 1949-55, treas., 1956—, v.p., 1962—. Served with AUS, 1942-45. Mason (Shriner). Optimist (pres. Mpls. 1977-78). Club: Breakfast (pres. 1973) (Mpls.). Home: 5833 Zenith Ave S Minneapolis MN 55410 Office: 1129 Currie Ave Minneapolis MN 55403

CALLAHAN, CLARENCE HENRY, realtor; b. Wayne County, Mich., May 14, 1907; s. Ward and Anna Katherine (Provey) C.; B.A., Mich. State U., 1931; postgrad., Indsl. Coll. Armed Forces, 1950-51, Air U. Staff and Command Sch., 1958-60, Air U. Adminstrn. Sch., 1956-60, Air War Coll., 1960-66, John Marshall Law Sch. Career Inst., 1963; m. Helen Ann Smith, July 14, 1934. Asst. controller Netherlands Plaza Hotel, Cin., 1933-34; asst. to v.p., gen. mgr. Hotel Cleve., 1934-37; exec. v.p. Downtown Club, Detroit, 1937-42, Meadowbrook Country Club, Northville, Mich., 1940-42; owner Food Services and Cons. Services Co., Detroit, 1946-55; mgr. corporate food services Chrysler Corp., Highland Park, Mich., 1956-60; cons., dir. food services No. Ill. U., 1962-63; dir. food services Receiving, Keifer and Maybury hosps., Detroit, 1964-65; cons., dir. food services Children's Hosp. Mich., Detroit, 1965-69; owner Callahan Realty, Birmingham, Mich., 1968—. Served to lt. col., USAAF, 1942-46; ETO, MTO. Mem. Mich. Assn. Realtor Bds., Nat. Bd. Realtors, Detroit Bd. Realtors (chmn. arbitration com.), Am. Legion, Hotel, Restaurant and Instl. Mgmt. Alumni Assn. Mich. State U. (co-founder), Mich. State U. Alumni Assn., Blue Key, Sigma Alpha Epsilon. Home: 690 Alter Rd Detroit MI 48215 Office: 725 S Adams Rd Birmingham MI 48011

CALLAHAN, DOUGLAS JAMES, lawyer; b. Ann Arbor, Mich., June 5, 1949; s. Albert Herford and Eileen Virginia (Wismer) C.; B.A., Mich. State U., 1971; J.D., Detroit Coll. Law, 1975. Coordinator defective materials Chevrolet Flint Truck Assembly, Flint, Mich., 1971-72; admitted to Mich. bar, 1975; individual practice law, Fenton, Mich., 1975—; asst. city atty. City of Fenton. Mem. Mich., Genesee County bar assns., Blue Key. Roman Catholic. Home: 1109 S Adelaide St Fenton MI 48430 Office: 242 W Caroline St Fenton MI 48430

CALLAHAN, GILBERT RAY, dentist; b. Vermilion Grove, Ill., Mar. 10, 1932; s. Bert Otha and Elsie (Gorman) C.; B.S., U. Ill., 1955, D.D.S., 1957; M.S., Northwestern U., 1962; m. Karen Kae Clark, Aug. 9, 1958; children—Kenda Sue, Bert Clark, William Clark. Practice dentistry specializing in orthodontics, Champaign, Ill., 1962—; guest lectr. dept. speech and theater U. Ill., 1966—. Served to capt. Dental Corps, AUS, 1956-60. Diplomate Am. Bd. Orthodontics. Mem. Am. Dental Assn., Am. Assn. Orthodontists, Ill. Assn. Orthodontics (trustee 1972), Delta Sigma Delta. Republican. Methodist. Mason (Shriner), Elk. Home: 36 Golf Dr Mahomet IL 61853 Office: 507 S 2d St Champaign IL 61820

CALLAHAN, HARRY LESLIE, cons. civil engr.; b. Kansas City, Mo., Jan. 11, 1923; s. Frank Benjamin and Myrtle Lou (Andersen) C.; B.S., U. Kans., 1944; m. Venita June Yohn, Dec. 16, 1944; children—Michael Thomas, Maureen Lynn, Kevin Leslie. With Black & Veatch, Kansas City, Mo., 1946—, div. mgr. spl. project div., 1970-71, partner, div. mgr., 1971—. Served to 1st lt. AUS, 1944-46. Mem. Am. Nuclear Soc., Am. Soc. C.E., Nat. Soc. Profl. Engrs., Water Pollution Control Fedn., Am. Concrete Inst., Engrs. Club Kansas City, Combustion Inst., Kappa Sigma. Club: Leawood South Golf, Homestead Tennis. Home: 7180 Cherokee St Prairie Village KS 66208 Office: 1500 Meadow Lake Kansas City MO 64114

CALLAHAN, JOHN CONRAD, educator; b. Owosso, Mich., May 27, 1923; s. Leo Francis and Bess (Conrad) C.; B.S., Mich. State U., 1947; M.F., Duke U., 1948; Ph.D., Purdue U., 1955; m. Jacqueline Harriet Gatet, Apr. 23, 1949; children—David Scott, James Campbell, Carol Ann. With U.S. Forest Service, 1948-50; mem. faculty Purdue U., West Lafayette, Ind., 1950—, asso. prof., 1960-64, prof. forest econs., 1964—, state extension coordinator forestry and natural resources, 1976—. Pres., Foresters, Inc., 1959—; cons. UN, FAO. Mem. Tippecanoe County Council, 1974—; mem. Area Plan Commn.; mem. Region IV Econ. Devel. Commn., 1976—. Served with AUS, 1943-45. Decorated Purple Heart. Mem. Soc. Am. Foresters (nat. chmn. div. forest econs. and policy, 1964-65), Am. Agrl. Econs. Assn., Sigma Xi, Xi Sigma Pi, Alpha Gamma Rho. Home: 301 Hollowood Dr West Lafayette IN 47906 Office: Dept Forestry and Natural Resources Purdue Univ West Lafayette IN 47907

CALLAHAN, KENNETH ROBERT, oral surgeon; b. Cleveland, Nov. 7, 1928; s. Nelson James and Mary Katherine (Mulholland) C.; B.Sc., John Carroll U., 1950; D.D.S., Case Western Res., 1955; m. Joan Patricia Reilly, Aug. 21, 1954; children—Kenneth Robert, Kevin, Christopher, Katherine, Collin. Intern, Cleve. Met. Gen. Hosp., 1955-56; resident Wheeling (W.Va.) Hosp., 1957-58, Grad. Sch. Medicine U. Pa., 1958-59; practice dentistry specializing in oral surgery, Cleve., 1958—. Clin. instr. oral surgery Case Western Res. U. Sch. Dentistry, 1966—. Trustee, John Carroll U., 1969-72. Diplomate Am. Bd. Oral Surgeons. Mem. Cleve. Soc. Oral Surgeons (pres. 1970-71), Cleve. Dental Soc. (bd. dirs. 1963—), John Carroll U. Alumni Assn. (nat. pres. 1969-72), Case Western Res. U. Dental Alumni Assn. (nat. pres. 1976-77), Cleve. Civil War Round Table (pres. 1970-71). Contbr. to profl. publs. in field. Home: 2620 Courtland Oval Shaker Heights OH 44118 Office: Southgate Med Arts Bldg Cleveland OH 44137

CALLIS, CLAYTON FOWLER, chem. co. ofcl.; b. Sedalia, Mo., Sept. 25, 1923; s. Edward and Mary (Fowler) C.; A.B., Central Methodist Coll., Fayette, Mo., 1944; M.S., U. Ill., 1946, Ph.D., 1948; m. Sara Rebecca Steele, Apr. 9, 1949; children—Joanne, Judy. Research chemist Gen. Electric Co., Hanford, Wash., 1948-51; research chemist Monsanto Co., Anniston, Ala., Dayton, Ohio, 1951-54, research group leader, Dayton, then St. Louis, 1954-60, asst. dir. research, 1960-62, mgr. research and devel., 1962-69, dir. research and devel., 1969-75; dir. tech. planning and evaluation Monsanto Indsl. Chems. Co., 1975—. Alt. del. Indsl. Research Inst. Recipient Distinguished Alumni award Central Meth. Coll., 1970, St. Louis award Am. Chem. Soc., 1971. Fellow Am. Inst. Chemists; mem. Am. Chem. Soc. (nat. councilor 1968—, dir. St. Louis sect. 1971-72, chmn. council com. program rev. 1975, 76, 77, dir. at large 1977—), Soap and Detergent Assn. (research com.), Sci. Research Soc. Am., AAAS, Alpha Chi Sigma, Phi Lambda Upsilon. Clubs: Clayton, Chemists N.Y. Author: (with R.R. Irani) Particle Size, Measurement, Interpretation and Application, 1963. Editorial adv. bd. Jour. Am. Chem. Soc., 1963-72. Contbr. articles to profl. jours. Home: 2 Holiday Ln St Louis MO 63131 Office: 800 N Lindbergh Blvd St Louis MO 63166

CALLIS, LANCE, lawyer; b. Norfolk, Va., Aug. 12, 1935; s. Felix L. and Nora T. (O'Halleran) C.; B.S., St. Louis U., 1959, J.D., 1959; m. Joan M. Wegrzyn, Nov. 23, 1963; children—Mona, Beth, Melissa, Philip. Admitted to Ill. bar, 1959, Mo. bar, 1959; practice law, Granite City, 1963—; with firm Callis, Schooley, Filcoff & Hartman. Guest lectr. Law Sch., St. Louis U., 1972. Mem. Local Air Pollution Commn.; mem. Community Resources Commn., Granite City; chmn. Madison County Judiciary Com., 1973; atty. Granite City; commr. Granite City Port Authority. Served with AUS, 1959-60. Mem. Am., Ill. (mem. med.-legal cooperation com.), Mo., Madison County (pres. 1976-77), Tri-City (pres. 1964) bar assns., Am. Trial Lawyers. Elk. Home: 3136 Harvard St Granite City IL 62040 Office: 2038 Edison Ave Granite City IL 62040

CALLOWAY, NATHANIEL OGLESBY, physician; b. Tuskegee, Ala., Oct. 10, 1907; s. James and Marietta (Oglesby) C.; B.S., Ia. State Coll., 1930, Ph.D., 1933; M.D., U. Ill., 1943; m. Doris Howes, 1946 (div.); children—David, Candace, Aubrey, Constance; m. 2d, Mary Ann Boruki; children—Kathlyn, Sharon, Roslyn. Instr. chemistry Tuskegee Inst. 1933-36; asst. prof. chemistry Fisk U., 1936-40; instr. pharmacology U. Chgo., 1940-42; intern U. Ill., 1944, resident physician, 1944-46, former asst. prof. medicine; dir. spl. heart studies, USPHS; prin. investigator OSRD, 1944-46; cons. U.S. Navy, U. Ill., 1946-49; dir. med. affairs, Provident Hosp., 1947-48, attending physician 1948—; engaged practice of internal medicine, 1946—; cons. physician VA, Chgo.; pres. Med. Assos. Chgo., 1949-63; chief med. service and acting chief labs. Tomah (Wis.) VA Hosp., 1963-66; practice medicine, Madison, Wis., 1966—, also attending physician Madison Gen. Hosp.; adminstr. Commodore Nursing Home, Madison, 1966-68. Owner Grand Marsh Wildlife Ranch, 1961—; lectr. Afro-Am. studies U. Wis., 1970—. Mem. adv. com. on aged Office Econ. Opportunity, 1964-70. Bd. dirs. Carver Research Found., Tuskegee Inst. Recipient Friends awards Nat. Urban League, 1959. Served to maj. M.C., AUS, 1951-53. Diplomate Am. Bd. Internal Medicine. Recipient Distinguished Alumni Achievement award Ia. State U., 1970. Fellow A.C.P.; mem. A.M.A., A.A.A.S., Am. Soc. Pharmacology and Exptl. Therapeutics, Nat. Med. Fellowships, Inc. (v.p.), Ill., Chgo. med. socs., Chgo. Soc. Internat. Medicine, Gerontology Soc. (chmn. clin. med. sect. 1971-72), Am. Geriatrics Soc., Inst. Medicine Chgo., Tb Inst. Chgo. and Cook County (dir.), Nat. (dir. 1959-62), Chgo. urban leagues, Wildlife Disease Assn., Sigma Xi, Phi Lambda Upsilon. Mem. editorial bd. Jour. Am. Geriatrics Soc., 1972—. Contbr. to med. publs. Home: 3310 Kingston Dr Madison WI 53713 Office: 1103 Regent St Madison WI 53715

CALTON, MELVIN LYLE, dentist; b. West Plains, Mo., Feb. 2, 1925; s. Paul Wesley and Lula Margaret (Dye) C.; A.A., S.W. Bapt. Coll., 1943; student Central Mo. State U., 1943-44; D.D.S., Washington U., 1947; m. Virginia Lee Koch, June 14, 1947; children—Timothy Lyle, Nancy Lee. Dental prosthetics resident Nat. Naval Med. Center, Bethesda, Md., 1957-58; pvt. practice dentistry, St. Louis, 1947-48, 66—. Tchr., Washington U. Sch. Dentistry, St. Louis, dir. dental assts. utilization program, 1966-72; mem. dental staff Barnes Hosp. Served to comdr. USN, 1948-66. Dental Asst. Utilization grantee USPHS, 1966-72. Fellow Am. Coll. Dentists; mem. Am. Dental Assn., St. Louis, Mo. dental socs., Barnes and Allied Hosp. Soc., Am. Prosthodontic Soc., Xi Psi Phi, Omicron Kappa Upsilon. Republican. Presbyterian (deacon 1969-71). Home: 1709 Greening Ln St Louis MO 63122 Office: 9929 Manchester Rd St Louis MO 63122

CALVERT, JAMES WILLIAM, dermatologist; b. Palmer, W.Va., Oct. 2, 1902; s. William Joseph and Lena Katherine (Staton) C.; B.S. in Medicine, W.Va. U., 1924; M.D., Ind. U., 1927; postgrad dermatology N.Y. U., 1947-50; m. Thelma G. Boone, Jan. 10, 1931; children—James, Richard, Diane Calvert Nelson, Connie Calvert Daughman. Intern, Maumee Valley Hosp., Toledo, Ohio, 1927-28; gen. practice medicine, W.Va., 1928-47; resident in dermatology N.Y. U., N.Y.C., 1947-50; practice medicine specializing in dermatology, Cin., 1950—; mem. staff dermatology Good Samaritan Hosp.; asst. clin. prof. Cin. U. Med. Sch. Trustee United Price Hill Methodist Ch., Cin. Mem. AMA, Am. Acad. Dermatology, Ohio Med. Soc., Cin. Acad. Medicine, Washington Dermatology Soc., Soc. Investigative Dermatology, Tropical Dermatology Soc. Democrat. Club: Shriners. Contbr. med. jours. Home: 2629 Falconbridge Dr Cincinnati OH 45238 Office: 1015 Carew Tower Cincinnati OH 45202

CALVIN, ROBERT MORRELL, banker; b. Ishpeming, Mich., June 14, 1916; s. Carl Justin and Lucille (Higgins) C.; student Northwestern U., 1934-36; B.B.A. cum laude, U. So. Cal., 1938; M.B.A., Harvard, 1940; m. Suzanne Nelson, June 30, 1951 (dec. 1957); children—Jeffrey Robert, Carlye Suzanne, Kim Elizabeth, Michael Van Buren. Corporate buyer, dept. mgr. R. H. Macy & Co., N.Y.C., 1940-49; mem. faculty N.Y. U. Sch. Retailing, 1946-49; asst. to pres. J. J. Haggarty Stores, Los Angeles, 1949-50; asst. div. mgr. Montgomery Ward & Co., Chgo., 1950-51; sr. v.p., dir. John Plain & Co., Chgo., 1951-71; chmn. bd., pres. Des Plaines Bank (Ill.), 1970—, State Bank Lombard, 1974—, Rochelle State Bank, 1974—; pres. First Service Bancorp., 1973—; v.p. Island Farm Creamery Co. (Minn.); dir. Farley Candy Co. Mem. Delta Sigma Pi, Phi Kappa Sigma. Clubs: Inverness Country; Eshquaguma Country (Minn.). Home: Sutton Rd Barrington Hills IL 60010 Office: 1223 Oakton St Des Plaines IL 60018

CAMARDO, VICTOR JOSEPH, holding co. exec.; b. Campbell County, Ky., June 19, 1928; s. Marco Joseph and Angelina Raffealo D'Erminio C.; B.B.A., U. Cin., 1951; m. Edda Josephine Fiorino, June 26, 1954; children—Mary Angela, Thomas, Carolyn, Paula, Lisa, Edward, Victoria. Sr. accountant Haskins & Sells, Cin., 1950-55; controller Koehl Box Co., Cin., 1955-56, Wadsworth div. Elgin Nat. Watch Co., Dayton, Ky., 1956-57; exec. v.p. Bardes Corp., Cin., 1957-68; controller KDI Corp., Cin., 1968—. Mem. St. Vincent Fin. Com. Mem. Nat. Assn. Accountants (dir. 1975—), Fin. Execs. Inst. (dir. 1974—). Clubs: Kenwood Country. Indian Hill. Home: 6577 Lisa Lane Cincinnati OH 45243 Office: 5721 Dragon Way Cincinnati OH 45227

CAMERON, ANSON WHEATON, retail store exec.; b. Chgo., July 2, 1922; s. Anson and Alta (Stevens) C.; B.S. in Mech. Engring., Northwestern U., 1946; m. Jean C. Granstrand, Feb. 26, 1944; children—David S., Dale S., Andrew W., Michael W.; m. 2d, Jeanne A. Kaiser, Oct. 12, 1974. With Charles A. Stevens & Co., Chgo., 1946—, sec., sr. v.p. charge operations, 1960—, also dir.; pres. Hanger-Tight Co. Mem. Better Bus. Bur. Chgo., Chgo. Crime Commn., Wabash Av. Assn., State Street Lighting Assn., Delavan Lake Improvement Assn. (dir. 1969-74). Bd. dirs. Chgo. Heart Assn., 1960-66, Northfield Community Fund, 1964-66. Served to lt. (j.g.) USNR, 1944-46. Mem. Nat. Retail Mchts. Assn. (dir. 1967-69). Clubs: Economic (Chgo.); Delavan Lake (Wis.) Yacht (commodore 1968-70); Northwestern (pres. 1969-70) (Chgo.). Home: 945 Manor Dr Wilmette IL 60091 Office: 25 N State St Chicago IL 60602

CAMERON, ROY EUGENE, scientist; b. Denver, July 16, 1929; s. Guy Francis and Ilda Annora (Horn) C.: B.S., Wash. State U., 1953 and 1954; M.S., U. Ariz., 1958, Ph.D., 1961; D.D. (hon.) Ministry of Christ Ch., Delavan, Wis., 1975; m. Margot Elizabeth Hoagland, May 5, 1956 (div. July 1977); children—Susan Lynn, Catherine Ann. Research scientist Hughes Aircraft Corp., Tucson, Ariz., 1955-56; sr. scientist Jet Propulsion Lab., Pasadena, Calif., 1961-68, mem. tech. staff, 1969-74; dir. research Darwin Research Inst., Dana Point, Calif., 1974-75; dep. dir. Land Reclamation Lab. Argonne (Ill.) Nat. Lab., 1975-77, dir. energy resources tng. and devel. 1977—; cons. Lunar Receiving Lab. Baylor U., 1966-68, Ecology Center Utah State U., Desert Biome, 1970-72, Tundra Biome, 1973-74, U. Maine, 1973-76. Served with U.S. Army, 1950-52; Korea, Japan. Recipient 3 NASA awards for tech. briefs; Paul Steere Burgess fellow U. Ariz., 1959; NSF grantee, 1970-74. Mem. AAAS, Soil Scientists Soc. Am., Ecol. Soc. Am., Phycological Soc. Am., Am. Soc. Agronomy, Antarctican Soc., Polar Soc. Am., Am. Scientist Affiliatian, World Future Soc., Soc. Study Origin of Life (intern), Ariz. Acad. Sci., Am. Inst. Biol. Scis., Sigma Xi. Baptist. Contbr. articles in field to sci. books. Home: 3433 Woodridge Dr Woodridge IL 60515 Office: 9700 S Cass Ave Argonne IL 60439

CAMERON, WILLIAM JOURDEN, obstetrician, gynecologist, educator; b. Lansing, Mich., Sept. 7, 1929; s. William D. and Verta Mae (Jourden) C.; B.S., Mich. State U., 1950; M.D., U. Mich., 1954; m. Mona Lou Hoedl, June 19, 1954; children—William Bruce, Amy Patricia, Julie Frances. Intern, St. Anthony Hosp., Denver, 1954-55; gen. practice medicine Burns Clinic, Petoskey, Mich., 1955-56; resident in gynecology and obstetrics U. Kans. Med. Center, 1958-62; instr. in gynecology and obstetrics, 1962-64, asst. prof. gynecology and obstetrics, 1964-66, asso. prof., 1967-73, prof., 1973—, asst. dean Med. Sch., 1967-70, dir. sect. gynecology, 1973—, vice chmn. gynecology and obstetrics, 1973—. Served as capt. M.C. USAF, 1956-58. Diplomate Am. Bd. Obstetrics, Gynecology. Mem. Am. Coll. Obstetricians, Gynecologists (chmn. Kans. sec. 1971-74), Am. Assn. Gynecol. Laparoscopists (advisory com. 1975), Am. Fertility Soc., AMA, Central Assn. Obstetricians, Gynecologists, Central Travel Club, Internat. Fertility Assn., Kansas City (Kans.) Gynecol. Soc. (pres. 1971-72), Kans. Obstetrical Soc., Wyandotte County (Kans.) Med. Soc., Nu Sigma Nu, Sigma Chi. Contbr. articles to profl. jours. Home: 6515 Overhill St Shawnee Mission KS 66208 Office: U Kans Med Center 39th and Rainbow Blvd Kansas City KS 66103

CAMMA, PHILIP, accountant; b. Phila., May 22, 1923; s. Anthony and Rose (LaSpada) C.; B.S., U. Pa., 1952; m. Anna Ruth Karg, July 21, 1956 (dec. Aug. 1960); 1 son, Anthony Philip. Accountant, Main and Co., C.P.A.'s, Phila., 1952-53; in charge accountant Haskins & Sells, C.P.A.'s, Phila., St. Louis, Cin. and Columbus, O., 1953-60; controller Marvin Warner Co., Cin., 1960-61; controller Leshner Corp., 1961-63; mng. partner Camma & Patrick, C.P.A.'s, 1963-66; founder Philip Camma & Co., C.P.A.'s, Cin., 1966—. Served with USAAF, 1942-45; ETO. Mem. Am. Legion, Am. Inst. C.P.A.'s, Ohio, Ky. socs. C.P.A.'s, Am. Accounting Assn., Nat. Assn. Accountants. Republican. Clubs: Cincinnati; University Pa.; Hamilton City. Home: Fenwick Club Cincinnati OH 45202 Office: Gwynne Bldg Cincinnati OH 45202

CAMP, HAROLD EMERSON, ceramic engr.; b. Hockingport, Ohio, Feb. 12, 1938; s. Vernon Harold and Verah Dolly (Lott) C.; student W.Va. U., 1956-58; A.B., Marietta Coll., 1962; M.S., Clarkson Coll., 1963; m. Betty Ann Richarson, Aug. 29, 1962. Process research engr. Corning Glass Works (N.Y.), 1963-67; project mgr. Owens Illinois Inc. Toledo, 1967-74; engring. mgr. Accu-Glass div. Becton Dickinson & Co., St. Louis, 1974—; instr. math Corning Community Coll., 1963-67. USAF teaching fellow, 1962-63. Mem. Am. Phys. Soc., Sigma Xi. Methodist. Patentee in field. Home: 12 Tower Hill St Louis MO 63132 Office: 10765 Trenton Ave St Louis MO 63132

CAMP, HERBERT LEE, otolaryngologist; b. Saginaw, Mich., May 27, 1940; s. Harper Lee and Agatha (Hardy) C.; B.S., Mich. State U., 1966; M.D., U. Mich., 1966; m. Jacqueline Nelson, June 17, 1961; children—Jeffrey, Susan, Patricia. Intern, Munson Med. Center, Traverse City, Mich., 1966-67; resident in surgery State U. N.Y., Syracuse, 1967-68, resident in otolaryngology, 1968-71; practice medicine specializing in otolaryngology, 1971—; mem. staffs Upstate Med. Center, Syracuse, 1971, Syracuse Meml.-Crous Irving Hosp., 1971, Syracuse Vets. Hosp., 1971, Wilford Hall, Lackland AFB, Tex., 1971-73, Ponce De Leon Infirmary, Atlanta, 1973-74, Grady Meml. Hosp., 1973-74, Midland (Mich.) Hosp. Center, 1974—, Bay Med.

LETTERS

DOES NOT COMPUTE?

For a man who single-handedly created a generation of blank-eyed, lobotomized video-game addicts, it's nice to see that Nolan Bushnell ("The Return of

King Pong," February) wants to plug his computerized wizardry into our sagging public-school systems. I'd put all my microchips on the table and bet that he can lure our impressionable youths away from Pac-land. Let's hope he keeps his word.

> *Barbara Romford*
> *New Britain, Connecticut*

What's this on your cover? Atari founder Nolan Bushnell with his arm draped over an *Apple* computer? I'd have been less surprised to see Ronald McDonald eating at Burger King.

> *Barry Tanagard*
> *Sacramento, California*

NO LADY-BIRDS

Thank you for your article about a wonderful man—an athlete, no less—who is certainly a hero in an hour when there are few. Larry Bird ("Rare Bird," February) is awesome. That he has talent and works hard can't be denied. However, I was disturbed by the notion of what a challenge it might be for *Success* magazine to find and publish a similar story about a woman. Are there no talented and hardworking women? Or are there simply talented, hardworking women without fame, fortune, or success?

> *Nancy Smith*
> *Panama City, Florida*

FAULKNER ON SUCCESS

A letter in your December issue drew an interesting parallel between last October's cover subject, Ted Turner, and fellow-southerner William Faulkner. I recently stumbled on a provocative quote of Faulkner's which may lend further credence to the comparison: "Success is feminine and like a woman; if you cringe before her, she will override you. So the way to treat her is to show her the back of your hand. Then maybe she will do the crawling."

> *George P. Lyon*
> *Chattanooga, Tennessee*

Please address your correspondence to: "Letters," *Success* **Magazine, 401 North Wabash Avenue, Chicago, IL 60611.**

P.S.

What's What at Who's Who

Marquis' *Who's Who in America,* now in its 42nd biennial edition, lists more than 75,000 prominent achievers in its pages. Kenneth H. Petchenik, president of Marquis Publications, directs the directory and offers the following hows and whys.

What does it mean to be cited in a Who's Who *volume?*

I think it's recognition, the fact that a person has achieved a sufficient amount of success to have become a subject of reference interest. The book is not a recorder of status. It's not a social register. It's a reference book.

How does a person get listed?

We have standards that cover every profession. Some of the standards are very obvious. If you're dealing with business managers as a category, one of the standards would involve looking at the top 500 companies as listed by *Fortune* or even the top 1,000 companies. We might take all of the corporate officers of the top 50, then take only

Petchenik . . . the game of the names.

senior vice presidents and up of the next 200, and so forth. Those kinds of identifications are fairly cut-and-dried. We've been doing it for 85 years now, and we think we have a very comprehensive, very effective blueprint for getting people in all sorts of fields.

What if you inadvertently left out somebody who deserves inclusion?

We encourage people to call our attention to the fact that they're not in it. We love it. It's one of the easiest ways to come up with a name. It doesn't mean they'll get in, but we'll always send them a data form to fill out and return.

Are there instances of someone getting into Who's Who *and not deserving it?*

It happens. For instance, a few years ago we sent a questionnaire to a woman who crossed out her name and put her dog's name down. Then she filled out a totally erroneous sheet, and we published it. That incident got a lot of publicity. While we all had a nice laugh over it, we tried to point out that it subverted the purpose of the book.

In recent editions, several listings end with the individual's life-achievement credo. Do you have a favorite?

My favorite is from the philosopher Brand Blanshard, a couple of editions ago: "The finest of all achievements, and the most difficult, I have come to think, is merely being reasonable. It is difficult because it runs counter to our love of the dramatic, the temperamental, the aggressive, and the spectacular, all of which we prize too highly. If men were reasonable, if they even tried to be reasonable, the world would be transformed overnight."

—B.Z.

How to have a "Goood" day every day!

Center, Bay City, Mich., 1975—; instr. in otolaryngology State U. N.Y., Syracuse, 1971; adj. asst. prof. Central Mich. U., 1974—. Served with USAF, 1971-73. Fellow Am. Acad. Ophthalmology and Otolaryngology, A.C.S.; mem. AMA, Mich. State, Midland County (Mich.) med. socs., Am. Council Otolaryngology, Soc. Mil. Otolaryngologists. Contbr. articles to profl. jours. Home: 16 Snowfield Ct Midland MI 48640 Office: 4007 Orchard Dr Midland MI 48640

CAMP, LUCILLE E., city ofcl., realtor; b. Goodland, Ind., Aug. 9, 1914; d. Joseph Leonard and Marie (Krintz) Camp; student Internat. Bus. Coll., Ft. Wayne, Ind., 1933, Ind. U. Extension, 1948-49; m. David B. McQuinn, Aug. 11, 1940 (div. Jan. 1946). Cosmetic sales William H. Block Co., Indpls., 1934; sec. Ind. Dept. Edn., 1935-36, Ind. Dept. Agr., Indpls., 1939-40; dental asst. Dr. William J. Stark, Indpls., 1945-47; lab technician, chair asst. Dr. Berkey, Ft. Wayne, 1947-48; surg. asst. Dr. J. B. Shaw, Ft. Wayne, 1948-49; sec. C.T. Foxworthy Co., automobile agy., 1948-51; owner, operator Dairy Queen Ice Cream Stores, Indpls., 1953-59; adminstrv. asst., office mgr. Ind. Commn. for Reorgn. Sch. Corps, Indpls., 1960-66; pvt. sec. to v.p. and dean Ind. Vocat. Tech. Coll., Indpls., 1966; personnel dir. City of Indpls., 1966-71; adminstr. Ind. Office Consumer Affairs, 1971—; corp. sec. Lawyer Realty, Inc.; ct. reporter Superior Ct. 2, Indpls. Vice committeeman Indpls. Republican Com., 1958, precinct committeeman, 1959-73, ward vice chmn., 1954—. Mem. Am. Bus. Women's Assn. (charter mem.; rec. sec. 1963), Clowes Hall Women's Com., Soc. Indpls. Symphony Orch., Internat. Platform Assn., Ind. U. Friends Music, Children's Mus., Indpls. Mus. Art, Indpls. Art Assn., Delta Theta Tau (pres. 1958-59, corr. sec. 1960-62). Methodist. Clubs: Hillcrest Country, Toastmistress (charter), Riviera, Soroptimist Internat. Home: 5928 Devington Rd Indianapolis IN 46226 Office: 7180 Castleton Rd Indianapolis IN 46226

CAMPBELL, ADRIEL DOWNEY, aluminum distbg. co. exec.; b. Evansville, Ind., Jan. 29, 1914; s. Walter M. and Linda (Saunders) C.; student pub. schs.; m. Dorothy Uht, Nov. 29, 1947; children—Robert, Richard, Susan. Investigator, Retail Credit Co., Atlanta, 1941-45; credit mgr. Good Year Tire & Rubber Co., Cleve., 1945-47; v.p. Wright Sales Co., Inc., Cleve., 1947-58, v.p., gen. mgr., 1960-75; v.p. Wrisco Inc., 1975—, nat. dir. La Petite Venetienne div.; pres. A. D. Campbell Supply Co., Cleve., 1958-60; dir. Wright Sales Cos., Inc., N.Y., Ill., Ohio, Ga., Tex.; ret. Republican. Roman Catholic. Home: 484 Oakton Circle Mayfield Village OH 44143 Office: 19620 Nottingham Rd Cleveland OH 44110

CAMPBELL, ALASTAIR MACINTOSH, advt. agy. exec.; b. Glasgow, Scotland, Feb. 13, 1940; s. Samuel and Donelda Eleanor (MacIntosh) C.; came to U.S., 1969; B.A., Sir George Williams U., Montreal, Que., Can., 1966; M.S. in Communications, Syracuse U., 1970; m. Allison Louise Simard, Oct. 1, 1966; children—Bonnie Louise, Rob Roy MacKinnon. Layout artist Weekend Mag., Montreal, 1959-62; asst. advt. mgr. Prudential Assurance Montreal, 1966-67; sr. copywriter, asst. circulation mgr. Reader's Digest, Montreal, 1967-69; v.p., creative dir. Maxwell Sroge Co., Chgo., 1970-75; gen. mgr. creative and prodn. G.R.I. Corp., Chgo., 1975-75; pres., creative dir. Alastair Campbell & Co., Inc., Chgo., 1976—. Mem. Chgo. Assn. Direct Mktg., Direct Mktg. Writers Guild, Clan Campbell Soc. U.S. Home: 736 Plum Tree Rd Barrington Hills IL 60010 Office: 919 N Michigan Ave #2305 Chicago IL 60611

CAMPBELL, BRUCE ALEXANDER, utility co. pub. relations exec.; b. Evanston, Ill., Oct. 19, 1929; s. Joseph Bruce and Ruth (Norcom) C.; B.S., U. Ill., 1951; M.A., Sangamon State U., 1977; m. Alice Jean Keller, July 25, 1953; children—Cynthia, Bruce, Craig, Thomas. Salesman Gen. Am. Life Ins. Co., St. Louis, 1953-55; with pub. relations depts. Ill. Bell Telephone Co., Chgo., 1955-62, pub. relations supr., 1965-69, pub. relations mgr., Springfield, 1970—; film prodn. supr. AT&T, N.Y.C., 1963-64; guest lectr. U. Ill., Bradley U., Sangamon State U. Pres. Family Services Assn., DuPage County, Ill., 1962-63, Wheaton (Ill.) Library Bd., 1969-70, Springfield Boys Club, 1975-77; bd. dirs. Meml. Med. Center, Springfield, 1976, Lincoln Library, Srpingfield, 1973, Sangamon County (Ill.) Good Will, 1972-74. Served with U.S. Army, 1951-53; Korea. Recipient Golden Boy award Boys Club, 1977. Mem. Ill. Press Assn., Ill. Broadcasters Assn., Publ. Relations Soc. Am. (accredited). Presbyterian. Clubs: Illini Country, Sangamo, (Springfield); Elks. Author: 200 Years: An Illustrated Bicentennial History of Sangamon County, 1976. Home: 1635 Ruth Pl Springfield IL 62704 Office: 406 E Monroe St Springfield IL 62721

CAMPBELL, CALVIN ARTHUR, JR., mining and tunneling equipment mfg. co. exec.; b. Detroit, Sept. 1, 1934; s. Calvin Arthur and Alta Christine (Koch) C.; B.A. in Econs., Williams Coll., 1956; B.S., Mass. Inst. Tech., 1959; J.D., U. Mich., 1961; m. Rosemary Phoenix, June 6, 1959; 1 dau., Georgia Alta. With Exxon Co., N.Y.C., 1961-69; chmn. bd., treas. John B. Adt Co., York, Pa., N.Y.C., 1969-70; with Goodman Equipment Corp., Chgo., 1971—, pres., 1971—. Bd. govs. Am. Mining Congress, Washington, 1972—. Mem. Am., N.Y. bar assns., Am. Inst. Chem. Engrs., Young Pres.'s Orgn., Psi Upsilon, Phi Delta Phi. Clubs: Saddle 4 Cycle, Racquet (Chgo.); Glen View Golf. Home: 1320 N State Pkwy Chicago IL 60610 Office: 4834 S Halsted St Chicago IL 60609

CAMPBELL, CHARLES GEORGE, banker; b. Andover, Eng., July 16, 1895; s. William T. and Grace (Calder) C.; came to U.S., 1901, naturalized, 1919; grad. Ind. Bus. Coll., 1916; student U. Chgo., 1920-22; m. Helen I. Thompson, June 14, 1926; children—Claire E. (Mrs. David Locke, Jr.), Joyce C. (Mrs. Rodney Beals). Sec.-treas. Kamp Motor Co., Mt. Carmel, Ill., 1923-26, pres., 1926-59; v.p. Vigo Motor Co., Terre Haute, Ind., 1944-50; v.p. Security Bank and Trust Co., Mt. Carmel, 1937-59, pres., 1959-64, chmn. bd., 1969—, also dir.; pres. Am. Savs. & Loan Assn., Mt. Carmel, 1939-59, dir., 1937—; dir. Camray, Inc., Mt. Carmel, Mt. Carmel Area Devel. Corp.; dir. Tri-Country Indsl. Com., 1965-67. Mem. Mt. Carmel City Commn., 1963—; mayor City of Mt. Carmel, 1965-67. Served with U.S. Army, 1917-19; AEF in France. Mem. Mt. Carmel C. of C. (dir. 1959-62, 65-68), Am. Legion (comdr. Wabash post 1937), 40 and 8, Wabash Valley Assn. Presbyterian. Mason (Shriner), Elk, Moose, Eagle, Kiwanian (pres. Mt. Carmel 1935, dir. 1936). Home: 323 Cherry St Mount Carmel IL 62863 Office: 400 Main St Mount Carmel IL 62863

CAMPBELL, CHARLES HOUSTON, chem. co. exec.; b. Nashville, Sept. 8, 1924; s. Hugh Graine and Alcenia (McMahon) C.; B.A., Vanderbilt U., 1949, M.S., 1950; m. Lou D. Puckett, Dec. 1, 1950; children—Terry Susan, Patricia Gail. Research chemist, purchasing mgr. Monsanto Co., 1950-70; v.p. adminstrn., sr. v.p. MC/B Mfg. Chemists, Cin., 1970-76; pres. Campbell Chem. Co., Cin., 1976—. Served with USAAF, 1942-46. Mem. Am. Chem. Soc., Cin. Drug and Chem. Soc. Contbr. articles to profl. jours. Patentee in field. Home: 7012 Golden Gate St Cincinnati OH 45244 Office: 2909 Highland Ave Cincinnati OH 45212

CAMPBELL, COLIN, obstetrician, gynecologist, med. sch. dean; b. Washington, June 24, 1927; s. Colin and Margaret (Kingsland) (Masters) C.; A.B., Stanford U., 1949; M.D., C.M., McGill U., Montreal, Can., 1953; Ed.M., Temple U., 1967; m. Catherine Marian Hayden, Aug. 20, 1952; children—Catherine, Janet, Philip. Gen. practice medicine, Perrine, Fla., 1955-57; practice medicine specializing in obstetrics and gynecology, Balt., 1960-61; instr. obstetrics gynecology, Temple U., Phila., 1961-64; asst. prof. obstetrics gynecology U. Mich., Ann Arbor, 1964-67, asso. prof., 1967-71, prof., 1971—, asst. dean, Med. Sch., 1972-76, asso. dean, 1976—. Diplomate Am. Bd. Obstetrics Gynecology. Fellow Am. Coll. Obstetricians Gynecologists. Contbr. numerous articles in obstetrics and med. edn. topics to sci. jours. Home: 381 Orchard Hills Dr Ann Arbor MI 48104

CAMPBELL, CRAIG BARTLETT, state legislator, lawyer; b. Anderson, Ind., July 22, 1938; s. Jack B. and Lois M. (Howerton) C.; A.B., DePauw U., 1960; LL.B., Ind. U., 1964; m. Joan C. Koebke, June 17, 1961; children—Scott B., Christine E. Admitted to Ind. bar, 1964; partner, Campbell, Campbell & Maitingly, Anderson, Ind., 1964—; mem. Ind. Ho. of Reps., 1971—, asst. minority floor leader, 1973-74, speaker pro tem, 1975—. Served with AUS, 1960-61. Mem. Am., Ind. bar assns., Nat. Soc. State Legislators, Beta Theta Pi. Democrat. Presbyn. Home: 915 Spring Valley Dr Anderson IN 46011 Office: 109 E 9th St Anderson IN 46016

CAMPBELL, DANIEL CURRIE, JR., thoracic surgeon, ret. air force officer; b. Jacksonville, Fla., Oct. 23, 1920; s. Daniel Currie and Georgia Bryan (Erwin) C.; B.A., U. Tenn., 1941, M.D., 1943; m. Margaret Jean Lindamann, Sept. 18, 1954; children—Georgia (dec.), Nancy, Jeanne. Intern, John Gaston Hosp., Memphis, 1944, asst. resident in pathology, 1944-45, asst. resident in surgery, 1945-46; resident in surgery Walter Reed Gen. Hosp., Washington, 1947, sr. resident in surgery, 1951-52; resident in thoracic surgery VA Hosp., Hines, Ill., 1952-53, sr. resident, 1953-54; commd. 1st lt. U.S. Army, 1946, advanced through grades to maj., 1949; chief of surgery, sta. hosps., Berlin, Heidelberg, Germany, 1949-51; commd. maj. U.S. Air Forrce, 1949, advanced through grades to col., 1962; ret., 1970; practice medicine specializing in thoracic surgery, Ft. Myers, Fla., 1970-76; chief of surgery Mo. Chest Hosp., Mt. Vernon, 1976—; asso. clin. prof. surgery U. Mo., Columbia and Kansas City. Decorated Air medal with 6 oak leaf clusters, Legion of Merit, Airmans medal for heroism, Vietnam campaign medal with 5 battle stars. Mem. AMA, Am. Assn. Thoracic Surgery, A.C.S., Am. Coll. Chest Physicians, Soc. Thoracic Surgeons, So. Thoracic Surg. Assn., Ozark, Mo. med. assns. Presbyterian. Clubs: Masons, Shriners. Home and Office: Box 66 Mo Chest Hosp Mount Vernon MO 65712

CAMPBELL, D'ANN MAE, historian; b. Denver, Dec. 30, 1949; d. Bernard Edward and Eleanor Louise (Mahoney) Campbell; B.A., Colo. Coll., 1972; postgrad. U. N.C., Chapel Hill, 1972—; m. Richard Jensen, July 16, 1976. Asst. dir. Family and Community History Center, Newberry Library, Chgo., 1976—; adj. prof. history U. Ill., Chgo. Circle, 1977—. Newberry Library fellow, 1975-76, Nat. Endowment for Humanities grantee, 1976-79. Mem. Orgn. Am. Historians (chair com. status women 1977—), Am., So., Social Sci. hist. assns., Nat. Hist. Communal Socs. Assn., Quantum Internat. Orgn., Phi Beta Kappa. Methodist. Contbr. articles to profl. jours. Editorial bd. Analytic Review of Utopia and Utopianism. Home: 400 E Randolph St Apt 3408 Chicago IL 60610 Office: 60 W Walton St Chicago IL 60610

CAMPBELL, DON PRESTON, lawyer; b. North Madison, Ind., July 6, 1938; s. Virgil B. and Betty June (Christie) C.; B.A., DePauw U., 1960; LL.B., Ind. U., 1963; m. Peggy Goiffinet, Aug. 23, 1975; children by previous marriage—Dawn Christie, Jodi-Beth. Admitted to Ind. bar, 1964; clk. Idaho Supreme Ct., 1963-64; practiced in Covington, Ind., 1964—; asso. firm Wallace & Wallace, 1964-67; mem. firm Wallace, Wallace, Campbell & Bunch, 1967—; atty. City of Covington, 1969-70, dep. pros. atty., 1972-74. Mem. Ind. Def. Lawyers Assn. (v.p. 1976-77), Covington Jr. C. of C. (pres. 1967-68), C. of C., Delta Theta Phi. Republican. Methodist. Mason, Lion (pres. 1970-71). Home: 1116 Commercial Circle Covington IN 47932 Office: 303 Washington St Covington IN 47932

CAMPBELL, GARY LEE, agrl. engr.; b. Harlan, Ia., Mar. 4, 1939; s. Clarence Clyde and Nina Irene (Potts) C.; B.S., Ia. State U., 1960; m. Daneen Lee Hensley, Oct. 15, 1960; children—Connie, Sonya. Engr. design grain drying and handling equipment Caldwell Mfg. Co., Kearney, Neb., 1960-62; agrl. engr., product engring. dept. John Deere Waterloo Tractor Works, Waterloo, Ia., 1962—. Registered profl. engr., Ia. Mem. Am. Soc. Agrl. Engrs., Soc. Automotive Engrs. Baptist (trustee 1971—). Patentee in field. Home: 8543 Hammond Av Waterloo IA 50701 Office: John Deere Waterloo Tractor Works Waterloo IA 50701

CAMPBELL, HELEN WOERNER (MRS. THOMAS B. CAMPBELL), librarian; b. Indpls., Oct. 17, 1918; d. Clarence Julius and Gertrude Elizabeth (Colley) Woerner; student Ind. U., 1935-38; B.S., Butler U., 1967; m. Thomas B. Campbell, Jan. 17, 1942; 1 dau., Martha (Mrs. L. Kurt Adamson). Asst. order librarian Ind. U., Bloomington, 1937-42; librarian Ind. U. Sch. Dentistry, Indpls., 1942-46, cataloger, part-time, 1960-65, asst. librarian, 1965-66, librarian, 1966—. Mem. Am. Assn. Dental Schs., Med. Library Assn., Spl. Libraries Assn. (chpt. pres. 1972-73). Home: 1865 Norfolk St Indianapolis IN 46224 Office: 1121 W Michigan St Indianapolis IN 46202

CAMPBELL, J. CHANDLER, psychologist; b. Detroit, Sept. 6, 1925; s. Harlin M. and Eva Lucile (Franks) C.; B.A., Coll. Wooster, 1950; M.Ed., Kent State U., 1952; Ph.D., Ind. U., 1959; m. Vivian Lee Albery, Aug. 1, 1954; children—Christine Lucile, Roger Scott. Tchr., pub. schs., Orrville, Ohio, 1950-51, Painesville, Ohio, 1952-53; chem. analyst Indsl. Rayon Corp., 1953-54; grad. asst. Bur. Ednl. Placement Ind. U., Bloomington, 1954-56; counselor, psychologist Bd. Coop. Ednl. Services, Westchester County, N.Y., 1956-59; state supr. Ohio Dept Edn., 1959-65; sr. cons. psychologist Rohrer, Hibler & Replogle, Inc., Southfield, Mich., 1965—. Mem. com. Cub Scouts and Boy Scouts Am., 1969—. Served with AUS, 1946-48. Mem. Am. Personnel and Guidance Assn. (life), Nat. Vocational Guidance Assn., Am. Psychol. Assn. Office: 200 Mark Plaza 21411 Civic Center Dr Southfield MI 48076

CAMPBELL, JOHN LAWTHER, psychologist; b. Alliance, Ohio, Nov. 11, 1921; s. John Floyd and Mary Frances (Lawther) C.; A.B., Muskingum Coll., 1947; M.A., Case Western Res. U., 1950; m. Arline Durkin, July 17, 1948; children—John Floyd, Jane Frances. Admissions counselor Cleve. Coll., Western Res. U., 1949-50, asso. in vocat. guidance, Med. Sch., 1954-59; psychologist, counselor, asso. dir. Vocat. Guidance Rehab Services, Cleve., 1950-75; dir. Vocat. Analysis Labs., Lakewood, Ohio, 1977—; pvt. practice psychology, Lakewood, 1975—; cons. Ohio State Bur. Vocat. Rehab., Bur. Hearings and Appeals, State Services for the Blind. Elder, Presbyn. Ch. Recipient Laymen's award Kiwanis, Rocky River, Ohio, 1968; nat. citation for service to handicapped in profession of rehab. counseling, San Diego, 1970; spl. award Guidance and Rehab. Services, 1975. Mem. Am. Psychol. Assn., Nat. Rehab. Assn., Nat. Rehab. Counseling Assn. Contbr. articles to profl. jours. Home: 19629 Shoreland Ave Rocky River OH 44116 Office: 14601 Detroit Ave Lakewood OH 44107

CAMPBELL, JOHN ROY, animal scientist, educator; b. Goodman, Mo., June 14, 1933; s. Carl J. and Helen (Nicoletti) C.; B.S., U. Mo., Columbia, 1955, M.S., 1956, Ph.D., 1960; m. Eunice Vieten, Aug. 7, 1954; children—Karen L., Kathy L., Keith L. Instr. animal sci., U. Mo., Columbia, 1960-61, asst. prof., 1961-65, asso. prof., 1965-68, prof., 1968—; asso. dean, dir. resident instruction Coll. Agr. U. Ill., Urbana, 1978—. Recipient Outstanding Tchr. award U. Mo., 1967; Superior Teaching award Gamma Sigma Delta. Mem. Am. Dairy Sci. Assn. (dir., Ralston Purina Distinguished Teaching award 1973), Nat. Assn. Coll. Tchrs. Agr. (Ensminger Interstate Distinguished Tchr. award 1973). Author: (with J.F. Lasley) The Science of Animals That Serve Mankind, 1969; In Touch with Students, 1972; (with R.T. Marshall) The Science of Providing Milk for Man, 1975. Home: 357 Crown Point St Columbia MO 65201 Office: Univ Illinois Coll Agriculture 104 Mumford St Urbana IL 61801

CAMPBELL, JULES DESLOGE, cons. engineer; b. St. Louis, Dec. 29, 1909; s. John Hayes and Marian (Desloge) C.; student Washington U., St. Louis, 1928-29, B.S., 1932, M.S., 1933; student Ga. Sch. Tech., 1929-30; m. Isabelle Kingsland Bonsack, Apr. 26, 1934; children—Helen Kingsland (Mrs. Robert Lewis Weise), Jules Desloge. Salesman Shell Petroleum Co., St. Louis, 1933; mech. engr. Internat. Shoe Co., St. Louis, 1934-42, 46-49, mgr. machinery and power dept., 1949-69; now gen. cons. engr. Mem. subdist. bd. commrs. St. Louis Museum Sci. and Natural History, 1972—, chmn., 1972-73. Bd. dirs. Chatillon-De Menil House Found., 1974—. Served to maj. AUS, 1942-46. Mem. St. Louis Acad. Sci. (v.p. 1964-69, dir. 1954—, chief operating officer 1969, pres. 1970—), Sigma Xi, Kappa Alpha. Republican. Roman Catholic. Clubs: Ambassadors Dinner, Town and Country, Clayton, Contemporary. Home: 4 Westerly Ln City of Ladue MO 63124

CAMPBELL, LYLE PAUL, commodity broker; b. Neola, Ia., Nov. 24, 1935; s. T. Marlowe and Verna Selma (Manhart) C.; B.S., Ia. State U., 1966; M.B.A., U. Chgo., 1971; m. Nancy Louise Felton, Aug. 16, 1953; children—Verna, Sheryl, Craig, Douglas, Scott, Cathleen. Real estate broker Byron Reed Co., Inc., Omaha, 1959-62; pres. Felcam, Inc., 1962-66; with No. Trust Co., Chgo., 1966-73, credit analyst, 1966-67, asst. cashier, 1967-69, 2d v.p., 1969-71, v.p., 1971-73; v.p. First Nat. Bank Chgo., 1973-74; chmn. bd. Peoples Bank Cambridge (Ill.), 1973—, First Nat. Bank of Westville (Ill.), 1976—, Peotone Bank and Trust Co. (Ill.); hedging specialist Conticommodity Services, Inc., Chgo., 1974—. Republican committeeman, Ames, Ia., 1964-66. Bd. dirs. U.S. Feed Grains Council. Mem. Phi Kappa Phi, Gamma Sigma Delta, Alpha Zeta. Conglist. Club: Bankers (Chgo.). Home: 4510 Downers Dr Downers Grove IL 60515 Office: 1800 Board of Trade Bldg Chicago IL 60604

CAMPBELL, M. ANNE, state ofcl.; b. Denver, Nov. 13, 1917; B.A., U. No. Colo., 1938; M.S., Wayne State Coll., 1959; Ed.D., U. Nebr., 1969. Commr. of edn. State of Nebr., Lincoln, 1975—. Republican. Office: 301 Centennial Mall S Lincoln NE 68509

CAMPBELL, MALCOLM DAVID, dentist; b. Detroit, Sept. 23, 1926; s. Malcolm Duncan and Mabel Edith (White) C.; B.A., Wayne State U., 1951, teaching certificate, 1951; D.D.S., U. Detroit, 1955, postgrad., 1962-63; m. Janet Cauhorn, Nov. 14, 1958; children—Mary Catherine, David, Elizabeth, Douglas. Pvt. practice dentistry, Dearborn, Mich.; mem. staff Harper Hosp., Detroit, 1957—; instr. Sch. Dentistry U. Detroit, 1961-65, U. Mich., 1966-74; adviser Wayne County Welfare Dept. Sponsor Detroit council Boy Scouts Am.; bd. dirs. Dearborn Community Health; deacon First Presbyterian Ch. of Dearborn. Fellow Am. Acad. Gen. Dentistry, Royal Soc. Health; mem. Southwestern Dental Club (treas., corr. sec. 1957, pres. 1960), Dental Aid Commn. (pres. 1959-61), Chgo., Detroit Dist. dental socs., Mich. Soc. Psychosomatic Dentistry (v.p. 1962-63, pres. 1964), Am. Acad. Dental Medicine (pres. elect Mich. sect. 1964-65), Am. Acad. Oral Medicine, Am. Assn. Dental Schs., Orgn. Tchrs. Dental Practice Adminstrn., Am. Acad. Dental Practice Adminstrn., Mich. Dental Assn. Office: 23601 Ford Rd Dearborn MI 48128

CAMPBELL, MILDRED FLORENCE, educator; b. Logansport, Ind., Apr. 5, 1906; d. Samuel Gilbert and Lottie Edith (Behmer) Campbell; A.B., Butler U., 1928; M.A., Woods Hole (Mass.) Marine, U. Mich. biol. stas., 1936; postgrad. Albion Coll., 1942, ecology, U. Ill., 1928—. Tchr. nat. sci. Shortridge High Sch., Indpls., 1928-68; nature counsellor, field trip guide various civic orgns., summers, 1928-68; lectr. conservation, ecology, dress and dolls of fgn. countries to various children's and civic groups, 1941—. Leader, counsellor, nature guide Campfire Girls, Girl Scouts U.S.A., chs. On program Talk of the Town, radio sta. WXLW. Recipient Opportunity Gift, Indpls. Mus. Art, 1974; outstanding services award for role as historian and naturalist Irvington community Indpls. Mayor, 1977. Mem. Nat. Audubon Soc. (took Christmas Count local plants and animals 1940-68), Ind. Audubon Soc. (past editor Yearbook), Irvington Hist. Soc. (mem. children's edn. commn. on hist. research 1962—, sci. editor 1966 Checklist Abstract), Guild of Community Hosp., Cranbrook Inst., NEA, Ind. Tchrs. Assn., Nat. Biology Tchrs. Assn., Am. Inst. Biology, Soc. Central Math. and Sci., Am. Ornithol. Union, Wilson Ornithology Soc., Ind. Acad. Sci. Republican. Presbyterian. Contbr. chpts. to biology texts, articles to profl. jours. Donated S.G. Campbell Bookbinding Display to Lilly Library, Bloomington. Home: 29 N Hawthorne Ln Indianapolis IN 46219

CAMPBELL, RICHARD AVANDER, automotive parts wholesale co. exec.; b. Toledo, Aug. 6, 1941; s. Avander John and Margaret Mae (Beller) C.; student Ohio U., 1959-60, Automotive Wholesalers Inst., 1971, 73, 74; m. Janet Joyce Kneffler, Oct. 3, 1964. With Toledo Auto & Truck Supply, Inc., 1957—, purchasing agt., 1962-64, v.p., 1964—; speaker at profl. meetings. Served with USCGR, 1963. Mem. Ohio Automotive Wholesalers Assn. (Membership award 1975), No. Wood County (Ohio) Area C. of C. (dir. 1977—), Automotive Service Industries Assn. (dist. dir. Young Execs. Forum), Nat. Fedn. Ind. Bus. Republican. Methodist. Home: 23834 W State St Route 579 Curtice OH 43412 Office: 5809 Woodville Rd Toledo OH 43619

CAMPBELL, ROLF CORYDON, landscape architect, city planner; b. Detroit, Jan. 5, 1930; s. Harold Lansing and Margaret Ann (Rolf) C.; B.S., Mich. State U., 1951, M.Urban Planning, 1953; m. Shirley E. Barr, Aug. 25, 1951; children—Sandra Lynn, Kevin Rolf, Douglas Brian, Scott Corydon, Darcy Ann. City planner City of Lansing (Mich.), 1953-62; prin. P.E.L.A., Assos., Lansing, 1955-62; div. head Tec-Search, Inc., Wilmette, Ill., 1952-70; pres., owner Rolf C. Campbell & Assos., Inc., Chgo. and Lake Bluff, Ill., 1971—. Served to 1st lt. USAF, 1953-55. Mem. Am. Inst. Planners, Am. Soc. Landscape Architects, Mich. State U. Alumni Club of Chgo. (pres. 1972-74, bd. dirs. 1972-77), Alpha Zeta, Beta Alpha Sigma, Sigma Alpha Epsilon. Home: 927 Cherokee Rd Lake Forest IL 60045 Office: 21 N Skokie Hwy Lake Bluff IL 60044

CAMPBELL, RONALD, coll. pres.; b. Detroit, Mar. 12, 1925; s. Samuel and Elizabeth (Campbell) C.; B.S., Bowling Green State U., 1950; M.Ed., U. Detroit, 1953; D.Ed., Wayne State U., 1965; m. Blondelle Bolding, Dec. 23, 1950; 1 son, Kevin. Instr. Dearborn (Mich.). Bd. Edn., 1950-55; dean instrn. Henry Ford Community Coll., 1955-64; pres. Monroe County (Mich.) Community Coll.,

1964—; vis. prof. Marygrove Coll., 1966. Chmn. Southeastern Mich. League Community Colls., 1975—. Bd. dirs. United Fund Monroe County, 1965-69; pres. YMCA, 1969-71. Bd. dirs. Monroe County, 1966—. Served with AUS, 1943-46. Mem. AAUP, Am. Acad. Polit. and Social Sci., Assn. Higher Edn., C. of C. (pres. 1970), Phi Delta Kappa. Home: 1525 Arbor Monroe MI 48161

CAMPBELL, TERENCE WARREN, psychologist; b. Chgo., Sept. 9, 1943; s. Jesse Frank and Dorothy Agnes C.; B.S. cum laude, Western Mich. U., 1965; Ph.D., U. Md., 1970; m. Constance Lee Martin, Aug. 20, 1966; children—Elisabeth Ann, Derek Martin. Asst. prof. Mercy Coll. Detroit, 1972—; cons. psychologist Madison Profl. Counseling Clinic (Mich.), 1972—, Macomb County (Mich.) Circuit Ct.; chief psychologist Md. Penitentiary, 1970-72; adj. asst. prof. Loyola Coll. Balt., 1970-72. Grant Found. fellow, 1967-68. Mem. Am., Mich. psychol. assns., Mich. Soc. Cons. Psychologists, Soc. Clin. and Exptl. Hypnosis, Nat. Register Health Service Providers in Psychology. Home: 18615 Birchcrest Detroit MI 48221 Office: 1200 E Twelve Mile Rd Madison Heights MI 48071

CAMPBELL, THOMAS CLARK, veterinarian; b. Laurel, Nebr., Nov. 27, 1917; s. John H. and Theresa (Allen) C.; student Wayne State Coll., 1937-38; D.V.M., Kans. State U., 1943; m. Eleanor Louise Ellis, Aug. 1, 1943; children—Thomas M., Kay (Mrs. Dave Harris), Timothy C., John O. Pvt. practice vet. medicine, Norfolk, Nebr., 1943, 46-52, sr. partner animal clinic, Norfolk, 1952—; insp. Norfolk Livestock Auction Market, 1949—. Founder, pres. Bel-Air Devel. Corp., 1962—; a founder Glenmore Devel. Corp., 1969—, v.p., 1969—. Mem. Norfolk Civil Service Commn., 1966—, chmn., 1968—; mem. Madison County Health Bd., 1966—; vice chmn. Madison County Red Cross, 1968—; sec., treas. Norfolk Fire Dist., 1950—; mem. adv. com. Lady Lourdes Hosp., Convent and Nursing Home, 1969—. Served to capt. Vet. Corps., AUS, 1943-46. Mem. Am., Nebr., Northeast Nebr. (pres. 1960-64) vet. med. assns., Norfolk C. of C. (dir. 1970-73). Methodist (trustee 1965-67). Lion. Home: 1305 Parkview Dr Norfolk NE 68701 Office: 1201 N 13th St Norfolk NE 68701

CAMPBELL, THOMAS HAROLD, credit union info. processing exec.; b. Grosse Pointe Farms, Mich., Oct. 6, 1937; s. Harold Timothy and Marian Elizabeth (Beaupre) C.; A.B., U. Detroit, 1959; M.B.A., Wayne State U., 1970; m. Jill Ellen Serino, Aug. 20, 1960; children—Andrew, Julie, Diane, Jeffrey, Jennifer. Tchr., St. Martin High Sch., Detroit, 1959-60; with Ford Motor Co., Detroit, 1963-74, systems analyst, 1968-72, computer specialist, 1972-74; mgr. data processing Dearborn (Mich.) Fed. Credit Union, 1974—. Active Cub Scouts Am. Detroit Area Council Boy Scouts Am., 1970-76; mem. parish council Christ the Good Shepherd Parish, Lincoln Park, Mich., 1974-77, com. chmn., 1974-77. Served with USN, 1960-63; comdr. Res. Mem. Naval Res. Assn., Mich. Automated Clearing House Assn. (mem. ops. com. 1976—). Roman Catholic. Club: Econ. of Detroit. Home: 905 Liberty St Lincoln Park MI 48146 Office: 21551 Oakwood Blvd Dearborn MI 48124

CAMPBELL, WILLIAM J., judge; b. Chgo., Mar. 19, 1905; s. John and Christina (Larsen) C.; grad. St. Rita Coll. Prep. Sch., 1922; J.D., Loyola U., 1926, LL.M., 1928, LL.D., 1955, Litt.D., 1965, J.C.D., 1967; m. Marie Agnes Cloherty, 1937; children—Marie Agnes (Mrs. Walter J. Cummings), Karen (Mrs. James T. Reid), Heather (Mrs. Patrick Henry), Patti (Mrs. Peter V. Fazio, Jr.), Roxane (Mrs. Wesley Sedlacek), William J., Christian, Thomas. Admitted to Ill. bar, 1927; Ill. adminstr. Nat. Youth Adminstrn., 1935-38; U.S. dist. atty. No. Dist. of Ill., 1938-40; judge U.S. Dist. Ct., 1940—, chief judge, 1959-70; asst. dir. Fed. Jud. Center, Washington, 1974—. Citizens bd. U. Chgo., Loyola U., Barat Coll. of Sacred Heart; bd. dirs. Catholic Charities Chgo.; co-founder Cath. Youth Orgn. Chgo., 1930; mem. exec. bd. Chgo. council, also nat. exec. bd. Boy Scouts Am. Mem. Am., Ill., Chgo., Fed. bar assns., Jud. Conf. U.S. (chmn. com. on budget 1955-69). Clubs: Law, Ill. Athletic, Union League, Saddle and Cycle, Standard (Chgo.). Home: 199 E Lake Shore Dr Chicago IL 60611 Office: US Court House Chicago IL 60604

CAMPBELL, WILLIAM STEWART, mech. engr.; b. Brooklyn, Ill., Jan. 30, 1931; s. Eugene T. and Mary Florence (Icnogle) C.; B.M.E., U. Ill., 1952; m. Carol Rose Colletti, Jan. 4, 1969; children—Cynthia Ann, Lori Ann. Power engr. Patten Industries, Elmhurst, Ill., 1964-70; mgr. pump sales Hydro Aire Co., Chgo., 1971-73; design engr. Austin Co., Des Plaines, Ill., 1973-74; engring. supr. Wilson Sporting Goods, River Grove, Ill., 1974—. Pres., Elmwood Park Civic Assn. Served with AUS, 1954-57. Registered profl. engr., Ill. Mem. Ill. Soc. Profl. Engrs. Democrat. Methodist. Club: Masons. Home: 1911 78th Ave Elmwood Park IL 60635 Office: 2233 West St River Grove IL 60171

CAMPION, MICHAEL ANDREW, psychologist; b. Mpls., Nov. 9, 1941; s. John Andrew and Ruth Vivian (Robertson) C.; B.S., U. Minn., 1963; M.A., St. Thomas Coll., St. Paul, 1968; Ph.D., U. Ill., 1971; m. Katherine Jean Smiley, Sept. 8, 1962; children—Matthew, Andrew, Christine, Thomas. Staff psychologist Decatur (Ill.) Mental Health Inst., 1971-73; dir. research project Indsl. Opportunities Inst., Decatur, 1973-74; pvt. practice psychology, Decatur, 1974—; cons., tchr. in field, Bd. dirs. For Here's Life, Closer to God Today. George Williams fellow, 1963. Mem. Am., Ill. psychol. assns., Nat. Rehab. Assn., Christian Med. Soc., Am. Sci. Affiliation. Methodist. Home: Rural Route 2 Box 49 Blue Mound IL 62513 Office: 132 S Water St Decatur IL 62523

CAMPLIN, FORREST RALPH, architect; b. Shirley, Ind., June 28, 1917; s. Russell and Mae (Lewman) C.; student pub. schs.; m. Viola Faye Reed, June 15, 1947; children—Gloria Jean, Mary Darlene, Rita Ann. With Russell Camplin, masonry contractor, 1936-42; with Gen. Motors Corp., Anderson, Ind., 1942-50; with Edward D. James, Inc. (now James Assos., Architects-Engrs., Inc.), Indpls., 1951—, architect, 1961—. Served with C.E., U.S. Army, 1942-45. Mem. A.I.A., Guild for Religious Architecture, Nat. Trust for Historic Preservation, Ind. Hist. Soc., Indpls. Mus. Art Methodist. Mason. Chief archtl. works include Faith Luth. Ch., Greenfield, Ind., 1963, First Baptist Ch., Plainfield, 1964, Calvary United Meth. Ch., Avilla, 1967, Good Shepherd Luth. Ch., South Bend, 1967, Phi Delta Theta frat. house, Hanover Coll., 1967, St. Thomas Episcopal Ch., Franklin, Ind., 1968, Central Nat. Bank, Greencastle, 1971, Chapel, Ft. Benjamin Harrison, 1976, Morgan County (Ind.) Courthouse, Martinsville, 1976, 1st United Meth. Ch., Crawfordsville, Ind., 1977. Home: PO Box 27 Wilkinson IN 46186 Office: 2828 E 45th St Indianapolis IN 46205

CANDELARESI, THOMAS ALEXANDER, foundry supply co. exec.; b. Cin., Feb. 26, 1950; s. Victor Robert and Evelyn Frances (Cooper) C.; student U. Cin., 1968-69; children—Arica Dawn, Amber Danielle. Programmer, First Nat. Bank of Cin., 1970-71; system analyst Manual Arts Furniture Co., Cin., 1972-73, 74-76; systems analyst T.S.C., Cin., 1973-74; data processing mgr. Scallan Supply Co., Cin., 1976-77, Hill & Griffith Co., Cin., 1977—. Vice pres. Miami Twp. Democrat Club, 1978—; mem. com. Miami Twp. Park Bd., 1977—; pres. Clermont County Young Democrat Club, 1978. Mem. Data Processing Mgmt. Assn., Milford Jaycees, Greater Milford Athletic Assn. Roman Catholic. Contbr. polit. column to local newspaper. Home: 5908 Cook Rd Milford OH 45150 Office: 4900 Cleves Rd Cincinnati OH 45238

CANDLER, JAMES NALL, JR., lawyer; b. Detroit, Jan. 25, 1943; s. James Nall and Lorna Augusta (Blood) C.; A.B., Princeton U., 1965; J.D., U. Mich., 1970; m. Jean Ward McKinnon, Mar. 8, 1974. Admitted to Mich. bar, 1970; asso. firm Dickinson, Wright, McKean, Cudlip & Moon, Detroit, 1970-77, partner firm, 1977—; adj. prof. U. Detroit Law Sch., 1975—; dir. Great Lakes Industries, World Investigations & Security Engrs., Inc.; prosecuting atty. City of Grosse Pointe Farms, Mich., 1971-74. Served to lt. USNR, 1965-67. Mem. State Bar of Mich., Am. Bar Assn., Maritime Law Assn. of U.S. Clubs: Country Club of Detroit; Grosse Pointe; Princeton of Mich. Office: 800 First Nat Bldg Detroit MI 48226

CANFIELD, CARL REX, JR., mfg. co. exec.; b. Oregon, Ill., May 15, 1923; s. Carl Rex and Edna Lucille (Wilde) C.; B.S. in Mech. Engring., Ill. Inst. Tech., 1950; postgrad. exec. tng. program U. Chgo., 1959; m. Mary Jane Butler, Jan. 3, 1952; children—Christopher Jay, Cynthia Ann, Laurie Lynn. Dir. engring. Marvel-Schebler div. Borg Warner Co., Decatur, Ill., 1959-63, v.p. engring. mechanics Universal Joint div., Rockford, Ill., 1965-68; mng. dir. Simms Marvel Schebler, London, 1963-65; mgr. engring. Warner Electric Brake & Clutch Co., Beloit, Wis., 1968-72; v.p., gen. mgr. Schwitzer div. Wallace Murray Corp., Indpls., 1972—; dir. Simms Marvel Schebler Joint Venture Co., London. Head fund raising Boy Scouts Am., Decatur, 1961-62. Served as ensign USNR, 1943-46. Registered profl. engr. Ill. Mem. Automotive Instrumentation Soc. (nat. dir. 1953-54), Soc. Automotive Engrs., Instrument Soc. Am., Nat. Free Lance Photographers Assn., Photog. Soc. Am. Presbyn. Mason (Shriner). Club: Camera (Indpls.). Patentee autofuel injection field. Home: 12317 Windsor Dr Carmel IN 46032 Office: 1125 Brookside Ave Indianapolis IN 46201

CANGI, ELLEN CORWIN, historian, educator; b. Lima, Ohio, July 18, 1942; d. Robert Joseph and Mary Louise (Artz) Corwin; diploma Good Samaritan Hosp. Sch. Nursing, 1963; B.A., Wright State U., 1973, M.A., 1976; postgrad U. Cin., 1976—; m. Joseph William Cangi, June 22, 1968; 1 dau., Anne Aiello. Instr. nursing Good Samaritan Hosp., Dayton, Ohio, 1970-72; grad. asst. Wright State U., 1975-76, adj. instr. history medicine, 1977—. Groesbeck scholar, 1976. Mem. Am. Hist. Assn., Orgn. Am. Historians, History of Medicine Soc., Phi Alpha Theta. Democrat. Roman Catholic. Home: 7865 Raintree Rd Centerville OH 45459 Office: Wright State Univ Dayton OH

CANISIA, SISTER MARY, hosp. adminstr.; b. Sindersfeld, Germany, Aug. 29, 1914; d. Joseph and Maria Anna (Balzer) Gerlach; came to U.S., 1935, naturalized, 1941; R.N., St. Francis Hosp., Peoria, Ill., 1940, certificate anesthesia, 1941; B.S., Creighton U., 1951; M.A. in Hosp. Adminstrn., St. Louis U., 1960. Joined Order of St. Francis, 1935; floor supr. St. Joseph's Hosp., Keokuk, Iowa, 1940-43; staff St. Francis Hosp., Peoria, 1945—, instr. Sch. Nursing, 1946-48, Sch. Anesthesia, 1944, 51-54, dir. Sch. Anesthesia, 1954-58, adminstr. hosp., 1960—; pres. St. Francis Community Clinic, Peoria, 1967—. Fellow Am. Coll. Hosp. Adminstrs.; mem. Am., Ill., Cath. hosp. assns. Home: St Francis Hosp Medical Center 530 NE Glen Oak St Peoria IL 61637

CANNADY, EDWARD WYATT, JR., physician; b. East St. Louis, Ill., June 20, 1906; s. Edward Wyatt and Ida Bertha (Rose) C.; A.B., Washington U., St. Louis, 1927, M.D., 1931; m. Diane W. Holt, Oct. 22, 1977; children by previous marriage—Edward Wyatt III, Jane Marie (Mrs. Starr). Intern internal medicine Barnes Hosp., St. Louis, 1931-33, resident physician, 1934-35, asst. physician, 1935—; asst. resident Peter Bent Brigham Hosp., Boston, 1933-34; fellow in gastroenterology Washington U. Sch. Medicine, 1935-36, instr. internal medicine 1935-74, emeritus, 1974—; cons. internal medicine Washington U. Clinics, 1942-74; physician St. Mary's Hosp., East St. Louis, 1935—, pres. staff, 1947-49, chmn. med. dept., 1945-47; physician Christian Welfare Hosp., 1935—, chmn. med. dept., 1939-53, dir. electrocardiography, 1936—; dir. electrocardiography Centreville Twp. Hosp., East St. Louis. mem. staff Meml. Hosp., Belleville, Ill., St. Elizabeth Hosp., Belleville. Dir. 1st Nat. Bank, East St. Louis; pres. C.I.F. Dir. health service East St. Louis pub. schs., 1936-37; chmn. med. adv. bd. Selective Service, 1941-45; pres. St. Clair County Council Aging, 1961-62; chmn. St. Clair County Home Care Program, 1961-68, St. Clair County Med. Soc. Com. Aging, 1960—; del. White House Conf. Aging, 1961, 71; mem. Adv. Council Improvement Econ. and Social Status Older People, 1959-66; bd. dirs., exec. com. Nat. Council Homemaker Services, 1966-73, chmn. profl. adv. com. 1971-73; bd. dirs. St. Louis Met. Hosp. Planning Commn., 1966-70; mem. Ill. Council Aging, 1966-74; mem. Gov.'s Council on Aging, 1974—; mem. Ill. Regional Heart Disease, Cancer and Stroke Com.; mem. exec. com. Bi-State Regional Com. on Heart Disease, Cancer and Stroke; pres. Ill. Joint Council to Improve Health Care Aged, 1959-61; dir. Ill. Council Continuing Med. Edn., 1972—, v.p., 1974—. Trustee McKendree Coll.; adv. bd. Belleville Jr. Coll. Sch. Nursing; bd. dirs. United Fund Greater East St. Louis, 1953-58. Recipient Distinguished Service Award Am. Heart Assn., 1957, Distinguished Achievement award, 1957. Diplomate Am. Bd. Internal Medicine. Fellow Am. Coll. Cardiology, Am. Geriatrics Soc., A.C.P. (gov. 1964-70); mem. AMA (ho. dels. 1961-71, mem. aging com.; editorial adv. bd. Chronic Illness News Letter 1962-70, chmn. Ill. delegation 1964-66, mem. council vol. health agys.), Am. (dir. 1956-62, personnel and personnel tng. com. 1956-60), Ill. (pres. 1950-51) heart assns., St. Clair County (pres. 1952, bd. censors 1953-57), Ill. (sec. cardiovascular sect. 1957, chmn. sect., 1958-59; chmn. com. on aging, 1959-69, speaker Ho. Dels. 1964-68, pres. 1969-70) med. socs., Beta Theta Pi, Nu Sigma Nu, Alpha Omega Alpha. Presbyn. Mason. Clubs: St. Clair Country, Mo. Athletic, Media; Palmbrook Country (Sun City, Ariz.). Contbr. sci. articles and papers to med. jours. Home: 43 Country Club Pl Belleville IL 62223 Office: 6600 W Main St Belleville IL 62223

CANNATTI, DOMINIC SAM, dentist; b. Youngstown, Ohio, May 5, 1922; s. Louis and Mary (Nigro) C.; D.D.S., Ohio State U., 1951; m. Diana Jean Clemons, Sept. 7, 1946; 1 dau., Nancy. Pvt. practice gen. dentistry, Battle Creek, Mich., 1951—. Dental cons. Peoples, Fed., Home life ins. cos., 1971—, Kellogg Community Coll., 1971-72. Chmn. profl. and finance com. United Fund, 1957. Trustee Kellogg Community Coll. Served with USAAF, 1942-46. Mem. Am., Mich. (chmn. com. dental edn. 1972-73), Southwestern Mich. Dist. (pres. 1953) dental assns., Acad. Gen. Dentistry, Mich. Assn. Professions, Pierre Fauchard Acad., Mich. Acad. Sci., Arts and Letters, Battle Creek C. of C., Delta Sigma Delta, Ohio State U. Alumni Club. Roman Catholic. Home: 136 Stafford Ave Battle Creek MI 49015 Office: 713 Capital Ave SW Battle Creek MI 49015

CANNON, CHARLES BERNARD, lawyer; b. Superior, Wis., Apr. 3, 1900; s. Dennis M. and Agnes (McCole) C.; B.S. in Chemistry, Marquette U., 1925; LL.B., Loyola U., Chgo., 1929, B.S.C. in Accounting, 1946; m. Blanche A. Reardon, June 29, 1935 (dec.); 1 dau., Patricia Reardon Willis; m. 2d, Helen O'Toole Meyer, Dec. 27, 1958. Instr. chemistry St. Ignatius High Sch., Chgo., 1925-29, Chgo. Coll. Dental Surgery, 1926-27; lectr. Loyola U. Law Sch., Chgo., 1935-64; partner law firm Fitzpatrick, Cella, Harper & Scinto, N.Y.C., 1964—. Served with U.S. Army, World War I. Recipient medal of Excellence, Loyola U. Law Sch., 1950. Mem. Am. Chem. Soc., Patent Law Assn. Chgo., Am., Ill., N.Y., Chgo. bar assns., Am. Patent Law Assn., Wis. Soc. of Chgo. (pres. 1955-56), Patent Law Assn. N.Y., N.Y. County Lawyers Assn. Clubs: Ill. Athletic, Chgo. Athletic Assn. (Chgo.); Chemists, N.Y. Athletic, Lotos (N.Y.C.). Home: 860 Lake Shore Dr Chicago IL 60611 Office: 135 S LaSalle St Chicago IL 60603 also 277 Park Ave New York City NY 10021

CANNON, HOWARD SUCKLING, packaging co. ofcl.; b. Chgo., Sept. 23, 1926; s. William A. and Margaret E. (Suckling) C.; B.S., Carnegie Inst. Tech., 1950; M.S., Rensselaer Poly. Inst., 1951, Ph.D. (Carboloy fellow), 1953; m. Helen Werder, May 27, 1947; children—Mary Cannon Schofield, Deborah, Timothy, Amy Cannon Pfeiler, Clare. Scientist, Linde Air Products, Buffalo, 1953-55; supr. phys. metal Am. Metal-Climax, Carteret, N.J., 1955-58; mgr. phys. metallurgy Continental Can Co., Chgo., 1958-64, dir. research in metallurgy, 1964-70, dir. research in new tech., 1970-73, asst. to v.p. research and engring., 1973-76; gen. mgr. Techno-Econs., 1976—. Tchr. metallurgy Ill. Inst. Tech., 1969-70. Vice pres. Crawford Gardens Civic Assn., 1964-65. Served with USAAF, 1945-46; PTO. Recipient award for best ednl. paper Packaging Inst., 1969. Mem. Am. Soc. Metals, Am. Inst. Metall. Engrs. Home: 12847 Ponderosa Dr Palos Heights IL 60463 Office: 1200 W 76th St Chicago IL 60620

CANNON, NANCY LOUISE, banker; b. Toledo, Jan. 14, 1940; d. Melvin Marcus and Ruth Virginia (Hatt) Schultz; B.S. in Mktg., Ball State U., 1973; diploma of distinction Inst. Fin. Edn.; m. Roger B. Cannon, Sept. 6, 1958; children—Bryan Douglas, Bruce Donald, Diane Louise. Teller Mutual Home Fed. Savings & Loan Assn., Muncie, Ind., 1973-74, teller in charge tng., 1974-75, mem. mktg. dept., 1975-76, asso. dir. mktg., 1977—. Solicitor United Way, Muncie, Ind., 1975-76; bd. sec. Delaware County (Ind.) chpt. March of Dimes, 1976-78. Recipient Certificate of Appreciation, March of Dimes, 1976-77. Mem. Inst. Fin. Edn., Am. Mktg. Assn. Lutheran. Home: 2804 W Woodbridge Dr Muncie IN 47304 Office: 110 E Charles St Muncie IN 47305

CANNON, RICHARD DAVID, nursing home exec.; b. Vincennes, Ind., Feb. 1, 1939; s. James and Alice Margaret (McCarty) C.; student Vincennes U., 1957-58; B.S. in Pharmacy, Purdue U., 1961; postgrad. in Bus., Ind. U., 1961-63; m. Carolyn Ann Phelps, Sept. 3, 1962; children—Mark, Danny, Scott, Amy. Pharmacist, mgr. Hook's Drugs, Bedford, Ind., 1961-62, Crowder's Pharmacy, Bedford, 1962-64; owner Cannon's Drug Store, Evansville, Ind., 1964-69; pres. Medco Centers Inc., Evansville, 1970—. Instr. first aid; mem. panel Nat. Council on Aging, 1975. Den father Cub Scouts, Buffalo Trace council Boy Scouts Am., 1971-72. Bd. dirs. Human Relations Commn., Tri-State Epilepsy Assn.; bd. dirs. Am. Cancer Soc., chmn., 1973. Mem. Am., Ind., Vanderburgh County, Lawrence County (pres. 1963-64) pharm. assns., Nat. Assn. Retail Mchts., Ind., Nat. nursing home assns., Am. Coll. Nursing Home Adminstrn., West Side Nut Club, West Side Mchts. Shopway Assn. Democrat. Roman Catholic (dir. Cath. Edn. Found.). Elk, Optimist, Rotarian. Home: 3119 E Blackford St Evansville IN 47714 Office: 405 Carpenter St Evansville IN 47708

CANNON, ZANE WILLIAM, educator; b. Kenyon, Minn., Nov. 18, 1922; s. William Joseph and Floreen (Sanders) C.; student Ball State U., 1940-43; B.S., Western Mich. U., 1960, M.A., 1966; m. Gloria Gene Phillips, July 4, 1943; children—Benjamin W., Russel J., Thomas F. Guest lectr. mktg. Western Mich. U., Kalamazoo, 1963-64, asso. prof. mktg., 1965—; art specialist Portage (Mich.) Pub. Schs., 1964-65; promotion dir. Jour. Advt., 1974-75. Vice-chmn. Kalamazoo Zoning Bd. Appeals, 1967-73. Served in U.S. Army, 1943. Recipient commendation USIS, 1958; Aid Advt. Edn. award, 1969; Bernstein Advisor award, 1971; Direct Mail Spokesman award Direct Mail Mktg. Assn., 1972; Teaching Excellence award, Western Mich. U., 1976; Silver medal award Am. Advt. Fedn., 1977. Mem. Am. Acad. Advt., Am. Advt. Fedn. (dir. 1974-75), AAUP, Am. Mktg. Assn., Am. Assn. Editorial Cartoonists, Direct Mail Advt. Assn., Internat. Assn. Printing House Craftsmen, Point-of-Purchase Advt. Inst., Mktg.-Advt. Roundtable, Kalamazoo Advt. Club, Western Mich. U. Ad Club. Republican. Presbyterian. Designed, illustrated Living in Kalamazoo, 1958. Home: 330 S Drake Rd M-12 Kalamazoo MI 49009 Office: Western Michigan U Coll Bus Mktg Dept Kalamazoo MI 49008

CANTER, ARTHUR, educator; b. Boston, July 8, 1921; s. Harry and Ida Sarah (Janofsky) C.; student Mass. Inst. Tech., 1938-39, U. Mich., 1943-45; B.A., U. Iowa, 1946, M.A., 1948, Ph.D., 1950; m. Miriam Louise Rosenbaum, Jan. 27, 1946; children—Andrea Sherril, Laurence Alan. Chief psychologist Inst. Psychol. Services, Ill. Inst. Tech., 1950-52; asst. prof. psychology Vanderbilt U., 1952-56; asst. prof. med. psychology John Hopkins Sch. Medicine, 1956-60; prof. psychiatry U. Iowa, 1960—; cons. U.S. Army Biol. Labs., Fort Detrick, Md., 1966-70, VA Hosp., Iowa City, Iowa, 1968—. Bd. dirs. Iowa City Municipal Library, 1970—; v.p., bd. dirs. Friends of Music, Inc., Iowa City, 1967-70. Served with AUS, 1942-45. Co-recipient ann. award Clin. Assos. in Psychiatry, 1957. Fellow Am. Psychol. Assn.; mem. Am. Psychosomatic Soc., Am. Orthopsychiat. Assn, AAUP, Sigma Xi. Jewish. Home: 30 Brookfield Dr Iowa City IA 52240

CANTON, IRVING DONALD, mgmt. cons.; b. N.Y.C., Feb. 10, 1918; s. Louis and Mollie (Wolf) C.; B.Chem. Engring., Coll. City N.Y., 1940; m. Shelly Terman, Sept. 28, 1958; children—Larry, Diana. Engr., U.S. Navy Dept., 1941-45; research group leader Foster D. Snell Inc., N.Y.C., 1945-49; chem. engring. cons. S.Am., 1949-53; asst. dir. Internat. div. Ill. Inst. Tech., Chgo., 1953-61; founding stockholder, v.p. Indsl. Research Mag., Beverly Shores, Ind., 1961-62; dir. comml. devel. and planning Internat. Minerals and Chem. Co., Skokie, Ill., 1962-67; founder, pres. Strategic Decisions Co. mgmt. cons., Chgo., 1968—. Mem. Am. Mktg. Assn. (dir.; v.p. mktg. mgmt. Chgo.), Midwest Planning Assn. (founding; v.p. 1975), Am. Chem. Soc., World Future Soc. Contbr. articles to profl. jours. Home: 4141 Grove St Skokie IL 60076 Office: 664 N Michigan Ave Chicago IL 60611

CANTONI, LOUIS JOSEPH, educator; b. Detroit, May 22, 1919; s. Pietro and Stella (Puricelli) C.; A.B., U. Calif. at Berkeley, 1946; M.S.W., U. Mich., 1949, Ph.D., 1953; m. Lucile Eudora Moses, Aug. 7, 1948; children—Christopher Louis, Sylvia Therese. Personnel mgr. Johns-Manville Corp., Pittsburg, Calif., 1944-46; social caseworker Detroit Dept. Pub. Welfare, 1946-49; counselor Mich. Div. Vocational Rehab., Detroit, 1949-50; conf. leader, tchr. psychology, coordinator family and community relations program Gen. Motors Inst., Flint, Mich., 1951-56; from asso. prof. to prof., dir. rehab. counseling Wayne State U., Detroit, 1956—. Judge Mich., regional and nat. essay and poetry contests, 1965—. Bd. dirs. Detroit Hearing Center, Detroit Met. Soc. for Blind. Served to 2d lt. AUS, 1942-44. Recipient award for leadership and service Mich. Rehab. Assn., 1964. Fellow A.A.A.S.; mem. Am. Philos. Assn., Council of Rehab. Counselor Educators (sec. 1957-58; chmn. 1965-66), Am. Psychol. Assn., Am. Personnel and Guidance Assn., Nat., Mich. (pres. 1963-64), Detroit (pres. 1958) rehab. assns., Poetry Soc. Mich., South and West, Phi Kappa Phi, Phi Delta Kappa. Democrat. Episcopalian. Author books including: (with Mrs. Cantoni) Counseling Your

Friends, 1961; With Joy I Called to You (poetry), 1969; editor: Placement of the Handicapped in Competitive Employment, 1957; contbr. articles to jours. Home: 2591 Woodstock Dr Detroit MI 48203 Office: Wayne State Univ Detroit MI 48202

CANTONI, LUCILE EUDORA MOSES (MRS. LOUIS J. CANTONI), social worker; b. Detroit, Aug. 20, 1924; d. Edgar I. and Alise (Rutland) Moses; B.S. in Edn., Wayne State U., 1946; M.S.W., U. Mich., 1949; m. Louis J. Cantoni, Aug. 7, 1948; children—Christopher Louis, Sylvia Therese. Social worker Florence Crittenton Home, Detroit, 1949-51, Mich. Children's Aid Soc., Flint, 1951-53, Merrill Palmer Inst., Detroit, 1961-62; social worker Family Service Met. Detroit, 1962—, dir. family life edn., 1968-75, area dir., 1975—; field instr. U. Mich. Sch. Social Work, Flint, 1952-53; field instr. Sch. Social Work, Wayne State U., Detroit, 1962-67, asso. grad. faculty, 1977—, practicum instr. family life edn. Coll. Edn., 1967-69. Mem. Nat. Assn. Social Workers, Assn. Certified Social Workers. Author: (with Louis Cantoni) Counseling Your Friends, 1961; Eighteen Family Life Education Groups, 1970; The First Two Years: Parents Anonymous of Michigan, 1974. Contbr. articles to profl. jours. Home: 2591 Woodstock Dr Detroit MI 48203 Office: 51 W Warren Ave Detroit MI 48201

CANTWELL, LOUIS YAGER, lawyer; b. Oak Park, Ill., Nov. 16, 1918; s. Robert Emmett and Anna Harrison (Yager) C.; B.S., Northwestern U., 1940, J.D., 1943; m. Janet Marie Hanssen, Nov. 9, 1956; children—Thomas (dec.), Andrea Lee, David Y. Admitted to Ill. bar, 1944; partner firm Cantwell & Cantwell, Chgo., 1946-63. Dir. Faith at Work mag., N.Y.C., 1965-67, 70—. Mem. Am. (interstate custody com. 1959-60), Ill. (mem. joint com. with Chgo. bar on codification family law), Chgo. (chmn. matrimonial law com. 1959-60) bar assns., Am. Acad. Matrimonial Lawyers, Phi Delta Phi, Phi Kappa Psi. Contbr. articles to mags. Office: 1 N LaSalle St Chicago IL 60602

CAPATINA, LIVIU IRIMIE, elec. engr.; b. Detroit, Mar. 14, 1925; s. Irimie N. and Victoria (Silca) C.; B.S.E.E., Mich. State U., 1951; m. Theresa J. Mileto, Apr. 23, 1956; children—Liviu, Michael P., Gene A. Designer, Austin Engrs., Detroit, 1951-52; devel. engr. Gen. Motors Corp., Livonia, Mich., 1952-53; asst. chief engr. Ford Motor Co., Dearborn, Mich., 1952-63, also sr. engr.; dir. Fairlane Devel. Co., 1958-60. Dir. Dearborn Youth Assn., 1967-75 (pres. 1971-75). Served with seabees USN, 1943-46, U.S. Army, 1951-52. Mem. IEEE, Am. Ordnance Assn. Greek Orthodox. Home: 415 S Melborn St Dearborn MI 48124 Office: Ford Motor WHQ Rm 687 Dearborn MI 48121

CAPEN, ROBERT BERNARD, architect; b. Kansas City, Mo., Dec. 14, 1924; s. Lester Edwin and Mae Cathern (Draney) C.; B.Arch., U. Kan., 1951; m. Mary Margaret Hurt, Mar. 14, 1953; children—Nancy Patrice, Ann Elizabeth, Melissa Ellen, Catherine Renee, John Edwin, Julie Christine. Architect, Burns & McDonnell Archtl. Engring. Co., Kansas City, Mo., 1953—. Served to lt. USAAF, 1942-45; PTO. Recipient hon. mention Morton Arboretum A.I.A. Internat. Archtl. Competition, 1956; 3d pl. award Burns & McDonnell interoffice TWA competition, 1954. Mem. A.I.A. (corporate), Scarab. Home: 2405 Red Bridge Rd Kansas City MO 64131 Office: PO Box 173 Kansas City MO 64141

CAPES, ROBERT MALCOLM, SR., distbg., mktg. co. exec.; b. Goodland, Ind., May 2, 1917; s. Jess Emmett and Iva (Harms) C.; student Milw. Sch. Engring., 1939-40, Marquette U., 1940-41; m. Florence Agnes Kessenich, Jan. 17, 1939; children—Barbara, Rita, Gregory, Mark, Robert Malcolm, Monica. Tool and die maker Manhattan Project, Allis-Chalmers Co., Milw., 1941-46; owner, operator Contemporary Wood Products Co., Marshfield, Wis., 1946-64; area mgr., Lytle Insulation Co., Marshfield, 1961-64; area mgr., v.p. Silvercote Products Inc. (Wis.), 1964-70; area sales mgr. Johns Manville Corp., Wis., Minn., and Iowa, 1970-75; owner, operator Automated Products Inc., Marshfield, 1966—; owner, pres. Suppliers Warehouse Ltd., Marshfield, 1960—. Adv. bd. Greater Marshfield Inc., 1970—. Roman Catholic. Clubs: Rotary, Elks, K.C. Home: 1402 Shawano Dr Marshfield WI 54449 Office: 1820 E 26th St Marshfield WI 54449

CAPLIS, MICHAEL EDWARD, biochemist; b. Ypsilanti, Mich., July 25, 1938; s. John Joseph and Marie Kathrine (Hochrein) C.; B.S., Eastern Mich. U., 1962; M.S., Purdue U., 1964, Ph.D., 1970; m. Lucille Marie Truitt, Feb. 11, 1956; children—Kathleen Ann, Michelle Marie, Maureen Marie, Therese Marie, Michael Edward, Matthew Clifford, Philip Patrick. Sci., math. tchr. St. John Prep Sch., 1958-62; analytical biochemist Ind. Chemist Office, 1962-67; grad. research asst. Purdue U., 1967-69; dir. clin. biochemistry St. Mary Mercy Hosp., Gary, Ind., 1969—. Asst. prof. Ind. U. Med. Sch. div. allied scis., 1969—; instr. Ind. Law Enforcement Tng. Bd., 1973—; asso. faculty N.W. Center for Med. Edn., Ind. U. Sch. Medicine; dir. N.W. Ind. Criminal Toxicology Lab., Gary, 1969—. Pres., Holy Angels Cathedral Sch. Home and Sch. Assn., 1972-73. Fed. grantee for establishment regional toxicology lab., 1970-74. Mem. Am. Assn. Clin. Chemists, Am. Acad. Clin. Toxicology, A.A.A.S., Am. Chem. Soc., Am., Midwest assns. forensic scis., Am. Assn. Crime Lab. Dirs., Am. Assn. Ofcl. Analytical Chemists, Sigma Xi. Roman Catholic. K.C. Home: Rural Route 7 Box 458 Valparaiso IN 46383 Office: 540 Tyler St Gary IN 46402

CAPO, OSCAR AGUSTIN, physician; b. Havana, Cuba, May 27, 1909; s. Agustin and Carmen (Jimenez de Cisneros) C.; M.D., U. Brussels, 1930-33, U. Havana, 1937; m. Berthe Gregoire, June 19, 1937; children—Suzanne (Mrs. Dejano Tavares Sobral), Oscar. Intern, Brugmann Hosp., St. Jean Hosp., Brussels, Belgium, 1932-33; resident in otolaryngology Univ. Hosp., Havana, 1946-50; practice medicine specializing in otolaryngology, Havana, 1946-60, Hamilton, Ohio, 1965—; mem. staffs Mercy Hosp., Hamilton, Ft. Hamilton Hosp., McCullaugh Hosp., Oxford, O., Childrens Hosp., Cin., Gral Hosp., Cin.; instr. otolaryngology U. Havana, 1950, U. Cin., 1967—. Mem. A.M.A., Am. Acad. Otolaryngology, Pan Am. Med. Assn., Ohio, Butler County med. assns., French, Belgian soc. otolaryngology, Am. Soc. Otolaryngology Allergy. Club: Big Five (Miami, Fla.). Home: 20 Pinecrest Ln Hamilton OH 45013 Office: 402 Main St Hamilton OH 45013

CAPPONE, MARGARET KATHLEEN, psychologist; b. Arnold, Pa., Feb. 26, 1940; d. Theodore Thomas and Josephine Florence (Lilli) C.; B.A., Marymount Coll., 1961; M.A., Fordham U., 1963, Ph.D., 1967. Vocat. counselor Cath. Charities, N.Y.C., 1964, 66; lectr. Pace Coll., Queens Coll., N.Y.C., 1966-67; instr. Marymount Coll., Tarrytown, N.Y., 1964-66; research asso. N.Y. Med. Coll., N.Y.C., 1967-68; chmn. bd. ARCS Corp., Holly, Mich., 1968-76; chmn., prof. psychology Saginaw Valley State Coll. (Mich.), 1976—; pres. Saginaw Psychol. Services, Inc., 1976—. Trustee Mich. Psychologists for Polit. Action Com., 1977. Mem. AAAS, Am., Mich. psychol. assns., Soc. Psychol. Study of Social Issues, Mich. Soc. Cons. Psychologists, Sigma Xi. Democrat. Roman Catholic. Office: 714 S Michigan Ave Saginaw MI 48602

CAPPS, RAYMOND HAUL, chem. co. ofcl.; b. Frogue, Ky., Nov. 15, 1913; s. Vester V. and Ora Maude (Bow) C.; A.A., Lindsey Wilson Jr. Coll., 1933; B.S., Western Ky. State U., 1950; student U. Louisville, 1942-45, U. Tenn., 1948-49, 52-53; m. Mary Louise Nell, Oct. 22, 1938; 1 son, Richard Eugene. Chemist, tech. supr. E.I. duPont de Nemours & Co., Charleston, Ind., 1941-45; research chemist Union Carbide Corp., Oak Ridge and Niagara Falls, N.Y., 1945-60, engr., supt. Niagara Falls and Marietta, Ohio, 1960—. Tchr. pub. schs. Adair County, Ky., 1933-40. Active Boy Scouts Am., 1957-64. Mem. Am. Chem. Soc. Republican. Methodist. Club: Lewiston Kiwanis (1st v.p. 1963), Elks, Advertisers. Contbr. articles sci. jours.; patentee liquid extraction of metals. Home: 1226 Glendale Rd Marietta OH 45750 Office: PO Box 299 Marietta OH 45750

CAPPUCCI, GABRIEL GERRARD, marketing exec.; b. New Haven, Aug. 1, 1934; s. Gabriel G. and Adele Ann (Anastasia) C.; B.S., Fordham U., 1956; m. Joan B. Tull, Sept. 27, 1958; children—Kathryne, Susan, Gabriel, Michael, Regina, Paul, Christopher, Gregory. Product mgr. Schering Corp., Kenilworth, N.J., 1960-69, sales tng. mgr. Dome Labs., West Haven, Conn., 1969-70; dir. sales and mktg. dermatology div. USV Pharm. Corp., Tuckahoe, N.Y., 1970-72; partner Kenrac Media, Inc., Yorktown Heights, N.Y., 1972-74; v.p. Danal Labs., Inc., Maryland Heights, Mo., 1974—. Mem. Am. Mktg. Assn., Fordham U. Alumni Assn., Pharm. Advt. Club. Home: 15683 Century Lake Dr Chesterfield MO 63017 Office: 42 Worthington Dr Maryland Heights MO 63043

CAPRINI, JOSEPH ANTHONY, surgeon; b. Upper Darby, Pa., Aug. 20, 1939; s. Joseph G. N. and Teresa C. (Cerra) C.; B.S., Villanova U., 1961; M.D., Hahnemann Med. Coll., 1965; M.S. in Surgery, Northwestern U., 1972; m. Stella Mary Evans, June 12, 1965; children—Michelle, Lara, Carol. Intern Evanston (Ill.) Hosp., 1965-66; resident Northwestern Univ. Med. Center, Evanston, Chgo., 1966-67, 69-73, Owen L. Coon Found. fellow in surg. hematology, 1973-74; practice medicine specializing in surgery, 1974—; instr. surgery Northwestern U., 1972, clin. asst. 1971, asst. prof. surgery, 1973—; mem. staff Evanston Hosp., dir. clin. admissions, 1972-74, asso. attending, 1974-76, attending, 1976—, dir. blood flow lab., 1975—, dir. surg. research, 1974—, attending surgical ward service, 1973-76, dir. coagulation research lab., 1970—; attending staff VA Research Hosp., Chgo., 1974—, Glenbrook Hosp. Served to capt. USAF, 1967-69. Diplomate Am. Bd. Surgery, Nat. Bd. Med. Examiners. Fellow A.C.S.; mem. AMA, Ill. State, Chgo. Med. socs., Am. Tramma Soc., Am. Heart Assn. (mem. council on thrombosis), Chgo. Heart Assn., MW Blood Club, Assn. for Academic Surgery, Am. Fedn. Clin. Research, N.Y. Acad. Scis., Chgo. Inst. Medicine, Chgo. Surg. Soc., MW Surg. Soc., Internat. Soc. Thrombosis Haemostasis. Producer movie: Repair of Giant Epigastric Hernia, 1973; contbr. articles to med. jours. Home: 28 Coventry Rd Northfield IL 60093 Office: 2100 Pfingsten Rd Glenview IL 60025

CARBERRY, JOHN J., clergyman; D.D., S.T.D., Ph.D., J.C.D., LL.D. Ordained priest Roman Cath. Ch., 1929; apptd. titular bishop of Elis, coadjutor cum lure successionis, 1956; consecrated, 1956, succeeded to See, 1957; bishop of Columbus, Ohio, 1965-68; archbishop St. Louis, 1968; created Cardinal, 1969. Address: Chancery Office 4445 Lindell Blvd St Louis MO 63108

CARBONE, ALFONSO ROBERT, constrn. exec.; b. Cleve., Jan. 17, 1921; s. Rosario P. and Carmela (Mandalfino) C.; student Sch. Architecture, Western Res. U. and Case Inst. Tech., 1940-42; B.Arch., Western Res. U., 1946; m. Anna Mae Simmons, June 16, 1945; children—Carmela, Florence Roberta, Rosario P. II, Anne Marie. Partner, v.p. estimator R.P. Carbone Constrn. Co., Cleve., 1940-77, owner, pres., 1977—. Alternate builder rep. mem. City of Cleve., Bd. Bldg. Standards and Bldg. Appeals, 1953-64, builder rep. mem., 1964-74, chmn., 1965-74; past chmn. Cleve. Air Pollution Appeals Bd. Mem. Business Men's Club, Central YMCA, Cleve.; mem. Nat. UN Day Com., 1971-73; trustee, chmn. resources com. Alta House. Served with U.S. Coast and Geodetic Survey, Washington, 1942-45. Recipient Alpha Rho Chi medal, 1946; decorated cavalier Order Star Solidarity (Italy). Mem. Cleve. Engring. Soc., Asso. Gen. Contractors Am., Builders Exchange Cleve., Holy Name Soc., Ohio Bldg. Insps. Assn., Citizen League Cleve., Greater Cleve. Growth Assn., Order Sons Italy Am. (pres. lodge, grand trustee officer), Epsilon Delta Rho. Roman Catholic (councilman; commd. extraordinary minister for adminstrn. Holy Communion 1974). Home: 3324 Aberdeen Rd Shaker Heights OH 44120 Office: 3185 E 79th St Cleveland OH 44104

CARBONE, HUBERT ALFRED, psychiatrist; b. Newark, Dec. 7, 1917; s. Francis N. and Lucy (Pollina) C.; A.B., Columbia, 1940; M.D., U. Rochester, 1943; m. Margaret E. Martin, Mar. 4, 1963; children—Paul, Robin, Charles, Patricia, David, Michael. Intern Orange (N.J.) Meml. Hosp., 1943-44; resident Norwich State Hosp.; resident, then asst. physician Foxboro State Hosp., 1946-47; asst. physician Norwich (Conn.) State Hosp., 1947-48, sr. physician, 1948-51, clin. dir., 1951-54, asst. supt., 1954-56; chief psychiatry VA Hosp., Sepulveda, Calif., 1957-58; clin. dir., dir. edn. and research Mental Health Inst., Cherokee, Iowa, 1958-62; clin. dir., dir. tng. and devel. Jamestown (N.D.) State Hosp., 1962-63; supt. N.D. State Hosp., 1963—; dir. N.D. div. Mental Health and Retardation; clin. instr. Yale, 1951-56, U. Calif. at Los Angeles, 1957-58; lectr. psychology Buena Vista Coll., 1959-62; asso. prof. psychiatry U. N.D. Med. Sch., 1963—, acting chmn. dept. psychiatry, 1973—. Cons. NIMH. Served to capt. AUS, 1944-46. Diplomate in psychiatry Am. Bd. Psychiatry and Neurology. Fellow Am. Psychiat. Assn., Royal Soc. Health; mem. Pan Am. Med. Soc., AMA, N.D. Med. Assn. (del.), 7th Dist. Med. Soc. (pres. 1966-67), Assn. Med. Supts. Mental Hosps. (pres. 1973). Home: PO Box 476 Jamestown ND 58401

CARDEY, KEITH ROYAL, mgmt. cons.; b. Potosi, Wis., Oct. 30, 1924; s. Arthur A. and Oramel R. (Schaal) C.; B.S., U. Wis., 1949; LL.B., U. Ky., 1952; m. Lorraine K. Morgan, June 30, 1943; children—Steve, Lynn. Cons., pres. Will County Water Co. (Ill.), 1967-77, Fla. Water Utilities Co., W. Palm Beach, 1975-77; exec. v.p. Consol. Water Co., Chgo., 1965-66; cons. mgmt. Middle W. Service Co., Chgo., 1957-59. Served with USNR, 1941-43. Admitted to Ky. bar, 1952. Mem. Ky., Am. bar assns. Republican. Clubs: Union League Chgo., Masons, Shriners. Home: 460 Oriole St Elmhurst IL 60126 Office: 2 N Riverside Plaza Chicago IL 60606

CARDILLO, JERRY E., mgmt. cons.; b. Rochester, N.Y., Nov. 24, 1920; s. Joseph D. and Josephine (Battaglia) C.; B.S. in Mech. Engring., U. Mich., 1944; m. Susan C. Cardillo. Sr. engr. Packard Aircraft Engine Div., Toledo, 1944-48; project engr. Dana Corp., Toledo, 1948-51; project engr., asst. chief engr. Willy Electronics Div., Toledo, 1951-53; tech. analyst mfg. operations Ford Div., Detroit, 1953-57; dir. engring. and mfg. staff Fed. Mogul Corp., Detroit, 1957, later v.p. mfg. engring. services; now pres. Cardillo Assos., Inc., mgmt. cons.; dir. E & E Engring. Co.; lectr. math. Mem. Nat. Soc. Profl. Engrs., Soc. Automotive Engrs. Republican. Roman Catholic. Patentee forging methods. Home: 28011 Weymouth Farmington Hills MI 48018

CARDIN, PAUL BUXTON, pharmacist; b. Winchester, Ky., June 28, 1924; s. John Jacob and Bernice Evelyn (Buxton) C.; student Wis. State U., Platteville, 1942, Ripon (Wis.) Coll., 1943; B.S., U. Wis., 1948; m. Helen Marie Anderson, May 28, 1947; children—Dennis Stuart, Kevin Dean, Paul Andrew. Pres., Cardins Pharmacy, Inc., Platteville and Cuba City, Wis., 1971—; cons. Platteville Municipal, Cuba City hosps.; dir. Mound City Bank. Mem. Platteville Bd. Health, 1955-77, health officer, 1969-77; mem. Grant County Bd. Suprs., 1966-76; Grant County supr. Five County Mental Health Clinic, 1966-73; chmn. Unified Bd. Alcoholism, Drug Abuse and Disabilities, 1974-76. Served with AUS, 1943-46. Named Wis. state pharmacist of year Wis. Travelers Assn., 1971. Mem. Nat. Assn. Retail Druggists, Am., Wis. (pres. 1970-71) pharm. assns., Wis. Alumni Assn., Wis. Pharmacy Alumni Assn. Republican. Methodist. Clubs: Platteville Country, Masons, Shriners. Home: 1010 7th Ave Platteville WI 53818 Office: 95 W Main St Platteville WI 53818

CARDINAL, JEFFREY LYNN, broadcasting exec.; b. Detroit, Mich., Aug. 10, 1948; s. Roy Edward and Nellie Ruth (Huston) C.; student Henry Ford Community Coll., 1967-69; diploma Inst. Broadcast Arts, 1968; B.A., Mich. State U., 1971; postgrad. Wayne State U., 1975—; m. Elizabeth Ann Butsch, Aug. 22, 1970; 1 dau., Margaret Elizabeth. Program and news dir. Sta. WHFC, Henry Ford Community Coll., Dearborn, Mich., 1967-69; news cons. Gamut Comments, Sta. WMSB-TV, WKAR-TV, E. Lansing, Mich., 1970; supr. Mich. State U. production agency, E. Lansing, 1971; asso. mgr. Cardinal & Worfel Productions, E. Lansing, 1971-72; coordinator Sta. WSDP, Plymouth, Mich., 1972—; guest lectr. Plymouth Salem High Sch., lectr. Kellogg Community Coll.; broadcasting cons. Meml. Christian Ch.; cons. Festivals com. Plymouth Bicentennial Com. Pres., Plymouth Cultural com.; rep. Plymouth Community Arts Council. Mem. Broadcast Edn. Assn., Nat. Assn. Ednl. Broadcasters, Nat. Assn. Broadcasters, Mich. News Broadcasters Assn., Mich. State U. Coll. of Communication Arts and Scis. Alumni Assn., Mich. State U. Alumni Assn., Mich. Assn. Ednl. Broadcasters (v.p.). Clubs: Kiwanis. Home: 936 Simpson St Plymouth MI 48170 Office: Station WSDP 46181 Joy Rd Plymouth MI 48170

CARDINAL, ROBERT J., mgmt. cons.; b. Springfield, Mass., Dec. 24, 1935; s. Alexander J. and Alice (Bellevance) C.; B.S., U.S. Coast Guard Acad., 1957; M.S., Ill. Inst. Tech., 1967; postgrad. Drexel Inst. Tech., 1961-63, Temple U. Sch. Law, 1960-61, Bklyn. Poly. Inst., 1963-65; m. Lois J. Perry, June 21, 1958; children—David, Suzette, Amy. Supr. engring., project adminstr. RCA, Moorestown, N.J., 1961-63; mgr. program control Grumman Corp., Bethpage, N.Y., 1963-65; mng. asso., dept. mgr. Lester B. Knight & Asso., Inc., Chgo., 1965-68, v.p., 1969-73, exec. v.p., 1973—; v.p., asst. gen. mgr. Walworth-Aloyco div. Walworth Co., Greensburg, Pa., 1968-69. Chmn. Bd. dirs. Jr. Achievement Chgo., 1975—; mem. finance com. New Trier Dist. Boy Scouts Am., 1971, 75—; mem. spl. task force Glencoe (Ill.) Sch. Bd., 1974; mem. Chgo. Crime Commn., 1975—; mem. Commn. on Future of Ill. Inst. Tech., 1976. Served with USCG, 1957-61. Registered profl. engr., Ill., Calif. Mem. Fairbanks Family in Am., Inc., I.E.E.E., Nat., Ill. socs. profl. engrs., Soc. Am. Mil. Engrs. (dir.), Inst. Mgmt. Cons., Ill. Inst. Tech. Alumni Assn. (dir. 1974—, v.p. 1975—). Republican. Methodist. Rotarian. Clubs: Army-Navy (Washington); Economic, Tower, Executives, Union League (Chgo.); Skokie (Ill.) Country. Home: 501 Grove St Glencoe IL 60022 Office: 549 W Randolph St Chicago IL 60606

CARDO, PHILIP THOMAS, mech. engr.; b. Jamaica, N.Y., May 26, 1929; s. Anthony Thomas and Rose (Nunziato) C.; B.S. in M.E., N.Y. U., 1952; m. Gloria R. Jiannette, Apr. 12, 1953; children—Philip A., Gerard P., Susan Mary. Design engr. Babcock & Wilcox Co., N.Y.C., 1952-59; tech. sales engr. Forster Wheeler Co., N.Y.C., 1959-61; regional sales mgr. John Wood Co., Florham Park, N.J., 1961-62, Detroit Stoker Co., Cleve., 1962-68, partner Schmidt Assos., Inc., Cleve., 1968—; dir. E.M.S. Corp. Mem. advisory com. Ohio bd. regents Energy Research Council. Mem. Am. Pub. Works Assn., ASME, Cleve. Engring. Soc. Contbr. articles to profl. jours. Home: 176 Forestwood Dr Northfield OH 44067 Office: 7333 Fairoaks Rd Cleveland OH 44146

CAREY, CARLTON FRANK, chiropractor; b. Anderson, Ind., Feb. 3, 1914; s. H. Fred and Bessie M. (Brandetburg) C.; grad. Palmer Coll. Chiropractic, 1938; m. Lorene C. Davis, Aug. 12, 1938; children—Sandra Darlene Carey Lucas, Gaye Carlene Carey Westerfield, Toni Davis Klanko. Pvt. practice chiropractic, Alexandra, Ind., 1939-41, Anderson, Ind., 1942—. Mem. Ind. Bur. Chiropractic (legis. chmn. 1939-58, pres. 1957-58), Fedn. Ind. Chiropractors, Ind. State Chiropractic Assn., Internat. Chiropractors Assn. Ind., Indpls. Press Club. Mason (Shriner). Club: Columbia. Patentee in field. Editor Ind. Laymens Monthly Jour., 1945-51. Home: 132 W 4th St Anderson IN 46011 Office: 221 Jackson St Anderson IN 46012

CAREY, EDWARD MARSHEL, JR., accounting co. exec.; b. Washington, Pa., June 12, 1942; s. Edward Marshel and Mildred Elizabeth (Bradley) C.; B.S. in Bus. Adminstrn., Greenville (Ill.) Coll., 1964; m. Naomi Ruth Davis, June 1, 1964; children—Martha Ann, Mary Louise. Accountant, Gen. Motors Corp., Anderson, Ind., 1964-68, supr. accounting, 1968-70; staff accountant Carter, Kirlin & Merrill, C.P.A.'s, Indpls., 1970-74, partner, 1974—. C.P.A., Ind. Mem. Am. Inst. C.P.A.'s (mgmt. of accounting practice com. 1976—, dir. Indpls. chpt. 1977—), Nat. Assn. Accountants, Am. Mgmt. Assn., Inst. Internal Auditors (dir.). Republican. Methodist. Club: Indpls. Athletic. Home: 4521 Brookshire Pkwy Carmel IN 46032 Office: 9102 N Meridian St Indianapolis IN 46260

CAREY, FREDERICK ARTHUR, lawyer; b. Bad Axe, Mich., Mar. 5, 1899; s. William Henry and Henrietta Louise (Des Jardins) C.; J.D., Detroit Coll. Law, 1920; m. Hazel Eleanor Whited, Sept. 1, 1922 (dec. Sept. 1949); children—Bruce D., Rolph D.; m. 2d, Margaret Y. Barbier, Nov. 29, 1969. Admitted to Mich. bar, 1920, U.S. Supreme Ct. bar, 1958; mem. firm Carey and Carey, Detroit, 1920—. Served with U.S. Army, World War I. Mem. Am., Detroit bar assns., State Bar Mich., Am. Judicature Soc., Lawyers Club U. Mich., Sigma Nu Phi. Episcopalian (past vestryman). Clubs: Detroit Golf, Detroit Athletic; Otsego (Mich.) Ski. Home: 2945 N Woodward Ave Bloomfield Hills MI 48013 Office: City Nat Bank Bldg Detroit MI 48226

CAREY, GEORGE LEE, dentist; b. Perry, Ill., May 7, 1906; s. George Baldwin and Celia (Vail) C.; student Western Ill. U., 1924-26; D.D.S., U. Ill., 1932; m. Dorothy Lee Pedigo, Apr. 2, 1931; children—Lee Pedigo, George Vail. Tchr. pub. sch., Barry, Ill., 1926-27; prin. grade sch., Pleasant Hill, Ill., 1927-28; instr. prosthetic dentistry U. Ill., 1932-35; pvt. practice dentistry, Park Ridge, Ill., 1935—; farm owner, subdiv. developer, office bldg. owner and mgr. Dental cons. Park Ridge Sch. Girls. Fellow Acad. Gen. Dentistry (Ill. pres. 1971-73, nat. dir. 1965-73, charter mem.), Am. Coll. Dentistry; mem. Chgo. Dental Soc. (dir. 1962-65), U. Ill. Alumni Assn. (dir. 1972-75). Park Ridge Community Ch. (pres. bd. dirs. 1958-59). Clubs: Park Ridge University, Park Ridge Country. Contbr. articles to profl. publs. Home: 643 Edgemont Ln Park Ridge IL 60068 Office: 112 S Northwest Hwy Park Ridge IL 60068

CAREY, GERALD EUGENE, veterinarian; b. St. Joseph, Mo., July 12, 1944; s. Earl Victor and Emma Jean (Ensign) C.; B.S., U. Mo.-Columbia, 1966, D.V.M., 1968; m. Donna Louise Graf, June 3, 1967; children—Jeffrey Jay, Mark Christopher. Unit head dog and cat quarantine unit NIH, Bethesda, Md., 1968-70; individual practice small animal medicine, surgery Kansas City, Mo., 1970-73, Blue Springs, Mo., 1973—. Served with commd corps USPHS, 1968-70. Recipient Pizer award, 1967. Mem. Kansas City (pres. 1977), Mo., Am. vet. med. assns. Mo. Acad. Veterinarians. Presbyterian (elder). Lion. Home: 1324 S 23d St Blue Springs MO 64015 Office: 938 S 7 Hwy Blue Springs MO 64015

CARHART, JAMES MILTON, internist; b. Youngstown, Ohio, June 7, 1928; s. Clarence Milton and Ruth L. (Sieg) C.; student Adelbert Coll., 1946-48; B.S., Western Res. U., 1949, M.D., Northwestern U., 1952; m. Sally Edith Rutherford, Sept. 9, 1950; children—Katherine Anne, Margaret Susan, John Rutherford. Intern, Wesley Meml. Hosp., Chgo., 1952-53; resident in internal medicine Ohio State U. Hosp., Columbus, 1955-58, Samuel J. Roessler fellow in renal disease, 1958-60; practice medicine specializing in internal medicine, Mt. Vernon, Ohio, 1968—; instr. dept. medicine Ohio State U. Hosp., 1960-63, asst. prof. internal medicine, 1963-66; bd. trustee Mercy Hosp. Served with M.C., U.S. Army, 1953-55. Diplomate Am. Bd. Internal Medicine. Mem. Am., Ohio State, Pan Am. med. assns., Am. Geriatric Soc., Am. Soc. Internal Medicine, Am. Heart Assn., Kidney Found. Central Ohio, AAAS, Knox County Health Council (dir.). Presbyterian. Home: 1 Brookwood Rd Route 3 Mount Vernon OH 43050 Office: 812 Coshocton Rd Mount Vernon OH 43050

CARICH, PETE ADAM, psychotherapist, counselor; b. Granite City, Ill., Dec. 14, 1930; s. Adam Carich and Theresa Delmonica (Delpuppo) C.; B.S., So. Ill. U., 1968, M.S., 1969; Ph.D., St. Louis U., 1973; m. Mary Adeline Craig, Feb. 4, 1950; children—Mark, Laura, Denise. Steelworker, Granite City (Ill.) Steel Co., 1950-68; tchr., Ritenour High Sch., Overland, Mo., 1968-73, counselor-therapist, 1973-76; pvt. practice as psychotherapist and marriage counselor, Belleville, Ill., 1976; coordinator, counselor Youth Counseling Center, Granite City, 1970, 74; instr. N.E. Mo. State U., St. Louis, 1972-74, So. Ill. U., Edwardsville, 1973-74, Tarkio Coll., St. Louis, 1974-75; drug and alcohol cons. USAF, Scott AFB, 1974; instr. Webster Coll., St. Louis, 1974-76. Adv. bd. St. John's Children's Home. Served with USN, 1951-55; ETO. Recipient Outstanding Scoutmaster award Boy Scouts Am., 1960, Silver Beaver award, 1970. Mem. Am. Assn. Marriage and Family Counselors, Nat. Alliance Family Life, Nat. Council Family Relations, Profl. Counselors Assn., Am., Ill., Mo. psychol. assns., Ill., Mo. personnel and guidance assns., Am. Soc. Clin. Hypnosis, Ill. Group Psychotherapy Soc., St. Louis Drug and Substance Abuse Counsel, So. Ill. U., St. Louis U. alumni assns. Roman Catholic. Clubs: K.C., Slavic and East European Friends. Home: 4735 Vincent St Granite City IL 62040 Office: 8601 W Main St Belleville IL 62223

CARL, EARL GEORGE, social worker; b. Wooster, Ohio, Sept. 14, 1924; s. Earl George and Effie (Weible) C.; B.S., Ohio U., 1951; M.S., Simmons Coll., 1955; m. Mary J. Sheehan, Dec. 25, 1950; children—Earl George III, Christopher T., Mary Lisa, Richard S. Boys's supr. Youth Service Bd., State Mass., Boston, 1952-54; psychiat. social worker VA Hosp., Coatesville, Pa., 1955-57, Family Service Chester County, West Chester, Pa., 1957-59; exec. dir. Family Service Pottstown, Pa., 1959-63; asst. dir. social service dept. Newberry (Mich.) State Hosp., 1963-66, dir. field offices, Marquette, Mich., 1966-70; dir. outpatient dept. Coldwater (Mich.) State Home and Tng. Sch., 1970-73; supr. admissions unit Kalamazoo State Hosp., 1973—; guest lectr. in social work No. Mich. U., supr. field lab. in social work, 1967-69; supr. field lab. in social work Western Mich. U., 1974—. Served with USNR, 1943-46. Mem. Nat. Assn. Social Work (dir. Mich. chpt.), Acad. Certified Social Workers, Certified Marriage Counselors Mich., Mich. Employees Assn. Home: 3815 Oakridge Rd Kalamazoo MI 49008 Office: Kalamazoo State Hosp Kalamazoo MI 49008

CARL, JOHN CHRIS, corp. exec.; b. East St. Louis, Ill., Aug. 31, 1927; s. J. Chris and Corinne (Stack) C.; B.S. in Elec. Engring., Purdue U., 1951; m. Suzanne Elizabeth Schuell, May 25, 1957 (dec. May 1971); children—John Gregory, Kathryn Ann; m. 2d, Margaret Ann Scanlan Connelly, Jan. 1, 1972 (div.). Sec.-treas. Carl Electric Co., East St. Louis, 1951-74; v.p.-treas. O'Neil Lumber Co., East St. Louis, 1965—; pres. So. Ill. Data Center Inc., East St. Louis, 1969—; v.p.-treas. Farm Structures Inc., 1969—; v.p., treas. Lyon Industries Inc., East St. Louis, 1971—; v.p. the Tacs Co., Belleville, Ill., 1970—; dir. So. Ill. Nat. Bank, Illini Fed. Savs. & Loan Assn., Fairview Heights, Ill., 1966-77. Served with USNR, 1946-48, 51-53. Mem. Ill. Soc. Profl. Engrs., Ill. Bus. Club. K.C. Clubs: St. Clair Country; Mo. Athletic, Serra, Kiwanis (pres. 1957-58). Home: 1 Sylvania Dr Belleville IL 62223 Office: PO Box 187 East St Louis IL 62202

CARLAND, MICHAEL, lawyer; b. Detroit, May 26, 1906; s. Major and Mabel (McQueen) C.; LL.B., U. Mich., 1931; m. Vera Johnson, July 16, 1934; children—Ann Kerastas, Patricia Burke, Mary Barrett. Admitted to Mich. bar, 1931; mem. firm Miner & Miner, Saginaw, Mich., 1931-33, Pulver & Bush, 1935; circuit judge 35th Jud. Circuit Mich., 1954-71; judge Mich. Ct. of Appeals, 1973-75; city atty., Owosso, Mich., 1942-47, Corunna, Mich., 1943-45; village atty., Laingsburg, Mich., 1944-46; dir. Owosso Savs. Bank, 1942-70. Pres., ARC, Owosso, 1970; chmn. bd. trustees First Congl. Ch., Owosso. Mem. Mich. Judges Assn. (pres. 1956), State Bar Mich., Shiawassee County Bar Assn. Clubs: City, Country (Owosso); Eagles, Rotary, Masons, Moose, K.P., Elks. Home: 300 E North St Owosso MI 48867

CARLEY, DAVID WILCOX, educator; b. Galesburg, Ill., June 21, 1922; s. Ralph F. and Ruth (Glover) C.; B.A., Knox Coll., 1943; M.S., U. Ill., 1947, Ph.D., 1952; m. Barbara Ann Campbell, June 8, 1945; children—William C., Karen (Mrs. Dennis A. Saphir). Research asso. George Washington U., 1944; chem. process engr. C.F. Braun & Co., Alhambra, Calif., 1947-49; sales mgr. Wilson Meyer Co., Los Angeles, 1952-60; spl. lectr. Whittier Coll., 1955-60; prof., chmn. dept. chemistry Ripon (Wis.) Coll., 1960—. Cons., dir. summer insts.; asso. program dir. acad. year insts. NSF; mem. Gen. Elec. Profs. Conf., 1970; mem. Research Corp. Conf. for Dept. Chmn.; vis. scholar Cambridge U. Mem. adv. council Gov.'s Air Pollution Control Commn.; congl. legis. counselor State of Wis., 1974. Mem. Ripon Sch. Bd. Served with USNR, 1944-46; PTO. NSF postdoctoral fellow, 1962; Schlitz Brewing Co. grad. fellow, 1951. Mem. Am. Inst. Chemists, Am. Chem. Soc., A.A.A.S., Sigma Xi, Phi Gamma Delta. Republican. Conglist. Club: Kiwanis (Ripon). Home: 527 Fairview St Ripon WI 54971

CARLILE, ROBERT LESLIE, accountant; b. Boswell, Ind., Oct. 2, 1924; s. Jasper Leslie and Mearl (Smith) C.; student Ind. State Tchrs. Coll., 1942-43; B.S., Ind. U. 1946-48; m. Olga E. Gize, Aug. 24, 1952; children—Byron, Bradley. Trainee, Goodyear Tire & Rubber Co., Akron, Ohio, 1948-49, office mgr., Moline, Ill., 1949-51, asst. store mgr., Waterloo, Iowa, 1951-52; cost accountant, chief timekeeper Burgess Battery Co., Freeport, Ill., 1952-55; sr. accountant William T. Bingham, C.P.A., Freeport, 1956-60; self-employed Robert L. Carlile, C.P.A., Freeport, 1960—. Mem. Forestry Commn., Freeport, 1960—. Treas. Freeport Community Chest, Winneshiek Theater; mem. adv. com. Highland Community Coll. Treas. Freeport Meml. Hosp. Served with USNR, 1943-46. Mem. No. Ill., Ill. socs. C.P.A.'s, Am. Inst. C.P.A.'s, Delta Sigma Pi. Methodist. Mason (32 deg.). Rotarian. Club: Freeport Country. Home: 1713 Manor St Freeport IL 60132 Office: 905 State Bank Center Freeport IL 61032

CARLIN, EDWARD AUGUSTINE, univ. dean; b. Gardiner, N.Y., Sept. 21, 1916; s. Edward A. and Mary (Mulligan) C.; B.S., N.Y. U., 1946, M.A., 1947, Ph.D., 1950; m. Eleanor Helen Bigos, Feb. 20, 1943; children—Mary Ellen, Edward Augustine. Instr. econs. and govt. Packard Bus. Coll., 1946-47; asst. prof. Mich. State U., 1947-51, asso. prof., 1952-56, asst. dean, prof., 1956, dean univ. coll., 1956—. Cons. Coll. Gen. Studies U. Nigeria. Served from pvt. to 1st lt., inf. AUS, 1942-46. Decorated Purple Heart. Mem. Am. Econ. Assn., Am. Acad. Polit. and Social Sci., A.A.U.P., Pi Gamma Mu. Author numerous articles in field. Co-editor: Curriculum Building in General Education, 1960. Home: 834 Rosewood St East Lansing MI 48823

CARLISLE, WILLIAM DONALD, dentist; b. Lakewood, Ohio, May 8, 1918; s. William Raymond and Viola Barbara (Hebebrand) C.; student U. Mich., 1936-38; D.D.S., Western Res. Dental Sch., 1942; m. Constance Ruth Snyder, Nov. 14, 1942; children—Gay Lynn, William Gary. Dentist, Cleve. Children's Clinic, 1942-44; pvt. practice dentist, Cleve., 1942-64, Rocky River, Ohio, 1964—. Vice pres., dir. Rocky River Savs. & Loan, 1960-68. Master, Cub Scouts Am., 1957. Precinct committeeman Republican party, 1954-60. Served to ensign USNR, 1940-43. Fellow Internat. Coll. Dentistry; mem. Am. Acad. Dental Practice Adminstrn., Am. Equilibration Soc., Am. Dental Assn. Methodist (mem. ofcl. bd. 1956-58). Lion. Clubs: Russel W. Bunting Periodontal Study (pres. 1971-72 U. Mich. Dental Study). Home: 19650 Parklane Dr Rocky River OH 44116 Office: 21010 Center Ridge Rd Rocky River OH 44116

CARLOCK, JOHN ROBERT, educator; b. Bloomington, Ill., July 30, 1921; s. Claud Byron and Myrtle Emma (Skelton) C.; student U. Ill., 1940; B.S., Ill. State U., Normal, 1942, M.S., 1951; postgrad. Harvard, 1943, Mass. Inst. Tech., 1944, (NSF fellow) U. Wis.-Madison, 1956-57, U. Mich., 1975. Tchr. pub. schs. Ill., 1943, 46-48; food technologist Libby, McNeill & Libby, Chgo., 1947-54; instr. Ill. State U., Normal, 1949-57, asst. prof., 1957-70, asso. prof. biol. scis., 1970-77, prof., 1978—; chemist Alpha Cellulose Corp., Bloomington, Ill., 1949-51; vis. prof. Central U. Iowa, 1978. Served to lt. USNR, 1943-46. Mem. Am. Inst. Biol. Sci., Assn. Midwestern Coll. Biology Tchrs. (pres. 1968, exec. dir. 1969-77, editor, 1969-77), Nat. Assn. Biology Tchrs., Ill. Acad. Sci., Ill. Assn. Higher Edn. (charter dir. 1966). Author: The Spectrum of Life, 1970; Hypothesis: A Simulation of Science, 1972. Editor Midwest Bioscene; photographer, arranger Life in Concert, multi-media nature presentations, N.Y.C., Indpls., Ind. state parks, Dubuque, Iowa, others, 1972—. Home: #1 2d St Greenwood Ct Bloomington IL 61701

CARLON, PATRICIA ALBINA HONSA (MRS. JOHN ALLAN CARLON), lawyer; b. Chgo., Oct. 20, 1938; d. Erwin John and Albina Marie (Urbancek) Honsa; B.S. in Edn., Ill. State U., 1960; LL.B., U. Ill., 1964; m. John Allan Carlon, June 6, 1959; children—Mark Allan, James Andrew. Admitted to Ill. bar, 1964; partner firm Carlon & Carlon, Normal, Ill., 1965—. Instr. bus. law Ill. State U., Normal, 1972—. Mem. adv. council Mennonite Hosp., Bloomington, Ill., 1972—, sec. adv. council, 1975—; bd. dirs. Salvation Army, 1974—. Mem. McLean County Bar Assn., McLean County Assn. Commerce and Industry, Normal C. of C. (dir. 1974—), Kappa Beta Pi. Home: 1110 E Emerson St Bloomington IL 61701 Office: 4 Citizens Sq Normal IL 61761

CARLSON, ALLAN EUGENE, optical co. exec.; b. Holdrege, Nebr., June 2, 1923; s. Ture Hjalmar and Lilith Mary Lee (Salgren) C.; student U. Nebr., 1940-42; B.S. in Geol. Engring., U. Utah, 1948, Ph.D., 1958; m. Millie Lou Foster, Sept. 7, 1946; 1 dau., Margaret Allyn. Scientist, Clevite Corp., Cleve., 1952-62, head crystal sect. Clevite Corp/Gould Inc., 1962-73; pres. Cleve. Crystals Inc., 1973—; lectr., cons. in field. Mem. Am. Phys. Soc., Am. Crystallographic Assn., Mineral. Soc. Am., Am. Soc. Crystal Growth, Materials Soc. Am., Am. Soc. Testing and Materials (head laser accessories sect. 1968-72), Sigma Xi. Contbr. articles to profl. publs. Patentee in field. Home: 1901 Wyandotte Rd Euclid OH 44117 Office: 19306 Redwood Ave Cleveland OH 44110

CARLSON, ANDREW RAYMOND, archivist; b. Ludington, Mich., Aug. 19, 1934; s. Louis Peter and Mable Pearl (Genter) C.; B.A., Western Mich. U., 1960, M.A., 1961; Ph.D., Mich. State U., 1970; m. Linda Inara Volfarts, Sept. 5, 1959; children—Sharon Lee, Andrew Arthur. Tchr., Galesburg-Augusta (Mich.) Schs., 1961-62, Kalamazoo Pub. Schs., 1965-67; faculty Eastern Ky. U., Richmond, 1967-70; asst. prof. Ferris (Mich.) State Coll., 1970-73; asst. prof. Western Mich. U., 1973-75; archivist Kalamazoo County (Mich.) Probate Ct., Kalamazoo, 1976—. Active Boy Scouts Am., 4-H Clubs, Civic Plyers. Served in U.S. Army, 1954-57; Korea. Mem. Am. Hist. Assn., Soc. European Historians, Historische Kommission zu Berlin, Pi Gamma Mu, Phi Alpha Theta, Deutsche Verein, Le Circle Francais, DAV, VFW. Author: German Foreign Policy 1890-1914, 1970; Anarchism in Germany, 1972; Wilhelm II and the Daily Telegraph Affair, 1977; also articles; author childdren's books under name Raymond Andrews. Home: 968 124th Ave Shelbyville MI 49344 Office: Room 106 County Bldg Kalamazoo MI 49007

CARLSON, ARTHUR, JR., pharm. co. exec.; b. Buffalo, Kans., June 5, 1922; s. Arthur and Olga Olive (Anderson) C.; D.V.M., Kans. State U., 1950; M.S., U. Mo., 1967; m. Kathleen May Chancy, Feb. 11, 1951; children—Janet, Diane, Nancy. Pvt. practice veterinary medicine, Humboldt, Kans., 1950-62; dir. pharm. research and control Cutter-Haver-Lockhart Labs., Shawnee Mission, Kans., 1962-68, v.p., 1968-74; dir. quality control Bayvet Corp., 1974—. Served with AUS, 1942-46. Inventor of adjuvant, prolonged-release medications, methods for convalescent nutrition and others. Home: 9205 W 89th St Overland Park KS 66212 Office: 12707 W 63d St Shawnee KS 66216

CARLSON, DAVID MARTIN, retail exec.; b. Marinette, Wis., July 15, 1940; s. Martin Algot and Ellen Lucille (Blom) C.; B.S., U. Mich., 1964, M.S., 1966, Ph.D., 1975; m. Sheri Phyllis Allen, Sept. 1, 1961 (div. Mar. 1970); 1 dau., Kristin Elizabeth; m. 2d, Jean Marie Furniss, May 1, 1971. Pres., Information Control Systems, Inc., Ann Arbor, Mich., 1964-70; data processing cons., Ann Arbor, 1970-71; v.p. systems Chatham Super Markets, Inc., Warren, Mich., 1971-75; v.p. mgmt. info. systems Allied Supermarkets, Inc., Livonia, Mich., 1975—. Chmn. Washtenaw County Citizens Com. for Social Services, 1969-70. Guest speaker London Sch. Econs., 1972, 73. Served with AUS, 1958-59, 61-62. Mem. Assn. for Computing Machinery, Assn. for Systems Mgmt., Soc. Certified Data Processors, Advanced Mgmt. Info. Systems Group (charter), Data Processing Mgmt. Assn., Alpha Pi Mu. Co-founder, tech. adviser Language and Language Behavior Abstracts, 1966-69. Home: 18116 Melrose St Southfield MI 48075 Office: 12425 Merriman Rd Livonia MI 48150

CARLSON, EDWARD ELMER, airline exec.; b. Tacoma, June 4, 1911; s. Elmer E. and Lula (Powers) C.; student U. Wash., 1928-32, alumnus summa laude dignatus, 1970; m. Nell Hinckley Cox, June 26, 1936; children—Edward Eugene, Jane Leslie. Mgr. Presdl. Hotel, Mt. Vernon, Wash., 1936-37, Rainier Club, Seattle, 1937-42; with Western Internat. Hotels, Inc., Seattle, 1946-70, exec. v,p., 1953-61, pres., 1961-69, chmn., chief exec. officer 1969-70, now dir.; pres., chief exec. officer UAL, Inc. and United Air Lines, 1970-74, chmn., chief exec. officer, 1975—, also dir.; dir. Seattle First Nat. Bank, Seafirst Corp., Safeco Ins. Corp., First Chgo. Corp., First Nat. Bank Chgo., Aluminum Co. Am. Pres. Century 21 Expn., Inc., Seattle, 1957-59, chmn. bd., 1959-61; chmn. Wash. World's Fair Commn., 1955-63, Wash. Oceanographic Study Commn.; mem. Pres.'s Industry-Govt. Spl. Task Force on Travel, 1968; mem. Undersec. Navy Adv. Commn. Navy Ship's Store Office; pres. Pacific Sci. Center Found., Wash., 1962-66, hon. chmn., 1964. Bd. dirs. Virginia Mason Found., Seattle Symphony, Virginia Mason Hosp., Museum Sci. and Industry, Chgo., Northwestern Meml. Hosp., Chgo.; adv. bd. Met. YMCA Chgo.; nat. citizens adv. bd. Eisenhower Med. Center; mem. bus. adv. com. Transp. Center Northwestern U. Mem. Air Transp. Assn. Am. (dir.), Order of St. John of Jeruselum, Nat. Alliance Businessmen (bus. adv. bd. Chgo. met. area), Com. Econ. Devel. (trustee). Rotarian (hon.). Clubs: Rainier, Seattle Golf, Seattle Yacht, (Seattle); Bohemian (San Francisco); Economic (Chgo. and N.Y.C.); Chicago Commercial (Chgo.); Tavern, Wings (N.Y.C.); Internat. (Washington). Home: 990 Lake Shore Dr Chicago IL 60611 Office: PO Box 66100 Chicago IL 60666

CARLSON, ERIC DUNGAN, astronomer, educator; b. Kansas City, Mo., Jan. 19, 1929; s. Harry Gustavus and Avis (Dungan) C.; A.B., Washington U., St. Louis, 1950; postgrad. U. Chgo., 1950-53; M.S., Northwestern U., 1965, Ph.D., 1968; m. Sandra Maria Ellzey, Oct. 11, 1970; children—Rebecca, Mark. Editor, asst. to editor-in-chief Consol. Book Pubs., Chgo., 1958-61; teaching and research asst. Northwestern U., Evanston, Ill., 1961-68, asst. prof. astronomy, 1969-76; sr. astronomer, edn. supr. Adler Planetarium, Chgo., 1968—. Cons. Ency. Brit. Films, World Book. Served with AUS, 1954-56. Mem. Am. Astron. Soc. Democrat. Episcopalian. Office: 1300 S Lake Shore Dr Chicago IL 60605

CARLSON, JON GORDON, lawyer; b. Wakefield, Mich., June 25, 1943; s. John Edwin and Irene Ann (Erickson) C.; A.B., U. Ill., 1965, J.D., 1967; m. Jane McCann, June 17, 1965; children—Christine, Eric, Susan. Admitted to Ill. bar, 1967; practiced in Belleville, 1967—; asso. Kassly, Bone, Becker & Carlson, 1968-70, partner, 1970—. Mem. Am., Ill. (tort council 1972—), St. Clair County (legis. chmn. 1972—, sec. 1974-76) bar assns., Am., Ill. (bd. mgrs. 1971—, treas. 1975-77) trial lawyer assns. Elk. Club: Mo. Athletic. Home: 25 Berkshire Dr Belleville IL 62223 Office: 7705 W Main St Belleville IL 62223

CARLSON, JON OLAF, educator; b. Harrisburg, Pa., Jan. 19, 1942; s. Joel Edwin and Faithe Marie (Brehm) C.; student Messiah Coll., 1959-61; Mus.B., Westminster Choir Coll., 1963, Mus.M., 1964; D.Mus. Arts, U. Ill., 1974; m. Anita Fay Hoke, June 20, 1964; children—Heather Lynn, Jennifer Sue. Minister music Covenant United Presbyn. Ch., Butler, Pa., 1964-66; activities coordinator Prairie View Community Mental Health Center, Newton, Kan., 1966-68; asst. prof. music Alaska Meth. U., Anchorage, 1971-75; faculty Ind. State U., Evansville, 1975—. Mem. Am. Choral Dirs. Assn. (pres. Alaska 1974-76), Assn. Choral Condrs., Am. Musicol. Soc., Coll. Music Soc., AAUP, Phi Kappa Lambda. Republican. Mem. Brethren in Christ. Address: Ind State U 8600 University Blvd Evansville IN 47712

CARLSON, KEITH VINCENT, microbiologist, educator; b. Perkins, Mich., Nov. 4, 1928; s. Ernest and Bertha (LeBresh) C.; student No. Mich. U., 1952-53; B.S., Mich. State U., 1956, M.S., 1961; postgrad. (NSF grantee) U. Wyo., 1959, U. Colo., 1960, Ind. U., 1961, Cornell U., 1967; m. Louise Jodocy, June 19, 1957; children—Dean Vincent, Connie. Tchr. high sch. biology and gen. sci. Iron Mountain, Mich., 1957-58; tchr. biology Roosevelt High Sch., Wyandotte, Mich., 1958-64; instr. microbiology, botany and biology Henry Ford Community Coll., Dearborn, Mich., 1964—, head dept., 1972-74. Served with USAF, 1948-52. Mem. Nat. Assn. Biology Tchrs., Am. Forestry Assn., Mich. Acad., Mich., Nat. sci. tchrs. assns. Roman Catholic. Home: 14232 Huntington Rd Riverview MI 48192 Office: Henry Ford Community Coll Dearborn MI 48128

CARLSON, KENNETH WILLIAM, periodontist; b. Topeka, Mar. 27, 1911; s. Gustave Elvin and Gertrude M. (Swanson) C.; student William Jewel Coll., 1932; D.D.S., U. Mo., 1937; m. Esther M. Griswold, May 28, 1940; 1 son, Gary K. Pvt. practice of dentistry, 1937-60; practice ltd. to periodontics, Topeka, 1961—. Asso. prof. clin. periodontology U. Mo., 1963-72; periodontal cons. VA Hosp., Topeka; hon. cons. Forbes AFB. Served with Dental Corps, AUS, 1942-44. Mem. 1st Dist. Dental Soc. Kan. (pres. 1962), Midwest Soc. Periodontology (pres. 1972). Presbyn. Elk. Clubs: Cosmopolitan, Topeka (Kans.) Country. Home: 2766 Boswell St Topeka KS 66611 Office: 512 Mills Bldg Topeka KS 66612

CARLSON, LEIGHTON EDWARD, mfg. and services co. exec.; b. Mpls., Nov. 19, 1948; s. Lester Albin Peter and Alva Marion (Thorson) C.; B.S., Mankato (Minn.) State U., 1971; dir. Fish Enterprises, Inc., 1971-76; dir. Christian Corps Research Center, Mpls., 1976—. Club: St. Anthony Athletic. Home: 1813 University Ave SE Minneapolis MN 55414 Office: 310 18th Ave SE Minneapolis MN 55414

CARLSON, MARTIN EVALD, educator; b. Saronville, Nebr., Nov. 5, 1905; s. Carl Anton and Clara (Monson) C.; A.A., Luther Coll., Wahoo, Nebr., 1933; B.A. summa cum laude, Augustana Coll., Rock Island, Ill., 1938; M.A., U. No. Colo., 1947; Ph.D., U. Nebr., 1963; m. Blanche Sylvia Johnson, Sept. 13, 1949; 1 son, Dale Roland. Tchr. Clay County (Nebr.) rural schs., 1924-29, Saronville, Nebr., 1933-36; prin. Palmer (Nebr.) High Sch., 1938-40; supt. schs. Palmer, 1940-42, 45-48; instr., coach Luther Coll., Wahoo, 1948-55, v.p., dean, 1955-62; prof. social sci. Kearney (Nebr.) State Coll., 1962-73, prof. emeritus, 1973—. Social sci., gen. edn. curriculum specialist Nebr. State Colls. Curriculum Devel. project, 1967-69; dir. History Insts., 1966, 67, 69. Served with USAAF, 1942-45. Apptd. Adm. Gt. Navy State Nebr., 1973. Mem. Nebr. Assn. Jr. Colls., Nebr. Assn. Colls. and Univs., Orgn. Am. Historians, Western Hist. Assn., Nat. Council for the Social Studies, Nat., Nebr. edn. assns., Am. Assn. Higher Edn., Nebr. Council Social Studies, Agrl. History Soc., Am. Assn. for State and Local History, Nebr. Ednl. Sales and Service Assn., Internat. Platform Assn., Nebr. Hist. Soc., Kearney Area Retired Tchrs. Assn. (pres. 1975-76), Assn. Profl. Ins. Agts., Kearney C. of C., Am. Security Council, Barbershoppers Chorus. Lutheran (lay preacher). Kiwanian (lt. gov. dist. 1968; Kiwanian of Yr., 1968; chmn. Nebr. New Club Bldg. 1971-72; sec.-treas. Kearney 1972—), Phi Alpha Theta. Contbr. articles to profl. jours. Home: 4216 Utah Ave Grand Island NE 68801

CARLSON, RICHARD GEORGE, chem. co. exec.; b. Chgo., Sept. 26, 1930; s. Gustav George and Mildred Elisabeth (Englund) C.; student Purdue U., 1948-49; B.S., Ill. Inst. Tech., 1956; m. S. Diane Russell, Oct. 10, 1948; children—Richard G., Pamela (Mrs. David Hoppe), Kurt D. With Waterway Terminal, Argo, Ill., 1949-56; with Dow Chem. Co., Midland, Mich., 1956—, production mgr. organic chems., 1968-71, bus. mgr. organic chems., 1971-73, dir. process research, 1973—. Pres., Midland Newcomers Club, 1957-58; scoutmaster Paul Bunyon council Boy Scouts Am., 1956-64; adviser Jr. Achievement, 1956-64; program chmn. P.T.A., 1962-63. Mem. adv. group dept. chem. engring. Ill. Inst. Tech., 1974—. Inst. Gas Tech. scholar, 1954-56. Mem. Am. Inst. Chem. Engrs., Mich. Energy and Resource Research Assn. (trustee 1974—), Tau Beta Pi. Methodist. Elk. Home: 1321 N Parkway Midland MI 48640 Office: Dow Chem Co Midland MI 48640

CARLSON, RICHARD WALTER, tax cons.; b. Mpls., Jan. 22, 1946; s. Hugo W. and Sylvia C. (Haugen) C.; B.A. magna cum laude (Coe scholar, Grace F. Tschirgi scholar), Coe Coll., 1968; M.A., U. Ill., 1969, postgrad., 1969—. Research asst. Edn. and Labor Com., U.S. Ho. of Reps., Washington, 1968; teaching and research asst. U. Ill., Urbana, 1968-69, 72, 74; legis. staff intern Office Pres. Pro Tem, Ill. State Senate, Springfield, 1969-70, staff cons. senate revenue com., 1970—; staff cons. Joint Senate-House Subcom. on Property Tax Reform, Springfield, 1970—; research dir. Tom Riley campaign U.S. Ho. of Reps. from 2d Dist. Ia., 1968; vis. asst. prof. pub. affairs Sangamon State U., 1976-77. Recipient Prof. Richard C. Spencer award Coe Coll., 1968. Therese Garner fellow in polit. sci. U. Ill., 1968-69. Mem. A.A.U.P., Am., Midwest polit. sci. assns., Am. Soc. Pub. Adminstrn., Nat. Tax Assn., Tax Inst. Am., Phi Beta Kappa. Author: (with Samuel K. Gove) The Illinois Legislature: Structure and Process, 1976. Home: 2420 Parkview Dr Springfield IL 62704 Office: 1013 State Office Bldg Springfield IL 62706

CARLSON, ROBERT GERALD, thoracic surgeon; b. Mpls., Dec. 22, 1929; s. Henry John and Agnes Emily (Fagerstrom) C.; B.A., U. Minn., 1951, M.D., 1954, M.S., 1969; m. Florence Ilene Fairbairn, Aug. 4, 1951; children—David, James, Diane, Joel. Intern, U. Oreg. Hosps., Portland, 1954-55; gen. practice medicine, Wadena, Minn., 1955-56; resident in gen. surgery Wayne County Gen. Hosp., Eloise, Mich., 1958-62; practice medicine specializing in gen. surgery, Willmar, Minn., 1962-65; resident in cardiovascular surgery U. Minn., Mpls., 1965-68; research fellow, dept. cardiac pathology Charles T. Miller Hosp., St. Paul, 1966; resident in cardiovascular surgery Cornell U., N.Y.C., 1968-69; instr. surgery Cornell U. Med. Center, 1968-69, asst. prof. surgery, 1969-73; practice medicine specializing in cardiovascular and thoracic surgery, Green Bay, Wis., 1974—; mem. staffs Bellin Meml. Hosp., St. Vincent's Hosp., St. Mary's Hosp.; mem. com. on coronary artery surgery Inter-Soc. Commn. for Heart Disease Resources. Publicity chmn. Friends of Garden City Library, 1961; active Boy Scouts Am.; publicity dir. Anoka County Republican Com., 1963; publicity chmn. Rep. Caucus, Anoka, Minn., 1966-67. Served with USAF, 1956-58. Diplomate Am. Bd. Surgery, Am. Bd. Thoracic Surgery, Nat. Bd. Med. Examiners. Fellow A.C.S. (certificate of appreciation 1971), Am. Coll. Cardiology, Soc. Thoracic Surgeons, Soc. Vascular Surgeons, Am. Coll. Chest Physicians (Regents' award 1971, certificate of merit 1971), Am. Coll. Angiology; mem. Am. Heart Assn., N.Y. Cardiol. Soc., Internat. Cardiovascular Soc., Internat. Surg. Soc., AMA (certificate of merit 1971, Billings silver medal 1972), AAAS, Brown County Med. Soc., Audubon Soc., Phi Beta Kappa, Alpha Omega Alpha. Republican. Lutheran. Clubs: Rotary, Oneida Country. Contbr. articles in field to profl. jours. Home: 2025 Lost Dauphin Rd DePere WI 54115 Office: 704 S Webster Ave Green Bay WI 54301

CARLSON, ROLAND DAVID, ophthalmologist; b. Cleve., Feb. 4, 1933; s. Einar Gunnar and Linnea Agnes (Westling) C.; A.B., Cornell U., 1954, M.D., 1958; m. Marjorie Lee Schreck, Apr. 10, 1965; children—Susan Lynn, David D., William R. Intern, Univ. Hosp., Cleve., 1958-59; resident in ophthalmology Cleve. Clinic, 1963-66; practice medicine specializing in ophthalmology, Lyndhurst, Ohio, 1966—; mem. staff. treas. Huron Rd Hosp.; asso. staff mem. St. Vincent Charity Hosp. Served with M.C., USAF, 1959-63. Decorated D.S.M. Fellow A.C.S., Am. Acad. Ophthalmology and Otolaryngology; mem. Acad. Medicine of Cleve. (dir.), Ohio Med. Assn., Cleve. Ophthal. Soc. Republican. Lutheran. Home: 32200 Fairmount St Pepper Pike OH 44124 Office: 29001 Cedar Rd Lyndhurst OH 44124

CARLSON, RONALD LEE, lawyer, educator; b. Davenport, Iowa, Dec. 10, 1934; s. Arthur A. and Louise (Sehmann) C.; B.A., Augustana Coll., 1956; J.D. (Clarion DeWitt Hardy law scholar), Northwestern U., 1959; LL.M. (E. Barrett Prettyman law scholar), Georgetown U., 1961; m. Mary Murphy, Feb. 10, 1965; children—Michael, Andrew. Admitted to Ill., Iowa bars, 1959, D.C. bar, 1960, U.S. Supreme Ct. bar, 1966; mem. firm Betty, Neuman, McMahon, Hellstrom & Bittner, Davenport, 1961-65; U.S. commr. So. Dist. Iowa, 1964-65; prof. law U. Iowa, Iowa City, 1965-73, Washington U., St. Louis, 1973—. Vis. prof. Wayne State U., Detroit, summers 1974, 76, 77; cons. Legis. Com. on Criminal Code Revision Ia., 1969-73; lectr. Nat. Coll. State Judiciary, Reno, 1974, Nat. Coll. Dist. Attys., Houston, 1974, Boston, 1976, Am. Acad. Jud. Edn., 1977. Vice pres. alumni bd. Augustana Coll., Rock Island, Ill., 1968. Mem. Am. Assn. Law Schs. (chmn. evidence sect., 1973), Am., Iowa, St. Louis bar assns., Am. Judicature Soc. Republican. Author: Criminal Justice for Police, 1970; (with M. Ladd) Cases on Evidence, 1972. Home: 401 Oakley St Clayton MO 63105 Office: Sch Law Washington U St Louis MO 63130

CARLYON, DON J., coll. pres.; b. Chambers, Neb., Aug. 14, 1924; s. Richard E. and Ruth (Wolters) C.; student Neb. Wesleyan U.; B.S., U. Neb.; LL.D., Saginaw Valley State Coll., 1975; m. Betty E. Hunley, June 13, 1946; children—Janette, David, Suzanne, Scott, Richard. Dir. U. Neb. Men's Residence Halls, 1953-56; asst. bus. mgr. U. Kansas City, 1956-57, bus. mgr., 1957-60, instr., 1956-60, acting dean Sch. Bus., 1958; bus. mgr. Delta Coll., Mich., 1960-64, pres., 1964—. Mem. Gov. Mich. Com. Comprehensive State Health Adv. Planning Council; mem. commn. adminstrn. Am. Assn. Jr. Colls.; pres. Mich. Community Coll. Assn. Served with USNR. Mem. Nat. Assn. Ednl. Buyers, Bay County Mental Health Assn., Phi Kappa Tau, Beta Gamma Sigma. Clubs: Torch, Rotary. Methodist. Home: 411 Park Av Bay City MI 48706 Office: University Center MI 48710

CARMEL, RICHARD JAY, lawyer; b. Chgo., July 5, 1936; s. Lester and Sally (Bright) C.; B.A., Northwestern U., 1958, LL.B., 1960, J.D., 1970; m. Elaine Kraus, June 25, 1967; children—Suzanne Lynn, Mark Thomas. Admitted to Ill. bar, 1960; clk. Ill. Appellate Ct., 1961-62; practiced in Chgo., 1962—; asso. Fink & Coff, 1962-64, Fischel, Kahn, Weinberg, Diamond & Brusslan, 1964-66; partner Fischel, Kahn, Weinberg & Brusslan, 1966-75; partner RGF & Assos., 1975-77; v.p. Balcor Co., Skokie, Ill., 1975-77; pres. Richard J. Carmel, Ltd., Chgo., 1977—. Served with AUS, 1960-61. Mem. Am., Ill., Chgo. bar assns. Home: 1665 Forest Av Highland Park IL 60035 Office: 4316 Mid Continental Plaza 55 E Monroe St Chicago IL 60603

CARMI, SHLOMO, educator, scientist; b. Cernauti, Rumania, July 18, 1937; s. Shmuel and Haia (Marcovici) C.; student Technion, Haifa, Israel, 1958-60; B.S. cum laude, U. Witwatersrand, Johannesburg, South Africa, 1962; M.S., U. Minn., 1966, Ph.D., 1968; m. Rachel Aharoni, Dec. 23, 1963; children—Sharon, Ronen-Itzhak. Came to U.S., 1963. Research engr. W. Rand Gold Mining Co., Krugersdorp, South Africa, 1962-63; research asst., research fellow U. Minn., 1963-68; asst. prof. mech. engring. Wayne State U., 1968-70, 72-73, asso. prof., 1973-78, prof., 1978—; sr. lectr. Technion, Israel Inst. Tech., 1970-72, sabbatical, I. Taylor chair, 1977-78; research specialist Ford Motor Co., summer 1973, 74, 76, 77; speaker sci. meetings, Israel, Can. and U.S. Served as sgt. inf., Israeli Army, 1956-58. South African Technion Soc. scholar, 1960-62; recipient prize Transvaal Chamber of Mines, 1961, faculty research award Wayne State U., 1970; research grantee ERDA, U.S. Army Research Office. Mem. Am. Phys. Soc., Am. Soc. M.E. (com. on heat transfer in energy systems), Am. Assn. U. Profs., Pi Tau Sigma (hon.). Contbr. articles and reviews to profl. jours. Home: 7380 St Auburn Dr Birmingham MI 48010 Office: Wayne State University Detroit MI 48202

CARMICHAEL, CHARLES WESLEY, plant engr.; b. Marshall, Ind., Jan 18, 1919; s. Charles Wesley and Clella Ann (Grubb) C.; B.S., Purdue U., 1941; m. Eleanor Lee Johnson, July 2, 1948; one dau., Ann Bromley Carmichael Biada. Owner, operator retail stores, West Lafayette, Ind., 1946-48, Franklin, Ind., 1950-53; mem. staff time study Chevrolet Co., Indpls., 1953-55; indsl. engr. Mallory Capacitor Co., Indpls., 1955-60, Greencastle, Ind., 1960-70, plant engr., 1970—; lectr. in field. Chmn. Greencastle dr. A.R.C., 1962-63; bd. dirs. United Way Greencastle, 1976—. Served to capt., F.A., U.S. Army, 1941-46; ETO. Decorated Bronze Star Medal, Purple Heart with oak leaf cluster. Mem. Greencastle C. of C. (dir. 1962-64), Am. Inst. Plant Engrs., Putnam County Bd. Realtors, Ind. Hist. Soc. Republican. Methodist. Clubs: Kiwanis (pres. Greencastle 1965), John Purdue, Soc. Ind. Pioneers, Windy Hill Country, Masons, Shriners, Am. Legion. Home: 702 Highwood Ave Greencastle IN 46135 Office: PO Box 273 Greencastle IN 46135

CARMICHAEL, ELEANOR JOHNSON (MRS. CHARLES WESLEY CARMICHAEL), librarian; b. Mooresville, Ind., Aug. 31, 1916; d. Howard Vinson and Cora Alta (Newman) Johnson; B.A., Earlham Coll., 1938; B.L.S., Columbia U., 1941; M.L.S., Ind. U., 1970; m. Charles Wesley Carmichael, July 2, 1948; 1 dau., Ann Bromley (Mrs. George H. Biada, Jr.). Librarian, Coll. Architecture, Cornell U., Ithaca, N.Y., 1942-46; librarian dept. physics Purdue U., Lafayette, Ind., 1946-49; librarian Indpls. Mus. Art, 1956-60; catalog librarian Roy O. West Library, DePauw U., Greencastle, Ind., 1960—. Mem. project task force Coop. Bibliographic Center for Ind. Libraries, 1972-74. Mem. AAUW, D.A.R., Am., Ind. library assns., Ohio Valley Group Tech. Service Librarians (sec. 1962-63), Beta Phi Mu, Alpha Phi, Tri Kappa. Author: (with K. Lark-Horowitz) A Chronology of Scientific Development, 1848-1948, 1948. Home: 702 Highwood Ave Greencastle IN 46135

CARMICHAEL, RALPH HARRY, biochemist; b. Freetown, Ind., Jan. 20, 1923; s. Sherman and Hazel Clove (Brock) C.; B.S., Ind. U., 1950, postgrad., 1960-62; M.S., Butler U., 1956; m. Nelly Elizabeth Fields, July 11, 1942; 1 son, Timothy Brett. Asso. biochemist Lilly Lab. for Clin. Research, Marion County Gen. Hosp., Indpls., 1950-56, supr. clin. chemistry, 1956-62, dept. head clin. chemistry, 1962-70, dept. head drug metabolism, 1970-76, sr. biochemist, 1976—. Served with AUS, 1943-45. Mem. Am. Chem. Soc., Am. Assn. Clin. Chemists, N.Y. Acad. Scis. Methodist. Contbr. articles to profl. jours. Home: 2732 Parkwood Dr Speedway IN 46224 Office: 1001 W 10th St Indianapolis IN 46202

CARMONY, MARVIN DALE, educator, linguist; b. nr. Richmond, Ind., Feb. 27, 1923; s. Harry Edgar and Ellen (Brown) C.; student Valparaiso Tech. Inst., 1941-42; A.B., Ind. State U., 1950, M.A., 1951; Ph.D., Ind. U., 1965; m. Mary Joan Nicholson, May 31, 1947; children—Ronald Dee, Kathryn Lynn. Radio operator Am. Airlines, Chgo., 1942-44; tchr. high schs., Pendleton and Shelbyville, Ind., 1953-59; instr. English, Ind. State U. at Terre Haute, 1959-63, asst. prof., 1963-66, asso. prof. English and linguistics, 1966-69, prof., 1969—, asso. dean Coll. Arts and Scis., 1970—. Dir. Ind. Place-Names Survey, 1968-70; co-founder Ind. Names (now Midwest Jour. Lang. and Folklore), 1970, gen. editor, 1970—. Trustee Olivet Nazarene Coll., 1967-70. Served with U.S. Mcht. Marine, 1944-46. Mem. A.A.U.P., Am. Dialect Soc. (adv. bd. publs. 1972—), Soc. Wireless Pioneers, Am. Name Soc. (mem. editorial bd. 1977), Linguistic Soc. Am., Modern Lang. Assn., Phi Delta Lambda. Author: (with D.F. Carmony) Indiana Dialects in Their Historical Setting, 1973; (with Ronald Baker) Indiana Place Names, 1975; also articles. Home: 227 Madison Blvd Terre Haute IN 47803

CARNAHAN, JOHN ANDERSON, lawyer; b. Cleve., May 8, 1930; s. Samuel Edwin and Penelope (Moulton) C.; B.A., Duke, 1953, LL.B., 1955, J.D., 1955; m. Katherine Halter, June 14, 1958; children—Peter Moulton, Allison Eads, Kristin Alexandra. Admitted to Ohio bar, 1955, pvt. practice law, Columbus, 1955—. Lectr. Ohio Legal Center Inst., 1969, 73, 74. Chmn. UN Day, Columbus, 1960. Pres. Capital City Young Republicans Club, 1960. Bd. dirs. Columbus Cancer Clinic; governing bd. Hannah Neil Mission, Inc. Named 1 of 10 Outstanding Young Men of Columbus, 1965. Mem. Am., Ohio State (council of dels. 1965-67), Columbus (bd. govs. 1970-72, sec.-treas. 1974-75, pres. 1976-77) bar assns., Duke Alumni Admissions Adv. Com. (chmn. 1965—), Phi Delta Theta, Phi Delta Phi. Presbyn. Club: University (Columbus). Editor: Duke Law Jour., 1954-55; contbr. to profl. publs. in field. Home: 872 Clubview Blvd N Worthington OH 43085 Office: 88 E Broad St Columbus OH 43215

CARNAHAN, ROBERT EDWARD, patent ofcl.; b. Kaukauna, Wis., Jan. 5, 1925; s. Elliot Z. and Mary Lucille (Robertson) C.; B.S., U. Wis., 1947; M.S., U. Ill., 1948, Ph.D. in Organic Chemistry, 1950; postgrad. in patent law N.Y. U., 1955; m. Anna Conner, Oct. 21, 1950; children—Barbara, Ellen, Janet. Research chemist Pfizer, Inc., Groton, Conn., 1950-55, patent agt., Bklyn., 1955-60; dir. patents Mead Johnson & Co., Evansville, Ind., 1960—. Served with USNR, 1944-46; PTO. Mem. Evansville C. of C., Phi Beta Kappa, Sigma Xi, Alpha Chi Sigma. Home: 5812 Twickingham Ct Evansville IN 47711 Office: 2404 Pennsylvania St Evansville IN 47721

CARNER, WILLIAM JOHN, banker; b. Springfield, Mo., Aug. 9, 1948; s. John Wilson and Willie Marie (Moore) C.; A.B., Drury Coll., 1970; M.B.A., U. Mo., 1972; m. Dorothy Jean Edwards, June 12, 1976. Mktg. rep. 1st Nat. Bank Memphis, 1972-73; asst. br. mgr. Bank of Am., Los Angeles, 1973-74; dir. mktg. Commerce Bank, Springfield, Mo., 1974-76; affiliate mktg. mgr. 1st Union Bancorp., St. Louis, 1976-78; prin. Long, Carner & Assos., St. Louis, 1977—; instr. Drury Coll., 1975. Publicity chmn. Am. Cancer Soc., Greene County, Mo., 1974-78; bd. dirs. Springfield (Mo.) Muscular Dystrophy Assn., 1975-76. Mem. Bank Mktg. Assn., Assn. M.B.A. Execs. Democrat. Mem. Disciples of Christ Ch. Clubs: Kiwanis, Mason, Shrine. Home: 3605 S Parkhill Springfield MO 65807 Office: PO Box 1482 SSS Springfield MO 65807

CARNES, GILES DERWOOD, psychologist; b. Neosho, Mo., June 1, 1927; s. Roy Kyle and Opal Emma (Bell) C.; m. Charlene Downs, June 12, 1954; children—Paul, Sharon. B.A., U. Mo., Columbia, 1952; M.A., 1954, Ph.D., 1958. Certified, Tex., 1962, Mo., 1973. Clinical, counseling psychologist VA Hosp., Houston, 1958-66; clin. asst. prof. psychiatry and rehab. medicine Baylor U., Houston, 1958-66; asst. prof. rehab. counseling U. Tex., Austin, 1966-68, asso. prof., dir., 1968-73; chief psychology service VA Hosp., Columbia, Mo., 1973—; asso. prof. psychiatry and rehab. medicine U. Mo., 1973—; vice-chmn. Gov.'s (Mo.) Com. on Employment of the Handicapped, 1976—. Mem. Council on Rehab. Edn. (pres. 1972), Am. Psychol. Assn., Nat. Rehab. Assn., Nat. Rehab. Counseling Assn., Am. Personnel Guidance Assn., Phi Beta Kappa. Recipient Nat. award Assn. for Physical and Mental Rehab., 1962; Spl. award, Tex. Rehab. Counseling Assn., 1972; Commendation, VA, 1973. Home: 2608 W Rollins Rd Columbia MO 65201 Office: 800 Stadium Rd Columbia MO 65201

CARNEY, CHARLES J., congressman; b. Youngstown, Ohio, Apr. 17, 1913; s. Michael G. and Florence Grogan (Grimm) C.; student Youngstown State U.; H.H.D., (hon.), Central State U., Cleve., LL.D., Coll. Osteo. Medicine and Surgery, Des Moines, 1972; m. Mary Lucille Manning, Nov. 12, 1938; children—Mary Ellen (Mrs. John Leshinsky), Ann (Mrs. James Murphy). Mem. United Rubber Workers Union, 1934-50, former pres. Local Union 102, pres. Dist. Council No. 1, 1940-43, staff rep., dist. dir., 1942-50; staff rep. United Steelworkers of Am., 1950-68; mem. 91st-95th Congresses from 19th Ohio Dist., mem. com. interstate and fgn. commerce, com. vets.' affairs, com. small bus., chmn. commodities and services subcom. Mem. Ohio State Senate, 1950-70, minority leader, 1969-70. Trustee Mahoning County CIO Indsl. Council. Mem. Farm Grange. K.C., Elk, Moose, Eagle. Home: 2405 Volney Rd Youngstown OH 44511 Office: Longworth Bldg US House of Representatives Washington DC 20515

CARNEY, JOHN PHILLIP, computer co. exec.; b. Sturgis, Mich., July 31, 1946; s. John Robert and Lulu May C.; student Kalamazoo Coll., 1964-65; A.B., Ind. U., 1973; m. Rosemary Theresa Sonneborn, Aug. 26, 1972; one dau., Sheila Elizabeth. Research asst. high energy physics lab. Ind. U., Bloomington, 1973; mathematician, model simulation project, Crane Naval Ammunition Depot, Crane, Ind., 1973-74; tech. rep. mainframe computers Burroughs Corp., Indpls., 1974-76; chief programmer/analyst On Line Data Base, Brulin & Co., Indpls., 1976-77; dist. computer facilities mgr. Burroughs Corp., Indpls., 1977—. Served with USAF, 1966-70. Decorated Air medal with 2 oak leaf clusters. Home: 2653 Cold Spring Ln Indianapolis IN 46222 Office: PO Box 270-B Indianapolis IN 46205

CARNICK, CRAIG EVANS, restaurant exec.; b. Detroit, June 20, 1946; s. Albert Lee and Geraldine (Bremen) C.; B.A., Wayne State U., 1966. Asst. catering mgr. Hotel Whittier, Detroit, 1962-65; asst. mgr. Roostertail Supper Club, Detroit, 1965-67; catering mgr. Trader Vic's Restaurants, Washington, 1967-69, maitre d' and catering mgr., Detroit, 1969-70; exec. asst. mgr. Top of the Tower Restaurant, Toledo, 1970-72; dir. food and beverage Leelanau Homestead Hotel, Glen Arbor, Mich., 1972-74; pres. Food ServCo., Inc., Glen Arbor, 1974—. Bd. dirs. Oakland County chpt. Big Brothers Am., Mid Am. Environ. Fund, 1977-80. Mem. Profl. Photographers Am., Am. Hotel-Motel Assn., North-Central Assn. Restaurant Execs. (pres. 1975-77). Office: Food ServCo Inc Glen Arbor MI 49636

CARNS, WILLIAM HULBERT, ins. exec.; b. Central City, Nebr., Apr. 18, 1912; s. James H. and Emma (Hulbert) C.; B.S. in Bus. Adminstrn., U. Nebr., 1933, J.D., 1935; m. Hazel Jane Eldridge, Sept. 10, 1938; children—William E., James O. Admitted to Nebr. bar, 1935; with firm Woods, Aiken & Aiken, Lincoln, Nebr., 1935-37; with Employers Group, Boston, 1937-48, Hartford A & I Co., Chgo., 1948-49; with Zurich-Am. Ins. Cos., Los Angeles, 1949-57, asst. U.S. mgr., sr. v.p., Chgo., 1962-77, chmn. bd., 1977—. Bd. govs. Ins. Crime Prevention Inst. Served to lt. USNR, 1942-45. Mem. Nat. Assn. Ind. Insurers, Phi Delta Phi, Beta Theta Pi. Clubs: Union League (Chgo.); Rolling Green Golf and Country (Arlington Heights, Ill.). Home: 106 S Stratford Rd Arlington Heights IL 60004 Office: 111 W Jackson Blvd Chicago IL 60604

CARON, E(DGAR) LOUIS, JR., chemist; b. Chgo., July 31, 1922; s. Edgar Louis and Ethyl Gertrude (Dame) C.; student Western Mich. U., 1940-43; B.S.E.E., A. & M. U. Tex., 1944; B.S. in Chem., Bradley U., 1947; M.S. in Organic Chem., U. Ill., 1948; m. Gladys Evelyn Weberg, Aug. 21, 1948; children—Paul Gregory, Kimberley Ruth, Jeffrey Mark, Melanie Anne, Gary Alan, Todd Louis. Lab. instr. Bradley U., 1946-47; research chemist, U. Ill., 1948; with Upjohn Co., Kalamazoo, Mich., 1948—, research chemist, 1948-66, sci. information systems analyst research asso., 1966—. Justice of the Peace, Kalamazoo, Mich., 1953-63; mem. Kalamazoo Co. Republican com., 1952—; del. Kalamazoo Co. Republican conv., Mich. State Republican conv. Served to Tech. 5th grade, AUS, 1943-46. Decorated Bronze Star medal. Accredited profl. chemist. Fellow Am. Inst. Chemists; mem. Am. Chem. Soc., Assn. Computing Machines, Assn. Systems Mgmt., Drug Information Assn. Patentee in field. Contbr. articles in field to profl. jours. Home: 1307 Coolidge Ave Kalamazoo MI 49007 Office: 301 Henrietta St Kalamazoo MI 49001

CAROZZA, DAVY ANGELO, educator; b. Monterenodomo, Italy, Oct. 10, 1926; s. Nicola and Maria A. (Mariotti) C.; came to U.S., 1947, naturalized, 1952; B.A. summa cum laude, Catholic U. Am., 1956, M.A. (Woodrow Wilson fellow), 1957, Ph.D. (Wilson fellow), 1964; m. Anna G. Carozza, Feb. 3, 1952; children—Daniel, Walter, Janet, Paolo. Tchr. Italian schs., 1943-47; grad. asst. in French, Catholic U. Am., Washington, 1957-58, lectr. summer sessions, 1957-65, lectr. in French, 1960-61; instr. Italian and French, U. Md., College Park, 1961-64, asst. prof. Italian, 1964-65; lectr. Sch. of Advanced Internat. Studies, Johns Hopkins, 1964-65; asso. prof. comparative lit. U. Wis., Milw., 1965-68, prof., 1968—. Vis. asso. prof. comparative lit. Northwestern U., Evanston, Ill., 1966; mem. panel discussion on Dante, Georgetown U. Forum radio program, 1965; adviser, coordinator Italian program for adults and children, Cardinal Stritch Coll., 1971-73. Served with AUS, 1948-52; Korea. U. Wis. grantee, 1966-69, 72, 73, 74. Mem. Midwest Modern Lang. Assn. (pres. 1969-70, exec. com. 1970-71), Modern Lang. Assn. Am. (exec. council 1969-70), Internat., Am. comparative lit. assns., Renaissance Soc. of Am., Dante Soc. of Am., Internat., Am. assns. tchrs. of Italian, Am. Assn. Tchrs. of French, Phi Beta Kappa, Delta Epsilon Sigma, Phi Kappa Phi. Author: European Baroque, 1976. Contbr. book revs. and articles to lit. jours. Home: 5549 N Berkeley Blvd Milwaukee WI 53217 Office: Dept Comparative Lit U Wisconsin Milwaukee WI 53201

CARPENTER, JAMES OSMER, gerontologist, educator; b. Brookings, S.D., Oct. 16, 1939; s. Osmer Sidney and Irene Esther Christine (Jacobson) C.; B.A. cum laude, Mich. State U., 1964; M.A. (NIH fellow), Ohio State U., 1966, Ph.D., 1970; m. Hannelore Charlotte Waldschmidt, Feb. 18, 1961; children—James, Christine, Lori. Asst. prof. pub. health adminstrn. U. Mich. Sch. Pub. Health, Ann Arbor, 1969—, asst. prof. health behavior and health edn., 1972—, asso. dir. program in health gerontology, 1972—; guest lectr. various univs., 1969—; chmn. Mich. Gov.'s Task Force on Health Edn. of the Pub., 1975—; mem. profl. advisory bd. Found Thanatology, Columbia U., 1972—; me. profl. tech. rev. com. Mich. Dept. Pub. Health, 1977—. Mem. Am. Statis. Assn., Gerontol. Soc., Nat. Council for Social Studies, North Central Sociol. Assn., Am. Pub. Health Assn., AAAS, Am. Acad. Polit. and Social Sci., Mich. Soc. Gerontology, Pi Gamma Mu, Alpha Kappa Delta, Kappa Delta Pi. Contbr. articles on med. gerontology to profl. jours. Home: 2163 Yorktown Dr Ann Arbor MI 48105

CARPENTER, JOHN DENNIS, banker; b. Stephen, Minn., Feb. 17, 1933; s. Oscar Dennis and Ingrid Marie (Nilsen) C.; student U. Wis. Sch. Banking, 1967; m. Peggy Eileen Pudil, Dec. 22, 1957; children—Denise, Scott, Daniel. Asst. cashier Grafton Nat. Bank (N.D.), 1956-62; asst. v.p. Northwestern State Bank, Luverne, Minn., 1962-68; v.p. Northwestern State Bank, Slayton, Minn., 1968-71; pres. First Nat. Bank, Hay Springs, Nebr., 1971-73; pres., chmn. bd.

Northwestern Bank, Hallock, Minn., 1973—, C-D-L Corp., Hallock. Served with U.S. Army, 1953-55; Korea. Mem. Minn. Bankers Assn., C. of C. (pres., sec.-treas.). Republican. Lutheran. Clubs: Lions (sec.-treas.), Elks, Masons. Home: 217 N 5th St Hallock MN 56728 Office: 302 S 2d St Hallock MN 56728

CARPENTER, RUSSELL PHELPS, office supply and art products co. exec.; b. Chgo., Sept. 6, 1900; s. William W. Seymour and Viola (Phelps) C.; B.A., Dartmouth, 1923; m. Mary Howe, Dec. 28, 1927; children—William, Carlisle C. Jones, Virginia. With Sanford Corp., Bellwood, Ill., 1923—, chmn. bd., 1950—. Pres., YMCA, Oak Park, Ill., 1956, bd. dirs., 1935—; pres. Chgo. Council on Alcoholism, 1967-68, 72-73, bd. dirs., 1967—, chmn. bd., 1977. Mason, Rotarian. Home: 1017 N Euclid St Oak Park IL 60302 Office: 2740 Washington Blvd Bellwood IL 60104

CARPENTER, WILL DOCKERY, agrl. chem. co. exec.; b. Moorhead, Miss., July 13, 1930; s. Horace Aubrey and Celeste (Brian) C.; B.S., Miss. State U., 1952; M.S., Purdue U., 1956, Ph.D., 1958; m. Hellen E. Dodd, Mar. 26, 1960; children—Celeste, Billy. With Monsanto Co., St. Louis, 1958—, beginning as research biochemist plant and animal nutrition, successively agrl. research, agrl. devel. in herbicides, mgr. herbicide devel., mgr. market devel., 1958-71, dir. market devel., 1971-75, dir. product devel., 1975—. Mem. adv. com. Internat. Plant Protection Center, 1968; chmn. new herbicide sect. So. Weed Conf., 1969-70; mem. tech. service adv. bd. Am. Cotton Grower, 1970; mem. Western interstate com. agr. Western Conf. of Council of State Govts., 1970; juror Kenneth A. Spencer award, 1976. Served to capt., arty., AUS, 1952-54. Mem. N.Y. Acad. Scis., Am. Soc. Plant Physiology, Weed Sci. Soc. Am. (treas. 1975-78), North Central Weed Control Conf. (pres. 1977). Home: 427 Monticello Dr Ballwin MO 63011 Office: 800 N Lindbergh Blvd St Louis MO 63166

CARPENTER, WILLIAM WARREN, assn. mgmt. co. exec.; b. Crawfordsville, Ind., Apr. 27, 1924; s. Guy Osmend and Estel Charlotte (Duncan) C.; B.A., DePauw U., 1948; m. Dorothy Susan Jacobs, Oct. 1, 1949; children—David, Stephen (dec. 1972), Carol, Donald, Douglas. Trainee, Continental Ill. Nat. Bank & Trust Co., Chgo., 1948-50; sales rep. IBM, Chgo., 1950-58; account exec. Smith, Bucklin & Assos., Inc., Chgo., 1958-64, v.p., 1964-71, pres., 1971—, also dir.; pres. Vanguard Reprodns. Co., Inc., Chgo. Sec., Wallcovering Industry Bur., N.Y.C., 1973—. Sec., Hinsdale (Ill.) Com. of One Hundred, 1960-62. Served to 2d lt. USAAF, 1942-45. Mem. Am. Soc. Assn. Execs., Am. Mgmt. Assn., N.A.M., Beta Theta Pi. Clubs: Ruth Lake Country (Hinsdale); Ill. Athletic, University, Executives (Chgo.). Home: 127 E 4th St Hinsdale IL 60521 Office: 111 E Wacker Dr Chicago IL 60601

CARR, BOB, congressman; b. Janesville, Wis., Mar. 27, 1943; s. Milton Raymond and Edna (Blood) C.; B.S., U. Wis., 1965, J.D., 1968; postgrad. Mich. State U., 1969. Admitted to Mich. bar, 1969; staff Mich. Senate, Lansing, 1968-69; asst. atty. gen. Mich., 1969-72; com. counsel Mich. Legislature, 1971-72; mem. 94th-95th Congresses from 6th Mich. dist. Office: 332 Cannon House Office Bldg Washington DC 20515

CARR, DONALD STEVENS, mech. engr.; b. Penacook, N.H., Nov. 3, 1924; s. George Amasa and Grace Esther (Farley) C.; B.S., Northeastern U., Boston, 1953; m. Marjorie Evelyn Buck, Nov. 24, 1951; 1 son, David Brian. With Fellows Corp., Springfield, Vt., 1947—, chief engr. Cutting Tool div., 1968-76, sales engr., 1976—. Chmn., Planning Com., Springfield, 1974-76. Registered profl. engr. Mem. Am. Gear Mfg. Assn., Soc. Mfg. Engrs., Am. Def. Preparedness Assn., Smithsonian Instn. Club: Masons. Office: PO Box 399 Springfield VT 05156

CARR, GENE EMMETT, supt. schs.; b. Madison, S.D., Dec. 6, 1937; s. Emmett A. and Phyllis E. (Heitman) C.; B.S., Dakota State Coll., 1961; M.S., U. Utah, 1964; Edn. Specialist, U. S.D., 1975; m. Carolyn Riley, May 25, 1961; children—Catherine, Robert, Michael, Mark, Patricia, Bradley. Tchr. pub. schs., Garretson, S.D., 1961-63, Dell Rapids, S.D., 1964-70; supt. schs., Oldham, S.D., 1970-76, Hamlin Schs., Hayti, S.D., 1976—. Vice pres. Oldham Fire Dept., 1972-76; mem. agr. com. Sioux Empire Farm Show, 1964—. Mem. Sch. Adminstrs. S.D., S.D. Sch. Supts. Assn. (v.p.), Am. Quarter Horse Assn. Club, Center of Nation Appaloosa Horse Club (pres. 1972-74), Pony of Ams. Club. Contbr. articles to equine mags. Home: Box 246 Bryant SD 57221 Office: Box 298 Hayti SD 57241

CARR, HAROLD NOFLET, airline exec.; b. Kansas City, Kans., Mar. 14, 1921; s. Noflet B. and Mildred (Addison) C.; B.S., Tex. A & M U., 1943; postgrad. Am. U., 1944-46; m. Mary Elizabeth Smith, Aug. 5, 1944; children—Steven Addison, Hal Douglas, James Taylor, Scott Noflet. Asst. dir. route devel. Trans World Airlines, Inc., 1943-47; exec. v.p. Wis. Central Airlines, Inc., 1947-52; mem. firm McKinsey & Co., 1952-54; pres. North Central Airlines, Inc., 1954-69; chmn., 1965—, chief exec. officer, 1969-76, dir., 1952—; dir. Detection Scis., Inc., Ross Industries, Inc., Stange Co., Stange Pesa S.A. de C.V., Temp Con, Inc., Westland Capital Corp. Professorial lectr. in mgmt. engring. Am. U., 1952-62. Bd. dirs. Minn. Safety Council; councilor Tex. A & M Research Found.; bd. nominations Nat. Aviation Hall of Fame; mem. adv. com. Tex. Transp. Inst., Tex. A & M U. System. Mem. World Bus. Council, Nat. Def. Transp. Assn., Air Transport Assn., Assn. Local Transport Airlines, Am. Econ. Assn., Minn. Execs. Orgn., Greater Mpls., St. Paul Area chambers commerce, Am. Assn. Airport Execs., Nat. Aero Assn., Smithsonian Assos., Tex. A. and M. Former Students Assn. Clubs: Midway (St. Paul); Aero, Nat. Aviation (Washington); Stearman Alumnus (Wichita, Kans.); Mpls.; Century, Aggie (College Station, Tex.); Briarcrest Country (Bryan, Tex.); Racquet (Miami, Fla.); Wings (N.Y.C.); Gull Lake Yacht (Brainerd, Minn.). Address: 7500 Northliner Dr Minneapolis MN 55450

CARR, JAMES CHARLES, physician; b. New Hampton, Iowa, Mar. 28, 1939; s. Hubert B. and Anna Mary (McKone) C.; B.A. in English, Loras Coll., 1957-61; M.D., U. Iowa, 1965; m. Mary Kay Peters, June 17, 1961; children—Barbara, Robert, Jane, Susan, David. Intern, Broadlawns Polk County Hosp., Des Moines, 1965-66; resident in family practice, 1966-67; practice medicine specializing in family medicine Med. Assos., New Hampton, Iowa, 1967—; chief staff St. Joseph's Community Hosp., New Hampton, 1972, 1975; instr. family medicine Mayo Med. Sch., U. Minn., Rochester, 1975—. Served to major Iowa N. G., 1966-72. Recipient Distinguished Service Award Jaycees, 1971; recipient Outstanding Young Mem of Am. Award, 1974; diplomate Am. Bd. Family Practice. Fellow Am. Acad. Family Practice; mem. AMA, Chickasaw County, Iowa Med. Socs., Assn. Am. Physicians and Surgeons. Roman Catholic. Home: 414 N Chestnut Ave New Hampton IA 50659 Office: 201 S Linn Ave New Hampton IA 50659

CARR, JAMES EDWARD, JR., mfg. co. exec; b. New Castle, Pa., Mar. 31. 1938; s. James Edward and Kathryn E (Ango) C.; B.S. In Bus., U. Tenn., 1961, postgrad., 1961-62; Transp. Mgmt. Degree, Coll. Advanced Traffic, 1968; m. Carol E. Franke, Sept. 2, 1961; children—Cathy, Julie, Wendy. Asst. traffic mgr. Ceco Corp., Chgo., 1962-68; corporate transp. mgr. Nalco Chem. Co., 1968-78; mgr. Corporate transp. Internat. Harvester Co., Chgo., 1978—; practitioner at law ICC; vice chmn., dir. ITOFCA, Inc. Mem. chem. sect. United Settlement Appeal Charity, 1972-74; adminstr. LaGrange Methodist Ch. Served with U.S. Army, 1956-57. Mem. Chgo. Assn. Commerce and Industry (exec. com. indsl. traffic counsel), Am. Soc. Traffic and Transp. (certified; bd. govs. Ill. chpt.), Mfg. Chemists Assn. (distbn com.), Nat. Indsl. Traffic League, Nat. Counsel Phys. Distbn. Mgmt. Clubs: LaGrange Field, Chgo. Traffic, Delta Nu Alpha. Contbr. articles to profl. jours. Home 535 Catherine Ave LaGrange IL 60525 Office: Internat. Harvester Co 401 N Michigan Ave Chicago IL 60611

CARR, JOHN JOSEPH, marketing cons.; b. Chgo., Aug. 5, 1924; s. John J. and Louise (Nowak) Ciezarek; student So. Ill. U., 1946, Ill. Inst. Tech., 1946-47; B.S. in Math., Roosevelt U., 1952; postgrad. Loyola U. at Chgo.; grad. Air Univ.; Ph.D. in Mktg., Dallas U., 1974; m. Betty Graczyk, Sept. 19, 1954; children—John E., Julie A., James E. Researcher, Argonne Nat. Lab., 1949-52; sales and market analyst Zenith Radio Corp., 1952-55; sales statis. analyst Am. Cyanamid Co., 1955-56; dir. sales analysis Helene Curtis Industries, Inc., 1956-61; dir. mktg. research Alberto Culver Co., Melrose Park, Ill., 1961-64; v.p., exec. dir. cosmetic services IMS Internat. Inc. (formerly DKK), Des Plaines, Ill., 1964—. Lectr., cons. mfg. cos. Served as radio operator on B-29, USAAF, World War II, 35 missions from Saipan to Japan. Decorated D.F.C., Air Medal with 6 clusters. Mem. Am. Statis. Assn., Am. Marketing Assn. K.C. Author: The Thunderstorm, 1949. Author research reports, articles on marketing and innovations in cosmetics, toiletries, health-beauty aids. Composer, writer of lyrics and music. Home: 9323 N Central Park Av Evanston IL 60203 Office: Butler and Maple Avs Ambler PA 19002

CARR, JOSEPH PATRICK, lawyer; b. Pitts., Mar. 27, 1918; s. James Alexander and Margaret (Lundy) C.; student U. Notre Dame, 1936-40; LL.B., Columbia, 1948; m. Patricia Ellen Conway, Feb. 14, 1953; children—Maureen P., James J., Sharon M., Kevin J. Admitted to N.Y. bar, 1948, Ill. bar, 1951; asso. Davis, Polk, Wardwell, Sunderland & Kiendl, N.Y.C., 1948-51; asso. Gardner, Carton, Douglas, Chgo., 1951-61, partner, 1961—. Pres., Holy Ghost Sch. Bd., South Holland, Ill., 1970-72. Served with USAAF, 1941-45. Decorated D.F.C., Air medal. Mem. Am., Ill. (gov. 1964-70), Chgo. bar assns., Am. Judicature Soc., Soc. Trial Lawyers, Nat. Assn. R.R. Trial Counsel. Roman Catholic. Clubs: Mid-Day, Klinger Lake. Home: 942 E 172d St South Holland IL 60473 Office: 1 First Nat Plaza Chicago IL 60603

CARR, LEON CLEMENT, pub. relations exec.; b. lMilbank, S.D., Sept. 11, 1924; s. Frank B. and Laura A. (Kohl) C.; B.A. in Journalism, U. Minn., 1951; m. Donnie M. Cronin, May 19, 1956; 1 son, John. Wire editor St. Cloud (Minn.) Daily Times, 1951-52; staff writer Asso. Press, Sioux Falls, Pierre, S.D., 1952-56; copy editor St. Paul Pioneer Press, 1956-57; copy editor St. Paul Dispatch, 1957-60, asst. news editor, 1960-61; with 3M Co., St. Paul, 1961—, staff publicist, 1965-71, pub. relations coordinator, 1971-73, supt. media relations, 1973-76, mgr. br. pub. relations, 1976—. Mem. Pub. Relations Soc. Am. (accredited), U. Minn. Sch. Journalism Mass Communication Alumni Assn. (charter, past pres.), Sigma Delta Chi (life). Roman Catholic. Club: Minn. Press (charter). Home: 21 E Logan Ave West St Paul MN 55118 Office: 3M Center Box 33600 St Paul MN 55133

CARR, RALPH WILLIAM, physician, surgeon; b. N.Y.C., Jan. 2, 1903; s. William Montgomery and Mellie (Dyer) C.; A.B., Wesleyan U., 1925; M.A., U. Minn., 1927; M.D., Johns Hopkins, 1934; m. May Sterrett Irvine, Mar. 12, 1936 (dec. 1956); children—Betsy Craig (Mrs. Jack Meeks), Alansa (Mrs. Leonard Bates), Bruce M., Susan Shelby (Mrs. J. Roger Gildersleeve); m. 2d, Luella Jane Weber, Nov. 27, 1957; children—Patricia, Barbara, Jennifer. House officer Johns Hopkins Hospital, 1934-35; asst. resident Long Island College Hospital, 1935-36; assistant, passed asst. surgeon U.S. Marine hosps., N.Y., New Orleans, San Francisco, 1936-40; med. officer charge out-patient office USPHS, Ketchikan, Alaska, 1940, sr. surgeon, 1956-74; mem. staff Ketchikan Gen. Hosp., 1940-74; pvt. practice, Ketchikan, 1943-74; mem. staff Harry S Truman Meml. VA Hosp., Columbia, Mo., 1974—; Med. dir. USPHS. Chmn. Ketchikan chpt. A.R.C., 1966-74. Mem. Ketchikan Library Bd., 1960-74. Fellow Internat. Coll. Surgeons (vice regent for Alaska 1969-74); mem. Alaska State Med. Assn. (pres. 1963-64), Alaska Pub. Health Assn., A.M.A., Assn. Mil. Surgeons U.S., Assn. Res. Officers USPHS, Ketchikan Med. Soc. (pres. 1951-52, 59-60), U.S. Power Squadron (dist. staff capt. 1954-74). Internat. Order Blue Gavel, Sigma Xi, Delta Upsilon, Nu Sigma Nu, Gamma Alpha. Republican. Methodist. Clubs: Toastmasters, Washington Athletic, Elks, Ketchikan Yacht (commodore 1964-65). Home: 1-E Burnam Rd Columbia MO 65201 Office VA Hosp 800 Stadium Rd Columbia MO 65201

CARR, ROBERT ALLEN, counselor; b. Kosciusko, Miss., Jan. 24, 1943; s. Junius E. and Gertrude (Grantham) C.; B.S., Jackson State U., 1964; M.Ed., DePaul U., 1975; m. Mae R. Wadlington, June 20, 1965; 1 son, Robert Allen. Tchr., Chgo. Bd. Edn., 1964-71, guidance counselor, 1971—, dept. chmn. higher edn. guidance center, counselor, 1975—; counselor project upward bound Loyola U., Chgo. Bd. dirs. South Avalon Improvement Assn. Mem. Am., Ill., Chgo. guidance and personnel assns., Council Coll. Attendance, Mid Am. Assn. Ednl. Opportunity, Personnel Assn. for Non White Concerns, Alpha Phi Alpha, Jackson State U. Alumni Assn. Democrat. Baptist. Home: 8606 Blackstone St S Chicago IL 60619 Office: 2039 Orchard St Chicago IL 60614

CARR, WILLIAM CLIFFORD, civil engr.; b. St. Louis, Feb. 22, 1945; s. William and Hazel Ester (Hughes) C.; B.C.E., Ga. Inst. Tech., 1968; M.S., Northwestern U., 1970; m. Pamela Gay Fontaine, July 3, 1975; children—William Clifford, Patricia Lynn. Engr., Monsanto Co., St. Louis, 1969-72; group leader Bendy Engring. Co., Earth City, Mo., 1972-74; project engr. LeMessurier Assos./SCI, St. Louis, 1974-76; prin. William C. Carr cons. structural engr., St. Louis, 1976—; lectr. Washington U., St. Louis. Registered profl. engr., Calif., Ill., Mo., Tex. NSF trainee, 1968-69. Mem. ASCE, Am. Concrete Inst., Structural Engring. Assn. Ill., Phi Kappa Phi, Tau Beta Pi, Chi Epsilon. Home and Office: 842 Lordshill St A-2 Shrewsbury MO 63119

CARRAHER, CHARLES JACOB, JR., profl. speaker; b. Cin., Sept. 22, 1922; s. Charles Jacob and Marcella Marie (Hager) C.; grad. pub. schs., Norwood, O.; m. Joyce Ann Root, June 13, 1947; children—Cynthia A., Craig J. With Cin. Enquirer, 1937-72, office mgr., circulation mgr., adminstrv. asst. to exec. v.p., 1947-66, dir. employee community relations, 1966-72; exec. v.p., Cin. Suburban Newspapers Inc., 1973-77. Mem. bd., v.p. Cin. Conv. and Visitors Bur., 1966-72; mem. Cin. Manpower Planning Council, 1972. Bd. dirs. Central Psychiatric Clinic, 1970—, Mental Health Assn., 1970-72, Great Rivers Girl Scout Council, 1969-74; v.p. bd. dirs. Neediest Kids of All, 1969-72; bd. dirs. Greater Cin. Urban League, 1971-74, 75—. Served to lt., USAAF, World War II, ETO. Decorated Air medal with cluster. Mem. Greater Cin. C. of C. (chmn. human resources devel. com. 1972), Beta Gamma Sigma. Republican. Methodist. Home: 10479 Cinderella Dr Cincinnati OH 45242 Office: 4415 Montgomery Rd Norwood OH 45212

CARRIER, WILFRED PETER, elec. engr.; b. Faulkton, S.D., July 14, 1923; s. Wilfred P. and Mary (Mundy) C.; E.E., Ill. Inst. Tech., 1952; m. Mary M. Mulcahy, July 17, 1943; children—Patrick, Timothy. Dir. quality Standard Coil Products Co., Chgo., 1951-59; dir. quality, reliability Mallory Capacitor Co., Indpls., 1958-74, dir. engring., 1974—. Served with AUS, 1942-46; CBI. Mem. Electronic Industries Assn., Am. Soc. Quality Control (regional award), IEEE, Am. Def. Preparedness Assn., Nat. Security Indsl. Assn. Roman Catholic. Clubs: Indpls. Athletic, K.C. Home: 9861 Chesterton St N Indianapolis IN 46280 Office: 3029 Washington St E Indianapolis IN 46206

CARRINGTON, FRANK GAMBLE, JR., legal orgn. ofcl.; b. Paris, France, May 11, 1936 (parents Am. citizens); B.A., Hampden-Sydney Coll., 1952; LL.B., U. Mich., 1960; LL.M. (police legal adviser fellow), Northwestern U., 1970; m. Mary Nymoen Olson, May 11, 1968; children—Christine Margaret, Claire Lynn. Admitted to Ohio bar, 1966, Colo. bar, 1969, Ill. bar, 1973, U.S. Supreme Ct. bar; spl. agt. U.S. Treasury Dept., Cin., 1960-67; legal adviser Chgo. Police Dept., 1967-68, Denver Police, 1968-70; exec. dir. Am. for Effective Law Enforcement, Inc., Evanston, Ill., 1970—. Guest lectr. criminal law U. Mich., Northwestern U. Bd. advs. Young Am. for Freedom, Am. Conservative Union; bd. dirs. Nat. Assn. Victim Assistance. Served with USMCR, 1967. Mem. Am. Bar Assn. (victims com.), Internat. Assn. Chiefs Police, Nat. Sheriff's Assn., Colo., Ill. assns. chiefs police. Author: (with others) Evidence Law for the Police, 1972; The Victims, 1975; The Defenseless Society, 1976; Neither Cruel nor Unusual: The Case for Capital Punishment, 1978. Home: 1341 Chestnut St Wilmette IL 60091 Office: Americans Effective Law Enforcement 960 State Nat Bank Plaza Evanston IL 60201

CARRITTE, JOHN PRIMROSE, JR., foundry exec.; b. Spokane, Wash., Aug. 26, 1894; s. John Primrose and Ellen Cameron (Knapp) C.; B.S. in Chem. Engring., U. Mich., 1917; m. Barbara Lee Marquis, Nov. 3, 1920; children—Barbara (Mrs. Carl J. Oxford, Jr.), Nita (Mrs. Jerome Regnier), Ellen (Mrs. Frank C. Huft). With Canadian Aluminum & Brass Co., 1922-26, Detroit Aluminum & Brass Corp., 1927-34; with True Alloys Inc., Detroit, 1934—, pres., 1935—. Served to 2d lt. U.S. Army, World War I. Mem. Detroit Exec. Assn. (past dir.), Ridgedale Players (past pres.), Ferndale Stamp Club (past pres.), Monk frat., Chi Phi. Republican. Mem. Anglican Ch. Rotarian, Mason. Club: Detroit Athletic. Home: 57 Oakdale Blvd Pleasant Ridge MI 48069 Office: 29955 Groesbeck Hwy Roseville MI 48066

CARROLL, CARMAL EDWARD, educator; b. Grahn, Ky., Oct. 8, 1923; s. Noah Washington and Jessie Laura (Scott) C.; Ph.B., U. Toledo, 1947, M.A., 1950, B.Edn., 1951; M.L.S., U. Calif. at Los Angeles, 1961; Ph.D., U. Calif. at Berkeley, 1969; m. Greta E. Seastrom, June 11, 1960. Edn. librarian, U. So. Calif., 1961-62; reference librarian U. Calif. at Berkeley, 1962-65; dir. library So. Oreg. Coll., Ashland, 1965-67; dir. libraries Wichita (Kans.) State U., 1967-70; prof. library sci. U. Mo. at Columbia, 1970—. Named Ky. col. Mem. A.A.U.P., A.L.A., Assn. Am. Library Schs., Mo. Library Assn., Nat. Micrographics Assn., Internat. Platform Assn., Phi Delta Kappa, Beta Phi Mu. Democrat. Episcopalian. Author: Professionalization of Education for Librarianship, 1970. Home: 2001 Country Club Dr Columbia MO 65201

CARROLL, FRANK EDWIN, constrn. co. exec.; b. Dorchester, Mass., Dec. 2, 1922; s. Henry Francis and Sarah (Sheehan) C.; B.S., Mass. Inst. Tech., 1947; m. Kathleen B. Dunn, Sept. 21, 1946; children—Sheila, Robert, Frank, Brian, Kathleen, Michael. Engr., Timber Engring. Co., Washington, 1947-48; br. mgr. Anning Johnson Co., Mpls., 1948-53; pres. Decks, Inc., Rolling Meadows, Ill., 1953—; pres. Carroll Research, Inc., Rolling Meadows. Chmn. troop 123 Boy Scouts Am., Park Ridge, Ill., 1965-66; mem. indsl. steering com. Harper Coll. Mem. Rolling Meadows (Ill.) Bd. Health. Bd. dirs. Rolling Meadows Crusade of Mercy. Served to 1st lt. AUS, 1943-46. Mem. ASCE, Chgo. Met. Subcontractors (pres. 1974—, dir.), Am. Subcontractors Assn. (dir., sec. 1976-77, treas. 1977-78), Internat. Platform Assn., Pub. Adult and Continuing Edn. Assn. Ill., Northwest (Ill.) Indsl. Council, Chgo. Bldg. Congress, Gypsum Roof Deck Found., Rolling Meadows C. of C. (dir., pres. 1973), Sigma Xi, Tau Beta Pi, Chi Epsilon. Roman Catholic. Rotarian. Clubs: Toastmasters Internat. (Park Ridge); Executives, Union League, M.I.T. (pres. 1975-76, dir.) (Chgo.); Barrington Hills Country. Home: 237 Maple Rd Barrington IL 60010 Office: 3960 Industrial Ave Rolling Meadows IL 60008

CARROLL, VALEREE SUE, speech pathologist; b. Kansas City, Mo., Aug. 29, 1946; d. Middleton Scott and Patricia Pauline (Anderson) C.; B.S. in Edn., U. Kans., 1968, M.A. in Speech Pathology, 1970. Speech pathologist Clay County Health Dept., Liberty, Mo., 1970-71, Kansas City (Mo.) Pub. Schs., 1971—. U.S. Office Edn. fellow, 1968-70. Mem. Am., Greater Kansas City speech hearing assns. Republican. Home: 8886 Juniper St Prairie Village KS 66207 Office: 1211 McGee St Kansas City MO 64106

CARRON, MALCOLM, univ. pres.; b. Detroit, May 15, 1917; s. Harold Gregory and Florence Irene (McLeod) C.; A.B., U. Detroit, 1939; Ph.L., W. Baden Coll., West Baden Springs, Ind., 1945, S.T.B., 1952; M.A., Loyola U., Chgo., 1949; Ph.D., U. Mich., 1956. Joined Soc. of Jesus, 1939, ordained priest Roman Catholic Ch., 1951; instr. English, St. Ignatius High Sch., Cleve., 1945-48; faculty U. Detroit, 1956—, asso. prof. edn., dean Coll. Arts and Scis., 1960-63, acad. v.p., 1963-66, pres. univ., 1966—; dir. City Nat. Bank. Past chmn. New Detroit Inc., Georgetown U.; commr. mem. North Central Accrediting Assn.; mem. Detroit Bd. Police Commrs. Bd. dirs. Detroit Pub. TV Found., Detroit Urban League, Met. Fund, United Found., Wayne County Health Found.; regional chmn. Rhodes Scholarship Selection Com. Fellow Philosophy Edn. Soc.; mem. Assn. Jesuit Colls. and Univs., Nat. Cath. Edn. Assn., Newcomen Soc., Econ. Club Detroit (dir.), Greater Detroit C. of C., Inst. Econ. Edn. (dir.), Alpha Sigma Nu, Phi Delta Kappa, Phi Kappa Phi. Club: Economic (Detroit). Author: The Contract Colleges of Cornell University, 1958; Readings in the Philosophy of Education, 1960. Address: U Detroit Detroit MI 48221

CARROON, ROBERT GIRARD, clergyman, historian; b. Kansas City, Mo., May 24, 1937; s. Matthew Arnold and Agnes Girardeau (Squire) C.; B.A., Ind. State U., 1959; M.Div., Nashotah House Theol. Sem., 1962; M.A., U. Wis., 1970; postgrad. Marquette U., 1970—. Ordained to ministry Episcopal Ch., 1962; curate St. Luke's Episcopal Ch., Racine, Wis., 1962-64; canon pastor, dean All Saints Cathedral, Milw., 1964-68; curator Milw. County Hist. Soc., historiographer Episcopal Diocese of Milw., 1968—. Teaching asst. U. Wis., Milw., 1964-67; instr. Inst. Geneal. Research, Samford U., Birmingham, Ala., 1974. Fellow Soc. Antiquaries Scotland; mem. Greater Milw. Council Chs., Milw. Ministerial Assn. (treas. 1967-69), Clan Donald Soc. Edinburgh, Clan Donald Soc. U.S.A. (Midwestern commr. 1974—), Stair Soc., Scottish History Soc., Scottish Ch. History Soc., An Commun Gaelic, St. Andrew Soc. Milw. (historian 1977—), Black Watch Regimental Assn., 1745 Assn., SAR (genealogist gen. 1977—), Huguenot Soc. (Wis. pres. 1977—). Contbr. articles to various publs. Home: 1100 W Wells St Milwaukee WI 53233 Office: 910 N 3d St Milwaukee WI 53203

CARROW, LEON ALBERT, physician; b. Chgo., Jan. 18, 1924; s. Charles and Mollie (Sachs) C.; B.S., U. Chgo., 1945, M.D., 1947; m. Joan Twaddell, June 21, 1974; children by previous marriage—Elizabeth, James. Intern Cook County Hosp. and Chgo. Lying-In Hosp., 1947-48; resident Chgo. Wesley Meml. Hosp., Chgo. Maternity Center, 1949-51; sr. attending physician in obstetrics and gynecology Northwestern Meml. Hosp., 1954—; asso. prof. obstetrics and gynecology Northwestern U. Med. Sch., 1967-73, prof. clin. obstetrics and gynecology, 1973—. Served with AUS, 1944-46; to capt. USAF, 1952-53. Fellow A.C.S.; mem. Ill., Chgo. med. socs., AMA, Chgo. Gynecology Soc., Am. Soc. Cytology, Central Assn. Obstetrics and Gynecology. Contbr. articles to profl. jours. Home: 566 Cedar St Winnetka IL 60093 Office: 251 E Chicago Ave Chicago IL 60611

CARRUTHERS, MARY MCNEIL, physician, med. educator; b. Detroit, Oct. 9, 1936; d. Thomas Francis and Ann Clare (Kobe) McNeil; B.S., U. Detroit, 1957; M.D., Wayne State U., 1962; m. Thomas Carruthers, July 25, 1959; children—Karen, Neil, Eileen. Intern, Detroit Gen. Hosp., 1962-63, resident in internal medicine, 1963-64, trainee in infectious diseases, 1965-68; resident in internal medicine, Henry Ford Hosp., Detroit, 1964-65; trainee in infectious diseases, Wayne State U., 1965-68; attending physician, med. service and chief, infectious diseases service, Mt. Sinai Hosp., Chgo., 1968-72, VA Lakeside Hosp., Chgo., 1972—; vis. physician, Northwestern Meml. Hosp., Chgo., 1974; instr. medicine, Wayne State U., 1966-68; asst. prof. medicine, Chgo. Med. Sch., 1968-72, Sch. Medicine, Northwestern U., 1972—. Diplomate Am. Bd. Internal Medicine. Fellow A.C.P.; mem. Infectious Diseases Soc. Am., Am. Soc. Microbiology, Am. Fedn. Clin. Research, Alpha Omega Alpha. Home: 510 Sheridan Rd Winnetka IL 60093 Office: 333 E Huron St Chicago IL 60611

CARSELLO, CARMEN JOSEPH, educator; b. Chgo., July 16, 1915; s. Joseph Anthony and Mary Domenica (Tomassone) C.; B.P.E., DePaul, 1938, M.A., 1953; A.B., Central YMCA Coll., 1943; postgrad. U. Chgo., 1954-64, Ill. Inst. Tech., 1965-69; Ph.D., Laurence U., 1971; m. Nicoletta Dalesio, June 18, 1939; children—Camille Drab, Stanley Drab, Frank, Robert. Tchr., Chgo. parochial schs., 1939-42, Cicero pub. schs., 1942-43; tchr. Chgo. pub. schs., 1950-57, reading specialist Bur. Child Study, 1957-63; prof. edn., reading specialist U. Ill., Chgo., 1963—, dir. Reading Center; lectr. U. Chgo., Northwestern U., Roosevelt U., DePaul U., Chgo. State Coll., Triton Coll.; cons. Chgo. Reading and Speech Clinic, Cal Test Bur., 1966, dept. mental health Chgo. Bd. Health, 1966, Lyon and Carnahan, 1967, Scott Foresman, Fed. Trade Commn.; presented paper World Congress Reading, Singapore, 1976. Active Boy Scouts Am., 1938-57; mem. Water Safety and First Aid Inst. ARC, 1938-57; mem. Right to Read Com.; mem. arrangements com. Ill. Psychol. Assn., 1968; mem. pub. relations com. Midwest Psychol. Assn., 1968-69; mem. Near West Side Community Com., 1939—; mem. Joint Civic Com. of Italian Americans, 1965—; election judge, 1970. Served with USN, 1943-45. Recipient citation for service West Side Community Com., 1966; Service award Chgo. Fedn. Community Coms., 1967; commendation for service Loyola U., 1969-77. Mem. Chgo. Area Reading Assn. (pres. 1971-72), Am. Psychol. Assn., Am. Ednl. Research Assn., Internat. Reading Assn., Internat. Council on Edn. for Teaching, Nat. Soc. for Study Edn., Alpha Phi Omega (chmn. faculty advisers, service award U. Ill. chpt. 1971). Inventor adjustable light shield. Contbr. articles to profl. jours. Home: 2154 N Nordica Ave Chicago IL 60635 Office: Box 4348 Chicago IL 60680

CARSON, HAROLD RUHL, store fixture co. exec.; b. Tecumseh, Mich., Aug. 10, 1942; s. Alexander and Barbara (Ruhl) C.; Jr. Accountant degree, Davis Bus. Coll., 1961; student Internat. Accounts Soc., 1963-64; m. Karen Ann Drodt, July 28, 1962; children—Dawn Marie, Christine Ann. Office mgr. Bulman Corp., Toledo, 1961-62; chief accountant Ida (Mich.) Farmers Co-Operative, 1962-64; asst. to owner Crown State Equipment Co., Toledo, 1964-65, sec., treas., 1965-71, controller, 1971—. Treas. E. Ida Immanuel Lutheran Ch., 1967-71, elder, 1974—. Mem. Toledo Area C. of C. Home: 421 Substation Rd Temperance MI 48182 Office: Call Box 402 1302 Kittle Rd Holland OH 43528

CARSON, RAYMOND DOW, optometrist; b. Portsmouth, O., Feb. 9, 1930; s. Eugene Isaac and Harriet Edith (Spohn) C.; student Ohio U., 1949-50; D. Optometry, Ohio State U., 1954, postgrad., 1954; postgrad., Ind. U., 1955; m. Marjorie Winifred Milward, Oct. 1, 1961; children—Scott, Kelly. Pvt. practice optometry, Portsmouth, 1955—; pres. Ramaro Inc., Portsmouth, 1968—, Ramaro Leasing Co., 1972—; pres. Shawnee Marine Inc., 1972—; dir. Taylor Sound Inc., Columbus, O.; pres. Greenery Outlet, 1976—; v.p. Newark Gardens, Inc., 1976—. Pres. Portsmouth Little Theater, 1957; pres. Scioto County Cancer Soc., 1959; dir. Scioto County chpt. A.R.C., 1972-75; dir. Scioto County Mental Health Assn., 1956—; mem. exec. com. River Days Festival, 1965-77, chmn., 1974-77; active Boy Scouts Am. Pres. Portsmouth Bd. Health, 1970—; chmn. Scioto Environmental Health, 1971-72; mem. exec. com. Scioto County Comprehensive Health Planning, 1971-77. Pres., Young Republican Club, 1960; finance chmn. Scioto County Rep. Party, 1972-73, mem. adv. com. 1972-73. Served with AUS, 1948-49. Fellow Eye Research Found., Royal Soc. Health, Internat. Coll. Ocular Sci.; mem. Am., Ohio, S. Ohio (pres. 1960), Tri State (dir. 1971—) optometric assns., Internat. Platform Assn., Bus. and Profl. Men's Club (dir. 1970—), Portsmouth Area C. of C. (v.p. 1966-75), Ohio Jaycees (state v.p. 1961-62), Methodist (exec. bd.). Lion (past state gov.), Elk, Mason. Home: 3638 Sheridan Rd Portsmouth OH 45662 Office: 1915 Scioto Trail Portsmouth OH 45662 also 8200 Gallia St Wheelersburg OH 45662

CARSON, SANDRA MARIE, sch. counselor; b. Maryville, Mo., Feb. 5, 1948; d. Charles Wesley and Marcia Jean (Martin) Cornell; B.M.E., Kans., U., 1970, M.S.E., 1975; m. David Eugene Carson, July 1, 1973; 1 son, Kyle David. Instrumental music tchr. elementary and secondary schs. Shawnee Mission (Kans.) Pub. Schs., 1970-73; substitute manpower tchr., counselor Kansas City (Kans.) Schs., 1974; elementary counselor Title 111 Spice Program, Ottawa (Kans.) Pub. Schs., 1975—; counselor, tutor minority high sch. students. Mem. Am., Kans., N.E. Kans. Area personnel and guidance assns., NEA. Contbr. Career Edn. Learning Packet, 5th grade, 1975. Home: Route 3 Box 56C Lawrence KS 66044

CARTER, ANNA CURRY (MRS. E. KEMPER CARTER), civic worker; b. Kansas City, Mo.; d. William Adams and Susan Maud (Machette) Curry; B.S., U. Mo., 1918; M.A., Columbia, 1930; postgrad. Oxford (Eng.) U., 1935; m. E. Kemper Carter, Feb. 22, 1936 (dec. Dec. 1951); 1 son, E. Kemper (dec.). Tchr., researcher Kansas City pub. schs., 1919-21; dir. speech and dramatics Westport Jr. High Sch., Kansas City, 1921-26; head speech dept. S.W. High Sch., Kansas City, 1926-36. Bd. govs. Kansas City Mus. History and Sci., 1960—, trustee, 1967-76; parliamentarian women's div. Kansas City Philharmonic Assn., 1964-76; mem. exec. and adv. bds. Community Children's Theatre, 1955, bd. dirs., mem. at large, 1958-76; mem. Soc. Fellows William Rocktrell Nelson Gallery Art, 1966-76; mem. Nat. Com. for Citizens Rights in Broadcasting, 1970-76; Freedoms Found. at Valley Forge, 1968—; hon. fellow Harry S. Truman Library; sponsor Winston Churchill Meml., Fulton, Mo. Hon. bd. dirs. Kansas City Art Inst. and Sch. Design; trustee Conservatory of Music, U. Mo. at Kansas City, Kansas City Philharmonic Orch. Assn., 1973-76. Recipient citations Skowhegan Sch. Art, N.Y.C., Kansas City Art Inst., 1976, Rockhurst Coll., Kansas City, 1974-76. Mem. A.A.U.W., Alliance Francaise (exec. bd.), English Speaking Union, Gen. Assembly Sci. Pioneers (past pres.), Alpha Phi. Baptist. Clubs: College, Woman's City, Carriage (charter mem.), Mission Hills Country, River, Kansas City, Rockhill Tennis; Capitol Hill (Washington). Home: Wornall Plaza 310 W 49th St Kansas City MO 64112

CARTER, BURDELLIS LAVERNE, univ. dean; b. Cloverland, Ind., Sept. 5, 1932; d. Charles Lionel and Dosia Vernice (Slack) Carter; B.A., Ind. Central Coll., 1954; diploma Methodist Hosp. Ind. Sch. Nursing, 1957; M.S. in Nursing Edn., Ind. U., 1961, Ed.D., 1965. Supr. Meth. Hosp., Indpls., 1957-60; instr. Coll. Nursing, U. Iowa, 1961-63; with Ind. U. Sch. Nursing, Indpls., 1964—, asst. prof., 1965-68, asso. prof., 1968-72, prof., 1972—, asst. dean student services, 1971—. Recipient award for outstanding teaching and community service Indpls. Field chpt. Pi Lambda Theta, 1969; named one of Outstanding Young Women, 1965. Mem. Am. Nurses Assn., Nat. League Nursing, Am. Assn. Higher Edn., Am. Assn. U. Profs., Council Nurse Researchers, Am. Personnel and Guidance Assn., Am. Assn. Collegiate Registrars and Admission Officers, Pi Lambda Theta, Sigma Theta Tau. Methodist (ch. choir). Office: 1100 W Michigan St Indianapolis IN 46202

CARTER, CHARLES BENJAMIN, physician; b. Tillman, S.C., Sept. 15, 1937; s. Samuel Marvin and Letha (Sanders) C.; B.S., Coll. Charleston (S.C.), 1959; M.D., Med. Coll. of S.C., 1963; m. Eleanor Collins, June 18, 1960; children—Charles Benjamin, Allyson, Geoffrey, Stuart. Intern. U. Va. Hosp., Charlottesville, 1963-64, resident in internal medicine, 1964-66, renal fellow, 1966-68; co-dir. kidney transplant program Meth. Hosp., Indpls., 1971—, chmn. sect. internal medicine, 1976—. Served with U.S. Army, 1968-71. Diplomate Am. Bd. Internal Medicine. Mem. Am. Soc. Nephrology, Am. Soc. Artificial Internal Organs, A.C.P., AMA, Nat. Kidney Found., Am. Fedn. Clin. Research, Porsche Club Am. Methodist. Contbr. articles to med. jours. Home: 35 Maple Crest Dr Carmel IN 46032 Office: Meth Hosp 1604 N Capitol Ave Indianapolis IN 46202

CARTER, CHRISTIE HEISTAND, dentist; b. Springfield, Ohio, June 18, 1923; s. Christie D. and Leona D. (Moore) C.; student Wittenberg U., 1946-48; D.D.S., Ohio State U., 1952; m. Vivian Hehl, Aug. 2, 1952; children—Lisa, Christie Neal, Terri. Dental intern Marine Hosp., Balt., 1952-53; pvt. dental practice, Springfield, Ohio, 1953—; mem. dental staff Mercy Hosp., 1953—. Served with USNR, 1942-46, USPHS, 1952-53. Fellow Acad. Internat. Dentistry, Acad. Gen. Dentistry; mem. Am. Soc. Dentistry for Children, Dental Inst. U.S., Am. Soc. Preventive Dentistry, Fedn. Dentaire Internationale, Am. Dental Soc. Anesthesiology, Mad River Valley Dental Soc. (pres. 1960-61), Am., Ohio dental assns., Springfield C. of C., Phi Gamma Delta, Psi Omega. Republican. Lutheran. Club: Springfield Country. Home: 1927 Fairway Dr Springfield OH 45504 Office: 1209 N Plum St Springfield OH 45504

CARTER, EARL THOMAS, physician, educator; b. Baltimore, Md., July 7, 1922; s. Earl and Thelma Eva (Bernheim) C.; B.S., Northwestern U., 1945, M.D., 1948; Ph.D. in Physiology, U. Tex., 1955; m. Barbara Carol Williamson, Aug. 16, 1947; children—Carol Lynn, Janice Gail, Steven Earl, Jeffrey Frank. Research physiologist, flight surgeon USAF, 1951-55; asst. prof. preventive medicine, physiology, instr. in medicine Ohio State Univ. Med. Sch., Columbus, 1956-60; mem. staff dept. medicine Mayo Clinic, 1960—, prof., chmn. div. preventive medicine, 1975—; prof. preventive medicine Mayo Sch. Medicine, 1974—; Med. dir. Northwest Airlines, Inc., 1968—. Diplomate Am. Bd. Preventive Medicine. Fellow A.C.P., Am. Coll. Preventive Medicine; mem. Am., Minn. State lMed. Assn., Aerospace Med. Assn. (pres. 1974-75), Airline Med. Dir's. Assn. (pres. 1976-77), Assn. Tchr's. of Preventive Medicine, Internat. Acad. Aerospace Medicine, Soc. Prospective Medicine. Methodist. Contbr. sci. publs. to med. jours. Home: 907 13th Ave SW Rochester MN 55901 Office: 200 Second St SW Rochester MN 55901

CARTER, EVERETT BARTON, nursing home adminstr.; b. Douglas County, Ill., Sept. 13, 1919; s. Hascue Barton and Bessie Luella (Foster) C.; student Union Bible Sem., 1940; Certificate in Accounting, LaSalle Extension U., 1956; m. Julia Winifred Riley, Aug. 8, 1940; children—Jon Geoffrey, Brian Frederick, Anne Riley (Mrs. Terry Cobbs). Minister, Pilgrim Holiness Ch., 1935-40, Friends Ch., 1940-52; asst. cashier Union State Bank, Carmel, Ind., 1945-50; accountant Flesch-Miller Tractor Co., Indpls., 1951, Apex Tool & Die Co., Indpls., 1952; accountant Gt. Commissions Schs., Anderson, Ind., 1953-55; bookkeeping supr. Citizens Banking Co., Anderson, 1955-62; denominational treas. Wesleyan Methodist Ch., Marion, Ind., 1962-68; sr. accountant L.A. Easterday C.P.A., Kokomo, Ind., 1968-73; adminstr. Wesleyan Nursing Home, Marion, 1973—. Trustee Marion Coll., 1963-72, Frankfort Bible Coll., 1968-71, Owosso (Mich.) Coll., 1968-71, Ind. North Dist. Wesleyan Ch., 1968—; bd. dirs. subarea III Central Ind. Health Systems Agy., 1976-77, mem. fin. feasibility com., 1976-77, long term advisory com., 1976-77. C.P.A., Ind. Mem. Am. Inst. C.P.A.'s, Ind. Assn. C.P.A.'s, Nat. Assn. Accountants, Am. Accounting Assn., Am. Coll. Nursing Home Adminstrs., Ind. Health Care Assn. (dist. chmn. 1976-77). Wesleyan (sec. Bd. Pensions gen. ch. 1968—). Home: 4002 S Boots St Marion IN 46952 Office: 518 W 36th St Marion IN 46952

CARTER, GEORGE EDWARD, educator; b. Leominster, Mass., Sept. 16, 1934; s. Lester Earl and Anita (Bourque) C.; B.A., Calif. State U., 1960; lM.A., 1962; Ph.D., U. Oreg., 1970; m. Carmen Ophelia Vazquez, Nov. 13, 1954; children—Lydia, David, Russell, Douglas. Asst. prof. St. Cloud (Minn.) State Coll., 1965-66; asst. prof. Bishops U., Lennoxville, Que., Can., 1966-68; asso. editor Papers of Daniel Webster, Dartmouth Coll., Hanover, N.H., 1968-70; dir. minority studies U. Wis., LaCrosse, 1970—, editor Black Abolitionist Papers project, 1976—; reviewer Nat. Endowment Humanities, 1976—. Mem. Wis. Humanities Com., 1973—. Served with U.S. Army, 1953-56. Nat. Hist. Pubs. Commn. fellow, 1966-67; Nat. Endowment for the Humanities fellow, 1973-74. Mem. Nat. Assn. for Interdisciplinary Ethnic Studies (sec.-treas. 1975—), ACLU, Wis. Civil Liberties Union, Am. Hist. Assn., Orgn. Am. Historians, Canadian Hist. Assn., Assn. for Canadian Studies in U.S., Nat. Assn. for Interdisciplinary Ethnic Studies. Soc. Friends. Contbr. articles in field to profl. jours. Home: 101 S 17th St LaCrosse WI 54601 Office: 101 Main Hall Univ of Wis LaCrosse WI 54601

CARTER, GEORGE EDWARD, ret. newspaper exec.; b. Kenton, O., Aug. 24, 1910; s. Lloyd Denver and Sarah Lucretia (Quayle) C.; A.B. Western Res. U., 1932, A.M., 1933, student law sch., 1933-34; m. Harriette Withington, Aug. 19, 1944; children—William (dec.), Cornelia (Mrs. Earl Miller), Sarah (Mrs. Charles L. West). With Scripps-Howard Newspapers, 1934—, sales rep., Times Press, Akron, O., 1934-37, sales rep., gen. office, Chgo., 1937-45, pres., bus. mgr. Ft. Worth Press, 1945-52, bus. mgr. Cleve. Press, 1952—, asst. v.p. E. W. Scripps Co. Mem. Phi Gamma Delta. Clubs: Union, Chagrin Valley Hunt. Home: Berkshire Rd Gates Mills OH 44040

CARTER, JACK FRANKLIN, agronomist, educator; b. Lodgepole, Nebr., Oct. 1, 1919; s. Thomas Baker and Mary Lee (Watkins) C.; B.S., U. Nebr., 1941; M.S., Wash. State U., 1947; Ph.D., U. Wis., 1950; m. Iris Imogene Smith, Oct. 19, 1941; children—Nancy (Mrs. Eric Svendsen), Stephen, Jeffrey, Joel, Brian. Grad. asst. Wash. State U., 1941-42, 45-47; grad. research asst. U. Wis., 1947-50; asso. prof., prof., chmn. dept. agronomy N.D. State U., Fargo, 1950—. Served with USNR, 1941-45. Fellow Am. Soc. Agronomy (dir.); mem. Crop Sci. Soc. Am. (pres.), Council Agrl. Sci. and Tech. (dir., pres.-elect), Sigma Xi, Alpha Zeta. Methodist. Home: 1345 N 11th St Fargo ND 58102

CARTER, JERRY RALPH, feed ingredient co. exec.; b. Springfield, Mo., Jan. 11, 1930; s. Lloyd Ralph and Atrelle (Ward) C.; B.S., Drury Coll., 1951; m. Blanchelen Campbell, June 15, 1951; children—Cheri Ellen, Thomas Lloyd, Timmithoy James. Salesman, Nat. Biscuit Co., Springfield, 1954-59; mgr. Southwest Rendering Co., Inc., Springfield, 1959—; mgr. Southwest By-Products, Inc., Springfield, 1959—, pres., 1961—. Served with USAF, 1951-54. Mem. Nat. Renderers Assn. (regional pres. 1971-72), Drury Coll. Alumni (pres. 1975). Episcopalian (vestry 1964-65). Mason (K.T., Shriner, Jester). Home: 2732 E Seminole St Springfield MO 65804 Office: PO Box 2876 CSS Springfield MO 65803

CARTER, JOHN SAMUEL, structural engr.; b. Corning, N.Y., June 9, 1920; s. John Quincy and Sarah (Gardner) C.; student Ball State U., Muncie, Ind., 1939; B.S. in Civil Engring., Mich. State U., 1949; m. Betty Jean Jones, Dec. 6, 1941; children—Elizabeth Ann (Mrs. David Luther), John Edwin, Robert Christopher, Brian David. Draftsman, insp. Am. Bridge div. U.S. Steel Corp., Gary, Ind., 1949-53, designer, Chgo., 1953-63; chief engr. Allied Structural Steel Co., Hammond, Ind., 1963-66, v.p. engring. 1966-69, asst. to pres., 1969-70, exec. v.p., 1970-73; gen. mgr. Inryco, Inc., Milw., 1973—. Served with AUS, 1940-45. Mem. Am. Soc. C.E., Tau Beta Pi. Mason. Home: 13430 Commons Dr Brookfield WI 53005 Office: 4101 Burnham St Milwaukee WI 53201

CARTER, LEON ARTHUR, accountant; b. Childress, Tex., Jan. 2, 1910; s. James Frank and Madge (Taylor) C.; B.A., Abilene Christian Coll., 1931; M.A., U. Tex., 1937; m. Marie Andrews, June 30, 1935; children—Martha Anne (Mrs. Robert A. Baker), William James, David Leon. Prin. high schs. Kirkland, Tex., 1931-34, Quail, Tex., 1935-41; mgr. office Nutrena Mills, Kansa City, Kan., 1942-46; practice pub. accounting, Mission, Kan., 1947—; sec. Kentucky Hills, Inc., Independence, Mo., 1957—. Chmn. liaison com. IRS, 1964-68. Mem. Pub. Accountants Assn. Kan. (pres. 1961-63), Nat. Soc. Pub. Accountants. Mem. Ch. of Christ (elder). Optimist (v.p. Kansas City 1960). Home: 6433 Woodson Dr Mission KS 66202 Office: 5800 Foxridge Dr Suite 619 Mission KS 66202

CARTER, SIDNEY EVANS, chiropractor; b. Burlington, Iowa, June 18, 1944; s. Ned Neal and Thyrel Evalyn (Driskel) C.; student Burlington Jr. Coll., 1962-63; D.C., Palmer Coll. Chiropractic, 1971; Certificate in Acupuncture, Nat. Coll. Chiropractic, 1975; m. Peggy Lee Mumme, June 9, 1974. Intern, Palmer Coll. Chiropractic Out-Patient Clinic, Davenport, Iowa, 1970-71; practice chiropractic, Burlington, 1973—. Recipient Leviathan award Clinic Masters, 1974, Badge of Honor, Am. Found. for Chiropractic Edn., 1975. Diplomate Nat. Bd. Chiropractic Examiners. Mem. Am. Chiropractic Assn., Iowa Chiropractic Soc., Am. Inst. Chiropractic (charter mem.), Am. Council Mental Health, Profl. Chiropractic Assn. Ins. Rev., Burlington C. of C. Mason (32 deg.), Rotarian, Eagle, Elk. Club: Burlington Golf and Country. Address: 903 N 7th St Burlington IA 52601

CARTER, THOMAS LEE, mech. engr.; b. Charleston, W.Va., Mar. 6, 1943; s. James Garner and Virginia Mae (Reed) C.; B.S. in Mech. Engring., U. Tenn., 1965; postgrad., 1965-68; postgrad. Pa. State U., 1969-73, Iowa State U., 1975—; m. Brenda Lynn Chambers, July 2, 1965; children—Thomas Craig, Gina Leann. With Aluminum Co. Am., 1961—, group leader Alcoa Labs., Alcoa Center, Pa., 1971-75, div. engr. Davenport Works (Iowa), 1975-76, chief mech. engr., Davenport Works, 1976-78, engring. mgr. Lafayette Works (Ind.), 1978—. Adviser Jr. Achievement, Tarentum, Pa., 1971-72; youth guidance counselor Youth Guidance Inc., Pitts., 1972-75. Registered profl. engr., Pa. Mem. ASME. Democrat. Baptist. Home: 5246 Surrey Dr Bettendorf IA 52722 Office: PO Box 500 Lafayette IN 47902

CARTWRIGHT, CHARLES BERT, dentist, univ. ofcl.; b. Mesilla Park, N.Mex., Aug. 10, 1923; s. Charles Abel and Margaret Julia (Elgin) C.; student Cleary Coll., 1941-42; student Eastern Mich. U., 1946-48; D.D.S., U. Mich., 1952, M.S., 1960; m. Jo Anne Virginia Draper, Aug. 12, 1950; children—Jane, Nancy, Suzanne, James. Pvt. practice dentistry, Ypsilanti, Mich., 1952-69; mem. faculty U. Mich. at Ann Arbor, 1958-72, asst. dean, Sch. Dentistry, 1972—. Mem. Mich. State Bd. Dentistry. Served with USNR, 1942-46. Mem. med. bd. Project Hope. Mem. Mich. Dental Assn. (chmn. sci. com.), Psi Omega (v.p.), Omicron Kappa Upsilon. Republican. Presbyn. (elder, deacon). Author: (with Louis C. Schultz and others) Operative Dentistry, 1966; (with G.T. Charbineau and others) Restorative Dentistry. Contbr. articles to profl. jours. Home: 4 Westbury Ct Ann Arbor MI 48104

CARUSO, SAVERIO, psychiatrist; b. Plati, Italy, Apr. 1, 1925; s. Giuseppe and Francesca (Scarfo) C.; M.D., U. Turin (Italy), 1955; m. Domenica Margaret Zappia, Oct. 24, 1953; children—Josephine, Rosemary, Joseph Michael, Michelle, Cynthia. Came to U.S., 1955, naturalized, 1958. Intern, Mercy Hosp., Hamilton, O., 1956-57, resident, 1957-58; resident in psychiatry Ohio State U., 1958-63; staff psychiatrist Cambridge (O.) State Hosp., 1963-64; clin. dir. Massillon (O.) State Hosp., 1964-66, supt., 1966-72, cons., 1972—; practice medicine specializing in psychiatry, Canton, O., 1972—; chmn. dept. psychiatry Timken Mercy Hosp., Canton, 1976-77. Mem. com. on urban edn. Ohio State Bd. Edn., 1969-71; mem. Stark County Mental Health Retardation Bd., 1968-72, Urban League of Massillon, 1970-71, Stark County Cath. Bd. Edn., 1970. Fellow Royal Soc. Health, Am. Psychiat. Assn.; mem. A.M.A., Stark County Med. Soc. K.C., Elk. Club: Unique (Canton). Home: 3886 Croydon Dr NW Canton OH 44718 Office: 1445 Harrison St Canton OH 44708

CARUTHERS, WILLIAM CLARK, photography studio exec.; b. Cape Girardeau, Mo., Apr. 27, 1913; s. William Pickney and Ada Maude (Norwine) C.; A.B., Southeast Mo. State U., 1930-34; m. Ellen Frances Tatum, Aug. 28, 1939; children—William Clark, Sally Kay (Mrs. Randolph Johnson), Mary Gail (Mrs. George Edward Schenk), Thomas Tatum. Profl. musician and tchr. music, Cape Girardeau, 1930-44; tchr. history, music, English, Perryville (Mo.) High Sch., 1934-42; instr. USAAF, Scott Field, Ill., 1943-46, coordinator of tng., 1944-46; sales mgr. Todd Studios, Inc., St. Louis, 1946-50, pres. and chmn. bd., 1950—. Guest soloist with John Philip Sousa Band, 1930; dir. music French Line Steamship Co., Paris, France, 1937-39; dir. Perryville (Mo.) Municipal Band, 1936-42; asst. dir. Cape Girardeau, Municipal Band, 1932-42; asst. dir. Southeast Mo. State U. Men's Glee Club, 1933-34; dir. Inst. on Advt., St. Louis U. and Advt. Club of St. Louis, 1950-62; lectr. adult classes St. Louis U. and Washington U., St. Louis, 1950-72; job opportunity cons. to St. Louis High Schs. Dist. commr. St. Louis chpt. Boy Scouts Am., 1961-71. Recipient

Civilian citations for Meritorious Service, USAAF, Army Air Force, 1944, 45, President's award Advt. Club of St. Louis, 1953, 54, 55. Mem. Indsl. Mktg. Club St. Louis (v.p., dir. 1948-58), Advt. Club St. Louis (v.p., dir. 1956-60). Republican. Presbyn. Home: 9 Black Oak Dr St Louis MO 63127 Office: Todd Studios Inc 4243 Lindell Blvd St Louis MO 63108

CARVER, CHARLOTTE MAHR, coll. adminstr.; b. Cleve., Feb. 17, 1925; d. Harry S. and Anna (Luntz) Mahr; student Case Inst. Tech., 1942-43, U. Dayton, 1943-45, Ohio State U., 1946-48; B.S. in Edn., Kent State U., 1964, M.Ed., 1966, postgrad., 1966-72; Ph.D. in Edn., U. Sarasota, 1972; 1 son, Christopher James. Mem. staff U.S. Govt. Signal Corps, Dayton, Ohio, 1942-46, civilian in charge identification and correlation unit, 1945-46; indsl. engr. Seagrave Fire Engine Co., Columbus, Ohio, 1948-49; co-founder Pneu-Hydraulics, Inc., Cleve., 1954-57; tchr. St. Barnabas Sch., Northfield, Ohio, 1959-61; head math. dept. Woodridge High Sch., Peninsula, Ohio, 1962-66; elementary guidance counselor North Royalton (Ohio) schs., 1966-67; dir. guidance Brecksville (Ohio) city schs., 1967-74; asst. dean arts, sci. and profl. edn. Rio Grande (Ohio) Coll., 1974—; reporter Cleve. Press, part-time 1956-59; mem. grad. faculty St. John Coll., Cleve., part-time 1970-74; spl. lectr. Ursuline Coll., Cleve., 1969; cons. Richland County Sch. System, 1969, 71-73. Mem. nat. adv. com. Coll. Admission Center, Chgo., 1968-71; governing bd. Southeastern Ohio Regional Edn. service Agency, 1974—; hon. admissions counselor U.S. Naval Acad., Annapolis, Md., 1968—; mem. Cleve. Commn. Higher Edn., 1970-74; chmn. evaluation teams accreditation North Central Assn. and Ohio Dept. Edn., 1970—; chmn. evaluation teams Cosmetology Accrediting Commn., 1977—; Midwest and nat. rep. adv. com. coll. testing Am. Coll. Testing Program, 1969-71, Nat. Com. Coll. Testing, 1971. Recipient certificate recognition U.S. Signal Corps, 1944, USAF, 1945, 70, DECA Clubs Am., 1968; named Hon. Citizen, Lexington, Ky., 1969. Mem. Ohio Vocat. Assn., Nat. (state rep. 1969-74), Ohio (exec. com. 1969-74, editor quar. 1971-72) assns. coll. admissions counselors, Assn. Colls. Tchr. Edn., Assn. Tchr. Educators (regional coordinator 1976-77), Southeastern Ohio Council Tchrs. English (coordinator 1975), Nat., Ohio, Northeastern Ohio, Brecksville edn. assns., Am. Assn. Higher Edn., Kappa Delta Pi, Delta Kappa Gamma. Founder, editor Voice of Hills Community Newspaper, 1956-59, Brecksville Sr. High Sch.'s Guidance Newsline, 1967-74. Patentee automated scheduler. Home: 630 Jay Dr Gallipolis OH 45631 Office: Rio Grande Coll Rio Grande OH 45674

CARVER, GERFORD CHESTER, mech. engr.; b. Battle Creek, Mich., July 11, 1929; s. Chester Gerford and Gertrude Marguerite (Stock) C.; B.M.E., Mich. Technol. U., 1950; M.S., Chrysler Inst., 1956; m. Eleanor Anne Dunne, June 25, 1955; children—John, James, Marguerite, Elizabeth, William, Sara. Shop liaison engr., detailer Clark Equipment Co., Battle Creek, 1950; test engr. Chrysler Corp., Highland Park, Mich., 1952-55, welding engr., 1955-56; div. project engr. Midland Ross Corp., Cleve., 1956-62; chief engr. R.S.L. Corp., Cleve., 1962; account engr. A.O. Smith Corp., Milw., 1962—. Served in arty. U.S. Army, 1950-52. Registered profl. engr., Ohio. Mem. Soc. Automotive Engrs., Am. Welding Soc., Am. Soc. Metals, Engring. Soc. Milw. Clubs: Snowstar Ski (asst. head instr.) (Milw.); Fairlane (Dearborn, Mich.). Home: 880 E Birch St Milwaukee WI 53217 Office: 3533 N 27th St Milwaukee WI 53216

CARVER, RICHARD GLEASON, engr.; b. Battle Creek, Mich., Feb. 2, 1938; s. Chester Gerford and Gertrude Marguerite (Stock) C.; student U. Mich., 1954-55; B.C.E., with honors, Mich. Tech. U., 1972, B.S. in Engring. Adminstrn. with honors, 1972; postgrad. in Pub. Adminstrn., Western Mich. U., 1976—; 1 son, Mark Richard. Instrumentman, design div. Mich. Bur. Hwys., Mich. Dept. State Hwys. and Transp., Lansing, 1954, 55-56, 60-63, 65-68, office engr., sr. instrumentman constrn. div., 1972-75, asst. project engr., 1975, hazard and environ. engr., bur. aeros., Capital City Airport, 1975—; survey crew chief Mich. Dept. Natural Resources, 1968; electronics insp. autonetics div. N. Am. Aviation, Southgate, Calif., 1960; engring. aid. Peckham Engring., Lansing, 1963-65. Served with USN, 1956-60. Mem. ASCE, Tau Beta Pi, Chi Epsilon. Clubs: Elks, Moose. Office: Bur Aeronautics Capital City Airport Lansing MI 48906

CARY, HOWARD BRADFORD, welding engring. exec.; b. Columbus, Ohio, May 24, 1920; s. Harley Bradford and Mildred Emiley (Eckhart) C.; B.S., Ohio State U., 1942; m. Harriet Francis Harmony, Oct. 3, 1942; children—Robert Bradford, Janet Elizabeth (Mrs. Dennis Laabs). Welding engr. Fisher Body div. Gen. Motors Corp., Flint, Mich., 1942-44; research engr. Battelle Meml. Inst., Columbus, 1946-48; welding engr. to asst. works mgr. Marion Power Shovel Co. (Ohio), 1948-58; from tech. center dir. to v.p. Hobart Bros. Co., Troy, Ohio, 1958—; pres., dir. Hobart Sch. Welding Tech. Mem. exchange mission to USSR, 1962, welding trade mission to Australia and Thailand, 1968. Served with USNR, 1944-46; PTO. Recipient Meritorious certificate Am. Welding Soc., 1956, Samuel Wylie Miller Meml. medal, 1971; A.F. Davis Silver medal, 1963, Nat. Safety Council award, 1965. Registered profl. engr., Ohio. Mem. Am. Soc. M.E., Nat. Soc. Profl. Engrs., Am. Welding Soc. (v.p. 1977), Am. Soc. Metals, Brit. Welding Inst., French Inst. Welding, Troy C. of C. (dir.). Club: Sailing. Author: Modern Welding Technology, 1977. Contbr. articles to tech. jours. Patentee in field. Home: 1492 Surrey Rd Troy OH 45373 Office: Hobart Brothers Co W Main St Troy OH 45373

CARY, JOHN MILTON, physician; b. Ewing, Mo., July 11, 1932; s. Milton Madison and Alice (Sells) C.; A.B., Central Coll. Mo., 1954; M.D., St. Louis U., 1958; m. Barbara Ann Dorsey, June 4, 1955; children—Kimberly Anne, John Madison. Intern, Barnes Hosp., St. Louis, 1958-59, resident in internal medicine, 1959-60, subsequently mem. staff; resident in internal medicine St. Lukes Hosp., St. Louis, 1961-62, subsequently mem. staff; fellow in hematology Washington U., St. Louis, 1960-61; practice medicine specializing in internal medicine, St. Louis, 1962—; mem. staff St. Johns Mercy Med. Center; clin. instr. Washington U., 1966—. Mem. ACP, St. Louis Soc. Internal Medicine, Mo. Med. Assn., St. Louis Med. Soc., Alpha Omega Alpha. Presbyterian. Home: 801 Mason Wood Dr St Louis MO 63141 Office: 2821 N Ballas Rd St Louis MO 63131

CARYER, JANE HATHEWAY, interior designer; b. Ottawa, Ill., Apr. 15, 1924; d. Elanathan P. and Vera (O'Connell) Hatheway; B.A., U. Wis., 1946; postgrad. Madison Bus. Coll., 1946-47. Sr. interior designer Hendrickson's, Inc., Madison, Wis., 1946-59; sr. interior designer, mgr., pres., treas. Jane H. Caryer, Inc., Madison, 1959—. Mem. Dane County Community Welfare Council, 1966-69; pres. Madison Opportunity Center, Inc., 1969-73; bd. dirs. West Side YMCA, 1975—, house chmn., 1977. Mem. Am. Soc. Interior Designers, D.A.R., U. Wis. Alumni Assn., Madison C. of C., Madison Art Assn., Aircraft Owners and Pilots Assn. Republican. Clubs: Altrusa International (treas. 1970-72, dir. 1976—; dist. 7, membership chmn.), Blackhawk Country (Madison). Home: Route 5 Box 37 Stoughton WI 53589 Office: 801 S Gammon Rd Madison WI 53719

CASE, ARTHUR B., gerontol. counselor; b. Red Oak, Ia., Jan. 18, 1937; s. Arthur Dale and Hester (Branan) C.; B.A., Doane Coll., Crete, Neb., 1962; postgrad. Inst. Gerontology, Mich. U.-Wayne State U., 1969; M.Ed., U. Neb., 1975; m. E. Maxine Radin, Mar. 23, 1967; children—Bonnie, Donald, Dale. Counselor, Neb. Rehab. Services for Visually Impaired, Lincoln, 1967-75, counselor to aged, 1973—. Bd. dirs. Lincoln Retirement Hotel; Inc., Neb. Commn. on Aging, 1972. Mem. Am. Assn. Workers for Blind (membership chmn. 1972-73), Nat. Rehab. Counseling Assn. (membership chmn. 1973-74), Neb. Vocat. Evaluation and Work Adjustment Assn. (pres. 1971-72), Gerontol. Soc., United Comml. Travelers (sr. counselor Lincoln council 104 1969-70), Antique Automobile Club Am. Home: 6412 Adams St Lincoln NE 68507 Office: 412 Anderson Bldg Lincoln NE 68508

CASE, HARRY EDGAR, newspaper exec.; b. Mansfield, Ohio, May 12, 1916; s. Edgar Hayes and Verna (Collier) C.; grad. Mansfield High Sch., 1934; m. Elizabeth Loch, Aug. 24, 1940; children—Robert Case, Jane. With Mansfield News-Jour., 1935-48, classified advt. mgr., 1943-48; bus. mgr. Elwood (Ind.) Call-Leader, 1948-53; bus. mgr. Kenton (Ohio) Times, 1953—, Upper Sandusky (Ohio) Chief Union, 1971—; gen. mgr. Morgan County Herald, McConnelsville, Ohio, 1969—. Past pres. Ohio League Home Dailies, Ohio Advt. Execs. Assn. Past pres. Hardin County Airport Authority. Mem. Inland Daily Press Assn., Ohio Newspaper Assn., Kenton Area C. of C. (past pres.). Republican. Roman Catholic. Elk, Rotarian (past pres. Kenton). Home: 693 N Wayne St Kenton OH 43326 Office: 201 E Columbus St Kenton OH 43326

CASERIO, MARTIN JOSEPH, automobile mfg. co. exec.; b. Laurium, Mich., July 18, 1916; s. Joseph and Mary (Michela) C.; B.S. in Metall. Engring., Mich. Technol. U., 1936, D.Sc. in Engring. (hon.), 1961; m. Josephine Spolarich, Oct. 7, 1944; children—Richard, Kathleen, Joseph, Patricia. With AC Spark Plug div. Gen. Motors Corp., Flint, Mich., 1937-57, gen. mgr., 1964-66, mgr. AC Milw. ops., 1957-58, gen. mgr. Delco Radio div., 1958-64, gen. mgr. GMC Truck & Coach div., Pontiac, Mich., 1966-72, gen. mgr. Pontiac Motor div., 1972—, v.p. parent co., 1964—. Active numerous civic orgns.; mem. exec. com. Mich. United Fund; mem. Pontiac Urban Coalition, Oakland County Traffic Improvement Assn. Bd. dirs. Mich. Crippled Children's Soc., 1956-57, United Way Mich.; trustee Pontiac Area United Fund; trustee Mich. Technol. U. Devel. Fund, mem. univ. bd. control; mem. nat. com. sponsors Verrazzano Coll.; trustee, chmn. finance com. St. Joseph Hosp.; exec. com. Meadow Brook Theatre Oakland U. Served to 1st lt. C.E., AUS, World War II. Recipient Silver Knight award Nat. Mgmt. Assn., 1963, Distinguished Service award Mich. Technol. U., 1970. Fellow Am. Soc. Metals (chmn. Saginaw Valley chpt. 1956, mem. finance com.); mem. Inst. Aero. Scis., Am. Ordnance Assn., Am. Rocket Soc., Navy League, Air Force Assn., Soc. Automotive Engrs. (chmn. Mid-Mich. sect. 1955), Am. Mgmt. Assn. (motor truck mfrs. com.), Am. Soc. Quality Control, Engring. Soc. Detroit, Flint Automobile Club (dir. 1954), Flint Indsl. Execs. Club (dir. 1955), Nat. Sheriffs Assn. (hon. life), Tau Beta Pi, Phi Kappa Phi. K.C., Elk. Clubs: Bloomfield Hills Country; Card Sound Golf, Ocean Reef (Key Largo, Fla.); Otsego Ski. Home: 246 Barden Rd Bloomfield Hills MI 48013 Office: Pontiac Motor Division General Motors Corp 1 Pontiac Plaza Pontiac MI 48053

CASEY, FREDERICK JOSEPH, III, lawyer; b. Brainerd, Minn., Apr. 30, 1942; s. Frederick Joseph and Irene Effie (Crawford) C.; B.A., Concordia Coll., 1964; J.D., U. Minn., 1967; m. Mary Lea Brooks, June 13, 1964; children—Paul, Kari, Jill. Admitted to Minn. bar, 1967; mem. firm Erickson & Casey, Brainerd, 1967—; asst. atty. Crow Wing County, Minn., 1967-75. Recipient Reverence for Law award Fraternal Order of Eagles, 1973. Mem. Am., Minn., Crow Wing County bar assn. (pres. 1977), Brainerd Area C. of C. (dir. 1974-76, pres. 1976). Lutheran (councilman 1970-72). Mason (Shriner), Elk, Kiwanian (pres. 1971-72). Home: 2104 Graydon Ave Brainerd MN 56401 Office: 319 S 6th St Brainerd MN 56401

CASEY, PATRICK MICHAEL, computer co. exec.; b. Cazanovia, Wis., Nov. 21, 1930; s. William Robert and Anastasia Veronica (Walsh) C.; grad. Indsl. Mgmt., U. Minn., 1959, Asso. in Adminstrv. Mgmt., 1966; m. Donna Rae Robushin, Apr. 13, 1953; children—Michele Ann, Timothy William, Patrick Sean, Kevin Matthew, Kathleen Marie, Colin Brian, Maureen Bridget. With Sperry Univac, St. Paul, 1956—, dir. operations Univac Tech. Services Div., 1975—; tchr. adult vocational classes in data processing; cons. on computer aided instrn. systems to sch. dists. Chm. Sch. Dist. 272, 1964-70; dir. Hennepin County Vocational Tech. Dist. 287, 1971-76; mem. Eden Prairie Planning and Zoning Bd., 1974. Served with USN, 1948-52. Republican. Roman Catholic. Club: Lions. Home: 17308 Padons Dr Eden Prairie MN 55343 Office: PO Box 3525 Saint Paul MN 55165

CASEY, WILLIAM JERRY, III, steel foundry exec.; b. Highland Park, Ill., Jan. 20, 1925; s. William J. and Mae (Brandt) C.; B.S. in Mech. Engring., Mass. Inst. Tech., 1946; m. Dawn Florence Muriel Benson, Aug. 31, 1951; children—William J., Nigel Bryan, Kathleen Elizabeth. With Am. Steel Foundries and Amsted, 1946—, successively engring. trainee, mech. designer, project engr., engr. analyst, asst. to v.p., tech. asst. fgn. sales, 1946-58, asst. v.p. Amsted Industries Internat. (formerly Am. Steel Foundries, Internat.), 1959-61, v.p., 1962-76, pres., 1976—. Served with USNR, 1943-46. Registered profl. engr., Ill. Mem. Chgo. Athletic Assn., ASME, Western Ry. Club Chgo., Mass. Inst. Tech. Club Chgo., Sigma Xi, Tau Beta Pi, Sigma Chi. Clubs: Internat. Trade, Mid-Am., Executives (Chgo.). Home: 622 Mulberry Pl Highland Park IL 60035 Office: 3700 Prudential Plaza Chicago IL 60601

CASHMARK, JOE JUNIOR, pub. exec.; b. Moulton, Iowa, Jan. 1, 1925; s. Joseph Everett and Zelda (Stansberry) C.; B.C.S., Drake U., 1950; m. Bette Jane Geneva, July 23, 1942; children—Debra Jean, Melanie Jo, Daryn Joel, Rita Diane. With Estherville (Iowa) Daily News, 1950-53, Mchts. Trade Jour., 1954-55, Midwest Farm Paper Unit, 1955-59; with Farm Jour., Inc., 1959—, mgr. office, Kansas City, Mo., 1961-65, v.p., 1965—; pres. C & S, Inc., Albia, Iowa, 1966—, King Communications, Inc., Benton, Ark., 1971—; dir. Cable Communications Corp., Phoenix, 1972—. Served with AUS, 1942-43. Mem. Advt. Fedn. Am. Clubs: Masons, Shriners, Kansas City (Mo.). Home: 8028 Granada Ln Prairie Village KS 66208 Office: Farm Jour Inc 7830 State Line Rd Prairie Village KS 66208

CASJENS, DAVID WILLIAM, lawyer; b. Hull, Iowa, Nov. 15, 1939; s. Floyd M. and Veda H. (Hindt) C.; B.B.A., U. Iowa, 1961, J.D., 1970; m. Charlene Roark, Feb. 5, 1964. Admitted to Iowa bar, 1970; partner firm Hindt & Casjens, Rock Rapids, Iowa, 1970—; atty. Lyon County, Iowa, 1973—; dir. George State Bank (Iowa). Served to capt. USAF, 1962-68. Mem. Am., Iowa, Lyon County, Lawyer-Pilots bar assns., Jr. C. of C., Am. Legion, Alpha Tau Omega. Kiwanian (dir. 1972-73). Home: 701 S Carroll St Rock Rapids IA 51246 Office: 122 S Story St Rock Rapids IA 51246

CASMEY, HOWARD BIRDWELL, state ednl. ofcl.; b. Euclid, Minn., Feb. 4, 1926; s. George and Gladys (Birdwell) C.; B.A., Concordia Coll., 1949; M.A., U. N.D., 1956; m. Eva Mae Lee, Aug. 14, 1949; children—Michael, Kim. Tchr. pub. schs., Plummer, Minn.; supt. schs., Lake Bronson, Minn., Herman, Minn., Ada, Minn., Golden Valley, Minn.; now commr. edn. State of Minn.; dir. Audio Sine Mfg. Co. Served with Armed Forces, World War II. Mem. Chief State Sch. Officers (pres. 1975-76). Home: 7519 Harold Ave Golden Valley MN 55427 Office: State Dept Edn 4th Floor Centennial Bldg St Paul MN 55101

CASPALL, FREDRICK CHARLES, educator; b. McDonough County, Ill., Sept. 24, 1935; s. Ralph and Kathryn (Kelso) C.; B.S., Western Ill. U., 1964, M.S., 1966; Ph.D., U. Kan., 1970; m. Barbara Eloise Holstine, June 1, 1963; children—Debra, Laura. Farmer, McDonough County, Ill., 1952-62; research asst., cons. Center for Research in Engring. Sci., Lawrence, Kan., 1966-69; from asst. prof. to asso. prof. Western Ill. U., 1969—; vis. asst. prof. Pa. State Coll., 1973. Land reclamation cons. Midland Coal Co., Trivoli, Ill., 1974—; environ. cons. AMAX Coal Co., Indpls., 1974, Western Ill. Regional Council, Macomb, 1973—. Mem. Assn. Am. Geographers, Am. Geog. Soc., Nat. Council Geog. Edn., Am. Quaternary Assn., Ill. Acad. Sci. Contbr. articles to profl. jours. Home: 525 E Washington St Macomb IL 61455 Office: Dept Geography Western Ill U Macomb IL 61455

CASPER, DALE EDWARD, librarian, educator; b. Mt. Clemens, Mich., Feb. 24, 1947; s. Edward Lawrence and Shirley May (Harms) C.; B.A., Mich. State U., 1969; M.A., U. of Minn., 1972, M.A. in Library Sci., 1974, postgrad., 1976—; m. Helen M. Haley, July 17, 1970; 1 child—Jared Anthony. Teaching asst. U. Minn., Mpls., 1969-71; tchr. lang. arts Incarnation Elementary Sch., Mpls., 1971-72; tchr., librarian Maternity of Mary Sch., St. Paul, Minn., 1972-75; librarian Dakota County Area Vocat. Tech. Sch., Rosemont, Minn., 1975-76, Mpls. Public Library, 1974-76, St. Clair County (Mich.) Community Coll., 1976—. Mem. Am., Mich. library assns., Am. Historical Assn., Phi Kappa Phi, Phi Beta Kappa. Republican. Roman Catholic. Contbr. research paper on parliaments of Henry VII, translation of Henry VII from Latin. Home: 4794 Emmett Rd Emmett MI 48022

CASPER, HUBERT ALFRED, mfg. co. exec.; b. St. Paul, Mar. 29, 1931; s. Hubert Michael and Mary (Hadd) C.; grad. high sch.; m. Marlene F. Vadnais, Oct. 8, 1949; children—Roxanne, Sherrie, Debra, Michael, Julie, Gary, Peter, Becky. Salesman, 3-M Co, Omaha, St. Louis, 1949-59; sales, advt. mgr. Waterous Pump Co., St. Paul, 1959-69; v.p. Farwell, Ozmun Kirk, St. Paul, 1969-77; mktg. dir. Remmele Engring. Co., St. Paul, 1977—. Mem. White Bear Lake Human Rights Commn., Minn., 1967—. Chmn. bd. dirs. YMCA, White Bear Lake, 1968-72. Mem. Jr. C. of C., Nat., Minn. indsl. distbrs. assns., St. Paul Sales and Mktg. Execs. Club (pres. 1976-77). Home: 1711 3d St White Bear Lake MN 55110 Office: 1211 Pierce Butler Rd St Paul MN 55104

CASSEL, CHARLENE ANN, psychologist, clin. dir.; b. Hershey, Pa., Sept. 16, 1939; d. Charles Henry and Beatrice Irene (Feidt) Cassel. A.A., Hershey Jr. Coll., 1958; B.A., Lebanon Valley Coll., 1967; Ph.D., U. Toledo, 1975. Intern, Crownsville (Md.) State Hosp., 1970-71. Lic. psychologist, Ohio. Staff psychologist Court Diagnostic Treatment Center, Toledo, Ohio, 1971-74, clin. dir., 1974—; instr. psychology U. Toledo, 1972—. Mem. exec. bd. Toledo Area Assn. Correctional Workers. Mem. Am. Psychol. Assn. NDEA fellow, 1967-68. Author, Proceedings Am. Psychol. Assn., 1971. Home: 2429 Cheyenne Blvd Toledo OH 43614

CASSELL, FRANK H., educator; b. Chgo., Oct. 12, 1916; s. Frank and Alicia (Robinson) Seymour; A.B., Wabash Coll., 1939; postgrad. U. Chgo., 1946-47; m. Marguerite Ellen Fletcher, Mar. 24, 1940; children—Frank Allan, Thomas Watts, Christopher, Bernard. With Inland Steel Co., Chgo., 1948-68, dir. personnel adminstrn. and labor relations, 1957-63, asst. v.p. adminstrn., 1963-68; pres. Frank H. Cassell & Assos., Washington and Chgo., 1968—; prof. indsl. relations Grad. Sch. Mgmt., Northwestern U., 1968—, dir. studies pub. mgmt., 1972-74, also cons.; vis. prof. Inst. Am. Studies, Salzburg, Austria, 1957, Bergenstock, Switzerland, 1971. Chmn. Ill. Gov.'s Com. on Unemployment, 1961-63; dir. Chgo. Urban league; dir. U.S. Employment Service, 1966-68; dir. Nat. Social Welfare Assembly, 1970-74; mem. Nat. Task Force on Income Maintenance, 1970-73; chmn. Chgo. Com. Urban Policy, 1972-74; mem. study on trades and crafts NRC, 1975—; mem. staff pensions study Nat. Planning Assn., 1976—. Mem. Am. Econ. Assn., Indsl. Relations Research Assn. Clubs: University (Chgo.); Internat. (Washington). Home: 128 Church Rd Winnetka IL 60093 Office: 104 S Michigan Av Chicago IL 60603

CASSELL, MARGUERITE ELLEN FLETCHER (MRS. FRANK H. CASSELL), civic worker; b. Crawfordsville, Ind., Apr. 18, 1918; d. Russell and Marguerite (Watts) Fletcher; student Butler U., 1936-39, Ind. U., 1942-43, Am. U., 1967-68; m. Frank H. Cassell, Mar. 24, 1940; children—Frank Allan, Thomas Watts, Christopher. Social worker Welfare Dept., Montgomery County, Ind., 1966—. Bd. dirs. YWCA Met. Chgo., 1963-72, v.p., 1969; bd. dirs. Winnetka Community Chest; mem. womans bd. Chgo. Urban League, 1965—. Mem. Nat. Democratic Womens' Club. Mem. Nat. Council Negro Women (life), United World Federalists, League Women Voters, Northwestern U. Circle (treas. 1972, pres. 1975). Congregationalist. Home: 128 Church St Winnetka IL 60093

CASSELS, DONALD ERNEST, physician, educator; b. Ellendale, N.D., Sept. 9, 1906; s. Ernest Eber and Louise Larsher (Chambers) C.; B.A., U. N.D., 1932; M.D., Harvard U., 1936; m. Isabella Collins, Oct. 8, 1938. Intern, Buffalo Gen. Hosp., 1936-37; resident in pediatrics U. Chgo., Hosps., 1937-38, instr., 1938-39; practice medicine specializing in pediatrics, 1941-43; asst. prof. pediatrics U. Chgo., 1943-48, asso. prof., 1948-54, prof., 1954—; mem. staffs Wyler Children's Hosp., Ill. Services for Crippled Children. Served to maj. M.C., AUS, 1943-46. Decorated Bronze Star; recipient Gold Key U. Chgo. Med. Alumni Assn., 1974. Diplomate Am. Bd. Pediatrics. Mem. Am. Acad. Pediatrics, Am. Pediatrics Soc., Soc. Pediatrics Research, Am. Coll. Cardiology, Am. Coll. Chest Physicians. Clubs: Quadrangle, Sturgeon Bay Yacht. Author: Heart and Circulation in Newborn and Infant, 1966; Electrocardiography in Infants and Children, 1966, others; contbr. articles, papers to med. jours. Home: 5617 Dorchester Ave Chicago IL 60637 Office: 950 E 59th St Chicago IL 60637

CASSIDY, DWANE ROY, insulation contracting co. exec.; b. Bedford, Ind., Oct. 20, 1915; s. Leo Clayton and Lilly Fay (Robbins) C.; student Roscoe Turner's Sch. Aviation, 1944; m. Mary Catherine Shrout, Aug. 28, 1937; children—Gail (Mrs. Gordon Everling), Cheryl, Duane, Nina (Mrs. Robert McAnulty). With L. C. Cassidy & Son, Inc., Indpls., 1934—, now v.p.; v.p. L.C. Cassidy & Sons, Inc. of Fla., 1963—. Served with USN, 1944-45; PTO. Mem. Gideons Internat. Methodist. (dir.). Club: Optimist (Indpls.). Home: 644 Lawndale St Plainfield IN 46168 Office: 1918 S High School Rd Indianapolis IN 46241

CASSIDY, GERALD JOSEPH, fast food co. exec.; b. Chgo., Aug. 16, 1941; s. Joseph Patrick and Mary Rita (Gleason) C.; B.S. in Indsl. Econs., Purdue U., 1964; M.B.A., Old Dominion U., 1970; m. Kay McCarty; children—Lisa Kathleen, Mary Elizabeth, Darrin Christopher, Angela Rhonda, Gerald Joseph II. Mdse. mgr. Dave Keen Music, Lafayette, Ind., 1964-66; fin. analyst Gen. Foods Corp., Lafayette, 1971-72; owner/operator 3 McDonald's Restaurants, Cassidy Restaurants, Inc., Tipton, Ind., 1973—, charter mem.

McDonal... ...v. Bd., 1973, 74; lectr. Purdue U., 1969. F... ...ublican Party, 1976—. Served to lt. U... ...of C., Ind. Restaurant Assn. Re... ...ks, Jaycees.

...N.Y.C., Aug. 4, 1934; s. ...oll. City N.Y., 1961; ...ol Mauer, Aug. 31, ...aden Alan. Asst. ...ntral Mo. State ...52-57. Mem. ...Am., Mo. ...hot. genus

...er,

...

Ps...

CASTI... Apr. 7, 1... Cosmopoli... 1962-63, De... Shirley Ann Ri... Rae, Alex Arthu... pvt. tchr. music, Fo... Ridge (Ill.) Pub. Sch... 1960-63, Forrest (Ill.) ... Highland Community Co... Arts, 1972-74. Guest con... Mid-West Music Festivals; adj... Elementary Sch. Assn. mus... Competitions, Stephenson County... 1973; music adviser, host Commu... 1967—; music dir. Soc. for Preservatio... Quartet Singing in Am., Freeport, 19... 1951-53. Mem. Livingston County Mu... 1963-64), Ill. Jr. Coll. Music Educators As... com. 1967-70), Music Edn. Nat. Conf., Coll. B... Am. Fedn. Musicians, Modern Music Masters. ... 1969; Behold the Savior of Mankind, 1971; Fugue ... Passacaglia, 1973; An Anthem for Ecology, 19... numerous art songs, instrumental works, incidental ... music, numerous arrangements of classical, jazz, popu...ed music for vocal and instrumental soloists, groups. Home: ...6 W Knox Dr Freeport IL 61032

CASTINE, CHARLES, power generation sales engr.; b. Los Angeles, Mar. 26, 1949; s. Edwin L. and Anne Marie (Cox) C.; B.S. in Mech. Engring., Tex. A. and M. U., 1970; m. Sandra Gail Hopson, June 23, 1973; 1 dau., Evita Marie. Power capacitor proposal engr. Gen. Electric Co., Hudson Falls, N.Y., 1971-72, large steam turbine-generator proposal engr., Schenectady, 1972-73, gas turbine proposal engr., 1973-74, nuclear sales engr., San Jose, Calif., 1974-75, power generation sales engr., Cedar Rapids, Iowa, 1975—; dir. Oakhill Engring. Co. Bd. dirs. Linn County Health Center. Mem. Am. Nuclear Soc., ASME (asso.), Omega Psi Phi. Republican. Methodist. Club: Rotary (Cedar Rapids). Home: 3805 Sue Lane NW Cedar Rapids IA 52405 Office: 210 2d St SE Cedar Rapids IA 52401

CASTLE, DONALD LAMPERT, lawyer; b. Urbana, Ill., Apr. 18, 1904; s. Charles Bailey and Katherine Elinore (Lampert) C.; A.B., U. Mich., 1926; J.D., Detroit Coll. Law, 1936; m. Edna S. Plageman, Aug. 13, 1932; children—William R., Katherine A. Castle Grein. Admitted to Mich. bar, 1936; with real estate dept. J.L. Hudson Co., Detroit, 1929-40, with personnel relations, 1940-46, asst. personnel dir., 1946-47, exec. dir. Hudson-Webber Found., 1948-69, pension adminstrn. dir., 1948-69; individual practice law, Birmingham, Mich., 1969—; sec.-treas. Hudson-Webber Found., 1958-69. Commr. Detroit Commn. Children Youth, 1956-65; trustee Detroit Coll. Law, 1943—; bd. Detroit YMCA, 1952—, pres., 1954-57, nat. bd., 1969—, nat. council, 1951—, Great Lakes regional bd., 1971—; trustee Webber Founds., 1977—. Mem. State Bar of Mich., Detroit Bar Assn., Am. Judicature Soc., Fin. Analysts Soc. of Detroit. Presbyterian. Clubs: Detroit Athletic, Noontide, Masons, Shriners. Home: 397 Chalfonte Rd Grosse Pointe Farms MI 48236 Office: 960 E Maple St Suite 120 Birmingham MI 48011

CASTLE, JACK BURTON, JR., banker; b. Lincoln, Nebr., Feb. 29, 1948; s. Jack Burton and Laraine Mardelle (Chant) C.; B.B.A., U. Iowa, 1974. Pub. finance officer Continental Ill. Nat. Bank & Trust Co. of Chgo., 1974—. Mem. U.S. Trampoline and Tumbling Assn. (sec.-treas. 1974, v.p. 1976), Nat. Trampoline and Tumbling Judges Assn. (nat. exec. dir. 1976—). Author: International Tumbling Rules, 1974. Certified tumbling judge. Home: 21 Kristin Dr Schaumburg IL 60195 Office: 231 S LaSalle St Chicago IL 60693

CASTLE, LON WAYNE, physician; b. York, Pa., Dec. 17, 1939; s. John Phillip and Charlotte Emma (Stoner) C.; B.S., Temple U., 1961, M.D., 1965; m. Dolores Camille Clauser, July 9, 1960; children—Lon A., Lynn M., Laura L., Lisa J., Lance W., Lee A. Intern, Geisinger Med. Center, Danville, Pa., 1965-66, resident in internal medicine, 1966-69; fellow in cardiology Cleve. Clinic, 1971-73, mem. cardiology staff, 1973—, chief of cardiac pacing sect., 1974—. Mgr. Little League baseball team, Chesterland, Ohio; commr. girls softball league, Chesterland. Served with USAF, 1969-71. Diplomate Am. Bd. Internal Medicine. Mem. AMA, Ohio Med. Assn., Cleve. Acad. Medicine. Republican. Roman Catholic. Club: Lions (Chesterland). Contbr. articles in field to med. jours. Home: 8052 W River Dr Novelty OH 44072 Office: 9500 Euclid Ave Cleveland OH 44106

CASTLE, VERNON CHARLES, recording co. exec.; b. Whitewater, Wis., May 17, 1931; s. Erwin Ellesworth and Anne Bertha (Nelson) C.; B.Ed., U. Wis., Whitewater, 1951; m. Jeanette C. Travis, Aug. 4, 1950. Profl. entertainer, musician, 1956-65; owner Castle Productions, Lake Geneva, Wis., 1966—, Castle Recording, 1972—, pres. Recreational Recordings, Ltd., 1972-77. Served with Adj. Gen. Corps, U.S. Army, 1952-55. Home: 642 Birches Dr Lake Geneva WI 53147 Office: PO Box 628 Lake Geneva WI 53147

CASTLEBERG, ROBERT LEE, real estate broker; b. Durand, Wis., July 15, 1930; s. Lutzie Michael and Ruth Ann (Gibson) C.; student Mt. San Antonio Jr. Coll., 1949-50; B.S., U. Wis., 1953, postgrad., 1955-56; m. Jeanette J. Brandon, Aug. 2, 1969; children—Sheila, Pamela, Eric; children (by previous marriage)—Michael, Steven, Cynthia, Suzanne. Realtor, property mgr. Stark Co., Madison, Wis., 1955-72, head dept., 1965-72, salesman, 1972—. Mem. real estate adv. com. Madison Area Tech. Coll., 1970—. Team capt. United Way, 1966-70; com. pack chmn. Boy Scouts Am., 1965-67. Served to 1st lt., Signal Corps, AUS, 1953-55. Bd. dirs. Northside Community Council, 1973-74, treas., 1975; bd. dirs. YMCA Central Br., 1974-75. Mem. Nat. Apt. Owners Assn. (dir. 1974—), C. of C. (mem. membership com. 1960-73). Lutheran (council pres. 1970-74). Home: 1714 Windom Way Madison WI 53704 Office: 117 Monona Av Madison WI 53703

CASTLEMAN, RICHARD LAVERN, corp. exec., b. Taylorville, Ill., Aug. 10, 1934; s. Roy David and Evelyn (Mason) C.; B.S., Millikin U., 1956; 1 dau., Kelly Gale. Clk., Office Ill. Sec. of State, Springfield, 1953-55; sr. accountant firm Gauger & Diehl, C.P.A.'s, Decatur, Ill., ...956-65; pvt. practice as C.P.A., Decatur, 1965—; comptroller ...likin U., Decatur, 1965-66; controller Progress Industries, Inc., ...r, Ill., 1966-67, v.p. finance, sec., 1967-72; v.p., gen. mgr., dir. ...co Acceptance Corp., Arthur, 1967-70, exec. v.p., dir., ...sst. sec. Capital City Casket Co., Little Rock, 1967-72; sec., ...R.A.S., Inc., Decatur, 1968-76; pres., dir. Comtemporary ...Inc., Decatur, 1969—, Contemporary Enterprises, Inc., ...—; owner Contemporary Vending Amusements, ...v. asst. logistics plans and tng. Signal Research and ... Army, Ft. Monmouth, N.J., 1957-59; cons. ...indsl. cos., 1965. Bd. dirs. Smith-Dickerson ...hi Bldg. Corp. (both Decatur). C.P.A. Mem. ...c. C.P.A.'s, Ill. Mfgrs. Assn. (legis. com. ... Merchandising Assn., Order DeMolay ...n of Honor award 1960), Delta Sigma ...fice: 2690 E Garfield Ave Decatur IL

...ysician; b. Dallas, S.D., Feb. 1, ...st) C.; student Albia Jr. Coll., ... Mildred Alyce Owen, Apr. ...William Albert II. Intern St. ...35-30; resident Mo. Pacific R.R. ...ce family medicine, Rippey, Iowa, ...1946—; mem. staff Iowa Luth. Hosp., ...oines; staff physician Midwestern area ...Recreational Vehicles Inc., Des Moines, ...uncil, Dallas Center, 1948-52. Served from lt. ...S. 1941-46. Mem. Iowa Med. Soc. (ho. dels. ...ad. Family Practice (dir. 1956-60, pres. 1963-64), ...County Med. Soc. (pres. 1958), Am. Acad. Family ...of dels. 1964-76, commn. membership and credentials). ...res. 1959-60). Home: 105 Rhinehart Ave Dallas Center IA ...ffice: 515 Sycamore St Dallas Center IA 50063

...STNER, CLARENCE LLOYD, city ofcl.; b. Auburn, Nebr., Sept. ...6, 1935; s. Clarence and Dorothy Z. (Hall) C.; B.S., U. Nebr., 1957; m. Emilie Kay Whitney, May 17, 1958; children—Ralph, Clarence, Anna. Asst. city mgr., Eugene, Oreg., 1958-65; city mgr., Ontario, Oreg., 1965-71; city adminstr., Bellevue, Nebr., 1971-76, Columbus, Nebr., 1976—. Mem. bd. Delta Upsilon Bldg. Corp., Lincoln, Neb., 1971-73. Served with AUS, 1957. Recipient Distinguished Service award Ontario Jr. C. of C., 1970, named Boss of Year, 1968. Mem. Nebr. (v.p. 1973), Oreg. (pres. 1970) city mgrs. assns., Am. Soc. Pub. Adminstrn., Internat. City Mgmt. Assn. Presbyterian. Kiwanian. Home: 3004 29th St Columbus NE 68601 Office: 2424 15th St Columbus NE 68601

CASTO, CHARLES EVERETT, physician; b. Akron, Ohio, Oct. 27, 1925; s. Jennings Bryan and Ruth Victoria (Newmyer) C.; B.S., U. Akron, 1947; M.D., Western Res. U., 1950; m. Virginia Dare Lee, June 18, 1948 (div. May 1974); children—Gail (Mrs. Michael McCabe), David, Susan (Mrs. Bruce Coe), Beth (Mrs. James Adams), John, Paul, James, Amy; m. 2d, Dorothy Jean Marconi, Nov. 1, 1974. Intern Akron City Hosp., 1950-51; resident Akron Gen. Hosp., 1951-52; practice medicine specializing in family medicine, Cuyahoga Falls, Ohio, 1952—; mem. staff Akron City Hosp., St. Thomas Hosp., Children's Hosp., Akron; missionary Laymen's Overseas Service, Bolivia, 1967; missionary Christian Med. Soc., Dominican Republic, 1973, 75, Haiti, 1974. Mem. exec. com. United Fund, 1960-63; chmn. camp com. YMCA, 1963; chmn. camp com. United Community Council, 1966; mem. Cuyahoga Falls Bd. Edn., 1973-74. Fellow Am. Acad. Family Practice; mem. Am., Ohio med. assns., Summit County Med. Soc. (sec. 1960-62, editor 1962-64), Summit County Acad. Gen. Practice (pres. 1963), Flying Physicians Assn., Lambda Chi Alpha, Nu Sigma Nu. Mem. United Ch. of Christ (mem. bd. World Ministries, elder 1956—). Club: Lofloner Fishing (Akron). Home: 4469 Deauville Ave Stow OH 44224 Office: 1630 Schiller Ave Cuyahoga Falls OH 44223

CASTRO, ROBERT RAYMOND, physician, surgeon; b. San Miguel, Peru, Sept. 16, 1929; s. Hector and Eloisa Maria (deSerrano) C.; came to U.S., 1957, naturalized, 1967; B.Sc., U. Toulouse (France), 1951; M.D., U. Paris, 1958; m. Nicole Godin, Oct. 10, 1959; children—Isabelle, Michael. Intern, Augustana Hosp., Chgo., 1957; resident in surgery McGill U., Montreal (Que. Can.) Gen. Hosp., 1958-60, fellow in cardiovascular surgery, 1960-61; resident in surgery U. Wis., U. Hosp., Madison, 1961-65; practice medicine specializing in gen. and thoracic surgery, Ottawa, Ill., 1967—; attending surgeon Norwest Hosp., Roosevelt Hosp., Chgo., 1965-66; attending physician Ottawa (Ill.) Community Hosp., 1967—. Diplomate Am. Bd. Surgery. Fellow A.C.S., Am. Coll. Chest Physicians. Home: 210 Forest Park Pl Ottawa IL 61350

CASWELL, ROBERT LEROY, pub. co. exec.; b. Cherokee, Iowa, Mar. 7, 1923; s. Carl Clark and Hazel Martha (Gates) C.; student Clarinda Jr. Coll., 1940-41, Iowa State Coll., 1941-43, U. Mich., 1943; B.S., Iowa State Coll., 1945; postgrad. U. So. Calif., 1947; m. Norma Jean Walker, June 4, 1944; children—Steven R., John R., Christopher C. Aircraft structural designer Douglas Aircraft Co., El Segundo, Calif., 1946-47; editor Clarinda (Iowa) Herald Jour., 1947-61; asst. sales mgr. Lisle Corp., Clarinda, 1961-68; pres. Express Pub. Co., Red Oak, Iowa, 1968—, Southwest Iowa Printing Corp., Red Oak, 1970—. Pres. Clarinda Community Theater, 1966-68; pres. Keep Iowa Clean, Inc., 1973; chmn. Montgomery County chpt. ARC, 1976—. Bd. dirs. Iowa Western Achievement Corp., 1971-72, Red Oak Indsl. Found., 1971-77. Served with USNR, 1943-46, 52-54. Mem. Iowa Press Assn. (dir.), Nat. Newspaper Assn., Red Oak C. of C. (dir. 1971), Aircraft Owners and Pilots Assn., Am. Legion, Sigma Delta Chi, Phi Gamma Delta. Republican. Lion (dist. gov. 1960-61). Author: Launch Jets, 1966. Home: 1609 Eastern Ave Red Oak IA 51566 Office: 2012 Commerce Dr Red Oak IA 51566

CATANESE, ANTHONY JAMES, educator; b. New Brunswick, N.J., Oct. 18, 1942; s. Anthony James and Josephine Marlene (Barone) C.; B.A., Rutgers U., 1963; Ph.D., U. Wis., 1968; M.Urban Planning, N.Y. U., 1965; m. Sara Jean Phillips, Oct. 27, 1968; children—Mark Anthony, Michael Scott, Mark Alexander. Asst. prof. city planning Ga. Inst. Tech., Atlanta, 1967-68, asso. prof. city planning, 1968-73, chmn. doctoral studies com., 1970-73; mem. faculty U. Miami, Coral Gables, Fla., 1973-75, James A. Ryder prof. transp. and planning, 1973-75, dir. Ryder program in transp., 1973-75; dean Sch. Architecture and Urban Planning U. Wis.-Milw., 1975—. Sr. cons. State Wis., 1965-67; sr. planner State N.J., 1963-64; pres. A.J. Catanese & Assos., Inc., Cons. Planners, Atlanta, also Miami, 1967—; sr. Fulbright prof. Colombia, 1971-72. Mem. Ga. Dunes Study Commn., 1972-73; bd. dirs. Agrl. Research Centers Consortium, 1976—. Chmn. Middle DeKalb County Dem. Party, 1969-71; mem. 5th Congl. Dist. Dem. caucus, 1971; Aide-de-Camp Govs. Office, State Ga., 1971-72; mem. Urban Policy Task Force, Carter Presdl. Campaign, 1976. Served with AUS, 1961-63. Recipient fellowships State N.J. Act, 1927, Werner Hegemann, 1964-65, Wis. Alumni Research Found., 1965-66, Richard King Mellon Trust, 1966-67, Ford Found., 1967. Mem. Am. Inst. Planners (v.p. bd. govs. 1971-74; mem. exec. com. 1971-74), Am. Soc. Planning Ofcls., Hwy. Research Bd., Regional Sci. Assn., Am. Acad. Polit. and Social Scis., Assn. Collegiate Schs. Planning, Jee Do Kwan Assn., Japanese Karate Assn. Author: Scientific Method of Urban Analysis, 1972; New Perspectives on Urban Transportation Research, 1972; Systemic Planning-Theory and Application, 1970; Planners and Local Politics; Impossible Dreams, 1973; Urban Transportation in South Florida, 1974. Contbr. articles to profl. jours. Office: Sch Architecture and Urban Planning U Wis-Milw Milwaukee WI 53201

CATERINE, JAMES MICHAEL, surgeon; b. Milw., Feb. 23, 1935; s. James A. and May Elizabeth (Marasco) C.; student Creighton U., 1952-55; M. D., U. Iowa 1959; m. Barbara Ann Bauer, July 9, 1961; children—Anthony, Rebecca, John Paul, Matthew, Gina. Intern, County Hosp., San Bernardino, Calif., 1959-60; resident Univ. Hosp., VA Hosp., Iowa City, 1960-61, VA Hosp., Des Moines, 1964-66; practice medicine specializing in gen. surgery, Des Moines, 1967—; mem. staffs Mercy, Luth., Meth., N.W., Broadlawns hosps., Des Moines, Mary Greely Hosp., Ames, Iowa; surgery teaching chmn. Mercy Hosp., Des Moines, 1970—, chief surgery, 1976—; asst. clin. prof. surgery Coll. Osteo. Medicine and Surgery, Des Moines, 1970—. Served with USAF, 1961-64. Recipient Excellence in Teaching award Coll. Osteo. Medicine and Surgery, 1974; certificate of recognition Broadlawns Hosp., Des Moines, 1975. Diplomate Am. Bd. Surgery. Fellow A.C.S., Am. Soc. Abdominal Surgeons; mem. Iowa Acad. Surgery, Pan-Am. Med. Assn., Am. Burn Assn., Iowa, Polk County med. socs., AMA (Physicians Recognition award 1977), Med. Forum Club, Am. Med. Tennis Assn. Roman Catholic. Clubs: Embassy, Des Moines Golf and Country, Des Moines Racquet. Contbr. articles to med. jours. Home: 7500 Benton Dr Des Moines IA 50322 Office: 1041 5th St Des Moines IA 50314

CATES, JOSEPH RICHARD, accountant; b. Mattoon, Ill., Oct 3, 1931; s. Joseph Raymond and Myrtle W. (O'Connell) C.; B.S., Eastern Ill. State Coll., 1955; m. Nancy Givan Deetz, Nov. 24, 1955; children—Joseph, Elizabeth, Cathy, Mary, John, Thomas. Auditor, Caterpillar Tractor Co., Decatur, Ill., 1955-57; loan dept. Northtown Bank, Decatur, 1957-61; revenue agent Internal Revenue Service, Decatur, 1961-65, Springfield, 1965-66, appellate conferee appellate div., Springfield, 1967-69; tax supr. Ernst & Ernst, C.P.A.'s, Springfield, 1969-71; individual practice C.P.A., Springfield, 1971-72, 75—; mgr. Klein, Brown & Carter, C.P.A.'s, Springfield, 1972-75. Mem. exec. com. Sangamon Valley Estate Planning Council, 1974-76. Served with U.S. Army, 1951-52. C.P.A., Ill. Mem. Am. Inst. C.P.A.'s, Ill. Soc. C.P.A's (mem. com. on fed. taxation 1970-74). Roman Catholic. K.C. Home and Office: 1924 Fairmont Dr Springfield IL 62702

CATHRO, DAVID METHVEN, pediatrician, clin. dir., educator; b. Dundee, Scotland, May 5, 1930; s. William Middleton and Margaret (Methven) C.; M.B., Ch.B., U. Edinburgh (Scotland), 1954, M.D. with high distinction, 1964; came to U.S., 1970; m. Christine Mary Lancaster Kerr, Aug. 30, 1963; children—David Methven, John Kerr, Michele Margaret. Rotating intern Hairmyres Hosp., Glasgow, Scotland, 1954-55; resident in internal medicine and pediatrics Royal Infirmary, Stirling, Scotland, 1957-58; resident in pediatrics Maryfield Hosp., Dundee, Scotland, 1958; research fellow in pediatric endocrinology Dept. Child Health U. St. Andrews, Dundee, 1958-63; lectr. child health, 1963-67; charge de recherches Hopital Debrousse, Lyon, France, 1967-70; resident in pediatrics Howard U. Hosp., Washington, 1970-71; chief resident in pediatrics, 1971-72; fellow in adolescent medicine Childrens Hosp., Washington, 1972-73, pediatrician, comprehensive care program, 1973-75; asst. clin. prof. child health George Washington U., Washington, 1975-77; asst. prof. pediatrics Wright State U., Dayton, Ohio, 1975-77, dir. adolescent services, 1975-77, asso. prof., 1977—. Scottish Hosp. Endowments Research Trust Fellow, 1958-61; Med. Research Council fellow, 1961-63; French Nat. Insts. Health research fellow, 1967-70. Fellow Am. Acad. Pediatrics (asso.). Contbr. articles to med. jours. Home: 60 Colonial Ln Dayton OH 45429

CATION, PAUL CURTIS, lawyer; b. Peoria, Ill., Nov. 16, 1924; s. Nathaniel Curtis and Dena M. (Meindirs) C.; B.S., U. Ill., 1948, LL.B., 1950; m. Muriel M. Sunderlin, Dec. 27, 1947; children—Richard C., Nancy Jean. Admitted to Ill. bar, 1950; partner firm Vonachen, Cation, Lawless, Trager, Slevin, Peoria, 1965—; asst. atty. gen. State of Ill., 1968—. Dir., Dunlap State Bank (Ill.), Bartonville Bank (Ill.). Treas. Peoria County Republican Central Com., 1968-74. Trustee, Methodist Hosp., Peoria, 1970—, mem. exec. com., 1970—, chmn. bd. trustees, 1974-77; bd. dirs. Forest Park Found., Peoria, 1958—, YMCA, Peoria, 1968—. Served with AUS, 1943-45. Decorated Purple Heart, Bronze Star. Mem. Am., Ill., Peoria County bar assns., Phi Delta Phi, Delta Upsilon. Republican. Methodist. Rotarian. Club: Mt. Hawley Country (Peoria). Author: Commercial Real Estate Transactions, 1972; Day to Day Banking Operations, 1974. Home: 417 W Giles Ln Peoria IL 61614 Office: 200 NE Adams St Peoria IL 61602

CATRON, DAVID LEE, musician; b. Butler, Mo., June 22, 1936; s. Mc Kinley and Martha Belle (Yoder) C.; B.A., Western State Coll., 1958, M.A. (grad. fellow), 1959; m. Nancy Lynn Empkie, Mar. 24, 1973; 1 dau. Angela Gayle. Dir. music pub. sch., Satanta, Kan., 1959-62; dir. bands Hugoton, Kan., 1962-67, Lawrence, Kan., 1967-70; asst. dir. bands Mich. State U. at East Lansing, 1970-74; dir. bands Wichita (Kan.) State U., 1974—. Active many marching band clinics; band chmn. State of Kan. Named Outstanding Young Tchr., 1965. Mem. Nat. Band Assn., Coll. Band Dirs. Nat. Assn., Mich. Band and Orch. Assn., N.E.A., Kan. Music Educators Assn. (dist. pres. 1965-68). Home: 8720 Lockmoor Circle Wichita KS 67207

CATT, NEAL EMERY, educator; b. Decker, Ind., Dec. 10, 1943; s. John W. and Fern A. (Marchino) C.; B.S., Oakland City Coll., 1967; M.A., Ind. State U., 1972. Lab. instr. Vincennes (Ind.) U., 1971-72, 74-75, asst. prof. earth scis., 1975—. farmer, Decker, 1974—. Mem. Gamma Theta Upsilon. Home: Rural Route 1 Decker IN 47524 Office: Vincennes U Vincennes IN 47591

CATTELINO, JOHN ANTHONY, savs. and loan exec.; b. Hurley, Wis., June 24, 1942; s. John Lawrence and Angeline Norma (Patritto) C.; B.S., U. Wis., Whitewater, 1964; M.B.A., No. Ill. U., 1967; m.

Derilyn Ruth Dean, June 7, 1969; children—Deborah Dean, Beth Allison. Retail mgr. Spurgeon Mercantile Co., Newton, Iowa, 1964-65; mktg. instr. No. Mich. U., Marquette, 1967-71, U. Wis., Platteville, 1971-74; v.p. mktg. Anchor Savs. & Loan Assn., Madison, Wis., 1974—; vis. lectr. U. Wis., Whitewater, 1976—; dir. Anchor Fin. Corp., Craft House '55; mem. adv. bd. mktg. Madison Area Tech. Coll., 1975—; chmn. mktg. com. Wis. Alumni Assn., 1975—. Mem. Sales and Mktg. Execs. Madison (dir. 1975—), Pi Sigma Epsilon (bus. advisor 1976—), Savs. Instns. Mktg. Soc. Am., AAUP, Assn. M.B.A. Execs., Am. Mktg. Assn., Vilas Park Zool. Soc. (bd. dirs. 1978—). Club: Mendota Boosters. Home: 2710 Mason St Madison WI 53705 Office: 25 W Main St Madison WI 53703

CAUDILL, GEORGE GRAY, pediatric allergist; b. Des Moines, Nov. 15, 1921; s. Wilburn Tyre and Dorothy Margaret (Gray) C.; M.D., U. Iowa, 1952; m. Dorothy May Swendsen, Sept. 5, 1948; children—Kimberly, Marci, Vicki, Catherine, Tamera, George. Intern, Broadlawns Hosp., Des Moines, 1951-53; gen. practice medicine, Newton, Iowa, 1953-54; resident in pediatrics Blank Meml. Hosp., Des Moines, 1954-56; gen. practice pediatrics, Des Moines, 1956-64; fellowship in allergy U. Iowa, Iowa City, 1964-65; individual practice medicine specializing in pediatric allergy, Des Moines, 1965—; guest lectr. Coll. Osteo. Medicine and Surgery, Des Moines; asst. clin. prof. pediatric dept. U. Iowa; dir. South Des Moines Nat. Bank, 1974—. Bd. dirs. Mid-Iowa Ednl. Computer Service, 1972—, Des Moines Ind. Sch. Dist., 1964—. Served with USN, 1942-45. Diplomate Am. Bd. Pediatrics, Am. Bd. Allergy and Immunology, recipient awards Cystic Fibrosis Found., 1958, Adult Edn. for the Des Moines Pub. Sch. in Health Edn., 1970, State Dept. Health, 1976. Mem. Am. Acad. Pediatrics, Am. Acad. Allergy, Am. Assn. for Clin. Immunology and Allergy, Iowa, Polk County med. socs., AMA, Iowa Soc. Immunology and Allergy. Republican. Clubs: Lions. Author revised edit. Better Homes and Gardens Baby Book, 1965-70; contbr. articles to profl. jours. Home: 3900 SW 28th Street Pl Des Moines IA 50321 Office: 1212 Pleasant St Des Moines IA 50309

CAUDILL, RODNEY CHAPPLE CLARK, psychiatrist; b. Moorehead, Ky., Sept. 28, 1923; s. Rodney and Eleanor (Kimbrell) C.; student Miami U., 1941-42; M.D., Ohio State U., 1948; m. Vivian Jean Morrison, July 29, 1943; children—Carla Dee, Cristin Morrison, Rodney Curt, Brent Kimbrell. Intern, St. Monica Hosp., Phoenix, 1949-50; resident, Topeka VA Hosp., 1962-63, C.F. Menninger Meml. Hosp., Topeka, 1964-65; family practice medicine, Middletown, Ohio, 1950-62; now practice medicine, specializing in psychiatry; staff Menninger Clinic, Topeka, 1962-65; staff psychiatrist Palm Beach Psychol. Clinic, West Palm Beach, Fla., 1965-66; dir. psychiat. services, also tchr., cons. Anderson (Ind.) Coll., 1966-69; founder, dir. Meramec Psychiat. Center, Yorktown, Ind., 1970—. Tchr., cons. Ball State U., 1972-75; cons. Aquarius House, Muncie, Ind., 1971-74; psychiat. cons. Family Practice Residents, Ball Meml. Hosp., 1973-75. Served to capt. USAF, 1954-56. Menninger Sch. Psychiatry fellow, 1962-65, NIMH grantee, 1962-65. Mem. AMA, Am., Ind. psychiat. assns., Ohio State, Ind. State med. assns., Sigma Alpha Epsilon, Nu Sigma Nu. Address: Box 427 Yorktown IN 47396

CAUSA, ALFREDO GUILLERMO, polymer scientist; b. Montevideo, Uruguay, June 25, 1928; s. Alfredo and Emilia (DeBenedetti) C.; came to U.S., 1959, naturalized, 1975; B.Sc. with honors, Montevideo Sch. Chemistry and Chem. Engring., 1958; M.S., Case Inst. Tech., Cleve., 1962; Ph.D. in Polymer Sci., U. Akron, 1968. Chemist, S.Am. subs. Courtaulds, Ltd., 1952-58; research chemist textile fibres div. Canadian Industries, Ltd., Millhaven Research Lab., Kingston, Ont., 1961-64, Tarrytown, Tech. Center, Union Carbide Corp., Tarrytown, N.Y., 1968-70; prin. chemist Goodyear Tire & Rubber Co., Akron, Ohio, 1970—. Fulbright scholar, 1959-61; Phillips Petroleum fellow, 1964-67. Mem. Am. Chem. Soc., AAAS, Sigma Xi, Alpha Chi Sigma. Contbr. articles to profl. jours. Home: 1255 Ashford Ln Akron OH 44313 Office: 1144 E Market St Akron OH 44316

CAVANAUGH, GERALD DANIEL, orthodontist; b. Manitowoc, Wis., Sept. 4, 1935; s. William Theodore and Veronica (Bartz) C.; student St. Mary's Coll., 1953-55, U.S. Mil. Acad., 1955-57; B.S. in Math. cum laude, Loras Coll., 1958; D.D.S., U. Minn., 1967, postgrad. in Orthodontics (NIH fellow), 1967-69, Ph.D. in Anatomy (NIH fellow), 1972; m. Grace Pollock Wooten, Aug. 24, 1963; children—Shannon, Michael, Meggan, John Patrick. Asso. engr. ITT, Chgo., 1958-60; engr. Lockheed Missile & Space Co., Sunnyvale, Calif., 1960-61, Philco Western Devel. Lab., Palo Alto, Calif., 1961-63; practice dentistry specializing in orthodontics, Mpls., 1969—; asst. prof. anatomy U. Minn., 1972-73, asst. prof. orthodontics, 1973—; dir. orthodontics Children's Health Center, Mpls., 1973—; dir. 1st Minn. Investment Co. NIH grantee, 1973. Mem. Minn. Internat. assns. dental research, Am., Minn. dental assns., Mpls. Dist. Dental Soc., Am. Assn. Orthodontics, Midwestern, Minn. socs. orthodontics, Gopher State, Minn. Orthodontic, Bloomington (Minn.) study clubs, Delta Sigma Delta, Omicron Kappa Upsilon. Democrat. Roman Catholic. Clubs: St. Anthony Athletic, King's Ct., Madeline Island Yacht, Pres's. of U. Minn., Alumni-St. Mary's Coll., Alumni-Loras Coll., Alumni-U. Minn., K.C., Elks. Office: 3604 Cedar Ave Minneapolis MN 55407

CAVANAUGH, JAMES LEWIS, JR., psychiatrist; b. Washington, May 13, 1941; s. James Lewis and Gladys (Welsh) C.; B.A., Williams Coll., 1963; M.D., U. Pa., 1967; m. Stephanie von Ammon, Mar. 26, 1968; children—Brendan James, Margaret Welsh. Intern, Cook County Hosp., Chgo., 1967-68; resident psychiatry U. Pa., 1968-71; clin. asst. Maudsley Hosp., London, 1970; practice medicine, specializing in psychiatry, Chgo., 1973—; asst. prof. psychiatry Rush Med. Sch., Chgo., 1973—; clin. dir. dept. psychiatry Rush Med. Coll., Chgo., 1973—. Served to lt. comdr. USNR, 1971-73. Diplomate Am. Bd. Psychiatry and Neurology (asst. examiner). Fellow Am. Psychiat. Assn. (mem. joint com. govt. relations 1976—), Inst. Medicine Chgo.; mem. AMA, Royal Coll. Psychiatry (London), Ill. Psychiat. Soc. (chmn. legislative liaison com. 1973—), Ill. Med. Soc. Clubs: Racquet, University (Chgo.). Home: 1210 Spruce St Winnetka IL 60093 Office: 1753 W Congress Pkwy Chicago IL 60612

CAVANAUGH, JOHN J., congressman; b. Omaha, Aug. 1, 1945; s. John J. and Kathleen (Munnelly) C.; m. Kathleen Ann Barrett, Aug. 2, 1969; children—Patrick, Colleen, Maureen; B.A., Regis Coll., Denver, 1967; J.D., Creighton U., 1972. Admitted to Nebr. bar, 1972; partner firm Leahy, Washburn, Render & Cavanaugh, 1972-76; mem. Nebr. Senate, 1972-76; mem. 95th Congress from 2d Nebr. Dist. Mem. Am. Legion, Jaycees. Clubs: K.C., Eagles, Cornhuskers Cosmopolitan. Recipient James A. Doyle award Creighton U. Sch. Law, 1975; named Outstanding Legislator, Eagleton Inst. Politics, Rutgers U., 1975. Office: 424 Cannon House Office Bldg Washington DC 20515

CAVANAUGH, THOMAS FRANCIS, accountant; b. Mpls., Dec. 24, 1933; s. Thomas H. and Ann (Sinnott) C.; B.B.A., U. Wis., 1955; m. Kathleen A. Daly, Dec. 28, 1956; children—Kerry L., Thomas F., Patrick D., Timothy M., Kathleen A. Internal auditor Minn. Mining & Mfg. Co, St. Paul, 1955-58; sec.-treas. Nekoosa Corp. (Wis.), 1958-77; pvt. practice accounting, Wisconsin Rapids, Wis., 1977—; owner T.F.C. Enterprises, mfr.'s rep., 1977—; sec., dir. Sr. Services Diversified, Tomahawk, Wis., 1974—; dir. Cath. Family Life Ins. Co., Milw., Stensberg Printing Inc., Wisconsin Rapids, Wis. Bd. dirs. Assumption High Sch. Found. Inc., treas., 1968-70. Served with U.S. Army, 1967. C.P.A., Wis. Mem. Am., Wis. insts. C.P.A.'s, Wisconsin Rapids Area C. of C. (dir. 1967-70, treas. 1968-70), Beta Alpha Psi. Roman Catholic. Home: 941 Elm St Wisconsin Rapids WI 54494 Office: 240 7th St S Wisconsin Rapids WI 54494

CAWLEY, LEO PATRICK, physician; b. Oklahoma City, Aug. 11, 1922; s. Patrick B. and Mary (Forbes) C.; B.S., Okla. State U., 1948; M.D., U. Okla., 1952; m. Joan Mae Woods, June 20, 1948; children—Kevin Patrick, Karin Patricia, Kary Forbes. Intern, Wesley Med. Center, Wichita, Kans., 1952-53, resident in pathology, 1953-54, clin. pathologist asso. dir. labs. 1957-69, dir. lab. medicine, 1969-76, dir. research and devel., 1976—; resident in pathology Wayne County Gen. Hosp., Eloise, Mich., 1954-56, chief resident, 1956-57; sci. dir. Wesley Med. Research Found. Served with USMCR, 1942-45; PTO. Diplomate Am. Bd. Pathology. Mem. AAAS, Am. Assn. Blood Banks, Am. Soc. Clin. Pathologists (dir. 1968-71), Am. Soc. Human Genetics, N.Y. Acad. Scis., Fedn. Am. Socs. Exptl. Biology, Am. Soc. Exptl. Pathology, Am. Assn. Clin. Chemists, Am. Chem. Soc., Soc. Exptl. Biology and Medicine, Internat. Platform Assn., Alpha Omega Alpha, Phi Lambda Upsilon. Author: Electrophoresis and Immunoelectrophoresis, 1969. Editor: Series of Monograms on Laboratory Medicine, 1965—; asso. editor Clin. Biochemistry, 1968—. Home: 60 Via Verde Wichita KS 67230 Office: 550 N Hillside St Wichita KS 67214

CAWOOD, ALBERT MCLAURIN, editorial writer; b. Harlan, Ky., Nov. 10, 1939; s. Frank Finley and Eugene (Barwick) C.; B.A. in English, Union Coll., Barbourville, Ky., 1962; M.A. in Journalism, Ohio State U., 1966; m. Sonia Barreiro, July 3, 1965; children—Romy Haydee, Shuly Xochitl. Columnist, Harlan Daily Enterprise, 1954-57; tchr. English, Harlan High Sch., 1962; secondary sch. tchr. Peace Corps, Sierra Leone, West Africa, 1962-64; grad. asst. Sch. Journalism, Ohio State U., 1964-66; editorial writer Dayton (Ohio) Daily News, 1966—; pres. Am. Syndicate Inc., 1973-77. Mem. Ohio Com. Crime and Delinquency, 1968—. Author stories, poetry, satire. Home: 211 S Winter St Yellow Springs OH 45387 Office: Dayton Daily News Dayton OH 45401

CAWTHORNE, DENNIS OTTO, lawyer, state legislator; b. Manistee, Mich., Apr. 29, 1940; s. Clifford Haney and Marie (Schimke) C.; A.B., Albion Coll., 1962; LL.B., Harvard, 1965. Asst. to Rep. Robert P. Griffin, Washington, 1957-58; mgr. Mackinac Island (Mich.) C. of C., 1962-65; instr. polit. sci. Muskegon County (Mich.) Community Coll., 1965-66; admitted to Mich. bar, 1966; mem. Mich. Ho. of Reps., 1966—, Republican leader, 1975—. Mem. Mich. Intergovtl. Cooperation Commn., 1967-73. Trustee Albion Coll., Mich. YMCA. Named among Outstanding Young Men of Mich., 1970. Mem. Mich. Bar Assn., Sigma Chi. Home: 510 Browning Ave Manistee MI 49660 Office: Capitol Bldg Lansing MI 48901

CAYLOR, HAROLD DELOS, surgeon; b. Nottingham, Ind., Aug. 19, 1894; s. Charles E. and Bessie (Ferree) C.; B.S., U. Chgo., 1916; M.D., Rush Med. Coll., 1918; M.S., U. Minn., 1927; m. Ella Leora Carey, Nov. 11, 1919 (dec. Jan. 1969); children—Rebecca (Mrs. Don Meier), Patricia (Mrs. James Niblick); m. Henrietta Louise Noe, Jan. 17, 1972. Intern, Presbyn. Hosp., Chgo., 1918, Evanston (Ill.) Hosp., 1919-20; partner, gen. surgeon Caylor-Nickel Clinic, Bluffton, Ind., 1922-24; asst. prof. surg. pathology Mayo Clinic Found., Rochester, Minn., 1927-29; gen. surgeon partner Clinic Hosp., Bluffton, Ind., 1929—. Chmn. bd. dirs. Caylor-Nickel Research Found.; trustee Caylor-Nickel Hosp., 1922-75, v.p., mem. exec. com., 1972-75. Diplomate Am. Bd. Surgery. Mem. A.C.S., Am. Group Practice Assn. (pres. 1962-63), Ind. Lung Assn. (pres. 1951-52), Ind. Bone and Joint Club (pres. 1954), Mpls. Surg. Soc., Sigma Xi, Phi Chi, Delta Upsilon. Republican. Methodist. Mason (Shriner), Elk. Clubs: Athletic (Indpls.); Sagamore of the Wabash. Home: 411 W Market St Bluffton IN 46714 Office: 303 S Main St Bluffton IN 46714

CAYLOR, TRUMAN E., physician; b. Pennville, Ind., Jan. 10, 1900; s. Charles E. and Bessie (Ferree) C.; student Ind. U., 1917-1919; B.S., Wis. U., 1921; M.D., Rush Med. Coll., 1924; m. Julia Gettle, June 28, 1923 (dec. June 6, 1960); m. Eva Abbott, May 29, 1961; children—Carolyn (Mrs. Herman Waddington), Charles H., Constance (Mrs. Joseph Carney). Intern, Evanston (Ill.) Gen. Hosp.; practice medicine specializing in urology, Bluffton, Ind., 1924—; mem. staff Caylor Nickel Clinic, Bluffton, mem. staff Caylor Nickel Hosp., Bluffton, 1939—, exec. com., 1939-75, also dir.; dir. Mut. Security Life Ins. Co. Mem. adv. com. Ind. Commn. on Aging, 1972-74; mem. adv. com. Grace Coll., Winona Lake, Ind., 1970—. Bd. dirs. Yorkfellow Inst., Caylor Nickel Research Found. Served with AUS, 1918. Mem. Ind. Council Sagamores, Ind. State Med. Soc. (50th Year Certificate of Distinction 1974), A.C.S., Am. Urol. Assn., Delta Upsilon. Mason (Shriner), Rotarian (dist. gov. 1965-66). Home: 920 River Rd Bluffton IN 46714 Office: 303 S Main St Bluffton IN 46714

CAYWOOD, THOMAS ELIAS, educator; b. Lake Park, Iowa, May 9, 1919; s. Harry E. and Alice A. (Bollenbach) C.; A.B., Cornell Coll., Mt. Vernon, Iowa, 1939; M.A., Northwestern U., 1940; Ph.D. (Shattuck scholar), Harvard U., 1947; m. Mary E. Miller, June 6, 1941; children—Ann, Beth, Kay Dee. Teaching fellow Harvard U., 1941-42, spl. research asso. in physics, 1942-46, research asst. in math., 1946-47; sr. mathematician Inst. Air Weapons Research, U. Chgo., 1947-50, coordinator research, 1950-52; supr. ops. research Armour Research Found., Chgo., 1952-53; partner Caywood-Schiller Assos., Chgo., 1953-70; v.p. Caywood-Schiller div. A.T. Kearney & Co., Chgo., 1971-78; professorial lectr. in mgmt. sci. and prodn. mgmt. Grad. Sch. Bus., U. Chgo., 1978—; pres. Investigacion de Operationes S.A. (Mexico), 1959-60; lectr. Sch. Bus., U. Chgo., 1953-58; mem. research and devel. bd. Dept. Def., 1952-53, chmn. panel on ordnance transp. and supply, 1959-64, mem. def. sci. bd., 1960-64. Alumni bd. dirs. Cornell Coll., 1962-65, trustee, 1964—, pres. bd. trustees, 1970-72. Mem. Inst. Mgmt. Sci., Am. Math. Soc., Am. Math. Assn., Inst. Indsl. Engrs., Ops. Research Soc. Am. (pres. 1969-70). Clubs: Flossmoor (Ill.) Country; Cosmos (Washington). Editor Ops. Research, 1961-68. Home: 704 Argyle Ave Flossmoor IL 60422 Office: U Chgo Grad Sch Bus Chicago IL 60637

CECCATO, ALDO, music dir.; b. Italy, Feb. 18, 1934; s. Antonio and Elena (Bertini) C.; came to U.S., 1968; grad. Verdi Conservatory, Milan, 1955, Hochschule fur Musik, Berlin, 1964, L'Accademia Chigiana, Siena, Italy, 1963; m. Eliana de Sabata, Dec. 1966; children—Cristiano, Francesco. Guest condr. maj. European and Am. orchs., 1969—; prin. condr. Detroit Symphony Orch., 1973-74, music dir., 1974—; gen. music dir. Hamburg (Germany) Philharmonic, 1975—; music dir. Meadow Brook Festival, 1975—; recordings include La Traviata with Beverly Sills, Arias with Grace Bumbry, Rachmaninoff with Augustin Anievas (Angel Records); Strauss and Mozart Arias with Beverly Sills, Maria Stuarda with Beverly Sills (ABC Records); The Four Seasons by Vivaldi with Franco Gulli, Old Italian Arias with the La Scala Singers (Audio Fidelity); Music of Liszt and Saint Saens with M. Campanella (Philips). lHome: 770 Pemberton Grosse Pointe MI 48230 Office: Detroit Symphony Orch Ford Auditorium Detroit MI 48226

CECIL, LAWRENCE KEITH, water pollution control cons.; b. Homer, Ill., Jan. 17, 1895; s. James Harvey Lawrence and Nellie (Beebe) C.; A.B., U. Ill., Urbana, 1924; m. Jennie Anderson, Dec. 23, 1918; children—Elizabeth (Mrs. John Landrum Brownewell), Patricia (Mrs. Patrick Errett Welch). Chemist Base Hosp. Lab., Camp Custer, Mich., 1917-18; asst. to dir. labs. Battle Creek (Mich.) Sanitarium 1919; chemist U. Okla. Hosp., Oklahoma City, 1919-21; bacteriologist Okla. State Bd. Health Lab., Oklahoma City, 1922, state chemist, dir. labs., 1923; commn. agt. Refinite Co., Permutit Co., Graver Co., Oklahoma City, 1924-25; sales engr. Infilco Inc. (formerly Internat. Filter Co.), Tulsa, 1926-29, southwestern mgr., 1930-50, sales mgr., Tucson, 1951-53, v.p., product mgr., 1954, v.p., mgr. Pacific Coast and Asia Operations, 1955-61; cons. environ. pollution control, Champaign, Ill., 1962—. Dir. Wapora, Inc., Washington. Chmn. Boneyard Inter-agy. Adv. Com., 1974—. Served with M.C., AUS, 1917-19. Registered profl. engr. Okla., Ariz., Ill., Ohio. Diplomate Am. Acad. Environ. Engrs. Fellow Am. Inst. Chem. Engrs. (environ. award, 1972, award for service to soc. 1973, chmn. water sect. environ. div. 1964-76, Founders award 1976), Am. Inst. Chemists; mem. Am. Chem. Soc., (life), Am. Water Works Assn. (life), Am. Pollution Control Fedn., Nat. Assn. Corrosion Engrs., Internat. Assn. Water Pollution Research, A.A.A.S., Izaak Walton League Am., Sierra Club. Contbr. articles to profl. publs. Patentee in field. Home: 805 LaSell Dr Champaign IL 61820

CECIL, STEPHEN RONALD, mfg. co. exec.; b. Balt., Nov. 5, 1942; s. Joseph Franklin and Jessie Henrietta (Cook) C.; student Ohio State U., 1961-62, 63-64; m. Marilyn Hover, Aug. 24, 1963; children—Robyn, Errin, Kelli, Karri, Ashle, Rhett. Sales trainee Galion Allsteel Body Co., Galion, Ohio, 1964-67; regional sales mgr. Hercules Galion Products, Roanoke, Va., 1967-70; product mgr. Peabody Galion Corp., 1970-71, product mgr. body and hoist div., 1970-72, gen. sales mgr., 1972, v.p. mktg. Peabody Galion div., 1972—. Bd. dirs. Jr. Achievement, Galion. Mem. Truck Body and Equipment Distbrs. Assn. (dir. 1973-74, mfrs. adv. council 1973—), Nat. Alliance Businessmen, Sigma Chi. Mason, Elk. Home: 1215 Cherington Dr Galion OH 44833 Office: 500 Sherman St Galion OH 44833

CEDAR, WARREN RICHARD, dentist; b. Chgo., June 28, 1920; s. Carl W. and Sarah (Hallberg) C.; A.A., North Park Coll., 1940; D.D.S., Northwestern U., 1943; m. Ursula Schmidt, Aug. 12, 1969; 1 dau., Candice (Mrs. Bruce Tideman). Pvt. practice dentistry, Evanston, Ill., 1945-70; faculty Northwestern U., Evanston, Ill., 1945—, prof. operative dentistry 1970—, chmn. dept., 1973—. Served with AUS, 1943-45. Fellow Internat., Am. colls. dentists; mem. Northwestern U. Dental Alumni Assn. (pres. 1958-59), Omicron Kappa Upsilon, Xi Psi Phi. Republican. Lutheran. Home: 9000 Parkside Morton Grove IL 60053 Office: 636 Church St Evanston IL 60201

CEDERBERG, ELFORD ALBIN, congressman; b. Bay City, Mich., Mar. 6, 1918; s. Albin and Helen (Olson) C.; student Bay City Jr. Coll., 1935-37. Mgr. Nelson Mfg. Co., 1946-52; mem. 83d-95th Congresses, 10th Mich. Dist., mem. appropriations com. Mayor of Bay City, 1949-53. Served as maj. inf., U.S. Army, 1941-45. Decorated Bronze Star. Mem. Am. Legion, V.F.W. Mem. Evang. Ch. Mason (33 deg.), Elk, Odd Fellow, Lion. Home: 2504 Abbott Rd Midland MI 48640 Office: Rayburn House Office Bldg Washington DC 20515

CEDERQUIST, STANLEY GUSTAF, food broker; b. Chgo., May 13, 1917; s. G. E. and Esther (Uron) C.; student U. Ill., 1936-40; m. Eleanor Nicholas, May 10, 1942; children—Eric S., Robert A. Chmn., Nicholas Co., Inc., Indpls., 1946—; pres. Indpls. Broadcasting Inc., 1970—; sec., dir. Instl. Life Ins. Co.; chmn. Indpls. Pub. Transp. Corp., 1973—. Served with USAAF, 1941-46; to capt. USAF, 1950-52. Mem. Nat. (past nat. chmn., exec. com.), Indpls. (past pres.) food brokers assns., Indpls. Assn. Mfrs. Reps., Ind., Indpls. chambers commerce, Contemporary Art Soc., Art Assn. Indpls., 500 Festival Assos., Mil. Order World Wars, Phi Kappa Tau. Kiwanian. Episcopalian. Clubs: Columbia, Indpls. Athletic, Meridian Hills Country, Sertoma (past pres.) (Indpls.). Home: 240 Williams Dr Indianapolis IN 46260 Office: 2500 E 46th St Indianapolis IN 46205

CELEBREZZE, ANTHONY J., fed. judge; b. Anzi, Italy, Sept. 4, 1910; s. Rocco and Dorothy (Marcoguiseppe) C.; student John Carroll U.; LL.B., Ohio No. U., 1936; D.D., Wilberforce University, 1955; LL.D., Fenn Coll., 1962, Boston Coll., 1963, La Salle coll., 1963, Ohio No. U., 1963; Pd.D., R.I. Coll., 1964; D. Pub. Service, Bowling Green State U., 1964; L.H.D., Miami U., 1965; m. Anne Marco, May 7, 1938; children—Anthony J., Jean Ann, Susan Marie. Admitted to Ohio bar, 1938, engaged in practice of law. Senator Ohio State Legislature, 1952-53; mayor of Cleve., 1953-62; sec. Dept. Health, Edn. Welfare, 1962-65; judge 6th Circuit Ct. of Appeals, 1965—. Mem. President's Adv. Commn. on Intergovtl. Relations 1959—; pres. U.S. Conf. Mayors, 1961-62. Served as seaman USN, World War II. Brotherhood award Nat. Conf. Christians and Jews, 1955, Nat. Human relations award, 1962; Order of Merit of the Republic, Italy, 1955; citation United Negro Coll. Fund, 1956. Nat. Fiorello LaGuardia award, 1961, Nat. Catholic Resettlement Council Ward, 1962, Pub. Service award YMCA, 1962, Gulick award Camp Fire Girls, Inc., 1962, Peter Canisius medal Canisius medal Canisius Coll., 1963, gold medallion City of Rome, 1963; Eleanor Roosevelt Humanities award, 1965. Mem. Am. Municipal Assn. (pres. 1958-59, distinguished service award 1960), Order of Merit. Home: 17825 Lake Rd Lakewood OH 44107 Office: Federal Bldg Cleveland OH 44114

CELESTE, RICHARD F., lt. gov. Ohio; b. Cleve., Nov. 11, 1937; s. Frank P. Celeste; B.A. in History magna cum laude, Yale U., 1959; Ph.B. in Politics (Rhodes scholar), Oxford U., 1962; m. Dagmar Braun, 1962; children—Eric, Christopher, Gabriella, Noelle, Natalie. Staff liaison officer Peace Corps, 1963; spl. asst. to U.S. ambassador to India, 1963-67; mem. Ohio Ho. of Reps., 1970-74, majority whip, 1972-74; lt. gov. Ohio, 1974—. Chmn. Cuyahoga County Democratic del. Ohio Ho. Reps., 1972-74. Methodist. Office: Office of the Lt Gov State House Columbus OH 43215

CELLA, PAUL, civil engr.; b. Chgo., Mar. 27, 1937; s. Louis B. and Harriet (Smith) C.; B.S., Rose Hulman Inst. Tech., 1958; postgrad. Northwestern U., 1958, DePaul U., 1959, U. Chgo., 1963; m. Joan Jacobson, Dec. 28, 1963; 1 dau., Catherine. Various engring. positions Met. San. Dist. Greater Chgo., 1958-74, adminstrv. engr., 1974—. Registered profl. engr., Ill. Mem. ASCE, Am. Pub. Works Assn. Contbr. articles to profl. jours. Home: 328 N Edgewood Ave LaGrange Park IL 60525 Office: 100 E Erie St Chicago IL 60611

CELMS, THEODORE, philosophic scholar, educator; b. Pedele, Latvia, June 14, 1893; s. Peteris and Liene (Kukis) C.; came to U.S., 1949, naturalized, 1956; Ph.D., U. Freiburg, Germany, 1923, U. Riga, Latvia, 1936; m. Vera nee Vichrovs, Jan. 21, 1920 (dec.); children—Izolde, Dagmara, Peter. Asst. prof. philosophy U. Riga, Latvia, 1927-35, asso. prof., 1935-36, prof., 1936-44, dean faculty of philology and philosophy, 1942-44; prof. philosophy U. Goettingen (Germany), 1944-49; vis. prof. U. Koenigsberg (Germany), 1935; asso. prof. philosophy Augustana Coll. Rock Island, 1949-50, prof., 1950-63, emeritus prof., 1963—. Recipient 3 Stars decoration Latvia;

Wilhelm von Humboldt medal, Germany. Author: Der phaenomenologische Idealismus Husserls, 1928; Truth and Illusion, 1939; Subjekt und Subjektivierung, 1943; numerous publs. in field. Home: 3420-9 1/2 Ave Rock Island IL 61201

CELUSTA, GEORGE ROBERT, ins. cons.; b. Duluth, Minn., Mar. 26, 1923; s. Stanley Martin and Sophie (Wozniak) C.; B.S., U. S.C., 1946; m. Elizabeth Mae Gustafson, Aug. 24, 1946; children—Timothy G., Jeffrey R. Office clk., agt. Provident Mut. Life Ins., Duluth, 1940-42; office clk., asst. to v.p. Barnes-Duluth Shipbldg. Co., Duluth, 1942-43; retail sales and mgmt. staff A & E Supply Co., Duluth, 1946-52, owner, mgr., 1952-57; agt., mgr. Conn. Gen. Life Ins. Co., Duluth and Mpls., 1957-66; dir. pension and advanced underwriting North Am. Life & Casualty Co., Mpls., 1966-68, exec. v.p., 1968-73, pres. subsidiary Nalac Financial Plans, Inc., 1971-73, v.p. agys. parent co., 1972-73; ins. cons., 1973—. Served with USNR, 1943-46. Presbyn. Rotarian. Club: Eshquaguma Country. Home: Box 149 Gilbert MN 55741 Office: PO Box 318 Virginia MN 55792

CENTANNI, RONALD PAUL, sch. counselor; b. Chgo., Nov. 7, 1942; s. Paul Francis and Ida Irene (DeMuro) C.; B.S., So. Ill. U., 1965, M.S., 1967. English instr. Coll. of DuPage, Glen Ellyn, Ill., 1971; tchr. English Bremen High Sch., Midlothian, Ill., 1972-73; guidance counselor Hillcrest High Sch., Country Club Hills, Ill., 1973-74; guidance counselor, asst. varsity baseball coach Tinley Park (Ill.) High Sch., 1974—; admissions counselor for USAF Acad., 1974—. Mem. Tinley Park Youth Commn., 1974-76, chmn., 1976-77, youth week chmn., 1976. Served with USAF, 1967-71. Recipient Most Outstanding Citizen award So. Ill. U., 1965; Air Force Times award of Merit, 1965; Certificate of Appreciation for Service to Tinley Park, 1976. Mem. Am. Personnel and Guidance Assn., Nat. Vocational Guidance Assn., Ill. Personnel and Guidance Assn., Ill. Vocational Guidance Assn., Res. Officers Assn., S. Suburban Inter-Conf. Guidance Assn. (treas. 1977—). Home: 7923 164th Ct Tinley Park IL 60477 Office: 6111 W 175th St Tinley Park IL 60477

CENTNER, JAMES LEO, auto co. exec.; b. Newport, Ky., June 28, 1922; s. Alexis F. and Mary Anne (Cloud) C.; Ph.B., Xavier U., 1942, M.B.A., 1954; postgrad. Chase Coll. Law, 1952-54; m. Naomi Anne Schlosser, Oct. 19, 1946; children—James L., Marsha Anne, Anne Marie. With First Nat. Bank Cin., 1946-47; with Hess & Eisenhardt Internat. Ltd., Cin., 1947—, v.p. finance and adminstrn., 1966-68, exec. v.p., 1968-75, pres., 1975—; adj. asso. prof. bus. adminstrn. Grad. Sch., Xavier U., Cin., 1954—, chmn. exec. adv. com., 1965—; pres. Cin. Indsl. Inst., 1971—. Pres. council Our Lady of Cin. Coll., 1965—; co-chmn. Edgecliff Found., Cin., 1964—; mem. United Appeal coms. Edgecliff Acad. Fine Arts, Cin., 1960—. Regent Sisters of Mercy, Cin. Provincialate; trustee Edgecliff Coll., 1974—. Served with CIC, AUS, 1942-46, col. Res. Fellow Internat. Acad. Mgmt.; mem. Internat. Soc. for Advancement Mgmt. (pres.) Am. Mgmt. Assn. (trustee 1972—), Am. Soc. for Personnel Adminstrn. Adminstrv. Mgmt. Soc. Republican. Roman Catholic. Author: Management-Labor Case Studies, 1959. Contbr. articles to profl. jours. Home: 2915 Alpine Terrace Cincinnati OH 45208 Office: 8959 Blue Ash Av Cincinnati OH 45242

CENTNER, ROSEMARY LOUISE, chemist; b. Newport, Ky., Sept 23, 1926; d. Alexis F. and Mary Anne (Cloud) Centner; B.A., Our Lady of Cin. Coll., 1947; M.S., U. Cin., 1949. Library asst., tech. library Procter & Gamble Co., 1949-52, br. librarian Miami Valley labs., Cin., 1952-56, tech. librarian, 1956-66, mgr. tech. info. service, 1966-72, mgr. div. info. cons., 1972-73, mgr. NDA coordination, 1973-75, mgr. biomed. communications, 1975—. Trustee, Edgecliff Coll., 1975—. Mem. Am. Soc. Info. Sci., Am. Chem. Soc., AAAS, Spl. Libraries Assn., Am. Med. Writers Assn. Iota Sigma Pi. Roman Catholic. Home: 2678 Byrneside Dr Cincinnati OH 45239 Office: Miami Valley Labs PO Box 39175 Cincinnati OH 45274

CERNEY, JAMES VINCENT, med. and health services co. exec.; b. Detroit, Jan. 27, 1914; s. James and Anna (Hein) C.; student Hiram Coll., 1935; A.B., Miami U., 1939; Dr. Podiatric Medicine, Ohio Coll. Podiatric Medicine, 1943; Dr. Mechanotherapy, Central States Coll. Physiatrics, 1948, D. Chiropractic, 1953; m. Martha Elizabeth French, Nov. 2, 1940; children—James F., Lee Carol (Mrs. John Spitler), Patricia Kay (Mrs. Raymond McIntire), Jeffrey Lynn, Kimberle Laine. Leader dance band, 1931-32; dancer Jack Lynch Revue, 1932-33; writer Northwest Sch. of Air series, stas. WLW, WHK, WCLE, 1939; publicity, promotion and merchandising mgr. radio sta. WING, Dayton, 1940; practice podiatric medicine, Dayton, 1943—; pres. Profl. Research, Dayton, 1944—. Pres. Dayton Triangle Profl. Football Team, 1958. Dir. pub. info. CD, Dayton, 1957-58. Recipient first prize award Nat. Podiatry Assn., 1952, meritorious award Civil Defense, 1954; named Ky. col. Mem. Central States Coll. Physiatrics (pres. 1960-61). Ohio Mechanotherapists (pres. 1960-61), County Podiatry Soc. (pres. 1962), Authors Guild, Nat. Athletic Trainers Assn., Internat. Platform Assn., Am. Coll. Sports Medicine Acad. Chinese Medicine, C. of C. (various coms. 1958-59), Dayton Purple Mask Theatre (pres. 1958), Dayton Ballet Guild (pres. 1958), Phi Kappa Tau. Mason. Author: Athletic Injuries, 1963; How to Develop a Million Dollar Personality, 1964; Confidence and Power for Successful Living, 1966; Dynamic Laws of Thinking Rich, 1967; Stay Younger-Live Longer, 1968; Talk Your Way to Success with People, 1968; Thirteen Steps to New Personal Power, 1969; Complete Book of Athletic Taping Techniques, 1971; Acupuncture Without Needles, 1974; Modern Magic of Natural Healing with Water Therapy, 1974; A Handbook of Unusual and Unorthodox Healing Methods, 1975; Prevent-System for Football Injuries, 1975; Touch-for-Health, 1977; Cerney System of Miracle Weight Loss, 1977; (novel) Flame Durrell, 1971; (stage plays) Blues in the Night, 1939, Fury, 1960, History of the Shiloh' Church, 1959. Editor Ohio Podiatry Jour., 1944. Contbr. articles to popular mags. Inventor throw away toothbrush, 1945, whirlpool bath system, 1946. Creator Skip Holiday series for radio, 1957. Home: 5225 N Main St Dayton OH 45415 Office: 5235 N Main St Dayton OH 45415

CERNEY, MARY ELLEN, clin. psychologist; b. Detroit, Apr. 23, 1929; d. Stephen Simon and Mary Anne (Neigoot) Cerney; B.A. summa cum laude, Coll. St. Francis, Joliet, Ill., 1960; M.A., Cath. U. Am., 1962, Ph.D., 1965; postgrad. Topeka Inst. Psychoanalysis, 1976—. Tchr. music pub. and parochial elementary schs., Northwestern Ohio, 1948-62; student Cath. U. Am., Washington, 1963-65, instr. psychology, 1964-67; instr. ednl. psychology Mary Manse Coll., Toledo, Ohio, 1965-66; directress juniorate, Sisters St. Francis, Tiffin, Ohio, 1965-69; instr. ednl. psychology Coll. St. Francis, Joliet, 1966-67; Madonna Coll., Livonia, Mich., 1967-69; postdoctoral clin. psychology Topeka (Kans.) State Hosp., 1969-70; postdoctoral clin. psychology Menninger Found., Topeka, 1970-72, clin. psychologist, psychotherapist, hosp. therapist, supr. psychotherapy vocat. assessment program, 1972—; cons. vocation program, Toledo Diocese, also permanent deacon program. Diplomate Am. Bd. Profl. Psychology; certified clin. psychologist, Ohio, Kans. Mem. Am., Ohio psychol. assns., Soc. Personality Assessment. Contbr. articles to psychol. jours. Home: 900 Lincoln St Topeka KS 66606 Office: Menninger Foundation Box 829 Topeka KS 66601

CERVENKA, BARBARA, artist, educator; b. Cleve., Sept. 28, 1939; d. James Joseph and Florence (Balzer) Cervenka; A.B., Siena Heights Coll., 1964; postgrad. Wayne State U., 1967-69; M.F.A., U. Mich., 1971. Joined Adrian Dominican Order, 1957; tchr. St. Joseph Sch., Maybee, Mich., 1959-62, St. Lawrence Sch., Detroit, 1962-66; tchr. art Bishop Borgess High Sch., Detroit, 1966-67, Bishop Foley High Sch., Madison Heights, Mich., 1967-69; teaching fellow U. Mich., Ann Arbor, 1970-71; asst. prof. art Siena Heights Coll., Adrian, Mich., 1971—; one-woman shows: U. Windsor (Ont., Can.), 1973; J. Walter Thompson Gallery, Detroit, 1972; Creative Arts Gallery, Central Mich. U., Mt. Pleasant, 1976; Art Gallery Windsor, 1977; also exhibited in group shows; represented in permanent collections: Eastern Mich. U., U. Mich. Mus., Watercolor U.S.A. Collection. Recipient 3d prize Mid-Mich. Show, 1971, 2d prize Scarab Watercolor Show, 1972, 1st prize Toledo Artists Show, 1973, Toledo Area Artist Show, 1976. Mem. Common Cause, Network, Amnesty Internat., Mich. Watercolor Soc. Home: 614 Oakwood St Adrian MI 49221 Office: Siena Heights College Adrian MI 49221

CERVON, LAWRENCE JOHN, electronics mfg. co. exec.; b. Lozisce, Yugoslavia, Jan. 27, 1922; s. Victor and Dinka (Lucic) C.; came to U.S., 1928, derivative citizenship; B.S., Coll. City N.Y., 1943; postgrad. Fordham, U. Law Sch., 1946-47; m. Louise K. Bossler, Apr. 26, 1953; children—Kathryn L., Lawrence J. With RCA Internat., N.Y.C., 1945-46, Westinghouse Electric Internat., N.Y.C., 1946-47; with Gates Radio Co. div. Harris-Intertype Corp., Quincy, Ill., 1947-74, v.p., gen. mgr., 1967-74; v.p., gen. mgr. Communications Equipment div. Microwave Assos. Inc., 1975-76; pres. Broadcast Electronics Inc. subs. Filmways Inc., Quincy, Ill., 1976—; dir. Ill. State Bank of Quincy. Pres. Indsl. Assn. Quincy, 1969-71; mem. exec. bd. Saukee area council Boy Scouts Am., 1965-67; mem. Ill. Export Council, 1974-76; mem. bd. advisers Quincy Coll. Bd. dirs. Quincy YMCA, 1964-67; bd. dirs. St. Mary Hosp., Quincy 1968-75, pres., 1973-74. Served with USMCR, 1943, USNR, 1944-45. Mem. Am. Mgmt. Assn., Sales and Mktg. Execs. Quincy (pres. 1958-59), Navy League U.S. Club: Quincy Country. Home: 70 E Lincoln Hill Quincy IL 62301 Office: 4100 N 24th St Quincy IL 62301

CESSNA, JOHN CURTIS, research chemist; b. Johnstown, Pa., Apr. 15, 1926; s. John Curtis and Virginia Claire (Lingenfelter) C.; A.B. cum laude, Augustana Coll., 1950; M.S., Ia. State Coll., 1952; m. Virginia B. Anderson, June 20, 1947; children—Alan, Bonnie. Research chemist Nat. Carbon Research Lab., Cleve., 1952-64; sr. research chemist consumer products div. Union Carbide Corp., Parma, O., 1964-72, battery products div. Parma Tech. Center, 1972—. Served with USNR, 1943-46. Mem. Am. Chem. Soc., Electrochem. Soc., Nat. Assn. Corrosion Engrs., Phi Lambda Upsilon. Contbr. articles profl. jours. Patentee in field. Home: 8066 Spieth Rd Litchfield OH 44253 Office: 12900 Show Rd Parma OH 44130

CHABERT, HENRI LOUIS, educator; b. Paris, May 8, 1913; s. Jean and Madeleine C. (Lejeune) C.; B.A., U. Paris, 1937, M.A., 1941, Ph.D., 1965. Admitted to Paris bar, 1942; corr., fgn. editor Carrefour and Le Parisien, London, 1944-49; revisor, Selection of Reader's Digest; prof. lycee, Versailles, France, 1950-57; translator, precis writer UN, N.Y.C., 1957-60; prof. French lit. and civilization Ohio Wesleyan U., 1960-61, U. Kans., 1964-65, U. No. Iowa, Cedar Falls, 1961—. Ministry Edn. Nationale grantee, 1950-51; Brit. Council grantee, 1949-50. Mem. Am. Assn. Tchrs. French, Assn. Professeurs Amerique. Clubs: Racing (Paris). Contbr. numerous articles profl. revs. Home: 524 W Seerley Blvd Cedar Falls IA 50613 Office: U No Iowa Cedar Falls IA 50613

CHADIMA, WARREN KAY, dentist; b. Cedar Rapids, Iowa, Oct. 9, 1938; s. George Edward and Gladys Ann (Charipar) C.; B.A., U. Iowa, 1961, D.D.S., 1965; m. Joan Louise Nagel, July 15, 1961; children—Laura Marie, Ann Louise. Pvt. practice dentistry, Cedar Rapids, 1965—; mem. faculty U. Iowa, Coll. Dentistry, Iowa City, 1967-72. Dir. Hubbard Ice and Fuel Co., Cedar Rapids. Mem. Am., Iowa dental assns., Delta Sigma Delta, Omicron Kappa Upsilon. Presbyn. Home: 3607 Terrace Hill Dr NE Cedar Rapids IA 52402 Office: 1956 1st Ave NE Cedar Rapids IA 52402

CHADWICK, JOHN LLOYD, mobile home mfg. co. exec.; b. Windsor, Ont., Can., Aug. 14, 1922; s. Charles H. and Susan M. (Sullivan) C.; student Inst. Chartered Accountants Ont., 1950; B.A. in Bus. Adminstrn., U. Western Ont., London, 1944; m. Bernice Danaher, Sept. 8, 1945; children—Donald, Cherilynn (Mrs. Lyle Baugh). Came to U.S., 1951, naturalized, 1957. Auditor, Clarkson, Gordon & Co., Hamilton, Ont., 1945-51, Peat, Marwick & Mitchell, Detroit, 1951-52; internal auditor Parke Davis & Co., Detroit, 1952-56; controller, treas. Goebel Brewing Co., Detroit, 1956-64; controller Champion Home Builders Co., Dryden, Mich., 1966-68, treas., 1968-71, sec., treas., 1971-72, v.p. finance, dir., 1972-77, sr. v.p. subsidiaries, sec., 1977—; pres. Champion Ventures, Inc. Served with Canadian Navy, 1944. Mem. Chartered Accountants Ont. K.C. Office: 5573 E North St Dryden MI 48228

CHADWICK, ROBERT REID, JR., banker; b. Mineola, N.Y., Apr. 28, 1944; s. Robert Reid and Lois Irene (Klein) C.; B.A., Beloit Coll., 1966; grad. Nat. Lending Sch., 1976; m. Lindsay McCormac, July 27, 1976; children from previous marriage—Kimberly Edith, Mark Robert; stepchildren—Christine Jo and Michael David Coppin. Asst. to v.p., cashier DuPage Bank & Trust Co., Glen Ellyn, Ill., 1969-70, auditor, 1971-74, v.p., cashier, 1975—, sec. bd. dirs., 1975—. Treas., Glen Ellyn United Fund, 1970—; mem. Central DuPage Hosp. Devel. Council, 1970. Served with U.S. Army, 1967-69: Vietnam. Mem. Bank Adminstrn. Inst. (chartered bank auditor), Am., Ill., DuPage County bankers assns. Clubs: Glen Ellyn Jr. C. of C., DuPage. Home: 301 Bryant Ave Glen Ellyn IL 60137 Office: 466 Main St Glen Ellyn IL 60137

CHAFFEE, JAMES LEONARD, city ofcl.; b. Green, Kans., June 23, 1941; s. Leonard Harrison and Eulah (Bergstrom) C.; B.S. in Civil Engring., Kans. State U., 1964; m. Shirley Kay Calvin, June 2, 1963; children—Mark, Wendy. Jr. civil engr. Calif. Hwy. Dept., Marysville, 1964-66; asst. civil engr. Tracy (Calif.) Dept. Water Resources, 1966; asst. city engr., Tracy, 1966-69; city engr., Pendleton, Oreg., 1969-72; dir. pub. works City of Manhattan (Kans.), 1972—. Registered profl. engr., Calif., Oreg., Kans. Mem. Am. Soc. C.E., Am. Pub. Works Assn., Am. Water Works Assn., Pi Kappa Alpha. Home: 1519 Highland Dr Manhattan KS 66502 Office: City Hall Manhattan KS 66502

CHAFFEE, JAMES RALPH, ins. agt.; b. Detroit, June 27, 1936; s. Warren Vern and Irene Frances (Piotrowski) C.; student Am. Coll. Life Underwriters, 1973-77; m. Jean Elissa Ford, Sept. 21, 1957; children—Michael, Timothy, Paula, Karen, Christopher. Supr., tchr. Arthur Murray Inc., Detroit, 1954-57; credit sales mgr. Goodyear Tire & Rubber Co., Detroit, 1957-62; special agt. Purdential Ins. Co. of Am., Southfield, Mich., 1962-72; gen. agt. James R. Chaffee & Assoc., Indpls. Life Ins. Co., Washington, Mich., 1972—. Dir. Shelby Township Parks and Recreation Bd., 1977—. Served with USNG, 1954-62. Recipient numerous ins. agts., sales awards, 1963—. Mem. Nat. Assn. Life Underwriters, Mich. State (bd. dir. 1976-77), Macomb County (pres. 1976-77) life underwriters assn. Roman Catholic. Clubs: K.C., Utica (Mich.) Kiwanis (pres. 1965-66). Home: 53727 Kristin Court Utica MI 48087 Office: 55500 Van Dyke St Washington MI 48094

CHAKIRIS, KENNETH MILTON, marketing exec.; b. Detroit, Dec. 11, 1925; s. Nicholas and Irene (Cloud) C.; B.A., Mich. State U., 1950; postgrad. Loyola U. (Chgo.), 1970-71; m. Betty June Hughes, Sept. 10, 1950; children—Kenneth N., James L., Carolyn A. Dir. mktg. TRW/United Greenfield Group, Northbrook, Ill., 1955-70; v.p. sales Rust-Oleum Internat., Evanston, Ill., 1970-74; sales/mktg. cons. Binswanger Glass div. Nat. Gypsum Co., Memphis, 1974—; mktg. cons. Orgn. Renewal, Inc., Washington, 1977—. Mem. distbn. council W. Tex. State U., 1971-72; pres.'s council Luth. Sch. Theology Chgo., 1970—. Served with USAF, 1944-46. Decorated Air medal with bronze oak leaf cluster. Mem. Am. Supply and Machinery Mfrs. Assn. (dir. 1971-74), Am. Mktg. Assn., Sales and Mktg. Execs. Assn. Chgo., Sales and Mktg. Execs. Assn. Internat., Internat. Cons. Found. Lutheran. Club: Rotary. Address: 755 Lincoln Ave Winnetka IL 60093

CHAKRABORTY, JYOTSNA, educator, physiologist; b. Calcutta, India, June 1, 1934; s. Mahadev and Anila (Benerjee) Mukherjee; came to U.S., 1969, naturalized, 1971; I.Sc., Bethune Coll., Calcutta, 1952; B.Sc., City Coll., Calcutta, 1954; M.Sc., Sci. Coll. of U. Calcutta, 1956; Ph.D., Saha Inst. Nuclear Physics of U. Calcutta, 1962; m. Ajit Chakrabarti, Apr. 28, 1954; 1 dau., Mala. Lectr. biophysics Inst. Nuclear Physics, Calcutta, 1965-69; asst. prof. physiology Med. Coll. Ohio, 1973-75, asso. prof., 1975—, dir. EM lab. of dept. physiology, 1970—; tchr. med. and nursing students Toledo U., Med. Coll. Ohio, Toledo, Bowling Green State U. Postdoctoral fellow Ford Found., 1969-70, Ia. State U., 1962-63; research tng. scholar Govt. of India, 1957-60. Mem. Electron Microscope Soc. India (exec. com. 1964-69), Electron Microscopy Soc. Northwestern Ohio (sec. 1973-75), Biophys. Soc. India (founder mem.), Soc. Study of Reprodn., A.A.A.S. Contbr. articles sci. jours. Office: Dept Physiology Med Coll Ohio PO Box 6190 Toledo OH 43614

CHALFANT, CLYDE, lawyer; b. Steubenville, Ohio, May 18, 1905; s. Frank and Anna (Driscoll) C.; B.S., Washington and Jefferson Coll., 1928; postgrad. Western Res. U., 1928-29, Harvard, 1929-31; m. Mary Peterson, Feb. 1, 1937; children—R. Peterson, Caroline. Admitted to Ohio bar, 1932; mem. firm Chalfant, Chalfant & Morrow, Steubenville, 1932—; pres., dir. First Steubenville Savs. & Loan Assn., 1956—; dir. First Nat. Bank & Trust Co., Steubenville, Bank of Weirton (W.Va.), Peoples Bank of Weirton, Weinman Pump & Supply Co., Marine Hydraulics Co. (both Pitts.). Mem. adv. bd. Coll. of Steubenville, 1966—, Small Bus. Adminstrn. Ohio, 1970—. Mem. finance com. Ohio Republican Com., 1964—. Presbyn. (trustee 1960-70). Clubs: Williams Country (Weirton); Country (Steubenville); University, Duquesne (Pitts.); Capitol Hill (Washington). Home: 646 Ross Park Blvd Steubenville OH 43952 Office: 913 1st Nat Bank Bldg Steubenville OH 43952

CHALFANT, JAN L., lawyer; b. Portland, Ind., Aug. 14, 1942; s. Ralph O. and Clarice Ann (Woodard) C.; A.B., DePauw U., 1964; J.D., Ind. U., 1968; m. Mary Ann Grobey, Aug. 21, 1965; children—Jeffrey, Amy. Admitted to Ind. bar, 1968; practiced in Winchester, Ind., 1968—; partner firm Sullivan & Chalfant; dep. pros. Randolph County, 1969-72; prosecutor 25th Jud. Circuit of Ind., 1975—. Bd. dirs. United Fund, Winchester, 1971—, pres., 1972; vice chmn. Golden Eagle dist. Boy Scouts Am. Mem. Am., Ind., Randolph County (pres. 1973) bar assns., Am. Judicature Soc., Ind. Pros. Attys. Assn. (dir. 1976—), Winchester C. of C. (pres. 1973). Republican. Methodist. Mason, Kiwanian (pres. 1972). Home: 212 E Washington St Winchester IN 47394 Office: 203 W Washington St Winchester IN 47394

CHALFANT, JOSEPH SHAW, mgmt. cons.; b. Richmond, Ind., Apr. 12, 1936; s. Ray King and Margaret (Shaw) C.; B.S., Ind. U., 1958; postgrad. U. Louisville Sch. Law, 1959-62; m. Harriet Vaughan Strange, June 6, 1959; children—Martin Joseph, Matthew Christopher. Sales, Colgate-Palmolive Co., 1958, merchandising rep., 1959-61; sales mgr. Mid-Continent Carton Corp., Louisville, 1961-63, pres., 1963-72; pres. Shaw Internat., 1972—; spl. mgmt. cons. Touche, Ross & Co., Louisville; past dir. for mfg. Ky. Fried Chicken Corp. Active March of Dimes. Served with AUS, 1958-59. Mem. Sigma Alpha Epsilon, Alpha Delta Sigma. Republican. Methodist. Club: Ad. Home: Trimingham Rd New Albany IN 47150 Office: PO Box 375 New Albany IN 47150

CHALIAN, VAROUJAN ASADOUR, prosthodontist; b. Beirut, Lebanon, Aug. 29, 1927; s. Asadour and Yeranouhi (Chamsarian) C.; B.S., Armenian Coll., Beirut, Lebanon, 1945; D.D.S., Ecole de Chirurgie Dentaire et de Stomatologie, Paris, France, 1955; D.D.S., Ind. U. Sch. Dentistry, 1964, M.S.D., 1968; m. Zarouhi Izmirlian, Oct. 15, 1961; children—Ara, Vicken, Luci, Sona. Came to U.S., 1956, naturalized, 1967. Dir. maxillofacial prosthetics clinic Ind. U. Sch. Dentistry, Indpls., 1960-65, asst. prof., dir., 1965-68, asst. prof., chmn., 1968-70, asso. prof. 1970-73, chmn., 1970—, prof. maxillofacial prosthetics and otolarngology, 1973—. Chief comprehensive dental sect. St. Vincent Hosp., Indpls., 1973; maxillofacial prosthetics cons. Walter Reed Hosp., Washington, Wright-Patterson AFB, Ohio, Nat. Cancer Inst. Bd. dirs. Little Red Door, Marion County Cancer Soc. Little Red Door, Marion County Cancer Soc. grantee, 1970-73. Diplomate Am. Bd. Prosthodontics. Fellow Am. Coll. Dentists; mem. Am. Acad. Maxillofacial Prosthetics (pres. 1973-74), Internat. Assn. for Study Dento-Facial Abnormalities (v.p. 1972-74). Author: Maxillofacial Prosthetics-Multidisciplinary Practice, 1971. Home: 5333 E 75th St Indianapolis IN 46250 Office: 1121 W Michigan St Indianapolis IN 46202

CHALKLEY, LEWIS MERIDETH, savs. and loan assn. exec.; b. Peru, Ind., Apr. 23, 1924; s. Lewis Baily and Nellie Mae (Pleasant) C.; B.S., Ind. U., 1950; m. Patricia Ann Butt, Apr. 7, 1948; children—Curryanne, Gregrey John, Roger Stacy, Janny Letitia, Jeffrey Lewis (dec.). With Peru Fed. Savs. & Loan Assn., 1946—, pres., 1961—, also dir.; chmn. bd. Ind. Financial Service Corp., 1971—. Trustee Dukes Meml. Hosp., YMCA; bd. dirs. United Fund, Miami County Crippled Children and Adults Assn.; treas. 1st Bapt. Ch., Peru, 1976, 77. Served with AUS, 1942-46. Recipient Award of Merit, Peru C. of C., 1969; Outstanding Leadership award Miami County United Fund, 1968. Mem. U.S., Ind. (dir.) savs. and loan leagues, Peru C. of C. (dir. 1968-71), Beta Gamma Sigma. Mason, Elk, Rotarian. Home: 5 Golden Hills Peru IN 46970 Office: 20 22 W 5th St Peru IN 46970

CHALKLEY, THOMAS HENRY FERGUSON, ophthalmic surgeon; b. N.Y.C., Nov. 3, 1933; s. Lyman and Katherine (Ferguson) C.; B.A., U. Wis., 1955, M.D., 1959; m. Cynthia Carroll, Nov. 21, 1975; children—Ellen Elizabeth, Deborah Katherine. Intern, Ed. J. Meyer Hosp., Buffalo, N.Y., 1958-59; resident physician Northwestern U. Med. Sch., 1960-62; practice medicine specializing in ophthalmic surgery, Chgo., 1962—; attending physician Passavant Meml., Children's Meml., VA Lakeside hosps., Chgo., 1962—; asso. prof. dept. ophthalmology Northwestern U. Med. Sch., 1962—. Served to comdr. USNR, 1966-68. Mem. Internat. Strabismological Soc., Am. Acad. Ophthalmology and Otolaryngology, Chgo. Ophthal. Soc. (pres. 1977—). Author: Your Eyes, 1973. Editorial bd. Am. Jour.

Ophthalmology, 1965—. Home: 3200 Lake Shore Dr Chicago IL 60657 Office: 700 N Michigan Ave Chicago IL 60611

CHALLMAN, JEAN CARSON (MRS. ROBERT CHESTER CHALLMAN), ret. librarian; b. Oakland, Calif., Jan. 5, 1912; d. Francis Leveridge and Armor Jean (Deamer) Carson; B.A., Stanford U., 1933; M.A., Ohio State U., 1936; M.A., U. Minn., 1962; postgrad. U. Calif. at Berkeley, 1934, Vassar Coll., 1945; m. Robert Chester Challman, Dec. 20, 1932; children—Jerome Alan, Martha Carson Challman Mayer. Caseworker Fed. Emergency Relief Adminstrn., San Francisco, 1934; parole officer Conn. State Reformatory for Women, Niantic, 1944; bookmobile librarian Anoka County Library, Spring Lake Park, Minn., 1962-65; librarian, Met. Community Coll., Mpls., 1965-77. Aide, Norwich (Conn.) State Hosp., 1944, Topeka State Hosp., 1949-50, Anoka (Minn.) State Hosp., 1957-59. Mem. AAUW (pres. Norwich, Conn., 1944-46), LWV (pres. Topeka 1949-50), ACLU, Am. Minn. library assns., Pi Beta Phi. Unitarian. Home: 3915 Beard Ave S Minneapolis MN 55410

CHALMERS, E(DWIN) LAURENCE, JR., museum adminstr.; b. Wildwood, N.J., Mar. 24, 1928; s. Edwin Laurence and Carolyn (Smith) C.; A.B., Princeton U., 1948, M.A., 1950, Ph.D., 1951; m. Hannah Kamp, June 1, 1973; 1 son, Timothy Blair; children by previous marriage—Edwin Laurence III, Thomas H. Instr. psychology Princeton U., 1951-52; asst. prof., then prof. psychology, asst. dean faculties Fla. State U., 1962-64, dean Coll. Arts and Scis., 1964-66, v.p. acad. affairs, 1966-69; chancellor U. Kan., Lawrence, 1969-72; pres. Art Inst. Chgo., 1972—. Served from 2d lt. to 1st lt. USAF, 1953-56. Mem. Phi Beta Kappa, Sigma Xi, Omicron Delta Kappa, Phi Kappa Phi. Home: 1301 N Astor St Chicago IL 60610

CHAMBERLAIN, WEBB PARKS, JR., ophthalmologist; b. Cleve., July 19, 1910; s. Webb Parks and Lucy Belle (Libbey) C.; m. Elizabeth Harker Newell, Dec. 4, 1948; children—Marilyn, Ann, Charlotte, Lucy, John. Intern, Univ. Hosps., Cleve., 1936-38; resident N.Y. Eye and Ear Infirmary, N.Y.C., 1938-41; practice medicine specializing in ophthalmology, Cleve., 1946—; ophthalmologist Luth. Med. Center, Cleve., 1946—; clin. prof. ophthalmology, dept. surgery Case Western Res. U. Sch. Medicine, 1958—. Mem. del. assembly United Torch Drive, Cleve. 1973. Trustee Great Lakes Shakespear Festival, 1965—, v.p., 1969-72; trustee pres. Cleve. Met. YMCA, 1977—; pres. Cleve. Med. Library Assn., 1961, bd. trustees, 19——; bd. trustees Cleve. Christian Home, 1965—, pres., 1968-69; trustee Hiram (O.) Coll. Served to maj. M.C., AUS, 1941-46. Fellow Am. Bd. Ophthalmology, Am. Acad. Ophthalmology and Otolaryngology (Honor award 1967), A.C.S. Clubs: Union Hermit, Chagrin Valley Hunt (Gates Mills, O.). Editor: Am. Orthoptic Jour., 1955-71; asso. editor Archives of Ophthalmology, 1961-63. Contbr. articles to various publs. Home: 19100 S Woodland Rd Shaker Heights OH 44122 Office: 1422 Euclid Av Room 1324 Cleveland OH 44115

CHAMBERLIN, LAWRENCE EUGENE, newspaper publisher; b. Mapleton, Iowa, July 21, 1933; s. Francis Joseph and Bessie Grace (Beymer) C.; B.S., Iowa State U.; m. Margaret McFerran Cole, Aug. 14, 1955; children—Catherine Rilla, Steven Charles. Advt. mgr. Monticello (Iowa) Express, 1957-60; editor, mgr. Sioux Valley News, Canton, S.D., 1960-64; editor, pub. Mobridge (S.D.) Tribune, 1964—. Served with AUS, 1955-57. Recipient state community service in field of journalism award Cons. Engrs. Council S.D., 1965, 74. Mem. Nat. Newspaper Assn. (chmn. better newspaper contest com. 1977), S.D. Press Assn. (dir. 1969-75, pres. 1974-75), Sigma Delta Chi (pres. S.D. chpt. 1966-68). Rotarian (pres. Canton 1963-64). Home: 1006 3rd Ave W Mobridge SD 57601 Office: 111 W 3d St Mobridge SD 57601

CHAMBERLIN, LESLIE JOSEPH, educator; b. St. Louis, Aug. 16, 1926; s. George Albert and Margaret Mary (Cassidy) C.; A.A., Harris Tchrs. Coll., 1948; B.S., Washington U. at St. Louis, 1951, M.A., 1953; D.Ed. (Parson Blewett Meml. scholar), U. Mo., 1960; m. Virginia Rose Schauer, Apr. 19, 1947; children—Veronica (Mrs. Paul Gold), Barbara (Mrs. Michael Youther), Linda (Mrs. Philip Newgent), Mark, Theresa, Matthew. Tchr., prin., Brighton, Ill., 1948-51; tchr., St. Louis, 1951-56, adminstrv. asst., 1956-60, prin. elementary schs., 1960-63; dir. admissions So. Ill. U., Carbondale, 1963-67; prof. ednl. adminstrn. and supervision Bowling Green (Ohio) State U., 1967—, chmn. ednl. adminstrn. and supervision, 1976—. Served with inf. AUS, 1945-46. Mem. Phi Delta Kappa. Lion. Author: Team Teaching Organization and Administration, 1969; Effective Instruction Through Dynamic Discipline, 1971; Administration, Education and Change: An Introduction, 1972; Improving School Discipline, 1974. Contbr. articles to profl. jours. Home: 11934 Sugar Ridge Rd Bowling Green OH 43402

CHAMBERS, DAVID ARTHUR PRYTHERCH, educator; b. Lloydminster, Sask., Can., Feb. 13, 1923; s. Thomas Griffith and Florence Emily (Greetham) C.; B.A., U. B.C. (Can.), 1951; M.Sc., McGill, U., 1957, Ph.D., 1963; m. Elizabeth Jean Carr, May 10, 1958. Mgr., Western Auto Supply, Red Deer, Alta., Can., 1940-43; research statistician Hudson's Bay Co., Vancouver, B.C., 1951-53, Dept. of Health, Province of B.C., Victoria, 1953-55; research psychologist Provincial Mental Hosp., Saint John, New Brunswick, 1959-62; asst. prof. psychology U. Sask., Saskatoon, 1962-65; asst. prof. psychology U. Western Ont., London, 1965-67, asso. prof., 1967—, asst. dean faculty of social sci., 1969—, asso. dean faculty of social sci., 1972-74, acting dean faculty of social sci., 1974-75, registrar, 1975—. Chief psychologist London (Ont.) Psychiat. Hosp., 1968-69; cons. psychologist, 1969-73; cons. psychologist Goderich (Ont.) Psychiat. Hosp., 1967—; chmn. bd. Cragsman Ltd., London, Ont., 1975—. Served with Royal Can. Navy, 1944-46. Ont. Mental Health Found. grantee, 1966-69, Can. Dept of Labour grantee, 1966-67, Fanshawe Coll. Applied Arts and Tech. grantee, 1967. Mem. N.Y. Acad. Scis., Sigma Xi. Home: 1571 Ryersie Rd London ON N6G 2S2 Canada

CHAMBERS, DUWAYNE LEROY, accountant; b. Hancock County, Ohio, Oct. 18, 1937; s. Park L. and Doris M. (Litzenberg) C.; student Findlay Coll., 1956; B.C.S., Internat. Coll., 1958; m. Kathleen Grace Woerner, Dec. 24, 1958; children—Douglas Lane, Deborah Kay, Kenneth Park, Karla Marie. Chief accountant Findlay (Ohio) Pub. Co., 1963-66; accountant Marathon Oil Co., Findlay, 1967-70; controller Seneca Wire & Mfg. Co., Fostoria, Ohio, 1970-73, asst. sec., 1972-73; pvt. practice accounting, Findlay, 1973—. Mem. Nat. Soc. Pub. Accountants, Nat. Assn. Accountants (chpt. pres. 1973), Findlay Optimist Club (treas., dir. 1960-62). Mem. Ch. of God (treas. 1965-70, chmn. bd. Youth for Christ, 1974-76). Elk, Rotarian. Home: 620 Frank St Findlay OH 45840 Office: 601 Tiffin Ave Findlay OH 45840

CHAMBERS, EARL RICHARD, personnel adminstr.; b. Wyoming, Ill., Nov. 4, 1916; s. John Thomas and Margaret Jane (Lawless) C.; B.Ed., Ill. State Normal U., 1938; M.A., U. Ill., 1947, postgrad., 1948-53; m. Jane Margaret Petersen, May 8, 1954; 1 son, Robert. Profl. personnel work Ill. Civil Service Commn., 1947-53, chief of exams. adminstrng., employee selection, 1951-53; personnel dir. St. Louis County, Mo., 1953—. Mem. Gov. Mo. Citizens Adv. Council Higher Edn. Act, 1972-73. Served from pvt. to tech. sgt. AUS, 1942-46; Philippines, New Guinea. Mem. Pub. Personnel Assn. (exec. bd. local chapter, 1952-53, regional sec.-treas., 1956-57, regional 1st v.p. 1963-64, regional chmn. 1964-65), Am. Soc. Personnel Adminstrn. (accredited); Am. Soc. Pub. Adminstrn. (exec. bd. local chpt. 1951-52, 59-63, 64-65, 70-71, pres. Met. St. Louis 1963-64), Internat. Personnel Mgmt. Assn. (v.p. St. Louis chpt. 1973-74, pres. 1974-75), Kappa Delta Pi, Pi Gamma Mu. Contbr. articles, abstracts and revs. to profl. jours. Home: 12 Armstrong Dr Glendale MO 63122 Office: 7900 Forsyth Blvd Clayton Mo 63105

CHAMBERS, LAURANCE GEORGE, univ. adminstr.; b. Kulm, N.D., Nov. 28, 1923; s. Giles Edward and Emma (Roedel) C.; m. Marjorie Louise Sommerdorf, Sept. 2, 1952; children—Debra Mary, Marc Giles, Timothy Paul; Ph.B., B.S., U. N.D., 1950; M.S., N.D. State U., 1970. Pub. weekly newspaper, editor daily newspaper Hazen (N.D.) Star, Wishek (N.D.) Star, Jamestown (N.D.) Daily Sun, 1951-53; editor Bar North (N.D.) State Cattlemans mag., 1952-53; asst. editor N.D. State Extension Service, 1962-67; mgr. dept. communication services Mich. Technol. U., Houghton, 1967—; communications and pub. relations cons.; tchr. parent and leader effectiveness tng. Mem. Pub. Relations Soc. Am., Toastmasters Internat. (area gov. 1972, Able Toastmaster), Kiwanis Internat. (lt. gov. Wis.-Upper Mich., pres. Copper Country Club 1975). Home: 1008 E Houghton Ave Houghton MI 49931

CHAMBERS, MERRITT MADISON, educator; b. Mount Vernon, Ohio, Jan. 26, 1899; s. Rufus Ward and Etta Amelia (Miller) C.; student U. Fla., Harvard; B.A., Ohio Wesleyan U., 1922; M.A., Ohio State U., 1927, Ph.D., 1931; Litt.D (hon.), Eastern Ky. U., 1969. Tchr., prin. high schs., 1922-26; with Am. Council on Edn., 1935-42, 45-51; cons. U.S. Office Edn., 1952-53; resident, propr. Lafayette Farms, Mt. Vernon, 1951-58; vis. prof. higher edn. U. Mich., 1958-63; exec. dir. Mich. Council State Coll. Presidents, 1961-62; prof. higher edn. Ind. U., 1963-69, Ill. State U., Normal, 1969—; summer prof. Memphis State U., 1970. Participated in surveys of higher edn., Mass. and Ill., 1949, Conn., Wis., Iowa, 1950, N.Y.C., 1961, Ky., 1962, Md., 1963; cons. Com. on Govt. and Higher Edn., 1957; chmn. Long-Range Study Higher Edn. Ky., 1965-66; cons. So. Ill. U. and Mich. Bd. Edn., 1966. Served to maj. USAAF, 1942-46. Decorated Army Commendation ribbon; recipient ann. award Nat. Orgn. Legal Problems Edn., 1970; award Nat. Colloquium Higher Edn., 1971; Presdl. citation Am. Coll. Pub. Relations Assn., 1972. Fellow A.A.A.S.; mem. Knox County Farm Bur. (pres. 1957-58), N.E.A. (life), Delta Sigma Rho, Phi Delta Kappa, Alpha Sigma Phi. Author: Youth-Serving Organizations, rev. edit., 1947; The Campus and the People, 1960; Voluntary Statewide Coordination in Public Higher Education, 1961; Chance and Choice in Higher Education, 1962; Financing Higher Education, 1963; The Colleges and the Courts Since 1950, 1964; Freedom and Repression in Higher Education, 1965; Bibliography of Higher Education, 1966; The Colleges and the Courts, 1962-66, 1967; Higher Education: Who Pays? Who Gains?, 1968; Higher Education in the Fifty States, 1970; The Developing Law of the Student and the College, 1972; Faculty and Staff Before the Bench, 1973; Higher Education and State Governments, 1974; The Colleges and the Courts: Entity, Property and Finance, 1975; Keep Higher Education Moving, 1976. Editor various works including: Charters of Philanthropies, 1948; Universities of the World Outside U.S.A., 1950. Contbr. ednl., legal publs. Home: 311 S Main St Normal IL 61761

CHAMBERS, ROBERT ORVILLE, lawyer; b. Washington, Ind., May 24, 1925; s. Orville and Vivian (Arnold) C.; LL.B., Ind. U., 1949; m. Jo Ann Larrick, June 21, 1947; children—Jeffry, Blake, Grant. Admitted to Ind. bar, 1949; spl. agt. FBI, Newark, Boston, 1950-51; practiced in Washington, 1951—; mem. firms Fitzpatrick, Chambers & Waller, 1956—; atty. City of Washington, 1958-67. Dir., Home Bldg. Savs. & Loan Assn., Washington, Washington Industries, Inc., Hoosier Magnetics, Inc. Served with USAAF, 1943-45. Mem. Am., Ind., Daviess County bar assns., Am. Quarter Horse Assn., Washington Saddle Horse Assn. Home: 24 Edwardsport Rd Washington IN 47501 Office: Peoples Bank Washington IN 47501

CHAMIS, CHRISTOS CONSTANTINOS, aerospace engr.; b. Sotira, Greece, May 16, 1930; s. Constantinos and Anastasia Gianos (Kyriakos) C.; came to U.S., 1948, naturalized, 1954; B.S. in Civil Engring., Fenn Coll., 1960; M.S., Case Inst. Tech., 1962; Ph.D., Case Western Res. U., 1967; m. Alice Margaret Yanosko, Aug. 20, 1966; children—Crysanthie Diane, Anna Lisa, Constantinos Andy. Engr., designer, draftsman cons. engring. firms, Cleve., 1955-60; grad. asst. Case Inst. Tech., 1960-62, 64-67; research mathematician B.F. Goodrich Research Center, Brecksville, O., 1962-64; research asso. Case Western Res. U., 1967-68; aerospace engr. NASA Lewis Research Center, Cleve., 1968—; adj. prof. Cleve. State U., 1969—. Served with USMC, 1952-53. Recipient Soc. Plastics Industry Reinforced Plastics Composites Best Paper award, 1969, 73, 75; NASA technology utilization awards, 1970-76, Spl. Achievement award, 1976; registered profl. engr., Ohio. Mem. Am. Inst. Aeros. and Astronautics, Am. Soc. C.E., Am. Soc. Testing Materials, Epirotic Soc. Dodona. Greek Orthodox. Editor: Treatises of Composite Materials: Structural Design and Analysis, 1975. Contbr. articles to profl. jours. Home: 24534 Framingham Dr Westlake OH 44145 Office: 21000 Brookpark Rd Cleveland OH 44135

CHAMNESS, WILLIAM BETHEA, leaf tobacco co. exec.; b. Florence, S.C., Nov. 17, 1927; s. Earle and Essie (Bethea) C.; student Clemson Coll., 1947-51; m. Zoe Parker, Nov. 15, 1952; children—Peter Bethea, Morri Cochran, Alex Parker, Dixie Kay. With Parker Tobacco Co., Inc., Maysville, Ky., 1953—, v.p., 1955-76, pres., 1976—; pres. Parker Internat., 1973—; owner C & H Homes; pres. Maysville Realty & Investment Co.; v.p. Extaho, Honduras, Hemisphere Tobacco & Trading Corp. Pres. Aberdeen Bd. Pub. Affairs, 1968—; chmn. bd. Brown County Airport Commn., 1967—. Co-chmn. Ohioans for Rhodes, 1966. Bd. dirs. Boys Club, Humphrey Playground, Maysville Players, Hayswood Hosp. Served with USNR, 1945-46, with AUS, 1951-53. Presbyn. (elder). Home: Huntington Park Aberdeen OH 45101 Office: PO Box 428 Maysville KY 41056

CHAMP, NORMAN BARNARD, JR., mfg. co. exec.; b. St. Louis, Sept. 20, 1928; s. Norman Barnard and Elizabeth (Trigg) C.; B.S., Mass. Inst. Tech., 1950; M.B.A., Harvard, 1952; m. Anne A. VanAnden, June 7, 1952 (div. 1970); children—Deborah Anne, Norman Barnard III; m. 2d, Judy Smith Zander, Oct. 1, 1977. Vice pres., dir. Midwest Piping Co., 1953-61; group v.p. Crane Co., 1961-62; mgr. mfg. St. Louis Car Co., 1962-68; v.p. Champ Spring Co., St. Louis, 1968-71, pres., 1971—; v.p. Champ Realty Investment and Finance Co., 1968; v.p. Edmu Realty Co., 1968-71, pres., 1971—; dir. Mark Twain Parkway Bank. Mem. St. Louis County Bd. Jail Visitors, 1962; co-chmn. Finance Com. Eagleton For Senator 1968; Mo. finance chmn. for Jimmy Carter, 1976; Clayton Twp. (Mo.) Democratic committeeman, 1976—; bd. mgrs. So. Side YMCA, 1958—; treas. Washington U. Child Guidance Clinic, 1971-74, trustee Webster Coll., 1973—. Served to 2d lt. USAF, 1952-53. Mem. Mass. Inst. Tech. Alumni Assn. (v.p. 1971, mem. nat. alumni club bd. 1967-70), Sigma Xi, Tau Beta Pi. Rotarian. Home: 22 Clermont Ln St Louis MO 63124 Office: 2107 Chouteau Ave St Louis MO 63103

CHAMPINE, GEORGE ALLEN, computer scientist; b. Fairmont, Minn., May 16, 1934; s. Ashley Floyd and Genevieve (Northway) C.; B.S., U. Minn., 1956, M.S. in Physics, 1959, Ph.D. in Bus. Adminstrn., 1975; m. Barbara Joan Nelson, Mar. 17, 1956; children—Renee, Mark, Lisa. Programming supr. UNIVAC div. Sperry Rand, St. Paul, 1958-63, mgr. radar data processing studies, 1964-68, mgr. advanced system applications, 1968-70, group mgr. advanced system design, 1970-73, staff scientist, 1974-77, dir. advanced systems, 1977—; systems analyst Bell Telephone Labs., Whippany, N.J., 1962-63; instr. Hamline U., 1959-61; adj. prof. Inst. Tech., U. Minn., 1976—; lectr. computer tech., Asia, Africa, Europe. Mem. Soaring Soc. Am., Am. Phys. Soc., I.E.E.E., Am. Mgmt. Assn., Internat. Platform Assn., Assn. Computing Machinery, Nat Acad. Sci. (adv. com.), Inst. Tech. Alumni Assn. (v.p.), Beta Gamma Sigma. Methodist. Author: Error Recovery for Nike Zeus Target Intercept Computer; Computer Control of Array Radar. Contbr. articles to profl. jours. Home: 11006 Radisson Dr Burnsville MN 55337

CHAMPLIN, ALBERT LOUIS, JR., food co. exec.; b. Chariton, Iowa, Sept. 15, 1918; s. Albert Louis and Angeline (Culbertson) C.; B.S. in Tech. Journalism, Iowa State U., 1941, B.S. in Animal Husbandry, 1941; m. Grace Mae Barnhill, Mar. 21, 1943; children—Steven Kirk, Lynn Champlin Lloyd. Dir. publs. Gen. Mills Research Labs., 1946-52; dir. publs. and publicity, dept. pub. relations Gen. Mills, Inc., lMpls., 1952-54, asst. mgr. dept. pub. relations, 1954-56, asst. to dir. pub. relations, asst. dir. pub. relations, 1965-73, dir. pub. relations, 1973—, dir. consumer affairs, 1977—. Mem. pub. relations com. Met. Mpls. YMCA; past v.p. pub. information Mental Health Assn. Minn. Served with USCGR, 1942-45. Mem. Pub. Relations Soc. Am. (pres. Minn. chpt. 1961), Minn. Press Club (treas. 1964), Farm House Frat. Republican. Mem. United Ch. of Christ. Home: 3124 Edgewood Ave S Minneapolis MN 55426 Office: 9200 Wayzata Blvd Minneapolis MN 55440

CHAMS, ALBERT NESSIM, obstetrician, gynecologist; b. Beirut, Lebanon, July 24, 1934; s. Nessim A. Alegra (Matalon) C.; came to U.S., 1962; naturalized, 1977; M.D. with high honors, Faculté Française de Medecine, Beirut, 1961; m. Huguette Totah, Apr. 4, 1962; children—Joyce Gail, Roger Nessim, Danielle. Intern, Central Maine Gen. Hosp., Lewiston, 1962-63; resident Mt. Sinai Hosp., Chgo., 1963-67; practice medicine specializing in obstetrics and gynecology, Chgo., 1967—; mem. staff Mt. Sinai Hosp., Edgewater Hosp., Gottleib Meml. Hosp. Recipient Abbie Norman award Mt. Sinai Hosp., 1967; diplomate Am. Bd. Obstetrics and Gynecology. Fellow A.C.S., Am. Coll. Obstetrics and Gynecology; mem. AMA, Am. Fertility Soc., Am. Assn. Gynecologists and Laparoscopists, Chgo. Med. Soc. Jewish. Clubs: Health (Chgo.) Touhy Tennis, B'nai B'rith. Home: 4450 W Lunt Lincolnwood IL 60646 Office: 30 N Michigan Ave Chicago IL 60601 also 3425 W Peterson Chicago IL 60621

CHAN, GER AU, physician; b. Swatow, Kwangtung, China, May 21, 1916; s. Tiau Tong and Sok Ching (Ling) C.; M.D., Lingnan U., 1942; M.P.H., Nat. Central U., China, 1946; m. Corinne Wu, May 18, 1946; children—Samuel, Audrey, Lester. Resident physician Nassau County Sanatorium, Farmingdale, N.Y., 1946-49; sr. resident physician Provincial Sanatorium, Charlottetown, P.E.I., Can., 1951-55; resident psychiatry U. Western Ont. (Can.), London, 1956-58; clin. dir. male service Ont. Hosp., Woodstock, 1959-69; dir. psychiat. unit Oxford Mental Health Centre, 1970-71; dir. employee health service St. Thomas (Ont.) Psychiat. Hosp., 1972—; pres. Oxford County Tb. and Respiratory Disease Assn., 1968-69. Fellow Am. Coll. Chest Physicians, Am. Geriatric Soc.; mem. Canadian, Ont. med. assns., Ont. Psychiat. Assn., Ont. Thoracic Soc. Presbyn. (elder 1965—). Home: 189 McMaster Court London ON N6K 1J8 Canada Office: St Thomas Psychiatric Hosp St Thomas ON N5P 3VP Canada

CHAN, MICHAEL MING-SUI, research scientist; b. Hong Kong, Feb. 17, 1924; s. Tse Seng and Wei Che (Tsang) C.; came to U.S., 1947; B.S. in Chemistry, U. Wash., 1949; postgrad. Columbia, 1950; M.S. (Indsl. Research fellow) in Food Tech., U. Mass., 1952, Ph.D. in Food Tech. and Biochemistry, 1956. Asso. scientist Fisheries Research Bd. Can., Ottawa, 1956-61; research officer Can. Dept. Agr., Ottawa, 1961-64; sr. food scientist N.B. Research and Productivity Council, Fredericton, Can., 1964-67, acting head food sci. and tech. dept., 1966-67; sr. research scientist Kraft, Inc., Glenview, Ill., 1967—; research instr. U. Mass., 1956; adv. com. food sci. and tech. Republic of China, 1977—. Recipient Can. Patents and Devel. Corp. award Nat. Research Council, 1964. Fellow Royal Soc. Health (U.K.); mem. Inst. Food Technologists (profl.), Am. Oil Chemists Soc. Home: 1204 Waukegan Rd Glenview IL 60025 Office: Kraft Inc 801 Waukegan Rd Glenview IL 60025

CHANDICK, GEORGE JOHN, educator; b. Cleve., Dec. 1, 1929; s. George Peter and Geraldine (Andrs) C.; B.A., Baldwin Wallace Coll., 1954; postgrad. Kent State U., 1964, Cleve. State U., 1972; m. Arlene Charlotte Schorpp, June 25, 1955; children—Janine, Lorian, Alaina. Phys. edn. tchr., Cleve., 1954—. Playground supr., Cleve., 1955—; community center dir. Cleve. Bd. Edn., 1955—; recreation dir., Seven Hills, Ohio, 1973—. Recipient Outstanding Community Service citation City of Seven Hills, 1974. Mem. A.A.H.P.E.R. (chmn. Midwest sector 1965), Lake Erie Amateur Athletic Union (chmn. boys track and field 1964-71), Sokol Tyrs Gymnastic Org. Democrat. Russian Orthodox. Home: 7295 Cricket Ln Seven Hills OH 44131 Office: City Hall Seven Hills OH 44131

CHANDLER, ANDERSON, banker; b. Wichita, Kans., Jan. 21, 1926; s. Charles Q. and Alice (Throckmorton) C.; B.S., Kans. U., 1948; postgrad. U. Wis. Sch. Banking, 1953, Harvard Bus. Sch., 1967; m. Patricia Hinshaw, June 14, 1948; children—Cathleen, Cynthia, Corliss Colette. Pres. Farmers State Bank, Sterling, Kan., 1950-60; pres., dir. Fidelity State Bank & Trust Co., Topeka, 1961—; v.p., dir. First Nat. Bank Newton (Kans.); dir. First Nat. Bank, Ottawa, Farmers State Bank, Sterling, Farmers State Agy., Inc., Kans. Bankers Surety Co., Chandler Nat. Bank, Lyons, Nebr. Mem. faculty Intermediate Sch. of Banking, U. Nebr. Active Girl Scouts U.S.A.; pres. Jayhawk council Boy Scouts Am.; pres. Topeka United Way, 1974-75; mem. adv. bd. Bus. Sch., U. Kans., also pres. Meml. Corp.; bd. dirs. Family Service and Guidance Center, Topeka Welfare Planning Council; pres. Downtown Topeka, PTA; bd. dirs., treas. Family Service and Guidance Center. Served to lt. USAAF, 1944-45. Mem. Topeka C. of C. (dir.), Kans. Native Sons and Daus. (pres.), Beta Gamma Sigma, Delta Tau Delta, Alpha Phi Omega. Presbyn. (treas. ch.). Mason (32 deg., Shriner), Elk. Clubs: Knife and Fork (pres.), Topeka Country. Home: 4718 West Hills Dr Topeka KS 66606 Office: 600 Kansas Ave Topeka KS 66601

CHANDLER, B.J., univ. dean; b. Bluffton, Ark., July 23, 1921; s. J. V. and Edna (McCreight) C.; B.A., U. Tex., 1948, M.Ed., 1949; Ed.D., Columbia, 1951; m. Marjorie Barger, Mar. 7, 1942; children—Brenda (Mrs. Thomas Dexter Barbour), Robert W.N., Cynthia (Mrs. E. Patrick Bost). Asst. prof. edn. U. Va., Charlottesville, 1951-54, asso. prof., 1954-56; asso. prof. edn. Northwestern U., Evanston, 1956-59, prof. edn., 1959-62, dean Sch. Edn., 1962—; ednl. cons. State Farm Ins. Cos., 1953-70. Co-chmn. Gov. Ill. Com. Literacy and Learning, 1963-68; mem. Gov. Ill. Task Force Edn., 1965-68; chmn. task force tchr. edn. Ill. Bd. Higher Edn., 1972-75; cons. Skidmore Owings & Merrill, 1972-73; mem. Ill. Tchr. Certification Bd., 1973-76. Chmn. adv. council and mem. bd. trustees Aerospace Edn. Found.; mem. adv. council Kellogg Found., 1965-68; trustee YMCA Community Coll. Chgo., 1968, Roycemore Sch., 1970—, N. Shore Country Day Sch., 1972-75; mem. Carter-Mondale Task Force on Edn., 1976. Served with USAAF, 1942-44. mem. Nat. Cath. Edn. Assn. (dir. 1972).

Author: Education and the Teacher, 1961; Education in Urban Society, 1962; (with Lindley J. Stiles and John I. Kitsuse) Personnel Management in School Adminstration, 1955; (with D. Powell and W. Hazard) Education and the New Teacher, 1972. Editor: Introduction to Teaching, 12 vols. Contbr. articles in field to profl. jours. Home: 2322 Central Park Evanston IL 60201

CHANDLER, CHARLES DANA, food service exec.; b. Indpls., Aug. 21, 1936; s. George Dana and Wilma Rankin (Dunkle) C.; student Butler U., 1954-56; B.S., Mich. State U., 1958; m. Annetta Lou Robinson, Apr. 9, 1960; children—Deborah Anne, Diane Marie. With MCL, Inc., food services, Indpls., 1954—, exec. v.p., 1968-73, pres., 1973—, dir., 1962—. Guest lectr. U. Ind., Indpls., Purdue U. Served with AUS, 1958-64. Recipient Triple Key award Nat. Food Service Exec. Assn., 1973, Outstanding Restaurant award Purdue U. chpt. Food Service Exec. Assn., 1972. Mem. Food Service Execs. Assn. (br. pres. 1972-74), Ind. Restaurant Assn. (program chmn. 1973), Nat. Restaurant Assn., Young Presidents Orgn., Phi Kappa Phi, Sigma Chi. Presbyn. (ruling elder 1970-73). Kiwanian. Home: Rural Route 2 Box 91 JV Coatesville IN 46121 Office: 2730 E 62d St Indianapolis IN 46220

CHANDLER, SCOTT STONER, bus. exec.; b. Kansas City, Mo., Dec. 6, 1932; s. Edwin and Sarah (Stoner) C.; B.S. with honors, Kans. State U., 1954, M.S., 1957; postgrad. U. Wis., 1958-60; m. Marjorie Kay Pinther, Sept. 22, 1962; children—Scott Stoner, Holly Ann. Tech. sales Armour Indsl. Chem. Co., Chgo., 1960-62, market devel., 1962-63, industry mgr., 1963-65; sr. mktg. analyst Internat. Minerals & Chem. Corp., Libertyville, Ill., 1965-67, mgr. sales analysis, 1967-68, product mgr., 1968-70, dir. supply and devel., 1970-74, dir. comml. devel., 1974-75, now v.p., gen. mgr. Veterinary Products div. Chem. Group, also pres., dir. subs. Brae Labs., Inc.; mem. steering com. Agri-Bus. Advisory Bd. Nat. Am. Indian Cattlemen's Assn.; bd. dirs. Animal Health Inst., 1977—. Mem. exec. bd. N.E. Ill. council Boy Scouts Am., 1974—. Served to 1st lt. USAF, 1954-56. Fellow Am. Inst. Chemists; mem. Midwest Chem. Mktg. Assn. (chmn. 1968-69, dir. 1969-70), Am. Chem. Soc., Midwest Planning Assn., Beta Theta Pi, Gamma Sigma Delta, Alpha Zeta, Alpha Phi Omega. Republican. Mem. Evang. Covenant Ch. Am. Patentee in field. Home: 911 N Glenayre Dr Glenview IL 60025 Office: IMC Plaza Libertyville IL 60048

CHANDRAN, SATISH RAMAN, educator; b. Quilon, Kerala, India, Oct. 6, 1938; s. Raman Govind and Ponnamma Pillai; B.S., Sree Narayana Coll., Quilon, 1955; M.S., Univ. Coll., Trivandrum, Kerala, 1958; Ph.D. (NSF grantee), U. Ill., Urbana, 1965; m. Judith Gail Urban, Oct. 1, 1966; children—Pamela, Anjali. Came to U.S., 1961, naturalized, 1970. Research asso. dept. entomology U. Ill., Urbana, 1965-66; asst. prof. biology U. Ill., Chgo., 1966-72; prof. Kennedy-King Coll., Chgo., 1972—. USPHS grantee, 1965. Mem. Am. Inst. Biol. Sci., Entomol. Soc. Am., Nat. Assn. Biology Tchrs., Sigma Xi, Phi Sigma, Omega Beta Pi. Research, publs. microsomal oxidases and musculature of insects. Home: 1648 Western Ave Flossmoor IL 60422

CHANEY, REECE, educator; b. Rowdy, Ky., July 27, 1938; s. Roy and Lola (Hays) C.; B.S., Ohio U., 1962, M.Ed., 1965, Ph.D., 1968; m. Phyllis Ann Bailey, Nov. 24, 1957; children—Tammy Kaye, Ronald Dean. Tchr., Scioto Valley Schs., Piaketon, Ohio, 1959-64; NDEA Title IV fellow Ohio U., 1964-68; elementary counselor South Western City Schs., Grove City, Ohio, 1965-66; prof. edn. Ind. State U., Terre Haute, 1968—; cons. career edn. and pupil personnel services Ind. Dept. Pub. Instrn. Licensed psychologist, Ind. Mem. Am., Ind. (pres. 1977-78) personnel and guidance assns., Assn. Counselor Edn. and Supervision, Nat. Vocat. Guidance Assn., Assn. Measurement and Evaluation in Guidance, Am. Sch. Counselor Assn., Phi Delta Kappa. Home: 4 Doe Dr Terre Haute IN 47802 Office: School of Education Indiana State University Terre Haute IN 47809

CHANEY, THOMAS JOHN, electronic circuits design engr.; b. Woodward, Okla., Mar. 19, 1940; s. John Everett and Evelyn Marie (Winfrey) C.; B.S.E.E., Kans. State U., 1962; M.S.E.E., Washington U., St. Louis, 1969; m. Carol Lee Johanning, Nov. 17, 1962; children—Scott Thomas, Suzanne Lee. Engr., Westinghouse Electric Co., Lima, Ohio, 1962-64, McDonnell-Douglas Co., St. Louis, 1964-65; sr. research engr. Computer Systems Lab., Washington U., St. Louis, 1965—. Past chmn. adminstrv. bd. Arlington United Methodist Ch.; cubmaster Boy Scouts Am., 1976-77. Mem. IEEE (chmn. St. Louis area computer group 1975-76), Sigma Xi. Reviewer IEEE Computer Transactions, Assn. of Computer Machinery. Contbr. articles to profl. jours. Home: 12633 Brumley Dr Bridgeton MO 63044 Office: 724 S Euclid St Saint Louis MO 63110

CHANG, CHAE HAN JOSEPH, physician, educator; b. Seoul, Korea, July 7, 1929; s. B.I. and E.D. (Min) C.; M.D., Severance Union Med. Coll., Seoul, 1953; Ph.D., Nagoya U., Japan, 1966; m. Chung Sook Chun, Nov. 24, 1956; children—Paul, Marian, Deborah, Linda. Came to U.S., 1954, naturalized, 1963. Intern, St. Joseph's Hosp., Phoenix, 1954-55; resident Emory U. Hosp., Atlanta, 1955-58; practice medicine, specializing in radiology, Morgantown, W.Va., 1964-70, Kansas City, Kans., 1970—; asso. prof. radiology W.Va. U. Sch. Medicine, 1964-69, prof., acting chmn. dept. radiology, 1969-70; prof. radiology, head div. roentgenology Kans. U. Med. Center, 1970—. Recipient Excellence in Teaching award W.Va. U. Sch. Medicine, 1970. Fellow Am. Coll. Radiology; mem. Assn. U. Radiologists, Soc. Pediatric Radiology, Am. Roentgen Soc., Radiol. Soc. N.Am., A.M.A., Kans., Wyandotte County med. socs. Contbr. articles profl. jours. Home: 2000 W 63d St Shawnee Mission KS 66208 Office: U Kans Med Center 39th and Rainbow Blvd Kansas City KS 66103

CHANG, CHERNG, chemist, educator; b. An Hei, China, May 17, 1942; came to U.S., 1966; s. Hui Tom and Shiou Yu (Lee) C.; B.S., Nat. Cheng Kung U., 1965; Ph.D., U. Fla., 1970; postgrad. U. Houston, 1970-72; m. Jean Shu-Jen Hwang, June 24, 1969; children—Steve, Wayne. NRC research asso. Wright-Patterson AFB, Ohio, 1972-74; sr. chemist Systems Research Lab., Dayton, Ohio, 1974-75; research asst. prof. Wright State U., Dayton, 1975—. Mem. Am. Chem. Soc., Am. Soc. Mass Spectrometry, Sigma Xi. Recipient Outstanding Alumni Academic Accomplishment award Nat. Cheng Kung U., 1965. Contbr. articles to profl. jours. Home: 3065 Maginn Dr Xenia OH 45385 Office: Wright State U Dayton OH 45431

CHANG, DAE HONG, educator; b. Nara, Japan, Jan. 9, 1928; s. Chun Bal and Kum I. (Kim) C.; B.A., Mich. State U., 1957, M.A., 1958, Ph.D., 1962; m. Seung Hi Cho, Aug. 20, 1964; children—Morris Bosang, Richard Jaesang. Chmn. dept. sociology Olivet (Mich.) Coll., 1962-66; asst. prof. dept. sociology No. Ill. U., DeKalb, 1966-69, asso. prof., 1968-69; prof., chmn. dept. sociology-anthropology U. Wis.-Whitewater, 1969-74; chmn. dept. adminstrn. justice Wichita (Kans.) State U., 1975—. Cons., Ill. Atty. Gen., 1968-69; resource person Mich. State Gov., 1964-66. Smith-Mundt fellow, 1954-55; NSF grantee, 1969-75. Mem. Am. Sociol. Assn., Am. Soc. Criminology, Midwest Sociol. Soc., Wis. Sociol. Assn. Author: Sociology: A Syllabus and Workbook, 1970; The Prison: Voices From the Inside, 1972; Sociology: An Applied Approach, 1973; Criminology: A Cross-Cultural Approach, 1975: Crime and Delinquency Prevention, 1977; Fundamentals of Criminal Justice: A Syllabus and Workbook, 1977. Home: 4809 Ethel St Wichita KS 67220 Office: Box 95 Wichita State U Wichita KS 67208

CHANG, JAE CHAN, hematologist, oncologist; b. Chong An, Korea, Aug. 29, 1941; s. Tae Whan and Kap Hee (Lee) C.; came to U.S., 1965, naturalized, 1976; M.D., Seoul (Korea) Nat. U., 1965; m. Sue Young Chung, Dec. 4, 1965; children—Sung Jin, Sung-Ju, Sung-Hoon. Intern, Ellis Hosp., Schenectady, 1965-66; resident in medicine Harrisburg (Pa.) Hosp., 1966-69; instr. in medicine U. Rochester, N.Y., 1970-72; chief hematology sect. VA Hosp., Dayton, Ohio, 1972-75; hematologist, dir. oncology unit, coordinator of med. edn. Good Samaritan Hosp., Dayton, 1976—; asst. clin. prof. medicine Ohio State U., Columbus, 1972-75; asso. clin. prof. medicine Wright State U., Dayton, 1975—; cons. in hematology VA Hosp. Mem. med. adv. com. Greater Dayton Area chpt. Leukemia Soc. Am., 1977—; trustee Montgomery County Soc. for Cancer Control, Dayton, 1976—. Nat. Cancer Inst. fellow, 1970-72; diplomate Am. Bd. Internal Medicine. Fellow A.C.P.; mem. Am. Soc. Hematology, Am. Fedn. Clin. Research, Am. Soc. Clin. Oncologists. Contbr. articles on leukemic cell metabolism to med. jours. Home: 898 Thorndale Dr Centerville OH 45429 Office: 2222 Philadelphia Dr Dayton OH 45406

CHANG, KIAN KOONG, physician; b. Sumatra, Indonesia, Nov. 7, 1935; s. Chee Chy and Fam Wan (Nio) Chang; M.D., Nat. Taiwan U., 1965; came to U.S., 1974; m. Theresa K. Chiang, July 30, 1965; children—Kenneth, Kevin. Intern, Victoria Gen. Hosp., U. Dalhousie, Halifax, N.S., Can., 1965-66; research fellow U. Ottawa (Ont., Can.), 1973; chief resident in pediatric surgery Children's Hosp., Winnipeg (Man. Can), 1974; chief surgery Good Samaritan Hosp., Rugby, N.D., 1975-76; pvt. practice medicine specializing in gen. and pediatric surgery, Minot, N.D., 1977—; mem. staff St. Joseph Hosp., Trinity Hosp. Diplomate Am. Bd. Surgery. Mem. AMA, N.D. Med. Assn., Gen. Med. Council Eng., Med. Assn. Malaysia. Buddhist. Home: 1000 15 1/2th Ave SW Minot ND 58701 Office: Trinity Profl Bldg Minot ND 58701

CHANG, NATHAN CHONG-TSAU, gen. and thoracic surgeon; b. Ningpo, China, July 15, 1919; s. Joseph Pu-Yung and Lily (Shue) C.; B.S., Nat. Kweiyang Med. Coll. (China), 1940; M.B., West China Union U., 1944, M.D., 1945; m. Mildred Irma Krueger, Oct. 28, 1950; 1 dau., Emily K. Came to U.S., 1948, naturalized, 1954. Intern U. Hosp., Chengtue, China, 1944-45, No. Westchester Hosp., Mt. Kisco, N.Y., 1950-52; resident gen. surgery Army Hosp., 1945-47; chief resident Puyang Hosp., Soochaw, 1947-49; fellow thoracic surgery Nat. Jewish Hosp., Denver, Tubora Hosp., Jamaica, N.Y., 1948-49; gen. surgery Norfolk (Va.) Gen. Hosp., 1952-55; resident thoracic surgery B.S. Pollak Hosp., 1955-57; practice medicine specializing in gen. and thoracic surgery, Windham, Ohio, 1957—; surg. staff Robinson Meml. Hosp., Ravenna, Ohio, 1957—, pres. med. staff, 1973, 74, chmn. dept. surgery, 1977-78; surg. staff Fairview Gen. Hosp., Cleve., 1967—; dir. Windham Clinic, 1959—. Served as surgeon, to maj. with Nationalist Chinese Army, 1945-47. Decorated Bronze Star. Diplomate Nat. Bd. Med. Examiners, Bd. Gen. Surgery. Fellow A.C.S., Am. Coll. Chest Physicians; mem. Portage County, Ohio med. socs., Ohio Surg. Assn., AMA. Home: 9652 Wolfe Rd Windham OH 44288 Office: 9250 N Main St Windham OH 44288

CHANG, PETER HON, elec. engr.; b. Shanghai, China, Feb. 19, 1941; s. Pao En and Loo (Wong) C.; B.S. in E.E., U. Calif., Berkeley, 1964, M.S. in E.E., 1966, Ph.D., 1970; diploma mech. engring. Hong Kong Polytech. Inst., 1962; m. Eppie O.P. Sheng, Aug. 24, 1968; children—Philip D., Jason D. Research engr. Sondell Sci. Instruments, Palo Alto, Calif., 1965-70; tech. staff Hewlett Packard Co., Palo Alto, 1970-71; sect. head research and devel. Miles Labs., Elkhart, Ind., 1971-74, product mgr., 1975-77; mgr. quality assurance Ames Co. div. Miles Labs., 1977—. Dir. Nike Enterprises Ltd., Hong Kong, VIR Electronics, Hong Kong. Mem. Am. Soc. Quality Control, IEEE. Roman Catholic. Patentee in field. Home: 2624 Jackson St E Elkhart IN 46514 Office: 1127 Myrtle St Elkhart IN 46514

CHANG, TEH-KUANG, educator, polit. scientist; b. Changting, Fukien, China, Sept. 15, 1925; s. Tsan-Yao and Mantii (Chang-Wu) C.; came to U.S., 1956; B.A., Nat. Taiwan U., 1950; M.A., U. Wash., 1968; Ph.D., Am. U., 1966; m. Grace Kuo-chang Chin, Oct. 1, 1959; children—Angelo, Angelin, Angelina. Asst. prof. polit. sci. Ball State U., Muncie, Ind., 1966-70, asso. prof., 1970-74, chmn. Asian Studies com., 1970-72, 76-77, prof., 1975—, prof. London Centre, winter 1975-76. Nat. vis. prof. Nat. Chengchi U., Nat. Taiwan U., Taiwan, Republic China, 1972-73. Mem. Am., Internat. (chmn. Asian polit. study group) polit. sci. assns., Assn. Asian Studies, Pi Sigma Alpha, Pi Gamma Nu. Author: Organization and Achievement of United Nations, 1953; Foreign Ministers' Conference of Four Powers after World War II, 1955; The Cultural Revolution and Political Modernization of Communist Chine, 1970; The Party Congress and the Political Development: A Comparison of National and Communist China, 1971; Political Science: United States of America and China, 1973; Special Feature of Communist China's 1975 Constitution, 1975; Presidential Power in Foreign Policy: Expansion and Contraction, 1977. Home: 615 Wayne St Muncie IN 47303

CHANNER, FREDERICK WYNDHAM, investment banker; b. Chgo., Nov. 23, 1909; s. George Stanton and Laura (Parsons) C.; Ph.B., U. Chgo., 1932; m. Georganne Gibson Dunshee, Oct. 12, 1944; children—Penelope, Christopher, Kendall. Engaged in investment business, Chgo., 1933—; with Channer Securities Co., 1936-59, pres., 1957-59; pres. Channer Newman Securities Co., Chgo., 1959-72, chmn. bd., chief exec. officer, 1972—. Served from pvt. to capt., Combat Intelligence, USAAF, 1942-45. Republican. Presbyn. Clubs: Mid-Day, Bond, Municipal Bond (Chgo.); Inverness Golf (Palatine). Home: 1894 W Stuart Ln Inverness Palatine IL 60067 Office: 39 S La Salle St Chicago IL 60603

CHANY, DREW LOUIS, civil and structural engr.; b. Cleve., Oct. 30, 1949; s. Walter Carl and Irene (Trizse) C.; B.S., Mich. State U., M.S., 1973; m. Deborah Joy Abel, June 18, 1971; 1 dau., Rebecca. Structural design engr. Gilbert/Commonwealth Co., Cons. Engrs., Jackson, Mich. Registered profl. engr., Mich. Mem. ASCE. Home: 1027 S Wisner St Jackson MI 49203 Office: 209 E Washington St Jackson MI 49201

CHAO, MARSHALL S., chemist; b. Changsha, China, Nov. 20, 1924; s. Hen-ti and Huey-ying C.; m. Patricia Hu, July 20, 1968; 1 dau., Anita. B.S., Nat. Central U., China, 1947; M.S., U. Ill., 1958, Ph.D., 1961. Teaching asst. Nat. Central U., 1947-49; tech. asst. Taiwan Fertilizer Co., 1949-55; research chemist The Dow Chem. Co., Midland, Mich., 1961-72, research specialist, 1973—. Deacon First Baptist Ch., Midland, 1974-76. Fellow Am. Inst. Chemists; mem. Am. Chem. Soc., Electrochem. Soc. (chmn. Midland sect. 1973, councilor 1974-76), Alpha Chi Upsilon, Sigma Xi. Author: Taiwan Fertilizers, 1951; contbr. articles to profl. jours. Patentee in field. Home: 1206 Evamar Dr Midland MI 48640 Office: Inorganic Lab Central Research Dow Chem USA Midland MI 48640

CHAPIN, EDWARD BARTON, banker; b. N.Y.C., July 1, 1914; s. Francis Stuart and Nellie Estelle (Peck) C.; B.B.A., U. Minn., 1936; M.B.A., U. Pa., 1940; m. Mary Olyn Kingbay, Aug. 9, 1940; children—Edward Barton, Charles Bradford. Investment clk. First Nat. Bank, Mpls., 1936-38; statistician Fed. Res. Bank Phila., 1940-42; with First Nat. Bank St. Paul, 1946—, successively adminstrv. asst., asst. cashier, asst. v.p., 1952-56, v.p., 1956—; instr. Minn. Sch. Banking. Mem. thesis rev. com. Stonier Grad. Sch. Banking. Active Community Chest, Boy Scouts Am. Served as lt. USN, 1942-45, lt. comdr. USNR, 1946-54. Mem. Am. Bankers Assn. (exec. com. bank investment div.), Investment Bankers Assn., Minn. Econ. Club, Am. Inst. Banking, C. of C., U. Minn. Alumni Assn., Minn. Taxpayers Assn. (treas.). Clubs: Minnesota; Twin City Bond; St. Paul Athletic. Author articles on money and banking. Home: 1728 Highland Pkwy St Paul MN 55116 Office: 332 Minnesota St St Paul MN 55101

CHAPLER, FREDERICK KEITH, obstetrician and gynecologist, educator; b. Kankakee, Ill., Apr. 6, 1932; s. Robert Frederick and Annetta Beatrice (Carpenter) C.; B.A., U. Calif., Berkeley, 1957, M.D., 1960; m. Gretchen Ellen Long, Apr. 27, 1955; children—Ted Robert, Susan Patricia. Intern, Los Angeles County Hosp., 1960-61; resident in obstetrics and gynecology U. Calif. Hosps., San Francisco, 1961-65, asst. clin. prof. obstetrics and gynecology, 1965-70, asst. dean students, 1965-67; chief gynecology San Francisco Gen. Hosp., 1967-70; asst. prof. obstetrics and gynecology U. Iowa, Iowa City, 1970-72, asso. prof., 1972-76, prof., 1976—. Served with USMC, 1952-54. Named Tchr. of Year U. Iowa Coll. Medicine, 1971, 73. Diplomate Am. Bd. Obstetrics and Gynecology. Mem. Am. Coll. Obstetricians and Gynecologists, Am. Fertility Soc., Am. Assn. Gynecol. Laparoscopists. Methodist. Contbr. articles to profl. jours., chpts. in books. Home: Rt 6 Box 144 Iowa City IA 52240 Office: Univ Hosps Iowa City IA 52242

CHAPMAN, C. CARL, real estate broker; b. Markleville, Ind., Feb. 28, 1902; s. Marion Alvin and Emma Luella (Van Duyn) C.; student Central Normal Coll., 1921-23; m. Goldie Ann Keller, July 30, 1925; children—Mary (Mrs. Donald Shepherd), Lois (Mrs. Richard Pippin), Dennis, Lola (Mrs. Thomas Lane). Salesman, Polk San. Milk Co., Indpls., 1923-37; mgr., Polk Products, Inc., Indpls., 1937-62; salesman, Spencer Realty, Greenfield, Ind., 1964-70; pres., partner, Chapman-Carmichael Realty, Inc., Greenfield, Ind., 1971—. Mem. Ind. State, Hancock County bds. realtors. Methodist. Mason (Shriner), Rotarian. Home: Rural Route 1 Greenfield IN 46140 Office: 1221 W Main St Greenfield IN 46140

CHAPMAN, DOUGLAS KENNETH, office equipment exec.; b. Toronto, Ont., Can., Jan. 10, 1928; s. Alfred D. and Isabel (Jones) C.; student U. Toronto, 1946-48, Victoria Coll., 1946-48; m. Doreen E. Lowe, June 29, 1950; children—Laura Chapman Kohler, Dawna, Kevin. Pres. ACCO Internat., Inc., Chgo., 1971—; chmn. bd., pres., dir. ACCO Canadian Co. Ltd., Toronto; chmn. bd., dir. ACCO Co. Ltd., Eng., ACCO Nederland B.V., Holland; v.p., dir. ACCO Mexicana, S.A. de C.V., Mexico; dir. ACCO Jamaica Ltd., Kingston, v.p., dir. ACCO mfg. C.A., Venezuela. Mem. Canadian Office Products Assn. (past pres.), Toronto Stationers Assn. (past pres.), Bus. Record Mfrs. Assn. (bd. dirs.), Nat. Office Products Assn. (v.p.), Wholesale Stationers Assn. (bd. dirs.). Clubs: North Shore Country (Glenview, Ill.); Mission Hills Country (Northbrook, Ill.); Scarboro Golf and Country (Toronto, Ont., Can.); Mid-Am., Metropolitan (Chgo.); East India, Pub. Sch. (London, Eng.). Home: 175 Dickens Rd Northfield IL 60093 Office: ACCO Internat Inc 770 S Acco Plaza Wheeling IL 60090

CHAPMAN, EDWARD ELDRED, pub. relations exec.; b. Toledo, Aug. 7, 1925; s. Edlred M. and Esther L. (Mix) C.; B.B.S., U. Toledo, 1948; postgrad Ohio State U., 1959-61; m. Jaclyn Beth King, July 26, 1947;children—Ryan, Joan, Laura. With Ohio Bell Telephone Co., 1948—, asst. mgr., Toledo, 1948-52, customer relations supr., Columbus, Ohio, 1953-62, pub. relations mgr., Cleve., 1963—; chief instr. pub. relations course Cleve. Advt. Club, 1970-76; instr. Kent State U. Sch. Journalism; prof. Ursuline Coll. Mem. pub. relations com. Kent State U., 1969-71; mem. adv. bd. Salvation Army, Lake Erie council Girl Scouts U.S.A. Mem. Pub. Relations Soc. Am. (N.E. Ohio chpt. dir., edn. chmn. 1968-71, nat. del. 1972-74, sec. 1977), Ohio State U., U. Toledo alumni. assns. Mason (32 deg., Shriner). Club: Advertising (Cleve.). Home: 26711 Bruce Rd Bay Village OH 44140 Office: 100 Erieview Plaza Cleveland OH 44114

CHAPMAN, EUGENIA SHELDON, state legislator; b. Fairhope, Ala., Jan. 10, 1923; d. Chauncey Bailey and Rose (Donner) Sheldon; B.Ed., Chgo. State U., 1944; m. Gerald M. Chapman, Nov. 24, 1948; children—George, John, Katherine, Andrew. Tchr. pub. schs., Cicero, Ill., 1944-47, Chgo., 1947-51; mem. Ill. Ho. of Reps., 1964—. Mem. Dist. 214 Bd. Edn., Cook County, Ill., 1961-64, sec., 1962-64; mem. exec. com. Tri-County div. Ill. Assn. Sch. Bds., 1964. Recipient Best Freshman and Best Legislator awards Ind. Voters Ill.; Golden award Ill. League Conservation Voters, 1974; Spl. award United Auto Workers, 1973; Presdl. citation Ill. Assn. Sch. Adminstrs., 1974. Mem. League Women Voters (pres. Arlington Heights 1957-59). Democrat. Address: 16 S Princeton Ct Arlington Heights IL 60005

CHAPMAN, GABRIEL PAUL, plastics mfg. co. exec.; b. Mobile, Ala., Sept. 25, 1946; s. Clarence P. and LaMoria A. (Jarvis) C.; B.S. in Indsl. Engring., Auburn U., 1969; postgrad. E. Tenn State U., 1970; M.S. in Bus. Adminstrn., Ind. U., 1977; m. Dianne R. Laube, June 9, 1972; children—G. Paul, Ryan H. Sales trainee Eastman Chem. Products, Inc., Kingsport, Tenn., 1970; sales rep., Milbourn, N.J., 1971-72; Indsl. Plastics Corp., Elkhart, Ind., 1972, process improvement mgr., 1973-74, mktg. devel. mgr., 1974-75, plant mgr., 1975-76, corp. mfg. mgr., 1977, v.p mfg., 1977—. Co. chmn. United Way, 1977; pres. Northside Residents Assn., 1974—. Mem. Inst. Indsl. Engring., Soc. Plastics Engrs., Rotary Internat. Republican. Roman Catholic. Club: Elks. Home: 826 N Main Elkhart IN 46514 Office: PO Box 2269 Elkhart IN 46514

CHAPMAN, (GEORGE) BRAINERD (III), lawyer; b. Louisville, Oct. 18, 1911; s. George B. and Kathryn (Schneiderhan) C.; B.A., Amherst Coll., 1933; J.D., Harvard, 1936; m. Martha McCaig, June 11, 1948; 1 son, George Brainerd, IV. Admitted to Ill. bar, 1936; asso., then partner Lord, Bissell & Brook, and predecessors, 1936-58; pvt. practice, 1959-62; partner Chapman, Pennington, Montgomery, Holmes & Sloan, Chgo., 1962-70, Vedder, Price, Kaufman & Kammholz, Chgo., 1971—. Dir. various corps. and founds. Former chmn. bd. Presbyn. Home. Served from capt. to col. JAG'S Dept., AUS, 1942-46. Decorated Bronze Star (U.S.); knight officer of Crown (Italy); recipient medal for Eminent Service, Amherst Coll., 1969. Mem. Am. Bar Assn., Harvard Law Soc., Beta Theta Pi. Presbyn. (elder, trustee). Clubs: Chgo., University, Law, Ephraim (Wis.) Yacht; Great Lakes Cruising (past dir.); Glen View (Golf, Ill.). Home: 990 Lake Shore Dr Chicago IL 60611 Office: 115 S LaSalle St Chicago IL 60603

CHAPMAN, GEORGE COURTNEY, educator; b. Chgo., Nov. 18, 1929; s. Harold Potter and Ella Mae (Field) C.; B.S. in Mech. Engring., U. Ill., 1952; m. Jane Bittermann, May 22, 1971; children—Mark, Beth. Instr., U. Ill. Inst. Aviation, Urbana, 1956-59;

asso. prof. dept. aviation Ohio State U., Columbus, 1959-66, 68—; dir. research/devel. Sanderson Films, Wichita, Kans., 1966-68. Cons., Gillespie Instructional Systems, 1968-73, Columbus (Ohio) Police Dept., 1971-72, Accelerated Tng. Programs, 1973-74. Mem. city council, Worthington, Ohio, 1965-66. Served with USNR, 1952-56. Recipient Meritorious award Aircraft Owners and Pilots Assn., 1965, award for creative excellence U.S. Film Festival, 1968, Achievement Wheatley award Univ. Aviation Assn., 1970. Mem. Soc. Automotive Engrs. (chmn. cockpit/cabin standarization for gen. aviation aircraft com. 1973-77), Nat. Assn. Flight Instrs. (dir. 1968-70), Univ. Aviation Assn. (dir. 1970-73), Quiet Birdmen. Lutheran (dir. 1962-65). Home: 488 Greenglade Ave Worthington OH 43085 Office: Box 3022 Columbus OH 43210

CHAPMAN, JAMES PINKSTON, pub. relations co. exec.; b. Macon, Ga., Jan. 24, 1916; s. Robert Browning and Clara (McCray) C.; B.A., U. Fla., 1937; children by former marriage—Sheryl Lynn Kammer, James Pinkston, Caprice K., Randall K. Sports editor Sanford (Fla.) Herald, 1937; city editor Daytona Beach (Fla.) Sun-Record, 1938; editor Valdosta (Ga.) Sun, 1939-40; sports editor Macon (Ga.) Telegraph, 1940-42; editorial staff N.Y. Times, N.Y.C., 1945-47; regional pub. relations dir. Ford Motor Co., Detroit, 1947-50; pres. James P. Chapman Inc., pub. relations counselors, Detroit, 1950—; lectr. in field; dir. Am. Pres.'s Life Ins. Co., 1965-69. Pres. Boys Com. Detroit, 1965-66, Mich. Population Council, 1970-72. Served with USAAF, 1943-45. Mem. Mich. Assn. Psychiat. Clinics (pres. 1970-73), Pub. Relations Soc. Am. (accredited) (pres. Mich. chpt. 1969-71), Bloomfield Open Hunt Club, University Club, Otsego Ski Club, Founders Soc., Detroit Press Club. Episcopalian. Home: 899 Lone Pine Rd Bloomfield Hills MI 48013 Office: 550 Washington Blvd Bldg Detroit MI 48226

CHAPMAN, LOREN JAMES, psychologist; b. Muncie, Ind., Jan. 5, 1927; s. Herbert Lee and Lurana Gertrude (Treff) C.; B.A. cum laude, Harvard U., 1948; M.A., Northwestern U., 1952, Ph.D., 1954; m. Jean Paulsen, June 6, 1953; children—Nancy, Laurence. Instr., asst. prof. psychology U. Chgo., 1956-59; asso. prof. U. Ky., 1959-62; asso. prof. Southern Ill. U., Carbondale, 1962-65, prof., 1965-66; prof. U. Wis., Madison, 1966—. NIMH fellow, 1954-56, research scientist awardee, 1970-75. Mem. Am., Midwestern psychol. assns., Am. Psychopathological Assn., AAAS. Author: (with J.P. Chapman) Disordered Thought in Schizophrenia, 1973. Contbr. articles to profl. jours. Asso. editor Jour. Abnormal Psychology, 1971-74. Home: 129 Richland Ln Madison WI 53705 Office: Dept Psychology Univ Wis Madison WI 53706

CHAPMAN, MARVIN JOHN, psychiatrist; b. Milw., Dec. 31, 1935; s. George Matthew and Martha Louise (Baehr) C.; B.S. (Ford Found. scholar), U. Wis., 1955, M.D., 1959; m. Marie Louise Olson, May 9, 1959; children—Nancy Lynn, Michael John, Eric Christopher. Clin. dir. Central State Hosp., Waupun, Wis., 1970-72; adminstr. State Wis. Sex Crimes Law Program, 1970-72; dir. adult programs Mendota Mental Health Inst., Madison, Wis., 1972-74, cons., 1975-76; dir. Forensic programs Wis. Div. Mental Hygiene, 1976—; med. dir. Rock County Mental Health System, Janesville, Wis., 1975—; pvt. forensic cons., Madison, 1967—. Lectr., U. Wis. Law Sch., 1972-76, clin. instr. Med. Sch., 1972-76, clin. asst. prof., 1977—; cons. Pine View Health Care Center, 1972—; mem. Lt. Gov.'s Task Force on Nursing Home Staff Tng. and Edn., 1975; lectr., Wis. State Sch. for Judges, 1975. Adv. bd. Reintegration Project Center Pub. Representation, Madison, Wis. Served with USN, 1958-67. Mem. Am. Acad. Psychiatry and Law, Am., Wis. (chmn. patient rights com. 1974) psychiat. assns. Home: 5907 Winnequah Rd Monona WI 53716 Office: Box 351 Janesville WI 53545

CHAPMAN, MORRIS BROADWAY, lawyer; b. Granite City, Ill., Mar. 31, 1919; s. Robert Evans and Gladys Margaret (Broadway) C.; student Westminster Coll., 1938-39; J.D., St. Louis U., 1942; m. Thelma Hoggett, Jan. 27, 1947; children—Morris, Martha, Melissa Chapman Rheinecker, Robert, Amy, James. Admitted to Ill. bar, 1942, since practiced in Granite City and St. Louis; prin. Morris Chapman & Assos., Granite City, 1942-64; mem. firm Chapman & Chapman, Granite City and St. Louis, 1942—. Chmn. Baha'i Nat. Spiritual Assembly, Guatemala, 1970-71. Fellow Internat. Soc. Barristers; mem. Am., Ill. State bar assns., Am. (nat. committeeman 1972-74), Ill. (dir., trustee 1972-73, committeeman 1972-73, pres.-elect 1976) trial lawyers assns. Home: Rural Route 3 Marione Rd Edwardsville IL 62025 Office: 722 Chestnut St St Louis MO 63101 also 1406 Niedringhaus Ave Granite City IL 62040

CHAPMAN, ROBERT EDWIN, psychiatrist; b. Newcomerstown, Ohio, May 30, 1932; s. Bernard W. and Helen I. (Shaffer) C.; B.S., Mt. Union Coll., 1954; M.D., Ohio State U., 1961; m. Sharon Joyce Stanfil, Apr. 6, 1962; children—Brett, Tracie, Bart. Intern, St. Josephs Hosp., Phoenix, 1961-62; fellow, Menninger Sch. Psychiatry, Topeka, 1965-68; med. dir. McLean County Mental Health Center, Bloomington, Ill., 1968-70; pres. Neuropsychiatry Service Corp., Normal, Ill., 1970—; asso. clin. prof. Med. Sch., U. Ill., Champaign; pres. med. staff Brokaw Hosp., Normal, 1977—. Served with M.C., U.S. Army, 1954-56, USN, 1962-65. Fellow Am. Bd. Psychiatry and Neurology; mem. Ill., Am. Psychiatric Assns., Ill., McLean County Med. Socs., AMA. Lodge: Shrine. Home: 2218 E Lincoln St Bloomington IL 61701 Office: 900 Franklin Ave Normal IL 61761

CHAPMAN, WILLIAM FRANCIS, newspaper editor; b. Powersville, Mo., Mar. 28, 1925; s. William Bryant and Esther (Coddington) C.; student jr. coll., St. Joseph, Mo., 1942-43, Central Mo. State Coll., 1946, Wayne State U., 1955; m. Lillian Louise Fyler, Aug. 10, 1945; children—Robert Earl, Karen Louise, Sharon Frances. News editor Warrensburg (Mo.) Daily Star-Jour., 1946-47; mgr. U.P.I., Jefferson City, Mo., 1949, war corr., Korea, 1950-51, mgr. Seattle, 1952-53; asst. city editor Detroit Free Press, 1954-61; exec. editor Daily Times, Chester, Pa., 1961-63; mng. editor The Times, Hammond, Ind., 1964-75, exec. editor, 1975—; editorial dir. Howard Publs., Oceanside, Cal., 1971—. Founding dir. Mid-Am. Press Inst., So. Ill. U. Carbondale (chmn. 1971); mem. Internat. Press Inst. Served with USMCR, 1943-46; PTO. Mem. Am. Soc. Newspaper Editors, A.P. Mng. Editors. Home: 7818 Marshall Pl Merrillville IN 46410 Office: 417 Fayette St Hammond IN 46325

CHAPPELLE, AUSTIN BEMIS, elec. products co. exec.; b. Dierks, Ark., Jan. 28, 1924; s. Case C. and Beatrice V. (Thornton) C.; B.S., U. Ark., 1949, M.S., 1950; postgrad. Mass. Inst. Tech., 1951; m. Patricia Ann Benny, June 29, 1950; children—Tersa Marie, Clifford Austin, Mark Elliott. Asso. prof. Miss. So. U., 1950-51; rocket devel. Hercules Powder Co., Wilmington, Del., 1953-56; research physicist propulsion Gen. Electric Co., Cin., 1956-59; sr. tech. staff Northrop Aircraft Co., Hawthorne, Calif., 1960-64; mgr. product devel. Govt. Electronics div. Motorola, Inc., Scottsdale, Ariz., 1964-74; mgr. WSG-3 programs office, Communications div. Electronic Communications Inc., subsidiary Nat. Cash Register, St. Petersburg, Fla., 1974-75; with govt. telecommunications div. Collins Radio, Cedar Rapids, Iowa, 1975—; dir. Chemseal Corp., 1965. Committeeman, Roosevelt council Boy Scouts Am., 1969-74. Served with USAAF, USAF, 1941-56. Asso. fellow Am. Inst. Aeros. and Astronautics; mem. Am. Inst. Physics, Am. Rocket Soc. (past pres.), Navy League, Old Crow Assn. (charter mem.), Tailhook Assn. Mason. Patentee electronic blasting machine. Home: 6537 Brookview Ln NE Cedar Rapids IA 52402 Office: Govt Telecommunications Group Collins Radio Cedar Rapids IA 52405

CHARAK, IRA, nuclear engr.; b. Bklyn., Mar. 8, 1936; s. Sol and Esther (Uchitel) C.; B.M.E., Ga. Inst. Tech., 1957; M.S., 1958; M.B.A., U. Chgo., 1976; m. Rita Gail Skott, Nov. 27, 1958; children—David, Jonathan. Nuclear engr., Chance Vought Corp., Dallas, 1961, Internuclear Co., Clayton, Mo., 1961-62; with Argonne Nat. Lab. (Ill.), 1958-60, 62—, mem. staff of dir. reactor analysis and safety div., 1975-77, coordinator fusion reactor safety research, 1976-77, mgr. site environ. statement project, 1977—. Judge, high sch. sci. fair, Chgo. Served with AUS, 1960-61. Registered profl. engr., Ill.; Schlumberger fellow 1957-58. Mem. Am. Nuclear Soc. Dir., Oak Park (Ill.) Temple. Contbr. articles to profl. jours. Home: 5220 Lawn Ave Western Springs IL 60558 Office: 9700 S Cass Ave Argonne IL 60439

CHAREWICZ, DAVID MICHAEL, photographer; b. Chgo., Feb. 17, 1932; s. Michael and Stella (Pietrzak) C.; student DePaul U., 1957, Northwestern U., 1952; m. Catherine Uccello, Nov. 8, 1952; children—Michael, Karen, Daniel. Trainee, Merill Chase, Chgo., 1950-51; dark room technician Maurice Seymour, Chgo., 1951-52; photographer Oscar & Assos., Chgo., 1955-63; owner Dave Chare Photography, Park Ridge, Ill., 1963—. Pres. Oakton Parent Tchr. Club, 1968-69, del. dist. 64 caucus, 1970, 73; mem. centennial photo com., Park Ridge, Ill., 1973. Served with AUS, 1952-54. Mem. Profl. Photographers Assn., Midstate Indsl. Photographers Assn. Home: 739 N Northwest Hwy Park Ridge IL 60068 Office: 1045 N Northwest Hwy Park Ridge IL 60068

CHARLES, ALLAN G., physician; b. N.Y.C., Nov. 15, 1928; s. Harry G. and Alice (Grotzky) C.; A.B. cum laude, N.Y. U., 1958, M.D., 1952;; m. Phyllis V.J. Vail, June 28, 1957; children—Della Marie, Aaron Joseph, David Jonathan. Intern Phila. Gen. Hosp., 1952-53; resident in obstetrics and gynecology Mt. Sinai Hosp. N.Y.C., 1955-57; resident in obstetrics and gynecology Michael Reese Hosp., Chgo., 1957-60, clin. asst., 1960-61, asso. attending physician, 1961-69, attending physician, 1969—, co-dir. Rh-Investigative Clinic, 1963—, vice chmn. dept. obstetrics and gynecology, 1971; practice medicine specializing in obstetrics and gynecology, Chgo., 1960—; courtesy staff Chgo. Lying-In-Hosp.; clin. asst. prof. obstetrics and gynecology U. Ill. Coll. Medicine, Chgo., 1960-64, Chgo. Med. Sch., 1964-72; clin. prof. Pritzger-Sch. Medicine, U. Chgo., 1972—. Diplomate Am. Bd. Obstetrics and Gynecology. Fellow Am. Coll. Obstetricians and Gynecologists, Internat. Coll. Surgeons, Central Assn. Obstetricians and Gynecologists, Am. Fertility Soc.; mem. A.M.A., Ill., Chgo. med. socs., Chgo. Gynecol. Soc. Author: Rh Iso Immunization and Erythroblastosis Fetalis, 1969. Contbr. articles to profl. jours. Developer substitute for uterine tube, Rh-sensitization. Home: 6854 S Bennett Ave Chicago IL 60649 Office: 30 N Michiagn Ave Chicago IL 60602

CHARLES, ANDREW VALENTINE, psychiatrist; b. Chgo., Nov. 5, 1939; s. George and Carol Claire (Goettel) C.; B.A. cum laude, U. Mich., 1961; M.D., U. Ill., 1965. Rotating intern Ill. Masonic Hosp., Chgo., 1965-66; psychiatry resident Presbyn. St. Luke's Hosp., Chgo., 1966-69; practice medicine specializing in psychiatry, Chgo., 1969—; mem. attending staff Presbyn. St. Lukes, Chgo. Lakeshore hosps.; med. dir. Ridgeway Hosp., Chgo., 1976—; instr. psychiatry Rush Med. Sch., Chgo., 1970—; psychiatrist Chgo. Bd. Edn., 1970—; clin. dir. Exec. Assessment Corp., 1976—. Diplomate Am. Bd. Psychiatry and Neurology. Mem. A.M.A., Am. Group Psychotherapy Assn., Am., Ill. psychiat. assns., Chgo. Med. Soc., Am. Acad. Med. Dirs., Am. Assn. Utilization Rev. Physicians, Phi Rho Sigma. Office: 8 S Michigan Ave Suite 3102 Chicago IL 60603

CHARLES, ISABEL, coll. dean; b. Bklyn., Mar. 10, 1926; d. James Patrick and Isabel (Roney) Charles; B.A., Manhattan Coll., 1954; M.A., U. Notre Dame, 1960, Ph.D., 1965; postgrad. U. Mich., 1968-69. Chmn. dept. English, Bishop Watterson High Sch., Columbus, Ohio, 1954-59, St. Mary of The Springs Acad., Columbus, 1959-62; asst. prof. English, Ohio Dominican Coll., Columbus, 1965-68, acad. dean, exec. v.p., 1969-73; asst. dean Coll. Arts and Letters, U. Notre Dame, 1973-75, acting dean, 1975, dean, 1976—. Mem. Modern Lang. Assn., Am. Assn. Acad. Deans, Am. Assn. Higher Edn. Contbr. articles to profl. jours. Home: Apt D 1661 N Riverside Dr South Bend IN 46616

CHARLES, PETER CHAPOTON, lawyer; b. Columbus, O., Aug. 12, 1940; s. James Patrick and Isabel Marie (Roney) C.; B.S., Xavier U., 1962; J.D., St. Louis U.. 1965; m. Kathryn Louise Ahlf, June i0, i964; children—Daniel Patrick, Timothy Michael, Kathleen Louise, Christine Isabel. Tax specialist Lybrand, Ross Bros. & Montgomery, Columbus, St. Louis, 1962-64; admitted to Mo. bar, 1965, Kans. bar, 1966; estate and gift tax examiner Internal Revenue Service, Kansas City, Mo., 1965-67; practiced in Springfield, Mo., 1967-69; partner firm Miller, Fairman, Sanford & Carr, Springfield, 1969—. Tchr. taxation Drury Evening Coll., 1967-70. Chmn. St. John's Hosp. Devel. Council, 1972—. Mem. Greene County Estate Planning Council, 1967—, pres., 1973-74. Bd. dirs. Vis. Nurses Assn., 1969-72, pres., 1971-72. Mem. Am., Kan., Mo. (vice-chmn. probate and trust com. 1972-74), Greene County bar assns. Rotarian. Home: 1523 S Clay St Springfield MO 65804 Office: 926 Woodruff Bldg Springfield MO 65805

CHARLES, REID SHAVER, urban planner, adminstr.; b. Wichita, Kans., Sept. 16, 1940; s. Harry Lytton and Margaret Virginia (Shaver) C.; B.A., U. Wichita, 1964, postgrad., 1964-65; postgrad. Tulane U., 1968-69; M.A., Wichita State U., 1970; m. Mary Elizabeth Rouland, June 1, 1963; children—Reid Shaver, Rouland Shannon. Grad. fellow Wichita State U., 1965; adminstrv. asst. to city mgr. Newton (Kans.), 1965-66; planning asso., New Orleans, 1966-69; adminstrv. asst. to exec. sec. devel. Town of Brookline (Mass.), 1969-73; chief systems planning City of Kansas City (Mo.), 1973-74, acting dep. dir. city devel., 1974-75; prin. CHJ Assos., Kansas City, Mo., 1975—; adminstrv. dir. City of Lincoln (Nebr.), 1976—; lectr., cons. in field; participant Nat. Urban Policy Roundtable IV, 1977; mem. tech. adv. group Urban Econ. Policy and Mgmt. Group, U.S. Conf. Mayors-Nat. League Cities, 1977—. Served with USAAF, 1961. Mem. Am. Polit. Sci. Assn., Am. Inst. Planners, Am. Acad. Polit. and Social Scis., Internat. City Mgmt. Assn., Am. Soc. Planning Ofcls., Am. Soc. Pub. Adminstrn., Pi Sigma Alpha. Mem. Soc. of Friends. Author municipal budgeting manuals. Home: 1961 Garfield St Lincoln NE 68502 Office: Office of Mayor 555 S 10th St Lincoln NE 68508

CHARLIER, ROGER HENRI, oceanographer, geographer; b. Antwerp, Belgium, Nov. 10, 1921; came to U.S., 1946, naturalized, 1948; Ph.D., U. Erlangen, 1947; Litt.D., U. Paris, 1956, Sc.D., 1957. Prof. geography and history Coll. Baudouin, Brussels, Belgium, 1941-42; student asst. U. Liege (Belgium), 1943-44; newspaper corr., Europe, 1945-50; dep. dir. assembly centers UNRRA, 1946-48; research analyst Internat. War Crimes Commn., Nuernberg, Germany, 1948-49; tchr. Berlitz Sch., Newark, 1950-51; asso. prof. dept. geography, chmn. dept. Polycultural U., Washington, 1951-52; chmn. dept. phys. scis. Finch Coll., N.Y.C., 1952-55; tchr. Brunswick (N.J.) Sr. High Sch., 1955; chmn. dept. geology and geography Hofstra U., N.Y.C., 1955-58; professeur suppléant U. Paris (France), 1958-59; vis. prof. edn. U. Minn., 1959-60; prof. earth scis. Parsons Coll., Fairfield, Iowa, 1960-61; prof. geology, geography and oceanography Northeastern Ill. U., Chgo., 1961—, research scholar in oceanography, 1962-64, vice chmn. dept. geography, 1964-70, dir. oceanography program, 1962—; prof. extraordinary U. Brussels, 1971—; vis. prof. U. Bordeaux, 1970-74; exchange scientist Internat. Research Exchange Com., 1968-69, Nat. Acad. Sci., 1967-68. Belgian Nat. Found. for Sci. Research grantee, 1977-78; Belgian Govt. grantee, 1976-78; Inst. for River and Estuarine Studies grantee, 1976-78; Fulbright scholar, 1975-76; NATO grantee, 1969-70; French Govt. fellow, 1967-69; Institut Oceanographique de Monaco grantee, 1967-68. Office: Northeastern Ill U 5500 N St Louis Ave Chicago IL 60625

CHARLTON, CLARENCE DEAN, banker, lawyer; b. Chgo., Nov. 14, 1903; s. George and Carrie (Kyger) C.; LL.B., J.D., U. Ill., 1926; m. Donna Cooley, Mar. 27, 1927 (dec. Mar. 8, 1935); m. 2d, Florence Brown, July 3, 1936 (dec. Mar. 31, 1938); m. 3d, Phyllis Boston, Apr. 8, 1939; children—Kenody J., Diane Ahlgrim. Admitted to Ill. bar, 1926; atty. Western Clock Co., LaSalle, Ill., 1926-28; gen. practice law, LaSalle, 1928-29, 74—; trust officer, dir., v.p. LaSalle Nat. Bank (Ill.), 1929-63, pres., 1959-74. Mem. City of La Salle Plan Commn. Pres. Tri-Cities chpt. A.R.C., 1942; mem. exec. bd. W.D. Boyce council Boy Scouts Am. Bd. dirs. mem. exec. bd. Tri-City Tb Soc.; trustee Oakwood Cemetery Assn.; sec., bus. mgr., trustee Hygienic Inst. LaSalle-Peru and Oglesby; mem. finance com. St. Mary Hosp. Mem. Am., Ill., LaSalle County, Tri-City bar assns., Ill. Bankers Assn. (pres. trust div.), Ill. Valley Theatre Guild, Community Concert Assn., C. of C. Methodist. Mason (Shriner), Rotarian. Clubs: Bankers, Union League (Chgo.); Deer Park Country, Deer Park Fishing, South Bluff Country. Home: 1427 Argyle Rd LaSalle IL 61301 Office: 105 Marguette St LaSalle IL 61301

CHARLTON, MICHAEL JOHN, mfg. co. exec.; b. Alliance, Ohio, July 1, 1949; s. Chester J. and Martha R. (Stranges) C.; grad. USAF Programming Tech. Sch., 1969. Maitre d' Lays Restaurant, Omaha, 1973-75; owner Mickey's Restaurant, Canton, Ohio, 1975; supr. programming Bellows Internat., Akron, Ohio, 1976—; v.p. FMP Mgmt., Inc., 1975-76; vice chmn. N.E. Ohio Cube, 1976—. Served with USAF, 1968-73. Mem. Nat. Cooperating Users of Burroughs Equipment. Home: 2305 Parkway Alliance OH 44601 Office: 200 W Exchange St Akron OH 44309

CHARLTON, RICHARD GEORGE, pub. relations exec.; b. Schenectady, N.Y., Mar. 26, 1934; s. Henry C. and Irene F. (DiLallo) C.; B.A., Syracuse U., 1955; m. Diana V. Carver, Aug. 7, 1954; children—Lincoln, Faith, Jennifer. Information specialist Gen. Elec. Co., Utica, Schenectady and Syracuse, N.Y., 1958-62; dir. pub. affairs and information Calspan Corp., Buffalo, 1962-74; dir. communications and pub. affairs J.I. Case Co., Racine, Wis., 1974—. Co-chmn. Tenn. State U. Cluster, 1978—; bd. dirs. Racine Urban League. Served with USAF, 1955-58. Mem. Internat. Assn. Bus. Communicators (accredited, pres. 1975-76, Gold Quill award 1970), Farm and Indsl. Equipment Inst., Pub. Relations Soc. Am. (accredited, pres. Niagara Frontier chpt. 1970). Methodist (ofcl. bd.). Author: (with others) Machines of Plenty, 1976. Contbg. editor Pub. Relations Jour., 1968-72. Home: 832 Hialeah Dr Racine WI 53402 Office: 700 State St Racine WI 53404

CHARNICKI, WALTER FRANCIS, pharm. co. exec.; b. Haverhill, Mass., Mar. 6, 1921; s. Francis and Mary (Shimanski) C.; B.S., Mass. Coll. Pharmacy, 1943, M.S., 1948; Ph.D., Purdue U., 1951; m. Eileen Donahue, Apr. 28, 1946; children—Claire A. (Mrs. Thomas Mingey), Michael L. Control chemist E.L. Patch Co., Stoneham, Mass., 1943, 46; retail pharmacist, Lawrence, Mass., 1943, 46-48; instr. Franklin Tech. Inst., Boston, 1946-47; teaching fellow Mass. Coll. Pharmacy, 1947-48; research asso. Merck, Sharp & Dohme Research Lab., West Point, Pa., 1951-59; dir. product devel. Dorsey Labs. div. Sandoz-Wander, Inc., Lincoln, Nebr., 1959-67, dir. pharm. devel. and control, 1967-71, v.p. research, devel. and prodn., 1971—. Served with USNR, 1943-46; PTO. Fellow Am. Found. Pharm. Edn.; mem. Am. Chem. Soc., Am. Pharm. Assn. (chmn. sci. sect. 1963, chmn. indsl. pharmacy sect. 1965), Lincoln C. of C., Sigma Xi, Rho Chi. Club: University. Home: 2601 Rathbone Rd Lincoln NE 68502 Office: PO Box 83288 Lincoln NE 68501

CHARPENTIER, DONALD ARMAND, psychologist; b. Bklyn., Mar. 8, 1935; s. Joseph Roche and Grace Viola (Adrience) C.; B.A., Hope Coll., 1956; M.A., Ohio U., 1958; Ed.S., George Peabody Coll., 1964; Ph.D., U. Minn., 1972; m. Janice Lee Getting, May 21, 1961; children—Jennifer Diane, Ian Lee. Burke. Asso. dir. Westminster Found. Ohio, 1956-57, acting dir., 1957-58; psychologist, probation officer Cook County Family Court, Chgo., 1961-62; asst. prof. psychology State U. N.Y., Fredonia, 1964-65; asst. prof. U. Wis., River Falls, 1965-72, asso. prof., 1974—. Vis. research fellow, Harvard U., 1973-74. Lic. psychologist, Wis. Mem. AAAS, Am. Assn. Advancement Social Psychology, Am. Psychol. Assn., Am. Sociol. Assn., Internat. Soc. History of Behavioral and Social Scis., Soc. Psychol. Study Social Issues. Home: Rt 4 River Falls WI 54022 Office: Dept Psychology Univ Wis River Falls WI 54022

CHARTIER, CHARLES ARDEN, lawyer; b. Concordia, Kans., May 1, 1938; s. Delbert Raymond and Merna (Cyr) C.; B.S., Kans. State Coll., 1960; J.D., U. Kans., 1963; children—Cheryl, Douglas; m. 2d, Janice R. Hobgood, May 31, 1967; 1 son, Darren; stepchildren—Shelley, Rick. Admitted to Kans., bar, 1963; asso. firm Weary, Weary & Barnhill, Junction City, Kans., 1963-64, Nuss & Nuss, Great Bend, Kans., 1964-65; partner Weary, Weary, Medley & Chartier, Junction City, 1965-68, Weary, Weary & Chartier, 1968-70; individual practice law, Junction City, 1970—; pub. hearing officer, Junction City, 1967—; asst. county atty., Geary County, 1966-68. Sec., Geary County March of Dimes, 1966-68, pres., 1968-70, bd. dirs., 1966—; chmn. Junction City and Geary County Joint Planning Commn., 1966—. Recipient Distinguished Service award Junction City Jr. C. of C., 1968; Charles Davis award Kans. Jr. C. of C., 1969; M. Keith Upson award U.S. Jr. C. of C., 1969. Mem. Am., Kans., Geary County bar assns., Am., Kans. trial lawyers assns., Junction City C. of C. (dir. 1966-67), Kans. (v.p. 1968-69, legal counsel 1969-71), Junction City City (pres. 1966-67, legal counsel 1970-71) jaycees, Order of Coif, Phi Delta Phi. Republican. Mem. Christian Ch. Address: 7261/2 N Washington St Junction City KS 66441

CHASE, EDWIN DUBOIS, finance co. exec.; b. Bklyn., May 18, 1921; s. Edwin D. and Grace (Cole) C.; student Washington and Lee U., 1938-39, U. Miami (Fla.), 1939-41; M.B.A., U. Chgo., 1948; m. Shirley Ann Schellenberg, Apr. 20, 1946; children—Wendy Ann, Mark Dubois. Bus. mgmt. rep. Studebaker Corp., South Bend, Ind. and N.Y.C., 1948-53; bus. mgmt. program Cessna Aircraft Co., Wichita, Kans., 1953-55; v.p., gen. mgr. Cessna Finance Corp. (formerly Nat. Aero Finance Co.), 1955-69, pres., gen. mgr., 1969—, dir., 1955—. Served to capt. USAAF, 1942-46. Mem. Aircraft Finance Assn. (v.p. 1971-76), Pi Kappa Alpha, Phi Eta Sigma. Club: Crestview Country. Home: 7723 Killarney Ct Wichita KS 67206 Office: 3900 E McArthur Rd Wichita KS 67201

CHASE, ERNEST ARTHUR, accountant; b. Galien, Mich., Apr. 10, 1931; s. Samuel M. and Mildred Irene (Morley) C.; student Internat. Corr. Schs., Lake Michigan Coll., 1974-75; m. Joyce Elaine Winney, July 21, 1951; children—Ernest L., Arthur M., Robert J., William R., James R. Assembly insp. David Products Co., Niles, Mich., 1951; gen. accountant Warren Featherbone Co., Three Oaks, Mich., 1953-55; cost accountant Bendix Products Co., South Bend, Ind., 1955-56; officer mgr. Babbitt Lumber Co., Niles, 1956-57; cost accountant Curtiss Wright Corp., South Bend, 1957-58; mgr. credit office Am. Home and Gray Aretz Co., South Bend, 1958; chief accountant Millburg Growers Exchange (Mich.), 1958-59; sales mgr. S.W. Mich. dist. Nat. Fedn. Ind. Bus., 1959-60; owner Chase Pub. Accounting Service, Galien, 1958—, Chase Ins. Service Center, Galien, 1960—, Family Everyday Clothing and Shoe Store, Three Oaks, 1963-65; salesman Kiefer Real Estate, Berrien Springs, Mich., 1962—. Leader, Boy Scouts Am., 1957-72; sec., treas., coach Galien Little League, 1964—; clk. Village of Galien, 1963-64; mem. adv. com. Galien Twp. Schs., 1963-70, chmn., 1966-70; mem. tax allocation bd. Berrien County, 1971-72, mem. key man com., 1971-72, chmn. finance com., 1971-72, chmn. budget com., 1969-70, dist. commr., 1969-72, 77-78; mem. regional key man com. Mich. Assn. Counties, 1971-72. Mem. Berrien County Republican Exec. Com., 1969-72. Served with USNR, 1949-50, 52-53. Mem. Ind. Accountants Mich., Mich. Assn. Mut. Ins. Agts., Nat. Soc. Pub. Accountants, Galien Jr. C. of C., Am. Legion. Methodist. Lion. Home: Hwy US 12 E Galien MI 49113 Office: 112 N Main St Galien MI 49113

CHASE, FREDRIC LEWIS, bldg. supplies co. exec.; b. Sun Prairie, Wis., Feb. 2, 1915; s. Frederick William and Edith May (Hecker) C.; student Frank Wiggins Trade Sch., Los Angeles, 1936-37; m. Helen Marie Bunker, May 30, 1942; 1 son, Neal. With Chase Lumber & Fuel Co., 1939—, mgr. br., De Forest, Wis., 1942-44, owner, 1944—; v.p., chief exec. Chase Inc., Windsor, Wis., 1975—; chmn. bd., officer Chase Fitzpatrick Ltd., Portage (Wis.) Lumber Co., Oreg. Lumber Co., F.L. Chase Lumber. Pres. DeForest Devel. Corp., 1956. Trustee Village of DeForest, Chase Trust. Mem. De Forest Investment Club. Roman Catholic (sec. parish 1952-54). Lion (merit award 1959), Elk. Home: 313 S Main St DeForest WI 53532 Office: Box 258 Windsor WI 53598

CHASE, JOSEPH EDWARD, psychologist, mental health adminstr.; b. Cleve., Sept. 24, 1941; s. Joseph Edward and Ruth Agnes (Bebout) C.; B.A., Hiram Coll., 1963; M.A., Western Mich. U., 1965; postgrad. U. Mich., 1967; Ph.D., Internat. Grad. Sch., 1978; m. Julia Ann Woodall, July 3, 1964; children—Joseph Edward III, Evan Andrew. Teaching fellow Western Mich. U., Kalamazoo, 1964-65; psychol. technician Battle Creek (Mich.) VA Hosp., 1965; psychology instr. Mott Community Coll., Flint, Mich., 1965-70; dir. outpatient service Genesee County Community Mental Health Services, Flint, 1970—; cons. Flint Police Dept., Goodwill Industries, Citizens Probation; adj. prof. Mich. State U.; instr. Mott Community Coll. Mem. Am. Psychol. Assn., Gestalt Inst. Cleve., Internat. Grad. U. Student Assn. (past pres.). Author: Existential Theory, the Gestalt Approach, 1975. Home: 950 Welch Blvd Flint MI 48504 Office: 808 N Grand Traverse St Flint MI 48503

CHASE, ROBERT HENRY, dentist; b. Evansville, Ind., Oct. 30, 1923; s. John Randall and Hilda Frances (Moutoux) C.; student St. Mary's Coll., 1941-44; D.D.S., U. Detroit, 1947; m. Gerry Ann Campbell, May 28, 1945 (dec. July 1970); children—Sue (Mrs. Michael Holthaus), Claudia (Mrs. Dennis Calus), Terese, Brigid, Heidi; m. Betty Eileen Krause, Feb. 19, 1972; stepchildren—Thomas, Michael, Katie (Mrs. James Karczewski), Robert, Richard, Jack, William, Janice, Julie. Pvt. practice dentistry, Detroit, 1947-50, Traverse City, Mich., 1953—. Lectr. dental asst. program N.W. Mich. Coll., 1962—; mem. Mich. Bd. Dentistry. City commr., Traverse City, Mich., 1961-69, mayor, 1962-63. Served with USNR, 1941-45, 51-53. Fellow Internat. Coll. Dentists; mem. Acad. Gen. Dentistry, Am. Soc. Preventive Dentistry, Am. Soc. Dentistry Children, Mich. Dental Assn., Mich. Assn. Professions. Elk, K.C., Kiwanian. Contbr. articles to profl. jours.; lectr. nat. pro life movement. Home: 757 Wilson Rd Traverse City MI 49684 Office: 876 1/2 E Front St Traverse City MI 49684

CHASE, ROBERT MERRILL, art gallery and pub. co. exec.; b. Chgo., Dec. 5, 1940; s. Merrill and Ann (Nickoll) C.; B.S., U. Wis., 1962; m. Moya Watson, July 3, 1965; children—Lara Sue, Robert Merrill. Co-founder, Merrill Chase Galleries, Ltd., Chgo., 1964, pres., chief exec. officer, 1968—; chief exec. Merrill Chase Pub. Assos., Chgo., 1974—. Mem. Chgo. Art Inst., Am. Soc. Appraisers. Club: Variety (Chgo.). Office: 620 N Michigan Ave Chicago IL 60611

CHASING HAWK, SHARON MARIE, counselor; b. Hazen, N.D., Nov. 9, 1951; d. Mathew Micah and Louise Millicent (Starr) Holding Eagle; B.S., U. N.D. at Grand Forks, 1976; M.A., U. S.D., Vermillion, 1977; m. Everette Wayne Chasing Hawk, Feb. 20, 1971; children—Everette Lance, Dace James. Tchr. intern Standing Rock Community Elementary Sch., Ft. Yates, N.D., 1974-76; minority counselor Acad. Counseling Center, U. S.D., Vermillion, 1977—. Bd. dirs. Vermillion Day Care Center. Am. Indian scholar, 1976-77. Mem. S.D., Nat. Indian edn. assns., Am., S.D. personnel and guidance Assns., S.D. Indian Counselor Assn. Congregationalist. Home: 325 Franklin St Vermillion SD 57069 Office: Slagle Hall Room 12 U SD Vermillion SD 57069

CHASZEYKA, MICHAEL ANDREW, govt ofcl.; b. Youngstown, Ohio, July 28, 1920; s. Michael and Anastasia (Klim) C.; B. in Mech. Engring., Ohio State U., 1943; M.S. in Mech. Engring., Ill. Inst. Tech., 1959; postgrad. U. Chgo., 1959-63; m. Libuse Panosh, Nov. 30, 1946. Jr. engr. Truscon div. Republic Steel Corp., Youngstown, 1947; design detailer, process engr. electromotive div. Gen. Motors Corp., McCook, Ill., 1947-51; research engr. Armour Research Found., Research Inst., Ill. Inst. Tech., Chgo., 1953-61; phys. sci. coordinator Midcontinental office Office Naval Research, Chgo., 1961—. Served to lt. USNR, 1944-46, 51-53. Fellow Am. Inst. Aeros. and Astronautics (asso. fellow; mem. nat. tech. com. underwater propulsion 1966-69, sect. chmn. 1965-67), Marine Tech. Soc. (chmn. Gt. Lakes sect. 1972-74); mem. ASME, Ohio State U. Alumni Assn., Ill. Inst. Tech. Alumni Assn. (bd. dirs.), Sigma Xi (asso.) Home: 4147 Grove Ave Western Springs IL 60558 Office: 536 S Clark St Chicago IL 60605

CHATHANATT, MATHEW MATHAI, chemist; b. Panthathala, India, July 6, 1942; s. Mathai and Annamma; B.S., Kerala U., 1963, M.S., 1966; Ph.D., U. Detroit, 1975; m. Alamma Joseph, May 29, 1971; children—Annie, Jason. Tchr., Our Lady of Grace High Sch., Bicholim, Goa, 1963-64; lectr. St. Thomas Coll., Palai, India, 1966-69; chemist Fabricon Automotive Products div. Eagle Picher Industries, River Rouge, Mich., 1972—. Mem. Kerala Assn. Recipient Outstanding Alumnus award Sacred Heart Coll., Thevara. Home: 4140 Jackson St Dearborn Heights MI 48125 Office: 1900 W Pleasant Ave River Rouge MI 48218

CHATMAN, DONALD LEVERITT, obstetrician, gynecologist; b. New Orleans, Dec. 27, 1934; s. Aristotle Lorenzo and Eulacie (Shamberger) C.; B.A., Harvard, 1956; M.D., Meharry Med. Coll., 1960; m. Eleanor Mae Scrutchions, Jan. 15, 1957; children—Lynn Ann, Eleanor Louise, Eric Leveritt. Intern, Cooper Hosp., Camden, N.J., 1960-61; gen. practice medicine, Lake Charles, La., 1961-63; resident in obstetrics-gynecology Michael Reese Hosp. and Med. Center, Chgo., 1965-69; practice medicine specializing in obstetrics gynecology, Chgo., 1969—; clin. asst. prof. Pritzker Sch. Medicine U. Chgo., 1974—. Diplomate Am. Bd. Obstetrics Gynecology. Mem. Am. Coll. Obstetricians Gynecologists, Ill., Chgo. med. socs. Home: 9122 S Constance St Chicago IL 60617

CHATTAWAY, DWIGHT NELSON, bottled water co. exec.; b. Monongahela, Pa., Mar. 30, 1936; s. John Nelson and Bertha Ellen (Mashinsky) C.; student U. Calif. at Riverside, 1958-60; B.A., Los Angeles State Coll., 1962; M.A., Calif. State Coll., 1966; postgrad. U. So. Calif., 1969-70; m. Lynda Louise Verguson, Jan. 15, 1974; children—Chat Nelson, Blake Nelson, Sonny Julaine. With Kaiser Steel Corp., Fontana, Calif., 1954-58, Arrowhead Puritas Waters, Los Angeles, 1958-69, corporate retail sales mgr., 1968-70; dir. sales and marketing Hinckley & Schmitt, Chgo., 1970-74, v.p. sales and marketing, 1974—, dir., 1975—. Mem. Am. Bottled Water Assn., Am. Marketing Assn., Sales and Marketing Execs. Assn. Republican. Methodist. Home: 1041 W Ogden St Naperville IL 60540 Office: 6055 S Harlem St Chicago IL 60638

CHEATHAM, DENNIS HAROLD, banker; b. Madison, Ind., May 27, 1943; s. John Harold and Callie Elizabeth (Hughes) C.; A.B., Ind. U., 1965; m. Quindaro Anne Groth; children—Theodore Chase, Quindaro Elizabeth. Sales mgr. charge card div. Indpls. Morris Plan, 1966-67; successively investment officer, asst. v.p., v.p. Am. Fletcher Nat. Bank & Trust Co., Indpls., 1967-72; asst. treas. Am. Fletcher Corp., Indpls., 1970-72; pres., dir., chief exec. officer State Bank Lapel (Ind.), 1972—, Pendleton Banking Co. (Ind.), 1973—; pres. dir. Pendleton Co., Inc., 1975—; dir. Mgmt. Advisers, Inc. and subs.'s, Anderson, Ind., 1973—; trustee Underwriters Nat. Assurance Co., Indpls., 1977—; adviser S. Madison County Bldg. Trades, Inc., 1975. Mem. allocations and rev. com. Madison County United Way, 1973; bd. dirs. Pendleton Festival Symphony, 1975—. Mem. Ind. Bankers Assn., Delta Upsilon (nat. treas., dir. 1974, 75, 76, nat. chmn. bd. dirs. 1977—). Home: PO Box 205 Pendleton IN 46064 Office: 100 E State St Pendleton IN 46064

CHEATHAM, MARGARET JOSEPHINE, psychologist; b. Amarillo, Tex., May 29, 1920; d. Josiah Hunter and Gertrude Malone (Boyd) C.; B.A., U. Tex., Austin, 1941; M.A., So. Methodist U., 1948; Ph.D., Western Res. U., 1953; postgrad. Moreno Inst., 1969. Pvt. practice psychology, Nashville, 1951-54; chief psychologist Guidance Center, Piqua, Ohio, 1955-56, San Antonio, Tex., 1956-57; staff psychologist VA Mental Health Center, Phila., 1957-61, VA Hosp., Waco, Tex., 1961-62, Prairie View Mental Health Center, Newton, Kans., 1963-72; pvt. group practice Wichita Psychiat. Center, 1972—. Served with USN, 1943-47. Certified psychologist, Kans., Tenn. Mem. Am., Kans., Tenn., Tex., Wichita, Southwestern psychol. assns., Moreno Inst., Am. Assn. Group Psycotherapy and Psychodrama, Am. Assn. Psychotherapists. Baptist. Home: 1006 Blackwill St Wichita KS 67207 Office: PO Box 8037 Wichita KS 67208

CHEATHAM, WALTER MALCOLM, corporate pub. affairs exec.; b. Toccoa, Ga., May 17, 1932; s. Jess Bailey and Eleanor Irene (Johnson) C.; B.A., Emory U., 1956, J.D., 1956; postgrad. Temple U., 1957-58; student Presbyn. Coll., 1950-51, U. Ga., 1951-54; m. Harriet Ann Craig, Jan. 6, 1973; 1 dau., Elinor Dallas. Mgr. govt. dept. Ga. C. of C., Atlanta, 1958-59; exec. staff rep. The Coca-Cola Co., Atlanta, 1959-62, mgr. mktg., San Antonio, 1962-64, mgr. pub. relations, Chgo., 1964-65; gen. mgr. Southeastern opns. Ruder & Finn Co., Atlanta, 1965-67; prin. Cheatham Pub. Relations/Advt., Atlanta, 1967-71; mktg. cons. N.W. Ayer ABH Internat., Dallas, 1971-74, account exec. Midwest, Chgo., 1974-75; dir. pub. affairs Midwest Union Carbide Corp., Chgo., 1976—. Trustee Ill. 2000 Found., 1977—. Mem. advisory bd. Civic Fedn. Chgo., 1975—; bd. dirs. Pub. Service Communications Council Chgo., 1976—, Christopher House United Christian Community Services Chgo., 1975-76; dir. Better Govt. Assn. Chgo., 1977—. Served with U.S. Army, 1956-58. Named One of Georgia's Five Outstanding Young Men, Ga. Jr. C. of C., 1962. Mem. Emory U. Alumni Assn. (v.p. 1967-71), Pub. Relations Soc. Am., Chgo. Area Pub. Affairs Group, Ill. Mfrs. Assn. (pub. relations/econ. edn. com.), Pub. Affairs Forum Ill. C. of C., Sigma Alpha Epsilon. Presbyterian. Club: Illinois Athletic. Home: 1000 Shambliss Ln Buffalo Grove IL 60090 Office: 120 S Riverside Plaza Chicago IL 60606

CHEATUM, ELWYN DALE, real estate broker; b. Watson, Ill., Nov. 25, 1928; s. Ervin Byron and Nina Merle (Norris) C.; student Mid-State and Ill. Central Coll., 1971; grad. Real Estate Inst., State of Ill., 1972; m. Louise Marie Green, Apr. 15, 1950; children—Daniel Stewart, Janice Louise. Telegrapher, train dispatcher Ill. Central R.R., Champaign, 1946-61; area mgr., instr. Dale Carnegie courses, Peoria, Ill., 1961-70, instr., Trinidad, Barbados, West Indies, 1969; sales rep. Ken Rau Realtor, Peoria, Ill., 1970-71; pres., sales mgr. Capitol Real Estate Co., Peoria, 1971—. Vice-chmn. Ill. Speakers Bur., 1974-75; mem. adv. council Peoria (Ill.) Sch. Dist. 150. Bd. dirs., sec. Peoria Christian Bus. Men Com., 1974-75; chmn. bd. dirs. Chapel Vision Ministries, 1968-73. Mem. Ill. (state regional chmn. real estate polit. and ednl. affairs 1975, state chmn. polit. action dept. 1976), Peoria (dir. 1975-76) bds. realtors, Peoria Heights C. of C. (dir. 1974). Mason (Shriner). Presbyn. Kiwanian. Home: 7113 Manning Dr Peoria IL 61614 Office: 4701 N University St Peoria IL 61614

CHEEVER, GENE G., clay products co. exec.; b. Brookings, S.D., Dec. 30, 1928; s. Herbert E. and Margaret (Williams) C.; B.S., S.D. State U., 1951; M.S., U. Ill., 1952; m. JoAnn Coughlin, June 18, 1952; children—Patrick, Dan, Todd, Timothy. Football coach, dir. phys. edn. Dakota Wesleyan U., 1952-54; football coach, dir. athletics Watertown (S.D.) High Sch., 1954-56; with Black Hills Clay Products Co., Belle Fourche, S.D., 1956-74, v.p., 1962-73, pres., 1973—; pres. Hebron Brick Co. (N.D.), 1973—; v.p. Dacco Inc. and Hebron Dacco, Fargo, N.D. Mem. regional adv. council Small Bus. Adminstrn., 1970—; adv. council S.D. State U., 1969—; mem. Municipal Swimming Pool Bd., Belle Fourche, 1957-73; council mem. Boy Scouts Am., 1968-73. State committeeman Butte County (S.D.) Republican Party. Mem. Western S.D. Traffic Bur. (dir.), Belle Fourche C. of C. (pres. 1970-71). Roman Catholic (mem. ch. bldg. com. 1959-73). Elk. Club: Belle Fourche Country (dir.). Home: 1079 5th Av W Dickinson ND 53601 Office: Hebron Brick Co Hebron ND 58638

CHEEVER, GORDON DALE, chemist; b. McAllen, Tex., Oct. 6, 1932; s. George Valentine and Edna Isma (Roger) C.; A.B., Johns Hopkins U., 1955, M.A., 1958; Ph.D., Case Inst. Tech., 1963; m. Leonore Germuth, June 4, 1955; children—Gordon Dale, Brian, Eric, Mark. With Glidden Paint Co., Balt., 1958-65; with Gen. Motors Research Labs., Warren, Mich., 1965—, sr. research chemist, 1966—. Mem. faculty Johns Hopkins, 1956-57, Case Inst. Tech., 1961-62. Mem. com. pack 257 Cub Scouts Am., Rochester, Mich., 1970-73. Mem. Fedn. Paint Soc., Sigma Xi. Editor: (with P. Weiss) Interface Conversion for Polymer Coatings. Home: 53417 Bellamine Dr Rochester MI 48063 Office: Gen Motors Technical Center Warren MI 48090

CHEEVER, RAYMOND CRAIG, editor; b. Bozeman, Mont., Dec. 25, 1926; s. Hurlbert Craig and Myrtle (Hollier) C.; B.S., Northwestern U., 1950; m. Grace Caroline Wiprud, Dec. 28, 1947; children—Sheryl Lynn, Richard Craig, Julie Caroline. Supr. sales promotion State Farm Ins. Co., Bloomington, Ill., 1950-58, editor agts. sales mag., 1958-68; pres. Accent on Info., Inc., 1956—, Cheever Pub., Inc., 1976—; owner Ray Cheever Enterprises. Mem. Pres. Com. on Employment Handicapped, 1962—; chmn. Bloomington-Normal Mayor's Com. on Employment Handicapped. Bd. dirs. Occupational Devel. Center. Served with USNR, 1944-46. Recipient citation for meritorious service Pres. Com. Employment Handicapped, 1958, 68. Mem. Delta Sigma Pi. Methodist. Mason (32 deg., Shriner). Founder, pub., editor quar. mag. Accent on Living (edited for physically handicapped). Home and office: 9 High Dr Box 700 Bloomington IL 61701

CHEKOURAS, CARL CHRISTOPHER, cons.; b. Beloit, Wis., Apr. 16, 1916; s. George A. and Sophie Theresa (Pierson) C.; student U. Wis. Extension, Beloit Coll., 1943-45; m. Geraldine A. Wolfe, Mar. 2, 1946; children—David, Carl, Susan. Product design and devel. wood-working industry, 1942-54; plant mgr. Agerstrand Corp., Freeport, Ill., 1954-56; organizer, pres. Ackrit Machine Co., Inc., South Beloit, Ill., 1954-56; dist. sales mgr. Atwood, Rockford, Ill., 1963-71; mgmt. staff Morris Midwest, Inc., Wausau, Wis., 1971-74; sales dir. Crown div. Steel King Industries. Mem. Am. Soc. Agr. Engrs., Farm Equipment Mfg. Assn., Soc. Automotive Engrs., Serra Internat. Contbr. articles to trade publs. Home: 42 Pleasant Acres Route 1 Stevens Point WI 54481 Office: 3000 Welsby Stevens Point WI 54481

CHELOHA, KENNETH LEO, publishing exec.; b. Columbus, Nebr., July 30, 1943; s. Frank Casmir and Helen Leocodia (Ziemba) C.; A.A. magna cum laude, Norfolk Jr. Coll., 1962; B.S. cum laude, U. Nebr., 1964; m. Patricia A. Stutesman, June 15, 1963; children—Kenneth J., Daniel L. Staff accountant Peat, Marwick, Mitchell & Co., C.P.A.'s, Lincoln, Nebr., 1964; sr. accountant Philip G. Johnson & Co., C.P.A., Lincoln, 1964-70; controller Mid-Am. Webpress, Inc., Lincoln, 1970-71, v.p. finance, 1971-76, chief operating officer, 1976—; cons. Mgmt. Services & Systems, Lincoln, 1968-72. Recipient Platte County Agrl. Soc. fellowship, 1960-64. C.P.A., Nebr. Mem. Am. Inst. C.P.A.'s, Nebr. Soc. C.P.A.'s, Lincoln Jr. C. of C. Catholic (trustee 1970-72; chmn. finance com. 1970-72). Home: 7400 Briarhurst Circle Lincoln NE 68505 Office: PO Box 81608 Lincoln NE 68501

CHELSETH, ARCHIE DONALD, mgmt. cons.; b. Duluth, Minn., Apr. 18, 1942; s. Osmund H. and Myrtle A. (LaTour) C.; B.A. cum laude (U.S. Steelworkers scholar 1960-61), U. Minn., 1963, M.A. in Pub. Adminstrn., 1968; m. Andrea L. Lundberg, Dec. 16, 1967 (div. 1973); m. 2d, Gretchen J. Kaufmann, Dec. 31, 1977. Research asst. League Minn. Municipalities, Mpls., 1963-64; adminstrv. fellow Office of Dean, Inst. Agr., U. Minn., St. Paul, 1964-65; asst. dir. civic affairs H.B. Fuller Co., St. Paul, 1965-66; adminstrv. asst. Assn. Minn. Counties, St. Paul, 1966; dir. research Forsythe U.S. Senate campaign, 1966, Office of Gov. Minn., 1966-69; adminstrv. asst. to pub. Mpls. Star and Tribune, 1969; exec. sec. Minn. Exptl. City Legis. Subcoms., 1969-70; asst. to majority leader Minn. Senate, 1971-72; asst. commr. Minn. Dept. Natural Resources, 1972-76; mem. Minn. Gov.'s River Basin Commn., 1976-77; instr. polit. sci. Coll. St. Thomas, 1968, 70, 76; cons. NSF, 1977—; Mem. exec. com. Gov.'s Council Health, Welfare and Rehab., 1967-69, 77, steering com. Gov.'s Council Exec. Reorgn., 1967-68; mem. Minn. Exptl. City Authority, 1971-72; chmn. Minn. Water Resources Council, 1973-77; vice-chmn. Upper Mississippi River Basin Commn., 1974-76, Mo. River Basin Commn., 1976-77, Gt. Lakes Basin Commn., 1975-77. Bd. dirs., asst. sec. Voyageurs Nat. Park Assn., 1968-75; bd. dirs. Civic Orch. Mpls. Mem. Am. Soc. Pub. Adminstrn. (mem. chpt. governing bd. 1968-70), Am. Polit. Sci. Assn., St. Paul Civic Symphony Assn. (pres. 1976-77), Minn. Hist. Soc., U. Minn. Alumni Assn. Republican. Presbyn. Home: 946 Carmel Ct Shoreview MN 55112

CHEN, MING CHIH, automotive co. exec.; b. Foochow, China, Aug. 15, 1920; s. Bing H. and Sue G. (Wong) C.; B.S., Fukien Christian U., 1942; Ph.D., U. Buffalo, 1950; postgrad. Purdue U., 1950-52; m. Hsiao Mei Cheng, May 3, 1943; children—Co Co Hugo, Yvonne. Came to U.S., 1948, naturalized, 1955. Research asst. U. Buffalo, 1948-50; research fellow Purdue U., 1950-52; research asso. O-Cel-O div. Gen. Mills Corp., Buffalo, 1952-57; group leader Simonize Co., Chgo., 1957-62; mgr. product devel. Sheller-Globe Corp., Detroit, 1962-73, dir. mfg. Devel. Center, 1973—. Mem. Am. Chem. Soc., Soc. Plastics Engrs., Soc. Plastics Industries, Soc. Automotive Engrs., Sigma Xi. Patentee in field. Home: 22530 Benjamin St St Clair Shores MI 48081 Office: 1641 Porter St Detroit MI 48216

CHEN, PAUL E., scientist; b. Hangchow, China, June 29, 1925; s. Johnson T.F. and Von N. (Kao) C.; B.S., Nat. Chiao Tung U., China, 1947; M.S., Purdue U., 1953; D.Sc., Washington U., St. Louis, 1962; m. Lydia S.M. Chung, Dec. 1, 1952; children—Susan, Michael. Came to U.S., 1951, naturalized, 1963. Instr., Nat. Taiwan U., Taipei, 1947-51; engr. Miss. Valley Structural Steel Co., Melrose Park, Ill., 1953-55; sr. engr. Sverdrup & Parcel Engring. Co., St. Louis, 1955-59; research scientist Monsanto Co., St. Louis, 1959-70; group supr. Bell Labs., Naperville, Ill., 1970—; dir. Unisystems, Inc., 1969—. Affiliate prof. materials sci. Washington U., 1965-69; prof. engring. mechanics U. Mo. at Rolla St. Louis Grad. Engring. Center, 1966-70; adj. prof. Ill. Inst. Tech., 1975—. Dir., Chinese Christian Ch., River Forest, Ill., 1976—. Mem. ASME, ASCE, Am. Inst. Physics, Soc. Rheology, Sigma Xi, Tau Beta Pi. Contbr. articles to profl. jours., chpts. to books. Designer bridges, U.S. and abroad. Home: 22W131 Glen Park St Glen Ellyn IL 60137 Office: Bell Labs Naperville IL 60540

CHEN, PETER FU MING, surgeon; b. Medan, Indonesia, Dec. 3, 1941; s. Ah Sok and Oei Tan; came to U.S., 1968, naturalized, 1977; M.D., Nat. Def. Med. Center, Taiwan, 1968; m. Shueh-Yen Tien, Apr. 9, 1968; children—Vivian, Calvin. Intern, Barberton (Ohio) Citizens Hosp., 1968; resident in surgery Fairview (Ohio) Gen. Hosp., 1969-73; practice medicine specializing in surgery, Mantua, Ohio; staff Robinson Meml. Hosp., Ravenna, Ohio. Recipient Scholar award Chinese Govt., 1968. Diplomate Am. Bd. Surgery. Fellow A.C.S.; mem. Ohio Med. Assn., Cleve. Surg. Soc., Portage County Med. Soc. Baptist. Home: 4692 Streeter Rd Mantua OH 44255 Office: 10683 Maple St Mantua OH 44255

CHEN, SIMON K., mfg. co. exec.; b. Shanghai, China, Oct. 13, 1925; s. Hoshien and Lin Sie (Chao) Tchen; came to U.S., 1948, naturalized, 1955; B.S.M.E., Nat. Chiao-Tung U., Shanghai, 1947; M.S.M.E., U. Mich., 1949; Ph.D. in Mech. engring., U. Wis., 1952; M.B.A., U. Chgo., 1964; m. Rosemary Ho; children—Margie, Lillian, Vivian, Victor. Div. chief engr. diesel engine div. Internat. Harvester Co., Melrose Park, Ill., 1952-69; v.p., gen mgr. large engine operation, then v.p. engring. and application power systems ops. Colt Industries, Beloit, Wis., 1969-73; pres. Beloit Power Systems, Am. Laminate Products subs. Tang Industries, Beloit, 1973—, also dir. Tang Industries Inc. Mem. Greater Beloit Com. Recipient Alumni Distinguished Service award U. Wis., 1973, Achievement and Service award Chinese Inst. Engrs., 1976, Arch T. Colwell award, 1966. Mem.

Soc. Automotive Engrs. Family Service Assn., ASME, Soc. Naval Architects and Marine Engrs., Sigma Xi, Beta Gamma Sigma. Republican. Club: Janesville (Wis.) Indoor Tennis. Home: 325 Racine Delavan WI 53115 Office: 555 Lawton Ave Beloit WI 53511

CHENEA, PAUL FRANKLIN, automobile mfg. co. exec.; b. Milton, Oreg., May, 17, 1918; s. Paul Francis and Gladys Martha (Welch) C.; B.S., U. Calif., 1940; M.S., U. Mich., 1947, Ph.D., 1949; D.Eng., Purdue U., 1968, Drexel U., 1971; D.Sc., Rose-Hulman Inst. Tech., 1968; D.Engring Sci., Tri-State Coll., 1968; D.H.L., Clarkson Coll. Tech., 1971; m. Katherine Louise Bullock, Jan. 17, 1941; children—Susanne, Paul Franklin. Project engr. contractors Pacific naval air bases, 1940-41; from instr. to asso. prof. engring. mechanics U. Mich., 1946-52, prof., chmn. dept. engring. mechanics, 1952-54, head div. engring. sci., 1954-57, asst. dean engring., 1954-56; asso. dean engring. Purdue U., 1956-58, acting head dept. gen. engring., 1954, acting head Sch. Elec. Engring. 1957-58, head Sch. Mech. Engring., 1959-61, acting head div. math. scis., 1960-61, v.p. acad. affairs, 1961-67, acting dean Sch. Sci., Edn. and Humanities, 1962-63; Edwin Sibley Webster prof. elec. engring. Mass. Inst. Tech., 1958-59; sci. dir. research lab. Gen. Motors Corp., Warren, Mich., 1967-69, v.p. research labs., 1969—. Mem. adv. panel engring. scis. NSF, 1956-59, chmn., 1958-59; mem. pres. com. Nat. Medal Sci., 1966-68; dir. Commn. Engring. Edn., 1960-70, chmn., 1960-63; chmn. steering com. Kanpur Indo-Am. Program, 1960-63; civilian cons. Army Sci. Adv. Panel, 1968-71; mem. energy research and devel. adv. council U.S. Energy Policy Office, 1973-75; mem. tech. adv. bd. U.S. Dept. Commerce, 1974-76; bd. govs. Com. for Institutional Cooperation and Midwestern Program for Minorities in Engring., 1975—; mem. roster of consultants to adminstr. ERDA, 1976—. Mem. vis. com. dept. mech. engring. Mass. Inst. Tech., 1966-77, div. engring. and applied sci. Calif. Inst. Tech., 1970—, Sch. Engring., Oakland U., 1968—, dept. mech. engring. U. Mich., 1968—, Sch. Engring., Purdue U., 1973-75; mem. engring. bd. visitors Duke, 1973—. Bd. dirs. Indsl. Research Inst., 1972—; trustee Thomas Alva Edison Found., 1971, Rensselaer Poly. Inst., 1972—, Hutzel Hosp., Detroit, 1975—. Served from 2d lt. to lt. col. Ordnance Dept., AUS, 1941-46. Recipient Outstanding Achievement award U. Mich., 1968. Fellow Am. Acad. Arts and Scis., ASME; mem. Soc. Automotive Engrs., Engring. Soc. Detroit (dir. 1970-76), Am. Inst. Physics, Am. Soc. Engring. Edn., Nat. Acad. Engring. Clubs: Cosmos (Washington); Detroit Athletic. Author: Mechanics of Vibration, 1952. Contbr. tech. papers, articles to profl. jours. Address: Research Labs Gen Motors Corp Warren MI 48090

CHENERY, FREDERICK LINCOLN, III, librarian; b. Monmouth, Maine, Apr. 8, 1927; s. Frederick Lincoln and Lelia Rebecca (Davis) C.; A.B. cum laude, Bates Coll., 1949; M.Div., Yale U., 1953; postgrad. Columbia U. Sch. Library Service, summer, 1953; M.L.S., U. Tex., 1960; postgrad. (Lilly Found. scholar), Oxford U., 1965-66; m. Lucie Emma Marie Böttcher, June 26, 1959; children—Mark-Andrew, Marie-Louise, Charlotte-Ann. Serials cataloger Yale Div. Sch. Library, 1952-53; librarian Episcopal Theol. Sem. of S.W., Austin, Tex., 1953-67, asso. prof., 1962-67; librarian Ch. Hist. Soc., Austin, 1957-59; librarian, asso. prof. bibliography U. Dubuque (Iowa) Theol. Sem., 1967-77; librarian Aquinas Dubuque Theol. Libraries, 1972-77. Mem. Am. Theol. Library Assn. (exec. sec. 1958-65). Home: 1100 S Grandview St Dubuque IA 52001

CHENEY, THOMAS WARD, ins. co. exec.; b. Union, Nebr., Dec. 17, 1914; s. Gilbert Ward and Vernie (Barnum) C.; B.S., U. Nebr., 1936; student Life Ins. Mktg. Inst., U. Kans., 1950; m. E. Margaret Phillippe, Oct. 15, 1938; children—Patricia Kay (Mrs. Lawrence E. Keim), Thomas Charles. With Modern Woodmen of Am., 1935—, dir., asst. to pres., Rock Island, Ill., 1954-60, pres., 1960—, also dir.; dir. 1st Nat. Bank Rock Island. Active various community drives; v.p. Blackhawk Indsl. Devel. Assn., Rock Island County, Ill., 1959. Mem. lay adv. bd. St. Anthony's Hosp., Rock Island, 1965-72; bd. govs. Rock Island Found., 1967-76; bd. govs. Rock Island Franciscan Hosp., 1969—, chmn. bd., 1974-75; bd. dirs. Augustana Coll., 1971—; mem. adv. com. Coll. Commerce and Bus., U. Ill., 1969—, YMCA, Rock Island, 1965-69. Served to lt. col. USAAF, 1941-46. Decorated Legion of Merit; recipient Distinguished Service award U.S. Jr. C. of C., 1940. Mem. Fraternal Ins. Counsellors Assn., Life Underwriters Assn., Gen. Agts. and Mgrs. Conf., Nat. Fraternal Congress of Am. (mem. exec. com. 1961-62, pres. 1967-68), Ill. Fraternal Congress, Ill. (dir.), Rock Island (pres. 1965) chambers commerce, Jr. C. of C. (pres. 1940), Delta Upsilon. Republican. Presbyn. (elder, trustee, deacon). Club: Rock Island Arsenal Golf (bd. govs. 1976—). Home: 2205 22 1/2 Ave Rock Island IL 61201 Office: Modern Woodmen of Am Rock Island IL 61201

CHENG, AYLMER PAO-SHENG, civil engr.; b. Hankou, China, Sept. 4, 1936; s. Shao Liang and Hui Lien (Liang) C.; came to U.S., 1961, naturalized, 1971; B.S., Nat. Taiwan U., 1959; M.S., U. Mo.-Rolla, 1962; Ph.D., Tex. A. and M. U., 1967; m. Mary Jo Wen-ying Ting, Sept. 2, 1967. Sr. structural engr. Brown & Root, Inc., Houston, 1963-65, chief structural dynamist, 1965-66; mech. engr. Shell Devel. Co., Houston, 1966-70; adj. lectr. U. Houston, 1968-69; sr. petroleum engr. Amoco Internat. Oil Co., Chgo., 1970-73, staff engr. sr. grade, 1973-75, engring. group leader, 1975—. Mem. spl. com. on single point moorings Am. Bur. Shipping, 1974—. Mem. ASCE (Spl. Achievement award 1973), Soc. Petroleum Engrs., Sigma Xi, Kappa Mu Epsilon. Contbr. articles to profl. jours.; editorial adv. bd. Ocean Engring. mag., 1976—. Home: 1671 Minnesota Elk Grove IL 60007 Office: 200 E Randolph Dr Chicago IL 60601

CHENG, FRANK HSIEH-FU, immunochemist, educator; b. Shanghai, China, Nov. 16, 1923; s. T.S. and Z.T. (Chien) C.; came to U.S., 1949, naturalized, 1970; B.S. cum laude, St. John's U., China, 1946; M.S., U. Tenn., 1950; Ph.D., Ind. U., 1957; m. Margareth King-Jan Liu, Aug. 9, 1958; children—Pearl, Tina, Teresa. Chemist, asso. supt. T.W. Wu & Co. Pharm. Lab., Shanghai, 1946-49; cancer research fellow U. Tenn., Knoxville, 1950-53; postdoctorate U. Wis., McArdle Meml. Lab. for Cancer Research, 1956-58; biochemist Toledo Hosp. Inst. Med. Research, 1958-63; asst. prof. U. Iowa, Iowa City, 1964-69, asso. prof., 1969—. Mem. Coralville (Iowa) Park and Recreation Commn., 1972-74. Chmn. bd. dirs. Wesley Found., Iowa City, 1970-71. Recipient Silver Shield award in chemistry St. Johns U., 1946. China Inst. in Am. scholar, 1955-56. Mem. AAAS, Am. Chem. Soc., Chinese Biochem. Soc., N.Y., Ohio acads. scis., Am. Acad. Allergy, Soc. Nuclear Medicine, Radiation Research Soc., Sigma Xi, Phi Lambda Upsilon, Phi Kappa Phi. Methodist. Optimist (Man of Year award Coralville 1969-71, dir. 1970-71, 74-75) (Coralville). Contbr. articles to profl. jours. Home: 1002 16th Ave Coralville IA 52241 Office: Nuclear Medicine Dept U Iowa Hosps Iowa City IA 52242

CHENG, FRANKLIN YIH, educator; b. Shanghai, China, July 1, 1936; s. Jai Ho and Pai-lam (Ho) C.; B.S., Taiwan Nat. Cheng-Kung U., 1960; M.S., U. Ill., 1962; Ph.D., U. Wis., 1966, hon. fellow, 1968; m. Pi-Yu Chang, Sept. 15, 1962; children—George Chen-Hsin, Deborah Wen-Hsin. Came to U.S., 1960, naturalized, 1973. Structural engr. Sargent & Lundy, C.F. Murphy, Chgo., 1962-63; research asst. U. Wis., 1963-66; asst. prof. civil engring. U. Mo. at Rolla, 1966-69, asso. prof., 1969-74, prof., 1974—. Cons. engr. Buchmueller, Whitworth & Foust, Inc., Mo., Arnold & O'Sheridan Engrs., Wis. Dir. insts. computer methods of optimum structural design and matrix computer methods in structural mechanics sponsored by U. Mo., Rolla; dir. Internat. Symposium of Structural Earthquake Engring. Served with Chinese R.O.T.C., 1956-60. Research grantee NSF and U. Mo., 1967—. Mem. Am. Soc. C.E., Am. Soc. Engring. Edn., Sigma Xi, Chi Epsilon. Author: Dynamic Structural Analysis, 1973. Contbr. articles profl. jours. Home: 1307 Highland Dr Rolla MO 65401

CHENG, KUANG LU, educator; b. Yangchow, China, Sept. 14, 1919; s. Fong Wu and Yi Ming (Chiang) C.; came to U.S., 1947, naturalized, 1955; Ph.D., U. Ill., 1951; children—Meiling, Chiling, Hans Christian. Microchemist, Comml. Solvents Corp., Terre Haute, Ind., 1952-53; instr. U. Conn., Storrs, 1953-55; engr., Westinghouse Electric Corp., Pitts. 1955-57; asso. dir. research, metals div. Kelsey Hayes Co., New Hartford, N.Y., 1957-59; mem. tech. staff RCA Labs., Princton, 1959-66; prof. chemistry U. Mo., Kansas City, 1966—. Recipient Achievement award RCA, 1963. Fellow AAAS, Chem. Soc. London; mem. Am. Chem. Soc., Electrochem. Soc., Soc. Spectroscopy, Am. Inst. Physics. Home: 2209 W 69th St Shawnee Mission KS 66208 Office: Dept Chemistry Univ Mo Kansas City MO 64110

CHENG, LESLEI YU-LIN, neurologist, psychiatrist; b. Soochow, China, May 27, 1905; s. James H. and Mary Chung (Chou) C.; came to U.S., 1950, naturalized, 1956; student Soochow U., 1920-22; M.D., Peking Union Med. Coll., 1928; postgrad. State U. N.Y., 1928; m. Mary M. Chan, June 2, 1945; children—Alfred K., Barbara Jane Cheng Neunes, Clara Joan Cheng Mok, Joyce Cheng Schlessinger, Elaine Cheng Lin, Marian Leslie. Intern, Peking Union Med. Coll. Hosp., 1927-28, resident, 1928-30; resident in neurology and psychiatry Deutsche Forschungsanstalt für Psychiatrie, Munich, Germany, 1932, Boston Psychopathic Hosp., 1932-33; practice medicine specializing in neurology and psychiatry, 1933—; chmn. dept. neuro-psychiatry United Univs., Chengtu, Szechuan, China, 1938-46, Central Hosp., Canton, China, 1946-47; dir. Nat. Neuro-psychiatry Inst., Nanking, China, 1947-49; supt. Taiwan Provincial Mental Hosp., 1949-50; staff psychiatrist, chief neurology service Topeka State Hosp., 1950-58; clin. dir. No. State Hosp., Sedro Wooley, Wash., 1958-59; clin. dir. Kans. Neurol. Inst., Topeka, 1960-65; founder, supt. med. dir. Broadview Center, Cleve., 1966-72; chmn. dept. psychiatry Mich. State U., 1973-75; med. dir. Gen. County Community Mental Health Services, Flint, Mich., 1975-76; staff psychiatrist family practice residency tng. St. Joseph Hosp., Flint., 1977—; prof. neuropsychiatry Nat. Central U., Nanking and Chengtu, China, 1938-46; prof. neuro-psychiatry Lingnan U. Med. Sch., 1946-47, Nat. Taiwan U., 1949-50; clin. asst. prof. psychiatry U. Wash., 1959; clin. prof. Mich. State U., 1971-73, prof., 1973-75. Diplomate Am. Bd. Psychiatry and Neurology. Fellow Am. Psychiat. Assn., Am. Acad. Neurology; mem AMA, Chinese Med. Assn., Chinese Mental Hygiene Assn., Am. Child Neurology Soc. Methodist. Clubs: Masons, Rotary. Author: Textbook of Neurology (Chinese), 1947; Textbook of Psychiatry (Chinese) 1949. Home: 1926 Woodslea Dr Apt 7 Flint MI 48507 Office: Family Practice St Joseph Hosp 302 Kensington Ave Flint MI 48502

CHENG, PAUL HUNG-CHIAO, civil engr.; b. China, Dec. 1, 1930; s. Yen-Teh and Shu-Yin (Tsou) C.; came to U.S., 1958, naturalized, 1973; B.S. in Civil Engring., Nat. Taiwan U., 1951; M.S. in C.E., U. Va., 1961; m. Lucial Jen Chen, Aug. 1, 1964; children—Maria, Elizabeth, Deborah, Samuel. Structural engr. Swift & Co., Chgo., 1963-67; sr. structural designer P & W Engring., Inc., Chgo., 1967; sr. structural engr. A. Epstein & Son, Inc., Chgo., 1967-68; staff engr. Interlake, Inc., Chgo., 1968-71, supervising engr., 1971-73, chief structural engr., 1973—; cons. Kawatetsu/Interlake, Ltd. (Tokyo). Registered structural engr., Ill.; registered profl. civil engr., Calif. Mem. ASCE, Am. Concrete Inst., Am. Mgmt. Assn. Home: 1620 Lawrence Crescent Flossmoor IL 60422 Office: Interlake Inc 135th and Perry Ave Chicago IL 60627

CHENG, WILLIAM JEN-PU, chem. co. exec.; b. Changsha, China, Sept. 26, 1915; s. Shao-Chien and Chao (Ling) C.; B.S., Tsing Hua U., 1939; M.S., Washington U., St. Louis, 1951, Heermans fellow, 1952; m. Chuan-Huan Wu, Sept. 25, 1954; children—Elizabeth, James, Nancy, Helen. Came to U.S., 1948, naturalized, 1973. Plant supt. China Vegetable Oil Corp., 1941-44; chem. engr. Chinese Army, 23d Arsenal, 1944-46; with Petrolite Corp., St. Louis, 1952—, head pilot plant, 1960-63, engring. research mgr., 1963-67, dir. engring. Tretolite div., 1967—. Mem. Am. Inst. Chem. Engrs., Am. Chem. Soc., N.Y. Acad. Sci. Patentee in field. Home: 705 Louwen Dr St Louis MO 63124 Office: 369 Marshall Ave St Louis MO 63119

CHENOWETH, ROBERT DUANE, machinery co. exec.; b. Bedford, Ind., Oct. 10, 1923; s. Henry Carl and Elizabeth Jane (Barrett) C.; engring. student Internat. Corr. Schs., 1946-48; grad. Approved Supply Pastor's Sch., Garrett Theol. Sch., 1959; B.A., Miami U., 1962, postgrad., 1962-64; m. Shirley Ellen Woods, Sept. 17, 1949; children—Steven Carl, Mark Duane, Paula Jane. Cons. engr. J.E. Novotny Co., Dayton, Ohio, 1956-60; ordained elder United Methodist Ch., 1960, ordained to ministry, 1958; pastor Brookville and Miamitown (Ohio) Meth. Chs., 1958-67; chief tool engr. OPW div. Dover Corp., Cin., 1963-64; chief mfg. engr., mgr. mfg. Campbell-Hausfeld Co., Harrison, Ohio, 1964-68; plant mgr. Sheffer Corp., Blue Ash, Ohio, 1968—. Cons. prodn. engring. Helipebs, Ltd., County of Gloucester (Eng.), 1972. Sec., Brookville Planning Com., 1960-63; mem. adv. com. Great Oaks Joint Vocat. Sch., Warren County (Ohio) Joint Vocat. Sch. Sec. bd. trustees Thomas Meml. Med. Center, Brookville. Recipient Service award City of Brookville, 1963. Mem. Soc. Mfg. Engrs. (2d vice chmn.). Optimist. Home: 1759 Maplewood Dr Lebanon OH 45036 Office: 6990 Cornell Rd Blue Ash OH 45242

CHEPAK, ROBERT MICHAEL, computer mfr.; b. N.Y.C., June 11, 1942; s. Michael and Hedwig Julia (Zazulak) C.; B.S., C.W. Post Coll., 1964; m. Barbara Kae McNees, Apr. 16, 1966; children—Robert Michael, Michelle Nicole. Account mgr. Burroughs Corp., Boston, 1968-70, dist. product mgr. EDP, Boston, 1970-72, product planning mgr. large systems, Detroit, 1972-74, Detroit fin. br. mgr., 1974-77, dir. industry systems planning fin., Detroit, 1977—, also v.p. advisory council, 1975, 76. Active Troy (Mich.) Youth Sports Program, 1976—. Served to capt. USAF, 1964-68. Decorated AF Commendation Medal; recipient Legion of Honor, Burroughs Corp., 1970, 75. Republican. Roman Catholic. Home: 5121 Shrewsbury Dr Troy MI 48098 Office: Burroughs Pl Detroit MI 48232

CHERENZIA, BRADLEY JAMES, radiologist; b. Niagara Falls, N.Y., Aug. 22, 1931; s. Peter and Myrna (Bradley) C.; B.S., U. Buffalo, 1953; M.D., Upstate Med. Center, State U. N.Y., 1957; m. Mary Jeanne Lombard, June 16, 1956; children—Kevin Paul, Lori Myrn, David Bradley, Robert James. Rotating intern State U. N.Y. Upstate Med. Center, Syracuse, affiliated hosps., 1957-58; resident in radiology Detroit Receiving Hosp., 1960-63; mem. dept. radiology Henry Ford Hosp., Detroit, 1963-65; mem. Drs. Otto, Kurtzman & Assos., P.C., Warren, Mich., 1965—; mem. staff Detroit Macomb Hosp., 1965—; clin. instr. radiology Wayne State U., Detroit, 1965—. Served as capt., M.C., U.S. Army, 1958-60. Diplomate Am. Bd. Radiology, Am. Bd. Nuclear Medicine. Mem. AMA, Mich., Wayne County med. socs., Am. Coll. Radiology, Radiol. Soc. N. Am. Roman Catholic. Home: 7437 Wellbourne Ct Birmingham MI 48010 Office: 11800 Twelve Mile Rd Warren MI 48093

CHERNEY, ARTHUR BERNARD, dentist; b. Milw., Dec. 8, 1911; s. Anthony Benjamin and Frances (Cechal) C.; D.D.S., Marquette U., 1936; m. Doris H. Gronert, Apr. 30, 1938; children—Claudia (Mrs. Frank DeGuire), Mary (Mrs. John McDivitt), Ann (Mrs. Thomas S. Ryder), Michael G. Pvt. practice dentistry, Milw., 1936—. Instr. oral histology and embryology Marquette U., 1937-38, part time lecturer and lab. instr., 1947-53, asst. prof., 1953-58, asso. prof., 1958-65, head oral histology dept., 1956-65, dir. dept. histology, 1958-65, prof. emeritus, 1965—; chief oral medicine St. Michael Hosp., Milw., 1939—, chief dental staff, 1951-62. Adv. bd. St. Charles Home for Boys. Served to lt. USNR, 1943-46. Fellow Am. Coll. Dentists, Royal Soc. Health (Eng.); mem. A.A.A.S., Greater Milw. Dental Assn. (v.p. 1955), Am. Dental Assn., Am. Assn. Hosp. Dentists, Am. Med. Writers, Am. Acad. Oral Medicine, Am. Legion, Omicron Kappa Upsilon. K.C. (4 deg.). Home: 2804 N 98th St Milwaukee WI 53222 Office: 6201 W Center St Milwaukee WI 53210

CHERNIACK, SAUL MARK, Canadian provincial ofcl.; b. Winnipeg, Man., Can., Jan. 10, 1917; s. Joseph Arthur and Fannie (Golden) C.; LL.B., U. Man., 1939; m. Sybil Claire Zeal, July 10, 1938; children—Howard David, Lawrence Allan. Called to Man. bar, 1939, created Queen's counsel, 1963; mem. firm Cherniack, Cherniack, Weinberg & Co., Winnipeg, 1939-69; mem. Man. Legislative Assembly, 1963—; Man. provincial minister of finance, minister of urban affairs, dep. premier, until 1975. Sch. trustee, Winnipeg, 1950-54; alderman, Winnipeg, 1959-60; mem. 1st Council of Met. Corp. of Greater Winnipeg, 1961-62. Past pres. Jewish Welfare Fund, past nat. v.p. Canadian Jewish Congress. Bd. dirs. Community Chest, Welfare Planning Council, Winnipeg Pub. Library. Served with Canadian Army, 1943-46. Recipient Centennial medal, 1967. Mem. Winnipeg Art Gallery, Man. Hist. Soc., Man. Alumni Assn. U. Man. Mem. New Democratic party. Home: 333 St John's Ave Winnipeg MB R2W 1H2 Canada Office: Legislative Bldg Winnipeg 1 MB Canada

CHERNICK, VICTOR, educator, pediatrician; b. Winnipeg, Man., Can., Dec. 31, 1935; s. Jack and Mina (Tapper) C.; M.D., U. Man., 1959; m. Norma Fordman, May 19, 1957; children—Marla, Sharon, Richard, Lisa. Intern, Winnipeg Gen. Hosp., 1959-60; postdoctoral tng. in pediatrics John Hopkins U., 1960-64, instr. dept. pediatrics, 1964-65, asst. prof., 1965-66; asst. prof. depts. pediatrics and physiology U. Man. Med. Sch., 1966-67, asso. prof., 1967-71, prof., chmn. dept. pediatrics, 1971—; vis. prof. dept. pediatrics Harvard U. and Children's Hosp. Med. Center, Boston, 1976-77; dir. respiratory service Winnipeg Children's Hosp., 1966-71, physician-in-chief, 1971—. Mem. cardiorespiratory grant rev. com. Med. Research Council Can., 1974—; mem. med. adv. bd. Canadian Found. for Sudden Infant Death, 1973-75. Trustee Queen Elizabeth Research Fund, 1973—. Recipient Queen Elizabeth II scientist award for research, 1967-73. Fellow Am. Acad. Pediatrics; mem. Royal Coll. Physicians and Surgeons Can. (council 1974—), Soc. Pediatric Research, Am. Physiol. Soc., Canadian Pediatric Soc. (medal for research 1970), Canadian Soc. for Clin. Investigation, Am. Thoracic Soc. Mem. editorial bd. Pediatrics, 1971—, Jour. Applied Physiology, 1973-76. Contbr. articles in field to profl. jours. Home: 14 Montcalm Crescent Winnipeg MB R2V 2N4 Canada Office: Childrens Centre 685 Bannaty NE Ave Winnipeg MB R3E 0W1 Canada

CHERNISH, STANLEY MICHAEL, physician; b. N.Y.C., Jan. 27, 1924; s. Michael B. and Veronica (Hodon) C.; B.A., U. N.C., 1945; M.D., Georgetown U., 1949; m. Lelia M. Higgins, June 19, 1949; 1 son, Dwight. Intern Washington Gen. Hosp., 1949-51; resident Marion County Gen. Hosp., Indpls., 1953-55; clin. research div. Eli Lilly & Co., Indpls., 1954—, staff physician, 1955-63, sr. physician, 1963-74, clin. pharmacologist, 1974—; clin. research in internal medicine, specializing in gastroenterology; vis. staff Marion County Gen. Hosp., 1965—, also mem. dietary com.; mem. staff Lilly Labs. Clin. Research; clin. asso. prof. medicine Ind. U. Sch. Medicine, 1976—. Served with USNR, 1943-45, 50-53; comdr. Res.; commandant's rep. Ind. U. Sch. Medicine, 1965—. Diplomate Nat. Bd. Med. Examiners, Am. Bd. Internal Medicine. Fellow A.C.P., Am. Coll. Gastroenterology, Am. Coll. Clin. Pharmacology and Therapeutics; mem. AMA (Physicians Recognition award in continuing med. edn. 1976), Ind. (mem. com. conv. arrangements, chmn. future planning com.), Marion County (mem. govt. liaison com.) med. socs., Am. Pancreatic Study Group, Assn. Am. Physicians and Surgeons, Am. Fedn. for Clin. Research, Am. Gastroent. Assn., Am. Soc. for Gastrointestinal Endoscopy. Contbr. articles to profl. jours. Home: 4403 Radnor Rd Indianapolis IN 46226 Office: 307 E McCarty St Indianapolis IN 46206

CHERRY, JOSEPH, research scientist; b. Chgo., Dec. 19, 1947; s. Joseph Vaughn and Mafalda (DiSomma) C.; B.S. in Math. and Chemistry, Roosevelt U., Chgo., 1975. Research technician Ill. Inst. Tech. Research Inst., Chgo., 1968-69; med. technician Michael Reese Hosp., Chgo., 1972-74; research scientist Continental Can Co., Chgo., 1970—. Mem. Am. Chem. Soc. Author: Marvin Gaye, 1973; poet: Black King, 1972. Home: 10644 S Wabash Ave Chicago IL 60628

CHERTACK, MELVIN M., internist; b. Chgo., June 19, 1923; s. Nathan and Anna (Wadoplan) C.; B.S., U. Ill., 1944, M.D., 1946, M.S., 1948; m. Orabelle Lorraine Melberg, May 26, 1948; children—Pamela, Craig, Rhonda. Intern, U. Ill. Hosp., Chgo., 1946-47, fellow and resident in internal medicine, 1947-50; practice medicine specializing in internal medicine, Skokie, Ill., 1950—; mem. attending staff Luth. Gen. Hosp., Park Ridge, Ill.; mem. courtesy staff Skokie Valley Hosp.; adj. staff Glenbrook Hosp., Glenview, Ill.; clin. asso. prof. U. Ill. Abraham Lincoln Coll. Medicine; advisor Harper Jr. Coll.; bd. health Skokie; advisor Diabetes Screening Program Lions Club. Mem. caucus com., Northfield, Ill. Served with U.S. Army, 1943-45. Recipient Research award Aaron Fox Found. for Diabetes Screening Program, 1976. Diplomate Am. Bd. Internal Medicine. Fellow A.C.P.; mem. Am. Diabetes Assn. (dir. Chgo. chpt., v.p. Chgo. affiliate, mem. coordinating com. juvenile diabetes, com. drugs and therapeutics), Chgo. Diabetes Assn. (chmn. detection and edn. program), Chgo., Ill. med. socs., AMA, Chgo. Soc. Internal Medicine, Chgo., Am. heart assns. Club: Anvil (Dundee). Contbr. articles to profl. jours. Home: 440 Whittier Ln Northfield IL 60093 Office: 64 Old Orchard Skokie IL 60076

CHESHIER, STEPHEN ROBERT, elec. engr., educator; b. Logan, O., Feb. 21, 1940; s. Joseph Mason (stepfather) and Pauline Fraser (Magle) C.; B.S. cum laude, Memphis State U., 1970; M.S.E., in Elec. Engring., Purdue U., West Lafayette, Ind., 1972; Ph.D. in Tech. Edn., U. Ill., 1975; m. Katherine Joyce Hadley, June 5, 1960; children—David Mark, John Michael. Enlisted USN, 1958, advanced through grades to chief petty officer, 1970; technician Naval Air Sta., Quonset Point, R.I., U.S.S. Wasp, 1958-61; tchr. Avionics Sch., Memphis, 1961-66; maintenance chief VP-56, Norfolk, Va., 1966-68; engr. Naval Avionics facility, Patuxent River, Md., 1968-70, chief air crew, 1968-70, dir. quality assurance, 1968-70; specialist in computer, communications and navigation Naval Air Sta., Patuxent River, 1968-70; ret., 1970; prof. head dept. elec. engring. tech. Purdue U., 1971—; speaker in field. Tchr., cons. Ind. Vocat./Tech. Coll.,

Lafayette, 1972—; editorial cons. Prentice-Hall Inc., Houghton-Mifflin Co., John Wiley & Son; mem. Lafayette Area Indsl. Adv. Com., 1973—. Recipient Tchr. of Year award Sch. Tech. Purdue U., 1973, 75. Mem. IEEE, Am. Soc. Engring. Edn., Sigma Pi Sigma, Eta Kappa Nu, Kappa Delta Pi, Phi Delta Kappa, Phi Kappa Phi, Chi Gamma Iota. Mem. Ch. of Christ (tchr.). Research, publs. on electronics communications and linear integrated circuits, microprocessors, recruiting minorities into tech. careers, engring. tech. edn. Home: 3036 W St Rd 26 West Lafayette IN 47906

CHESLEY, STANLEY MORRIS, lawyer; b. Cin., Mar. 26, 1936; s. Frank and Rachel (Kinsburg) C.; B.A. in Econs., U. Cin., 1958, LL.B., 1960; m. Suellen Kaufmann, Aug. 15, 1959; children—Richard Alan, Lauren Beth. Admitted to Ohio bar, 1960; mem. firm Waite, Schindel, Bayless & Schneider, Cin., 1960—; adj. prof. Salmon Chase Law Sch., No. Ky. State, 1973—. Mem. Citizens Com. on Youth, Cin., 1963-64; pres. Camp Livingston, Am. Jewish Com., 1966—. Mem. Am., Ohio, Cin. bar assns., Assn. Trial Lawyers (state committeeman 1968-70; 2d vice chmn. torts sect. 1969-70; vice chmn. torts sect. 1972-73, nat. chmn. torts sect. 1974—, program chmn. 1974—). Jewish (bd. dirs. temple 1964-73). Contbr. articles to various publs. Home: 2930 Belkay Ln Cincinnati OH 45241 Office: 1318 Central Trust Tower Cincinnati OH 45202

CHESS, ROBERT HUBERT, psychiatrist; b. Greenville, Miss., May 20, 1930; s. James and Barbara C.; A.B., Tenn. State U., 1953, M.S., 1954; M.D., Meharry Med. Coll., 1959; M.B.A., Xavier U., 1976; m. Gloria Faye Thompson, Dec. 27, 1960; children—Faye Rosalind, Robert Hubert. Intern, Wayne County Gen. Hosp., Eloise, Mich., 1959-60; resident in psychiatry Rollman Psychiat. Inst., Cin., 1965-68; practice family medicine, Meridian, Miss., 1960-62, Laurel, Miss., 1962-65; resident psychiatrist Rollman Psychiat. Inst., Cin., 1965-68, chief male inpatient service, 1968-71, dir. community services unit, 1971—; asst. clin. prof. psychiatry U. Cin., 1972-77, asso. clin. prof., 1977—; individual practice medicine, specializing in psychiatry Cin., 1968—. Bd. dirs. Children's Psychiat. Center, SW Regional Council Alcoholism, Assn. Home Care Agencies. Diplomate Am. Bd. Psychiatry and Neurology. Fellow Am. Psychiat. Assn.; mem. AMA, Nat. Med. Assn., Am. Orthopsychiat. Assn., Am. Assn. Social Psychiatry, Am. Mgmt. Assn., Sigma Pi Phi, Kappa Alpha Psi. Methodist. Clubs: Masons (32 deg.), Shriners. Home: 3280 N Whitetree Circle Cincinnati OH 45236 Office: 3009 Burnet Ave Cincinnati OH 45219

CHESSER, AL H., union ofcl.; b. Pettis County, Mo., Feb. 26, 1914; s. James A. and Mary Pearl (Dirck) C.; grad. high sch.; m. Rose Burns. Brakeman-condr. Santa Fe Ry., Amarillo, Tex., 1941; sec.-treas., legis. rep. Brotherhood R.R. Trainmen, Local 608, 1945-56, chmn. Tex. legis. bd., 1956-62, nat. legis. rep., Washington, 1962-69; nat. legis. rep. United Transp. Union, 1969-71, pres., Cleve., 1971—. Vice pres., mem. exec. council AFL-CIO; chmn. Congress of Ry. Unions, 1972-75. Chmn., Amarillo Labor Polit. Council, 1954-56; mem. Gov.'s Indsl. Commn., 1957-61; mem. Fed. Task Force on R.R. Safety, 1964-69, Pres.'s Consumers Adv. Council, 1964-68, Greater Cleve. Growth Bd. and Transp. Study Group of Domestic Affairs Task Force, 1973; adv. panel U.S. Congress Office Tech. Assessment, 1976; hon. co-chmn. Internat. Guiding Eyes, 1976. Bd. dirs. Democratic Nat. Com., 1973—; mem. transp. adv. com. Fed. Energy Adminstrn., 1975—; co-chmn. R.R. Safety Research Bd., 1975—. Chmn. bd. Civil Service Commn.; bd. dirs. Amarillo Community Chest, Maverick Boys Club. Hon. staff mem. U.S. Army Transp. Sch. Mem. Nat. Def. Execs. Res. Mason (Shriner). Author: Transportation and Energy, 1975; Economic Advantages of Transporting Coal by Rail, 1976. Office: 14600 Detroit Ave Cleveland OH 44107

CHESTER, EDWARD MILTON, educator, physician; b. Queens, N.Y., Jan. 26, 1912; s. Jacob and Anna (Rifkin) C.; B.S., N.Y. U., 1932; M.D., State U. Iowa, 1936; m. Mary Hogan, July 25, 1938; children—Carol Susan, James William. Intern, Cleve. City Hosp., 1936-37, resident in internal medicine, 1938-41; resident in internal medicine, Montefiore Hosp., N.Y.C., 1937-38; practice medicine specializing in internal medicine, Berea, Ohio, 1941-58; asso. prof. medicine Cleve. Met. Gen. Hosp./Case Western Res. U. Med. Sch., 1958-74, prof., 1974—, dir. ambulatory medicine clerkship, 1963—. Recipient Kaiser Permanente award for excellence in teaching, 1975. Fellow A.C.P.; mem. Am. Heart Assn., Am. Diabetes Assn., Am. Fedn. Clin. Research, Cleve. Acad. Medicine, Cleve. Diabetes Assn., Alpha Omega Alpha. Author: The Ocular Fundus in Systemic Diseases: Clinical Patholical Correlation, 1973. Home: PO Box 304 Berea OH 44107 Office: 3395 Scranton Rd Cleveland OH 44109

CHESTERFIELD, JOHN LAWRENCE, aluminum co. exec.; b. Seattle, Oct. 26, 1942; s. John Morris and Erma-Jeanne C.; B.A. in Math., DePauw U., 1964; children—David Christopher, Daniel Lawrence. With Aluminum Finishing Corp., Indpls., 1968—, v.p. ops., 1970-77, pres., 1977—. Trustee St. Luke's United Methodist Ch., 1971. Served from ensign to lt. j.g. USNR, 1964-68; Vietnam. Mem. Am. Electroplaters Soc., Naval Res. Assn. Republican. Methodist. Club: Econ. (Indpls.). Office: 1012 E 21st St Indianapolis IN 46202

CHESTNUT, JOSEPH LOUIS, publishing co. exec.; b. Hamtramck, Mich., July 9, 1927; s. Joseph Alexander and Natalie (Kaminski) C.; B.S. in Mech. Engring., U. Mich., 1951; m. Esther Teresa Delgado, Sept. 9, 1950; children—David, Alex, Andrew. Engr., Delco Products div. Gen. Motors Corp., Dayton, Ohio, 1951-52; office mgr. Dayton Tech Art Co., Detroit, 1952-58, v.p., Dayton, 1958-71, pres., 1971—. Served with USAAF, 1945-47. Home: 488 E Dale Dr Dayton OH 45415 Office: 1329 Stanley Ave Dayton OH 45404

CHESTON, SHARON HUTSON, counselor; b. Balt., Mar. 19, 1947; d. Hugh Maynard and Margaret Elizabeth (Beck) Hutson; B.A. in Psychology, Roanoke Coll., 1969; M.Ed., N.C. State U., 1975; m. James Cheston, Jan. 23, 1969; children—Shannon Elizabeth, Kelly Christine. Counselor, Christ the King Luth. Ch., Cary, N.C., 1975-76; psychol. counselor, cons. Christian edn. Bethany Luth. Ch., Batavia, Ill., 1976—; Psychologist Luth. Welfare Services of Ill. Mem. Am. Personnel and Guidance Assn. Lutheran. Research on marital communications. Home: 1041 Pueblo Dr Batavia IL 60510 Office: 8 S Lincoln St Batavia IL 60510

CHEVERIE, CARROLL L., SR., advt. exec.; b. Eastport, Me., Sept. 19, 1909; s. Carroll and Iva M. (Hunt) C.; student Northeastern U. Sch. Law, 1931; grad. Bentley Coll., 1933; m. Virginia Howard, July 24, 1937; children—Jean, Carroll L., William H., Gina, Richard. With Chase Bank, N.Y., 1929-31; with Washington and Suburban Utilities Cos., 1931-41; treas. Consol. Investment Trust, Boston, 1941-51; treas., dir. H.B. Humphrey, Alley & Richards, Boston and N.Y., 1951-59; treas., dir., mem. exec. com. Clinton E. Frank, Inc., Chgo., 1959-72, exec. v.p., dir. finance, mem. exec. com., 1969—, also dir.; chmn. bd., dir. Cheverie & Levinson, Inc., Boston, C. & W. Imports, Inc. Ltd., Dubuque, Ia.; dir. Hartford Plaza Bank, Chgo., L & K Corp., Inc., Boise, Ida. Bd. dirs. Am. Acad. Art, Chgo. Home: Gin Cove Rd Perry ME 04667 Office: 120 S Riverside Plaza Chicago IL 60606

CHHABRA, ROSHAN LAL, elec. engr.; b. Gujaranwala, India, Mar. 1, 1941; s. Sardari Lal and Maya (Dora) C.; came to U.S., 1966, naturalized, 1976; B.S., Uttar Pradesh Agrl. U., 1966; M.S., Iowa State U., 1969, Ph.D., 1973. m. Suman Satiya, Nov. 25, 1969; children—Monica K., Paul N. Project engr. Winpower Corp., Newton, Iowa, 1972-73, chief elec. engr., 1973-75, dir. research and devel., 1975—. Mem. planning com. Des Moines Area Community Coll., 1975-77; tchr. for merit badges Boy Scouts Am. Presdl. scholar, 1962-66. Mem. IEEE, Am. Soc. Agrl. Engrs., Engine Generator Systems Mfrs. Assn.; Sigma Xi, Phi Kappa Phi, Tau Beta Pi, Alpha Epsilon, Gamma Sigma Delta. Contbr. articles to profl. jours. Home: 510 E 4th St S Newton IA 50208 Office: 1207 1st Ave E Newton IA 50208

CHI, RICHARD SEE-YEE, educator; b. Peking, China, Aug. 3, 1918; s. Mi Kang and Pao (Ten) C.; B.S., Nankai U., China, 1937; M.A., Oxford (Eng.) U., 1962, D.Phil., 1964; Ph.D., Cambridge (Eng.) U., 1964. Came to U.S., 1965. Exec. industry China and Hong Kong, 1938-56; inst. Air Ministry, Eng., 1957-60; lectr. Cambridge U., 1960-62, U. London, summer 1961; univ. lectr. Oxford U., 1962-65; curator City Art Gallery, Bristol, Eng., 1965; asso. prof. Ind. U., Bloomington, 1965-71, prof., 1971—, acting chmn., summer 1972; asso. adviser Centro Superiore di Logica e Scienze Comparate, Italy, 1972—; vis. asso. prof. U. Mich., summer 1968; fellow-participant Linguistic Inst., U. Calif., Los Angeles, 1966; contbg. specialist Summer Faculty Seminar on Buddhism, Carleton Coll., Minn., 1968; mem. Workshop on Problems on Meaning and Truth, Oakland U., 1968; adviser for film Buddhism in China, New York, 1972; cons. Inst. Advanced Studies World Religions, 1972—; session chmn. East-West Philosophers' Conf., 1973; panelist Internat. Conf. on Indian Philosophy, U. Toronto, 1974, 5th Internat. Symposium Multiple-valued Logic, Ind. U., 1974, Internat. Seminar on History of Buddhism, U. Wis., 1976, 30th Internat. Congress Human Scis. in Asia, Mexico City, 1976; mem. sub-com. Buddhist philos. materials Nat. Endowment for Humanities, 1974; rep. of State of Ind., Nat. Reconstrn. Conf., China, 1975. Fellow China Acad., 1969. Mem. Cambridge U. Buddhist Soc. (v.p. 1961-62), Royal Asiatic Soc., Aristotelian Soc., Mind Assn., Assn. Brit. Orientalists, Assn. for Symbolic Logic, Linguistic Soc. Am., Soc. for Asian and Comparative Philosophy (bd. mem.-at-large 1975—), Oriental Art Soc. (founding mem.), Kings Coll. Assn. (Eng.), Asian Studies Inst. (mem. adv. com. 1975—), Indpls. Mus. Art. Club: Lake Havasu Golf and Country. Author: A General Theory of Operators, 1967; Buddhist Formal Logic, 1968; A Comparative Study of Propositions in the Western and Indian Logic, 1972; Topics on Being and Logical Reasoning, 1974; A Semantic Study of Propositions, East and West, 1976; The Art of Chinese Calligraphy, 1977. Home: 3650 E Will Sowders Rd Bloomington IN 47401

CHIANG, HUAI CHANG, educator, entomologist; b. Sunkiang, China, Feb. 15, 1915; s. Wentse Chiang and Hsiu Hsiu Chiang; came to U.S. 1945, naturalized 1953; B.S., Tsing Hua U., Peking, China, 1938; M.S., U. Minn. 1946, Ph.D. 1948; m. Zoh Ing Shen, Sept. 8, 1946; children—Jeanne, Katherine, Robert. Asst. instr. entomology Tsing Hua U., Peking, 1938-40, instr. 1940-44; asst. prof. U. Minn., St. Paul, 1954-57, asso. prof. 1957-60, prof. 1960—; cons. FAO, U.S. Dept. Agr.; mem. sci. del. Nat. Acad. Sci.; sci. panel Council Environ. Quality. Recipient Guggenheim fellowship, 1955; named Tchr. of Yr., Student Assn., U. Minn. 1961. Mem. Am., Canadian, Royal (London) entomol. socs., Japanese Soc. Population Research, Internat. Assn. Ecologists, Internat. Organization Biol. Control, AAAS, Minn. Acad. Sci., Sigma Xi, Gamma Sigma Delta. Editor 3 books, and Jour. of Entomology Research, India; contbr. over 150 research papers in field to profl. jours. Home: 1896 Carl St St Paul MN 55113 Office: U Minn St Paul MN 55108

CHIARO, A. WILLIAM, mgmt. cons.; b. Chgo., July 12, 1928; s. Anthony Joseph and Marie Anne (Bonario) C.; B.S., U. Ill., 1954; m. Lyne LaVerne Franke, Aug. 27, 1961; children—David Huntington, Caroline Elizabeth. Accountant, IBM, Chgo., 1954-55; with Black & Skaggs Assos., Glen Ellyn, Ill., 1955—, v.p., 1967—; dir. P.M. Illinois, Inc. Served with U.S. Army, 1946-47, USAF, 1950-52. Mem. Soc. Advancement Mgmt., Soc. Profl. Bus. Cons. Presbyn. Club: Lake Shore of Chicago. Contbr. articles to med. and profl. jours. Home: 722 Kent Rd Kenilworth IL 60043 Office: 799 Roosevelt Rd W Glen Ellyn IL 60137

CHIASSON, MARSHALL, housing industry cons.; b. Chgo., Feb. 27, 1918; s. Placid Nelson and Marie Anna (Chiasson) C.; student U. Ill., 1936-40, St. Louis Sch. Aeros.; Ceramic Engr., Miliken U., 1945; m. Jane Cosgrove, June 15, 1941; 1 son, Marshall II. Owner Readimix Concrete Co., land developer, gen. contractor, 1948-65; regional sales mgr. A.B.C. Co., Miami, Fla., 1965-72; nat. account mgr. Hydro-Air Engring. Co., St. Louis, 1972; now exec. v.p. Universal Enterprises, Inc., Springfield, Ill. prodn. cons. Alpine Engineered Products, Inc., Pompano Beach, Fla., 1976—. Served with USNR, 1942-44. Mem. Am. Soc. Agrl. Engrs. Elk. Home: 643 W Washington St Pittsfield IL 62363 Office: 2440 Production Dr St Charles IL 60174

CHICOINEAU, JACQUES CHARLES, educator, puppeteer; b. Mantes-la-Jolie, France, Sept. 17, 1919; s. Henri A. and Jeanne (Obitz) C.; certificate U. Paris, 1961; B.S., Washington U., St. Louis, 1964, M.A., 1968; m. Odette M. Ravel, Sept. 23, 1950; children—Philippe Francois, Frederic Henri. Technician research lab. Rhone-Poulenc Corp., 1946-59; from instr. to prof. French, Webster Coll., St. Louis, 1960—, now also chmn. modern lang. dept. Served with French Army, 1940-42. Decorated chevalier des Palmes Academiques. Mem. Assn. U. Profs., Societe Professeurs Francais en Amerique, Alliance-Francaise (past pres.), Societe Francaise de St. Louis (pres.), Am. Assn. Tchrs. French (past pres.), Puppet Guild St. Louis (past pres.), Puppeteers of Am., Phi Delta Phi (nat. v.p. 1965—). Home: Ile de France 760 Tuxedo St St Louis MO 63119

CHIEN, ROBERT I., mgmt. cons.; b. Tietsin, China, Nov. 29, 1922; s. Yueh-Chiao and Mary (Hsu) C.; LL.B., Nat. S.W. Asso. U., Kumming, China, 1944; M.B.A., U. Denver, 1947; M.A., U. Minn. 1953, Ph.D., 1953; m. Nancy Liu, June 30, 1948; children—Agnes, Bruce, Grace Lynn. Came to U.S., 1947, naturalized, 1958; Instr. econs. and statistics U. Minn., 1949-51; sr. market research analyst Wyandotte Chems. Corp. (Mich.), 1951-54, mgr. market research, 1954-57; dir. marketing research G.D. Searle & Co., Skokie, Ill., 1957-66, dir. marketing research and devel., 1966-68, dir. econ. and operations research, 1968-69, dir. sweetener projects and corp. econ. research, 1969-72, dir. corporate bus. research and devel. div., 1973-74; pres. Robert I. Chien & Assos., 1974—; asso. prof. mktg. Roosevelt U.; lectr. Wayne State U., 1956-57; cons. to vice-chancellor Chinese U., Hong Kong, 1964. Decorated Outstanding Services commendations Nat. Chinese Air Force. Mem. Am. Marketing Assn. (merit award 1963-64). Inst. Mgmt. Scis., Midwest Pharm. Advt. Club, Western Pharm. Marketing Research Group, Operations Research Soc. Am., others. Contbr. articles to profl. jours. Home: 545 Willow Rd Winnetka IL 60093 Office: PO Box 1045 Skokie IL 60076

CHILCOTE, ROBERT RALPH, physician, educator; b. Cleve., Oct. 8, 1941; s. Ralph E. and Margaret A. (Fisher) C.; A.B., Cornell U., 1963; M.D., U. Rochester, 1969; m. Sherrill Smith, Jan. 23, 1964; children—Kelly, Krista, Ryan. Intern in pediatrics Strong Meml. Hosp., U. Rochester (N.Y.), 1969-70, resident in pediatrics, 1970-71, chief resident in pediatrics, 1971-72; fellow in pediatric hematology James Whitcomb Riley Hosp. for Children, Ind. U. Sch. of Medicine, Indpls., 1972-75; practice medicine specializing in pediatrics, Chgo., 1975—; dir. div. pediatric hematology Michael Reese Hosp. and Med. Center, Chgo., 1975-77; co-dir. div. pediatric hematology-oncology Wyler Children's Hosp., 1977—; asst. prof. dept. pediatrics Pritzker Sch. of Medicine, U. Chgo., 1975—. Diplomate Am. Bd. Pediatrics. Mem. Am. Acad. Pediatrics (mem. sect. on oncology-hematology 1974—), AAAS, Am. Cancer Soc., Am. Soc. Clin. Oncology. Contbr. articles on pediatric hematology to profl. jours. Home: 20600 Hellenic Dr Olympia Fields IL 60461 Office: Wyler Children's Hosp 5801 Ellis Ave Chicago IL 60637

CHILDRESS, JOHN SAVAGE, insurance exec.; b. St. Louis, Nov. 12, 1932; s. Wade Turner and Josephine (Bates) C.; student Canterbury Sch., 1946-50; grad. Lawrenceville Sch., 1951; student U. Va., 1955; m. Lillian Tuttle Sheldon, June 22, 1957; children—John Bates, William Bixby, Frank Sheldon, Lillian Sheldon, L. Wade. With Charles L. Crane Agy., 1955-72, exec. v.p., 1958-72, mem. exec. com., 1968-72; v.p., sr. account exec. Marsh & McLennan, St. Louis, 1972—. Active United Fund. Bd. dirs. St. Louis Children's Hosp. Devel. Bd., pres., 1976; past bd. dirs. Jr. Kindergarten, Vocational Counseling and Rehab. Services, Edgewood Children's Center. Recipient citation St. Louis Police Dept., 1969; recipient citations from various ins. orgns., also Mo. Div. Ins. Mem. Ins. Bd. Greater St. Louis (pres. 1967-68), Mo. Assn. Independent Ins. Agents (pres. 1968-69), Ins. Council Greater St. Louis (chmn. 1969), Midwest Territorial Conf. (1st vice chmn. 1966), Nat. Assn. Casualty and Surety Agts. (dir. 1967-75, exec. com. 1971-75, treas. 1975-76, sec. 1976-77), Nat. Assn. Ins. Agts. (dir. 1969-70), U. Va. Alumni Assn. (pres. 1962), St. Louis Amateur Boxing Assn. (pres. 1971-76). Roman Catholic. Clubs: St. Louis Country, Noonday, Stadium (St. Louis). Home: 2 Deer Creek Hill Ladue MO 63124 Office: 515 Olive St St Louis MO 63101

CHILDRESS, NANCY ULLMAN, owner pub. relations agy.; b. Youngstown, Ohio, Nov. 14, 1926; d. Bert J. and Agnes G. (Riley) Ullman; B.A., Allegheny Coll., 1948; m. Fred J. Childress, Jr., Oct. 11, 1952; children—John F. III, Kevin J. Reporter, The Vindicator, 1948-54; stringer, Steering Wheel, Fairchild Publs., 1956-57; dir. pub. info. Mahoning chpt. ARC, 1956-57; dir. pub. relations Youngstown Symphony Soc., 1967-70; owner Nancy Childress, Pub. Relations, Youngstown, 1971—; mem. faculty, advt. and pub. relations Youngstown State U. Bd. dirs. Youngstown Hearing and Speech Center, 1975—, William Holmes McGuffey Hist. Soc., 1974—, Jr. Achievement, 1977—; trustee Youngstown Bd. Trade, 1975—. Mem. Pub. Relations Soc. Am. (charter pres. Western Res. chpt.). Club: Quota (pres. Youngstown club 1975-77, dir. 1977—). Home: 6631 Harrington Ave Youngstown OH 44512 Office: 418 Home Savs & Loan Bldg Youngstown OH 44503

CHILDS, GAYLE BERNARD, educator; b. Redfield, S.D., Oct. 17, 1907; s. Alva Eugene and Dora Amelia (Larsen) C.; A.B., Nebr. State Tchrs. Coll., 1931; M.A., U. Nebr., 1936, Ph.D., 1949; M.Ed., Harvard, 1938; m. Doris Wilma Hoskinson, Dec. 22, 1930; children—Richard Arlen, George William, Patricia Ann (Mrs. Ronald Bauers). Tchr. sci. Wynot (Nebr.) High Sch., 1928-30; tchr. sci. Wayne (Nebr.) High Sch., 1930-38, prin., 1938-41; supt. Wakefield (Nebr.) pub. schs., 1941-44, West Point (Nebr.) pub. schs., 1944-46; curriculum specialist U. Nebr. extension div., Lincoln, 1946-49, instr. secondary edn. Tchrs. Coll., also curriculum specialist extension div., 1949-51, asst. prof., 1951-53, asso. prof., 1953-56, prof., head class and corr. instrn., 1956-63, prof., asso. dir. extension div., 1963-66, prof., dir. extension div., 1966-74. Lectr., Sr. Fulbright-Hays Program, Haile Sellassie I U., Addis Ababa, Ethiopia, 1974. Mem. Nebr. Edn. Assn. (dist. III sec. 1941-42), Nat. U. Extension Assn. (mem. adminstrv. com., div. corr. study 1952-68, dir. 1963-65, mem. joint com. minimum data and definitions 1965-70, chmn. 1970-73; Walton S. Bittner award 1971; establishment Gayle B. Childs award div. ind. study 1969; Gayle B. Childs award 1973), Internat. Council on Corr. Edn. (chmn. com. on research 1961-69), Nebr. Schoolmasters Club, Phi Delta Kappa (dist. rep. 1957-63, dir., 1963-69, mem. commn. on edn. and human rights and responsibilities 1963-74, mem. adv. panel on commns. 1970-72; Distinguished Service award 1970). Kiwanian. Contbr. articles to profl. jours. Home: 4530 Van Dorn St Lincoln NE 68506 Office: 901 N 17th St Lincoln NE 68508

CHILDS, GEORGE RICHARD, food co. exec.; b. Terra Alta, W.Va., Oct. 9, 1924; s. Solomon Wosley and Lulu Grace (Bucklew) C.; B.S., W.Va. U., 1950; M.S., Purdue U., 1951; Ph.D., U. Md., 1964; m. Mildred Evelyn Braham, July 16, 1949; children—Mark, Gregory, Bradley, Eric. Poultry research specialist Central Soya Co., Inc., Decatur, Ind., 1951-61, mgr. poultry feeds, 1964-68, dir. feed research, 1968—; animal husbandman Bur. Comml. Fisheries, Dept. Interior, 1961-64. Served with USAAF, 1943-46. Mem. Am. Feed Mfrs. Assn. (chmn. nutrition council 1976-77), Sigma Xi, Alpha Zeta, Alpha Gamma Rho. Methodist. Home: Route 4 Box 129 Decatur IN 46733 Office: Central Soya Co Inc 1200 N 2d St Decatur IN 46733

CHILDS, ROBERT EDWARD, lawyer, educator; b. Hammond, Ind., Sept. 1, 1915; s. Julius and Ella Charlotte (Hamer) C.; B.S. with honors cum laude, Northwestern U., 1936, J.D., 1939; LL.M., U. Mich., 1947; m. Evelyn H. Falk; children—Robert Edward, Donald R. Admitted to Ind. bar, 1939, Mich. bar, 1950, also U.S. Supreme Ct. bar; practiced in Hammond, Ind., also Detroit; mem. firm Childs, DeLand & Hackett; prof. law Wayne State U., Detroit, 1946-76, prof. emeritus, 1976—. Cons. Ford Motor Co., major oil cos. Campaign mgr. Republican party, 1954; candidate Mich. Supreme Ct., 1957. Served with USNR, 1943-46; PTO. Mem. Am., Ind. bar assns., State Bar Mich., Am. Judicature Soc., Phi Beta Kappa, Phi Eta Sigma. Conglist. (chmn. bd. trustees 1971-73). Mason (32 deg., Shriner). Club: Ford Yacht (Grosse Isle, Mich.). Contbr. articles to profl. jours. Home: 301 Riverlane St Dearborn MI 48124 Office: 468 W Ferry St Wayne State U Detroit MI 48202

CHILSON, HERMAN PALMER, mcht.; b. Webster, S.D., Sept. 27, 1905; s. Chil H. and Julia (Dalager) C.; student St. Olaf Coll., 1923-25; m. Agnes Helen Hanson, Mar. 31, 1930; children—Joan (Mrs. James Iverson), Charles H. Dept. mgr. Elevator Store Co., Webster, 1925-30, pres., 1930-71, sec., 1971—. Mem. small bus. adv. com. U.S. Dept. Commerce, 1948-49; mem. S.D. Gov.'s Com. Small Bus., 1951-53. Pres. Pickerel Lake Park Assn., 1948-49, Webster Sch. Bd., 1944-52; v.p. S.D. Historic Sites Commn. Bd. regents Augustana Coll., 1945-64, now fellow. Recipient Dean Akeley award U. S.D., 1976; named Jaycee Boss of Year, 1963. Mem. Nat. Mchts. Assn. (pres. 1943-45), S.D. Retail Mchts. Assn. (dir. 1940-42), U.S. (nat. councilor), Webster (pres. 1938-39, dir. 1960-63) chambers of commerce, Izaak Walton League (pres. Webster 1950-51), S.D. Ornithologist Union (pres.), S.D. Hort Soc. (pres.), Day County Hist. Soc. (pres. 1963-65), N.E. Lake Region Assn. (pres.), Minn. Hist. Soc. (mem. exec. council), Am. Penstemon Soc. Republican. Lutheran (pres. 1961-62). Mason (Shriner), Kiwanian (pres. Webster 1938-39). Club: Minneapolis Athletic. Contbr. daily and local papers, S.D. Bird Notes mag. Home: 325 W 8th Ave Webster SD 57274 Office: 505 Main St Webster SD 57274

CHING, JAMES CHRISTOPHER, educator; b. Honolulu, Oct. 12, 1926; s. James I. and Elsie (Ching) Motoyama; B.A., Wabash Coll., 1951; M.A., U. Hawaii, 1953; Ph.D., U. Mo., 1962; m. Won May Lee, Dec. 15, 1950; 1 son, James Michael. Instr. speech U. Mo., 1953-56, U. Hawaii, 1956-58; mgr. C-D Advt. Honolulu, 1958; mng. editor Voice of East Oahu, Honolulu, 1959; asst. prof. speech and theater Wabash Coll., Crawfordsville, Ind., 1960; asst. prof. Tulane U., New Orleans, 1960-64, asso. prof., 1964-67; prof. speech Ill. State U., Normal, 1967; later chmn. dept. speech and theatre arts U. Bridgeport (Conn.); then vis. prof. dept. speech and dramatic art U. Mo., Columbia; now chmn. dept. theatre and communication arts Hamline U., St. Paul. Served with AUS, 1944-46. Mem. Speech Communication Assn., Am. Theatre Assn., So. Speech Assn., Univ. and Coll. Theatre Assn. (v.p.), Phi Kappa Phi, Tau Kappa Alpha, Phi Kappa Psi, Blue Key. Author: Advanced Public Speaking, 1966. Home: 1641 Eleanor Ave St Paul MN 55116

CHINN, KENNETH CAMERON, accountant; b. Plover, Iowa, Aug. 28, 1904; s. William Stanley and Charlotte Elizabeth Cameron (Jones) C.; B.A., Morningside Coll., 1926; postgrad. Am. Inst. Banking, 1926-28, LaSalle Sch. Higher Accountancy, 1930-31, Nat. Bus. Tng. Sch., 1938; m. Phyllis Margaret Jahde, June 24, 1970. Transit clk., loan teller First Nat. Bank, Toy Nat. Bank, Sioux City, Iowa, 1924-30; accounting clk. Strauss Nat. Bank; checker Central Proof div. Continental Nat. Bank & Trust Co., Chgo., 1929-30; sales and budget accountant Cities Service Oil Co., Sioux City, 1930-33; bookkeeper U.S. Regional Agrl. Credit Corp., Sioux City, 1933-35; cashier, accountant Michael-Leonard Seed Co., Sioux City, 1935-46; gen. bookkeeper Simpson Insulation Co., Sioux City, 1946-49; office mgr. Nat. Bookkeeping and Tax Service, Sioux City, 1949-50; self-employed accountant, tax and bus. cons., Sioux City, 1950—; partner, cons. staff mem. Asso. Investors, Sioux City, 1956-61; v.p. Nord Co., Inc., Sioux City, 1962; notary pub., Iowa. Sioux City rep. Woodbury County Grand Jury, 1955. Precinct committeeman Republican party, 1943-45; del. Woodbury County Conv., 1957. Mem. Nat. Assn. Credit Men, Am. Assn. Ret. Persons, Nat. Soc. Pub. Accountants, Alpha Tau Delta. Methodist (mem. ofcl. bd. 1936-54, auditor). Clubs: Masons, Order Eastern Star, Adventurers Travel; Sioux City Auto; Morningside College M. Address: 2537 S Maple St Sioux City IA 51106

CHINN, ROBERT CARSON, computer co. exec.; b. Biloxi, Miss., July 30, 1916; s. Roy and Lula (Carson) C.; B.A., La. State U., 1939, J.D., 1942; postgrad. U. Mich., 1963-64; m. Eleanor Wyatt Walker, Aug. 31, 1957; children—Robert Carson, Bennett T., Elizabeth W., Meredith W. Admitted to La. bar, 1942; practiced in Baton Rouge, 1945-46; with Ford Motor Co., 1946-69, labor relations rep., 1946, indsl. relations mgr., 1947, mgmt. devel., 1953-57, planning and engring. mgr. Ford div., 1957, asst. mgr. Kansas City (Mo.) Assembly Plant, 1959-62, asst. mgr. Wixom (Mich.) Assembly Plant, 1962, mgr., 1963-67, mgr. Twin Cities Ford Assembly Plant, St. Paul, 1967-68; v.p. mfg. operations staff Control Data Corp., Mpls., 1969-73, sr. v.p. indsl. group, 1973-75, sr. v.p. corp. programs, 1975—, mem. corp. policy com., 1976—; chmn. bd. Elbit Computers Ltd., Haifa, Israel; dir. Eden Land Co., Mid-Am. State Bank, St. Paul, H. & Val J. Rothschild Co. Div. chmn. Atlanta and St. Paul United Fund Campaign, 1956-68; gen. chmn. Atlanta A.R.C. campaign; mem. adv. bd. U.S.-Israel Bi-Nat. Research Found., 1977—. Served to maj., inf., AUS, 1942-46. Mem. Am., La. bar assns., Bus. Equipment Mfrs. Assn., Engring. Soc. Detroit, Soc. Automotive Engrs., Am. Soc. Mfg. Engrs., St. Paul C. of C. (pres. 1972; chmn. bd. 1973), Minn. Assn. Commerce and Industry (dir.). Presbyn. Mason (Shriner), Kiwanian, Rotarian. Home: 4905 Poppy Ln Edina MN 55435 Office: 8100 34th Ave S Minneapolis MN 55440

CHIPAIN, GEORGE CHRIS, orthodontist; b. Oak Park, Ill., Apr. 24, 1935; s. Chris George and Christine (Karales) C.; B.S., U. Ill., 1955; D.D.S., Northwestern U., 1959; M.S.D., Fairleigh Dickinson U., 1969; children—Chris, Georgia. Pres. G. Chipain, D.D.S., M.S.D., Ltd., Elmhurst, Ill., 1969—, Chipain Sports Store, 1974—. Mem. Am. Dental Assn., Ill., Chgo. dental socs., Am. Assn. Orthodontists, Ill. Soc. Orthodontists. Greek Orthodox. Club: Kiwanis (Elmhurst). Office: Thorn Bldg West Suite 3 135 Addison Ave Elmhurst IL 60126 also 1634 S Ardmore Villa Park IL 60181

CHIPLEY, JOHN RAYMOND, microbiologist; b. Athens, Ga., Nov. 10, 1944; s. John Wesley and Rosalie (Thornton) C.; B.S., U. Ga., 1966, M.S., 1967, Ph.D., 1969; m. Miriam Culpepper, Dec. 19, 1970. Research microbiologist Ga. Expt. Sta. U. Ga., 1969-71; research microbiologist Ohio State U., Columbus, 1971—; cons. in field. Recipient Henry Garren award U. Ga., 1969; NDEA fellow, 1966-69; Ohio State U. grantee, 1974-75; U.S. Dept. Agr. grantee, 69—. Mem. Am. Soc. Microbiology, Sertoma Club, Sigma Xi (Distinguished Research award 1969), Gamma Sigma Delta, Phi Tau Sigma. Democrat. Baptist. Reviewer Assn. Ofcl. Analytical Chemists, 1975—, Jour. Food Sci., 1973—. Contbr. articles to profl. jours. First to show definite distbn. of fungal toxins in animal tissues, to show definite enhancement of fungal toxin prodn. by gamma irradiation, and to show role of lipids in microbial transport studies; research includes studies of transport mechanisms and physiology of bacteria, steroid metabolism by bacteria, effects of irradiation upon microorganisms, others. Home: 2158 Ridgecliff Rd Columbus OH 43221

CHISHOLM, DONALD HERBERT, lawyer; b. Kansas City, Mo., Sept. 25, 1917; s. Herbert C. and Bessie M. (Osborne) C.; A.A., Kansas City Jr. Coll., 1932-35; LL.B., U. Mo., 1938; m. Mildred Ruth Ice, Dec. 1, 1940; children—William L., Nan Elizabeth. Admitted to Mo. bar, 1938, Fed. bar, 1938; since practiced in Kansas City, Mo.; mem. firm Wright, Rogers & Margolin, 1938-41; partner firm Stinson, Mag, Thomson, McEvers & Fizzell, 1947—. Dir. Park Nat. Bank, Schooley Printing Stationery Co., Standard Linen Supply Co., Rockhill Fed. Savs. & Loan Assn., Kansas City Bridge Co. (all Kansas City, Mo.). Bd. dirs. Truman Med. Center, Richard Cabot Clinic, Jacob L. and Ellac Loose Found., Kansas City, Clearing House for MidContinent Founds.; chmn. bd. trustees Park Coll. Served from pvt. to capt., AUS, 1942-46. Regent Am. Coll. Probate Counsel; mem. Am. Judicature Soc., Am., Kansas City bar assns., The Mo. Bar, Lawyers Assn. Kansas City (mem. estate planning council). Republican. Presbyn. Clubs: University, Mission Hills. Home: 1015 W 64th Terrace Kansas City MO 64113 Office: 2100 Tenmain Center Kansas City MO 64105

CHISHOLM, GEORGE NICKOLAUS, dentist; b. Pullman, Wash., Sept, 21, 1936; s. Leslie L. and Lila Rene (Cates) C.; D.D.S., U. Nebr., 1960; 1 son, Andrew M.; m. 2d, Debbie Jean Carder, Nov. 11, 1976. Practice dentistry, Lincoln, Nebr., 1963—; clin. instr. Coll. Dentistry, U. Nebr., 1976—. Served to capt. Dental Corps, USAF, 1960-63. Mem. Am., Nebr. dental assns., Lincoln Dist. Dental Assn. (sec. treas. 1976—), Sigma Alpha Epsilon, Xi Psi Phi. Mason (32 deg., Shriner). Asst. editor Nebr. State Dental Jour., 1967-69. Home: 1230 Manchester Dr Lincoln NE 68528 Office: 1025 Stuart Bldg Lincoln NE 68508

CHISHOLM, TAGUE CLEMENT, pediatric surgeon, educator; b. E. Millinocket, Maine, Nov. 6, 1915; s. George James and Victoria Mary (Tague) C.; A.B. cum laude, Harvard U., 1936, M.D., 1940; m. Verity Burnett, 1940 (div. 1975); children—Christopher Tague, Penelope Ann, Robin Francis; m. 2d, Johanna Lyon Meyers, Aug. 6, 1975. Intern, Peter Bent Brigham Hosp., Boston Children's Hosp., Boston, 1940-41, resident in gen. and pediatric surgery, 1941-46; Arthur Tracy Cabot fellow in surgery Harvard Med. Sch., 1946; practice medicine specializing in pediatric surgery, Mpls., 1947—; mem. faculty U. Minn. Sch. Medicine, Mpls., 1947—, clin. prof. surgery, 1965-77; trustee Mpls. Children's Health Center Hosp. Trustee Bishop Whipple Schs., Faribault, Minn.; bd. dirs. Wells Found., Mpls. Diplomate Am. Bd. Surgery. Recipient Merit medal U. Rio Grande Norte, Brazil, 1976; Charles Bowles Rogers award Hennepin County (Minn.) Med. Soc., 1976. Editorial bd. Jour. Pediatric Surgery, 1965-76, Pediatric Digest, 1962—, Jour. Minn. Med. Assn., 1957—; contbr. articles in pediatric surgery to profl. jours. and books. Home: 16617 Black Oaks Ln Wayzata MN 55391

CHISHOLM, WILLIAM LEE, med. photographer; b. Kansas City, Mo., July 2, 1947; s. Donald Herbert and Mildred Ruth (Ice) C.; student Westminster Coll., 1965-67; B. Profl. Arts, Brooks Inst. Photography, 1973; m. Susan Elizabeth Lilley, Dec. 8, 1974. Med. photography intern Parkland Meml. Hosp., Dallas, 1973; chief med. photographer U. Mo. Sch. Medicine, Kansas City; owner Graphis 2, Indsl. Comml. Photography, Prairie Village, Kans.; lectr. photography, 1973—. Served with USNR, 1967-68. Mem. Profl. Photographers of Am., Biol. Photog. Assn., Brooks Inst. Alumni Assn. Home: 4808 W 70th St Prairie Village KS 66208 Office: 4808 W 70th St Prairie Village KS 66208

CHISM, JAMES ARTHUR, data processor; b. Oak Park, Ill., Mar. 6, 1933; s. William Thompson and Arema Eloise (Chadwick) C.; A.B., DePauw U., 1957; M.B.A., Ind. U., 1959. Mgmt. engr. consumer and indsl. products div. Uniroyal, Inc., Mishawaka, Ind., 1959-61, sr. mgmt. engr., 1961-63; systems analyst Miles Labs., Inc., Elkhart, Ind., 1963-64, sr. systems analyst, 1965-69, project supr., distbn. systems, 1969-71, project mgr. systems and programming for corporate finance and adminstrv. depts., 1971, mgr. adminstrv. systems and staff services, 1973—. Asso. instr. bus. adminstrn. Ind. U., South Bend, 1964-66; mem. systems and data processing curriculum com. Ind. Vocational Tech. Coll., South Bend Campus, 1969-74; mem. systems curriculum adv. com. Southwestern Mich. Coll., 1974—. Served with AUS, 1954-56. Mem. Assn. Systems Mgmt. (chpt. pres. 1969-70, div. dir. 1972-77, recipient Merit, Achievement awards), Am. Mgmt. Assn., Internat. Communications Assn., Assn. Internal Mgmt. Cons., DePauw U., Ind. U. alumni assns., Delta Kappa Epsilon, Sigma Iota Epsilon. Republican. Episcopalian. Club: Summit (South Bend, Ind.). Home: 504 Cedar Crest Ln Mishawaka IN 46544 Office: 1127 Myrtle St Elkhart IN 46514

CHITWOOD, JULIUS RICHARD, librarian; b. Magazine, Ark., June 1, 1921; s. Hoyt Mozart and Florence (Umfrid) C.; A.B. cum laude, Quachita Baptist Coll., Arkadelphis, Ark., 1942; M.Mus., Ind. U., 1948; M.A., U. Chgo., 1954; m. Aileen Newsom, Aug. 6, 1944. Music supr. Edinburg (Ind.) pub. schs., 1946-47; music and audio-visual librarian Roosevelt Coll., Chgo., 1948-51; humanities librarian Drake U., 1951-53; spl. cataloger Chgo. Tchrs. Coll., 1953; asst. circulation librarian Indpls. Pub. Library, 1954-57, coordinator adult services, 1957-61; dir. Rockford (Ill.) Pub. Library 1961—, No. Ill. Library System, Rockford, 1966-76. Chmn. subcom. library system devel. Ill. Library Adv. Com., 1965—; adv. com. Grad. Sch. Library Sci., U. Ill., 1964-68; program adv. com. Sauk Valley Jr. Coll., 1967; cons. in field, participant workshops. Mem. history com. Ill. Sesquicentennial Commn.; mem. Mayor Rockford Com. for UN, 1962—. Sect. chmn. Rockford United Fund, 1966—; exec. bd. Rockford Civic Orch. Assn., 1962—; pres. Rockford Regional Acad. Center, 1974—. Served to maj., inf. AUS, 1942-45; ETO. Mem. Am. (chmn. standards adult services com., adult services div. 1961-66, chmn. subcom. revision standards of materials, pub. library div. 1965-66, pres. bldg. and equipment sect. library adminstrn. div. 1966-67, chmn. staff devel. com. personnel adminstrn. sect., library adminstr. div. 1964-68, pres. library adminstrn. div. 1969-70), Ill. (v.p. 1964-65, pres. 1965-66, Librarian of Year award 1974) library assns., Rockford C. of C. (mem. bd. Rockford area 1967-69). Unitarian (pres. 1965-67). Rotarian (exec. bd. Rockford 1965-66). Clubs: Professional Men's, Rockford University. Home: 916 Paris Av Rockford IL 61107 Office: 215 N Wyman St Rockford IL 61101

CHIU, LIAN-HWANG, educator; b. Taoyuan, Taiwan, China, Aug. 22, 1935; s. Chin-Ting and Hsiang-Mei (Sung) C.; came to U.S., 1963, naturalized, 1974; B.S., Nat. Taiwan Normal U., 1959; M.Ed., Nat. Chengchih U., 1963; M.A., Columbia, 1965, Ed.D., 1968; m. Fusiang, Chiang, Jan. 6, 1963; children—Kenneth, Benjamin, Catherine. Tchr., San Chi Tech. High Sch., Taiwan, 1958-59, 61-62; research asst. City U. N.Y., 1965-66; lectr. ednl. psychology Ind. U., Kokomo, 1967-68, asst. prof., 1968-72, asso. prof., 1972—. Cons., Mental Health Center, Howard Community Hosp., Kokomo, 1971-72; NSF fellow Ednl. Testing Service, Princeton, N.J., 1976, cons., 1977—. Served to lt. Chinese Army, 1959-61. Govtl. fellow Republic China, 1963-65, Arthur I. Gates fellow Columbia U., 1965-66. Mem. Am. Assn. Ednl. Research, AAUP (chpt. pres. 1970-72), Am. Psychol. Assn., Phi Delta Kappa. Contbr. articles to profl. jours. Home: 2921 Bagley Dr Kokomo IN 46901 Office: 2300 W Washington St Kokomo IN 46901

CHLEBICKI, GEORGE JOSEPH, cons. engr., human ecologist; b. Chgo., Apr. 24, 1913; s. Andrew and Jozefa (Mrukowicz) C.; student Thornton Jr. Coll., 1953-56; M.A. in Environ. Planning, Governor's State U., 1976; m. Helen Wolinski, Apr. 18, 1936; children—Sylvia Ann Chlebicki Junius, Cynthia Marie Chlebicki Collazo, Georgi, Gregory. Forging insp., chief die designer Wyman-Gordon Co., Harvey, Ill., 1939-52; municipal cons. engr., Harvey, 1945—; owner, mgr. George J. Chlebicki & Assos., until 1975; tchr. engring. Thornton Community Coll., 1970—. Chmn. Harvey Planning Commn., 1953-59; mem. advisory com. bldg constrn. tech. program Thornton Community Coll.; trustee Chgo. South Suburban Mass Transit Dist., 1968—, Harvey United Fund, 1972—. Fellow Am. Congress on Surveying and Mapping; mem. Cons. Engrs. Council Ill., Am. Water Works Assn., Ill. Land Surveyors Assn. (past pres., mem. examining com. 1972-74), Ill. Soc. Profl. Engrs. (past pres. Chgo. chpt.), Ill. Engring. Council (past pres.). Clubs: Elks (past exalted ruler), Optomists Internat. (past lt. gov.), Optomists (past pres. local chpt.). Contbr. articles to mags. and newspapers. Address: 15305 Broadway Ave Harvey IL 60426

CHLUP, JOSEPH FRANK, mfr.; b. Chgo., Sept. 16, 1928; s. Joseph J. and Beatrice M. (Belina) C.; B.S. in Indsl. Engring., U. Ill., 1951; m. Jean R. DeDera, Feb. 18, 1951; children—Ruth Ann, Mary Louise, Joseph D., John. Mgr. mgmt. engring. U.S. Rubber Co., Mishawaka, Ind., 1955-58; sr. systems analyst Fed. Res. Bank of Chgo., 1958-66; mgr. systems and programming Trans Union Corp., Chgo., 1966-69; v.p. mfg. operations Fearn Internat., Inc., Franklin Park, Ill., 1969—, also dir. Served with AUS, 1946-48, 51-53. Mem. Am. Inst. Indsl. Engrs., Am. Assn. Systems and Procedure. Home: 1581 N Columbia St Naperville IL 60540 Office: 9353 W Belmont Ave Franklin Park IL 60131

CHO, ANDREW YOONHA, pathologist; b. Chejudo, Korea, Nov. 10, 1934; s. Byeongeon and Seeon (Moon) C.; came to U.S., 1965, naturalized, 1976; M.D., Cath. Med. Coll., 1963; m. Veronica Soonsuk Son, Feb. 17, 1965; children—Paul Henry, Julianna Monica, Ann Mary, Susan C. Intern, St. Joseph Mercy Hosp., Detroit, 1965-66; resident in pathology, Wayne State U. Hosps., Detroit, 1966-70, instr., 1970-72; asso. pathologist St. Mary Hosp., Livonia, Mich., 1973—, also dir. hematology and blood bank. Served with Army of S. Korea, 1950-54. Diplomate Am. Bd. Pathology. Mem. AMA, Mich., Wayne County med. socs., Mich. Soc. Pathologists, Coll. Am. Pathologists, Internat. Acad. Pathology. Roman Catholic. Home: 1733 Bellwood Ct Bloomfield Hills MI 48013 Office: 36475 Five Mile Rd Livonia MI 48154

CHO, CHENG TSUNG, physician; b. Kaohsiung, Taiwan, Dec. 2, 1937; s. R.E. and S.M. (Chou) C.; came to U.S., 1964, naturalized, 1976; M.D., Kaohsiung Med. Coll., 1962; Ph.D., U. Kans., 1970; m. Chiou-shya Chen, Dec. 14, 1968; children—Jennifer, Julie. Intern, Norwegian-Am. Hosp., Chgo., 1964-65; resident U. Kans. Med. Center, 1965-67, fellow, 1967-70, asst. prof. pediatrics, microbiology, 1970-74, asso. prof., 1974—, chief sect. of pediatric infectious disease, dept. pediatrics, 1972—. Recipient Outstanding Pediatric Teaching award U. Kans. Med. Center, 1975; diplomate Am. Bd. Pediatrics. Fellow Am. Acad. Pediatrics; mem. AAAS, Am. Soc. Microbiology, Soc. Pediatric Research, Soc. Exptl. Biology and Medicine, Kans. Med. Soc., Midwest Pediatric Research Soc. Author articles on virology and infectious diseases. Home: 10215 Howe Ln Leawood KS 66206 Office: Dept Pediatrics U Kans Med Center Kansas City KS 66103

CHOBAN, MITCHELL ANTONE, realty co. exec.; b. St. Paul, July 19, 1941; s. Michael and Helen (Hoover) C.; B.A., Hamline U., 1966; postgrad. U. Minn., 1973—. Owner, mgr. Ken Rose Shopping Center, Rosemount, Minn., 1964—, Oakview Apt. Complex, Newport, Minn., 1969—; systems mgr. Control Data Corp., St. Paul, 1966-72; sec.-treas. Choban Realty Co., St. Paul, 1972—. Bd. dirs. Manit Corp., Southvue Assn. Served with AUSNR, 1959-62. Mem. South St. Paul C. of C., St. Paul Home Builders Assn. Home: 2111 5th St S St Paul MN 55075 Office: 1315 Southview Blvd South St Paul MN 55075

CHOCKLEY, FREDERICK WILSON, JR., lawyer; b. Joliet, Ill., Jan. 23, 1923; s. Frederick W. and Vera (Barrowman) C.; student Duke, 1941-42; B.S., U. Pa., 1947; LL.B., Western Res. U., 1949; m. Nancy Young, July 20, 1945; children—Nancy (Mrs. William R. Seelbach), Lizabeth A., Frederick Wilson III, Laurel Y.; m. 2d, Jean Schilling, June 16, 1972. Admitted to Ohio bar, 1949; mem. firm Walter, Haverfield, Buescher & Chockley, Cleve., 1949—; acting judge Lakewood (Ohio) Municipal Ct., 1968, 69, 70; spl. counsel to atty. gen State of Ohio, 1953. Mem. Ohio Bd. Bar Examiners, 1960-65. Mem. Lakewood Library Bd., 1969-70. Mem. Lakewood City Council, 1953-61, pres., 1960-61. Served with U.S. Army, 1943-45. Mem. Am., Ohio, Cleve. (mem. exec. com. 1964-66) bar assns., Am. Arbitration Assn., Sigma Alpha Epsilon, Phi Delta Phi. Republican. Presbyn. Clubs: Westwood Country, University of Pa. (pres. 1956) (Cleve.). Home: 1443 E Melrose St Westlake OH 44145 Office: Terminal Tower Cleveland OH 44113

CHODERA, TIMOTHY RAY, mfg. co. engr.; b. Medina, Ohio, Mar. 24, 1952; s. Joseph John and Marcella Elaine (Damon) C.; B.S. in Mech. and Nuclear Engring., Purdue U., 1970-74; postgrad. in internat. mgmt., U. Santa Clara, 1977—. Production engr. Allen-Bradley Co. Milw., Wis., 1973; dir. show for USO, U.S. Armed Forces, 1974; dir. sales United Consumers Club West Lafayette, Ind., 1974-75; project engr. Arthur G. McKee & Co., Independence, Ohio and Buenos Aires, Argentina, 1975-77; mfg. engr. Signetics Corp. Sunnyvale, Calif., 1977—. Mem. ASME, Tau Beta Pi, Pi Tau Sigma. Home: 9240 Highland Dr Brecksville OH 44141 Office: 811 E Arques St Sunnyvale CA 94086

CHOE, SUNKI, educator; b. Kang Won Do, Korea, Nov. 10, 1937; s. Chang Kil and Soon Chul (Chung) C.; came to U.S., 1957, naturalized, 1974; A.B. (Faculty honor scholar), Wagner Coll., 1961; M.A., U. Mass., 1964; m. Hyun Joo An, June 25, 1966; children—Jennifer, Kenneth, Jonathan. Tchr. social studies Middlesex Sch., Concord, Mass., 1964-65; instr. polit. sci. Barrington (R.I.) Coll., 1967-70; asst. prof. polit. sci. Taylor U., Upland, Ind., 1970—. Cons., Intellex Corp., 1972—, Staran Trading Corp., 1972—. Henry Kendall Found. fellow U. Mass., 1965-66. Mem. Am. Polit. Sci. Assn., Ind. Acad. Social Scis., Pi Sigma Alpha, Phi Sigma Kappa. Home: 1013 S 1st St Upland IN 46989 Office: Taylor U Upland IN 46989

CHOI, CHAN-KYOO, physicist; b. Seoul, Korea, Nov. 19, 1942; s. Hongki and Oksoon (Chang) C.; came to U.S., 1966, naturalized, 1976; B.S., Sogang Jesuit Coll. (Korea), 1965; M.S. (Grad. fellow), So. Ill. U., 1969, Ph.D., 1973. Research asst. So. Ill. U., 1973-74, asst. prof. physics, 1974-75; research asst. prof. nuclear engring. U. Ill., 1975—; participant Curriculum Devel. in Fusion, Argonne (Ill.) Nat. Lab., 1975-77, Internat. Atomic Energy Agy. Fusion Reactor Design Conf. and Workshop, 1977. Mem. Am. Phys. Soc., Am. Nuclear Soc., IEEE, AAAS, Korean Phys. Soc., Sigma Xi. Roman Catholic. Contbr. articles to sci. jours. Home: 1606 Kingston Dr Urbana IL 61801 Office: 214 Nuclear Engring Lab U Ill Urbana IL 61801

CHOI, SEUNG HOON, nuclear engr.; b. Seoul, Korea, Aug. 12, 1943; s. Maeng Soon and Hwa Jin (Lee) C.; came to U.S., 1973; B.S., Han Yang U., Korea, 1969; certificate Westinghouse Nuclear Tng. Center, Zion, Ill., 1974; M.S., Northwestern U., 1977; m. Chang Soon Kim, Nov. 28, 1970; children—Eun Hye, Mindulla. Nuclear engr. Korea Electric Co., Seoul, 1969-73, Sargent & Lundy Engrs., Chgo., 1974-77, Gilbert/Commonwealth Co., Jackson, Mich., 1977—; cons. in field. Mem. Am. Nuclear Soc., ASME. Home: 2630 Chapel Rd Parma MI 49269 Office: Gilbert/Commonwealth Co 209 E Washington St Jackson MI 49201

CHOI, YUNG-IN, physician; b. Seoul, Korea, May 18, 1942; s. Myung-Jin and Keum-Joo (Lee) C.; M.D., Yonsei U., Korea, 1967; m. Shee Khang, Sept. 30, 1968; children—Peter, Paul. Intern, Ellis Hosp., Schenectady, N.Y., 1969-70; resident in internal medicine Henry Ford Hosp., Detroit, 1970-73, fellow in endocrinology and metabolism, 1973; fellow in hypertension and hyperlipidemia U. Mich. Med. Center, 1973; attending physician Meml. Hosp. Mason County, Ludington, Mich., 1974—. Diplomate Am. Bd. Internal Medicine. Mem. A.C.P., AMA, Am. Soc. Internal Medicine, Am. Heart Assn. Home: 1409 Ivanhoe Rd Ludington MI 49431 Office: 12 Atkinson Dr Ludington MI 49431

CHOITZ, JOHN FRANK, educator; b. nr. Carneiro, Kans., Jan. 19, 1911; s. Fred F. and Helena (Pflughoeft) C.; diploma St. Johns Coll., 1930, Concordia Theol. Sem., 1936; M.S., Ft. Hays (Kans.) State Coll., 1941; Ph.D., U. Iowa, 1952; m. Florence Holm, July 26, 1936; children—Patricia, Dorothy, Carol. Ordained to ministry Lutheran Ch., 1936; pastor Luth. chs., Bazine, Kans., State U. Iowa, Chgo.; tchr. Bazine High Sch., 1937-44, Detroit Luth. High Sch., 1944-46; asso. prof. English and humanities Concordia Tchrs. Coll., River Forest, Ill., 1951-58; asst. editor mag. Luth. Edn., 1952-58; supt. Luth. high schs. Greater Detroit, also dep. supt. schs. Mich. dist., 1958-67; pres. Mich. Luth. Coll., Detroit, 1962-70; dir. devel. Lawrence Inst. Tech., Southfield, Mich., 1970-74, prof. humanities, 1973-77; asst. pastor St. John's Luth. Ch., Taylor, Mich., 1970-77. Mem. Mayor's Youth

Employment Com., Detroit, 1962; schs. program com. United Community Services, Detroit, 1962; mem. Citizens for Ednl. Freedom, Detroit, 1962; mem. Mayors Adv. Com. Total Action Against Poverty, 1965-70; chmn. bd. Saratoga Gen. Hosp., Detroit, 1967-77. Bd. dirs. Jr. Achievement, Detroit, 1961. Mem. Detroit Ednl. TV Found., Asso. Luth. Secondary Schs. (mem. gen. com. 1960-70, chmn. curriculum commn.), Luth. Edn. Assn. Clubs: Detroit Athletic, Lutheran Luncheon, Economic (Detroit). Home and Office: 1559 Pleasant Valley Dr Newark OH 43055

CHOJNOWSKI, EUGENE FRANCIS, mfg. co. exec.; b. Chgo., Apr. 23, 1929; s. Leo C. and Stella (Werner) C.; m. Jean Kostka, Apr. 16, 1949; children—Robert, Thomas, Barbara, Mark. B.S., Purdue U., 1951. Registered profl. engr., Mich., 1958. Foundry technician Internat. Harvester Co., 1951-53; served with U.S. Army, 1953-55; technician, research metallurgist, chief metallurgist, research and devel. mgr., plant engr. Hayes-Albion Corp., Albion, Mich., 1955-67; partner Heat Transfer Systems Co., Jackson, Mich., 1967-69, pres., 1969—. Chmn. Albion chpt. March of Dimes, 1961-62; chmn. Albion chpt. Red Cross, 1962; asst. advisor explorer scouts Boy Scouts Am., 1958-60. Mem. Am. Soc. Metals (dir. Jackson chpt. 1966-68), Am. Foundrymans Soc., Soc. Automotive Engrs., Purdue Alumni Assn., Jackson Outdoor Club, Mich. Tuberculosis and Respiratory Disease Assn., Arbor Hills Country Club. Recipient Distinguished Service award, 1960. Author: (with others) Am. Soc. for Metals Handbook, Vol. 2., 1965. Home: 1934 S West Ave Jackson MI 49203 Office: 1934 S West Ave Jackson MI 49203

CHOLLAR, ROBERT GANUN, found. exec.; b. Syracuse, N.Y., Feb. 10, 1914; s. Walter Edward and Estelle Augusta (GaNun) C.; student Dartmouth Coll., 1932-33; A.B., Antioch Coll., 1935; D.Sc. (hon.), Ind. Inst. Tech., 1972; m. Thelma Lucille Holt, Sept. 22, 1934; children—Charles Edward, Brian Holt, Richard Robert. With Nat. Cash Register Co., Dayton, Ohio, 1933-71, v.p. research and devel., 1959-64, v.p. and group exec. research, devel. and mfg., 1964-71; chmn. bd., pres. Charles F. Kettering Found., Dayton, 1971—; dir. Dayton Power & Light Co.; trustee Sloan-Kettering Inst. for Cancer Research; advisory mem. bd. trustees, mem. sci. policy com. Sloan-Kettering Cancer Center; bd. dirs. Dayton-Miami Valley Consortium. Recipient Internat. Statesman award Sister Cities, 1974; Ohio Commodore. Mem. Council Fgn. Relations, Internat. Standards Orgn. (chmn. 1961-73), Indsl. Research Inst. (pres. 1960-61), Am. Chem. Soc., Tau Beta Pi, Chi Phi. Clubs: Moraine Country (Dayton); Univ. (N.Y.). Patentee synthetic rubber, plastics, printing. Home: 4472 Lotz Rd Dayton OH 45429 Office: 5335 Far Hills Ave Dayton OH 45429

CHOONTANOM, SAMAN, physician; b. Nakornpathom, Thailand, Aug. 14, 1939; s. Ta and Chalam (Bho Ragsa) C.; came to U.S., 19—, naturalized, 1977; M.D., Chengmai Hosp., Thailand, 1964; m. Wadhana Karoun, Jan. 30, 1968; children—Prichaya, Darlene. Intern, Wayne County Gen. Hosp., Eloise, Mich., 1965-66; resident in surgery, 1966-70; staff surgeon Metro-Electric Authority Hosp., Bangkok, Thailand, 1970-72, Keokuk County Hosp., Sigourney, Iowa, 1973-74; chief of staff Hegg Meml. Hosp., Rock Valley, Iowa, 1976—. Diplomate Am. Bd. Surgery. Fellow Am. Soc. Abdominal Surgeons; mem. AMA, Iowa Med. Soc. Club: Rotary. Home: 1011 17th Ave Rock Valley IA 51247 Office: 1200 21st Ave Rock Valley IA 51247

CHOPE, HENRY ROY, automation and controls co. exec.; b. Louisville, July 19, 1921; s. Henry Roy and Amelia Louise (Gutermuth) C.; B.E.E., Ohio State U., 1948; M.S. in Applied Physics, Calif. Inst. Tech., 1948; S.M. in Engring. Scis., Harvard U., 1950; m. Lois Elizabeth Sherman, June 11, 1954; children—Elizabeth Ann, David Roy, Amelia Louise, Charles Sherman. Electronic scientist in rocket devel. U.S. Air Force Cambridge (Mass.) Research Lab., 1949-50; co-founder, dir., exec. v.p. Indsl. Nucleonics Corp., Columbus, Ohio, 1950—; dir. Solidstate Controls, Inc., 1967—. Vice pres., trustee Riverside Meth. Hosp., Columbus, 1969—; trustee Ohio Wesleyan U., 1971—. Served to 1st lt. USAAF, 1943-46. Recipient Distinguished Alumnus award Ohio State U., 1961, Alumni Centennial award, 1970. Fellow Instrument Soc. Am. (Albert F. Sperry award 1972); mem. IEEE (sr., Morris E. Leeds award 1967), Am. Nuclear Soc., Nat. Soc. Profl. Engrs., Ohio C. of C. (dir.), Tau Beta Pi (pres. and chmn. exec. com. 1966-70). Lutheran. Club: Scioto Country (Columbus). Contbr. articles to profl. jours; patentee nuclear energy, instrumentation, process control. Home: 3885 Woodbridge Rd Columbus OH 43220 Office: 650 Ackerman Rd Columbus OH 43202

CHORMANN, RICHARD FREDERICK, bank and trust co. exec.; b. Adrian, Mich., Nov. 13, 1937; s. Frederick T. and Anna M.(Blohm) C.; B.S., Western Mich. U., 1959; postgrad U. Wis., 1968-70; m. Caroyn Ann Curtis, Sept. 7, 1957; children—Gregory, James, Cynthia. Exec. v.p. First Nat. Bank & Trust Co. of Mich., Kalamazoo, 1959—; v.p. First Nat. Fin. Corp., Kalamazoo; dir. Gt. Lakes Computer Center, Inc., Kalamazoo, 1967—, First Nat. Bank Saulte St. Marie. Bd. dirs. Big Bros. of Greater Kalamazoo, bd. pres., 1970; bd. dirs. Jr. Achievement of Kalamazoo, chmn., 1976-77. Named One of Five Outstanding Local Presidents by Michigan Jaycees, 1968. Mem. Mich. Bankers Assn., Mich. Automated Clearing House Assn. (dir.), Bank Adminstrn. Inst., Mich. (v.p. 1970-71), Kalamazoo (pres. 1967-68, chmn. bd. 1968-69) Jaycees. Lutheran (chmn. ch. council 1970). Home: 5257 E F-G Ave Kalamazoo MI 49004 Office: 108 E Michigan St Kalamazoo MI 49006

CHOS, LOUIS JOHN, JR., chem. co. exec.; b. Cleve., Sept. 22, 1951; s. Louis John and Ellen Virginia (Carlson) C.; B.S. in Chem. Engring., Case Western Res. U., 1973. Chem. engr. Dow Chem. Co., Midland, Mich., 1972-74, prodn. engr., 1974-77, prodn. supr., 1977-. Adviser Jr. Achievement, Midland, 1975-76; active Big Brother Orgn., Gladwin-Clare counties, 1975—. Mem. Am. Youth Hostels. Lutheran. Home: 5451 Oak Ridge Dr Beaverton MI 48612 Office: 730 Bldg Dow Chem Co Midland MI 48640

CHOU, CLIFFORD CHI FONG, research engr.; b. Taipei, Taiwan, Dec. 19, 1940; s. Ching piao and Yueh li (Huang) C.; came to U.S., 1966; Ph.D., Mich. State U., 1972; m. Chu hwei Lee, Mar. 23, 1968; children—Kelvin Lin yu, Renee Lincy. Research asst. Mich. State U., E. Lansing, 1967-70, Wayne State U. Detroit, 1970-72, research asso., 1972-76, research engr. Ford Motor Co., Dearborn, 1976—; tchr. part time dynamics, engring. systems analysis; asst. tchr. auto safety related courses; project engr. auto safety research programs. Soc. Automotive Engrs. grantee. Mem. ASME, AIAA, Sigma Xi. Clubs: Detroit Chinese Am. Assn. Contbr. numerous articles to profl. jours. Office: PO Box 2053 Rm 1007 Automotive Safety Center Dearborn MI 48121

CHOU, DAVID HUNG-EN, food scientist; b. Nantou, Taiwan, Dec. 2, 1940; s. Chien-tsai and Shin (Chen) C.; B.S., Nat. Taiwan U., 1966; M.S., U. Minn., 1970, Ph.D., 1973; m. Shuh-Mei Chen, Sept. 18, 1969; children—Cindy. Research asst., Nat Taiwan U., 1967-68; research asst. U. Minn., 1968-71, research fellow, 1971-73; project leader Ralston Purina Co., St. Louis, 1973-76, sr. project leader, 1976—. Served to 2d lt. Nationalist Chinese Army, 1966-67. Mem. Chinese Agrl. Chemistry Assn., Inst. Food Technologist, Am. Assn. Cereal Chemists, Soc. Rheology, Am. Chem. Soc., Sigma Xi, Gamma Sigma Delta. Club: American Formosan. Home: 9250 Arban Dr St Louis MO 63126 Office: Checkerboard Sq St Louis MO 63188

CHOUINARD, EDWARD FRANCIS, chem. co. exec.; b. Chgo.; s. Alfred Francis and Hannah Georgia (Klein) C.; B.S., Purdue U., 1963; M.S., U. Ia., 1964; Ph.D., Ill. Inst. Tech., 1968; M.B.A., Central Mich. U., 1973; m. Sharon Ann Dettre, Aug. 27, 1966; children—Melissa Lynne, Jennifer Kristen. Research scientist, sect. head Owens Corning Fiberglas Co., Granville, Ohio, 1967-70; research specialist Environ. Research Lab., Dow Chem. Co., Midland, Mich., 1970-73, tech. sales specialist, Chgo., 1973-77; v.p., treas., dir. ARC Securities, Inc., Atlanta, 1970-74; dir. mktg. internat. ops. Gt. Lakes Chem. Corp., West Lafayette, Ind., 1977—. Mem. Am. Chem. Soc., Am. Inst. Chem. Engrs., Sigma Xi, Phi Lambda Upsilon, Sigma Iota Epsilon. Home: 3523 Canterbury West Lafayette IN 47905 Office: Gt Lakes Chem Corp PO Box 2200 West Lafayette IN 47906

CHOUKAS, NICHOLAS CHRIS, dental educator; b. Chgo., Sept. 5, 1923; s. Chris and Ethel (George) C.; student Wright Jr. Coll., 1941-43, U. Chgo., 1943-44; D.D.S., Loyola U., Chgo., 1950, M.S. in Oral Anatomy, 1958; m. LaVerne Tumosa, Apr. 19, 1951; children—Janet Lynn, Chris Nicholas, Michael John, Nicholas Chris II. Fellow in oral surgery Loyola U., 1953; resident in oral surgery Cook County Hosp., Chgo., 1954-55; practice specializing in oral and maxillofacial surgery, Elmwood Park, Ill., 1956—; asst. prof. Loyola U. Dental Sch., 1957-64, asso. prof., 1964—, chmn. dept. oral surgery, 1962—, asso. prof. oral biology Grad. Sch., 1968-69, prof. dept. oral biology, 1969—, prof. dept. oral and maxillofacial surgery, 1969—; attending oral surgeon Hines (Ill.) VA Hosp., 1958-60; asso. attending surgeon Cook county Hosp., 1959-62; cons. VA Hosp., Hines, Ill., 1960—. Served to lt. (j.g.), USNR, 1951-53. Research grantee NIH, 1961, 62, 63. Diplomate Am. Bd. Oral Surgery. Fellow Internat. Assn. Oral Surgeons, Am. Coll. Dentists, Inst. Medicine of Chgo., Pan Am. Med. Assn., Internat. Coll. Dentists, Internat. Assn. Maxillofacial Surgeons, Am. Coll. Stomatologic Surgeons; mem. Chgo. Soc. Oral Surgeons, Am. Soc. Oral Surgeons, Odontographic Soc., Logan Brophy Meml. Soc., Sigma Xi, Omicron Kappa Upsilon, Delta Sigma Delta. Contbr. articles to profl. jours. Home: 230 Oakdene Rd Barrington Hills IL 60010 Office: 7310 North Ave Elmwood Park IL 60635

CHOW, BRIAN GEE-YIN, physicist; b. Macau, Aug. 10, 1941; s. Kai-Chuen and Chi-Shiu (Miao) C.; came to U.S., 1964, naturalized, 1976; B.S., Chung Chi Coll., Hong Kong, 1963; Ph.D., Case Western Res. U., 1969; M.B.A., U. Mich., 1977; m. Pauline Pui-Lam Chou, June 14, 1969; 1 dau., Kira. Research asso. Case Western Res. U., Cleve., 1969; postdoctoral scholar U. Mich., Ann Arbor, 1972-73; asst. prof. physics Saginaw Valley State Coll., University Center, Mich., 1969-73, chmn., 1970-74, asso. prof., 1973—, dir. obs., 1974-76. Recipient grants Am. Enterprise Inst. for Pub. Policy Research, 1974-75, HEW, 1975, 76. Mem. Am. Phys. Soc. Contbr. articles to profl. jours. Home: 3136 Columbine Dr Saginaw MI 48603 Office: Dept Physics Saginaw Valley State Coll University Center MI 48710

CHOYKE, ARTHUR DAVIS, JR., luminous ceiling co. exec.; b. N.Y.C., Mar. 13, 1919; s. Arthur Davis and Lillian (Bauer) C.; A.B., Columbia, 1939, B.S., 1940; m. Phyllis May Ford, Aug. 18, 1945; children—Christopher Ford, Tyler Van. With indsl. engring. dept. Procter & Gamble Co., S.I., N.Y., 1940-43; instr. Pratt Inst., Bklyn., 1942-45; chief indsl. engr. M & M, Ltd., Newark, 1943-47; partner Ford Distbg. Co., Chgo., 1947-57; incorporator, pres., treas., dir. Artcrest Products Co., Inc., Chgo., 1951—; dir. Gallery Series, Harper Sq. Press. Club: Arts (Chgo.). Home: 29 E Division St Chicago IL 60610 Office: 401 W Ontario St Chicago IL 60610

CHOYKE, PHYLLIS MAY FORD (MRS. ARTHUR DAVIS CHOYKE, JR.), ceiling systems co. exec.; b. Buffalo, Oct. 25, 1921; d. Thomas Cecil and Vera (Buchanan) Ford; B.S. summa cum laude, Northwestern U., 1942; m. Arthur Davis Choyke, Jr., Aug. 18, 1945; children—Christopher Ford, Tyler Van. Reporter, City News Bur., Chgo., 1942-43, Met. sect. Chgo. Tribune, 1943-44; feature writer OWI, N.Y.C., 1944-45; sec. corp. Artcrest Products Co., Inc., Chgo., 1958—, v.p., 1964—, founder-dir. Harper Sq. Press div., 1966—. Mem. Phi Beta Kappa. Clubs: Arts, Colony (Chgo.). Editor: Gallery Series One, 1967; Gal-Series Two—Poems of the Inner World, 1968; Gallery Series Three—Poets: Levitations and Observations, 1970; Gallery Series Four-I am Talking About Revolution, 1973; Gallery Series Five/Poets—To An Aging Nation (with occult overtones), 1977. Home: 29 E Division St Chicago IL 60610 Office: 401 W Ontario St Chicago IL 60610

CHRISMAN, JAMES EDWARD, dentist; b. Newton, Ill., Dec. 5, 1916; s. Edward Wesley and Clara Ann (Crowley) C.; B.S., Davidson Coll., 1934-38; student N.C. Sch. for Deaf Tchr. Tng., 1938-39, Ill. Wesleyan U., 1946; D.D.S., Northwestern U., 1949; m. Ruth Catherine Henebry, Sept. 4, 1941; children—James C., Daniel P., Robert A. Instr., Schs. for Deaf, N.C., Neb., S.D., 1938-41; field exec. Boy Scouts Am., Sioux Falls, S.D., 1941; pvt. practice dentistry, Bloomington, Ill., 1949—. Instr., Mennonite Hosp. Sch. Nursing, 1950-65; cons. Mennonite Long Term Care Unit, 1970—, Heritage Manor, 1970—. Mem. state bd. Am. Cancer Soc., 1963-64; mem. adv. bd. Mennonite Hosp., 1956—; active A.R.C., Boy Scouts Am. Served with USCGR, 1942-46. Recipient Silver Beaver award Boy Scouts Am., 1953. Mem. U.S. Power Squadron (comdr. 1973—), Xi Psi Phi. Lutheran. Mason (Shriner). Club: Exchange (pres. 1957-58) (Bloomington). Home: 906 Randall Dr Normal IL 61761 Office: 710 N East St Bloomington IL 61701

CHRISTEN, JACK ROBERT, fasteners mfg. co. exec.; b. Fort Wayne, Ind., July 12, 1941; s. Harold William and Margaret Ellen (Holmes) C.; student Purdue U. extension, 1968-72; m. Linda Sue George, Apr. 8, 1967; 1 son, Anthony William. Printer, Standard Packaging Corp., 1960-63; with Peter Eckrich & Sons, Fort Wayne, 1966-73, computer programmer, 1968-70, programmer system analyst, 1970-73; mgr. data processing and info. services Gripco Fasteners div. Mite Corp., South Whitley, Ind., 1973—. Supt. Sunday Sch., Our Hope Luth. Ch., 1975-76. Served with U.S. Army, 1963-65. Mem. Systems Three and Thirty Two Users Soc. (co founder, 1st program chmn.), Data Processing Mgmt. Assn. (dir.). Republican. Club: American Turners of Fort Wayne. Home: 2042 Apollo Dr Huntertown IN 46748 Office: Broad at Maple St South Whitley IN 46787

CHRISTENSEN, BARLOW FORBES, lawyer; b. Shelley, Idaho, Oct. 21, 1928; s. Joseph Cortez and Lenore Gardner (Forbes) C.; B.S. with high honors Brigham Young U., 1955; J.D., Columbia, 1960; m. Anne Elizabeth Kirk, Aug. 9, 1957; children—Susan Anne, Sharon, Kirk Barlow, Marcia, Joseph, Thomas Arthur. Admitted to Idaho bar, 1960; asso. firm Robert M. Kerr, Jr., Blackfoot, Ida., 1960; law clk. State Idaho Supreme Ct., 1960-62; adminstrv. asst. Am. Bar Assn., Chgo., 1962-65; research atty. Am. Bar Found., Chgo., 1965—. Served with AUS, 1951-53. Mem. Idaho State, Am. bar assns., Scribes, Phi Kappa Phi. Republican. Mem. Ch. Jesus Christ of Latter-day Saints (missionary 1948-50, patriarch Chicago Heights, Ill. Stake 1975—). Author: Lawyers for People of Moderate Means, 1970. Home: 156 Algonquin St Park Forest IL 60466 Office: 1155 E 60th St Chicago IL 60637

CHRISTENSEN, CHARLES, zool. soc. adminstr.; b. Chgo., Aug. 20, 1912; s. Ludwig Theodore and Emma Minna (Reinhold) C.; B.S., U. Ill., 1933; postgrad. Northwestern U., 1940-58, Dartmouth, summers 1955-57; m. Jean Joynt, June 21, 1947; children—Sandra Love, Mary Lee (Mrs. James Ray Kahl), Rose Ann (Mrs. William Witherspoon), Charles. Accountant firm Jahn & Ollier, Engraving Co., Chgo., 1933-41; systems engr. IBM Sales, Chgo., 1941-42; payroll mgr. Fed. Res. Bank, Chgo., 1942-45; asst. controller, credit mgr. Hotpoint div. Gen. Electric Corp., Chgo., 1946-64; credit mgr. Norge div. Borg-Warner Corp., Chgo., 1964-68; asso. dir. adminstrn. Chgo. Zool. Soc., Brookfield, Ill., 1968—. Treas., Westchester (Ill.) Park Dist., 1961-71; mem. Westchester Zoning Bd. Appeals, 1955-65. Recipient U. Ill. Hosp. Outstanding Contbns. award, 1973. Mem. Proviso Twp. Municipal League, Nat. Assn. Credit Mgmt. Roman Catholic (Holy Name Soc.). Home: 927 Hull Av Westchester IL 60153 Office: Chgo Zool Park 3300 Golf Rd Brookfield IL 60513

CHRISTENSEN, DON EDWARD, systems design engr.; b. Springfield, Ohio, Aug. 7, 1927; s. Otto M. and Ruth Harriet (Melvin) C.; grad. Machine Accountants Tng. Assn., 1963; student Ind. U.-Purdue U., Indpls., 1974; m. Wanjean Christensen, July 30, 1949; children—Ivan G., Bruce O., Laura M., Phyllis M. With Am. Dist. Telegraph Co., 1944-51, Indpls. Power & Light Co., 1951-56, RCA, Indpls., 1956-59, Acousticon of Indpls. div. Dictograph Corp., 1959-64; systems design engr. RCA, 1964—. Pres., dir. Marion County chpt. Com. to Restore the Constn.; chmn. 11th dist. Am. Party, 1973-74, chmn. Am. Party, 1974-76. Recipient Liberty awards Congress of Freedom Inc., 1975, 76. Mem. IEEE. Republican. Lutheran. Clubs: Ind. Order of Foresters. Patentee TV control circuits. Home: 1016 N Drexel Ave Indianapolis IN 46201 Office: 600 N Sherman Dr Indianapolis IN 46201

CHRISTENSEN, DONN DOUGLAS, lawyer; b. St. Paul, June 30, 1929; s. Jonas Jergen and Hildur Minerva (Lundeen) C.; B.S., U. Minn., 1950, LL.B., 1952; m. Renee E. Pinet, Aug. 31, 1970; children—Keith, Catherine, Eric. Admitted to Minn. bar, 1952, U.S. Fed. Ct., 1955; practiced in St. Paul, 1954-68, 70—; dep. atty. gen. State of Minn., 1968-70; justice of peace, Village of Mendota Heights, Minn., 1961-66; instr. bus. law Macalester Coll., St. Paul, 1960-67. Served with AUS, 1952-54. Mem. Am., Minn. (chmn. environmental law sect. 1972-73), Ramsey County bar assns., Execs. Assn. St. Paul (pres. 1966), Mendota Heights C. of C. (sec. 1965), Delta Theta Phi. Club: Athletic (St. Paul). Home: 676 Schifsky Rd St Paul MN 55112 Office: 1210 Commerce Bldg St Paul MN 55101

CHRISTENSEN, EVERETT M., personnel cons.; b. New Ulm, Minn., Mar. 15, 1935; s. Everett M. and Hildegard F. (Amann) C.; A.B. in Econs., Mich. State U., 1957; M.A. in Psychology, U. Minn., 1965; m. Sybil A. Burreson, May 5, 1962; children—Brent, Dawn, Glenn, Sue. Personnel rep., Josten's, Inc., Owatonna, Minn., 1960-61; personnel adminstr., Honeywell, Inc., Mpls., 1961-65; personnel dir., F and M Savs. Bank, Mpls., 1965-70, dir. adminstrn., 1970-72; pres. PPSD, Inc., Mpls. and Ft. Lauderdale, Fla., 1972—; dir. Madelia, Minn., Telephone Co., 1962—; instr. St. Thomas Coll. Grad. Sch. Bus., St. Paul, 1976-77, St. Olaf Coll., Northfield, Minn., 1976. Served to lt. USAF, 1957-59. Mem. Soc. Personnel Adminstrn., Am. Soc. Tng. and Devel. Roman Catholic. Club: Kiwanis (Mpls. Downtown). Author: Dynamic Supervision, 1971.

CHRISTENSEN, HAROLD LEWIS, electronics co. exec.; b. Turton, S.D., Mar. 29, 1916; s. John Lewis and Elsie Maria (Teska) C.; LL.B., Blackstone Sch. Law, 1960; M.B.A., U. Chgo., 1949; m. Edna Doris Lively, Dec. 23, 1945 (dec. Aug. 1972); children—Carol (Mrs. James Stamborski), Kay (Mrs. August Yount), Kurt Lewis; m. 2d, Judy Sikes Rickher, Dec. 28, 1972. Pres., Kearney Clark & Assos., Park Ridge, Ill., 1971-74, Exertia Electronics, Inc., Des Plaines, Ill., 1972—. Asst. prof. Wittenberg U. (O.), 1949-51, U. Ill., Chgo., 1957-58. Served with AUS, 1934-46. Decorated Purple Heart. Mem. A.A.U.P., Assn. Automotive Engrs., V.F.W. Mason. Club: Rolling Green Country. Home: 925 Marshall St Des Plaines IL 60016 Office: 1001 E Touhy St Des Plaines IL 60018

CHRISTENSEN, HOWARD ALAN, utility co. exec.; b. Atlantic, Iowa, Aug. 15, 1933; s. J. Chris and Stena (Gustafsen) C.; B.S., State U. Iowa, 1959; m. Verla Ann Suhr, May 10, 1953; children—Debra, JoElyn, Jeffrey. Mgr., Arthur Andersen & Co., Kansas City, Mo., Birmingham, Ala., 1959-65; with St. Joseph Light & Power Co. (Mo.), 1965-76, v.p., sec., 1965-76; treas. Mich. Wis. Pipe Line Co., Detroit, 1976—. Bd. dirs. St. Joseph Area United Way, 1970-75, Jr. Achievement, 1975. Served with AUS, 1953-55. Mem. Am. Inst. C.P.A.'s, Nat. Assn. Accountants (dir. 1971-73), St. Joseph Area C. of C. (dir., sec. 1971, v.p. 1972, 1st v.p. 1973-75), Beta Gamma Sigma, Beta Alpha Psi. Lutheran. Rotarian (dir. 1970-71, sec. 1971-72, pres. 1974-75). Home: 2845 Woodcreek Way Bloomfield Hills MI 48013 Office: One Woodward Ave Detroit MI 48226

CHRISTENSEN, J. GORDON, music specialist; b. Grand Island, Neb., Sept. 19, 1942; s. Elmer Erling and Eva Valentine (Stroud) C.; B.Mus., Hastings Coll., 1965; Mus.M., U. Neb., 1971, postgrad., 1971—; student U. Colo., 1965-66. Music tchr. Palisade (Neb.) Pub. Schs., 1966-68; music specialist Imperial (Neb.) Elementary Schs., 1968—. Developer, Pilot Projects in Humanities Edn. for U. Neb., 1971-72; cons. humanities edn. Hastings Coll., 1972-73, U. Neb., 1972-74, U. Ia., 1972, Neb. Dept. Econ. Devel., 1974, Nat. Council Tchrs. English, 1972. Elementary Secondary Edn. Act research grantee, 1972; Nat. Endowment for Arts funding, 1973-74. Mem. N.E.A., Am. Guild Organists (dean Central Neb. chpt. 1974—), Nat. Assn. Humanities Edn. (Neb. State chpt. pres. 1972-73, nat. bd. dirs. 1974—), Music Educators Nat. Conf., Pi Kappa Lambda. Lutheran. Club: Imperial Jaycees (chmn. internat. relations com. 1974-75). Home: Box 711 Imperial NE 69033 Office: 723 Broadway Imperial NE 69033

CHRISTENSEN, JERRY MELVIN, agrl. engr.; b. Volga, S.D., May 5, 1949; s. Melvin Nicholi and Louise (Werner) C.; B.S., S.D. State U., 1972. Engr., Morton Bldgs., Spencer, Iowa, 1972-73, Morton, Ill., 1973—. Registered profl. engr., Ill. Mem. Am. Soc. Agrl. Engrs. Democrat. Lutheran. Home: 636 S 4th Ave Morton IL 61550 Office: Morton Bldgs Inc 252 W Adams St Morton IL 61550

CHRISTENSEN, JULIEN MARTIN, psychologist, educator; b. Capron, Ill., Sept. 3, 1918; s. Martin and Lucille Marie (Edson) C.; B.S. in Accounting, U. Ill., 1940; M.A. in Exptl. Psychology, Ohio State U., 1952, Ph.D. in Exptl. Psychology, 1959; m. Imogene Elaine Willis, Mar. 23, 1954; children—Kimberly Elaine, Kyle Elise, Karen Lucille. Project engr. Aerospace Med. Research Lab, Wright-Patterson AFB, Ohio, 1946-50, br. chief, 1950-52, asst. div. chief, 1952-56, dir., 1956-74; chmn. dept. indsl. engring. qnd ops. research Coll. Engring., Wayne State U., Detroit, 1974-77, prof., 1977—; cons. Standard Oil, N.Y.C., 1965, Nat. Acad. Sci., 1965-66, United Air Lines, Chgo., 1966, Nat. Safety Council, Chgo., 1968—; lectr. U. Mich., 1960—, Wittenberg U., 1950-57, U. Dayton, 1959-65; adj. prof. Wright State U., 1965-74; pub. speaker Wright-Patterson AFB Pub. Information Office, 1950-74. Served with USAAF,

1943-46. NSF fellow, 1957; recipient Franklin V. Taylor award Am. Psychol. Assn., 1969; Exceptional Civilian Service award USAF, 1966. Fellow Am. Psychol. Assn., Human Factors Soc.; mem. Air Force Assn. (citation of honor 1966), Tau Beta Pi, Pi Mu Epsilon, Alpha Kappa Psi, Psi Chi. Lutheran (pres. vestry 1971). Clubs: Explorers (N.Y.C); Pole Vaulters (Fairbanks, Alaska). Contbr. articles to profl. jours. Office: Dept Indsl Engring and Ops Research Coll Engring Wayne State U Detroit MI 48202

CHRISTENSEN, MARGUERITE ALICE, librarian; b. Trout Lake, Wis., Aug. 24, 1917; d. Peter Carl and Alice (Cady) Christensen; B.A., U. Wis., 1938, B.L.S., 1939. Librarian, high sch. and Pub. Library, Bloomer, Wis., 1939-41; asst. librarian Wis. State U., Superior, 1941-43, Carroll Coll., Waukesha, Wis., 1943-45; asst. reference librarian U. Wis.-Madison, 1945-66, head gen. reference dept., 1967—. Mem. ALA, Assn. Coll. and Research Libraries. Home: 4469 Hillcrest Dr Madison WI 53705

CHRISTENSEN, NORMAN ANTON, physician, educator, med. research; b. Brigham City, Utah, Mar. 8, 1915; s. Orson Anton and Rae (Noble) C.; student Weber Coll., 1930-35; B.S., U. Utah, 1937; M.D., U. Chgo., 1941; M.S. in Medicine, U. Minn., 1948; m. Kathleen Bowen, Sept. 1, 1939; children—Carol Rae, Norman Anton, Paul Bowen, Steven Ross. Intern in medicine and surgery Presbyn. Hosp., Chgo., 1941-42; fellow in internal medicine Mayo Grad. Sch., Rochester, Minn., 1942-44, 46-47, cons. internal medicine, 1947-76, instr., 1949-54, asst. prof. internal medicine, 1954-63, asso. prof. clin. medicine, 1963-71, prof. clin. medicine, 1971-73, prof. internal medicine, 1973-76, emeritus, 1976—; practice medicine specializing in internal medicine, Mayo Clinic, Rochester, Minn., 1942-44, 46-76; mem. staffs St. Marys, Meth. hosps., 1942-44, 46-76; mem. Rochester Bd. Health, 1954-60, pres., 1956-60. Served with M.C. USNR, 1944-46. Decorated Bronze Star (3); recipient Sci. Exhibit award Chgo. Med. Soc., 1958, Spl. Lecture award Japan chpt. Am. Coll. Chest Physicians, 1963, Spl. Lecture Participation award Pan Am. Med. Assn., 1967; diplomate Am. Bd. Internal Medicine. Fellow AMA (Billing's Silver medal 1957, Spl. certificate for movie 1969), A.C.P., Am. Coll. Chest Physicians, Royal Soc. Medicine (London); mem. World Med. Assn. (Spl. award for movie 1963), Minn. State Med. Assn. (exec. com.), Zumbro Valley Med. Soc., Minn. Soc. Internal Medicine, Pan Am. Med. Assn. (diplomate internal medicine), Alumni Assn. May Found. for Med. Edn. and Research, Am. Med. Writers Assn., Sigma Xi; hon. mem. Ecuadorian chpt. Pan Am. Med. Assn., Dental Forum of Milw. Club: Rotary (dir. chpt. 1968-69) (Rochester). Contbr. numerous articles to profl. jours. Home: 9304 Glen Oaks Circle Sun City AZ 85351 Office: Mayo Clinic Rochester MN 55901

CHRISTENSEN, PAUL MANDELL, elec. engr.; b. Cannon Falls, Minn., Nov. 23, 1931; s. Mandell Paul and Stella (Johnson) C.; B.E.E., Iowa State U., 1959; m. Mary Kathleen Shannon, Dec. 23, 1952; children—Kathleen Ann, Karen Jean, John David. Clk., Standard Oil Co. (Ind.), Iowa City and Sioux City, Iowa, 1950-52, 54-55; with Fisher Controls Co., Marshalltown, Iowa, 1959—, head dept. electronics design, 1961-68, mgr. elec. engring., 1969-72, dir. electronics technology, 1972-76, dir. research and engring., 1976—. Served with U.S. Army, 1952-54. Mem. IEEE, Instrument Soc. Am. Address: Fisher Process Equipment Ltd Brenchly House Week St Maidstone Kent ME14 1RF England also 205 S Center St Marshalltown IA 50158

CHRISTENSEN, ROBERT WAYNE, civil engring. exec.; b. Omaha, Aug. 16, 1932; s. Peter Christian and Agnes Francis (Dolezal) C.; B.S. in Civil Engring., Northwestern U., 1955, M.S., 1956; m. Mary Ellen Clark, June 15, 1957; children—Sheila Ann, Peter Clark. Dir. capital improvement program div. Chgo. Dept. City Planning, 1959-61; exec. dir. Pub. Bldg. Commn. Chgo., 1961-74; v.p. Seay & Thomas Inc. real estate, Chgo., 1974-76; dir. Globe Engring. Co., chmn. Globecon Inc., chmn. Globe Services Internat., Inc., Chgo., 1976—; mayor's adminstrv. officer, Chgo., 1965-68; dep. commr. Chgo. Dept. Devel. and Planning, 1968-70. Named as One of Ten Outstanding Young Men Chgo., Jr. C. of C., 1961; recipient Service award Northwestern U., 1971. Mem. ASCE, Northwestern U. Engring. Alumni Assn. (pres. 1970-72), Delta Tau Delta, Tau Beta Pi. Democrat. Roman Catholic. Clubs: Mid Day, Tavern, Economic of Chicago, Ridgemoor Country. Home: 5642 N Newark St Chicago IL 60631 Office: 222 N Dearborn St Chicago IL 60601

CHRISTENSEN, WALLACE M., radio sta. mgr.; b. Tyler, Minn., June 21, 1946; s. Verner W. and Iva (Sharp) C.; grad. Brown Inst. Broadcasting and Electronics, 1965; m. Diane Louise Sween, Feb. 3, 1965; children—Carmen Cyril, Collin Charles, April Heather. Announcer, KYNT radio sta., Yankton, S.D., 1965-66; announcer YLOH, Pipestone, Minn., 1966-72, salesman, 1966-70, sales mgr., 1970-72, gen. mgr., 1972-76, owner, 1976—. Home: Route 2 Box 173 Lake Benton MN 56149 Office: KLOH Radio Pipestone MN 56164

CHRISTENSON, CHRIS, photographer; b. Bedford, O., Nov. 13, 1925; s. Chris and Ilah (Fivecoate) C.; grad. high sch.; m. Eunice McAdoo, Sept. 1, 1957; children—Jeffrey, Joan, Susan. Photographer, Bedford Pictorial Studio, 1948-58; pres., Chris Christenson Photographer, Inc., Bedford, 1958—; track photographer, Thistledown, Randall Park, Cranwood, Summit, 1961; staff photographer Ohio Thoroughbred mag., 1971—. Home: 719 Johnson St Bedford OH 44146 Office: 39 Woodrow St Bedford OH 44146

CHRISTGAU, MERTON ALBERT, elec. engr.; b. Mpls., Aug. 10, 1920; s. Albert William and Ruth (Swenson) C.; B.E.E., U. Minn., 1946. Draftsman Audio Devel. Co., Mpls., 1941-42; radar trainee Civilian Signal Corps, Omaha, 1942; elec. and radio insp. Glenn L. Martin-Nebr. Co., 1942-45; draftsman, engr. Engring. Research Asso., St. Paul, 1946-52; engr. Autonetics div. N. Am. Aviation, Downey, Calif., 1852-58, Maico, Mpls., 1958-60; elec. engr. audio/visual magnetic products 3M Co., St. Paul, 1960—. Alternate radio officer Dist. 4, Los Angeles County Disaster Civil Def. Communications. Mem. Aircraft Owners and Pilots Assn., IEEE, Standards Engrs. Soc. (sec.-treas. 1962-65), Audio Engring. Soc., Am. Inst. Aero. and Astronautics, Radio Amateur Satellite Corp., 3M Amateur Radio Club (pres. 1976), Am. Radio Relay League, Minn. Alumni Assn. Home: 1843 Berkeley Ave St Paul MN 55105 Office: 3M Center St Paul MN 55101

CHRISTIAN, EDWARD KIEREN, radio sta. exec.; b. Detroit, June 26, 1944; s. William Edward and Dorothy Miriam (Kieren) C.; student Mich. State U., 1962-64; B.A., Wayne State U., 1966; m. Judith Dallaire, Nov. 21, 1966; children—Eric, Dana. Mgr., John C. Butler Co., Detroit, 1968-69; nat. sales mgr. WCAR Radio, Detroit, WSUN Radio, St. Petersburg Fla., 1969-70; v.p., gen. mgr. WCER Radio, Charlotte, Mich., 1970-74; exec. v.p. WNIC AM-FM Radio, Detroit, 1974—. Pres., United Way, Charlotte, 1973-74, Charlotte Community Nursery Sch., 1973-74. Del. Republican State Conv., 1974. Bd. dirs. Greater Detroit Safety Council. Mem. Dearborn C. of C. (dir.). Kiwanian. Home: 795 Lakeland St Grosse Pointe MI 48230 Office: 15001 Michigan Ave Dearborn MI 48126

CHRISTIAN, JOE CLARK, physician; b. Marshall, Okla., Sept. 12, 1934; s. Roy John and Katherine Elizabeth (Beeby) C.; B.S., Okla. State U., 1956; M.S., U. Ky., 1959, Ph.D., 1960, M.D., 1964; m. Shirley Ann Yancey, June 5, 1960; children—Roy Clark, Charles David. Intern, resident Vanderbilt Hosp., Nashville, 1964-66; practice medicine specializing in med. genetics, Indpls., 1966—; asst. prof. med. genetics Ind. U. Med. Sch., Indpls., 1966-69, asso. prof., 1969-74, prof., 1974—, dir. Human Genetics Center, 1975—. Served with AUS, 1956. Mem. Am. Soc. Human Genetics, Am. Oil Chemists Soc., Am. Heart Assn., Internat. Soc. Fat Research, Am. Forestry Assn., Am. Dermatoglyphics Assn., Internat. Soc. Twin Studies (chmn. working group on methodology), Sigma Xi, Alpha Omega Alpha. Contbr. articles to profl. jours. Home: 4738 Jennys Rd Indianapolis IN 46208 Office: 1100 W Michigan St Indianapolis IN 46202

CHRISTIAN, RICHARD CARLTON, advt. exec.; b. Dayton, Ohio, Nov. 29, 1924; s. Raymond A. and Louise (Gamber) C.; B.S. in Bus. Adminstrn., Miami U., Oxford, O., 1948; M.B.A., Northwestern U., 1949; student Denison U., The Citadel, Biarritz Am. U.; m. Audrey Bongartz, Sept. 10, 1949; children—Ann Carra, Richard Carlton. Mktg. analyst Nat. Cash Register Co., Dayton, 1948, Rockwell Mfg. Co., Pitts., 1949-50; exec. v.p. Marsteller Inc., Chgo., 1951-60, pres., 1960-75, chmn. bd., 1975—; dir., chmn. Bus Publs. Audit of Circulation, Inc., 1969-75; dir. Wilmette Bank; speaker, author mktg., sales mgmt., mktg. research and advt. Trustee Nat. Coll. Edn., Northwestern U., 1970-74; chmn. exec. com. James Webb Young Fund Edn., U. Ill., 1962-75; adv. bd. Sch. Journalism U. Ga. Served with inf., AUS, 1942-46; ETO. Decorated Bronze Star, Purple Heart. Mem. Am. Mktg. Assn. (dir. 1953-54), Indsl. Mktg. Assn. (founder, chmn. 1951), Bus./Profl. Publs. Advt. Assn. (life mem. Chgo.; pres. Chgo. 1954-55, nat. v.p. 1955-58, G.D. Crain Jr. award 1977), Northwestern U. Bus. Sch. Alumni Assn. (founder, pres.), Am. Mgmt. Assn., Am. Assn. Advt. Agys. (dir., chmn. 1976-77), Nat. Advt. Rev. Council (pres. 1976-77), Northwestern U. Alumni Assn. (nat. pres. 1968-70), Better Bus. Bur. Chgo. (council, dir.), Chgo. Assn. Commerce and Industry, Council Fgn. Relations, Alpha Delta Sigma, Beta Gamma Sigma, Delta Sigma Pi, Phi Gamma Delta. Baptist (trustee). Clubs: Sky (N.Y.C.); Chicago, Mid-America, Executives, Economic (Chgo.); Kenilworth; Westmoreland Country (Wilmette, Ill.); Pine Valley Golf (Clementon, N.J.). Home: 132 Oxford Rd Kenilworth IL 60043 Office: Marsteller Inc 1 E Wacker Dr Chicago IL 60601

CHRISTIANSEN, CHARLES LESTER, dentist; b. Manitowoc, Wis., May 26, 1906; s. Charles Peter and Emma Jane (Houghton) C.; B.S., Marquette U., 1928, D.D.S., 1928; m. Elizabeth Sarah Baccus, May 25, 1946; children—Janet Rose, Charles Dittloff. Pvt. practice dentistry, Milw., 1928—. Pres., trustee Almarc Realty Corp., 1935—. Served with USNR, 1943-46. Mem. Am., Wis., Greater Milw. (del. 1956-57) dental assns., Civil Air Patrol (comdr. Milw. 1941-43), Psi Omega. Mem. De Molay. Home: High Point Beach Rd Port Washington WI 53074 Office: 6114 W Capitol Dr Milwaukee WI 53216

CHRISTIANSEN, CLARENCE HERBERT, lawyer, ins. exec.; b. Inwood, Iowa, July 2, 1923; s. Andrew and Ruth (Renshaw) C.; B.A., State U. Iowa, 1947, J.D., 1948; student Purdue U., 1943; m. Donna Mae Geertz, Mar. 20, 1943; children—Joan Lee (Mrs. John Green), Dana Andrew, Scott Charles. Admitted to Iowa bar, 1948, U.S. Supreme Ct. bar, 1960; practice law, Davenport, Iowa, 1948—; partner law firm Christiansen & Lowry, Lambach, Kopf, & Berger, 1949-53, partner, 1953-54; sr. partner Kopf & Christiansen, 1954-64; sr. partner Lambach, Christiansen, Stevenson & Goebel, 1964-70; sec., treas., dir. Profl. Arts Bldg., Ltd,, 1961-65, sec., 1965-71; sec., treas., dir., mem. mgmt. com. Life Securities Iowa, Inc., 1964-73, gen. counsel, 1964—, v.p., 1977—; pres., treas,, dir. Kopf & Assos., Ltd., 1959-72, gen. counsel, 1959—; pres., treas., dir. Mid-Am. Securities Co.; pres., dir. Am. Security Life Ins. Co., 1968-70; exec. v.p., sec., treas., dir., gen. counsel Regency Nat. Ltd., 1969-72, gen. counsel, 1969—, v.p., 1977—; sec., gen. counsel, dir. BEC Products, Inc., BEC Pressure Controls Corp., Electro-Plasma, Inc.; sec., gen. counsel, dir., mem. mgmt. com. BEC Industries, Ltd., 1975—; sec.-treas., dir. Kolar Corp., Main at Locust Pharmacy, Inc.; exec. v.p. Regency Life Ins. Co., 1967-70; sec., dir. Audio Odyssey, Ltd., 1975—; sec. Security State Trust & Savs. Bank, 1968-69; gen. counsel Financial Security Life Ins. Co., 1970—, v.p., 1977—. Sect. chmn. Community Chest, 1951, 52. Pub. chmn. Young Republicans, 1953-54. Served to capt. USMC, 1943-46, 50-51. Mem. Fed., Am. (vice chmn. automobile com. of ins. sect. 1964-67, mem. life ins. com. 1970—), Iowa, Scott County bar assns., Fedn. Ins. Counsel (life ins. com. 1976—), Delta Tau Delta, Gamma Eta Gamma. Lutheran. Mason (32 deg., Shriner), Optimist (pres. Davenport 1949-50, pres. Moline 1974-75). Home: Apt 4 Carriage Club 3215 E Locust St Davenport IA 52803 Office: Profl Arts Bldg Davenport IA 52803

CHRISTIANSEN, H. DOUGLAS, employment agy. exec.; b. Chgo., Aug. 1, 1940; s. Henry and Berneice May (Manz) C.; B.A., U. Colo., 1967; m. Jill Pomeroy, May 27, 1966; children—Amy Christiansen, John Douglas. Counselor, mgr. Chem. Industries Personnel, Chgo., 1967-73; pres. Chem. Personnel Search, Westchester, 1973—; dir. Buntrock Industries Inc., Chgo. Served with U.S. Army, 1959-62. Republican. Methodist. Home: 129 S Madison St LaGrange IL 60525 Office: 1127 S Mannheim St Westchester IL 60153

CHRISTIE, LAURIE MARY, leasing corp. exec.; b. Boston, Apr. 10, 1932; d. Wellman Blake and Mary Lily (Sheridan) C.; A.B., Regis Coll., 1953; postgrad. Boston U. Sch. Social Work, 1955. Caseworker, N.H. Dept. Pub. Welfare, Portsmouth, 1953-54, New Eng. Home for Little Wanderers, Boston, 1954-57; personnel asst., wage, salary and ins. adminstr. Itek Corp., Lexington, Mass., 1958-60, div. adminstr. facilities and planning, 1960-63; with Chandler Leasing Corp. subs. Walter E. Heller & Co., Chgo., 1963—, v.p. nat. mktg. programs, 1971-73, v.p. ops., 1973-76, v.p. adminstrn., 1976—, asst. sec. parent co., 1977—. Mem. Regis Coll. Alumnae Assn. (dir. 1961-64). Home: 1615 E Central Rd Arlington Heights IL 60005 Office: 105 W Adams St Chicago IL 60603

CHRISTIN, VIOLET MARGUERITE, ret. banker; b. Chgo., Oct. 4, 1903; d. Charles A. and Eva M. (Bosse) Christin; student Northwestern U., 1936-37, Am. Inst. Banking, 1955—; Ph.D., Colo. State Christian Coll. With Nat. Bank Austin, 1922—, asst. sec., 1953-57, sec., 1957-65, sec., asst. v.p., 1965-75, also cons., sec. marketing com. Mem. Am. Inst. Banking, Ill. Bankers Assn. (50 yr. club), Assn. Chgo. Bank Women, Nat. Assn. Bank Women, Bank Marketing Assn., Chgo. Financial Advertisers (dir., treas.). Clubs: Executives, Advertising, Press (Chgo.). Home: 805 N Grove Ave Oak Park IL 60302 Office: 5645 W Lake St Chicago IL 60644

CHRISTISON, WILLIAM HENRY, III, lawyer; b. Moline, Ill., Aug. 30, 1936; s. William Henry and Gladys Evelyn (Matherly) C.; B.A., Northwestern U., 1958; LL.B., U. Iowa, 1961; m. Mary Proctor Stone, Sept. 16, 1958; children—William Henry IV, Elizabeth S., Caroline S. Admitted to Ill. bar, 1961; partner firm Baymiller & Christison, Peoria, Ill., 1961—; permanent trustee in bankruptcy U.S. Dist. Ct., So. Dist. of Ill., Peoria, 1967—. Vice pres., dir. W.H.C., Inc., Moline, 1958—; dir., mem. exec. com., trust investment com. 1st Nat. Bank, Peoria, 1967—. Mem. Peoria Sesquicentennial Commn., 1968. Bd. dirs. John C. Proctor Endowment, 1964—, pres. 1972—; bd. dirs. Meth. Med. Center Found., Ill. Masonic Youth Found. Mem. Am., Ill. (dist. sec. 1966), Iowa, Peoria (dir. 1968-69) bar assns., Greater Peoria Legal Aid Soc. (dir. 1971-74), Peoria Hist. Soc., Phi Gamma Delta, Phi Delta Phi. Mason (Shriner, Jester), Rotarian (dir. 1972-75). Clubs: Ill. Valley Yacht and Canoe, Country (Peoria) Home: 3217 W Prince George Ct Peoria IL 61614 Office: 700 1st Nat Bank Bldg Peoria IL 61602

CHRISTMAN, FRANK LEO, advt. agency exec.; b. St. Joseph, Mo., Mar. 28, 1947; s. Leo J. and Emma (Thompson) C.; B.J., U. Mo., 1969; m. Martha May Morgan, May 7, 1971; children—Kelly Ann, Glenn Scott. Media dir. Fletcher/Mayo/Assos., St. Joseph Mo., 1969-71, copy writer, 1971-73, account exec., 1973-75, account supr., 1975-76, v.p., 1976—. Served with U.S. Army, 1969-70. Recipient Curators award U. Mo., 1965. Mem. Nat. Agri-Mktg. Assn.

CHRISTMAN, PHILIP W., savs. and loan co. exec.; b. Barnesville, Ohio, Sept. 5, 1942; s. Philip M. and Kathryn L. (Herbert) C.; B.S.B.A., Franklin U., 1967; m. Judith K. Fought, Sept. 14, 1963; 1 son, Erik James. Asst. mgr. Crown Finance Corp. Columbus, Ohio, 1963-66; asst. mgr. pub. relations, Atty. Gen's Office State of Ohio, Columbus, 1966-67; treas. Columbus (Ohio) Savings Loan Assn., 1967-70, v.p., 1970-75, pres., 1975—, also dir.; pres., dir. Columbus Service & Mortgage Co., 1975—; dir. Community Devel. Corp. Republican. Clubs: Masons. Home: 490 Cherrington Rd Westerville OH 43081 Office: 155 N High St Columbus OH 43215

CHRISTMAN, RICHARD HENRY, computer specialist; b. Chgo., July 8, 1944; s. Henry and Ruth (Hutnik) C.; student Am. Acad. Art, 1962-63; Asso. Sci., Triton Coll., 1967; B.S. in Bus. Adminstrn., Roosevelt U., 1971; m. Sandra O. Lodding, Oct. 18, 1969; children—Noel, Christine. Computer ops. staff Automatic Electric Co., 1965-66; programmer Triton Coll., River Grove, Ill., 1966-67, lead analyst, 1967-69, exec. dir. info. systems, 1975—; analyst, asst. dir. College of Lake County, 1969-71; sr. account mgr. Burroughs Corp., Milw., 1971-75, dist. product mgr., 1975; lectr. and cons. computer sci. Mem. Assn. System Mgmt., Data Processing Mgmt. Assn., Ill. Assn. Ednl. Data Systems. Club: Lions. Patentee in field. Home: 330 W Morse St Bartlett IL 60103 Office: 2000 5th Ave River Grove IL 60171

CHRISTNER, GEORGE EDWARD, JR., mfg. co. exec.; b. Wadsworth, Ohio, Jan. 17, 1935; s. George Edward and Donna (Evans) C.; B.S. in Bus. Adminstrn. cum laude, Kent State U., 1956, M.B.A., 1963; m. Marilyn Jean Husak, June 29, 1957; children—Laura Jean, Kenneth Ward. Prodn. control specialist Babcock & Wilcox Co., Barberton, Ohio, 1956-59, product specialist, 1959-61, market analyst, 1961-64; asst. to pres. Beasley Industries, Inc., Columbus, Ohio, 1965, controller, Hilliard, Ohio, 1966-70, v.p., gen. mgr. Central region, 1970-72, v.p., gen. mgr. automotive operations, 1973-76, exec. v.p., 1976-77; exec. v.p., gen. mgr. Zero Mfg. Co., Washington, Mo., 1977—. Mem. Am. Marketing Assn., Am. Prodn. and Inventory Control Assn., Delta Upsilon. Home: 22 Seven Oaks Dr Chesterfield MO 63017 Office: 811 Duncan Ave Washington MO 63090

CHRISTOFFEL, EVERETTE THOMAS, chief engr.; b. Bradford, S.D., Feb. 16, 1918; s. Walter Frederick and Regina (Raether) C.; grad. high sch., 1936; m. Helen Josephine Johnson, Jan. 12, 1946; children—Thomas Joseph, Diane (Mrs. Thomas Voight), Penny Lynn. With Metal Ware Corp., Two Rivers, Wis., 1939-41, 45—, purchasing agt., 1945-55, product engr., 1955—. Treas. Two Rivers chpt. A.R.C., 1956-58; pres. P.T.A., 1957-58. Served with USNR, 1941-45. Home: 2827 Forest Ave Two Rivers WI 54241 Office: 1700 Monroe St Two Rivers WI 54241

CHRISTOPHER, GLENN AUBREY, pub. co. exec.; b. St. Louis, Dec. 17, 1921; s. James William and Grace Belloit (Crews) C.; student Washington U., St. Louis, 1949-55; m. Betty L. Stoerk, July 30, 1943; children—Judith (Mrs. Michael L. McDermott), Nancy (Mrs. O.R. Oberheuser). Asst. controller Pulitzer Pub. Co., St. Louis, 1955-65, mgr. info. systems, 1966-69, sec.-treas., dir., 1969—; sec.-treas., dir. Star Pub. Co., Tucson, KOAT-TV, Inc., Albuquerque, KETV, Omaha. Trustee Pulitzer Pub. Co. Voting Trust; bd. dirs., sec.-treas. St. Louis Post-Dispatch Found.; bd. dirs. Blue Cross Hosp. Services, Inc., St. Louis, Better Bus. Bur., St. Louis. Served with AUS, 1942-45. Mem. Inst. Newspaper Controllers and Finance Officers. Republican. Presbyn. (elder 1955—, trustee 1957—). Home: 10022 Charoin Way St Louis MO 63128 Office: 900 N 12th Blvd St Louis MO 63101

CHRISTOPHER, NORMAN FRANKLIN, physicist; b. Irvine, Ky., Sept. 23, 1930; s. Thomas Ashcraft and Anna Maude (Turner) C.; m. Jane Anne Dean, June 16, 1952; children—Paula, Phyllis. B.A., Ky. Wesleyan Coll., 1952; M.S., Ohio U., 1969. Shift chemist Liberty Powder Def. Corp., Baraboo, Wis., 1952-54; shift supr. Goodyear Atomic Corp., Piketon, Ohio, 1954-57, sect. head mass spectrometry dept., 1957—. Mem. Am. Soc. Mass Spectrometry. Home: 406 S Market St Waverly OH 45690 Office: PO Box 628 Piketon OH 45661

CHRISTOPHERSON, CHARLES ARCHIBALD, lawyer; b. Sioux Falls, S.D., Aug. 21, 1907; s. Charles Andrew and Abbie (Deyoe) C.; B.A., U. S.D., 1929, LL.B., 1931; postgrad. George Washington U., 1929-30; m. Dorothy Leone Robinson, Jan. 15, 1938; 1 dau., Margaret Ellen. Admitted to S.D. bar, 1931; practiced in Sioux Falls, 1931—; mem. firm Christopherson & Christopherson, 1936-51, Christopherson, Bailin & Anderson, and predecessor, 1952—. Vice consul for Norway in S.D., 1953—. Bd. dirs. S.D. Childrens Home, 1956-72, S.D. Scottish Rite Ednl. Found., 1960-68. Served with USNR, 1944-47. Mem. Am., Minnehaha County bar assns., State Bar S.D., Phi Delta Theta. Republican. Congregationalist. Mason (33 deg.), Kiwanian. Home: 809 Ridge Rd Sioux Falls SD 57105 Office: 509 S Dakota Ave Sioux Falls SD 57105

CHRISTOPOULOS, ANGELOS CONSTANTINE, psychiatrist; b. Raptopoulo, Greece, Aug. 18, 1939; s. Constantine Efstathios and Katerina Harry (Synadinos) C.; came to U.S., 1966, naturalized, 1975; M.D., Nat. U. Athens, 1963; m. Maria Balkoura, July 26, 1969; 1 dau., Katerina. Intern, Cook County Hosp., Chgo., 1966-67; resident psychiatry U. Mo. Med. Center, Columbia, 1967-69; resident psychiatry Ill. State Psychiat. Inst., Chgo., 1969-70, staff psychiatrist, 1970—; attending psychiatrist Presbyn.-St. Lukes Hosp., Chgo.; asst. prof. psychiatry U. Ill. Med. Sch., 1973—, Rush Med. Coll., Chgo., 1973—. Served with Greek Air Force, 1963-66. Mem. AMA, Am. Psychiat. Assn. Office: 1601 W Taylor St Chicago IL 60612

CHRISTY, DONALD, banker, state ofcl.; b. Scott City, Kans., Nov. 23, 1909; s. Marion Estes and Effice (Ater) C.; B.S., Kans. State U., 1933; M.S., Tex. A. and M. U., 1938; m. Helen G. Shedd, May 28, 1933; children—Donald O., Arthur E., Alice. Mem. faculty Tex. A. and M. U., 1933-42; with First Nat. Bank, Scott City, Kans., 1946—, pres., 1961—; mem. Kans. Senate, 1968-77. Mem. adv. com. equipment and structures U.S. Dept. Agr., 1959-63; mem. Kans. Bd. Agr., 1951-63, Kans. Water Resources Bd., 1955-69, Kans. Watershed, 1953-57. Bd. dirs. Kans. State Fair, 1951-63, Scott County Fair, 1945-68. Mem. Bd. Edn., 1943-46. Recipient Outstanding

Individual of Yr. award Am. Soc. Agrl. Engrs., 1972. Mem. Farm Bur., C. of C. Mem. Christian Ch. Lion. Home: 1005 Washington St Scott City KS 67871 Office: 501 Main St Scott City KS 67871

CHRISTY, JOHN JAMES, rehab. center adminstr.; b. Cranston, R.I., Sept. 1, 1914; s. Anthony Frank and Frances Mary (Zito) C.; B.S., U. R.I., 1938; m. Yolande Jeanne Morin, Aug. 1, 1944; children—Robert M., Thomas A., Rena F., Marla J., Susan E. Reporter Providence Jour., 1932-38; grad. asst. U. R.I., Kingston, 1938-39; with Atlantic Refining Co., Providence, R.I., 1939-41, comml. salesman, New Haven, 1946-47; commd. maj., U.S. Army, 1947, advanced through grades to col., 1961, ret. 1969; exec. dir. Ind. Cath. Conf., Indpls., 1969-73; exec. dir. Crossroads Rehab. Center, Indpls., 1973—; sec. Indpls. Healing Community Project, 1975—. Chmn. pub. relations com. Indpls. Red Cross, 1970-74, recipient volunteer award, 1974; mem. Indpls. 500 festival com., 1966-77. Bd. dirs. Cath. Communications Center, Indpls., 1970-74. Decorated D.S.C., D.S.M., Silver Star, Bronze Star medal, Purple Heart. Mem. Assn. U.S. Army (pres. Ind. chpt. 1973-75), Pub. Relations Soc. Am., Am. Legion, V.F.W., Mil. Order World Wars, Indpls. C. of C., Indpls. Athletic Club. K.C., Rotarian (dir. 1972-74). Home: 7216 Brompton Ct Indianapolis IN 46250 Office: 3242 Sutherland Ave Indianapolis IN 46205

CHRON, GUSTAV NICHOLAS, ednl. adminstr.; b. Chgo., June 6, 1926; s. Nicholas Constantine and Jennie (Athans) C.; B.A., DePaul U., 1952; M.A., Northwestern U., 1954; B.A. in Aeros., Stanton U., 1965, Ph.D., 1976; M. Ed., Loyola U., Chgo., 1969; J.D., Clinton U., 1971; Ph.D., Met. Coll. Inst., London, 1974; m. Helen Hoegerl, Sept. 18, 1948; children—Edward, Karen, Timothy. Mem. staff Chgo. Better Bus. Bur., 1954-58; tchr. Northbrook (Ill.) elementary schs., 1958-60, Northbrook Jr. High Sch., 1960-63, Glenbrook South High Sch., Glenview, Ill., 1963-64; adminstrv. asst. Comsat div. Trust Dept. Continental Ill. Nat. Bank, Chgo., 1964-65; prin. Westmoor Sch., Northbrook, 1966—; dir. Northbrook Dist. 28 Summer Sch., 1971, 77; asst. prof. aeros. Grad. Research Inst., East Coast U., 1975—. Served with USNR, 1943-46. Decorated Air medal, Purple Heart, Navy Commendation medal. Mem. Nat., Ill. elementary sch. prins. assns., Am. Judicature Soc., Navy League, Navy Inst., Am. Legion, Assn. Naval Aviation, U.S. Parachute Assn., Nat. Eagle Scout Assn., Am. Philatelic Soc., Phi Delta Kappa, Delta Theta Phi, Pi Gamma Mu. Home: Chicago IL Office: 2500 Cherry Ln Northbrook IL 60062

CHU, JOHNSON CHIN SHENG, physician; b. Peiping, China, Sept. 26, 1918; s. Harry S. P. and Florence (Young) C.; M.D., St. John's U., 1945; m. Sylvia Cheng, June 11, 1949; children—Stephen, Timothy. Came to U.S., 1948, naturalized, 1957. Intern U. Hosp., Shanghai, 1944-45; resident, research fellow N.Y.U. Hosp., 1948-50; resident, physician in charge State Hosp. and Med. Center, Weston, W.Va., 1951-56; chief services, clin. dir. State Hosp., Logansport, Ind., 1957—. Fellow Am. Psychiatric Assn., Am. Coll. Chest Physicians; mem. A.M.A., Ind. Med. Assn., Cass County Med. Soc., A.A.A.S. Research in cardiology and pharmacology. Contbr. articles profl. jours. Home: E 36 Lake Shafer Monticello IN 47960 Office: State Hosp Logansport IN 46947 also Southeastern Medical Center Walton IN 46994

CHUA, CHENG LOK, educator; b. Singapore, Jan. 5, 1938; s. Yew Cheng and Kuo Hui (Tan) C.; came to U.S., 1956, naturalized, 1965; B.A., DePauw U., 1960; M.A., U. Conn., 1962, Ph.D., 1968; m. Gretchen Taeko Sasaki, July 26, 1965; children—Iu-Hui Jarrell, Poh-Pheng Jaime. Part-time instr. English, U. Conn., Storrs, 1960-65; asst. prof. English, U. Mich., Ann Arbor, 1965-72; lectr., sr. lectr. English, U. Singapore, 1972-74; lectr. English, Calif. State U. at Fresno, 1974—; Nat. Endowment Humanities postdoctoral fellow Yale U., 1976-77, vis. fellow comparative lit., 1976-77; vis. asso. prof. Moorhead (Minn.) State U., 1977-78. Australasian Univs. Lang. and Lit. Assn. grantee, 1975. Mem. Modern Lang. Assn., Multi-Ethnic Lit. of U.S., AAUP. Home: 1102 S 16th St Moorhead MN 56560

CHUCK, KENNETH CHARLES, restaurant exec.; b. Sheboygan, Wis., Jan. 28, 1927; s. Charles and Jessie (Spendal) C.; student pub. schs.; m. Mary Ann Susan, Apr. 15, 1950; children—Karen, Nancy, Kenneth L. Formed Chuck's Supper Club, Oconomowoc, Wis., 1947—, pres., 1968—; pres. Hospitality Industry Inc., 1975—, So. Gateway Inc., 1973—. Town constable Oconomowoc, 1965-73, mem. Planning Bd., 1968—; officer Summit Vol. Fire Dept., 1971, 72, 73. Served with AUS, 1945-47. Recipient Golden Knife award Am. Dairy Assn., 1976. Mem. U.S. Trotting Assn., Tavern League Wis., Nat., Wis. (dir.) restaurant assns., Oconomowoc C. of C. (dir.). Roman Catholic. Club: Kiwanis. Home: 37304 Valley Rd Oconomowoc WI 53066 Office: 37238 Valley Rd Oconomowoc WI 53066

CHUKWU, ETHELBERT NWAKUCHE, mathematician; b. Mbano, Nigeria, Nov. 22, 1940; s. Nwachukwu Uwa-ezoke and Ihejere Teresa Chukwu; came to U.S., 1962; B.S.; Brown U., 1965; M.S., U. Nigeria, 1973; Ph.D., Case Western Res. U., 1972; m. Regina Chifo-anozo Chukwunyere, Dec. 26, 1966; children—Ezeigwe, Uchenna, Obioma. Asst. lectr. U. Nigeria, Nsukka, 1970; lectr. in math. Cleve. State U., 1972, asst. prof., 1972-76, asso. prof., 1976—. Nigerian State scholar, 1954-60; African Scholarship Program for Am. Univs., 1962-65; Univ. fellow, 1970-72; recipient research initiation award, 1974, 77. Mem. Am. Math. Soc. Roman Catholic. Contbr. writings to profl. publs. in Nigeria and U.S. Home: 2104 Renrock Rd Cleveland Heights OH 44118 Office: Dept Math Cleveland State U Cleveland OH 44115

CHUNG, CHAI-SIK, educator; b. Wonju, Korea, July 14, 1930; s. Young-hun and Ae-dok (Hahn) C.; M.Th., Yonsei U., 1957; B.D., Harvard, 1959; Ph.D., Boston U., 1964; m. Soon Ria Paik, Dec. 17, 1962; children—Eugene, Warren Euwon. Instr. social studies Emory U., Oxford, Ga., 1962-63; asst. prof. sociology Bethany Coll., Bethany, W.Va., 1963-65; Fla. Atlantic U., Boca Raton, Fla., 1965-66, Boston U., 1966-69; asso. prof. Heidelberg Coll., Tiffin, Ohio, 1969-72, prof., 1972—, chmn. dept., 1969—. Vis. scholar Center for Japanese and Korean Studies, U. Calif. at Berkeley, 1974. Social Sci. Research Council research grantee. Mem. Assn. Asian Studies, Soc. for Sci. Study Religion, Am. Sociol. Assn. Contbr. articles to profl. jours. Home: 229 Main St Tiffin OH 44883

CHUNG, FRANK HUAN-CHEN, chemist; b. Kiangsi, China, July 20, 1930; s. Koe-yie and Chi-ming (Hsu) C.; came to U.S., 1964, naturalized, 1974; B.S. in Chem. Engring., Chung Cheng Inst. Tech., Taiwan, 1953; M.S. (NSF fellow), Kent State U., Ohio, 1966, Ph.D. (NASA fellow), 1968; m. Doris Chu-feng Wen, Dec. 26, 1959; children—Susan, Shirley, Sonia. Instr. indsl. chemistry Chung Cheng Inst. Tech., 1954-57, lectr., 1960-63; liaison officer, guided missile sch., U.S. Army, Tex., 1958-59; research fellow phys. chemistry Kent State U., 1964-68; sr. scientist Sherwin-Williams Research Center, Chgo., 1968—. Recipient Internat. Achievement award Kent State U., 1967; Commendation letter U.S. Army, 1959. Mem. Am. Chem. Soc., Soc. Applied Spectroscopy, Am. Crystallographic Assn., Midwest Assn. Chinese Engrs. Scientists. Formulator of Matrix-Flushing Theory for quantitative interpretation of x-ray diffraction patterns of mixtures; contbr. articles to sci. jours. Office: Sherwin Williams Research Center 10909 S Cottage Grove Ave Chicago IL 60628

CHUNPRAPAPH, BOONMEE, physician, educator; b. Songkhla, Thailand, Nov. 23, 1938; s. Yen Far and Chou Sou Chen; came to U.S., 1966; M.D., Chulaongkorn U., 1964; m. Kaysorn Soottajit, Jan. 29, 1974; children—Benj, Kabil. Intern, Samaritan Hosp., Troy, N.Y., 1966-67; resident Univ. Hosp., U. Ala., Mobile, 1968-71; attending physician Oak Forest (Ill.) Hosp., 1973-74, Cook County Hosp., Chgo., 1973—; asst. prof. U. Ill. Hosp., Chgo., 1974—; cons. West Side VA Hosp., Chgo., 1975—; asst. prof. dept. orthopaedic surgery Abraham Lincoln Sch. Medicine. Diplomate Am. Bd. Orthopaedic Surgery. Mem. Am. Soc. Hand Surgery, A.C.S., Med. Assn. Thailand, Chgo., Ill. State med. socs., AMA. Buddhist. Contbr. articles to profl. jours. Home: 10 S 308 Birnam Trail Hinsdale IL 60521 Office: 840 S Wood St Chicago IL 60612

CHURCH, DOUGLAS DENTON, lawyer; b. Indpls., Jan. 22, 1944; s. Meredith Merrill and Lois Anne (Denton) C.; B.A., Ind. U., 1966, J.D., 1970; m. Kathleen Ann Gilpatrick, Aug. 20, 1966; children—Julia Justine, Jordan Douglas. Admitted to Ind. bar, 1970; practiced in Noblesville, Ind., 1970—; law clk. Appellate Ct. Ind., 1968-70; mem. firm Church, Roberts & Beerbower, Noblesville, Ind., 1970—; dir. Tipton Bldg. and Loan Assn. Chmn. Noblesville Community Forum, 1971-73; nat. co-chmn. Ind. U. Indpls. Law Sch. Fund Drive, 1972-73; profl. div. chmn. Hamilton County United Fund Drive, 1972-73, 73-74. Del. Ind. Republican Conv., 1972-76. Bd. dirs. Hamilton County Cancer Soc., 1970-72; chmn. membership campaign Riverview Hosp. Meml. Found., 1976-77. Mem. Am. (7th circuit gov. law student div., 1969-70), Ind. (mem. young lawyer sect. council 1973-77), Hamilton County (sec. 1974-75) bar assns., Noblesville Jr. C. of C., Noblesville Area C. of C. (dir., area beautification chmn. 1972), Ind. U. Indpls. Law Sch. Alumni Assn. (dir. 1974-75, sec. 1976-77), Phi Delta Phi. Elk. Home: 307 N 9th St Noblesville IN 46060 Office: 938 Conner St Noblesville IN 46060

CHURCH, JAY KAY, psychologist, educator; b. Wichita, Kans., Jan. 18, 1927; s. Kay Iverson and Gertrude (Parrish) C.; B.A., David Lipscomb Coll., 1948; M.A., Ball State U., 1961; Ph.D., Purdue U., 1963; m. Dorothy Agnes Fellerhoff, May 21, 1976; children—Karen Patrice, Caryn Annice (Mrs. Ronald Wayne Casey), Rex Warren, Max Roger. Chemist, Auburn Rubber Corp. (Ind.), 1948-49; salesman Midwestern United Life Ins. Co., Fort Wayne, Ind., 1949-52; owner, operator Tour-Rest Motel, Waterloo, Ind., 1952-66; tchr., guidance dir. Hamilton (Ind.) Community Schs., 1955-61; counselor Washington Twp., Indpls., 1961-62; faculty Ball State U., Muncie, Ind., 1963—, prof. psychology, 1971—, chmn. dept., 1970-74, chmn. bd. dirs. Fed. Credit Union, 1973-74. Pvt. practice psychol. counseling, Muncie, 1963—. Mem. Am., Midwest, Ind. psychol. assns. Home: Rural Route 6 77 E Balsam Dr Muncie IN 47302

CHURCH, MARGARET, educator; b. Boston, Apr. 8, 1920; d. Joseph W. and Sophy (Phillips) Church; A.B., Radcliffe Coll., 1941, Ph.D., 1944; M.A., Columbia, 1942. Instr. English, Temple U., 1944-46, Duke, 1946-53; asst. prof. English, Purdue U., Lafayette, Ind., 1953-61, asso. prof. English, 1961-65, prof. English, 1965—, also chmn. comparative lit. Mem. Am. Comparative Lit. Assn., Midwest Modern Lang. Assn. (pres. 1977), Modern Lang. Assn. Am., Phi Beta Kappa (hon.). Episcopalian. Author: Time and Reality: Studies in Contemporary Literature, 1963; Don Quixote, The Knight of La Mancha, 1971; also articles in field. Editorial bd. Modern Fiction Studies, 1968, co-editor, 1971—. Home: 808 N Rd 400 W West Lafayette IN 47906

CHURCHILL, COLIN WALTER, health assn. exec.; b. La Tuque, Que., Can., Jan. 24, 1918; s. Wendall Herman and Elsie Stuart (Ritchie) C.; A.B., Dartmouth, 1939; postgrad. Johns Hopkins, 1939-41, Harvard, 1949; m. Jane Burch Athey, May 20, 1961; children—Colin Walter, Wendall S. Clk., Boston & Maine R.R., Boston, 1944-45; research asso. NRC, Washington, 1945-47; with Johns Hopkins U. and Hosp., Balt., 1939-41, 45-63; dir. Hosp. Research and Ednl. Trust, Chgo., 1963—. Cons. HEW, 1968-73. Served with USNR, 1941-44. Clubs: University (Washington); Canadian (N.Y.C.); Skokie Country (Glencoe, Ill.). Home: 958 Grove St Winnetka IL 60093 Office: 840 N Lake Shore Dr Chicago IL 60611

CHURCHILL, DONALD WALTER, SR., educator; b. Carlton, Neb., Nov. 29, 1912; s. Walter A. and Gepha J. (Fox) C.; A.B., Neb. State Coll., 1935; M.Ed., U. Neb., 1952; Ed.D. (fellow), U. No. Colo., 1960; m. Bernice Mary Thomas, July 8, 1940; children—Patricia Anne Churchill Hollo, Donald Walter. Tchr., coach Milburn (Neb.) Consol. Sch., 1935-39; tchr., coach, supt., Berwyn (Neb.) Pub. Schs., 1939-45; supt. Loup County Pub. Schs., Taylor, Neb., 1945-49; teaching fellow U. No. Colo. Greeley, 1959-60; prof. edn. Bemidji (Minn.) State U., 1960—, also dir. edn. adminstrn., coordinator grad. studies. Vis. prof. U. South Fla., Tampa, 1968; cons. pub. schs., Montevideo, Minn., 1970-71, Pipestone, Minn., 1971-72; chmn. visitation team Nat. Council for Accreditation of Tchr. Edn., 1968, 69, 71. Hon. life mem. USAF Air Def. Team; hon. adm. Neb. Navy. Mem. Nat., Minn. edn. assns., A.A.U.P., Smithsonian Asinn. Elementary Prins. Assn., Bemidji C. of C., Minn. Assn. for Student Teaching (pres. 1966-68), Izaak Walton League (pres.), Phi Delta Kappa. Mason (Shriner), Elk; mem. Order Eastern Star. Home: 2514 Bemidji Av Bemidji MN 56601 Office: Dept Student Teaching Bemidji U Bemidji MN 56601

CHURCHILL, RUEL VANCE, mathematician; b. Akron, Ind., Dec. 12, 1899; s. Abner Cain and Meldora (Friend) C.; B.S., U. Chgo., 1922; Ph.D., U. Mich., 1929; m. Ruby Sicks, 1922 (dec. 1969); m. 2d, Alice Baldwin Warren, 1972; children—Betty Churchill McMurray, Eugene S. Instr. to prof. U. Mich., Ann Arbor, 1922-65, prof. emeritus, 1965—; researcher U. Freiburg, Germany, 1936; researcher Calif. Inst. Tech., 1950; vis. lectr. U. Wis., Madison, 1941; mathematician USAF, 1944. Mem. Math. Assn. Am., Am. Math. Soc., Phi Beta Kappa. Author: Complex Variables and Applications, 3d edit., 1974; Fourier Series, 3d edit., 1977; Operational Mathematics, 3d edit., 1972. Home: 1231 Wisteria Dr Ann Arbor MI 48104 Office: U Mich Dept Math Ann Arbor MI 48109

CHURCHMAN, CAROLYN MARGARET HAUGHT (MRS. RAY E. CHURCHMAN), broadcaster; b. Indpls., June 9, 1927; d. Edgar L. and Lillian (Ilg) Haught; student Jordan Coll. Music, 1941-43, Ohio State U., 1944-46; m. Ray E. Churchman, Mar. 6, 1954. Musician, WCOL, Columbus, O., 1944; woman's dir. WBNS, Columbus, 1946-48; announcer WFBM TV, Indpls., 1956; free lance radio and TV commls., N.Y.C., 1956; hostess daily interview program WTTV, Indpls., 1957-73; interviewer, hostess WFBM Radio, Indpls., 1961-73; account exec., hostess daily interview show WXLW Radio, 1973—; free lance writer, producer radio and TV commls., 1950—; account exec. Bill Henke Advt. Agy., Indpls., 1961-74. Chmn. fund raising dr. Am. Cancer Soc., 1967; chmn. campaign Cystic Fibrosis, 1965-66, Retarded Olympics, 1969, Easter Seals, 1970; pres. Ind. Cystic Fibrosis, 1971-72. Recipient Ind. Boys Sch. award, 1967, Sr. Citizens Center award Indpls. Sr. Citizen Center, 1966, Community Blood Bank award, 1966, 67, Am. Cancer Soc. award for leadership in campaign, 1967, Casper award Community Service Council, 1967; Ind. Health Assn. award, 1969. Mem. Indpls. Community Service Council, Am. Women in Radio and TV, Indpls. Advt. Club, Chi Omega. Author: World's Fare Cookbook. Home: 4888 Kesslerview Dr Indianapolis IN 46220 Office: WXLW 3003 Kessler Blvd Indianapolis IN 46222

CHUTE, ROBERT DONALD, elec. engr., educator; b. Detroit, Nov. 29, 1928; s. George Maynard and Josephine Chute; B.S. in Elec. Engring., U. Mich., 1950; M.S., Wayne State U., 1966; m. Marion Louise Price, June 17, 1950; children—Janet Louise, Lawrence Robert. Control engr. indsl heating div. Gen. Electric Co., Shelbyville, Ind., 1950-57; group leader Chrysler Corp., Warren, Mich., 1957-59; chief product engr. internat. div. Burroughs Corp., Detroit, 1959-73; asso. prof. elec. engring. Lawrence Inst. Tech., Southfield, Mich., 1973—; cons. in indsl. controls, 1969—. Instl. rep. Detroit Met. Area council Boy Scouts Am., 1964-68. Registered profl. engr., Ind. Mem. IEEE, Engring. Soc. Detroit. Presbyterian. Club: Just Right. Author: (with George M. Chute) Electronics in Industry, 1971; patentee in field. Office: 21000 W Ten Mile Rd Southfield MI 48075

CIAMBRONE, ANGELO ANSELMO, lawyer; b. Chicago Heights, Ill., Oct. 16, 1929; s. Angelo and Rose Francesca (Mazza) C.; B.S., DePaul U., 1951, J.D., 1954; postgrad. U. Notre Dame, 1952-53; m. Jean C. Del Giudice, June 16, 1962; children—Rosanne, Gregory. Admitted to Ill. bar, 1955; practiced in Chgo., 1957-60, Chicago Heights, 1961—; partner Wilczynski, Wilczynski, Ciambrone, Karwoski & Bransky, Ltd., Chicago Heights, 1961—; dir. First Nat. Bank, Chicago Heights, Ill., Bank, Italo-Am. Nat. Union. Pres., Chicago Heights Symphony Orch., 1966-72; treas. Mental Health and Family Service Center South Cook County, 1972-73, v.p., 1974-76, pres., 1976—; mem. Ill. Racing Bd. Served with AUS, 1955-56. Mem. Am., Ill., Chgo. bar assns., Am. Judicature Soc., Justinian Soc., Chicago Heights C. of C. (v.p. 1967), Phi Alpha Delta. K.C., Kiwanian (pres. Chicago Heights club). Home: 860 D'Amico Dr Chicago Heights IL 60411 Office: 1515 Halsted St Chicago Heights IL 60411

CIATTEO, CARMEN THOMAS, psychiatrist; b. Clifton Heights, Pa., May 25, 1921; s. Ralph and Grace (Manette) C.; A.B. in Chemistry, U. Pa., 1947; M.D., Loyola U. (Chgo.), 1951; m. Lucille Dolores Ranum, Nov. 1, 1957; children—William, Jane, Thomas. Intern, Mercy Hosp., Chgo.; resident Fitzsimons Army Hosp., Denver, 1952-53, Hines (Ill.) VA Hosp., 1957-59; practice medicine specializing in psychiatry, Joliet, Ill., 1959-72; cons. Ill. Dept. Corrections, Joliet; psychiatrist VA hosps., 1959; cons. Dept. Vocat. Rehab., 1959-72, Matrimonial Tribunal Diocese Joliet, 1959-76, Bur. Prisons, U.S. Dept. Justice, Chgo., 1975-76, 77—; tchr. nursing tng. Hines VA Hosp., 1957-59. Served with USAF, 1942-46, 51-56. Mem. AMA, Ill. Psychiat. Soc., Am. Psychiat. Assn., Am. Correctional Assn. Democrat. Roman Catholic. Home: Rt #2 135 Little Creek Lockport IL 60441

CICALA, JOHN ANTHONY, psychol. counselor; b. Norristown, Pa., July 14, 1944; s. John J. and Beatrice (Salerio) C.; B.S., U. Nev., Reno, 1974; M.S. in Psychology, Pittsburg (Kans.) State U., 1977. Veteran's counselor U. Nev., Reno, 1975; family counseling Pittsburg State U., 1976, grad. asst., 1976—. Served with USAF, 1962-67. Included among 50 Outstanding Am. Poets, J. Mark Press. Mem. Nutrition Today Soc., Am. Personnel and Guidance Assn., Nat. Vocational Guidance Assn., Nat. Council on Family Relations, New Writers Club, Alpha Epsilon Delta, Phi Delta Kappa. Contbr. poetry to popular mags. and small press publs.

CICCIARELLI, FRANCIS EUGENE, pathologist; b. Peoria, Ill., Apr. 22, 1934; s. Frank and Elvira (Matarelli) C.; B.S., U. Notre Dame, 1955; M.D., Loyola U., 1959; m. Theresa Marie Murphy, May 20, 1963; children—Thomas, Michael, Monica. Intern, St. Francis Hosp., Peoria, Ill., 1959-60; resident in pathology Mayo Clinic, Rochester, Minn., 1961-65; asso. pathologist St. John's Hosp., Springfield, Ill., 1965-66; pathologist, co-dir. labs. Finley Hosp., Dubuque, Iowa, 1966—, Mercy Med. Center, Dubuque, 1966—, Xavier Hosp., Dubuque, 1966—; co-dir. Med. Services Lab., Dubuque, 1967—; dir. Dubuque Tri-Hosp. Sch. Med. Tech. Mem. Dubuque Plumbing Bd., 1976—. Diplomate Am. Bd. Pathology. Mem. Am. Soc. Clin. Pathologists, Coll. Am. Pathologists, AMA. Home: 205 Hill St Dubuque IA 52001 Office: 543 W 8th St Dubuque IA 52001

CILKE, ROBERT HENRY, educator; b. Petoskey, Mich., June 27, 1941; s. Robert Emil and Eleanor (Baines) C.; diploma music N. Central Bible Coll., Mpls., 1962; B.Mus. Edn., MacPhail Coll. Music, 1963; M.A., Central Mich. U., 1969; m. Barbara Eleene Hatch, Dec. 28, 1963; children—Debra, Brenda, Robert F. Supr. music pub. schs., New Underwood, S.D., 1963-64, Mackinaw City, Mich., 1964-65, Rogers City, Mich., 1965-72; chmn. music dept N. Central Bible Coll., Mpls., 1972-76; prin. Brookdale Christian Center Sch., 1976—. Ordained to ministry Assemblies of God Ch., 1966; pastor Assembly of God, Cheboygan, Mich., 1964-65, Faith Assembly of God, Rogers City, 1965-72; minister of music Gospel Tabernacle, Mpls., 1974-76; asso. pastor Brookdale Assembly of God, Mpls., 1976—; mem. nat. com. Nat. Ch. Music Fellowship, 1973-74. Mem. Cultural Activities Com. Mpls., 1974-76. Bd. dirs. King's Acad., Brooklyn Center, Minn., 1974. Mem. C. of C. Brooklyn Center. Home: 6012 Washburn Ave N Brooklyn Center MN 55430 Office: 6030 Xerxes Ave N Brooklyn Center MN 55430

CIOCCI, PETER LOU, data processing mgr.; b. Rome, Italy, May 1, 1941; s. George and Ruth (Berger) C.; came to U.S., 1947, naturalized, 1957; B.S. in Psychology, Loyola U., 1970; m. Hedy Jean Schoeman, Mar. 20, 1966; children—Leslie Kim, Michelle Suzanne. Programmer trainee to lead analyst, project leader First Nat. Bank of Chgo., 1965-74; fin. systems mgr. to mgr. systems and programming Powers Regulator Co., Skokie, Ill., 1974—. Active Walker PTA, North Shore Community Orgn. Mem. Assn. for Systems Mgmt. (co. rep.), Loyola Alumni Assn., Powers Mgmt. Club. Clubs: N. Suburban Bowlers. Revised and edited Standards Manual for First Nat. Bank, 1969-72. Office: 3400 W Oakton St Skokie IL 60076

CIOCH, JOSEPH JOHN, dietitian; b. W. Lafayette, Ind., Feb. 5, 1933; s. John Joseph and Mary (Snyder) C.; B.S. in Hotel Adminstrn., Pa. State U., 1958, M.A., 1970, Ed.D., 1974; m. Doris, July 16, 1955; children—John Joseph, Susan Jean. Lab. asst. dept. foods and nutrition Pa. State U., University Park, 1954-58; exec. asst. mgr. Stouffer Food Corp., N.Y.C., 1958-63; asso. dir. Instl. Food Research and Services Program, Pa. State U., 1963-71, instr. food service housing adminstrn., 1971-73; prof. restaurant-hotel and instl. mgmt. Purdue U., West Lafayette, Ind., 1974—, dept. head, 1962—. Mem. Am. Dietetic Assn. (com. profl. registration 1966), Western Ind. Dietetic Assn., Ind. (ednl. dir. 1974), Nat. restaurant assns., Soc. Advancement Food Service Research, Pa. State Hotel and Restaurant Soc. (dir. 1964-65). Editorial adv. bd. Cahners Books Internat. 1976; contbr. articles to profl. jours. Recipient Community Leaders Am. award, 1976; Spl. Service award Commonwealth Pa., 1973. Home: 2601 Darwin Dr West Lafayette IN 47906 Office: Purdue U West Lafayette IN 47907

CIOFFARI, MARIO SALVATORE, physician; b. Calitri, Italy, Dec. 1, 1906; s. Constantino and Antoinetta (Armiento) C.; came to U.S., 1917, naturalized, 1922; A.B., Cornell U., 1928, M.D., 1933; m. Kathleen L. Mahoney, June 18, 1938 (dec. Oct. 1968); children—Richard John, Ann Lucia. Intern, New Rochelle (N.Y.)

Hosp., 1933-34; resident in pediatrics N.Y. Foundling Hosp., N.Y.C., 1934-36; practice medicine specializing in pediatrics, Yonkers, N.Y., 1936-42, Detroit, 1942-69, Southfield, Mich., 1969—; sr. attending physician in pediatrics Mt. Carmel Hosp., Detroit, 1943, dir. pediatrics, 1954-56. Mem. Am. Acad. Pediatrics, Detroit Pediatrics Soc. (past pres.), Mich., Wayne County med. socs., Mich. Allergy Soc., Detroit Mus. Arts Founders' Soc., Am. Automobile Assn., Automobile Club Mich., Cranbrook Inst. Sci., Mich. Assn. Professions, Am. Mus. Natural History, Am. Heart Assn., Detroit Zool. Soc., Caduceus Soc. Cornell, Cornell U. Alumni Assn., Cornell U. Med. Coll. Assn., Alpha Kappa Kappa. Roman Catholic. Contbr. articles to profl. jours. Home: 2325 W Thirteen Mile Rd Royal Oak MI 48073 Office: 21819 W Nine Mile Rd Southfield MI 48075

CIPOLLA, LAWRENCE JOHN, ednl. co. exec.; b. Hartford, Conn., Nov. 30, 1943; s. Anthony Francis and Rose Marie (Alesi) C.; A.A. with honors, Manchester Community Coll., 1968; B.A. with high honors, U. Conn., 1970; M.A. with honors U. Minn., 1972; m. Judith L. Peterka, June 24, 1972. Spencer Found. research asso. U. Minn., Mpls., 1971-72; sr. instructional system analyst 3M Co., St Paul, 1972-74, instructional systems analyst, 1974-76; dir. real estate learning systems div. Golle & Holmes Corp., Mpls., 1976—; cons., lectr. in field. Served with USAF, 1961-65; ETO. Regent's Fund scholar, 1971-72; Spencer Found. research fellow, 1971-72. Mem. Am. Soc. Tng. and Devel.; Nat. Assn. Realtors, Realtors Nat. Mktg. Inst., Greater Mpls. Bd. Realtors, Profl. Picture Framers Am., Profl. Photographers Am., Photog. Soc. Am., Royal Photog. Soc. Gt. Britain, Phi Beta Kappa. Club: Sports and Health (Mpls.). Home: 7021 Comanche Ct Edina MN 55435 Office: One Appletree Sq Minneapolis MN 55420

CIRIACY, EDWARD WALTER, physician, educator; b. Phila., Feb. 12, 1924; s. William Frederick and Elizabeth Jane (McGettigan) C.; B.S., Pa. State Coll., 1948; M.D., Temple U., 1952; m. Adele Large Wallis, Sept. 9, 1942; children—Adele, Edward Walter, Deborah, Melissa Jane, Timothy. Intern, Frankford Hosp., Phila., 1952-53, surg. resident, 1953-54; surg. resident Temple Hosp., Phila., 1953-54; practice medicine specializing in family practice, Ely, Minn., 1954-57, 58-71, Miami, Fla., 1957-58; mem. staffs Ely-Bloomenson Community Hosp.; prof. U. Minn., 1971—, chmn. dept. family practice, 1971—. Mem. adv. panel for subcom. on patient care Cancer Coordinating Com. for Health Scis. Served with USAAF, 1944-46. Recipient Merit award Minn. Acad. Gen. Practice, 1963. Diplomate Nat. Bd. Med. Examiners, Am. Bd. Family Practice (chmn. recertification com. 1972-76). Fellow Am. Acad. Family Physicians (charter); mem. Minn. Acad. Family Physicians (pres. 1967-68, com. on med. sch. relations and tng. programs), AMA, Pan Am. Med. Assn., Soc. Tchrs. of Family Medicine (pres. 1975—), Minn. Med. Assn. (mem. com. med. services 1970—), Range Med. Soc. (pres. 1961), Babcock Surg. Soc., Assn. Am. Med. Colls., Alpha Omega Alpha. Mason. Contbr. numerous articles to med. jours. Home: 17 E Beacon Hill Rd Ely MN 55731 Office: Mayo Meml Bldg U Minn Minneapolis MN 55455

CISLAK, PETER JOHN, chem. co. exec.; b. Indpls., June 26, 1931; s. Francis Edward and Jeannette (Huling) C.; B.S., Purdue U., 1958, M.S., 1958; m. Margaret Frances Noble, June 6, 1953; children—Gregory Noble, Carol Margaret, David John, Susan Marie. Instr. Purdue U., 1958-62; statistician Reilly Tar and Chem. Corp., Indpls., 1962-63, data processing mgr., 1964-69, prodn. mgr. chem. div., 1969-77, sr. mgr. ops. research and long-range planning, 1977—; lectr. Purdue U., 1970. Active Boy Scouts. Bd. mem. Honeywell H-200 Users Assn., 1966-69. Served with AUS, 1953-57. Mem. Am. Chem. Soc., Am. Statis. Assn., Operations Research Soc. Am., Data Processing Mgmt. Assn., Assn. Computing Machinery, Am. Mgmt. Assn. (co-chmn. computers in research seminar), Soc. Chem. Industry (Eng.), Soc. Mayflower Descs. (dep. gov. Ind. chpt.), Am. Inst. Chem. Engrs. K.C. (4th deg.). Home: 8065 Morningside Dr Indianapolis IN 46240 Office: 151 N Delaware St Indianapolis IN 46204

CISNEROS, LEE, tire and rubber co. exec.; b. Mission, Tex., Apr. 19, 1921; s. Alfred and Rose (Mendoza y Cisneros) C.; student traffic mgmt., La Salle Extension U., 1946-47; student courses Am. Mgmt. Assn., Stanford Grad. Sch. Transp. Mgmt. Program, Northwestern U. Transp. Scis. Program and Advanced Mgmt. Program; m. Dorothy V. Farmer, Dec. 7, 1941; children—Ronald L., Kenneth Ray, Timothy Lynn. Shipping supr. Cabot Corp., Pampa, Tex., 1945-50, asst. traffic mgr., Boston, 1950-52, traffic mgr., 1952-56, gen. traffic mgr., 1957-59, dir. traffic and sales services, 1960-64, mgr. phys. distbn., 1964-68; dir. transp. Firestone Tire & Rubber Co., Akron, Ohio, 1968-75, dir. phys. distbn., 1976—. Mem. Town Meeting, Braintree, Mass. Served with USAAF, 1942-45. Mem. Nat. Indsl. Traffic League (dir., exec. com.), New Eng. Shippers Adv. Bd. (exec. com.), New Eng. Indsl. Traffic League (exec. com.), Assn. Traffic Clubs Am. (regional v.p.), Akron (chmn. transp. com.), Boston (transp. com.), Braintree Jr. (dir., v.p.) chambers commerce, New Eng. Council (transp. com.), Asso. Industries of Mass. (transp. com.), Nat. Def. Transp. Assn. (nat. v.p.), New Eng. Traffic Club (pres., bd. govs.), Am. Soc. Traffic and Transp. (founder mem.), Nat. Freight Traffic Assn., Exec. Reservists (regional dir.), Transp. Assn. Am. (dir., user panel, fuel council). Home: 2520 Shade Park Dr Bath Township Akron OH 44313 Office: 1200 Firestone Pkwy Akron OH 44317 also Grants Hill Rd Center Ossipee NH

CISSIK, JOHN HENRY, air force officer, aerospace physiologist; b. Great Neck, N.Y., Aug. 18, 1943; s. John Peter and Gladys Lucille (Moore) C.; B.A., U. Tex., Austin, 1965, M.A., 1967; Ph.D. in Physiology, U. Ill., 1972; m. Dorothy Paulette Allen, Dec. 21, 1965; 1 son, John Mark. Commd. 2d lt. USAF, 1967, advanced through grades to maj., 1977; aerospace physiologist, physiol. tng. unit Wright-Patterson AFB, O., 1967-69, Andrews AFB, Washington, 1969-70; aerospace physiologist, lab. officer USAF Med. Center, Scott AFB, Ill., 1972—, coordinator USAF Phase II Cardiopulmonary Lab. Specialist Tng. Course, 1972—; cons. in field. USAF rep. to Fed. Interagy. Com., 1975—, Am. Assn. Respiratory Therapists, 1974—, Bd. Schs., 1975—, Nat. Soc. Cardiopulmonary Technologists, 1973—. Mem. equipment repair com. Our World Pre-sch., O'Fallon, Ill., 1975-76. Certified instr. in cardiopulmonary resuscitation. Mem. Nat. Soc. Cardiopulmonary Technologists (editorial adv. com. 1975—, chmn. editorial adv. com. 1977—), Am. Soc. Respiratory Care Adminstrs., Aerospace Med. Assn., Am. Thoracic Soc., Am. Assn. Physicians Assts., Chi Gamma Iota, Phi Sigma. Editorial adv. bd. Jour. Cardiovascular and Pulmonary Tech., 1975—. Research, publs. on respiratory nitrogen prodn. in man and pulmonary physiology. Home: 301 Dartmouth Dr O'Fallon IL 62269 Office: USAF Med Center (SGHT) Scott AFB IL 62225

CITIPITIOGLU, ERGIN, research engr.; b. Ankara, Turkey, Feb. 18, 1937; s. Mehmet Ali and Belkis (Pornek) C.; came to U.S., 1962; M.C.E., Istanbul Tech. U., 1960; Ph.D., Okla. State U., 1965; m. Gul Ataman, Mar. 11, 1971; children—Lale, Ahmet. Bridge design engr. Turkish State Hwy. Directorate, 1960-62; asst. prof. civil engring. U. Louisville, 1965-67, asso. prof., 1967-68; research asso. mech. engring. dept. U. Cin., 1968-69; tech. v.p. Hypermation, Inc., 1969-70; asso. prof. civil engring. Middle East Tech. U., 1970-74; mem. tech. staff Structural Dynamics Research Corp., Cin., 1975—. Registered profl. engr., Ohio, Ky. Mem. Am. Acad. Mechanics, ASCE, Am. Concrete Inst., Am. Soc. Engring. Edn., Internat. Assn. Housing Sci. Club: Masons. Home: 10215 Pendery Dr Cincinnati OH 45242 Office: 5729 Dragon Way Cincinnati OH 45227

CITRIN, PHILLIP MARSHALL, lawyer; b. Chgo., Nov. 1, 1931; s. Mandel Hirsch and Birdie (Gulman) C.; B.S., Northwestern U., 1953, J.D., 1956; m. Judith Goldfeder, Dec. 23, 1967; 1 son, Jeffrey Scott Levin. Admitted to Ill. bar, 1957; partner firm Davis, Jones & Baer, Chgo., 1961—. Republican candidate judge circuit ct., Cook County, Ill., 1976. Served with USNR, 1956-58. Fellow Am. Acad. Matrimonial Lawyers (founding); mem. Chgo. (bd. mgrs. 1974-76), Ill. (mem. assembly of dels. 1972-73), Am. (gavel awards com.) bar assns., Phi Delta Phi. Clubs: Monroe, Arts (Chgo.). Home: 423 Greenleaf Ave Wilmette IL 60091 Office: 120 S LaSalle St Chicago IL 60603

CITRON, RICHARD IRA, employee benefit cons.; b. Chgo., Apr. 1, 1944; s. Irving T. and Ruth (Katz) C.; B.S., U. Ill., 1966; M.S., Ill. Inst. Tech., 1968, Ph.D., 1972; m. Phyllis Kalifey, Dec. 26, 1971; 1 son, Brian Todd. Asst. prof. math. Ind. U. at Glen Park, 1970-72; cons., actuary A.S. Hansen Inc., Chgo., 1972—. Grantee Blum Kolver Found., 1963-66, NSF, 1968-70. Mem. Am. Math. Soc., Soc. Indsl. and Applied Math, AAAS, Am. Acad. Actuaries (affiliate). Contbr. articles to profl. jours. Home: 4730 Enfield Skokie IL 60076 Office: 150 N Wacker Dr Chicago IL 60606

CLAGUE, THOMAS EUGENE, personnel edn. exec.; b. Earlham, Iowa, July 20, 1923; s. Glenn and Hazel Bessie (Bell) C.; B.S., Iowa State U., 1949; m. Ann F. Eliason, Aug. 6, 1950; children—Karen, Brian, Candace (Mrs. Pedro Garza, Jr.), Kevin. Direct salesman C.W. Humphrey Co., Des Moines, 1949-50; blockman Allis Chalmers Mfg. Co., Des Moines, 1950-54; exptl. engr. John Deere Dubuque Tractor Works, Dubuque, Iowa, 1954-56; copywriter, account exec. Aubrey, Finlay, Mariey & Hodgson, Inc., advt. agy., Chgo., 1956-63; dir. sales relations Gandy Co., Owatonna, Minn., 1963-72; v.p. Shaklee Distbrs., Owatonna, 1970—; pres. SMI Distbrs., Motiv-Action Unltd., Owatonna, 1974—; cons. engr. to agrl. chem. industry, 1971—; free-lance agr. writer, 1957-64. Active Owatonna United Fund, 1965-70; chmn. sustaining drive Boy Scouts Am., 1969; publicity dir. school bond issue, 1968. Bd. dirs. Owatonna Concert Assn., 1969-75, Community Music, Inc., Owatonna, 1968-72. Served with AUS, 1943-46. Mem. Am. Soc. Agrl. Engrs. (chmn. Chgo. sect. 1958-59), Knights St. Patrick, Alpha Zeta, Phi Mu Alpha, Farm House. Republican. Address: 1001 Van Buren St Owatonna MN 55060

CLAIRMONT, WILLIAM EDWARD, hwy. constrn. exec.; b. Walhalla, N.D., Jan. 2, 1926; s. Emil O. and Mae E. (Bisenius) C.; student N.D. State U., 1948-49; m. Patricia Ann Filben, Oct. 7, 1950; children—Stephen, Julie, Cynthia, Nancy. Pres. William Clairmont, Inc., hwy. heavy contractor, Bismarck, N.D., 1949—; chmn. bd., chief exec. officer Mandan Security Bank (N.D.); land developer, Bismarck; owner cattle-farming operation, Costa Rica. Mem. Walhalla (N.D.) City Council, 1955-56. Bd. regents Mary Coll., Bismarck, 1974—. Served with USMC, 1944-46. Mem. N.D. Asso. Gen. Contractors (pres. 1971, bd. dirs. 1964-67). Elk. Club: Apple Creek Country (Bismarck). Home: 821 1st St Bismarck ND 58501 Office: Box 1074 Bismarck ND 58501

CLAMPITT, RICHARD ROY, psychologist; b. New Providence, Iowa, Dec. 7, 1925; s. Roy Justin and L. Pauline (Felt) C.; B.S., Iowa State U., 1951, M.S., 1954; Ph.D. (USPHS fellow), State U. Iowa, 1955; m. Joan Lucile Utzinger, June 30, 1956; children—Christopher Alan, Carolyn Elaine, Susan Lucinda. Clin. psychologist, asst. prof. Columbus (Ohio) Psychiat. Inst., Ohio State U. Med. Sch., 1956-61; clin. psychologist Central Minn. Mental Health Center, St. Cloud, 1961—. Coordinator, Counselin Services to Clergy, Minn. Conf. United Meth. Ch., 1969—. Chmn. Civil Service Bd., City of St. Cloud, Minn., 1968-69, 71-72, 74-75; bd. dirs. Family Planning Center, 1971-76, chmn. founding bd., 1971-73; bd. dirs. United Cerebral Palsy Central Minn., 1965—, chmn., 1969-70. Diplomate Am. Bd. Profl. Psychology. Mem. Am. (Minn. rep. council reps. 1974-76, pres. div. state assns. 1977—), Minn. (mem. exec. council 1970—) psychol. assns., Common Cause, St. Cloud Area C. of C. (chmn. municipal affairs div. 1966), Sigma Xi, Phi Kappa Phi, Phi Mu Alpha Sinfonia, Pi Mu Epsilon, Psi Chi. Democrat. Methodist (mem. adminstrv. bd. 1963—). Home: 39 Pandolfo Pl St Cloud MN 56301 Office: 1321 13th St N St Cloud MN 56301

CLANCY, DANIEL FRANCIS, journalist; b. Logansport, Ind., May 8, 1918; s. Joseph Francis and Daisy C. (Strecker) C.; student pub. schs.; m. Okodell Glads Salyer, Apr. 12, 1947; children—Cassandra Sue, Holly Eve. Reporter Logansport Press, 1942-46, Springfield (Ohio) Daily News, 1946-47, Springfield Sun, 1947-56; reporter, Columbus (Ohio) Dispatch, 1956—. Dir. Nat. Com. Against Limiting the Presidency, 1949-54; trustee More Agrl. Prodn. Served to lt. col. Ohio Def. Corps. Decorated French Nat. Merit, Gold medal, La Renaissance Francaise, medal Honor and Merit, knight Order of Lion of Ardennes, Cross of Lorraine and Compains of Resistance, Soc. Encouragement Arts, Scis., Letters Silver medal (France); knight Order of Crown of Stuart (Eng.); Assn. Am. Friendship Bronze medal, Trieste; count Ho. of Deols (Italy); knight Delcassian Order (Ireland); medal Institute of Libertador Ramon Castilla (Peru); medal Internat. Eloy Alfaro Found. (Panama); silver medal spl. membership Japanese Red Cross Soc.; Ohio Faithful Service ribbon; recipient Nat. Headliner award, 1948, 49; 1st place award for editorial columns Nat. Found. for Hwy. Safety, 1970; Appreciation plaque Ohio N.G., 1976; Meritorious service medal SSS; Ky. col., adm. Nebr. Navy, La. col., hon. adm. Tex. Navy, N.Mex. col., Miss. col., lt. col. Ala., Ga., lt. gov. Ohio, Ind. Sagamore; commodore Okla., Ohio. Mem. Am. Mil. Inst., Orders and Medals Soc. Am., Ohio Def. Officers Assn., Am. Flag Assn., Ohio Valley Mil. Soc., Am. Internat. Acad., Brazilian Acad. Polit. and Social Sci., Nat. Citizens for State 51; (P.R.), Inst. Heraldry (Spain), Internat. Inst. Study and Devel. Human Relations, Brazilian Acad. Econs. and Adminstrv. Scis., Sons Union Vets. Civil War (past state comdr.), Continental Confedn. Adopted Indians (v.p. 1954—), Assn. U.S. Army, Am. Indian Lore Assn. (hon.), My Country Soc. Clubs: National Headliners; Honolulu Press. Author: Two Term Tradition, 1940; Collected Poems, 1937-47, 1948. Contbr. articles to mags. Home: 2420 Zollinger Rd Columbus OH 43221 Office: Columbus Dispatch 34 S 3d St Columbus OH 43216

CLANCY, WILLIAM GERARD, orthopedic surgeon; b. N.Y.C., Apr. 10, 1941; s. William G. and Mary C. (Courneen) C.; B.S., Manhattan Coll., 1963; M.D., State U. N.Y., 1967; m. Geraldine Walsh, Apr. 20, 1968; children—Elise Ann, Christopher Todd, Kerry Lynn. Intern, St. Luke's Hosp., N.Y.C., 1967-68, resident in surgery, 1968-69, resident in orthopedic surgery, 1969-72; practice medicine specializing in orthopedic surgery and sports medicine, Madison, Wis.; chief, orthopedic surgery U.S. Naval Hosp., Annapolis, 1973-74; asst. prof. orthopedic surgery U. Wis., Madison, 1974—, head sports medicine div., team physician, 1974—. Diplomate Am. Bd. Orthopedic Surgeons. Fellow Am. Acad. Orthopedic Surgeons, Am. Orthopedic Soc. for Sports Medicine, Am. Coll. Sports Medicine, Univ. Soc. Orthopedic Sports Medicine. Contbr. articles to profl. jours. Home: 202 Blue Ridge Pkwy Madison WI 53706 Office: 1300 University Ave Madison WI 53706

CLAPP, CHESTER DILLINGHAM, educator; b. Ecorse Twp., Mich., Apr. 26, 1920; s. Chester Dillingham and Olga Theresa (Adkinson) C.; B.S., Wayne State U., 1942; M.S.W., U. Mich., 1947, M.A., 1948, Ph.D., 1952; m. Margaret Rose Cavanaugh, June 30, 1966; children—Pamela, Jennifer, Mark. Asst. prof. psychology Merrill-Palmer Inst., Detroit, 1951-54; dir. Macomb Child Guidance Clinic, Utica, Mich., 1955-66, Valley Counseling Center, Morgantown, W.Va., 1966-68; asso. prof. psychology Jacksonville (Fla.) U., 1968-69; prof. psychology Calumet campus Purdue U., Hammond, Ind., 1969—. Asso. prof. psychology W.Va. U., Morgantown, 1966-68. Chmn. N.W. Ind. Welfare Reform Coalition, Hammond, 1974. Bd. dirs. Purdue Calumet Devel. Found., East Chicago, Ind., 1971—. Served with USNR, 1942-45. Mem. A.A.U.P., Ind. Psychol. Assn., N.W. Ind. Conf. on Social Welfare (dir. 1971—), Sigma Xi. Home: 2141 Ridgewood Ave Highland IN 46322 Office: 2233 171st St Hammond IN 46323

CLAPP, THOMAS REID, concrete co. exec.; b. Washington, June 11, 1947; s. Roger Alvin and Harriet (Reid) C.; student Monmouth Coll.; m. Linda Mae Kinkaid, Apr. 14, 1967; children—Thomas Charles, Barbara Ellen. Asst. dist. mgr. Atlantic Mobile Corp., Chgo., 1971-75; pres. Anchor Concrete Service, Inc., Chillicothe, Ill., 1975—, also dir. Trustee Plymouth Congregational Ch. Served with U.S. Army, 1969-71. Decorated Bronze Star medal, Army Commendation medal. Mem. Am. Rental Assn., Chillicothe C. of C. Home: 907 Santa Fe Chillicothe IL 61523 Office: PO Box 482 Route 29 Chillicothe IL 61523

CLARDY, JESSE V., educator; b. Olney, Tex., Feb. 15, 1929; s. Jesse Ellis and Tiny (Pringle) C.; B.S., Tex. Arts and Industries U., 1949, M.S., 1951; Ph.D., U. Mich., 1961. Faculty, U. Tex., Arlington, 1961-62; faculty U. Mo., Kansas City, 1963—, asso. prof. Russian, 1964-68, prof., 1968—. Served with AUS, 1951-54. Mem. S.W. Slavic Assn. (pres. 1964-65), Bi-Slavic Assn. (sec. 1970-71), Assn. for Advancement Slavic Studies. Republican. Author: Philosophical Ideas of Alexander Radishchev, 1964; G.R. Derzhavin a Political Biography, 1967. Home: 1004 Broad St Warrensburg MO 64093 Office: Dept History U Mo Kansas City MO 64110

CLARE, STEWART, educator, research biologist; b. nr. Montgomery City, Mo., Jan. 31, 1913; s. William Gilmore and Wardie (Stewart) C.; B.A., U. Kans., 1935; M.S., Iowa State U., 1937; Ph.D., U. Chgo., 1949; m. Lena Glenn Kaster, Aug. 4, 1936. Student asst. entomology, also William Volker scholar U. Kans., 1931-35; Rockefeller Research fellow Iowa State U., 1935-36, teaching fellow, 1936-37; Univ. fellow zoology U. Chgo., 1937-40; dist. survey supr. entomology U.S. Civil Service Commn. Bur. Entomology and Plant Quarantine, 1937-40, tech. cons., 1941-42; instr. meteorology USAAF Weather Sch., 1942-43; research biologist Midwest Research Inst., Kansas City, Mo., 1945-46; spl. study, research Kansas City Art Inst., U. Mo., 1946-49; instr. zoology U. Alta., 1949-50, asst. prof. zoology, lectr.-instr. sci. color, dept. fine arts, 1950-53; research grantee Alberta Research Council, 1951-53; asst. prof. Kansas City Coll., 1953; lectr. zoology U. Adelaide, S. Australia, 1954-55; sr. research officer entomology Sudan Govt. Ministry Agr., Khartoum, Sudan and Gezira Research Sta., Wad Medani, Sudan, N.Africa, 1955-56; sr. entomologist Klipfontein Organic Products Corp., Johannesburg, Union S.Africa, 1957; prof., head dept. biology Union Coll., 1958-59, chmn. sci. div., prof., head biology, 1959-61, spl. study grantee, 1960; prof., head dept. biology Mo. Valley Coll., Marshall, 1961-62, research grantee, 1961-62; lectr., instr. biology, meteorology, sci. of color Adirondack Sci. Camp div. edn. N.Y. State U. Coll. summers 1962-66, dir. acad. program 1963-66, research facilities grantee, 1963-66; Buckbee Found. prof. biology Rockford (Ill.) Coll., lectr. biology eve. coll., 1962-63, spl. research grantee, 1962-63; prof., chmn, dept. biochemistry, mem. research div. Kansas City (Mo.) Coll. Osteopathy and Surgery, 1963-67, also NIH basic research grantee, 1963-67; prof. biology Coll. of Emporia (Kans.), 1967-74, dir. biol. research, 1972-74, prof. emeritus, 1974—, research study grantee, 1967-74, research biologist, cons., 1974—, spl. research grantee study in Arctic, 1970, 72, Central Am. and Mexico, 1973; cons. in field, 1962—. Served with USNR, 1943-45. Recipient certificate service Vols. Internat. Tech. Assistance, 1970; creativity recognition award Internat. Personnel Research, 1972; Distinguished Achievement and Service awards for edn. and research in biology, Certificate of Merit in Art, Internat. Biog. Centre, 1968, 72, 73. Life fellow Intercontinental Biog. Assn.; mem. Brit. Assn. Adv. Sci. (life), Am. Entomol. Soc. (life), Nat. Assn. Biology Tchrs., Arctic Inst. N.Am., Am. Polar Soc., N.Y. Acad. Scis. (life), Inter-Soc. Color Council, Sigma Xi, Phi Sigma, Psi Chi, numerous others. Contbr. monographs in capillary movement in porous materials, physiology and biochemistry of anthropoda; also articles to profl. jours. Home: 405 NW Woodland Rd Indian Hills in Riverside Kansas City MO 64150

CLARESON, THOMAS DEAN, educator; b. Austin, Minn., Aug. 26, 1926; s. Thomas Albert and Ruth (Dalager) C.; B.A., U. Minn., 1946; M.A., Ind. U., 1949; Ph.D., U. Pa., 1955; m. Alice Jane Super, Dec. 23, 1954; 1 son, Thomas Frederic Reade. Grad. asst. in English, Ind. U., 1947-49, U. Pa., 1950-53; instr. N.Mex. A. & M. U., 1949-50, U. Md. Overseas Program, 1953-54, Norwich U., 1954-55; faculty Coll. of Wooster (Ohio), 1955—, prof. English, 1967—. Chmn. Sci. Fiction Research Assn., Inc., 1970-76. Danforth grantee, 1959; Am. Philos. Soc. research grantee, 1960, 64, 66-67; Nat. Endowment for Humanities summer grantee, 1976. Mem. Modern Lang. Assn. (exec. council sect. popular culture 1976-80), Am. Studies Assn., Coll. English Assn. of Ohio (exec. com. 1969-71, v.p. 1975, pres. 1976), Popular Culture Assn. Presbyn. Author: Science and Society: Readings at Midcentury, 1961; Victorian Essays: A Symposium, 1967; SF: The Other Side of Realism, 1971; SF Criticism: An Annotated Checklist, 1972; A Spectrum of Worlds, 1972; Science Fiction: A Dream of Other Worlds, 1973; Voices for the Future: Major SF Authors, 1976; Many Futures, Many Worlds, 1977. Editor: Extrapolation, 1959—; mem. editorial bd. Victorian Poetry, 1963—; adv. editor Greenwood Press reprint series of sci. fiction mags. Home: 2223 Friar Tuck Circle Wooster OH 44691

CLARIDGE, RICHARD T., educator; b. St. Louis, Feb. 27, 1922; s. William Roy and Mamie Harriet (Kowaleski) C.; student Washington U., 1940-43; M.A., St. Louis U., 1951; postgrad. Columbia, 1957, So. Ill. U., 1970-74. Tchr. drama, asso. dir. children's theatre St. Louis YMCA, 1946-51; dir. drama and speech E.Alton-Wood River (Ill.) High Sch., 1951—, chmn. dept. English and speech, 1964—. Mem. Internat. Thespian Soc. (state dir. 1955-68), Nat. Council Tchrs. English, Ill. Assn. Tchrs. English, Ill. Speech and Theatre Assn. Home: 260 Norwood Dr East Alton IL 62024 Office: 777 Wood River Ave Wood River IL 62095

CLARK, AVRIL MARIE, microbiologist; b. Quincy, Ill., Jan. 26, 1924; d. Wallace Edward and Marie A. (Recker) Heberling; B.S., Quincy Coll., 1945; student St. John Hosp. Sch. of Med. Tech., 1946-47; 1 dau., Joan Marie Clark Queen. Microbiologist, St. John's Mercy Hosp., St. Louis, 1948-52; med. technologist St. Frances Hosp. Lab., Peoria, Ill., 1956-58; lectr. in microbiology Quincy Coll. (Ill.), 1966-70; adminstrv. technologist, ednl. coordinator St. Mary Hosp., Quincy, 1959—. Pres. Altrusa Club, 1974-76; bd. govs. for Dogwood Festival, C. of C., 1975-77, bd. dirs. Quincy Soc. Fine Arts; active United Fund, 1975; bd. dirs. Quincy Community Little Theatre,

Quincy Art Club, ESA World Center Found. Named Outstanding Woman of Ill., ESA Orgn., 1968; Outstanding Woman of Quincy, 1970. Mem. Am. Soc. Med. Tech.; Am. Soc. Clinical Pathologists. Republican. Catholic. Club: Elks Aux. Home: 2236 Vermont St Quincy IL 62301 Office: 1415 Vermont St Quincy IL 62301

CLARK, BURR, JR., editor; b. Howell, Mich., Jan. 20, 1924; s. Walter Burr and Hazel Lydia (Ferguson) C.; B.S., Mich. State U., 1952; M.S., U. N.H., 1960; Ph.D., W.Va. U., 1966; m. Mary Margaret Chubb, Apr. 5, 1947; children—Carol (Mrs. Linwood A. Clements), Janet Margaret, Brian Burr. Dairy farmer, Howell, 1952-56; research asst. W.Va. U., Morgantown, 1960-63; editor Chem. Abstracts Service, Columbus, O., 1963—. Mem. Am. Chem. Soc., AAAS, Sigma Xi, Alpha Zeta, Phi Sigma. Republican. Methodist. Home: 200 Larrimer Ave Worthington OH 43085 Office: 2540 Olentangy River Rd Columbus OH 43210

CLARK, C. KENNETH, JR., lawyer; b. Youngstown, Ohio, Mar. 11, 1930; s. C. Kenneth and Katharine (Griswold) C.; A.B., Oberlin Coll., 1951; J.D., Harvard U., 1954. Admitted to Ohio bar, 1954; partner firm Harrington, Huxley & Smith, Youngstown, 1963—; dir. WKBN Broadcasting Corp., Youngstown, others. Pres. Vol. Service Bur. Youngstown, 1965-68; Trustee Youngstown Health and Welfare Council, Youngstown Playground Assn., Asso. Neighborhood Centers Youngstown, pres., 1969. Mem. Am., Ohio State bar assns., U.S. Jud. Conf. for Sixth Circuit, Youngstown Area C. of C. Presbyn. Clubs: Torch (Youngstown, dir.), Cambium (pres. 1967-68), Youngstown. Home: 1637 Tanglewood Dr Youngstown OH 44505 Office: Mahoning Bank Bldg Youngstown OH 44503

CLARK, CURTIS VAUGHN, dentist; b. Lenoir City, Tenn., Nov. 21, 1929; s. Charles Hobart and Minnie J. (Cardwell) C.; B.M. (Rector scholar), DePauw U., 1952; postgrad. Vienna Acad., 1952; D.D.S., Ind. U., 1964; m. Mary Josephine Morton, June 17, 1953 (div. Mar. 1956); 1 dau., Catherine Elizabeth (dec.). Pub. relations Fund Raising Assn., Indpls., 1955-59; pvt. practice dentistry, Indpls., 1964—. Instr. crown and bridge Ind. U. Sch. Dentistry, 1964-66. Bd. dirs., gen. chmn. audience devel., vice chmn. condr. search com. Indpls. Symphony, 1974—, chmn. season tickets subscriptions, 1975. Served with AUS, 1953-55. Recipient award Delta Sigma Delta nat. essay competition, 1963. Mem. Am., Ind. (alternate del. ho. dels. 1969—) dental assns., Indpls. Dist. Dental Soc. (bus. mgr. jour. 1967-69, bd. dirs. 1974-76, chmn. ad hoc forum), Fedn. Dentaire Internationale, Delta Tau Delta, Phi Mu Alpha, Pi Kappa Lambda, Delta Sigma Delta, Omicron Kappa Upsilon. Republican. Presbyn. Club: Manor House (Indpls.). Home: 5440 Hedgerow Dr Indianapolis IN 46226 Office: 3901 N Meridian St Suite 336 Indianapolis IN 46208

CLARK, DAVID WILLARD, hosp. adminstr.; b. Rockford, Ill., May 17, 1930; s. Willard Wilbur and Arline Marie (Anderson) C.; m. Barbara Ardel Boyd, June 18, 1955; children—Deborah Jean, Alan Boyd; B.S., Beloit Coll., 1952; M.B.A., U. Chgo., 1955. Adminstrv. resident Univ. Hosps. of Cleve., 1955-56, adminstrv. asst., 1956-60, asst. adminstr., 1960-66, asso. adminstr., 1966-67, adminstr., 1967—; pres. Hosp. Finance Corp., Med. Center Co. Chmn. hosp. div. United Torch, 1976. Mem. Am., Ohio (trustee, dist. chmn.), Greater Cleve. (chmn.) hosp. assns., Am. Coll. Hosp. Adminstrs., Univ. Hosps. Exec. Council, Council Teaching Hosps., Phi Beta Kappa. Club: Masons. Recipient Kate Baron Service award, 1952. Home: 18906 Scottsdale Blvd Cleveland OH 44106 Office: 2065 Adelbert Rd Cleveland OH 44106

CLARK, DOROTHY J. FOX (MRS. ROBERT I. CLARK), editor, columnist, historian, former curator; b. Terre Haute, Ind., July 3, 1919; d. George A. and Grace (Powell) Fox; student Santa Rosa Jr. Coll., Ind. State U.; m. Robert I. Clark, June 3, 1939; children—James Powell (dec.), Dennis Andrew. Sec., Vigo County Hist. Soc., Inc., Terre Haute, 1960—; curator Hist. Mus. Wabash Valley, Terre Haute, 1960-73, Paul Dresser Birthplace, Terre Haute, 1963-73; hist. columnist Sunday Terre Haute Tribune-Star, 1956—, Woman's editor, 1973—. Cons. history Wabash Valley Supplementary Ednl. Center, Ind. State U., 1965-68. Mem. adv. council Vigo County Park and Recreation Bd., 1967-71; pres. Vigo County Cemetery Commn., 1969—; county chmn. Ind. Sesquicentennial, 1966; sec., Terre Haute Heritage, Inc., 1966-67; mem. regional council Ind. State Mus., 1970-73; mem. Ind. Commn. Am. Revolution Bicentennial; county chmn. Vigo County Bicentennial. Sch. trustee Vigo County, 1960. Bd. dirs. Banks of the Wabash Festival Assn. Mem. D.A.R. (chpt. regent 1959-61), Daus. Am. Colonists, Magna Charta Dames, Soc. Genealogists (London, Eng.), Terre Haute C. of C. (recreation and tourism com.). Home: 2032 N 8th St Terre Haute IN 47804 Office: 721 Wabash Ave Tribune Bldg Terre Haute IN 47808

CLARK, ERNEST LYNN, state agency exec.; b. St. Louis, May 12, 1947; s. John C. and Ella Mae (Baker) C.; A.A., St. Louis Jr. Coll. Dist., 1973; B.S. in Bus. Adminstrn., B.S. in Law Enforcement and Corrections, N.E. Mo. State U., 1975. Dep. clk., then asst. chief clk. Ct. Criminal Causes, St. Louis, 1969-70; cons. Ct. Adminstrv. Office, St. Louis, 1971-72; data processor Gen. Bancshares Service Corp., St. Louis, 1971-75, N.E. Mo. State U., Kirksville, 1973-74; research analyst Mo. Ho. of Reps., Jefferson City, 1975-76, 76-77; statewide campaign coordinator candidate for lt. gov. Mo., 1976; personnel specialist Bi-State Devel. Agency, St. Louis, 1977—; cons. data processing, fed. funding, mgmt. and personnel relations; fed. funding specialist Mo. Ho. of Reps., 1975. Co-organizer 1st Nat. Alliance of Businessmen's Job Fair for Vets., St. Louis, 1971; mem. revised policy manual com. St. Louis Jr. Coll. Dist., 1971. Served with USCG, 1965-69. Recipient letter of commendation for community service St. Louis Mayor, 1972; citation Mo. Ho. of Reps., 1977. Mem. Collegiate Vets. Mo. (founder), St. Louis Council Collegiate Vets. (a founder), Am. Criminal Justice Assn., Am. Mgmt. Assn., Mo. Sheriff's Assn. Clubs: Moose, Odd Fellows. Home: 2929 Magnolia Ave Saint Louis MO 63118 Office: 3869 Park Ave Saint Louis MO 63110

CLARK, GEORGE ALEXANDER, ophthalmologist; b. Indpls., Dec. 14, 1927; s. Cecil Pratt and Isabella Marie (Brodie) C.; B.S., Ind. U., 1951, M.D., 1954; postgrad. Wayne State U., 1957-60; m. Shirley Lee Sprague, June 14, 1953; children—George Gregory, James Sprague, Karin Lee. Intern, Marion County (Ind.) Gen. Hosp., Indpls., 1954-55; resident Detroit Receiving Hosp., 1957-60; fellow in ophthalmology Kresge Eye Inst. Wayne State U., Detroit, 1957-60; practice medicine specializing in ophthalmologic surgery, 1960—; mem. staff Community Hosp. Indpls., Winona Hosp. Indpls., St. Francis Hosp.; instr. medicine Ind. U., 1960—; cons. in ophthalmology USPHS, 1959-60. Served with USMC, 1946-47; USAF, 1955-57. Mem. Ind., Indpls. opthalmological otolaryngology socs., Am., Ind. med. assns., Marion County Med. Soc., Am. Acad. Ophthalmology Otolaryngology, Internat. Inteaocular Lens Soc., Kiwanis. Republican. Presbyterian. Club: Meridian Hills Country. Home: 620 Forest Blvd Indianapolis IN 46240 Office: 50 E 91st St #214 Indianapolis IN 46240

CLARK, GERALD EUGENE, power plant engr.; b. Holmes County, Ohio, Apr. 21, 1939; s. Herbert William and Peral L. (McCaughey) C.; G.E.D., Akron U., 1966; student Internat. Corr. Schs., 1968-72; m. Ruth Ellen Bernard, Aug. 6, 1960; children—Alan, Bradley, Curtis, Deanna, Elena, Foster. Elec. generation power plant engr. Buckeye Holmesville Mfg. Co., Holmesville, Ohio, 1961-64; engr. Goodyear Tire and Rubber Co., Akron, Ohio, 1964-68; inspector Comml. Union Engring. Co., N.Y.C., 1968-69; plant supt. Orrville (Ohio) Municipal Utilities Co., 1970—. Served with USN, 1957. Certified Am. Social Mech. Engr. Mem. ASME. Roman Catholic. Home: 957 N Main St Orrville OH 44667 Office: PO Box 207 N Main St Orrville OH 44667

CLARK, GERTRUDE JOSEPHINE, ry. equipment mfg. co. exec., writer; b. Chgo.; d. George W. and Helen (Cooper) C.; grad. Moser Bus. Coll., 1937, Boulevard Modeling Sch., 1949; student Northwestern U., 1948-69, Central YMCA Coll., Chgo., 1969. Sec. Cardwell Westinghouse Co., Chgo., 1941-63, dir. advt. and pub. relations, 1964—; also subs.'s; feature writer articles Chgo. Tribune, 1957—, Chgo. Daily News, 1969—, Greek Press, Chgo. Tribune, 1962—, numerous other mags. Bd. dirs. Friends of Lit., Chgo., 1969—. Recipient 2d place award Medill Sch. Journalism, Northwestern U., 1962. Mem. Nat. Secs. Assn. Chgo., Met. Bus. and Profl. Women's Club, Ill. Woman's Press Assn. (chmn. publicity 1975-76), Women's Advt. Club Chgo. (membership com. 1968-69, chmn. scholarship com. 1970-71), Iota Sigma Epsilon (sec. 1951, pres.-elect 1967-68), Women in Communications, Nat. League Am. Pen Women, Chgo. Symphony Soc., Smithsonian Instn., Am. Bible Soc., Chgo. Evening Club, Nat. Geog. Soc., Methodist (adminstrv. bd., mem. fin. com., mem. United Meth. Women). Clubs: Zonta (dir. 1966-67) (Chgo.); Toastmistress (pres.). Contbr. articles to profl. jours.

CLARK, JACK PROW, physician; b. Bloomington, Ind., June 15, 1932; s. Fred Orlin and Beulah Alice (Prow) C.; M.D., Ind. U., 1956; m. Carolyn Elizabeth Shaffer, June 26, 1966; children—Cathy Ann, Susan Kay, David Allan, Bruce Lee. Intern USPHS Hosp., Seattle, Navajo Indian Hosp., Ft. Defiance, Ariz., 1956-57; family practice medicine, Syracuse, Ind., 1959—; active staff Goshen (Ind.) Gen. Hosp.; preceptor in family practice Ind. U. Sch. Medicine; pres. Syracuse Family Practice, Inc. Active Boy Scouts Am. Served with USPHS, 1957-59. Diplomate Am. Bd. Family Practice. Fellow Am. Geriatric Soc., Am. Acad. Family Physicians (recipient Ross award 1961); mem. Ind. Acad. Family Physicians (dist. pres. 1968), Ind. Med. Assn. Methodist (chmn. missions commn. 1970-71, trustee bldg. com. 1966-69, chmn. Key 73, 1973, chmn. evangelism 1973, chmn. ofcl. bd. 1973, lay leader 1975-77). Home: Rural Route 3 Box 312 Syracuse IN 46567 Office: 303 S Huntington St Syracuse IN 46567

CLARK, JAMES GORDON, cons. engr.; b. Kansas City, Mo., Dec. 23, 1913; s. John Arthur and Stella (Wright) C.; A.S., Kansas City Jr. Coll., 1933; B.S. with honors, U. Ill., 1935, M.S., 1939; m. Jeannette Hazel McKinstry, May 8, 1937 (dec. Dec. 2, 1951); children—Nannette Kay, Diana Jean; m. 2d, Janice Elizabeth Winters, Nov. 28, 1952; children—Mary Elizabeth, Jane, James. Instr. civil engring. Ore. State Coll., 1935; jr. engr. U.S. Bur. Reclamation, Denver, 1936; from instr. to prof. civil engring. U. Ill., 1936-55; interim profl. work structural engring. Am. Bridge Co., Bethlehem Steel Co., Howard, Needles, Tammen & Bergendoff, Curtiss Wright Corp.; structural engr. Consol. Vultee Aircraft Corp., 1944-45; partner Balke & Clark, 1953-54; asso. Harry Balke Engrs., 1955; partner Clark & Daily, 1956, partner Clark, Daily & Dietz, 1957-63; pres. Clark, Dietz & Assos., engrs., Urbana, Ill., Memphis, Sanford, Fla., Jackson, Miss., Carbondale, Ill., Chgo. and St. Louis, 1963-75, cons., 1975—; partner Clark, Altay & Assos., 1965—. Mem. profl. engrs. license com. State Ill.; chmn. James F. Lincoln Arc Welding Found. Award Programs, 1949, 50, 52, 58. Trustee Ill. Bapt. Student Found., 1954—. Mem. Nat., Ill. socs. profl. engrs., Am. Soc. C.E. (past pres. Central Ill. sect.), Am. Soc. Engring. Edn., Am. Ry. Engring. Assn., Am. Soc. Testing Materials, Am. Welding Soc., Hwy. Research Bd., Am. Ry. Bridge and Bldg. Assn., Sigma Xi, Tau Beta Pi, Chi Epsilon. Author: Elementary Theory and Design of Flexural Members (with J. Vawter), 1950; Welded Deck Highway Bridges, 1950; Welded Highway Bridge Designs, 1952; Comparative Bridge Designs, 1954; Welded Interstate Highway Bridges, 1959. Home: 716 W Florida Ave Urbana IL 61801 Office: 211 N Race St Urbana IL 61801

CLARK, JAMES RICHARD, JR., lawyer; b. Cin., Nov. 14, 1921; s. James Richard and Helen H. (Herschede) C.; student Notre Dame U., 1943; J.D., U. Cin., 1947; m. Helen E. Magers, June 9, 1973; children by previous marriage—Cynthia Jane, Carol Ann. Admitted to Ohio bar, 1947; partner firm Clark, Hellebush, Cunningham & Kepley Co. L.P.A. and predecessor, Cin., 1947—. Former chmn. Community Health and Welfare Council; former trustee Community Chest and Council; former pres. Ohio Citizens Council; adv. bd. Hamilton County Welfare Dept.; lay adv. bd. Our Lady of Mercy Hosp.; mem. Ohio Ho. of Reps., 1951-53; commr. Hamilton County, 1953-60. Served to lt. inf., AUS, 1943-46; PTO. Mem. Am., Ohio, Cin. bar assns., Am. Legion, DAV. Republican. Roman Catholic. Clubs: Cincinnati, Hyde Park Country. Home: 6895 Farmbrook Dr Cincinnati OH 45230 Office: 2800 Carew Tower Cincinnati OH 45202

CLARK, JOHN DAVIS, JR., food service co. exec.; b. Orange, N.J., Oct. 21, 1948; s. John Davis and Rosella Faith (Machey) C.; B.S. in Bus. Adminstrn., U. Md., 1972, M.B.A., 1972; m. Elaine Leavitt, July 13, 1970. Mgmt. devel. Quality Inns Internat., Silver Springs, Md., 1973; dir. mktg. Rodeway Inns Am., Dallas, 1973-75; v.p. mktg. Arthur Treacher's Fish & Chips, Columbus, Ohio, 1975—. Nat. Defense fellow, 1972. Mem. Am. Mktg. Assn. Home: 10647 Riverside Dr Powell OH 43065 Office: 1328 Dublin Rd Columbus OH 43215

CLARK, JOHN WILLIAM, med. technologist; b. Aurora, Ill., May 17, 1947; s. Clarence William and Helen Marie (Fairbanks) C.; B.S. in Med. Tech., No. Ill. U., 1970; m. Marsha M. Hennig, Feb. 26, 1972; 1 dau., Sarah. Med. tech. intern Copley Meml. Hosp., Aurora, 1968-69, gen. med. technologist, 1969-70, supr. microbiology and serology, 1970-77; microbiology cons. Med. Technomics, Oak Brook, Ill., 1976—; lab. supr. Dreyer Med. Clinic, Aurora, Ill., 1977—. Mem. Am., Ill. socs. microbiology, Am. Soc. Clin. Pathologists. Club: Kiwanis. Inventor in field. Home: Rural Route 3 Box 326 Aurora IL 60504 Office: Dreyer Med Clinic 1870 W Galena Blvd Aurora IL 60506

CLARK, KENNETH RAYMOND, lawyer; b. Knoxville, Ia., Feb. 6, 1909; s. Lawrence Otis and Jennie (Ver Ploeg) C.; B.A., Coe Coll., 1930, LL.D., 1965; LL.B., Columbia, 1933; LL.M., U. Mich., 1935. Admitted to Ill. bar, 1935, since practiced in Chgo., 1935—; past lectr. in law Northwestern U. Sch. Commerce. Trustee Coe Coll. Served to capt. AUS, World War II. Presbyn. Clubs: Saddle and Cycle, Racquet (Chgo.). Author: Profit Sharing and Pension Plans, 1946; Taxation of Life Insurance and Annuities, 1942. Home: 1449 Astor St Chicago IL 60610 Office: 135 S LaSalle St Chicago IL 60603

CLARK, LARRY DALTON, civil engr.; b. Sask., Can., May 12, 1942; s. Albert Ray and Christina Emily (Marum) C.; B.S. in Civil Engring., S.D. Sch. Mines, Rapid City, 1971; m. Janice Martina Kettleson, Aug. 16, 1969; children—Tamara Dayrie, Laura Janelle. Engr. in tng. Iowa Hwy. Commn., Ames, 1971-75; asst. resident engr. Iowa Dept. Transp., New Hampton, 1975-76, acting resident engr., 1977—. Active local United Way campaign, 1976-77. Registered profl. engr., Iowa. Mem. ASCE, Nat., Iowa socs. profl. engrs., Sigma Tau. Lutheran. Home: 511 Wilson St New Hampton IA 50659 Office: Box 89 New Hampton IA 50659

CLARK, M.R., supt. schs.; b. Union, Iowa, Aug. 10, 1904; s. Fred C. and Elizabeth Frances (Hansen) C.; A.B., Iowa State Tchrs. Coll., 1931; M.A., State U. Iowa, 1936; LL.D., Upper Iowa Coll., 1967; m. Dorothy A. Cunliffe, June 20, 1931; 1 dau., Barbara Ann. Classroom instr., Randalia, Iowa, 1925-31, supt. schs., 1931-37, West Branch, Iowa, 1937-40, Sac City, Iowa, 1940-46, Dubuque, Iowa, 1946-66; supt. Area One Vocational Tech. Sch. Dist., Calmar, Iowa, 1966-75. Dir. Iowa High Sch. Ins. Co. Pres. Cummunity Chest, 1952-53, Ia. Community Chests and Councils, 1953; pres. N.E. Iowa Boy Scout Council (Silver Beaver award). Bd. dirs. Dubuque County Mental Health, Dubuque Cancer Soc., A.R.C., United Fund Iowa. Recipient Alumni Service award State Coll. Iowa; classroom and lab. named in his honor. Mem. N.E.A., Am. Assn. Sch. Adminstrs., Am., Iowa assns. adult edn., Iowa Edn. Assn. (past pres. N.E. dist.), Iowa Supts. Club (pres. 1956-57), Iowa Area Sch. Adminstrs. (pres. 1971-73), Dubuque C. of C. (dir.), Epsilon Pi Tau, Phi Delta Kappa. Republican. Methodist. Mason (32 deg., Shriner); mem. Order Eastern Star. Clubs: Rotary (pres.; dist. gov. 1957-58), Dubuque Auto (dir.). Contbr. to jours. Home: 102 Sunset Dr Decorah IA 52101

CLARK, MARTIN ELLIOTT, counselor; b. Mattoon, Ill., July 14, 1945; s. Glen Edward and Ellen Iline (Faubion) C.; B.A., Bob Jones U., 1967, M.A., 1968; Ed.D., Va. Poly. Inst. & State U., 1974; m. Bonni-Jean Garrison, July 31, 1966; children—Cherish Christina, MacKensie Diahann. Instr., Bob Jones U., 1967-68; ordained to ministry, Baptist Ch., 1967; asst. minister Calvary Bapt. Ch., Landrum, S.C., 1967-68; minister United Bapt. Ch., Easton, Me., 1968-70, College Bapt. Ch., Blacksburg, Va., 1970-74; dir. counseling service Cedarville (Ohio) Coll., 1974—; vis. prof. Bapt. Bible Sem., Manila, Philippines, 1975; vis. prof. Christian Heritage Coll., San Diego, 1976; chaplain Va. Poly. Inst. & State U., 1970-74. Mem. Evang. Theol. Soc., Am., Ohio personnel and guidance assns., Am. Ohio coll. personnel assns. Bapt. Author: The Bible Has The Answer, 1976; contbr. articles to religious periodicals. Home: 111 Creamer Dr PO Box 77 Cedarville OH 45314 Office: Cedarville Coll Cedarville OH 45314

CLARK, MARY ROMAYNE SCHROEDER (MRS. DONALD ARTHUR CLARK), educator, civic worker; b. Fergus Falls, Minn.; d. Christian Frederick and Dorothy Genevieve (Miller) Schroeder; B.A., Coll. St. Teresa, 1944; diploma fine arts Conservatory St. Cecelia, 1944; postgrad. Marquette U., U. Salzburg (Austria); m. Donald Arthur Clark, Aug. 24, 1946 (dec. Jan. 1975); children—Donald Arthur, Anne Elizabeth, Christopher John. Instr., Ottumwa (Iowa) Heights Coll., 1944-46; instr. U. N.D., Grand Forks, 1946-48, Marquette U., Milw., 1948-52, Milw. Area Tech. Coll., 1962-66, Mt. Mary Coll., Milw., 1976—. Mem. com. on edn. U.S. Cath. Conf., Washington, 1971-75; state vol. adviser Nat. Found., 1971—; mem. adv. bd. Sickle Cell Disease Center, Deaconess Hosp., Milw., 1970-73; mem. nat. alumnae bd. Coll. St. Teresa, Winona, Minn., 1970—; mem. bd. edn. Archdiocese Milw., 1965-71, pres., 1967-71. Named Wis. Woman of Year, Wis. Cath. War Vets., 1963, Alumna of Year, Coll. St. Teresa, 1969, Outstanding Vol. Nat. Found., 1974, Vol. Activist Germaine Monteil, 1974. Mem. Archdiocesan Confraternity Christian Mothers (pres. 1961-63), Archdiocesan League Cath. Home and Sch. Assns. (pres. 1963-65), Archdiocesan Council Cath. Women (dist. pres. 1965-67), Nat. Forum Cath. Parents Orgns. (v.p. 1977), Internat. Fedn. Cath. Alumnae, AAUW, Marquette U. Faculty Wives (pres. 1959). Home: 317 N Story Pkwy Milwaukee WI 53208

CLARK, MONTAGUE GRAHAM, JR., coll. pres.; b. Charlotte, N.C., Feb. 25, 1909; s. Montague G. and Alice C. (Graham) C.; student Ga. Inst. Tech. Sch. Engring.; LL.D., Drury Coll., 1957; Ed.D., S.W. Baptist Coll., 1972; Litt.D., Sch. of the Ozarks, 1975; m. Elizabeth Hoyt, May 2, 1933; children—Elizabeth (Mrs. Joe Embser), Alice (Mrs. Harold Davis), Margaret (Mrs. William Miller), Julia (Mrs. Cecil Hampton). Vice pres. Hoyt & Co., Atlanta, 1934-46; v.p. Sch. of Ozarks, Point Lookout, Mo., 1946-52, pres., 1952—, sec. bd. trustees, 1957-71, now trustee; ordained to ministry Presbyn. Ch., 1950; dir. Bank of Taney County; dir., mem. exec. com., sec. corp. Blue Cross. Past mem. Commn. on Colls. and Univs., North Central Assn. Colls. and Secondary Schs.; former moderator Lafayette Presbytery and Synod of Mo., Presbyn. Ch. of U.S. Past mem. nat. adv. council on health professions edn. NIH; mem. Nat. council Boy Scouts Am., also mem. adv. bd. Ozarks Empire Area council; mem. Wilson's Creek Battlefield Nat. Commn., 1961—; hon. mem. Mo. Am. Revolution Bicentennial Commn.; former v.p. Am. Heart Assn., also dir.; mem. exec. com., chmn. fund raising adv. and policy com., Gt. Plains regional chmn.; chmn. Mo. Heart Fund, mem. adv. council Council on Am. Affairs. Chmn. bd. Mo. Heart Assn.; trustee Patriotic Edn., Inc.; mem. South Central/Lakes County Med. Services System; v.p. Thomas Hart Benton Homestead Meml. Commn. Served to maj. Internal Security, World War II. Named Ark. traveler, 1962; recipient Silver Beaver award Boy Scouts Am., Gold Heart award Am. Heart Assn., George Washington certificate Freedoms Found., 1974, numerous other awards; named to Ozark Hall of Fame. Mem. S.A.R. (past pres. gen. nat. soc., hon. v.p. Mo. Soc.; Nat. Soc. Good Citizenship medal, Patriot medal, Minute Man award, Va. Soc. medal), Navy League U.S., Branson C. of C. (econ. devel. com.), Mo. Pilots Assn. (1st chmn. bd.), Civil Air Patrol (dir., adv. bd.), White River Valley Hist. Soc. (past pres.), Soc. Colonial Wars, Acad. Mo. Squires, Order Founders and Patriots Am., Air Force Assn., Internat. Assn. Chiefs of Police. Clubs: Mason (33 deg., Shriner, K.T.), Rotary (past local pres., dist. gov. 1966-67), De Molay, Shrine. Address: The Sch of the Ozarks Point Lookout MO 65726

CLARK, PATSY SUE, pub. relations dir.; b. Vernon, Tex., Aug. 6, 1934; d. Henry Devrick and Christine B. (Barrett) Hays; B.A. in Communications, Baylor U., 1955; m. John D. Clark; children—Russell Devrick, Susan Patricia. Copy writer Alexander McKenzie Advt., Dallas, 1966-67; concept dir. Vic Lundberg, Inc., Advt., Grand Rapids, 1967-70; dir. pub. relations Williams & Works, Inc., Cons. Engrs., Planners, Architects, Surveyors, Geologists, Grand Rapids, 1970—. Pres., Forest Hills (Mich.) No. High Sch. Music Assn. Recipient Excellence awards Advt. Council Grand Rapids, 1969, Rockford, Ill., 1969, Springfield, Ohio, 1969, Midwest Advt. Council, 1969. Mem. Soc. Tech. Communications (dir., Merit award 1974), Pub. Relations Soc. Am. (exec. bd. govt. sect.), Mich. Assn. Design Profls. (polit. action com.). Republican. Home: 4243 Greenbrier Ct SE Grand Rapids MI 49506 Office: 611 Cascade West Pkwy SE Grand Rapids MI 49506

CLARK, PAUL EDWARD, pub.; b. Metropolis, Ill., Mar. 7, 1941; s. Paul E. and Lillie Jean (Melcher) C.; B.A., So. Ill. U., 1963, M.A., 1965; M.Div., Northwestern U., 1970; D.Mus., Inst. Musical Research (London), 1973; Ph.D., U. Ill., 1978. Staff accompanist The Story (TV series) and White Sisters (Word Records), 1959-62; staff accompanist voice faculty So. Ill. U., Carbondale, 1961-65; ordained to ministry, Meth. Ch., 1966; pastor Stockland (Ill.) United Meth. Ch., 1966-70; minister of music First United Meth. Ch., Watseka, Ill., 1972-76; dir. choral activities Unit 3, Donovan (Ill.) schs., 1970—; studio musician Chgo., Nashville, Los Angeles, 1966—; pres. Clark

Music Pub. and Prodn., Watseka, 1973—; cons. for workshops, univs. Named Piano Tchr. of the Year, So. Ill. U., 1970; Gospel Music Instrumentalist award, 1971; Ill. Chess Coach award, 1973, 74; U. Calif. at Los Angeles fellow, 1971. Mem. Am. Choral Dirs. Assn. (dist. chmn. 1977-80), Am. Fedn. Musicians, Music Educators Nat. Conf., Ill. Music Educators Assn., U.S. Chess Fedn., So. Ill. U. Alumni Assn., NEA, Broadcast Music Inc., Phi Mu Alpha, Mu Alpha Theta. Republican. Methodist. Contbr. articles in field to profl. jours. music reviewer, critic, columnist The Illiana Spirit (newspaper), 1976—; composer; The Voice That Calls His Name, 1961; Spring Was Just A Child, 1977; Country Living, 1976; Losing is the Hurting Side of Love, 1977; Jesus Dear Jesus, 1971. Home: 115 W Locust St Watseka IL 60970 Office: PO Box 299 Watseka IL 60970

CLARK, PERCY, JR., ednl. adminstr.; b. Chgo., July 21, 1942; s. Percy and Mary (Carson) C.; B.A., Western Mich. U., 1964, M.A., 1969; m. Carol Sue Christophersen, Mar. 19, 1964; children—Mark, Michelle, Nicole. Elementary and secondary classroom tchr. Portage (Mich.) pub. schs., 1964-68; inservice coordinator Kalamazoo Valley Intermediate Sch. Dist., 1968-69; prin. Northglade Elementary Sch., Kalamazoo, 1969-72; dir. student services Kalamazoo pub. schs., 1972—; cons. in field. Bd. dirs. Northside Assn. Community Devel., Kalamazoo Jr. Achievement, Kalamazoo Boys Club, Kalamazoo County Vol. Services Program, Kalamazoo Goodwill Industries, Kalamazoo Child Guidance Clinic, Kalamazoo Family Health Center, Kalamazoo chpt. NAACP; mem. outreach com. Boy Scouts Am. Recipient various certificates of appreciation. Mem. Am., Mich. personnel and guidance assns., Assn. Supervision and Curriculum Devel., Nat. Assn. Pupil Personnel Adminstrs., Mich. Assn. Elementary Sch. Prins., Mich. Soc. Mental Health. Home: 1723 Carlsbrook St Portage MI 49081 Office: 1220 Howard St Kalamazoo MI 49008

CLARK, PETER BRUCE, newspaper exec.; b. Detroit, Oct. 23, 1928; s. Rex Scripps and Marian (Peters) C.; B.A., Pomona Coll., 1952, LL.D., 1972; M. Pub. Adminstrn., Syracuse U., 1953; Ph.D., U. Chgo., 1959; H.H.D., Mich. State U., 1973; LL.D. (hon.), U. Mich., 1977; m. Lianne Schroeder, December 21, 1952; children—Ellen Lianne, James Bruce. Research asso. polit. sci. U. Chgo., 1957-58, instr., 1958-59; asst. prof. polit. sci. Yale, 1959-61; with Eve. News Assn., Detroit, 1960—, sec., 1960-61, v.p., asst. pub., 1961-63, pres., publisher Detroit News, 1963—, chmn. bd., dir., 1969—; chmn. Fed. Res. Bank Chgo., 1975—. Bd. dirs. United Found., United Hosps. Detroit. Served with Signal Corps, AUS, 1953-55. Mem. Am. Newspaper Pubs. Assn. (dir. 1966-74), Am. Soc. Newspaper Editors, Am. Polit. Sci. Assn., Pi Sigma Alpha. Clubs: Adcraft, Economic, Detroit, Detroit Athletic, Country (Detroit). Office: Detroit News 615 Lafayette Blvd Detroit MI 48231

CLARK, PHILLIP THEODORE, travel exec., writer; b. St. Cloud, Minn., May 27, 1921; s. Harry Brooks and Mabel (Lundgren) C.; B.A., U. Minn., 1945. Garden editor Living for Young Homemakers mag., N.Y.C., 1957; editor Hort. mag. Mass. Hort. Soc., Boston, 1958-60; garden editor The News, Mexico City, 1951—; pub. relations dir. N.Y. Bot. Garden, N.Y.C., 1962-66; pub. relations counsel Field Mus. of Natural History, Chgo., 1966-69, chief museum's worldwide natural history tours, 1966-71; chief Phil Clark's Natural History Tours, Chgo., 1971—. Bd. dirs. Outdoor Ethics Guild; hon. bd. dirs. Historia Natural y Pro Natura (Guatemala). Fellow Royal Horticulture Soc. Gt. Britain; mem. Hort. Soc. Am., Am. Philatelic Soc., Pan-Am. Council of Chgo., La. Soc. Hort. Research (hon.), Bot. Soc. Mexico, Bombay Natural History Soc. Lutheran. Author: A Guide to Mexican Flora, 1964; A Flower Lover's Guide to Mexico, 1971; articles in various mags., garden writer World Book Ency. Yearbook, 1975-77. Home: Sherry Apts 5300 S Shore Dr Chicago IL 60615

CLARK, RICHARD, U.S. senator; b. Paris, Iowa, Sept. 14, 1929; s. Clarence and Bernice (Anderson) C.; student U. Md., in Wiesbaden, Germany, 1950-52, U. Frankfurt (Germany), 1950-52; B.A., Upper Iowa U., 1953; M.A., U. Iowa, 1956; m. Jean Gross, June 6, 1954; children—Julie, Tom. Asst. prof. history and polit. sci. Upper Iowa U., 1959-64; adminstrv. asst. to Congressman John C. Culver, 1965-72; mem. U.S. Senate, 1972—. Chmn., Ia. Office Emergency Planning, 1963-65, Iowa Civil Def. Adminstrn., 1963-65. Served with AUS, 1951-52. Mem. Am. Hist. Assn., Conf. on European History, Am. Assn. for Advancement Slavic Studies, A.A.U.P., Conf. on Slavic and East European History. Office: 404 Old Senate Office Bldg Washington DC 20510

CLARK, ROBERT LOY, human services adminstr.; b. Kansas City, Mo., July 2, 1937; s. Robert William and Donna Lavonna (Loy) C.; A.B., No. Colo. U., 1959; postgrad. Syracuse U., 1959; M.S. in Psychology, Ft. Hays (Kans.) State U., 1963; postgrad. U. Nebr., 1963; m. Connie Lou Davis, Sept. 3, 1960; children—Vicki Marie, Robert Scott, Angie Linn. Vocational rehab. counselor Hays (Kans.) Div. Rehab. Services, 1960-62, Lincoln (Nebr.) Div. Rehab. Services, 1964-65, Glenwood (Iowa) Hosp.-Sch. for Mentally Retarded, 1965-66; exec. dir. Greater Omaha Assn. Retarded Citizens, 1966-71; dir. Douglas County (Nebr.) Dept. Mental Health Resources, Omaha, 1971-74; asst. dir. human services Eastern Neb. Human Services Agy., Omaha, 1974-75; adminstr. human services Lincoln-Lancaster County (Nebr.), 1975—. Community services cons. U. Nebr. Coll. Medicine, 1971-74, instr. med. psychology, dept. psychiatry, 1975—; adv. mem. governing bd. Eastern Nebr. Community Office of Retardation, 1970-74; mem. Nebr. Gov.'s Citizens' Study Com. Mental Retardation, 1967-69; bd. dirs. Nebr. Assn. Mental Health, 1972—, treas., 1974-76; bd. dirs. Lincoln Action Program, 1976—. Mem. Rehab. Assn. Nebr. (past dir., treas. 1964-72). Democrat. Home: 1681 Woodsview Lincoln NE 68502 Office: 555 S 10th St Lincoln NE 68508

CLARK, ROLAND REXFORD, health and safety co. exec.; b. Rockford, Ill., Nov. 21, 1925; s. Harry E. and Myrtle (Jaeger) C.; student Rockford Sch. Bus., 1947, extension courses No. Ill. U.; m. Eileen A. Watts, Sept. 22, 1945; children—Susan Marcia, Christie Eileen. Prodn. supr. Med. Supply Co., Rockford, 1948-50, prodn. mgr., purchasing agt., 1950-58, v.p., asst. gen. mgr., 1958-63, exec. v.p., gen. mgr., 1963-68, pres., chief exec. officer, 1968-74; pres., chief exec. officer Marion Health and Safety, Inc., 1974—; v.p. Marion Labs., Inc., Kansas City, Mo. Active A.R.C. Served with USAAF, 1944-45. Decorated Air medal. Mem. Am. Soc. Safety Engrs., Vets. Safety, Indsl. Safety Equipment Assn., Rock River Valley Safety Engrs. (past pres.), Rockford C. of C. Mason, Elk. Home: 4717 Quarry Ridge Trail Rockford IL 61103 Office: 3703 N Main St Rockford IL 61101

CLARK, SAMUEL SMITH, physician, educator; b. Phila., Sept. 2, 1932; s. Horace E. and Jane (Mullin) C.; B.S., McGill U., 1954, M.D., 1958, C.M., 1958; m. Heather Jean Ogilvy, June 21, 1957; children—Ross Angus, Erin, Brian Mullin. Intern, Bethesda (Md.) Naval Hosp., 1958-59; resident Royal Victoria Hosp., Montreal, Que., Can., 1962-67; practice medicine, specializing in urology, Munster, Ind., 1967-68, Chgo., 1969—; attending urologist St. Catherines Hosp., East Chicago, Ind., 1967, Our Lady of Mercy Hosp., Dyer, Ind., 1967, St. Margarets Hosp., Hammond, Ind., 1967; asst. prof. urology Abraham Lincoln Sch. of Medicine, U. Ill., Chgo., 1968-71, asso. prof., 1971-73, prof., 1973—, head div. urology, 1971—; chief urology West Side VA Hosp., Chgo., 1969—, U. Ill. Hosp., Chgo., 1971—; cons. urology Kankakee State Hosp., 1969-75, Ill. State Pediatric Inst., 1970—, Dixon State Sch., 1971—, Chgo. Read Mental Health Center, 1972—. Served to lt. M.C., USN, 1958-62. Diplomate Am. Bd. Urology, Fellow A.C.S., Inst. of Medicine of Chgo.; mem. Am. (exec. com. North Central sect. 1974—), Canadian urol. assns., Soc. Univ. Urologists, Am. Assn. U. Profs., Ind., DuPage med. socs., A.M.A., Warren H. Cole Soc., Chgo. Urol. Soc. (sec. treas. 1974). Episcopalian. Club: Chicago Athletic. Contbr. articles to profl. jours. Home: 592 Turner St Glen Ellyn IL 60137 Office: 840 S Wood St Chicago IL 60680 also 399 Schmale Rd Wheaton IL 60187

CLARK, STEPHEN, cons. co. exec.; b. St. Louis, Mo., Dec. 27, 1936; s. Eldridge and Mattie Ardena (Lumpkin) C.; B.B.A., Washington U., 1971; m. Shirley Lyons, Apr. 26, 1959; children—Stephen, Stanford, Sidney. Histopathol. technician Hosp. div., City of St. Louis, 1956-64; asst. product mgr. Chuck Wagon div. Ralston Purina Co., St. Louis, 1968-70, sr. mktg. research analyst, 1970-71; exec. dir. Bus. Resource Center, St. Louis, 1972—. Bd. dirs. St. Louis Health Systems Agy. Served with AUS, 1959-68. Mem. N.A.A.C.P., Urban League. Home: 730 Lantern Ln St Louis MO 63132 Office: 112 N 4th St Suite 1054 St Louis MO 63102

CLARK, THOMAS ROLFE, clin. psychologist; b. Detroit, Oct. 30, 1941; s. Edward Rolfe and Ruth Ann (Spurr) C.; m. Mary Franzen, July 15, 1972. A.B. magna cum laude, Greenville Coll., 1963; Ph.D. (Robards Doctoral fellow), U. Windsor (Can.), 1972; intern Wayne County Psychiat. Hosp., Detroit, mem. staff, 1972—; pvt. practice clin. and med. psychology and psychotherapy, Detroit, 1972—; faculty Henry Ford Community Coll., Dearborn, Mich., 1972—; part-time staff Met. Guidance Center, Farmington Hills, Mich., 1974-76. Organist 1st United Methodist Ch., Dearborn, 1965—; concert organist, 1975—; bd. dirs. Meth. Children's Village, Livonia, Mich., 1974—; mem. adminstrv. bd. Clarenceville United Meth. Ch., Livonia, 1974—. Mem. Am., Southeastern, Western, Mich. psychol. assns., Am. Orthopsychiat. Assn., Christian Assn. Psychol. Studies, Internat. Therapy Behavior Assn., Am. Assn. Sex Edn. Counselors, Mich. Soc. Cons. Psychologists, Am. Guild Organists. Contbr. articles to profl. jours.; rec. artist. Recipient awards in music, psychology. Home: 26347 Sims Dr Dearborn Heights MI 48127 Office: Suite 302 26206 W Twelve Mile Rd Southfield MI 48034

CLARK, WALTER HILL, savs. and loan exec.; b. Athens, Ga., June 5, 1928; s. John Quincy and Beulah Bernice (Hill) C.; B.B.A., So. Ill. U., 1951; M.B.A., De Paul U., 1958; grad. Advanced Mgmt. Program Harvard, 1971; m. Juanita E. Dillard, July 13, 1957; children—Hilton Pierre, Jaunine Charise. With First Fed. Savs. and Loan Assn. Chgo. (Ill.), 1962—, treas., 1967—, v.p., 1969-74, sr. v.p., group mgr., 1974-75, exec. v.p., 1975—. Vice pres. Travelers Aid Soc.-Immigration Service League, Chgo., 1967-76, pres., 1976—, bd. mem., 1967—; bd. dirs. Community Renewal Soc., Chgo., 1961—. Bd. dirs. adv. council bus. adminstrn. U. Ill., Chgo. campus, 1969—. Served with AUS, 1952-54. Mem. Nat. Soc. Controllers and Financial Officers Savs. Instns., Alpha Phi Alpha. Conglist. (financial sec. 1956—, trustee). Clubs: Economic, Union League, (Chgo.), 71. Home: 1235 E Madison Park Chicago IL 60615 Office: 1 S Dearborn St Chicago IL 60603

CLARK, WARREN SEELEY, JR., food assns. exec.; b. Torrington, Conn., Apr. 13, 1935; s. Warren Seeley and Martha Anna (Weingart) C.; B.S. in Dairy Mfg. with honors and distinction, U. Conn., 1956; M.S. (Dairy Industry Supply Assn. fellow), Iowa State U., Ames, 1959, Ph.D., 1963; m. Virginia A. Manning, June 14, 1958; children—Drew Bradley, Gail Elizabeth, Neal Brian. Instr. Iowa State U., 1961-63, asst. prof. dairy and food industry, 1964-66; dir. lab. Anderson-Erickson Dairy Co., Des Moines, 1966-67; mgr. tech. services Am. Dry Milk Inst., Chgo., 1967-71, dir. research, 1971-75, asst. exec. dir., 1976, exec. dir., 1976—; dir. research Whey Products Inst., Chgo., 1971-75, asst. exec. dir., 1976, exec. dir., 1976—. Mem. Dairy Industry Com. Task Force on Environ. Problems, 1967—, mem. subcom. sanitary standards, 1967-68. Chmn. bd. rev., Addison, Ill., 1969-70, chmn. hosp. com., 1972-73. Vice chmn. bd. trustees 3-A Sanitary Standards Symbol Adminstrv. Council, 1968-77, chmn., 1977—. Served with AUS, 1956-58. Recipient Tall Corn award Iowa State U. chpt. Alpha Zeta, 1966. Mem. Intersoc. Council Am. Pub. Health Assn., Am. Dairy Sci. Assn., Inst. Food Technologists, Internat. Assn. Milk, Food, Environ. Sanitarians, Dairy Soc. Internat., N.Y. Acad. Scis., Dairy Shrine Club, Sigma Xi, Alpha Zeta, Gamma Sigma Delta. Contbg. author: Standard Methods for the Examination of Dairy Products, 13th edit., 1972; Ency. Food Tech., 1974. Contbr. articles to profl. jours. Home: 253 N Friars Ct Addison IL 60101 Office: 130 N Franklin St Chicago IL 60606

CLARK, WILLIAM MERLE, sportswriter; b. Clinton, Mo., Aug. 18, 1932; s. Merle William and Beulah (Wilson) C.; student George Barr Umpire Sch., 1950, Central Mo. State U., 1950-51; B.J., U. Mo., 1958; postgrad. Somers Umpire Sch., 1962; m. Dolores Pearl Denny, Aug. 11, 1955; children—Patrick Sean, Michael Seumas, Kelly Kathleen, Kerry Maureen, Casey Connor. Umpire, Central Mexican League, Neb. State League, 1956; sportswriter, Lexington (Ky.) Leader, 1958, Columbia (Mo.) Missourian, 1958-60, Columbia (Mo.) Tribune, 1963—; recreation dir. City of Columbia, Mo., 1962-68. Umpire, Pioneer League, 1962; partner J.C. Stables, Columbia, Mo., 1965—; scouting supr. Pitts. Pirates, 1968, Seattle, 1969, Milw., 1970, Cin., 1971—. Served with AUS, 1951-54. Mem. Amateur Athletic Union (life), Mo. Sportswriter's Assn. (pres. 1958), Mo. Archeol. Soc., Mo. Hist. Soc., Columbia Audubon Soc. Unitarian-Universalist. Address: 3906 Grace Ellen Dr Columbia MO 65201

CLARKE, CHARLES FENTON, lawyer; b. Hillsboro, Ohio, July 25, 1916; s. Charles F. and Margaret (Patton) C.; A.B. summa cum laude, Washington and Lee Coll., 1938; LL.B., U. Mich., 1940; LL.D., Cleve. State U., 1971; m. Virginia Schoppenhorst, Apr. 3, 1945; children—Elizabeth, Margaret, Jane, Charles Fenton IV. Admitted to Mich. bar, 1940, Ohio bar, 1946; pvt. practice law, Detroit, 1942; asso. Squire, Sanders & Dempsey, Cleve., 1946-57, partner, 1957—. Dir. Found. Equipment Corp., W.M. Brode Co. Trustee Legal Aid Soc., 1959-67; pres. Nat. Assn. R.R. Trial Counsel, 1966-68; pres. Alumni bd. dirs. Washington and Lee U., 1970-72; pres. bd. dirs. Free Med. Clinic Greater Cleve., Inc.; life mem. Sixth Circuit Jud. Conf.; chmn. legis. com. Cleve. Welfare Fedn., 1961-68; trustee Cleve. Citizens League, 1956-62; dir. Citizens adv. bd. Cuyahoga County Juvenile Ct., 1970-73; dir. George Jr. Republic, Greenville, Pa., 1970-73; vice chmn. Cleve. Crime Commn., 1974-75. Mem. exec. com. Cuyahoga County Rep. Orgn., 1950—; councilman, Bay Village, Ohio, 1948-53. Pres., trustee Cleve. Hearing and Speech Center, 1957-63; trustee Laurel Sch.; bd. dirs. Bowman Tech. Sch. Served to 1st lt. C.I.C., AUS, World War II. Fellow Am. Coll. Trial Lawyers; mem. Cleve. Civil War Round Table (pres. 1968), Cleve. Zool. Soc. (dir. 1970), Phi Beta Kappa. Republican. Presbyn. (sec. bd. trustees 1965-74, elder). Clubs: Skating, Union (Cleve.); Tavern. Home: 2262 Tudor Dr Cleveland Heights OH 44106 Office: Union Commerce Bldg Cleveland OH 44115

CLARKE, CHARLES PATRICK, electronics co. exec.; b. Chgo., Oct. 3, 1929; s. James Patrick and Elizabeth (McLaughlin) C.; student U. Ill., 1948-50; B.S., DePaul U., 1953. Auditor, Baumann Finney Co., C.P.A.'s, Chgo., 1953-55; with Cuneo Press, Inc., Chgo., 1955-66, successively asst. gen. accounting supr., asst. chief corp. accountant, gen. auditor, 1955-61, systems, procedures and audit mgr., 1961-64, asst. to treas., 1964-66; comptroller Internat. Couriers Corp. (formerly Bankers Utilities Corp.), Chgo., 1966-69, treas., 1969-72, financial v.p., 1972-75; pres. C.P. Charles & Assos., 1975-76; treas., corp. controller DC Electronics, Inc., 1976—. C.P.A., Ill. Mem. Am. Inst. C.P.A.'s, Ill. Soc. C.P.A.'s, Am. Mgmt. Assn., Nat. Assn. Accountants, Ill. Assn. Professions, Internat. Acad. Profl. Bus. Execs., Adminstrv. Mgmt. Soc., Nat. Mgmt. Assn., Financial Execs. Inst. Democrat. Roman Catholic. Home: 36 Parliament Dr W Palos Heights IL 60463 Office: 544 N Highland Aurora IL 60506

CLARKE, ELVIRA FARENTHEA WIERMAA (MRS. WILLIAM O. CLARKE), educator; b. Aurora, Minn.; d. John and Elizabeth (Wiermaa) Wiermaa; B.S., U. Minn., 1937, M.A. 1948; m. William O. Clarke, Nov. 27, 1935 (dec. June 1946). Tchr. pub. schs., Mpls., 1935-39, prin., 1939-40; tchr., St. Paul, 1951-57, counselor, 1957—; dean women Central Mo. State Coll., 1948-51. Pres. Palo Real Estate, Inc., 1971—. Mem. Am. Personnel and Guidance Assn., Am. Sch. Counselors Assn., Am. Coll. Personnel Assn., Minn. Counselors Assn., Assn. Coll. Admissions Counselors, Am. Fedn. Tchrs., Nat. Vocational Guidance Assn. (nat. credentials chmn. 1968-69), Twin City Vocational Guidance Assn. (pres. 1969-70), Minn. Assn. Coll. Admissions Counselors (membership chmn. 1970-71), Nat., Minn. edn. assns., Minn. Assn. Secondary Sch. Counselors and Coll. Admissions Officers (sec.-treas. 1971-73). Mem. Order Eastern Star. Home: 1254 Raymond Ave St Paul MN 55108

CLARKE, IRVING VANT, investment co. exec.; b. St. Joseph, Mo., Feb. 12, 1924; s. Kenton Harper and Dorothy Irene (Vant) C.; B.A., Williams Coll., 1947; M.B.A., Harvard Bus. Sch., 1949. Investment mgr. Swift & Co., Chgo., 1949-64, asst. treas., 1964-71, dir. investments, 1971-73; pres. Penmark Investments, Inc., Chgo., 1973—; mem. Investment Policy Panel Pension Benefit Guaranty Corp., Washington, 1975—; dir. Globe Life Ins. Co., 1965-77, Life Ins. Co., Fla., 1965-76. Served with USN, 1943-46. Mem. Investment Analyst Soc. Chgo., Harvard Bus. Sch. Club, Chgo. Republican. Mem. Union Ch. Clubs: Chgo. Athletic Assn., Dairymen's Country Wis., Williams NYC. Home: 635 S Oak St Hinsdale IL 60521 Office: 222 N Dearborn St Chicago IL 60601

CLARKE, OSCAR WITHERS, physician; b. Petersburg, Va., Jan. 29, 1919; s. Oscar Withers and Mary (Reese) C.; B.S., Randolph Macon Coll., 1941; M.D., Med. Coll. Va., 1944; m. Susan Frances King, June 18, 1949; children—Susan Frances, Mary Elizabeth, Jennifer Ann. Intern Boston City Hosp., 1944-45; resident internal medicine Med. Coll. Va., 1945-46, 48-49, fellow in cardiology, 1949-50; practice medicine specializing in internal medicine, cardiology Gallipolis (Ohio) Holzer Med. Center, 1950—. Dir. Ohio Valley Devel. Co., Gallipolis, Community Improvement Corp. Vice pres. Tri-State regional council Boy Scouts Am., 1957. Pres. Gallipolis City Bd. Health, 1955—, Gallia County Heart Council, 1955—. Trustee Med. Meml. Found.; bd. dirs., sec., treas. Med. Advances Inst. Served as capt. M.C., AUS, 1946-48; ETO. Recipient John Stewart Bryant pathology award Med. Coll. Va., 1943. Fellow A.C.P., Royal Soc. Medicine; mem. Gallia County Med. Soc. (pres. 1953), A.M.A., Am., Central Ohio (recipient medal of merit 1960, trustee) heart assns., Ohio Med. Assn. (pres. 1973-74), Am., Ohio (trustee) socs. internal medicine, Am. Fedn. Clin. Research, Tri-State Community Concert Assn. (pres. 1957-59), Alpha Omega Alpha, Sigma Zeta, Chi Beta Phi. Presbyn. Rotarian (pres. 1953-54). Contbr. articles in field to profl. jours. Home: Spruce Knoll Gallipolis OH 46531 Office: Box 344 Holzer Med Clinic Gallipolis OH 45631

CLARKE, RICHARD STEWART, mfg. co. exec.; b. Louisville, Aug. 23, 1934; s. Jesse Edward and Sarah Mary Elizabeth (Pilkerton) C.; student St. Procopius Coll., 1955-56, DePaul U., 1956-57; B.S., Ill. State Normal U., 1958; postgrad. N.E. Mo. State Tchrs. Coll., 1959, U. Chgo., 1960, Northwestern U., 1961-63, 69; m. Constance Jean Koga, Sept. 29, 1956; children—Stewart, Stephen, Susan. Floor salesman Sears, Roebuck & Co., Downers Grove, Ill., machine operator Shaffer Bearing Co., Downers Grove, 1956; salesman Seven-Up Bottling Co., Chgo., 1956; salesman Ency. Brit., Chgo., 1956; asst. gen. mgr., methods engr. Autoquip Corp., Chgo., 1956-57, indsl. engr., scheduling and data processing mgr., 1962-64, prodn. mgr., personnel mgr., 1964-67, engring. and mfg. mgr., 1967-69, v.p. mfg., 1969-73, gen. mgr., 1975-76; mgmt. cons. Albert Ramond & Assos., 1976—; real estate broker, 1973-74; planning mgr. Bell & Howell Corp., 1974; tchr. sci., audio/visual dir., student tchr. supr. Wilmette (Ill.) Bd. Edn., 1958-62; pub. lectr. on sci. teaching techniques in Midwest, 1959-62; encyclopedist Childrens Press Sci. Ency., 1961-62. Group leader, sect. pres. Christian Family Movement, 1967-70; tchr. Confraternity of Christian Doctrine, 1971-74. Pres. Northtown Fair Housing Com., 1967-68. Mem. Purchasing Mgmt. Assn. Chgo., N.E.A., Ill. Classroom Tchrs. Assn., Chgo. Area Tchrs. Sci. Assn. (past dir.), N.A.A.C.P., Holy Name Soc., Catholic Assn. for Internat. Peace, Kappa Delta Pi, Pi Gamma Mu, Gamma Phi. Republican. Home: 2453 W Morse St Chicago IL 60645 Office: Suite 1615 Tribune Tower Chicago IL 60611

CLARKE, ROBERT FRANCIS, educator; b. Portsmouth, Va., Oct. 8, 1919; s. Walter A. and Jane E. (Tucker) C.; B.S. in Edn., Kans. State Tchrs. Coll., 1955, M.S., 1957; Ph.D., U. Okla., 1963; m. Annetta Elaine McNabb, May 25, 1947; children—Linda, John. Clk., sign painter, 1937-40; apprentice and machinist Norfolk Navy Yard, 1940-43; stationary engr. Santa Fe R.R., 1948-55; instr. edn. Kans. State Tchrs. Coll., 1956-58; faculty biology dept. Emporia (Kans.) State U., 1958—, asst. prof., 1960-65, asso. prof., 1965-68, prof., 1968—, chmn. dept., 1972—. Served with U.S. Maritime Commn., 1943-48. NSF fellow and grantee. Mem. Am. Inst. Biol. Scis., Southwestern Assn. Naturalists (pres. 1972), Herpetologists League, Am. Soc. Ichthyologists and Herpetologists, Kans. Acad. Sci. (v.p. 1977), Kans. Assn. Biology Tchrs., Animal Behavior Soc., Kans. Herpetology Soc. (pres. 1977). Eagle. Home: 2331 Arrowhead Dr Emporia KS 66801

CLARKE, THOMAS JOHN, veterinarian; b. Glendale, Ohio, Feb. 12, 1938; s. Thomas John and Margaret Mary (Rowley) C.; student Xavier U., 1956-57; D.V.M., Ohio State U., 1962; m. Joyce Ann Anger, Sept. 1, 1962; children—Beth Ann, Victoria Lynn, Thomas John 4th. Intern Angell Meml. Animal Hosp., Boston, 1962-63; practice vet. medicine, Cin., 1964—. Pres. profl. corp. Montgomery Animal Hosp., 1964—, Milford Vet. Clinic, 1964—, Wyoming Vet. Clinic, 1970—; adviser vocational sch. system Hamilton County (Ohio) Schs., 1969—; mem. Hamilton County Bd. Health. Recipient Mary Mitchell Research award Mass. Soc. Prevention of Cruelty to Animals, 1963. Mem. Am. (dir.), Ohio, Cin. (pres. 1972—) vet. med. assns., Phi Zeta, Omega Tau Sigma. Republican. Roman Catholic. Contbr. articles to publs. Address: 7700 Montgomery Rd Cincinnati OH 45236

CLARKE, WALDO HALLETT, civil engr.; b. Franklin, N.J., Dec. 12, 1927; s. Waldo Joseph and Gertrude Margaret (Cougle) C.; B.Sc., Rutgers U., 1953; m. Eunice Mildred Skillman, Oct. 27, 1951; children—Jonathan Hall, Elizabeth Carol, Rebecca Jane. Chief design engr. Levitt & Sons, Hyattsville, Md., 1967-73; project engr. Larwin-Atlantic, Chevy Chase, Md., 1973-74; dir. engring. Murray-McCormick Environ. Group, Atlanta, 1974-77; asso. Henderson & Bodwell, Cin., 1977—. Served with USN, 1945-48. Registered profl. engr., N.J., Md., Va., N.C., Ala., Ga., Ohio. Mem. Nat. Soc. Profl. Engrs., Am. Congress Surveying and Mapping, Am. Water Works Assn., Water Pollution Control Fedn. Home: 11618 Mount Holly Ct Cincinnati OH 45240 Office: 1132 W Kemper Rd Cincinnati OH 45240

CLARKE, WESLEY ALLEN, ret. city ofcl.; b. Kalamazoo, Mich., Dec. 11, 1912; s. William Edward and Margurite A. (Gunther) C.; student U. Mich., 1928-30, Western Mich. U., 1959-60; m. Marie Jane Mitchell, July 11, 1933; children—Sally (Mrs. Alfred L. Snow), Kay (Mrs. Richard E. Anderson), John M. Publicity aide J.L. Hudson Co., Detroit, 1931-40; buyer Ingersoll div. Borg-Warner Corp., 1941-45; purchasing agt. Norge-Heat div., Detroit, 1945-48; purchasing agt. Burroughs Mfg. Co., Kalamazoo, 1948-56; ct. adminstr. City of Kalamazoo, 1956-63; city mgr. City of Otsego (Mich.), 1963-77. Treas., Brucker Sch. P.T.A., Kalamazoo, 1948-50; mem. Kalamazoo County Safety Council, 1956-60. Recipient Certificate of Merit, Western Mich. U., 1960. Mem. Otsego C. of C. Presbyn. Elk, Rotarian. Home: 721 Brookside Dr Otsego MI 49078 Office: 117 E Orleans St Otsego MI 49078

CLARY, JACK RAY, lawyer; b. Piggort, Ark., Sept. 8, 1932; s. Shella R. and Audra (Binkley) C.; B.S. cum laude, Central Mich. U., 1954; J.D., U. Mich., 1959; m. Joellen K. Donnelly, June 11, 1955;children—Jack C., John R., Jennifer J. Admitted to Mich. bar, 1960, since practiced in Grand Rapids; clk. for labor arbitrator David A. Wolfe, 1956-59; asso. firm Warner, Norcross & Judd, 1959-64, partner, 1964-69; partner Clary, Nantz, Wood & VanOrden, 1970—. City commnr., E. Grand Rapids, 1973—. Chmn. devel. bd. Central Mich. U. Served with AUS, 1954-56. Mem. Central Mich. U. Alumni Assn. (past pres.), Am., Mich., Grand Rapids bar assns. Contbr. articles to profl. jours. Home: 336 Manhattan SE Grand Rapids MI 49502 Office: 700 Commerce Bldg Grand Rapids MI 49502

CLASEN, GEORGE HENRY, newspaper publisher; b. Washington, Kans., Jan. 26, 1916; s. George Henry and Elizabeth (Bogue) C.; A.B., U. Kans., Lawrence, 1939; m. Margaret Anita West, Oct. 28, 1939; children—Richard, David. Editor, Norborne (Mo.) Democrat-Leader, 1939-42, Florence (Kans.) Bull., 1946-64; pub. Garnett (Kans.) Rev., 1964—. Mem. Florence City Council, 1948-50, Florence Sch. Bd., 1956-64. Served with USAAF, 1942-46. Mem. Nat. Editorial Assn., Kans. Press Assn. (past pres.), Kans. C. of C. Republican. Methodist. Clubs: Masons, Rotary (past pres. Garnett), Kansas Day (pres. 1977). Home: 344 Monroe St Garnett KS 66032 Office: 112 W 6th St Garnett KS 66032

CLAUDSON, WILLIAM DOLAN, musician, educator; b. Arnold, Nebr., Nov. 1, 1932; s. Charles Byron and Ruby Ethel (Maxson) C.; Mus.B., Colo. State U., 1955; Mus.M. Northwestern U., 1958; Ph.D., 1965; m. Katherine M. Solomon, Aug. 18, 1973; children—Marcus, Christine. Prof. music, dean State U. Coll., Potsdam, N.Y., 1963-66; prof. music Fla. State U., Tallahassee, 1966-70; prof. music, chmn. music edn. So. Ill. U., Edwardsville, 1970—. Choral adjudicator, cons., evaluator Ill. Dept. Edn., 1970—. Served to 1st lt. AUS, 1954-56. Mem. A.A.U.P., Music Educators Nat. Conf., Ill. Music Educators Assn., Am. Choral Dirs. Assn., Pi Kappa Lambda, Pi Mu Alpha, Phi Delta Kappa. Christian Scientist, Presbyn. (dir. choir). Author numerous publs. in field. Home: 1320 Gloucester Edwardsville IL 62025

CLAUER, CALVIN ROBERT, cons. engr.; b. South Bend, Ind., Sept. 8, 1910; s. Calvin Kingsley and Etta (Fiddick) C.; B.S. in Civil Engring., Purdue U., 1932; postgrad. Columbia U., 1944-45; m. Rosemary Y. Stultz, June 23, 1934; 1 son, Calvin Robert. Project engr. Ind. State Hwy. Commn., 1932-35; engr. Erie R.R. Co., 1935-36; dist. chief engr. Truscon Steel Co., Indpls., 1936-42; chief engr. United Steel Fabricators, Inc., 1945-55, div. sales mgr., 1955-57; pres. Clauer Assos., Engrs. for Industry, Wooster, Ohio, 1957-60, chief product engr. Mfg. group Republic Steel Corp., Youngstown, Ohio, 1960-75; prin. Clauer Assos., Youngstown, 1975—. Chmn. civil engring. tech. indsl. adv. com. Youngstown State U., 1971-76. Served to col. USAR, 1932-60. Fellow ASCE; mem. Internat. Assn. for Bridge and Structural Engring., ASTM, Am. Iron and Steel Inst. Republican. Christian Scientist. Clubs: Rotary, Tippecanoe Country, Masons, Shriners. Holder patent on sheet metal box beam. Home and Office: 7401 W Parkside Dr Youngstown OH 44512

CLAUSIUS, GERHARD PAUL, optometrist; b. Chgo., Dec. 18, 1907; s. Robert Adolph and Margaret (Reutlinger) C.; Dr. Optometry, Ill. Coll. Optometry, 1932; m. Ella Marie Carlson, July 22, 1933; children—Gerhard Paul, Donald Robert, Doris Constance (Mrs. Donald Allan Mosser). Practice optometry, Belvidere, Ill., 1932—; lectr., writer on Lincoln and Civil War, 1948—. Mem. Belvidere Bd. Edn., 1939-42; mem. Ill. Sesqui-Centennial Commn. Mem. Am. Optometric Found., Am., Ill. (dir. 1948) optometric assns., No. Ill. Optometric Soc. (v.p. 1958-59), Ill. (v.p.), Ky., Vicksburg-Warren County, Boone County (life), Chgo. hist. socs., Chgo. Civil War Round Table (past pres.), Phi Theta Upsilon. Lutheran. Rotarian (past pres. Belvidere). Club: Buena Vista (past dir., v.p.) (Fontana, Wis.). Home: 929 Garfield Ave Belvidere IL 61008 Office: 601 S State St Belvidere IL 61008

CLAUSSEN, DONAVON DWAYNE, dentist; b. Jasper, Minn., Dec. 3, 1931; s. Sophus and Irene (Thill) C.; student Augustana Coll., 1950-52; B.S., U. Minn., 1954, D.D.S., 1956; m. Charlotte A. Eifert, Sept. 5, 1954; children—Stephen J., Jeffrey S., Bradley J., Thomas A. Gen. practice dentistry, Austin, Minn., 1958—; dir. Sterling State Bank. Pres. bd. dirs. Austin Symphony Orch., 1966-68; pres. Austin Male Chorus, 1961, Austin Fine Arts Group, 1963-66, Austin Coordinating Council, 1968-69; mem. nat. bd. for ch. extension Luth. Ch. Mo. Synod. Dir. Austin Artist series. Served to capt. USAF, 1956-58. Mem. Alumni Assn. U. Minn. Dental Sch. (bd. dirs.), Austin Dental Soc., Am., Minn. (del.), S.E. Minn. Dist. (v.p.) dental assns., Austin C. of C., Psi Omega. Republican. Lutheran (choir dir., pres. congregation). Asso. editor Northwest Dentistry. Home: 402 22d St NW Austin MN 55912 Office: 1431 W Oakland Ave Austin MN 55912

CLAUSSEN, VERNE EVERETT, JR., optometrist; b. Wilson, Kans., Aug. 10, 1944; s. Verne E. and Dorothy Louise (Soukup) C.; student (Santa Fe scholar, Union Pacific scholar), 1962-65; B.S., U. Houston Coll. Optometry, 1966, certificate in optometry, 1968; certificate (Gesell fellow) in pediatrics, 1969; D.Optometry, U. Houston, 1970; m. Patricia Mary Williams, Aug. 26, 1966; children—Verne Everett III, Mary Chris. Practice optometry U. Houston Coll. Optometry, mem. clin. staff, 1970; optometrist, Wamego and St. Mary's, Kans., 1970—. Lectr. optometry Eastern Seaboard Conf., Washington, U. Houston, 1969; vision cons. Briarwood Sch. for learning problems, Houston, 1967-69. Councilman, Alma City (Kans.), 1971-73. Bd. dirs. Optometric Extension Program Found. Recipient Contest award Kans. Optometric Jour., 1971. Mem. Am., Kans. optometric assns., Heart of Am. Contact Soc., Alma, Wamego (dir.), St. Mary's (v.p.) chambers commerce, Farm House Assn. (v.p. 1976-77), Phi Theta Upsilon, Farm House Frat. (dir.). Republican. Methodist. Club: Dutch Mill Swingers Square Dance. Home: Route 2 Alma KS 66401 Office: 5th and Elm Wamego KS 66547

CLAVIN, TERRY JOHN, SR., distillery exec.; b. Mpls., Mar. 13, 1927; s. Bernard James and Frances Marcella (Harrington) C.; student St. Thomas Coll., 1947-48, U. Minn., 1948-49; m. Sally Arlet Beach, Sept. 18, 1947; children—Terry John II, Candace (Mrs. Steve Hoffman), Jayme, Timothy, Melisa. Owner, Midwest Industries, Inc., Long Prairie, Minn., 1947-55; partner, Jet Oil Co., Long Prairie, 1956-70; owner, pres. Minn. Distillers, Inc., Long Prairie, 1970—; Minn. coordinator J.F. Kennedy campaign, 1960, Hubert H. Humphrey campaign, 1964. Served with USNR, 1945-46. Decorated Bronze Star medal. Mem. V.F.W., Am. Legion, K.C., Elk. Home: 212 3d St N Long Prairie MN 56347 Office: 609 6th St NE Long Prairie MN 56347

CLAWSON, JOHN ADDISON, chem. co. exec.; b. Monaco, Pa., June 4, 1922; s. Ralph S. and Elsie (Winnett) C.; B.S., Miami U., 1943; postgrad. Harvard, 1968; m. Patricia Harmon, July 5, 1947; children—Christine (Mrs. Deane P. Higgs), Hunter Winnett. Vice-pres., nat. mgr. bus. and labor reports div. Prentice-Hall, 1948-55; with DuBois Chemicals div. Chemed Corp., 1955—, dist. mgr. N.Y.C., 1955-60, regional mgr. eastern div., 1960-64, divisional mgrs. v.p., 1964-66, exec. v.p., dir. sales, 1966-70, gen. mgr., 1968-70, pres., chief exec. officer, dir. sales, 1970—; dir., v.p. Chemed Corp., 1971—; pres., group exec. DuBois Group, 1975—; dir. DuBois of Can., Ltd., Dubois Chemicalien, N.V., Amsterdam, Holland. Dean's asso. Miami U., 1973—. Served to lt (j.g.) USNR, 1943-46. Mem. Soap and Detergent Assn. (chmn., chief exec. officer 1974-76, exec. com., bd. dirs. 1976—), Delta Sigma Phi, Sigma Alpha Epsilon. Presbyn. Clubs: Queen City, Kenwood Country (Cin.); Bankers; John's Island. Home: 974 Pavillion St Cincinnati OH 45202 Office: DuBois Tower Cincinnati OH 45202

CLAY, WILLIAM LACY, congressman; b. St. Louis, Apr. 30, 1931; s. Irving C. and Luella (Hyatt) C.; B.S., St. Louis U., 1953; m. Carol Ann Johnson, Oct. 10, 1953; children—Vicki Flynn, William Lacy Jr., Michelle Katherine. Real estate broker, St. Louis, 1955-59; mgr. Supreme Life Ins. Co., St. Louis, 1959-61; bus. rep. State and County Municipal Union, St. Louis, 1961-64; edn. coordinator Steamfitters Local 562, St. Louis, 1966-67; mem. 91st-95th congresses from 1st Dist. Mo. Mem. exec. bd. N.A.A.C.P., St. Louis, 1955-60; dist. chmn. Friends of Scouts, St. Louis, 1961. Committeeman Democratic party, 1964—, alderman, St. Louis, 1959-64. Served with AUS, 1953-55. Recipient distinguished citizens award Alpha Kappa Alpha, 1969; Argus award, St. Louis, 1969. Mem. CORE. Roman Catholic. Author: Anatomy of Economic Murder, 1963. Home: 633 Whitingham Dr Silver Spring MD 20904 Office: 1209 Longworth Office Bldg Washington DC 20015

CLAYBAUGH, GLENN ALAN, pharm. co. exec.; b. Lincoln, Nebr., Dec. 10, 1927; s. Joseph H. and Helen (Krause) C.; B.Sc., U. Nebr., 1949; M.Sc., Mich. State U., 1950; Ph.D., Iowa State U., 1953; m. Mary Lou Graham, Aug. 29, 1950; children—Lloyd, Cynthia. Microbiologist, Mead Johnson & Co., Evansville, Ind., 1953-60, sect. leader, 1960-63, mgr. mktg., 1963-65, asso. dir. mktg., 1965-72, dir. profl. services, 1972—. Vis. prof. Purdue U., 1972, U. Miss., 1973, U. Calif. at Irvine, 1974. Served with AUS, 1946-47. Fellow Am. Pub. Health Assn., Royal Soc. Health; mem. Am. Dairy Sci. Assn., Am. Soc. Microbiology, Sci. Research Soc. Am., Sigma Xi, Alpha Zeta. Kiwanian (lt. gov. 1972-73, gov. Ind. dist. 1975-76, internat. chmn. citizenship services 1977-78). Patentee in field. Home: 1612 Russell St Evansville IN 47712 Office: Mead Johnson & Co Evansville IN 47721

CLAYBORNE, CALVIN COOLIDGE, counselor; b. Wahallop, Miss., Aug. 28, 1931; s. Jesse Phillip and Indiana (Stemmis) C.; B.S., Ark. A. M. and N. Coll., 1957; M.S., So. Ill. U., 1969; m. Aritha Parks, May 5, 1965; 1 dau., Alicia. Counselor, E. St. Louis Sr. (Ill.) High Sch., 1972-77; youth adv. Ill. Dept. Children and Family Services, E. St. Louis, 1976—. Served with U.S. Army, 1953-54. Recipient Distinguished Tchr. award youth dept. Baptist Gen. Conv. Ill., 1975. Mem. Am. Personnel and Guidance Assn., Arkansas Alumni Assn., S. Ill. U. Alumni Assn. Baptist. Clubs: So. Cross, Masons. Home: 730 N 24th St East Saint Louis IL 62205 Office: 4901 State St East Saint Louis IL 62205

CLAYBURG, JOHN FRANKLIN, veterinarian; b. Carroll, Iowa, June 28, 1946; s. Frank Thomas and Claribel J. (Anderson) C.; D.V.M., Iowa State U., 1971; m. Karen S. Fenney, June 13, 1968; children—Gary, Roger, Kathy. Practice veterinary medicine, Coon Rapids, Iowa, 1971—; mem. faculty Des Moines (Iowa) Community Coll., 1977; cons. to local swine farms, 1974—. Mem. Coon Rapids Bd. Adjustment, 1977, mem. Planning and Zoning Commn., 1975—, chmn., 1977—; vol. ambulance attendent, Coon Rapids, 1974—, mem. Vol. Fire Dept., 1974—; mem. council on ministries United Meth. Ch., Coon Rapids, 1973—, pres., 1975-77, mem. adminstrv. bd., 1971-77. Mem. Am., Iowa veterinary med. assns., Am. Assn. of Swine Practitioners, Coon Rapids C. of C., Tomahawk, Gamma Sigma Delta, Phi Zeta. Club: Rotarian. Home: 409 4th Ave Coon Rapids IA 50058 Office: 114 6th Ave Coon Rapids IA 50058

CLAYBURGH, BEN JAMES, physician; b. Scobey, Mont., Jan. 31, 1924; s. Mark J. and Anna (Horvick) C.; B.A., U. N.D., 1946, B.S., 1947; M.D., Temple U., 1949; M.S. in Orthopedic Surgery, U. Minn., 1956; m. Mina Tennison, June 26, 1948 (dec. Feb. 1968); children—James, Robert, John, Richard; m. 2d, Beverly Manternach, Jan. 3, 1970. Intern, St. Paul, 1949-50; resident Mayo Found., Rochester, Minn., 1953-56; practice medicine, specializing in orthopedic surgery, 1956—; orthopedic surgeon Grand Forks (N.D.) Clinic, 1956-66, Orthopedic Clinic, Grand Forks, 1966—; clin. prof. Sch. Medicine, U. N.D., Grand Forks, 1956—; cons. orthopedic surgery USAF, 1962—. Chmn. N.D. Republican Com., 1964-65; Republican nat. committeeman for N.D., 1968-76; mem. exec. com. Rep. Nat. Com., 1971—. Served to capt. USAFR, 1951-53. Diplomate Am. Bd. Orthopedic Surgery. Mem. Am. Acad. Orthopedic Surgery (bd. councilors), Clin. Orthopedic Soc., AMA, N.D. Med. Assn. Home: 1626 Belmont Rd Grand Forks ND 58201 Office: 960 Columbia Rd S Grand Forks ND 58201

CLAYCAMP, HENRY JOHN, marketing exec.; b. Ogallah, Kan., Mar. 12, 1931; s. Henry John and Jenny Katherine (Armbruster) C.; B.A., Washburn U., 1956; Ph.D., U. Ill., 1961, M.A., 1957; m. Joanne Hillman, Aug. 20, 1950; children—Eric, Gregg, Jan, Jill. Asst. prof. marketing Mass. Inst. Tech., Cambridge, 1961-65; asso. prof. marketing Stanford (Calif.) U., 1965-69; vis. prof. IMEDE Mgmt. Devel. Inst., Lausanne, Switzerland, 1969-70; dir. advanced methods and research N.W. Ayer & Son, N.Y.C., 1970-73; v.p. corporate marketing Internat. Harvester Co., Chgo., 1973-77, v.p. corporate planning, 1977—. Mem. Am. Marketing Assn. (v.p. 1975-76), Inst. Mgmt. Sci. (chmn. coll. marketing 1973). Editorial bd. Jour. Marketing Research, 1972-76; researcher Consumer Behavior Jour., 1974-76; contbr. articles in field to profl. jours. Home: Route 1 Indian Trail Rd Barrington IL 60010 Office: 401 N Michigan Ave Chicago IL 60611

CLAYMAN, CHARLES B., physician, educator; b. Detroit, Feb. 22, 1926; s. Harry S. and Belle (Schwartz) C.; A.B., Wesleyan U., Middletown, Conn., 1945; M.D., Ind. U., 1949; m. Edith L. Stump, May 21, 1956; children—Joseph L., Diane R., Adam M., Linda C. Intern, U. Chgo. Clinics, 1949-50, resident, 1950-54; instr. U. Chgo. Sch. Medicine, 1954-56, asst. prof., 1956-62, research asso., 1962-68; practice medicine specializing in internal medicine, Chgo., 1962—; mem. staff Weiss Meml. Hosp.; asso. prof. U. Ill. Sch. Medicine, 1973—; sr. scientist, dept. drugs AMA, 1974—. Diplomate Am. Bd. Internal Medicine. Fellow A.C.P.; mem. Am. Gastroenterol. Assn., AMA (contbg. editor jour. 1977—), Chgo. Soc. Internal Medicine, Ill., Chgo. med. socs., Sigma Xi. Contbr. articles in field to profl. jours. Home: 8801 Golf Rd Des Plaines IL 60016 Office: 4640 Marine Dr Chicago IL 60640

CLAYTON, CHARLES BERNARD, dentist; b. Saline Mines, Ill., Feb. 6, 1929; s. Henry Stanford and Hattie Jane (Baker) C.; A.B., U. Evansville, 1952; D.D.S., Ind. U., 1959. Chief dental services Beatty Meml. Hosp., 1959-60; pvt. practice dentistry, Seymour, Ind., 1960-65, Indpls., 1965—. Served with USMCR, 1952-54. Mem. Am. Dental Assn., Am. Analgesia Soc., Am. Acad. Gnathologic Orthopedics, Am. (pres. elect 1972-73), Ind. socs. preventive dentistry, Am. Acad. Gen. Dentistry, Am. Endodontic Soc. Roman Catholic. K.C. Clubs: Meridian Hills Country, Nat. Health Spa (both Indpls.). Address: Suite 63 1010 E 86th St Indianapolis IN 46240

CLAYTON, WILLIAM FRANCIS, lawyer; b. Charles City, Iowa, Sept. 20, 1923; s. Frank William and Louise Marie (Krause) C.; B.A., U. Calif. at Berkeley, 1948; J.D., U. S.D., 1951; m. Sally R. Renden, Aug. 22, 1946; children—Stuart D., Kristin M. (dec.), William R., Thomas W., Robert M. Admitted to S.D. bar, 1951, since practiced in Sioux Falls; asso. firm Claude Hamilton & Thomas Barron, 1951-54; pvt. practice, 1954-69; U.S. atty., Sioux Falls, 1969—; states atty. Minnehaha County, 1958-65; negotiator for Justice Dept. at Wounded Knee, 1973. Chmn. Minnehaha County Young Republicans, 1956, dist. dir., 1958; mem. S.D. Ho. of Reps., 1966-69. Bd. dirs. S.D. Home for Handicapped Children, 1954-58, S.D. Sch. for Mentally Retarded, 1964-70. Served with USAAF, 1942-46; ETO. Mem. Northwestern Tennis Assn. (regional v.p. 1956), States Attys. Assn. (pres. 1962), Am., Fed. (v.p. S.D. chpt. 1970-71), bar assns., State Bar S.D. (chmn. pub. information com. 1962-64), Am. Legion, (comdr. Post 15, 1954), Phi Alpha Delta. Mason (Shriner), Lion, Elk. Home: 510 E 21st St Sioux Falls SD 57105 Office: Security Bldg Suite 616 Sioux Falls SD 57102

CLEARY, FRANK JOSEPH, food mfg. co. exec.; b. Phila., July 6, 1930; s. Frank J. and Rebecca C. (Carbrey) C.; B.S., U. Pa., 1952; M.B.A., Rutgers U., 1957. Asst. treas. Aerojet Gen. Corp., Los Angeles, 1959-67; asst. comptroller ITT Gilfillan Inc., Los Angeles, 1967-69; v.p., treas. Capital Estates, Reno, Nev., 1969; v.p. fin., treas. Lucky Breweries, San Francisco, 1969-71; cons. J. Labatt Ltd., London, Ont., Can., 1971-72; pres. DeMets Inc., Melrose Park, Ill., 1972—. Dir. Calif. Survey on Govt. Efficiency, 1967-68. Served to 1st lt. U.S. Army, 1952-54. Registered profl. engr., Calif. Mem. Fin. Execs. Inst., Am. Inst. Indsl. Engrs., Assn. Systems Mgmt. Republican. Roman Catholic. Home and office: 2100 N 15th Ave Melrose Park IL 60160

CLEARY, MICHAEL JOHN, athletic assn. exec.; b. Cleve., Nov. 12, 1934; s. Michael and Bertha (Reape) C.; student John Carroll U., 1952-56; m. Suzanne C. Williams, Aug. 7, 1954; children—Mary Kathleen, Michael, Brian, Kevin, Anne, Elizabeth, Margaret, Owen, Daniel. Asst. to exec. dir. Nat. Assn. Intercollegiate Athletics, Kansas City, Mo., 1960-63; dir. events Nat. Collegiate Athletic Assn., Kansas City, 1963-66; exec. dir. Nat. Assn. Collegiate Dirs. Athletics, Mpls., 1966-69, Cleve., 1969—, mem. coll. football centennial coordinating com., 1968-69. Bd. regents St. Mary Plains Coll., Dodge City, Kan., 1963-67. Served with USNR, 1956-58. Mem. Am., Cleve. (dir.) socs. assn. execs., Coll. Sports Information Dirs. Assn., Nat. Assn. Expn. Mgrs. Home: 18935 Colahan Dr Rocky River OH 44116 Office: 21330 Center Ridge Rd Cleveland OH 44116

CLEARY, PATRICK JAMES, newspaper editor; b. Momence, Ill., Jan. 20, 1929; s. James Augustine and Nellie DeWitt (Liston) C.; student U. Chgo., 1946-48; m. Alice Marie Duval, Oct. 1, 1955; children—Mary Elizabeth, James Augustine, Michael John. Reporter, wire editor, city editor Kankakee (Ill.) Daily Jour., 1945-52; reporter Gary (Ind.) Post-Tribune, 1952-53; staff asst. Ill. Senate, 1953-57; dir. pub. relations Plumbing Contractors Assn. Chgo. Cook County (Ill.), 1957-59; city clk. City of Kankakee, 1955-57, clk., county and probate cts. County of Kankakee, 1959-63; editor Farmers Weekly Rev., Joliet, Ill., 1963—; cons. editor Compass Newspapers Inc., Kankakee, 1977—, Herscher (Ill.) Rev., 1963-69; co-editor Crete (Ill.) Record, Steger (Ill.) News, 1963-64; chmn. bd. rev. Ill. Dept. Labor, 1969-73. Home: 1905 E Oak St Kankakee IL 60901 Office: 458 N Chicago St Joliet IL 60434

CLEMA, JOE KOTOUC, computer scientist; b. Omaha, Sept. 23, 1938; s. Joseph Arthur and Sylva Marie (Kotouc) C.; B.S., U. Nebr., 1963; M.S., U. Miami, 1969; Ph.D., Colo. State U., 1973; m. Mary Arta Chipman, May 10, 1963; 1 dau., Jennifer Arta. Mathematician, systems analyst Gen. Electric Co., Louisville, 1969-70; head sci. applications group Colo. State U., Ft. Collins, 1970-73; project engr. Gen. Dynamics Co., Ft. Worth, 1973-77; sr. software devel. mgr. Simulation Tech., Inc., Dayton, Ohio, 1977—; v.p. bd. dirs. Ann. Simulation Symposium, 1976—. Served with U.S. Army, 1963-67. Mem. AAAS, IEEE, Assn. for Computing Machinery (vice chmn. spl. interest group on simulation), Am. Inst. Indsl. Engr. (sr.), Assn. for Computer Programmers and Analysts, Air Force Assn., Nat. Mgmt. Assn., Soc. for Simulation. Republican. Home: 6128 Martingale St Dayton OH 45459 Office: Simulation Tech Inc 4124 Linden St Dayton OH 45432

CLEMANS, THEODORE VAUGHN, personnel and labor relations cons.; b. Springfield, Ohio, Dec. 29, 1946; s. Frank E. and Norma M. (Smith) Wells; A.A., Urbana Coll., 1969; B.S. in Bus. Adminstrn., Wright State U., 1970, postgrad., 1971-72; m. Karen Sue Roach, June 21, 1969. Field rep. Ohio Assn. Pub. Sch. Employees, Columbus, 1972-73; state coordinator Am. Fedn. State, County and Municipal Employees, Columbus, 1973-75; dir. elections Ind. Employment Relations Bd., Indpls., 1975; exec. dir. Physicians Alliance div. State Med. Soc. Wis., Madison, 1976; pres. Labor Relations Bur., Inc., Columbus, 1976—; instr. United Auto Workers Family Edn. Center, Black Lake, Mich., 1970-71; guest speaker at various univs. on labor relations, 1971-77; participant, panel mem. Labor-Mgmt. Arbitration Conf., 1974, 75, 76. Mem. Indsl. Relations Research Assn., Am. Soc. for Personnel Adminstrn., Am. Arbitration Assn. (mem. labor panel), Soc. of Profls. in Dispute Settlement, Internat. Personnel Mgmt. Assn., Am. Inst. Profl. Consultants. Democrat. Lutheran. Editor Mgmt. Negotiators Digest, 1976-77. Home: 2329 Pawnee Dr London OH 43140 Office: PO Box 192 Columbus OH 43216

CLEMENS, ANTON HUBERT, life sci. instrument co. exec.; b. Gerolstein, Germany, Nov. 19, 1928; s. Mathias and Maria Appolonia (Pohs) C.; M.S., Polytechnicum, Bingen, Germany, 1951; m. Elfie Marie Marschallik, Dec. 20, 1952; children—Martina, Viviane, Caroline. Came to U.S., 1965. With various x-ray cos., Germany, 1952-59; resident rep. Picker Internat., Lausanne, Switzerland, 1959-62; cons. research and devel., mfg. and marketing med. instruments, Belgium, Germany, Switzerland, 1962-65; dir. research and devel. Ames Co., Miles Labs., develop new instrument program for clin. medicine, Elkhart, Ind., 1965-71, dir. life sci. instrument program for med. and biol. research, 1971—. Mem. Am. Mgmt. Assn., N.Y. Acad. Sci., Assn. Advancement Med. Instruments, Instrument Soc. Am., Nuclear Medizinische Gesellschaft, Gesellschaft für Automation and Daten Verarbeitung in der Medizin. Patentee in field. Contbr. articles to profl. publs. Home: 3435 Calumet Ave Elkhart IN 46514 Office: Miles Labs Inc Elkhart IN 46514

CLEMENS, JAMES RITTENHOUSE, educator, librarian; b. Lansdale, Pa., June 2, 1913; s. Jacob Cassel and Hanna (Rittenhouse) C.; student Temple U., 1931-32; B.A., Goshen Coll., 1935; M.S. in L.S., Columbia, 1950; postgrad. U. Pa., 1939-49; m. Eva M. Moyer, May 25, 1946; children—James William, Frederick Paul. Tchr., Montgomery County Sch., Kulpsville, Pa., 1936-42, Bucks County Sch., Chalfont, Pa., 1946-47; ednl. dir. Civilian Pub. Service Camps, Luray, Va. and Denison, Ia., 1942-46; librarian Goshen (Ind.) Coll., 1950—, asst. prof. library sci., 1953—. Pres., Goshen Community Chorus, 1973-74; circulation mgr. Gospel Evangel, 1974—. Mem. A.L.A. Home: 117 River Vista Dr Goshen IN 46526

CLEMENS, JOSEPH BERNARD, museum designer, artist, mural artist, sculptor; b. Greensburg, Pa., Oct. 25, 1920; s. Joseph John and Catheryn (Popovich) C.; student Cleve. Inst. Art., 1948-49, Cooper Sch. Art, 1958-59; m. Mary Lucille Coyne, Aug. 10, 1942; children—Judith Ann (Mrs. Glenn Robinson), Mary Lou (Mrs. George Hoffmann), Suzann, Janine. Freelance fine art, mus. designer Noblesville, Ind., 1972—; pres. J.B. Clemens Assos., mus. planning and constrn., Noblesville, 1972—; pres. Am. Edit. Inc., Noblesville, 1972—. Served with AUS, 1942-46. Mem. Midwest Museums Conf., Am. Assn. Museums. Mus. dioramas, murals, exhbts. Milw. Pub. Mus., Conner Prairie Pioneer Settlement, Noblesville, Ind. State Mus., Oshkosh (Wis.) Pub. Mus., Beloit (Wis.) Coll., Children's Mus., Indpls., art works in pvt. collections. Home: 14875 Allisonville Rd Noblesville IN 46060

CLEMENS, LEROY SIMON, newspaper editor; b. Hennepin, Ill., Oct. 16, 1922; s. Simon Peter and Marie (Munks) C.; student Henry Ford Tech. Sch., Dearborn, Mich., 1941; m. Ruth Frances Johnsen, Feb. 7, 1945; children—Donald Leroy, Karen Ruth, Mark Simon. Reporter Daily Republican-Times, Ottawa, Ill., 1946-49, city editor, 1949-60; mng. editor Elgin (Ill.) Daily Courier-News, 1960-73; exec. editor Elgin-Wheaton-Schaumburg (Ill.) divs. Copley Newspapers, 1973—. Served with USN, 1940-46. Mem. Ill. AP Editors Assn., Kane County Press Assn., Asso. Press Mng. Editors, U.P. Internat. Ill. Newspaper Editors, Sigma Delta Chi. Republican. Home: 1131 Blackhawk Dr Elgin IL 60120 Office: 300 Lake St Elgin IL 60120

CLEMENT, PAUL PLATTS, JR., edn. devel. co. exec.; b. Geneva, Ill., Aug. 30, 1935; s. Paul P. and Vera Elizabeth (Dahlquist) C.; A.B., Coe Coll., 1957; m. Susan Alice Aikins, June 7, 1958; children—Paul Platts IV, Kathleen Elizabeth. Sales tech. rep. Burroughs Corp., Chgo., 1960-63; mgr. EDP, Harding-Williams Corp., Chgo., 1963-65; edn. coordinator Standard Oil Co., Chgo., 1965-69; mgr. product planning Edutronics Systems Internat., Chgo., 1969-71; dir. edn. Advanced Systems Inc., Chgo., 1971—; cons. in field. Served to capt. USAF, 1958-60. Mem. Assn. Computer Machinery, Nat. Soc. Performance and Instrn. Home: 4942 Linscott St Downers Grove IL 60515 Office: 1601 Tonne Rd Elk Grove IL 60007

CLEMENTS, WALTER SAMUEL, real estate exec.; b. Tawas City, Mich., Oct. 16, 1949; s. Laurence Edward and Gertrude Mae (Bessey) C.; B.S. in Bus. Adminstrn., Central Mich. U., 1971; certificate in real estate U. Mich., 1975; m. Janet Ruth Sheldon, Aug. 8, 1970; children—Lisa Mae, Tyler Sheldon, Sales asso. Fister & Clements, Realtors, St. Joseph, Mich., 1971, v.p., co-owner, 1972—; instr. Lake Mich. Coll., Benton Harbor, 1973-75, real estate div. U. Mich., 1977—; cons. in field. Chmn. blood bank ARC, Berrien County, 1974. Recipient Presidents Cup, Bd. Realtors SW Mich., 1976. Mem. Southwestern Mich. Bd. Realtors, multiple listing systems SW Mich. and S. Bend, Kalamazoo, S. Bend and Mishawaka bds. realtors, Nat. Assn. Realtors, Realtors Nat. Mktg. Inst. (certified comml. investment mem.), Internat. Real Estate Fedn., Kiwanis. Republican. Lutheran. Club: Moose. Home: 4474 Flora Ln St Joseph MI 49085 Office: 815 Main St Joseph MI 48085

CLEMONS, SAMUEL HOUSTON, govt. ofcl.; b. Chattanooga, Oct. 5, 1924; s. Samuel Houston and Cora Fritts (Durrah) C.; B.A., Roosevelt U., 1950, M.Pub. Adminstrn., 1974; children—Jan Lynn, Sybil Roxanne. Tchr. pub. schs. Chgo., 1952-54; various govt. positions, 1955—, successively HEW, Social Security Adminstrn.; dir. area office housing mgmt. div. HUD, Milw., 1971—. Instr. polit. sci. Marquette U., 1974—, also Alverno Coll. Mem. Wis. Humanities Com., 1973—. Bd. dirs. Wis. Kidney Found. Served with AUS, World War II. Mem. Kappa Alpha Psi. Episcopalian. Home: 1256 E Chambers Ave Milwaukee WI 53211 Office: 744 W 4th Milwaukee WI 53203

CLENDENAN, RAY CHARLES, social service adminstr.; b. Detroit, May 24, 1928; s. Charles C. and Mildred M. (Clothier) C.; A.A. in Agr., Mich. State U., 1948; m. Hilda Marie Hager, June 19, 1948; children—Connie, Clif, Chris, Carol. Founder, adminstr. Youth for Christ, Marlette, Mich., 1952—, Teen Ranch, boys home, Marlette, Mich., 1966—; cons. mgmt. boys home facilities. Mem. United Fund Com., North Branch, Mich., 1953-54; active Tall Pine council Boy Scouts Am., 1941-47. Bd. dirs. Youth for Christ Internat., recipient pres.'s award, 1971. Recipient Outstanding Young Farmer award Jr. C. of C., 1954. Mem. Mich. Assn. Childrens Agys. (exec. sec. 1971-74), Marlette C. of C. Mem. Christian Missionary Alliance Ch. (dir. 1960—). Home: 6679 Clifford Rd Marlette MI 48453 Office: 3041 Main St Marlette MI 48453

CLENDENEN, HOWARD E., ins. co. exec.; b. nr. Milton, Iowa, July 9, 1923; s. Robert S. and Anna F. (Lipsett) C.; student Simpson Coll., 1946-47; m. Mardell Fetters, Aug. 2, 1944; children—James, Mary (Mrs. Francis H. Boyd Jr.), Paul, Tom. Field adjuster Iowa Home Mut. Casualty Co., 1948-51; claim examiner State Automobile and Casualty Underwriters, Des Moines, 1951-54, asso. prodn. supr., 1954-56, agy. asst., 1956-59, v.p., also agy. mgr., 1959-60; exec. v.p. Automobile Underwriters Corp., Des Moines, 1960-61, pres., 1961-71, chmn. bd., 1971; pres. The Statesman Group., Inc., Des Moines, 1969—, dir., also v.p. affiliate cos., 1969—. Chmn. Ins. Iowa Coll. Found., 1972—. Bd. dirs. Greater Des Moines United Way, v.p., 1972, pres. 1974; trustee Iowa Found. Ins. Edn., pres., 1974-75; trustee Marycrest Coll., Davenport, Iowa, 1976—. Served with AUS, 1943-46; ETO, PTO. Mem. Nat. Assn. Ind. Insurers (chmn. bd. govs. 1971-73), Greater Des Moines C. of C. Mason (32 deg., Shriner). Clubs: Wakonda Country, Des Moines, Embassy, Bohemian. Home: 501 S 1st St Indianola IA 50125 Office: 1400 Des Moines Bldg Des Moines IA 50309

CLENDENIN, ROBERT JAMES, lawyer; b. Monmouth, Ill., Oct. 12, 1904; s. J. W. and Louvisa (Stevenson) C.; A.B., Leland Stanford, 1926; J.D., U. Mich., 1930; L.H.D., Coll. of Ozarks, 1971; m. Louise Velde, Dec. 6, 1941; children—Robert J., John V., William H., Thomas. Admitted to Ill. bar, 1931; practice of law, 1930—; mem. firm Clendenin Burkhard & Butler, Monmouth, 1934—. Dir., chmn. bd. Monmouth Trust & Savs. Bank; dir. Bud Rowlett, Inc., Monarch Engring. Co., Martha Brown Ltd., asst. U.S. dist. atty. So. dist. Ill., 1935-39; referee in bankruptcy and master in chancery So. dist. Ill., 1939-53. Bd. dirs. Monmouth Coll., 1972—, U.S. Naval Acad. Found.; pres. Mellinger Ednl. Found.; adv. dir. Culver Ednl. Found., 1959-60; trustee Coll. Ozarks Alumni Found. Recipient Alumni Service award Culver Mil. Acad., 1967. Served to lt. USNR, 1943-45; capt. Res. ret. Mem. Am., Fed., Ill., Chgo., Peoria, Warren County bar assns., Soc. of Barristers (U. Mich.), Am. Legion, S.A.R., Tau Kappa Alpha, Alpha Sigma Phi. Democrat. Presbyn. Mason (32 deg., Shriner), Elk. Clubs: University (Chgo.); Creve Coeur; Army-Navy (Washington). Home: 1111 E Euclid Ave Monmouth IL 61462 Office: First Nat Bank Bldg Peoria IL 61602

CLEVELAND, JOSEPH CORNELIUS, heart surgeon; b. Birmingham, Ala., Oct. 10, 1936; s. Edward Farrell and Lula Gladys (Moore) C.; B.A., DePauw U., Greencastle, Ind., 1957; M.D., Case Western Res. U., 1961; m. Ester Georgienne Burow, June 22, 1958; children—Joseph Cornelius, Jonathan Burow. Intern and resident in surgery Univ. Hosps., Cleve.; resident in surgery Hahnemann Hosp., Phila.; asst. prof. surgery Yale Sch. Medicine, 1967-69; practice medicine specializing in gen. and vascular surgery, Danville, Ill., 1969-73; cardiothoracic resident surgeon Tufts New Eng. Med. Center, Boston, 1973-75; cardiac surgeon Carle Clinic, Urbana, Ill., 1975—; clin. asso. U. Ill. Med. Sch. Fellow A.C.S., Am. Coll. Chest Physicians, Am. Coll. Cardiology; mem. Central Surg. Soc., AMA, Ill. Med. Soc. Methodist. Clubs: Champaign Country; Masons (32 deg). Contbr. med. jours. Home: 3210 Stoneybrook St Champaign IL 61820 Office: 602 W University St Carle Clinic Urbana IL 61801

CLEVELAND, WILBUR ARTHUR, mfg. co. exec.; b. Mpls., Dec. 24, 1921; s. Wilbur Critchfield and Ella Ann (Menard) C.; student Dunwoody Indsl. Inst., 1946-47, U. Minn., 1957; m. Evelyn Claire Veilleux, Aug. 14, 1943; children—David, Rena, Alan, Martha, Thomas. Tool designer Minn. Engring. Co., Mpls., 1948-52, v.p. tool design and engring., 1953-58; with Deep Draw Corp., Mpls., 1959—, gen. mgr., 1966—, v.p., 1968-77, pres., chief exec. officer, chmn. bd., 1977—. Mem. exec. dist. com. Viking Miniwicota Dist. council Boy Scouts Am., 1934-45, 58—, dist. commr., 1974-77, dist. chmn., 1977—, Silver Beaver award, 1974, Order of Arrow, Vigil of Honor, 1974, Dist. Award of Merit, 1975, Wood badge, 1977. Served with USNR, 1942-45. Home: 5920 Interlachen Blvd Edina MN 55436 Office: 712 W Ontario Ave Minneapolis MN 55403

CLEVENGER, HORACE MARSHALL, operations research analyst; b. Manhattan, Kans., Dec. 21, 1913; s. Charles Henry and Edna (Warren) C.; B.S.A., Purdue U., 1938; M.S., Ohio State U., 1952; postgrad. Harris Tchrs. Coll., St. Louis, 1956-57, So. Ill. U., Alton, 1961, Washington U., 1962-71; m. Roberta Walter, June 8, 1941; children—John Walter, Robert Marshall, Donna Jean. Clk., Bur. Census, Washington, 1940-41; agrl. statistician Bur. Agr. Econs., Trenton, N.J., 1941-42; analytical statistician Bur. Agrl. Econs., Columbus, 1942-52, Doane Agrl. Service, St. Louis, 1953-54; acting asst. traffic mgr. Stix, Baer & Fuller, St. Louis, 1954-56; tchr. St. Louis Bd. Edn., St. Louis, 1956-57; analytical statistician U.S. Army Transp. Materiel Command, St. Louis, 1957-60, operations research analyst, 1960-64; math. statistician U.S. Army Aviation Systems Command, 1964-69; ops. research analyst U.S. Army Troop Support and Aviation Materiel Readiness Command, 1969—. Mem. Ops. Research Soc. Am., Am. Soc. Quality Control, Am. Statis. Assn., Am. Econ. Assn. Contbr. articles to profl. jours. Home: 21 Almeda Pl Ferguson MO 63135 Office: 4300 Goodfellow Blvd St Louis MO 63120

CLEVENGER, ROBERT VINCENT, lawyer; b. Hancock, Mich., July 23, 1921; s. Arthur W. and Yolande (Elwood) C.; student Earlham Coll., Richmond, Ind., 1939-41; A.B., U. Ill., 1942, J.D., 1947; m. Dorothy Jean Marsh, Sept. 18, 1943; children—Arthur Eugene, Darley Yolande, Mary Marsha. Admitted to Ill. bar, 1947, since practiced in Pekin; asst. state's atty., Tazewell County (Ill.), 1951-52, spl. asst. state's atty., 1956-57; pub. guardian, conservator of Tazewell County, 1961-69. Dir., sec. Pekin Devel. Corp., 1970-74, Future Horizons, Inc., Pekin, 1972—; sec. Celestial Investors, Pekin, 1966—. Vice chmn. Creve Coeur council Boy Scouts Am., 1967-68, recipient Order of Arrow, 1960, Silver Beaver award, 1967; dean of merit badge counselors, 1969—; explorer adviser Explorer Post 1776, 1976—; chmn. Tazewell Citizens Com. on Human Relations, 1967; pres. Pekin Edison Sch., P.T.A., 1954-55, Pekin council, 1955-56; pres. Greater Peoria area chpt. World Federalists, U.S., 1967-69, sec., 1969—; chmn. Pekin Safeguard Against Crime Com., 1976—. Mem. Town Bd. of Pekin Twp., 1949-53; pres. Champaign County (Ill.) Young Democrats, 1946-47; Tazewell County chmn. Ill. Com. for Constl. Revision, 1950; Pekin Twp. chmn. Dem. Com., 1950-52; Dem. precinct committeeman, 1972-74; mem. Tazewell County Dem. Central Com., 1972-74. Served as master sgt. AUS, 1942-46, 50-53. Recipient Citation for Outstanding Contbn. to Human Relations, Tazewell Citizens Com. on Human Relations, 1968. Mem. Am., Ill., Tazewell County (pres. 1955-56, chmn. legal aid com. 1971—) bar assns., Fedn. Local Bar Assns. (pres. 3d dist. 1963), Pekin C. of C. (chmn. edn. com. 1955-56, chmn. local affairs com. 1959-60), Tri-County Urban League, Internat. League for Rights of Man, Alpha Kappa Lambda, Phi Alpha Delta. Methodist (chmn. Christian social concerns commn. 1967-70). Kiwanian (pres. 1956, sec. 1963-64, lt. gov. Ill.-Eastern Iowa dist. 1965, mem. internat. relations com. Ill.-Eastern Iowa dist. 1967, chmn. support chs. in spiritual aims Ill.-Eastern Iowa dist. 1966, chmn. citizenship services com. Pekin club 1976—). Club: Pekin Boat (judge advocate 1957—). Home: 1011 Monroe St Pekin IL 61554 Office: 342 St Mary Pekin IL 61554

CLEVENGER, THOMAS RUSSELL, JR., mfg. co. exec.; b. Camden, N.J., Mar. 14, 1930; s. Thomas Russell and Maud Lillian (Butler) C.; B.Sc., Rutgers U., 1956; D.Sc., Mass. Inst. Tech., 1961; m. Doris Harvey Johnson, Aug. 25, 1956; children—Matthew Russell, Douglas Arnold. Instr. ceramics Mass. Inst. Tech., Cambridge, 1959-60, asst. prof., 1961-64, Ford Found. postdoctoral fellow, 1961-63; with Owens-Ill., Inc., Toledo, 1964—, v.p., tech. dir. Consumer and Tech. Products div., 1968-72, v.p., tech. dir. Internat. div., 1972—, gen. mgr. Far East/Pacific, 1975—. Tech. attache Matshshita Electric Co., Osaka, Japan, 1961-62. Served with USN, 1950-54. Mem. Am. Ceramic Soc., Am. Mgmt. Assn. (research council), Keramos, Sigma Xi. Clubs: Inverness, North Cape Yacht. Home: 3030 Hopewell Pl Toledo OH 43606 Office: 405 Madison Ave Toledo OH 43666

CLIFFORD, JOHN WILLIAM, writer, lyricist; b. Springfield, Ill., Oct. 19, 1918; s. John Bernard and Rose (Collins) C.; B.S., Kan. State Tchrs. Coll., 1952; m. Carol Deane Cline, Apr. 3, 1943; children—Christine, John Shannon. Freelance writer, 1946-49; tchr. journalism Lawrence (Kans.) High Sch., 1952-53; copy editor Topeka Daily Capitol, 1953-56; copy chief Turner Advt. Agy., Topeka, 1956-60; writer-producer Centron Corp., Inc., Lawrence, 1960—; song lyricist, novelist. Served with AUS, 1941-45. Mem. ASCAP, Am. Guild Authors and Composers. Author: (novel) The Shooting of Storey James, 1962. Writer original script for feature film Carnival of Souls; To Touch a Child, many other ednl.-information films. Home: 801 Mississippi Lawrence KS 66044 Office: 1621 W 9th St Lawrence KS 66044

CLIFFORD, LARRY WILLIAM, accountant; b. Duluth, Minn., Jan. 3, 1948; s. Louis A. and Betty Jean (Clifford) C.; A.A., Waukesha County Tech. Inst., 1977. Pres. Clifford-Schwarz & Assos., Inc., New Berlin, Wis., 1976—. Bd. dirs., treas. Hellman Research Found. Mem. Nat. Assn. Accountants. Republican. Lutheran. Home: 4401 N 84th St Milwaukee WI 53225 Office: 13825 W National Ave New Berlin WI 53151

CLIFFORD, SYLVESTER, educator, speech pathologist, audiologist; b. Forgan, Okla., May 17, 1929; s. William L. and Ella (Street) C.; B.A., No. State Tchrs. Coll., Okla., 1951, M.A., U. Denver, 1957, Ph.D., 1959; m. Betty Alice Gregory, June 10, 1947; children—Bradford William, Opal Alice. Tchr. Hazelton (Kan.) Pub. High Sch., 1951-52, Anthony (Kan.) High Sch., 1952-53, 55-57, Wallace Sch. for Brain Damaged Children, Denver, 1958-61; tchr. speech pathology dir. Speech and Hearing Clinic, U.S.D., Vermillion, 1961—, dir. dept. communication, 1969—; prof. Sch. Medicine, U. S.D., Harrington lectr., 1976. Mem. S.D. Cleft Palate Evaluation Team, 1964—; cons. S.D. Dept. Edn., S.D. Cancer Soc., 1961—, S.D. Heart Assn., 1962-66, VA Hosp., Sioux Falls. Chmn. Clay County Easter Seal Soc., Vermillion, 1962-68, bd. dirs. S.D., 1966—. Served with AUS, 1953-55. Mem. Am., S.D. (sec., treas. 1963, pres. 1964, editor Jour. 1969-71) speech and hearing assns., Central States Speech Assn., Am. Cleft Palate Assn., Nat. Assn. Retarded Children, Assn. Depts. and Adminstrs. in Speech Communication, Alpha Psi Omega, Tau Kappa Delta. Methodist. Rotarian. Home: 424 E Main St Vermillion SD 57069

CLIFFORD, THOMAS JOHN, univ. pres.; b. Longdon, N.D., Mar. 16, 1921; s. Thomas Joseph and Elizabeth (Howitz) C.; B.C.S., U. N.D., 1942, J.D., 1948; M.B.A., Stanford, 1957, Stanford exec. fellow, 1958; m. Florence Marie Schmidt, Jan. 25, 1943; children—Thomas John, Stephen Michael. Instr. accounting U. N.D., 1946-47, counselor men, 1947-49, head accounting dept., 1948-49, dean sch. commerce, 1950—, pres., 1971—. dir. Red River Nat. Bank, Grand Fords, N.D., Ottertail Power Co. Pres., N.D. Research Council; bd. dirs. United Hosp.-Grand Forks, Greater N.D. Assn., Bush Found., St. Paul; pres. N.D. Council Econ. Edn., 1969—. Served from 2d lt. to capt. USMC, 1942-45. C.P.A. Decorated Purple Heart, Bronze Star, Silver Star. Mem. N.D. C.P.A. Soc. (pres. 1953-54), AIM, Am. Inst. Accountants, Am. Bar Assn., Order of Coif, Blue Key, Beta Gamma Sigma, Beta Alpha Psi, Phi Etu Sigma, Kappa Sigma. K.C. Home: Yale Dr Grand Forks ND 58201

CLIFTON, DONALD O., psychol. research co. exec.; b. Butte, Nebr., Feb. 5, 1924; s. Kem A. and Pearl (Hoscheit) C.; B.S., U. Nebr., 1948, M.A., 1949, Ph.D., 1953; m. Shirley May Roush, Oct. 15, 1945; children—Connie, James, Mary, Jane. Prof. U. Nebr., Lincoln, 1950-69; pres. Selection Research, Inc., Lincoln, 1969—; asso. dir. Nebr. Human Resources Research Found., Inc. Bd. dirs. Father Flanagan's Boys Town. Served with USAF. Decorated D.F.C., Air Medal. Certified psychologist, Nebr. Mem. Am., Nebr. psychol. assns., Newcomen Soc. Republican. Methodist. Clubs: Rotary (pres. NE Lincoln, dist. gov.). Author: The Magnificence of Management, 1970; The Agent Perceiver, 1971. Home: 630 Cottonwood Dr Lincoln NE 68510 Office: 2646 S 48th St Lincoln NE 68506

CLIFTON, KELLY HARDENBROOK, biologist, educator; b. Spokane, Wash., July 22, 1927; s. John Minton and Nora Marie (Toole) C.; B.A., U. Mont., 1950; M.S., U. Wis., 1951, Ph.D., 1955; m. Mayre-Lee Harris, Aug. 27, 1949; children—Kelly Hardenbrook, William Harris, Brice Minton. Am. Cancer Soc. postdoctoral fellow Childrens Cancer Research Inst., Boston, 1955-56, research asso., 1956-59; research fellow Harvard Med. Sch., 1957-59; mem. faculty U. Wis.-Madison, 1959—, prof. human oncology and radiology, 1975—, asst. dean for pre-med. affairs, 1972-77, acting chmn. pathology, 1977—; mem. radiology com. NRC, 1968-72; mem. prevention-detection therapy research com. Am. Cancer Soc., 1977—. Served with USCGR, 1945-46. Nat. Cancer Inst. spl. research fellow Karolinska Inst., Stockholm, Sweden, 1970-71; Am. Cancer Soc., Nat. Cancer Inst. research grantee, 1960—. Mem. Soc. Exptl. Biology and Medicine (sect. chmn. 1963-65, editorial bd. procs. 1976-79), Am. Assn. Cancer Research (asso. editor Cancer Research, 1968-71), Radiation Research Soc. (editorial bd. Radiation Research 1977-80), Am. Soc. Exptl. Pathology. Contbr. articles to profl. jours. Home: 1218 University Bay Dr Madison WI 53705

CLIKEMAN, FRANKLYN MILES, nuclear engr., educator; b. Havre, Mont., Mar. 6, 1933; s. Bert Marion and Celia Dora (Klingler) C.; B.S. in Engring. Physics, Mont. State U., 1955; Ph.D. in Nuclear Physics, Iowa State U., 1962; m. Janice Anita Moe, Aug. 18, 1958; 2 children, Paul, Mary. Postdoctoral appointee, Ames (Iowa) Lab., Iowa State U., 1962-63; asst. prof. nuclear engring., Mass. Inst. Tech., Cambridge, 1963-65, asso. prof., 1965-70; asso. prof. nuclear engring., Purdue U., W. Lafayette, Ind., 1970—. Mem. Am. Nuclear Soc., Am. Physics Soc., Am. Soc. Engring. Edn., Sigma Xi, Phi Eta Sigma, Tau Beta Pi, Phi Kappa Phi. Lutheran. Home: 2801 Ashland St West Lafayette IN 47906 Office: School lluclear Engring Purdue Univ West Lafayette IN 47907

CLIMER, JAMES HUBERT, utility exec.; b. Akron, Ohio, Jan. 31, 1926; s. Edgar N. and Dorothea (Hawkins) C.; student U. Notre Dame, 1943-44; B.S., Ia. State U., 1947; m. Geraldine Mary Bourdon, Sept. 11, 1948; children—Linda, Lisa, Paul, Kelly, Caroline. With Consumers Power Co., Jackson, Mich., 1947—, successively trainee, sr. gen. engr., nuclear power devel. engr., staff asst. exec., 1947-64, market research supr., 1964-69, dir. market research, 1969-72, dir. rate research, 1972-75, dir. rates and rate research, 1975—. Active Girl Scouts U.S., Boy Scouts Am. Mem. Jackson Pub. Sch. Bd., 1967-74, treas., 1968-70, pres., 1970-72; bd. dirs. Jackson Community Concert Assn. Served with USNR, 1943-46. Registered profl. engr., Mich. Mem. Am. Gas Assn. (chmn. market research com. 1971-73, Distinguished Service award 1974), Elec. Utility Market Research Council (chmn. council 1966-67). Home: 315 S Bowen St Jackson MI 49203 Office: 212 W Michigan Ave Jackson MI 49201

CLINE, ARTHUR RAYMOND, lawyer; b. Barr Mills, Ohio, Aug. 20, 1898; s. Alvin Arthur and Clara (Froelich) C.; student Coshocton County (Ohio) Normal Sch., 1916-17; A.B., Ohio State U., 1923, J.D., 1925; m. Christine D. Wippel, Sept. 2, 1924. Tchr. rural schs., Ohio, 1917-18; brakeman Pa. R.R., 1920; supt. maintenance and repair Athens County, Ohio Dept. Hwys., 1925-28; admitted to Ohio bar, 1925; practiced in Toledo, 1928—; mem. firm Cline, Bischoff & Cook Co., L.P.A., 1941—. Sec., dir. Dundee Truck Line, Inc., Toledo, Funk Motor Transp., Inc., Grand Rapids, Ohio, Auto-Tronic Control Co., Toledo, Dundee Motor Express, Inc., Toledo, Airport Mobile Homes, Inc., Swanton, Ohio; v.p., dir. Progress Nat. Bank, Toledo, 1965-73.

Chmn., Toledo citizens com. Lake Erie Water Works, 1938, mem. citizens adv. com. constrn., 1938-41, exec. chmn. dedication com., 1941; mem. Toledo City Plan Commn., 1937-74, chmn., 1941-74; mem. Lucas County (Ohio) Plan Commn., 1941-74, chmn., 1942-74; chmn. coordination com. Toledo Regional Plan for Action, 1963-73. Trustee, U. Toledo, 1967-75, trustee emeritus, 1975—. Served with U.S. Army, 1918-19. Mem. Am., Ohio (v.p. 1942-44; redrafting constn. com.), Toledo (past pres.), Lucas County (past pres.) bar assns., Ohio State U. Alumni Assn. (life; Alumni Citizenship award 1977), Am. Soc. Planning Ofcls. (life), Toledo C. of C. (past trustee), Am. Legion (life), Sphinx, Gamma Eta Gamma. Methodist. Mason (33 deg. Shriner). Clubs: Toledo, Maumee River Yacht (life) (Toledo); South Side Toledo Exchange (past pres.). Home: 2720 Medford Dr Toledo OH 43614 Office: Cline Bischoff & Cook Co LPA Security Bldg Toledo OH 43604

CLINE, CHARLES WILLIAM, poet; b. Waleska, Ga., Mar. 1, 1937; s. Paul Ardell and Mary Montarie (Pittman) C.; A.A., Reinhardt Coll., 1957; student Conservatory of Music, U. Cin., 1957-58; B.A., George Peabody Coll. for Tchrs., 1960; M.A., Vanderbilt U., 1963; m. Sandra Lee Williamson, June 11, 1966; 1 son, Jeffrey Charles. Asst. prof. English, Shorter Coll., Rome, Ga., 1963-64; instr. English, W. Ga. Coll., Carrollton, 1964-68; manuscript procurement editor Fiedler Co., Grand Rapids, Mich., 1968; asso. prof. English, Kellogg Community Coll., Battle Creek, Mich., 1969-75, prof. English and resident poet, 1975—; condr. poetry readings and workshops; chmn. creative writing sect. Midwest Conf. on English, 1976. Recipient poetry awards from Weave Anthology, 1974, Modus Operandi, 1975, Internat. Belles-Lettres Soc., 1975, Poetry Soc. of Mich., 1975, N.Am. Mentor, 1976. Founding fellow Internat. Acad. of Poets; mem. Nat. Council of Tchrs. of English, Midwest Conf. on English, Soc. for Study of Midwestern Lit., Nat. Mich. edn. assns., Mich. Assn. of Higher Edn., World Poetry Soc. Intercontinental, Internat. Poetry Soc. Presbyterian. Author: Crossing the Ohio, 1976. Editor: Forty Salutes to Mich. Poets, 1975. Contbr. poems to jours. and anthologies. Home: 3529 Romence Rd Kalamazoo MI 49002 Office: 450 North Ave Battle Creek MI 49016

CLINE, DONALD WELLER, physician; b. Sioux City, Iowa, Mar. 21, 1932; s. James Alexander and Emma (Weller) C.; B.A., U. Omaha, 1953; M.D., U. Nebr., 1957; m. Patricia Laura Hineline, Mar. 12, 1974; children by a previous marriage—Kathryn, Donald, John; stepchildren—Michael, Penelope, Mary Patrice, Martha, Mark, Matthew. Intern, Sacred Heart Hosp., Yankton, S.D., 1957-58, resident, 1958-61; resident Yankton State Hosp., Yankton Clinic, 1958-61; clin. asso. anatomy State U. of S.D., 1959-61, instr., 1961-62, NIH postdoctoral fellow, 1962-63; preceptee surgery C.B. McVay, Yankton, 1963-64; asso. Yankton Clinic, 1963-64; asso. Creston (Iowa) Med. Clinic, 1965-66, partner, 1966—, dir. clinic lab., 1967-73, pres. Clinic Bldg. corp., 1971, chief of staff, 1972; asso. staff mem. Sacred Heart Hosp., Yankton, 1963-64, active staff mem., 1964; active staff mem. Greater Community Hosp., Creston, Iowa, 1965—; staff physician emergency div. Henry Ford Hosp., Detroit, Mich., 1974-75, W. Bloomfield (Mich.) Center, 1975-76, physician in charge, 1976—; founding mem., bd. dirs. Union County Health Planning Council, 1972-73. NIH fellow, 1962. Fellow Am. Coll. of Surgeons; mem. AMA, Iowa, Union-Taylor County med. socs., Sigma Xi. Roman Catholic. Home: 7471 Jackson Park Dr Birmingham MI 48010 Office: 6777 W Maple Rd West Bloomfield MI 48033

CLINE, DOROTHY MAY STAMMERJOHN (MRS. EDWARD WILBURN CLINE), educator; b. Boonville, Mo., Oct. 19, 1915; d. Benjamin Franklin and Lottie (Walther) Stammerjohn; grad. nurse U. Mo., 1937; B.S. in Edn., 1939, postgrad., 1966-67; M.S., Ark. State U., 1964; m. Edward Wilburn Cline, Aug. 16, 1938 (dec. May 1962); children—Margaret Ann (Mrs. Rodger Orville Bell), Susan Elizabeth (Mrs. Gary Lee Byrns), Dorothy Jean. Dir. Christian Coll. Infirmary, Columbia, Mo., 1936-37; asst. chief nursing service VA Hosp., Poplar Bluff, Mo., 1950-58; tchr.-in-charge Tng. Center No. 4, Poplar Bluff, 1959-66, State Sch. No. 53, Boonville, 1967—; instr. U. Mo., Columbia, 1973-74; cons. for workshops for new tchrs., curriculum revision Mo. Dept. Edn. Mem. Butler County Council Retarded Children, 1959-66; v.p. Boonslick Assn. Retarded Children, 1969-72; sec.-treas. Mo. chpt. Am. Assn. on Mental Deficiency, 1973-75. Mem. Mo. Tchrs. Assn., Am. Assn. on Mental Deficiency, Council for Exceptional Children, A.A.U.W. (v.p. Boonville br. 1968-70, 75-77), Bus. and Profl. Women's Club, Smithsonian Assn., U. Mo. Alumni Assn., Ark. State U. Alumni Assn., Internat. Platform Assn., Boonslick Hist. Soc., Eastern Center Poetry Soc. (London), Friends Historic Boonville, Creative Writers Groups, Delta Kappa Gamma. Mem. Christian Ch. Home: 603 E High St Boonville MO 65233

CLINE, JAMES CLEVELAND, chemist; b. Racine, Ohio, May 17, 1933; s. Russell M. and Seva (Beaver) C; certificate chem. tech., Marietta (Ohio) Coll., 1955; m. Margaret E. Martin, Sept. 25, 1952; children—James R. Martha Sue, Darla Jean. With Globe Metall. Co. (div. Interlake Inc.), Beverly, Ohio, 1955—, lab. tech., 1955-56, research and devel. chemist, 1956-59, lab. supr., 1959-63, asst. chief chemist, 1963-65, chief chemist, 1965—; cons. water chemist to instrument co. U.S. del. Internat. Standard Orgn. meeting, Moscow, 1972, Stockholm, 1973, Zaporozhie, USSR, 1974. Pres. Ft. Frye Taxpayers Assn. Trustee Mt. Vernon (Ohio) Nazerene Coll., 1972-75. Served with USMC, 1952-55; Korea. Decorated Korean Service, UN, Nat. Def. medals. Mem. Am. Soc. for Metals, Am. Soc. for Testing Materials, Soc. for Applied Spectroscopy. Mem. Ch. of Nazarene (chmn. bd. trustees, mem. dist. adv. bd., home missions bd.). Lion. Home: Box 453 Beverly OH 45715 Office: Box 157 Beverly OH 45715

CLINE, JAYSON HOWARD, retailer, numismatist; b. Richlands, Va., Sept. 21, 1934; s. George Henry and Rachel Elizabeth (Ray) Johnson; student pub. schs. Richlands; children—Carlotta Bernard, Quinton, Carmellia. With Sunshine Biscuit Co., Dayton, 1954-55; apprentice Nat. Cash Register Co., Dayton, 1955-65; owner, operator Cline's Rare Coins, Dayton, 1955—; lectr. Wilberforce (Ohio) Coll. Mem. Am., Blue Ridge, Greene County, Penn-Ohio, So. Calif., Tex. State, Tenn. State numismatic assns. Republican. Mem. Christian Missionary Alliance Ch. Author: Standing Liberty Quarters, 1976. Home: 2850 Stonequarry Rd Dayton OH 45416 Office: 4421 Salem Ave Dayton OH 45416

CLINE, WILBUR JAMES, ednl. adminstr.; b. Centerville, Iowa, May 28, 1918; s. Thomas C. and Nadie (Maring) C.; B.S., Iowa Wesleyan Coll., 1940; M.S. in Edn., Drake U., 1954; Specialists Degree, U. Colo., 1959; m. Olive Lucille Jones, Oct. 25, 1942; 1 dau., Marjorie Anne Cline Holland. Tchr. Centerville (Iowa) Pub. Schs., 1939-41, Ottumwa (Iowa) Pub. Schs., 1941-42, Mason City (Iowa) Pub. Schs., 1942-43; tng. officer VA, Des Moines, Iowa, 1946-53; guidance counselor Davenport High Sch., Iowa, 1954-60; dir. guidance services Davenport (Iowa) pub. schs., 1960-63; dir. data processing services Scott County (Iowa) schs., 1963-66; dir. Area 9 Schs. Info. Center, Bettendorf, Iowa, 1966-70; v.p. Kempton-Cline Data Systems, Davenport, Iowa, 1970-74; asst. to dir. Bi-State Met. Computer Commn., 1974-75; guidance counselor Pleasant Valley Community Schs., Pleasant Valley, Iowa, 1975—; vocat. cons. to Social Security Adminstrn., 1963-64. Mem. Citizens Advisory Com., Scott County Mental Health Center, 1977; elder Newcomb Presbyn. Ch., Davenport, 1957-58. Served with USAAF, 1942-46, to lt. col. USAF, 1950-52; Korean War. Mem. Am. Personnel and Guidance Assn., NEA, Iowa, Pleasant Valley edn. assns., Nat. Vocat. Guidance Assn., Am. Sch. Counselors Assn., Res. Officers Assn., Assn. for Measurement and Evaluation in Guidance, Beta Beta Beta. Club: Masons. Home: 1555 W Garfield St Davenport IA 52804 Office: Belmont Rd Pleasant Valley IA 52767

CLINEFELTER, JAMES WALTER, corp. exec.; b. Akron, Ohio, Oct. 3, 1927; s. James Claude and Gladys Madora (Fraze) C.; B.A., U. Akron, 1950, M.A., 1951; m. Barbara Joan Baugh, Apr. 13, 1957; children—James Christopher, Joan Lucinda, Laura Mélitine, Barbara Claudia. With J. C. Clinefelter Co., rubber and plastics extrusion machinery sales, Akron, O., 1950—, sales rep., 1950-56, owner, 1956-66; pres., chmn. bd. J. C. Clinefelter Co., Inc., 1966—; partner C-Z Equipment Co., Burke & Hare; pres. Wayne Equip. Corp., Akron, 1963—, chmn. bd., 1963—; Midwest sales agt. John Royle & Sons, Paterson, N.J., 1956-72, regional sales mgr., 1972—; sales rep. Gem Gravure Corp., 1976—, Videx Equipment Corp., 1976—; owner Pigeon Run Farm, 1955—; asst. instr. U. Akron, 1948-49, grad. asst. instr., 1949-50. Vice pres. Empathy Internat., 1972—. Mem. Summit County Democratic Exec. Com., 1953-66, treas. Central Com., 1959-66, del. to state convs., 1956, 58, 60, 62, 64. Mem. Wire Assn., Monarchist League (life), Summit County, Wayne County hist. socs., Nat. Rifle Assn. (life), Akron Rubber Group, Am. Chem. Soc., Pi Sigma Alpha, Phi Alpha Theta. Episcopalian. Mason (32 deg., Shriner). Clubs: Cascade (life), University (Akron); Lakeview Country (Morgantown W.Va.); Hamilton (Paterson, N.J.); Banyan Soc. (Toronto, Ont., Can.); Whatley Hall (Banbury, Oxon). Patentee in field. Home: 618 Ridgecrest Rd Akron OH 44303 also Route 1 Apple Creek OH Office: 572 W Market St Akron OH 44303

CLINTON, FRANK LEE, assn. exec.; b. Chgo., July 29, 1937; s. Francis Ring and Eva (Strohl) C.; B.S., U. Ill., 1960. Credit analyst Marshall Field & Co., Chgo., 1961-62; with trust dept. Edgar County Nat. Bank, Paris, Ill., 1962-64; purchasing mgr., accountant Bastian-Blessing Co., Chgo., 1965-71; production mgr. McCann Engring. & Mfg. Co., Glendale, Calif., 1971-74; exec. dir. Paris C. of C., Paris, Ill., 1975—. Dir. Edgar County Fair Assn., 1966, v.p., 1970-73; pres. Young Republican Orgn., Edgar County, 1964. Served to sgt. Army N.G., 1960-66. Mem. Ill. Assn. of C. of C. Execs. Presbyterian. Clubs: Sycamore Hills Country, Paris Booster, U.S. Auto, Mason. Sports announcer for Paris Broadcasting Corp., 1953—. Home: 1002 S Main St Paris IL 61944 Office: Room 22 Ken More Bldg Paris IL 61944

CLINTON, WILLIAM CHRISTOPHER, physicist; b. Dubuque, Iowa, Aug. 19, 1937; s. William Milford and Mary Avo (Thorpe) C.; B.A., William Jewell Coll., 1966; student Ill. Inst. Tech., 1967, Mass. Inst. Tech., 1968. Med. lab. technician U.S. Air Force, Aeromed. Research Lab., Holloman AFB, N.Mex., 1961-65; physicist U.S. Bur. Mines, Rolla (Mo.) Metallurgy Research Center, 1966—. Chmn., Rolla Combined Fed. Campaign, 1976—; bd. dirs. Rolla Civic Theatre, 1976—. Mem. Microbeam Analysis Soc., Internat. Metallographic Soc., Sigma Xi. Club: Rolla Lions (treas. 1971—). Contbr. articles to tech. jours. Home: PO Box 1125 Rolla MO 65401 Office: Bur Mines PO Box 280 Rolla MO 65401

CLIPPERT, DUANE JOHN, diversified co. exec.; b. Beloit, Wis., Oct. 7, 1925; s. John David and Gyneth Elizabeth (Hendricks) C.; B.A., St. Ambrose Coll., 1950; m. Charlene Joy Cook, Aug. 16, 1947; children—Karen, Allyn, Dana, Terry, Christie, David, Steven, Jeffrey, Charlene, Amy. Programming mgr. Ordnance Weapons Command, Rock Island, Ill., 1952-61; mgr. data processing H.K. Porter, Pitts., 1961-65; dir. mgmt. info. systems Nat. Lock Co., Rockford, Ill., 1965-71, Hillenbrand Industries, Batesville, Ind., 1971—. Pres., Harvard Players, 1969-70; commr. Harvard Boys Baseball, 1965-71; active Boy Scouts Am. Served with AUS, 1944-46. Decorated Purple Heart. K.C., Moose. Home: Vine St Oldenburg IN 47036 Office: Hwy 46 Batesville IN 47006

CLIPSON, ADDISON HENDRICKSON, JR., architect; b. Sandusky, Ohio, Apr. 3, 1932; s. Addison Hendrickson and Mildred Leona (Stickreth) C.; B.S., U. Cin., 1953; m. Jeraldyne Mae Beets, Dec. 19, 1953; children—Randall, Brian. Engr., Mead Corp., Cin., 1952-55; designer, Elliston & Hall-McAllister-Stockwell, Cin., 1957-63; partner, Fisk-Rinehart & Hall-McAllister-Stockwell, Cin., 1970-75; pres. Addison Clipson Architects, Cin., 1975—. Mem. adv. bd. Indian Hill Historic Mus. Assn., 1974—; mem. exec. com. Glendale (Ohio) Heritage Preservation, Inc., 1974—. Served with CIC, AUS, 1955-57. Recipient Honor award A.I.A., 1974, 76. Mem. Nat. Assn. Watch and Clock Collectors (sec. Buckeye chpt. 1973-74), Early Am. Industries Assn., Am. Clock and Watch Mus., Nat. Trust Historic Preservation, Miami Purchase Assn. A.I.A., Ohio Geneal. Soc., Ohio Soc. Architects, English Speaking Union, Cin. Hist. Soc., Scarab, Caledonian Soc. (historian), Ohio Tool Collectors Soc. Club: Glendale Lyceum. Home: 905 Greenville Ave Glendale OH 45246 Office: 24 Village Sq Cincinnati OH 45246

CLOE, WILLIAM ELLSWORTH, govt. ofcl.; b. Danville, Ill., Aug. 19, 1915; s. Elmer F. and Pearl (Lane) C.; A.B., U. Ill., 1940; m. Vera L. Orr, Aug. 23, 1940; children—William Ellsworth, John M. With U.S. Dept. Commerce, Washington, 1940-41; biologist, Ill. Dept. Conservation, Springfield, 1941-43; refuge mgr. Ill. Conservation Dist., Jacksonville, 1945-49, biologist, 1949-55, asst. supt., 1955-63, fed. aid coordinator, 1963-73; grants coordinator U.S. EPA, Chgo., 1973—. Served with USNR, 1943-45; PTO. Mem. Ill. Parks and Recreation Assn. Republican. Presbyn. Moose. Home: 1645 Warbler Dr Naperville IL 60540 Office: 230 S Dearborn St Chicago IL 60604

CLOKE, THOMAS HENRY, mech. engr.; b. Chgo., Oct. 17, 1921; s. Thomas Henry and Lillian Clara (Krez) C.; B.S., U. Ill., 1943; m. Frances Irene Fox, Dec. 19, 1942; children—Deborah (Mrs. Wayne R. Kalbow), Thomas Myron. With Shaw, Naess & Murphy and Naess & Murphy, architects, Chgo., 1946-62, chief mech. engr., 1954-62; chief engr. Jensen & Halstead, architects, Chgo., 1962-64; prin. Neiler, Rich & Bladen, Inc., cons. engrs., Chgo., 1964-68, Gritschke & Cloke, Inc., cons. engrs., Chgo., 1968—. Cons. engr. U.S. Air Force in Japan, 1963. Mem. Glen Ellyn (Ill.) Park Bd., 1957-60, pres., 1961; mem. Recreation Commn., Village of Glen Ellyn, 1965-74, chmn., 1974-75, mem. Bldg. Bd. of Appeal, 1973—. Served to capt. AUS, 1943-46. Decorated Bronze Star medal. Registered profl. engr., Ill. Fellow Am. Soc. Heating, Refrigerating and Air Conditioning Engrs. (mem. research promotion com. 1969-75, research and tech. com. 1976—); mem. Air Pollution Control Assn., Nat. Fire Protection Assn., Am. Mgmt. Assn., Soc. Am. Mil. Engrs., U.S. Power Squadron, U.S. Naval Inst., Chgo. Athletic Assn., U. Ill. Alumni Assn., Theta Chi. Home: 950 Roslyn Rd Glen Ellyn IL 60137 Office: 221 N LaSalle St Chicago IL 60601

CLOPTON, WILLARD CARADINE, JR., psychologist; b. Washington, Nov. 7, 1929; s. Willard Caradine and Alta (Orrell) C.; B.A., George Washington U., 1956, 64; M.A., U. Cin., 1971, Ph.D., 1972; m. Lauretta K. Heilmayer, June 29, 1957 (div.); children—Carolyn, Catherine. Reporter Cin. Post & Times-Star, 1956-60; reporter Washington Post, 1960-68, columnist, 1969; dir. counseling service Raymond Walters Coll., Cin., 1972—. Served with AUS, 1951-53. Mem. Phi Beta Kappa, Psi Chi. Home: 789 Danvers Dr Cincinnati OH 45240 Office: Raymond Walters College 9555 Plainfield Rd Cincinnati OH 45236

CLOSE, CAMERON MICHAEL, wine import and wholesaling exec.; b. Cin., Oct. 7, 1946; s. Charles Richard and Marian Hazel (Berhalter) C.; B.S. in Pharmacy, U. Cin., 1969, M.S. in Pharm. Adminstrn. (Grad. Studies scholar), 1972; m. Kristine Lynne Hanni, June 24, 1972; children—Lydia Allison, Megan Hanni, Cameron Michael Jr. Pharmacist Bob's Pharmacy, Cin., 1969-71; grad. teaching asst. pharmacy U. Cin., 1969-71; pharmacist Walgreen's, Cin., 1971-73; adminstrv. asst. exec. dir. Ohio Pharm. Assn., Columbus, 1973, exec. dir., 1973-76, treas. Ohio Pharmacy Polit. Action Com., 1973-76; pres. Bauer and Foss Inc., internat. wine mchts., 1976—. Instr. wine appreciation. Recipient Johnson and Johnson award, 1969. Mem. Am. Pharm. Assn., Ohio State Pharm. Assn., Am. Wine Soc. Contbr. articles in field to profl. jours. Home: 553 Clotts Rd Gahanna OH 43230 Office: 354 Lowery Ct Groveport OH 43125

CLOSSON, ALFRED BURTON, JR., art gallery adminstr., interior design exec.; b. Cin., Oct. 20, 1930; s. Alfred Burton and Lucinda Winwood Rodgers C.; B.A., Yale, 1952; children—Lucinda, Laura Gurley. Asst. buyer John Shillito Co., Cin., 1955-56; buyer A.B. Closson Jr. Co., Cin., 1956—, pres., 1966—. Trustee Cin. Playhouse in the Park, Contemporary Art Center; trustee Determined Young Men, Queen City Assn. Served as sgt. AUS, 1952-54. Mem. Young Presidents Orgn., Cin. Retail Mchts. Assn. (pres. 1973). Republican. Episcopalian. Clubs: Racquet and Tennis (N.Y.C.); Camargo, Cin. Racquet. Home: 9665 Shawnee Run Rd Cincinnati OH 45203 Office: 403 Race St Cincinnati OH 45202

CLOUGH, JOHN WENDELL, geophysicist; b. Oak Bluffs, Mass., Jan. 3, 1942; s. Wendell Bradford and Marjorie Holbrook (Potter) C.; B.E.E., Northeastern U., 1965; M.S., U. Wis., 1970, Ph.D., 1974; m. Jean Elizabeth Rex, July 6, 1968; 1 son, Asa Bradford. Various positions Woods Hole (Mass.) Oceanographic Instn., 1961-65; staff geophys. and polar research center U. Wis., Madison, 1965-75, chief scientist RIGGS-II Antarctic survey, 1974-75; asst. prof. geology U. Nebr., Lincoln, also sci. dir. Ross Ice Shelf Project Mgmt. Office, 1975—. Mem. Am. Geophys. Union, Internat. Glaciological Soc., Soc. Exploration Geophysicists. Methodist. Home: 3425 N St Lincoln NE 68510 Office: 135 Bancroft Hall U Nebr-Lincoln Lincoln NE 68588

CLOUSE, JOHN DANIEL, lawyer; b. Evansville, Ind., Sept. 4, 1925; s. Frank Paul and Anna Lucile (Frank) C.; A.B., U. Evansville, 1950; J.D., Ind. U., 1952. Admitted to Ind. bar, 1952; asso. firm James D. Lopp, Evansville, 1952-56; practiced in Evansville, 1956—; asst. atty. City of Evansville, 1954-55. Pres. Civil Service Commn., Evansville Police Dept., 1961-62; pres. Ind. War Memls. Commn., 1963-69; mem. Vandenburgh County Jud. Nominating Com., 1976—. Served with AUS, 1943-46. Decorated Bronze Star medal. Mem. Ind., Evansville bar assns., Pi Gamma Mu. Clubs: Evansville Petroleum, Travelers Century. Home: 1127 Lincoln Ave Evansville IN 47714 Office: 1004 Hulman Bldg Evansville IN 47708

CLOUSE, RAYMOND EDWARD, architect; b. East Liverpool, Ohio, Oct. 5, 1913; s. Ernest Edward and Belle (Bucher) C.; student Ohio U., 1934-35; B.Arch., Ohio State U., 1939; student Moody Bible Inst., 1955-57; B.D., No. Bapt. Sem., 1962; m. Mary Elizabeth Havird, June 30, 1960. Estimator, Ohio Fuel Gas Co., Columbus, 1939-46; estimator Goodyear Aircraft, Akron, Ohio, 1946-48; pvt. archtl. practice, East Liverpool, 1948-55; with U.S. P.O., Chgo., 1962-67; ordained to ministry Am. Bapt. Ch., 1968; pastor 1st Bapt. Ch., Lamoille, Ill., 1967-69; architect Brethren Archtl. Service, Winona Lake, Ind., 1969—. Mem. Nat. Council Archtl. Registration Bds. Mem. A.I.A. Home: RD 6 Wayside Terr Warsaw IN 46580 Office: 1401 Kings Hwy Winona Lake IN 46590

CLOUSSON, JERRY PAIGE, lawyer; b. Clarksburg, W.Va., May 31, 1932; s. French Walker and Garnette Mae (Pitts) C.; A.B., W.Va. U., 1954, J.D., 1956; LL.M., Georgetown U., 1959; m. Carolyne Ann Smith, Aug. 22, 1954; children—Mark Steven, Dana Lynne, Kirk Bradley. Admitted to Ill. bar, 1960; litigation specialist NLRB, Chgo., 1960-62; counsel Am. Newspaper Pubs. Assn., Chgo., 1965-70; pvt. labor law practice, Chgo., 1970-76; dir. negotiations AMA, 1976—. Labor law instr. Loyola Law Sch., Chgo., 1972—; bus. law instr. Triton Jr. Coll., Maywood, Ill., 1968-71; hearing examiner Ill. Fair Employment Practices Commn., 1974—; lectr. continuing edn. program Ill. Bar Assn.; mem. labor panel Am. Arbitration Assn. Pres., Glen Ellyn (Ill.) United Fund, 1972-73. Commr., Glen Ellyn Capital Improvements Commn., 1973—; treas. Olgivee Campaign Commn., 1972. Bd. dirs. Glen Ellyn Youth Center, 1973—; bd. dirs., sec. Glen Ellyn Jr. C. of C. Ednl. Trust Fund, 1969-72. Served to capt. USAF, 1956-60. Recipient Merit award Chgo. chpt. Fed. Bar Assn., 1973; named Jaycee of the Year, 1968. Mem. Nat. Occupational Safety and Health Inst. (sec. 1973-74), Fed. (nat. v.p. 1973-74, pres. Chgo. chpt. 1972-73), Ill. (chmn. labor law sect. 1972-73) bar assns., Glen Ellyn Jr. C. of C., (sec. 1969-70), Glen Ellyn Civic Betterment Party (treas. 1972-73), Nat. C. of C. (labor relations com.). Mason. Club: Glen Ayre Racquet. Editor: Labor Law Newsletter, Ill. Bar Assn., 1969-72. Home: 355 N Park Blvd Glen Ellyn IL 60137 Office: 105 W Adams Chicago IL 60603

CLUGSTON, RICHARD MARTIN, coll. ofcl.; b. Ft. Wayne, Ind., Aug. 4, 1925; s. Herbert A. and Ethel (Martin) C.; B.S. with honors in Mathematics, State Tchrs. Coll., 1948; M.A. in Ednl. Psychology, U. Minn., 1950; postgrad. State Coll. Iowa, 1964, 66; m. Charlotte H. Follensbee, Jan. 2, 1970; children—Richard Martin, David A., Mary K., Richard J., Robert J., Pamela J., Daniel S., Kevin M. Tchr. mathematics Minneota (Minn.) High Sch., coach track football, 1948-49; counseling intern Excelsior (Minn.) High Sch., 1949-50; guidance dir., asst. prin. White Bear (Minn.) High Sch., 1950-52; asst. dir. student personnel, instr. edn. psychology, N.D. State Coll., Fargo, 1952-54; counselor, asst. prof. dept. edn., S.D. State Coll., Brookings, 1954-57; dir. guidance and testing Cedar Falls (Iowa) Community Sch. Dist., 1957-62, 64-66; elementary counselor Karlsruhe Am. Elementary Sch., Germany, 1962-64; dean students Rochester (Minn.) State Jr. Coll., 1966—; dir. of summer guidance workshop, No. State Tchrs. Coll., Aberdeen, S.D., 1958; asst. prof. of edn. and psychology NDEA Guidance Inst., State Coll. of Iowa, Cedar Falls, summer, 1960, 61, 62, 66; mem. research com. Minn. Continuing Edn. For Women Program, 1967-68; mem. State Research Com., State Dept. of Pub. Instruction, State of Iowa, 1959-60. Chairperson Cedar Falls Community Youth Study Com., 1968-69. Served with USAAF, 1943-45. Mem. Nat. Vocat. Guidance Assn., Am. Social Health Assn. (family life cons. for state Iowa 1957-66), Am. Sch. Counselors Assn., Minn. Assn. of State Community Coll. Adminstrs. (pres. 1973-74), Minn. Coll. Personnel Assn. (pres. 1974-75), Am., Minn. personnel and guidance assns., Phi Delta Kappa, Kappa Delta Pi. Club: Lions. Home: 1408 4th St SE Rochester MN 55901 Office: Rochester Community College Rochester MN 55901

CLUM, JAMES AVERY, educator; b. Sidney, N.Y., July 7, 1937; s. Moore Preston and Nettie Mae (Miles) C.; B.Metall. Engring., Ohio State U., 1960; M.S., Carnegie-Mellon U., U., 1963, Ph.D., 1968; m. Cynthia Marie Spoerl, Aug. 4, 1962; 1 dau., Kimberly Ann. Research metallurgist Battelle Meml. Inst., 1964-67; vis. research asso. Ohio State U., 1967, 68; researcher Cambridge (Eng.) U., 1968, 69; asst. prof. metall. engring. U. Wis., Madison, 1969-77, asso. dir. univ-industry research program, 1970-72; operating steel metallurgist Ford Motor Co., 1973, 74; research asso. prof. metall. engring. Vanderbilt U., Nashville, 1977—. Am. Soc. Engring. Edn./Ford Found. fellow, 1973-74. Fellow Am. Inst. Chemists; mem. Am. Soc. Engring. edn. (sec.-treas. materials div.), Am. Soc. Metals (dir. Milw. chpt.), Am. Inst. Mining, Metall. and Petroleum Engrs. (dir. Chgo. sect. Iron and Steel Soc.), Am. Ceramic Soc., AAAS, Am. Vacuum Soc., N.Y. Acad. Sci., Edward Daniel Clark Soc., Sigma Xi, Sigma Nu, Tau Beta Pi, Alpha Sigma Nu, Sigma Gamma Epsilon. Home: 5110 South Hill Dr Madison WI 53705 Office: 1509 University Ave Madison WI 53706

CLYDE, GRACE KATHERINE, employment counselor; b. Oak Park, Ill., Jan. 31, 1919; d. Joel Albert and Cora Myrtle (Hinds) Johnson; B.A. in Sociology, Beloit (Wis.) Coll., 1941; postgrad. Am. Acad. Art, 1942-60, Ohio State U., 1973; m. Henry B. Clyde, Jr., Sept. 13, 1947; children—Henry B., Bruce William, Carol Diane. Admissions counselor Beloit Coll., 1942-44; fashion store mgr. Montgomery Ward & Co., Ann Arbor Mich., 1944; asst. buyer, mgr. infants and children's wear The Fair Store, Oak Park, 1945-49; adminstrv. asst. GI Builders, Downers Grove, Ill., 1952-62; rep., cons. Scholastic Mag., Inc., N.Y.C., 1963-66; social worker Franklin County Welfare Dept., Columbus, Ohio, 1967-68; employment counseling supr. Ohio Bur. Employment Services, Columbus, 1968—, also vocat. expert Bur. Hearings and Appeals, Social Security Adminstrn., Washington, 1977—; mem. Gov.'s Com. on Employment of Handicapped, Columbus Met. Area Com. Employment of Handicapped; pub. speaker on employment counseling. Adv. com. Columbus Pub. Schs. Adult Edn.; mem. Linkage Com. for Developmentally Disabled; ednl. dir. Lima (Ohio) PTA Council. Mem. Am., Ohio (commn. licensure of counselors) personnel and guidance assns., Nat. Employment Counselors Assn., Internat. Assn. Personnel in Employment Services, Central Ohio Weavers Guild, Delta Gamma. Editor: (with John Rowe and Valerie Wickham) Midwest Colleges and Universities: Data and Entry Requirements, 1943; (with others) Let's Talk, 1965; (with others) Access—Columbus, 1978. Home: 634 Morning St Worthington OH 43085 Office: Ohio Bureau of Employment Services 309 S 4th St Columbus OH 43215

CLYDE, MAX NEWTON, hwy. engr.; b. Bellaire, Mich., Apr. 14, 1927; s. John Joseph and Lottie (Corey) C.; B.S. in Civil Engring., U. Mich., 1949; certificate Bur. Hwy. Traffic, Yale, 1952; m. Connie Marie Fountain, Dec. 26, 1951; children—Kathryn Anne, John David, Julia Lynne. With Mich. Dept. State Hwys. and Transp., Lansing, 1949—, engr. geometrics, 1957-62, engr. traffic ops., 1962-65, engr. design, 1966-71, engr. testing and research, 1971-73, engr. traffic and safety, 1973-74, asst. dep. dir. hwys., 1974—; guest lectr. Mich. State U., 1955-62, Northwestern U., 1964-66; ofcl. rep. of Mich. Dept. Hwys. on Hwy. Research Bd., 1971-74. Mem. Meridian Twp. Zoning Bd. Appeals, 1963-66; mem. Meridian Twp. Planning Commn., 1966-70, vice chmn., 1968-70; commr. Mich. Water Resources Commn., 1975—. Served with AUS, 1944-46. Fellow Inst. Traffic Engrs. (asst. div. chmn. sts. and hwys. div. dept. 5, 1965-72), Am. Assn. State Hwy. Ofcls. (com. on materials 1971-73), U.S. Ski Assn., A.P.-U.S. Power Squadron (chmn. seamanship tng. 1972-73, chmn. advanced pilot tng. 1976-77). Club: Lansing Ski. Home: 1442 Roxburgh Dr East Lansing MI 48823 Office: PO Box 30050 Lansing MI 48909

CLYMER, WAYNE KENTON, bishop; b. Napoleon, Ohio, Sept. 24, 1917; s. George Arnold and Grace Susan (Hulvey) C.; A.B., Asbury Coll., 1939; M.A., Columbia, 1942; B.D., Union Theol. Sem., 1944; Ph.D., N.Y.U., 1950; LL.D., Westmar Coll., 1969; D.Litt., Hamline U., 1975; m. Helen Eloise Graves, Sept. 3, 1939; children—Kenton James, Richard George. Ordained to ministry Evang. Ch., 1942; pastor Emanuel Ch., Ozone Park, N.Y.C., 1939-41, St. Paul's Ch., Forest Hills, N.Y.C., 1941-46; prof. Evang. Theol. Sem., Naperville, Ill., 1946-57, dean, 1957-67, pres., 1967-72; bishop United Meth. Ch., Mpls., 1972—; lectr. St. Andrews Theol. Coll., Manila, 1966, Trinity Coll., Singapore, 1967. Pres. Coll. Bishop United Meth. Ch., 1975. Pres. Naperville Sch. Bd., 1959-63. Bd. dirs. Naperville Community Fund, 1966; pres. Chgo. Pastoral Counseling Center. Mem. Soc. for Sci. Study Religion, Kappa Delta Pi. Kiwanian. Author: Affirmation, 1971; Membership Means Discipleship, 1976. Contbr. to Ency. Religious Edn. Home: 12207 Mari Ln Minnetonka MN 55343 Office: 122 W Franklin Ave Minneapolis MN 55404

COADY, JOHN MARTIN, assn. exec.; b. Minooka, Ill., Apr. 2, 1927; s. John Jay and Mildred S. (Brinckerhoff) C.; A.S., Joliet Jr. Coll., 1949; D.D.S., Loyola U., Chgo., 1953, M.S., 1960; Pvt. practice dentistry, Morris, Ill., 1954-57, Chgo., 1957-63; asst. prof. Loyola U. Sch. Dentistry, Chgo., 1954-60; asst. sec., council on dental edn. Am. Dental Assn., Chgo., 1963-70, sec. council on dental edn., 1970-72, asst. exec. dir. edn. and hosps., 1972—. Mem. Am. Dental Assn., Am. Soc. Oral Surgeons (hon.), Ill., Chgo. dental socs., Am. Acad. Oral Pathology, Am. Legion, Blue Key, Omicron Kappa Upsilon, Delta Sigma Delta. Contbr. articles to profl. jours. Home: 1550 N Lake Shore Dr Chicago IL 60610 Office: 211 E Chicago Ave Chicago IL 60611

COAKLEY, JAMES FRANCIS, educator; b. Pitts., Dec. 12, 1933; s. James Francis and Elizabeth (Bartus) C.; B.F.A., Carnegie Inst. Tech., 1955; M.A., U. Minn., 1959; Ph.D., Northwestern U., 1964. Asst. prof. speech Loyola U., 1964-66; with U. Mich., 1966-71; prof. theatre Northwestern U., 1971—; vis. lectr. The Goodman Sch., Chgo., 1965-66; asst. critic music and theatre, Chicago Today, 1971-74. Served with AUS, 1956-58. Mem. Am. Theatre Assn. Contbr. to drama, ednl. theater jours. Home: 912 Greenwood St Evanston IL 60201 Office: Dept Theatre Northwestern U Evanston IL 60201

COAN, WARREN RONALD, bus. cons. exec.; b. Oak Park, Ill., Nov. 29, 1941; s. Warren A. and Charlotte C. (Sigler) C.; student Ill. Inst. Tech., Chgo., 1971; m. Janis Ruth Plapp, June 17, 1961; children—David, Robert, Sharon. Project leader Consol. Foods Corp., Chgo., 1972-73; systems designer Kennecott Copper Corp., Salt Lake City, 1973-75; systems analyst Fuller Brush Co., Chgo., 1975; systems analyst Infotek Corp., Milw., 1975-76; pres., Consol. Mgmt. Cons., Waukesha, Wis., 1976—; cons in field. Cub master Boy Scouts Am., Waukesha, 1975-77. Lutheran. Office: 21490 Sierra Dr Waukesha WI 53186

COATES, GLENN EDWARD, contractor; b. Milw., Aug. 31, 1930; s. Harry Edwards and Daisy Glen (LaPlante) C.; student Bernie Robbins Real Estate Sch., 1974; m. Irene K. Drazgowski, Sept. 16, 1950; children—Glenn M., David G., James E., Kevin L., Brian P., Duane A. Constrn. supt., various contractors, Wis., 1952-57; v.p. Superior Cast Stone Co., Sussex, Wis., 1957-63; pres. Glenco Industries Inc. contractor, Franklin, Wis., 1963—. Unit leader Potawatomi Council Boy Scouts Am., 1963-66. Bd. dirs. Peshtigo Preserve, 1968-72. Named Boss of Year, Nat. Assn. Women in Constrn., 1972-73. Mem. Allied Constrn. Employers Council, Wis. Employers Council (dir., 1970-75), Nat. Investment Real Estate Brokers, Constrn. Specifications Inst. Elk, Lion, Eagle. Clubs: Milw. Traders; Wis. Exchange. Home: 6810 S Lovers Ln Franklin WI 53132 Office: Box 383 Franklin WI 53132

COATES, GLENN RICHARD, lawyer; b. Thorp, Wis., June 8, 1923; s. Richard and Alma (Borck) C.; student Milw. State Tchrs. Coll., 1940-42, N.M. A. and M.A., 1943-44; LL.B., U. Wis., 1948, D.Juridicial Scis., 1951; m. Dolores Milburn, June 24, 1944; children—Richard Ward, Cristie Joan. Admitted to Wis. bar, 1949; atty. Mil. Sea Transp. Service, Dept. Navy, 1951-52; pvt. law practice, Racine, Wis., 1952—; dir. Pioneer Savings & Loan Assn., Racine Federated, Inc. Lectr., U. Wis. Law Sch., 1955-56. Chmn. bd. St. Luke's Meml. Hosp. Served with AUS, 1943-46. Mem. State Bar Wis. (bd. govs. 1969-74, chmn. bd. 1973-74), Wis. Jud. Council (chmn. 1969-72), Am. Bar Assn., Am. Law Inst., Order of Coif. Methodist (chmn. finance com. 1961-67). Mason. Club: Racing Country. Contbr. to profl. publs. in field. Author: Chattel Secured Farm Credit, 1953. Home: 2830 Michigan Blvd Racine WI 53402 Office: 840 Lake Ave Racine WI 53403

COATS, NORMAN MURRY, feed and food co. exec.; b. Borden, Ind., Nov. 26, 1925; s. Ernie and Laura (Blankenbaker) C.; B.S., Purdue U., 1950, postgrad., 1950-51; postgrad. Washington U., St. Louis, 1951-58; m. Phyllis Mae Prien, Nov. 11, 1950; children—Timothy Wayne, Paul Andrew, Janet Rose. Research analyst Purdue U., 1950-51; research analyst Ralston Purina Co., St. Louis, 1951-64, dir. econ. and marketing research dept., 1965—. Cons. Office of Emergency Preparedness, 1971—, Nat. Def. Exec. Reservists; mem. adv. com. for agr. U.S. Census, 1973, chmn., 1975; chmn. agr. com. Fed. Statis. Users Conf., 1975—. Loaned exec. United Fund, St. Louis, 1957, 62. Served with USAAF, World War II. Decorated Air medal. Recipient Key Man award St. Louis Jr. C. of C., 1953, Pres.'s award, 1957; Century Club award St. Louis C. of C., 1966, award of merit. Mem. Am. Mktg. Assn., Nat. Assn. Bus. Economists (chmn. 1977—), Am. Feed Mfrs. Assn. (chmn. marketing research com. 1969—, chmn. feed statistics com. 1969, mem. econ. adv. com. 1966-69, chmn. wage and price control com. 1971-74), St. Louis C. of C. (membership com. 1961-75), Am. Agrl. Econs. Assn. Presbyn. (clk. of session, chmn. bldg. com. 1969). Clubs: Agribusiness of St. Louis, St. Louis Agricultural Economics (chmn. 1961-69). Home: 9 Forest Glen Ln Kirkwood MO 63122 Office: 835 S 8th St St Louis MO 63199

COBB, CHARLES ERNEST, ret. sch. adminstr.; b. New Athens, Ohio, Apr. 26, 1908; s. Charles Buchannon and Minnie O'Dell (Baer) C.; B.S. in Edn., Ohio State U., 1932; M.Ed., U. Pitts., 1942; m. Kathryn Virginia Jones, Nov. 18, 1933; children—Frederick Ernest, Marilyn Kathryn (Mrs. Don Hall). Elementary tchr., Martin's Ferry, Ohio, 1932-34; high sch. tchr., Martin's Ferry, 1934-39, Warren Consol. Schs., Tiltonsville, Ohio, 1940-42; prin. Rushcreek Meml. High Sch., Bremen, Ohio, 1942-45; exec. head Summit Schs., Summit Station, Ohio, 1945-48; supt. Bremen (Germany) Enclave Sch., 1948-49, Jefferson Union Schs., Richmond, Ohio, 1949-57, Fairport Exempted Village Schs., Fairport Harbor, Ohio, 1957-69; pres. C.E. Cobb Realty Inc., Perry, Ohio, 1970—. Mem. Am., Ohio assns. sch. adminstrs., N.E.A., Ohio Edn. Assn., Northeast Ohio Tchrs. Assn., Ohio Sch. Bds. Assn., Am. Overseas Educators Orgn., Nat., Ohio, Lake County realty assns., Ohio State U. Alumni Assn. Republican. Methodist Mason (32 deg.). Club: Fairport Men's Civic. Home: 230 Ridgecrest Dr Painesville OH 44077 Office: 3500 Dayton Rd Madison OH 44057

COBB, JEANNE LEE (MRS. ELMER MACDONALD COBB), ret. librarian; b. Aberdeen, S.D., Mar. 14, 1914; d. Lars Guren and Marion Irene (Hay) Lee; student No. State Tchrs. Coll., 1931-33, U. Minn., 1946-47, U. N.D., 1964, U. Utah, 1964—; m. Elmer MacDonald Cobb, June 29, 1946; 1 dau., Judith Elizabeth. Tchr., Clark, S.D., 1933-34, Castlewood, S.D., 1934-37, Sisseton, S.D., 1937-44; code clk. Signal Corps, U.S. Govt., Washington, 1944-46; head librarian Jamestown (N.D.) Pub. Library, 1962-77. Mem. Jamestown Bicentennial Com., 1974-76. Named Jamestown Woman of Distinction, Jamestown Sun, 1970. Mem. P.E.O., Sigma Delta Epsilon. Episcopalian. Clubs: Portfolio, Cultural Interests. Home: 405 2d Ave SW Jamestown ND 58401

COBLE, PAUL ISHLER, advt. co. exec.; b. Indpls., Mar. 17, 1926; s. Earl and Agnes Elizabeth (Roberts) C.; A.B., Wittenberg U., 1950; postgrad. Case-Western Res. U., 1950-53; m. Marjorie M. Trentanelli, Jan. 27, 1951; children—Jeff, Sarah Anne, Doug. Reporter, Springfield (Ohio) Daily News, 1944; reporter, feature writer Rockford (Ill.) Register-Republic, 1947-48; account exec. Fuller & Smith & Ross, Inc., Cleve., 1949-57; dir. sales promotion McCann Erickson, 1957-63; dir. sales devel. Marschalk Co., 1963-65, v.p., 1965-70, sr. v.p., 1970-73; pres. Coble Group, 1973—; chmn. bd., sec.-treas. Hahn & Coble. Inc., advt., mktg. and pub. relations, 1977—; pub. Islander mag., Hilton Head Island, S.C., 1973—. Chief instr. Cleve. Advt. Club Sch., 1961-73. Active fund raising drives for various charitable and youth orgns. Served with AUS, 1944-46. Mem. Sales and Marketing Internat., Assn. Indsl. Advertisers, Cleve. Advt. Club, Newcomen Soc. Clubs: River Oaks Racquet; Sea Pines (Hilton Head Island, S.C.). Contbr. articles to profl. pubs. Home: 22683 Meadowhill Ln Rocky River OH 44116 Office: Hanna Bldg Cleveland OH 44115

COBLER, LOIS BEULAH, educator; b. Garrett, Ind., June 1, 1899; d. Thomas C. and Ida M. (Van Zile) Cobler; grad. Tri State U., 1923; B.S., Ind. U., 1937; postgrad. Manchester Coll., Clark U., Western Mich. U., Ball State U., Ind. U., 1938-58. Tchr. pub. schs., Garrett-DeKalb County, Ind., 1918-56; tchr. Garrett Jr. High Sch., 1927-28; librarian J.E. Ober Elementary Sch., Garrett, 1956-66; now librarian Garrett Ch. of Christ. Bd. dirs. Garrett Hosp. Aux. Chmn. nat. projects Northeastern Ind. Garden Clubs, 1970—, parliamentarian, 1972—; co-chmn. steering com. DeKalb County Internat. Christian Leadership Prayer Breakfast, 1972, sec., chmn. pub. relations county prayer breakfast, 1973, chmn. county breakfast, 1974; monthly radio commentator Garrett Hosp. Aux.; bd. dirs. Garrett Community Hosp. Aid Found., 1974—; chmn. nominations com. for Ind. Mother of Year, 1974. Named Bus. and Profl. Hoosier Lady of Year, 1965; Alumni Distinguished Service award Tri State Coll. and Alumni Assn., 1969; Sr. Citizen Queen, DeKalp County (Ind.), 1976-77. Mem. Nat., Ind. ret. tchrs. assns., DeKalb County Ret. Tchrs., Garrett Hosp. Assn., Ind. Sch. Librarians, Assn., Ind. State Tchrs. Assn. (life), Garrett Hist. Soc., Bus. and Profl. Women's Club (hon.; pres. 1932-34, 65-66), Delta Kappa Gamma, Tri Kappa (pres. 1974-76). Mem. Ch. of Christ (organist). Club: Garrett Roadside Garden (sec.). Author: History of Garrett Church of Christ, 1967; contbr. biographies of Nancy Hanks Lincoln and Gene Stratton Porter to Mothers of Achievement in American History, 1776-1976, 1976. Co-editor: So Grows A City—Greater Garrett Centennial 1875-1975. Contbr. articles to profl. jours. Home: 301 W King St Garrett IN 46738

COBLITZ, SANFORD E., mfg. exec.; b. Scranton, Pa., July 10, 1921; s. D. Monte and Rae (Grodin) C.; student Fenn Coll., 1939-40, Rutgers U., 1943; m. Leah P. Shapiro, July 15, 1944; children—Mark A., David B., Gary R. With Ward Products Corp., Cleve., 1938-48, supt., Ashtabula, Ohio, 1946-48; chmn. bd. A. Louis Supply Co., Ashtabula, 1948—, pres. dir. Wheeler Mfg. Corp., Ashtabula, 1957—; dir. Glenn Arden Corp., Ronway Transcraft Corp., Mandrake Advt. Co.; chmn. bd., dir. Pilot Mfg. Corp. Served with Signal Corps, AUS, 1943-46. Mem. Am. Supply Assn., Nat. Indsl. Distbrs. Assn., Am. Water Works Assn. Patentee pipe tools. Home: 567 Knollwood St Ashtabula OH 44004 Office: 3744 Jefferson Rd Ashtabula OH 44004

COCHRAN, DONALD EARL, lawyer; b. Chgo., Sept. 17, 1939; s. John Roy and Ruth (Miller) C.; B.S. in C.E., Ind. Inst. Tech., 1961; M.S., Mich. State U., 1963; J.D., DePaul U., Chgo., 1972; m. Susan Tanner, Mar. 21, 1970. Engring., surveying cons., 1964—; dir. engring. and legal depts. Suburban Homes Corp., Valparaiso, Ind.; engr. Drainage Bd. Adams County (Ind.), 1966-68; asst. prof. Ind. Inst. Tech., 1962-68; asst. prof. constrn. tech. Calumet campus Purdue U., Hammond, Ind., 1968-73. Vice pres., mem. bd. Power-Tech, Inc., cons. engrs., Ft. Wayne, 1968—; owner Cochran Enterprises Co., Gary; pvt. practice law, Gary and Westville, Ind., 1972—. Registered profl. engr., Ind., Ohio; profl. land surveyor, Ind. Mem. Am. Soc. C.E., Nat. Soc. Profl. Engrs., Am. Congress on Surveying and Mapping, Ind. Soc. Profl. Land Surveyors (chmn. com. on edn. and registration exams 1966-70, v.p. 1968, pres. 1970 Ill., Ind. bar assns. Home: 576 Fargo Rd Jackson Farm Westville IN 46391

COCHRAN, DWIGHT EDWIN, II, veterinarian; b. East Chicago, Ind., May 18, 1948; s. Dwight Edwin and Laura Eileen (Meyer) C.; student Baylor U., 1966-68; D.V.M., Purdue U., 1973; m. Glenda Kay Boyd, May 19, 1973. Gen. practice veterinary medicine, Boswell, Ind., 1973—; cons. Ind. Dairy Goat Assn. Pres. Benton County (Ind.) Res. Dep. Sheriffs' Assn., 1976. Recipient Leadership award 4-H Clubs, 1974. Mem. Ind. Acad, Veterinary Medicine (Continuing Edn. award 1975—), Am. Assn. Swine Practitioners, Am. Assn. Sheep, Goat Practitioners, Am. Assn. Bovine Practitioners, Am., Ind., West Central Ind. veterinary med. assns. Presbyterian. Author: Common Diseases of Dairy Goats, A Guide to Their Prevention, Treatment, and Control For the Herdsman, 1977. Home: 405 E Main St Boswell IN 47921 Office: 104 E Main St Boswell IN 47921

COCHRAN, MALCOLM LOWELL, psychologist; b. Crawfordsville, Iowa, Oct. 17, 1941; s. Vaun Wesley and Pearl Ida (Robertson) C.; B.A., Iowa Wesleyan Coll., 1963; M.S., Municipal U. of Omaha, 1965; m. Barbara Sue Stotts, Apr. 17, 1966; children—Teresa Marie, Gary Lowell, Debra Sue, Patricia Diane. Intern sch. psychometrist, Child Study Service Municipal U. of Omaha, 1963-64; research psychometrist, sch. psychologist Glenwood State Hosp.-Sch., Glenwood, Iowa, 1964-68, cons. psychologist, diagnostic and evaluation clinic, 1968-74, dir. employee testing program, 1968-72, dir. psychol. testing center, 1974—, lectr.,-in-service training, child devel., 1968-72. Cubmaster Boy Scouts Am., Glenwood, 1976-77. Served with Army N.G., 1961. Recipient Explorer Scouts Silver Award Boy Scouts Am., 1958; certified sch. psychologist, Iowa; licensed psychologist, Iowa. Fellow Am. Assn. Mental Deficiency. Republican. Methodist. Contbr. articles to profl. jours. Home: 225 W Florence Ave Glenwood IA 51534 Office: 711 S Vine St Glenwood IA 51534

COCKENBACH, PHILIP ANDREW, fin. corp. exec.; b. Columbus, Ohio, Sept. 5, 1946; s. Harold C. and Mary Jo (Smith) G.; B.A. in Econ. Geography, Ohio State U., 1970; grad. diploma Ohio Savs. and Loan Acad., 1974; m. Sheila E. Jennings, June 15, 1969; children—Sara, Amy, Gail, Elizabeth (dec.). Dir. research and devel., Dollar Savs. Assn., Columbus, 1965-73, exec. v.p., 1973—; exec. v.p., dir. Dollar Fin., Inc. Dir. Central Ohio Camp Fire Girls. Served with USMC, 1965-67. Mem. Ohio Savs. and Loan League, Soc. Real Estate Appraisers, Urban Land Inst., Bldg. Owners and Mgrs. Assn., Fin. Execs. Inst., Columbus Apt. Assn. (dir.), Builders Exchange of Ohio. Republican. Roman Catholic. Club: Bexley Lions (dir.). Home: 121 N Remington St Columbus OH 43209 Office: 1 E Gay St Columbus OH 43215

COCKERHAM, WILLIAM CARL, sociologist, educator; b. Oklahoma City, Mar. 31, 1939; s. Carl Reese and Eva Louise (Purdum) C.; student Washburn U., 1957-59; B.A., U. Okla., 1962; postgrad. U. Hawaii, 1965, Stanford U., 1969; M.A., U. Calif. at Berkeley, 1968, Ph.D., 1971; m. Cynthia Francane Ross, Apr. 2, 1969; children—Laura Louise, Geoffrey Bruce, Sean Alan. Asst. prof. sociology U. Wyo., Laramie, 1971-75, U. Ill., Champaign-Urbana, 1975—. Served with AUS, 1962-66. Wyo. Gov.'s Planning Com. on Criminal Adminstrn. grantee, 1973-74. Mem. Am., Midwest, Pacific sociol. assns., Western Social Sci. Assn. Contbr. articles to profl. jours. Home: 4 McDonald Ct Champaign IL 61820

COCKRELL, RONALD SPENCER, scientist, educator; b. Kansas City, Mo., June 26, 1938; s. Robert Spencer and Jean (Hammond) C.; B.S., U. Mo., 1960, B.Med.Sci., 1964; Ph.D., U. Pa., 1968; m. Florence Barbara Hanline, June 17, 1960; children—Richard, Synthia. Asst. prof. biochemistry St. Louis U. Sch. Medicine, 1969-74, asso. prof., 1974—. Nat. Cancer Inst. grantee, 1970—. Mem. Am. Soc. Biol. Chemists. Home: 9540 Hale Dr St Louis MO 63123 Office: 1402 S Grand St Louis MO 63104

COCKS, ANNA PEARL RHODES (MRS. RICHARD E. COCKS), librarian; b. Moscow, Mich., July 18, 1918; d. Wilfred G. and Florence (Moulton) Rhodes; B.A. in Chemistry, Western Mich. U., 1940; B.L.S., George Peabody Coll. for Tchrs., 1941; m. Richard E. Cocks, June 20, 1943; children—Valerie Ann (Mrs. Ronald E. Roughton), Margaret Ann (Mrs. Michael A. Row). Asst. librarian Pa. State U. Agr. Library, State College, 1941-42; librarian Lincoln Sch. br. pub. library, Kalamazoo, 1942-43; tech. services librarian Miles Lab., Inc., Elkhart, Ind., 1957—. Pres., PTA, 1955; active Concert Club, 1955-56, YMCA membership drives, 1956-57. Mem. AAUW, Am. Chem. Soc., Spl. Libraries Assn., Am. Soc. Info. Sci., Med. Library Assn., ALA, AAAS, Phi Sigma Alpha (pres. chpt.). Episcopalian (sec. bd. Women of Ch. 1957). Clubs: Order Eastern Star, Zonta Internat. Contbg. editor COPNIP List, 1958-71, editor-in-chief, 1964-65. Home: 1622 Victoria Dr Elkhart IN 46514 Office: 1127 Myrtle St Elkhart IN 46514

COCKS, RICHARD ERNEST, chem. engr.; b. Coldwater, Mich., Aug. 1, 1917; s. Harry A. and Harriette Nina (Hall) C.; A.B., Western Mich. U., 1939, B.S. in Chem. Engring., U. Ill., 1942; m. Anna Pearl Rhodes, June 20, 1943; children—Valerie A. (Mrs. Ronald Roughton), Margaret (Mrs. Michael A. Row). Supr., Hercules Powder Co., Radford, Va., 1942-45; research chem. engr. Victor Chem. Works, Chicago Heights, Ill., 1945-48, div. supt., Nashville, 1948-49; dept. head Panelyte div. St. Regis Paper Co., Kalamazoo, 1950-53, plant mgr. plant food div. Farm Bur. Services, Kalamazoo, 1953-55; with Miles Labs., Inc., Elkhart, Ind., 1955—, adminstr. engring. services and real estate, 1968-75, mgr. corp. real estate and facilities planning, 1976—. Adviser, Jr. Achievement, 1962-63; active United Way. Registered profl. engr., Ohio, Ind. Mem. Ind. Soc. Profl. Engrs., Nat. Soc. Profl. Engrs., Am. Chem. Soc., Am. Inst. Chem. Engrs., ASTM, Indsl. Devel. Research Council, Nat. Assn. Corp. Real Estate Execs. Episcopalian. Mason (32 deg.), Lion. Home: 1622 Victoria Dr Elkhart IN 46514 Office: 1227 Myrtle St Elkhart IN 46514

CODDINGTON, JOHN LEROY, magnetic shielding mfg. co. exec.; b. Indpls., Sept. 2, 1930; s. Roy Harry and Katherine Evelyn (Wallace) C.; B.E.E., Rose Hulman Inst. Tech., 1953; postgrad. U. Cin., 1957,

Drexel U., 1955; m. Gallant B. Broussand, June 7, 1952; children—Sheryl, Denise, Mike, Mark, Nick, Christina, Robert. With RCA, various locations, 1953-55, Avco Corp., 1955-59; asst. mktg. mgr. Tex. Instruments, Dallas, 1959-64; mktg. mgr. Perfection Mica Co., Bensonville, Ill., 1964-70; pres. Eagle Magnetic Co., Inc., Indpls., 1970—, also dir.; dir. Med. Devices Corp. Served with U.S. Army, 1953-55. Mem. Export Club, Ind. Optical Soc., Soc. Info. Displays. Roman Catholic. Club: K.C. Patentee in displays and data processing. Home: 1936 Cunningham Rd Indianapolis IN 46224 Office: PO Box 24283 Indianapolis IN 46224

CODDINGTON, THOMAS TUCKER, automotive co. exec.; b. Columbus, Ohio, Jan. 1, 1938; s. Gilbert Harold and Louise (Hazen) C.; B.M.E., Ohio State U., 1961; M.Automotive Engring., Chrysler Inst., Highland Park, Mich., 1964; m. Cecelia Ann McLaughlin, Aug. 31, 1968; children—Maureen Louise, Kevin Ward. With Chrysler Corp., Detroit, 1961—, engring. coordinator, spl. vehicle devel., 1969-74, supr. fuel metering systems, engring. office, 1974—. Served in USAF, 1961-62. Mem. Soc. Automotive Engrs., Ohio State U. Alumni Assn., SAR. Patentee fuel filter and rollover valve. Home: 6179 Herbmoor St Troy MI 48098 Office: 12800 Lynn Townsend Dr Highland Park MI 48203

CODDINGTON, VAN TYLE WILLIAM, steel co. exec; b. Milw., 1917; grad. Purdue U., 1939. Chmn., pres. Lakeside Bridge & Steel Co., Milw.; dir. Audax Fund, Wis. Fund., Milw. Western Bank. Past pres., past dir. Citizens Govtl. Research Bur.; past pres. Employers Assn. Milw., Milwaukee County council Boy Scouts Am., St. John's Home for the Aged, Milw.; past pres., chmn. United Community Services Milwaukee County, Wauwatosa (Wis.) Sch. Bd.; past v.p. Greater Milw. com.; chmn. adv. com. Coll. Engring., Marquette U. Vice chmn. dir. Milw. Childrens Hosp.; bd. dirs. Milw. Psychiat. Hosp. Mem. Milw. C. of C. (dir., past pres.), Steel Plate Fabricators Assn. (dir.), Am. Inst. Steel Constrn. (dir., pres.). Home: 2062 S Shore Dr Lake Beulah Route 3 East Troy WI 53120 Office: 5300 N 33d St Milwaukee WI 53209

CODY, JOHN CARDINAL, clergyman. Ordained priest Roman Catholic Ch., 1931; aux. bishop Diocese St. Louis, 1947-54; co-adjutor with right of succession to bishop St. Joseph, Mo., 1954; bishop St. Joseph, 1955; coadjutor to Bishop Kansas City-St. Joseph, 1956, bishop, Oct. 1956; coadjutor with right of succession to Archdiocese New Orleans, 1961, apostolic adminstr., 1962-64, archbishop, 1964-65; archbishop Chgo., 1965—; elevated to cardinalate, 1967. Mem. Nat. Conf. Cath. Bishops, Sacred Congregation for Evangelization of Nations, Sacred Congregation for Clergy; chancellor Cath. Ch. Extension Soc.; mem. regional bd. Boy Scouts Am.; nat. chaplain Nat. Cath. Soc. Foresters; high spiritual dir. Cath. Order Foresters. Home: 1555 N State Pkwy Chicago IL 60610 Office: PO Box 1979 Chicago IL 60690

COE, RALPH TRACY, mus. ofcl.; b. Cleve., Aug. 27, 1929; s. Ralph M. and Dorothy T. C.; B.A., Oberlin Coll., 1953; M.A., Yale U., 1957. Asst. curator Nat. Gallery Art, Washington, 1957-59; curator paintings and sculpture Nelson Gallery Art, Kansas City, Mo., 1959, asst. dir., 1965-77, dir., 1977—. Lectr. art history U. Kans., Lawrence, 1969—; vis. research asst. Victoria and Albert Mus., London, Eng., 1956-57. Mem. IRS commr. art adv. panel, Washington, 1973-77, NEA Mus. Panel, 1977—; trustee Am. Fedn. Arts, 1977—. Mem. Coll. Art Assn. Am., Am. Assn. Mus., Soc. Archtl. Historians. Club: Rockhill (Kansas City, Mo.). Contbr. articles to profl. jours., exhbn. catalogs. Home: 4511 Holmes St Kansas City MO 64110 Office: 4525 Oak St Kansas City MO 64111

COE, ROBERT WILLIAM, state ofcl.; b. Johnston City, Ill., Feb. 19, 1927; s. Myron John and Lola Oneida (Cothern) C.; B.S., No. Ill. U., 1965, M.S., 1966; m. Dorothy L. Thorson, June 8, 1947; children—Sandra (Mrs. Michael Freedman), Ronald, Cheryl, Dena. Sanitarian Ill. Dept. Pub. Health, Carbondale, 1950-54, Rock Island, 1954-64, Aurora, 1964-71, Springfield, 1971-72, exec. adminstr., Chgo., 1972—; prof. mgmt. No. Ill. U. at DeKalb, 1966-67. Asst. scoutmaster Cub Scouts Am., 1957-59; asst. scoutmaster Boy Scouts Am., 1959-61, scoutmaster, 1961-64, dist. commr., 1964-66. Served with AUS, 1945-47. Mem. Ill. Pub. Health Assn., Assn. Ill. Milk, Food and Environmental Sanitarians (sec., treas. 1968—), A.A.U.P. Author: A Study to Determine the Effect of Appropriations Upon Program Administration, 1966. Editor: Office Management (Clarence Sims), 1965. Home: 206 Boulder Hill Pass Aurora IL 60538 Office: Ill Dept Pub Health 2121 W Taylor St Chicago IL 60612

COELHO, RICHARD JOSEPH, univ. ofcl.; b. Newark, Ohio, July 26, 1913; s. Joseph Arthur and Marguerite (Kuster) C.; A.B., Denison U., 1935; M.A., U. Denver, 1954, Ph.D., 1955; m. Helen C. Lindquist, June 4, 1945; children—Joseph R., David F., Christine A., Carl A. Chief clk. freight traffic dept. Pa. R.R., Pitts., 1935-41; gen. office mgr. Lucien Lelong, Inc., Chgo., 1946-48; credit, traffic mgr. Robbins Incubator Co., Denver, 1950-52; dir. conf. leadership tng. Ford Motor Co., Dearborn, Mich., 1956-57; communications cons. nursing staff Sparrow Hosp., Lansing, Mich., 1957-58; faculty Mich. State U., East Lansing, 1955—, dir. residence halls acad. programs, 1962-71, asso. dean U. Coll., 1971—; dir. Binational Cultural Center, Juiz de Fora, Brazil on grant from USIA, 1960-61. Commr., East Lansing council Boy Scouts Am., 1962-64; lay rep. edn. div. Mich. Catholic Conf. Bishops, 1962—. Served to col. AUS, 1941-46. Decorated Bronze Star medal with cluster. Mem. Speech Assn. Am., Assn. Gen. and Liberal Studies, Sigma Alpha Epsilon, Pi Delta Epsilon, Omicron Delta Kappa, Phi Mu Alpha. Republican. Home: 1103 Old Hickory Ln East Lansing MI 48823

COEN, GEORGE WEBER, lawyer; b. Lancaster, Ohio, Mar. 26, 1914; s. Noble Price and Georgia Sproat (Weber) C.; student Inter Am. U. Panama, 1933-34, J.D., U. Va., 1938; postgrad. La. State U., 1946, Ohio State U., 1948; m. Dorothy Kirn, Dec. 13, 1941; children—Rush, Andrew. Admitted to Ohio bar, 1938, U.S. Supreme Ct. bar, 1946; practice law, Lancaster, 1938—; mem. firm Coen, Turpin & Wexler; dir., sec. First Bremen Bank; dir. Lancaster Nat. Bank, Am. Bancorp., Ohio Bar Title; instr. Columbus Coll. Art and Design, 1960—; Supreme Ct. commr. on grievances and discipline. Chmn., Lancaster Tax Rev. Bd., 1966, Ohio Library Bd., 1950-72; chmn. endowment com. Am. Library Trustees Assn., 1968; chmn. bldg. com. Fairfield County Handicapped Center; mem. Mental Health and Retardation Bd.; sec.-treas. Lancaster Community Action, 1966—; mem. Fairfield County Health Planning Council; former law mem. Ohio Commn. Aging; past mem. bd. dirs. Fairfield County chpt. ARC; bd. dirs. Council Retarded Children, Lancaster; participant Columbus Area Leadership Program. Served with AUS, 1940-46. Mem. Am., Fed., Ohio bar assns., ALA (mem. council 1970—), Nat. Assn. Coll. and Univ. Attys. Home: 209 E Mulberry St Lancaster OH 43130 Office: 234 Equitable Bldg Lancaster OH 43130

COFFELT, JOHN J., univ. pres.; b. Neosho, Mo., Dec. 26, 1924; s. Roscoe John and Estella Matilda (Turner) C.; m. Anne Marie Nelson, Feb. 27, 1945; children—Susan Ann (Mrs. Robert Lyon), Margaret Jean (Mrs. Duane Spatar), Janet Lee (Mrs. Robert Bannon), John Byron; B.S., U. Denver, 1948; M.A., Northeastern State U., Greeley, Colo., 1951; Ed.D., U. Colo., 1962. Aircraft mechanic Boeing Aircraft Corp., Seattle, 1942-43; bookkeeper Colo. Nat. Bank, Denver, 1946-48; dir. accounts and records, registrar, instr. State Tchrs. Coll., Dickinson, N.D., 1948-52; dir. research Colo. Dept. Edn., Denver, 1952-56; dir. Colo. Legis. Com. on Edn., 1956-58; dir. Colo. Sch. Bd. Assn., Boulder, 1958-62; coordinator research Okla., 1962-65; vice chancellor research and planning Okla. State Regents for Higher Edn., Oklahoma City, 1965-68; v.p. adminstrv. affairs Youngstown (Ohio) State U., 1968-73, pres., 1973—. Bd. dirs. N.E. Med. Edn. Devel. Center of Ohio; trustee N.E. Ohio U. Coll. Medicine, N.E. Television of Ohio, Butler Inst. Am. Art, Youngstown Hosp. Assn.; mem. exec. bd. Mahoning Valley council Boy Scouts Am. Mem. Assn. for Higher Edn., Am. Assn. State Colls. and Univs., Alpha Kappa Psi, Phi Delta Kappa, Phi Kappa Phi, Masons (32 deg.), Lions Club (dir. Youngstown). Home: 1010 Colonial Dr Youngstown OH 44505 Office: 410 Wick Ave Youngstown OH 44555

COFFEY, CECIL RAYMOND, banker; b. New Salem, Kans., Sept. 9, 1910; s. Wade R. and Hallie J. (Hiett) C.; A.B., Southwestern Coll., 1932; m. J. Eleanor Sturm, Dec. 25, 1938; children—Bruce C., Roger D., John R. Asst. cashier Farmers & Mchts. State Bank, Dexter, Kans., 1934-40; loan examiner RFC, 1946-51; v.p., cashier State Bank, Winfield, Kans., 1953—. Active ARC; mem. Winfield Bd. Edn., 1958-64; mem. Winfield City Commn., 1965-74. Served with AUS, 1940-46, 51-53. Mem. VFW, Am. Legion., C. of C. Mason, Kiwanian. Home: 111 Red Bud Dr Winfield KS 67156 Office: 823 Main St Winfield KS 67156

COFFEY, JOHN LOUIS, judge; b. Milw., Apr. 15, 1922; s. William L. and Elizabeth (Walsh) C.; B.A., Marquette U., 1943, LL.B., 1948, LL.D., 1948, M.B.A. (hon.), 1963; m. Marion Kunzelmann, Feb. 3, 1951; children—Peter, Lisa. Admitted to Wis. bar, 1948; asst. city atty. Milw., 1949-54; judge Civil Ct., Milw., 1954-60, Milw. Municipal Ct., 1960-61; judge Br. 12, Circuit Ct., Milw., 1961-74; sr. felony judge Circuit Ct. Milw. County, 1974—; mem. Wis. Bd. Criminal Ct. Judges, 1960—, Wis. Bd. Circuit Ct. Judges, 1962—. Chmn. adv. bd. St. Joseph's Home for Children, 1958-64; mem. adv. bd. St. Mary's Hosp., 1964-70; mem. Milwaukee County council Boy Scouts Am.; chmn. St. Eugene's Sch. Bd., 1967-72; chmn. St. Eugene's Parish Council, 1974; mem. vol. services adv. com. Milwaukee County Dept. Pub. Welfare; bd. govs. Marquette U. High Sch. Served with USNR, 1943-46. Named Outstanding Young Man of Year, Milw. Jr. C. of C., 1951; One of Five Outstanding Young Men in State, Wis. Jr. C. of C., 1957. Mem. Am., Wis., Milw. bar assns., Am. Judicature Soc., Am. Legion (Distinguished Service award Cudworth post, 1973), Marquette U. Law Alumni. Roman Catholic. Club: M Club (Marquette U., dir.). Home: 1015 E Churchill Lane Milwaukee WI 53217

COFFEY, RICHARD JAMES, state ofcl.; b. Omaha, Dec. 22, 1920; s. Raymond Thomas and Elizabeth Evans (Nields) C. Radio news announcer, editor Radio Stas. KORN, Fremont, Neb., 1944-46, KFOR, Lincoln, Neb., 1946-47, KRCB, Council Bluffs, Ia., 1947-51, KLNG, Omaha, 1951-53, WOW-TV, Omaha, 1957-62; account exec. Catholic Voice, Omaha, 1959-62; employment service rep. Nebr. Dept. Labor, Omaha, 1962—. Vice-chmn. Democratic Central Com., Douglas County, Neb., 1958; mem. Dem. State Central Com., 1958; pres., Dem. Club, 1956-60. Recipient First Place award Toastmaster Speech Contest, 1955, Citizenship award City of Omaha, 1972. Mem. Internat. Assn. Personnel in Pub. Employment, Omaha Press Club. Home: 1010 Glenwood Ave Omaha NE 68131 Office: 5404 Cedar St Omaha NE 68106

COFFIN, ROBERT PARKER, architect, engr.; b. Chgo., Aug. 6, 1917; s. Charles Howells and Irene Borden (Parker) C.; B.Engring., Yale, 1939; m. Emily Elizabeth Magie, Jan. 7, 1944; children—Emily Elizabeth, Robert Parker, Barbara Ann, John Magie. Sr. engr. Commonwealth Edison Co., Chgo., 1939-49; with Sham Metz & Dolio, architects, Chgo., 1950-56; owner Robert Parker Coffin, architect, engr., Barrington, Ill., 1956—; dir. Bank of Buffalo Grove (Ill.). Trustee, Village of Long Grove (Ill.), 1957-60, pres., 1960—. Bd. dirs. St. Leonards House, Chgo. Served with USNR, 1942-46. Mem. Am. Soc. Ch. Architecture, A.I.A., Am. Soc. C.E., Soc. Archtl. Historians, Bensenville Howe Soc. (dir.), prin. works include North Shore Country Day Sch., Winnetka, Ill., 1960, St. Marks Ch., Barrington, 1965, Turnberry Country Club, Crystal Lake, Ill., 1971, Woodcreek Cts., Lincolnshire, Ill., 1973. Home: Box 181 Long Grove IL 60047 Office: 119 North Ave Barrington IL 60010

COFFMAN, FLOYD HURST, lawyer, judge; b. Overbrook, Kans., July 6, 1918; s. Clyde Wilson and Minerva (Bragg) C.; B.S., Kans. State Tchrs. Coll., 1940; J.D., Washburn Coll., 1947; m. Geraldine E. Crawford, Jan. 11, 1942; children—Bruce C., H. Hurst, Martha Jane, Geraldine Ann. Admitted to Kans. bar, 1947, practice in Ottawa, 1947-53; probate judge Franklin County, Kans., 1949-53; judge 4th Jud. Dist. Kans., 1953—. Conf. lay leader Kans. Conf. Methodist Ch., 1958-60. del. gen. conf., 1960, 64, 66, 68, 70, 72, 76; mem. Commn. Interjurisdictional Relations, Meth. Ch., 1960-64, mem. Gen. Bd. Christian Social Concerns, 1964-68, mem. Gen. Council on Ministries, 1972-76, mem. Gen. Bd. Pensions, 1976—; pres. Kans. Council Chs., 1971. Served with AUS, 1942-45. Recipient Univ. citation Baker U., Baldwin, Kans., 1967. Mem. Am., Kans. bar assns., Kans. Probate Judges Assn. (pres. 1952), Kans. Dist. Judges Assn. (pres. 1959), C. of C. (pres. 1959). Mason (master). Home: Route 3 Ottawa KS 66067 Office: Ct Bldg Ottawa KS 66067

COFFMAN, KENNETH MORROW, mech. contractor; b. Ann Arbor, Mich., Aug 3, 1921; s. Harold Coe and Aletha (Morrow) C.; B.S., Lawrence U., 1943; m. Barbara Ann Porth, Dec. 30, 1943; children—Gregory, Deborah Coffman Greene, Jenifer. Exec. v.p. Stanley Carter Co. Ohio, Toledo, 1957-59; v.p. sales Wenzel & Henoch Co., Milw., 1959-64; exec. v.p. Milw. W & H Inc., 1964-70; exec. v.p Azco Downey Inc., Milw., 1970-76, pres., 1977—. Bd. dirs. YMCA, Milw., 1968-72, Tri County, 1973-77; chmn. bd. mgrs. Camp Minikani, 1965-77. Served with USMC 1943-46. Named Layman of year, Tri County YMCA, 1973. Mem. Nat. Certified Pipe Welders Bur. Wis. (dir. 1973-77), Mech. Contractors Assn. South East Wis. (dir. 1970-77), Mech. Contractors Devel. Fund. (dir., pres. 1972-73), Wis. Constrn. Employers Council (dir. 1973-77), MCA of Wis. (dir. 1977), Nat. Fire Protection Assn., Nat. Assn. Plumbing, Heating, Cooling Contractors, Sheet Metal and Air Conditioning Contractors Nat. Assn. Congregationalist. Home: 925 E Wells St Milwaukee WI 53202 Office: Box 1155 Milwaukee WI 53201

COFFMAN, PHILLIP HUDSON, educator; b. Lincoln, Nebr., Nov. 27, 1936; s. Rowland Francis and Elberta (Hudson) C.; B. Music Edn., U. Nebr., 1958; M. Music, U. Idaho, 1962; Ph.D., U. Toledo, 1971; m. Karen M. Preston, Aug. 14, 1958; children—Phillip C., Catherine L. Tchr. pub. schs., Rushville, Neb., 1958-59; instr. Doane Coll., Crete, Nebr., 1959-60; teaching asst. U. Idaho, Moscow, 1960-62, instr., 1962-65; asso. prof., chmn. dept. music Jamestown (N.D.) Coll., 1965-68; adminstrv. intern U. Toledo, 1968-71; asso. prof., head dept. music U. Minn., Duluth, 1971-76, dean Sch. Fine Arts, 1976—. Mem. Lincoln Symphony, 1954-60, Toledo Symphony, 1969-71; guest artist Ednl. TV, 1964; instr. Internat. Music Camp, 1967-68. Pres. Civic Music Assn., 1967, University Artist Series Bd., 1971—, Campus Ministry Bd., 1972-75. F.E. Olds scholar, 1963, Bush Found. fellow, 1973. Mem. Coll. Music Soc., Am. Assn. Higher Edn., Internat. Council Fine Arts Deans, Theta Xi, Phi Mu Alpha, Pi Kappa Lambda, Kappa Kappa Psi. Home: 4601 Woodland Ave Duluth MN 55803

COFFMAN, WILLIAM EUGENE, ednl. psychologist; b. Belington, W. Va., June 13, 1913; s. Walter E. and Mary (Thornhill) C.; B.S. in Edn., Wittenberg U., 1934; M.A., W.Va. U., 1938; Ed.D., Columbia, 1949; m. Eloise Clarke, Dec. 21, 1939; children—Mary Eloise, Judith Ann (Mrs. David Piche). Tchr., Mineral County (W.Va.) Schs., 1934-37, prin., 1937-44; asso. prof. Okla. State U., 1949-52; asst. dir. test devel. div. Ednl. Testing Service, Princeton, N.J., 1952-54, asso. dir., 1954-57, dir., 1957-60, dir. research and devel. CEEB Program, 1960-66, research adviser, 1966-69; E.F. Lindquist prof. ednl. measurement, dir. Iowa testing programs U. Iowa, Iowa City, 1969—. Vis. prof. edn. Syracuse U., 1966; vis. lectr. Princeton Theol. Sem., 1964-69; cons. Nat. Assessment Ednl. Progress, Systems Devel. Corp., Ford Found. Served with AUS, 1944-45. Fellow Am. Psychol. Assn.; mem. Am. Ednl. Research Assn., Nat. Council Measurement in Edn. (pres. 1972-73), Alpha Tau Omega. Author: (with Fred Godshalk, Frances Swineford) The Measurement of Writing Ability, 1966; Developing Tests for the Culturally Different, 1965. Editor: Frontiers of Educational Measurement and Information Systems, 1973. Contbr. to Ency. Ednl. Research, Educational Measurement, 2d edit. Home: Apt 406 201 N 1st Ave Iowa City IA 52240

COFMAN, PHILIP NAST, community center exec.; b. Fitchburg, Mass., June 2, 1933; s. Benjamin Nast and Florence (Polman) C.; B.S., Boston U., 1959; M.S.W., Hunter Coll., 1969; m. Marsha Dorothy Karsh, June 15, 1958; children—Kathy Ann, Mitchell Alan, Shira Beth. Dir. phys. edn. Gloversville (N.Y.) Jewish Community Center, 1959-61; dir. activities Portland (Maine) Jewish Community Center, 1961-62; exec. dir. Jewish Community Center Lewiston, Auburn, Maine, 1962-64; program dir., exec. dir. part time Jewish Community Center, Norwalk, Conn., 1964-69; asst. exec. dir. Jewish Community Center, Dallas, 1969-76; exec. dir. Jewish Community Center, Omaha, 1976—. Field work supr. U. Tex. at Arlington, 1971-73. Served with AUS, 1951-53. Decorated Combat Infantryman Badge, Bronze Star; 92d St YM YWHA scholar, 1963-64. Mem. Assn. Jewish Center Workers, Nat. Assn. Social Workers, Acad. Certified Social Workers, N. Tex. Jewish Communal Workers Group (pres., 1973-76). Home: 13824 Marinda St Omaha NE 68144 Office: 333 S 132d St Omaha NE 68154

COGNATA, DONALD JASPER, police officer; b. St. Louis, Oct. 20, 1941; s. Frank and Francine (Caldwell) C.; A.S., Forest Park Community Coll., 1965; B.S., U. Mo., 1971; M.A., St. Louis U., 1974; grad. Nat. Crime Prevention Inst., 1973, Mo. U. Crime Prevention Workshop, 1974; m. Eileen Beverly Schultz, July 17, 1965; children—Donald Antoin, Christina Lee, Troy Dominic. With St. Louis Met. Police Dept., 1965—, precinct sgt., 1975, project coordinator geo-coding system, 1975-77, supr. mgmt. service sect., 1977—; lectr., cons. geo-coding, computer security, police mgmt., crime prevention, psychodeterence; bd. dirs. Aid to Victims of Crime; bd. advisers South St. Louis Alcoholism Council. Comml. exec. vol. SBA. Served with USMC, 1958-62. Certified probation and parole bd. vol., Mo. Mem. Internat. Assn. Police Officers, St. Louis Police Officers Assn., Am. Statis. Soc. Home: 6964 Marquette St Saint Louis MO 63139 Office: 1200 Clark St Saint Louis MO 63103

COHEN, ALLAN RICHARD, lawyer; b. Chgo., Feb. 25, 1923; s. Louis and Ruth (Cohen) C.; B.A., U. Wis., 1947, J.D., 1949; postgrad. Northwestern U., 1953-54; m. Audrey Doris Levy, Oct. 14, 1960; children—Joseph, David, Gale. Admitted to Ill. bar, 1950, since practiced in Chgo. Served with AUS, 1943-45. Decorated Presdl. citation with oak leaf cluster. Mem. Fed., Ill. (vice chmn. sect. comml. bankruptcy and banking laws 1977-78), Chgo. (vice chmn. com. bankruptcy 1972-73, chmn. 1973-74; panelist seminar on bankruptcy, 1968, 72, 74) bar assns., Zeta Beta Tau, Tau Epsilon Rho. Lion. Club: Elms Swim and Tennis (Highland Park, Ill.). Home: 1986 Dale St Highland Park IL 60035 Office: 100 W Monroe St Chicago IL 60603

COHEN, ARMOND EMANUEL, rabbi; b. Canton, Ohio, June 5, 1909; s. Samuel and Rebecca (Lipkowitz) C.; B.A., N.Y. U., 1931; rabbi, Jewish Theol. Sem. Am., N.Y.C., 1934; M.A. in Hebrew Lit., 1945, D.D., 1966; LL.D. (hon.), Cleve. State U., 1969; m. Anne Lederman, 1934; children—Rebecca Cohen Long, Deborah (dec.), Samuel J. Sr. rabbi Park Synagogue, Cleve., 1934—; vis. prof. pastoral psychiatry Jewish Theol. Sem. Am.; adj. prof. Am. Coll., Jerusalem; bd. dirs. Inst. Religion and Health; editorial bd. Jour. Religion and Health. Trustee Council World Affairs; bd. dirs. Cuyahoga unit Am. Cancer Soc.; mem. bd. Consumers League Ohio. Hon. fellow Hebrew U., Jerusalem, 1969. Author: All God's Children; Selected Readings in Zionism; Outline of Jewish History; Readings in Medieval Jewish Literature; also articles, monographs. Home: 3273 Euclid Heights Blvd Cleveland Heights OH 44118 Office: 3300 Mayfield St Cleveland Heights OH 44118

COHEN, AVERY SAMUEL, lawyer; b. Youngstown, Ohio, Nov. 29, 1936; s. Maxwell Warren and Ann (Mirkin) C.; A.B., Adelbert Coll., 1958; J.D., Harvard, 1961; m. Susannah Ruth Rosenthal, June 11, 1958; children—Adam, Ethan, Dorit. Admitted to Ohio bar, 1961; asso. atty. Lane, Krotinger, Santora, Cleve., 1961-62; law clerk Hon. Frank J. Battisti, 1962; asso. Guren, Merritt, Sogg & Cohen, Cleve., 1963-67, partner, 1967—; sec., gen. counsel, dir. Computer Resources, Inc., Cleve., 1969—; pres. Clevak Corp., Cleve., 1969-72. Lectr., Cleve. State U. Coll. Law, 1965—, Practicing Law Inst., 1970—. Mem. Ohio Securities Law Adv. Bd., 1970-74. Mem. vis. com. Adelbert Coll., 1964-72, chmn. 1971-72; mem. vis. com. Western Res. Coll., 1972—; bd. overseers Case Western Res. U., 1971-77; trustee Hebrew Free Loan, 1968-74; trustee, pres. Hattie Larlham Found. Mem. Cleve. Bar Assn. (chmn. securities law com. 1971-72, chmn. securities law inst. 1971-72, chmn. corp., banking and bus. law com. 1974-75), Zionist Orgn. Am. (chpt. v.p. 1971—). Jewish (temple trustee 1970-77). Home: 4096 Carroll Blvd University Heights OH 44118 Office: 650 Terminal Tower Cleveland OH 44113

COHEN, IRVING, med. adminstr., educator; b. Toronto, Ont., Can., Oct. 30, 1924; s. Joseph and Esther (Rosen) C.; came to U.S., 1947, naturalized, 1957; M.D., U. Toronto, 1947; m. Orpha Jane Servies, Oct. 22, 1948; children—Michael Alan, Lawrence Milton, Sara Jane. Intern, St. Vincent Hosp., Plainfield, Ind., 1947-48, resident in pathology, 1948-49, resident in internal medicine, 1949-50, asst. dir. family practice residency program, 1977—; gen. practice medicine, Plainfield, Ind., 1950-57, 59—; asso. prof. family medicine Ind. U. Served as maj. M.C., U.S. Army, 1957-59. Diplomate Am. Bd. Family Practice. Fellow Am. Acad. Family Practice, Am. Diabetes Assn., AMA. Home and office: 645 E Main St Plainfield IN 46168

COHEN, LESLIE JAY, personnel exec.; b. Chgo., June 19, 1931; s. Jack and Sylvia Thelma (Sanders) C.; B.S. in Commerce, Roosevelt U., 1952. Asst. to pres. Jay Mills Co., Chgo., 1954-60; founder EDP Personnel, Inc., Chgo., 1960, pres., 1960-64; founder, pres. Secretaries Inc., Chgo., 1964—; mem. industry liaison com. Better Bus. Bur., 1970—. Served with U.S. Army, 1952-54. Decorated Bronze Star. Mem. Nat. (Pres.'s award 1973, treas. 1973-74, dir. 1972—), Ill. (Lincoln Meml. award 1976, treas. 1970, dir. 1971-72) employment assns., Temporaries Ind. Profl. Soc. (treas. 1977—), Nat., Chicagoland assns. temporary services. Jewish. Home: 20 E Cedar St Chicago IL 60611 Office: 130 E Randolph St Chicago IL 60601

COHEN, MAXIM M., port and harbor exec.; b. Maroopol, Russia, Jan. 1, 1900; s. Joseph and Elizabeth (Kushner) C.; came to U.S., 1903, naturalized, 1907; grad. high sch.; m. Florence R. Witashkis, Sept. 2, 1923; children—Donald, Lois (Mrs. Robert Adelman). Exec. mgr. East Chgo. Dock Terminal Co., 1928-41; part-owner Lake Port Shipping Co., Chgo., 1933-41, Lakes-Overseas Shipping Co., Chgo., 1936-41; gen. mgr. Chgo. Regional Port Dist., 1953—. Home: 55 E Elm St Chicago IL 60611 Office: 12800 Butler Dr Lake Calumet Harbor Chicago IL 60633

COHEN, MELVIN SAMUEL, mfg. co. exec.; b. Mpls., Jan. 16, 1918; s. Henry Benjamin and Mary (Witebsky) C.; B.S. in Law, U. Minn., 1939, J.D., 1941; m. Eileen Phillips, Aug. 16, 1947; children—Amy Rebecca, Mary-Jo Rose. Admitted to Minn. bar, 1941, U.S. Supreme Ct. bar, 1944; practiced in Mpls. until 1942; with legal div., rationing sect. OPA, Washington, 1942-43; pub. counsel CAB, 1943-44; with Nat. Presto Industries, Inc., Eau Claire, Wis., 1944—, treas., 1950-51, v.p., adminstr., treas., 1951-54, exec. v.p., 1954-60, pres., 1960-75, chmn. bd., 1975—; also dir.; chmn. bd., dir. Century Metalcraft Corp., Los Angeles, Guardian Service Security Systems, Los Angeles, Presto Mfg. Co., Jackson, Miss., Johnson Printing, Eau Claire, United Truck Leasing, Inc., Mpls., Lawrence Motors, Inc., Red Wing, Minn., Red Wing Transp. Co., Red Wing Truck Rental, Inc., World Aerospace Corp., Mpls., 1963—; pres., dir. Master Corp. Tex., Abilene, 1965, Jackson Sales & Storage Co. (Miss.), Presto Parts and Service Corp., Mineola, N.Y., Presto Parts and Service, Inc., Los Angeles, Presto Parts & Service Corp., Atlanta, Nat. Presto Industries Export Corp., Eau Claire, Presto Internat. Ltd., Hong Kong, Canton Mfg. Co. (Miss.); v.p., dir. Nat. Pipeline Co., Cleve. Nat. Automatic Pipeline Ops., Inc., Escanaba, Mich.; dir. 1st Wis. Nat. Bank, Eau Claire. Mem. industry advisory com. for aluminum industry and internat. combustion engine industry Nat. Prodn. Authority, Korean War. Club: Eau Claire Country. Editor Minn. Law Rev., 1939-41. Home: 1703 Drummond St Eau Claire WI 54701 Office: Presto Area Eau Claire WI 54701

COHEN, MILLARD STUART, diversified mfg. co. exec.; b. Chgo., Jan. 17, 1939; s. Lawrence Irmas and Myra Paula (Littmann) C.; B.S. in Elec. Engring., Purdue U., 1960; m. Judith E. Michel, Aug. 2, 1970; 1 dau., Amy Rose. Design engr. GTE Automatic Electric Labs., Northlake, Ill., 1960-66; chief elec. engr. Nixdorff Krein Industries, St. St. Louis, 1966-68, dir. data processing, 1968-72, treas., 1970—, exec. v.p. Nixdorff Chain, 1972-76, pres. Grape Expectations, 1976—, also dir. Dist. commr. Boy Scouts Am., 1968-72; judge Mo. State Fair. Recipient award of merit French Wine Commn., 1972. Mem. Nat., Mo. restaurant assns., Assn. Computing Machinery, IEEE, Mensa, Les Amis du Vin, Chaine des Rotisseurs, Commanderie de Bordeaux. Jewish (trustee temple). Club: Mo Athletic. Home: 561 Bonhomme Forest Olivette MO 63132 Office: PO Box 27479 St Louis MO 63141

COHEN, MURRAY, pub.; b. Bklyn., Aug. 30, 1929; s. Nathan and Ethel Rose (Nassofer) C.; B.A., Transylvania Coll., 1951; M.A., U. Mo., 1953; m. Jacquelyn Gertrude Schwartz, Oct. 23, 1955; children—Roberta Louise, Jennifer Eileen. Reporter-photographer Terrell (Tex.) Tribune, 1955, Tyler Morning Telegraph, 1955-57; editor, pub. Crossroads Chronicle, Vandalia, Ohio, 1957-62, 73-76; editor, pub. Delphos (Ohio) Daily Herald, 1962—, pres. Delphos Herald, Inc., owner Gahanna (Ohio) Rocky Fork Enterprise, Paulding (Ohio) Progress, Mercer County (Ohio) Chronicle, Highland (Ill.) News-Leader, Beardstown (Ill.) Illinoian-Star, Bolivar (Tenn.) Bull., 1962—, Trotwood (Ohio) Argus, Woodsfield (Ohio) Monroe County Beacon, Wautoma (Wis.) Argus; pres. Vandalia-Butler Pub. Co. Mem. Ohio Hwy. Safety Com., 1964-70. Served with AUS, 1953-55. Recipient Gov.'s Conservation Writer's award, Ohio, 1968. Mem. Am. Newspaper Pubs. Assn., Ohio Newspaper Assn., Inland Daily Press Assn., C. of C., Am. Legion, V.F.W. Jewish. Elk; mem. B'nai B'rith. Home: 403 W 5th St Delphos OH 45833 Office: 405 N Main St Delphos OH 45833

COHEN, MYRON AARON, musician; b. Denver, Mar. 28, 1918; s. Goodman and Rose (Cohen) C.; student De Paul U. Sch. Music, 1936-38, Am. Conservatory of Music, Chgo., 1939-42, Juilliard Sch. Music, 1947; B.A., U. Omaha, 1947; Mus.M., U. Neb., 1960; violin student with Richard Czerwonky, Scott Willits, Louis Persinger, others. Concertmaster following orchs.: Omaha Symphony Orch., 1947-77, Omaha Opera Co. Orch., 1959—, Lincoln (Nebr.) Symphony Orch., 1951-60; asst. condr. Omaha Youth Orch., 1958-66; part-time faculty U. Omaha, 1951-52, U. Neb. at Lincoln, 1958-59; soloist radio, TV; pvt. violin tchr., Omaha, 1946—. Served with AUS, 1943-45. Winner commencement contest for violinists Am. Conservatory Music, 1940. Mem. Omaha Musicians Assn. (past mem. exec. bd.), Neb. Music Tchrs. Assn. (past pres.), Am. String Tchrs. Assn., Pi Kappa Lambda. Democrat. Jewish religion. Author: The Beginning Violinist's Left Hand Technique, 1956; Finger Relationships through Patterns and Keys for Violin, 1964; also revs. and articles. Home: 3925 S 24th St Omaha NE 68107

COHEN, PAUL G(ERSON), import co. exec.; b. N.Y.C., July 23, 1938; s. Henry A. and Esther (Reiner) C.; B.A., Union Coll., Schenectady, 1960; m. Jeanne A. Hurwitz, June 17, 1962; children—David Mark, Deborah Esther. With Northwestern Bell Tel. Co., Omaha, 1966-74, revenue supr. long distance and WATS, 1971-74; asst. v.p., sec. S. Riekes & Sons, Inc., Omaha, 1974-75, gen. ops. mgr., 1975-76; v.p. ops., Riekes Crisa Corp., Omaha, 1976—. Treas., youth sports program Omaha Suburban Athletic Assn., 1976—; bd. dirs. Cystic Fibrosis Assn. Nebr., 1977—; bd. dirs. Jewish Fedn. Omaha, 1973-76, v.p., 1977—. Served with USAF, 1960-66; lt. col. Nebr. Air NG, 1967—. Mem. Air Force Assn., Nebr. NG Assn. (dir. 1973-76). Jewish. Clubs: B'nai B'rith (past pres.; regional pres. 1974-75, dist. bd. govs., 1976—). Home: 1855 S 130th St Omaha NE 68144 Office: 1818 Leavenworth St Omaha NE 68102

COHEN, PHILLIP, wholesale and retail trade exec.; b. Milw., Apr. 5, 1919; s. Jacob E. and Anna (Kurman) C.; B.A. in Bus. Adminstrn., U. Wis., 1942; m. Mildred Kaminsky, Aug. 5, 1945; children—Phyllis, Jay. Pres., Wis. Toy & Novelty Co., Milw., 1946—; v.p. Unicare Health Service, Milw., 1969—; chmn. bd. Union Prescription Centers, Inc., Milw., 1964—, mem. bd. of exec. com. Unicare, 1964—. Bd. dirs. Union Toy and Prescription Found., Milw., 1963—; trustee Union Toy Profit Sharing Trust, Milw., 1964—. Served to capt. USAAF, 1941-45. Democrat. Jewish (temple bd. 1967-69). Clubs: Masons, B'nai B'rith, Brynwood Country (Milw.); Bonaventure Country (Ft. Lauderdale, Fla.). Home: 11724 Shorecliff Ln Mequon WI 53092 Office: 105 W Michigan St Milwaukee WI 53203

COHEN, ROGER LEE, real estate exec.; b. St. Joseph, Mo., Oct. 4, 1935; s. Joseph A. and Esther L. (Wienstock) C.; B.S. in Bus. Adminstrn., U. Mo., 1957; m. Marjorie Critten, May 2, 1974; children—Robin, Cynthia, Bradley. Exec. trainee Sears, Roebuck & Co., Chgo., 1957; partner Karbank & Co., realtors, Kansas City, 1959-68; pres. Roger L. Cohen & Co., realtors, Kansas City, Mo., 1969—; dir. Robert Esrey & Co., realtors, Empire State Bank, Kansas City, Mo. Bd. dirs. Kansas City (Mo.) Real Estate Bd. Chmn. Jackson County (Mo.) Indsl. Commn., 1969; chmn. March of Dimes, Jackson County, 1965-66. Mem. bd. govs. Menorah Med. Center, Jewish Fedn., Kansas City, Mo.; bd. dirs. Performing Arts Found.; bd. assos. Trinity Luth. Hosp. Served with F.A., AUS, 1957-59. Mem. Soc. Indsl. Realtors (pres. Western Mo.-Kans. chpt. 1974-76, nat. dist. v.p. 1976—), Young Pres.'s Orgn. Jewish religion (v.p. bd. trustees temple). Clubs: Oakwood Country, Homestead Country, Kansas City. Home: 3700 W 64th Mission Hills KS 66208 Office: 15 W 10th St Kansas City MO 64105

COHILL, DONALD FRANK, surgeon; b. Darby, Pa., Dec. 1, 1934; s. Raymond Harris and Agnes Mae (Smith) C.; A.B. in Chemistry, Haverford (Pa.) Coll., 1956; M.D., U. Pa., 1960; m. Lorna Westcott, Feb. 15, 1957; children—Karen Lea, Linda Lea, Julie Lea, Andrew Scott. Intern, U. Pa.-Presbyn. Hosp., Phila., 1960-61; surg. resident Abington (Pa.) Meml. Hosp., 1966-70, asso. surgeon, 1969-70; practice medicine specializing in gen. surgery, Racine, Wis., 1970—; surgeon St. Mary's, St. Luke's hosps.; dir. med. edn. St. Mary's Hosp.; exec. com. Kurten Med. Group; adv. bd. Life Line, Racine. Served with M.C., USAF, 1962-64. Decorated Commendation medal. Fellow A.C.S., Milw. Acad. Surgery; mem. AMA, Wis., Racine County med. socs., Racine Acad. Medicine, Wis. Surg. Soc. Mem. Evang. Ch. Home: 1902 Crestwood Dr Caledonia WI 53108 Office: 2405 Northwestern Ave Racine WI 53404

COHN, LUCILE MAE KOHN, psychol. counselor, nurse; b. Kokomo, Ind., Apr. 17, 1924; d. Jacob and Anna (Kaplan) Kohn; grad. Jewish Hosp. Sch. Nursing, 1944; B.S. in Nursing, U. Wis., 1964, M.S. in Guidance and Counseling, 1966, postgrad., 1966-70; Ph.D., Marquette U., 1971; m. Norman Cohn, Apr. 20, 1947; children—Richard A., Robert I. Head psychiat. nurse Cin. Gen. Hosp., 1944-45; nurse, instr. Columbia Hosp., Milw., 1954-65; employee counselor Mt. Sinai Hosp., Milw., 1966—; staff psychologist Pychiat. Clinic Mt. Sinai Med. Center, 1972—, asst. adminstr., dir. patient care services, 1973—; chmn. dept. psychiat. tng. Milw. County Gen. Hosp. Sch. Nursing, 1974—; practice psychol. counseling, 1971—; lectr. in field; cons. dying patients and grieving families, nursing homes, hosps.; vol. co-therapist med. students Med. Coll. Wis.; guest lectr. Pres., Guardian chpt. Women's Am. Orgn. Rehab. Through Tng., 1951-52, regional v.p., 1953-55; sec., v.p., pres. P.T.A., 1952-58; mem. Jewish Home for Aged, 1972—; mem. ladies aux. Mt. Sinai Hosp., 1966—; weekly vol. Milw. Counseling Center, 1972—. Bd. dirs. Gerontol. Research and Services Corp., 1974—. Served as 1st lt. Nurse Corps, AUS, 1945-47. Mem. Am., Wis., Milw. Dist. (Service award 1977) nurses assns., Am. Personnel and Guidance Assn., Internat. Assn. Vocat. Guidance, Am. Coll. Personnel Assn., Hadassah, Milw. Urban League, Gerontol. Soc. (dir.), Pi Lambda Theta, Phi Kappa Phi. Jewish (religious sch. tchr. 1954-68, pres. temple sisterhood 1955-58). Contbr. articles to profl. jours. Home: 136 E Mall Rd Milwaukee WI 53217 Office: 8900 W Wisconsin Ave Milwaukee WI 53226

COHN, ROBERT ALLEN, editor, lawyer; b. St. Louis, Sept. 4, 1939; s. Harold and Lillian (DeWoskin) C.; A.B., Washington U., 1961, J.D., 1964, B.S. in Polit. Sci., 1965, B.S. in Philosophy, 1967; m. Barbara Florence Berg, Dec. 19, 1965; children—Scott Harold, Julie Francine. Dormitory adminstr. Washington U., St. Louis, 1961-64; admitted to Mo. bar, 1964; adminstrv. asst. to St. Louis County supr., 1964-69; editor-in-chief St. Louis Jewish Light, 1969—. Chmn., St. Louis County Human Relations Commn., 1970—; chmn. Regional Forum, Met. St. Louis, 1972—; personal health com. Alliance for Community Health, 1971. Mem. Am., Mo., St. Louis County bar assns., Bar Assn. St. Louis, Am. Jewish Press Assn. (pres. 1972—), Omicron Delta Kappa, Alpha Sigma Lambda, Phi Delta Phi, Pi Lambda Phi. Jewish religion (v.p., dir. temple). Author: The History and Growth of St. Louis County, 1969. Home: 629 S Central Ave Clayton MO 63105 Office: Railway Exchange Bldg 611 Olive St St Louis MO 63101

COHNBERG, ROSELLEN ELAINE (MRS. JOHN F. MEYERS II), physician; b. St. Louis, Aug. 1, 1922; d. Lee Jay and Sylvia (Broude) Cohnberg; A.B., Washington U., 1944, M.D., 1947; M.S. in Pub. Health, Mo. U., 1968; m. John F. Meyers II, July 11, 1963; children—John F. Meyers III; Cheryl Lynn Meyers. Intern internal medicine Sinai Hosp., Balt., 1947-48; jr. resident pediatrics St. Louis Children's Hosp., 1949-49, asst. resident pediatrician, 1949-50; pvt. practice specializing in pediatrics, Monett, Mo., 1950-63, Neosho, Mo., 1963-67; staff St. Vincent Hosp., Monett, sec. med. staff, 1953-55, pres., 1955-56; staff St. Johns Hosp., Joplin, Mo., 1963-67; pediatrics Washington U., 1948-50; med. field dir. Mo. Crippled Children's Service, 1967-68; med. cons. State of Ill., Region VI, East St. Louis, 1968-69; cons. pediatrics Mt. Vernon Tb Sanitorium, 1952-54; med. cons. poverty Ill. Dept. Pub. Health, Chgo., 1970-71, dir. inter-agy. tech. assistance team, 1971-72; med. dir. student health center U. Mo., St. Louis, 1968; chief of staff Cedar Vale (Kans.) Regional Hosp., 1972—; med. dir. Cedar Vale Clinic and Hosp., 1972—; pvt. pediatric and family practice, Cedar Vale, 1972—. Mem. Adv. Com. on Crippled Children State Mo., 1958-65; asst. mem. Adv. Com. Rheumatic and Congenital Heart Diseases, 1958-63. Mem. bd. Ozark Region Heart Assn., 1956-58, co-chmn. Barry County (Mo.) Heart Fund drive, 1954-56. Diplomate Nat. Bd. Med. Examiners, Am. Bd. Pediatrics, Am. Bd. Family Practice. Fellow Am. Acad. Pediatrics, Am. Acad. Family Practice, N.Y. Acad. Sci.; mem. League Women Voters (mem. bd. 1959-63), AMA, Phi Beta Kappa, Sigma Xi. Home: PO Box 398 Cedar Vale KS 67024

COLAKOVIC, BRANKO MITA, geographer, educator; b. Surduk, Yugoslavia, Feb. 10, 1940; s. Mitar Zivan and Bogdanka (Djuric) C.; came to U.S., 1967, naturalized, 1975; B.A., U. Belgrade, Yugoslavia, 1962, M.A., 1965; Ph.D., U. Minn., Mpls., 1970; m. Paula Marie Johnson, June 12, 1968; children—Kenneth Mita, Zora Ida. Regional planner Zavod za Urbanizam Vojvodine, Novi Sad, Yugoslavia, 1966-67; research asst. U. Minn., 1967-70; asst. prof. geography Mankato (Minn.) State U., 1970-73, asso. prof., 1973—. Mem. Assn. Am. Geographers, Upper Midwest Ethnic Studies Assn., Am. Geog. Soc. N.Y., Minn. Council for Geog. Edn., Blue Earth County Geog. Soc. (treas. 1971-73, sec. 1973—). Serbian Orthodox. Author: Atlas of Minnesota School Districts, 1972; Yugoslav Migrations to America, 1973; Minnesota Region 9-Lakeshore Development, 1973; Minnesota Region 9—Population Forecast 1990. Editor: Geog. Survey quar. jour., 1972-75. Contbr. articles, revs. to profl. jours. Home: 1023 N 6th St Mankato MN 56001

COLBER, RUSSELL HOWARD, pub. relations exec.; b. Milw., June 21, 1938; s. Ralph Howard and Margaret Marie (Hoppens) C.; B.A. (WLOL Broadcasting scholarship), U. Minn., 1965; M.S. (Nat. Acad. of TV Arts and Scis. fellowship), Syracuse U., 1966; m. Bonita Elizabeth Cheesebrough, Sept. 1, 1963; children—Newell Howard, Geoffrey Howard. Asst. to v.p. corp. communications Dayton Hudson Corp., Mpls., 1966-70; v.p., Advertisers Diversified Services, Mpls., 1970-73; chmn. communications div. The Mpls. Inst. of Arts, 1973-75; pres., Russ Colber & Assos., Mpls., 1975—; prin. Colber/Williams Agy., 1977—; convenor, Twin Cities Journalism Conf.; chmn. communications com. Nat. Model Cities Conf.; instr. journalism Normandale Community Coll. Bd. dirs. Minn. Dance Theatre; arts com. chmn. Twin Cities Ednl. TV Fund-Raising, 1972, 73. Accredited in Pub. relations. Mem. Pub. Relations Soc. of Am. (counselors and health sects.), Minn. Arts Forum, Walker Art Center, Lowry Hill Residents Assn., The Nat. Trust (Gt. Britain). Pantheist. Clubs: Minn. Press. Editorial bd. MPLS. Mag., 1974—; contbr. articles and stories to Minn. newspapers and mags. Home: 1805 Irving Ave South Minneapolis MN 55403 also North Shore Dr Waverly MN 55390 Office: 3959 28th Ave South Minneapolis MN 55406

COLBERT, EUGENE JOSEPH, govt. ofcl.; b. Washington, Dec. 23, 1927; s. Eugene and Addie Lee (Moyler) C.; student Cortez Peters Bus. Coll., 1948-50; m. Hazel Young, Aug. 18, 1948; children—Michael H., Darrel W., Montez (Mrs. Clarence Gillis), Khamula, Shawn, Qefiri. Site supr. Nat. Park Service Lincoln Meml., Washington, 1966-68, Restored Ford's Theater, Washington, 1968-70, coordinator Nat. Park Service supervisory tng., 1970-71, supt. George Washington Carver Nat. Monument, 1971, Wilson's Creek Nat. Battlefield, 1971—, Spl. Achievement award, 1971. Exec. sec. George Washington Carver Birthplace Dist. Assn. Served with AUS, World War II; PTO. Home: Box 184 Diamond MO 64840 Office: Box 38 Diamond MO 64840

COLBERT, MARVIN JAY, physician, educator; b. Spokane, Nov. 6, 1923; s. John B. and Elizabeth (Peters) C.; B.S., Yale U., 1946; M.D., Boston U., 1949; m. Eleanor Ruth Rott, June 2, 1951; children—Janet Lee, James Lee, Lawrence Jay. Intern, Presbyn. Hosp., Chgo., 1949-50, resident, 1950; resident VA Hosp., Boston, 1953-55, U. Ill. R. and E. Hosp., 1954-55; practice medicine specializing in internal medicine, Belmond, Iowa, 1955-56; coordinator clerkship program U. Ill. Coll. Medicine, 1956-59, dir. Health Service U. Ill. at Med. Center, Chgo., 1959—, instr., 1956-59, prof., 1969—; vis. prof. internal medicine Chiengmai Med. Sch. and Hosp., Chiengmai, Thailand, 1965-66. Served with U.S. Army, 1943-46; to capt., 1950-52. Recipient Golden Apple Teaching Award Students at U. Ill. Coll. Medicine; diplomate Am. Bd. Internal Medicine. Mem. A.C.P., Chgo. Soc. Internal Medicine, Am. Fedn. for Clin. Research, Am. Assn. for Automotive Medicine, Sigma Xi. Methodist. Home: 5600 Plymouth Ct Downers Grove IL 60515 Office: Health Service PO Box 6998 Chicago IL 60680

COLBY, JOY HAKANSON, art critic; b. Detroit; d. Alva Hilliard and Eleanor Louise (Radtke) Hakanson; B.F.A., Wayne State U.; m. Raymond L. Colby, Apr. 11, 1953; children—Sarah, Katherine, Lisa. Art critic Detroit News, 1947—; Detroit corr. Art News, 1973-76; partner Kasle Colby Art Cons., Birmingham, Mich., 1976—; mem. advisory panel Mich. Council Arts; art com. New Detroit, Inc.; mayor's appointee Detroit Council Arts, 1974. Recipient Art Alumni award Wayne State U., 1967. Author: Art and a City, 1956; contbr. articles to art jours. Home: 1145 Lenox St Bloomfield Hills WI 48013 Office: 251 Merrill St Birmingham MI 48011

COLBY, PETER JAMES, aquatic biologist; b. Grand Rapids, Mich., Mar. 26, 1933; s. J. Emerson and Jessie Elizabeth (Slater) C.; B.S., Mich. State U., 1955, M.S., 1958; Ph.D., U. Minn., 1966; m. Dorothy Ann Jacobson, Dec. 27, 1957; children—James Eric, Craig Alan, Scott Norman. Grad. asst., dept. fisheries and wildlife Mich. State U., East Lansing, 1955-56; food technologist, research dept. Gen. Foods Corp., Battle Creek, Mich., 1957-62; research asst., dept. entomology, fisheries and wildlife U. Minn., St. Paul, 1962-66; aquatic biologist, project leader U.S. Bur. Comml. Fisheries, Ann Arbor, Mich., 1966-70; aquatic biologist, project leader U.S. Bur. Sport Fisheries and Wildlife, also research asso., dept. environmental and indsl. health Sch. Pub. Health, U. Mich., Ann Arbor, 1970-71; unit leader Walleye unit, research scientist Ont. (Canada) Ministry Natural Resources, Thunder Bay, 1971—. Served as 2d lt. AUS, 1956-57. Mem. Am. Fisheries Soc., Am. Inst. Fishery Research Biologists., Internat. Assn. Great Lakes Research, Am. Soc. Zoology. Home: 134 Hinton Ave Thunder Bay ON P7A 7E2 Canada Office: Box 5000 Thunder Bay F ON P7C 5G6 Canada

COLBY, ROBERT LESTER, psychologist; b. N.Y.C., Jan. 21, 1941; s. Allan M. and Beatrice D. (Kalkut) C.; B.A., N.Y. U., 1963; M.S., L.I. U., 1965. Psychiat. technician St. Vincent's Hosp., N.Y.C., 1963-64; psychometrist Vocational Service Center, N.Y.C., 1964-65; counselor N.Y. State Dept. of Labour, div. of employment, N.Y.C., 1965; ednl. counselor, vocational counselor Vocat. Service Centre, N.Y.C., 1965-66; teaching fellow, research asst. U. Waterloo (Ont., Can.), 1966-67; lectr. Wellington Coll., U. Guelph (Ont.), 1967-69, clin. and research fellow Centre for Ednl. Disabilities, 1967-69; chief behavioral cons. Brant County Bd. of Edn., Brantford, Ont., 1969—; cons. Assn. Children with Learning Disabilities. Rep. Ont. Anti-Poverty Coalition, 1975—. Bd. dirs. Workers Task Force, 1974-75; chmn. Inter-Agy. Coordinating Com., 1975-77. Mem. Am., Can. psychol. assns., Assn. for Psychol. Study Social Issues, Adminstrv. Psychologists in Edn., Regional Assn. Profls. in Psychology (treas. 1975-76), Assn. Psychologists N.S., Can. Mental Health Assn. (chmn. sci. adv. com. 1973-75, dir. 1969—, pres. 1975-76). Home: 50 Blenheim Rd Cambridge ON N1S 1E8 Canada Office: 349 Erie Ave Brantford ON N3S 2H7 Canada

COLDSMITH, DONALD CHARLES, physician; b. Iola, Kans., Feb. 28, 1926; s. Charles Irwin and Sarah Ethel (Willett) C.; B.A., Baker U., 1949; M.D., U. Kans., 1958; children by previous marriage—Carol Jean, April Teresa (adopted), Glenna Lynn, Leslie Ann; m. Edna Emma Howell, Nov. 6, 1960; 1 dau., Connie Lee. Youth sec. YMCA, Topeka, 1949-53; intern Bethany Hosp., Kansas City, Kans., 1958-59; practice medicine, specializing in family practice, Emporia, Kans., 1959—; mem. staff Newman Meml., St. Mary's hosps., Emporia. Breeder, exhibitor registered Appaloosa horses. Served with AUS, 1944-46. Diplomate Am. Bd. Family Practice. Fellow Am. Acad. Family Physicians; mem. AMA, Kans. Flint Hills med. socs., Western Writers Am., Appaloosa Horse Club Am. Republican. Methodist. Kiwanian. Author: Horsin' Around. Contbr. articles to mags.; free lance writer, newspaper columnist. Home: Route 5 Emporia KS 66801 Office: 1024 W 12th St Emporia KS 66801

COLE, A(NNA) RUTH, former educator; b. Eaton, Ohio; d. George Washington and Esther (Akel) Cole; student U. Colo., summer 1937, B.S., Miami U., Oxford, Ohio, 1939; M.A., Ohio State U., 1953; postgrad. Vassar Coll., 1963. Tchr., Morris Sch., Hamilton, Ohio, 1921-23, 24-25, Edison Elementary Sch., Columbus, Ohio, 1925-26, Robert Louis Stevenson Sch., Columbus, 1926-71. Mem. Buckeye Fed. Savs. & Loan Assn. Mem. mission work area Trinity United Meth. Ch., 1973-76. Martha Holden Jennings Scholar, 1968-69. Mem. Republican Womens' Clubs. Mem. Grandview Heights Tchrs. Assn. (pres. 1954-56, profl. activities com. 1966-67), Franklin County Hist. Soc., Center Sci. and Industry, Assn. for Childhood Internat. (pres. 1958-60), N.E.A. (life), Ohio Edn. Assn., Central Ohio Tchrs. Assn., Wesleyan Service Guild (pres. 1943-45, 62-65, dist. sec. 1957-61, v.p., program chmn. 1968-69), Ohio Ret. Tchrs. Assn. (life), Am. Assn. Ret. Persons, Kappa Phi (life), Phi Delta Gamma (pres. 1955-57; life), Delta Kappa Gamma (membership chmn. 1962-64; mem. initiation com. 1966-68, 69—, chmn. initiation com. 1973—), European Spa (life). Methodist (mem. edn. commn. 1966-68, dist. sec. program resources United Meth. Women 1973-77, chmn. Christian Global Concerns 1974—, mem. adminstrv. bd. 1978—, coordinator prayer circles 1978—). Home: 1314 W 7th Ave Columbus OH 43212

COLE, BRUCE HERMAN, advt. exec.; b. Chgo., July 22, 1928; s. Leo L. and Kate (Mandelkern) C.; student U. So. Calif., 1948-50; A.B., Grinnell Coll., 1953; m. Jane Renwick Bagby, June 7, 1953; children—Rosemary, Dorothy, Robert Bagby, Frances. Advt. mgr. Gen. Electric Co., Schenectady, 1953-59; account exec., Reincke, Meyer & Finn, Inc., Chgo., 1959-60; v.p., gen. mgr. Marsteller, Inc., Chgo., 1960-74, exec. v.p., 1974—, also dir. Lectr., U. Wis. Mgmt. Center, Medill Sch. Journalism Northwestern U.; instr. advt. Northwestern U. Evening Div. Extension at Coll. DuPage. Served with USN, 1946-48. Mem. Am. Mgmt. Assn. (lectr.), Am. Assn. Advt. Agys. (chmn. Chgo. council), Grinnell Coll. Alumni Assn. Chgo. (chmn. bd.), Chgo. Advt. Club (dir.), Sigma Delta Chi. Clubs: University, Off the Street (dir.), Economic (Chgo.); LaGrange Country; Oak Brook (Ill.) Polo. Home: 3830 Woodland Ave Western Springs IL 60558 Office: 1 E Wacker Dr Chicago IL 60601

COLE, CLARENCE RUSSELL, coll. dean; b. Crestline, Ohio, Nov. 20, 1918; s. Arthur Leroy and Anita Emma (Stephan) C.; student pre-med. Otterbein Coll., Westerville, Ohio, 1937-39; D.V.M., Ohio State U., 1943, M.S., 1944, Ph.D., 1947; m. Mary Piper, Mar. 15, 1945; children—Carol Ann, Larry Lee, Pamela Sue. Instr. dept. vet. pathology Ohio State U. Coll. Vet. Med., asst. prof., 1947-49, chmn., 1947-67, asso. prof. 1949-54, prof., 1954-67, asst. dean, 1960-67, dean, 1967—, prof. comparative pathology Coll. Medicine, 1952—, Grad. Sch., 1954—; Regents prof. Ohio Bd. Regents, 1966—; chmn. Mershon Center Nat. Security, Ohio State U., 1965-67, mem. U. Council Research, 1960-67; adminstr. cons. Vet. Research, Archtl., Engring Planning, Animal Med. Center, N.Y.C.; cons. nat. adv. res. resources council NIH, 1968—, NIH Health Manpower Grants Br.; mem. nat. adv. com. Nat. Center for Primate Biology, 1967-70; mem. com. on comparative pathology NRC-Nat. Acad. Sci., 1971—; mem. fellowship com. NATO, 1958. Recipient Herzfeld lectr. award Auburn U., 1954; 1st award sci. exhibit Ohio State Med. Assn., 1956; 2d award AMA, 1966. Mem. Men and Women of Sci., Internat. Acad. Pathologists (exec. council), Internat. Toxoplasmosis Com. (vice-chmn. 1959—), AVMA (Gold award 1957, chmn. adv. bd. vet. med. spltys. 1960-64, 68-75), Am. Coll. Vet. Pathologists (citation 1967, pres. 1967), Assn. Am. Vet. Med. Colls. (sec., treas. 1969—), Ohio Vet. Med. Assn. (trustee), Sigma Xi, Phi Zeta, Omega Tau Sigma. Club: Torch Internat. Address: 1925 Coffey Rd Columbus OH 43210

COLE, DAVID JOHN, village ofcl.; b. Racine, Wis., Jan. 1, 1949; s. Harold Louis and Pearl Julia (Chobodie) C.; B.A., U. Wis., 1970; M.A. in Pub. Adminstrn., No. Ill. U., 1976; m. Marie Hartwig, Aug. 28, 1971. Research aide Southeastern Wis. Regional Planning Commn., Waukesha, 1969; adminstrv. intern Village of Maywood (Ill.), 1971-72, adminstrv. asst., 1972-73; administrv. asst. Village of Brown Deer (Wis.), 1973-76; village adminstr. Village of Sussex (Wis.), 1976, Village of Butler (Wis.), 1976—. Ams. Abroad chmn. Am. Field Service, Brown Deer, 1974—; mem. Brown Deer Sch. Dist. Safety Com., 1974-75, outdoor areas chmn., 1974-75; mem. adv. com. Brown Deer High Sch. Vocational Tng. Program, 1974-75; alternate mem. Milw. County Manpower area Planning Council, 1974-76. Mem. Internat. City Mgmt. Assn., Am. Soc. Pub. Adminstrn., Sigma Pi. Lutheran. Home: 8390 N Grandview Dr Brown Deer WI 53223 Office: 12621 W Hampton Ave Butler WI 53007

COLE, DICK TAYLOR, JR., counselor; b. Panama City, Fla., Dec. 19, 1950; s. Dick Taylor and Dorothy (Baxter) C.; B.S. in Edn., The Citadel, 1973; M.A. in Religion and Counseling cum laude, Covenant Theol. Sem., 1977; m. Deborah Lynn Jowers, Mar. 2, 1974. Tchr., First Bapt. High Sch., Charleston, S.C., 1974-75; asst. to counseling program Covenant Theol. Sem., St. Louis, 1977—; profl. counselor Christian Counseling Service, St. Louis, 1977—. Named Youth of Year, Charleston Exchange Club, 1972. Mem. Nat. Assn. Christians in Social Work, Am. Personnel and Guidance Assn., Christian Assn. Psychol. Studies, Evang. Tchrs. Tng. Assn. Presbyterian. Home: 1226 Meyer Ave University City MO 63130 Office: 12330 Conway Rd Saint Louis MO 63141

COLE, DONALD WHEELER, mgmt. psychologist; b. Cleve., Dec. 30, 1929; s. Lawrence Chester and Mabel Louise (Wheeler) C.; A.B., U. R.I., 1950; M.S., Boston U., 1952; D.S.W., Washington U., St. Louis, 1964; m. Norma Gale Skoog, July 11, 1953; 5 children. Dir. Yakima (Wash.) Guidance Center, 1955-56; asst. dir. Western State Hosp., Tacoma, 1956-57; dir. casework Family and Children's Service, Pittsfield, Mass., 1959-62; dir. West office Cleve. Family Service, 1962-63; mgmt. devel. TRW, Inc., Cleve., 1963-71; mgmt. psychologist, cons. Don Cole & Assos., Cleve., 1968—; dir. personnel and orgn. devel. Bobbie Brooks, Cleve., 1974-76; staff analyst Cleve. Little Hoover Commn., 1966-68; mem. sci. and tech. council Am. Industries Corp., Cleve., 1969-71; mem. faculty Cleve. State U., 1966-73; dir. Orgn. Devel. Inst. and Internat. Registry Orgn. Devel., Cleve., 1968—, Midwest Orgn. Devel. Network, 1968—. Licensed psychologist, Ohio. Fellow Am. Orthopsychiat. Assn.; mem. Am. Group Psychotherapy Assn., Am. Mgmt. Assn., Am. Psychol. Assn., Orgn. Devel. Network (trustee). Home: 11234 Walnut Ridge Rd Chesterland OH 44026 Office: 6151 Wilson Mills Rd Suite 102 Cleveland OH 44143

COLE, EDYTH LUTICIA, state govt. ofcl.; b. Chgo., Dec. 3, 1942; d. Alfred Jackson and Helen Louise (Dixon) Cole; B.S., Wilberforce U., 1967; M.Ed., U. Ill., 1969; 1 adopted son, Cary Calvin. Asst. dean of students LeMoyne-Owen Coll., Memphis, 1969-70; field rep. Ill. Fair Employment Commn., Chgo., 1970-72; affirmative action officer Sangamon State U., Springfield, Ill., 1972-75; personnel dir. Ill. Office of Edn., Springfield, 1975—. Rehab. fellow, 1967-69. Mem. Am. Personnel and Guidance Assn., Ill. Affirmative Action Officers Assn. (v.p.), Nat. Assn. Affirmative Action Officers (dir.), Delta Sigma Theta (2d v.p.). Methodist. Home: 856 Independence Ridge Springfield IL 62702 Office: 100 N 1st St Springfield IL 62777

COLE, EUGENE ROGER, clergyman, author; b. Cleve., Nov. 14, 1930; s. Bernard James and Mary Louise (Rogers) C.; B.A., St. Edwards Sem., 1954; student John Carroll U., 1957; M.Div., Sulpician Sem. N.W., 1958; A.B., Central Wash. State Coll., Ellensburg, 1960; M.A., Seattle U., 1970. Ordained priest Roman Catholic Ch., 1958; Newman moderator and cons. Central Wash. State Coll., Ellensburg, 1958-59; chaplain St. Elizabeth Hosp., Yakima, Wash., 1959-61; chmn. English dept. Yakima Central Cath. High Sch., 1959-66, Marquette High Sch., Yakima, 1966-68; poetry critic Nat. Writers Club, Denver, 1969-72; poet in service Poets & Writers Inc., N.Y.C., 1974—; freelance writer, editor, researcher, 1958—; researcher Harvard, 1970. Religious counselor. Recipient Lorraine Harr Haiku award, 1974; Ann. Mentor Poetry award, 1974; Pro Mundi Beneficio award, 1975. Mem. Authors Guild, Poetry Soc. Am., Western World Haiku Soc., Acad. Am. Poets, World-Wide Acad. Scholars, Internat. Poetry Soc., Internat. Platform Assn., Nat. Fedn. State Poetry Socs., Poetry Soc. (London), Am. Contract Bridge League, Kappa Delta Pi. Author: April Is the Cruelest Month, 1970. Editor: Grand Slam: 13 Great Short Stories about Bridge, 1975. Guest editor Experiment: An Internat. Rev., 1961. Author religious monograph, also contbr. articles, poetry and drama to numerous lit. jours. and anthologies. Home and office: PO Box 272 Whiting IN 46394

COLE, THOMAS ALAN, biologist, educator; b. Harrisburg, Ill., Jan. 9, 1936; s. Samuel John and Pearle Mae (Fritts) C.; B.A., Wabash Coll., 1958; Ph.D., Calif. Inst. Tech., 1963; m. Lynda Ryan, July 29, 1967 (div. Dec. 21, 1976); children—Michelle, Julie, Thomas Jonathan, Jennifer. Mem. faculty Wabash Coll., Crawfordsville, Ind., 1962—, asso. prof. biology, 1967-68, chmn. dept., 1968-76, Treves prof. biology, 1976—. Mem. exec. com. undergrad. edn. biol. sci., 1969-71. Mem. Commn. on Undergrad. Edn. in Biol. Scis., 1968-71; cons.-examiner North Central Assn. Accrediting Commn.; mem. edn. directorate panel NSF; reader in biology advanced placement program Ednl. Testing Service, 1975, 77. Recipient Outstanding Young Man of Am. award U.S. Jr. C. of C., 1970. Fellow A.A.A.S.; mem. Ind. Coll. Biology Tchrs. Assn. (pres. 1973), N.Y. Acad. Scis., Phi Beta Kappa, Delta Tau Delta (v.p. home assn., Beta Psi chpt.). Republican. Co-author: Biology, 3d edit., 1966, 4th edit., 1972; Essentials of Biology, 1969, 2d edit., 1974; Principles of Zoology, 1969, 2d edit., 1977; lab. manuals, 1966, 72, 74, study guide, 1975. Home: 1000 S Grant Ave Crawfordsville IN 47933

COLEMAN, CLARENCE WILLIAM, banker; b. Wichita, Kans., Mar. 24, 1909; s. William Coffin and Fanny Lucinda (Sheldon) C.; degree U. Kans., 1928-32; LL.D. (hon.), Ottawa U., 1973; m. Emry Regester Inghram, Oct. 2, 1935; children—Rochelle, Pamela, Kathryn Sheldon. Dir., The Coleman Co., Inc., Wichita, 1932—, v.p. mfg., 1944-51, asst. gen. mgr., 1951-54, vice chmn. bd., 1971—; pres. Union Nat. Bank of Wichita, 1957-72, vice chmn. bd., 1972—; chmn. bd. Cherry Creek Inn, Denver, 1961-69. Bd. dirs. Found. for Study of Cycles, Pitts., 1966—; bd. dirs. Inst. Logopedics, Wichita, 1940—, chmn. bd., 1947-48; bd. dirs. Wichita Symphony Soc., Inc., 1965—; trustee Wichita Symphony Soc. Found., 1966—; bd. dirs. United Fund Wichita and Sedgwick County, 1957-70; trustee Friends U., 1956-65; bd. dirs. Wichita Crime Commn., 1953—, pres., 1958-59. Mem. NAM, Wichita C. of C. dir. 1947-60, pres. 1956), Phi Kappa Psi. Club: Rotary. Home: 530 Broadmoor Ct Wichita KS 67206 Office: 1005 Union Center Wichita KS 67202

COLEMAN, DENNIS JOHN, real estate broker; b. Wichita, Kans., Dec. 6, 1939; s. George T. and Mary K. (Curtin) C.; A.A., St. Gregory's Coll., 1960; B.B.A., Wichita State U., 1963; grad. Realtors Inst., Kans. Assn. Realtors, 1974; m. Jeanne M. Farrell, June 26, 1965; children—Maura H., Daniel F. Sales rep. R.T. French Co., food mfrs., Rochester, N.Y., 1963-65; market research analyst Kansas City (Mo.) Star Co., 1965-66; sales rep. Eugene D. Brown, realtors, Overland Park, Kans., 1966-70; broker-realtor Deffenbaugh & Assos. (name changed to Coleman & Assos. 1974), Overland Park, 1970—; chmn. Johnson County Multiple Listing Service, 1976. Bd. dirs. Johnson County (Kans.) Bd. Realtors, 1974-76, v.p., 1974, pres., 1975—, dir. multiple listing service, 1974—, Realtor of Yr., 1976. Named An Outstanding Young Man of Am., 1972. Mem. Kans. Assn. Realtors (sec. bd. govs. grad. realtors inst. 1974—, zone v.p. 1977), Nat. Realtors Mktg. Inst., Nat. Assn. Realtors, Home Builders Assn. Kansas City (Mo.), Overland Park C. of C., Wichita State Univ. Alumni Assn. (dir. 1969-72). Home: 9541 Granada Ln Overland Park KS 66207 Office: 3500 W 75th St Suite 102 Shawnee Mission KS 66208

COLEMAN, DONALD PATRICK, constrn. co. exec.; b. Buffalo, N.Y., Sept. 10, 1939; s. L.C. and A.M. (Heiderman); student Cornell U., 1957-59; B.S. (Maytag Scholar in Commerce) U. Mo., 1964; m. Diane J. De Luca, Fab. 1, 1964. Vice pres., gen. mgr. Garney Co's, Inc. Kansas City, Mo., 1970-77; pres. Weatherby Lake Improvement Co. Kans. City, Mo., 1977—, treas., 1972-74, v.p., 1974-77, chmn. environ. protection com., 1973-75, dir., 1970—. Mem. Kans. City Heavy Contractors Assn., Kans. City Mech. Contractors Assn. Home: 7902 NW Scenic Dr Kansas City MO 64152 Office: 1331 NW Vivion Rd Kansas City MO 64118

COLEMAN, E. THOMAS, congressman; b. Kansas City, Mo., May 29, 1943; s. Earl T. and Marie (Carlson) C.; A.B. in Econ., William Jewell Coll., 1965; M.P.A., N.Y. U., 1969; J.D., Washington U., 1969; m. Marilyn Anderson, June 8, 1968; children—Julie Anne, Emily Catherine, Megan Marie. Admitted to Mo. bar, 1969; practiced in Gladstone, 1973—; asst. atty. gen. Mo., 1969-73; mem. Mo. Ho. of Reps., 1973-77; mem. 95th Congress for 6th Mo. Dist. Home: 2919 NE Russell Rd Kansas City MO 64117 Office: US House of Representatives Washington DC 20515

COLEMAN, HAROLD KENNETH, electro-optics engr.; b. Roscoe, Tex., Nov. 19, 1949; s. Harry Hoyt and Addie Lucile (Kinney) C.; A.S., Tex. State Tech. Inst., 1974; A.A.S., U. Tenn., 1975; m. Linda M. Erwin, July 30, 1972; children—Teresha, Marcy. Staff project engr. electro-optics devel. Caterpillar Tractor Co., Peoria, Ill., 1974—. Licensed radiotelephone engr. Mem. Soc. Photographic and Instrumentation Engrs., Laser Inst. Am. Home: 119 Cedar St Morton IL 61550 Office: 600 W Washington St East Peoria IL 61630

COLEMAN, JEAN MACMICKEN, lawyer; b. Rochester, N.Y., Dec. 2, 1907; d. Kenneth Bruce and Ada Louise (Chase) McMicken; B.A., U. Rochester, 1929; student Law Sch., Cornell U., 1929-32; m. John Edward Coleman, May 16, 1931; children—George Leidigh II, Chase (Mrs. Davies). Admitted to Ohio bar, 1932; practice law, Dayton, O., 1932—. Third v.p. YWCA, 1951-52, treas., 1952-56, 1st. v.p., 1959-62, pres., 1962-64; mem. steering com. United Health Found., 1965-67, bd. dirs., 1967—, v.p., 1967-68, chmn. budget panel, 1967-73, 1st v.p., 1972-74, pres. 1974-76; bd. dirs. Community Welfare Council, 1951-67, 68-73, chmn. group work div., 1959-61; trustee Dayton and Montgomery County Library, 1962—, pres. bd., 1968-71, 73-76, v.p., 1971-73, 76—; mem. budget com. Community Chest, 1954-61, bd. dirs., 1960-69. Recipient Trustee of Year award Ohio Library Assn., 1971, named to Hall of Fame, 1976; recipient Service to Mankind award Sertoma Club, 1976. Mem. Am., Ohio State, Dayton bar assns., Am. (program vice chmn. 1969-70, program vice chmn. 1970-71, sec. 1971-72, regional rep. 1971-73, pres. 1974-75, legis. com. 1975—), Ohio (exec. com. 1966-72, pres. 1968-70, legis. com. 1973—) library trustee assns., Nat. Assn. Women Lawyers, Kappa Beta Pi. Club: Dayton Womans. Home: 191 Folsom Dr Dayton OH 45405 Office: Third National Bldg Dayton OH 45402

COLEMAN, JOHN EDWARD, lawyer; b. Dayton, Ohio, May 28, 1907; s. George Leidigh and Verrell (Chaffin) C.; B.A. with honors, Cornell U., 1929; J.D., 1932; m. Jean MacMicken, May 16, 1931; children—George L. II, Chase C. (Mrs. Chase C. Davies). Admitted to Ohio bar, 1932, since practiced in Dayton; pres. Central Finance Co., Dayton, 1932-40, Central Mortgage Co., Dayton, 1935-40, Coleman Mortgage Co., Dayton, 1932-68. Served with AUS, 1940-46. Decorated Legion of Merit. Mem. Res. Officers Assn. (nat. pres. 1951-52), Nature Conservancy (Ohio chpt. pres. 1960), Dayton Soc. Natural History (treas. 1964—), Am., Ohio, Dayton bar assns., Phi Beta Kappa, Delta Chi, Phi Delta Phi. Mason (Shriner). Clubs: Army and Navy (Washington); Dayton Racquet (Dayton). Home: 191 Folsom Dr Dayton OH 45405 Office: 634 3d Nat Bldg Dayton OH 45402

COLEMAN, LESTER EARL, JR., chem. co. exec.; b. Akron, Ohio, Nov. 6, 1930; s. Lester Earl and Ethel Angeline (Miller) C.; B.S., U. Akron, 1952; M.S., U. Ill., 1953, Ph.D., 1955; m. Jean Goudie Moir, Aug. 31, 1951; children—Robert Scott, Kenneth John. With Goodyear Tire & Rubber, Akron, 1951-52; with Lubrizol Corp., Cleve., 1955—, asst. dir. head research and devel., 1968-72, v.p. internat. ops., asst. to pres., 1972-74, exec. v.p., 1974-76, pres., 1976—, also dir.; dir. Ferro Corp., Cleve. Pres., exec. bd. N.E. Ohio council Boy Scouts Am.; mem. Euclid Gen. Hosp. Assn. Served to capt. USAF, 1955-57. Mem. Am. Chem. Soc. (local chmn. 1973), Sigma Xi, Alpha Chi Sigma, Phi Lambda Upsilon, Phi Delta Theta. Methodist. Contbr. articles to profl. jours. Patentee organic and polymer chemistry. Home: 35850 Eddy Rd Willoughby Hills OH 44094 Office: PO Box 3057 Cleveland OH 44117

COLEMAN, MARY STALLINGS, justice; b. Tex.; d. Leslie C. and Agnes B. (Huther) Stallings; B.A., U. Md., 1935; J.D., George Washington U., 1939; H.H.D., Nazareth Coll., 1973; LL.D., Olivet Coll., 1973, Alma Coll., 1973, Eastern Mich. U., 1974, Western Mich. U., 1974, Detroit Coll. Law, 1975, Adrian Coll., 1976; m. Creighton R. Coleman, June 24, 1939; children—Leslie (Mrs. Donald Jackson Hagan), Carol. Admitted to D.C. bar, 1940, Mich. bar, 1950; practice law, Washington, 1940-46; partner Wunsch & Coleman, attys., Battle Creek, Mich., 1950-61; probate and juvenile ct. judge, Calhoun County, Mich., 1961-73; justice Mich. Supreme Ct., 1973—. Mem. Mich. Gov.'s Commn. on Crime, 1964-68, Gov.'s Commn. on Delinquency, 1968-70, Gov.'s Commn. on Youth, 1964-70, Gov.'s Commn. on Law Enforcement and Criminal Justice, 1968-72; mem. Pres.'s Commn. Internat. Women's Year, 1975. Trustee Albion Coll. Recipient awards Calhoun County Assn. Sch. Bds., 1964, Frat. Order Police, 1967, Enquirer and News, 1969, Young Adult Council, NAACP, 1969; Distinguished mem. Phi Kappa Phi, 1973; Profl. Achievement award George Washington U. Alumni Council, 1973; Outstanding Woman Mich. Bus. and Profl. Women, 1973; Distinguished Alumnus award U. Md., 1973; Religious Heritage Am. award, 1974; Woman of Year award Mich. Assn. Professions, 1976; Woman of Year award Soroptomists, 1976; Distinguished Citizen award Mich. State U., 1977; Resolution Mich. Legislature, 1977. Fellow Am. Bar Found.; mem. Am., Mich., Calhoun County bar assns., Am. Judicature Soc., Nat. Assn. Juvenile Ct. Judges, Nat., Mich. assns. women lawyers, AAUW, Mich. Probate and Juvenile Ct. Judges Assn. (award 1973, pres. 1971-72), Altrusa Internat., Bus. and Profl. Women, Jr. League, P.E.O., Am. Legion Aux., Order of Coif (hon.), Beta Sigma Phi, Alpha Delta Kappa, Alpha Omicron Pi (Outstanding Alumni award 1975). Episcopalian. Club: Battle Creek Country. Home: 355 E Hamilton Ln Battle Creek MI 49015 Office: Law Bldg Box 30052 Lansing MI 48909

COLEMAN, RAYMOND JAMES, educator; b. Bethel, Kans., Jan. 8, 1923; s. Leonard George and Jo Hannah (Poulsen) C.; B.S., U. Kans., 1948; M.A., Central Mo. State U., 1963; Ph.D., U. Ark., 1967; m. Katherine Elizabeth Dietrich, Apr. 8, 1945; children—Katherine Anne Coleman Morehead, Jayne Elaine, Christopher Lynn. With Gen. Mills, Inc., Kansas City, Mo., 1949-56; owner Osceola Flour & Feed (Mo.), 1950-54, Sure Mix Feed, Clinton, Mo., 1954-56; supr. Investors Diversified Services, Mpls., 1957-63; prof. Kans. State U., Manhattan, 1965—. Cons. Research Found. Kans., McCalls, Inc.; asso. Devel. Planning & Research Assos., Manhattan, 1971—. Republican precinct committeeman, Manhattan, 1969-72. Chmn., Westminster Found., Synod of Kans., Topeka, 1968-70. Served to lt. (j.g.) USNR, 1943-46; PTO. Mem. Am. Marketing Assn., Kansas City Soc. Financial Analysts, Kansas City Sales and Marketing Execs., Ozarks Econ. Assn., S.W. Marketing Assn., Beta Gamma Sigma, Delta Mu Delta. Contbr. articles to profl. jours. Home: 1924 Blue Hills Rd Manhattan KS 66502

COLEMAN, RICHARD WALTER, educator; b. San Francisco, Sept 10, 1922; s. John Crisp and Reta (Walter) C.; B.A., U. Calif., Berkeley, 1945, Ph.D., 1951; m. Mildred Bradley, Aug. 10, 1949, (div. Oct. 1951); 1 dau., Persis C. Research asst. div. entomology and parasitology U. Calif., Berkeley, 1946-47, 49-50; ind. research, 1951-61; prof. biology, chmn. dept. Curry Coll., Milton, Mass., 1961-63; chmn. div. scis. and math. Monticello Coll., Godfrey, Ill., 1963-64; vis. prof. biology Wilberforce U., Ohio; 1964-65; prof. sci. Upper Iowa U., Fayette, 1965—, head dept. biology, 1972. Collaborator natural history div. Nat. Park Service, 1952; spl. cons. Arctic Health Research Center, USPHS, Alaska, 1954-62; apptd. explorer Commr. N.W. Ty., Yellowknife N.W. Ty., Can., 1966. Mem. Iowa Acad. Sci., A.A.A.S., A.A.U.P., Am. Inst. Biol. Scis., Nat. Sci. Tchrs. Assn., Ecol. Soc. Am., Am. Soc. Limnology and Oceanography, Am. Bryological and Lichenological Soc., Arctic Inst. N.Am., N.Am. Benthological Soc., Am. Malacological Union, Assn. Midwestern Coll. Biology Tchrs., Société de Biologie de Montréal, Nat. Assn. Biology Tchrs., Sigma Xi. Methodist. Contbr. articles to profl. reports. Home: PO Box 156 Fayette IA 52142

COLEMAN, ROBERT EDWARD, orthodontist; b. Detroit, Jan. 16, 1915; s. Edward M. and Kathryn J. (Bolton) C.; B.S., U. Detroit, 1936, D.D.S., 1937; M.S., U. Mich., 1939; m. Marion Purdy, Nov. 20, 1940; children—Carolyn, Edward Michael, Mary, Janet. Practice orthodontics, Detroit, 1937—; head dept. orthodontics Dental Sch., U. Detroit, 1951-63. Served as capt. Dental Corps, AUS, 1943-46. Diplomate Am. Bd. Orthodontics. Fellow Am. Coll. Dentistry (pres. Mich. chpt. 1974); mem. Am. Dental Assn., Mich., Detroit Dist. dental socs., Am. Assn. Orthodontists, Great Lakes Soc. Orthodontists (pres. 1964), Edward H. Angle Soc. Orthodontists (pres. Midwest chpt. 1962), A.A.A.S., Charles H. Tweed Found. Orthodontic Research, U. Detroit Alumni Assn. (past dir.), U. Detroit Dental Alumni Assn. (past pres., sec. 1939-49), U. Mich. Orthodontic Alumni Soc. (pres. 1965-66), Omicron Kappa Upsilon (past pres.), Delta Sigma Delta (past grand master). Lion (past dir.). Clubs: Detroit Dental Clinic, Downtown Dental (past pres.), Detroit Athletic, Country of Detroit. Contbr. articles to profl. jours. Home: 69 Webber Pl Grosse Pointe Shores MI 48236 Office: 20166 Mack Ave Grosse Pointe MI 48236

COLEMAN, THEODORE LESLIE, SR., journalist, pub. relations ofcl.; b. N.Y.C., Oct. 19, 1906; s. Thomas Henry and Sarah (Shelton) C.; ed. high sch.; m. Frances Virginia Moore, Dec. 13, 1944; children—Theodore L., Iris B. (Mrs. Arthur Brown). Reporter, columnist Pitts. Courier, 1936-44, reporter, editor, mgr. Chgo. bur., 1944-54; editor N.Y. Age, N.Y.C., 1954-57; reportor-editor Ohio Sentinel, Columbus, 1957-62; polit. reporter Chgo. Defender, 1962-64; reporter writer WBBM-TV, Chgo., 1964-66; asst. to dir. pub. relations mayor's office City of Chgo., 1966—. Mem. com. pub. relations local YMCA. Coordinator spl. activities Chgo. Citizens for Eisenhower, 1952. Mem. N.A.A.C.P., Urban League, Chgo. Headline Club, Chgo. Press Club, Sigma Delta Chi. Democrat. Office: Room 412 121 N La Salle St Chicago IL 60602

COLEMAN, THOMAS JAMES, physician; b. Wichita, Kans., June 3, 1918; s. Thomas James and Marguerite (Crummey) C.; student Kans. State U., 1940-41, U. Va, 1946-47; M.D., U. Rochester, 1951; m. Amy Desmond Jones, Aug. 27, 1949; children—Thomas James, Pamela Jane, Patricia Lynn, Richard Cahill, Martha Sue, Robert Bruce. Intern, U. Kans. Med. Center, 1951-52, resident, 1952-55; practice medicine specializing in internal medicine; mem. staffs St. Francis Hosp., Wesley Med. Center, St. Joseph Hosp. and Rehab. Center; clin. asst. prof. medicine Wichita State U. br. U. Kans. Sch. Medicine, 1977—; NIH fellow in endocrinology U. Kans., 1954-55. Served to capt. USAAF, 1942-46. Decorated D.F.C., Air medal with oak leaf cluster. Diplomate Am. Bd. Internal Medicine, Nat. Bd. Med. Examiners. Mem. A.C.P., Am. Coll. Cardiology, AMA, Flying Physicians Assn., Am. Heart Assn. (dir. Kans, affiliate), Kans. Heart Assn. (pres. 1974-75), Am. Soc. Internal Medicine. Republican. Club: Wichita State U. Shocker. Home: 155 N Crestway Wichita KS 67208 Office: 959 N Emporia St Wichita KS 67214

COLEMAN, WILLIAM LUTHER, lawyer; b. Paris Twp., Ohio, Feb. 7, 1914; s. John Henry and Marie (Zacharias) C.; student Ohio No. U., 1934-35; J.D., Ohio State U., 1939; m. Rose Anna Green, Nov. 23, 1940; children—William Henry, Thomas Hewitt, Charlotte Coleman Eufinger, Stephen Green, Rose Ann, Michael Stuart. Admitted to Ohio Bar, 1939, U.S. Supreme Ct. bar, 1961, since practiced in Marysville; pros. atty. Union County, 1941-49. Active Boy Scouts of Am.; mem. nat. council Ohio State U. Coll. Law; bd. dirs. Blue Cross Hospitalization Bd., Columbus, Ohio; chmn. Ohio Democratic Exec. Com., 1966—; chmn. Nat. Young Dems. Conv., 1946, Bi-ann. Conv. League Young Dems. Ohio, 1940-44, 46, 50, 52; mem. state exec. com. League Young Dems. Clubs, 1939-54; mem. Dem. Nat. Com., 1960-64; Dem. candidate for lt. gov. Ohio, 1966. Mem. Am., Ohio, Union County bar assns., Am. Trial Lawyers Assn., Ohio Game Assn., Union County Tb Health Assn., Newcomen Soc. N. Am. Lutheran. Home: 19349 Coleman Broke Rd Milford Center OH 43045 Office: 110 S Court St Marysville OH 43040

COLEMAN, WILLIAM SIDNEY, mfg. co. exec.; b. Grand Rapids, Mich., Aug. 26, 1924; s. William S. and Cathleen Ruth (Gilleland) C.; B.S. in Mech. Engring., Mich. State U., 1945; M.S., Mass. Inst. Tech., 1946; m. Janet R. McRae, June 4, 1949; children—David, Richard, Judith. With Gen. Motors Research Labs., Warren, Mich., 1946-61, supr. strength of materials, 1954-57, sr. engr., 1957-61; with Mpls. Moline div. White Motor Corp., Hopkins, Minn., 1961-71, v.p. engring., 1969-70, pres., 1971; dir. product group adminstrn. Am. Motors Corp., Detroit, 1972-75; gen. mgr. Eaton Engring. and Research Center, Southfield, Mich., 1976—. Mem. Soc. Automotive Engrs. (nat. dir. 1970-73), Engring. Soc. Detroit (Engr. of Year award 1954), Tau Beta Pi. Republican. Presbyn. (deacon 1968-70). Contbr. articles to profl. jours. Home: 6771 Cottonwood Knoll West Bloomfield MI 48033 Office: 26201 Northwestern Hwy Southfield MI 48076

COLES, JAMES MICHAEL, photographer; b. Centralia, Ill., May 30, 1945; s. Herbert Eugene and Betty Vee (Ledbetter) C.; certificate in Spanish, So. Ill. U., 1970; m. Maria de las Angeles Zavala Sanchez, Apr. 3, 1971; children—Maria Elizabeth, Michael Francisco. Teller, Anna Nat. Bank (Ill.), 1969-72; salesman Met. Life Ins. Co., Carbondale, Ill., 1972-74; owner, photographer J.M.C. Photo Service, Anna, 1974—. Served with USN, 1965-68. Mem. Profl. Photographers of Am., Ill. Press Assn. Baptist (audio visual dir. 1970). Address: 512 S Main St Anna IL 62906

COLES, RICHARD WARREN, biologist, univ. adminstr.; b. Phila., Sept. 16, 1939; s. Henry Braid and Katharine Baker (Warren) C.; B.A. with highest honors (open scholar), Swarthmore Coll., 1961; M.A., Harvard, 1967, Ph.D. (NSF, NIH fellow), 1967; m. Mary Minier Sargent, June 16, 1962; children—Christopher Sargent, Deborah Walton. Teaching fellow Harvard, 1961-65; asst. prof. biology Claremont (Calif.) Colls., 1965-70; dir. Tyson Research Center, Washington U., Eureka, Mo., 1970—, also faculty asso. biology; cons. ednl. film loops Ealing Corp., Cambridge, Mass., 1963, Nat. Geog. mag., 1973-74, Nat. Geog. Book Service, 1975-76. Vice pres. House Springs Elementary Sch. Parent-Tchrs. Orgn., 1975-76. NSF grantee; NIH grantee. Mem. Am. Soc. Mammalogists (life), Am. Soc. Zoologists, Ecol. Soc. Am., Rocky Mountain Biol. Labs., Webster Grove Nature Study Soc., Mo. Prairie Found., Wilderness Soc., AAAS (life), Am. Ornithologists Union (life), Orgn. Biol. Field Stas. (sec.-treas.), Am. Inst. Biol. Scis., Phi Beta Kappa, Sigma Xi. Home: Route 1 Box 726C Eureka MO 63025 Office: PO Box 258 Eureka MO 63025

COLES, ROBERT WILLIAM, JR., govt. ofcl.; b. Richmond, Va., Aug. 15, 1929; s. Robert William and Marie Theresa (Washington) C., Sr.; B.S., Va. Union U., 1952; 1 son, Gregory Eric. Accountant, M.A. Motley Plumbing & Heating, Inc., Richmond, 1952-55; with IRS, U.S. Treasury Dept., Cleve., 1955—, internal revenue agt., conferee, 1964—. C.P.A., Ohio. Mem. Am. Inst. C.P.A.'s, Ohio Soc. C.P.A.'s, Phi Beta Sigma (chpt. pres. 1962-63). Congregationalist (ch. accountant 1966—). Home: 4400 Clarkwood Pkwy Apt 325 Warrensville Heights OH 44128 Office: 1240 E 9th St Cleveland OH 44199

COLETTA, RALPH JOHN, lawyer; b. Chillicothe, Ill., Dec. 13, 1921; s. Joseph and Assunta (Aromatario) C.; B.S., Bradley U., 1943; J.D., U. Chgo., 1949; m. Ethel Mary Meyers, Nov. 19, 1949; children—Jean Christine, Marianne, Suzanne, Joseph, Robert, Michele, Renee. Admitted to Ill. bar, 1949; since practiced in Peoria. Chmn. bd. Founders Preferred Mgmt. Corp., Modern Income Life Ins. Co.; incorporator, promoter Gt. Heritage Life Ins. Co.; pres. White Star Corp. Div. chmn. United Fund; active ch. fund-raising. Republican precinct committeeman, 1953-59; asst. state's atty., 1953-56. Served from pvt. to 1st lt. AUS, 1943-46; PTO. Mem. Am., Ill., Peoria, Chgo. bar assns, Am. Legion (judge adv.), Am. Trial Lawyers Assn. K.C. Clubs: Mount Hawley Country, Creve Coeur. Home: 301 W Crestwood Dr Peoria IL 61614 Office: Savings Center Tower Peoria IL 61602

COLGROVE, ALBERT F., III, retail mktg. exec.; b. Frankfort, Ind., Feb. 2, 1938; s. Albert F. and Ferol Venus (Wright) C.; student Ball State U., 1955-56; B.A., Franklin Coll. Ind., 1960; m. Karen Lorraine Hibner, Jan. 30, 1960; children—Kathlene Jo, Amy Elizabeth, Alissa Lynn. Advt. prodn. mgr. H.P. Wasson's Dept. Store, Indpls., 1961; copywriter L.S. Ayres & Co., Ayr-Way Stores, Inc., Indpls., 1961-63, asst. advt. dir., 1963-67; asst. advt. dir. Ayr-Way Stores, Inc., 1967-71, advt. dir., 1971-74, dir. mktg., 1974—. Active United Fund Greater Indpls. Bd. dirs. Indpls. Christmas Com. Mem. Advt. Club Indpls., Am. Mgmt. Assn., Sales Mktg. Execs., Ind. Retail Council, Indpls. C. of C., Hon. Order Ky. Cols., Alpha Phi Gamma. Elk (Elk of year 1968). Home: Rural Route 2 Box 193 Zionsville IN 46077 Office: 8250 Zionsville Rd Indianapolis IN 46268

COLLEN, SHELDON ORRIN, lawyer; b. Chgo., Feb. 7, 1922; s. Jacob Allen and Ann (Andalman) C.; B.A. cum laude, Carleton Coll., 1944; J.D., U. Chgo., 1948; m. Ann Blager, Apr. 8, 1946; 1 son, John O. Admitted to Ill. bar, 1949; practiced in Chgo., 1949—; asso. Adcock, Fink & Day, 1948-51; mem. firm Simon & Collen, 1952-57, Friedman & Koven, 1958—. Specialist, Fed. Antitrust Litigation. Sec., Jupiter Industries, Inc., Chgo., 1961—. Mem. bd. edn. U. Chgo. Law Rev., 1948-49. Bd. dirs. Lower Northcenter, Chgo. Youth Centers. Served with AUS, 1943-46. Mem. Am., Chgo. (antitrust law and securities law coms., chmn. 1976-77), Ill. (counsel corp. and securities law sect.) bar assns., Bar Assn. 7th Circuit, Am. Judicature Soc., Art Inst. Chgo., Mus. Contemporary Art, Chgo. Council Fgn. Relations. Clubs: Union League (Chgo); Lafayette (Minnetonka Beach, Minn.). Home: 3750 Lake Shore Dr Chicago IL 60613 also Meadville Rd Excelsior MN Office: 208 S LaSalle St Chicago IL 60604

COLLEY, RAYMOND DEAN, indsl. engring. exec.; b. Mt. Vernon, Mo., Dec. 21, 1942; s. Quentin Roosevelt and Jaunita Winnie (Schwebel) C.; B.S., S.W. Mo. U., 1964; m. Betty Ann Wheeler, Aug. 1, 1964; 1 dau., Tisha Lynn. Instr., U.S. Bur. Prisons, 1961-64; designer, engring. planner McDonnell Douglas Aircraft, 1964-66; sr. program planner, prodn. engr., maintainability engr. Emerson Electric, St. Louis, 1966-69; sr. producibility engr. Sangamo Electric, Springfield, Ill., 1969-73; supr. methods and standards-indsl. engring. Fiat Allis, Springfield, 1973—; mem. adv. staff Area Vocational Tech. Sch., Machine Shop and Labs., 1974—. Mem. Springfield Underwater Search and Rescue Team, 1970-76, sec., 1974-75. Served with USAF, 1967. Mem. Am. Machinists Adv. Panel, Am. Inst. Indsl. Engrs., Soc. Mfg. Engrs., Am. Inst. Design and Drafting (pres. coll. chpt. 1964). Episcopalian. Home: 143 Lost Tree St Springfield IL 62704 Office: 3000 S 6th St Springfield IL 62703

COLLIER, DAVID C., automotive co. exec.; b. Hardisty, Alta., Can., Oct. 28, 1929; s. William G. and Helene E. C.; certificate tchg. U. Alta., 1948; B.S., U. Mont., 1956; M.B.A., Harvard U., 1958; m. Eleanor G. Beacom, Sept. 1, 1953; children—Carol E., William G., Kimberly E., Catherine M. With Gen. Motors Corp., 1958—, with comptroller's staff, Detroit, 1958-65, asst. comptroller Gen. Motors of Can., Oshawa, 1965-68, dir. product programs, Detroit, 1968-69, asst. comptroller, 1969-70, gen. asst. treas., N.Y., 1970-71, treas., N.Y., 1971-73, pres. Gen. Motors of Can., Ltd., Oshawa, 1973-75; v.p., gen. mgr. Buick Motor div., Flint, Mich., 1975—. Mem. Fin. Execs. Inst. Office: 902 E Hamilton Ave Flint MI 48550

COLLIER, DAVID SWANSON, orgn. exec.; b. Balt., Sept. 28, 1923; s. John Pouder and Anna (Swanson) C.; B.S., Northwestern U., 1947, M.A., 1949, Ph.D., 1952. Mil. intelligence officer, U.S. Army, 1943-44; govt. specialist Dept. Army, 1945-46, 50-51; fgn. trade cons., 1947-48; instr. Northwestern U., 1948-50; Smith-Mundt vis. prof. internat. relations Am. U. Beirut (Lebanon), 1952-53; Fulbright research prof. Tokyo U., 1953-54; exec. dir. Midwest region Am. Friends of Middle East, 1954-57; exec. dir. Found. Fgn. Affairs, Chgo., Inc., 1957—, editor fgn. policy series, 1967—, pres., 1972—; exec. dir. Inst. for Philos. and Hist. Studies; alternate del. Gen. Assembly, U.S. Mission to UN, 1977. Trustee Intercollegiate Studies Insr., Bryn Mawr, Pa., 1976—. Recipient Order Golden Emblem, Parliament South Africa, 1974. Mem. Am. Polit. Sci. Assn., Am. Soc. Pub. Adminstrn., Am. Assn. Higher Edn., Am. Econ. Assn., Slavic, Asian studies assns., Far Eastern Assn., Middle East Inst. Clubs: Union League, Executives (Chgo.). Author: The Politico—Economic Position of Japan, 1955. Co-author: Radicals and Conservatives, 1957, Western Policy and Eastern Europe, 1965; Strategy for Accelerated Development, 1975. Pub., asso. editor Modern Age, A Quar. Rev., 1958-70, editor, 1970—; co-editor Berlin and the Future of Eastern Europe, 1963; Western Integration and the Future of Eastern Europe, 1964; Elements of Change in Eastern Europe, 1968; The Conditions for Peace in Europe, 1969; Accelerated Devel. in Southern Africa, 1973. Home: 2810 NE 23d St Pompano Beach FL 33062 Office: 743 N Wabash Ave Chicago IL 60611 also 14 S Bryn Mawr Ave Bryn Mawr PA 19010

COLLIER, HELEN VANDIVORT, counseling psychologist; b. Nagpur, India, June 16, 1928; d. William Boardley and Stephena Ruth (Hecker) Collier; came to U.S., 1929; A.B., Ohio Wesleyan U., 1950; M.Ed., U. Toledo, 1968, Ed.D., 1974; children—Keith Vandivort, Daniel Vandivort, Heidi Vandivort. Tchr. elementary schs., Itasca, Ill., 1950-53; ednl. cons., Toledo Bd. Edn., 1960-67; elementary counselor, pub. schs., Toledo, 1968; counseling psychologist, asst. prof., U. Toledo, 1968-74; asst. dir. adult counseling project Sch. Continuing Studies Ind. U., Bloomington, 1975-76; pvt. practice psychotherapy and counseling, cons., Bloomington, 1974—; cons. orgnl. devel.; student San Diego Gestalt Tng. Center. Women's Ednl. Equity Act, Office of Edn. grantee, 1977—; licensed psychologist, Ohio. Mem. Am. Psychol. Assn., Assn. for Women in Psychology, Assn. for Humanistic Psychology, Am. Personnel and Guidance Assn., Nat. Vocat. Guidance Assn., Assn. for Counselor Edn. and Supervision, Am. Soc. Tng. and Devel., Women's Equity Action League, Nat. Women's Polit. Caucus. Co-editor: Meeting the Educational and Occupational Planning Needs of Adults, 1975; Counseling and Motivating Adults: A Training Manual, 1977. Home: 3801 Morningside Dr #6 Bloomington IN 47401 Office: Box 464 Bloomington IN 47401

COLLIER, WILLIAM JEWELL, physician; b. Albany, Mo., Apr. 25, 1925; s. Ora and Mabel (Adkisson) C.; student U. Chgo. Sch. Medicine, 1945-46; B.S., Tulane U., 1947; M.D., Bowman Gray Sch. Medicine, Wake Forest Coll., 1949; m. Mary Evelyn Fisher, Mar. 29, 1952; children—William Jewell II, Sherry Lynn, Terri Lee, Linda Lorraine. Intern, U.S. Naval Hosp., Great Lakes, Ill., 1949-50; resident internal medicine VA Hosp., Wadsworth, Kans., 1950-51, resident gen. surgery, 1951-52, 54-57; asst. chief surgery VA Hosp., Wichita, Kans., 1957-58; pvt. practice gen. and thoracic surgery, McPherson, Kans., 1958—. Dir. Home State Bank & Trust. Mem. aviation adv. bd. McPherson City-County Airport. Served from lt. (j.g.) to lt. M.C., USNR, 1952-54. Diplomate Am. Bd. Surgery. Fellow Southwestern Surg. Congress, A.C.S., Internat. Coll. Surgeons; mem. C. of C. Mem. Christian Ch. Rotarian. Home: 302 S Walnut St McPherson KS 67460 Office: 400 W 4th St McPherson KS 67460

COLLINGS, DELORES ELOISE, artist; b. Putnam County, Ind., Jan. 24, 1933; d. Alton Lowell and Laverne (Presslor) Cunningham; student Marshall (Ind.) pub. schs.; m. Dallas Wendell Collings, Oct. 24, 1952; children—Bradley, Brian, Tracy, Frank. Bookkeeper, Phillips & Mull DX Service, Rockville, Ind., 1951-52, Rockville Nat. Bank, 1956; co-operator Palette Art Studio, Bridgeton, Ind., 1974—; dir. Covered Bridge Festival of Parke County, Inc., Billie Creek Village. Recipient awards Kappa Kappa Kappa, 1968, Paris Art League, 1968, best of show award Parke County Art Exhibit, 1972, 77, hon. mention Brown County Asso. Show, 1969. Mem. Covered Bridge, Brown County art assns., DAR. Democrat. Methodist. Home: Rural Route 2 Rosedale IN 47874

COLLINGSWORTH, ARTHUR JAMES, teenage exchange program exec.; b. Jackson, Mich., Feb. 2, 1944; s. Neri and Ruby Maxine (Van Sickel) C.; B.A. (regents-alumni scholar), U. Mich., 1967; M.A. (Earhart Found. fellow, Center for Strategic and Internat. Studies fellow), Georgetown U., 1971. Brazilian Govt. rep. to Mich. and Ohio, 1958-62; mem. Brazilian del. Chgo. Internat. Trade Fair and Mpls. Aquatennial, 1962; mem. staff Congressman George Meader, 1964; resource person Internat. Commn. U.S. Nat. Student Assn. Nat. Congress, 1966—; nat. coordinator participation politics research United Citizens for Nixon-Agnew, Washington, 1968; mem. White House transition staff, 1968-69; dir. pub. affairs Youth for Understanding Internat. Teenage Exchange Program, Ann Arbor, Mich., 1969-75, v.p., 1975—. Founder, chmn. bd. dirs. Niels Hansen Meml. Found., 1966—. Am. Friends of Vietnam travel grantee, 1965. Mem. Japan Soc., Center Inter-Am. Relations, Detroit Com. on Fgn. Relations, Nat. Inst. Social Scis., Mich. Hist. Soc., Univ. Mus. Soc. Clubs: Met., Capitol Hill (Washington). Home: 2111 Devonshire St Ann Arbor MI 48104 Office: 3501 Newark Ave Washington DC 20016

COLLINS, ALBERT VINCENT, chem. co. exec.; b. Cleve., Sept. 10, 1912; s. Thomas G. and Dorothy A. (Desson) C.; B.Ch.E., Case Sch. Applied Sci., 1934; m. Helen M. Schaller, Dec. 29, 1945; 1 son, James Brendon. With McGean Chems., Cleve., 1937-45, U.S. Steel Corp., Lorain, Ohio, 1935-37; lab. mgr. Chemetron Co., Cleve., 1938-63; asst. chief chemist Shell Chems., Houston, 1945-48; tech. dir. Mooney Chem. Co., Inc., Cleve., 1964—. Mem. Am. Chem. Soc., Am. Inst. Chem. Engrs., ASTM, Sigma Lambda. Democrat. Roman Catholic. Clubs: First Friday, K.C. Patentee in field. Home: 4189 W214 Fairview Park OH 44126 Office: 2301 Scranton St Cleveland OH 44113

COLLINS, ARTHUR F., former coll. ofcl.; b. Hinsdale, Ill., July 28, 1891; s. Sydney T. and Anna (Farquhar) C.; B.S., Beloit Coll., 1913; m. Dorothy Densmore, Sept. 10, 1927; children—Densmore B. (dec.), Theodore B. Salesman, Am. Radiator Co., 1913-17; asst. cashier Bank of New Richmond, Wis., 1919-20; western advt. mgr. Country Home mag. Crowell-Collier Pub. Co., 1920-47; western advt. mgr. Parade Sunday Mag., Parade, 1947-54, western sales supr., 1954-59; with Chgo. Assn. Commerce and Industry, 1959; with devel. div. Beloit Coll., 1959-66. Chmn., Hinsdale Community Service, 1961-63. Trustee Beloit Coll., 1939-59, life trustee, 1959—. Served as 1st lt. F.A., U.S Army, World War I. Episcopalian (mem. vestry 1943-49, jr. warden 1950). Mem. Am. Legion (charter, post comdr. Chgo. 1936-37), Newcomen Soc. N. Am., Phi Kappa Psi. Episcopalian (chmn. planning com.). Mason (32 deg.). Clubs: Executives, Union League, Beloit Coll. Alumni (pres.). Home: 513 S Garfield Ave Hinsdale IL 60521

COLLINS, CARDISS, Congressman; b. St. Louis, Sept. 24, 1931; student Northwestern U.; m. George W. Collins; 1 son, Kevin. Stenographer, Ill. Dept. Labor; sec. Ill. Dept. Revenue, then accountant, revenue auditor; mem. 93d-95th congresses from 7th Ill. Dist., mem. Com. on Govt. Ops., subcoms. legal and monetary affairs and govt. activities, majority whip at large. Bd. dirs. Greater Lawndale Conservation Commn., Chgo. Mem. NAACP. Baptist. Democrat. Office: Room 113 Cannon House Office Bldg Washington DC 20515*

COLLINS, CHARLES WALTER, geographer, educator; b. Antigo, Wis., Apr. 23, 1938; s. James Marvin and Augusta M. (Fank) C.; student U. Wis. at Fox Valley Extension Center, 1959-61; B.S., U. Wis. at Oshkosh, 1963; M.S. (Stickney fellow 1964-66, 68-69), U. Wis. at Milw., 1966, postgrad. (Univ. fellow), 1968-69; postgrad. U. Minn., 1966; m. Joan Ellen Gossen, Sept. 7, 1957; children—Guy Allen, Jaime O., Michael Trevor. Faculty asst. geography and geology U. Wis. at Oshkosh, 1963-64; grad. asst. U. Wis. at Milw., 1964-66; faculty U. Wis. at Platteville, 1966—, asst. prof. geography, 1968—. Cub Scout leader Boy Scouts Am., Platteville, 1966-68. Candidate, U.S. Third Congressional Dist., Wis., 1974. Served with USNR, 1955-63. Mem. Assn. Am. Geographers, Wis. Council Geographic Edn., Wis. Acad. Arts and Scis., Nat. Geographic Soc., Gamma Theta Upsilon. Democrat. Club: Optimist. Author: An Atlas of Wisconsin, 1968, 2d edit. 1972; Atlas of Iowa, 1974; Atlas of Ohio, 1975; Illinois, An Atlas, 1976; New York, An Atlas, 1977. Home: PO Box 423 Platteville WI 53818

COLLINS, DAVID RAYMOND, educator, author, lectr.; b. Marshalltown, Iowa, Feb. 29, 1940; s. Raymond Amby and Mary Elizabeth (Brecht) C.; B.S., Western Ill. U., 1962, M.S., 1966. Instr. English, Woodrow Wilson Jr. High Sch., 1962—; founder, dir. Miss. Valley Writers Conf., 1973—. Sec., Quad Cities Arts Council, 1971-75; pres. Friends of Moline Pub. Library, 1965-66. Recipient writing award Writer's Digest, 1967, writer of the year award Writers' Studio, 1971, award Bobbs-Merrill Pub. Co., 1971, writer of the year award Quad-Cities Writers Club, 1972, writing awards Judson Coll., 1971. Mem. Nat., Ill., Moline (dir. 1964-67) edn. assns., Ill. Parent Tchr. Assn. (life mem., Outstanding Ill. Educator award 1975), Ill. Hist. Soc., Black Hawk Div. Tchrs. English (pres. 1967-68), Writers' Studio (pres. 1967-71), Children's Reading Roundtable, Authors' Guild, Soc. Children's Book Writers, Juvenile Forum, Quad-Cities Writers Club (pres. 1973-75, 77—), Am. Amateur Press Assn., Western Ill. U. Alumni (dir. 1968-74, Outstanding Achievement award 1973), Kappa Delta Pi, Sigma Tau Delta, Alpha Delta, Delta Sigma Phi. Democrat. Roman Catholic. Author: Kim Soo and His Tortoise, 1970, Great American Nurses, 1971, Walt Disney's Surprise Christmas Present, 1972, Linda Richards, America's First Trained Nurse, 1973; Harry S. Truman, People's President, 1975; I, Abraham Lincoln, 1976; Illinois Women: Born to Serve, 1976; Joshua Poole Hated School, 1977; Charles Lindbergh, Flying Ace, 1978; George Washington Carver, 1978; A Spirit of Giving, 1978. Home: 3403 45th St Moline IL 61265 Office: 1301 48th St Moline IL 61265

COLLINS, DENVER, JR., constrn. co. exec.; b. Akron, Ohio, Oct. 2, 1932; s. Denver and Blanche Vella (Hilliard) C.; student Kent State U., 1950-52; B.S., Ohio State U., 1956; m. Mary Helen Hanson, Jan. 29, 1955; children—Denver Dean, Karen Kay, Sharen Sue. Operating engr. Marshall C. Rardin & Sons, Inc., Akron, 1949-56, chief estimator bidding and estimating, 1957-62, gen. supt., 1962-67, gen. mgr., 1967—, v.p., 1962—, also dir., Mem. Stow (Ohio) Community Council, 1962. Served to 1st lt. C.E., AUS, 1956-57. Am. Soc. C.E., Soc. Am. Mil. Engrs. (Gold medal 1956), Ohio Contractors Assn. (chmn. pub. relations com. 1968-69), Grange. Club: Golf Country (Aurora, O.). Home: 79 State Route 303 Streetsboro OH 44240 Office: 2715 Mogadore Rd Akron OH 44312

COLLINS, DON CARY, lawyer; b. Christopher, Ill., Sept. 10, 1951; s. Everett Hugh and Evelyn Lorraine (Wootton) C.; student Western Ky. U., 1969-70; B.A., Ill. State U., Normal, 1972; J.D., So. Ill. U., 1976. Admitted to Ill. bar, 1976, U.S. Dist. Ct. bar, 1976, Mo. bar, 1977; asso. firm Meyer & Kaucher, Belleville and Highland, Ill., 1976—. Mem. Am., Ill., Mo., St. Clair County, St. Louis Met. bar assns., Am. Trial Lawyers Assn. Home: 405 Williamsburg Dr Apt 8 Belleville IL 62221 Office: 4517 W Main St Belleville IL 62223

COLLINS, EDWARD JAMES, JR., assn. exec.; b. Lawrence, Mass., Mar. 17, 1933; s. Edward James and Mary Elizabeth (Rogers) C.; m. Dorothy Jane McCann, Sept. 19, 1964; 1 son, Edward James; 1 stepdau., Dorothy Lorraine; A.B. in Journalism, U. Calif., Berkeley, 1959. Mng. editor Brawley (Calif.) Daily News, 1959-62; asso. exec. dir. Calif. Veterinary Med. Assn., Moraga, Calif., 1962-66; asst. dir., prof., pub. relations Calif. Med. Assn., San Francisco, 1966-68; v.p. Assn. Western Hosps., San Francisco, 1968-76; exec. dir. Am. Assn. Med. Soc. Execs., Chgo., 1977—. Mem. Am., No. Calif. (pres. 1973), Chgo. socs. assn. execs., Greater Chgo. Conf. Med. Soc. Execs., Am. Radio Relay League. Recipient Agrl. Writers award, 1961, Key Man award Oakland (Calif.) Jaycees, 1964. Home: 617 Indian Hill Rd Deerfield IL 60015 Office: 535 N Dearborn St Chicago IL 60610

COLLINS, EDWARD RUSSELL, accounting exec.; b. Rochester, N.Y., Oct. 15, 1935; s. Ambrose Frank and Margaret Adelaide (Pritchard) C.; B.S. in Bus. Adminstrn., Xavier U., 1958, M.A., 1961; m. Catherine Jean Thiem, Nov. 11, 1967; children—Stephen Edward, Ryan Patrick. Accountant, Alco Bldg. Products Co., Cin., 1959-60; auditor Butler, Lamping & Ramey, Cin., 1960-69; audit mgr. Arthur Young & Co., Cin., 1969-71; pvt. practice auditing and tax accounting, Cin., 1971-72; adminstrv. partner Bernhardt, Showalter & Collins, C.P.A.'s, Cin., 1972—. Instr. accounting Evening Coll., Thomas More

Coll., Fort Mitchell, Ky., 1971—; dir. Centarus, Inc., Mgmt. Recruiters Cin., Inc., Babst Photography Co.; dir. service bur. Cin. Assn. Credit and Fin. Mgmt., 1968—. Troop treas. Boy Scouts Am., Cin., 1967-70. Bd. dirs. Dominican Sisters of Sick Poor-Home Health Agy., Cin. C.P.A., Ohio. Mem. Am. Inst. C.P.A.'s, Ohio Soc. C.P.A.'s, Cin. Assn. Credit Men, Nat. Assn. Investment Clubs (dir. Cin.-Dayton chpt. 1971—). K.C. Clubs: Delta Assn. Investment (treas. 1964—), Buckeye. Home: 779 Woodfield Dr Cincinnati OH 45231 Office: 4811 Vine St Cincinnati OH 45217

COLLINS, ERNEST HAMMOND, savs. and loan exec.; b. N.Y.C., Jan. 1, 1911; s. Ernest H. and Margaret (Casell) C.; B.S., U. Colo., 1932; M.B.A., Harvard, 1934; m. Margaret Louise Lucas, Dec. 21, 1935; children—Patricia (Mrs. J.D. Thompson), Sue (Mrs. C.J. vonBaeyer), Ernest Hammond III, Jean. Accountant, Washington Gas Light Co., 1934-36; developer REA, 1936-38; chmn. bd. Greencastle Fed. Savs. & Loan Assn., 1940—; adv. council Fed. Home Loan Bank Bd., 1972-76. Mem. City Council Greencastle, 1964-72. Trustee Ind. Savs. and Loan Group Ins. Served to lt. USNR, 1944-46. Mem. U.S. (exec. com. 1969-72), Ind. (pres. 1965) savs. and loan leagues. Methodist. Home: 618 Highwood Ave Greencastle IN 46135 Office: 2 S Jackson St Greencastle IN 46135

COLLINS, EVA MAE LOMERSON, ins. agency exec.; b. Lake Orion, Mich., July 10, 1930; d. J.M. and Thelma Marie (Kimmery) Lomerson; student U. Mich., 1948-49, Wayne State U., 1954-55; m. John Armstrong Collins, Feb. 24, 1968. Divisional mgr. Sears Roebuck & Co., Pontiac, Mich., 1951-69; underwriter personal lines Bingham & Bingham Inc., Birmingham, Mich., 1970-73, comml. lines, 1973-74, agency mgr., 1974-77, v.p. InterCEDE Group, 1977—. Named woman of year Land-O-Oak chpt. Am. Bus. Women's Assn., 1965. Mem. DAR (chpt. regent-gen. 1967-69, state chmn. pages and jr. membership 1967-70, state outstanding jr. mem. 1966), Detroit Soc. Geneal. Research, Hist. Soc. Mich., Ins. Women Met. Detroit (rec. sec. 1977—), U. Mich. Alumni Assn. (life), Daus. Colonial Wars, Nat. Trust for Historic Preservation, Nat. Wildlife Fedn. Republican. Clubs: Club on Hill, Gt. Oaks Country (Rochester, Mich.). Home: 1122 Mill Valley Rd Rochester MI 48063 Office: 30400 Telegraph Rd S-364 Birmingham MI 48010

COLLINS, GARY ROSS, educator; b. Hamilton, Ont., Can., Oct. 22, 1934; s. Harold A. and Vera (Stanger) C.; B.A., McMaster U., 1956; M.A., U. Toronto, 1958; Ph.D., Purdue U., 1963; postgrad. U. London, 1958-59, Western Bapt. Sem., 1963-64; m. Julie Ann Heinz, July 18, 1964; children—Marilynn, Janice Carolyn. Came to U.S., 1964. Psychol. intern U. Oreg. Med. Sch., 1962-63; counselor Portland (Oreg.) State Coll., 1963-64; asst. prof. psychology Bethel Coll., St. Paul, 1964-66, asso. prof., 1966-68, chmn. dept., 1966-68; prof. psychology Conwell Sch. Theology, Phila., 1968-69; prof. psychology, chmn. div. pastoral counseling and psychology Trinity Evang. Div. Sch., Bannockburn, Ill., 1969—. Served with Royal Canadian Navy Res., 1953-63. Fellow Am. Sci. Affiliation (nat. v.p. 1973, nat. pres. 1974—); mem. Am. Psychol. Assn. Author: Search for Reality, 1969; Living in Peace, 1970; Our Society in Turmoil, 1970; A Psychologist Looks at Life, 1971, reprinted as Overcoming Anxiety, 1973; Man in Transition, 1971; Effective Counseling, 1972; Fractured Personalities, 1972; Man in Motion, 1973; The Christian Psychology of Paul Tournier, 1973; Coping with Christmas, 1975; How to be a People Helper, 1976; The Rebuilding of Psychology, 1977. Editor several books. Office: Trinity Divinity Sch Bannockburn IL 60015

COLLINS, HARKER, bus. exec.; b. Denver, Nov. 24, 1924; s. Clem Wetzel and Marie (Harker) C.; B.S., U.S. Naval Acad., 1945; m. Emily Harvey, Aug. 23, 1957; children—Catherine Emily, Cynthia Lee, Constance Marie. Asst. buyer Montgomery Ward & Co., N.Y.C., 1947-51; prodn. mgr. Diamond Hosiery Mills, High Point, N.C., 1953-55; v.p. Vanette Hosiery Mills, Dallas, 1955-59; v.p., dir. Grote Mfg. Co., Madison, Ind., Power Brake Parts Mfg. Co., Chgo., Monarch Tool & Machine, Chgo., Grote of Can. Ltd., 1959-71; group v.p., gen. mgr. Bendix Corp., South Bend, Ind., 1971-73; pres., dir. Bandag, Inc., Muscatine, Iowa, 1973—, chief exec. officer, 1974—; dir. Bandag Europe N.V. (Belgium), Bandag Can. Ltd., Vakuum Vulk U.S., Shrader's Inc., Master Processing Corp., VV System AG (Switzerland), Gardner-Denver Corp.; Heavy Duty Parts, Inc.; instr. U. Denver, 1948. Bd. dirs. Hwy. Users Fedn., 1970—; chmn. automotive industry liaison com. with Dept. Transp., 1968—, automotive industry excise tax com., 1964-70, automotive industry tariff com., 1964-70, joint operating com. for automotive trade shows, 1969-77; mem. Pres.'s Com. Hwy. Safety, 1966-68. Republican county chmn. Jefferson County, Ind., 1963-65; bd. dirs. Iowa Coll. Found., 1976—; bd. fellows Northwood Inst., 1974—. Served to ensign USN, 1945-47; to lt. USNR, 1951-53. Recipient Automotive Industry Leadership award, 1965, 74; award for most outstanding chief exec. officer tire and rubber industry Fin. World, 1975, 77. Mem. Automotive Service Industry Assn. (v.p. 1966-67, pres. 1968-69, dir. heavy duty exec. com. 1969-71, chmn. safety and environ. protection com. 1962-67, 70—), Automotive Sales Council (dir. 1966-67, sec. 1971-72, v.p. 1972-73, pres. 1973-74), Am. Nat. Standards Inst. (chmn. task force on used vehicle standards 1966-74), Home Products Safety Council (pres. 1960-63, dir. 1960-68), Medicine Cabinet Mfg. Council (pres. 1960-63, dir. 1960-68), Truck Safety Equipment Inst. (pres. 1960-63, dir. 1960-68), Muscatine C. of C. (dir. 1975—). Clubs: Rotary, 33 (treas. 1977—). Office: Bandag Center Muscatine IA 52761

COLLINS, JAMES SLADE, II, lawyer; b. St. Louis, June 9, 1937; s. James S. and Dolma Ruby (Nielsen) C.; B.S. in Bus. Adminstrn., Washington U., 1958, J.D., 1961; m. Neva Frances Guinn, June 27, 1959; children—Shari Lynn, Camala Ann. Admitted to Mo. bar, 1961, U.S. Supreme Ct., 1969, U.S. Dist. Ct. for Eastern Mo., 1972; asso. Whalen, O'Connor, Grauel & Sarkisian, St. Louis, 1961-70; partner Whalen, O'Connor & Byrne, 1970-72; partner Whalen, O'Connor, Collins, & Danis, 1972-75; asso. Hullverson, Hullverson & Frank, Inc., 1975—. Dir. Design 500, Inc., Sten-Com, Inc., L.M.L. Enterprise, Inc. Trustee, Village of Hanley Hills, Mo., 1966-69, mayor, 1967, municipal judge, 1967-68, 69-70. Mem. Am. Bar Assn., Bar Assn. Met. St. Louis, Lawyers Assn. St. Louis, Am. Trial Lawyers Assn., Phi Delta Phi. Republican. Baptist. Home: 916 Park Watch Dr St Louis County MO 63011 Office: 722 Chestnut St St Louis MO 63101

COLLINS, JOHN SHERMAN, bus. exec.; b. Elmira, N.Y., Jan. 2, 1929; s. Jerry Bernard and Anna Jeanette (Sherman) C.; B.S., Bucknell U., 1950; m. Eileen Marie Mulcahy, Sept. 15, 1951; children—Elizabeth Anne, John J., Patricia Marie, Rosemary, Carol, David Patrick, Maureen, Mary Ellen, Jerry Bernard II. Civil engr. Pa. R.R., Altoona, Pa. and N.Y.C., 1950-54, track supr. various locations, 1954-65; engr., maintenance of way Lehigh R.R., Bethlehem, Pa., 1965-68; chief railroad engr. DeLeuw, Cather & Co., Washington, 1968-70, dir. bus. devel., Chgo., 1971-73, v.p., 1973—. Served with AUS, 1951-53. Registered profl. engr. N.Y., Pa., Ill., D.C., Va., Ky. Mem. Nat. Council Engring. Examiners, Nat. Soc. Profl. Engrs., ASCE, Am. Ry. Engring. Assn., Roadmasters Assn., Western Soc. Engrs., Am. Legion. Republican. Roman Catholic. Clubs: N.Y. Railroad, Met. Ry. (v.p. 1967-68) (N.Y.C.); Western Ry. (Chgo.). Home: 1576 Surrey Dr Wheaton IL 60187 Office: 165 W Wacker Dr Chicago IL 60601

COLLINS, LESLIE WAYNE GRANT, test engr.; b. Regina, Sask., Can., Feb. 1, 1937; s. Wayne and Leona (Sudom) C.; came to U.S., 1965; B. Engring., U. Sask., 1960; m. Barbara Louise Wallerman, July 6, 1961; children—Lisa Louise, Garth Leslie. Asst. prodn. engr. Redi-Mix Concrete Ltd., Moose Jaw, Sask., summer 1958; staff irrigation project dept. agrl. engring. U. Sask., summer 1959; service engr. John Deere Ltd., Regina, Sask., 1961-65, test engr. John Deere Dubuque Works (Iowa), 1965—. Mem. Am. Soc. Agrl. Engrs., Canadian Soc. Agrl. Engring., Soc. Automotive Engrs. Congregationalist. Club: Toastmasters. Home: 2440 Briarwood Dr Dubuque IA 52001 Office: PO Box 538 Dubuque IA 52001

COLLINS, MARY BETH HUGHES (MRS. TABER LOREE COLLINS), health care adminstr.; b. Detroit, Jan. 3, 1925; d. James Edward and Mildred Ina (Barding) Hughes; student Marymount Acad., 1942; B.A., Manhattanville Coll., 1947; M.A., Ariz. State U., 1970; m. Taber Loree Collins, Aug. 7, 1947; children—Louise (Mrs. Conwell D. Ponath), James, Suzanne (Mrs. Lance Giroux), Marybeth, Mildred, Marquerite, Miriam, Frank, Jesse, Kathleen, Martha. Community services coordinator Alcohol and Drug Abuse div. Ariz. Health Dept., Phoenix, 1967-68, acting dir., 1968-70; coordinator City of Phoenix Drug Control, 1970-73; exec. dir. Drug Action Coalition, Md., 1973-74; exec. dir. Community Orgn. for Drug Abuse Control, Phoenix, 1974-76; exec. v.p. Internat. Assn. Prevention Programs, after 1976; now head Mich. Substance Abuse Program; cons. Drug Abuse Workshop, Ariz. State U. and Ariz. Western Coll., 1969; cons. Pyramid Project, 1975—; mem. state task force on alcohol, narcotics and drug abuse Ariz. Justice Planning, 1970—. Pres., Ariz. Family, Inc., 1970-71. Bd. dirs. Community Orgn. for Drug Abuse Control, Nat. Coordinating Council on Drug Edn., Alcoholism and Drug Abuse Programs of N.Am., Nat. Drug Abuse Conf. Mem. Internat. Council on Alcoholism and Addictions, Ariz. Alumnae of Sacred Heart (founding pres. 1963-64), Pi Lambda Theta. Home: 6417 McCue Rd Holt MI 48842

COLLINS, MICHAEL ROBIN, sanitary engr.; b. Radford, Va., Aug. 16, 1948; s. Joseph Elmer and Mary Kate (Hutton) C.; B.S. in Civil Engring. with honors, Va. Tech. U., 1970, M.S. in Sanitary Engring., 1972; m. Linda Kay Grossnickle, July 25, 1975; 1 dau., Jennifer Lynn. Sanitary engr. Anderson & Assos., Blacksburg, Va., 1975; dist. engr. Kans. Dept. Health and Environment, Chanute, 1975—; instr. in ecology Neosho County (Kans.) Community Jr. Coll., 1976—. Served with U.S. Army, 1972-75. Registered profl. engr., Kans., Va. Mem. ASCE, Water Pollution Control Fedn., Nat. Soc. Profl. Engrs., Kans. Engring. Soc. Baptist. Club: Elks. Home: 1212 W Sycamore Chanute KS 66720 Office: PO Box 566 Chanute KS 66720

COLLINS, RAYMOND ELSTON, chem. corp. exec.; b. Cin., Aug. 17, 1931; s. Lee and Sadie Blanche (Bartley) C.; B.S. in Bus. Adminstrn., Miami U., Oxford, Ohio, 1958; m. Mary Rose Blackwell, July 31, 1954; children—Deborah Rae, Jeffrey Todd. Indsl. salesman Nat. Cylinder Gas div. Chemetron Corp., Cin., 1958-62; dist. rep. Thermice Corp. subsidiary Publicker Industries, Inc., St. Louis, 1962-65; sales rep. pigments div. Sun Chem. Corp., Cin., 1965-73; pigments div. rep. maj. accounts Hilton Davis Chem. Co. div. Sterling Drug, Inc., 1973—. Mem. Indian Hill Home Owners Assn., Naperville Welcome Wagon New Comers Club. Served with AUS, 1952-54. Decorated Bronze Star, other medals. Mem. St. Louis Paint and Varnish Assn., Chgo. Soc. for Paint Tech., Chgo. Printing Ink Prodn. Club, Asst. Scout Master Assn. Presbyn. Mason (Shriner). Club: Sheiks. Home: 1521 Chippewa Dr Naperville IL 60540 Office: 200 E Oakton St Des Plaines IL 60018

COLLINS, RICHARD ANTHONY, trade assn. exec.; b. Lake Forest, Ill., Sept. 19, 1931; s. Anthony D. and Alice A. (Luedke) Czaikowski; B.A. magna cum laude, Augustana Coll., 1956; M.B.A., U. Wis., 1957, postgrad., 1966-70; m. Joan V. Krapfel, Apr. 17, 1965; children—Craig R., Clark A. Econ. statistician Eastman Kodak, Rochester, N.Y., 1957-59; mgr. mktg. research Ritter Co., mfr. dental and med. equipment, Rochester, N.Y., 1959-63; mktg. research supr. Oscar Mayer & Co., meat packing, Madison, Wis., 1964-66; mktg. program coordinator U. Wis. Extension, Madison, 1966-68; prof. U. Wis., Whitewater, 1968-72; marketing exec. Anchor Savs. & Loan Assn., Madison, 1972-73; EFTS project dir. Fed. Home Loan Bank Bd., 1973-74; dir. EFT projects Credit Union Nat. Assn., Madison, 1974-76, v.p. fin. systems, 1976—. Ad hoc prof. mktg. programs for small bus. U. Wis. Extension, 1970-73; instr. Savings and Loan Inst. courses, 1965-72; numerous cons. assignments for various firms in Wis., Ill. Mem. Madison Housing Consortium, 1972-73. Served with AUS, 1949-53. Mem. Wis. Savs. and Loan League (vice chmn. electronic funds transfer systems com. 1972-73), Am. Mktg. Assn. (chpt. seminar chmn. 1972-73), Savs. Instns. Mktg. Soc. Am. Clubs: Madison Press, Madison Advertising. Author: (with George L. Herpel) Specialty Advertising in Marketing, 1972. Home: 2812 Waunona Way Madison WI 53713 Office: 1617 Sherman Ave Box 431 Madison WI 53701

COLLINS, RICHARD JOHN, sales exec.; b. Gary, Ind., June 24, 1921; s. Frank H. and Aileen Mary (Cary) C.; student Gary Coll., 1939-42; B.S., Ind. U., 1947; m. Betty Ann Cogswell, Sept. 21, 1946; children—Cary, Thomas, Libby A., Timothy, Theodore, Cathleen. Sales cons. Met. Life Ins. Co., 1960-70; field mgr. mgmt. sales Commonwealth Life & Accident & Ins., 1967-69; cons. sales engr. Batestor (now Batesco), Gary, Ind., 1969-75, field sales engr., research and devel., 1975—; cons. Mespeco, Inc. Treas. Gary Republican Central Com., 1966-70; precinct capt. Gary Rep. Com., 1964-70, Crown Point (Ind.) Rep. Com., 1971-75. Served with USMC, 1942-46. C.L.U. Mem. Am. Foundry Soc., Metall. Soc., Iron and Steel Soc. of Am. Inst. Mining, Metall. and Petroleum Engrs., Molten Metals Testing Assn., Research and Devel. Guild, Am. Legion. Roman Catholic. Patentee. Home: 306 Northeast St Crown Point IN 46307 Office: PO Box 8115 Gary IN 46410

COLLINS, ROLAND DEAN, civil engr.; b. Champaign, Ill., Mar. 17, 1927; s. Floyd Sterling and Lela Mae (Roland) C.; B.S. in Civil Engring., U. Ill., 1949, M.S. in Structural Engring., 1951; m. Barbara Ruth Thomasson, Sept. 9, 1950; children—Susan Lee, Gregory Dean, Jeffery Craig. Research asso. U. Ill., 1949-50; instr. Cornell U., 1951-52; bridge designer State Ill., 1952-54; pvt. practice as cons. engr., Springfield, Ill., 1954—. Mem. Sangamon County Bd. Suprs., 1966-74; chmn. Sangamon County Bd., 1973-74. Precinct committeeman Republican party, 1966-76, vice-chmn., sec. Sangamon County Rep. central com., 1970-76. Bd. dirs. Boys Club, United Community Services. Served with USAAF, World War II. Named Outstanding Young Man of Year, Jr. C. of C., 1961; recipient Pres. award Cons. Engrs. Council Ill., 1973. Registered profl. engr., Ill. Mem. Am. Soc. C.E., Am. Concrete Inst., Internat. Assn. Bridge and Structural Engrs., Ill. Soc. Profl. Engrs. (pres. Capitol chpt. 1960-61; Distinguished Service award 1975), Cons. Engrs. Council Ill., Beta Theta Pi, Chi Epsilon. Presbyn. (deacon trustee). Clubs: Sangamo, Island Bay Yacht (Springfield). Home: 77 W Hazel Dell Springfield IL 62707 Office: 431 S Grand Ave W Springfield IL 62704

COLLINS, WALTON ROBERT, editor, univ. ofcl.; b. Phila., Feb. 15, 1930; s. Walton R. and Margaret M. (Missett) C.; A.B., U. Notre Dame, 1951; M.Pub.Adminstrn., Ind. U., 1976; m. Carolyn A. Huebner, June 11, 1952; children—W. Robert, Mary Carol, Jeanne, John, Margaret. Writer, Indsl. Maintenance mag., Phila., 1951-53; reporter, news editor Alexandria (Ind.) Times-Tribune, 1953-56, gen. mgr., 1956-57; gen. assignment reporter South Bend (Ind.) Tribune, 1957-61, asso. editor, 1963-69, book editor, 1961—; lectr., U. Notre Dame, 1963, 77, St. Mary's Coll., Notre Dame; lectr. Ind. U., South Bend, 1968—, asst. to chancellor, 1969—. Mem. Council Advancement and Support Edn. Club: South Bend Press. Home: 2201 Riverside Dr South Bend IN 46616 Office: 1825 Northside Blvd South Bend IN 46615

COLLINS, WILLIAM THOMAS, pathologist; b. Omaha, Feb. 21, 1922; s. John Maurice and Elizabeth (Ewing) C.; B.S., U. Ky., 1942; M.D., U. Mich., 1944; m. Ann E. Adams, May 30, 1942; children—William Thomas, Carol Ann, John Mark, Donald Brian. Intern, Good Samaritan Hosp., Cin., 1944-45; resident in pathology Cin. Gen. Hosp., 1945-46, asst. attending pathologist, 1948-51; pathologist, dir. labs. Good Samaritan Hosp., Cin., 1952-56; fellow in exfoliative cytology Free Hosp. for Women, Brookline, Mass., 1949; asso. pathologist Blodgett Meml. Hosp., Grand Rapids, Mich., 1956-57; asso. pathologist Lima (Ohio) Meml. Hosp., 1957-58, pathologist, dir. lab., 1958—; asso. clin. prof. pathology Med. Coll. Ohio, Toledo, 1972—; instr. in pathology Coll. Medicine, U. Cin., 1948-51, asst. prof. pathology, 1951-56; pres. med. staff Lima Meml. Hosp., 1968-70; chmn. adv. group Northwestern Ohio Regional Med. Program, 1970-71; mem. certified lab. assts. com. Nat. Accrediting Agy. for Clin. Lab. Scis., 1974-76. Bd. dirs. Allen County chpt. ARC, pres., 1972-73; bd. dirs. Allen County unit Am. Cancer Soc., pres., 1973-75; exec. com. Ohio div. Am. Cancer Soc.; bd. dirs. Lima Area C. of C., 1962-65, Lima Symphony Orch., 1963-69, United Fund of Greater Lima, 1970-72. Served to lt. M.C., USNR, 1946-48. Diplomate Am. Bd. Pathology. Mem. Lima and Allen County Acad. Medicine (sec., treas.), Ohio State Med. Assn., AMA, Ohio Soc. Pathologists (pres. 1970-71), Am. Assn. Pathologists, Am. Soc. Clin. Pathologists, Coll. Am. Pathologists (rep. to ho. of dels.), Internat. Acad. Pathology, AAAS, Ohio Acad. Sci., Sigma Xi. Republican. Presbyterian. Clubs: Rotary (pres. 1964-65), Elks. Home: 1524 Fairway Dr Lima OH 45805 Office: Lima Meml Hosp Lima OH 45804

COLLINSON, JOHN THEODORE, railroad exec.; b. Pitts., July 29, 1926; s. John Gordon and Katherine (Bicky) C.; B.S. in Civil Engring., Cornell U., 1946; m. Patricia Ann Davison, Nov. 15, 1947; children—John G., Donald L., Nancy Ann. With engring. dept. B. & O. R.R. Co., Balt., 1946-63, B. & O.-C. & O. R.R., 1963-73; with operating dept. Chessie System, Balt., 1974—, exec. v.p., 1976—; dir. Trailer Train, Belt Ry. of Chgo., K. & I.T. R.R. Served with USNR, 1943-46. Presbyterian. Clubs: Country (Cleve.), Masons (Shriners). Home: 30003 Fairmount Blvd Pepper Pike OH 44124 Office: Terminal Tower Cleveland OH 44124

COLLOTON, JOHN WILLIAM, hosp. adminstr.; b. Mason City, Iowa, Feb. 20, 1931; m. Loras C. With U. Iowa Hosps. and Clinics, Iowa City, 1956—, dir. and asst. to univ. pres., 1971—. Served with Armed Forces, 1953-55. Mem. Am., Iowa (dir., pres. 1977) hosp. assns. Contbr. articles to profl. jours. Office: U Iowa Hosps and Clinics Newton Rd Iowa City IA 52240*

COLOMBO, FREDERICK, lawyer; b. Detroit, Dec. 7, 1916; s. Louis J. and Irene Elizabeth (McKenney) C.; A.B., U. Mich., 1938; J.D., 1940; m. Francis Fisher, June 12, 1947; children—William, Joan, Richard, John. Admitted to Mich. bar, 1940; asst. atty. gen. Mich., 1940-42; mem. firm Colombo & Colombo, Birmingham, Mich., 1942—; dir. Uniroyal, Inc. Trustee Harper Grace Hosp.; bd. dirs. Music Hall Detroit; chmn. Roman Catholic Archdiocese Devel. Fund Detroit, 1966; mem. various Republican financial coms. Mem. Am., Mich., Detroit, Oakland County bar assns., Am. Judicature Soc. Clubs: Bloomfield Hills Country (pres. 1968), Detroit Athletic (pres. 1974), Country of Fla. (Delray Beach). Home: 1115 Country Club Dr Bloomfield Hills MI 48013 Office: 1500 Woodward St N Suite 209 Birmingham MI 48011

COLON, RONALD WARREN, advt. exec.; b. Elmwood Park, Ill., Dec. 10, 1931; s. Leroy Lewis and Sylvia Gwendolyn (De Prey) C.; B.A., Oberlin Coll., 1953; postgrad. U. Mich., 1955-56; m. Arlene Evans, May 29, 1969; 1 son, Lewis; adopted children—Leslie, Robin, Lenora. Broadcast dir. Beeson-Reichert Advt., Toledo, 1959-63; writer-producer W.B. Doner Advt., Detroit, 1963-70; broadcast dir. Creative House Advt., Detroit, 1970-74; advt. mgr. Art Van Furniture Warren, Mich., 1975—. Free lance TV producer; speaker advt. conf. of rotogravure Sunday mags., 1976. Corp. rep. Council Christians and Jews, 1964-65; asst. chief, historian YMCA Indian Princesses, 1972-74. Served with Armed Forces, 1953-55. Recipient Retailer of Year award Brand Names Found., 1976. Mem. NAACP (council 1965-66), Adcraft Club Detroit. Home: 23840 Ithaca St Oak Park MI 48237 Office: Art Van Furniture Warren MI

COLONDER, FRED EDWARD, wholesale co. exec.; b. St. Louis, Dec. 4, 1925; s. Fred Edward and Bessie Maudell (Rivers) C.; student Xavier Coll., 1944, S.E. Mo. State Coll., 1946-48, U. Nev., 1948-50; m. Margaret Louise Houston, Sept. 5, 1953; children—Fred Edward III, John Houston. Asst. advt. mgr. Hollander & Co., St. Louis, 1951-52, asst. sales mgr., 1952-56, sales mgr., 1956-66, v.p., 1967—. Served with USAAF, 1944-45. Mem. Sigma Nu. Office: 600 Brown Rd St Louis County MO 63042

COLONESE, JOSEPH SAL, architect, auto. engr.; b. Cleve., Dec. 22, 1921; s. Vincent and Irene (Ross) C.; B.S., Kent State U., 1950; m. Jean Melick, Sept. 16, 1950; children—Mark Gary, Jo-Ean. Engr., architect, Union Carbide & Carbon, Cleve., 1950-51; engr., architect N.Y. Central R.R., Cleve., 1951-53; architect, engr. Chrolet Gen. Motors Corp., Cleve., 1953-65, sr. project engr., architect Detroit, 1965—; pres. Col-Lam Enterprises engring. cons., 1974—. Active in Unreached Youth, 1955-75. Chief engr., Soap Box Derby, 1955-65. Served with USN, 1942-45, U.S. Army, 1945-58. Recipient Best Design award Mfrs. Assn., 1955-64. Mem. Detroit Engring. Soc. Home: 4894 Haddington Dr Bloomfield Hills MI 48013 Office: 30007 Van Dyke St Warren MI 48090

COLSON, DONALD LEE, food co. exec.; b. Neenah, Wis., May 9, 1931; B.S., U. Wis., 1954; postgrad. (scholar) Am. Inst. Baking, 1954; m. Patricia M. Hanson, June 27, 1975; children by previous marriage—Carla Jan, Cheryl Lee, David Jay, Christy Kay. Prodn. foreman Am. Bakeries Co., 1954-57; dept. mgr. Kroger Co., 1958-60; bakery mix formulator, 1960-68; dir. cereal mix div., dir. research and devel. J.W. Allen Co., Chgo., 1968—. Mem. Am. Assn. Cereal Chemists, Am. Soc. Bakery Engrs. Club: Chgo. Prodn. Home: 129 S Harvard St Arlington Heights IL 60005 Office: 110-118 N Peoria St Chicago IL 60607

COLTMAN, BERTRAM WILLIAM, JR., plastics mfg. co. exec.; b. Chgo., Sept. 29, 1926; s. Bertram William and Agnes Harriet (Swanson) C.; B.S., Northwestern U., 1949; m. Michelle B. Simmone, Nov. 26, 1964; children—Kevin Kendall, Bertram William III,

Rudyard John. Pres., chmn. Rep. Molding Corp., Chgo., 1946—, Ajax Plastic Products, Chgo., 1949—, Des Plaines Molding Corp. (Ill.), 1952—; dir. Packaging Products Corp., Berland, Inc., Kenland, Inc. Bd. dirs. YMCA, Chgo. Served with USNR, 1943-46, AUS, 1951-54. Mem. Soc. Plastic Engrs., Midwest Plastic Assn. (pres., dir. 1972), Am. Legion, Delta Sigma Pi. Roman Catholic. Elk, Moose. Clubs: Michigan Shores Country (Wilmette, Ill.); Kenosha (Wis.) Yacht. Home: 1620 Tower Rd Winnetka IL 60093 Office: 6330 W Touhy Ave Chicago IL 60648

COLTON, FRANK BENJAMIN, chemist; b. Bialystok, Poland, Mar. 3, 1923; s. Rubin and Fanny (Rosenblat) C.; brought to U.S., 1934, naturalized, 1934; B.S., Northwestern U., 1945, M.A., 1946; Ph.D., U. Chgo., 1949; m. Adele Heller, Mar. 24, 1950; children—Francine, Sharon, Laura, Sandra. Research fellow Mayo Clinic, Rochester, Minn., 1949-51; with G.D. Searle & Co., Chgo., 1951—, asst. dir. chem. research, 1961-70, research adviser, 1970—. Recipient Discovery medal for first oral contraceptive Nat. Assn. Mfrs., 1965. Mem. Am. Chem. Soc., Chgo. Chemists Club. Contbr. profl. jours. Pioneer in organic and steroid chemistries. Pioneer work in oral contraception. Home: 3901 Lyons St Evanston IL 60203 Office: G D Searle Co Searle Pkwy Skokie IL 60203

COLVIN, WAYNE SCOTT, personnel adminstr.; b. Boston, Apr. 2, 1951; s. Kenneth Crawford and Gem (Moore) C.; B.A., Ohio Wesleyan U., 1974; M.A., Ohio State U., 1976. Dir. residence life, area IV, Bowling Green (Ohio) State U., 1976—; pres. Ohio Epsilon Alumni Assn., ednl. found., 1974—. Mem. Am. Personnel and Guidance Assn., Am. Coll. Personnel Assn., Nat. Assn. Student Personnel Adminstrs., Ohio Assn. Student Personnel Adminstrs., Nat. Assn. Fraternity Advisors (nat. bd. dirs. 1977—), Sigma Phi Epsilon. Home: 1608 Clough St Bowling Green OH 43402 Office: 425 Student Services Bldg Bowling Green State Univ Bowling Green OH 43403

COLWELL, WILLIAM BURNETT, bank exec.; b. Chgo., May 28, 1934; s. William H. and Vera (Klintz) C.; B.A. magna cum laude, Beloit Coll., 1956; postgrad. U. Ill. Grad. Sch. Journalism, 1957; m. Jeanette Weitman, June 20, 1959; children—Catherine Ann, Hunter William. Reporter, U.P.I., summer 1956; staff reporter Wall Street Jour., 1957-59; dir. pub. relations, advt. Amsted Industries, Inc., Chgo., 1959-76; v.p. press and pub. relations 1st Nat. Bank of Chgo., 1976—. Bd. dirs., chmn. pub. relations Mid-Am. chpt. ARC, 1969-71, mem. pub. relations com., 1977; chmn. spl. services div. Met. Chgo. Crusade Mercy, 1964-65; area chmn. fin. campaign Chgo. council Boy Scouts Am., 1964; pub. relations chmn. capital fund drive Salvation Army, 1962; mem. pub. relations com. Chgo. Heart Assn., 1972-75. Mem. Pub. Relations Clinic Chgo. (pres. 1966), Pub. Relations Soc. Am. (pres. Chgo. chpt. 1976), Assn. for Modern Banking in Ill. (chmn. pub. info. com. 1977-78), Chgo. Assn. Commerce and Industry (pub. relations com. 1966—), Nat. Alliance Businessmen (Chgo. met. pub. relations bd. 1972-74), Beloit Coll. Alumni Council, Phi Beta Kappa, Phi Eta Sigma, Sigma Alpha Epsilon. Clubs: Chgo. Press; Park Ridge (Ill.) Country. Home: 314 Cuttriss Pl Park Ridge IL 60068 Office: One First Nat Plaza Chicago IL 60670

COMAN, EDWARD JOHN, JR., financial-accounting exec.; b. Chgo., Dec. 7, 1939; s. Edward John and Agnes (Martin) C.; B.S., Walton Sch. Commerce, 1961; C.P.A., U. Ill., 1964; M.B.A., U. Chgo., 1969; m. Maxine M. Mikols, Dec. 29, 1962; children—Martin, Daniel, Timothy, Amy. Sr. accountant Glenn Ingram & Co., C.P.A.'s, Chgo., 1962-67; mgr. internal cons. Jewel Food Stores, Melrose Park, Ill., 1967-68, controller mfg. and distbn., 1968-69; pres. Edward J. Coman & Assos. - C.P.A.'s, 1969—. Mem. faculty U. Ill. at Circle Campus, 1970-72. Scoutmaster Boy Scouts Am., Glen Ellyn. Mem. Am. Inst. C.P.A.'s, Ill. Soc. C.P.A.'s, Am. Mgmt. Assn., Accounting Research Assn., Am. Accounting Assn. C. of C. Rotarian. Office: 1100 S Main St Lombard IL 60148

COMATY, JOSEPH EDWARD, JR., psycho-pharmacologist; b. Trenton, N.J., Dec. 31, 1949; s. Joseph Edward and Mary Jane (Mooney) C., Sr.; A.B. Villanova U., 1971, M.S., 1976; m. Claire Diane Advokat, July 8, 1978. Research scientist N.Y. State Research Inst. Neurochemistry and Drug Addiction, Ward's Island, 1973-74, research scientist dept. pharmacology, 1974-76; research asso. pharmacology Chgo. Med. Sch., 1976—. Sigma Xi grantee, 1977-78. Mem. Am., Eastern psychol. assns., AAAS, N.Y. Acad. Sci., Mid-Atlantic Acetyl-Choline Discussion Group. Roman Catholic. Club: K.C. Contbr. numerous articles in field to profl. jours., chpts. to textbooks; author 13 abstracts. Home: 1471 Brown St Apt 1 Des Plaines IL 60016 Office: 2020 W Ogden Ave Dept Pharmacology Chgo Med Sch Chicago IL 60612

COMBRINK, DAVID O., JR., agrl. assn. stockman; b. Hazelton, Kans., Oct. 21, 1919; s. David Oscar and Bertha Lucy (Smith) C.; student Ark. City Jr. Coll., 1938; m. Wilma Jewel Emmele, July 1, 1941; children—Carmen (Mrs. James K. Stoneking), Dennis David. Farmer wheat, cattle and sheep, Kiowa, Kans., 1946—; pres. Farmers Coop. Bus. Assn., 1965—, also dir. Mem. adv. com. Union Equity Coop. Exchange, Enid, Okla., 1971-76; mem. ASCS com. U.S. Dept. Agr., 1963-72. Mem. Barber County Planning Bd., 1969—, Fire Dist. Bd., 1968-69, Water Dist. No. 2 Bd., 1969-75. Served with USAAF, 1943-45; ETO. Mem. Farm Bur. Fedn., Kans. Wheat Growers Assn. Methodist. Mason. Home: Rural Route 1 Kiowa KS 67070 Office: Highway k-14 Hazelton KS 67061

COMBS, DOROTHY JENKINS, singer, civic worker; b. Aulander, N.C., Sept. 9, 1931; d. Abram Jackson and Katie (Ward) Jenkins; A.B in Edn., Duke U., 1953; M.S. in Psychology, Winona State U., 1975-76; m. Joseph John Combs, Jr., June 26, 1953; children—Dorothy Wrenn, Joseph John, III, Jennifer Jenkins. Tchr., E.K. Powe Sch., Durham, N.C., 1953-54, Child Centered Sch., Durham, 1954-55, Lakewood Elementary Sch., Durham, 1955-56, Child Centered Sch., 1956-57; substitute tchr. pub. schs., Chesterfield, Mo., 1964-67, Rochester, Minn., 1968-72; soprano soloist with Duke Men's Glee Club, 1951-52; soprano soloist with various civic chorales and ch. choirs in N.C., 1940-58, Colo., 1958-61, Tex., 1962-64, Mo., 1964-67, Minn., 1967—; appeared as soprano soloist Sta. KTTC-TV, Rochester, Minn., 1969, Sta. WCCO-TV, Mpls., 1969; debut in opera as Despina in Cosi Fan Tutte, Rochester Symphony, 1969; leading role in Kiss Me, Kate, Rochester, 1975; appeared in Shakespeare's The Hollow Crown, 1975; producer organizer music festival, Rochester, 1969; youth counselor Christ United Meth. Ch., Rochester, 1970-75, pres. chancel choir, 1975-76; mem. Bi-Centennial Com. for Rochester and Olmsted County, Minn., 1975-76, producer dir. interpretation of Godspell, 1975; mem. adv. bd. Zumbro Valley Mental Health Center, 1977—; asso. Selection Research, Inc., Lincoln, Nebr., 1977—; coordinator certified programs Program Dynamics, Inc., Mpls., 1977—; bd. dirs. Rochester Area Student Housing, 1974-76. Mem. Am. Personnel and Guidance Assn. Address 1103 7th St SW Rochester MN 55901

COMBS, JUDITH ZITELMAN, clin. psychologist; b. Appleton, Wis., Oct. 19, 1939; d. George Edward and Laura Elizabeth (Boldt) Zitelman; B.S., Carroll Coll., 1961; M.A., Bradley U., 1962; m. William Robert Combs, Feb. 1, 1964; children—W. Bradford, Susan Lynn. Intern psychology Peoria (Ill.) State Hosp., 1962-63, staff psychologist, 1963-66; clin. psychologist St. Vincents Hosp., Jax, Fla., 1971-73, Inst. Phys. Medicine and Rehab., Peoria, Ill., 1976—; supr. psychology dept., 1977—. Mem. Am. Psychol. Assn. (asso.), Peoria Area Assn. Psychologists, Ill. Psychol. Assn., Ill. Assn. Psychologists in Rehab., Ill. Valley Mental Health Assn. (dir. 1976—, pres. 1977-78). Home: 507 Sunset Way East Peoria IL 61611 Office: 619 NE Glen Oak Ave Peoria IL 61603 also 2900 N Knoxville Ave Peoria IL 61603

COMER, JAMES MICHAEL, educator; b. Cin., Aug. 3, 1941; s. Wallace George and Mary Elizabeth (Fitzmaurice) C.; A.B., U. Cin., 1963, M.B.A., 1965; Ph.D. (Ednl. fellow), Northwestern U., 1971; m. Dorie J. Jusk, Apr. 18, 1970; children—Kevin Fitzmaurice, Melissa Ann. Sales rep. market research E.I. duPont de Nemours & Co., Wilmington, Del., 1965-66; asst. prof. DePaul U., Chgo., 1969-74, asso. prof. mktg., 1974—, chmn. dept., 1974-77. Office Sci. and Info. Systems research grantee, 1975. Mem. Am. Inst. Decision Scis., Am. Mktg. Assn., Sales and Mktg. Execs. (v.p. 1974—), Inst. Mgmt. Scis. Office: 25 E Jackson Blvd Chicago IL 60604

COMMENATOR, RALPH WILLIAM, banker; b. Rudyard, Mich., Apr. 13, 1922; s. George Henry and Irene M. (O'Connell) C.; B.A., Mich. State U., 1950; m. Rita E. Rickey, Sept. 16, 1943; children—Patricia, W. Rickey, Catherine, Marianne, Karen, Ralph. With Mich. Banking Dept., 1950-61; v.p. Citizens State Bank, Ontonagon, Mich., 1961-63; br. mgr., v.p. First Comml. Savs. Bank, Constantine, 1963-67; v.p. Thompson Savs. Bank, Hudson, 1967-68, exec. v.p., dir., 1968-71; exec. v.p., cashier Iron River Nat. Bank, 1972—, also dir. Bd. dirs. Hannon-Colvin Am. Legion Post 180 Home Found. Served with AUS, 1943-46. Mem. Am. Legion, Hudson Area C. of C. (pres. 1970). K.C., Lion (charter pres.). Home: 430 Maple St Iron River MI 49935 Office: Iron River Nat Bank Iron River MI 49935

COMPTON, JAMES KELLEY, charitable fund exec.; b. Winfield, Kans., Oct. 26, 1935; s. Donald C. and Gladys F. (Gardenhire) C.; B.S., Kans. State Coll., 1960; m. Karen L. Wohlschlegel, Oct. 30, 1939; children—Kim Allen, Kari Ann. Dept. head C.R. Calvert Co., Inc., dept. store, Winfield, 1959-60, store mgr., Harper, 1960-62; dist. rep. Blue Cross Blue Shield, Hutchinson, Kans., 1962-68, profl. relations rep., Topeka, 1968-70; exec. dir. United Way of Reno County, Hutchinson, 1970—; asst. mgr. Hutchinson C. of C., 1970—; exec. dir. Combined Fed. Campaign of Reno County, 1970—. Mem. Mayor's Com. on Police and Fire Protection, 1974; mem. Hutchinson Human Relations Commn., 1974-75; mem. Gov.'s Com. on Manpower Devel., 1975—; mem. Hutchinson Sch. Bd. Com. on Bldg. Needs, 1976, Kans. Citizens Adv. Group for Social and Rehab. Services, 1977. Served with USNR, 1954-56; mem. Res. Home: 1820 N Main St Hutchinson KS 67501 Office: 15 E 2d St Hutchinson KS 67501

COMPTON, TED ARTHUR, pub. relations cons., writer; b. Indpls., May 14, 1938; s. Russell Leist and Marjorie Ellenor (Maas) C.; B.A., Carleton Coll., 1959; m. Christine Anne Schroeder, July 1, 1961; children—Lynn Elizabeth, Glenn Russell. Tech. writer Western Electric Co., Inc., Winston-Salem, N.C., 1959-60, advt. and mktg. writer, N.Y.C., 1960-61, mktg. coordinator, 1962-65, pub. relations supr., Atlanta, 1965-67, pub. relations mgr., Cicero, Ill., 1967-69, film and graphics mgr., Chgo., 1969-74; pres. Compton Communications, Oak Brook, Ill., 1974—; columnist Back Stage, 1976—; juror Chgo. Internat. Film Festival, 1970-77, U.S. TV Commls. Festival, 1974—; juror U.S. Film Festival, 1971—, bd. advisors, 1976—; bd. dirs. Midwest Seminar on Videotape and Film, 1975—. Recipient Silver Screen award U.S. Indsl. Film Festival, 1975. Mem. Pub. Relations Soc. Am. (accredited), Asso. Bus. Writers Am., Chgo. Film Council (dir. 1975-76, program chmn. 1977—), Info. Film Producers Am., Chgo. Unltd., Oak Brook Assn. Commerce and Industry. Served with AUS, 1961-62. Home: 112 N Washington St Hinsdale IL 60521 Office: 800 Enterprise Dr Oak Brook IL 60521

COMSTOCK, JOHN WILLIAM, county ofcl.; b. Grygla, Minn., Mar. 22, 1923; s. William and Rosamond Mary (Warner) C.; B.S., Mich. State U., 1951, M.S., 1967; m. June Marie Rigby, Sept. 30, 1944; children—Sharon (Mrs. Richard VanLoocke), Christine (Mrs. Robert Schaedler), Deborah. Vocational agrl. instr. Reading (Mich.) High Sch., 1951-54; tchr. Mich. Co-op. Extension Service, 4-H, Hillsdale County, Mich., 1954-57, 4-H youth agt. agr., Lenawee County, Mich., 1957-60, extension dir. Lenawee County, Adrian, Mich., 1960-75, Washtenaw County, Ann Arbor, Mich., 1975—. Sec., Twp. Zoning Bd., 1969—; pres. Non-Profit Housing Corp., 1973—. Served with AUS, 1942-45; PTO. Recipient Presdl. citation, Mich. Assn. County Agrl. Agts., 1963, Distinguished Service award Nat. Assn. County Agrl. Agts., 1973. Kellogg Found. fellow, 1973-74. Mem. Nat., Mich. (state dir. 1973-76) assns. county agrl. agts., Am. Soc. Animal Sci. Mason, Kiwanian. Home: 2525 Ogden Hwy Adrian MI 49221 Office: PO Box 8645 Ann Arbor MI 48107

CONANT, ROBERT SCOTT, harpsichordist, educator; b. Passaic, N.J., Jan. 6, 1928; s. Frederick B. and Bessie (Scott) C.; B.A., Yale, 1949, Mus.M., 1956; m. Nancy Lydia Jackson, Oct. 10, 1959; children—Elizabeth Scott, Andrew Frederick. Concert harpsichordist N.Y. Town Hall recital debut, 1953; ann. tours as recitalist, chamber music player U.S., Europe, 1956—; appeared with Pitts. Symphony, 1961; soloist Casals Festival, 1963; lectr., performer numerous colls., univs.; asst. prof., curator Yale Collection Mus. Instruments Sch. Music Yale, 1961-66, fellow Silliman Coll., 1961-66, asso. fellow, 1966-71; asso prof. music history and harpsichord Chgo. Mus. Coll., Roosevelt U., 1967-71, prof., 1971—. Founder, pres. Festival of Baroque Music, Greenfield Center, N.Y. Served with AUS, 1951-53. Mem. Coll. Music Soc. (treas. 1971-74). Recorded for Decca, Columbia, RCA Victor. Contbr. articles to profl. jours. Home: 154 Maple St Wilmette IL 60091 Office: 430 S Michigan Ave Chicago IL 60605 also Wilton Rd Greenfield Center NY 12833

CONCANNON, DONALD OWEN, lawyer; b. Garden City, Kans., Oct. 28, 1927; s. Hugh and Margaret (McKinley) C.; A.A., Garden City Jr. Coll., 1948; A.B., J.D., Washburn U., 1952; m. Patricia June Davis, Nov. 23, 1952; children—Chris Owen, Debra Lynne, Craig Alan. Admitted to Kans. bar, 1952; individual practice law, Hugoton, Kans., 1952—; sec.-treas. Spikes, Inc., Hugoton, 1958-74; pres. Fortune Ins. Co., Inc., 1972-74, chmn., 1974—; county atty. Stevens County, Kans., 1953-57; city atty., Satanta, Kans., 1956-62; dir. 1st Nat. Bank Attica. State chmn. Republican party, 1968-70; chmn. Kans. Presidential Electors, 1960. Mem. Am., Kans., SW Kans. bar assns., Hugoton C. of C. (man of yr., 1971). Club: Masons. Home: 129 N Jackson St Hugoton KS 67951 Office: 120 W 6th Hugoton KS 67951

CONCANNON, MICHAEL DENNIS, elec. engr.; b. Cook County, Ill., June 21, 1941; s. Milton H. and Jean (Pauly) C.; student U. Ill., 1959; B.S. in E.E., Western Mich. U., 1969; m. Suzanne K. Pearson, Feb. 10, 1962; children—David Michael, Cynthia Ann. Project engr. Johnson Corp., Three Rivers, Mich., 1967—. Served with USAF, 1961-65. Richard and Hilda Rosenthal scholar, 1965. Mem. IEEE, Fluid Controls Inst. Club: Elks. Home: Route 1 Box 81B Three Rivers MI 49093 Office: 805 Wood St Three Rivers MI 49093

CONDO, WILLARD JOHN, provincial govt. ofcl.; b. Moline, Ill., Oct. 29, 1913; s. John Adam and Grace (Stafford) C.; B.A., Augustana Coll., 1934; grad. staff course Royal Mil. Coll., 1945; LL.D., U. Man., 1975; m. Patricia Gordon Collard, Nov. 11, 1944; children—Richard Stafford, Rosemary (dec.). Asst. sec.-treas. Seversky Aircraft Corp., 1934-36; export dept. Tex. Co., 1936-39; jr. officer Gt. West Life Assurance Co., 1947-52; asst. comptroller U. Man., Winnipeg, Can., 1952-54, comptroller, 1954-60, comptroller, v.p. adminstrn., 1960-74; chmn. Univ. Grants Commn., Province of Man., 1975—. Vice chmn. Man. Health Services Commn., 1962—; mem. adv. bd. Royal Winnipeg Ballet, 1960. Served to capt. Canadian Army, 1940-47. Chartered Inst. Secs. fellow, 1963. Recipient Centennial medal Govt. Can., 1967; Man. Good Citizenship award, 1971; Outstanding Alumni award Augustana Coll., 1973. Mem. Inst. Pub. Adminstrn., Canadian Assn. U. Bus. Officers (pres. 1959-60), U. Man. Alumni Assn. (hon. life), Alpha Delta, Alpha Psi Omega, Omicron Kappa Upsilon. Clubs: Manitoba, Canadian (Winnipeg). Home: 202 Lamont Blvd Winnipeg MB R3P 0E9 Canada Office: 11-395 Berry St Winnipeg R3J 1N6 MB Canada

CONDON, GAYLE DEAN, wholesale trade exec.; b. nr. Hampton, Nebr., Feb. 26, 1919; s. Walter S. and Emma E. (Kaeding) C.; student U. Nebr., 1938-41; m. Vivian Splain, June 1, 1941; children—Carolyn Gail (Mrs. Walden), William Dean. Mechanic, Chris Beck Tire & Rubber Co., Lincoln, Nebr., 1945-48; pres., owner Condon Auto Electric Co., Lincoln, 1949—. Cons. J.C. Distbg. Co. Served with USAAF, 1942-45. Decorated Bronze Star medal. Mem. United Automobile Assn., Automotive Electric Assn., United Comml. Travelers, Woodmen of the World, V.F.W., Am. Legion. Lutheran. Mason (32 deg., Shriner). Home: 4520 Vandorn St Lincoln NE 68506 Office: 1821 N St Lincoln NE 68508

CONDON, RICHARD FRANCIS, banker; b. Chgo., July 5, 1929; s. Joseph F. and Myrtle (Kunau) C.; A.B., Loyola U., Chgo., 1949; J.D., John Marshall Law Sch., 1959; m. Evelyn Wickstrand, Oct. 20, 1962; 1 son, Thomas E. Tax accountant U.S. Gypsum Co., Chgo., 1953-56; pension cons. Marsh & McLennan, Inc., Chgo., 1956-62; asst. trust officer Crocker Nat. Bank. Los Angeles, 1962-65; trust officer, v.p. Chgo. City Bank & Trust Co., 1965-68, Naperville Nat. Bank & Trust Co. (Ill.), 1969—. Served with AUS, 1951-53. Mem. Cook County Corp. Fiduciaries Assn., Land Trust Council Ill., Midwest Pension Conf., Mensa, Phi Alpha Delta. Club: Cress Creek Country. Home: 915 Edgewater Dr Naperville IL 60540 Office: 136 S Washington St Naperville IL 60540

CONDON, ROBERT EDWARD, surgeon; b. Albany, N.Y., Aug. 13, 1929; s. Edward A. and Catherine (Kilmartin) C.; A.B., U. Rochester, 1951, M.D. (N.Y. Bd. Regents scholar), 1957; M.S., U. Wash., 1965; m. Marcia Jane Pagano, June 16, 1951; children—Sean Edward, Brian Robert. Intern King Co. Hosp., Seattle, 1957-58; resident dept. surgery U. Wash. Sch. Medicine and affiliated hosps., 1958-65; postdoctoral research fellow Nat. Heart Inst., 1961-63; asst. prof. surgery Baylor Coll. Medicine, Houston, 1965-67; asso. prof. surgery U. Ill. Coll. Medicine, Chgo., 1967-69, prof., 1969-70; prof. and head dept. surgery, U. Iowa Coll. Medicine, Iowa City, 1971-72; prof. surgery Med. Coll. Wis., Milw., 1972—; chief surgical service VA Hosp., Wood, Wis., 1972—; attending surgeon Milw. County Gen. Hosp., Columbia Hosp., 1972—; cons. Deaconess, St. Luke's, Luth., St. Joseph hosps., Milw. Served with USMCR, 1951-53. Recipient sr. class award as Outstanding Faculty Member Baylor U. Coll. Medicine, 1966, Excellence in Teaching award Phi Chi, 1967, Certificate of Appreciation U. Iowa Coll. Medicine, 1971, Tchr. of Year award Jr. Class U. Iowa Coll. Medicine, 1972; Guggenheim fellow, 1963-64. Diplomate Am. Bd. Surgery, Nat. Bd. Med. Examiners. Mem. A.C.S., AAAS, AMA, Am., Central, Western surg. assns., Wis., Chgo. surg. socs., Soc. U. Surgeons, Soc. Clin. Surgery, Med. Research Soc. (London), Royal Soc. Medicine, N.Y. Acad. Scis., Assn. Am. Med. Colls., Milw. Acad. Surgery, Assn. for Acad. Surgery. Author: (with others) Abdominal Pain: A Guide to Rapid Diagnosis, 1969, Manual of Surgical Therapeutics, 3d edit., 1975. Asso. editor Rev. of Surgery; editorial bd. Jour. Surg. Oncology, Archives of Surgery, Surgery. Home: 2300 E Kensington Blvd Milwaukee WI 53211 Office: 8700 W Wisconsin Ave Milwaukee WI 53226

CONFORTI, MICHAEL DOMINIC, JR., metal fabrication co. exec.; b. Torrington, Conn., Sept. 27, 1929; s. Michael Dominic and Elizabeth M. (Downey) C.; B.S. in Mech. Engring., U. Conn., 1952; m. Mary T. Stolicny, Feb. 26, 1949; children—Mary Beth (Mrs. David Hale), Donna (Mrs. David Moore), Michael Dominic III. Mech. engr. Torin Mfg. Co., Torrington, 1952-58, sales engr., 1958-60, regional tech. service mgr., Chgo., 1960-65; product mgr. Medart div. Jackes Evans Mfg. Co., St. Louis, 1965-67, gen. mgr., 1967-76, v.p., 1970-74, exec. v.p. Jackes Evans, 1974-76; pres. Medart, Inc., Rosemont, Ill., 1976-77; pres. Hydro Air Engring., Inc., St. Louis, 1977—. Served with AUS, 1946-48. Mem. ASME, Am. Soc. Heating, Refrigeration and Air Conditioning Engrs., Sons of Italy (pres. 1960-61). Home: 686 Applewood St Kirkwood MO 63122 Office: 9701 Higgins Rd Rosemont IL 60018

CONGER, DUANE HENRY, hydrologist; b. Oxford, Wis., Feb. 5, 1930; s. Henry Fern and Lena Emma (Groskreutz) C.; B.S. in Civil Engring., U. Wis., 1954; m. Joanne Rose Anderzon, Aug. 26, 1967; 1 son, Dennis Duane. Hydraulic engr. U.S. Geol. Survey, Madison, Wis., 1954, 1956—. Served with USAF, 1954-56. Registered profl. engr. Wis., Fellow Am. Soc. Civil Engrs. Home: 4321 Herrick Ln Madison WI 54711 Office: 1815 University Ave Madison WI 53706

CONGER, IVAN ALBERT, periodical publisher, editor; b. Owosso, Mich., Aug. 7, 1929; s. Frank Lybrock and Hattie Evelyn (Barker) C.; grad. high sch.; m. Dorothy Esther Stanton, June 27, 1953; 1 dau., Dianne Kaye. Clk. typist Ann Arbor R.R., 1946-49; operator pasting machine Electric Auto-Lite (now Globe-Union, Inc.), battery mfg., Owosso, 1949—; pres. Shiawassee County (Mich.) Hist. Soc., Durand, 1966-69, dir., 1965-69, dir. ex officio, 1969—, editor Shiawassee Gazette, 1967-77; pub. editor The Curwood Collector, Owosso, 1972—. Asst. scoutmaster, treas. Boy Scouts Am., 1959-71. Served with AUS, 1951-52. Recipient Good Citizen award Ford Motor Co., 1966. Mem. Shiawassee County Geneal. Soc., Hist. Soc. Mich., Mich. Mus. Assn., Shiawassee Arts Council, Shiawassee River Assn., V.F.W., Lincoln Soc. Philately. Methodist. Address: 1825 Osaukie Rd Owosso MI 48867

CONGLETON, ROBERT CURTIS, indsl. relations exec.; b. Terre Haute, Ind., July 23, 1920; s. George Curtis and Bertha Mae (Walker) C.; B.S. in Edn. and Biology, Ind. State U., 1947; M.S. in Indsl. Psychology, Purdue U., 1949; postgrad. clin. psychology U. Ill., 1954-56; m. Barbara Lee Hunt, Mar. 7, 1942; children—Karen (Mrs. Kenneth Williams), Greg, Cynthia. Psychol. counselor, prof. psychology various univs., 1947-57; sect. engr. manpower Gulf States Paper Corp., Tuscaloosa, Ala., 1957-60, head manpower, 1961-64, personnel dir. subsidiary E-Z Packaging Co., Maplesville, Ala., 1960-61; asst. corporate mgr. indsl. relations St. Joe Paper Co., Port St. Joe, Fla., 1964-66; dir. indsl. relations AVCO Aerostructures, Nashville, 1966-69; dir. indsl. relations indsl. chem. div. PPG Industries, Inc., Barberton, Ohio, 1969—. Mem. Employers Assn. Summit County, Am. Psychol. Assn., Profl. Speakers Assn., Bur. Nat.

Affairs, Am. Mgmt. Assn., Barberton Area C. of C., Phi Delta Kappa, Beta Beta Beta. Home: 493 Farr Ave Wadsworth OH 44281 Office: PO Box 31 Barberton OH 44203

CONGREVE, WILLARD JOHN, supt. schs.; b. Chgo., Aug. 16, 1921; s. Willard and Anna M. (Johannsen) C.; Ed.B., Chgo. Tchrs. Coll., 1942; Mus.M., Northwestern U., 1947; Ph.D., U. Chgo., 1957; m. Beth Olsen, June 6, 1950; children—Judith Ann, Linda Sue. Asst. prof. music Midland Luth. Coll., Fremont, Nebr., 1947-49; tchr. music Chgo. Pub. High Schs., 1949-58, prin. Foster and Von Humboldt Elementary Schs., 1958-60; prin. U. Lab. High Sch., U. Chgo., 1960-69, asso. prof. edn., 1960-69; supt. Newton (Iowa) community schs., 1969-72, Washington Twp. (N.J.) pub. schs., 1972-75; supt. schs., City of Hammond, Ind., 1975—. Chmn. Red Cross Youth, Chgo., 1961-64; bd. dirs. Lake Area United Way, Jr. Achievement Served with USAAF, 1943-45, U.S. Army, 1951-52. Decorated Bronze Star. Mem. Am. Assn. of Sch. Adminstrs., Nat. Sch. Bds. Assn., Phi Delta Kappa, Phi Mu Alpha. Presbyterian. Contbr. numerous articles on edn. to profl. jours. Home: 2050 171st St Hammond IN 46323 Office: 5935 Hohman St Hammond IN 46320

CONKLIN, JEAN D., hosp. adminstr.; b. Mpls., Jan. 28, 1913; d. Earl R. and Hazel (Davis) Conklin; grad. Meth. Kahler Sch. Nursing, 1940; B.S., U. Minn., 1948, M.H.A., 1951. Gen. duty nurse Worrall Hosp., Rochester, Minn., 1940, Sartori Hosp., Cedar Falls, Iowa, 1940-41; pediatric supr. Gillette Children's Hosp., St. Paul, 1941-42, relief supervisory nurse, dir. nursing, 1946, pediatric instr., 1948-49, hosp. adminstr., 1949-77, cons. to bd., 1977—; pres. Upper Midwest Hosp. Conf., 1963-64; adv. mem. Gov.'s Commn. on Handicapped; bd. dirs., mem. exec. com., mem. rehab. services com. Minn. Soc. Crippled Children and Adults. Recipient Citizen of Year award Greater St. Paul Area Council Employment of Handicapped. Mem. Minn. Hosp. Assn. (pres. 1957), Am. Coll. Hosp. Adminstrs., Quota Internat., Nat. Assn. Children's Hosps. and Related Instns. Home: 1455 Salem Church Rd Bldg 1465 Apt 203 Inver Grove Heights MN 55075 Address: Gillette Children's Hosp 200 E University Ave St Paul MN 55101

CONKLIN, RICHARD LOUIS, educator; b. Rockford, Ill., Dec. 9, 1923; s. Paul Stanley and Edna Aline (Bartholomew) C.; m. Barbara Hahn, Aug. 6, 1950; children—Nancy, Bonnie, Paul, Scott. B.S., U. Ill., 1944, M.S., 1949; Ph.D., Colo. U., 1957. Jr. scientist Los Alamos Sci. La., 1944-46; asst. prof. Huron (S.D.) Coll., 1949-53; instr. Colo. U., Boulder, 1953-57; asso. prof. Hanover (Ind.) Coll., 1957-58, prof., 1958—; NSF faculty fellow U. Hawaii, Honolulu, 1967-68. Fellow Ind. Acad. Sci.; mem. Am. Assn. Physics Tchrs. (pres. Ind. sect. 1966), Ind. Acad. Sci. (program chmn. 1969, chmn. physics sect. 1969, 75), Am. Phys. Soc., AAAS, Sigma Xi, Tau Beta Pi, Sigma Tau, Sigma Pi Sigma. Recipient Distinguished Teaching award Hanover Coll., 1973. Home: PO Box 24 Hanover IN 47243 Office: Hanover Coll Hanover IN 47243

CONLEE, JAMES KENT, corp. exec.; b. White Hall, Ill., Jan. 2, 1934; s. Thomas Harrison and Gussie (DeHart) C.; B.S., Western Ill. U., 1956; postgrad. in organic chemistry Washington U., St. Louis, 1956-57; m. Joan Cardwell, June 28, 1953; children—Teresa, Mark, Michael, Andrew, John. Research chemist Alton Box Board Co. (Ill.), 1956-58, Universal Match Corp., Ferguson, Mo., 1958-61; process engr. and project mgr. Union Starch & Refining Co., Granite City, Ill., 1961-66; chief engr. milling div. Cargill, Inc. and Corn Starch & Syrup Co., Cedar Rapids, Iowa and Dayton, Ohio, 1966-73; pres., dir. Modern Process Design, Inc., Dayton, 1973—; v.p., dir. NEMCO, S.A. (Mexico City). Registered profl. engr., Ohio. Mem. Nat., Ohio socs. profl. engrs., Order of Engrs., Am. Assn. Oil Chemists, Dayton Engrs., Full Gospel Businessmen's Fellowship Internat. Mem. Ch. of God. Developed new methods for producing corn syrups and starches. Home: 6437 Westford Rd Dayton OH 45426 Office: 4977 Northcutt Pl PO Box 1400E Dayton OH 45414

CONLEY, FAY OLIVER, cons. engr.; b. Hastings, Mich., Mar. 28, 1889; s. George and Catherine (Troyer) C.; student Detroit Inst. Tech., 1917-18; m. Pauline Oulette, Mar. 20, 1948. Owner, F. Conley Co., cons. engrs. in plastics and pressure castings to automotive industry, Detroit, 1919-57; cons. engr. Active Boys Club Detroit, 1939—. Decorated knight Sovereign Mil. Order Temple Jerusalem; knight comdr. Internat. Constantinian Order; recipient Distinguished Service award Automotive Old Timers, 1964. Fellow Augustan Soc. (life mem.); mem. Order Crown Charlemagne (life), Baronial Order Magna Charta (life), Mil. Order Crusaders (life), Descs. Knights Garter Eng. (life), Soc. Mayflower Descs. (life), Alden Kindred Am. (life), United Indian War Vets., Huguenot Soc. Mich., Ams. Amorial Ancestry, New Eng. Historic Geneal. Soc., Soc. Plastics Engineers (founder 1942, also the 1st pres., life mem., mem. past pres.'s adv. bd.; recipient distinguished mem. award), Engrs. Soc. Detroit, Soc. Plastic Pioneers, Automotive Old Timers (life), Am. Soc. Metals, Iron and Steel Inst., S.A.R. (bd. mgrs. Mich. soc.), S.R., Sons Union Vets. Civil War (commandery-in-chief), Nat. Soc. Sons Spanish-Am. War Vets., Scotch-Irish Soc. U.S.A., Sons and Daus. of Pilgrims, Nat., Ohio geneal. socs., Scotish Genealogy Society of Edinburgh, Scotland. Elk. Clubs: Aztec of 1847; Detroit Yacht. Designer, developer plastic radio cabinet, 1932, automobile inside sun visor, 1916, automobile cowl ventilator, 1916, numerous other plastic items. Address: 4869 Ridgewood St Route 2 Richland MI 49083

CONLEY, JAMES EDWARD, surgeon; b. Harrisville, R.I., Aug. 10, 1913; s. Edward James and Emily Rachel (Davies) C.; B.S. cum laude, Providence Coll., 1935; M.D. cum laude, Harvard, 1939; m. Lillian Brandt Quirk, Sept. 16, 1941; children—Emily, James, Robert, Bruce, Ellen, William, Katherine. Intern, resident Mass. Gen. Hosp., Boston, 1939-43; practice gen. and vascular surgery, Milw., 1946—; mem. staff Columbia, Milw. Children's, County Gen. hosps., Milw. Prof. surgery Med. Coll. Wis., 1946—. Pres., Quirk Found., 1968—; v.p. Florentine Opera Assn., 1971. Served with USNR, 1943-46. Decorated Bronze Star (2). Diplomate Am. Bd. Surgery. Fellow A.C.S.; mem. Internat. Cardiovascular Soc., Soc. Vascular Surgery, Midwestern Vascular Surgery Soc. (founder mem.), Central Surg. Assn., Milw. Surg. Soc. (pres. 1966-67), Milw. Acad. Medicine (pres. 1959-60), Royal Soc. Medicine. Club: University Milwaukee. Recipient Distinguished Service award Am. Cancer Soc., 1966. Mem. edit. adv. bd. Cancer Bull. Cancer Program, 1957-62. Contbr. articles to profl. jours. Home: 1406 E Fox Ln Milwaukee WI 53217 Office: 425 E Wisconsin Ave Milwaukee WI 53202

CONLIN, JAMES CLYDE, real estate broker; b. Ft. Dodge, Iowa, Aug. 12, 1940; s. Clyde Elwin and Evelyn (Olson) C.; student Wentworth Mil. Acad., 1959-61; m. Roxanne Elizabeth Barton, Mar. 21, 1964; children—Jacalyn Rae Alice, James Barton, Debra Ann. Agt., Cooper Realty Inc., Des Moines, 1966-68, Stanbrough Realty, Des Moines, 1968-72; pres. Mid-Iowa Equities, Inc., Des Moines, 1971—; sales mgr. Iowa Realty, Des Moines, 1972—; owner Gen. Services Co., Des Moines, 1973—; pres. Mid-Iowa Mgmt. Co. Mem. Nat. Assn. Realtors, Nat. Inst. Real Estate Brokers, C. of C. Home: 6116 SW 48th Ave Des Moines IA 50315 Office: Iowa Realty 5661 Fleur Dr Des Moines IA 50321

CONLON, JAMES RUSSELL, JR., optometrist; b. Oak Park, Ill., July 5, 1927; s. James R. and Marie A. (Sweeney) C.; D.Optometry, Monroe Coll. Optometry, 1948. Practice optometry specializing in contact lenses, Lombard, Ill., 1948-50, Chgo., 1952-68, St. Charles, Ill., 1968—. Contact lens cons. Precision Cosmet Co., Mpls., 1958-60, Allergan Pharms., Los Angeles, 1960-61, Mueller-Welt Co., Chgo., 1964-69, Contact Lens Clinic, Ill. Coll. Optometry, Chgo., 1971—; lectr. in field. Bd. dirs. Nat. Eye Research Found., Chgo. Served with USNR, 1944-46, 50-52. Fellow Nat. Eye Research Found., Am. Acad. Optometry (diplomate contact lens sect.); mem. Am. Optometric Assn., Ill., Fox Valley optometric socs., Internat. Contact Lens Soc. London, St. Charles C. of C. Roman Catholic. Elk. Clubs: Antique Auto, Classic Car, Mercedes Benz U.S. and Internat., Four Cylinder, Sports Car. Contbr. to profl. publs. in field. Co-designer bifocal contact lenses. Address: 115 S 2d St St Charles IL 60174

CONLON, JEROME WILLARD, ry. co. exec.; b. Denver, Oct. 2, 1939; s. John Willard and Elizabeth Agnes (Fisher) C.; A.A., Springfield Jr. Coll., 1960; B.B.A., Loyola U., 1962, J.D., 1965; m. Josephine Charlene Giuliano, June 20, 1964; children—Catherine, Elizabeth, Margaret. Admitted to Ill. bar, 1965; auditor Skoner & Skoner, Chgo., 1965; atty. George Wiesbard, Chgo., 1966-67; auditor taxes C. & N.W. Ry. Co., Chgo., 1968-69, asst. dir. taxation, 1969-70, dir. taxation, 1970-75, treas., 1975-76, v.p. pub. affairs, 1976—. Mem. Ry. Income Tax Accounting Conf. C.P.A., Ill. Mem. Ill. Bar Assn., Ill. C. of C., Nat. Assn. Ry. Commrs., Internat. Assn. Assessing Officers. Home: 3738 W Eddy St Chicago IL 60618 Office: 400 W Madison St Chicago IL 60606

CONLON, JOSEPH T., JR., lawyer, educator; A.B. in English magna cum laude, Notre Dame U., 1952; J.D., Harvard, 1957. Admitted to Mo. bar; asst. counsel subcom. Ho. of Reps., Washington, 1958-59; asso. firm Keefe, Schlafly, Griesedieck and Ferrell, St. Louis, 1959-60; law faculty U. Notre Dame, 1960-62; pros. atty. Lincoln County (Mo.), 1963-64; faculty bus. law U. Mo., St. Louis, 1965-66, asst. prof. bus. law, 1966-69; asso. prof. mgmt. scis. St. Louis U., 1971—. Served with AUS, 1953-55. Mem. Am., Mo., St. Louis bar assns., Am. Judicature Soc., Harvard Law Sch. Assn., C. of C. Clubs: Harvard of St. Louis, Notre Dame of St. Louis (dir.), Missouri Athletic, Press of St. Louis. Office: Sch Bus Adminstrn 3674 Lindell Blvd St Louis MO 63108

CONN, ARTHUR LEONARD, chem. engr., oil co. exec.; b. N.Y.C., Apr. 5, 1913; s. Nathan Avram and Jennie (Harmel) C.; S.B. in Chem. Engring., Mass. Inst. Tech., 1934, S.M. (Thorp fellow 1935), 1935; postgrad. Inst. Mgmt. Northwestern U., 1959; m. Bernice Robbins, Sept. 2, 1937 (dec. May 1970); children—Robert Harmel, Elizabeth (Mrs. J. Geoffrey Magnus) Alex Paul; m. 2d, Irene Sekely Farkas, June 10, 1972. Asst. dir. Sch. Chem. Engring. Practice, Mass. Inst. Tech., Boston sta., 1935; asst. to dir. research Blaw-Knox Co., Pitts., 1936; chemist Alco products div. Am. Locomotive Co., Dunkirk, N.Y., 1936-39; with Standard Oil Co. (Ind.), 1939—, chem. engr., Whiting, Ind., 1939, group leader, 1943, sect leader, 1945, div. dir., 1950, supt. tech. service, 1959, dir. process devel. Amoco Oil Co. subsidiary, 1960, research coordinator, 1962-64, sr. cons. engr., 1964, dir. govt. contracts, 1967—. Cons., AEC, 1951-53, Office Coal Research, 1969—, ERDA; mem. indsl. adv. com. U. Ill. at Chgo., 1973—, adv. com. on coal research City U. N.Y., 1972—; mem. Nat. Research Coms. on Coal Liquefaction and Processing Coal Liquids. Fellow AAAS (dir. 1970-73), Am. Inst. Chem. Engrs. (chmn. nat. program com. 1965, dir. 1966-71, v.p. 1969, pres. 1970, Founders award); mem. Am. Chem. Soc., Am. Petroleum Inst., Tau Beta Pi. Contbr. articles to profl. jours. Patentee in field. Home: 1469 E Park Pl Chicago IL 60637 Office: Amoco Oil Co PO Box 400 Naperville IL 60540

CONNAUGHTON, JACK FLOYD, entertainment co. exec.; b. Waukesha, Wis., July 2, 1945; s. John Joseph and Marion Virginia (Dunbar) C.; B.A., U. Wis., LaCrosse, 1968; M.S., 1971; m. Georgeann S. Phillipps, Aug. 15, 1970; 1 dau., Stacey Lea. Profl. bowler, 1968-69; adminstrv. asst. U. Wis., LaCrosse, 1969-71, asst. dir. Cartwright Student Center, Milw., 1971-76; gen. mgr. Bowling Enterprises, Sheboygan, Wis., 1976—; dir. Dick Ritgers Profl. Bowlers Camp, 1977—. Elected to Hall of Fame Nat. Assn. Intercoll. Athletics, 1977; recipient Wis. Gov.'s award, 1968, award Assn. Coll. Unions, 1968, Bowler of Year award, Milw., 1975. Mem. Am. Bowling Congress, Bowling Proprietors Wis., Assn. Coll. Unions, Sheboygan C. of C., Delta Sigma Phi. Roman Catholic. Nat. collegiate bowling champion, 1967, 68; winner World Cup, Paris, 1967. Home: 3920 15th St S Sheboygan WI 53081 Office: 2022 North Ave Sheboygan WI 53081

CONNAUGHTON, PETER JAMES, physician, surgeon; b. Chgo., Jan. 29, 1932; s. James and Mary (Gavin) C.; M.S., Northwestern U., 1960; M.D., Loyola U. Stritch Sch. Medicine, 1955; m. Jeannine Cunningham, Aug. 25, 1956; children—Peter J., William J., Jeannine M., Maureen B. Intern, Cook County Hosp., Chgo., 1955-56; resident gen. surgery Northwestern U., 1956, 59-61; attending surgeon Little Traverse Hosp., Petoskey, Mich., chief of surgery, 1965-72; bd. dirs. Burns Clinic, Petoskey, 1972-75, chmn. bd., pres., 1973-75. Served as capt. USAF, 1957-59. Diplomate Am. Bd. Surgery. Fellow A.C.S. (councillor Mich. chpt. 1974—); mem. Mich., Pan Am., No. Mich. (sec. 1965-68, v.p. 1969, pres. 1970) med. socs., AMA. Home: 630 Spencer St Petoskey MI 49770 Office: Burns Clinic Petoskey MI 49770

CONNELL, ROGER JOHN, mfg. co. exec.; b. Swampscott, Mass., July 4, 1914; student Boston U., 1933-38; J.D., Northeastern U., 1939; m. Mary Bonner Pearson, Oct. 11, 1944; children—Elizabeth Jane, Susan Ellen, Mary Bonner, Roger John. Partner, Connac Products Co., Saugus, Mass., 1949-51; specialist govt. contracts to mgr. large jet engines contract adminstrn. Aircraft Engine Group, Gen. Electric Co., Evendale, Ohio, 1951-77; cons. govt. contracts to def. oriented industries, 1977—; lectr. in field. Chmn. Retirement Bd. City of Swampscott, 1938-39, selectman, 1946-50; active fund-raising Community Chest; mem. nat. adv. bd. Am. Security Council. Served to col. U.S. Army, 1939-45. Mem. Mil. Order World Wars, Res. Officers Assn., Ret. Officers Assn., Nat. Contract Mgmt. Assn., Delta Sigma Phi. Roman Catholic. Home: 399 W Galbraith Rd Apt 210 Cincinnati OH 45215

CONNELLAN, THOMAS KENNEDY, JR., business exec.; b. Wyandotte, Mich., June 15, 1942; s. Thomas Kennedy and Florence Irene (Rhea) C.; B.B.A., U. Mich., 1964, M.B.A., 1966, Ph.D., 1973; m. Sandra J. Sherlock, Dec. 27, 1969; 1 dau., Avis Murphy. Program dir., research asso. Bur. Indsl. Relations, Grad. Sch. Bus. Adminstrn., U. Mich., 1966, editorial dir., div. Mgmt. Edn., 1968-73; pres. The Mgmt. Group, Inc., Ann Arbor, Mich., 1973—; dir. Standard Realty Corp; cons. Hudson's Bay Co., Kellogg-Salada Co., Clark Equipment Co., Gould Inc., Ford Co., Gen. Motors Corp., Jacobsen Mfg. Co., Piper Aircraft Co., Honeywell Ltd. Bd. dirs. Inst. for Behavior Change. Served with U.S. Army, 1966-68. Mem. Acad. of Mgmt., Am. Soc. Tng. and Devel. Author: The Brontosaurus Principle: A Manual for Corporate Survival, 1976. Office: 3125 Geddes Ave Ann Arbor MI 48104

CONNELLY, BRIAN ROBERT, advt. exec.; b. Evanston, Ill., Aug. 17, 1935; s. Will Henry and Jane (Kaye) C.; student Mich. State U., 1953-58; m. Janet Lou Harris, Nov. 23, 1958; children—Patrick, Michael, Kelly. Announcer various radio-tv stas., Mich., 1954-60; v.p. Connelly Co., Ann Arbor, 1960-65; pres. Brian Connelly Advt., Inc., Ann Arbor, 1965—. Chmn., Mich. Republican State Central Campaign Com., 1969-72; mem. City Council Ann Arbor, 1967-69. Served with AUS, 1958-59. Recipient Silver Elephant award Ann Arbor Rep. party, 1969; Outstanding Young Man of Ann Arbor award, 1971. Mem. Ann Arbor C. of C. (dir.), Pi Kappa Phi. Episcopalian. Club: Civitan Internat. (dist. gov. 1970-71, internat. v.p. 1972-74, internat. pres.-elect 1977-78, Honor Key Ann Arbor club 1970, Mich. dist. club 1971, internat. club 1973). Home and office: 500 Parklake Ave Ann Arbor MI 48103

CONNELLY, JOHN PETER, physician, educator; b. Boston, May 12, 1926; s. Thomas J. and Bridget (Finnigan) C.; B.S., Boston Coll., 1951; M.D., Georgetown U., 1955; m. Martha T. Cronin, June 24, 1950; children—Maureen, Martha, Eileen, Marie, Cathleen, John, Michael. Intern, Royal Victoria Hosp., Montreal, Que., Can., 1955-56; jr. resident children's service Mass. Gen. Hosp., Boston, 1956-57, asst. resident, 1957-58, chief resident, 1964-68, co-dir., 1968-73, chief pediatric resident Mass. Gen. Hosp., sr. resident in pediatrics Johns Hopkins Hosp., Balt., 1957-58; practice medicine, specializing in pediatrics, Boston, 1958-73; asst. pediatrician children's service Mass. Gen. Hosp., Boston, 1962-64, chief children's ambulatory clinic, 1963-64, chief ambulatory div., 1964-69, pediatrician, 1967-73, med. dir. pediatric nurse practitioner program, 1964-73, exec. dir. Bunker Hill Health Center, 1967-73; vis. physician Lying-In div. Boston Hosp. for Women, 1961-69, cons. maternal and child health, 1968-69; teaching fellow pediatrics Harvard, 1957-58, 61-62, instr., 1962-64, asso. in pediatrics, 1964-67, asst. clin. prof. pediatrics, 1967-69, asso. prof. pediatrics, 1969-73; chief pediatrics Foster McGaw Hosp., Loyola U., Maywood, Ill., 1972-76, prof., chmn. dept. pediatrics Loyola U. Stritch Sch. Medicine, Maywood, 1972-76; chmn. dept. health services devel. Am. Acad. Pediatrics, Evanston, Ill., 1976—; dep. asst. commr. health City of Boston, 1969-73; cons. Boston Children's Service Assn., 1966-73; cons. Nat. Center for Health Services Research and Devel., HEW, and Welfare, 1970-72; cons. Office Asst. Sec. Health and Sci. Affairs, HEW, 1971-73; civilian cons. pediatrics U.S. Naval Hosp., Chelsea, Mass. Dir. Mass. Dental Service Corp., 1971-73. Mem. Mass. Gov.'s Adv. Council, Comprehensive Health Planning Agy., 1971-73; mem. Harvard Center for Community Health and Med. Care, 1968-73; bd. dirs. Mass. Soc. Prevention Cruelty Children, 1967-73, Orphans of Italy, Inc., 1962-73; bd. dirs. Catholic Charitable Bur., Boston, 1968-70, cons., 1970-73; bd. adv. B.S. in Pediatrics program, U. Colo., Denver, 1969-70; mem. community resources com. Interinstl. Cardiovascular Center, Chgo., 1973-75; mem. Ill. Sudden Infant Death Syndrome Study Commn., 1975—. Served with AUS, 1944-45; to capt. M.C., USAF, 1958-61; capt. M.C., USNR ret. Decorated Knight Order of Malta. Diplomate Am. Bd. Pediatrics. Mem. Mass., Chgo. med. socs., New Eng., Chgo. pediatric socs., Am. Fedn. for Clin. Research, Am. Acad. Pediatrics (council on practice, chmn. liaison com. with Am. Nurses Assn. 1970-72), Assn. for Ambulatory Pediatric Services, Logan-Brophy Soc. Oral Surgery (hon.), Am., New Eng. diabetes assns., Royal Coll. Medicine (London), Irish and Am. Pediatric Soc. (sec.-treas. 1968-70, exec. council 1970—, pres. 1976-77), D.A.V., U.S. Naval Inst., Am. Legion, Alpha Omega Alpha. Clubs: Union Boat, Appalachian Mountain (Boston); Harvard; Chicago Athletic. Author: (with L. Berlow) You're Too Sweet—A Manual for Juvenile Diabetics, 1969; (with J.D. Stoeckle, R.M. Farrisey) The Nurse Clinician, 1974. Contbr. numerous articles in field to profl. jours., chpts. to books. Home: 147 Herrick Rd Riverside IL 60546 Office: 1801 Hinman Ave Evanston IL 60204

CONNELLY, RILEY WILLIAM, lawyer; b. Yankton, S.D., Oct. 1, 1926; s. Riley Cornelius and Florence Lucille (Thompson) C.; student Augustana Coll., 1946-47, N.D. State Coll., 1947-48; LL.B., Creighton U., 1952; m. Suzanne Marie Ament, Dec. 29, 1956; children—Todd R., Craig J., Cheryl Ann, JoAnne M. Admitted to S.D. bar, 1961; claims mgr. Security Gen. Ins. Co., Sioux Falls, S.D., 1955-62; partner Zimmer & Connelly, attys., Parker, S.D., 1962-67; prin. Riley W. Connelly, Atty., Parker, 1967—. Dep. states atty., Turner County, S.D., 1962-66, states atty., 1966-76; city atty., Parker, 1968-76; law trained magistrate 1st Circuit, 1976—. Bd. dirs. Problems in Living Center, 1972—, pres., 1975-76. Served with USAAF, 1945. Mem. S.D. Bar Assn., S.D. States Attys. Assn. (pres. 1976-77), S.D. Claims Assn. (pres. 1961-62), Delta Theta Phi. Republican. Lutheran. Mason (Shriner). Home: Box 337 Parker SD 57053 Office: Madsen Bldg Parker SD 57053

CONNELLY, THOMAS JOSEPH, lawyer; b. Kansas City, Mo., Jan. 31, 1940; s. Edward Joseph and Mary Costello (McCallum) C.; A.B., U. Detroit, 1963, J.D., 1970; m. Barbara Marciniak, Aug. 1, 1964; children—Catherine, Jennifer. Admitted to Mich. bar, 1970; individual practice law, Plymouth, Mich., 1970-74; partner firm Bulgarelli Allen and Connelly, Walled Lake, Mich., 1974—; prosecutor, city atty., Wixom, Mich., Milford (Mich.) Village and Twp., Wolverine Lake, Mich., 1974—. Pres. parish council St. Mary's Ch. Mem. Am. Judicature Soc., Am., Mich., Oakland County bar assns., Mich. Arabian Horse Assn., Blue Key Honor Fraternity. Republican. Home: 1635 Garner Rd Milford MI 48042 Office: 2410 S Commerce Rd Walled Lake MI 48088

CONNER, DONALD GENE, banker; b. Muncie, Ind., Aug. 7, 1936; s. Chalmer Amos and Alpha Mae (Corkwell) C.; student Bank Adminstrn. Inst., Am. Inst. Banking; m. Donna Sue Scott, Jan. 25, 1975; children—Bruce Allen, David Wayne. With Farmers State Bank, Mooreland, Ind., 1956-58; with Indsl. Trust & Savs. Bank, Muncie, Ind., 1958—, asst. cashier, 1962-65, auditor, 1965-76, comptroller, 1976—. Pres. bd. dirs. Children's Home, 1972—; bd. dirs. Yorktown (Ind.) Jr. Athletic Assn., 1972-73. Mem. Bank Adminstrn. Inst. (chartered bank auditor, pres. E. Central Ind. 1970-71), Inst, Internal Auditors (certified internal auditor, gov. Indpls. chpt. 1977-78), C. of C. Clubs: Lions (pres. Yorktown 1970-71, zone chmn. 1971-72), Elks. Home: 2 Buckingham Rd Yorktown IN 47396 Office: 117 E Adams St Muncie IN 47305

CONNER, E. DAVID, contract engring. co. exec.; b. N.Y.C., Aug. 15, 1934; s. Emerson D. and Melitta (Guske) C.; student N.Y. U., 1952-55, U. N.C. at Chapel Hill, 1957-58; m. Elizabeth Krell, July 9, 1956; children—Christopher, Lori, Lisa, Ann. With Vestal Modern Design Co. (N.Y.), 1955-72, sales mgr., 1962-65, dir., v.p., 1965-72; br. mgr. TAD Tech. Services Corp., Cambridge, Mass., 1972-74, div. mgr., v.p., Mt. Prospect, Ill., 1974—, pres. Alpha Tech. Services div. 1975—. Mem. Nat. Tech. Services Assn. (Pres.'s award Midwest chpt. 1976; dir. 1975—, pres. Midwest chpt. 1976), Psi Upsilon. Asst. scoutmaster Boy Scouts Am., various locations. Presbyterian. Home: 4 Linda Ln Streamwood IL 60103 Office: 800 W Central Rd Mt Prospect IL 60103

CONNER, JOHN ROBERT, metals co. exec.; b. Evansville, Ind., Oct. 5, 1924; s. George and Luella (Sandefur) C.; B.S. in Mech. Engring., U. Cin., 1948; m. Bettye J. Lashley, Apr. 17, 1949; children—Linda, Robert, Kevin. Purchasing engr. Servel, Inc., Evansville, 1948-51, div. mgr. plastics plant Cambridge Molded

Plastics Co., Richmond, Ind., 1951-57, purchasing engr., 1957-58; div. mgr. Lancaster Pa. div. R.R. Donnelley Co., Chgo., 1959-60, staff asst. to sr. v.p. mfg., 1961-62; gen. mgr., exec. v.p. McCormick Armstrong Co., Wichita, Kans., 1963-66; exec. v.p. Alden Press, Inc., Chgo., 1966-68; pres., owner Modern Light Metals, Inc., Coloma, Mich., 1968—. Mem. Tau Beta Pi. Republican. Author: Performance Charts for Management, 1966. Home: 3003 Bluffwood Terr St Joseph MI 49085

CONNER, WARREN J., market research co. mktg. exec.; b. Woodbury County, Iowa, June 2, 1938; s. Warren Thomas and Evelyn Francis (Petersen) C.; B.A., Morningside Coll., 1960; M.S.T., Drew U, 1963; m. Doris May Sadler, June 14, 1959 (dec.); children—Stephen Andrew, Sheryl Lynn. Ordained to ministry United Meth. Ch., 1963; pastor chs., Iowa, 1963-70; prodn. mgr. Majers Corp., Omaha, 1970-76, mktg. dir., 1976—. Democrat. Home: 5526 Jaynes St Omaha NE 68104 Office: 10179 J St PO Box 549 Omaha NE 68129

CONNOLLY, L. WILLIAM, lawyer; b. Gary, Ind., June 14, 1923; s. Leo W. and Lauretta E. (Feely) C.; student Miss. State U., City U N.Y.; Ph.B., Marquette U., 1948, J.D., 1951; m. Suzanne M. Irving, Sept. 2, 1950; children—Thomas A., Charles D., Alicia M., James J., Charlene, Susan, John J., Robert P. With Am. Automobile Ins. Co., Milw., 1951-52; admitted to Wis. bar, 1952, U.S. Supreme Ct. bar, 1967; practiced in Milw.; mem. firms Rummel & Connolly, 1952-55, Spence, Rummel & Connolly, 1955-59, Spence & Connolly, 1959-64. Trustee Village of Thiensville, Wis., 1957-61. Served with AUS, 1943-46. Fellow Internat. Acad. Lex et Scienta; mem. Am., Wis., Milw. bar assns., Am. Arbitration Assn. (nat. panel arbitrator 1973—), Am. Judicature Soc., Delta Theta Phi. Home: 830 Wood Dr Oconomowoc WI 53066 Office: 3106 W 80th St Milwaukee WI 53222

CONNOR, JAMES RICHARD, univ. ofcl.; b. Indpls., Oct. 31, 1928; s. Frank E. and Edna (Felt) C.; B.A. with highest distinction, U. Iowa, 1951; M.S. (Woodrow Wilson fellow), U. Wis., 1954, Ph.D. (fellow), 1961; m. Zoe Ezopov, July 7, 1954; children—Janet Kay, Paul Andrew. Asst. prof. history Washington and Lee U., Lexington, Va., 1956-57, Va. Mil. Inst., Lexington, 1958-61; asst. dir. Salzburg (Austria) Seminar in Am. Studies, 1961-62; asst. prof. history U. Va., Charlottesville, 1963-66, dir. of Inst. Analysis, 1963-66; asso. prof. history No. Ill. U., Dekalb, 1966-69, asso. provost, 1966-69; prof. history Western Ill. U., Macomb, 1969-74, provost, acad. v.p., 1969-74; prof. history, chancellor, U. Wis., Whitewater, 1974—; asso. dir. Va. Higher Edn. Commn., 1964-65; intern in acad. adminstrn., Stanford U., Calif., 1965-66; mem. Commn. on Institutions of Higher Edn., 1970-75. Served with U.S. Army, 1946-47, 51-53. Mem. Am. Hist. Assn., AAUP, Phi Beta Kappa, Phi Delta Kappa, Beta Gamma Sigma, Delta Sigma Pi, Phi Kappa Phi, Phi Eta Sigma, Phi Alpha Theta. Contbr. articles to Ency. Brit. Home: Route 2 Linden Dr Whitewater WI 53190 Office: Univ Wisconsin Whitewater WI 53190

CONNOR, JOHN THORP, II, accountant; b. Omaha, Feb. 6, 1944; s. John Thorp and Margaret M. (Hensley) C.; B.S., U. Nebr., 1966, J.D., 1969; m. Janice Kay Blazek, Aug. 27, 1967; children—Meredith Ann, John Thorp, III. Admitted to Nebr. bar, 1969, Kans. bar, 1970; tax supr. Touche Ross & Co., Kansas City, Mo., 1969-72, dir. tax ops., partner, Omaha, 1972-77, asso. partner-in-charge, 1977—. C.P.A., Nebr., Iowa, Kans., La., Mo. Mem. Am. Inst. C.P.A., Omaha Estate Planning Council, Nebr. Soc. C.P.A., Nebr. Bar Assn., Am. Bar Assn., Omaha C. of C. Home: 901 Bayberry Court Bellevue NE 68005 Office: 2000 First National Center Omaha NE 68102

CONNOR, LAWRENCE STANTON, journalist; b. Indpls., Aug. 31, 1925; s. Nicholas John and Agnes (Peelle) C.; student Butler U., summers 1943, 47, U. Ky., 1943, Miss. State U., 1944; A.B., U. Notre Dame, 1949; m. Patricia Jean Alandt, Nov. 3, 1956; children—Carolyn, Julia, Lawrence Stanton, Maureen, Janet, Michael Connor. With Indpls. Star, 1949—, chief copy desk, news editor, city editor, 1963—. Served with USAAF, 1943-46. Roman Catholic. Office: 307 N Pennsylvania St Indianapolis IN 46206

CONNORS, CHARLES WILLIAM BALDRIDGE, lawyer; b. Chgo., Oct. 30, 1937; s. James Joseph and Mary Elizabeth (Baldridge) C.; B.S. in Ceramic Engring., U. Ill., 1960; J.D., DePaul U., 1967; m. Ann McCabe, June 11, 1960; children—Colleen, Charles, Susan, George. Metall. trainee U.S. Steel Corp., Chgo., 1963; research chemist, product mgr. Nalco Chem. Co., Chgo., 1963-65; mem. legal dept., 1965-72, gen. mgr. metal industry chems., 1972—. Admitted to Ill. bar, 1967. Served to lt. (j.g.) USNR, 1960-63. Mem. Ill., Chgo. bar assns., Am. Ceramic Soc., Nat. Inst. Ceramic Engrs., Keramos. Roman Catholic. Home: 1121 Ashland Ave Wilmette IL 60091 Office: Nalco Chem Co 9165 S Harbor Ave Chicago IL 60617

CONNORS, DORSEY (MRS. JOHN E. FORBES), TV and radio commentator, newspaper columnist; b. Chgo.; d. William J. and Sara (MacLean) Connors; B.A. cum laude, U. Ill.; m. John E. Forbes; 1 dau., Stephanie. Appeared on Personality Profiles, WGN-TV, Chgo., 1948, Dorsey Connors Show, WMAQ-TV, Chgo., 1949-58, 61-63, Armchair Travels, WMAQ-TV, 1952-55, Home Show, NBC, 1954-57, Haute Couture Fashion Openings, NBC, Paris, France, 1954, 58, Dorsey Connors program, WGN, 1958-61, Tempo Nine, WGN-TV, 1961, Society in Chgo., WMAQ-TV, 1964; floor reporter WGN-TV, Rep. Conv., Chgo., Dem. Conv., L.A., 1960; writer column Hi! I'm Dorsey Connors, Chgo. Sun Times, 1965—. Founder Ill. Epilepsy League; mem. exec. bd. Chgo. Beautiful Com.; mem. woman's bd. Ill. Children's Home and Aid Soc. Mem. AFTRA, Screen Actor's Guild, Nat. Acad. TV Arts and Scis., Soc. Midland Authors, Chgo. Hist. Soc., Chi Omega. Author: Gadgets Galore, 1953; Save Time, Save Money, Save Yourself, 1972. Address: care Chgo Sun Times 401 N Wabash Chicago IL 60611

CONNORS, JOHN PHILLIP, cardiothoracic surgeon, educator; b. Worcester, Mass., Dec. 27, 1939; s. John Phillip and Marquerite Marie C.; A.B., Holy Cross Coll., Worcester, 1961; M.D. magna cum laude, Georgetown U., 1965; m. Ruth Ann Connors; children—John, Kathy, David. Intern in surgery Barnes Hosp., St. Louis, 1965-66, asst. resident in surgery, 1966-67, 69-71, chief resident in surgery, 1971-72, sr. resident in cardiothoracic surgery, 1972-73, chief resident in cardiothoracic surgery, 1973-74; asso. prof. surgery Washington U., St. Louis, 1974—; dir. div. cardiothoracic surgery Waldheim dept. surgery Jewish Hosp. of St. Louis, 1975—. Served with M.C. USN, 1967-69; Vietnam. Named Man of Year, Scholar-Athlete, Holy Cross Coll., 1961; diplomate Am. Bd. Surgery, Am. Bd. Thoracic Surgery. Mem. St. Louis Med. Soc., St. Louis Surg. Soc., St. Louis Thoracic Surg. Soc., Mo. State Med. Assn., A.C.S., Am. Coll. Cardiology, Alpha Sigma Nu, Alpha Omega Alpha. Contbr. articles to profl. publs. Home: 511 Hunter Creek Ct Des Peres MO 63131 Office: Waldheim Dept Surgery Jewish Hosp Saint Louis 216 S Kingshwy Saint Louis MO 63110

CONOMY, JOHN PAUL, physician; b. Cleve., July 31, 1938; s. John James and Marie Elizabeth (Bimbea) C.; B.S., John Carroll U., 1960; M.D., St. Louis U., 1964; m. Jeanette Melchior, Oct. 19, 1963; children—John, Lisa, Christopher. Intern, St. Louis U. Hosps., 1964; resident in neurology Univ. Hosps. Cleve., 1965-68; fellow in neuropathology Case Western Res. U., 1968; postdoctoral research fellow U. Pa., 1970-71; clin. instr. neurology U. Tex. Southwestern Med. Sch., 1971-72, also sr. staff neurologist Scott and White Clinic & Hosp.; practice medicine specializing in neurology; mem. staff Cleve. Met. Gen. Hosp., Univ. Hosps. Cleve., Cleve. VA Hosp.; chmn. dept. neurology Cleve. Clinic Found., 1977—; asso. prof. Case Western Res. U., 1972—. Served with USAF, 1968-70. Recipient grants Mary B. Lee Fund, Reinberger Found., NIH, Mellen Fund. Fellow A.C.P.; mem. Am. Acad. Neurology (chmn. membership com., chmn. ethics com., asst. sec.-treas.), Soc. Neurosci. (pres. Cleve.), AMA (vice chmn. sect. neurology), Am. Assn. History Medicine, Assn. Research in Nervous and Mental Diseases, Assn. Univ. Profs. Neurology, Alpha Omega Alpha. Roman Catholic. Contbr. articles to profl. jours. Office: Dept Neurology Cleveland Clinic 9500 Euclid St Cleveland OH 44106

CONOVER, DONALD PAUL, ins. co. exec.; b. Loveland, Ohio, Jan. 29, 1916; s. Lee E. and Clara (Beckman) C.; B.S., B.A., Ohio State U., 1938; m. Velva DeFosset, Apr. 26, 1941 (dec. July 1974); children—Phillip Lee, Michael Craig. Former agt. Northwestern Mutual Fire Assn., Allied Fire Ins. Co.; with Am. States Ins. Group, Indpls., 1943—, pres., 1976—, also dir.; v.p., dir. Lincoln Nat. Equity Sales Corp. Mem. Soc. Chartered Property and Casualty Underwriters. Home: 7440 Dean Rd Indianapolis IN 46240 Office: 500 N Meridian St Indianapolis IN 46206

CONRAD, EDWARD GEORGE, apiarist; b. Dunlap, Iowa, Sept. 20, 1917; s. George Alexander and Lucy Marian (Miles) C.; grad. high sch.; m. Ellen Elizabeth Holmes, June 8, 1945; 1 son, Melvin E. Apiarist, Woodbine, Iowa, 1924-59, Hoffman, Minn., 1954—; field assessor, Woodbine, 1949-59; salesman Mass. Protective, also Paul Revere Life Ins. Co., Woodbine, 1951-53; pres. Runestone Honey Co., Inc., Hoffman, Minn., 1962—. County finance chmn. Am. Cancer Soc., 1953; adult leader Swan Lake 4-H Club, 1960-64. Republican precinct chmn., Woodbine, 1938-48. Mem. Internat. Platform Assn. Methodist (ofcl. bd. 1945-55, chmn. Christian social concerns 1961-62, lay leader 1964-69, supt. Sunday sch. 1971-75). Mason (32 deg.); mem. Order Eastern Star. Home: Rural Free Delivery 1 Kensington MN 56343 Office: Kensington MN 56343

CONRAD, JEROME ARTHUR, surgeon; b. Grand Rapids, Mich., Dec. 18, 1938; s. Conrad J. and Adele (Graff) C.; B.S., Aquinas Coll., 1960; M.D., Georgetown U., 1964; m. Rita A. Laberteaux, July 28, 1962; children—Amy T., Christopher J., Caroline A. Intern, San Francisco Gen. Hosp., 1964-65; orthopedic resident Henry Ford Hosp., Detroit, 1965-69; fellow in orthopedics Harvard U., 1969; practice medicine specializing in orthopedic surgery Community Hosp., Big Rapids, Mich., 1971—; mem. staff Reed City, Kelsey Meml. hosps., Lakeview, Mich. Served to lt. comdr. USNR, 1969-71. Diplomate Am. Bd. Orthopedic Surgery. Fellow Am. Acad. Orthopedic Surgery, A.C.S.; mem. AMA, Am. Trauma Soc., Mich. Orthopedic Soc., Mich. State, Tri-County med. socs. Clubs: Lions, Elks. Home: 523 Ridgeview St Big Rapids MI 49307 Office: 413 Mecosta St Big Rapids MI 49307

CONRAD, JESSE LEE, accountant; b. Magnetic Springs, Ohio, Apr. 12, 1936; s. Jesse M. and Leona (Rogers) C.; B.S., Bowling Green State U., 1958; m. Charlene F. Blue, Nov. 21, 1959; children—Brad E., Carl D., Kristi D., Robert L. With French & Riddle accountants, Delaware, Ohio, 1958; self employed accountant, Marysville, Ohio, 1958—; sec.-treas. Sheilds Pharmacy, Inc., Marysville, 1971—; v.p. Union Enterprises, Inc., Plain City, Ohio, 1972—. Mem. Leesburg Magnetic P.T.A., 1962—, North Union Athletic Boosters, 1968—; treas. Union County Salvation Army, 1974—; mem. North Union Sch. Bd., 1970—, pres., 1972—; mem. Magnetic Springs Council, 1968-70. Trustee Union County Meml. Hosp. Mem. Leesburg Magnetic Alumni Club, Nat. Soc. Pub. Accountants, Marysville C. of C., Pub. Accountants Soc. Ohio, Ohio Young Farmers, Phi Delta Theta. Methodist (trustee). Home: 83 E Park St PO Box 147 Magnetic Springs OH 43036

CONRAD, JOHN JOSEPH, editor; b. Red Bud, Ill., Mar. 3, 1950; s. Roy Peter and Georganne Louise (Ries) C.; B.A. in Mass Communications, So. Ill. U., Edwardsville, 1974; m. Denise Schmidt, Aug. 18, 1973; 1 dau., Sarah. With Clarion Printing Co., Columbia, Ill., 1969—, news editor, 1971-75, partner, 1975—, editor publs., Columbia Star and Monroe County Clarion, 1975—, sec.-treas., 1975—; v.p. Conrad Press, Ltd. Founding mem. Columbia Bus. Dist. Devel. and redevel. Commn.; pres. bd. dirs. Monroe County (Ill.) Mental Health Services, Inc. Served with USAR, 1969-75. Recipient Am. Press certificate of appreciation U.S. Jaycees, 1976, 77. Mem. So. Ill. Editorial Assn. (dir.), Ill. Press Assn., Nat. Newspaper Assn., Columbia Gymnastic Assn., Columbia C. of C. (dir., treas.), Am. Legion. Roman Catholic. Clubs: Lions (Columbia); K.C. Home: Route 2 Box 6 Gilmore Lakes Columbia IL 62236 Office: 212 W Locust St Columbia IL 62236

CONRAD, JOHN ROBERT, mfg. co. exec.; b. Chgo., Dec. 3, 1915; s. Nicholas J. and Irene (Billups) C.; student Yale, 1934-36; B.S., U. Chgo., 1937; postgrad. Boeing Sch. Aeros., Calif., 1938; m. Arlys M. Streitmatter, Apr. 11, 1958; children by previous marriage—Lynn, Catherine (Mrs. Bruce Anglin), Joanne (Mrs. Frederick A. Herrick). Properties mgr. engring. and mfg. divs. Douglas Aircraft Co., 1938-45; v.p. S & C Electric Co., Chgo. 1945-52, pres., 1952—; chmn. bd. S & C Electric Can., Ltd. Mem. CIGRE. Trustee Orchestral Assn. Mem. IEEE, Power Engring. Soc. Home: 505 N Lake Shore Dr Chicago IL 60611 Office: 6601 N Ridge Blvd Chicago IL 60626

CONRAD, LARRY ALLYN, state ofcl.; b. Harrison County, Ind., Feb. 8, 1935; s. Marshall and Ruby (Rooksby) C.; m. Mary Lou Hoover; children—Jeb Allyn, Amy Lou, Andrew Birch, Jody McDade. Chief counsel U.S. Senate Subcom. Constl. Amendments, 1964-69; sec. state State of Ind., Indpls., 1970—. Bd. dirs. P.A.C.E., Ind. Am. Revolution Bicentennial Commn., Mus. Indian Heritage; mem. adv. bd. N.W. Ind. Sickle Cell Found.; former hon. state chmn. March of Dimes; Democratic nominee for gov. of Ind., 1976. Mem. NAACP (life). Office: State House Indianapolis IN 46204

CONRAD, ROGER ALLEN, civil engr.; b. Flint, Mich., Sept. 12, 1944; s. Harry Lester and Elaine Francis (Knierer) C.; B.S. in Civil Engring., Mich. State U., 1967; m. Shelia Brannon, Jan. 27, 1973; children—Matthew Allen, John Lester. Field layout engr. The Christman Co., Lansing, Mich., 1967—. Elder United Presbyterian Ch., Lansing, 1972—. Registered profl. engr., Mich. Mem. ASCE, Nat. Soc. Profl. Engrs. Republican. Clubs: Kiwanis, Elks. Home: 1617 Ravenswood Dr Lansing MI 48917 Office: 408 Kalamazoo Plaza Lansing MI 48933

CONRADS, EDWARD CHARLES, banker; b. Kewanee, Ill., Aug. 8, 1928; s. Paul Edward and Beatrice Alice (Holzbach) C.; B.A., Lawrence U., 1950; postgrad. Occidental Coll., 1953-54. Teller, escrow clk. Bank of Am., Glendale and Montrose, Calif., 1954-55; personnel asst. Gen. Motors, Van Nuys, Calif., 1955-56; underwriter Hartford Ins. Co., Los Angeles, 1956-64; asst. trust officer Security Pacific Nat. Bank, Los Angeles, Pomona and Pasadena, Calif., 1964-73; trust officer First Nat. Bank & Trust Co., Rockford, Ill., 1973—. Mem. Am. Inst. Banking (basic and gen. certificates, former instr.), Lawrence U. Alumni Assn., Phi Kappa Tau. Clubs: Masons, Mayan Order. Home: 186 Flintridge Dr Rockford IL 61107 Office: 401 E State St Rockford IL 61101

CONRATH, RICHARD CRANMER, educator, clergyman; b. Cambridge, Ohio, June 23, 1937; s. Carl W. and Marguerite (Doughty) C.; B.A., St. John Vianney Coll., 1959; B.S. in Edn., Coll. of Steubenville, 1965; Licentiae Sacrae Theologiae, Catholic U. of Am., 1963; Ed.M., Kent State U., 1970, Ph.D., 1975; m. Carmeline Mary Mangano, Jan. 21, 1967 (div. Feb. 1975); children—Christine Marie, Carrie Margaret, Cathleen Mary. Ordained priest Roman Catholic Ch., 1963, later laicized; asst. pastor St. Mary's Ch., Shadyside, Ohio, 1963-65, Ohio U., Athens, 1965-66; tchr. English Allen East High Sch., Lafayette, Ohio, 1966-67, Mentor (Ohio) pub. schs., 1967-69; instr. philosophy Lakeland Community Coll., Mentor, 1969-72, asst. prof. philosophy 1972-74, asso. prof., 1974-77, prof., 1977—, acting chmn. dept. of philosophy, 1969—; tennis coach, 1975—. Bd. dirs. Lake County Youth Fedn., 1969-71. Am. Studies fellow, 1967. Mem. Ohio, Tri-State philos. assns., Nat. Orgn. on Legal Problems of Edn., Am. Classical League, Ohio Assn. of Two-Year Colls. (dir. 1970-73), Phi Delta Kappa. Democrat. K.C. Contbr. poetry and articles to various publs. Home: 7927 Richwood Dr Mentor Lake OH 44060 Office: Lakeland Community College Mentor OH 44060

CONROY, ROBERT JOSEPH, mgmt. info. systems dir.; b. Toledo, May 6, 1931; s. Martin John and Ethelyn Nina (McGill) C.; B.B.A. with honors, U. Toledo, 1955; grad. Ind. Exec. Program; m. Donna B. Grindle, May 7, 1952; 1 dau., Cathleen Ann. Orgn. and methods examiner Army Ordnance, Rossford Ordnance Depot, 1955-57, computer programmer, 1957-59; with Owens Corning Fiberglas, Inc., Toledo, 1959—, beginning as computer programmer, successively sr. programmer, EDP methods supr., systems and procedures mgr., mgr. computer systems, dir. corporate data processing services, 1973-76, dir. mgmt. information systems planning and control, 1976—; data processing adv. com. U. Toledo Community and Tech. Coll.; former lectr. Am. Mgmt. Assn.; past speaker RCA Users Assn. Served with USNR, 1951-53; Korea. Certified data processor. Mem. Data Processing Mgmt. Assn., Internat. Communicators Assn., Am. Legion, U. Toledo Alumni Assn. (bd. trustees), Toledo Mus. Art, Toledo Humane Soc., Toledo Orch. Assn. Republican. Episcopalian. Home: 1986 Cherrylawn Dr Toledo OH 43614 Office: Fiberglas Tower Toledo OH 43659

CONROY, THOMAS HYDE, lawyer; b. Beloit, Kans., Feb. 6, 1922; s. Thomas Emmett and Ida Ruth (Hyde) C.; A.B., U. Kans., 1945, LL.B., 1949; m. Helen Regina Supple, Nov. 27, 1952; children—Thomas William, Sheila Anne, Regina Marie, Joseph Patrick. Admitted to Kans. bar, 1949; asso. Ralph H. Noah, Beloit, 1949-52; city atty., City of Beloit, 1953-55; county atty., County of Mitchell, 1957-65; partner Hamilton & Conroy, 1965; practice, 1965—; city atty., Beloit, 1967—; owner, developer Conroy Place, 1965—; dir. First Nat. Bank, Beloit. Bd. dirs. Mitchell County Hist. Soc., Inc., 1972—, 1st v.p., 1972—; trustee Mitchell County Hosp., 1965—, pres., 1965-73. Mem. Am. Legion, Phi Kappa, Phi Delta Phi. K.C. (state adv. 1958-59), Elk, Lion. Home: 721 E 3d St Beloit KS 67420 Office: 209 E Main St Beloit KS 67420

CONROYD, W. DANIEL (WALTER FRANCIS), univ. ofcl., lawyer; b. Oak Park, Ill., Oct. 1, 1920; s. Walter Earl and Lucille Mary (McCabe) C.; B.S. in Commerce, Loyola U., Chgo., 1942; J.D., DePaul U., 1947; m. Margaret Ann McAuliff, Feb. 13, 1943; children—Colleen (Mrs. Michael C. Strening), Maureen (Mrs. Thomas Fitzgerald), Michael, Sheila (Mrs. William Hogan), Alicia. Clk., FBI, 1942-44; wage adminstr. Montgomery Ward & Co., 1944-45; with Loyola U., Chgo., 1945—, dir. pub. relations, 1945-50, dir. fulfillment fund, 1950-55, asst. to pres., 1955-59, v.p. devel. and pub. relations, 1959—; admitted to Ill. bar, 1947. Sec. lay bd. trustees Loyola U.; bd. dirs. St. Francis Hosp. Served with USNR, 1943. Mem. Pub. Relations Soc. Am., Am., Chgo. bar assns., Am. Coll. Pub. Relations Assn., Pub. Relations Clinic, Am. Alumni Council, Delta Theta Phi, Tau Kappa Epsilon. Clubs: Economic, Chgo. Athletic Assn., Whitehall (Chgo.); North Shore Country (Glenview, Ill.). Home: 3108 Walden Ln Wilmette IL 60611 Office: 820 N Michigan Ave Chicago IL 60611

CONSENGCO, DIONISIO SANTOS, JR., physician; b. Orion, Bataan, Philippines, Dec. 31, 1940; s. Dionisio E. and Marcosa R. (Santos) C.; came to U.S., 1964, naturalized, 1976; M.D., U. Santo Tomas, Philippines, 1964; m. Elizabeth Gatus, Oct. 28, 1966; children—Vincent T., Arnold G., Josephine A. Intern, Md. Gen. Hosp., Balt., 1964-65; resident in internal medicine Providence Hosp., Southfield, Mich., 1965-67, Harper Hosp., Detroit, 1967-68; practice medicine specializing in internal medicine, Jackson, Mich., 1974—; mem. staff W.A. Foote Meml. Hosp., Jackson. Mem. Am. Coll. Physicians, Am., Mich. socs. internal medicine, Mich. State, Jackson County med. socs. Roman Catholic. Home: 2450 Glengarry St Jackson MI 49203 Office: 306 W Washington Ave Suite 102 Jackson MI 49201

CONSOLAZIO, PETER CARMINE, food co. exec.; b. Mt. Vernon, N.Y., May 30, 1944; s. A. Nino and Lola A. (Manzione) C.; B.S., Fordham U., 1968, M.B.A., 1971; m . Emily Norris, June 26, 1965; children—Lori Ann, Amy Patricia. Fin. analyst Gen. Foods Corp., White Plains, N.Y., 1968-70, fin. mgr., 1970-73, asso. mgr. promotion, 1973-76; promotion mgr. Foods div. Quaker Oaks Co., Chgo., 1976—. Mem. Promotion Mktg. Assn. Am. (dir. 1976—). Club: Premium Industry. Home: 602 S Knollwood Dr Wheaton IL 60187 Office: Mdse Mart Plaza Suite 345 Chicago IL 60654

CONTARSY, GEORGE SULTAN, holding co. exec.; b. Oak Park, Ill., Oct. 1, 1932; s. Edward Eli and Sara (Berkson) C.; student U. Ill., 1950-52, John Marshall Law Sch., 1952-54; m. Carole Ruth Freed (dec.); children—Laurence, Elise T.; m2d, Joyce Koransky, May 30, 1976. Credit mgr. Fairbanks Morsen Co., Chgo., 1954-57; gen. mgr. Marshalls Inc., Gary, Ind., 1957-61; v.p., Comml. Discount Corp., Chgo., 1961-69; v.p., treas. LIBCO Corp., Lincolnwood, Ill., 1969-73. pres., 1973, also dir.; dir. Union Linen Supply Co., Greater Chgo. Auto Auction, Reliable Mfg. Co., Teleo Mktg. Services. Mem. bd. edn. dist. 219 Niles Twp., 1977. Mem. Nat. Assn. Fleet Adminstrs., Nat. Auto Auction Owners Assn. Democrat. Jewish. Home: 4712 Greenwood St Skokie IL 60076 Office: 625 N Michigan Ave Chicago IL 60611

CONVERSE, JAMES LEONARD, illustrator; b. Jackson, Mich., Jan. 19, 1937; s. Orrin Leonard and Clara Estella (Snow) C.; student Am. Acad. Art Chgo., 1956-57, Art Center Coll. Design, Los Angeles, 1963-64; m. Gloria Jean Stevens, July 3, 1956; children—Errol B., Jennifer D. Illustrator, Pacific Press Pub. Assn., Mountain View, Calif., 1960-63; owner, art dir. Converse Illustrations, Los Angeles, 1963-67, Columbus, Ohio, 1967-70, Midland, Mich., 1970—; illustrator Dow Chem. Co., Midland, 1969-73; art dir. Worthington Foods (Ohio), 1967-69. Executed numerous sci. and ednl. art projects, also artwork in conjunction with Walt Disney for movie Mary Poppins, 1964. Home: 213 Sinclair St Midland MI 48640

CONVERY, NEIL PATRICK, lawyer; b. N.Y.C., Nov. 22, 1931; s. Michael and Ellen (Hansberry) C.; B.A., St. Thomas Coll., 1959; J.D. cum laude, William Mitchell Coll. Law, 1964; m. Catherine Eileen Pohl, Aug. 25, 1962; children—Maureen, Michael, Margaret, Kathleen, John, Sheila, Brian. Admitted to Minn. bar, 1964; spl. investigator for corp. counsel City of St. Paul, 1961-64, asst. corp. counsel, 1964-65; asst. U.S. atty. for Dist. Minn., 1965-68; partner firm Riverd, Convery & Assos., St. Paul, 1968—. Dist. chmn. Indianhead council Boy Scouts Am., 1972-73; bd. dirs. St. Paul-Ramsey County Council Alcohol Problems and Drug Abuse, 1970-74, v.p., 1970-72; bd. dirs. Nativity Parish Sch., 1972-74. Served with USAF, 1952-56. Mem. Am., Fed., Minn., Ramsey County bar assns. Home: 662 Sibley Meml Hwy St Paul MN 55118 Office: 1220 Northern Fed Bldg St Paul MN 55102

CONWAY, DONAL FALLER, physician; b. Dublin, Ireland, Nov. 29, 1924; s. William Francis and Mona (Faller) C.; M.B., B.A.O., B. Ch., Univ. Coll. Dublin, 1950; diploma tropical medicine and hygiene London (Eng.) U., 1960, diploma pub. health, 1961; m. Joan Dowling, Apr. 2, 1950; children—Shannon, Fiona, Gavin. Intern, St. Luke's Hosp., Bradford, Eng., 1950-51; practice medicine, specializing in family medicine, Bradford, 1951-53, Sask., Can., 1966-70, Lancaster, Ont., Can., 1970—; mem. active staff Cornwall (Ont.) Gen. Hosp., Hotel Dieu Hosp.; coroner United Counties of Stormont, Dundas and Glengarry, 1970—; med. examiner Ont. Dept. Transport, 1970—. Served to lt. col. M.C., Brit. Army, 1953-65. Mem. Canadian, Ont. med. assns., Assn. Coroners Ont., Assn. Family Physicians Can. Club: Cornwall Flying. Address: Box 340 Lancaster ON Canada

CONWAY, JACK GORDON, structural steel co. exec.; b. Indpls., Nov. 1, 1928; s. Robert M. and Pauline (Perkins) C.; B.S. in Civil Engring., Ind. Inst. Tech., 1956; m. Anne Palangian, Aug. 11, 1951; children—Gary, Craig. Project mgr. Am. Tel. & Tel., Cin., 1956-61; asst. product mgr. U.S. Gypsum Co., Chgo., 1961-69; v.p., div. mgr. Anchor Concrete Products Co., Buffalo, 1969-74; gen. mgr. Spancrete N.E., Inc., Aurora, 1974-76; gen. mgr. Nilcon Minn., Inc., St. Paul, 1977; gen. structural contracts mgr. Crown Iron Works, 1977—. Served with Army Security Agy., 1948-52. Mem. ASCE. Recipient Order of Silver Slide Rule, 1962. Inventor in field. Home: 13100 Harriet Ave S Burnsville MN 55337

CONWAY, JOHN, commuter airline exec.; b. Appleton, Wis., Sept. 10, 1924; s. John and Jane (Evans) C.; B.S., Northwestern U., 1949; m. Carole Steiner, Nov. 28, 1966; children—Lydia Jane, John, Vickie, Caterine. Founding v.p. Air Wisconsin, Appleton, 1964—; pres. Conway Hotel Co., Appleton, 1962—, Camp-tel, Inc., Appleton, 1971—. Chmn., Wis. Council Aeronautics, 1968-73. Chmn., 8th Dist. Republican Party, 1963-67, finance chmn., 1968—. Served with USAAF, 1943-46. Decorated Bronze Star medal. Mem. Wis. Innkeepers Assn. (pres.-elect 1976—). Rotarian (dir. 1960-71). Home: 1530 Reid Dr Appleton WI 54911 Office: 103 E Washington St Appleton WI 54911

CONWAY, NEIL MICHAEL, lawyer; b. Madison, Wis., Apr. 9, 1926; s. Neil Michael and Marie Anna (Paltz) C.; A.B., U. Wis., 1949, LL.B., 1950; m. Marilyn Therese Sauer, Sept. 8, 1951; children—Anne Marie, Jeffrey Thomas, Mary Rose. Admitted to Wis. bar, 1950; asso. Knoll & Wells, Beaver Dam, Wis., 1950; partner Genrich, Terwilliger, Wakeen, Piehler & Conway, Wausau, 1951-72; dir. Terwilliger, Wakeen, Piehler, Conway & Klingberg, S.C., 1972—; dir. Marathon County Savs. & Loan Assn. Spl. hearing officer U.S. Dept. Justice, Western Dist. Wis., 1958-69; mem. Wis. Gov.'s Tax Adv. Com., 1966-70. Bd. dirs. Marathon County Social Welfare Coordinating Council, 1959-64, pres., 1963-64; bd. dirs. Cath. Welfare Bur. Mem. Wis. (pres. bd. dirs. taxation sect. 1959-66), Marathon County (pres. 1972-73) bar assns., Phi Alpha Delta. Elk, Rotarian (past pres.). Home: 729 Eau Claire Blvd Wausau WI 54401 Office: 401 4th St Wausau WI 54401

CONWAY, ROBERT MARTIN, banker; b. St. Louis, July 9, 1933; s. Alphonses Henry and Leota (Martin) C.; B.B.A., St. Mary's U., 1955; M.S. in Commerce, St. Louis U., 1967; m. Patricia A. Forrestal, June 27, 1959; children—Kathy, Robert, Carolyn. Salesman Johnson Foil Co., St. Louis, 1957-60, Dolan Co., realtors, St. Louis, 1960-61; sr. investment analyst Prudential Ins. Co. Am., St. Louis, 1961-70; exec. v.p., sr. loan officer Tower Grove Bank & Trust Co., St. Louis, 1971-76, pres., chief exec. officer, 1976—; asst. prof. finance jr. coll. dist., St. Louis. Bd. dirs. Landmarks Assn. Greater St. Louis, United Student Aid Fund. Served with AUS, 1955-57. Mem. Mo. Realtors Inc., Nat. Realtors Inc., St. Louis Realtors Inc., Mortgage Holders Assn., Homebuilders Assn. Home: 40 Midpark Ln St Louis MO 63124 Office: 3134 S Grand St St Louis MO 63118

CONYERS, JOHN JAMES, JR., congressman; b. Detroit, May 16, 1929; s. John and Lucille (Simpson) C.; B.A., Wayne State U., 1957, LL.B., 1958. Admitted to Mich. bar, 1959; legis. asst., State of Mich., 1958-61; practiced law Detroit, 1962-64; referee Workmen's Compensation Dept., State Mich., Detroit, 1962-64; mem. 89th-95th Congresses from 1st Mich. Dist. Mem. NAACP (bd. Detroit chpt.), ACLU (Mich. adv. bd.). Served to 2d lt. Corps Engrs., AUS, 1951. Baptist. Club: Cotillion (comm. police relations com.). Home: 19970 Canterbury Rd Detroit MI 48221 Office: Rayburn House Office Bldg Room 2444 Washington DC 20515

COOHON, DONALD BURNS, veterinarian; b. Sturgis, Mich., May 14, 1921; s. Leo G. and Velva (Burns) C.; D.V.M., Mich State U., 1943; M.P.H., U. Mich., 1954; m. Ruthmary Veen, Sept. 11, 1943; children—Carolyn Boyd, William James, Claudia Ann Nightingale, Catherine Louise Baird. Practice vet. medicine, Dowagiac, Mich., 1944-46; veterinarian Grand Rapids Health Dept., 1946-51, Kalamazoo County Health Dept., 1951-55, Mich. Dept. Pub. Health, Lansing, 1955—. Vis. lectr. epidemiology U. Mich., 1963; mem. Mich. Health Resource Mgmt., 1968—. Mem. exec. com. orgn. and extension, area council Boy Scouts Am., Kalamazoo, 1955. Mem. Am., Mich. (certificate appreciation 1966), Midstate vet. med. assns., Mich. Pub. Health Assn. (pres. 1963-65), Conf. Pub. Health Vets., Assn. State and Territorial Pub. Health Vets., AAAS, Mich. Health Officers Assn., Alpha Tau Omega. Lutheran. Contbr. articles to profl. publs. Home: 3641 E Arbutus Dr Okemos MI 48864 Office: 3500 N Logan St Lansing MI 48914

COOK, ALEXANDER BURNS, educator; b. Grand Rapids, Mich., Apr. 16, 1924; s. Gorell Alexander and Harriette Florence (Hinze) C.; B.A., Ohio Wesleyan U., 1949; M.S., Case Western Res. U., 1967. Editorial cartoonist, artist Cleve. Plain Dealer, 1949-55; account exec. Edward Howard & Co., Cleve., 1955-61; spl. art tchr. Cleve. Pub. Schs., 1964—; curator exhibits Gt. Lakes Mus., Vermilion, Ohio, 1970—. Served with AUS, 1943-45. Recipient award of honor Ohio Wesleyan U., 1955; Distinguished Achievement award Gt. Lakes Hist. Soc., 1973. Mem. Gt. Lakes Hist. Soc. (exec. v.p. 1959-64, v.p. 1964—, trustee, mem. exec. com. 1959—), Akron Art Inst., Cleve. Mus. Art, Delta Tau Delta, Pi Delta Epsilon, Pi Sigma Alpha. Republican. Episcopalian. Contbr. editorial cartoons to Reid Cartoon Collection, U. Kan. Jour. Hist. Center; editorial adviser, numerous articles to Inland Seas, 1957—, The Chadburn, 1976—. Paintings represented in pvt. collections, 1960—; executed mural depicting Gt. Lakes shipping Gt. Lakes Mus., 1969. Home: 11850 Edgewater Dr Lakewood OH 44107

COOK, DAVID RAY, engr.; b. Tulsa, June 19, 1936; s. Artie Wrothal and Nellie Mae (Miller) C.; m. Benetta Borne, May 26, 1959; children—Kathryn, Karlene, Kristine. B.M.E., Okla. State U., 1959; M.S. in Systems Mgmt., Fla. Inst. Tech., 1969, M.S. in Contract Mgmt., 1970. Registered profl. engr., Ala. Design engr. Douglas Aircraft Co., Santa Monica, Calif., 1959-60; sr. design engr. Gen. Dynamics, Omaha, 1960-62; design engr. Boeing Co., Huntsville, Ala., 1962-65; mgr. Bendix Corp., Troy, Mich., 1965—; v.p. Profl. Consultants, Inc., 1974—. Pres. Brevard Symphony Orch., Cocoa, Fla., 1973-74. Mem. Am. Mgmt. Assn., ASME, Nat. Soc. Profl. Engrs., Soc. Automotive Engrs. Club: Masons (32 deg.). Home: 2551 Armstrong Dr Lake Orion MI 48035 Office: 900 W Maple St Troy MI 48084

COOK, DENNIS CALVYN, civil engr.; b. Washington, Aug. 11, 1940; s. Calvin Elvere and Mary Delores (Keyes) C.; B.S., U. Wis., 1962, M.S., 1964; m. Sara Lynn Curran, Dec. 26, 1964; children—Christopher, Jennifer. Engr. trainee Bur. of Pub. Rds., 1962-65, asst. area engr., asst. planning engr., St. Paul, 1965-69, planning engr., Kansas City, Mo., 1969-73; staff asst. U.S. Dept. Transp., Kansas City, 1973-74; asst. planning dir. Fed. Hwy. Adminstrn., Chgo., 1974-75, asst. div. adminstr., Ames, Iowa, 1975—. Mem. Monticello Twp. (Kans.) Planning Commn., 1971-72, mem. Monticello Twp. Zoning Bd., 1972-73. Registered profl. engr., Minn. Mem. ASCE. Methodist. Club: Ballard Country (Huxley, Iowa). Home: Rural Route 1 Kelley IA 50134 Office: 105 E 6th St Ames IA 50010

COOK, JACK, computer specialist; b. Pitts., July 20, 1937; s. John Joseph and Mary Josephine (Schmitt) C.; student Duquesne U., 1955-57; B.S., U. Pitts., 1959; postgrad. Bowling Green State U., 1970-72; m. Barbara Ann Kahn, Oct. 25, 1969; children—Joe, Judy, Jann, Jerry, Doug, Steve. Programmer analyst Republic Steel Corp., Cleve., 1960-63; senior systems rep. Honeywell EDP Co., Cleve., 1963-64; data processing mgr. Tel. Services Inc., Lima, Ohio, 1964-67; computer services mgr. Nat. Family Opinion, Toledo, Ohio, 1967—; mem. bus. advisory com. Penta County Vocat. Sch., 1975—. Republican precinct committeeman, 1970-73. Mem. Computer Mgmt. Assn. (bd. dirs. 1976—), Assn. for Computing Machinery. Roman Catholic. Clubs: Catawba Island, K. of C. Home: 374 Colony Rd Rossford OH 43460 Office: PO Box 315 Toledo OH 43691

COOK, JAMES ARNOLD, physician; b. Muskegon, Mich., Mar. 9, 1934; s. Marinus and Ella (Sieplinga) C.; A.B., Calvin Coll., 1955; M.D., Wayne State U., 1959; m. Sandra J. Rop, Sept. 24, 1954; children—Cathy Joan, James A., Robert Charles. Intern, Oakwood Hosp., Dearborn, Mich., 1959-60, resident, 1960-61; staff physician Rehoboth Hosp. (N.Mex.), 1961-62; practice medicine specializing in family practice, Wheaton, Ill., 1962—; attending physician Central Dupage Hosp., Winfield, 1962—, pres. staff, 1970-71, bd. dirs., 1970-71, 72—. Mem. AMA, Ill., Dupage County med. socs., Am. Acad. Gen. Practice. Republican. Mem. Christian Ref. Ch. Home: 409 E Prairie St Wheaton IL 60187 Office: 1530 N Main St Wheaton IL 60187

COOK, JAMES HARRISON, iron co. exec.; b. Red Wing, Minn., Sept. 6, 1920; s. Harry Cleveland and Alvida Caroline (Lillyblad) C.; B.M.E., U. Minn., 1942; postgrad. Ohio State U., 1947, United Theol. Sem., New Brighton, Minn., 1975—; m. Elizabeth Hamilton Hull, Dec. 28, 1946; children—James Harrison, Edward H., Caroline E. Jr. engr. Red Wing Potteries, Inc., 1940-42; plant layout N.Am. Aviation Co., Kansas City, Mo., 1942-43; research engr. Battelle Meml. Inst., Columbus, Ohio, 1946-47; pres. Red Wing Iron Works, 1947—; pres., dir. North Star Mech. Contractors. Mem. Bd. Pub. Works, Red Wing, 1955-61, Library Bd., 1964-69. Served with USNR, World War II. Registered profl. engr., Minn., Wis. Mem. Minn. Soc. Profl. Engrs., Sigma Chi, Pi Tau Sigma. Episcopalian (priest). Mason, Elk, Improved Order Redmen. Home: 317 Franklin St Red Wing MN 55066 Office: 2109 W Main St Red Wing MN 55066 also Box 23 Hertel WI 54845

COOK, JOHN PHILLIP, educator; b. Washington, Aug. 24, 1924; s. Patrick Michael and Lavinia (Gaskins) C.; B.C.E., Cath. U., 1951. B.Archtl. Engring., 1952; M. Civil Engring., Rensselaer Poly. Inst., 1955, D. Engring. Sci., 1963; m. Margaret Roos, Sept. 6, 1952; children—Jacqueline, Lawrence, Thomas, James, Jerome, Mary, Daniel, Joseph. Instr., Rensselaer Poly Inst., 1952-55, asst., asso. prof., 1958-67; bridge designer McEnteer Assos., 1955-58; prof. civil engring. U. Cin., 1967—, Jacob Lichter prof. engring. constrn.; cons. Dartworth, Inc., Simsbury, Conn., FAA, Washington, Thiokol Chem. Co., Trenton, Procter & Gamble, Watson-Bowman Assos. Mem. troop com. Boy Scouts Am., Cin., 1968—. Served with USNR, 1942-46. Recipient Tau Beta Pi Teaching Excellence award U. Cin., 1971; Distinguished Service citation Hwy. Research Bd., 1973. Mem. Hwy. Research Bd. (chmn. paving joint seal com. 1967—), ASCE local sect. award 1951), Am. Concrete Inst., Sigma Xi, Chi Epsilon, Tau Beta Pi. Author: Construction Sealants and Adhesives; Composite Construction Methods. Home: 1449 Wolfangle Rd Cincinnati OH 45230

COOK, KENNETH JOHN, tech. pub. co. exec.; b. Milw., Sept. 4, 1941; s. Kenneth Alfred and Ruth Louise (Tetzlaff) C.; B.S. in Elec. Engring., Purdue U., 1964; M.Bus. Econs., Claremont Grad. Sch., 1967; m. Sandra Taylor, July 3, 1964. Engring. writer Collins Radio, Cedar Rapids, Iowa, 1963; specifications analyst Gen. Dynamics, Pomona, Calif., 1964-67; officer, v.p. mktg. Ken Cook Co., Milw., 1967-70; v.p. U.S. ops. Planaprint Internat., Inc., Deerfield, Ill., 1970-73; v.p. global mktg. communications group Time/Access, Inc., Northfield, Ill., 1973-75; v.p. indsl. tng. systems Ken Cook Co., Milw., 1975—. Recipient Robert G. Frank award for outstanding contbns. in tech. communication, 1975. Mem. Internat. Trade Club, Soc. Tech. Communications (nat. and local officer 1972—), Am. Soc. Tng. and Devel., Sons of Bosses Internat., Triangle, Tau Kappa Alpha, Delta Sigma Rho. Methodist (choir pres. 1970-71, 76-77). Home: 3195 Deerfield Rd Deerfield IL 60015 Office: 9929 W Silver Spring Rd Milwaukee WI 53225

COOK, NOEL ROBERT, mfg. co. exec.; b. Houston, Mar. 19, 1937; s. Horace Berwick and Leda Estelle (Houghton) C.; student Iowa State U., 1955-57; B.S. in Indsl. Engring., U. Mich., Patricia Jane Henny, Aug. 17, 1962; children—Laurel Jane, David Robert. Engr. in tng. Eaton Mfg., Saginaw, Mich., 1960-61; mgr. mfg. and contracting J. N. Fauver Co., Madison Heights, Mich., 1961-65; pres. Newton Mfg., Royal Oak, Mich., 1965—; soc. Indsl. Piping Contractors, Birmingham, Mich., 1969-75; pres. RNR Metal Fabricators, Inc., Royal Oak, Mich., 1974—. Served with U.S. Army, 1960-61. Mem. Fluid Power Soc., Nat. Fluid Power Assn., Birmingham Jr. C. of C. (past bd. dirs.). Patentee in field. Home: 1903 Wickham Rd Royal Oak MI 48073 Office: 4249 Delemere Blvd Royal Oak MI 48073

COOK, ROBERT WILCOX, educator, lawyer; b. Providence, Dec. 1, 1943; s. Irving Howes and Joyce (Wilcox) C.; B.E.E., Rensselaer Poly. Inst., 1968, M.S., 1968; Ph.D., Northwestern U., 1970; J.D. with honors, Chgo. Kent Coll. Law, 1977; m. Elizabeth Stoneman, Apr. 11, 1976; children—Paul Wilcox, Peter DeVaney. Tech. staff Bell Telephone Labs., Naperville, Ill., 1966-73, mem. patent staff, 1973-76; vis. asst. prof. Roosevelt U., Chgo., 1976-77; asst. prof. econs. and bus. North Central Coll., Naperville, Ill., 1977—; admitted to Ill. bar, 1977; individual practice law, Naperville, Ill., 1977—. Village trustee Village of Weston (Ill.), 1967-69, chmn. planning commn., 1967-69. Mem. IEEE, Assn. Computing Machinery, Am. Bar Assn. Mem. Reorganized Ch. of Jesus Christ of Latter Day Saints. Patentee in field; also articles, chpt. in book. Home: 25W178 39th St Naperville IL 60540 Office: North Central Coll Naperville IL 60540

COOK, STANTON R., newspaper pub.; b. Chgo., July 3, 1925; s. Rufus Merrill and Thelma Marie (Bogerson) C.; B.S. in Mech. Engring., Northwestern U., 1949; m. Barbara Wilson. Dist. sales rep. Shell Oil Co., 1949-51; prodn. engr. Chgo. Tribune, 1951-60, asst. prodn. mgr., 1960-65, prodn. mgr., 1965-67; v.p. Chgo. Tribune Co., 1967-70, exec. v.p. gen. mgr., 1970-72, pres., 1972-73, chmn., pub., 1973—; v.p., dir. Tribune Co., Chgo., 1973-74, pres., chief officer, 1974—; dir. Newspaper Advt. Bur., Inc., AP, Am. Newspaper Pubs. Assn.; trustee U. Chgo., Mus. Sci. and Industry, Field Mus. Nat. History, Orchestral Assn. Chgo. Symphony (all Chgo.), Am. Newspaper Pubs. Assn. Found., Robert R. McCormick Trusts and Founds. Office: 435 N Michigan Ave Chicago IL 60611

COOK, THOMAS EDWARD, environ. control cons., chem. engr.; b. Fresno, Calif., Jan. 10, 1925; s. Francis William and Josephine Agatha (Sakalauskas) C.; student Bradley U., 1946-47, 51; B.S. in Chem. Engring., Columbia, 1949; postgrad. Ohio State U., 1961, 67; m. Shirley Caroline Mackie, May 30, 1943. Phys. technologist Caterpillar Tractor Co., Peoria, Ill., 1949-52; prin. chem. engr. Battelle Meml. Inst., Columbus, Ohio, 1952-61; project engr., chief chemist Tectum Corp., Columbus, 1961-63; self-employed in cons. and fundamental research, Columbus, 1963-66; design and sales engr. Harrop Precision Furnace Co., Columbus, 1966-68; cons. energy conservation and environ. control processes, Columbus, 1968—; customer service rep. Swift Chem. Co., Columbus, 1971-76. Merit Badge counselor Boy Scouts Am., 1963—; pres., Cat Welfare Assn., 1970-71. Mem. Greater Clintonville Community Council, 1967—, pres., 1974. Served with USNR, 1942-45. Mem. Am. Chem. Soc. (pub. relations and community affairs chmn. 1975-76), Am. Inst. Chem. Engrs. (mem. exec. com. 1967-68), Engrs. Found. Ohio (com. for continuing profl. edn.), Am. Chem. Soc., Air Pollution Control Assn., No. Bus. and Profl. Assn., Ohio Acad. Scis., Bradley Fedn. Scholars. Patentee in field. Address: 3570 Maize Rd Columbus OH 43224

COOK, VESPER WILKINSON (MRS. HORACE D. COOK), museum curator; b. Peru, Ind., June 21, 1917; d. John Elmer and Mary (Stickel) Wilkinson; grad. high sch.; m. Horace D. Cook, June 27, 1965. Research worker Ind. Hist. Soc., Indpls., 1952-53; curator two museums Miami County, Peru, Ind., 1961—. Mem. Miami County Bicentennial Com. Mem. Miami County Hist. Soc. (sec.), Peru Drama League (1st v.p. 1956, pres. 1957-58, dir. 1958-59), Ind. Hist. Soc., Midwest Museums Conf., Am. Numis. Assn., Miami County Steam Locomotive Assn. (chmn. gen. bus. div.), Bus. and Profl. Womens Club, Circus Hist. Soc. Circus Fans Assn. Am., Miami County (sec.), North Central Ind. (sec. 1973—) geneal. socs. Republican. Methodist. Clubs: Miami Lens (sec. 1940, 46-51), Monday Night Literary (sec. Peru). Contbr. to Indiana Houses of the Nineteenth Century, 1962; Furniture Makers of Indiana, 1972. Research homes in Miami County built before 1860. Contbr. articles to Peru Daily Tribune. Home: 327 E 6th St Peru IN 46970 Office: 11 N Huntington St Peru IN 46970

COOK, WAYNE RALPH, lawyer, former state ofcl.; b. Danville, Ill., Aug. 13, 1912; s. Charles A. and Grace (Massey) C.; A.B., U. Ill., 1934; LL.B., Ind. U., 1944; J.D., 1945; M.A., Georgetown U., 1946; m. Maryla Karpin, June 4, 1934 (dec. Dec. 1969); 1 dau., Bonnie Karen (Mrs. Herbert L. Tallitsch); m. 2d, Irene G. Samuel, Apr. 17, 1976. Admitted to Ill. bar, 1945, Ind. bar, Ark. bar, 1977, U.S. Supreme Ct.; practiced in Danville, 1947-51, St. Charles, Ill., 1970—; asst. Ill. atty. gen., Springfield, 1949-53; mem. firm Hubachek & Kelly, Chgo., 1953-59; spl. counsel Bankers Life & Casualty Co., Chgo., 1959-69; past pres., dir. Okla. Oil Co., Denver; former v.p., dir. Nat. Drilling Co., Inc., Property Investment Co., Inc., Ponderosa Paper Products, Inc., Ariz.; past dir. Forum Record Sales Corp., N.Y., Artia Records Corp., N.Y., Home Lockers, Inc., Parliament Records Corp.; asst. U.S. atty., No. dist. Ill., Chgo., 1969-70; dep. atty. gen. State of Ind., 1970-71, asst. atty. gen. in charge environ. law, 1971-73, chief counsel depts., 1973-77. Served to lt. col. AUS, 1941-43, 45-47. Decorated Purple Heart, Bronze Star medals. Mem. Am., Ill., Ind., Ark., 7th Fed. Circuit, Chgo. (chmn. judiciary com. 1966-67), Indpls. bar assns., Am. Soc. Internat. Law, Am. Judicature Soc., Selden Soc., U.S. Armor Assn., 1st Armored Div. Assn. (pres. 1970-71), Sigma Delta Kappa. Mem. Christian Ch. Clubs: Army and Navy (Washington); Ill. Athletic (Chgo.); Capitol (Little Rock); Columbia (Indpls.). Home: 108 Nicklas Ave Danville IL 61832 also 8 Pinnacle Point Little Rock AR 72205 Office: 303 State Bank Bldg St Charles IL 60174 also 436 National Old Line Bldg Little Rock AR 72201

COOKSON, DAVID UPJOHN, physician; b. Orange, N.J., Sept. 4, 1932; s. Leonard Theodore and Rhoda (Upjohn) C.; student U. Mich., 1952; M.D., Harvard U., 1956; m. Christine Elizabeth Morrison, Sept. 11, 1954; children—David, Daniel, Sondra, Matthew. Intern, Ancker Hosp., St. Paul, 1956-57; resident in internal medicine Univ. Hosp., Madison, Wis., 1957-59, 61-62, fellow in allergy, 1962-63; practice specializing in internal medicine, Madison, 1963—; mem. staff Madison Gen. Hosp., Univ. Hosps. Served with USAF, 1959-61. Diplomate Am. Bd. Internal Medicine. Fellow Am. Coll. Physicians; mem. AMA, Am. Acad. Allergy, Am. Soc. Internal Medicine, Wis. State, Dane County med. socs., Wis. State Golf Assn. (pres. 1976—). Clubs: Aesculapian (Boston); Maple Bluff Country (past pres.), Madison. Home: 4910 Lake Mendota Dr Madison WI 53705 Office: 4410 Regent St Madison WI 53705

COOLEY, ADELAIDE NATION, artist; b. Idaho Falls, Idaho, Apr. 18, 1914; d. Carl DeLos and Ivo Ethel (Miller) Nation; student Stephens Coll. Women, 1931-33; B.S., U. Wis., 1935; m. William Cooley, Jr., Aug. 24, 1937; children—Marcia Jean, Susan Adelaide, William Carl. One-woman shows (11), Chgo., Springfield, Quincy, Peoria, Ill., 1958-74; numerous group shows, Ill., Mich., Calif., Iowa, N.Y., Mass.; juror, art exhbns., 1971—; pres. Peoria Art Center, 1962-63; art cons. exhibits Carson Pirie Scott Co., Peoria, 1967-68; announcer daily art news Sta. WIVC-FM (now WIRL Radio), E. Peoria, 1968; founder pub. art com., Peoria, 1974. Recipient Outstanding Woman in Art award Peoria Y.W.C.A., 1973. Author published biographies of two sculptors. Home: 3308 N Bigelow St Peoria IL 61604

COOLEY, DONALD LEE, mech. and elec. engr.; b. Portsmouth, Ohio. Sept. 1, 1926; s. Lawrence H. and Myrtle H. (McQuillen) C.; student U. Cin., 1947-49, Marshall Coll., 1967-68, Pace Coll., 1968; B.A. in Math., Ohio U., 1971; m. Virginia J. Schwamberger, Sept. 17, 1948; children—Michael L., John E. Draftsman, Selby Shoe Co., Portsmouth, 1946-47; cataloger Wright-Patterson AFB, Dayton, Ohio, 1950-52; engr.'s asst. Ohio Power Co., Portsmouth, 1947-49, air conditioning specialist, 1955-68; purchasing agt. Atomic Plant, Portsmouth, 1952-55; air conditioning specialist Am. Elec. Power Co., N.Y.C., 1968-69; engr.'s asst. William Lewis & Assos.,

Portsmouth, 1969-73; engr. Hayes, Donaldson, Wittenmyer & Partners, Portsmouth, 1973—; tchr. Shawnee State Coll., 19—. Adviser troop Scioto County council Boy Scouts Am., 1955-59; player agt. Little League, 1953-59. Served with USNR, 1944-46; PTO. Registered profl. engr., Ohio, Ariz. Mem. Nat. Soc. Profl. Engrs., Am. Soc. Heating, Refrigerating and Air Conditioning Engrs., Order of the Engr. Club: Kiwanis. Home: 1245 Coles Blvd Apt 11 Portsmouth OH 45662 Office: 601 8th St Portsmouth OH 45662

COOLEY, FLETCHER EARL, counselor; b. Montgomery, Ala., May 25, 1935; s. William Edward and Frankie (Armstead) C.; B.S., Ala. State U., 1961; M.Ed., Tuskegee Inst., 1965; certificate Urban Edn., U. Chgo., 1970; postgrad. U. Minn., 1975—. Recreational dir. Ft. Bragg (N.C.), 1966-67, Ft. Gordon (Ga.), 1967-68; counselor Ralph Bunche Sch., Canton, Ga., 1965-66, Clam Lake (Wis.) Civilian Job Corps Center, 1968, Central High Sch., Mnpls., 1968—. Active Bancroft Neighborhood Assn. Served with USN, 1953-58, USNR, 1958—. Recipient YMCA Century Club Award, 1976; Minn. Masonic Meritorious Award for Counselors, 1975; named Central High Sch. Counselor of Year, 1972; Gen. Elec. fellow vocat. guidance U. Louisville, 1972. Mem. Am. Personnel and Guidance Assn., Am. Sch. Counselor Assn., Am. Coll. Personnel Assn., Minn., Mnpls. edn. assns., Phi Delta Kappa. Democrat. Roman Catholic. Clubs: Tuskegee Minn., Holy Name Soc., K.C., Knights of Peter Claver. Home: 3924 Elliot Ave S Minneapolis MN 55407 Office: 3416 4th Ave S Minneapolis MN 55408

COOLEY, RICHARD EUGENE, lawyer; b. Flint, Mich., Apr. 28, 1935; s. Eugene J. and Helen (Lumbert) C.; A.B., Albion Coll., 1957; J.D., Duke, 1960; m. Wanda Lee Ford, Feb. 20, 1965; children—Scott Richard, Courtney Ann. Admitted to Mich. bar, 1960; since practiced law in Flint; asst. pros. atty. Genessee County, Flint, 1962-64; partner firm Bellairs, Dean, Cooley & Siler, Flint, 1964—; atty. Linden Village, 1964—, Fenton Twp., 1971—; spl. asst. atty. gen for State of Mich., 1975—. Mem. exec. com. Tall Pine council, also v.p. Sowegen Dist. council Boy Scouts Am.; bd. dirs. Flint br. Child and Family Services Mich., pres., 1975-77; bd. dirs. Flint Inst. Health, 1975—. Mem. Am., Genesse County (dir. 1972-75, v.p. 1976-77, pres. 1977-78) bar assns., State Bar Mich., Flint Jr. C. of C. (dir. 1965-67), Flint Inst. Arts, Flint Inst. Music, Flint Power Squadron, Delta Theta Phi. Republican. Presbyn. (deacon). Clubs: University Elks, Masons, Rotary, Warwick Hills Golf and Country. Home: 6079 Plantation Dr Grand Blanc MI 48439 Office: Genesse Bank Bldg Flint MI 48502

COOLEY, WILLIAM, JR., obstetrician, gynecologist; b. Peoria, Ill., Aug. 29, 1910; s. William and Ella Victoria (Engstrom) C.; B.S., Northwestern U., 1932, M.D., 1936; m. Adelaide Nation, Aug. 24, 1937; children—Marcia Cooley Blevins, Susan Cooley Fargo, William C. Intern, Michael Reese Hosp., Chgo., 1935-36, resident, 1937; resident Free Hosp. for Women, Boston, 1938; practice medicine specializing in obstetrics, gynecology, Peoria, Ill., 1938—; staff Meth. Hosp. Central Ill., Peoria, 1938—, pres. 1952. Dir. Sheridan Bank of Peoria; faculty Peoria Sch. Medicine U. Ill., 1971—; cons. for maternal welfare Ill. Dept. Health, 1969—. Bd. dirs. Peoria City Bd. Health, 1966—, pres., 1969-73. Served to lt. col. (flight surgeon) USAAF, 1942-46. Decorated Army Commendation Medal. Diplomate Am. Bd. Obstetrics and Gynecology. Fellow A.C.S., Am. Coll. Obstetrics and Gynecology; mem. Central Assn. Obstetrics and Gynecology, Creve Coeur Club, Beta Theta Pi, Phi Rho Sigma. Republican. Methodist. Rotarian. Clubs: Country of Peoria, Creve Coeur. Home: 3308 N Bigelow St Peoria IL 61604 Office: 1101 Main St Peoria IL 61606

COOLIDGE, EDGAR DAVID, III, investment banker; b. Evanston, Ill., Apr. 27, 1943; s. Edgar David and Elaine Montague (Hutchins) C.; B.A., Williams Coll., 1965; M.B.A., Harvard U., 1967; m. Constance Bennett Howard, Sept. 8, 1973; children—Lisa, Stephanie. Volunteer, Peace Corps, Colombia, S.A., 1967-69; asso. William Blair & Co., Chgo., 1969-75, partner, 1975-76, partner, mgr. corporate fin. dept., 1977—. Pres. bd. dirs. Youth Guidance, Chgo., 1976—; chmn. Assocs. Rush Presbyterian St Lukes Med. Center, Chgo., 1973-77; bd. dirs. Better Govt. Assn., 1973—; exec. dir. fin. com. Citizens for Percy, 1971-72; mem. fin. com. Citizens for Thompson, 1976. Mem. Economic Club Chgo. Presbyterian. Clubs: Racquet (chgo), Sunset Ridge Country. Home: 1320 N State St Chicago IL 60610 Office: William Blair & Co 135 S LA Salle St Chicago IL 60603

COOLIDGE, MRS. JAMES H., III, club woman; b. Atlanta, May 16, 1915; d. William Olin and Lucia A. (Cromer) Mashburn; student U. Cin., 1933-35; m. James Henry Coolidge III, Feb. 20, 1948; children—Carlton Cromer, James Henry IV, William Mashburn. Dir. Coca-Cola Bottling Co., Cin. Sec., Garden Center, Cleve., 1959—; mem. womans com. MacDonald House, U. Hosps.; Cleve., 1953—, Northeastern Ohio Opera Assn., 1967—; mem., past pres. Friends of Univ. Hosps.; pres. women's adv. bd. Fenn Coll. Trustee Soc. for Blind, Cancer Soc.; trustee, chmn. women's com. Cleve. Zool. Garden. Mem. Kappa Kappa Gamma. Clubs: Intown (asst. treas., dir. 1958—), Sundial Garden (past pres.), Kirkland Country, Union (Cleve.); Rolling Rock (Ligonier, Pa.); Gulfstream (Del Ray Beach, Fla.) Home: 18100 S Park Blvd Cleveland OH 44120

COOLLEY, RONALD BRUCE, lawyer; b. Manchester, N.H., Feb. 15, 1946; s. Mace A. and Ruth A. (Foote) C.; B.S., Iowa State U., 1964; M.B.A., J.D., U. Iowa, 1972; m. Nancy E. Chase, May 20, 1969. Financial analyst engring. Ford Motor Co., Dearborn, Mich., 1972-73; admitted to Ill. bar, 1973; partner firm Mason, Kolehmainen, Rathburn & Wyss, Chgo., 1973—; lectr. patent law. Mem. Am., Chgo. bar assns., Patent Law Assn. Chgo. Home: 534 Deerfield Rd Deerfield IL 60015 Office: Mason Kolehmainen Rathburn & Wyss 20 Wacker Dr Chicago IL 60606

COON, JOSEPH WALTER, JR., fire protection cons.; b. Westfield, N.J., Oct. 28, 1922; s. Joseph Walter and Violet (Kettelwell) C.; student Rutgers U., 1940-42, U. Cin., 1944-45; m. Patricia Jane Bailey, Feb. 12, 1944; children—Anthony T., Joseph Walter, III, Anne C., Kathleen P. Registered profl. engr., Calif., Pa.; certified fire sci. tech. and vocational ednl. instr., Kans. Engr., dist. mgr. Rockwood Sprinkler Co., Kansas City, Mo., 1945-61; chief engr. Viking Fire Protection Co., Kansas City, 1962-70; mgr. fire protection div. Smith & Boucher, Cons. Engrs., Kansas City, 1970-74; fire protection cons. Burns & McDonnell, Architects and Engrs., Kansas City, Mo., 1974—; fire protection cons. City of Merriam (Kans.), Shawnee Mission Hosp. Mem. Internat. Conf. Bldg. Ofcls., Soc. Fire Protection Engrs., Nat. Soc. Profl. Engrs., Am. Soc. Safety Engrs., Nat. Fire Protection Assn. (adv. council). Home: 9120 W 73d St Apt 202 Merriam KS 66204 Office: 4600 E 63d St Kansas City MO 64141

COONEY, GEORGE AUGUSTIN, lawyer; b. Detroit, July 12, 1909; s. Augustin W. and Mary (McBride) C.; A.B., U. Detroit, 1932, J.D., 1935; m. Julia Grace Starrs, Oct. 26, 1940; children—George Augustin, Michael Edward, Timothy John. Admitted to Mich. bar, 1935; since practiced in Detroit. Lectr., U. Mich. Inst. Continuing Legal Edn. Recipient Tower award U. Detroit, 1972. Fellow Am. Coll. Probate Counsel; mem. Am., Mich., Fed., Detroit bar assns., Cath. Lawyers Soc. Detroit (dir.), Selden Soc., Mich. Assn. Professions, State Bar Mich. (dir. probate and trust law sect., assemblyman), Mich. Conf. Bar Officers (chmn.). Served as warrant officer USAAF, 1943-46. K.C. Clubs: Detroit Golf, Nat. Lawyers (Washington); Stoney Point (Ont.) Sportsmens. Home: 17177 Parkside Ave Detroit MI 48221 Office: 2329 Commonwealth Bldg Detroit MI 48226

COONS, DAVID JAY, advt. exec.; b. Peoria, Ill., May 7, 1943; s. Harold LeRoy and Norma Charlotte (Brauer) C.; B.S., Northwestern U., 1965, M.S., 1966; m. Ann Louise McCallister, Dec. 28, 1975. Instr., Valparaiso (Ind.) U., 1966-67, asst. dean Coll. Bus. Adminstrn., 1967-71; market analyst Biddle Advt., Chgo., 1971, account exec., 1972-75, v.p. marketing, 1976—; lectr. Purdue U., Westville, Ind., 1970-71, Ill. State U., Normal, 1971-72. Mem. Am. Marketing Assn. Office: 875 N Michigan Ave Chicago IL 60611

COONS, ELDO JESS, mfg. co. exec.; b. Corsicana, Tex., July 5, 1924; s. Eldo Jess and Ruby (Allison) C.; student engring. U. Calif., 1949-50; m. Betty June Muntz, June 1, 1954; children—Roberta Ann, Valerie, Cheryl. Owner C & C Constrn. Co., Pomona, Calif., 1946-48; sgt. traffic div. Pomona Police Dept., 1948-54; nat. field dir. Nat. Hot Rod Assn., Los Angeles, 1954-57; pres. Coons Custom Mfg., Inc., Oswego, Kans., 1957-68; chmn. bd. Borg-Warner Corp., 1968-71; pres. Coons Mfg., Inc., Oswego, 1971—. Mem. Kans. Gov.'s Adv. Com. for State Architects Assn. Served with C.E., AUS, 1943-46. Named to Exec. and Profl. Hall Fame. Mem. Oswego C. of C. (dir.), Nat. Juvenile Officers Assn., Municipal Motor Officers Assn., Am. Legion, AIM (fellow pres.'s council), Young Pres.'s Orgn. Mason (K.T., Shriner), Rotarian (pres. Oswego 1962-63). Originator 1st city sponsored police supervised dragstrip. Home: 1315 North St Oswego KS 67356 Office: 2300 W 4th St Oswego KS 67356

COOPER, CALVIN GORDON, constrn. co. exec.; b. Richland County, Wis., Sept. 10, 1925; s. William Ray and Edna Florence (Adams) C.; B.S., U. Wis., 1950; m. Avadele Thompson; children—Vicki Lynn, Scott William. Elec. engr. Underwriters Labs., 1950-52; project engr. Askania Regulator Co., 1952-54; elec. engr. Revere Copper & Brass Co., 1954-56; with Kelso-Burnett Electric Co., Chgo., 1956—, v.p., 1968-75, exec. v.p., 1975-76, pres., 1976—, also dir.; pres., dir. Schmidt Electric Inc., Ft. Wayne, Ind., 1972—. Served with USNR, 1943-46. Mem. Nat. Electric Contractors Assn., Rock River Valley Electric Assn. Home: 9809 Partridge Ln Crystal Lake IL 60014 Office: 5200 Newport Dr Rolling Meadows IL 60008

COOPER, C(HARLES) E(DWARD), artist; b. Chgo., Nov. 5, 1922; s. Sam and Rose (Achtman) C.; student Corcoran Gallery Art, 1944-45, Inst. Design, 1946-47, Roosevelt Coll.. 1948-52, Sch. Art Inst. Chgo., 1948-51; B.Art Edn., Loyola U. Chgo, 1964; I.D., Ill. Inst. Tech. 1966. With Jan Smith Gallery, 1950-51, House of Arts, 1952-56, Robert North Gallery, 1958-60, Kerrigan Hendrick Gallery, 1961 (all Chgo.); exhibited one man shows Club St. Elmo, Morris B. Sachs North Side, 1949, Northwestern U. Hillel Found., Evanston, Ill., 1960, 64, Fisher Hall Gallery, Chgo.; exhibited in group shows Momentum shows, 1948, 49, 51, 52, 54, Am. Jewish Art Club, 1951—, Ill. Inst. Tech., 1963, Navy Pier No-Jury Show, Chgo., 1957, Art Inst. Chgo. Vicinity shows, 1947, 52, 53, 58, 63, Art Inst. Chgo. Rental Gallery, 1960—, Chgo. Soc. Artist Gallery, 1967-69, Alpha Gallery, 1977; high sch. art tchr. Chgo. Pub. Sch. System, 1952—; lectr. art pvt. orgns.; art cons. Bd. Jewish Edn., Chgo.; cons. pvt. collectors. Mem. planning com. for arts Am. Jewish Com.; exec. bd. Lane Tech. PTA. Served with USMCR, 1942-45; PTO. Recipient Raymond Schiff Realtors award, 1961; Morris DeWoskin award 1965. Mem. Chgo. Soc. Artists (dir., 1st v.p.), Artists Guild Chgo., Chgo. New Art Assn. (dir.), Am. Jewish Arts Club (Maurice Spertus award 1964, Nathan A. Schwartz award 1970, exhbn. chmn. 1965, 69. rec. sec. 1963, v.p. 1972, 73, co-chmn.), Chgo. Artists Coalition (dir., mem. fair practices com.), Artists Equity. Home: 712 W Diversey Ave Chicago IL 60614 Office: care Lane Technical High School Chicago IL 60618

COOPER, CHARLES RAYMOND, radio announcer; b. Wheeling, W.Va., May 13, 1952; s. Clarence Robert and Mary Ellen (West) C.; diploma Inst. Broadcast Arts, 1970. Announcer radio sta. WEIR, Weirton, W.Va., 1970-72; announcer, prodn. mgr. radio sta. WDAO, Dayton, Ohio, 1972-75; announcer sta. WYLD, New Orleans, 1975; announcer, music librarian radio sta. WBMX-FM, Oak Park, Ill., 1975—. Feature editor newspaper Smithfield High Sch., 1970, photographer year book, 1970. Speaker local elementary and high schs.; master ceremonies community fund raising. Recipient Golden Microphone award Inst. Broadcast Arts, 1970, Pub. Service award Optimists, 1974, Outstanding Contbn. placque Radio Sta. WEIR, 1972; Gold album from rec. artists Brass Construction, 1977. Home: 425 S Kenilworth Ave Apt 1 NW Oak Park IL 60302 Office: 408 S Oak Park Ave Oak Park IL 60302

COOPER, CHARLES ROSCOE, JR., constrn. co. exec.; b. Scandia, Kans., Mar. 15, 1930; s. Charles Roscoe and Alice (Nylund) C.; B.S., U. Nebr., 1958; m. Gwen M. Monson, June 23, 1951. Vice pres. Beatrice Constrn. Co. (Nebr.), 1958-69, pres., gen. mgr., 1969—, also dir.; founder C. & R. Engring., Inc., Beatrice, 1969, pres., gen. mgr., dir., 1969—; pres. Country Club Estates, 1965-71, dir. 1965-73; v.p., dir. Hastings Inn, Inc., 1974-75, Werco Inc., 1975—, Beatrice Devel. Corp., 1975—; dir. Beatrice State Bank, Beatrice Nat. Bank. Dir. laison com. Nebr. Dept. Roads, 1969—. Served with USN, 1951-54. Mem. Asso. Gen. Contractors (nat. dir., state dir., mem. nat. safety com.), Nebr. Assn. Gen. Contractors (pres. 1975). Republican. Presbyterian (deacon 1967-69). Club: Beatrice Country (pres. 1963-64). Home: 1315 S 3d St Beatrice NE 68310 Office: 2620 Lincoln St Box 641 Beatrice NE 68310

COOPER, CLAYTON HAROLD, mfg. co. exec.; b. Marshalltown, Iowa, Dec. 8, 1914; s. Harold M. and Edna M. (Anderson) C.; B.S. in Mech. Engring., Iowa State U., 1936; m. Virginia Barbara Cobb, Sept. 28, 1940; children—David C., Stephen C. Sales engr. Ingersoll Rand Co., 1936-41; with Cooper Mfg. Co., Marshalltown, 1945—, pres., 1972—; dir. Comml. State Bank, Marshalltown, 1958—. Mem. adv. bd. Boy Scouts Am., 1955-58; mem. Marshalltown, Sch. Bd., 1952-55. Trustee Marshalltown Area Hosp., 1961-76. Served to maj., Corps Engrs., AUS, 1941-45. Decorated Legion of Merit, Croix de Guerre. Mem. Outdoor Power Equipment Inst. (dir., treas. 1966-69), Marshalltown C. of C., Am. Legion, Kappa Sigma. Conglist. (past deacon, chmn. trustees). Elk. Club: Elmwood Country (past dir., pres.). Home: 510 Highland Dr Marshalltown IA 50158 Office: Cooper Mfg Co Marshalltown IA 50158

COOPER, CRAVEN LEROY, counselor; b. Chgo., Nov. 10, 1937; s. Craven Lafayette and Leona Naomie (Sykes) C.; B.A., Chgo. State U., 1974; m. Judith Ann Williams, Nov. 8, 1958; children—Gregory, Craven, Brenda Ellen. Banquet houseman Morrison Hotel, Chgo., 1957-58; shipping clk. M. Smolerl & Sons, Chgo., 1958-60; head shipping clk. L. Klein Mfg. Co., Chgo., 1960-68; career instr. City of Chgo., 1968-70, spl. instr., 1970-71, master instr., 1971-73, counselor, 1973—; ex-offender vol. counselor, 1971-78; vol. counselor and group leader Cook County Jail, 1973-78. Recipient Vol. of Year award City of Chgo., 1970, Pace Inst., 1976; named Great Guy of Day, Radio Sta. WGRT, 1973; certificate of appreciation Safer Found., 1973. Mem. Am., Ill. personnel and guidance assns. Baptist. Home: 1428 S Sawyer St Chicago IL 60623 Office: 3146 W Roosevelt Rd Chicago IL 60612

COOPER, DENNIS ROGER, lawyer; b. Cin., Mar. 16, 1940; s. Jack Valet and Hazel Louise (Brown) C.; B.B.A., U. Cin., 1968; J.D., Chase Law Sch., 1974; m. Auri Esther Rosado, Aug. 6, 1965; children—Jeffery M., Michael P., Allison J. Specialist info. systems Cin. Gas & Electric Co., 1968-69; mgr. systems and programming Kenner Products Co., Cin., 1970-73; mgr. prodn. control systems, 1973-74, project mgr. MIS Dept., 1977—; asso. prof. W. Ger. U. Md. and U. Chgo., 1974-76; admitted to Ohio bar, 1974. Served with USMCR, 1959-64, U.S. Army, 1965-66, 74-77; Vietnam. Mem. Am., Ohio, Cin. var assns., Assn. Trial Lawyers Am., Pi Alpha Delta. Republican. Home: 1410 Meadowbright Ln Cincinnati OH 45230 Office: 1014 Vine-Kenner St Cincinnati OH 45202 also 5205 N Bend Rd Cincinnati OH 45239

COOPER, DUNCAN BROWN, III, lawyer; b. Chgo., June 24, 1940; s. Duncan Brown and June (Cosme) C.; B.S. in Mktg., U. Ill., 1962; J.D., Creighton U., 1968; m. Elizabeth Jane Nowlin, Dec. 26, 1964; 1 dau., Mary Elizabeth. Admitted to Ill. bar, 1968; mem. firm Heyl Royster Voelker & Allen, Peoria, Ill., 1968—, mng. partner, 1976—. Served to lt. USN, 1962-65. Mem. Am., Ill. State (chmn. labor law sect. council 1974), Nebr. State, Peoria County bar assns., Ill. Def. Council. Methodist. Club: Country (Peoria). Contbr. articles to legal jours. Home: 444 High Point Rd Peoria IL 61614 Office: 300 Central Bldg Peoria IL 61602

COOPER, GEORGE KILE, educator; b. Bushnell, Ill., Apr. 5, 1920; s. George Kile and Lula Robison C.; B.Ed., Western Ill. U., 1942; M.B.A., Ind. U., 1951; Ph.D., U. Mich., 1962; m. June Anna Cardell, June 12, 1948; children—Kyle, Ernest, Ruth Anne, William, Lula Jean, Andrew. Tchr. bus. Reynolds (Ill.) Community High Sch., 1946-47; coordinator student teaching bus. subjects Western Mich. U., Kalamazoo, 1948-55, head dept. bus. edn., 1955-62; head dept. bus. edn. and adminstrv. office mgmt. Eastern Ill. U., Charleston, 1962-73, prof. bus., 1962—, vis. research and devel. specialist Center for Vocat. and Tech. Edn., Ohio State U., Columbus, 1973-74. Adviser state dir. vocat. edn. in devel. Ill. State Plan Vocat. Edn., 1964-65. Served to 1st. lt. AUS, 1942-46. Mem. Ill. (pres. 1971-72), North Central (dir. 1976—) bus. edn. assns., Am. (mem. resolutions com. 1975-77), Ill. (treas. 1965-69) vocat. assns., Pi Omega Pi (nat. pres. 1966-68), Delta Pi Epsilon (pres. Kappa chpt. 1960-61), Phi Delta Kappa, Phi Kappa Phi. Home: 708 Taft Ave Charleston IL 61920

COOPER, GEORGE LESTER, coll. dean; b. Hobart, Okla., Feb. 11, 1927; s. John Calvin and Sarah Celestine (Kincaid) C.; B.A., Okla. State U., 1950, M.S., 1959; Ed.D. (NDEA Fellow), 1975; m. Wilma Irene Chalfant, Oct. 10, 1953; children—Guy, Kevin, Leslie, David. Instr., Fairfax (Okla.) High Sch., 1950-51, 52-53, Classen High Sch., Oklahoma City, 1953-54, No. Okla. Jr. Coll., 1954-56, Stroud (Okla.) High Sch., 1956-60; mem. faculty Okla. State U., 1951-52, summer 1963-64; sch. psychologist Hutchinson (Kans.) Pub. Schs., 1962-66; acad. dean Hutchinson Community Jr. Coll., 1966—. Cons., Ednl. Mgmt., Hutchinson, 1972—; council chmn., participant completion Community Coll.-Regents Transfer Agreement, State Kans., 1975. Pres., Reno County Assn. Mental Health, 1964-66. Bd. dirs. Reno County YMCA. Served with AUS, 1945-47. Mem. Kans. Assn. Sch. Psychologists (pres. 1964-66), Kans. Council Deans and Dirs. Instrn. (chmn. 1972-73), Kans. Council Instructional Deans (chmn. 1973), Am. Assn. Higher Edn., Kans. Assn. Acad. Deans (pres. 1969-70), Nat. Council Resource Devel., Assn. Sch., Coll., Univ. Staffing, Kans. Juco Jayhawk Athletic Conf. (pres. 1972), Phi Kappa Phi, Phi Delta Kappa. Home: 616 Molly Mall Hutchinson KS 67501 Office: 1300 N Plum Hutchinson KS 67501

COOPER, GLENN CLAYTON, JR., accountant; b. Lebanon, Ind., Oct. 7, 1922; s. Glenn and Myrtle Mae (Logan) C.; student Ind. Central Bus. Coll., 1948; m. Mary Ellen Large, June 20, 1942. Bookkeeper, salesman Fred Siess Co., Inc., Lebanon, 1948-55; office mgr. East Side Mercury, Inc., Indpls., 1956-57; auditor for dealer devel. Ford Motor Co., Detroit, 1957-63; accounting rep. Var Heil Ford, Indpls., 1963; office mgr. Crossroads Lincoln-Mercury, Inc., Indpls., 1964-67; self-employed pub. accountant, Lebanon, 1967—. Bd. dirs. Oak Hill Cemetery Assn. Served with AUS, World War II. Decorated Bronze Star medal (2). Mem. Nat., Ind. socs. pub. accountants, Boone County C. of C. (dir.). Mason, Rotarian; mem. Order Eastern Star. Home: Rural Route 6 State Rd 39N Lebanon IN 46052 Office: 124 E Washington St Lebanon IN 46052

COOPER, HARRY PRESTON, JR., ins. co. exec.; b. Yountsville, Ind., Dec. 5, 1911; s. Harry Preston and Josephine Missouri (Long) C.; A.B., Ind. U., 1934, J.D., 1936; m. Elizabeth Louise Browning, Nov. 24, 1933; children—Carol (Mrs. Arthur Otis Miles), Harry Preston III, Linda (Mrs. John Steven Etherton). Admitted to Ind. bar, 1936; with Nat. Assn. Mut. Ins. Cos., 1936-61, exec. sec., 1946-61; with Ind. Farmers Mut. Ins. Co., Indpls., 1936—, pres., 1968—; a founder Town & Country Mut. Ins. Co., Indpls., 1954—, pres., 1961—; dir. Ind. Farmers Town & Country Mut. Ins. Cos. Bd. govs. Ind. Insurors' Assn.; bd. dirs. Ins. Inst. Ind. Served as lt. (j.g.) USNR, 1944-46. Mem. Am., Ind. bar assns., Am. Mgmt. Assn., Phi Beta Kappa, Beta Theta Pi, Phi Delta Phi. Republican. Presbyn. (trustee). Mason (Shriner), Kiwanian. Home: 9145 Springmill Rd Indianapolis IN 46260 Office: 10 W 106th St at N Meridian St Indianapolis IN 46290

COOPER, JERRY WILLIAM, oil co. exec.; b. Joplin, Mo., Aug. 16, 1937; s. Troy and Iris (Brigance) C.; B.J., U. Mo., 1959; A.A., Mo. So. Coll., 1957; m. Sharon Downie, Jan. 1, 1966; children—Kimberly Jo, Jason Andrew. Corporate communications supr. Great Lakes Pipeline Co. Kansas City, Mo., 1961-66; asst. to pres. Williams Companies, Tulsa. Okla., 1966-71; cons. Amoco Production Co., subs. Standard Oil Corp.. Tulsa, 1971-74; dir. pub. and govt. affairs Standard Oil Co. of Ind., Chgo., 1974—. Bd. dirs. Hinsdale Wholistic Health Center, chmn., 1976-77; bd. dirs. Okla. Lung Assn., 1968-71. Recipient Distinguished Service award Radio Free Europe Fund, 1968. Mem. Pub. Relations Soc. Am., World Future Soc. Republican. Clubs: Masons, Hinsdale Tennis. Home: 17 Orchard Place Hinsdale IL 60521 Office: 200 E Randolph Dr Chicago IL 60601

COOPER, JOHN ARNOLD, chartered financial analyst, investment mgr., educator; b. Detroit, Oct. 27, 1917; s. Gage Whitman and Helen (Danger) C.; A.B., Williams Coll. 1939; M.B.A., Mich. State U., 1968; m. Virginia Bailey Svagr, 1977; 1 dau., Maud (Mrs. Maud Cooper Granzow). Treas., Cooper Supply Co., 1941-44, sec., 1944-56, pres., 1956-65, also dir.; pres., dir. Cooper Family Corp., 1961-65, Cooper Equipment Co., 1960-65; v.p. Tex. Industries, Inc., 1963-67; pres. John Cooper Assos. (formerly A & W Cooper Co.), Birmingham, Mich., 1967—; sessional instr. portfolio mgmt. U. Windsor, 1977—. Dir. Transit Mixed Concrete Inst. Met. Detroit, 1952-53, 55-60, 63-66, pres., 1952-53, 59-60; dir., treas. Builders Exchange, Detroit, 1965-66, dir. pres., 1967-68. Patron mem. Founders Soc., Detroit Inst., Arts; mem. Oakland County Planning Commn., 1968-70. Bd. dirs. Friends Bloomfield Twp. Library, 1967-69; mem. investment com. U. Detroit. Served from ensign to lt. (j.g.) USNR, 1944-46. Recipient Outstanding Alumni award Mich. State U., 1973. Mem. Mich. (bd. govs. 1958-63), Am. (dir. 1961-63) trucking assns., Am. Mgmt. Assn. Episcopalian. Clubs: Bloomfield Hills (Mich.) Country; University (Detroit); The Williams of New York; Hillsboro (Pompano

Beach, Fla.); Mich. Polar Equator. Home: 1660 Apple Ln Bloomfield Hills MI 48013 Office: 1100 N Woodward Ave Birmingham MI 48011

COOPER, JOHN WILLIAM, banker; b. Kokomo, Ind., Oct. 29, 1925; s. Gayl Emerson and Ruth Morgan (Haynes) C.; B.S. with distinction, Ind. U., 1949; M.B.A., Northwestern U., 1955; postgrad. Rutgers U., 1964-66; m. Catherine Jeanne Haug, Aug. 7, 1954; children—Catherine Jeanne, Peter Stephen. With credit dept. Glidden Co., 1949, Continental Can Co., 1950-52; with Harris Trust & Savs. Bank, Chgo., 1952—, asst. sec., 1961-66, asst. v.p., 1966-69, v.p., 1969—; lectr. Nat. Trust Sch. Active Boy Scouts Am.; treas. exec. com., trustee Profit Sharing Research Found. Republican precinct committeeman, 1966. Served with USNR, 1944-46. Named Eagle Scout, Boy Scouts Am., 1939. Mem. Midwest Pension Conf., Am. Bankers Assn. (employees trusts com.), Corp. Fiduciaries Assn. Ill. (chmn. employees trust com.), Assn. Pvt. Pension and Welfare Plans (regional chmn.), Phi Gamma Delta, Beta Gamma Sigma, Alpha Kappa Psi, Alpha Phi Omega. Republican. Episcopalian. Club: Ind. Univ. Alumni (pres. 1958-59) (Chgo.). Contbr. articles to profl. jours. Home: 639 Wilmot Rd Deerfield IL 60015 Office: 111 W Monroe St Chicago IL 60690

COOPER, REGINALD RUDYARD, orthopaedic surgeon, educator; b. Elkins, W.Va., Jan 6, 1932; s. Eston H. and Kathryn (Wyatt) C.; B.A. with honors, W.Va. U., 1952, B.S., 1953; M.D., Med. Coll. Va., 1955; M.S., U. Ia., 1960; m. Jacqueline Smith, Aug. 22, 1954; children—Pamela Ann. Douglas Mark, Christopher Scott, Jeffrey Michael. Orthopedic surgeon U.S. Naval Hosp., Pensacola, Fla., 1960-62; asso. in orthopedics U. Iowa Coll. Medicine, Iowa City, 1962-65, asst. prof. orthopaedics, 1965-68, asso. prof. orthopedics, 1968-71, prof. orthopedics, 1971—, chmn. orthopedics, 1973—; research fellow orthopedic surgery Johns Hopkins Hosp., Balt., 1964-65; exchange fellow to Britain for Am. Orthopedic Assn., 1969. Served to lt. comdr. USNR, 1960-62. Diplomate Am. Bd. Orthopedic Surgeons (examiner 1968—). Mem. Iowa, Johnson County med. socs., Orthopedic Research Soc. (sec.-treas. 1970-73, pres. 1974-75), Am. Acad. Orthopedic Surgeons (Kappa Delta award for outstanding research in orthopedics 1971), Canadian, Am. orthopedic assns., Am. Acad. Orthopedic Surgeons (dir. 1973-74), N.Y. Acad. Sci., Assn. Bone and Joint Surgeons, AMA, Am. Rheumatism Assn., Am. Fedn. Clin. Research. Home: 201 Ridgeview Ave Iowa City IA 52240

COOPER, ROYAL OWEN, assn. exec.; b. Kansas City, Kans., Aug. 3, 1929; s. Herbert Bryan and Mildred (Owen) C.; B.S. in Pub. Adminstrn., U. Mo., 1955; m. Deborah Bucher, 1976. Grad. asst. dept. polit. sci. U. Mo., Columbia, 1954-55; claims rep. Equitable Life Assurance Soc. U.S., Chgo., 1955-57; asst. state purchasing agt., Jefferson City, Mo., 1957-61, state purchasing agt., 1961-65; commodity broker Clayton Brokerage Co., Jefferson City, Mo., 1965-68; asst. exec. sec. Mo. State Med. Assn., Jefferson City, 1969-77, exec. sec., 1977—. Served with AUS, 1948-52. Mem. Am. Soc. Assn. Execs., A.M.A. (affiliate), Am. Assn. Med. Soc. Execs., Mo. Soc. Assn. Execs. (pres. 1973-74), Profl. Conv. Mgmt. Assn., Phi Sigma Alpha, Alpha Kappa Psi. Democrat. Episcopalian (lay reader 1961-71). Home: 2138 Tanner Bridge St Jefferson City MO 65101 Office: 113 Madison St Jefferson City MO 65101

COOPER, STEVEN JON, hosp. adminstr., educator; b. Oct. 19, 1941; B.A., U. Calif., Los Angeles, 1966; M.Ed., Loyola U., 1973; postgrad. Union Sch., 1977—; m. Sharon M. Lepack; children—Robin E., Erik S. Ednl. coordinator dept. radiology Mt. Sinai Hosp. Med. Center, Chgo., 1969-72; chmn. dept. radiol. scis. U. Health Scis., Chgo. Med. Sch., VA Hosp., North Chicago, 1972—; cons. HEW; lectr. in field. Served with USAF, 1960-64, USAFR, 1964-66. Mem. W.K. Kellogg Found. grantee. Mem. Am. (mem. edn., curriculum review coms., task force), Ill. (chmn. annual meeting 1976, program Midwest conf., 1977) socs. radiol. tech., Coll. Radiol. Scis., Am. Hosp. Radiology Adminstrs. (mem. edn. com., treas. Midwest region, nat. v.p.), AMA (com. on allied health edn. and accreditation), Sigma Xi. Author numerous publs. in field. Home: 346 Colony Green Dr Bloomingdale IL 60108 Office: Sch Related Health Scis Bldg 51 VA Hosp North Chicago IL 60064

COOPER, THOMAS DAVID, metall. engr.; b. Dayton, Ohio, Apr. 7, 1932; s. Arnold Leroy and Edna Catherine (Guthrie) C.; Met. E., U. Cin., 1955; M.S., Ohio State U., 1964; m. Katherine Ann Ambrose, Dec. 26, 1953; children—Theresa Deborah, Michael Bruce, Stephen Jeffrey. Engr., Westinghouse Electric Co., Pitts., 1955-56; various positions, Air Force Materials Lab., Wright-Patterson AFB, Ohio, 1956—, chief materials integrity br., 1976—. Served to lt. USAF, 1956-58. Recipient Distinguished Alumnus award U. Cin. Coll. Engring., 1972. Registered profl. engr., Ohio. Fellow Am. Soc. for Metals (mem. tech. divs. bd., chmn. materials testing and quality control div.), Am. Inst. Aeros. and Astronautics (asso. fellow; chmn. materials tech. com.); mem. Am. Inst. Metall. Engrs. (chmn. structural materials com.), Am. Soc. for Nondestructive Testing, Dayton YMCA, Sigma Xi, Tau Beta Pi, Phi Lambda Upsilon, Alpha Tau Omega. Mason. Co-editor Oxide Dispersion Strengthening, 1968; Prevention of Structural Failure, 1975. Contbr. articles to tech. jours. Home: 542 Rader Dr Vandalia OH 45377 Office: Air Force Materials Laboratory Wright-Patterson AFB OH 45433

COOPER, WAYNE, artist; b. Depew, Okla., May 7, 1942; s. Orval and Mary Ellen (Harrington) C.; student Valparaiso U., 1962-64; m. Clara Marie Beck, Mar. 26, 1962. Group shows include: The Naples (Fla.) Art Gallery, Collectors Showroom, Chgo., Lewis Gallery, Willow Tree, Omaha, Cotton Terry Gallery, Austin, Tex., Sloan McKinney Gallery, Tulsa, Walton St. Gallery, Chgo., Carolyn Summers Gallery, Chgo., Dorer Gallery, Marietta, Ga., Circle Gallery, Chgo., N.Y.C., Los Angeles; represented in permanent collections: Park View Hosp., Ft. Wayne, Ind., Olson Collection, Fredriksberg Castle, Copenhagen, Andrews Collection, Kilchberg, Switzerland, Williams Co., Japan, also numerous pvt. collections; owner gallery and studio, Hebron, Ind., 1968—. Recipient Best of Show award Indian Art Exhbn., Gilcrease Mus., Tulsa, 1976. Mem. Gary Artists League, Fla. Fedn. Artists, Ind. Artists and Craftsmen, Green County Art Assn. (Tulsa), Mid-Am. Art Assn. (Chgo.), N. Shore Art League (Chgo.), Huntsville (Ala.) Art League, Am. Artists Profl. League, Inc. Home and Office: Box 361 Hebron IN 46341 also Box 106 Depew OK 74028

COOPER, WYLOLA, counselor, educator; b. Cleve., Feb. 12, 1926; d. William and Leola (Anderson) Wilkins; B.E., Chgo. State U., 1967; M.A., Roosevelt U., 1974; m. Henry Julius Cooper, Apr. 4, 1948; children—Henry Julius, Wylola, Antigone, Yolanda Lee. Tchr., counselor Southwest Coop. for Spl. Edn., Chgo., 1967—, Dist. 117 Pub. Schs., Chgo., 1967—. Mem. Am. Fedn. Tchrs., NEA, Ill. Educators Assn., Am. Personnel and Guidance Assn., Council Exceptional Children, Chgo. State, Roosevelt U. alumni assns. Roman Catholic. Home: Chicago IL 60615

COOPERRIDER, TOM SMITH, botanist; b. Newark, Ohio, Apr. 15, 1927; s. Oscar Harold and Ruth Evelyn (Smith) C.; B.A., Denison U., 1950; M.S., U. Iowa, 1955, Ph.D. (NSF fellow), 1958; m. Miwako Kunimura, June 13, 1953; children—Julie Ann, John Andrew. With Kent (Ohio) State U., 1958—, instr. biol. scis., 1958-61, asst. prof., 1961-65, asso. prof., 1965-69, prof., 1969—, dir. exptl. programs, 1972-73, curator herbarium, 1968—, dir. Bot. Gardens and Arboretum, 1972—, mem. editorial bd. Univ. Press, 1976—; on leave as asst. prof. dept. botany U. Hawaii, 1962-63; NSF researcher Mountain Lake Biol. Sta., U. Va., summer 1958; cons. endangered and threatened species U.S. Fish and Wildlife Service, Dept. Interior, 1976—. Served with AUS, 1945-46. NSF research grantee, 1965-72. Fellow Ohio Acad. Scis. (v.p. 1967); mem. Am. Soc. Plant Taxonomists, Internat. Assn. Plant Taxonomists, AAAS, Bot. Soc. Am. Author: Ferns and Other Pteridophytes of Iowa, 1959; Vascular Plants of Clinton, Jackson and Jones Counties, Iowa, 1962. Home: 548 Bowman Dr Kent OH 44240

COOPERSMITH, BERNARD IRA, physician, surgeon; b. Chgo., Oct. 19, 1914; s. Morris and Anna (Shulder) C.; B.S. cum laude, U. Ill., 1936, M.D. cum laude, 1938; m. Beatrice Klass, May 26, 1940; children—Carol, Cathie. Intern, Michael Reese Hosp., Chgo., 1938-39, resident in obstetrics and gynecology, 1939-42; practice medicine specializing in obstetrics and gynecology, Chgo., 1942—; mem. staff Prentice Women's Hosp. of Northwestern Meml. Hosp., Michael Reese Hosp., Mt. Sinai Hosp., Chgo. Maternity Center; asst. prof. obstetrics and gynecology Northwestern U. Med. Sch., Chgo., 1948—. Pres. Barren Found. Chgo., 1971-73. Diplomate Am. Bd. Obstetrics and Gynecology. Recipient Service awards Michael Reese Hosp., 1972, Northwestern U. Med. Sch., 1973, Chgo. Maternity Center, 1968. Fellow A.C.S.; mem. Chgo., Ill. med. socs., AMA, Chgo. Gynecol. Soc., Central Assn. Obstetrics and Gynecology, Am. Coll. Obstetrics and Gynecology, Alpha Omega Alpha. Jewish. Clubs: Bryn Mawr Country, Carleton. Contbr. articles to profl. jours. Home: 1110 N Lake Shore Dr Chicago IL 60611 Office: 333 E Superior St Suite 444 Chicago IL 60611

COORTS, GERALD DUANE, educator; b. Emden, Ill., Feb. 3, 1932; s. Ralph Albert and Hannah Tena (Wubben) C.; B.S. (Danforth fellow), U. Mo., 1954, M.S., 1958; Ph.D., U. Ill., 1964; m. Annette Bosman, Sept. 14, 1957; children—David Jonathan, Charles Frederick, Cynthia Anne. Instr. horticulture Purdue U., 1959-61; asst. prof. horticulture U. R.I., 1964-68; asso. prof. plant and soil sci. So. Ill. U., Carbondale, 1968-72, prof., 1972—, chmn. dept., 1973—. Bd. dirs. Jackson County YMCA, Green Earth, Inc. Served to 1st lt., Chem. Corps, AUS, 1954-56. Recipient Obelisk award for Outstanding Teaching, 1972. Mem. U.S. Jr. C. of C. (chpt. v.p. 1966-67), Am. Soc. Hort. Sci., Am. Soc. Agronomy, Am. Hort. Soc., Council for Agrl. Sci. and Tech., Plant Growth Regulator Working Group, Internat. Plant Propagators Soc., Sigma Xi, Alpha Zeta, Gamma Sigma Delta, Pi Alpha Xi, Phi Mu Alpha, Phi Sigma, Phi Kappa Phi, Farmhouse. Home: 1714 Colonial Dr Carbondale IL 62901

COPE, DAVID HOWELL, educator, composer; b. San Francisco, May 17, 1941; s. Howell Nicholson and Charlotte Evlyn (Schleicher) C.; B.Mus., Ariz. State U., 1963; M.Mus., U. So. Calif., 1965; m. Mary Jane Stluka, Aug. 12, 1967; children—Timothy, Stephen, Brian, Gregory. Mem. faculty Kans. State Coll., Pittsburg, 1966-68, Calif. Lutheran Coll., 1968-69; mem. faculty Cleve. Inst. Music, 1970-73; asst. prof. music Miami U., Oxford, Ohio, 1973—; pres. Composers' Autograph Publs., Cleve., 1968—. Mem. A.S.C.A.P. (panel composition awards 1971, 72), Assn. Ind. Composers and Performers, Phi Mu Alpha. Editor: The Composer Mag., 1969—. Author: New Directions in Music, 2d edit., 1976; Notes in Discontinuum, 1970; New Music Composition, 1976; New Music Notation, 1976. Composer numerous published works. Address: Dept Music Miami U Oxford OH 45056

COPE, HAROLD CARY, coll. ofcl.; b. Westtown, Pa., Aug. 9, 1918; s. Joshua A. and Edith (Cary) C.; B.S., Cornell U., 1941; student U. Omaha, 1953-54, U. Mich., 1959; m. Ann Elizabeth Reeves, Apr. 17, 1943; children—David Harold, Sarah Ann, Elizabeth R., Hannah Sue. Supr. student union cafeteria Cornell U., 1941-42; dietitian Earlham Coll., Richmond, Ind., 1946-49, mgr. resident halls, 1949-52, mgr. resident halls, accountant, 1952-55, asst. comptroller, 1955-58, bus. mgr., 1958-67, v.p. bus. affairs, 1967-72; instr. instl. mgmt., 1948-58; pres. Friends U., Wichita, Kans., 1972—. Cub master Boy Scouts Am., 1947-51; chmn. stewardship and fin. bd. 5 Years Meeting, Soc. of Friends, 1960-66, mem. exec. council, 1960-70, nat. bd. com., 1966-74; bd. dirs., treas. Friends Fellowship Retirement Home, 1964-70; clk. White Water Monthly Meeting of Friends, 1963-66; clk. Ind. Yearly Meeting of Friends, 1965-71; mem. nat. bd. Am. Friends Service Com., 1968-74, mem. exec. com., 1970-74; chmn. Richmond Housing Authority, 1968-72; adv. bd. Sedgwick County Zoo, 1972—; mem. Alcohol Task Force for Sedgwick County, 1972-74; bd. dirs., sec. Quaker Hill Found.; bd. dirs., treas. Partnership for Productivity Found., 1970-73; bd. dirs., mem. exec. com. Richmond YMCA; trustee Channel 8 TV Sta. Mem. Ind. (pres. 1960-61), Central (mem. exec. com. 1970-71) assns. bus. officers. Kiwanian, Rotarian. Club: Y's Mens (treas. 1956-57, pres. 1959-60, dist. gov. 1960-61). Home: 522 Hiram St Wichita KS 67213

COPELAND, ELAINE JOHNSON, ednl. adminstr.; b. Catawba, S.C., Mar. 11, 1943; d. Aaron Jasper and Roberta Lucille (Hawkins) Johnson; B.S., Livingstone Coll., 1964; M.A. in Teaching, Winthrop Coll., 1971; Ph.D., Oreg. State U., 1974; m. Robert M. Copeland, Sept. 26, 1964; 1 son, Robert. Tchr. sci. Florence (S.C.) Pub. Schs., 1964-65; tchr. biology York (S.C.) Pub. Schs., 1965-70; counselor Oreg. State U., 1970-74; research asso. U. Ill., Champaign, 1974-75, asst. dean, dir. minority affairs grad. coll., 1975—; project supr. Title 1, Black Elderly Project, 1974-75; co-organizer Black Elderly Conf. of Champaign County, 1975. Chmn. bd. dirs. Univ. YWCA, 1976-77; bd. dirs. Ill. Children's Home and Aid, 1975—. Recipient award for service to elderly Telecare, 1975. Mem. Am. Psychol. Assn., Am. Personnel and Guidance Assn.. for Non-White Concerns in Personnel and Guidance, Coll. Student Personnel Assn., Phi Kappa Phi, Delta Sigma Theta. Methodist. Clubs: Urban League Guild, Champaign County. Home: 34 Ashley Ln Champaign IL 61820 Office: 337 Administration Bldg University of Illinois Urbana IL 61801

COPELAND, WILLIAM EDGAR, physician; b. Huntington, W.Va., Nov. 22, 1920; s. Orville Edgar and Clara Gertrude (Naylon) C.; M.D., Med. Coll. Va., 1945; m. Carolyn Ann Varin, Jan. 31, 1948; children—William Edgar, Christopher Marsh, Stephen Jeffrey. Intern, Stuart Circle Hosp., Richmond, Va., 1945-46; resident in obstetrics gynecology Hosp. U. Pa., Phila., 1948-51; practice medicine specializing in obstetrics and gynecology, Phila., 1951-53, Columbus, Ohio, 1953—; mem. staff Ohio State U. Hosp., Columbus, Childrens Hosp., VA Hosp., Dayton, Riverside Meth. Hosp., Columbus, Wright Patterson AFB Hosp., Dayton; mem. faculty Ohio State U., 1953—, prof. obstetrics and gynecology, 1970—, dir. clin. div., dept., 1971-73. Mem. adv. com. Planned Parenthood, YMCA. Served with USN, 1943-47. Fellow Am. Coll. Obstetricians and Gynecologists, ACS, Am. Soc. Study Fertility; mem. Central Assn. Obstetricians and Gynecologists, AMA, N. Am. Obstet. and Gynecol. Soc., Ohio Med. Soc., Ohio State U. Health Center Med. Soc., Assn. Am. Med. Colls. Clubs: Scioto Country, Faculty, Zanesfield Rod and Gun, Grand Hotel Hunt, Ohio State U. Pres., League Ohio Sportsmen. Contbr. articles to profl. jours. Home: 2495 Sherwin Rd Columbus OH 43221 Office: 1800 Zollinger Rd Columbus OH 43221

COPELAND, WILLIAM JAMES, paper co. exec.; b. Fort Edward, N.Y., May 19, 1922; s. John H. and Frances Olive (Saunders) C.; B.S., Cornell U., 1948; m. Dorothy Elizabeth Reid, June 17, 1950 (dec. May 1975); children—Jennifer L., Heather R., W. John; m. 2d, Barbara Ann Clapp Dayton, July 31, 1976. Chemist research div. Internat. Paper Co., 1948-53, sales engr. sales dept., 1953-55, sales rep. wood pulp, 1956-58; asst. sales mgr. Beckett Paper Co., Hamilton, Ohio, 1958-65, sales mgr., 1965-70, asst. v.p., 1971-72, v.p. sales, 1972—. Chmn., Multiple Sclerosis chpt. Butler County, 1966-67; mem. civic adv. bd. Mercy Hosp., Hamilton, 1971—, chmn., 1976-77; bd. dirs. Am. Cancer Soc., Hamilton, Butler County Children's Home, Greater Cin. chpt. Nat. Multiple Sclerosis Soc.; mem. Republican Exec. Com. Butler County, 1958—; trustee Lane Pub. Library, Hamilton, pres., 1976-77. Served with USMCR, 1943-46, 51-52. Mem. Salesmen's Assn. of Paper Industry (pres. 1965). Presbyn. (elder). Mason, Elk. Clubs: Hamilton City; Cornell (N.Y.C.). Home: 1465 Eaton Rd Hamilton OH 45013 Office: 4th and Buckeye Sts Hamilton OH 45012

COPES, MARVIN LEE, ednl. adminstr.; b. Connersville, Ind., Sept. 19, 1938; s. Kenneth Edward and Frances Gertrude (Bean) C.; B.S., Purdue U., 1961, M.S., 1962, Ph.D., 1975; postgrad., Ind. State U., 1967-68, Ind. U., 1967-68; m. Luretta Ann Grenard, Aug. 26, 1961; children—Bradley Alan, Brian Keith, Brent Lee. Grad. asst. agr. edn. Purdue U., 1961-62, grad. instr., 1968-69; tchr. vocat. agr. Tri-County Sch. Corp., Walcott, Ind., 1964-65; vocat. dir. Met. Sch. Dist. Vernon Twp., Crothersville, Ind., 1965-68, also dir. Ind. Vocat. Agr. Demonstration Center; asst. exec. sec. Kappa Delta Pi Hdqrs., West Lafayette, Ind., 1969-70; dir. Blue River Vocat.-Tech. Center, Shelbyville, Ind. 1970—. Pres., Loper Parent Tchr. Orgn., 1974—; leader 4-H, 1964—; adviser Future Farmers Am., 1964—; cubmaster Cub Scouts Am., 1976; active Boy Scouts Am.; bd. dirs. Shelbyville Boys Club Am., 1976, Northeast India Christian Mission, 1974. Served to 1st lt., AUS, 1962-64. Mem. Am., Ind. vocat. assns., Ind., Nat. councils local adminstrs., Future Farmers Am. Alumni Assn., Shelby County C. of C., Pershing Rifles, Gideons Internat., Alpha Tau Alpha, Kappa Delta Pi, Phi Delta Kappa. Mem. Christian Ch. (elder). Mason; mem. Order Eastern Star. Author: A Curriculum Guide for Training in Agricultural Supply, 1968, Student Handbook for Cooperative Progress in Agricultural Occupations, 1968, A Predictability of Career Choices of High School Seniors, 1975. Home: Rural Route 2 Box 370 Fairland IN 46126 Office: 789 St Joseph Shelbyville IN 46176

COPPOC, GORDON LLOYD, educator; b. Larned, Kans., Nov. 11, 1939; s. Louis Albert and Mary Eleanor (Rudd) C.; B.S., Kans. State U., 1961, D.V.M., 1963; postgrad. Tufts U., 1964; Ph.D., Harvard, 1968; m. Harriet Jo Kagay, June 9, 1962; children—Laura Jean, Elizabeth Ann. Instr. pharmacology U. N.C. Sch. Medicine, 1966-67; research asso. Ben May Lab. Cancer Research, U. Chgo., 1969-71; asst. prof. pharmacology Purdue U., Lafayette, Ind., 1971-73, asso. prof., 1973-77, prof., 1977—. Pres., Bach Chorale Singers. Served to capt. USAF, 1967-69. Mem. AAAS, AVMA, Am. Soc. Vet. Physiologists and Pharmacologists, Assn. Am. Vet. Med. Colls. (sec. council of educators), Vet. Cancer Soc., Am. Fedn. Wildlife, Am. Coll. Vet. Pharmacology and Therapeutics, Common Cause, Sierra Club, Sigma Xi, Phi Zeta, Phi Kappa Phi, Gamma Sigma Delta. Baptist. Home: 636 Vine St West Lafayette IN 47906 Office: Purdue U Lafayette IN 47907

CORAN, ARNOLD GERALD, pediatric surgeon, educator; b. Boston, Apr. 16, 1938; s. Charles and Anne (Cohen) C.; B.A. cum laude, Harvard U., 1959, M.D. cum laude, 1963; m. Susan Williams, Nov. 17, 1960; children—Michael, David, Randi Beth. Intern, Peter Bent Brigham Hosp., Boston, 1963-64, resident in surgery, 1964-68, chief surg. resident, 1969, resident in surgery Children's Hosp. Med. Center, Boston, 1965-66, sr. surg. resident, 1966, chief surg. resident, 1968; instr. surgery Harvard, Cambridge, Mass., 1967-69; asst. clin. prof. surgery George Washington U., Washington, 1970-72; head physician pediatric surgery Los Angeles County-U. So. Calif. Med. Center, 1972-74; asst. prof. surgery U. So. Calif., 1972-73, asso. prof., 1973-74; prof. surgery U. Mich., Ann Arbor, 1974—, head sect. pediatric surgery U. Mich. Hosp., 1974—. Served to lt. comdr. M.C., U.S. Army. Diplomate Am. Bd. Surgery, Am. Bd. Thoracic Surgery. Fellow A.C.S.; mem. Am. Acad. Pediatrics, Soc. Univ. Surgeons, Am. Pediatric Surg. Assn., Western, Central surg. assns. Contbr. numerous articles in field to profl. jours. Home: 3450 Vintage Valley Rd Ann Arbor MI 48105 Office: Mott Children's Hosp Ann Arbor MI 48109

CORBALLY, JOHN EDWARD, univ. pres.; b. South Bend, Wash., Oct. 14, 1924; s. John Edward and Grace (Williams) C.; B.S., U. Wash., 1947, M.A., 1950; Ph.D., U. Calif. at Berkeley, 1955; LL.D., U. Md., 1971, Blackburn Coll., 1972, Ill. State U., 1977; m. Marguerite B. Walker, Mar. 12, 1946; children—Jan Elizabeth, David William. Tchr., Clover Park High Sch., Tacoma, 1947-50; prin. Twin City High Sch., Stanwood, Wash., 1950-53; asst. prof. edn., asso. prof. Ohio State U., Columbus, 1955-60, prof., 1960-69, dir. personnel budget and exec. asst. to pres., 1960-64, v.p. adminstrn., 1964-66, provost, v.p. acad. affairs, 1966-69; chancellor, also pres. Syracuse U., 1969-71; pres. U. Ill., Chgo. and Urbana, 1971—. Dir. Ill. Bell Telephone Co., AMA Tax Exempt Fund. Mem. commn. on govtl. relations Am. Council on Edn.; mem. exec. com. Assn. Am. Univs.; mem. governing bd. Ill. Council on Econ. Edn.; bd. dirs. Ill. Ednl. Consortium; chmn. nat. council ednl. research Nat. Inst. Edn., 1973-79; mem. bd. nominators Am. Inst. for Pub. Service. Trustee Mus. Sci. and Industry, Chgo.; bd. dirs. Council for Financial Aid to Edn.; acad. trustee Lincoln Acad. Ill. Served to lt. (j.g.) USNR, 1943-46. Mem. Chgo. Council on Fgn. Relations (Chgo. com.), Phi Beta Kappa, Phi Kappa Sigma, Phi Delta Kappa, Phi Kappa Phi, Omicron Delta Kappa, Chi Gamma Iota, Beta Gamma Sigma. Clubs: Mid-America, Executives, Tavern (Chgo.). Author: Introduction to Educational Administration, 4th edit., 1971; Educational Administration: The Secondary School, 2d edit., 1965; School Finance, 1962. Home: 711 W Florida Ave Urbana IL 61801

CORBET, WARREN HARDING, agrl. engr.; b. Severance, Kans., Oct. 20, 1920; s. Henry L. and Rosene (Laverna) C.; student Highland Jr. Coll., 1938-40; B.S. in Agrl. Engring., Kans. State Coll., 1943; m. Alice V. Doll, Apr. 11, 1952; 1 dau., Catherine Luetta. Engr., John Deere Waterloo Tractor Works, Waterloo, Iowa, 1943-48; with U.S. Dept. Interior Bur. Reclamation specializing in hydrology, 1948—. Recipient Superior Performance awards. Mem. Grand Island Engrs. Club, Am. Soc. Agrl. Engrs., Grand Island Leiderkranz, Tau Beta Pi. Presbyn. (elder). Mason (32 deg., Shriner). Home: 204 W 18th Grand Island NE 68801 Office: Box 1607 Grand Island NE 68801

CORBETT, DENNIS DALE, advt. exec.; b. Evansville, Ind., Apr. 11, 1944; s. Cecil W. and Gertrude M. (Jackson) C.; B.S. in Bus., U. Evansville, 1966; B.S. in Econs., Henry George Sch., 1969; theol. certificate Ambassador Coll., 1970; m. Dwana Sue Yates, Jan. 27, 1973; 1 dau., Koelle Kristen. Spl. investigator Research Assos., 1963-65; detective Internat. Films, 1968-71; owner Corbett Enterprises, Evansville, Ind., 1963—. Probation counselor Vanderburgh County Vol. Probation Counselors Program, 1972—; campaign dir. March of Dimes, 1968; mem. nat. adv. com. Am. Security Council; mem. citizens adv. com. for Right to Keep and Bear Arms; founder Archtl. Barriers Research. Bd. dirs. Evansville Area

Council Chs., mem. mass media com.; bd. dirs. Concern for Haiti (orphanage); mem. Republican Citizens Finance Com. Ind., Recipient Key Man award Jr. C. of C., 1966. Mem. Am. Mgmt. Assn. (presidents assn.), Nat. Rifle Assn., Nat. Wildlife Fedn., ACLU, Direct Selling Legion, Internat. Speakers Network, Ams. Against Union Control of Govt., Council on Religion and Internat. Affairs, Conservative Caucus, Security and Intelligence Fund, Council Inter-am. Security, Interam. Soc. OAS, Nat. Right to Work Com., Am. Film Inst., Assn. Supervision and Curriculum Devel., Inst. Soc., Ethics and Life Scis., Target '76, Jr. C. of C. Methodist (dir., mem. council ministries, chmn. action task force 1973-74). Home: 2005 N Harding St Evansville IN 47711 Office: 150 Broadway New York City NY 10038 also 1639 N California St Chicago IL 60647

CORBETT, JULES JOHN, educator; b. Natrona, Pa., Apr. 12, 1919; s. Anthony and Theodosia (Kuczynski) C.; A.A., North Park Coll., 1947; student Franklin Sch. Sci. and Arts, 1946; B.S., U. Chgo., 1950; M.S., Ill. Inst. Tech., 1956; m. Gabrielle Ann Wengel, June 24, 1950; children—Brian Lee, Alan Jeffrey, Christine Marie. Bacteriologist, instr. Englewood Hosp., 1950; dir. labs., Beverly Med. Arts Bldg., 1954; bacteriologist, The Borden Co., 1955-64; instr. biology Roosevelt U., Chgo., 1956-58, asst. prof., 1958-64, asso. prof., 1964-72, prof., 1972—, chmn. biology dept., 1974—. Served with AUS, 1937-39, USNR, 1941-45. Mem. Am., Ill. socs. microbiologists, Ill., N.Y. acads. sci., A.A.A.S., Am. Legion (comdr. 4th dist. 1974), 40 and 8, Sigma Xi. Roman Catholic. Home: 8318 S Komensky Ave Chicago IL 60652 Office: 430 S Michigan Ave Chicago IL 60605

CORBIN, ROBERT MCCARTNEY, entertainer; b. Barnesville, Ohio, Apr. 9, 1908; s. Walter Dent and Rose (Pryor) C.; student pub. schs.; m. Isabelle Neptune, June 3, 1937; children—Jean (Mrs. Charles Hannon, Jr.), Robert II, Richard Ricton. With various vaudeville shows, 1926-30; calliope player, clown, with various fair attractions, 1930—; advt. promotion man Ohio State Fair, Columbus, 1958-59; advance rep. Ringling Bros. Barnum & Bailey Circus, Venice, Fla., 1961; press agt., comml. clown Deggeller Magic Midway, Stuart, Fla., 1962-71. Named Ky. col. Mem. Am. Fedn. Musicians, A.F.T.R.A., Internat. Platform Assn., Internat. Ind. Showmens Assn., Circus Hist. Soc., Nat. Rifle Assn., Mgrs. Round Table Club of Motion Picture Hearld, Greater Ohio Showmens Assn., Soc. Am. Magicians (asso.). Eagle, Elk. Author: A Lifetime in Show Business, 1968. Address: 318 E South St Barnesville OH 43713

CORBOY, PHILIP HARNETT, lawyer; b. Chgo., Aug. 12, 1924; s. Harold Francis and Marie (Harnett) C.; student St. Ambrose Coll., 1942-43, U. Notre Dame, 1945; J.D., Loyola U., 1948; m. Doris Marie Conway, Nov. 26, 1949; children—Philip Harnett, Joan Marie, John, Thomas, Robert. Admitted to Ill. bar, 1949; asst. corp. counsel City Chgo., 1949-50; pvt. practice, 1950—. Trustee Roscoe Pound Found. Served with AUS, 1943-45. Fellow Am. Coll. Trial Lawyers, Am. Bar Assn. (mem. commn. on jud. standards, ho. of dels.); mem. Ill., Chgo. (pres. 1972-73) bar assns., Law Sci. Acad., Am. Judicature Soc., Am., Ill. trial lawyers assns., Nat. Inst. Trial Advocacy (vice chmn. 1971-72), Internat. Acad. Trial Lawyers, Internat. Soc. Barristers, Inner Circle Advocates. Clubs: Evanston Golf, Chicago Athletic Assn. Contbr. articles to profl. jours. Home: 9519 Monticello Evanston IL 60203 Office: 33 N Dearborn St Chicago IL 60602

CORCORAN, JAMES MARTIN, JR., lawyer; b. Evanston, Ill., Nov. 12, 1932; s. James M. and Ethel M. (Fitzgerald) C.; A.B., U. Notre Dame, 1955, J.D., 1956; m. Catherine F. Howland, Aug. 6, 1955; children—Mary Carol, John Kevin, Lawrence T., Rosemary C., Pauline M., Moira E., Daniel P. Admitted to Ill. bar, 1956, since practiced in Evanston; partner Corcoran & Corcoran, attys., Evanston, 1957-63, sr. partner, 1964-72; pres., Corcoran & Corcoran, Profl. Corp., Evanston, 1973—; lectr. in field. Mem. sch. bd. St. Mary's Sch., 1969-72. Recipient Harrison Tweed award Assn. Continuing Legal Edn. Adminstrs., 1975; Distinguished Service award Chgo. Estate Planning Council, 1975. Fellow Am. Coll. Probate Counsel (editorial bd. Probate Notes 1975—); mem. Am., Ill. (bd. govs. 1972-75), Chgo. bar assns. Roman Catholic. Author: (with others) Drafting Wills and Trust Agreements, rev., 1977; Alternatives to Probate, 1972; Suggested Will and Trust Clauses, 1973; In the Office—A Form Book for Lawyers, 1974; Estate and Gift Taxation for the General Practitioner, 1977; Probate Forms for Estates of Minors, Incompetents and Decedents, 1977. Contbr. chpts. to continuing legal edn. books, articles to profl. jours. Home: 929 Sheridan Rd Evanston IL 60202 Office: 1603 Orrington Ave Evanston IL 60201

CORCORAN, MAURICE FRIDOLIN, elec. engr.; b. New Bedford, Mass., Dec. 15, 1926; s. Charles S. and Norma (Bartholomeus) C.; B.S. in Elec. Engring., Tufts U., 1951; m. Irene Helen McDonald, June 17, 1951; children—Christine, Valerie, Sandra, Gregory. With Allis Chalmers, various locations, 1951-73, field engr., Cleve., 1953-59, sr. engr. indsl. systems, Milw., 1959-62, sr. elec. engr. project ops., Milw., 1962-66, mgr. elec. engring. project ops., Milw., 1966-73; staff cons. engr. Doyen & Assos., Inc., Chgo., 1973—. Served with AUS, 1945-46. Registered profl. engr., Wis. Mem. IEEE (sr.), Assn. Iron and Steel Engrs. Home: 2833 Fern Ave Northbrook IL 60062 Office: 222 W Adams St Room 381 Chicago IL 60606

CORCORAN, THOMAS EDWARD, pathologist, educator; b. Rock Rapids, Iowa, Feb. 16, 1914; s. Louis Leonard and Myrtle Louise (Early) C.; B.S., State U. Iowa, 1938, M.D., 1938; m. Florence Virginia McLean, July 3, 1941; children—Thomas M., Becky Ann. Intern, St. Mary's Hosp., Kansas City, Mo., 1938-39; resident VA Hosp., Des Moines, 1946-48, chief lab. service, 1951—; resident State U. Iowa, 1949; practice medicine specializing in pathology, Des Moines, 1946-74, chief of staff, 1974—; clin. asso. prof. pathology State U. Iowa, 1956—. Served to capt. M.C., AUS, 1941-46. Fellow Am. Soc. Clin. Pathologists; mem. Phi Delta Theta, Nu Sigma Nu. Home: 3328 Douglas St Des Moines IA 50310 Office: VA Hosp 30th and Euclid Sts Des Moines IA 50310

CORCORAN, THOMAS JOSEPH, Congressman; b. Ottawa, Ill., May 23, 1939; s. Thomas F. C.; m. Helenmarie Anderson; children—Camilla, Evan, Philip, Steven, Monica; grad. U. Notre Dame, 1961; postgrad. U. Ill., 1961-62, Northwestern U., 1966-68, U. Chgo., 1962-63. Legis. asst. Ill. Senate Pres. Pro Tem W. Russell Arrington, 1966-69; dir. State of Ill. Office, Washington, 1969-72; v.p. Chgo. & North Western Transp. Co., 1974-76; mem. 95th Congress from 15th Ill. Dist. Home: Ottawa IL 61350 Office: 1107 Longworth House Office Bldg Washington DC 20515

CORDANO, DONALD LAVERNE, accountant, educator; b. Joliet, Ill., Aug. 5, 1934; s. Joseph S. and Louise M. (Brusatti) C.; B.S., Lewis U., 1956; M.B.A., DePaul U., 1962; postgrad. U. Ill., 1963-65, No. Ill. U., 1967-68; m. Suellen K. Brehn, Aug. 29, 1959; children—Marysue, James. Vice pres., gen. mgr. Bryant Bldgs., Inc., Plainfield, Ill., 1956-65; prof. accountancy Lewis U., Lockport, Ill., 1965—; owner, accountant Donald L. Cordano & Assos., Joliet, 1965—. Bd. dirs., treas. Cath. Charities. Served with USNR, 1952-60. Mem. Am. Mgmt. Assn., Am. Accounting Assn., Nat. Assn. Accountants, Nat. Soc. Pub. Accountants, Ind. Accountants Assn. Ill., Am. Interprofl. Inst., Assn. Enrolled Agts., Delta Mu Delta, Delta Sigma Pi, Delta Epsilon Sigma. Clubs: Moose, Tiger, Moran Athletic. Home: 1601 Arden Pl Joliet IL 60435 Office: Lewis University Route 53 Lockport IL 60441 also 625 N Hickory St Joliet IL 60435

CORDONIER, LOUIS HARAN, educator; b. Troy, Kans., July 28, 1921; s. Alfred Edward and Lucy Lorraine (Kirby) C.; student U. Kans., 1939-41; D.D.S., U. Mo., 1945; postgrad. USN Dental Sch., 1954-55; m. Patricia Ann Woods. Dec. 23, 1944; children—Judith (Mrs. Troy Keith Endsley), Alan Edward. Individual practice dentistry, Troy, Kans., 1946-51; commd. lt. (j.g.) USN, 1945, advanced through grades to capt., 1960; asst. dental officer Treasure Island, San Francisco, 1945-46, Gt. Lakes, Ill., 1951; asst. dental officer USS Boxer, Korea, 1951-52, NTC, San Diego, 1952-53, dental officer Naval Air Sta., San Juan, P.R., 1955-57, Amphibious Base, Coronado, Calif., 1957-60; sr. dental officer USS Oriskany, 1961-63, Naval Air Sta., Olathe, Kans., 1963-65, 68-69; comdg. officer 3d Dental Co., 3d Marine div., Vietnam, 1966-67, ret., 1969; asst. prof. comprehensive dentistry U. Mo. at Kansas City Sch. Dentistry, 1973—. Scoutmaster Pony Express council Boy Scouts Am., 1949-51, chmn. health and safety, 1950-51. Pres. city council, Troy, Kans., 1950-51. Mem. Am. Dental Assn., Vietnam Service Dental Soc. (mem. bd. govs. 1966-67), Zi Psi Phi. Republican. Mem. Christian Ch. Mason, Kiwanian. Club: Optimist (Lake Quivira, Kans.). Home: Lake Quivira Kansas City KS 66106 Office: Sch Dentistry U Mo 650 E 25th St Kansas City MO 64108

CORE, HARRY MICHAEL, mental health adminstr.; b. Core, W.Va., Oct. 7, 1933; s. Earl L. and Freda (Garrison) C.; B.A., W.Va. U., 1955; M.S.W., U. N.C., 1957; m. Jane Ann Boggs; children—Kevin Michael, Brian David. Psychiat. social worker Lake County Mental Health Center, Mentor, O., 1960-63, dir. social services 1963-67, asst. dir., 1967-72, dir., 1972—; family counselor Lake County Juvenile and Domestic Relations Ct., 1963-66; practice psychiat. social work, 1966—; adj. faculty Case Western Res. U., 1966—; psychiat. social work cons. Ridgecliff Hosp., Euclid, Ohio, 1971—. Served with Med. Service Corps, AUS, 1957-60. Fellow Am. Orthopsychiat. Assn.; mem. Nat. Assn. Social Workers, Acad. Certified Social Workers. Contbr. articles to profl. jours. Home: 6707 Stratford Rd Painesville OH 44077 Office: 8935 Mentor Ave Mentor OH 44060

COREY, GORDON RICHARD, utilities co. exec.; b. Osceola, Wis., Sept. 27, 1914; s. Ralph Watson and Bessie Mabel (Simpson) C.; B.A., U. Wis., 1936, M.B.A., Northwestern, 1940; C.P.A., Ill., 1940; m. Margarete Grenn, 1967; children—(by previous marriage), Eleanor (Mrs. Geo. Tatge), Margaret (Mrs. Ross Amundson), Ralph, Martha. Vice pres. Commonwealth Edison Co., 1953-62, exec. v.p., 1962-64, chmn. finance com., 1965-73, vice chmn., 1973—, also dir.; dir. Continental Ill. Bank, Chgo., Inland Steel Co. Clubs: Economic, Commercial, Wayfarers, Mid-town Tennis. Home: 2511 Park Pl Evanston IL 60201 Office: 1 First Nat Plaza Chicago IL 60690

COREY, PAUL A., govt. ofcl.; b. Youngstown, Ohio, Aug. 16, 1926; s. Phillip P. and Effie (Coury) C.; B.A., U. Notre Dame, 1949; M.A., Case Western Res. U., 1955; m. Marie A. Cercek, June 16, 1951; children-Denis, Janet, David. Supr., Cleve. Recreation Dept., 1949-57; tchr. div. adult edn. Cleve. Bd. Edn., 1950-61; pres. Cleve. Tchrs. Union (AFL-CIO), 1956-61; exec. asst. Cuyahoga County Commrs., Cleve., 1961-71; dir. State Personnel, State of Ohio, Columbus, 1971-73; dir. Ohio Selective Service System, 1973—. Chmn. adv. com. Foster Grandparents, 1967-71; county sector chmn. Nat. Alliance Businessmen Job Program, 1967-71; mem. adminstrv. com. Bell Neighborhood Center, 1959-71; mem. Citizens League Greater Cleve., 1956-71; mem. Fed. Exec. Bds., 1973—; chmn. central Ohio chpt. Fed. Exec. Assn. Mem. exec. com. Cuyahoga County Democratic Com., 1955-71. Recipient Shaveyco award as Young Democrat of Year, 1958; Sign Mag. award as one of Ten Outstanding Cath. Leaders Under 35, 1961; Human Relations award St. Jude Children's Research Hosp., 1971; Pub. Service award Am.-Lebanese Nat. Com., 1972; Exemplary Leadership award Am. Cancer Soc., 1972; Exceptional Service medal Selective Service, 1975. Mem. Internat. Personnel Mgmt. Assn. (pres. Ohio chpt.), Pub. Personnel Assn. (pres. Ohio chpt.), County Commrs. Assn. Ohio, Ohio Soc. Archivists, Ohio Order of Commodores, Phi Delta Kappa. K.C. Clubs: Agonis, Syntaxis (adv. bd.). Home: 7755 Candlewood Ln Worthington OH 43085 Office: 127 Federal Bldg 85 Marconi Blvd Columbus OH 43215

CORMANEY, PATTY JOHNSON, journalist; b. Cedar Falls, Iowa, Nov. 3, 1921; d. Vivian Wells and Bernice Maurine (McClain) Johnson; B.A., U. Iowa, 1943; m. Elmer E. Cormaney, Aug. 29, 1957. Women's editor Waterloo (Iowa) Daily Courier, 1944-57; columnist Family Weekly, 1954-69; free-lance writer, 1944—. Recipient Jane Arden award Theta Sigma Phi, 1958; award Nat. Fedn. Press Women, 1955; Sweepstakes award A.P., 1960. Mem. P.E.O., Kappa Kappa Gamma. Presbyn. Author: I Was Just Thinking, 1962. Home and office: 2217 Rownd St Cedar Falls IA 50613

CORMIER, ROMAE J(OSEPH), mathematician, educator; b. N.Y.C., May 17, 1928; s. Arthur Joseph and Marie-Anna (Richard) C.; student Loyola Coll., 1947-48; B.S., U. Chattanooga, 1951; postgrad. U. S.C., 1953; M.A., U. Tenn., 1956; M.A., U. Mo., 1963; m. Sue Lee Stacks, May 16, 1954; children—Ivan Cormier, Richard, Landall, Darrin Vernon Cormier. Asso. mathematician Vitro Corp. Am., Eglin AFB, 1955; asst. instr. U. Mo., Columbia, 1961-63; cons. DeKalb, Ill., 1965; math. prof. No. Ill. U., DeKalb, 1956—, dir. univ. employees credit union; exec. v.p. Success Dynamics Corp., N.Am. Mineral. Exporations, 1970—; realtor. Served with AUS, 1952-54. Mem. Am., Austrian, Indian, 1952-54. Mem. Am., Glasgow, Edinburg math. socs., Math. Assn. Am., Tensor Soc., Socs. Mathematiques de Belgique and France, Real Sociedad Matematica Espanola, Unione Matematica Italiana, Math. Soc. Japan, Nat. Council Tchrs. Math., Nat. Assn. Real Estate Bds., DeKalb County Bd. Realtors, German Am. Nat. Congress, Stage Coach Players. Contbr. articles to profl. jours. Home: 125 Delcy Dr DeKalb IL 60115

CORN, ROBERT MARION, mech. engr.; b. Emington, Ill., Feb. 12, 1940; s. William Prentice and Viola Helen (Hewson) C.; B.M.E., Bradley U., 1962; m. Nancy Ann Carlson, June 6, 1964; 1 son, Dennis Robert. Trainee Ford Motor Co., Dearborn, Mich., 1964-67, design analyst, 1967-69, design engr., 1969-74, sr. design engr., 1974—. Registered profl. engr., Mich. Mem. Soc. Automotive Engrs. Home: 33824 Tawas Westland MI 48185 Office: PO Box 2053 Dearborn MI 48124

CORNELL, JOSIAH HART, JR. (SI), journalist; b. Cin., May 11, 1922; s. Josiah Hart and Annette Lasseter (Patton) C.; student Eastern Ky. U., 1940-41, U. Cin., 1941-42; m. Patricia Helen Hardy, Dec. 27, 1974; children—Josiah Hart III, William Patton, Carroll Lee (Mrs. Malcolm A. Merritt). With Scripps Howard, 1940—, corr. Life Mag., columnist Cin. Post, 1957—. Instr. U. Cin., evenings, 1956-68. Bd. dirs. Vols. Am., 1965—. Served to capt. AUS, 1942-45. Mem. Christophr Gist Hist. Soc., Lexington Civil War Round Table. Republican. Episcopalian. Mason. Clubs: Cincinnati, Fort Mitchell Country. Home: 5036 Collinwood Pl Cincinnati OH 45227 Office: 800 Broadway Cincinnati OH 45202

CORNELL, ROBERT JOHN, congressman; b. Gladstone, Mich., Dec. 16, 1919; s. Ralph Florman and Veronica Elizabeth (Sullivan) C.; B.A., St. Norbert Coll., 1941; M.A., Catholic U. Am., 1947, Ph.D., 1957. Ordained priest Roman Catholic Ch., 1944; asso. prof. history St. Norbert Coll., DePere, Wis., 1947-74; mem. 94th-95th congresses from 8th Wis. Dist. Chmn. Dist. Democratic Com., Wis., 1969-74; mem. Wis. Dem. Adminstrv. Com., 1969-74. Mem. Am., Cath. hist. assns., Acad. Polit. Sci., Labor Historia ns, Orgn. Am. Historians. Author: The Anthracite Coal Strike of 1902, 1957. Home: 103 Grant St DePere WI 54115 Office: US Ho of Reps Washington DC 20515

CORNING, BLY ARGLE, mfg. co. exec.; b. nr. Buckley, Mich., Feb. 22, 1917; s. Clark E. and Nina B. (Milliman) C.; student Eastern Mich. U., 1937-40; m. Audrey Tuttle, Sept. 27, 1940; 1 dau., Jenifer Blye. With AC Spark Plug div. Gen. Motors, Flint, Mich., 1940-45; owner Corning Mfg. Co., Swartz Creek, Mich., 1949—. Bd. govs. William C. Clements Lib-Assos., U. Mich. Served with AUS, 1946-47. Mem. Music Library Assos., Sheet Music Collectors, Kappa Phi Alpha. Mason. Clubs: Presidents (U. Mich.); Flint Golf. Home: 1902 Hampden Rd Flint MI 48503 Office: 7501 Wade St Swartz Creek MI 48473

CORNING, ROBERT NATHAN, chemist; b. Cedar Falls, Iowa, Aug. 19, 1923; s. Robert Henry and Ruth Marie (Johnson) C.; student Iowa State Tchrs. Coll., 1941-42; B.S. in Chem. Tech., Iowa State Coll., 1947; postgrad. civil engring. Oreg. State Coll., 1945-46, in analytical chemistry U. Ill., 1949-50; m. Mary Jane Simmon, Sept. 3, 1950; children—James, John, Kathryn Jane. Analytical chemist Monsanto Chem. Co., St. Louis, 1947-49, 50-55; chief chemist Micro Switch div. Honeywell Corp., Freeport, Ill., 1955-64, Tee Pak Corp., Danville, Ill., 1964-66; chief chemist, chem. cons. Doerfer Engring., Cedar Falls, 1966-70; pres., owner, chief chemist Corning Labs., Cedar Falls, 1970—. Served with AUS, 1944-46. Registered profl. engr., Iowa, Ill., N.Y. Fellow Am. Inst. Chemists; mem. Am. Chem. Soc., Air Pollution Control Assn., Water Pollution Control Assn., Am. Council Ind. Labs. (nat. exec. com. 1976-79), Nat. Soc. Profl. Engrs., Iowa Engring. Soc. (pres., Chpt. of Year award 1977), Alpha Chi Rho, Alpha Chi Sigma, Phi Mu Alpha. Club: Rotary (leader group study exchange team to Norway 1977). Home: 1811 W 4th St Cedar Falls IA 50613 Office: 1922 Main St Box 625 Cedar Falls IA 50613

CORNWELL, DAVID LANCE, Congressman; b. Paoli, Ind., June 14, 1945; student Hillsdale Coll., 1964, Am. Coll. Monaco, 1969, Ind. U., 1974; m. R. Jane Bogardus, 1974. Engaged in mfg. bus.; sec. bd. dirs. Cornwell Co., Inc., Paoli; mem. 95th Congress from 8th Ind. Dist. Mem. Orange County Young Democrats, Friends of Music of Ind. U. Mem. VFW, Jaycees, Am. Legion. Served in U.S. Army, 1966-68. Office: Room 1609 Longworth House Office Bldg Washington DC 20515*

CORNYN, JOHN EUGENE, accounting co. exec.; b. San Francisco, Apr. 30, 1906; s. John Eugene and Sara Agnes (Larkin) C.; B.S., St. Mary's Coll., 1935; M.B.A., U. Chgo., 1936; m. Virginia R. Shannahan, Sept. 10, 1938 (dec. Dec. 1964); children—Virginia R., Kathleen R. Cornyn Arnold, John Eugene III, Madeleine A., Carolyn G. Cornyn Clemons; m. 2d, Marian C. Fairfield, Aug. 21, 1965. Accountant, George Rossetter & Co., Chgo., 1937-40, George Black & Co., Portland, Oreg., 1941-42, Columbia Steel Co., Geneva, Utah, 1942-43, Am. Appraisal Co., Milw., 1943-44, Doty & Doty, Chgo., 1944-47, Murphy, Lanier & Quinn, Chgo., 1947-51; partner John E. Cornyn & Co., C.P.A.'s, Winnetka, Ill., 1951-73; pres. John E. Cornyn & Co. Ltd., 1973—. Exec. sec. North Shore Property Owners Assn., 1953—. C.P.A., Ill. Mem. Am. Inst. C.P.A.'s, Ill. Soc. C.P.A.'s, Am. Accounting Assn., Am. Tax Assn. Home: 126 Bertling Ln Winnetka IL 60093

CORRELL, HOWARD LEROY, physician; b. Spring Green, Wis., Nov. 2, 1908; s. Washington Greville and Marie (Clement) C.; B.S., U. Wis., 1930, M.D., 1935; m. Ellen Vivian, Apr. 20, 1940; children—John, Paul, Timothy, Rebecca. Intern, Anchor Hosp., St. Paul, 1935-36; resident internal medicine State U. Ia., Iowa City, 1936-37; resident and research instr. in neuropsychiatry, U. Wis., Madison, 1937-38; resident in medicine Milw. Co. Gen. Hosp., 1938-40; pvt. practice internal medicine, Milw., 1940—; instr. in medicine to clin. prof. medicine Med. Coll. Wis., Milw., 1946-73; chief cardiology Marquette Sch. Medicine, 1948-58; cons. cardiology VA Hosp., Wood, Wis., 1947-73. Pres. Wis. Heart Assn., 1956-57. Served with USNR, 1942-46. Diplomate Am. Bd. Internal Medicine. Fellow A.C.P., Am. Coll. Cardiology, Clin. Cardiology Am. Heart Assn.; mem. Med. Soc. Milw. Co. (pres. 1969-70, dir. 1970-74), State Med. Soc. Wis. (pres. 1975—). Home: Rural Free Delivery 1 Arena WI 53503 Office: 6745 W Wells St Milwaukee WI 53212

CORRELL, ROBERT JACK, audio visual co. exec.; b. Adair, Iowa, Dec. 16, 1930; s. Karl Stewart and Zura Grace (Harry) C.; B.S., State U. Iowa, 1956; m. Carol Jean Graham, June 15, 1952; children—Douglas Stewart, Carol Sue, Christen Grace. Salesman, Swank, Inc., St. Louis, 1956-60, dir. sponsored films, 1961-64; salesman Correll Engring. Co., St. Louis, 1960-61; owner Cor-rell Communications Co., St. Louis, 1964—. Instr. Nat. Audio Visual Inst., Ind. U., Bloomington, 1964; cons. audio visual design Hemis-Fair, San Antonio, 1970. Served with USN, 1951-55. Mem. Nat., Mo. audio visual assns., Sales and Marketing Execs. Assn., Am. Soc. Tng. Dirs., St. Louis Regional Commerce and Growth Assn., Alpha Kappa Psi. Presbyn. (deacon 1970—). Home: 32 Oak Terr Webster Groves MO 63119 Office: 5316 Pershing Ave St Louis MO 63112

CORRIGAN, EARL JAMES, ednl. adminstr.; b. Carroll, Iowa, June 25, 1931; s. William Joseph and Lillian Veronica (Duffy) C.; B.A., U. No. Iowa, 1966; M.A., Roosevelt U., 1973; m. Lavon Marie Martin, Mar. 28, 1969. In sales and managerial positions with Brady Motorfrate, Inc., Iowa, Nebr., Mass., Fla., Ill., 1951-64; tchr. bus. edn. Oak Park-River Forest (Ill.) High Sch., 1966-76, dir. career edn., 1976—; planner-specialist Equal Employment Opportunity Program, 1975—. Mem. Mem. Am. Personnel and Guidance Assn., Ill. Guidance Assn., Ill. Council Local Adminstrs., Bus. Leaders Am., Phi Delta Kappa, Phi Beta Lambda. Author: Your Job Application, 1977; author high sch. materials. Home: 228-C S Maple Ave Oak Park IL 60302 Office: 201 N Scoville Ave Oak Park IL 60302

CORRIGAN, HUGH ANTHONY, county ofcl.; b. Cleve., May 30, 1921; s. Patrick and Mary (Cusick) C.; student John Carroll U.; J.D., Cleve.-Marshall Coll. Law, 1954; m. Kathleen Richards, Aug. 4, 1962; children—Michael J., Patricia A., Coleen A., Kathleen M., Mary E., Hugh A. Admitted to Ohio bar, 1954; mem. Ohio Ho. of Reps., 1957-60; judge Cleve. Mcpl. Ct., 1960-63, Ct. Common Pleas, Cleve., 1963-68; commr. Cuyahoga County, Ohio, 1968—. Mem. Regional Planning Commn. Cleve., N.E. Ohio Areawide Coordinating Council, Met. Health Planning Corp., Trustee Matt Talbot Inn, Helping-Hand Halfway House. Served with USAF. Mem. Cleve., Cuyahoga County bar assns., Am. Legion. K.C. Club: Anchor. Home: 3492 Colletta Ln Cleveland OH 44111 Office: 1219 Ontario St Cleveland OH 44113

CORRIGAN, JOHN RAYMOND, pharm. co. scientist; b. Fargo, N.D., Apr. 28, 1919; s. Hilary Francis and Mary Frances (Hogan) C.; student Gonzaga U., 1936-38; B.S., U. Portland, 1940; M.S. U. Notre

Dame, 1942, Ph.D., 1949; m. Barbara Barrett, Sept. 22, 1951 (dec. Oct. 1971); children—Ann, Martha, John, Stephen. Research asso. Frederick Stearns & Co., Detroit, 1943-47, Sterling-Winthrop Research Inst., Rensselaer, N.Y., 1947-51, Merck, Sharp & Dohme, Inc., West Point, Pa., 1951-55; dept. dir. Mead Johnson & Co., drugs and nutritional products, Evansville, Ind., 1955—. Abstractor, Chem. Abstracts Service, 1960-72. Vice pres., McCutchanville Community Assn., 1971-73, pres., 1973-75, dir. 1966-76; judge Tri-State Sci. Fair, 1957—. Pres. Mead Johnson Active Republican Club, 1969-70. Recipient Mead Johnson Pres.'s award, 1966. Fellow Am. Inst. Chemists, A.A.A.S.; mem. Am. Chem. Soc. (past chmn. Ind.-Ky. border sect.), Am. Inst. Chem. Engrs. Contbr. articles to chem. jours. Patentee in field. Home: 2251 Cherry Ln Evansville IN 47711 Office: 2404 Pennsylvania St Evansville IN 47721

CORRIGAN, SAMUEL WALTER, educator; b. St. Boniface, Man., Can., Oct. 19, 1939; s. Cecil Edwin and Viola Angelice (Corrigan) C.; B.A., U. Man., 1962; M.A., U. B.C., 1964; Ph.D., U. Cambridge, 1970; 1 adopted son, Elwood Henry Episkenew. Asst. prof. dept. anthropology U. Man., 1969-70; research in applied social anthropology, 1970—, lectr. anthropology and Indian studies Brandon (Man.) U., 1970-71, asst. prof., 1971-77, asso. prof., 1977—, dir. native studies, 1972. Co-ordinator spl. programs for 3 univs. Man., spl. mature student program Brandon U., 1970-71. Can. sec. state, 1971; mem. Brandon adv. group Man. Police Commn., 1972—. Fellow Can. Council, 1965, 66; research grantee Can. Council, 1970, Brandon U., 1971, U. Man., 1970. Fellow Royal Anthrop. Inst.; mem. Am. Anthrop. Assn., Canadian Ethnology Soc., Delta Kappa Epsilon. Roman Catholic. Home: 111-1712 Portage Av Winnipeg MB R3J 0E3 Canada Office: Brandon U Brandon MB Canada

CORRY, ROBERT JOHN, surgeon; b. Cleve., Dec. 3, 1934; s. Robert Milton and Isabel Catherine (Gledhill) C.; student Univ. Sch., 1951-53; A.B. magna cum laude, Yale, 1957; M.D., Johns Hopkins, 1961; m. Linda Sally Selin, June 5, 1965; children—Robert, Sara, Catherine. Intern, Johns Hopkins Hosp., 1961-63; surg. asst. resident Mass. Gen. Hosp., Boston, 1965-67, chief resident, 1968-69, asst. surgery, 1969-73; attending surgeon, asso. prof. surgery U. Iowa Coll. Medicine, Iowa City, 1973-76, prof. surgery, 1976—, dir. transplantation, 1973—. Teaching fellow Harvard Med. Sch., 1968-69, instr., 1969-72, asst. prof. surgery, 1972-73; cons. Iowa City VA Hosp., 1973—. Bd. dirs., med. adv. com. Kidney Found. Iowa, 1973—. Diplomate Am. Bd. Surgery. Mem. A.M.A., A.C.S., Transplantation Soc., Am. Soc. Transplant Surgeons, Soc. U. Surgeons, Assn. for Acad. Surgery, Soc. Surgery of Alimentary Tract, Mass., Iowa Johnson County med. socs., Iowa Acad. Surgery, Iowa Clin. Surg. Soc., Collegium Internationale Chirurgiae Digestivae, Am. Assn. Tissue Banks. Contbr. articles to profl. jours. Home: 319 Hutchinson Ave Iowa City IA 52240 Office: Univ Hosps Iowa City IA 52242

CORSON, ROSALIE P., marketing cons.; b. Elkhart, Ind., Jan. 4, 1938; d. Carl Woodard and Charlotte Louise (Keyser) Corson; student Butler U., 1955-56, Ind. U., 1957; B.A., Purdue U., 1960. Asst. editor Tool and Mfg. Engr., Am. Soc. Tool and Mfg. Engrs., Detroit, 1960-62; social investigator Wayne County Dept. Social Welfare, Detroit, 1963-64; exec. dir. Camp Fire Girls, Inc., Adrian, Mich., 1964-66; asst. v.p. Coachmen Industries, Middlebury, Ind., 1966-71; founder, pres. Corson Pub. Co., Middlebury, Ind., 1970-74; editor, pub. Progressive Woman News Mag., 1971-73, The Middlebury Independent, 1971-74; mktg. cons.; dir. INTERTEC, Inc., Elkhart, Ind.; officer, dir. Polynesian Electro-genic Devel. Co., Honolulu; co-owner Country Craftsman gallery, Middlebury. Mem. Nat. Orgn. for Women, Ind. Women's Polit. Caucus, Women's Press Club. Home: 57377 S Route 15 Goshen IN 46526 Office: PO Box 62 Middlebury IN 46540

CORSON, THOMAS HAROLD, recreational vehicle mfg. co. exec.; b. Elkhart, Ind., Oct. 15, 1927; s. Carl W. and Charlotte (Keyser) C.; student Purdue U., 1945-46, Rensselaer Poly. Inst., 1946-47, So. Meth. U., 1948-49; m. Dorthy Claire Scheide, July 11, 1948; children—Benjamin Thomas, Claire Elaine. Pres., chmn. bd. Coachmen Industries, Inc., Middlebury, Ind., 1965—; dir. St. Joseph Valley Bank, Elkhart, First State Bank; chmn. bd., sec. Greenfield Corp. Viking Boat Co. Inc., Middlebury; chmn. bd., Henco Enterprises, Inc., Niles, Mich.; chmn. bd. Space Age Camper Co., Inc., Middlebury. Sustaining mem. Republican Nat. Com.; chmn. Elkhart County Rep. Finance Com. Bd. dirs. Michiana Econ. Devel. Found.; trustee Interlochen Arts Acad. and Nat. Music Camp; mem. adv. bd. Goshen (Ind.) Coll. Served with USNR, 1945-47. Mem. Ind. Mfrs. Assn. (dir.). Methodist. Mason (Shriner). Club: Elcona Country (past dir.). Home: PO Box 504 Skyview Dr Middlebury IN 46540 Office: Coachmen Dr PO Box 30 Middlebury IN 46540

CORTESE, EDWARD FORTUNATO, mag. pub. co. exec.; b. Phila., Jan. 11, 1922; s. Bernard Joseph and Luigina (Ulivieri) C.; B.F.A., Temple U. and Phila. Coll. Art, 1951; m. Theresa A. Radano, May 31, 1948; children—Bernard Joseph, Joseph Edward, Judith Louise. Book designer, illustrator John C. Winston Co. (name changed to Holt, Reinhart & Winston), N.Y.C., 1951-60; art dir. Edraydo, Inc., Phila., 1960-61; free lance artist, Phila., 1961-62; art dir. Penn Lithographic Co., Phila., 1962-63; exec. dir. art Saturday Evening Post Co., Inc., Phila. and Indpls., 1963—. Lectr. advanced illustration Phila. Coll. Art, 1966-71. Served with USAAF, 1943-47. Mem. Ednl. Press Assn. Am. Home: 2719 Embassy Row Indianapolis IN 46224 Office: 1100 Waterway Blvd Indianapolis IN 46206

CORTESE, THOMAS ANTHONY, surgeon; b. Mesoraca, Italy, Feb. 20, 1908 (parents Am. citizens); s. Joseph and Mary (Schipani) C.; A.B., Ind. U., 1930, B.S., 1931, M.D., 1933. Intern, resident in surgery Columbus Hosp., Chgo., 1933-34; intern St. Francis Hosp., Indpls., 1932-33; practice medicine specializing in surgery, Indpls., 1935—; mem. staff St. Francis, Community, Univ. Heights hosps.; mem. Pres. Johnson's Commn. on Cardiovascular Disease, 1966-67. Mem. Pres. Johnson's Council on Youth Opportunity, 1966-67. Served with M.C., U.S. Army, World War II. Recipient Cavaliere di Merito, Republic of Italy, also commendatore. Diplomate Am. Bd. Surgery, Am. Bd. Abdominal Surgery, Internat. Coll. Surgeons. Fellow Internat. Fertility Assn.; mem. Indpls., Marion County med. socs., Am. Soc. Contemporary Medicine and Surgery, Am. Soc. Study of Sterility, Am. Fedn. Scientists, N.Y. Acad. Scis., Am. Assn. Clinics, AAAS, World Med. Assn. (founder), Ind. State Med. Assn., AMA, Fedn. of Italian Am. Socs. Ind. (pres., founder), Am. Legion, St. Francis Pathol. Soc., Am. Atomic Scientists. Club: Indpls. Athletic. Author: Hiatus Hernia, 1947; contbr. articles in field to profl. jours. Home: 3901 S East St Indianapolis IN 46227 Office: 3901 SE St Indianapolis IN 46227

CORUSY, PAUL VINCENT, assn. exec.; b. Canton, Ohio, May 20, 1925; s. Paul and Mary (Kufta) C.; B.Sc., Ohio U., 1949; J.D., Cleve. State U., 1961; m. Maxine Joyce McKellips, Aug. 30, 1947; children—Lynne Denise, Paul Martin, Mark Allyn. With Glidden Co., Cleve., 1949-60, mgr. local taxes, until 1960; mgr. local taxes Minn. Mining & Mfg. Co., 1960-64; exec. dir. Interat. Assn. Assessing Officers, Chgo., 1964—. Trustee Pub. Adminstrn. Service, 1964-75, Govt. Affairs Inst. Served with USNR, 1943-46. Mem. Am. Soc. Assn. Execs. (vice chmn., chmn. 1977-78), Am., Ill., Chgo. bar assns. Home: 5520 Grand Ave Western Springs IL 60658 Office: 1313 E 60th St Chicago IL 60637

CORWIN, BERT CLARK, optometrist; b. Rapid City, S.D., Oct. 4, 1930; s. Meade C. and Adeline (Clark) C.; A.A., S.D. State U., 1952; B.S., Ill. Coll. Optometry, 1956, D.Optometry, 1957; m. Lydia Maxine Forehand, Oct. 10, 1959; children—Clark, Kelley. Optometric practice, Rapid City, S.D., 1957—; dir. S.D. Vision Service Corp. Chmn. adv. bd. S.D. Dept. Pub. Social Services, 1971—; regional adv. bd. S.D. Regional Med. Planning and Comprehensive Health Planning, 1971—. Pres., Black Hills Service Club, 1963, Cleghorn P.T.A., 1968-69. Named Lion of the Year, Rushmore Lions Club, 1965, distinguished service award Black Hills Service Club, 1967. Fellow Am. Acad. Optometry; mem. Optometric Found, S.D. Sight and Service Found., Am. (chmn. optometric practice com. 1972-74, mem. exec. council of profl. devel. div. 1974—), S.D. (pres. 1970-71) optometric assns. Methodist. Mason (Shriner), Lion, Toastmaster (pres. Rapid City 1973). Contbr. articles to profl. publs. in field. Address: 5436 Timberline Rapid City SD 57701

CORYELL, FRANKLIN MERCER, librarian; b. Cleve., June 9, 1927; s. Schofield Michael and Mae (Shaw) C.; B.A., Western Res. U., 1950; M.L.S., Kent State U., 1968; m. Giuliana Sarrocco, Oct. 19, 1950; children—May Margaret, Julian Frank. Pub. relations Curtis Pub. Co., Cleve., 1950-51; stockbroker Wm. J. Mericka & Co., Cleve., 1952-57; resident mgr. Eastman Dillon, Union Sec. & Co., Cleve., 1958-63; v.p. sales Group Securities, Inc., Cleve., 1963-66; br. librarian Cleve. Pub. Library, 1968; dir. Wickliffe (Ohio) Pub. Library, 1969—. Div. chmn. bldg. fund campaign Case Inst. Tech., 1958; chmn. Cleve. Press Ann. Investment Forum, 1960. Served with USAF, 1944-45. Mem. Am., Ohio (library devel. com. 1970), Lake County (pres. 1970-71) library assns., Bond Club Cleve., Am. Assn. Security Analysts. Mason, Kiwanian. Club: Cleveland Athletic. Home: 26241 Lakeshore Blvd Euclid OH 44132 Office: 1713 Lincoln Rd Wickliffe OH 44092

COSENTINO, MICHAEL ANTHONY, lawyer; b. Aurora, Ill., June 12, 1935; s. Anthony James and Justine Ann (Gentry) C.; student Beloit Coll., 1954; B.A., U. Wis., 1958, LL.B., 1963; m. Mary Dianne Farrell, Jan. 18, 1964; children—Michael James, Thomas Anthony. Admitted to Ind. bar, 1963, since practiced in Elkhart; partner firm Slabaugh & Cosentino. Dir., sec., C/P Products Corp., 1969—; pros. atty. 34th Jud. Circuit, Elkhart, 1975—. Served with AUS, 1958-60. Mem. Ind., Elkhart City, Elkhart County bar assns. Republican. Home: 153 Manor Ave Elkhart IN 46514 Office: 115 W Lexington Ave Elkhart IN 46514

COSKEY, RALPH JOSEPH, dermatologist; b. Detroit, July 29, 1929; s. Leo A. and Hedwig D. (Felner) C.; B.A., U. Mich., 1951; M.D., Wayne State U., 1955; m. Carol Goldenberg, July 6, 1952; children—Laura, Larry. Intern Sinai Hosp., Detroit, 1955-56; resident in dermatology Henry Ford Hosp., Detroit, 1958-61; practice medicine specializing in dermatology, 1961—; mem. staff Sinai Hosp., Providence Hosp., Detroit Gen. Hosp.; clin. asso. prof. dermatology Wayne State U., 1975—. Served with USAF, 1956-58. Mem. AMA, Mich. State., Oakland County med. socs., Am. Acad. Dermatology, Soc. Investigative Dermatology, Mich. Dermatol. Soc. Republican. Jewish. Contbr. articles to med. jours. Office: 23133 Orchard Lake Rd Farmington MI 48024

COSMAN, ERMAL GLEN, chemist; b. Pittsburg, Kans., Jan. 18, 1924; s. William Lee and Addie Marguerite (Korb) McClung; B.S., Kans. State Coll. Pittsburg, 1949; m. Kathleen Marie Cooper, Sept. 4, 1943; children—Jeanette Maxine, Ronald Dale. Mem. sales staff Montgomery Wards Co., Marysville, Kans., 1949-50; chemist Phillips Petroleum Co. (Tex.), 1950-53; corrosion engr. Coop. Farm Chem. Assn., Lawrence, Kans., 1953-61; chief chemist, supr. tech. services Farland Industries, Hastings. Nebr., 1961—; lectr. in field. Served with USN, 1941-42. Mem. Am. Inst. Chem. Engrs., Am. Soc. Lubrication Engrs. Clubs: Mason, Shriners. Home: 1417 Webster St Hastings NE 68901 Office: PO Box 949 Hastings NE 68901

COSSABOOM, EWING ORVILLE, lawyer, farm mgr.; b. Millersburg, Ky., Mar. 17, 1917; s. Charles O. and Lillian (Young) C.; A.B., Transylvania U., 1939; J.D., U. Cin., 1942; m. Joy G. Ferdon, July 20, 1962. Chief purchase and claims sect., real estate div. Ohio River div. U.S. Army Engrs., 1942-45; practiced law in Cin., 1945—; mem. firm Dickerson, Ahrens, Cossaboom & Burns, 1954—; farm mgr. J.M. Ewing Farm, Morgan, Ky., 1952-73; sec., treas. College Hill Realty Co.; v.p. Whitney Corp., 1965—, treas., 1967—; dir. Mt. Healthy Savs. & Loan Co. Chmn., Mt. Healthy Civil Service Commn., 1968—. Mem. Christian Ch. Contbr. articles to profl. jours. Home: 1623 Madison Ave Mount Healthy OH 45231 Office: Am Bldg 30 E Central Pkwy Cincinnati OH 45202

COSSITT, HENRY DELA, orthodontist; b. Homestead, Pa., Sept. 24, 1899; s. Henry DeLa and Nettie Pomeroy (Truesdall) C.; B.A., U. Mich., 1923; D.D.S., U. Pitts., 1929; postgrad. Dewey Sch. Orthodontia, 1929; m. Lois Ann Hackett, June 25, 1931; children—Annette (Mrs. Arthur Levy), Henry DeLa IV. Pvt. practice orthodontics, Toledo, 1930—. Adviser to commr. of health City of Toledo, 1938-40; mem. health sect. Council of Social Agys., Toledo, 1935-52. Bd. dirs. Lucas County Chpt. Am. Cancer Soc., 1961-63, Toledo Dental Scholarship Fund, 1960—; trustee Rowe Sch. Organic Edn., 1941-51. Fellow Am. Coll. Dentists, Acad. Internat. Dentistry, Royal Soc. Health (Gt. Britain); mem. Am. Dental Leaders, Am. Assn. Dental Editors, Toledo Dental Soc. (pres. 1938-39, E.N. Bach Meml. award 1969), Fedn. Dentaire Internat., Am., Ohio (del. 1940-51) dental assns., Gt. Lakes Soc. Orthodontists (pres. 1942-44), Am. Assn. Orthodontists (sect. editor 1946-69), Toledo Dental Dispensary Assn. (trustee 1940-71), Am. Soc. Dentistry for Children, Pierre Fauchard Assn., Soc. Mayflower Descs., Am. Legion, Delta Sigma Pi, Psi Omega, Omicron Kappa Upsilon, Omicron Delta Kappa, Pi Tau Phi. Republican. Presbyn. Editor: Toledo Dental Soc. Bull., 1951-74, editor emeritus, 1974—. Home: 5679 Monroe St Apt 1020 Sylvania OH 43560 Office: 4352 Sylvania Ave Toledo OH 43623

COSTANTINI, WILLIAM PAUL, lawyer; b. N.Y.C., July 6, 1947; s. James Geremia and Alma Elaine (Massina) C.; B.A., U. Notre Dame, 1969; M. Urban Planning (fellow), U. Mich., 1971; J.D. (fellow), St. John's U., 1974; m. Susan Ann Duffy, May 25, 1974; 1 son, Ryan Duffy. Admitted to N.Y. bar, 1975, Ill. bar, 1976; atty., corporate hdqrs. IBM, Armonk, N.Y., 1974-75, data processing div. hdqrs., 1975-76, regional counsel data processing div., Midwest region, Chgo., 1976—; lectr. in field. Bd. dirs. Townhomes of River's Edge, Naperville, Ill. Recipient Ned D. Frank award St. John's U. Sch. Law, 1974. Mem. Am., Ill., Chgo., DuPage County bar assns. Home: 1675 Cove Ct Naperville IL 60540 Office: One IBM Plaza Chicago IL 60611

COSTELLO, HARRY GEORGE, lawyer; b. St. Paul, Aug. 11, 1915; s. Harry G. and Estelle M. (Jerue) C.; student Coll. St. Thomas, St. Paul, 1932-33, 35-36; LL.B. cum laude, William Mitchell Coll., 1940; children—Patricia M., Cynthia A., Michele M., Suzanne M. Admitted to Minn. bar, 1940; since practiced in St. Paul; mem. firm, Moore, Costello & Hart, 1947—. Vis. instr. Macalester Coll., 1946-51; mem. State Bd. Law Examiners, 1961—, pres. bd., 1964-67. Served to maj. AUS, 1942-46. Decorated Legion of Merit (U.S.); Croix de Guerre (France). Mem. Am., Minn., Ramsey County bar assns. Clubs: St. Paul Athletic, Town and Country. Office: Northwestern Nat Bank Bldg 5th and Cedar Sts St Paul MN 55101

COTE, DENIS ANDRE, mktg. co. exec.; b. Montreal, Que., Can., Sept. 5, 1941; s. Philippe A. and Aurea (Allie) C.; came to U.S., 1959, naturalized, 1965; student McGill U., Montreal; m. Kathleen L. Jacoby, July 7, 1962; 1 son, Stephan. Tool and die maker Ford Motor Co., Sandusky, Ohio, 1963-69; mfg. rep. Plant Life Industries, Sandusky, Ohio, 1969-71, gen. mgr., 1971-75; pres. DC Chem. Co., Sandusky, 1975—, (merged with Plant Life Co. 1976, name changed to DC Chem.), v.p. mktg. DC Filters & Chem., 1976—. Mem. Erie County Bd. Realtors, 1970—. Recipient Boy Scouts Am. award of leadership, 1970; named Outstanding Jaycee Sandusky chpt., 1973, 74. Mem. Mfg. Agents Nat. Assn., Mfrs. Nat. Assn., Nat. Assn. Ind. Businessmen, Internat. Fabricare Inst. Republican. Lutheran. Clubs: Southwood Racket, Elks. Patentee filter related products. Home: 1910 Adrian Circle Sandusky OH 44870 Office: 1517 5th St Sandusky OH 44870

COTHREN, ROBERT MACK, supt. schs.; b. Paragould, Ark., June 8, 1932; s. R. Macon and Hazel (Gregory) C.; B.S., Ark. State U., 1953 M.Ed., U. Ark., 1956; D.Ed., U. Nebr., 1968; m. Lurabeth Kilgo, Aug. 26, 1956; children—Robert Mack, D. Craig. Supt. pub. schs., Parks, Nebr., 1956-62, Shelton, Nebr., 1962-66, Aurora, Nebr., 1966-72, Beatrice, Nebr., 1972—. Mem. Shelton Pub. Library Bd., 1962-66; scholarship chmn. U.P. R.R., 1964-66; state del. North Central Assn., 1962-66, mem. State Profl. Practices Commn., 1972—. Served with AUS, 1953-55. Recipient Gideon's Dignitary award, 1968, 73. Mem. Am., Nebr. assns. sch. adminstrs., NEA (state del. 1969-72), Nebr. (state dir. 1969-72, dist. pres. 1968-69), Dundy County (pres. 1961-62) edn. assns., Nebr. Activities Assn. (vice chmn. 1965-66, state del. 1968-69), North Central Assn. (state committeeman 1969—), C. of C. Mason (32 deg., Shriner), Rotarian, Lion (pres. 1964-65). Home: 1122 Dorsey Beatrice NE 68310

COTTER, PATRICK DAVID, med. psychologist; b. Brewster, Minn., Jan. 29, 1947; s. Vincent Richard and Dorothy (Tibodeau) C.; B.A., U.S.D., 1969, M.A., 1971, Ph.D., 1973; m. Kay Delores Lillig, Aug. 18, 1972. Intern, then resident in psychology U. Oreg. Med. Sch., Portland, 1973-75; med. psychologist Children's Meml. Hosp., Chgo., 1975—; asso. psychology Northwestern U. Med. Sch., 1977—; pvt. practice psychology, Chgo., 1976—. Mem. Am., Ill. psychol. assns., Am. Assn. Mental Deficiency, Midwestern Assn. Behavior Analysis, Soc. Pediatric Psychology, Psi Chi. Democrat. Roman Catholic. Home: 2335 W Touhy Ave Chicago IL 60645 Office: 2300 Children's Plaza Chicago IL 60614

COTTON, WILLIAM PHILIP, JR., architect; b. Columbia, Mo., July 11, 1932; s. William Philip and Frances Barbara (Harrington) C.; A.B., Princeton, 1954; M.Arch., Harvard, 1960. Archtl. designer Darby-Bogner & Assos., Milw., 1960-62; draftsman, job capt. Hellmuth, Obata, & Kassabaum, St. Louis, 1962-64; pvt. archtl. practice, 1964—. Asst. prof. Washington U. Sch. Architecture, fall 1966. Bd. dirs. Pub. Revenue Edn. Council, Assn. St. Louis U. Libraries; trustee Steedman Archtl. Library; sec. Mo. Heritage Trust, Inc. Served to 1st lt. AUS, 1954-56. Mem. A.I.A. (state preservation coordinator 1972—), Soc. Archtl. Historians, New Music Circle (pres. 1966-68), Landmarks Assn. St. Louis (v.p. 1967-69). Roman Catholic. Designer, editor, photographer: 100 Historic Buildings in St. Louis County, 1970. Home: 5145a Lindell Blvd St Louis MO 63108 Office: 806 Chestnut St St Louis MO 63101

COTTRELL, GRACE GRIGGS, communications dir., writer; b. Gadsden, Ala.; d. Rhodum L. and Maude (Turner) Griggs; Ph.B., Northwestern U., 1971. Editor, Covenant Club News, Chgo., 1952-64, Uptown Topics, Chgo., 1955-56, The Record, Chgo., 1954-76; dir. communications Glenmary Home Missioners, Cin., 1972—; contbr. articles and stories to golf, garden, women's and religious periodicals, daily and weekly press. Mem. Women in Communications, Pub. Relations Soc. Am., Iota Sigma Epsilon. Democrat. Methodist. Club: Woman's City (Cin.). Home: 102 W Sharon Rd Glendale OH 45246

COUCH, ALBERT EDWARD, III, clergyman, coll. adminstr.; b. Eagle Mills, N.Y., Mar. 19, 1929; s. Albert Edward and Alicia (Lindroth) C.; grad. Taft Sch., 1947; B.A., Yale, 1951; M.A., Oberlin Coll., 1954, B.D., 1955; M.Div., Vanderbilt U., 1973; postgrad. Mansfield Coll., Oxford U., Union Theol. Sem., Am. Found. Religion and Psychiatry, N.Y.C., Philanthropy Tax Inst.; m. Marguerite Penner, Aug. 31, 1952; children—Pamela Jane, Jennifer Anne, Heather Ellen, Gwendolyn Joy. Ordained to ministry U.P. Ch. U.S.A., 1955; dir. summer recreation, Rocky Hill, Conn., 1947-48; dir. Camp Cheerful Soc. for Crippled Children, Cleve., 1949-52; student pastor Remsen Christian Ch., Medina, Ohio, 1952-54; minister pastoral care Forest Hill Presbyn. Ch., Cleve., 1954-57; pastor 1st Presbyn. Ch., Freeport, L.I., 1957-65; sr. pastor 1st Presbyn. Ch., San Pedro, Cal., 1965-69; asso. dir. devel., gen. faculty mem. Oberlin (Ohio) Coll., 1969-71; asst. supt., dir. devel., cons. chaplain Culver Mil. Acad. and Culver Acad. for Girls, Culver, Ind., 1971-74; v.p., cons. chaplain, asso. prof. Simpson Coll., Indianola, Iowa, 1974—. Pres., Interfaith Council, Freeport, N.Y., 1964-65, Greater Peninsula Council Chs., Cal., 1968-69. Mem. Soc. Bibl. Lit., Cum Laude Soc., Yale, Oberlin alumni assns., Council for Advancement and Support Edn., C. of C. (exec. bd.). Mason, Rotarian. Contbr. to religious, ednl. publs. Home: 811 North B St Indianola IA 50125

COUGHLIN, WILLIAM JOSEPH, air products co. exec.; b. Boston, July 14, 1918; s. Cornelius Steven and Mabel Josephine (McMahon) C.; m. Lucille Margaret Mary Kerr, Aug. 31, 1940; children—Michael, Daniel, Constance Coughlin Hardy, Kathleen Coughlin Jeffers, Patrick, Eileen; student Internat. Corr. Schs., 1949-53, Ohio State U., 1969-71. Welder, Puget Sound Naval Shipyard, Bremerton, Wash., 1940-43, 48-49, welder supr., 1949-53, welding engring. technician, 1953-56; welder Keyes Tank Co., Casper, Wyo., 1945-46, Standard Oil of Ind., Casper Refinery, 1946-48; devel. engr. Arcair Co. div. Air Products & Chems. Corp., Lancaster, Ohio, 1956-58, tech. service mgr., 1958-62, indsl. mgr., 1962-67, v.p. mfg., 1967-70, v.p. ops., 1970—, also v.p. ops. Gas Equipment div., Emmaus, Pa.; tchr. fundamentals of welding to mgrs. Lancaster cos., 1957. Certified mgr. Inst. Certified Profl. Mgrs. Mem. Am. Welding Soc. (dir. Columbus sect. 1957-58, 63-64), Fairfield County Engrs. Soc. (pres. 1965-66), Lancaster C. of C. Club: K.C. Contbr. articles to profl. jours. Home: 248 Seneco Dr Lancaster OH 43130 Office: PO Box 406 N Memorial Dr Lancaster OH 43130

COULOLIAS, SPYRO PHILIP, electronic mfg. co. exec.; b. Melrose Park, Ill., June 25, 1940; s. Philip Spyro and Bessie Philip (Zakos) C.; B.A., Lawrence U., 1962; M.S., Roosevelt U., 1965; m. Mary Mercury, July 8, 1967; children—Betty, Philip. Staff accountant Lybrand, Ross Bros. & Montgomery, 1965-66; founder, chief exec. officer Sperry Electronics, Ltd., 1967—; co-founder, sec.-treas. Comfab, Inc., Franklin Park, Ill.; pres., chmn. Parkland Internat. Ltd., Chgo. Served with USNR, 1963-68. Mason. Home: 424 Wilson Ln Addison IL 60101 Office: 129 Broadway St Melrose Park IL 60160

COULSON, ALAN JAMES, land surveyor; b. Glasgow, Scotland, Feb. 22, 1936; s. David and Catherine Francis (Cameron) C.; came to U.S., 1947, naturalized, 1956; student Elgin Community Coll., 1953-55, Chgo. Tech. Coll., 1962-63, U. Wis., 1971; m. Carol Yvonne Aurand, Apr. 12, 1938; children—David Andrew, Jeanne Catherine, Georgia Carol. Field engr. L.W. Besinger, Carpentersville, Ill., 1954-60, Whitehouse Engring. Co., Carpentersville, 1960-62, H.L. Uteg & Assos., Dundee, Ill., 1962-63; gen. agt. State Farm Ins., Elgin, Ill., 1963-66, Sentry Ins., Elgin, 1966-68; pres. A.J. Coulson, Land Surveyor, Dundee, 1974—. Bd. dirs. Elgin Area Family Service Assn., 1970-72. Served with AUS, 1955-57. Recipient Presidents award Elgin Jaycees, 1970. Mem. Elgin Scottish Soc. (v.p. 1971-72), Ill. Land Surveyors Assn., Nat. Soc. Profl. Engrs., Wis. Soc. Land Surveyors, Am. Judicare Soc., Nat. Assn. Small Businesses, J.C. Internat. (senator 1975—). Home: 1500 Erie St Elgin IL 60120 Office: 116 W Main St Dundee IL 60118

COULTER, KENNETH EUGENE, chem. co. exec.; b. Auburn, Mich., Feb. 4, 1917; s. Fred Louis and Cathryn (Thomas) C.; B.S., M.S., U. Mich., 1941; m. Eleanor Mina Kohler, Oct. 24, 1942; children—Beverly (Mrs. Norman Cameron), Janet A., Donald, Jean E., Cathryn. With Dow Chem. Co., 1942—, asst. chief engr., 1955-59, mgr. engring. constrn. and maintenance dept., 1959-63, dir. Midland div. research and devel., 1963-67, mgr. plants and hydrocarbons, Bay City 1967-73, mgr. Gulf Coast Olefin project, 1973—. Industry com. Coll. Engring. U. Mich., 1968; tchr. Midland Adult Edn. Program, 1954-55. A.H. White Meml. fund com. U. Mich., 1967; chmn. Sch. Bd. Bay County, Mich., 1945-54; mem. Midland Police and Fire Protection Study Com., 1963-64. Mem. Am. Inst. Chem. Engrs. (nat. dir. 1970-73, v.p. 1974, pres. 1975), Am. Chem. Soc., Am. Mgmt. Assn., Am. Petroleum Inst., Nat. Soc. Profl. Engrs., U. Mich. Alumni Assn. (sec. Midland chpt. 1950-51). Mason. Patentee in field. Contbr. articles to profl. publs. Home: 511 W Meadowbrook Dr Midland MI 48640 Office: Dow Chemical Co Midland MI 48640

COULTER, THOMAS H(ENRY), assn. exec.; b. Winnipeg, Man., Can., Apr. 21, 1911; s. David and Sarah Anne (Allen) C.; B.S., Carnegie Inst. Tech., 1933; M.A., U. Chgo., 1935; m. Mary Alice Leach, Nov. 24, 1937; children—Sara, Anne, Jane, Thomas II. Investment analyst Shaw & Co., Chgo., 1935-36; sales engr. Universal Zonolite Insulation Co., Chgo., 1936-39, sales promotion mgr., 1939-40, gen. sales mgr., 1940-41, v.p., 1941-45; mgr. devel. div. Booz, Allen & Hamilton, Chgo., 1945-48, partner, 1948-50; pres. Am. Bildrok Co., 1950-54; chief exec. officer Chgo. Assn. Commerce and Industry, 1954—; pub. Commerce mag.; lectr. mktg., exec. program U. Chgo. Mem. State Dept.'s Top Mgmt. Seminar Team, Israel, 1956, Japan, 1958; mem. Dist. Export Council. Mem. Mayor's Commn. Rehab. Persons; mem. Chgo.-Cook County Criminal Justice Commn., Cook County Real Estate Tax Study Commn., Ill. Gov.'s Council on Health and Fitness, Revenue Study Commn. on Legalized Gambling, Chgo. Dept. Human Services Bd. dirs. Chgo. Crime Commn.; bd. dirs. Chgo. chpt. A.R.C. 1953-59; mem. citizens bd., council Sch. Bus. Assn.; bd. govs. Internat. House, U. Chgo.; mem. citizens com. U. Ill.; exec. council Chgo. Civil Def. Corps; exec. com. Ill. Council Econ. Edn.; trustee Skokie Valley Community Hosp., pres., 1955-57, 66-70; bd. dirs. Better Bus. Bur. Met. Chgo., Hosp. Planning Council Met. Chgo., Chgo. Council Fgn. Relations; mem. Northwestern U. Assos.; trustee Village of Golf, Ill., 1951-55; mem. nat. adv. bd. Am. Security Council Edn. Found.; mem. adv. bd. Chgo. Area council Boy Scouts Am.; mem. Cook County Home Rule Commn.; mem. Rehab. Inst. Chgo. Assos.; mem. adv. com. U. Chgo. Met. Inst.; mem. nat. adv. council Nat. Legal Center for Pub. Interest; mem. Cook County Econ. Devel. Adv. Com. Decorated comdr.'s cross Order of Merit (Germany); knight Order of Merit (Italy); knight Order of Lion (Finland); knight 1st class Royal Order of Vasa (Sweden), comdr. Royal Order Vasa, 1972; recipient Silver Ann. All-American award Sports Illustrated, 1957; Outstanding Civilian Service medal U.S. Army, 1961; Gold Badge of Honor for Merits (Austria), 1962, (Province of Vienna), 1971; citation pub. service U. Chgo.; Alumni merit award for outstanding profl. achievement Carnegie Inst. Tech.; Indsl. Statesman award U.S.-Japan Trade Council, 1976; Citizen Fellowship award Inst. Medicine, 1976. Mem. Nat. Sales Execs., Newcomen Soc. N. Am., U.S. C. of C., Nat. Planning Assn., U.S. Olympians (dir. Midwest chpt.), Midwest-Japan Assn., Japan-Am. Soc. Chgo. (dir.), Midwest/U.S. France Assn., Am. Austrian Soc. of Midwest, Finnish Am. C. of C. of Midwest, Royal Hort. Soc., Chgo. Hist. Soc., Field Mus. Natural History, Art Inst. Chgo., Chgo. Council on Fgn. Relations (Chgo. com.), Lambda Alpha. Clubs: Mid-Am., Commercial, Executives (pres. 1950-51), Sales Mktg. Execs. (pres. 1953-54), Canadian Univ., Economic (Chgo.); Glenview (Golf, Ill.). Home: 58 Overlook Dr Golf IL 60029 Office: 130 S Michigan Ave Chicago IL 60603

COUPLIN, JAMES RONALD, hotel exec.; b. Palouse, Wash., Aug. 31, 1909; s. Charles Allan and Madge (Callahan) C.; Ph.B., U. Chgo., 1931; m. Marie Corrine Franklyn, Aug. 3, 1936. Gen. mgr. Hotel Waldorf, Toledo, 1934-42, Hotel Chain, Chgo., 1946-60; exec. v.p., dir. Cedar Hotel Co. Inc., 1958-72; partner, mgr. Hotel Douglas, Elgin, Ill., 1960-72, now ret. Fellow Harry S. Truman Library, Independence, Mo., 1974-75. Served from 1st lt. to maj. AUS, 1942-46; ETO. Decorated Bronze Star. Mem. Humane Soc. U.S., U. Chgo. Alumni Assn., Am., Ill. hotel assns., Elgin Assn. Commerce, S.A.R., Nat., N.J. geneal. socs., Conn. Soc. Genealogists (charter), Am. Legion, N.M. Mil. Inst. Alumni Assn. (sec.-treas. Chgo. area), Nat. Humane Soc., Soc. Lost Chord, Orange County (N.Y.) Geneal. Soc., Phi Kappa Sigma. Republican. Unitarian. Mason (32 deg., Shriner). Contbr. articles to geneal. quars.: Edsall, Winfield, Simpson, Ferris lines. Home: 1170 Dundee Ave Elgin IL 60120 Office: PO Box 345 Elgin IL 60120

COURTEAU, ELMER JOSEPH, JR., newspaperman, writer; b. Mpls., May 7, 1921; s. Elmer Joseph and Laura (Rivard-Dufresne) C.; B.A., Coll. of St. Thomas, 1947; postgrad. U. Md., 1948, U. Paris (Sorbonne), 1949, U. Wis., 1952; U. Minn., 1961-63; m. Constance Ann Dobmeyer, June 26, 1948; children—Michele, Gregory, Marc, Jeffrey, Jennifer, Gretchen, Kristin. With Duluth News-Tribune and Herald, 1947-48, Hibbing (Minn.) Daily Tribune, 1950-61, St. Paul Pioneer-Press & Dispatch, 1961-66, Mpls. Tribune, 1966—, Cath. Digest, 1969—. Mem. Am. Hist. Assn., Am. Acad. Polit. Sci., Am. Name Soc., Cath. Hist. Soc. Phila., La Societe Historique de Que. Democrat. Roman Catholic. Home: 201 Liberty Pl South St Paul MN 55075 Office: 425 Portland Ave Minneapolis MN 55415

COURTNAGE, LEE EDMUND, educator; b. Lead, S.D., Mar. 5, 1932; s. Ted Roosevelt and Edna Mae (Dyson) C.; B.A., Wayne State Coll., 1956; M.A., U. No. Colo., 1957, Ed.D., 1967; m. Elaine M. Schreurs, June 30, 1956; children—Steve, Kelly, Kara, Shawn. Tchr. sci. Newman Grove (Nebr.) pub. schs., 1956-57; regional sch. psychologist Iowa Dept. Pub. Instrn., Des Moines, 1957-58; sch. psychologist Blackhawk County Schs., Waterloo, Iowa, 1958-62, dir. spl. edn., 1963-65; dir. spl. edn. Blackhawk-Buchanan County Schs., Waterloo, 1967-68; prof., dir. spl. edn. U. No. Iowa, Cedar Falls, 1968—. Cons. Iowa's Title III, 1971-75, adv. com. specific learning disabilities, 1972-74; adv. mem. Iowa State Com. Title VI, 1970-75. Served with AUS, 1953-55. Recipient award Hearing Assn. Iowa, 1965, Distinguished Achievement award for excellence in tchr. edn. Am. Assn. Colls. Tchr. Edn., 1974. Mem. Council for Exceptional Children (life mem., pres. Blackhawk County chpt. 1965-66), Iowa Edn. Assn. (pres. dept. spl. edn. 1970-71), Am. Assn. Mental Deficiency, Iowa Assn. for Children with Learning Disabilities (dir. 1972—), Aligned Community of Epileptics (dir. 1972—), Phi Delta Kappa. Home: 1912 Sunnyside Dr Cedar Falls IA 50613

COUSERT, EARL MAURICE, supt. schs.; b. Francisco, Ind., Aug. 31, 1929; s. Charles William and Lettie Mae (Hutchinson) C.; B.S. magna cum laude, Oakland City Coll., 1951; M.S., Ind. U., 1957, Ed.S., 1965; m. Bonnie Carol Wallace, Mar. 24, 1956; children—Alan, Debra, Jill. Tchr. math., chemistry Bicknell City Schs., 1951-55; tchr. chemistry, social studies Washington City Schs., 1955-60; prin. Plainville Schs., 1960-62; prin. Odon High Sch., 1962-66; supt. Sunman (Ind.) Consol. Schs., 1966-68, Sunman-Dearborn Community Sch. Corp., 1968-74, South Madison Community Sch. Corp., 1974—. Chmn., Ind. Beta Club Council, 1977—. Sec., Sunman Community Assn., 1968, pres., 1970; pres. Sunman Recreation Com., 1968-74. Served to maj. AUS, 1948—. Mem. Res. Officers Assn., NEA (life), Ind. Schoolmen's Club, Ind. Assn. Pub. Sch. Supts., Am. Assn. Sch. Adminstrs., Mu Tau Kappa. Home: 1007 Lancashire Ln Pendleton IN 46064

COUSINO, JOE ANN, sculptress; b. Toledo, Nov. 17, 1925; d. George Carl and Lucille Carolyn (Kocher) Bux; B.A., U. Toledo, 1947; postgrad. U. So. Ill., 1954, U. Mex., 1946, 49, Pratt Inst., 1947; children—Paula Rene and Richard Nils (twins). One-woman shows: Toledo Mus. Art, 1949, Newman Town Gallery, Toledo, 1957, Frank Ryan Gallery, Chgo., 1962, Ohio State U. Gallery, 1963, San Giuseppi Gallery Mt. St. Joseph, Cin., 1964, Chiara Gallery, Cleve., 1967, Tadlow Gallery Goldcoast Mich., 1972, Arndt Art Mus., Elmira, N.Y., 1977; numerous invitationals including U.S.A. Dept. Commerce Exposition in Rio de Janerio, Brazil, 1963, Akron Art Inst. Sculptural Internat., 1966, Bolssom Center Invitational Kent State U., 1968-70; lectr., instr. in field; mem. Mayor's Com. Arts Toledo, 1974-77; instr. art adult dept. YWCA Toledo, 1944-57, YMCA 1945-57; feature artist Univ. workshops, 1966-77; dir. Lighting Fixtures, Inc., Toledo, 1958, Cousino Metal Products, 1960-72. Bd. dirs. Friends Univ. Toledo Library, 1974-77; trustee Fedn. Art Soc., 1954-77, pres., 1964-66. Recipient numerous art awards including: Ohio State Ceramic Sculpture award, 1955; Jr. League Best in Show, Toledo Mus., 1956; Gold Metal best in show, Religious Art Am., Chgo., 1960; purchase award Toledo Fedn. Lending Collection, Toledo Mus. Art, 1970. Mem. Nat. Craftsmens Council (Ohio del. 1962-65; Ohio Designer Craftsman (trustee 1964-66), Toledo Potters Guild (founder, pres. 1951-53), Am. Archaeology Soc. Episcopalian. Address: 3717 Indian Rd Toledo OH 43606

COUSINS, LLOYD WILLIAM, ednl. adminstr.; b. Scales Mound, Ill., June 27, 1915; s. John Edward and Martha Rebecca (Hicks) C.; student U. Dubuque, 1934-36; B.Mus. Edn., Northwestern U., 1938, M.Mus., 1943; postgrad. Roosevelt U. (Chgo. Mus. Coll.), 1949-51; m. Miriam M. Mills, Aug. 6, 1938; children—Lloyd William, Michael G., Stephen M. Supr. music Evanston (Ill.) Pub. Schs., 1938-43; dir. dept. music Nat. Coll. Edn., Evanston, 1943—, chmn. humanities dept., 1964-68, also founder, dir. Internat. Edn. Program. Lectr., European, world tours, 1951—; pres. Cousins Tours & Travel, Inc., Evanston, 1951—; dir. music Trinity Ch. N. Shore, Wilmette, Ill., 1950-73, Bahai Temple, Wilmette, 1953-72; condr. all maj. oratorios with mems. Chgo. Symphony Orch. and Community Chorus of Nat. Coll. Edn., 1949-73; piano soloist Chgo. Symphony String Quartet; lectr. Chgo. Symphony series, 1975; humanities lectr. maj. museums, colls., galleries and artistic monuments of world. Served with U.S. Army, 1945. Mem. Music Educators Nat. Conf., Pi Kappa Lambda, Phi Mu Alpha. Republican. Methodist. Kiwanian, Mason (32 deg.). Clubs: Mich. Shores (Wilmette); Univ. (Evanston). Home: 819 Milburn St Evanston IL 60201

COUSINS, WILLIAM, JR., judge; b. Swiftown, Miss., Oct. 6, 1927; s. William and Drusilla (Harris) C.; B.A. with honors in Polit. Sci., U. Ill., 1948; LL.B., Harvard, 1951; m. Hiroko Ogawa, May 12, 1953; children—Cheryl Akiko, Noel William, Yul Vincent, Gail Yoshiko. Admitted to Ill. bar, 1953; title examiner, atty. Chgo. Title and Trust Co., 1953-57; asst. state's atty. Cook County, Chgo., 1957-61; mem. firm Turner and Cousins, Chgo., 1961-69, Stradford, LaFontant, Gibson, Fisher, Cousins, 1969-72, Rivers, Cousins, Clayter and Lawrence, 1972-76; judge Circuit Ct., Chgo., 1976—. Mem. exec. council Northeast Assn. of Ill., 1969-73; mem. Stony Island Park Civic Assn., pres. Chatham Avalon Park Community Council, 1962-65. alderman 8th ward City of Chgo., 1967-76, del. Democratic Nat. Conv., 1972. Bd. dirs. Parkway Community House, 1963-70, Chgo. Area Planned Parenthood Assn., 1967-75, Americans for Democratic Action, Com. for Ill. Govt., PUSH; bd. dirs. Ind. Voters Ill., 1963-67, v.p., 1966-67. Served with AUS, 1951-53; lt. col. JAG's Corps Res. Mem. Am., Nat., Ill., Cook County (dir., Edward N. Wright award 1968, William R. Ming award 1974), Chgo. bar assns., Delta Sigma Rho, Kappa Alpha Psi. Conglist. (chmn. spl. bldg. fund drive 1963-65; outstanding layman of the year 1958). Office: 29 S LaSalle St Chicago IL 60603

COUTCHIE, SIDNEY TRUMAN, apparel mfg. co. exec.; b. Fremont, Mich., Feb. 13, 1928; s. Sidney Napoleon and Lucy Marion (Mattice) C.; profl. accounting grad. Davenport Bus. Coll., 1953; m. Roena Mae Conner, May 4, 1951; children—Randall Lee, Darla Rae. Staff accountant McEwan & Kauffman, C.P.A.'s, Grand Rapids, Mich., 1954-58; sec., treas. H.H. Cutler Co., Grand Rapids, 1958—, Cutler Mfg. Corp., Grand Rapids, 1972—, Midwest Fashions, Inc., Grand Rapids, 1973—. Served with USN, 1945-49, 51-52. Mem. Nat. Assn. Accountants, Am. Legion. Home: 1265 Royal Oak St SW Wyoming MI 49509 Office: 120 Ionia Ave SW Grand Rapids MI 49501

COUTS, CHARLES RAYMOND, lawyer; b. Wellsville, Ohio, May 28, 1911; s. Charles and Birdie (Penn) C.; A.B. cum laude, Ohio Wesleyan U., 1933; J.D., Harvard, 1936, LL.M., 1937; m. Clara Browne, June 5, 1943. Admitted to Ohio bar, 1937, Mass. bar, 1938, to practice U.S. Supreme Ct., 1960; gen. practice law, Boston, 1937-38; with B.F. Goodrich Co., Akron, Ohio, 1939-75, asst. counsel, 1939-58, counsel, 1958-60, asst. sec., counsel, 1960-70, corp. sec., 1971-74, past officer, dir. several subsidiaries. Mem. Friends Akron U. Trustee Ohio No. U. Mem. Am. Soc. Corp. Secs., Am., Akron, Boston bar assns., Am. Arbitration Assn. (arbitrator 1975—), Ohio Wesleyan Alumni Assn. Akron (past pres.), Phi Beta Kappa, Omicron Delta Kappa, Theta Alpha Phi, Phi Kappa Tau. Methodist (del. ann. conf. 1951—). Clubs: Akron City, Portage Country (Akron); Harvard (N.Y.C. and Boston). Home: 255 N Portage Path Akron OH 44303

COUTTS, SHIRLEY SUE WEBB, educator; b. Pensacola, Fla., Jan. 1, 1930; d. Quilla Clifford and Mary Gertrude (McCumber) Webb; B.S., Fla. State U., 1951; M.A., N.E. Mo. State U., 1975; m. Robert L. Coutts, Feb. 19, 1951 (div. Oct. 1973); children—Candila Sue, Robert L., William C., R. Christopher. Elementary classroom tchr., Pensacola. Fla., 1952-53, 58-59, Tallahaassee, Fla., 1959-62, Fairfield, Iowa, 1967-74; elementary guidance cons. Arrowhead Area Edn. Agy. 5, Ft. Dodge, Iowa, 1975—. Trainer Help Line, Ft. Dodge, 1976, 77. Mem. Am., Iowa personnel and guidance assns., Iowa Sch. Counselors Assn. (v.p. elementary), Phi Delta Kappa. Methodist. Home: 607 11th Ave N Fort Dodge IA 50501 Office: 1909 1st Ave N Fort Dodge IA 50501

COUTTS, WARREN HALL, JR., lawyer, rancher; b. El Dorado, Kans., Nov. 6, 1900; s. Warren Hall and Ida Frances (Whitehead) C.; student Kans. State U., 1920-21, U. Kans., 1921-23; J.D., Washburn U., 1924; 1 son, Warren Hall III (dec.). Admitted to Kans. bar, 1924, U.S. Supreme Ct. bar; sr. partner Coutts, Coutts & Metcalf, El Dorado, 1967—; pres. Pan Am. Commerce, Inc.; pres., owner Pine Forest Ranch, Inc., Hall Mar Ranches; breeder registered Herefords. Municipal judge, El Dorado, 1926-30. Founder, Warren Hall Coutts III Meml. Art Gallery, Inc.; mem. forestry com. Conservation Fedn. Mo. Trustee Washburn U. Mem. Am. Hereford Assn., Am. Saddle Horse Breeders' Assn., El Dorado, Wichita (soc. fellows art) art assns., Shetland Pony Club Am., Am. Quarterhorse Breeders Assn., Kappa Sigma, Phi Alpha Delta, Theta Nu Epsilon. Episcopalian. Elk. Clubs: Washburn U. W., El Dorado Country. Contbr. to Am. Saddle and Bridle mag., Southwestern Horseman mag. Home: Hall Mar Pl El Dorado KS 67042 Office: 110 N Main El Dorado KS 67042

COVAN, BURL LEE, ednl. adminstr.; b. Chgo., June 2, 1931; s. Morris and Ollie (Prelutsky) C.; B.S., U. Ill., 1953, A.M., 1954; A.M., Northeastern Ill. U., 1970. Tchr. English, Spanish, guidance counselor, pub. schs., Chgo., 1955-67, guidance cons., 1967-71; asst. prin. Mather High Sch., Chgo., 1971—. NDEA summer guidance Inst. grantee, 1962, 65. Mem. Am. Personnel and Guidance Assn. Jewish. Club: B'nai B'rith. Home: 1033 W Loyola Ave Chicago IL 60626 Office: 5835 N Lincoln Ave Chicago IL 60659

COVEY, FRANK MICHAEL, JR., lawyer; b. Chgo., Oct. 24, 1932; s. Frank M. and Marie B. (Lorenz) C.; B.S. with honors, Loyola U., 1954, J.D. cum laude, 1957; S.J.D., U. Wis., 1960; m. Patricia Ann McGill, Oct. 7, 1961; children—Geralyn, Frank M. III, Regis Patrick. Admitted to Ill. bar, 1957, U.S. Supreme Ct. bar, 1965; practiced law, Chgo., 1957—; law clk. Ill. Appellate Ct., 1959; asso. Belnap, Spencer, Hardy & Freeman, 1959-60; asso. McDermott, Will & Emery, 1960-65, partner, 1965—. Instr., Northwestern U. Sch. Law, 1958-59, Loyola U. Coll., 1958-69. Research asso. Wis. Gov.'s Com. on Revision of Law of Eminent Domain, 1958; asso. gen. counsel Union League Civic and Arts Found., 1967-69, mng. dir., 1975—, v.p., 1969-72, 73-75, pres., 1972-73; co-dir. Grant Park study team Nat. Commn. on Causes and Prevention of Violence, 1968. Mem. Better Govt. Assn., Chgo. Art Inst.; mem. Chgo. Mus. Natural History, also mem. com. cts. and justice, com. legis. reform; mem. bd. athletics Loyola U., 1970-72, estate planning com., 1969—, mem. com. future law sch., 1975-76. Recipient award Conf. Personal Finance Law, 1955; Founder's Day award Loyola U., 1976. Mem. Am., Ill. (Lincoln award 1963), Chgo., 7th Fed. Circuit bar assns., Am. Judicature Soc., Cath. Lawyers Guild, Chgo. Council Lawyers, Legal Club Chgo., Law Club Chgo., Loyola U. Alumni Assn. (pres. 1965-66, bd. govs. 1966-70), Evanston-North Shore Bd. Realtors (asso.), Law Alumni Assn. (award 1957, v.p. 1968-69, pres. 1969-70, chmn. fund campaign 1967-68, bd. govs. 1972-73), Thomas More Club (chmn. 1973-75), Ill. Hist. Soc., Air Force Assn., Blue Key, Phi Alpha Delta, Alpha Sigma Nu, Pi Gamma Mu, Delta Sigma Rho. Roman Catholic (parish council 1973-75). Clubs: Monroe, Union League (dir. 1977—) (Chgo.). Author: Roadside Protection Through Access Control, 1960; also articles, speeches. Contbg. author: Federal Civil Practice in Illinois, 1974. Home: 1104 W Lonnquist Blvd Mount Prospect IL 60056 Office: 111 W Monroe St Chicago IL 60603

COVEY, ROBERT OTIS, lawyer; b. Oshkosh, Wis., Jan. 21, 1921; s. David L. and Bessie V. (Otis) C.; B.A., U. Wis., 1942; J.D., Northwestern U., 1948; m. Mary E. Karlen, June 3, 1943; children—Karlen R., Kathleen M. (Mrs. David Waggoner), Carol Ann (Mrs. Miles J. Beard), Christopher. Admitted to Ill. bar, 1948, since practiced in Crystal Lake; sr. partner firm Covey, Covey & Waggoner, Crystal Lake, Ill.; pres., chmn. bd. First Fed. Savs. and Loan, Crystal Lake, 1970—. Pres., Sch. Bd. Dist. 47, 1951-61. Chmn., Citizens for Eisenhower, McHenry County, 1952. Mem. McHenry County (pres. 1962), Chgo., Ill., Am. bar assns. Congregationalist (moderator, chmn. ch. 1970-72). Mason, Lion. Club: Crystal Lake (Ill.) Country. Home: 970 S Shore Dr Crystal Lake IL 60014 Office: 88 Grant St Crystal Lake IL 60014

COVINGTON, CHARLES J., mfg. co. exec.; b. Farmington, Mo., Jan. 8, 1914; s. Mabry J. and Ethel Ann (Covington) C.; student Wichita (Kans.) U.; m. Lois Ellen Combs, Dec. 9, 1939; children—Joe J., Patricia Ann, Jon Scott. With Dowzer Electric div. Sola Basic Industries, Mt. Vernon, Ill., 1938—, pres., 1948—, chmn. bd., 1973—; pres. Elec. Apparatus Service, 1956-57, Power Cores, Inc., 1960-72; dir. Security Bank of Mt. Vernon; chmn. bd. King City Fed. Savs. & Loan Assn., Mt. Vernon. Pres. Greater Egypt Planning Commn., 1976—; chmn. Buffalo Trace council Boy Scouts Am., 1948-53, canoe base, regional chmn., recipient Silver Beaver award 1951, Silver Antelope award, 1960. Chmn. bd. trustees Rend Lake Conservancy Dist. Recipient award Nat. Elec. Mfrs. Assn., Community Service award, 1969. Mem. Nat. Indsl. Service Assn. (pres.), Ill. Mfrs. Assn., Mt. Vernon C. of C. (Best Citizen award 1954, pres.). Lion, Elk. Clubs: Union League (Chgo.); Missouri Athletic (St. Louis). Home: 1818 Isabella Ave Mount Vernon IL 62864 Office: First & Castleton Sts Mt Vernon IL 62864

COVINGTON, CONSTANCE JOAN (MRS. WILLIAM C. DALLMANN), physician; b. Miles City, Mont., Aug. 13, 1936; d. Elbert Gorton and Juliana Clara (Richter) Covington; student Chico State Coll., 1953-54; A.B., U. Calif. at Berkeley, 1957; M.D., U. Calif. at San Francisco, 1960; m. William C. Dallmann, June 12, 1960; children—Shane Morgan Alan Nathanael, Lara Catherine. Intern, U. Calif. Children's Hosp., San Francisco, 1960-61, resident pediatrics, 1961-63; asst. dir. pediatric outpatient clinic San Francisco Presbyn. Hosp., 1963-64; asst. dir. Valparaiso (Ind.) U. Student Health Service, 1964-72; practice medicine, specializing in pediatrics, Valparaiso, 1970—; mem. staff Porter Meml. Hosp., Valparaiso. Bd. dirs. Porter County Guidance Clinic, 1971-72. Mem. Porter County Med. Soc. Lutheran. Home: 1905 Rock Castle Park Dr Valparaiso IN 46383 Office: 1101 E Glendale St Valparaiso IN 46383

COVINGTON, MCCORMICK ROYALL, investment co. partner; b. Cleve., Apr. 4, 1932; s. Herbert Hunt and Eleanor Blanche (McCormick) C.; student Yale, 1950-52; B.A., Centre Coll. Ky., 1955; postgrad. U. Va. Law Sch., 1955-56; m. Mary Katherine Seabury, Mar 4, 1961; children—Mary Melinda, McCormick, Herbert Hunt III, Millicent. Salesman, Acme Quality Paints, Detroit, 1958-59, Omaha, 1959-60, Dallas, 1960-62; salesman McDonald & Co., Cleve., 1962-69, partner, 1969—. Cons., Moore Enterprises, Dyke Coll., Cuyahoga Community Coll. Pres., Shaker Heights Republican Club, 1967-72. Trustee, Shaker Boys League, 1964—, pres., 1973-74. Served with AUS, 1956-58. Presbyn. Clubs: Bond (Cleve.); Country (Pepper Pike, O.). Home: 2957 Eaton Rd Shaker Heights OH 44122 Office: 2100 Central National Bank Bldg Cleveland OH 44114

COWAN, JOHN DESMOND, mfrs. rep.; b. Cleve., Apr. 20, 1931; s. John Joseph and Christina Mary (Johnston) C.; grad. high sch.; 1 son, Scott Johnston. With sales dept. Hinde & Dauch div. W.Va. Pulp & Paper Co., Sandusky, Ohio, 1960-62; product mgr. Jayhawk Fibre Form div. Lawrence Paper Co. (Kans.), 1962-64; pres. John D. Cowan

& Assos., Inc., Columbus, Ohio, 1965—; product inventor, partner Conasco Plastics Co., Lanco Industries, Columbus; partner Patterson & Cowan Assos., Columbus and Phila. Served with USN, 1950-54. Mem. Ohio Prestressed Concrete Assn. (exec. dir.), Prestressed Concrete Inst. (Asso. Mem. award), Quiet Birdmen, U.S. Naval Inst., Cousteau Soc. Methodist. Clubs: Columbus Athletic, Catawba Island. Patentee in field. Home: 2804 Chateau Circle Columbus OH 43221 Office: 30 E Columbus St Columbus OH 43206

COWAN, LAWRENCE, clin. psychologist; b. Detroit, July 23, 1932; s. Benjamin Julian and Dorothy (Eisenstadt) C.; B.A., Mich. State U., 1954; M.A., U. Mo., 1958; Ph.D., Wayne State U., 1967; m. Patricia Ruth Pennington, June 24, 1956; 1 son, David Michael. Sch. psychologist Cherry Hill Sch. Dist., Inkster, Mich., 1958-68; psychol. dir. Midwest Mental Health Clinic, Dearborn, Mich., 1968-69; cons. Center for Forensic Psychiatry, Ann Arbor, Mich., 1969-70; clin. psychologist Southfield, Mich., 1969—; lectr. U. Mich., Dearborn, 1973-74; cons. Redford (Mich.) Union Schs., 1971—. Served with U.S. Army, 1954-56. Certified cons. psychologist, Mich.; certified marriage counselor, Mich. Mem. Mich. Psychol. Assn. (v.p. profl. affairs 1974-76; pres. 1976), Mich. Soc. Cons. Psychologists, Mich. Assn. Marriage Counselors, Am. Psychol. Assn., Am. Psychology-Law Soc., Mich. Assn. Sch. Psychologist. Home: 28262 Greencastle Farmington Hills MI 48018 Office: 24555 Southfield Rd Southfield MI 48075

COWDEN, JAMES ELIAS, psychologist; b. Green Bay, Wis., Jan. 18, 1934; s. Calvin Thomas Dawson and Irene Ingeborg (Tossava) C.; B.A. in Psychology with honors (Levi Strauss scholar), U. Calif. at Berkeley, 1955; Ph.D. (USPHS fellow), U. Wis., 1960. Staff clin. psychologist Wis. Sch. for Boys, Wales, 1960-62; counseling psychologist VA Hosp., San Francisco, 1962-63; chief psychologist, supr. research sect. Bur. of Clin. Services, Madison, Wis., 1964—. Clin. psychologist part-time, Madison, 1968—; research cons. to U. Ill. Med. Center, 1968-74; prin. investigator mental health service study Dane County, Wis., 1974; research cons. Minn. Dept. Corrections, N.H. Dept. Corrections, 1976, R.I. Dept. Corrections, 1977. Mem. Mendota/Monona Lake Property Owners Assn., 1971—. Mem. Am., Wis. State, Western, Dane County psychol. assns., Sigma Xi. Club: Four Lakes Yacht. Contbr. articles on delinquency and psychotherapy to profl. jours. Home: 1116 Pocahontas Dr Monona WI 53716 Office: 2700 Marshall Ct Madison WI 53705

COWDEN, WILLIAM DEE, food service co. exec.; b. McPherson, Kans., Mar. 29, 1937; s. Roy Max and Esther Marie (Dodd) C.; student (Univ. scholar) Kans. U. Sch. Bus., 1958-61; m. Joan Dolores Skeet, Mar. 15, 1958; children—Michael, Michelle, Barry, Amy, Judy. Asst. to pres. Agrl. Bus. Co., Inc., Lawrence, Kans., 1961-62; pres. Kaw Valve & Fitting Co., Lawrence, 1962-67; pres., founder Inventrol Services, Kansas City, Mo., 1966-67, Kansas City Controls Co. (Kans.), 1967-70; pres., founder, dir. Convenience Systems, Inc., Overland Park, Kans., 1970—. Served with USAF, 1957-58. Mem. Nat., Mo. restaurant assns. Republican. Baptist. Inventor, patentee, distbr. Save-A-Life Poison Antidote Kit, 1962. Home: 7017 Johnson Dr Mission KS 66202 Office: Suite 311 95th and Nall Sts Cap Fed Bldg Overland Park KS 66207

COWLES, JOHN, JR., publisher; b. Des Moines, May 27, 1929; s. John and Elizabeth (Bates) C.; grad. Phillips Exeter Acad., 1947; A.B., Harvard Coll., 1951; Litt.D. (hon.), Simpson Coll., 1965; m. Jane Sage Fuller, Aug. 23, 1952; children—Tessa Flores (Mrs. David Radin), John, Jane Sage, Charles Fuller. With Mpls. Star and Tribune Co., 1953—, editor, 1961-69, pres., 1968-73, chmn., 1973—; pres. Harper's Mag. Co., 1965-68, chmn., 1968-73; dir. Harper & Row, Pubs., Inc., 1965—, chmn. bd., 1968—; dir. Des Moines Register and Tribune Co., 1960—, A.P., 1966-75, 1st Bank System, Inc., 1964-68. Trustee Farmers & Mechanics Savs. Bank Mpls., 1960-65, Equitable Life Ins. Co. Ia., 1964-66. Campaign chmn. Mpls. United Fund, 1967; bd. dirs. Walker Art Center, 1960-69, Urban Coalition of Mpls., 1968-70, German Marshall Fund of U.S., 1975—; bd. dirs. Guthrie Theatre Found., 1960-71, pres., 1960-63, chmn., 1964-65; trustee Phillips Exeter Acad., 1960-65. Served from pvt. to 2d lt. AUS, 1951-53. Named one of ten outstanding young men U.S. Jr. C. of C., 1964. Mem. ACLU (Minn. dir. 1956-61), Am. Newspaper Pubs. Assn. (dir. 1975-77). Clubs: Century Assn. (N.Y.C.); Minneapolis, Woodhill (Mpls.). Home: 1418 Mt Curve Ave Minneapolis MN 55403 Office: 425 Portland Ave Minneapolis MN 55488

COWLES, WARREN HARDING, research engr.; b. Goodells, Mich., Jan. 27. 1922; s. Artemus William and Blanche Juanita (Pester) C.; B.S. in Aero. Enging., U. Mich., 1945; m. Elizabeth Jane Bannon, Oct. 20, 1973; 1 son. Dennis Michael. Aerodynamicist, McDonnel Aircraft Co., 1945-46; project engr. Chrysler Corp., Highland Park, Mich., 1946-48; dir. tech. programs Holley Carburetor div. Colt Industries Op. Corp., Warren, Mich., 1948—. Mem. Soc. Automotive Engrs. Republican. Roman Catholic. Author: Advanced Fuel Metering Demonstration, 1977. Patentee 29 inventions. Home: 1871 Spring Grove Bloomfield Hills MI 48013 Office: 11955 E Nine Mile Rd Warren MI 48090

COWLIN, EUGENE DU PONT, steel co. exec.; b. N.Y.C., Aug. 9, 1889; s. James Steedman and Maude (du Pont) C.; student N.Y.C. pub. schs.; m. Eda Hardinbergh, 1910 (dec. 1968); children—Sydney Eugene, Kenneth Steedman, Alice du Pont; m. 2d, Marcia Laver, Feb. 14, 1970. With Eaton Corp., Massillon, Ohio, 1923-57, mgr. N.Y. office, 1923-30, mgr. sales, Massillon, 1930-44, gen. div. mgr., Massillon, 1944-57; v.p. Moore & Steele Corp., Tioga County, N.Y., 1957—. Served with U.S. Army, World War I. Mem. Nat. Ry. Appliance Assn. (pres. 1937, dir.), Farm Equipment Inst. (life), ASME (chmn. B18 com.), Am. Ry. Enging. Assn. (life), Am. Ordnance Assn. (mem. small arms com. 1940—), Soc. Automotive Engrs., Canadian R.R. Club, Toronto R.R. Club, Am. Security Council. Republican. Episcopalian. Clubs: Masons; Lake Shore, Chgo. Yacht, Carleton, Whitehall (Chgo.); Langmoor Country (Ohio); Diners. Address: 3914 Willow Dell Dr NE Canton OH 44714

COWLIN, JOHN LEADLEY, lawyer; b. Crystal Lake, Ill., Sept. 3, 1937; s. Henry L. and Emily M. (Gillooley) C.; B.A., U. Mich., 1960; J.D., Wayne State U., 1967; m. Edith Andrews, Apr. 20, 1968; children—John Leadley II, Catherine Laura. Admitted to Ill. bar, 1968, U.S. Supreme Court, 1971; mem. firm Cowlin, Cowlin and Unguarsky, Crystal Lake, 1968—; city atty. City of Crystal Lake, 1968—; atty. Crystal Lake Park Dist., 1968—, Grafton (Ill.) Park Dist., 1968-69, Morengo (Ill.) Park Dist., 1976—; asst. states atty. McHenry County, Ill., 1968-75; field counsel Farmers Home Adminstrn., McHenry County, 1972—, Fed. Nat. Mortgage Assn., McHenry County, 1972—. Bd. dirs. McHenry State Bank, 1974—. Rep. precinct committeeman, 1968-72; v.p. McHenry County 4-H Youth Fedn., 1976—. Served with AUS, 1962-64. Decorated Army Commendation medal. Mem. Nat. Dist. Atty's. Assn., Am., Ill., McHenry County (treas. 1977-78) bar assns., Ill. States Attys. Assn., Am. Trial Lawyers Assn., Ill. Municipal League, Commercial Law League, Woodstock Fine Arts Assn., C. of C., Kappa Sigma, Delta Theta Phi. Roman Catholic. Clubs: U. Mich. Club of Chgo.; Woodstock (Ill.) Country. Home: 95 McHenry Ave Crystal Lake IL 60014 Office: 20 Grant St Crystal Lake IL 60014

COX, CLARENCE ALBERT, dentist; b. Eldorado, Ill., Sept. 10, 1922; s. William Luther and Maudie Leona (Tuggle) C.; student Washington U., St. Louis, 1947; B.S., Shurtleff Coll., 1949; B.S., U. Ill., 1953, D.D.S., 1955; m. Bernice Leona Fisher, June 18, 1949; children—Katherine Louise, William Clarence, Janice Elaine. Med. technologist Alton (Ill.) Meml. Hosp., 1945-51; individual practice dentistry, Wood River, Ill., 1955—. Tchr. Community Coll., Alton. Served with AUS, 1942-45, USMCR, 1950-51. Mem. Alton Dental Soc. (pres.). Baptist (chmn. diaconate). Lion, Rotarian. Home: 4239 Chantel Dr Alton IL 62002 Office: 22 S 2d St Wood River IL 62095

COX, DAVID JACKSON, biochemist; b. N.Y.C., Dec. 22, 1934; s. Reavis and Rachel (Dunaway) C.; B.A., Wesleyan U., 1956; Ph.D., U. Pa., 1960; m. Joan M. Narbeth, Sept. 6, 1958; children—Andrew Reavis, Matthew Bruce, Thomas Jackson. Instr. biochemistry U. Wash., 1960-63; asst. prof. chemistry U. Tex., 1963-67, asso. prof., 1967-73; prof., head dept. biochemistry Kans. State U., 1973—; vis. prof. U. Va., 1970-71. NSF Predoctoral fellow, 1956-59; NSF Sr. Postdoctoral fellow, 1970-71. Mem. Am. Soc. Biol. Chemists, Am. Chem. Soc., AAAS, N.Y. Acad. Scis., Phi Beta Kappa, Sigma Xi. Democrat. Presbyterian. Home: 2846 Oregon Ln Manhattan KS 66502 Office: Dept Biochemistry Kans State U Manhattan KS 66506

COX, EARL EDWIN, leasing co. exec.; b. Herman, Ark., Sept. 5, 1917; s. John William and Etta Mae (Crossley) C.; student Franklin Inst., 1936-37; m. Mary Elizabeth Reine, Sept. 5, 1938; children—Elizabeth (Mrs. Cyril Francis Schrage), Patricia (Mrs. James Edward McNeely). Salesman, Automobile Club Southwestern Ind., Evansville, 1938-40, George Koch Sons Mfrs., Evansville, 1940-41, H.J. Heinz Co., Denver, 1941-44; gen. mgr. Wyo. div. Am. Automobile Assn., Cheyenne, 1946-53; regional dir. Nat. Hwy. Users Conf., Portland, Oreg., 1953-54; registered rep., broker Foster & Marshall, N.Y.C., 1958-60; asst. mng. dir. Constrn. League, Bldg. Constrn. Assn., Bldg. Congress and Asso. Gen. Contractors, Indpls., 1961-68; exec. v.p. Ind. Subcontractors Assn., Indpls., 1968-76; account exec. Kepco Leasing, 1976—. Chmn. Constrn. Industry Legal Found., 1976—. Served with USMCR, 1944-46. Mem. Am. Subcontractors Assn. (nat. dir. 1972-74), Constrn. Employers Council, Constrn. Industry Round Table, Ind. Soc. Assn. Execs., Am. Arbitration Assn. (Ind. constrn. arbitration com.). Republican. Elk. Author: Subcontractors Handbook, 1973. Home: 50 Pine Dr Indianapolis IN 46260 Office: 5650 W 86th St Indianapolis IN 46278

COX, FORREST CURTIS, II, dentist; b. Trenton, Mo., May 22, 1929; s. Forrest Curtis and Judson Lillian (Ritzenthaler) C.; student Culver-Stockton Coll., 1947-49, U. Mo. Lynotype Sch. 1949, Kirksville State U., 1950-51; D.D.S., U. Mo., 1958; m. Bonnie Fay Wilson, Feb. 5, 1950; children—Cathie Sue (Mrs. Hubert Michael Lowrey), Paul Curtis. Practice gen. dentistry, Trenton, 1958—; mem. med. staff Wright Meml. Hosp., 1958—. Mem. laymens adv. bd. Culver Stockton Coll., 1962-64; active Boy Scouts Am. Mem. Trenton Planning and Zoning Commn., 1968—. Served with USNR, 1951-52; Korea. Mem. Am., Mo., N.W. Mo. Dist. dental assns., Grandriver Dental Study Group (pres. 1965—), Internat. Platform Assn., Pierre Fachard Acad., Past Comdrs. Assn. Mo., Trenton C. of C. (pres. 1961). Mem. Christian Ch. (deacon 1961, elder 1962—, pres. bd. 1962-65). Mason (Shriner). Home: 713 Town and Country Ln Trenton MO 64683 Office: 1011 Cedar St Trenton MO 64683

COX, HARDIN CHARLES, state senator; b. Rock Port, Mo., Mar. 4, 1928; s. Hardin Charles and Frieda (Stapel) C.; B.A., U. Mo., 1951; m. Virginia Ann Heifner, Jan. 3, 1952; children—Charles Bryan, Mark Hardin. Sec., treas. Farmers Mut. Ins., Rock Port, 1959; treas. Farmers Mut. Hail Ins. Co. Mo., 1959—, Columbia Mut. Ins. Co. Mo., 1960—, Mo. Farmers Mut. Hail Ins. Co. Mo., 1960—; mem. Mo. Senate, 1975—, chmn. legis. research com., mem. coms. agr., conservation, parks and tourism; roads and hwys., accounts, edn.; realtor Hardin Cox Real Estate, Rock Port, 1963. Chmn. council Boy Scouts Am., 1958-69. Mem. Mo. Ho. of Reps., 1964-75, chmn. legis. research com., 1965-73, chmn. Meml. Bldg. Commn., 1964-69; Served with AUS, 1945-48. Recipient 4-H Meritorious Service award, 1966; award for best personal column in weekly newspaper Mo. Press Assn., 1969; Legislators Conservation award Mo. chpt. Nat. Wildlife Assn., 1971. Mem. Am. Legion, Realtors Assn., Sigma Chi. Democrat. Mason. Club: Group Millionaires. Home: 602 W Calhoun St Rock Port MO 64482 Office: 300 Main St Rock Port MO 64482

COX, HARRY SEYMOUR, business exec.; b. Covington, Ky., Mar. 23, 1923; s. Harry S. and Rebecca E. (Wolfe) C.; B.A., Ohio Wesleyan U., 1947; m. Sally I. Stoneburner, Aug. 31, 1946; children—Inga C. (Mrs. Terryl Q. Walker), Sally (Mrs. Michael Sattler), Christopher. Accountant, Barrow, Wade, Guthrie & Co., Cleve., 1947-55; accountant White Consol. Industries, Inc. Cleve., 1956-68, v.p., treas., 1973—; chmn. bd. Laub Baking Co., Cleve., 1968-72. Served to lt. USNR, 1942-46. Mem. Sigma Alpha Epsilon. Methodist (chmn. trustees 1962-68). Clubs: Westwood Country (Rocky River, Ohio); Country of Ashland, Clifton (Lakewood, Ohio); Union (Cleve.). Home: 20252 Westhaven Ln Rocky River OH 44116 Office: 11770 Berea Rd Cleveland OH 44111

COX, HENRY HOYT, JR., editor; b. Chgo., Apr. 29, 1922; s. Henry Hoyt and Ruth (Griffin) C.; B.A. in English, DePauw U., 1949; B.J., U. Mo., 1951; m. Ethel Margaret Lindemann, Sept. 21, 1951; children—Sherry (Mrs. R. Craig), Gary Robert. Free lance writer, 1949-51; asst. to editor employee mag. Pure Oil Co., Chgo., 1951-52, asst. editor, 1952-56, editor, 1956-66; editor UARCO, Inc., Barrington, Ill., 1966-70; mng. editor Profl. Safety mag., Am. Soc. of Safety Engrs., Park Ridge, Ill., 1970—. Committeeman Northwest Suburba, council Boy Scouts Am., 1963—, merit badge counselor, 1963—. Served to 1st. lt., inf., AUS, 1942-46; PTO. Recipient Trade Fair Coverage award Jr. Achievement of Chgo., 1959, George Washington Honor Medal award Freedoms Found., 1963. Mem. Internat., Chgo. (award 1953) assns. bus. communicators, U. Mo. Alumni Assn., Fedn. Fly Fishermen. Club: Northern Illinois Flytyers (dir. 1971-75). Contbr. articles on petroleum industry to various publs. Home: 255 N Ashland Ave Palatine IL 60067 Office: 850 Busse Hwy Park Ridge IL 60068

COX, LAWRENCE KOSSUTH, II, dentist; b. Adrian, Mich., Mar. 12, 1936; s. Lawrence Kossuth and Georgian (Wood) C.; B.A., Albion Coll., 1959; D.D.S., U. Detroit, 1963; m. Joan Gurdjian, Aug. 16, 1958; children—Terry, Laura, Steven. Gen. practice dentistry, Adrian, 1965—; mem. dental staff Bixby Hosp., 1965—, sec., treas. 1969-72, chief of dental staff, 1973—. Clin. examiner Mich. Dental Assistance Assn., 1966; adviser Lenawee County Vocat. Inst., 1968—; chmn. and instr. dental div., 1968-75; v.p. Kiwanis Riverview Terrace Corp., 1971-73; instr. U.S. Dental Inst., Chgo., 1977—. Served to capt. Dental Corps, USAF, 1963-65. Mem. U. Detroit Alumni Assn. (pres. 1973—), Alpha Tau Omega, Psi Omega (pres. 1962-63, Achievement award 1963). Elk, Kiwanian (pres. 1970-71, Kiwanian of Year 1975). Club: Circle K (dist. chmn. 1972-75). Home: 165 Orchard Dr Adrian MI 49221 Office: 225 S Main St Adrian MI 49221

COY, JAMES RICHARD, physician; b. Cleve., Oct. 5, 1923; s. Dale L. and Nina Florence (Browneller) C.; student Duke, 1941, Santo Thomas U., Manila, P.I., 1945; B.S., Northwestern U., 1947; M.D., Western Res. U., 1951; m. Ellen Kroehle, June 18, 1949; children—James Richard II, Dale L. II. Intern, St. Luke's Hosp., Chgo., 1951-52; resident anesthesiology Univ. Hosps., Cleve., 1954-56; vis. anesthesiologist Lakewood (Ohio) Hosp., 1956—. Served with AUS, 1941-46, USAF, 1952-54. Decorated D.S.M., Purple Heart, Bronze Star. Mem. Am., Ohio, Cleve. socs. anesthesiologists, Cleve. Acad. Medicine, Phi Gamma Delta, Nu Sigma Nu. Mason (Shriner, Jester). Clubs: Westwood Country (Rocky River, Ohio); Rockwell Springs Trout. Home: 17814 Lake Ave Lakewood OH 44107 Office: Lakewood Hosp Lakewood OH 44107

COYER, WILLIAM FRANK, physician; b. Denver, Apr. 22, 1941; s. Elmer William and Helen Mae (Bacon) C.; B.S., U. N.Mex., 1963; M.D., U. Tenn., 1967. Intern pediatrics U. Tenn. and City of Memphis hosps., 1967-68, resident pediatrics, 1968-69; chief resident pediatrics U. Colo., Denver, 1969-70, perinatal medicine fellow, 1970-71; teaching cons. Kauikeolani Children's Hosp., Honolulu, 1972-74; clin. asst. prof. pediatrics U. Hawaii, 1973—; asst. prof. pediatrics Loyola U. Stritch Sch. Medicine, Maywood, Ill., 1974—, asst. prof. anesthesiology, 1975—; dir. newborn medicine and pediatric intensive care Foster G. McGaw Hosp., Maywood, 1977—; dir. perinatal referral center Foster G. McGaw Hosp. and Loyola U. Med. Center, Maywood, 1974—. Served to maj., M.C., U.S. Army, 1971-74. Diplomate Am. Bd. Pediatrics. Fellow Am. Acad. Pediatrics; mem. AMA, Ill. Assn. Maternal and Child Health, Perinatal Group Ill., Chgo. Med. Soc., Chgo. Pediatric Soc. Home: 2S531 Emerald Green Dr Warrenville IL 60555 Office: 2160 S 1st Ave Maywood IL 60153

COYLE, LEO PERRY, telephone co. exec., b. Union City, N.J., Mar. 27, 1925; s. Leo Francis and Marie (Perry) C.; B.S., St. Peter's Coll., 1949; M.A., Western Res. U., 1950, Ph.D., 1959; postgrad. Rutgers, The State U., 1950-53; m. Betty Marie Hengesbaugh, June 30, 1951; children—Martha Lee, Susan Jane. Reporter, Jersey Jour., Jersey City, 1948-49; English master Rutgers Prep. Sch., New Brunswick, N.J., 1951-53; instr. John Carroll U., 1953-57, research fellow, 1957—; dir. employee communications Ohio Bell Telephone Co., Cleve., 1957—; editorial cons., 1962—. Served with AUS, 1943-46. Mem. Indsl. Audio Visual Assn. (pres.), Council on Internat. Non-Theatrical Events (v.p.). Author: George Ade, 1964. Contbr. to Popular Lit. in Am., 1972. Contbr. articles to profl. jours. Home: 3405 Hollister Rd Cleveland OH 44118 Office: 100 Erieview Plaza Cleveland OH 44114

COYLE, WILLIAM ROBERT, retail exec.; b. Columbus, Ohio, Mar. 16, 1928; s. Avard Robert and Gladies Vella (Marsh) C.; B.Sc., Ohio State U. 1948; m. Marjorie Alden Coyle, June 13, 1956; 1 son, Jeffrey Alan. Tchr., pub. sch. Columbus, 1949-51; founder, pres. Coyle Music Inc., Columbus, 1952—; vice pres. Buckeye Music Publ. Inc., 1958—. Named Outstanding Young Man in Music Industry, 1966. Mem. Nat. Assn. Music Mchts. (chmn., past pres.), Nat. Assn. Sch. Music Dealers (past pres.), Am. Music Conf. (dir.), Music Industry Council, Nat. Music Council, Am. Bandmasters Assn., Ohio State U. Alumni Assn. (adv. bd.), Alpha Tau Omega. Republican. Clubs: Presidents Ohio State U., Faculty Ohio State U., Newcomen, Mason, Shriners. Contbr. articles to musical publs. Home: 4944 Sharon Hill Dr Worthington OH 43085 Office: 2864 High St N Columbus OH 43202

COYNE, JOHN MARTIN, city ofcl.; b. Cleve., Nov. 11, 1916; s. Edward and Katherine (Coyne) C.; student Ohio U., 1936-37, LaSalle Extension U., 1955; m. Ruth Jean Brophy, Nov. 30, 1940; children—John Martin, Penny Jean (Mrs. James Dixon), Edward, James P. Village treas., Brooklyn, Ohio, 1940-41, village clk., 1942-47, mayor City of Brooklyn, 1948—. Bd. dirs. Deaconess Hosp. of Cleve.; exec. bd. Cuyahoga County Democratic Com. Mem. Ohio, Cuyahoga County mayors assns. Kiwanian. Home: 6620 Glencoe Ave Brooklyn OH 44144 Office: 7619 Memphis Ave Brooklyn OH 44144

COYNE, JOHN THOMAS, marketing and communications exec.; b. St. Paul, Mar. 29, 1934; s. Martin Thomas and Mary Alice (Brodle) C.; B.A., U. Minn., 1957; m. Constance Marie Kowaliw, Aug. 3, 1963; children—Christopher, Eileen, Thomas, Margaret. With Theodore Hamm Brewing Co., St. Paul, 1964-68, mgr. advt. media, 1966-68; with Ellerbe Architects/Engrs./Planners, Bloomington, Minn., 1968-75, dir. marketing and communications, 1971-73, v.p. marketing and communications, 1973-75. With Coyne & Associates (marketing and communications consultants) 1975—, president. Served to lt. AUS, 1957-58. Mem. Nat. Assn. Catholic Alumni Clubs (nat. men's pres., 1962-63), Mpls. C. of C., Pub. Relations Soc. Am. (state dir., 1973-74), Sales and Marketing Execs. (chapter dir. 1975-77), Soc. Marketing Profl. Services. Office: 1398 Cherry Hill Rd Mendota Heights MN 55118

COYNE, MARY JEANNE, lawyer; b. Mpls., Dec. 7, 1926; d. Vincent Mathias and Mae Lucille (Steinmetz) Coyne; B.S.L., U. Minn., 1955, J.D., 1957. Admitted to Minn. bar 1957, U.S. Supreme Ct., 1964; law clerk for Justice Leroy E. Matson, Minn. Supreme Ct., St. Paul, 1956-57; partner Meagher, Geer, Markham, Anderson, Adamson, Flaskamp & Breenan, Mpls., 1957—. Dir. Brown Photo Co. Instr. appellate advocacy U. Minn. Law Sch., 1964-68; mem. nat. panel arbitrators Am. Arbitration Assn., 1967—. Trustee Hennepin County Law Library. Mem. U. Minn. Law Alumni Assn. (sec. 1966-72, dir. 1971-74), Am., Minn., Hennepin County bar assns., Nat. Assn. Women Lawyers (rec. sec. 1968-69, assembly del. 1969-71, treas. 1972-74), Minn. Women Lawyers, Order of Coif, Phi Delta Delta, Beta Sigma Phi. Clubs: Minneapolis Golf. Editor: Women Lawyer Jour., 1971-72. Home: 5405 York Ave S Edina MN 55410 Office: 2250 IDS Center Minneapolis MN 55402

CRABB, KENNETH WILLARD, publisher, ch. ofcl.; b. Ottumwa, Iowa, July 9, 1920; s. Kenneth C. and Mary (Elliott) C.; student Albia (Iowa) Jr. Coll., 1938-40; B.J., U. Mo., 1942; m. Marjorie Jane Martin, Aug. 15, 1948; children—Kenneth Wayne, Martin Donald, Renee Louise. News editor Chariton (Iowa) Newspapers, 1942; editor Taylor County News, Bedford, Iowa, 1943; v.p. Herald-Register Pub. Co., Grinnell, Iowa, 1943; co-owner, editor Alamosa (Colo.) Daily Courier, 1945-47; make-up editor Salt Lake City Tribune, 1947-49; pub. Dawson County Rev. and Glendive (Mont.) Daily News, 1949-52; pres. Dawson County Publs., Glendive, 1949-52; comml. printer Indianola (Iowa) Record & Tribune Co., 1952-54, Des Moines Register & Tribune Co., 1954-57; ins. cons., rep. State Farm Ins. Cos., Indianola, 1957-74; pub. Citizen-Patriot, Atwood, Kans., 1974—; pres. Rawlins County Pub. Co., Atwood, 1974—. City councilman Indianola, Iowa 1962-70, chmn. finance com., 1963-70, mayor pro-tem, 1967-70; mem. Rawlins County Area Promotional Council, pres., 1975—. Mem. dist. com. Yellowstone Valley (Mont.) council Boy Scouts Am., 1949-52, Tall Corn (Ia.) Area council, 1952-71, exec. bd. to Mid-Ia. Council, 1971-74. Served with USNR, 1944-45. Recipient Silver Beaver award Boy Scouts Am., 1962; Nat. Quality award for quality life underwriting service, 1974. Mem. Life Underwriters Tng. Council, Kans. Press Assn., D.A.V., Am. Legion, Atwood C. of C. (exec. council 1975—), Sigma Delta Chi, Delta Tau Delta. Methodist (lay leader local ch. 1962-65, treas. local ch. 1975—, lay leader Des Moines dist. 1969-71, asso. lay leader Iowa Conf. 1971-73, lay leader 1973-74, lay mem. Kans. West Ann. Conf. 1975—, Kans. West bd. pensions 1976—). Rotarian (pres. 1971-72). Home: Box 26 Atwood KS 67730 Office: 510 Main St Atwood KS 67730

CRABB, ROBERT JOSEPH, retail co. exec.; b. Portland, Ore., Apr. 25, 1915; s. Earl Evan and Bess (Alexander) C.; A.B., Dartmouth, 1937; M.B.A., Tuck Sch., 1938; m. Catherine Boucher, Oct. 4, 1939; children—Earl II, Robert, John. With Green Giant Co., 1938-50, Investors Diversified Services, 1950-51; partner Larry Smith & Co., real estate cons., Seattle, Wash., 1951-55; with Dayton-Hudson Corp., Mpls., 1956—, sr. v.p., 1968—; pres. Dayton-Hudson Properties, coml. property devel. co., Mpls., 1970-77; dir. Pako Corp., First Southdale Nat. Bank, Title Ins. Co. of Minn. Trustee Fairview Community Hosps., Whipple Schs. Mem. Internat. Council Shopping Centers (trustee). Clubs: Minneapolis, Minikahda. Home: 6625 Dakota Trail Minneapolis MN 55435 Office: 777 Nicollet Mall Minneapolis MN 55402

CRABTREE, JOE, financial exec.; b. Tompkinsville, Ky., Mar. 1, 1922; s. Chester and Cecil (Seay) C.; B.S., U. Ill., 1943; m. Carolyn West, May 13, 1972; children—Joel John, Pamela Jean, Wendy Anne. Asst. treas. Pyle Nat. Co., Chgo., 1943-47; cons. Cutler Hammer Inc., Milw., 1947-50; dir. applications Univac div. Sperry Rand Corp., Blue Bell, Pa., 1950-63; controller AIL, Deer Park, N.Y., 1963-69; v.p. Mohawk Data Scis. Corp., Herkimer, N.Y., 1969-71; v.p. finance, treas. Midland Cooperatives, Inc., Mpls., 1971—; dir. Seaway Pipeline Inc., Gibble Oil Co., Claims Recovery, Inc.; v.p., treas. Petroleum Resources Co., Trade Credit Corp., Midland Credit Corp. Bd. dirs. Chessea Woods Assn. Mem. Am. Inst. Accountants, Financial Execs. Inst., Am. Accounting Assn., Assn. Govt. Accountants, Nat. Assn. Accountants, Nat. Soc. Accountants for Coops., Ill., N.Y. socs. C.P.A.'s, North Central Credit Assn., Delta Sigma Pi, Phi Eta Sigma, Beta Gamma Sigma. Episcopalian. Clubs: Mpls. Athletic, Lions. Home: 16235 18th Ave N Minneapolis MN 55391 Office: 2021 Hennepin Ave E Minneapolis MN 55413

CRADDOCK, WILLIAM JOHN, economist; b. Rosetown, Sask., Can., Mar. 20, 1938; s. William H. and Margaret (Carstaris) C.; diploma in Agr., U. Sask., 1958, B.S.A., 1962, M.S.A., U. Toronto, 1963; Ph.D., Ia. State U., 1966; m. Doreen L.L. Hoehn, July 9, 1960; children—Colin Trevor, Lisa Marlana, Sheldon William. Research asso. U. Sask., Saskatoon, 1962; research asst. Iowa State U., Ames, 1963-65, research asso., 1966; faculty agrl. econs. U. Man., Winnipeg, Can., 1966—, prof., 1972-76; v.p., dir. United Grain Growers Ltd., Winnipeg, 1975—, W.J. Craddock Ltd., Winnipeg, 1975—. Mem. Winnipeg Commodity Exchange, Palliser Wheat Growers Assn., Agrl. Inst. Can., Canadian Agrl. Econs. Soc., Am. Agrl. Econs. Assn. Home: 35 Laval Dr Winnipeg MB R3T 2X8 Canada Office: 1108-330 Portage Ave Winnipeg MB Canada

CRADEN, MICHAEL DENNIS, sports ofcl., zool. soc. adminstr.; b. Toledo, Ohio, May 16, 1938; s. Max and Norma B. (Boyles) C.; B.S. in Edn., Defiance Coll., 1960; M.S. in Edn., Bowling Green State U., 1961; Re.D. in Recreation, Ind. U., 1975; m. Sally Sims Matheney, July 30, 1966; children—Michael Dennis, Scott M. Phys. edn. tchr. schs., Toledo, 1957-59, athletic dir., 1957-59; coach at St. Mary's Sch.; tchr. of English Bowling Green Jr. High Sch., Ohio, 1960, Jefferson Jr. High Sch., Toledo Whitmer Sch. Dist., 1960-61, Sylvania (Ohio) High Sch., 1961-67, coach of cross country track team, Hi-Y adviser, 1961-67; summer playground dir. City of Toledo, 1956-61; football ofcl., Toledo City League, 1957—, basketball ofcl., 1957—, track ofcl., 1962—, track ofcl. at State Track Meet in Columbus, Ohio, 1970-76; dir. of recreation City of Sylvania, 1966—; commr. of recreation, City of Toledo, Ohio, 1968-70; tchr. Am. history Maumee High Sch., 1970-71, tchr. Am. lit. and English, 1971-72; athletic commr. No. Lakes League, 1975—; instr. arts and crafts, recreation Ind. U., 1967-68; dir. of program Toledo Zool. Soc., 1972—, coordinator of Toledo pub. sch. tchrs. at the zoo. Mem. Bd. Edn. Washington local schs., Toledo, 1974—, pres., 1976; Sunday sch. tchr. Olivet Luth. Ch., 1963. Named to Defiance Coll. Athletic Hall of Fame, 1977. Mem. Nat. Recreation and Park Assn., Am. Assn. of Zool. Parks and Aquariums, Toledo Zool. Soc., Northwest Dist. Track Ofcls. Assn. (pres. 1976-77), Old Newsboy Goodfellow Assn., East African Wild Life-Soc., Whitmer Athletic Club, Kappa Sigma Kappa, Phi Epsilon Kappa. Democrat. Lutheran. Author: (John M. Cooper) Beginning Track and Field for Men and Women; contbr. articles on the zoo to periodicals and books; editor Safari mag., Toledo Zoo Guide Book; sports editor Oraculum, 1957-58; organized Sylvania High School's first cross country team. Home: 4205 Marlaine Dr Toledo OH 43606 Office: 2700 Broadway Toledo OH 43609

CRAFT, PEARL SARAH DIECK SERBUS, newspaper editor; b. Riverdale, Ill.; d. Emil Edwin and Pearl (Kaiser) Dieck; student Bryant and Stratton Bus. Coll., 1935; m. Gerald Serbus, Jan. 26, 1946 (dec. Aug. 1969); children—Allan Lester, Bruce Alan, Curt Lyle; m. 2d, James E. Craft, Jan. 16, 1974. Mem. home econs. staff Chgo. Herald Examiner, 1934-39; operator test kitchen Household Sci. Inst., Mdse. Mart, Chgo., 1940-45; free-lance writer grocery chains, Chgo., 1945-49; Riverdale-Dolton corr. Calumet Index, Chgo., 1953-58, editorial asst., 1958-69, asst. editor, 1960—; with Suburban Index, Chgo., 1959—, editor, 1960-68, editor in chief Calumet and Suburban Index, 1968—; mng. editor Index Publs., 1972-74; v.p. Haines-Craft; free-lance writer. Bd. dirs. Roseland Mental Health Assn. Recipient Distinguished Service Member scroll P.T.A., 1959, Sch. Bell award Ill. Edn. Assn., 1965. Mem. bd. Suburban Community Concert Assn. Mem. Ill. Woman's Press Assn. (past pres.; 44 Mate Palmer awards in ann. writing contest, 1958-74; named woman of distinction for 1968, outstanding citizen award 1972), Nat. Fedn. Press Women (3 awards), Ill. Congress Parents and Tchrs. Assn. (life), Riverdale (bd. dirs., past v.p.), Chgo. South (v.p., dir.) chambers commerce. Address: 111 W 144th St Riverdale IL 60627

CRAIG, FORREST FIELD, JR., petroleum engr.; b. Homestead, Pa., Feb. 24, 1926; s. Forrest Field and Helena (Goeddel) C.; B.S., in Chem. Engring., U. Pitts., 1947, M.S., 1948, Ph.D., 1951; m. Elizabeth Jane Menk, July 8, 1949; children—Forrest Field III, Elizabeth Anne. With Amoco Prodn. Co., Tulsa, 1951-71, spl. research assoc., 1965-71; chief petroleum engr. Amoco Internat. Oil Co., Chgo., 1971-75, mgr. petroleum engring., 1975—. Campaign team capt. Community Chest, Tulsa, 1960-65; chpt. adviser Order of DeMolay, Tulsa, 1969-71. Served with USNR, 1944-46. Registered profl. engr., Okla., Tex. Mem. Soc. Petroleum Engrs. (sect. chmn. 1967-68, 73-74, chmn. transactions editorial com. 1966, chmn. continuing edn. com. 1969-70, distinguished lectr. 1971-72, bd. dirs. 1973-76, pres. 1977, John Franklin Carll award 1977), Am. Inst. Mining, Metall. and Petroleum Engrs. (dir. 1976-78, mem. exec. com. 1977, v.p. 1978), Am. Inst. Chem. Engrs., Sigma Xi, Phi Gamma Delta. Republican. Presbyn, Mason (Shriner). Author: (monograph) Reservoir Engineering Aspects of Waterflooding, 1971; co-author: Secondary and Tertiary Oil Recovery Processes, 1974. Patentee in field, U.S. and Can. Home: 3940 West End Rd Downers Grove IL 60515 Office: PO Box 8368 Chicago IL 60680

CRAIG, GEORGE BROWNLEE, JR., educator; b. Chgo., July 8, 1930; s. George Brownlee and Alice M. (McManus) C.; student U. Chgo., 1946-48; B.A., Ind. U., 1951; M.S., U. Ill., 1952, Ph.D., 1956; m. Elizabeth Ann Pflum, Aug. 7, 1954; children—James F., Mary C., Patricia A., Sarah L. Research asst. dept. entomology U. Ill., 1951-53; entomologist Des Plaines Valley Mosquito Abatement Dist., Ill., 1951-53; research entomologist U.S. Army Chem. Research and Devel. Labs., Md., 1954-57; faculty biology U. Notre Dame (Ind.), 1957—, prof., 1964—, George and Winifred Clark prof. biology, 1974—; cons. WHO, Swift & Co., USPHS, Environ. Def. Fund, Pan Am. Health Orgn.; research dir. Internat. Centre Insect Physiology and Ecology, Nairobi, Kenya; mem. tropical medicine and parasitology study sect. NIH, 1969-74; mem. exec. com. Western Hemisphere, World Orgn. Biol. Control. Fellow AAAS, Am. Acad. Arts and Scis.; mem. Entomol. Soc. Am. (chmn. med. and vet. entomology 1964, mem. governing bd. 1969-74, recipient medal for distinguished teaching 1975), Am. Genetics Soc., Am. Soc. Parasitologists, Am. Mosquito Control Assn. (award for research achievement 1976), Am. Soc. Tropical Medicine and Hygiene, Sigma Xi (chpt. pres. 1964-65). Contbr. articles to profl. jours. Research in field genetics of insects vectors of disease, especially Aedes mosquitoes. Home: 19645 Glendale Ave South Bend IN 46637 Office: Notre Dame IN 46556

CRAIG, JAMES LYNN, physician, med. service adminstr.; b. Columbia, Tenn., Aug. 7, 1933; s. Clifford Paul and Annie (Harris) C.; student Middle Tenn. State U., 1953; M.D., U. Tenn., 1956; M.P.H., U. Pitts., 1963; m. Suzanne Anderson, July 21, 1957; children—James Lynn, Margaret Ann. Intern, U. Tenn. Meml. Hosp., 1957; resident U. Pitts. Hosps., 1962-64; practice medicine specializing in preventive medicine, Chattanooga, 1964-74, Mpls., 1974—; mem. med. staff Baroness Erlanger Hosp., Chattanooga, Tenn., 1964-74, Meml. Hosp., Chattanooga, 1968-74, Parkridge Hosp., 1970-74; physician TVA, 1961-66, chief health officer, 1966-68, med. dir., 1968-74; med. dir. Gen. Mills, Inc., Mpls., 1974—; clin. instr. dept. preventive medicine U. Tenn., Memphis, 1970-74, Meharry Med. Coll., Nashville, Tenn., 1972-74; vice chmn. advisory group Tenn. Mid-South Regional Med. Program, 1972-73. Bd. dir. Chattanooga Area Council Alcoholism and Other Drug Abuse, Alcoholic Rehab. Inc., Louise Currey Opportunity Home for Girls. Served with M.C., USAF, 1958-60. Diplomate Am. Bd. Preventive Medicine. Fellow Am. Acad. Occupational Medicine; mem. Am. Nuclear Soc., AMA. Alpha Omega Alpha. Clubs: Kiwanians. Contbr. articles in preventive medicine to profl. jours. Home: 4410 Tyrol Crest Minneapolis MN 55416 Office: 9200 Wayzata Blvd Minneapolis MN 55440

CRAIG, ROBERT BRUCE, chem. mfg. co. exec.; b. Chgo., Mar. 21, 1930; s. Herbert and Vivian Segrid (Solberg) C.; student Goodman Theatre, Chgo., 1949-50; spl. courses U. Wis., U. Mich., U. Minn.; m. Mary Kathleen McConkey, June 8, 1962; children—Robert Bruce, Victoria Jean. Salesman, 3M Co., Chgo., 1953-64, tng. mgr., St. Paul, 1964-73; v.p. Varn Products Co., Inc., Addison, Ill., 1973—; lectr. sales mgmt., chem. safety. Congressional adviser, 1978. Served in U.S. Army, 1951. Mem. Chgo. Club Printing House Craftsmen (pres. 1977-78). Republican. Club: Itasca Country. Home: 254 N Brookdale Ln Palatine IL 60067 Office: 905 S Westwood Ave Addison IL 60101

CRAIG, ROBERT GEORGE, educator; b. Charlevoix, Mich., Sept. 8, 1923; s. Harry Allen and Marion Ione (Swinton) C.; B.S., U. Mich., 1944, M.S., 1951, Ph.D. (E.I. du Pont research fellow), 1955; m. Luella Georgine Dean, Sept. 29, 1945; children—Susan Georgine, Barbara Dean, Katherine Ann. Research chemist Linde Air Products Co., 1944-50, Texaco, Inc., Beacon, N.Y., 1954-55; research asso. U. Mich. Engring. Research Inst., 1955-57; faculty dept. dental materials Sch. Dentistry, U. Mich., Ann Arbor, 1957—, asst. prof., 1957-60, asso. prof., 1960-64, prof., 1964—, chmn. dept., 1969—; mem. exec. com. U. Mich. Sch. Dentistry, 1972-75; cons. Walter Reed Army Hosp., 1969-75. Research grantee Nat. Inst. Dental Research, 1965-76, Nat. Sci. Service tng. grantee, 1976—. Mem. Am. Nat. Standards Inst. (chmn. spl. com.), Internat. Assn. Dental Research (pres.-elect dental materials group 1972-73, pres. 1973-74, Wilmer Souder award 1975), Am. Assn. Dental Schs. (chmn. biomaterials sect. 1977—), Am. Chem. Soc., ASTM, Soc. Exptl. Stress Analysis, Am. Assn. Dental Schs., ADA, Soc. Biomaterials, Phi Kappa Phi, Phi Lambda Upsilon, Sigma Xi, Omicron Kappa Upsilon. Author: (With F.A. Peyton) Restorative Dental Materials, 1975; (with K.A. Easlick, S.I. Seger and A.L. Russell) Communicating in Dentistry, 1973; (with W.J. O'Brien, J. M. Powers) Dental Materials-Properties and Manipulation, 1975. Editor, contbr. Dental Materials Review, 1977; cons. editor Jour. Dental Research, 1971-73, Jour. Dental Edn., Jour. Oral Rehab., Mich. State Dental Jour. Contbr. articles to profl. jours. Home: 1503 Wells St Ann Arbor MI 48104

CRAIG, ROLLAND EUGENE, accountant, former city ofcl.; b. Danville, Ill., Jan. 6, 1902; s. Wilbur Palmer and Lulu (Johnson) C.; student U. Chgo., 1919-21, Ind. U., 1945-47; C.P.A., U. Ill., 1947; m. Mary A. Yeazel, Feb. 8, 1931. Pvt. practice, C.P.A., Danville, Ill., 1947-65; partner Clifton Gunderson, Coker and DeBruyn, C.P.A.'s, 1965-73; pvt. practice, Danville, 1975—; commr. finance City Danville, 1963-71, mayor, 1971-75. Methodist. Dist. dep. Order Demolay. Mason (33 deg.), Kiwanian. Home: 15 Fletcher Pl Danville IL 61832 Office: 41 On The Mall Danville IL 61832

CRAIG, WILLIAM ELLWOOD, children's homes exec.; b. Chester, Pa., June 26, 1915; s. William Ellwood and Josephine Worthington (Willard) C.; B.A., U. Calif. at Berkeley, 1937; B.D., Ch. Div. Sch. of Pacific, 1940; Ph.D., U. Calif. at Los Angeles, 1949; m. Mary Elizabeth Ellis, July 17, 1941; children—Mary Catherine (Mrs. Karl A. Selby), Charlotte Elizabeth, Margaret Ellis (Mrs. John D. Graver). Ordained priest Episcopalian Ch., 1940; rector, Los Angeles, 1940-48, Grand Island, Nebr., 1948-52, Oklahoma City, 1952-54; dean Christ Cathedral, New Orleans, 1954-56; dir. St. Francis Boys' Homes, Salina, Kans., 1956—. Mem. nat. council Episcopal Ch., 1949-55, Living Church Found., 1958—. Mem. Nat. Assn. Homes for Boys (exec. sec., 1973—), Nat. Assn. Tng. Schs., Conf. Tng. Schs. Supts., S.R. (Calif. chaplain, 1948). Republican. Elk, Kiwanian. Club: Salina Country. Editor Book of Proc., Nat. Assn. Homes for Boys, 1965—. Home: 107 W Prescott Ave Salina KS 67401 Office: Box 1348 Salina KS 67401

CRAIGHEAD, RODKEY, banker; b. Pitts., July 24, 1916; s. Ernest S. and Florence L. (Rodkey) C.; B.S., U. Pitts., 1942; postgrad. Grad. Sch. Banking, U. Wis., 1959-61; m. Carol M. Price, June 26, 1943; children—Rodkey, Virginia, Corinne. With Mellon Nat. Bank, Pitts., 1936-41; with Detroit Bank & Trust Co., 1946—, v.p., 1961-67, sr. v.p. comml. loans, 1967-69, exec. v.p., 1969-73, pres., 1974—, chmn., chief exec. officer, 1977—, also dir.; pres., dir. Detroitbank Corp., 1974—; dir. Pinon Valley Ranch, Weston, Colo., Winkelman Stores, Inc., Detroit. Bd. dirs. Jr. Achievement Mich., Met. Fund, Detroit Symphony Orch.; trustee Cranbrook Schs. Served to capt. AUS, 1942-46. Mem. Robert Morris Assos., Greater Detroit C. of C. (dir. 1977—), Assn. Res. City Bankers. Presbyterian (trustee). Clubs: Detroit Athletic, Economic, Detroit (Detroit); Orchard Lake Country; Bloomfield Hills Country. Home: 3912 Maple Hill E West Bloomfield MI 48033 Office: Detroit Bank & Trust Co Fort at Washington Sts Detroit MI 48321

CRAIN, ADA ELIZABETH, ret. librarian; b. Goltry, Okla., Sept. 18, 1904; d. Ernest B. and Maudie H. (Owens) Crain; B.S., Southwest Mo. State U., 1928; postgrad. Nat. U. Mexico, 1937, Mich. State U., 1960; M.Ed., U. Mo., 1940. Prin., Brandsville (Mo.) High Sch., 1928-30, Atlanta (Mich.) High Sch., 1930-42; tchr. Harbor Beach (Mich.) High Sch., 1942-43; prin. Blissfield (Mich.) High Sch., 1943-44; tchr. Big Rapids (Mich.) High Sch., 1944-57; librarian Fowlerville (Mich.) High Sch., 19S7-69, Fowlerville Pub. Library, 1960-65; ret. Recipient award of Appreciation Fowlerville Bd. Edn., 1969; named Fowlerville's Most Outstanding Citizen, VFW, 1976. Mem. Mich. Edn. Assn., NEA, Am. Assn. of Ret. Persons, Mo. Alumni Assn., SW Mo. State U. Alumni Assn. Methodist. Club: Garden. Address: 400 Cedar River Dr Lot 21 Fowlerville MI 48836

CRAIN, CHARLES BERNARD, controller; b. Kansas City, Mo., Nov. 1, 1947; s. William Clifford and Rita Marie (Fessler) C.; B.S. in Bus. Adminstrn., U. Mo., Columbia, 1969; M.B.A., Central Mo. State U., 1974; m. Barbara Jean Wiederkehr, Jan. 3, 1969; children—Bryce Eric, Michelle Regan, Melissa Megan. Mem. audit staff Elmer Fox & Co., C.P.A.'s, Kansas City, Mo., 1969-70, 71-72; staff accountant Forum Restaurants, Inc., Kansas City, 1972-73, divisional controller, 1973-74, corporate controller, 1974-75; chief financial officer, controller Topsy's Internat., Inc., Kansas City, 1975—. Served with AUS, 1970-71. Decorated Army Commendation Medal; recipient Gen. Mills Outward Bound grant, 1964. Mem. Nat. Assn. Accountants, U. Mo. Alumni Assn., Central Mo. State U. Alumni Assn., Outward Bound Alumni Assn. Republican. Roman Catholic. Club: Mo. Brittany. Home: Rt 2 Box 293K9 Belton MO 64012 Office: 215 E 18th St Kansas City MO 64108

CRAINE, JOHN PARES, bishop; b. Cleve., June 28, 1911; s. John Lee and Hilda B. (Wright) C.; A.B., Kenyon Coll., 1932, D.D., 1952; B.D., Bexley Hall, 1935; D.D., Wabash Coll., 1975; m. Esther Judson Strong, May 31, 1940 (dec. Apr. 1973); children—Susan Lee, Elizabeth Burnaby, John Pares II. Student minister St. Mark's, Cleve., 1933-35; ordained to ministry P.E. Ch., 1935; minister-in-charge St. Philip's Ch., Cleve., 1935-36; curate Trinity Ch., Santa Barbara, Calif., 1936-38; rector Trinity Ch., Oakland, Calif., 1938-41; canon Grace Cathedral, San Francisco, 1941-44; rector Trinity Parish Ch., Seattle, 1944-50, Christ Ch., Indpls., 1950-57, also dean Christ Ch. Cathedral, Indpls., 1953-57; consecrated bishop-coadjutor Diocese of Indpls., 1957, diocesan, 1959—. Mem. Greater Indpls. Progress Com. Chmn. bd. trustees Kenyon Coll.; chmn. bd. Episcopal Radio-TV Found.; hon. bd. dirs. Howe Mil. Sch.; mem. nat. bd. Urban League. Mem. Riley Meml. Assn., Loyal Legion, Newcomen Soc., Phi Beta Kappa. Clubs: Woodstock, Ind. Academy, Columbia (Indpls.). Home: 4164 Washington Blvd Indianapolis IN 46205 Office: 1100 W 42d St Indianapolis IN 46208

CRANE, FRANK MELVIN, agrl. co. exec.; b. Mankato, Minn., June 10, 1923; s. Lucas Melvin and Marie (Lindquist) C.; B.S., U. Minn., 1948, M.S., 1949, Ph.D., 1954; m. Audrey May Kraus, June 26, 1948; children—Carolyn Marie, Keith William, Suzanne Blanche, Debora Ann. Instr., U. Minn., 1948-51; research dir. Land O'Lakes Creameries, Inc., Mpls., 1951-69, v.p. mktg. activities Agrl. Service div., Fort Dodge, Iowa, 1969-74, v.p. research, 1974—. Served with USNR, 1942-46. Decorated Air medal. Mem. Am. Soc. Dairy Sci., Am. Soc. Animal Sci., Poultry Sci. Assn., N.W. (pres.), Am. (chmn. nutrition council, dir. 1972—, exec. com. bd. dirs. 1973) feed mfrs. assns., Alpha Gamma Rho, Alpha Zeta. Contbr. articles to profl. jours. Home: 2625 Woodland Dr Fort Dodge IA 50501 Office: 2827 8th Ave S Fort Dodge IA 50501

CRANE, JOHN KAIL, civil engr., computer analyst; b. Chgo., Aug. 20, 1925; s. John Bryan and Pearl L. (Bair) C.; B.S. in Civil Engring., Mass. Inst. Tech., 1948; student Bendix Computer Machine Lang. Sch., 1958. With structural div. Cook County Hwy. Dept., Chgo., 1948-58, head, computer div., 1958-69, head bur. engring. services and pub. affairs, 1969—. Chmn., Exchange, computer users orgn., 1965; mem. profl. engrs. exam. com. Ill. Dept. Registration and Edn., 1976—. Served with USNR, 1944-46. Registered profl. engr., Ill.; registered structural engr., Ill. Mem. Am. Pub. Works Assn., Mass. Inst. Tech. Alumni Club Chgo, Ill. Soc. Profl. Engrs. (chmn. Chgo. PEG com. 1971, v.p. Chgo. chpt. 1973, pres. 1975, chmn. Ill. ethics and practice com. 1976), ASCE, Ill. Assn. Structural Engrs., Western Soc. Engrs., Am. Concrete Inst., Order Engr. Ringholder, Nat. Assn. County Engrs. Club: Illinois Athletic. Home: 4976 N Milwaukee Ave Chicago IL 60630 Office: Cook County Hwy Dept Chgo Civic Center Chicago IL 60602

CRANE, KATHARINE ELIZABETH, editor, writer; b. Kenton, Ohio; d. George Edward and Kate (Rhodes) Crane; A.B., Smith Coll., 1916; Ph.D., U. Chgo., 1930. Tchr., St. Katherine's Sch., Davenport, Iowa, 1916-17, Shippen Sch., Lancaster, Pa., 1920-22, Women's Coll., U. N.C., 1925-26; asst. editor Ency. Social Scis., 1929-30; asst. editor Dictionary Am. Biography, 1930-36, Social Studies and Social Edn., 1936-39; state supr., state guide, Va. Hist. Survey. Library Services, 1940-43; officer Dept. State, 1943-50; historian Mil. Air Transport Service, 1950-60; free-lance writer, 1960—. Author: Status of Countries in Relation to the War, 1944; Blair House, 1946; Mr. Carr of State, 1960. Contbr. articles to profl. jours. Home: 500 N Main St Kenton OH 43326

CRANE, PHILIP MILLER, congressman; b. Chgo., Nov. 3, 1930; s. George Washington and Cora (Miller) C.; student DePauw U., 1948-50; B.A., Hillsdale Coll., 1952; postgrad U. Mich., 1952-54, U. Vienna (Austria), 1953, 56; M.A., Ind. U., 1961, Ph.D., 1963; LL.D., Grove City (Pa.) Coll.; m. Arlene Catherine Johnson, Feb. 14, 1959; children—Catherine Anne, Susanna Marie, Jennifer Elizabeth, Rebekah Caroline, George Washington V, Rachel Ellen, Sarah Emma, Carrie Esther. Advt. mgr. Hopkins Syndicate, Inc., Chgo., 1956-58; teaching asst. Ind. U., Bloomington, 1959-62; asst. prof. history Bradley U., Peoria, Ill., 1963-67; dir. schs. Westminster Acad., Northbrook, Ill., 1967-68; mem. 91st-95th congresses from 12th Ill. Dist. Pub. relations dir. Vigo County (Ind.) Republican Orgn., 1962; dir. research Ill. Goldwater Orgn., 1964; chmn. Ill. Citizens for Reagan Com., 1975; mem. nat. adv. bd. Young Ams. for Freedom, 1965—. Bd. dirs. Intercollegiate Studies Inst.; chmn. Am. Conservative Union; trustee Hillsdale Coll. Served with AUS, 1954-56. Recipient Distinguished Alumnus award Hillsdale Coll., 1968, Independence award, 1974; William McGovern award Chgo. Soc., 1969; Freedoms Found. award, 1972. Mem. Am. Hist. Assn., Orgn. Am. Historians, Acad. Polit. Sci., Am. Acad. Polit. and Social Scis., Phila. Soc., A.S.C.A.P., Phi Alpha Theta, Pi Gamma Mu. Methodist. Author: Democrat's Dilemma, 1964; The Sum of Good Government, 1976. Contbr. to Crisis in Confidence, 1974, Continuity in Crisis: The University at Bay, 1974. Office: Longworth House Office Bldg Washington DC 20515

CRATES, FREDERICK JOE, water mgmt. products mfg. co. exec.; b. Findlay, Ohio, May 3, 1932; s. Don F. and Maxine E. (Deaunee) C.; B.S., Findlay Coll., 1954; postgrad. City Coll. N.Y., 1963; M.S., No. Mich. U., 1968; postgrad. Bowling Green State U., 1967-70; m. Kathleen Louise Child, June 15, 1964; children—James, Krista. Tchr. biology Arcadia (Ohio) High Sch., 1954-57, Findlay (Ohio) High Sch., 1957-70; mgr. quality control Hancor, Inc., Findlay, 1970—, dir. research and devel., corp. dir., 1974—; mem. U.S.-USSR Tech. Exchange Com. for Plastic Products for Irrigation and Drainage, 1976-80. NSF grantee, 1963. Mem. Am. Soc. Testing and Materials, Soc. Plastic Engrs., Soc. Quality Control, Nat. Environ. Health Assn., Am. Soc. Agrl. Engrs. Odd Fellow, Rotarian. Home: Rural Route 3 Findlay OH 45840 Office: Box 1047 Findlay OH 45840

CRAVEN, JAMES CLETUS, appellate judge; b. Greenfield, Tenn., Aug. 7, 1925; s. James A. and Addie (Huggins) C.; B.S., U. Ill., 1948, J.D., 1949; m. Gloria Pheney, Nov. 24, 1951; children—William J., Nancy, Donald, Rebecca. Admitted to Ill. bar, 1950; asst. atty. gen. Ill., 1950-52; gen. practice Springfield, Ill., 1952-64; judge Appellate Ct., 4th Dist. Ill., Springfield, 1964—. Home: Rural Route 6 Springfield IL 62707 Office: Supreme Ct Bldg Springfield IL 62702

CRAVENS, JERE ALAN, newspaper pub.; b. Milaca, Minn., May 1, 1932; s. Ab R. and Ruth S. (Sholin) C.; B.A., U. Minn., 1954, M.A., 1957; m. Dort Millam, July 3, 1954; children—Deb, Ellen, Sandy. Salesman advt. Mille Lacs County Times, Milaca, 1955-74, publisher, editor, 1974—; pres. ECM Publs., Princeton, Minn., 1973-78. Home and office: PO Box 9 Milaca MN 56353

CRAWFORD, BETTY JEAN, counselor; b. Chattanooga, Oct. 22, 1932; d. Marshall and Olivia Crawford; B.S., Wayne State U., 1960, M.E., 1964, M.A., 1974. Clk., City of Detroit, 1951-60; tchr. Detroit Bd. Edn., 1960-76, counselor, 1976—; cons. Systematic Tng. for Effective Parenting, 1976—. Treas., Courville Sch. PTA, 1970-71. Mem. Detroit Fedn. Teachers. Am. Personnel and Guidance Assn., Women of Wayne, Assn. Tchr. Educators, Wayne State U. Alumni Assn. Democrat. Roman Catholic. Club: League of Cath. Women. Home: 20501 Keystone Detroit MI 48234 Office: 2001 Myrtle St Detroit MI 48208

CRAWFORD, DARNELL ALLEN, import and export co. exec.; b. Lockland, Ohio, Apr. 15, 1937; s. Arnell and Minnie (Allen) C.; student pub. and trade schs., Meridian, Miss., and Forest City, Ark.; m. Florence Coleman, Jan. 1957; children—Derrick, David, Jacqueline, Racheal, Jeffery Darnell, Jr. Pres. Crawfords Import Export, Cin., 1975—. Past pres. Arlington Ridge Corp.; community action chmn. CORE; chmn. local chpt. SCLC; chmn. welfare com. Mid-town Young Democratic Incorp.; bd. dirs. St. Louis Human Devel. Corp., 1966-70, St. Louis Comprehensive Health Center. Served with U.S. Army and USMC Res., 1954-57; Korea. Mem. NAACP, Urban League, Fgn. Policy Assn. (asso.). Office: Crawfords Import Export Box 15412 Cincinnati OH 45215

CRAWFORD, DEAN ERNEST, accountant; b. Topeka, Jan. 15, 1940; s. Ernest Percy and Beulah Marie (Jones) C.; student U. Kans., 1959-60; m. Peggy Marie Huffman, Nov. 23, 1966; children—Kelly, Karla, Kevin. Accountant, J.T. Weatherwax, Lawrence, Kans., 1963-65, Lesh, Bradley, Barrand, Lawrence, 1965-72; pvt. practice accounting, Lawrence, 1972-78; v.p. bus. mgmt. Native Am. Research Assos., Inc. and Native Am. Research Inst., Inc., Lawrence, 1978—. Treas. Achievement Place, Inc., 1973-77. C.P.A.. Kans. Mem. Am. Inst. C.P.A.'s, Kans. Soc. C.P.A.'s. Club: Optimist. Home: RFD 4 Box 76A Lawrence KS 66044 Office: 932 Massachusetts St Lawrence KS 66044

CRAWFORD, DEWEY BYERS, lawyer; b. Saginaw, Mich., Dec. 22, 1941; s. Edward Owen and Ruth (Wentworth) C.; B.A. with distinction, Dartmouth Coll., 1963; J.D. with distinction, U. Mich., 1966; m. Nancy Elizabeth Eck, Mar. 24, 1973. Admitted to Ill. bar, 1967; asso. firm Gardner, Carton & Douglas, Chgo., 1969-74, partner, 1975—; dirl. Ithaca (Mich.) Roller Mills. Dir. Ill. Assn. Retarded Citizens, 1975—. Served with U.S. Army, 1966-68. Mem. Am., Chgo. bar assns. Republican. Congregationalist. Office: 4600 One First National Plaza Chicago IL 60657

CRAWFORD, EDWIN MCNEILL, ednl. adminstr.; b. Montgomery, Ala., May 14, 1929; s. William H. and Mary (Thomas) C.; B.S., Auburn U., 1951; m. Mary Jean Barrett, Mar. 5, 1955; children—Ellen McNeill, Edwin Barrett, Graham Thomas. Reporter, Decatur (Ala.) Daily, 1951; editor Auburn (Ala.) U. Alumnews, 1952, Montgomery Examiner, 1953-54; account exec. Sparrow Advt. Agy., Birmingham, 1954-58; exec. asso. So. Regional Edn. Bd., Atlanta, 1958-62; dir. univ. relations Auburn U., 1962-66; asso. dir., dir. Office Instl. Research, Nat. Assn. State Univs. and Land-Grant Colls., Washington, 1966-70; v.p. for pub. affairs U. Va., Charlottesville, 1970-75; v.p. pub. affairs Ohio State U., Columbus, 1975—. Mem. Ala. Civil War Centennial Commn., 1962-64. Del., Democratic Nat. Conv. from 9th Dist. Ala., 1956; mem. Jefferson County Dem. Exec. Com., 1958. Recipient Silver Anvil awards Pub. Relations Soc. Am., 1962, 64. Mem. Am. Coll. Pub. Relations Assn. (certificate of exceptional achievement 1963, trustee 1971-74, chmn. 1974-75), Assn. Am. Univs. (council fed. relations 1971-75), Nat. Assn. State Univs. and Land-Grant Colls. (exec. com. 1977—), Newcomen Soc., Council for Advancement and Support of Edn. (chmn. 1974-75), Edn. Writers Assn., Mid-South St. Andrews Soc., Phi Delta Kappa, Omicron Delta Kappa, Sigma Nu. Presbyterian. Clubs: Rotary, Scioto Country. Home: 2338 Tremont Rd Columbus OH 43220

CRAWFORD, FERRIS NATHAN, educator; b. Frankfort, Mich., Nov. 1, 1912; s. Nathan Jennings and Elizabeth (Lentz) C.; A.B., Central Mich. U., 1935; M.A., U. Mich., 1940; D.Ed., Mich. State U., 1959; m. Eileen Bessie Icheldinger, June 25, 1941; children—Douglas Nathan, Barbara Ann (Mrs. David E. Ellies), Susan Marie, Thomas Alfred. Tchr. high schs., Rose City, Mich., 1935-36, Fairgrove, Mich., 1936-37, Dearborn, Mich., 1939-42; prin. Fairgrove High Sch., 1937-39; adminstr. Ford Airplane Sch., Willow Run, Mich., 1942-45; dir. selective psychol. testing Ford Motor Co., Dearborn, Mich., 1945-46; dir. community sch. service program Mich. Dept. Edn., Lansing, 1946-54, chief higher edn., 1954-58, asst. supt. for gen. edn., 1958-65, asso. supt. for ednl. services, 1966-76; dir. Mid-Am. Cons. Assos., 1977—. Lectr., U. Mich., Mich. State U., 1960-65, U. Tex., 1963; exec. sec. Mich. Commn. on Coll. Accreditation, 1961-66. Recipient Distinguished Pub. Service award Mich. Congress Parents and Tchrs., 1959, Mich. Council Community Coll. Presidents, 1963, Gov.'s Awards Commn. for Distinguished Pub. Employees, 1974, Mich. Council for Exceptional Children, 1975; Distinguished Service awards Mich. Legislature, 1976, Mich. Assn. Sch. Bds., 1976, Mich. Assn. Sch. Adminstrs., 1976, Mich. Community Coll. Assn., 1976. Mem. Phi Delta Kappa. Author: (with Maurice Seay) The Community School and Community Self-Improvement, 1954. Contbr. numerous articles to profl. jours. Home and office: 2958 Mayfair Dr Lansing MI 48912

CRAWFORD, FRANK PARKER, lawyer, judge, assn. ofcl.; b. Washington, Sept. 25, 1915; s. Frank Joseph and Cecelia Anne (Parker) C.; student Ind. State U., 1933-37; LL.B., Ind. U., 1940; m. Margaret Olivia Green, Oct. 4, 1946; children—Frank Parker, Margaret C., Loretta J., Hugh G. Admitted to Ind. bar, 1940, since practiced in Terre Haute; mem. firm Cooper, Royse, Gambill and Crawford, 1940-46, Gambill, Dudley, Cox and Crawford, 1946-48, Crawford and Crawford, 1948—; atty. City of Terre Haute, 1957-68; judge City Ct., Terre Haute, 1972—. Instr. Judge Adv. Gen. Dept., Ft. Sheridan, Ill., 1955-64; chmn., legal advisor legal com., region 7, div. on alcoholism, Ind. Dept. Mental Health. Mem. bd. lay advisors St. Anthony Hosp., pres., 1971-73; bd. dirs. Goodwill Industries, Terre Haute, 1970—; mem. adv. bd. Vis. Nurse Assn., Child Welfare Assn.; founding mem. bd. dirs. Terre Haute Med. Edn. Found., 1969, sec., 1969-74; mem. adv. council, counsel Terre Haute Center for Med. Edn., Ind. State U., 1971—. Served to maj. AUS, 1942-46. Mem. Terre Haute (pres. 1957-58), Ind. (bd. mgrs. 1958-59), 6th Dist. (pres. 1958-59) bar assns., Ind. Assn. City and County Attys. (pres. 1964-65), Am. Arbitration Assn. (nat. panel arbitration 1973—). Elk, Rotarian (dir. 1971-76). Clubs: Terre Haute Country, Aero (Terre Haute); Strawberry Hill Cannoneers. Home: 1613 S 6th St Terre Haute IN 47802 Office: 221 Mchts Savings Bldg Terre Haute IN 47807 also 105 City Hall Terre Haute IN 47808

CRAWFORD, GEORGE GAVER, journalist; b. Kenosha, Wis., Aug. 5, 1898; s. Charles Luther and Edith (Gaver) C.; student U. Wis., 1919-21; m. Mary D. Burnett, June 15, 1925; children—Joan Burnett, George Seeber. Newspaper reporter, 1922-28; telegraph editor Waukegan News-Sun, 1928-31, city editor, 1931-35, mng. editor 1935-53, editor, v.p., dir., 1953—; dir. Keystone Printing Co. Served with U.S. M.C., 1918. Mem. Taxpayers Fedn. Ill. (v.p., exec. com.), Lake County Civic League (organizer), AP Mng. Editors Assn., Ill. Asso. Press Editors (past pres.), Inland Daily Press, Am. Legion, Lake County Art League, Waukegan C. of C., Am. Soc. Newspaper Editors, Chi Phi, Sigma Delta Chi. Republican. Episcopalian (vestryman). Mason, Rotarian. Clubs: Chgo. Headline, Chgo. Press. Home: 1414 N Jackson St Waukegan IL 60085 Office: Waukegan News-Sun Waukegan IL 60085

CRAWFORD, GEORGE LEROY, JR., civil engr.; b. Davenport, Iowa, Mar. 6, 1928; s. George LeRoy and Florence (Gadient) C.; student U. Wyo., 1945-46; B.S., U. Ill., 1950; m. Patricia Ann Schumann, Aug. 15, 1948; children—George LeRoy III, Catherine Ruth, Nancy Jo; m. 2d, Patareka Kerbly, Apr. 6, 1974. Field traffic engr. Ill. Div. Hwys., East St. Louis Dist., 1950-62, dist. traffic engr., 1962-63, sr. field engr. Bur. Traffic, Springfield, 1963-64; prin. G.L. Crawford & Assos., 1964-66; pres. Crawford, Bunte, Roden, Inc., Springfield, 1966-72; v.p. Alan M. Voorhees & Assos., Inc., St. Louis, 1972-73; pres. George L. Crawford & Assos., Inc., Maryland Heights, Mo., 1973—. Served with C.E., AUS, 1945-47. Presbyn. (elder). Mason (Shriner). Home: 1707 Featherwood Dr Creve Coeur MO 63141 Office: 140 Weldon Pkwy Maryland Heights MO 63043

CRAWFORD, H(ENRY) GERALD, musician, educator; b. West Frankfort, Ill., Apr. 18, 1937; s. Henry S. and Beula (Adams) C.; B.Music, Eastman Sch. Music., 1959, M.Music, 1971; m. Marianna Mitchell, Aug. 23, 1958; children—Jerry Michael, Lisa Erin, Maria Belen. With N.Y.C. Opera Co., 1961-63; asst. prof. Southeastern La. U., Hammond, 1966-74; asst. prof. applied music Western Ill. U., Macomb, 1974—; dir. choral activities Wesley United Methodist Ch., Macomb, 1974—. Danforth asso. 1974—. Mem. Nat. Assn. Tchrs. Singing, Pi Kappa Lambda, Phi Mu Alpha. Operatic roles New Orleans Opera House Assn., Rochester (N.Y.) Opera Under the Stars, Chautauqua Opera; soloist, recitalist. Home: 506 Meadow Dr Macomb IL 61455

CRAWFORD, JAMES CARROLL, state ofcl.; b. Goldthwaite, Tex., June 15, 1928; s. Dean O. and Doris (Welch) C.; student Macalester Coll., 1948-51, U.S. Army War Coll.; B.A., Minn. Metro State Coll., 1974; student FBI Nat. Acad., 1974; m. Barbara Jean Hall, Dec. 27, 1950; children—James Carroll, Jodie (Mrs. Ronald David Moulton), Jeffrey Garnet. Patrol officer Minn. State Patrol, Forest Lake, 1952-61, sgt. in charge ops. 1961-67, capt. in charge tng., 1967-70, chief, St. Paul, 1973—; dir. motor vehicles Minn. Dept. Pub. Safety, St. Paul, 1970-73; chmn. curriculum com. Minn. Police Tng. Bd. Mem. Washington County Adv. Com., 1970—, Forest Lake Police Commn., Stillwater Twp. Joint Planning Commn.; chmn. Forest Lake Planning Commn., 1962; Community Fund chmn. Indianhead council Boy Scouts Am., 1973. Served with USNR, 1946-49, USAF, 1949-50; now brig. gen. U.S. Army Res. Recipient Gov.'s Distinguished Service citation, 1957, Police Service award SAR, Distinguished Service award Minn. Optometric Assn. Mem. Minn. Hwy. Patrol Suprs. Assn. (pres. 1969-70), Minn. Peace and Police Officers Assn., FBI Acad. Assos., Midwest Fleet Safety Suprs. Assn. (hon.), Internat. Assn. Chiefs Police (hwy. traffic safety com.), Minn. Chiefs Police (legis. com.), Minn. Safety Council, Am. Legion. Mason (Mason of Year 1977). Home: 980 SE 10th Ave Forest Lake MN 55025 Office: Hwy Dept Bldg St Paul MN 55155

CRAWFORD, JAMES WELDON, psychiatrist, educator; b. Napoleon, Ohio, Oct. 27, 1927; s. Homer and Olga (Aderman) C.; A.B., Oberlin Coll., 1950; M.D., U. Chgo., 1954, Ph.D., 1961; m. Susan Young, July 5, 1955; 1 son, Robert James. Intern Wayne County Hosp. and Infirmary, Eloise, Mich., 1954-55; resident Northwestern U., Chgo., 1958-59; practice medicine specializing in psychiatry, Chgo., 1961—; mem. staff Mt. Sinai Hosp., Chgo., George F. Lundon Hosp., Ravenswood Hosp., Louis A. Weiss Meml. Hosp., Chgo. clin. asso. prof. dept. psychiatry Abraham Lincoln Sch. Medicine, U. Ill., 1970—; chmn. dept. psychiatry Ravenswood Hosp. Med. Center, 1973—. Mem. com. on nat. health ins. Council Community Services Met. Chgo., 1973-75. Bd. dirs. Ravenswood Hosp. Med. Center, 1971-73, Chase House Episcopal Diocese Chgo. Served with M.C., AUS, 1945-46. NIH, Inst. Neurol. Diseases postdoctoral fellow, 1955-59. Fellow Am. Psychiat. Assn.; mem. A.M.A., A.A.A.S., Assn. Am. Med. Colls., Ill. Psychiat. Soc., Chgo. Med. Soc., AAUP, Sigma Xi. Contbr. articles to profl. jours. Home: 2418 Lincoln St Evanston IL 60201 Office: Field Clinic Chicago IL 60640

CRAWFORD, JEAN ANDRE, counselor; b. Chgo., Apr. 12, 1941; d. William Moses and Geneva Mae (Lacy) Jones; student Shimer Coll., 1959-60; B.A., Carthage Coll., 1966; M.Ed., Loyola U., Chgo., 1971; postgrad. Nat. Coll. Edn., Evanston, Ill., 1971-77, Northwestern U., 1976-77; m. John N. Crawford, Jr., June 28, 1969. Med. technologist, Chgo., 1960-61; primary and spl. edn. tchr. Chgo. Pub. Schs., 1966-71, counselor maladjusted children, 1971—; counselor juvenile first-offenders, 1968—. Vol., Sta. WTTW-TV. Certified in spl. edn., pupil personnel services, Ill. Mem. Am.. Ill. personnel and guidance assns., Am., Ill. sch. counselors assns., Coordinating Council Handicapped Children, Phi Delta Kappa. Club: Mid-Town Tennis. Home: 601 E 32d St Chicago IL 60616 Office: 1801 S Ashland Ave Chicago IL 60608

CRAWFORD, LESLIE WILLIAM, educator; b. Scobey, Mont., July 29, 1934; student Am. U., Washington, 1952-53; B.S., Eastern Mont. U., Billings, 1956, M.S., 1962; postgrad. Colo. State Coll., Greeley, 1961; Ed.D., U. Calif., Berkeley, 1967. Tchr. pub. schs., Lewistown, Mont., 1955-58, Douglas, Ariz., 1958-59; supr. Eastern Mont. Coll. Campus Sch., 1960-62, vis. lectr. reading and early childhood edn., 1966; curriculum coordinator and supr., lectr. elementary edn. Western Wash. State Coll., 1964-65; research asst. Primary Reading Project, U. Calif., Berkeley, 1966; asst. prof. reading and lang. arts U. Victoria, B.C., 1967-69; asst. prof. Reading Center, Ohio U., 1969-70; vis. asst. prof. U. Wash., 1970; asst. prof., coordinator undergrad. reading and lang. arts Bowling Green State U., 1970-72; asso. prof., dir. elementary edn. Moorhead (Minn.) State U., 1972-74, prof., chairperson dept. edn., 1974—; cons. Queen of Angels Sch., Duncan, B.C., 1968-69, Athens City Title I Program, 1969-70, Fed.-Hocking Title I Program, 1969-70, Lincoln Internat. Sch., San Jose, Costa Rica, 1973-74, Am. Coop. Sch., Monrovia, Liberia, 1975; asso. dir. Crim Sch. Team Teaching and Individualizing Project, 1971-72; co-chmn. Minn. Conf. on Preparation Program for Elementary Tchrs. in Next Decade, 1976. Mem. Internat. Reading Assn. (pres. elect Martha G. Weber chpt. 1971-72, mem. exec. com. Ohio Council), Nat. Council Tchrs. English, Minn. Intercollegiate Faculty Assn., Phi Delta Kappa. Author: (with Morris Finder) Structural View of English, 1966. Contbr. articles to ednl. jours. Home: 426 Horn Ave Moorhead MN 56560 Office: Edn Dept Moorhead State U Moorhead MN 56560

CRAWFORD, PAUL KERRINS, parliamentarian, former educator; b. Cameron, Mo., Nov. 15, 1906; s. William Thomas and Mary Ellen (Devenney) C.; B.A., Baker U., 1928; Ph.M., U. Wis., 1936; Ph.D., Northwestern U., 1949; m. Christine O'Neal, Aug. 19, 1930; 1 dau., Rosalyn (Mrs. Robert Santilli). Tchr., Cameron, 1928-29, Freeport, Ill., 1929-40; faculty speech communication No. Ill. U., DeKalb, 1940-74, emeritus, 1974—; parliamentarian with short courses, lectures to various groups, 1962—. Mem. adv. bd. Newman Found., 1960—. Mem. No. Ill. U. Found. Recipient Cardinal Newman award 1960; Oustanding Service award No. Ill. U. Alumni Assn., 1971, Pres.'s award No. Ill. U. Found., 1974. Life fellow Internat. Inst. Arts and Letters; mem. Am. Inst. Parliamentarians (adv. council), Ill. Speech and Theater Assn. (life), Speech Communication Assn. Am. (life mem., rep. legis. assembly). Author: An Outline of Parliamentary Law, 1935; The Lincoln Douglas Debate at Freeport, 1958; (with W. Buys, etal), Communication in the High School Curriculum: Speaking and Listening, 1961. Contbr. articles to various jours. Editor: Ill. Speech News, 1935-39; asso. editor Masque and Gavel mag., 1940-44. Home: 231 Fairmont Dr DeKalb IL 60115

CRAWFORD, RAYMOND CLARKE, dentist; b. Adena, Ohio, Apr. 4, 1912; s. Homer Campbell and Virgie Emma (Townsend) C.; student Duke, 1932-33; D.D.S., Ohio State U., 1937; m. Hazel Rittenhouse, Dec. 28, 1939 (dec. June 1968); children—Judith Lynn (Mrs. Gerald E. Ingle), Lee Campbell, m. Lou Wilson Stewart, Sept. 19, 1970. Pvt. practice dentistry, Adena, 1937—; dir. First Nat. Bank, Cadiz, Ohio. Mem. sch. bd., Adena, 1939-43. Served with USAAF, 1943-46. Fellow Internat. Coll. Dentists; mem. Pierre Fauchard Acad., Am., Ohio dental assns., Eastern Ohio Dental Soc., Harrison County Hist. Soc., Psi Omega. Mason. Home: 600 Dewey Ave Cadiz OH 43907 Office: 111 Main St Adena OH 43901

CRAWFORD, RAYMOND MAXWELL, JR., nuclear engr.; b. Charleston, S.C., July 28, 1933; s. Raymond Maxwell and Mary Elizabeth (Bates) C.; B.S., Wayne State U., 1958, M.S., 1960; Ph.D., U. Calif. at Los Angeles, 1969; m. J. Denise LeDuc, Mar. 10, 1951; children—Denis, Michael, Deborah, Peter, Elizabeth. Instr. Wayne State U., 1960-63; asst. prof. Cal. State U. at Northridge, 1963-66; tech. staff Atomics Internat., 1969-71; nuclear engr. Argonne (Ill.) Nat. Lab., 1971-74; asst. head nuclear safeguards and licensing div. Sargent & Lundy, Chgo., 1974—. Tech. cons. Atomic Power Devel. Assn., 1962-63; summer fellow NASA Lewis Research Center, 1965-66. Scoutmaster and counsellor Boy Scouts Am., 1963-66; active YMCA, 1966-69; active Recs. for Blind, 1964-65. Recipient numerous awards. Mem. Analog Computer Ednl. Users Group (dir.), Am. Nuclear Soc., Am. Inst. Chem. Engrs., Am. Chem. Soc., Am. Soc. Engring. Edn., Am. Sci. Affiliation, N.Y. Acad. Scis., A.A.A.S., Sigma Xi, Tau Beta Pi, Phi Lambda Upsilon. Contbr. articles to tech. jours. Home: 1005 E Kennebec Ln Naperville IL 60540 Office: 55 E Monroe St Chicago IL 60603

CRAWFORD, ROBERT ADELBERT, civil engr.; b. Lead, S.D., Oct. 23, 1925; s. Robert Fulton and Laura Olive (Wagner) C.; B.S., U. N.Mex., 1950; m. Dorothy Lee Sloss, Jan. 26, 1946 (dec.); children—Lawrence Douglas, Connie Lee (Mrs. James Larson), Esther Ann. Supervisory civil engr., U.S. Navy, Guam, Marinas Island, 1951-56; research engr. S.D. Dept. Transp., Pierre, 1956—. Served with USNR, 1943-46, 50-51. Home: 202 S Taylor St Pierre SD 57501 Office: Div Hwys SD Pierre SD 57501

CRAWFORD, WILLIAM BASIL, JR., newspaper reporter; b. Waukegan, Ill., June 22, 1941; s. William Basil and Jane Elinore (Murray) C.; m. Joan Ellen Plaushines, Sept. 3, 1965; 1 dau., Kirsten Jane; B.A. in History, U. Chgo., 1963. Asst. fiscal officer Chgo. Truck Drivers Union, 1964-68; asst. news editor City News Bur. Chgo., 1968-72; reporter Chgo. Tribune, 1972—; tchr. advanced reporting and basic writing Medill Sch. Journalism, Northwestern U., Evanston, Ill. Mem. Chgo. Reporters Assn., Chgo. Press Club, U. Chgo. Alumni Assn. Recipient Hon. mention Ill. U.P.I., 1974, 2d Place award for investigative reporting, 1975, First Place awards for best investigative story Ill. A.P., 1975, 76, Sweepstakes award for best story in all categories, 1976, 3d Place award for investigative, 1976; Pulitzer prize for Spl. Local Reporting, 1976. Home: 322 Devonshire Ave Barrington IL 60010 Office: 435 N Michigan Ave Chicago IL 60010

CRAYTON, BILLY GENE, physician; b. Holden, Mo., May 15, 1931; s. John Reuben and Carrie Zona (Head) C.; student Central Mo. State Coll., 1948-49; B.S., Stetson U., 1958; postgrad. U. Kansas City, summer 1955; M.D., U. Mo., 1962. Intern, Mound Park Hosp., St. Petersburg, Fla., 1962-63; practice gen. medicine Latham Hosp., California, Mo., 1963-64, Kelling Clinic and Hosp., Waverly, 1964—; preceptor in community health and med. practice U. Mo. Sch. Medicine, Waverly, 1968—; sec., dir. Kelling Hosp., Inc., 1969-71; pres. Kelling Clinic, 1971—; pres. Riverview Heights, 1972—. Adviser, Mo. chpt. Am. Assn. Med. Assts., 1973—. Adviser, Explorer Post Boy Scouts Am., 1968-70. Served with AUS, 1952-54. Mem. Am. Acad. Family Practice, Am., So., Mo. med. assns. Baptist. Home: PO Box 41 Waverly MO 64096 Office: Kelling Clinic and Hosp Waverly MO 64096

CREBS, DONALD EUGENE, bldg. contractor; b. West Salem, Ohio, May 25, 1923; s. Claude Eugene and Viola Alice (McBride) C.; Accountant degree Oberlin Sch. Commerce, 1942; m. Wilma Louise Burdette, July 24, 1943; children—Thomas, Richard, David, Kenneth, Joanne, Kathy. Sec. to gen. supt. E.B. Badger & Sons, Point Pleasant, W.Va., 1942-43; cost accountant B.F. Goodrich Co., Akron, Ohio, 1943-47; owner D.E. Crebs-Contractor and Builder, West Salem, 1947—; real estate broker, West Salem, 1964—; dir. Holmes-Wayne Rural Electric Coop., Millersburg. Active Boy Scouts Am. Mayor, Village of West Salem, 1972—. Bd. dirs. Lodi Community Hosp. Served with AUS, 1943. Recipient Silver Beaver award Boy Scouts Am., 1967. Methodist (pres. trustees 1950-70). Mason. Home: 140 Britton St West Salem OH 44287 Office: 140 Britton St West Salem OH 44287

CREDEN, JOHN THOMAS, banker; b. Chgo., Oct. 25, 1936; s. Samuel G. and Edith B. (Bullen) C.; B.A., Williams Coll., 1958; grad. Stonier Grad. Sch. Banking, 1970; m. Meta Evelyn Till, July 23, 1960; children—Stephen T., Anne T. Data processing sales IBM, 1958-62; with First Nat. Bank of Southwestern Mich., Niles, 1962—, trust officer, 1963-68, sec., 1966-75, v.p., 1972-76, exec. v.p., dir., 1972—; pres., dir. Western Mich. Corp., 1976—. Sec.-treas. Greater Niles Indsl. Devel. Corp., 1968—; mem. Bd. Edn. Niles Community Schs.; pres. Jeanne Griffin Found. Served with AUS, 1959-65. Clubs: Pickwick, Signal Point, Orchard Hills Country (Niles). Home: 1000 Weesaw Rd Niles MI 49120 Office: 210 E Main St Niles MI 49120

CREESE, WALTER LITTLEFIELD, educator; b. Danvers, Mass., Dec. 19, 1919; s. Guy Talbot and Avis (Littlefield) C.; A.B. magna cum laude, Brown U., 1941; M.A., Harvard, 1945, Ph.D., 1950; m. Eleanor Roberts, June 16, 1945; 1 son, Guy. Tutor, teaching fellow Harvard, 1944-45; instr. Wellesley Coll., 1945; from instr. to prof.

Hite Art Inst., U. Louisville, 1956-58, acting head, 1953-54, 56-57; prof. architecture U. Ill., 1958-63; dean Sch. Architecture and Allied Arts, U. Oreg., 1963-68; prof. Coll. Fine and Applied Arts, U. Ill., Urbana, 1968—; vis. summer prof. Harvard, 1961; vis. asso. Mass. Inst. Tech.-Harvard Joint Center, 1969-70. Chmn., Louisville and Jefferson County Planning and Zoning Commn., 1952-55. Fulbright postdoctoral fellow U. Liverpool (Eng.), 1955-56; Smithsonian Research fellow, 1969-70; Guggenheim fellow, 1972-73; Rockefeller Found. fellow, 1976-77. Mem. AIA (hon.), Soc. Archtl. Historians (editor jour. 1950-53, pres. 1958-60), Coll. Art Assn., Sphinx Soc., Phi Beta Kappa, Phi Kappa Phi. Author: The Search for Environment, 1966; The Legacy of Raymond Unwin, 1967. Contbr. numerous articles to archtl., art mags. Address: U Ill 103 Architecture Urbana IL 61801

CREHORE, CHARLES AARON, lawyer; b. Lorain, Ohio, Sept. 15, 1946; s. Charles Case and Catherine Elizabeth (Kurtz) C.; B.A., Wittenberg U., 1968; postgrad. (Delta Sigma Phi Found. scholar), U. Mich., 1968-69, Cleve. State U., 1972-73; J.D., U. Akron, 1976; m. Kathy Louise Stoecklin, June 28, 1969. Asso. chemist B.F. Goodrich Co., Akron, chemist, 1970-72, sr. chemist, 1972-75, patent agt., 1975-76, patent atty., 1976—; admitted to Ohio bar, 1976. Kennedy Found. grantee, 1968-69. Mem. Am., Ohio bar assns., Am. Patent Law Assn., Licensing Execs. Soc., Phi Alpha Delta. Mem. Gen. Ch. New Jerusalem. Home: 314 Misty Ln Akron OH 44321 Office: 500 S Main St Akron OH 44318

CREIGH, DOROTHY WEYER, educator, writer; b. Hastings, Nebr., Dec. 4, 1921; d. Frank E. and Mabelle (Carey) Weyer; A.B., Hastings Coll., 1942; M.S., Columbia, 1945; m. Thomas Creigh, Jr., July 17, 1948; children—Mary Elizabeth, Thomas III, John Weyer, James Carey. Soc. editor Hastings Daily Tribune, 1941-42; tchr. Central City (Nebr.) High Sch., 1942-43; editor weekly newspaper Naval Ammunition Depot, Hastings, 1943-44; with AP, Richmond, Va., 1945-46, UNRRA, Hankow and Shanghai, China, 1946-48; tchr. Hastings Coll., 1952, 61-68; garden editor Hastings Daily Tribune, 1960; editor Stringing Along, music mag., 1966-67. Dir. Nebr. Arts Council, 1966—, Central Nebr. Heart Assn., 1966-69; Mem. Gov.'s Conf. on Higher Edn.; mem. State Bd. Edn., 1974—. Mem. Nebr. Hist. Found., Adams County Hist. Assn. (dir. 1965—), Nat. Trust for Historic Preservation (bd. advisers 1976—). Presbyn. Club: Lochland Golf. Author: (with C. Brock) Journalism for Nebraska High Schools, 1943; (with F.E. Weyer) Hastings College, 75 Years, 1958; Bellevue College, 1962; Tales from the Prairie, vol. I, 1970, vol. II, 1973, vol. III, 1976; The People, 1971; Adams County (Nebr.) A Story of the Great Plains, 1972 (Merit award Am. Assn. State and Local History 1973); (casettes) How to be An Effective Public Official, Exec. Inst., 1973; The First Hundred Years, 1973; Where in the World Have We Been?, 1973; A Primer for Local Historical Societies, 1976; Nebraska State Bicentennial History, 1977. Editor: Hastings Coll. Alumni Quar., 1949-51; Hist. News, monthly hist. mag. Author scripts for movie documentaries on Great Plains, 1977. Contbr. to mags., newspapers. Address: 1650 N Elm St Hastings NE 68901

CREIGH, THOMAS, JR., utility co. exec.; b. Evanston, Ill., Jan. 3, 1912; s. Thomas and Frances (Connor) C.; grad. Mercersburg (Pa.) Acad., 1929; A.B., Wabash Coll., 1933; m. Dorothy Claire Weyer, July 17, 1948; children—Mary Elizabeth, Thomas III, John, James. With No. Natural Gas Co., 1933-36; with Kans.-Nebr. Natural Gas Co., Inc., 1936—, v.p., 1951-61, pres., 1961—, also dir.; v.p., dir. Excelsior Oil Corp., 1955—, Helium, Inc., 1960—, Dunne Gardner Drilling Co., 1960-70; sec., dir. Western Plastics Corp., 1953-67; pres., dir. Western Gas Corp.; dir. Cap-Con Internat., Inc., Western Alfalfa Corp., Energy Transmission Systems, Inc. Trustee Hastings Coll. Mem. Am. Gas Assn. (dir. 1969-73), Ind. Natural Gas Assn. Am. (dir. 1967—), Nebr. Assn. Commerce and Industry (pres. 1966), Presbyn. (trustee). Home: 1650 N Elm St Hastings NE 68901 Office: Kans-Nebr Natural Gas Co Hastings NE 68901

CRESS, JOSEPH NICHOLAS, clin. psychologist; b. Adrian, Minn., Feb. 16, 1944; s. Nicholas Arnold and Dorothea Monica (Hartman) C.; A.B., St. Louis U., 1968; M.A., So. Ill. U., 1972, Ph.D. (Univ. Grad. Sch. Dissertation fellow), 1974; m. Elaine Marie Peaslee, July 21, 1974. Co-founder, mem. staff Sophia House, Inc., Exptl. High Sch., St. Louis, 1966-68; tchr., dir. Oglala Sioux Indian Culture Center, Red Cloud Sch., Pine Ridge, S.D., 1968-70; clin. psychologist Community Mental Health Center, Rock Island, Ill., 1974—; mem. adj. faculty psychology, Augustana Coll., Rock Island, St. Ambrose Coll., Davenport, Iowa, U. Iowa, 1975—; psychol. cons. Head Start Programs, various ednl. agys., 1974—. Fellow preparation profl. personnel in edn. of handicapped children, 1970-72. Mem. Am., Upper Mississippi Valley psychol. assns. Contbr. articles in field to profl. jours. Home: 2329 Southview Dr Bettendorf IA 52722 Office: 2701 17th St Rock Island IL 61201

CRESWELL, DOROTHY ANNE, coll. adminstr.; b. Burlington, Iowa, Feb. 6, 1943; d. Robert Emerson and Agnes Imogene (Gardner) Mefford; A.A., Burlington Community Coll., 1963; B.A., U. Iowa, 1965; M.S. in Math., Western Ill. U., 1970; m. John Lewis Creswell, Aug. 28, 1965. Bus. computer programmer Mason & Hanger-Silas Mason Co., Inc., Burlington, 1965-70, sci. computer programmer, 1970-74; system programmer Computer Resources div. Contractors Hot Line, Ft. Dodge, Iowa, 1974; dir. data processing Iowa Central Community Coll., 1975—. Mem. Data Processing Mgmt. Assn. (sec. Mississippi Valley chpt. 1968-69), Rockwell City Bus. and Profl. Womens Club, Assn. Computing Machinery, Iowa Assn. Ednl. Data Systems. Democrat. Methodist. Home: 845 Court St Rockwell City IA 50579 Office: 330 Ave M Fort Dodge IA 50501

CRESWELL, THOMAS JAMES, educator; b. Chgo., July 22, 1920; s. Samuel Joseph and Mary (Daley) C.; B.E., Chgo. Tchrs. Coll., 1943; M.A., U. Chgo., 1952, Ph.D., 1974; m. Beverly Grace Nielsen, Dec. 19, 1953; step-children—Rachel Eve (Mrs. James Eriksson), Peter Lawrence Beilman. Tchr., Chgo. Pub. Schs., 1946-52; regional dir. Papermate Pen Co., 1952; tchr. English, Wilson Jr. Coll., 1953-58; instr. English, Chgo. Tchrs. Coll., 1958-63, asst. prof., 1963-71; dir. lang. arts and lit. Sci. Research Assos., Inc., 1966-68, editorial cons., 1965—; dir. ednl. experimentation Chgo. State U., 1968-69, dean instrn., 1968-71, asso. prof. English, 1971-75, prof. English, 1975—; editorial cons. Holt, Rinehart & Winston, Inc., 1965—, Sci. Research Assos., Inc., 1973. Mem. Save the Dunes Council, 1955—. Served with AUS, 1943-46. Am. Council Learned Soc. fellow linguistics, 1964-65. Mem. Conf. on Coll. Composition and Communication, Linguistic Soc. Am., Modern Lang. Assn., Nat. Conf. Tchrs. English (editorial bd. 1977—), Am. Dialect Soc., Dictionary Soc. N.Am. Asst. editor Chgo. Schs. Jour., 1958-63, mng. editor, 1964, 65; chmn. editorial bd. Ill. Sch. Jour., 1971-74. Contbr. articles to profl. jours. Home: Rural Route 2 Box 184 Michigan City IN 46360 Office: 9500 S King Dr Chicago IL 60628

CRETSOS, JAMES MIMIS, sci. info. co. exec., chemist; b. Athens, Greece, Oct. 23, 1929; s. Basil D. and Chrissa B. (Thomaidou) Kretsos; came to U.S., 1946, naturalized, 1955; B.S. in Chemistry, Am. U., 1960, postgrad., 1960-62; m. Barbara Ann Deitz, Mar. 10, 1952; children—Maurice William, Christopher James. Research chemist Melpar, Inc., Falls Church, Va., 1961-63, info. scientist, 1963-64, head tech. info. center, 1964-65, mgr. info. services lab., 1965-67, dir. instructional materials center, Tng. Corp. of Am., Falls Church, 1966-67; dir. info. systems lab., Litton Industries, Bethesda, Md., 1967-69; head sci. info. systems dept., Merrell-Nat. Labs., Cin., 1969—. Dir. Infoflow, Inc. Cons to OEO, Ohio, Ky. Ind. Regional Library and Info. Council; lectr. U. Cin., 1973-74, U. Ky., 1976-77. Mem. Creative Edn. Found., Buffalo, 1967—. Served with M.C., AUS, 1954-56. Mem. Am. Chem. Soc., Am. Mgmt. Assn., Am. Soc. Info. Sci. (chmn. So. Ohio chpt. 1973-74, chmn. SIG/BC 1973-74 chmn. profl. enhancement com. 1974-75, chmn. 5th mid-year meeting 1976, Watson Davis award 1976), Assn. for Computing Machinery, Drug Info. Assn., Med., Spl. (pres. Cin. chpt. 1974-75, consultation officer 1976-77) libraries assns., Pharm. Mfrs. Assn., A.A.A.S., Nat. Micrographics Assn. Club: Indoor Tennis. Editor Health Aspects of Pesticides Abstract Bull., 1967-69. Home: 10701 Adventure Ln Cincinnati OH 45242 Office: 110 E Amity Rd Cincinnati OH 45215

CRILLY, BETSY J. GOODER, broadcasting exec.; b. Chgo., Dec. 1, 1925; d. Seth M. and Jean (McMullen) Gooder; grad Roycemore Sch., 1944; m. Edgar D. Crilly, Aug. 22, 1947; children—Marilyn Joan, Jeanne Claire. Asst. to pres. Gooder-Henrichsen Co., Inc., civil engrs., Chgo., 1945-49, dir., sec., 1955—; sec., treas. Triple R., Inc., 1965-78, Twin C., Inc., 1972—; dir. pub. affairs WQTC-AM-FM, Two Rivers, Wis., 1971—, KSJB-AM and KSJM-FM, Jamestown, N.D., 1971—. Mem. women's bd. Northside Chgo. Heart Assn., 1950-53; chmn. Deerfield (Ill.) Heart Fund, 1955-58; pres. Chgo. Service Club, 1958, dir. benefit, 1957, 62, 65, mem. bd., adv. bd., 1957-66; pres. Deerfield div. Arden Shore, 1961; chmn. Roycemore Sch. Benefit, 1965; mem. women's aux. bd. Jamestown Hosp., 1967-69; pres. Stutsman County chpt. Am. Cancer Soc., 1969. Pres., Deerfield Twp. Women's Republican Club, 1958-59. Recipient Service award Am. Heart Assn.; Spl. Service award Service Club Chgo. Mem. Ill. Opera Guild. Episcopalian. Club: Jamestown Country. Home: 1500 N Lake Shore Dr Chicago IL 60610

CRIPPEN, JOHN KENNETH, chem. co. exec.; b. Buchanan, Mich., July 8, 1908; s. Stuart S. and Charlotte (Allen) C.; student Northwestern U., 1932; m. Lida Genevieve Jayne, Apr. 23, 1932; children—Charlotte Jayne (Mrs. Raymond D. Drake), Katherine (Mrs. Carl Marich), Margaret G. (Mrs. Stephen Roney), Lida G. (Mrs. Michael Nelson), John Allen, Paul Dwight. Mgr. advt. and sales promotion Barry Asphalt Co., Chgo., 1932-36; asst. advt. mgr. Devry Corp., 1936-40; mgr. advt. and sales promotion Bantam Bearings Corp., South Bend, Ind., 1940-44; cons. L.B. Allen Co., Inc., Schiller Park, Ill., 1944—. Faculty, Austin Evening Coll., 1936-40. Exec. sec. Anti-communist League Am. Mem. Hong Kong Christian Evangelistic Soc. (hon. pres.-gen.), Continental Research Inst. (cons. editor, dir.), S.A.R. Author: Successful Direct-Mail Methods and Advertising Salesmanship, 1936. Home: Box 365 Park Ridge IL 60068

CRIPPIN, KENT EVERETT, cons.; b. Kansas City, Mo., Nov. 14, 1936; s. Charles Cecil and Anna Louise (Skiles) C.; student Kans. U., 1954-55; A.A., Kansas City Jr. Coll., 1957; B.S., Iowa State U., 1960; postgrad. U. Mo., 1963-64; m. Christine Catherine Ruf, Aug. 24, 1957; children—Jeffrey Steven, Christine Elise, Todd Daniel. City planning cons. Henningson-Durham-Richardson, Omaha, 1960-61; city planning cons./dir. Kansas City (Kan.)/Wyandotte County Plan Commn., 1962-66; dep. dir. Kansas City Met. Plan Commn., 1966-69; v.p., dir. Lawrence-Leiter & Co., mgmt. cons., Kansas City, Mo., 1969—. City councilman, Leawood, Kan., 1975—. Bd. dirs. YMCA, Kansas City, Kans., 1964-73, West Branch YMCA, Kansas City, Kans., 1967-72, A.R.C., Kansas City, Kans., 1964-67; trustee Notre Dame de Sion Sch. Recipient Distinguished Service award Jr. C. of C., Kansas City, Kans., 1964, Man of Merit award YMCA, Kansas City, Kans., 1969. Mem. Am. Inst. Planners, Nat. Bd. Examiners (chmn. Kansas City sect. 1969-70), Am. Soc. Landscape Architects (sec.-treas. Mo. Valley chpt. 1970-72), Inst. Mgmt. Cons. Presbyn. (elder 1965—). Home: 8605 Mohawk Rd Leawood KS 66206 Office: 427 W 12th St Kansas City MO 64105

CRISLER, RICHARD CARLETON, broker; b. Cin., Nov. 30, 1907; s. Carleton Graves and Elizabeth (Cropper) C.; B.A., Yale, 1929; m. Lucy Hagin Howard, July 10, 1948; children—Richard Carleton, Lucy H. (Mrs. Arther Tallas); 1 stepson, C. Alexander Howard. With Guaranty Trust Co., N.Y., 1929-32; agy. supt. Western & So. Indemnity, 1932-35; v.p. Field Richards & Co., Cleve., Cin., 1935-41; pres. Transit Radio Inc., Cin., 1948-52; pres. R.C. Crisler & Co., Inc., Cin., 1952—; chmn. bd. Greater Cin. Cablevision Inc.; dir. Ky. Jockey Club, Inc. (Latonia Race Track), Christine Valmy, Inc., Reeves Telecom Corp. Bd. dirs. City Charter Com., 1937—; trustee WGUC-FM; mem. Yale Devel. Com., 1950—. Served to capt. USAAF, 1942-46. Mem. Ky. Livestock Improvement Assn. (dir.). Home: 2444 Madison Rd Cincinnati OH 45208 Office: 580 Walnut St Cincinnati OH 45202

CRIST, CLAUDE KENNETH, retail food co. exec.; b. Clarence, Iowa, Nov. 2, 1918; s. Harry H. and Ruth R. (Berryhill) C.; B.S. in Commerce, U. Iowa, 1940; m. Atha Kincaid, Sept. 11, 1948; children—Ron, Marlys. Auditor, Iowa Tax Commn., Des Moines, 1940-42; with Hy Vee Food Stores, Inc., Chariton, Iowa, 1946—, sec., controller, 1970—. Mem. Chariton Library Bd., 1964—, chmn., 1972-74; bd. dirs. Chariton Area Devel. Corp., 1972-76, Lucas County Jud. Magistrate Appointing Commn., 1973—; mem. Lucas County Sheriff's Posse, 1968—; bd. dirs. Lucas County chpt. ARC, 1958—. Bd. dirs. Lucas County Meml. Hosp., chmn., 1975-76. Mem. Adminstrv. Mgmt. Soc. (Diamond Merit award 1975, pres. Des Moines chpt. 1973-74). Republican. Methodist (adminstrv. bd. 1970-76, finance com., trustee). Mason (Shriner), Rotarian. Home: Route 5 Chariton IA 50049 Office: 1801 Osceola Ave Chariton IA 50049

CRISWELL, CHARLES HARRISON, environ. chemist, engr.; b. Springfield, Mo., Jan. 9, 1943; s. John Philip and Elba Anne (Denton) C.; A.B., Drury Coll., Springfield, 1967; postgrad. U. Mo., 1967-68; m. Joyce LaVonne Louth, Apr. 26, 1968; children—Christina Rachel. San. chemist, dir. water pollution control labs. City of Springfield, 1968-72, asso. environ. engr.. chief water pollution control sect., 1972—; lectr. Springfield Pub. Schs., S.W. Mo. State U. and U. Lab. Sch., Drury Coll. Ruling elder, treas. John Calvin Union Presbytery, 1975—. Mem. Am. Chem. Soc. (com. environ. analytical methodology), Am. Inst. Biol. Scis., Mo. Acad. Sci., Mo. Water and Sewerage Conf., Mo. Water Pollution Control Assn. (asso. editor newsletter, 1976—, chmn. program com. 1977—, v.p. 1977-78, pres. elect 1978-79), Water Pollution Control Fedn. (indsl. waste com. 1975-80, govt. affairs-indsl. liaison task group 1976-81, govt. affairs com. 1977-82), Beta Beta Beta, Phi Mu Alpha. Contbr. articles to profl. jours. Home: 2108 E Montclair St Springfield MO 65804 Office: Room 210 830 Boonville St Springfield MO 65802

CRITSER, JERRY JOSEPH, govt. ordnance specialist; b. Rensselaer, Ind., Sept. 25, 1932; s. Joseph Merrill and Mabel Berniece (Wallace) C.; student St. Josephs Coll., Collegeville, Ind., 1950-51. Purchasing agt. Miniature Train Co. div. P.A. Sturtevant Co., Rensselaer, 1951-52; equipment specialist ordnance electronics U.S. Army Munitions Command, Joliet, Ill., 1956-73, Ordnance Advanced Armament Systems, Rock Island, Ill., 1973—. Pres., Ventures in Sound Recordings, London and Joliet, Ill., 1952—; producer British theatre pipe organ recs. Served with USAF, 1952-56. Mem. Am. Def. Preparedness Assn., Soc. Logistic Engrs., Chgo. Symphony Soc., Audio Engring. Soc., Ind. Hist. Soc., Am. Theatre Organ Soc., Automatic Mus. Instrument Collectors Assn. Republican. Episcopalian. Mason (Shriner). Curator collection master record library, M. Welte & Sohn, Freiburg, Germany, N.Y., and Kimball-Welte, Chgo. Contbr. to theatre organ publs. Home: 411 Hickory St Joliet IL 60435 Office: US Army Armament Materiel Readiness Command Rock Island IL 61201

CRNKOVICH, STEVEN ANTHONY, realtor; b. Chgo., May 18, 1941; s. Steve Lawrence and Antonia Elizabeth (Jerkovic) C.; student Monmouth Coll., 1959, Morton Jr. Coll., 1960-61, Grad. Realtors Inst. Ill., 1969; m. Karen Helen Puike, Nov. 21, 1964; children—Christopher Steven, Gregory Joseph. Cost accountant Best Foods, Chgo., 1962; gen. accountant Gen. Foods, 1963-65; salesman Baird & Warner, real estate, Crystal Lake, Ill., 1966-70, sales mgr., 1970-75, asst. v.p., 1972—, Pres.'s Club, 1973, 74. Pres., St. Thomas Bowling League, 1970. Adv. bd. Catholic Social Services Rockford Diocese. Mem. McHenry County Bd. Realtors (dir., 1970-71, 74-75, sec.-treas. 1972, pres. 1973) Crystal Lake C. of C. (dir.) Ill. (Million Dollar Club, life), Nat. assns. realtors, Nat. Inst. Real Estate Brokers. Roman Catholic. Lion. Office: 386 Virginia St Crystal Lake IL 60014

CRNOKRAK, JOHN R., electronic weighing and force measurement co. exec.; b. Chgo., Jan. 4, 1940; s. Nicholas and Mildred (Milosevich) C.; B.S., Loyola U., Chgo., 1962; M.S., Mich. State U., 1962-65; m. Kathleen Gail Boyle, Aug. 17, 1961; children—Patty, Kelly, Christopher. Tchr., coach W. Catholic High Sch., Grand Rapids, Mich., 1962-65; with Eagle-Picher Industries, Inc., Cin., 1965-70, regional sales mgr., 1970; nat. sales mgr. Consumer Products div. Westinghouse Electric Corp., Pitts., 1970-74; nat. sales mgr. Nat. Computer Systems, Mpls., 1974-75; nat. sales mgr., dir. mktg. Weigh-Tronix, Inc., Fairmont, Minn., 1975—. Mem. Nat. Scale Men's Assn. Republican. Roman Catholic. Club: Rotary. Home: 1105 Albion St Fairmont MN 56031 Office: 1000 Armstrong Dr Fairmont MN 56031

CROAK, MARTIN LEO, lawyer; b. Albany, Wis., Dec. 5, 1915; s. Martin Anthony and Margaret Cecilia (Dunphy) C.; Ph.B., U. Wis., 1937, LL.B., 1940; m. Catherine Mary Barry, May 29, 1941; children—Maureen, Sheila, Cathleen (Mrs. Thomas M. Smith), Kevin, Kerry. Admitted to Wis. bar, 1940; legal counsel FHA, Milw., 1940-42; spl. agt. FBI, 1942-65; mem. firm Croak Law Offices, Monona, Wis., 1966—. Legal and legis. counsel Wis. Chiefs of Police, 1967-72. Pres., Blessed Sacrament Sch. P.T.A., Madison, Wis., 1958-59, Edgewood High Sch. P.T.A., Madison, 1963-65; chmn. adv. bd. Edgewood High Sch., 1971-73. Mem. Monona Grove Businessmens Assn. (pres. 1970). Roman Catholic (mem. ch. council 1967-68, 71-73). K.C., Elk. Club: Optimist (Madison). Home: 5009 Dorsett Dr Madison WI 53711 Office: 4715 Monona Dr Monona WI 53716

CROCKER, EDWARD D., lawyer; b. Fostoria, O., Oct. 21, 1915; s. Charles P. and Edna G. (Ohl) C.; A.B., Wittenberg U., 1937; student U. Munich, 1937-38; LL.B., Harvard, 1941; m. Ida L. Roderick, Apr. 3, 1943; children—Stephen Roderick, Sharyn (Mrs. John M. Frisbie), David Roderick, Sara Lynne (Mrs. James J. Stafford, Jr.). Admitted to Ohio bar, 1941, U.S. Supreme Ct. bar, 1955; practiced in Cleve., 1941—; partner firm Arter & Hadden, 1954—; atty. OPA, Washington, 1942. Trustee Cleve. Inst. Art; mem. adv. bd. Musical Arts Assn. Served to lt. (s.g.), aviator, USNR, 1942-45; PTO. Decorated D.F.C., Air Medal with 2 gold stars, Philippine Campaign ribbon with gold star. Mem. Am., Ohio, Cleve. bar assns., Am. Coll. Trial Lawyers, Internat. Assn. Ins. Counsel, U.S. Jud. Conf. 6th Circuit (life). Republican. Presbyn. Clubs: Mayfield Country (Lyndhurst, O.); Union, Mid-Day (Cleve.). Author 5 articles pub. legal periodicals. Contbr. legal treatises. Home: Saddleback Ln Gates Mills OH 44040 Office: 1144 Union Commerce Bldg Cleveland OH 44115

CROCKETT, RICHARD CALWELL, c. of c. exec., farmer; b. Langdon, N.D., Aug. 30, 1919; s. Nathaniel J. and Lillian M. Crockett; B.S., N.D. State U., 1942; postgrad. Harvard Sch. Bus., 1942; m. Janice Adair Nelson, Dec. 28, 1942; children—Richard Boyd, Douglas David. Extension agt. State of N.D., 1946-48; ty. mgr. Agrl. Supply Co., Grand Forks, N.D., 1948-49; owner, mgr. Langdon Farm Supply, 1949-64; owner, operator farm, nr. Fargo, N.D., 1947-68; owner Crockett Ins. Agy., Langdon, 1958-64; exec. v.p. Greater N.D. Assn.; exec. v.p. N.D. C. of C., Fargo, 1964—, now pres.; dir. Sundeen Grain Co. Past pres. N.D. Chamber Execs.; mem. bd. N.D. Devel. Credit Corp., Central Livestock Shipping Assn., St. Paul. Precinct committeeman, county chmn. Cavalier County Republican party, 1960-64, mem. state platform com., 1958-60; mem. Langdon Park Bd., 1957-64. Served with USAAF, 1943-45. Mem. U.S. Durum Growers Assn. (pres. 1958-62, dir. 1956-68, chmn. durum wheat industry adv. com. 1962-64), Am. Soc. Farm Mgrs. and Rural Appraisers, Am. Legion, Airplane Owners and Pilots Assn. Presbyn. (trustee ch.). Mason (Shriner), Elk, Eagle. Home: 1519 Elm St Fargo ND 58102 Office: 303 N 5th St Fargo ND 58102

CROFT, ANITA BELLE BROWN (MRS. THOMAS L. CROFT), educator, civic worker; b. Wichita, Kans., Nov. 1, 1911; d. Harry Benton and Mabel May (Smith) Brown; A.B. cum laude, U. Wichita, 1932; A.M., U. Mich., 1936, postgrad., 1937-38; postgrad. U. So. Ill., 1971-72; m. Thomas L. Croft, Aug. 23, 1934; children—Terrence Lee, Timothy Lent, Ann Kristin (Mrs. William John Harrison), Thomas Albert. Asst. prof. psychology Lindenwood Coll., St. Charles, Mo., 1949-52; student counselor, tchr. psychology John Burroughs Sch., St. Louis, 1952-54; ednl. adviser Central Presbyn. Ch., St. Louis, 1955-56; tchr. psychology Maryville Coll. St. Louis, 1972-74. Bd. dirs. Women's Assn. St. Louis Symphony Soc., 1962—, Grace Hill Settlement House, St. Louis, 1963-70, Friends of St. Louis City Hosp. Sch. Nursing, 1959-66; chmn. bd. Central Sch. for Young Years, St. Louis, 1957-70; v.p. bd. St. Louis Municipal Sch. Nursing, Freedoms Found., St. Louis, 1967. Mem. Am., Midwest psychol. assns., Inter-Soc. Color Council, Nat. Soc. Arts and Letters, Mortar Bd., Sigma Xi, Tri Delta. Club: Wednesday (chmn. edn. sect. 1969-72, dir.). Home: 9393 Ladue Rd St Louis MO 63124

CROFT, ARTHUR RONALD, dentist; b. Omaha, May 3, 1935; s. Arthur Harry and Margaret Ruth (Dudley) C.; B.S., U. Omaha, 1959; D.D.S., U. Nebr., 1968; m. Geraldine Adelaide Welsh, Mar. 2, 1957; children—Arthur Ronald, Mark, Rhonda, Douglas. Stockbroker, Francis I. Dupont & Co., Omaha, 1959-64; pvt. practice dentistry, O'Neill, Nebr., 1968—; cons. oral maxilo-facial surgery Niabrara Valley Hosp., Lynch, Nebr.; mem. staff St. Anthony's Hosp., O'Neill, Niabrara Valley Hosp., Lynch. Mem. O'Neill C. of C. Republican. Episcopalian. Mason. Home: 722 Londonberry Dr O'Neill NE 68763 Office: 832 N 8th St O'Neill NE 68763 also 119 N 51st St Suite 302 Omaha NE 68132

CROFT, DUANE EUGENE, newspaperman; b. Richmond, Ind., June 5, 1926; s. Marion Eugene and Josephine (Atwell) C.; student U. Miss., 1945-46; B.S. in Journalism, Northwestern U., 1949, M.S. in Journalism, 1950; m. Elizabeth Joan Guyan, Sept. 3, 1949; children—Robert Lory, Martha Susan, Stephanie Gail, Timothy

Peter, Todd Eric, Carrie Christine. Edn. editor Evanston (Ill.) Mail, 1950; reporter McCook (Neb.) Daily Gazette, 1950-51, editor, 1951-53; makeup editor Nashville Tennessean, 1953-55; asst. telegraph editor Canton (Ohio) Repository, 1955-58, legis. corr., polit. writer, asst. editorial writer, 1958-62; editorial writer Toledo Blade, 1962-63, asso. editor, 1963-68, editorial dir., 1968—. Served with USNR, 1944-46. Recipient Headliner award Ohio Press Club, 1959, 60; 1st place award for editorial writing AP Soc. of Ohio, 1965, 66. Mem. Internat. Press Inst., Nat. Conf. Editorial Writers, Ohio Legis. Corr. Assn., Alpha Phi Gamma, Sigma Delta Chi (Distinguished Service award for editorial writing 1966), Beta Theta Pi. Home: 2332 Cheltenham Rd Toledo OH 43606 Office: 541 Superior St Toledo OH 43604

CROFT, THOMAS L(UVERNE), lawyer; b. Mpls., Feb. 2, 1913; s. Albert J. and Anna (Williams) C.; A.B., Wichita State U., 1934; J.D., U. Mich., 1937; m. Anita Belle Brown, Aug. 23, 1934; children—Terrence Lee, Timothy Lent, Ann Kristin (Mrs. William J. Harrison), Thomas Albert. Admitted Mo. bar, 1937; asso. Thompson, Mitchell, Thompson and Young, St. Louis, 1937-42; Igoe, Carroll, Keefe & Coburn, St. Louis, 1942, 1945-49; partner Coburn, Croft, Shepherd, Herzog & Putzell and predecessor firms, 1949—; lectr. St. Louis U. Sch. of Law, 1948-50. Mem. Mo. State Bd. Law Examiners, 1956-64, pres., 1960-62. Sec. the Character com. for St. Louis and St. Louis County, 1947-56; pres. bd. trustees Presbyn. Home for Children of Mo., 1959-60, mem. exec. com.; pres. bd. dirs. Community Sch., 1959-60. Mem. com. visitors U. Mich. Law Sch., 1964—. Served as lt. USNR, 1942-45. Mem. Am., St. Louis, Mo., bar assns., C. of C. Met. St. Louis (dir. 1964-66), Mo. Hist. Soc. Republican. Presbyterian. Clubs: University, Noonday, Bellerive Country. Home: 9393 Ladue Rd St Louis MO 63124 Office: One Mercantile Center Suite 2900 St Louis MO 63101

CROFT, TILLIE VICTORIA SWANSON (MRS. FRED WILEY CROFT), corp. exec., civic worker; b. nr. Joy, Ill., Jan. 29, 1899; d. Swan Erick and Lena (Monson) Swanson; student Western Ill. U., 1918-20; m. Frederick Wiley Croft, June 23, 1921; children—Lena Marie (Mrs. William Oscar Wissman), Fredrick Eugene. Tchr. pub. schs., nr. Joy, 1920-21, nr. New Boston, Ill., 1921-22; bookkeeper Fred's Service, Inc., Pontiac, 1925-40, partner, 1940-58, sec.-treas., dir., 1958—, also co-owner; dir. Humiston Haven Corp., Pontiac. Trick or Treat chmn. UNICEF, Pontiac, 1958—; v.p. Bapt. Missionary Soc., love and service class 1st Bapt. Ch., Pontiac; fgn. mission speaker Am. Baptist Conv. Great Rivers Region, Area III, Bloomington, Ill.; bd. dirs. Bloomington Bapt. Student Found., 16 yrs. Named Mother of Year, Pontiac Bapt. Mission Soc., 1947; recipient distinguished service awards in commerce, community, church work, UNICEF. Mem. Am. Legion Aux. (1st v.p., membership chmn. 1966-67), United Ch. Women (pres. Pontiac council 1958-60, v.p. 1975—, internat. relations chmn.), Ch. World Service (area contact person clothing appeal 1965—), Royal Neighbors Am., C. of C. (city beautification com.), Internat. Platform Assn., Am. Security Council, People to People. Republican. Baptist (deaconess, publicity chmn. 1972—). Clubs: Zonta (dir. Pontiac 1961-65, pres. 1967-69, safety chmn. 1969-71, internat. relations chmn. 1971—), Pontiac Woman's. Home: 711 S Locust St Pontiac IL 61764 Office: 426 W Madison St Pontiac IL 61764

CROLL, ROBERT FREDERICK, educator, economist; b. Evanston, Ill., Feb. 3, 1934; s. Frederick Warville and Florence (Campbell) C.; B.S. in Bus. Adminstrn., Northwestern U., 1954; M.B.A. (Burton A. French scholar) with high distinction, U. Mich., 1956; D.B.A., Ind. U., 1969; D.Litt., John F. Kennedy Coll., 1970; m. Sandra Elizebeth Bell, June 15, 1968; 1 son, Robert Frederick. Instr. Ind. U. Sch. Bus., Bloomington, 1956, researcher in bus. econs., 1960-62; mng. dir. Motor Vehicle Industry Research Assos., Evanston, 1962-63; personal asst. to speaker Ill. Ho. of Reps., 1963-65; asst. prof. bus. adminstrn. Kans. State U., 1965-66; asst. prof. Inst. Indsl. Relations, Loyola U. Chgo., 1966-70; asso. prof. Sch. Bus. Adminstrn., Central Mich. U., 1970-76, prof., 1976—. Mem. platform committee Ind. Republican Com., 1958; Ind. del. Young Rep. Nat. Conv., 1959; nat. chmn. Youth for Goldwater Orgn., 1960-61; chmn. coll. clubs Young Rep. Orgn. Ill., 1960-62; asst. chief page Rep. Nat. Conv., 1964; mem. Mt. Pleasant City Charter Commn., 1973—. Trustee estate of F.W. Croll, Chgo., 1959—. Recipient Grand prize Gov. of Ind., 1958. Accredited personnel diplomate Am. Soc. Personnel Adminstrn. Accreditation Inst. Mem. Soc. Automotive Engrs., A.I.M., Soc. Advancement Mgmt., Am. Econ. Assn., Mt. Pleasant C. of C., Young Ams. for Freedom (founder 1960, vice chmn. 1962-63), Phila. Soc. (founder 1964), Beta Gamma Sigma, Delta Sigma Pi Key, Phi Delta Kappa, Phi Kappa Phi, Pi Sigma Alpha, Delta Mu Delta, Sigma Pi, Alpha Kappa Psi, Sigma Iota Epsilon, Phi Chi Theta. Episcopalian. Club: Mount Pleasant Country. Author: Fall of an Automotive Empire: A Business History of the Packard Motor Car Company, 1945-1958, others. Contbr. articles to profl. jours. Address: 1224 Glenwood Dr Mount Pleasant MI 48858

CROM, ROBERT LOUIS, univ. dean; b. Hampton, Iowa, Feb. 15, 1926; s. Lloyd Martin and Alice May (Froning) C.; B.S., Iowa State U., 1950; M.S., N.D. State U., 1956; Ph.D., Mich. State U., 1967; m. Lucille Maxine Ritter, June 9, 1950; children—Penny, Linda, Randall, Richard. 4-H Youth asst. Ia. State Extension Service, Grundy County, 1947; farm service asst. Radio Sta. WMT, Cedar Rapids, Iowa, 1949; farm service dir. Radio Sta. KGLO, Mason City, Iowa, 1950-51; radio and TV specialist U.S. Dept. Agr., Washington, 1951-53; dir. communications N.D. State U., Fargo, 1953-58, asst. to pres., 1962-66; asso. dir. alumni affairs Iowa State U., Ames, 1966-68, dir., 1968-71, asst. dean extension, 1971—. Spl. asst. N.D. Commr. Higher Edn., 1958; adv. cons. Gov.'s Conf. on Iowa in the Year 2000, 1973-77. Trustee Nat. Farmhouse Found., Iowa 4-H Found., Iowa State Meml. Union, Faculty Policy Com., World Food Inst., Iowa State U.; trustee Iowa Bd. Pub. Programs in Humanities, pres., 1976-77. Served with USNR, 1944-46. Mem. AAAS, Council Agrl. Sci. and Tech., Nat. U. Extension Assn., FarmHouse, Blue Key, Cardinal Key, Alpha Zeta, Gamma Sigma Delta. Methodist. Rotarian. Home: 1418 McKinley Dr Ames IA 50010

CROMBIE, LANCE BRIAN, cons., farmer; b. St. Paul, Mar. 31, 1939; s. Francis Joseph and Veronica (Zankl) C.; B.S., St. John's U., 1961; M.S., U. Minn., 1965, Ph.D., 1968; m. Eleanor M. Dufault, Sept. 1, 1962; children—Kathleen, Daniel, Brent, Ross. Scientist, Glenwood Hills Hosp., Golden Valley, Minn., 1967-68; dir. labs. Kallestad Labs., St. Louis Park, Minn., 1968-71; pres., chmn. bd. Bio-Tec, med. diagnostic products mfg. co., Mpls., 1971-75. Asst. prof. dept. pharm. U. Minn., 1970—; cons. Cancer Research Lab., Northwestern Hosp., Mpls. Mem. exec. com. Minn. Heart Assn., 1971-75; mem. reaffiliation com. Am. Heart Assn., 1974—. Recipient Key award Minn. Jr. C. of C., 1971. Mem. A.A.A.S., Am. Soc. Microbiology, N.Y., Minn. acads. scis., Brooklyn Center (dir. 1969-71), Minn. (state environment chmn. 1970-71) jr. chambers commerce. Contbr. articles to profl. jours. Patentee in field. Home: Route 1 Webster MN 55088

CROMLEY, JON LOWELL, lawyer; b. Riverton, Ill., May 23, 1934; s. John Donald and Naomi M. (Mathews) C.; B.S., U. Ill., 1958; J.D., John Marshall Law Sch., 1966. Real estate title examiner Chgo. Title & Trust Co., 1966-70; admitted to Ill. bar, 1966; practiced in Genoa, Ill., 1970—; mem. firm O'Grady & Cromley, Genoa, 1970—. Bd. dirs. Genoa Day Care Center, Inc. Mem. Am., Ill., Chgo., DeKalb County bar assns. Home: 130 Homewood Dr Genoa IL 60135 Office: 213 W Main St Genoa IL 60135

CROMWELL, EVALYN TETSU-SEI, librarian; b. Mazon, Ill., Mar. 14, 1915; d. John Sebastian and Ann Marie (Dunlop) Cromwell; diploma, Wright Jr. Coll., 1938, library certificate, 1941; student Art Inst., evenings 1945-47; Ph.B., Northwestern U., 1961. With Chgo. Pub. Library, 1941—, jr. library asst. Taft High Sch. Library, 1941-42, Albany Park br. library, 1942-43, children's library asst. Norwood Park sub-br., 1943-54; adult service librarian Hild Library, 1954-75, catalog dept., 1975—. Instr. first aid A.R.C., 1961—, vol. first aid stas., 1961—. Recipient citation A.R.C., 1970. Mem. AAUW (resolutions chmn. bd. dirs. Chgo. br.), Ill. Audubon Soc., ALA, Ill. Library Assn., Sierra Club, Art Inst. Chgo., Field Mus. Natural History (life), Labsum Shedrub Ling, UN Assn. U.S.A., Oceanic Soc. Club: Apollo Musical. Home: PO Box 11074 Chicago IL 60611 Office: 425 N Michigan Ave Chicago IL 60611

CROMWELL, RONALD EUGENE, family sociologist; b. Dodge City, Kans., Oct. 15, 1946; s. Norman A. and June E. (Stauth) C.; B.S., Kans. State U., 1968, M.S., 1969; Ph.D. (NIMH Family Sociology fellow), U. Minn., 1972; m. Vicky L. Thomas, July 27, 1975; children—Angela, Aron; stepchildren—Gaylan, Valarie. Grad. asso. Kans. State U., Manhattan, 1967-68, instr., 1968-69, asst. prof., 1969-70; NIMH fellow U. Minn., Mpls., 1970-72; dir. Family Study Center, U. Mo., Kansas City, 1972—, also asst. prof. sociology. NIMH family cons. Mem. planning and budgeting com. United Way, Kansas City, 1972—. Bd. dirs. Family and Children's Service, Kansas City, Youth Adv. Bd.; chmn. bd. dirs. Family Study Center, Kansas City, 1972—. Urban Family Life grantee, 1972-73. Mem. Mo. Extension Homemakers Assn., Mo. (pres. 1974-75), Nat. (asso. editor Monograph series 1973—) councils on family relations, Midwest Sociol. Soc., Am. Sociol. Assn., Adult Edn. Assn., Am. Assn. Marriage and Family Counselors, Phi Theta Kappa, Omicron Nu. Author: Power in Families, 1975. Contbr. articles to profl. jours. Home: 10237 Cedarbrooke Ln Kansas City MO 64131 Office: 1020 E 63d St Kansas City MO 64110

CRONENWETT, WILSON ROBERTSON, pub. relations cons.; b. Butler, Pa., Jan. 11, 1913; s. Carl Emmanuel and Lola Bess (Robertson) C.; B.A., Capital U., 1936; m. Agnes Elizabeth Martin, July 31, 1943 (dec. 1973); children—Corinne Martin, Christine; m. 2d, Mary Fisher, June 6, 1975. Reporter, Butler (Pa.) Eagle, 1940-42; enlisted U.S. Navy, 1942, advanced through grades to comdr., 1962; dir. pub. relations Studio 5 Advt., Muskegon, Mich., 1963; pres., cons. pub. relations Cronenwett Assos., Holton, Mich., 1963—; instr. career action Aquinas Coll., Grand Rapids, Mich., 1973—; instr. Grand Valley State Coll., Allendale, Mich., 1977—. Exec. dir. Seaway Festival, 1964; bd. dirs. Port City Playhouse, 1964-66; mem. exec. council Boy Scouts Am., 1963-66; bd. dirs. A.R.C., 1967-69; bd. dirs. West Shore Symphony, 1974—, pres., 1975-77; bd. dirs. Hackley Heritage Assn., 1974—, v.p., 1976-78; asst. treas. Episcopal Diocese Western Mich., 1967-78. Named Mich. Distinguished Fellow to Upper Gt. Lakes Regional Commn., 1968. Mem. Mich. Profl. Indsl. Devel. Assn. (state pres. 1966), Am. Soc. Hosp. Pub. Relations Dirs., Mich. Hosp. Pub. Relations Assn. (dist. chmn. 1969—, state pres. 1973—), Naval Inst., Pub. Relations Soc. Am. (pres. W. Mich. chpt. 1972), Friends of Hackley Pub. Library (pres. 1976-78). Clubs: Sitka Community (sec., treas. 1968—) (Holton); Toastmasters (pres. 1968) (Muskegon, Mich.). Address: 8092 Ryerson Rd Holton MI 49425

CRONIN, JOSEPH MARR, supt. edn. Ill.; b. Boston, Aug. 30, 1935; s. Joseph and Mary (Marr) C.; A.B., Harvard U., 1956; M.A.T., 1957; Ed.D., Stanford U., 1965; m. Marie Whalen, June 21, 1958; children—Maureen, Kathleen, Elizabeth, Anne, Joseph, Timothy, Patricia. Prin., E.W. Broome Jr. High Sch., Rockville, Md., 1961-64; asst. prof., then asso. prof. Harvard U., 1965-70, asso. dean Grad. Sch. Edn., 1970-71; sec. ednl. affairs State of Mass., 1972-75; supt. edn. State of Ill., Springfield, 1975—. Mem. steering com. Edn. Commn. of States, 1971-75; mem. tchr. programs adv. bd. Ednl. Testing Service; mem. adv. bd. Mass. Council for Children; trustee Trust for Environ. Edn.; bd. overseers Com. to Visit Summer Sch., Harvard U., 1973-75; active, Ill. Council on Aging, Ill. Dangerous Drugs Commn. Recipient Secondary Sch. Prin. of Year award Crofts Edn. Service, 1963, Outstanding Mag. Editorial award Ednl. Press Writers Am., 1969. Mem. Am. Assn. Sch. Adminstrs., Am. Arbitration Assn., Am. Ednl. Research Assn., Nat. Edn. Com., Jr. Achievement, Inc. Author: The Control of Urban Schools, 1973; (with Richard Hailer) Organizing an Urban School System for Diversity, 1973. Contbr. articles to profl. jours. Home: 3129 Lochridge Ln Springfield IL 62704 Office: 100 N 1st St Springfield IL 62777

CROOK, BRIAN MANNING, data processing mgr.; b. Mpls., Apr. 20, 1935; s. Norris A. and Ethel Albine (Dunn) C.; B.S., U. Minn., 1964; postgrad. U. Mich., 1974-76; m. Kay Noreene Forester, Sept. 25, 1970. Analyst, U. Minn., Mpls., 1964-66; systems programmer Schlumberger-EMR Computer Div., Mpls., 1966-67; data processing supr. and quality assurance coordinator Com-Share Inc., Chgo. and Ann Arbor, Mich., 1967-68; v.p. Com-Tel Inc., Chgo., 1968-69; v.p. Nat. Computer Franchise Corp., Chgo., 1969-70; software devel. mgr. Computer Operations Inc., Costa Mesa, Calif., 1970; mgr. special systems Com-Share Inc., Ann Arbor, 1971-72; mgr. info. systems Mfg. Data Systems Inc., Ann Arbor, 1972-73; data processing mgr. U.S. Postal Service, Allen Pk., Mich., 1973—. Served with U.S. Army, 1957-59. Mem. Assn. for Computing Machinery. Home: 22735 Cranbrooke Dr Novi MI 48050 Office: 17500 Oakwood Blvd Allen Park MI 48101

CROSBY, ELEANOR RAUCH (MRS. THOMAS M. CROSBY, JR.), civic worker; b. Bryn Mawr, Pa., Mar. 9, 1942; d. R. Stewart and Frances (Brewster) Rauch Jr.; B.A., Smith Coll., 1963; M.A., U. Wash., 1965; m. Thomas M. Crosby, Jr., June 12, 1965; children—Stewart French, Brewster McKnight, Grant Pillsbury, Brooke Sturgis. Research asst. Fed. Res. Bank Mpls., 1965-68; research aid to Walter Heller, U. Minn., 1966-69; dir. Tonkawood Ski Sch., SkiTonka, Minn., 1968—; mem. woman's assn. for Minn. Symphony Bd., 1968-70; asst. vice chmn. of Mpls. United Fund, 1968-71; bd. dirs. Center Opera Assn., 1965-74, KTCA-KTCI TV twin cities Ednl. TV sta.; chmn. bd. Assn. for Pub. TV, 1971-73; bd. dirs. Nat. Friends of Pub. Broadcasting, 1967-77, Jr. League of Mpls., 1968-71, Dynamy Minn., 1976—, Blake Sch. Parents Council, 1974—; chmn. Minn. Orch. Symphony Ball, 1977—; class sec. Smith Alumni Assn., 1973—. Club: Long Lake (Minn.) Hounds (sec. 1971—). Home: 1612 Willow Dr Long Lake MN 55356

CROSBY, JAMES LEROY, county ofcl.; b. Grand Blanc, Mich., Oct. 16, 1921; s. Harry C. and Nellie E. (Proctor) C.; B.S., Mich. State U., 1949, M.S., 1968; m. Betty J. Sockman, June 24, 1950; children—Robert J., Scott W., Janet L. Farm partner, Grand Blanc, 1941-46; vocational agrl. tchr., Coldwater, Mich., 1950-53; 4-H youth agt. Mich. State U. Coop. Extension, Branch County, 1953-55, asst. agrl. agt., Lapeer County, 1955-58, county extension dir. Ogemaw County, 1958-62, Montcalm County, 1962—. Trustee Montcalm Community Coll., 1962-68, chmn. bd., 1964-68. Recipient Presdl. award Mich. Assn. County Agrl. Agts., 1962, Citation of Honor, Mich. Minuteman, 1969, Distinguished Service award Nat. Assn. County Agrl. Agts., 1970, Distinguished Service award Montcalm Community Coll., 1973, Montcalm County Rural-Urban award Montcalm County Farm Bur. Young Farmers, 1974. Dow travel scholar, 1964. Mem. Nat., Mich. (pres. 1973) assns. county agrl. agts., Epsilon Sigma Phi. Mason. Home: 906 Alexander St Greenville MI 48838 Office: 617 N State Rd Stanton MI 48888

CROSBY, JOHN RICHARD, fabricated metal products co. exec.; b. Cleve., Apr. 22, 1924; s. Ernest Raymond and Eleanor Louise (Leppert) C.; B.S. in Chem. Engring., Case Inst. Tech., 1945; m. Audrey Carol Kronquist, Mar. 21, 1970; children—Cynthia, Barbara, Lisa, Jennifer. With Standard Oil Co. (Ohio), Cleve., 1946-58, asst. to v.p., 1953-58; exec. dir. Cleve. Devel. Found., 1958-59; chief exec. officer Joseph Dyson & Sons, Inc., Eastlake, 1960—, also dir.; dir. Dependable Appliance Parts Co., Inc., Eastlake, Ohio, Pres. Univ. Christian Movement of Cleve., 1969-73; pres. Arthritis Found., N.E. Ohio, 1972-76; v.p. Health Fund Cleve., 1974-76. Served to lt. (j.g.) USNR, 1942-46. Mem. Cleve. Engring. Soc., Newcomen Soc. Republican. Mem. United Ch. of Christ. Club: Canterbury Golf (Shaker Heights, Ohio). Home: 30650 W Landerwood Dr Pepper Pike OH 44124 Office: 33300 Lakeland Blvd Eastlake OH 44094

CROSBY, KENNETH GERALD, psychologist; b. Rochester, N.H., May 13, 1928; s. Samuel Adams and Audrey Marie (Perreault) C.; A.B., Bates Coll., 1949; M.A., Syracuse U., 1958; Ed.D., Boston U., 1968. Psychologist, dir. tng. Laconia (N.H.) State Sch., 1949-65; fellow in mental retardation Boston U., 1965-68; research scientist N.Y. State Inst. for Basic Research in Mental Retardation, S.I., N.Y., 1968-69; dir. Accreditation Council for Services for Mentally Retarded and Other Developmentally Disabled Persons, Joint Commn. on Accreditation of Hosp., Chgo., 1970—. Cons. numerous and various vol. and govt. groups on standards for programs for mentally retarded and developmentally disabled. Fellow Am. Assn. Mental Deficiency; mem. Am., Ill. psychol. assns., Council Exceptional Children, Assn. Advancement Psychology, Nat. Soc. Autistic Children, A.A.A.S. Compiler-editor Standards for Residential Facilities for the Mentally Retarded, 1971, 5th edit., 1975; Standards for Community Agencies Serving Persons with Mental Retardation and Other Developmental Disabilities, 1973; Standards for Services for Developmentally Disabled Persons, 1977. Contbr. to profl. jours. Home: 3540-A N Pine Grove Chicago IL 60657 Office: 875 N Michigan Ave Chicago IL 60611

CROSBY, THOMAS MANVILLE, JR., lawyer; b. Mpls., Oct. 9, 1938; s. Thomas Manville and Ella Sturgis (Pillsbury) C.; B.A., Yale, 1960, LL.B., 1965; m. Eleanor Grant Rauch, June 12, 1965; children—Stewart French, Brewster McKnight, Grant Pillsbury, Brooke Sturgis. Admitted to Minn. bar, 1965; practiced in Mpls., 1965—; mem. firm Faegre & Benson, Mpls., 1965—; Bd. dirs. Walker Art Center, pres., 1973-76, chmn., 1976—; bd. dirs. Minn. Orch. Served to 1st lt. USNR, 1960-62. Mem. Am., Minn., Hennepin County bar assns. Clubs: Woodhill Country (Wayzata, Minn.); Minneapolis. Home: 1612 Willow Dr Long Lake MN 55356 Office: Northwestern Bank Bldg Minneapolis MN 55402

CROSBY, (ZELMA) JEAN, educator; b. Toledo, Dec. 31, 1929; d. Gifford and Zeola Anna (Killan) Lewis; B.M.E., North Central Coll., Naperville, Ill., 1951; postgrad. Wright State U., 1968-69, U. Cin., 1970-75; M.Ed., Xavier U., 1976; m. Burton LeRoy Crosby, Aug. 30, 1947; children—Steven, Michael, Christina. Tchr., pub. schs., Hillside, Ill., 1951-53, Fulton, Ohio, 1955-56, North Baltimore, Ohio, 1956-57, Weston Ohio, 1958-60, Antwerp, Ohio, 1962-65, Celina and St. Henry, Ohio, 1965-66, Rockford, Ohio, 1966-67, Celina, Ohio, 1967-70, Cin., 1970—. Mem. NEA, Ohio Edn. Assn., Am. Personnel and Guidance Assn. Methodist. Home: 2179 Broadhurst Ave Cincinnati OH 45240 Office: 3310 Compton Rd Cincinnati OH 45239

CROSS, GILBERT HALL, state ofcl.; b. Dahlgren, Ill., Aug. 23, 1919; s. Roland Robert and Isabel (Hunter) C.; B.A., Washington U., St. Louis, 1941; student U. Colo., summers, 1937, 38, 39; govt. certificate Queens Coll., 1943; m. Grace Caroline Goodwin, July 20, 1946; 1 dau., Clara. Mem. corp. dept. State of Ill., 1949-56; supr. Ill. Narcotic Rehab., 1958-63; personnel dir. City Water, Light and Power Co., Springfield, Ill., 1963-72; equal employment opportunity tng. coordinator Ill. Dept. Transp., 1972—. Treas. Sangamon County Community Action Com., 1964-66. Chmn. finance bd. Lincoln Library, Springfield, 1964-67. Served with AUS, 1941-45. Decorated Bronze Star. Mem. Internat. Narcotic Officers Enforcement Assn. (charter), Am. Pub. Power Assn. (mgmt. com. 1965—), Ill. League Municipal Employees, A.L.A., Ill. Hist. Soc. (life), Ill. Assn. Hwy Engrs. (life), D.A.V., Am. Legion, V.F.W. Republican. Mem. Christian Ch. (bd. dirs.). Home: 639 W Vine St Springfield IL 62704 Office: Springfield IL 62764

CROSS, JOHN RICHARD, printing co. exec.; b. Birmingham, Eng., Feb. 1, 1930; s. Bert Smith and Bernice (Fischer) C.; brought to U.S., 1930, naturalized, 1948; student U. Minn., 1947-51; B.A., Hamline U., 1954; m. Karlyn Mari Nordgaard, Aug. 28, 1954; children—Jeffrey, James, William. Sr. accountant Haskins & Sells, C.P.A.'s, Mpls., 1956-66; treas. Deluxe Check Printers, Inc., St. Paul, 1966—. Treas. St. Paul Assn. for Retarded Children, 1961-63; mem. mgmt. com. Northwest Suburban YMCA, 1964-67; councilman Village of Dellwood, Minn., 1971-73. Served with USAF, 1949. C.P.A., Minn. Mem. Minn. Soc. C.P.A.'s, Am. Inst. C.P.A.'s, Minn. Field Trial Assn. (dir. 1971-77). Home: 90 Many Levels Rd White Bear Lake MN 55110 Office: 1080 County Rd F St Paul MN 55112

CROSS, SHERMAN TRACY, power and gas co. exec.; b. Madison, Wis., July 15, 1924; s. Sherman Tracy and Asenath Jeanette (Montgomery) C.; student Wayne State U., 1947-49; m. Nancy Gail Smith, Apr. 11, 1947; children—Constance (Mrs. Paul E. Harper), Douglas M., Cameron T. Reporter, asst. picture editor Detroit Times, 1942-50; with pub. relations staff Consumers Power Co., Jackson, Mich., 1950—, pub. info. dir., 1971—. Served with AUS, 1942-45. Decorated Bronze Star. Mem. Pub. Relations Soc. Am., Pub. Utilities Advt. Assn. Clubs: Nat. Press (Washington), Detroit Press. Home: 2351 Lindsey Rd Jackson MI 49201 Office: 212 W Michigan St Jackson MI 49201

CROSSAN, JOHN ROBERT, lawyer; b. Beckley, W.Va., May 31, 1947; s. Thomas Benjamin and Margaret Windsor (Hicks) C.; B.S. with honors, U. Va., 1969; J.D., U. Chgo., 1973; m. Monique Margaretha Scheen-Weyer, Dec. 22, 1973. Asst. program mgr. Urban Mass Transp. Adminstrn., Washington, 1969-70; admitted to Ill. bar, 1974; staff atty., cons. Ill. Dept. Transp. and Gov.'s Task Force on N.E. Ill. Pub. Transp., Chgo., 1971-73; asso. atty. Hill, Gross, Simpson, Van Santen & Assos., Chgo., 1974-77; asso. firm Cook, Wetzel & Egan, Ltd., Chicago, 1978—. Sec. bd. dirs. 73 E. Elm Condominium Assn., 1976—. Mem. Am., Ill., Chgo. bar assns., Patent Law Assn. Chgo., Tau Beta Pi. Club: Chicago Yacht. Contbr. editor Young Lawyer Jour., 1976-77. Home: 73 E Elm St Chicago IL 60611 Office: 135 S La Salle St Chicago IL 60603

CROSSLEY, RICHARD PRICE, physician, surgeon; b. Webberville, Mich., Oct. 19, 1920; s. William R. and Clara M. (Price) C.; B.S., Mich., State Normal Coll., 1943; M.S., U. Mich., 1947; A.B.,

Eastern Mich. U., 1948; D.O., Chgo. Coll. Osteopathy; m. Alice Marie Urbin, Aug. 23, 1953; children—Kathleen (Mrs. Raymond Jamrock), Robinson Marshall, Lawrence Curtis, Alyson Dru (Mrs. Alan Kortas). Intern, Chgo. Osteo. Hosp., 1952-53, mem. staff, staff sec., sec. exec. com., 1953—; gen. practice osteo. medicine, Chgo., 1953—; asst. prof. medicine Chgo. Coll. Osteo. Medicine, 1959—. Capt., Calumet City Police Dept., 1966-75; commr. health, Calument City, 1975—. Served with USNR, 1943-45. Decorated Silver Star; recipient Service award Chgo. Osteo. Hosp., 1967, 70, 74; 5th Annual Police Sci. award Internat. Assn. Chiefs Police and Am. Express Co., 1972. Fellow Am. Acad. Forensic Scis. (chmn. gen. sect.); mem. Internat., Ill. assns. chiefs of police, Fraternal Order Police, Ill. Osteo. Assn. (past trustee). Republican. Methodist. Club: Atlas (nat. v.p. 1962—). Home: 435 Clyde Ave Calumet City IL 60409 Office: 3206 W 83d St Chicago IL 60652

CROSSON, JAMES D., judge; b. Newberry, S.C., Mar. 8, 1909; s. Henry H. and Sallie (Spearman) C.; A.A., Jewish Peoples Inst., Chgo., 1934; student Lewis Inst. Tech., 1936; LL.B., John Marshall Law Sch., 1940, LL.M., 1947; certificate traffic, Northwestern U. Law Sch., 1956, Fordham U. Law Sch., 1957; grad. Nat. Coll. State Trial Judges, U. Colo.; m. Jane T. Garland, Dec. 31, 1948; 1 son, J. David. Admitted to Ill. bar, 1942; practice in Chgo., 1942, 46-54; mem. firm Gassaway, Crosson, Turner and Parsons, 1955-59; referee Municipal Ct. Chgo., 1954-61, adminstrv. asst. to chief justice, 1961-62; judge Circuit Ct. Cook County (Ill.), Chgo., 1962—. Law mem. panel 111, Bd. Appeals, SSS of No. Ill., 1954—. Active N.A.A.C.P. Trustee John Marshall Law Sch., 1963—, treas. 1967—; trustee Met. YMCA, Chgo., 1969—, 1st v.p., 1970—. Served to capt. AUS, 1942-46; ETO. Recipient citation of merit John Marshall Law Sch., 1966. Mem. Am., Fed., Cook County (dir.), Chgo. bar assns., Am. Judicature Soc., Kappa Alpha Psi. Conglist. Mason. Club: Original Forty (Chgo.). Home: 1055 E Hyde Park Blvd Chicago IL 60615 Office: Chgo Civic Center Bldg Chicago IL 60602

CROSSWHITE, BOB H., ins. co. exec.; b. Kansas City, Mo., Feb. 21, 1929; s. Carleton L. and Esther (Herbert) C.; B.S., Rockhurst Coll., 1952. Vice pres. Old Security Ins. Cos. and Wide World Underwriters, Kansas City, Mo., 1948-69; pres., dir. Life Ins. Co. of Kans., 1969-72; pres. Insured Contracts, Inc., Shawnee Mission, Kans., 1972—. Served with USMCR, 1951-52. C.L.U. Mem. Kans. Life Assn., Life and Health Service Assn. (pres. 1960-61), Am. Soc. C.L.U.'s, Nat. Assn. Life Underwriters, Risk Selectors Club (pres. 1959-60). Clubs: Kansas City Ski, Flatland Ski Assn. (Kansas City). Home: Lake Lotawana Box 11485 Kansas City MO 64112 Office: PO Box 8108 Shawnee Mission KS 66208

CROUCH, FRANKLIN MADISON, lawyer; b. Richmond, Va., June 29, 1920; s. Crawford Curry and Mattie Madison (Bowie) C.; B.S., U. Richmond, 1940; J.D., Chgo. Kent Coll. Law, 1950; m. Lucy Bailey White, Aug. 15, 1942; children—Bruce, Ellen (Mrs. Terrence A. Reed), Rupert, Richard, Deborah (Mrs. George Smith), Julia (Mrs. Kevin Conroy), David, John. Instr. physics and aeros. U. Richmond, 1940-41; admitted to Ill. bar, 1950, U.S. Patent Office, 1951; law clk. Carlson Pitzner Hubbard & Wolfe, Chgo., 1945-50; asso. atty. Wolfe Hubbard Voit & Osann, 1950-62; partner firm Wolfe Hubbard Leydig Voit & Osann, 1962-71; mem. firm Leydig, Voit, Osann, Mayer & Holt, Ltd., 1971—. Commr. Glen Ellyn (Ill.) Park Dist., 1962-75, pres. bd., 1967-73, v.p., chmn. finance com., 1973-75. Served to lt. (s.g.) USNR, 1941-45. Recipient outstanding service awards Chgo. Girl Scouts, 1957, 58, 59. Mem. Am., Chgo. bar assns., Am., Chgo. patent law assns., U.S. Trademark Assn., Assn. Internat. pour la Protection de la Propriete Industrielle, Internat. Patent and Trademark Assn., Phi Delta Phi, Sigma Pi Sigma. Club: West Suburban Swim (dir. 1968-72) (Glen Ellyn). Home: 545 N Park Blvd Glen Ellyn IL 60137 Office: 1 IBM Plaza Chicago IL 60611

CROUSE, EARL FREDERICK, publisher; b. Newton, Ill., Jan. 6, 1914; s. E. Sherman and Lillian (Smallwood) C.; B.S., U. Ill., 1938; m. Frances L. Fuson, June 25, 1939; children—Kenneth, David, Annetta, Shirley. Editor farm mgmt., v.p. in charge econ. dept. Doane Agrl. Service, Inc., 1938-58; founder, pres. Farm Bus. Council, Inc., Champaign, Ill., 1958-75, Bank Services, Inc., 1967-76 (companies now merged to become BankVertising Co. pubs. newsletters The Farm Picture, MoneyWise, MoneyWise II); chmn. bd. Bank Vertising Co., 1976—. Mem. Am. Soc. Farm Mgrs. and Rural Appraisers, Am. Farm Econs. Soc., Urbana, Champaign chambers commerce, Bank Marketing Assn. Kiwanian. Baptist. Co-author: Rural Appraisals, 1956. Contbr. articles to profl. jours. Home: 43 Sherwin Dr Urbana IL 61801 Office: 1300 Hagan St Champaign IL 61820

CROUTHER, MELVIN SYLVESTER MANSON, JR., state ofcl.; b. Nov. 22, 1926; s. Melvin S.M. and Anna Marie (Taylor) C.; B.S. in Biology, Lincoln U., 1956; M.S.W., Washington U., St. Louis, 1960; m. Betty Madison, Jan. 27, 1953; 1 dau., Lou-Ann. Cartographer, Aeronautical Chart and Information Service, St. Louis; social worker Bd. of Children's Guardians, St. Louis, 1957-61; social worker Tng. Instn. Central Ohio, Columbus, 1961-62, supr. social work regional office, 1962, regional dir., regional office, Cleve., 1962-66; asso. dir. Neighborhood Opportunity Centers, Cleve., 1966-67; project dir. Neighborhood Youth Corps, Cleve., 1967-68; dep. supt. Ohio Youth Commn., Cuyahoga Hills, 1968-71; supt. Cuyahoga Hills Boys Sch., Warrensville Twp., Ohio, 1971-74; asst. chief instl. services, chmn. parole bd. Ohio Youth Commn., Columbus, 1974—. Guest tchr. Kent (Ohio) State U.; guest tchr. Cuyahoga Community Coll., 1972—; guest tchr. med.-law tng. Case Western Res. U., Certificate Merit, 1974; pres. Milverton Rd. Street Club, Cleve., 1964; cochmn. st. club com., mem. exec. com. Mt. Pleasant Community Council, Cleve.; admission chmn. local housing improvement program. Vice pres. Cleve. YMCA-YWCA, 1973-74; active Boy Scouts Am. Served with USMCR, 1945-46. Recipient Citation for Youth Work in Neighborhood Youth Corps by Cleve. City Council, 1968; Citation for Starting 1st Boys Group Home Subsidized State, 1964. Mem. Acad. Certified Social Workers, N.A.A.C.P. (Cleve. exec. com.), P.T.A., Hampshire Parks Estates Assn., Nat. Council Crime Delinquency, Ohio Correctional Cts. Services Assn., Alpha Phi Alpha. Baptist (mem. ch. bd.). Kiwanian (pres.). Clubs: Ambassadors, Gaylords, Masons (32 deg., K.T., Shriner). Home: 3719 Concord Dr Beachwood OH 44122

CROW, GLENN SHATFORD, printing co. exec.; b. Cleve., May 31, 1925; s. Ralph Earl and Fern Lydia (Shatford) C.; B.A., Mt. Union Coll., 1949; m. Anne Marie Deutschmann, Nov. 26, 1955; 1 son, Keith. Salesman, Ohio Mattress Co., Cleve., 1949-54; chief exec. Mercantile Research Co., Cleve., 1955-70, Wishford Co., Cleve., 1962-69; pres. Auburn Industries, Inc., Cleve., 1969—. Sec., treas. B-R Industries, Inc., Cleve., 1973—. Served to 1st lt. AUS, 1943-46. Mem. Phi Kappa Tau. Home: 2919 Warrington Rd Shaker Heights OH 44120 Office: 1260 W 4th St Cleveland OH 44113

CROW, RICHARD RONALD, chem. co. exec.; b. Point Marion, Pa., Aug. 19, 1915; s. Benjamin K. and Alice (Richards) C.; B.S., California (Pa.) Coll., 1936; M.A., Ohio State U., 1938; m. Mary Grace Jessup, Aug. 16, 1951; children—Megan Leslie, Philip Edward. Tng. dir. Curtiss-Wright Corp., Columbus, Ohio, 1941-45; corporate tng. dir. U.S. Rubber Co., N.Y.C., 1945-53; mgmt. devel. dir., asst. mgr. indsl. relations, regional mgr. indsl. relations Continental Oil Co., Houston and Ft. Worth, 1953-59; v.p. personnel Stouffer Foods Corp., Cleve., 1959-68; corporate dir. personnel Sherwin-Williams Co., Cleve., 1968-69, v.p. personnel, 1969-76, v.p. human resources, 1977—; dir. Gordon Pred Assos. Mem. council on devel., edn. and tng. Nat. Indsl. Conf. Bd., mem. manpower planning and devel. commn. Accredited personnel exec. Recipient Laureate citation award Epsilon Pi Tau, 1946. Mem. Am. Mgmt. Assn. Home: 3858 W Surrey Ct Rocky River OH 44116 Office: 101 Prospect Ave Cleveland OH 44115

CROWELL, EDWARD PRINCE, assn. exec.; b. Chillicothe, Ohio, Sept. 17, 1926; s. Harrison P. and Jeannette (Sturtevant) C.; student U. Maine, 1946-48; D.O., Kirksville (Mo.) Coll. Osteopathy and Surgery, 1952; m. Elaine Kittelberger, Apr. 14, 1956. Intern Waterville (Maine) Osteo. Hosp., 1952-53; chief resident physician hosps. Phila. Coll. Osteo. Medicine, 1953-56; sr. attending internist Waterville Osteo. Hosp., 1956-63, chmn. dept. medicine, med. dir., 1958-63; asst. exec. dir. Am. Osteo. Assn., Chgo., 1964-66, asso. exec. dir., 1966-68, exec. dir., 1968—, bur. convs., 1968—, chmn. dept. bus. affairs, 1968—. Mem. adv. council Maine Hosp. Constrn. Com., 1959-64. Served with USNR, 1944-46. Diplomate Am. Osteo. Bd. Internal Medicine. Fellow Am. Coll. Osteo. Internists. Home: 3245 Prestwick Ln Northbrook IL 60062 Office: 212 E Ohio St Chicago IL 60611

CROWLEY, ANNE STAHL, advt. exec.; b. Independence, Mo., Aug. 21, 1921; d. William Thomas and Nellie (Carey) Couser; student pub. schs.; m. David Warren Stahl, Aug. 30, 1941 (div. 1971); children—John Mitchell, Charlotte Anne (Mrs. Russell K. Ameter), Margaret Ailsa (Mrs. Thomas Greer), Barbara Lynn; m. 2d, Joseph A. Crowley, Jan. 5, 1974. Copywriter, prodn. mgr. Robert L. Wilson Co., Tulsa, 1938-41; copy and girl Friday Ritchie-Safford Advt., 1941; clk. Airco, Houston, 1942-43; pres. Stahl Assos., Inc., Bryan and Maumee, Ohio, 1959—; partner Hofstal Co., toy designer, 1959—. Mem. Am. Advt. Fedn., Advt. Club Toledo, Toledo Press Club, M.B.L.S., Internat. Platform Assn., Mem. Reorganized Ch. of Jesus Christ of Latter-day Saints. Club: Zonta Internat. Home: 4144 River Rd Toledo OH 43614 Office: 2340 Detroit Ave Maumee OH 43537

CROWLEY, JEREMIAH ALOYSIUS, welding engr.; b. Babylon, N.Y., Mar. 3, 1921; s. Jeremiah Aloysius and Mary Agnes (Tighe) C.; B.S., Nat. U. Ireland, 1950; m. May 21, 1954; children—Patricia Crowley Maguire, Margurite, Jeremiah Aloysius, John, Mary Pat, Kathleen, Elizabeth, Eileen. Nuclear welding engr. Gen. Dynamics Corp., Groton, Conn.; sr. welding engr. Grumman Aircraft Corp.; welding engr. republic Aviation Corp.; chief engr. Avco-Lycoming Co., Charleston, S.C.; now chief welding engr. Morrison Constrn. Co., Hammond, Ind.; tchr.-cons. Greater Charleston Tech. Center. Democratic committeeman, 1953-56. Served with USNR, 1942-46. Mem. Am. Welding Soc. (past sect. chmn.). Roman Catholic. Club: K.C. (4 deg.). Home: 4341 N Lake Shore Dr Crown Point IN 46307 Office: 2700 E Dunes Hwy Gary IN 46403

CROWLEY, LEONARD VINCENT, pathologist; b. Binghamton, N.Y., Jan. 12, 1926; s. Frank Lawrence and Florence Cecelia (Belanger) C.; student Coll. Holy Cross, 1943-45; M.D., U. Vt., 1949; M.S., Ohio State U., 1956; m. Jane F. McNeill, July 14, 1951; children—Leonard Vincent, Jane, Karen, Nancy, Susan. Instr. pathology Columbia U. Coll. Physicians and Surgeons, N.Y.C., 1952-54; Ohio State U. Med., 1954-56; asst. prof. U. Vt., 1956-58, asso. prof., 1958-60; clin. asst. prof. pathology and laboratory medicine, U. Minn., Mpls., 1960—; attending pathologist St. Mary's Hosp., Mpls., 1960—. Served to lt. M.C., USNR, 1950-52. Author: Introductory Concepts in Pathology, 1972, A Syllabus of Visual Aids in Pathology, 1972; An Introduction to Clinical Embryology, 1974; Introductory Concepts in Anatomy and Physiology, 1976. Contbr. articles to sci. jours. Home: 5337 Kellogg Ave Minneapolis MN 55424 Office: 2414 S 7th St Minneapolis MN 55406

CROWN, HENRY, business exec.; b. Chgo., June 13, 1896; s. Arie and Ida (Gordon) C.; student pub. schs., Chgo.; m. Rebecca Kranz, Aug. 12, 1920 (died Oct. 1943); children—Robert (dec.), Lester, John Jacob; m. 2d, Gladys Kay, Mar. 1946. Clk., Chgo. Fire Brick Co., 1910-12; traffic mgr. Union Drop Forge Co., 1912-16; partner S.R. Crown & Co., 1916-19; treas. Material Service Corp., bldg. materials, 1919-21, pres., 1921-41, chmn. bd., 1941-59; chmn. exec. com., dir. Gen. Dynamics Corp., 1959-66, 70—; chmn. bd. Henry Crown and Co., 1967—; dir. Waldorf Astoria Corp.; v.p., dir. 208 S. LaSalle St. Bldg. Corp. Mem. Chgo. CD Corps; bd. dirs. Chgo. Boys Clubs: mem. nat. council Boy Scouts Am.; trustee U. Chgo. Cancer Research Found., DePaul U.; mem. U. Ill. Citizens Com.; mem. Northwestern U. Assos.; fellow St. Joseph's Coll., Rensselaer, Ind.; mem. citizens bd. Loyola; asso., fellow Brandeis U. Served as col. C.E., AUS, World War II. Decorated Legion of Merit; chevalier de la Legion D'Honneur (France); Gold Cross Royal Order Phoenix (Greece); Order Ruben Dario (Republic Nicaragua); recipient Horatio Alger award Am. Schs. and Colls. Assn.; Damen award Loyola U., Chgo.; Humanitarian Service award for industry Eleanor Roosevelt Cancer Research Found.; Julius Rosenwald Meml. award Jewish Fedn. and Welfare Fund, Chgo. Mem. Mil. Order World Wars. Mason (Shriner, 33 deg.). Clubs: Mid-Day, Standard, Executives, Tavern (Chgo.); St. Louis. Home: 900 Edgemere Ct Evanston IL 60202 Office: 300 W Washington St Chicago IL 60606

CROWN, IRVING, business exec.; b. Chgo., Dec. 9, 1894; s. Arie and Ida (Gordon) C.; student pub. schs., Chgo.; m. Rose Seltzer, Jan. 10, 1928; 1 dau., Suzanne (Mrs. Charles H. Goodman). Pres. Material Service Corp., Chgo., 1955-60; vice chmn. material service div. Gen. Dynamics Corp., 1960-67, Henry Crown & Co., Chgo., 1967—; v.p. Freeman Coal Mining Co. 1947-67, Marblehead Lime Co. 1948-67. Mem. Western Soc. Engrs. Mason (Shriner). Clubs: Covenant, Propeller, Mid Am., Internat., Carlton, Standard (Chgo.); Bryn Mawr Country. Home: 1040 Lake Shore Dr Chicago IL 60611 Office: 300 W Washington St Chicago IL 60606

CROWNER, DAVID WELLS, dentist; b. Toledo, Oct. 28, 1935; s. Harold Penninan and Jeanette Helen (Bremer) C.; student Purdue U., 1953-55, U. Toledo, 1955-56; D.D.S., Ohio State U., 1960; m. Barbara Ann Prickman, Dec. 27, 1958; children—Susan Lynne, John David. Pvt. practice dentistry, Toledo, 1962-72, Sylvania, Ohio, 1972—. Pres., Renwore, Inc., Sylvania, 1969—. Finance chmn. Sylvania Sch. Bd. Levy, 1973; 1st v.p. St. Paul's Lutheran Sch., Toledo. Served with Dental Corps, USNR, 1960-62, comdr. Res. Decorated Navy Commendation medal. Mem. Am., Ohio, Toledo (program chmn. 1971-72, clinic day chmn. 1968-69, chmn. continuing edn. 1976-77) dental assns., Beta Beta Beta, Alpha Epsilon Delta. Club: International Torch (membership chmn. 1975-77) (Toledo). Home: 4634 Carskaddon Toledo OH 43615 Office: 6419 Monroe Sylvania OH 43560

CROWSON, WALTER COLLON, dentist; b. Detroit, Oct. 12, 1932; s. Walter Stanley and Leone (Collon) C.; B.A., Mich. State U., 1957; D.D.S., U. Mich., 1958; m. Bonnie Lou Kremer, Nov. 30, 1974; 1 dau. by previous marriage, Jony Collon. Practice dentistry, Ferndale, Mich., 1958—. Dental dir. Detroit Orthopaedic Clinic, 1959—; chmn. Dental Adv. Bd. to Ferndale, 1968—; chmn. Oakland County Dental Vocational Adv. Com.; cons. Dept. Edn. State of Mich.; cons. dental hygiene program Oakland Community Coll., 1975-76. Pres. Graefield Condominium Assn., Birmingham, Mich., 1972—; bd. dirs. Tri-County Dental Health Council, 1975—. Recipient Citizen of Year award Clawson Troy Elks Club, 1974. Sigma Gamma Found. grantee, 1972. Mem. Am., Mich. dental assns., Mich. Assn. Professions, Oakland County Dental Soc. (chmn. aux. personnel 1974-76), Birmingham Power Squadron, Lambda Chi Alpha, Delta Sigma Delta. Elk. Club: Huron Pointe Yacht (Mt. Clemens, Mich.). Home: 1970 Graefield St Birmingham MI 48008 Office: 26789 Woodward St Huntington Woods MI 48070

CROWTHER, HAROLD FRANCIS, lawyer; b. Colorado Springs, Colo., July 26, 1920; s. Willis B. and Lillian (Baird) C.; B.A., Washburn U., Topeka, 1947, J.D., 1950. Admitted to Kans. bar, 1950, since practiced in Salina; juvenile ct. probation officer Saline County, 1956-59. Sec.-treas. Salina Municipal Band, 1960—; prin. flute Salina Civic Orch. Served with USN, 1939-45. Mem. Saline County Bar Assn. (sec.-treas. 1954, v.p. 1955, pres. 1956), Am. Fedn. Musicians (pres. local 207 1956-57), Pearl Harbor Survivors Assn. (life). Author: The Oblique Equalizer or Some for Me, 1965. Home: 646 E Iron Ave Salina KS 67401 Office: Great Plains Bldg Salina KS 67401

CROWTHER, ROBERT HAMBLETT, cons. in energy, tech. and econs.; b. Amherst, N.H., Mar. 17, 1925; s. Louis Everett and Julia Emeline (Hamblett) C.; B.Chem. Engring., Fenn Coll., 1950; M.S., Kans. State Coll., 1952; m. Mary Nan McKeever, Sept. 8, 1946; children—Philip Everett, Deborah Marie, Hugh Gordon. Process engring. supr. Standard Oil Ind., Whiting, 1951-59; research projects mgr. Am. Oil Co., Whiting, 1959-65; computer applications div. mgr. Amoco Chems. Corp., Chgo., 1965-69; comml. devel. mgr. C.W. Nofsinger Co., Kansas City, Mo., 1969—; founder Centrecon Corp., Shawnee Mission, Kans., 1976—. Pres., Civic Assn., Olympia Fields, Ill., 1968-69. Served with USAAF, 1943-46. Decorated Air medal. Mem. Am. Inst. Chem. Engrs., Am. Petroleum Inst., Sigma Xi, Phi Lambda Upsilon. Patentee in field. Home: 4205 W 91st St Prairie Village KS 66207

CRUICKSHANKS, BRYAN, eye surgeon; b. Northumberland, Eng., Oct. 11, 1935; s. William Blackwood and Jessie McLachlan (Brown) C.; M.B., B.S., U. Durham, 1961; m. Mary Watson, May 31, 1962; children—Lindsey Fiona, Giles Fraser. Intern, Royal Victoria Infirmary, Newcastle upon Tyne, Eng., 1961-62; resident Royal Infirmary of Edinburgh (Scotland), 1962-66; sr. registrar Birmingham and Midland Eye Hosp., Eng., 1967-70; tutor ophthalmology U. Birmingham, England, 1967-70; practice medicine specializing in eye surgery, Sarnia, Ont., Can., 1971—; chief eye dept. Sarnia Gen. Hosp.; courtesy staff St. Joseph's Hosp., Sarnia. Served with RAF, 1954-56. Diplomate Am. Bd. Ophthalmology. Fellow A.C.S., Royal Coll. Surgeons (Can.), Royal Coll. Surgeons (Eng.), Royal Coll. Surgeons (Edinburgh), Soc. Eye Surgeons; mem. Internat. Intraocular Implant Club, Am. Intraocular Implant Soc. (founding mem.). Office: 160 Essex Sarnia ON N7T 4R7 Canada

CRUM, MARK, library exec.; b. Pitts., May 28, 1922; s. Mark and Elizabeth (Musser) C.; B.A., U. Pitts., 1943; B.S. in L.S., Carnegie Inst. Tech., 1948; M.B.A., Western Mich. U., 1966, Ed.D., 1970; m. Margaret Ellen Peterson, June 3, 1943; children—Faith Elisabeth (Mrs. Mark Bryan Van Liere). First asst. Carnegie Library of Pitts., 1948, adminstrv. asst. 1949-50; dir. Kanawha County (W.Va.) Pub. Library, 1952-56, Kalamazoo Library System, 1956—. Served to 1st lt. AUS, 1943-47, 51-52. Mem. Am., Mich. assns. Home: 1315 Homecrest Ave Kalamazoo MI 49001 Office: 315 S Rose St Kalamazoo MI 49006

CRUMB, LAWRENCE NELSON, librarian, clergyman; b. Palo Alto, Calif., May 19, 1937; s. Fred Wells and Esther Carol (Nelson) C.; B.A. magna cum laude, Pomona Coll., 1958; M.A., U. Wis., 1967; M.Div., Nashotah (Wis.) House Sem., 1961, S.T.M., 1973; postgrad. Gen. Theol. Sem., N.Y.C., 1961-62; m. Ellen Adele Locke, July 31, 1968; 1 dau., Sarah Elisabeth. Ordained deacon Protestant Episcopal Ch., 1961, priest, 1962; curate St. John's Ch., Elkhart, Ind., 1962-64, Lafayette, 1964-65; asst. librarian, instr. Greek, Nashotah House, 1965-70, instr. homiletics, 1968-70, registrar, 1969-70; library staff U. Wis.-Parkside, 1970—, head of serials, 1972-74, chief info. services, 1974—; librarian-observer Princeton Theol. Sem., 1968. Mem. Wis. Hist. Soc., Wis. Library Assn., Phi Beta Kappa, Beta Phi Mu. Episcopalian. Contbr. to Racine: Growth and Change in a Wisconsin County, 1977. Home: 3524 Washington Ave Racine WI 53405 Office: U Wis Library Wood Rd Kenosha WI 53141

CRUMBAUGH, JOHN HOWARD, bldg. research cons.; b. Sidney, Ohio, Sept. 17, 1918; s. Forrest and Bessie (Sollenberger) C.; m. Edna Oberndorfer (dec.); m. 2d, Ardeth Ahlstrom, Oct. 15, 1974; children—Lee, Cris. B.S., Iowa State U., 1946; student Wayne State U., 1966, U. Wis., 1968, DuPage Sch. Real Estate, 1970. Engr., Iowa Hwy. Commn., Ames, 1940-42; designer H. R. Green Co., Cedar Rapids, Iowa, 1942-43; architect MHKCB Co., Edmonton, Alta., Can., 1943-44; designer The Austin Co., Chgo., 1946-47; with U.S. Gypsum Co., Chgo., 1947—, structural engr., 1947-57, research mgr., 1957-67, mgr. advanced planning, 1967-71, mgr. cons. services, 1971—. Mem. Brookfield (Ill.) Planning Commn., 1949-55; committeeman Chgo. W. Suburban council Boy Scouts Am., 1961-65; mem. Des Plaines (Ill.) Environ. Control Commn., 1976—. Mem. Gypsum Assn., Am. Nat. Standards Inst., ASTM. Club: Des Plaines Elks. Patentee bldg. systems. Home: 900 Center St Des Plaines IL 60016 Office: US Gypsum Research Center Des Plaines IL 60016

CRUMLEY, RICHARD DAVID, educator; b. Lancaster, Ohio, Nov. 24, 1921; s. Leroy Elsworth and Eva Mabel (Gwartney) C.; B.S., Ohio U., 1942; M.S., U. Chgo., 1950, Ph.D., 1956; m. Mary Louise Stanhagen, Aug. 24, 1947; children—William Stanhagen, Catherine Louise. Instr. Ohio U., Athens, 1946-48; asst. prof. edn. U. S.C., Columbia, 1953-56; asso. prof. math. State Coll. Iowa, Cedar Falls, 1956-62; asso. prof. math. Ill. State U., Normal, 1962—. Vis. asso. prof. math. U.S. AID, Kano, Nigeria, 1964-66; mem. NEA tchr. corps Nepal, summer 1975. Served with AUS, 1942-46. Recipient Holzinger prize U. Chgo., 1956. Mem. Sch. Sci. and Math. Assn. (dir. 1963-64, v.p. 1968-69, pres. 1973-74), Nat., Ill. (dir. 1966-69, pres. 1970-71) councils teachers math., Math. Assn. Am., Kappa Mu Epsilon, Phi Delta Kappa. Democrat. Lutheran. Home: 906 N School St Normal IL 61761

CRUMMETT, WARREN B., chem. co. exec., scientist; b. Moyers, W. Va., Apr. 4, 1922; s. Elmer and Virginia Maude (Smith) C.; B.A., Bridgewater Coll., 1943; Ph.D., Ohio State U., 1951; m. Elizabeth Anne Stathers, Feb. 28, 1948; children—Allan Warren, Daniel David. Chemist, Solvay Process Co., Hopewell, Va., 1943-46; with Dow Chem. Co., Midland, Mich., 1951—, lab. tech. mgr., 1971—; mem. environ. measurements adv. com. EPA, 1976—. Faculty adult edn. Washington U., 1966. Mem. "Com. of 100" to establish Delta Coll., 1953-56; chmn. curriculum com. Re-look at Midland Schs., 1958; mgr. Little League Team, 1961-67. Fellow Am. Inst. Chemists; mem. Am. Chem. Soc., Research Soc. Am., A.A.A.S., N.Y. Acad. Sci. Republican. Methodist (chmn. commn. on missions, 1962-65). Mem. editorial adv. bd. Analytical Chemistry, 1974-76. Home: 808 Crescent Dr Midland MI 48640 Office: 574 Bldg Dow Chem Co Midland MI 48640

CRUMP, PATRICIA ANNE, charitable orgn. exec.; b. Birmingham, Ala., Feb. 2, 1939; d. Joseph Alfred and Matilda Jane (Craven) Ward; student Auburn U., 1958-61; children—William Todd, Stephanie Trent. Pub. relations asst. Samford U., Birmingham, 1965-67; pub. relations dir. United Way of Jefferson, Shelby and Walker Counties, Birmingham, 1967-73; communications dir. United Way of Mpls. Area, 1973—, nat. communications adv. com. United Way of Am., 1973—. Mem. Goals for Birmingham Com., 1972. Recipient photog. awards United Way Am., 1970-71, 69-70, also awards in graphics, radio prodn., TV. Mem. Birmingham Assn. Indsl. Editors (v.p. 1969-70), Pub. Relations Soc. Am., Mpls. C. of C. Clubs: Minn. Advt., Minn. Press. Office: United Way 404 S 8th St Minneapolis MN 55404

CRUMPACKER, SHEPARD J., JR., lawyer, judge, ex-congressman; b. South Bend, Ind., Feb. 13, 1917; s. Shepard J. and Grace (Dauchy) C., Sr.; B.S., Northwestern U., 1938; J.D., U. Mich., 1941; m. Marjorie Patton, Feb. 18, 1950; 1 son, Richard Owen. Admitted to Ind. bar, 1941, practiced in South Bend, 1946-50, 1956-77; judge St. Joseph Superior Ct., 1977—; city atty. South Bend, 1969-71. U.S. del. NATO Parliamentary Conf., Paris, 1955; mem. 82-84th Congresses from 3d Ind. Dist.; mem. U.S. delegation Internat. Copyright Conv., 1952. Bd. dirs. Mich. Coll. Commerce, chmn., 1977—, Jr. Achievement of South Bend, 1976—. Served to 1st lt. AUS, 1941-46, now maj. USAF Res. ret. Mem. Air Force Assn. (local past comdr., past chmn. No. Ind. chpt.), Izaak Walton League Am. (past pres. St. Joseph County chpt.). Republican. Mason, Rotarian. Home: 237 Timber Ln South Bend IN 46615 Office: 224 W Jefferson Blvd South Bend IN 46601

CRUMPTON, CARL F., state ofcl.; b. Ogden, Kans., Nov. 14, 1924; s. Eddie H. and Mary Ann (Nelson) C.; B.S., Kans. State U., 1949, M.S., 1951; m. Joan Roblyer, Feb. 18, 1964; children—Curtis M., Carla F., Jeffry A.; stepchildren—Paul A. Hungerford, Sheryl A. Hungerford. Grad. asst. Kan. State U., 1949-50; geologist U.S. Geol. Survey, Manhattan, Kans., 1950-51; with State Hwy. Commn. Kans., Topeka, 1951—, chief phys. research, 1965-70, asst. engr. planning and devel. research div., 1970—. Lectr. geology, Evening Coll., Washburn U., 1967-72, adj. asst. prof., 1972—. Asst. scoutmaster Boy Scouts Am., Topeka, 1965-68; judge Topeka Regional Sci. and Engring. Fair, 1968—. Pres. Ogden City Council, 1955-57. Served with USMCR, 1942-45. Decorated D.F.C., Air medal with three gold stars. Mem. Hwy. Research Bd. Com., Nat. Coop. Hwy. Research Program Adv. Panels, Clay Minerals Soc., Clay Soc. Japan, Kans. Acad. Sci., Flint Hills Geol. Soc., Am. Legion, Phi Kappa Phi, Sigma Gamma Epsilon. Contbr. articles to profl. jours. Home: 4728 W 18th St Terr Topeka KS 66604 Office: 2300 Van Buren St Topeka KS 66611

CRYER, EUGENE EDWARD, editor; b. Morris, Ill., Sept. 9, 1935; s. Ralph Claypool and Lucy Marguerite (Garner) C.; B.S., So. Ill. U., 1957; m. Catherine Lynn Buchholz, Aug. 18, 1971; children—Michael, Patricia, Cathleen, Scott. Reporter, So. Illinoisan, Carbondale, Ill., 1956-57, Kankakee (Ill.) Jour., 1960-64; asst. city editor Rockford (Ill.) Register-Republic, 1964-68; sports editor Rockford Morning Star and Register-Republic, 1968-71; city editor Morning Star, Rockford, 1971, news editor, 1972-73; mng. editor Morning Star and Register-Republic, 1974-77, exec. editor, 1977—. Mem. exec. bd. Ill. A.P., 1974—, pres., 1977-78; bd. dirs. Mid-Am. Press Inst., 1968-71. Recipient various newswriting awards, 1967, 73. Mem. A.P. Mng. Editors Assn., Sigma Delta Chi. Lutheran. Home: 5764 Vineyard Ln Rockford IL 61107 Office: 97 E State St Rockford IL 61105

CUBBON, FRANK WALLACE, JR., lawyer; b. Cleve., Sept. 14, 1926; s. Frank Wallace and Eunice Viola (Baker) C.; A.B., Allegheny Coll., 1949; J.D., U. Toledo, 1953; m. Barbara Ann Davies, Dec. 28, 1948; children—Frank Wallace III, Kay, Kyle, William, Stuart, Richard, Barbara, Amy, Thomas. Admitted to Ohio bar, 1953, Mich. bar, 1959; individual practice law, Toledo, 1953—; owner Cubbon Properties; lectr. personal injury seminars; tchr. trial practice U. Toledo. Served with U.S. Army, 1946-48. Mem. Am., Toledo, Lucas County, Mich., Ohio bar assns., Assn. Trial Lawyers Am., Phi Gamma Delta. Methodist. Contbr. articles to legal jours. Home: 7955 Dorr St Toledo OH 43617 Office: 335 N Superior St Toledo OH 43604

CUBRIA, JOSE LUIS, wholesale florist exec.; b. Havana, Cuba, Apr. 12, 1945; s. Jose Luis and Ondina Teresa (Bezanilla) C.; came to U.S., 1961, naturalized, 1968; student accounting Roosevelt U.; m. Mary Ellen Egan, Oct. 23, 1971; children—Anne Marie, Margaret Mary, Kathleen. Operations supr./programmer Montgomery Wards Co., Chgo., 1968-73; programmer/analyst Aldens Inc., Chgo., 1973-74; sr. programmer Am. Nat. Bank & Trust Co., Chgo., 1974-76; treas./controller Stuppy Inc., St. Joseph, Mo., 1976—. Served with U.S. Army, 1966-68. Mem. Am. Mgmt. Assn. Roman Catholic. Club: Rotary. Home: 5 Allen Ct Saint Joseph MO 64506 Office: 4801 N 169 Hwy Saint Joseph MO 64506

CUDDY, C. VICKI FORSTER-CLARKE (MRS. WILLIAM T. CUDDY), pub. relations cons.; b. N.Y.C., May 2, 1914; d. Alvanley H. and Irene (Dossor) Forster-Clarke; student Ohio State U., 1963-64; m. William T. Cuddy, Dec. 29, 1933; children—William Herbert, John Clarke. Sec., King Features Syndicate, N.Y.C., 1932-35; co-owner Columbus (Ohio) Light Opera Co., 1947-52; owner Portrait & Comml. Photography Studio, Columbus, 1952-59; audio-visual instr. Arlington Camera Center, Columbus, 1959-61; asst. dir. vol. services Riverside Meth. Hosp., Columbus, 1961-62, dir. pub. relations, 1962-72; dir., corp. sec. Man-Data Corp., Columbus, 1972-74; pub. relations cons., 1974—. Mem. pub. relations com. Boy Scouts Am., 1965-69; v.p. Project Hope, 1975-76. Bd. dirs. Riverside Meth. Hosp. Vols., 1960-62; v.p., trustee Maryhaven, Inc., 1968—, pres., 1970-71. Fellow Acad. Hosp. Pub. Relations Dirs.; mem. Pub. Relations Soc. Am. (dir.), Am. Soc. Hosp. Pub. Relations Dirs., Am. Hosp. Assn., Internat. Platform Assn., Zonta Internat. (pres. Columbus 1972-74), Profl. Photographers of Ohio (officer, dir. 1953-61), Columbus Soc. Profl. Photographers (officer, dir. 1953-61), Women in Communication (officer, dir. 1970-72). Republican. Episcopalian. Home: 642 Beautyview Ct Columbus OH 43214

CUGELL, DAVID WOLF, physician; b. New Haven, Sept. 19, 1923; s. Abel George and Rose (Weiss) C.; B.S., Yale U., 1945; M.D. L.I. Coll. Medicine, 1947; m. Christina Enroth, Sept. 5, 1955. Intern, Bronx Hosp., N.Y.C., 1947-48; intern, resident in medicine Albany (N.Y.) Hosp., 1948-50; fellow Thorndike Meml. Lab., Harvard Med. Sch., 1950-51, 53-55; attending physician Northwestern Meml., Cook County, VA Research hosps. (all Chgo.); from asso. in medicine to prof. Northwestern U. Med. Sch., 1955—, chief pulmonary disease sect. medicine dept., 1966—. Served with AUS, 1951-53. Diplomate Am. Bd. Internal Medicine (exam. bd. pulmonary diseases). Fellow A.C.P., Am. Coll. Chest Physicians; mem. Am. Thoracic Soc., Central Soc. Clin. Research, Am. Fedn. Clin. Research, Chgo. Lung Assn. (pres.). Office: 303 E Chicago Ave Chicago IL 60611

CUISINIER, FRANCIS XAVIER, lawyer; b. Chgo., Nov. 1, 1906; s. Francis Xavier and Catherine (Hansen) C.; student Georgetown U., 1926; B.A., U. Wis., 1929; J.D., Loyola U., 1933; m. Helen Catherine Eulberg, Apr. 12, 1947; children—Francis Patrick, Margo Ann. Asst. football coach U. Wis., 1929-31; admitted to Ill. bar, 1934; practiced in Chgo., 1934—; mem. firm Murphy, Lilliander & Gemmill, 1938-41, Stephan, Cuisinier and Gillespie, 1950-56. Pres., Ridge Civic Council, Chgo., 1962, trustee, 1962—. Served to lt. comdr. USNR, 1942-45. Mem. Ill., Chgo. bar assns., Iron Cross, Pi Kappa Alpha, Phi Delta Phi. Roman Catholic. Club: University of Wis. (dir. 1952—, trustee Scholarship Trust) (Chgo.). Home: 10307 S Leavitt St Chicago IL 60643 Office: 208 S LaSalle St Chicago IL 60604

CULBERTSON, ALBERT LUDLUM, constrn. co. exec.; b. Peoria, Ill., Sept. 5, 1924; s. Albert Ludlum and Hazel (Harrington) C.; student U. Mich., 1942; B.S., U. Ill., 1948; m. Shirley A. Dunbar, Dec. 28, 1945; children—Janet Culbertson Varnon, Karen Culbertson Boddy, Leigh Culbertson Woda, Clark, Martha. With Dunbar Constrn. Co., Cleve., 1948—, treas., 1962—, pres., 1962-75, chmn. bd., 1975—. Trustee, chmn. property com. Cleve. YMCA. Served with USAAF, 1943-46. Decorated Air medal with 2 oak leaf clusters, D.F.C. Mem. U. Ill. Alumni Assn., Asso. Contractors Ohio (pres.), Am. Inst. Constructors, Asso. Gen. Contractors Am. (chmn. edn. com.). Home: 85 N Strawberry Ln Chagrin Falls OH 44022 Office: 5095 Taylor Dr Bedford Heights OH 44128

CULBERTSON, JACK ARTHUR, edn1. exec.; b. Nickelsville, Va., July 16, 1918; s. Otto Cecil and Lola (Fuller) C.; A.B., Emory and Henry Coll., 1943; M.A., Duke, 1946; Ph.D., U. Cal. at Berkeley, 1955; m. Mary Virginia Pond, Aug. 12, 1952; children—Karen Anne, Margaret Lynne. Tchr. elementary schs., Scott County, Va., 1937-41; tchr. Wilson Jr. High Sch., El Centro, Calif., 1949-51, Mineral Springs High Sch., Winston-Salem, N.C., 1943-44; prin. Jewell Ridge Community Sch., Tazewell County, Va., 1947-49; supt. Ellwood Sch. Dist., Santa Barbara, Calif., 1951-53; grad. asst. Duke, 1944-46; teaching asst. U. Calif. at Berkeley, 1953-54; asst. prof. edn. U. Oreg., 1955-59; exec. dir. U. Council for Ednl. Adminstrn., Columbus, Ohio, 1959—; cons. Ford Found.; adviser W.K. Kellogg Found. Mem. NEA, Am. Assn. Sch. Adminstrs (commn. adminstrv. tech. 1966—), Assn. for Supervision and Curriculum Devel., Am. Ednl. Research Assn. (v.p. 1966-68), Nat. Conf. Profs. Ednl. Adminstrn. (mem. exec. com. 1957-60), Nat. Soc. Study of Edn. (mem. yearbook commn. 1964), Phi Delta Kappa. Editor: Social Science Content for Preparing Educational Administrators; editorial bd. Ednl. Adminstrn. Quar. 1965—, Jour. Ednl. Adminstrn. Contbr. profl. jours. and books. Home: 145 Montrose Way Columbus OH 43214 Office: 29 W Woodruff Ave Columbus OH 43210

CULBERTSON, SAMUEL ALEXANDER, II, business exec.; b. Louisville, June 2, 1915; s. Alexander Craig and Florence (McFatrich) C.; student U. Va., 1934-37, Law Sch. U. Va., 1937-40; m. Nancy Madlener, June 18, 1957; children—Samuel III, Catherine, Edward. Former chmn. exec. com. Murine Co., Inc.; dir. mem. exec. com. McIntosh Corp.; dir., chmn. exec. com. Computer Bus. Mgmt., Inc.; former chmn. bd. Pet-Tel; now chmn. bd. Investment & Capital Mgmt.; pres. Utah Shale Land & Minerals, Commodity Partners, Inc.; dir. Pengo Petroleum. Former pres. John Howard Assn., Northtown Vocat. Council; chmn. Isham Meml. YMCA; former mem. Ill. Bldg. Authority; bd. dirs. Civic Fedn., N. Michigan Ave. Assn., Citizens Assn., Harris Sch., Chgo., Chgo. Youth Centers; now chmn. bd. dirs. Grant Hosp. Republican. Episcopalian. Clubs: Masons (32 deg.), Shriners, Racquet, Tavern (Chgo.); Glen View; Lake Geneva (Wis.); Riomar Golf, Riomar Bay Yacht (Fla.); John's Island (Fla.); Augusta (Ga.) Nat. Home: 71 E Division St Chicago IL 60610 Office: 135 S LaSalle St #2600 Chicago IL 60603

CULL, ALAN CLIVE KENYON, headmaster; b. Standlake, Oxford, Eng., July 1, 1920; s. Frank and Florence Emma (Cantwell) C.; came to U.S., 1951, naturalized, 1956; edn. diploma Newland Park Tchrs. Coll., 1948; B.A. magna cum laude, Yankton (S.D.) Coll., 1952; M.A., U. S.D., 1955; m. Prisca Lois Graf, Feb. 20, 1946; children—Joy (Mrs. Dennis Johnson), Bruce. Tchr. English, Palmer Central Sch., Reading, Eng., 1946; head history dept. Caversham Secondary Sch., Reading, 1948-51; tchr. English and speech, Central Sch., Yankton, S.D., 1952-55; headmaster St. Mary's Episcopal Sch. for Indian Girls, Springfield, S.D., 1955—. Served with Brit. Army, 1940-46. Recipient Freedoms Found. award, 1954, Amerianism medal D.A.R., 1966, Alumni award for profl. excellence Yankton Coll., 1972. Mem. Nat. Assn. Episcopal Schs. (bd. govs., 1969-72). Episcopalian (lay vicar, 1956—). Mason (Shriner); mem. Order Eastern Star. Address: Box 468 Springfield SD 57062

CULLEN, FRANK JOSEPH, export sales co. exec.; b. Chgo., Feb. 25, 1937; s. Frank P. and Josephine (Barrett) C.; B.S.M.E., U. Notre Dame, 1959; m. Virginia Ruth Gaul. May 29, 1965; children—Elizabeth, Catherine, Frank J., Patrick. Pres., Cullen-Friestedt Co., Chgo., 1962-68, 75—; v.p., gen. mgr. Fed. Signal Corp., Chgo., 1968-71; v.p., export sales mgr. Engring. Equipment Co., Chgo., 1971; pres. So. Wis. Farms Inc., Chgo., 1977—, Ill. Farms, Inc., Chgo., 1977—. Chmn. nominating com. U.V.P. Party, Village of River Forest, Ill., 1976-77. Mem. Assn. Iron & Steel Engrs., A.S.M.E., Am. Ry. Engrs. Assn., Roadmasters & Maintenance and Way Engrs. Assn. Roman Catholic. Clubs: Union League (Chgo.), Butterfield Country. Office: 1515 W 22d St Oakbrook IL 60521

CULLEN, WILLIAM JOSEPH, elec. contracting co. exec.; b. Chgo., Nov. 7, 1929; s. Philip Francis and Catherine (Giroux) C.; grad. Washburne Trade Sch.; m. Mary Ann Lucas, Jan. 6, 1951; children—Mary Louise, William Joseph, Margaret, Kathleen, James. Electrician, Calumet Electric Co., Chgo., 1949-52, 1954-55; estimator John W. Breslin Elec. Co., Chgo., 1955-60; pres. Cullen Electric Co., Chgo., 1960—; pres. Arrow Ill. Trucking Co.; bd. dir. E. Side Bank & Trust Co. Active St. Cajetan's Holy Name Soc. Served with USMC, 1952-54; Korea. Recipient Gold Key Award De LaSalle High Sch. Alumni, 1976. Mem. Nat. Elec. Contractors Assn., De LaSalle Alumni Assn. (v.p. 1973-74). Democrat. Roman Catholic. Clubs: K.C., Ridge Country. Home: 2142 W 115th St Chicago IL 60643 Office: 9534 S Torrence Ave Chicago IL 60617

CULLEY, JOHN BRITT, real estate co. exec.; b. Augusta, Ga., Oct. 29, 1919; s. Fenton Bayard and Emily Britt C.; student Evansville (Ind.) Coll. 1938-39; grad. Lockyear's Bus. Coll., Evansville; m. Mary Parker Nov. 4, 1944; children—John Britt, Mary Gail. Exec. v.p. Terminal Warehouse Co. Inc., Evansville, 1945-76; gen. mgr. Ingle St. Warehouse Co., Evansville, 1945-76; partner, mgr. M. & J. Co., Evansville, 1958—; owner, mgr. Culley Realty Co., Evansville, 1966—. Vice pres. Community Chest, Evansville; a founder Evansville United Fund; sr. warden St. Pauls Episcopal Ch., Evansville; pres. Evansville Heart Assn; pres. Vanderburgh County Tb Assn. Licensed real estate broker, Ind. Mem. Nat., Ind. assns. realtors, Ind. Warehousemens Assn. (sec.-treas.). Clubs: Kiwanis (past pres.), Evansville Country (past v.p., bd. dirs.), Elks (past exalted ruler). Home: 2334 E Chandler Ave Evansville IN 47714 Office: Suite 100 Executive Park E 101 Plaza Blvd Evansville IN 47715

CULLEY, WILLIAM JAMES, biochemist; b. Peoria, Ill., Nov. 13, 1928; s. Thomas Henry and Helen (Reed) C.; B.S., Bradley U., 1953; Ph.D., Purdue U., 1959; m. Bonnie Louise Young, May 2, 1959; children by previous marriage—Barbara (Mrs. George Iceberg), Angela (Mrs. Donald Kingen); children—Bonnie, Connie. Head of research Muscatatuck State Hosps., Butlerville, Ind., 1959—. Chmn., Ripley County Red Cross, 1973. Served with AUS, 1946-49. Mem. Versailles C. of C. (pres. 1973), A.A.A.S., Am. Chem. Soc., Am. Assn. Clin. Chemists, Am. Assn. Mental Deficiency. Lion. Contbr. articles to research jours. Home: Route 1 Versailles IN 47042 Office: Box 77 Muscatatuck State Hosp Butlerville IN 41223

CULLIGAN, JOHN AUSTIN, surgeon; b. St. Paul, Oct. 21, 1926; s. John Maurice and Margaret Ellen (McGovern) C.; B.S., U. Notre Dame, 1948; M.B., U. Minn., 1950, M.D., 1951, M.S., 1959; m. Sheila Elizabeth Spriggs, Dec. 27, 1952; children—John, Kathleen, Sheila, Thomas, Elizabeth, Shannon, Paul. Intern, U. Pa. Grad. Hosp., Phila., 1950-51; resident Mayo Found., Rochester, Minn., 51-52, 55-58, Glen Lake Sanitarium, Mpls., 1958-59; practice medicine specializing in thoracic and cardiovascular surgery, St. Paul, 1959—; mem. staff St. Joseph's Hosp., United Hosps., St. Paul, St. Mary Hosp., Mpls.; clin. prof. surgery U. Minn., 1977—. Served with USNR, 1952-54. Recipient E. Starr Judd award Mayo Clinic, 1958. Diplomate Am. Bd. Surgery, Am. Bd. Thoracic Surgery. Fellow A.C.S., Am. Coll. Chest Physicians; mem. St. Paul (pres. 1975), Minn. (pres. 1976—) surg. socs., Soc. Thoracic Surgery. Roman Catholic. Clubs: St. Paul Athletic, Town and Country St. Paul. Home: 976 Summit Ave St Paul MN 55105 Office: Lowry Med Arts Bldg St Paul MN 55102

CULLIGAN, MICHAEL WILLIAM, fuel and light co. exec.; b. Two Rivers, Wis., Mar. 13, 1939; s. William Joseph and Grace Alice (Abel) C.; B.B.A., U. Wis., 1962; m. Mary Lea Stangel, May 19, 1960; children—Cynthia, Timothy Kristin. Staff accountant Haskins & Sells, C.P.A.'s, Milw., 1961-64, Harold Kugler, Manitowoc, Wis., 1964-65; treas. Wis. Fuel & Light Co., 1977—; Treas., dir. WFL, Inc.; part time instr. Lakeshore Tech. Inst., Manitowoc. Advance gifts chmn. Heart Fund, Manitowoc County, 1967; mem. Manitowoc County New Health Planning Council; mem. rev. com. Green Bay Regional New Health Planning Council; mem. fin. com., capital expenditures com. Manitowoc-Two Rivers YMCA; chmn. Nixon for Pres. campaign, Manitowoc County, 1968, 72. Served with USAF Res., 1957-62. C.P.A., Wis. Mem. Am. Inst. C.P.A.'s, Wis Soc. C.P.A.'s, Wis Natural Gas Agy., Wis. Utilities Assn., Taxation, Internal Auditing and Property Accounting Tasks Force (gen. accounting exec. com.), Manitowoc Jr. C. of C. (bd. dirs. 1968-69, sec. 1966-67). Elk. Home: 1308 Ahrens St Manitowoc WI 54220 Office: 402 N 10th St Manitowoc WI 54220

CULP, ARCHIE WILLIAM, JR., nuclear engr., educator; b. St. Joseph, Mo., Jan. 20, 1931; s. Archie William and Johanna (Lutz) C.; A.S., St. Joseph Jr. Coll., 1950; B.S., U. Mo. Sch. Mines and Metallurgy, 1952, M.S., 1954; Ph.D., U. Mo., Columbia, 1970; m. DonaFay Belle Miller, Apr. 20, 1957; children—Craig Randall, Brian Scott, Eric Ross. Nuclear engr. Convair, Fort Worth, 1955-56; cons. engr. ASTRA, Inc., Milford, Conn. and Raleigh, N.C., 1956-61; mem. faculty U. Mo., Rolla, 1961—, asso. prof. mech. engring., 1964—. NSF fellow, 1967-68. Mem. Am. Nuclear Soc., Sigma Xi, Tau Beta Pi, Phi Kappa Phi, Pi Tau Sigma. Lutheran. Home: 2 Curtis Dr Rolla MO 65401 Office: Dept Mech Engring U Mo Rolla MO 65401

CULVER, GORDON FRANKLIN, educator; b. Pawnee, Okla., Feb. 2, 1923; s. William Penn and Mary Belle (Hetherington) C.; B.S., Okla. State U., 1948, M.S., 1949; D.Ed., U. Nebr., 1958; m. Erma Josephine Mitchell, Oct. 3, 1942; children—Alan Gordon, Janis Lynn, Stephen Franklin, Robert Wayne, Gregg Mitchell. With U.S. Civil Service, 1942-43; bus. tchr. Stillwater (Okla.) High Sch., 1949-51; mem. faculty Okla. State U. Coll. Bus., Stillwater, 1951-61; mem. faculty, chmn. dept. bus. edn. U. Nebr. Tchrs. Coll., Lincoln, 1961—, prof., 1965—; cons. to ednl. instns., state depts. edn.; dean Inst. for Certifying Secs., Nat. Secs. Assn., 1968-69. Mem. Policies Commn. Bus. and Econ. Edn., 1973-76, chmn., 1975-76; bd. dirs. Future Bus. Leaders Am., 1973-76. Served with AUS, 1943-45. Decorated Bronze Star. Mem. Nat. (exec. bd. 1973-75, pres. 1977-78) Mountain-Plains (pres. 1970-71, Leadership award 1971) bus. edn. assns., Adminstrv. Mgmt. Soc. (hon. chpt. mem., chmn. edn. com. 1966-78), Nat. Secs. Assn., Delta Pi Epsilon (nat. pres. 1974-75), Pi Omega Pi, Phi Delta Kappa. Republican. Methodist. Asso. editor Nat. Bus. Edn. Forum, 1966-68. Contbr. articles to profl. jours. Home: 1705 Janssen Dr Lincoln NE 68506

CULVER, JOHN CHESTER, senator; b. Rochester, Minn., Aug. 8, 1932; s. William C. and Mary (Miller) C.; A.B. cum laude, Harvard, 1954, LL.B., 1962; postgrad. (Lionel de Jersey Harvard scholar), Emmanuel Coll., Cambridge (Eng.) U., 1954-55; m. Ann Cooper, June 15, 1958; children—Christina, Rebecca, Catherine, Chester John. Admitted to Ia. bar, 1963; legis. asst. to Mass. senator, Washington, 1962-63; mem. law firm McGuire, Bernau, & Culver, Cedar Rapids, Ia., 1963-64; mem. 89th-93d congresses, 2d Iowa Dist., chmn. sub. com. fgn. econ. policy; mem. U.S. Senate from Iowa, 1974—; dean of men Harvard Summer Sch., 1960. Bd. overseers Harvard U., 1975—. Served to maj. USMCR, 1955-59. Mem. Linn County, Iowa bar assns. Home: 6800 Connecticut Ave Chevy Chase MD 20015 also McGregor IA Office: US Senate Office Bldg Washington DC 20515

CUMBERWORTH, JAMES EMMET, accountant, business exec.; b. Detroit, July 7, 1917; s. Charles S. and Alice Marie (Walsh) C.; B.S., Marist Coll., 1939; m. Hazel Aline Lathrop, Dec. 24, 1938; children—Patricia (Mrs. William Duchaine), Michael, Bridget (Mrs. Frank Abbott), James Emmet, Timothy, Terence, Robert, Colleen (Mrs. Harlan Morgan), Matthew, Margaret (Mrs. Jessie McGee), Kathleen, Theresa, Daniel, Elizabeth. Pvt. practice tax law, Moline, Ill., 1955—; pres., dir. LeClaine Hotel, Inc., Moline, 1960—; exec. v.p., dir. Moline Consumers Co., 1955—; sec.-treas., dir. Settle Constrn. Co., Moline, 1967—; pres., dir. Appanoose Salvage Co., Centerville, Ia., 1970—. Cons. Western Ready Mixed Co., Gem City Ready Mix Co., Quincy, Ill., Bussen Quarry Co., St. Louis, Central Stone Co., Huntingdon, Mo., Mo. Gravel Co., La Grange, Mo. Trustee Leo L. Henkel Found. Served with AUS, 1943-45. Mem. Nat. Soc. Pub. Accountants. Elk. Home: 3702 7th St Moline IL 61265 Office: 313 16th St Moline IL 61265

CUMMINGS, CHARLES THERON, pub. utility exec.; b. Wolf Summit, W.Va., June 22, 1917; s. Alexander Charles and Gladys Alma (Logue) C.; B.A., Salem (W.Va.) Coll., 1939; m. Norma June Bargerhuff, Aug. 26, 1961; children—Alma Jane Cummings Office, John Charles, Kimberly June. With Hope Natural Gas Co., Clarksburg, W.Va., 1939-60, mech. engr., 1948-50, safety dir., 1950-60; gen. mgr. River Gas Co., Marietta, Ohio, 1960-67, v.p., gen. mgr., 1967-74, pres., 1974—, chief exec. officer, 1976—, also dir. Trustee ARC, 1963-68, Marietta Meml. Hosp., 1963—; pres. Community Improvement Corp., Marietta, 1968-71. Served with U.S. Army, 1942-46. Recipient Outstanding Citizen award, Marietta, 1976. Mem. Ohio, Am. gas assns., Ohio Oil & Gas Assn., Rotary. Marietta Area C. of C. (v.p. 1971-72, pres., 1972-73, dir., 1963-75). Republican. Club: Shriners, Masons. Home: 211 Rathbone Rd Marietta OH 45750 Office: 324 4th St Marietta OH 45750

CUMMINGS, FREDERICK JAMES, museum exec.; b. Floydayda, Tex., Aug. 19, 1933; s. James Sidney and Dollie (Clark) C.; B.A., Willamette U., 1954; M.A., Harvard U., 1956; postgrad. Courtauld Ins., London, 1960-61; Ph.D., U. Chgo., 1966. m. Judith Church, July 30, 1955; children—Elihu Clark, Eleanor Louise, Leslie Elizabeth, Fred James Church, Diana Margaret. Grad. instr. U. Chgo., 1959-60; instr. U. Mo., 1961-64, acting dir. Mus. Art and Archeology, 1963-64; curator European art Detroit Inst. Arts, 1964-66, asst. dir., 1966-73, dir., 1973—, exec. dir. Founders Soc., 1973, also trustee; ex-officio mem. Arts Commn., City of Detroit; adj. prof. history of art Wayne State U., 1965; curator, coordinator Bicentennial exhbn. Nat. Gallery Art, Washington, 1973-74. Mem. Council on Museums and Edn. in Visual Arts, 1973, Gov.'s Commn. on Art in Pub. Bldgs., 1975, Spl. Commn. on Maintenance and Preservation Meadowbrook Hall, Oakland U., 1976—; bd. dirs. Detroit Artists Market; chmn. bd. trustees Mich. Workshop Fine Prints; trustee Center for Creative Studies, Detroit, Channel 56 Ednl. Television. Mem. Am. Soc. Eighteenth Century Studies (chmn. visual arts com. 1971-72), Coll. Art Assn. Am. (chmn. com. on museum-univ. relations 1972, exec. com. 1972), Am. Assn. Museums, Nat. Council on Mus. Edn. Decorated officer Order of Merit (Italian), Order of Merit (French); recipient Fine Arts Silver medal Mich. Acad. Sci., Arts and Letters, 1972; Author: Art in Italy, 1600-1700, 1965; American Decorative Arts, from the Pilgrims to the Revolution, 1967; (with Allen Staley) Romantic Art in Britain: Paintings and Drawings, 1760-1860, 1967; co-organizer Twilight of the Medici, Late Baroque Art in Florence 1670-1743, 1974; co-organizer, author Painting in France 1774-1830: The Age of Revolution, 1974-75; editor: (with Charles H. Elam) The Detroit Institute of Arts Illustrated Handbook, 1971; mem. editorial bd. The Art Quarterly, 1966-74, editor, 1966-69; contbr. articles to profl. pubs. Home: 18652 Fairway Dr Detroit MI 48221 Office: Detroit Inst Arts 5200 Woodward Ave Detroit MI 48202

CUMMINGS, JOHN PATRICK, lawyer, ecologist; b. Westfield, Mass., June 28, 1933; s. Daniel Thomas and Nora (Brick) C.; B.S. cum laude, St. Michael's Coll., 1955; Ph.D. (Pub. Health fellow), U. Tex., 1968; J.D., U. Toledo, 1973, M.S. in Civil Engring., 1977; m. Dorothy June D'Ingianni, Dec. 27, 1957; children—John Patrick, Mary Catherine, Michael Brick, Kevin Andrew, Erin Christine, Colleen Elise. Engr., Frauhauf Trailer Co., Westfield, 1955; with Hamilton Mgmt. Corp., brokers, Austin, Tex., 1960-70; teaching asso. U. Tex., Austin, 1964-68; chemist Owens-Ill. Glass Co., Toledo, 1968-71, ecologist, 1971-76, mgr. product safety, 1976—. Cons. EPA, Glass Containers Mfrs. Inst., Nat. Center for Resource Recovery; adj. prof. U. Toledo, 1977—; admitted to Ohio bar, 1973, U.S. Ct. Mil. Appeals, 1974. Served to capt. USAF, 1955-62. Recipient H.R. Henze award for teaching excellence U. Tex., 1968. Fellow Chem. Soc.; mem. Am., Ohio, Toledo bar assns., Am. Ceramic Soc. (chpt. chmn. 1972-73), Tech. Soc. Toledo (v.p. 1969-70), AAAS, Am. Chem. Soc., Soc. Applied Spectroscopy, Am. Crystallographic Assn., Inst. Chemists, Air Force Assn., Res. Officers Assn. (Tex. v.p. 1965-67, Mich. v.p. 1973-75, Mich. pres. 1976-77) Sigma Xi, Phi Alpha Delta. K.C. (4 deg.). Patentee in field. Home: 1980 Rose Arbor Toledo OH 43614 Office: 1700 N Westwood Ave Toledo OH 43607

CUMMINGS, LARRY LEE, educator; b. Indpls., Oct. 28, 1937; s. Garland R. and Lillian P. (Smith) C.; A.B. summa cum laude, Wabash Coll., 1959; postgrad. (Woodrow Wilson fellow) U. Calif. at Berkeley, 1959-60; M.B.A., Ind. U., 1961, D. Bus. Adminstrn. (Ford Found. fellow, Richard D. Irwin Dissertation fellow), 1964; children—Lee Anne, Glenn Nelson. Asst. prof. Sch. of Bus., Ind. U., Bloomington, 1964-67, asso. prof., 1967; asso. vis. prof. Columbia, N.Y.C., 1967-68; asso. prof. organizational behavior U. Wis., Madison, 1968-70, prof. Grad. Sch. Bus. and Indsl. Relations Inst., 1970—, Romnes Fellow, asso. dean Grad. Sch., 1975—, lectr. dept. of psychology, 1971—. Vis. prof. U. B.C., Can., 1971-72; cons. to Eli Lilly and Co., Eli Lilly Internat. in London, Bundy Corp., Samsonite Corp., Touché, Ross, Bailey & Smart, Inc., World U., San Juan, P.R.; research proposal reviewer, Can. Council, 1971-74. Bd. dirs. Center for the Study of Organizational Performance, Madison. Recipient McKinsey Found. Mgmt. Research award, 1970. Ford Found. Sr. Research fellow, 1969-70; Richardson Found. Research grantee, 1969. Fellow Acad. of Mgmt. (mem. publs. planning com. 1973-74), Am. Psychol. Assn. (mem. sci. affairs com. div. 14 1973-76); mem. Midwestern Psychol. Assn., Am. Sociol. Assn., Am. Soc. Personnel Adminstrn. (com. chmn. research com. 1969-70), Soc. Personnel Adminstrn., Indsl. Relations Research Assn., Sigma Xi, Phi Beta Kappa, Beta Gamma Sigma, Sigma Iota Epsilon, Tau Kappa Alpha, Delta Phi Alpha. Author: (with W.E. Scott) Readings in Organizational Behavior and Human Performance, 1969, 2d edit., 1973; (with F.A. Shull and A.L. Delbecq) Organizational Decision Making, 1970; (with D.P. Schwab) Performance in Organizations, 1973. Cons. editor Richard D. Irwin Series in Mgmt. and Behavioral Sci., 1972—. Editor Acad. Mgmt. Jour., 1975—; asso. editor Decision Scis., 1972—; mem. editorial bd. Organization and Adminstrv. Scis., 1973—. Contbr. numerous research articles on organizational psychology and personnel mgmt. to profl. jours. Office: Grad Sch Bus U Wis 1155 Observatory Dr Madison WI 53706

CUMMINGS, OLIVER WILLIAM, editor; b. Cairo, Ill., Sept. 2, 1946; s. William Lawrence and Nellie Marie (Kerr) C.; B.A., So. Ill. U., 1968, M.S., 1969, Ph.D. (fellow), 1972. Intern dept. psychology and research A.L. Bowen Children's Center, Harrisburg, Ill., 1970; instr. So. Ill. U., Carbondale, 1972; test service coordinator Midwest, Houghton Mifflin Co., Geneva, Ill., 1972-76, sr. editor test dept., Iowa City. Iowa, 1976—. Mem. Am. Personnel and Guidance Assn., Nat. Council Measurement in Edn., Assn. Measurement and Evaluation in Guidance, Nat. Vocat. Guidance Assn., Assn. Counselor Educators and Suprs., Phi Delta Kappa. Baptist. Home: PO Box 2022 Iowa City IA 52240 Office: PO Box 1970 Iowa City IA 52240

CUMMINS, GEORGE MANNING, JR., physician; b. Davenport, Iowa, May 24, 1914; s. George Manning and Edna Eugenia (Eckstein) C.; B.S., St. Ambrose Coll., 1935; M.D., Rush Med. Sch., 1941; M.S., Northwestern U., 1947; m. Merlene Virginia Anderson, June 11, 1941; children—George Manning III, Gregory M., Gilbert M., Cynthia H., Geoffrey M. Practice medicine, specializing in internal medicine, Chgo., 1946; chief gastrointestinal sect. Chgo. Wesley Meml. Hosp; asst. prof. medicine Northwestern U. Sch. Medicine, 1955—. Served with AUS, 1942-46. Diplomate Am. Bd. Internal Medicine. Fellow A.C.P.; mem. A.M.A., Ill., Chgo. med. socs., Chgo. Inst. Medicine, N.Y. Acad. Scis., Alpha Omega Alpha. Clubs: Mid-Am. (Chgo.); Kenosha (Wis.) Country. Contbr. articles to profl. jours. Home: 505 N Lake Shore Dr Chicago IL 60611 Office: 251 E Chicago Ave Chicago IL 60611

CUNLIFF, ALBERT EDWARD, lawyer; b. St. Louis, Nov. 6, 1905; s. Charles and Elizabeth Jeanette (Lewis) C.; student Washington U., St. Louis, 1925-29; LL.B., Benton Coll. Law, 1931; m. Elizabeth Semple, Aug. 7, 1936; children—Elizabeth C. (Mrs. M. Edward Kinkade), Albert Edward. Admitted to Mo. bar, 1930, Fed. bar, 1936; practiced in St. Louis, 1930—; sr. partner firm Luke, Cunliff, Herr, Chavaux, Hilgendorf, McCluggage & DeYong, St. Louis, 1933—; lectr. workmen's compensation law Benton Coll. Law., 1931-37. Chmn. Eagle reviewers and presentors St. Louis area council Boy Scouts Am., 1955—. Bd. dirs., pres. backstoppers, Policemen and Firemen Relief Assn., 1977-78. Served to capt. USNR, 1942-45; chief justice High Ct. Am. Samoa, 1943-44; comdg. officer St. Louis Navy Law Co., 1948-64. Mem. Am., Mo., St. Louis bar assns., Phi Alpha Delta, Beta Theta Pi. Conglist. Mason (Shriner), Rotarian. Clubs: Mo. Athletic (St. Louis); Algonquin Golf (Webster Groves, Mo.). Author: Missouri Workmen's Compensation Digest, 1931—. Home: 14 Holiday Ln St Louis MO 63131 Office: 706 Chestnut St St Louis MO 63101

CUNNINGHAM, BRYCE ALLEN, educator; b. Brainerd, Minn., June 21, 1932; s. Henry Allen and Gerda Lillian (Peterson) C.; B.A., U. Minn., 1955, B.S., 1958, Ph.D., 1963; m. Marilyn Frances Berge, June 17, 1956; children—Catherine, John, Robert, James. Asst. prof. Kans. State U., Manhattan, 1963-72, asso. prof. biochemistry, 1972—. Mem. Am. Chem. Soc. Home: 400 Oakdale Dr Manhattan KS 66502

CUNNINGHAM, DAVID REA, trading corp. exec.; b. Camp Douglas, Wis., Mar. 9, 1936; s. Chester M. and Lorraine J. (Rea) C.; grad. N.Y. Inst. Photography, 1961, Inst. Applied Sci., 1954. With U.S. Postal Dept. Transp., 1953-58; pres., mgr. African Trading Corp. Wis., Camp Douglas, 1960—; bd. dirs. Fgn. Trade Devel., Farrell Lines. Active Midwest Chpt. on Epilepsy. Served with U.S. Army, 1958-60. Mem. Am. Mgmt. Assn. (Internat. Div.), Soc. Advanced Mgmt., Nat. Assn. Better Bus. Burs., Direct Selling Legion, Specialty Advt. Info. Bur., Made in Europe. Democrat. Christopher. Club: World Wide Cycling Assn. Contbr. articles to Rehabilitation Gazette. Office: Main St Box 294 Camp Douglas WI 54618

CUNNINGHAM, DONALD FREDRICK, photographer; b. Jackson, Mich., Jan. 27, 1922; s. Fredrick John and Ruth Elizabeth (Uphouse) C.; grad. high sch.; m. Bernice R. Snider, Apr. 3, 1948; children—Patrick John, James Allen, William Lloyd. Staff photographer Jackson (Mich.) Citizen Patriot Newspaper, 1941-55, 60-70; program dir. WWTV-TV, Cadillac, Mich., 1956-59; chief photographer Consumers Power Co., Jackson, 1970—. Served with AUS, 1942-45. Mem. Profl. Photographers Am., Mich. Press Photographers Assn. Club: Clark Lake Yacht. Home: 11985 Strait Rd Hanover MI 49241 Office: 115 W Trail St Jackson MI 49201

CUNNINGHAM, FLOYD FRANKLIN, geographer; b. Flat Rock, Ill., Dec. 24, 1899; s. Carl Homer and Lillie Alberta (Seitzinger) C.; student Eastern Ill. U., Charleston, 1916-18; B.E., Illinois State University at Normal, Ill., 1926; student U. Chgo., summer, 1927; A.M., Clark U., 1928, Ph.D., 1930; m. Helen Blanche Espy, Sept. 1, 1925; children—Jo Ann (Mrs. Jack Jungers), Floyd Espy. Tchr. rural schs., Crawford County, Ill., 1918-22; prin. Emerson Sch., Berwyn, Ill., 1925-27; prof., head dept. geography U. Ala. at Florence, 1929-47; chmn. dept. geography So. Ill. U., 1947-58, prof. geography, dir. Lab. of Climatology, 1959-66, prof. emeritus geography, 1966—; distinguished vis. prof. geography Western Ky. U., 1966—; vis. prof. Peabody Coll. for Tchrs., summer, 1935; instr. geography, Biarritz, Am. U., Biarritz, France, 1945-46; U.S. Army lecture bur., Frankfurt, Germany; lectr. geography, Berlin, Munich, Frankfurt, Bremen, Wiesbaden, Mannheim, Karlsruhe, Kassel, Giessen, Augsburg (all Germany), Salzburg, Vienna (Austria), 1947; rep. State of Ala., Internat. Geog. Congress, Warsaw, Poland, 1934; Fulbright lectr. geography Ain Shams U., Am. U., Cairo, 1953-54. Recipient distinguished service awards Western Ky. U., 1970, dept. earth sci. and community planning So. Ill. U., Edwardsville, 1975, Ill. Geog. Service, 1977. Fellow Nat. Council Geog. Edn. (sec. 1937-40, pres. 1942-44), Am. Geog. Soc.; mem. AAUP (pres. So. Ill. U. chpt. 1956-60), Ill. Acad. Sci., Ill. Geog. Soc. (pres. 1948-49), Nat. Travelers Club, Am. Assn. for the UN, Soil Conservation Soc. Am., Am. Forestry Assn., Am. Platform Assn., Assn. Am. Geographers, Kappa Delta Pi, Gamma Theta Upsilon. Democrat. Club: Kiwanis (life mem., pres. Florence 1932; lt. gov. 1st div. Ala. dist. 1941, distinguished service award Carbondale 1973). Author: Laboratory Manual in the Geography of North America, 1930; (with C.F. Jones) Laboratory Manual in the Geography of South America, 1932; (with Samford and McCall) You and Regions Near And Far, 1964, You And The United States, 1964, You And The Americas, 1965, You and the World, 1966; 1001 Questions Answered About Water Resources, 1967. Contbr. articles to Jour. Geography, Ala. Sch. Jour. Home: PO Box 267 Carbondale IL 62901

CUNNINGHAM, JAMES BERNARD, county ofcl.; b. Cleve., Apr. 25, 1939; s. James Proudfoot and Eileen Mary (Davey) C.; student John Carroll U., Cleve., 1960-63; m. Dorothy E. Smith, June 22, 1963; children—James, Kelly, Sean, Michael, Daniel, Ryan. Estimator, field engr. Republic Steel Corp., Cleve., 1960-67; sales estimator E.F. Donley & Sons, Inc., Cleve., 1968-71; pres., prin. J.B. Cunningham & Assos., Euclid, Ohio, 1971-72; asst. project engr. Turner Constrn. Co., Cleve., 1972; exec. commr. Cleve. Dept. Pub. Utilities, 1972-76; exec. adminstr. Cuyahoga County Engr.'s Office, Cleve., 1977—. Past mem. Citizens Adv. Com. E. Cleve.; mem. exec. com. Cuyler County Republican Orgn. Mem. Cleve. Commrs. Assn., Civil Service Employees Assn., Am. Water Works Assn., Cleve. Water Assn. Roman Catholic. Clubs: Cleve. K.C. (4th deg.), W. Side Irish-Am., Lithuanian-Am. Citizens, Italian-Am. Home: 1374 S Lyn Circle South Euclid OH 44121 Office: 1928 Standard Bldg 1370 Ontario St Cleveland OH 44113

CUNNINGHAM, JOHN EDWARD, cons. elec. engr.; b. Arlington, Mass., Mar. 13, 1923; s. Michael E. and Mary E. C.; Engr., Gen. Electric Co., Lynn, Mass., 1947-56; chief spl. project engr. Canoga Electronics Inc., Fort Walton Beach, Fla., 1956-65; project engr. Smith Electronics, Cleve., 1963-67; project mgr. Cleve. Inst. Electronics, Cleve., 1967-76; cons. electronic engr., Lakewood, Ohio, 1976—. Registered profl. engr., Ohio. Author: Security Electronics, 1970; Building and Installing Electronic Intrusion Alarms, 1972; Understanding and Using the VOM and EVM, 1973; Cable Television, 1976; Broadcast Antennas, 1977. Contbr. articles to profl. jours. Mem. cable TV advisory com. FCC; lectr. Case Western Res. U., Lakeland Community Coll., Kent State U., Miami Dade Community Coll. Mem. IEEE (sr.), Cleve. Engring. Soc., Audio Engring. Soc.

CUNNINGHAM, MARCUS EDDY, engring. exec.; b. Lynn, Mass., Jan. 16, 1907; s. Daniel and Susie (Goad) C.; B.S. Yale, 1928; postgrad. Boston U., 1929; m. Mary Eloise Baird, Feb. 14, 1931 (dec. Nov. 1964); children—Charles Baird, Marcus Eddy; m. 2d, Marilyn Alice Eneix, Oct. 1, 1966. Gen. supt. Daniel Cunningham Constrn. Co., Boston, 1928-32, Austin Co., Cleve., 1932-40; pres., treas., dir. Brady Hill Co., Detroit, 1940—; pres., treas., dir. Cunningham-Limp Co., Detroit, 1948-70, chmn. bd., chief exec. officer, 1970—; chmn. bd., chief exec. officer, treas., dir. Cunningham-Limp, Ltd., Toronto, Ont., Can., 1959—; chmn. bd. Cunningham-Limp Internat. S.A., 1963—, Cunningham-Limp Co. de las Americas, S.A., 1966—, Cunningham-Limp de Espana, S.A., 1966—, Cunningham-Limp (France) SARL, 1967—, Cunningham-Limp Deutschland, Gmbh, 1970—. Dir., v.p. Gulfstream Park Racing Assn., Hallandale, Fla., 1963—. Bd. dirs. Detroit, Nat. councils Boy Scouts Am. Mem. Engring. Soc. Detroit, A.I.M. (president's council). Clubs: Yale (Detroit); Bloomfield Hills Country; Oakland Hills Country (Birmingham, Mich.); Indian Creek Country, Kenilworth (Bal Harbour, Fla.); Jockey (Miami Beach, Fla.); Brickell Bay (Miami, Fla.); Le Mirador Country (Mont Peierin, Switzerland). Home: 104 Brady Ln Bloomfield Hills MI 48013 (winter) Ocean Blvd Golden Beach FL 33160 Office: 1400 N Woodward Ave Birmingham MI 48011

CUNNINGHAM, MARILYN ALICE ENEIX (MRS. MARCUS E. CUNNINGHAM), business and advt. exec.; b. Warren, Minn., Mar. 8, 1917; d. Frederick C. and Mary (Boman) Eneix; B.A., U. Mich., 1937; m. Marcus E. Cunningham, Oct. 1, 1966. Account supr. Grant Advt., Inc., Chgo. and N.Y.C., 1945-60; dir. advt. Cunningham-Limp Co., Detroit, 1960-69, v.p., dir., Birmingham, Mich., 1969-71, dir., vice chmn. bd. 1972—; vice chmn. bd., v.p., dir. Cunningham-Limp Internat., 1971—; vice chmn. bd., dir. Cunningham-Limp des las Americas (S.A.), 1972—, Cunningham-Limp Ltd., 1972—, v.p., dir. Brady Hill Co., Detroit, 1960—. Active in civic and philantropic activities. Mem. Fine Arts Soc. Detroit (chmn. script com.), Internat. Platform Assn., Smithsonian Inst. Assos., Alpha Phi. Republican. Presbyn. Clubs: Bloomfield Hills Country, Oakland Hills Country (Birmingham); Indian Creek Country, Kenilworth (Bal Harbour, Fla.); Jockey (Miami Beach, Fla.); Brickell Bay (Miami, Fla.); Le Mirador Country (Mont Peierin, Switzerland). Author: The Right Plant on The Right Site for Maximum Profit, 1962; The Comprehensive Approach to Facility Expansion, 1967; Design and Engineering, 1970; The Facility Planning Services of Cunningham-Limp, 1973; Total Responsibility in Facility Expansion, 1975. Author, publ. SCOPE mag. Contbr. articles to nat. mags., bus. publs., tech. periodicals. Home: 104 Brady Ln Bloomfield Hills MI 48013 also Ocean Blvd Golden Beach FL 33160 Office: 1400 N Woodward Ave Birmingham MI 48011

CUNNINGHAM, SARAH JANE, lawyer; b. Des Moines; d. Paul Harvey and Harriett (Plummer) Cunningham; A.B., Sterling Coll., 1944; LL.B., U. Nebr., 1959; postgrad. U. Iowa, 1947, U. Nebr., 1948-49. Pub. sch. tchr., Kans., 1944-46, Nebr., 1946-52; owner, mgr. McCook (Nebr.) Bus. Service, 1952-56, Sally's Gift Shop, McCook, 1953-56; admitted to Nebr. bar, 1959, since practiced in McCook. Mem. Gov.'s Commn. Status Women, 1962-71, chmn., 1962-64; mem. Citizens Adv. Council on Status of Women, 1968-76; bd. dirs. McCook City Library, 1967-76, pres., 1970-73; mem. legis. com. Nebr. Heart Assn., 1966-68; vice chmn. Red Willow County (Nebr.) Rep. Central Com., 1967-69; trustee Bus. and Profl. Women's Found., Washington, 1963-71, pres., 1966-67; trustee Sterling Coll., Community Hosp. Assn., McCook, 1973—. Named Woman of Achievement, Nebr. Fedn. Bus. and Profl. Women's Clubs, 1966. Mem. McCook C. of C. (indsl. com. 1967), Nat. Assn. Parliamentarians, D.A.R., Internat. (v.p. 1968-71), Nat., Nebr. fedns. bus. and profl. women's clubs (Nebr. pres. 1957-59, nat. pres. 1966-67), Am., Nebr. bar assns., P.E.O., Order Eastern Star. Conglist. (moderator 1960-62, 75). Home: 201 Park Ave McCook NE 69001 Office: 116 West E St McCook NE 69001

CUNNINGHAM, VICKI SUE, educator; b. Wyandotte County, Kans., July 28, 1951; d. John Joseph and Marjorie Arleen (McKee) Cunningham; B.S. in Edn., Kans. State Tchrs. Coll., 1973; M.S., Emporia State Coll., 1976; postgrad. Kans. U., 1977—. Clk. Bd. Edn., Kansas City, Kans., 1967; tchr. bd. Edn., North Kansas City, Kans., 1973—. Vol. Channel 19 Fund Raising Auction, 1977. Mem. NEA, Mo. State Tchrs. Assn., Am. Personnel and Guidance Assn., PTA, Psi Chi, Pi Lambda Theta. Republican. Methodist. Home: 111 Brentwood Apt 201 Liberty MO 64068 Office: Pleasant Valley Sch Pleasant Valley and Sobbie Rds Liberty MO 64068

CURLETT, ARTHUR SIMISON, city ofcl.; b. Xenia, Ohio, June 22, 1926; s. James Jacob and Imogene (Simison) C.; student Miami U., Oxford, Ohio, 1946-47, Sinclair Coll., 1947-50, U. Dayton, 1975—; 1 dau., Vicki Lynne. Clk., Fetz Bros. Grocery, 1943-45; mgr. shoe dept. J.C. Penney Co., 1947-48; dep. county auditor Greene County, 1948-55; gen. mgr. Community Bowling, Inc., 1955-57 (all Xenia); dir. finance City of Xenia, 1957—. Served with USNR, 1945-46. Mem. Municipal Fin. Officers Assn., Municipal Clks. Assn., Greene County Hist. Soc. (treas. 1973-74), Am. Soc. Pub. Adminstrn., Pi Alpha Alpha. Methodist. Mason (32 deg.), Rotarian (dir. 1967-71, pres. 1970-71, chmn. dist. community service com. 1971-73). Club: Xenia President's (pres. 1970-71). Home: 6749 Swissway Dr Dayton OH 45459 Office: 101 N Detroit St Xenia OH 45385

CURNOW, JOHN WAYNE, mech. engr.; b. Port Huron, Mich., Mar. 31, 1935; s. Gordon Earl and Lillian Ruth (Burgett) C.; B.S.M.E., U. Mich., 1958; m. Nancy R. Crawford; children—Kevin John, Alan Wayne. Design, devel. engr. indsl. group Sperry Vickers div. Sperry Rand Corp., Troy, Mich., 1965-66, mgr. lab., 1967-70, engring. supr., 1970-72, sect. chief indsl. valve group, 1972-73, chief engr. N.Am. group controls, 1973-75, dir. engring. N.Am. group Controls, Elect. Products, 1975—. Bd. govs. Nat. Conf. Fluid Power. Served with U.S. Army, 1958. Mem. Soc. Automotive Engrs. Nat. Fluid Power Assn. Patentee in field. Home: 7000 Gunlock Bay Utica MI 48078 Office: 1401 Crooks Rd Troy MI 48084

CURRAN, CON PATRICK, III, advt. agency exec.; b. St. Louis, Oct. 3, 1928; s. Con Patrick and Cecelia (Hogan) C.; B.S., Regis Coll., 1951; m. Joan Nuetzel, Apr. 30, 1955; children—Con, Joan, Chris, Craig, Jenny. Salesman, Con P. Curran Printing Co., St. Louis, 1955-60, sales mgr., 1960-63; pres. Ross-Curran Co., 1963-68; pres. Graphic Assos., Inc., Clayton, Mo., 1973—. Served with USNR, 1951-53. Mem. Direct Mail Assn., Am. Mktg. Assn., Sales and Mktg. Execs. Assn. Club: University. Office: 7908 Bonhomme Ave Clayton MO 63105

CURRAN, DANIEL ROONEY, elec. mfg. co. exec.; b. Homestead, Pa., Mar. 6, 1925; s. John P. and Anna P. (Rooney) C.; B.S., Pa. State U., 1949, M.S., 1950; postgrad. Brown U., 1950-53; m. Martha Jane Stoudnour, Aug. 30, 1945; children—Judith Ann, Deborah Lee, Jennifer Louise. Research asst. physics Pa. State U., 1948-50, Brown U., 1950-53; research staff mem. Raytheon Mfg. Co., Waltham, Mass., 1953-55; project engr. transducers Bendix Aviation Co., Davenport, Iowa, 1955-56; sr. physicist Clevite Research Center, Cleve., 1956-57, head electronic devices sect., 1958-65; mgr. filter products Instrument Systems div. Gould Inc., Cleve., 1965-69, operations mgr. magnetics dept., 1969-70, market planning mgr., 1970—. Cons. ultrasonics. Served with USMCR, 1943-46. Recipient C.B. Sawyer Meml. award, 1968. Mem. I.E.E.E. (ann. paper award 1966), Acoustical Soc. Am., Sigma Xi, Sigma Pi Sigma. Contbg. author Physical Acoustics (W.P. Mason), 1964. Contbr. articles to profl. jours. Patentee in field. Home: 695 Briarcliff Dr Aurora OH 44202 Office: 3631 Perkins Ave Cleveland OH 44114

CURRAN, JOHN DAVID, editor; b. Sault Ste. Marie, Ont., Can., Apr. 7, 1942; s. John Albin and Phyllis Margaret (Hone) C.; B.A., U. Toronto, 1964; B.J., Carleton U., 1967; m. Joan Maureen Douglas, July 8, 1967; children—Bruce John, Andrea Maureen, James Andrew. Reporter Sault Daily Star, Sault Ste. Marie, 1964-66; reporter Kitchener Waterloo (Ont.) Record, 1967-68; with Sault Daily Star, 1968—, city editor, 1969-74, news editor, 1974—, spl. adviser to pres., 1973-75. Part-time instr. Sault Coll. Applied Arts and Tech., 1971-74. Pres., Assn. Mentally Retarded, 1971-72; chmn. Adult Services Com., 1968-70; mem. land use com. Sault Region Conservation Authority, 1972-74; chmn. Operation Placement Com., 1968-70. Club: Soo Curlers' Assn., Sault Golf. Home: 18 Linstedt St Sault Ste Marie ON Canada Office: 369 Queen St E Sault Ste Marie ON P6A 5M5 Canada

CURRENT, JAMES REVEL, dentist; b. Farmland, Ind., Dec. 7, 1904; s. Orpheus Erasmus and Esther Anola (McProud) C.; student Ind. U., 1924-26, Ball State U., 1930-32; D.D.S., Northwestern U., 1936; m. Florence Lenore Wilbur, June 6, 1936. Farmer, east central Ind., 1920—; individual practice dentistry, Tell City, Ind., 1936—. Pres. governing bd. Perry County Meml. Hosp., 1964-72; sec. Tell

City Schweizer Fest com., stage and sound mgr., 1959-73; sec. Perry County Sesquicentennial Com., 1964-67; sec. Civil War Centennial Com., 1960-65; v.p. Perry County Civil Def. Adv. Council, 1956—; mem. Tri-state Area Health Planning Council, 1968-73; mem. Perry County Health Planning Council, 1968-73; mem. Tell City String Ensemble, 1959—, Lincoln Hills Symphony Orch., 1959—. Served to lt. USNR, 1944-46; PTO. Mem. Am. Legion, Tell City Hist. Soc. (pres. 1968-71), Civil War Round Table Vanderburg County Courthouse, Triangle, Theta Chi, Psi Omega. Republican. Methodist. Mason (Shriner), K.P. Clubs: Fine Arts Camera (Evansville, Ind.); Filson (Louisville). Address: 515 Main St Tell City IN 47586

CURRENT, RICHARD LEE, mortgage banking co. exec.; b. Sidney, Ohio, Dec. 23, 1935; s. Weldon Marion and Ruth Emelyn (Archer) C.; B.S., Ohio State U., 1960, M.S., 1961; m. Gloria Ann Young, June 15, 1958; children—Wade Alan, Layne Alison, Chad Alex, Leigh Ann. Research analyst Federated Dept. Stores, Inc., Cin., 1961-62; with Kissell Co., Springfield, Ohio, 1962—, v.p. mktg. div., 1968-72, sr. v.p., 1972-75, exec. v.p., 1975—. Served with AUS, 1954-56; ETO. Lutheran. Mason. Home: Route 2 DeGraff OH 43318 Office: 30 Warder St Springfield OH 45501

CURRIE, LAWRENCE EVERETT, psychologist; b. Chgo., Aug. 18, 1945; s. Clarence Clifton and Violante Earlscort (Robertson) C.; B.A., Drake U., 1967; M.A., Iowa, 1969; Ph.D., Syracuse U., 1973; m. June 6, 1970 (div. 1975); children—Jamál Lawrence, Táhirih Louise. Personnel specialist Owens Illinois Corp., Toledo, 1968; staff devel. specialist Hutchings Psychiat. Center, Syracuse, 1972-73; rehab. counselor Iowa Div. Rehab. Edn. and Services, Oakdale, 1969-70; asst. prof. U. Wis. at Stout, Menomonie, 1973-75; asso. exec. dir. research and program devel. Goodwill Rehab. Center, Milw., 1975-77; pvt. practice clin./cons. psychology, Milw., 1977—; adj. prof. DePaul U., 1976—; cons. psychologist, 1975—. Bd. dirs. Urban Media, Milw. Recipient grants Rehab. Services Adminstrn.; licensed psychologist; certified rehab. counselor. Mem. Am., Wis. psychol. assns., Am. Soc. Clin. Hypnosis, Soc. for Clin. and Exptl. Hypnosis, Am. Assn. Sex Educators, Counselors and Therapists, Nat., Wis. rehab. assns. Contbr. articles to profl. jours. Home: 9088 N 75th St Milwaukee WI 53223 Office: 9001 N 76th St Suite 303 Milwaukee WI 53223

CURRIER, THOMAS RICHARD, state ofcl., pub. health adminstr.; s. Augustus Bernard and Irene M. (Allen) C.; M.A., Western Mich., U., 1974; m. Frances Gram, Sept. 22, 1973. Ordained to ministry Roman Catholic Ch., 1957; dir. pastoral mission office Diocese of Lansing (Mich.), 1957-70; pres. World Communications, Inc., Lansing, 1971-73; social researcher Mich. Gov.'s Office, Lansing, 1973-74; health adminstr. Mich. Dept. Pub. Health, Lansing, 1974—; mem. faculty social sci. dept. Jackson Community Coll., Jackson, Mich., 1974—; cons. to Health Services Research Inst., U. Tex., San Antonio, 1976—. Recipient Gold Camera award Chgo. Film Festival, 1972. Author: Restructuring the Parish, 1967, Agony and Ecstasy in Building a Christian Community, 1969, The Future Parish, 1970, God As My Other Self, 1972; contbr. articles on pub. health to profl. publs.; producer film programs. Home: 7004 N River Hwy Grand Ledge MI 48837 Office: 3423 N Logan Lansing MI 48906

CURRIN, MONTELL, JR., savs. and loan exec.; b. Saginaw, Mich., Oct. 23, 1944; s. Montell Lovelace and Nancy (McClaine) C.; A.A., Delta Coll., Mich., 1969; B.S., Saginaw Valley State Coll., 1977; 1 son, Montell Hugh. Mail dispatcher Consumers Power Co., Bay City, Mich., 1964-65; loan processor First Savs. & Loan Assn., Saginaw, 1970-71, mgmt. trainee, 1971-73, br. mgr., 1973, asst. v.p., 1973-75, v.p., 1975—. Bd. dirs. Saginaw Econ. Devel. Corp., 1976—; indsl. adv. bd. Opportunities Industries Center Am., 1977—; bd. dirs. Saginaw chpt. Big Sisters Am., 1974-75; mem. Saginaw City Council, 1977—. Served with USAF, 1965-69. Recipient certificate of recognition Saginaw Model Cities Program, 1976. Office: 124 S Jefferson St Saginaw MI 48607

CURRY, CARLTON EUGENE, automotive mfg. co. exec.; b. Lizton, Ind., Mar. 4, 1935; s. William Daniel Harrison and Minnie Eulalia (Trammel) C.; B.S. in Aero. Engring., Purdue U., 1958; m. Ann Estelle Merritt, July 3, 1957; children—Charles Lynn, Kimberly Sue. Jr. engring. aide Allison div. Gen. Motors Corp., Indpls., 1956, supr. program adminstrn. Detroit Diesel Allison div., Indpls., 1966-73, staff systems analyst, 1973—; gen. engr. U.S. Naval Avionics Facility, Indpls., 1957-66. Mem. Indpls. License Rev. Bd., 1972, Indpls. Bd. Transp., 1973-77; Republican precinct committeeman, 1970, 72, ward chmn., 1972-73, area chmn., 1973-77; bd. dirs. Community Action Against Poverty, 1976-77. Recipient Citizenship award Am. Legion, 1953; John Bernall Starr scholar, 1953. Mem. Am. Inst. Aeros. and Astronautics, Army Aviation Assn. Mem. Christian Ch. Clubs: Lions (pres. Chapel Hill 1977), Toastmasters Internat. Contbr. analytical articles to profl. jours. Home: 8406 Model Sq Indianapolis IN 46234 Office: PO Box 894 U4 Indianapolis IN 46206

CURRY, ERNESTINE DIXSON (MRS. GROVER C. CURRY), ednl. adminstr.; b. Canton, Miss., Jan. 1, 1919; d. Robert Benjamin and Estella Missouri (Foote) Dixson; student Wilson Jr. Coll., 1937; B.E., Chgo. Tchrs. Coll., 1941; M.A., Northwestern U., 1952; Ed.M., Chgo. State Coll., 1964; m. Grover C. Curry, Mar. 5, 1944; children—Neil, Gary. Tchr., Chgo. Pub. Schs., 1941-65, elementary sch. prin., 1965-75, secondary sch. prin., 1975—. Mem. Joint Negro Appeal Bd. Mem. Nat. Assn. Elementary Sch. Prins., Nat. Council Adminstrv. Women in Edn., Ill., Chgo. (1st v.p. 1971—) prins. assns., Nat. Assn. Secondary Sch. Prins., Samuel Stratton Edn. Assn., Northwestern U. Alumni Assn., N.A.A.C.P. (life), Zeta Phi Beta. Baptist (minister music, chmn. bd. religious edn. 1951-75). Clubs: 67th and Indiana Block (pres. 1963-65), Ella Flagg Young (Chgo.). Home: 6740 S Indiana Ave Chicago IL 60637 Office: 244 E Pershing Rd Chicago IL 60653

CURRY, JAMES CHRISTOPHER, physician; b. Baraboo, Wis., Dec. 5, 1926; s. James Michael and Florence Anne (Nichol) C.; student Marquette U., 1944-46, M.D., 1949; m. Kathleen M. Devine, June 18, 1949; children—Kathleen Therese, Christopher James, Eileen Mary. Intern, St. Agnes Hosp., Fond du Lac, Wis., 1949-50; gen. practice medicine, Mt. Calvary, Wis., 1950-52; mem. staff St. Agnes Hosp.; resident internal medicine Milwaukee County Hosp., Wauwautosa, Wis., 1952-54, Wood County VA Hosp., Milw., 1954-55; NIH fellow in allergy, clin. instr. U. Va. Hosp., Charlottesville, 1955-56; practice medicine, specializing in allergic diseases, Appleton, Wis., 1956—; mem. staffs Appleton Meml. Hosp., St. Elizabeth Hosp., Theda Clarke Hosp. Mem. adv. com. Sch. Medicine, U. Va., 1960—; mem. bd. advisers Wis. div. Am. Automobile Assn., 1974—. Pres. Valley council Boy Scouts Am., 1970-73, v.p. Bay Lakes council, 1973-74, mem. exec. bd., rep. to nat. council, 1974—. Recipient Silver Beaver award Boy Scouts Am., 1973, Leadership award, 1974. Diplomate Am. Bd. Clin. Immunology and Allergy. Fellow Am. Coll. Allergy, Am. Assn. Clin. Immunology and Allergy (pres. region 1969-70, chmn. com. edn. 1970—); mem. A.M.A., Wis. State, Outagamie med. socs., S.W. Allergy Forum, Wis. Allergy Soc., Phi Chi. Elk, Rotarian. Clubs: Tennessee Squires, Riverview Country. Home: 1112 E Moorpark Ave Appleton WI 54911 Office: 436 E Longview Dr Appleton WI 54911

CURRY, JAMES MELVIN, univ. ofcl.; b. Breckenridge County, Ky., Nov. 25, 1923; s. Jesse M. and E. Katherine (Vessels) C.; grad. high sch.; Asso. in Sci., Vincennes (Ind.) U., 1976; student Ind. State U., 1975—; m. M. June Preusz, Apr. 19, 1945. With E. Bierhaus & Sons, Vincennes, Ind., 1946-53; bus. mgr. Drs. Anderson, Smith & Anderson, Vincennes, 1953-60; with Tresslar Co., Inc., Vincennes, 1960—, treas., dir., 1968-71, purchasing agt., 1971-72, advt. mgr., 1973-74, mgr. warehouse div., 1974-77; treas., dir. Bicknell Wholesale Co., Inc., Vincennes, 1968-71; sec.-treas. Tresslar, Inc., Vincennes, 1969-71; dir. purchasing Vincennes U., 1977—. Recipient Outstanding Alumnus award Ind. Assn. Distributive Edn. Clubs Am. Mem. Distributive Edn. Clubs Am. (Nat. 1st award in mgmt. decision-making-merchandising 1973), Mensa. Republican. Roman Catholic. Elk. Home: 2002 Main St Vincennes IN 47591

CURRY, LEONARD ONEY, X-ray co. exec.; b. Sheldon, Mo., May 17, 1922; s. Denver Oney and Bertha (Rapp) C.; grad. high sch.; m. Nancy Ellen Brown, Oct. 19, 1946; children—David Leonard, Donald Max, Sue Ellen, Ronda Lea, Catherine Ann. Welder for various firms, Leavenworth, Kans., San Pedro, Calif., Kansas City, Mo., Kansas City, Kans., 1942-49; X-ray technician Indsl. X-ray Engrs., Seattle, 1949-51, Tulsa Testing Lab., 1952, Richardson X-ray, Alhambra, Calif., 1952; owner, founder Modern X-ray Co., Nevada, Mo., 1953—; partner Welding & Radiography Cons., Leawood, Kans. Mayor of Milo, Mo., 1967-77. Served with USNR, 1944-46. Mem. Indsl. Radiographic Service Assn. (charter; pres. 1967), Am. Legion, D.A.V. Mem. Christian Ch. Mason (Shriner), Elk; mem. Order Eastern Star. Club: Nevada Country. Home: Milo MO 64767 Office: PO Box 152 Nevada MO 64772

CURTIN, MICHAEL DANIEL, food co. exec.; b. N.Y.C., Feb. 8, 1938; s. Michael Daniel and Mary (Smashe) C.; B.S., Lafayette Coll., 1959; M.S. in Chem. Engring., Carnegie Mellon U., 1961; postgrad Xavier U., 1968-69; m. Mary Elizabeth Davidson, Sept. 8, 1962; children—Rebecca Ann, Laura Lee. Project engr. Procter & Gamble Co., Cin., 1960-65, group leader, 1965-71, tech. brand mgr., 1971-72; tech. dir. Miracle White Co. div. Beatrice Foods Co., Chgo., 1972-73, dir. operations, 1973-76, v.p. operations, 1976-77, asst. to exec. v.p. Beatrice Food Co., 1977—. Shell fellow, 1960, Alcoa fellow, 1955-59. Recipient Boy Scout Lunch-O-Ree Fund Raiser award, 1975. Mem. Packaging Inst. Am., Am. Inst. Chem. Engrs., Merchandising Execs. Club, Tau Beta Pi. Clubs: Internat. Snipe Yacht Assn., Fairwinds Tennis, Four Lakes Tennis, Ohare Racquet, Four Lakes Ski. Home: 1575 Leabrook Ln Wheaton IL 60187 Office: 1111 E Touhy Ave Des Plaines IL 60018

CURTIS, ALICE READY PARTLOW (MRS. JOHN M. WALMSLEY), pub. relations exec.; b. Keystone, W.Va.; d. Ira Judson and Andrea B. (Martin) Partlow; A.B., Marshall Coll., 1928; postgrad. King's Coll., U. London (Eng.), 1932, Columbia U., 1933; m. Hal L. Curtis, Apr. 15, 1939 (dec.); m. 2d, John M. Walmsley, Oct. 30, 1975. Writer, Jam Handy Orgn., Detroit, 1941-43; newspaper editor Ft. Wayne Army Post, Detroit, 1943-44; asst. pub. relations dir. Mich. Blue Cross, Detroit, 1944-50; pub. relations dir. YWCA Met. Detroit, 1950-66; pub. relations officer Merrill-Palmer Inst., Detroit, 1966-70; owner Alice Curtis Pub. Relations, Grosse Pointe, Mich., 1970—; pub. relations dir. Cottage Hosp., Grosse Pointe, 1972—. Recipient citation, journalism dept. Mich. State U., 1950; award Women's Advt. Club Detroit, 1950. Mem. Mich. Hosp. Pub. Relations Assn. (bd. mem. 1971), Pub. Relations Soc. Am. (mem. bd. 1966-68), Mich. Humane Soc., Am. Soc. Hosp. Pub. Relations Dirs., Founders Soc. Detroit Inst. Arts, Fine Arts Soc. Detroit, Theta Sigma Phi. Democrat. Episcopalian. Clubs: Detroit Press. Author: Is Your Publicity Showing, 1949. Home: 16826 Cranford Ln Grosse Pointe MI 48230 Office: 159 Kercheval Ave Grosse Pointe Farms MI 48236

CURTIS, ARTHUR WINBERG, III, communications cons.; b. Hartford, Conn., July 11, 1944; s. Arthur Winberg, Jr., and Margaret Mary (Hille) C.; B.A., Johns Hopkins U., 1966; postgrad. Miami U., 1970-73; m. Cynthia Taylor, Mar. 25, 1967. Tchr. English, Baltimore County Schs., 1966-67; program cons. Md. Tuberculosis and Respiratory Disease Assn., 1967-70; staff mem. Miami U., 1970-72; operations and prodn. mgr. Sta. WMUB-FM, Miami U., 1972-73; communications cons., Cheboygan, Mich., 1974—. Mem. bd., pub. relations chmn. Cheboygan County chpt. Am. Cancer Soc., 1976-77; mem. rev. com. No. Mich. Health Systems Agency; mem. bd., sec. Cheboygan Pub. Library; mem. Republican State Central Com., Md., 1966-70; mgr. 10 polit. campaigns. Home and Office: 344 S Huron St Cheboygan MI 49721

CURTIS, CARL THOMAS, U.S. senator; b. Minden, Nebr., Mar. 15, 1905; s. Frank O. and Alberta Mae (Smith) C.; grad. Minden High Sch., 1923; student Nebr. Wesleyan U., LL.D., 1958; m. Lois Wylie-Atwater, June 6, 1931 (dec. Sept. 1970); children—Clara (Mrs. James Hopkins) (dec.), Carl; m. 2d, Mildred G. Baker, Dec. 1, 1972. Tchr. Minden Schs., 1927; admitted Nebr. bar, 1930 and began practice at Minden; county atty., 1931-34; mem. 76th to 83d Congresses; mem. U.S. Senate, 1955—. Mem. Nebr. Bar Assn., Theta Chi. Republican. Presbyn. Mason, Odd Fellow, Elk, Rotarian. Home: Minden NE 68959 Office: Senate Office Bldg Washington DC 20510

CURTIS, GENE A., realtor; b. Braggadocio, Mo., July 30, 1932; s. Austin and Edith Blanche (Hatley) C.; B.S., U. Mo. at Columbia, 1958; m. Marjorie Jones, Aug. 25, 1957; children—David J., Stephen A. Credit mgr. Continental Oil Co., Kansas City, Mo., 1958-63, Lincoln, Nebr., 1963-64; owner Centennial Agy., Lincoln, 1968—; organizer Union Real Estate, 1977—. Courier, Southwest Bapt. Coll., Bolivar, Mo., 1974-75; Neb. rep. Home Mission Bd., So. Bapt. Conv., Atlanta. Served with USMCR, 1953-56. Mem. Lincoln Bd. Realtors (chmn. edn. com., 1971-73), Nebr. Realtors Assn. (dean realtors inst., 1974-75, pres. ednl. trust fund 1974-75). Baptist. K.P. Home: 4301 S 46th St Lincoln NE 68516 Office: 4733 Prescott St Lincoln NE 68506

CURTIS, GEORGE WARREN, JR., lawyer; b. Merrill, Wis., Sept. 24, 1936; s. George Warren and Rose E. (Zimmerman) C.; B.A., U. Minn., 1959; J.D., U. Wis., 1962; m. Mary Kersztyn, Dec. 27, 1973; 1 dau., Emily Jennifer; children by previous marriage—George, Kathy, Eric, Greg, Paul, David. Admitted to Wis. bar, 1962, Fla. bar, 1968; practiced in Merrill, 1962-68, Oshkosh, Wis., 1968—; mem. firms Russell & Curtis, 1962-68, Nolan, Engler, Yakes & Curtis, 1968-74, Curtis, MacKenzie, Haase & Brown, 1974—. Active YMCA. Mem. Delta Sigma Rho. Democrat. Home: 5996 Hwy 21 Omro WI 54963 Office: 429 Algoma Blvd Oshkosh WI 54901

CURTIS, WILLIAM KNOX, educator; b. Perryopolis, Pa., Sept. 29, 1937; s. Earle Edwin and Elizabeth (Knox) B.; B.A., Kent State U., 1961, M.S., 1964; postgrad. Bowling Green State U., 1972-75; m. Lynne Louise Loushine, June 15, 1963; children—Kimberly Ann, Aimee Lynne. Tchr. Portage County Schs., Brimfield, Ohio, 1964-65; reporter Medina (Ohio) County Gazette, 1965; account exec. Bracy & Bracy Advt., Cleve., 1966; prof. speech and theatre Defiance (Ohio) Coll., 1966—. Exec. dir., actor, play writer Community Theater, Cleve., 1965-66. Mem. Speech Communication Assn., Am. Theater Assn., N.E.A., A.A.U.P., Alpha Psi Omega. Author plays: The Place, Lester Sims Retires Tomorrow, The Bowling Alley Press Conference. Home: 1196 Fallen Timbers Dr Defiance OH 43512

CURTLER, HUGH MERCER, JR., educator; b. Charlottesville, Va., Dec. 31, 1937; s. Hugh Mercer and Nancy Daingerfield (Elsraod) C.; certificate Balt. Poly. Inst., 1955; B.A., St. John's Coll., 1959; M.A., Northwestern U., 1962, Ph.D., 1964; m. Linda Edith Lockwood, June 15, 1962; children—Hugh Mercer III, Ralph Rudolph Hirsch. From instr. to asst. prof. U. R.I., at Kingston, 1964-66; asst. prof., chmn. dept. humanities Midwestern Coll., Denison, Iowa, 1966-68; asso. prof. philosophy Southwest State U., Marshall, Minn., 1968—, chmn. dept. 1968—. Md. State scholar, 1955-59; Northwestern U. fellow, 1961-64; Young Humanist fellow, 1971-72; vis. fellow Center Study Democratic Instns., 1972. Mem. Am. Philos. Assn., A.A.U.P., Soc. Philosophy and Pub. Affairs, Soc. Polit. and Legal Philosophy, Common Cause, A.C.L.U., SANE, Ams. for Democratic Action. Home: Box 102 Cottonwood MN 56229 Office: Dept Philosophy Southwest State U Marshall MN 56258

CUSACK, JOHN FRANCIS, lawyer; b. Chgo., Dec. 13, 1904; s. James Joseph and Eileen Nellie (Fitzgerald) C.; Ph.B., U. Chgo., 1928, J.D., 1930; m. Magdalene M. Hanousek, Dec. 29, 1937; children—John Francis, Judith (Mrs. John G. Ryan), James J., Raymond R., Richard W., Thomas E., Magdalene H., Ana C. Admitted to Ill. bar, 1931; partner Cusack & Cusack, 1931—; dir. Hazeltine Research, Inc., Chgo. Chmn., Motion Picture Appeal Bd. Chgo., 1968-75; mem. Dept. Urban Renewal, 1969—; chmn. Friends of Chgo. Schs. Com., 1966-70; mem. Comml. Dist. Devel. Commn., 1972—, Neighborhood Devel. Commn., 1973—; bd. dirs. South Shore Commn. Fellow Am. Matrimonial Acad.; mem. Am., Ill., Chgo. bar assns., Catholic Lawyers Guild Chgo. (gov. 1960—), Am. Trial Lawyers Assn., Am. Judicature Soc. Home: 9401 S Hoyne St Chicago IL 60620 Office: 11 S LaSalle St Chicago IL 60603

CUSHENBERY, DONALD CLYDE, educator; b. Sharon, Kans., Sept. 24, 1925; s. Jesse Clyde and Lillian May (Schloetzer) C.; B.S., Fort Hays (Kans.) State Coll., 1948; M.S., Kans. Tchrs. Coll. at Emporia, 1954; D.Ed., U. Mo. at Columbia, 1964; m. Elfrieda Berg, Aug. 10, 1951; children—Barbara, Donna, Linda. Tchr., Sharon, Kans., 1944-45, Argonia, 1945-46; prin. coach, Plains, Kans., 1948-53; prin. Lincoln Jr. High, Anthony, Kans., 1953-55; asst. prof. Kans. State Coll., Pittsburg, 1955-64; prof. edn. U. Nebr. Omaha, 1964—, Found. prof., 1971-77. Reading workshop dir., tech. cons. Right to Read Program. Recipient Great Tchr. award, 1971. Mem. Nebr. Reading Council (pres.), Phi Delta Kappa, Kappa Delta Pi. Baptist. Lion. Author: Reading Improvement in the Elementary Sch., 1969; Remedial Reading in the Secondary School, 1972; (with Kenneth Gilreath) Effective Reading Instruction for Slow Learners, 1972; (with Helen Howell) Reading and the Gifted Child, 1974. Home: 919 N 69th St Omaha NE 68132 Office: 60th and Dodge Sts Omaha NE 68101

CUSTER, HARRY RICHARD, surgeon; b. Los Angeles, June 30, 1923; s. Harry John and Anna Marie (Bouchie) C.; B.A., Ohio State U., 1945, M.D., 1948; postgrad. U. Mich., 1950-51; m. Dorothy Marie Bott, June 25, 1948; children—Marc Joseph, Laura, Michael. Intern U.S. Naval Hosp., Phila., 1948-49; resident Leila Y. Post Montgomery Hosp., Battle Creek, Mich., 1949-52; chief resident Ohio State U. Hosp., 1952-53; pvt. practice Colby, Kans., 1954-67, Charlevoix, Mich., 1967—; past mem. staff, chmn. dept. surgery St. Thomas Hosp., Colby; now chief Charlevoix Hosp. Chmn., Mem. City Council, Colby. Mem. adv. bd. Marymount Coll., Salina. Served as lt. (j.g.) M.C., USN, 1948-49. Decorated knight St. Gregory, 1963. Diplomate Am. Bd. Abdominal Surgery (regent Kans.), Pan. Am. Med. Assn. (surg. sect.), Am. Bd. Surgery. Fellow Internat. Coll. Surgeons (vice regent Kan.); mem. Nat. Council Cath. Men (Gold Cross asso.). Democrat. K.C. (4 deg.), Lion. Home: PaBaShan Trail Charlevoix MI 49720 Office: 723 Park Charlevoix MI 49720

CUTHBERT, THOMAS WILLIAM, mfg. co. exec.; b. Cicero, Ill., Jan. 22, 1938; s. Gordon Norman and Eleanor Mae (Johnson) C.; student U. Wis., Oshkosh, 1972-73, Oakland Community Coll., 1974—; m. Judith Ann Lader, Apr. 27, 1963; children—Scott Thomas, Amy Ann. Programmer, Wilson Sporting Goods Co., River Grove, Ill., 1963-65; office mgr., instr. Electronic Machine Accounting Coll., Chgo., 1965-66; programmer analyst Rockwell Internat., Oshkosh, 1966-73, systems analyst, div. hdqrs., Troy, Mich., 1973-74, supr. corp. mgmt. systems devel., 1976—. Served with USN, 1956-60; Taiwan. Mem. Am. Prodn. Inventory Control Soc. (dir. sec. Fox Valley, Wis., chpt. 1971-73). Home: 1366 W Selfridge St Clawson MI 48017 Office: 2135 W Maple Rd Troy MI 48017

CUTLER, GRANVILLE BERRY, educator; b. Mattoon, Ill., Nov. 22, 1919; s. Granville R. and Margaret A. (Berry) C.; B.S., Western Mich. U., 1942; M.A., U. Mich., 1949; m. Betty J. Erickson, Apr. 21, 1946; 1 dau., Mary Louise. Supr. music Three Oaks (Mich.) Twp. schs. 1942, 46-52; music instr. Holland (Mich.) pub. schs., 1953-54; instr. brass Hope Coll., 1952-54; asst. supt., secondary prin. Sheridan (Mich.) Rural Agrl. schs., 1954-57; high sch. prin. Plainwell (Mich.) pub. schs., 1957-68; nat. comdr. All Am. Drum and Bugle Corps and Band Assn., 1964—; nat. commr. All Am. Assn. Contest Judges, 1965-68. Served with AUS, 1942-45. Named Hon. Citizen New Orleans, 1965, Jefferson Parrish, La., 1964, Hon. Col. La., 1964. Mem. Mich. (regional pres.), Nat. edn. assns., Am. Fedn. Musicians, Am. Legion (comdr. 1950), V.F.W., Phi Delta Kappa, Alpha Phi Omega, Phi Mu Alpha. Lion (pres. chpt. 1964; sec. 1972), Mason. Home: 1627 Lay Blvd Kalamazoo MI 49001

CUTLER, IRVING HERBERT, educator; b. Chgo., Apr. 11, 1923; s. Zelig and Frieda (Wopner) C.; A.A., Herzl Jr. Coll., 1942; student Dartmouth, 1943; M.A., U. Chgo., 1948, Ph.D., Northwestern U., 1964; m. Marian Horovitz, Aug. 31, 1951; children—Daniel, Susan. Investigator, Dept. Labor, 1946-47; tchr. high schs., Mich. and Ill., 1948-57; transp. economist C.E., U.S. Army, 1957; instr. Chgo. City Colls., 1957-60; teaching asst. Northwestern U., 1960-61; prof. geography Chgo. State U., 1961—, chmn. dept. geography, 1974—; film cons. Ginn and Co., 1964-65, Altschuler Films, 1967-70; cons. OEO, 1966-67. Mem. Wilmette Human Relations Com., 1966-73; mem. mass transp. com. Chgo. Assn. Commerce and Industry, 1967-68; mem. adv. bd. Explore Your Am. Program, 1976—. Served to lt. (j.g.) USNR, 1943-46; PTO. Haas Research Fund grantee Northwestern U., 1964. Mem. Assn. Am. Geographers (mem. transp. com. 1968-72), Am. Profs. for Peace in Middle East, Nat. Council for Geog. Edn., Ill. Geog. Soc., Internat. Geog. Union, Geog. Soc. Chgo. (mem. excursions com. 1976—), Chgo. Hist. Soc., Chgo. Jewish Hist. Soc. (dir.), Sigma Xi. Author: The Chicago-Milwaukee Corridor: A Geographic Study of Intermetropolitan Coalescence, 1965; Chicago: Metropolis of the Mid-Continent, 1973, 2d edit., 1976; co-author: Chicago: Transformations of an Urban System, 1976; Urban Communities, 1977; Illinois: Land and Life in the Prairie State, 1977. Editor: The Chicago Met. Area: Selected Geographic Readings, 1970. Contbr. chpts. to A Modern City—Its Geography, 1970, Mass Transportation, 1967. Home: 3217 Hill Ln Wilmette IL 60091 Office: Chicago State U 95th and King Dr Chicago IL 60628

CUTLER, KENNETH LANCE, lawyer; b. Davenport, Iowa, Aug. 8, 1947; s. Ben M. and Shyrlee (Gibberman) C.; B.A., M.B.A., U. Chgo., 1970; J.D., U. Tex., 1973; m. Linda Susan Lefstein, June 22, 1969. Admitted to Ga. bar, 1973, Minn. bar, 1973; atty. law firm Powell,

Goldstein, Frazer & Murphy, Atlanta, 1973; atty. law firm Dorsey, Windhorst, Hannaford, Whitney & Halladay, Mpls., 1973—; adj. prof. Hamline U. Sch. Law; lectr. Minn. Practice Inst. Mem. U. Chgo. Twin Cities Alumni Schs. Com., 1974—. Mem. Am., Minn., Hennepin County bar assns., Alpha Delta Phi. Jewish. Clubs: Minneapolis Athletic, Calhoun Beach. Home: 1630 W 26th St Minneapolis MN 55405 Office: 2300 1st National Bank Bldg Minneapolis MN 55402

CUTLER, ROBERT PORTER, psychiatrist, psychoanalyst; b. Chgo., Nov. 13, 1917; s. Percival Nelson and Mary Asenath (Butler) C.; A.B., Princeton U., 1940; B.M., Northwestern U., 1943, M.D., 1944; certificate Chgo. Inst. Psychoanalysis, 1950; m. Patricia Ann Pickett, Apr. 26, 1950; children—Robert, David, Mary, Elliot. Intern, Cook County Hosp., Chgo., 1944-45, Northwestern U. Preble fellow, 1945-46; resident in psychiatry Ill. Neuropsychiat. Inst., Chgo., 1946-48; fellow Ill. Inst. Juvenile Research, Chgo., 1948-49; practice medicine specializing in psychiatry and psychoanalysis, Kenilworth, Ill., 1949—; asst. prof. psychiatry Northwestern U., 1950-73; asso. clin. prof. psychiatry U. Ill., 1973—. Pres. Kenilworth Caucus, 1968-69, Kenilworth Hist. Soc., 1968-70. Served with USPHS, 1954-56. Fellow Am. Psychiat. Assn.; mem. AMA, Ill., Chgo. med. socs., Ill. Psychiat. Soc., Chgo. Psychoanalytic Assn., Central Neuropsychiat. Assn. Republican. Presbyterian. Clubs: Mich. Shores (Wilmette, Ill.); Elm, Triangle (Princeton). Contbr. articles to sci. jours. Home and Office: 256 Woodstock Ave Kenilworth IL 60043

CUTSHAW, JOHN WILLIAM, JR., lawyer; b. Cambridge City, Ind., Jan. 5, 1932; s. John William and Marian (Butler) C.; B.S., Purdue U., 1953; J.D., Ind. U., 1960; m. Ann Kay Davis, Feb. 19, 1961; children—Linda Ann, Nancy Jane. Admitted to Ind. bar, 1960, since practiced in Cambridge City; sr. partner Cutshaw & Holtsclaw, Cambridge City, 1967-75; dir., atty. Peoples State Bank, Cambridge City; atty. Western Wayne Sch. Corp., Cambridge City, 1963—, Centerville-Abington Sch. Corp., Centerville, Ind., 1972—, Towns of Cambridge City, Dublin, Milton, East Germantown, Greens Fork, Ind., 1963—. Mem. local bd. SSS, 1971-75. Served with USNR, 1953-57. Mem. Am., Ind. State, Wayne County bar assns., Alpha Sigma Phi, Delta Theta Phi. Republican. Methodist. Mason, Kiwanian. Home: Rural Route 1 Wagner Rd Cambridge City IN 47327 Office: 15 N Foote St Cambridge City IN 47327

CUTSINGER, JOHN MARIS, lawyer; b. Indpls., Jan. 8, 1914; s. Floyd and Mary (Lacy) C.; student Franklin Coll., 1934-35; B.A., U. Va., 1937; LL.B., Ind. Law Sch., 1941; m. Martha Lee Smith, Sept. 30, 1942 (dec. May 25, 1967); 1 dau., Martha Elizabeth; m. 2d, Genevieve Clauson Van Liew, July 12, 1972. Admitted to Ind. bar, 1941; clk. Ind. Dept. Pub. Welfare, Indpls., 1936-41, atty., 1941-42; atty. OPA, 1946, VA Regional Office, Indpls., 1946-53; practice in Franklin, Ind., 1953—; mem. firm Cutsinger and Schafstall; pros. atty. 8th Jud. Circuit Ct. Ind., 1959-63. Dist. dir. Boy Scouts Am., 1954; treas. Johnson County Cancer Soc., 1955-65; mem. Johnson County Sesqui-Centennial Commn., 1971-73. Served with AUS, 1942-45. Recipient alumni citation Franklin Coll., 1966. Mem. Am., Ind., Johnson County (sec.-treas. 1954-55, v.p. 1961, pres. 1965) bar assns., Johnson County Hist. Soc. (pres. 1955-59, trustee 1959-67, 70—), Ind. Hist. Soc., Soc. Ind. Pioneers, S.A.R. (state treas. 1964), Huguenot Soc. Ind. (pres. 1958-60), Am. Legion, Am. Judicature Soc., Order Symposiarchs, Phi Delta Theta (trustee 1956-62), Sigma Delta Kappa. Presbyn. (elder). Mason (32 deg.); mem. Order Eastern Star (worthy patron 1959-60), Elk, Kiwanian (sec. 1954-56, trustee 1959-62, v.p. 1964, pres. 1965, lt. gov. 9th div. 1968). Clubs: 100; Hillview Country. Author: History of Bench and Bar in Johnson County, Ind. Home: 1410 E Jefferson St Franklin IN 46131 Office: 98 N Jackson St Franklin IN 46131

CUTTING, DAVID MARK, chem. co. exec.; b. Windsor, Ont., Can., Oct. 3, 1942; s. Donald John and Norma (Garwood) C.; B.S., No. Ill. U., 1968; m. Kathryn Louise Heavilin, Aug. 18, 1962; children—Jennifer Renee, Jeannene Marie, Joscelyn May. With Pierce Chem. Co., Rockford, Ill., 1968—, ops. mgr., 1973-74, v.p., 1974—. Bd. dirs. Rockford Christian Elementary Sch., 1975—; vol. Peace Corps, Costa Rica, 1964-66. Mem. Am. Chem. Soc. Republican. Baptist. Home: 2107 Melrose St Rockford IL 61105 Office: PO Box 117 Rockford IL 61105

CUTTS, JAMES HARRY, educator; b. Barnesly, Yorkshire, Eng., June 12, 1926; s. James Harry and Emma (Smith) C.; B.A., U. Sask., 1948; M.S., Dalhousie U., 1956; Ph.D., U. Western Ont., 1958; m. Margaret Edith Lynden, Sept. 22, 1952; children—Janet Lynn, James Harry. Sr. technician in hematology, Grey Nun's Hosp., Regina, and St. Paul's Hosp., Vancouver, 1948-53; demonstrator in pathology and provincial hematologist, Dalhousie U., Halifax, N.S., Can., 1953-56; research fellow Nat. Cancer Inst. Can., 1958-62; asst. prof. med. research U. Western Ont., London, Can., 1962-66, asso. prof. anatomy, 1966-68; prof. anatomy U. Mo., Columbia, 1968—, chmn. pro tem anatomy dept., 1973-74. Served with Canadian Army, 1943-45. Recipient SAMA Golden Apple award, 1972-73. Martin Ross Meml. fellow in cancer research, 1960-62. Mem. Canadian Assn. Anatomists, Canadian Soc. for Cell Biologists, Am. Assn. Anatomists, Am. Assn. for Cancer Research, Am. Soc. Zoologists, Anat. Soc. Ireland and Gt. Britain, N.Y. Acad. Scis. Author: Cell Separation, Methods in Hematology, 1970. Home: 1021 Lakeside Dr Columbia MO 65201

CYNAR, WALTER PETER, circuit judge; b. Hamtramck, Mich., Nov. 14, 1919; s. Andrew and Josephine (Bawol) C.; A.B., Western Mich. U., 1943; postgrad. Am. U., 1945, Georgetown U. Law, 1946; LL.B., U. Detroit, 1949; postgrad. Wayne State U., 1951; m. Toni Ezersky, Aug. 28, 1943; children—Christopher, David, Mark, Mary, John. Admitted to Mich. bar, 1949; practice as trial lawyer, Mich., 1949-66; circuit judge Macomb County, Mich., 1967—. Chmn. Warren (Mich.) Crime Commn., 1968-70; vice chmn. Big Bros. Macomb County, 1971-73; dist. chmn. Michigami dist. Boy Scouts Am., 1971-73, mem. exec. bd., asst. counsel Detroit Area Council, 1970; mem. Mich. 500th Kopernik Anniversary com.; corporate leader Boys' Club Met. Detroit; chmn. Boys Club Met. Detroit, Warren, 1969-72, recipient Friend of Boy award, 1974, Outstanding Vol. Leader award, 1975-76, Corporate Key award; mem. Macomb County Law Enforcement and Criminal Justice Planning Council; past mem. Clinton Twp. Civil Service Commn.; mem. Clinton Twp. Goodfellows, Warren Goodfellows, Polish Festival of Detroit Com., Warren Polka Boosters. Bd. dirs. Mt. Clemens (Mich.) Symphony, 1967-68, Warren Symphony Soc., Macomb County Hist. Soc.; chmn. bd. trustees St. Mary's Coll.; bd. regents Orchard Lake schs., Hamtramck High Alumni Varsity Club, Hamtramck High Hall of Honor. Served to lt. USNR, 1943-46. Recipient Silver Beaver award Boy Scouts Am.; St. George scouting emblem; Award of Merit, Michigami Scouting Dist.; Outstanding Citizen award Macomb Country, hon. alumnus Orchard Lake Schs. Alumni Assn.; Central Citizens Com. Polonia award. Mem. Mich. Judges Assn., Macomb County Bar (past dir.), State Bar Mich. (council negligence law sect.; treas. family law sect. council), Nat. Coll. State Judiciary, Mich. Bar Assns., Mich. Inter-Profl. Assn., Nat. Adv. Soc., Advs. Club, Amvets (life), Am. Legion, Polish Legion Am. Vets, Am. Polish Action Council, Mich. Acad., Kosciuszko Found., Alliance of Poles, Polish Falcons, Friends Polish Art, Polish Nat. Alliance, Polish Am. Congress, Rotarian, K.C., Eagle. Clubs: Am. Polish Century (life), Polish Century, Mich. Polish Century. Home: 32012 Aline St Warren MI 48093 Office: County Bldg Mt Clemens MI 48043

CYROL, EDMUND ALEXANDER, mgmt. cons., indsl. engr., labor arbitrator; b. Detroit, Oct. 20, 1915; s. Thomas and Marie Teresa (Bach) C.; B.S. in Mech. Engring., U. Mich., 1939; m. Alyce Tarlo, July 4, 1942. Indsl. engr., Murray Corp. of Am., Detroit, 1939-41; tool engr. Packard Motor Car Co., Detroit, 1941-42; pres. of E.A. Cyrol & Co., mgmt. consultants, Chgo., 1950—; exec. reservist Bus. and Defense Services Adminstrn., U.S. Dept. of Commerce, 1964-74; labor arbitrator Weyenberg Shoe Co., Milw., 1976—, Boot & Shoe Workers Union, 1976—, Fed. Mediation and Conciliation Service, Am. Arbitration Assn.; dir. Bushnell Ill. Tank Co., 1975—, Hetrzberg-New Method, Inc., 1976—; pres. Computerized Standards, Inc., Chgo., 1972—; chmn. Nat. Time & Motion Study and Mgmt. Clinic, 1950-54; tchr. mathematics shop theory various evening schs., Detroit, 1939-42. Registered profl. engr., Ill. Mem. Soc. of Indsl. Engrs., Midwest Indsl. Mgmt. Assn. Club: Illinois Athletic. Author: Standard Data for Turret Lathes and Hand Screw Machines, 1952; contbr. numerous articles on indsl. engring. to profl. and tech. jours. Home: 1444 Sequoia Trail Glenview IL 60025 Office: 120 S LaSalle St Chicago IL 60603

CZAPLICKI, ROMAN, chiropractic physician; b. Grudziadz, Poland, Aug. 12, 1931; s. Antoni Konstanty and Dominika (Lojewski) C.; came to U.S., 1945; D.Chiropractic, Nat. Coll. Chiropractic, 1960; Diploma in Acupuncture Medicine, Nat. Chinese Taiee Acupuncture Coll., 1971; asso. degree Chinese medicine, Hon Hing Inst. Chinese Medicine, Hong Kong, 1971; diploma in osteopathy, New South Wales Osteopathic Coll., Sydney, Australia, 1977; certified chiropractic acupuncturist, Nat. Coll. Chiropractic, Chgo., 1977; m. Marrieta Surowka, Mar. 17, 1969; 1 dau., Tatiana Dominika. Pvt. practice chiropractic Chgo., 1960-68, Sydney, Australia, 1968-71, Warren, Mich., 1972—; instr. Chinese medicine Am. Coll. Chiropractic Internists, Detroit, 1972—. Served with AUS, 1950-52. Fellow Am. Coll. Chiropractic Internists; mem. Am., Mich. (dir. dist. 1, bd. appeals peer review, chmn. com. acupuncture research) chiropractic assns., Am. Assn. Chiropractic Medicine. Author: Acupuncture—5000 Years of Healing Art, 1975. Office: 30925 Schoenherr St Warren MI 48093

CZARNECKI, GENEVIEVE ANN, city ofcl.; b. Detroit, Feb. 20, 1932; d. Edward Francis and Mary Ann (Galazka) Czarnecki; B.S. in Nursing, Wayne State U., 1963, M.S. in Nursing, 1965, postgrad., 1972. Mem. staff, supr. St. Joseph Mercy Hosp., Detroit, 1953-65; instr. Henry Ford Community Coll., Dearborn, Mich., 1965-73; chmn. Region 2 Detroit Bd. Edn., 1970-75, vice chmn. central region Detroit Bd. Edn., 1973—; cons. Henry Ford Hosp., Detroit, 1969-71; adviser Detroit dist. Student Nurse Assn. Trustee New Detroit Inc., 1972-76. Recipient Outstanding Service to Polish Community award Polish Am. Congress. Mem. Mich. (instr. 1967, mem. adv. com. on refresher courses for nurses), Detroit (v.p., mem. edn. com.) nurses assns., Nat. League for Nursing, Wayne State U. Alumni Assn., Wayne State U. Coll. Nursing Alumni Assn., Mich. Assn. Sch. Bds., Am. Fedn. Tchrs., Detroit Women Sch. Adminstrs., Am. Assn. Sch. Adminstrs., AAUP, Internat. Platform Assn. Roman Catholic. Author: (with others) (audio-visual program) Observations of Mother in Labor and Delivery. Home: 8106 Dayton St Detroit MI 48210 Office: 5101 Evergreen Dearborn MI 48128

CZERWINSKI, JOHN ROBERT, educator; b. Chgo., July 30, 1937; s. John Casimir and Nanette Silvia (Wohlers) C.; B.M.E., De Paul U., 1960; M.S. in Ednl. Adminstrn., No. Ill. U., 1974; m. Maggie Elaine Sanders, July 30, 1966; children—John Robert II, Peter Paul. Tchr., Oscar Meyer Elementary Sch., Chgo., 1961-62, Senn High Sch., Chgo., 1962-63; tchr. Ill. Youth Center, St. Charles, Ill., 1963—, editor Hour Glass, 1970—. Served as 2d lt. AUS, 1960-61; now maj. Res. Law Enforcement Ednl. Program grantee, 1967-74. Mem. Res. Officers Assn., Beta Pi Mu. Roman Catholic. Office: Box 122 St Charles IL 60174

DABAGIA, LEE WARREN, lawyer; b. Michigan City, Ind., Mar. 22, 1937; s. George M. and Mary (Eaise) D.; B.A. cum laude, Beloit Coll., 1959; postgrad. N.Y. U., 1959; J.D., Ind. U., 1962; m. Dana Polomcak, July 31, 1967; children—Lee Warren, Lincoln Dana. Admitted to Ind. bar, 1962, since practiced in Michigan City; law clk. U.S. Dist. Ct., Hammond, Ind., 1962-64; lectr. bus. law Ind. U., Gary, 1963-67; mem. firm Winski & Dabagia, 1964-71, Sweeney, Fox, Sweeney, Winski & Dabagia, 1971—; chief dep. pros. atty., LaPorte County, Ind., 1965-70; dir. Citizens Bank, Michigan City, Ind., Bus. Investments, Inc., Dwyer Products Co., Stanley Knight Corp. Bd. dirs. Walters Hosp. Found., Inc., Jr. Achievement, Inc.; trustee, pres. Islamic Center of Michigan City, 1973—. Served with USMCR, 1962-68. Recipient Distinguished Service award Michigan City Jr. C. of C., 1967. Mem. Am., Ind., Michigan City, LaPorte County bar assns., Michigan City C. of C. (dir. 1975—). Elk. Club: Pottawattomie Golf Course and Country (dir., sec. bd. 1972—, v.p. 1974). Home: 2211 Oriole Trail Michigan City IN 46360 Office: 709 Franklin Sq Michigan City IN 46360

DABNEY, JACK LEE, psychologist; b. Dubuque, Iowa, Jan. 27, 1929; s. Claude Orvin and Naomi Helen (Stoker) D.; B.S., U. Nebr., 1951, M.A., 1957; m. Lucille Marie Clarence, June 7, 1952. Psychologist, Douglas County Hosp., Omaha, 1955—, mental health coordinator, 1961-71, supr. Hosp. Annex Alcoholism Treatment Program, 1956-57. Served with AUS, 1953-55. Mem. Am. (asso.), Nebr. (affiliate) psychol. assns. Home: 7072 Spencer St Omaha NE 68104 Office: 4102 Woolworth Ave Omaha NE 68105

DACHMAN, ROBERT, found. exec.; b. Chgo., Aug. 22, 1926; s. Harry Louis and Rose (Schuffler) D.; student U. Ill.; B.A., Roosevelt U., 1949; m. Jeanne Marie Marantz, Aug. 21, 1961; 1 son, Alan Jay. Staff, Maj. Gen. Julius Klein, 1949-50; area dir. City of Hope, 1950-60; dir. pub. relations and devel. Chgo. Med. Sch., 1960-62; exec. dir. Little City Found., Chgo., 1962—. Trustee Orchard Mental Health Center, Better Boys Found. Served with Armed Forces. Mem. 52 Assn. Club: Variety of Ill. (v.p.), B'nai B'rith. Home: 2305 Greenwood St Northbrook IL 60062 Office: 625 N Michigan Ave Chicago IL 60601

DACIO, SOCORRO LARDIZABAL, ret. educator; b. Tagudin, Ilocos Sur, Philippines, Sept. 23, 1907; s. Juan Dacio and Martina Lardizabal; came to U.S., 1966, naturalized, 1972; B.S. Edn., U. Philippines, 1930; M.A., Loyola U., Manila, Philippines, 1958; LL.B., Francisco Law Sch. (Philippines), 1960. Prin., Lubao High Sch., Pampanga, Philippines, 1930-33; tchr. Tagudin St. Augustine's High Sch., Philippines, 1933-46; tchr. Francisco Coll., Manila, 1950-60; instr., head edn. dept. Columban Coll., Olongapo City, Zambales, Philippines, 1960-66; instr. English, world lit., head. English dept. Emmetsburg (Iowa) Community Coll., 1967-70; reading, lang. arts tchr. Donoghue Pub. Sch., Chgo., 1970-77. English Program Devel. Act grantee to Simpson Coll., Indianola, Iowa, 1967, U. Chgo., 1968, Kans. State U., 1969, U. W. Fla., 1970. Mem. Chgo. Tchrs. Union, AAUW, Community Coll. English Assn., Iowa State Ednl. Assn., Modern Lang. Assn. Author: Rowena (a musical drama), 1938; Nabay-bay-an (play), 1939; The Horrors of the Japanese War in the Philippines (satire), 1946; Is the Noli Me Tangere a Novel?, 1958; Influence Peddling-A Crime Punishable By Law, 1960. Home: 2970 N Lake Shore Dr Apt 5E Chicago IL 60657 also Tagudin ILocos Sur Philippines

DAEMMRICH, HORST SIGMUND, educator; b. Pausa, Germany, Jan. 5, 1930; s. Arthur M. and Gertrud A. (Orlamünde) D.; A.B. (C. Allen Harlan scholar), Wayne State U., 1958, M.A., 1959; Ph.D. (Petersen Kochs fellow, Goethe fellow), U. Chgo., 1964; m. Ingrid H. Guenther, June 10, 1962; children—JoAnn, Arthur. Instr., U. Chgo., 1961-62; asst. prof. Germanic langs. and lits. Wayne State U., Detroit, 1962-66, asso. prof., 1967-70, prof., 1971—; resident dir. Jr. Year Inst. at U. Freiburg (Germany), 1972-73. Mem. Am. Soc. Aesthetics, Am. Lessing Soc., Am. Assn. Tchrs. German (mem. commn. on higher edn. 1974—), Modern Lang. Assn. Am. (sec. and chmn. 19th century lit. 1972-73), Midwest Modern Lang. Assn. (sec. and chmn. modern Germanic lit. 1966-67). Author: The Shattered Self, 1973; Literaturkritik in Theorie und Praxis, 1974. Author (with Diether Haenicke), editor: The Challenge of German Literature, 1971. Contbr. articles to profl. jours. Home: 14531 Stahelin Blvd Detroit MI 48223 Office: Dept Romance and Germanic Langs Wayne State U Detroit MI 48202

DAESCHNER, RICHARD WILBUR, food co. exec.; b. Preston, Nebr., July 5, 1917; s. Richard T. and Elma (Beckenhauer) D.; B.S. in Edn., Kans. State Tchrs. Coll., 1937; J.D., Washburn U., 1941; m. Prudence Armstrong, June 6, 1942; children—Richard, Rebecca, Martha. Admitted to Kans. bar, 1941; spl. agt. FBI, Washington, Boston, N.Y.C., Chgo., 1941-48; with employee relations dept. Beatrice Foods Co., Chgo., 1948—, dir. employee relations, 1963-68, dir. personnel and indsl. relations, asst. sec., 1968-73, asst. v.p., 1973—. Bd. dirs. Chgo. Better Bus. Bur. Mem. Bar Assn. Kans., Chgo. Bar Assn., Grocery Mfrs. Assn., Ill. C. of C., Chgo. Assn. Commerce and Industry, Phi Delta Theta. Republican. Presbyn. (trustee). Elk. Clubs: Chicago Executives, Inverness Golf. Home: 1700 Appleby Rd Inverness Palatine IL 60067 Office: 120 S LaSalle St Chicago IL 60603

DAGEN, RAYMOND DAVID, social service adminstr.; b. Troy, N.Y., June 24, 1942; s. Elmer F. and Gertrude L. (Stockwell) D.; student various univs.; m. Norma May Noble, Feb. 1, 1964; children—Daniel Ray, Timothy Ray, Bethany Rae. Accountant, Sunoco Oil Co., Boston, 1963-64; student officers tng. sch. Salvation Army, N.Y.C., 1964-66, corps officer, 1966-71, adult rehab. officer, 1971-73, dir. adult rehab. center, 1973—. Participant mem. Downtown Area Ch. Council, 1976—; mem. Columbus Pub. Inebriate Task Force, 1973—; coordinator regional alcoholism programs, Columbus, 1973—; bd. dirs. Columbus Area Council on Alcoholism, Ohio Assn. Alcoholism Programs. Served with USNR, 1960-63. Mem. Holiness Soc., Regional Assn. Alcoholism Workers. Clubs: Kiwanis, Masons (32 deg.). Home: 5453 Redwood Rd Columbus OH 43229 Office: 570 S Front St Columbus OH 43215

DAHL, DAVID SELMER, neurologist, educator; b. Albert Lea, Minn., Mar. 17, 1936; s. Selmer J. and Dorothy (Lee) D.; B.A., St. Olaf Coll., 1958; M.S., State U. Iowa, 1961, M.D., 1963; m. Janet Helen Orr, June 15, 1963; children—Sarah, Elizabeth, Christopher. Intern, Bellevue Med. Center, N.Y.C., 1963-64; resident in neurology U. Hosps., Iowa City, 1964-66; surgeon USPHS, Bethesda, Md., 1966-68; asst. prof. neurology U. Wis., Madison, 1968-74; asso. prof. clin. neurology, chief sect. neurology Mt. Sinai Med. Center, Milw., 1974—. Diplomate Am. Bd. Neurology. Mem. Muscular Dystrophy Assn. Am. (grantee 1968), Sigma Xi, Alpha Omega Alpha. Democrat. Mem. United Ch. of Christ. Contbr. articles on neuromuscular diseases to sci. jours. Home: 2428 E Beverly Rd Shorewood WI 53211 Office: 950 N 12th St Milwaukee WI 53201

DAHL, HARRY WALDEMAR, lawyer; b. Des Moines, Aug. 7, 1927; s. Harry Waldemar and Helen Gerda (Anderson) D.; B.A., U. Iowa, 1950; J.D., Drake U., 1955; m. Bonnie Sorensen, June 14, 1952; children—Harry Waldemar, Lisabeth, Christina. Admitted to Iowa bar, 1955, Fla. bar, 1970; practiced in Des Moines, 1955-59, 70—, Miami, Fla., 1972—; mem. firm Steward & Crouch, Des Moines, 1955-59; Iowa dep. indsl. commr., Des Moines, 1959-62, commr. 1962-71; mem. Dahl law firm, Des Moines, 1970—; mem. firm Underwood, Gillis and Karcher, Miami, 1972—; adj. prof. law Drake U., 1972—. Exec. dir. Internat. Assn. Indsl. Accident Bds. and Commns., 1972-77, dean Coll. Workmen's Compensation, 1972-76; pres. Workers' Compensation Studies, Inc., 1974—, Hewitt, Coleman & Assos. Iowa, Inc., 1975—; mem. adv. com. Second Injury Fund, Fla. Indsl. Relations Commn. Served with USNR, 1945-46. Recipient Adminstrs. award Internat. Assn. Indsl. Accident Bds. and Commns., 1967. Mem. Assn. Trial Lawyers Am. (chmn. workers compensation sect. 1974-75), Am. (chmn. workers compensation com. 1976—), Iowa bar assns., Fla. Bar, Am. Soc. Law and Medicine (mem. council 1975—), East High Alumni Assn. (pres. 1975-76), Order of Coif. Methodist. Mason (Shriner). Club: Sertoma (chmn. bd. 1974-75). Author: Iowa Law on Workmen's Compensation, 1975; contbr. articles to legal jours. Editor ABC Newsletter, 1964-77. Home: 3005 Sylvania Dr Des Moines IA 50365 Office: 5600 Grand Ave Des Moines IA 50312

DAHL, IRWIN ALPHY, coll. adminstr.; b. Mpls., Aug. 13, 1912; s. Ole Ingebretsen and Inga Marie (Svengaard) D.; B.S., U. Minn., 1935, M.A., 1939; grad. Command and Gen. Staff Coll., 1953; m. Marion Catherine Tuttle, June 7, 1939; 1 dau., Mary Katheryn. Instr., U. Minn., 1935-36; tchr. Becker (Minn.) High Sch., 1936-39; prin. Aitkin (Minn.) High Sch., 1939-41; commd. 1st lt. U.S. Army, 1941, advanced through grades to lt. col. 1950; instr. Inf. Sch., Ft. Benning, Ga., 1941-43; officer Inf., ETO, 1943-45; exchange staff officer Canadian Army Sch. Center, Camp Borden, Ont., 1947-49; assigned Q.M. Sch., Ft. Lee, Va., 1949-50; battalion comdr., Korea, 1950-52; exec. officer U.S. Graves Registration Service, Japan, 1952-53; dir. Office Procurement Policy Office of Q.M. Gen., Washington, 1954-57; student Logistics Mgmt. Inst., 1957; bn. comdr., ETO, 1957-60; asst. comdt. Armed Forces Food and Container Inst., Chgo., 1960-62; logistics officer U.S. Army Support Group, Vietnam, 1962-63; comdg. officer U.S. Army Subsistence Center, Chgo., 1963-65; ret., 1965; dept. mgr. Bank of Am., San Francisco, 1945-47; instr. Thornton Community Coll., 1965-68, dir. instl. resources and devel., 1968—. Decorated Bronze Star medal with 2 oak leaf clusters. Mem. U. Minn. "M" Club, Ret. Officers Assn., Alpha Sigma Pi, Phi Delta Kappa. Roman Catholic. Home: 418 Springfield St Park Forest IL 60466 Office: Thornton Community Coll South Holland IL 60473

DAHL, IVAN JUSTIN KEITH, univ. adminstr.; b. Milton, N.D., Aug. 25, 1930; s. Ivan and Alberta Mae (Morrison) D.; B.S., State Coll., Mayville, N.D., 1957; M.S., Ind. U., 1963; Ph.D., U. N.D., 1968; postdoctoral study Stanford, 1970; m. Mary Louise Kiewel, June 28, 1968; children—Elizabeth Claire, Kathryn Michele. Prin., LaKota (N.D.) High Sch., 1956-60, Meeteetse (Wyo.) High Sch., 1960-62; supt. Cooperstown (N.D.) Pub. Schs., 1963-67; asst. prof. edn. Ball State U., Muncie, Ind., 1968-69; prof. edn. U. N.D., Grand Forks, 1969-72, asso. dean Coll. Edn., 1972—. Evaluator, North Central Assn., Nat. Council Accreditation Tchr. Edn.; cons. U.S. Office Edn., N.D. Dept. Pub. Instrn. U.S. Office of Edn. grantee, 1970-71. Mem. Am. Assn. Colls. Tchr. Edn. (evaluator), N.E.A., Assn. Supervision and Curriculum Devel. (dir.), Phi Delta Kappa, (chpt. pres. 1973—). Presbyn. Elk, Kiwanian. Contbr. articles to profl. jours. Address: 3622 10th Av North Grand Forks ND 58201

DAHLBERG, CARL JULIUS, lumber co. exec.; b. Effie, Minn., Dec. 15, 1905; s. John Carl and Hanna Christine (Johnson) D.; student pub. schs.; m. Huldah Ann Sandquist, Dec. 25, 1924; children—Waldo, Delyane (Mrs. Truman Schoaf), Marlene (Mrs. Nathan Petersen), Karen (Mrs. Herb Schenk). Self employed in logging, lumbering, 1924-77; founder Dahlberg & Son, Effie, 1940—; inc. No. Constrn. Co. Keewatin, Minn., 1946-49; founder Keewatin Sawmill Co., 1949, pres., 1949—; founder Dahlberg Timber Co., Keewatin, 1963, pres., 1963—; dir. Security State Bank, Hibbing, Minn., 1968-77. Mayor Effie, Minn., 1940-54. Mem. Timber Producers Assn., (pres. 1955-57, dir. 1937-77), Northern Hardwood & Pine Assn. (dir. 1959-75). Mason (Shriner, Jester), Elk. Club: Algonquin (Hibbing, Minn.). Home: 203 Access Dr Hibbing MN 55746 also 5201 E Butte Mesa AZ Office: Keewatin MN 55753

DAHLJELM, HARVEY DOUGLAS, air force officer; b. Highland Park, Mich., Feb. 12, 1946; s. Irving LeRoy and Ellen Ann (Mandel) D.; B.S. in Elec. Engring., Mich. State U., 1968; postgrad. No. Mich. U., 1972-75, Mich. Technol. U., 1974-75; M.S. in Elec. Engring., Air Force Inst. Tech., 1976. Commd. 2d lt. USAF, 1968, advanced through grades to capt., 1971; various assignments including electronic warfare officer spl. ops. squadron Ubon RTAF, Thailand, 1971-72, 644th Bombardment Squadron, Sawyer AFB, Mich., 1972-75; assigned Air Force Inst. Tech., Wright-Patterson AFB, Ohio, 1975-76, devel. engr. aero. systems div. Air Force Systems Command, 1976—; with Giant Strike Task Force Hdqrs., Marham AFB, Eng., 1973, 43d Strategic Wing Anderson AFB, Guam, 1973, 307th Strategic Wing U-Tapao RTAF, Thailand, 1973; grad. Naval War Coll., 1973, Indsl. Coll. Armed Forces, 1973. Chief cons. Mich. State U. Computer Lab., 1965-68. Asst. dist. commr. Piere Marquette Boy Scouts Am., 1972-75. Decorated D.F.C. (2), Air medals (12); recipient award Detroit Free Press, 1968. Mem. I.E.E.E. (pres. Mich. State U. chpt. 1968, pres. Air Force Inst. Tech. chpt. 1975-76, Outstanding Leadership and Service award 1977), Assn. Computing Machinery (pres. Mich. State U. chpt. 1967), Nat., Mich. socs. profl. engrs., Soc. Am. Mil. Engrs., A.A.A.S., Armed Forces Communication and Electronics Assn., Nat. Eagle Assn., Assn. Old Crows (Snow Crows pres. 1972-74, chmn. bd. 1974-75), Delta Sigma Phi, Alpha Pi. Club: Mich. State University Alumni (East Lansing, Mich.). Home: 341 Lexington Ave East Lansing MI 48823 Office: Box 2058 Wright-Patterson AFB OH 45433

DAHLKE, NORBERT ARNOLD, veterinary feeder co. exec.; b. Fond Du Lac, Wis., Sept. 24, 1923; s. Arnold Carl and Bernice Mae (Dilts) D.; educated U. Wis., 1942-43, Iowa State U., 1943-46; m. Louise Mary Stuckert, Sept. 7, 1946; children—Louis Mary Stucket, Sept. 7, 1946; children—Charles Norbert, Sandra Rita, Cynthia Nita. Gen. practice veterinary medicine, Waupaca, Wis., 1946-63; production mgr., Waupaca br., Wis. Feeder Pig Mktg. Co-op., Francis Creek, Wis., 1963-69, asst. mgr., 1969, gen. mgr., 1969—; v.p. White River Power Co. Dir. Waupaca Riverside Community Hosp.; pres. Coop. outreach objective Politics, 1976. Served with AUS, 1943-44. Mem. Nat. Feeder Pig Dealers Assn. (pres. 1976-77), Wis.-Valley Vet. Assn. (past pres.), Wis., Am., N.E. Wis. vet. med. assns., Wis. Swine Health Council. Clubs: Lions, Elks. Home: 858 N 8th St Manitowoc WI 54220 Office: 200 Norwood Dr Francis Creek WI 54214

DAHN, CARL JAMES, aero. engr.; b. Chgo., June 22, 1936; s. Carl E. and Genevieve (Bardon) D.; B.S. in Aero. Engring., U. Minn., 1959; m. Rose E. Kucenski, May 25, 1974. Rocket propulsion devel. engr. Aerojet Gen. Corp., Azusa, Calif., 1959-61, propulsion and explosives devel. engr., 1961-62; chief engr. Omega Ordanace Co., Azusa, 1961-62; propulsion and explosives specialist Honeywell, Inc., Mpls., 1964-69; system safety research engr. IIT Research Inst. Systems Hazard Analysis, Chgo., 1969-74; hazards engring. specialist Polytechnic, Inc., Chgo., 1974-77; pres. Safety Cons. Engrs., Inc., Rosemont, Ill., 1977—; instr. explosives, guns and ballistics; cons. in same field. Asst. scout master Mpls. St. Paul council Boy Scouts Am., 1962; area dir. Parents Without Partners, 1973; ward chmn. Republican party, 1964; ward chmn. Democratic party, 1973. Mem. Am. Soc. Safety Engrs., Am. Soc. Test Methods (com. sec.), System Safety Soc., Soc. Explosives Engrs., Nat. Soc. Profl. Engrs. Democrat. Methodist and Roman Catholic. Club: N.W. Divorced Catholic Group. Researcher, patentee in explosives field. Home: 6118 W Melrose St Chicago IL 60634 Office: 5240 Pearl St Rosemont IL 60018

DAI, DAVID WEI-YANG, educator; b. China, Apr. 5, 1942; s. Jun-Dei and Lang-In (Yaug) D.; came to U.S., 1972; B.A., Nat. Taiwan Normal U., 1966; M.A., Tam Kang Coll. Arts and Scis., 1972; M.A. in Bibl. Lit., Olivet Nazarene Coll., 1974, M.A. in Secondary Edn., 1975; postgrad. U. Ill., 1975; m. Meme F. Wang, Jan. 18, 1971; 1 dau., Amy. Tchr. English, Taipei First Girls' High Sch., 1966-72; chmn. English tchrs. Tam-Kang Coll., 1968-72; instr. Tamsui Coll., 1970-72; prof. Chinese history, oriental philosophy, folk lit. Olivet Nazarene Coll., Kankakee, Ill., after 1972—, librarian, lab. asst., 1972-73; now faculty U. Ill., Urbana. Served with M.P., AUS, 1967-68. Mem. Kappa Delta Pi, Sigma Tau Delta. Contbr. articles to newspapers and mags. Translator: Caligula (Camus), 1970. Home: 1115 W Green St 218 Urbana IL 61801 Office: 2070 Fgn Langs Urbana IL 61801

DAILY, BRUCE EDWARD, hosp. lab. adminstr.; b. Columbus, Ohio, Dec. 6, 1928; s. Ezra Riley and Carol Leona (Sheridan) D.; B.S. in Microbiology, Ohio State U., 1958; m. Julianne Mary Drugan, May 2, 1970; stepchildren—Cynthia Brock (Mrs. William Mackin), Susan Brock, Sally Brock. Bacteriologist, Children's Hosp., Columbus, 1952-54; co-owner, pres. Dayfield Labs., Columbus, 1954-72; adminstrv. lab. dir. Grady Meml. Hosp., Delaware, Ohio, 1972—; cons. in field. Mem. adv. com. Columbus Tech. Inst., 1969—. Served with AUS, 1947-48, 50-52. Mem. Am. Soc. Microbiology, South Central Assn. Clin. Microbiologists, Ohio Assn. Bioanalytical Lab. Dirs. (pres. 1966-68). Mason, Elk. Researcher use of acridine dyes in detection of pathogenic E. Coli. Home: 608 Heritage Blvd Delaware OH 43015 Office: 561 Central Ave Delaware OH 43015

DAILY, EUGENE JOSEPH, civil engr.; b. Rolla, Mo., Aug. 18, 1913; s. John J. and Anne Helen (Hanefin) D.; B.S., U. Mo., 1936; M.S., U. Ill., 1951; m. Jewell Norris, May 1, 1937; children—Carolyn J., Kathleen (Mrs. Larry Wachowiak), John E. Civil engr. constrn., mil. cons., 1936-46; prof. civil engring., U. Ill., 1946-56; now pres. Daily & Assos., Engrs., Inc., Champaign, Ill. Served with USNR, 1943-46. Mem. Cons. Engring. Council Ill. (dir. 1971-74, sec. 1974, v.p. 1975, pres. 1977), Am. Pub. Works Assn. (dir. 1970-73), ASCE (pres. sect. 1973), Acad. Civil Engrs., Nat. Soc. Profl. Engrs., Cons. Engr. Council U.S., Am. Ry. Eng. Assn., Am. Roadbuilders Assn. K.C. Club: Champaign (Ill.) Country. Home: 1114 Lincolnshire St Champaign IL 61820 Office: 816 Dennison Dr Champaign IL 61820

DAISLEY, EDWIN TRAYES, JR., mortgage banker; b. Indpls., Aug. 11, 1928; s. Edwin Trayes and Frankie Mae (Nichols) D.; B.A., U. Iowa, 1950; postgrad. Northwestern U., 1955, 57, 58, Mich. State U., 1961, 62, 68; certificate in real estate U. Omaha, 1964; m. Zaida Virginia Wells, Oct. 9, 1954; children—Dana W., Rebecca C., Edwin T., III, Robert C. Sales trainee Continental Can Co., Chgo., 1950-53; v.p. Don J. Murray Co., Omaha, 1953—. Served with AUS, 1950-52. Mem. Nebr. Mortgage Bankers Assn., Mortgage Bankers Assn. Am., Met. Omaha Builders Assn. (dir. 1964-77, treas. 1970-73, life dir.), Nebr. State Home Builders Assn., Nat. Assn. Home Builders, Omaha Bd. Realtors, Neb. Realtors Assn., Nat. Assn. Realtors, Soc. Residential Appraisers (pres. 1962-63), Omaha Assn. Ins. Agts., Rho Epsilon. Episcopalian. (vestry 1959-61, 75-77, treas. 1960-61). Club: Happy Hollow Country (Omaha). Home: 1121 S 79th St Omaha NE 68124 Office: 10407 Devonshire Circle Omaha NE 68114

DAKSHINAMURTHI, ARUMUGHAM, physician; b. Siraimeettam Palayam, India, Nov. 20, 1939; s. S.R. Arumugham and Sellammal Gounder; M.B.B.S., Stanley Med. Coll. Madras U., 1964, D.C.H., 1966; m. Valliammal Palanisamy, Sept. 8, 1967; children—Uma, Anandamurugan, Arathi. Asst. surgeon Madras Govt. Hosps., 1966-69; intern, Worcester (Mass.) City Hosp., 1969-70; resident in pediatrics St. Vincent Hosp., Worcester, 1970-72; fellow in neonatology, Wesson Womens Hosp. Springfield, Mass., 1972-73; practice medicine specializing in pediatrics, Ashland, Ohio, 1974—; mem. staff Samaritan Hosp. Mem. Ashland County Bd. Mental Health Retardation, 1977—. Diplomate Am. Bd. Pediatrics. Mem. Ashland County, Ohio med. assns. Home: 1005 Thomas Dr Ashland OH 44805 Office: 350 Hillcrest Dr Ashland OH 44805

DALE, RICHARD, educator; b. Columbus, Ohio, Oct. 22, 1932; s. Edgar and Elizabeth Cullen (Kirchner) D.; m. Doris Mae Cruger, Aug. 18, 1967; A.B., Bowdoin Coll., 1954; postgrad. Columbia Coll. Physicians and Surgeons, 1954-55; M.A., Ohio State U., 1957; M.A., Princeton U., 1961, Ph.D., 1962. Instr. govt. U. N.H., 1962-63; asst. prof. polit. sci. No. Ill. U., 1963-66; adj. prof. polit. Sci. So. Ill. U., Carbondale, 1966-67, asst. prof., 1967-71, asso. prof., 1971—; mem. council and exec. com. S.African Inst. Race Relations, 1974-75; mem. adv. bd. Univ. Press Am., 1976—. Served with U.S. Army, 1957-59. Mem. Am., Midwest polit. sci. assns., Internat. Studies Assn., Inter-Univ. Seminar on Armed Forces and Soc., Group for Study of Nationalism, African Studies Assn., Western Assn. Africanists, Internat. African Inst. (London), Royal African Soc. (London), Botswana Soc., S.W. Africa Sci. Soc., Polit. Sci. Assn. S.Africa, S.African Mil. History Soc., Delta Tau Delta. Nat. Def. Fgn. Lang. fellow in Afrikaans, U. Calif., Los Angeles, summer 1964; Am. Philos. Soc. travel grantee, summer 1970. Author: Botswana and Its Southern Neighbor: The Patterns of Linkage and Options in Statecraft, 1970; The Racial Component of Botswana's Foreign Policy, 1971; co-editor, contbr. to Southern Africa in Perspective: Essays in Regional Politics, 1972; contbr. articles to profl. jours. Home: Union Hill Route 4 Carbondale IL 62901

D'ALEXANDER, WILLIAM JOSEPH, publisher; b. Cleve., Dec. 16, 1927; s. Silvio and Rose Margret DePhillips D'A.; B.S. in Bus. Adminstrn., Kent (Ohio) State U., 1951; m. Mary Jo Comella, Apr. 15, 1961; children—William, Michael, James, Robert. Asst. advt. mgr. Gen. Electric Supply Corp., Cleve., 1951-52; advt. mgr. No. Ohio Appliance Corp., Cleve., 1952-53; account exec. Fuller, Smith and Ross Advt. Agy., Cleve., 1953-55; pub. Penton Pub. Co., Cleve., 1955-73; pres. Delta Communications Inc., Cleve., 1973—. Served with AUS, 1947-48. Mem. T-F Club Chgo. (pres. 1966-67), Alpha Tau Omega (pres. 1950). Home: 23585 Duffield Rd Shaker Heights OH 44122 Office: 1120 Chester Ave Cleveland OH 44114

DALGLEISH, CHARLES HAULDEN, JR., retail automobile exec.; b. Detroit, June 14, 1925; s. Charles Haulden and Lillian (Carkner) D.; B.Sc., U. Mich., 1947; postgrad. Wayne U., 1948; m. Mary Jane Gilbert, Aug. 15, 1953; children—Sara Jane, Charles, Elizabeth. Pres. Charles Dalgleish Cadillac, Inc., Detroit, 1965—; pres. Dalgleish Leasing Corp., Detroit, 1963—. Served with USNR, 1943-45. Mason. Clubs: Athletic (Detroit); Orchard Lake Country. Home: 4885 N Harsdale Rd Bloomfield Hills MI 48013 Office: 6160 Cass Ave Detroit MI 48202

DALLARA, ROBERT FRED, JR., psychologist; b. Greensburg, Pa., June 1, 1949; s. Robert Fred and Rose Marie (Boccabella) D.; B.S., Xavier U., 1971, M.A., 1973, postgrad., 1973—; m. Jacqueline Sue Yeskey, June 14, 1975. Intern psychologist Longview State Hosp., Cin., 1972-73; psychologist Portage Path Community Mental Health Center, Akron, Ohio, 1974-75; pvt. practice psychology, also doctoral asst. Akron U., 1975-76; pvt. practice psychology, Cuyahoga Falls, Ohio, 1975—; v.p., sec. D. V. Ramani, M.D. and Assos., Inc., Cuyahoga Falls, Ohio, 1977—; cons. Support, Inc. Mem. Inst. for Advanced Study in Rational Psychotherapy, Inst. for Rational Living, Am. Personnel and Guidance Assn., Am. Coll. Personnel Assn. Roman Catholic. Lodge: Moose. Home: 1515 Brittain Circle Apt 6 Akron OH 44310 Office: 1350 Portage Trail Cuyahoga Falls OH 44222

DALLIANIS, HARRY THOMAS, real estate co. exec.; b. Tripolis, Greece, Dec. 13, 1934; s. Thomas William and Irene (Manzagriotakis) D. (parents Am. citizens); B.S., Loyola U., Chgo., 1957; m. Jean Demas, Dec. 8, 1962; children—Irene Lorraine, Thomas Harry. With Ideal Realty Co., Chgo., 1963—, pres., 1965—. Certified residential broker. Mem. Nat. Assn. Realtors, Nat. Mktg. Realtors Inst., Real Estate Securities and Syndication Inst., Nat., Ill. assns. realtors, Chgo. Real Estate Bd. (bd. govs. 1969-70), North Suburban Real Estate Bd. (dir. 1974-76, chmn. zoning 1975-76), Ind. Fee Appraisers, Am. Hellenic Progressive Assn. Greek Orthodox. Clubs: Lincolnwood Men's, St. Andrews (dir. 1969-75). Office: Ideal Realty Co 5695 N Lincoln Ave Chicago IL 60659

DALLIANIS, JEAN DEMAS, real estate co. exec.; b. Oak Park, Ill., Dec. 30, 1940; d. Charles William and Helen Alice (Kyriakopulos) Demas; B.A., Northwestern U., 1962; m. Harry T. Dallianis, Dec. 8, 1962; children—Irene Lorraine, Thomas Harry. Tchr., Von Steuben High Sch., Chgo., 1962-65; sec.-treas. Ideal Real Estate & Ins. Brokerage, Inc., Chgo., 1965-72, v.p., exec. dir., 1972—, dir. corporate relocation, 1975—; dir. Ideal Realty Co. Mem. Lincolnwood (Ill.) Community Council, 1972—; treas. Lincolnwood Homeowners Assn., 1974-75. Precinct capt. Lincolnwood Citizens Action Party, 1977; mem. Lincolnwood Bicentennial Com.; tchr. Sunday sch. Saints Peter & Paul Greek Orthodox Ch., 1976—, dir. Sch. Bd., 1977—. mem. Lincolnwood PTA. Certified rev. appraiser. Mem. Nat. Assn. Realtors, Realtors Nat. Mktg. Inst., Ill. Assn. Realtors, Chgo. Real Estate Bd., North Side Real Estate Bd., Nat. Assn. Ind. Fee Appraisers, N. Suburban Chicagoland Real Estate Bd. (v.p. 1975-76, pres. 1976—), RELO/Inter-City Relocation Service (Chgo. metro area chairperson 1975-76), League Women Voters, Nat. Assn. Rev. Appraisers, Ind. Fee Appraisers. Zeta Tau Alpha. Greek Orthodox. Office: 5695 N Lincoln Chicago IL 60659

DALLMAN, WILLIAM HAROLD, penal instn. adminstr.; b. Cin., Sept. 13, 1942; s. Harold Frank and Lorene (Tudor) D.; B.A., Miami U., Oxford, Ohio, 1964, postgrad., 1964-67; postgrad. Xavier U., 1973-74; m. Dita Kaye Martin, Oct. 27, 1962; children—Sara, Elizabeth, Morgan. Staff psychologist Lebanon (Ohio) Correctional Instn., 1964-66, supervising psychologist, 1966-68, asso. supt., 1968-72, supt., 1972—. Asst. prof. grad. corrections program Xavier U., Cin., 1973—. Mem. Warren County Bd. Mental Retardation, 1967-69. Recipient Boss of Year award Miami Valley Jr. C. of C., 1972. Mem. Am. Correctional Assn., Am. Assn. Correctional Psychologists, Ohio Ct. and Correctional Services Assn. Rotarian. Address: Box 56 Lebanon OH 45036

DALLMANN, WILLIAM CHARLES, speech pathologist; b. Detroit, Nov. 16, 1929; s. Bertram and Lillian (Morgan) D.; A.B., San Francisco State U., 1957, M.A., 1963; Ph.D. (NDEA fellow), Purdue U., 1973; m. Constance Joan Covington, June 12, 1960; children—Shane, Alan, Lara. Underwriter, Liberty Mut. Ins. Co., San Francisco, 1957-62; pvt. investigator Kraut & Schneider San Francisco, 1963-64; instr. speech pathology Valparaiso U., 1964-65, asst. prof., 1966-72, asso. prof., 1973—, dir. speech and lang. clinic, 1964—; pvt. practice speech pathology, 1975—; pvt. investigator, 1977—. Served with USN, 1948-49, to 1st lt. U.S. Army, 1951-53; Korea. Fellow Counseling Assos. (dir.); mem. Am. Soc. Profl. Investigators (certified profl. investigator, exec. dir.), Am. Speech, Hearing Assn. (certified in clin. competence in speech pathology), Internat. Soc. Profl. Hypnosis (certified profl. hypnotist), Internat. Soc. Gen. Semantics, Am. Soc. Clin. Hypnosis. Lutheran. Author: Images of God: Excursions into Christian Semantics, 1977. Home: 1905 Rock Castle Park Dr Valparaiso IN 46383 Office: Speech and Lang Clinic Valparaiso U Valparaiso IN 46383

DALLOS, PETER JOHN, educator; b. Budapest, Hungary, Nov. 26, 1934; s. Ernest and Maria (Klein) D.; came to U.S., 1956, naturalized, 1962; student Technol. U., Budapest, 1953-56; B.S. in Elec. Engring., Ill. Inst. Tech., 1958; M.S., Northwestern U., 1959, Ph.D., 1962; married; 1 son, Christopher. Engr., Zenith Radio Corp., Chgo., 1957; with Am. Machine & Foundry Co., Niles, Ill., 1959-60; mem. faculty Northwestern U., Evanston, 1962—, asso. prof. elec. engring., audiology, 1966-69, prof., 1969—. Recipient Hearing Research award 12th Beltone Inst., 1977; Guggenheim fellow Karolinska Inst., Stockholm, 1977-78. Fellow Acoustical Soc. Am.; mem. Internat. Soc. Audiology (exec. com.), IEEE, AAAS, Soc. Contemporary Art (Chgo.), Soc. Neurosci., Sigma Xi, Eta Kappa Nu, Tau Beta Pi. Author: The Auditory Periphery: Biophysics and Physiology, 1973. Contbr. numerous articles to profl. jours. Home: 2719 Lawndale Ave Evanston IL 60201

DALSTON, JEPTHA WILLIAM, hosp. adminstr.; b. Longview, Tex., Mar. 18, 1931; B.A., Tex. A. and M. U., 1952; M.A., U. Okla., 1965, Ph.D. in Health Adminstrn. and Polit. Sci., 1970; postgrad. Columbia U., 1963-64; M.H.A., U. Minn., 1969; married. Controller, Reynolds Army Hosp., Ft. Sill, Okla., 1958-61; adminstr. USPHS Indian Hosp., Lawton, Okla., 1961-66; chief planning and evaluation Indian Health Service, USPHS, Oklahoma City, 1969-70; asst. adminstr. Univ. Hosp. and Clinics, Oklahoma City, 1970-73, adminstr., 1973-75; dir. Univ. Hosp., Ann Arbor, Mich., 1975—; asst. prof. U. Okla., 1970-73, asso. prof., 1973—; prof. U. Mich., 1976—; preceptor U. Minn. Served with Armed Forces, 1952-58. Mem. Am. Hosp. Assn., Am. Pub. Health Assn., Am. Coll. Hosp. Adminstrn., Am. Acad. Polit. Sci. Office: Univ Hosp 1405 E Ann St Ann Arbor MI 48104

DALTON, JOHN HENRY, mfg. co. mktg. exec.; b. Phila., May 27, 1926; s. John Ford and Marie Margaret (Sangmeister) D.; B.A. in Physics, Williams Coll., 1947; B.S. in Aero. Engring., B.S. in Bus. Adminstrn., Mass. Inst. Tech., 1950; certificate in def. weapons systems mgmt. Wright-Patterson AFB, 1969; m. Elizabeth Ann Wise, Sept. 2, 1950; children—Melinda Ann, Mark Richard, Amy Elizabeth. Supr. machine shop/test facility Parker-Hannifin Co., Cleve., 1950-53; plant start-up coordination Goodyear Atomic Corp., Portsmouth, Ohio, 1953-57, supr. process control, 1955-57, engr., supr. dept. mech. inspection, 1957-59; with def. systems div. Goodyear Aerospace Corp., Akron, Ohio, 1959—, staff sales engr., 1974-76, mgr. mktg. for anti-submarine warfare, 1977—. Instr., vol. ARC, Akron, 1970—; head No. Ohio sect. Nat. Ski Patrol System, 1975—. Served with USN, 1944-46. Registered profl. engr., Ohio. Mem. Am. Inst. Aeros. and Astronautics (vice chmn. Cleve.-Akron sect.), Nat. Security Indsl. Assn. (chmn. planning com.), Phi Beta Kappa, Phi Gamma Delta. Patentee submarine weapons launch. Home: 1900 Ashwood Dr Akron OH 44313 Office: 1210 Massillon Rd Akron OH 44315

DALTON, LEROY CALVIN, educator; b. Blue River, Wis., June 13, 1926; s. Edgar LeRoy and Lona Francis (Dyer) D.; B.S., U. Wis., 1950, M.S. in Edn., 1954; M.S. in Math., Marquette U., 1964; postgrad. U. Chgo., 1958; m. Evelyn Mae DeJean, Sept. 2, 1950; children—Steven LeRoy, Nanci Jean. Tchr. math. and sci. Spring Green (Wis.) High Sch., 1950-52, McHenry Community High Sch. (Ill.), 1952-53; tchr. math. Wauwatosa (Wis.) High Sch., 1953-61; tchr. math., chmn. math. dept. Wauwatosa West High Sch., 1961—; math. area chmn. Wauwatosa Secondary Schs., 1962-65, 71—. Mem. Wauwatosa Youth Commn., 1971-73; chmn. council on ministries Wauwatosa Ave. Meth. Ch., 1974-76. Named Math. Tchr. of Year, Wis. Soc. Profl. Engrs., 1975; NSF summer fellow Marquette U., 1959-63. Mem. Nat. Council Tchrs. Math. (life, dir. 1977—), NEA (honor award 1970), Math. Assn. Am. (com. on high sch. contests 1965-71), Wis. Math. Council (pres. 1962), Wis., Wauwatosa edn. assns., Milw.-Suburban Math. Council, Phi Delta Kappa, Mu Alpha Theta (nat. pres. 1962-65). Author: (with Laidlaw Bros.) Algebra I, 1967, Algebra 2 and Trigonometry, 1968; Geometry, 1971; Using Algebra, 1974; Using Advanced Algebra, 1975; editor Topics for Mathematics Clubs, 1973. Home: 938 N 115th St Wauwatosa WI 53226 Office: 11400 W Center St Wauwatosa WI 53222

DALTON, RAYMOND ANDREW, univ. adminstr.; b. Chgo., Jan. 15, 1942; s. Chester Mack and Dorothy Laveda (Mitchell) D.; B.S., Ill. State U. at Normal, 1964, M.S., 1966; postgrad. Calif. State U. at Los Angeles, 1967, Otis Art Inst., 1967, U. Ill., 1972-74. Tchr. art, English, Antelope Valley High Sch., Lancaster, Calif., 1965-67; tchr. Drew Jr. High Sch., Los Angeles, 1967; asst. dir. registration Office Admissions and Records, U. Ill. at Chgo. Circle, 1968; adminstrv. asst. to chmn. dept. of art, 1969-71, adminstrv. asst. to dean, 1970, asst. dean Coll. Architecture and Art, 1971—, instr. art, 1969-71, asst. prof., 1971—; adminstrv. leave U. P.R., 1977—. Cons. Camp Mendenhall, Lake Hughes, Calif., 1966; cons. Park Forest (Ill.) Schs., 1973; drawing tchr. Ill. Inst. Tech., 1973. Exhibited in group shows First Nat. Bank of Normal, 1965, Palmdale (Calif.) Art Gallery, 1967, Push Expo, Chgo., 1972, U. Ill. Faculty Exhibit, Chgo., 1972, 74, Joliet West High Sch., 1975. Co-chmn. art com. Push Expo, Chgo., 1972. Mem. Coll. Art Assn., Nat. Conf. Artists, Union Black Arts, Acad. Affairs Adminstrs., Nat. Council Art Adminstrs. Assn. Home: 3335 N Halsted Chicago IL 60657

DALTON, RUTH MARGARET, physician; b. Chgo., Apr. 30, 1926; d. Maurice Jewett and Madeline (Murphy) Dalton; diploma, Thornton Jr. Coll., 1946; student DePaul U., 1946-48; B.S., M.D., U. Ill., 1953. Intern, Madison (Wis.) Gen. Hosp., 1953-54, resident in pathology, 1954-57; resident in pathology Phila. Gen. Hosp., 1957-58; asso. pathologist St. Francis Hosp., La Crosse, Wis., 1958—. Pres., Wis. Assn. Blood Banks, 1963, bd. dirs., 1962; chmn. exec. bd. regional blood com. Badger Red Cross Blood Center, 1966-68; bd. dirs. Am. Assn. Blood Banks, 1969-72, dist. chmn. inspection and accreditation program, 1968-71; sec.-treas. La Crosse chpt. Cath. Physicians Guild, 1963. Sr. planning bd. advisor Girl Scouts U.S.A., 1965-71; bd. mem. La Crosse County chpt. ARC; bd. advisers Viterbo

Coll., pres., 1977—. Recipient Service award ARC. Badger Regional Blood Center, 1969. Fellow Am. Soc. Clin. Pathologists; mem. AAAS, AMA, State Med. Soc. Wis., La Crosse County Med. Soc. (sec.-treas. 1963-65), La Crosse Pediatric Soc. (sec.-treas. 1962-67), Wis. Soc. Pathologists, Wis. Assn. Blood Banks, Am. Assn. Blood Banks, U. Ill. Alumni Assn., Nat. Wildlife Assn., Sierra Club. Home: 1107 Nancy Ct La Crosse WI 54601 Office: 709 S 10th St La Crosse WI 54601

DALTON, TERRENCE BARNEY, health center adminstr.; b. Monroe, Wis., Sept. 7, 1949; s. Robert Joseph and Norine Evelyn (Barney) D.; B.S., U. Wis., Platteville, 1971; M.Ed., Boston U., 1974; m. Sharon Beth Stegner, May 7, 1977. Psychiat. social worker Dodge County Mental Health Center, Juneau, Wis., 1974-76; coordinator alcohol, other drug abuse, Dodge County Human Services Bd., Juneau, 1976-77, program dir. mental health, developmental disabilities, alcohol and other drug abuse, 1977—. Bd. dirs. Dodge County Council Alcohol and Other Drugs, 1976. Served with U.S. Army, 1971-74. Mem. Wis. Assn. Alcoholism, Other Drug Abuse, Assn. Halfway House Alcoholism Programs N.Am., Am. Personnel and Guidance Assn., Wis. Profl. Soc. Addictions, Alpha Phi Omega (life). Home: 303 S University Ave Beaver Dam WI 53916 Office: Box 68 Home Rd Juneau WI 53039

DALTON, WALTER WILLIAM, lawyer; b. Nevada, Mo., May 16, 1908; s. Frederick A. and Ida Jane (Poage) D.; student Westminster Coll.; A.B., U. of Mo., 1931, J.D., 1932, A.M., 1933; m. Margaret Clotilda Brown, June 6, 1959 (dec. Apr. 2, 1976). Admitted to Mo. State bar, 1931, practiced in Columbia, 1933-36; gen. atty. St. Louis-San Francisco Ry. Co., 1936-57, gen. solicitor, 1958-73; of counsel Fordyce & Mayne, 1973—; chmn. Mo. R.R. Assn., 1954-68; indsl.-traffic atty. War Dept., Washington, 1941-42. Trustee Mo. Law Sch. Found., State Hist. Soc. Mo., Jefferson Nat. Expansion Meml. Assn., St. Louis. Served as capt. to lt. col., USAAF, 1942-46; chief contracts U.S. Air Forces hdqrs. A.A.F., 1945-46; comdr. 9145th Air Res. Group, 1960-61; col. Air Force Res. (JA) Hdqrs. MAC, 1961-68; mem. Air Res. Forces Policy Com., 1961-65; col. USAF (ret.). Fellow Am. Coll. Trial Lawyers; mem. Am., Mo., St. Louis (chmn. trial sect. 1976-77) bar assns., English-Speaking Union (dir. St. Louis), Friends of Library Mo. (past pres.), S.R. (pres. St. Louis chpt. 1977—), Soc. Colonial Wars (gov. Mo. 1977), Phi Delta Phi, Phi Gamma Delta, Blue Key, Mystical Seven. Conglist. Mason (32 deg.). Clubs: Press, Mo. Athletic, University (St. Louis). Home: 4 Wakefield Dr St Louis MO 63124 Office: Suite 1100 120 S Central Ave St Louis MO 63105

DALY, DAVID GEORGE, graphic arts co. exec.; b. Cresco, Iowa, Oct. 7, 1936; s. Thomas W. and Ellen M. (Burgess) D.; B.B.A., State U. Iowa, 1963; m. Kay J. Jones, June 30, 1961; children—Kimberly, Pamela, John. Sr. accountant Arthur Andersen & Co., Chgo., 1963-66; asst. corporate controller Josten's, Inc., Owatonna, Minn., 1966-67, div. controller, Topeka, 1967-71; v.p. finance Herff Jones div. Carnation Co., Indpls., 1971-74, v.p. ops., 1974—. Served with AUS, 1959-61. C.P.A., Minn. Mem. Am. Inst. C.P.A.'s, Minn. Soc. C.P.A.'s, Alpha Kappa Psi. Home: 12404 Brookshire Pkwy Carmel IN 46032 Office: 1411 N Capitol St Indianapolis IN 46202

DALY, EUGENE PATRICK, JR., lawyer; b. Fargo, N.D., July 29, 1943; s. Eugene Patrick and Kathryn Lucille (Kennedy) D.; B.A., Coll. St. Thomas, 1965; J.D. cum laude, U. Minn., 1968; m. Bonnie Jean Heinen, Aug. 6, 1966. Admitted to Minn. bar, 1968, since practiced in Mpls.; law clk., chief justice Minn. Supreme Ct., St. Paul, 1968-69; mem. firm Mullin, Weinberg & Daly, Mpls., 1969—; instr. legal writing U. Minn. Law Sch., 1969-70; adj. prof. law, 1976—. Mem. Minn. (chmn. community relations com. 1974—). Hennepin County bar assns., Order of Coif. Tax editor Bench & Bar, 1971—; mem. bd. editors Minn. Law Rev., 1966-68. Contbr. articles to profl. jours. Office: 2200 Dain Tower Minneapolis MN 55402

DALY, JOEL THOMAS, TV news commentator; b. Great Falls, Mont., Aug. 21, 1934; s. Joseph Earl and Viola (Fenger) D.; B.A. magna cum laude, Yale, 1956; m. Suzon Kay Weis, Aug. 24, 1957; children—Douglas Victor, Scott Thomas, Kelly Kay. Announcer KVNI, Couer d'Alene, Idaho, 1952, WHBF-TV, Rock Island, Ill., 1954; newscaster WAVZ, New Haven, 1955-56, WGAR, Cleve., 1959, news dir. CFN, Panama, C.Z., 1957-59, WEWS, Cleve., 1960-64; newscaster WJW-TV, Cleve., 1964-67; news commentator WLS-TV, Chgo., 1967—. Foster parent Ill. Children's Home, 1968-71. Chmn., LaGrange (Ill.) Heritage and Archtl. Commn., 1970-72. Served with AUS, 1956-59. Recipient Panama C.Z. Gov.'s award, Best Documentary award Cleve. Press Club, 1964, Outstanding Coverage award Ohio A.P., 1966, Emmy award Chgo. Acad. TV Arts and Scis., 1968, 69, 76, commendation Ill. Police Assn., 1969, Best Editorial award Ill. A.P., 1970, 71, Human Relations award Am. Jewish Congress, 1971, Myrtle Leaf award Hadassah, 1974. Lutheran (youth counselor 1965-67). Home: 211 S LaGrange Rd LaGrange IL 60525 Office: WLS-TV 190 N State St Chicago IL 60601

DALY, MAGGIE (MRS. ARTHUR BAZLEN), writer, lectr.; b. Castle Caufield, County Tyrone, Ireland, July 2; d. Joseph and Margaret (Kelly) Daly; m. Arthur Bazlen, Aug. 31, 1939 (dec.); 1 dau., Brigid. Profl. actress; fashion coordinator radio, 1952-54; feature writer Ladies Home Jour., 1954; appeared on Home Show, TV, 1954; lectr. on fashions to womens, men's groups; formerly columnist for Chgo. Today, Chgo. Sunday Tribune; featured columnist Chgo. Tribune. Dir. Chgo. U.S.O.; hon. chmn. Chgo. Mental Health Assn. Mem. Adult Education Assn., Fashion Group of Chgo. Author: Guide to Charm, 1955; Kate Brennan, 1957. Address: Chicago Tribune 445 N Michigan Ave Chicago IL 60611

DALY, THOMAS JOSEPH, coatings co. exec.; b. Chgo., Jan. 25, 1929; s. James Thomas and Helen Veronica (Murphy) D.; B.S. in Chem. Engring., Ill. Inst. Tech., 1950, M.S. in Chem. Engring., 1954; m. Catherine Ann Radloff, Oct. 6, 1956; children—Thomas, Kevin, Timothy, Maura, Megan, Mary, Sean. Chemist, Great Lakes Solvents, Inc., Chgo., 1950; chemist Jewel Paint & Varnish Co., Chgo., 1951-62, chief chemist, 1962-68, asst. tech. dir., 1968-73; asst. tech. dir. Gen. Paint & Chem. Co., Cary, Ill., 1973-74, tech. dir., 1974-77, mgr. mfg., 1976—; cons. artist colors, 1966-73, bitumatic coatings, caulks and sealants, 1953-66. Pres. West Glen Community Assn., Glenview, Ill., 1960-68; v.p. Bel-Air Utility Co., Glenview, 1962-71. Recipient Outstanding Service award Chgo. Soc. Paint Tech., 1972, Service award Fedn. Socs. Coatings Tech., 64, 70. Mem. Chgo. Paint Coatings Assn. (chmn. joint ednl. com. 1966-67), Chgo. Soc. Coatings Tech. (pres. 1971), Chgo. Tech. Socs. Council (gov. 1962-68), Lake Forest (Ill.) Community Music Assn., Lake Forest Hist. Soc. (life). Club: Nifty Niblicks Golf. Contbr. articles to profl. jours.; developer paint products. Home: 943 Longwood Dr Lake Forest IL 60045 Office: Universal Chems & Coatings Inc 1124 Elmhurst Rd Elk Grove Village IL 60007

DALY, WILLIAM GERALD, pet products co. exec.; b. McKeesport, Pa., Sept. 12, 1924; s. William and Helen Jean (McGowan) D.; B.S. in Chem. Engring., Worcester Poly. Inst., 1946; B.S. in Indsl. Mgmt., Carnegie-Mellon U., 1951; grad. exec. program Columbia U., 1969; m. Jean F. Wandrisco, June 24, 1950; 1 dau., Kathleen Jean. Pilot plant devel. engr. Gulf Research & Devel. Co., Pitts., 1946-52; mfg. mgr. to plant mgr. Procter & Gamble, 1954-66; plant mgr., asst. v.p. mfg. Heublein, Inc., 1967-72; v.p. operations, pres. Hills div. Riviana Foods, Houston and Topeka, 1973—; dir. Mchts. Nat. Bank of Topeka. Served with USNR, 1944-46, 52-54; PTO. Mem. Pet Food Inst. (bd. dirs.), Topeka C. of C. (bd. dirs.), Nat. Freight Traffic Assn., Am. Mgmt. Assn., Nat. Aeros. Assn., Aircraft Owners and Pilots Assn. Republican. Home: 2329 Mayfair Pl Topeka KS 66611 Office: PO Box 148 Topeka KS 66601

D'AMBROSIO, DOMINICK, assn. exec.; b. Charleston, W.Va., Aug. 16, 1922; s. James and Rose D'A.; student U. Cin., 1941-44; certificate in radio Cin. Coll. Music, 1946; student Ohio Coll. Applied Scis., 1951-52, U. Wis. Labor Inst.; m. Mary, 1946; 1 child. Radio announcer, 1946-49; with Allied Indsl. Workers Am., Milw., 1957—, regional dir., 1957-70, internat. soc.-treas., 1970-75, internat. pres., 1975—; pres. local 820 United Auto Workers, 1942-46, regional rep., 1949-57. Office: Allied Indsl Workers Am 3520 W Oklahoma Ave Milwaukee WI 53215*

D'AMICO, DANIEL IGNATIUS, lawyer, city ofcl.; b. St. Paul, 1908; s. Angelo and Mary (Cashill) D'A.; B.A., U. Minn., 1931, LL.B., 1933; m. Harriet Beebe, Jan. 4, 1936; 1 dau., Mary (Mrs. DeWayne Capra). Admitted to Wis. bar, 1933, since practiced in Cumberland; Cumberland city atty., 1937-41, 43-50, 61-63, 68—. Dir. Northwestern State Bank, Cumberland, Bank of Turtle Lake (Wis.); pres. D'Amico Ltd., Cumberland. Clk. bd. Joint Sch. Dist. No. 2, Cumberland, 1943—. Mem. Am., Inter-County bar assns., Am. Judicature Soc. Roman Catholic. Elk, K.C., Kiwanian. Home: 1380 Comstock St Cumberland WI 54829 Office: 1316 2d Ave Cumberland WI 54829

DAMMAN, JAMES J., lt. gov. Mich.; b. Grosse Pointe Park, Mich., Jan. 16, 1933; s. Adolph Louis and Rose Cecelia (Goddeeris) D.; B.S. in Mktg., U. Detroit, 1954; m. Margaret A. Schulte, Oct. 6, 1956; children—James J., Joan E., Stephen, Susan, Mark, Sandra. Sec., treas.-controller A.L. Damman Co., retail hardware stores, Sterling Heights, Mich., 1964-71, later v.p.; now lt. gov. State of Mich., Lansing. Past chmn. study com. Troy Hosp.; past mem. Troy City Commn., Troy Zoning Bd. Appeals; mem. Troy Drug Alert Com., Oakland County Crippled Children's Soc. Mem. Jaycees. Club: Rotary. Home: 2751 Lake Charnwood Troy MI 48084 Office: Room 128 State Capitol Lansing MI 48903

DAMMANN, ROBERT DONALD, ednl. adminstr.; b. Chgo., Mar. 13, 1928; s. Henry William and Adela (Kaufmann) D.; student U. So. Calif., 1947-48; Mus. B., Northwestern U., 1949, B. Mus. Edn., 1950, M.B.A., 1959; m. Joanne Gubbins, Sept. 5, 1953; children—Kathleen Ellen, Donald Alan. Asst. mgr. imports Great Lakes Overseas, Inc., Chgo., 1953-60; researcher marketing Revere Elec. Mfg. Co., Chgo., 1960-64, advt. mgr., 1964-65, mgr. marketing services, 1965-68; mgr. marketing services MSL Steel Co., 1968-69; marketing mgr. Innovex div. Hammond Corp., 1969-70; adminstrv. mgr. dept. anesthesia Northwestern U. Med. Sch., Chgo., 1970-73, dir. adminstrv. services, 1973—. Served with AUS, 1951-53. Mem. Assn. Am. Med. Colls. (exec. com. bus. affairs group Midwest-Gt. Plains region 1974-75, chmn. bus. affairs group Midwest-Gt. Plains region 1976-77, mem. nat. steering com. 1976—), Phi Mu Alpha. Lutheran. Home: 7836 N Kildare Ave Skokie IL 60076

DAMON, ANDREW CHRIST, lawyer, govt. ofcl.; b. Milw., July 18, 1920; s. Christ and Nicoletta (Tzavaras) Demopoulos; Ph.B., U. Wis., 1946, LL.B., 1949; m. Katherine Vangalis, May 13, 1950; children—Christopher, John, Patricia. Admitted to Wis. bar, 1949; practiced in Milw.; legal counsel subsidiary 3M Co., Waukesha, Wis., 1953-60; atty./dep. sec. Wis. State Environ. Agy., 1963—. Served with AUS, 1943-45; ETO. Mem. Greek Orthodox Ch. (pres. ch. 1969-71, 74-75). Home: 4723 Tonyawatha Trail Monona WI 53716 Office: Box 7921 Madison WI 53707

D'AMOUR, WILLIAM GEORGE, dentist; b. Green Bay, Wis., July 2, 1921; s. George William and Albina Mary (Frechette) D.; student St. Norbert Coll., 1939-41, U. Wis., 1941-42; D.D.S., Marquette U., 1946; m. Mary Priscilla Sewall, Apr. 2, 1944; children—Marye Louise, George William, John Michel, Robert Joe, Rose Marye Jean, Kenneth Edward. Pvt. practice dentistry, Goodman, Wis., 1945-51, Kingsford, Mich., 1951—; mem. staff Dickinson County Meml. Hosp. Dir. Iron Mountain Kingsford Credit Union. Dep. sheriff, Dickinson County, Mich., 1953—. Served to lt. (j.g.) USNR, 1945-46; Mem. Am. Coll. Dentists, Am. Endodontic Soc., Am., Mich. dental assns., Am. Legion. Roman Catholic. Elk, K.C. (4 deg.). Clubs: Chippewa, (officer 1971—) Pine Grove Country (Iron Mountain). Home: 1824 Woodward Ave Kingsford MI 49801 Office: 373 Woodward Ave Kingsford MI 49801

DAMRAU, DAVID JAMES, EDP exec., cons.; b. Tigerton, Wis., Jan. 3, 1944; s. Herman Carl and Margaret (Bernarde) D.; A.D. in Applied Sci., N. Central Tech. Inst., 1972, B.A., 1972. Programmer, U. Ill. Med. Center, Chgo., 1972-75, systems-analyst U. Ill., Chgo. Circle, 1975-77; ednl. coordinator, EDP cons. Loyola U., Maywood, Ill., 1977—; dir. Dámrau Enterprises, Comprec Inc. Lutheran. Home: 3334 Ernst St Franklin Park IL 60131 Office: 2160 S 1st Ave Maywood IL 60153

DANCE, JAMES CALVIN, librarian; b. Knoxville, Tenn., May 30, 1929; s. Harry J. and Gladys L. (Tipton) D.; B.A., Maryville Coll., 1951; M.S., Sch. Library Service, Columbia, 1953. Psychology librarian Columbia U. Libraries, 1953-54; press relations officer Detroit Pub. Library, 1955, asst. coordinator community and group services, 1956-63, asst. coordinator book selection, 1963-67, coordinator community and group services, 1968-73, coordinator pub. relations, 1973—. Creator, host Library's Title Hunt TV program, 1956-63; mem. lit. adv. panel Mich. Council for Arts, 1973—. Recipient Detroit Pub. Library Staff Meml. and Fellowship award, 1966. Mem. Am., Mich. library assns., Adult Edn. Assn. Mich. Editor: (periodical) Among Friends, 1968-71; book reviewer Detroit Free Press, 1960-68, Detroit News, 1974-75. Home: 2405 Carson St Detroit MI 48209 Office: 5201 Woodward Ave Detroit MI 48202

DANCER, WILLIAM JENNINGS, JR., retial chain exec.; b. Stockbridge, Mich., Oct. 27, 1914; s. William Gurney and Winnalee Adella (Comstock) D.; B.S., Mich. State U., 1936; m. Betty Jean Terrell, June 29, 1950; children—Melissa Jean, William Terrell. Warehouse mgr. Dancer Co., dept. stores, 1936-45, warehouse and office mgr., 1945-58, treas. corp., 1958-67, pres., 1967—; dir. Stockbridge State Bank. Pres. Community Chest, 1940. Mem. Mich. Retailers Assn., Mich. Bankers Assn. Democrat. Presbyterian. Club: Masons. Home: 700 E Main St Stockbridge MI 49285 Office: 136 S Clinton St Stockbridge MI 49285

DANEK, TERRENCE JACOB, dentist; b. N.Y.C., Sept. 28, 1941; s. Casimir M. (dec.) and Lillian D. (Perchorowicz) D.; D.D.S., Loyola U. Dental Sch., Chgo., 1966; m. Ursula Stachowicz, June 18, 1966 (dec.); 1 dau., Annette Marie; m. 2d, Joyce M. Grabowski, Nov. 26, 1972; children—Brian Christopher, Christopher Edward. Individual practice dentistry, Morris, Ill., 1968—. Served with USAF, 1966-68. Mem. Am. Acad. Gen. Dentistry, Am., Ill. Valley dental assns., Grundy County C. of C., Ill. Dental Soc., Flying Dentist's Assn., Chgo. Dental Soc. (asso.), Am. Cancer Soc., Delta Sigma Delta. Rotarian (pres. 1971-72; govs. rep. 1972-73, 74-75). Home: 109 Briar Ln Morris IL 60450 Office: 316 Liberty St Morris IL 60450

DANENBERG, EMIL CHARLES, pianist, coll. pres.; b. Hong Kong, July 30, 1917; s. Emil F.X. and Elsie (Gardner) D.; m. Mary Ann Brezsny, June 23, 1951; came to U.S., 1926, naturalized, 1941; A.B., U. Calif., Los Angeles, 1942, A.M., 1944. Concert debut, 1922; New York debut, 1950; concert tours throughout U.S. and Europe; assistantship in music U. Calif., Los Angeles, 1942-44; faculty Oberlin (Ohio) Coll., 1944—, prof. pianoforte, 1960—, acting dean Conservatory Music, 1970-71, dean, 1971-75, pres. Coll., 1975—. Mem. Am. Fedn. Musicians (life), AAUP, Music Tchrs. Nat. Assn., Phi Mu Alpha, Pi Kappa Lambda. Home: 154 Forest St Oberlin OH 44074

DANFORD, ROBERT EUGENE, financial analyst; b. Cleve., Apr. 3, 1925; s. Cecil Everet and Alice Mary (Young) D.; student Drake U., 1943; B.B.A., Kent (Ohio) State U., 1949; M.B.A., Western Res. U., 1953; m. Jean Marie DePompei, Aug. 7, 1948; children—Deborah, William, Danette, James, Robert, Michael, Matthew, Mark, Christopher, Daniel, Thomas. Agt. IRS, Ashtabula, Ohio, 1949-51; accountant Motors Ins. div. Gen. Motors Corp., Cleve., 1951-53, cost accountant Fisher Body div., Cleve., 1954-56, cost analyst, Euclid, Ohio, 1957-64; sr. mem. Robert E. Danford & Assos., Willoughby, Ohio 1965—; lectr. personal, corp. taxes. Bd. dirs. Lake County Mental Health Assn.; trustee corp. trusts, retirement funds. Served with A.C., AUS, 1943-46. Mem. Nat. Soc. Pub. Accountants, Ohio Soc. Pub. Accountants. Roman Catholic (treas. ch. Holy Name Soc.). K.C. (4th deg.). Home: 7925 Stockbridge Rd Mentor OH 44060 Office: Robert E Danford & Assos 38107 2d St Willoughby OH 44094

DANFORTH, JOHN CLAGGETT, U.S. Senator; b. St. Louis, Sept. 5, 1936; s. Donald and Dorothy D.; B.A., Princeton U., 1958; B.D., Yale U., 1963, LL.B., 1963, M.A. (hon.); L.H.D. (hon.), Lindenwood Coll.; D.D. (hon.), Lewis and Clark Coll., Portland, Oreg.; LL.D. (hon.), Drury Coll., Maryville Coll., Rockhurst Coll., Westminster Coll. m. Sally Dobson; children—Eleanor, Mary, D.D., Jody, Thomas. Admitted to N.Y. bar, Mo. bar; asso. firm Davis, Polk, Wardwell, Sunderland & Kiendl, N.Y.C., 1963-66, Bryan, Cave, McPheeters & McRoberts, St. Louis, 1966-68; atty. gen. Mo., 1968-76; mem. U.S. Senate, 1976—, mem. Finance, Commerce and Govtl. Affairs coms.; chmn. Mo. Law Enforcement Assistance Council, 1973-74; ordained to ministry Episcopal Ch.; asst., asso. pastor various chs. in N.Y. and Mo.; hon. canon Christ Ch. Cathedral, St. Louis. Mem. Mo. Acad. Squires, Nat. Jesuit Honor Soc., Sigma Alpha Mu. Recipient Outstanding Young Man award Mo. Jr. C. of C., 1969. Office: 460 Russell Senate Office Bldg Washington DC 20510

DANFORTH, ROBERT CLARKE, physician, educator; b. Flint, Mich., Jan. 17, 1933; s. Herschel Clarke and Margaret Christine (Busby) D.; B.S., U. Wis., 1955, M.D., 1958; m. Phyllis Rae Robertson, June 30, 1956; children—Christine, Douglas. Intern, So. Pacific Gen. Hosp., San Francisco, 1958-59; resident neurology Univ. Hosps., Madison, Wis., 1959-62; practice medicine specializing in neurology, computerized tomography and electroencephalography, Milw., 1964—; mem. staff St. Joseph, Columbia, Milwaukee County, Family, St. Luke's, Milw. Luth., St. Anthony, St. Francis, St. Mary's, St. Michael hosps. (all Milw.); asso. clin. prof. neurology Med. Coll. Wis., 1969—. Pres. Wis. Epilepsy League, 1973-75, mem. adv. bd., 1975—; adv. bd. Myasthenia Gravis Found., Wis. Heart Assn.; mem. med. rev. bd. Wis. Motor Vehicle Dept. Served to lt. comdr. USNR, 1962-64. Mem. Central Assn. Electroencephalography, Assn. Research Nervous and Mental Disease, Am. Acad. Neurology, Am. Electroencephalography Soc., Wis. Neurol. Soc., A.M.A., Wis., Milwaukee County med. assns., Milw. Neuropsychiat. Soc., Am. Med. Electroencephalography Soc., Phi Chi, Sigma Alpha Epsilon. Mem. United Ch. Christ. Club: Lakeshore, Glendale Racquet. Home: 7450 N Pierron Rd Glendale WI 53209 Office: 161 W Wisconsin Ave Milwaukee WI 53203 also care Milw Neurodiagnostic Assos 3070 N 51st St Milwaukee WI 53210

DANFORTH, WILLIAM HENRY, physician, educator; b. St. Louis, Apr. 10, 1926; s. Donald and Dorothy (Claggett) D.; A.B., Princeton, 1947; M.D., Harvard, 1951; m. Elizabeth Anne Gray, Sept. 1, 1950; children—Cynthia, David, Ann, Elizabeth. Intern Barnes Hosp., St. Louis, 1951-52, resident, 1954-57, now mem. staff; asst. prof. medicine Washington U., St. Louis, 1960-65, asso. prof., 1965-67, prof., 1967—, vice chancellor for med. affairs, 1965-71, chancellor. 1971—, chmn. Med. Center Redevel. Corp., 1973—; pres. Washington U. Med. Sch. and Asso. Hosps., 1965-71; program coordinator Bi-State Regional Med. Program, 1967-69. Dir., Ralston Purina Co., Mallinckrodt, Inc., McDonnell Douglas Corp. Mem. nat. adv. heart and lung council Nat. Heart and Lung Inst., 1970-74; mem. council Nat. Inst. Allergy and Infectious Disease, 1976—. Trustee, chmn. bd. Danforth Found.; trustee Am. Youth Found., Princeton U., 1970-74. Served with USN, 1952-54. Mem. Am., Central socs. for clin. research, Nat. Acad. Scis. Inst. Medicine. Home: 10 Glenview Rd St Louis MO 63124 Office: Washington U St Louis MO 63130

DANHOF, CLARENCE HENRY, educator; b. Sully, Iowa, Sept. 12, 1911; s. Henry and Anna (Brouwer) D.; A.B., Kalamazoo Coll., 1932; M.A., U. Mich., 1933, Ph.D., 1939; postgrad. State U. Iowa, 1933-34; m. Gertrude M. Brussee, June 14, 1935 (dec. Dec. 1950); children—Sharon A. (Mrs. Lang D'Atri), Constance M. (Mrs. Tom Baker), Pamela J. (Mrs. Dan Benitez); m. 2d, Ruth I. Ingram, Oct. 2, 1951; 1 dau., Debra Clare; 1 stepdau., Leslie Augustine. Asst. prof. econs. Lehigh U., Bethlehem, Pa., 1937-42; staff various govt. agys., Washington, 1942-46; asst. prof. Princeton, 1946-51; dir. Office Def. History, U.S. Bur. Budget, Washington, 1951-53; prof. econs. Tulane U., New Orleans, 1953-61; sr. staff Brookings Instn., Washington, 1961-66; sr. scientist George Washington U., Washington, 1966-70; dep. dir. technology project Council of State Govts., Washington, 1971; prof. polit. economy Sangamon State U., Springfield, Ill., 1972—. Mem. faculty Columbia 1949, Am. U., Washington, 1962-63, Johns Hopkins, 1968-69. Mem. Econ. History Assn. (v.p. 1959), So. Econ. Assn. (v.p. 1965), Agrl. History Assn. (pres. 1972), Beta Gamma Sigma. Clubs: Cosmos (Washington); Nat. Potomac Yacht (treas. 1962-64). Author: Government Contracting and Technological Change, 1968; Change in Agriculture, the Northern United States, 1820-1870, 1968; (with William D. Carey) Power to the States, Mobilizing Public Technology, 1972. Home: 26 Beach View Ln Springfield IL 62707

DANIEL, DAVID LOGAN, welfare agy. dir.; b. Columbia, Tenn., Jan. 2, 1906; s. David and Mahalah (Lloyd) D.; B.A., Fisk U., 1928; M.A., U. Chgo., 1954, postgrad., 1955-56; m. Mary Beatrice Evins, Aug. 4, 1935. Caseworker, casework supr., dist. office asst. adminstr. Chgo. Relief Adminstrn., Cook County Bur. Welfare and Dept. Pub. Aid, 1933-48; asst. div. dir., pub. assistance div. Cook County Dept. Pub. Aid, Chgo., 1948-66, dir., services programs, 1966-67, dep. dept. dir., 1967-69, dir., 1969-74; asst. dir. Ill. Dept. Pub. Aid, 1974—. Mem. bd. mgrs. Youth Guidance, 1948—; bd. dirs. Chgo. Commons Assn., Big Bros./Big Sisters of Met. Chgo., Joint Negro Appeal. Served with AUS, 1943-46; capt. Res. ret. Recipient Service award Vets. Assistance Commn. Cook County, 1973, Chgo. Area Manpower Planning Council, 1974; Past Pres.'s award City Club Chgo., 1974;

Holy Angels award Holy Angels Catholic Ch., 1976; Stamps Service award Joint Negro Appeal, 1976. Mem. Nat. Assn. County Welfare Dirs. (pres. 1973-74), Nat. Assn. Social Workers, Acad. Certified Social Workers, Chgo. Urban League, Am. Pub. Welfare Assn., NAACP (life), Ill. Welfare Assn. (pres.), Amvets (sr. vice comdr. Chgo. post #1), Alpha Phi Alpha (life; past chpt. pres.). Methodist. Clubs: City of Chgo. (dir., past pres.), Chgo. Umbrian Glee (pres. 1946—). Home: 5839 S Michigan Ave Chicago IL 60637 Office: 624 S Michigan Ave Chicago IL 60605

DANIEL, DONNA MARY, librarian; b. Galion, Ohio, Oct. 19, 1932; d. Ambrose Louis and Gertrude (Daniel) Daniel; B.S., Ohio U., 1956; M.S. in L.S., Western Res. U., 1964. Librarian, Galion Jr. and Sr. High Schs., Galion, 1956-57; tchr. Northridge High Sch., Dayton, 1957-59; librarian Madison High Sch., Mansfield, 1959-66; asst. librarian Mansfield br. Ohio State U., 1966-67; librarian Shelby Jr. High Sch., 1967—. Edn. chmn. St. Joseph's Sch., Galion, 1969-71; sec. council St. Joseph Parish, 1969-71. Mem. N. Central Ohio Tchrs. Assn. Sch. Librarians (sec.-treas. 1962-66), Ohio Assn. Sch. Librarians (regional dir. 1965-67, 74-76), ALA, Ohio Library Assn., NEA, Richland County, Shelby tchrs. assns., Ohio Edn. Assn., Ch. Music Assn. Am., Delta Kappa Gamma. Roman Catholic. Home: 406 Fairview Galion OH 44833

DANIEL, JAMIE L., business cons.; b. Grand Junction, Tenn., Nov. 16, 1921; d. Doctor Newton and Helen Beatrice (Nabers) D.; student U. Miss., 1954-56; m. Paul J. Phyfer, Aug. 1940 (dec. 1954); m. 2d, Donald Lindenberg, June 1956 (div. 1974); children—Paul Jones Phyfer, Daniel Wade Phyfer, Kathryn Anne Phyfer, David Laird Phyfer, Jon Ward Lindenberg, James Frank Lindenberg. Pub. info. officer Mark VII Corp., Geneva, Ill., 1973-75; v.p. BASIC, Geneva, Ill. and Washington, Va., 1975—. Vice pres. Ill. LWV, 1967-71; sec. Landmarks Preservation Service, Chgo., 1975-77; chmn. daily procedures N. Ill. Conf., United Methodist Ch., 1972-77. Mem. Chgo. Assn. Commerce and Industry, Mid Am. Arab C. of C. Methodist. Club: Plaza. Contbr. Ill. Voters Handbook for LWV Ill., 1964-71. Home: 1016 Ray St Geneva IL 60134 Office: PO Box 145 Geneva IL 60134

DANIEL, LEWIS BROWER, banker; b. Cin., Sept. 21, 1916; s. William Abbot and Dorothy Ann (Werner) D.; A.B., Cornell U., 1939; spl. courses Stonier Grad. Sch. Banking, Nat. Trust Sch.; m. Marjorie Louise Gibson, Mar. 26, 1949; 1 dau., Deborah Daniel Long. Sec., gen. credit mgr. Early & Daniel Co., 1960-61; asst. trust officer The Fifth Third Bank, Cin., 1961-66, trust officer, 1966-71, v.p., trust officer, 1971-75, head trust div., sr. v.p., trust officer, chmn. trust com., 1975—; v.p. Fifth Third Bancorp; dir. Frank Herschede Co. Vice pres. Jr. Achievement; asst. treas. Deaconess Hosp.; dir. Cin. Ballet Co.; trustee Lake Placid Ednl. Found., Indian Hill Hist. Assn., Southwestern Ohio Sr. Services, Inc.; adv. bd. Zool. Soc. Served with USAAF, 1941-42. Fellow Nat. Inst. Credit; mem. Ohio Bankers Assn. (pres. trust div., exec. com.), Cin. Estate Planning Council, Ohio Trust Sch. (vice chmn. bd. regents). Republican. Episcopalian. Clubs: Carmgo, Cin. Country, Univ., Bankers, Lake Placid (treas.), Zanesfield (Ohio) Rod and Gun. Home: 8480 Fox Cub Ln Cincinnati OH 45243 Office: Fifth Third Center Cincinnati OH 45202

DANIEL, MARY REED (MRS. WILLIAM J. DANIEL), artist; b. East St. Louis, Ill.; d. William Henry and Willie (Fuller) Reed; student St. Dominic Coll., 1954-56, So. Ill. U., 1958; m. William J. Daniel, June 27, 1961; 1 son, William J. Works exhibited African Art Museum, Washington, 1965, Rockford (Ill.) Coll., 1965, Chgo. Pub. Library, 1968, Monroe Gallery, Chgo., 1968, U. Wis., 1969—, Atlanta U., 1969, Carrefour Gallery, N.Y.C., 1974, Crane Galleries, Chgo., 1976, U. Chgo., others; represented in permanent collections Borg-Warner Corp., Ill. Bell Telephone Co.; tutor art. Recipient awards art fairs. Mem. Mid-Am. Art Assn., North Shore Art League, Artists League Midwest, South Side Community Art Center Chgo., Artists Guild Chgo. Home: 1936 N Mohawk St Chicago IL 60614

DANIEL, T. (TEDD DANIEL HEAGSTEDT), actor; b. Chgo., Aug. 23, 1945; s. Theodore C. and Thelma L. (Soderlind) H.; B.S., Ill. State U., 1967, postgrad., 1967-69; certificate Ecole Internationale de Mime, Marcel Marceau, Paris, France, 1970. Owner, A World of Mime, 1971—, Studio of Mime, 1977—; performer of mime in colls., univs., tour P.R., children's programs/high sch. programs through Urban Gateways, tours of Midwest, U.S.A., Europe, Eastern U.S. Tchr. pedagogy of mime Kendall Coll., 1972-73, Ruth Page Found. Sch. Chgo. Ballet, 1974-75. Recipient 2d Place award Internat. Platform Assn., 1972. Mem. A.F.T.R.A., Internat. Mimes and Pantomimists, Am. Theatre Assn. Home: 313 A Ridge Rd Wilmette IL 60091 Office: 1056 Gage Winnetka IL 60093

DANIELS, CHARLES ANTHONY, polymer phys. chemist; b. Utica, N.Y., Jan. 1, 1943; s. Angele Vincent and Congetta Marie (Bonarrigo) D.; m. Jean Daniels, Sept. 5, 1964; children—Deana, Christopher, B.A., Utica Coll., Syracuse U., 1964; M.S., Case Western Res. U., 1967, Ph.D., 1969, postgrad., 1969. Asso. devel. scientist B.F. Goodrich Chem. Co., Avon Lake, Ohio, 1969, devel. scientist, 1971-77, sr. research and devel. scientist, research and devel. group leader, 1977—; adj. prof. chemistry, John Carroll U., Cleve., 1972-73. Mgmt. counseller Lorain County (Ohio) Jr. Achievement, 1972-76. Mem. Am. Chem. Soc., Soc. Plastics Engrs. (sub-com. on PVC pipe), Sigma Xi, Phi Kappa Phi. Contbg. author: Physical Aspects of Plastics, Physical and Chemical Structures and Properties, 1977; contbr. chpt. Physical Contents of PVC; articles in field. Home: 242 Sunset Rd Avon Lake OH 44012 Office: BF Goodrich Tech Center PO Box 122 Avon Lake OH 44012

DANIELS, JAMES VINCENT, electronics co. exec.; b. Chgo., May 23, 1909; s. James Patrick and Mary Ellen (Burke) D.; student Northwestern U., 1925-27, Curtis-Wright Flying Service, 1928; m. Marilou Juhnke, Sept. 23, 1939 (dec.); children—Nancy (Mrs. Thomas D. Mahar, Jr.), Barbara, James Vincent, Paul; m. 2d, Rosemary Murnighan Nilson, Nov. 6, 1975. Airplane pilot, instr. Sky Harbor, Northbrook, Ill., 1928-32; sales mgr. Flashtric Neon Signs, Chgo., 1932-36; co-founder Kemlite Labs., Chgo., 1936, pres., dir., 1958—; pres. Electronic Lights, Inc., Chgo., 1965—; dir. 1819 West Grand Bldg. Corp. Mem. Illuminating Engring. Soc., Soc. Photog. Scientists and Engrs., Ill. Mfg. Assn., Chgo. Assn. Commerce and Industry (aviation com.). Patentee in field. Home: 1140 Michigan Ave Wilmette IL 60091 Office: 1819 W Grand Ave Chicago IL 60022

DANIELS, ROGERS CUSHING, mfg. co. exec., veterinarian; b. Boston, Apr. 8, 1924; s. James William and Katherine Alden (Nash) D.; D.V.M., Tex. A. and M. U., 1953; certificate, Northeastern U., 1946; m. Cresta Marie Reidy, Jan. 1, 1947 (div. Aug. 1952); children—Ericka Jo (Mrs. Wayne Nesbitt), Paula Sue; m. 2d, Phyllis Irene Fishel Houlihan, Mar. 31, 1960; children—Charles Cushing, Lola Kay, Michael Elbert. Pvt. practice vet. medicine, Shreveport, La., 1953-55, Ft. Worth, 1955-60, Springtown, Tex., 1961-68; v.p., dir. tech. services Triple F Feeds, Brownwood, Tex., 1968-71; dir. inhalation therapy, cardiology and central services Brownwood Community Hosp., 1971-73; dir. profl. and tech. services Philips Roxane, Inc., St. Joseph, Mo., 1973—. Cons. in food animal health mgmt., 1966—. Served with AUS, 1943-45. Decorated Purple Heart medal. Mem. Am. Soc. Agrl. Consultants, Acad. Vet. Consultants, Tex. Acad. Vet. Practitioners, Am., Tex., Mo. vet. med. assns., Philips Roxane Mgmt. Club, Phi Kappa Phi, Phi Zeta. Mason. Home: 3802 N 29th St St Joseph MO 64506 Office: 2621 N Belt Hwy St Joseph MO 64502

DANIELS, RONALD LEE, real estate investment, catalog showroom chain exec.; b. Des Moines, Jan. 17, 1940; s. Daniel T. and Selma Sylvia (Stoll) D.; B.S. in Econs., U. Pa., 1961; grad. Gemological Inst. Am., 1962; m. June Ellen Lang, Aug. 6, 1965; children—Jeffrey Aaron, Tanya Lynn, Danylle Beth. With Ardan Wholesale Inc., Des Moines, 1962—, merchandise mgr., 1962-67, v.p., 1967-70, pres., 1970—; pres. Daniels Investment Co., comml. realty, Des Moines, 1972—. Chmn. United Jewish Appeal Des Moines, 1973. Exec. bd. Des Moines Jewish Welfare Fedn., 1973. Mem. Des Moines Jr. C. of C. Mason (Shriner, 32 deg.); mem. B'nai B'rith. Home: 139 37th St Des Moines IA 50312 Office: 2320 Euclid Ave Des Moines IA 50310

DANIELS, STUART FREDERICK, elec. engr., electronics co. exec.; b. Framingham, Mass., Jan. 12, 1941; s. Charles F. and Lotta (Crowell) D.; B.S. cum laude in Elec. Engring., U. N.H., 1963; Ph.D. in Elec. Engring., Case Inst. Tech., 1970, M.S., 1966; m. Sandra Quimby, June 16, 1963; children—Charles F., Catherine. Research and teaching asst. Case Inst. Tech., Cleve., 1963-68; chief engr. Digital Gen. Corp., Cleve., 1968-73, v.p., 1973—; mem. computer tech. advisory com. Cuyahoga Community Coll., Cleve., 1974—; cons. in numerical control and digital systems engring. to various firms in midwestern region, 1965—. Goodyear fellow, 1967-68. Mem. IEEE, Sigma Xi, Phi Kappa Phi, Tau Beta Pi. Clubs: Mentor Harbor Yachting; National Skeet Shooting. Author tech. manuals on digital computers; patentee in field. Home: 3277 Kenmore Rd Shaker Heights OH 44122 Office: 11000 Cedar Ave Cleveland OH 44106

DANIELSKI, JOHN JULIUS, ophthalmic surgeon; b. Mt. Clemens, Mich., July 10, 1931; s. Julius Sylvester and Helena Lila (Kasprick) D.; B.S. magna cum laude, Wayne State U., 1952, M.D. cum laude, 1955; m. Donna Lou Smith, July 29, 1961; children—Tamara, Ann, John. Intern, Wayne County Gen. Hosp., Eloise, Mich., 1955-56, resident in pathology, 1958-60, in ophthalmology, 1956; pvt. practice medicine, specializing in ophthalmic surgery, Detroit, 1963-65, Garden City, Mich., 1966—; asst. to chief of staff, dir. dept. ophthalmology William Beaumont Hosp., Royal Oak, Mich., 1963-65; staff ophthalmic surgeon Peoples Community Hosp., Wayne, Mich., 1966-75, Met. Hosp. West, Westland, Mich., 1972—; mem. faculty Wayne State U. Coll. Medicine, Detroit, 1964—; FAA med. examiner, 1966-72. Served with M.C., USAF, 1956-58. Diplomate Am. Bd. Ophthalmology. Mem. Am. Acad. Ophthalmology and Otolaryngology, AMA, Mich. State, Wayne County med. assns., Mich. Ophthal. Assn., Civil Aviation Med. Assn., Nat., Mich. Music Tchrs. Assn., Mich. State U. Alumni Assn., Phi Beta Kappa, Sigma Xi, Alpha Omega Alpha. Democrat. Roman Catholic. Club: NW Alano (Westland). Contbr. articles in field to med. jours. Home: 15988 Westmore Ct Livonia MI 48154 Office: 30900 Ford Rd Garden City MI 48135

DANIELSON, CHARLES IRVIN, chem. co. exec.; b. Decorah, Iowa, June 22, 1931; s. Carl Ole and Ida Marie D.; B.A., Luther Coll., 1953; m. Virginia Ruth Perau, Feb. 27, 1956; children—Michael, Allison, Lori. Staff accountant Wolf and Co., C.P.A.'s, 1957-61; treas., dir. Am. Lithographing Corp., Des Moines, 1961-64; mfg. accounting mgr. Sheller-Globe Corp., Keokuk, Iowa, 1964-69; asst. treas. Midwest Carbide Corp., Keokuk, Iowa, 1969—; dir. Bell Ave Realty Co., 1961-64. Pres. bd. dirs. Jr. Achievement of Keokuk, Inc., 1970-72. Served with U.S. Army, 1953-55. C.P.A. Mem. Am. Inst. C.P.A.'s, Iowa Soc. C.P.A.'s, C. of C. Republican. Lutheran. Clubs: Kiwanis, Elks. Home: 311 Hawthorne Place Keokuk IA 52632 Office: PO Box 607 Keokuk IA 52632

DANIELSON, CHESTER HAROLD, mfg. co. exec.; b. Fairfield, Iowa, Jan. 4, 1926; s. Frank Raymond and Martha (Bauer) D.; B.S., Iowa State U., 1950; m. Lorene W.; children—Ronald, Janet, Barbara, Steven. Automobile dealer, Fairfield, 1950—; pres., gen. mgr. Streator Products Corp., Fairfield, 1964—. Mem. Fairfield City Council, 1958-61; v.p. Fairfield Community Fund, 1964-72, pres., 1972-73; trustee Fairfield Waterworks, 1963-73. Served in USAF, 1943-45. Named Man of Year, Fairfield, 1964. Mem. Motor Club Iowa (dir. 1967—), C. of C. (pres. 1964), Jr. C. of C. (pres. 1955), Newcomen Soc. N.Am., Am. Legion, Delta Upsilon. Republican. Methodist. Clubs: Elks, Lions (pres. 1966), Golf and Country (v.p. 1971) (Fairfield). Home: 204 Highland Ave Fairfield IA 52556 Office: 121 E Broadway Fairfield IA 52556 also 408 Lowe St Box 398 Fairfield IA 52556

DANIELSON, DORIS ANDRESEN (MRS. PHILIP M. DANIELSON), pub. relations exec.; b. Chgo., Aug. 6, 1940; d. August Arnold and Lillian Mae (Rice) Andresen; B.A., Ill. Wesleyan U., 1961; postgrad. Roosevelt U., 1963-65; m. Philip M. Danielson, June 10, 1961. Editorial clk. Argonne (Ill.) Nat. Lab., 1961-62; asst. editor No. Trust Bank, Chgo., 1962-64, editor, 1964-66, supr. pub. relations, 1966-68, asst. mgr. advt. and pub. relations, 1968-73; dir. pub. relations Manpower, Inc., Milw., 1973-76; dir. pub. relations and communications Arthur Young & Co., Chgo., 1976—. Recipient Golden Trumpet awards Publicity Club Chgo., 1965, 66. Mem. Pub. Relations Soc. Am. Home: 5620 Main St Downers Grove IL 60515 Office: One IBM Plaza Chicago IL 60611

DANIELSON, PHILIP MICHAEL, vacuum cons.; b. Champlain, Minn., Sept. 11, 1936; s. Carl Emil Theodore and Estelle Eleanor (Berkeland) D.; B.S. in Chemistry, Ill. Wesleyan U., 1960; m. Doris Karen Andresen, June 10, 1961. Nuclear research scientist Argonne Nat. Lab., 1960-72; vacuum cons. Danielson Assos., Milw., 1972—. Mem. Am. Vacuum Soc. (chmn. sect. 1970—, treas. chpt. 1975), Council Wis. Writers, Windy City Sci. Fiction Writer's Conf., Sierra Club, Appalachian Mountain Club. Contbr. articles to profl. jours. Address: 5620 Main St Downers Grove IL 60515

DANIELSON, RUTH FLORENCE, banker; b. Atwater, Minn., June 1, 1917; d. Louis A. and Kristine Anna (Blohm) Rosenquist; m. Thomas C. Danielson, Aug. 14, 1936; children—Lou Ann, Suzanne; student St. Cloud Tchrs. Coll., 1935-36, 61. With Atwater State Bank, 1936—, v.p., cashier, 1962-74, pres., 1975—, also dir.; agt. Northwest Nat. Ins. Co., 1955-62; propr. Atwater State Agy., 1962—; dir. Ind. State Bank of Minn. Sec., treas., Ladies Aid, Immanuel Lutheran Ch., 1940-45, pres., 1949, treas. congregation, 1977—; pres. PTA, 1947-48; mem. Kandiyohi County Library Bd., 1964-65; organizer Nutrition for Elderly Program, Atwater, 1977—. Licensed ins. agt. Mem. Am. Ind. Bankers, Minn. Bankers Assn., Eastern Star. Address: Atwater MN 56209

DANILEVICIUS, ZENONAS, physician, editor; b. Petrograd, Russia, May 13, 1915; s. Boleslovas and Martha (Paliunas) D.; M.D., Vyt. D. U. Kaunas, Lithuania, 1938; m. Joana Sakevicius, Oct. 3, 1937; children—Rita Maria, Daina Maria, Linas Zenonas. Came to U.S., 1947, naturalized, 1953. Intern, U. Hosp., Kaunas, 1937-38; resident in internal medicine Mil. Hosp., Kaunas, 1938-41; dir. Second. City Policlinic, Kaunas, 1941-44; intern St. Anthony Hosp., Chgo., 1947-48; pvt. practice medicine, Chgo., 1949-63; sr. editor Jour. of A.M.A., Chgo., 1963—, also sci. dir. fgn., European and Latin Am. edits.; dir. Nursing Sch., UNRRA, Schwaebisch Gmuende, Bavaria, 1946-47. Expert witness at hearings Ways and Means Com., U.S. Congress, 1961. Chmn. sci. program. com. Hosp. St. Anthony, Chgo., 1960-63. Mem. Am. Med. Writers Assn., Catholic Lithuanian Acad. Science Roma (Italy), Ill., Chgo. med. socs., A.M.A., Am. Soc. History Medicine, Am. Soc. Internal Medicine, Internat. Platform Assn. Author: Zmogus, Physiology, 1943. Contbr. articles and translations to profl. jours. Home: 6635 S Talman Ave Chicago IL 60629 Office: 535 N Dearborn St Chicago IL 60610

DANIS, CHARLES WHEATON, bldg. and constrn. co. exec.; b. Dayton, Ohio, Mar. 20, 1915; s. Benjamin George and Grace Esther (Bunce) D.; B.S. in Mech. Engring., Cornell U., 1937; m. Elizabeth Jane Sliter, June 21, 1947; children—Richard Ralph, Charles Wheaton, Amy Louise, Julie Marie, John Sliter. Engr., Armco Steel Co., Middleton, Ohio, 1937-38; engr. B.G. Danis Co., Dayton 1938-42, v.p., gen. mgr., 1945-66, pres., 1966-71; chmn., chief exec. officer Danis Industries Corp., Dayton, 1971—; chmn., dir. Home Savs. & Loan Assn., Dayton, 1950—; dir. 1st Nat. Bank, Dayton. Bd. dirs., treas. Dayton YMCA, 1966-73, Jr. Achievement, Dayton, 1970—; v.p., bd. dirs. Goodwill Industries, Dayton, 1956-64; pres., bd. dirs. Dayton Better Bus. Bur., 1954-60, Engring Found. Dayton, 1966-71; trustee Siena Home for Aged, Dayton, 1967-70, U. Dayton, 1975—; trustee, pres. Dayton Catholic Social Services, 1971-72. Served with C.E., AUS, 1942-44. Mem. Dayton C. of C. (dir. 1954-55, 75-77). K.C. Clubs: Dayton Bicycle, Dayton Racquet, Engineers, Sycamore Country, Moraine Country. Home: 629 Evans Ln Dayton OH 45459 Office: 1801 E 1st St Dayton OH 45403

DANNEWITZ, DEAN VINCENT, cons. employee relations; b. Emmetsburg, Iowa, May 23, 1928; s. John Earl and Edna Irene (Pendlebury) D.; A.A., Worthington Community Coll., 1948; B.B.A., U. Minn., 1956, M.A., 1966; m. Geneva Lavone Clark, June 21, 1953; children—Debra Lynn, Duane Alan, Brian David. Asst. wage and salary dir. Consumers Power Co., Jackson, Mich., 1956-60; asst. to v.p. indsl. relations Xerox Corp., Rochester, N.Y., 1960-65; mgr. personnel and adminstrn. Control Data Corp., Mpls., 1967-69; v.p. Elmer R. John Assos., Inc., Mpls., 1969-72; pres. Employee Relations Cons., Inc., Mpls., 1972—; exec. dir. Minn. State Adv. Council for Vocat. Edn.; lectr. St. Thomas Coll., Augsburg Coll. Mem. long range planning com. Bloomington Bd. Edn., 1976-77. Served with USAF, 1950-54. Mem. Am. Psychol. Assn., Am. Mgmt. Assn., Am. Soc. Personnel Adminstrn., Am. Compensation assn., Assn. Mgmt. Cons., Twin Cities Personnel Assn., U. Minn. Alumni Club. Methodist. Club: Decathlon Athletic. Home: 2701 96th St W Bloomington MN 55420 Office: 2850 Metro Dr Suite 315 Minneapolis MN 55420

DANZY, RICHARD L., city ofcl.; b. Chgo., Apr. 29, 1923; s. Eugene H. and Pearlie (Archer) D.; certificate Wilson Jr. Coll., 1943; B.S., Roosevelt U., 1949; M.Ed. in Spl. Edn., Chgo. Tchrs. Coll., 1963; M.S. in Edn., Ill. State U., 1968; m. Marilyn Render, Apr. 20, 1963; children—Michael, Richard, Diane (Mrs. Rufus Grady), Keith. Tchr., Carver Sch., Chgo., 1950-56; tchr. sci. Deneen Sch., Chgo., 1956-61; spl. edn. tchr., counselor Moseley Social Adjustment Sch., Chgo., 1961-67; learning resource specialist Woodlawn Exptl. Sch. Dist. Project, Chgo., 1968-71; staff asst. Neighborhood Youth Corps, Chgo., 1971-73; adminstrv. staff asst. Elementary and Secondary Edn. and Head Start med. programs Chgo. Bd. Edn., 1973—. Instr. George Kennedy King Jr. Coll., 1967-68; instr. human relations Chgo. Bd. Edn., 1971-73. Pres. Black Econ. Devel. Corp., 1967-69. Chmn. local draft bd., 1968-72. Mem. adv. bd. Ill. Council Exceptional Children. Served with AUS; ETO. Mem. ACLU, Chgo. Tchrs. Union, Afro Am. Tchrs. Assn., Common Cause. Conglist. Home: 9044 Bennett St Chicago IL 60617 Office: Chgo Bd Edn 228 N LaSalle St Chicago IL 60606

DAPKUS, WILLIAM VINCENT, elec. engr.; b. Saginaw, Mich., Mar. 2, 1920; s. Frank and Anna Hursulis (Slogaritus) D.; B.E.E., Bucknell U., 1947; m. Margaret Patricia Paralis, Jan. 29, 1948; children—William, Lynn, Theodore. Engr. aide Tenn. Eastman Co., Oak Ridge, 1944-46; engr. Consumers Power Co., Jackson, Mich., 1948-51; elec. designer Smith Hinchman & Grylls, Detroit, 1953-57; job capt. Cunningham-Limp Co., Birmingham, Mich., 1974—. Activities chmn. local Boy Scouts Am., 1960-65. Served with AUS 1943-46. Registered profl. engr., Mich. Mem. U.S. Soc. Scientists and Engrs. Democrat. Roman Catholic. Home: 13520 Dixie St Detroit MI 48239 Office: 1400 N Woodward Ave Birmingham MI 48011

DAPRON, ELMER JOSEPH, JR., advt. exec.; b. Clayton, Mo., Jan. 14, 1925; s. Elmer Joseph and Susanna (Kruse) D. m. Sharon Kay Neuling. Employed in constrn. bus., Fairbanks, Alaska, 1947-48; tech. writer-editor McDonnell-Douglas Corp., St. Louis, 1948-57; free-lance writer, Paris, France, 1957; with Gardner Advt. Co., St. Louis, 1960—, v.p. 1969—. Producer, commentator nationally-syndicated radio show Elmer Dapron's Grocery List; communications cons. to govt. and industry. Served with USMCR, 1943-45; PTO; 50-51; Korea. Recipient advt. awards including New Filming Techniques award Internat.-Film Festival, 1969. Hon. fellow Harry Truman Library Inst. Mem. Nat. Agrl. Mktg. Assn. (v.p. 1970—, trustee, Miss. Valley Farm Mktg. Man of Year 1974), Marine Corps League (nat. vice comdt. 1967-69). Clubs: Media, Arena, Four Seasons. Democrat. Contbr. articles to publs. Home: 300 Mansion House Center St Louis MO 63102 Office: 10 Broadway St Louis MO 63102

DARBY, HARRY, former U.S. senator, industrialist, farmer, stockman; b. Kansas City, Kans., Jan. 23, 1895; s. Harry and Florence Isabelle (Smith) D.; B.S. in Mech. Engring., U. Ill., 1917, M.E., 1929; LL.D. (hon.), Kans. State U., Manhattan, St. Benedict's Coll., Atchison, Kans., Westminster Coll., Fulton, Mo., Washburn U., Topeka; D.Comml. Sci., Baker U., Baldwin City, Kans.; m. Edith Marie Cubbison, Dec. 17, 1917; children—Harriet (Mrs. Thomas H. Gibson, Jr.), Joan (Mrs. Roy A. Edwards), Edith Marie (Mrs. Ray Evans), Marjorie (Mrs. Eugene D. Alford). With Mo. Boiler Works Co., Kansas City, 1911-19; with Darby Corp., 1920—, now chmn. bd., owner; founder, chmn. bd. dirs. Leavenworth Steel, Inc., Darby Ry. Cars, Inc.; dir. numerous corps. U.S. senator from Kans., 1949-50; mem. Republican Nat. Com. for Kans., 1940-64. Active 4-H Club; chmn. Kans. Hwy. Commn., 1933-37; mem. at large nat. council, mem. regional exec. com. Boy Scouts Am. Trustee Nat. Cowboy Hall Fame; exec. com. Agrl. Hall Fame; chmn. Eisenhower Presdl. Library Commn.; chmn. emeritus Am. Royal Livestock and Horse Show; chmn. bd. Eisenhower Found., Abilene, Kans.; dir. U. Kans. Research Found., Kan. Heart Assn. Served from 2d lt. to capt., F.A., U.S. Army, 1917-19; AEF. Recipient awards for civic activities. Fellow Am. Soc. M.E.; mem. Navy League U.S., Kansas City Crime Commn., Kans. Registration Bd. Profl. Engrs., U. Ill. Found., Am. Soc. C.E., Nat., Kans. socs. profl. engrs., Am. Hereford Assn., Am. Nat. Livestock Assn., Kans. Livestock Assn. (exec. com.), Am. Soc. Agrl. Engrs., V.F.W., Am. Legion, 40 and 8, Military Order World Wars. Episcopalian. Mason (32 deg., Shriner, Jester). Clubs: Kansas City, Automobile of Missouri, Saddle and Sirloin, Rotary, River, Terrace, Man of The Month (Kansas City, Kans.); Chicago; Chevy Chase, Capitol Hill (Washington); Cherry Hills (Denver), Burning Tree (Bethesda, Md.). Home: 1220 Hoel Pkwy Kansas City KS 66102 Office: 1st St and Walker Ave Kansas City KS 66110

DARBY, RALPH LEWIS, chem. engr.; b. Youngstown, Ohio, Nov. 13, 1918; s. Ralph Emerson and Anita (Goodridge) D.; B.Chem. Engring., Ohio State U., 1942; certificate of meteorology U. Chgo., 1943; m. Marian Louise Pflaum, Dec. 6, 1942; children—Ralph Russell, Margaret Lynn. Research engr. Commonwealth Engring. Co., Dayton, Ohio, 1946-47; research engr. Battelle Meml. Inst., Columbus, Ohio, 1947-63, group dir., 1963-65, div. chief dept. econs. and information research, 1965-70, chief projects mgmt. dept. social and mgmt. scis., 1970-75, sr. research engr. dept. def., transp. and space systems, 1975—. Served to capt. USAAF, 1942-46; ETO; with USAF, 1952. Decorated Bronze Star medal. Registered profl. engr., Ohio. Fellow Am. Inst. Chemists; mem. Am. Chem. Soc., Am. Soc. for Information Sci., A.A.A.S., Spl. Libraries Assn., Sigma Phi Epsilon. Methodist. Mason. Contbr. articles profl. jours. Home: 3112 Leeds Rd Columbus OH 43221 Office: 505 King Ave Columbus OH 43201

DARBY, RICHARD DURHAM, oral surgeon; b. Lowrys, S.C., Jan. 19, 1916; s. James Simpson and Lois (Durham) D.; student Belmont Abbey, 1933-35, Davidson U., 1935; D.D.S., Emory U., 1939; m. Joanne Woodward Reed, Feb. 8, 1942; children—Joanne (Mrs. John Novak), Richard Durham, Jr., Lucy. Intern Walter Reed Gen. Hosp., Washington, 1939-40; oral surgeon, dentist, Bloomington, Ind., 1948—; mem. staff Bloomington Hosp. Served to col. AUS, 1940-47. Decorated Bronze Star medal. Fellow Royal Soc. for Promotion of Health; mem. Am., Ind., South Central (sec., treas. 1953-56) dental socs., Ind. Acad. Dental Practice Adminstrn., Ind. State Dental Assn. (bd. 1956-58), Delta Sigma Delta, Club: Country (pres., dir. 1953-56) (Bloomington). Home: 1327 Sheridan Rd Bloomington IN 47401 Office: 111 S Lincoln St Bloomington IN 47401

D'ARCY, DENNIS THOMAS, financial exec.; b. Detroit, Oct. 29, 1929; s. Harry Dennis and Mabel Winifred (Wooding) D'A.; student Wayne State U., 1952-53; m. Anne E. Porta; children—Glenn, Dale, Denise, Paul, Myung, Bridget, Harry, Kevin. Mgmt. cons., auditor for credit unions Mich. Credit Union League, 1953; asst. sec.-treas. Service Savs. & Loan Assn., 1954; treas., mgr. Wayne (Mich.) Westland Fed. Credit Union, 1955—. Owner internat. wholesale and retail bus. Pres., Wayne Assn. for Retarded Children, 1956-58; pres. West Wayne County Com. for State Constl. Conv., 1962; chmn. City of Wayne CSC, 1962-64, Wayne Human Relations Commn., 1970—. Served with AUS, 1947-51. Decorated Bronze Star medal; recipient certificate merit Detroit Com. for Observance of Human Rights, 1975. Mem. Wayne C. of C. (pres. 1961-64), Credit Union Exec. Soc. (exec. com. chpt.), Mich. Credit Union League (dir. 1958-60). Western Wayne First Friday Club (pres. 1958). Roman Catholic. Club: Rotary (pres. 1976-77) Home: 3315 Clark St Wayne MI 48184 Office: 34646 Sims St Wayne MI 48184

D'ARCY, LEO PAUL, radio news dir.; b. Cleve., Apr. 7, 1936; s. Michael and Julia (Madden) D'A.; grad. high sch.; m. Joanne Brick, Jan. 18, 1958; children—Lee Ann, Lauri, Raymond, David, Douglas, John, Matthew. Sales and announcer radio sta. WSRS, Cleve., 1959-62; free lance news announcer Radio and TV Broadcasting, Cleve., 1962-67; sales and news announcer radio sta. WPVL, Painesville, Ohio, 1967-68; news dir. WELW Radio AM & FM, Cleve., 1968-76, gen. mgr., 1976—, host daily talk shows, 1970-77; communications instr. Tri-County Police Sch., Willoughby, Ohio, 1970-73. Clubs: Exchange of the Heights (pres. 1973-74). Home: 266 E 150th St Cleveland OH 44110 Office: 36913 Stevens Blvd Willoughby OH 44094

DARE, EDWARD DAVID, med. service adminstr.; b. Evansville, Ind., Apr. 9, 1939; s. Sherman Edward and Anna Marie (Baker) D.; student Vincennes U., 1958-60; B.S., U. Evansville, 1963; m. Lawanda Joyce Steffey, June 20, 1960; children—Scott, Daniel, Steven. Teaching supr. Sch. Tech., Carle Clinic, Urbana, Ill., 1964-66; dir. nursing and personnel mgr. Marshfield (Wis.) Clinic, 1966-73; regional mgr. Hyland div. Baxter-Travenol, Costa Mesa, Calif., 1973-76; clinic adminstr. Med. Arts Clinic, Emporia, Kans., 1976—; exec. sec. Med. Equipment, Inc., 1976—; cons. to Emporia State U., 1976—; coroner Wood County, Wis., 1968-73. Alderman, Marshfield City Council, 1970-73. Named Outstanding Young Man, Marshfield Jaycees, 1972. Mem. Am. Soc. Clin. Pathologists, Med. Group Mgmt. Assn., Emporia C. of C., Registry of Med. Technologists, Nat. Rifle Assn., Nat. Muzzle Loading Rifle Assn. Club: Masons. Author: Guidebook to Laboratory Procedures, 1970; Sixty-Three Hours, 1977. Home: Rural Route 2 PO Box 136C Emporia KS 66801 Office: 1601 State St Emporia KS 66801

DARGUSCH, CARLTON SPENCER, cons.; b. Batavia, N.Y., Aug. 19, 1900; s. Julius Herman and Etta (Burnham) D.; student Ind. U., 1921-22 and 1924, Ohio State U., 1922-25; m. Genevieve Johnston, Nov. 6, 1923; children—Carlton Spencer (dec.), Evelyn Byrd (Mrs. Charles A. Lanphere). Legislative draftsman for Ohio Gen. Assembly, 1925; atty. Tax Commn. of Ohio, 1925-33; tax commr. of Ohio, 1933-37; mem. firm Dargusch & Hutchins, Columbus, Ohio; dir. Clark Grave Vault Co. Cons., Engrs. Joint Council. Helped draft plans for Selective Service also Universal Mil. Tng.; past asst. director for manpower ODM; mem. Am. del. Conf. for Applied Research, Vienna, 1956, India, 1958, USSR, 1960. Trustee Ohio State Univ., 1938-59, 63-65, chmn. bd., 1944-45, 51-52, 58-59; dir. Ohio State U. Research Found., 1951-60. Served U.S. Army, 1940-47, through grades to brig. gen. Awarded D.S.M., 1946, Army Commendation Medal with cluster. Recipient award Ohio State U., 1960. Mem. Mil. Order W.W., Am. Legion, Omicron Kappa Upsilon (hon.). Kappa Sigma, Phi Delta Phi. Mason. Clubs: Army and Navy (Washington); Sphinx (Ohio State U.); Columbus, Columbus Country; Queen City (Cin.); Union (Cleve.); Engineers (N.Y.C.); Chevy Chase (Md.). Author: Estate and Inheritance Taxation (with John Cassidy), 1930, rev. (with Jack H. Bertsch), 1956; Operation of Selective Service in World War II, 1956; also articles. Home: 271 N Columbia Ave Bexley OH 43209 Office: 218 E State St Columbus OH 43215

DARKINS, CHARLES JOHN, chem. co. exec., b. Joliet, Ill., Jan. 27, 1921; s. Charles William and Helen Victoria (Hollsten) D.; D.A., U. Iowa. Salesman Comml. Solvents Corp., Peoria, Ill., 1949-51; with Stauffer Chem. Co., Chgo., 1952—, regional sales mgr., 1969—. Served with USAAF, 1942-45, USAF, 1951-52. Decorated D.F.C., Air medal. Mem. Chgo. Drug and Chem. Assn., Chgo. Perfumery, Soap and Extract Assn., Am. Chem. Soc., Ill. C. of C., Chgo. Athletic Assn., Alpha Chi Sigma. Home: 730 N Hicks Rd Apt 713 Palatine IL 60067 Office: 120 S Riverside Plaza Chicago IL 60606

DARLING, HAROLD WILLIAM, educator; b. Boston, Mar. 8, 1926; s. Lester Ernest and Theodora Steele (Spencer) D.; A.B., Eastern Nazarene Coll., 1950; M.S., Purdue U., 1951, Ph.D., 1958; m. Ollie Cora Black, Aug. 5, 1950; children—Barbara, Terry. Acad. dean Spring Arbor (Mich.) Coll., 1953-55, registrar, 1955-57, dir. student affairs, 1957-58, dean acad. affairs, 1960-66, prof. psychology, 1967—; head dept. psychology and edn. Eastern Nazarene Coll., Wollaston, Mass., 1958-60. Vis. prof. Pasadena (Cal.) Coll., 1966-67. Served with inf. AUS, 1944-46. Mem. Common Cause, N.A.A.C.P., Soc. Christian Action (pres. 1974-75), Kappa Delta Pi. Kiwanian. Author: Man in Triumph, 1969 (also pub. as paperback with title Man in His Right Mind, 1972). Home: 182 Harmony St Spring Arbor MI 49283

DARNLEY, JAMES DANA, neurologist; b. Bridgeport, Conn., Sept. 27, 1918; s. James Aloysius and Marion Bernadette (Johnson) D.; A.B. summa cum laude, Dartmouth Coll., 1940, postgrad. med. sch., 1939-41; M.D., C.M., McGill U., 1943; m. Eloise Agnes Knight, Dec. 28, 1952; children—Brenda, Deborah, James Dana. Resident Mary Hitchcock Meml. Hosp., Hanover, N.H., 1946-47, Royal Victoria Hosp., Montreal, 1947-48, Bronx VA Hosp., 1948-50; neurologist Miss. Baptist, St. Dominic's hosps., Jackson, Miss., 1950-52; neurologist Ford Hosp., Detroit, 1952-63; chief neurology and electroencephalography William Beaumont Hosp., Royal Oak, Mich., 1963—. Served to capt. M.C., AUS, 1944-46; PTO. Named Tchr. of Year Beaumont Hosp., 1969-70. Diplomate Am. Bd. Psychiatry and Neurology. Fellow Am. Acad Neurology; mem. Am. EEG Soc. (asso.), Phi Beta Kappa. Republican. Roman Catholic. Home: 31306 Cline Dr Birmingham MI 48009 Office: 3535 W 13 Mile Rd Royal Oak MI 48072

DARR, DAVID LLOYD, dentist; b. Sioux Falls, S.D., Jan. 31, 1935; s. Glenn David and Eleanor Beatrice (Ribstein) D.; B.S., St. Louis U., 1957, D.D.S., 1961; m. Patricia Jean Scheldrup, Feb. 3, 1964; children—Debora, James. Pvt. practice dentistry, Mpls., 1961—. Fellow Augustana Coll., Sioux Falls, 1970. Fellow Acad. Gen. Dentistry (v.p. Twin Cities 1975); mem. N.E. Mpls. Dental Assn. (pres. 1971), Am., Minn. dental assns., Xi Psi Phi, Tau Kappa Epsilon. Kiwanian (pres. elect N. Suburban Mpls. 1975). Home: 5115 Rainier Pass NE Minneapolis MN 55421 Office: 4150 Central Ave NE Minneapolis MN 55421

DARRAGH, BARBARA ANN, personnel interviewer; b. Chgo., Sept. 18, 1947; d. Stanley Robert and Antonette Therese (Borkowski) Cisek; B.S., Loyola U., Chgo., 1969, M. Ed., 1976; m. Robert Darragh, Sept. 11, 1976. Statistician, clerical Nelson Market Research Co., Chgo., 1965-69; editorial aide, advt. rep. Am. Congress Rehab. Medicine, Chgo., 1969-76; adminstrv. asst. to personnel dir. Central Nat. Bank, Chgo., 1976; personnel interviewer Am. Coll. Surgeons, Chgo., 1976—. Mem. Am. Personnel and Guidance Assn., Am. Psychol. Assn. Home: 5820 S Austin Ave Chicago IL 60638 Office: 55 E Erie St Chicago IL 60611

DARRAGH, HELEN ALICE, psychiat. social worker; b. Cedar Rapids, Iowa, July 12, 1915; d. John William and Frances (Hurych) Darragh; B.A., U. Mo., 1938; M.Social Service, Smith Sch. Social Work, 1942; postgrad. U. Mich., 1943, Inst. Psychoanalysis, 19S5, Therapist, Family Consultation Service, Wichita, Kans., 1938-64, Consultation Bur., Detroit, 1943-44, Family Service, Chgo., 1950-51, Chgo. Child Care Soc., 1951-52; therapist dept. psychiatry Jewish Hosp., St. Louis, 1956-64, chief psychiat. social worker, 1958-64; casework supr. Family Welfare Assn., Scranton, Pa., 1944-46; dist. sec. Children's Services, Cleve., 1946-48; dist. dir. United Charities Chgo., 1952-56; exec. dir. Met. Commn. on Aging, Chgo., 1956-59, also children's instl. cons. Social Planning and Welfare Council; dir. profl. services Family and Children's Service Greater St. Louis, 1964—; practicum instr. Wayne U., Detroit, 1943-44, U. Mich., Detroit, 1943-44, Smith Coll., Northampton, Mass., 1944-46, Western Reserve U., Cleve., 1946-48, 53-55, U. Chgo., 1948-56, Washington U., St. Louis, 1957; asst. prof. dept. psychiatry St. Louis U., 1968—; Ford Found. for Aging fellow; intern Eloise State Hosp., Detroit, 1941. Bd. dirs. Day Care Nursery, 1955, Housing Project, 1956. Fellow Am. Orthopsychiat. Assn.; mem. Nat. Assn. Social Workers, Council on Social Work Edn., Family Service Assn. Am., Council Family Relations, Mo. Assn. Social Welfare, Alpha Gamma Delta. Democrat. Clubs: University, St. Louis University Women's, Washington University Women's. Home: 1 Whitehall Ct Brentwood MO 63144 Office: 2650 Olive St St Louis MO 63103

DARST, MARIE ROENA (MRS. HARRY WALTER DARST), civic worker; b. Davisville, Mo., Dec. 13, 1919; d. John Leonard and Allie (Wilkinson) Britton; student Central Bapt. Coll., 1953-54; pvt. music studies, 1962-63; m. Harry Walter Darst, May 21, 1938; 1 dau., Marilyn Ruth (Mrs. Roy G. Orr). Saleslady, Fine Bros. Matison Dept. Store, Hattiesburg, Miss., 1963, Belk-Whitney Dept. Store, Hattiesburg, 1964-65. Pres., Ala. Bapt. Women's Missionary Assn., 1960-61; pres. Miss. Bapt. Women's Missionary Assn., 1964-66, Mo. Bapt. Women's Missionary Assn., 1970-71, Nat. Womens Missionary Aux., 1969-71; nat. dir. Youth Auxs. Baptist Missionary Assn. Am., 1971—; editor youth aux. page Golden Words, Bapt. Publs. Com., 1970—; corr. sec. Nat. Women's Missionary Aux. of Bapt. Missionary Assn. Am., 1972—. Home: 1169 Whispering Wind Dr Arnold MO 63010

DARTER, MICHAEL ISAAC, civil engr.; b. Salt Lake City, June 8, 1943; s. Francis Michael and Bertha (Van Mondfrans) D.; B.C.E., U. Utah, 1966, M.C.E., 1968; Ph.D. in Civil Engring., U. Tex., 1973; m. Shona Olsen, Dec. 23, 1965; children—Michelle, Michael, Paul, Sonya, Rebecca. Hwy. designer Utah Dept. Transp., 1963-65, structural engr., 1966, materials engr., 1967-70; sr. engr. Austin Research Engrs. Inc. (Tex.), 1971-73; research engr. Center for Hwy. Research, U. Tex., Austin, 1970-73, Transp. Research Lab., U. Ill., Urbana, 1973—; asst. research prof. civil engring. U. Utah, winter 1973; asst. prof. U. Ill., Urbana, 1973—; cons. U.S. Army C.E., 1974—. Mem. ASCE, Transp. Research Bd., Assn. Asphalt Paving Technologists, Sigma Xi, Chi Epsilon, Phi Kappa Phi. Contbr. articles to profl. jours. Home: 100 W George Huff Dr Urbana IL 61801 Office: 111 Talbot Lab Urbana IL 61801

DARY, DAVID ARCHIE, educator, author; b. Manhattan, Kans., Aug. 21, 1934; s. Milton Russell and Ruth Engel (Long) D.; B.S. in Humanities, Kans. State U., 1956; M.S. in Journalism, Kan. U., 1970; m. Carolyn Sue Russum, June 2, 1956; children—Catherine Lee, Carol Ann, Cynthia Kay, Cristina Sue. Reporter, editor CBS News, Washington, 1960-63, mgr. local news, NBC News, Washington, 1963-67; dir. pub. affairs Kans. Rep. State Com., Topeka, 1968; mem. faculty U. Kans., Lawrence, 1969—, prof. journalism, 1970—. Cons. broadcast journalism, 1967—. Mem. Kans. State Hist. Soc. (bd. dirs. 1972—), Western History Assn., Assn. for Edn. in Journalism, Sigma Delta Chi, Kappa Tau Alpha. Mason. Author: Radio News Handbook, 1967; Manual De Noticias Radiofonicas, 1970; Television News Handbook, 1970; How To Write News for Broadcast and Print, 1973; The Buffalo Book, 1974. Contbr. numerous articles to various mags. and newspapers. Home: 1101 W 27th St Lawrence KS 66044

D'ASARO, JOHN JOSEPH, accounting co. ofcl.; b. Chgo., May 16, 1936; s. Joseph Anthony and Cynthia Rosalie (Damiani) D'A.; B.S. in Accounting with honors, U. Ill. at Urbana, 1958; m. Virginia Ann Haley, June 21, 1958; children—James Alan, John Anthony, Cathy Ann; m. Barbara Grogan Driggs, Oct. 7, 1972. Staff accountant Ernst & Ernst, Chgo., 1958-69, supr. mgmt. cons. services, 1969-73, mgr., 1973—. Treas. Oak Park Mus. Theatre, Ill., 1967-69, pres., 1969—; tour adminstrv. dir. Oak Park River Forest Concert Tour Assn., 1970-71, pres., 1971—. Served with AUS, 1959. Mem. Am. Inst. C.P.A.'s, Ill. Soc. C.P.A.'s, Beta Gamma Sigma, Sigma Iota Epsilon, Beta Alpha Psi, Phi Eta Sigma. Mem. United Ch. of Christ (financial sec. 1962-66, pres. 1969-72). Home: 1106 Jackson Ave River Forest IL 60305 Office: Ernst & Ernst 150 S Wacker Dr Chicago IL 60606

DASHNER, RICHARD FRANCIS, coating co. exec.; b. Oak Park, Ill., Sept. 26, 1931; s. Francis J. and Margaret T. (Tompkins) D.; student Knox Coll., 1949-50; B.S., U. Ill., 1953; m. Alice T. Turner, July 11, 1954; children—Margaret Ruth, John Robert. Indsl. salesman U.S. Gypsum Co., Chgo., 1955-59; indsl. sales engr. Nat. Gypsum Co., Buffalo, 1959-68; constrn. salesman Gen. Electric Silicones, Oak Brook, Ill., 1968-73, constrn. market devel. specialist, 1973-77; pres. A & D Coating Co., Westchester, Ill., 1977—. Active DuPage council Boy Scouts Am., recipient Scouter's Keys, 1970, 73. Served from 2d lt. to 1st lt. inf. AUS, 1953-55. Mem. Archtl. Aluminum Mfg. Assn. (energy conservation com., sealant com. 1975, reflective insulating glass com.) Constrn. Specifications Inst. (student com. 1970-75, mem. tech. papers com. 1977), Phi Sigma Kappa. Presbyn. (deacon 1972-75). Contbr. articles to profl. jours.; patentee structural glazing systems, dry silicone glazing, silicone in thermal breaks. Home: 919 N Washington St Wheaton IL 60187 Office: 9930 Derby Ln Westchester IL 60153

DAS VARMA, RANENDRA LAL, physician; b. Bihar, India, Oct. 18, 1935; s. Sachindra Lal and Pari Rani (Mitra) DasV.; came to U.S., 1959, naturalized, 1971; B. Medicine, Prince of Wales Med. Coll. India, 1958, M.D., 1958; m. Janet Wassity Aug. 28, 1965; children—Julie, Jay, Robby. Intern, Perth Amboy (N.J.) Gen. Hosp., 1960; resident Akron (Ohio) City Hosp., 1961-65; mem. staff Permanente Med. Group, Parma, Ohio, 1968-72; dir. div. medicine, dir. coronary care and intensive care units St. Thomas Hosp., Akron, 1972—; clin. asst. prof. medicine Case Western Res. U., 1974—; mem. council chiefs of internal medicine, asso. prof. medicine North East Ohio U., 1975—; vis. physician Cleve. Met. Gen. Hosp. Trustee N.E. Ohio chpt. Am. Heart Assn. Diplomate Am. Bd. Internal Medicine. Fellow Am. Coll. Cardiology, A.C.P., Royal Coll. Physicians and Surgeons Can.; mem. Am., Ohio State med. assns., Am. Soc. Internal Medicine. Hindu. Home: 661 Beaverbrook Dr Akron OH 44313 Office: 444 N Main St Akron OH 44310

DASWICK, PETER NICHOLAS, furniture corp. exec.; b. Wilmington, Del., Sept. 1, 1917; s. Nicholas C. and Mary K. (Kosloff) D.; student U. Chgo., 1937-38; B.S., Ill. Inst. Tech., 1949; m. Beverley L. Rippel, Sept. 21, 1939; 1 son, Richard Jonathon. Partner R.C. Harris, P.N. Daswick, Architects, Chgo., 1949-52; pvt. archtl. and engring. practice, Chgo., 1952-60; with Am. Mart Corp., Chgo., 1960—, sr. v.p., 1965—, bd. dirs., 1962—. Mem. A.I.A. Republican. Unitarian. Club: Tavern (Chicago). Home: 237 Walden Dr Glencoe IL 60022 Office: 666 N Lake Shore Dr Chicago IL 60611

DAUBENDIEK, GENE RUSSELL, utilities co. exec.; b. Cylinder, Iowa, Mar. 12, 1923; s. Carl Henry and Bertha K. (Krecji) D.; B.E.E., Iowa State U., 1944; m. Mary Matilda Phillips, Feb. 18, 1945; children—James Louis, Sarah Ann. Mgr., West Iowa Telephone Co., Osceola, 1943-45; engr. Jefferson (Iowa) Telephone Co., 1943—, sec.-mgr., 1962—; pres. Telephone Constrn., Inc., Jefferson, 1950-64; dir. West Iowa Telephone Co., Remsen, Iowa State Bank, West Bend; trustee W.H. Daubendiek Trust, West Bend. Chmn. Jefferson Airport Commn., 1960-72, Indsl. Bur., 1966; mem. Jefferson City Council, 19S6-58, Jefferson Indsl. Devel. Co., 1960. Mem. Jefferson C. of C., Ind. Telephone Pioneers Assn. (life), Iowa Telephone Assn. (hon. dir.), Orgn. Protection and Advancement Small Telephone Cos. (pres. 1969-71), U.S. Ind. Telephone Assn. (dir.), Theta Xi. Republican. Methodist. Clubs: Green County Golf and Country (past pres.), Elks, Lions (past pres.). Home: PO Box 51 Jefferson IA 50129 Office: PO Box 267 Jefferson IA 50129

DAUBENSPECK, ROBERT DONLEY, advt. exec.; b. Butler, Pa., Nov. 5, 1926; s. Frank and Virginia (Donley) D.; A.B., Princeton, 1949; m. Susan Mary Alcorn, Oct. 28, 1967; children—Nancy, Joan, Jean, Thorne. Supr., Benson & Benson, Mktg. Research, Princeton, N.J., 1949-51; sales analyst Lever Bros., N.Y.C., 1951; mgr. sales devel. NBC, Chgo., 1952-61; with Foote, Cone & Belding, Chgo., 1961—, v.p., 1964—, media dir., 1974—, v.p. in charge media and programming, 1977—. Campaign mgr. Congresswoman Florence Dwyer, 1956. Served with USAAC, 1945. Mem. Broadcast Advt. Club. Episcopalian. Clubs: Executive, Whitehall, Boyer, Barclay, St. Charles Country. Author: Recall Technique as Measurement of Broadcast Audiences, 1950. Home: 966 Sunset Rd Geneva IL 60134 Office: 401 N Michigan Ave Chicago IL 60611

DAUBERT, LEROY LINCOLN, engring, co. exec.; b. Lebanon, Pa., Nov. 30, 1911; s. Clarence Elizer and Virginia Ellen (Miller) D.; B.S. in Archtl. Engring., Iowa State U., 1934, B.S. in Mech. Engring., 1936; m. Ruth Thelma Feroe, July 20, 1935; 1 dau., Susan Ann. Engr., Carrier Corp., 1937-41; chief engr. Des Moines Ordnance Plant, 1942-47; engr. Delavan Engring. Co., 1947-52; pres. Deco Engring. Products, Inc., Des Moines, 1952-74, Deco Internat., Inc., Des Moines, 1952—, Daubert Co., Inc., Des Moines, 1974—, Clive Ag Supply, Des Moines, 1974—, D & D Properties, Des Moines, 1974—; chmn. bd. Deco Engring. Products, Inc., 1974—. Chmn. Bd. of Assessment and Review, City of Des Moines, 1958—; pres. Des Moines Sch. Bd., 1961, 66; bd. dirs. Des Moines C. of C., 1969-74, chmn. civic affairs com., 1965-68; chmn. Des Moines Sch. Constrn. Com., 1970—. Recipient Civic award Des Moines Youth Orgn., 1967; Mayors award Mayors Task Force, 1970. Mem. Internat. Assn. Assessing Officers, Nat. Assn. Assessors, Internat. Producers Council, Am. Soc. Heating and Ventilating Engrs. Presbyterian. Clubs: Des Moines, Embassy, Wakonda Country, Elks, Masons, Shriners. Designed and constructed world's first all brick and tile swimming pool; developed electrostatic spray equipment. Home: 3200 Wauwatosa Dr Des Moines IA 50321 Office: 1904 NW 92d St Ct Des Moines IA 50322

DAUER, JAMES ALAN, electronics co. exec.; b. Chgo., July 16, 1947; s. Alvin Joseph and Cecelia Marie (Wisniski) D.; B.S., U. Ill., 1969; M.B.A., Loyola U., 1974. Engr., Electro-Motive div. Gen. Motors, 1969-71; operations research analyst McDonald's Corp., Oakbrook, Ill., 1971-75; dir. operations research Beltone Electronics Corp., Chgo., 1975—; cons. Marvin H. Frank Advt. Agy., Chgo., 1975—. Served with U.S. Army, 1971-72. Recipient Gen. Motors Excellence award, 1969, 70. Mem. Am. Marketing Assn., Operations Research Soc. Am., Engring. Alumni Bd. U. Ill. Home: 756 W Algonquin Rd Apt 11 Des Plaines IL 60016 Office: 4201 W Victoria St Chicago IL 60606

DAUGHERTY, CHARLES HOYL, JR., designer; b. Washington, Feb. 2, 1940; s. Charles Hoyl and Clara (Schorfheide) D.; B.A., So. Ill. U., 1966; m. Judith Ann Runyon, Dec. 29, 1959; children—Amanda Kay, Karen Kay. Student worker, tech. asst. coop. research in design, environ. planning So. Ill. U., Edwardsville, 1961-64, design asst. Inst. Bahavioral Research, Carbondale, 1964-65, staff asst., asst. to coordinator coop. research in design Center for Study of Crime, Delinquency and Corrections, Univ. Relations and Exhibits, Communications Media Services div., 1965-67, comml. artist II Univ. Exhibits, 1967-68, instructional materials programmer III, 1968-73, asst. coordinator, 1973-74, asst. dir., 1974-75, coordinator, 1975—; project dir. Ill. Dept. Bus. and Econ. Devel., 1975, 76, Ill. Div. Vocat. and Tech. Edn., 1975, 76, Fed. Energy Adminstrn., 1976. Active, So. Ill. U. Bicentennial Commn., 1975-76. Served with USAF, 1958-59, Res., 1959-64. Recipient award of merit Indsl. Designers Soc. Am., 1966; Eagle Scout, Boy Scouts Am.,

1950—, Order of Arrow, 1954-58. Mem. Nat. Audio Visual Assn., Aircraft Owners and Pilots Assn., Nat. Pilots Assn. Democrat. Methodist. Clubs: So. Ill. U. Flying Salukis (hon.); Crab Orchard Lake Sailing (harbor master 1976—). Home: 802 1/2 W Walnut St Carbondale IL 62901 Office: Anthony Hall So Ill U Carbondale IL 62901

DAUL, ROGER RAYMOND, equipment mfg. co. exec.; b. Green Bay, Wis., Aug. 2, 1938; s. Raymond and Senarita Helen (Manders) D.; B.A., U. Wis., 1970, B.S., 1972; m. Harriet Newville, Nov. 7, 1959; children—Randolph, Richard, Scott. Mem. mfg. mgmt. staff, staff engr. Aosmith Corp., Milw., 1960-73; plant mgr. Triple P Inc., Necedah, Wis., 1973-75; dir. mfg. Howard Rotavator Co., Harvard, Ill., 1975-76, v.p. mfg., Muscoda, Wis., 1976—. Local chmn., Young Republicans, 1963-65; chmn. physician search com., Muscoda; mem. Muscoda Devel. Com., 1977—. Mem. Indsl. Mgmt. Soc., Am. Prodn. and Inventory Control Soc. Republican. Presbyterian. Lion. Home: 323 S Wisconsin Ave Muscoda WI 53573

DAULT, RAYMOND ARTHUR, educator; b. Muskegon, Mich., June 30, 1923; s. Joseph F. and Eloise M. (Gosselin) D.; A.B., Mich. State U., 1950; M.B.A., Ind. U., 1969; m. Joyce J. Martin, Oct. 19, 1946; 1 dau., Suzanne Raye. Asst. reservation mgr. Bismarck Hotel, Chgo., 1950; asst. mgr. Ind. Meml. Union, Ind. U., Bloomington, 1950-53, mgr. Union Bldg. Med. Center, Indpls., 1953-70; asso. prof. restaurant, hotel and instl. mgmt. Ind.-Purdue U., Indpls., 1970-74, prof., 1974—. Cons. Nat. Sanitation Found., Ann Arbor, Mich., 1970-72, Com. for a Quality Environment, 1970-73, Am. Hotel and Motel Assn., 1968-73. Pres. Bd. Zoning Appeals, Speedway, Ind., 1959-63. Served with AUS, 1943-46. Recipient Keys to N.Y.C., 1968, New Orleans, 1968, Elizabethtown, Ky., 1968, Oklahoma City, 1974, Indpls., 1974, Cleve., 1975, Cin., 1975, Louisville, 1975; named Coll. and Univ. Food Operator of Year, Internat. Foodservice Mfrs. Assn., 1970; Alumnus of Year, Mich. State U. Sch. Hotel, Restaurant and Instl. Mgmt., 1972; recipient Outstanding Faculty Mem. award Purdue U. Sch. Engring. and Tech., Indpls., 1976. Mem. Ind. (exec. v.p. 1972—), Indpls. (exec. sec. 1972—) hotel and motel assns., Mich. State U. Alumni Assn. (pres. 1970-73), Am. Legion. K.C., Lion. Home: 2312 N Fisher St Speedway IN 46224 Office: 799 W Michigan Indianapolis IN 46202

DAUM, CHARLES AUGUST, sch. adminstr.; b. Evansville, Ind., Feb. 17, 1931; s. Adam August and Louise Elizabeth (Fischer) D.; B.S., Evansville Coll., 1953; M.S., Ind. U., 1957; m. Mary Elizabeth Phillips, Nov. 26, 1953; children—Laura Lynn, Brian Kevin, Jennifer Leigh. Tchr., Baker Sch., Evansville, 1955-68; prin. Newburgh (Ind.) Elementary Sch., 1968—; coordinator media Warrick County Sch. Corp., 1968—. Asst. prof. grad. div. U. Evansville, 1965-72. Pres., Warrick County United Fund, 1969-71. Bd. dirs. Southwestern Ind. United Way. Served with AUS, 1953-55. Mem. N.E.A., Nat. Elementary Prins. Assn., Ind. Prins. Assn., Phi Zeta, Lambda Chi. Mem. United Ch. Christ (pres. 1960-62). Eagle (life). Home: 621 Bartlett Dr Newburgh IN 47630 Office: 306 State St Newburgh IN 47630

DAUM, HUGH WARNER, frozen food cons.; b. Sioux Falls, S.D., Apr. 7, 1919; s. Henry Frank and Margaret Leona (Callahan) D.; student N.D. State Coll., 1936-37, U. Minn., 1937-38, U. Santa Clara (Cal.), 1941; m. Kathryn Ann Townsend, Dec. 17, 1949; 1 son, Hugh Warner. Dist. sales mgr. Union Sales Corp., Columbus, Ind., 1938-40, Libby, McNeill & Libby, Seattle, 1940-41; pres. Hugh W. Daum Co., Chgo., 1946-48; nat. sales and advt. mgr. John H. Dulany & Son, Fruitland, Md., 1949-50; pres. Hugh W. Daum Co., Crete, Ill., 1950-76; frozen food cons. Louis Hilfer Co., Chgo., 1976—. Commr. Calumet council Boy Scouts Am., 1973—, mem. nat. council, 1972—, recipient Silver Beaver award; active Ill. Assn. for Crippled. Served to maj. AUS, 1941-46. Mem. Midwestern (dir., past v.p., Frozen Gavel, Igloo awards), Nat., Central States (past pres.) frozen foods assns., Merchandising Execs. Club, Nat., Chgo. food brokers assns., Aircraft Pilots and Owners Assn., Ducks Unlimited, Nat. Pilots Assn., Alpha Tau Omega. Clubs: K.C., Lincolnshire Country (Crete). Home and Office: 585 Aberdeen Dr Crete IL 60417

DAUME, HAROLD CHARLES, JR., marketing exec.; b. Jersey City, N.J., Apr. 5, 1942; s. Harold Charles and Eda (Biber) D.; student Union Coll., 1960-62; B.A., Drew U., 1964; children—David, Lori A., Patricia W. Research analyst McGraw-Hill, Hightstown, N.J., 1964-65, sr. research analyst, 1965-68; research account exec. Gallup & Robinson, Inc., Princeton, N.J., 1968-69; v.p. Audits & Surveys, Inc., N.Y.C., 1972-75; dir. research Marschalk Co., Inc., Cleve., 1975-76; account rep. ASI Market Research, Inc., Chgo., 1969-70, dir. print studies, 1970-71, dir. sales devel., 1971-72, vp, 1977—; guest lectr. Baldwin-Wallace Coll., Cleve. State U., 1975—; speaker Am. Marketing Assn. confs., 1972. Mem. Am. Marketing Assn. (v.p. 1976), N.Y. Soc. Gen. Semantics, U.S. Badminton Assn., Nat. Pilots Assn. Episcopalian. Co-inventor in field of TV comml. pre-testing. Home: 716 Fullerton Pkwy Chicago IL 60614 Office: 180 N Michigan Ave Chicago IL 60601

DAUW, DEAN CHARLES, psychologist, educator; b. Rock Island, Ill., July 31, 1933; s. Charles J. and Frances M. (Heffran) D.; Ph.D. (Vocat. Rehab. Services Adminstrn. fellow 1962-64, NIMH fellow 1964-65), U. Minn., 1965. cons. psychologist McMurry Co., Chgo., 1965-66; dir. orgn. devel. CNA Fin. Co., Chgo., 1966-68; pres. Human Resource Developers, Chgo., 1968—; asso. prof. behavioral scis. DePaul U. Grad. Sch. Bus., 1969—. Mem. Am. Psychol. Assn., Assn. Humanistic Psychology, Am. Personnel and Guidance Assn., Nat. Vocat. Guidance Assn., Am. Assn. Sex Educators, Counselors and Therapists, Acad. Mgmt., AAUP. Author: Creativity and Innovation in Organizations, 3d rev. edit., 1976; Up Your Career, 2d rev. edit., 1977. Home: 1212 Lake Shore Dr Chicago IL 60610 Office: 112 W Oak St Chicago IL 60610

DAVENPORT, JAMES VERTIE, dentist; b. Cin., Aug. 24, 1930; s. Andrew Jackson and Pearl May (Meadows) D.; B.S., Wilmington Coll., 1952; D.D.S., Ohio State U., 1959; m. Jane Glancy, Dec. 20, 1952; children—Beth Louise, Scott Vertie. Asst. engr. Gen. Electric A.N.P. Project, Cin., 1952-55; practice gen. dentistry, Lebanon, Ohio, 1960—. Pres., Warren County chpt. Am. Cancer Soc., 1961-62. Mem. Am. Dental Assn., Ohio, Cin. dental socs. Mason, Kiwanian. Home: 923 McBurney Dr Lebanon OH 45036 Office: 18 N East St Lebanon OH 45036

DAVENPORT, JOHN BRIAN, archivist; b. Grand Forks, N.D., June 5, 1951; s. Willard Eugene and Margaret Jane (Burnham) D.; student U. N.D., 1969-70; B.A., Macalester Coll., 1973; M.A., U. Denver, 1974. Asst. curator spl. collections Chester Fritz Library, U. N.D., 1974-76; archivist O'Shaughnessy Library Coll. of St. Thomas, St. Paul, 1977—. Mem. Am. Hist. Assn. Irish Am. Cultural Inst. Democrat. Club: Elbert Hubbard Soc. Home: 25 S Wheeler St 3 Saint Paul MN 55105 Office: O'Shaughnessy Library College Saint Thomas Saint Paul MN 55105

DAVES, MARTHA MARISE, educator; b. Cullman, Ala., Aug. 5, 1923; d. James Gordon and Louise (James) Daves; B.S., Ala. Coll., 1944; M.A., N.Y. U., 1946, Ed.D., 1963. Tchr., Fairview High Sch., Cullman, 1944-45; faculty State Tchrs. Coll., Florence, Ala., 1946-51; faculty Eastern Ill. U., Charleston, 1951—, prof. phys. edn., 1968—, asso. chmn. dept., 1977—. Mem. Am., Ill. assns. for health, phys. edn. and recreation, Nat., Midwest assns. phys. edn. for coll. women. Home: Rural Route 1 Greenup IL 62428

DAVID, KEITH RAYMOND, educator; b. Arkansas City, Kans., Aug. 20, 1929; s. Floyd M. and Edna G. (Wommack) D.; B.A. in Sociology, Okla. Baptist U., 1954; M.A. in Philosophy, Wichita State U., 1962; Ph.D. in Philosophy, So. Ill. U., 1969; postgrad. Oxford (Eng.) U., 1977; m. Donnaretha Aduddell, Apr. 2, 1949; children—Kevin Lee, Gerald Lynn, Kim Alan, Philip Brian. Detail engr. Boeing Co., Wichita, Kans., 1948-51; liaison engr. dept. of engring. research Wichita State U., 1954-60; instr. ethics and logic So. Ill. U., Carbondale, 1964-68; asso. prof. dept. philosophy William Jewell Coll., Liberty, Mo., 1969—, research asst. Morris Library Archives, 1969. Ordained to ministry Bapt. Ch., 1954; pastor (part-time) various Bapt. Chs., Kans., 1954-62, Ill., 1962-69; participant 4th symposium Am. Philosophy, Winterthur, Switzerland, 1973; instr. Maple Woods Community Coll., Kansas City, Mo., 1974. Pilot, Civil Air Patrol, Coffeyville, Kans., 1948-51; committeeman Heart of Am. council Boy Scouts Am., 1970-73; mem. Citizen's Com., Liberty, 1970; mem. Community Devel. Com., Kansas City, Mo., 1974; mem. planning com. Mental Health Assn., Clay County (Mo.), 1975, bd. dirs., 1976-77. Mem. Am., Mo. philos. assns., Soc. for Advancement of Am. Philosophy, AAAS, AAUP, So. Soc. for Philosophy and Psychology, Am. Hist. Soc., Ill. State Bapt. Assn. (dir. 1967), Kansas City Area Philosophy Tchrs. Assn. (chmn. 1976-77), Phi Sigma Tau, Phi Kappa Phi. Contbr. chpt. to book, articles to profl. jours. Home: 1029 Broadmore Ln Liberty MO 64068

DAVID, PAUL P(ETER), psychiatrist; b. Rumania, Aug. 31, 1921; s. Mihaly David and Margit (Dajbukat) D.; came to U.S., 1951, naturalized, 1956; M.D., U. Heidelberg, 1948; m. Rose Patay, Dec. 20, 1947; 1 son, Raymond. Intern Hackensack (N.J.) Hosp., 1951-52; resident Elgin (Ill.) State Hosp., 1952-53, Mt. Sinai Hosp., 1963-65; practice medicine specializing in psychiatry, Riverdale, Ill., 1965—; chmn. psychiat. dept. Christ Hosp., Oak Lawn, Ill., 1974—; clin. asst. prof. Chgo. Med. Sch., 1968—. Recipient Abbie N. Prince award, 1965. Mem. A.M.A. (Physician's Recognition award 1969, 75), Ill., Chgo. med. socs., Am. Psychiat. Assn. Home: 1100 Cambridge Rd Flossmoor IL 60422 Office: 159 E 144th St Riverdale IL 60627

DAVIDSOHN, ISRAEL, pathologist; b. Tarnopol, Austria, Apr. 20, 1895; s. Jacob and Rachel (Halpern) D.; came to U.S., 1923, naturalized, 1930; M.D., U. Vienna (Austria), 1921; postgrad. U. Berlin, 1921-23; m. Clara Freud, Oct. 10, 1923; children—Ellen Doris, Samuel James. Intern, Mt. Sinai Hosp., Phila., 1923-24, resident, 1924-25, pathologist, dir. labs., 1926-30; research fellow Research Inst. Cutaneous Medicine, Phila., 1926-30; dir. dept. pathology Mt. Sinai Med. Center, Chgo., 1930-65, dir. dept. exptl. pathology, 1965—; cons. dept pathology Rush Med. Coll., Chgo., 1965—, instr. pathology, 1932-34, asso. prof., 1934-47, asst. and asso. prof. pathology Rush Med. Coll. U. Ill., 1941-47, prof. emeritus, 1975—; prof. pathology Chgo. Med. Sch., 1947-74. chmn. dept. pathology, 1947-68, chief div. exptl. pathology, 1969-74. Recipient Gold Medal, Am. Soc. Clin. Pathologists, 1943; Ward Burdick award, 1954; Morris Parker award, Chgo. Med. Sch., 1956; John Elliott award Am. Assn. Blood Banks, 1958; City of Hope award, 1961; Distinguished Service award Am. Cancer Soc., Ill. div., 1967; Philip Levine award. Am. Soc. Clin. Pathologist, 1971, Distinguished Service to the Commn. on Continuing Edn. award, 1976. Mem. Am. Bd. Pathology (trustee 19S2-66, life trustee, 1967, v.p., 1961-63, pres. 1965), Am. Coll. Am. Pathologists (bd. govs. 1956-58), Ill. Soc. Pathologists (pres. 1943), Am. Soc. Clin. Pathologists (pres. 1951-52), Ill. (pres. 1951-52), Am. (pres. 1952-53) assns. blood banks, Royal Soc. Medicine. Jewish. Co-editor, conthg. author: Clinical Diagnosis by Laboratory Methods (Todd and Sanford), 1962; contbr. articles to med. jours. and texts. Home: 3150 N Lake Shore Dr Chicago IL 60657 Office: California Ave at 15th St Chicago IL 60657

DAVIDSON, EUGENE MERLE, chiropractor; b. Horton, Kans., Mar. 24, 1938; s. Francis Newton and Mildred Elizabeth (Schober) D.; student Central Mo. State Coll., 1956-58; Dr. Chiropractic, Cleveland Chiropractic Coll., 1967; postgrad. in Roentgenology, Nat. Coll. Chiropractic, 1970-71; m. Myrna Jane Daugherty, Jan. 11, 1957; children—Carol Jane, Eric Eugene, Patricia Ann, Kevin Ray. Sr. engring. asso. Bendix Corp., Kansas City, Mo., 1958-67; gen. practice chiropractic medicine, Russell, Kans., 1967—. Scoutmaster, Boy Scouts Am., 1972—. Mem. Am. (mem. Peer Review com. 1972-74; mem. Council on Roentgenology 1971-74), Kans. (mem. Peer Review com. 1972-75, sec. N.W. dist. 1968-70, pres. N.W. dist. 1970-72, named Chiropractor of Year 1972-73) chiropractic assns., Acacia, Russell C. of C. (dir. 1970-72), Beta Chi Rho (sec. 1965). Methodist (pres. Adminstrv. Council local ch. 1970-71). Elk, Kiwanian. Club: Internat. On-the-Beam. Home: 136 W 5th St Russell KS 67665 Office: 20 S Maple St Russell KS 67665

DAVIDSON, GEORGE MORTON (MORT), cons.; b. Indpls., Aug. 3, 1916; s. George William and Mary Elizabeth (Welch) D.; A.B., Ind. U., 1938; m. Jane Suiter, Oct. 6, 1939; children—Karen Lee, Kathy Lynn. Sales rep. T. M. Crutcher Dental Depot, Inc., Indpls., 1938-42, asst. to the pres., 1946-53, sec.-treas. 1953-69, pres., 1969—; chief exec. officer George M. Davidson & Assos., Indpls., 1971—. Mem. Indpls. Com. Fgn. Relations, participant Fgn. Policy Confs., 1950-53; participant in the Joint Civilian Orientation Conference, 1959. Mem. of Indiana House Reps., 1953-58, chmn. mil. and vets. affairs com., 1954-58; mem. Ind. Econ. Council, 1955-57; mem. Com. on Continuity of State Govt., 1956-57. Mem. Marion County Civil Def. Adv. Council, 1957-59; civilian Aid to Secretary of Army, State Ind., 1953-61. Vice chmn. U.S.O., Indpls., 1960—, mem. nat. council, 1961—. Served to 1st lt., AUS, 1942-45; ETO; asst. dir. med. dept. Indpls. Organized Res. Corp Sch., 1950-51. Decorated Bronze Star, Oak Leaf Cluster, Combat Med. Badge, Meritorious Service Unit Citation, 3 major campaign Battle Stars, Outstanding Civilian Service medal. Mem. Indpls. C. of C. (chmn. nat. def. com. 1951-53), Ind. State C. of C., Indpls. Hosp. Devel. Assn. (asso. bd. dirs. 1955-57), Assn. U.S. Army (Ind. pres. 1962-63, nat. adv. dir. 1958-71), Navy League U.S., 500 Festival Assos. Inc., 75th Div. Vets. Assn., Am. Legion, V.F.W., Ind. U. Alumni Assn., Res. Officers Assn. U.S. (rep. Indpls. chpt. 82d Congress, 1951, past pres., Indpls., chmn. pub. relations com. Ind. dept. 1951), Rep. Vets. Ind. (treas. 1953-57), Mil. Order of World Wars (Indpls. comdr. 1960-62, Ind. State comdr. 1961-62; nat. membership com.), Marion Co. Rep. Vets. World War II, Def. Orientation Conf. Assn., Newcomen Soc. N.Am., Sigma Chi. Presbyterian. Clubs: Columbia; Armed Forces Officers (gov. 1955-57); 300; Indiana Univ. (Indpls.); Indiana State Legislators. Author Ind. Returning Vets. Program; Armed Forces Res. Leave of Absence for Tng. Act. of Ind. Office: 2625 N Meridian St Indianapolis IN 46208

DAVIDSON, HARLAN LEE, pub. co. exec.; b. Bloomington, Ill., Dec. 7, 1927; s. Claude Charles and Emma Martha (Von Fuseling) D.; B.A., Columbia U., 1952; m. Angela T. Ercole, Mar. 30, 1963; children—Harlan Lee, Francesca, Andrew, Claudia. Dir. bookstore, library and spl. sales McGraw-Hill Co., N.Y.C., 1958-63; dir. mktg. Holt, Rinehart & Winston Co., N.Y.C., 1963-68; dir. U. Chgo. Bookstores, 1968-74; v.p. AHM Pub. Corp., Arlington Heights, Ill., 1974-75, pres., 1976—, chmn. bd., 1976—, owner, 1977—; pres. Metro Books, Inc., 1976—; cons. to pub. cos., colls., univs., 1969-75. Served with USCG, 1945-48. Recipient Russell Reynolds award Nat. Assn. Coll. Stores, 1962. Mem. Am., So. hist. assns., Assn. Am. Pubs., Orgn. Am. Historians, St. Andrews Soc. Democrat. Presbyterian. Clubs: Ill. Athletic, Deer Creek. Home: 1394 Sheridan Rd Highland Park IL 60035 Office: 3110 N Arlington Heights Rd Arlington Heights IL 60004

DAVIDSON, HAROLD EUGENE, clergyman; b. West Jefferson, Ohio, Sept. 13, 1927; s. Henry G. and Mable Maurine (Brown) D.; B.A., Otterbein Coll., 1949; B.D., Union Theol. Sem. N.Y.C., 1952; M.Div., Ashland Coll., 1970; D.Min., Meth. Theol. Sch., Ohio, 1974. Nat. pres. Evang. U.B. Youth, 1947-52; ordained to ministry United Meth. Ch., 1952; asst. pastor Avondale United Meth. Ch., Columbus, Ohio, 1951-52; pastor Como United Meth. Ch., Columbus, 1952-54; chaplain Buckeye Youth Center, Columbus, 1954—. Clin. asso. in pastoral care Meth. Theol. Sem., Delaware, Ohio, 1968—; cons. Buckeye Boy's Ranch, Grove City, Ohio, 1965-74; clin. counselor Hirsch Hall halfway house for boys, Columbus, 1974-77; del. White House Conf. on Children and Youth, 1970. Mem. Nat. Assn. Chaplains for Youth Rehab. (pres. 1962). Author: Adolescence and Juvenile Delinquency, 1960; Understanding Teens, 1965. Home: 2794 Woodstock Rd Columbus OH 43221 Office: 2280 W Broad St Columbus OH 43204

DAVIDSON, HELEN LAHMAN (MRS. STEPHEN POWELL DAVIDSON), archivist; b. Springfield, Mo., Jan. 27, 1918; d. Oren Obra and Lula (Julian) Lahman; student Drury Coll., 1935-38; B.S., S.W. Mo. State Tchrs. Coll., 1939; postgrad. Am. U., summer 1958; m. Stephen Powell Davidson, Feb. 24, 1945. Asst. archivist Eli Lilly & Co., Indpls., 1956-59, archivist, 1959—. Mem. Regional Archives Adv. Council, 1969-74; mem. Ind. adv. bd. Nat. Hist. Publs. and Records Commn., 1976—. Mem. Am. Records Mgmt. Assn. (exec. v.p. chpt. 1970-71), Spl. Libraries Assn. (sec. Ind. chpt. 1963-64, dir. picture div. 1965-68, vice-chmn. picture div. 1968-69, chmn. picture div. 1969-70), Soc. Am. Archivists (mem. bus. archives com. 1960-63, chmn., 1963-66, mem. bus. archives com. 1972-74), Ind. Mus. Soc. (dir., sec. 1971-74), Ind. Hist. Soc. (mem. com. on library 1973—), Delta Delta Delta. Baptist. Contbr. articles to profl. jours. Home: 3329 W 42d St Indianapolis IN 46208 Office: 307 E McCarty St Indianapolis IN 46206

DAVIDSON, JOHN KENNETH, SR., family sociologist, survey researcher educator; b. Augusta, Ga., Oct. 25, 1939; s. Larcie Charles and Betty (Corley) D.; student Augusta Coll., 1956-58; B.S. Ed., U. Ga., 1961, M.A., 1963; Ph.D., U. Fla., 1974; m. Josephine Frazier, Apr. 11, 1964; children—John Kenneth Jr., Stephen Wood. Asst. prof. dept. psychology and sociology Armstrong State Coll., Savannah, 1963-67; asst. prof. dept. sociology Augusta Coll., Augusta, Ga., 1967-74; acting chmn., asst. prof. dept. sociology Ind. U., South Bend, 1974-76; asso. prof., chmn. dept. sociology U. Wis.-Eau Claire, 1976—; research cons. dept. obstetrics and gynecology Med. Coll. Ga., Augusta, 1969-74, pediatrics, 1972-73, also asso. dir. health care project, 1971-73, research instr., summer 1971, research asso., summer 1972-73, research cons. dept. community dentistry, 1974—. Program coordinator Community Devel. in Process Phase II and III, Title I Higher Edn. Act of 1965, 1970; mem. sociology and anthropology Univ. System Ga., 1970-74, chmn. curriculum sub-com., 1970-72; dir. Sex Edn. The Pub. Schs. and You project Ind. Com. on The Humanities, 1975; mem. Nat., Wis., Southeastern councils on family relations; past state chmn. pub. affairs Ind. Assn. Planned Parenthood Affiliates, 1975-76; mem. Eau Claire Coordinating Council. Past bd. dirs. Planned Parenthood North Central Ind., also past chmn. pub. affairs com., 1975-76; bd. dirs., 1st v.p. Wis. Family Planning Coordinating Council. Mem. Am. Sociol. Assn., So., Midwest sociol. socs., Am. Assn. U. Profs., Augusta Coll. Alumni Soc., U. Fla., U. Ga. alumni socs., Groves Conf., Pres.'s Club U. Wis.-Eau Claire, Kappa Delta Pi, Phi Kappa Phi, Phi Theta Kappa, Alpha Kappa Delta (pres. Beta chpt. 1971-72, nat. exec. com. 1972—). Episcopalian. Asso. editor Jour. Marriage and the Family, 1975—; contbr. articles to profl. jours. Home: 1305 Nixon Ave Eau Claire WI 54701 Office: Dept Sociology Univ Wis Eau Claire WI 54701

DAVIDSON, JOSEPH BRIAN, veterinarian, business exec., author; b. Dumas, Tex., July 7, 1923; s. Robert Barney and Daisy Lelia (Baker) D.; student West Tex. State U., 1941-43; D.V.M., Mich. State U., 1946; m. Lucile Jessie Linton, June 13, 1948; children—Pamela, Deborah, Lucinda. Gen. vet. practice, Brown City, Mich., 1946-59; founder, pres. Hemo-Blend Research, Brown City, 1959—; nutritional field cons. Hill's div. Riviana Foods, Topeka, Custom Blend Feeds, Wheatley, Ont., Can., 1965-70; organizer North Plains Land Devel. Corp., Amarillo, Tex., 1971—; organizer, pres. Horse Publs., Canton, Ohio, 1967—, Davidson Pub. Co., Canton, 1970—, Multi-Dent, Inc., Canton, 1971—, Multi-Commerce, Inc., Canton, 1972—, United Cattle Producers, Inc., Canton, 1973—; asso. Vaught Oil Co., Canton, 1966-71; partner Davidson Agri-Bus., Tex., 1972—; co-founder Animal Research Labs., 1974, Profile Mgmt., 1977, Square Circle Devel. Co., Inc., 1977—, Gasoil Energy, 1977—; state veterinarian Mackinac Island, Mich., 1951-57. Mayor of Brown City, 1953-57; county chmn. Citizens for Eisenhower, 1952-53; del. county and state Republican convs., 1951-57. Served with AUS, 1943-44. Recipient numerous plaques, certificates for pub. speaking appearances, service clubs, library assns., others. Mem. Am., Ohio, Mich. vet. med. assns., Ohio Writers, U.S. Trotting Assn., Thoroughbred Racing Protective Bur., Nat. Assn. Watch and Clock Collectors, C. of C. Methodist. Lion, Mason, Elk; mem. Order Eastern Star. Author: Horsemen's Veterinary Adviser, 1967; All Horse Races are Fixed, 1968; Amelia Earhart Returns from Saipan, 1970. Editor Mich. State U. Veterinarian 1946. Home: 2775 Eversholt Circle NW Canton OH 44709 Office: 4450 Belden Village St Canton OH 44718

DAVIDSON, PAUL ROBERT, educator; b. Waterbury, Conn., Aug. 29, 1942; s. Robert Arnold Elliott and Christine Kirk (Hathaway) D.; A.B., Bard Coll., 1964; postgrad. Trinity Coll., Hartford, Conn., 1965, 67-68, N.Y. U., 1965-66; M.A., U. Pitts., 1971, Ph.D., 1976; m. Mary Joan Penland, Oct. 25, 1969 (div. Apr. 1977); children—Christiaan David, Garth Edward; m. 2d, Ernesta Ellen Cunningham, Nov. 8, 1977. Math. tchr. Cheshire (Conn.) Acad., 1966-68, Watkinson Sch., Hartford, 1968-69, Rockland Country Day Sch., Congers, N.Y., 1969-70; teaching fellow, asst. instr. U. Pitts., 1970-76; asst. prof. math. U. Wis., Green Bay, 1976-77; lectr. math. U. Wis. Center, Baraboo-Sauk County, 1977—; cons. Limbach Co., Pitts., 1972-76. Andrew Mellon predoctoral fellow U. Pitts., 1972-74. Mem. Am. Math. Assn. Republican. Episcopalian. Home: 325 13th St Baraboo WI 53913 Office: Math Program U Wis Center Baraboo WI 54313

DAVIDSON, ROBERT LIPPARD, plastics co. exec.; b. Dayton, Ohio, Mar. 22, 1918; s. Walter George and Lillian Blanche (Lippard) D.; B.A., Dartmouth, 1939; m. Catherine Bradley Vilas, July 5, 1943; children—Robert Lippard, Roger V., Anne (Mrs. Thomas P. Sealy), Susan. With Breskin Pub. Corp., N.Y.C., 1939-41; with Kurz-Kasch, Inc., Dayton, O., 1946—, pres., 1961—, chmn. bd., 1974—. Mem. Oakwood Bd. Edn. Trustee Aviation Hall of Fame. Served with USNR, 1942-45. Mem. Soc. Plastics Industries (v.p. 1960-61, dir. 1958-61), Ohio Mfrs. Assn. (trustee 1972—), Theta Delta Chi.

Republican. Episcopalian. Club: Moraine Country (Dayton). Home: 49 Alpine Ln Dayton OH 45419 Office: 1421 S Broadway Dayton OH 45408

DAVIDSON, WILLIAM, clergyman; b. Miles City, Mont., July 20, 1919; s. Thomas and Catherine (Gold) D.; B.S., Mont. State U., 1940; S.T.B., Berkeley Div. Sch., 1946, D.D., 1966; m. Mary Ernestine Shoemaker, June 3, 1942; children—Carol (Mrs. Ronald Carpenter), Thomas, George, Robert. Tchr. agr. Sidney (Mont.) High Sch., 1940-43, ordained to ministry Episcopal Ch., 1947; minister, then rector various chs. in Mont., 1946-56; asso. sec. nat. council div. town and country, home dept. Episcopal Ch., 1956-62; rector Grace Ch., Jamestown, N.D., 1962-65; bishop of Western Kans., 1966—. Chmn. trustees St. John's Mil. Sch., Salina, Kans., 1966—, St. Francis' Boys' Homes, Salina, 1966—. Named Young Man of Year, Lewistown (Mont.) Jr. C. of C., 1954. Mem. Salina C. of C. Home: 1004 Manor Rd Salina KS 67401 Office: PO Box 1383 Salina KS 67401

DAVIDSON, WILLIAM LESLIE, mgmt. cons.; b. Milw., Nov. 22, 1917; s. William Leslie and Sarah Lay (Coffin) D.; B.A., Beloit (Wis.) Coll., 1939; m. Alice Brewer, Feb. 4, 1943; 1 dau., Ann Leslie (Mrs. Terry Robert Peel). Dir. personnel adminstr. Crane Co., mfg., Chgo., 1960-62; co-owner, partner Manplan Cons., Chgo., 1962—; dir. Tower Fed. Savs. and Loan Assn., Western Springs, Ill. Seminar leader Midwest Indsl. Mgmt. Assn., Aurora (Ill.) Coll., 1964—. Pres., Forest Hills Assn., Western Springs, Ill., 1957-58; mem. labor relations com. Ill. C. of C., 1951—. Served with AUS, 1941-45. Mem. Am. Mgmt. Assn., Am. Compensations Assn., Inst. Mgmt. Consultants, Phi Kappa Psi. Episcopalian. Mason (Shriner). Club: University (Chgo.). Contbr. articles to profl. jours. Home: 4909 Woodland Ave Western Springs IL 60558 Office: 20 N Wacker Dr Chicago IL 60606

DAVIDSON, WILLIAM M., basketball team exec. Chief exec.-operation Detroit Pistons. Office: Suite 3000 Cobo Hall Detroit MI 48226*

DAVIES, GRAHAM OVERBY, oral surgeon; b. Chgo., Aug. 9, 1923; s. Clarence Hoover and Lillian (Overby) D.; student Lawrence Coll., 1941-42, U. Chgo., 1948-50; D.D.S., Loyola U., Chgo., 1946; M.S.D., Northwestern U., 1954; m. Suan M. Hartman, Oct. 7, 1957; children—Laura Ann, Julie, Jennifer. Pvt. practice oral surgery, Chgo., 1948—; asso. prof. oral surgery Chgo. Coll. Osteo. Medicine, 1974-77, prof., 1977—; pres. Dagar Products, Inc., 1975; guest lectr. U. Ill.; spl. cons. Ill. Cancer Detection Program. Bd. dirs. Miss Ind. Scholarship Pageant Corp., 1972-74; trustee Town of Michiana Shores (Ind.), 1960-62; trustee Town of Long Beach (Ind.), 1967—, pres. bd., 1973, 76; adv. com. Ind. Coastal Zone Mgmt. Program. Served with AUS, 1942-45; capt. USAAF, 1946-48. Mem. Am., Ill., Chgo., Kenwood-Hyde Park (pres. 1958) dental assns., N.W. Ind. Dental Soc., Ill. (charter), Chgo. socs. oral surgeons, Odontographic Soc., Chgo. Inst. Medicine (gov.), Delta Tau Delta, Delta Sigma Delta. Club: Long Beach Country (dir. holding corp. 1972). Author: The Comparative Effects of Various Local Anesthetics on Pulse Wave and Rate, 1954; co-author Phosphate in Lake Michigan, 1974. Home: 2751 Floral Trail Long Beach Michigan City IN 46360 Office: 111 N Wabash Ave Chicago IL 60602

DAVIES, JAMES GERALD, coll. adminstr.; b. Johnstown, Pa., Oct. 18, 1947; s. Glyndur James and Maletha Margret (Harker) D.; B.S., Evangel Coll., 1970. Computer operator Univac, Oak Brook, Ill., 1970-71; programmer AT&T, Cleve., 1973-74; systems analyst/programmer Evangel Coll., Springfield, Mo., 1974-75, dir. data processing, 1975—; lectr. in field. Served with U.S. Army, to sgt., 1971-73, with USAR, 1977—. Mem. Data Processing Mgmt. Assn. (dir. 1977-78), Nat. NCR Ednl. Users Group (dir.-at-large). Republican. Mem. Assemblies of God. Home: 1360 E Pythian St Springfield MO 65802 Office: 1111 N Glenstone St Springfield MO 65802

DAVIES, JOHN ARTHUR, assn. exec.; b. Cleve., Feb. 29, 1920; s. William Richard and Florence Christina (Koch) D.; B.A., Wesleyan U., 1943; certified profl. mgr. Inst. Profl. Mgrs., Trinity Coll. m. Una Ruth Keeter, Oct. 27, 1951; children—Janet C., Nancy S. Mgr., Flint Ink Corp., Atlanta, 1953-58; materials devel. mgr. Champion Papers Corp., Hamilton, Ohio, 1959-66; exec. v.p. Internat. Assn. Printing House Craftsmen, Inc., Cin., 1966—; dir. edn. council Graphic Arts Tech. Found., Pitts. Mem. Nat. Watch and Clock Collectors Assn. Clubs: Elks, Cin. Lions (sec.). Patentee in field. Home: 5462 Schiering Dr Fairfield OH 45014 Office: 7599 Kenwood Rd Cincinnati OH 45236

DAVIES, ROBERT, mathematician; b. Omaha, May 5, 1917; s. Harold Nathan and Losia (Sheppard) D.; Ph.B., U. Wis., 1939, M. Philosophy, 1946, Ph.D., 1949; m. Frances Noe, June 16, 1956; children—Kenneth, Ralph. Research physicist Taylor Instrument Cos., Rochester, N.Y., 1940-42; research asso. radiation lab. Mass. Inst. Tech., 1942-45; asso. engr. Rand Corp., Santa Monica, Calif., 1949-53; sr. engr. research labs. Gen. Motor Corp., Warren, Mich., 1953-56, asst. dept. head, 1956-62, tech. dir. math. scis., 1962-69, spl. asst. for planning, 1969—. Bd. dirs. Friends Kresge Library, Rochester, Mich.; research com. Sinai Hosp. Bd., Detroit. Fellow AAAS; mem. Am. Math. Soc., Math. Assn. Am., Ops. Research Soc. Am., Indsl. Math. Soc., Soc. Engring. Scis., Am. Soc. M.E., Am. Mgmt. Assn., Sigma Xi. Editor: Friction and Wear, 1959; Cavitation in Real Liquids, 1964. Contbr. articles to profl. jours. Patentee in field. Home: 1601 Kirkway Bloomfield Hills MI 48013 Office: 12 Mile and Mound Rds Warren MI 48090 Died Sept. 7, 1977.

DAVIS, ALVIN GEORGE, internat. trade cons.; b. Chgo., May 10, 1918; s. Isadore and Mary (Wasserman) D.; m. Rose Lorber, Dec. 14, 1940; children—Fred Barry, Glenn Martin. With Sears Roebuck & Co., 1936-40; gen. partner, sales mgr. Ritz Mfg. Co., 1940-41; buyer hobby dept. The Fair, 1941-43; mgr. hobby div. Central Camera Co., wholesalers, 1944; pres., gen. mgr. Nat. Model Distbrs., Inc., 1945-63; dir. internat. operations Aurora Plastics Corp., 1963-70, v.p. internat. div., 1966-70; v.p. Aurora Plastics Can., Ltd., 1963-70; mng. dir. Aurora Plastics Nederland N.V., 1964-70, Aurora Plastics Co. U.K. Ltd., Croydon, Eng. IBM internat. mdse. and distbn. cons.; now internat. trade cons. Mem., chmn. People to People Com.; scoutmaster, past mem. fin. com. Chgo. council Boy Scouts Am.; active, info. officer Civil Air Patrol. Recipient Berkeley award, 1957, Hobbies award of merit Hobby Industry Assn., 1960, Meritorious award of honor, 1975. Fellow Inst. Dirs. (London, Eng.); mem. Nat. Rifle Assn. (life), Soaring Soc. Am., Airplane Owners and Pilots Assn., Acad. Model Aeros. (contest dir. 1936-70), Nat. Model R.R. Assn. (life), Model Industry Assn. (dir. 1952-60, sec. 1954-57, pres. 1957-59), Hobby Industry Assn. (pres. 1957-59), Chgo. Aeronuts (hon.), Internat. Execs. Assn., Am. Soc. Internat. Execs., PCC Publicity Club. Mason (32 deg., Shriner). Club: Chicago Press. Contbr. articles on merchandising to trade mags. Contbg. editor Model Aviation, Brittanica Jr., 1949. Office: 3601 W Devon St Suite 300 Chicago IL 60659

DAVIS, A(NDREW) PAUL, lapidist; b. St. Charles, Mo., Mar. 3, 1895; s. William James and Lydia Edith (Bates) D.; B.Pd. in Edn., S.E. Mo. State Coll., 1915; B.S. in Edn., U. Mo., 1924, M.S. in Edn., 1928; m. Lula May Pierce, May 25, 1916; children—Douglas Courtland, Mildred Louise (Mrs. Ralph W. Kunce). Tchr., supt. schs., Mo., Iowa, 1915-33; bus. mgr. Nine Cent Shoe Repair and Davis Cleaners chain, St. Louis, 1933-60; lapidist, goldsmith, 1954—; numismatist, 1940—; painter, works exhibited one-man shows, St. Louis, 1966, Cape Girardeau, Mo., 1967, Lafayette (Ind.) Art Center, 1968. Mem. Am. Numis. Assn., Am. Art Alliance (pres. St. Louis chpt. 1965), St. Louis Mineral and Gem Soc. (pres. 1962). Baptist (trustee). Mason. Author: Aaron's Brestplate, 1960. Contbr. articles lapidary jours. Address: 1501 Blue Bell Ln Rock Hill MO 63119

DAVIS, ANN, curator; b. Ottawa, Can.; d. Henry Francis and Isobel Margaret (O'Reilly) Davis; B.A., Bishop's U., 1968; M.A., U. Toronto, 1969; Ph.D., York U., 1974. Curator, Canadian art, Winnipeg Art Gallery, Man., Can., 1973—; asso. prof. U. Winnipeg, 1976—; advisor Manitoba Art Council. Man. Dept. Edn., Man. Environ. Council; bd. mem. Canadian Conf. of the Arts, 1974—. Recipient Ont. grad. fellowship, 1968, York U. Grad. fellowship, 1970, Can. Council grad. fellowships, 1971, 72. Mem. Canadian Museums Assn., Canadian Conf. Arts. Office: Winnipeg Art Gallery 300 Memorial Blvd Winnipeg MB R3C 1V1 Canada

DAVIS, ANNETTA CAROLYN, speech pathologist; b. Wichita, Kans., Dec. 8, 1914; d. Lawrence Leslie and Lessie Lelia (Kelly) Davis; A.B., U. Wichita, 1938; M.S., U. Mich., 1941. Clinician, Inst. Logopodics, Wichita, 1938-40; tchr. speech therapy Augusta (Kans.) Elementary Sch., 1940-46, Leavenworth, Kans., 1946-50; speech therapist Eureka Dist., Kans., 1950-51, Spastioville Sch., Wichita, 1951-52; speech clinician, instr. Coll. of Emporia (Kans.), 1952-58; speech pathologist N. Kansas City Sch. Dist., Leavenworth, 1960—. Mem. Am. Speech and Hearing Assn., Mo., North Kansas City tchrs. assns., Alpha Delta Kappa. Presbyterian. Mem. Order Eastern Star, White Shrine of Jerusalem. Address: 811 S 3d St Leavenworth KS 66048

DAVIS, ARVIN LEE, lawyer, county ofcl.; b. Menominee, Mich., Feb. 10, 1938; s. Ferdie and Lillian (Lessin) D.; B.B.A., Western Mich. U., 1961; J.D., Ind. U., 1966; m. Leslie Arden Heyward, Aug. 23, 1964; children—Andrew Jon, Laura Michelle. Admitted to Mich. bar, 1966, U.S. Supreme Ct. bar, 1972; tax atty. Ernst & Ernst, C.P.A.'s, Kalamazoo, 1966-68; mem. firm Brown, Colman & DeMent, Kalamazoo, 1969-74; pros. atty. Kalamazoo County, 1968-69, asst. pros. atty., 1974—. Tchr. accounting and bus. Parsons Bus. Sch., Kalamazoo, 1971-75; dir. Midwest Fish Farming Enterprises, Inc., Kalamazoo, 1971—. Served to capt. Finance Corps, AUS, 1961-63. Decorated Army Commendation medal. Mem. Am., Ind., Mich. bar assns. Republican. Home: 844 Boswell Ln Kalamazoo MI 49007 Office: Kalamazoo County Bldg Kalamazoo MI 49007

DAVIS, BOBBY JOE, supt. schs.; b. Springfield, Mo., Mar. 23, 1931; s. Hillis Wilbur and Ethel Mae (Wright) D.; B.S. in Edn., Southwest Mo. State Coll., 1952; M.S. in Ednl. Adminstrn., Mo. U., 1958; m. Loydene Waters, Dec. 26, 1955; children—Cynthia Suzanne, Michael Wayne. Tchr. Chadwick (Mo.) Pub. Schs., 1953-55, Salem (Mo.) Pub. Schs., 1955-58; elementary prin. Mexico (Mo.) Pub. Schs., 1958-60; jr. high sch. prin. Community Unit Sch. Dist. 9, Granite City, Ill., 1960-64, adminstrv. asst., 1964-67, supt. schs., 1967—. Active Cahokia Mound council Boy Scouts Am., 1970—; mem. lay bd. St. Elizabeth Hosp., 1972—. Mem. Am. Assn. Sch. Adminstrs., Madison County Sch. Adminstrs. (pres. 1969-70), Large Sch. Dist. Council Supts. Ill. (dir.), C. of C. (dir.), Phi Delta Kappa. Club: Kiwanis Breakfast (charter mem.). Home: Route 2 Box 791 Granite City IL 62040 Office: 20th and Adam Sts Granite City IL 62040

DAVIS, BRUCE ALLEN, psychologist; b. Monett, Mo., Aug. 13, 1948; s. William Lester and Mable Caroline (Frederickson) D; A.B. in Psychology with honors, Drury Coll., 1970; M.S. in Guidance and Counseling, Southwest Mo. State U., 1974; m. Sherri Ellen Gallagher, May 31, 1973. Staff psychologist and marriage counselor Greene County Guidance Clinic, Springfield, Mo., 1974-76, 77—; asso. psychologist U.S. Fed. Prison Med. Center, Springfield, 1976; marriage counselor, psychodiagnostician Davis Psychol. Testing Service, Springfield, 1975—; cons. in field. Licensed psychologist, psychol. examiner, Mo. Mem. Am. Psychol. Assn., Am. Assn. Marriage and Family Counselors, Am., Mo. personnel and guidance assns., Mo. Guidance Assn., Kappa Alpha Order. Mem. Disciples of Christ. Home and Office: 1240 S Saratoga Springfield MO 65804

DAVIS, CALEB ABNER, JR., accountant; b. Memphis, Jan. 31, 1933; s. Caleb Abner and Reola (Wiley) D.; Ph.B., Northwestern U., 1961; M.B.A., Govs. State U., 1976; children—Karen, Shari. Civil engr. City of Chgo., 1961-69; accountant, auditor Washington, Pittman & McKeer, Chgo., 1969-71; pvt. practice accounting, Chgo., 1971—; instr. accounting Central YMCA Community Coll., Chgo., 1971—, chmn. bus. dept., 1977—. Bd. dirs. Afro Am. Hosp. Found., chmn., 1967—. Mem. Nat. (dir. 1974-75), Ill. (dir. 1976—) assns. of enrolled agts., Northwestern U., Govs. State U. alumni assns. Home: 8825 S Cottage Grove Ave Chicago IL 60619 Office: 18 S Michigan Ave Suite 920 Chicago IL 60602

DAVIS, CORNELIA HAVEN CASEY (MRS. FRANK V. DAVIS), club woman, ret. bus. exec.; b. Greenville, Ill., Sept. 17, 1909; d. George Farnum and Cornelia (Ravold) Casey; A.B., Millikin U., 1931; m. Frank V. Davis, May 9, 1936; children—James Casey, Thomas Wait (dec. Apr. 1952), Andrew Waggoner. Bond County statistician Ill. Emergency Relief Commn., 1934-36; sec.-treas. E.H. Paul Co., Hookdale, Ill., 1957-67, Davis & Royer, Inc., Greenville, Ill., 1967-73. Pres. Greenville P.T.A., 1944-45; charter mem. Utlaut Meml. Hosp. Found., 1957; historian Utlaut Meml. Hosp. Aux., 1958-59, pres., 1966-67, rec. sec., 1969-70; pres. Greenville Garden Club, 1954-56; chmn. Bond County chpt. A.R.C., 1962-64, Ill. fund vice chmn., 1966, territorial fund chmn., 1967-68, 69, mem. resolutions com. Bd. dirs. Bond County Tb Assn., 2d v.p., 1965-67, pres., 1969-70; 1st v.p. and fund drive chmn. (Christmas Seals) Heritage Trail Tb and Respiratory Disease Assn., 1970-71; chmn. Greenville and Bond County Bicentennial Commn.; bd. dirs. Greenville Sesquicentennial, 1965. Recipient various citations for service, Good Citizenship medal S.A.R., 1962. Mem. Audubon Soc., Nat. Trust for Historic Preservation, Ill. (life mem.), Bond County (charter, pres., dir.) historic socs., Bond County Fair Assn. (life), DAR (regent Benjamin Mills chpt. 1952-54, 68-70, registrar 1964-66, 1st vice regent 1966-68, dir. 6th Ill. div. 1955-56, Ill. corr. sec., 1956-58, nat. def. com. state chmn. 1963-65), Children Am. Revolution (organizing sr. pres. Hills Ft. Soc. 1955, sr. state pres. 1960-63, nat. life promoter, nat. officers club), U.S. Daus. War of 1812 (pres. Kaskaskia chpt. 1963-66, corr. sec. 1966-69, Ill. 2d v.p. 1963-66, 1st v.p. 1966-70, pres. 1970-73, nat. chmn. nat. def. com., 1967-73, hon. state pres.), Ill. Ct. Women Descs. Ancient and Hon. Arty. Co. (Ill. librarian 1963-64, nat. chmn. nat. def. and resolutions com.), Daus. Am. Colonists (chmn. Ill. colonial heritage com.), Col. Daus. 17th Century (charter Ill. chpt., treas.-registrar 1961-66, chpt. pres. 1966-69, chmn. corr. secy. gen. 1970-73, nat. chmn. nat. def. and resolutions com. 1967-76, 2d v.p. gen. 1973-76, pres. gen. 1976—), Colonial Dames of Am. (rec. sec. chpt. XII 1969-71, 77—, 1st v.p. 1974-75), Nat. Soc. Magna Charta Dames, Soc. Descs. Colonial Clergy, Ill. Geneal. Soc., Bond County Art and Cultural Assn. (dir., sec.), Sons and Daus. Pilgrims (chmn. constn. and bylaws com. 1977), Nat. Gavel Soc., Nat. Soc. Daus. Colonial Wars, S. Central Ill. Woman's Golf Assn. (chmn. 1953, 66, 71), Delta Delta Delta. Republican. Episcopalian (regional chmn. ch. women Springfield diocese 1966-68). Address: Rural Route 2 Box 49-A Greenville IL 62246

DAVIS, DANIEL LEIFELD, counselor; b. Columbus, Ohio, July 18, 1951; s. David W. and Jane L. (Leifeld) D.; B.A., Otterbein Coll., Westerville, Ohio, 1973; M.Ed., Kent (Ohio) State U., 1975; postgrad. Ohio State U., 1977; m. LeAnn K. Rhoden, July 6, 1974. Dir. Concord Counseling Service, Westerville, 1972-74; juvenile justice planner, adminstrn. justice div. Ohio Dept. Econ. and Community Devel., 1976—; psychology resident Columbus Psychol. Services, 1977—; vol. counselor Huckleberry House Runaways, Columbus, 1970-72; mem. Westerville Task Force Youth, 1973, North Area Mental Health Assn., 1974; adv. com. Ohio Drug Studies Inst., 1977—; mem. Ohio Drug Treatment Adv. Council, 1977—. Recipient Outstanding Male Sr. award Otterbein Coll., 1973, commendation Ohio Gen. Assembly, 1974. Youth deacon First Community Ch., Columbus, 1970. Mem. Am. Personnel and Guidance Assn. Author manuals. Home: 112 E Broadway Westerville OH 43081 Office: 24 E Weber Rd Columbus OH 43202

DAVIS, ERWIN LLOYD, supt. schs.; b. St. Cloud, Minn., Aug. 13, 1921; s. Erwin John and Loretta (DeZelar) D.; B.S., St. Cloud State Coll., 1947; M.A., U. Minn., 1951; m. Patricia Ervin, June 5, 1946;children—Judith, Margaret, Nancy, Lawrence. Tchr., Forest Lake (Minn.) High Sch., 1947-49; asst. prin., 1949-54; prin. Mahtomedi (Minn.) High Sch., 1954-58, Kaiserslautern (Germany) Am. High Sch., 1958-59; coordinator secondary schs., dependents schs., U.S. Army, Germany, 1959-61; dir. secondary edn. Flint (Mich.) schs., 1961-66; supt. schs. Genesee Intermediate Sch. Dist., Flint, 1966—. Mem. Human Relations Commn., Flint, 1964-68, United Fund Speakers Bur., 1963-69; pres. Flint Goodwill Industries, 1973. Served with USAAF, 1943-46; PTO. Decorated Air medal. Mem. Am., Mich. assns. sch. adminstrs. (pres. 1976), Mich. Congress Sch. Adminstrs. Assns. (pres. 1973), Mich. Assn. Intermediate Sch. Adminstrs. (pres. 1972), Internat. Toastmasters, N.E.A., Phi Delta Kappa. Kiwanian. Home: 500 Dorset Circle Grand Blanc MI 48439 Office: 2413 W Maple Ave Flint MI 48507

DAVIS, F(RANCIS) GORDON, pub. relations exec.; b. Bloomfield, Ind., May 21, 1908; s. Francis Gordon and Grace (Bryan) D.; student Wayne State U., 1925-27, postgrad., 1929-30; B.A., U. Mich., 1929, postgrad., 1930, 42; postgrad. Cleve. Inst. Art, 1936-37, Western Res. U., 1938-39; m. Margaret Aletha Smith, July 13, 1931; children—Margaret Jayne (Mrs. Edward A. Johnson), Marilyn Grace (Mrs. Richard Karl Johnston). Reporter, aviation editor, editorial writer Buffalo Times, 1930-33; feature, editorial sci. writer Cleve. Press, 1934-42; pub. relations dir. Mich. Blue Cross-Blue Shield, Detroit, 1942-46; exec. dir. Mich. Health Council, Detroit, 1943-46; owner F. Gordon Davis & Assos., Royal Oak, Mich., 1946—. Mem. Pub. Relations Soc. Am., Am. (chmn. pub. relations adv. com. 1964-65, pres. conf. pres.' affiliated socs. 1968-69), Ohio (hon. life) hosp. assns., Am. Soc. Hosp. Pub. Relations (chmn. organizing com. 1965, pres. 1968-69), Mich. (pres. 1975-76), Southeastern Mich. (pres. 1973-74) hosp. pub. relations assns. Club: Higgins Lake Boat. Contbr. articles to profl. jours; pub. relations columnist, 1956-71. Home: 1152 Buckingham Rd Birmingham MI 48008 Office: 3601 W Thirteen Mile Rd Royal Oak MI 48072

DAVIS, F(RANCIS) KEITH, civil engr.; b. Bloomington, Wis., Oct. 23, 1928; s. Martin Morris and Anna (Weber) D.; B.S. in Civil Engring., S.D. State U., 1950; m. Roberta Dean Anderson, May 25, 1957; 1 son, Mark Francis. With firm Howard, Needles, Tammen & Bergendoff, Kansas City, Mo., 1950—, asst. chief structural designer, 1960-65, project mgr., sect. chief, 1965-76, dep. chief structural engr., 1976—. Bd. advisers N.W. Kans. Area Vocational Tech. Sch., 1977—. Served with AUS, 1951-53. Registered prof. engr., Mo., Iowa. Fellow Am. Soc. Civil Engrs.; mem. Nat., Mo. socs. profl. engrs. Clubs: Homestead Country, Johnson County Outdoor. Home: 5024 Howe Dr Shawnee Mission KS 66205 Office: 1805 Grand Ave Kansas City MO 64108

DAVIS, FRANK WELLS, JR., lawyer; b. Des Moines, Sept. 5, 1937; s. Frank Wells and Elizabeth (Moore) D.; student Grinnell Coll., 1955-57; LL.B., U. Iowa, 1962; m. Janice Kupfer, Aug. 27, 1960; children—Frank Wells, III, Margaret Anne. Admitted to Iowa bar, 1962; asso. Davis, Huebner, Johnson & Burt, Des Moines, 1962-67; partner Davis, Johnson, Burt & Davis, Des Moines, 1967-73, Gamble, Riepe, Burt, Webster & Fletcher, Des Moines, 1974—. City atty., Windsor Heights, Iowa, 1966—. Mem. exec. com. Central Iowa Regional Crime Commn., Des Moines, 1969-72, vice chmn., 1970-72; mem. citizen adv. bd. Hickman Mental Health Clinic, Des Moines, 1971—; mem. bd. dirs. Greater Des Moines Amateur Hockey Assn., 1971—. Mem. Iowa Def. Counsel Assn., Iowa Municipal Attys. Assn., Nat. Assn. Railroad Trial Counsel, Am., Iowa (mem. com. 1969—), Polk County bar assns., Order of Coif, Sigma Chi, Phi Delta Phi. Republican. Episcopalian (mem. vestry 1964-67). Clubs: Des Moines; University Athletic (Iowa City, Iowa). Home: 7205 Colby Ave Des Moines IA 50311 Office: 2600 Ruan Center Des Moines IA 50309

DAVIS, GARY LEE, mfg. co. exec.; b. Winchester, Ind., Feb. 5, 1950; s. Gayland A. and Mable (Bousman) D.; assos. certificate in mech. design Tri State Coll., 1970, B.S. in Mech. Engring., 1973; postgrad. Purdue U., Fort Wayne, 1974—; m. Kathy S. Roberts, June 12, 1971; 1 dau., Jessica Jean. Product engr. Spicer Axle div. Dana Corp., 1975—. Mem. Soc. Automotive Engrs. (sec., treas.). Roman Catholic. Home: Rt 1 Yoder IN 46798 Office: PO Box 1209 Fort Wayne IN 46801

DAVIS, GARY STEPHEN, clay products mfg. co. exec.; b. Atlantic, Iowa, July 2, 1941; s. Glen McKnight and Carrie Mae (Anderson) D.; B.S., Iowa State U., 1963; m. Sharon Elaine Anderson, Nov. 24, 1962; children—Stephanie Renee, Jill Suzanne. With Wilson & Co., Cedar Rapids, Iowa, 1963-66; regional dir. Structural Clay Products Inst., Ames, Iowa, 1966-69; dir. tech. services Can Tex Industries, Des Moines, 1969-72; dir. archtl. mktg. Endicott Clay Products Co., Fairbury, Nebr., 1972—. Mem. adv. bd. bldg. trades dept. Des Moines Area Community Coll., Ankeny, Iowa, 1970—. Mem. City Council, Huxley, Iowa, 1968-70. Sears Roebuck Co. scholar, 1959, Elks scholar, 1959. Mem. Agrl. Engring. Soc. Am., Constrn. Specifications Inst. (sec. Central Iowa chpt.), Huxley Jr. C. of C. Contbr. profl. jours. Home and office: 303 W 5th St Huxley IA 50124

DAVIS, HELEN LEE (MRS. JOHN RICHELIEU DAVIS), polygraphist; b. Mobile, Ala.; d. James Homer and Frances Esther (Johnson) Lee; B.S., U. Ala., 1946; A.B., Lake Forest Coll., 1956; M.S., Loyola U., Chgo., 1967; m. John Richelieu Davis, Mar. 7, 1947; children—Jennifer Lee, Susan, Helen K., John Richelieu, Thomas Ruff. Singer, Jimmy Dorsey, Tex Beneke, Les Brown, NBC-TV, N.Y.C., CBS Radio and TV, Chgo., 1940-59; polygraphist, 1958—; v.p., dir. testing John R. Davis Assos., Inc., Lincolnwood, Ill., 1959—; tchr., guidance counselor pub. schs., Ill., Ala., 1966-70. Mem. Vol. Bur. Winnetka-Northfield Area, 1973-74. Mem. exec. com. Evanston (Ill.) Caucus. Fellow Am. Acad. Forensic Scis., Am. Assn. Polygraph Examiners; mem. Am. Personnel and Guidance Assn., Am. Sch. Counselors Assn., Nat. Assn. Parliamentarians, AAUW (v.p.), U. Ala.

163 WHO'S WHO IN THE MIDWEST

Alumni Assn. (pres.). Club: Woman's (dir.) (Evanston). Home: 71 Coventry Rd Northfield IL 60093 Office: 7101 N Cicero Ave Lincolnwood IL 60646 also 120 S LaSalle St Chicago IL 60603

DAVIS, HERBERT HEYER, JR., lawyer, title co. exec.; b. Pitts., June 23, 1918; s. Herbert and Victoria C. (Griser) D.; J.D., U. Va., 1941; m. Jean Hamilton Abernethy, Jan. 30, 1971; children—Jill, Vickie, Deborah, David. Admitted to Va. bar, 1941, Ohio bar, 1945; legal officer V.A., Cleve., 1945-49; escrow officer Lawyers Title Ins. Corp., Cleve., 1949-53; pres. Lake County Title, Co., Painesville, Ohio, 1953—; instr. real estate law Lakeland Community Coll.; dir. Wyman Asso's., Inc.; trustee Lake County R.C., 1973. Served with US Army, 1941-45. Recipient Purple Heart. Mem. Ohio, Lake County bar assns., Ohio Land Title Assn. (pres. 1974), Am. Land Title Assn. Republican. Episcopalian. Clubs: Rotary, Grand River Yacht (sec., treas. 1974-77), Madison Country. Home: 7 Wintergreen Hill St Painesville OH 44077 Office: 66 Mentor Ave Painesville OH 44077

DAVIS, JACK CARLSON, bus. exec.; b. Kansas City, Mo., Dec. 30, 1925; s. William G. and Lila (Carlson) D.; B.F.A., Kansas City Art Inst., 1953; asso. in bus. Kansas City Jr. Coll., 1957; student Acadamie Julian, Paris, France, 1948; m. Phyllis Ileana Lakin, Nov. 21, 1947; children—Brett Carlson, Normandy Marie, Glen Barry, Kathryn Lorraine, Edgar Bearn. Asst. advt. mgr. Davis Paint Co., Kansas City, Mo., 1952-55; advt. mgr. Keystone Trailer Co., Kansas City, 1955-57, Central Tech. Inst., Kansas City, 1957-63; exec. v.p. Atlantic Sch., Kansas City, 1963-71, pres., 1971-73; v.p. Nat. Systems Corp., Newport Beach, Calif., 1969-73; founder, exec. v.p. Westervelt Travel Inst. Ltd., London, Ont., Can., 1973-76; founder, pres. Westport Tng. Corp., Inc., Kansas City, Mo., 1976—. Served with USNR, 1943-46. Mem. C. of C. Home: 721 Westwind Dr Lee's Summit MO 64063

DAVIS, JAMES ALLAN, JR., educator, psychiatrist; b. Nebraska City, Nebr., Mar. 21, 1942; s. James Allan and Dorothy Inez (Hood) D.; student U. Iowa, 1960-63; B.S., U. Nebr., 1967, M.D., 1968; m. Joyce Ann Pearson, Aug. 31, 1963; children—Katherine Jo, Jennifer Jo. Intern, Immanuel Hosp., Omaha, 1968-69; resident Nebr. Psychiat. Inst., Omaha, 1969-72, asst. prof. psychiatry, 1972-75, dir. residency tng., 1975—, asso. prof. psychiatry, 1976—; cons. Clarkson Hosp., Omaha, 1975—; attending psychiatrist VA Hosp., Omaha, 1972-75. Mem. adv. com. Youth Service System, chmn., 1973-74. Named Outstanding Resident in Psychiatry, 1971; Outstanding Instr., U. Nebr. Med. Center, 1974, Outstanding Clin. Instr. by psychiat. residents, 1977. Mem. Am., Sioux psychiat. assns., Beta Theta Pi, Phi Rho Sigma. Author: (with Merrill T. Eaton and Margaret Peterson) Psychiatry, Medical Outline Series, 3d edit., 1976. Home: 2015 S 127th Omaha NE 68144 Office: 602 S 45th Omaha NE 68105

DAVIS, JAMES ROBERT, mgmt., cost control services co. exec.; b. Columbus, Ohio, Aug. 21, 1934; s. Robert C. and Vivian M. (Purcell) D.; B.S., Ohio State U., 1956; m. Alice Sullivan Vincent, June 9, 1956; children—James Robert, Jeffrey P., Lucretia J., Linda M. Salesman, Internat. Silver Co., N.Y.C., 1958-61; field rep. Gates, McDonald & Co., Columbus, 1961-65, v.p. mktg., 1965-69, exec. v.p., 1969-70, pres., 1971—, also dir. Treas., trustee Buckeye Boys Ranch, Columbus. Served with USN, 1956-58. Mem. Sales, Mktg. Execs. Internat., Am. Mgmt. Assn. Republican. Clubs: Rotary, Optimists. Home: 2166 N Parkwy Dr Columbus OH 43221 Office: 1261 Dublin Rd Columbus OH 43221

DAVIS, JIMMIE MARTIN, analytical biochemist; b. Abingdon, Ill., Aug. 26, 1936; s. Howard E. and Portia (Simpson) Davis; B.S., Eureka Coll., 1958; M.S., Western Ill. U., 1969; m. Roberta Cowling, June 30, 1957; children—Ginger Roberta, Jennifer Sue, Martin Dale, Derry Tad. Med. research asso. Galesburg (Ill.) State Research Hosp., 1961-69, research scientist I, 1969-71, research scientist II, 1971-73; lab. supr. Galesburg Cottage Hosp. Lab., 1973—. Mem. John Mosser Library Bd., 1977; asst. dist. commr. Prairie council Boy Scouts Am., 1977. Mem. Am. Physiol. Soc., Soc. Neurosci., Lambda Chi Alpha, Sigma Zeta. Club: Kiwanis (interclub chmn., v.p. 1967-68, pres. 1968-69, trustee 1968—, sec.-treas., lt. gov. div. 19 I-I dist. 1976-77). Contbr. articles to sci. jours., books. Home: 500 W Latimer St Abingdon IL 61410 Office: Cottage Hosp 695 N Kellogg St Galesburg IL 61401

DAVIS, JOHN BYRON, surgeon; b. Omaha, Aug. 8, 1922; s. Herbert H. and Olga (Metz) D.; student Yale, 1941-43, 46-47; M.D., Nebr. Med. Coll., 1951; m. Cornelia Alexander Cowan, July 27, 1946; children—Dana Alexander (Mrs. William Miskell II), John Byron, Cynthia Elise. Intern, Presbyn. Hosp. Chgo., 1951-52; resident U. Ill. Research and Ednl. Hosps., Chgo., 1952-56; practice medicine specializing in surgery, Omaha, 1956—; mem. staff Children's Meml., Immanuel, Bishop Clarkson Meml., Meth. hosps., Omaha. Pres. med. staff Immanuel Hosp., 1964; asso. prof. surgery Nebr. Med. Coll., Omaha, 1968—. Served with USNR, 1943-46; ETO, PTO. Fellow A.C.S.; mem. Western Surg. Soc., Am. Thyroid Assn., Am. Geriatrics Soc., N.Y. Acad. Sci., Soc. for Surgery Alimentary Tract. Soc. Head and Neck Surgeons, Pan Am. Med. Assn., Warren H. Cole Surg. Soc., Omaha Mid-West Clin. Soc., Omaha-Douglas County, Nebr. med. socs., Omaha Research Club, Am. Heart Assn., Omaha Clin. Club, Collegium Internationale Chirurgiae Digestivae (titular mem.), Royal Soc. Medicine (affiliate mem.). Contbr. profl. jours. Home: 9937 Devonshire St Omaha NE 68114 Office: West Dodge Med Center Suite 422 8300 Dodge St Omaha NE 68114

DAVIS, JOHN CALVIN, JR., ret. physician; b. Omaha, Nov. 9, 1890; s. John Calvin and Alice (Overton) D.; student Harvard, 1911-13; A.B., B.S., U. Nebr., 1914, M.D., 1917; m. Elizabeth K. Nelson, Apr. 9, 1921 (dec. May 1968); 1 son, John Calvin III; m. Hazel F. Hawes, June 27, 1969. Intern, Methodist Hosp., Omaha, 1917; practice medicine specializing in ear, nose and throat, Omaha, 1922-74; mem. staff Meth., Univ., Luth. Immanuel hosps., Omaha. Tchr., U. Nebr. Coll. Medicine, 1920-57, head dept. otolaryngology, 1949-57; med. cons. U.P. R.R., 1948-74; sr. cons., prof. otolaryngology U. Nebr. Coll. Medicine, Omaha, 1950-74. Served from 1st lt. to capt., M.C., AUS, 1917-19. Diplomate Am. Bd. Otolaryngology. Fellow A.C.S.; mem. Triological Soc., A.M.A., Am. Soc. Study Headaches, Am. Soc. Study Allergy, Alpha Omega Alpha, Phi Rho Sigma. Republican. Presbyn. Mason (Shriner, Jester), Elk, Rotarian. Club: Cornhusker Motor (1st v.p. 1971—) (Omaha). Home: 801 S 52d St Apt 1609 Omaha NE 68106

DAVIS, JOSEPH, ednl. adminstr.; b. McKeesport, Pa., Oct. 24, 1942; s. Jesse James and Daisy Lucille (Williams) D.; B.S., U. Cin., 1964; M.A., Oakland U., 1977. Tchr. adult edn., Cin., 1964; coach jr. high sch., Cin., 1964-65; asst. registrar U. Cin., 1967-69; admissions advisor Oakland U., Rochester, Mich., 1969-70, asst. dir. admissions and scholarships, 1970-71, asso. dir., 1971—; adv. bd. Raised Aspirations for Youth and Adults, 1974—. Mem. Assn. Coll. Registrars and Admissions Officers, Mich. Assn. Coll. Registrars and Admissions Officers, Am., Mich. personnel and guidance assns., Nat., Mich. assns. coll. admissions counselors, Assn. Non-White Concerns, Mich. Assn. Edn. Options, Mich. Council Ednl. Opportunity Programs, Oakland Area Counselors Assn., Mich. State U. Employees Credit Union (adv. com.). Home: 33 Perry Pl Dr Pontiac MI 48058 Office: Admissions Office Oakland University Rochester MI 48063

DAVIS, JUANITA MELBA LAWRENCE, educator; b. Belle Plaine, Kans., May 1, 1936; d. Ulysses Andrew and Carrie Melba (Lawless) Lawrence; student Okla. Christian Coll., 1954-55; B.A. in Speech, Harding Coll., 1960; M.A. in Edn., Kans. State U., 1974; postgrad. Wichita State U.; m. Darrel E. Davis, Aug. 6, 1961 (div. Apr. 1967); children—Brent Thomas, Brian Lane. Sec. Boeing Co., Wichita, Kans., 1957-58; tchr. high sch., Claremore, Okla., 1960-61, Augusta, Kans., 1961-62, 64, Andover, Kans., 1967-69; tchr. jr. high sch., Manhattan, Kans., 1969-74; counselor Carlton Jr. High Sch., Derby, Kans., 1974—. Mem. sch. adv. com. Curtis Jr. High Sch., Wichita. Mem. Am., Kans., South Central Kans. (pres. 1977-78) personnel and guidance assns., Am. Sch. Counselors Assn. Democrat. Mem. Ch. of Christ. Home: 5820 E Skinner St Wichita KS 67218 Office: 4900 S Clifton St Wichita KS 67216

DAVIS, KENT DEL MONCE, med. technologist; b. Rice Lake, Wis., Sept. 22, 1940; s. Owen Del Monte and Theresa Naoma (Larson) D.; student Coll. of William and Mary, 1960, York Coll., 1965; m. Beryl Phillips, Aug. 19, 1961; children—Lisa Ann, Kent Del Monce. Supr. animal research Norfolk Gen. Hosp., 1961-62; lab. specialist Mendota State Hosp., Madison, Wis., 1962-64; supr. dept. spl. hematology and coagulation York (Pa.) Hosp., 1964-69; clin. adminstrv. and research technologist, supr. hematology, coagulation, and radioisotopes Harrisburg (Pa.) Hosp., 1969-70; supr. spl. hematology lab. Gundersen Clinic, Ltd., La Crosse, Wis., 1970—; supr. radioimmunoassay Lab., Lutheran Hosp., La Crosse, 1975-76. Served with USN, 1958-61. Mem. Am. Bd. Bioanalysis, AAAS, Internat. Soc. Clin. Lab. Technologists. Baptist. Contbr. articles to profl. jours. Home: Route 3 Box 159C La Crosse WI 54601 Office: 1836 South Ave La Crosse WI 54601

DAVIS, LAWRENCE, educator; b. Blossburg, Pa., Aug. 17, 1932; s. Harold Irving and Carrie Mae (Rude) D.; B.S., Black Hills State Coll., 1957; M.A., U. S.D., 1958; m. Shirley Leone Blodgett, May 24, 1957; children—Shirleen Deanna (dec.), Darrell Eugene. Speech therapist Sioux City (Iowa) Pub. Schs., 1958-68; asst. prof. speech and hearing sci. Briar Cliff Coll., Sioux City, 1968-74; instr. gen. and related instruction Western Iowa Tech. Community Coll., Sioux City, 1974—; cons. N.W. Hearing Aid Center, Sioux City. Past pres. Sioux City Lions, 1971, zone chmn., 1977. Served with USAF, 1950-54. Certificate of clin. competence, Am. Speech and Hearing Assn. Mem. Am., Iowa vocat. assns., Iowa Higher Edn. Assn., Am. Legion, Phi Delta Kappa. Methodist. Home: 3416 Pierce St Sioux City IA 51104 Office: Box 265 Sioux City IA 51106

DAVIS, LELAND LOWELL, mfg. co. exec.; b. Marlin, Tex., Feb. 2, 1930; s. Lowell L. and Blanche (Amos) D.; student U. Corpus Christi, 1948-50; M.B.A., U. Md., 1964; m. Kathryn V. Phillips, July 6, 1956; children—George Robert, Stephen Dwain, Susan Renee. Joined USMC, 1951, advanced through grades to maj., 1962; mem. U.S.-Japanese Mil. Indsl. Council, 1953-54; maintenance and logistics specialist, 1956-60; research and devel. mil. vehicles, 1960-64; ret., 1964; mgr. mil. sales Avco Lycoming, Williamsport, Pa., 1964-66, mgr. indsl. engines, 1966-70, dir. indsl. products, 1970-71; dir. marketing Am Gen. Corp., Wayne, Mich., 1971-72; v.p. Irvin Industries Inc., Detroit, 1972—. Recipient commendation for devel. programs on Okinawa, Ryukan Govt., 1960. Mem. Soc. Automotive Engrs., Am. Mgmt. Assn. Home: 5385 Saline-Ann Arbor Rd Saline MI 48176 Office: 31120 W 8 Mile Rd Farmington MI 48024

DAVIS, LEORN JAMES, realtor, ins. agt.; b. Amo, Ind., Oct. 18, 1923; s. Henry Wilson and Mapal Fern (Hamilton) D.; student Purdue U., 1963; m. Barbara Jane Hillman, Sept. 22, 1962; children—Ronald James, James Perry, Kent James. Owner, L.J. Davis Ins. Agy., Davis Realty, Plainfield, Ind., 1948—. Mem. Hendricks County Bd. Realtors (pres. 1969), Plainfield, Ind. C. of C. Lion, Rotarian, Mason; mem. Order Eastern Star. Home: PO Box 127 Amo IN 46103 Office: 2420 E Main St Plainfield IN 46168

DAVIS, LESTER WILLIAM, JR., travel exec.; b. Indpls., Dec. 12, 1924; s. Lester W. and Geraldine (Gregory) D.; B.S., Eastern Ill. U., 1947; m. Virginia M. Smith, Feb. 2, 1943; children—Shirley Ann Davis Casey, Debra Diann. Radio, TV announcer-news dir. WLBH, Mattoon, Ill., WPRS, Paris, Ill., WFRL, Freeport, Ill., WREX-TV, Rockford, Ill., 1947-57; del. leader dir. coordinator People to People Internat., Winnebago, Ill., Maupintour, Lawrence, Kans., 1957—; trustee, mem. exec. bd. People to People, 1975—. Bd. dirs. Ill. Growth Enterprises. Served with Paratroop Corps, U.S. Army, 1942-45. Mem. VFW. Republican. Presbyterian. Clubs: Lions, Elks, Moose, Masons, Shriners, Germania of Freeport. Home and Office: PO Box 32 306 N Elida St Winnebago IL 61088

DAVIS, MARY-AGNES MILLER (MRS. EDWARD DAVIS), social worker; b. Montgomery, Ala.; d. George Joseph and Mollie (Ingersol) Miller; B.A., Wayne State U., 1944; postgrad. U. Mich., 1946. Family caseworker marriage counsellor Cath. Charities, Detroit, social worker Youth Service Bur., Detroit, 1951, 1957-59, foster homes dept. Juvenile Ct., Detroit, 1953-57, Community Action for Detroit Youth, 1963-64; asst. dir. community relations Ed Davis, Inc., Chrysler Agy. Lectr., instr. Madonna Coll. for Girls, Livonia, Mich.; pub. relations dir. James Fraziers Symphony concert. Founder Co-ette Club, Inc., 1942, nat. sponsor, cons., 1955—, also mem. nat. bd. dirs.; mem. speakers bur. Nat. Conf. Christians and Jews; chmn. Women's com. United Negro Coll. Fund; mem. fgn. visitors com. Internat. Inst.; mem. Catholic Inter-racial com.; pres. Mayor's Com. Keep Detroit Beautiful, Inc., 1973—; mem. adv. bd. Women for Detroit Symphony Orch., 1974-75. Bd. dirs., adult membership com. Campfire Girls; exec. com. vol. bur. Women's Com. United Community Services, 1947-50, mem. governing bd.; mem. Mich. Adv. Council on Day Care; dir., 2d v.p. Franklin Settlement; bd. dirs., v.p. Neighborhood Service Orgn., United Found., 1955-56; bd. dirs. Detroit Red Cross, Women's Assn. of Detroit Symphony Orch., Nat. Council U.S. Women, Inc. Recipient vol. award United Community Services, YWCA Ann. award, 1963, Nat. award United Negro Coll. Fund, 1964, Heart of Gold award United Found., 1968, Keep Detroit Beautiful medal of honor, 1976. Mem. AIM (asso.), Nat. Assn. Social Workers, Acad. Certified Social Workers, Nat. Council Women U.S. Inc. (sustaining), St. Joseph's Indian Mission (sustaining), Girl Friends Inc. (local editor 1958—, nat. mag. editor 1961-63), League Women Voters (unit sec. 1964), Am. Assn. UN, Founders Soc. Detroit Inst. Arts, League Catholic Women, NAACP (life), Alpha Kappa Alpha. Home: 2020 W Chicago Blvd Detroit MI 48206 Office: 11825 Dexter Blvd Detroit MI 48224

DAVIS, MICHAEL STEPHEN, counselor; b. Steubenville, Ohio, Feb. 27, 1947; s. Dushan G. and Mary Agnes (Mulrooney) D.; B.A., Kent State U., 1969; M.S. in Edn., U. Dayton, 1975. Tchr., Holy Rosary Central Grade Sch., Steubenville, 1969-72; playground supr., adult leisure edn. dir. City of Steubenville, 1972-73; counselor, chief transitional services Jefferson County Comprehensive Mental Health Center. Steubenville. 1973-77; sr. counselor Family Service Assn., Steubenville, 1977—; cons. social work Jefferson County Headstart Program. Trustee, Jefferson County Young Democrats, 1972. Mem. Am. Personnel and Guidance Assn., Am. Rehab. Counselors, Internat. Assn. Psychosocial Rehab. Democrat. Roman Catholic. Developed psychiat. transitional services program. Home: 216 Opal Blvd Steubenville OH 43952 Office: 725 N 4th St Steubenville OH 43952

DAVIS, MORRIS, polit. scientist; b. Boston, Oct. 9. 1933; s. Hyman William and Mary (Goldstein) D.; A.B., Harvard Coll., 1954; A.M., Ph.D., Princeton U., 1958; m. Ruth Phyllis Miller, June 21, 1958; children—Jonathan Miller, Melissa Anne, William Atticus. Research asst. Center Internat. Studies, Princeton U., 1958; instr. polit. sci. U. Wis., Madison, 1958-59; asst. prof. polit. sci. Dalhousie U., Halifax, Can., 1960-62; asst. prof. polit. sci. Tulane U., New Orleans, 1962-64, asso. prof., 1964-65; asso. prof. polit. sci. U. Ill., Urbana-Champaign, 1965-68, prof., 1968—. Panelist com. internat. disaster assistance Nat Acad. Scis., 1977. Research tng. fellow, Social Sci. Research Council, 1959-60; USPHS research grantee, 1964-67; John Simon Guggenheim Meml. Found. fellow, 1967-68; Ford Found. fellow, 1969-70; NSF research grantee, 1971-74; Killam sr. fellow, 1972-73. Mem. Peace Sci. Soc., Assn. Can. Studies in U.S. Democrat. Jewish. Author books: Iceland Extends Its Fisheries Limits: A Political Analysis, 1963; (with M.B. Weinbaum) Metropolitan Decision Processes: An Analysis of Case Studies, 1969; (with J.F. Krauter) The Other Canadians: Profiles of Six Minorities, 1971; editor: Civil Wars and the Politics of International Relief: Africa, South Asia, and the Caribbean, 1975; Interpreters for Nigeria: The Third World and International Public Relations, 1977. Contbr. articles to profl. publs. Home: 3 Burnett Circle Urbana IL 61801 Office: 361 Lincoln Hall U Ill Urbana IL 61801

DAVIS, OWEN ROBERT, tractor mfg. co. exec.; b. San Antonio, May 11, 1931; s. Owen Ulmont and Lucille (Nottingham) D.; student S.W. Tex. State Tchrs. Coll., 1951; B.S. in Agrl. Engring., Tex. A. and M. U., 1952; m. Mary Jane McDonald, June 6, 1953; children—Robert Owen, Daniel Charles, Cindy Jane. With Allis-Chalmers Co., Milw., 1954—, chief engr. agrl. equipment div., 1966-70, mgr. engring., 1970-74, gen. mgr. agrl. tractor div., 1974—. Pres. P.T.A. Northview Elementary Sch., Waukesha, Wis., 1961. Served to 1st lt. arty. AUS, 1952-54; Korea. Registered profl. engr., Wis. Mem. Am. Soc. Agrl. Engrs., Soc. Automotive Engrs., Farm and Indsl. Equipment Inst. Home: 638 S Greenfield Ave Waukesha WI 53186 Office: PO Box 512 Milwaukee WI 53201

DAVIS, PERRY LAWRENCE, educator; b. Bay St. Louis, Miss., Jan. 25, 1912; s. Earl Kenneth and Beatrice Marie (LeBlanc) D.; B.S., Spring Hill Coll., 1940; M.A., Miss. So. U., 1949; Ph.D., La. State U., 1954; m. Jean Ann Fiesler, Nov. 2, 1973; children—Lawrence P., Thomas Earl, Pamela Mae, Donald David. Tchr., St. Rose Elementary Sch., Bklyn., 1933-34; tchr., Baton Rouge, 1934-42; guidance dir. pub. schs., Ponchatoula, La., 1947-54; supr. guidance services Ascension Parish, Donaldsonville, La., 1954-55; dir. mental health clinic, Donaldsonville, 1955-58; prof. edn.-guidance Bradley U., Peoria, Ill., 1958—. Home: 823 Rebecca Pl Peoria IL 61606

DAVIS, PETER ANTHONY, lawyer, author, photographer; b. Ludington, Mich., Nov. 7, 1936; s. Alexander Wilberforce and Helen Alvina (Peterson) D.; B.A., Miami U., 1960; M.A., U. Kans., 1962; postgrad. Syracuse U., 1962-63; J.D., Northwestern U., 1966; m. Ann Margaret Weber, Nov. 26, 1960. Admitted to Mich. bar, 1966; practiced in Detroit, 1966-70, Ann Arbor, Mich., 1970—; mem. firm Clark, Klein, Winter, Parsons & Prewitt, Detroit, 1966-70; partner Hooper, Hathaway, Fichera, Price & Davis, Ann Arbor, 1970—; instr. polit. sci. U. Kans., 1961-62. Served with AUS, 1956-58. Fellow Grad. Overseas Tng. Program in India, Maxwell Grad. Sch. Citizenship and Pub. Affairs, Syracuse U., 1962-63. Life fellow Am. Trial Lawyers Found.; mem. Am. Arbitration Assn. (nat. panel labor arbitrators 1968—), Def. Research Inst., Am. Judicature Soc., Am., Washtenaw County (chmn. fed. ct. com., mem. judiciary com.), Detroit bar assns., State Bar Mich., Am. (labor arbitration and med. malpractice com.), Mich. trial lawyers assns., Pi Sigma Alpha. Author: Discovery Techniques: A Handbook for Michigan Lawyers; contbr. numerous articles to profl. jours. Home: 3167 Wagner Rd Ann Arbor MI 48103 Office: Tenth Floor First Nat Bldg Ann Arbor MI 48108

DAVIS, PHILLIP RAY, agrl. engr.; b. Danville, Ill., May 7, 1946; s. Lloyd and Mary Alice (Parliament) D.; B.S. in Agrl. Engring., U. Ariz., 1969, M.S., 1972; m. Andrea Lee Taft, June 8, 1968; children—Melanie Diane, Gabrielle Lynn, Phillip Nathaniel. Instr. U. Ariz., 1969-74; agrl. engr. Hill Cons. Engring., Redding, Calif., 1974; agrl. engr., partner Davis Fertilizer & Grain, Georgetown, Ill., 1974—. Mem. Am. Soc. Agrl. Engrs. (chmn. Ariz. sect. 1973-74). Address: Rural Route 1 Georgetown IL 61846

DAVIS, REED ELLSWORTH, real estate broker; b. Humboldt, Nebr., Aug. 29, 1893; s. Adonirum Judson and Elizabeth Jane (Hurley) D.; grad. Chillicothe Bus. Coll., 1916; student Grand Island Coll., 1916-18; m. Myrtle Dorothy Kenworthy, Sept. 1, 1923; 1 son, Reed Ellsworth. Tchr. bus. adminstrn. Grand Island (Nebr.) Acad., 1916-18; motion picture stunt flyer, 1919-20; supr. constrn. of 1st cabin airplane built in U.S., 1921; real estate salesman Burt Fowler Co., Realtors, Omaha, 1922-34; comdr. Civilian Conservation Corps, Cloquet, Minn., 1934-35; real estate salesman Stuht-Bedford Co., Realtors, Omaha, 1936-41; v.p. Hargleroad-Davis Co., Realtors, Omaha, 1949-59; pres. Reed Davis Co., Realtors, Omaha, 1959—. Served with U.S. Army, 1918-19, USAAF, 1941-48, USAF, 1951-52; now col. ret. Mem. Omaha Bd. Realtors (profl. standards com. 1971-75), Add Sell League Omaha, S.A.R., Am. Legion (life), Am. Assn. Ret. Persons, Nat. Assn. Uniformed Services, Air Force Assn. (charter), Res. Officers Assn. (life mem., chpt. sec. 1938-49, state v.p. for air 1953-54), Ret. Officers Assn. (life mem., chpt. pres. 1970-71), Omaha C. of C., Order Daedalians (life). Mason (Shriner), Nat. Sojourner. Clubs: OX-5 (life mem.), Press, Statesman, Offutt Air Base Officers. Home: 3724 Mason St Omaha NE 68105 Office: 159 N 72d St Omaha NE 68114

DAVIS, RICHARD BRADLEY, physician; b. Iowa City, Iowa, Nov. 6, 1926; s. Bradley Nelson and Gladys Mae (Fairbanks) D.; B.S., Yale U., 1949; M.D., State U. Iowa, 1953; Ph.D., U. Minn., 1964; m. Jean Nixeen Anderson, June 22, 1957; children—Janet, Stephen, Catharine. Intern, Mary Fletcher Hosp., Burlington, Vt., 1953-54, resident, 1954-56; instr. U. Minn., Mpls., 1959-64, asst. prof. medicine, 1964-69; vis. investigator Sir William Dunn Sch. Pathology, Oxford, Eng., 1964-65, MRC Blood Coagulation Research Unit, Churchill Hosp., Oxford, 1965; asso. prof. medicine U. Nebr., Omaha, 1969-73, prof. medicine, 1973—, acting dir. div. hematology, 1974-76, prof. pathology, 1976—, dir. hematology div., 1976—, fellow grad. faculty, mem. exec. grad. council, exec. com. U. Nebr. Hosps., Med. Center. Served with U.S. Army, 1945-46. Borden Undergrad. Med. Research awardee, 1960; USPHS career devel. awardee, 1961-69. Fellow A.C.P.; Central Soc. Clin. Research, Am. Fedn. Clin. Research, Am. Soc. Exptl. Pathology, N.Y. Acad. Scis., Am. Assn. History of Medicine, Soc. Exptl. Biology and Medicine, Am. Soc. Hematology, Royal Micros. Soc., Internat. Soc. Haemostasis and Thrombosis, Omaha Mid-West Clin. Soc., Sigma Xi, Alpha Omega Alpha, Phi Beta Pi, Theta Kappa Psi. Contbr. articles to sci. publs. Home: 3514 S 94th St Omaha NE 68124 Office: 42nd St and Dewey Ave Omaha NE 68105

DAVIS, RICHARD FRANCIS, govt. ofcl.; b. Providence, Aug. 18, 1936; s. Walter Francis and Mary Elizabeth (Gearin) D.; B.S., U. Ark., 1964; postgrad. Mass. Inst. Tech., 1964; m. Virginia Catherine Oates, Aug. 27, 1960; children—Walter Douglas, John Richard, Theresa Catherine. Planner, Met. Area Planning Commn. Little Rock, 1964-66; mem. Met. Planning Commn. Kansas City, Mo., 1966-67, dir. econs., 1967-69, dir. ops., 1969-71; exec. dir. Mid-Am. Regional Council, Kansas City, 1972-77; gen. mgr. Kansas City Area Transp. Authority, 1977—; instr. city planning U. Mo., Kansas City, 1973-74. Planning commr. City of Gladstone, Mo., 1967-69, city councilman, 1969-71, mayor, 1971-72, chmn. park bd., 1972-76; mem. Clay County Mo. Indsl. Devel. Commn., 1972—; mem. Council on Edn. Kansas City, Mo., 1974—. Served with USAF, 1955-59. Mem. Am. Pub. Works Assn., Am. Soc. Pub. Adminstrn. (Pub. Adminstr. of Year 1973), Am. Soc. Planning Ofcls., Internat. City Mgmt. Assn. (certified planner in charge Mo.), Ad Club Kansas City. Home: 3612 N Brooktree Circle Gladstone MO 64119 Office: 1350 E 17th St Kansas City MO 64108

DAVIS, ROBERT EARL, research pharmacist; b. Jackson, Miss., Mar. 7, 1942; s. F. Earl and Agnes Gloria (Simmons) D.; B.S. in Pharmacy, U. Miss., Ph.D. in Pharmaceutics; m. Patricia Moak, Sept. 14, 1961; children—Diana Lynn, Robert Earl, Karen Leigh. Research pharmacist CIBA Pharm. Corp., Summit, N.J., 1966; chief pharmacist Oxford-Lafayette County Hosp., Oxford, Miss., 1967; instr. pharmacy U. Miss., 1967-68; sr. research asso. pharm. product devel. Mead Johnson & Co., Evansville, Ind., 1968—. Am. Found. Pharm. Edn. fellow, 1965-68. Mem. Am. Pharm. Assn., Acad. Pharm. Scis., Basics and Indsl. Sects. Acad. Pharm. Scis., Omicron Delta Kappa, Rho Chi. Baptist. Contbr. articles to profl. jours. Home: 900 Hartford Ct Evansville IN 47710 Office: 2404 Pennsylvania Ave Evansville IN 47721

DAVIS, ROBERT LOUIS, lawyer; b. Wichita, Kans., June 16, 1927; s. Carl H. and Maria (Francisco) D.; A.B., U. Kans., 1950, J.D., 1952; m. Marian Frances Larson, June 26, 1955; children—Martha F., Alison L., Carl B., Janet E. Admitted to Kans. bar, 1952, Utah bar, 1953; atty. Gulf Oil Corp., 1952-53; partner firm Davis & Davis, Wichita, 1954-61, Davis, Bruce & Davis, 1962-70, Davis, Bruce, Davis & Cather, 1971-72, Davis, Bruce, Davis & Winkler, Wichita, 1973-77, Bruce, Davis & Gilhousen, Wichita, 1977—; lectr. bus. law Friends U., Wichita, 1967. Pres. Goodwill Industries Greater Wichita, 1965-66, 71-73; mem. Wichita Bd. Edn., 1963-71, also pres., 1969-70; bd. dirs. Wichita Guidance Center, 1964-70, Friends Com. on Nat. Legis., Washington, 1970—, Community Planning Council Wichita, 1972-76; trustee Friends U., 1959-77, chmn. bd., 1965-74; trustee Kans. Found. Pvt. Colls., Kans. Yearly Meeting Friends. Served with USNR, 1945-46. Mem. Wichita, Kans., Utah, Am. bar assns., Assn. Governing Bds. Univs. and Colls., Nat. Assn. Coll. Attys., Phi Beta Kappa, Omicron Delta Kappa. Clubs: Masons (33 deg.), Shriners, Lions; Keystone High-Twelve, Petroleum, Univ., Knife and Fork (Wichita). Mem. Soc. of Friends. Editor The Logos jour. Alpha Kappa Lambda, 1950-60. Home: Route 1 Box 66A Colwich KS 67030 Office: 1022 Union Center Wichita KS 67202

DAVIS, STUART ALAN, realtor; b. Denver, Mar. 15, 1930; s. Elwyn J. and Laurene (Freeland) D.; B.S., Washington U., 1952; m. Dorris Helen Fleck, June 21, 1952; children—Stuart Alan, Jay Brian. Sales asso. Laurene Davis, Inc., 1951-57, gen. partner, 1957-62, v.p., 1962-65, pres., 1965—. Mem. real estate faculty Forest Park Community Coll., St. Louis, 1968-73. Chmn., Webster Groves (Mo.) Bd. Adjustment, 1963—; vice-chmn. Webster Groves Community Youth Council, Citizen's Adv. Council and Bus. Devel. Commn., 1962-67; pres., PTA, 1968; active Boy Scouts Am. Real estate chmn. 2d congl. dist. campaign Republican party, 1972-76. Trustee F.S. Plant Park and Wildlife Sanctuary; bd. dirs. South County region ARC, 1964-68; mem. exec. com. Better Bus. Bur. Greater St. Louis, 1975—. Served as 2d lt. AUS, 1953-54. Recipient citation Nat. Inst. Real Estate Brokers, 1967, Distinguished Service citation City of Webster Groves, 1968. Mem. Nat. Assn. Realtors (dir. 1977), Realtors' Nat. Mktg. Inst., Mo. Realtors Assn. (pres. 1977, chmn. exec. com.), Real Estate Bd. Met. St. Louis (pres., chmn. exec. com. 1974—), Navy League, Webster Groves C. of C. (pres. 1961-62). Lion. Club: Annapolis Parents (pres. 1972—) (St. Louis). Home: 228 Jefferson Rd Webster Groves MO 63119 Office: 127 W Lockwood Ave Webster Groves MO 63119

DAVIS, THOMAS JORDAN, advt. and pub. relations exec.; b. Memphis, Apr. 22, 1908; s. Cleveland and Amy Lee (Hazlet) D.; ed. pub. schs., spl. classes in pub. relations and advt.; m. Dahl Jean Hollingsworth, Sept. 3, 1929; children—Thomas L., Beryl Jean. Investigator, State of Ohio, 1934-38; columnist Ohio State News, Columbus, 1936-40, advt. dir., 1941-43; pres. Tom Davis Agy., bus. and mktg. cons., Cleve., 1958—. Mem. Cleve. City Council, 1938-40; chmn. Ohio Statewide Polit. Orgn., 1937-44; Mem. Ohio and Cuyahoga County Democratic Coms. Recipient Distinguished Contbn. award Ohio Ho. of Reps., 1968, Distinguished Service award Nat. Assn. Mktg. Developers, 1962, Distinguished Service award Mich. State Hwy. Assn., 1969. Mem. Greater Cleve. Growth Assn., NAACP (life), Cleve. Bus. League, USCG Aux. Roman Catholic. Clubs: Recess (Detroit), Great Lakes Cruising. Home: 14616 Onaway Rd Shaker Heights OH 44120 Office: 1940 E 6th St Cleveland OH 44114

DAVIS, VICTOR JOSPEH, bus. exec.; b. St. Louis, Dec. 30, 1936; s. Victor Kenneth and Dorothy Rose (Andrews) D.; B.B.A., U. Mo., 1959; m. Rose Marie Bartelow, May 9, 1964; children—Victor, Paul, Jennifer, Catherine. Sales mgr. Procter & Gamble, Los Angeles, to 1977; dir. personnel devel. The Drackett Co., Cin., 1977—, also dir. tng. dept.; cons. communications and tng. to various bus. firms, 1973—. Active United Appeal of Cin., 1977—; vol. United Negro Coll. Drive, 1977. Served with USN, 1959-63. Mem. Am. Soc. Personnel Adminstrs. Roman Catholic. Club: Harper's Point Racquet. Home: 10611 Orinda Dr Montgomery OH 45242 Office: 5020 Spring Grove Ave Cincinnati OH 45230

DAVIS, WAYNE PITMAN, publisher, editor; b. Phillipsburg, Mo., Sept. 9, 1920; s. William Riley and Alice (Pitman) D.; B.A., Principia Coll., 1939; B.J., U. Mo., 1941; m. Jeanne Frances West, May 28, 1944 (dec. June 1975); children—Kenneth Wayne, Polly Jeanne. News editor Albia (Iowa) Newspapers, 1941-42; pub. Moravia (Iowa) Union, 1942-45; mgr. Mille Lacs Messenger, Isle, Minn., 1946-47; pub. Seymour (Iowa) Herald, 1947-77; pub. relations coordinator Iowa State Center, Iowa State U., Ames, 1977—; mng. editor, gen. mgr. Centerville Daily Iowegian, 1967. Sec. Seymour Community Club, 1949-68, 70-72, pres., 1969; chmn. Seymour Utility Bd., 1969-75. Served as 2d lt. AUS, 1945-46. Recipient with wife Master Editor-Publisher award Iowa Press Assn., 1971. Mem. Pi Kappa Alpha, Sigma Delta Chi. Republican. Christian Scientist. Home: 133 Beedle Dr Apt 3 Ames IA 50010 Office: Iowa State Center Scheman Bldg Iowa State U Ames IA 50011

DAVIS, WILLIAM ACKELSON, farmer, mcht.; b. Kirk, Colo., Aug. 5, 1903; s. Elias Griffith and Zelma May (Ackelson) D.; student U. Colo., 1922-23; m. Jessie Marian Shaw, Oct. 26, 1926; children—Jack Presley, William Shaw, Eugene Griffith. Partner, Reed Motor Co., Burlington, Colo., 1927-29, D & M Motor Co., Cheyenne Wells, Colo., 1929-34; founder, owner Davis Motor Co., Goodland, Kans., 1934-47, Davis Implement Co., Goodland, 1941—; sr. partner William A. Davis & Sons, Goodland, 1945—; dir., v.p. Esch Lumber Co., Burlington, 1965—; dir. Gt. Western Producers, Inc.; sec. Davis Cattle Co., Inc., Davis Bros. Farms, Inc.; chmn. Dept. Agr. Farmer's Home Adminstrn., Kans., 1962-65. Mem. State Banking Bd. Kans., 1967-73, past chmn.; mem. Sherman Community Sch. Bd., Goodland, 1942-48, N.W. Kans. Free Fair Bd., 1954-56; chmn. Kans. Gov.'s Sugar Beet Com., 1962—, Sch. Unification Planning Bd., Goodland, 1963-66; mem. Kennedy-Johnson Water Resources Com., 1959; chmn. Kennedy-Johnson Colo.-Kans. Beet Com., 1959; mem. Pres.'s Council on Youth Opportunity, 1964. Del., Democratic Nat. Conv., 1964, 68. Recipient pub. service citations Comml. Credit Corp., 1964, Sperry Rand Corp., 1965, Farm Power and Equipment Mag., 1967, Kiwanian, 1968, Community Leaders Am., 1968, New Holland Machine Co., 1968. Hon. fellow Truman Library Inst. (Independence, Mo.); mem. Goodland C. of C. (pres. 1957-58), Am. Hampshire Soc., Nat. Fedn. Beet Growers, Phi Gamma Delta. Elk, Rotarian. Home: 1500 E 10th St Goodland KS 67735 Office: 620 Caldwell St Goodland KS 67735

DAVIS, WILLIAM EUGENE, architect; b. Terre Haute, Ind., Sept. 4, 1921; s. William Eugene and Anne (Reese) D.; B.S., U. Ill., 1948, M.Arch., 1966; m. Carolyn Elaine Thompson, Oct. 23, 1964; children—Elizabeth Anne, John William. Structural designer Allen & Kelly, architects, Indpls., 1948; field design engr. Girdler Corp., Louisville, 1950-52; constrn. engr. U.S. Army C.E., Chgo. dist., 1952-53; chief engr. design Liberty Powder Co., Newport, Ind., 1953-57; architect, prin., owner W.E. Davis, architect, Rockville, Ind., 1957—. Lectr. archtl. tech. Ind. U.-Purdue U., Indpls., 1959-63, asst. prof., 1963-68, asso. prof., 1968-73, prof., 1973—, chmn. dept. constrn. tech., 1966—. Served with USAAF, 1943-46. Mem. A.I.A., Soc. Archtl. Historians, Nat. Trust Hist. Preservation, Am. Assn. U. Profs., Ind. Soc. Architects. Rotarian. Prin. archtl. works include Holy Cross Luth. Ch., Crawfordsville, Ind., Southeastern Ch. Christ, Indpls., Billie Creek Village, Rockville, Ind. Home: 411 Jackson St Rockville IN 47872 Office: Box 61 Rockville IN 47872

DAVIS, WILLIAM FRANCIS, lawyer; b. Omaha, Nov. 26, 1932; s. Frank J. and Marie (Snyder) D.; B.A., U. Omaha, 1956; LL.B., Creighton U., 1960; m. Elizabeth Lee Hickman, Aug. 22, 1959; children—Denise Marie, Diane Marie, Donna Marie, Doreen Marie, Mark William. Admitted to Nebr. bar, 1960, since practiced in Nebraska City; legal mem. Otoe County Bd. Mental Health, 1965-70; city atty., Nebraska City, 1970—; county atty. Otoe County, 1971—. Commr. Nebraska City Housing Authority, 1962-65; mem. Nebraska City Park Bd., 1964-70, chmn., 1966-70; chmn. Nebraska City Planning Commn., 1966-70. Named Young Man of Year, Nebraska City Jr. C. of C., 1966, Optimist of Year, 1969. Mem. Am., Nebr., Otoe County bar assns., Alpha Sigma Nu, Sigma Phi Epsilon (dist. gov. 1965-68). Republican. Roman Catholic. Eagle, Elk (exalted ruler 1968-69). Home: 1402 1st Ave Nebraska City NE 68410 Office: 804 Central Ave Nebraska City NE 68410

DAVIS, WILLIAM WALTER, SR., vocat. adminstr.; b. Omaha, Oct. 20, 1928; s. John and Mildred Edona (Forbush) D., Jr.; B.A., Omaha U., 1972, M.A., 1974; m. Elaine Francine Smith, May 29, 1949; 1 son, William Walter, Jr. Neuropsychiat. nursing asst. VA Hosp., Omaha, 1955-66; sr. resident advisor Lincoln Job Corps Center, Lincoln, Nebr., 1966-67; counselor Omaha Opportunities Industrialization Center, Omaha, 1967-68, dep. dir., 1968—; cons. Teaching Tchrs. to Teach Task Force U. Nebr., Lincoln, 1970—, Urban Center, 1971, Child Care Tng. Center, Omaha, 1973-74; chmn. project rev. com. Human Resource Task Force Riverfront Devel., Omaha, 1973-74. Vice pres. Omaha United Methodist Assn., 1974. Served with USAF, 1951-55. Mem. Am. Personnel and Guidance Assn., Omaha Musician Assn. Democrat. Home: 3828 N 19th St Omaha NE 68110 Office: 2802 N 24th St Omaha NE 68110

DAVISON, BURNS HARRIS, II, lawyer; b. Des Moines, Sept. 15, 1931; s. Burns Harris and Dorothy Margaret (Johnson) D.; B.S., Ind. U., 1953; LL.B., Drake U., 1958; m. Susan Jean Morris, Aug. 28, 1958; children—Burns Harris III, Anna Sue, William M., Robert W. Admitted to Iowa bar, 1958; U.S. Dist. Ct. for Iowa, 1958, U.S. Tax Ct., 1959, U.S. Ct. Appeals bar, 1964; asso. firm Holliday & Myers, Des Moines, 1958-59; partner firm Jones, Hoffmann & Davison, Des Moines, 1959—. Pres. Hubbell Sch. PTA, Des Moines, 1976-77; vestryman St. Andrew's Episcopal Ch., Des Moines, 1972-75, 76—; pres. Des Moines Community Playhouse, 1967. Served to capt. U.S. Army, 1953-55; lt. col. USAR Ret. Decorated Purple Heart. Mem. Am., Iowa State, Polk County bar assns., Res. Officers Assn., Assn. U.S. Army, Am. Law Inst., Info. Council on Fabric Flammability, Am. Judicature Soc., Phi Kappa Psi, Phi Alpha Delta. Republican. Episcopalian. Clubs: Kiwanis (pres. Des Moines chpt. 1970-71), Spirit Lake Yacht. Home: 4812 Algonquin Rd Des Moines IA 50311 Office: 900 Des Moines Bldg Des Moines IA 50309

DAVISON, KENNETH EDWIN, educator; b. East Cleveland, May 4, 1924; s. Gordon Edwin and Mildred K. (Smith) D.; A.B., Heidelberg Coll., 1946; A.M., Western Res. U., 1951, Ph.D., 1953; m. Virginia Nell Rentz, June 14, 1959; children—Robert Edwin, Richard Allen. Asst. prof. history, polit. sci. Heidelberg Coll., Tiffin, Ohio, 1952-56, asso. prof. polit. sci., 1956-59, prof., 1959-64, prof. history, dir. Gen. Edn. Program, 1964-67, prof., chmn. Am. studies dept., 1967—; vis. prof. Am. studies Bowling Green State U., 1972, 73, 74, 75; supr. Regional Preservation Office, 1976—; cons. Tiffin Historic Trust, 1976—. Chmn., Heidelberg Community Lecture and Concert Series, 1956-63; mem. Ohio com. for pub. programs in humanities, 1973—; chmn. Tiffin-Seneca Bicentennial Commn., 1974-77. Recipient Ohioana Library Book award, 1973. Mem. Orgn. Am. Historians, Western History Assn., Ohio-Ind. Am. Studies Assn. (pres. 1965, 66), Am. Assn. State and Local History, Nat. Trust Historic Preservation, Soc. Ohio Archivists (exec. council 1970-73, v.p. 1972-73), Oral History Assn., Soc. Hist. Archaeology, So. Hist. Assn., Ohio Acad. History (editor newsletter 1971-74), Popular Culture Assn. (adv. bd. 1972-75), Am. Assn. Museums, Am. Studies Assn. (nat. exec. council 1968—, nat. treas. 1973—, editor newsletter 1974-75), Ohio Hist. Soc. (research adviser 1968-75), Soc. Archtl. Historians, Canadian Am. Studies Assn., Center for Study of Presidency (bd. educators 1974—), Pi Kappa Delta, Phi Alpha Theta. Presbyn. (elder, del. to Presbytery). Author: Cleveland and the Civil War, 1962; The Presidency of Rutherford B. Hayes, 1972. Guest editor Ohio History, 1968; editor Hayes Hist. Jour., 1976—. Contbr. to Collier's Ency., 1964, 68, Am. Educator's Ency., 1965, articles to profl. jours. Home: 125 Hampden Park Tiffin OH 44883

DAVY, MICHAEL FRANCIS, cons. civil engr.; b. Springfield, Mo., Mar. 24, 1946; s. Philip Sheridan and Caecilia Magdalen (Thiemann) D.; B.S. in Civil Engring., U. Wis., 1969; m. Joyce Kaye Young, Aug. 17, 1968; children—Mark Sheridan, Katherine Ann, Jennifer Mary. Engring. aide Wis. Dept. Natural Resources, Madison, 1969; project engr. Davy Engring. Co., La Crosse, Wis., 1969-71, 2d v.p., 1971-74, v.p., 1974—; mgr. Davy Water Quality Lab., La Crosse, 1975—; mem. civil engr. adv. bd. U. Wis., Platteville, 1973-75. Mem. exec. bd. Gateway Area council Boy Scouts Am., 1973-77. Registered profl. engr., Wis., Minn., Ill., Iowa, Mich. Mem. Nat., Wis. (Young Engr. of Year 1976) socs. profl. engrs., Wis. Soc. Land Surveyors, Water Pollution Control Fedn., AAAS, Profl. Engrs. in Pvt. Practice, ASCE. Home: 615 N 23d St La Crosse WI 54601 Office: 115 S 6th St La Crosse WI 54601

DAVY, PHILIP SHERIDAN, civil engr.; b. Madison, Wis., July 12, 1915; s. Francis Joseph and Mathilda Sarah (Femrite) D.; B.S. in Civil Engring., U. Wis., 1937, M.S. in Civil Engring., 1938; m. Caecilia Magdalen Thiemann, Feb. 8, 1939; children—Katherine Agnes (Mrs. William Bathurst), Patricia Mary (Mrs. Steven Sciborski), Michael Francis, Barbara Jean (Mrs. John Salassa), Thomas Henry, Margaret Theresa. Engr., Frank J. Davy & Son, cons. engrs., La Crosse, Wis., 1938-41, Permutit Co., N.Y.C., 1946; v.p. Davy Engring Co., cons. engrs., La Crosse, 1947-56, pres., 1956—; lectr. U. Wis., 1950—, Wis. Dept. Natural Resources, 1970-77. Mem. Gov.'s Com. on Wis. Water Resources, 1965-66; mem. regional adv. bd. to Dept. Resource Devel., State Wis., 1966-68, chmn., 1968. Campaign chmn. United Fund, LaCrosse, 1961, 72; com. chmn. Gateway area council Boy Scouts Am., 1948-52, bd. mem., 1953-66, v.p., 1967-70, pres., 1971-73; bd. dirs., pres. United Fund, La Crosse, 1962-65; bd. dirs., chmn. fin. and adminstrn. com. Diocese of LaCrosse. Served from 2d lt. to lt. col., C.E., AUS, 1937-46. Decorated Papal Knight of Holy Sepulchre, Diocese of LaCrosse; recipient Silver Beaver, St. George and Distinguished Eagle awards Boy Scouts Am. Registered profl. engr., Wis., Minn., Iowa, Mich., Ill., Ind. Fellow ASCE; mem. Am. Water Works Assn. (trustee, chmn. Wis. sect. 1957, 60), AAAS, Water Pollution Control Assn., Nat. (dir. 1967-70, Engr. of Yr. 1967), Wis. (v.p. 1965-67, pres. 1974-75) socs. profl. engrs., Am. Pub. Works Assn., Greater LaCrosse C. of C. (dir. 1959-62, exec. bd. 1964-67, pres. 1968). Scabbard and Blade, Tau Beta Pi, Chi Epsilon, Phi Kappa Phi. Home: 1230 King St La Crosse WI 54601 Office: 115 S 6th St La Crosse WI 54601

DAWDY, HARRY M., assn. exec.; b. Topeka, Aug. 22, 1905; s. Fred F. and Nina (Wilson) D.; B.S., Washburn U., 1927; postgrad. U. Chgo., 1937, U. Kans., 1950-51; M.S.P.H., Mo. U., 1968; m. Maureen Lee, Aug. 30, 1931; children—William F., Sondra (Mrs. B. Ross Moen). Hi-Y sec. Kan. YMCA, 1928-29; boys' work sec. Wichita YMCA, 1929-35; chief probation officer Sedgwick County Juvenile Ct., 1935-39; coordinating dir. Kans. Children's Instns., 1939-41; dir. Kans. Vocational Rehab. Service, 1941-46; exec. dir. Am. Cancer Soc., Kans., 1946-52, exec. v.p. Mo., 1952-72; exec. sec. Mo. Pub. Health Assn., Jefferson City, 1972—. Instr. community orgn. Kans. U. Sch. Social Work, 1949-50; instr. social group work Mo. U. Sch. Social Work, 1954. Vice pres. Kans. Congress Parents and Tchrs., 1939-50. Mem. bd. Cancer Research Center, Columbia, Mo. Fellow Am. Pub. Health Assn.; mem. Nat. Assn. Social Workers, Mo. Pub. Health Assn. (pres. 1960), Mo. Council Health Careers (pres. 1958), Mo. Health Council (pres. 1959), Mo. Acad. Sci. Kiwanian, Mason (K.T.). Mem. Disciples of Christ Ch. Home: 511 Meier Dr Jefferson City MO 65101 Office: PO Box 275 Jefferson City MO 65101

DAWES, WAYNE LEE, pedodontist; b. Wabash, Ind., Apr. 1, 1940; s. Wilbur Calvin and Nada Mary (Shultz) D.; D.D.S. cum laude, Ind. U., 1966; m. Judith Carol Tucker, June 19, 1966; children—Jennifer Lynn, Julia Ann, Janel Nicole. Intern Riley Hosp., Indpls., 1966-67, resident, 1967-68; practice dentistry specializing in pedodontics, Fort Wayne, Ind., 1968—; mem. staff Lutheran Hosp., Fort Wayne, 1971—, St. Joseph's Hosp., 1969—. Served with AUS, 1958-62. Mem. Am., Ind., Isaac Knapp dental assns., Ind. Univ. Alumni Assn., Assn. Dentistry for Children, Ind. Pedodontic Soc., Omicron Kappa Upsilon, Delta Sigma Delta (pres. 1964-65, recipient Outstanding Achievement award 1966). Presbyn. Home: 1111 Dodane Rd Fort Wayne IN 46819 Office: 223 E Tillman Road Fort Wayne IN 46816

DAWSON, THERESA SHEAHEN, speech pathologist; b. Cleve., Sept. 28, 1934; d. Allan Newman and Virginia Lillian (Dougherty) Sheahen; B.A. cum laude, Marygrove Coll., 19S8; M.A., Western Reserve U., 1960; m. Robert H. Dawson, Apr. 4, 1959; children—Dawn, Deborah, Angela, Jennifer, Elizabeth. Speech pathologist cleft palate team Mt. Sinai Hosp., Cleve., 1960-62; speech pathologist Fairview Gen. Hosp., Cleve., 1960-62; dir. parent edn. United Cerebral Palsy Assn., Cleve., 1960-73; speech pathologist Lakewood (Ohio) Hosp., 1960—; cons. to nursing homes; speaker in-service meetings at nursing homes and hosps. Treas., St. Raphael Sch. Bd., 1973-76. Certified clin. competence in speech pathology. Mem. Am. Speech and Hearing Assn., Marygrove Alumnae Assn. Republican. Roman Catholic. Clubs: St. Raphael Women's Guild, Lakewood Country. Home: 29317 Lincoln Rd Bay Village OH 44140 Office: 14701 Detroit Ave Lakewood OH 44107

DAY, CLARA BELLE TAYLOR, labor union ofcl.; b. Northport, Ala.; d. George and Belle (Baylom) Taylor; student Crane Jr. Coll., Chgo., 1960-62; m. Joseph Henry Day; 1 dau., Georgia (Mrs. Irie Dell Grant). Br. office mgr. warehouse and mail order employees Internat. Brotherhood Teamsters, Chgo., 1955-61, asst. bus. rep., 1961-68, dir. community affairs, labor rep., 1968—; trustee, bus. rep. Local Union 743 Teamsters, 1976—. Commr., Ill. Commn. on Status of Women, 1972—; mem. Chgo. Commn. Human Relations, 1967—, Ill. Commn. Human Relations, 1964—, Nat. Assn. Inter-group Relation Ofcls., 1968—, Greater Lawndale Conservation Commn., 1953—; vol. worker Sears YMCA, Chgo., 1968—; del. Internat. Women's Year Conf., Houston, 1977. Recipient Woman of Distinction award Chgo. Citizens' Com., 1965, Civil Rights award Jewish Labor Com., 1968, citation Greater Lawndale Assn., 1964, Beautiful People award Chgo. Urban League, 1971, award Operation P.U.S.H., 1974, award as Labor's Outstanding Black Woman, Black Labor Leaders, 1973, others. Mem. League Women Voters, Chgo. Urban League (cons. bd. 1966—), N.A.A.C.P. (mem. bd. Chgo. West Side), Coalition of Labor Union Women (midwest v.p. 1974—). Presbyn. Home: 1856 S Lawndale Ave Chicago IL 60623 Office: 300 S Ashland Blvd Chicago IL 60607

DAY, JOHN EDWARD, real estate broker; b. Saginaw, Mich., Mar. 8, 1908; s. Thomas and Margaret Ann (Cavanaugh) D.; B.A., Central Mich. U., 1931; m. Marian McDonagh, Aug. 25, 1934; children—Thomas Bruce, Patricia Ann, John Edward, Marilyn Jane Day Zaetta. Instr. social sci. Arthur Hill High Sch., Saginaw, 1932-59; partner John Day Realty, Saginaw, 1955—; pres. John Day Co., Saginaw, 1966-73; farmer, Saginaw, 1936—. Mem. Am. Soc. Appraisers, Nat., Saginaw (dir. 1960-66) bds. realtors, Saginaw Agrl. Soc. (pres., dir.), Mich. Real Estate Assn. Roman Catholic. Clubs: Fordney, Germania (Saginaw). Home: 1591 Short St Saginaw MI 48603 Office: 4474 Bay Rd Saginaw MI 48603

DAY, JOHN MACLEISH, food co. exec.; b. Orange, N.J., May 14, 1935; s. Lewis Andrew and Isabel Gilette (Williamson) D.; B.A., U. Wash., 1957; M.B.A., Stanford U., 1962; m. Janet Barbara Brinkman, June 16, 1957; children—Daniel, Christopher, Elizabeth. With Gen. Mills Inc., Mpls., 1962-69, product mgr., 1965-68, sr. product mgr., 1968-69; with Green Giant Co., Mpls., 1969-75, dir. corp. devel., 1971-73, v.p. mktg., 1973-75; v.p. mktg., mfg. div. Beatrice Foods Co., Park Ridge, Ill., 1975—. Served with USAF, 1958-60. Mem. Assn. Nat. Advertisers, Am. Mktg. Assn. Republican. Episcopalian. Home: 251 Donlea Rd Barrington Hills IL 60010 Office: 2015 Spring Rd Suite 600 Oak Brook IL 60521

DAY, MARIAN MCDONAGH, realtor; b. Saginaw, Mich., Nov. 27, 1907; d. Thomas Blakely and Eleanor (Hill) McDonagh; B.S. in Home Econs., Mich. State U., 1931; m. John Edward Day, Aug. 25, 1934; children—Thomas, Patricia, John E. II, Marilyn J. Partner, John Day Constrn. Co., Saginaw, 1947-65; founder, partner John Day Realty, Saginaw, 1955-75; dir., sec. treas. John Day Co., Saginaw, 1966-74; Brokers Investment Inc., Saginaw, 1968-73; dir., v.p. Saginaw Leasing Corp., 1967-72. Chmn. edn. com., bd. dirs. Women's Nat. Farm and Garden Show, Saginaw, 1963-67; co-developer real estate curriculum Delta Coll., Bay City, Mich., 1970, mem. edn. com. real estate, 1958-72. Named Realtor of Year, Saginaw Bd. Realtors, 1967. Mem. Mich. Real Estate Assn. (chmn. edn. com.), Saginaw Bd. Realtors (dir. 1965-71, v.p. 1971), D.A.R. (bd. dirs. 1959-62), Home Econs. Alumni Assn. Mich. State U. (bd. dirs. 1959-65), Real Estate Alumni U. Mich. (bd. dirs. 1966-72), Soc. Mayflower Descs., Nat. Soc. Colonial Daus. 17th Century. Roman Catholic. Club: Saginaw Culture. Home: 1591 Short Rd Saginaw MI 48603 Office: 6225 Gatiot Rd Saginaw MI 48603

DAY, SISTER MARY AGNITA CLAIRE, educator; b. Osage, Iowa, Aug. 22, 1906; d. Bert A. and Florence (Fiddick) Day; B.S., State U. Iowa, 1928; M.S., St. Louis U., 1942; postgrad. Kellogg Found., research seminar in nursing service administrn. U. Chgo., 1951. Gen. pvt. duty, supervision in nursing, 1928-34; joined Congregation of Sisters of St. Mary, 1934, novitiate, 1934-37; clin. instr. med. nursing St. Mary's Hosp., St. Louis, 1937-38; instr. St. Louis U. Sch. Nursing, 1938-43, asst. prof., 1943-51, dir. dept. nursing, 1946-51, asso. prof., 1951-63, prof., 1963-74, prof. emeritus, 1974—, acting dean, 1956-58, dean Sch. Nursing and Allied Health Professions 1958-61; now engaged in hist. and sci. research; USPHS grantee for research related to rehab. nursing; dir. nursing service and personnel St. Mary's Hosp., Kansas City, Mo., also dir. field work for nursing service administrn. majs. St. Louis U. Sch. Nursing, 1951-54; dir. St. Mary's Hosp. Sch. Nursing, Madison, Wis., 1954-56. Recipient St. Louis U. Alumni Merit award, 1974. Mem. Mo. League for Nursing (pres. 1952-54, 59-61, editor publ., named Nurse of Year 1974), Am. Nurses Assn., Nat. League for Nursing, St. Louis Regional League for Nursing (past pres.), Internat. Soc. Posturography. Author: Principles and Techniques of Nursing Procedures, 1943; Basic Science in Nursing Arts, 1947; also articles. Contbr. to textbook, 1971. Home: 1465 S Grand Blvd St Louis MO 63104

DAY, RICHARD LEROY, dentist; b. Gas City, Ind., Mar. 24, 1935; s. Grandville M. and Della (Owen) D.; A.B., Taylor U., 1958; D.D.S., Ind. U., 1962; m. Anne E. Ineson, July 17, 1958; children—Lori Ann, Lisa Ellen. Gen. practice dentistry, Wabash, Ind., 1962—. Mem. Wabash County Bd. Health, 1964—, vice chmn., 1968-70, chmn., 1970-77. Mem. Wabash C. of C., Wabash Valley Dental Soc. (past pres.), Ind. State (dist. del. 1969), Am. dental assns., Grant County Dental Soc., Nat. Rifle Assn. (life), Ind. Sportsmen's Council, Nat. Wildlife Fedn., Wabash Wildlife and Sportsman Assn., Nat. Exchange Club, Xi Psi Phi. Mem. Christian and Missionary Alliance Ch. Contbr. articles in field to profl. jours. Home: 1047 St James Ct Wabash IN 46992 Office: 812 Manchester Ave Wabash IN 46992

DAY, ROBERT GEORGE, lawyer, state representative; b. Peoria, Nov. 30, 1913; s. George and Myrtle (Entwistle) D.; B.S., U. Ill., 1938; m. Marthann Judy, Apr. 19, 1940; children—Susan Wallace, Robert George, Douglas Stephen. Admitted to Ill. bar, 1939, U.S. Supreme Ct. bar, 1957; practiced in Peoria, 1939—; mayor, Peoria, 1961-65; mem. Ill. Ho. of Reps., 1966—, mem. judiciary, higher edn. coms.; instr. bus. law and polit. sci. Bradley U., Peoria, 1948-49. Cons. U.S. Conf. Mayors, Kansas City, 1965. Mem. Ill. Constnl. Study Commn. Gen. Chmn. sch. referendum, Peoria, 1956. Served with AUS, 1943-45; ETO. Recipient Peoria Jr. C. of C. Good Govt. award, 1964. Mem. Ill. Bar Assn., Ill. Congress Parents and Tchrs. (life). Republican. Kiwanian. Home: 2601 N Kingston Dr Peoria IL 61604 Office: Jefferson Bldg Peoria IL 61602

DAY, ROGER FOREST, lawyer; b. Sunbury, Ohio, Nov. 17, 1929; s. Forest M. and Luretta M. (Haycook) D.; B.A., Otterbein Coll., 1951; J.D., Ohio State U., 1957; m. Evelyn Joyce Kormes, Dec. 17, 1955; 1 son, Michael. Admitted to Ohio bar, 1957, since practiced in Columbus; asso. firm Dargusch & Dargusch, 1957-62; partner firm Dargusch & Day, 1962-75, Porter, Wright, Morris & Arthur, 1975—; gen. counsel Ohio Trucking Assn., 1967—, Ohio Assn. Cemeteries, 1962—, Ohio Florists Assn., 1970—, Methods Time Measurement Assn., 1970—. Served with CIC, AUS, 1951-54. Mem. Am., Ohio, Columbus bar assns., Phi Delta Phi, Zeta Phi. Mason. Club: Scioto Country. Home: 2501 Lytham Rd Columbus OH 43220 Office: Porter Wright Morris & Arthur 37 W Broad St Columbus OH 43215

DAY, ROLAND BERNARD, state supreme ct. justice; b. Oshkosh, Wis., June 11, 1919; s. Peter Oliver and Joanna King (Wescott) D.; B.A., U. Wis., 1942, J.D., 1947; m. Mary Jane Purcell, Dec. 18, 1948; 1 dau., Sarah Jane. Admitted to Wis. bar, 1947; trainee Office Wis. Atty. Gen., 1947; asso. mem. firm Maloney & Wheeler, Madison, 1947-49; 1st asst. dist. atty. Dane County, 1949-52; partner Day, Goodman, Madison, 1953-57; legal counsel, staff Sen. William Proxmire, Washington, 1957-58; partner Wheeler, Van Sickle, Day & Anderson, Madison, 1959-74; justice Wis. Supreme Ct., 1974—. Mem. Madison Housing Authority, 1960-64, chmn., 1961-63. Regent U. Wis. System, 1972-74. Served with AUS, 1943-46. Mem. Am. Bar Assn., State Bar Wis., Am. Trial Lawyers Assn., Am. Judicature Soc., Ygdrasil Lit. Soc. (pres. 1968). Conglist. Clubs: Madison, Madison Literary. Home: 4806 Sherwood Rd Madison WI 53711 Office: Supreme Ct Chambers 214 E State Capitol Madison WI 53702

DAY, WILLIAM FRANK, JR., lawyer; b. White River, S.D., Sept. 22, 1930; s. William Franklin and Pearl Susan (Coash) D.; J.D., U. S.D., 1956; m. Donna Mae Hansen, Sept. 4, 1955; children—Michael William, Lori Ann. Admitted to S.D. bar, 1956, since practiced in Winner; states atty. Tripp and Todd County (S.D.), 1958-61; trial judge Rosebud Sioux Tribe, Rosebud, S.D., 1964-70. Past chmn. Tripp County Democratic Com. Served to 1st lt. inf. AUS, 1953-55, capt. 1960-61. Fellow Internat. Soc. Barristers; mem. Am., S.D. (pres. 1974), S.D. Jr. Bar Assn. (past pres.), 10th Circuit (pres. 1960) bar assns., S.D. (past pres.) Am. trial lawyers assns., Am. Bd. Trial Advocates, Winner C. of C., Delta Tau Delta. Episcopalian. Mason (Shriner), Elk (past dist. dep.). Home: 601 E 7th St Winner SD 57580 Office: Box 690 Winner SD 57580

DAY, WILLIS FRANKLIN, III, storage co. exec.; b. Toledo, Feb. 4, 1923; s. Willis F. and Ernestine (Kirchmaier) D.; student Northwestern U., 1943; B.S., Miami U., Oxford, Ohio, 1945; m. Rosemary Claypool, Sept. 15, 1944; children—Jane Louise, Deborah Ann, Willis F. IV, John Edward. With Willis Day Storage Co., Toledo, 1939—, pres., 1957—; pres. Willis Day Indsl. Park, Toledo, 1964—; dir. Ohio Citizens Trust Co., Toledo, Mayflower Warehousemen's Assn. Bd. dirs. St. Vincent Hosp., Toledo. Served to lt. (j.g.) USNR, 1943-46. Mem. Am. Legion, Phi Delta Theta. Mason (32 deg.). Clubs: Toledo, Toledo Yacht; Catawba Island (Port Clinton, Ohio); North Cape Yacht (Monroe, Mich.). Home: 3422 Indian Rd Toledo OH 43606 Office: 801 Washington St Toledo OH 43601

DAYANANDA, MYSORE ANANTHAMURTHY, educator, engr.; b. Mysore City, India, July 1, 1934; s. Tekhalli Srinivasarao Anantha Murthy and Kapila Ananthamurthy; came to U.S., 1958, permanent resident, 1968; B.Sc. with honors, Mysore U., 1955; D.I.I.Sc., Indian Inst. Sci., 1957; M.S., Purdue U., 1961, Ph.D., 1965; m. Prema Kumari Rao, July 5, 1972. Sr. research asst. Indian Inst. Sci., Bangalore, 1957-58; postdoctoral research asso. Purdue U., 1965-66, asst. prof. materials engring., 1966-70, asso. prof., 1970-75, prof., 1975—. Cons. Catalytic Pollution Control, Inc., N.J., 1971-72. Fellow Am. Inst. Chemists; mem. Am. Inst. Mining, Metall. and Petroleum Engrs., Am. Soc. Metals, Microbeam Analysis Soc., Am. Soc. Engring. Edn., Sigma Xi. Contbr. articles to profl. jours. Home: 461 Cumberland Ave West Lafayette IN 47906 Office: Sch Materials Engring Purdue U Lafayette IN 47907

DAYE, GEORGE WASHINGTON, microbiologist; b. Ore City, Tex., Sept. 23, 1923; s. George Washington and Annie L. (Smith) D.; B.S., Tex. Coll., 1949. Technician, ITT Serium Center, Michael Reese Hosp., Chgo., 1949-51; lab. technician, media div. Ill. Dept. Pub. Health, Chgo., 1951-55; with U. Ill. Med. Sch., 1955—; adminstrv. supr. labs., head microbiology Oak Forest (Ill.) Hosp. of Cook County, 1955-77; dir. clin. microbiology Garfield Park Community Hosp., Chgo., 1977—. Mem. adv. com. Morraine Valley Coll., Malcolm X Coll.; chmn. award com. United Negro Coll. Fund. Served with AUS, 1943-46. Mem. AAAS, Ill. (chmn. speakers bur. 1978), Am. socs. microbiology, Chgo. Mycological Soc., S. Central Assn. Clin. Microbiology, Alpha Phi Alpha. Presbyterian. Home: 7447 S Shore Dr Chicago IL 60649 Office: 3821 W Washington Blvd Chicago IL

DAYTON, CHARLES ARTHUR, dentist; b. Hanna, Alta., Can., Mar. 10, 1917 (parents Am. citizens); s. Charles and Mae (Nichols) D.; student U. Minn., 1938, St. Olaf Coll., 1942; B.A., Northwestern U., 1945 then D.D.S.; m. Frances Bernetta Kapusinski, May 27, 1952. Practice gen. dentistry, Galesburg, Ill., 1947—. Served with AUS, 1941-43, USNR, 1945-47. Mem. Knox County Dental Soc. (past pres.), Am., Ill., Prairie Valley dental assns., Fedn. Dentaire Internat., Acad. Gen. Dentistry, Delta Sigma Delta. Elk. Club: Soangetaha Country (Galesburg). Home: 1987 N Broad St Galesburg IL 61401 Office: 501 Bank of Galesburg Bldg Galesburg IL 61401

DAYTON, ROBERT JACKSON, splty. store exec.; b. Mpls., Feb. 4, 1942; s. Donald Chadwick and Lucy (Jackson) D.; B.A., Yale U.; P.M.D. certificate, Harvard Bus. Sch., 1972; m. Joan Gardiner Layng, June 19, 1964; children—James, Tobin, Scott. Pres., Harold Corp., Mpls. Mem. trust com. Northwestern Nat. Bank of St. Paul; dir. Gt. No. Ins. Co. Bd. dirs., v.p. Guthrie Theatre Found., 1971-77; bd. dirs. Abbott-Northwestern Hosp., 1977—, Jr. Achievement, 1977—; trustee Blake Schs., 1973—. Presbyn. Clubs: Minneapolis; Woodhill Country (Wayzata, Minn.); Yale (N.Y.C.). Home: 2663 Woodbridge Rd Wayzata MN 55391 Office: 818 Nicollet Mall Minneapolis MN 55402

DCAMP, CHARLES BARTON, educator, musician; b. Fairfield, Iowa, Feb. 16, 1932; s. Glenn Franklin and Nina Clarice (Larson) DC.; student Bradley U., 1950-51; B.S., U. Ill., 1956, M.S., 1957; m. Ruth Joyce MacDonald, June 27, 1953; children—James Charles, Douglas Kevin, David Michael, Richard Manley, Paul Frederick, Jon Barton. Tchr., Watervliet (Mich.) Pub. Sch., 1958-61; tchr. music United Twp. High Sch., East Moline, Ill., 1961-63; band dir. Pleasant Valley (Iowa) Schs., 1963-74; dir. bands St. Ambrose Coll., Davenport, Iowa, 1974—, also chmn. dept. music; guest dir., adjudicator festivals, music contests Iowa, Ill.; producer Quad-City Music Guild, 1973-77; tchr. woodwinds Bemidji State Coll. Band Camp. Mem. Riverdale Vol. Fire Co., 1966-75, pres., 1971-73. Served with AUS, 1952-55. Mem. Iowa (past pres.), Nat. Cath. bandmasters assns., Coll. Band Dirs. Nat. Assn., Music Educators Nat. Conf., Iowa Music Educators, Am. Fedn. Musicians, Am. Sch. Band Dirs. Assn., Nat. Band Assn., N.E.A. (life), Phi Mu Alpha Sinfonia, Phi Delta Kappa, Tau Kappa Epsilon. Republican. Methodist. Contbr. articles to profl. jours. Home: 301 Circle Dr Riverdale Bettendorf IA 52722 Office: St Ambrose Coll Davenport IA 52804

DCAMP, LUAN JEANETTE, psychologist; b. Fairfield, Iowa; d. Glenn Franklin and Nina (Larson) Dcamp; R.N., St. Francis Hosp. Sch. Nursing; B.S., U. Ill.; M.A. (Ruth Kirk scholar), Ph.D., U. Chgo. Formerly nurse, St. Francis Hosp., Peoria, Ill., A.R.C. Disaster Service, Peoria; nurse Augustana Hosp., Chgo., 1957-59, Grant Hosp., Chgo., 1959-61; with Ill. Dept. Mental Health, Chgo., 1955-68, dir. psychol. services Grant Hosp., 1963-70; basic sci. staff Luth. Gen. Hosp., Park Ridge, Ill., 1966—; mng. dir. Incentives, Des Plaines, Ill., 1967—; individual practice psychology, Chgo., 1968—. Instr. psychology, biology Crane Jr. Coll., Chgo., 1961-68. Mem. Am., Ill. psychol. assns., Am. Group Psychotherapy Assn., Ill. Group Psychotherapy Soc., Psychologists Interested in Advancement Psychotherapy, Assn. Women Psychologists, Internat. Platform Assn., Am. Assn. Biofeedback Clinicians. Contbr. articles to profl. lit. Office: 2424 Dempster St Des Plaines IL 60016

DEACON, GORDON KENNETH, mgmt. cons.; b. Markham, Ont., Can., June 26, 1943; s. Kenneth Emmerson and Mary Grace (Perkin) D.; B.Sc. in Engring., U. Guelph (Ont.), 1967. With Ontario Hydro Co., London, Ont., 1967-73, marketing exec., 1967-68, agrl. sales supr., 1968-73; asst. v.p. prodn. Simmons Ltd., Bramalea, Ont., 1974-75; pres. Mgmt. Sci. Research Assos. Inc., Toronto, Ont., 1975—. Lectr. farm power Centralia Coll. Agrl. Tech., Huron Park, Ont. Registered profl. engr., Ont. Mem. Assn. Profl. Engrs. Ont., Am., Canadian socs. agrl. engring., Engring. Inst. Can. Club: High Park Ski (v.p., dir. skiing). Home: Glenburn Farms Unionville ON Canada Office: Suite 603 44 Eglinton Ave W Toronto ON M4R 1A1 Canada

DEADRICK, ELDON JAY, dentist; b. Paynesville, Minn., Sept. 13, 1923; s. John Ernest and Augusta Louise (Kelm) D.; student Hamline U., 1947-49; B.S., U. Minn., 1951, D.D.S., 1953; m. Norma Lea Penningroth, Sept. 23, 1950; children—Thomas John, Karen Louise. Pvt. practice dentistry, Kimball, S.D., 1953-58, Platte, S.D., 1958—. Mem. Kimball City Council, 1956-58; mem. Platte Community Sch. Dist. Bd., 1963—, pres., 1969—. Served with AUS, 1942-46; PTO. Mem. So. Dist. Dental Soc., Am., S.D. dental assns., Acad. Gen. Dentistry, Platte Comml. Club (pres. 1963), V.F.W., Am. Legion. Republican. Presbyn. Mason (Shriner), Elk, Odd Fellow; mem. Order Eastern Star. Address: Platte SD 57369

DEADY, MICHAEL JOSEPH, dentist; b. Terre Haute, Ind., June 9, 1940; s. James Michael and Audrey Claire (Windley) D.; B.S., Ind. State U., 1962; D.D.S. Ind. U., 1965; div.; children—Kevin Michael, Mark Andrew, Chad Matthew. Intern, Ind. U. Med. Center, Indpls., 1965-66, resident, 1966-68; pvt. practice dentistry, limited to oral surgery, Terre Haute, Ind., 1968—. Mem. faculty Ind. U. Med. Center, part time, 1965-68. Mem. Am., Ind. dental assns., Western Ind. Dental Soc., Am., Ind., Great Lakes socs. oral surgeons. Home: 2612 N 13th St Terre Haute IN 47806 Office: 1630 Poplar St Terre Haute IN 47808

DEAHL, WARREN ANTHONY, lawyer; b. South Bend, Ind., Sept. 18, 1918; s. Floyd Anthony and Sarah (Rosenbury) D.; A.B., U. Notre Dame, 1941, J.D. cum laude, 1943; m. Marjorie Katherine Sears, Nov. 29, 1941; children—Floyd Richards, John Orlo. Admitted to Ind. bar, 1943, practiced law in South Bend, 1946—; sr. partner firm Thornburg, McGill, Deahl, Harman, Carey & Murray; counsel South Bend Community Sch. Corp., South Bend Civic Center Bldg. Authority; dir. Albion Nat. Bank, South Bend Lathe, Inc., Western Rubber Co. Past trustee YMCA; past mem. advisory bd. Vis. Nurse Assn. Served with U.S. Army. 1943-46. Decorated Bronze Star medal. Fellow Am. Coll. Probate Counsel; mem. Am., Ind., St. Joseph County (past pres.) bar assns., Am. Judicature Soc., South Bend-Mishawaka Area C. of C. (past pres., past dir.), Estate Planning Council, Ind. Soc. of Chgo. Clubs: Summit, Pickwick. Home: 5422 Abshire Dr South Bend IN 46614 Office: 6th Floor First Bank Bldg South Bend IN 46601

DEAK, CHARLES KAROL, chemist; b. Budapest, Hungary, Sept. 26, 1928; s. Karoly and Ida (Benes) D.; came to U.S., 1955, naturalized, 1961; B.S., Eotvos Coll., Budapest, 1948; student Sorbonne, Paris, 1949; postgrad. Wayne State U., 1957-61; m. Jenny Bocinski, Apr. 9, 1958; children—James, Christine. With Frankel Co., Inc., Detroit, 1957-74, quality control mgr., 1968-71, mgr. tech. services, 1971-74; mgr. Analyatical Assos., Detroit, 1974—. Mem. Am. Chem. Soc., ASTM, Am. Soc. Metals, Assn. Analytical Chemists, Photog. Soc. Am. Roman Catholic. Patentee in chem. firefighting agts. and dense metal separation. Club: Internat. Brotherhood Magicians. Home: 29844 Wagner St Warren MI 48093 Office: 19380 Mount Elliott St Detroit MI 48234

DEAL, JERRY M., grain farmer; b. Wheaton, Minn., Mar. 15, 1932; s. Philip Louis and Katherine Mary (Hunder) D.; grad. high sch.; m. Frances Marie Carlson, Apr. 27, 1952; children—Julie (Mrs. Gary Lee Miller), Joni, Jacqueline, Philip. Grain farmer, Wheaton, 1950—. Mem. Traverse Soil and Water Conservation Dist., 1955—, chmn., 1959-60, 67-68, 74—. Founder, Minn. Real Estate Taxpayers Assn., 1970, pres., exec. officer, 1971—. Named Oustanding Young Farmer in Traverse County, 1963. Mem. Nat. Farmers Orgn., Farmers Union. Roman Catholic. Editor: Minn. Taxpayer, 1971—. Home: Route 2 Box 164 Wheaton MN 56296 Office: 1002 Broadway Wheaton MN 56296

DEAL, LEO V., educator; b. Parker, Ind., June 16, 1930; s. Fred L. and Mildred L. (Cecil) D.; A.B., DePauw U., 1951; M.A., Ohio State U., 1958; Ph.D., Mich. State U., 1965; m. Nola Jene Arndt, July 5, 1952; children—Eric, Nancy. Tchr., Wellington (Ohio) High Sch., 1955-57, Olmsted Falls (Ohio) High Sch., 1958-59; speech pathologist Lima (Ohio) Hosp., 1959-60; asst. prof. Mich. State U., E. Lansing, 1963-68, asso. prof., 1968-70, prof., 1970—, chmn. dept. audiology and speech scis., 1971—; pres. Lansing Oral Cleft Clinic, 1969-71. Chmn., Lansing Coordinating Com. for Handicapped. 1973-74; bd. dirs. United Ministry of Higher Edn., Mich. State U., 1970—, chmn. Wesley Found. Bd., 1976—. Served with USAF, 1951-55. Certified Am. Speech and Hearing Assn. Mem. Am., Mich. speech and hearing assns., Am. Cleft Palate Assn.. Internat. Assn. Logopedics and Phoniatrics, Phi Kappa Phi. Methodist. Contbr. articles to profl. jours, chpts. to books. Home: 1249 Ivanhoe Dr East Lansing MI 48823 Office: Mich State U East Lansing MI 48824

DEAN, ALICE ROGERS, physician; b. Clearfield, Pa.; d. Charles Calvin and Minerva (Dunlap) Rogers; student U. Rochester, 1955-56; M.D., Case-Western Res. U., 1962; m. Robert Stanley Dean, Sept. 3, 1956 (div. Dec. 1967); children—Alice Kathryn, Lisa Carol. Research, child devel. Case-Western Reserve U., Cleve., 1962-65; intern Milw. Children's Hosp., 1965-66; resident adult psychiatry Marquette U., Milw., 1966-68; resident child psychiatry Milw. County Gen. Hosp., Wauwatosa, Wis., 1968-70, dir. adolescent girls div., dept. psychiatry, 1970-71; pvt. practice psychiatry, Milw., 1971—; cons. Milw. County Children's Ct. 1970—. Mem. AMA, Am., Wis. psychiat. assns. Home: 5426 N Lake Dr Milwaukee WI 53217 Office: Bockl Bldg 2040 W Wisconsin Ave Milwaukee WI 53233

DEAN, GERALD STANLEY, pathologist; b. Spokane, Wash., July 22, 1921; s. Roy Gerald and Winzie (Dahleen) D.; B.S., Whitworth Coll., 1944; B.M., Northwestern U., 1946, M.D., 1947; m. Patricia Goller, July 1, 1944; children—Julie Eugenie, Leslie Patricia. Intern, St. Lukes, Hosp., Chgo., 1946-47, resident in pathology, 1947-48; resident in pathology Passavant Meml. Hosp., Chgo., 1950-52; dir. labs. Highland Park (Ill.), Lake Forest (Ill.) hosps., 1952—; chief of staff Highland Park Hosp., 1972-75; asst. prof. pathology Northwestern U. (Chgo.). Served from 1st lt. to capt. M.C., AUS, 1948-50. Fellow N.Y. Acad. Scis., Inst. Medicine, Coll. Am. Pathologists, Am. Soc. Clin. Pathologists; mem. Am. Assn. Blood Banks, Am. Soc. Cytology, AMA, Ill. Med. Soc., Ill. Soc. Pathologists (past pres.). Presbyterian (elder). Club: Highland Park Rotary (past pres.). Home: 2371 Saint Johns Ave Highland Park IL 60035 Office: Highland Park Hospital Highland Park IL 60035

DEAN, MICHAEL LEWIS, educator; b. Stamford, Conn., Feb. 9, 1942; s. Stanley R. and Belle (Katzman) D.; B.A., U. Mich., 1963; M.B.A., Ohio State U., 1965, Ph.D., 1971; m. Carol Lois Hoffman, Mar. 21, 1965; children—Jeffrey Brian, Julie Ellen. Staff asst. food products div. Procter & Gamble, Cin., 1965-66, asst. brand mgr., 1967-68; economist, econ. planning and analysis div. Battelle Meml. Inst., Columbus, Ohio, 1968-70; asst. prof. mktg., mem. grad. faculty Coll. of Bus. Adminstrn., U. Cin., 1971-74, asso. prof., mem. grad. faculty, 1974—, coordinator mktg. M.B.A. program, 1975—; bus. adviser Great Oak Vocat. Sch. Dist., Ohio, 1976—; pres. Action Data Mktg. Research, Inc., Cin., 1977—. Cons., adviser Lotspeich Schs., Cin., 1975—. Mem. Assn. for Consumer Research, Am. Mktg. Assn., Product Research and Devel. Assn., Soccer Assn. for Youth, Beta Gamma Sigma. Republican. Jewish. Contbr. articles on bus. research and mktg. to profl. jours. Home: 7614 Carriage Ln Cincinnati OH 45242 Office: Mail Location 20 Univ of Cincinnati Cincinnati OH 45221

DEAN, ROBERT KELLY, hosp. adminstr.; b. Toledo, May 11, 1916; s. Ira Kelly and Berneice (Armstrong) D.; B.S. in Bus. Adminstrn., Ohio State U., 1939; M.S. in Hosp. Adminstrn., Northwestern U., 1956; m. Mary Straub, July 30, 1939; children—Merrybelle (Mrs. Samuel England), Robert Kelly, Jr., Kerry Richard, Mark Loren. Exec. sec. VA Bd. Civil Service Examiners, Columbus, Ohio, 1946-50; personnel officer VA Hosp., Fort Wayne, Ind., 1950-51; supervisory personnel officer VA Hosp., Cleve., 1951-54; adminstrv. asst. City Hosp., Springfield, Ohio, 1955-56; hosp. adminstr. Longview State Hosp., Cin., 1956-57; asst. dir. Ohio Dept. Mental Hygiene and Correction, Columbus, 1956-62, acting dir., 1962-63; hosp. adminstrv. officer St. Elizabeths Hosp., Washington, 1963-67; supt. Winfield (Kans.) State Hosp. and Tng. Center, 1967—. Lectr. hosp. adminstrn. George Washington U., Washington, 1965-66. Bd. dirs. Cowley County Assn. Retarded Citizens. Served with Hosp. Corps, USNR, 1944-46. Fellow Assn. Mental Health Adminstrs.; mem. Am. Assn. Mental Deficiency, Nat. Assn. Retarded Citizens, Kans. Hosp. Assn., Winfield C. of C., Northwestern U. Hosp. Adminstrn. Alumni Assn. Methodist. Elk, Rotarian. Home: care Winfield State Hosp Winfield KS 67156 Office: Winfield State Hosp and Training Center Winfield KS 67156

DEAN, WANDA ELIZABETH, counselor; b. Richmond, Va.. Jan. 29, 1953; d. Abel and Dorothy Beatrice (Parker) Dean; B.A., Lincoln U., 1974; M.A., Washington U., St. Louis, 1974-75; postgrad., Mich. State U., 1975—. Research asst. Inst. Black Studies, St. Louis, 1974-75; counselor intern Halter High Sch., St. Louis, 1974-75; counselor Lynch Elementary Sch., Detroit, 1975-76; grad. asst. urban counseling Mich. State U., East Lansing, 1975—, adminstrv. asst. student services, 1976—; cons. in field. Recipient William H. Madella award, 1974; NIMH grad. fellow, 1975—. Mem. Am., Mich. personnel and guidance assns., Assn. Non White Concerns, Mich. Assn. Non White Concerns, Assn. Black Psychologists, Mich. Assn. Black Psychologists, Nat. Assn. Black Sch. Educators, Delta Sigma Theta. Club: Order Eastern Star. Home: 2415 E Jolly Rd Apt 7 Lansing MI 48910 Office: W-37 Owen Hall Mich State U East Lansing MI 48823

DEARDEN, JOHN FRANCIS, cardinal; b. Valley Falls, R.I., Oct. 15, 1907; s. John S. and Agnes (Gregory) D.; grad., St. Mary's Sem., Cleve., 1929, N. Am. Coll., Rome, Italy, 1933; S.T.D., Gregorian U., Rome, 1934. Ordained priest, R.C. Ch., Rome, Dec. 8, 1932; rector of St. Mary's Sem., Cleve., 1944-48; apptd. Papal Chamberlain with title of Very Rev. Monsignor, 1945; consecrated coadjutor bishop Pitts. and titular bishop of Sarepta, May 18, 1948; became Bishop Pitts., Dec. 22, 1950; archbishop Archdiocese of Detroit, 1959—; named to College of Cardinals, 1969. First pres. U.S. Nat. Conf. Cath. Bishops, 1966-71. Address: 1880 Wellesley Dr Detroit MI 48203

DEARDORFF, EARL WILLIAM, JR., appliance and tool co. exec.; b. Johnstown, Pa., Feb. 23, 1938; s. Earl William and Carolyn Marie (Forespring) D.; B.B.A., U. Mich., 1960, M.B.A., 1963; m. Barbara Elaine Hrebar, Aug. 17, 1963; children—Nanette Suzanne, Joshua Andrew. Marketing trainee Gen. Electric Co., 1964, dist. rep. houseware div., St. Louis, 1964-65, dist. rep., housewares div., N.Y.C., 1966-68, mgr. marketing recruiting, corporate office, N.Y.C., 1969-70, mgr. manpower devel. and communication, Brazil, 1970-72, mgr. marketing adminstrn. and planning, maj. appliances, electronics, housewares, Sao Paulo, Brazil, 1972, mgr. product planning and market research, maj. appliance and TV, 1973-74, mgr. bus. planning, maj. appliances and TV, 1974-75, mgr. marketing, housewares and radio, 1975-76; v.p. internat. div., portable appliance and tool group McGraw-Edison Co., Columbia, Mo., 1976-77, v.p. pvt. label tools, portable appliance and tool group, 1977—. Sr. fellowship adviser First Reformed Ch., Pompton Plains, N.J., 1968-69; founding mem., bd. dirs. Pompton Family Ski Club, 1968; v.p. PTA, Sao Paulo, Brazil, 1975-76. Mem. Am. Soc. Sao Paulo (dir. 1972-73, 75-76). Served to lt. USNR, 1960-62. Republican. Clubs: Masons, Country Club of Mo. Home: 3207 Honeysuckle Dr Columbia MO 65201 Office: 1801 N Stadium Blvd Columbia MO 65201

DEATLEY, GERTRUDE DARLING (MRS. JULE R. DEATLEY), artist; b. Indpls., Jan. 9, 1911; d. Harry and Luzena (Hayworth) Darling; student pvt. tutors; m. Jule R. DeAtley, June 14, 1938. Exhibited group shows Ind. State Fair, 1961, 62, Hoosier Salon, Indpls., 1962; represented permanent pvt. collections. Owner, The DeAtleys, antiques, Indpls., 1948-66; columnist, owner DeAtley Appraisal Service, 1966—; regular columnist Indpls. Star. Adv. bd. Children's Mus. Indpls.; ceramist, artist in residence, in charge ceramic dept. Little Sisters of Poor, Indpls. Fellow Internat. Inst. Arts and Letters; mem. Ind. State Museum Assn., Indpls. Mus. Art, Ind. Hist. Soc., Ind. Pioneer Soc. Am., Smithsonian Assos. Club: Indpls. Press. Home: 2345 W 86th St Indianapolis IN 46260 Office: 307 N Pennsylvania St Indianapolis IN 46206

DEATLEY, JACK HINDS, gen. contractor; b. Champaign, Ill., Nov. 13, 1941; s. Jack Carter and Hilah Maxine (Hinds) DeA.; B.S., So. Ill., U., 1965; m. Judith Ann Reisinger, Aug. 13, 1966; children—Edward Neal, Laura Ann. Staff accountant Haskins & Sells, C.P.A.'s, St. Louis, 1965-69; v.p. Barber & DeAtley, Inc., Urbana, Ill., 1969—, also dir.; dir. Lancer Corp., Bowie, Md., Ms. America Tennis, Bowie, Md., L.S.I., Inc., Bowie, Md. C.P.A., Mo., Ill. Mem. Champaign County Contractors Assn., Mo. Soc. C.P.A.'s, Champaign C. of C. Republican. Disciples of Christ. Clubs: Champaign Country, Kiwanis, Elks. Home: 1003 Harrington St Champaign IL 61820 Office: 611 N Goodwin St Urbana IL 61801

DEATON, CHARLES RAY, economist, pub. co. exec.; b. Des Moines, Oct. 19, 1928; s. Carl and Dorothy (Schroeder) D.; B.S. in Bus. Adminstrn., Drake U., 1951; m. Patricia Ruth Giese, Aug. 29, 1958; children—Valerie Lynne, Lisa Ann. Supervisory M.I. analyst Hdqrs. 500th M.I. Group, Dept. Army, Tokyo, Japan, 1951-55; mgr. editorial research Better Homes & Gardens mag., Apt. Life mag., also Spl. Interest Publs., Des Moines, 1956-76, group dir. editorial research, 1976—. Lectr., Coll. Journalism Drake U., 1969. Chmn. Bd. dirs. Meredith Credit Union 1968-72, v.p., 1971-72. Served with AUS, 1946-48. Mem. Des Moines Alumni Assn. of Pi Kappa Phi (pres. 1965-74), Pi Kappa Phi, Alpha Kappa Psi. Republican. Presbyn. Mason. Club: Pioneer. Home: 3923 Maquoketa Dr Des Moines IA 50311 Office: 1716 Locust St Des Moines IA 50336

DEBATES, JAMES RONALD, sch. adminstr.; b. Neponset, Ill., Apr. 24, 1933; s. Frank Harry and Mary (Thomas) DeB.; B.S., Western Ill. U., 1955, M.S., 1956; certificate advanced study U. Ill., 1967; m. Marie Darlene Nielsen, Apr. 10, 1955; children—Jaye Ronald, Janet Marie. With Community Unit Sch. 210, Williamsfield, Ill., 1956, 58-62; bus. mgr. Putnam County Unit Sch. 535, Cranville, Ill., 1962—. Commr. Starved Rock council Boy Scouts Am., LaSalle, Ill., 1962-74. Served with AUS, 1956-58. Recipient Scouters award Boy Scouts Am., 1964, Commr.'s Honor award 1966, Scouters Key, 1967; named hon. chpt. farmer Future Farmers Am., 1965. Mem. Ill. Assn. Sch. Bus. Ofcls. (state com. mem. 1968—, dir. 1973-75), Assn. Sch. Bus. Ofcls. U.S. and Can., N.E.A., Ill., Putnam County (past pres.) edn. assns., Tri County Conf. (past pres., sec.), Soc. Study Edn., Beta Beta Beta, Chi Gamma Iota, Delta Sigma Phi. Methodist (lay leader, trustee). Mason. Home: Rural Route 1 Box 17 McNabb IL 61335 Office: Centerville Adminstrn Center Granville IL 61326

DE BELLIS, ANTHONY CARMINE, SR., educator; b. Vallemaio, Italy, Apr. 21, 1920; s. Salvatore and Josephine (D'Alessandro) DeB.; came to U.S., 1936, naturalized, 1947; B.Sc. in Edn., Ohio State U., 1946, B.A., 1947, M.A., 1948; certificate exam. Italian lit. Royal U. Palermo (Italy), 1945; m. Raffaelina Mary Linsalata, Nov. 16, 1942; children—Deanna M. (Mrs. William H. Lynch II), Anthony Carmine, Jr., Barbara Jo (Mrs. Lawrence J. Zaino). Asst. Ohio State U., 1946-47, instr., 1947-48; instr. Washington and Jefferson Coll., 1948-49; instr. Romance langs. U. Mo., 1966-72, asst. prof., 1972—, also dir. undergrad. studies in Italian. Served with AUS, 1942-46, 50-66; personal asst. to chief civil affairs Allied Commn. Italy, 1944-45; gen. staff officer, 1950-66. Decorated Bronze Star medal, Army Commendation with clusters; Gold Medal (Greece); Cavaliere Order Merit Italy. Mem. Am. Assn. Tchrs. Italian, Modern Lang. Assn., Renaissance Soc. Am., Midwest Modern Lang. Assn., Sigma Delta Pi, Phi Sigma Iota. Roman Catholic. K.C. Author: Italian Verbs, 1972; (with Wallace Craft) Basic Elements of Italian Poetry, 1975. Contbr. articles, revs. to profl. jours. Home: 2204 Ridgemont Columbia MO 65201

DEBENKO, EUGENE, educator, librarian; b. Szaszregen, Hungary, June 2, 1917; s. Jeno and Vilma (Simon) D.; B.A., Reg. Ferdinand U., Cluj, Rumania, 1939, M.A., 1940; Ph.D., Ferenc Jozsef U., Kolozsvar, Hungary, 1943; M.A., Ind. U., 1956. Came to U.S., 1950, naturalized, 1956. Jr. officer econ. affairs Hungarian Civil Service, 1940-47; instr. lang., newspaper reporter, Austria, 1947-50; bus. operations analyst Assos. Investment Co., South Bend, Ind., 1952-55; mem. faculty Mich. State U., East Lansing, 1956—, head Internat. Library, 1964—, prof. social sci., 1970—. Lectr., cons. library U. Ryukyus, 1961-63; library cons. AID, India, 1963, Thailand, 1967, Africa, 1966, 70-71, 77. Mem. Am. Hungarian Fedn., Washington, 1951—. Rockefeller Found. grantee, 1961-63, Midwest Univs. Consortium for Internat. Activities grantee, 1966, 1970-71, several research grants Mich. State U. Mem. Nat. Council Cath. Men, A.L.A., African Studies Assn. (mem. com. archives 1967-70), Asian Studies (mem. com. Asian libraries 1964), Beta Phi Mu. Club: Michigan State University Faculty (East Lansing). Author: Research Sources for South Asian Studies in Economic Development, 1966; Research Sources for African Studies, 1969. Contbr. articles to profl. jours. Home: 312 Lee Circle East Lansing MI 48823

DEBES, CHARLES NELSON, structural engr., investment co. exec.; b. Chgo., Mar. 2, 1913; s. Edward Harry and Cora I. (Nelson) D.; S.B. in Elec. Engring., Mass. Inst. Tech., 1935; m. Phyllis Elizabeth Reinert, Mar. 2, 1940; children—Cheryl Lynn, Mary Brent Debes Depth, Robin Jeanne. Plant engr. Woodward Governor Co., Rockford, Ill., 1938-44; pres. Charles N. Debes Asso., Inc., cons. engrs., Rockford, 1944—, Park Strathmoor Corp., Rockford, Chambro Corp., Rockford, Debes Fin. Corp., Rockford, Rockford Convalescent Center, Inc., Rockford; chmn. bd. Alma Nelson Manor Inc., Rockford, Debes Corp., Rockford. Pres. Rockford Health Care Council. Registered profl., structural engr. Ill., Wis., Iowa, Minn., Ohio. Mem. Am., (Ill. del. 1958-60), Ill. (state pres. 1957-59) cons. engrs. councils, Am. Interprofl. Inst. Patentee in field. Home: 1414 Brown Hills Rd Rockford IL 61107 Office: 550 S Mulford Rd Rockford IL 61108 also 5668 Strathmoor Dr Rockford IL 61107

DE BLAISE, ANTHONY WALTER, pub. works co. exec.; b. Racine, Wisc., Apr. 28, 1928; s. Anthony and Ella Julia (Lockhart) DeB.; B.C.E., U. Wis., Madison, 1952; student Marquette U., 1954; m. Laura Stasieluk, Apr. 19, 1952; children—Ronald Klassen, Renee, Amy. Staff engr. Kenosha (Wis.), 1952-55, asst. city engr., 1955-59, dir. pub. works, 1959-64; dir. pub. works and utilities Flint (Mich.), 1964—; surveyor, engr. DC Surveying Co., 1953-59. Mem. Mass Transp. Authority, Flint Tech. Adv. Com., Genesee Metro Planning Com., Flint Planning Com., Harbor Com. Kenosha. Recipient Outstanding Service award Flint Planning Com., 1974; Engr. of Year award Mich. Soc. Profl. Engrs. (Flint chpt.), 1975. Mem. Wis. Soc. Profl. Engrs. (v.p. 1964), Am. Pub. Works Assn. (pres. Inst. Municipal Engring. 1977-78), Am. Road Builders Assn. (bd. airport div. 1973), Profl. Engrs. Wis. Club: Kiwanis (dir.). Home: 1602 Linwood Ave Flint MI 48503 Office: Dir Pub Works and Utilities 1101 S Saginaw Flint MI 48502

DEBOER, JOHN H., farmer; b. Corona, S.D., May 2, 1911; s. Hisko and Jennie (Vust) DeB.; student pub. schs.; m. Amelia Louise Sprung, Nov. 4, 1937; children—Roy Duane, Elaine Irene (Mrs. Mark Lynn Wilde). Farmer, Corona, 1937—; owner DeBoer Trucking Co., 1949-57; carpenter; city policeman, Corona, 1957-73. Coach, Jr. Leaguers, 1956-58, Teener Baseball, 1967-69; chmn. Rental Housing Project, 1974; nominee S.D. Sch. Bd., 1974. Recipient award of merit Asso. Sch. Bd. S.D., 1974. Club: Community. Home: PO Box 1093 Corona SD 57227

DE BOER, RONALD PETER, psychologist; b. Grand Rapids, Mich., Nov. 12, 1937; s. Peter and Eleanor (Van Oostendorp) DeB.; B.A., Mich. State U., 1960, M.A., 1962; children—Laurel Lynne, Ronald Scott, Michael Jon, Michele Ann. Sch. psychologist Harper Creek and Springfield Pub. Schs., Battle Creek, Mich., 1962-66; counseling psychologist, dept. psychology State Tech. Inst. and Rehab. Center, Plainwell, Mich., 1966—; pvt. practice clin. psychology, Battle Creek, 1970—. Pres., Local Council for Exceptional Children, 1965-66, dir., 1964-65; pres. Shrion, Inc., Battle Creek, 1967-70, treas.. 1967-70. HEW grantee, 1960-62. Mem. S.W. Mich. Sch. Psychologist Council (past treas.), Mich. Assn. Profl. Psychologists, Am. Personnel and Guidance Assn. Presbyterian (elder). Home: 715 Ave A Battle Creek MI 49015 Office: Alber Dr Plainwell MI 49080

DEBOER, RUTH MAE, postal clk.; b. Chicago Heights, Ill., June 4, 1942; d. Simon and Alice (Oostman) DeBoer; A.B., Hope Coll., 1964; M.A., Bowling Green State U., 1965; postgrad. U. Denver, 1968, Programming Inst. Denver, 1969-70. Grad. asst. speech Bowling Green (O.) State U., 1964-65; instr. speech communication U. No. Colo., Greeley, 1965-72; vis. instr. speech Hiram Scott Coll., Scottsbluff, Nebr., 1967; farmer De Boer Farms, Chicago Heights, Ill.. 1973; with U.S. Post Office, 1974—; customer relations rep. Rosalee Lincoln Corp., 1974—. Theatre apprentice Huron Playhouse (Ohio), 1965; dir. Readers Theatre Troupe, U. No. Colo., 1967-72; substitute tchr. Illiana Christian, 1973. Recipient 4-H award Danforth Found. Mem. Am. Theatre Assn., Speech Communication Assn., Interpretation Theatre Alliance (Colo. rep. 1967-72), Central States Speech Assn., Pi Epsilon Delta, Pi Kappa Delta, Alpha Gamma Phi. Democrat. Roman Catholic. Address: Rural Route 2 Box 391 Chicago Heights IL 60411

DE BRUIN, JACK PETER, photographer; b. The Hague, Netherlands, May 8, 1923; s. Franciscus Laurentius and Lucy (Pronk) de B.; came to U.S., 1957, naturalized, 1964; B.S., Coll. Chem. Tech., Netherlands, 1941; A.A., Netherlands Art Inst., 1948; diplomas Dutch Sch. Profl. Photography, 1948, U. Cambridge, 1955, McCrone Research Inst., Chgo., 1972; m. Rosamund Hamre-Mertes, Nov. 26, 1977. Owner portrait studio, The Hague, 1948-50; head sect. photography Central Bur. Standards, The Hague, 1950-53; dir. photography Med. Biol. Lab., Nat. Def. Research Council, Netherlands, 1953-57; asst. photographer U. Ill. Med. Center, Chgo., 1957; dir. dept. med. illustration Presbyn.-St. Luke's Hosp., Chgo., 1957-64, Mt. Sinai Hosp., Chgo., 1964-68; bio-med. photographer U. Health Scis./Chgo. Med. Sch., 1968—, instr. med. photography, 1973—, instr. med. communications, 1974-76, asst. prof. med. communications, 1976—; instr. U. Ill. at Chgo., 1961-65, adj. prof., 1970; photog. cons. Chgo. Med. Soc. Quar., 1971. Served with Dutch Resistance, 1940-45, Netherlands Army, 1944-45. Recipient 1st prize in research photography, Netherlands, 1954, 1st prize in gen. photography, 1954-56; cups in research photography, 1955, 56; gold medal for motion picture, 1964. Mem. Biol. Photographers Assn. (registered biol. photographer 1966, Evelyn Palmer award 1961, mem. nat. ho. of dels.), Profl. Photographers Am., Health Scis. Communications Assn., Sci. Research Soc. N.Am., Sigma Xi (asso.). Home: 515 S Clarence Ave Oak Park IL 60304 Office: 2020 W Ogden Ave Chicago IL 60612

DE CABOOTER, PHILIP HAROLD, civil engr.; b. Waukesha, Wis., Oct. 10, 1941; s. Adolph Fredrick Charles and Ruth Johnette Elanora DeC.; B.S. cum laude, Marquette U., 1967, M.S., 1971; m. Patricia Elizabeth Sauer, June 8, 1968; children—Steven, Daniel, Kevin. With Wis. Dept. Transp., 1961—, civil engr., Madison, 1967-73, asst. contracts and estimates engr., 1973—; instr. civil engring. Marquette U., 1970, 72, U. Wis., 1971; cons. Limnetics, Inc., Milw., 1972. Recipient Fred Burggraf award Hwy. Research Bd. of Nat. Acad. Scis., 1973. Mem. ASCE, Nat., Wis. socs. profl. engrs., Sigma Xi, Tau Beta Pi, Chi Epsilon. Contbr. articles to profl. jours. Home: 944 Derby Dr Sun Prairie WI 53590 Office: 4802 Sheboygan Ave Madison WI 53702

DE CAMARA, RICHARD PAUL, automotive mfg. co. adminstr.; b. Ventnor, N.J., Mar. 6, 1917; s. Alfonso Solis and Mary Helena (Conly) de C.; A.B., George Washington U., 1949, M.B.A., 1950, D.B.A., 1966; m. Marguerite Pauline Willey, Feb. 15, 1941; children—Joan (Mrs. Dennis Shea), Richard, Donna Lyn, Donald, Robert. Vice pres. St. L. S.F. R.R., Springfield, Mo., 1963-66; v.p. adminstrn. I.C.R.R., Chgo., 1966-72; v.p., gen. mgr. recreational vehicle group Midas Internat., Chgo., 1972-76, exec. v.p., 1976—; dir. Lakeside Bank, Chgo., 1968-71. Instr. bus. courses George Washington U., Washington, 1961-62, Drury Coll., Springfield, 1965-66. Served with U.S. Army, 1941-62. Decorated Bronze Star medal with oak leaf cluster. Mem. Phi Beta Kappa, Phi Eta Sigma. Home: 465 South St Elmhurst IL 60126 Office: 222 S Riverside Plaza Chicago IL 60606

DECENSO, DONALD DANIEL, dentist; b. Youngstown, Ohio, June 16, 1929; s. Frank Alexander and Rachael Margaret (Lambert) DeC.; student Youngstown U., 1947-49; B.S., Ohio State U., 1951, D.D.S., 1957; m. Patricia Kay Thompson, Aug. 20, 1955; children—Diane Marie, Donna Lee, Deborah Sue. Intern, Fla. State Hosp., Chattahoochee, 1957-58; mem. staff Orient Mental Hosp. (Ohio), 1958-59; pvt. practice dentistry, Upper Arlington, Ohio, 1958-59; dentist, Mansfield (Ohio) Reformatory, 1959-61; pvt. practice dentistry, Mansfield, 1959—. Med.-dental adviser Pioneer Vocational Sch., 1969—; mem. active staff Mansfield Gen. Hosp.; mem. adv. bd. Geriatric Center Mansfield. Served with USMCR, 1951-53. Mem. Am. Acad. Gen. Dentistry (dist. dir. 1973—, sec.-treas. Ohio chpt.), Am. Acad. Periodontology, Am. Dental Soc. Anesthesiology, Ohio Acad. Practice Adminstrn., Am., Ohio, Central Ohio (v.p. 1974-75, pres. 1976-77) dental assns., Mansfield Dental Soc. (pres. 1965-66), Mansfield-Richland County Dental Clinic Assn. (dir.). Republican. Roman Catholic (chmn. liturgy com. 1974-75). K.C. (4 deg.), Elk. Clubs: Serra (pres. 1970-71), University (Mansfield). Home: 579 Edgewood Rd Mansfield OH 44907 Office: 425 W Cook Rd Mansfield OH 44907

DECHAIRO, THOMAS, physician; b. Arma, Kans., May 26, 1913; s. Joe and Pasquala (Police) D.; B.S., Kans. U., 1934, M.D., 1936; m. Margaret V. Roberts, Mar. 8, 1936; children—Thomas Carl, Douglas Clark, Margaret Joyce (Mrs. Larry Joe Licthenegger), Roger Richard. Intern Kansas City Gen. Hosp., 1936-37; practice medicine, specializing in family practice, Westmoreland, Kans., 1937—; owner, operator 20 bed pvt. hosp., 1942—; health officer Pottawatomi County, 1962—; coroner Pottowatomi County, 1944-50. Active Boy Scouts Am. for 33 years; mem. and trustee High Sch. Ednl. Bd., 1944-56. Mem. Am. Acad. Family Physicians, Alpha Omega Alpha. Methodist (trustee 1954—). Mason; mem. Order Eastern Star. Club: Westmoreland Service. Address: Westmoreland KS 66549

DECK, ROBERT ANDREW, accountant cons.; b. Massillon, Ohio, Jan. 2, 1910; s. Andrew Auth and Mary Ann (Kennedy) D.; student Kent State U., 1932-33; m. Dorothy Mary Harvey, Oct. 27, 1931; children—Robert Edward, Joseph Charles. Accountant, Milcor Steel Co., Canton and Milw., Wis., 1932-40; with Am. Electric Switch & Goods Roads Machinery, Minerva, Ohio, 1941-66, controller, sr. adminstr., 1957-66; pvt. practice cons. accountant, Minerva, Ohio, 1966—. Pub. accountant, Ohio. Mem. Nat. Soc. Accountants, Nat. Soc. Bus. Budgeting. Clubs: Rotary, K.C. Home and Office: 323 East Line St Minerva OH 44657

DECKER, DOUGLAS RICHARD, window mfg. co. computer programmer; b. Chgo., Oct. 17, 1946; s. Van Joseph and Vera Bertha (Pohl) D.; student Central Bus. Coll., 1969; m. Betsy Annette Smith, Aug. 29, 1969; children—Deanna, Paul Martin. Asst. mgr. Shopeze Food Stores, Newton, Kans., 1968-69; prodn. control Hehr Internat., Newton, 1969-75, programming coordinator, 1975—. Served with U.S. Army, 1966-68. Mem. Data Processing Mgrs. Assn. Clubs: Am. Legion, Moose. Home: 507 E 3d St Newton KS 67114 Office: PO Box 189 Newton KS 67114

DECKER, JOSEPH CHARLES, pharmacist, pharm. chain exec.; b. Highland Park, Mich., Sept. 2, 1936; s. Josef Peter and Maria Theodora (Gerwert) D.; B.S. in Pharmacy, U. Mich., 1958; m. Nannette Sue Emerick, Dec. 27, 1972; children by previous marriage—Joel, Jeffrey, James. Pharmacist, Richardson's Pharmacy, Ann Arbor, Mich., 1958-62, mgr., 1962-68, partner, 1965-68; chmn. bd., pres. Richardson's Pharmacy Inc., Ann Arbor, 1968—; dir. Nat. Bank of Ypsilanti. Bd. dirs., treas. Ypsilanti Area Indsl. Devel. Corp., 1968-70. Mem. Nat. Assn. Chain Drug Stores, Am., Mich., Washtenaw County Pharm. assns., Phi Delta Chi. Home: 3207 Hayes Ct Ann Arbor MI 48104 Office: 2215 W Stadium Rd Ann Arbor MI 48103

DECKER, LEONARD LLEWELLYN, heavy equipment mfg. co. exec.; b. Lansing, Mich., May 2, 1941; s. Llewellyn Irvin and Alma (Schultz) D.; B.S. in Commerce and Marketing (J.W. Knapp Co. retailing scholar, 1966-67, achievement scholar, 1967), Ferris State Coll., 1967; M.B.A., Eastern Ill. U., 1972; m. Joanne Marie Damon, Aug. 1, 1964. Salesman, Fed. Dept. Stores, Lansing, 1959-63; insp. Oldsmobile div. Gen. Motors Corp., Lansing, Mich., 1963-65; salesman Burton Bootery, Big Rapids, Mich., 1965-67; market analyst Blaw-Knox Constrn. Equipment, Inc. div. White Consol. Industries, Mattoon, Ill., 1967-73, mgr. marketing research, 1973-75, internat. sales mgr., 1975—. Mem. Am. Marketing Assn. (chpt. sec. 1973, talk-in chmn.). Lutheran (bd. dirs.). Club: Internat. Trade (Chgo.). Home: 1819 Phillips Pl Charleston IL 61920 Office: East Route 16 Mattoon IL 61938

DECKER, PETER W., chem. found. exec.; b. Grand Rapids, Mich., Mar. 20, 1919; s. Charles B. and Ruth E. (Thorndill) D.; B.S., Wheaton Coll., 1941; postgrad. Northwestern U., 1942-43; D.Sc. (hon.), London Inst. Applied Research, 1973; m. Margaret I. Stainthorpe, June 10, 1944; children—Peter, Marilyn, Christine, Charles. Advt. dept. Hotels Windermere, Chgo., 1942, Princess Pat Cosmetics, Chgo., 1943; market research investigator A.C. Nielson Co., Chgo., 1944-48; pres. Peter Decker Constrn. Co., Detroit, 1948-60; sales mgr. Century Chem. Products Co., Detroit, 1961-62, v.p., 1962-63, pres., 1963-75; sr. partner G & D Advt. Assos., 1967—; v.p., treas., exec. dir. Christian Edn. Advancement, Inc., 1975-77; registrar, instr. N.T. Greek and Theology Birmingham (Mich.) Bible Inst., 1973—. Neighborhood commr. Boy Scouts Am., 1961-66, now merit badge counselor. Mem. Bd. Rev., Beverly Hills, Mich., 1957-63; chmn. bd. review Southfield Twp., Mich., 1964-67; bd. dirs., past pres. Beverly Hills Civic Assn. Bd. dirs. Mich. Epilepsy Center and Assn., 1957-71, exec. com., 1962-67. Mem. Detroit Soc. Model Engrs. (pres. 1958, 62, dir. 1955-71), Chem. Splty. Mfg. Assn., AAAS, Nat. Geog. Soc., Internat. Platform Assn., Am. Soc. Testing and Materials. Republican (sustaining mem. Oakland County, Mich.). Baptist (trustee, instr. Bible Inst.). Home: 33210 Rosevear Dr Beverly Hills Birmingham MI 48009 Office: 280 E Lincoln Birmingham MI 48009

DECKERT, JAMES ROBERT, lawyer; b. Great Bend, Kans., Sept. 22, 1940; s. Albun P. and Mabel (Miller) D.; B.S. in Accounting, U. Kans., 1962, J.D., 1965; m. Dianne Lee Turner, July 3, 1965. Admitted to Kans. bar, 1965, Mo. bar, 1968; with tax dept. Arthur Andersen & Co., Kansas City, Mo., 1965-68; asso. firm Morris Sanders King & Stamper, Kansas City, 1968; partner firm Davidson, Hentzen, Deckert & Haitbrink, Kansas City, Mo., 1968-74, Davidson, Deckert & Schutter, 1974—. Mem. exec. com. Guild of Friends of Art, 1972—. Bd. dirs. Bacchus Found. Served to 1st lt. Judge Adv. Gen. Corps, AUS, 1966-72. Mem. Mo. (mem. taxation com.), Am. bar assns., Kans. U. Alumni Assn. Kansas City (pres.), Delta Upsilon (pres. alumni assn.). Clubs: University (Kansas City, Mo.); Indian Hills Country (Mission Hills, Kans.). Home: 1232 W 61st Terr Kansas City MO 64113 Office: 2520 Commerce Tower Kansas City MO 64105

DE CLUE, JOSEPH ANTHONY, personnel exec.; b. Richwoods, Mo., Dec. 19, 1928; s. Joseph Daniel and Mary Elma (Cordia) DeC.; B.S., U. Mo., 1956; m. Jennie Maude Roussin, Sept. 11, 1951; children—Nancy Elizabeth, John Anthony, Suzanne Marie, Stephanie Joan. Personnel asst. Mo. Hwy. Dept., Jefferson City, 1956, asst. personnel dir., 1957-66, dir. employee relations, 1966-70, personnel dir., 1970—. Mem. mayor's spl. adv. com. on finance, Jefferson City, 1970-72; adv. bd. Tri-County Tech. Sch., Eldon, Mo., 1970-72; scoutmaster Boy Scouts Am., Jefferson City, 1960-61; liaison man for non-merit system agys. Loaned Exec. Action Program, 1974. Served with AUS, 1951-52; ETO. Mem. Mo. Inst. Pub. Adminstrs. (dir. 1975—), Mo. Personnel Mgmt. Council (exec. com., chmn. 1975), Am. Mgmt. Assn. Roman Catholic. K.C. Home: 1101 Lee St Jefferson City MO 65101 Office: PO Box 270 Capitol at Jefferson Jefferson City MO 65101

DECOSSE, JEROME JOSEPH, physician, educator; b. Valley City, N.D., Apr. 19, 1928; s. Edmund and Gertrude (Anderson) DeC.; B.S., Coll. of St. Thomas, 1948; M.D., U. Minn., 1952; Ph.D., State U. N.Y. Upstate Med. Center, 1969; m. Sheila Marie Flynn, June 22, 1957; children—Stephen, Carol, David, Philip, Sarah. Intern, resident Roosevelt Hosp., N.Y.C. 1952-60; resident Meml. Hosp., N.Y.C., 1960-62; asst., asso. prof., then prof. Case Western Res. U., 1966-71; prof., chmn. div. surgery Med. Coll. Wis., Milw., 1971—; chief surgery Milw. County Gen. Hosp. Mem. pub. adv. coms. NIH, 1968-72, 74—. Mem. Wis. Legis. Commn., 1973-74. Served to capt. M.C., AUS, 1956-58. Decorated Commendation Medal. Markle scholar in acad. medicine, 1964-69. Diplomate Am. Bd. Surgery. Fellow A.C.S. (gov.). Clubs: Milw. Athletic, Milw. Country. Editorial bd. Archives of Surgery, 1973, Surgery, 1976. Contbr. articles to sci. jours. Home: 1510 E Goodrich Ln Fox Point WI 53217 Office: 8700 W Wisconsin Ave Milwaukee WI 53226

DECOURSEY, CHARLES JOSEPH, JR., psychologist; b. Edina, Mo., Aug. 5, 1912; s. Charles Joseph and Frances Rebecca (Blessington) DeC.; A.B., St. Ambrose Coll., 1934, A.M. in Psychology, St. Louis U., 1955. Dir. Youth Guidance Nat. Youth Adminstrn., City of St. Louis, 1937; vocat. adviser VA Guidance Center, St. Louis U., 1946-50; pvt. practice psychol. counseling; dir. DeCoursey Psychol. Services and Reading Improvement Lab., St. Louis, 1950—. Served from pvt. to maj., AUS, 1940-46; lt. col. Res. ret. Diplomate Am. Bd. Psychol. Services; nat. certified rehab. counselor. Mem. Internat. Reading Assn., Profls. Interested in Religious Issues, Am., Midwestern, Southwestern, Mo. (certified) psychol. assns., Nat. Rehab. Assn., Nat. Vocat. Guidance Assn., Adult Edn. Council Greater St. Louis, S.R., U.S. Flag Assn. Roman Catholic. K.C. (4 deg.). Home: Route 1 Box 202 Gray Summit MO 63039 Office: 4326 Lindell Blvd St Louis MO 63108

DEDECKERE, DORIS C., pub. relations exec.; b. Grosse Pointe, Mich., Aug. 21, 1926; d. George Joseph and Lillian Anna (Pipper) Clutterbuck; ed. Wayne State U.; student U. Mich. Extension, Detroit Inst. Musical Arts; m. Robeert O. DeDeckere, Sept. 9, 1950; children—Robeert, David, James, Adrienne. Exec. sec. Recorder's Court, Detroit, from 1968; vice chmn. Mayor's Narcotics Com., Detroit; chmn. Pub. Health Commn.. Detroit, 1970-73; asso. dir. Mayor's Com. Human Resources Devel., 1973-74; dir. pub. relations Metro Detroit March of Dimes, 1974-77, Detroit Inst. of Tech., 1977—; coordinator Ethnic Classroom Project at Wayne State U.; pub. relations cons. to community theatre groups; free lance writer, 1965—. Chmn. Housing Poor Peoples March for Eastside of Detroit, 1967; chmn. Christian Services St. Matthews Ch., 1969-72; trustee Detroit Community Music Sch., Project Headline. Recipient Spirit of Detroit medal, 1973. Mem. Women in Communication, Pub. Relations Soc. Am., Univ. Cultural Center Assn., Detroit Press Club, Econ. Club of Detroit, Friends of Detroit Library, Women's Economic Club, Friends of Natural History Mus. Roman Catholic. Club: Breakfast of Detroit. Contbr. poetry to various mags. and articles to community publs. Home: 4S42 Audubon Detroit MI 48224 Office: Detroit Inst of Technology 2727 2nd Ave Detroit MI 48201

DEDERICK, ROBERT GOGAN, bank economist; b. Keene, N.H., Nov. 18, 1929; s. Frederic Van Dyck and Margaret (Gogan) D.; A.B., Harvard, 1951, M.A., 1953, Ph.D., 1958; postgrad. Cornell U., 1953-54; m. Margarida N. Magalhaes, Aug. 24, 1957; children—Frederic, Laura, Peter. Econ. research mgr. New Eng. Mut. Life Ins. Co., 1957-64; asso. economist No. Trust Co., Chgo., 1964, v.p., asso. economist, 1965-69, v.p., economist, 1969-70, sr. v.p., economist, 1970—. Mem. econ. adv. bd. U.S. Dept. Commerce, 1969-70, 75-76. Fellow Nat. Assn. Bus. Economists (pres. 1973-74); mem. Am. Econ. Assn., Conf. Bus. Economists, Am. Bankers Assn., Am. Statis. Assn., U.S. C. of C. (bank, monetary, fiscal com. 1975—), Chgo. Assn. Commerce and Industry (dir. policy com.), Am. Inst. Banking, Nat. Economists Club, Am. Finance Assn., Nat. Bur. Econ. Research (dir.), Phi Beta Kappa. Clubs: Economic, Metropolitan, Bankers, Harvard (Chgo.); Oak Brook (Ill.), Hinsdale (Ill.) Golf Club. Home: 133 S County Line Rd Hinsdale IL 60521 Office: No Trust Co 50 S LaSalle St Chicago IL 60675

DEDMON, ROBERT ERNEST, physician; b. Fairbury, Nebr., Jan. 6, 1931; s. Roy E. and Cora C. (Frank) Deadman; A.B., Ind. U., 1953, M.D., 1956; m. Helen Ann Boudry, June 23, 1957; children—Sharon, MaryDee, Susan. Intern, Presbyn. Hosp., Chgo., 1956-57, resident internal medicine, 1961-62, 57-59; research fellow NIH, 1959-60; practice medicine specializing in internal medicine, Chgo., 1962-64, Neenah, Wis., 1964—; fellow sect. endocrinology and metabolism Presbyn.-St. Luke's Hosp., Chgo., 1960-61, dept. medicine and dept. microbiology, 1962-64; instr. medicine U. Ill. Coll. Medicine, Chgo., 1961-64; clin. asst. prof. medicine U. Wis., Madison, 1964-72; chmn. internal medicine com. Theda Clark Meml. Hosp., Neenah, 1969-71, chmn. intensive care com., 1971-72, pres. med. staff, 1974-75; mng. partner, pres. Twin City Clinic, Neenah, 1965-74; staff v.p. med. affairs, corporate med. dir. Kimberly-Clark Corp., Neenah, 1976—; cons. Nat. Center for Health Statistics, 1965. Bd. dirs. Nicolet Clinic, 1974-76. Diplomate Am. Bd. Internal Medicine. Fellow A.C.P. (life mem.); mem. Am., Wis. socs. of internal medicine, AMA, Wis. State, Winnebago County (pres. 1974-75), Am. Fedn. Clin. Research, Ill., Chgo. med. socs., Am. Fedn. Clin. Research, AAAS, Am. Rheumatism Assn., Chgo. Rheumatism Soc., Arthritis Found., N.Y., Fox Valley acads. of sci., Am. Guild Organists (dean Northeastern Wis. chpt.), Sigma Xi. Presbyterian (elder 1966—, choir mem. 1964—, asso. organist 1964—). Contbr. articles to profl. jours. Home: 333 Park Dr Neenah WI 54956 Office: 2100 Winchester Rd Box 999 Neenah WI 54956

DEDRICK, DOUGLASS ALAN, nuclear engr.; b. Chicago Heights, Ill., Aug. 26, 1950; s. Donald Clark and Norama (Ekstedt) D.; m. Dorothy Fliter, Feb. 20, 1971; certificate radiographic interpretation Mass. Inst. Tech., 1972-75; asso. design tech. Ohio State U., 1975-76; student in Metall. Engring., Purdue U., 1976. Nuclear engr., supr. Graver Tank & Mfg. Co., East Chicago, Ind., 1974-76; nuclear engr. Stone & Webster Engring. Corp., Boston, 1973-74; nuclear engr. Pub. Service Ind., Plainfield, 1976—. Mem. Am. Nuclear Soc., Am. Soc. Quality Control, Am. Welding Soc., ASCE, Am. Soc. Non-Destructive Testing, ASME. Patentee electroslag welding suspension units. Home: 3440 Leatherbury Ln Indianapolis IN 46222 Office: Pub Service Ind 1000 E Main St Plainfield IN 46168

DEE, ARTHUR EMIL, banker; b. Coloma, Wis., Jan. 20, 1932; s. Arthur Louis and Alma Louise (Mueller) D.; grad. Oshkosh Bus. Coll., 1952, U. Wis. Sch. Banking, 1963; m. Dorothy Virginia Bucholz, June 4, 1955; children—Carla, Paula. Accounting dept. Allis Chalmers Accounting Office, Milw., 1953; bookkeeper Brakebush Bros., Westfield, Wis., 1953-55; v.p. M & I Peoples Bank Coloma, 1955—. Sec. Coloma Municipal Water Utility, 1958-65; dir., treas. Westfield (Wis.) Integrated Sch. Dist., 1963—; pres. central Wis. chpt. Bank Adminstrn. Inst., 1967, Coloma Businessmen, Inc., 1970-71; pres. Village of Coloma, 1975—; bd. dirs. Internat. Luth. Laymen's League, 1966-70, S. Wis. Dist., Luth. Ch.-Mo. Synod, 1976—. Mem. Wis. Bankers Assn. (group pres. 1977—). Home: Box 197 Coloma WI 54930 Office: M & I Peoples Bank Coloma WI 54930

DEE, PAUL EDWARD, surgeon; b. Canton, Ohio, Sept. 2, 1909; s. Fred Charles and Zetta O. (McGregor) Drungenbolz; B.A., Ohio State U., 1934, M.D., 1937; m. Eileen Kathryn Durr, June 30, 1938; children—Tom, Jerry. Intern, Akron (Ohio) City Hosp., 1937-38; orthopedic fellow orthopedic surgery Cleve. Clinic, 1942-47; pvt. practice medicine, Forest, Ohio, 1938-42, specializing in orthopedic surgery, Rockford, Ill., 1947—; mem. staff Swedish-Am. Hosp., 1947—; cons. staff St. Anthony Hosp., Rockford Meml. Hosp. Pres. Rockford Profl. Bldg. Corp., 1956—. Mem., treas. Rockford Airport Authority, 1968—. Diplomate Am. Bd. Orthopedic Surgery. Fellow A.C.S.; mem. Am. Acad. Orthopedic Surgeons, AMA, Chgo. Orthopedic Soc., Latin Am. Soc. Orthopedics and Traumatology. Mason (Shriner, Jester). Club: Pyramid. Home: 5704 Springbrook Rd Rockford IL 61111 Office: 1221 E State St Rockford IL 61108

DEER, E. DOROTHY, occupational therapist, rehab. counselor; b. Pitts., Apr. 1, 1920; d. Lewis Hutchinson and Martha (Caughey) Deer; certificate in occupational therapy Richmond Profl. Inst., 1945; B.S., San Jose State Coll., 1964, M.S., 1966. Dir. music and recreation N.H. State Hosp., Concord, 1946-47; asst. to exec. dir. Am. Occupational Therapy Assn., N.Y.C., 1947-48; asst. dir. occupational therapy Eastern State Hosp., Williamsburg, Va., 1948-50; therapist VA Hosp., Vancouver, Wash., 1950-54; dir. occupational therapy U. Okla. Med. Center, Oklahoma City, 1954-57; dir. occupational therapy Central State Hosp., Norman, Okla., 1957-59; indsl. therapist Agnews State Hosp., San Jose, Calif., 1964-67; counselor Santa Clara County Welfare Dept., San Jose, 1967-68, Clay County Health Dept., Liberty, Mo., 1968-70; vocat. rehab. counselor Kansas City (Kans.) Dist. Office, 1970-72; work evaluator Indsl. Rehab. Center, Merriam, Kans., 1972-74; supr. evaluation Jewish Vocat. Services, Kansas City, Mo., 1974—. Cons. Juvenile Ct., Clay County, 1968-70, Clay County Rural Schs., 1968-70. Mem. exec. bd. Clay-Platte Health and Welfare Council, Clay County, 1968-71, Mental Health Services Corp., Clay County, 1968-72. Mem. AAUW, Nat. Rehab. Assn., Am. (del. ho. of dels. 1955-58, sec. 1957-58), Mo. occupational therapy assns., Nat. Assn. Rehab. Counselors, Nat. Vocat. Evaluation and Work Adjustment Assn. (dir.), Vocat. Evaluation and Work Adjustment Assn. (bd. Mo. chpt.), N.E. Kans. Rehab. Assn., Kans. Rehab. Assn. (membership sec. 1971-72). Office: 1516 Grand Ave Kansas City MO 64108

DEERE, CYRIL THOMAS, computer co. exec.; b. Rockville, Conn., Apr. 28, 1924; s. Albert Bertram and Belle Murdie (King) D.; B.S., Yale, 1949; m. Shirley Ann Scheiner, June 2, 1945; children—Sandra Deere Leinz, Kathryn Deere Bailey. With Lee Paper Co., Vicksburg, Mich., 1949-50, Addressograph-Multigraph Corp., Hartford, Conn., 1950-55, Cleve., 1955-69; with Data Card Corp., Mpls., 1969—, v.p. mktg., 1969-75, sr. v.p., 1975—, dir. Plastics div., 1974—; pres., dir. Canadian Data Card Ltd., Toronto, Ont., 1974—; chmn. bd. Data Card Internat., 1977—. Served with USMCR, 1943-44. Decorated Purple Heart. Mem. Am. Nat. Standards Inst. (1st chmn. credit card standards com. 1968-73), Input/Output Systems Assn. (pres. 1975). Clubs: Interlachen Country; Yale of N.W.; Normandale Tennis. Home: 5646 Interlachen Circle Edina MN 55436 Office: 7625 Parklawn Ave Minneapolis MN 55435

DEETER, ALLEN C., educator; b. Dayton, Ohio, Mar. 8, 1931; s. Raymond Coate and Elizabeth Flora (Petry) D.; B.A. cum laude, Manchester Coll., 1953; B.D. magna cum laude, Bethany Theol. Sem., 1956; M.A., Princeton, 1958, Ph.D., 1963; postgrad. Garrett Sem., 1954-55, Marburg U. (Germany), 1965-66, Harvard, 1968-69; m. Joan Sue George, Aug. 31, 1952; children—Michael Allen, Daniel Paul, David Kevin. Ordained to ministry Ch. of Brethren, 1953; minister edn. Chgo. 1st Ch. of Brethren, 1954-56; faculty Manchester Coll., North Manchester, Ind., 1959—, asso. prof. religion and philosophy, 1966-72, prof., 1972—; dir. Peace Studies Inst. and Program in Conflict Resolution, 1967—, asso. dean coll., 1969—. Dir. Brethren Colls. Abroad, Marburg and Strasbourg U., 1965-66, worldwide coordinator, 1975—; vis. lectr. Punjabi U., Dibrugahr U., USIS, Madras and Calcutta, India, 1969. Leader, Boy Scouts Am., 1966-68; mem. film rev. bd. Chgo. Council Chs., 1954-56; vice chmn. bd. dirs. John F. Kennedy Haus, Marburg, 1965-66; bd. dirs. Council on Intercultural Studies and Programs, vice chmn., 1974—. Danforth asso., 1960—. Lilly Found. fellow., 1957; Soc. for Religion in Higher Edn. fellow, 1968-69. Mem. Ind. Acad. Religion (pres. 1970-71), Am. Acad. Religion, AAUP, Am. Soc. Ch. History, Internat. Studies Assn. Author: In His Hand, 1965; Kagawa, 1970; Heirs of a Promise, 1971. Editor: Bull. Peace Studies Inst., 1970—. Home: 714 N Bond St North Manchester IN 46962 Office: Manchester College Box 184 North Manchester IN 46962

DEETHARDT, DOROTHY ELLA PIKE, home economist; b. Aurora, S.D., May 29, 1914; d. Willis Lloyd and Grace Mae (Van Cleve) Pike; m. Harold I. Deethardt, Sept. 7, 1939; children—Virgil, Ronald, Shirley. B.S., S.D. State Coll., 1937; M.S., S.D. State U., 1966. Home mgmt. supr. Farm Security Adminstrn., Winner and Kadoka, S.D., 1938-39; research technician Dept. Home Econs., Agr. Expt. Sta., S.D. State U., 1955-69, research asst., 1969—. Regent, John Kerr chpt. Daus. of Am., 1950-52, 74—. Mem. Inst. Food Technologists, Bus. and Profl. Women's Club, DAR, United Methodist Women, Sigma Xi. Contbr. articles to Expt. Sta. bulls.; papers given tech. meetings. Home: Rural Route 1 Aurora SD 57002 Office: Coll Home Econs SD State U Brookings SD 57006

DEETS, SAMUEL EDWIN, business exec.; b. Cochranton, Pa., July 28, 1934; s. Samuel Edgar and Vera Marie (Gheres) D.; Th.B., God's Bible Sch. and Coll., Cin., 1958, A.B., 1959; B.S., U. Cin., 1961, M.A., 1963, Ph.D., 1970; m. Carolyn May Benninger, June 1, 1957; 1 dau., Michelle Benninger. Instr., God's Bible Sch. and Coll., Cin., 1961-63, pres., 1965-75; asst. to pres. Ballou Office Service, Inc., Cin., 1975—. Lectr., U. Cin., 1963-65. Mem. Cin. Charter Com. Mem. Am. Polit. Sci. Assn., Data Processing Mgmt. Assn., Am. Acad. Polit. and Social Sci. Republican. Methodist. Author: The Anti-Poverty Program-A Study in Professionalized Reform, 1970. Editor: God's Revivalist, 1965-75. Home: 4715 Sycamore Rd Cincinnati OH 45236 Office: 307 E 4th St Cincinnati OH 45202

DEETZ, ROBERT LEO, supt. sch.; b. Modena, Wis., May 18, 1929; s. Leo Thomas and Vera Mae (Kezar) D.; B.S., U. Wis., Eau Claire, 1957; M.Ed., Winona State Coll., 1960; m. Lois Dorothy Larson, May 9, 1952; children—Jacqueline Rae, Lon Arlan. Tchr., pub. schs., Taylor, Wis., 1957-59; prin. high sch., Hixton, Wis., 1959-60, Whitehall, Wis., 1960-61; supt. schs., Elk Mound, Wis., 1961-63, Spring Valley, Wis., 1963-68, Mayville, Wis., 1968—. Chmn., Mayville Salvation Army Com., 1973—; sec. Dodge County Soil and Water Dist., 1972—, Dodge County Agr. Com., 1972—, Wis. State Soil and Water Com., 1974—, Com. on Youth and Edn. Wis., 1974—; mem. Mayville Library Bd., 1969—. Served with USNR, 1950-51. Kettering fellow, 1969. Mem. Am. Legion. Rotarian. Clubs: Mayville Golf, Mayville Trapshooting. Home: 433 Seitz Ave Mayville WI 53050 Office: 500 N Clark St Mayville WI 53050

DEEVER, M. LAWRENCE, newspaper exec.; b. Hutchinson, Kans., May 10, 1918; s. Azell L. and Grace (Banks) D.; A.B., York Coll., 1939; B.D., Bonebrake Theol. Sem., 1942; m. Carol L. Owings, Apr. 14, 1966. Spl. events mgr., promotion dept. Chgo. Daily News, 1948-60; asst. personnel mgr. newspaper div. Field Enterprises Inc., Chgo., 1960-65, personnel mgr., 1965-76; pension mgr. Chgo. Tribune, 1976—. Mem. Newspaper Personnel Relations Assn., Indsl. Relations Assn. Chgo. Home: 1406 Washington St Wilmette IL 60091 Office: 435 N Michigan Ave Chicago IL 60611

DEFFENBAUGH, ROBERT WARREN, lawyer; b. Rochelle, Ill., Oct. 28, 1920; s. Roy A. and Elizabeth K. (Struck) D.; B.A., U. Ill., 1942, J.D., 1948; m. Eleanor K. Mathis, Dec. 16, 1960. Admitted to Ill. bar, 1948; asst. atty. gen. State Ill., 1948-49, legislative reference bur., 1949; asst. legal adv. Office Supt. Pub. Instrn., 1950-58, 67-69; practiced in Springfield, Ill., 1948—; mem. firms Drach, Terrell and Deffenbaugh, Springfield; part owner, dir. radio sta. WFMB, Springfield. Bd. dirs. Ill. United Cerebal Palsy, 1958-65. Served with AUS, 1942-45. Mem. Am., Ill., Sangamon County (v.p. 1973-74, pres. 1974-75) bar assns., Am. Judicature Soc., Phi Delta Phi, Phi Gamma Delta. Republican. Presbyn. Mason (32 deg., K.T.), Elk, Kiwanian (pres. 1971-72, dir. 1951-54, 69-73). Home: 912 Williams St Springfield IL 62704 Office: 804 Myers Bldg Springfield IL 62701

DEFOREST, JULIE MORROW, artist, poet; b. N.Y.C.; d. Cornelius W. and Rosalie Caroline Morrow; A.B., Wellesley Coll.; M.A., Columbia U.; studied with Jonas Lie, Charles W. Hawthorne, John Carlsen; m. Cornelius Wortendyke De Forest, Mar. 9, 1929. Painter in oil; one-man shows including N.A.D., N.Y. World's Fair, Cin. Art Mus., Pa. Acad., Corcoran Gallery, Allied Artists Am., Nat. Arts Club, Profl. Artists Cin., Cin. Mac Dowell Soc., Bklyn. Mus., U. Cin., Jersey City Mus., Farnsworth Mus. Wellesley Coll., several others; numerous group exhbns.; represented in permanent collections Wellesley Coll., Cin. Art Mus., U. Cin., Hillforest Hist. Found., Columbia, Slater Meml. Mus., Howard U., Fisk U., Xavier U., ARC, Cin., Am. Christian Coll., Tulsa, Christ Hosp., Cin., Clovernook Home for Blind, Cin., Hillforest Mus., Aurora, Ind. Recipient purchase prize, painting Federated Women's Clubs, 1936; two medals for patriotic service Women's Theodore Roosevelt Meml. Assn.; two poetry awards, Coll. Club Cin., also citation for attainment in art, literature, patriotic service, 1963. Fellow Royal Soc. Arts (life); mem. D.A.R., Minute Women Allied Artists Am., Cin. Art. Mus. Assn., Theodore Roosevelt Assn. (2 citations for patriotic service for cooperation in nat. centennial celebration), Cin. MacDowell Soc., Internat. Platform Assn. Congregationalist. Clubs: Nat. Arts, Women's University (N.Y.C.); Wellesley, Women's College, Cincinnati Country, Town (Cin.). Author: Belfry Chimes and Other Rimes, 1974. Address: Vernon Manor Hotel Oak St and Burnet Ave Cincinnati OH 45219 also Nat Arts Club 15 Gramercy Park New York City NY 10003

DEFOSSET, DONALD, wholesale paper sales co. exec.; b. Cin., Nov. 12, 1921; s. Joseph Gustav and Alice (Sandman) DeF.; student U. Cin., 1945-46; m. Marilyn Herzog, Aug. 24, 1946; children—Donald, Daniel. Salesman Phillips Glass Co., Cin., 1945-46; dist. mgr. Ft. Howard Paper Co., St. Louis, 1947-67; exec. v.p. Royal Papers, Inc., St. Louis, 1967—. Active P.T.A., Boy Scouts Am. Served with AUS, 1941-45. Presbyn. (deacon). Home: 10228 Thornwood Dr Ladue MO 63124 Office: 801 Spruce St St Louis MO 63102

DE FRANCESCO, JOHN BLAZE, JR., pub. relations exec.; b. Stamford, Conn., May 22, 1936; s. John B. and Mae (Matyscyk) DeF.; B.S., U. Conn., 1958; m. Louise C. Terlizzo, Nov. 1, 1958; children—Daryl, Jay, Dana, Dorian. Commd. ensign U.S. Navy, 1958, advanced through grades to lt. comdr., 1967, with reserves, 1967-77; sr. v.p. Daniel J. Edelman, Inc., Chgo., 1967-77; v.p. Harshe-Rotmont Druck, Inc., Chgo., 1977—; dir. Fanani Builders Inc., Deerfield, Ill., 1977—. Mem. bd. Div. Vocational Rehab., Gov. of Ill., 1976—. Served with USN, 1958-67. Recipient Silver Anvil awards, Pub. Relations Soc. Am., 1966-75; Publicity Club of Chgo. Golden Trumpet award, 1976. Mem. Am. Marketing Assn., Marketing Communications Execs. Internat., Navy League of U.S. Naval Reserve Assn. Roman Catholic. Club: Tennaqua. Home: 1222 Laurel Ave Deerfield IL 60015 Office: 444 N Michigan Ave Chicago IL 60601

DEFRANK, CLAIRE MARIE, profl. musician, educator; b. Chgo., Feb. 9, 1951; d. Carlo and Clara (Cottone) DeFranco; Mus.B., Roosevelt U., 1973; m. Gary Charles Van Horn, July 24, 1977. Tchr., Elementary Schs. Instrumental Music Program, Chgo., 1973—; pvt. instrumental tchr.; tchr. vocal, gen. music Gen. Pershing Sch., Berwyn, Ill., 1974—. Recipient DAR Good Citizenship award, 1968. Ill. State grantee, 1968; Mayor Daley Youth Found. scholar, 1968, Gregorian Assn. scholar, 1968, Roosevelt Competitive Music scholar. Mem. Women Band Dirs. Assn., Am. Theater Assn., Internat. Platform Assn., Joint Civic Com. of Italian Ams. Youth Group. Home: 7233 Woodward St Woodridge IL 60515

DE FRIEZE, HAROLD RAYMOND, govt. ofcl.; b. Rock Island, Ill., June 5, 1936; s. Louis and Pauline Matilda (Minnig) DeF.; student Command and Gen. Staff Coll., 1967-72, Army Indsl. Coll., 1970-72, Air War Coll., 1976-77; B.S., U. Okla., 1974; M.S., Fla. Inst. Tech., 1976; m. Molly Ann Linder, Feb. 19, 1955; children—Laurel Ann, Harold Royce, Susan Beth, David Charles. With Mgmt. Information Systems Directorate, HQ ARRCOM, Rock Island, Ill., 1961—, chief sci. and engring. systems div., 1974—; instr. Command and Gen. Staff Coll. U.S. Army Res., Davenport, Iowa, 1973—; tech. asst. to area vocat. centers, East Moline, Ill. and St. Cloud, Minn. Coach, East

Moline Little League Baseball Team, 1962, YMCA Grade Sch. League Basketball Team, 1971. Recipient Recongition certificate HQ Wecom, 1972, Army Res. Component Achievement medal, 1973. Mem. DARCOM Sci. and Engring. Computing Council, Res. Officers Assn. Club: Eagles. Home: 2820 9 1/2 St East Moline IL 61244 Office: Comdr ARRCOM DRSAR-MSE Rock Island IL 61201

DEGEN, BERNARD JOHN, II, assn. exec.; b. Washington, July 6, 1937; s. Bernard E. and Pearl (Freeman) D.; A.B., George Washington U., 1959; postgrad. Temple U., 1959-61; m. Evelyn A. Cocosis, Nov. 24, 1963; children—Stephanie Lisa, Bernard John, III. Asst. bibliographer Biol. Abstracts, Phila., 1961-63; med. and surg. editor Lea & Febiger Publs., Phila., 1963-66; exec. dir. Am. Soc. Oral Surgeons, Chgo., 1966—, exec. sec. bd. trustees Edn. Found., 1966—. Sec. Oral Surgery Polit. Action Com., 1970—. Served to 1st lt. AUS, 1961-62. Fellow Internat. Coll. Dentists (hon.); mem. Am. Pub. Health Assn., AMA (affiliate mem.), Alumni Assn. Valley Forge Mil. Acad., Am. Soc. Assn. Execs., Profl. Conv. Mgmt. Assn., Am. Hosp. Assn., Am. (hon.), Southeastern (hon.), Rocky Mountain (hon.), S.C. (hon.) socs. oral surgeons, Delta Tau Delta. Clubs: Whitehall, Internat. (Chgo.). Office: 211 E Chicago Ave Chicago IL 60611

DE GIROLAMO, DALE ALLEN, sch. adminstr.; b. Cleve., Sept. 13, 1946; s. Michael Peter and Betty Jeanne (Holland) DeG.; B.S. in Edn., Kent State U., 1969, M.A., 1972; m. Elaine Marie Burke, Apr. 14, 1973; 1 dau., Amy Marie. Speech lang. pathologist Elyria (Ohio) City Schs., 1969-74, Lorain County Health Dept., Elyria, 1969-74; coordinator speech, language and hearing therapy services Lorain County Bd. Edn., Elyria, 1974—; instr. speech language pathology Baldwin-Wallace Coll., Berea, Ohio, 1974—. Mem. Am. Speech and Hearing Assn. (certificate of clin. competence), No. Ohio Language Speech and Hearing Assn., Ohio Speech and Hearing Assn. (pres. elect 1977), Council for Exceptional Children, A.G. Bell Assn. for Deaf, N. E. Ohio, Speech and Hearing Assn., Ohio Sch. Suprs. Assn., Ohio Assn. Spl. Edn. Adminstrs., Buckeye Assn. Sch. Adminstrs., Phi Delta Kappa. Editor: Journal of the Association for Precision Speech Therapy and Communications Technology, 1976—. Office: R D 1 Route 58 Box 286 Oberlin OH 44074

DE GRAFFENRIED, VELDA MAE CAMP (MRS. THOMAS P. DE GRAFFENRIED), clin. lab. exec.; b. Kirwin, Kans.; d. George Robert and Laura (Woodward) Camp; student No. Ill. U., 1959-60; m. Thomas P. de Graffenried, May 23, 1942; children—Donna Rae (Mrs. Kenneth George Pigott), Albert Lawrence II, Nicholas Thomas. With De Graffenried & Fisher Clin. Labs., DeKalb, Ill., 1957—, office mgr., 1957-64, exec. sec., 1964—, also dir. pub. affairs. Vice-pres. Haish Sch. PTA, DeKalb, 1958-59; den mother cub scouts Chief Shabbona council Boy Scouts Am., 1957-60; supr. Teen Age Club, Louisville, 1949-50; county crusade chmn. Am. Cancer Soc., 1965, exec. bd. DeKalb County, 1964—, chairwomen, 1970—; sec. DeKalb County Soc., 1969-70, chmn., 1970-72. Recipient commendation Am. Cancer Soc., 1965, 75, spl. award, 1974; commendation Boy Scouts Am., 1955. Mem. DeKalb County Med. Soc. Women's Aux. (pres. 1973) DeKalb Hosp. Aux. Methodist. Home: 1208 Sunnymeade Trail DeKalb IL 60115

DEGRAVELLES, WILLIAM DECATUR, JR., physician; b. Jennings, La., Feb. 20, 1928; s. William Decatur and Ara May (Zenor) deG.; B.S., S.W. La. Inst., 1949; M.D., Tulane U., 1952. Intern Charity Hosp. La., New Orleans, 1952-53; splty. tng. in phys. medicine, rehab. N.Y. U., Bellevue Med. Center, N.Y.C., 1953-56; practice medicine, specializing in phys. medicine and rehab.; dir. rehab. service Duke Med. Center, Durham, N.C., 1956-58; chief phys. medicine and rehab. Iowa Meth. Hosp., Des Moines, 1958—; chief phys. medicine and rehab. Younker Meml. Rehab. Center, Des Moines, 1958—, med. dir., 1958—. Med. cons. Easter Seal's Camp Sunnyside, Des Moines; chmn. med. adv. com. Polk County (Iowa) Nat. Found., 1958-65; mem. Gov.'s Com. on Employment Handicapped, 1964. Bd. dirs. Goodwill Industries, Inc., Des Moines, Iowa Easter Seal Soc. Named Physician of Year Gov.'s Com. on Employment Handicapped, 1968; recipient Cotton award Iowa chpt. Arthritis and Rheumatism Assn., 1965; award Ia. Parks and Recreation Assn., 1974. Diplomate Am. Bd. Phys. Medicine and Rehab. Mem. A.M.A., Iowa, Polk County med. socs., Muscular Dystrophy Assn. Am. (med. adviser Polk County chpt.), Nat. Multiple Sclerosis Soc. (chmn. med. adv. com. central Iowa chpt., 1958-66), Ia. Rehab. Assn. (bd. dirs., past pres.), Internat. Assn. Rehab. Facilities (dir. 1973-76). Home: 6024 Ronwood Dr Des Moines IA 50312 Office: 1200 Pleasant St Des Moines IA 50308

DEGROOT, DON FERDINAND, ret. TV exec.; b. Holland, Mich., Aug. 17, 1911; s. Ferdinand H. and Wilhelmina (Knopf) DeG.; A.A., Flint (Mich.) Jr. Coll., 1930; m. Iola Shirley, Oct. 20, 1934; children—Ted E., Douglas A., John D. With WFDF, Flint, Mich., 1930-41; radio dir. Holden-Graham-Clark Advt. Agy., 1941; with WWJ AM-FM-TV, Detroit, 1941-46, 49-76, asst. gen. mgr., 1952-69, v.p., 1971-76, gen. mgr., 1969-76; program mgr. sta. WBAL, Balt., 1946-47; sta. mgr. WTAC, Flint, 1948-49. Bd. dirs. Broadcast Music; trustee Detroit Inst. Arts, 1973—. Chmn. Mich. Industry adv. com. CONELRAD, 1960-61; v.p. Mich. Radio and TV Brotherhood Week, 1961; pres. Farmington Area Community Fund, 1954-56; TV chmn. Detroit United Found. Torch Dr., 1954, media chmn., 1975. Mem. Mich. Assn. Broadcasters (pres. 1961), Broadcast Pioneers (chmn. Mich. chpt. 1958-59), Mich. Asso. Press Broadcasters (pres. 1957-58), Mich. Assn. Broadcasters (v.p. 1952), Broadcast Music Inc. (dir. 1971—), Eve. News Assn. Detroit (v.p. broadcast div. 1974-76). Club: Orchard Lake Country (Detroit). Home: 30225 Ardmore St Farmington Hills MI 48018

DE HAAS, HERMAN TONY, pub. relations exec.; b. Harrison, Ark., Mar. 27, 1940; s. Herman and Golda Belle (Langston) DeH.; B.A., U. S.D., 1963; postgrad. Boston U., 1966; m. Coleene Rae Engle, July 17, 1965; children—Kyle Tony, Kourtney Ray. Pub. relations rep. Reynolds Metals, Richmond, Va., 1970-71; sr. pub. info. asst. Newport News Shipbldg. (Va.), 1971-72; pub. relations mgr. Dayco Corp., Dayton, Ohio, 1973-77; dir. pub. relations Fromm, Inc., Kansas City, Mo., 1977; mgr. corporate info. Tenneco Inc., Houston, 1978—. Served to capt. USAF, 1963-70. Mem. Pub. Relations Soc. Am. (pres. Dayton-Miami Valley chpt. 1977), Automotive Pub. Relations Council. Home: 7118 Halsey Shawnee KS 66216 Office: PO Box 2511 Houston TX 77001

DEHAMEL, JOHN BELLEAU, JR., constrn. cons.; b. Cleve., Sept. 27, 1923; s. John Belleau and Josephine Brainard (Enright) deH.; B.S.C.E., Case Inst. Tech., 1948; m. Ann Gaither, June 22, 1946; children—Joanne, Corinne. Field engr. Jennings-Lawrence Co., Columbus, Ohio, 1941; design engr. Smith-Hinchman & Grylls, Inc., Detroit, 1946; design engr., field supt. George S. Rider, Co., Cleve., 1948-50; engr. estimator deHamel Constrn. Co., Cleve., 1938-41, 50-65; v.p., dir. Demac Investment Co., Lathrup, Mich., 1965—; pres., treas., dir. J.B. deHamel, Jr. & Assos., Chagrin Falls, Ohio, 1965—. Mem. Chagrin Falls Bd. Edn. Rev. and Planning Com., 1960; arbitrater Am. Arbitration Assn., 1951—. Mem. bldg. and grounds com. Case Western Res. U., 1972—. Served with USNR, 1943-46. Recipient Am. Arbitration Assn. service award, 1965. Mem. Constrn. Specifications Inst., Nat., Ohio, Cleve. socs. profl. engrs., Profl. Engrs. in Pvt. Practice, Chagrin Valley C. of C., Cousteau Soc., Smithsonian Instn., Mystic Seaport Hist. Soc., Internat. Oceanographic Found., Great Lakes Hist. Soc., Archaeol. Inst. Am., Am. Inst. Nautical Archaeology. Clubs: Tanglewood Country, Chagrin Valley Racquet, Hillbrook, Pine Lake Trout, Deep Springs Trout, Cleve. Playhouse. Home: 8502 Tanglewood Chagrin Falls OH 44022 Office: 23 N Franklin Chagrin Falls OH 44022

DEHART, WILMA JOYCE, behavioral therapist; b. Twin Branch, W.Va., May 26, 1930; d. Wilbur C. and Mabel Florence (Slusher) Jackson; B.A. in Psychology, Oakland U., 1974, M.A. in Guidance and Counseling, 1975; m. Arnold O. DeHart, June 26, 1951; children—Barry, Thomas, Ronald. Assertiveness tng. instr. West Bloomfield (Mich.) Community Schs., 1977—; behavior modification therapist Assn. for Geriatric Psychology, Inc., Bloomfield Twp., Mich., 1977—. Mem. Am., Mich. personnel and guidance assns., Mich. Assn. for Specialists in Group Work. Club: Internat. Toastmistresses. Home: 777 Brantford St Rochester MI 48063 Office: 202 Walnut St Rochester MI 48063

DEHAVEN, WILLIAM KENNETH, mech. engr.; b. Beloit, Wis., Apr. 21, 1924; s. Chester Clayton and Helen Elizabeth (Hare) DeH.; student Carleton Coll., 1943-44; B.S. with honors, U. Wis., 1948; m. Mary Alice Malone, Sept. 22, 1947; 1 son, Patrick William. Stress Analyst Babcock & Wilcox, Co., boiler mfr., Barberton, Ohio, 1948-51; with Beiswenger & Hoch, cons. engrs., Akron, Ohio, 1951-61; v.p., chief hwy. engr. Glaus, Pyle, Schomer, Burns & DeHaven, Akron, architect and cons. engrs., partner, 1961—; pres. Kentwood Corp., Akron, 1968—. Chmn., Urban Design and Fine Arts Commn., Akron, 1964—. Served with USAAF, 1943-46. Registered profl. engr., Ohio. Mem. Am. Soc. C.E. (sect. pres. 1969, state council pres. 1974), Ohio Soc. Profl. Engrs. (pres. Akron dist.), Inst. Traffic Engrs., Am. Soc. M.E. Clubs: Sharon Golf, Fairlawn Country. Home: 942 Genesee Rd Akron OH 44303 Office: 341 White Pond Dr Akron OH 44320

DEHNEL, MARGARET ANNE LEWIS, psychologist; b. Ottawa County, Ohio, Apr. 24, 1915; d. Charles Edward and Lulu Anne (Kamke) Lewis; B.Ed., U. Toledo, 1939, M.Ed., 1960; postgrad. George Washington U., U. Mich., Wayne State U.; m. John E.E. Dehnel (div.). Instr. U. Toledo, 1945-47; chief sch. psychologist Bedford Pub. Schs., Temperance, Mich., 1960-67; chief psychol. services Project PUPIL, Fremont, Ohio, 1967-70; dir. Child Study Auglaize County (Ohio) Schs., Wapakoneta, 1970—; individual practice as psychologist, Temperance, also Toledo, 1965-70; U.S. del. Internat. Assn. Spl. Edn., London, 1966. Bd. dirs. Regional Spl. Edn. Center. Served as officer USNR, 1943-45. Mem. Nat. (charter), Ohio (program com.) sch. psychologists assns., Council on Mental Retardation (charter), Council on Children with Learning Disorders (charter), Council for Exceptional Children, Ohio Assn. Children with Learning Disabilities (state legis. com.), Council Adminstrs. Spl. Edn., Toledo Mus. Art, Phi Kappa Phi, Kappa Delta. Congregationalist. Home: 326 Stinebaugh Dr Apt 1 Wapakoneta OH 45895 Office: Courthouse Wapakoneta OH 45895

DEHNKE, CARL BENJAMIN, indsl. valve co. exec.; b. Harrisville, Mich., Oct. 3, 1930; s. Herman and Maude Frances (Dodge) D.; B.S. summa cum laude in Aeronautics, Parks Coll., St. Louis U., 1957; children—Denise, Robert, Mary, James. Systems engr. IBM, Washington, 1959-60, Flint, Mich., 1961-62; dir. of mgmt. services FWD Corp., Clintonville, Wis., 1962-69; dir. info. tech. Dezurik unit Gen. Signal Corp., Sartell, Minn., 1969—. Served with U.S. Army, 1950-53; Korea. Mem. Assn. for Systems Mgmt., Data Processing Mgmt. Assn. Republican. Presbyterian. Home: 1455 3rd St SE St Cloud MN 56301 Office: Dezurik Corp Riverside Ave North Sartell MN 56377

DEINARD, AMOS SPENCER, lawyer; b. Terre Haute, Ind., Mar. 10, 1898; s. Samuel Nathaniel and Rosa D.; B.A., U. Minn., 1920; LL.B., 1921; S.J.D., Harvard, 1922; m. Hortense Honig, Mar. 15, 1933; children—Amos, Miriam J. (Mrs. Erwin A. Kelen). Admitted to Minn. bar, 1922, since practiced in Mpls.; partner firm Leonard, Street & Deinard, Mpls., 1922—; dir. Electro-Craft Corp., Fiberite Corp., La Maur Inc., Napco Industries, Inc., Salkin & Linoff, Inc. Chmn., Mpls. Fair Employment Practices Commn., 1949-64; gov. Mt. Sinai Hosp. Assn. Mpls., 1945—, v.p., 1957—; bd. dirs. North Central region NCCJ, Am. Orgn. Rehab. Through Tng., Am. Jewish Joint Distbn. Com., Inc.; bd. dirs. Minn. Soc. Prevention Blindness, pres., 1946-49; bd. dirs. Mpls. Fedn. Jewish Service, pres., 1935-40; trustee Temple Israel, 1926—, v.p., 1930—. Mem. Am., Minn. State, Hennepin County bar assns., Phi Beta Kappa. Clubs: Harvard of Minn., B'nai B'rith. Home: 1729 Morgan Ave S Minneapolis MN 55405 Office: 1200 National City Bank Bldg Minneapolis MN 55402

DEINZER, GEORGE WILLIAM, coll. exec.; b. Tiffin, Ohio, Nov. 1, 1934; s. Harvey Charles and Edna Louise (Harpley) D.; A.B., Heidelberg Coll., 1956; postgrad. Washington U., 1956-57. Asst. to dir. phys. plant Heidelberg Coll., 1957-58, admissions counselor, 1958-60, dir. admissions, 1960-7l, dir. financial aids, asso. dir. admissions, 1971—. Voting rep. Coll. Entrance Examination Bd., 1963—; cons. Ohio Scholarship Funds, 1960-61. Chmn. allocations com., 1st v.p., bd. dirs. United Way. Mem. Assn. Coll. Admissions Counselors, Ohio Assn. Coll. Admissions Counselors, Am. Assn. Coll. Registrars and Admissions Officers, Nat., Ohio (regional coordinator, treas., state trainer, chmn. needs analysis com.) assns. student financial aid adminstrs., Ohio Athletic Conf. Financial Dirs. (chmn.), Internat. Platform Assn., Am. Personnel and Guidance Assn., Am. Coll. Personnel Assn., U.S. Naval Inst., Beta Beta Beta. Republican. Rotarian (dir.). Contbr. articles to profl. jours. Home: 197 Jefferson St Tiffin OH 44883

DEITCH, ROBERT DAVID, ophthalmologist; b. Indpls., Oct. 18, 1932; s. Victor and Marjorie (Miller) D.; M.D., Ind. U., 1957; m. Sylvia Scott Pritchard, May 2, 1970; 1 dau., Denise Lynn. Intern Marion County Gen. Hosp., Indpls., 1957-58; resident ophthalmic plastic surgery Methodist Hosp., Birmingham, Ala., 1963, Hempstead (N.Y.) Hosp., 1964; resident ophthalmology Ind. U. Med. Center, 1960-63, dir. ophthalmic plastic surgery service, 1964-68; practice medicine specializing in ophthalmology and ophthalmic plastic surgery, Indpls., 1964—; mem. staff Ind. U., Marion County Gen., St. Vincent's, Winona, St. Francis, Community, Univ. Heights hosps., Indpls.; asst. dept. ophthalmology Ind. U. Med. Sch., 1963—; ophthalmologist MEDICO, Algiers, Algeria, 1966. Served to capt. USAF, 1958-60. Diplomate Am. Bd. Ophthalmology. Fellow Am. Acad. Ophthalmology and Otolaryngology, A.C.S., Assn. Research Ophthalmology, Am. Soc. Ophthalmic Plastic and Reconstructive Surgery; mem. Am. Acad. Facial Plastic and Reconstructive Surgery, Nat. Parks Assn., Am. Forestry Assn., Brit. Sub-Aqua Club, Aircraft Owners and Pilots Assn., Sierra Club, Nat. Audubon Soc., Indpls. Mus. Art, Nat. Soc. Preventive Blindness, YMCA, Wilderness Soc., Am. Legion, Smithsonian Assos., Internat. Oceanographic Found., Am. Mus. Natural History, Indpl. Zool. Soc., Field Mus. Natural History, Ind. U. Alumni Assn., S.A.R., Alpha Tau Omega, Nu Sigma Nu Mason (Shriner). Contbr. articles to profl. publs. Home: 32 Red Oak Ln Carmel IN 46032 Office: 1500 Albany St Beach Grove IN 46107

DEITCHER, JOSEPH, rabbi; b. Montreal, Que., Can., June 6, 1938; s. Lionel and Sarah (Golub) D.; B.A., Yeshiva U., 1959, M.H.L., 1962; m. Leah Ingber, Feb. 7, 1960; children—Menahem, Zipora, Devora. Ordained rabbi, 1962; rabbi Beth Israel Synagogue, Halifax, N.S., Can., 1962-67; dir. Hillel counselorship, Jewish chaplain Dalhousie U., Halifax, 1962-67; chaplain Hillel Found. McGill U., Montreal, 1967-69; rabbi Young Israel Val Royal, Montreal, 1967-70; ednl. coordinator Hebrew Acad., Montreal, 1970-73; exec. dir. Eastern Can. region Union Orthodox Jewish Congregations, Montreal, 1973-76; dir. Nat. Conf. Synagogue Youth; rabbi Anshe Sholom B'nai Israel Congregation, Chgo., 1976—. Mem. bd. edn. Arie Crown Hebrew Day Sch., Chgo.; mem. youth commn. Greater Chgo. region Nat. Conf. Synagogue Youth. Mem. Chgo. (edn. com.) Rabbinical Council, Rabbinical Council Am., Chgo. Bd. Rabbis; Yeshiva U. Rabbinic Alumni. Contbr. articles to religious jours. and secular newspapers. Home: 525 Roscoe St Chicago IL 60657

DEITZ, MICHAEL RICHARD, ophthalmologist; b. Woodhaven, N.Y., Jan. 5, 1932; s. Richard F. and Maryetta (Beddow) D.; B.S., Ursinus Coll., 1954; M.D., U. Pa., 1958; M.S., U. Mich., 1962; m. Mildred Jeanette McNally, Aug. 23, 1953; children—Kathryn, Richard, Suzanne. Intern Phila. Gen. Hosp., 1958-59; resident U. Mich. Hosp., Ann Arbor, 1959-62; practice medicine, specializing in ophthalmology, Kansas City, Kans., 1962—; mem. staff Bethany Hosp., Kansas City, Kans., Providence-St. Margaret Med. Center, Kansas City, Kans.; instr. Kans. U. Med. Center, 1963—; pres. chmn. bd. various small bus. corporations.; one of founders Kan. Interprofl. Com., 1957, co-chmn., 1970—. Mem. A.M.A. (Billings gold medal 1962), Wyandotte County Med. Soc. (legislative chmn. 1967—), Kans. Med. Soc. (county chmn. delegation 1968-71), K.C. Soc. Ophthalmology and Otolaryngology, Am. Acad. Ophthalmology and Otolaryngology., Nat. Train Collectors Assn. (div. pres. 1973). Home: 5211 W 64th Terr Prairie Village KS 66208 Office: 155 S 18th St Kansas City KS 66102

DEJARLD, RICHARD LEE, dentist; b. Joliet, Ill., Nov. 5, 1929; s. Norman Levern and Kathryn Mabel (Heyer) DeJ.; student Joliet Jr. Coll., 1948-50; B.S., U. Ill., 1952, B.S., D.D.S., 1956; m. Zaharoula Rousonelos, May 26, 1951; children—Tina, Lisa, Dina. Pvt. practice dentistry, Joliet, 1958-60, Wilmington, Ill., 1960—. Served with USAF, 1956-58. Mem. ADA, Will County Dental Soc. (pres. 1968-69), Sports Car Club Am. Elk. Home: 1311 West Acres Rd Joliet IL 60435 Office: 101 Fulton St Wilmington IL 60481

DEKAM, DAVID KENNETH, paper co. exec.; b. Kalamazoo, Aug. 7, 1946; s. George Alexander and Naomi Christine (Cox) DeK.; B.S. in Paper Sci., Western Mich. U., 1964; m. Barbara Ann Francisco, Apr. 4, 1970; children—Monica Marie, Gabriel David. Papermaking team mgr. Charmin Paper Co., Green Bay, Wis., 1969-70; process engr. Georgia Pacific Corp., Kalamazoo, 1971-72, tech. asst. to prodn. mgr., 1973-74, tech. dir., 1975—. Active YMCA, Kalamazoo, 1973-76. Mem. Paper Ind. Mgmt. Assn., Tech. Assn. Pulp and Paper Ind. (local sect. sec. 1976, vice chmn. 1977, chmn. 1978, mem. additives com. 1975—, papermaking com. 1975—). Democrat. Roman Catholic. Club: Kalamazoo Rod & Gun. Contbr. articles to profl. jours., papers to profl. confs. Home: 5160 Riverview Dr Parchment MI 49004 Office: Georgia Pacific Corp 2425 King Highway Kalamazoo MI 49003

DEKANY, JOHN PETER, govt. ofcl.; b. Gyor, Hungary, Apr. 14, 1935; s. John and Gisele (Nemes) DeK.; B.S. summa cum laude (Interchem. Corp. scholar), Poly. Inst. N.Y., 1956; M.S. (univ. fellow), Princeton, 1957; m. Bernadette Koke, Sept. 5, 1959; children—John C., Mark T., Gisele F., Paul A., Charles L. Chem. engr., Argonne (Ill.) Nat. Lab., 1957-61; nuclear engr. U.S. ABC, Washington, 1961-66; venture analyst Gulf Oil Corp., Pitts., 1970-71; nuclear engr. Westinghouse Electric Corp., Pitts., 1966-71; div. dir. U.S. EPA, Ann Arbor, Mich., 1972—. Active Boy Scouts Am. Trustee Murrysville (Pa.) Library, 1970-71. Served with C.E., AUS, 1960. Mem. Am. Inst. Chem. Engrs., Sigma Xi, Tau Beta Pi, Phi Lambda Upsilon. K.C., Rotarian. Contbr. articles to profl. jours. Home: 4356 Dillingham Dr Tecumseh MI 49286 Office: 2565 Plymouth Rd Ann Arbor MI 48105

DEKOCK, WILLIAM HENRY, dentist, orthodontist; b. Manson, Iowa, Jan. 27, 1938; s. Henry Cornelius and Edith (Cathcart) DeK.; B.A. cum laude, U. Iowa, 1959; D.D.S., 1963, M.S., 1967; m. Margaret Ann Ladd, June 30, 1962; children—Nicholas, Gregory, Edith. Pvt. practice dentistry specializing in orthodontics, Cedar Rapids, Iowa, 1967—. Adj. asso. prof. orthodontics U. Iowa, 1967—. Served to lt. USNR, 1963-65. Recipient grant Grad. Coll. U. Iowa, 1968—. Diplomate Am. Bd. Orthodontists. Mem. Am. Dental Assn., Am. Assn. Orthodontists, Linn County Dental Soc. (pres. 1976—), Phi Eta Sigma, Sigma Phi Epsilon, Psi Omega. Democrat. Methodist. Club: Thursday Noon Optimist (pres. 1974—). Contbr. to profl. publs. in field. Home: 2404 Grande Ave Cedar Rapids IA 52403 Office: 2727 1st Ave SE Cedar Rapids IA 52403

DEKOSTER, LUCAS JAMES, state senator; b. Hull, Iowa, June 18, 1918; s. John and Sarah K. (Poppen) DeK.; student Kan. State Coll., 1935-36; B.S. in Mech. Engring., Iowa State Coll., 1939; J.D. cum laude, Cleve.-Marshall Law Sch., 1949; m. Dorothea L. Hymans, Dec. 30, 1942; children—Sarah Kay, Jacqueline Anne, John Gordon, Claire Ellen, Mary Denise. Aero. research scientist NACA, 1940-48; admitted to Ohio bar 1949, Iowa bar, 1952; asso. J. Darrell Douglass, patent atty., Cleve., 1948-52; pvt. practice law, Hull, 1952—; mem. Iowa Senate, 1964—. Pres. Hull Bldg. & Loan Assn. (Iowa); v.p. Mut. Fire and Automobile Ins. Co., Cedar Rapids. Mem. Am., Iowa, Sioux County bar assns., Hull Bus. and Profl. Men's Club (past pres.). Home: 404 Center St Hull IA 51239 Office: 1106 Main St Hull IA 51239

DEKOWSKI, WILLIAM ANTHONY, religious educator; b. Peru. Ill., Dec. 18, 1947; s. Anthony Valentine and Marie Elizabeth (Kolterman) D.; student Ill. Valley Community Coll., 1965-67; B.A. in Scholastic Philosphy, Immaculate Conception Sem. (Mo.), 1971; M.A. in Counseling, No. Ill. U., 1977. Substitute tchr. La Salle-Peru Twp. (Ill.) High Sch., 1971-73; religion instr. Marquette High Sch., Ottawa, Ill., 1973—. Mem. dist. and council exec. bd. Boy Scouts Am., 1963—; state chaplain Ill. State Columbian Squires, 1976—; mem. dist. exec. bd. Ill. Student Council Assn., 1976-78; regional mem., regional adviser Internat. Knights of the Altar. Recipient Vigil of Honor, Order of the Arrow, Boy Scouts Am., 1976, Dist. Merit award, 1975, Eagle award, 1961. Mem. Am., Ill. personnel and guidance assns.. Nat. Audubon Soc., Nat. Geog. Soc., Nat., Internat. wildlife assns. Roman Catholic. Club: K.C. Home: 510 6th St Peru IL 61354 Office: 1000 Paul St Ottawa IL 613S0

DELANEY, JOHN PETER, instnl. adminstr.; b. Hartford, Conn., Mar. 15, 1943; s. John Falvey and Mary Ellen (Brecker) D.; B.A., Providence Coll., 1965; M.Ed., U. Hartford, 1969; Ed.D., U. Mass., 1971; children—Kelly Elizabeth, John Timothy. Dir. adult recreation G.H.O.A.R.C., Hartford, Conn., 1968-70; cons. New Eng. Media Center for Deaf, 1970-71; asst. prof. spl. edn. U. Mass., 1971-76; asst. commr. Ohio Div. Mental Retardation, 1976-77; supt. Apple Creek (Ohio) State Inst., 1974—. Mem. Am. Assn. on Mental Deficiency, Council for Exceptional Children, Common Cause. Home and Office: Box 148 Apple Creek OH 44606

DELANEY, MARTIN T., packaging co. exec.; b. St. Joseph, Mo., Feb. 11, 1922; s. John P. and Blanche (Burns) D.; student bus. coll., 1946-47; m. Ellen McHenry, Feb. 16, 1946; children—Beverly, Catherine, Michele, Dennis, Deborah, Maureen, Daniel. With St. Joseph Paper Products Inc., St. Joseph, Mo., 1947—, sec., 1972-74, v.p., 1974—. Served with inf. AUS, 1942-46. Decorated Silver Star, Purple Heart. Mem. Nat. Assn. Accountants (dir.), Am. Legion. Democrat. Roman Catholic. Clubs: Elks, K.C., South Side Commerce, Litton Congressional. Home: Rt 4 St Joseph MO 64507 Office: 4515 Easton Rd St Joseph MO 64503

DELANGE, JOHN ROGER, JR., dentist; b. St. Paul, Feb. 12, 1938; s. John Roger and Ruth Eleanor (Damm) DeL.; B.A., U. Minn., 1959, D.D.S., 1963; m. Susan Angela Stahel, Dec. 26, 1966; children—Jon Christopher, Giselle Gabrielle. Practice gen. dentistry, St. Paul, 1963—; advisor dental products div. 3M Corp. Mem. Found. for Advancement Implants and Transplants, 1972—. USPHS grantee, 1962. Mem. Andahazy Ballet Borealis Co. Mem. Am. Dental Assn., St. Paul Dist. Dental Soc., Minn. Alumni Assn., Am. Soc. Dental Anesthesiology, Internat. Congress Oral Implantologists, Am. Acad. Implant Dentistry, North Star Study Club, U. Minn. Sch. Dentistry Century Club, Psi Omega. Lutheran. Home: 4622 Glabe Ln Minneapolis MN 55406 Office: 2233 Hamline Ave N Roseville MN 55113

DELANGE, KENNETH ALLEN, advt. exec.; b. Girard, Kans., Jan. 20, 1935; s. Joseph Leo and Ruby (Kennedy) DeL.; B.S., Kans. State Coll., 1956; m. Margaret Schnackenberg, Apr. 18, 1954; 1 dau., Lisa Michelle. Purchasing agt., accountant Pittcraft, Inc., Pitts., 1953-56, sales, advt. agy. dir., 1956-63; advt. prodn. mgr. Travel Industries, 1963-65, advt., pub. relations dir., Oswego, Kans., 1965-69; v.p., dir. Communications Concepts, Inc., Joplin, Mo., 1969-70; pres. ADventures, Inc. Advt. Agy., Joplin, 1970-77, Delange Industries, Inc., 1977—; exec. v.p. Pittcraft Printing, Inc., Pittsburg, Kans., 1977—, Meml. Pub. Co., Joplin; dir. S.E. Kans. Outdoor Recreation Assn., Four State Advt. Club, Joplin. Served with USMCR, 1954-55. Named Advt. Man of Year, Printers Ink mag., 1966. Mem. Am. Legion, Am. Vets, C. of C., Advt. Fedn. Am., Okla., Kans. outdoor writers assns., Outdoor Writers Assn. Am. Mason (Shriner). Clubs: Exchange, Big Four Advt. (dir., pres.), Kansas City Advt. and Sales Execs. Home: 306 1/2 E 32d St Joplin MO 64801 Office: 306 E 32d St ADventures Plaza Joplin MO 64801

DELAP, MICHAEL HAVEN, fastener mfg. co. exec.; b. Detroit, Aug. 21, 1945; s. Ralph H. and LaVerne R. (Smothers) DeL.; A.A. in Bus. Adminstrn., Cleary Coll., 1968, B.B.A. in Accounting, 1970; postgrad. Eastern Mich. U., 1969; m. Caral H. Rubens, June 25, 1967. Accountant Long Transp. Co., Detroit, 1966-67, chief financial officer, Prestyle Mfg. Co., Detroit, 1967-70, also dir.; controller Paramount Plywood Co., Royal Oak, Mich., 1970-73; exec. v.p., sec., treas. Zelda Fastener Co., Walled Lake, Mich., 1972—, also dir.; sr. partner DeLap & Assos., Oak Park, Mich., 1970—, Mic Carde & Co., Oak Park, 1970—. Mem. Am. Numismatic Assn., Nat. Soc. Pub. Accountants. Jewish religion (past dir. temple). Home: 14814 Bassett St Livonia MI 48154 Office: 2175 W Maple Rd Walled Lake MI 48088

DE LAPP, ALBERT A., ret. ins. exec.; b. Auburn, Ind., Nov. 29, 1891; s. Erwin T. and Emma (Ashley) De L.; A.B., Hillsdale (Mich.) Coll., 1914; post graduate work at Northwestern U., 1914-15; m. Dorothy Kearney, June 18, 1921; children—Dorothy W. (Mrs. Keith Van Buskirk), Joan A., Gwendolyn (Mrs. Milton Nielsen), Joseph K., Albert A. Indsl. engr., 1915-17, 1925; in ins. bus., 1925-71; mgr. Mo. State Life Ins. Co., Gen. Am. Life, 1931-34, Union Mutual Life Ins. Co., 1934-37; city comptroller, Evanston, 1937-41; pres. Stearns Electric Paste Co. Trustee, Hillsdale Coll., 1940-72, past vice chmn.; past pres. Hillsdale Coll. Alumni Assn. Capt. U.S. Army, 1917-19; comdg. officer Chicago Ordnance Depot, 1917, Middletown Ordnance Depot (Harrisburg, Pa.), 1918-19. C.L.U. Mem. Evanston Hist. Assn., Nat. Assn. of Life Underwriters, Evanston 4th of July Corporation (trustee, past pres.), Alpha Tau Omega. Republican. K.C. (4DEG.). Clubs: Interfraternity (pres.), North Evanston Men's (past pres.). Home: 2319 Hartzell Evanston IL 60201 Office: 220 S State St Chicago IL 60604

DELAVAN, JOSEPH MILTON, lawyer; b. Chgo., June 24, 1934; s. Joseph Milton and Eleanor (O'Sullivan) de La Van; B.S., Northwestern U., 1957, J.D., 1960; m. Patricia Rae Leary, June 11, 1960; children—Mary Margert, Kathleen Ann. Admitted to Ill. bar, 1960; mem. staff T.J. McCracken & Co., C.P.A.'s, 1960-63; v.p. finances Cordin & Co., freight consolidators, 1964-67; partner McCracken, Callfield & Delavan, Chgo., 1968—; dir. Mager & Gougelman, Inc., 1968—; developer Suntide Motel, Sarasota, Fla., 1971. Fund dir. Girl Scouts U.S., Chgo., 1970; auditor Community Chest, Chgo., 1970-71. Mem. Ill. Bar Assn., Am. Inst. C.P.A.'s, Ill. Soc. C.P.A.'s, Beta Alpha Chi. Club: University (Chgo.). Home: 45 S Park St Hinsdale IL 60521 Office: 134 N LaSalle St Chicago IL 60602

DE LAY, THOMAS SHUTER, lawyer; b. Columbus, Ohio, Feb. 3, 1923; s. Frank and Edythe (Shuter) DeL.; B.A., Ohio Wesleyan U., 1948; J.D., U. Cin., 1952; m. Lila Lee Hawk, Aug. 9, 1952; children—Linda Susan, Janet Lynn, David Reeder. Admitted to Ohio bar, 1953; mem. firm Frank & Thomas DeLay, Jackson, Ohio, 1953-64; pros. atty., Jackson County, 1963—. Served with AUS, 1943-45; ETO. Mem. Am. Legion, Phi Delta Theta, Phi Delta Phi. Mason, Elk. Home: 99 N High St Jackson OH 45640 Office: 262 Main St Jackson OH 45640

DEL CASTILLO, JULIO CESAR, neurosurgeon; b. Havana, Cuba, Jan. 21, 1930; s. Julio Cesar and Violeta (Diaz de Villegas) Del C.; came to U.S., 1961, naturalized, 1968; B.S., Columbus Sch., Havana, 1948; M.D., U. Havana, 1955; m. Rosario Freire, Sept. 18, 1955; children—Julio Cesar, Juan Claudio, Rosemarie. Intern, Michael Reese Hosp., Chgo., 1955-56; resident Cook County Hosp., Chgo., 1957, Lahey Clinic, Boston, 1957-58, U. Pa. Grad. Hosp., 1958-60; research asst. dept. gen. surgery Jackson Meml. Hosp., Miami, Fla., 1962-64; practice medicine, specializing in neurosurgery, Havana, 1960-61, Quincy, Ill., 1965—; mem. staff Blessing Hosp., Quincy, pres. staff, 1972-74; mem. staff St. Mary's Hosp., Quincy. Bd. dirs. Western Ill. Found. for Med. Care, 1970—; trustee Blessing Hosp., 1972-74. Mem. Am. Acad. Model Aeros., Congress Neurol. Surgeons, A.M.A., A.C.S., Adams County Med. Soc. (sec., treas. 1966—), Ill. Med. Soc., Exptl. Aircraft Assn. Rotarian (dir. 1970-72, pres. 1976-77). Home: 14 Curved Creek Quincy IL 62301 Office: 1124 Broadway Quincy IL 62301

DE LERNO, MANUEL JOSEPH, elec. engr.; b. New Orleans, Jan. 8, 1922; s. Joseph Salvador and Elizabeth Mabry (Jordan) DeL.; B.E. in Elec. Engring., Tulane U., 1941; M.E.E., Rensselaer Poly. Inst., 1943; m. Margery Ellen Eaton, Nov. 30, 1946; children—Diane, Douglas. Devel. engr. indsl. control dept. Gen. Electric Co., Schenectady, 1941-44; asst. prof. elec. engring. Newark Coll. Engring., 1946-47; test engr. Maschinenfabrik Oerlikon, Zurich, Switzerland, 1947-48; application engr. Henry J. Kaufman Co., Chgo., 1949-55; pres. Del Equipment Co., Chgo., 1955-60; v.p. Del-Ray Co., Chgo., 1960-67; pres. S-P-D Services Inc., Forest Park, Ill., 1967—; mem. standards making coms. Nat. Fire Protection Assn. Internat. Served as lt. (j.g.) USNR, 1944-45, to lt. comdr., 1950-52. Registered profl. engr., Ill. Mem. IEEE (sr.), Ill. Soc. Profl. Engrs., Soc. Fire Protection Engrs., Am. Water Works Assn. Mem. Kenilworth Union Ch. Home: 147 Robsart Pl Kenilworth IL 60043 Office: 7719 W Van Buren St Forest Park IL 60130

DELEVIE, JACOB BRAM, ophthalmologist; b. Amsterdam, Netherlands, May 1, 1927; s. Herman and Leonie (Serphos) D.; M.D., U. Amsterdam, 1951; m. Margaretha Agatha Blyham, Oct. 24, 1953; children—M. Carey, Hugo A., Jacqueline D. Came to U.S., 1953, naturalized, 1955. Intern, University Hosp., Amsterdam, 1951-53, Grace Hosp., Detroit, 1954; resident neurol. surgery Henry Ford Hosp., Detroit, 1957-58, resident ophthalmology, 1958-61; practice medicine, specializing in ophthalmology, Pontiac, Mich., 1961—; chief sect. eye-ear-nose-throat Pontiac Gen. Hosp., 1967-70, 72; clin. instr. dept. ophthalmology Wayne State U., Detroit, Mich., 1966—. Treas., Pontiac Area Urban League, 1968-70; pres. br. Mich. Children's Aid Soc., Pontiac, 1967-69, mem. bd., 1963-72. Trustee Family and Children's Service of Oakland, 1971-72. Served to capt. AUS, 1955-57. Recipient Liberty Bell award Bar of Oakland County, Mich., 1969, merit award Pontiac United Found., 1970. Diplomate Am. Bd. Ophthalmology. Mem. A.M.A., Mich. Ophthalmol. Soc., Am. Acad. Ophthalmology and Otolaryngology. Rotarian. Home: 534 Wooddale St Birmingham MI 48010 Office: 700 Riker Bldg Pontiac MI 48058

DELGADO, CHARLES BENJAMIN, city ofcl.; b. Waco, Tex., Apr. 17, 1939; s. Charles Cardel and Nakayah (Bright-Delgado) Delton; student West Point, 1960-62; B.A., Lamar Coll., 1964; M. Pub. Adminstrn., U. Kans., 1966; m. Karen Ann Mishler, Apr. 22, 1962; children—Charles Kevin, Christopher Wayne, Melissa Ann. Asst. to city mgr., Beaumont, Tex., 1962-64; research asst. U. Kans., 1964-65; asst. to city mgr., Salina, Kans., 1965-66; city mgr., Newport, Ark., 1966-70, Winfield, Kans., 1970-76, Shawnee, Kans., 1976—. Mem. exec. bd. Kans. Blue Shield Assn., 1974—. Pres., North Central Ark. Econ. Devel. Dist., 1967-69; treas. Health Planning Council South Central Kans., 1972-74. Served with USAF, 1957-62. Mem. Internat. City Mgmt. Assn., Kans. Assn. City Mgrs. Home: 11311 W 51st Terr Shawnee KS 66203 Office: 11110 Johnson Dr Shawnee KS 66203

DELGADO, JOSEPH RAMON, business exec.; b. Chgo., Mar. 4, 1932; s. Joseph Ramon and Florence (Nelson) D.; B.A. in English, U. Ill., 1958. With Campbell-Mithun Advt., Chgo., 1960-68, purchasing agt., dir. office services, 1964-68; purchasing agt., asst. to pres., asst. to treas. Maxant Button & Supply Co., Chgo., 1968-70; asst. purchasing agt., adminstrv. asst. Soiltest, Inc., Evanston, Ill., 1970—. Mem. Lyric Opera Subscription Com., 1957. Observer, Joint Civic Com. on Elections, 1965; election judge primary and gen. elections, 1968, 70. Served with AUS, 1952-54. Mem. Purchasing Agts. Assn. Chgo. (co-chmn. publicity and pub. relations com. 1963-64), U. Ill. Alumni, Illiniweks, Chgo. Symphony Soc. (charter). Lutheran. Republican. Clubs: Whitehall, Barclay, Ltd., International (Chgo.). Dance choreographer for various groups and individuals. Home: 700 Bittersweet Pl Chicago IL 60613 Office: 2205 Lee St Evanston IL 60202

DELHAUER, ROBERT ALLAN, merchandising exec.; b. Chgo., July 23, 1926; s. William H. and Elfrieda (Hill) D.; student Ill. Inst. Tech., 1947-48; B.A., Midwestern Conservatory, 1951; postgrad. N.Y. U., 1969—; m. Sarah Elizabeth Horton, Oct. 1, 1949; children—Mark Stuart, Paul Quinn, Rebecca Joyce. Mem. staff food mktg. div. Libby McNeil & Libby, Chgo., 1948; dept. mgr. consumer goods, buyer Biddle Purchasing Co., Chgo., 1949-54, mdse. mgr., 1957-64, asst. v.p. merchandising, N.Y.C., 1964-67, v.p. div. mgr., 1967-74, sr. v.p. sales and merchandising, 1974-76, sr. v.p., gen. mgr. Midwest, 1976—, mem. exec. com., 1969—, dir., 1968—; exec. v.p., dir. Harben Co. subsidiary, 1972—; chmn., mng. dir. Biddle Purchasing Co., Ltd., 1971—; cons. Nat. Am. Wholesale Grocers Assn., 1969—. Served to 1st lt. AUS, World War II; ETO. Republican. Presbyn. Mem. Chgo. Housewares Club. Club: Executives (Chgo.); Mchts. and Mfrs. Home: 5 Pembrook Dr Indian Head Park IL 60525 Office: 309 W Washington Ave Chicago IL 60606

DELHEY, RICHARD WALTER, appliance mfg. co. exec.; b. Chgo., Feb. 9, 1932; s. Marie Lucy (Rohl) D.; B.S., U. Ill., 1956; m. Jean Marie Horrigan, Aug. 8, 1958; children—Jonathan, David, Elizabeth, Susan, Daniel, Judith. Asst. v.p. Ethicon, Somerville, N.J., 1956-65; mgr. mktg. services Glidden-Durkee, Cleve., 1965-71; v.p. ops. Mgmt. Recruiters, Cleve., 1971-72; mgr. food ingredients Swift Edible Oil Co., Chgo., 1972-75; pres. Candel, Inc., Arlington Heights, Ill., 1975—. Mem. Am. Mktg. Assn. Democrat. Roman Catholic. Club: Cleve. Ad. Patentee disposable salt and pepper shakers for restaurants, spice packaging, thermostat clock for saving home heating and cooling fuel. Home: 328 Dale St S Arlington Heights IL 60004 Office: 500 Higgins Rd E Elk Grove Village IL 60007

DELIMAN, JOSEPH RONALD, dentist; b. Lorain, Ohio, Jan. 23, 1941; s. Joseph J. and Mary (Barbuscak) D.; student Kent State U., 1959-62; D.D.S., Ohio State U., 1966; m. Rita M. Skorupa, July 14, 1962; children—Tracy Elayne, Scott Martin, Eric Joseph. Pvt. practice dentistry, Lorain, 1968—; mem. staff St. Joseph Hosp., also mem. screening and evaluation bd. Methadone Maintenance Clinic. Served as capt. Dental Corps, USAF, 1966-68. Mem. Am., Ohio, Lorain County dental assns., Delta Sigma Delta. Rotarian. Home: 3801 Windsor Ct Lorain OH 44053 Office: 209 6th St Lorain OH 44052

DELISLE, BETTY ANN, ins. co. exec.; b. Milw., Apr. 11, 1928; d. Ernst A. and Hilda (Preuss) Krombholz; m. Leo A. DeLisle, Feb. 21, 1948; children—James (dec.), Kenneth, David. Various positions Mut. of N.Y., Milw., 1955-72; asst. sec, asst. to pres. R.W. Houser & Assos. Ltd., Milw., 1972—, also subsidiaries Midwestern Nat. Inst. Corp., Milw., and Funding Inc., Phoenix, 1974—. Mem. Ins. Women Milw. (dir. 1968-69). Republican. Roman Catholic. Office: R W Houser & Assos Ltd 11430 W Bluemound Rd Wauwatosa WI 53226

DELLETT, KENNETH BAKER, physician; b. LaCrosse, Kans., Aug. 15, 1930; s. Louis A. and Elizabeth (Koochel) D.; M.D., U. Kans., 1955; postgrad. U. Nebr., 1965; m. Margaret Field, June 5, 1953; children—Kenneth R., Tamara S. Intern U.S. Naval Hosp., Pensacola, Fla., 1955; resident U. Nebr., Omaha, 1963-65; practice gen. medicine, El Dorado, Kans., 1958-63; practice medicine, specializing in ophthalmology, El Dorado, 1963—; pres. staff Susan B. Allen Hosp., El Dorado. Served to lt. comdr. M.C., USNR, 1955-58. Mem. A.M.A., Kans. Med. Soc., Kans. Eye and Ear Assn. Home: 1830 Chelsea Dr El Dorado KS 67042 Office: 5th and Main Plaza El Dorado KS 67042

DELLORTO, JOHN ARTHUR, psychotherapist; b. Chgo., Sept. 20, 1931; s. Frank Anthony and Myrtle (Noak) D.; B.A., Maryknoll Coll., 1954; M.R.E., Maryknoll Sr. Coll., 1956; M.S.W., Loyola U. Chgo., 1958; M.A. in Counseling/Psychology, Tavistock Inst. Human Relations (London, Eng.), 1961; postgrad. No. Ill. U.; m. Barbara Ann Kozak, Sept. 7, 1957; children—John, Michael, James, Mary, Daniel. Chief psychiat. social worker St. Francis Hosp., Evanston, Ill.; exec. dir. Kane-Kendall County Mental Health Center, Aurora, Ill., 1964-76; pvt. practice psychotherapy, Aurora, 1976—. Cons. Ill. Dept. Pub. Health, 1969—. Mem. Aurora Area Cath. Sch. Bd., 1970—, pres., 1973-75; mem. Mayor's Human Relations Commn., Aurora, 1973—. Bd. dirs. Marie Wilkinson Child Devel. Center, Aurora, 1973—. Served with USAF, 1958-61; ETO; comdr. 36th Med. Service Squadron, 1976—. Mem. Ill. Assn. Mental Health Center Adminstrs. (pres. 1968-70), Res. Officers Assn. Home: 404 S LaSalle St Aurora IL 60505 Office: 1240 Highland Ave Aurora IL 60506

DELOACH, GEORGE ROBERT, JR., real estate co. exec.; b. Columbia, S.C., Jan. 17, 1943; s. George Robert and Madeline (Smith) D.; A.B., U. S.C., 1965, J.D., 1968; m. Ann Willen, Sept. 24, 1971. Admitted to S.C. bar, 1968, Ind. bar, 1969, U.S. Supreme Ct. bar, 1973; atty. Midwestern United Life Ins. Co., Ft. Wayne, Ind., 1969-70; v.p., gen. counsel, corporate sec. Oxford Devel. Corp., Indpls., 1970-75; exec. v.p. Charter Oak Devel. Co., Peoria, Ill., 1975—. Mem. Ind., S.C. bar assns., Phi Kappa Sigma, Phi Delta Phi. Republican. Methodist. Home: 6007 N Inwood Pl Peoria IL 61614 Office: Charter Oak Rd Peoria IL 61614

DE LOACHE, MARY BOYLSTON, banker; b. Spartanburg, S.C., June 24, 1945; d. Mims Workman and Sarah (Boylston) DeLoache; A.B. in English, U. S.C., 1967. Adminstrv. asst., teller Wachovia Bank, Charlotte, N.C., 1967-69; credit analyst, adminstrv. asst. Chem. Bank, London, 1970-72; mgmt. trainee Chem. Bank, N.Y.C., 1972-73, asst. mgr., 1974; asst. sec. Chem. Bank Internat. Chgo., 1975-76, asst. v.p., 1976—. Mem. Pi Beta Phi. Episcopalian. Home: 450 W Briar Pl Apt 12H Chicago IL 60657 Office: Suite 9300 233 S Wacker Dr Chicago IL 60606

DELONG, DWIGHT MOORE, entomologist; b. Corning, Ohio, Apr. 6, 1892; s. George Washington and Addie (Moore) DeL.; B.S., Ohio Wesleyan U., 1914, D.Sc., 1941; M.S., Ohio State U., 1916, Ph.D., 1922, D.Sc. (hon.), 1977; D.Sc. (hon.), Bowling Green State U., 1971; m. Fanny Merchant, Dec. 22, 1917 (dec. June 1974); m. Aileen Selman, Apr. 1975; children—Joan Elizabeth (Mrs. Robert L. Snouffer), Eleanor Jane (Mrs. David A. Wiedie), George Wesley. Grad. asst., asst. zoology, entomology Ohio State U., 1914-17, instr., 1918, asst. prof., 1921-23, prof., 1923-62, prof. emeritus, 1962—, dir. Franz Theodore Stone Lab., 1936-37; entomologist Pa. Dept. Agr., 1918-21; sci. expdns. to Mexico, 1939, 1941, 1945, 1954; entomologist Nat. Sci. Found., Europe, 1960, Alaska, 1964, Panama, 1967. Recipient Distinguished Tchg. award Ohio State U., 1962. Mem. AAAS, Ohio Acad. Sci. (v.p., 1930, 1932, pres. 1959), Entomol. Soc. Am. (chmn. North Central br. 1960, Founder's Meml. award, 1964), Washington Entomol. Soc., Soc. Systematic Zoology, Sigma Xi. Author: (with D. J. Borror) An Introduction to the Study of Insects, 1958, 4th edit. (with Borror and C.A. Triplehorn). Contbr. numerous articles to sci. jours. Formulation, publs. recommended controls for several field and household economic insect pests; described several genera and several hundred species of leafhoppers new to sci. Home: 1967 Collingswood Rd Columbus OH 43221 Office: 1735 Neil Ave Columbus OH 43210

DE LONG, LAWRENCE WARREN, elec. mfg. co. exec.; b. Allentown, Pa., May 6, 1937; s. Warren F. and Florence (Calkins) DeL.; student Lehigh U., 1955-57; B.S., Wyomissing Poly. Inst., 1960; postgrad. Villanova U., 1960-62; m. Joyce H. DeLong, July 12, 1958; children—Mark, Julianne. Mktg. specialist, systems engr. Honeywell Inc., Ft. Washington, Pa., 1960-67; product mgr. Foxboro Co. (Mass.), 1967-69; mgr. mktg. regional sales Ferroxcube Corp., Saugerties, N.Y., 1969-72; mgr. product mktg. Allen-Bradley Co., Highland Heights, Ohio, 1972—. Mem. Instrument Soc. Am., Numerical Control Soc., Nat. Elec. Mfrs. Assn., Programmable Computer Com. Contbr. articles to profl. publs. Home: 519 Treeside Dr Stow OH 44224 Office: 747 Alpha Dr Highland Heights OH 44143

DELOR, CAMILLE JOSEPH, physician; b. Sandusky, Ohio, Jan 24, 1907; s. Charles J. and Amelia (Biron) D.; A.B., U. Mich., 1928; M.S., Ohio State U., 1934, M.D., 1934; m. Eleanor B. Diltz, Sept. 2, 1932; children—Nancy (Mrs. David Bringardner), Susan (Mrs. Jacob Baas, Jr.). Intern St. Francis Hosp., Columbus, Ohio, 1934-35; resident Ohio State U. Hosp., Columbus, 1935-37; practice medicine, specializing in gastroenterology, Columbus, 1937—; mem. staff Ohio State U. Hosp., Pomerene prof. medicine Ohio State U., 1948—, dir. div. gen. medicine, 1974—. Fellow A.C.P.; mem. Am. Fedn. Clin. Research, Am. Gastroent. Assn., Alpha Omega Alpha, Alpha Kappa Kappa, Sigma Xi. Contbr. articles to profl. jours. Home: 2404 Kensington Dr Columbus OH 43221 Office: U Hosp Clinics 456 Clinic Dr Columbus OH 43210

DELOREAN, JOHN ZACHARY, motor co. exec.; b. Detroit, Jan. 6, 1925; s. Zachary R. and Katherine (Pribak) DeL.; B.S. in Indsl. Engring., Lawrence Inst. Tech., 1948; M.M.E., Chrysler Inst., 1952; M.B.A., U. Mich., 1957; m. Cristina Ferrare; 1 son, Zachary. Engr., Chrysler Corp., 1948-52, Packard Motor Co., 1952-56; dir. advanced engring. Pontiac Motor div. Gen. Motors Corp., 1956-59, asst. chief engr., 19S9-61, chief engr., 1961-65, gen. mgr. Gen. Motors Corp., 1965-69, v.p., 1965-73, gen. mgr. Chevrolet div., 1969-72, v.p., group exec. N.Am. car & truck ops., 1972-73; pres. Nat. Alliance Businessmen, 1973-74; prin. John Z. DeLorean Corp., Bloomfield Hills, Mich., 1974—; chmn. bd. DeLorean Motor Co., 1974—. Chmn. housing task force Urban Coalition; chmn. Mich. Council for Arts, Police Athletic League Detroit. Bd. dirs. Mich. United Fund, Oakland U.; bd. govs. William Beaumont Hosp. Mem. Soc. Automotive Engrs., Am. Soc. Body Engrs., Engring. Soc. Detroit, Indsl. Math. Soc., Mich. Profl. Engrs., Detroit Inst. Arts. Clubs: Bloomfield Hills Country; Detroit Athletic, Recess (Detroit); Augusta (Ga.) Nat. Golf (dir.); Pauma Valley Country. Author: Black Capitalism. Home: PO Box 427 Bloomfield Hills MI 48013 Office: 100 W Long Lake Rd Bloomfield Hills MI 48013

DELPH, THOMAS LEE, hardware co. exec.; b. Anderson, Ind., June 26, 1933; s. Everett William and Marjorie Isabell (Cookman) D.; B.S., Ind. U., 1955; m. Marylu Merrill, June 13, 1969; children by previous marriage—Beth Miller, Carol, Deborah (Mrs. Rick Talley), Kimberly, William, Stephanie, Angela. Asst. sports editor Bloomington (Ind.) Herald-Telephone, 1954-55; asso. editor Hardware Retailing, Indpls., 1958-61, mng. editor, 1961-64, sales promotion mgr., 1964-66, marketing mgr., 1966-68, gen. sales mgr., 1968-69, dir. sales and marketing, 1973—. Mem. Media Comparability Council, 1970—. Active Delaware Trails Little League, Jordan YMCA. Precinct del. Republican party, 1961-64, mem. nat. speakers' bur., 1962-64. Served with AUS, 1956-57. Recipient award for article Indsl. Marketing, 1960. Mem. Indpls. Ad Club, Am. Hardware Mfg. Assn. Young Execs., Ind. U. Alumni Assn., German Shepherd Dog Club Central Ind. (pres. 1976-77), German Shepherd Dog Club Am., Owners-Handlers Assn., Ind. U. Varsity Club. Methodist. Club: Toastmasters (Dist. Speaker of Year 1960). Home: 8339 Trace Circle Indianapolis IN 46260 Office: 770 N High School Rd Indianapolis IN 46224

DE LUCA, ARNOLD ARTHUR, newspaper exec.; b. Chgo., Jan. 11, 1939; s. Arthur Giatino and Ida E. (Bottigiliero) DeL.; children—Arthur Dominic, Adrianna Marie; B.S., No. Ill. U., 1965; M.B.A., U. Chgo., 1975. Regional sales rep. Diebold, Inc., Canton, Ohio, 1960-62; display advt. sales rep. Calumet Pub. Co., Lansing, Ill.,

1961-63; regional sales mgr. Olympic Home Food Service, Chgo., 1963-65; display advt. mgr. Daily Jour., Dear Publs., Washington, 1965-67, advt. dir., 1967-71, gen. mgr., 1971; promotion mgr. Copley Newspapers, Elgin div., Wheaton, Ill., 1972-74, dir. sales, 1974—; instr. Coll. of DuPage, 1973—; instr. to newspaper industry, sales seminars and workshops. Chmn., Wheaton Sister City Commn., 1970—; founder Bicentennial Freedom Forest, 1976, Operation Help, 1970, Operation Helping Hand, 1972, Operation Friendship, 1973; bd. dirs. Wheaton United Fund, Jr. Achievement. Mem. Ill., No. Ill., Inland Daily press assns., Nat. Newspaper Assn., Internat. Newspaper Advt. Execs., Chgo. Press Club, Glen Ellyn, Wheaton (pres., dir.) chambers commerce, No. Ill. U. Alumni Assn. (dir., mem. exec. bd.), Theta Chi, Lions Club, Glen Oak Country Club, DuPage County Exec. Club, U. Chgo. Exec. Club. Recipient numerous awards from profl. assns., also Outstanding Young Am. award Jr. C. of C., 1974; Author: The Idea Machine, 1973; contbr. articles to trade publs. Home: PO Box 173 Wheaton IL 60187 Office: 362 S Schmale Rd Wheaton IL 60187

DE LUCA, JOSEPH, beauty-barber co. exec.; b. Columbus, Ohio, Apr. 14, 1939; s. Joseph Anthony and Augusta Mary (Lombardo) DeL.; B.S., St. Charles Bormarro Coll., 1960; A.B., Ohio State U., 1962; m. Dixie M. Mason, June 22, 1972; children—Richard, Carolyn, Jacquelyn, Jodie, Debbra Ann. Pres., acting mgr. DeLuca's Salons and Beauty Colls.. Columbus, Ohio, 1977—; pres. sales coordinator, Spair Hair, div. Elizabeth Arden, Inc., N.Y.C., 1972—; pres. Aculed Enterprise, Ohio, 1977—; pres., dir. Clothes Galleries of Ohio, 1974—; dir. Contentint Mcht. Assn.; dir., prof. cosmetology Ohio State U. Mem. Jr. C. of C.; hon. mem. Columbus Firefighters Assn.; mem. Young Republicans of Franklin County. Recipient vocat. edn. award Ohio Dept. Edn., 1975; HEW grantee, 1966-77; recipient Community Service award Columbus radio stas., 1976. Mem. Nat. Assn. Hairdressers and Cosmetologists (award of achievement 1974). Roman Catholic. Clubs: Horsemen's Benevolent Assn., Thoroughbred Horsemen's Assn., Columbus Athletic. Author book, articles in field. Home: 35 S Stanwood Rd Bexley OH 43209 Office: 1443 S Hamilton Rd Columbus OH 43227

DELUKA, CHARLES EDWARD, JR., sch. prin.; b. Witt, Ill., Mar. 9, 1927; s. Charles Edward and Josephine Minnie (Westbrook) DeL.; B.S., Ill. State U., 1950, M.S., 1956; m. Janette Rose MacIntyre, June 17, 1950; children—David, Beth, Heather. 7-Up distbr., Bloomington, Ill., 1950-58; pub. relations man Builder's Supply Co., Bloomington, 1958-60; salesman, tchr. Dale Carnegie Courses, Bloomington, 1960-62; trainee Montgomery Ward Store, Burlington, Wis., 1962-64, store mgr., 1964-68; phys. edn. tchr. pub. schs., Bristol, Wis., 1968-71; supt. dist. 2, Salem, Wis., 1971-75; prin. Saybrook (Ill.)-Arrowsmith High Sch., 1975—. Vice pres. Wis. P.T.A., 1974-75. Trustee Brookmire-Hastings Scholarship, Wis. P.T.A. Served with USNR, 1945-46. Presbyn. Lion, Mason (Shriner). Home: PO Box 347 Saybrook IL 61770 Office: High Sch N Main St Saybrook IL 61770

DELVALLE, HELEN CYNTHIA, artist; b. Chgo., Sept. 22, 1933; d. Andrew Jack and Mary Texanna (Cohen) DelValle; student Pa. Acad. Fine Arts, 1952; B.J., Northwestern U., 1960. Tchr. art, math., history, Fla., 1952-54; artist, designer, Chgo., 1954-59; free-lance artist, 1959—; group exhbns. include: Municipal Art League of Chgo.; U. State Mus.; Mid Am. Art Assn.; Am. Soc. of Artists; Northshore Art Guild; one woman shows include: Balzekas Mus., Chgo., 1973; Chgo. Pub. Library, 1972, 73, 75; Combined Insurance Co. of Am., Chgo., 1970, 71, 72, 74, 75; Am. Soc. of Artists, Chgo., 1971, 1977; others. Recipient Portraiture award, 1961; Dingle award, N.L.A.P.W., Chgo., 1971; Traditional in Oil. N.L.A.P.W., 1971; hon. mention, Municipal Art League, 1973; Landscape in water color, N.L.A.P.W., Chgo., 1973; Internat. award Landscape Painting, Switzerland, 1975. Mem. Am. Soc. Artists (membership chmn. 1970—), Nat. League Am. Pen Women, Municipal Art League Chgo. Author poems. Address: PO Box 958 Chicago IL 60690

DELVES, EUGENE LOWELL, accountant; b. Chgo., July 16, 1927; s. Clarence and Marie (Zopf) D.; A.B., DePauw U., 1950; M.B.A., Northwestern U., 1952; m. Sue Howard, Mar. 27, 1954; children—Donald, Robert, Sarah. Mem. staff Arthur Andersen & Co., Chgo., 1951-54, mgr., 1954-62, partner, 1962—; speaker. Dir. Beverly Improvement Assn. Mem. accounting adv. com. Northwestern U.; dir. Balzekas Mus.; dir., finance chmn. Meth. Found. of U. Chgo., 1965-69. Served with USAF, 1946-47. C.P.A., Ill. Mem. Am. Inst. C.P.A.'s, Am. Accounting Assn., Ill. Soc. C.P.A.'s (v.p.), DePauw Alumni Assn. (nat. pres.), Phi Beta Kappa, Sigma Nu, Beta Gamma Sigma. Methodist (finance com. No. Ill. conf., trustee). Clubs: DePauw Alumni (past pres.), Beverly Country, Chicago Athletic Assn. (Chgo.). Contbr. articles to profl. jours. Home: 9142 S Winchester Ave Chicago IL 60620 Office: 69 W Washington St Chicago IL 60602

DELZELL, ROBERT FREDRIC, librarian; b. Independence, Kans., Sept. 4, 1918; s. William Andrew and Myrtle (Bearden) D.; A.B., Drury Coll., 1940; postgrad. Northwestern U., 1940-41; B.S., Washington U., St. Louis, 1950; M.S. in L.S., U. Ill., 1951. Asst. to editorial librarian Prentice-Hall, Inc., N.Y.C., 1946-48; acquisitions asst. library Washington U., 1948-49, reference asst., 1949-50, chief acquisitions dept. 1951-53; bibliog. asst. Air U. Library, Maxwell AFB, Ala., 1953, chief acquisitions br., 1953-55, asst. to dir., 1955; adminstrv. asst. rank asst. prof. U. Ill. Library, Urbana, 1955-58, asso. prof., 1958-67, personnel librarian, 1967-68, dir. personnel, prof. library adminstrn., 1968—; mem. nonacad. personnel adv. com. to chancellor U. Ill., 1969—; faculty rep. Univ. Theatre Bd., 1963-67, 70-74; mem. Campus Round Table, 1960—; faculty adviser U. Ill. Film Soc., 1961-62. Served with AUS, 1941-45; ETO. Mem. Am. (chmn. Scarecrow Press award 1967-68, Grolier award jury 1968-69, J.W. Lippincott award jury 1975-76, chmn. awards com. 1970-73), Ill. (chmn. fgn. exchange program com. 1964-66) library assns., Beta Phi Mu (nat. pres. 1969-70), Sigma Nu. Editor: Book of Beta Phi Mu, 1954, U. Ill. Library Sch. Assn. News Letter, 1956-67. Contbr. articles profl. jours. Home: 401 N Prairie St Apt 4C Champaign IL 61820 Office: 305 Library U Ill Urbana IL 61801

DEMAAGD, RONALD UECKER, city mgr.; b. Grand Rapids, Mich., Aug. 19, 1938; s. Louis John and Minnie (Uecker) DeM.; B.A. with honors, Mich. State U., 1962, M. Pub. Adminstrn., 1963; m. Marilou Strickland (div. May 1972); children—Mark, Christopher. Adminstrv. intern City East Lansing, Mich., 1961-63; asst. city mgr. Muskegon, Mich., 1963-67; city mgr. Whitewater, Wis., 1967-70, Ferndale, Mich., 1970—. Chmn. Whitewater Plan Commn., 1967-70; mem. Ferndale Plan Commn., 1970—. Bd. dirs. South Oakland County Incinerator Authority, vice chmn., 1974-75, chmn., 1976-78. Mem. Mich. Municipal League (trustee 1977—, mem. employees relations com., legis. com.), Internat., Oakland County (pres.1974-75) city mgmt. assns., Am. Soc. Pub. Adminstrn., Internat. Personnel Mgmt. Assn., Mich. Soc. Planning Ofcls. (dir.), Mich. Pub. Employer Labor Relations Assn., Ferndale C. of C. Home: 575 E Troy St Ferndale MI 48220 Office: 300 E Nine Mile Rd Ferndale MI 48220

DEMANN, MICHAEL MARCUS, psychologist; b. Mpls., June 1, 1932; s. George S. and Mary Hazel (Short) DeM.; B.A., U. Minn., 1955, M.A., 1958, Ph.D., 1960; m. Carol L. Knutson, Feb. 10, 1961; children—James G., Susan M., John P. Mem. staff VA Hosp., Mpls., 1960-61; with Rohrer, Hibler & Replogle, 1961-65; pvt. practice psychology, St. Paul, 1965—; cons. Social Security Adminstrn., Mpls., 1966-67. Dir. Internat. Graphics Corp., Mpls. Bd. dirs. Opportunity Workshop, Mpls., 1962-69; bd. govs. St. Mary's Jr. Coll., Mpls. Served with Med. Service Corps, AUS, 1950-52. Mem. Am., Minn. (exec. council 1971-73) psychol. assns., Am. Legion. Episcopalian (sr. warden). Home: 6513 Stauder Circle Edina MN 55436 Office: 6600 France Ave S Minneapolis MN 55435

DE MAO, PETER ROBERT, coal co. exec.; b. Arnold, Pa., June 16, 1937; s. Domenic and Helen (Sylak) De M.; B.A., U. Pitts., also B.S., 1967; M.B.A., Ind. No. U., 1974; m. Sandra Marie Wvycheck, Sept. 5, 1959; children—Randall Lee, Lisa Marie, Cynthia Lynn. Project mgr. new plant planning Westinghouse Electric Co., Pitts., 1965-70; v.p., adminstrn.-fin. Marion Power Shovel Co. (Ohio), 1970-74; v.p. ops. Rohr-Flexible Co., Delaware, Ohio, 1974-75; v.p. planning Amax Coal Co., Indpls., 1975—; chmn. Common Surface Mining Equipment Troubleshooting, Indpls., 1976—. Active United Way. Mem. Fin. Execs. Inst., Am. Mining Congress, Prodn. and Inventory Control Soc., Am. Mgmt. Assn. Club: Columbia (Indpls.). Home: 11715 Rolling Springs Dr Carmel IN 46032 Office: 105 S Meridian St Indianapolis IN 46225

DEMARAY, LEONARD ALLEN, army officer; b. Chgo., Aug. 23, 1946; s. Lynne Earl and Lois (Richard) D.; student Sparten Sch. Aeros., 1971-72, Central Tex. Coll., 1973-74, Am. Tech. U., 1975—; Asso. in Sci., N.Y. U., 1977. Enlisted U.S. Army, 1963, advanced through grades to staff sgt., 1967, discharged, 1970, re-enlisted, 1972—, stationed Republic Vietnam, 1966-70, 72-73, Alaska, 1975—. Decorated Silver Star with cluster, D.F.C. with 2 clusters, Bronze Star with cluster, Air medal with 88 clusters, Purple Heart with three clusters, Vietnam Cross Gallantry with palm, Army Commendation medal with five clusters. Mem. VFW (life), Ill. (life), Nat. (life) rifle assns., Nat. Geog. Soc. (life), Assn. U.S. Army, Aircraft Owners and Pilots Assn., Exptl. Aircraft Assn. Democrat. Home: 1622 Winnemac Ave Chicago IL 60640 Office: Box 421 242d Avn Co Fort Wainwright AK 99703

DE MARCO, THOMAS JOSEPH, periodontist, univ. dean; b. Farmingdale, N.Y., Feb. 12, 1942; s. Joseph Louis and Mildred Nora (Cifarelli) De M.; B.S., U. Pitts., 1962, D.D.S., 1965; Ph.D., certificate in Periodontology, Boston U., 1968; C.F.P., Coll. for Fin. Planning, 1976; m. Virginia Hill, Jan. 22, 1966; children—Todd Gordon, Kristin Alice, Lisa Anne. Practice dentistry specializing in periodontics, Cleve., 1968—; mem. staff Highland View, Univ., VA hosps., Cleve.; asst. prof. periodontics, pharmacology Case Western Res. U., 1968-70, asso. prof., 1970-73, prof., 1973—, asso. dean Sch. Dentistry, 1972—. Air Force Office Sci. Research grantee, 1969; Upjohn Co. grantee, 1970; Columbus Dental grantee, 1971. Certificate in clin. hypnosis. Mem. Am. Acad. Periodontology, Internat. Assn. Dental Research, Am. Soc. for Preventive Dentistry (pres. Ohio chpt. 1971-73). Contbr. articles on periodontics, pharmacology to sci. jours. Home: 12800 Westchester Trail Chesterland OH 44026 Office: 2123 Abington Rd Cleveland OH 44106

DEMARS, ROBERT ALPHONSE, city ofcl.; b. Chgo., Apr. 30, 1930; s. Alphonse I. and Annabel (Erickson) DeM.; A.A., Flint Jr. Coll., 1951; B.A., Eastern Mich. U., 1953; M.A., U. Mich., 1954; m. Doris Faye Lockard, Nov. 28, 1963. Tchr. pub. schs. Chelsea, Mich., 1953-54, Garden City, Mich., 1954-56, Lincoln Park, Mich., 1956—. City councilman Lincoln Park, 1965-67, mayor, 1967—. Pres., Lincoln Park Community Council, 1961. Bd. dirs. Peoples Community Hosp. Authority. Served with USN, 1945-49. Mem. Fedn. of Tchrs., Mich. Assn. Suprs., Mich. Mental Health Assn., C. of C., Am. Legion, V.F.W. Democrat. Mason (32 deg., Shriner), Eagle, Moose, Kiwanian (sec.-treas. 1958-59). Home: 833 Mayflower Ct Lincoln Park MI 48146 Office: 1355 Southfield St Lincoln Park MI 48146

DEMAS, THEODORE JOHN, dentist; b. Detroit, Dec. 29, 1933; s. John and Catherine (Liabotis) D.; B.S., U. Detroit, 1956, D.D.S., 1960; m. Joyce Viole Yannaki, June 28, 1958; children—John, Michael, William. Pvt. practice dentistry, Taylor, Mich., 1960—. Recipient achievement award Acad. Gold Foil Operators, 1960. Mem. Am., Mich. dental assns., Oakland County, Detroit Dist. dental socs., Omicron Kappa Upsilon, Psi Omega. Mason. Home: 3855 Burning Tree St Bloomfield Hills MI 48013 Office: 20420 Ecorse Rd Taylor MI 48180

DEMELLO, FRANK JOHN, epidemiologist, dentist; b. Jerusalem, Palestine, Mar. 12, 1939; s. John Miguel and Samiyeh (Naddaf) D.; came to U.S., 1961, naturalized, 1971; B.A., St. John's U., Collegeville, Minn., 1965; Ph.D. (Univ. scholar), U. Ky., 1972; D.D.S., U. Minn., 1977; m. Sharon Jean Ahlers, Aug. 23, 1966; children—John Robert, Jean Frances. Banker Ottoman Bank, Nablus, Jordan, 1956-61; research asso. Mpls. Med. Research Found., 1968—; epidemiologist Hennepin County (Minn.) Med. Center, Mpls., 1972—; pvt. practice dentistry, Mpls., 1977—; dir. clin. lab. Hennepin County Gen. Hosp., Mpls., 1970-71. Chmn. St. Joan of Arc Sch. P.T.A., Mpls., 1973-74. Hartford Found. grantee, 1968-70. Mem. Am. Soc. Microbiology, Am. Dental Assn., Am. Soc. Dentistry for Children. Contbr. articles to profl. jours. Research on treatment of gas-gangrene. Home: 6134 Woody Ln NE Fridley MN 55432 Office: 619 S 5th St Minneapolis MN 55415

DEMENT, JAMES W., III, mgmt. cons.; b. Mobile, Ala., May 7, 1942; s. James W. and Pauline O. (Boult) D.; B.S., Fla. State U., 1965; M.B.A., U. Chgo., 1977; m. Ellen S. Dement, Aug. 26, 1967; children—Ward, David. Mgr., Marriott Corp., Washington, 1965-68; franchise ops. mgr. McDonalds Corp., Oakbrook, Ill., 1968-70; owner, pres. Roth Young Assos., Chgo., 1970—. Mem. Ill. Assn. Personnel Cons. (pres.), Nat. Assn. Personnel Cons. (bd. dirs.), Ill. Employment Assn. (dir.). Republican. Episcopalian. Clubs: Tower, Whitehall, Exec. Home: 21653 Andover Rd Kildeer IL 60047 Office: 150 S Wacker Dr Chicago IL 60606

DEMENT, KENNETH LEE, lawyer; b. Poplar Bluff, Mo., Feb. 13, 1933; s. Charles K. and Ada (Hudson) D.; B.S., Southeast Mo. State Coll., 1955; D.Juridicial Sci., Washington U., 1961. Admitted to Mo. bar, 1961; practiced in Sikeston, Mo., 1961—; city atty., Sikeston, 1972—. Govt. appeal agt. Scott County Draft Bd., 1965-72; mem. City of Sikeston Bd. Housing Appeals, 1969—; commr. Sikeston Housing Authority, 1973—. Treas., Young Democratic Clubs Mo., Inc., 1963; pres. Scott County Young Democrats, 1964. Served as capt. USMCR, 1955-57. All-Am. Football player, 1953, 54. Mem. Scott County Bar Assn. (pres. 1963). Address: 310 W North St Sikeston MO 63801

DEMET, FRANCIS JOSEPH, lawyer; b. South Milwaukee, Wis., Sept. 11, 1923; s. Thomas John and Margaret Veronica (Vogt) D.; A.B., Loras Coll., 1948; LL.B., Georgetown U., 1951; m. Margadette Moffatt, Nov. 27, 1954; children—Donal, Maura, Kerry, Michael, Barry, Kevin, Brigid, Deirdre. Admitted to Wis. bar, 1952; practiced in Milw., 1952—; partner, officer Demet & Demet, Milw., 1954—. Pres., Saints Peter and Paul Council, 1976—; mem. bd. Milw. East Side Organizing Com., 1972-73; pres. bd. St. Joan Antida High Sch., 1972-73. Mem. Milwaukee County Republican Com., 1954-56. Served with USAAC, 1942-45. Mem. Am., Wis., Milw., 7th Circuit (dir. 1971-78) bar assns., St. Robert's Athletic Assn. (sec. 1971-73). Clubs: Athletic, Serra, Civil War Roundtable (Milw.). Contbr. articles to profl. jours. Home: 2415 E Wyoming Pl Milwaukee WI 53202 Office: 815 N Cass St Milwaukee WI 53202

DEMHARTER, DOROTHY ELIZABETH CROW, hosp. adminstr.; b. Akron, Ohio, Jan. 28, 1927; d. Edmond Daniel and Dorothy Josephine (Starner) Crow; grad. City Hosp. of Akron Sch. Nursing, 1948; m. William Charles Damharter, Feb. 14, 1948; children—William Michael, Sharon Lee, Cynthia Louise. Pvt. duty nurse, 1951-53; staff nurse Massillon Ohio State Hosp., 1959-60, supr., 1961-68, Medicaid/Medicare coordinator, geriatric program, 1968-72, adminstrv. asst. to supt., 1972-76, acting supt., 1975-76, asst. supt., 1976—. Asst. leader, then leader 4-H Clubs, 1969-74. Mem. Am. Nurses Assn., Stark County Mental Health Profls. Office: Massillon State Hosp 3000 Erie St SW Box 540 Massillon OH 44646

DEMING, CHARLES ROBERT, veterinarian; b. Anthony, Kans., July 26, 1920; s. Loren Strong and Lois Edna (Dixon) D.; D.V.M., Iowa State U., 1952; postgrad. pub. health orientation for veterinarians U. Ill., 1970; m. Jeanne Boyd, Oct. 10, 1948; children—Charles Robert, Loren Dale, Jeanne. Asso. Av. Vet. Hosp., St. Joseph, Mo., 1952-59; individual practice vet. medicine, St. Joseph, 1959—; asso. Reptile Garden and Zoo, St. Joseph, 1959-63; cons. Hog Builders Internat., Hemple, Mo., 1964-69; dir. Productores Internacional De Cerdo, Monterey, Mexico. Bd. dirs. Concerned Taxpayers Assn., St. Joseph, 1969—. Served with USMC, 1940-46. Fellow Royal Soc. Health, London; mem. Kansas City, Mo., Am. vet. med. assns., VFW, Iowa State U. Vet. Med. Alumni Assn. Optimist, Mason. Home: 2509 Jule St St Joseph MO 64501 Office: 1531 Savannah Ave St Joseph MO 64505

DEMKE, RICHARD STEVEN, dentist; b. Hillsboro, Wis., Aug. 9, 1950; s. Robert L. and Francis L. (Moutoux) D.; B.S., Wis. State U., 1971; D.D.S., Marquette U., 1975; m. Linda Lou Hillmer, Aug. 4, 1974. Gen. practice dentistry, Princeton, Wis., 1975—. Home: 328 Farmer St Princeton WI 54968 Office: Route 1 Princeton WI 54968

DEMONS, LEONA MARIE, counselor; b. Townsend, Ga., Jan. 6, 1928; d. Stephen and Rosa Lee (Wilson) Carter; B.S., Savannah State Coll., 1949; M.A. (NDEA fellow), Atlanta U., 1965; postgrad. (NDEA fellow) Kans. State U., 1967-68; children by previous marriage—Wynette, John, Chris, Donna; 1 foster son, Clinton Drummond. Asst. to dir. pub. relations Savannah State Coll., 1949-52; tchr. pub. schs. Washington County (Ga.), 1952-62; asst. in personnel Morehouse Coll., 1962-64; counselor, instr. in edn. Albany State Coll., 1964-69; counselor, coordinator human devel., adviser fgn. students Lincoln Land Community Coll., 1970—. Mem. Am., Ill. personnel and guidance assns., Am. Psychometric Assn., NAACP, Springfield Urban League, Alpha Kappa Alpha. Baptist. Home: 2101 E Cornell St Springfield IL 62703 Office: Room 185 Lincoln Land Community Coll Springfield IL 62708

DEMOSS, THURMAN MILLARD, lawyer; b. Westfield, Ind., Nov. 23, 1918; s. Otto E. and Oma Edna (Thompson) DeM.; student Franklin Coll., 1937-40; LL.B., Ind. U., 1951; m. Bethel Louise McFadden, Nov. 19, 1941; children—Suzanne, James, Thomas. Mgr., Snyder's Restaurant, Franklin, Ind., 1945-48; dep. ins. commr. State of Ind. 1949-53; admitted to Ind. bar, 1951; practice law, Franklin, 1951—. City atty., Franklin, 1955-59; mem. State Election Bd., 1966—; county atty., Johnson County, Ind., 1960-62. Chmn. Gettysburg Meml. Commn. Served with AUS, 1942-45. Decorated Purple Heart, Bronze Star medal. Recipient outstanding profl. Man of the Year award Franklin C. of C., 1969. Mem. Am. Judicature Soc., Kappa Delta Rho. Democrat. Presbyn. Mason, Elk, Odd fellow. Clubs: Indianapolis Athletic; Hillview Country (Franklin). Home: 1150 E Adams Dr Franklin IN 46131 Office: 103 E Monroe St Franklin IN 46131

DEMOTT, ROBERT WARMSLEY, JR., diversified mfg. co. exec.; b. N.Y.C., June 21, 1921; s. Robert Warmsley and Bertha Dorothy (Fix) DeM.; B.S. in Mech. Engring., Duke U., 1947; postgrad. exec. program U. Calif. at Los Angeles, 1968; m. Jacqueline Quinn, Dec. 23, 1946; children—Diane Painter, Robert Knox, Denise, Roy McMillan. Dist. mgr. Rexnord, Inc., Los Angeles, 1958-61, regional sales mgr., Phila., 1961-66, western div. mgr., Los Angeles, 1966-69, v.p. sales, Milw., 1969-73, pres. conveying equipment div., 1973—. Exec. bd. Milwaukee County council Boy Scouts Am., 1973-74; bd. dirs. Blue Cross Wis. Served to lt. USNR, 1949-59. Mem. Sales and Mktg. Execs. Milw. (pres. 1972-73), Phi Beta Kappa, Omicron Delta Kappa, Tau Beta Pi, Pi Sigma Epsilon, Phi Delta Theta. Presbyn. (ruling elder 1963-69). Clubs: Lake Shore (dir. 1969-73); Greater Milw. Swim (dir. 1970-73), Milw. Athletic. Home: 9575 N Sequoia Dr Milwaukee WI 53217 Office: 4701 W Greenfield Ave Milwaukee WI 53214

DE MOURA, LUIZ FERNANDO PEREZ, surgeon; b. Maceio, Brazil, Feb. 24, 1938; s. Alvaro A. and Elena Perez DeM.; came to U.S., 1965, naturalized, 1970; B.A., U. Recife, Brazil, 1955, M.D., 1961; m. Anne Bohn, Feb. 7, 1970; children—Kristina, Luiz Robert, Monica. Intern, U. Hosp., Recife, 1960-61; resident in surgery Bon Secour Hosp., Grosse Pointe, Mich., 1969-70; chief resident in otolaryngology Vanderbilt U., Nashville, 1971-72; fellow in otology Memphis Found. Otology, 1965, Harvard Med. Sch., Boston, 1965-66, Henry Ford Hosp., Detroit, 1966-69; practice medicine specializing in otolaryngology, Mount Clemens, Mich., 1972—; vice chief dept. otolaryngology William Beaumont Hosp., Troy, Mich.; mem. staff St. Joseph, Harrison hosps. Served as lt. Brazilian Army, 1958. Recipient Joaquim Amazonas award U. Recife Med. Sch., 1959. Fellow A.C.S.; mem. Mich. State, Macomb County (sec.) med. socs., AMA, Am. Acad. Ophthalmology and Otorhinolaryngology. Roman Catholic. Home: 575 Wellington Crescent Mount Clemens MI 48043 Office: 39960 Garfield Rd Mount Clemens MI 48044

DEMPSEY, TERENCE MARK, lawyer; b. Henderson, Minn., Feb. 17, 1932; s. Mark Vincent and Mabel Margaret (Stehly) D.; B.A., Coll. St. Thomas, 1954; J.D., U. Calif. at Hastings, 1962; m. Janet Helm, Dec. 8, 1963; 1 son, Matthew Jerome. Admitted to Minn. bar, 1963; mem. firm, McGuire & Dempsey, Montgomery, 1963-64, Somsen, Dempsey & Schade, New Ulm, Minn., 1964—; asst. pub. defender 5th Jud. Dist., 1967-69; city atty., New Ulm, 1969—. Mem. Minn. Gov.'s Commn. on Crime Prevention and Control. Served with USAF, 1955-58. Mem. State Bar Calif., Minn. State Bar, Am. Judicature Soc., 9th Jud. Dist. Bar Assn. (pres. 1976-77), Minn. City Attys. Assn. (pres. 1973-74), Phi Alpha Delta. Lion. Home: 309 S Minnesota St New Ulm MN 56073 Office: State Bond Bldg New Ulm MN 56073

DEMUTH, PAUL EMMANUEL, transp. co. exec.; b. Louisville, Sept. 12, 1934; s. Clarence Joseph and Carolyn Ann (Schoenbachler) DeM.; B.S. in Commerce, U. Louisville, 1960; m. Dixie Sherman, July 3, 1970; children by previous marriage—Karen Ann, Paula Jean, Steven Michael, Joan Marie, Gregory Alan, Christopher Joseph. Commerce agt. Central & So. Motor Freight, Louisville, 1952-60; asst. to gen. traffic mgr. Chemetron Corp., Louisville, 1960-65; exec. v.p. Coldway Carriers, Inc., Clarksville, Ind., 1965-70; pres. Midwest Emery Freight System, Inc., Chgo., 1970-74, Lowery Trucking Co.,

1972-74, Catalina Industries, Inc. Exec. v.p. Kentuckiana World Commerce Council, 1965—. Chmn. bd. trustees City of Devondale (Ky.), 1963-64. Served with USAF, 1968-69; Korea. Mem. Assn. ICC Practitioners (pres. Louisville chpt. 1966-67), Am. Trucking Assn. (dir. 1971-72), Ky. Motor Transport Assn. (legislative com. 1967-68), Fall City Football Assn. (treas. 1964-65), Toastmasters (treas. 1959-60). Address: 1130 Maple Ln Western Springs IL 60558

DENADEL, RAYMOND LEE, educator; b. Pella, Iowa, Apr. 23, 1932; s. John J. and Nellie (DeGeus) DenA.; B.A. magna cum laude, Central Coll., Pella, 1954; M.A., State U. Iowa, 1959; Ph.D., U. Ill., 1971; postgrad. Drake U., N.C. State Coll., Am. Acad. in Rome, Italy, Vergilian Sch., Cumae, Italy, Am. Sch. Classical Studies, Athens, Greece. Asst. Latin instr. Central Coll., Pella, 1954; Latin instr. Pella High Sch., 1954-55; Latin and English instr. Proviso West High Sch., Hillside, Ill., 1958-62; grad. Latin instr. U. Iowa, 1962-63; grad. instr. classics U. Ill., 1963-67; asst. prof. classics, chmn. dept. Rockford (Ill.) Coll., 1967-71, asso. prof., 1971-75, prof., 1975—, chmn. div. lang. and lit., 1971-74; pvt. piano instr., 1949-54; mem. evaluation team North Central Assn., 1976. Mem. Rockford Arts Council, 1973-74. Served with AUS, 1955-57. Recipient Fulbright grant, 1960, Distinguished Alumnus award Central Coll., 1972. Mem. Am. Philol. Assn. (life), Classical Assn. Middlewest and South (life; v.p. Ill. 1974-78), Am. Classical League, Vergilian Soc. Am., Archaeol. Inst. Am. (nat. exec. com. 1976—), Oriental Inst. Chgo., AAUP, Ill. Classical Conf. (mem. exec. bd. 1965-71, pres. 1969-70), Ill. Fgn. Lang. Tchrs. Assn., Overseas Educators Assn., Rockford Archaeol. Soc. (pres. 1968-70, 72-74, sec.-treas. 1974-78), Dutch Immigrant Soc., Nat. Geog. Soc. (life), Smithsonian Assos., State Hist. Soc. Iowa (life), Sigma Tau Delta, Chi Gamma Iota, Eta Sigma Phi (nat. exec. sec. 1974-78). Mem. Reformed Ch. Am. (organist). Club: Classical (pres. 1977—) (Chgo.). Contbr. articles to profl. jours. Home: 701 Broadway Pella IA 50219 Office: 5050 E State St Rockford IL 61101

DENBROOK, MYRON ELWOOD, JR., architect; b. Orrville, Ohio, June 22, 1922; s. Myron Elwood and Ida Anna (Henselman) D.; student Ohio State U., 1940-43; B.Arch., U. Wash., 1945; m. Eva Mae Carter, Apr. 14, 1945; children—Myron Elwood III, Mark. With Wash. State Coll., Pullman, 1945-47; designer, draftsman Daniel R. Huntington, Architect, Pullman, 1946-47; chief draftsman H. B. Gessel, Pullman, 1947; designer, chief draftsman T. B. Wells, Architect, Grand Forks, N.D., 1947; partner Wells & Denbrook, Architects, Grand Forks, 1948-60; pres. Wells, Denbrook, Adams, Wagner, P.C., Grand Forks, 1960—. Mem. Urban Renewal Agy., Grand Forks, 1963-64, chmn., 1964-69; mem. Citizens Com., Grand Forks, 1966—, chmn., 1970-71. Mem. AIA (chpt. dir. 1954-56, 60-62), Constrn. Specifications Inst. (tech. chmn. N.D.-Red River Valley chpt. 1963-72), N.D. (v.p. 1949, 50-51, pres. 1973-75), Grand Forks (dir. 1970-71, v.p. 1973) chambers commerce. Mem. Federated Ch. (bd. deacons 1966-75, chmn. 1967-68, trustee 1956-59, 60-62, chmn. 1975). Lion, Mason (Shriner), Elk. Prin. archtl. works include Lake Region Jr. Coll., Devils Lake, N.D., 1965-71, Gamble Hall, U. N.D., Grand Forks, 1967, Chester Fritz Auditorium, 1970. Home: 2718 Belmont Rd Grand Forks ND 58201 Office: 1420 24th Ave S Grand Forks ND 58201

DENEEN, JAMES FRANCIS, lawyer; b. St. Joseph, Mo., Nov. 27, 1938; s. Frank Vernon and Mary Bernadine (McLaughlin) DeN.; B.S., U. Mo., 1961; LL.B., J.D., 1964; m. Suzan Ann Kraft, Mar. 30, 1964; children—James Scott, Mary Susan. Admitted to Mo. bar, 1964; asst. atty. gen. State Mo., 1964-65; practiced in Joplin, 1965—. Asst. city atty., Joplin, 1969-73. Home: 1338 Sheridan Dr Joplin MO 64801 Office: 4th and Main St Joplin MO 64801

DENELSKY, GARLAND Y., psychologist; b. Des Moines, Nov. 13, 1938; s. Isadore Albert and Minnie (Landman) DeN.; B.A. (Yonker honor acad. scholar), Grinnell Coll., 1960; M.S. (U.S.P.H.S. fellow), Purdue U., 1962, Ph.D., 1966; m. Ellen Patricia Weitz, Aug. 19, 1962; children—Rebecca Lee, Stephen Joel, Jeffrey Stuart. Grad. teaching asso. Purdue U., 1962-63, 64-65; intern U. Oreg. Med. Sch., 1963-64; assessment psychologist, acting chief psychol. research C.I.A., Washington, 1966-71; staff psychologist, dir. psychology tng. program Cleve. Clinic Found., 1971—. Alumni rep. Grinnell Coll., 1967—; mem. Onaway Community Assn., 1973—. Recipient research grant, Cleve. Clinic, 1973. Mem. Am., Midwestern, Ohio (trustee), Cleve. (exec. bd.) psychol. assns., Cleve. Acad. Consulting Psychologists (exec. bd., pres. 1976-78), Ohio Acad. Cons. Psychologists (pres.). AAAS, Sigma Xi. Jewish. Contbr. articles profl. jours. Home: 3327 Aberdeen Rd Shaker Heights OH 44120 Office: 9500 Euclid Ave Cleveland OH 44106

DENGLER, HARRY OSCAR, III, hosp. adminstr.; b. St. Louis, Dec. 22, 1944; s. Harry Oscar and Marie Frances (Harrigan) D.; A.A., Meramec Community Coll., 1971; certificate in bus. adminstrn. Washington U., St. Louis, 1975; m. Lynn Dorothy Sperreng, Apr. 12, 1969; 1 son, Robert Harry. Jr. cost accountant Kearney Electric Co., St. Louis, 1962-64; sr. billing clk. Emerson Electric Co., St. Louis, 1964-66; sales agt. Prudential Life Ins., St. Louis, 1966-67; customer relations cost accountant Gen. Electric Co., St. Louis, 1967-70; accounting supr. Hamilton Life Ins. Co. div. ITT, St. Louis, 1970-72; dir. accounting St. Francis Hosp., Washington, Mo., 1972-74; asst. adminstr. Lindell Hosp., St. Louis, 1974—. Mem. Nat. Assn. Accountants, Hosp. Financial Mgmt. Assn., Am. Mgmt. Assn. Home: 9563 Pine Spary St Saint Louis MO 63126

DENHAM, HARRY WELTON, JR., foundry exec.; b. Litchfield, Mich., Jan. 5, 1905; s. Harry Welton and Theodana (Lovejoy) D.; student U. Mich., 1924-25; grad. Cleary Bus. Coll., 1926-27; student Sch. Bus. Adminstrn., Harvard, 1931; m. Virginia Drury, Feb. 17, 1960; children—Janet Mary (Mrs. J. Robert Sarrinen Swanson), Thomas Menno. Accountant, Am. Foundries Co. and Am. Boiler & Foundry Co., Milan, Mich., 1927-31, asst. to pres., 1931-46, exec. v.p., 1946—, gen. mgr., 1948-49, v.p. Am. Foundries Co., 1950-62, v.p., gen. mgr., 1963—. Recipient spl. award merit Nat. Foundry Assn. Mem. Nat. Foundry Assn. (membership chmn. 1966-67, 74-75, pres. 1969-71). Club: Barton Hills Country (Ann Arbor). Home: 9741 Liberty Rd Chelsea MI 48118 Office: 330 2d St Milan MI 48160

DENHART, PAUL RAYMOND, veterinarian; b. Findlay, Ohio, Feb. 11, 1924; s. Raymond and Esther Lucille (Presnell) D.; D.V.M., Ohio State U., 1947; m. Ruth Ann Ford, Oct. 9, 1948; children—Charles Ford, Deborah Ann, Christine, Susan. Individual practice vet. medicine, Zanesville, Ohio, 1947—; sec. PDH FARMS, Inc., Zanesville, 1970—. Pres. Pleasant Grove Sch. Bd., 1965-68; mem. Zanesville Bd. Edn., 1970—; bd. dirs. Muskingum County (Ohio) Joint Vocat. Sch. Bd., 1970—, Zanesville-Muskingum County Bd. Health, 1962-71, Muskingum County Fair Bd., 1962-71. Served with USNR, 1945-46. Mem. Ohio Vet. Med. Bd. (pres.), Southeastern Ohio Acad. Vet. Medicine, Ohio, Am. vet. med. assns., Alpha Tau Omega. Republican. Episcopalian (vestryman). Mason, Rotarian. Home: 355 Parkway Dr Zanesville OH 43701 Office: 2058 E Pike St Zanesville OH 43701

DEN HARTOG, JOHN GILBERT, surgeon; b. Hospers, Iowa, Oct. 26, 1929; s. Walter and Mary (Vande Steeg) DenH.; student Northwestern Jr. Coll., 1947-49; B.A., State U. Iowa, 1956; B.S., U. S.D., 1958; M.D., State U. Iowa, 1960; m. Marilyn S. Pfeifer, Dec. 6, 1952; children—Daniel John, Steven James. Intern, St. Mary's Hosp., Grand Rapids, Mich., 1960-61, resident in surgery, 1961-63, 67-69; med. missionary to Ethiopia, 1963-67, 70-74; practice medicine specializing in gen. surgery, Hastings, Mich., 1974—; mem. active staff Pennock Hosp.; co-founder Mehireta Yesus Hosp., Ghinda, Ethiopia, 1965, med. dir., 1970-74. Served with USN, 1951-55. Diplomate Am. Bd. Surgery. Fellow A.C.S.; mem. AMA, Mich., Barry County med. socs., Mich. Soc. Gen. Surgeons, Southwestern Mich. Surg. Soc., Alpha Omega Alpha. Republican. Home: 907 N Glenwood Dr Hastings MI 49058 Office: 1005 W Green St Hastings MI 49058

DE NINNO, JOHN LOUIS, electronics mfg. co. exec.; b. Pitts., July 6, 1933; s. Louis Peter and Suzanne P. (Maurice) DeN.; B.S., U. Pitts., 1956; M.S., Case Western Res. U., 1973; m. Patricia Ann Gaughan, June 6, 1959; children—Karen L., Lynn S., Lisa A., Gregory J. Sr. indsl. engr., Jones & Laughlin Steel Corp., Pitts., 1956-61; mgr. of indsl. engring. Cyclops Corp., Pitts., 1961-65; plant mgr. The Stanley Works, Conn., 1965-70; dir. mfg. engring., Warner & Swasey Co., Cleve., 1970-72; pres. Reliable Products Co., Cleve., 1972-76, Crystaloid Elctronics Co., Stow, Ohio, 1976—, Investors Growth Corp., Akron, Ohio, 1976—. Chmn. Library Bd., Scott Twp., 1963. Served to capt., USAF, 1957-60. Mem. Am. Inst. Indsl. Engrs. Roman Catholic. Clubs: Country (Hudson); Cleveland Athletic; University (Pittsburgh). Home: 2259 Danbury Ln Hudson OH 44236 Office: PO Box 671 Hudson OH 44236

DENISON, GENE WILLIAM, educator; b. Virgil, S.D., July 14, 1929; s. William Carl and Ingabelle Dona (Evenson) D.; B.A., Huron Coll., 1951; M.A., U. S.D., 1960; m. Norma Jeanne Bonesteel, June 10, 1951; children—Jeffry Gene, Matthew Gene. Faculty polit. sci. Huron (S.D.) Coll., 1954—, asso. prof., 1967—, chmn. sci. and social sci. div., 1973. Democratic precinct committeeman Beadle County, S.D., 1964-68; mayor City of Huron, 1960-65, cited for distinguished pub. service, 1965. Mem. S.D. Gov.'s Com. Exec. Reorgn., 1971-72, trustee Huron Pub. Library, 1974-75, pres., 1974-75; Huron Planning Commn., 1973-75, S.D. Acad. Resources Council, 1971-73. Served with AUS, 1951-53. Decorated Bronze Star medal. Named Tchr. of Year, Huron Coll., 1965. Mem. Pi Gamma Mu. Presbyn. Home: 611 14th St Huron SD 57350

DENK, DANIEL BERNARD, lawyer; b. Kansas City, Mo., Mar. 9, 1943; s. Bernard Peter and Betsy (Blucher) D.; B.A., Kans. State U., 1965; J.D., Kans. U., 1968; m. Jacqueline Lee Caesar, Feb. 11, 1966; children—Laura, Ryan. Admitted to Kans. bar, 1968; mem. firm Cross & Kancel, Kansas City, 1968-70, Cross, Serra & Denk, 1970-71; atty. City of Kansas City, 1971-75, Kansas City Bd. Pub. Utilities, 1976—; prof. bus. law. Rockhurst Coll., 1970—. Mem. Am., Kans., Wyandotte County (sec. 1973, v.p. 1976, pres. 1977) bar assns., Kans. Trial Lawyers Assn., Phi Delta Phi. Home: 2037 Tauromee St Kansas City KS 66102 Office: New Brotherhood Bldg Kansas City KS 66101

DENLINGER, ELMER LOUIS, chiropractor; b. South Bend, Ind., Dec. 16, 1927; s. Jacob Hershey and Gladys Barbara (Helfrich) D.; B.A. in Anthropology and Spanish and Religion, Beloit Coll., 1950; D.C., Nat. Coll. Chiropractic, Chgo., 1959; m. Myrle Neill, Sept. 1959; children—Jacob, Rebecca, Jonathan, Benjamin, David. Archaeol. field worker, dept. cultural history U. Chgo., 1946, Beloit (Wis.) Coll., 1947; archaeol. field worker Bur. Reclamation Smithsonian Instn., Columbia River Basin Surveys, 1949, Missouri River Basin Surveys, 1950; practice chiropractic specializing in nutrition, Elkhart, Ind., 1959—; mem. Gonstead Chiropractic Seminars, Mt. Horeb, Wis.; program chmn. Edgar Cayce Found. Chiropractic Div. Seminars, 1975-76. Active Boy Scouts Am. Served with CIA, AUS, 1954-55. Recipient Merit award Am. Coll. Chiropractic, 1971, Chiropractor of Yr. award, 1971; Eagle Scout award Boy Scouts Am., also God and Country award. Mem. Am., Ind. State (dist. dir. N.W. dist. 1975-78) chiropractic assns., Nat. Coll. Chiropractic Alumni Assn., Spiritual Frontiers Fellowship, Liberty Lobby, Parker Chiropractic Research Group, Laubach's Congress on Research for Chiropractors, Nat. Health Fedn. (life), Assn. for Research and Enlightenment, Am. Badminton Assn., others. Clubs: Century Nat. Coll. Chiropractic, Elkhart Racquet. Home: 25909 Lake Dr Elkhart IN 46514 Office: 23888 E US 33 Elkhart IN 46514

DENNER, MELVIN WALTER, educator; b. North Washington, Iowa, Aug. 27, 1933; s. Norbert William and Petronella Nettie (Eischeid) D.; B.S. (NSF fellow), Upper Iowa U., 1961; M.S., U. Ky., 1963; Ph.D., Iowa State U., 1968; m. N. Anne Greer, June 19, 1966; children—Mark Andrew and Michael Alan (twins). Asst. prof. life scis. Ind. State U., Evansville, 1968-71, chmn. dept., 1969—, asso. chmn. div. scis. and math., 1975—, asso. prof., 1971-76, prof., 1976—, acting chmn. div. scis. and math., 1976-77. Vice chmn. Iowa Young Democrats, 1958-60. Bd. dirs. Evansville Zool. Soc., Campus Ministry and Allied Health Programs. Served with USNR, 1953-57. NIH fellow, 1966-67; Alumni Achievement fellow, 1967-68. Mem. Internat. Soc. Invertebrate Pathology (founding), Am. Soc. Parasitologists, Am. Micros. Soc., A.A.A.S. (film critic), Am. Inst. Biol. Sci., Sigma Xi, Sigma Zeta. Contbr. articles to profl. jours. Home: 100 S Peerless Evansville IN 47712 Office: Dept Life Scis Ind State U Evansville Evansville IN 47712

DENNEY, ARTHUR HUGH, educator; b. Rosendale, Mo., Sept. 25, 1916; s. Frank M. and Cora L. (Beatie) D.; B.S., U. Mo., 1938, M.A. Econs., 1950; Diploma in Community Devel., U. London, 1969; m. A. Ilene Tucker, Aug. 5, 1939; children—Charles Hugh, Jo Ann (Mrs. Raymond Fisher). Technician, U.S. Forest Service, Mo., 1938; state coordinator Mo. Conservation Commn., Jefferson City, 1938-44; recreation dir. Mo. Dept. Resources and Devel., Jefferson City, 1944-45, dir. 1945-48; owner, operator Blue Springs (Mo.) Lodge Resort, 1948-50, 54-57; adminstrv. asst. McDonald Aircraft, St. Louis, 1950-54; instr. regional and community affairs U. Mo., Columbia, 1958-67, asso. prof., 1967-70, prof., 1970—, chmn. dept., 1968, 73-75. Cons., USDA, U.S. Dept. Labor, U.S. Dept. Commerce, Purdue U., U. Ark., Govt. of Indonesia. Chmn. civic improvement com. Columbia Indsl. Commn., 1966-68; chmn. Greater Columbia Planning Com., 1960-62. Danforth fellow, 1937. Mem. Community Devel. Soc. N. Am. (dir. 1973—, pres. 1976-77), A.A.A.S., World Futures Soc., Nat. Univ. Ext. Assn. (adminstrv. bd. 1975—), Alpha Gamma Rho, Alpha Zeta. Mason. Author: Decongesting Metropolitan America, 1972. Contbr. articles to profl. jours. Home: 208 Westridge Columbia MO 65201

DENNING, BERNADINE NEWSOM (MRS. BLAINE DENNING), ednl. adminstr.; b. Detroit, Aug. 17. 1930; d. William Charles and Evelyn Tyler (Pembrook) Newsom; B.S. (Faculty Women's scholar, Joseph Doyle scholar, State Bd. Edn. scholar), Eastern Mich. U., 1951; M.Ed., Wayne State U., 1956, Edn. Specialist, 1966, Ed.D., 1970; m. Blaine Denning, Aug. 26, 1956. Tchr., Jefferson Jr. High Sch., Detroit, 1951-59; coordinator Great Cities Sch. Improvement Project, 1959-62; counselor Winship Jr. High Sch., Detroit, 1962-65; intercultural coordinator Detroit pub. schs., 1965-68; asst. dir. Parent-Tchr.-Student Activities, Detroit, 1968-72; dir. Dept. Sch. Vols., Detroit pub. schs., 1971, Title IV Civil Rights Office, 1977—; dir. urban program in edn. U. Mich., Ann Arbor, 1971, dir. spl. studies and projects Sch. Edn., 1972—. Instr. swimming Wayne County chpt. A.R.C., 1947—; asst. dir. Christmas Seal Camp, Chelsea, Mich., 1952-64, Burt R. Shurly Camp, Chelsea, 1964-66; membership chmn. Met. Detroit, YWCA, 1968-69, salute to youth chmn., 1969, chmn. bd. mgmt., 1970-73, mem. met. bd., 1970-73, nat. bd. dirs., chmn. health and environment, 1973; v.p. YWCA of U.S.A., Mich. Women's Commn.; vice chmn. Central dist. Camp Fire Girls, Detroit, 1968-72; chmn. fashion extravaganza March of Dimes, Wayne County, 1972-73; mem. Detroit Library Commn.; chmn. Detroit div. United Community Services. Bd. dirs. Detroit council Camp Fire Girls, 1968—; mem. alumni bd. Wayne State U., 1970—; bd. dirs. Delta Home for Girls, Detroit, 1971-73, Homes for Black Children, Detroit, 1973. Recipient Nat. Found. award, 1972, 73; Charlotte Farnsworth award Campfire Girls, 1972; March of Dimes, 1972; named Woman of Year, Zeta Phi Beta, 1975, Iota Phi Lambda, 1975. Mem. AAUW, (chpt. dir. 1969-70), Assn. Supervision and Curriculum Devel., Am. Edn. Research Assn., Detroit Women Sch. Adminstrs., Met. Edn. and Cultural Activities Assn., Met. Detroit Soc. Black Ednl. Adminstrs. (dir. 1968-73), Mich. Assn. Supervision and Curriculum Devel. (sec. 1970-71), Nat. Assn. Intergroup Relations Ofcls., Nat. Council Negro Women, NAACP (life), Nat. Soc. for Study Edn., Nat. Community Sch. Edn. Assn., Orgn. Suprs. and Adminstrs., Nat. Sch. Pub. Relations Assn., Nat. Conf. Social Welfare, Delta Kappa Gamma, Beta Sigma Phi, Delta Sigma Theta. Clubs: Health and Phys. Edn., Women's Econ. (Detroit); Faculty Women's (U. Mich.). Home: 3309 Leslie St Detroit MI 48238 Office: 453 Myrtle St Detroit MI 48201

DENNIS, DAVID STUART, dentist; b. Oak Park, Ill., Aug. 9, 1939; s. Dwight Louis and Pauline Gertrude (O'Brien) D.; A.B., Ind. U., 1969, D.D.S., 1972, resident oral medicine, 1972-74; m. Cherri Lynne Federle, Nov. 30, 1968; children—Katherine Corrine, David Ben, Ryan Ben. Research asst. Ind. U., 1968-72, clin. instr., 1972-74, research asso., 1972-74; pvt. practice clin. dentistry, research oral health H.J. Limp Clinic, Kentland, Ind., 1974—. Sec. Kentland Bd. Aviation Commrs., 1975—. Served with USAF, 1960-65. Decorated D.F.C., Air medal with oak leaf cluster. Mem. Am. Dental Assn., Internat. Assn. Dental Research, Aerospace Med. Assn., A.A.A.S. Roman Catholic. Research on human saliva and immunology as related to periodontal disease, human pulpal response to exptl. material. Home: 210 E Washington St Kentland IN 47951 Office: Box 127 H J Limp Clinic Kentland IN 47951

DENNIS, LUCILLE, artist; b. Terre Haute, Ind., Feb. 10, 1910; d. Max and Anna (Shatsky) Shower; Ph.B., U. Chgo., 1931; diploma Chgo. Acad. Fine Arts, 1932; m. Albert Dennis, Feb. 17, 1946; 1 dau., Martha Lynn. Designer, Edson Novelty Co., Chgo., 1933-40; exhibited in one-person shows Rose-Hulman Inst., Terre Haute, Ind., Ind. State U., Terre Haute, 1945; group shows Hoosier Salon, Indpls., Ind. Artists Club, Inc., Indpls., Evansville Tri-State, 1977, Sheldon Swope Art Gallery, many others; represented in permanent collections including Ind. U., Bloomington. Bd. dirs. Y-Teen Activities, YWCA, 1966-67. Recipient E. Kirk McKinney merit award Hoosier salon, Indpls., 1967, Psi Iota Purchase award, 1971. Mem. Ind. Artists Club, Nat. Lit. Soc., Fedn. Jewish Women, Hoosier Salon Patron's Assn., U. Chgo. Alumni Assn. (life). Home: 710 S 8th St Terre Haute IN 47807

DENNIS, RALPH EMERSON, JR., lawyer; b. Marion, Ind., Dec. 19, 1925; s. Ralph Emerson and Martha (Bahr) D.; A.B., Dartmouth Coll., 1946; J.D., Ind. U., 1950; m. Virginia Lea Harter, June 19, 1949; children—Nancy (Mrs. William Barefoot), Kathleen, Amel, Mary, Ralph III. Admitted to Ind. bar, 1950; since practiced in Muncie; partner firm Dennis, Cross, Raisor, Jordan & Marshall and predecessor firms, 1956—. Dir., sec. Lift-A-Loft Corp, Muncie, Creviston Steel Co., Inc., Muncie; judge city ct., Muncie, 1950-59; atty. City Muncie, 1964-67. Mem. Muncie Community Sch. Bd., 1960-63. Served with USNR, 1944-46. Recipient distinguished service award Jr. C. of C., 1960, good govt. award, 1960. Mason, Elk; mem. Blue Lodge. Home: 411 Wildwood Ln Muncie IN 47303 Office: 200 E Washington St Muncie IN 47305

DENNISON, KUMPOL, surgeon; b. Pattani, Thailand, Feb. 20, 1939; s. Kamol and Payom (Poonsombat) Dhanasene; came to U.S., 1966, naturalized, 1976; M.D., U. Med. Sci., Bangkok, Thailand, 1963; m. Lourdes G. Madayag, Feb. 16, 1967; children—Paul, Marissa, Gary. Intern, Grace Hosp., Detroit, 1966-67, resident in gen. surgery, 1967-71; fellow in cardiovascular surgery William Beaumont Hosp., Royal Oak, Mich., 1971-72; practice medicine specializing in surgery, Merrillville, Ind., 1972—. Fellow A.C.S.; mem. Ind. State, Lake County med. socs. Buddhist. Club: Youche Country. Home: 12603 Van Buren St Crown Point IN 46307 Office: 8695 Connecticut St Suite D Merrillville IN 46410

DENNY, FREDERICK GAIL, stone co. exec.; b. Harrisburg, Ill., Mar. 22, 1940; s. James Gail and Nell M (Nagle) D.; student So. Ill. U., 1957; m. Sherra Lynn Geltosky, Dec. 12, 1959; children—Jeffery Gail, Frederick Brett. Operator Fred Denny Trucking Co., Harrisburg, 1958-68; partner Denny & Church Excavating Co., 1967—; sec.-treas. Gail Denny Trucking Co., Inc., Harrisburg, 1970—, Denny & Simpson Stone Co., Inc., 1960—; partner Colonial Devel. Co., 1971—; chmn. bd. Colonial Recreation and Mobil Home Sales, Inc., Harrisburg, 1972-76; pres. D and S Coal Co. Inc., Madisonville, Ky., 1976—; pres. Tri-Lakes Investment, Inc., 1973—; v.p. Horses Unltd. mag., 1973-74; dir. Hardin County Materials, Inc., 1973—. Pres. Egyptian Truck Owners Assn., 1970. Elk. Home: 10 Dogwood Pl Harrisburg IL 62946 Office: Rural Route 2 Harrisburg IL 62946

DENOYER, ARSENE J., community relations exec.; b. Limestone Twp., Kankakee County, Ill., Dec. 21, 1904; s. Arsene and Julia (Clark) D.; student parochial schs. of Kankakee and Bourbonnais, Ill. Field dir. Am. Nat. Red Cross, 1943-48; sales United Educators, Inc., 1932-42, community relations, 1948-63, asst. treas., community relations director, 1963—; asst. treas. Book House for Children, 1963—. Cons. Carmel High Schs. Exec. bd. Nat. Conf. Christians and Jews. Served as 1st sgt. USAAF, 1942-43. Mem. Am. C. of C. Execs., Am. Legion, D.A.V., Am. C. of C., Ill. Assn. C. of C. Execs., Chgo. Pubs. Assn., Milw., Chgo. (govtl. affairs com.), assns. commerce and industry, Waukegan-Lake County C. of C. (nat. affairs com.), Chgo. Pubs. Assn. (chmn. reference book sect.). Club: Swedish Glee (Waukegan). Home: 805 Baldwin Ave Waukegan IL 60085 Office: 801 Green Bay Rd Lake Bluff IL 60044

DENSER, CLARENCE HUGH, JR., pathologist; b. Chillicothe, Ohio, Feb. 27, 1927; s. Clarence Hugh and Clara (Mider) D.; B.S., Millsaps Coll., 1947; M.D., Tulane U., 1948. Intern, Charity Hosp. La., New Orleans, 1948-49, resident in pathology, 1949-53; pathologist Armed Forces Inst. Pathology, Washington, 1954-55; practice medicine specializing in pathology, Clin. Pathology Lab., Des Moines, 1957—; Served with M.C., USAF, 1955-57. Mem. Coll. Am. Pathologists, Am. Soc. Clin. Pathologists, AMA, Am. Acad. Forensic Scis., Am. Soc. Cytology, Am. Pub. Health Assn., Am. Cancer Soc. (pres. Iowa div. 1976-78), Iowa Assn. Blood Banks (pres. 1968), Iowa Assn. Pathologists (sec.-treas. 1964-68), Iowa Acad. Sci., Iowa, Polk County med. socs., Alpha Omega Alpha. Club: Des Moines. Address: 1073 5th St Des Moines IA 50314

DENSLOW, JOHN STEDMAN, osteopath; b. Hartford, Conn., Dec. 19, 1906; s. George H. and Maud (Stedman) D.; D.O., Kirksville (Mo.) Coll., 1929; D.Sc. (hon.), Chgo. Coll. Osteopathy, 1941; m. Mary Jane Laughlin, Aug. 22, 1934; children—Martha, George, Peter. Asst. dir. clinic, Chgo. Coll. Osteopathy, 1930-32, dir. clinic, 1932-38; prof. osteo. technic, Kirksville Coll. Osteopathy and Surgery, 1938—, chmn. dept. osteo. technic., dir. research affairs, 1938-65, v.p., 1965—; dir. Still Meml. Research Trust. Chmn. Mo. State Bd. Health. Cons. USPHS Nat. Health Survey; vice chmn. project rev. com. Mo. Reg. Med. Program. Mem. Gov.'s Adv. Council for Comprehensive Health Planning. Project dir. N.E, Mo. Coop. Stroke Pilot Project. Mem. Am. Physiol. soc., Am. Assn. Colls. Osteopathic Medicine (vice chmn.), Am. Osteopathic Assn., Mo. Assn. Osteopathic Physicians and Surgeons, New York Academy of Science. Episcopalian (warden). Club: Rotary. Home: Thousand Hills Farm Kirksville MO 63501 Office: 704 W Jefferson St Kirksville MO 63501

DENTON, JOHN CHARLES, chem. co. exec.; b. Sapulpa, Okla., June 16, 1919; s. Joseph Olney and Alice Carroll (McCray) D.; B.S., U. Tulsa, 1941; m. Bobette Joan Holm, Sept. 20, 1941; children—Barba Joan Denton Wahl, Cynthia Susan Denton Smith. Engring. trainee, Gulf Oil Corp., 1941-42; shift foreman to v.p. div. Spencer Chem. Co., Pittsburg, Kans., 1942-57; pres. Spencer Chem. Co., Kansas City, Mo., 1957-60; pres. Spencer Chem. div. Gulf Oil Corp., Kansas City, 1963-65; pres., chief exec. officer Chemplex Co., Rolling Meadows, Ill., 1966—; dir. Palatine Nat. Bank (Ill.). Acting pres. Village of Barrington Hills, 1975-77; Mem. Nat. Soc. Profl. Engrs., Kans. Engring. Soc. Clubs: Kansas City, Barrington Hills Country; Meadow (bd. govs.); Oak Hills Country (San Antonio), Carlton (Chgo.),; Missionm Hills Country (Shawnee Mission, Kans.); River (Kansas City); Clinton Country (Iowa). Home: 251 Steeplechase Rd Barrington Hills IL 60010 Office: 3100 Golf Rd Rolling Meadows IL 60008

DENTON, LIONEL ARTHUR, electronics co. exec.; b. Columbus, Ohio, Dec. 1, 1922; s. Arthur Samuel and Florence Nathalia (Harrington) D.; B.S., Ohio State U., 1948; m. Frances Louise Vaughan, Apr. 7, 1943. Sec.-treas. Ohio Semiconductors, Inc., Columbus, 1956-62; pres., Halmar Electronics, Inc., Columbus, 1962—; dir. Ohio Semitronics, Inc., Columbus. Vice chmn. United Way Franklin County, 1973. Bd. dirs. Multiple Sclerosis Soc. Franklin County; treas., trustee Mercy Hosp., Columbus; exec. bd. Central Ohio council Boy Scouts Am.; adv. council Columbus dist. SBA. Served with USAF, 1943-45. Mem. N.A.M., Ohio Mfrs. Assn., Newcomen Soc. N.Am., Columbus Indsl. Assn. (pres. 1973-74), Columbus C. of C., Ohio State U. Assn., Delta Sigma Pi. Presbyn. Rotarian. Home: 1071 Sunbury Rd Columbus OH 43219 Office: 1544 W Mound St Columbus OH 43223

DENTON, RAY DOUGLAS, ins. co. exec.; b. Lake City, Ark., May 16, 1937; s. Ray Dudney and Edna Lorraine (Roe) D.; B.A., U. Mich., 1964, postgrad., 1969-70; J.D., Wayne State U., 1969, postgrad., 1964-65; m. Cheryl Emma Borchardt, Mar. 9, 1964; children—Ray D., Derek St. Clair, Carter Lee. Claims rep. Hartford Ins. Co., Crum & Forster, Detroit, and Am. Claims, Chgo., 1962-73; partner Chgo. Metro Claims, Oak Park, Ill., 1974-75; founder, pres. Ray D. Denton & Assos., Hinsdale, Ill., 1975—. Mem. Pi Kappa Alpha, Phi Alpha Delta. Home: 413 W Haven St New Lenox IL 60451 Office: 120 E Ogden St Hinsdale IL 60521

DENZER, HAROLD FREMONT, JR., financial exec.; b. Marion, Ohio, Dec. 22, 1919; s. Harold F. and Hannah Bernice (Manahan) D.; B.A., Ohio Wesleyan U., 1941; student Pitts. Inst. Mortuary Sci., 1948-49; B.Mus., Capital U., 1963. Sec.-treas. Denzer Funeral Home, Inc., Marion, 1944-75, Denzer Co., Marion, 1975—. Pipe organ tchr.; organist First Presbyn. Ch., Marion, 1966—. Served with AUS, 1941-43. Mem. Am. Legion, Presbyn. Assn. Musicians, Am. Guild Organists, Am. Theater Organ Soc., Aircraft Owners and Pilots Assn., DAV, Am. Fedn. Musicians, Beta Theta Pi, Phi Mu Alpha. Lutheran. Mason (Shriner), K.T., Elk, Odd Fellow, Order Eastern Star, Lion. Clubs: Marion Country; Univ. (Columbus, Ohio). Home: 760 Leetonia Circle Marion OH 43302 Office: 360 E Center St Marion OH 43302

DEPAPE, ALBERT DESIRE, pediatrician; b. Bruxelles, Man., Can., Aug. 19, 1918; s. August Edward and Augusta (Lombaert) DeP.; B.A., U. Man., 1942; M.D., 1948; postgrad. McGill U., 1950-52, Harvard, 1953; m. Mary Elizabeth Peters, July 22, 1953; children—Joanne, Wanda, Brent, Carla, Darcy, Trevor. Intern St. Boniface Gen. Hosp., Winnipeg, 1947-48, resident, 1948-50, head dept. pediatrics and pediatric pathology, 1955-71, head dept. pediatric pathology, 1972—; resident Children's Meml. Hosp., Montreal, 1950-52, Children's Med. Center, Boston, 1953; practice medicine specializing in pediatrics, Winnipeg, 1954—; asso. prof. pediatrics U. Man., 1970—. Dir. Kenaston Holding Co., Winnipeg. Pres. Amateur Swimming Assn. Man., 1970-71, Canadian Amateur Swimming Assn., 1972-74; mem. sports med. com. Fedn. Internationale De Natation Amateur Internat., 1972-76, sec., 1976—, chmn. aquatic drug control 1976 Olympics; chmn. sports medicine com. Amateur Swimming Unions of Ams., 1971—. Fellow Royal Coll. Physicians and Surgeons Can. K.C. Club: Winnipeg Winter (dir. 1969-71). Home: 128 Lawndale Ave Winnipeg MB R2H 1T3 Canada Office: St Boniface Gen Hospital Winnipeg MB R2H 2A6 Canada

DEPEW, EDDIE GERALD, chem. co. exec.; b. East Bernstadt, Ky., Aug. 13, 1940; s. Charles Hughes and Nannie Kathleen (Hibbard) D.; B. Indsl. Engring., Gen. Motors Inst., 1963; M.B.A., Miami U., Oxford, Ohio, 1967; m. Carolyn Lee Stoppiello, May 16, 1964; children—Dawn Annette, Deena Marie. Process engr., methods engr. Delco Moraine div. Gen. Motors Corp., Dayton, Ohio, 1958-67; indsl. engr. Monsanto Research Corp., Miamisburg, Ohio, 1967-71, data processing sr. systems analyst, 1971-75, applications devel. mgr., 1975—; mgr. industries group, applications systems div. Guide Internat. Corp., Chgo., 1977—. Mem. Am. Production Inventory Control Soc. Republican. Home: 1302 McGuire St E Miamisburg OH 45342 Office: PO Box 32 Miamisburg OH 45342

DEPEW, FRANK SMITH, mfg. co. exec.; b. Palmerton, Pa., Oct. 27, 1931; s. Harlan Armstrong and Mary Louis (Gardner) D.; student Earlham Coll., 1949-50; B.S., U. Mo., 1954, M.B.A., 1955; m. Beverly Jean Church, Aug. 8, 1953; children—Jeff, Jill, Jana, Julie. Sales engr. Doane Agrl. Service, St. Louis, 1954-60, div. mgr., 1960-63; mgr. mktg. research, Massey Ferguson Co., Toronto, Ont., Can., 1963-66, mktg. mgr., Des Moines, 1966-69; v.p. mktg. subs. W.R. Grace Co., Buffalo, N.Y., 1969-71; with Hesston (Kans.) Corp., 1972-76, v.p., gen. mgr. agr. products group, 1976; exec. v.p. Jacobsen Mfg. Co., Racine, Wis., 1976, pres., 1977—. Served to 1st lt. AUS, 1955-57. Mem. Am. Mktg. Assn., Am. Mgmt. Assn., Phi Gamma Delta. Presbyterian. Club: Kiwanis. Home: 507 Cambridge St Lake Bluff IL 60044 Office: 1721 Packard Ave Racine WI 53403

DEPREE, MAX O., furniture mfg. co. exec.; b. Zeeland, Mich., Oct. 28, 1924; s. Dirk J. and Nellie (Miller) DeP.; student Wheaton Coll. (Ill.), 1942-43, Sorbonne, U. Paris (France), 1945, Hope Coll. (Holland, Mich.), 1946-47; m. Esther Mae Kaat, Dec. 6, 1946; children—Jody Ann, Charles, Nancy, Kris. With Miller Herman Inc. and subsidiary cos., various locations, 1947—, exec. v.p. internat. operations, 1968-71, chmn. bd., 1971—, also mem. exec. com., 1962—. Trustee Fuller Theol. Sem., Pasadena, Calif. Served with AUS, 1943-46. Home: 2967 Lakeshore Holland MI 49423 Office: 8500 Byron Rd Zeeland MI 49464

DEPRIT, ANDRE ALBERT, educator; b. St. Servais, Belgium, Apr. 10, 1926; s. Max Francois and Anne-Marie Caroline (Vasse) D.; L.Ph., U. Louvain (Belgium), 1948, L.Sc., 1953, D.Sc., 1957; m. Andree Jeanne Bartholome, Sept. 5, 1959; 1 son, Etienne. Came to U.S., 1964, naturalized, 1974. Sr. research asso. Nat. Bur. Standards, Gaithersburg, Md., 1977—; asso. prof. U. Kinshassa (Zaire), 1957-59, U. Louvain, 1957-61, prof., 1961-64; staff mem. Boeing Sci. Research Labs., Seattle, 1964-71; sr. research fellow NASA, Greenbelt, Md., 1971-72; prof. U. Cin., 1972-77; cons. Charles Stark Draper Lab., Cambridge, Mass., 1977—, Naval Research Lab., Washington, 1976—, Nat. Bur. Standards, Boulder, Colo., 1974—; vis. prof. U. Wis., Madison, 1975, Yale U., New Haven, 1965-66, U. Liege, Belgium, 1970; vis. lectr. U. Wash., Seattle, 1965-66; resident visitor Bell Telephone Labs., 1968. Recipient Nat. Acad. Scis. Watson medal, 1972; Royal Acad. Scis. (Belgium) Agathon De Potter prize, 1957, Wettrems Prize, 1971. NATO fellow, 1963; Nat. Acad. Sci., NRC fellow, 1971-72. Mem. Internat. Astron. Union, Am., Royal astron. socs., Am. Inst. Aeros. and Astronautics, AAAS, Sigma Xi. Editor Celestial Mechanics, 1969-73. Contbr. articles to profl. jours. Home: 7475 Demar Rd Cincinnati OH 45243 Office: Dept Math Scis U Cin Cincinnati OH 45221

DERGE, DAVID RICHARD, educator; b. Kansas City, Mo., Oct. 10, 1928; s. David Richard and Blanche (Butterfield) D.; A.B., U. Mo., 1949; A.M., Northwestern U., 1951, Ph.D., 1955; LL.D., Hanyang (Korea) U., 1973; m. Elizabeth Anne Greene, Sept. 4, 1951 (dec. Mar. 1970); children—David Richard III, Dorothy Anne; m. 2d, Patricia Jean Williams, Sept. 2, 1972; children—William David, Mary Jennifer. Instr. U. Mo., 1954-56, Northwestern U., summer 1955; asst. prof. polit. sci. Ind. U., Bloomington, 1956-60, asso. prof., 1960-65, prof., 1965-72, also acad. coordinator Peace Corps Tng. Programs, asso. dean Grad. Sch., 1965-67, asso. dean of faculties, 1967-69, exec. v.p., dean adminstrn., 1969-72, dir. bur. instl. research, 1968-70; pres. So. Ill. U., Carbondale, 1972-74, prof. polit. sci., 1974—, prof. Sch. Tech. Careers, 1977—. Pres. Behavioral Research Assos.; sec., dir. Midwest Univ. Consortium for Internat. Activities, Inc., 1967; mem. U.S. Adv. Commn. on Internat. Edn. and Cultural Affairs; cons. Exec. Office of Pres., White House, 1970-72, HEW, 1971-72. Mem. Bloomington City Council, 1964-67. Served with AUS, 1944-48, USNR, 1952-73; comdr. Res. ret. Grantee Social Sci. Research Council, 1957, Eagleton Inst. Practical Politics, 1959, Citizenship Clearing House, 1961; Sigma Delta Chi Distinguished Teaching award Ind. U., 1963; Weatherly Distinguished Teaching award Ind. U., 1964; named Outstanding Young Man Ind., Ind. Jr. C. of C., 1963. Mem. Am. Polit. Sci. Assn., U.S. Naval Inst., Phi Beta Kappa, Pi Sigma Alpha, Alpha Pi Zeta, Kappa Sigma. Club: Bloomington Squash Racquets; La Table Six. Author numerous books and articles on govt. Home: Route 1 Spring Arbor Lake Carbondale IL 62901

DERIJK, WALDEMAR GERARDUS, dental researcher; b. Venlo, The Netherlands, Mar. 5, 1945; s. Joseph Franciscus and Anna Catherina (Verhezen) DeR.; came to U.S., 1968; m. Marilyn Frances Bohling, July 26, 1974; children—Julie-Jo, Daisun-Elrond. B.A., U. Amsterdam, 1968; M.S., U. Nebr., 1970, Ph.D., 1974, D.D.S., 1977. Research asst. Behlen Lab. Physics, Lincoln, Nebr., 1968-74; research asso. Coll. Dentistry U. Nebr., Lincoln, 1974-77; with Boyne Sch. Dental Medicine Creighton U., Omaha, 1977—. NSF grantee, 1968-74. Mem. Internat. Assn. Dental Research (recipient Edward H. Hatton award 1976), Am. Phys. Soc., Internat. Assn. Dental Research, AAAS. Research in testing dental silver analgems using a laser. Home: 2444 N 74th St Lincoln NE 68507 Office: Boyne Sch Dental Medicine Creighton U Omaha NE 68131

DERJANECZ, JANOS JOHN, surgeon; b. Peterhida, Hungry, Dec. 11, 1927; s. Derjanecz and Gerdelus (Margit) D.; came to Can., 1960, naturalized, 1966; M.D. (hon.) U. Pecs; m. Brenda Bellamy, Feb. 1st. 1963; children—Anna, Catherine Suzanne. Intern, St. George Hosp., 1953-54; resident, Eng. and Can., 1959-63; practice gen. surgery; mem. staff Stvenson Meml. Hosp. Alliston, Ont., Can., 1966—; demonstrator Inst. Physiology U. Pecs, 1950-54. Fellow Internat. Coll. Surgeons. Diplomate Internat. Bd. Proctology. Mem. Can., Ont. med. assns. Roman Catholic. Author numerous publs. in field. Home: 142 Victoria St W Alliston ON Canada Office: 146 Victoria St W Alliston ON Canada

DERMOTT, JON ALAN, lawyer; b. Lamar, Mo., Jan. 19, 1938; s. Charles Elgin and Marjorie Fra (Washburn) D.; J.D., U. Ark., 1963; m. Courtney Ann Stevens, Jan. 26, 1963; children—Lyter, Sharrock, Seth. Admitted to Ark. bar, 1963, Tex. bar, 1964, Mo. bar, 1967; landman Texaco Inc., Dallas, 1963-64; atty. So. Union Gas Co., 1964-65; asso. firm Wright, Lindsey & Jennings, Little Rock, 1965-67; mem. firm Blanchard, Van Fleet, Martin, Robertson & Dermott, Joplin, Mo., 1967—. Bd. dirs. Arthur H. Barnett Meml. Kiwanis Found., Freeman Hosp., Joplin; bd. dirs. Joplin United Fund, 1967-75, pres., 1974; bd. dirs. Joplin YMCA, 1976—. Served with USMCR, 1955-63. Mem. Am., Ark., Tex. bar assns., Mo. Bar, Mo. Young Lawyers Sect. Council, Sigma Nu, Delta Theta Phi, Blue Key. Episcopalian. Kiwanian (pres. 1976, bd. dirs. 1968—). Home: 634 Jaccard Pl Joplin MO 64801 Office: 502 Pearl St Joplin MO 64801

DERNER, CAROL ANN NIEDHAMMER (MRS. GEORGE B. DERNER), librarian; b. Evansville, Ind., May 12, 1934; d. Jacob Christopher and Catherine Loretta (Grant) Niedhammer; B.A. in Am. Lit., Ind. U., 1956, M.A. in Library Sci., 1958; m. George B. Derner, May 4, 1957. Bookmobile librarian Gary (Ind.) Pub. Library, 1956-57, young adult librarian, head popular library, head extension dept., 1963-67; children's librarian Bloomington (Ind.) Pub. Library, 1958-59, Pub. Libraries Lake County, Ind., 1959-60; high sch. librarian Valparaiso (Ind.), 1960-63, then librarian Gary Pub. Library; head librarian Elmwood Park (Ill.) Pub. Library, 1968-76; asst. dir. Lake County Pub. Library, Merrillville, Ind., 1976—. Pres., YWCA, Gary, 1966-67; bd. dirs. League Women Voters, Elmwood Park, 1970-76. Mem. Am., Ill. (sec. pub. library sect. 1973-74), Ind. library assns., Library Adminstrs. Conf. No. Ill. (sec. 1971-72). Club: Altrusa of No. Cook (dir. 1975-76). Home: 6871 Fillmore Dr Merrillville IN 46410 Office: 1919 W Lincoln Hwy Merrillville IN 46410

DEROSA, ANTHONY SALVATORE, restaurant chain exec.; b. Chgo., Jan. 1, 1928; s. Salvatore and Margherita (Sanmarco) DeR.; grad. high sch.; m. Gloria Jean Garapolo, Jan. 28, 1967; children—Salvatore, Anthony, Ross. Asst. supt. Globe Auto Glass, 1951-53; sales mgr. Bunge Bros. Fuel Co., 1955-59; supr. Amfood Industries, Inc. (formerly Henry's Drive-In, Inc.), 1959-60, v.p., 1960-68, exec. v.p., 1968—, pres., 1970, chmn bd., 1972—. Served with USNR, 1945-46. Mem. Nat. Assn. Rev. Appraisers, Am. Assn. Certified Appraisers. Inventor ventilating system. Home: 2617 Knob Hill Rd McHenry IL 60050 Office: 505 W Algonquin Rd Arlington Heights IL 60005

DE ROSSET, ARMAND JOHN, chemist, oil products co. exec.; b. N.Y.C., Jan. 10, 1915; s. William Green and Ruth Haseltine (Dame) deR.; B.S., Lafayette Coll., 1936; Ph.D. in Chemistry, U. Wis., 1939; m. Ruth Wilson Bailey, Sept. 2, 1939; children—Gabrielle Marguerite, William Steinle, James Bailey, Marie Victoire, Richard Dame. Research chemist Universal Oil Products Co. (name changed to UOP Inc. 1975), Des Plaines, Ill., 1939-42, 46-58, research coordinator, 1958-64, asst. research dir., 1964-75, dir. separations research, 1975—. Pres. Clarendon Blackhawk Mosquito Abatement Dist., DuPage County, Ill., 1969—; park commr. Village of Clarendon Hills (Ill.), 1975—. Served with Chem. Corps USAAF, 1942-46; Col. res. Ret. Mem. Am. Chem. Soc., Newcomen Soc. N.Am., Chgo. Catalysis Club, Chgo. Physics Club (sec. 1970—). Democrat. Episcopalian. Club: Cosmos (Washington). Contbr. numerous articles on petroleum refining and petrochemistry to profl. jours.; patentee in field. Home: 270 Holmes Ave Clarendon Hills IL 60514 Office: Ten UOP Plaza Des Plaines IL 60016

DERR, GILBERT SIMS, ednl. adminstr.; b. Gastonia, N.C., Apr. 22, 1917; s. Gilbert Cornelius and Iva Beatrice (Sims) D.; B.S., Hampton Inst., 1939; M.A., DePaul U., 1948, Spl. Edn., 1961; Ed.D., U. Sarasota, 1976; m. Verrona Williams, Mar. 31, 1945. Tchr., Nat. Youth Adminstrn., Forsyth, Ga., 1939, Durham (N.C.) City Schs., 1941-42, 46-47; tchr., adminstr. Bur. Socially Maladjusted Children, Chgo. Pub. Schs., 1948—. Lectr., DePaul U., 1969—. Pres., Central Southside Community Workers, 1968; co-chmn. Dusable Heritage Com., 1966; mem. Ill. Sesquicentennial Commn., 1968. Trustee, pres. Henry Booth House, 1969. Served with USNR, 1942-46. Recipient Alumni award DePaul U., 1972, Forensic award Delta Sigma Rho-Tau Kappa Alpha, 1966, Service to Youth award YMCA, 1955, Civic award Ickes Prairie Archer Cts. Action Com., 1969, award Ill. Hist. Soc., 1969, award Phi Beta Sigma, 1966. Mem. Ill. Hist. Soc. (v.p. 1970), Kappa Delta Pi. Home: 7654 Calumet St Chicago IL 60619 Office: 228 N LaSalle St Chicago IL 60601

DERR, RICHARD LUTHER, educator; b. Hughesville, Pa., Dec. 27, 1930; s. Luther and Nora (Hanlon) D.; B.S., State U. N.Y. at Brockport, 1951; M.Ed., U. Ill., 1955, Ed.D., 1959; m. Evelyn Frances Musielak, Apr. 11, 1953; children—Stephanie, Christopher. Elementary sch. tchr., Niagara Falls, N.Y., 1951, St. Louis, 1957-59; asst. prof. Western Reserve U., Cleve., 1959-65, asso. prof. Case Western Reserve U., Cleve., 1966-75, prof., 1975—, acting chmn. dept. edn., 1977-78; cons. curriculum and philosophy sch. dists. Served with U.S. Army, 1951-53. Mem. Am. Ednl. Research Assn., Philosophy Edn. Soc., Am. Ednl. Studies Assn. Roman Catholic. Author: A Taxonomy of Social Purposes of Public Schools: A Handbook 1973; contbr. articles in edn. to profl. jours. Home: 4280 Lander Rd Orange Village OH 44022 Office: 2040 Adelbert Rd Cleveland OH 44106

DERRY, CHARLES DALE, TV exec.; b. Detroit, Dec. 13, 1941; s. Charles Louis and Samuella Stanley (Dale) D.; B.A., U. Detroit, 1965; postgrad. Wayne State U., 1966-67; m. Patricia Ann Sitek, Aug. 8, 1969. Chief photographer, producer, dir. U. Detroit TV Centre, 1961-65; engr. WXYZ-TV, Detroit, 1964, stage mgr., 1968—; asso. dir. audio visual communication U. Detroit Sch. Dentistry, 1965-66; engr. WKBD-TV, Detroit, 1966-68. Freelance dir., producer, photographer; TV cons., instr. Madonna Coll., 1970—. Mem. Dirs. Guild Am., Profl. Photographers Am., Indsl. Photographers Mich., Nat. Press Photographers Assn., Soc. Motion Picture and TV Engrs., AAUP, Detroit Puppeteers Guild, Dexter Hist. Soc., Alpha Epsilon Rho. Roman Catholic. Home: 8660 Merkel Rd Dexter MI 48130 Office: 20777 W Ten Mile Rd Southfield MI 48075

DERWINSKI, DENNIS ANTHONY, dentist; b. Chgo., Oct. 18, 1941; s. Anthony Joseph and Julia Donata (Pochron) D.; D.D.S., Marquette U., 1965; m. Mary Pamela Butler, Feb. 11, 1964 (div. Dec. 8, 1975); children—Julie Elizabeth, Nancy Carol, John Christopher, Amy Stuart, Mollie Maureen, Courtney Marie; m. 2d, Gayle Marie Sondelski, Oct. 8, 1977. Resident Cook County Hosp., Chgo., 1967-68; practice dentistry, Wausau, Wis., 1968—. Pres., chmn. bd. Riverview Dental Assos. Service Corp., 1968—, Riverview Dental Bldg. Ltd., 1968—; cons. hosp. com. Wis. Dental Soc., 1972-75. Mem. com. Samoset Council Boy Scouts Am., 1971-75. Bd. dirs. Montessori Sch. Wausau, 1971-75, pres. 1976-77. Served with USAF, 1965-67. Mem. Am. Dental Assn., Wis. Dental Soc., North Central Acad. Dental Group Practice, Central Wis. Dental Soc. Roman Catholic. Home: 1209 E Crocker St Wausau WI 54401 Office: 630 1st St Wausau WI 54401

DERWINSKI, EDWARD JOSEPH, congressman; b. Chgo., Sept. 15, 1926; s. Casimir Ignatius and Sophia (Zmijewski) D.; B.Sc. in History, Loyola U., 1951; m. Patricia Van der Giessen. Rep. 24th Dist., Ill. Gen. Assembly, 1957-58; mem. 86th-95th Congresses. from 4th Dist. Ill., mem. Internat. Relations Com., P.O. and Civil Service Com. Served with inf. U.S. Army, 1945-46. Mem. Polish Highlanders Alliance Am. (past nat. dir.), Cath. War Vets., Polish Alma Mater, Am. Legion, Polish Legion Am. Vets. (past state vice comdr.), VFW, Polish Nat. Alliance, Alpha Delta Gamma. Republican. Roman Catholic. Moose, K.C. Kiwanian. Home: 12236 S Harlem Ave Palos Heights IL 60463 Office: 1401 Longworth House Office Bldg Washington DC 20515

DERZON, GORDON M., hosp. adminstr.; b. Milw., Dec. 28, 1934; B.S., Dartmouth Coll., 1957; M.A., U. Mich., 1961; married. Adminstrv. resident Bklyn. Hosp., 1960-61, adminstrv. asst., 1961-63, asst. exec. dir., 1963-65, exec. dir., 1966-67; exec. dir. State U. Hosp., Bklyn., 1967-68, Kings County Hosp. Center, Bklyn., 1968-74; supt. U. Wis. Hosps., Madison, 1974—; asso. prof. State U. N.Y., 1967-74; asst. clin. prof. U. Wis., Madison. Mem. Am. Hosp. Assn. (del.-at-large), Am. Coll. Hosp. Adminstrs. Contbr. articles to profl. jours. Home: 3421 Circle Close Madison WI 53705 Office: 1300 University Ave Madison WI 53706

DESANTIS, ANTHONY, theatre, restaurant owner; b. Gary, Ind., Jan. 5, 1914; s. Sam and Maria (DiVergilo) DeS.; student Armour Inst.; m. Lucille Cuzeli, Feb. 12, 1945; children—Deborah, Diane. With research lab. staff Sherwin-Williams Paint Co., 1934-39; owner Embassy Club, 1940-45; owner Martinique Restaurant, Chgo., 1946—, Drury Lane Theatre, Chgo., 1951—; dir. Heritage Pullman Bank & Trust Co., Chgo.; pres. Martinique Co., Evergreen Park Motel Corp., Drury Lane Prodns., Inc., (all Chgo.); treas. Martinique-Drury Lane Theatre Corp., Chgo.; dir., vice chmn. bd. Standard Bank & Trust Co.; dir. Heritage Bank Corp., pres. Watertower Entertainment Inc.; v.p. Indian Creek Investment Co. Fire Marshall, Evergreen Park. Mem. citizens bd. U. Chgo.; bd. assos. De Paul U., Chgo.; adv. bd. Little Flower Soc. (Humanitarian award 1966), Bd. Catholic Charities; Decorated comdr. Order Holy Sepulchre, comdr. Order St. Augustine Filius Ordinis, Order St. John of Jerusalem; knight Sovereign Order Malta, Order St. Gregory; named Man of Yr., Men of Tolentine, 1971; Man of Yr., Oak Lawn C. of C., 1965; Man of Decade, Evergreen Park C. of C. Mem. Chgo. Police Capts. Assn. (Distinguished Service award 1970), Chgo. Patrolmen's Assn. (life mem.). Clubs: Carlton, Chgo. Variety, Executive, Mid America, Beverly Country, (Chgo.); Del Safari Country (Palm Springs, Calif.); Mount Kenya Safari, Africa. Address: 2500 W Drury Ln Evergreen IL 60642

DESCHNER, REINHART PHILLIP, engr.; b. Bebe, Tex., May 4, 1927; s. Henry and Hannah (Seipman) D.; B.S., Southwestern U., 1949; m. Rebecca Ann Tittle, Dec. 17, 1949; children—William, Robert, Monte, Rose Ann, Mary Janette. Shift chemist Stanolind Oil & Gas Co., Brownsville, Tex., 1951-57; tech. service rep. Amoco Chem. Corp., Chgo., 1957-59, tech. asst. to plant supt., Seymour, Ind., 1959-66, asst. project chem. engr., 1966-67, project chem. engr., 1967-71, devel. engr., 1971-72, project engr., 1972-76; environ. engr. Humko Products div. Kraftco Corp., Champaign, Ill., 1976-77, engring. mgr., 1976—; cons. Northrup Ventura, Philippines, 1967, Saudi Arabia, 1969, Seymour Chem. Recycling, Seymour, Ind., 1971-76; owner, mgr. Renshed Tech. Cons., Seymour, 1971—. Precinct committeeman Republican party, 1960-76; active Boy Scouts Am., 1949-76; starter for state meets, judge Jr. Olympics, pres. Seymour Swim Club; chmn. edn. com. Seymour C. of C., 1969-74. Served with USNR, 1945-47. Certified wastewater operator; recipient Dist. Statuette, Boy Scouts Am., 1966; Good Samaritan award, City of Seymour, 1971. Mem. Am. Chem. Soc., Am. Rocket Soc., Am. Inst. Aeros. and Astronautics, Water Pollution Control Fedn. Republican. Methodist. Contbr. research for patents held by Amoco Chem. Corp. Home: 805 Lincoln Dr Monticello IL 61856 Office: 710 N Mattis St Champaign IL 61820

DESENBERG, BILL RAE, lawyer; b. Buchanan, Mich., Feb. 5, 1909; s. Louis M. and May (Belvel) D.; A.B. cum laude, Notre Dame U., 1931, LL.B. cum laude, 1933; m. Marjorie Hetler, May 5, 1940; children—Margaret Ann, Louis Arthur, James Henry. Admitted to Mich. bar, 1933; individual practice law, Buchanan, 1936—; partner Desenberg & Desenberg, Buchanan, Mich., 1970-73, Desenberg, Moses & Desenberg, P.C., 1973—; dir. Inter-City Bank. Active Boy Scouts Am. Pres. Meml. Field, Inc., Buchanan, 1940-73. Trustee Buchanan Library Bldg. Corp., 1945-50. Recipient Selective Service medal. Fellow Am. Coll. Probate Counsel; mem. Mich. State Bar (comr. probate and trust law sect. 1971; mem. com. specialization legal practice 1973), Am., Mich., Berrien County bar assns., Notre Dame Law Assn. Mason. Mich. chmn. joint editorial bd. Uniform Probate Code, 1972. Home: 609 River St Buchanan MI 49107 Office: 118 Main St Buchanan MI 49107

DESHAZOR, ASHLEY DUNN, retail co. exec.; b. Blackstone, Va., May 28, 1919; s. Francis Bertram and Carrie Lee (Joyner) DeS.; B.S. in Bus. Adminstrn., U. Richmond, 1941; m. Margot Joy Best, Sept. 18, 1943 (dec. June, 1966); children—Margot Joy (Mrs. N. Coleman Brydon, Jr.), Nancy Lee, Linda Louise; m. 2d, Shirley Dean, June 1, 1968; 1 son, Dean Laffey. With Sears Roebuck & Co., Sears Roebuck de Colombia, 1941-63; mgr. nat. mdse. dept. Montgomery Ward & Co., Chgo., 1963, 65, procurement asst. to v.p. and gen. mdse. mgr., 1963-65, v.p., corp. credit mgr., 1966—, also dir.; dir. Montgomery Ward Credit Corp.; mem. Ill. Electronic Funds Transfer Systems Study Commn. Mem. bd. of assos. U. Richmond. Bd. dirs. Chgo. Boys Clubs; trustee, mem. exec. com. Nat. Found. Consumer Credit; mem. governing bd. Credit Research Center, Purdue U. Served to lt. comdr., USNR, 1941-46; ETO, PTO. Mem. Nat. Retail Mchts. Assn. (past chmn. credit mgmt. div.), Sigma Alpha Epsilon. Episcopalian. Clubs: Economic, Mid-America (Chgo.); Westmoreland Country (Wilmette, Ill.); Camelback Country (Scottsdale, Ariz.). Home: 155 Woodley Rd Winnetka IL 60093 Office: 619 W Chicago Ave Chicago IL 60607

DE SHIELDS, ROBERT W., dentist; b. Cleve., May 29, 1935; s. William Henry and Leila Pearl (Hanna) DeS.; D.D.S., Ohio State U., 1959, M.S., 1964; children by previous marriage—Dana Lynn, William Douglas, Richard Walter. Practice dentistry specializing in clin. orthodontics, Cleve., 1964—; dental missionary to Guatamala, Allied Dental Med. Missions Youngstown, Ohio, 1975-77, to Nicaragua, 1976. Served with USAF, 1959-62. Mem. Am., Ohio, Cleve. dental assns., Cleve. Soc. Orthodontists, Ohio Assn. Orthodontists, Am. Assn. Orthodontists, Am. Cleft Palate Assn. Club: Vermilion Boat. Contbr. articles in field to profl. jours. Home: 17270 Akita Ct Strongsville OH 44136 Office: 7155 Pearl Rd Cleveland OH

DE SILVA, PARAKRAMA, cardiologist; b. Matara, Sri Lanka, Sept. 19, 1933; s. Sugathadasa and Wimala (Sahabandu) de S.; M.D., U. Hiroshima, 1960; m. Chizuko Shimizu, May 11, 1958; children—Rohan Tissa, Ajit Gemunu, Kumari Rupika. Came to U.S., 1960, naturalized, 1971. Intern, Glens Falls (N.Y.) Hosp., 1960-61; resident Medfield (Mass.) State Hosp., 1961-62, St. Mary's Hosp., Rochester, N.Y., 1962-63, Ottawa (Ont.) Gen. Hosp., 1963-66; asst. in medicine U. Chgo., 1966-70, staff physician, 1966-70; cardiologist Perco Med. Group and Holy Cross Hosp., Chgo., 1970-73; pvt. practice specializing in cardiology, Chgo., 1973—; mem. staff Holy Cross Hosp. Fellow Royal Soc. Health, Royal Soc. Medicine; mem. Am. Coll. Cardiology, Am. Heart Assn. (councils on clin. cardiology and cardiovascular surgery), Am., Chgo. socs. internal medicine, Assn. Am. Physicians and Surgeons. Home: 5129 S Cornell Ave Chicago IL 60615 Office: 4255 W 63d St Chicago IL 60629

DESLEY, JOHN WHITNEY, med. illustrator; b. Old Mystic, Conn., May 17, 1925; s. Clifford James and Hester (Walbridge) D.; B.F.A., U. Conn., 1950; M.Med.Illustration, Mass. Gen. Hosp., 1953; m. Janice C. Reed, Dec. 22, 1951; children—Christopher, Rebecca, Timothy, Rachel, Leah and Louisa (twins). Asst. med. artist Mass. Gen. Hosp., Boston, 1953-54; chief med. artist VA Hosp., Birmingham, Ala., 1954-58, Med. Art Dept., U. Minn. Hosp., Mpls., 1958-63; med. artist Mayo Clinic, Rochester, Minn., 1963—. Cons. to postgrad. medicine jour. 1963-73. Chmn. Bamber Valley Sch. Bd., Rochester, Minn., 1970-73. Served with USNR, 1943-46. Recipient Superior Performance award VA, 1956, others. Mem. Assn. Med. Illustrators (bd. govs. 1968-73, rec. sec. 1972-73), Nat. Exchange Club, Newt Holland Drawing and Painting Club. Contbr. numerous med. drawings to profl. jours. Home: 3245 18th Ave SW Rochester MN 55901 Office: Mayo Clinic Rochester MN 55901

DESPRES, PAUL FRANCOIS-COULLIARD, advt., printing co. exec.; b. Grand Rapids, Mich., July 30, 1932; s. Stanislas Joseph and Eulalie (Peters) M.; student St. Norbert Coll., 1951-54, extension div. U. Mich., 1954, Aquinas Coll., 1968-69; m. Martha L. Nischan, Jan. 25, 1958; children—John, Anne, Suzanne, Michael. Owner, Despres Dowel Mfg. Co., Grand Rapids, 1954—; pres., treas. Dorr Raceway, Inc., (Mich.), 1964-70, Despres, Inc., Grand Rapids, 1968—; with Despres Charities, Grand Rapids, 1962—, pres., 1964—; owner Now Printing, 1974-77, Visu-Graphics, 1975-77, Stylized Creations, 1975-77. Vol. probation officer, 1972-77. Home: 860 Maryland St Grand Rapids MI 49505 Office: 1419 Coit NE PO Box 2389 Grand Rapids MI 49501

DE STASIO, MICHAEL BARTHOLOMEW, mktg. engr.; b. Phila., Aug. 9, 1946; s. Bartholomew Thomas and Josephine Dolores (Orlando) DeS.; B.S., Aero-Space Inst., 1972; m. Lois Welker, Nov. 29, 1975. Cons. elec. draftsman A & T Engring., Chgo., 1970-72; computer programmer No. Trust Bank, Chgo., 1973; mktg. engr. Telemed Corp., Hoffman Estates. Ill., 1973—. Served with U.S. Army, 1966-69. Decorated Purple Heart, Bronze Star medal, Air medal. Home: 1813 N Raleigh Ln Hoffman Estates IL 60195 Office: 2345 Pembroke St Hoffman Estates IL 60195

DE STEPHEN, ALBERT MICHAEL, mech. engr.; b. Canton, Ohio, Feb. 17, 1920; s. Anthony and Jennie (DeGiacomo) DeS.; B.M.E., Internat. Corr. Schs., 1960; m. Helen Marie Skivolocke, Sept. 19, 1943; 1 dau., Norma Jean. With research and devel. div. Babcock and Wilcox Co., Alliance, Ohio, 1950-52, 54—, asst. supt. welding mills div. tubular products, 1965-73, supt. welding mills div. tubular products, 1973—. Served with USAAF, 1942-46. Mem. ASME (sec. Canton Alliance Massilon sect. 1961—), Assn. Iron, Steel Engrs. Republican. Roman Catholic. Patentee non-destructive testing welded steel tubing. Home: 1774 Federal St Alliance OH 44601 Office: 640 Keystone St Alliance OH 44601

DESY, ADDIE LUELLA PIERCE, ednl. counselor; b. Levering, Mich., Mar. 29, 1905; d. Clarence and Adelia Ann (Mitchell) Pierce; student Central Mich. U., 1923-27; B.S., Wayne State U., 1956, M.Ed., 1957; postgrad., Mich. State U., 1957-61; m. Everett E. Desy, May 31, 1930 (dec.). Tchr., Indian River, Mich., 1923-25, Dimondale, Mich., 1926-30, Lafayette Sch., Lincoln Park, Mich., 1946-60; counselor Huff Jr. High Sch. and Lincoln Park High Sch., Lincoln Park, Mich., 1971-77; part time counselor, Mackinaw City (Mich.) High Sch., 1971-77; tchr., Lincoln Park, summers, 1950-59. Mem. Huff Scholarship Bd., 1963-70. Recipient honor award, Mich. Edn. Assn., 1970, pub. service award, Lincoln Park Bd. Edn., 1970. Mem. Am., Mich. personnel and guidance assns., N.Central Counselors Assn. Roman Catholic. Club: Mackinaw City Woman's. Address: Box 435 Mackinaw City MI 49701

DETERT, DAVID GLASCOCK, graphic co. exec.; b. Billings, Mont., Mar. 15, 1938; s. Donald Apperson and Nancye Reed (Glascock) D.; S.B. in Elec. Engring., Mass. Inst. Tech., 1960; M.S. in Elec. Engring., U. Ill., 1962, Ph.D., 1965; m. Joyce Ruth Felten, Aug. 30, 1960; children—Christine, Jonathan, Lisa. Staff scientist Avco Corp., Wilmington, Mass., 1965-68, chief geophysics sect., 1968-71; prin. scientist Raytheon Co., Sudbury, Mass., 1971-73; group mgr. air force mktg. Univac Corp., Eagan, Minn., 1973-76; gen. mgr. Dolphin Graphics Inc., Edina, Minn., 1976—. Mem. Am. Geophys. Union, Am. Meteorol. Soc., Sigma Xi, Eta Kappa Nu. Home: 1324 Wilderness Run Dr Eagan MN 55123 Office: 11931 12th Ave South Burnsville MN 55337

DETRICH, ARTHUR JUDD, assn. exec.; b. Chgo., Nov. 29, 1944; s. Richard Charles and Audrey Alice (Olsen) D.; A.A., Chgo. City Jr. Coll., 1966; B.S., So. Ill. U., 1969. Foreman research and devel. div. Perma-Line Co., Chgo., 1966-69; audio visual producer A.M.A., Chgo., 1970—. Communications cons. to U.S. corps.; freelance producer, cinematographer, photojournalist, indsl. photographer; speaker; guest lectr. So. Ill. U.; cons. multi-media presentation Nat. Found. March of Dimes, 1972. Juror bus. and indsl. jury Chgo. Internat. Film Festival, 1970-76, recipient hon. mention in pub. relations, 1974. Mem. Univ. Film Assn., Jaguar Assn. Greater Chgo., Classic Jaguar Assn., Jaguar Drivers Club, BMW Motorcycle Owners Am., Chgo. Region BMW Owners Assn. Developer, thermo-epoxy striping machine for hwys.; designer unique living environment. Home: 2127 N Sedgwick St Chicago IL 60614 Office: 535 N Dearborn St Chicago IL 60610

DETRICH, WILLIAM BENTON, camp and conf. center exec.; b. Hagerstown, Md., Oct. 13, 1926; s. Clarence Lee and Mable Grace (Reath) D.; student pub. schs.; m. Maxine Louise Bonebrake, Oct. 30, 1948; children—Susan (Mrs. James M. DeVos), Sheila Kae. Store reorganizer McCrory Corp., 1950-70; exec. dir. East Bay Camp-Conf. Center, Hudson, Ill., 1970—. Mem. adv. council on youth camp act Ill. Dept. Health, 1972—. Mem. adv. bd. Mennonite Hosp., 1972-74. Served with USNR, 1943-47; PTO. Mem. Am. Camping Assn. (pres. Ill. sect.), Nat. Audubon Soc., Smithsonian Assos., Christian Camping Internat., Open Lands Project. Kiwanian (Internat. Pres.'s award 1972, Distinguished Service award 1973). Address: Rural Route 2 Hudson IL 61748

DETROY, BENJAMIN FORREST, agrl. engr.; b. Dexter, Mo., Nov. 28, 1923; s. Benjamin and Mary (Tate) D.; B.S. in Agrl. Engring., U. Ill., 1950; M.S., U. Wis., 1964; m. Marjorie Anne Neidy, Feb. 26, 1949; children—Marx, Michael, Mary, Benjamin J., Linda, Katherine. Research engr. U.S. Dept. Agr., Stoneville, Miss., 1950-53, research leader, Madison, Wis., 1956—; test engr. Internat. Harvester Co., East Moline, Ill., 1953-56. Scoutmaster, Four Lakes council Boy Scouts Am., 1964-74. Served with USMCR, 1945-46, 50-51. Registered profl. engr., Wis. Recipient Statuette award Boy Scouts Am., 1969. Mem. Nat., Wis. socs. profl. engrs., Am. Soc. Agrl. Engrs., Bee Research Assn., V.F.W. Mason. Home: 6704 Maywood Ave Middleton WI 53562 Office: 436 Russell Labs-ENT U Wis Madison WI 53706

DETTMAN, RONALD ROBERT, union ofcl.; b. Cheboygan, Mich., Aug. 24, 1922; s. Robert and Pearl D.; student Sch. Labor, U. Mich., 1968-70; m. Opal M. Dettman, July 18, 1942; 1 child. Chief steward Constrn. and Gen. Laborers Local Union 1329, 1947-50; steward local 324 Internat. Union Operating Engrs., 1950-52, now mem.; pres. Sault Ste. Marie AFL-CIO Trades and Labor Council, 1950-52; sec.-treas. local 1600 Flint Gen. City Employees, Am. Fedn. State, County and Municipal Employees, 1960-74; fin. sec. Council 29, Am. Fedn. State, County and Municipal Employees, 1962—, Greater Flint AFL-CIO, 1967—; employed with Gen. Services Adminstrn. City of Flint. Bd. dirs. Central Methodist Ch., 1947-49; trustee City of Flint Employee Retirement System, 1968-70; bd. dirs. Nat. Conf. Pub. Retirement Systems, 1970—. Served with USNR, 1942-45. Mem. In-Plant Printing Mgmt. Assn. (Reprodns. Mgr. of Year 1976), C. of C. Club: Masons. Home: 205 Douglas St Montrose MI 48457 Office: G4101 Clio Rd Flint MI 48504

DETWEILER, JOHN ADAM, physician; b. Pine Grove, Pa., Apr. 16, 1924; s. John A. and Bessie (Philips) D.; B.S., Lebanon Valley Coll., 1948; M.D., Tufts U., 1952; m. Elaine Wedemeyer, Sept. 26, 1946; children—Judith, Joan, Jeanne. Intern, St. Francis Hosp., 1952-53; med. resident Hines VA Hosp., Hines, Ill., 1953-56; internist, Arlington Heights, Ill., 1956—; chief of staff N.W. Community Hosp., Arlington Heights, 1956; clin. asso. prof. medicine. U. Ill. Coll. Medicine, 1963—. Chmn. Bd. Health, Village Arlington Heights. Served with AUS, 1946-48. Diplomate Am. Bd. Internal Medicine. Fellow A.C.P., Am. Coll. Chest Physicians; mem. Phi Rho Sigma. Home: 1201 Sunset Terr Arlington Heights IL 60005 Office: 1430 N Arlington Heights Rd Arlington Heights IL 60004

DEUBNER, RUSSELL LEIGH, electronic mfg. co. exec.; b. Jamestown, Ohio, Aug. 10, 1919; s. Otto Theodore and Ida Mae (LeVeck) D.; B. Metall. Engring., Ohio State U., 1942; m. Irene C. Schuetter, Jan. 21, 1944; children—Scott, Cheryl. Maintenance technician Columbus (Ohio) Bolt and Forging Co., 1939-40; lab. tech. Ohio State U., 1941-42; with Battelle Meml. Inst. and Battelle Devel. Corp., 1945-58, mgr. devel. corp., 1952-57, chief bus. cons. div., 1958; gen. mgr. chromium plating div. Gen. Devel. Corp., Miami, Fla., 1958-61; mgmt. cons. Ohio Semiconductors, Inc., Columbus, 1960-62, asst. to pres., 1961-62, dir. standard products group, 1962; bd. chmn., exec. v.p., treas. Scientific Columbus, Inc., 1963-69; pres. Scientific Columbus div. Esterline Corp., 1969—; dir. Basic Electric Corp. Served with USNR, 1942-45. Decorated Bronze Star. Club: Scioto Country (Columbus). Home: 2420 Donna Dr Columbus OH 43220 Office: 1035 W 3d Ave Columbus OH 43212

DEUR, GORDON, optometrist; b. Fremont, Mich., Mar. 12, 1926; s. Harry Daniel and Bertha (Van Goor) D.; student Mich. State Coll., 1944; Calvin Coll., 1947-48; D. Optometry, No. Ill. Coll. Optometry, 1950; m. Ruth Vogel, Oct. 11, 1950; children—Cheryl, Evonne, Delwyn, Lonette. Pvt. practice optometry, Zeeland, Mich., 1951—. Visual cons. low vision clinic Western Mich. U.; adv. bd. Ferris State Coll. on Optometric Technician. Mem. Am., Mich. (Emil Arnold Sci. award 1959), Western Mich. optometric assns., Better Vision Inst., Coll. Optometrists on Vision Devel. (state dir.), Beta Sigma Kappa. Republican. Author: (with others) Pre-school Vision Screening Manual, 1959, (with others) Out of Office Vision Training Manual, 1961. Home: 1890 S Maple St Zeeland MI 49464 Office: 1989 96th Ave Zeeland MI 49464

DEUTSCH, FREDERICK MORAN, lawyer; b. Talmage, Nebr., Sept. 4, 1898; s. Fred and Mary Eleanor (Moran) D.; LL.B., J.D., U. Nebr., 1921; m. Catherine Lawlor, July 28, 1938. Admitted to Nebr. bar, 1921; individual practice law, Norfolk, Nebr., 1921—; dir. DeLay First Nat. Bank & Trust Co., 1950—. Trustee U. Nebr. Found. Served with USNR, 1918. Mem. Am., Nebr. State, 9th Jud. Dist. bar assns., Am. Coll. Trial Lawyers, Am. Coll. Probate Counsel, Internat. Assn. Ins. Counsel, Fedn. Ins. Counsel, Am. Legion, Norfolk C. of C. (pres. 1931). Democrat. Roman Catholic. Clubs: Omaha, Lincoln Univ., K.C., Elks. Home: 200 Bridge Rd Norfolk NE 68701 Office: 125 Norfolk Ave Norfolk NE 68701

DEUTSCH, OWEN CHARLES, mag. pub. exec.; b. Chgo., Jan. 9, 1936; s. Conrad Alexander and Betty (Liebermann) D.; student U. Mich., 1956-57; B.A., Roosevelt U., 1960, postgrad., 1960-61; postgrad. Loyola U. Sch. Law, 1961-62. Advt. rep. Commerce mag., Chgo., 1962-70; advt. dir. Chicago mag., Chgo., 1970—; cons. in field. Active Hyde Park-Kenwood Community Orgn. Mem. Chgo. Advt. Club, Sales and Marketing Execs. Assn. Chgo. (Distinguished Sales award 1968). Home: 1700 E 56th St Apt 1205 Chicago IL 60637 Office: 500 N Michigan Ave Chicago IL 60611

DEVEBER, LEVERETT LEBARON, physician; b. Toronto, Ont., Can., Jan. 27, 1929; s. Leverett Sandys and Ruth (Quain) deV.; M.D., U. Toronto, 1953; postgrad. pediatrics U. Manchester (Eng.), 1957, U. Liverpool (Eng.), 1958; m. Iola Aline Plaxton, June 17, 1954; children—George, Gabrielle, Christine, Michele, Eileen, Barrie. Intern St Michael's Hosp., Toronto, 1954, Shaugnessy Hosp., Vancouver, B.C., Can., 1955; practice gen. medicine, Sudbury, Ont., 1955-56; resident Bellevue Hosp., N.Y.C., 1959, Hosp. Sick Children, Toronto, 1960; immunohaematology fellow U. Man. (Can.), Winnipeg, 1961; practice medicine, specializing in pediatric haematology, London, Ont.; dir. haematology lab. Children's Hosp., London, 1961—; dir. Rh research lab. and immunohaematological div. blood bank, both Victoria Hosp., London; mem. staff St. Joseph Hosp., Univ. Hosp., London; mem. faculty dept. pediatrics U. Western Ont., London, 1961—, asst. prof., 1966-69, asso. prof., 1969-75, prof., 1975—, also acting chmn. dept., 1973—. Mem. animal house com., research coordinating com. Victoria Hosp. Med. adviser Right to Life, London, also before N.Y. Supreme Ct., Conn. Supreme Ct. Bd. dirs., pres. Alliance for Life Can. Can. Life Ins. med. fellow, 1961-64. Fellow Royal Coll. Physicians (Can.); mem. Western Immunology Club (founding mem.), Canadian Assn. Advancement Health Services, Med. Edn. Club (founding mem.), Canadian Haemophilia Soc. (chmn. med. adv. bd.). Roman Catholic. Contbr. articles to profl. jours. Home: 815 Talbot St London ON Canada Office: 392 South St London ON Canada

DEVENOW, CHESTER, mfg. co. exec.; b. Detroit, Mar. 3, 1919; s. Samuel E. and Bessie (Aronow) D.; B.A., N.Y. U., 1941; postgrad. Harvard Law Sch.. 1941-42; m. Marilyn S. Fruchtman, Apr. 20, 1947; children—Mark Stephen, Jeffrey, Sara, Susan. Pres., dir. Globe-Wernicke Industries, Inc., 1954-67; pres., chief exec. officer, chmn. bd., dir. Sheller-Globe Corp.; chmn. bd. Superior Coach Corp.; pres. Community Improvement Corp. Toledo; dir., mem. exec. com. GAC Corp. Mem. 1st Nat. Automotive Safety Adv. Council; former U.S. rep. to UN Council on Trade and Devel. Trustee Blue Cross N.W. Ohio, Riverside Hosp., Toledo, Toledo Labor-Mgmt.-Citizens Com., Ohio State U., Siena Heights Coll., Adrian, Mich. Served to 1st lt. AUS, 1942-45. Decorated Bronze Star. Clubs: Glengarry Country (Holland, Ohio); Belmont Country, Brynwyck Country (Perrysburg, Ohio); Toledo, Country (Toledo); Recess (Detroit). Home: 3000 Valleyview Dr Toledo OH 43615 Office: 1505 Jefferson Ave Toledo OH 43624

DEVER, DANIEL EUGENE, orthodontist; b. Washington, Apr. 2, 1946; s. Lewis A. and Ruthe (Gerwig) D.; B.A., Ohio State U., 1968, D.D.S., 1971, M.S., 1976; m. Nancy Ann O'Brien, Dec. 19, 1970; children—Jonathan Tyler, Lorene Beth. Practice dentistry specializing in orthodontics, West Chester, Ohio. Served with U.S. Army, 1971-73. Mem. ADA, Ohio Dental Assn., Cin. Dental Soc., Am. Assn. Orthodontists. Home: 8230 Julie Marie Dr West Chester OH 45069 Office: 9319 Cincinnati Columbus Rd West Chester OH 45069

DEVEREAUX, DUANE LOREN, engring. co. exec.; b. Tuttle, N.D., Feb. 13, 1928; s. Robert Allen and Selma Hattie (Olson) D.; grad. sr. indsl. and mech. engr. U. Minn., 1956; m. Sylvia Ann Kovach, Aug. 13, 1950; children—Denise, Darcy, Diana. Method engr. Donaldson Co., St. Paul, 1953-56; engring. mgr. Bur. Engring, Inc., Mpls., 1956-63; owner, mgr. Qualitek Engring. and Mfg. Co., Mpls., 1963—; mgr., owner Devco Rentals, 1968—; chmn. bd. Partech, 1972—; owner Devco Properties, 1977—. Served with C.E. AUS, 1950-52. Mem. Soc. Mfg. Engring., Am. Legion. Republican. Lutheran. Mason. Club: Interlachen Country. Home: 6100 Jeffrey Ln Edina MN 55436 Office: 2455 Louisiana Ave North Minneapolis MN 55427

DEVEREUX, PATRICK RICHARD, bus. mgr., cons.; b. St. Louis, Apr. 1, 1949; s. Joseph F. and Patricia (Leonard) D.; A.B., St. Louis U., 1971, M.B.A., 1975; m. Karen Ann Wedepohl, May 31, 1975. Admissions counselor St. Louis U., 1971-73, bus. mgr., 1973—; cons. Devereux & Assos., Clayton, Mo., 1975—; instr. Webster Coll., 1976, St. Louis U., 1976-77. Served with USAR, 1971. Mem. St. Louis U. Alumni Assn. (pres. arts and scis. 1977), Med. Group Mgmt. Assn., Am. Mgmt. Assn. Home: 255 Cedar Village Ballwin MO 63011 Office: 1325 Grand Blvd S St Louis MO 63104

DEVI, TRIPURANENI ANJANA, surgeon; b. Tenali, India, June 14, 1937; s. Ghatamaneni Raghavaiah and Ghatamaneni Varamalleswaramma; came to U.S., 1964; M.B.B.S., Andhra (India) U., 1961; m. Tripuraneni L. Perumallu, M.D., June 20, 1973; 1 dau., Tripuraneni Deepa. Resident house officer Govt. Gen. Hosp., Guntur Med. Coll., Andhra U., 1961-62, tutor anatomy, 1963-64; surg. intern Rochester (N.Y.) Gen. Hosp., Strong Meml. Hosp., 1964-65; resident gen. surgery Mercy-Douglass Hosp., U. Pa., 1965-67, chief resident, 1968-69; surg. preceptor Wilmington Med. Center, Jefferson Med. Coll., Phila., 1969-70; attending pediatric surgeon King George Hosp.; asst. prof. pediatric surgery Andhra Med. Coll., 1971-73; attending surgeon Guntur Gen. Hosp., asst. prof. surgery Guntur Med. Coll., 1973-74; sr. staff surgeon VA Hosp., Danville, Ill., 1974—.

Diplomate Am. Bd. Surgery. Fellow A.C.S., Royal Coll. Surgeons (Edinburgh). Home: 1014 Hillside Dr Danville IL 61832 Office: VA Hosp 1900 E Main St Danville IL 61832

DEVINE, SAMUEL LEEPER, congressman; b. South Bend, Ind. Dec. 21, 1915; s. John Francis and Kittie Marie (Leeper) D.; student Colgate U., 1933-34, Ohio State U., 1934-37; J.D., cum laude, U. Notre Dame, 1940; m. Betty Galloway, Aug. 24, 1940; children—Lois (Mrs. George H. Collins), Joyce (Mrs. R.W. Morrell), Carol (Mrs. Matt Miller). Spl. agt. FBI, Dept. Justice, 1940-45; admitted to Ohio bar, 1940; with Hamilton & Kramer Law Offices, Columbus, 1948-55; pros. atty. Franklin County, Ohio, 1955-58; mem. Ohio Legislature, 1951-55; mem. 86th to 95th Congresses, 12th Dist., Ohio. Past chmn. Ohio Un-American Activities Commn. Mem. Charity Newsies, Soc. Former FBI Agts., Ohio Assn, Football Ofcls., Varsity O Assn. Republican. Methodist. Mason (33 deg., Shriner). Club: Columbus Country Home: 386 S Merkle Rd Columbus OH 43209 Office: Federal Bldg 85 Marconi Blvd Columbus OH 43216 also Rayburn Office Bldg Washington DC 20515

DEVINEY, MARVIN LEE, JR., chem. co. exec.; b. Kingsville, Tex., Dec. 5, 1929; s. Marvin Lee and Esther Lee (Gambrell) D.; B.S. in Chemistry and Math., S.W. Tex. State U., San Marcos, 1949; M.A. in Phys. Chemistry, U. Tex. at Austin, 1952, Ph.D. in Phys. Chemistry, 1956; m. Marie Carole Massey, June 7, 1975; children—Marvin Lee III, John H., Ann-Marie K. Devel. chemist Celanese Chem. Co., Bishop, Tex., 1956-58; research chemist Shell Chem. Co., Deer Park, Tex., 1958-66; sr. scientist, head group phys. and radio-chemistry Ashland Chem. Co., Houston, 1966-68, mgr. sect. phys. and analytical chemistry, 1968-71, mgr. sect. phys. chemistry div. research and devel., Columbus, Ohio, 1971—. Mem. sci. adv. bd. Am. Petroleum Inst. Research Project 60, 1968-74. Mem. ednl. adv. com. Columbus Tech. Inst., 1974—, Central Ohio Tech. Coll., 1975—. Served to lt. col., USAR. Humble Oil Research fellow, 1954. Fellow Am. Inst. Chemists (chmn. elect Ohio 1978); mem. N.Y., Tex. acads. scis., Am. Def. Preparedness Assn., Am. Carbon Soc., Am. Assn. Textile Chemists, Colorists, Am. Chem. Soc. (chmn. chpt. exec. bd. 1969, Best Paper award rubber div. 1967, 70. Honorable Mention awards 1968, 69, 73; symposium co-chmn., book editor 1975), Engr.'s Council Houston (sr. councilor 1970-71), Sigma Xi, Phi Lambda Upsilon, Alpha Chi, Sigma Pi Sigma. Contbr. articles to profl. jours. Home: 3538 Chowning Ct Columbus OH 43220 Office: Box 24 Dublin OH 43017

DEVISE, PIERRE ROMALN, educator, city planner; b. Brussels, Belgium, July 27, 1924; s. Victor Pierre and Madeleine (Cupers) deV.; B.A., U. Chgo., 1945, M.A., 1958; m. Betty Jeanne Jacobsen, Nov. 17, 1966; children—Peter Charles, Daniel Romain. Came to U.S., 1935, naturalized, 1958. Chancellor, Belgian Consul, Chgo., 1945-47, comml. attache, 1947-56, Belgian Consulate Gen., Chgo.; planning dir. Hyde Park-Kenwood Conf., 1956-57; research planner Northeastern Ill. Planning Commn., 1958-60; sr. planner Chgo. City Planning Dept., 1961-63; asst. dir. Hosp. Planning Council for Met. Chgo., 1964-70; asst. dir. Ill. Regional Med. Program, 1971-73; prof. urban scis. U. Ill., 1972—. Lectr., De Paul U., 1962—; vis. lectr. U. Mich., 1966, U. Hawaii, 1968, U. Ill., 1969, 70, U. Ia., 1971, U. Chgo., 1972; prin. investigator Chgo. Regional Hosp. Study, 1966—; exec. dir. Chgo. Commn. to Study Conv. Week Disorders, 1968-70; cons. Chgo. Commn. on Human Relations, 1966—, Chgo. Model Cities Program, 1968—, Cook County Council of Govts., 1968—, Comprehensive Health Planning, Inc., 1971—; Census Bur., 1973—, U.S. Senate Health Subcom., 1974, HEW, 1975—, House Ways and Means Com., 1975—, Senate Banking Com., 1976—. Mem. Am. Statist. Assn., Chgo. Assn. Commerce and Industry, Am. Pub. Health Assn., Assn. Am. Geographers. Author monographs including Suburban Factbook, 1960; Social Geography of Metropolitan Chicago, 1960; Chicago's People, Jobs and Homes, 1963; Chicago's Widening Color Gap, 1967; Chicago's Apartheid Hospital System 1968; Chicago: 1971, Ready for Another Fire, 1971; Misused and Misplaced Hospitals and Doctors, 1973; Chicago's Future, 1976; Chicago: Transformations of an Urban System, 1976. Home: 2058 N Dayton Chicago IL 60614 Office: U Ill Box 4348 Chicago IL 60680

DEVITO, ROBERT ALEXANDER, psychiatrist; b. Portsmouth, N.H., July 19, 1935; s. Alexander and Ethel (Barnett) deV.; A.B., Harvard, 1957; M.D., Loyola U., Chgo., 1961; m. Joan Jenette Pratte, May 23, 1964; 1 dau., Stefani. Intern St. Elizabeth's Hosp., Boston, 1961-62; resident Ill. State Psychiat. Inst., Chgo., 1962-65; chief Mil. Community Mental Health Center, Sheppard AFB, Tex., 1966-67; dir. jr. clerkship in psychiatry Loyola U. Med. Sch., Chgo., 1967-69; supt. John J. Madden Zone Center, Hines, Ill., 1969-77; dir. Ill. Dept. Mental Health and Developmental Disabilities, 1977—; practice medicine specializing in psychiatry, 1967—; clin. prof. psychiatry Loyola U. Med. Sch., 1977—; lectr. Pfizer Labs. Speaker's Bur., 1972—, Squibb Pharms. Speakers' Bur., 1975, Lederle Labs. Speakers Bur., 1976—; cons. Inpatient Alcoholism Treatment programs Chgo. Alcoholic Treatment Center, 1967-69, Hines Alcoholism Treatment Program, 1967-72; organizer Internat. Symposium on Schizophrenia, Chgo., 1977. Served with USAF, 1965-67. Decorated Air Force commendation medal. Named clin. tchr. of the year Loyola U. Stritch Sch. Medicine, 1969, hon. mem. of the class award, 1970; Faculty Initiate award Epsilon chpt. Alpha Omega Alpha, 1973. Diplomate Am. Bd. Psychiatry and Neurology. Fellow Am. Psychiat. Assn. (certified adminstrv. psychiatrist); mem. Ill. Psychiat. Assn. (chmn. constn. revision com. 1972-73, treas. 1974—, chmn. edn. com. 1976-77), AMA, Ill., Chgo. med. socs. Editor: Ill. Psychiat. Soc. Newspaper, 1970-72. Sr. editor, contbr: A View Into A Modern, State-Operated Mental Health Facility, 1975. Contbr. articles to profl. publs. Home: 4129 Saratoga Ave Apartment 215A Downers Grove IL 60515 Office: 1200 S 1st Ave Hines IL 60141

DEVITT, EDWARD JAMES, judge; b. St. Paul, May 5, 1911; s. Thomas Phillip and Catherine Ethel (McGuire) D.; LL.B., U. N.D., 1935, B.S., 1936; m. Marcelle M. LaRose, Apr. 22, 1939; children—Marcelle Terese, Timothy Patrick. Admitted to D.C., Minn., Ill., N.D. bars; practiced law, E. Grand Forks, Minn., 1935-39; municipal judge, 1935-39; asst. atty. gen. Minn., 1939-42; instr. law U. N.D., 1935-39, St. Paul Coll. Law, 1945—; practice law, St. Paul, 1946—; mem. 80th Congress from 4th Minn. Dist.; probate judge Ramsey County (Minn.), St. Paul, 1950-54; U.S. dist. judge Dist. Minn., 1954—, now chief dist. judge. Served as intelligence officer USN, 1942-46. Decorated Purple Heart. Mem. Am., Minn., Ramsey County bar assns., Am. Legion, VFW, DAV, St. John's U. Alumni Assn. (pres.), Order of Coif, Phi Delta Phi, Beta Gamma Sigma, Delta Sigma Rho, Blue Key. Republican. Roman Catholic. Clubs: K.C., St. Paul Athletic. Home: 1676 S Mississippi River Blvd Saint Paul MN 55116 Office: 734 Federal Bldg 316 N Robert St Saint Paul MN 55101*

DEVITT, JAMES CLEMENT, state senator; b. LaCrosse, Wis., Oct. 12, 1929; s. John J. and Mary (Mullen) D.; grad. Holy Name Sch., 1943, St. John's Cathedral, 1947; student Marquette U., 1947-50; m. Rita M. Kosmicki, Oct. 16, 1950; children—Patricia Ann, Brian James. Pres. Devitt Cartage Co., Inc., 1964-65, STC Leasing Corp., 1968-69; pres., chmn. bd. Devitt Leasing, Inc., 1965-68; partner S.D.& H. Co., real estate 1969-74; mem. Wis. State Assembly, 1966-68; Wis. state senator, 1968—, senate majority caucus sec., 1969, 71, 72, chmn. com. on health and social services, 1971-72, chmn. com. on health, edn. and welfare, 1973-74. Wis. rep. to Four-State Legis. Com. on Pollution Lake Michigan, 1967-71. Capt., St. Charles Boys Home Bldg. Fund, 1963; chmn. March of Dimes, 1965; mem. Whitnall Sch. Bd. Planning Com., 1965-66; mem. Gov.'s Task Force on Uniform Bldg. Code, 1970-72, Gov.'s Task Force on Offender Rehab., 1971-72, Gov.'s Health Planning and Policy Task Force, 1971-72, Gov.'s Hwy Safety Task Force, 1971-72. Bd. dirs. United Assn. Retarded Children, 1965-75, David A. Hellman Found., 1973-75, Wis. Spl. Olympics. Named one of Five Outstanding Young Men in Wis., 1964, Law Enforcement Man of Year, Milw. Police Officers, 1970, Republican of Year, Wis. Coll. Republicans, 1971; recipient Distinguished Service award City of Greenfield, 1965, Nat. Distinguished Service award to Am. Small Bus., 1970, Individual and Outstanding Service award United Assn. Retarded Children, 1972. Mem. Nat. Def. Transp. Assn. (v.p. Wis. 1966-69), Assn. U.S. Army (membership chmn. 1963), Am. Legion (life), Wis. (internat. dir. 1963, state v.p. 1961), Greenfield (pres. 1961, life) Jaycees, Greenfield C. of C. (pres. 1964-67), Farm Bur. Republican. Roman Catholic. K.C., Lion. Home: 8565 W Waterford Ave Greenfield WI 53228 Office: Room 415 SE State Capitol Madison WI 53702

DE VOE, E. DAVID, rehab. center exec.; b. Columbus, Ohio, Apr. 23, 1931; s. Ensign David and Fonda Venita (Delp) De V.; B.A., Ohio State U., 1953; m. Shirley May Collier, Feb. 21, 1965; children—Denise Buyaky, Harold, Dawn Butler, Douglas, Daphne, Diedre. Asst. dir. pub. relations United Appeals of Franklin County, Columbus, 1954-56; dir. pub. relations United Fund of Allen County, Ft. Wayne, Ind., 1956-59; pres. Concord Counsellors, Inc., pub. relations, fund raisers, advt., Ft. Wayne, 1959-71; asso. dir. Anthony Wayne Rehab. Center for Handicapped and Blind, Ft. Wayne, 1971—. Classical record columnist News-Sentinel, Ft. Wayne, 1968—; producer weekly radio program The Kaleidoscope of Sound, Sta. WPTH-FM, Ft. Wayne, 1967—; producer Classic Nights, Sta. KDKA-FM, Pitts., 1972—. Mem. Allen County Republican Com.; del. Ind. Rep. Conv., 1972-74. Bd. dirs. Coordinating Council for Handicapped; bd. dirs. Community Coordinating Center for Rehab. and Health Services, Inc., 1968-70, pres., 1970; bd. dirs. Adult Psychiat. Center of N.E. Ind., 1961-67, v.p., 1967. Mem. Am. Council for Blind, Ind. Assn. Rehab. Facilities, Pub. Relations Soc. Am., Nat. Assn. Social Workers, Acad. Certified Social Workers (nat. pub. relations com. 1966-68), Ft. Wayne Advt. Club (dir. 1966-69, publicity chmn. 1964), Sigma Delta Chi, Chi Phi, Phi Mu Alpha Sinfonia. Unitarian. Club: Ft. Wayne Press. Creator ballet Out of Darkness, premier, 1964. Home: 902 W Wildwood Ave Fort Wayne IN 46807 Office: 2826 S Calhoun St Fort Wayne IN 46807

DE VOE, RAYMOND MINERT, farm coop. adminstr.; b. Sparta, Wis., Aug. 11, 1941; s. Minert B. and Pauline Catherine (Dutton) De V.; Asso. Edn., Juneau County Tchrs. Coll., 1971; m. Sharon Jean Ablemann, Sept. 2, 1972; one dau., Susan Raye. With Midland Retail Dept., Scandia, Minn., 1971-72; with Suring Co-op. Assn. (Wis.), 1972—, gen. mgr., 1972—. Sunday Sch. supt., bd. dirs. Maple Valley Community Ch., Suring, 1974—. Served with USAF, 1961-69; Vietnam. Mem. Dist. Mgrs. Assn. (sec. dist. 1976—), Wis. Fedn. Coops., Midland Coops. Mgrs. Assn. Clubs: Suring Civic (dir. 1974—), Masons. Home: 116 Krueger St Suring WI 54174 Office: 223 Heasley St Suring WI 54174

DE VOTO, DONALD EDWIN, mgmt. cons.; b. Marshall, Ind., Feb. 27, 1918; s. William Michael and Grace (Tague) DeV.; A.B., Wabash Coll., 1939; postgrad. Purdue U., 1939, McGill U., 1940; m. Madonna Warner, Sept. 26, 1942; children—Eric, Craig. Instr. Romance langs., English, Wabash Coll., 1939-41; with R.R. Donnelley & Sons Co., Chgo., 1941-57; sr. cons. Booz, Allen & Hamilton, Chgo., 1957-58; pres. DeVoto, Sullivan & Berry, Ltd. (and predecessor firms), Chgo., 1959—; dir. MOP Corp. Pres., bd. dirs. Zion-Benton Hosp. Mem. Assn. Exec. Recruitive Cons. (pres. 1971-72, dir.), Chgo. C. of C., Phi Beta Kappa. Presbyn. (elder). Clubs: University (Chgo.), Ruth Lake Country (Hinsdale, Ill.). Home: 100 Ann St Clarendon Hills IL 60514 Office: 120 S Riverside Plaza Chicago IL 60606

DEVOY, ROBERT SEWARD, cons. city planning, real estate; b. Delevan, Wis., Aug. 27, 1935; s. Harold and Mary Jane (Ripley) DeV.; B.S., U. Wis., 1958, M.S., 1960; m. Ethel Rockwell Miller, July 20, 1957; children—Patricia Lynn, Sally Jo. Planner, City Madison, Wis., 1957-59; research analyst Citizens Govtl. Research Bur., Inc., Milw., 1959-61; dir. community renewal program City Milw., 1961-64; sr. v.p. Real Estate Research Corp., Chgo., 1964-76; dir. Canadian Real Estate Research Corp., Toronto; pres. DeVoy Collaborative, 1976—. Instr. Am. instns. Milw. Inst. Tech., 1960-64; guest lectr. univs. Wis., Mich., Minn., Ill., Ind., Chgo. Commr., Planning Commn., Glen Ellyn, Ill., 1966-71; trustee Village Glen Ellyn, 1971-74; mem. commn. on housing and urban growth Am. Bar Assn. V.F.W. scholar, 1953-54. Mem. Am. Inst. Planners, Am. Soc. Planning Offcs., Econ. Club Chgo., League New Community Developers, Jr. C. of C., Lambda Alpha. Contbr. articles to profl. jours. Home: 737 Forest Ave Glen Ellyn IL 60137 Office: 1749 Hobart St NW Washington DC 20009

DEVRIES, BERNARD JERIN, architect; b. Chgo., June 21, 1909; s. Christian W.B. and Johana (Zicterman) DeV.; student Mich State U., 1929-30; B.S. in Architecture, U. Mich., 1934; m. Jean Ann Frissel, June 27, 1936; 1 dau., Jo-Ann C. Jaehnig. Asst. engr. City of Ann Arbor (Mich.), 1934-37; designer Lewis J. Sarvis, architect, Battle Creek, Mich., 1937-38; pvt. practice architecture Bernard J. DeVries (now DeVries Assos., Inc.), Muskegon, Mich., 1938—; architect Gen. Telephone Co. Mich., Master City Plan Muskegon, CBD Redevel. Plan Muskegon, Muskegon Marquette Urban Renewal Project. Chmn. Mich. State Bd. Registration for Architects, Mich. State Bd. Registration for Land Surveyors; mem. bd. examiners Nat. Council Archtl. Registration Bds. Commr., Muskegon City Planning Comm., 1944-67, chmn., 1947-67; commr. Muskegon Bd. Appeals, 1954-67; charter mem. Muskegon Community Services Planning Council, 1963—, dir., 1963; founder, charter mem. Lake Michigan Region Planning Council, Inc., 1960—, vice chmn., 1964—, chmn. Mich. delegation, 1961—. Recipient Distinguished Service award Junior C. of C., 1943, hon. mention Am. Gas Assn. Residence Competition, 1939, Mich. Sch. Bds. Sch. Design Competition, 1963; named Muskegon's Mr. Planner, Muskegon Chronicle, 1963. Registered architect, Mich., Ill., Ind., Ohio, Mass., Conn., N.J., Ga., Tex. Fellow A.I.A. (sec., dir. Western Mich. chpt. 1945-47, v.p. Grand Valley chpt. 1963, president 1964); mem. Mich. Soc. Architects (urban renewal and design com. 1962, dir. 1967-74, gold medal 1966), Am., Mich. (founder, charter, dir. 1956, dir. 1967-74, pres. 1970) socs. planning ofcls., Mich. Assn. of Professions (charter), Muskegon C. of C. (urban renewal com., Builders award 1956). Kiwanian (pres. Muskegon 1952). Clubs: Muskegon Century, Muskegon Yacht. Prin. works include: schs., hi-rise apts., indsl., instl. Co-author: Dunes Area Regional Planning, 1962, Regional Highways and Population Growth Report, 1963. Home: 1907 Hoyt St Muskegon MI 49442 Office: Hackley Union Nat Bank Muskegon MI 49440

DEVRIES, PAUL DAMPMAN GARRETT, food co. exec.; b. Balt., Sept. 18, 1944; s. Van Beuren Wright and Marjorie Jane (Dampman) De V.; B.S., Yale U., 1966; M.B.A., U. Pa., 1971; m. Emily Melody Doudine, June 6, 1970; children—Christopher, Matthew. Line supr. Procter & Gamble, N.Y.C., 1969; brand mgr. Quaker Oats Co., Chgo., 1972-73; mgr. mktg. Stouffer Foods, Cleve., 1974—; dir. Nat. Frozen Pizza Inst. Deacon Ch. of Western Res., Presbyn. Ch., Gates Mills, Ohio, 1977—. Served with C.E., U.S. Army, 1966-68. Mem. Am. Mktg. Assn. Republican. Home: 7109 Wilson Mills Rd Gates Mills OH 44040 Office: 5750 Harper Rd Solon OH 44139

DEVRIES, ROBERT KEITH, publisher; b. Sully, Iowa, July 6, 1932; s. Fred G. and Lena (Willetts) DeV.; student Central Coll., Pella, Iowa, 1950-51; B.A., Wheaton Coll., 1954; Th.M., Dallas Theol. Sem., 1958, Th.D., 1969; m. Carolyn Schroeder, June 2, 1962; children—Steven Robert, Suzanne Mishael. Instr., So. Bible Tng. Sch., Dallas, 1957-60; asst. registrar Dallas Theol. Sem., 1959-63; editor Moody Press, Chgo., 1963-66, editor-in chief, 1967-68; dir. publs. Zondervan Pub. House, Grand Rapids, Mich., 1968-69, v.p. publs., 1969-72; exec. v.p. Book div. Zondervan Corp., 1972—. Mem. Evang. Covenant Ch. Club: Lotus (Grand Rapids). Home: 7554 Lime Hollow SE Grand Rapids MI 49506 Office: 1415 Lake Dr SE Grand Rapids MI 49506

DEW, DANIEL CHING-YEE, surgeon; b. Hong Kong, Apr. 10, 1940; s. Arthur Boon-Seng and Rosalind (Lui) D.; came to U.S., 1960; A.B., Taylor U., Ind., 1964; M.D., U. Ind., 1968; m. Cynthia Yuet-Man, June 15, 1968; children—Nathaniel, Timothy. Practice medicine specializing in surgery, Elkhart, Ind., 1973—; gen. surgeon, active staff Elkhart Gen. Hosp., 1973—. Diplomate Am. Bd. Surgery. Fellow A.C.S.; mem. AMA, Ind. Med. Assn., Christian, Elkhart County med. socs. Office: Elkhart Clinic 303 S Nappanee St Elkhart IN 46514

DEWAAY, DONALD GENE, lawyer; b. Sheldon, Iowa, Oct. 5, 1916; s. Jason and Nelle (Pearson) DeW.; student Sheldon Jr. Coll., 1934-36; B.A., U. Ia., 1938, J.D. with distinction, 1940; m. Lola Marie Snyder, July 12, 1958; children—Robert S., Donald G. Jr. Admitted to Iowa bar, 1940; partner firm Fisher & DeWaay, Rock Rapids, 1941—; atty. County of Lyon, 1942-50, City of Rock Rapids, 1954-70. Dir. Lyon County State Bank, Rock Rapids, Hawkeye Bancorp., Des Moines; mem. 21st Dist. Judicial Nominating Commn., 1960-70. Mem. bd. curators Iowa State Hist. Soc., 1969-71. Del. Iowa Republican Convs., 1942-50. Served with AUS, 1942-45; PTO, ETO. Fellow Iowa Acad. Trial Lawyers; mem. Iowa Conf. of Bar Assn. Pres.'s (pres. 1962-63), Lyon County (pres.), 21st Dist. (pres.), Iowa (gov.) bar assns., Am. Trial Lawyers Assn., Rock Rapids C. of C. (bd. dirs.), V.F.W., Am. Legion, Gamma Eta Gamma. Republican. Conglist. Mason (Shriner, Jester), Elk, United Comml. Traveller. Club: Rock River Country (Rock Rapids). Mem. rev. staff Ia. Law Rev., 1938-40. Home: 601 S Union St Rock Rapids IA 51246 Office: Profl Bldg Rock Rapids IA 51246

DEWALD, ERNEST LEROY, landscape architect; b. Cleve., Oct. 15, 1907; s. Frank Ernest and Bessie Mary (Stutzman) D.; B.F.A., Ohio State U., 1931; postgrad. (scholar) Lake Forest Found. Architects and Landscape Architects, 1931; m. Edna E. Kummer, Oct. 9, 1935. Landscape architect U.S. Forest Service, Nat. Park Service, 1933-38, Cleve. City Parks, 1938-41, Albert D. Taylor, Cleve., 1941-43; engr. Fisher Body, Cleve., 1943-45; landscape architect City of Cleve., 1945-56, Outcalt-Guenther & Assos., Cleve., 1956-59; pvt. practice landscape architecture, Cleve., 1959—; cons., lectr.; vis. critic Ohio State U., 1966-67, U. Ga., 1968; mem. Ohio Bd. Landscape Architects Examiners, 1965-72, pres., 1968-70; pres., Nat. Council Landscape Archtl. Registration Bd., 1968-69, 72-73; exec. sec. Ohio Roadside Council, 1959-67, vice chmn., 1968—; dir. Am. Soc. Landscape Architects Found., 1969-71. Registered landscape architect, Calif., N.Y., Ohio, Pa. Fellow Am. Soc. Landscape Architects (nat. 2d v.p. 1969-71, sec. council fellows 1972-74, Ohio chpt. medal for service 1974); mem. Ohio Planning Conf., Cleve. Mus. Art (life), Ohio State U. Alumni (life). Author: (with Thomas H. Jones) Cleveland Region Airport Plan, 1946. Works include sch. site devel. plans, Hudson, Elyria and Lorain, Ohio; bldgs. Case Western Res. U., Akron (Ohio) U., Cuyahoga Community Coll., Cleve.; engring. bldgs. NASA, Plumbrook, Ohio and Cleve.; mfg. cos. site plans for Ohio Machinery, Brecksville, Ohio, Nat. Screw Mfg., Mentor, Ohio, others. Home: 12910 Fairhill Rd Shaker Heights OH 44120 Office: 3570 Warrensville Center Rd Shaker Heights OH 44122

DEWALD, PAUL ADOLPH, physician; b. N.Y.C., Mar. 12, 1920; s. Jacob Frederick and Elsie (Wurzburger) D.; B.A., Swarthmore Coll., 1942; M.D., U. Rochester Sch. Medicine, 1945; certificate psychoanalysis State U. N.Y., 1960; m. Eleanor Whitman, Sept. 1, 1961; children—Jonathan S., Ellen F. Intern, Strong Meml. Hosp., Rochester, N.Y., 1945-46, resident, 1948-52; instr. U. Rochester, 1952-57, asst. prof. psychiatry, 1957-61; pvt. practice psychoanalysis, St. Louis, 1961—; asst. clin. prof. psychiatry Washington U., St. Louis, 1961-65; asso. clin. prof. St. Louis U., 1965-69, clin. prof. psychiatry, 1969—. Dir. treatment service Psychoanalytic Found. St. Louis, 1961-72, med. dir., 1972-73; med. dir. St. Louis Psychoanalytic Inst., 1973—, supervising and tng. analyst, 1973—; mem. faculty Chgo. Inst. Psychoanlysis, 1961—, supervising and tng. analyst, 1965—; vis. prof. U. Cin., 1968—. Served to capt., M.C., AUS, 1946-48. Fellow Am. Psychiat. Assn.; mem. Mo. (pres. 1970-71), Eastern Mo. (pres. 1969-70) psychiat. assns., Am., St. Louis (pres. 1970-71), Chgo. psychoanalytic socs. Author: Psychotherapy: A Dynamic Approach, 1964, 2d. edit. 1969; The Psychoanalytic Process, 1972. Home: 60 Conway Ln St Louis MO 63124 Office: 4524 Forest Park St Louis MO 63108

DEWALD, RONALD L., physician, educator; b. Aurora, Ill., Oct. 4, 1934; s. Lee H. and Elsie (Kellen) DeW.; B.S., U. Ill., 1955, M.D., 1959; m. Mary Lee Johnstone, July 21, 1956; children—Ann Elise, Lee Fraser, Christopher James, Ronald Lee. Intern, Presbyn. St. Lukes Hosp., Chgo., 1959-60; resident U. Ill. Hosp., Chgo., 1960-62, 64-65; asst. prof. orthopaedic surgery, 1965-67, asso. prof., 1967-71; prof., chmn. dept., Stritch Sch. Medicine Loyola at Chgo., 1972-73; prof. Rush Med. Coll., Chgo., 1973—. Cons. surgeon Ill. Div. Services for Crippled Children, 1967—, Ill. Childrens Hosp. Sch., Chgo., 1968—, Holy Family Hosp., Des Plaines, 1972—, Hines (Ill.) VA Hosp., 1972—; asso. surgeon Shriners Hosp. for Crippled Children, Chgo., 1972—. Served to capt. M.C., AUS, 1962-64. Diplomate Am. Bd. Orthopaedic Surgery (bd. examiners 1973—). Fellow A.C.S.; mem. A.M.A. (Hektoen Silver medal 1971), Chgo., Ill. med. socs., Chgo., Clin. orthopaedic socs., Scoliosis Research Soc. (founding, dir.), Am. Acad. Orthopadic Surgeons (regional admissions chmn. 1975—), Ill. Orthopaedic Assn., Am. Orthopaedic Assn. Contbr. articles to profl. jours. Office: 1725 Harrison St W Chicago IL 60612

DE WALT, ARTHUR RALPH, architect; b. Cleve., Jan. 13, 1938; s. Augustus Ralph and Augusta Mae (Rishel) DeW.; student Rensselaer Poly. Inst., 1955-58; B. Arch., Western Res. U., 1963. Partner William B. Morris, Architect, Shaker Heights, Ohio, 1963-65; partner Morris and DeWalt, Architects, Shaker Heights, 1965-68; partner Morris, DeWalt, Cullen, Whitley & Whitley, Architects and Planners, Shaker Heights, 1968-70; individual practice architecture, Cleve., 1970—; cons. architect The H.L. Vokes Co., Cleve. and Detroit, Simon & Co., Cleve. Instr. Cuyahoga Community Coll., 1967-71. Chmn. Archtl. Bd. of Review, Eastlake, Ohio, 1973—; chmn. Archtl. Bd. of Review, Mayfield Heights, Ohio, 1974—, city architect, 1977—. Scoutmaster Greater Cleve. Council Boy Scouts Am., 1971. Registered architect,

Ohio, Ill., N.J., Pa. Mem. A.I.A. (corporate mem.), Architects Soc. Ohio (recipient design honor award, 1965, 66, 67, 68), Soc. Archtl. Historians, Nat. Council Archtl. Registration Bds., Delta Kappa Epsilon. Presbyn. Club: University (Cleve.). Office: 35555 Curtis Blvd Eastlake OH 44094

DEWAR, NORMAN ELLISON, chem. spltys. co. exec.; b. Rochester, N.Y., Nov. 14, 1930; s. Donald C. and Agnes M. (McLean) D.; B.S. in Chemistry, Syracuse U., 1952; M.S. in Microbiology (AEC fellow), Purdue U., 1955, Ph.D. in Microbiology (NIH fellow), 1959; m. Joan E. Lehman, Jan. 2, 1955; children—Harold, Joyce, Carol. Group leader microbiology Vestal Labs. div. W.R. Grace & Co. chem. specialities, St. Louis, 1959-60, sect. leader microbiology and product devel. solns, 1960-62, dir. research, 1962-69, v.p., dir. research, 1969—. Mem. antimicrobial program adv. com. EPA. Fellow Royal Soc. Health, Gt. Britain; mem. N.Y. Acad. Scis., Chem. Spltys. Mfrs. Assn. (chmn. disinfectant, sanitizers div. 1971-72), Inst. Environ. Scis., Am. Pub. Health Assn., Am. Soc. Microbiology (nat. counselor Mo. br. 1970-74), ASTM, Sigma Xi, Phi Lambda Upsilon. Contbr. chpt. disinfectants Clinical Laboratory Methods, 1970 (Gradwohl). Patentee in field. Home: 7145 Westmoreland St St Louis MO 63130 Office: Vestal Labs 4963 Manchester St St Louis MO 63110

DEWAR, ROBERT EARL, chain store exec.; b. Traverse City, Mich., Nov. 20, 1922; s. Floyd C. and Irlene (Nash) D.; student Alma Coll., 1940-42; LL.B., Wayne State U., 1948; student U. Mich. Grad. Sch. Bus Adminstrn., 1963; m. Nancy Jane Miller, Sept. 26, 1944; children—Robert Earl, Jane Elizabeth, John. Admitted to Mich. bar, 1948; gen. practice law, Detroit, 1948-49; with S. S. Kresge Co., 1949—, asst. v.p. finance, 1963-65, v.p. finance, 1965-66, adminstrv. v.p., 1966-68, exec. v.p. adminstrn. and finance, 1968-70, pres., chief adminstrv. officer, 1970-72, chmn. bd., chief exec. officer, 1972—. Served as pilot USNR, 1942-45. Decorated Air Medal (2). Presbyn. Home: 1931 East Valley Bloomfield Hills MI 48013 Office: 3100 W Big Beaver Troy MI 48084

DEWEY, CHARLES SHERMAN, cons. indsl. psychologist; b. Fairbanks, Alaska, Oct. 22, 1905; s. Sherman and Mary (Gosa) D.; Ph.D., Stanford, 1944; m. Rebecca Arnell, Dec. 26, 1942. Instr., indsl. arts, vocat. subjects, Seattle, schs., 1934-41; instr., U. Wash., 1939-40; dir. state vocat. survey, Tucson, 1938; indsl. psychologist, Joshua Hendy Iron Works, Sunnyvale, Calif., 1943; tng. specialist, Army Service Forces, Fort Mason, Calif., 1943-44; indsl. psychologist, Stevenson, Jordan & Harrison, Inc., Chgo., 1944-46; owner, Charles S. Dewey and Assos., cons. indsl. psychologists, Chgo., 1946—; asso. prof. Chgo. Tchrs. Coll., 1961-64, chmn. dept. psychology, 1963-66, prof., 1964-66; asso. prof. psychology Ill. Inst. Tech., 1966-71. Recipient Good Am. award Com. 100, Chgo., 1966. Fellow Am. Soc. Clin. Hypnosis Found., AAAS, Am. Psychol. Assn.; mem. Ill. (pres. 1968-69), Midwestern psychol. assns., Nat. Acad. Econs. and Polit. Sci., Indsl. Relations Research Assn., AIM, Am., Chgo. (v.p. 1965) Chgo. Guidance and Personnel Assn. (pres. 1964-65), Midwest Human Factors Soc. (dir. 1961-63, pres. 1964-65), Am. Mgmt. Assn., Am. Mktg. Assn., Soc. Am. Mil. Engrs., Interam. Soc. Psychology, Internat. Assn. Applied Psychology, Ill. Guidance and Personnel Assn. (dir. 1966-68), Phi Delta Kappa. Mason (32 deg., Shriner). Clubs: Chgo. City (chmn. mental health com. 1964-65), Chgo. Psychol. (sec. 1958-60, pres. 1961-62). Contbr. articles to profl. jours. Home: 3130 Lake Shore Dr Chicago IL 60657 Office: 135 S La Salle St Chicago IL 60603

DEWEY, REBECCA ARNELL (MRS. CHARLES SHERMAN DEWEY), cons. psychologist; b. Auburn, Wash., Oct. 11, 1902; d. John Robert and Emma (Hanson) Arnell; Ph.D., Stanford U., 1946; m. Charles Sherman Dewey, Dec. 26, 1942. Tchr. pub. schs. Auburn, Aberdeen, Seattle, Wash., 1921-38; instr. Stanford, 1941-44; instr. U. Nev., summer 1941; asst. prof. U. Ill., Chgo., 1946-49; cons. psychologist Charles S. Dewey and Assos., 1946—. Fellow AAAS; mem. A.I.M., Am., Midwestern, Ill. (sec. 1964-69) psychol. assns., Modern Lang. Assn., Indsl. Relations Research Assn., Chgo. Psychol. Club (pres. 1964-65), Am., Ill. personnel and guidance assns., Chgo. Guidance and Personnel Assn., Interam. Soc. Psychology, Internat. Assn. Applied Psychology, Women's Share in Pub. Service (v.p. 1966-67), Pi Lambda Theta. Contbr. articles to profl. jours. Home: 3130 Lake Shore Dr Chicago IL 60657 Office: 135 S LaSalle St Chicago IL 60603

DEWIRE, NORMAN EDWARD, religious ofcl.; b. Cin., Mar. 5, 1936; s. Ormsby and Lucille (Binder) D.; B.S. in Edn., Ohio U., 1958; S.T.M., Boston U., 1962; D.D., Adrian (Mich.) Coll., 1976; m. Shirley Woodman, June 16, 1957; children—Cathy Lynn, Deborah Kay. Ordained to ministry Methodist Ch., 1959; pastor, Jacksonville, Ohio, 1957-58, Charlton City (Mass.) Meth. Ch., 1958-62, Central Meth. Ch., Detroit, 1962-67; exec. sec. Detroit Conf. Bd. Missions and Ch. Extension, United Meth. Ch., 1967-69, exec. dir. Joint Strategy and Action Com., 1969-75, gen. sec. Gen. Council on Ministries, United Meth. Ch., Dayton, Ohio, 1975—; bd. dirs. Center for Parish Devel.; del. 5th Assembly World Council Chs., Nairobi; governing bd. Nat. Council Chs. of Christ in U.S.A.; former pres., founding bd. Offenders Aid Restoration of U.S. Bd. trustees United Theol. Sem.; bd. dirs. Nat. Rural Housing Coalition, Grafton Hills Assn. Recipient award for pub. service Dept. Justice and U.S. Atty. Gen., 1974. Mem. N.Am. Acad. Ecumenists, Asso. Ch. Press, Kappa Delta Pi. Club: Dayton Racquet. Author: (with others) Discovering God's Mission in Our Community, 1968. Contbr. to New Occasions, 1975. Home: 34 W Dixon Ave Dayton OH 45419 Office: 601 W Riverview Ave Dayton OH 45406

DEWITT, JESSE R., clergyman; b. Detroit, Dec. 5, 1918; s. Jesse A. and Bessie G. (Mainzinger) DeW.; B.A., Wayne State U., 1950; B.D., Garrett Theol. Sem., 1948; D.D., Adrian Coll., 1965; m. Annamary Horner, Apr. 19, 1941; children—Donna Lea (Mrs. William Wegryn), Darla Jean (Mrs. William Inman). Ordained deacon, received in full membership Methodist Ch., Detroit conf., 1945, ordained elder, 1948; student pastor, 1944-46; minister Aldersgate Ch., Detroit, 1946, Faith Ch., Oak Park, Mich., 1953-58; exec. sec. Detroit Conf. Bd. Missions, 1958-67; asst. gen. sec. Ch. Extension Nat. Bd. Missions, 1970-72; now bishop United Meth. Ch., resident bishop Wis. area; del. gen. conf. Meth. Ch., 1964, 66, 68, 70, 72; chmn., dean Midwest Conf. Christian World Missions, other coms. and task forces. Bd. dirs. Ch. and Soc., Evergreen Manor, Oshkosh, Wis., Madison (Wis.) Meth. Hosp., Meth. Man., West Allis, Wis., Wis. United Meth. Found; trustee North Central Coll., Naperville, Ill., Evang. Theol. Sem., Naperville. Home: 702 Morningstar Lane Madison WI 53704 Office: 324 Emerald Terrace Sun Prairie WI 53704

DEWITT, JOAN MARIE, chemist; b. St. Louis, June 16, 1935; d. Daniel Harry and Adele Mary (Kottenstette) DeW.; B.S., St. Louis U., 1959. Lab technician LaFrance Mfg. Co., St. Louis, 1956-59, chemist, 1959—. Mem. evangelization com. Archdiocese St. Louis, 1977—; nat. treas. Christian Life Communities, 1967-71. Recipient award Nat. Fedn. Christian Life Communities, 1971, John XXIII Christian Life Community Leadership award, 1971. Mem. Soc. Die Casting Engrs. (nat. dir., Service award 1971), Am. Chem. Soc., AAAS, Am. Soc. Metals. Roman Catholic. Club: Eagles. Home: 9 Godfrey Ln Ferguson MO 63135 Office: 10256 Page Industrial Blvd Saint Louis MO 63132

DEWITT, WILLIAM ORVILLE, baseball exec.; b. St. Louis, Aug. 3, 1902; s. William Joseph and Lulu May (Sowash) D.; student St. Louis U., 1925-27, Law Sch., 1928-31, Washington U., St. Louis, 1927-28; m. Margaret Holekamp, Mar. 21, 1936; children—Joan, Donna Dorothy, William O. Office boy for St. Louis Browns, 1916; stenographer St. Louis Cardinals, 1917-25, treas., 1926-35, v.p., 1936; v.p., gen. mgr. St. Louis Browns, 1936-48, pres., 1949-51, v.p., 1952-53; asst. gen. mgr. N.Y. Yankees, 1954-56; baseball coordinator, 1957-59; pres. Detroit Baseball Co., 1959-60; v.p., gen. mgr. Cin. Baseball Club Company, 1960-61, pres., gen. mgr., owner, 1961-66; baseball cons., 1967-72; pres. William O. DeWitt & Assos.; chmn. bd. Cin. Coliseum Corp., Cin. Hockey Club, 1972—, Chgo. White Sox, 1975—; admitted to Mo. bar, 1931, Fed. bar, 1958, U.S. Supreme Ct. bar, 1972. Mem. Major League Exec. Council, 1948-50, 77—; mem. com. to select vet. players to Baseball Hall of Fame, 1972—. Named major league exec. of year, 1944. Mem. Mo. Bar Assn., Bar Assn. St. Louis, Delta Theta Phi, Alpha Sigma Nu. Presbyn. Mason (33 deg., Shriner). Clubs: University (St. Louis); Queen City, One Hundred, Cincinnati Country, Recess, Commonwealth (Cin.); Little (Gulfstream, Fla.); Ocean (DelRay Beach, Fla.); Thoroughbread of Am. Home: 2841 Ambleside Pl Cincinnati OH 45208 also 1465 Lands End Rd Point Manalapan FL 33462

DEWOLF, ALIDOR JOSEPH, machine tool co. exec.; b. Chgo., Mar. 19, 1916; s. Louis Joseph and Gabrella (LaGrou) DeW.; student DePaul U., 1935-36; B.S., Loyola U., 1936-38; m. Geraldine Ann Dreis, Aug. 21, 1944; children—Debra, Richard, Linda, Peggy. With Dreis and Krump Mfg. Co., Chgo., 1945—, controller, 1945-50, sec., also gen. sales mgr., 1950-55, pres., 1955-76, chmn., 1976—. Served to lt. (j.g.), USNR, 1941-45. Mem. Nat. Machine Tool Builders Assn. (dir. 1961-66, pres. 1966-67). Clubs: Beverly Country (pres. 1968-69, dir. 1952-55, 58-59) (Chgo.); Country of Florida, Ocean of Florida, The Little Club (Fla.); Butterfield Country (Hinsdale, Ill.). Home: 4 Oak Brook Club Dr G107 Oak Brook IL 60521 Office: 7400 S Loomis Blvd Chicago IL 60636

DE WOLFE, JOHN CHAUNCEY, III, lawyer; b. Oak Park, Ill., July 24, 1944; s. John Chauncey and Dorothy Sinclair (Fulton) De W.; A.B., Brown U., 1965; J.D., Cornell U., 1968; m. Dianne Douglas, July 28, 1973; children—Geoffrey, Warren, Lucinda. Admitted to Ill. bar, 1968; since practiced in Chgo.; mem. firm De Wolfe, Mills & Markley and predecessor firms, 1968—, partner, 1970—; dir. Oak Hill Farms, Chgo., 1st DuPage Corp., Hinsdale, Ill., Eascom Corp., Oak Brook, Ill. Mem. ednl. evaluation commn. Sch. Dist. 208, Cook County (Ill.), 1968-70. Mem. DuPage County (Ill.) Rep. Orgn., 1973—, committeeman, 1973—. Trustee St. Leonard House, Episcopal Diocese of Chgo., pres., 1975—; trustee Pop Warner Little Scholars, 1975—. Served as midshipman USNR, 1961-65. Recipient Cornelius W. Wickersham award Fed. Bar Council, 1968. Mem. Am., Ill. State, Chgo., Du Page County bar assns., Chgo. Estate Planning Council, Chgo. Hist. Soc., Art Inst. Chgo., Phi Alpha Delta. Republican. Episcopalian (vestryman). Club: Union League (Chgo.). Home: 805 W Hickory St Hinsdale IL 60521 Office: 135 S La Salle St Chicago IL 60603

DE WOODY, CHARLES, lawyer; b. Chgo., Oct. 18, 1914; s. Charles and Oneta (Ownby); student U. Fla., 1931-33, U. Mich., 1933-35, Columbia, 1935-36, Western Res. U., 1936-38; m. Nancy Tremaine, June 15, 1940; children—Charles, Nancy. Office atty. Oglebay, Norton & Co., Cleve., 1939-43; partner Arter, Hadden, Wykoff & Van Duzer, 1943-61; pvt. practice, 1961—; v.p., sec., dir. Ferry Cap and Set Screw Co., Nat. Extruded Metal Products Co., Internat. Rock Bit Co.; sec., dir. Tubecraft; dir. Direct Digital Industries, Ltd., Meteor Crater Enterprises, Inc. Bar-T-Ranch. Mem. Am., Ohio, Cleve. bar assns., Cleve. Law Library Assn. Episcopalian. Clubs: Union, Country (Cleve.); Cleve. Racquet Club (Pepper Pike, Ohio); Chagrin Valley Hunt (Gates Mills, Ohio). Address: Hunting Valley Chagrin Falls OH 44022

DEWOSKIN, IRVIN SAMUEL, health products co. exec.; b. St. Louis, Oct. 27, 1909; s. Leon and Fannie (Prensky) DeW.; B.S., Washington U., St. Louis; m. Eleanor Ritchie, Apr. 10, 1961; children—Steven, Kenneth, Nancy, Robert. Pres., Beltx Corp., 1943—, Orthoband Corp., 1957—, Erex Health Products, Barnhart, Mo., 1959—. Mem. St. Louis Planning Com., 1968; mem. adv. bd. St. Louis U. Med. Center, dept. orthodontics, 1972. Bd. dirs. Mo. State Tech. Services, 1969. Mem. Nation Round Table, Alpha Epsilon Pi, Beta Gamma Sigma, Omicron Delta Gamma. Jewish. Mason (32 deg., Shriner). Patentee in field. Home: 726 Knickerbacker Dr Manchester MO 63011 Office: PO Box 278 Barnhart MO 63012

DEWYER, GARY ALTON, farm equipment mfg. co. exec.; b. Cleve., Mar. 22, 1940; s. Harris James and Sally Wilma (Johnson) D.; B.M.E., Cleve. State U., 1963; M.B.A., Case Western Res. U., 1970; m. Helen Cecilia Kill, June 15, 1968; 1 dau., Marta Lynn. Sr. design engr. Addressograph Multigraph Corp., Cleve., 1963-67, systems analyst, 1968, staff asso. corp. mktg. research, 1969; exec. v.p., Kill Bros. Co., Delphos, Ohio, 1970—; dir. Comml. Bank Delphos. Dir. Jr. Achievement Delphos. Registered profl. engr. Ohio. Catholic. Clubs: Delphos Country, Shawnee Country. Home: Route #1 Circle Dr Delphos OH 45833 Office: State Route 697 W Delphos OH 45833

DEXHEIMER, WALLACE DANIEL, structural engr.; b. Sheboygan, Wis., Sept. 9, 1929; s. Ralph Eugene and Minnie Ilene (Mongando) D.; B.S. in Civil Engring., S.D. Sch. Mines and Tech., 1953; m. Wanda Arlene Vance, Aug. 17, 1952; children—Douglas Dale, Steven Gene, Dawn Marie, Nancy Kay. Civil engr. Brady Cons., Spearfish, S.D., 1955-57, structural engr., 1972—; structural engr. Johnson & Nielsen, Riverside, Cal., 1957-70, Zeiler & Gray, Inc., Denver, 1970-72. Served with AUS, 1953-57. Mem. Am. Concrete Inst., Prestressed Concrete Inst., Structural Engrs. Assn. of Calif., Triangle frat. Home: 1216 W Jackson St Spearfish SD 57783 Office: 1216 W Jackson Spearfish SD 87783

DEXTER, DONALD HARVEY, surgeon; b. Maywood, Ill., Apr. 8, 1928; s. Harry Malcolm and Theodora Jane (Trelawny) D.; B.S., Tulana U., 1948; M.D., Northwestern U., 1950; m. Esther Ruth Reeve, May 16, 1953; children—Donald H., Jr., Scott Reeve, Bryce Malcolm, Margaret Helen. Intern, Cook County Hosp., Chgo., 1950-51; resident in surgery Ill. Central Hosp., Chgo., 1951-52, Cook County Hosp., Chgo., 1955-58; practice medicine specializing in surgery, Macomb, Ill., 1958—, sr. mem. Macomb Clinic; prof. dept. health scis. Western Ill. U., 1975—, team physician; coroner McDonough County, Ill., 1964-76. Mem. Western Ill. U. Found. Served with USN, 1953-54. Named Outstanding Citizen of Macomb, Jaycees, 1972, Macomb Area C. of C., 1973; recipient award of recognition Devel. Center at Western Ill. U. and Macomb Area C. of C., 1977; diplomate Am. Bd. Surgery. Fellow A.C.S. (pres. Ill. chpt. 1972); mem. AMA, Ill. State Med. Soc., Ill. Surg. Soc., MW Surg. Assn., Internat. Assn. Coroners and Med. Examiners, Phi Beta Kappa. Republican. Episcopalian. Club: Rotary. Home: Tower Rd Rural Route #1 Macomb IL 61455 Office: Macomb Clinic 505 E Grant St Macomb IL 61455

DEY, SUHRIT KUMAR, educator; b. Calcutta, India, May 15, 1939, came to U.S., 1966, naturalized, 1976; s. Gokul Das and Manimala (Bose) D.; B.A. with honors, Calcutta U., 1958, M.A., 1960; Ph.D., Miss. State U., 1970; m. Sabita Kumar, Feb. 9, 1963; children—Sujata, Charlie. Lectr. in math. Calcutta U. affiliates, West Bengal, 1961-66; research asst. in aero. engring. Miss State U., Mississippi State, 1966-70; asst. prof. math Eastern Ill. U., Charleston, Ill., 1970-73, asso. prof., 1973—; vis. prof. Indian Inst. Mgmt., Calcutta, 1973; faculty research participant and faculty asso. Argonne Nat. Lab., Argonne, Ill., 1976-77. NSF grantee 1972, Heineman Found. grantee, 1977, Calcutta U. fellow, 1977; recipient award Ill. Acad. Sci., 1977. Mem. Am. Math. Soc., Phi Kappa Phi. Hinduism. Club: Math. Author: Outlines of Astronomy, 1966. Home: 717 Olean Place Charleston IL 61920 Office: Dept Math Eastern Ill U Charleston IL 61920

DEZA, ERNEST CABANGAL, psychiatrist; b. Iloilo City, Philippines, Aug. 6, 1923; s. Honorio Donasco and Ursula Diamante (Cabangal) D.; A.A., U. San Agustin, 1946; M.D., U. Santo Tomas, 1951; m. Mary Brillantes, Nov. 12, 1949; children—Alfonso, Edmundo, Zenaida (Mrs. Federico Pastelero Jr.). Came to U.S., 1953, naturalized, 1976. Intern, St. Mary's Hosp., Knoxville, Tenn., 1953-54; resident, Taunton (Mass.) State Hosp., 1954-56, Mental Health Inst., Cherokee, Iowa, 1956-57; practice medicine, specializing in psychiatry, 1960—; clin. dir. Blackfoot (Idaho) State Hosp., 1958-60, Western State Hosp., Hopkinsville, Ky., 1970-72, State Hosp., Richmond, Ind., 1972—; professorial guest lectr. psychiatry Riverside Hosp., Bacoalod City, Philippines, 1968-70. Served with USAF, 1942-45. Recipient UST Poetry 1st prize, Gold medal abstract oil painting, 1970. Mem. Am. Group Psychotherapists, Cath. Psychiatrists Guild, Am. Psychiat. Assn., Ind. Philippine Med. Assn., Lyrical Guild Ia., Am. Med. Psychiatrists Assn., Holy Family Parish Soc. Roman Catholic. Club: Readers Digest Book. Author: Book of Satire, 1948; Laugh Poems, 1970; Psychiatry in the Philippines, 1970; New Laugh Poems, 1975; Depression, 1975. Home: 11522 Templar Dr St Louis MO 63141

DIAMANT, ROBERT, architect; b. Budapest, Hungary, Apr. 2, 1922; s. Nandor and Margaret S. (Spitzer) D.; came to U.S., 1947, naturalized, 1957; student Hungarian Polytech. Inst., 1945-47; B.Arch. (Hillel Found. scholar), Miami U., 1949; m. Charlotte L. Block, Oct. 8, 1950 (dec. 1972); children—Steven, Laura Jo, Adam; m. 2d, Rochelle Portman, 1975. Designer, participating asso. Skidmore, Owings & Merrill, architects and engrs., Chgo., 1949-57, sr. designer, 1957-63, asso. partner, 1963-73, gen. partner, 1973—. Lectr., archtl. juror Miami U., Oxford, O., U. Minn., Pa. State U., U. Balt. Recipient awards, including citation of merit A.I.A., 1961, 62, honor award, 1967, Distinguished Bldg. and Honor award, 1968 (2), Distinguished Bldg. award, 1970, 71. Mem. A.I.A., Nat. Council Archtl. Registration Bds. Clubs: Arts (Chgo.). Prin. archtl. works include O'Hare Plaza Complex, Chgo., Bond Ct. Complex, Cleve., Gateway Center, Chgo., Lake Meadows Housing Project, Chgo., One Marine Midland Plaza, Rochester, N.Y., John Hancock Center, Chgo. Office: 30 W Monroe St Chicago IL 60603

DIAMOND, ARTHUR M., lawyer; b. South Bend, Ind., Jan. 3, 1925; s. Arthur M. and Mary (Kietzer) D.; J.D. magna cum laude, U. Notre Dame, 1947; m. Dagny Marie Lenon, June 17, 1950; children—Arthur M., David Andrew, Eric Lenon. Admitted to Ind. bar, 1947; since practiced in South Bend; partner firm Diamond & Miller, South Bend, 1947-71; partner firm Diamond & Perry, South Bend, 1971—. Merit badge counsellor Boy Scouts Am., 1950-62. Republican precinct committeeman, 1962-65; del. Rep. State Conv., 1964, 68, 74. Bd. dirs. Community Corp. Ednl. Rev. Mem. Am., Ind. (ho. of dels. 1974-77), St. Joseph County (pres. 1975-76) bar assns., Am. Judicature Soc. Clubs: South Bend Knife and Fork (dir., officer 1960-65); Toastmasters International (dir. 1964-68, pres. 1970-71). Home: 2726 Erskine Blvd South Bend IN 46614 Office: Lafayette Bldg South Bend IN 46601

DIAMOND, BERNARD, surgeon; b. N.Y.C., Feb. 12, 1912; s. George and Ida (Fishbein) D.; B.S., Coll. City N.Y., 1932; M.D., U. Edinburgh, 1937; m. Ruth Thelma Freedman, July 17, 1941; children—Sydney (Mrs. Sydney Diamond Ratner), Norman. Intern, Albany (N.Y.) Meml. Hosp., 1937-38; resident U. Iowa Hosps., Iowa City, 1945-48; practice medicine specializing in orthopedic surgery Waterloo, Iowa, 1949—; mem. staff St. Francis, Allen, Schoitz hosps., Waterloo. Served to 1st lt. M.C., AUS, 1941-43. Diplomate Am. Bd. Orthopedic Surgery. Fellow A.C.S., Internat. Coll. Surgeons; mem. Am. Acad. Orthopedic Surgeons. Author: The Obstructing Acromion, 1964; (play) The Contest, 1971 (recipient Per Se award from Per Se, Smith mags. 1970); (plays) Time Span, 1977. Home: 200 Windsor Dr Waterloo IA 50701 Office: 304 South St Waterloo IA 50701

DIAMOND, DIANA LOUISE, editor; b. Floral Park, N.Y., Feb. 4, 1937; d. Louis Bartholomew and Helen Stephanie (Strzelecki) Chmielewski; student Middlebury Coll., 1954-56; B.A. in English, U. Mich., 1958; m. Horace Williams Diamond, Jr., June 29, 1958 (div. 1975); children—Bruce Williams, Scott Kenneth, Kent Christopher, Mark Patrick. Editorial asst. dept. higher edn. NEA, Washington, 1958-59; pvt. tchr. art, Sunnyvale, Calif., 1964-68; reporter Pioneer Press, Highland Park, Ill., 1969-70; reporter Lerner Newspapers, Highland Park, 1970—, mng. editor, 1972—, suburban coordinator, 1974—; corr. (part-time) The N.Y. Times, 1975—; moderator, co-producer League Women Voters TV show Left, Right and Center, 1968. Mem. Sunnyvale Citizens Bond Com., 1966, Sunnyvale Citizens Adv. Com., 1967; exec. sec. Midpeninsula Citizens for Fair Housing, 1966-68; chmn. Art for San Francisco Peninsula, 1967; pres. Deerfield (Ill.) Area Human Relations Com., 1968-70; mem. Deerfield Human Relations Commn., 1969-70; bd. dirs. YWCA, Highland Park, 1977—, Chgo. Philharmonic Soc., 1977—, Calif. Republican League, 1962-64. Recipient Nat. Blue Ribbon Newspaper award, 1976, 77, 78; 3d pl. Ill. Editorial of Year contest, 1974; 1st pl. for Best Feature Story, Ill. Press Assn., 1974, and Suburban Newspapers Am., 1977; 2d pl. for Best Column, Nat. Newspaper Assn., 1977. Mem. League Women Voters Deerfield (dir. 1968-70), Sigma Delta Chi. Club: Zonta Internat. Home: 990 Summit Dr Deerfield IL 60015 Office: 1908 Sheridan Rd Highland Park IL 60035

DIAMOND, JESS, pediatrician, educator; b. N.Y.C., Sept. 18, 1918; s. Sol and Rose (Lopin) D.; M.D., Royal Coll. Physicians and Surgeons, Glasgow, 1942; m. Ann Kessler, June 20, 1948; children—Jayne Lee, Steven Franklin, Donna Lynn. Intern, Fordham Hosp., 1942-43, resident in pediatrics, 1946-48; resident in contagious diseases Kingston Ave. Communicable Hosp., N.Y.C., 1948; clin. asst. prof. pediatrics Albert Einstein Coll. Medicine, N.Y.C., 1967-71; clin. asso. dept. pediatrics So. Ill. U. Coll. Medicine, Springfield, 1972-75, clin. asst. prof., 1975—; lectr. pediatrics, emergency med. technician program Lincoln Land Coll.; guest lectr. Sangamon State U.; cons. pediatrician Andrew McFarland Zone Center, Springfield; mem. staff Meml. Med. Center, Springfield, 1969—; chmn. dept. pediatrics St. Johns Hosp., Springfield, 1969—; mem. perinatal adv. com. State of Ill.; pres. Found. for Med. Care of Central Ill.; mem. regional perinatal steering com. City of Springfield. Diplomate Am. Bd. Pediatrics. Fellow Am. Acad. Pediatrics, N.Y. Acad. Medicine. Contbr. articles to pediatrics jours. Home: 2320 Sylvan Rd Springfield IL 62704

DIAMOND, JOHN LEROY, mfg. co. exec.; b. Anthony, Kans., Jan. 8, 1913; s. Daniel Eugene and Mary Etta (Studebaker) D.; B.S., U. Ill., 1938; student Ill. State Normal U., 1935-37, Greenville Coll., 1933-34; m. Violet Chloe Kanady, Aug. 28, 1938; children—Janet (Mrs. Fred Craddick), Jerry M., Marcia L. Tchr. vocation agr. Greenville (Ill.) High Sch., 1938-42; asst. agrl. extension adviser Peoria County, 1942-43; extension adviser Edwards County, Albion, Ill., 1943-46, Peoria County, 1946-53; with Caterpillar Tractor Co., Peoria, 1953-78, agr. market devel. specialist, until 1978; ret., 1978. Mem. Am. Soc. Agrl. Engrs., Soil Conservation Soc. Am. Land Improvement Contractors Am. (hon., life). Home: 3117 N Parish St Peoria IL 61604 Office: 100 NE Adams Peoria IL 61629

DIARA, SCHAVI MALI, ednl. adminstr.; b. Detroit, Apr. 30, 1948; d. William Earl and Margaret Ruis (Walton) Ross; B.A., Wayne State U., 1970, M.A., 1977; m. Agadem L. Diara, July 25, 1969. Tchr., English and life sci. Highland Park (Mich.) High Sch., 1970-71; tchr. English, Upward Bound Program, Wayne State U., Detroit, 1971-72; tchr. English and social studies urban extension, 1972-73; tchr., head English dept. Roeper City Country Sch., Bloomfield Hills, Mich., 1973-77; now English tchr. Wayne State U.; dir. Diara Inst., Detroit, 1977—; guest lectr. Oakland Community Coll., Feb. 1977. Mem. Nat. Council Tchrs. of English, Assn. Study of Afro-Am. Life and History, Associated Black Pubs. Detroit, Animal Protection Inst. Am., Pan African Congress, Mid-Western Assn. Black Profl. Women. Author: (poems) Growing Together, 1973; (novella) Song for My Father, 1975. Home: 4095 Kendall St Detroit MI 48238 Office: PO Box 38063 Detroit MI 48238

DIAZ, GREGORIO, computer scientist; b. Sao Paulo, Brazil, June 24, 1947; s. Fernando E. and Martha C. (Fernandez) D.; came to U.S., 1969; student Universidad Central de Venezuela, 1968-69; B.A., U. Kans., 1972, M.S., 1974; m. Ann H. Albrecht, Aug. 13, 1974. Computer systems analyst Bur. of Child Research, U. Kans., Lawrence, 1972-74, coordinator for computer applications, 1974—, lectr. dept. computer sci., 1977—; cons. Center for Project Follow Through, 1976—. Mem. Assn. for Computing, Digital Equipment Users Soc. Contbr. papers in field to profl. meetings and jours. Home: YY-316 Meadowbrook St Lawrence KS 66044 Office: Bureau Child Research Univ Kansas Lawrence KS 66045

DIAZ-PEREZ, RODRIGO, pathologist, lab. dir., educator; b. Asuncion, Paraguay, June 16, 1924; s. Viriato Diaz-Perez and Leticia Godoi; came to U.S., 1957, naturalized, 1962; M.D., Universidad Nacional Asuncion, 1954; m. Nivia Molinero, Mar. 29, 1958; children—Leticia, Roland. Instr. pathology U. Va., Charlottesville, 1960-61; clin. prof. pathology U. W.Va., 1962-64; asso. pathologist St. Joseph Mercy Hosp., Ann Arbor, Mich., 1964-69; dir. labs. Annapolis Hosp., Wayne, Mich., 1969—; clin. prof. med. tech. Mercy Coll., Detroit, 1974—; bd. dirs. Profl. Corp. Pathology. Fellow Am. Soc. Clin. Pathology, Coll. Am. Pathologists. Recipient commendation VA Hosp., Clarksburg, W.Va., 1964. Roman Catholic. Contbr. articles to med. jours. and editor books in lit. field. Home: 2959 Hickory Ln Ann Arbor MI 48104

DI BONA, JAMES RICHARD, r.r. and grain trade supply co exec.; b. Quincy, Mass., Apr. 4, 1934; s. Guido Ralph and Helen Elizabeth (Pangraze) DiB.; B.S. in Bus. Adminstrn. cum laude, Boston U., 1959; m. Ann Olga Brigalli, Nov. 27, 1958; children—Helen Anne, James Richard, Hope Angela, Anne Olga. With Gen. Elec. Co., 1959-76, beginning as trainee, Everett, Mass., successively traveling auditor, Schenectady, N.Y., financial analyst, N.Y.C., mgr. finance, Decatur, Ill., dir. financial operations, Bilbao, Spain, 1959-74, mgr. bus. planning, Lynchburg, Va., 1974-76; pres., chief exec. officer Internat. Stanley Corp. of Internat. Paper Co. and Stanley Works, Omaha, 1976—. Bd. dirs., treas. Am. Sch. of Bilbao, 1971-73; pack leader Boy Scouts Am., Decatur, Ill., 1969. Served with AUS, 1953-55. Mem. Nat. Inst. Accountants, Spanish Inst. Financial Execs. Democrat. Roman Catholic. Club: Omaha Kiwanis. Home: 1541 S 109th St Omaha NE 68144 Office: 8401 W Dodge St Omaha NE 68114

DICK, HERMAN JUSTUS, pathologist, laboratory dir.; b. Syracuse, N.Y., June 22, 1913; s. Edward Joseph and Anna Bertha (Dias) D.; A.B., Syracuse U., 1934, M.D., 1937; m. Mary Agnes Gannon, Oct. 19, 1938; children—Mary Ann, Dorothy, Edward W., Herman J., Gannon J., Lawrence R. Gen. practice medicine, Syracuse, 1938-42; asst. prof. pathology Syracuse U. Coll. Medicine, 1946-50; dir. pathology labs. Crouse Irving Hosp., Syracuse, 1946-50, St. Joseph Hosp., Syracuse, 1950-61, Oswego County (N.Y.) Lab., 1961, Sheboygan (Wis.) Meml. Hosp., 1961—; mem. vol. faculty pathology State U. N.Y., Upstate Med. Center, 1950-61, Marquette U., Milw., 1961—, Med. Coll. Wis., 1961—. Served from 1st lt. to maj. M.C. AUS, 1942-46. Diplomate Am. Bd. Pathology. Mem. AMA (Physician Recognition award), Soc. Health and Human Values, Am. Soc. Quality Control. Contbr. articles to pathology jours. Home: 4630 Superior Ave Sheboygan WI 53081

DICK, JOHN HOWARD, office products co. exec.; b. Chgo., Dec. 29, 1946; s. Albert Blake, III, and Elisabeth (York) D.; B.A., Nasson Coll.; M.S., Lake Forest Coll.; m. Brenda Johnson, Oct. 3, 1970; children—Elisabeth G., Phoebe A. With A.B. Dick Co., Chgo., 1969—, mktg. mgr., 1978—. Bd. govs. Lake County Republican Fedn., 1974—; treas. A.B. Dick Found.; mem. mgmt. devel. program U. Chgo., 1972. Clubs: Exec., Economic, Chgo., Racquet, Onwentsia (bd. govs.). Home: 455 Oakwood Ave Lake Forest IL 60045 Office: 5700 W Touhy Ave Chicago IL 60648

DICK, MARVIN EDGAR, dentist; b. LaHarpe, Kans., Jan. 25, 1918; m. Arthur Clarence and Altie (Wardell) D.; student Madison Coll., 1940; D.D.S., Emory U., 1943; m. Emma Laura Canfield, Dec. 23, 1940; children—Doyle M., Milton L., Helen Elaine. Practice dentistry, Wichita, Kans., 1944-54, 56—; lectr. in field; established dental clinic, Philippines, 1967; mem. splty. adv. com. Kans. Diabetes Research Center. Sponsor CAP. Served to maj. Dental Corps, USAF, 1954-56. Mem. ADA, Kans., Wichita Dist. dental assns., Flying Dentists Assn. (charter mem.), Acad. Gen. Dentistry, Acad. Dentistry for Children (charter mem. Kans. chpt.), Aircraft Owners and Pilots Assn. Republican. Seventh Day Adventist (elder). Home: Rte 2 111 Douglass KS 67039 Office: 536 S Bluff St Wichita KS 67218

DICKENMAN, ROBERT CHARLES, pathologist; b. Beatrice, Nebr., Nov. 7, 1926; s. Charles and Edith (Felthauser) D.; B.S., U. Nebr., 1952; M.D., Creighton U., 1952; M.S., Wayne State U., 1957. Intern, St. Mary's Hosp., San Francisco, 1952-53; resident Detroit Gen. Hosp., 1953-57; practice medicine specializing in pathology; mem. staff South Macomb Hosp., Warren Mich., dir. labs., 1966—; mem. staffs Cottage Hosp., Grosse Pointe Farms, Mich., Detroit Meml. Hosp., Alexander Blain Hosp., Jennings Meml. Hosp.; asst. clin. prof. pathology Wayne State U., 1966—. Mem. Am. Soc. Clin. Pathologists, Coll. Am. Pathologists, Internat. Soc. Hematology, Internat. Acad. Pathology, Am. Soc. Hematology, Am. Assn. Blood Banks (insp.), Ama, Calif. Soc. Pathologists, Founders Soc., Detroit Inst. Art, English Speaking Union, Alpha Sigma Mu, Sigma Xi. Republican. Club: Detroit Athletic. Contbr. articles to med. jours. Home: 815 Ellair Pl Grosse Pointe Park MI 48230 Office: South Macomb Hosp 11800 Twelve Mile Rd Warren MI 48093

DICKENS, HAL GEORGE, advt. agy. exec.; b. Chgo., Mar. 1, 1932; s. Harry and Betty (Ziv) D.; student Sorbonne, Paris, 1946; B.A.E., Art Inst. Chgo., DePaul U., 1950; children by previous marriage—Kim, Craig, Hal G.; m. Laima Jakutis, June 17, 1974. Vice pres. E.H. Weiss, 1954-59, McCann Erickson, 1959-61, Grant Advt. Agy., 1961-63, North Advt. Agy., 1965-66; dir. marketing Coca-Cola Bottling Co. of Chgo., 1963-64; pres. Dickens Advt., Inc., Park Ridge, Ill., 1966—; dir. North Community State Bank (Chgo.). Served with AUS, 1952-53. Mem. Merchandising, Marketing exec. clubs. Republican. Roman Catholic. Contbr. articles to trade publs. Home and office: 500 Poplar Ln Glenview IL 60025

DICKERSON, BETTY EMILY, artist, educator; b. Nashville, Kans., Feb. 11, 1908; d. Arthur Herbert and Grace Emily (Carpenter) Millard; A.B., U. Kans., 1929; postgrad. Wichita (Kans.) Art Assn. Sch., 1931-45; pvt. study with various artists. Instr. painting drawing Wichita Art Assn., 1931—; instr. Hutchinson (Kans.) Recreational Center, 1965—; instr. spl. color class Grad. Sch. Kans. State U., Emporia, 1950-74; assembler nat. decorative and graphic arts exhbns; art workshop lectr.; color. cons. to designers; commd. portrait artist. Home: 509 N Martinson St Wichita KS 67203

DICKERSON, DENNIS MERLE, elec. engr.; b. Kearney, Nebr., Mar. 8, 1943; s. Merlyn Clyde and Audree A. (Datus) D.; B.S. in Elec. Engring., U. Nebr., 1966; m. Carol Jean Moore, Sept. 27, 1969; 1 dau., Sarah Elizabeth. Prodn. engr. Am. Stores Packing Co., Lincoln, Nebr., 1969-70; elec. engr. C.E., U.S. Army, Omaha, 1971-75; facilities engr. Lima (Ohio) Army Modification Center, 1975—. Co-chmn. law enforcement sub-group Pub. Safety Task Force of Riverfront Devel. Com., Omaha, 1973-75. Served with USCGR, 1966-69. Registered profl. engr., Nebr., Calif. Mem. Iowa Engring. Soc. (sec. 1974-75, pres.-elect chpt. 1975-76), IEEE, Ohio Soc. Profl. Engrs., Res. Officers Assn. Elk. Home: 2150 W Wayne St Lima OH 45805 Office: Lima Army Modification Center Lima OH 45804

DICKINSON, DARRELL RAY, warehouse exec.; b. New Virginia, Iowa, Feb. 20, 1927; s. Alva Ray and Doris Lenore (Taylor) D.; student N.D. State U., 1944-45, Drake Community Coll., 1952-53; m. Merlene Elaine Cadwell, Sept. 1947; children—Carrell, Gregory, Jeffrey, Eric. With Brady Motorfrate, 1947-55; partner Hogan Freight Service, 1955-65; gen. mgr. White-Line Transfer & Storage, Mchts. Transfer & Storage, Des Moines, 1965-73; v.p. warehouse div. Mid Am. Lines, Inc., Des Moines, 1973-77; owner, pres. Mchts.-White Line Warehousing, Inc., Des Moines, 1977—. Pres. Urbandale Sch. Bd., 1972-73. Served with U.S. Army, 1944-46. Mem. Am., Iowa (dir.) warehousemens assns., Am. Chain Warehouses (bd. dirs.), Iowa Motor Truck Assn. (bd. dirs.), Nat. Council Phys. Distbn. Mgrs. Club: Masons. Home: 6903 Oliver Smith Dr Urbandale IA 50322 Office: 1350 W Market St Des Moines IA 50304

DICKINSON, GLEN WOOD, JR., motion picture exhibitor, hotel exec.; b. Brookfield Mo., May 29, 1914; s. Glen W. and Adda B. (Campbell) D.; B.A., U. Kans., 1936, LL.B., 1938; m. Georgia Faye Dent, Aug. 18, 1940; children—Scott, Kent, Woody. Owner, Dickinson, Inc., Mission, Kans., 1939—; pres. Glenwood Manor Motor Hotel, Overland Park, Kans., 1961—; dir. Southgate State Bank, Prairie Village, Kans. Trustee Glen W. Dickinson Found. Served to lt. (j.g.) USNR, 1942-46. Mem. United Theatre Owners of Heart Am., Nat. Assn. Theatre Owners, Phi Gamma Delta, Phi Delta Phi. Home: 4015 W 57th St Mission KS 66205 Office: 5913 Woodson St Mission KS 66202

DICKINSON, WAYNE ALFRED, photographer; b. Chgo., June 4, 1921; s. Walter Luke and Elsie (Reinsch) D.; grad. parochial schs.; m. Margaret O'Dishoo, July 23, 1955. Radio actor, Chgo., 1937-50; owner Mar-Wayne Studio, specialists in portrait, wedding photography, Highland, Ind., 1950—; tape recording engr.; free lance photographer UPI, 1946-60. Mem. Profl. Photographers Am. Address: 8006 Richard St Highland IN 46322

DICKINSON, WAYNE GAYMAN, metals co. exec.; b. LaCrosse, Wis., Jan. 18, 1918; s. Ray Levi and Eva Lucina (Gayman) D.; student LaCrosse State U., 1935-39; m. Mildred Irene Nelson, Sept. 26, 1944; children—Nancy S., David W., Ray A. With No. Engraving Co. and divs., 1941—, asst. chemist, LaCrosse, Prairie Du Chien, and Sparta, Wis., 1941-42, processing engr., Sparta, 1943-45, process mgr., 1946-50, process, cost sales service mgr. 1951-56, factory mgr., 1957-58, sales engr., 1959-63, sales mgr., 1964-68, v.p. sales, 1968—. Treas. Sparta Concert Assn. Mem. Electrochem. Soc., Am. Electroplaters Soc. Republican. Elk, Kiwanian, Rotarian. Home: 400 E Oak St Sparta WI 54656 Office: 803 S Black River St Sparta WI 54656

DICKS, ROBERT EVAN, physician; b. Chgo., Sept. 10, 1943; s. Lawrence E. and Ruth E. (Essington) D.: A.B., Ind. Central Coll., 1965; M.D., Ind. U., 1969; m. Marceline A. Essington, Aug. 17, 1963; children—Emily S., Robert E. Intern, Meth. Hosp., Indpls., 1969-70, resident in family practice, 1973; pvt. practice family medicine, Indpls. Served with AUS, 1973-75. Decorated Army Commendation Medal. Mem. Ind., Marion County med. assns., Am. Acad. Family Practice. Methodist. Home: 756 Sunshine Ct Greenwood IN 46142 Office: 8242 S Madison Ave Indianapolis IN 46227

DI DENTE, STANLEY PAUL, electronics and leasing co. exec.; b. Waynesburg, Ohio, Dec. 11, 1946; s. Louis and Anne Mae (Pennese) DiD.; B.S., Kent State U., 1968; Tchr., Akron (Ohio) Pub. Schs., 1969-71; salesman, sales mgr. Midwest Region Assos., Akron, 1971-72; salesman, program devel. Blum Enterprises, St. Louis, Mo., 1972-73, Meridian Waterproofing Corp., Cleve., 1973; nat. sales coordinator Novar Electronics Corp., Barberton, Ohio, 1973-75, gen. mgr. Leasing Services Corp. subs. Novar Electronics, Barberton, 1975-76, adminstrv. v.p. Leasing Services Corp. and Novar Corp. subs. Novar Electronics Corp., 1976—. Roman Catholic. Home: 2073 Penguin Dr Akron OH 44319 Office: 24 Brown St Barberton OH 44203

DIEDERICHS, JANET WOOD, pub. relations exec.; b. Libertyville, Ill.; d. J. Howard and Ruth (Hendrickson) W.; B.A., Wellesley Coll., 1950; m. John Kuensting Diederichs, 1953. Sales agt. Pan Am. Airways, Chgo., 1951-52; regional mgr. pub. relations Braniff Internat., Chgo., 1953-69; pres. Janet Diederichs & Assos., Inc., pub. relations cons., Chgo., 1970—. Pres. Jr. League, Chgo., 1968-69; mem. pub. affairs com. Nat. Trust for Historic Preservation, 1973—; mem. regional com. on Marshall scholars for Brit. govt., 1975—; dir. Chgo. Conv. and Tourism Bur. Mem. Nat. Acad. TV Arts and Scis., Soc. Am. Travel Writers, Am. Newspaper Women's Club, Pub. Relations Soc. Am., Publicity Club Chgo., Chgo. Press Club. Clubs: Economic, Mid-America (dir.), Casino, Woman's Athletic (Chgo.). Home: 229 E Lake Shore Dr Chicago IL 60611 Office: 333 N Michigan Ave Chicago IL 60601

DIEHL, PAUL EUGENE, optometrist; b. Belleville, Ill., Sept. 23, 1936; s. Carl and Lucille (Bell) D.; A.A., Belleville Area Coll., 1954-56; O.D. (fellow), Ill. Coll. Optometry, 1959; m. Sharon Lee Busekrus, Apr. 8, 1961; children—Deborah Paulette, David Paul, Jonathan Brian. Individual practice optometry, St. Louis, 1959, Belleville and Cahokia, Ill., 1962—. Pub. speaker numerous civic orgns. and parent-tchr. groups. Served with USAF, 1959-62. Recipient John Marsh music award Belleville Area Coll., 1955. Mem. Am., Ill., Southwestern optometric assns., Optometric Extension Program, Tomb and Key, Phi Theta Kappa. Mem. First Assembly of God Ch. (deacon bd. 1970-72). Club: Rotary (dir. 1977—). Research on soft contact lenses. Home: 21 Andora Dr Belleville IL 62220 Office: 20 E Main St Belleville IL 62220 also 1020 Camp Jackson Rd Cahokia IL 62206

DIEMAND, EUGENE AUGUST, printing co. exec.; b. York, Pa., Feb. 23, 1925; s. Eugene Paul and Alice (Hauser) D.; student Western Res. U., 1943-44; diploma Charles Morris Price Sch. Advt., Phila., 1954; Grad. Indsl. Coll. Armed Forces, 1972, Air Command and Staff Coll., Air U., 1972, Air War Coll., 1975; m. Ruth Jane Maute, Sept. 1, 1951; children—Kim, Steven, Jeffrey, Christopher. Apprentice chef John Wanamaker, Phila., 1942; supr. prodn. Gen. Accident F & L Co., Phila., 1946-56; advt.-sales promotion mgr. Am. Casualty Co., Reading, Pa., 1956-65; mgr. advt. Marsh & McLennan, Inc., ins. brokers, Chgo., 1965-73; pres. Diemand Printing Co., Chgo., 1973—. Mem. Palmyra (N.J.) City Council, 1962-65. Served with USAAF, 1943-46; PTO; and USAF, 1951-53; Korea; lt. col. Res. ret. Mem. Ins. Advt. Conf. (dir.). Mason. Home: 625 S Wheaton Ave Wheaton IL 60187 Office: 323 S Franklin St Chicago IL 60606

DIENER, BETTY JANE, sch. adminstr.; b. Washington, D.C., Sept. 15, 1940; d. Edward George and Minnie Chambliss (Feild) Diener; A.B., Wellesley Coll., 1962; M.B.A., Harvard Bus. Sch., 1964, D.B.A., 1974. Account mgr. Young & Rubicam Inc., N.Y.C., 1964-70; sr. product mgr. Am. Cyanamid Co., Wayne, N.J., 1970-72; asst. prof. mktg. Grad. Sch. Mgmt. Case Western Res. U., Cleve., 1974—, asst. dean, 1976—; bd. dir. Revco Drug Stores Inc.; cons. Bonne Bell Inc., Richman Bros. Inc. Bd. dir. Womens City Club of Cleve., 1977—, Karamu House, 1976—; indsl. coordinator Internat. Women's Year activities, 1975, chairperson, 1976; mem. Ohio Coordinating Com., 1977. Mem. Am. Mktg. Assn., Assn. Consumer Behavior. Contbr. articles to Mktg. Sci. Inst., Jour. Mktg., 1973—. Home: 12900 Lake Ave #1623 Lakewood OH 44107 Office: Sch Mgmt Sears 624 Case Western Res U Cleveland OH 44107

DIENHART, ARTHUR VINCENT, utility co. exec.; b. Sioux Falls, S.D., July 23, 1920; s. Arthur Peter and Mae Agnes (Donahue) D.; B.C.E. magna cum laude, U. Minn., 1942: m. Rose Mary McCartan, Sept. 2, 1946; children—Paul Edward, Mark Charles. Engr., Dravo Corp., Pitts., 1942-45, 46; with No. States Power Co., Mpls., 1946—, mgr. engring., 1965-69, v.p. facility engring. and constrn., 1970—. Served as officer USNR, 1945-46; PTO. Registered profl. engr., Minn., Wis., N.D. Fellow ASCE; mem. Nat., Minn. socs. profl. engrs., Am. Nuclear Soc., Am. Concrete Inst., U. Minn. Alumni Assn., Tau Beta Pi, Chi Epsilon. Home: 5740 Morgan Ave S Minneapolis MN 55419 Office: 414 Nicollet Mall Minneapolis MN 55401

DIERINGER, HENRY WILLIAM, judge; b. Chgo., Jan. 26, 1910; s. Henry W. and Louise (Bartz) D.; student U. Ill., 1931-33; J.D., John Marshall Law Sch., 1936; m. Helen M. Rutkowski, Aug. 15, 1970; children—Henry William, Sharon M. Admitted to Ill. bar, 1936, practiced in Chgo., 1936-56; judge Superior Ct. (now part of Circuit Ct. Ill.), Chgo. 1956-70; justice Appellate Ct. Ill., 1970—. Pres. Greater Chgo. Churchmen, 1952-55. Bd. dirs. Ch. Fedn. Greater Chgo., 1948-72; trustee John Marshall Law Sch., 1967-70. Recipient award for services as Protestant chmn. Brotherhood Christians and Jews, 1953, Distinguished Alumnus Merit citation John Marshall Law Sch., 1968. Mem. Am., Ill., Chgo. bar assns., Am. Judicature Soc., Delta Theta Phi. Mason (33 deg., Shriner), Odd Fellow, Elk. Clubs: Executives, Ill. Athletic (Chgo.). Office: Richard J Daley Center Chicago IL 60602

DIERKS, JACK CAMERON, literary agent; b. Evanston, Ill., June 1, 1930; s. Wilford Rudolph and Margaret Mae (MacLaren) D.; student North Park Jr. Coll., 1947-49; A.B., Beloit Coll., 1951; M.S., Northwestern U., 1957. With pub. relations Prudential Ins. Co., Chgo., 1957-59, Allstate Ins. Co., Skokie, Ill., 1959-60, Trans Union Corp., Chgo., 1961-62; editor Food Business mag., 1962-63; partner Porter, Gould & Dierks, 1972—; free lance writer, 1965—. Advt. cons. Sweetwood Corp., Houston, Tex., 1964. Served with USNR, 1951-55. Mem. Sigma Delta Chi. Presbyn. Clubs: Chicago Headline, Chicago Press. Author: A Leap to Arms: The Cuban Campaign of 1898, 1970; (with others) The Writer's Manual, 1977. Home: 1360 N Lake Shore Dr Chicago IL 60610 Office: 1236 Sherman Ave Evanston IL 60202

DIERKSEN, CAROL ANN, educator; b. Hull, Iowa, Mar. 5, 1943; d. Edward Gustav and Frances Jeanette (Becker) Stange; B.A. in Elementary Edn. and Deaf Edn. magna cum laude, Augustana Coll., Sioux Falls, S.D., 1965; postgrad U. Minn., 1966, 75; M.A. in Speech Pathology, Northwestern U., 1968; postgrad. U. N.Mex., 1971, Mankato State U., 1972, U. Wis., 1974; m. Eugene Alvin Dierksen, Nov. 21, 1970. Spl. tchr. Minn. Sch. for the Deaf, Faribault, 1965-67, speech therapist, 1968-71, curriculum coordinator, 1971-72, coordinator Title I, 1972-74, supr. middle sch., 1974-77, supr. lower and middle sch., 1977—; lectr. in field. Certified elementary tchr., hearing impaired tchr., speech pathology, supr. speech, supr. hearing empaired, Minn. Mem. Am. Speech and Hearing Assn. (certificate of clin. competence in speech pathology), Minn. Assn. Educators of Hearing Impaired, NEA, Minn. Edn. Assn., Uniserv, Minn. Sch. Deaf Edn. Assn. (sec. 1966-67, pres. 1974), Conf. Am. Instrs. of the Deaf, AAUW (chairperson world affairs study group 1972—), Owatonna C. of C. Lutheran. Home: 209 N Elm St Owatonna MN 55060 Office: Minnesota School for the Deaf Faribault MN 55021

DIESEL, WILLIAM GARDNER, pub. co. exec.; b. Bloomington, Ill., Feb. 18, 1918; s. William Edward and Lucy (Murfey) D.; B.E., Ill. State Normal U., 1939; m. Mary Louise Naffziger, Sept. 5, 1948; children—John William, Ann Marie, Holly Jean. Reporter, Daily Pantagraph, Bloomington, 1940-50, state editor, 1950-52, news editor, 1952-67, asst. to pub., 1967-71, bus. mgr., 1971-74, gen. mgr., 1974—; sec. Evergreen Communications, Inc., 1972—. Del. seminar for pubs., editors, chief news execs. Am. Press Inst., N.Y.C., 1960. Served with USAAF, 1941-45. Mem. Assn. Commerce and Industry McLean County (dir. 1976—). Episcopalian. Home: 1221 E Washington St Bloomington IL 61701 Office: 301 W Washington St Bloomington IL 61701

DIETER, RAYMOND ANDREW, JR., thoracic and cardiovascular surgeon; b. Chebanse, Ill., June 19, 1934; s. Raymond Augustus and Emma Rose (Witt) D.; student U. Ill., 1952-56, Sch. Vet. Medicine, M.A., 1966; M.D., Loyola U., Chgo., 1960; m. Bette Renée Myers, Sept. 29, 1961: children—Raymond Andrew, David Lowell, Lisa Renée, Lynn Marie, Robert Sean, Deanna Lyn. Intern, Cook County Hosp., Chgo., 1960-61; resident in gen. surgery VA Hosp., Hines, Ill., 1963-67, sr. resident cardiopulmonary surg. sect., 1967-69; extern Chgo. Contagious Disease Hosp., 1958-60; house physician Alexian Bros. Hosp., Chgo., 1960; asst. surgeon USPHS, Mt. Edgecumbe, Alaska, 1961-63; clin. asst. instr. Loyola U. Sch. Medicine, Maywood, Ill., 1967-77, asst. clin. prof., 1977—; insr. examiner ins. cos., 1963-69; thoracic, cardiovascular, and gen. surgeon Central DuPage Hosp., Winfield, Ill., 1969—; pres. elect Good Samaritan Hosp., 1977; staff Elmhurst (Ill.) Meml. Hosp., Glen Ellyn (Ill.) Clinic, Hines VA Hosp.,

Loyola U. Hosp., Maywood, Delnor Hosp., St. Charles, Ill., Geneva (Ill.) Community Hosp., Alexian Bros. Hosp. Diplomate Am. Bd. Surgery, Am. Bd. Thoracic Surgery, Nat. Bd. Med. Examiners. Fellow A.C.S., I.C.S.; mem. Charles B. Puestow Surg. Soc., Chgo., DuPage County (pres. 1977), Ill. State med. socs., AMA, Nat. Assn. Residents and Interns, Assn. Res. Officers USPHS, Assn. Acad. Surgeons, Assn. Mil. Surgeons, Am. Coll. Chest Physicians, Suburban Surg. Soc., Soc. Critical Care Medicine, Soc. Thoracic Surgeons, Surburan Thoracic Soc., Am. Heart Assn., Ill. Geneal. Soc. Roman Catholic. Lion. Author: Mickelson-Peterson Family Sketch, 1970; Sorensen-Jensen Family Sketch, 1975. Contbr. articles to profl. jours. Office: Glen Ellyn Clinic 454 Pennsylvania Ave Glen Ellyn IL 60137

DIETRICH, ERNEST RAY, social worker; b. Hannibal, Mo., Jan. 30, 1936; s. Ernest LeRoy D. and Mary Elizabeth (Griffin); student Hannibal-LaGrange Jr. Coll., 1954-55; B.A., U. Ark., 1958; m. Anastasia Marie Piel, June 20, 1963; children—Natelle Rae, Robert Jay, James Kevin, Maryellen, Elizabeth Anne. With Neighborhood Assn., St. Louis, 1961-71; dir. youth and child devel. div. Consol. Neighborhood Services, Inc., 1972—; youth counselor St. Louis Police Dept., 1973—. Sponsoring mem. St. Louis Women's Crusade Against Crime, 1973—; solicitor St. Louis United Fund, 1961-71; mem. troop 745 com. Boy Scouts Am.; dir. Overthere Youth Center, 1971—. Served with AUS, 1959-61. Mem. Mo. Assn. Social Workers, Am. Forestry Assn., Am. Camping Assn. (dir. St. Louis sect.), Phi Delta Theta. Club: Optimist (St. Louis). Home: 915 Mark Twain St Florissant MO 63031 Office: 2930 N 21st St St Louis MO 63107

DIETRICH, RICHARD VINCENT, geologist; b. LaFargeville, N.Y., Feb. 7, 1924; s. Roy Eugene and Mida Amy (Vincent) D.; A.B., Colgate U., 1947; M.S., Yale U., 1950, Ph.D., 1951; m. Frances Elizabeth Smith, Dec. 28, 1946; children—Richard Smith, Kurt Robert, Krista Gayle. Geologist, Iowa Geol. Survey, 1947, N.Y. State Sci. Service, summers 1949-50; asst. prof. geology Va. Poly. Inst., Blacksburg, 1951, asso. prof., 1952-56, prof., 1956-69, asso. dean arts and scis., 1966-69, dean, 1969; prof. geology. also dean arts scis. Central Mich. U., Mt. Pleasant, 1969—; dir. Econ. Geol. Pub. Co., 1966-72. Organizer N.Am. for Mineral. Abstracts, 1976—. Served with USAAF, 1943-46. Fulbright research prof. U. Oslo, 1958-59. Fellow Geol. Soc. Am.; mem. Am. Mineral. Soc., Soc. Econ. Geol., Norsk Geologisk Forening, Geol. Soc. Finland, Am. Geol. Inst. (gov. 1972-74), Phi Beta Kappa. Presbyterian. Author books; contbr. articles to profl. publs.; editor Mineral Industries Jour., 1953-61; mng. editor Bull. Econ. Geology, 1966-73; author poems. Home: 2499 E Broomfield Rd Mt Pleasant MI 48858 Office: 311 Brooks Hall Central Mich U Mt Pleasant MI 48859

DIETRICH, SUZANNE CLAIRE, instructional designer; b. Granite City, Ill., Apr. 9, 1937; d. Charles Daniel and Evelyn Blanche (Waters) D.; B.S. in Speech, Northwestern U., 1958; M.S. in Pub. Communication, Boston U., 1967; postgrad. So. Ill. U., 1973—. Intern, prodn. staff Sta. WGBH-TV, Boston, 1958-59, asst. dir., 1962-64, asst. dir. program Invitation to Art, 1958; cons. producer dir. dept. instructional TV radio Ill. Office Supt. Pub. Instruction, Springfield, 1969-70; dir. program prodn. and distbn., 1970-72; instr. faculty call staff, speech dept. Sch. Fine Arts So. Ill. U., Edwardsville, 1972—, grad. asst. for doctoral program office of dean Sch. Edn., 1975—; exec. producer, dir. TV programs Con-Con Countdown, 1970, The Flag Speaks, 1971. Home: 1011 Minnesota Ave Edwardsville IL 62025

DIETRICH, WILLIAM CARL, food co. exec.; b. Le Sueur, Minn., Mar. 16, 1932; s. William Frederick and Dolores Geraldine (Moran) D.; grad. Mercersburg (Pa.) Acad., 1950; B.S. in Biochemistry, U. Minn., 1955; m. Corinne Jean Borchert, Oct. 3, 1964; children—Mary Elizabeth, Dolores Jean. With Green Giant Co., Le Sueur, 1955—, v.p. prodn., 1970-75, v.p. ops., mem. mgmt. com., 1975-77, sr. v.p., 1977—; dir. First State Bank Apple Valley (Minn.), Community Investment Enterprises, Mpls.; mem. Minn. Economic Devel. Commn.; gen. chmn. campaign United Way, Green Giant Co.; chmn., Dodge County Heart Fund. Bd. dirs. Dolores G. Dietrich Meml. Found. Mem. Nat. Canners Assn. (dir. 1968-70), Minn. Canners and Freezers Assn. (pres., dir. 1968-69), Phoenix, Gray Friars, Phi Gamma Delta. Roman Cath. Club: Le Sueur Country (pres. 1971). Home: 548 S Main St Le Sueur MN 56058 Office: 1100 N 4th St

DIETRICK, HARRY JOSEPH, rubber co. exec.; b. Cleve., Aug. 15, 1922; s. Joseph Michael and Anna (Prystasz) D.; B.S. cum laude, Western Res. U., 1948, M.S., 1950, Ph.D., 1951; advanced mgmt. program Harvard, 1965; m. LaVerne Juell Maier, Dec. 9, 1943; children—Laurel (Mrs. Thomas Wik), Karen (Mrs. Carl Soeder). Page, Fed. Res. Bank of Cleve., 1940; analytical chemist Cosma Labs. Co., 1941-43, chemist, part time, 1946-49; research asst. Office Naval Research project Western Res. U., 1949-51, grad. asst. phys. and gen. chemistry, part time, 1949-51, research asso., 1951-53; tech. man B.F. Goodrich Research Center, Brecksville, Ohio, 1953-55, sr. tech. man, 1955-57, project leader, 1957-59, section leader, 1959-63, mgr. indsl. prodns. and aerospace research, 1963-65, mgr. tire research, 1965-73; spl. assignment, B.F. Goodrich Tire Co., Akron, Ohio, 1973-74, dir. tech. adminstrn., spl. asst. to v.p. tech., 1974—. Served to capt., Chem. Warfare Service, AUS, 1943-46. Recipient jr. tech. award. Cleve. Tech. Soc. Council, 1958. Fellow A.A.A.S., Am. Inst. Chemists; mem. Cleve. Tech. Soc. (pres. council 1963), Am. Chem. Soc. (Nat. councilar 1957-59, sect. trustee 1966—), Am. Rocket Soc. (v.p. sect. 1962-63), Accoustical Soc. Am., Am. Inst. Physics, Western Res. U. Alumni (council 1957-61), Phi Soc. Sigma Xi. Contbr. articles to profl. jours. Home: 7354 Brookside Pkwy Cleveland OH 44130 Office: BF Goodrich Tire Co. 500 S Main St Akron OH 44318

DIETZ, ALBERT ARNOLD CLARENCE, biochemist, educator; b. Port Huron, Mich., Aug. 15, 1910; s. Frederick W. and Sophia (Klenk) D.; B.S., U. Toledo, 1932, M.S., 1933; postgrad. U. Heidelberg (Germany), summer 1934, U. Mich., summer 1935; Ph.D., Purdue U., 1941; m. Lelah May Johnstone, Nov. 27, 1937; children—William A.J., Robert J.M. Biochemist, Enza-Vita Labs., Toledo, 1933-39, U.S. Rubber Co., Detroit, 1942-43, Inst. Med. Research, Toledo Hosp., 1943-59, Armour and Co., Chgo., 1959-60; NDRC fellow Purdue U., 1941-42; with VA Hosp., Hines, Ill., 1960—; research asst. prof. biochemistry Chgo. Med. Sch., 1962-69; asso. prof. Loyola U. Stritch Sch. Medicine, 1969-74, prof., 1974—. Pres. Toledo PTA, 1951-53. Recipient Chgo. Clin. Chemist award, 1977. Fellow AAAS; mem. Am. Chem. Soc. (past chmn. Toledo sect.), Am. Assn. Clin. Chemists (chmn. Chgo. sect., 1969-71, dir. 1975—, pres. elect 1978), N.Y. Acad. Scis., Ill. Acad. Sci., Sigma Xi. Club: Torch (pres. 1963-64) (Chgo.). Contbr. numerous articles to profl. jours. Home: 1618 W 54th St LaGrange IL 60525 Office: VA Hosp Box 54 Hines IL 60141

DIETZ, NORBERT WILLIAM, ins. co. exec., ret. army officer; b. Botkins, Ohio, May 9, 1921; s. Frank George and Mary Kathryn (Wesbecher) D.; m. Jeanie Belle Reedy, Apr. 19, 1947; children—Norbert, Joyce, Wayne. Served as pvt. U.S. Army, 1944-52, commd. 2nd lt., 1952, advanced through grades to maj., 1962; ret., 1964; with SAFECO Ins. Co. Am., Cin., 1964—, supt. services dept., 1975—. Pres. Mom and Dads Club, St. Rita Sch. for Deaf, 1966-72, pres. Festival, 1972-75, chmn., 1973-77, mem. fin. com., 1975—, mem. gov. bd., 1977—; mem. fin. bd. St. Matthias Parish, Cin., 1973—. Decorated Bronze Star medal, Army Commendation medal. Named Man of Year Tri-County Sertoma Club, Cin., 1975. Home: 11526 Ivyrock Ct Cincinnati OH 45240 Office: 5901 E Galbraith Rd Cincinnati OH 45236

DIETZ, ROWLAND ERNEST, realty exec.; b. Cin., Oct. 26, 1920; s. William C.F. and Bertha (Stephens) D.; B.A., Swarthmore Coll., 1942; M.A., Columbia, 1946, Ph.D., 1962; div.; children—Christopher P., Brian L. Asst. prof. polit. sci. Western Coll., Oxford, Ohio, 1962-67; pres. R.E. Dietz Co., Inc., Cin., 1955—. Lectr. polit. sci. No. Ky. State Coll., 1973. Vice-pres., bd. dirs. Cin. Council on World Affairs; bd. dirs. Cin. Charter Com.; trustee, sec. Ft. Washington Trust. Mem. Am. Music Scholarship Assn. (v.p., dir. 1973—), Cin. Inst. Real Estate Mgmt. (pres. 1970-71). Clubs: University, Bankers (Cin.). Home: 3302 Nash Ave Cincinnati OH 45226 Office: 225 E 6th St Cincinnati OH 45202

DIFFENDAL, ANNE ELIZABETH POLK, historian, curator; b. Charlotte, N.C., Jan. 3, 1943; d. John Willard and Alyce Pyburn (Montague) Polk; B.A., Barry Coll., Miami, Fla., 1964; M.A., Emory U., 1965; Ph.D., U. Nebr., 1974; m. Robert Francis Diffendal, Jr., June 5, 1967; Archivist, Ga. Dept. Archives History, Atlanta, 1965-66; asst. prof. history St. Dominic Coll., St. Charles, Ill., 1966-70; instr. history Doane Coll., Crete, Nebr., 1971-72; also cons. archives program; instr. history U. Nebr., Lincoln, 1972-73; curator manuscripts Nebr. Hist. Soc., Lincoln, 1974—. Contbr. articles to hist. jours. Home: 1242 Hawthorne Ave Crete NE 68333 Office: 1500 "R" St Lincoln NE 68508

DIGGS, CHARLES C., JR., congressman; b. Detroit, Dec. 2, 1922; s. Charles C. and Mayme Ethel (Jones) D.; student U. Mich., 1940-42, Fisk U., 1942-43, Wayne U. Sch. Mortuary Sci., 1945-46, Detroit Coll. Law, 1951-52; m. Janet Hall, Nov. 6, 1971; children—Charles III, Denise, Alexis, Douglass, Carla, Cindy. State senator, Mich., 1951-54; mem. 84th-95th Congresses from 13th Mich. Dist. Served with USAAF, 1943-45. Mem. Am. Legion. Democrat. Baptist. Mason, Elk. Home: 8401 Woodward Detroit MI 48202 Office: Rayburn Office Bldg Washington DC 20515

DIGGS, OLIVE MYRL, city ofcl.; b. Mound City, Ill.; d. Charles George and Blanche (Chambers) Diggs; student U. Ill., 1926-29; B.Sc., Northwestern U., 1940, postgrad., 1940-41; M.A., Roosevelt U., 1957; M.A., U. P.R., 1958; postgrad. Loyola U., Los Angeles, 1954. Auditor, Chgo. Bee newspaper, 1929-32, gen. mgr., 1932-34, editor, 1934-47; asst. dir. Ill. Com. Human Relations, Chgo., 1952-55; adminstrv. asst. Dept. Urban Renewal, City of Chgo., 1955—. Cons. Nat. Youth Adminstrn., 1940-43; race relations adviser City Chgo., 1943-49; mem. Chgo. Land Clearance Com., 1949-52; tech. adviser White House Conf. on Children. Prof. Roosevelt U., Chgo., summer 1964. Bd. dirs. YWCA, Bensenville Home and Soc., Jane Dent Home, Chgo. Heart Assn. Recipient citizen's certificate of merit Wilberforce U., 1956, achievement award, Roosevelt U., 1959. Mem. The Links, AAUW, Nat. Assn. Housing and Redevel. Ofcls., Nat. Assn. Human Rights Workers, Nat. Assn. Coll. Women, Alpha Gamma Pi, Delta Sigma Theta. Author: Non-White Housing in Illinois, 1953; Desegregation by Court Decision, 1955; Upper Class Negro Woman in Chicago, 1957. Home: 3001 Martin Luther King Dr Chicago IL 60616 Office: 320 N Clark St Chicago IL 60610

DILGARD, JAMES LEROY, savs. and loan exec.; b. Ashland, Ohio, Apr. 8, 1936; s. Waldo R. and Josephine (Stover) D.; B.A., Ohio Wesleyan U., 1959; postgrad. Ohio State U. Coll. Law, 1960, Franklin U., 1961-62; diploma Am. Savs. and Loan Inst., 1967, grad. diploma 1970; certificate in mgmt. Grad. Sch. Bus. N.Y. U., 1968; m. Joyce Bally, June 11, 1960 (div. 1969); children—Jon Kenneth, Jo Delores; m. 2d, Anita Clarke, Mar. 31, 1972. With Central Savs. and Loan Co., Columbus, Ohio, 1960—, asst. treas., 1962-66, treas., 1966—, appraiser, 1966-76, sr. v.p., 1977—, also dir. Bd. dirs. Delta Tau Delta Ohio Wesleyan House Corp., 1968—; trustee Central Ohio chpt. Multiple Sclerosis Soc., 1976—. Mem. Fin. Mgrs. Soc. (pres. chpt. 1975-76). Republican. Club: Sertoma (dir. 1969-75, pres. 1973-74) (Columbus, O.). Home: 2060 Glenmere Rd Columbus OH 43220 Office: 37 N High St Columbus OH 43215

DILL, CHARLES ALBERT, creative advt. art dir.; b. Chgo., Apr. 11, 1922; s. Charles Albert and Florence Janet (Wang) D.; student Am. Acad. Art, Chgo., 1946; B.F.A., Bradley U., 1952; m. Ruth Helen Knott, May 5, 1945; children—Stephen Dill, Carol (Mrs. Robert Bro), Rebecca (Mrs. Max Custer), Elizabeth (Mrs. Jeffrey Symmonds), Timothy, David. Artist apprentice J. Walter Thompson, Chgo., 1946-47; comml. artist Grimm Advt., Chgo., 1947-48, Hosler Advt., Peoria, Ill., 1949-50; owner Dill Art Studio, Peoria, 1950-65; creative art dir. Mace Advt. Agy. Inc., Morton, Ill., 1965—; instr. Bradley U., 1954-55. Served with USAAF, 1942-45. Decorated Air medal. Mem. Bradley U. Fedn. Scholars, Peoria Advt. and Selling Club, Alpha Delta. Home: 2806 W Greenbrier Ln Peoria IL 61614 Office: 632 W Jefferson St Morton IL 61550

DILL, JOEL STANDISH, educator; b. St. Marys, Ohio, Sept. 20, 1940; s. Joel Wesley and Virginia Muriel (Frey) D.; B.A., Capital U., 1962; M.A., Wittenberg U., 1967; Ed.D., Ball State U., 1970; m. Janet Marie Gress, Aug. 23, 1969; children—Darin Wesley, Sarah Gress. Tchr., coach Buckeye Valley High Sch., Delaware Valley, Ohio, 1962-64; tchr., head basketball coach Riverdale High Sch., Mt. Blanchard, Ohio, 1964-66; dean students, head baseball and asst. basketball coach Urbana (Ohio) Coll., 1966-68; asst. prof. psychology, counseling Ball State U., Muncie, Ind., 1970-71; asst. prof. higher edn. U. Evansville, Ind., 1971—, mem. athletic bd. Cons. area dentists; vocat. expert HEW; research cons. Evansville Blind Assn. Bd. dirs. St. Vincent's Day Care and Nursery Sch. Mem. Am., Ind. psychol. assns., Am. (v.p. profl. devel. Assn. Humanistic Edn. and Devel.), Ind. (chmn. ethics com.) personnel and guidance assns., Student Personnel Assn. Tchr. Edn. (nat. exec. bd.), Phi Delta Kappa. Lutheran. Clubs: Tri-State Racquet, Evansville Tennis. Research on blind adolescent, coll. students. Home: 6408 Arcadian Hwy Evansville IN 47715

DILL, J(OSEPH) ANTHONY, state legislator, lawyer; b. nr. St. Louis, Aug. 31, 1939; s. Alfred J. and Helen (Reibestein) D.; A.B. magna cum laude, Rockhurst Coll., 1961; J.D., St. Louis U., 1964; m. Donna Mae Raskevice, 1972. Admitted to Mo. bar, 1964; pvt. practice, 1964—; mem. Mo. Ho. of Reps., 1966—, chmn. minority caucus, 1975-76; dir. Gravois Bank, St. Louis County, Mo. Active Boy Scouts Am.; del. Mo. Republican Conv., 1964, 68, 72, 76; 2d dist. dir. Mo. Assn. Reps., 1966-72. Mem. Mo. Air N.G., 1964-70. Recipient Honor citation St. Louis Suburban Tchrs. Assn., 1968, Distinguished Service award South County Jaycees, 1971. Mem. Am., St. Louis bar assns., Mo. Bar, Alpha Sigma Nu, Phi Delta Phi, Alpha Phi Omega. Roman Catholic (bd. dirs. parish lay bd. 1967-71). Home: 7723 Ravenhill Dr Affton MO 63123 Office: 8507 Gravois St Louis MO 63123

DILLER, JAMES GORDON, plastic surgeon; b. Allen County, Ohio, May 23, 1929; s. Clarence D. and Ruth M. (Claudon) D.; student Wheaton (Ill.) Coll., 1947-51; M.D., Ohio State U., 1955; m. Jean Miller, June 21, 1952; children—Collette, Janelle, Christopher, Jeanine, Nicole. Intern, Blodgett Meml. Hosp., Grand Rapids, Mich., 1955-56; med. missionary, Belgian Congo, 1957-60; resident in gen. surgery Cleve. Clinic, 1960-64, resident in plastic surgery, 1964-66; practice medicine specializing in plastic surgery Toledo Clinic, 1966—, mem. exec. com. Toledo Clinic, Inc., 1969-70, pres. Toledo Clinic Corp., 1970; chief plastic surgery dept. Flower Hosp., St. Luke's Hosp., Toledo Hosp. Founding mem. Christian Counseling Center Toledo, 1974-76. Diplomate Inst. Tropical Medicine, Antwerp, Nat. Bd. Med. Examiners, Am. Bd. Surgery, Am. Bd. Plastic Surgery. Fellow Am. Coll. Surgeons; mem. AMA, Ohio State Med. Assn., Lucas County Med. Soc., A.C.S., Toledo Surg. Soc., Ohio Valley Plastic Surg. Soc., Am. Soc. Plastic Reconstructive Surgery. Contbr. articles in field to profl. jours. Office: 4235 Secor Rd Toledo OH 43623

DILLER, MARY ANN, univ. adminstr.; b. Kansas City, Mo., Sept. 13, 1924; d. Edward and Willa Vaughn (Gates) Diller; A.B., MacMurray Coll., 1945; A.M., U. Ill., 1948; Ph.D., Mich. State U., 1973. Tchr. history Roxana High Sch., 1945-46; asst. in rhetoric and history U. Ill., 1946-48; tchr. history and English, Belleville (Ill.) Twp. High Sch. and Jr. Coll., 1948-49; tchr. social sci. Danville (Ill.) Jr. Coll., 1949-66, head social sci. dept., 1958-66, dean adult edn., 1966-75; regional program dir. for continuing edn. and pub. service U. Ill., 1975—. Vice pres. Vermilion County Citizens for Community Action, 1964-66; mem. bd. Children's Home of Vermilion County, 1969-75; mem. faculty adv. com. Ill. Bd. Higher Edn., 1968-70. Mem. Nat., Ill., Danville (pres. 1959-60, 63-64) edn. assns., Ill. Adult Edn. Assn. (mem. exec. bd. 1965-70, 71—, pres. 1973), Pub. Sch. Adult and Continuing Educators of Ill., Nat. Assn. Pub. Continuing and Adult Edn. Assn. (publ. com. 1975-77, higher edn. com. 1975-76), Adult Edn. Assn. U.S.A., Am. Assn. for Higher Edn., Nat. Univ. Extension Assn., AAUW (Danville pres. 1969-70, Ill. bd. mem. 1967-73), Sigma Phi Gamma (pres. 1961-62), Pi Alpha Theta, Delta Kappa Gamma, Kappa Delta Pi, Phi Kappa Phi, Phi Delta Kappa. Presbyn. Author: (with Violet Malone) The Guidance Function and Counseling Roles in an Adult Education Program, 1978. Home: 1426 Mayfair Rd Champaign IL 61820

DILLEY, JAMES WILLIAM, JR., assn. exec.; b. Evergreen Park, Ill., Oct. 13, 1936; s. James William and Josephine (Strands) D.; ed. Northwestern U., 1954-58. Adminstrv. asst. Student Health Service, Northwestern U., 1958-66; project coordinator Am. Coll. Health Assn., Evanston, Ill., 1966-67, exec. sec., 1967-70; exec. dir., 1970—. Mem. A.A.A.S., Am. Pub. Health Assn., Am. Sch. Health Assn., Am. Sociol. Assn., Royal Soc. Health, Am. Soc. Assn. Execs. Contbr. articles to profl. jours. Home: 4229 86th St Kenosha WI 53140 Office: 2807 Central St Evanston IL 60201

DILLING, DIANA JEAN, lawyer; b. Miami, Fla., Aug. 1, 1943; d. Kirkpatrick W. Dilling and Betty Ellen (Bronson) Dilling Curtiss; student Newcomb Coll., 1961-62; B.B.A., Tulane U., 1965; J.D., U. Fla., 1968. Admitted to Ill. bar, 1969, Fla. bar, 1969; mem. firm Dilling and Dilling, Chgo., 1969-71; asst. atty. gen. State of Ill., Chgo., 1971—; v.p. Midwest Medic-Aide, Inc., Chgo., 1969-71; treas., dir. P.E.P. Inventions, Inc., Chgo., 1971—; sec. Ry. Devel. Corp., 1975—; dir. Dillman Labs., Ltd., Chgo. Mem. Am., Ill., Fla., Chgo. bar assns., Phi Delta Delta. Republican. Episcopalian. Office: 134 N LaSalle St Chicago IL 60602

DILLING, KIRKPATRICK WALLWICK, lawyer; b. Evanston, Ill., Apr. 11, 1920; s. Albert W. and Elizabeth (Kirkpatrick) D.; engring. student Cornell U., 1939-40; B.S. in Law, Northwestern U., 1942; student DePaul U., 1946-47, L'Ecole Vaubier, Montreux, Switzerland; Degré Normal, Sorbonne, Paris, France; m. Betty Ellen Bronson, June 18, 1942 (div. July 1944); m. 2d, Elizabeth Ely Tilden, Dec. 11, 1948; children—Diana Jean, Eloise Tilden, Victoria Ely, Albert Kirkpatrick. Def. work Am. Steel Foundries, East Chicago, Ind., 1942-43: admitted to Ill. Bar, 1947; mem. firm Dilling and Dilling 1948—; gen. counsel Am. Massage and Therapy Assn.; dir. P.E.P. Industries, Ltd., Ry. Devel. Corp., Chgo. Truck Leasing Co., Mgmt. Info. Center, Inc., Harbil Inc.; v.p. Dillman Labs., Ltd. Dir., gen. counsel Nat. Health Fedn. Bd. dirs. Nat. Safety Council; mem. Religious Leaders Conf. Served from pvt. to 1st lt. AUS, 1943-46. Mem. Am., Ill., Chgo. bar assns., Am. Trial Lawyers Assn., Cornell Soc. of Engrs., Pharm. Advt. Club, Am. Legion, Air Force Assn., Delta Upsilon. Republican. Episcopalian. Clubs: Lake Michigan Yachting Assn.; Cornell U. Club of Chicago; Northbrook (Ill.) Tennis. Contbr. articles to pub. health publs. Home: 1120 Lee Rd Northbrook IL 60062 also Casa Dorado Indian Wells CA Office: 188 W Randolph St Chicago IL 60601

DILLON, DELPHIN DELMAS, publishing co. exec.; b. Youngwood, Pa., June 9, 1907; s. Oliver Laver and Sadie Myrtle (Griffin) D.; B.A., Duquesne U., 1938; S.T.B., Pitts. Theol. Sem., 1940, M.Div., 1972; postgrad. Oxford U., 1964; m. Lucille Peck, Sept. 23, 1930; children—Dwight, Carole Dillon Lockhart, Wendell, Barbara Dillon Gadke, Betty Dillon Mezget. Ordained to ministry, Presbyn. Ch., 1940; pastor Ripley, N.Y., 1946-47, Crestline, Ohio, 1948-52, Beachland Presbyn. Ch., Cleve., 1952-64; asso. editor World Pub. Co., Cleve., 1964-68; founder Dillon Liederbach Pub. Co., Lakewood, Ohio, 1969, pres., chief exec. officer, 1969—. Bd. dirs. YMCA, Crestline, 1948-51. Served to lt. col., AUS, 1942-46; ETO. Decorated Bronze Star medal. Mem. Am. Hist. Assn., Ch. History Soc., Delta Theta Phi. Republican. Presbyn. Mason (32 deg.), Kiwanian. Author: Notre Abri, 1948; Manual of the Christian Faith, 1962; History of the English Bible, 1966. Home: 20201 Lorain Rd Fairview Park OH 44126 Office: 14591 Madison Ave Lakewood OH 44107

DILLON, JAMES RICHARD, corp. exec.; b. Alliance, Ohio, Nov. 4, 1922; s. Howard R. and Pauline I (Nelson) D.; B.S. in Elec. Engring., Ind. Inst. Tech., 1943; postgrad. Sch. Law, Hawaii U., 1946; m. Marjorie M. Watson, May 24, 1947; 2 sons, Robert W., Richard N. Pres. Alliance (Ohio) Elec. Co., 1947—; treas. Alliance Industries, Inc., 1972—; treas. Pump Systems Inc., Alliance, 1974—; dir. Alliance First City Nat. Bank, Union Ave. Plaza. Pres. United Fund; pres. YMCA. Served with USN, 1943-46. Fellow of engring., Ind. Inst. Tech.; named Man of Year, city of Alliance, 1976. Episcopalian. Clubs: Masons, Shrine. Home: 387 Linwood Dr Alliance OH 44601 Office: Box 744 Alliance OH 44601

DI MARTINO, DAVID ROSS, educator; b. Rochester, N.Y., Feb. 28, 1947; s. Salvatore Joseph and Rose Mary (Bilotti) DiM.; B.A., State U. N.Y., Albany, 1969; M.A., State U. N.Y., Binghamton, 1970; Ph.D., Syracuse U., 1975; m. Lorraine A. Seidel, Aug. 26, 1967; 1 son, Kris David. Instr., Ohio State U., Marion, 1971-74, asst. prof., 1975—; cons. Urban Systems Research, Engring., Inc., OEO project, 1973. Mem. Citizen's Adv. Com. to Ohio EPA, Scioto River basin, 1976—; mem. Commn. on Nat. Settlement Systems, Internat. Geog. Union, 1976—. Dell Plain fellow Syracuse U., 1970-71; Nat. Acad. Sci./NRC grantee, 1976, Midwestern Univs. Consortium for Internat. Activities grantee, 1976, Ohio State Faculty research grantee, 1975-76. Mem. Internat. Geog. Union, Assn. Am. Geographers, Am. Geog. Soc., Conf. Latin Americanist Geographers, Nat. Council Geog. Edn., Socially and Ecologically Responsible Geographers, Soc. N.Am. Cultural Survey, Ohio Acad. Sci. Contbr. articles to profl. jours. Home: 310 Lafayette St Marion OH 43302 Office: 1465 Mount Vernon Ave Marion OH 43302

DIMBILOGLU, MUSTAFA EKREM, physician; b. Cankiri, Turkey, May 14, 1927; s. Mehmet and Emine D.; came to U.S., 1969; M.D., Istanbul U., 1952; m. Muazzez Güler, Apr. 29, 1953; children—M. Haluk, H. Melih, A. Mermin. Intern, Wheeling (W.Va.) Hosp., 1958-59; resident, Leila Hosp., Battle Creek, Mich., 1960-63, Med. Coll. Pa., Phila., 1963-65; practice medicine specializing in surgery, Battle Creek, 1970—. Served with M.C. Turkish Army, 1953-54. Diplomate Am. Bd. Surgery, Turkish Bd. Surgery. Fellow Internat. Soc. Univ. Colon and Rectal Surgeons, A.C.S., Am. Soc. Abdominal Surgeons; mem. AMA, Turkish Med. Assn., Acad. Surgery of Detroit, Mich. State, Calhoun County med. socs., Southwestern Mich., Frederick A. Collor surg. socs. Home: 254 Central St Battle Creek MI 49017 Office: 1010 North Ave Battle Creek MI 49017

DIMENZA, SALVATORE, psychologist; b. Chgo., May 2, 1938; s. Salvatore and Bartalomea (Gallina) diM.; A.B., DePaul U., 1960, M.A., 1964; postgrad. Loyola U., 1961-64, Ill. Inst. Tech., 1964, 72; m. Greta Van der Meer, Aug. 4, 1973. Dir. research Ill. Drug Abuse Program, Chgo., 1972-73; dir. mgmt. systems Ill. Drug Abuse Program, 1973; dir. drug abuse div. Joint Commn. Accreditation of Hosps., Chgo., 1973-76, asso. program dir. for planning and devel., 1976—; cons.; developer nat. standards for providing mental health treatment services. Recipient Superior Achievement award State of Ill., 1972. Fellow Royal Soc. Health; mem. Am. (asso.), Ill. psychol. assns., Am. Pub. Health Assn., Alcohol and Drug Problems Assn. N.Am., Am. Health Planning Assn. Contbr. articles to profl. jours. Home: 1516 N State Pkwy Chicago IL 60610 Office: 875 N Michigan Ave Chicago IL 60611

DIMICK, RUSSELL ALLEN, city ofcl.; b. Montfort, Wis., Dec. 19, 1926; s. Loys Vertner and Mabel Olive (Schneyer) D.; student Wis. Inst. Tech., 1946-49; B.S., U. Mo., 1950; m. Margaret Virginia Marklien, Aug. 12, 1950; children—Michael, Mary, Margurite, Margaret. Civil engr. Ill. Hwy. Commn., Springfield, 1950-51; with Milw. R.R., 1951-52; asst. city engr. City Waukesha, Wis., 1952-54; dir. pub. works City Cedarburg, Wis., 1954-58, 60—; city engr. City Mequon, Wis., 1958-60. Vol. fireman Cedarburg, 1954—. Served with USNR, 1944-46. Registered profl. engr., Wis. Mem. Am., Wis. pub. works assns., Holy Name Soc. K.C. Home: W69 N521 Margie Ln Cedarburg WI 53012 Office: PO Box 41 Cedarburg WI 53012

DIMMICK, WILLIAM ARTHUR, bishop; b. Paducah, Ky., Oct. 7, 1919; s. James Oscar and Annis Amanda (Crouch) D.; B.A., Berea Coll., 1946; M.Div., Yale U., 1949, D.D., Berkeley Divinity Sch., 1975; M.A., George Peabody Coll., 1955. Ordained priest Episcopal Ch., 1955; rector St. Philips Ch., Nashville, 1955-60; dean St. Marys Cathedral, Memphis, 1960-73; rector Trinity Ch., Southport, Conn., 1973-75; bishop Episcopal Diocese No. Mich., Marquette, 1975—. Pres., Memphis and Shelby County Health and Welfare Planning Council, 1970-73. Mem. Standing Liturgical Commn., Episcopal Ch. Asso. Parishes. Home: PO Box 129 Marquette MI 49855 Office: 131 E Ridge St Marquette MI 49855

DINEEN, ROBERT JOSEPH, elec. mfg. co. exec.; b. Cin., Dec. 3, 1929; s. Thomas Leo and Stella Patricia (Finnegan) D.; B.E.E., U. Cin., 1952; m. Marilyn Kamp, May 4, 1957; children—Brian, Lynn, Erin, Kerrie, Kevin, Mary Shannon, Patricia. With Allis-Chalmers Corp., Milw., 1951—, group exec., v.p. power generation and transmission group, 1971-76; pres. Allis-Chalmers Power Systems, Inc., Fiat-Allis Constrn. Machinery Inc., Deerfield, Ill., 1976—. Bd. dirs. Cin. Indsl. Inst. Served with AUS, 1952-54. Recipient distinguished alumnus award, U. Cin., 1971. Mem. Nat. Elec. Mfrs. Assn. (gov.), IEEE, Am. Mgmt. Assn. Home: 2122 Middlefork Rd Northfield IL 60093 Office: 104 Wilmot Rd Deerfield IL 60015

DING, GAR DAV, architect; b. Canton, China, Nov. 14, 1929; s. Chew Cheung and Ngan She (Ho) D.; came to U.S., 1966; B.Arch., U. Auckland (N.Z.), 1953; B.Engring., U. Canterbury (N.Z.), 1959; M.Engring. Sci., U. New S. Wales, 1961; m. Maisie Young, Aug. 24, 1954; children—David, Judy, Derek, Walter. Lectr., then sr. lectr. archtl. sci. U. Sydney (Australia), 1959-66; prof., chmn. environ. systems studies Va. Poly. Inst. and State U., Blacksburg, 1966-72; prof., dir. grad. studies in architecture Miami U., Oxford, Ohio, also U. Cin., 1972-73; prof. architecture, head dept. U. Ill., Urbana, 1973—; mem. bldg. research adv. bd. Nat. Acad. Sci., 1976—; housing com. New River Dist. Valley Planning Commn., 1970-72; cons. in field. Humes Industries scholar, 1956; C.S. McCilly scholar, 1957; recipient Research award Royal Inst. Brit. Architects, 1966; research grantee Dept. Army, 1968, NSF, 1976. Fellow N.Z., Royal Australian insts. archietects; mem. ASCE, Instn. Engrs. Australia. Co-author: Models in Archiyecture, 1968; contbg. author: Metropolitan Transportation Planning, 1975. Home: 10 Forest View St Mahomet IL 61853 Office:

DINGELL, JOHN DAVID, congressman; b. Colorado Springs, Colo. July 8, 1926; s. John D. and Grace (Bigler) D.; B.S. in Chemistry, Georgetown U., 1949. J.D., 1952. Admitted to D.C. bar, 1952, Mich. bar, 1953; asst. pros. atty., Wayne County (Mich.), 1953-55: mem. 84th to 88th Congresses from 15th Dist. Mich., 89th-95th Congresses from 16th Dist. Mich., chmn. subcom. on energy and power Interstate and Fgn. Commerce Com., mem. Small Bus. Com., Mcht. Marine and Fisheries Com. Served as 2d lt. inf. AUS. 1945-46. Mem. Delta Theta Phi. Office: House of Representatives Washington DC 20515

DINGER, ROLAND VERNEIL, photographer; b. Hecla, S.D., Aug. 6, 1920; s. Irving Henry and Anna Viola (Hungerford) D.; M. Photography, Winona Sch. Photography, 1964; m. Pamela Mae Yeoman, Apr. 28, 1974; children by previous marriage—Faithe (Mrs. Larry Hoyt), Hope (Mrs. Roger Kahler), Rita, Dwight, Mary. Photographer, Flouretone Studios Inc., St. Paul, 1945-47; owner Dinger Studio, Britton, S.D., 1947-58; founder, pres. Dinger-Graf Corp., Aberdeen, S.D., 1958-72, Dinger, Inc., Bismarck, N.D. and Aberdeen, S.D., 1973—. Mem. city council City of Britton, 1953-58. Served with USAAF, 1939-45. Mem. Profl. Photographers Am. (vice chmn. 1969-72), S.D. (pres. 1962), N.D., Minn. profl. photographers assns., Am. Legion, V.F.W. Mason (Shriner), Odd Fellow, Elk. Home: 318 S 9th St Bismarck ND 58501 Office: 318 S 9th St Bismarck ND 58501 also 717 S Main St Aberdeen SD 57401

DINGFELDER, STEVEN PETER, psychologist, social service adminstr.; b. Mpls., May 9, 1944; s. Sigbert and Elizabeth (Neu) D.; B.A., U. Minn., 1966; M.A., Ind. State U., 1968, Ph.D., 1971; m. Claire Elaine Shechter, Dec. 19, 1965; children—Jennifer Ann, Scott Allen. Psychologist, Moore-Porter Evaluation Clinic, Terre Haute, Ind., 1968; sch. psychologist Vigo County (Ind.) Sch. Corp., Terre Haute, 1969-70; clin. psychologist Katherine Hamilton Mental Health Center, Terre Haute, 1970-72, program dir., 1972-74; chem. dependency coordinator No. Pines Unified Services Center, Cumberland, Wis., 1974—. Chmn. Vigo County Coordinating Council on Alcohol and Drug Abuse, 1972-74; adj. prof. psychology Ind. State U., Terre Haute, 1972; mem. drug abuse com. Ind. State Dept., 1972-74; cons. psychologist Gibault Sch. for Boys, Terre Haute, 1974. Mem. Mayor's Com. on the Problems of Youth, Terre Haute, 1970-74; mem. Gov.'s Adv. Council on Alcohol and Drug Abuse, State of Ind., 1974. Recipient Becker award Ind. State U., 1968. Mem. Am., Ind. (chmn. div. sch. psychology 1973-74) psychol. assns., Council for Exceptional Children, Ind. Assn. of Counselors on Alcohol and Drug Abuse (v.p. 1973-74), Wis. Assn. on Alcohol and Other Drug Abuse (edn. subcom. 1974—), Wis. Assn. Community Human Services Program, Wis. Assn. Chem. Abuse Coordinators (chmn. 1976), Lambda Psi Sigma, Phi Delta Kappa. Home: Route 3 PO Box 253A Cumberland WI 54829 Office: Northern Pines Unified Services Center Cumberland WI

DINGLEDINE, EUGENE W., constrn. co. exec.; b. Washington, Ill., Feb. 1, 1920; s. Walter J. and Clara E. (Hagenstoz) D.; B.S. in Civil Engring., U. Ill.; m. Doris J. Dorward, Aug. 1 1943; children—Donald, Linda Gable, Edward, Jon, Civil engr. Patrick Warren Inst., Chgo., 1948-50, Mercury Builders, Chgo., 1950-55; with Del Constrn. Co., Washington, 1955—, pres., 1956—. Mem. Washington Sch. Bd. Served to capt. USAAF, 1942-45. Decorated Purple Heart, Air medal. Mem. Asso. Gen. Contractors Am., Central Ill. Builders (sec.-treas.). Mason (Shriner), Rotarian. Club: Washington Civic. Home: 129 Irish Ln Washington IL 61571 Office: 130 Irish Lane Washington IL 61571

DINGWALL, ROBERT JOHN, horticulturist; b. Grandview, Man., Can., Sept. 5, 1925; s. Peter Robert and Muriel Olivia (Brigham) D.; came to U.S., 1964; student Niagara (Ont.) Sch. Horticulture, 1944-47; children—Lewis, Laura, Peter, Susan. Chief horticulturist U. Toronto, 1947-55; supr. South Shore Nursery, Bridgewater, N.S., Can., 1955-64; adminstr. Duke Gardens Found., Somerville, N.J., 1964-69; chief horticulturist Mo. Bot. Garden, St. Louis, 1969—. Cons.; columnist St. Louis Globe Democrat. Mem. Am. Hort. Soc., Nat. Wildlife Fedn., St. Louis Herb Soc. (hon.), Boxwood Soc. (hon.), Rose Soc. (hon.). Author: Pesticides, A Guide to Safe Garden Use, 1971. Home: 9260 F Ft Sumter Ln St Louis MO 63126 Office: 2345 Tower Grove Ave St Louis MO 63110

DINKEL, JOSEPH WILLARD, elec. engr.; b. Galion, Ohio, Aug. 19, 1918; s. LeRoy Frederick and Jessie Edna (Barr) D.; B.S. in Elec. Engring., Case Inst. Tech., 1949; B.A. in Math, Wittenberg U., 1943; m. Eleanor Jane Dickson, Sept. 7, 1947; children—Barbara Jane, Betty Ann. Drug clk., Seemann's Drug Store, Galion, 1936-39; research engr. Jack & Heintz, Bedford, Ohio, 1949; elec. engr. Taylor Elevator Co., Inc., Cleve., 1949-58, v.p., chief engr., 1958—. Mem. adv. bd. Trade Sch. Served with USN, 1943-46, 50-52. Mem. IEEE (sr.), Am. Def. Preparedness Assn., Cleve. Engring. Soc. Republican. Lutheran. Home: 22269 Berry Dr Rocky River OH 44116 Office: 2011 St Clair Ave Cleveland OH 44114

DINKINS, THOMAS ALLEN, III, systems analyst; b. St. Louis, Dec. 29, 1946; s. Thomas Allen and Catherine (Fabick) D.; student St. Louis U., Christian Bros. Coll., 1964; m. Donna Berra, Apr. 29, 1967; 1 son, Thomas Allen IV. Field engr. Honeywell Info. Systems, St. Louis, 1970-74; parts clk. John Fabick Tractor Co., St. Louis, 1962-66, systems analyst, 1974—. Served to sgt., USAF, 1966-70. Mem. Nat. Model R.R. Assn. Home: 9123 Hatton Dr St Louis MO 63126 Office: 1 Fabick Dr Fenton MO 63026

DINSE, ALBERT ERNEST, mgr. city testing lab.; b. Chgo., Apr. 24, 1903; s. August Henry and Augusta (Zoellner) D.; student parochial schs.; m. Evelyn M. Plath, Nov. 29, 1923; m. 2d, Bertha D. Findeisen, Aug. 12, 1972. Analyst Gen. Chem. Co., Chgo., 1917-20; with Sinclair Refining Co. Testing Lab., 1920-24; testing engr. Wacker Dr. constrn. City of Chgo., 1924-27; testing engr. Carnegie Ill. Steel Co., Chgo., 1929-31; mgr. Walter H. Flood Co. Testing Lab., Kalamazoo, 1954-62; mgr. city testing lab. City of Kalamazoo, 1962—. Mem. Am. Fedn. Musicians. Lutheran. Club: Twin City Camera of St. Joseph (past sec.). Home: 3009 Cameron St Kalamazoo MI 49001 Office: 822 Schuster Ave Kalamazoo MI 49001

DINWIDDIE, FAYE LOVE (MRS. BENJAMIN F. DINWIDDIE), ret. social worker, author; b. Paris, Tenn.; d. Nelson Watson and Willa (Muzzall) Love; student U. Toledo, 1933-34, U. Denver, 1937-38, U. Mich., 1946; m. John S. Foster, May 23, 1925 (div. 1938); 1 son, John Love Foster (dec.); m. 2d, Benjamin F. Dinwiddie, Oct. 22, 1942 (dec. Mar. 1964). Supr., Dunbar Community Center, Toledo, 1934, dir., 1935-37; newspaper columnist Ohio State Press, Colo. Statesman, Ohio State News, 1937-41; field worker health edn. Toledo and Lucas County Tb Soc., 1944-54; case worker Lucas County Welfare Dept., 1955-62; family counselor Office Econ. Opportunity for Greater Toledo, acting dir. econ. opportunity center, 1965-71; dir. recruitment Women's Job Corps. Mem. met. planning commn. Toledo C. of C., 1943-46; mem. exec. com. health and welfare sect. Toledo Council Social Agys., 1951-54, chmn. social hygiene com., 1952-54; mem. Toledo Recreation Commn., 1947-52; pres. Coterie Study Group, 1940-41; mem. Study Hour Club. News specialist, editor newsletter Community Orbit; writer column Like It Is. Trustee Toledo YMCA, 1953-59. Recipient certificate of merit, Toledo C. of C., 1953, Ohio Pub. Health Assn., 1954; Key to City of Cleve., 1972; Certificate for service Creative Arts Workshops, 1972. Mem. Am. Pub. Health Assn., N.A.A.C.P. (life), Royal Soc. Health (life), Internat. Platform Assn., Am. poets Fellowship Soc., Black Writers Conf., Nat. Writers Club, Ohio Soc. N.Y., Centro Studi Internazionali Baptist. Author: (poetry) Song of the Mute, 1970. Contbr. poetry to various publs. Home: 1908 Washington St Toledo OH 43624

DIPERT, MERLIN HARRY, mathematician; b. Govertown, Ind., Sept. 19, 1918; s. Jasper P. and Atta (Boots) D.; A.B., Ind. Central Coll., 1940; M.S., Ind. U., 1948; postgrad. Ill. Inst. Tech., 1965-67; m. Eugenia Kuklinski, July 27, 1940; children—Judy Kay (Mrs. Charles Schmidt), Jerry Justin. Prof. math. Westmar Coll., LeMars, Iowa, 1947-52; exptl. technician Bendix Products Div., South Bend, Ind., 1953-57; mathematician-computers Argonne (Ill.) Nat. Lab., 1957-71; chief systems devel. sect., mathematician computers EPA, Chgo., 1971—. Mem. Am. Statis. Assn., A.A.A.S., Biometrics Soc., Radiation Research Soc. Home: 235 W Adams Villa Park IL 60181 Office: 230 S Dearborn St Chicago IL 60604

DIPRIZIO, CHRISANN SCHIRO, rehab. counselor; b. Chgo., Dec. 31, 1946; d. Joseph Frank and Ethel (Fortunato) Schiro; B.S., Loyola U., Chgo., 1967, M.Ed., 1970; Ph.D. (research grantee), Northwestern U., 1974; children—Jennifer, Daniel. Sci. tchr. Northbrook (Ill.) Jr. High Sch., 1967-70; dir. career counseling and placement Mundelein Coll., Chgo., 1972-74; human devel. counselor Regional Service Agy., Skokie, Ill., 1974-75; asst. prof. psychology, rehab. counselor Ill. Inst. Tech., Chgo., 1975—. Certified sex edn. cons.; registered psychologist, Ill. Mem. Am. Personnel and Guidance Assn., Nat. Rehab. Assn., Nat. Council Rehab. Edn. Kappa Beta Gamma Alumnae Assn. (nat. officer). Roman Catholic. Office: Psychology Dept Ill Inst Tech 3101 S State St Chicago IL 60616

DIRKSCHNEIDER, EUGENE FRANCIS, supt. schs.; b. Dodge, Nebr., Nov. 27, 1927; s. Frank and Otillia (Bazata) D.; student U. N.Mex., 1946, U. Nebr., 1946-48; B.A., Wayne State Tchrs. Coll., 1950; M.S., U. Omaha, 1957; m. Minnie Bertha Anderson, Mar. 7, 1953; children—Diane Sue, Dawn Marie, Scott Eugene, Todd Alan, Kip Michael. Tchr. pub. schs., Platte Center, Nebr., 1950-52, 55-56, supt. schs., 1956-59; supt. Paxton (Nebr.) Pub. Schs., 1959-62, Valley (Nebr.) Pub. Schs., 1962-65, Wilber (Nebr.) Pub. Schs., 1965—. Served with USNR, 1946-48, AUS, 1952-54. Mem. NEA, Nebr., Wilber-Clatonia edn. assns., Nat., Am., Nebr. assns. sch. adminstrs., Nebr. Sch. Activities Assn. (chmn. state bd. control), Nebr. Schoolmasters, Am. Legion (past vice comdr.), Wilber C. of C., Nebr. Czechs of Wilber (pres.), Ak-Sar-Ben. Roman Catholic. Elk, Rotarian. Home: 524 E 1st St Wilber NE 68465 Office: 9th and Franklin Sts Wilber NE 68465

DISKANT, MARION WHILE (MRS. ANDREW DISKANT), educator; b. Cleve., Mar. 13, 1933; d. Stephen W. and Anne (Bridgwater) While; B.A., Baldwin Wallace Coll., 1955; M.S., Case Western Res. U., 1967; m. Andrew Diskant. Tchr. math. John Adams High Sch., Cleve., 1955-66; chmn. math. dept. Harry E. David Jr. High Sch., Cleve., 1966-67; asst. prin. Robert H. Jamison Jr. High Sch., Cleve., 1967-72; unit prin. Lincoln Jr. High Sch., Cleve., 1972-73; asst. prin. James F. Rhodes High Sch., Cleve., 1974-77; unit prin. East Tech. High Sch., Cleve., 1977—. Mem. Ohio Assn. Classroom Tchrs., Cleve. Edn. Assn. (sec. 1963-64), Ohio Edn. Assn., N.E.A., Northeastern Ohio Tchrs. Assn., Cleve. Math Club, Inst. Math. Statistics, Nat. Hist. Soc., Am. Statis. Assn., Biometric Soc., Delta Kappa Gamma (pres. Alpha chpt.). Home: 4948 E 81st St Garfield Heights OH 44125 Office: E 55th St and Scovill Ave Cleveland OH 44104

DISKERUD, CLAYTON L., social scientist; b. Mpls., Mar. 23, 1937; s. David L. and Helma P. (Nelson) D.; B.S., Carthage Coll., 1955; M.A., U. Minn., 1963; postgrad. Reed Coll., 1964, U. Minn., 1973-74; m. Shirley L. Eller, Aug. 22, 1959; children—William David, Debra Jean. Research asst. U. Minn., 1959-61, instr. social sci., 1964-65; tchr., Anoka, Minn., 1960-62; instr. Carthage Coll., Kenosha, Wis., 1962-64, asst. prof., 1965-67, dir. spl. schs., 1967-74, chmn. social sci. program, 1974—; adj. prof. Pepperdine U., Los Angeles, 1975—. Supr., Protestant Youth council, 1962-63; specialist Kenosha County Schs., 1962-63; cons. Racine Pub. Schs., 1966. Partner, Diskerud Resort Annandale, Minn., 1969—. Precinct chmn. Democratic party, 1960-62; campaign cons., 1966-72; delegate Dem. Farm Labor Conv., 1962. Asia Soc. fellow; Martin Luther Faculty fellow; Ill. Synod Scholar, grantee Luth. Bd. Coll. Edn. Mem. Annandale Resort Owners Assn., Nat., S.E. Wis. (chmn. 1965-69) councils social studies, Adult Edn. Assn. Wis., Nat. Assn. Summer Sessions, Alumni Council Carthage Coll. (chmn. continuing edn. 1966-69), Phi Alpha Theta, Phi Delta Kappa, Tau Sigma Chi. Lutheran. Contbr. numerous articles to profl. publs. Home: 2136 24th Ave Kenosha WI 53140

DI SPIGNO, GUY JOSEPH, adminstrv. psychologist; b. Bklyn., Mar. 6, 1948; s. Joseph Vincent and Jeanne Nina (Renna) DiS.; B.S., Carroll Coll., 1969; M.A. (fellow), No. Ill. U., 1972; M.Ed., Loyola U., 1974; Ph.D., Northwestern U., 1977. Instr., No. Ill. U., DeKalb, 1969-70; chmn. Humanities Dept., Quincy (Ill.) Boys' High Sch., 1970-71; dir. religious edn. St. Mary's Ch., DeKalb, 1971-72; dir. edn. Immaculate Conception Parish, Higland Park, Ill., 1972-77; dir. program and staff devel. Am. Valuation Cons., Des Plaines, Ill., 1977—; sr. cons. Alpha Ednl. Cons., 1972-76. Mem. Highland Park Human Relations Commn., 1975-77, Home Owners and Businessmen's Assn., Highland Park 1976-77; vol. Chgo. Area Advance Team - Jimmy Carter for Pres., 1976; vol. coordinator Citizens for Dan Walker for Gov. Ill., 1972; mem. Pres.'s Club Democratic Party. Clifford B. Scott scholar, 1967. Mem. Community Religious Edn. Dirs. (nat. vice chmn. 1971-73), Am. Psychol. Assn., AAUP, Am. Personnel and Guidance Assn., Phi Alpha Theta, Sigma Phi Epsilon. Roman Catholic. Contbr. articles in field to profl. jours. Home: 2090 Hassell Rd Apt 308 Hoffman Estates IL 60195 Office: 2200 E Devon Ave Des Plaines IL 60018

DISTELDORF, DONALD NICHOLAS, accountant; b. Chgo., Sept. 26, 1927; s. Nicholas J. and Lillian (Doether) D.; B.S. in Accounting, DePaul U., 1951; m. Therese Boettger, June 17, 1950; children—Joan, Susan, Janet, Donald J. Jr. accountant Marshall Berman & Co., Chgo., 1950-51; sr. accountant P. L. Crawford & Co., Chgo., 1952-56; pvt. practice accounting, Oak Lawn, Ill., 1956—. Treas. Evergreen Park (Ill.) Swimming Pool Orgn., 1956-58, pres., 1960-61. Served with U.S. Army, 1945-46. C.P.A., Ill. Club: Elks. Home: 3157 W 101st St Evergreen Park IL 60642 Office: 4961 W 95th St Oak Lawn IL 60453

DITTMANN, JOHN FRED, engring. mgr.; b. Frontenac, Kans., Nov. 8, 1920; s. Gus and Veronica (Fecho) D.; B.S., Dickinson Coll., 1943; M.Sc., U. Kans., 1949; m. Iris Glee Tyler, Aug. 3, 1942; children—Dr. J. Paul, Jay T. Chemistry instr., football coach Southwestern Coll., 1946-48; mgr. lead-acid battery labs. Eagle-Picher Industries, Inc., Joplin, Mo., 1952-61, mem. engring. staff, dir. battery research and devel., 1962-65, mgr. reliability Apollo Program, 1966-68, mgr. engring., 1969—. Served to capt., USAAF, 1944-46; ETO. Mem. Electrochem. Soc., AAAS, Am. Ordnance Assn., Am. Soc. Quality Control, Am. Chem. Soc., Spiva Art Center, Omicron Delta Kappa, Sigma Alpha Epsilon. Republican. Methodist. Contbr. articles on batteries to profl. jours. Patentee in field. Home: 531 Park Ave Joplin MO 64801 Office: PO Box 130 Seneca MO 64865

DITZLER, THOMAS FREDERICK, psychotherapist; b. Flint, Mich., Aug. 28, 1946; s. Thomas Edward and Mary Margaret (McLinden) D.; B.A., Hillsdale Coll., 1968; certificate in edn. U. Mich., 1975, M.A. in Counseling, 1976; m. Ann Marie Herrick, Feb. 20, 1971. Indsl. accounts mgr. F.P.A. Inc., Flint, 1971-74; retail sales mgr. Goodyear Tire & Rubber Co., Flint, 1974; psychotherapist PsycholTherapeutic Treatment Clinic, Flint, 1976—; dir. Midwest Inst. Obesity Research, 1977. Mem. AAUP, Am. Personnel and Guidance Assn., Assn. Specialists in Group Work. Home: 3842 Park Forest Dr Flint MI 48507 Office: 300 Phoenix Bldg Flint MI 48502

DIVELY, GEORGE SAMUEL, communications and info. handling equipment mfg. exec.; b. Claysburg, Pa., Dec. 17, 1902; s. Michael A. and Martha A. (Dodson) D.; B.S. in Elec. Engring., U. Pitts., 1925; M.B.A., Harvard U., 1929; D.Engring (hon.), Case Inst. Tech., 1961; D.Sc. in Engring. (hon.), U. Pitts., 1962; D.Sc. (hon.), Fla. Inst. Tech., 1972; m. Harriett G. Seeds, June 30, 1933 (dec. 1968); 1 son, Michael A.; m. 2d, Juliette Gaudin, Feb. 1969. With Harris Corp., 1937—, successively asst. to sec.-treas., asst. treas., sec.-treas., dir., mem. exec. com., v.p., gen. mgr., 1937-47, pres. 1947-61, chief exec. officer, 1952-68, chmn. bd., 1954-72, chmn. exec. and finance com., 1972-75, hon. chmn. bd., chmn. fin. policy com., 1975—; hon. dir. Central Nat. Bank Cleve. Bd. dirs. Nat. Council for Fin. Aid to Edn.; mem. vis. com. Harvard U. Grad. Sch. Bus. Adminstrn.; hon. trustee Case Western Res. U.; trustee Ednl. TV Assn. Met. Cleve. Fellow Am. Mgmt. Assn. (life mem.). Mason. Clubs: Cleve. Country, Union, Harvard, Pepper Pike (Cleve.); Harvard (N.Y.C.), Royal Palm Yacht and Country (Boca Baton, Fla.). Author: The Power of Professional Management. Home: 20776 Brantley Rd Shaker Heights OH 44122 Office: 55 Public Sq Cleveland OH 44113

DIVINA, HENRY DUKE, accountant, mgmt. cons.; b. Sorsogon, Philippines, July 30, 1940; s. Gregorio E. and Roberta D. (Detablan) D.; came to U.S., 1968, naturalized, 1975; A.C.S., Philippine Coll. Commerce, 1959; B.S.B.A., U. East Manila (Philippines), 1962; postgrad. Ind. U., 1975—; m. Caridad P. Barroga, Sept. 6, 1969; 1 dau., Caryn Gemma. Cost estimator Sherwin Williams Co., Dayton,

Ohio, 1968-70; accountant firm Joseph F. Glotzbach, C.P.A., Hammond, Ind., 1970-71; auditor Ind. Blue Cross, Indpls., 1971-75; accountant Ind. Dept. Pub. Welfare, 1976—; ltd. practice pub. accounting, Indpls., 1973—. Vol. cons. Indspls. Bus. Devel. Found., 1974. C.P.A., Philippines. Mem. Am. Accounting Assn., Ind. Soc. Pub. Accountants, Philippine-Am. Accounting Assn. (founder, pres. 1974), Barangay Club of Ind. Inc. (auditor 1974, pres. 1976). Home: 3263 Acacia Dr Indianapolis IN 46224 Office: 3422 W 30th St Indianapolis IN 46222

DIVNEY, HERBERT PHILLIPS, clin. psychologist; b. Columbus, Ohio, Apr. 3, 1923; s. James and Narelle (Phillips) D.; B.A., Kent State U., 1948; M.A., Cath. U. Am.; m. Dorothy Smith; 1 son, James. Clin. psychology tng. program intern Perry Point VA Hosp. (Md.), 1950-51; mem. staff Apple Creek State Hosp., Apple Creek, Ohio, 1952-66, chief psychologist, 1956-66, dir. Psychol. Service, 1973—; psychologist Hampshire Country Sch., Rindge, N.H., 1955-56; cons. psychologist Boys Village, Smithville, Ohio, 1955-65; cons., therapist Ashland (Ohio) Family Services, 1966-68; psychologist, therapist Dr. Abdon Villalba, Cuyahoga Falls, Ohio, 1967-68; dir. Alcohol Edn. and Tng. Program, Fallsview Mental Health Center, Cuyahoga Falls, 1966-68; psychologist, adminstr. S.E. Colo. Family Guidance Center, LaJunta, 1968-73; dir. psychol. services Tiffin (Ohio) Mental Health and Mental Retardation Center; cons. Tuscarawas Comprehensive Community Health Center, Dover, Ohio, 1976—. Mem. exec. bd. So. Colo. region Boy Scouts Am., 1971-72. Mem. Am., Ohio psychol. assns., Ohio State Assn. Psychologists and Psychol. Assts. (treas. 1976-77). Home and Office: 56-B Siesta Dr Tiffin OH 44883

DIX, RAYMOND EUGENE, publishing co. exec.; b. Wooster, Ohio, Aug. 5, 1908; s. Emmett C. and Edna Marian (Voorhees) D.; student Ohio Wesleyan U., 1926-28; B.J., U. Mo., 1930; H.H.D., Coll. Wooster, 1966; L.H.D., Defiance Coll., 1968; m. Carolyn Victoria Gustafson, Oct. 15, 1932; children—R. Victor, Edna C. (Mrs. David Crocker), Ellen (Mrs. Francis Love). Editor Ravenna (Ohio) Record, 1930-31; advt. mgr. Daily Record, Wooster, 1931-40, mng. editor, 1940-53, pub., 1953—; pres. Ashland Pub. Co., Wooster, 1966—; dir. Wayne County Bank. Trustee Methodist Theol. Inst., Del. Mem. Ohio Newspaper Assn. (past pres.), Inter-Am. Press Assn. (dir. treas. 1968-73, 2d v.p. 1973—), Wooster C. of C. (pres. 1942-43). Rotarian (pres. 1945-46). Home: 647 Northwestern St Wooster OH 44691 Office: E Liberty St Wooster OH 44691

DIXON, ALAN JOHN, lawyer, state ofcl.; b. Belleville, Ill., July 7, 1927; s. William G. and Elsa (Tebbenhoff) D.; B.S., U. Ill., 1949; LL.B., Wash. U., 1950; m. Joan Louise Fox, Jan. 17, 1954; children—Stephanie Jo, Jeffrey Alan Dixon, Elizabeth Jane Dixon. Admitted to Illinois bar, 1950, since practiced in Belleville; police magistrate, Belleville, 1949; asst. atty. St. Clair County, 1950; mem. Ill. Ho. Reps., 1950-62; mem. Ill. Senate, 1962-70, minority whip senate; chmn. Jud. Adv. Council; treas. State of Ill., 1971-76, sec. of state, 1977—. Mem. C. of C., Am. Legion. Club: Democratic (St. Clair County). Home: 7528 Claymont Ct Belleville IL 62223 Office: 25 W Main St Belleville IL 62220

DIXON, BARBARA JANE, interior designer, cons.; b. South Bend, Ind., Dec. 6, 1933; d. Vincent Alan and Wanda Anita (Rapell) Dixon; student Mich. State U., 1951-55; postgrad. St. Mary's Coll., 1956-57, N.Y. Sch. Design, 1956-58; m. Erwin Delton VanGilder, May 25, 1959; children—Eric Dalton, Marc David. Factory color cons. Smith-Alsop Paint Co., Terre Haute, Ind., 1955-56; archtl. design cons., Mishawaka, Ind., 1956-58; residential-comml. designer, South Bend, Chgo., 1958-63; designer industrialized housing industry, Ga., Fla., Ind., Mich., 1962—; v.p. design Treasure Chest Corp., Sturgis, Mich., 1969, also dir.; pres., dir. Sandpiper Art, Inc.; v.p. T.C.I. Ltd.; v.p. design C.O. Smith Ind. Peachtree Housing, Moultrie, Ga., Nobility Homes, Ocala, Fla.; also coordinator trade show displays; writer series on decorating for 2 Mich. newspapers, 1961-63; hostes TV show Know Your Decorator. Officer, Shoreham Village (Mich.) Bd. Zoning, 1960-63. Named Woman of Year, Profl. Model's Club, 1952; Miss South Bend, 1956; Miss Chgo. Photoflash, 1958; Miss All-Star Chgo., 1958; recipient 1st pl. furniture design hardwoods Nat. Hardwoods Assn., 1956; 1st pl. Best in Show award, Louisville, Atlanta, 1964-65, 66, 69, 70-74; others. Mem. Design Council Industrialized Housing (award 1974), Nat. Soc. Interior Designers, Mich. State U. Alumni Assn., Internat. Platform Assn., Writers Guild, Internat. Biog. Assn. Permanent guest editor, conbtr. Today's Home mag., 1974—. Home: 4212 S Lakeshore Dr Saint Joseph MI 49085 Office: 3630 S Lakeshore Dr Shoreham Saint Joseph MI 49085

DIXON, EARL, educator; b. Detroit, Aug. 17, 1949; s. Elgie and Sallie Sue Dixon; B.S. in Phys. Edn. and Recreation Adminstrn., Eastern Mich. U., 1973, M.A. in Guidance and Counseling, 1976; m. Loretta Lynn Mansel, Sept. 23, 1972; 1 dau., Keisha Nichol. Unit dir. Ypsilnti (Mich.) Boys' Club, 1972-73; project coordinator cons. New Detroit, Inc., 1975; program dir. Highland Park (Mich.) YMCA, 1974-75; tchr., coach Highland Park Sch. Dist., 1976—; propr. specialized tax service, 1977—. Active local polit. camapaigns. Winner honorable mention-All Am., Nat. Assn. Intercollegiate Athletics, 1971. Mem. Am. Personnel and Guidance Assn., Mich. Social Workers Assn., Human Potential Workshop Cons. Home: 126 Puritan St Highland Park MI 48203 Office: David Whitney Bldg Suite 1041 Detroit MI 48226

DIXON, ERNEST THOMAS, JR., clergyman; b. San Antonio, Oct. 13, 1922; s. Ernest Thomas and Ethel Louise (Reese) D.; B.A. magna cum laude, Samuel Houston Coll., 1943; B.D., Drew Theol Sem., 1945; D.D., Huston-Tilotson Coll., 1962; m. Lois Freddie Brown, July 20, 1943; children—Freddie Brown, Ernest Reese, Muriel Jean, Leona Louise. On trial W. Tex. Conf. United Methodist Ch., 1943; ordained deacon, 1945, full connection, elder, 1946; asst. minister East Calvary Meth. Ch., N.Y.C., 1943-44, Wallace Chapel A.M.E. Zion Ch., Summit, N.J., 1944-45; dir. religious extension service Tuskegee (Ala.) Inst., 1945-51; vis. instr. rural ch. work Gammon Theol. Sem., Atlanta, 1949-51; travelling sec. Student Vol. Movement for Ministerial Tng. and Qualifications, West Tex. Conf., from 1956; mem. Nashville regional missionary personnel com. Bd. Missions, United Meth. Ch., 1953-65, chmn. inter-div. music com., Bd. Edn., 1956-60; now bishop United Meth. Ch., Topeka, Kans. Pres. bd. dirs. Bethlehem Center, Nashville, 1956-59, 63-65; trustee St. Paul Sch. Theology-Meth., 1964—, Morgan Christian Center, Morgan State Coll., Balt., 1964—. Mem. Alpha Phi Alpha. Home: 4201 W 15th St Topeka KS 66604

DIXON, FREDERICK WILLIAM, physician; b. Columbus, Ohio, Mar. 18, 1912; s. Charles Roy and Louise (Beck) D.; B.A., Ohio State U., 1933, M.D., 1936; m. Ruth Fern Hankins, July 14, 1936; 1 dau., Barbara Ruth (Mrs. Gale James Eastwood). Intern, Harper Hosp., 1936-37; gen. practice medicine, Dearborn, Mich., 1938—; indsl. physician Murray Corp., Detroit, 1937-42, 46-48; mem. staff Oakwood Hosp. Troop committeeman Detroit Area council Boy Scouts Am., 1948—; mem. adv. com. League Women Voters, 1950-54; contbg. mem. Detroit Symphony Orch. Served to maj. M.C., AUS, USAAF, 1942-46; col. Res., staff specialist SSS; comdg. officer Detroit Moblzn. Unit, 1961-72. Ret. from Army Res. as Col., M.C., 1972. Meritorious Service award Selective Service System. Mem. A.M.A., Mich., Wayne County, Dearborn (past pres.) med. socs., Assn. Mil. Surgeons U.S., Res. Officers Assn., Air Force Assn. (charter mem.), Mich. Assn. Professions (organizer, charter mem.), Am. Acad. Gen. Practice, Alpha Kappa Kappa, Alpha Sigma Phi. Republican. Mason (32 deg., Shriner). Club: Dearborn Country. Home: 245 S Martha St Dearborn MI 48124 Office: 530 N Telegraph Rd Dearborn MI 48128

DIXON, JAMES JASON, physician; b. Kansas City, Mo., July 6, 1920; s. Otto Jason and Olive (Robertson) D.; A.B., U. Kans., 1943, M.D., 1947; m. Kathryn May Hanna, May 2, 1948; children—David Jason, William Nelson, Robert Grant, Mary Christine. Intern, Toledo Hosp., 1947-48, resident, 1948-50; resident Henry Ford Hosp., Detroit, 1950-52; pathologist, dir. labs. Ashtabula (Ohio) Gen. Hosp., 1952—, Lake County Meml. Hosp., Painesville, Ohio, 1952-58; pathologist Brown Meml. Hosp., Conneaut, Ohio, 1961-70; cons. pathologist Geneva (Ohio) Meml. Hosp., 1961-68; mem. regional adv. com. Cleve. Red Cross Blood Program; dep. sheriff Ashtabula County. Past v.p. Ashtabula Fine Arts Center; active ARC. Diplomate Am. Bd. Pathology. Mem. Ohio, Ashtabula County (sec., treas. 1956, pres. 1960) med. socs., Am. Soc. Clin. Pathologists, Coll. Am. Pathologists, Ohio, Cleve. socs. pathologists, Am. Cancer Soc. (med. dir. Ashtabula County), Am. Assn. Blood Banks, AAAS, Ashtabula Power Squadron (comdr. 1966), Nat. Rifle Assn. (life), Nat. Assn. Federally Licensed Firearms Dealers, Ohio Gun Collectors Assn., Smith and Wesson Collectors Assn., Ohio Rifle and Pistol Assn. (life), Tau Kappa Epsilon, Nu Sigma Nu. Republican. Episcopalian (sr. warden 1960-63). Elk, Rotarian. Clubs: Ashtabula Country, Ashtabula Yacht; Redbrook Boat, Ashtabula Rod and Gun. Home: 1724 Highland Ln Ashtabula OH 44004 Office: Ashtabula Gen Hosp Ashtabula OH 44004

DIXON, KENT DARKLEY, advt. agy. exec.; b. Duluth, Minn., Sept. 27, 1926; s. Robert and Florence (Darke) D.; B.A., U. Minn., 1950; m. Marilyn L. Blair, Oct. 1, 1953. Various sales, advt. positions Internat. Milling Co., 1950-53; copy writer, account exec. Ruthrauff & Ryan Agy., Inc., 1953-55; marketing mgr. Rap-In-Wax Paper Co., Mpls., 1955-57; founder Kent Dixon Advt. Agy., Mpls., 1957, owner 1957—. Lectr. advt., pub. relations Mgmt. Center, Coll. St. Thomas, St. Paul, 1960—; lect. advt. U. Minn.; speaker numerous food merchandising convs. Founder Ernie Swift Meml. Conservation Com., 1969. Founding dir. Northern Environmental Council, Duluth, Minn., 1970. Served with AUS, World War II. Mem. Mpls. Advt. Club, Aircraft Owners and Pilots Assn., Young Men of Minn. Club: Minn. Press. Home: 4709 Meadow Rd Minneapolis MN 55424 Office: 711 W Lake St Minneapolis MN 55408

DIXON, WESLEY MOON, JR., pharm. mfg. co. exec.; b. Evanston, Ill., Oct. 18, 1927; s. Wesley Moon and Katherine (Strawn) D.; student Hotchkiss Sch., 1941-45; B.A., Yale, 1950; m. Suzanne Searle, May 23, 1953; children—Katherine Suzanne, Carolynn Frances, John Wesley. Salesman Owens-Ill., 1950-54; with G.D. Searle & Co., Chgo., 1954—, became pres., 1971, now vice chmn., also dir.; dir. No. Trust Co., A.B. Dick Co. (both Chgo.). Trustee, Art Inst. Chgo., 1969—, Lake Forest Coll.; bd. dirs. Lake Forest Hosp., Rehab. Inst. Chgo. Republican. Episcopalian. Clubs: Onwentsia, Shoreacres (Lake Forest, Ill.); University, Chicago, Casino, Mid-Am. Commercial, Economic, Commonwealth (Chgo.). Home: 70 W Laurel Ave Lake Forest IL 60045 Office: PO Box 1045 Skokie IL 60076

DIZZONNE, MICHAEL FRANK, psychometrist; b. Chgo., Feb. 28, 1941; s. Frank and Angeline Catherine (Pisano) D.; B.A., Roosevelt U., 1965; M.Ed., Loyola U. At Chgo., 1975. Psychometrist, VA Hosp., North Chicago, Ill., 1968—; pvt. practice as psychometrist, 1977—. Mem. Am., Ill., Midwest psychol. assns., Am. Personnel and Guidance Assn. Roman Catholic. Home: 2321 W Washington St Waukegan IL 60085 Office: VA Hospital North Chicago IL 60064

DOAN, RANDALL LOREN, banker; b. Paoli, Ind., Sept. 27, 1932; s. Russell and Marie S. (Busick) D.; grad. Wis. Sch. Banking, 1963; m. Marilyn Lamon, Nov. 3, 1950; children—Dan, Lisa A., Rusty. With Orange County Bank, Paoli, Ind., 1956—, asst. v.p., 1959-62, v.p., 1962—, dir., 1967—. Treas. Orange County Easter Seal Assn., 1967-71; chmn. Orange County chpt. ARC, 1961-63; bd. dirs. Orange County Retarded Sch., 1969-71. Served with USAF, 1951-55. Mem. Paoli C. of C. (dir. 1970—). Mason, Lion. Clubs: Green Acres Country, Hoosier Bankers. Home: Rural Route 2 Paoli IN 47454 Office: Orange County Bank W Court St Paoli IN 47454

DOANE, DAVID STEPHEN, psychologist; b. Cleve., Apr. 24, 1945; s. Steve and Anne Marie (Balenchin) D.; B.A., Duquesne U., 1967; M.A., Bowling Green State U., 1969; Ph.D., Kent State U., 1976. Instr. psychology Lakeland Community Coll., Mentor, O., 1969-72; asst., Kent (O.) State U., 1972-74; instr. psychology Owens Tech. Coll., Toledo, O., 1975-76; pvt. practice psychology Psychol. Services, Toledo, 1974—; cons. psychologist Lucas County Drug Abuse Program, Toledo, 1974—. Mem. Am., N.W. Ohio psychol. assns. Office: 5445 Southwyck Blvd Toledo OH 43614

DOBBS, DONALD EDWIN ALBERT, elec. products co. exec.; b. Ft. Wayne, Ind., Oct. 8, 1931; s. Edmund F. and Agnes (Stempnick) D.; B.S., Marquette U., 1953; m. Beatrice A. Spieker, July 27, 1957; children—Margaret L., Christopher E.J., Laura C. Reporter, Cath. Chronicle, Toledo, 1953; indsl. editor, pub. relations Nat. Supply Co., Toledo 1955-59; employee communications exec. Prestolite Co., an Eltra Co., Toledo, 1959-61, pub. relations dir., 1961—. Past chmn. Maumee Valley Hosp. Sch. Nursing Com. Pres. Internat. Inst., Toledo, 1970-73; past chmn. Child Nutrition Center, Toledo; mem. Ohio Adv. Council Vocat. Edn.; vice chmn. Mayor's Citizen Devel. Forum. Bd. dirs. Mercy Hosp., Frederick Douglass Community Assn., Toledo chpt. A.R.C., Crosby Gardens; chmn. Salvation Army; pres. Toledo Council of World Affairs; past pres. Toledo Hearing and Speech Center; pres. bd. dirs. Internat. Park. Served with AUS, 1953-55. Mem. Marquette U. Alumni Assn. N.W. Ohio (past pres., area dir.), Soc. Profl. Journalists, Pub. Relations Soc. Am., Cath. Interracial Council (past pres.), Sigma Delta Chi. Democrat. (past nat. com. Wis. Young Dems.). Roman Catholic. K.C. (4 degree), Kiwanian (past pres. Toledo, Mid-City Athletic League, Kiwanis Youth Found.; lt. gov. 1974-75). Clubs: Toledo Press, Toledo Mud Hens Diamond (charter). Home: 2433 Meadowwood Dr Toledo OH 43606 Office: 511 Hamilton St Toledo OH 43694

DOBECK, RUDOLF JOHN, dept. store exec.; b. Bazine, Kans., Feb. 15, 1926; s. Robert and Dora R. (Rall) D.; A.A., Yankton Coll., 1948; B.S., Denver U., 1950; M.A., Highlands U., 1952; m. Daisy Dickenson, Aug. 16, 1952; children—Robert, Vicky, Peggy. Tchr. pub. high sch., Sterling, Colo., 1950-51; instr. Highlands U., Las Vegas, N.Mex., 1952-54; with J.C. Penney Co., Albuquerque, Los Angeles and N.Y.C., 1954-70, v.p. ops. Asso. Dry Goods Co., N.Y.C., 1970-73; v.p. ops., constrn. and planning Federated Dept. Stores, Cin., 1973—. Served with AUS, 1944-46. Mem. DAV. Presbyterian. Clubs: Toastmasters (sec.), Cin. Home: 2868 Saddleback Dr Cincinnati OH 45244 Office: 222 W 7th St Cincinnati OH 45202

DOBIN, NORMAN BENJAMIN, physician; b. Kherson, Russia, July 20, 1911; s. Noah and Frieda (Goldman) D.; came to U.S., 1923, naturalized, 1933; B.S., U. Ill., 1933, M.D., 1936; M.S., Northwestern U., 1940; m. Ora Jane O'Neill, Oct. 10, 1957; children—Stella, Nora, David, Jacqueline, Norman, Michael, Intern, Cook County Hosp., Chgo., 1935-36; research and teaching fellow Northwestern U., 1939-49; dept. neurology and psychiatry Cook County Hosp., Chgo, 1939-41, Passavant Meml. Hosp., Chgo., 1947-49; attending physician neurology and psychiatry Michael Reese Hosp., Chgo., 1950—, VA Hosp., Hines, Ill., 1951—; attending physician St. Joseph Hosp.; cons. neurologist Shriners Hosp. Crippled Children, Chgo., 1956—; mem. faculty Northwestern U., 1939-67, U. Ill. Coll. Medicine, 1967—. Served with M.C., AUS, 1941-45, Mem. AMA, Ill., Chgo. med. socs., Chgo. Neurol. Soc., Ill. Psychiat. Soc., Central Neuropsychiatric Soc., Am. Psychiat. Soc., Sigma Xi. Contbr. articles to profl. jours. Home: Rural Route 1 Box 68 Beecher IL 60401 Office: 104 S Michigan Ave Chicago IL 60603

DOBOGAI, JOHN EDWARD, JR., tax analyst; b. Milw., Oct. 14, 1941; s. John Edward and Betty Jean (Holzman) D.; B.S. in Bus. Adminstrn., U. Va., 1968; m. Suzanne Lee Rouse, Mar. 25, 1970; children—Deborah Lee, John Edward, III, Michael Edward, Sarah Lee. Pres., John E. Dobogai & Co. Inc., tax analysts, Medford, Wis., 1974—; dir. numerous corps. U.S. tax expert liaison to Can., 1968. Chmn. United Givers Fund Medford, 1974-76; del. U.S. Bicentennial Com., 1975. Scoutmaster, Boy Scouts Am. Trustee Boys to the Woods Found. Served with USAF, 1960-64. Mem. Am. Legion, Medford Jaycees, Va. Life Underwriters Assn. Democrat. Mormon. Lion. Home: Box 354 Abbotsford WI 54405 Office: 319 E Broadway St Medford WI 54451

DOBRICK, JO-ANNE SHAYE, art gallery exec.; b. Detroit, Sept. 19, 1945; d. Nathan and Lillian (Davis) Shaye; student Ohio State U., 1963-65, Art Inst. Chgo., 1970-71; B.A., Roosevelt U., 1972; m. Howard Dobrick, Dec. 9, 1968; 1 dau., Rebecca Ellen. With United Air Lines, 1966-67, retail advt. dept. Chgo. Tribune, 1968-70; tchr. Evanston (Ill.) Dist. 65, 1970-72; dir. Dobrick Gallery, Chgo., 1974—, pres. Dobrick Gallery Ltd., 1974—; lectr. to charitable, interest groups. Participant, Art in Pub. Places, 1975; chmn. art com. Channel 11 Pub. Broadcasting, 1975—. Sec. for Park Art div. Friends of the Park. Mem. Chgo. Art Dealers Assn. Office: 161 E Erie St Chicago IL 60611

DOBROVOLNY, JERRY STANLEY, engring. educator; b. Chgo., Nov. 2, 1922; s. Stanley and Marie (Barone) D.; B.S. in Mech. Engring., U. Ill., 1943, M.S., 1947; m. Joan Gretchen Baker, June 14, 1947; children—James Lawrence, Janet Lee. Mem. faculty U. Ill., Urbana, 1945—, asso. prof. Coll. Engring., 1957—, prof., head dept. gen. engring., 1959—; geophys. research engr. Ill. Geol. Survey, summers 1949-52; design and traffic surveys engr. Ill. Div. Hwys., summers 1948, 53, 54; cons. soil mechanics, 1955—. Mem. Ill. Adv. Council on Vocational Edn., 1969-72, Nat. Council on Vocational Edn., 1970-73. Past pres. Champaign County Young Republican Club; past faculty adviser Illini Young Rep. Club; mem. Champaign County Rep. Central Com. Served to sgt., C.E., AUS, 1942-44. Recipient Arthur L. Williston award, 1970. Registered proft. engr. Fellow A.A.A.S.; mem. Am. Legion, 40 and 8, Soc. for History and Tech., Ill. Acad. Sci., Am. Soc. Engring. Edn., Am. Assn. Petroleum Geologists, ASCE, Am. Tech. Edn. Assn. (trustee 1964-67, 69-74, pres. 1967-69), Champaign County (pres. 1964-65), Ill. (pres. 1974-75), Nat. socs. profl. engrs., Newcomen Soc. N.Am. Scabbard and Blade, Sigma Xi, Sigma Iota Epsilon, Tau Nu Tau. Author: (with others) Basic Drawing for Engineering Technology; (with R. P. Hoelscher and C. H. Springer). Graphics for Engineers, 1968. Home: 1104 S Prospect Ave Champaign IL 61820 Office: Coll Engring U Ill Urbana IL 61801

DOBSON, JOHN MCCULLOUGH, historian; b. Las Cruces, N.Mex., July 20, 1940; s. Donald Duane and Carolyn Margaret (Van Anda) D.; B.S., Mass. Inst. Tech., 1962; M.S., U. Wis., 1964, Ph.D., 1966; m. Cynthia Davis, Aug. 29, 1963; children—David, Daniel. Asst. prof. history Calif. State U., Chico, 1966-67; fgn. service officer U.S. Dept. State, Washington, 1967-68; asst. then asso. prof. history Iowa State U., Ames, 1968—; vis. asso. prof. history U. Md., summer 1972, spring 1976. U.S. Internat. Trade Commn. grantee, 1976. Mem. Am. Hist. Assn., Orgn. Am. Historians, Soc. Historians of Am. Fgn. Relations, AAUP. Author: Politics in the Gilded Age: A New Perspective on Reform, 1972; Two Centuries of Tariffs: The Background and Origins of the U.S. International Trade Commn., 1977; America's Ascent, 1978. Home: 2019 Kildee St Ames IA 50010 Office: Dept History Iowa State U Ames IA 50011

DOCKHORN, ROBERT JOHN, physician; b. Goodland, Kans., Oct. 9, 1934; s. Charles George and Dortha Mae (Horton) D.; B.A., U. Kans., 1956, M.D., 1960; m. Beverly Ann Wilke, June 15, 1957; children—David, Douglas, Deborah. Intern, Naval Hosp., San Diego, 1960-61, resident in pediatrics, Oakland, Calif., 1963-65; resident in pediatric allergy and immunology U. Kans., 1967-69, asst. adj. prof. pediatrics, 1969—; resident in pediatric allergy and immunology Children's Mercy Hosp., Kansas City, Mo., 1967-69, chief allergy-immunology div., 1969—; practice medicine specializing in allergy and immunology, Prairie Village, Kans., 1969—; clin. asso. prof. pediatrics U. Mo., Kansas City, 1972—. Diplomate Am. Bd. Pediatrics. Fellow Am. Acad. Pediatrics, Am. Coll. Allergists (bd. regents 1976—), Am. Acad. Allergy; mem. AMA, Kans., Johnson County med. socs., Kans. (pres. 1976-77), Mo. (sec. 1975-76) allergy socs., Joint Council of Socio-Economics of Allergy (dir. 1976—). Contbr. articles to med. jours. Home: 8510 Delmar Ln Prairie Village KS 66208 Office: 5300 W 94th Terr Prairie Village KS 66207

DOCKINS, GLENN, JR., librarian; b. Scopus, Mo., Dec. 29, 1925; s. Glen and Stella Lee (Teeters) D.; student U. Nebr., 1965; B.S. in Edn., S.E. Mo. State Coll., 1951; M.L.S., George Peabody Library Sch., 1964; m. Cleta Mae Rolf, July 26, 1958; children—Maria Antonia, Tammy Leigh, Rebekah Kaye. Librarian, Flat River (Mo.) Jr. High Sch., 1961-65; library dir. Mexico (Mo.)-Audrain County Library, 1965-67; exec. library dir. Cumberland Trail Library System, Flora, Ill., 1967—; cons. library bldgs. Served with USNR, 1944-46. Mem. Ill., Am. library assns., Mo. State Tchrs. Assn., Alpha Beta Alpha. Baptist. Clubs: Masons, Elks. Contbr. articles to profl. jours. Home: 427 E 6th St Flora IL 62839 Office: Cumberland Trail Library System 12th and McCawley Flora IL 62839

DOCKTER, JAMES EUGENE, book distbn. co. exec.; b. Chgo., Oct. 30, 1943; s. Eugene J. and Christine M. (Nienager) D.; B.S. in Commerce, U. Ky., 1965; m. Rebecca L. Miller, Aug. 26, 1944; children—Scott, Gregory, James A. Regional mgr. CNA Ins. Co., Chgo., 1968-70; dir. sales Mdse. Warehouse Co., Columbus, O., 1970-72; gen. mgr. V.R. Ednl. Services Co., Columbus, 1972-73, v.p., 1973-74, pres., 1974-76; pres. Profl. Book Distbrs., Inc., Columbus, 1976—. Served with U.S. Army, 1966-68; Vietnam. Decorated Army Commendation medal. Mem. Nat. Assn. Life Underwriters, Ins. Co. Edn. Dirs. Soc., Am. Soc. Tng. and Devel. Club: Swim and Racquet (pres.) (Columbus). Office: 563 E Hudson St Columbus OH 43211

DODD, GEORGE TRAVIS, lawyer; b. Bklyn., Apr. 16, 1937; s. Fred Orville and Josephine (Morrison) D.; A.B. with honors (Rector Scholar 1955), DePauw U., 1959; J.D., Northwestern U., 1962; m. Barbara Alspaugh, Aug. 6, 1977; children—Lisa Lee, Andrea Lynn, Brian Travis. Admitted to Ind. bar, 1962; asso. Shoaff, Keegan & Baird, Fort Wayne, Ind., 1962-66; partner Shoaff, Keegan, Baird & Simon, 1967—. Chmn., United Arts Fund Drive, Fort Wayne, 1969;

mem. com. mgmt. YMCA, 1968-73; mem. Election Canvass Bd., 1963-71. Bd. dirs. Fort Wayne Philharmonic Orch., v.p., 1973-75, pres., 1975-77; bd. dirs. Allen County Cancer Soc., 1965-76, v.p., 1975-76; sec. Ft. Wayne Fine Arts Found., 1973-74, v.p., 1975—. Mem. Am., Ind. bar assns., Phi Beta Kappa, Phi Eta Sigma, Phi Delta Phi, Ft. Wayne C. of C. (treas. 1971-73). Conglist. (deacon 1968-71). Contributing author Depositions and Discovery, 1967. Home: 7009 Inverness Dr Fort Wayne IN 46804 Office: 2400 Fort Wayne Nat Bank Bldg Fort Wayne IN 46802

DODD, JAMES ARTHUR, library dir.; b. N.Y.C., Feb. 17, 1925; s. Charles Allen and Florence (Warner) D.; B.A. cum laude, Northland Coll., Ashland, 1950; M.S. in L.S., U. Wis., 1951; postgrad. Wayne State U., 1958; m. Nancy Ann Hoecker, Oct. 20, 1951; children—Elizabeth, Paul Henry. Youth librarian, adult asst. Detroit Pub. Library, 1951-56, br. library 1st asst., 1956-59; br. librarian Grosse Pointe (Mich.) Pub. Library, 1959-64; library dir. Adrian (Mich.) Coll., 1964—; cons. Siena Heights Coll., Adrian, 1975—. Bd. dirs. Lenawee County United Fund, pres., 1973; bd. dirs., exec. bd., sec. Goodwill Industries; trustee Mich. Library Consortium; hon. chmn. United Way Lenawee County. Mem. ALA, Mich. Library Assn. (exec. bd. acad. div. 1973, sec.-treas. acad. div.), Midwest Acad. Librarians Assn., Mich. Archives Assn. (dir.), U. Wis. Library Sch. Alumni Assn. (pres. 1972-73), AAUP (past sec., treas. local chpt.). Methodist (past pres. men's club, sec. council on ministries). Kiwanian. Clubs: Economic of Detroit; Lenawee Country. Contbr. articles to profl. jours. Home: 4771 Devonshire Dr Adrian MI 49221

DODDERIDGE, RICHARD WILLIAM, advt. co. exec.; b. Council Grove, Kans., Oct. 3, 1926; s. Russell Reubin and Rachel Augusta (Jacobs) D.; B.S., Kansas State U., 1947; student Harvard Grad. Sch. Bus. Advanced Marketing Seminar, 1968; m. Cornelia Ann Thornberry, Oct. 25, 1952; children—Richard William, John Russell, Daniel James. Sports dir. KFBI, Wichita, Kans., 1947; account exec. Bruce B. Brewer Co., Inc., Kansas City, Mo., 1947-67, exec. v.p., 1967-72, pres., 1972-74; pres. Brewer Advt. Inc. div. Young & Rubican Inc., 1974—. Vice chmn. Better Bus. Bur., Kansas City, 1964-66; vice-chmn. Citizens Assn., Kansas City, Mo., 1959-60; mem. Camp Gravois com. YMCA, Kansas City, 1963-68; mem. Starlight Theatre Assn., 1964—; mem. Kansas City (Mo.) Motion Picture Bd. Appeals, 1951; pres. Mission Woods Homes Assn., 1966-67. City council, Mission Woods, Kans., 1969-75. Bd. trustees Kansas City Mus.; bd. dirs. Kansas Art Center Found., Pub. TV 19, 1973—; bd. govs. Kansas City Art Inst., 1977—. Served with USAAF, 1944-45. Named man of the year Am. Advt. Fedn., 9th Dist., 1967; recipient Silver medal award Am. Advt. Fedn. Printers' Ink, 1967; named Mem. of the Year, Advt. and Sales Execs. Club., 1959. Mem. Advt. and Sales Execs. Club (bd. govs. 1961-73, pres. 1969-70, trustee 1973-76), Am. Advt. Fedn. (dist. gov., 1961-62; nat. dir. 1968-72, chmn. pub. affairs com. 1972-73), Am. Assn. Advt. Agys. (com. govt. and pub. relations 1967-74, chmn. Mo. council 1975-76), Kansas City C. of C. (prime time steering com. 1973-75). Republican. Episcopalian (vestryman 1969-74). Rotarian. Clubs: Kansas City Press, Kansas City, Carriage (dir. 1972-75, v.p. 1974-75), Midnighters, Woodside Racquet. Home: 5333 Mission Woods Rd Shawnee Mission KS 66205 Office: 3 Crown Center 2440 Pershing Rd Kansas City MO 64108

DODDS, HARRY WILLIAM, elec. products co. exec.; b. McKeesport, Pa., Nov. 26, 1911; s. Harry Edward and Winifred (Lawrence) D.; student Case Sch. Applied Sci.; m. Eleanor Jane Doll, July 2, 1935 (div. 1971); children—Vivian (Mrs. Dean Hull), Valorie (Mrs. Larry Lephart), Vickie (Mrs. Franklin Urban), Harry William. Vice pres. Brush Labs., Cleve., 1948-56; exec. v.p. Sawyer Research Products, Inc., Cleve., 1956-68, pres., 1968—; chmn. bd. Merriam Instrument Co., Cleve., 1961-69. Bd. dirs. Lake County (Ohio) Found. Served to comdr. USCG Aux., 1974-75. Mason (Shriner). Home: 2250 Parlane Dr Apt 5 Willoughby Hills OH 44094 Office: 35400 Lakeland St Eastlake OH 44094

DODERER, MINNETTE FRERICHS (MRS. FRED H. DODERER), state senator; b. Holland, Iowa, May 16, 1923; d. John A. and Sophie (Sherfield) Frerichs; student U. No. Iowa, 1944; B.A. in Econs., U. Iowa, 1948; m. Fred H. Doderer, Aug. 5, 1944; children—Dennis H.J., Kay Lynn. Vice chmn. Johnson County Democratic Central Com., 1956-59; sec. Iowa Citizens for a Constl. Conv., 1959-60; mem. Johnson County Jury Commn., 1962-64; mem. Iowa Ho. of Reps., 1964-68; mem. Iowa Senate, 1969—, pres. pro tem, 1975-77. Mem. adv. com. on gen. operation and policy Ia. Ednl. Broadcasting Network; nat. committeewoman Iowa Dem. party, 1968-70, mem. Dem. nat. policy council, 1973—. Trustee U. Iowa Sch. Religion, Iowa City. Mem. UN Assn., League Women Voters, Nat. Conf. State Legislatures, Iowa Civil Liberties Union, Iowa Women's Polit. Caucus, Nat. Orgn. for Women, Women's Equity Action League, Delta Kappa Gamma. Home: 2008 Dunlap Ct Iowa City IA 52240

DODSON, JOHN ROBERT, burial services adminstr.; b. Cheyenne, Wyo., Mar. 2, 1949; s. Donald R. and Dorothy Jean (Downey) D.; grad. Worsham Coll., 1973-74, m. Pamela Sue Bertels, Nov. 30, 1974. Intern, Abts Mortuary, Pekin, Ill., 1974-75; asso. with Marks Funeral Home, Edwardsville, Ill., 1975-76; propr., dir. Stumpf Funeral Home, Pana, Ill., 1976—. Served with U.S. Army, 1969-71; Vietnam. Decorated Bonze star. Mem. Ill. Funeral Dirs. Assn., Nat. Funeral Dirs. Assn., Internat. Order of Golden Rule, Pana Jaycees (pres. 1977-78), Pana C. of C. (dir. 1976—), Am. Legion, VFW. Lutheran. Clubs: Rotary, Lions. Address 112 Kitchell Ave Pana IL 62557

DODSON, OSCAR HENRY, museum dir., numis. cons.; b. Houston, Jan. 3, 1905; s. Dennis Seth and Maggie (Sisk) D.; B.S., U.S. Naval Acad., 1927, postgrad., 1936; M.A., U. Ill., 1953; m. Pauline Wellbrock, Dec. 17, 1932; 1 son, John Dennis. Commd. ensign USN, 1927, advanced through grades to rear adm., 1957, ret. 1957; asst. prof. history U. Ill., 1957-59; dir. Money Museum, Nat. Bank of Detroit, 1959-65, World Heritage Mus., U. Ill., Urbana, 1966-73. Mem. Ann. Assay Commn., 1948. Decorated Silver Star, Fellow Am. Numis. Soc., Royal Numis. Soc. London; mem. Am. Mil. Inst., Am. Archaeol. Inst., Am. Numis. Assn. (pres. 1957-61; Farren Zerbe award 1968), Am. Assn. Museums, Internat. Banknote Soc. London (hon.), U.S. Naval Acad. Alumni Assn. (life), U.S. Naval Acad. Found., U. Ill. Found., U. Ill. Alumni Assn. (life mem., Loyalty award 1966). Clubs: Torch, Rotary (pres. Champaign, Ill. 1972-73); Army-Navy (Washington); New York Yacht (N.Y.C.); Champaign Country; Circumnavigators. Author: Money Tells The Story, 1962. Contbr. articles to profl., numismatic jours. Office: 484 Lincoln Hall Urbana IL 61801

DOEMENY, LAURENCE JAMES, adminstrv. chemist; b. San Diego, Aug. 11, 1942; s. E. Paul and Dorothy Irene (Burke) D.; A.B., San Diego State U., 1965, M.S., 1968; Ph.D. (Am.-Chem. Soc. petroleum research fund fellow), Calif., Santa Barbara, 1970; m. Jane Susan Rankine, Aug. 9, 1969; 1 son, Emmerich John. Research asso., chemistry dept. U. Minn., Mpls., 1970-71, instr. Sch. Pub. Health, 1971-73; aerosol physicist Nat. Inst. Occupat. Safety Health USPHS, Cin., 1973-74, chief, measurements systems sect., 1974—. Mem. Am. Chem. Soc. (exec. com. div. chem. health safety), Am. Phys. Soc., AAAS. Contbr. articles to sci. jours.

DOENCH, THOMAS JUDSON, dentist; b. Dayton, Ohio, June 12, 1943; s. Harold Frank and Thelma Regina (Price) D.; D.D.S., Ohio State U., 1967; m. Patricia June Steffen, Dec. 17, 1966; children—Adam Thomas and Katherine Angela (twins). Pvt. practice dentistry, Kettering, Ohio, 1969—; pres. Omnifac Corp. Clin. instr. dentistry Ohio State U., 1970-74. Served with USMC, 1967-69. Mem. AAUP, Am., Ohio dental assns., Dayton Dental Soc. (asso. editor Bull. 1971-75, dir. 1974-77), Psi Omega. Club: Bootheads Men's (pres. Dayton 1973). Patentee in field. Home: 760 Bickleigh Rd Centerville OH 45459 Office: 1700 E Whipp Rd Kettering OH 45440

DOERMANN, PAUL EDMUND, surgeon; b. Kodaikanal, India, Aug. 3, 1926 (parents Am. citizens); s. Carl M. and Cora (Knupke) D.; student Ohio State U., 1944; B.S., Capital U., 1947; M.D., U. Mich., 1951; m. W. Ernestine McPherson, May 3, 1953; children—William McPherson, Marcia, Paula Michelle, Diana, Charles. Intern, Louisville Gen. Hosp., 1951-52, resident in surgery, 1952-53; resident in surgery Milw. County Hosp., 1955-58; med. missionary Luth. Mission Hosp., Madang, New Guinea, 1958-59; surgeon Linvill Clinic, Columbia City, Ind., 1960-61; practice medicine specializing in surgery, Huntington, Ind.; pres. med. staff, chief surg. service Huntington Meml. Hosp.; pres. Huntington Surg. Corp. Served from 1st lt. to capt., AUS, 1953-55. Luth. Acad. scholar. Diplomate Am. Bd. Surgery. Fellow A.C.S.; mem. A.M.A., Huntington County, Christian med. socs., Huntington C. of C., Am. Platform Assn. Lutheran. Rotarian. Home: Rural Route 8 Box 325 Grimm Rd Huntington IN 46750 Office: 1751 N Jefferson Huntington IN 46750

DOERNER, ROBERT CARL, physicist; b. St. Cloud, Minn., Sept. 26, 1926; s. Carl A. and Marcella (Krieger) Doerner; m. Elizabeth Dalton, Oct. 16, 1954; children—Katherine, Mary, Joanne, David, James. B.S. in Physics, St. Johns U., 1949; M.S., St. Louis U., 1952, Ph.D., 1954. Resident research asso. Argonne Nat. Lab., (Ill.), 1955-56, asst. physicist, 1956-60, asso. physicist, 1960-72, physicist, 1972—; visiting prof. engring. physics, Cornell U., Ithics, N.Y., 1962. Chmn. Edn. Com., 1966-68, bd. dirs., 1970-72; bd. dirs., Dixon State Sch. Assn. for the Retarded; advisory com. Ill. Com. Mental Health, Devel. Disabilities; chmn. Govt. Affairs Com. Mem. Am. Nucl. Soc. (Chgo., section sec., 1968-69, vice-chmn., 1969-70, chmn., 1970-72), Am. Phys. Soc., Inst. Radio Engr., Sigma Xi, Pi Mu Epsilon. Published papers in Nucl. Sci., Engr., Phys. Rev., Int. Conf. Atomic Energy (Geneva), React. Dev. Prog. Repts. Home: 615 S Knollwood St Wheaton IL 60187 Office: Reactor Analysis Safety Division Argonne National Laboratory 9700 S Cass Ave Argonne IL 60439

DOETSCH, GUNTER HUGO KARL WILHELM, film co. exec.; b. Frankfurt/Main, West Germany, Mar. 4, 1926; s. Hugo Karl Wilhelm and Wilhelmine Margarete (Barth) D.; grad. Real Gymnasium of Frankfurt, 1945; LL.M., U. Frankfurt, 1951; m. Joyce M. Utz, Dec. 20, 1975; children—Hugo IV, Günter Alexander II. Came to U.S., 1956, naturalized, 1959. Legal cons. copyright and patent law Dr. Wolff & Tritschler Studio, Frankfurt/Main, Germany, 1952-55, asst. to pres., 1955-56, photo-journalist, Algiers, Italy, Switzerland, France, Eng., 1956-57; with foto-doetsch films, Chgo., 1957-63; pres., chief exec. officer LaRue Communications, Inc., Chgo., 1963—, pres., chief exec. officer Scientificom div., 1969—, Artcom div., 1971—, H.B. Assos. div., 1976—. Instr. advanced motion picture techniques Sch. of Art Inst. Chgo., 1968—. Chmn. design com. Biol. Photog. Assn. Congress Biocommunications 72, Chgo. Recent films include: Continuous Monitoring in the Critically Ill Patient (Am. Film Festival award 1973), Calcium Metabolism: The Consequences of Dietary Deficiency (U.S. Indsl. Film Festival award 1974), Serious Burn Management in the Office, 1974, Cyclic AMP and Drug Interaction in Vascular Smooth Muscle, 1974, Fire in the Patient Care Facility: Rehearsal for Survival, 1975, Apexcardiography: A Consideration for Early Detection, 1975, SST for All-in-One Blood Collection and Analysis, 1975, Horizons: Oral Surgery (Chgo. Internat. Film Festival award), 1975, TMO: Travenol Membrane Oxygenator, 1976, The Photrax System, 1976, Milestones in Veterinary Medicine, 1976, Techniques in Blood Culturing, 1976, Modern Methods of Venous Blood Collection, 1976, The Drug Selection Illusion, 1977. Office: 708 N Dearborn St Chicago IL 60610

DOGGETT, JOHN NELSON, JR., ch. adminstr.; b. Phila., Apr. 3, 1918; s. John Nelson and Winola (Ballard) D.; B.A., Lincoln U., 1942; M.Div., Union Theol. Sem., N.Y.C., 1945; D.D., Bethany Sch. Religion (Calif.), 1948; M.Ed., St. Louis U., 1969, Ph.D., 1971; m. Juanita Toley, Aug. 2, 1973; children by previous marriage—Lorraine, John, William, Kenneth. Ordained minister United Methodist Ch., 1943; civilian chaplain S. Gate Community Ch., San Francisco, 1945-47; organizing pastor Downs Meml. Meth. Ch., Oakland, Calif., 1947-49; pastor Scott Meml. Meth. Ch., Pasadena, Calif., 1950-53, Hamilton Meml. Meth. Ch., Los Angeles, 1953-64, Union Meml. United Meth. Ch., St. Louis, 1964-76; dist. supt. United Meth. Ch., St. Louis, 1976—; staff Pastoral Counseling Inst., St. Louis, 1968—; instr. foundations of edn. Harris Tchrs. Coll., St. Louis, 1971-75; asso. prof. practical theology Met. Coll., St. Louis, 1976—. Pres. bd. dirs. Central Med. Center Hosps., St. Louis, 1973—; pres. St. Louis NAACP, 1973—; bd. dirs., also exec. com. United Way St. Louis, 1974—; mem. Citizens Com. Mo. Dept. Corrections, 1974—. Named Minister of Year, St. Louis Argus Newspaper, 1971. Mem. Am. Assn. Pastoral Counselors, Am. Personnel and Guidance Assn., Met. Ministerial Alliance, St. Louis Police-Clergy Assn., Human Devel. Corp. (Met. Bicentennial award 1976), Aid to Victims of Crime, Phi Delta Kappa, Alpha Phi Alpha. Democrat. Mason, Shriner. Home: 126 Glen Cove Dr Chesterfield MO 63017 Office: 4625 Lindell Blvd Suite 416 St Louis MO 63108

DOGLIO, JAMES JOSEPH, supt. schs.; b. Tovey, Ill., Aug. 26, 1927; s. James and Lena A. (Fassero) D.; B.S., Ill. State U., 1951, Ed.D., 1974; M.S., James Millikin U., 1957; m. Elizabeth Ann Ford, Aug. 12, 1950; children—Kay Ann, Anita, James Diana, Kevin, Carol. Coach, Kincaid (Ill.) High Sch., 1952-58; prin. Donovan (Ill.) Unit Schs., 1958-64, supt. schs., 1964-68; supt. schs. Woodland Unit Schs., Streator, Ill., 1968-76, Unit 10 Schs., Auburn, Ill., 1976—; cons. in field. Served with AUS, 1946-47, 51-52. Mem. Livingston County Assn. Sch. Adminstrs. (v.p. 1960-61), Iroquois County Adminstrn. Assn. (pres. 1964-65), Ill. Assn. Sch., Coll. and Univ. Staffing, Ill. (pres. Corn Belt div. 1975-76), Am. assns. sch. adminstrs., Am., Ill. assns. supervision and curriculum devel., Am. Legion, VFW, Phi Delta Kappa. Democrat. Roman Catholic. K.C., Lion, Kiwanian. Contbr. articles to profl. jours. Address: 4 Isabelle Dr Auburn IL 62615

DOHENY, DONALD ALOYSIUS, lawyer, business exec.; b. Milw., Apr. 20, 1924; s. John Anthony and Adelaide (Koller) D.; student U. Notre Dame, 1942-43; B.Mech. Engring., Marquette U., 1947; J.D., Harvard, 1949; postgrad. indsl. engring. and bus. adminstrn. Washington U., 1950-56; m. Catherine Elizabeth Lee, Oct. 25, 1952; children—Donald Aloysius, Celeste Hazel, John Vincent, Ellen Adelaide, Edward Lawrence II, William Francis, Madonna Lee. Asst. to civil engr. Shipbuilding div. Froemming Bros., Inc., Milw., 1942-43; draftsman, designer The Heil Co., Milw., 1944-46; admitted to Wis. bar, 1949, Mo. bar, 1949; mem. firm Igoe, Carroll & Keefe, St. Louis, 1949-51; asst. to v.p. and gen. mgr., chief prodn. engr., gen. adminstr., dir. adminstrn. Granco Steel Products subsidiary Granite City Steel, Granite City, Ill., 1951-57; asst. to pres. Vestal Labs., Inc., St. Louis, 1957-63; exec. v.p., dir. Moehlenpah Engring., Inc., Hydro-Air Engring., Inc., 1963-67; pres. dir. Foamtex Industries, Inc., St. Louis, 1967-75; exec. v.p., dir. Seasonal Industries, Inc., Portsmouth, Va., 1973-75; mem. law firm Donald A. Doheny, St. Louis, 1967—; mem. firm Doheny & Assos., Mgmt. Counsel, St. Louis, 1967—; pres., dir. Mktg. & Sales Counsel, Inc., St. Louis, 1975—; pres., dir. Mid-USA Sales Co., St. Louis, 1976—; lectr. bus. orgn. and adminstrn. Washington U., 1950-74. Served as pvt. AUS, 1943-44; 1st lt. Res., 1948-52. Registered profl. engr., Mo. Mem. Am. Judicature Soc., Am. Marketing Assn. (nat. membership chmn. 1959), Am., Mo., Wis., Milw. bar assns., Bar Assn. St. Louis (gen. chmn. pub. relations 1955-56, vice chmn., sec.-treas. jr. sect. 1950, 51), Marquette Engring. Assn. (pres. 1946-47), Engring. Knights, Am. Legion, Tau Beta Pi, Pi Tau Sigma, K.C. Clubs: Notre Dame (pres. 1955, 56), Marquette (pres. 1961) (St. Louis); Stadium, Mo. Athletic, Arena. Home: 10906 Conway Rd Frontenac MO 63131 Office: 2324 Weldon Pkwy St Louis County MO 63141 also 408 Olive St Suite 400 St Louis MO 63102

DOHERTY, JOHN DOUGLAS, research neurobiologist; b. Everett, Mass., May 1, 1943; s. Joseph P. and Rose Ann D.; B.S., U. N.H., 1965; M.S., George Washington U., 1968; Ph.D., U. Wis., 1973; m. Yoshiko Gotoh, Oct. 14, 1972; 1 dau., Hanako Stephanie. Research chemist FDA, 1965-69; postdoctoral fellow pharmacology dept. Yale U., New Haven, Conn., 1973-77; faculty U. Chgo., 1977—. Marine Biol. Lab., Woods Hole, Mass., travel fellow, 1970, NIH postdoctoral fellow, 1975-76. Mem. Entomol. Soc. Am., Am. Soc. Neurosci., Sigma Xi, Alpha Zeta. Contbr. articles to profl. jours. Home: 120 Willard St New Haven CT 06515

DOHERTY, RICHARD PAUL, educator; b. Ottawa, Ill., July 30, 1932; s. Paul A. and Rita (Bonges) D.; B.S. magna cum laude, St. Joseph Coll. (Ind.), 1954; M.S. Ed., No. Ill. U., 1957; Ph.D. (fellow), Ball State U., 1970; m. Teresa Ann Donahue, Dec. 27, 1958; children—Thomas, Barbara, John, Kathleen, James. Tchr., Marseilles, Ill., 1957-60, Fenton High Sch., Bensenville, Ill., 1961-69; chmn. dept. social scis. Rend Lake coll., Ina, Ill., 1970-76. Served with AUS, 1954-56. Mem. Phi Delta Kappa, Phi Alpha Theta. Roman Catholic. Democrat. Author: The Origin and Development of Chicago-O'Hare International Airport, 1970. Home: 2904 Apple St Mount Vernon IL 62864 Office: Rend Lake Coll Ina IL 62846

DOHLMAN, DENNIS RAYE, oil co. exec.; b. Iowa Falls, Iowa, Mar. 16, 1946; s. Lowell L. and Harmena (Ploeger) D.; B.S., Iowa State U., 1968; m. Mary Ilene Ontjes, Sept. 2, 1966; children—John Bradley, Rebecca Ralene. Process engr. No. Petrochem. Co., Morris, Ill., 1968-70, maintenance engr., 1970-72, asst. utility area supt., 1972-74, utility area supt., 1974-76; plant supt. Aminoil USA, Inc., Tioga, N.D., 1977—. Mem. Am. Inst. Chem. Engrs., Gideons. Home: 322 Hanson St Tioga ND 58852 Office: Box 457 Tioga ND 58852

DOHMEN, FREDERICK HOEGER, wholesale drug co. exec.; b. Milw., May 12, 1917; s. Fred William and Viola (Gutsch) D.; B.A. in Commerce, U. Wis., 1939; m. Gladys Elizabeth Dite, Dec. 23, 1939 (dec. 1963); children—William Francis, Robert Charles; m. 2d, Mary Alexander Holgate, June 27, 1964. With F. Dohmen Co., Milw., 1939—, successively warehouse employee, sec., v.p., 1944-52, pres., 1952—; dir. The F. Dohmen Co., 1947—, chmn. bd., 1952—. Bd. dirs. St. Luke's Hosp. Ednl. Found., Milw., pres., 1969-72, chmn. bd., 1972-73; bd. dirs. U. Wis.-Milw. Found., 1976—; industry chmn. Nat. Bible Week, Laymen's Nat. Bible Com., N.Y.C., 1968—. Mem. Nat. Wholesale Druggists Assn. (chmn. resolutions com. 1963, mem. of bd. control 1963-66), Nat. Assn. Wholesalers (trustee 1966-75), Druggists Service Council (dir. 1967-71), Wis. Pharm. Assn., Miss. Valley Drug Club, Beta Gamma Sigma, Phi Eta Sigma, Delta Kappa Epsilon. Presbyn. Clubs: University (Milw.). Home: 3903 W Mequon Rd 112 N Mequon WI 53092 Office: 2738 S 13th St Milwaukee WI 53201

DOHRMAN, GARY LEE, publishing co. exec.; b. Columbus, Ohio, Aug. 19, 1940; s. Lee Winifred and Mary Maria (Norton) D.; B.R.E., Piedmont Bible Coll., Winston-Salem, N.C., 1962; postgrad. Northwestern U., Chgo., 1964-65; m. Barbara Blake, June 30, 1961; children—Allison, Rebecca, Melanie. With customer service div. Sears, Roebuck & Co., Winston-Salem, 1958-62; C.L.U., Am. Nat. Ins. Co., Winston-Salem, 1962-63; mgr. mail order div. Moody Bible Inst., Chgo., 1963-66; mgr. Piedmont Gospel Bookstore, Winston-Salem, 1967-70; dist. mgr., catalog cons. Zondervan Corp. of Nashville, Grand Rapids, Mich., 1970-78, mgr. mail order div., family bookstore div., 1978—; radio announcer Sta. WMBI, Chgo., 1964-65; minister of music 1st Bapt. Ch., Whiting, Ind., 1963-64, Oak Park Ave. Bapt. Ch., Oak Park, Ill., 1964-66, Cedar Forest Bapt. Ch., Winston-Salem, 1967-70; v.p. Louis Rideout Evang. Assn. (Nashville). Mem. Am. Mktg. Assn., Internat., Nat. wildlife assns., Gideons Internat. Office: 1415 Lake Dr SE Grand Rapids MI 49506

DOHRMANN, RUSSELL WILLIAM, paper co. exec.; b. Clinton, Iowa, June 29, 1942; s. Russell Wilbert and Anita Doris Miller D.; B.S., Upper Iowa U., 1965; M.B.A., Drake U., 1971; children—Angela, Michelle, Sarah. Jr. accountant Chamberlain Mfg. Corp., Clinton, 1965, sr. accountant, 1966, plant controller, Derry, Pa., 1967-68; acting mgr. Wheelabrator Frye Inc., Des Moines, 1968-75, cost and procedures mgr., financial cost analyst, v.p., controller, 1971—, group controller Internat. div., 1974—. Mem. Des Moines C. of C., Am. Inst. Corp. Controllers, Nat. Assn. Accountants, Nat. Audubon Soc. Home: 1810 78th St Windsor Heights IA 50322 Office: Wheelabrator Frye Inc PO Box 4947 Des Moines IA 50309

DOISY, EDWARD ADELBERT, biochemist; b. Hume, Ill., Nov. 13, 1893; s. Edward Perez and Ada (Alley) D.; A.B., U. Ill., 1914, M.S., 1916; Ph.D., Harvard U., 1920; D.Sc., Washington U., 1940, Yale U., 1940, U. Chgo., 1941, Central Coll. 1942, U. Ill., 1960, Gustavus Adolphus Coll., 1963; LL.D., St. Louis U., 1955; Docteur honoris causa, U. Paris, 1945; m. Alice Ackert, July 20, 1918 (dec. 1964); children—Edward Adelbert, Robert Ackert, Philip Perez, Richard Joseph; m. 2d, Margaret McCormick, Apr. 19, 1965. Asst. in biochemistry Harvard Med. Sch., 1915-17; instr., asso. and asso. prof. biochemistry Washington U. Sch. Medicine, St. Louis, 1919-23; prof. biochemistry, dir. dept. St. Louis U. Sch. Medicine, 1923-65, Distinguished Service prof. biochemistry, emeritus, also dir. emeritus Edward A. Doisy dept. biochemistry, 1965—, adminstrv. bd.; dir. dept. biochemistry, biochemist St. Mary's Hosp., St. Louis, 1924—. Served to 2d lt. U.S. Army, 1917-19. Several named lectures at various univs. and soc. meetings. Recipient Gold medal St. Louis Med. Soc., 1935; Philip A. Conne medal Chemists Club N.Y., 1935; St. Louis award, 1939; Willard Gibbs medal, 1941; Am. Pharm. Mfg. Assn. award, 1942; Squibb award, 1944; Barren Found. medal, 1972; shared Nobel Prize in Physiology and Medicine with Dr. Henrik Dam, 1943. Mem. League of Nations com. for standardization sex hormones, London, 1932, 35. Mem. Am. Soc. Biol. Chemists (council 1926-27, 34-37, 40-45, pres. 1943-45), Am. Chem. Soc., Nat. Acad. Scis., Am. Philos. Soc., Pontifical Acad. Scis., Am. Acad. Arts and Scis., Phi Beta Kappa, Sigma Xi, Phi Kappa Phi, Alpha Omega Alpha. Author: Sex and Internal Secretions (with Edgar Allen and Charles H. Danforth), 1939. Contbr. articles on blood buffers, sex hormones, vitamin K. and antibiotic compounds to profl. jours. Home: 4B Colonial Village Ct

Webster Groves MO 63119 Office: 1402 S Grand Blvd St Louis MO 63104

DOKKEN, STEPHEN ISAAC, lawyer; b. Faribault, Minn., Dec. 21, 1934; s. Walter George and Blanche (Paulson) D.; B.A., Carleton Coll., 1956; LL.B. cum laude, U. Minn., 1964; m. Geneva Elizabeth Dahle, Dec. 30, 1960; children—Terrance Peter, Tracy Alana. Admitted to Ohio bar, 1964, Minn. bar, 1966; asso. firm Squire, Sanders & Dempsey, Cleve., 1964-66; partner Cook & Dokken, Faribault, 1966—; spl. municipal judge, Faribault, 1967-70; guest lectr. Sch. Agr., U. Minn., 1970-71. First vice chmn. Rice County Republican Com., 1968-70; bd. dirs. Faribault Area Family YMCA, Inc., also co-chmn. fund dr., 1972. Served with USN, 1956-61; comdr. Res. Mem. Minn., Am., 5th Dist. (pres. 1974-75) bar assns., Am. Judicature Soc., Res. Officers Assn. Lutheran. Elk, Toastmaster. Clubs: Exchange, Sertoma (Faribault). Home: 1100 NE 3d St Faribault MN 55021 Office: 331 NW 2d Ave Faribault MN 55021

DOLACK, LEROY JOSEPH, mfg. exec.; b. Chgo., Feb. 24, 1933; s. Thomas Casimir and Catherine (Mushinski) D.; B.S.C., Loyola U., Chgo., 1955; M.B.A., U. Chgo., 1960; m. Dorothy Anne Roman, Feb. 11, 1956; children—Mari-Anne, Carol, Elizabeth. Various positions in accounting, engring., finance and mfg. Bell & Howell, Chgo., 1956-61; v.p. DuPage Die Casting Co., Niles, Ill., 1961—. Mem. Soc. Advancement Mgmt., Soc. Automotive Engrs., Soc. Die Cast Engrs., Am. Die Cast Inst., Soc. Mfg. Engrs. Home: 525 Circle Ln Lake Forest IL 60045 Office: 6100 Gross Point Rd Niles IL 60648

DOLAN, JAY PATRICK, educator; b. Bridgeport, Conn., Mar. 17, 1936; s. Joseph Thomas and Margaret (Reardon) D.; A.B., St. John's Sem., 1958; S.T.L., Gregorian U., Rome, 1962; Ph.D., U. Chgo., 1970; m. Patricia McNeal, May 26, 1973; children—Patrick Joseph, Mark McNeal. Asst. prof. U. San Francisco, 1970-71; asso. prof. dept. history U. Notre Dame, 1971—, also dir. Center for Study Am. Catholicism, 1977—; cons. Nat. Endowment Humanities, 1976—, Elkhart (Ind.) Bicentennial Commn., 1975-76. Fellow Rockefeller Found., 1969-70, Shelby Cullom Davis Center Hist. Studies, Princeton U., 1973-74. Mem. Am. Cath. Hist. Assn. (John Gilmary Shea award 1975), Am. Soc. Ch. History (exec. council 1977—), Orgn. Am. Historians. Author: The Immigrant Church: New York's Irish and German Catholics 1815-1865, 1975; Heritage of '76, 1976; Catholic Revivalism, 1977. Home: 16130 Brockton Ct Granger IN 46530 Office: Dept History Univ Notre Dame Notre Dame IN 46556

DOLAN, LILLIAN GABEL, librarian; b. Fond du Lac, Wis., Dec. 9, 1911; d. Ferdinand William and Rose (Hollinger) Gabel; B.S. in Elementary Edn., Marian Coll., 1963; M.S. in L.S., U. Wis., 1966; m. Gerald William Dolan, June 9, 1937 (dec. May 1975); children—Mary (Mrs. Donald C. Thelen), Janet (Mrs. Nolan Sauerbreit), Alice (Mrs. Robert Cornett). Tchr. pub. schs., Wis., 1929-37, St. Joseph's Sch., Fond du Lac, 1955-65; librarian Moraine Park Tech. Inst., Fond du Lac, 1966-76; ret., 1976. Mem. Am., Wis., Fox Valley (pres. 1974-75) library assns., Wis. Edn. Assn., Bus. and Profl. Womens Assn., Daus. Isabella. Roman Catholic. Home: 118 W Cotton St Fond du Lac WI 54935 Office: Arthur & Assos Inc 548 Prairie Rd Fond du Lac WI 54935

DOLAN, R. EDMUND, coll. adminstr.; b. Butte, Mont., Mar. 26, 1941; s. Edmund R. and Madelon (Thomas) D.; B.A., U. Santa Clara, 1963; Ph.D., Loyola U. (Chgo.), 1970; m. Helen Marie Cronin, June 3, 1967; children—John Kevin, Melissa Marie. Asst. dean City Colls. of Chgo., 1967-71; asso. prof. Oakton Community Coll., Morton Grove, Ill., 1971-72, dean, 1972—. Loyola U. Pres.'s scholar, 1966; NDEA fellow, 1968. Mem. Am. Assn. Higher Edn., Humanistic Psychology Assn. Club: Chgo. Ambassador. Home: 2108 McDaniel St Evanston IL 60201 Office: 7900 Nagle St Morton Grove IL 60059

DOLCE, JOHN LEONARD, oral surgeon; b. Chgo., Apr. 26, 1935; s. John and Mae Catherine (Seaton) D.; D.D.S., Loyola U., Chgo., 1959; m. Mary Alice McCarthy, Apr. 23, 1960; children—Marcia, John, Edward, Helene, Matthew. Dental Intern, Hines (Ill.) VA Hosp., 1960; resident oral surgery U. Okla. Med. Center, Oklahoma City, 1961-63; individual practice oral surgery, Mundelein, Ill., 1963—; clin. asst. prof. dept. oral surgery Loyola U., Chgo., 1963—; partner Century Qual-I-Cast, Libertyville, Ill., 1971—. Vice chmn. Lake County Health Planning Council, 1973-74, chmn., 1974—; vice chmn. Kane Lake McKenry County Health Systems Agy., 1976—. Bd. dirs. Puerta Abierta, social service orgn., 1969—. Mem. ADA, Am. Soc. Oral Surgeons, Mundelein C. of C. (v.p. 1973, pres. 1974). Home: 11 Martha Ln Evanston IL 60102 Office: Route 1 Box 256C Mundelein IL 60060

DOLD, HELEN SHUMAKER (MRS. C. NORMAN DOLD), civic worker; b. Prospect, Pa., Oct, 8, 1898; d. Elwood Curtis and Effie (Gailey) Shumaker; A.B., and B.Mus., Denison U., 1921; M.A., U. Wis., 1925; m. Charles Norman Dold, Sept. 24, 1927 (dec. Aug. 1965); children—Charles Norman, John Allen, Robert James, Mary Ann. Instr. English, U. Wis., 1923-25, Rockford (Ill.) Coll., 1925-27. Dir., Rose Exterminator Co., Chgo. Bd. mgrs. Woman's Am. Baptist Home Mission Soc., 1942-53, Midwestern v.p., 1951-53; chmn. bd. mgrs. Bapt. Missionary Tng. Sch., 1951-53; corr. sec. Woman's Club of Wilmette (Ill.), 1954-56; regent Skokie Valley chpt. DAR, 1958-60; pres. Woman's Bapt. Mission Union of Chgo., 1960-62; mem. North Shore Republican Women's Club. Mem. Mortar Bd. (hon.), Phi Beta Kappa (hon.), Delta Delta Delta, Delta Omicron. Co-author anthology The World Unfolding, 1927. Home: 1350 Greenwood Ave Wilmette IL 60091

DOLE, PHILIP SANFORD, educator; b. Lewiston, Idaho, May 4, 1925; s. Ira Stanley and Bessie Lulu (Perkins) D.; student U. Calif. at Los Angeles, 1945-50; B.S., Roosevelt U., 1966, M.S., 1968; m. Doris Yates, Nov. 5, 1950; children—Steven, Jennifer, Nancy. Staff accountant Brunswick Corp., 1958-61; div. controller Hwy. Trailers, Chgo., 1961-62; staff accountant Oak Mfg. Co., Crystal Lake, Fla., 1962-65; asso. prof. accounting Rock Valley Coll., Rockford, Ill., 1966—. C.P.A., Ill. Home: 3301 N Mulford Rd Rockford IL 61111

DOLE, ROBERT J., U.S. senator; b. Russell, Kans., July 22, 1923; s. Doran R. and Bina Dole; student U. Kans., U. Ariz.; A.B., Washburn Municipal U., Topeka, 1952, LL.B., 1952. Admitted to Kans. bar; mem. Kans. Ho. of Reps., 1951; pvt. practice law, Russell, 1953-61; Russell County atty., 1953-61; mem. 87th Congress 6th Dist. of Kans., mem. 88th-90th congresses, 1st Dist. Kans.; now mem. U.S. Senate from Kans. Chmn., Republican Nat. Com., 1971-73; Rep. candidate for v.p., 1976. Served with AUS, World War II. Decorated Bronze Star with cluster. Mem. Am. Legion, V.F.W., 4-H Fair Assn., Kappa Sigma. Methodist. Mason (Shriner), Elk, Kiwanian. Home: Russell KS 67665 Office: New Senate Office Bldg Washington DC 20510

DOLEZAL, WILBUR FRANCIS, dentist; b. Chgo., July 23, 1928; s. John and Mathilda Anna (Benes) D.; B. Gen. Edn., Morton Jr. Coll., 1948; B.S., U. Ill., 1950; D.D.S., Loyola U., Chgo., 1954; m. Geraldine Clara Viskocil, Dec. 26, 1953; 1 son, Stephen John. Individual practice dentistry, Franklin Park, Ill., 1956-57, Morris, Ill., 1957—; mem. staff Morris Hosp., 1957—; instr. prosthetics, crown and bridge, operative dentistry Loyola U. Dental Sch., Chgo., 1957-59. Mem. profl. adv. com. Grundy County Health Dept., 1971—, Home Health Care Task Force, 1972-74; mem. Bd. Edn., Dist. 101, Morris Community High Sch., 1974—. Bd. dirs. Am. Cancer Soc., 1959—; chmn. lay adv. com. Morris Community High Sch., 1972-73. Served to capt. USAF, 1954-56. Fellow Am. Coll. Dentists, Internat. Coll. Dentists; mem. Am. Dental Assn., Ill. (com. on relations with affiliated groups 1974-79), Ill. Valley (pres. 1971-72), Chgo. dental socs., Ill. Acad. Practice Adminstrn., Pierre Fauchard Acad., Morris C. of C. (dir. 1959-61), Omega Beta Pi, Phi Kappa Theta, Psi Omega. Republican. Roman Catholic (mem. parish council 1967-70, mem. liturgy com. 1976—, minister extraordinaire 1977—). K.C. Club: Morris Country (dir. 1967-71). Home: 200 Briar Ln Morris IL 60450 Office: 417 W Jefferson St Morris IL 60450

DOLL, DIXON RAYMOND, systems engring. cons.; b. San Angelo, Tex., Nov. 19, 1942; s. Raymond Joseph and Mary Clare (Dixon) D.; B.E.E. cum laude, Kans. State U., 1964; M.S. in Engring., U. Mich., 1965, Ph.D. (NSF fellow 1965-68), 1969; m. Carol Ann Pucci, June 19, 1965; children—Dixon Raymond, Alexander Pucci, Andrew James. Systems engr. Datamax Corp., Ann Arbor, Mich., 1969-70; mem. faculty, Grad. Sch. Bus., Eastern Mich. U., Ypsilanti, 1970-72; vis. faculty mem. IBM Systems Research Inst., N.Y.C., 1972—; pres., dir. Mich. Communications Group, Inc., Ann Arbor, 1972—; chmn., dir. DMW Telecommunications Corp., Ann Arbor, Mich., 1973—; tech. dir. Internat. Communications Corps ICC Inst., Miami, Fla., 1972—; dir. Graphic Scanning Corp., N.Y.C., 1972. Mem. I.E.E.E., Assn. for Computing Machinery, Assn. for Systems Mgmt., Sigma Xi, Phi Kappa Phi. Club: Racquet (Ann Arbor). Contbg. author, editor Data Communications, 1972—; tech. editor Data Processing Mag., 1969-71. Home: 2975 Hickory Ln Ann Arbor MI 48104

DOLNEY, DENNIS DEAN, veterinarian; b. St. Paul, Sept. 8, 1946; s. Jerome and Sylvia Marie (Block) D.; student S.D. State U., 1964-66; D.V.M., Iowa State U., 1970; m. Betty Lee Dargatz, Aug. 19, 1967; children—Andrea Michele, Christine Evalyn. Veterinarian, Howard (S.D.) Veterinary Clinic, 1970-71, Groton (S.D.) Veterinary Clinic, 1971-73; veterinary animal health and meat insp. Animal and Plant Health Inspection Service, Sioux Falls, S.D., 1973; partner Milbank (S.D.) Veterinary Clinic, 1973—. Health officer, Milbank, 1974-76. Mem. Northeast S.D. Veterinary Assn. (pres.), S.D., Minn. veterinary med. assns., AVMA. Roman Catholic. Office: 221 3d Ave E Milbank SD 57252

DOLNICK, NORMAN, pub. relations exec.; b. Chgo., Jan. 24, 1918; s. Benjamin and Bertha (Balter) D.; student U. Chgo., 1940, Northwestern U., 1936; m. June Blythe, Jan. 2, 1948; children—Don, David. Info. specialist Nat. War Labor Bd., Washington, 1944-46; pub. relations dir. United Packinghouse Workers, Chgo., 1946-53; v.p. Harshe-Rotman & Druck, 1953-62; pres. Norman Dolnick & Assos., 1962—; lectr. U. Chgo., Roosevelt U. Exec. com. Citizens of Greater Chgo., 1958-68; communications com. Welfare Council Met. Chgo., 1969—. Bd. dirs. Chgo. Urban Corps, Catalyst for Youth. Mem. Pub. Relations Soc. Am. (Silver Anvil award 1947, Distinguished Service award Chgo. chpt. 1966; chpt. pres. 1966), Art Inst. Chgo. Club: Press (Chgo.). Home: 1418 E 54th Place Chicago IL 60615 Office: 333 N Michigan Ave Chicago IL 60601

DOLNICK, SAMUEL LOUIS, ednl. adminstr.; b. Chgo., May 28, 1918; s. Philip and Ida (Ganetzky) D.; B.E., Chgo. Tchrs. Coll., 1940; M.A., Northwestern U., 1951; Asso. degree, U. Ill., 1953; m. Edith Neidorf, May 28, 1942; 1 son, Gene. Tchr., Stockton Elementary Sch., Chgo., 1940-42, Schurz High Sch., 1947-55, Chgo. Tchrs. Coll., 1955, U. Ill., 1952-53, 76—; prin. Belding Elementary Sch., Chgo., 1955-59, Medill Elementary Sch., Chgo., 1959-61, Carver High Sch., Chgo., 1961-63, Von Steuben High Sch., Chgo., 1963-74. Cons. ednl. evaluation Am. Peoples Ency., 1955, 57; cons. Journ. Films, Inc., 1955-69. Served with AUS, 1942-46. Decorated 3 Bronze Stars. Mem. Chgo. Prins. Assn. (pres. 1967-69, 73—), Electric Shop Tchrs. Chgo. (pres. 1953-54), Am. Fedn. Sch. Adminstrs. (exec. bd. 1973-76), Nat., Ill. assns. secondary sch. prins., N.E.A., Audio-Visual Edn., Phi Delta Kappa. Mem. B'nai B'rith. Home: 2626 Lakeview Ave Chicago IL 60614 Office: 221 N La Salle St Chicago IL 60601

DOMBROSKI, ALEX ANTHONY, microbiologist; b. Nanticoke, Pa., May 10, 1924; s. Alex and Elizabeth (Stigora) D.; B.S., Kings Coll., 1953; M.S., Wayne State U., 1957; m. June 19, 1954; children—Alendria Jean, Lori Jane. Bacteriologist, Henry Ford Hosp., Detroit, 1957-59; microbiologist St. Joseph Hosp., Lorain, Ohio, 1959—. Certified med. technologist, Am. Soc. Clin. Pathologists, 1957. Mem. Am. Soc. Clin. Pathologists. Home: 42813 Haven Dr Elyria OH 44035 Office: Microbiology Dept Saint Joseph Hosp 205 W 20th St Lorain OH 44052

DOMEK, JOHN ANTHONY, mech. engr.; b. Chgo., Aug. 22, 1930; s. John Stanley and Victoria (Bitto) D.; student U. Ill., 1949-51, Ill. Inst. Tech., 1952—; m. Rosemary Bibbings, Jan. 25, 1958; children—John Steven, Malyn Catherine. Detail draftsman Henry Pratt Co., Chgo., 1951-52, checker, 1952-53, squad leader, 1953-55, design engr., 1955-60, project engr., 1960-62; design engr. Parker Hannifin Co., Des Plaines, Ill., 1962-63, project engr., Ellis Fluid Dynamics Corp., Chgo., 1963-65, asst. chief engr., 1965-66; asst. chief engr. Efdyn Corp. subsidiary Miner Enterprises, Inc., Chgo., 1966-68, chief engr., 1968-74, v.p. engring., 1974—. Registered profl. engr., Ill. Mem. Nat. Soc. Profl. Engrs. Inventor hydraulic resonance impulse modulator for vehicle suspensions, hydro-elastic energy absorbing system for vehicle bumpers, adjustable hydraulic shock absorber with rotatable reservoir. Home: 1497 McCormick Pl Wheaton IL 60187 Office: 8700 S Dobson Ave Chicago IL 60619

DOMINICAK, ROBERT HARRY, civil engr.; b. Pukwana, S.D., Feb. 26, 1941; s. Harry Michael and Virginia June (Mesnard) D.; B.S. in Civil Engring., S.D. Sch. Mines and Tech., 1968; m. Sharon Faye Faller, Nov. 26, 1960; children—Bradley Robert, Curtis Leigh. Vice pres., engr. Thomas & Lockwood cons. engrs., Rapid City, S.D., 1968-76; v.p. Thomas, Erickson, Dominicak & Crow cons. engrs. Inc., Rapid City, 1976—. Mem. adminstrve. bd., past chmn. finance com. Methodist Ch.; active Boy Scouts Am., 1970-74, mem. unit com. Penjahame Dist. Com., 1975-77, dist. chmn., council exec. bd., 1971—, v.p. ops. Black Hills Area council, 1977—, recipient Dist. Merit award, 1973. Registered profl. engr., S.D., Mont., Wyo.; registered land surveyor, S.D. Mem. Am. Concrete Inst., ASCE (past br. pres., v.p. S.D. Sect.), S.D. Engring. Soc., Nat. Soc. Profl. Engrs. Republican. Methodist. Clubs: Optimist, Elks. Home: 222 Stanley Ct Rapid City SD 57701 Office: 2202 Jackson Blvd Rapid City SD 57701

DOMMERMUTH, WILLIAM P., educator; b. Chgo., June 29, 1925; s. Peter R. and Gertrude (Schnell) D.; B.A., U. Ia., 1948; Ph.D., Northwestern U., 1964: m. H. Joan Hasty, June 6, 1959; children—Karin Jo, Margaret, Jean. Advt. copywriter Sears, Roebuck & Co., Chgo., 1949-51, sales promotion mgr., 1951-58; asst., then asso. prof. mktg. U. Tex. at Austin, 1961-67; asso. prof. U. Iowa, Iowa City, 1967-68; prof. So. Ill. U., Carbondale, 1968—. Cons. bus. firms. Mem. Am. Mktg. Assn., Am. Inst. Decision Scis., Phi Beta Kappa, Beta Gamma Sigma, Theta Xi, Delta Sigma Pi. Democrat. Roman Catholic. Club: Jackson Country. Author: (with Kernan and Sommers) Promotion: An Introductory Analysis, 1970; (with Andersen) Distribution Systems, 1972; (with Marcus and others) Modern Marketing, 1975. Contbr. articles to profl. jours. Home: Six Rolling Acres Murphysboro IL 62966 Office: Dept Marketing So Ill Univ Carbondale IL 62901

DOMPKE, NORBERT FRANK, photography studio exec.; b. Chgo., Oct. 16, 1920; s. Frank and Mary (Manley) D.; grad. Wright Jr. Coll., 1939-40; student Northwestern U., 1946-49; m. Marjorie Gies, Dec. 12, 1964; children—Scott, Pamela. Cost comptroller, budget dir. Scott Radio Corp., 1947; pres. TV Forecast, Inc., 1948-52, editor Chgo. edit. TV Guide, 1953, mgr. Wis. edit., 1954; pres. Root Photographers, Inc., Chgo., 1955—. Served with USAAC, 1943-47. C.P.A., Ill. Mem. United Photographers Orgn. (pres. 1970-71), Profl. Photographers Am., Am. Assn. Sch. Photographers (v.p. 1966-67, sec. treas. 1967-69, pres. 1969-70, dir. 1971—), Ill. Small Bus. Men's Assn. (dir. 1970), Ill. Assn. Profl. Photographers, Chgo. Assn. Commerce and Industry (edn. com. 1966—), NEA, Nat. Sch. Press Assn., Ill. High Sch. Press Assn., Nat. Collegiate Sch. Press Assn., Ill. C. of C. Co-founder T. Guide, 1947. Clubs: Carlton; Whitehall; International; Tonquish Creek Yacht. Home: 990 N Lake Shore Dr Chicago IL 60611 Office: 1131 W Sheridan Rd Chicago IL 60660

DON, DANIEL ARTHUR, lawyer; b. Chgo., Feb. 2, 1932; s. Edward and Irene (Kinzelberg) D.; B.A. cum laude, Yale U., 1953, LL.B., 1958. Admitted to Ill. bar, 1958; since practiced in Chgo.; atty. Arvey, Hodrs & Martynband, 1958-71; partner firm Kallen, Don & Schneider, Chgo., 1972—; lectr., author Ill. Inst. Continuing Legal Edn., 1965—. Bd. dirs. young peoples div. Jewish Fedn. Chgo., 1962-66, Bur. Jewish Employment Problems, 1966—, Park View Home for Aged, 1968—. Served to 1st lt. AUS, 1953-55. Mem. Chgo. (mem. comml. law com.), Ill. (chmn. uniform comml. code com. 1969), Am. (mem. com. consumer class actions) bar assns., Phi Beta Kappa. Club: Standard (Chgo.).

DONAHUE, JAMES J., JR., bedding co. exec.; b. Pueblo, Colo., Dec. 16, 1919; s. James J. and Sarah E. (Bryden) D.; student Lawrence U., 1938-40, U. Minn., 1940-41, 46-47, U. Md., 1957-63, Am. U., 1957-63; B.A.; m. Laura L. Sherman, Sept. 7, 1968; children by previous marriage—James J. III, Thomas M.; step-children—Pamela (Mrs. Thomas DeWall), Brien Peterson. Salesman Am. Brass Co., Mpls., 1940-41, 46-47; sales and advt. mgr. Skellet Van & Storage Co., 1947-50; dir. research and devel. Conwed Corp., St. Paul, 1967-71; v.p., gen. mgr. Anderson Machine, Inc., Chaska, Minn., 1971-73; exec. v.p., treas. U.S. Bedding Co., St. Paul, 1973—. Mem. staff and faculty Command and Gen. Staff Coll., Fort Leavenworth, Kans., 1953-57. Bd. dirs. United Fund, Mpls., 1948-50, ARC, Mpls., 1948-50. Served to col. U.S. Army, 1942-46, 51-66. Decorated Legion of Merit, Joint Services Commendation, Bronze Star medal with 3 oak leaf clusters. Mem. Ret. Officers Assn. Mason (32 deg.), Rotarian. Clubs: Dellwood Hills Golf (White Bear Lake, Minn.); Pool and Yacht (St. Paul); St. Croix Yacht (V.I.). Patentee in field. Home: 1889 29th Ave NW St Paul MN 55112 Office: US Bedding Co 558 Vandalia St St Paul MN 55114

DONAHUE, JEROME G., biomed. engring. co. exec.; b. Milw., Dec. 21, 1937; s. Ignatius J. and Margaret (Thiel) D.; B.S., Marquette U., 1960; M.A., U. Neb., 1967; grad. Harvard Mgmt. Program, 1975. m. Barbara Leivermann, Apr. 4, 1970. Broker, agt., claims adjuster Crawford & Co., Mpls., 1960-63; dir. continuing edn. U. Minn. at Mpls., 1963-68; with Medtronic, Inc., Mpls., 1968—, dir. investor relations, 1973-74, dir. communications and employee devel., 1974-75, gen. mgr. neurol. products div., 1976—; dir. Saucier Inc., Mpls., instr. U. Minn. at Mpls., 1963-68; cons. Med. Devices Inc., Mpls., 1972-73. Sports event coordinator, Mpls. Aquatennial, 1965-68; athletic event coordinator Pan Am. trials, 1967. Kellogg Found. fellow, 1965-67; Butler Found. grantee, 1968. Mem. Nat. Investor Relations Inst., Am. Soc. Tng. Dirs., Am. Assn. Advancement Med. Instrumentation, Health Industries Mfrs. Assn., Pub. Relations Soc. Am., Catholic Order Foresters, Iota Rho Chi. Clubs: Mpls. Athletic, Kings Court Racquet. Contbr. articles to profl. jours. Office: 3055 Old Hwy 8 Minneapolis MN 55418

DONALD, WILLIAM CLYDE, II, clergyman; b. Battle Creek, Mich., Nov. 28, 1918; s. William Clyde and Louella (Shattuck) D.; A.B., Albion Col, 1940; B.D., Garrett Bibl. Inst., 1943; D.D., Northwestern U., 1947; m. Carolyn Marie Fosberg, July 28, 1943; 1 dau., Pamela Marie (Mrs. Larry Ward). Chaplain Deaconess Hosp., Milw., 1948-56; pastor Bethel Evangelical and Reformed Ch., Milw., 1949-57, Bethel Evangelical and Reformed Ch., Detroit, 1957-70, Peoples Ch. Chgo., 1970-73; sr. minister 1st Congl. Ch., Benton Harbor, Mich., 1973-77, Plymouth Congl. Ch., Mpls., 1977—; part-time faculty Wayne State U., 1950-70. Chmn. bd. Third Securities Corp., Rockford, Ill., 1965-77. Mem. Am. Protestant Hosp. Assn. (fellow coll. chaplains). Tau Kappa Epsilon. Mem. B'nai B'rith (hon.). Home: 2611 Kyle Ave Golden Valley MN 55422 Office: 1900 Nicollet Ave Minneapolis MN 55403

DONALDSON, FRANK COOMBS, obstetrician, gynecologist; b. Lebanon, Ind., May 25, 1922; s. Fred Raymond and Esther Ann (Coombs) D.; A.B., DePauw U., 1943; M.D., Ind. U., 1946; m. Loraine A. Kalow, May 21, 1948; children—Frederick, Frank Coombs, Thomas, Susan Jane, David. Intern, St. Elizabeth Hosp., Lafayette, Ind., 1946-47, resident, 1949-52; resident Ind. U. Med. Center, Indpls., 1950-51; staff obstet.-gynecol. service William Beaumont Hosp., El Paso, Tex., 1947-49, chief service, 1949; practice medicine specializing in obstetrics, gynecology, Anderson, Ind., 1951—; staff pres. St. Johns Hosp., Anderson, 1962, chief staff, 1963-65; staff pres. Community Hosp., Anderson, 1972, chief staff, 1974—; vol. physician Frances Newton Mission Hosp., Punjab, India, 1968. Chmn. profl. div. United Fund, Anderson, 1969. Served to capt. M.C., AUS, 1943-49. Diplomate Am. Bd. Obstetrics-Gynecology. Fellow A.C.S., Am. Coll. Obstetricians-Gynecologists; mem. Anderson C. of C. (dir.), Ind. Obstet.-Gynecol. Soc. (pres. 1972), Ind. Med. Assn. (chmn. gynecol. sect. 1968), A.M.A., Beta Theta Pi. Presbyn. (elder 1969—). Club: Anderson Country. Home: Route 2 Windridge St Anderson IN 46011 Office: 2009 Brown St Anderson IN 46014

DONALSON, JAMES RYAN, real estate broker; b. Kansas City, Mo., Jan. 7, 1945; s. Joseph Elmer and Betty Lee (Cousins) D.; B.S. (Mo. Real Estate Assn. scholar), U. Mo., 1967; m. Sandra Lynn Yockey, Dec. 26, 1964; children—Kimberly Kay, Debra Lynn, Jennifer Lee. Loan officer City Wide Mortgage Co., Kansas City, 1967; interviewer personnel Panhandle Eastern Pipe Line Co., Kansas City, 1968; partner Donalson Realtors, Kansas City, 1969—; pres. Classic Homes, Kansas City, 1973—; bd. dirs. Multiple Listing Service Greater Kansas City, 1971-75, treas., 1972-73. Bd. dirs. Platte County unit Am. Cancer Soc., 1973-75. Mem. Nat. Assn. Real Estate Bds., Mo. Assn. Realtors (dir. 1974-75), Real Estate Bd. Kansas City (dir. 1978—), Platte County Bus. and Profl. Mens Assn., U. Mo. Alumni Assn. Baptist. Lion (dir. 1974-76). Office: 7526 NW Prairie View Rd Kansas City MO 64151

DONATI, ROBERT MARIO, physician, educator; b. Richmond Heights, Mo., Feb. 28, 1934; s. Leo S. and Rose Marie D.; B.S. in Biology, St. Louis U., 1955, M.D., 1959. Intern St. Louis City Hosp., 1959-60; asst. resident John Cochran Hosp., St. Louis, 1960-62; fellow nuclear medicine St. Louis U., 1962-63; practice medicine specializing in nuclear medicine, St. Louis, 1963—; mem. staff John Cochran

Hosp., also St. Louis U., 1963—, mem. faculty Sch. Medicine, 1963—, asst. prof. internal medicine, 1965-68, asso. prof., 1968-74, prof., 1974—, dir. div. nuclear medicine, 1968—; chief nuclear medicine services St. Louis VA Hosp., 1968—. Served to capt. AUS, 1966-68. Diplomate Am. Bd. Nuclear Medicine. Mem. A.M.A., St. Louis Med. Soc., Am. Fedn. for Clin. Research (counciler 1967-70), Central Soc. Clin. Research, A.A.U.P., N.Y. Acad. Scis., Soc. for Exptl. Biology and Medicine, Soc. Nuclear Medicine (acad. council 1970—), Am. Coll. Nuclear Physicians (asso. chmn. sci. program 1978), Am., Internat. socs. hematology, Sigma Xi. Roman Catholic. Editor: (with W.T. Newton) Radioassay in Clinical Medicine, 1974. Contbr. articles to profl. jours. Research in clin. investigative nuclear medicine and humoral control of cellular proliferation. Home: 5335 Botanical Ave St Louis MO 63110 Office: St Louis VA Hosp 115JC St Louis MO 63125

DONEGAN, GEORGE JOSEPH, lawyer, state legislator; b. St. Louis, May 23, 1923; s. Samuel Patrick and Anna (Cunningham) D.; B.A. cum laude, Drury Coll., 1947; J.D., Georgetown U., 1950; m. Elizabeth Sheppard, Jan. 15, 1943; children—George J., Elizabeth Ann, Cecilia, Michael, Kathleen, Mary Darby, Patrick, Laura, Timothy, Sean, Charles Kerry. Credit reporter Dun & Bradstreet, Greene County, Mo., 1947; law clk. Covington & Burling, Washington, 1948-50; admitted to D.C., Mo. bars, 1950; asst. dist. counsel OPS, D.C., 1951; trial atty. criminal div. Justice Dept., 1952-54; U.S. atty., D.C., 1954-56; mem. firm Miller, Fairman, Sanford, Carr & Lowther, Springfield, Mo., 1956-65; partner Donegan & Holden, Springfield, 1965-67; practiced in Springfield, 1967-76; partner firm Donegan & Bolton, 1976—; faculty, Drury and Evangel Colls., Springfield, 1956-60. Chmn. City of Springfield Housing Authority, 1967-70. Mem. Mo. Ho. of Reps., 1967-70, 72—. Bd. dirs. United Fund of Springfield and Greene County, pres., 1964; bd. dirs. S.W. Mo. Ecumenical Center, v.p., 1969-71, treas. 1971-73. Served with USAAF, World War II. Mem. Am., Mo., Greene County (pres. 1961) bar assns., Am. Assn. for UN, Sigma Nu. Republican. Roman Catholic. K.C., Rotarian. Home: 1471 E Meadowmere St Springfield MO 65804 Office: 1714-18 E Meadowmere St Springfield MO 65804

DONER, MARY FRANCES, author; b. Port Huron, Mich.; d. James and Mary Jane (O'Rourke) Doner; ed. Immaculate Heart Convent and Western High Sch., Detroit, St. Clair (Mich.) High Sch., Columbia. Began writing for pulps after leaving coll.; staff writer Dell Pub. Co., N.Y.C., 8 yrs.; music reporter, Boston Traveler, 2 yrs.; contract writer for several pulps in N.Y.C., for Alfred H. King, for Penn Pub. Co.; contract writer Doubleday & Co., 1940—, for novels of Great Lakes country; speaker Boston Book Fair, 1938, Living Literature, Boston U., 1939, Meet the Author series, Boston Pub. Library, 1946; tchr. creative writing Boston Center for Adult Edn., 1943-45, Ludington (Mich.) High Sch., Jr. High and Pub. Library, 1964—, also West Shore Community Coll., Ludington. Hon. mem. Ladies Library Assn., Port Huron, Mich., Women's Lit. Club, Ludington, League Catholic Women; mem. Internat. Inst. of Arts and Letters, Author's League, Pen and Brush Club (N.Y.C.), Smithsonian Instn. (asso.). Author: numerous novels including: Blue River, 1946; Ravenswood, 1948; Cloud of Arrows, 1950; The Host Rock, 1952; The Salvager, 1958; The Shores of Home, 1961; While the River Flows, 1962; The Wind and the Fog, 1963; On Creative Writing, 1967; Cleavenger Vs. Castle, 1968; Pere Marquette—Soldier of the Cross, 1969; Return a Stranger, 1970; Thine Is the Power, 1971; Not By Appointment, 1972; The Darker Star, 1974. Contbr. over 250 short stories and serials to mags. some transcribed into Braille. Home: 210 N Lewis St Ludington MI 49431

DONESA, ANTONIO BRAGANZA, neurosurgeon; b. Manila, Philippines, July 27, 1935; s. Alfonso Pinson and Flora (Braganza) D.; B.S., U. Philippines (Manila), 1956, M.D., 1959; m. Barbara Louise Quinn, Nov. 30, 1962; children—Carmen, Christopher. Came to U.S., 1959, naturalized, 1969. Intern St. Mary's Hosp., Waterbury, Conn., 1959-60; resident U. Ala. Med. Center, Birmingham, 1961-65; practice medicine specializing in neurosurgery, Ft. Wayne, Ind., 1966—; pres. Neurosurgery, Inc., Ft. Wayne, 1971—, also dir.; mem. staff Parkview, St. Joseph's, Lutheran hosps. (all Ft. Wayne); cons. Marion (Ind.) Gen. Hosp., VA Hosp., Ft. Wayne. Recipient Certificate Leadership award March Dimes, 1972, Certificate Appreciation award Heart Fund, 1971. Mem. AMA, Assn. Philippine Practicing Physicians in Am., Ft. Wayne Acad. Medicine and Surgery, Ind. Philippine Med. Assn. (past pres.), Am. Coll. Internat. Physicians (founder), Council Philippine Med. Assn. (dir.), Ind., Allen County med. socs., Congress Neurol. Surgeons, Soc. Philippine Neurol. Surgeons in Am. (pres.). Clubs: Masons (32 deg.), Shriners, Summit (Ft. Wayne). Home: 8215 Tranquilla Pl Fort Wayne IN 46815 Office: 3030 Lake Ave Fort Wayne IN 46805

DONIHUE, DAVID LEE, accounting firm exec.; b. Sturgis, Mich., Mar. 22, 1947; s. Robert Carl and Dorothy Louise (Rawles) D.; B.B.A., Western Mich. U., 1969; m. Yolanda Margarita Monroy, July 1, 1972. Audit mgr. firm Seidman & Seidman, C.P.A.'s, Grand Rapids, Mich., 1968-75; audit mgr. specializing in banking firm Conley, McDonald, Sprague & Co., C.P.A.'s, Milw., 1975—. Asst. treas. Camp Tall Turf, inner-city youth camp, Grand Rapids, 1970-75; co-founder, treas. Recycle Unlimited, Grand Rapids, 1972—, also dir. Bd. dirs., treas., chmn. budget, alt. del. Kent County Unit Mich. Heart Assn., 1973-75. C.P.A., Mich., Wis. Mem. Am., Wis. (banking com.), Mich. insts. C.P.A.'s, Western Mich. U. Hon. Accounting Soc. Home: 2545 Brookside Ln Brookfield WI 53005 Office: 2825 N Mayfair Rd Milwaukee WI 53222

DONLON, WILLIAM JAMES, labor union ofcl.; b. Colorado Springs, Colo., Apr. 22, 1924; s. John A. and Kathleen M. (Neer) D.; student Colo. Coll., 1941-45; B.S., U. Denver, 1949, J.D., 1950; m. Jo Anne Janssen, July 19, 1946; children—William James, Gregory A., Michele L., DruAnn M. Admitted to Colo. bar, 1950, Ohio bar, 1964, Ill. bar, 1969; gen. chmn. Brotherhood Ry. and Airline Clks., Denver, 1953-64, gen. counsel, Rosemont, Ill., 1964—. Instr. ry. labor matters U. Ill. Served with USAAF, 1942-45. Decorated Air medal with 2 oak leaf clusters. Mem. Am., Ill., Chgo. bar assns., Am. Legion, Phi Delta Theta, Phi Alpha Delta. Democrat. Roman Catholic. Home: 1806 Boulder Dr Mt Prospect IL 60056 Office: 6300 River Rd Rosemont IL 60018

DONNAN, THOMASIA BATTEN, club woman; b. Palestine, Tex., May 29, 1912; d. John R. and Myrtle Lee (Washburn) Batten; student Tex. State Women's U., 1929-30, Washington U., St. Louis, 1947-48; m. William Varis Donnan, June 24, 1951; 1 dau., Nancy (Mrs. W.O. Beans, Jr.); stepchildren—Marybelle (Mrs. Harry Recker), Carol (Mrs. Thomas Holling), Dwight A. Tchr. rural sch., Cherokee County, Tex., 1931-32; salesman, cashier, Famous-Barr, St. Louis, 1932-41; with St. Louis Globe-Democrat, 1941-52. Mem. St. Louis Beautification Commn., 1967-69; mem. Glendale Park Bd., 1963-64; landscape design critic, 1966—, master flower show judge, 1969—. Mem. bd. Federated Garden Clubs Mo., 1961-73, asst. dir. East Central Dist., 1961-62; writer, editor The Nat. Gardener, 1969—; pres. Glendale Garden Club, 1960-61, 68-69; pres. St. Louis County Garden Club, 1969-70. Mem. Asso. Garden Clubs Kirkwood (pres. 1957-59), Nat. Council State Garden Clubs, Glendale Women's Club. Methodist. Editor The Garden Forum, 1965-69. Home: 995 Kirkham Ave Glendale MO 63122 Office: 4401 Magnolia Ave Saint Louis MO 63110

DONNELL, JAMES C., II, business exec.; b. Findlay, Ohio, June 30, 1910; s. Otto Dewey and Glenn (McClelland) D.; A.B., Princeton, 1932; m. Dolly Louise DeVine, July 2, 1932; 1 dau., Susan (Mrs. Harry W. Konkel). With Marathon Oil Co., Findlay, 1932-36, mgr. crude oil sales, 1932-36, v.p., 1937-48, pres., 1948-72, chmn., 1972-75; ret., 1975; dir. 1st Nat. Bank, Findlay, Nat. City Bank of Cleve., Armco Steel Corp., Phelps Dodge Corp., N.Y. Life Ins. Co., Libby-Owens-Ford Co. Mem. world council nat., council YMCA. Mem. Am. Petroleum Inst., Am. Assn. Petroleum Geologists, Phi Beta Kappa, Sigma Xi. Republican. Presbyn. Elk. Clubs: Country (Findlay); Princeton, Links, University (N.Y.C.); Duquesne (Pitts.); Union (Cleve.); Inverness (Toledo); Bohemian (San Francisco). Home: 839 S Main St Findlay OH 45840

DONNELLY, GORDON CHARLES, banker; b. Olivia, Minn., Aug. 22, 1915; s. Charles A. and Elizabeth H. (Young) D.; B.S., U. Minn., 1940; m. Harriet Siewert, Oct. 2, 1944; children—Kathleen (Mrs. Robert Ahlbrecht), Diane, Drew. With State Bank of Wheaton (Minn.), 1945—, pres., 1966—; pres. Ind. State Bank of Minn. Served with USAAF, 1942-45. Mem. Ind. Bankers Minn. (pres. 1966). Republican. Presbyn. Mason (32 deg. Shriner). Home: 405 9th St N Wheaton MN 56296 Office: State Bank of Wheaton Wheaton MN 56296

DONNELLY, JOHN SCRIVER, retail food exec.; b. Mpls., Aug. 12, 1935; s. John Martin and Eileen (Scriver) D.; A.B. magna cum laude, Dartmouth, 1957; M.B.A. highest distinction, Amos Tuck Sch. Bus. Adminstrn., 1958; m. Karen Anne Severson, Dec. 19, 1959; children—John Bernt, Thomas Martin, Jane Elizabeth, Anne Leslie. Financial mgmt. Honeywell, Inc., 1958-62, market mgr., 1962-65; with Graco Inc., Mpls., 1965-75, sales mgr. internat. div., 1965-66, dir. internat. operations, 1966-70, v.p. operations, 1970-75; pres., chief exec. officer Anchor Inn Promotions, Inc., 1975—. Mem. trade delegation to Russia, Yugoslavia, Hungary, 1969; coach Edina Hockey Assn., 1968—, bd. dirs., 1976—. Trustee Minn. Outward Bound Sch., 1971-74, sec., 1973; trustee Dynamy Minn., 1975—. Served with AUS, 1958-59. Gen. Motors Aldebaran fellow, 1956-57. Mem. Mpls. C. of C. (world trade com. 1965-70), Phi Beta Kappa. Clubs: Edina Country; Mpls. Athletic. Home: 4523 Drexel Ave S Minneapolis MN 55424 Office: 60 11th Ave NE Minneapolis MN 55413

DONNELLY, RICHARD MORRILL, advt. co. exec.; b. St. Louis, Nov. 10, 1926; s. Richard Morrill and Helen (Schreiber) D.; student U. Wyo., 1944, Yale, 1945; B.S. in Bus. and Pub. Adminstrn., Washington U., St. Louis, 1950; children from previous marriage—Lisa Anne, Jeffrey Scott, Jana Lynne. Account supr. Gardner Advt., 1954-64; pres. Donnelly & Toben, St. Louis, 1964-65, Donnelly & Dolen, advt., 1965-66, Ridgway Advt. Agy., 1966-67, Rutledge Advt., 1967-68, Donnelly & Weston Advt., Inc., 1968-70, Donnelly & Stanton Advt., 1970-74, Donnelly Advt. Co., 1975—; dir. Burlen Industries, Inc., Jack and Jill Products, Inc., Hatter Pub. Co., The Garrett, John Simmons & Assos. Alumni bd. govs. Washington U. Served with AUS, 1944-46. Mem. Beta Theta Pi (dir. 1968-71), Delta Sigma Pi. Clubs: Washington University (bd. govs. 1969-70, pres. 1970-71), Racquet (dir. 1975—), Media (St. Louis); Strathalbyn Farms (dir. 1976—); Lake Shore (Chgo.). Home: 9373 Ladue Rd St Louis MO 63124 Office: 8007 Clayton Rd St Louis MO 63117

D'ONOFRIO, PETER JOSEPH, paramedic, firefighter; b. Bronx, N.Y., Sept. 20, 1947; s. Elia Danato and Concetta Chella (Diorio) D'O.; Asso. Applied Sci. in Mktg., Sinclair Community Coll., 1973, Asso. Applied Sci. in Nursing, 1979; B.S. in Bus., U. Dayton, 1974, M.B.A., 1975, B.S. in Edn., 1975. Coordinator software documentation and distbn., internat. div. N.C.R. Corp., Dayton, Ohio, 1971; program dir. young adult dept. YMCA, Dayton, 1972-74; salesman Elder Beerman Inc., Dayton, 1974-75; adminstrv. asst. Kettering (Ohio) Fire Div., 1976; instr. bus. tech. div. Sinclair Community Coll., 1976; paramedic, firefighter Wayne Twp. Fire Dept., Dayton, 1976—. Vice pres., treas. Cath. Youth Orgn., 1961-65; pres. young adult council YMCA, 1970-71, chmn. young adult program com., 1971-72. Served in USAF, 1967-71. Certified cardiopulmonary instr. ARC. Mem. Am. Mktg. Assn., AAUP, Hamilton Civil War Round Table, 9th Va. Revolutionary War Reenactment Group, Phi Theta Kappa. Home: 3108 E Stroop Rd Kettering OH 45440 Office: 7008 Brandt Pike Dayton OH 45424

DONOHUE, CARROLL JOHN, lawyer; b. St. Louis, June 24, 1917; s. Thomas M. and Florence (Klefisch) D.; A.B., Washington U., St. Louis, 1939, LL.B. magna cum laude, 1939; m. Juanita Maire, Jan. 4, 1943 (div. 1973); children—Patricia Carol Stevens, Crhistine Ann Smith, Deborah Lee. Admitted to Mo. bar, 1939; asso. law firm Hay and Flanagan, St. Louis, 1939-42, firm Salkey and Jones, St. Louis, 1946-49; partner firm Husch, Eppenberger, Donohue, Elson and Jones, St. Louis, 1949—. Mayor, Olivette, Mo., 1953-56. Campaign chmn. ARC, St. Louis County, Mo., 1950; mem. adv. com. Child Welfare, St. Louis, 1952-55, exec. com. Slum Clearance, 1949, bond issue com., 1955, St. Louis County Bond Issue screening and supervisory coms., 1955-61, county citizen's com. for better law enforcement, 1953-56; chmn. com. on immigration policy, 1954-56. Chmn. County Bd. Election Commrs., St. Louis County, Mo., 1960-65. Served from apprentice seaman to lt. USNR, 1942-45. Decorated Bronze Star, Navy and M.C. medal. Mem. Mo. Bar (mem. bd. govs., 1948-50, 52, 54, 56; chmn. ann. meeting), St. Louis Bar Assn., (pres. 1954-55, v.p. 1948-49, treas. 1951-54), Order of Coif, Omicron Delta Kappa, Sigma Phi Epsilon, Delta Theta Phi. Club: Missouri Athletic. Office: 100 N Broadway St Louis MO 63101

DONOHUE, JOHN ROBERT, dentist; b. Antigo, Wis., Aug. 27, 1919; s. Matthew C. and Rose C. (O'Hara) D.; B.S., St. Norbert Coll., 1942; D.D.S., Marquette U., 1952; m. Joan G. Hanousek, Mar. 2, 1957; children—Matthew J., Mary Margaret, Elizabeth Ann. Gen. practice dentistry, Antigo, 1952—; mem. staff Langlade County Meml. Hosp. Bd. dirs. Am. Cancer Soc., 1966-73. Served with AUS, 1942-47. Mem. ADA. K.C. (4 deg.). Home: 739 Langlade Rd Antigo WI 54409 Office: 700 1/2 5th Ave Antigo WI 54404

DONOVAN, JAMES, lawyer; b. Napoleon, Ohio, Mar. 13, 1927; s. James and Mary Elizabeth (Kerr) D.; A.B., U. Mich., 1950, LL.B., 1953; m. Louise Zbylot, Feb. 11, 1956; children—James, John, Mary E. Admitted to Ohio bar, 1953; mem. firm Meekison & Donovan, Napoleon, 1953—. Served with USNR, 1945-46. Mem. Am., O. bar assns. elk. Home: 635 W Washington St Napoleon OH 43545 Office: 609 N Perry St Napoleon OH 43545

DONOVAN, JAMES LAWRENCE, engring. mgr.; b. Binghamton, N.Y., Mar. 21, 1926; s. Cyril Lawrence and Helen Mildred (Phair) D.; B.A., Syracuse U., 1954; postgrad. Bridgeport Sch. Engring., 1967, N.Y. U., 1970; m. Shirley Sliter, Dec. 7, 1947; m. 2d, Bee H. Houghton, July 4, 1968; children—Kathleen, John, James, Thomas, William, Nancy. Process engr. Columbia Nat. Corp., Pace, Fla., 1957-60; project engr. Gulf States Paper Co., Demopolis, Ala., 1960-64; chief process engr. Dorr-Oliver, Stamford, Conn., 1964-68; project mgr. Hoechst-Unde Corp., Englewood Cliffs, N.J., 1968-70, BASF Corp., Ludwigshafen, West Germany, 1970; dir. projects-teller Environmental Systems, N.Y.C., 1971; chief design V.A. Hosp., Bronx, 1972; project mgr. Processes Research, Cin., 1973—; cons. chem. plant design. Pres. local P.T.A., 1958-59. Served with AUS, 1943-46. Registered profl. engr., N.Y., N.J., Conn. Mem. Am. Inst. Chem. Engrs., Nat. Soc. Profl. Engrs., V.F.W. Club: Makatewah Country. Home: 350 Compton Rd Cincinnati OH 45215 Office: Vernon Pl Cincinnati OH 45220

DONOVAN, JOHN ANTHONY, bishop; b. Chatham, Ont., Can., Aug. 5, 1911; s. John J. and Mary C. (O'Rourke) D.; B.A., Sacred Heart Sem., 1932; student N.A. Coll., Rome (Italy), 1936; J.C.L., Pontificial Athenaeum of Lateran, Rome, 1947; LL.D., U. Detroit, 1952 Ordained priest Roman Cath. Ch., 1935, domestic prelate, 1949; pastor St. Aloysius' Ch., Detroit, also chancellor Archdiocese Detroit, 1951-58, St. Veronica's Ch., East Detroit, 1958-67; titular bishop of Rhasus and aux. bishop of Detroit, 1954-67; vicar gen. Archdiocese Detroit, 1959-67; bishop of Toledo, 1967—. Address: 2116 Parkwood St Toledo OH 43620

DONOVAN, JOHN VINCENT, bus. and tech. internat. cons.; b. Chgo., May 13, 1924; s. Timothy Vincent and Mable Elizabeth (Hederman) D.; A.B., DePauw U., 1947; m. Patricia Helen Hasselhorn, Dec. 29, 1950; children—James D., Timothy J., Walter C. Mem. adminstrv. staff Swiftdo Brazil, 1947-50; asst. treas. Mid State Corp., mobile homes mfr., Union City, Mich., 1951-55; sales mgr. Dole Corp., Honolulu, 1958-61; gen. mgr. Bailey Corp., cosmetics, Chgo., 1955-58; pres. Intercon Research Assos. Ltd., Evanston, Ill., 1961—, also dir. Bd. dirs. Ind. Voters Ill., 1942-45. Served with USNR, World War II. Mem. Licensing Execs. Soc., AAAS, Assn. Corp. Growth, Midwest Planning Assn., World Future Soc., U.S./France Exchange Club. Club: Chgo. Athletic Assn. Home: 431 Laurel Ave Wilmette IL 60091 Office: 1219 Howard St Evanston IL 60202

DONOVAN, JOSEPH PATRICK, lawyer; b. Waxahachie, Tex., Sept. 12, 1941; s. Joseph Bertrand and Ursula Kathleen (Ratchford) D.; m. Eileen Rosemarie Donovan, Dec. 30, 1967; children—Joseph Patrick, Brian Thomas, Daniel Brendan, Thomas Jefferson; B.A., U. Dallas, 1966; J.D., U. San Diego, 1975. Admitted to Ill. bar, 1976. Trust adminstr., tax specialist So. Calif. First Nat. Bank, San Diego, 1972-75; asso. firm Kralovec, Sweeney, Marquard & Doyle, Chgo., 1976—. Mem. Am., Fed., Ill., Chgo. bar assns., Am. Trial Lawyers Assn., Marine Corps Res. Officers Assn. Named Aviator of Year, Am. Helicopter Soc., 1971. Home: 8955 S Hoyne St Chicago IL 60620 Office: 39 S LaSalle St Chicago IL 60603

DONOVAN, SANDRA STERANKA, scientist; b. Cleve., Sept. 20, 1942; d. William and Clare Marie (Foresta) Steranka; m. Paul C. Donovan, July 16, 1966; 1 son, Todd Christopher. B.A. magna cum laude, Case Western Res. U., 1964, M.S., 1966, Ph.D., 1969. Research chemist, materials sci. dept. Hercules, Inc., Wilmington, Del., 1969-70; sr. research asso. applied materials sci. dept. Horizons, Inc., Cleve., 1971-73, group leader, 1973-76, mgr., 1976—. Mem. bd. overseers Case Western Res. U., 1972—, mem. vis. com to sch. mgmt., 1973—. Mem. Flora Stone Mather Coll. Alumnae Assn. (dir. 1973—), Western Res. Coll. Alumni Assn. (dir. 1975—), Electrochem. Soc., Phi Beta Kappa, Sigma Xi, Iota Sigma Pi. Contbr. articles to profl. jours. Home: 246 Hawthorne Dr Chagrin Falls OH 44022 Office: 23800 Mercantile Rd Cleveland OH 44122

DOODY, JAMES RAYMOND, ednl. adminstr.; b. Murphysboro, Ill., Mar. 28, 1937; s. Ashton Raymond and Vera Naoma (Schumacher) D.; student So. Ill. U., 1955-61; m. Mary Kay Squires, Aug. 20, 1960; children—Michael Raymond, Jane Ann. Substitute tchr., Madison County, Ill., 1961; asst. dir. pub. relations and advt. Boatmen's Nat. Bank, St. Louis, 1962-65; asst. mgr. advt. and sales promotion Presstite div. Interchem. Corp., St. Louis, 1965-67; dir. pub. info. Monticello Coll., Godfrey, Ill., 1967-69; dir. pub. relations North Central Coll., Naperville, Ill., 1969—; pres. Ill. Coll. Relations Conf., 1977. Bd. dirs. Naperville Community Fund, 1972—, v.p., 1976—; founder Naperville-North Central Coll. Community Concert Assn., 1974, v.p., 1974-77, pres., 1977—; mem. Naperville Bicentennial Commn., 1974-76. Served with U.S. Army, 1959-60. Mem. Pub. Relations Soc. Am. (accredited), Council for Advancement and Support of Edn. (2 pub. leadership awards), Publicity Club of Chgo. Methodist. Home: 80 Waxwing Ave Naperville IL 60540 Office: 30 N Brainard St Naperville IL 60540

DOOLEY, DALE ALLEN, electronic banking co. exec.; b. Hartington, Nebr., May 8, 1941; s. Ted Raymond and Jessie Adel (Bobenmeyer) D.; student Wayne State Tchrs. Coll., 1958-59; m. Margie May Short, Sept. 21, 1963; children—Kelly Alan, Terry Dean, Todd Michael. Programmer, Dial Financial, Des Moines, 1968-70, systems analyst, 1970-72, mgr. systems and programming, 1972-75, sr. mktg. rep. mktg. research and devel., 1975-76; exec. dir. Iowa Transfer System, Inc., Des Moines, 1976—. Office: Iowa Transfer System Inc 430 Liberty Bldg Des Moines IA 50309

DOOLEY, DONALD JOHN, editor; b. Des Moines, Aug. 16, 1921; s. Martin and Anne Marguerite (Barger) D.; B.A., State U. Iowa, 1947; postgrad. Drake U., 1949-50; m. Beverly Frederick, Dec. 21, 1955; children—Nancy Elizabeth, Katherine Anne (dec.), Mary Bridget, Robert Frederick. Gen. promotion and pub. relations mgr. Meredith Corp., Des Moines, 1953-59, dir. pub. relations, 1960-65; editorial and art dir. Better Homes and Gardens Books, also Creative Home Library, 1965-77, dir. editorial planning and devel., 1977—. Chmn. bd. adv. com. Sch. Volunteer Program, Des Moines; adv. bd. Pub. Relations Council, Des Moines Schs.; mem. steering com. Des Moines Sch. Dist. Program to Desegregate Schs., 1974-75; treas., bd. dirs. Parents Assn. U. Iowa, 1974-78; trustee Citizen's Scholarship Found. Am., 1976—; trustee Iowa Freedom of Info. Council. Served with USAAF, 1942-46. Mem. Pub. Relations Soc. Am. (accredited, chpt. pres. 1969, bd. dirs. chpt. 1966-72), Sigma Nu (chpt. comdr. 1946-47). Democrat. Home: 2727 Stanton St Des Moines IA 50321 Office: 1716 Locust St Des Moines IA 50336

DOOLEY, J. GORDON, food scientist; b. Nevada, Mo., Nov. 15, 1935; s. Howard Eugene and Wilma June (Vanderford) D.; B.S. with honors in Biology, Drury Coll., Springfield, Mo., 1958; postgrad. (NSF grantee) U. Mo., Rolla, 1961, (NSF grantee) Kirksville (Mo.) State Coll., 1959; M.S. in Biology (NSF grantee), Brown U., 1966; postgrad. bus. mgmt. Alexander Hamilton Inst., 1973-75, No. Ill. U., 1964. Tchr. sci. Morton West High Sch., Berwyn, Ill., 1963-64; dairy technologist Borden Co., Elgin, Ill., 1964-65; project leader Cheese Products Lab., Kraft Corp., Glenview, Ill., 1965-73; sr. food scientist Wallerstein Co. div. Travenol Labs., Inc., Morton Grove, Ill., 1973-77; mgr. food sci. GB Fermentation Industries, Inc., Des Plaines, Ill., 1977—; sci. lectr. seminars, Mexico, 1975. Recipient Spoke award Nevada (Mo.) Jr. C. of C., 1960. Mem. Am. Dairy Sci. Assn., Inst. Food Technologists, Am. Chem. Soc., Cousteau Soc., Am. Inst. Biol. Scis., Nat. Sci. Tchrs. Assn., Beta Beta Beta, Phi Eta Sigma. Republican. Presbyterian. Club: Toastmasters Internat. (pres. Baxter Labs. club 1976-77). Patentee in food and enzyme tech. field; contbr. sci. articles to profl. jours. Home: 990 Browning Ln Lake Zurich IL 60047 Office: 1 N Broadway Des Plaines IL 60016

DOOLEY, ROBERT DANIEL, radiologist; b. Alameda, Calif., Aug. 6, 1923; s. Daniel Raymond and Anna Nora (Shannon) D.; student Loyola U., Chgo., 1941-43; B.S., U. Ill., 1944, M.D., 1946; m. Dorothy Jane Klink, June 8, 1946; children—Michael, Karen, Dorian, Joyce. Intern, U.S. Marine Hosp., S.I., N.Y., 1946-47, resident in radiology, Balt., 1947-50; radiologist U.S. Marine Hosp., Chgo., 1950-52; asst. radiologist Little Co. of Mary Hosp., Evergreen Park, Ill., 1952-53; radiologist Garfield Park Hosp., Chgo., 1953-55, 57-62, Community Meml. Gen. Hosp., La Grange, Ill., 1955—; asst. prof. radiology Rush Med. Sch., Chgo., 1971—. Trustee La Grange Village Library, 1968-74. Served with USPHS, 1946-52. Diplomate Am. Bd. Radiology. Fellow Internat. Coll. Surgeons, Am. Coll. Radiology (councilor); mem. AMA, Ill. State, DuPage County (pres. 1974-75) med. socs., Ill. (pres. 1976-78), Chgo. (trustee 1971—) radiol. socs. Club: Les Gourmets (Chgo.). Home: 6 Oak Brook Club Dr J-108 Oak Brook IL 60521 Office: 40 S Clay St Hinsdale IL 60521

DOOLEY, THOMAS HENRY, banker; b. Cin., Jan. 29, 1931; s. Edward M. and Elfrieda M. (Mayer) D.; B.B.A., U. Mich., Feb., 1954, M.B.A., June 1954; m. Patricia D. McCoy, Aug. 23, 1952; children—Roger, Dennis, Alyce, Kathleen, Jennifer, Thomas. Sr. accountant Peat, Marwick, Mitchell & Co., Detroit, 1956-63; 1st. v.p., comptroller, Am. Nat. Bank & Trust Co., Kalamazoo, 1963-68, dir. Gt. Lakes Computer Center, Inc., 1963-68; sr. v.p. controller Mfrs. Nat. Corp., 1968—; dir. Graham Mortgage Corp., 1968—; controller Mfrs. Detroit Internat. Corp., 1968—; dir. Mfrs. Bank of Livonia, 1974—, Mfrs. Bank of the Shores, 1977—, Saline Bank, 1977, Bay City Bank & Trust Co., 1977—, Nat. Bank of Southfield, 1977—, Mfrs. Detroit Internat. Corp., 1977—; v.p., dir. Manubank Leasing Corp., 1974—. Served to 1st lt., AUS Audit Agy., 1954-56. C.P.A., Mich. Mem. Bank Adminstrn. Inst. (accounting commn. 1967-70), Am. Banking Assn. (task force on accounting 1973-75), Am. Inst. C.P.A.'s, Mich. Assn. C.P.A.'s, Fin. Execs. Inst., C. of C. Club: Forest Lake Country (Bloomfield Hills, Mich.) (dir.). Office: Mfrs Bank Tower Renaissance Center Detroit MI 48243

DOOLITTLE, JANET SNOOK (MRS. JOHN RUSSELL DOOLITTLE, SR.), artist, bookend co. exec., club woman; b. Aurora, Ill.; d. Albert Melville and Jane (Kelley) Snook; student Sarah Lawrence Coll., 1929-30, Northwestern U., 1931-32, Art Inst. Chgo., 1940, 41, 42; m. John Russell Doolittle, Sr., Feb. 1, 1932; children—Jane Kelley (Mrs. Karl Herigot Velde), David Drysdale, Lauren Grace (Mrs. Eduardo Jorge Ansaldo), John Russell. Exhibited in group show Rental Gallery of Art Inst. Chgo., 1964; owner, operator Jandoo, Northbrook, Ill., 1962—; pres. Doolittle Stationery Specialities Co., Chgo., 1970-75, Doolittle & Co., 1970-75; ret., 1975. Chmn., New Horizons in Sculpture competition, Chgo., 1961, 62. Chmn., Children's Hour Program, Winnetka, 1948; mem. original com., 1st aux. annual benefit Plantation Polka; sec. Ill. Children's Home and Aid Soc., Winnetka, Ill., 1949; sec. Jr. Aux. Infant Welfare, Winnetka, 1953—; life mem. Chgo. Art Inst., 1944—. Recipient prize Winnetka Woman's Club, 1958, 2d place prize U.S.A. Woman's Curling Championship Competition, 1963. Clubs: Winnetka Women's (art chmn. 1955), Winnetka Woman's Golf; 100, Arts (Chgo.), University, Chgo. Curling (Northbrook, Ill.). Home: 1400 Lake Shore Dr Chicago IL 60610

DOOLITTLE, JOHN ELDON, obstetrician, gynecologist; b. Mulliken, Mich., June 14, 1930; s. Frank E. and Ruth (Collins) D.; student U. Mich., 1948-51; M.D., 1955; m. Marilyn Yvonne Snyder, July 12, 1952; children—Frank Jeffrey, Nancy Lynn, Jean Michelle, James Eric. Intern, J.D. Munson Hosp., Traverse City, Mich., 1955-56; resident Miami Valley Hosp., Dayton, Ohio, 1959-63; pvt. practice medicine specializing in obstetrics and gynecology Niles, Mich., 1963—; chief staff Pawating Hosp., Niles; dir. Clinique des Femmes. Trustee March of Dimes of Berrien County. Served with USAF, 1956-58. Diplomate Am. Bd. Obstetrics and Gynecology. Fellow A.C.S., Am. Coll. Obstetrics and Gynecology; mem. S.W. Mich. Perinatal Assn. (past pres.). Republican. Unitarian. Clubs: Signal Point Paddle Tennis; Summit (South Bend, Ind.). Home: 1601 Echo Valley Niles MI 49120 Office: 9 S St Joseph Ave Niles MI 49120

DOOLITTLE, RICHARD IRVING, ednl. adminstr.; b. Oceanside, N.Y., Feb. 4, 1933; s. Irving Warren and Helen Landon (Clampit) D.; B.S., Syracuse U., 1954; M.B.A., N.Y. U., 1965; m. Lorraine Ann Francois, June 29, 1958; children—Donna Claire and Caren Marie (twins). Asso. sec. N.Y. chpt. banking sch. Am. Inst. Banking, 1956-65; dir. ops. Am. Inst. Banking ednl. div. Am. Bankers Assn., Washington, 1965-74; asso. dir. Stonier Grad. Sch. Banking, Rutgers U., 1965-74; adminstr. Grad. Sch. Banking, U. Wis.-Madison, 1974—; asso. dir. Internat. Banking Summer Sch., Brown U., 1972. Served with AUS, 1954-56. Mem. Am. Mgmt. Assn., Am. Soc. Assn. Execs., Am. Inst. Banking (dist. council 1977—), Kappa Sigma, Omega Gamma Delta; hon. mem. N.Y. chpt. Am. Inst. Banking Alumni Assn. Episcopalian. Clubs: Madison, Rotary. Home: 3014 Pelham Rd Madison WI 53713 Office: 122 W Washington Ave Madison WI 53703

DOORNBOS, ROY, JR., educator; b. Grand Rapids, Mich., Sept. 14, 1926; s. Roy and Johanna Elizabeth (Ciereman) D.; B.S., Central Mich. U., 1949; M.A., U. No. Colo., 1953, Ed.D., 1962; postgrad. Ind. U., 1956; m. Gayle J. Scott, Aug. 17, 1955. Athletic coach Sandusky (Mich.) High Sch., 1949-51; athletic dir., coach, instr. phys. edn. Plainwell (Mich.) High Sch., 1951-53; instr. phys. edn. Coolidge Elementary Sch., Flint, Mich., 1953-55; instr., coach Flint Community Jr. Coll., 1955-56, chmn. dept. phys. edn., athletic dir., 1956-64; chmn. dept. phys. edn. Wis. State U. at Whitewater, 1964-69; athletic dir., div. chmn. Adams State Coll., Alamosa, Colo., 1969-71, dir. community and recreational devel., 1971-72; dir. student service, athletic dir., chmn. dept. recreational mgmt. Ind. Inst. Tech., Ft. Wayne, 1972-75, chmn. dept. recreational mgmt. and athletics, 1975-77; cons. jr. coll. phys. edn., Rochester, Minn., 1970, Colo. Community and Recreation Devel., 1971-72; regional dir. Wis. Gov.'s Council on Fitness, 1965-69; mem. Colo. Gov.'s Com. Developmental Disabilities, 1970-72; mem. Ft. Wayne Mayor's Recreation Coordinating Com., 1972—. Bd. regents Wis. State Univs., 1965-69; bd. dirs. Limberlost council Girl Scouts U.S.A., 1977—. Named Toastmaster of Year, Flint, 1963. Mem. Nat. Jr. Coll. Athletics (regional dir. 1958-63), AAHPER (life) (Mid-West v.p. recreation), Nat. Assn. Intercollegiate Athletics (chmn. dist. 21, 1975—), Phi Epsilon Kappa, Kappa Delta Pi, Phi Delta Kappa. Club: Rotary (dir. 1976). Home: 5136 Truemper Way Apt 6 Fort Wayne IN 46815

DORAN, JAMES GOLDEN, ednl. camp exec.; b. Madison, Wis., Apr. 12, 1919; s. John Harry and Nora (McCooey) D.; Ph.B., Marquette U., 1947; postgrad. Loyola U. at Chgo., 1954, U. Ill. at Urbana, 1965; m. Joyce Gail Cole, Feb. 8, 1954; children—Charles Cole, Mary Noreen, Sean Patrick. Tchr., Pub. Sch. Dist. 15, McHenry, Ill., 1952-68; reading specialist, 1968—; dir. Arrowhead Reading Camp for Boys, Minocqua, Wis., 1967-74; owner, dir. Algonquin Reading Camp for Boys, Rhinelander, Wis., 1975—. Bd. dirs. The Little Sch., Crystal Lake, Ill., 1970-74, YMCA, Crystal Lake, 1967-68. Served with USAAF, 1941-45. Mem. N.E.A., Assn., Am. Camping Assn., Midwest Assn. Pvt. Camps., Wis. Tennis Assn., Cath. Order Foresters (youth dir. 1955-68, award 1973), Phi Delta Kappa. Address: Route 3 Rhinelander WI 54501

DORATHY, ROBERT G., mfg. co. exec.; b. Prophetstown, Ill., July 16, 1918; s. John L. and F. Leona (Given) D.; B.A., Grinnell Coll., 1940; m. Emma Lou Cushing, Apr. 26, 1947; children—Steven R., Julia R. Prodn. mgr. Eclipse Lawn Mower Co., Prophetstown, 1941-54, controller, 1954-59; controller Penberthy div. Houdaille Industries, Inc., Prophetstown, 1959—; dir. Rock River Lumber & Grain Co., Inc., Prophetstown, 1971-76, chmn. bd. dirs., 1976—. Sec., elementary bd. edn. Prophetstown, 1959-65, community high sch. bd. edn., 1966-69. Served with AUS, 1943-46; ETO. Mem. Am. Legion (comdr. 1951-52, chmn. exec. bd. 1948-68). Republican. Home: 414 Johnson Ave Prophetstown IL 61277 Office: PO Box 112 Prophetstown IL 61277

DOREMUS, JOHN, television and radio performer; b. Sapulpa, Okla., Aug. 3, 1932; s. John W. and Arie M. (Crumley) D.; B.A., U. Tulsa, 1953; m. Joellen Casler, Dec. 27, 1953; children—David, Fred, Deidre, Paul. Host, John Doremus Show, also Patterns in Music, WMAQ Radio and TV, Chgo., 1959-65; adminstv. exec., sales, host John Doremus Show, WAIT, Chgo., 1965-71; host music and talk show WGN Radio, Chgo., 1971-73; chmn. John Doremus, Inc., 1973—; producer, narrator Spirit of '76. Chmn., March of Dimes, 1958-59, United Cerebral Palsy, 1964-68. Chmn. bd. dirs. Roycemore Prep. Sch., 1968-69, Arden Shores Sch. for Boys, 1967-70. Served with USMCR, 1950-51, USAF, 1954-57. Named Distinguished Alumnus, U. Tulsa, 1973; One of 10 Outstanding Young Men, Jaycees, 1964; Best Chgo. Radio Personality, 1967; recipient citation of merit Chgo. Father's Day Council, 1966. Mem. Chgo. Press, Execs. clubs, Chgo. Assn. Commerce and Industry, Chgo. Athletic Assn., Kappa Sigma. Episcopalian (vestryman). Rotarian. Clubs: Lake Shore, Tavern, Thorngate Country. Home: 460 Thornmeadow St Deerfield IL 60015 Office: 875 N Michigan Ave Chicago IL 60611

DORENFEST, SHELDON I., corp. exec.; b. Chgo., May 10, 1935; s. Bernard and Frieda (Patt) D.; B.S., U. Ill., 1956; M.B.A., Northwestern U., 1963; m. Mary Ellen Hill, Jan. 4, 1959; children—Laura, Lisa. Sr. accountant, cons. Peat, Marwick, Mitchell, 1956-62; asst. corporate controller, asst. to pres. hosp. div., dir. corporate bus. cons. services Abbott Labs., North Chicago, Ill., 1962-69; pres. Compucare, Inc., Chgo., 1969—. Adviser minority enterprises. Served with AUS, 1957. C.P.A., Ill. Mem. Am. Inst. C.P.A.'s, Ill. Soc. C.P.A.'s. Home: 416 W Sheridan Pl Lake Bluff IL 60044 Office: 1230 Park Ave W Highland Park IL 60035

DORFMAN, ISAIAH S., lawyer; b. Kiev, Russia, Mar. 17, 1907; s. Samuel and Ella (Kite) D.; brought to U.S., 1913, naturalized, 1931; Ph.B., U. Chgo., 1927, J.D., 1931; m. Lilliam Schley, Oct. 6, 1934; children—Paul, Tom, John. Admitted to Ill. bar, 1931; regional atty. Region 13, NLRB, Chgo., 1937-42, chief spl. litigation unit, Washington, 1942-43; chief analyst Office Strategic Services, U.S. Govt., London, Eng., 1943-44; attache U.S. legation, Stockholm, Sweden, 1944-45; sr. partner firm Dorfman, DeKoven & Cohen, Chgo., 1945—. Instr. labor law Law Sch., Nat. Univ., Washington, 1942-43. Mem. Chgo. (chmn. com. unauthorized practice law 1966-67), Ill., Am. bar assns. Jewish religion. Mem. B'nai B'rith. Club: Standard (Chgo.). Home: 260 E Chestnut St Chicago IL 60611 Office: 1 IBM Plaza Chicago IL 60611

DORGAN, BYRON LESLIE, state ofcl.; b. Dickinson, N.D., May 14, 1942; s. Emmett P. and Dorothy (Bach) D.; B.S. in Bus. Adminstrn., U. N.D., 1964; M.B.A., U. Denver, 1966; children—Scott, Shelly, Nathan. Exec. devel. trainee Martin Marietta Corp., Denver, 1966-67; dep. tax commr. of N.D., Bismarck, 1967-69, tax commr., 1969—. Instr. econs. Bismarck Jr. Coll., 1968-70. Chmn., Multistate Tax Commn., 1972-74; mem. nat. adv. bd. Tax Action Campaign, 1973—; mem. Gov.'s Planning Adv. Bd., 1969—, N.D. Bd. Equalization, 1969—, Gov.'s Com. on Data Processing, 1972—; mem. adv. com. Coll. Bus. Adminstrn., Mary Coll., 1969—, U. N.D., 1971—. Mem. N.D. exec. com. Democratic party, 1969—. Mem. Nat. Assn. Tax Adminstrs. (exec. com. 1969—). Home: 224 Apollo Ave Bismarck ND 58501 Office: Office Tax Commr State Capitol Bismarck ND 58505

DORGAN, ROBERT THOMAS, agrl. tractor mfg. exec.; b. Chgo., Apr. 22, 1925; s. Walter H. and Juanita M. (Corbett) D.; student Sch. Profl. Supr. U. Chgo., 1958-60; B.A., Roosevelt U., 1976; m. Shirley M. Schomer, May 10, 1947; children—Robert Thomas, Linda Lee. With Internat. Harvester Co., 1946—, machine operator, 1946-48, mgmt. trainee, 1948-49, mgr. various positions, Chgo. and Louisville, 1949-73, mgr. mfg. ops. Farmall Plant, Rock Island, Ill., 1973—. Jr. Achievement advisor, Chgo., 1953-55; active Big Bro. program, Chgo., 1958-59; dir. Jr. Holy Name Soc., Chgo., 1959-63; mem. adv. bd. Salvation Army, Rock Island, Ill., 1976—. Served with U.S. Army, 1943-46. Named Man of Year for youth work St. Turibius Cath. Ch., Chgo., 1961; named Father of Year Chgo. Tribune, 1962. Mem. Am. Soc. Quality Control (sr.), Soc. Automotive Engrs., Soc. Mfg. Engrs. (certified mfg. engr.). Roman Catholic. Home: 3507 21st St Rock Island IL 61201 Office: 500 42d St Rock Island IL 61201

DORHEIM, FREDRICK HOUGE, geologist; b. Badger, Iowa, Nov. 12, 1912; s. Fredrick and Elsie Irene (Houge) D.; B.S., Iowa State U., 1938, M.S., 1950; student U. Iowa; m. Eleanora Amanda Linn, Nov. 29, 1939; 1 dau. Karen Irene Dorheim Spenner. Chief geologist Iowa State Highway Commn., 1946-50; geologist B.L. Anderson, Inc., Cedar Rapids, Iowa, 1950-56; econ. geologist, Iowa Geol. Survey, Iowa City, 1975, chief geologist, 1975—; cons., lectr. in field. Served with USN, 1944-46. Mem. Am. Assn. Petroleum Geologists, Am. Inst. Profl. Geologists, Iowa Conservation Edn. Council, Geol. Soc. Am., Geol. Soc. Iowa, Iowa Acad. Sci., Sigma Xi. Republican. Lutheran. Club: Iowa City Engrs. Contbr. articles to profl. jours. Home: 430 Upland Ave Iowa City IA 52240 Office: 123 N Capitol St Iowa City IA 52242

DORIA, HELEN E. DANN (MRS. RAMON G. DORIA), educator; b. East Chicago, Ind., Feb. 2, 1915; d. Roman and Magdeline (Darlson) Dann; B.S., Ind. U., 1950, M.S., 1953; postgrad. Purdue U., 1955, Internat. U. (San German, P.R.), 1964, Ind. U., 1956-65; m. George A. Umbarger, May 5, 1940 (dec. 1944); 1 son, George Alfred; m. 2d, Ramon G. Doria, Jan. 4, 1969. Sec., Community Recreation Dept., East Chicago, 1932-36, Ind. Employment Div. Unemployment Compensation Office, East Chicago, 1936-39; with Signal Corps Office War Dept., Wright Field, Dayton, Ohio, 1939-43; tchr. pub. schs., East Chicago, 1950—, kindergarten-primary supr., 1963-75, ret., 1975. Program cons. Lowell R. Robertson Child Care Centers, 1963—, dir., 1963—; mem. adv. council Hoosier Boys Town; pres. Community Child Care Adv. Council, 1970-71, 73-74. Mem. N.E.A., Am., Ind. assns. for supervision and curriculum devel., East Chgo. Tchr. Assn. (v.p. 1958), Conf. on Supervising Tchrs. (chmn. 1968), Nat. Soc. for Study of Edn., Assn. for Childhood Edn. (pres. 1954), Transylvania Soc. (aux. pres. 1977), Am. Edn. Research Assn., Nat. Council Adminstrv. Women in Edn., Ind. U. Alumni Assn., Nat. Council Encouragement Patriotism, Pi Lambda Theta, Delta Kappa Gamma (pres. Beta Delta chpt. 1972-74), Beta Delta. Byzantine Rite Catholic. Home: 3144 Ridge Rd Highland IN 46322 Office: 210 E Columbus Dr East Chicago IN 46312

DORIWALA, BAQARALI AHMADALI, project engr.; b. Bhadsura, India, Apr. 10, 1950; s. Ahmadali Safderali and Bhuribai Ahmadali (Hasanali) D.; came to U.S., 1971, naturalized, 1975; B.M.E. cum laude (Open Merit scholar), Villanova U., 1973; M.M.E., Ill. Inst. Tech., 1977; postgrad. bus. adminstrn. Baldwin Wallace Coll., 1977—; m. Jophin Khokawala, Mar. 11, 1976; 1 son, Moiz B. Salesman Sherwin-Williams Co., Phila., 1971-73, project engr., Chgo., 1973-76, Cleve., 1976—. Registered profl. engr., Ohio, Calif. NSF research fellow, 1972. Mem. Tau Beta Pi, Pi Tau Sigma. Moslem. Contbr. articles in field to profl. jours. Home: 6418 Stumph Rd Parma Heights OH 44130 Office: 1370 Ontario St Cleveland OH 44113

DORLAND, DOUGLAS MASON, educator; b. Wahoo, Nebr., Dec. 7, 1944; s. Edward Luther and Eula (Bader) D.; B.A., Nebr. Wesleyan U., 1967; M.A., U. Nebr., 1968; postgrad. U. Ark., 1969-70, Ind. U., 1971; m. Brenda Kay Becker, Dec. 17, 1967; children—Chad, Melanie, Megan. Guidance counselor, tchr. social studies Davenport (Nebr.), High Sch., 1968-69; with First Nat. Bank, Winter Park, Fla., 1969-70; instr. bus. Ind. Central U., Indpls., 1970-74; asst. dir. mgmt. devel. Ind. Central U., Indpls., 1974-75, asst. prof. bus., 1974—; mktg. cons. Herron Assoc., Indpls., 1977—. Bd. dirs. Baxter YMCA, 1975-76. Recipient Small Bus. Inst. Dist. award, 1975-76. Mem. Indpls. Jaycees (chmn. forums and speakers program, nat. conv. 1976), Am. Mktg. Assn., Soc. for Advancement of Mgmt., Nat. Council for Small Bus. Mgmt. Devel., Small Bus. Inst. Dirs. Assn., Ind. Acad. Social Sci., Phi Beta Lambda. Methodist. Clubs: Southside Optimists, Masons. Author: The Small Business Problem Solver, 1977. Home: 5205 S Linwood St Indianapolis IN 46227 Office: 1400 E Hanna Ave Indianapolis IN 46227

DORMAN, JAMES LEE, business exec.; b. Jerome, Idaho, Dec. 10, 1932; s. James E. and Ilena (Johnson) D.; B.B.S., Idaho State U., 1955; M.B.A., U. Denver, 1960; m. Beverly Charlotte Owen, Dec. 19, 1953;children—Dee Ann Lynn, James Lee, Michelle Jean. Comml. audit mgr. Arthur Andersen & Co., Chgo., 1960-66; corporate controller Foote, Cone & Belding, Inc., Chgo., 1966-68; controller UIP Corp., Milw., 1968—, exec. v.p., 1969-71, pres., 1971-74; v.p. dir. Super Steel Products Corp., Milw., 1974-76, now dir.; pres., Marquette Capital Co., Milw., 1974-76; dir. Automatic Fire Protection Corp. Wis., Inc., Buckstaff Co., Oshkosh, Wis. Bd. dirs. Lakeland Coll., Sheboygan, Wis. Served to lt. AUS, 1955-59. Recipient Armed Forces Chem. Assn. award, 1953. Mem. Ill., Wis. socs. C.P.A.'s, Am. Inst. C.P.A.'s, Wis. Mfrs. Assn. Club: Western Racquet (Elm Grove, Wis.). Home: 2140 Elm Tree Rd Elm Grove WI 53122

DORN, ALVA LOUIS, newspaper editor; b. N.Y.C., Nov. 16, 1911; s. George Alva and Janet (Schmidt) D.; student U. Mo., 1929-31; m. Edna May Lucas, July 11, 1936; 1 dau., Maryrose (Mrs. Roger E. Hopkins). City editor Schenectady Union-Star, 1940-43, news editor, 1943-46; mng. editor Monroe (Mich.) Evening News, 1946-48; picture editor Kalamazoo Gazette, 1948—, photo columnist, 1959—; photography columnist Ann Arbor (Mich.) News, Muskegon (Mich.) Chronicle; instr. photography Kalamazoo Community Sch. for Adults, 1952-74, Kalamazoo Valley Community Coll., 1974—; photog. writer, lectr., exhibitor, judge. Bd. dirs. Kalamazoo Home for Aged, 1954-60, Kalamazoo Inst. Arts, 1960-64. Winner black and white print competition U.S. Camera mag., 1960. Fellow Photog. Soc. Am. (editor Camera Club Bull. 1959-61, chmn. Western Mich. chpt. 1962-63), New Pictorialist Soc.; mem. Photo Guild Kalamazoo (pres., founder), Mich. Press Assn. (pres. editorial div. 1949-50), Kalamazoo Camera Hobbyists (pres., founder 1952), Nat., Mich. press photographers assns., Pi Kappa Alpha. Episcopalian. Mason. Home: 3823 Dale St Kalamazoo MI 49001 Office: 401 S Burdick St Kalamazoo MI 49006

DORN, CHARLES RICHARD, veterinarian; b. London, Ohio, June 12, 1933; s. Howard Field and Lucille Margaret (Bethard) D.; D.V.M., Ohio State U., 1957; M.P.H., Harvard, 1962; postdoctoral studies U. Calif. at Berkeley, 1963; m. Barbara Monroe, Dec. 20, 1964; children—Michael L., Lorissa L., Margot L. Staff veterinarian Stark Animal Hosp., Canton, Ohio, 1957-58; vet. insp. Cin. Health Dept., 1960-61; postdoctoral trainee USPHS, 1961-62; research specialist cancer Calif. Dept. Pub. Health, Berkeley, 1962-68; prof. vet. microbiology and community health and med. practice U. Mo., Columbia, 1968-75; prof., chmn. dept. vet. preventive medicine Ohio State U., Columbus, 1975—; cons. vet. pub. health WHO, India, 1975; vis. scientist epidemiology Nat. Cancer Inst., 1975; lectr. vet. medicine U. Cal. at Davis, 1967-68. Mem. bd. health, Columbia, Mo., 1969-71. Served to lt. col. USAF, 1958-60. Fellow Am. Pub. Health Assn., Am. Bd. Vet. Pub. Health; mem. Am., Ohio, vet. med. assns., Conf. Pub. Health Vets., Am. Assn. Food Hygiene Vets., Assn. Tchrs. Vet. Pub. Health and Preventive Medicine, Conf. Research Workers Animal Disease, Am. Pub. Health Assn., Am. Assn. Vet. Med. Colls., Vet. Cancer Soc., Internat. Assn. Comparative Research Leukemia and Related Diseases, Soc. Environmental Geochem. Health, Sigma Xi, Gamma Sigma Delta, Phi Eta Sigma, Phi Zeta. Contbr. articles to profl. jours. Office: Dept Vet Preventive Medicine Coll Vet Medicine Ohio State U 1900 Coffey Rd Columbus OH 43210

DORN, GARY RAYMOND, printing co. exec.; b. Chgo., Apr. 8, 1933; s. Fred H. and Freida H. (Wagner) D.; student Western Res. U., 1961-62; m. Elsie Marie Walledom, June 5, 1953; children—Lynn, Karen, Bradley, Robert, Paul. Salesman, Redson-Rice Corp., Chgo., 1952-56; v.p., sales mgr. D.F. Keller Co., Chgo., 1956-64; pres. Bradley Printing Co., Elmhurst, Ill., 1964—. Bd. dirs. Summit Sch., Dundee, Ill., 1972-75. Served with USAF, 1950-52. Mem. Printing Industry of Ill. Club: Elgin Country. Home: PO Box 41 Dundee IL 60118 Office: 730 Oak Lawn Elmhurst IL 60126

DORN, HERMAN WILLIAM, biochemist; b. N.Y.C., Sept. 14, 1911; s. David Frances (Schnaper) D.; A.B., Clark U., 1935, M.A., 1936; Ph.D., 1938; m. Mary Alice McDermott, Apr. 2, 1934; children—Cynthia (Mrs. James D. Witt), Prescott M., Juliet (Mrs. James E. Walden), Barrett E. Prin. chemist Internat. Minerals & Chem. Corp., Libertyville, Ill., 1939-45; dir. biochemistry and nutrition Owens-Ill. Glass Co., Toledo, 1945-47; dir. research foods and drugs Neisler Labs., Decatur, Ill., 1947-52; owner Dorn & Co. food and drug research, St. Louis, 1952-72, Glen Ellyn, Ill., 1973-77; instr. Clark U., 1935-38, State U. Iowa, 1942-44, U. Toledo, 1946-47. Chmn. Council Social Agys., Decatur, 1955-58; dep. dir. Civil Def., Decatur, 1951-58. Bd. dirs. DuPage council Boy Scouts Am., Silver Beaver award, 1954. Served to col. AUS, 1942-45. Decorated Meritorious Service medal; recipient Civic Service award Decatur, 1952. Registered profl. engr., Ohio, Ill., Tex., Calif.; certified Nat. Registry Clin. Chemists. Fellow Am. Inst. Chemists, N.Y. Acad. Scis., AAAS, Am. Chem. Soc.; mem. Ill. Soc. Profl. Engrs. (pres. 1956), Am. Chem. Soc. Elk, Rotarian. Contbr. articles to profl. jours. Patentee in field. Address: 2906B Helen Ct Champaign IL 61820

DORN, RUSSELL LAWRENCE (LARRY), securities co. exec.; b. Fergus Falls, Minn., Feb. 9, 1942; s. Russell Lee and Dorothy Mae (Knoff) D.; B.A., St. Cloud (Minn.) State Coll., 1964; m. Jeanette May, July 27, 1963; children—Jennifer Ann, Matthew Lawrence.

Divisonal mgr. Financial Programs, Inc., Denver, 1965-66; self-employed securities sales, 1966-68; partner Olson Securities Co., Fergus Falls, 1968-71; pres. Dorn & Co., Inc., Fergus Falls, 1970—. Chmn. Young Republican's, 1967, dist. chmn., 1968-69; Served with AUS, 1966-71. Mem. C. of C. (dir.), Am. Legion, Ind. Broker Dealer Trade Assn., Twin City Bond Club, YMCA (dir.), Ducks Unltd. Lutheran (ch. council). Kiwanian (dir.), Elk. Club: Fargo Country (N.D.). Home: 205 W Vasa St Fergus Falls MN 56537 Office: 129 S Mill St Fergus Falls MN 56537

DORNBROCK, WILLIAM LEE, mech. engr.; b. Detroit, Feb. 25, 1942; s. William C. and Margaret A. (Ettle) D.; B.M.E., Lawrence Inst. Tech., 1966; M.B.A., Wayne State U., 1977. Project engr. Pioneer Engring. Co., 1959-64; owner, pres. Maranco Co., Sterling, Mich., 1964-66; sr. design engr. Fisher Body div. Gen. Motors Corp., Warren, Mich., 1966-69; sales application engr. Eaton Corp., Southfield, Mich., 1969-72; engring. mgr. Chrysler Corp., Detroit, 1972—. Bd. commrs. Lennox County, Mich., 1970-74. Mem. Soc. Automotive Engrs., Am. Soc. Body Engrs., Am. Soc. Plastics Engrs. Club: Chrysler Yacht. Home: 11825 Seaton St Sterling Heights MI 48077 Office: Chrysler Corp CIMS 425-11-08 Detroit MI 48288

DORNER, JOSEPH LAWRENCE, vet. clin. pathologist, educator; b. Dover, Del., Mar. 2, 1936; s. Joseph Matthew and Margaret (Maga) D.; A.A.S., State U. N.Y., 1954; B.S., U. Ill., 1962, M.S., 1965, D.V.M., 1964, Ph.D., 1968; m. Marianne Nachum, Aug. 30, 1958; children—Joseph Philip, Kurt Matthew. Clinician, Small Animal Medicine, U. Ill. Coll. Veterinary Medicine, 1968, clin. pathologist, 1969—. Recipient Distinguished Teaching award, 1972, Alumni Merit award, 1973. Mem. Am., Ill. State, Eastern Ill. vet. med. assns., Am. Soc. Vet. Clin. Pathologists (chmn. consultation com. 1970-71), Am. Assn. Vet. Clinicians, Omega Tau Sigma, Phi Zeta (pres. 1971), Gamma Sigma Delta, Sigma Xi. Contbr. articles to sci. jours. Office: Sch Veterinary Medicine U Ill Urbana IL 61801

DOROSCHAK, JOHN Z., dentist; b. Solochiw, Ukraine, Feb. 11, 1928; s. William and Anna (Stroczan) D.; came to U.S., 1950, naturalized, 1954; student U. Minn., 1955-57, B.S., 1959, D.D.S., 1961; m. Nadia Zahorodny, June 30, 1962; children—Andrew, Michael, Natalie, Maria. Pvt. practice dentistry, Mpls., 1961—. Cons. St. Joseph's Home for Aged, Mpls., 1974-77, St. Paul, 1977—. Mem. steering com. St. Anthony West Neighborhood, Mpls., 1971-72; chmn. Mpls. dentists com. Little Sisters of the Poor Devel. Program, 1975; Webelos leader troop 50, Boy Scouts Am., 1975-76; pres.-elect N.E. Regional Sch. Assn. Parents and Tchrs., 1977; bd. dirs. East Side Neighborhood Service, 1972. Served with AUS, 1953-55. Mem. Am. Dental Assn., Minn. Soc. Preventive Dentistry (dir. 1977—), Am. Soc. Dentistry for Children, Mpls. Dist. Dental Soc. (nursing home subcom. 1974—), Ukrainian Med. Assn. (sec. treas. 1971-75), Ukrainian Profl. Club. Ukrainian Catholic Ch. (campaign chmn. 1966—, mem. ch. com. 1965—). Club: University Minnesota Alumni (charter mem.). Home: 919 Main St NE Minneapolis MN 55413 Office: Broadway and University Profl Bldg 230 NE Broadway Minneapolis MN 55413

DOROSHOW, HERBERT S., urol. surgeon; b. Phila., June 24, 1919; s. I. N. and Clara (Rosenthal) D.; B.A., Pa. State U., 1940; M.D., Jefferson Med. Sch., 1944; children—Carol, James, William. Intern, Jefferson Hosp., Phila., 1944; resident in urology Johns Hopkins Hosp., Balt., 1944-47; practice medicine specializing in urology, Chgo., 1950—; urologist Michael Reese Hosp., Chgo., S. Chgo. Community Hosp., St. James Hosp., Chgo. Heights, Ill., Ingalls Meml. Hosp., Harvey, Ill.; mem. faculty Northwestern U. Med. Sch. Mem. AMA, Am., Chgo. urol. assns., Chgo. Med. Soc., Johns Hopkins Med. and Surg. Soc., Phi Beta Kappa. Clubs: Univ., Mid-Am., Ravisloe Country. Home: 1200 N Lake Shore Dr Chicago IL 60610 Office: Suite 1927 25 E Washington St Chicago IL 60602

DOROTHY, LOU ANN, lawyer; b. Mt. Vernon, Ill., July 19, 1925; d. Obe A. and B. Eva (Milburn) Grant; B.S in Law, U. Ill., 1947; m. Morton F. Dorothy, Jr., Dec. 7, 1946 (dec. May 1963); children—Morton F. III, Syren Jo (Mrs. Claude R. McElvain), John J., Sarah F. Admitted to Ill. bar, 1949; since practiced in Mt. Vernon; mem. firm Dorothy & Dorothy, 1949-67, Lou Ann Dorothy, 1971-76; partner in firm with son, 1976—; asst. dir. Womble Mountain Legal Aid, Harrisburg, Ill., 1967-68; info. rep. to Dir. Personnel State of Ill., 1968; asst. dir. Peoria (Ill.) Legal Aid, 1968-69; asst. and acting dir. Legal Aid Jackson and Williamson County (Ill.), 1969-71; exec. dir. Jefferson County Housing Authority, 1975—; asso. firm Dorothy & Woodruff; various positions in fields law, bus., journalism and investigation; certified housing dir. Bd. dirs. Jefferson County Found. for Vision and Learning Disorders. Mem. Ill., Jefferson County bar assns., Nat. Assn. Housing and Redevel. Authorities, Ill. Assn. Redevel. Authorities, Ill. Sheriff's Assn., various local housing groups, Internat. Platform Assn., Am. Legion Aux. (pres. 1950), Bus. and Profl. Women's Club (sec. luncheon group 1969), U. Ill. Alumni Assn. (life), Smithsonian Instn., Am. Contract Bridge League, Alpha Xi Delta. Presbyterian. Mem. Ancient Mystical Order Rosae Crucis. Home and Office: Route 1 Texico IL 62889

DORRANCE, WILLIAM HENRY, engr., corp. exec.; b. Highland Park, Mich., Dec. 3, 1921; s. William Henry and Bernice (Updike) D.; B.S.E., U. Mich., 1947, M.S.E., 1948; m. Janet Rogers, Aug. 30, 1946; children—Cynthia Ann, Rebecca Hall, William Henry, Jay Bolton. Chief, aerodynamics Aero. Research Center, U. Mich., Ann Arbor, 1947-51, Convair Div. Gen. Dynamics Corp., San Diego, 1951-55; sr. staff scientist Convair Gen. Offices, San Diego, 1955-61; group dir. Aerospace Corp., Los Angeles, 1961-64; v.p. Conductron Corp. Ann Arbor, 1964-69, dir., 1965-69; chmn., chief operating officer Interface Systems Corp., 1967-70; pres. Orgn. Control Services Corp., Ann Arbor, 1970—. Div. leader United Fund Drive, Northridge, Calif., Ann Arbor, 1964-65. Vice pres. San Diego Young Republicans, 1952-53. Mem. vestry St. Dustan's Ch., 1952-55. Served with USAF, 1943-45. Decorated air medal, 5 oak leaf clusters, presdl. unit citation. Recipient citation Am. Rocket Soc. San Diego sect., 1958. Mem. Ann Arbor C. of C. (dir.), Nat. Fedn. Ind. Bus's. Episcopalian. Clubs: Barton Hills Country (dir., treas. 1976—), Sigma Xi, Theta Chi, Phi Kappa Phi. Author: Viscous Hypersonic Flow, 1962. Contbr. numerous articles to profl. jours. Patentee in field. Home: 11 Heatheridge St Ann Arbor MI 48104 Office: OCS Inc 1925 Pauline Blvd Ann Arbor MI 48103

DORSCHEL, QUERIN PETER, lawyer; b. Green Bay, Wis., Feb. 8, 1898; s. Peter Frank and Pauline (Schumacher) D.; B.S., Marquette U., 1920; LL.B., U. Chgo., 1934; m. Philemene Connell, Aug. 15, 1927; m2d Gertrude Reiss Corbett, Feb. 21, 1939. Pvt. practice pub. accounting, auto financing, Milw. and Chgo., 1920-32; admitted to Ill. bar, 1934; counsel and sec. Ill. Power Co., and subsidiaries, 1934-39; partner Pam, Hurd & Reichmann, now Schiff, Hardin & Waite, Chgo., 1939-75. Mem. Am., Ill. State, Chgo. bar assns. Clubs: Chicago, University, Glen View Country; Tucson Country. Home: 1242 Lake Shore Dr Chicago IL 60610 Office: 233 S Wacker Dr Chicago IL 60606

DORSEY, DENNIS BASIL, pathologist; b. Braymer, Mo., Mar. 3, 1912; s. Claude Purdue and Mary Allce (Lankford) D.; student Mo. Wesleyan Coll., 1929-30; A.B., Baker U., 1933; M.D., Kans. U., 1937; m. Hazel Louise Overley, Mar. 11, 1939; children—Alice Louise, Carol Ann, David Christopher. Intern, Augustana Hosp., Chgo., 1937-38, resident in surgery, 1939-40, resident in pathology, 1947-50; dir. pathology Lakeview Meml. Hosp., Danville, Ill., 1950-64, Central DuPage Hosp., Winfield, Ill., 1964—; staff mem. Copley, St. Joseph Mercy hosps., Aurora, Ill., Edward Hosp., Naperville, Ill., Community Hosp., Geneva, Ill., Delnor Hosp., St. Charles, Ill.; past pres. med. staff Central DuPage Hosp. Bd. dirs. Avery Cooney Sch., Downers Grove, Ill., 1965-68, pres., 1967-68; past mem. bd. dirs. and exec. com. Aurora area Blood Bank. Served to maj. AUS, 1942-46. Recipient Sci. Exhibit gold award Joint Ann. Meeting, Coll. Am. Pathologists and Am. Soc. Clin. Pathologists, 1962; named Pathologist of Year, Coll. Am. Pathologists, 1969; recipient Govs. award Central DuPage Hosp., 1975. Fellow Coll. Am. Pathologists (pres. 1975-77), Am. Soc. Clin. Pathologists; mem. Am., Ill. State, DuPage County med. assns., Ill. (past pres.), Am. assns. blood banks, Inst. Medicine Chgo., Ill. Soc. Pathologists (past pres.), Alpha Omega Alpha. Presbyterian. Clubs: St. Charles Country. Editor bull. Coll. Am. Pathologists, 1960-61, Adminstrn. in the Pathology Lab., 1969; contbr. articles to med. jours. Home: 1S333 Edgewood Walk West Chicago IL 60185 Office: 0N025 Winfield Rd Winfield IL 60190

DORSEY, GEORGE CHARLES, physician; b. Clinton, Ia., Jan. 19, 1895; s. Edward William and Annie Elizabeth (Looney) D.; B.S., Northwestern U., 1921, M.D., 1921; postgrad. U. Minn., 1944-48, Ariz. State Hosp., 1960-65; m. Erma Kimbal, Apr. 28, 1924; children—George, John K., William, Robert, Mary Ann (Mrs. Gordon Sundin). Intern, Evanston (Ill.) Hosp., 1920, Henrotin Hosp., Chgo., 1921; gen. practice medicine and surgery, Chgo., 1922-24, Mpls., 1924-59. Mem. 50 Year Club Am. Medicine, 50 Year Club Northwestern U. Address: 5300 Vernon Ave S Minneapolis MN 55436

DORSEY, PHYLLIS SWAN, civic leader; b. Dallas, Nov. 2, 1923; d. Hugo and Joy (Hervey) Swan; A.B., Stanford U., 1945; m. Robert Treat Dorsey, Dec. 29, 1944; 1 dau., Carol Joy (Mrs. William Earl Bushek). Civic devel. chmn. Garden Club of Ohio, 1964-66; founder, chmn. Port Enhancement Com., 1964—; roadsides chmn. Nat. Council State Garden Clubs, 1975-77; chmn. Ohio Roadside Council, 1969—. Mem. Floralia Arrangers, Ohio Council Nationally Accredited Flower Show Judges. Republican. Club: Coll. (Cleve.). Home: 3726 Tolland Rd Shaker Heights OH 44122

DORSTE, THOMAS CHARLES, architect; b. Anderson, Ind., Feb. 12, 1923; s. Louis Thomas and Mary Samantha (Haughton) D.; student Ball State U., 1939; B.Arch., Mass. Inst. Tech., 1947; m. Eleanor Claire Edwardson, Apr. 8, 1944; children—Robert Edwardson, Sarah Haughton, Craig Thomas. Designer, draftsman Anderson & Beckwith, Boston, 1947-50; chief draftsman Burns & Burns Indpls., 1950-53; partner Dorste & Pantazi, Indpls., 1953-59; owner Thomas C. Dorste, Indpls., 1959-61; v.p., treas. James Assos., Indpls., 1961—; pres. James & Berger, architects, engrs., economists, Indpls., 1964— (dir. both firms); dir. JA Constrn. Mgmt. Corp., James Assos., Vincennes and Fort Wayne, Ind. Mem. econ. devel. com. City Indpls., 1972-75, adv. com. Indpls. Dept. Devel., 1960-65, policy com. City Market, 1974. Mem. ednl. council Mass. Inst. Tech., 1965—, Nat. Trust for Historic Preservation, 1974—, Indpls. Mus. Soc., 1971—, Indpls. Symphony Soc., 1971—. Pres., bd. dirs. Indpls. Leadership Com., 1970—. Served with C.E., AUS, 1942-46. Mem. A.I.A., Ind. Soc. Architects, Mass. Inst. Tech. Club Ind., Amateur Fencers League Am. Club: Indpls. Fencing. Architect: Ind. U. Univ. Schs., 1963; Greenwood Shopping Center, 1966; Indpls. Regional Postal Facility, 1971; Indpls. Conv. Center, 1972; others. Home: 5319 Whisperwood Ln Indianapolis IN 46226 Office: 2828 E 45th St Indianapolis IN 46205

DORUS, ELIZABETH, psychologist, geneticist; b. Parsons, Kans., Dec. 6, 1940; d. Ronald Oscar and Ethel (Lane) Bankson; B.A., Valparaiso U., 1962; Ph.D., U. Chgo., 1971; M.A., U. Pa., 1975; m. Walter Dorus, Jr., June 30, 1968; children—Stephen. Intern clin. psychology Duke U. Med. Center, 1964-65; consulting psychology Mental Health div. Chgo. Bd. Health, 1967-71; instr. psychology U. Pa., 1972-73, research fellow Found. Fund for Research in Psychiatry, 1972-73; research fellow Ill. State Psychiatric Inst., Chgo., 1974-75; research fellow Nat. Inst. Health dept. medicine U. Chgo., 1975-76, research asso., asst. prof. dept. psychiatry, 1977—. NIMH Research Scientist Devel. award, 1977—. Mem. Am. Psychol. Assn., Am. Soc. Human Genetics, Behavioral Genetics Assn., Soc. Social Biology. Contbr. articles to Archives of Gen. Psychiatry, British Journal of Psychiatry and others. Office: Dept Psychiatry U Chgo 950 E 59th St Chicago IL 60637

DORWEILER, PAUL LAWRENCE, electronic engr.; b. Mpls., Jan. 11, 1934; s. Peter Paul and Dora (Peterson) D.; student U. Minn., 1957-58, Mankato State Coll., 1963-64; B.S., Northwestern Electronics, 1959; m. Jean C. Dorweiler, June 6, 1959; children—Kevin, Pamela, Lisa, Kimberly. Fed. electric radician Fed. Elec. Co., Dewline, Alaska, 1959; mgr. Minn. Airmotive Radio-Flying Cloud Fld., Hopkins, Minn., 1960-63; supr. tech. publs. E.F. Johnson Co., Waseca, Minn., 1966-67; mgr. Ben's Aircraft Radio, Waterloo, Iowa, 1967; editor Ojibway Press, Duluth, Minn., 1967-70; free lance writer, 1967—; owner Paul Lawrence & Assos., 1972—; mgr. publs. Telex Corp., Mpls., 1972-76; prodn. engr. S.C. Electronics, Inc., Mpls., 1976-77; mgr. publs. Microcomponent Technology, 1977—. Served with USNR, 1954-56. Mem. IEEE, Soc. Tech. Communication (certificate of achievement 1975), Am. Legion, Pilots Internat. Clubs: Elks, K.C. Home and Office: 4106 Woodbine Ln Brooklyn Center MN 55429

DOSEMAGEN, GILBERT JAMES, camera shop exec.; b. Kenosha, Wis., Jan. 21, 1936; s. Edward Frank and Bernice Alma Hein D.; student U. Wis.-Kenosha, 1953-55; B.E., Whitewater State Coll. (became U. Wis.-Whitewater), 1958. Clk., Maxwell's Inc., Kenosha, 1952-55, office mgr., 1955-58, store mgr., 1958-63, gen. mgr., 1963-69, pres., 1969—. Alderman, City of Kenosha, 1962—; chmn. City of Kenosha Parking Commn., 1969, transit commn, 1971-74. Recipient Page 1 award Kenosha Newspaper Guild, 1974. Pres. Kenosha Taxpayers Assn. Inc., 1970-71. Roman Catholic. Elk, Rotarian (sec. Kenosha 1973-76). Home: 923 45th St Kenosha WI 53140 Office: PO Box 577 Kenosha WI 53141

DOSLAND, CHESTER ALLEN, lawyer; b. Fargo, N.D., June 14, 1928; s. Chester Arthur and Edna (Baker) D.; student S.D. State Coll., 1945-46; B.S. in Law, U. Minn., 1953, LL.B., 1953; m. Mary Lou Hunting, Dec. 26, 1953; children—Thomas Allen, Catherine Ann, Beth Mary. Admitted to Minn. bar, 1953; law clk. Minn. Supreme Ct., St. Paul, 1953-54; practice law, New Ulm, Minn., 1954—; dir. Citizens Bank New Ulm; mem. Minn. Bd. Law Examiners, 1963-71, pres., 1971—. Pres. New Ulm chpt. United Fund, 1964. Served with AUS, 1946-48. Diplomate Am. Bd. Trial Advs. Fellow Am. Coll. Trial Lawyers; mem. Delta Theta Phi. Mem. United Ch. Christ. Home: 36 Woodland Dr New Ulm MN 56073 Office: 1 S State St New Ulm MN 56073

DOSLAND, WILLIAM BUEHLER, lawyer; b. Chgo., Nov. 10, 1927; s. Goodwin L. and Beatrice (Buehler) D.; B.A., Concordia Coll., 1949; J.D., U. Minn., 1954; m. Donna Mae Mathison, Sept. 15, 1956; children—David William, Susan Elizabeth. Admitted to Minn. bar, 1954; gen. partner firm Dosland, Dosland & Nordhougen, Moorhead, Minn., 1954-68; sr. partner firm Dosland, Dosland, Nordhougen & Mickelberg, Moorhead, 1968—; dir. Am. Bank & Trust Co., Moorhead, 1969-74, chmn. bd., 1974—; gen. counsel, corporate sec. Am. Crystal Sugar Co. Mem. Minn. Senate from 56th dist., 1959-72. Served with USNR, 1945-46, 51-53. Mem. Minn. Bar Assn. Mason, Lion. Home: 929 21st Ave S Moorhead MN 56560 Office: Am Bank & Trust Co Bldg Moorhead MN 56560

DOSSETT, JON LOREN, heat treating co. exec.; b. Terre Haute, Ind., Jan. 28, 1940; s. Ota Lewis and Grace Ann (Tatlock) D.; B.S. in Metall. Engring., Purdue U., 1965; m. Gwendolyn Jane Brown, Jan. 28, 1961; children—Melissa Jane, Jon Loren, Jennifer. Asst. chief metallurgist Link Belt div. FMC Corp., Indpls., 1965-69; metallurgy mgr. Warner Gear div. Borg Warner Co., Muncie, Ind., 1970-74; supr. metall process control Internat. Harvester Corp., Hinsdale, Ill., 1974-76; div. mgr. Lindberg Heat Treating Co., Melrose Park, Ill., 1977—. Registered profl. engr., Ind., Ill. Mem. Am. Soc. Metals (advisory tech. awareness council 1975—, chmn. div. heat treating 1976—, tech. divs. bd. 1976—), Soc. Automotive Engrs., Am. Foundryman's Soc. Republican. Methodist. Contbr. articles to profl. jours.; chmn. editorial bd. Jour. Heat Treating, 1977—. Home: 355 Western Ave Clarendon Hills IL 60514 Office: 1975 N Ruby St Melrose Park IL 60160

DOST, RAYMOND MATTHEW, mech. engr.; b. Chgo., Dec. 3, 1920; s. Edward Julius and Anne Marie (Dier) D.; student Armour Inst. Tech., Chgo., 1939-40; student U. Mich., 1940-41, postgrad., 1973; B.S. in Mech. Engring., Northwestern U., 1947; M.S., Western Mich. U., 1970; m. Barbara Jean Letts, June 22, 1946; children—Matthew Charles, Susan Marie, Sally Jean. Project engr., draftsman Bendix Research Lab., Detroit, 1941-43; aero. engr. Affiliated Engring. Co., Detroit, 1943-44; design engr. Engring. Research Asso., St. Paul, 1947-48; petroleum engr. Pan Am. Petroleum Corp., Ft. Worth, 1948-55; prodn. mgr. Kingwood Oil Co., Mt. Vernon, Ill., 1955-61; engr. Brazos Oil & Gas Co., Houston, 1963-65; pvt. practice engring. cons., Mt. Vernon, 1961-63, Colon, Mich., 1965-67; tchr. physics and phys. sci. Colon Community schs., 1967; project engr. Wheelcamper Corp., Centreville, Mich., 1971-73; instr. drafting and indsl. studies Glen Oaks Community Coll., Centreville, 1967-73, coordinator apprenticeship tng., 1970-72, chmn. technology div., 1973; engr., dir. planning St. Joseph County (Mich.), Centreville, 1974—. Sec. Colon Community Schs. Bd. Edn., 1968-72. Served with U.S. Navy, 1944-45. Registered profl. engr., Tex., Ill., Mich. Mem. Mich. Soc. Planning Ofcls., Water Pollution Control Fedn., Nat., Mich. socs. profl. engrs. Clubs: Lions, Optimists, Mason, Elks. Home: PO Drawer 0 Colon MI 49040 Office: PO Box 277 Centreville MI 49032

DOTSON, CHARLES EDWARD, mayor; b. Central Station, W.Va., Aug. 19, 1916; s. Harold and Nellie Gay (Hart) D.; grad. high sch.; student Alexander Hamilton Inst., 1962; m. Carolyn Alverta Flickinger, Oct. 3, 1948; children—Ruth (Mrs. Timothy Jay Van Horn), Carol. Sales and service engr. Columbiana Engring. Co. (Ohio), 1951-60; plant engr. N.R.M. Corp. div. Condec Corp., Columbiana, 1960-76; mem. Columbiana Village Council, 1972, mayor, 1973—. Served with AUS, 1944-46. Named Citizen of Year, Columbiana C. of C., 1974. Methodist. Mason (K.T.). Home: 61 Ray Ave Columbiana OH 44408 Office: City Bldg W Friend St Columbiana OH 44408

DOTTERER, LEWIS LEROY, sch. psychometrist; b. Kokomo, Ind., Apr. 8, 1952; s. Lewis Jacob and Marjorie Pauline (Henry) D.; B.S., Ball State U., Muncie, Ind., 1974, M.A., 1976; postgrad. counseling psychology Mich. State U., 1977—; m. Phoebe Beth Shotton, Nov. 24, 1974. Orderly, Logansport (Ind.) State Hosp., 1971; grad. asst. ednl. psychology Ball State U., 1974-75, grad. asst. counseling center, 1975-76; intern in sch. psychometry, Anderson and Muncie, Ind., also police screening, Muncie, psychometric tester physically handicapped children Isanogel Rehab. Center, 1975-76; sch. psychometrist Whitley County Schs., Columbia City, Ind., 1976-77; cons. Whitley County Assn. Mentally Retarded; teaching asst. Mich. State U., 1977-78; researcher adult adjustment patterns. Mem. Am. Psychol. Assn., Am. Personnel and Guidance Assn., Phi Delta Kappa. Mem. Ch. of God-Anderson, Ind. Home: 1448 F Spartan Village East Lansing MI 48823 Office: Coll Edn Erickson Hall Mich State Univ East Lansing MI 48824

DOTY, FRANK ARTHUR, research co. exec.; b. Chgo., July 10, 1933; s. Warner W. and Rose (Buttlar) D.; B.S., Monmouth Coll., 1955; m. Mary K. Brehen, June 20, 1959; children—Carl W., Elizabeth R., Kathleen M., Deborah L., Cynthia A. With Chgo. Ink & Research Co., 1949—, research dir., 1955-59, mgr., dir., 1959—, treas., 1962—. Fellow Am. Inst. Chemists; mem. Am. Chem. Soc., Marking Device Assn. Club: Chgo. Marking Device (pres. 1964). Home: Route 3 Box 624 Antioch IL 60002 Office: 97 Ida Antioch IL 60002

DOTY, JAMES TRUMAN, charitable assn. exec.; b. Manning, Ia., June 15, 1912; s. Birch Homer and Blanche Sarah (Mauldin) D.; student Drake U., 1931-34; m. Eunice H. Morrison, June 21, 1941. Regional sales mgr. Ansco Film div. Gen Aniline & Film Corp., 1946-54; pres. Bear Photo Service, San Francisco, 1954-60; chmn. bd. Crown-Bremson Industries, 1960-62; pres. People-to-People Internat., Kansas City, Mo., 1969—, trustee, 1967—. Served with USMCR, 1942-46. Mem. Palm Desert C. of C. (pres. 1967-68). Rotarian. Clubs: Indian Wells Country (Palm Desert); Internat. (Washington). Home: 4545 Wornall Rd Kansas City MO 64111 Office: 3 Crown Center Kansas City MO 64108

DOUB, JACK ROWLAND, test instruments mfg. co. exec.; b. St. Charles, Mo., Sept. 19, 1943; s. John Jacob and Georgia (Rowland) D.; B.S.E.E., Northwestern U., 1966, M.B.A., 1969; m. Martha Irene Slusser, June 25, 1977. Market planning analyst Franklin Electric Co., Bluffton, Ind., 1969-71; sales research analyst Columbia Gas System Service Corp., Wilmington, Del., 1971-72; market analyst Sears, Roebuck & Co., Chgo., 1972-75; product mgr. Dynascan Corp., Chgo., 1975—. Mem. Am. Mktg. Assn., Am. Mgmt. Assn., Soc. Advancement of Mgmt., Alliance Française Chgo. Presbyterian. Home: 737 Fairfield Ave Elmhurst IL 60126 Office: 6460 W Cortland Ave Chicago IL 60635

DOUGHTY, WILLIAM HOWARD, realtor; b. Williamstown, Mass., June 7, 1907; s. W. Howard and Lydia S. (Vail) D.; grad. Deerfield (Mass.) Acad., 1925; A.B., Williams Coll., 1929; m. Elizabeth P. Sargent, Jan. 2, 1932; children—William Howard, Helen S. (Mrs. Robin D. Lester), Anthony R., Stephen V. Pres. Chinnock & Doughty, Inc., Chgo., 1969-74. Chmn. traffic com. Chgo. Central Area Com., 1956-59; mem. central city council Urban Land Inst., 1960. Trustee Williams Coll., 1967-72, Bradley Real Estate Trust. Mem. Bldg. Mgrs. Assn Chgo. (pres. 1952-55), Nat. Assn. Real Estate Investment Trusts (pres. 1967), Nat. Assn. Bldg. Owners and Mgrs. (chmn. Downtown com. 1955-58), Kappa Alpha. Clubs: Realty (pres. 1950), Digest, University, Commonwealth (Chgo.); Indian Hill (Winnetka, Ill.); Williams (N.Y.C.). Home: 829 Westerfield Dr Wilmette IL 60091 Office: 134 S LaSalle St Chicago IL 60603

DOUGLAS, BRUCE EDWARD, splty. mfg. co. exec.; b. Plainwell, Mich., Nov. 30, 1946; s. Charles E. and Winifred E.; B.A., Mich. State U., 1969, M.A. in Communication Arts, 1974; m. Gail M. Folsom, Nov. 1977. Dir. offsite sales Swiss Alpine Devel. Corp., Lansing, Mich., 1972-74; plant mgr. Art Card Shop (now assumed by Harco Graphic Arts Supply, Inc.), Grand Rapids, Mich., 1974—, also cons.; instr. bus. communications Vets. Outreach Program, Davenport Coll. Bus. Active Heritage Hill Assn. of Grand Rapids. Recipient ann. award Mich. State U. Broadcasters Guild, 1972. Mem. Nat. Assn. Ednl. Broadcasters. Home: 337 Baltimore St NE Grand Rapids MI 49503 Office: 405 Douglas St NW Grand Rapids MI 49502

DOUGLAS, HERBERT DWIGHT, lawyer, judge; b. Joplin, Mo., Sept. 2, 1943; s. Herbert Hinton and Thelma (Breshears) D.; student Tex. Christian U., 1961-63; B.A., U. Mo., 1965; J.D., 1968; m. Bonnie Ann Douglass, Aug. 20, 1966; children—Steven Dwight, Rebecca Ann. Admitted to Mo. bar, 1968; partner firm Douglas, Douglas & Dougals, Neosho, Mo., 1968—; municipal judge City of Neosho, 1976—. Mem. Kansas City dist. adv. council SBA, 1972-75. Mem. Lawyers State Com., Bond for Gov. campaign, 1972; coordinator Danforth for U.S. Senator campaign, Newton County, 1976; mem. Neosho City Council, 1976; mem. adv. com. to Mo. atty. gen., 1977; bd. dirs. Youth Woodcraft Enterprises, Inc. project OEO, Neosho, Mo., 1975-76. Served with AUS, 1969-71. Decorated Army Commendation medal. Mem. Newton County (pres. 1975-76), Mo. bar assns., Mo. Assn. Republicans (v.p. 7th Congl. dist.), Phi Delta Phi. Republican. Mem. Christian Ch. (deacon). Rotarian. Club: Grand Lake Sailing (gov.). Home: 1012 Bond St Neosho MO 64850 Office: 206 S Wood St Neosho MO 64850

DOUGLAS, LESLIE A., govt. ofcl.; b. Martins Ferry, Ohio, Feb. 18, 1931; s. Jess H. and Helen Elizabeth (Ward) D.; A.B., West Liberty State Coll., 1958; M.Ed., Kent State U., 1962; m. Betty L. Briggs, Aug. 12, 1959; children—Charles, Richard, Kathryn, James. Tchr. social studies, basketball coach Stanton Local High Sch., 1958-60; dir. guidance Barnesville Exempted Village Schs., 1960-63; dir. pupil personnel services Martins Ferry City Schs., 1963-70; dir. job counseling Model Cities Project, Martins Ferry, 1970-74; dir. Easter Seals Camp for Handicapped, Camp Pittenger, 1975-76. Sec., Belmont County Jobs for Vets. Com., 1970-74; pres. Belmont County Easter Seal Soc., 1972-73. Bd. dirs. Ohio Soc. Crippled Children and Adults, Upper Ohio Valley United Way. Served with USAF, 1951-55. Recipient Schoolman medal Freedoms Found., 1971; named Elk of Year for Ohio, 1971. Fellow Am. Sch. Health Assn., Internat. Biog. Assn.; mem. Ohio Edn. Assn. (life), Nat. Vocat. Guidance Assn., N.E.A., Am. Vocat. Assn., Council Exceptional Children, Am. Personnel and Guidance Assn., V.F.W., Am. Legion. Elk, Mason (Shriner). Home: 606 Monroe St Martins Ferry OH 43935 Office: Hanover St Martins Ferry OH 43935

DOUGLAS, PAUL LOUIS, state ofcl.; b. Sioux Falls, S.D., Sept. 19, 1927; s. Louis Paul and Victoria (Karavaselis) D.; B.S., U. Nebr., 1951, J.D., 1953. Admitted to Nebr. bar, 1953; individual practice law, Lincoln, 1953-56; with County Atty.'s Office, Lancaster County, Lincoln, 1956-74, chief dep. county atty., 1959-60, county atty., 1960-74; atty. gen. Nebr., Lincoln, 1975—. Served with USMC, 1945-47. Mem. Nebr., Lincoln bar assns., Nat. Assn. Attys. Gen., Midwest Attys. Gen. (chmn.), Am. Legion, Lincoln C. of C. Republican. Greek Orthodox. Clubs: Masons (32 deg.), Shriners, Order Eastern Star, Elks. Office: Office of Atty Gen Dept of Justice State House Lincoln NE 68509

DOUGLASS, JEAN HALL, realtor; b. St. Louis, Oct. 23, 1946; s. Jean Hall and Helen Regina (Walsh) D.; A.B., St. Louis U., 1968; m. Mary Constance Dulle, Dec. 28, 1968; children—Michael Christopher, Elizabeth Anne, Gregory John. Tchr. Am. Govt., McCluer High Sch., St. Louis, 1968-69; asso. Ira E. Berry, Inc., St. Louis, 1969-74, v.p., 1972-74; founder, pres. J.H. Douglass, Realtor, St. Louis, 1974—; instr. real estate licensing courses Real Estate Bd. Met. St. Louis Pre-License Sch., 1975—, dean faculty, dir., 1977—. Mem. Nat., Mo. assns. realtors, Realtors Nat. Mktg. Inst., Farm and Land Inst., Nat. Assn. Ind. Fee Appraisers. Office: 730 Crab Thicket Ln Des Peres St Louis MO 63131

DOUTY, RICHARD THOMAS, civil engr.; b. Williamsport, Pa., July 12, 1930; s. Richard Otis and Helen Anna (Sauter) D.; B.C.E., Lehigh U., 1956; M.S., Ga. Tech. Inst., 1957; Ph.D., Cornell U., 1964; m. Patricia Marie Hopkins, June 27, 1959; children—Richard Keith, Eric Thomas, Ellen Marie, Christopher Brandon. Mgmt. trainee fabricated steel div. Bethlehem Steel Co. (Pa.), 1957-58; asst. prof. civil engring. U. Mo., Columbia, 1962, prof. civil engring., 1970—; sabbatical leave sr. research fellow U. Pa., Phila., 1969-70; cons. in field. Mem. NRC Selective Bd. Research Associateship. Served with USN, 1950-54. NSF research grantee. Mem. ASCE (com. electronic computation). Contbr. numerous articles to profl. jours. Home: 1412 Ridgemont Ct Columbia MO 65201 Office: Dept Civil Engring U Mo Columbia MO 65201

DOVEL, THOMAS DELWIN, educator; b. Clinton, Iowa, Jan. 8, 1937; s. Myles Delwin and Ethel (Palmer) D.; student Roanoke Coll., 1955-57; B.S., Miami U., Oxford, O., 1959, M.B.A., 1961; postgrad. Ohio State U., 1961-62; m. Nella Poteet, Apr. 27, 1963; children—Linda Marie, Thomas David. Owner, operator Dovel Distbg. Co., Roanoke, Va., 1955-57; mgmt. asst. Federated Dept. Stores, Dayton, O., 1962-63; mktg. intelligence coordinator Frigidaire div. Gen. Motors Corp., Dayton, 1963-68; mgr. mktg. research Mead Corp., Dayton, 1968-69; mgr. sales tng. Hobart Mfg. Co., Troy, Ohio, 1970; asso. prof. mktg. Wright State U., Dayton, 1970—, asst. dean Coll. Bus. and Adminstrn., 1974-77, exec. dir. Inst. Community and Orgn. Devel., 1976—; v.p. Research Team, Inc., 1973-76. Mem. Am. Mktg. Assn. (sec. 1969-70, v.p. 1970-71, pres. 1971-72), Am. Mgmt. Assn., Sales Mktg. Execs. Internat., Delta Sigma Pi, Omicron Delta Gamma. Home: 1572 Lindenhurst Dr Dayton OH 45459

DOVERSBERGER, RICHARD ARTHUR, indsl. engr.; b. Warren, Ind., July 19, 1926; s. Jacob Ezra and Orpha Nadean (Bardsley) D.; B.S., Ball State U., 1947, M.A., 1965; m. Jacqueline Anne Stroup, July 22, 1950 (div. Jan. 1973); children—Debra Anne, Cynthia Kay; m. 2d, Connie Jo Ford Davidson, May 28, 1976 (div. Dec. 1976). Tchr., coach Richland Twp. High Sch., Larwill, Ind., 1947-48; cost estimator Beaver Machine Corp., Warren, 1948-50; with Caswell-Runyon Corp., Huntington, Ind., 1950-55, with RCA Corp., Marion, Ind., 1953-72, econ. analyst, 1963-72, facilities planner, plant layout, 1965-72; indsl. engr. Gatke Corp., Warsaw, Ind., 1972; with Square D Corp., Huntington, 1972-73; with Wofac Co., cons. engring., Ft. Wayne, Ind., 1973-75; indsl. engr., Wabash Magnetics, Huntington, 1975—. Mem. Huntington County Draft Bd., 1970—; vol. A.R.C., 1973. Bd. dirs., treas. Salamonie Summer Festival, Warren, 1971, 72. Served with AUS, 1948-49, 50-51. Inducted into Huntington County (Ind.) Sports Hall of Fame, 1976. Mem. Am. Inst. Indsl. Engrs., Am. Econ. Assn., Nat. Hist. Soc., Am. Wildlife Fedn., Phi Delta Kappa (pres. 1972, 73, 76), Alpha Phi Gamma. Mason (past master, sec.), Kiwanian (dir. 1972, 73). Home: Rural Route 8 Crampton Ave Columbia City IN 46725 Office: Wabash IPM 200 E Daniels Rd Palatine IL 60067

DOW, ALDEN BALL, architect; b. Midland, Mich., Apr. 10, 1904; s. Herbert Henry and Grace A. (Ball) D.; student U. Mich., 1923-26. Dr. Architecture (hon.), 1963; B. Arch., Columbia, 1931; A.F.D. (hon.), Hillsdale Coll., 1960, Albion Coll., 1964; LL.D., Mich. State U., 1966; Dr. Hum., Saginaw Valley State Coll., 1969, Northwood Inst., 1969; m. Vada Bennett, Sept. 16, 1931; children—Michael Lloyd, Mary Lloyd, Barbara Alden. Practicing architect, Midland, 1933—. Awarded Diplome de Grand Prix for residential architecture in U.S., Paris Internat. Expn., 1937. Fellow A.I.A. (award of merit); mem. Nat. Council Archtl. Registration, Am. Soc. Architects (past pres., mem. bd., award of merit 1967), Mich. Engring. Soc., Ch. Archtl. Guild of Am., Archl. League N.Y., Theta Delta Chi, Alpha Rho Chi. Clubs: Country (Midland, Mich.); Saginaw (Mich.); Saginaw Bay Yacht (Bay City, Mich.). Bldgs. include 1st Meth. Ch., Northwood Inst., Midland Center for the Arts, Ann Arbor City Hall, Inst. Social Research Bldg., also adminstrv. office bldg. at U. Mich.; 1970 facility, Kalamazoo Valley Community Coll. Author: Reflections, 1970. Home: 315 Post St Midland MI 48640

DOW, DEAN ASHTON, dental supply co. exec.; b. Seattle, July 26, 1926; s. Raymond Earl and Eleanor Fay (Zentner) D.; B.B.A., U. Wash., 1949; m. Merrillyn Mills Goodnow, Aug. 25, 1950; children—Dale, Laura, Mary. Salesman, Patterson Dental Co., Seattle, 1949-56, mgr., Lincoln, Nebr., 1956-59, mgr., Los Angeles, 1959-61, v.p., Bloomington, Minn., 1961-73, pres., 1973—. Served with USAAF, 1945. Mem. Am. Dental Trade Assn. (chmn. dealers sect. 1968), Sigma Alpha Epsilon. Home: 6418 Hill-A-Way Ct Edina MN 55435 Office: 1100 E 80th St Bloomington MN 55420

DOW, MICHAEL LLOYD, pub. co. exec.; b. Saginaw, Mich., Feb. 14, 1935; s. Alden B. and Vada B. (Bennett) D.; student Williams Coll., 1953-56; B.S., Mich. State U., 1961; m. Rhea A. Acker, Dec. 17, 1960; children—Michael, Diane. Exec. v.p., treas. Panax Corp., East Lansing, Mich., 1963-74, treas., 1969—; Kalamazoo Printing Machinery Co., Inc., Asso. Newspapers, Inc., Wayne, Mich., 1969—; v.p., treas. The Mellus Newspapers, Inc., Lincoln Park, Mich., 1970—; partner Central Mich. Inns, Inc., Mt. Pleasant, 1965—, No. Mich. Inns, Inc., Traverse City, 1967—, Gen. Aviation, Inc., Lansing, 1965—. Trustee Leelanau Schs., Glen Arbor, Mich. Served with AUS, 1956-58. Mem. Lansing C. of C. (dir. 1971—). Office: Gen Aviation Bldg Capital City Airport Lansing MI 48906

DOWD, GERI ANDREA HACKER, author, editor; b. Chgo., Feb. 6, 1902; d. Frederick William and Selma (Petersohn) Hacker; student Northwestern U., 1935-36, 46, Chgo. Tchr's. Coll., 1958-59; A.A., Wright Jr. Coll., 1958; B.A., Roosevelt U., 1961, postgrad. Sch. Sociology, 1968—; m. Lawrence Bernard Dowd, Apr. 14, 1934. Author: Circus Parade, 1950, Bonny and Barry, Busy Scientists, 1951, Discussion on the Etiology and Chemotherapy of Cancer and Other Virus Diseases, 1952, Suzy Sewzy, 1953, Lunar Glass: A Possible Key to a New Selenology, 1969; author play: The First Easter, 1962; contbr. stories, articles, revs. to newspapers, popular mags., profl. jours., 1914—; credit mgr., legal counsel to firms, 1928-39; columnist, founder woman's page Elm Leaves, Oak Park, Ill., 1941-44; pub., editor World Arts & Sci. Pub. Co., Elmwood Park, Ill., 1945—; playwright, producer, dir. local theatre groups. First chief of staff Elmwood Park Emergency Feeding and Housing, 1942-66; founder, librarian tchr. Westwood Evang. Luth. Ch. Library, Elmwood Park, 1961-66; active ARC. Recipient German Scholar of Year award Wright Jr. Coll., 1958; certified tchr. kindergarten through 12th grade, Ill. Mem. Chgo. Assn. Credit Men, Children's Reading Profl. Round Table, Women's Nat. Book Assn., Am. Acad. Arts and Scis., Center Study Democratic Instns., Am. Judicature Soc., Am. Acad. Polit. and Social Sci., Psychotherapy, Social Sci. Rev., Forum of Contemporary History, World Future Soc., Ill. State Acad. Sci., AAAS, Astron. Soc. Pacific, Fedn. Am. Scientists, Union Concerned Scientists, Am. Inst. Physics, Roosevelt U. Alumni Assn., Elmwood Park Women's Club (pres. emeritus 1941-43, hon.), Ill. Fedn. Women's Clubs (dist. Past Pres's. Club 1944—). Home and Office: 7922 Oakleaf Ave Elmwood Park IL 60635

DOWD, THOMAS MICHAEL, judge; b. La Rue, O., June 2, 1915; s. Michael T. and Etta (Caulfield) D.; student U. Minn., 1943-44, S.W. Tex. U., 1944-45; J.D., Ohio No. U., 1951; m. Mary Trudell, June 5, 1950; 1 dau., Lisa Anne. Admitted to Ohio bar, 1951; then practiced, Kenton, O.; judge Ct. Common Pleas, Hardin County, O., 1973—. Bus. mgr. The Linking Ring Mag. of Magic, Kenton, 1955—. Former pres. bd. trustees Hardin Meml. Hosp., Kenton. Served with USAAF, 1941-45. Mem. Ohio Bar Assn., Internat. Brotherhood Magicians (internat. treas. 1955—). K.C. (state dep. 1961-63), Elk. Home: Magic Meadow Farm Kenton OH 43326 Office: Court House Kenton OH 43326

DOWDING, NANCY ELSIE, psychologist, counselor, educator; b. Canton, Ohio, Aug. 16, 1924; d. Richard Alexander and Tena (Wise) D.; A.B. cum laude, Western Res. U., 1948, M.A., 1959, Ph.D., 1962; M.A., Columbia U., 1952. Counselor, Cuyahoga Community Coll., Cleve., 1963—. Pres., Women's Equity Action League, 1970. Licensed psychologist, Ohio. Mem. Am. Psychol. Assn., Delta Kappa Gamma. Author: The Greatest Minority of All, Civil Rights Digest, summer 1971. Home: 6100 Laurent Dr 801-B Parma OH 44129

DOWELL, MICHAEL BRENDAN, chemist; b. N.Y.C., Nov. 18, 1942; s. William Henry and Anne Susan (Cannon) D.; B.S., Fordham U., 1963; Ph.D., Pa. State U., 1967; m. Gail Elizabeth Renton, Mar. 16, 1968; children—Rebecca, Margaret. Physicist, U.S. Army Frankford Arsenal, Phila., 1967-69; research scientist Parma (Ohio) Tech. Center, Union Carbide Corp., 1969-74, devel. mgr. carbon fiber applications, 1974-76, group leader metals and ceramics research, 1976—. Chmn. 14th Congressional Dist. steering com. Common Cause, 1974-76; officer, trustee Hudson Montessori Assn., 1974—. Served to capt. ordnance, AUS, 1967-69. Mem. Am. Chem. Soc., Am. Phys. Soc., Am. Carbon Soc., Phi Lambda Upsilon. Roman Catholic. Contbr. articles to profl. jours. Home: 368 N Main St Hudson OH 44236 Office: PO Box 6116 Cleveland OH 44101

DOWELL, ROBERT WILSON, constrn. co. exec.; b. Omaha, July 7, 1929; s. Robert and Nina M. (Young) D.; B.S. in Mech. Engring., Iowa State U., Ames, 1952; m. Patricia Perry, Aug. 4, 1950; children—Mark C., Pamela M., Jennifer L. Head dept. prodn. Union Carbide Olefins Co., South Charleston, W.Va., 1952-60; staff engr. No. Natural Gas Co., Omaha, 1960-64; mgr. constrn. purchasing Olin Corp., N.Y.C., 1964-68, Stamford, Conn., 1968-69; v.p. Design & Devel. Corp. div. ITT Sheraton Corp. Am., Boston, 1969-74; v.p., dir. Constrn. Gen. Growth Devel. Corp., Des Moines, 1974—. Served with AUS, 1947-49, 52-53. Registered profl. engr., W.Va., Nebr., Iowa, Mass. Mem. ASME, Iowa Engring. Soc., Nat. Soc. Profl. Engrs. Mason. Home: 4711 Aspen Dr W Des Moines IA 50265 Office: 1055 6th St Des Moines IA 50305

DOWLING, RUTH NAOMI APKING, educator; b. Daykin, Neb., Apr. 22, 1918; d. William Henry and Twila (Moody) Apking; student Drury Coll., 1955-56, U. Mo., summers 1960-61; B.S. cum laude, S.W. Mo. State U., 1957; M.A., U. Neb., 1962; M.S. in Journalism, Ohio U., 1965; Ph.D., So. Ill. U., 1973; m. Paul Henry Dowling, July 30, 1942 (div. 1955). With advt. dept. Denver Post, 1947-48, Springfield (Mo.) Newspapers, 1948-49; head accounts payable dept. Heer's, Inc., Springfield, 1950-57; head English dept. Brentwood (Mo.) High Sch., 1957-60; asso. prof. English S.W. Mo. State U., Springfield, 1961—. Mem. S.W. Mo. Tchrs. Assn. (dept. sec.-treas. 1967-68), A.A.U.W. (group chmn. 1963-64, 66-71, 73-74, state pub. information officer 1975—), A.A.U.P. (state conf. sec. 1973-75, pres. local chpt. 1974-75), Nat. Council Tchrs. of English, Nat. Fedn. Press Women, Mo. Press Women, Journalism Edn. Assn., N.E.A., Kappa Tau Alpha, Theta Sigma Phi. Home: 1323 E Stanford St Springfield MO 65804

DOWN, (WILLIAM) JACK, ednl. adminstr.; b. Lansing, Mich., July 22, 1924; s. Eldon Eugene and Frankie (Kuhlman) D.; B.A., Mich. State U., 1946, M.A., 1954, Ph.D., 1974; m. Marilyn Elaine Burley, Aug. 31, 1946; children—Elaine Lenore Down Angstman, Eugene Thomas, Evan Jack. Tchr. pub. schs., Holt, Mich., 1949-51, Lansing, Mich., 1954-55; dir. Vocat. Sch., Am. Samoa, 1951-53; prin. K-12, Webberville, Mich., 1955-56; guidance dir. East Lansing, Mich., 1956-66; dir. Am. Coop. Sch., Santa Cruz, Bolivia, 1965-66; ednl. adviser Dept. State U.S., Vietnam, 1966-68; asst. guidance dir., pub. schs. St. Johns, Mich., 1968-70; coordinator vocational tests State Prison So. Mich., Jackson, 1972-74; dir. guidance Colegio Nueva Granada (Bogota), 1974-75; prin. Am. Coop. Sch., Monrovia, Liberia, 1976—; partner, v.p. SNARB Realty Co., 1965—. Bd. dirs. Lansing Child Guidance Clinic, 1957-61, Friends of the East Lansing Library, 1959-61. Recipient Social Service medal Premier Vietnam, 1968, Ford Found. grantee, 1970; So. Ill. U. grantee, 1970-71; Dissemination of Knowledge Found. grantee 1970. Mem. Am. Personnel and Guidance Assn., Am. Psychol. Assn., Assn. Emotion Disturbed, Nat. Edn. Assn. Research on fatalism among religious groups, especially Buddhist and Christian, France, Vietnam and U.S.; contbr. articles to edn. and travel jours. Home: 2510 Haslett Rd East Lansing MI 48823 Office: American Coop School Box 98 American Embassy Monrovia Liberia

DOWNARD, WILLIAM LOUIS, historian; b. Cin., Dec. 28, 1940; s. William A. and Mildred (Drees) D.; B.A., St. Joseph's Coll. Ind., 1963; M.A., U. Cin., 1964; Ph.D., Miami U., Ohio, 1969; m. Sue Winblad, Aug. 24, 1963; children—Becky, David, Mary Beth, Steven. Tchr., high schs., Greenhills, Ohio, 1968-69; instr. Mt. St. Joseph's Coll. Ohio, 1968-69; mem. faculty St. Josephs Coll., Rensselaer, Ind., 1969—, asso. prof. history, 1973—, chmn. dept., 1977—. Named Prof. of Year, St. Josephs Coll., 1975; Nat. Endowment Humanities grant, summer 1975. Mem. Am. Hist. Assn., Orgn. Am. Historians. Author: The Cincinnati Brewing Industry: A Social and Economic History, 1973. Home: 115 Park Ave Rensselaer IN 47978 Office: Box 897 St Josephs Coll Rensselaer IN 47978

DOWNE, RICHARD BRONSON, nuclear products mfg. co. exec.; b. Binghamton, N.Y., July 11, 1920; s. Charles and Alice May (Bronson) D.; Quality Control Tech. degree, Applied Tech. Inst., 1976; m. Marjory Lena Darling, Dec. 6, 1941; children—Patricia, Barbara, Joann, Paul, John, Steven. Inspector, IBM, Endicott, N.Y., 1941-51, Gen. Motors Tank Plant, Cleve., 1951-55; quality engr. Barth Corp., Cleve., 1956-61; quality control mgr. McDowell Wellman Engring. Co., Cleve., 1961-67; chief inspector Leece Neville Co., Cleve., 1967-72; quality control engr. Picker Corp., Cleve., 1972-75; chief inspector Ohio Nuclear, Inc., Solon, 1975—; instr. Cleve. State U., 1972-73. Pres. Riverside Boys Baseball League, 1965-67, Riverside Recreation Council, 1962-66; precinct committeeman North Olmstead Republican Party, 1965-70. Served to sgt., U.S. Army, 1941-45; ETO. Recipient Silver Beaver award Boy Scouts Am., 1966. Mem. Am. Soc. for Quality Control (sr.), Soc. of Mfg. Engrs. Roman Catholic. Clubs: K.C. (4 deg.), Lin Par. Home: 1606 Elston Ave Cleveland OH 44109 Office: 29100 Aurora Rd Solon OH 44139

DOWNEN, MADELINE ELIZABETH MORGAN, hosp. librarian; b. Pontiac, Mich., Aug. 17, 1930; d. Albert Oran and Hazel Marie (Fisk) Morgan; student Ind. U., 1948-50, St. Josephs Calumet Coll., 1968—; certificate hosp. librarianship Am. Hosp. Assn. Inst., 1964; certificate media mgmt. Med. Library Assn., 1972; m. Evan Ray Downen, Dec. 3, 1949 (div. 1968); children—Charles Albert, Linda Carol (Mrs. Dennis Smith), Gregory Lyn. Apprentice med. librarian St. Catherine Hosp., East Chicago, Ind., 1947-50, med. librarian, 1962-65, supr. McGuire Meml. Library, 1965—. Med. library cons. Our Lady of Mercy Hosp., Dyer, Ind., 1969-70; mem. state med. library cons. com. Ind. U. Sch. Medicine, 1973; coordinator Midwest Health Sci. Library Network Interlibrary Loan Consortia, 1975—; chmn. N.W. Ind. Health Sci. Library Consortium, 1975—. Pres. East Chicago Mothers Club, 1966-67. Mem. Med. Library Assn., Regional Med. Library Council (by-laws com. representing hosp. library 1971). Mem. Christian Ch. Home: 6730 Alexander Ave Hammond IN 46320 Office: 4321 Fir St East Chicago IN 46312

DOWNEND, PAUL EUGENE, accountant; b. Toledo, Aug. 16,, 1907; s. William Joseph and Della M. (Keller) D.; student pub. schs.; m. Mary B. Butler, Nov. 27, 1952. Supr., Ernst & Ernst, Toledo, 1930-42; sec., controller, dir. Ohio Locomotive Crane Co., Bucyrus, 1942; pres., dir. Superior Equipment Co., Bucyrus, 1943; pres., dir. Channel Grove Land Improvement Co.; mgr. Mar-Nol Co.; sec. Peneagle Corp.; dir. Second Nat. Bank, Bucyrus, Ohio, Oakwood Cemetery Assn. Chmn. Bucyrus City Planning Commn.; chmn. Crawford County Republican Exec. Com.; mem. Crawford County Bd. Electors. Pres., bd. dirs. Bucyrus Community Hosp.; chmn. bd. dirs. Crawford County Soc. Crippled Children. C.P.A., Ohio. Mem. Am. Inst. Accountants, Ohio Soc. C.P.A.'s, Am. Ordnance Assn. (life), Mason (Shriner, Jester), Rotarian (past pres.), Elk (past trustee). Clubs: Columbus Athletic, Catawba Cliffs Beach, Crawford Country Auto (v.p., dir.). Home: 325 Joan Dr Bucyrus OH 44820 Office: Hopley Ave Bucyrus OH 44820

DOWNER, ROBERT NELSON, lawyer; b. Newton, Ia., July 15, 1939; s. Lowell William and Mabel (Hannon) D.; B.A., U. Ia., 1961, J.D., 1963; m. Jane Alice Glafka, May 29, 1971; children—Elise Michelle, Andrew Nelson. Admitted to Ia. bar, 1963; asso. mem. firm Meardon, Sueppel, Downer & Hayes and predecessor firms, Iowa City, 1963-68, partner, 1969—. Sec., dir. Dubuque Forge, Inc. (Ia.), 1972—. Trustee Christian Retirement Services, Inc., Iowa City, 1967—; spl. adviser Ia. Crime Commn., 1967-68; vice chmn. Citizens Better Iowa City, 1968-69, chmn., 1969-70; mem. Alumni Council U. Ia., 1971—. Pres. bd. trustees Iowa City Pub. Library, 1973-74, chmn. finance, 1974-77. Mem. Central Com., Johnson County Republican party, 1972-74; mem. Ia. Supreme Ct. Continuing Legal Edn. Com., 1975—. Named Outstanding Young Religious Leader Ia. Jr. C. of C., 1970. Mem. Ia. City C. of C. (v.p. 1977), Johnson County (pres. 1976), Ia. (chmn. com. continuing legal edn.), Am. bar assns., Ia. Hist. Soc., Phi Delta Phi, Omicron Delta Kappa, Phi Kappa Sigma, U. Ia. Alumni Assn. (life mem.). Rep. Methodist. Optimist. Clubs: University Athletic (Iowa City). Home: 126 Potomac Dr Iowa City IA 52240 Office: 100 S Linn St Iowa City IA 52240

DOWNEY, DANIEL ROBERT, architect; b. St. Louis, May 13, 1927; s. Daniel Peter and Elsie Lillian (Horton) D.; A.A., Harris Jr. Coll., 1949; B.Arch., Washington U. (St. Louis), 1954; m. Norma Jean Stallings, Sept. 3, 1954; children—Kevin Michael, Karen Lynn, Keith Bryan, Kimberley Gail. With Maguolo & Quick, Architects & Engrs., St. Louis, 1954-56, Drake-O'Meara Assos., 1956-58; in charge specification writing and office mgmt. Murphy, Downey, Wofford &

Richman/Architects (formerly Murphy & Mackey, Inc.), St. Louis, 1958-71, pres., treas., 1971—. Bd. dirs. Boy's Club of St. Louis, Inc. Served with USNR, 1944-46; with USMCR, 1950-51. Mem. A.I.A. (pres. St. Louis chpt. 1973), Profl. Constrn. Specifications Inst. (dir. St. Louis chpt. 1963-64, pres. 1966-67), Bldg. Ofcls. Conf. Am., Kappa Alpha. Presbyn. Mason. Archtl. works include: Queeny Tower-Barnes Hosp., St. Louis, Children's Hosp., various coll. and sch. bldgs., La Salle Park Redevel. Area, St. Louis. Home: 13006 Musket Ct St Louis MO 63141 Office: 6124 Enright St St Louis MO 63112

DOWNEY, JOHN WILHAM, composer, educator; b. Chgo., Oct. 5, 1927; s. James Bernard and Augustina (Haas) D.; Docteur es Lettres (Ph.D.), U. Paris-Sorbonne, 1956; Prix de Composition (scholar), Paris Conservatory, 1956; m. Irusha Czuczak; children—Lydia, Marc. Chmn. humanities dept., Mayfair Br., Chgo. City Coll., 1958-64; prof. theory and composition, U. Wis., Milw., 1964—; instr. music theory, De Paul U., 1960-64, Roosevelt U., 1961; composer: Cello Sonata, recorded CRI label, 1968; Agort, woodwind quintet, recorded Orion label, 1973; Adagio Lyrico for two pianos, Octet for Winds, What If?, for mixed choir, solo tympany and brass octet, A Dolphin, voice and chamber ensemble, 1977; resident artist MacDowell Colony, summers 1971, 75-77. Bd. dirs., Rondel Arts Studio. Fulbright Scholar to France, 1952-54; scholar, French Govt., 1954-55, teaching fellow, 19S5-56; teaching fellow, German Govt., 1956-57; Copley Found. grantee, 1956-57, 57-58; recipient awards U. Wis., 1971, 73, 75, 77, Ford Found., 1976, Nat. Endowment for the Arts, 1977. Mem. Am. Soc. Univ. Composers, Am. Music Center, ASCAP (awards, 1974-77), Am. Fedn. Musicians, Wis. Contemporary Music Forum (founder, chmn., 1970—), Center Twentieth Century Studies, Rondel Arts Studio, Phi Kappa Phi, Delta Omicron. Office: Univ of Wisconsin School of Fine Arts - Music Milwaukee WI 53201

DOWNING, JAMES SNAPP, coal co. exec.; b. Cleve., Aug. 4, 1936; s. Richard and Irma (Huguenard) D.; grad. high sch.; m. Cynthia Hurst, Sept. 9, 1961; children—David, Elizabeth, Jeffrey. With Downing Coal Co., Cleve., 1959—, v.p., sec., 1966—; pres. Gt. Lakes Coal Co., 1972—; v.p., sec. Freeport Gas Coal Co., Sewell River Coal & Land Co., Ohio Mining Co. Republican. Home: 31931 Meadowlark Way Pepper Pike OH 44124 Office: 2412 Terminal Tower Cleveland OH 44113

DOWNING, ROBERT WOODLING, r.r. ofcl.; b. Sewickley, Pa., Sept. 18, 1913; s. James A. and Hattie (Wragg) D.; B.S. in Civil Engring., Yale, 1935; m. Mary A. Matthews, Aug. 7, 1937; children—Nancy J., Robert M., Susan E. Asst. on engr. corps, asst. supr. track Pa. R.R., 1935-38; rodman C.M. St.P. & P. R.R., 1938; asst. to supt., dist. roadmaster, trainmaster, div. supt., asst. to pres. G.N. Ry., 1938-58, v.p., 1958, exec v.p. 1967-70; exec. v.p. Burlington No., Inc., 1970-71, pres. 1971-73, vice chmn., chief operating officer, 1973—; chmn. Colo. & So. Ry., Ft. Worth & Denver Ry., 1971—. Pres. Portal Pipe Line Co.; trustee Minn. Mut. Life Ins. Co.; dir. N.W. Bancorp., Northwestern Nat. Bank St Paul, Nat. R.R. Passenger Corp. Served from ensign to lt. comdr., USNR, 1941-45. Home: 2028 Upper St Dennis Rd St Paul MN 55116 Office: 176 E 5th St St Paul MN 55101

DOWNING, ROGER NEALE, accounting exec.; b. Waukon, Iowa, Apr. 10, 1931; s. Vern E. and Bernice R. (Stafford) D.; B.A. cum laude, Luther Coll., 1957; postgrad. U. Iowa, 1957-58; m. Carol Pyron, Oct. 12, 1974. Sr. auditor Arthur Andersen, Chgo., 1958-62; comptroller O'Leary Contractors & Equipment Co., 1962-63; sr. v.p. LaGrange (Ill.) State Bank, 1963-77; propr. Downing's Accounting & Tax Service, Western Springs, Ill., 1977—; officer, dir. West Suburban Telephone Answering Service, Inc.; v.p., dir. Systems Leasing Co. Served with USAF, 1951-54. C.P.A., Ill. Mem. Ill. Soc. C.P.A.'s, Am. Inst. C.P.A.'s. Rotarian. Home: 1730 W 60th St LaGrange IL 60525 Office: 1023 Burlington Ave Western Springs IL 60558

DOWNS, RICHARD FAUNCE, artist, photographer; b. Grove City, Pa., June 16, 1924; s. Herbert Grant and Hilda Adams (Faunce) D.; student Los Angeles Art Center Sch., 1947-50, Winona Lake Sch. Photography, 1953; m. Genevieve Madelin Johnson, Aug. 24, 1946; children—Sheldon, Lamont, Cheryl (Mrs. Michael Venetta), Valerie. Employee, Downs Studio, Warren, Ohio, 1950-58, owner, 1958—. Painter oil portraits various local persons. Served with USNR, 1943-46. Mem. Gideons Internat. (pres. Trumbull County chpt. 1960-63). Republican. Mem. Christian and Missionary Alliance. Home: 8482 Old Farm Trail NE Warren OH 44484 Office: 120 E Market St Warren OH 44481

DOYLE, ARTHUR JAMES, lawyer; b. Boston, June 19, 1923; s. M. Joseph and Grace M. (McPhee) D.; J.D., Boston Coll., 1949; m. Glenda M. Luehring, Oct. 14, 1950; children—Teresa, Kevin, Kelley, Conaught, Briana, Michael, Brian, Christopher. Admitted to Mo. bar, 1949, Mass. bar, 1949; asso. Johnson, Lucas, Graves & Fane, attys., Kansas City, Mo., 1949-51; asso. Spencer, Fane, Britt & Browne, attys., Kansas City, 1951-57, partner, 1957-73; v.p., gen. counsel Kansas City Power & Light Co., 1973-77, dir., 1976—, exec. v.p., 1977—; dir., asst. sec. Centennial State Bank, 1969—, dir., sec., 1970—, exec. com., 1971—. Served to lt. (j.g.), USNR, 1942-46. Mem. Mo. (vice-chmn. adminstrv. law sect. 1969—, chmn. 1973-74), Kansas City bar assns., Lawyers Assn. Kansas City, Fed. Power Bar Assn., Mo. C. of C. (bd. dirs. 1968-70, chmn. social and labor com. 1968-70). Roman Catholic. Clubs: The Kansas City, The Carriage. Home: 1060 W 55th St Kansas City MO 64113 Office: Power & Light Bldg 1330 Baltimore Ave Kansas City MO 64141

DOYLE, DAVID CHARLES, computer programmer adminstr.; b. Cheboygan, Mich., Sept. 28, 1952; s. Orlando and Jeanne (St. Amand) D.; A.S. in Data Processing, Ferris State Coll., 1973, B.S. in Data Processing, 1974. Computer programmer, State of Mich., Lansing, 1974-75, sr. programmer, 1975-76, acting programming supr., 1977, programming supr., 1977—; cons. in field.; instr. Lansing Community Coll. Mem. Assn. Systems Mgmt. Home: 4175 Vanetter Rd Williamston MI 48895 Office: Allegan Treas Bldg Lansing MI

DOYLE, DONALD ROBERT, educator; b. Aberdeen, S.D., Feb. 11, 1939; s. Robert Joseph and Florence Esther (Gardner) D.; B.S. in Edn., No. State Coll., S.D., 1961, M.S. in Guidance and Counseling, 1965; Ed.D. in Adminstrn., Guidance and Counseling, U. Mont., 1971; m. Betty Jane Marzolf, July 8, 1962; children—Scott Robert, Patricia, Esther. Tchr. and guidance specialist Bur. of Indian Affairs, Eagle Butte, S.D., 1960-61; dir. of guidance Elkton (S.D.) Schs., 1961-63; prin. elementary schs. of Todd County, Lakeview, S.D., 1963-65, Lanark (Ill.) Schs., 1965-67; instr. psychology Austin (Minn.) State Jr. Coll., 1967-68; grad. research asso. and cons. in project talent U. Mont., Missoula, 1968-70; asso. prof. social sci. Sauk Valley Coll., Dixon, Ill., 1970-76, 77—; dir. of pupil services Lander (Wyo.) Schs., 1976-77. Bd. dirs. Sinnissippi Mental Health Center, Dixon. Mem. NEA, Ill. Edn. Assn., Rock River Personnel and Guidance Assn., Phi Delta Kappa. Republican. Congregationalist. Clubs: Masons, Elks, Order Eastern Star. Contbr. articles on edn. to profl. jours. Home: 1305 11th Ave Sterling IL 60131

DOYLE, FRANCIS PATRICK, physician; b. St. Boniface, Man., Can., Feb. 28, 1922; s. Joseph Pierce and Margaret (King) D.; B.Sc., St. Paul's Coll., U. Man., 1943; M.D., Laval U., Quebec, Can., 1948; m. Marie Therese Arbez, Dec. 27, 1949; children—Rosemary, Patricia, Elaine, Paul. Intern St. Francois d'Assise Hosp., Quebec, 1947-48; practice gen. medicine, Ste. Anne, Man., 1948—; mem. staff St. Boniface Hosp., Ste. Anne Hosp. Med. examiner, Province of Man., 1953—; dir. CBC, 1977—. Mem. Man. Hosp. Commn., 1962-70, Man. Health Services Commn., 1970-72, spl. adviser, 1972-74. Chmn. Seine River Sch. Div., 1963-69. Bd. dirs. Can. Council Christians and Jews, Catholic Found. Man., St. Boniface Hosp. Mem. Catholic Physicians Guild Man. (past pres.), Catholic Health Assn. Can. (v.p.). Home: 259 Central St Ste Anne MB Canada Office: 142 Central St Ste Anne MB Canada

DOYLE, JAMES EDWARD, judge; b. Oshkosh, Wis., July 6, 1915; s. James Edward and Agnes Catherine (McCarthy) D.; A.B., U. Wis., 1937; LL.B., Columbia, 1940. m. Ruth Bachhuber, Aug. 10, 1940; children—Mary, James Edward, Catherine, Anne. Admitted to Wis. bar, 1940; asso. firm LaFollette, Sinykin & Doyle, Madison, 1948-65; U.S. dist. judge Western Dist. Wis., 1965—. Mem. Am., Wis., Dane County bar assns., Am. Law Inst. Home: 1114 Mohican Pass Madison WI 53711 Office: Fed Bldg Monona Ave Madison WI 53701

DOYLE, JOHN VINCENT, mktg. exec.; b. Oak Park, Ill., Oct. 31, 1922; s. J. Frederick and Elizabeth (Meyers) D.; student Northwestern U., 1941-42, Internat. Corr. Schs., 1942-44, Columbia U., 1945-46, N.Y.U., 1947-48; m. Frances G. Jiranek, Feb. 10, 1945; children—Kathleen Frances, Virginia Marie, Frederick Charles. Promotion copywriter Chgo. Tribune-N.Y. News Syndicate, N.Y.C., 1946-47; copywriter O.S. Tyson, Inc., N.Y.C., 1947-48, Batten, Barton, Durstine & Osborn, N.Y.C., 1948-51; sr. v.p., dir. account mgmt. Campbell-Ewald Co., Detroit, 1951-68; dir. mktg. Florists Transworld Delivery Assn., 1968-71; exec. v.p. Thomas Murray & Austin Chaney Advt., Hudson, Ohio, 1971—. Bd. dirs. United Community Services, Detroit, 1963-70; trustee Cranbrook Inst. Sci., Bloomfield Hills, Mich., 1964-73. Served with USCGR, 1942-45. Clubs: Walden Golf and Tennis, Western Res. Racquet (Aurora, Ohio). Home: 530-28 Russet Wood Ln Aurora OH 44202 Office: 55 Atterbury Blvd Hudson OH 44202

DOYLE, RUSSELL RICHARD, civil engr., municipal ofcl.; b. Cin., June 28, 1942; s. Russell Dawkins and Laverna Helen (Dasch) D.; B.S., U. Cin., 1968; postgrad. U. Pitts., 1973—; m. Ann Marie Casner, July 2, 1971. Asst. hwy. engr. Calif. Div. Hwys., Los Angeles, 1968-69; form and design, also office engr. Peter Kiewit Sons Inc., Pasadena, Calif., 1969-70; redevel. engr. City of Muskegon (Mich.), 1971-72; dir. pub. works, bldg., also village engr. Village of Hanover Park (Ill.), 1976—. Am. Pub. Works Assn. fellow U. Pitts., 1973—; registered profl. engr., Ill. Mem. Am. Pub. Works Assn., (historian Chgo. met. chpt. 1977—), Park Forest (Ill.) (pres. 1975-76, Jaycee of Year 1974-75), NE Region (dist. dir. 1976-77), Ill. (dir. 1977-78) Jaycees, Nat. Soc. Profl. Engrs., ASCE. Methodist. Home: 8116 Kingsbury Dr Hanover Park IL 60103 Office: 2121 W Lake St Hanover Park IL 60103

DOYLE, THOMAS EDWARD, constrn. co. exec.; b. Hartford City, Ind., Jan. 29, 1930; s. Raymond L. and Blanche E. (Getz) D.; B.S., Ind. U., 1958; m. Patricia Lou Selby, Dec. 6, 1954; children—Marta Lynn, Karen Kay, Daniel Raymond, Mark Selby. Asst. dir. personnel Days Transfer, Inc., Elkhart, Ind., 1958-60; v.p. operating services Brady Motorfrate, Inc., Des Moines, 1960-68; mgr. personnel, safety and compliance Green Constrn. Co., Des Moines, 1969—. Mem. adv. council Center for Indsl. Research and Service, Iowa State U. Bd. dirs., treas. Industries Council of Des Moines. Served with USNR, 1948-52. Certified exec. in personnel. Mem. Am. Soc. for Personnel Adminstrn. (state dir. Iowa, pres. Central Iowa chpt.), Iowa Council Safety Suprs. (past chmn., dir.), Am. Soc. Safety Engrs., Asso. Gen. Contractors of Iowa (accident prevention com.), Indsl. Relations Research Assn. Home: 2712 Madison Ave Des Moines IA 50310 Office: 2015 Grand Ave Des Moines IA 50312

DOYLE, THOMAS MICHAEL, lawyer; b. Lansing, Mich., June 6, 1938; s. Maurice Joseph and Helen (O'Neill) D.; student Notre Dame U., 1956-58; B.A. cum laude, Mich. State U., 1960; J.D., U. Mich., 1963; m. Nan Hunter, Nov. 30, 1963; children—Tom, John, Bill. Admitted to Mich. bar, 1963, D.C. bar, 1972; asso. firm Snyder, Loomis & Ewert, Lansing, 1963-66, partner, 1966-67; officer firm Doyle, Whitmer, Carruthers & Hess, P.C., Lansing and Washington, 1967—; lectr. labor Mich. State U., East Lansing, 1964-65, lectr. bus. law, 1966—; dir. Systems Research Inc., Lansing. Co. chmn. Fire Bd. City Lansing, 1966. Mem. Am., Mich., D.C., Ingham County bar assns., Am. Judicature Soc., Am. Arbitration Assn. (mem. panel), Alpha Tau Omega. Roman Catholic. Home: 924 Tanglewood St East Lansing MI 48823 Office: 427 S Capitol Ave Lansing MI 48933 also 520 S Union St Traverse City MI 49684 also 1629 K St NW Suite 520 Washington DC

DRABEK, ANTHONY STEPHEN, trade assn. exec.; b. Oak Park, Ill., July 19, 1924; s. Peter Paul and Margaret (Pollok) D.; B.A., Ohio State U., 1951; postgrad. Mich. State U., 1963-65; m. Betty Louise Amsden, July 8, 1948 (dec. May 1976); children—Stephen Wayne, Patricia Eilleen, Charles Paul, Deborah Kim; m. 2d, Jackie H. Booth, Feb. 26, 1977. Asst. to sec. treas. Builders Exchange of Columbus (O.), 1951-57, exec. sec., treas., exec. dir., 1957—. Chmn., Ohio Constrn. Industry Legislative Council, 1972-75. Served with USNR, 1943-45. Recipient Boss of Year award Columbus chpt. Women in Constrn., 1973; named Ky. col. Mem. Internat. Builders Exchange Execs. (pres. 1964-65, dir. internat. hdqrs.; recipient Dan Patrick award 1972), Ohio Congress Builders Exchanges (chmn. adv. council 1966-72, exec. coordinator Ohio offices), Columbus C. of C., Am. Soc. Assn. Execs., Am. Legion (post comdr. 1957-58), Sertoma Internat. (life mem.; recipient Distinguished Gov.'s award 1968; sec. Sertoma Charities of Ohio 1973-74, pres. 1974-76). United Methodist. Club: Maennerchor (Columbus). Home: 5498 Satinwood Dr Columbus OH 43229 Office: 1175 Dublin Rd Columbus OH 43215

DRACH, DUDLEY, realtor, lawyer; b. Cleve., Dec. 14, 1900; s. Jacob W. and Ellen (O'Brien) D.; B.A., Baldwin Coll., 1922; LL.D., Cleve.-Marshall Law Sch., 1922, Dr. Law, 1968. Admitted to Ohio bar, 1922; practiced in Lakewood, 1930—; pres., co-owner West Side Realty Co., 1931—; fee appraiser govt. agys., 1935—. Pres. Cleve. Real Estate Bd., 1944; chmn. Bd. Valuation, 1957, 63, 67. Served with U.S. Army, 1917-18. Recipient Real Estate Dean Valuation awards, 1966. Mem. Am. Soc. Appraisers, Nat., Ohio, Cleve. real estate bds., Soc. Real Estate Appraisers, Am. Legion, Am. Turners. Elk. Club: Westwood Country (Rocky River, Ohio). Home: 2089 Wooster Rd Rocky River OH 44116 Office: 15600 Madison Ave Lakewood OH 44107

DRACHE, HIRAM MAX, educator; b. Waseca, Minn., Aug. 18, 1924; s. Paul A. and Anna (Schultz) D.; B.A., Gustavus Adolphus Coll., 1948; M.A., U. Minn., 1951; Ph.D., U. N.D., 1963; m. Ada Marie Nelson, Feb. 28, 1948; children—Kay Ellen, David Bryan, Paul Arthur. Tchr. high sch., Owatonna, Minn., 1948-50; asst. to treas. Federated Mut. Ins. Co., Owatonna, 1953-55; prof. Concordia Coll., Moorhead, Minn., 1952-53, 55—; owner, operator farms, 1950—. Bd. dirs. Minn. Humanities Commn. Served to maj. USAAF, 1943-45. Decorated D.F.C. Mem. Northwest Farm Mgrs. Assn. (exec. chmn.), Clay County Farm Bur., Agrl. History Soc., Minn. Hist. Soc. (dir), Phi Alpha Theta, Pi Gamma Mu. Republican. Lutheran. Author: The Day of the Bonanza, 1964; The Challenge of the Prairie, 1970; Beyond the Furrow, 1976; contbg. author North Dakota Decision Makers; Two Centuries of American Agriculture. Contbr. articles to profl. jours. Home: Baker MN 56513 Office: Moorhead MN 56560

DRAEGER, KENNETH WILFRED, computer co. exec.; b. Wyandotte, Mich., July 30, 1940; s. Wilfred Arthur and Marjorie (Rapp) D.; student Mich. Technol. U., 1958-60; B.S. in Math., Western Mich. U., 1962; M.B.A., Wayne State U., 1967; m. Carol Ann Ahola, Sept. 7, 1963; children—Kimberley Carol, Tracey Lynn. With Ford Motor Co., Dearborn, Mich., 1963-68, data processing mgr., 1965-66, supr. tech. computer center, 1966-68; dir. marketing and operations Graphic Controls Corp., Buffalo, 1968-70; v.p. mktg. The Cyphernetics Corp., Ann Arbor, Mich., 1970-72, v.p. ops., communications and systems programming, 1972-76; pres. ADP Network Services, Inc.-Domestic, Ann Arbor, 1976—; instr. computer, data processing Wayne State U., Detroit, 1964-65, Henry Ford Community Coll., Dearborn, 1963-65. Mem. Assn. Computing Machinery, Delta Sigma Phi. Club: Washtenaw Country (Ypsilanti, Mich.). Home: 3321 Alton Ct Ann Arbor MI 48105 Office: 175 Jackson Plaza Ann Arbor MI 48106

DRAFFEN, GARY THOMAS, electronics co. ofcl.; b. Paducah, Ky., Sept. 13, 1943; s. John Thomas and Mary (Wallace) D.; student Paducah Community Coll., 1961-63, Murray State U., 1963-65; m. Paula Jean Bell, June 20, 1965. Asst. plant supt. CTS of Paducah (Ky.), 1962-65, product engr., 1965-70, distributor sales mgr., 1972-75, product mgr., Brownsville, Tex., 1971-72; with U.S. Pioneer Electronics, Elk Grove, Ill., v.p. div., Moonachie, N.J., 1975—. Mem. Am. Mgmt. Assn. Republican. Methodist. Home: 1611 Waxwing Ct Schaumburg IL 60195 Office: 737 Fargo St Elk Grove Village IL 60007

DRAGISIC, BRANISLAV MIHAILO, physician; b. Titograd, Yugoslavia, Apr. 6, 1932; s. Mihailo R. and Mileva J. (Sakovic) D.; M.D., U. Belgrade, Yugoslavia, 1959; m. Stanislava Mikic, July 21, 1962; children—Peter, Phillip. Came to U.S., 1962, naturalized, 1971. Intern Gen. Hosp., Valjevo, Yugoslavia, 1959-60; resident in anesthesia St. Joseph's Hosp., Joliet, Ill., 1963-66; resident Asso. Anesthesiologists of Joliet, 1963-66; dir. Chicago Heights, Anesthesia Assn. S.C., 1966—; mem. staff St. James Hosp., Chicago Heights, Ill.; dir., chmn. dept. anesthesiology Good Samaritan Hosp., Downers Grove, Ill., 1976—. Served with Yugoslavian Army, 1959-60. Mem. AMA, Ill., Chgo. socs. anesthesiology, Internat. Research Soc. of Anesthesia, World's Soc. Anesthesiologists. Home: 700 Valley Rd Itasca IL 60143 Office: 1423 Chicago Rd Chicago Heights IL 60411

DRAGOO, JOHN ROBERT, physician; b. Franklin, Ind., Feb. 11, 1926; s. Arthur Reese and Nola Ethyelene (Mullikin) D.; B.S., Ind. U., 1948, M.S., 1956, M.D., 1960; postgrad. Franklin Coll., 1948, U. Minn., 1961; m. Jane Hinkle Dye, June 17, 1956; children—Mary Anne, Arthur Russell. Teaching fellow dept. anatomy, Ind. U. Med. Center, 1948-56; intern Orange County Gen. Hosp., Orange, Calif., 1960-61; practice medicine specializing in family practice The Wabash Clinic, Wabash, Ind., also Urbana (Ind.) Med. Center, 1961—; med. dir. Merriweather Convalescent Center, Wabash, 1969—; mem. staff Wabash County Hosp., chief of staff, 1978—; sch. physician Northfield, 1962-73; bd. physician Wabash Police Dept.; cons. family practice residency program Ind. U. Sch. Med., Ft. Wayne; dir. Frances Slocum Bank & Trust Co., Wabash. Pres. Wabash County Cancer Soc., 1965-68; mem. Ind. DeMolay Found. Recipient of Temple Jewel, Mizpah Shrine, Fort Wayne, Ind., 1967. Mem. A.M.A., Am. Acad. Gen. Practice, Wabash County Med. Soc. (pres. 1964), Ind. State Med. Assn., Am. Profl. Practice Assn., Ind. Acad. Gen. Practice, Nat. Rifle Assn., Isaak Walton League, Indiana Soc. Chgo., Ky. Cols., Nu Sigma Nu, Kappa Delta Rho. Mason (K.T., 32 deg. Shriner), Elk. Clubs: Khyber Rifle (Ft. Wayne, Ind.); Wabash Wildlife. Home: 1021 St James Ct Wabash IN 46992 Office: 400 Ash St Wabash IN 46992 also Urbana Med Bldg Urbana IN 46990

DRAGOS, STEPHEN FRANCIS, redevelopment co. exec.; b. Chgo., Aug. 30, 1936; s. Stephen William and Philomena Genevieve (Cihlar) D.; B.Arch., U. Notre Dame, 1961; m. Donna Jean Polivka, June 24, 1961; children—Pamela, Stephen, Christian. Chief planner City Planning Assos., Inc., Mishawaka, Ind., 1960-63; sr. planner Candeub Fleissig Assos., N.Y.C., 1963-65; exec. dir. Valley Devel. Found., Binghamton, N.Y., 1968-73; gen. mgr. planning and design Mondey Ltd., Montreal, Que., Can., 1973-74; exec. v.p. Milw. Redevel. Corp., 1974—; adj. prof. U. Wis., Milw., 1975—; cons. in field.; mem. exec. council Urban Land Inst., Washington, 1972—; founder, chmn. Broome County Archtl. Adv. Commn., 1971-73; mem. Binghamton (N.Y.) Commn. Arch. Urban Design, 1967-73, chmn., 1971-73; sec. community advisory com., local partner Ely Park Housing, N.Y. State Urban Devel. Corp., 1969-71. Vice pres. Friends of Art, Milw., Art Center, 1975—; v.p. bd. govs. Roberson Center for Arts and Scis., Binghamton, 1972-73. Mem. Wis. Soc. Architects, AIA, Nat. Trust for Historic Preservation, Am. Soc. Planning Ofcls., Internat. Downtown Execs. Assn. Roman Catholic. Club: Univ. (Milw.). Home: 9570 N Lake Dr Bayside WI 53217 Office: 735 N Water St Milwaukee WI 53202

DRAISEY, HENRIETTA HELEN, realty co. exec.; b. Ethan, S.D., Aug. 18, 1918; d. James Arthur and Ellen Frances (Moore) Grady; student Notre Dame Jr. Coll., Mitchell, S.D., 1936, Mitchell Bus. Coll., 1936; m. Glenn Leo Draisey, June 4, 1947; children—Patrick James, Margaret Ann Draisey Schroeder. Sec. Mitchell Abstract Co., 1937-48; salesman Asmussen Real Estate Co., Mitchell, 1966-69; pres. Draisey Realty, Inc., Mitchell, 1969—; past pres. Mitchell Bd. Realtors. Mem. Housing and Redevel. Commn., City of Mitchell; vice chmn. Adjustment Tng. Center, Mitchell; mem. citizens adv. com. Brady Meml. Home, Mitchell; trustee Dakota Wesleyan U., Mitchell. Licensed real estate broker, S.D. Mem. Nat. Assn. Realtors, Mitchell C. of C., Am. Legion. Roman Catholic. Home: 413 E 2d Ave Mitchell SD 57301 Office: 220 E 5th Ave Mitchell SD 57301

DRAKE, DONALD ANSON, II, orthodontist; b. Mitchell, S.D., Mar. 13, 1948; s. Don A. and Barbara (Maurice) D.; B.A., U. of South Dakota, 1970; D.D.S., Loyola U., Maywood, Ill., 1974; M.S.D., St. Louis U., 1976; m. Cecelia E. Hearne, Apr. 15, 1968; children—Donald A. Drake, III, Courtland Michael Drake. Resident in orthodontics St. Louis U. Med. Center, (Mo.), 1974-76; gen. practice dentistry, Sioux Valley Hosp., (S.D.), 1976-77, McKennan Hosp., 1976-77. Advisory bd. Clift Palate, S.D., 1977; coach Little League, Sioux Falls, 1977. Recipient ROTC award, 1967. Mem. Am. Dental Assn., Am. Orthodontic Assn., Midwestern Soc. of Orthodontists, South Eastern S.D. Dental Soc., Orthodontic Research Found., Tweed Found., Polit. Sci. Club (sec., v.p.), Hipprocatis (v.p.), Delta Tau Delta, Xi Psi Phi (sec.), Omicron Kappa Upsilon, Blue Key. Episcopalian. Clubs: Elks, Rotary, Masons. Contbr. articles in field. Home: 2417 S 2d Ave Sioux Falls SD 57105 Office: 3307 S Lincoln St Sioux Falls SD 57105

DRAKE, FRANK MELVIN, civil engr.; b. Lyons, Kans., Nov. 23, 1912; s. Jacob Alfred and Olive May (Jones) D.; B.S., U. Kans., 1938; m. Mary Eleanor Erwin, June 25, 1939; children—Sherryn Schultz, Frank Marion, Dona Gene Gerhart. Inspector Kans. Hwy. Commn., Constrn. dept., 1938-57, asst. constrn. engr., 1957-63; dist. engr. The Asphalt Inst., Lenexa, Kans., 1963-65, regional engr., 1965—. Mem. Lyons Sch. Bd., 1955-57. Served to capt., USAAF, 1942-45. Mem. ASCE, Assn. Asphalt Paving Tech., Kans. Engr. Soc., Kans. Nat. Def. Exec. Res. Presbyn. (elder 1949-75). Home: 12904 Piccadilly St Apt 5 Lenexa KS 66215 Office: 13001 W 95th St Lenexa KS 66215

DRAKE, JUSTIN RIGGS, metall. engr., corporate materials research dir.; b. Sullivan, Ind., Nov. 14, 1921; s. Roy Calvin and Hazel (Riggs) D.; m. Helen Benedict, June 19, 1942; children—Justin, Philip Roy. B.S., in Metall. Engring., Purdue U., 1950. Foundry tech. Harrison Steel Casting Co., Attica, Ind., 1940-42; research metall. engr., metall. lab. Caterpillar Tractor Co., Peoria, Ill., 1950-55, research supr., 1955-60, project leader, 1961-65; mgr. metall. research Cummins Engine Co., Columbus, Ind., 1966-72, dir. materials research, 1973—. Pres. P.T.A., Morton, Ill., 1963-64; trustee Meth. ch., Morton, 1963-65; Republican precinct committeeman, 1973-77. Mem. Am. Soc. Metals (Indpls. exec. com. 1975-77). Author tech. papers in field.

DRAKE, ROBERT TUCKER, lawyer; b. Wilmette, Ill., Feb. 16, 1907; s. Lyman M. and Jennie (Keith) D.; A.B., Dartmouth Coll., 1929; LL.B., Columbia, 1934; m. Martha B. Swan, Sept. 14, 1929; children—Janet D. (Mrs. Robert H. Morris), Helen (Mrs. John E. Sanford). Admitted to N.Y. bar, 1934, D.C. bar, 1935, Ill. bar, 1937; atty. NLRB, 1942-47; partner Foss, Schuman & Drake, 1960—; dir. Wilmette Bank, 1970-77, Bank of North Shore, Northbrook, Ill., 1976—; asso. prof. law U. Idaho, 1947-49; labor arbitrator Fed. Mediation and Conciliation Service-Am. Arbitration Assn., 1950—. Chmn. Ill. div. ACLU, 1954-57, Ind. Voters of Ill., 1965-67; bd. dirs. Sierra Club Legal Def. Fund, 1977—, Fund for Justice, 1975—. Mem. UN Assn. (dir. Ill. div.). Home: 1225 Whitebridge Ln Winnetka IL 60093 Office: 11 S LaSalle St Chicago IL 60603

DRANE, WALTER HARDING, publisher; b. Clarksville, Tenn., Feb. 18, 1915; s. William McClure and Mary Stacker (Luckett) D.; A.B., U. of South, 1935; postgrad. bus. Case Western Res. U., 1936-38; m. Maud Carson Tucker, Aug. 30, 1941; children—Eleanor Drane Christensen, Roberta Drane Siegler, Walter Harding, Beverley Drane Coughlin. Pres. Banks-Baldwin Law Pub. Co., Cleve., 1960—, also dir.; founder, pres. Walter H. Drane Co. municipal code compilers and pubs., Cleve., 1955—, chmn., 1960-76. Bd. dirs. Univ. Circle Br. YMCA, Cleve., 1958-69. Served with USN, 1940-45. Episcopalian. Home: 2312 Delamere Dr Cleveland Heights OH 44106 Office: 1904 Ansel Rd Cleveland OH 44106

DRANNAN, WALTER THEODORE, grain co. exec.; b. St. Joseph, Mo., Oct. 4, 1922; s. James and Elizabeth (Sauer) D.; B.A. in Art, Mo. Western Coll., 1977; student Heatherly Sch. (London, Eng.), 1969, Academie de La Grande Chauniere (Paris, France), 1971; m. Martha Jane Neudorff, Aug. 7, 1942 (div. Oct. 1964); children—James A., Martha (Mrs. Rudy J. Clark), John A., Thomas G., Daniel W.; m. 2d, Marilyn L. Parks, May 17, 1974. Traffic mgr., grain buyer Russell Miller Milling Co., St. Joseph, 1950-52; partner W.S. Geiger Grain Commn. Co., St. Joseph, 1952-54; traffic mgr. Schreiber Mills, Inc., St. Joseph, 1954-59; v.p. traffic Crouch Bros., Inc., St. Joseph, 1959-64; exec. sec. St. Joseph Grain Exchange, 1964—; pres., chmn. bd. Bi-State Transfer, Inc., St. Louis, 1964-71. Tchr. adult edn. Hillyard Tech. Sch., St. Joseph, 1962-70; design artist Icarus jour., St. Joseph, 1972-75; columnist Livestock Jour. newspaper, 1967-69; broadcaster grain market broadcasts sta. KFEQ, St. Joseph, 1964—. Served with AUS, 1942-45; ETO. Decorated Bronze Star; notary pub. Mem. St. Joseph Traffic Club (bd. dirs.), Am. Soc. Traffic and Transp. (treas. Mo. chpt.), Am. Artists Profl. League, VFW, Am. Legion, Delta Nu Alpha. Artist; represented numerous permanent collections, U.S., Italy, Eng. Home: 633 N 20th St St Joseph MO 64501 Office: 1404 Corby Bldg St Joseph MO 64501

DRAZKOWSKI, FRANK ANTHONY, hosp. adminstr.; b. Ironwood, Mich., Feb. 13, 1921; s. Frank Anthony and Bonita Loretta (Orchowski) D.; grad. high sch.; certificate corr. course Internat. Accountants Soc., 1948; Kellogg Found. scholar, 1950-53; certificate instnl. mgmt. course VA, 1952; m. Edith M. Paull, Feb. 4, 1942; children—Janice, Bernadine (Mrs. Matt Rouker), Jerry. Sales rep. Mich.-Wis. Beverage Corp., Bessemer, Mich., 1939-42; agt. N.Y. Life Ins. Co., Ironwood, Mich., 1945-47; city clk. City Bessemer (Mich.), 1947-50; laborer Pickands-Maher Mining Co., Bessemer, 1950; asso. adminstr. Grand View Hosp., Ironwood, 1950-52, exec. dir., 1952—. Mem., chmn. numerous coms. Upper Peninsula Hosp. Council, 1950—, sec., 1956-57, v.p., 1957-58, pres., 1958-59; mem., chmn. several coms. Western Upper Peninsula Health Council, 1969—, v.p., 1970-72, exec. bd., 1970—; mem. Dist. VI hosp. relations com. Blue Cross Mich., 1961—, chmn. dist. VI hosp. relations com., 1962-64, 68-72, mem. state hosp. relations com., 1962-64, 68—, trustee, 1964-67, 72—. Trustee Tri-State Hosp. Assembly, 1971—, sec., 1973—; trustee Mich. Health Planning Adv. Council, 1971—; bd. dirs. Upper Peninsula Areawide Comprehensive Health Planning Assn., 1970—, mem. exec. com., 1970-72, mem. health information and edn. com., 1972—. Served to 1st. lt. inf. AUS, 1942-45. Decorated Silver Star medal with oak leaf cluster, Bronze Star medal; recipient award of merit Tri-State Hosp. Assembly, 1975. Mem. Am. Coll. Hosp. Adminstrs., Am. (ho. of dels. 1972—), Mich. (com. numerous coms.; trustee 1963-69, 71-74, pres. 1972-73; numerous other coms.) hosp. assns., Am. Legion, V.F.W. K.C., Elk. Home: Box 708 US 2 Ironwood MI 49938

DRENIK, DOUGLAS JAY, flooring co. exec.; b. Cleve., May 6, 1943; s. Felix and Rose (Kranz) D.; B.S., Ohio State U., 1961; m. Bonnie Michel, Sept. 24, 1966; children—Douglas Jay, Jason Patrick. With Foster & Kleiser Outdoor Advt. Co., Cleve., 1966-68; salesman recreation and athletic products Minn. Mining & Mfg. Co., Cin., 1968-69, Cleve., 1969-70; with Cin. Floor Co., Cin., 1970-73, v.p., Indpls., 1973—. Mem. Constrn. Specifications Inst. Home: Rural Route 3 Box 36 Greenfield IN 46140 Office: 2555 E 55th Pl Indianapolis IN 46220

DRENNER, DON VON RUYSDAEL, poet, ret. librarian; b. Mound Valley, Kans., Nov. 17, 1915; s. Robert Samples and Freda Pearl (Christy) D.; student Parsons Jr. Coll., 1933-35; U. Kans., 1935-36, RAF Sch., 1941-42, BBC Engring. Sch., 1943, Cambridge, 1943-44; m. Anna Augusta Davenport, Jan. 24, 1945; children—Ann Leora (Mrs. Larry Don Murrow), Elizabeth Katherine (Mrs. Vincent P. De Sandro). Profl. radio engr. Midwest Broadcasting Co., Coffeyville, Kans., 1938-45, 45-59, librarian, 1961-77; ret., 1977; head librarian Carnegie Pub. Library, Coffeyville, 1959-77; systems engr., librarian S.E. Kans. Library System; communications engr. City Coffeyville, 1957-68; biomed. cons. engr. Coffeyville Meml. Hosp., 1970—. Served with RAF, 1941-43, psychol. warfare div., SHAEF, 1943-45. Mem. Am., Kans. library assns. Author: The Vault of Night, 1951; Text Book on Radio, 1958; Letter to Sheila Ann, 1945; Usage of The Past, 1954; Anna. Anna!, 1955; Faustus, 1957; Concerning Kansas, 1958; Fibril, 1960; Graphics of Love, 1961; The Anna Book, 1964. Contbr. articles to profl. jours. Home: 503 Highland Rd Coffeyville KS 67337

DRESNER, SAMUEL HAYIM, rabbi; b. Chgo., Nov. 7, 1923; s. Julius and Maude (Handmacher) D.; B.A., U. Cin., 1945; rabbi, Jewish Theol. Sem., 1951; D.H.L., 1954; m. Ruth Rapp, June 17, 1951; children—Hannah, Miriam, Nehama, Rachel. Dir., Hillel Found., Coll. City N.Y., 1951-54; asso. rabbi Har Zion Temple, Phila., 1954-57; rabbi Beth El Congregation, Springfield, Mass., 1957-69, North Suburban Synagogue Beth El, Highland Park, Ill., 1969-77, Moriah Congregation, Deerfield, Ill., 1977—. Adj. prof. Spertus Coll. Judaica, Chgo., 1977. Chmn., Springfield Human Relations Commn., 1963-65. Chmn. Synagogue Council Am. on Jewish Community Center, 1963-67. Scholar in residence Brandeis Inst., summer 1973. Author: Prayer Humility and Compassion, 1957; Jewish Dietary Laws, 1959; Three Paths of God and Man, 1960; The Zaddik, 1960; The Jew in American Life, 1963; God, Man and Atomic War, 1966; The Sabbath, 1970; Between the Generations, 1971; Levi Yitzhak, 1974; Agenda for American Jews: Federation and Synagogue, 1976. Editor: Conservative Judaism, 1955-64. Home: 115 Eastwood Dr Deerfield IL 60015 Office: 200 Hyacinth Ln Deerfield IL 60015

DREVENSTEDT, JEAN, psychologist; b. Louisville, July 13, 1927; d. Eduard A. and Suretta (Redmon) Drevenstedt; B.S. with distinction, Ind. U., 1949; Ph.D., Vanderbilt U., 1965. With prodn. dept. Zimmer-McClaskey-Lewis Advt. Agy., Louisville, 1949-58; USPHS fellow dept. psychiatry and neurology Northwestern U. Med. Sch., Chgo., 1962-63; psychologist Children's Asthma Research Inst. and Hosp., Denver, 1964-65; clin. psychologist, asst. prof. Ohio U., Athens, 1965-71, asso. prof., 1971—. Mem. Am., Midwest, Ohio psychol. assns., AAAS, Mortar Bd., Sigma Xi, Beta Gamma Sigma, Alpha Omicron Pi. Republican. Presbyn. Contbr. articles to profl. jours. Home: 1 Monticello Dr Apt 102 Athens OH 45701 Office: Psychology Dept Ohio Univ Athens OH 45701

DREWES, MENKE, govt. scientist; b. Hannover, Germany, Mar. 27, 1912; s. Menke and Anna (Brammer) D.; B.S., U. Hannover, 1931, M.S., 1933, Dr. Engring., 1955; m. Ann Wibmer, Dec. 21, 1943. Came to U.S., 1933, naturalized, 1938. Operating engr. Standard Oil N.Y., Buffalo, 1938-41; devel. and design engr. Internat. Harvester Co., Chgo., 1945-48; dir. engring. Payswell Products, Chgo., 1948-54; asso. dir. air conditioning devel. Crane Co., Chgo., 1954-58; mgr. devel. and projects Space Tech. div. Guardite Co., Wheeling, Ill., 1958; mem. staff engring. devel. and products Newman-Green; mem. staff Gov.'s office Sci. and Tech., Springfield, Ill., 1970—. Trustee Bateman Sch., Chgo. Mem. Am. Vacuum Soc. Republican. Mason (Shriner); mem. Order Eastern Star (past grand patron). Home: 470 St Moritz Dr Glen Ellyn IL 60137

DREWS, HERBERT RICHARD, retail co. exec.; b. Mpls., May 3, 1924; s. Herbert H. and Zola (Howard) D.; B.S., U. Minn., 1948, J.D., 1950; m. Marlys Corinne Olson, Apr. 10, 1952; children—Pamela Kay, Richard Earl. Admitted to Minn. bar, 1950; spl. agt. FBI, N.Y.C., 1950-52; atty., Walgreens, Chgo., 1952-56, asst. dir. employee relations, 1956-59, dir. employee relations, 1959-69, v.p. human resources, 1969—. Mem. adv. com. Coll. Commerce and Bus. Adminstrn., U. Ill. at Urbana, 1973—. Served with USAAF, 1943-46. Mem. Am. Mgmt. Assn. (human resources council), Ill. C. of C., Nat. Restaurant Assn., Phi Delta Theta, Phi Delta Phi. Republican. Lutheran. Rotarian. Club: Economic (Chgo.). Home: 62 Fox Trail Lincolnshire IL 60015 Office: 200 Wilmot Rd Deerfield IL 60015

DREWS, ROBERT CARREL, physician; b. St. Louis, Sept. 9, 1930; s. Leslie Charles and Sally (Carrel) D.; A.B., Washington U., 1952, M.D., 1955; m. Lorene Ruth Loewenguth, June 12, 1951; children—Pamela, Belinda, Carl, Jeanmarie. Intern, St. Luke's Hosp., St. Louis, 1955-56; resident McMillan Hosp., St. Louis, 1956-59; practice medicine specializing in ophthalmology, St. Louis, 1961—; mem. staff Barnes Hosp. Group, Bethesda Gen., St. Luke's, St. Mary's, St. Louis County, St. Louis Children's hosps. (all St. Louis); lectr. ophthalmology Sch. Medicine, Washington U., St. Louis, 1956-66, asst. prof., 1966-73, asso. prof., 1973—; vis. prof. U. P.R., San Juan, 1970-71, U. Fla., Gainsville, 1973, U. Mich., Ann Arbor, 1974, U. Tex., San Antonio, Southwestern Med. Sch., Dallas, Downstate U. N.Y., N.Y.C., McGill U.; cons. Faith, Frisco Employees hosps., both St. Louis, Spl. Sch. Dist. St. Louis County, 1967—; supervising ophthalmologist Mo. Div. Welfare, 1963—. Chmn. computer tng. div. com. profl. activities blind Washington U., 1965-72; mem. adv. council medicine St. Louis Lions, 1966—. Bd. dirs. Pan. Am. Assn. Opthalmology Found., Bethesda Gen. Hosp., St. Louis Soc. Blind, Eye Research Found., Columbia; mem. alumni bd. govs. Washington U., 1971—. Served to lt. comdr., M.C., USNR, 1959-61. Diplomate Nat. Bd. Med. Examiners, Am. Bd. Ophthalmology. Fellow Am. Acad. Ophthalmology, A.C.S.; mem. St. Louis (pres. 1971-72), Mo. (pres. 1971-72) ophthal. socs., St. Louis (mem. speakers bur. com. 1967-75), Mo. med. socs., Mo. Assn. Ophthalmology (pres.), Assn. Research Ophthalmology, Assn. Mil. Surgeons, So. Med. Assn. (pres. ophthalmology sect.), Am. Intra-Ocular Implant Soc. (pres.), Mil. Ophthalmologists Soc., AMA, Optical Soc. Am., Washington U. Med. Sch. Alumni Assn. (exec. council 1965-71, 77—), Washington U. Alumni Fedn. (exec. council 1965-71), Internat. Assn. Prevention Blindness (exec. com. 1974). Author books, numerous articles. Home: 7361 Cornell Ave University City MO 63130 Office: 211 N Meramec Ave Clayton MO 63105

DREWS, ROBERT SEYMOUR, psychiatrist; b. Bklyn., Dec. 25, 1900; s. Jacob and Ida (Singer) D.; B.M., Wayne State U., 1925, M.D., 1926; M.D., U. Mich., 1935, D.P.H., 1938; postgrad. Johns Hopkins Inst. Med. History, Temple U., Psychiat. Inst. Columbia, Wayne County Gen. Hosp.; m. Josephine Sandorf; 1 dau., Sonia. Extern, Receiving Hosp., 1924-25; intern Western Pa. Hosp., 1925-26; pvt. practice, gen. medicine, 1926-46, psychiatry, 1946—; psychiat. cons. Rayswift Gables; asso. dir. Inst. for Group Psychotherapy and Psychodrama, N.Y.C., 1954—; dir. group psychotherapy St. Philip Neri Church; psychiat. lectr. Parents Without Partners Met. Detroit; spl. lectr. Hillsdale Coll.; con. psychiatrist Juvenile Ct., Ferndale, Mich.; dir. group psychotherapy St. Philip and St. David chs. Vice chmn. sect. on psychodrama Internat. Congress of Psychotherapy, Barcelona, 1958. Founder, pres., dir. Mich. Inst. of Psychodrama. Recipient Charles Burlingame award Am. Soc. Social Psychiatry, 1960. Founding fellow Acad. Psychosomatic Medicine; fellow Royal Soc. Health (London, Eng.), Am. Geriatric Soc., Am. Soc. for Group Psychotherapy and Psychodrama (pres. 1959; Am. del. to Internat. Congress of Group Psychodrama, Zurich, 1957, Paris, 1960), Am. Assn. Advancement Psychotherapy, Am. Sociol. Soc.; mem. Am. Acad. Psychotherapy, Assn. Physicians and Surgeons, Am. Psychiat. Assn., Am. Psychosomatic Soc., Mich. Soc. for Group Psychotherapy and Psychodrama (pres. 1958-59, 1961), Internat. Council Group Psychotherapy, Am. Assn. Group Psychotherapy, Am. Soc. Clin. Research in Hypnosis, AAAS, Am. Ontoanalytic Soc. (co-founder), Am. Inst. Archeology, Detroit Philos. Soc. (sec. 1956, dir., pres. elect 1970), Am. Assn. for UN (bd. govs.), Internat. Soc. Gen. Semantics (pres. Detroit br. 1955), Internat. Platform Assn., Phi Delta Epsilon. Clubs: Bohemian, Fact Finders, International Date Line, Cornelian Corner. Contbg. editor Group Psychotherapy. Address: 16300 W Nine Mile Rd Charterhouse Route 111 Southfield MI 48071

DREYFUS, LEE SHERMAN, univ. chancellor; b. Milw., June 20, 1926; s. Woods Orlo and Claire (Bluett) D.; B.A., U. Wis., 1949, M.A., 1952, Ph.D., 1957; m. Joyce Mae Unke, Apr. 5, 1947; children—Susan Lynn, Lee Sherman. Radio actor sta. WISN, Milw., 1933-49; instr. U. Wis., 1949-52; gen. mgr. radio sta. WDET, Detroit, 1952-56; asst. prof. speech Wayne State U., 1956-60, asso. prof. speech, asso. dir. mass communications, 1960-62; gen. mgr. sta. WHA-TV, Madison, Wis., 1962-65; dir. instructional resources U. Wis., 1965-67, prof. speech, chmn. radio-TV and films, 1962-67; chancellor U. Wis., Stevens Point, 1967—; cons. in field. Chmn. Army adv. panel on R.O.T.C. affairs, 1969-73; chmn. Gov.'s Blue Ribbon Commn. on cable TV, 1971; ednl. cons. to sec. defense and sec. Army; chief mission under Vietnam contract for Higher Edn., U. Wis., Stevens Point Found. Inc.; dir. Sentry Broadcasting Corp. Bd. dirs. Am. Assn. State Colls. and Univs., del. to Poland, 1973, Peoples Republic China, 1975, Taiwan, 1976. Bd. dirs. Wis. Ballet Co., Birmingham (Mich.) Young People's Theatre, St. Michael's Hosp., Stevens Point, Sentry Found. Served with USNR, 1944-46. Recipient citation for mental health Gov. Mich.; Pres.'s medallions Assn. U.S. Army, 1973, 74. Mem. Nat. Assn. Ednl. Broadcasters (dir.), Speech Assn. Am. (chmn. radio-TV film com.), Broadcast Pioneers Am., N.O.R.A.D. (hon.), Phi Beta Kappa, Phi Eta Sigma, Phi Kappa Phi, Kappa Sigma, Phi Tau Phi. Episcopalian. Mason. Author: Televised Instruction, 1962; World's First Intercontinental Video Classroom Connection via Earlybird Satellite, 1965. Home: 408 W Maple Ridge Dr Stevens Point WI 54481

DREYFUSS, MARK STEVEN, microbiologist; b. Dayton, Ohio, July 21, 1952; s. Arnold Howard and Lenore Ruth (Schulman) D.; B.S., Ohio State U., 1973, M.S., 1978; m. Linda Nan Brucker, Sept. 9, 1973. Research asst. dept. poultry sci. Ohio State U. and Ohio Agrl. Research and Devel. Center, Columbus, 1974—, also tchr. lab. class in poultry microbiology, Grad. Sch. rep. Univ. Senate, 1976-77. Active Boy Scouts Am., Troop 192 in N.J., 1964-70. Mem. Am. Soc. Microbiology, Phi Tau Sigma. Office: 674 W Lane Ave Columbus OH 43210

DREZDZON, WILLIAM LAWRENCE, educator; b. Milw., Feb. 19, 1934; s. Edward Kenneth and Mildred Mary (Schneider) D.; B.S. in Math., St. Mary's U., 1957; M.S. in Math. (Esso Oil Co. fellow), Ill. Inst. Tech., 1964; m. Elaine Marie Dal Santo, Nov. 21, 1959; children—Gregory Francis, Andrea Louise. Tchr. math., chemistry, St. Michael's High Sch., Chgo., 1957-59, Lane Tech. High Sch., Chgo., 1959-66; software design engr. A.C. Electronics div. Gen. Motors, Oak Creek, Wis., 1966-67; prof. math., chmn. dept. Kennedy-King Coll., Chgo., 1967-71; prof. math. and learning lab. coordinator Oakton Community Coll., Morton Grove, Ill., 1971—; cons. nat. calculus survey, 1975. NSF grantee, 1961-65; Chgo. Bd. Edn. grantee, summer 1964; NSF coop. program, 1971, 72; Chautauqua Course grantee, 1975—. Mem. Math. Assn. Am. (chmn. jr. coll. com. Ill. Sect., 1971-74), No. Ill. Math. Assn. Community Colls. (founding pres., 1971, 72), Am. Math. Assn. Two-Yr. Colls. (chmn., 1975), Nat., Ill. Councils Tchrs. of Mathematics, Met. Mathematics Club of Gtr. Chgo., Ill. Math Assn. Community Colls., Adler Planetarium Soc., Ill. Assn. Personalized Learning Programs, Analytic Psychology Club of Chgo., Delta Epsilon Sigma. Regional editor Math. Assns. of Two-Year Colleges Jour., 1970—; author: Curriculum Guide of Transfer Courses for the Ill. Community College Board, 1974; Math. Research and Teaching Techniques, 1973, 76; contbr. articles td jours. Home: 1006 N Lombard Ave Oak Park IL 60302 Office: 7900 N Nagle St Morton Grove IL 60053

DRICHTA, CARL E., univ. adminstr.; b. Milw., Oct. 30, 1948; s. Erwin A. and Florence M. (Kleczka) D.; B.A. in Psychology, U. Wis., 1971; M.A. in Clin.-Exptl. Psychology, Wichita State U., 1973, Ph.D. in Speech Pathology (Univ. fellow), 1976. Instr., grad. asst. in psychology Wichita State U., 1971-73, mem. grad. faculty, 1974, 75; instr. Kans. Newman Coll., 1973; speech and lang. pathologist, early environment enrichment program Inst. Logopedics, Wichita, Kans., 1975, speech and lang. pathologist, 1975-76; project coordinator, dir. U. Wis.-Milw. Sch. Allied Health Professions, 1976—. Mem. Am. (certificate of clin. competence in speech pathology), Wis., Kans. speech and hearing assns., Am., Midwestern, Southwestern psychol. assns., Council Exceptional Children, Am. Soc. Allied Health, Psi Chi. Mng. editor Allied Health and Behavioral Scis., 1976—. Home: 3001 S Howell Ave Milwaukee WI 53207 Office: Sch Allied Health Professions U Wis Milwaukee WI 53201

DRISCOLL, DANIEL DELANO, photographer; b. Williamsburg, Iowa, Mar. 19, 1946; s. Vincent Edmund and Hilda Gertrude (Schmidt) D.; student U. Iowa, 1964-66; B.A., Loras Coll., 1969; student Winona Sch. Profl. Photography, summers 1969-71: m. Constance Elizabeth Kelleher, Feb. 28, 1970; children—Duree Danielle, Darren Daniel. With Hilda's Photography, Williamsburg, Ia., 1969-72; owner Driscoll Gallery, Williamsburg, 1973—, Kent Studio, Iowa City, 1975-76. Named Iowa Photographer of Year, 1975, 76, 77; Iowa fellow of photography, 1975; named Heart of Am. Photographer, 1976, 77; recipient Frank W. Medlar Meml. trophy for best portrait, 1975, 76, 77. Mem. Minn. (sweepstakes winner 1973, 74), Neb. (photographer of year 1974), Pa. (top out of state photographer 1974), Va., Am. (Master of Photography degree 1977) profl. photographers assns. Contbr. articles to profl. jours. Home: 302 W State St Williamsburg IA 52361 Office: 521 Court St Williamsburg IA 52361

DRISCOLL, GLEN ROBERT, univ. pres.; b. Sligo, O., Apr. 29, 1920; s. William Arthur and Jennie Mabel (Smith) D.; student DePauw U., 1938-41; B.A., U. Louisville, 1947, L.L.D., 1973; M.A., U. Minn., 1949, Ph.D., 1952; m. Dorothy June Little, Nov. 9, 1941; children—David Arthur, Robert Earl, Nancy Lee (Mrs. Russell Husted). Instr. history U. S.D., Vermillion, 1949-52, asst. prof., 1952-56, prof., 1956-64; prof. history, chmn. div. social scis. U. Mo., St. Louis, 1964-65, dean Coll. Arts and Scis., 1965-68, dean faculties, 1968-69, chancellor, 1969-72; pres. U. Toledo, 1972—. NSF lectr. U. Neb., U. Tex.; dir. WGTE-TV, Toledo, First Nat. Bank, Toledo. Mem. Woodrow Wilson Found. Regional Bd., 1969-72; bd. dirs. Toledo Symphony Orch. Assn.; trustee Boys Club Toledo. Served with USAAF, 1942-46. Mem. Am. Hist. Assn., A.A.U.P., Am. Council Edn. (com. on urban affairs), Ohio Acad. Scis., Societe d'Histoire Moderne, Soc. French Hist. Studies, Am. Assn. Higher Edn., Toledo Area C. of C., Phi Alpha Theta, Delta Chi. Methodist. Clubs: Toledo Press, Belmont Country. Home: 3425 W Bancroft St Toledo OH 43606

DRISCOLL, ROBERT THOMAS, radio network co. exec.; b. Tyler, Minn., Aug. 17, 1943; s. Thomas and Margery Pearl (Polesky) D.; 1st Class License, Brown Inst. Broadcasting & Electronics, 1964; m. Jeanette Darleen Bednaryczk, May 29, 1965; children—Patrick Thomas, Nicole Marie. Engr., announcer Sta. WLEW, Bad Axe, Mich., 1964-65; production mgr. Sta. WBCM, Bay City, Mich., 1965-67; field rep., adminstrv. supr. Mich. Farm Bureau, Lansing, 1967-69, mgr. press relations, 1969-74; co-owner, gen. mgr. Great Lakes Radio Network, Milan, Mich., 1974—; broadcast cons., mktg.-advt. cons. Mem. Nat. Assn. Farm Broadcasters, Mich. Assn. Broadcasters, Nat. Assn. Agrl. Marketers. Developer mktg. concept for advt. sales. Home: 13281 Dennison Rd Milan MI 48160 Office: 231 Hurd St Milan MI 48160

DRISCOLL, THOMAS FRANK, editor; b. Chgo., June 16, 1925; s. Edward Joseph and Helen (Brozicek) D.; B.S. in Journalism, Northwestern U., 1948, M.S., 1949; m. Margaret Mae Wagner, Dec. 28, 1946; children—Carol, Paul, David, Jane, Peter, Mary Anne, Joseph, Elizabeth, Daniel, Ellen. Reporter Peoria Jour. Star 1949-54, asst. city editor, 1954-56, city editor, 1956-70, asst. mng. editor, 1970-73; mng. editor, 1973—. Served with USNR, 1943-45. Roman Catholic. Contbr. articles in field to profl. jours. Home: 222 S Menard St Metamora IL 61548 Office: War Memorial Dr Peoria IL 61601

DRISKELL, CLAUDE EVANS, dentist; b. Chgo., Jan. 13, 1926; s. James Ernest and Helen Elizabeth (Perry) D., Sr.; B.S., Roosevelt U., 1950; B.S. in Dentistry, U. Ill., 1952, D.D.S., 1954; m. Naomi Roberts, Sept. 30, 1953; 1 dau., Yvette Michele; stepchildren—Isaiah, Ruth, Reginald, Elaine. Practice dentistry, Chgo., 1954—. Adj. prof. Chgo. State U., 1971—; dean's aide, adviser black students Coll. Dentistry U. Ill., 1972—; dental cons., supervising dentist, dental hygienists supportive health services Bd. Edn., Chgo., 1974. Vice pres. bd. dirs. Jackson Park Highlands Assn., 1971-73. Served with AUS, 1944-46; ETO. Fellow Internat. Biog. Assn., Royal Soc. Health (Gt. Britain), Acad. Gen. Dentistry; mem. Lincoln (editor), Chgo. dental socs., Am., Nat. (editor pres.'s newsletter; dir. pub. relations, publicity; recipient pres.'s spl. achievement award 1969) dental assns., Am. Assn. Dental Editors, Acad. Gen. Dentistry, Soc. Med. Writers, Soc. Advancement Anesthesia in Dentistry, Omega Psi Phi. Author: The Influence of the Halogen Elements upon the Hydrocarbon, and their Effect on General Anesthesia, 1962. Asst. editor Nat. Dental Assn. Quar. Jour., 1977—. Contbr. articles to profl. jours. Home: 6727 S Bennett Ave Chicago IL 60649 Office: 11139 S Halsted St Chicago IL 60628

DROEGEMUELLER, ARTHUR CLARENCE, pub. accountant; b. Chgo., June 6, 1904; s. William A. and Ida W. (Lannefeld) D.; Ph.B., U. Chgo., 1925; C.P.A., U. Ill., 1930; m. Katherine H. Meyer, Nov. 19, 1927 (div.); children—Joan Louise (Mrs. Richard J. Wilke), Katherine Ellen (Mrs. R. Thomas Saether); m. 2d, Marjorie Adams Aldrich, 1954; 1 stepson, Frederick B. Aldrich. Pub. accountant, 1923—; with Frazer and Torbet, C.P.A.'s, 1930-54, partner, 1941-54; sr. partner Droegemueller, Brady & Nelson, C.P.A.'s, 1955-56; partner Main & Co., C.P.A.'s, 1956-63, Main Lafrentz & Co., C.P.A.'s, 1963-65; individual practice, 1965—; treas. Eppi Precision Products, Inc., 1968-76. Treas. Chgo. Luth. Theol. Sem., 1939-60; mem. bd. mgmt. Onward Neighborhood House, pres., 1950-51. C.P.A., Ill., Tex., Wis. Mem. Am. Inst. C.P.A.'s, Ill. Soc. C.P.A.'s (sec.-treas. 1946-48), Phi Pi Phi (nat. treas. 1933-39), Alpha Sigma Phi. Lutheran. Club: Union League. Home: 309 Tanglewood Ln Naperville IL 60540 Office: Suite 1400 100 W Monroe St Chicago IL 60603

DRONEK, LAWRENCE GERARD, mfg. co. exec.; b. South Milwaukee, Wis., Feb. 4, 1951; s. Chester Thomas and Eugenia Ann (Behr) D.; B.A., Dominican Coll. Racine, 1973; m. Lori Ellen Peterka, Jan. 19, 1974. Graphic designer, photographer, writer Shoreline Leader, Racine, Wis., 1973-74; mng. editor S. Milw. Voice Jour./Cudahy-St. Francis Free Press, S. Milwaukee, 1974; advt. and pub. relations asst. NCR Appleton (Wis.) Papers, 1974-76; sales promotion asst. Wacker Corp., Milw., 1976-77; mktg. communications mgr. Utility Products Co., Milw., 1977—. Home: 514 Brookdale Ct South Milwaukee WI 53172 Office: 6565 N 60th St Milwaukee WI 53223

DROTNING, PHILLIP THOMAS, oil co. exec.; b. Deerfield, Wis., July 4, 1920; s. Edward Clarence and Martha (Skaar) D.; student U. Wis., 1937-41; m. Loretta Jayne Taylor, Nov. 3, 1964; children—Meredith Anne, Maria Kristina, Misya Kerri. Reporter, Wis. State Jour., Madison, 1943-44; editorial page writer Milw. Jour., 1944-45; freelance author, 1945-47; exec. sec. to gov., Wis., 1948-55; v.p. Northwest Airlines, Inc., 1956-61; spl. asst. to adminstr. NASA, Washington, 1961-65; exec. communications cons. Standard Oil Co. (Ind.), 1965-66; mgr. communications Am. Oil Co., Chgo., 1967-68; dir. urban affairs Standard Oil Co. of Ind., Chgo., 1968-72, dir. pub. affairs ops., 1973, dir. corporate social policy, 1973—. Dir. Highland Community Bank, Chgo., 1973—, Council Population and Environment, 1973—. Bd. dirs., first v.p. Child Care Assn. Ill., 1973-76, pres., 1976—. Served with USMCR, 1941-43. Mem. Pub. Relations Soc. Am., Nat. Assn. Mfrs. (chmn. urban affairs com. 1969-71), Nat. Minority Purchasing Council (pres. 1972—). Clubs: National Press, International, Federal City (Washington); Lake Forest (Ill.); Plaza (Chgo.). Author: A Guide to Negro History in America, 1968; Black Heroes in our Nation's History, 1969; A Job with a Future in the Petroleum Industry, 1969; Up from the Ghetto, 1970; New Hope for Problem Drinkers, 1977; Taking Stock: A Woman's Guide to Corporate Success, 1977. Editorial advisory bd. The Chicago Reporter, 1971—; contbr. numerous articles to pubs. Home: 400 N Washington Rd Lake Forest IL 60045 Office: 200 E Randolph Dr Chicago IL 60601

DROUBIE, GEORGE BARAKAT, state edn. adminstr.; b. St. Paul, Dec. 1, 1935; s. George and Marie (Bab) D.; B.S., U. Minn., 1958, B.S. in Elementary Edn., 1961, M.A. in Ednl. Adminstrn., 1959, Ed.D. in Ednl. Adminstrn., 1972; m. JoAnne Carol Capeti, July 25, 1959; children—Karen, Alan, Michael. Elementary tchr., Nekoosa, Wis., 1959-61, Wayzata, Minn., 1961-67; dir. tchr. licensing and placement Minn. Edn. Dept., St. Paul, 1967—. Mem. NEA, Minn., Wayzata (pres. 1966-67) edn. assns., Minn. Assn. Sch. Personnel Adminstrs., Minn. Instl. Tchr. Placement Assn., Nat. Assn. State Dirs. Tchr. Edn. and Certification, Toastmasters Internat. (treas.). Mem. Syrian Orthodox Ch. (pres.). Home: 55 Langer Circle West St Paul MN 55118 Office: Edn Dept Capitol Sq St Paul MN 55101

DRUCKER, DANIEL CHARLES, univ. dean; b. N.Y.C., June 3, 1918; s. Moses Abraham and Henrietta (Weinstein) D.; B.S., Columbia, 1937, C.E., 1938, Ph.D., 1940 (Illig medal); m. Ann Bodin, Aug. 19, 1939; children—R. David, Mady Drucker Upham. Instr. Cornell U., 1940-43; supvr. Armour Research Found., Chgo., 1943-45; asst. prof. Ill. Tech., 1946-47; asso. prof. Brown U., Providence, 1947-50, prof., 1950-64, L. Herbert Ballou University prof., 1964-68, chmn. div. engring., 1953-59, chmn. phys. scis. council, 1961-63; dean Coll. Engring. U. Ill., Urbana, 1968—. Engring. cons. in theoretical and expt. applied mechanics; mem. U.S. Nat. Com. on Theoretical and Applied Mechanics; treas. Internat. Union Theoretical and Applied Mechanics; Marburg lectr. Am. Soc. Testing Materials, 1966; mem. Materials Research Council, 1969—; chmn. NSF Adv. Com. Engring., 1969-70; mem. ship research com. NRC. Guggenheim fellow, 1960-61; recipient von Karman medal ASCE, 1966, Lamme award Am. Soc. Engring. Education, 1967, NATO Sr. Sci. fellowship, 1968, Fulbright award, 1968. Fellow ASME (past pres.), Am. Acad. of Arts and Scis., Am. Acad. Mechanics (past pres.), Institute Aeros. Astronautics (asso. fellow), ASCE (past chmn. exec. com. engring. mechanics div.); mem. Nat. Soc. Profl. Engrs., Soc. Exptl. Stress Analysis (past pres., Murray lectr. 1967, M.M. Frocht award 1971, hon. chmn. 3d Internat. Congress Exptl. Mechanics), Am. Technion Soc. (past pres. So. N.E. chpt.), Soc. for Rheology, Am. Soc. for Engring. Edn. (past 1st v.p., past chmn. engring. coll. council), Western Soc. Engrs., Nat. Acad. Engring., Sigma Xi (past pres. Brown U. chpt.), Tau Beta Pi, Pi Tau Sigma, Phi Kappa Phi, Sigma Tau. Club: Cosmos. Author: Introduction to Mechanics of Deformable Solids, 1967. Past tech. editor Jour. Applied Mechanics. Contbr. chpts. in tech. books; also tech. papers mech. and sci. jours. Office: U Ill Urbana IL 61801

DRUKKER, BRUCE HIGHSTONE, obstetrician, gynecologist, clin. adminstr.; b. Passaic, N.J., Sept. 8, 1934; s. Henry L. and Sylvia V. (Highstone) D.; B.S., Calvin Coll., Grand Rapids, Mich., 1957; M.D., Cornell U., 1959; m. Esther Verna VanManen, June 19, 1956; children—Stephen, Cynthia, Jeffery. Intern, Henry Ford Hosp., Detroit, 1959, resident in obstetrics gynecology, 1960-64, sr. staff physician, 1966-73, chmn. dept. gynecology obstetrics, 1973—; clin. asso. prof. obstetrics gynecology U. Mich. Med. Sch., 1976—. Served with M.C. U.S. Army, 1964-66. Diplomate Nat. Bd. Med. Examiners, Am. Bd. Obstetrics Gynecology. Mem. Am. Coll. Obstetrics Gynecology, Am. Soc. Clin. Oncology. Office: Henry Ford Hosp Detroit MI 48202

DRUMMY, WILLIAM WALLACE, JR., physician; b. Omaha, Jan. 3, 1923; B.S., Villanova Coll.; M.D., Harvard U., 1948. Intern, then resident in internal medicine Boston City Hosp., 1948-49, 51-52; research fellow in endocrinology New Eng. Med. Center Hosp.-Ziskind Meml. Lab., Boston, 1952-53; practice medicine specializing in internal medicine, Terre Haute, Ind., 1972—; mem. staff Union, Terre Haute Regional hosps.; asso. prof. Ind. U. Med. Sch., 1972-76. Served as officer M.C., USAF, 1950-56. Diplomate Am. Bd. Internal Medicine. Office: 436 S 30th St Terre Haute IN 47803

DRUMRIGHT, ARTHUR LEE, accountant; b. Springfield, Mo., Aug. 3, 1919; s. Dosey L. and Clara C. (Eslinger) D.; Southwest State U., 1937-40; m. Bernadine M. Bartels, June 19, 1948; 1 son, Arthur Lee. Accountant, A.P. Green Fire Brick Co., Mexico, Mo., 1942-54; sr. partner Drumright, Smith and Robinson, Mexico, Mo., 1955—; mem. Illiamo Estate Planning Council, 1976-77. Mem. Conservation Assn. of Mo. Mem. Nat. Assn. of Pub. Accountants, Ind. Accountants Soc. of Mo. (legis. com. 1969-72, pres. 1973-74, chmn. accountants ednl. seminar 1974-77), Mexico Investment Club (treas. 1958-71). Methodist (ch. bd. 1964-68). Mason (Shriner), Kiwanian (pres. 1959). Home: 1504 Webster Dr Mexico MO 65265 Office: 108 N Jefferson Mexico MO 65265

DRURY, JAMES WILFRID, health care co. exec.; b. Carbondale, Ill., Oct 3, 1931; s. Lafayette and Oma Opal (Wright) D.; B.A., So. Ill. U., 1953; m. Jane Elinor Barco, Mar. 8, 1952; children—Mathew, John, Susan, David. Surety underwriter Safeco Ins. Group, St. Louis, also Kansas City, Mo., 1955-63, surety mgr. central div. St. Louis, 1963-69; v.p. sales Hosp. Bldg. and Equipment Co., St. Louis, 1969-71, exec. v.p., 1971-75; v.p. sales Minner Constrn. Co., Inc., Kirkwood, Mo., 1976-77; nat. sales mgr. BBC Health Care, St. Louis, 1977—. Served to 1st lt., USMCR, 1953-55. Presbyn. (elder 1968-72). Home: 12624 Big Bend Rd Kirkwood MO 63122 Office: 1144 Hampton Ave St Louis MO 63139

DRURY, JOHN, TV journalist. Reporter, newscaster WLS-TV, Chgo. Bd. dirs. Summit Sch., East Dundee, Ill. Recipient award for best enterprize reporting A.P., 1971; Best Documentary award U.P.I., 1973; Med. Journalism award State Med. Soc., 1973. Mem. Sigma Delta Chi (bd. dirs.). Club: Headline of Chgo. (bd. dirs.). Office: WLS-TV 190 N State St Chicago IL 60601

DRVOTA, MOJMIR, cinema scientist, author; b. Prague, Czechoslovakia, Jan. 13, 1923; s. Jan and Zdenka (Krejcikova) D.; came to U.S., 1958, naturalized, 1963; student Charles U., 1945-48; Ph.D., Palacky U., 1953; M.S., Columbia U., 1961; m. Jana Kratochvilova, May 18, 1957; 1 dau., Monica. Script writer Czechoslovak State Film, Prague, 1948-52; stage dir. state theaters Czechoslovakia, 1952-56; librarian Bklyn. Pub. Library, 1958-62; asst. prof. dramatic arts Columbia U., 1962-69; asso. prof. cinema N.Y. U., N.Y.C., 1969-72; prof. cinema Ohio State U., Columbus, 1972—. Mem. Univ. Film Assn., Phi Kappa Phi. Author: Short Stories, 1946; Boarding House for Artists, novel, 1947; The Constituents of Film Theory, 1973; Solitaire, novel, 1974. Home: 5140 N High St Columbus OH 43214 Office: 156 W 19th Ave Columbus OH 43210

DUBI, LEONARD ALLEN, clergyman; b. Chgo., July 9, 1942; s. Stephen John and Henrietta Barbara (Rzegocki) D.; B.A., St. Mary of the Lake Sem., 1964, S.T.B., 1966, S.T.L., 1968; student Saul Alinsky Inst., 1970-71. Asso. deacon St. John De La Salle Ch., Chgo., 1967-68; asso. pastor St. Andrew Ch., Chgo., 1968-69, St. Daniel the Prophet Ch., Chgo., 1969-74, Our Lady of the Angels Ch. Chgo., 1974—. Co-chmn. Campaign Against Pollution, 1970-71, Citizens Action Program, 1971-73. Recipient Chicagoland 100 award, 1971. Address: 3808 W Iowa Chicago IL 60651

DUBIN, ARTHUR DETMERS, architect; b. Chgo., Mar. 14, 1923; s. Henry and Anne (Green) D.; student Lake Forest Coll., 1943-44; B.Arch., U. Mich., 1949; m. Lois Amtman, Mar. 10, 1951; children—Peter Arthur, Polly Louise. Architect, partner Dubin & Dubin, architects and engrs., Chgo., 1950-65, Dubin, Dubin & Black, architects and engrs., 1965-66, Dubin, Dubin, Black & Moutoussamy, 1966—; v.p., dir. 7337 South Shore Dr. Corp., 7345 South Shore Dr. Corp.; v.p. DDBM, Inc., constrn. mgmt. cons. Chmn. Highland Park (Ill.) Civic Beautification Com., 1965-74; adviser Amtrak, 1972—; gen. partner 340 Wellington Assos., 1962-73; hon. research asso. Smithsonian Instn., 1975—; mem. Ill. Commn. on High Speed Rail Transit, 1966-68; mem. Met. Housing and Planning Council of Chgo., Nat. Council Archtl. Registration Bds., 1971—. Mem. Highland Park Bicentennial Commn., 1974—. Served with inf., AUS, 1943-46. Decorated Bronze Star medal with cluster, Purple Heart. Mem. AIA, Ill. Soc. Architects, Ry. and Locomotive Hist. Soc. (dir. 1960—), Train Collectors Assn., Am. Pub. Transit Assn., Western Soc. Engrs., Art Inst. Chgo. (life). Clubs: Cliff Dwellers (dir. 1972-75), Builders (dir. 1972—, pres. 1970-71), Arts (Chgo.). Author: Some Classic Trains, 1964, More Classic Trains, 1974. Editor: North America: Great Trains, 1973. Contbr. to mags. Archtl. works include govt. bldgs., mil. installations, transp. facilities, banks, indsl. plants, schs. and colls., hosps., housing and urban renewal planning. Home: 229 Park Ave Highland Park IL 60035 Office: 55 W Wacker Dr Chicago IL 60601

DUBLIN, ELVIE WILSON, psychotherapist; b. Athens, Greece, May 18, 1937; d. Anthony John Nicolopoulos and Rosa Protecdicos; student Nat. Capodistrian U. Athens, Greece, 1956-58; B.A., Ind. U., 1966, Ph.D., 1972; m. James E. Dublin, Dec. 21, 1973; children by previous marriage—David A., Toni R. Came to U.S., 1959, naturalized, 1966. NSF research trainee, 1965-67; USPHS trainee in clin. psychology, 1967-70; cons., Hospitality House Nursing Home, Bedford, Ind., 1972-73; psychotherapist Choice Inc., 1973—, sec./treas., 1973—. Am. Field Service Internat. scholar, 1954-55. Mem. Am., Ind. psychol. assns., Assn. for the Advancement of Psychology, Eastern Primal Assn. (clin.). Home: Tall Oaks 9401 E State Rd 46 Bloomington IN 47401 Office: 1205 S Walnut St Bloomington IN 47401

DUBOIS, JOHN RENE, JR., child psychiatrist; b. Detroit, May 16, 1931; s. John Rene and Madlyn (Callan) D.; B.S., U. Mich., 1956, M.D., 1956; m. Mary Lou Dettinger, June 23, 1956; children—John Rene III, Patrick Joseph, Lou Anne. Intern, Denver Gen. Hosp., 1956, Presbyn. Hosp., Denver, 1957; resident Colo. Psycopathic Hosp., Denver, 1957-59, Henry Ford Hosp., Detroit, 1962-64, Hawthorn Center, Northville, Mich., 1964-66; practice psychiatry, London, Ont., Can., 1966—; dir. Mme. Vanier Childrens Services, London, 1966—; mem. staff Victoria Hosp., London. Clin. asst. prof. psychiatry and pediatrics U. Western Ont., London, 1972—. Served with USAF, 1959-62. Diplomate Am. Bd. Psychiatry and Neurology. Fellow Royal Coll. Physicians and Surgeons. Home: 1454 Corley Dr London ON N6G 2K4 Canada Office: 871 Trafalgar St London ON N5Z 1E6 Canada

DU BOIS, LAURENCE ROBERT, aluminum co. exec.; b. Bellaire, Ohio, July 20, 1927; s. Charles Lorain and Marie (Stratter) D.; B.S., Ohio State U., 1948; m. Irene Patricia Milash, June 19, 1954; children—Laurence Gregory, Karen Patricia, Linda Marie, Brian Robert. C.P.A. with Haskins & Sells, Chgo., 1949-55; comptroller Detroit Brass & Malleable Co., Wyandotte, Mich., 1955-57; chief gen. accountant Ormet Corp., Hannibal, Ohio, 1957-63, asst. controller, 1963-66, controller, 1966-67, treas., controller, 1967—; treas., controller Ormet Shipping Corp., 1966—, Ormet Ship Finance Corp., 1966—, Ore Shipping Corp., 1966—; treas. Conalco Revere Realty Co., 1966—. Trustee Ohio Pub. Expenditures Council, 1966—. Mem. Marshall County Taxpayers Assn., 1963—, Monroe County Taxpayers Assn., 1963—; trustee Ormet Found., Monroe County Bd. Mental Retardation. Served with USMCR, 1945-46. C.P.A., D.C., Ill. Mem. Nat. Assn. Accountants, Ohio State U. Alumni Assn. Club: Switzerland of Ohio Country. Home: 112 Hillcrest Dr Woodsfield OH 43793 Office: PO Box 176 Hannibal OH 43931

DUBOIS, LOREN ARTHUR, retail co. exec.; b. Putnam, Conn., June 3, 1928; s. Joseph Paul and Edna Pearl (Lavigne) DuB.; B.A., Yale, 1950; M.B.A., U. Pa., 1955. With Marshall Field & Co., Chgo., 1955—, mgr. silverware, 1963-69, mgr. foods and restaurants div., 1969-71, v.p., gen. operating mgr., 1971—; dir. Jonadco System Inc. Bd. dirs. Easter Seal Soc. Met. Chgo., Inc. Served to lt. (j.g.) USNR, 1951-54. Mem. Nat. (ops. bd. dirs. 1972—), Ill. (dir.) retail mchts. assns. Club: University (Chgo.). Home: Box 322 Ogden Dunes Portage IN 46368 Office: 111 N State St Chicago IL 60690

DUBOIS, WILLIAM, JR., pub. relations specialist, state ofcl.; b. Hartford City, Ind., Mar. 19, 1933; s. William L. and Marian M. (Cline) DuB.; B.S., Ball State U., 1961; m. Treva M. Boise, Apr. 2, 1955; children—Janice Lea and Janelle Lynn (twins), Teresa Ann, Steven Dean. Reporter, sportswriter Hartford City (Ind.) News-Times, 1952-53, 55-56; reporter, sports editor Portland (Ind.) Comml.-Review, 1956-57, editor, 1957-60; reporter, copy editor Muncie (Ind.) Star, 1960-61, city editor, 1961-65, mng. editor 1967-74; exec. asst. to Ind. Republican state chmn., 1974-76; adviser to gov. Ind., 1974-76, exec. asst., 1977—; info. dir. Ind. C. of C., Indpls., 1965-67; reporter, copy editor Indpls. News, 1967; editor Graphic, Portland, Ind., 1959-60. Bd. dirs., exec. v.p. Eastern Ind. Community TV, 1973-74; chmn. pub. relations com. Delaware County United Fund, 1968-70, bd. dirs., 1970-73. Served with AUS, 1953-55. Mem. Muncie-Delaware County C. of C. (dir., exec. com. 1969-71), Ball State U. Journalism Alumni Assn. (pres. 1969-70), Huguenot, Ind. hist. socs., Du Bois Family Assn., Sigma Delta Chi (former pres. Ind. east chpts.). Republican. Club: Indpls. Press. Home: 1 Hellis Dr Muncie IN 47304 Office: Room 210 Statehouse Indianapolis IN 46204

DUCHESNEAU, PAUL MCLEAN, physician; b. Auburn, Mass., June 9, 1923; s. A. P. and Gladys (McLean) D.; B.S., U. R.I., 1948; M.D., Boston U., 1952; m. Renate Elizabeth Halley, May 23, 1953; 1 son, David. Intern, Percy Jones Army Hosp., Battle Creek, Mich., 1952-53; resident in radiology Roosevelt Hosp., N.Y.C., 1954-57; adj. radiotherapist Hosp. for Spl. Surgery, N.Y.C., 1957-58; staff radiologist Meml. Hosp., N.Y.C., 1958-60; staff radiologist Cleve. Clinic, 1960—, head neuroradiology, 1965—. Scoutmaster Boy Scouts Am., 1967-72. Served to capt. USAF, 1943-46, 52-54. Mem. Am. Soc. Neuroradiology, Radiologic Soc. N.Am., Am. Coll. Radiology, Ohio State Med. Assn., AMA. Clubs: Mentor Harbor Yachting, Cleve. Ski. Home: 2977 Fonenay Rd Shaker Heights OH 44120 Office: 2020 E 93d St Cleveland OH 44106

DUCOMB, ROBERT JAMES, JR., state legislator; b. South Bend, Ind., Sept. 3, 1943; s. Robert James and Lucy Azelia (Cotter) DuC.; A.B., Ind. U., 1964, J.D., 1967; m. Jane Jackson, Aug. 27, 1966; children—Darby Nicole, Dana Marie. Admitted to Ind. bar, 1967; mem. firm DuComb, Nimtz & DuComb, South Bend, Ind., 1969—; mem. Ind. Ho. of Reps., 1972—, majority caucus chmn., 1976—; dep. city atty., South Bend, 1969-71. Pres., Clay Twp. Republican Club, 1972; precinct committeeman, 1970-75; del. Ind. Rep. Conv., 1970, 72. Adv. bd. Ind. U. at South Bend, 1973—; bd. dirs. Alcoholism Council of St. Joseph County, 1974—. Served to lt. AUS, 1967-69. Mem. St. Joseph County, Ind. bar assns., South Bend Jr. C. of C. (dir. 1970-71). Rep. Home: 16146 Brockton Ct Granger IN 46530 Office: 511 W Colfax St South Bend IN 46601

DUDAS, JOSEPH EDWARD, lift truck mfg. engr., mayor; b. Josephine, Pa., Dec. 10, 1917; s. Stephen and Elizabeth (Nagy) D.; B.A., Fenn Coll., 1964, certificate Mgmt., 1958; certificate Mining Engring., U. W.Va., 1941, Case Western Res. U., 1976; m. Veronica Tira, June 10, 1939; children—Bernadette, Edward, Deborah Ann. Sect. foreman Island Creek Coal Co., Holden, W.Va., 1940-46; indsl. relations Cleve. Hardware & Forging, 1946-56; planning engr. Towmotor Co., Mentor, Ohio, 1956—. Mayor, Lakeline Village, Ohio, 1971—. Chmn. membership com., v.p. Lake County Consumers Council. Mem. Mayors and City Mgrs. Assn. (pres.). Democrat. Roman Catholic. Home: 33601 Lakeshore Blvd Willoughby OH 44094 Office: 7111 Tyler Blvd Mentor OH 44090

DUDEK, BERNARD JOSEPH, computer specialist; b. Chgo., Dec. 30, 1941; s. Barney Joseph and Essie Pauline (Carter) D.; B.S. in Math., U. Ill., 1972; M.B.A., DePaul U., 1976; m. Jane Pierce Rood, May 6, 1967; 1 son, Bernard Joseph. Computer operator Argonne (Ill.) Nat. Lab., 1966; mgr. data processing U. Ill., Chgo., 1966-74, Bell and Howell Corp., Chgo., 1974-76, Morton Norwich Corp., Chgo., 1976—; instr. bus. adminstrn. Elmhurst (Ill.) Coll., 1973—; cons. in field. Served with U.S. Army, 1964-66. Mem. Assn. Computing Machinery, Soc. Certified Data Processors, Data Processing Mgmt. Assn. (certified data processor 1973). Home: 786 S Swain St Elmhurst IL 60126 Office: 110 N Wacker Dr Chicago IL 60606

DUDEK, NORMAN DEAN, industry exec.; b. Hastings, Nebr., May 5, 1928; s. Otto Vincent and Marie Bonita (Rehn) D.; student Hastings Coll., 1946-47, U. Neb., 1970-71; m. Pauline Marie Brungardt, May 15, 1948; children—James Allen, Beverly Joanne (Mrs. Bill Fintel), Jane Marie, Robert Vincent. Photographer, photo-engraver Hastings Daily Tribune, 1950-65; tng. supr. Ordnance, Grand Island, Nebr., 1966-73; personnel mgr. Ag-Tronic, Inc., Hastings, 1973—; tchr. mgmt. courses Central Tech. Community Coll.; lectr. drug problems, indsl. supervision. Mem. City Council Hastings, 1970-75; chmn. bd. Hastings/Adams County R.R. Transp. Safety Dist. Mem. Am. Hist. Soc. Germans from Russia, Assn. for Visual Arts (treas., dir.), United Comml. Travelers. Lutheran. Mason, Kiwanian (past lt. gov., Distinguished Lt. Gov. 1972-73, Life Fellow award Kiwanis Found.). Writer, producer numerous tng. cassettes, slide programs. Home: Route 1 Box 18A Bladen NE 68928 Office: 1801 W B St Hastings NE 68901

DUDEWICZ, EDWARD JOHN, educator; b. Jamaica, N.Y., Apr. 24, 1942; s. Edward George and Adele (Drula) D.; S.B., Mass. Inst. Tech., 1963; M.S., Cornell U., 1966, Ph.D., 1969; m. Patricia Anne Scott, July 6, 1963; children—Douglas, Robert, Carolyn. Asst. engr. AVCO Corp., Wilmington, Mass., 1963; asst. prof. statistics U. Rochester, 1967-72, asst. prof. biostatistics, 1971-72; asso. prof. statistics Ohio State U., 1972-77, prof., 1977—, chmn. grad. com. statistics, 1973-75; vis. scholar, vis. asso. prof. Stanford U., 1976; cons. in field. Office Naval Research grantee, 1967-72, U.S. Army grantee, 1972-74; NSF fellow, 1966-67. Fellow N.Y. Acad. Scis.; mem. Inst. Math. Statistics, Am. Statis. Assn., Math. Assn. Am., A.A.U.P., Japan Statis. Soc., Am. Soc. Quality Control. Author: Introduction to Statistics and Probability, 1976. Contbr. articles to profl. jours. Home: 2524 Dorset Rd Upper Arlington OH 43221 Office: Dept Statistics Ohio State U Columbus OH 43210

DUDICK, THOMAS MICHAEL, constrn. materials mfr.; b. Cleve., Sept. 10, 1946; s. Michael Mark and Bernadette Marie (Long) D.; B.A. in Economics, Cleve. State U., 1970; m. Katherine Anne Hunt, Nov. 24, 1973; children—Susan Margret, Thomas Michael II. Project leader Ceilcote Co., Inc., 1965-69; owner, pres. Dudick Corrosion-Proof Mfg., Inc., Macedonia, Ohio, 1970—. Served with U.S. N.G., 1966-72. Mem. Nat. Assn. Corrosion Engrs. Roman Catholic. Home: 6605 Elmcrest St Hudson OH 44236 Office: 576 E Highland Rd Macedonia OH 44056

DUDLEY, DURAND STOWELL, librarian; b. Cleve., Feb. 28, 1926; s. George Stowell and Corinne Elizabeth (Durand) D.; B.A., Oberlin Coll., 1948; M.L.S., Case Western Res. U., 1950; m. Dorothy Woolworth, July 3, 1954; children—Jane Elizabeth, Deborah Anne. Librarian, Marietta (O.) Coll. Library, 1953-55, Akron (O.) Pub. Library, 1955-60; librarian Marathon Oil Co., Findlay, O., 1960—, sr. law librarian, 1974—. Mem. Spl. Libraries Assn. Presbyn. (deacon). Home: 304 Hancock St Findlay OH 45840 Office: Marathon Oil Co 539 S Main St Findlay OH 45840

DUDLEY, HORACE CHESTER, scientist, educator; b. St. Louis, June 28, 1909; s. Horace Chester and Rhoda Olivette (Mc Adoo) D.; A.B., Mo. State Coll., 1931; Ph.D. in Chemistry, Georgetown U., 1941; postgrad. U. Calif., 1948, USN Corr. Course, 1948-49, Oak Ridge Inst. Nuclear Studies, 1949, U.S. Army Tng. Center, 1949, N.Y. U., 1957; m. Thelma Avis Scott, June 13, 1935 (dec.); children—Jeanette, David; m. 2d, Joan Marie Kallenback, Nov. 6, 1954; children—Robert, Susan. Lab. asst. U.S. Bur. Standards, Washington, 1931-32; jr. chemist bur. chemistry Dept. Agr., Washington, 1933-34; asst. chemist div. med. research Chem. Warfare Service, Edgewood Arsenal, Md., 1934-36; biochemist USPHS, Bethesda, Md., 1936-42; commd. lt. USN, 1942, advanced through grades to capt., 1955; explosives specialist, comdg. officer USN units, PTO, 1942-47; head div. biochemistry USN Med. Research Inst., Bethesda, 1947-52; head sect. allied sci. Med. Service Corps, Washington, 1949-52; head radioisotope lab. dept. radiology U.S. Naval Hosp., St. Albans, N.Y., 1952-62; ret., 1962; prof. physics, chmn. dept. physics U. So. Miss., 1962-69; prof. radiation physics U. Ill. Med. Center, Chgo., 1969—; cons. in field. Decorated Bronze Star, Sec. Navy medal; AEC grantee, 1963-64; NSF grantee, 1963, 65; U. So. Miss. grantee, 1965, 66, 67; U. Ill. grantee, 1970, 72. Fellow AAAS; mem. Am. Phys. Soc., Health Physics Soc., Am. Assn. Physics Tchrs., Am. Assn. Physicists in Medicine, Am. Bd. Health Physics (certified), Sigma Xi. Club: Masons. Author: New Principles in Quantum Mechanics, 1959; Morality of Nuclear Planning, 1976; contbr. articles to profl. jours.; patentee in field. Home: 405 W 8th Pl Hinsdale IL 60521 Office: U Ill Med Center PO Box 6998 Chicago IL 60680

DUDLEY, JOHN HENRY, floriculture-horticulture co. exec.; b. Detroit, Nov. 17, 1912; s. Henry Augustus and Margaret Helen (Bigelow) D.; grad. Detroit U. Sch. 1932; B.A., Mich. State U., 1937; student Am. Mgmt. Assn. seminars; m. Elizabeth Baird Dean, June 21, 1940; children—John Henry, Thomas Dean. With John Henry Co., 1937—, gen. mgr., 1939-62, pres., 1939-72, chmn. bd., 1972—; judge Bicentennial Rose Parade, Pasadena, Calif., 1976; speaker to florist meetings. Former v.p., chmn., bd. dirs. Mich. United Fund; past pres., campaign chmn. United Community Chest Greater Lansing Area; past area chmn. Project Hope; past chmn. Ingham County Rehab. Centers; past mem. Mich. Gov.'s Com. Traffic Safety; past mem. state bd. Am. Cancer Soc., past campaign chmn., past pres. Ingham County unit; past chmn. United Negro Coll. Fund, YMCA; chmn. spl. study and adv. com. YMCA-YWCA; mem. Pres.'s Commn. White House Fellowships, 1976—; bd. dirs. Student Loan Mktg. Assn., 1975—. Served from lt. (j.g.) to lt. comdr., USNR, 1942-45. Decorated Navy Marine medal, Bronze Star; named to Floriculture Hall of Fame, 1966. Mem. Soc. Am. Florists (past pres., past chmn. nat. advt. council, nat. edn. com.), Florists Telegraph Delivery Assn. (dir. 1950, nat. award), All Florist Industry Congress (founder, co-chmn.), Mich. Florists Assn. (past pres., dir., chmn. prizes, awards com., mem. com., publs. com., Outstanding Service award, nat. award), Wholesale Florists and Florist Suppliers Am. (past treas., dir., Lee Kintzele award 1973), Florists Transworld Delivery Assn. (past dir.), Soc. Am. Florists Endowment (charter, founder, trustee, v.p., treas., now chmn.), Am. Inst. Floral Designers (hon.). Rotarian. Clubs: Lansing City (pres. 1959), Lansing Automobile, Lansing Country (past pres., bd. govs.); Detroit, Detroit Economic; Los Angeles Country; Capitol Hill (Washington); New York Metropolitan. Home: 610 W Ottawa St Lansing MI 48933 also 875 Comstock Ave Apt 17-F Los Angeles CA 90024 Office: PO Box 17099 Lansing MI 48901

DUDLEY, WILFRED GEORGE, ednl. adminstr.; b. Elwood, Ind., Mar. 26, 1931; s. Wilfred and Lillian Ellen (Miller) D.; B.S., Ball State U., 1953, M.S., 1960; m. Susan Baker, Dec. 28, 1952; children—Brenda, Pamela. Tchr., La Crosse (Ind.) Pub. Schs., 1955-56, Elwood Pub. Schs., 1956-63; asst. prin. Wendell L. Wilkie High Sch., Elwood, 1963-68; prin. Oakland Elementary Sch., Elwood, after 1968, now asst. supt. Elwood Pub. Schs. Dir. Elwood YMCA, 1959-62. Served with AUS, 1953-55. Mem. Elwood C. of C. (dir.), Ind., Elwood Classroom tchrs. assns., N.E.A., Nat. Assn. Elementary Sch. Prins. Mason (Shriner), Elk. Home: 1223 Dulee Dr Elwood IN 46036

DUEL, WARD CALVIN, sanitarian; b. Fond du Lac, Wis., Mar. 13, 1924; s. Myrton H. and Matie (Tidyman) D.; B.S., U. Wis., 1950; postgrad. Marquette U., 1957; M.P.H., U. Calif. at Berkeley, 1959; m. Madelyn M. Kressin, Oct. 1, 1950; children—Ward Rick, Christine Selma, Roxanne Matie, Beth Dawn. In quality control Green Giant Corp., Rosendale, Wis., 1940-42; later with DeSchipper Canning Co., Carthage, Ind.; sanitarian City of Kenosha (Wis.), 1950-57, City of Berkeley (Calif.), 1957-58; office adminstr. Lake County, Ill., 1959-65; health dir. Village of Skokie (Ill.), 1965-68, McHenry County (Ill.), Woodstock, 1968-70; dir. environ. health AMA, Chgo., 1970—; cons. to adminstrs. bds. health, Palatine, Morton Grove, Arlington Heights, Des Plaines, Schaumberg (all Ill.); curriculum cons. Ind. State U., 1967. Mem. Underwriters Lab. Standards Com. Active Boy Scouts Am.; founding pres. McHenry County Youth Services Bur. Served with AUS, 1944-46; ETO. Decorated Bronze Star; recipient Samuel J. Crumbine award, 1963, Theta award Defenders of Environment, 1970; award for ednl. excellence Ill. Office Edn., 1975; Editors award Jour. Environ. Health, 1977. Fellow Nat. Environ. Health Assn. (pres. 1967-68), Ill. (pres. 1962-64), Wis. (pres. 1956-58) assns. sanitarians, Am. Pub. Health Assn., ASME (mem. 5 standards coms.), Delta Omega, Pi Kappa Alpha. Home: 4907 West St McHenry IL 60050 Office: 535 N Dearborn St Chicago IL 60610

DUENWEG, LOUIS, utility exec.; b. Terre Haute, Ind., July 26, 1915; s. Louis and Marie Catherine (Coons) D.; B.S. in E.E., Rose Poly. Inst., 1936; exec. devel. courses U. Mich., Columbia U.; m. Mary G. Thompson, Oct. 28, 1960. Cons. Orgn. European Econ. Coop., Paris, 1956-57; with Detroit Edison Co., 1936—, acting asst. supt. Detroit div. overhead lines, 1965, dir. tng. and communications, 1946-69, mgmt. devel. coordinator, 1970—; instr. Dartmouth Coll., 1952-60, U. Detroit, 1954-55, Grad. Sch. Credit Fin. Mgmt.; comdt. U.S. Army Res. Sch., Ft. Wayne, Mich., 1954-55, mem. staff and faculty Command Gen. Staff Coll. Republican precinct del., 1960-61. Served with C.E. and AGC, AUS, 1940-46. Decorated Army Commendation Medal. Registered profl. engr., Ind. Mem. Mil. Order World Wars, Am. Def. Preparedness Assn., Am. Soc. Tng. and Devel., Soc. Advancement Mgmt. (past officer), Adult Edn. Assn. U.S.A. (past bd. dirs.), Nat. Indsl. Conf. Bd., Grosse Pointe War Meml., Detroit Inst. Arts, Alpha Tau Omega, Tau Beta Pi, Blue Key, Tau Nu Tau. Clubs: Power, Edison Bus. (past pres.), Meridian Luncheon, Fine Arts. Contbr. articles on mgmt. to profl. jours. Home: 1111 Devonshire Rd Grosse Pointe Park MI 48230 Office: 2000 Second Ave Detroit MI 48226

DUERRE, JOHN ARDEN, microbial physiologist, biochemist; b. Webster, S.D., Aug. 21, 1930; s. Dewey H. and Stella M. (Barber) D.; B.S., S.D. State U., 1952, M.S. (Lederle fellow), 1956; Ph.D., U. Minn., 1960; m. Benna Bee Harris, June 16, 1957; children—Gail, Dawn, Arden. Research asso., AEC fellow Argonne (Ill.) Nat. Lab., 1960-61; research bacteriologist NIH Rocky Mountain Lab., Hamilton, Mont., 1960-63; asst. prof. microbiology U. N.D. Med. Sch., 1963-65, asso. prof., 1965-71, prof. microbiology, 1971—; vis. scientist neuropsychiat. research unit. Research Council Lab., Carchalton, Surrey, Eng., 1969-70. Chmn. Grand Forks County (N.D.) Wildlife Fedn., 1965-67, 77, Grand Forks (N.D.) chpt. Ducks Unltd., 1970, 77; dist. dir. N.D. Wildlife Fedn., 1976-77. Served with U.S. Army, 1953-55. Recipient Career Devel. award NIH, 1965-75; NIH grantee, 1966, 71-78; NSF grantee, 1963-71. Mem. N.Y., N.D. acads. scis., Am. Soc. Microbiologists, Fedn. Am. Soc. Exptl. Biology, Henrici Soc., Sigma Xi (Outstanding Grad. Conduct and Research award 1977). Democrat. Clubs: Grand Forks Curling, Grand Forks Gun, Elks. Contbr. numerous articles to profl. publs. Home: 918 N 26th St Grand Forks ND 58201 Office: U ND Med Sch Grand Forks ND 58201

DUESENBERG, RICHARD WILLIAM, lawyer; b. St. Louis, Dec. 10, 1930; s. (John August) Hugo and Edna Marie (Warmann) D.; B.A., Valparaiso U., 1951, J.D., 1953; LL.M., Yale, 1956; m. Phyllis Evelyn Buehner, Aug. 7, 1955; children—Karen, Daryl, Mark, David. Admitted to Mo. bar, 1953; prof. law N.Y. U. Sch. Law, 1956-62, dir. Law Center Publs., 1960-62; sr. atty. Monsanto Co., St. Louis, 1963-70, asst. gen. counsel, asst. sec., 1975-77, v.p., sec., gen. counsel, 1977—; dir. law Monsanto Textiles Co., St. Louis, 1971-75; corp. sec. Fisher Controls Co., Marshalltown, Iowa, 1969-71; corp. sec. Olympia Industries, Inc., Spartanburg, S.C., 1974-75. Vis. prof. law U. Mo. Sch. Law, 1970-71; faculty Banking Sch. of South La. State U., 1967—; mem. legal adv. council Mfg. Chemists Assn., Washington. Bd. dirs., vice chmn. Luth. Med. Center, St. Louis, bd. dirs. Valparaiso U. also chmn. bd. visitors Law Sch.; bd. dirs. Bach Soc. of St. Louis, also pres. Served with AUS, 1953-55. Recipient Distinguished Alumnus award Valparaiso U., 1976. Mem. Am. Law Inst., Luth. Acad. for Scholarship, Am. Arbitration Assn. (mem. nat. panel arbitrators 1960), Am. (chmn. subcom. on sales, bulk transfers and title documents 1970-76, com. on uniform comml. code 1976—), Mo., St. Louis, Internat. bar assns., Am. Judicature Soc., Order of Coif. Lutheran. Author (with L. King) Sales and Bulk Transfers Under the Uniform Commercial Code, 2 vols., 1966, rev. edits., 1977; New York Law of Contracts, 3 vols., 1964; Missouri Forms and Practice Under the Uniform Commercial Code, 2 vols., 1966. Editor: Ann. Survey of Am. Law, N.Y. U., 1961-62. Contbr. articles to law revs., jours. Home: 9124 Glencrest Dr St Louis MO 63126 Office: 800 N Lindbergh Blvd St Louis MO 63166

DUESENBERG, ROBERT HENRY, lawyer; b. St. Louis, Dec. 10, 1930; s. Hugo John August and Edna (Warmann) D.; B.A., Valparaiso U., 1951, LL.B., 1953; LL.M., Harvard, 1956; m. Lorraine F. Hall; children—Lynda Renee, Kirsten Lynn, John Robert. Admitted to Mo. bar, 1953; practiced in St. Louis, 1956-58; became counsel Wabash R.R. Co., St. Louis, 1958 (merged into N. & W. Ry. 1964), gen. atty., until 1965; counsel, then asst. gen. counsel Pet, Inc., 1965—; dir. Gerber-Barthel Truck & Tractor Corp., Inc., Gerber-Barthel, Inc. Sec., treas., legal adviser Am. Kantorei. Bd. dirs. Luth. Publicity Orgn. Chmn., Young Republican Club, Porter County, Ind., 1948. Mem. adv. bd. Southwestern Legal Found. Served with Judge Adv. Gen. Corps., AUS, 1953-55. Mem. Am. (mem. membership com.), Mo., St. Louis (chmn. antitrust com. 1971-73, v.p. bus. law sect. 1972-73, chmn. sect. 1973-74) bar assns., Am. Judicature Soc., Valparaiso U. Alumni Assn. (dir.), Pi Gamma Mu, Pi Sigma Alpha. Lutheran. Club: Harvard (St. Louis). Contbr. articles to legal publs. Home: 9026 Whitehaven St St Louis County St Louis MO 63123 Office: 400 S 4th St Louis MO 63166

DUFAUX, DONALD WARREN, sch. counselor; b. St. Louis, July 17, 1935; s. William Frederick and Thelma Irene (Stricklin) D.; B.A., Belmont Abbey Coll., 1967; M.Ed., U. S.C., 1969; Ph.D., St. Louis U., 1976. With Mesker Bros. Iron Co., Hazelwood, Mo., 1956-59, Citizen and So. Nat. Bank Columbia, S.C., 1966-67, Vocat. Rehab., Columbia, 1969-70; coordinator Stanford U. Research Inst., Columbia, 1970-71; night counselor Whealy Halfway House, Columbia, part-time, 1971; guidance counselor Juvenile Corrections Center, Columbia, 1971-72; coordinator Vocat. Careers Inc., Pine Lawn, Mo., 1972-73; acad. counselor Met. Coll., St. Louis, 1973; with Essex Cryogenics, St. Louis, 1973-74; rehab. counselor Jewish Employment and Vocat. Service, St. Louis, 1974-76; counselor Briar Cliff Coll., Sioux City, Iowa, 1976—; lectr. in field. Vol. St. Vincent DePaul Soc., St. Peter's Ch., Columbia, S.C., 1968-72; active Dem. Re-Election campaign, 1968—. Served with U.S. Army, 1957-59. U. S.C. assistantship, 1967. Mem. Nat. Cath. Guidance Conf., Am. Personnel and Guidance Assn., Assn. for Counselor Edn. and Supervision, Assn. for Specialists in Group Work. Roman Catholic. Club: Maranatha. Home: 217 19th St Apt 401 Sioux City IA 51105 Office: 3303 Rebecca St Sioux City IA 51104

DUFEK, RONALD DWANE, service sta. owner; b. Geddes, S.D., Oct. 20, 1939; s. Ernest and Rose (Sejnoha) D.; student So. State Coll., 1965; m. Maureen Neihus, Nov. 22, 1969; children—Ernest, Terry, Mike, Tammy, Stacey. Owner, operator Dufs Standard Sta., Geddes, S.D., 1966—. Pres. Geddes (S.D.) Devel. Corp., 1969—; sec. Geddes Hist. Soc., 1970—; state dir. Geddes Jaycees, 1973. Served with U.S. Army, 1959-62. Mem. Common Cause, Nat. Small Bus. Assn., Nat. Fedn. Ind. Bus. Methodist. Clubs: Geddes Commercial (pres. 1970, 71), Geddes Baseball (bd. dirs. 1966—). Home and Office: Box 297 Geddes SD 57342

DUFF, DONALD LEE, ins. co. exec.; b. Middletown, Ohio, Sept. 27, 1934; s. Glenn Edward and Lennie (Spencer) D.; B.S. in Bus. Adminstrn., Olivet Coll., 1958; postgrad. Ind. U., 1968, Fort Wayne Art Sch., 1972; m. Donna M. Lanman, July 20, 1957. With Mut. Security Life Ins. Co., Fort Wayne, 1958-62, asst. supt. agys., 1962-64, dir. group and pension sales, 1964-68, asst. v.p., 1968-70, v.p. dir. mktg. services, 1970—; instr. Am. Coll., 1971-72. Fund solicitor United Arts Fund Drive Fort Wayne, 1977; trustee Huntington Coll., 1972—, mem. exec. com., 1974—, vice-chmn., 1974—, pres. 1974—; ambassador Asso. Colls. Ind., 1976-77; mem. bd. adminstrn. Nat. Assn. Evangelicals. Served with USAF, 1961-63. C.L.U. Mem. Life Ins. Mktg. Research Assn., Am. Soc. C.L.U.'s (pres. Fort Wayne 1969-70). Republican. Mem. United Brethern in Christ. Home: 1824 Old Lantern Trail Fort Wayne IN 46825 Office: 3000 Coliseum Blvd Fort Wayne IN 46805

DUFF, JEROME JAMES, lawyer; b. St. Louis, Sept. 30, 1926; s. James William and Helen Theresa (Egan) D.; LL.D., St. Louis U., 1952; m. Dolores Amalia D'Alto, Sept. 10, 1949; children—Christine M., Susan J., James G. Admitted to Mo. bar, 1952, U.S. Dist. Ct. bar, U.S. Supreme Ct. bar; asst. claims mgr. Zurich Ins. Co., St. Louis, 1949-55; partner firm Katcher, Roche, Cloyd and Duff, St. Louis, 1955-62; partner firm Jerome J. Duff & Assos., Inc., St. Louis, 1962—; lectr. St. Louis U., Washington U., U. Mo. Served with USMCR, 1944-46. Decorated Purple Heart. Mem. Am., Mo., St. Louis, Teamster Union bar assns. Democrat. Roman Catholic. Home: 6001 Deerwood Dr Saint Louis MO 63123 Office: 1139 Olive St Saint Louis MO 63101

DUFFETT, NICHOLAS DECKER, microbiologist, lab. adminstr.; b. Henrietta, Mo., Mar. 28, 1909; s. Henry Edgar and Mary Ellen Decker D.; B.S., Central Mo. State Tchrs. Coll., 1931; M.S., U. Colo., 1933, Ph.D., 1938; m. Mattie Ethel Williams, May 25, 1935; children—Mary Frances (Mrs. Gilbert L. Dryden), Phyllis Ellen (Mrs. Paul L. Beck), Margaret Elizabeth (Mrs. James R. Gormly). Instr. bacteriology and pub. health U. Colo., Denver, 1938-39; bacteriologist C.B. Dolge Co. Labs., Westport, Conn., 1939-44; prin. bacteriologist Pub. Health Labs., St. Louis Health div., 1944-48, asst. dir., 1948-53, dir., 1953-64; lectr. bacteriology Washington U., St. Louis, 1953-64; dir. div. labs., Kans. State Dept. Health and Environment, Topeka, 1964-74, dir. Office Labs. and Research, 1974-76; adj. prof. microbiology U. Kans., Lawrence, 1971—. Chmn. Conf. State and Provincial Pub. Health Dirs. 1966-67. Diplomate Am. Bd. Med. Microbiology. Fellow Am. Acad. Microbiology, Am. Pub. Health Assn., A.A.A.S. Mem. Am. Soc. Microbiology, Am. Inst. Biol. Scis., Am. Soc. Clin. Pathologists, Conf. Pub. Health Lab. Dirs., Assn. State and Territorial Pub. Health Lab. Dirs., Kans., Mo. (pres. 1962-63) pub. health assns., Sigma Xi. Home: 2920 Gage Blvd Topeka KS 66614

DUFFIELD, THEODORE ALDEAN, newspaper editor; b. Henry, Ill., Dec. 29, 1912; s. William James and May (Wilson) D.; B.S., U. Ill., 1936; m. Helen Grace Forsyth, June 25, 1938; children—Dennis Wilson, Patricia Sue Duffield Albrecht. With Bureau County Republican, Princeton, Ill., 1936-41, editor, 1949—; with Champaign-Urbana Courier, Urbana, Ill., 1941-49. Mem., vice chmn. Princeton Planning Commn. Zoning Bd. Appeals, 1967—. Mem. Ill. Press Assn. Republican. Mem. United Ch. Christ. Home: 311 Boyd Ave Princeton IL 61356 Office: 316 S Main St Princeton IL 61356

DUFFY, CHARLES WILLIAM, automotive exec.; b. Buffalo, Oct. 20, 1915; s. Charles James and Elizabeth (Smith) D.; B.S., Georgetown U., 1939; m. Rosemary Edminster, Feb. 6, 1943; children—Margaret E., Charles J., John F., Ann O., Mark P., Elizabeth A. Dist. traffic mgr. Chesapeake & Potomac Telephone Co., Charleston, W.Va., 1939-46; asst. dir. indsl. relations Spencer Chem. Co., Kansas City, Mo., 1946-50; advt. mgr., account exec. Kelsey Hayes Co., Detroit, 1950-58; exec. v.p., dir. Standard Products Co., Cleve., 1958-61; asst. mgr. automotive internat. div. TRW, Inc., Cleve., 1961-65; pres., gen. mgr. Ramsey Corp. subsidiary TRW, Inc., St. Louis, 1965—; dir. Manchester Bank of St. Louis. Bd. dirs. St. Louis Assn. for Retarded Children, 1974—, ARC, St. Louis; vice chmn. St. Louis U. Pres.'s Council, 1972—; mem. Mo. adv. com. U.S. Commn. on Civil Rights; trustee St. Louis U. Served to 1st lt., Signal Corps, AUS, 1941-46. Mem. Soc. Automotive Engrs. Roman Catholic. Clubs: Algonquin Golf (St. Louis); Recess, Athletic (Detroit). Home: 12903 Topping Estates S St Louis MO 63131 Office: PO Box 513 St Louis MO 63166

DUFFY, GEORGE CHRISTOPHER, JR., television sta. exec.; b. Cleve., Aug. 15, 1936; s. George Christopher and Dorothy Cecelia (Rooney) D.; m. Roberta Hahn, Sept. 22, 1962; children—Maureen, Karen, Susan, Christopher; student U. Miami (Fla.), 1954-55, Ohio State U., 1955-58, U. So. Calif. Sch. of Cinema, summer 1957. Promotion rep. TV Guide mag., Cleve., 1959-62; asst. promotion dir. WJW-TV, Cleve., 1962-64; promotion dir. WCPO-TV, Cin., 1964-65; dir. advt. and promotion KYW-TV, Phila., 1965-66; dir. advt., promotion and press info. WLS-TV, Chgo., 1966-71, dir. programming, 1973-75; dir. broadcasting KMOX-TV, St. Louis, 1971-73; v.p., gen. mgr. WTHR, Indpls., 1975—. Bd. dirs. Indpls. Cath. Social Services, United Way, Greater Indpls. Progress Com., Jr. Achievement, Advt. Club Ill., Crossroads Rehab. Center. Mem. Nat. Assn. Broadcasters, Nat. Assn. Television Program Execs., Ind. Broadcasters Assn. (pres.-elect), USMC Combat Corrs. Assn., Marine Corps Res. Officers Assn. Recipient Clio award, 1970, Chgo. Film Festival award, 1969-70, Broadcast Promotion Assn. award, 1969-70; named USMC Reservist of Year, 1974. Home: 7075 N Pennsylvania St Indianapolis IN 46220 Office: WTHR 1401 N Meridian St Indianapolis IN 46220

DUFFY, PHILIP ANTHONY, orgn. exec.; b. Boston, Feb. 13, 1944; s. Donald Philip and Zita V. (Legner) D.; B.A., Marquette U., 1966; postgrad. Grad. Sch. Bus., L.I. U., 1969-72; m. Linda E. Bixler, Nov. 10, 1973; children—Joanna, Bryan, Matthew. With Pfizer, Inc., N.Y.C., 1969-71, Interracial Council for Bus. Opportunity, N.Y.C., 1971-73; with Nat. Minority Purchasing Council, Inc., Chgo., 1973—, now exec. dir.; cons. corporate minority purchasing programs. Served in U.S. Army, 1966-69. Decorated Bronze Star with oak leaf cluster, Army Commendation medal. Mem. Chgo. Council Fgn. Relations, Old Town Triangle Assn. Home: 4502 Prince St Downers Grove IL 60515 Office: 36 S Wabash Ave Chicago IL 60603

DUFFY, WILLIAM EDWARD, JR., educator; b. Fostoria, Ohio, Aug. 30, 1931; s. William Edward and Margaret Louise (Drew) D.; B.S., Wayne State U., 1958, M.Ed., 1960; Ph.D., Northwestern U., 1967; m. Sally King Wolfe, Nov. 21, 1958. Tchr., Detroit pub. schs., 1957-61; instr. social studies Northwestern U., Evanston, Ill., 1961-65; asst. prof. edn. U. Iowa, Iowa City, 1965-70, asso. prof., 1970—; lectr. in field. Fellow Philosophy of Edn. Soc. Editorial bd. Ednl. Philosophy Theory, 1969-71; contbr. book revs. and articles to profl. publs. Home: 300 Windsor Dr Iowa City IA 52240 Office: 224 LCM U Iowa Iowa City IA 52242

DUGAN, WILLIS EDWIN, ret. ednl. assn. exec.; b. Rippey, Iowa, Aug. 31, 1909; s. Thomas Edward and Ida Mathilda (Faulds) D.; B.S., St. Cloud State Tchrs. Coll., 1937; M.A., U. Minn., 1939, Ph.D., 1942; m. Hazel Clare Foster, June 15, 1935; children—Mary Clare, Patricia Ann, Margaret Louise, James William, Virginia Kay. Tchr. pub. schs., Minn., 1927-34; asst. dir. Nat. Youth Adminstrn., Minn., 1935-38; teaching asst., counselor, instr. U. Minn., 1938-42, asst. prof., dir. student personnel coll. edn., 1942-43, asso. prof. coll. edn., 1946-50, prof. ednl. psychology, 1950-66, dir. counselor edn. and student personnel work; exec. dir. Am. Personnel and Guidance Assn., 1966-72, emeritus, 1972—. Mem. state bd. examiners of psychologists, Minn. Asst. to dir. fgn. ops. ARC, 1943-44, asst. nat. dir. personnel, 1944-46; personnel cons. Nat. Found. Infantile Paralysis, 1946; state chmn. March Dimes campaign, Minn., 1949-57; mem. adv. council Bur. labor Statistics, U.S. Dept. of Labor, 1963—; mem. nat. adv. bd. Control Data Inst. Recipient Distinguished Alumni award St. Cloud State Coll., 1969, Regents award U. Minn., 1970. Mem. Am. Personnel and Guidance Assn. (exec. com., pres. 1963-64), Nat. Vocat. Guidance Assn. (trustee), Student Personnel Assn. Tchr. Edn. (past pres.), Am. Psychol. Assn., NEA, Assn. for Counselor Edn. and Supervision (pres. 1961-62), Phi Delta Kappa, Psi Chi. Author: Counseling Points of View, 1960; Guidance Procedures in High School (with C.G. Wrenn), 1950; (with others) Guidance Systems, 1971. Editor: Counseling Points of View, 1960. Home: Route 1 Little Birch Lake Grey Eagle MN 56336

DUGGAN, JEROME TIMOTHY, pub. utility exec., lawyer; b. Kansas City, Mo., Oct. 30, 1914; s. Jerry F. and Claire (Aaron) D.; A.B., U. Mo., 1936, LL.B., 1938; m. Dorothy Blanche Castle, May 4, 1940; children—Jerome Castle, Dorothy Lucinda. Admitted to Mo. bar, 1938; in gen. law practice, Kansas City, Mo., 1938-40; asso. Hook & Thomas, 1938-40; asst. city counselor, Kansas City, Mo., 1940-42; regional rationing atty. OPA, 1942-43; in gen. law practice, also mem. Gage, Hillix & Phelps, 1946-50; gen. counsel The Gas Service Co., 1950-56; v.p., gen. counsel, 1956-63, exec. v.p., gen. counsel, 1963-68, pres., 1968—, also dir. Chmn. Kansas City (Mo.) Housing Authority, 1947-50; dir. Indsl. Council Kansas City, Mo., 1951-55; mem. Municipal Services Commn., 1955-56; bd. dirs. Citizens Regional Planning Council, Greater Kansas City Area Safety Council; gov. Am. Royal Assn., 1960—; mem. Bus. and Indsl. Devel. Commn. Kansas City; vice chmn. Kansas City Tourist Commn.; mem. exec. com. Asso. Industries Mo., 1962—; trustee Mo. Pub. Expenditure Survey, 1962—; pres. Asso. Industries Mo., 1970-72. Pres. bd. trustees Research Hosp. and Med. Center, 1970-71; trustee Midwest Research Inst., Jacob Loose Found.; regent Rockhurst Coll.; bd. dirs. Downtown, Inc. Served as lt. USN, 1943-46. Mem. Mo. Bar Assn., Am. Gas Assn. (dir.), Greater Kansas City C. of C. (dir.), Kans. Assn. Commerce and Industry (dir.), Sigma Nu, Phi Delta Phi. Clubs: Kansas City (pres. 1976-77), Mission Hills Country. Home: 11215 Holly Kansas City MO 64114 Office: Scarritt Bldg Kansas City MO 42

DUKE, BRUCE EDWARD, counselor; b. Newark, Dec. 5, 1942; s. Vincent Edward and Ruth Louise (Goddard) D.; B.A., Paterson State Coll., 1965; M.A., Ohio State U., 1967; postgrad, 1976—; m. Janice Mosny, Aug. 21, 1965; children—Kelly, Rebecca. Tchr., high sch., Mechanicsburg, Ohio, 1965-66; counselor high sch., Hilliard, Ohio, 1967-69; dir. career planning and placement Albion (Mich.) Coll., 1969-74; counselor U. Dayton, 1974—. Mem. Kettering Bd. Community Relations, 1975-76. Mem. Am. Personnel and Guidance Assn., Am. Coll. Personnel Assn., Phi Delta Kappa. Home: 417 Winding Way Kettering OH 45429 Office: St Mary Hall Guidance Center Univ Dayton OH 45469

DUKES, HOWARD HENRY, orthodontist; b. Atchison, Kans., May 29, 1912; s. Henry Sylvester and Viola Frances (Hand) D.; B.S., U. Mo., 1936, D.D.S., 1936, M.S.D., 1949; m. Fleta Margaret Wilson, June 19, 1939; children—Howard Henry, David Wilson. Intern Kansas City (Mo.) Gen. Hosp., 1936-37; gen. practice dentistry Kansas City, Kans., 1938-48; practice orthodontics, Kansas City, 1949—. Tchr. U. Mo. Sch. Dentistry, 1939-48, U. Kans. Sch. Medicine, 1938-48. Vice chmn. drives United Fund, 1958-60; mem. exec. council KAW Council Boy Scouts Am., 1963-73. Bd. dirs. Cloisters Home Assn., 1970-73. Served with U.S. Army, 1942-46; ETO. Decorated Silver Star. Recipient Silver Beaver award Boy Scouts Am. 1968; Alumni Achievement award U. Mo., Kansas City, 1977. Diplomate Am. Bd. Orthodontists. Fellow Internat. Coll. Dentists, Am. Coll. Dentists; mem. Wyandotte County (past pres.), 1st Kans. Dist. (past pres.) dental socs. Kans. Orthodontic Assn. (past pres.), Southwestern Soc. Orthodontists (past pres., dir. 1960-70, Alfred P. Westfall Meml. award 1976), Dental Alumni Assn. U. Mo. (past pres., dir. 1968-73), Am. Assn. Orthodontists (librarian 1969—, Distinguished Service Scroll 1977), U. Mo.-Kansas City Alumni Assn. (past pres. nat. chpt., dir. 1975-77), Omicron Kappa Upsilon. Home: 3020 W 84th St Leawood KS 66206 Office: 754 Brotherhood Bldg Kansas City KS 66101

DUKES, JOHN ROBERT, scientist, engr.; b. Findlay, Ohio, Oct. 9, 1930; s. Orlo O. and Ruby K. (Kober) D.; m. Katherine L. Schaller, Aug. 30, 1953; children—Suzanne, David. B.S. in Physics, B.E.E., Ohio State U., 1954, M.B.A., 1971; B.S. in Liberal Arts, Bowling Green State U., 1954. Registered profl. engr., Ohio. Served to 1st lt. U.S. Army, 1954-56; elec. engr. Indsl. Nucleonics Corp., Columbus, Ohio, 1956-57, physicist, 1957-58, physics supr., 1958-61, mgr. applied physics, 1961-77, mgr. regulatory and staff ops., 1977—, radiological safety officer, 1960-69, corp. health physics officer, 1969—; mem. faculty Franklin U., Columbus, 1957-65; v.p. VIP Motel, Inc., Findlay, 1969-74, pres. 1974—. Mem. Am. Nat. Standards Inst., Internat. Electrotech. Commn., (U.S. rep. 1973—), Internat. Standards Orgn. (U.S. rep. 1974—), Health Physics Soc., Am. Nuclear Soc., Tau Beta Pi, Sigma Pi Sigma, Eta Kappa Nu, Kappa Alpha Mu. Holder numerous patents. Home: 236 Weydon Rd Worthington OH 43085 Office: 650 Ackerman Rd Columbus OH 43202

DUKES, PHILLIP EARL, psychologist; b. Chattanooga, Aug. 30, 1946; s. Bennie and Lillian Omega (Davis) D.; B.A., Central State U., 1968; M.S.S.A., Case Western U., 1971; M.A., U. Mich., 1973, Ph.D., 1974; m. Phyllis Jean Carmack, June 5, 1971. Counselor, Econ. Opportunity Program, Cleve., 1969-70; project dir. Garden Valley Neighborhood Center, Cleve., summer 1970; planning and evaluation specialist Model Cities Program, Ann Arbor, Mich., 1972-73; asst. study dir. U. Mich., 1972-74, lectr. in psychology, 1976—; house supr. Family Group Homes, Inc., Ann Arbor, 1974-75; research asso. Fanon Research Center, Los Angeles, 1975-76; cons. in field; instr. un-wed mothers edn. program Community High Sch., Ann Arbor, 1972—. NIMH fellow, 1969-72. Mem. Am. Psychol. Assn., Nat. Assn. Black Psychologists, Soc. Psychol. Study Social Issues, Omega Psi Phi. Home: 19465 Chesterfield St Detroit MI 48221 Office: 1100 S University St Ann Arbor MI 48109

DUKEWITS, WALTER CARL, educator; b. Newton, Kans., Aug. 12, 1904; s. John W. and Clara (Boerger) D.; B.A., Concordia Sem., St. Louis, 1929; M.A., U. Nebr., 1930; Ed.D., Columbia, 1949. Missionary in South India, 1930-56; prin. Concordia High Sch., Vadakangulam, Tin.Dt. South India, 1938-56; prof., dean students St. John's Coll., Winfield, Kans., 1956-60, prof. religion, dir. research, 1960—. Mem. A.A.A.S., St. John's Coll. Alumni Assn. (treas., dir. Ednl. Found.), Phi Delta Kappa. Home: 509 College St Winfield KS 67156

DULL, PAUL PHELLIS, ret. judge; b. Celina, Ohio, May 30, 1907; s. Edgar M. and May (Phellis) D.; A.B., Ohio Wesleyan U., 1929; A.M., Columbia, 1931; J.D., Ohio State U., 1937; m. Dorothy E. Anderson, Dec. 23, 1933 (dec.); children—Peter Phellis, Jill; m. 2d, Alberta B. Buerkle, Apr. 7, 1966. Instr. polit. sci. U. Ky., 1931-32; publicity and student promotion Kan. Wesleyan U., 1933; pvt. law practice, Celina, 1937-44, 46-47; judge Common Pleas Ct., Mercer County, Ohio, 1947-74, ret., 1974. Bd. dirs. Mercer County chpt. A.R.C., Soc. Crippled Children. Served with USAAF, 1944-45. Mem. Am., Ohio, Mercer County bar assns., Am. Legion, Am. Judicature Soc., Acad. Polit. Sci., Am. Acad. Polit. and Social Sci., Ohio Hist. Soc., Sigma Alpha Epsilon, Phi Delta Phi, Omicron Delta Kappa, Pi Sigma Alpha, Kappa Delta Pi, Pi Delta Epsilon. Mason, Moose, Eagle, Woodman of the World. Author (books of verse): Sprouts From A Small Potato, 1940; Salt To Taste, 1948; Letting Out the Seams, 1954; Unmarked Intersections, 1966; Back Track, 1976; also jud. opinions and legal articles. Home: 659 N Walnut St Celina OH 45822 Office: Court House Celina OH 45822

DULL, WILBUR ROBBINS, lawyer; b. Gallatin, Mo., Oct. 4, 1914; s. Albert Ross and Ola (Vipond) D.; B.A., U. Iowa, 1936, J.D. with distinction, 1938; m. Doris Lister, June 5, 1938; children—James, Mary Beth (Mrs. James Brockman), William. Admitted to Iowa bar, 1938, since practiced in Ottumwa; asso. Gilmore, Moon & Bannister, 1942-46; partner Gilmore & Dull, 1946-53, Gilmore, Dull & Keith, 1953-65, Dull & Keith, 1965-69, Dull, Keith & Beaver, 1969—. Served with USNR, 1943-46. Mem. Wapello County (pres.), Iowa (gov.), Am. bar assns. Methodist. Elk, Rotarian. Home: 1577 N Van Buren St Ottumwa IA 52501 Office: 211 E 4th St Ottumwa IA 52501

DULUDE, DONALD OWEN, electric co. exec.; b. Bay City, Mich., Oct. 13, 1928; s. Owen P. and Bertranda L. (LaLonde) D.; B.S. in Mech. Engring., U. Mich., 1950; m. Irene M. Blondin, July 8, 1950; 1 son, Timothy Donald. Design engr. Bay City Shovels, Inc., 1950-57; mech. engr. Kuhlman Electric Co., Birmingham, Mich., 1957-60; partner Barribeau-Dulude & Assos., Inc., Birmingham, 1960-68; pres. gen. mgr. Quality Spring Products, Inc., subs. Kuhlman Corp., Coldwater, Mich., 1968-72, also dir., now exec. v.p. ops., dir. Kuhlman Corp. Bd. dirs. Howe (Ind.) Mil. Sch. Fathers Assn. Served with AUS, 1953-55. Mem. Spring Mfrs. Inst. (nat. dir. 1970-76), Mich. Spring Mfrs. Assn. (pres. 1972-75), Detroit, Battle Creek engring. socs., Oakland Hills C. of C. Roman Catholic. Elk. Patentee in field. Address 3912 Oakland Dr Birmingham MI 48012

DUMAS, ROBERT HUGH, librarian; b. Presque Isle, Maine, Aug. 5, 1926; s. Romie Jean and Hazel (Boyle) D.; A.B., U. Maine, 1948, postgrad. (univ. scholar), 1948-49; postgrad. Boston U., 1952-53; S.M., Sch. Library Sci., Simmons Coll., 1954; m. Barbara Jane Morrison, July 16, 1954; children—Robert Hugh, Lisa Diane, Leith Tristan, Maurice Andre, James Romie. Br. asst. Enoch Pratt Free Library, Balt., 1954-57; regional reference asst. Los Angeles Pub. Library, 1957; coordinator young adult services Dallas Pub. Library, 1958-62; library dir. Dedham (Mass.) Pub. Library, 1962-66; city librarian Decatur (Ill.) Pub. Library, 1966—. Bd. dirs. Decatur Area Arts Council. Mem. Am., Ill. library assns., ACLU, Common Cause. Club: Swan Boat (Boston). Home: 1346 W Macon St Decatur IL 62522 Office: 247 E North St Decatur IL 62523

DUMELLE, JACOB DOMONICK, govt. ofcl.; b. Chgo., Apr. 12, 1925; s. Frank and Virginia (Rebman) D.; B.S. in Mech. Engring., Ill. Inst. Tech., 1947, M.S. in Pub. Engring. Adminstrn., 1950; m. Dorothy Jean Konieczny, Feb. 23, 1957; children—Grace Antoinette, Margo Ilona, Lili Anne, Christopher Jacob. Asst. engr. Armour Research Found. of Ill. Inst. Tech., 1947-48; adminstrv. asst. to village mgr. Brookfield, Ill., 1950-53; administrv. asst. to city mgr., dir. insp. Peoria, Ill., 1953-58; city mgr. Lebanon, N.H., 1958-60; administrv. asst. to U.S. Senator Norris Cotton of N.H., 1960; research dir. Dept. of Air Pollution Control, Chgo., 1961-62; asst. chief maintenance and operation Met. Sanitary Dist. of Greater Chgo., 1962, 66-67, asst. chief engr., 1967-68; dep. asst. administr. Accelerated Pub. Works Program, Area Redevel. Administrn., Washington, 1962-64; project dir. Air Resources Mgmt. Study, Northeastern Ill. Planning Commn., 1964-66; tng. officer, dir. Lake Michigan Basin Office, Fed. Water Quality Adminstrn., 1968-70; mem. Ill. Pollution Control Bd., 1970-73, chmn., 1973—. Mem. Environmental Adv. Commn., Village of Oak Park (Ill.), 1972—. Served with USNR, 1944-46; lt. comdr. Res. Recipient Environmental Quality award U.S. Environmental Protection Agy., 1975. Mem. Air Pollution Control Assn. (sec., treas., v.p., pres. Lake Michigan states sect.), Internat. City Mgmt. Assn., Naval Res. Officers Assn., Water Pollution Control Fedn., Chgo. Pub. Health Engrs. Club, Nat., Ill. socs. profl. engrs., Tau Beta Pi, Pi Tau Sigma. Democrat. Roman Catholic. Contbr. articles on pollution control and govt. adminstrn. to profl. jours. Home: 411 N Elmwood Ave Oak Park IL 60302 Office: 309 W Washington St Chicago IL 60606

DUMKE, MELVIN PHILIP, dentist; b. Sleepy Eye, Minn., Jan. 23, 1920; s. Herman Gustav and Else Ida (Battig) D.; D.D.S., U. Minn., 1943; m. Phyllis Lorraine Steuck, June 25, 1950; children—Pamela, Bruce, Shari. Practice dentistry, Sleepy Eye, 1946-50, Morgan, Minn., 1950-66, Mankato, Minn., 1966—. Lectr. dental assts. Mankato State Coll., 1967-69. Mem. Town Council, Morgan, 1960-65. Bd. control Martin Luther Acad., New Ulm, Minn., 1965—. Served to capt., Dental Corps AUS, 1943-46. Mem. Am., Minn. (chmn. peer rev. com. 1973—) dental assns., Royal Soc. Health, S. Central Dental Study Club (pres. 1970), Fedn. Dentaire Internationale, Mankato C. of C., U. Minn. Alumni Assn., V.F.W. (recipient Distinguished Service award 1966, comdr. 1965), Am. Legion, Psi Omega. Lutheran (pres. congregation 1970). Lion (pres. 1965, 74, zone chmn. 1975). Clubs: Mankato Golf, U. Minn. Sch. Dentistry Century. Home: 364 Carol Ct Mankato MN 56001 Office: 430 S Broad St Mankato MN 56001

DUMKE, RAY MICHAEL, accountant; b. St. Joseph, Mich., Jan. 10, 1918; s. Michael and Pauline (Huelsberg) D.; B.S., Ind. U., 1941; m. Inez Doescher, May 3, 1942; children—Michael, Julie (Mrs. Marion Johnson), Suzanne (Mrs. Elmer Taylor), Anne. Account exec. Merrell, Lynch, Pierce, Fenner & Smith, N.Y.C., 1946; prin. partner Dumke & Assos., St. Joseph, Mich., 1947—. Tchr., Benton Harbor (Mich.) High Sch., evenings 1947-49. Mem. St. Joseph Sch. Bd., 1963—, pres., 1973-74. Served to capt. CAC, AUS, 1941-45. Mem. Ind. Accountants Assn. Mich. (pres., 1967), Sigma Nu. Methodist (trustee). Lion. Club: Berrien Hills Country. Home: 900 GreenWood Ave St Joseph MI 49085 Office: 204 1/2 State St St Joseph MI 49085

DUMOUCHEL, PAUL, archbishop; b. Winnipeg, Man., Can., Sept. 19, 1911; s. Joseph and Josephine Dumouchel; student U. Man., 1929-30, Sem. Lebret, Sask., Can., 1931-36; grad. St. Boniface (Man.) Coll., 1930. Ordained priest Roman Catholic Ch., 1936; missionary to Indians of Man., 1936-50; retreat master, 1940-50; prin. sch., 1950-55; bishop of Keewatin, Man., Can., 1955-67; archbishop, LePas, Man., 1967—. Author: Saulteux Grammar, 1942. Address: 108 1st St West The Pas MB Canada

DUNAWAY, DONALD LEE, nuclear safety specialist; b. Raymond, Ind., Oct. 14, 1934; s. Russell Dwight and Ruth Irene (Johnson) Dunaway; m. Janice DeHoff, Sept. 4, 1955; children—Karla, Eric, Joel. B.S., Miami U., 1956, M.B.A., 1964. Analyst, Tech. Div., Nat. Lead Co. of Ohio, Cin., 1956-60, nuclear safety dept., 1960—, dept. chief, 1968—. Pres. bd. trustees, Brookville United Methodist Ch., 1966-72, treas., 1972-75; mem. Brookville Library bd., 1967—, pres., 1972—; pres. Franklin County Hist. Soc., 1970-71; v.p. Brookville Found., 1976—. Mem. Am. Nuclear Soc. (exec. com. nuclear criticality safety div., 1972-75, vice chmn., 1977—), Masons. Contbr. articles on nuclear criticality safety in transp. to publs. Home: Route 3 Box 87 Brookville IN 45239

DUNBAR, ROBERT ALEXANDER, cons. soil and found. engr.; b. Eveleth, Minn., Sept. 30, 1928; s. Robert George and Ethel Irene (Saari) D.; B.C.E., Cornell U., 1954, M.C.E., 1958; m. Wanda F. Kerr, May 2, 1959; 1 son, Douglas R. Project engr. Photog. Survey Corp., Toronto, Ont., Can., 1955-56; project civil engr. Canadian Colombo Plan (Ceylon), 1956-57; chief geol. engr. Photronix, Inc., Columbus, Ohio, 1958-60; owner, prin. engr. Dunbar Geotech. Engrs., Columbus, 1960—; lectr. air photo interpretation dept. geodetic sci. Ohio State U., 1960-64. Served with U.S. Army, 1946-48; Japan. Recipient Bausch & Lomb Photogrammetric award, 1955. Registered profl. engr. Ohio, W.Va., Ky., Ind., Pa., Ont. Mem. ASCE, Am. Cons. Engrs. Council, Nat. Soc. Profl. Engrs., ASTM, Geol. Soc. Am., Am. Arbitration Assn. (panel arbitrators). Mason. Clubs: Scioto Boat, Nat. Flyers Assn. (Columbus). Home: 2474 Buckley Rd Columbus OH 43220 Office: 1286 W Lane Ave Columbus OH 43221

DUNBAR, WANDA KERR (MRS. ROBERT A. DUNBAR), advt. agy. exec.; b. Mansfield, Ohio, Oct. 9, 1931; d. Martin Wayne and Blanche B. (Parker) Kerr; student Capital U., 1949-50; B.S. in Journalism, Ohio State U., 1953, postgrad., 1956, 61; student Columbus Sch. Arts and Design, 1957-58; m. Robert A. Dunbar, May 2, 1959; 1 son, Douglas. Pub. relations dir. Columbus Goodwill Industries (Ohio), 1952, Dayton Goodwill Industries Rehab. Center (Ohio), 1953-55; community relations officer, heading promotion of bond issue Slum Clearance Dept. City Columbus, 1955-57; editor internal mag., co. photographer Ross Labs., Columbus, 1957-60; pres., dir. Wanda Kerr Dunbar, Inc., Columbus, 1961—; editor, advt. mgr. Ohio Contractor, Ohio Contractors Assn., 1962—. Sec., Wing 41, Nightingale Cottage Convalescent Home for Children, 1965, pres., 1966. Recipient Mag. award Asso. Contractors Am., 1965; 1st pl. Dayton Community Chest contest in pub. relations, 1953. Mem. Women in Constrn. (charter), Women in Communications, Ohio Contractors Assn., Nat. Fedn. Ind. Bus., Columbus Council Communicating Arts. Republican. Mem. Community Ch. Club: Scioto Boat (Columbus). Home: 2474 Buckley Rd Columbus OH 43220 Office: 4645 Executive Dr Columbus OH 43220

DUNCAN, DONALD ROSS, lawyer; b. Kansas City, Mo., Nov. 22, 1935; s. Walter Fredrick and Lillie May (Medlock) D.; B.S., S.W. Mo. State U., 1957; J.D., Washington U., St. Louis, 1964; m. Melinda Ann Field, Aug. 16, 1963; children—Gregory Scott, Jonathan Field. Admitted to Mo. bar, 1964; mem. firm Turner, Reid & Duncan, Springfield, Mo., 1964—; spl. asst. atty. gen. Mo., 1969—. Instr. bus. law So. Mo. State U., 1965-72. Chmn. health task force Goals for Springfield, 1970-72; v.p. Lakes Country Comprehensive Health Plan Council, 1969—. Bd. dirs. Lester E. Cox Med. Center, Ozark Christian Counselling Service. Served with inf. AUS, 1957-61. Mem. Greene County Bar Assn. (chmn. cts. com. 1970-72). Baptist (deacon). Home: 3038 S Marlan St Springfield MO 65804 Office: Empire Bank Bldg Springfield MO 65804

DUNCAN, NEVIN JAMES, ednl. adminstr.; b. Oshkosh, Wis., June 15, 1933; s. James Francis and Gladys Irene (Killiam) D.; B.S., U. Wis., 1954; M.Ed., Seattle U., 1960; D.M.S., Wash. Mil. Inst., 1962; Ph.D., Northgate Grad. Sch., 1970; Ed.S., Mankato State Coll., 1972; m. Christel Baldzun, June 15, 1956; 1 dau., Sin-Jin. Tchr. history Franklin Pierce High Sch., Tacoma, 1960-64; prof. history Olympic Coll., Bremerton, Wash., 1964-67; supr. student tchrs. prof. edn. Bemidji (Minn.) State Coll., 1967-74; prin. Alvarado (Minn.) High Sch., 1974—. Cons. Chinese affairs Dept. State, 1973—, ednl. psychology Bemidji State Coll. Jury foreman Beltrami County, Minn., 1972-73; vol. Avarado Fire Dept. Served to col. AUS, 1954-56. Decorated Legion of Merit, D.F.C., Bronze Star medal, Air medal, Purple Heart, Army Commendation medal. Middle Eastern Inst. fellow Hamline U., 1968, East Asian fellow Hamline U., 1975. Mem. Minn., Nat. assns. secondary sch. prins., Am. Legion. Lutheran. Elk, Lion. Author: Relationship of Western Pragmatism to Contemporary Neo-Confucianism, 1970; Rectification of Names, An Attempt at Synthesis, 1975. Home: PO Box 85 Alvarado MN 56710

DUNCAN, RICHARD LEONARD, civic worker, fin. cons.; b. Hancock, Minn., Oct. 20, 1902; s. Walter L. and Nellie (Moe) D.; student Carleton Coll., 1923-25; A.B., Miami U., Oxford, Ohio, 1927; m. Dorothy C. Runyon, June 13, 1927. Asst. in bus. office Miami U., 1925-35, comptroller, 1935-47; v.p. in charge ops. Western Coll., 1947-50, v.p., 1950-51; past pres. Oxford Loan & Bldg. Assn., dir. emeritus First Nat. Bank and Trust Co. of Hamilton, Ohio; trustee, treas. Health Care Mut. Ins. Co. Trustee, treas. Hosp. Care. Corp., Cin.; trustee, treas. Theta Chi Found. Past asst. treas., controller United Appeal; pres. Friends of Library, Miami U.; past exec. sec. gen. budget com. Community Chest, past asst. treas. ARC Cin. area, also past mem. disaster com. Butler County chpt.; past trustee, treas. United Campus Ministry, Miami U., Oxford; trustee Westover Home for Aged, Health Planning Assn. Butler County Council on Aging; treas. bd. trustees Fort Hamilton Hosp.; gov., pres. bd. Cin. unit Shriners Hosps. for Crippled Children Insts. for Burns; asso. Coll.-Conservatory of Music of U. Cin.; trustee Greater Cin. Hosp. Council; treas., trustee Health Careers Assn. Cin.; past trustee, treas. Cin. Scholarship Found; past mem. area com. Girl Scouts U.S.A. Recipient Bishop medal Miami U., 1973. Mem. AAAS, Am., Ohio forestry assns., Am. Numismatic Assn., Soc. Philatelic Americans, Am., Washington philatelic socs., Oxford Museum Assn., Hist. and Philos. Soc. of Ohio, Archeol. Inst. Am., Am. Mgmt. Assn., Internat. Wood Collectors Soc. (treas.), Ohio Citizens Council, Ohio Acad. Sci., Am. Mus. Natural History, Cin. Zool. Soc. (cons.), Greater Cin. Safety Council, Ohio Soc. N.Y., Phi Beta Kappa, Theta Chi (pres. nat. trustee). Presbyterian. Mason (33 deg.), Odd Fellow, Kiwanian. Clubs: University, Cincinnati, Fraternity, U. Cin. Faculty, Butler County Torch, Bankers (Cin.); Basin Harbor (Vergennes, Vt.); Hamilton City; Oxford Men's. Home: 101 University Ave Oxford OH 45056 Office: 3400 Vine St Cincinnati OH 45220

DUNEA, GEORGE, physician; b. Craiova, Rumania, June 1, 1933; s. Charles L. and Gerda (Low) D.; came to U.S., 1964; M.D., U. Sydney (Australia), 1957; m. Mary Mills Barr, 1969; children by previous marriage—Mary Louise, John (Barr); 1 dau., Melanie. Intern, Royal N. Shore Hosp., Sydney, 1958-59; resident in internal medicine, Australia and Eng., 1959-63; nephrology fellow Cleve. Clinic, Presbyn.-St. Luke's Hosp., Chgo., 1964-66; practice internal medicine specializing in nephrology, Chgo., 1972—; attending physician Cook County Hosp., 1966—, dir. dept. nephrology-hypertension, 1969—; prof. medicine U. Health Scis.-Chgo. Med. Sch.; vis. prof. medicine Rush Med. Coll. Active various civic coms. Diplomate Am. Bds. Internal Medicine,

Nephrology. Fellow A.C.P.; mem. Royal Coll. Physicians (London, Edinburgh), AMA, Am. Soc. Nephrology, Brit. Med. Assn., Soc. Med. History. Author monthly letter Brit. Med. Jour.; contbr. chpts. to books, articles to profl. jours. Home: 209 E Lake Shore Dr Chicago IL 60611 Office: 1835 W Harrison St Chicago IL 60612

DUNHAM, HENRY HOWARD, physician; b. Galesburg, Kans., Aug. 16, 1912; s. Henry E. and Lelia (Magner) D.; B.S., Kans. State Coll., 1935; Sc.M., Brown U., 1937, Ph.D., 1939; M.D., U. Kans., 1944; m. Mary Clare Couch, Sept. 3, 1954. Research biologist Carnegie Instn. of Washington, Cold Spring Harbor, N.Y., 1939-41; intern Wis. General Hosp., Madison, 1944-45; resident U. Kans. Med. Center, Kansas City, Kans. 1948-51; practice medicine specializing in radiology, Wabash, Ind., 1962-77; dir. dept. radiology; Wabash County Hosp.; lectr. biology Evansville Coll., 1957-61. Served with M.C., USNR, 1945-46. Mem. Am. Coll. Radiology, Am. Soc. Zoology. Research on genetics of Cladocerans, avian genetics and reproductive physiology. Home: Rural Route 2 Box 139 A Neosho MO 64850

DUNHAM, JOHN LEE, assn. exec.; b. Charleston, W.Va., Mar. 4, 1939; s. George and Mary (Summers) D.; student Wilson Jr. Coll., 1956-59, Loop Coll. (Chgo.), 1962-63, Roosevelt U., 1963-68, U. Wash., 1967; m. Gloria Armstrong, Aug. 18, 1972. Data processing technician Social Security Adminstrn., Chgo., 1956-60; computer technician Chgo. Police Dept., 1961-64; dir. computer ops., membership services rep. U.S. Savs. and Loan League, Chgo., 1964—; lectr. in field; founder, pres. Skylite Enterprises, Inc. Bd. dirs. Bio-Med. Careers Assn. Mem. Systems Programmers Soc. (chmn. bd.), Am. Savs. and Loan Inst. (mem. grad. thesis rev. bd.), Cosmopolitan C. of C., Am. Bus. and Econ. Soc. Chgo., Black Execs. Chgo., Nat. Bus. League. Author: Someday I'm Going to Be Somebody, 1970. Club: Sno-Gophers Ski (Chgo.). Home: 8747 S Cornell St Chicago IL 60617 Office: 111 E Wacker Dr Chicago IL 60601

DUNKELBERG, ALBERT GIBBS, lawyer; b. Hull, Iowa, June 29, 1922; s. Elmer Cornelius and Mildred (Gibbs) D.; LL.B., Drake U., 1952; m. Leone Kathryn Schultz, Sept. 7, 1950; children—Kathryn Diane, Kermit Gibbs, Kendall Alan. Admitted to Iowa bar, 1952, U.S. Dist. Ct. bars, 1952, 53; partner firm Sams & Dunkelberg, Osage, Iowa, 1953-66, Dunkelberg & McKinley, Osage, 1966-68, Dunkelberg, McKinley & Folkers, Osage, 1968—; dir. Osage Farmers Nat. Bank. Sec., Osage Devel. Corp., 1960-61. Treas., City of Osage, 1960—; mem. 2d Jud. Dist. Iowa nominating com., 1972—; magistrate appointment commr., Mitchell County, Iowa, 1973—. Served with USNR, 1941-46; PTO. Mem. Am. Legion, C. of C. (pres. 1958), Iowa State, 2d Jud. Dist., 12th Jud. Dist. (pres. 1965-66) Mitchell County (pres. 1965-70) bar assns. Lutheran. Kiwanian (1st pres. 1963-64). Home: 804 Poplar St Osage IA 50461 Office: 515 State St Osage IA 50461

DUNKELBERGER, DENNIS ALAN, advt. agy. exec.; b. Dayton, Ohio, Dec. 17, 1946; s. Jack Edward and Evelyn Mae (Steiner) D.; B.F.A., Miami U., Ohio, 1969; m. Nancy Jo Nassif, Apr. 15, 1972; 1 son, Jeffery Alan. Artist, Standard Register Co., Dayton, 1969; designer E.F. MacDonald Incentive Co., Dayton, 1969-72; designer, illustrator Penny-Ohlmann-Neiman, Dayton, 1972-73, art dir., 1973-74, creative dir., 1974-75; pres., creative dir. Dennis Dunkelberger Advt., Dayton, 1975—. Bd. dirs. Dayton Sertoma Club, 1977; campaign planner Dayton Sch. Bd., 1970. Recipient many advt. awards including Best of Show, Dayton Advt. Club, 1975, 76, Champion Paper award, 1975, Chrysler-Plymouth Spl. award, 1971; logos pub. in Carter's Trademarks/5, Curtis 100 Best Letterheads, Mead Paper award, 1977. Mem. Dayton Advt. Club, Am. Mktg. Assn., Dayton Bus. Forum (pres. 1978), Dayton C. of C., 304 for Big Brothers Dayton. Democrat. Lutheran. Clubs: Dayton Racquet, Dayton Court House, Phi Kappa Tau. Office: 730 South Main Bldg Dayton OH 45402

DUNKLAU, RUPERT LOUIS, corp. dir.; b. Arlington, Nebr., May 19, 1927; s. Louis and Amelia (Gnuse) D.; B.S., U. Nebr., 1950; m. Ruth Eggert, June 4, 1950; children—Paul, Janet. With Valmont Industries, Inc., Valley, Nebr., 1950-72, now dir.; dir. Fremont Nat. Bank (Nebr.), Nebr. State Savs. and Loan, Fremont. Trustee Midland Lutheran Coll., Fremont, Dodge County Meml. Hosp., Fremont, Luth. Med Central, Wheatridge Found., Chgo., Luth. Ch.-Mo. Synod Found.; bd. dirs. Valparaiso U. Served with USNR, 1945. Lutheran (bd. dirs., mem. nat. body). Home: 2146 Phelps Ave Fremont NE 68025 Office: 1900 E Military St Fremont NE 68025

DUNLEVY, JAMES HENRY, physician; b. Hillsboro, N.D., July 17, 1926; s. James Henry and Ovidia Amanda (Thorstad) D.; B.A., U. Iowa, 1947; M.D., Washington U., 1951; L.H.D., Parsons Coll., 1972; m. Allie Lu Phelps, June 12, 1949; children—Lucinda Ann, Mary Jane, Amy Jo. Intern U. Minn., 1952; gen. practice resident U. Iowa, 1953; practice medicine and surgery, Fairfield, Iowa, 1953—; mem. staff Jefferson County Hosp., pres. 1969-70; med. edn. com. U. Iowa, 1970-71; continuing edn. com. U. Iowa Med. Sch., 1969-71. Mem. Fairfield Community Sch. Bd., 1951-70; v.p. Fairfield Community Concert Bd., 1965—; Fairfield Park & Recreation Bd., 1977. Served with USN, 1944-46. Diplomate Am. Bd. Family Practice. Mem. Am. Soc. Anesthesiologists, Jefferson County Med. Soc. (pres. 1976), Fairfield C. of C. (bd. dirs. 1955-57), Iowa Alumna Council. Lutheran (mem. exec. bd. Synod, 1968—; exec. council, 1970—). Rotarian (pres. 1958-59). Home: 808 North Ct Fairfield IA 52556 Office: 304 South Maple St Fairfield IA 52556

DUNLOP, ROBERT MITCHELL, banker, city ofcl.; b. Orange City, Iowa, Nov. 13, 1917; s. George and Florence Annie (Mitchell) D.; B.A., Coe Coll., 1941; grad. Grad. Sch. Banking U. Wis., 1965; m. Dorothy Louise Carr, Oct. 21, 1941; children—Mark Robert, Scott Carr, Deborah Louise. Owner, operator Dunlop Ins. Agy., Orange City, 1946-58; with Northwestern State Bank, Orange City, 1958—, v.p., 1963—, dir., 1959—. Pres., fire chief Orange City Vol. Fire Dept., 1950-62; bd. dirs. Sioux County Hist. Soc., 1969-70; active Boy Scouts Am.; mem. city council, Orange City, 1948-64, mayor, 1964—. Served to capt., AUS, 1942-46. Decorated Bronze Star. Mem. Northwest Iowa Mayor's Assn. (pres. 1969-70), C. of C., Am. Legion. Lion. Club: Sioux Golf and Country. Home: 404 2d St NE Orange City IA 51041 Office: 122 Central Ave NW Orange City IA 51041

DUNMIRE, RAYMOND VERYL, librarian; b. Vandergrift, Pa., Dec. 17, 1925; s. Robert Braden and Fay (Stubrick) D.; B.A., Thiel Coll., 1950; M.A., Fla. State U., 1957; m. Ruth March, Apr. 4, 1953; children—Perry Carl, Cary Allan, Barry Ivan. Prof., head librarian Thiel Coll., Greenville, Pa., 1953-65; dir. libraries Southeastern Community Coll., Whiteville, N.C., 1965-69; dir. libraries, asso. prof. Augustana Coll., Sioux Falls, S.D., 1969—; inter-library loan librarian U. Fla. at Gainesville, 1960-61, instr. Sch. Edn., 1961-62. Cons., evaluator So. Assn. Secondary Schs. and Colls., various locations, 1968—. Mem. com. Cub Scouts Am., Sioux Falls. Bd. dirs. Center Western Studies, Sioux Falls. Served with USAAF, 1943-46. Mem. ALA (life), Southeastern, S.D. library assns., N.C. Lit. and Hist. Soc., Assn. Ednl. Communications and Tech., AAUP, Beta Phi Mu, Phi Alpha Theta, Delta Sigma Phi. Lutheran (mem. ch. council). Contbr. articles to profl. jours. Office: Mikkelsen Library Augustana Coll Sioux Falls SD 57102

DUNN, ARTHUR ALEXANDER, credit corp. exec.; b. Boston, Mar. 23, 1914; s. Arthur Clarence and Isabelle (Hinckley) D.; B.S., Tufts U., 1937; m. Mary Tyler Spohn, July 21, 1945; children—Arthur Alexander, Tyler Cameron. Asst. to pres. State Mut. Ins. Co., Worcester, Mass., 1958-64, v.p., 1965; asst. chmn. bd. New Eng. Mut. Life Ins. Co., Boston, 1965-68; v.p. ops. U.S. Life Corp., N.Y.C., 1968-70, pres., chief exec. officer U.S. Life Credit Corp., Schaumburg, Ill., 1970—; dir. Nat. Consumer Fin. Assn., 1970—. Pres., Fairlawn Hosp., 1962-66. Served to comdr. USNR, 1942-46. Recipient several awards Am. Mgmt. Assn. Republican. Episcopalian. Home: 442 W Russell St Barrington IL 60010 Office: 1027 E State Pkwy Schaumburg IL 60195

DUNN, ARTHUR SEYMOUR, dentist; b. Chgo., Sept. 23, 1923; s. Morris Conrad and Hanna (Opper) D.; B.S., U. Ill., 1945, D.D.S., 1947; m. Lila Rosen, Mar. 10, 1946 (div. July, 1965); children—Fredrick, Daniel, Charlotte, Nancy; m. 2d, Elaine Smuckler Liebman, Nov. 11, 1965; stepchildren—Jeffrey, Vance. Intern Brooke Gen. Hosp., San Antonio, 1947-48; practice gen. dentistry, Chgo., 1948-51, 53-56, Glencoe, Ill., 1954—; mem. staff Highland Park (Ill.) Hosp.; instr. Research and Edn. Hosp., Coll. Medicine, U. Ill., Chgo., 1949-50. Served to capt. AUS, 1943-44, 47-48, 51-53; Korea. Fellow Royal Soc. Health (Gt. Britain); mem. Pierre Fauchard Acad., Chgo. (legal com. 1960-63, com. on geriatrics 1976—, patient relations com. 1976-77), Ill., Am., Israel dental assns., Am. Acad. Implant Dentistry (pres. central dist. 1975), Am. Acad. Oral Medicine, Am. Cleft Palate Assn., Am. Speech and Hearing Assn., Am. Soc. Preventive Dentistry, Am. Soc. Geriatric Dentistry, U.S. Power Squadrons, Alpha Omega. Jewish. Mem. B'nai B'rith. Club: Columbia Yacht. Home: 720 Oakton St Evanston IL 60202 Office: 333 Park Ave Glencoe IL 60022

DUNN, DOROTHY FAY, govt. ofcl.; b. Sidney, Ill.; d. Lafayette and Jeannettie (Thompson) Dunn; B.S., U. Ill., 1939; M.S. in Pub. Health, U. N.C., 1946; Ph.D., Purdue U., 1962; postgrad. U. Minn., U. N.C. summer, 1964. Home mgmt. supr. U.S. Dept. Agr., 1939-43; personnel utilization Fed. Civil Service, 1943-44; home econs. field rep. U. Wis., 1944-45; dir. health edn. Will County Health Dept., Ill., 1946-47; health edn. cons. Ill. Dept. Pub. Health, 1947-51; asso. prof. health sci. U. Ill., 1951-67; prof., head dept. home econs. Western Ky. U., Bowling Green, 1967-68; prof., chmn. home mgmt., econs. and equipment Stout State U., Menomonie, Wis., 1968-71; asst. to regional dir. for consumer affairs FDA, Chgo., 1971—. Recipient FDA commendable service award, 1975. Fellow Am. Pub. Health Assn., AAAS, Am. Coll. Health Assn. (chmn. health edn. sect., program chmn., health edn. chmn.), Am. Sch. Health Assn.; mem. Am., Ill. (past chmn. health com.) assns. home econs., Ill. Pub. Health Assn. (sec.-treas., mem. exec. bd., rep. to Am. Pub. Health Assn. governing council), AAUP, AAUW (past chmn. profl. sect.), Nat., Ill. socs. pub. health educators, Nat. Assn. Ednl. Broadcasters, Am. Council Consumer Interest, Internat. Platform Assn., Omicron Nu, Sigma Delta Epsilon, Kappa Delta Pi. Contbr. profl. publs. Research in domestic water demand, behavioral characteristics of smokers, Tb, non-teaching positions for home economists. Home: 504 E Chalmers St Champaign IL 61820 Office: Room A 1945 175 W Jackson Blvd Chicago IL 60604

DUNN, EVERETT WESLEY, cons. civil engr.; b. Summit, S.D., Aug. 1, 1892; s. Moncena and Lois (Woodward) D.; B.S. in Civil Engring., S.D. State U., 1913; m. Dorothea Hesse, Feb. 26, 1916; children—Mary Louise (Mrs. Robert Bartelt), Dorothy Jane (Mrs. Clare Vanden Broek), James E., Lois Ann (Mrs. Howard Jubinville). Dist. engr. Iowa Hwy. Commn., Sioux City, 1918-40; gen. mgr. Sioux Syndicate Contractors, Sioux City, 1941-43; industry mem. U.S. Wage Adjustment Bd., Washington, 1944-46; asst. gen. mgr. Birch Johnson Lytle, Alaska Mil. Constrn., Seattle, 1946-49; cons. Alaska Asso. Gen. Contractors, Anchorage, 1949-51; industry mem. Constrn. Industry Stblzn. Com., Washington, 1950-52; cons. engr. Peter Kewit Sons Co., Portsmouth, Ohio, 1952-53, iron ore devel. Lake Superior & Ishpening R.R., Marquette, Mich., 1956; cons. various projects, 1957-64; spl. cons. Nev. test site AEC Contractors, 1964-77. Trustee Eugene and Lottie Grove Trust. Named Distinguished Engr., S.D. State U. Coll. Engring., 1977. Fellow ASCE; mem. Nat. Soc. Profl. Engrs., Iowa Engring. Soc. (life mem.), Chi Epsilon (hon.), Tau Beta Pi (hon.). Republican. Methodist. Mason. Club: Meadowbrook Golf (Hartley, Iowa). Home and office: 530 W Maple St Hartley IA 51346

DUNN, FRANCIS GILL, state justice; b. Scenic, S.D., Nov. 12, 1913; s. Thomas Bernard and Mary (Gill) D.; student Dakota State Coll., 1931-34; LL.B., U. S.D., 1937; LL.M., George Washington U., 1948; m. Eldred Elizabeth Wagner, 1942; children—David, Rebecca Dunn Smith, Thomas, Carol Dunn Norbeck. Individual practice law, Madison, S.D., 1937-41, Sioux Falls, S.D., 1954-56; sec. to U.S. Senator W. J. Bulow, 1941-42; trial atty. U.S. Dept. Justice, Washington, 1946-50; asst. U.S. atty. for S.D., 1950-54; municipal judge, Sioux Falls, 1956-59, circuit judge, 1959-73; justice S.D. Supreme Ct., Pierre, 1973-74, chief justice, 1974—. Served to lt. USN, 1942-46. Mem. Am., S.D. bar assns., VFW, Delta Theta Phi. Roman Catholic. Club: Elks. Office: 1100 E Church St Pierre SD 57501*

DUNN, GILBERT BRUCE, supt. schs.; b. Port-Au-Prince, Haiti, Feb. 1, 1933; s. A. Orville and Florence Wilheminia (Puels) D.; B.A., Andrews U., 1955; M.A., U. Mich., 1956; Edn. Specialist, Mich. State U., 1967; m. Mary Faye Youngs, June 6, 1955; children—Scott, Greg, Rebecca, Shelley. Asst. supt. schs., Pinckney, Mich., 1965-68; supt. schs., New Lothrop, Mich., 1968-73, Cassopolis, Mich., 1973—. Mem. Shiawassee County Mental Health Bd., 1972-73, Livingston County Mental Health Bd., 1966-68. Mem. Am., Mich. assns. sch. adminstrs., Sch. Adminstrs. Polit. Action Com., Cassopolis C. of C., Mid Mich. Adminstrs. Assn. (v.p. 1971-72), Berrien-Cass Adminstrs. Assn. (sec.-treas. 1974-75). Mem. Seventh Day Adventist Ch. Clubs: Lions, Optimists. Home: Route 1 Cassopolis MI 49031 Office: Cassopolis Pub Schs Decatur Rd Cassopolis MI 49031

DUNN, HORTON, JR., chem. research co. information scientist; b. Coleman, Tex., Sept. 3, 1929; s. Horton and Lora Dean (Bryant) D.; B.A. summa cum laude, Hardin-Simmons U., 1951; M.S., Case Western Res. U. Research chemist Lubrizol Corp., Cleve., 1953-70, dir. tech. info. center, 1970—; chmn. bd. dirs., bus. mgr. Isotopics, Cleve., 1964-67, editor, 1961-63. Mem. Am. Chem. Soc. (chpt. treas. 1968-70), Am. Soc. for Info. Sci. (chpt. pres. 1973-74), A.A.A.S., Beta Phi Mu, Alpha Chi. Contbr. articles to profl. jours. Patentee in field. Home: 530 Sycamore Dr Cleveland OH 44132 Office: 29400 Lakeland Blvd Wickliffe OH 44092

DUNN, JOSEPH BRANNON, mfg. co. exec.; b. Cambridge, Ohio, Oct. 20, 1914; s. Frank Cleason and Golde (Brannon) D.; B.S. in Mech. Engring., Tri State Coll., 1935; m. Marjorie Beatrice Kelso, Apr. 19, 1934; children—Dea Rae, William B., John R., Christopher C. Tool design engr. to sr. project engr. Aeroproducts div. Gen. Motors Co., 1939-50; quality mgr. Master Vibrator Co., Dayton, Ohio, 1950-52, mgr. Decco Machine & Tool Co., Dayton, 1952-53; design and field rep. U.S. Lite Ray Co., Dayton, 1953-54; prodn. contact, sr. project engr. Fregidaire Co., Dayton, 1954-73; sr. project engr. Delco Air Conditioning Co., Dayton, 1973-75; dir. engring. Linton Industries Co., Dayton, 1975—. Mem. Soc. Automotive Engrs. Republican. Methodist. Clubs: Foremans, Masons. Home: 4160 Cloverleaf Rd Vandalia OH 45377 Office: 3490 S Dixie Dr Dayton OH 45439

DUNN, LEHMANN MAYNARD, cons. civil engr.; b. Port Huron, Mich., Mar. 1, 1914; s. Maynard E. and Hazel E. (Lehmann) D.; B.S. in Civil Engring., Mich. Technol. U., 1935; m. Annetta Jane Broeckaert, Aug. 17, 1940; children—David B., Daniel L., Deryl D. Commd. 2d lt. C.E., U.S. Army, 1935, advanced through grades to lt. col. Res., ret.; surveyor Detroit Dist., U.S. C.E., 1935-36, 2d lt. 6th Engrs., Ft. Lawton, Wash., 1936-37; constrn. insp. U.S. Bur. of Reclamation, Coulee Dam, Wash., 1937-38; mining engr. P.I.M. Co., Vulcan, Mich., 1938-41; with C.E., Erie Proving Ground, Ohio, 1942-42; partner Blue Water Concrete and Constrn. Co., Port Huron, 1947-48; pres. Dunn Constrn. Engring., Inc., Port Huron, 1948—. Dir. Indsl. Devel. Corp., Port Huron, 1950-52. Mem. City of Port Huron Code Rev. Com., 1951-53, City of Port Huron Bldg. Code Bd. of Appeals, 1955-57; mem. Mich. Housing Code Commn., 1956-57. Active Blue Water council Boy Scouts Am., 1948—, pres., 1960-63, 65-67; mem. Port Huron Found., 1951—, Port Huron Mus. of Arts and History, 1963—, Mich. Tb and Respiratory Disease Assn., 1952—, Mich. United Conservation Club, 1960—. Registered profl. engr. and land surveyor, Mich. Recipient Silver Beaver award, Boy Scouts Am., 1964. Mem. Nat. (dir. 1956-60), Mich. (dir. at large 1951-54, v.p. 1954-55, pres. 1955-56) socs. profl. engrs., Profl. Engrs. in Pvt. Practice, Profl. Engrs. in Constrn. (chmn. planning and ethics), Mich. Soc. Registered Land Surveyors, Mich. Assn. Professions (dir. 1970—), Port Huron C. of C. (dir. 1970-72, v.p. 1972-73), Metal Bldg. Dealers Assn. (chmn. ethics com. 1970-72, dir. 1970-74, pres. 1972-73). Presbyn. Clubs: Masons, Mich. Technol. U., Varsity, Alumni, Huskies, Rotary (pres. Port Huron 1959-60, gov. Dist. 633, 1976-77); Skippers Booster (St. Clair County Community Coll.). Home: 5690 Lakeshore Rd Port Huron MI 48060 Office: PO Box 884 2240 10th St Port Huron MI 48060

DUNN, LILLIAN JOYCE DANIELS, sch. counselor; b. Robbins, Ill., Aug. 9, 1938; d. Douglas Ivory and Margie (Moore) Daniels; B.A., St. Augustine's Coll., 1960; M.S., Chgo. State U., 1976, adminstrv. certificate, 1977; m. Kenneth Dunn, Apr. 25, 1965; children—Darrin Douglas. Librarian, Bookmobile, South Suburban Library System, Robbins, Ill., 1968-69; substitute tchr. Chgo. Pub. Schs., 1960-61; tchr. French, Phillips High Sch., Chgo., 1961; tchr., Marshall Elementary Sch., Chgo., 1961-62, Carver High Sch., Chgo., 1963-65, Parker High Sch., Chgo., 1965-66, Harlan High Sch., Chgo., 1966-68; tchr. English, grade advisor Simeon Vocat. High Sch., Chgo., 1969-76, secondary edn. counselor, 1976—. Mem. Simeon Vocat. Local Sch. Council, Chgo., 1974-77, PTA, 1970-74; mem. Ill. State Visitation Accreditation Team, Chgo., 1977—; sec. Missionary Union and Aid Soc., Chgo., 1960-76; exec. sec. Robbins Bicentennial Events, 1975-76; pres. New Idea Party, 1972-75. St. Augustine's Coll. scholar, 1956-60. Mem. Am. Personnel and Guidance Assn., Phi Delta Kappa, Phi Kappa Alpha, Alpha Kappa Alpha. Methodist. Club: Elks. Home: 13735 S Trumbull St Robbins IL 60472 Office: 8235 S Vincennes Ave Chicago IL 60620

DUNN, LYMAN, chem. engr.; b. Cherry Valley, Ark., June 6, 1907; s. William Dewitt and Augusta (Hicks) D.; student U. Ill., 1926-29, Ill. Inst. Tech., 1931-32; m. Elizabeth Hinckle, July 11, 1931. Chemist, Bowman Dairy Co., Chgo., 1929-38; head, alkali research Detrex Corp., Detroit, 1938-42; sales engr. and cons. engr. various firms, 1942-52; founder, mgr. spl. products div. City Products Corp., Chgo., 1952-61; founder, pres. Marlan Co., Chgo., 1961—; dir. Wittmore Mfg. Co. (Altoona, Pa.), Marco Finance Co. (Chgo.), Tastee Freez of Ariz. (Phoenix), Village Enterprises, Inc. (St. Louis). Patron, Sisters of Precious Blood, Rome City, Ind., 1964—. Club: Chicago Yacht. Patentee chem., mech., and food industry fields. Home: 535 N Michigan Ave Chicago IL 60611 Office: 325 W 25th Pl Chicago IL 60616

DUNN, MARVIN DALE, judge; b. Normal, Ill., June 4, 1930; s. Ollie E. and Ruby (Bradley) D.; B.S., U. Ill., 1954, J.D., 1957; m. Carole June Lirot, Apr. 8, 1961; children—Sarah Elizabeth, Bradley Paul. Admitted to Ill. bar, 1957; practiced in Aurora, Ill., 1957—; asso. Sears & Streit, attys., Aurora and Chgo., 1957-62; partner Paklin, Nelson & Dunn, Aurora, 1962-70, Nelson & Dunn, attys., Aurora, 1970-76; judge 16th Jud. Circuit Ct., Geneva, Ill., 1976—. asst. states atty., Kane County, Ill., 1966-76. Served with USNR, 1951-53. Mem. Am. Judicature Soc., Am. Legion, Am., Ill., Kane County (pres., dir. 1964—) bar assns., Ill. Trial Lawyers Assn., Navy League, Aurora Jr. C. of C. (dir. 1959-62), Aurora Union League. Elk, Rotarian. Home: Route 1 Box 633 Partridge Rd Batavia IL 60510 Office: Kane County Courthouse Geneva IL

DUNN, ROBERT SIGLER, electronics co. exec.; b. Cin., Aug. 13, 1926; s. John Wesley and Miriam (Sigler) D.; B.S. in Mech. Engring., Purdue U., 1949, B.S. in Elec. Engring., 1949; m. Barbara Rigdon, June 26, 1949; children—Anne Louise, John Robert, Mark Alan. With Collins Radio Co., 1949-72, mgr. indsl. engring., 1954-62, regional mfg. dir., Cedar Rapids, Iowa, 1965-69, v.p., asst. gen. mgr., 1969-70, gen. mgr., 1970-71, v.p. ops., 1971-72; v.p. ops. King Radio, Olathe, Kans., 1973—, also dir. Mem. Iowa State Bd. Engring. Examiners, 1969-72. Bd. dirs. Hawkeye Area council Boy Scouts Am., 1966-72, Jr. Achievement of Cedar Rapids, 1964-66. Served with USNR, World War II. Mem. IEEE, Am. Soc. Quality Control, Nat. Soc. Profl. Engrs., Cedar Rapids-Marion C. of C. (dir. 1969-72), Eta Kappa Nu, Pi Tau Sigma, Tau Beta Pi, Theta Xi. United Methodist. Home: 15320 Melrose Pl Shawnee Mission KS 66221 Office: 400 N Rogers Rd Olathe KS 66061

DUNN, WARREN HARVIE, accountant; b. Benkelman, Nebr., Nov. 30, 1920; s. Harvie Alvin and Nettie D. (Johnson) D.; student U. Nebr., 1938-39, U. Omaha; m. Betty Jane Shanon, Apr. 13, 1946 (div. 1974); children—Nancy Jo, Linda Diane, Robert Allen, David Scott. Loan clk. Dundy County Soil Conservation Service, 1939-40; with Farmers Nat. Co., Omaha, 1941-42, 46—, cashier, 1946-67, sec. treas., 1967-76, gen. mgr., 1975—, v.p., chief fin. officer, 1976—; cons. farm accounting. Mem. Ralston (Nebr.) City Planning Commn., 1952-62, chmn., 1960-62; treas. Iowa-Nebr. Midlands Multiple Sclerosis Soc., 1958—; active Boy Scouts Am., United Fund. Served to sgt., USAAF, 1942-46. Licensed real estate broker, Nebr., Iowa, Mo.; recipient certificate of recognition Sec. of Agr., 1968. Mem. Alpha Sigma Phi. Republican. Clubs: Omaha Exchange (past pres., past pres., dir. Midwest Exchange Clubs), Masons, Shriners. Home: 8633 Broadmoor Dr Omaha NE 68114 Office: 4820 Dodge St Omaha NE 68132

DUNN, WILLIAM EDWARD, dentist; b. Elkton, S.D., July 22, 1921; s. John Elijah and Jane (Horine) D.; student St. John's U., 1938-40; D.D.S., Creighton U., 1943; m. Charlotte Mary Walsh, Sept. 22, 1948; children—James, Thomas, Catherine, Patrick, Maureen, Michael. Practice dentistry Sioux Falls, S.D., 1948—; dir. Delta Dental Plan of S.D., 1971-74. Mem. policy com. HeadStart, Sioux Falls, 1971-74; mem. S.D. Gov.'s Emergency Health Services Com., 1970-73, S.D. Health Professions Loan Com., 1974-77. Served with

USNR, 1944-46. Fellow Am. Coll. Dentists; mem. S.D. Dental Assn. (pres. 1969-70, sec. 1974-77), Southeastern Dist. Dental Soc. (pres. 1960-61), Optimist. Roman Catholic. Editor S.D. Dental Newsletter, 1974-77. Home: 1312 S Center Ave Sioux Falls SD 57105 Office: 2200 S Minnesota Ave Sioux Falls SD 57105

DUNNE, GEORGE W., govt. ofcl.; b. Chgo.; ed. Northwestern U., Evanston, Ill.; married, 3 children. Asst. supt. Chgo. Park Dist., to 1955; mem. Ill. Ho. of Reps., 1955-61, majority leader, 1961; mem. Cook County Bd. Commrs., Chgo., 1961—, pres., 1969—; chmn. Cook County Dem. Party, 1976—. Served with U.S. Army, World War II, Korea. Democrat. Office: 118 N Clark St Chicago IL 60602*

DUNNING, LESLIE LEON, aero. engr.; b. Francisco, Ind., Oct. 31, 1922; s. David and Ruth Ellen (McEllhiney) D.; B.S. in Aero. Engring., Purdue U., 1950; M.B.A. in Engring. Adminstrn., Air Force Inst. Tech., 1959; m. Elaine Margie Loomis, Jan. 3, 1944; children—Daniel Duane, Deborah Dayl. Commd. 2d. lt. USAF, 1944, advanced through grades to col., 1968, project officer, Wright-Patterson AFB, Ohio, 1957-63, systems program dir., specialized aircraft, 1974-75, asst. dep. for systems, 1976, dep. for remotely piloted vehicles and air launched strategic missiles, 1976—; system project officer, Hdqrs. Air Force Systems Command, 1963-66; asst. for F/FB-111 DCS systems, 1970-71; dir. tactical units ops. center, Nakhon Phanom, Thailand, 1966-67; systems project officer, dir. aero. systems, Hdqrs. USAF, 1967-69, program element monitor, 1969, dir. prodn. DCASR, Phila., 1971-74. Served with USAAF, 1942-46. Decorated Air medal with six oak leaf clusters, Bronze Star, Legion of Merit; recipient certificates of achievement, 1972, outstanding achievement plaques, 1971, 73. Dayton. Asso. fellow, Am. Inst. Aeros. and Astronautics; mem. Aviation Hall of Fame Assn., Am. Def. Preparedness Assn., Nat. Assn. Remotely Piloted Vehicles, Air Force Assn. Presbyterian. Club: Wright-Patterson Officers'. Home: 3340 Beaumonde Ln Dayton OH 45409

DUNPHY, EUGENE VINCENT, JR., savs. and loan assn. exec.; b. Chgo., July 10, 1909; s. Eugene Vincent and Emma Theodora (Birdseye) D.; student DePauw U., 1928-29; m. Helen Abney, Dec. 26, 1933; children—Eugene Vincent, Frederick A. Underwriter, Hartford Fire Ins. Co., Chgo., 1929-35; ins. mgr. W.G. Ruggles and Co., Evanston, Ill., 1935-40; owner Dunphy Ins. Agy., Evanston, 1940-72; v.p. Dunphy-McKinley Assos., Evanston, Ill., 1972—; founder, also dir. and sec.-treas. Evanston Fed. Savs. and Loan Assn., 1950—. Mem. Evanston C. of C. (dir. 1964—), Chgo. DePauw Alumni Assn. (pres. 1959-60). Rotarian (dir. 1963—). Club: Skokie Country. Home: 727 Raleigh Ct Northbrook IL 60062 Office: 2530 Crawford Ave Evanston IL 60201

DUNPHY, WARD, lawyer; b. Milw., Apr. 26, 1909; s. William and Ellen (Murphy) D.; A.B., Marquette U., 1931, J.D., 1933; m. Ellen O'Shonessy, June 22, 1940; children—Richard, Lynn (Mrs. James Schindler), Patrick. Admitted to Wis. bar, 1933, Fed. Dist. bar, 1944, U.S. Supreme Ct. bar, 1961; mem. firms Minor, Jursik & Dunphy, 1933-40, Kay & Dunphy, 1940-46, Kay, Dunphy & Walstead, 1946-50, Kay, Dunphy & McNulty, 1950-57, Dunphy & McNulty, 1957-65; partner firm Kluwin, Dunphy, Hankin & McNulty, Milw., 1965—. Instr. Coll. Law Marquette U., 1946-52, U. Wis., Madison, 1970-71. Mem. Wis. Circuit Ct. Commn., 1966—. Bd. dirs. St. Rosa Orphanage, 1965-72, Multiple Sclerosis Soc., Milw., 1970-76. Mem. Am., Wis., Milw. bar assns., Am. Coll. Probate Counsel, Am. Judicature Soc., Inter Profl. Inst., Delta Theta Phi. K.C. Clubs: Wisconsin, Marquette "M" Home: 617 N 74th St Milwaukee WI 53213 Office: 1100 W Wells St Milwaukee WI 53233

DUNSKER, STEWART BEN, neurosurgeon; b. Cin., Aug. 12, 1934; s. Shiel and Tillie (Gelman) D.; A.B. cum laude, Harvard, 1956; M.D., U. Cin., 1960; m. Ellen Lothian Treiman, July 2, 1966; 1 dau., Shiela Lauren. Intern, U. Ill. Research and Edn. Hosp., Chgo., 1960-61; asst. resident medicine Cin. Gen. Hosp., 1961-62, asst. resident surgery, 1964-65; asst. resident neurosurgery Barnes Hosp., St. Louis, 1965-66, resident neurosurgery, 1967-68; fellow neurosurgery Wash. U., St. Louis, 1968-69; practice medicine specializing in neurosurgery, Mayfield Neurologic Inst., Cin., 1970—; asso. dir. neurosurgery residency program Good Samaritan, Christ hosps., Cin., 1970—; instr. surgery U. Cin., 1970—; dir. microsurgery symposium, Cin., 1972, 73, 75. Served to capt. AUS, 1962-64. Recipient Borden Research award Borden Co. Found., 1960. Diplomate Am. Bd. Neurol. Surgery. Fellow A.C.S.; mem. Am. Assn. Neurol. Surgery, Congress Neurol. Surgeons, Soc. U. Neurosurgeons, AMA, Ohio Med. Assn., Cin. Acad. Medicine. Jewish. Rotarian. Clubs: Literary; Queen City, Losantiville Country. Editorial bd. Spine, 1975, Neurosurgery, 1976. Office: 506 Oak St Cincinnati OH 45219

DUNTON, CHARLES RICHARD, paper co. exec.; b. Elmwood, Ill., Sept. 24, 1929; s. Loyde A. and Hazel R. (Corbett) D.; B.S., Whalton Sch. Commerce, Chgo., 1955; m. Starr O. Stapleton, Aug. 25, 1951; children—Pamela Sue, Cynthia Lee, Charles Richard. Auditor, Hall, Penn, Jackson & Co., Chgo., 1955-59; sr. auditor Arthur Young & Co., Chgo., 1959-63; v.p. Murnane Paper Co., North Lake, Ill., 1963—. Served with AUS, 1951-53; Korea. Home: 3745 Euclid Ave Berwyn IL 60402 Office: 607 Northwest Ave North Lake IL 60164

DUPIES, DONALD ALBERT, civil engr.; b. Waukegan, Ill., Apr. 17, 1934; s. Renie Bernard and Catharine Marie (Dowe) D.; B.C.E., Marquette U., 1957; m. Margaret T. McKibbin, Sept. 29, 1962; children—Mark, Patrick, Peggy, Colleen. With Howard, Needles, Tammen & Bergendoff, Milw., 1959—, office engr., 1969-71, engr. in charge, 1971-74, asso., 1974—. Bd. dirs. Centurions of St. Joseph Hosp., Milw., 1971-76; cubmaster Milwaukee County council Boy Scouts Am., 1973-75. Served with C.E., U.S. Army, 1957-59. Registered profl. engr., Wis., Ill. Mem. ASCE, Wis. Assn. Mfr. and Commerce, Wis. Council for Transp. Info., Engrs. and Scientists of Milw., Inst. Transp. Engrs., Am. Mgmt. Assn., Internat. Bridge, Tunnel and Turnpike Assn., Bicentennial Engring., Sci. and Tech. Exposition and Conf. Council, Am. Pub. Works Assn., Water Pollution Control Fedn., Transp. Research Bd., Assn. Wis. Planners, Marquette U. Engring. Alumni Assn. (dir. Milw. 1976—), Tau Beta Pi, Chi Epsilon. Roman Catholic. Home 4733 N Cumberland Blvd Whitefish Bay WI 53211 Office: 6815 W Capital Dr Milwaukee WI 53216

DUPUIS, WAYNE JOSEPH, ins. co. exec.; b. Detroit, Nov. 1, 1929; s. Arthur Joseph and Helen Marie (Buckley) D.; student Eastern Mich. U., 1947-50, U. Mich. Extension Sch., 1952-53; m. Josephine Ghidoli, July 3, 1952; children—Lynda Dupuis, Mark. Vice pres. James T. Barnes & Co., mortgage banking, 1956-62; pres. Gold Star Agy. Inc., Detroit, 1962—, Nat. Fin. Planning, Inc., Detroit, Various Markets Inc.; sec. Ajax Corp., P.R., 1965—; dir. Old Pioneer Life Ins. Co., 1967—. Mem. Detroit Assn. Ins. Agts., Builders and Trades Detroit, Greater Detroit Bd. Commerce. Clubs: Detroit Yacht (commodore), Detroit Athletic. Home: 789 Briarcliff St Grosse Pointe Woods MI 48236 Office: 300 First National Bldg Detroit MI 48226

DU PUY, ELBERT NEWTON, obstetrician and gynecologist; b. Parral, W.Va., Oct. 19, 1904; s. Elbert Stephenson and Lillian (Dixon) DuP.; B.S., U. W.Va., 1930; M.D., Duke U., 1932; m. Ruth Christine Griffenhagen, May 7, 1938; children—James Newton, Karl Frederick Griffenhagen, William Edwin Stuart. Intern, Ch. Home and Infirmary, Balt., 1933; resident in obstetrics Univ. Hosp., Balt., 1934-36; fellow Rotunda Hosp., Dublin, Ireland, 1931; practice medicine specializing in obstetrics and gynecology, Beckley, W.Va., 1936-42, Quincy, Ill., 1946—; mem. staff Blessing Hosp., 1946—, pres. staff, 1974-76, chief obstetrics and gynecology, 1973-75; mem. staff St. Mary Hosp., 1946—, chief obstetrics and gynecology, 1975-77. Mem. nat. council Boy Scouts Am., 1968—; trustee Robert Morris Coll., Carthage, Ill., 1964-69, Kiwanis Internat. Spastic Paralysis Research Found., 1956—; mem. Quincy Bd. Edn., 1958-63, pres., 1962-63. Served with MC, U.S. Army, 1942-46; MTO. Decorated Silver Star, Bronze Star; recipient Silver Beaver award Boy Scouts Am., 1972. Diplomate Am. Bd. Obstetrics and Gynecology. Fellow Am. Coll. Obstetrics and Gynecology (founder), A.C.S., Royal Soc. Medicine (Eng.), Am. Acad. Geriatrics, Am. Acad. Psychosomatic Medicine, Royal Soc. Health (Eng.), Edn. and Sci. Found. of Ill. Med. Soc. (founder); mem. AMA (Physicians' Recognition award), World, So. med. assns., Central Assn. Obstetricians and Gynecologists, Assn. Mil. Surgeons, Ill. (past pres., past chmn. bd. trustees), Adams County (past pres.) med. socs. Congregationalist. Clubs: Univ. (Chgo.); Quincy (Ill.) Country; Masons, Shriners, Jesters. Home: 18 Country Club Dr Quincy IL 62301 Office: 1101 Maine St Quincy IL 62301

DUPUY, JANICE MARIE, counselor-therapist; b. San Angelo, Tex., Aug. 13, 1945; d. Loranzia and Alice Josephine (Jones) Outin; student U. Alaska, 1963; B.S., Angelo State U., 1967; M.S., U. Nebr., 1972; m. Wardell Raymond Dupuy, Dec. 17, 1965. Instr., Kadena (Okinawa) Edn. Center, 1967; teen club coordinator Kadena Youth Center, 1969; counselor Omaha Opportunities Industrialization Center, 1970; tchr. Omaha Pub. Schs., 1971, counselor, 1975-77; asst. dir. Family Adv. Center, Taiwan, 1972-75; home-sch. liaison Bellevue (Nebr.) Pub. Schs., 1977—. Regional rep. Children's Mental Health Adv. Com., 1976—; v.p. Sarpy County Mental Health Adv. Bd., 1976—. Mem. Nebr., Am. personnel and guidance assns., Women of Omaha in Edn., Bellevue Edn. Assn., Nebr. Edn. Assn. Democrat. Methodist. Home: 1601 Cascio Dr Bellevue NE 68005 Office: Bellevue Pub Schs Spl Services Office Bellevue NE 68005

DURAN, ROBERT JACKSON, hand surgeon; b. McAlester, Okla., June 1, 1923; s. Samuel Montgomery and Fanny (Plunkett) D.; student Westminster Coll., 1941-42, Northeastern State U., 1942-43, Emory U., 1943; M.D., U. Okla., 1947; m. Joanne Kreisle, July 3, 1948; children—Martha Jane (Mrs. Richard E. Hennessey), William David, Samuel Montgomery. Intern, Meth. Hosp., Indpls., 1947-48; resident surg. pathology St. Elizabeth Hosp., Lafayette, Ind., 1948-49; resident gen. surgery Scott and White Clinic, Temple, Tex., 1949-50; resident gen. and plastic surgery Mayo Clinic, Rochester, Minn., 1953-56; practice medicine specializing in plastic, reconstructive and hand surgery, Columbus, Ohio, 1956—; mem. staffs Univ. Hosp., Children's Hosp., St. Anthony Hosp., Mount Carmel Hosp.; faculty Ohio State U., Columbus, 1957—, clin. prof., co-dir. hand service, 1968—. Served to capt. USAF, 1950-52. Diplomate Am. Bd. Plastic Surgery. Fellow A.C.S.; mem. A.M.A., Am. Soc. for Surgery of the Hand, Am. Soc. Plastic and Reconstructive Surgery, Am. Assn. Plastic Surgeons, Ohio Med. Assn., Ohio Valley Plastic Surgery Soc., Columbus Surg. Soc. (pres. 1968), Columbus Acad. Medicine, Ohio Acad. Sci., Phi Chi. Republican. Methodist. Clubs: Faculty; Scioto Country, Rotary. Contbr. articles to profl. jours. Office: 1275 Olentangy River Rd Columbus OH 43212

DURAND, JOSEPH CARROLL, savs. and loan exec.; b. Valparaiso, Ind., Aug. 12, 1914; s. Joseph Herschel and Myrtle (Carroll) D.; B.S., Ind. U., 1948; m. Doris Jean Peake, Jan. 10, 1942; children—Mary Carroll, Jeanne. Fed. examiner Fed. Home Loan Bank, Indpls., 1948-49; asst. sec. First Fed. Savs. and Loan Assn. of Valparaiso, 1949-58, treas. 1950-58, v.p., 1958-64, exec. v.p., 1964-66, dir., 1961—, pres., 1966—; dir. Fed. Home Loan Bank of Indpls., 1971-74; pres. Valparaiso Exchange, Inc., 1966—. Active Valparaiso Sch. Bd., 1957-70; mem. Valparaiso Park Bd., 1952-56, Valparaiso Planning Commn, 1952-56; bd. dirs. Valparaiso Improvement Assn., 1969—; dir. United Fund of Porter County, 1969-70. Served to capt. AUS, 1941-45. Mem. Savs. and Loan League Ind. (pres. 1971—), U.S. Savs. and Loan League (legis. com. 1969-71, dir. 1977—), Valparaiso C. of C. Methodist (trustee 1962-68). Kiwanian. Club: Valparaiso Golf. Home: 2306 Linden Dr Valparaiso IN 46383 Office: First Fed Savs and Loan Assn Washington at Lincolnway Valparaiso IN 46383

DURANT, PAUL DILLINGHAM, II, ins. co. exec.; b. Ann Arbor, Mich., Feb. 20, 1931; s. Wentworth Tenney and Katherine (Henning) D.; B.B.A., North Tex. State U., 1958; m. Carolyn Peterson, June 2, 1967; 1 son, Jon Paul. Staff accountant Peat, Marwick, Mitchell & Co., Dallas, 1958-59; comptroller Steere Tank Lines, Inc., Dallas, 1959-64; accountant Paul D. Durant, C.P.A., Dallas, 1964-65; v.p., controller, asst. treas. Gt. Commonwealth Life Ins. Co., Dallas, 1965-68; pres., dir. Investers Found. Life Ins. Co., Dallas, 1969; cons. Fin. and Acquisitions, Dallas, 1968-69; exec. v.p., treas., dir., co-founder Am. Bus. & Comml. Life Ins. Co., Dallas, 1969-73; treas., v.p. Southland Life Ins. Co., 1973-77, Sentry Life Ins. Co. Served with Signal Corps., U.S. Army, 1951-53. Mem. Am. Inst. C.P.A.'s, Am. Accounting Assn., Tex. Soc. C.P.A.'s. Methodist. Home: 3830 Robert St Stevens Point WI 54481 Office: 1800 North Point Dr Stevens Point WI 54481

DURBROW, BRIAN RICHARD, mgmt. cons.; b. Milw., Apr. 26, 1940; s. Robert James and Marianne Winifred (Pengelly) D.; A.A., U. Fla., 1961; B.B.A., U. Iowa, 1962; M.S., No. Ill. U., 1968; Ph.D., Ohio State U., 1971; diploma, Indsl. Coll. Armed Forces, 1972; m. Barbara Helen Mustine; children—Robert E., William D. Jr. accountant Buick-Oldsmobile-Pontiac div. Gen. Motors Corp., South Gate, Calif., 1962-64, sr. accountant Chevrolet div., Janesville, Wis., 1964-66; payroll supr. No. Ill. U., 1966-68; financial analyst Ohio State U., 1968-70; pres. B.R. Durbrow and Assos., Cin., 1969-72; asst. prof. mgmt. Wright State U., Dayton, 1970-71; prof. financial mgmt. Air Force Inst. Tech., 1972-73; pres. Barbrisons Mgmt. Systems, Inc., Cin., 1972—; v.p. PMC Assos., Cin., 1976—, Selindox, Inc., Tulsa, 1977—; vis. prof. mgmt. U. Ala., 1975; asso. prof. mgmt. Xavier U., Cin., 1975-77; speaker Nat. Mgmt. Assn. Active Young Republicans, Calif., Wis., Ill.; vice chmn. Young Reps., Janesville, Wis., 1964, chmn., 1965-66, county treas., 1964, vice chmn., 1965, chmn., 1966, 1st dist. vice chmn., 1965-66, mem. city, county, dist. and state exec. bd., 1965-66, conv. del., 1965; pres. Mgmt. Research and Devel. Inst., Cin., 1976. Mem. Acad. Mgmt., Nat. Mgmt. Assn., Nat. Platform Assn., Soc. Advancement Mgmt., Am. Soc. Tng. and Devel., Nat. Council for Small Bus. Mgmt. Devel., Nat. Small Bus. Assn., Assn. Mgmt. Consultants, Sigma Iota Epsilon, Beta Gamma Sigma, Delta Tau Delta, Delta Sigma Pi. Author: Inter-Firm Executive Mobility, 1971; Management Dynamics, 1974; editor various reference works. Contbr. articles to profl. jours. Office: 2957 Annwood St Cincinnati OH 45206

DUREL, THOMAS JAMES, elec. engr., educator; b. Thibodaux, La., Dec. 14, 1946; s. Francis Mederic and Marie Antonnette (Caillouet) D.; B.S.E.E., Christian Bros. Coll., 1969; M.Ed., U. N.C., Greensboro, 1973; m. Donna Frances Pate, Aug. 9, 1968; children—Jeremy, Katie, Mandi. Engr., Western Electric Corp., Winston Salem, 1969-70; grad. asst. in edn. U. N.C., Greensboro, 1970-71; asst. to v.p. Family Health Found., New Orleans, 1972-75; asst. mgr. edn. Commn. Profl. Hosp. Activities, Ann Arbor, Mich., 1975-77, mgmt. engr., 1977—. Mem. Am. Soc. Tng. Devel. Home: 1221 Westport Rd Ann Arbor MI 48103 Office: 1968 Green Rd Ann Arbor MI 48105

DUREN, PETER LARKIN, mathematician; b. New Orleans, Apr. 30, 1935; s. William and Mary (Hardesty) D.; A.B. cum laude (scholar 1952-56), Harvard U., 1956; Ph.D. (Ramo-Wooldridge Corp. fellow 1957-59, NSF fellow 1959-60), Mass. Inst. Tech., 1960; m. Grace Olcott Adkins, June 15, 1957; children—Elizabeth Adkins, William Larkin. Instr. Stanford U., 1960-62; asst. prof. U. Mich., 1962-66, asso. prof., 1966-69, prof. math., 1969—; temporary mem. Inst. Advanced Study, 1968-69; vis. scholar U. London, also U. Paris, 1964-65; Sloan Found. fellow, 1964-66; vis. lectr. Technion, Haifa, Israel, 1975. Mem. Am. (asso. editor procs. 1973-75, invited speaker 1976), London math. socs., AAUP, Math. Assn. Am. Author: Theory of Hp Spaces, 1970; also articles. Mng. editor Mich. Math. Jour., 1976-77. Home: 1225 Baldwin Ave Ann Arbor MI 48104

DURIC, MIODRAG, elec. engr.; b. Zagreb, Yugoslavia, Feb. 27, 1940; s. Aleksandar and Stevanka (Smud) D.; came to Can., 1968, naturalized, 1976; B.S., U. Zagreb, 1964; postgrad U. Windsor (Ont., Can.), 1975—; m. Vjekoslava Majer, Nov. 1, 1958; 1 son, Robert. Project engr., Rade Koncar electrification of railways, Zagreb, 1964-68; design engr. Detroit Edison Co., 1968-70; engring. supr. elec. dept. CDA Engring., Detroit, 1970—. Registered profl. engr., Ont., Mich. Mem. Assn. Profl. Engrs. Ont. Home: 440 Laporte Ave Windsor ON N8S 3R2 Canada Office: 220 Bagley Suite 800 Detroit MI 48226

DURKIN, JOHN S., data processing co. exec.; b. Monticello, N.Y., Oct. 16, 1945; s. John A. and Marion (Cross) D.; B.A., Mich. State U., 1967; m. L. Joan Ruof, June 29, 1968; children—John, Janeen. Auditor, Touche Ross & Co., Cleve., 1967-68; auditor Arthur Andersen & Co., Cin., 1970-71; v.p. Kanter Corp., Cin., 1971-75; pres. Econ. Data Processing Corp., Cin., 1975—, also dir.; dir. DCW Investments. Financial adviser, Cin. Assn. Children with Learning Disabilities, 1977. Served with AUS, 1968-70. C.P.A., Ohio. Mem. Ohio Soc. C.P.A.'s. Republican. Episcopalian. Clubs: Fenwick Athletic and Businessmens. Home: 5880 Winton Ridge Cincinnati OH 45232 Office: 580 Walnut St Cincinnati OH 45202

DURNIAK, JAMES DENNIS, aero. engr.; b. Sewickley, Pa., Oct. 24, 1946; s. Peter Richard and Nell Francis (Routh) D.; B.S., LeTourneau Coll., 1968; M.S., Air Force Inst. Tech., 1977; m. Sharon Marie Moore, Aug. 23, 1969. Heavy equipment engr. R.G. Le Tourneau Inc., Longview, Tex., 1967-68; commd. 2d lt. USAF, 1969, advanced through grades to capt., 1972; navigator Grand Forks AFB, 1974-75; project engr., turbofan engine, Wright Patterson AFB, Ohio, 1977—, F-107 liaison with USN, Washington, 1978—. Decorated DFC, Air medal with 4 oak leaf clusters. Mem. Am. Inst. Aeros. and Astronautics, Air Force Assn. Roman Catholic. Home: 1573 Etta Kable Dr Dayton OH 45432 Office: JCMPO-PM 3 Washington DC 20360

DURNO, JOHN DREGGE, banker; b. Grand Rapids, Mich., July 14, 1936; s. John G. and Barbara I. (Dregge) D.; A.B., Dartmouth, 1958; M.B.A., U. Mich., 1961; m. Eleanor F. Hawkins, Dec. 12, 1959; children—Geoffrey H., Amy G., Craig F. With Nat. Bank of Detroit, 1961—, asst. v.p., 1966-72, v.p., 1972-74, v.p., sr. internat. loan officer, 1974-77, v.p. adminstrn. overseas brs., London, Eng., 1977—. Served to lt. (j.g.), USNR, 1958-60. Clubs: Country, Dartmouth (Detroit). Home: 26 Parkside Wimbledon London SW19 England Office: National Bank of Detroit Adminstrv Offices Overseas Branches 15 Grosvenor Pl London SW1 England

DURWOOD, MAUREEN WOLKOFF, civic worker; b. Providence, June 14, 1931; d. William and Julianna (Schmelz) Wolkoff; student Pembroke Coll., Brown U., 1949-51; grad. U. of Mo. at Kansas City, 1968; m. Richard Mark Durwood, June 24, 1950; children—Keith James, Jan Leslie, Dana Ellen. Bd. dirs. women's div. Jewish Fedn. Greater Kansas City, 1961—, chmn. gen. soliciation women's div.; bd. dirs., pres. Kansas City chpt. Brandeis U. Nat. Women's Com., 1971-74, nat. bd., 1974—, regional v.p., 1974-77, mid-west region v.p., 1977-78; corr. sec. Am. Jewish Com., 1964—, v.p., 1969-71, 72-73, area co-chmn. Brown U.; chmn. Young Women's Community Workshop, 1964—; v.p. Kansas City Women's div. Jewish Fedn.; v.p. Kansas City Lyric Opera, sec., 1977-78; v.p. Kansas City Fedn. Mem. exec. bd. Kansas City Legal Aid and Guardian Soc., 1973—; bd. dirs., chmn. pub. relations Nat. Council Jewish Women of Greater Kansas City, 1965—, tour chmn., 1969-70; bd. dirs. Planned Parenthood Assn. of Kansas City, Menorah Hosp., 1977-78, New Reform Temple, womens div. Kansas City Philharmonic, 1977-78. Mem. Jr. Women's Philharmonic League (dir. 1965), Menorah Hosp. Aux., Kansas City Lyric Opera Assn. (pres. elect 1972), Kansas City Art Inst., Torch and Scroll. Home: 6100 Mission Dr Shawnee Mission KS 66208

DURZO, FRANK JOHN, mfg. co. exec.; b. Havre, Mont., Sept. 4, 1914; s. Bruno and Maria (Bonacci) D.; B.Sc. in Mech. Engring., U. Wis., 1942; m. Elizabeth Bennett, Aug. 30, 1947; children—John, Judith, Lisa, David. Sales engr. J.O. Ross Engring. Corp., Chgo., 1946-47; with Jeffrey Mfg. Co., Columbus, O., 1947-64, pres., dir., 1963-64; pres., dir., chief exec. officer Jeffrey Galion Inc., Columbus, 1965-74; pres. Jeffrey Galion Group of Dresser Industries, Inc., Columbus, 1974—, chmn., spl. asst. Jeffrey Galion Operating units, 1975—; dir. Columbia Gas Systems, Inc. (Wilmington, Del.), City Nat. Bank & Trust Co., Columbia Gas of Ohio Inc., Scientific Advances, Inc. Trustee Battelle Meml. Inst., Columbus; bd. dirs. Capital U. M.B.A. community adv. council; pres. Central Ohio Council Boy Scouts Am.; mem. governing com. Columbus Found. Served from ensign to lt. USNR, 1943-46. Recipient Presdl. citation for work with physically handicapped, 1960. Registered profl. engr., Ohio. Mem. Ohio Soc. Profl. Engrs., Columbus Area C. of C. (dir.). Republican. Rotarian. Clubs: Athletic, Scioto Country, Golf, University, Columbus Maennerchor; Green Valley Country, Poinsett (Greenville, S.C.). Home: 1220 Kenbrook Hills Dr Columbus OH 43221 Office: PO Box 2252 400 W Wilson Bridge Rd Columbus OH 43216

DUS, KARL MARIA, biochemist; b. Vienna, Austria, Jan. 2, 1932; s. Karl Arthur and Johanna (Novak) D.; came to U.S., 1958; Ph.D. in Chemistry, U. Vienna, 1958; m. Martha Mahler, June 5, 1971; children—Johanna, Melinda Mae. Research fellow in medicine Mass. Gen. Hosp., Harvard Med. Sch., Cambridge, 1958-60; research asso. biochemistry Brandeis U., Waltham, Mass., 1960-61; asst. research chemist U. Calif., San Diego, 1961-65, asso., 1965-68; asst. prof. biochemistry U. Ill., Urbana, 1968-73; asso. prof. St. Louis U. Med. Sch., 1974—; vis. maitre de recherches in genetics and physiology Centre National de la Recherche Scientifique, Gif-sur-Yvette, France, 1965-66. NIH, NSF grantee, 1969—. Mem. Am. Chem. Soc., Am. Soc. Biol. Chemists, AAAS, N.Y. Acad. Sci., Am. Soc. Photobiology. Roman Catholic. Patentee on instrument design. Contbr. articles in field to profl. jours. Home: 411 S Holmes St Kirkwood MO 63122 Office: 1402 S Grand Blvd Saint Louis MO 63104

DUSENBURY, RONALD JAN, lawyer; b. Bradley, Ill., July 2, 1934; s. Stafford and Carolyn Salome (Van Kuren) D.; B.A., So. Ill. U., 1956; J.D., Vanderbilt U., 1959; m. Christine Minckler, May 24, 1957; children—Marshall, Marc, Heidi. Admitted to Ill. bar, 1959; mem. firm Swaim & Dusenbury, 1959-65, Dusenbury & Lucas, 1965-70; sr. partner firm Dusenbury, Lucas, Berz & Yurgine, Kankakee, Ill., 1970—. Asst. state's atty., 1965-69; pub. defender, 1970-72. Dist. chmn. Boy Scouts Am., 1972-73. Bd. dirs. YMCA, 1960-62, 70—. Mem. Am., Ill. bar assns., Trial Lawyers Assn. Elk. Club: Exchange. Home: Rural Route 3 St Anne IL 60964 Office: 175 N Dearborn St Kankakee IL 60901

DUSH, JOSEPH FRANKLIN, lawyer; b. St. Louisville, Ohio, Aug. 28, 1915; s. Frank Aldan and Ada May (Parker) D.; B.A., Ohio State U., 1937, J.D., 1939, LL.D., 1939; m. Ruth Taylor, May 7, 1954. Admitted to Ohio bar, 1939, U.S. Fed. Cts., 1945; mem. firm Dush & Eckstein, 1968—. Law clk. U.S. Dist. Ct. So. Dist. Ohio, Columbus, 1945-47. Trustee Willard Meml. Library, 1958-77. Rotarian. Author, illustrator: History of Willard, Ohio, 1974. Home: 405 W Maple St Willard OH 44890 Office: Willard United Bank Bldg Willard OH 44890

DUTTA, SHIVNATH, physicist; b. Bihar, India, Jan. 4, 1944; s. Gowri Nath and Tatini Bala (Bose) Dutta; m. Uma Ghosh, July 11, 1968; 1 dau., Suma. B.Sc. with honors, Bihar U. (India), 1964; M.Sc., Jadavpur U. (India), 1966; M.S., U. Sask., Can., 1971. Research asst. Indian Assn. for Cultivation of Sci., India, 1967-68; research asst. U. Sask. (Can.), 1971-72; research asst. Ohio U., 1974—. Govt. India Merit scholar, 1959-66. Mem. Am. Phys. Soc. Home: 28 Wolfe St Athens OH 45701 Office: Physics Dept Ohio U Athens OH 45701

DUTTON, JAMES NEWTON, musician; b. Sioux City, Iowa, Mar. 10, 1921; s. Winfred A. and Edna (Hulett) D.; student U. Nebr., 1939-40, Morningside Coll., 1940-41; B.A. in Music, Northwestern U., 1947, M.A., 1948; m. Frances Hilliker, Oct. 15, 1967; children—Jon French, Rebecca Elizabeth, James Edwin, Linda Corinna, Mark. Head percussion dept. and chamber music program Am. Conservatory Music, Chgo., 1947—; music dir. Bethany Union Ch., Chgo., 1948-60, South Town Youth Concerts Assn., Chgo., 1958-66, Chgo. Artists Orch., 1958—; leader James Dutton Trio, 1948-70, concert tours, 1948-53, 1960-70, featured on Roger Williams Show, 1965-66; guest condr. St. Louis Philharmonic Orch., 1959; condr. Percussion Arts Orch., 1976—; founder, dir. Birchcreek Performing Arts Acad., Bailey's Harbor, Wis., 1976—; also lectr. Served to capt. USAAF, World War II; ETO. Decorated Air medal. Mem. Am. Symphony Orch. League, Music Educators Nat. Conf., Percussive Arts Soc., Am. Fedn. Musicians, Pi Kappa Lambda, Phi Mu Alpha. Contbr. articles to mags. Home: 505 N Lake Shore Dr Chicago IL 60611 Office: 116 S Michigan Ave Chicago IL 60603

DUTY, ALLENE BEAUMONT (MRS. SPENCER CUMMER DUTY), author; b. Cleve., Jan. 29, 1912; d. John Erwin and Grace Forbes (Allen) Beaumont; B.S., Western Res. U., 1935; diploma Cleve. Sch. Art, 1935; m. Spencer Cummer Duty, Dec. 29, 1936 (dec. June 1973); children—Nancy Allen (Mrs. James Douglas Campbell, Jr.), Spencer Beaumont. Mem. women's adv. council Western Res. Hist. Soc.; mem. jr. council Cleve. Mus. Art; past mem. sr. bd. Amasa Stone House. Author: The Kreider Family, 1953; The Duty Family, 1972; The Forbes Family, 1972; The Taylor Family, 1972; Addenda to Cummer Memoranda, 1972; The Allen Family, 1973; The Ancestors and Descendants of Ephraim Simmons, 1977. Clubs: Kirtland Country, Intown (Cleve.). Home: 3450 Green Rd Cleveland OH 44122

DUVALL, CHARLES STEVEN, health service adminstr.; b. Balt., Mar. 2, 1948; s. Charles Robert and Dorothy Simpson (Duncan) D.; B.S. in Biology and Chemistry, U. N.Mex., 1970; M.S. in Microbiology and Chemistry, S.D. State U., 1973, M.Ed. in Counseling and Adminstrn., 1976; postgrad. health services adminstrn. and health edn., U. Calif., Los Angeles, 1975, predoctoral cardiovascular training program Hahnemann Med. Coll. and Hosp., Phila., 1970. Asst. nuclear medicine Lovelace Found., Albuquerque, 1971; computerized inventory controller Ford Motor Co., Los Angeles and Albuquerque, summer 1969, 70; clin. lab. technician dept. biology U. N.Mex., Albuquerque, 1969-70; grad. research asst. dept. microbiology S.D. State U., Brookings, 1970-73, research asso., 1973-74, dir. infirmary Univ. Health Service, 1973-74, adminstrv. asst., 1974, acting adminstr., 1974-75; spl. asst. to dir. Student Health Service U. Calif., Los Angeles, 1975; dir. Univ. Health Service, S.D. State U., Brookings, 1975—; emergency room technician and asst. adminstr. Four Seasons Nursing Home and Univ. Heights Hosp., Albuquerque, 1970; emergency med. technician Brookings Hosp., 1973-74; instr. S.D. State U. Adult leader Boy Scouts Am.; first aid instr.; advisor Am. Red Cross Bloodmobile. Served to 1st lt. Med. Service Corp. U.S. Army, 1973-77. Recipient Franklin Joseph Schoen Meml. scholarship, 1966-68; Meyer Raeburn award nominee, ROTC, 1973. Mem. Am. Mgmt. Assn., Am. Acad. of Health Adminstrs., AAUP, Am. Coll. Health Assn. (mem. exec. bd. 1974-75, council of dels. 1976-79), Am. Coll. Hosp. Adminstrs., Am. Fedn. Hosps., Am. Pub. Health Assn., Inst. of Society, Ethics and the Life Scis., N. Central Coll. Health Assn. (pres. 1977-78), Soc. for Health and Human Values, S.D. Coll. Personnel Assn., S.D. Pub. Health Assn., Sigma Xi, Phi Kappa Phi, Phi Sigma. Patentee radioactive iodine labeling; contbr. articles to profl. jours. and chpts. to books. Home: 815 1/2 3rd Ave Brookings SD 57006 Office: Student Health Service South Dakota State University Brookings SD 57007

DUVALL, CORA LUCILLE, newspaper editor; b. Ohio County, Ind., Aug. 20, 1915; d. Leonard Carlysle and Jessie Frances (Bellman) Cofield; student pub. schs., Rising Sun, Ind.; m. Forrest Duvall, Apr. 21, 1946; children—Carole Lou, Steven, Diane. Mng. editor Ohio County Newspapers, Inc., Rising Sun, 1937-46; lab. technician, sec. to assay dept. Schenley Penicillin Mfg. Co., Lawrenceburg, Ind., 1946-52; mng. editor Rising Sun Recorder, 1958—. Methodist. Home: 730 Main St Rising Sun IN 47040 Office: PO Box 128 235 Main St Rising Sun IN 47040

DUXLER, BERL (WOODY), automotive parts co. exec.; b. Chgo., July 11, 1931; s. Samuel M. and Florence L. (Lichtenstein) D.; grad. high sch., 1948; m. Anita Brown, May 3, 1953; children—Michael, Larry, Susan. With S.M. Duxler Co., Chgo., 1949—, gen. mgr., 1962-75, pres., 1975—. Tire stud committeeman Ill. State Tire Safety Law, 1972. Served with AUS, 1951-52. Mem. Ill. State Tire Dealers (pres. 1971-73), Nat. Tire Dealers (dir. 1972-78). Jewish (trustee temple 1972-73). Home: 111 Rivershire Ln Lincolnshire IL 60015 Office: 1880 Busse Rd Elk Grove Village IL 60007

DUZY, ALBERT FRANK, cons. mech. engr.; b. Ambridge, Pa., Jan. 3, 1921; s. Frank Joseph and Julia (Koteles) D.; B.S. in Mech. Engring., Carnegie-Mellon U., 1955; m. Margaret Kathryn Meyer, Jan. 17, 1946; children—Adrienne M. Gill, Julianne M. Greenbank, Albert Frank. Fuels specialist Eastern Gas & Fuel Assos., Pitts., 1947-56, Babcock & Wilcox Co., Barberton, Ohio, 1957-71; v.p. Paul Weir Co., Chgo., 1971—. Chmn. Barberton United Fund, 1966. Served with USN, 1939-46; PTO, ETO, NATOUSA. Registered profl. engr., Ohio, Pa. Mem. ASME (Best Paper award 1967-68, certificate of appreciation jointly with IEEE and ASCE 1971-72, communications policy bd., power dept. policy bd., del. nat. nominating com., permanent rep. to Am. Power Conf., also coms., exec. com. Chgo. sect.), Nat. Soc. Profl. Engrs. Republican. Club: Tower (Chgo.). Contbr. numerous articles to profl. publs. Home: 1615 E Central Rd Apt 310P Arlington Heights IL 60005 Office: 20 N Wacker Dr Chicago IL 60606

DWORKIN, HOWARD JERRY, nuclear physician, educator; b. Bklyn., Oct. 29, 1932; s. Joseph Henry and Molly M. (Hodas) D.; B.S. in Chem. Engring., Worcester Polytech Inst., 1955; M.D., Albany Med. Coll., 1959; M.S. in Radiation Biology, U. Mich., 1965; m. Carole Joan Meyer, July 5, 1955; children—Rhonda Fran, Steven Irving, Paul J. Intern, Albany (N.Y.) Hosp., 1959-60; resident Rochester (N.Y.) Gen. Hosp., 1960-62, U. Mich. Hosps., 1962-64; asst. coordinator Nuclear Medicine Unit, 1963-66, instr. 1965-66; asst. prof. medicine U. Toronto (Ont., Can.), 1966, asso. prof., 1967; head dept. nuclear medicine Princess Margaret Hosp., Toronto, 1967; head nuclear medicine sect., radiology Nat. Naval Med. Center, Bethesda, Md., 1967-69; dir. sch. nuclear medicine tech. William Beaumont Hosp., Royal Oak, Mich., 1969—, dir. nuclear medicine resident tng. program, 1970—; clin. asst. prof. dept. medicine Wayne State U. Med. Sch., Detroit, 1970—. Served with USN, 1967-69. Diplomate Am. Bd. Internal Medicine. Fellow Am. Coll. Physicians, Am. Bd. Nuclear Medicine; mem. Soc. Nuclear Medicine (trustee 1973—), Am. Fedn. Clin. Research, Am. Thyroid Assn., Endocrine Soc., AMA Am. Coll. Nuclear Physicians (sec. 1974-77, pres. 1978—). Patentee radioactive labeled protein material process and apparatus; Author: (with N. Aspin, R.G. Baker) Clinical Use of Isotopes in the Physics of Radiology, 1969; Part Two, Clinical Procedures in Radioisotope Laboratory Procedures, 1969; contbr. articles and chapters to med. jours. and texts. Home: 5540 Northcote Ln West Bloomfield MI 48033 Office: Dept Nuclear Medicine William Beaumont Hosp Royal Oak MI 48072

DWYER, MARTIN CHARLES, indsl. exposition co. exec.; b. Cleve., Jan. 6, 1921; s. Martin Charles and Adelaide (Moran) D.; B.A., John Carroll U., 1942; postgrad. Ia., 1942-43, Columbia, 1943, Cleve. Coll., 1945-46; m. Gail Alberta Martin, June 15, 1946; children—Martin Charles III, Linda Gail, Patricia Anne. Editor sales promotion pieces lamp dept. Gen. Electric Co., 1946-48; mgr. Cleve. Conv. Bur., 1948-55; exhibit mgr. Nat. Retail Lumber Dealers, Washington, 1955-60; pres. Martin C. Dwyer, Inc., Chgo., 1960—, gen. mgr. NEFTA-GAZ EXPO 1973, U.S. petroleum equipment exposition, Moscow, USSR, 1973. Gen. chmn. March of Dimes, Chgo., 1965. Served to lt. AC, USNR, 1942-46. Recipient Excellence award Exhibitors Adv. Council, 1959, Constrn. Man of Year award Engring. & News Record, 1966. Mem. Am. Soc. Assn. Execs., Nat. Assn. Exhibit Mgrs. Rotarian. Clubs: North Shore Country (Glenview, Ill.); Tulsa; Kenwood Country (Bethesda, Md.). Home: 2946 Indian Wood Rd Wilmette IL 60091 Office: 400 N Michigan Ave Chicago IL 60611

DWYER, W. MICHAEL, mktg. exec.; b. Omaha, Oct. 1, 1938; s. Wendell R. and Ruth (Legg) D.; B.A., Princeton, 1959; M.B.A., U. Minn., 1963; m. Barbara Mary Jensen, Dec. 19, 1962; children—Mark, Timothy, David, Mary Wendell, Steven. With Pillsbury Co., Mpls., 1961-64, mgr. marketing services Batten, Barton, Durstines & Osborne, Mpls., 1965-67; with Gen. Mills Co., Mpls., 1968-77, planning and new products mgr., 1968-70, dir. mktg. research, 1970-77; dir. mktg. services Peavey Co., Mpls., 1977, v.p. mktg. services, 1977—; lectr. mktg. U. Minn., Mpls., 1968—. Active Big Bros., Mpls., 1962; active fund drs. Republican party, 1960—; mem. Hennepin County Health and Social Services Bd., 1974—. Served with USMCR, 1960-61. Recipient Mo. regional alumni award Princeton, 1955. Mem. Am. Mktg. Assn., World Future Soc., Mpls. Jr. C. of C. (bd. dirs.), Am. Assn. Pub. Opinion Research. Home: 4832 James Ave S Minneapolis MN 55409 Office: Peavey Bldg 730 2d Ave S Minneapolis MN 55402

DYCK, GEORGE, med. educator; b. Hague, Sask., Can., July 25, 1937; s. John and Mary (Janzen) D.; came to U.S., 1965; student U. Sask., 1955-56; B.Christian Edn., Canadian Mennonite Bible Coll., 1959; M.D., U. Man., 1964; postgrad. Menninger Sch. Psychiatry, 1965-68; m. Edna Margaret Krueger, June 27, 1959; children—Brian Edward, Janine Louise, Stanley George, Jonathan Jay. Fellow community psychiatry Prairie View Mental Health Center, Newton, Kans., 1968-70, clin. dir. tri-county services, 1970-73; prof., chmn. dept. psychiatry U. Kans. Sch. Medicine, Wichita, 1973—. Bd. dirs. Mennonite Mut. Aid, Goshen, Ind., 1973—, Mid-Kans. Community Action Program, 1970-73, Wichita Council on Drug Abuse, 1974-76. Diplomate Bd. Psychiatry and Neurology, Royal Coll. Physicians and Surgeons (Can.) in Psychiatry. Fellow Am. Psychiat. Assn. (sec. Kans. dist. br. 1976—); mem. A.M.A., Kans. Med. Soc. Mennonite. Home: 1505 Hillcrest Rd Newton KS 67114 Office: 1001 N Minneapolis St Wichita KS 67214

DYE, CALVIN CECIL, accountant; b. Marietta, Ohio, Nov. 10, 1926; s. Cecil Congleton and Leona Gladys (Roth) D.; student Ohio U., 1944, Stanford, 1945; A.B., Marietta Coll., 1949; m. Phyllis Maxine Dobbins, Apr. 24, 1949; children—Gary Lee, Joyce Elaine, Janet Maxine, Nancy Jayne. Staff accountant Cecil C. Dye, pub. accountant Marietta, 1946-58; partner Dye & Dye, Marietta, 1958—, Caroal Realty Co., Marietta, 1970—; sec. Marietta Royalty Co., F.J. Peavy Investment Inc., 1960—, Constn. Stone Co., Marietta, 1962-72; treas. Hub Freight Systems, Inc., Marietta, Valley Apts., Inc., 1974—; dir. Rejer Transport Inc., R.O. Wetz Inc., Marietta. Spl. agt. for ministerial land rental collection Ohio State Auditor, 1967—; clk. Marietta Twp., 1965-67; city auditor Marietta, 1972—; merit badge counselor Katooga council Boy Scouts Am., 1962—. Mem. Republican Central Com., 1974—; mem. exec. com. Washington County Republicans, 1972—. Served with AUS, 1944-45, USAAF, 1945-46. Mem. Pub. Accountants Soc. Ohio (pres. Marietta chpt. 1963-67, treas., 1967—), Nat. Soc. Pub. Accountants (Accreditation Council for Accountancy 1974—), Municipal Finance Officers Assn., Ohio Hist. Soc., Fraternal Order Police Assos. Methodist. Club: Marietta Bowling Assn. (treas. 1961—). Home: 611 3d St Marietta OH 45750 Office: 225 Putnam St Marietta OH 45750

DYE, LLOYD ARTHUR, III, finance co. exec.; b. Nowata, Okla., Feb. 1, 1935; s. Lloyd Arthur and Lily Florence (Whitson) D.; student pub. schs. Nowata; m. Karen Lovelle Price, July 2, 1965; 1 dau., Melissa Noelle. Adminstrv. asst. Coop. Refinery Assn., Wellington, Kans., 1953-62; mgmt. liaison Petroleum, Inc., Wichita, Kans., 1962-66; owner, mgr. Lloyd A. Dye & Assos., oil industry cons., Wichita, 1966-70; pres., owner Liberty Capital Corp., Wichita, 1970—. Democrat. Home: 6223 Peach Tree Ln Wichita KS 67218 Office: PO Box 18206 Wichita KS 67218

DYE, RICHARD OMAR, chem. co. exec.; b. Detroit, Feb. 5, 1932; s. Fred O. and Beatrice L. (Stone) D.; student Wayne State U., 1950-52, U. Detroit, 1956-58; m. Norma E. Johnson, Oct. 7, 1954; children—Jennifer S., Jeffrey R., Gregory D. Exec. v.p. Pressure Vessel Service, Inc., Detroit, 1958-69; pres. Dy-Chem Products Co., Inc., Warren, Mich., 1969—. Precinct capt. Republican Party, Royal Oak, Mich., 1958-62. Served with U.S. Navy, 1952-56. Mem. Econ. Club Detroit, Chem. and Allied Industries Assn. of Mich. Presbyterian. Club: Forest Lake Country. Home: 2204 Park Ridge Dr Bloomfield Hills MI 48013 Office: 21704 Hoover Rd Warren MI 48089

DYE, RUSSELL VINCENT, IV, pub. affairs ofcl.; b. Forest Hill, Liberty, Mo., Jan. 20, 1907; s. Alexander Vincent and Ida (Miller) D.; ed. Dulwich Coll., Eng. 1920-22, U. Berlin, Germany, 1922-23, U. Mexico, 1924-25. Formerly, diplomatic sec. Am. embassies in Berlin, Paris, Mexico City, Buenos Aires, since self employed in investments, real estate, oil properties, own inventions. Past pres. Clay County Council Chs.; chmn. bd. Clay County SSS, 1948-72. Past trustee Vets. Hall, Liberty, Mo. Served as interpreter AUS, 1940-45. Recipient certificate of appreciation for selective service duties Pres. Eisenhower, 1958, with lapel pin President Kennedy, 1963, Pres. Nixon, 1971. Mem. State (life, mem. exec. com., v.p. 1959—), Clay County (pres. 1959-68) hist. socs., Am. Legion (past post comdr.), Clay County Council Chs. (past pres.), 40 and 8 (past chef de gare), Assn. U.S. Army. Presbyn. Contbr. articles on history, selective service, vets. affairs to local publs. Home: Forest Hill Liberty MO 64068

DYE, WESLEY JOHN, recreation co. exec.; b. Denver, Oct. 21, 1944; s. John Wilmer and Alice (Shenk) D.; B.A., U. So. Calif., 1972; m. Tena Copeland, Mar. 5, 1969. Dir., Colorado City Recreation Dist., 1970-72; v.p. Creative Image, Inc., Denver, 1970-72; exec. v.p. Era, Inc., Ft. Wayne, Ind., 1972—, pres. Recreation Resources div., 1972—; dir. Yuma Civic Conv. Center, 1977—; cons. Am. Sports Arenas, Inc., Edn. Design Assos. Dist. rep. Conv. Visitors Bur., Mankato, Minn. Mem. Nat. Sporting Goods Assn., Nat., Minn. recreation parks assns., Internat. Assn. Auditorium Mgrs., C. of C., Colo., Ill. park recreation socs., Nat. Issues Com. Clubs: Yuma Racket, Colorado City Golf, Vacation Village Ill. Golf. Home: 2002 Hillside St Fort Wayne IN 46805 Office: 400 E Randolph St 3315 Chicago IL 60601

DYER, BYRON WILTON, mktg. exec.; b. Morris, Minn., Jan. 6, 1932; s. Charles Bernard and Harriet Zephyr (Pricket) D.; grad. Sch. Agr., U. Minn., 1947-51; m. Phyllis Lavaine Boen, June 20, 1952; children—Kevin, Debra, Keith, Karen. Farmer, Morris, 1955-58; salesman Golden Cream Dairy, Morris, 1958-60; ins. agt., Morris and Detroit Lakes, Minn., 1960-65; salesman farm equipment Minn. Harvestore Inc., Princeton, Minn., 1966-70; salesman, br. mgr. Huske-Bilt Structures, St. Cloud, Minn., 1970-72; livestock confinement specialist Morton Bldgs., Inc., Foley, Minn., 1972-76, dir. livestock housing, Morton, Ill., 1976—. Agrl. adviser Pine City Vo-tech., 1971-72; adv. com. Princeton Vets. Farm Tng. Program. Justice of the Peace, Princeton, 1971-72; chmn. Stevens County (Minn.) Young Republican League, 1960. Served with USMCR, 1951-54. Mem. Am. Soc. Agrl. Engrs., Am. Legion. Methodist (dir. 1967-72). Home: 718 Taylor St Morton IL 61550 Office: 252 W Adams St Morton IL 61550

DYER, LAWRENCE MATTHEW, real estate broker; b. O'Fallon, Mo., Apr. 13, 1932; s. Lawrence Matthew and Teresa Gertrude (Burkemper) D.; B.S., U. Mo., 1959; m. Martha Blondet, Apr. 20, 1953; children—Mary Jane, Holly Elizabeth, Amy Katherine. Owner L.M. Dyer Realty Co., St. Charles, Mo., 1970—. Served with AUS, 1953-55. Mem. Nat. Assn. Realtors (pres. Mo. chpt. farm and land inst. 1976—), Mo. Soc. Farm Mgrs. and Rural Appraisers (dir. 1974-76), St. Charles County Bd. Realtors (pres. 1973), Home Builders Assn. K.C., Rotarian. Home: 3028 W Adams St Charles MO 63301 Office: 1 Westbury Dr St Charles MO 63301

DYER, PETER HARRY, chiropractor; b. Bernardston, Mass., July 17, 1949; s. Edwin William Frances and Caryl Ann (Hopkinson) D.; student N.H. Coll., 1967-69, Lincoln Coll. of Chiropractic, 1969-71; D.C., Nat. Coll. Chiropractic, 1973; m. Linda Sharon Moore, Mar. 23, 1974. Practice chiropractic, Monticello, Ind., 1973—. Mem. Am. Chiropractic Assn., Ind. Soc. Chiropractic Physicians, Rotary Internat. Home: 211 S 425 E Monticello IN 47960 Office: 110 W Washington St Monticello IN 47960

DYER, TIMOTHY JAMES, sch. supt.; b. Ypsilanti, Mich., Dec. 29, 1937; s. John F. and Genevive (Lynn) D.; B.A. in Polit. Sci., Eastern Mich. U., 1961, M.A. in Ednl. Adminstrn., 1965; Ed.D. in Curriculum Devel., Wayne State U., 1974; postgrad. (East-West fellow scholar), U. Hawaii, 1971. Tchr. Wayne (Mich.) Meml. High Sch., 1961-66, asst. prin., 1966-68; asst. prin. Wayne Meml. High Sch., 1966-68; prin. Adlai E. Stevenson Jr. High Sch., Westland, Mich., 1968-73; supt. Wayne-Westland Community Sch. Dist., 1973—; cons. U. Mich. Sch. Edn., 1974—. Regent, Eastern Mich. U., Ypsilanti, 1973—. Pres. Nat. Newman Student Fedn., 1963-64, U.S. Youth Council, 1964-65, Nat. Council of Catholic Youth, 1966-67; mem. YMCA, western Wayne County, 1973—. Councilman, City of Ypsilanti, 1965-70, mayor pro tem, 1967-68, mayor, 1969-70; dir. Washtenaw County (Mich.) Bd. of Pub. Works, 1968-70, Washtenaw County Bd. of Canvassers, 1970-72. Trustee Peoples Community Hosp. Authority, 1966-72. Named Outstanding Young Man in Ypsilanti, 1967; named Outstanding Young Man in Mich., 1968; named One of the Ten Outstanding Young Men in Washtenaw County, 1970. Mem. Nat., Mich. assns. sch. adminstrs., Am. Acad. Sch. Adminstrs., Mich. Assn. Sch. Bds., Assn. Pub. Sch. Systems, Assn. Sch. Bus. Ofcls., Mich. Assn. Suprs. and Curriculum Devel., Wayne, Westland chambers commerce, Assn. Governing Bds. for Colls. and Univs., Phi Kappa Delta. Rotarian (Community Achievement Recognition award 1974). Club: First Friday Club of Wayne. Home: 32222 Woodbrook Dr Wayne MI 48184 Office: 3712 Williams St Wayne MI 48184

DYER, WILLIAM ALLAN, JR., newspaper exec.; b. Providence, Oct. 23, 1902; s. William Allan and Clara (Spink) D.; grad. Lawrenceville Sch., 1920; B.Ph., Brown U., 1924; LL.D., Ind. U., 1977; m. Marian Elizabeth Blumer, Aug. 9, 1934; children—Allan H., William E. Reporter, Syracuse (N.Y.) Jour., 1923; various advt. positions Syracuse (N.Y.) Post-Standard, 1925-41; v.p., gen. mgr. Star Pub. Co., Indpls., 1944-49; v.p. Indpls. Newspapers, Inc., 1949-75, gen. mgr., 1949-74, pres., 1975—; pres. Muncie Newspapers, Inc., 1975—; dir. Standard Life Ins. Co. Ind.; dir. Central Newspapers, Inc., Indpls., 1949—, exec. v.p. 1964-73; N.Y.C. dir. Met. Sunday Newspapers, 1951-75, pres., 1969-75; dir. Am. Newspaper Pub. Assn. bur. advt., 1963-69, Research Inst., 1955-62, pres., 1963-64; pres. Central Newspapers Found. Indpls., 1969-70. Mem. exec. com. United Fund Indpls., 1954-70, pres. 1970; v.p. Comm. Service Council, Indpls. 1967-68. Trustee Brown U., 1952-59; pres. Indpls. Community Hosp. Found., 1976—. Served to lt. comdr., USNR, 1941-44. Recipient Advt. Club Torch of Truth award, 1975; Am. Advt. Fedn. silver medal, 1971. Mem. Better Bus. Bur. Indpls. (dir. 1950-65, pres. 1958, 65), Nat. Better Bus. Bur. (dir. 1950-70), Council Better Bus. Burs. (dir. 1970), Indpls. C. of C. (dir. 1967—, v.p. 1970-71), Am. Newspaper Publishers Assn. (labor relations com. 1953-63), Indpls. Advt. Club (dir. 1952-54, pres. 1952-53), Indpls. Comm. Hosp. Assn. (dir. 1952-54, 66-69, v.p. 1954). Club: Brown U. Ind. (Brown Bear award, 1968, sec. 1946-52, pres. 1952-54). Home: 401 Buckingham Dr Indianapolis IN 46208 Office: 307 N Pennsylvania Ave Indianapolis IN 46206

DYER-BENNET, JOHN, educator; b. Leicester, Eng., Apr. 17, 1915; s. Richard Stewart and Miriam (Clapp) Dyer-B.; came to U.S., 1925, naturalized, 1942; A.B., U. Calif., Berkeley, 1936, A.M., 1937;

M.A., Harvard, 1939, Ph.D., 1940; m. Mary Abby Randall, June 14, 1951; children—David, Barbara. Instr. math. Vanderbilt U., 1940-41, 45-46; from instr. to asso. prof. Purdue U., 1946-51, 52-60; faculty Carleton Coll., Northfield, Minn., 1960—, prof. math., 1965—, chmn. dept. math. and astronomy, 1964-66, tennis coach, 1961—, soccer coach, 1963—; T.C. Wollan meml. distinguished lectr. math. Concordia Coll., Moorhead, Minn., 1972. Served to 1st lt. AUS, 1941-45, as capt., 1951-52. NSF sci. faculty fellow, 1958-59. Mem. Am. Math. Soc., Math Assn. Am., AAUP (nat. council 1967-70), ACLU, Phi Beta Kappa, Sigma Xi. Democrat. Home: 907 Winona St Northfield MN 55057

DYKEMA, HERMAN, mfg. co. exec.; b. Plainwell, Mich., Jan. 12, 1922; s. Peter and Susie (Hiemstra) D.; student traffic mgtm. LaSalle Extension U., 1947; m. Dorothy Lee Brower, Sept. 2, 1946; children—Cecily (Mrs. Richard Lee Cagle), C. Kevin. With KTS Industries, Inc., Atlanta and Kalamazoo, 1946—, dist. sales mgr., Atlanta, 1959-62, nat. sales mgr., Kalamazoo, 1962—; also dir. Served with AUS, 1942-45. Mem. Am. Supply and Machinery Mfrs. Assn., Nat. Machine Tool Builders Assn. Clubs: Kalamazoo Riding, Soc. Preservation Barbershop Quartet Singing Am. (dist. v.p. 1973). Elk. Home: 3008 Duchess Dr Kalamazoo MI 49008 Office: 500 Harrison St Kalamazoo MI 49001

DYKES, ANGELITA DEL MUNDO, coll. counselor; b. Angeles City, Philippines, Oct. 13, 1947; d. Maximo M. and Paula H. (Santiago) del Mundo; came to U.S., 1971; naturalized, 1973; B.A., U. Philippines, 1969; M.A. in Edn., U. So. Calif., 1976; m. John C. Dykes, Jan. 10, 1970; children—JoAnne, Jennifer. Instr. Edn. Service Center, U.S. Air Force, Clark AFB, Philippines, 1969-70; registration asst. U. So. Calif., Los Angeles, 1974-77; instr. Eng. for Japanese Nationals, Misawa, Japan, 1974-76; field rep. Los Angeles City Coll., 1974-77. Mem. Am. Personnel and Guidance Assn. Researcher in field of continuing edn. Home: 25 Knollwood Dr Apt J-98 Rapid City SD 57701

DYKES, ARCHIE REECE, univ. chancellor; b. Rogersville, Tenn., Jan. 20, 1931; B.S., East Tenn. U., 1952, M.A., 1956; Ed.D. (Ford Found. fellow), U. Tenn., 1959. Tchr., Church Hill Sch., 1952-55, prin., 1955-58; supt. Greenville City Schs., 1959-62; prof., dir. Center Advanced Grad. Studies, U. Tenn.-Memphis State U., 1962-66; Am. Council Edn. fellow U. Ill., 1966-67; chancellor U. Tenn. at Martin, 1967-71, U. Tenn. at Knoxville, 1971-73; chancellor U. Kans., Lawrence, 1973—; mem. Edn. Commn. States, 1973-76, Nat. Advisory Council Edn. Professions Devel., 1975-76; vice-chmn. Com. Operation U.S. Senate, 1975-76; dir. Mchts. Nat. Bank, Topeka, Security Benefit Life Ins., Esmark, 1st Nat. Bank, Kansas City. Trustee U. Mid-Am., 1973—, Nelson Gallery, Kansas City, 1973—, Harry S. Truman Library Inst., 1973—. Mem. Am. Council Edn., Am. Assn. Sch. Adminstrs. (co-chmn. com. sch. bd.-supt. relations), Kans. Assn. Commerce and Industry, Am. Assn. Higher Edn., Phi Kappa Phi. Author: School Board and Superintendent, 1965; (with others) Philosophic Theory and Practice in Educational administration, 1966; Faculty Participation in Academic Decision Making, 1968; Presidential Leadership in Academe, 1967; Faculty Participation in Governance, 1968. Office: Office of the Chancellor Univ Kans Lawrence KS 66044

DYKHOUSE, DAVID JAY, lawyer; b. Charlotte, Mich., Oct. 2, 1936; s. Jay and Mary (Carland) D.; B.A. with highest honors, Rutgers U., 1958; J.D., U. Mich., 1962; m. Caroline Dow, June 15, 1963; children—Mary Catherine, David J., Jay Douglas. Admitted to Mich. bar, 1962; asso. firm Honigman, Miller, Schwartz & Cohn, Detroit, 1962-65; dept. dir. Mich. Dept. Commerce, Lansing, 1965-66, Mich. commr. ins., 1966-69, legal adviser to Gov. Mich., 1969; partner Ziegler, Dykhouse & Wise, Detroit, 1970—; adj. prof. law Wayne State U., Detroit, 1970—; chmn. Mich. Adminstrv. Law Commn., 1970—. Woodrow Wilson fellow, 1958-59. Mem. Bar Assn. Mich., Detroit, Am. bar assns., Sons Whiskey Rebellion, Phi Beta Kappa. Republican. Presbyterian. Clubs: Detroit Athletic, Prismatic (Detroit); Bay View Boat (Mich.); Players (N.Y.C.). Author: Construction Surety Bonds-Their Adequacy and Availability, 1970; Cases and Materials on Regulated Industries, 1972. Contbr. articles to profl. jours. Office: 3000 Book Bldg Detroit MI 48226

DYKHOUSE, VANCE JACOB, orthodontist; b. Rock Rapids, Iowa, Aug. 25, 1941; s. Jacob and Hermina (Van Anken) D.; student Kans. State U., 1959-60, Okla. U., 1960-62; D.D.S., U. Mo., Kansas City, 1966, M.S., 1970; m. Judith Carlene Puckett, June 4, 1965; children—Diane Lynne, David Edward. Resident in orthodontics U. Mo., Kansas City, 1968-70, clin. instr. orthodontics, Dental Sch., 1976—; pvt. practice orthodontics, Kansas City, 1970—. Served with USNR, 1966-68. Mem. Am. Dental Assn., Am. Assn. Orthodontists, Midwest Soc. Orthodontists, St. Louis U. Orthodontic Research Found., Tweed Found., Omicron Kappa Upsilon. Republican. Methodist. Club: Kiwanis. Home: 5219 Pleasant St Kansas City MO 64133 Office: 4240 Blue Ridge Blvd Kansas City MO 64133

DYKMAN, HAROLD ALBERT, osteopathic physician; b. Grand Rapids, Mich., Oct. 8, 1914; s. Albert and Jennie (Datema) D.; A.B., Calvin Coll., 1938; D.O., Kirksville Coll. Osteopathy and Surgery, 1941; M.D., Kansas City U. Physicians and Surgeons, 1942, Dr.P.H., 1942; Ph.D., Trinity Coll. and Sem., 1960, Th.D., 1962, D.D., 1963, LL.D., 1966; grad. Hong Kong Coll. Chinese Acupuncture, 1971; postgrad. tng., Japanese Acupuncture, Tokyo, 1971; m. Lucille V. Hawkins, Aug. 31, 1937; children—Dwight A., Charlene A. Intern, Saginaw Osteo. Hosp., 1942, chief staff, 1966, later mem. staff; practice osteopathic med., specializing in internal med., Saginaw, 1942-74; sr. staff officer VA Hosp., Battle Creek, Mich., 1974—. Surgeon, staff officer U.S. Merchant Marine. Diplomate Am. Osteo. Bd. Psychiatry. Fellow Am., Internat. colls. angiology; mem. Am., Mich. osteo. assns., Saginaw Valley Assn. Physicians and Surgeons, Am. Coll. Gen. Practitioners, Am. Inst. Hypnosis, Am. Med. Soc. Vienna, Am. Ministerial Assn., Psi Sigma Alpha, Kappa Phi Epsilon. Congregationalist. Mason (32 deg., K.T., Shriner), Elk, Germania. Home: 108 Christopher Ln Battle Creek MI 49015 also VA Hosp 115 Battle Creek MI 49016

DYKSTRA, RICHARD ALLEN, electronics engr.; b. Cedar Grove, Wis., June 12, 1948; s. Henry and Elsie Mae (Janisse) D.; m. Linda Anzia, Aug. 31, 1968; children—Stacy, Christopher, Sally. B.S., Milw. Sch. Engring., 1971. Elec. engr. Engine Devel. Lab., Kohler Co. (Wis.), 1971-73, electronics project engr., 1973—. Alumni counselor Milw. Sch. Engring., 1971—, indsl. adv. com., 1975—; mem. Cedar Grove-Belgium Area Schs. Needs Assessment Com., 1975-76, mem. citizens adv. com., 1976—. Recipient award for outstanding achievement Milw. Sch. Engring. Alumni Assn., 1969. Mem. IEEE, Inst. Noise Control Engring., Engine Mfrs. Assn., Tau Omega Mu. Contbr. articles to profl. jours. Home: 169 Ramaker Ave Cedar Grove WI 53013 Office: Kohler Co Engine Devel Lab 44 High St Kohler WI 53044

DZIJA, JOHN DENNIS, lawyer; b. Chgo., Jan. 20, 1946; s. Theodore Casimir and Eleanore (Mikrut) D.; B.S., Loyola U. (Chgo.), 1973, J.D., 1976; m. Camille Cunico, Aug. 16, 1969. Customer service rep. 3M Bus. Products Co., Chgo., 1972-73; docket clk. Cook County (Ill.) Recorder of Deeds Dept., Chgo., 1973-75; admitted to Ill. bar, 1976; law clk. firm Jonas, Schey & Assos., Chgo., 1975-76, asso., 1976-78; asso. firm Elmore, Gowen & DeMichael P.C., Midlothian, Ill., 1978—. Served with USAF, 1968-72, USAF Res., 1977—. Mem. Am., Ill. State, Chgo. bar assns., Assn. Trial Lawyers Am., Ill. Trial Lawyers Assn., Advocates Soc., Suburban Aeroclub Chgo., Acad. Model Aeronautics. Roman Catholic. Home: 6945 W 64th Pl Chicago IL 60638 Office: 14735 S Crawford Midlothian IL 60445

EADES, CHARLES JOSEPH, bus. exec.; b. Cin., July 2, 1929; s. William Leonard and Faye Elvira (Arbogast) E.; Ph.B., U. Cin., 1954; postgrad. Chase Coll., m. Doris Lee Grimm, Sept. 6, 1947; children—Kathy Lynn, Charles Joseph, David Douglas; m. 2d, Darlene Ruth Johnson, June 20, 1975. Pub. accountant, Milford, Ohio, 1956-60; with Emery Industries, Inc., Cin., 1960—, asst. sec., 1966—; pres. Emery Ltd., Cin., 1971—, also dir.; dir. Cin. Turfgrass Nursery Inc., 1968—, Don Curless, Inc., 1966—, Vanlandingham Bros., Inc., 1969—. Mem. Clermont County Planning Commn., 1954-58; mem. Miami Twp. Zoning Commn., Milford, 1956-60. Mem. Clermont County (Ohio) Rep. Central Com., 1968—; mem. Ohio Rep. Central and Exec. Coms., 1972—; trustee Ohio Rep. Fin. Com., 1973—; trustee Ohio Rep. News, 1973—. Mem. Miami Twp. Bd. Edn., Milford, 1954-58. Trustee, sec. Clermont Care Center, Inc., 1971—. Served to maj., inf., U.S. Army, 1951-53; to lt. col. Res. Decorated Silver Star, Bronze Star (2), Army Commendation medal (3). Mem. Am. Soc. Ins. Mgmt., Tax Found., Internat. Tax Inst., Tax Execs. Inst., Council State Chambers Commerce (mem. com. on state taxation 1970—), Airborne Assn., Res. Officers Assn., Ohio Mfrs. Assn. (taxation com. 1976—), Nat. Soc. Pub. Accountants. Club: Masons (master, sec., trustee). Office: 1300 Carew Tower Cincinnati OH 45202

EADIE, GEORGE ROBERT, engr.; b. Eldorado, Ill., Sept. 24, 1923; s. Joseph Powell and Myrtle Olive (Bacon) E.; B.S., U. Ill., 1949, M.S., 1956; E.M., 1957; m. Ruth V. Butler, June 17, 1943; children—Carolyn Madge, Rosalyn Kay. Engring. and mgmt. positions in coal industry, Pa., Okla., Ill., 1949-54; asso. prof. mining engring. U. Ill., Urbana, 1954-62, prof. gen. engring., 1968-76; engring. and mgmt. positions, Freeman Coal Corp., W. Frankfort, Ill., 1962-65; asso. editor Coal Mining and Processing mag., Chgo., 1965-68; adminstr. Ill. State Geol. Survey, 1968-76; prof. mining engring. tech., Ind. State U. of Evansville, 1976—. Served to lt. col., USAFR, 1942-69. Decorated D.F.C., Air Medal with two oak leaf clusters, Purple Heart. Mem. Soc. Mining Engrs., Am. Inst. Mining Engrs., Ill. Mining Inst., Ind. Mining and Tech. Soc., Am. Soc. Engring. Edn. Contbr. tech. articles on mine safety, ventilation and edn. to publs. Home: 3234 N Red Bank Rd Evansville IN 47712 Office: Indiana State University Evansville 8600 W University Blvd Evansville IN 47712

EADON, JACK EDWARD, food co. exec.; b. Hammond, Ind., July 6, 1949; s. John Ramsay and Lois Pauline (Leek) E.; B.S. in Ops. Mgmt. with honors and highest distinction, U. Ill., 1973; M.B.A. in Fin. mktg. with honors, U. Chgo., 1974. Asst. sales mgr. Cock Robin Ice Cream Co., Naperville, Ill., 1972-74; mktg. asst. hot cereals Quaker Oats Co., Chgo., 1975, asst. brand mgr. hot cereals, 1975-76, asst. brand mgr. Aunt Jemima Frozen Foods, 1976-77, brand mgr. Celeste Frozen Foods, 1977—. Mem. Am. Mktg. Assn. Home: 1750 N Clark St Chicago IL 60614 Office: 345 Merchandise Mart Plaza Chicago IL 60654

EAGLETON, THOMAS FRANCIS, U.S. senator, lawyer; b. St. Louis, Sept. 4, 1929; s. Mark David and Zitta Louise (Swanson) E.; B.A. cum laude, Amherst Coll., 1950; LL.B. cum laude, Harvard, 1953; m. Barbara Ann Smith, Jan. 20, 1956; children—Terence, Christin. Admitted to Mo. bar, 1953; practiced in St. Louis, 1953—; past mem. firm Eagleton & Eagleton; circuit atty., St. Louis, 1957-60; became atty. gen., State of Mo., 1960; lt. gov. of Mo., 1964-68; U.S. senator from Mo., 1968—. Served with USNR, 1948-49. Home: 5313 Cardinal Ct NW Washington DC 20016 Office: 6235 New Senate Office Bldg Washington DC 20510

EAKIN, THOMAS CAPPER, sports promotion exec.; b. New Castle, Pa., Dec. 16, 1933; s. Frederick William and Beatrice (Capper) E.; B.A. in History, Denison U., 1956; m. Brenda Lee Andrews, Oct. 21, 1961; children—Thomas Andrews, Scott Frederick. Life ins. cons. Northwestern Mut. Life Ins. Co., Cleve., 1959-67; dist. mgr. Putnam Pub. Co., Cleve., 1968-69; regional bus. mgr. Chilton Pub. Co., Cleve., 1969-70; dist. mgr. Hitchcock Pub. Co., Cleve., 1970-72; pres. TCE Enterprises, Shaker Heights, Ohio, 1973—; trustee Newcomerstown (Ohio) Sports Corp. Founder, nat. chmn. Cy Young Centennial, 1967, Cy Young Golf Invitational, 1967—; mem. adv. bd. Cleve. Indian Old Timers Com., 1966-67; founder, pres. Golf Internat. 100 Club, Shaker Heights, 1970—, founder, pres. Ohio Baseball Hall of Fame, 1976—; hon. dir. Tuscarawas County (Ohio) Old Timers Baseball Assn., 1972—; (commendation award 1970); fund rep. Boy Scouts Am., Cleve., 1959-60, United Appeal, 1959-63, Heart Fund, 1963-64; mem. Cleve. Council Corrections, 1971-73; chmn. Class of 1952 money raising and reunion coms. Univ. Sch. Alumni Fund, 1966; mem. adv. bd. Cuyahoga Hills Boys Sch., Warrensville Heights, Ohio, 1971—, Camp Hope, Warrenville Twp., 1973; founder, dir. TRY (Target/Reach Youth), 1971—, Interact Club Shaker Heights, 1971—, Cy Young Mus., 1970—; mem. exec. com. Tuscarawas County Am. Revolution Bicentennial Commn., 1974—. Served with AUS, 1956-58. Recipient commendation awards Cy Young Centennial Com., 1967, Tuscarawas County C. of C., 1967, Sporting News, 1968, Gov. James A. Rhodes Ohio, 1968, 75, Gov. John J. Gilligan Ohio, 1972, 74, Newcomerstown C. of C., 1967; Outstanding Contbn. to Baseball award baseball commr. William Eckert, 1967; Sport Service award Sport mag., 1969; Civic Service award Cuyahoga Hills Boys Sch., 1970; citation of merit La. Stadium and Expn. Dist., 1972; Presdl. commendation Richard M. Nixon, 1973, Gerald R. Ford, 1977; Distinguished Service award Camp Hope, 1974; Founder's award Interact Club Shaker Heights, 1974; Proclamation award-Thomas C. Eakin Day, City of Cleve., 1974; Gov.'s award for community action State of Ohio, 1974; award of achievement Ohio Assn. Hist. Socs., 1975; Chief Newawatowes award Newcomerstown C. of C., 1975; Commendation award Ohio Senate, 1976; commendation Ohio Am. Revolution Bicentennial Adv. Commn., 1976; certificate of merit Tuscarawas County Am. Revolution Bicentennial Commn., 1976, appreciation award, 1977. Mem. Denison U. Cleve. Men's Club (v.p. 1964-65), Tuscarawas County Hist. Soc. (trustee 1978—), Phi Delta Theta (pres. Cleve. alumni club 1970, Appreciation award 1971, dir. 1971-75, exec. com. nat. Lou Gehrig award com. 1975—, Outstanding Alumnus award 1975). Baptist (mem. bd. 1966-69). Clubs: Rotary (Outstanding young Rotarian award, 1962, pres. Shaker Heights 1970-71, founder and chmn. club's Internat. student exchange program U.S. and Can. 1965-70); Wahoo (dir. 1975—). Address: 3706 Traynham Rd Shaker Heights OH 44122

EAKINS, EDWIN MILTON, broadcasting exec.; b. Walhonding, Ohio, Apr. 5, 1936; s. Cecil Pearl and Vera Delores (Matheny) E.; B.S. in Radio-TV and Speech, Ohio State U., 1966; m. Sandra Kay Cousino, Feb. 2, 1963; children—Jay Michael, Robin Lynn. Producer-dir. Sta. WBNS-TV, Columbus, Ohio, 1963-69, promotion dir., 1969-72; dir. programming Ohio Ednl. Broadcasting Co., Columbus, 1972—; mem. media panel Ohio Arts Council, 1976-78. Pres. West Jefferson (Ohio) Parent Tchr. Orgn., 1976-77. Served with U.S. Army, 1959-61. Mem. Nat. Assn. Ednl. Broadcasters, Nat. Acad. TV Arts, Scis. (pres. Columbus/Dayton/ Cin. chpt. 1974-76, nat. trustee 1976-78). Home: 295 Taylor Blair Rd West Jefferson OH 43162 Office: 2470 North Star Rd Columbus OH 43221

EARL, DAVID MAGAREY, former educator; b. St. Joseph, Mo., Oct. 23, 1911; s. Edwin Charles and Barbara (Thurtell) E.; A.B., Oberlin Coll., 1933; M.A., Wayne State U., 1950; Ph.D., Columbia U., 1957, certificate E. Asian Inst., 1952; m. Joy Natalie Hill, June 19, 1933. Personnel examiner Detroit CSC, 1941-50; instr. Meiji U., Tokyo, 1952-54, Yamaguchi (Japan) U., 1954-56; instr. U. Md. Overseas Program, Japan, Korea and Taiwan, 1957-63, asst. dir. for Korea, 1963-65; prof. Far Eastern history and comparative religion Eastern Mich. U., Ypsilanti, 1965-77, ret., 1977. Mem. Nat. Spiritual Assembly of Baha'is of N.E. Asia, 1958-59, rec. sec., 1959-61, chmn., 1961-64, chmn. Korea, 1964-65. Served in USN, 1942-45. Mem. AAUP, Acad. Polit. Sci., Am. Acad. Religion, Assn. Asian Studies, Asiatic Soc. Japan, Royal Asiatic Soc., Phi Beta Kappa. Author: Emperor and Nation in Japan: Political Thinkers of the Tokugawa Period, 1964; contbr. entries to Ency. Brit. and Kodansha Ency. of Japan; contbr. articles to profl. jours. Home: 128 W Green St Olivet MI 49076

EARL, LEWIS HAROLD, economist, educator; b. Guthrie, Tex., Dec. 17, 1918; s. Henry W. and Ruth (O'Neal) E.; B.A., Tex. Technol. Coll., 1939; student U. Tex., 1939-40, Am. U., 1941-42; J.D., Georgetown U., 1950; m. Patricia Miller, Mar. 5, 1943 (dec. Jan. 1973); children—William Lee, Patricia Lewise (Mrs. Nelson), Robert Charles, James Michael. Admitted to D.C. bar, 1950, U.S. Supreme Ct. bar, 1972; with Bur. Labor Statistics, Dept. Labor, 1940-42, 46-54; industry, commodity economist NPA, Dept. Commerce, 1951-53; productivity specialist, economist, program analyst, asst. program officer US Tech. Cooperation Program in Brazil, 1953-57, program officer, Argentina, 1957-59, El Salvador, 1959-61; internat. relations officer AID, Washington, 1961-63; chief internat. research Office Manpower Automation and Tng., U.S. Dept. Labor, Washington, 1963-65, chief fgn. manpower program staff Office Manpower Policy, Evaluation and Research, Dept. Labor, 1965-70; U.S. del. to chem. industries com. Internat. Labor Office, 1969; tech. dir. Seminar for Ministry Labor Tng. Coordinators, OAS, Mexico City, Mexico, 1970; asst. dir. for program devel. for Human Resources, U. Houston, 1970-75; manpower planning officer Gulf Coast CAMPS Secretariat, Mayor's Office, City of Houston, 1970-74; cons. Gov.'s Div. Planning Coordination, Austin, Tex., 1974; instr. econs., asso. dir. manpower program U. Mo., Columbia, 1975—. Mem. Boone County Community Services Adv. Commn. Served as lt. USNR, 1942-46. Mem. Acad. Polit. Sci., Am. Acad. Polit. and Social Sci., Soc. for Internat. Devel., Nat. Planning Assn., Am. Soc. for Tng. and Devel., Houston Personnel Assn., Indsl. Relations Research Assn., Nat. Economist Club, Alpha Chi, Pi Sigma Alpha, Omicron Delta Epsilon. Home: Columbia MO 65201 Office: Dept Econs Middlebush Hall Univ Missouri Columbia MO 65201

EARLE, ELINOR SOUTHGATE, librarian; b. Union City, Ind., Mar. 24, 1921; d. Thomas Evans and Elinor (Southgate) Earle; A.B., U. Ky., 1942; M.A., Ohio State U., 1946; B.S. in L.S., U. Ill., 1947. Tchr. English, McDowell County, W.Va., 1942-43; asst. reference librarian Lincoln Library, Springfield, Ill., 1947-48; asst. in reference Akron (Ohio) Pub. Library, 1948-51, head gen. reference, 1951-57, asst. librarian West Hill br., 1959-60, librarian, Kenmore br., 1961—; base librarian AFB, Phalsbourg, France, 1957-59. Chmn. research com. Summit County Com. for Peace, 1969-71. Corr. sec. Ohio Family Historians, 1967-73. Served with WAVES, 1944-45. Mem. Am., Ohio, Summit County library assns., Akron Assn. U. Women, Daus. Am. Colonists (vice regent 1964-68, regent 1968-70, sec. 1970-72, registrar 1976—), D.A.R., United Daus. Confederacy (state chmn. So. lit. 1974—), Ohio Soc. Dames Ct. Honor (registrar 1967—), Ohio Soc. Huguenots (librarian 1966-72, cons. genealogist 1972—). Home: 77 Fir Hill Akron OH 44304 Office: 2200 14th St Akron OH 44314

EARLEY, ARTHUR EDSEL, advt. exec.; b. Ahoskie, N.C., Mar. 28, 1923; s. James Lawrence and Nancy Catherine (Dilday) E.; A.B., Wake Forest U., 1943; M.A., U. N.C., 1947; m. Edith A. Black, Aug. 19, 1955. Instr., U. Va., 1947-48; mem. advt. and mktg. staff Gen. Electric Co., 1949-56, editor Light Mag., 1952-55; asso. media dir. Meldrum & Fewsmith, Inc., Cleve., 1956-60, v.p. marketing services, 1960-64, v.p. creative services, 1965, exec. v.p., 1969, pres., chief exec. officer, 1970—. Former chmn. bd. Bus. Publs. Audit of Circulation Inc., 1968-69. Mem. men's com. Cleve. Play House, 1961—, UN Day Com., 1970-77; trustee, former v.p. Cleve. Area Arts Council. Trustee Center Mktg. Communications, chmn., 1975-76; v.p., trustee Cleve. Play House Club; trustee Cleve. Hearing and Speech Center, pres., 1976-77; bd. visitors Wake Forest U., Winston-Salem, N.C.; former trustee Cleve. Better Bus. Bur. Served to 2d lt. AUS, 1943-46. Recipient, Distinguished Alumnus in Bus. award Wake Forest U., 1975; named Ad Man of Year, Am. Advt. Fedn., 1970, Cleve. Advt. Man of Year Cleve. Advt. Club, 1976; named to Cleve. Advt. Hall of Fame. Mem. Cleve. Indsl. Marketers, Cleve. Advt. Club (pres. 1966-67, trustee 1964-70), Am. Assn. Advt. Agys. (chmn. Cleve. council 1973-74, dir. 1974-77, sec.-treas. Central region 1974-75, chmn. 1976-77). Greater Cleve. Growth Assn. (mem. downtown council; chmn. regional devel. and competitive posture com.), Omicron Delta Kappa, Alpha Psi Omega. Baptist (former trustee). Clubs: Hermit (pres., dir.), Mayfield Country, Brathenahl, Mid-Day, Newcomen Soc. Contbr. articles to profl. jours. Home: 13720 Shaker Blvd Cleveland OH 44120 Office: 1220 Huron Rd Cleveland OH 44115

EARLY, BERT HYLTON, lawyer; b. Kimball, W.Va., July 17, 1922; s. Robert Terry and Sue Keister (Hylton) E.; student Marshall U., 1940-42; A.B., Duke, 1946; J.D., Harvard, 1949; m. Elizabeth Louise Henry, June 24, 1950; children—Bert Hylton, Robert Christian, Mark Randolph, Philip Henry, Peter St. Clair. Admitted to W.Va. bar, 1949, Ill. bar, 1963; asso. firm Fitzpatrick, Marshall, Huddleston & Bolen, Huntington, W.Va., 1949-57; instr. Marshall U., 1950-53; asst. counsel Island Creek Coal Co., 1957-60, asso. gen. counsel, 1960-62; dep. exec. dir. Am. Bar Assn., 1962-64, exec. dir., 1964—; mem. W.Va. Jud. Council, 1960-62; vice chmn. Conf. Nat. Orgns., 1971-73; mem. task force Twentieth Century Fund on Govtl. Regulation and Press Freedom, 1971. Mem. Huntington City Council, 1961-62. Bd. dirs. Huntington Pub. Library, 1951-60, Morris Meml. Hosp. Crippled Children, 1953-60, Huntington Galleries, 1961-62, W.Va. Tax Inst., 1961-62, Robert Crown Center for Health Edn., 1970-76, United Charities Chgo., 1972—; trustee Davis and Elkins Coll., 1960-63; bd. dirs. Community Renewal Soc., 1965-76; mem. vis. com. U. Chgo. Law Sch., 1975—. Served to 1st lt., pilot USAAC, 1943-45. Fellow Am. Bar Found.; mem. Am. Law Inst., Am. (ho. of dels. 1958-59, nat. chmn. Jr. Bar Conf. 1958), Internat. (asst. sec.-gen. 1967—), Inter-Am., W.Va., Chgo. bar assns., W.Va. State Bar (chmn. jr. sect. 1951), Am. Judicature Soc. Democrat. Presbyterian. Clubs: Economic (Chgo.); University (Washington and Chgo.); Hinsdale (Ill.) Golf. Home: 136 S Oak St Hinsdale IL 60521 Office: Am Bar Center Chicago IL 60637

EARLYWINE, JOSEPHINE LEWIS (MRS. LAYMAN J. WILKINSON), physician; b. Chgo., Feb. 21, 1920; d. Joseph L. and Elsie (Boradman) Earlywine; B.S., Northwestern U., 1940, M.B., 1943, M.D., 1943; m. Layman J. Wilkinson, Dec. 26, 1941; children—Wanda K., Joseph L. Intern Cook County Hosp., Chgo., 1943-44; resident Cook County Children's Hosp., 1944-46; pvt. practice Wilmette, Ill., 1946—; attending staff Evanston Hosp. Assn.; asso. in pediatrics Northwestern U. Med. Sch., 1946-66, asso. prof., 1966—; attending pediatrician The Cradle, Evanston, 1960-65, med. dir., 1965—; attending staff Wilmette Infant Welfare, 1950—, Children's Meml. Hosp., 1964—; med. dir. Grove Sch., 1975—; dir. 1st Nat. Bank of Wilmette. Recipient Citizens award City of Wilmette, 1974. Diplomate Am. Bd. Pediatrics. Fellow Am. Acad. Pediatrics (mem. com. on adoption 1969—); mem. Inst. Medicine Chgo., Chgo. Pediatric Soc., Chgo. Med. Soc., Delta Zeta. Club: Zonta. Home: 1221 Greenwood Wilmette IL 60091 Office: 1149 Wilmette Ave Wilmette IL 60091

EASH, ORUS ORVILLE, architect; b. Middlebury, Ind., Dec. 12, 1915; s. Clayton and Ivy Eash; Student Goshen Coll., 1934-36; B.Arch., U. Mich., 1939; m. Ruth Ganger, Apr. 13, 1941; 1 son, John. Mem. staff U.S. Govt. Housing, 1941-44, Bauer & Eash, Architects, 1944-49; practice architecture, Traverse City, Mich., 1939-41, 49-56, Ft. Wayne, Ind., 1956-76, Eash, Miller, White, Inc., 1977—. Bd. dirs., past chmn. Lake Michigan Region Planning Council, 1964—; chmn. Phys. Task Force, Ft. Wayne Future, 1971-76, vice chmn., 1977—. Registered profl. architect, Ind., Mich., Ohio, Fla., Va. Mem. A.I.A., Ft. Wayne Soc. Architects. Prin. works include Mut. Security Life Ins. Co. Bldg., 1959-70, University Park Med. Clinic, 1968, Immanuel Bapt. Ch., 1962, Simpson Meth. Ch., 1968, Indian Meadows Sch., 1972, Woodside Sch., 1976 (all Ft. Wayne), also numerous religious, ednl., comml. and apt. bldgs., and nursing homes. Home: 7515 Oak Ln Fort Wayne IN 46804 Office: 6110 Constitution Dr Fort Wayne IN 46804

EASLEY, JOHN HOAGLAND, ophthalmologist, otorhinolaryngologist; b. Otoe County, Nebr., Oct. 25, 1910; s. George and Bessie (Markle) E.; M.D., U. Nebr., 1939; m. Berenzce Emma Smith, June 10, 1939; children—John Hoagland, Joan (Mrs. Edward Burton Alcott), Jane (Mrs. Michael Seim), James Francis, Joseph Leo, Jerry Anthony, Jean Ann. Intern Hosp., Detroit, 1939-40, resident, 1940-41, 45-47; practice medicine, specializing in ophthalmology and otorhinolaryngology, Grand Island, Nebr., 1947—; mem. staff St Francis Hosp., Luth. Hosp. (both Grand Island). Cons. VA Hosp.; tchr. St. Francis Sch. Nursing, Grand Island, 1947—; mem. area hosp. adv. council, Grand Island, 1965—. Served to lt. col., flight surgeon USAAF, 1941-45. Mem. A.M.A., Nebr. Eye Ear Nose Throat Assn., Am. Soc. Clin. Hypnosis. Democrat. Roman Catholic. K.C. (4 deg.). Club: Riverside Country. Home: 2023 W Koenig Grand Island NE 68801 Office: 306 1st Nat Bank Bldg Grand Island NE 68801

EASLEY, RALPH ANDREW, JR., cons. civil engr.; b. Decatur, Ill., Mar. 3, 1934; s. Ralph Andrew and Roberta Lillian (Morehead) E.; A.A., Centralia Twp. Jr. Coll., 1954; B.S. (scholar), U. Ill., 1957; m. Marcia Ann Graebel, Nov. 23, 1956; children—David, Kimberly, Jamie. Dir. pub. works City Ojai (Calif.), 1961-62; asso. civil engr. City San Buenaventura (Calif.), 1962-64; chief engr., asso. Robert Martin & Assos., Ventura, Calif., 1964-66; chief asst. city engr. Evansville, Ind., 1966-72; pres. Andy Easley Engring., Evansville, Ind., 1972—; pres. Village Homebuilders, Inc., Elberfeld, Ind., 1972—, Easley-Raney Assos., cons. civil engr., Hartford, Ky., 1972-73; v.p. Utility Devel. Corp., Evansville, 1972-75; pres. Tech. Engring. Constrn. Corp., Evansville, 1975—. Served with C.E., USNR, 1957-61. Mem. Am. Soc. C.E., Nat. Soc. Profl. Engrs. Presbyn. Home: 9000 Petersburg Rd Evansville IN 47711 Office: 1133 W Mill Rd Evansville IN 47710

EASOM, HARRY AUGUST, ophthalmologist; b. Detroit, Feb. 4, 1933; s. William G. and Emmy Easom; B.A., U. Mich., 1954, M.D., 1958; m. Carolyn Heineke, Aug. 29, 1959; children—William, Katherine, Julie, Susan. Intern Colo. Gen. Hosp., Denver, 1958-59; resident Washington U. Hosp., St. Louis, 1959-62, Heed Ophthalmic fellow plastic surgery, 1962, Fight for Sight fellow ophthalmic pathology, 1963; pvt. practice ophthalmology, Milw., 1963—; mem. staff St. Mary's, Columbia, Children's, Luth. hosps. (all Milw.). Asso. clin. prof. ophthalmology Med. Coll. Wis., 1970—. Diplomate Am. Bd. Ophthalmology. Mem. Milw. Ophthal. Soc. (pres. 1972-73), Phi Beta Kappa, Phi Kappa Phi, Alpha Omega Alpha, Phi Eta Sigma. Home: 7400 N Longview Ave Milwaukee WI 53209 Office: 2266 N Prospect Ave Milwaukee WI 53202

EAST, JAMES HENRY, data processor; b. Clinton, S.C., Aug. 18, 1936; s. James Wesley and Helen Dorothy (Daly) E.; m. Mary Ann Miller, Feb. 11, 1961; children—Susan, Sandra, Christopher. Data processor Chrysler Corp., St. Louis, 1958-63, Pevely Dairy Co., St. Louis, 1963-69; mgr. data processing Intertherm, Inc., St. Louis, 1969-75; 2d v.p. Meyer Bros. Drug Co., St. Louis, 1975—. Served with AUS, 1955-58. Mem. Data Processing Mgmt. Assn. (dir. 1967-77, officer 1972-75, pres. 1977-78). Roman Catholic. Home: 11291 Bristolwood Dr St Louis MO 63126 Office: 1177 N Warson Rd St Louis MO 63132

EAST, THOMAS D., tenor, educator; b. Trinidad, Colo., Mar. 29, 1932; s. Thomas D. and Evelyn (Plested) E.; B.A., Colo. State Coll., 1954; postgrad. U. Colo., 1957, Hochschule Fuer Musik, Stuttgart, Germany, 1962-63; M.M., U. Ind., 1965; m. Joanne Orr, Oct. 1, 1954; children—Tommy, Michael. Vocal music tchr., Denver, 1954-59; lead tenor Hessisches Landestheater, Darmstadt, Germany, 1963-67; tenor soloist Stuttgart Philharmonik, 1963; soloist Central City Opera Assn., Colo., 1954, 57, 59; soloist Utah Symphony, Salt Lake City, 1967—; artist in residence U. Utah, Salt Lake City, 1967-71; soloist Denver Symphony, Greater Denver Opera Co., 1958, Denver Lyric Theater, 1958-60, Louisville Symphony, 1961, Utah Opera Co., Salt Lake City, 1967-71; dir. opera studies U. Toledo, 1971—. Soloist with Memphis Opera, 1972, Toledo Symphony, 1973, Toledo Opera Assn., 1975, 76, 77, Dayton Opera Assn., 1975, 76, 77. Recipient Fulbright award, 1962; Rockefeller grantee, 1963. Mem. Nat. Assn. Tchrs. Singing. Mason. Home: 6041 Gillingham Sylvania OH 43560

EASTERDAY, ALFRED LESTER, paint co. exec.; b. nr. Seville, Ohio, Sept. 8, 1913; s. Jett and Rena (Hottenstein) E.; ed. pub. schs., Ohio; m. Mildred Genevieve Dye, Dec. 15, 1934; children—Ronald, Allen, Cindria, Valene. Varnish plant supt. So. Coating & Chem. Co., Sumter, S.C., 1939-42; formulating chemist Thompson Co., Oakmont, Pa., 1942-45; research dir. Sewall Paint & Varnish Co., Kansas City, Mo., 1945-47; pres. Easterday Paint & Chem. Co., with factories in Kenosha, Racine, Milw., Wis., 1947—, chmn. bd., 1948—. Mem. Wis. Paint, Varnish & Lacquer Assn. (pres. 1971). Research and developer color changing heat sensor inks used in canning industry. Home: 11301 75th St Kenosha WI 53140 Office: 1306 E Bolivar Milwaukee WI 53207

EASTERDAY, MICHAEL JOSEPH, accountant; b. Salina, Kans., Apr. 14, 1941; s. Joseph Francis and Florence I. (Sandstrom) E.; B.S. cum laude, St. Benedict's Coll., 1963; M.S., U. Kans., 1964; m. Mary Alice Shea, Aug. 11, 1962; children—Mary Theresa, Anne Christine, Joseph Michael, Catherine Elizabeth. With Peat, Marwick, Mitchell & Co., 1964—, mgr., 1970-74, partner, 1973—, mng. partner, Wichita, Kans., Active various community drives; mem. pastoral council Diocese of Kansas City-St. Joseph, 1970-74, pres. pastoral council, 1971-73; mem. St. Thomas More Sch. Bd., Kansas City, 1970-72; mem., vice chmn. adv. bd. Cath. Family and Community Services Home Health Care Agy., 1969-72; mem. exec. com. Council Cath. Laity, Kansas City-St. Joseph, 1970-73; mem. U.S. Cath. Bishop Nat. Adv. Council, 1973-74. Bd. dirs. Catholic Family and Community Services, 1972-74, Wichita Area Devel., Kans. Found. Pvt. Colls.; bd. dirs. Benedictine Coll., Athison, Kans., 1971—, chmn. bd. govs., 1973-75; bd. dirs. United Way Wichita and Sedgwick County, NCCJ, Wichita Festivals; bd. advisers U. Kans. Sch. Bus., 1976—; mem. nat. finance com. Nat. Conf. Catholic Charities, 1977—. C.P.A., Mo., Kans. Mem. Am. Inst. C.P.A.'s, Mo., Kans. socs. C.P.A.'s, Nat. Assn. Accountants (Kansas City chpt. sec. 1970-71, v.p. 1971-73, pres. 1973-74), Hosp. Financial Mgmt. Assn., St. Benedict's Coll. Alumni (Kansas City pres. 1968-70), Wichita C. of C., Beta Gamma Sigma. Rotarian. Home: 126 Brendonwood Ct Wichita KS 67206 Office: 666 Fourth Financial Center Wichita KS 67202

EASTMAN, RICHARD DELL, concrete, sand and gravel co. exec.; b. Lansing, Mich., July 15, 1917; s. Howard W. and Clara Blenn (Dell) E.; student Western Mich. U., 1940-42, Mich. State U., 1946-49; m. Monna E. Fowler, July 17, 1959; children—Richard John, Renita Ruth, Russell Dell, Rand Dell, Gregory F. stepchildren-Tracy Ann Johnson, Jeffrey C. White. With Ireland & Lester Co., St. Joseph, Mich., 1949—, pres., gen. mgr., 1952—. Mem. Twin Cities Devel. Corp., Benton Harbor, Mich., 1965—. Cubmaster Southwestern Mich. council Boy Scouts Am., 1960—; coach Little League, 1969—; mem. St. Joseph Improvement Assn., 1965; mem. Sch. Bd., Coloma, 1970-78. Bd. dirs. A.R.C. Served with AUS, 1942-46. Mem. Twin City Symphonic., C. of C. Mason. Home: 6556 Paw Paw Ave Coloma MI 49038 Office: 220 N Wayne St St Joseph MI 49085

EASTMAN, ROGER WILLIAM, civil engr., steel mfg. co. exec.; b. Inwood, Iowa, Aug. 10, 1942; s. Harley Francis and Goldie Evelyn (Iseminger) E.; M.S. in Civil Engring., S.D. State U., 1970; m. Patricia Elaine Mize, June 21, 1968; children—Tricia Elaine, Judson William. Engring. trainee Pittsburgh-Des Moines Steel Co., Des Moines, 1970-72, project engr. for bridge in N.Y.C., 1972, resident field engr., constrn. depts., various locations, 1972, field project engr., N.Y.C., 1973-74, div. quality assurance mgr. central div., 1974—; cons. steel constrn. Ch.-sch. supt. Westover Bapt. Ch., 1972-78. Served with U.S. Army, 1962-65. Am. Inst. of Steel Constrn. grantee, 1969; registered profl. engr. Mem. ASCE, Am. Welding Soc., Am. Soc. Non-destructive Testing. Republican. Home: 409 NE Crestmoore St Ankeny IA 50021 Office: 1015 Tuttle St Des Moines IA 50308

EASTO, PATRICK CLIFFORD, educator; b. Detroit, July 19, 1940; s. Howard Grover and Mary Veronica (Russell) E.; B.S., Eastern Mich. U., 1966; M.A., Wayne State U., 1968; Ph.D., Syracuse U., 1973. Asst. prof. sociology Eastern Mich. U., Ypsilanti, 1970-75, asso. prof., 1975—; research asso. Inst. Labor and Indsl. Relations, U. Mich., 1974; court sociologist 3d Judicial Circuit Ct. Detroit, 1975. Served with USN, 1959-63. Mem. Am., Mich. sociol. assns. Contbr. articles to profl. jours. Home: 91 Potter Dr 3 Belleville MI 48111 Office: Dept Sociology Eastern Mich Univ Ypsilanti MI 48197

EASTON, GAIL RAYMOND, osteo. physician; b. Maywood, Nebr., Jan. 12, 1915; s. Ray Reuben and Delta Lydia (Dodson) E.; student Nebr. Sch. Agr., 1932-34, Hastings (Nebr.) Bus. Coll., 1935; D.O., Kirksville Coll. Osteopathy and Surgery, 1940; m. Martha Carolyn Lewis, July, 1939; children—Delta Anne Easton King, Patricia Gail Easton McClelland. Intern, Roswell (N.Mex.) Osteo. Hosp.; gen. practice osteo. medicine and surgery, Weaubleau, Mo., 1940—; mem. bd. Hickory County Health Dept. Founder, pres. bd. dirs. Golden Hours Found., Inc.; active Emphasis Elderly; bd. dirs. Mo. Div. of Blind, Mo. Bur. Blind; mayor City of Weaubleau, 1968-76. Served in U.S. Mcht. Marines, 1944-45. Mem. Am., Mo., Ozark osteo. assns., Internat. Platform Assn. Republican. Methodist. Clubs: Lions (past pres. Weaubleau, past dist. gov., chmn. bd. govs. Mo. 1971-72), Masons. Home: Weaubleau MO 65774 Office: PO Box 197 Weaubleau MO 65774

EATMON, MARY BETH, counselor, educator, ednl. adminstr.; b. Paragould, Ark., Jan. 11, 1922; d. Riley Hall and Mary Agnes (Spain) Johnson; B.S., Bradley U., 1966, M.A., 1971; m. Press Eatmon, Sept. 14, 1941; children—Carolyn, Pressie, Diane, Deborah, Cynthia. Tchr., Paragould Pub. Schs., 1941-48, Homewood Heights Schs., Creve Coeur, Ill., 1961-72; tchr., asst. prin. La Salle Sch., Creve Coeur, 1972—. Mem. Nat., Ill., Creve Coeur, edn. assns., Am. Personnel and Guidance Assn., Am. Sch. Counselor Assn., PTA (life), Pi Lambda Theta. Democrat. Baptist. Home: 200 W Summit St Washington IL 61571 Office: 300 N Highland St Creve Coeur IL 61611

EATON, JAMES WOODFORD, newspaper exec.; b. Indpls., Apr. 14, 1942; s. James Woodford and Genevee (Oliver) E.; B.A., Butler U., 1964; M.A., Kent State U., 1967, Ph.D., 1973; m. Linda McKinney, Aug. 27, 1966; 1 dau., Victoria Lynn. Grad. asst. in history Kent (Ohio) State U., 1964-66, teaching fellow in history, 1966-68, instr. history Tuscarawas campus, 1968-72; staff Dover-New Philadelphia (Ohio) Times-Reporter, 1972—. bus. editor, 1973—. Mem. Soc. Am. Bus. and Econ. Writers, Am. Hist. Assn., Conf. Brit. History, Research Soc. Victorian Periodicals, New Philadelphia Jaycees. Mem. Christian Ch. Home: 221 E 10th St Dover OH 44622 Office: 629 Wabash Ave New Philadelphia OH 44663

EATON, RICHARD ROE, educator, counselor; b. Festus, Mo., Jan. 22, 1939; s. Leo Glenman and Ruth Elizabeth (Sago) E.; B.S. in Edn., S.E. Mo. State U., 1962; M.Ed., U. Mo., Columbia, 1965; Ph.D. in Counselor Edn., St. Louis U., 1977. Tchr., Arcadia Valley Schs., Ironton, Mo., 1958-61; jr. high sch. tchr. Hazelwood Sch. Dist., St. Louis, 1962-67; high sch. counselor Ladue Sch. Dist., St. Louis, 1967—; adj. instr. St. Louis U., 1977; cons. in field. Certified rational emotive psychotherapist Inst. Advanced Study in Rational Emotive Psychotherapy. Mem. Am., St. Louis personnel and guidance assns., Mo. Guidance Assn., Nat. Assn. Humanist Educators, Ladue Community Tchrs. Assn., NEA, Mo. Nat. Ednl. Assn., S.E. Mo., U. Mo.-Columbia, St. Louis U. alumni assns. Methodist. Home: 1180 Moorlands Dr St Louis MO 63117 Office: 1224 S Warson Rd St Louis MO 63124

EATON, WILLIAM CHARLES, mech. engr.; b. Detroit, July 9, 1927; s. Earle and Bernice (Kyes) E.; B.S., Mich. State U., 1950; M.S., Iowa State U., 1954; m. Lavelle Grace Hauck, June 19, 1955; children—Patricia, Lawrence, Richard. Design engr. Ford Motor Co., Birmingham, Mich. 1954-57; chief engr. Midland-Ross Corp., Owosso, Mich., 1957-68, dir. reliability and safety, 1968-70; dir. engring. Omsteel Industries, Omaha, 1970-72; mgr. irrigation engring. Valmont Industries, Valley, Nebr., 1972-76, mgr. new products identification, 1977—; treas., dir. PLR Corp., Omaha, 1975—. Served with USNR, 1945; served with AUS, 1951-52. Mem. Soc. Automotive Engrs., Nat., Nebr. socs. profl. engrs., Mich. Assn. Professions. Republican. Methodist (trustee). Club: Omaha Exchange. Home: 2115 S 91st St Omaha NE 68124 Office: Valmont Industries Valley NE 68064

EBBERT, GEORGE CONRAD, artist, author, newsman; b. Pitts., Aug. 14, 1912; s. Conrad George and Josephine Katherine (Kellenberg) E.; student pub. schs. Springfield, Ill.; m. Jeannette Mae Harbert, Mar. 8, 1942 (dec.); 1 dau., Doris Mae. Reporter, N.Y.C. PM, 1937-41; war corr. Army News Service, Pisa-Rimini, Italy, 1942-43, Tripoli and Tunis, 1943-44, Tampa, Fla., 1944-45; mng. editor North Town Tattler, Chgo., 1946-53; copy editor Chgo. Sun, 1953-55; mgr. pub. relations Pabst Brewing Co., Chgo., 1955-60; dir. publicity Gourfain Loeff & Adler, advt. agy., Chgo., 1960-63; creative dir. Poole-Clarinda Co., Chgo., 1963-74; novels: Mephisto and the Eagle (Internat. Writers' Guild award), 1967; Satan Will Never Die, 1974; The Nymph who Hated Men, 1978; syndicated PM editorial May Your Light Never Be Extinguished, 1941; executed portrait Pres. Franklin D. Roosevelt, Little White House, Warm Springs, Ga., 1938, portrait Pres. John F. Kennedy, Kennedy Center, Washington, 1978. Served with AAC, 1942-45. Mem. Chgo. Press Club, DAV. Democrat. Roman Catholic. Represented in Artists/USA, 1977-78. Home and studio: 616 Rush St Room 622 Chicago IL 60611

EBEL, SUSAN LEWIS, counselor; b. South Bend, Ind., Nov. 12, 1939; d. Grant and Essie (Ayers) Lewis; B.S., Western Mich. U., 1961; M.A., U. Mich., 1975. Art tchr., Muskegon, Royal Oak and Ann Arbor, Mich., 1961-70; owner Hyperbole, Inc., women's boutique, Detroit, 1966-68; personnel mgr. Little Things Boutique, Ann Arbor, 1970-72; mgr. Circle Book Store, Ann Arbor, 1972-74; counselor, program specialist U. Mich. Center Continuing Edn. for Women, Ann Arbor, 1975—; staff and program devl. cons. St. Clair Coll., Windsor, Ont., Can., lectr., 1975-76; cons. Tecumseh (Ont.) Nursing Home, 1975-76. Mem. N.Am. Simulation and Gaming Assn., Am. Personnel and Guidance Assn., Am. Coll. Personnel Assn. Originator: (with Easterly) Access, interactive ednl. simulation, 1975; (with T. Anderson) The Name of the Game, interactive orgnl. simulation, 1977. Home: 1308 Geddes St Ann Arbor MI 48104 Office: 328 Thompson St Ann Arbor MI 48109

EBEREITER, THOMAS CHARLES, banker; b. Gillett, Wis., June 2, 1927; s. Charles Herman and Ruth Viola (Tasche) E.; B.B.A., U. Wis., 1950, M.B.A., 1952; m. Sally Ann Manley, Aug. 22, 1953; children—Sue Ann, Carol, Lisa. Mgr. Ebenreiter Sales Co., Gillett, Wis., 1954-64; asst. prof. U. Wis., Madison, 1964-65; with Gillett (Wis.) State Bank, 1966—, pres., 1968—, also dir.; dir. Gillett Indsl. Devel. Corp. Pres. Gillett Civic Club, 1968-69. Served with USNR, 1945-46. C.P.A., Wis. Mem. Wis. Soc. C.P.A.'s, Am. Legion. Republican. Lutheran. Mason (Shriner), Kiwanian. Home: 321 Orchard St Gillett WI 54124 Office: Main St Gillett WI 54124

EBERHARDT, DANIEL HUGO, lawyer; b. Milw., Feb. 19, 1938; s. Erwin M. and Hazel M. (Daley) E.; student U. Wis. at Milw., part-time 1956-58, Utah State U., 1959; B.S., Colo. State U., 1962; J.D., Marquette Law Sch., 1968; m. Josephine E. Jeka, Sept. 10, 1960; children—Daniel Hugo, Mark John. Sales and purchasing staff South Side Packing Co., Milw., 1956-58; admitted to Wis. bar, 1968; since practiced in Elkhorn; asso. mem. firm Morissy Morrissy Sweet & Race, Elkhorn, Wis., 1968-70; partner Sweet & Eberhardt, Elkhorn, 1970—; Commr. Walworth County Circuit and County Cts., 1975—. Dir. R-Way Constrn., Elkhorn, Palmer & Dunbar, Inc. Bd. dirs. Walworth County chpt. A.R.C., 1969-70. Served with Transp. Corps, AUS, 1963-65. Mem. Colo. State U. Alumni Assn., Wis., Am., Walworth County bar assns., Am. Trial Lawyers Assn., V.F.W., Phi Alpha Delta, Omicron Delta Kappa. Rotarian. Home: Route 4 Box 220 Elkhorn WI 53121 Office: 18 S Broad St Elkhorn WI 53121

EBERHARDT, LEE EUGENE, export-import co. exec.; b. Barberton, Ohio, Dec. 22, 1915; s. Leo Ernest and Lucy Pearl (Young) E.; student Akron U., 1932-34, Case Sch. Applied Sci., 1938-41; B.M.E., Ohio State U., 1937, M.S., 1940; Dr. Engr., U. Taiwan, 1954; m. Lahmee Wittbrock, Dec. 13, 1946; children—Robert Heath, Lawrence Heath. Rubber machinery, design engr. Goodyear Aircraft, Akron, Ohio, 1938-40, chief tool engr., 1940-41; asst. chief engr. Lone Star Ordnance Plant, Texarkana, Tex., 1942-43; chief designer Bauer Bros. Co., Springfield, Ohio, 1946-52, asst. to pres., 1952-58, pres. Bauer Internat.-Brussels and Tokyo, 1959-69; pres. Liasson Internat., Inc., Springfield, Ohio 1969—; mng. dir. Teknointer S/A, Geneva, Switzerland, 1975—; chmn. Matech. Engring., Saitama, Japan, 1976—; cons. India, Malaysia, Republic of China govts. Served with AUS, 1943-45. Mem. Japan Tech. Assn. Pulp and Paper Industry, Paper Industry Mgmt. Assn., Australian and N.Z. Pulp and Paper Industry Assn., Iris Soc. Am. (past pres., sr. judge). Clubs: Springfield (Ohio) Country, Shriner., Masons (32 deg.). Contbr. articles to tech. jours. Patentee pulp and paper industry. Home: 1440 N Fountain St Springfield OH 45501 Office: PO Box 481 Springfield OH 45501

EBERHART, PAUL DONALD, printing co. exec.; b. Gordon, Nebr., Nov. 27, 1933; s. Albert George and Carola Josephine (Peltz) E.; student U. Minn., 1952-60; children—Mark, David, Karl. With mech. dept. South St. Paul (Minn.) Reporter, 1949-51; with prodn. dept. St. Paul Pioneer Press, 1951-61; prodn. engr. Mergenthaler Linotype Co. div. Eltra Corp., Chgo., 1961-65; sales rep. Domtar Pulp & Paper Co., N.Y.C., 1965-69; Midwest rep. newsprint Boise Cascade Corp., Mpls., 1969-72; mktg. coordinator Mergenthaler div. Eltra Corp., Chgo., 1972-73; pres., gen. mgr. Security Blank Book & Printing Co., St. Cloud, Minn., 1973—; pres., Bankers Certified Service, St. Cloud, 1974—. Circuit del. Luth. Ch. Mo. Synod (Moderate) Conv., Dallas, 1977; coordinator Legis. Dist. 17A, 1976; Ind. Republican candidate Minn. Senate, 1976; chmn. Dist. 17 Ind. Rep. Com., 1977-78. Club: St. Cloud Boat (sec.-treas.). Home: PO Box 608 St Cloud MN 56301 Office: 500 1st St N St Cloud MN 56301

EBERIUS, KLAUS OTTO, machine tool import co. exec.; b. Koethen, Germany, Feb. 13, 1940; s. Otto and Gertrud (Marx) E.; came to U.S., 1972; engring. degree Akademie of Engring., Cologne, Germany, 1967; m. Amei Brauns, Apr. 17, 1964; children—Edda, Susanne. Asst. plant mgr. Anton Piller Kg., Osterode, Germany, 1967-68; mgr. tng. center VDF Corp., Hannover, Germany, 1968-72; tech. services mgr. Upton, Bradeen & James, Sterling Heights, Mich., 1972-73, mgr. metal cutting div., 1973-76; v.p., gen. mgr. Unitec Nat. Co., Broadview, Ill., 1976—; instr. programming night sch., Hannover. Recipient award NC-Research, 1969. Mem. Numerical Control Soc., Am. Mgmt. Assn., German Am. C. of C. Home: 3802 Richard Dr Elgin IL 60120 Office: 2805 S 19th Ave Broadview IL 60153

EBERSOLE, CLARE EVERED, ednl. adminstr.; b. Northville, Mich., Oct. 5, 1925; s. Clarence Howard and Gladys Irene (Herrick) E.; student Wright Jr. Coll., Chgo., 1943, Okla. A. and M. Coll., 1944; B.S., Eastern Mich. U., 1950; M.A., U. Mich., 1955; postgrad. Wayne State U., 1957-62, Mich. State U., 1964; m. Madelyn Virginia Durfey, Sept. 4, 1948; children—Thomas H., Douglas A., Beth E. Tchr. pub. schs. Wayne County (Mich.), 1950-54, supervising tchr., 1954-57, cons., 1957-62, dir. bus. affairs, 1963-66; dir. data processing Detroit Pub. Schs., 1966-69; asso. supt. Wayne County Intermediate Sch. Dist., Detroit, 1969—; cons. Lapeer State Home. Mem. Mich. Spl. Traffic Safety Commn. Served with USN, 1943-46, 50-52. Mem. Mich. Assn. Ednl. Data Systems (pres.), Am. Assn. Sch. Adminstrs.,

Mich. Sch. Bus. Ofcls., Engring. Soc. Detroit, N.E.A., Mich. Edn. Assn., Eastern Mich. U. Alumni Assn. (dir.). Presbyn. (mem. session). Club: Livonia Optimist (pres.). Home: 9816 Blackburn Ave Livonia MI 48150 Office: 33500 Van Born Rd Wayne MI 48184

EBERT, GEORGE HENRY, univ. adminstr.; b. Nevada, Iowa, Apr. 3, 1925; s. Clarence John and Nellie (Cooper) E.; B.S. in Forestry, Iowa State U., 1952, M.S. in Forest Economics, 1965, Ph.D. in Adult Edn., 1972; m. Gladys Eileen Meyer, Sept. 16, 1950; children—George Meyer, Ann Louise, Barbara Eileen. Rep., McDonald Lumber Co., Minn., 1952-61; dir. extension courses and confs., Iowa State U., Ames, 1966—, grad. instr. adult edn., 1974—. Deacon elder Collegiate Presbyn. Ch., Ames. Mem. Iowa (pres.), Mo. Valley (state rep.) adult edn. assns., Phi Delta Kappa, Xi Sigma Pi, Kappa Delta Pi. Home: 2114 Greenbriar Circle Ames IA 50010

EBERT, IAN OLERIA, elec. engr., educator; b. Mingo, Iowa, Mar. 13, 1920; s. Albert Jerome and Grace Mabel (Adkins) E.; B.S. in Elec. Engring., Iowa State U., 1942; M.S. in Elec. Engring., U. Ill., 1947; m. Doris Elizabeth Fuller, Oct. 18, 1945; children—James Ian, Barbara Elizabeth. Research scientist Naval Research Lab., Washington, 1943-48; asst. prof., asso. prof. elec. engring. Mich. State U., East Lansing, 1948-62; advisor, prof. telecommunications Engring. Coll., Poona, India, 1962-63; asso. prof. elec. engring. Mich. State U., 1963—; electronics cons. Mich. Industries, 1950—; con. on elec. and electronics safety for law firms and ins. cos. Mem. East Lansing Elec. Bd., 1970—. Served with USN, 1943-45. Mem. AAAS, AIEE. Home: 1842 Linden St East Lansing MI 48823 Office: Elec Engring Dept Mich State Univ East Lansing MI 48824

EBERT, ROGER JOSEPH, film critic; b. Urbana, Ill., June 18, 1942; s. Walter H. and Annabel (Stumm) E.; B.S., U. Ill., 1964; postgrad. U. Cape Town (South Africa), 1965, U. Chgo., 1966-67. Staff writer Champaign-Urbana News Gazette, 1958-66; film critic Chgo. Sun-Times, 1967—; instr. Chgo. City Coll., 1967-68; lectr. fine arts U. Chgo. extension, 1969—; lectr. film Columbia Coll., Chgo., 1972—. Recipient award Chgo. Headline Club, 1963, Overseas Press Club award, 1963; Chgo. Newspaper Guild award, 1973; Pulitzer prize distinguished criticism, 1975. Rotary fellow, 1965. Mem. Am. Newspaper Guild, Nat. Soc. Film Critics, U. Ill. Alumni Assn. (dir. 1975—). Phi Delta Theta. Clubs: Arts, Cliff Dwellers (Chgo.). Author: An Illini Century, 1967; (screen play) Beyond the Valley of the Dolls, 1970. Home: 509 W Dickens Chicago IL 60614 Office: 401 N Wabash Ave Chicago IL 60611

EBERT, TERRY WAYNE, dermatologist; b. Hammond, Ind., May 10, 1942; s. Walter Adam and Edna Henrietta (Yarck) E.; B.S., Stanford U., 1964; M.D., Ind. U., 1968. Intern, Cedars of Lebanon Hosp., Los Angeles, 1968-69; resident in dermatology Northwestern U. Med. Center, Chgo., 1971-74; practice medicine specializing in dermatology, Munster, Ind., 1974—. Served as capt. M.C., U.S. Army, 1969-71. Mem. AMA, Ind. Med. Assn., Am. Acad. Dermatology (asso.). Republican. Lutheran. Home: 505 N Lake Shore Dr Chicago IL 60611 Office: 509 Ridge Rd Munster IN 46321

EBY, CECIL DEGROTTE, educator; b. Charles Town, W.Va., Aug. 1, 1927; s. Cecil DeGrotte and Ellen Butler (Turner) E.; B.A., Shepherd Coll., 1950; M.A., Northwestern U., 1951; Ph.D., U. Pa., 1958; m. Patricia Ellen McQuire, June 16, 1956; children—Clare Virginia, Lillian Turner de Tormes. Instr. English, High Point (N.C.) Coll., 1955-56, asst. prof., 1956-57; asst. prof. Madison (Va.) Coll., 1957-59, asso. prof., 1959-60; asst. prof. Washington and Lee U., Lexington, Va., 1960-62, asso. prof., 1962-65; asso. prof. U. Mich., Ann Arbor, 1965-68, prof., 1968—. Fulbright lectr. Am. lit. U. Salamanca (Spain), 1962-63; Fulbright chmn. Am. studies U. Valencia (Spain), 1967-68. Mem. City of Tecumseh (Mich.) Hist. Commn., 1975—. Served with USNR, 1945-46. Rackham Research grantee, 1967, 71, 77. Mem. Research Club of Mich., Alpha Psi Omega, Pi Kappa Phi. Democrat. Episcopalian. Author: The Old South Illustrated, 1959; Porte Crayon: The Life of David H. Strother, 1960; A Virginia Yankee in the Civil War, 1961; The Siege of the Alcazar, 1965; Between the Bullet and the Lie, 1969; That Disgraceful Affair: The Black Hawk War, 1973. Home: 711 W Potawatomie St Tecumseh MI 49286 Office: Haven Hall U Mich Ann Arbor MI 48103

EBY, DONALD LYMAN, chem. co. exec.; b. Chariton, Iowa, Aug. 25, 1920; s. Charles Wiley and Blanche Elizabeth (Thompson) E.; B.S. in Mech. Engring., Iowa State U., 1942; M.S., Washington U., St. Louis, 1955; m. Miriam Lucille Stoddard, Feb. 14, 1942; children—Susan (Mrs. Gordon C. Piercy Jr.), Linda, Charles. Plant engring. supt. Monsanto Co., Sauget, Ill., 1946-58, asst. dir. engring., St. Louis, 1958-61, plant mgr. Bridgeport, N.J., 1961-64, mfg. dir., St. Louis, 1965—. Pres. Gloucester-Salem County council N.J. Boy Scouts Am., 1963-64. Bd. dirs. Gloucester City (N.J.) United Fund, 1962. Served to maj., C.E., AUS, 1942-46. Registered profl. engr., Ill., N.J. Mem. Nat. Soc. Profl. Engrs., Am. Inst. Chem. Engrs. Presbyn. (elder). Kiwanian (pres. Collinsville, Ill., 1954-55). Home: 42 Daryl Ln St Louis MO 63124 Office: 800 N Lindbergh Blvd St Louis MO 63166

EBY, JANE M., educator; b. Waterloo, Iowa, Apr. 25, 1916; d. Charles W. and Blanche E. (Thompson) Eby; B.S., U. No. Iowa, 1937; M.Mus., Northwestern U., 1943; D. Music Edn., Ind. U., 1969. Tchr. music, pub. schs., Edgewood, Iowa, 1937-39, Garwin, Ia., 1939-41; tchr. harmony, piano, organ Shimer Coll., Mt. Carroll, Ill., 1941-49; tchr. music Boxholm (Iowa) Consol. Sch., 1949-50; elementary music supr., Cedar Falls, Iowa, 1950-52; faculty Mankato State Coll. (Minn.) 1952—, asso. prof. music edn., 1968-72, prof. music edn., 1972—, acting chairperson dept. music, 1975-76. Named Outstanding Educator Am., 1973. Mem. Minn. Music Educators Assn. (v.p. elementary music 1967-69), A.A.U.W. (br. pres. 1962-64), Am. Assn. Higher Edn., Music Educators Nat. Conf., Delta Kappa Gamma, (pres. chpt. 1970-72, editor North Star News 1973-77), Kappa Delta Pi, Pi Kappa Lambda, Sigma Alpha Iota. Co-author: Minnesota Curriculum Guide for Elementary Music, 1973. Home: 234 Clover Ln Mankato MN 56001

EBY, LAWRENCE THORNTON, bldg. materials co. exec.; b. South Bend, Ind., May 3, 1916; s. Ralph C. and Edna May (Thornton) E.; B.S., U. Notre Dame, 1938, M.S., 1939, Ph.D., 1941; m. Claudine Isabelle Hart, June 8, 1941; children—Jan Sue Eby Korner, Claudia Ann Eby Norlin. Research chemist Esso Research & Engring. Co., Linden, N.J., 1941-57; asst. mgr. market devel. Enjay Chem. Co., Elizabeth, N.J., 1957-64; pres. Protective Treatments, Aeroplast Corp., Dellrose Industries, Dayton, O., 1964-65; dir. devel. Chrysler Corp., Trenton, Mich., 1965-67; mgr. polymer div. U.S. Gypsum Co., Des Plaines, Ill., 1967-73, asso. dir. research, 1973—. Lectr., 1st Symposium on Polymers Nat. Council Sci. and Tech., Mexico, 1972. Chmn. Mental Health Fund, Linden, N.J., 1954-55. Recipient Honor award U. Notre Dame, 1965. Mem. Am. Chem. Soc., Am. Inst. Chemists (Honor scroll 1961), Soc. Plastics Engrs., Comml. Devel. Assn., Chem. Market Research Assn., A.A.A.S., Am. Assn. Textile Chemists and Colorists, Tech. Assn. Pulp and Paper Industry, Akron Rubber Group, Assn. Iron and Steel Engrs., Alpha Chi Sigma. Presbyn. (elder 1946—, pres. bd. trustees 1961). Contbr. articles to profl. jours. Patentee in field. Home: 102 S Kennicott Ave Arlington Heights IL 60005 Office: 1000 E Northwest Hwy Des Plaines IL 60016

ECALE, HENRY, structural engr.; b. Champigneulles, France, Jan. 1, 1921; s. George Edward and Elise Marie (Bauermeister) E.; came to U.S., 1926, naturalized, 1931; B.S., U. Ill., 1946; m. Marian Frances Young, Oct. 14, 1944; children—David, Carol Lynn. Sales engr. Ceco Steel Products Corp., Indpls., 1946-51; design engr. Koppers Co., Pitts., 1951-54; chief bridge engr. dept. pub. Works City of Chgo., 1955—. Served with AUS, 1942-46. Registered profl. engr., Ind.; registered structural engr., Ill. Mem. Am. Pub. Works Assn. Home: 333 E Ontario St Chicago IL 60611 Office: 320 N Clark St Chicago IL 60610

ECHELBARGER, DENNIS MICHAEL, accountant; b. Muskegon, Mich., May 1, 1941; s. Charles Theron and Dorothy Marguerite (Kelly) E.; B.A., Aquinas Coll., 1964; m. Diane Jean Vink, June 20, 1964; children—Dennis E., David G., Deanna L., Daniel B., Deborah R. Accountant, Bayle & Norman, Grand Rapids, Mich., 1964-69; partner Bayle, Norman & Echelbarger, Grand Rapids, 1969-75; v.p., sec., mgr. F & A Cheese Corp., Grand Rapids, 1975-77; prin. Dennis M. Echelbarger, C.P.A., Grand Rapids, 1977—. Bd. dirs. Grand Valley Co-op Credit Union, 1974—, pres., 1977-78; sec. Kentwood Community Econ. Devel. Commn., 1975—; bd. dirs., treas. Princeton Estates Homeowners Assn., Grand Rapids, 1975—; mem. St. Mary Magdalen Bd. Edn., Grand Rapids, 1975-78. C.P.A., Mich. Mem. Am. Inst. C.P.A., Mich. Assn. C.P.A., Aquinas Coll. Alumni Assn. Home: 5297 Queensbury St SE Grand Rapids MI 49508 Office: 700 36th St SE Grand Rapids MI 49508

ECHOLS, FLOYD LESLIE, social work adminstr.; b. Marion, Va., May 13, 1927; s. Floyd L. and Mary (Andes) E.; student Pa. State U., 1944-45, B.S., 1949; M.S.W., U. Pa., 1954; m. Margaret Lillian Cleaver, Nov. 17, 1951; children—David, Michael. Social worker VA Mental Health Clinic, Phila., 1952-54; social worker Social Service, Lapeer (Mich.) State Home, 1954-57, asst. dir., 1957-58; dir. social work dept. Caro (Mich.) State Hosp., 1958—. Field instr. U. Mich. Sch. Social Work, Mich. State U., 1955—. Vice-pres. bd. advisers Flint Child Guidance Clinic, 1960; mem. Mich. Developmental Disabilities Council, 1975—, Mich. Health Code Council, 1975. Served with AUS, 1944-47, 50-51. Mem. Am. Assn. on Mental Deficiency (chmn. social work sect. 1965, chmn. 1970), Nat. Assn. Social Workers, Pa. State Alumni Assn., U. Pa. Alumni Assn. Clubs: Inter-relations (chmn. Mich. Jaycees, 1962); Exchange (Caro, Mich.). Home: 372 Cass River Dr Caro MI 48723 Office: Lock Box A Caro MI 48723

ECKBERG, ROBERT HANSEN, co-owner machine shop; b. Grand Rapids, Mich., Aug. 10, 1914; s. Oscar and Clara Peterine (Hansen) E.; student Grand Rapids Jr. Coll., 1931-33; m. Irene G. Swart, Dec. 20, 1941; children—William Robert, Donald Ralph. Partner, Eckberg Motor Rebuilding Co., Grand Rapids, 1941—, gen. mgr., 1965—. Served with U.S. Army, 1941-45. Mem. Nat. Assn. Engine Rebuilders, Better Bus. Bur., C. of C. Republican. Lutheran. Home: 1636 Lotus St SE Grand Rapids MI 49506 Office: 347 LaGrave St Grand Rapids MI 49503

ECKENROAD, JOHN HENRY, III, city ofcl.; b. Berwyn, Ill., Aug. 14, 1943; s. John H. and Mary (Lawler) E.; B.A., Loras Coll., 1965; M. Pub. Adminstrn. (Internship Program grantee), No. Ill. U., 1967; m. Margaret Mary Friedrich, June 24, 1967; children—Meg, Kathleen. Asst. mgr. Village of LaGrange Park (Ill.), 1966-67, mgr., 1967-69; mgr. Village of Northfield (Ill.), 1969—. Mem. Internat. City Mgmt. Assn. (Mgmt. Innovation award for intergovtl. cooperation), Municipal Finance Officers Assn., Ill. City Mgrs. Assn., Northfield C. of C. (co-founder 1970, dir. 1970—). K.C., Kiwanian. Office: 361 Happ Rd Northfield IL 60093

ECKERT, BERNARD GLENN, salesman; b. Royal Oak, Mich., Mar. 11, 1929; s. Frank Louis and Lillian Mable (Snyder) E.; student U. Detroit, 1960, Lansing Community Coll., 1975. Founder, owner, operator Eckert's Nursery, Mason, Mich., 1951-76; real estate salesman Carriage House Realty, Inc., Lansing, Mich., 1976—; dir. Eckert's Turf Nursery Inc. Mem. Aurelius Twp. (Mich.) Planning Commn., 1970—. Served with USAF, 1950. Mem. Lansing Bd. Realtors, Farm, Land Inst., Mich. Turfgrass Assn. Roman Catholic. Home: 4633 Curtice St Mason MI 48854 Office: 928 Jolly Rd Lansing MI 48910

ECKERT, HAROLD PROCTOR, elementary sch. prin.; b. Saginaw, Mich., July 16, 1926; s. Augustus and Blanche Aurilla (Clayberg) E.; B.S., Central Mich. U., 1951; M.A., 1964; m. Adeline Dorothy Arndt, July 12, 1947; children—Larry Lynn, Hal Edward. Tchr. Union Sch., Carrollton, Mich., 1952-55, jr. high sch., 1955-61; elementary prin. Carrollton Elementary Sch., 1961—. Dir. Title I Fed. Programs, Carrollton, 1970—. Carrollton Community adv. bd. Community Coordinated Child Care Assn. Saginaw County (Mich.), 1969—. Served with inf., AUS, 1944-46; PTO. Decorated Bronze Star medal. Mem. Council for Exceptional Children, Nat., Mich. assns. elementary sch. prins., Saginaw County Prins. Assn., Optimist (Saginaw, Mich.). Home: 920 Flint St Frankenmuth MI 48734 Office: 3211 Carla Dr Saginaw MI 48604

ECKERT, JOHN SAMUEL, cons. chem. engr.; b. Delta, Ohio, June 29, 1910; s. Gottleib Lee and Margaret (Schug) E.; B.Chem. Engring., Ohio State U., 1933; m. Adele E. Raxworthy, Sept. 24, 1939. Jr. compounder, jr. engr. Goodyear Tire & Rubber Co., Akron, Ohio, 1934-37; dept. supr. E.I. du Pont de Nemours & Co., Inc., Cleve., 1937-42; constrn. engr. area supt. B. F. Goodrich Co., Borger, Tex., 1942-44; dir. engring. Chem. Process Products div. The Norton Co., Akron, 1944-75; ret., 1976; cons. mass transfer ops. field, 1975—. lectr. chem. engring. Ohio State U., 1961—, adj. asso. prof., 1969-75; lectr. mass transfer various univs. Fellow Am. Inst. Chem. Engrs. (mem. speakers panel); mem. Air Pollution Control Assn., Nat. Assn. Corrosion Engrs., Am. Soc. Metals. Mason. Contbr. articles on mass transfer to profl. jours. Patentee in field. Address: 3000 Millboro Rd Cuyahoga Falls OH 44224

ECKERT, RALPH JOHN, ins. co. exec.; b. Milw., Mar. 12, 1929; s. John C. and Vlasta (Stauber) E.; B.S., U. Wis., 1951; m. Greta M. Allen, July 11, 1953; children—Maura, Peter, Thomas, Karen, Edward. With Benefit Trust Life Ins. Co., Chgo., 1954—, pres., chief exec. officer, 1971-72, pres., chmn. bd., 1972—, also dir. Pres. Ill. Life Ins. Council. Served with AUS, 1951-53. Fellow Soc. Actuaries; mem. Am. Acad. Actuaries, Chgo. Actuarial Club (pres. 1965). Lutheran. Mason. Clubs: Michigan Shores (Wilmette, Ill.); Cedar Lake Yacht (Slinger, Wis.). Office: 1771 W Howard St Chicago IL 60626

ECKHARDT, FERDINAND, museum cons.; b. Vienna, Austria; s. Ferdinand and Wilhelmine (Helmreich) E.; Dr.Phil., U. Vienna; LL.D., U. Man. (Can.), 1971, C.M., 1976; m. S.C. Gramatté, Feb. 24, 1934 (dec. 1974). Writer, publisher, critic; dir. emeritus Winnipeg (Man.) Art Gallery; now mus. cons. Austrian hon. consul for Man. and Sask., 1960—. Decorated Austrian Croix d'Honneur for Sci. and Art. Author books. Contbr. articles to profl. jours. Home: 54 Harrow St Winnipeg MB R3M 2Y7 Canada

ECKHARDT, HENRY THEODORE, mfg. co. exec.; b. Somers Point, N.J., Aug. 31, 1922; s. Henry T. and Jeremiah Eliza (Greer) E.; student Carnegie Inst. Tech., 1946-49; B.A., U. Pitts., 1953, M.Litt., 1958; m. Carol Ruth Kamman, Sept. 9, 1950; children—Susan Diane, Stephen Karl, Ellen Elizabeth, Alison Lynn. Rate clk. Alcoa, Pitts., 1949-51; advt. mgr. Miller Printing Machy Co., Pitts., 1952-56; account exec. Bond & Starr, Pitts., 1957-59; account supr., v.p. Erwin Wasey, Ruthrafff & Ryan, Pitts., 1960-62; dir. indsl. div. Vic Maitland & Asso. Pitts., 1962-64; with Harris Corp., Cleve., 1965—, dir. merchandising, 1968—. Pres. Cleve. Luth. High Parents Tchrs. League, 1974-75. Trustee Theta Xi Found., 1958-62. Served to 1st lt. U.S. Army, 1940-46. Mem. Assn. Indsl. Advertisers, Graphic Arts Advertisers Council (pres. 1969-71, sec.-treas. 1976-77). Lutheran. Club: Cleve. Ad. Home: 3859 Savoy Dr Fairview Park OH 44126 Office: 55 Public Sq Cleveland OH 44113

ECKHART, GERALD GEISSE, chem. co. exec.; b. Winnetka, Ill., June 14, 1929; s. Harold and Ruby A. (Geisse) E.; B.S., Ind. U., 1951; m. Mary Joyce Jones, June 23, 1951; children—Jeffrey Alan, Margery Robin. Pres. Aquamint Labs., Inc., St. Charles, Ill., 1959—; v.p. Purex Corp., Ltd., Batavia, Ill., 1964-75, mem. corp. devel. com., 1972-75; with Campana Corp., Batavia, 1964-75, v.p. advt., 1973-75. Vice pres. Wild Rose Assn., St. Charles, 1972—. Pres. Delnor Hosp. Men's Found., St. Charles, 1975-76, mem. bd. Delnor Hosp., 1975-76. Served with AUS, 1952-54. Mem. Acacia. Club: St. Charles Sports Boosters (pres. 1972-73). Home: 36W370 Ferson Creek Rd St Charles IL 60174 Office: 12 S 1st Ave St Charles IL 60174

ECKHOFF, HAROLD EUGENE, cons. engr.; b. Harvel, Ill., Apr. 20, 1925; s. Howard Edward and Matilda Albertina (Plunkett) E.; B.S., U. Ill., 1944, M.S., 1947; m. Dorothy Mae Call, Apr. 3, 1945; children—Dorothy Grace, Barbara Diane, Bruce David, Carolyn Ann. Instr., U. Ill., 1947-48; with Modjeski and Masters, cons. engrs., Harrisburg, Pa., 1948—, asso., 1972—. Pres., South Suburban Council for Mentally Retarded Children, Inc. 1967-70, 72-73. Served to ensign USNR, 1944-46. Home: 417 Watseka St Park Forest IL 60466 Office: 3612 Lincoln Hwy Olympia Fields IL 60461

ECKHOFF, NORMAN DEAN, educator; b. Meade, Kans., Apr. 10, 1938; s. Martin H. and Nora E. (Feldman) Eckhoff; m. Norma A. Cochran, July 20, 1959; children—Bradley, Nisa (dec.), Cindi. A.A., Pratt Jr. Coll., 1958; B.S., Kans. State U., 1961, M.S., 1962, Ph.D., 1968. Research engr. Boeing Co., Wichita, Kans., 1962-63; process engr. Litwin Corp., Wichita, 1963; reactor engr. AEC, Oak Ridge, Tenn., 1963-64; instr., asst. prof., asso. prof., prof., head dept. nuclear engring., Kans. State U., Manhattan, 1964—. Cons. USAEC, USDA (ERS), Kemin Corp., Des Moines, Systems Research Corp., Manhattan, Kans. Gas and Electric, Wichita, Devel. Planning and Research Assos., Manhattan. Mem. Manhattan City Planning Bd., 1972-76. Mem. Am. Nuclear Soc., AAAS, Kans. Acad. Sci., Am. Soc. Engring. Edn., Manhattan C. of C., Sigma Xi, Phi Kappa Phi, Tau Beta Pi, Recipient teaching excellence award Kans. State U., 1970, Western Electric award for contbns. to engring. edn., 1977. Home: 2508 Rogers Blvd Manhattan KS 66502 Office: Dept Nuclear Engring Ward Hall Kansas State Univ Manhattan KS 66506

ECKLOFF, MAURINE CHRISTINE NELSON, educator; b. Upland, Nebr., Apr. 18, 1928; d. Henry Victor and Christine (Raun) Nelson; student Hastings Coll., 1945-47; B.A., U. Denver, 1948; M.S., Kearney State Coll., 1961; Ph.D., U. Nebr., 1974; m. Warren Nathaniel Eckloff, Sept. 3, 1954; children—Nathan, Ann, Ward. Script writer radio sta. KNX-CBS, Los Angeles, 1949; tchr. speech, English pub. schs., Broken Bow, Nebr., 1949-50; program mgr., broadcaster radio sta. WGET, Gettysburg, Pa., 1951-52; traffic mgr. KBTV, Denver, 1953-54; telecaster Woman's Voice program KHOL-TV, Kearney, Nebr., 1954-61; prof. speech Kearney State Coll., 1962—, mem. senate, 1977—. Mem. Bd. edn. Minden (Nebr.) Pub. Schs., 1972—, pres., 1976-77. Kearney State Coll. research grantee, 1972, 73. Mem. Am. Women in Radio and TV (pres. Nebr. chpt. 1958), AAUW (first v.p. Nebr. div. 1962-64), Kearney State Coll. Edn. Assn. (pres. 1966-67), Nebr. Speech Communication Assn. (1st v.p. 1971-73, chmn. research 1976-78), Speech Communication Assn. Am., Internat. Communication Assn., Nebr. State Edn. Assn., Inst. Gen. Semantics, Kearney State Coll. Faculty Women (pres. 1977-78), Delta Kappa Gamma, Sigma Tau Delta, Gamma Phi Beta. Methodist (sec. TV, Radio and Film Commn., Nebr. conf., 1960-62). Contbr. articles to profl. jours. Home: Rural Route 1 Minden NE 68959 Office: Kearney State College Kearney NE 68847

ECKROSE, ROY ALFRED, city ofcl.; b. East Tawas, Mich., Feb. 16, 1941; s. Edwin Alfred and Marion Bernice (Nyberg) E.; student U. Wis., 1958-60, Western Ill. U., 1976-78; m. Janet Ellen Anderson, July 7, 1962; children—Andrea, Greta, Erik. Asst. city engr. City of Janesville, Wis., 1961-70, elec. supr., 1970—, asst. pub. works dir., 1970-75, dir., 1975—. Cons. in devel. and bldg. design, 1964-72; mem. spl. com. on solid waste mgmt. Wis. Legis. Council, 1976-77; mem. Rock County (Wis.) Solid Waste Mgmt. Bd., 1977—. Mem. youth com. Janesville YMCA, 1968-69, mem. camp com., 1968-69, mem. facilities com., 1965-67, chmn., 1966-67; mem. Janesville Concert Assn., 1970—. Mem. Am. Pub. Works Assn., Inst. for Municipal Engrs., Inst. for Solid Wastes, Inst. for Equipment Services, Internat. Assn. for Pollution Control, Wis. Soc. Profl. Engrs. (dir. 1971-73, named Young Engr. of Yr. 1973), Wis. Profl. Engrs. in Govt. (chmn. 1975-76), Y's Men's Internat. Lutheran (ch. council 1973—, pres. 1974—, dist. del. 1969, 74). Home: 3214 Windsor St Janesville WI 53545 Office: 18 N Jackson St Municipal Bldg Janesville WI 53545

ECKSTEIN, FRANKLIN DEAN, lawyer; b. Plymouth, Ohio, Mar. 14, 1939; s. Royal Wendell and Ethel Dorothea (Bilsing) E.; student Case Inst. Tech., 1957-59; B.S., Wittenberg U., 1962; J.D., Ohio State U., 1968; m. Janice Gertrude Mahnke, June 16, 1966; children—Brian Christopher, Carla Marie. Admitted to Ohio bar, 1968, U.S. Supreme Ct. bar, 1971; mem. firm Dush & Eckstein and predecessor firm, Willard, Ohio, 1968—. Asst. prosecutor Huron County, 1970-73; solicitor, Monroeville, 1977—, Shiloh and North Fairfield, Ohio, 1969—; law dir. City of Willard, 1970—. Pres., Community Choir, 1972-73. Bd. dirs. YMCA, 1969—, Jr. Achievement, 1970—, United Fund, 1971—; bd. dirs. Willard Area Hosp., 1973—, pres., 1974—. Served with AUS, 1963-65; Germany. Mem. Am., Ohio bar assns., Am. Trial Lawyers Assn. Lutheran. Kiwanian. Home: 953 Woodbine St Willard OH 44890 Office: 110 1/2 Myrtle Ave Willard OH 44890

ECKSTEIN, GREGORY THOMAS, physician; b. Chgo., July 7, 1937; s. George Charles and Grace (Blank) E.; student Loyola U., Chgo., 1955-58; M.D., Stritch Sch. Medicine, Chgo., 1962; m. Sandra Swinbanks, Oct. 20, 1962; children—Gregory Thomas, Michael Patrick. Intern, Milw. County Gen. Hosp., 1962-63; resident in internal medicine Henry Ford Hosp., Detroit, 1965-68; practice medicine specializing in internal medicine, McHenry, Ill., 1968—; mem. staff McHenry Hosp.; mem. McHenry Med. Group; clin. asst. Stritch Sch. Medicine, 1970-74; med. dir. McHenry-Lake County Emergency Med. Services Program, 1974-75. Pres. Montini Sch. Bd., 1972-74; pres. parish council St. Patrick's Roman Cath. Ch., 1976—. Served to capt. M.C., AUS, 1963-65. Decorated Army Commendation medal. Diplomate Nat. Bd. Med. Examiners, Am. Bd. Internal Medicine. Mem. AMA, Ill., McHenry County med. socs.

Home: 3706 W Young St McHenry IL 60050 Office: 1110 N Green St McHenry IL 60050

EDDY, BRET LAWRENCE, artist; b. Dubuque, Iowa, May, 23, 1913; s. Lawrence Henry and Ethel Maud (Scott) E.; grad. high sch. One-man shows at Crespi Gallery, N.Y.C., 1956-58, Artzt Gallery, N.Y.C., 1961-66; exhibited in group shows at Detroit Art Inst., 1943-44, 50, 63, Creative Gallery, N.Y.C., 1952-54, Caravan Gallery, N.Y.C., 1954-57, Audubon Soc., 1965, Detroit Artist Market, 1967-70, Kingsley Inn, Southfield, 1969, 70, Mich. Artrain, 1971, Grand Rapids Art Inst., 1974—, New Orleans Internat., 1976; represented in permanent collections at Gen. Electric Co. Offices, Southfield Mich., Univac Offices, Southfield. Recipient Mrs. Albert Kahn Watercolor award Detroit Art Inst., 1963. Mem. Detroit Artist Market, Theatre Hist. Soc., Am. Theatre Organ. Soc. Home: 8489 West Pkwy Detroit MI 48239

EDDY, RAYMOND ELDON, ednl. adminstr. b. Miller, S.D., Apr. 12, 1932; s. Eldon Adrian and Mabel Enid (Farmer) E.; student Huron Coll., 1953-54; B.A., Dakota Wesleyan U., 1957; M.A., U. S.D., 1961, postgrad. 1967-68; m. Janis Joan Smith, June 4, 1955. Tchr., Hawthorne Elementary Sch., Sioux Falls, S.D., 1957-59, Whittier Jr. High Sch., Sioux Falls, 1959-70; civics, math, bus. tchr. Cleve. Elementary Sch., 1969-72; asst. prin. Robert Frost Elementary Sch., Sioux Falls, 1972-74, prin., 1974—. Justice of Peace, Minnehaha County, S.D., 1962-67. Served with AUS, 1950-53. Mem. N.E.A., S.D. Edn. Assn., Sch. Adminstrs. S.D., S.D. Dept. Elementary Sch. Prins., V.F.W., Am. Leion, Phi Delta Kappa. Republican. Mason (Shriner), Elk. Home: 2608 W 29th St Sioux Falls SD 57105

EDELSON, DAVID, mental health center exec.; b. N.Y.C., Jan. 28, 1919; s. Max and Freida (Epstein) E.; B.A., N.Y. U., 1948; M.S.W., Columbia U., 1950; M.H.A., Northwestern U., 1958; m. Miriam Osnovitz, Apr. 3, 1943; children—Richard, Jeffrey. Dir., Nat. Travelers Aid Assn., Belleville, Ill., 1952-54; dir. social service Evansville (Ind.) State Hosp., 1954-56; psychiat. social work supr. Dixon (Ill.) State Sch., 1956-57; asst. supt., adminstr. East Moline (Ill.) State Hosp., 1958-62; supt. Dixon Developmental Center, 1962—; mem. Gov.'s Adv. Council on Mental Retardation, 1963. Licensed nursing home adminstr., Ill. Fellow Am. Assn. Mental Deficiency; mem. Nat. Assn. Pub. Residential Facilities, Nat. Assn. Supts. Pub. Residential Facilities for Mental Retardation (dir. 1976—), Ill. Council for Exceptional Children, Lee County Mental Health Assn., Dixon C. of C., Ill. Assn. for Mentally Retarded (Leadership award 1968). Office: 2600 N Brinton Ave Dixon IL 61021

EDELSTEIN, RODDEY NOEL, state ofcl.; b. Bklyn., Apr. 30, 1945; s. Hyman Julius and Antoinette (Kagan) E.; B.A., So. Ill. U., 1966, M.A. (Univ. resident fellow), 1968; m. Joyce Kay Evers, Nov. 27, 1968; children—Kenneth Mark, Kerny Michelle. Constl. conv. librarian State of Ill., Springfield, 1969-70, local govt. mgmt. officer, 1970-74, research dir., 1974, criminal justice exec. liaison, 1974-76; mem. Nat. Young Adult Conservation Corps Task Force, 1977—. Coordinator campaign United Fund Exec. Agy., Ill., 1973. Mem. Am. Pub. Works Assn., Am. Soc. Pub. Adminstrn., Nat. League Cities, Nat. Municipal League, Internat. City Mgmt. Assn. Author: Henry B. Stanton and His Role in the Abolitionist Movement, 1968; The New Illinois Constitution-Home Rule Powers, 1971; Illinois County Government—Constitutional Implementation, 1971. Home: 713 E Walnut St Chatham IL 62629 Office: Conservation Area Rural Route 5 Springfield IL 62707

EDELSTEIN, WARREN STANLEY, educator; b. Balt., June 11, 1937; s. Solomon and Cecile (Klaw) E.; B.A., Lehigh U., 1958; postgrad. Johns Hopkins, 1958-59; M.A., Duke U., 1961; Ph.D., Brown U., 1964; m. Rosalie Toby Kuperman, June 25, 1965; 1 dau., Francesca. Asst. prof. math Ill. Inst. Tech., 1965-71, asso. prof., 1971—. Postdoctoral fellow Johns Hopkins, 1964-65; grantee Office Naval Research, NSF, Argonne Nat. Lab. Mem. Soc. Indsl. and Applied Math, Soc. Engring. Sci. Contbr. articles to profl. jours. Home: 6218 N Campbell St Chicago IL 60659 Office: Dept Math Ill Inst Technology Chicago IL 60616

EDENS, B(ISHOP) DAVID, educator; b. Sumter, S.C., Feb. 11, 1926; s. Henry Timmons and Lila Mae (Edens) E.; A.A., Mars Hill Coll., 1948; B.A., Wake Forest U., 1950; M.Div., So. Bapt. Theol. Sem., 1953, Th.M., 1954; postgrad. (fellow) Merrill Palmer Inst., 1954-55; Ed.D., Columbia, 1957; m. Virginia Deane Buckner, July 7, 1950; children—Deena, Debra. Dir. counseling Trinity Bapt. Ch., San Antonio, 1957-67; prof. family life edn., dir. marriage and family program Stephens Coll., Columbia, Mo., 1967—. Pres. San Antonio Mental Health Assn., 1960-61, Mo. Council on Family Relations, 1968-69, Planned Parenthood Central Mo., 1969-70. Served with USNR, 1944-46. Fellow Am. Assn. Marriage and Family Counselors. Author: Sexual Understanding Among Young Adults, 1959; The Changing Me, 1973; Teen Sense, 1971; (with Virginia Buckner Edens) Why God Gave Children Parents, 1966, Making the Most of Family Worship, 1968. Contbr. articles to profl. jours. Home: 817 Colgate St Columbia MO 65201 Office: Stephens Coll 1200 E Broadway Columbia MO 65201

EDGAR, IRVING I., psychiatrist; b. Roswadow, Poland, July 4, 1902; s. Asher Laser and Bella Gitel (Schlussel) Itzkowitz; brought to U.S., 1910, naturalized, 1916; B.A., Wayne State U., 1925, B.M., 1926, M.D., 1927, M.A., 1933; m. Gertrude Forman, Nov. 6, 1971; children—David L., Richard S., Joyce Vronsky. Intern Grace Hosp., Detroit, 1926-27; practice medicine specializing in psychiatry, Detroit, 1927—; med. dir. Island View Adolescent Center, Detroit, 1971-74; cons. Grace, Sinai, Jennings Meml., Crittenton hosps. (all Detroit). Diplomate Am. Bd. Psychiatry and Neurology. Fellow A.C.P., Am. Psychiat. Assn.; mem. Jewish Hist. Soc. Mich. (pres. 1964-73), Am. Jewish Hist. Soc. (exec. council 1975—). Author: Shakespeare, Medicine and Psychiatry, 1970; Essays in English Literature and History, 1971. Editor Mich. Jewish History mag. Home: 29233 Wellington Ct Apt 61 Southfield MI 48076 Office: 1036 David Whitney Bldg Detroit MI 48226

EDGAR, JAMES HERBERT, JR., govt. ofcl.; b. Mobile, Ala., Feb. 15, 1942; s. James Herbert and Vivian Marie (Woodruff) E.; B.A., U. Ala., 1964; M.A. (NDEA fellow), U. Va., 1966, Ph.D. (NDEA fellow), 1972; M.B.A. summa cum laude, Central State U., 1976; m. Farideh Mohadjer-Ashjai, Oct. 29, 1970; 1 son, James Herbert, III. Instr. history U. Md. in Europe, Wuerzburg, Germany, 1969-70, Teheran, Iran, 1977—; asso. prof. history Ferrum Coll., 1971-72; sales rep. Met. Life Ins. Co., Mobile, 1972-73; procurement specialist U.S. Naval Supply Center, Norfolk, Va., 1973-74; mgmt. intern Oklahoma City Air Logistics Center, Tinker AFB, 1974-76; procurement analyst Hdqrs. U.S. Air Force Logistics Command, Wright-Patterson AFB, Ohio, 1976-77; contracting officer Project Peace Log U.S. Air Force Logistics Command, Teheran, 1977—; teaching asst. U. Va., 1967-68. Served with U.S. Army, 1969-71. Recipient Grover Cleveland Hall award U. Ala., 1963, Ann Inglett award, 1964, Katie Belle Harrison award, 1964; named Outstanding Third Year ROTC Cadet, U.S. Army, 1963. Mem. Nat. Contract Mgmt. Assn., Air Force Assn., Scabbard and Blade, Phi Alpha Theta, Pi Tau Chi, Pi Sigma Alpha. Asso. editor Essays in History, 1966-68. Home: 4731 Whitewood Ct Dayton OH 45424

EDGERLEY, EDWARD, JR., cons. engr.; b. Lancaster, Pa., Mar. 8, 1931; s. Edward and Mary (McNeal) E.; student Franklin and Marshall Coll., 1949; B.S., Pa. State U., 1952; S.M., Mass. Inst. Tech., 1954; Ph.D., U. Calif. at Berkeley, 1968; m. Mary Replogle, Nov. 6, 1954; children—Mark Edward, Dale Lee, Craig Alan, Darla Jean. Teaching asst. Mass. Inst. Tech., 1952-54; mem. faculty Washington U., St. Louis, 1957-73, asso. prof. civil and environmental engring., 1962-73, asso. dean engring., 1968-69, program chmn. environmental engring., 1969-73. Exec. v.p. Ryckman Edgerley Tomlinson & Assos., cons. engrs., St. Louis, 1957-75, pres., 1975—. Chmn. pack com. Cub Scouts Am., 1968-69, 75—; troop chmn. Boy Scouts Am., 1969-74. Bd. dirs. St. Louis Alliance for Regional Community Health, 1970-74. Served as officer USAF, 1954-57. Recipient Publ. award, Resources div. Am. Water Works Assn., 1962. Mem. Am. Soc. C.E., Greater St. Louis Air Pollution Assn. (pres. 1969), Am. Chem. Soc. Rotarian. Club: Mass. Inst. Tech. (pres. 1968-69) (St. Louis). Presbyn. (elder). Contbr. sci. articles to jours. Home: 582 Brookhaven Ct Kirkwood MO 63122 Office: 12161 Lackland Rd St Louis MO 63141

EDGERTON, WINFIELD DOW, gynecologist; b. Caruthersville, Mo., Nov. 8, 1924; s. Winfield Dow and Anna Kathryn (Hale) E.; student Central Coll., Fayette, Mo., 1942-44; M.D., Washington U., St. Louis, 1947; m. Rose Marie Cahill, June 24, 1945; 1 son, Winfield Dow. Intern, St. Luke's Hosp., St. Louis, 1947-48; resident Chgo. Lying-In Hosp., 1948-49, Free Hosp. for Women, Brookline, Mass., 1951, U.S. Naval Hosp., Chelsea, Mass., 1951-53; practice medicine specializing in obstetrics and gynecology, Davenport, Iowa, 1955—; mem. staff St. Luke's Hosp., also dir. obstetrics and gynecology; med. dir. Maternal Health Center, Davenport.; clin. asst. prof. obstetrics and gynecology U. Iowa Coll. Medicine, 1971—. Served to lt., M.C., USN, 1949-55. Fellow Am. Coll. Obstetricians and Gynecologists (chmn. Iowa sect.), Royal Soc. Medicine; mem. Central Assn. Obstetricians and Gynecologists, Am. Fertility Soc., Am. Assn. Gynecologic Laparoscopists (trustee), AMA, Iowa, Scott County (past pres.) med. socs. Republican. Congregationalist. Club: Davenport. Contbr. articles to med. jours. and texts. Home: 4 Lombard Ct Davenport IA 52803 Office: 121 W Locust St Davenport IA 52803

EDLUND, ROSCOE CLAUDIUS, ret. mgmt. and bus. cons.; b. Bklyn., July 30, 1888; s. Claudius and Emma (Anderson) E.; A.B., Cornell U., 1909; postgrad. N.Y. Sch. Social Work 1913-14; m. Esther Gillette Alling, May 2, 1916 (dec. Apr. 5, 1965); 1 son, Harold Alling. Sec. to pres., univ. pub. Cornell U., 1909-12; asst. to gen. dir. Russell Sage Found., 1912-14; asst. sec. Cleve. Community Chest, 1914-15; mng. dir. Balt. Community Chest, 1916-19, Hampden County Improvement League, Springfield, Mass., 1920-26; mgr. Soap and Detergents Assn., N.Y.C., 1927-48; plans bd. chmn. Fred Rudge, Inc., N.Y.C., 1948-50; ind. mgmt. cons., 1950-74; asso. Rogers, Slade & Hill, Inc., mgmt. cons., N.Y.C., 1954-65. Bd. dirs., sec. Eastchester (N.Y.) Community Fund, 1952-54, sec. Balt. Fund, 1916-19; chmn. McCoy Hall Recreation Commn. for Soldiers and Sailors, Balt., 1916-19; organizer, dir., treas. Am. Fat Salvage Com., N.Y.C., 1942-48; bd. govs. Lawrence Hosp., Bronxville, N.Y., 1954-59, v.p., 1959; mem. adv. bd. Christian Crusade; mem. men's com. Japan Internat. Christian U. Found., 1967—. Recipient Wisdom award of honor Wisdom Soc.; Roscoe C. Edlund Videotape Room, Mann Hall, Cornell U. named in his honor; named Hon. Alumnus, Coll. Agr. and Life Scis., Cornell U., 1976; Roscoe C. Edlund Library Bldg. at Armour Meml. Home for Aged named in his honor. Hon. fellow Truman Library Inst.; mem. Am. (past pres., hon. life), N.Y. (past pres., hon. life), Mid-Am. socs. assn. execs., N.A.M. (chmn. mfg. trade assns. group 1936), C. of C. U.S. (past mem. assns. com.), Assn. Mgmt. Consultants, (trustee 1970-72, hon. life), Britannica Soc., Am. Viewpoint Inc. (dir. 1945-75, sec. 1952-59). Laymen's Nat. Bible Com. (adv. com. 1945—), Am. Bible Soc. (bd. mgrs. 1952-65), Kansas City Internat. Relations Council, Kansas City People-to-People Council, Friends of Art of Nelson Gallery, Internat. Platform Assn., UN Assn., Common Cause, Phi Beta Kappa, Delta Sigma Rho, Alpha Chi Rho. Baptist (Mo. area dir. world mission campaign Am. Bapt. Conv. 1966-67). Clubs: Siwanoy Country (Bronxville, N.Y.); Tower (Cornell U., Ithaca, N.Y.); Scandinavian of Greater Kansas City (Mo.). Author: To-Day's Challenge to Trade Associations, 1938; Ratio of Members Dues to Members Sales in 243 Trade Associations, 1954. Address: 8100 Wornall Rd Kansas City MO 64114

EDMINSTER, RALPH RAY, pathologist; b. Muncie, Ind., Nov. 8, 1935; s. Leonard Ralph and Ruby Irene (Drumm) E.; B.A., DePauw U., 1958; M.D., Washington U., St. Louis, 1962; m. Nancy Susan Jameson, June 12, 1960; children—Susan Beth, Jean Marie, Ann Louise. Intern, Butterworth Hosp., Grand Rapids, Mich., 1962-63, resident in pathology, 1963-67; asso. pathologist, dermatopathologist E.W. Sparrow Hosp., Lansing, Mich., 1967—; asso. clin. prof. pathology Mich. State U. Coll. Human Medicine. Diplomate Am. Bd. Dermatology, Am. Bd. Pathology. Fellow Coll. Am. Pathologists, Am. Soc. Clin. Pathologists; mem. AMA. Republican. Office: Sparrow Hosp Box 30480 Lansing MI 48909

EDMONSON, HAROLD ARTHUR, editor; b. Chgo., Nov. 30, 1937; s. George R. and Letty F. (Werth) E.; A.A., Wright Jr. Coll., 1958; B.S., U. Ill., 1960. Publicity writer Zonolite Corp., Chgo., 1961-64; free lance writer, pubr., 1965-66; co. newspaper editor Rauland Corp., Melrose Park, Ill., 1967-68; asso. editor Trains mag., Milw., 1968-71; books editor Kalmbach Pub. Co., Milw., 1971—. Served with U.S. Army Reserves, 1960-66. Mem. R.R. Club Chgo. (pres. 1974—). Author: Steam on Q., 1960; Main Line Mexico, 1964; World Steam in Action, 1970; Journey to Amtrak, 1972; Trains Around the World, 1972; The Love of Trains, 1974. Home: 1040 E Knapp St Milwaukee WI 53202 Office: 1027 N 7th St Milwaukee WI 53233

EDMUNDS, PALMER DANIEL, lawyer; b. Terre Haute, Ill., Oct. 29, 1890; s. Amos and Mary Ann (Campbell) E.; A.B., Knox Coll., 1912, LL.D., 1945; LL.B., Harvard U., 1915; LL.D., Piedmont Coll., 1975; m. Margaret Burton, June 29, 1932 (dec. 1964); m. 2d, Sarah Shepard Brown, Nov. 13, 1970. Admitted to Ill. bar, 1915; practiced in Chgo., 1915-63; dir., counsel Ill. Service Recognition Bd., 1922-25; mem. firm Dodd, Matheny & Edmunds, 1925-29; commr. Supreme Ct. Ill., 1929-32; mem. Dodd & Edmunds, Chgo., 1932-58; lectr. on conflict of laws and Ill. practice John Marshall Law Sch., Chgo., 1926—, on fed. practice, 1938—, prof. law, 1958-76; vis. prof. law Knox Coll., 1944-58; compliance commr. WPB and Civilian Prodn. Adminstrn., 1944-47; hearing commr. NPA, 1951-53. Mem. Com. for Continuation of Congregational Christian Chs.; trustee John Marshall Law Sch. Served as 1st lt. A.E.F., 1917-19; capt., O.R.C. Mem. Am. Legion (past comdr. Black Hawk post Chgo.; past historian Dept. Ill.), Am. Acad. Polit. and Social Sci., Fgn. Policy Assn., Internat., Am., Ill., Chgo. bar assns., Ill. State Hist. Soc., Abraham Lincoln Assn., SAR, Nat. Sojourners, Am. Bantam Assn., Sebright Club Am., India Bar Assn., World Peace Through Law Center, 40 and 8, Soc. 28th Div., Phi Gamma Delta, Delta Sigma Rho, Democrat. Clubs: Masons, Elks, Harvard (Chgo.). Author: (with W.F. Dodd) Illinois Appellate Procedure, 1929; Edmunds Common Law Forms, 1931; Illinois Civil Practice Forms, 1933; Edmunds Federal Rules of Civil Procedure, 1938; Cyclopedia of Federal Procedure Forms, 1939; Law and Civilization, 1959; co-author: Encyclopedia of Federal Procedure, 2d edit., 1944; Edmunds Conflict of Laws, 1948; editor and compiler: Jones Illinois Statutes Annotated, vols. 18-22, 24. Home: PO Box 317 Gilman IL 60938

EDWALDS, ROBERT MANFRED, psychiatrist; b. Chgo., Mar. 26, 1925; s. Hjalmer Manfred and Eleanor (Brennan) E.; Ph.B., U. Chgo., 1947, B.S., 1949, M.D., 1953; m. Mary Jane Phillips, Jan. 27, 1951; children—Margaret Edwalds Swanson, Thomas Patrick, Michael Joseph, Loraine Elizabeth, Eric Richard, Paula Maureen, Gretchen Marie. Intern, Blodgett Meml. Hosp., Grand Rapids, Mich., 1953-54; resident psychiatry Northville (Mich.) State Hosp., 1954-57; fellow child psychiatry Worcester (Mass.) Youth Guidance Center, 1964-66; chief intensive treatment service Galesburg (Ill.) State Research Hosp., 1957-60; staff psychiatrist VA Hosp., Syracuse, N.Y., 1960-64; cons. child psychiatrist Devereaux Sch., Rutland, Mass., 1965-66, John J. Madden Zone Center, Hines, Ill., 1966-67; cons. East Moline (Ill.) State Hosp., 1967-74; cons. child psychiatrist Larkin Home, Elgin, Ill., 1968-73; med. dir. inpatient service Lakeview Health Center, West Salem, Wis., 1975-77; cons. psychiatrist Lakeview Health Center Nursing Service, 1975-77; pvt. practice psychiatry, Syracuse, N.Y., 1960-64, Oak Park, Ill., 1967-75, La Crosse, Wis., 1976—; attending staff Riveredge Hosp., Forest Park, Ill., 1967-75, clin. dir. Intensive treatment unit Riveredge Hosp., 1969-73, qualifying med. staff Mercyville Hosp., Aurora, Ill., 1973-75, cons. child psychiatrist, 1974-75; cons. staff psychiatrist St. Francis Hosp., LaCrosse, Wis., 1975—; cons. child psychiatrist La Crosse (Wis.) Home for Children, 1975—; clin. instr. psychiatry U. Ill. Coll. Medicine, Chgo., 1958-60; instr. psychiatry State U. N.Y., Upstate Med. Center, Syracuse, 1960-64. Served with AUS, 1943-45. Decorated Purple Heart with oak leaf cluster, Bronze Star medal. Recipient Research award, Mich. Soc. Neurology and Psychiatry, 1956. Diplomate Am. Bd. Neurology and Psychiatry. Fellow Am. Orthopsychiat. Assn.; mem. Am., Ill. psychiat. assns., Am. Soc. Adolescent Psychiatry, AAAS, Assn. Am. Med. Colls., Acad. Child Psychiatry, AMA, Wis., LaCrosse med. socs. Contbr. articles to profl. jours. Home: 639 N Cuyler Ave Oak Park IL 60302 Office: 615 S 10th St LaCrosse WI 54601

EDWARDS, DONALD MERVIN, agrl. engr., educator; b. Tracy, Minn., Apr. 16, 1938; s. Mervin B. and Helen L. (Halstenrud) E.; B.S., S.D. State U., 1960, M.S., 1961; Ph.D. in Agrl. Engring., Purdue U., 1966; m. Judith Lee Wilson, Aug. 8, 1964; children—John, Joel, Jeffrey, Mary. Agrl. engr. Soil Conservation Service, U.S. Dept. Agr., Marshall, Minn., 1957-62; research asst. S.D. State U., Brookings, 1960-62; research asst. Purdue U., West Lafayette, Ind., 1962-66, faculty adviser, 1962-64; asso. prof. agrl. engring. U. Nebr., Lincoln, 1966-70, asst. dean, asso. prof. Coll. Engring. and Architecture, 1970-71, prof., 1971—, asst. dean, 1971-73, asso. dean, dir. Engring. Research Center, 1973—, dir. Energy Research and Devel. Center, 1976—; cons., collaborator state and fed. agys., industry, 1960—; chmn. engring. div. Greater Nebr. Sci. and Engring. Fair, 1973—; mem. Nebr. Gov.'s Energy Adv. Com., 1976—; gov.'s rep. to Western Gov.'s Regional Energy Office, 1976—. Active Boy Scouts Am., Lincoln, 1974—; leader 4-H County Club, Lincoln, 1967—; active Am. Field Service, 1972—; bd. dirs. Lincoln Transp. System, 1975—; deacon Rosemont Christian and Missionary Alliance, 1976—, mem. ch. exec. bd., 1976—, tchr. Sunday sch., 1972—. Recipient Distinguished Teaching award U. Nebr., 1970; Outstanding Young Educators award Am. Soc. Agrl. Engrs., 1973. Registered profl. engr., Nebr. Mem. Profl. Engrs. Nebr. (pres. Southeastern chpt. 1974-75, state dir. 1974—, v.p. 1976-77), Nat. Soc. Profl. Engrs., Coop. Edn. Assn., Nebr. Acad. Sci. (co-chmn. engring. div.), AAAS, Nat. Assn. Coll. Tchrs. Agr., Am. Soc. Engring. Edn. (sec. profl. interest council I 1975-77, chmn. profl. devel. com. 1973-76), Am. Soc. Agrl. Engrs. (dir. 1977—), Engrs. Council for Profl. Devel. (dir. 1974—), Internat. Water Resources Assn. (charter), Sigma Xi, Tau Beta Pi, Gamma Sigma Delta, Sigma Tau, Alpha Epsilon, Alpha Gamma Rho, Farmhouse. Contbr. articles to profl. jours. Home: 6641 Cleveland Ave Lincoln NE 68507

EDWARDS, EUGENE O'BRIEN, electronics mfg. co. exec.; b. Bentonville, Ark., Apr. 21, 1925; s. Oscar and Elsie Marie (Pierce) E.; student Draughons Sch. Bus., 1946, Syracuse U., 1966-67; m. Perneiche Alice Hobbs, Apr. 18, 1946; children—William O., Richard L., Jerry O., Stephen L. Chief engr. KBIX and KBIX-FM Radio, Muskogee, Okla., 1947-54; engring. supr. Tulsa Broadcasting Co., Muskogee, 1954-57; with Gates div. Harris Intertype Corp., Quincy, Ill., 1957—, v.p. sales, 1971-77, v.p. mktg., 1977—. Served with USMCR, 1942-45. Mem. Nat. Assn. Broadcasters (asso.), Nat. Assn. Ednl. Broadcasters (asso.), Nat. Assn. FM Broadcasters (asso.), Sales and Mktg. Execs. Club Quincy (pres. 1966), Sales and Mktg. Execs. Internat., Armed Forces Communications and Electronics Assn., Am. Mgmt. Assn., Internat. Christian Broadcasters. Republican. Baptist. Clubs: Quincy Country, Bella Vista Country, Sheridan Swim, Quincy Rotary. Home: 2310 N Willmar St Quincy IL 62301 Office: 123 Hampshire St Quincy IL 62301

EDWARDS, HOMER FLOYD, JR., educator; b. Forsyth, Ga., June 25, 1918; s. Homer Floyd and Mary Beulah (Jay) E.; B.A., Emory U., 1947, M.A., 1948, Ph.D., 1964; m. Marjorie H. Duncan, Apr. 29, 1967; one son, Christopher B. Instr. classics Emory U., Atlanta, 1954-55, instr. French and German, Emory-at-Oxford, 1955-57; asst. prof. humanities Morehouse Coll., Atlanta, 1959-63, Wayne State U., Detroit, 1963-65; faculty, head dept. theoretical studies Cranbrook Acad. Art, Bloomfield Hills, Mich., 1967-75; asso. prof. humanities Wayne State U., 1965—, chmn. dept. humanities, 1964-75; dir. Passau program Mich. Consortium Medieval and Early Modern Studies, Detroit, 1977—. Served with AUS, 1943-45. Univ. fellow Emory U., 1958-59. Mem. AAUP, Am. Musicol. Soc., Am., Brit. socs. aesthetics, Assn. Gen. Studies, Coll. Art Assn., Mind Assn. (Eng.), Modern Lang. Assn., Am. Hist. Assn., Hist. Assn. (Eng.), Mich. Acad., Nat. Assn. Humanities Edn. Episcopalian. Club: Scarab. Home: 201 E Kirby St Apt 1204 Detroit MI 48202

EDWARDS, HOWARD MILTON, JR., physician; b. Lee, Ill., Sept. 29, 1920; s. Howard M. and Ila M. (Olson) E.; B.S., Northwestern U., 1942; M.D., Cornell, 1945; m. Ruth Ann Ganz, Jan. 19, 1946; children—Carol Ann, Susan Elizabeth, Mary Ellen, Howard Milton III Intern Methodist Hosp., Bklyn., 1945-46; resident Ill. Research Hosp., Chgo., 1948-49, Chgo. Lying-In Hosp., 1949-50; practice medicine, specializing in abdominal surgery, 1950—, Dixon, Ill., 1971—. Pres., Serend, Inc., Dixon, 1960—; treas. Edwards Bldg. Corp., Dixon, 1968—, pres., 1971—; med. dir. Edwards Clinic, Lee County Nursing Home. Mem. adv. com. practical nursing program Sauk Valley Coll. Served to capt. M.C., AUS, 1943-45, 46-48. Fellow Am. Coll. Anesthesiology, Am. Soc. Abdominal Surgeons, ICS; mem. A.M.A., Internat. Bronchoesophagological Soc., Acad. Med. Dirs. Patentee in field of respiration monitors. Contbr. articles to med. jours. Office: 144 North Ct Dixon IL 61021

EDWARDS, IAN KEITH, obstetrician, gynecologist, clin. dir.; b. Spartanburg, S.C., Mar. 2, 1926; s. James Smiley and Georgina (Waters) E.; A.B., Duke U., 1949, M.D., 1953; m. Glenda Melissa Joselyn, Dec. 27, 1968; children—Darien, Jennifer, Carol, Terry. Spl. study pediatrics St. Bartholomew's Hosp., London, 1952; resident in obstetrics and gynecology Grady Meml. Hosp., Atlanta, 1955-58; chief obstetrics and gynecology Valley Forge (Pa.) Army Hosp., 1958-61; practice medicine specializing in obstetrics gynecology, Olney, Ill., 1969—; partner Trover Clinic, Madisonville, Ky., 1961-68, Weber Med. Clinic, Olney, Ill., 1969—, dir. dept. obstetrics gynecology 1970-74, mem. exec. steering com., 1969-72; chief staff Hopkins County (Ky.) Hosp., 1967-68; chief staff Richland Meml. Hosp., Olney, 1975—; clin. instr. obstetrics gynecology U. Ky. Med. Center, Lexington, 1965-68; cons. Childbirth Edn. League. Served to capt. M.C., U.S. Army, 1954-55; Korea. Diplomate Am. Bd. Obstetrics Gynecology. Fellow Am. Coll. Obstetricians Gynecologists; mem. Phila. Obstet. Soc., Am. Legion, VFW, Hopkins County (pres. 1968), Richland (pres. 1974—) med. socs. Democrat. Methodist. Contbr. articles to med. jours. Clubs: Lions, Kiwanis. Office: Weber Med Clinic 1200 N East St Olney IL 62450

EDWARDS, KENNETH EARLE, mfg. co. exec.; b. Kansas City, Mo., Apr. 18, 1926; s. Earle L. and Julia (Patterson) E.; B.S., U. Colo., 1950; M.B.A., Northwestern U., 1953; m. Mary L. Stewart, June 20, 1950; children—John, Jay, Craig, Brett, Bruce. Advt. copywriter Montgomery Ward, Chgo., 1950-51; asst. advt. mgr. Culligan Internat. Co., Northbrook, Ill., 1951-56, mgr. advt., 1956-69, dir. marketing, 1969-71, v.p., dir. marketing, 1971—. Instr. mktg. Harper Coll., 1974-75, Northwestern U., 1975—. Bd. dirs. North Suburban YMCA, 1969-72. Named Internat. Sales Promotion Man Of Year, Sales Promotion Execs. Assn., 1964. Served with USNR, 1944-46. Mem. Sales Promotion Execs. Assn., Am. Mktg. Assn., Sales Mktg. Execs. Internat., Sigma Nu, Alpha Delta Sigma, Delta Sigma Pi. Presbyn. (trustee). Club: Newcomen. Home: 858 Woodbine Ln Northbrook IL 60062 Office: 1 Culligan Pkwy Northbrook IL 60062

EDWARDS, MAUDEST FREEMAN GENTRY, civic worker, former practical nurse; b. St. Louis, June 8, 1910; d. Dabbny and Rose (Johnson) Wilson; student Jackson Coll., 1931-32; grad. Chgo. Practical Nursing Program, 1952; m. Roy Edwards, May 14, 1973. Practical nurse Chgo. Meml. Hosp., 1952-72. Pres., Ladies Aux. Dining Car Employees Union, 1934-40, lobbyist 1953-77; div. 1st v.p. Licensed Practical Nurses Assn. Ill., 1965-68, dir. on bd., 1969-73; transp. driver A.R.C., 1959-65; election judge, 1943-74; out-reach worker Chgo. Mayor's Office for Sr. Citizens. Recipient Meritorious Service award in fight against heart disease; certificate of recognition YMCA, 1977. Home: 6135 S Vernon Ave Chicago IL 60637

EDWARDS, OTIS CARL, JR., sem. dean; b. Bienville, La., June 15, 1928; s. Otis Carl and Margaret Lee (Hutchinson) E.; B.A., Centenary Coll., 1949; S.T.B., Gen. Theol. Sem., 1952; postgrad. Westcott House, Cambridge, Eng., 1952-53; S.T.M., So. Meth. U., 1962; M.A. (Univ. fellow), U. Chgo., 1963, Ph.D., 1971; D.D., Nashotah House, 1976; m. Jane Hanna Trufant, Feb. 19, 1957; children—Carl Lee, Samuel Adams Trufant, Louise Reynes. Ordained priest Episcopal Ch., 1954; curate Episcopal ch., Baton Rouge, 1953-54, vicar, Abbeville, La., 1954-57, Waxachachie, Tex., 1960-61, rector, Morgan City, La., 1957-60, priest in charge, Chgo., 1961-63; instr. Wabash Coll., 1963-64; asst. prof. Nashotah (Wis.) House, 1964-69, asso. prof., 1969-72, prof., 1972-74, sub-dean, 1973-74, acting dean, 1973-74; dean Seabury-Western Theol. Sem., Evanston, Ill., 1974—. Chmn. Council for Devel. of Ministry, Episcopal Ch.; chmn. Council Sem. Deans; mem. Bd. for Theol. Edn.; mem. Gen. Bd. Examining Chaplains; chmn. campus affairs com., trustee Kendall Coll. Recipient Spl. award Mystery Writers Am., 1965. Mem. Soc. Bibl. Lit., Cath. Bibl. Assn., Am. Acad. Religion, Chgo. Soc. Bibl. Research. Democrat. Author: How It All Began, 1973; The Living and Active Word, 1975. Book rev. editor Anglican Theol. Rev., 1971-76, v.p. of corp., 1975—. Contbr. articles and book revs. to various jours. and mags. Home: 625 Garrett Pl Evanston IL 60201 Office: 2122 Sheridan Rd Evanston IL 60201

EDWARDS, RICHARD PIERRE, metallurgist; b. Muncie, Ind., July 17, 1928; s. Johnson Pierre and Gladys Ellen (Keever) E.; B.S. in Metall. Engring. Purdue U., 1950; m. Margaret Jean McClung, Mar. 9, 1952; children—James R., Jean A. Mgr. quality assurance Warner Gear, Muncie, 1971-73; mgr. mfg. services TEGA div. Borg Warner, Troy, Mich., 1973-77, mgr. metallurgy Warner Gear div., Muncie and Auburn, Ind., 1977—. Served to 1st lt. AUS, 1951-52; Korea. Registered profl. engr., Ind. Mem. Am. Soc. Metals, Soc. Automotive Engrs., Soc. Mfg. Engrs., Am. Soc. Quality Control. Presbyterian. Clubs: Masons, Purdue. Home: 2604 W Queensberry Dr Muncie IN 47302 Office: PO Box 2688 Muncie IN 47302

EDWARDS, RONALD KENNETH, educator; b. Lansing, Mich., Aug. 31, 1929; s. Renza Oscar and Lula Fay (LeBar) E.; B.S., Ferris State Coll., 1952; M.S., U. Tenn., 1953; Ph.D., Mich. State U., 1969; m. Ivanna Marie May, Mar. 21, 1953; children—Ronda May Edwards Rothermel, Rita Marie, Robert Dale. Tchr., Flat Rock (Mich.) High Sch., 1953-54, Reed City (Mich.) High Sch., 1954-60; adminstr. Ferris State Coll., Big Rapids, Mich., 1960-63; faculty Lansing (Mich.) Community Coll., 1963-66, prof., chmn. dept. bus., 1966—. Cons. Community Coll. Bus. Programs, 1969—; instr. Am. Assn. Community and Jr. Colls., 1971—. Bd. dirs. Ingham County, Mich. Jail Inmate Rehab. Program, Mason, 1968-74. Served with AUS, 1946-49. Grantee U.S. Office Edn., 1967, Mich. Vocat. Edn., 1968. Mem. Adminstrv. Mgmt. Soc., N. Central Bus. Edn. Assn. (bd. dirs. 1971-74), Nat., Mich. bus. edn. assns., Mich. Occupational Edn. Assn., Am. Vocational Assn., Delta Pi Epsilon. Inventor in field. Home: 7224 W Mount Hope St Lansing MI 48917 Office: 419 N Capitol Ave Lansing MI 48914

EDWARDS, ROY ANDERSON, III, banker; b. New London, Conn., Nov. 23, 1945; s. Roy A. and Joan C. (Darby) E.; B.S. in Bus. Adminstrn., U. Kans., 1968, M.B.A., 1973; m. Terry Kistler Beach, Sept. 5, 1970; children—Ross Darby, Roy Beach. Mem. audit staff of Arthur Young & Co., Kansas City, Kans., 1973-75; fin. cons. Clay Blair Services Corp., Kansas City, 1974-75, also v.p., 1974-75; v.p. in gen. mgmt. Douglas County State Bank, Lawrence, Kans., after 1975, now chief exec. officer bd. dirs.; propr. Mitchell-Hill Seed Co., St. Joseph, Mo., 1971—. Fin. chmn. Douglas County Republican Com., Kans., 1976-77; chmn. Kans. U. Affairs Com., 1977-78, Kans. Spl. Olympics Com., 1977— bd. dirs. Lawrence (Kans.) Art Center, 1976, The Lawrence Villages, 1976. Served to lt. USN, 1968-71. Mem. Young Bank Officers of Kans., Lawrence C. of C., Lawrence Humane Soc. (chmn. 1975-77), Kans. Bankers Assn., U. Kans. Alumni Assn., Phi Delta Theta, Alpha Kappa Psi. Republican. Episcopalian. Clubs: Lawrence Country, Rotarian. Contbr. articles on fin. to profl. jours. Home: 1136 Hilltop Dr Lawrence KS 66044 Office: 9th St and Kentucky Ave Lawrence KS 66044

EDWARDS, VERN DOWNING, lawyer; b. Superior, Wis., May 23, 1916; s. Verne R. and Alice (Gallagher) E.; LL.B., U. Wis., 1939, Ph.D., 1968, LL.D., 1968; m. Lee D. Harper, Feb. 8, 1941; children—Nancy (Mrs. Thomas McNamara), Mark D., Catherine A., Linda E. (Mrs. James Jenkins), Sara D. Admitted to Wis. bar, 1939; atty. tax dept. Wis. Dept. Revenue, Madison, 1940-45; owner firm Edwards, Becker, Lynch, Parke & Heim, Ltd., La Crosse, Wis., 1945—; chmn. bd. Coulee State Bank, La Crosse. Served with USNR, 1941-44. Mem. Am., Milw., Wis., La Crosse bar assns. Elk. Club: La Crosse. Home: 1327 Cass St La Crosse WI 54601 Office: 502 Exchange Bldg La Crosse WI 54601

EDWARDS, VERNE E(RVIE), JR., educator; b. Platteville, Wis., June 23, 1924; s. Verne Elgie and Arlie Julia (Stowell) E.; student Carleton Coll., 1942-43; B.S., Wis. State U., Platteville, 1947; M.S., U. Wis., 1949; m. Dolores Whitcher, June 13, 1947; children—Deborah Jane, Nancy Ellen. Corr., Wis. and Iowa dailies, 1939-43, 46-47; grad. asst. U. Wis., 1948-49; instr. Washington State U., 1949-52; asst. prof., asso. prof., prof. and dept. chmn. Ohio Wesleyan U., Delaware, 1952—. Chief editorial writer Detroit Free Press, 1962-63; summer fellow Milw. Jour., Rochester Times-Union, Columbus Citizen, Buffalo Evening News, Columbus Dispatch, Toledo Blade, 1951-72; cons. Fulfillment Corp. Am., 1958—; rep. Am. Council Edn. for Journalism, 1963—. Served with USAAF, 1943-46; PTO. Recipient 1st prize Sigma Delta Chi Found. Writing Awards, 1965. Mem. Am. Soc. Journalism Sch. Adminstrs. (past pres.), Assn. for Edn. in Journalism, Am. Assn. U. Profs. (past chpt. pres.), Sigma Delta Chi, Omicron Delta Kappa, Gamma Theta Upsilon. Asso. editor: Journalism Educator, 1966-69; mem. editorial adv. bd. Journalism Quar., 1972—. Author: Journalism in a Free Society, 1970. Contbr. various mags. Home: 23 Spencer St Delaware OH 43015

EDWARDS, WALTER HARRISON, JR., mfg. co. pres.; b. Nashville, Sept. 20, 1913; s. Walter Harrison and Pearl Reed (Williams) E.; B.S., Ind. U., 1935; m. Lucy Elisabeth Beasley, Apr. 25, 1936; children—Judith Ann (Mrs. James Clifford Riebe), Mary Ellen (Mrs. David Allen Harden). Pres. W.H. Edwards Engring. Corp., Indpls., 1935—; exec. v.p. Broady Edwards, Campbell & Tarrant, contractors, Indpls., 1963-68; pres. Edwards Machine & Tool Corp., Indls., 1947-55; Co-founder Nora Brook Civic League, 1941; organizer Windcombe Civic League, 1952. Del., Nat. Young Democrats, 1935. Served as officer, 83d Inf. Div., AUS, 1942-46; ETO. Decorated Silver Star, Bronze Star medal with oak leaf cluster, Purple Heart with cluster. Mem. Ind. Subcontractors (founding pres. 1967-68), Mason Contractors Assn. Ind. (pres. 1962-63), Constrn. League Indpls. (dir. 1950-53), Bldg. Contractors Assn. Ind. (dir. 1950-66), C. of C., 83d Inf. Div. Assn. (life), Alpha Tau Omega. Dem. Baptist (trustee, chmn., life deacon). Mason (Shriner, life mem. Legion Honor). Clubs: Indpls. Athletic, Southern Indpls. (pres. 1955), Rotary. Home: 611 Bryn Mawr Dr Indianapolis IN 46260 Office: 2353 Winthrop Ave Indianapolis IN 46205

EDWIN, ALLAN IRA, electronics co. exec.; b. N.Y.C., Nov. 10, 1942; s. Murray H. and Irene (Lebowitz) E.; M.S. in Elec. Engring., U. Mich., 1965, M.S. in Bio-Engring., 1970. Mem. tech. staff Bell Telephone Labs., Holmdel, N.J., 1963-65; NIH trainee in bioengring. U. Mich, Ann Arbor, 1965-68; chmn., chief exec. officer Interactive Systems Inc., Ann Arbor, 1969—. N.Y. State Regents scholar, 1960-64. Certified mfg. engr. Mich. Mem. IEEE, Soc. Mfg. Engrs. Home: 3855 Loch Alpine Dr W Ann Arbor MI 48103

EDYVEAN, RICHARD WHITLEY, electronics co. exec.; b. Evanston, Ill., Sept. 5, 1951; s. Alfred Rowe and Dorothy (Rogers) E.; B.S. in Elec. Engring., Purdue U., 1973, M.S. in Engring., 1977; m. Susan Jane Rose, Sept. 4, 1976. Multiplex systems engr. Frequency div. Microwave Communications, Inc., Washington, 1973-74; sr. tech. rep. Trace, Inc., Lafayette, Ind., 1975-76; v.p. engring. Automation Electronics Co., Lafayette, 1977—; cons. in field. Mem. IEEE. Home: 400 N River Rd #217 W Lafayette IN 47906 Office: 1000 South St Lafayette IN 47902

EELLS, WILLIAM HASTINGS, automobile co. exec.; b. Princeton, N.J., Mar. 30, 1924; s. Hastings and Amy (Titus) E.; B.A., Ohio Wesleyan U., 1946; M.A., Ohio State U., 1950. Asst. to dir. Inst. Practical Politics, Ohio Wesleyan U., 1948-50, asst. dir., 1952-53, dir., 1953-57; instr. dept. polit. sci., 1952-59; instr. polit. sci. Mt. Union Coll., 1950-51; coordinator Atomic Devel. Activities, State of Ohio, 1957-59; Midwest regional mgr. civic and govtl. affairs Ford Motor Co., Columbus, 1959—. Mem. Ohio Gov.'s Cabinet, 1957-59; chmn. bd. Blue Cross, 1967-72; chmn. bd. Blossom Music Center, Cleve., 1967-75; chmn. Gov.'s Council on Rehab., 1966-68; mem. exec. com. Met. Opera's Nat. Council, 1967—; pres. Nat. Council High Blood Pressure Research; v.p. Lake Erie Watershed Conservation Found.; mem. Nat. Council on Arts, Nat. Endowment for Arts, 1976—; bd. dirs. Am. Heart Assn.; trustee Cleve. Orch., Ednl. TV, Cleve., Cleve. Playhouse, Cleve. Ballet, Cleve. Zoo, Cleve. Luth. Hosp., Cleve. Inst. Music, Recipient awards including USCG Distinguished award, 1965, Ohio State U. Devel. award, 1967. Mem. Cleve. Growth Assn. (dir), S.A.R., Ohio C. of C. (v.p.), Ohio Mfrs. Assn. (trustee), Pi Sigma Alpha, Pi Gamma Mu, Omicron Delta Kappa, Delta Tau Delta. Republican. Presbyn. Clubs: Princeton (N.Y.); U. Columbus, Cleve. Union; Columbus. Author: Your Ohio Government, 1953, 6th edit., 1967. Contbr. articles to profl. publs. Home: Summit Chase Columbus OH 43212 Office: 808 Huntington Trust Bldg Columbus OH 43215

EGAN, RICHARD DENNIS, paper mfg. co. exec.; b. Evanston, Ill., Apr. 4, 1939; s.Charles Nickerson and Margaret Kathryn (Hubsch) E.; B.A., Yale, 1961; postgrad. Harvard, 1971; m. Anne Witteborg, Feb. 2, 1963; children—Timothy, Joseph, Daniel. Advt. rep. NW Publs., 1964-65; scheduling coordinator Shawano Paper Mills Inc. (Wis.), 1966-67, exec. v.p., 1975-77, pres., 1977—; sales mgr. Green Bay Tissue Mills Inc., Wis., 1967-72. gen. mgr., 1972-77, pres., 1977—; exec. v.p., Little Rapids Pulp Co., Green Bay, 1975-77, pres., 1977—, also dir.; dir. W. Bank & Trust Co., Wis. Paper Group, Tissue div. Am. Paper Inst., Wis. Paper Council. Surveyor Brown County, Wis., 1968; mem. pres.'s task force St. Norbert Coll., 1972—; pres. Abbot Pennings Found., 1974-76. Served to lt. (j.g.) USNR, 1961-63. Mem. Am. Transfer Printing Inst. Roman Catholic. Clubs: Oneida Golf; Yale (N.Y.C.); Harvard Bus. Sch. (Milw.). Home: 3755 S Webster Ave Green Bay WI 54301 Office: PO Box 3629 Green Bay WI 54303

EGANHOUSE, GERALD ROGER, orthodontist; b. Bellevue, Iowa, Sept. 25, 1933; s. Elmer George and Amelia Mary (Kiefer) E.; student Iowa State U., 1957-59; D.D.S., U. Iowa, 1963, M.S., 1965; m. Barbara Geraldine Johnson, Nov. 19, 1955; children—Michael, David, Kenneth, Jenifer, Paul. Pvt. practice orthodontics, Cedar Rapids, Iowa, 1965—; vis. lectr. U. Iowa, 1965-67; chmn. bd. Saint Luke's Dental Clinic, 1975—. Served with USAF, 1953-57. Diplomate Am. Bd. Orthodontics. Mem. ADA, Am. Orthodontic Assn., Iowa Dental Soc., Iowa Iowa Orthodontic Soc. (pres. 1972-73), Midwestern Soc. Orthodontists, Omicron Kappa Upsilon. Club: Cedar Rapids Country. Home: 295 30th St Cedar Rapids IA 52403 Office: 2727 1st Ave Cedar Rapids IA 52402

EGEKVIST, W. SOREN, former coll. pres., bus. cons.; b. Mpls., Dec. 9, 1918; s. Soren Andersen and Lillian (Anderson) E.; A.B., Carleton Coll., 1941; M.B.A., Harvard, 1943; Ph.D. candidate U. Chgo., 1948; LL.D., Jamestown Coll., 1975; m. Margaret Stang, Oct. 21, 1948. Chief economist, U.S. Civil Service, chief price control and rationing div. GHQ-SCAP-Tokyo, Japan, 1945-47; partner Robert Heller & Assos., Cleve., 1948-52; asst. to pres J. Kayser Co., N.Y.C., 1952-55; v.p., gen. mgr. Munsingwear, Inc., Mpls 1955-58; pres., dir. Sorenco, Inc., 1958—; interim pres. Jamestown (N.D.) Coll., 1974-76; hon. consul gen. of Japan, 1976—; del. United Nations FAO, India, 1947; mem. exec. res. U.S. C. of C., 1958-68. Trustee, Jamestown Coll.; Twin City dir. Internat. Exec. Service Corps. Served to capt. AUS, 1943-46. Decorated Legion of Merit, recipient meritorious civilian service medal War Dept., 1947, citation for distinguished service Internat. Exec. Service Corps. Mem. Japan Soc. Minn. (pres. 1975), Newcomen Soc., Beta Gamma Sigma, Mpls. C. of C. Mason (32 deg., Shriner), Rotarian. Lutheran. Clubs: Harvard (pres. 1962-63) (Mpls. and St. Paul); Mpls. Athletic, Mpls., Interlachen Country (gov. 1963-69)(Mpls.). Author: Economic Stabilization Plan for Japan, 1947, Legislation for Economic Stabilization Bd., 1947, Economic Controls During Occupation of Japan, 1952. Office: 5316 Dundee Rd Edina MN 55436

EGELAND, EUGENE CARROLL, data processor; b. Wallingford, Iowa, Nov. 27, 1930; s. Clarence Clifford and Susanna Hadie (Herke) E.; B.S., Iowa State U., 1954; m. Virginia Sue Larson, Mar. 18, 1951; children—Gloria Lee (Mrs. Paul Lewis Koll), Robert Gene, Bradley Jay. Operator data processing machine Iowa State U., Ames, 1951-52, asst. mgr. data processing, 1953-54; mgr. data processing Hy-Vee Food Stores, Inc., Chariton, Iowa, 1954—. Mem. data processing adv. bd. Indian Hills Community Coll., Ottumwa, Iowa, 1969—. Mem. Data Processing Mgmt. Assn. (dir. Des Moines chpt. 1961-63), Assn. for Systems Mgmt., Chariton C. of C. (dir. 1964-66, 72-74). Lutheran (treas. 1957-60). Mason (Shriner). Club: Lake View Golf and Country (pres. 1962, 63, 74). Home: 630 Osage Ave Chariton IA 50049 Office: 1801 Osceola Ave Chariton IA 50049

EGER, GEORGE WILLIAM, JR., adminstrv. mech. engr.; b. Springfield, Mass., July 1, 1918; s. George W. and Margaret (Mayer) E.; M.E., Stevens Inst. Tech., 1940; m. Ramona May Prina, Aug. 7, 1948; children—Cheryl Ann, Warren Blair, George W., Shawn Lee; m. 2d, Maree Lee Ahn, Jan. 8, 1977. With Caterpillar Tractor Co., Peoria, Ill., 1940-66, supervising engr. Peoria proving ground, 1950-52, engr. research staff, 1952-58, asst. chief engr. power shift transmissions, 1958-63, chief engr. East Peoria plant, 1963-66; mgr. engring. constrn. equipment div. Internat. Harvester Co., Melrose Park, Ill., 1967-72, v.p. engring. Pay Line div., 1972-77, v.p. World-wide Pay Line group, 1977—. Inventor power shift transmissions for crawler tractors, 1953, for rubber-tired tractors, 1965. Home: 3150 Illinois Rd Winnetka IL 60093 Office: 600 Woodfield Rd Schaumburg IL 60196

EGGAN, FRED R(USSELL), ret. educator; b. Seattle, Sept. 12, 1906; s. Alfred Julius and Olive M. (Smith) E.; Ph.B., U. Chgo., 1927, A.M., 1928, Ph.D., 1933 m. Dorothy Way, Aug. 9, 1938 (dec. 1965); m. 2d, Joan Rosenfels, June 29, 1969. Research asso. in Philippine ethnology U. Chgo., 1934-35, instr. anthropology, 1935-40, asst. prof., 1940-42, asso. prof., 1942-48, prof., 1948-74, emeritus, 1974—, chmn. dept., 1948-52, 61-63, dir. Philippine studies program 1953—, Harold H. Swift Distinguished Service prof., 1963-74; Morgan lectr. U. Rochester, 1964; vis. fellow All Souls Coll., Oxford, 1970; Frazer lectr., Cambridge, Eng., 1971; vis. prof. U. Calif. at Santa Cruz, winter 1976. Ofcl. U.S. del. to 8th Pacific Sci. Congress, Manila, 1953, 9th, Bangkok, 1957, 10th, Honolulu, 1961, 11th, Tokyo, Japan, 1966, 13th, Vancouver, 1975; mem. Pres.'s Com. on Scientists and Engrs., 1956-57; chmn. bd. Human Relations Area Files, Inc., 1964-67; research asso. Lab. Anthropology, Santa Fe, 1964—; adv. com. social scis. NSF, 1961-62; hon. cons. Bernice P. Bishop Mus., Honolulu; mem. Commn. on Coll. Geography, 1965-67; councillor Smithsonian Instn., 1966—; mem. adv. bd. Desert Research Inst., U. Nev.; bd. dirs. Founds. Fund for Research Psychiatry, 1966-69; mem. Pacific Sci. Bd., 1968—. Served as capt. AUS, 1943; dir. Civil Affairs Tng. Sch. for Far East, U. Chgo., 1943-45. Fulbright research scholar, Philippines 1949-50; Guggenheim fellow, 1953; fellow Center for Advanced Study in Behavioral Scis., Stanford, 1958-59; recipient Viking Fund medal and award, 1956; hon. curator Chgo. Natural History Mus., 1962. Fellow Royal Anthrop. Inst. (hon.), Brit. Acad., Am. Acad. Arts and Scis., AAAS; mem. Am. Philos. Soc., Nat. Acad. Scis. (mem. com. on scis. and pub. policy 1965-67, mem. council 1967-70), Assn. Asian Studies (dir. 1966-68), Am. Anthrop. Assn. (pres. 1953, Memoirs editor 1960-64), Am. Ethnol. Soc., NRC (chmn. com. Asian anthropology 1952-53), Social Sci. Research Council (chmn. bd. 1955-56), Phi Beta Kappa, Sigma Xi, Tau Kappa Epsilon. Club: Quadrangle. Author: Social Organization of the Western Pueblos, 1950; The American Indian, 1966; Essays in Social Anthropology and Ethnology, 1975. Editor: Social Anthropology of North American Tribes, 1937, enlarged edit., 1955. Supr. Handbook on The Philippines, 4 vols., 1956. Mem. adv. com. Ency. Brit., 1953—. Editorial bd. Sci., 1968-70. Home: 5752 S Harper Ave Chicago IL 60637 Office: 1126 E 59th St Chicago IL 60637

EGGEN, J(OHN) ARCHER, librarian; b. Virginia, Minn., May 4, 1915; s. John J. and Anne Marie (Berg) E.; student Va. Jr. Coll., 1932-35; B.A., U. Minn.; m. Eleanor Gray, Mar. 11, 1948 (dec. Feb. 1959); m. 2d, Trueda Monson, Jan. 14, 1961 (dec. July 1974). Design engr., co. librarian Continental Machines, Inc., Mpls., 1941-45; librarian Fergus Falls (Minn.) Pub. Library, also Ind. Sch. Dist. No. 21, 1945-49; head librarian Cedar Rapids (Iowa) Pub. Library, 1949-56; city librarian St. Paul Pub. Library, 1956—, also dir. Mem. Am., Minn., Iowa library assns. Mason, Rotarian. Club: Southview County. Contbr. articles to library periodicals. Home: 360 S Lexington Pkwy St Paul MN 55105 Office: 90 W 4th St St Paul MN 55112

EGGERS, MARIE ELIZABETH, guidance counselor; b. St. Louis, Dec. 1, 1918; d. Paul A. and Mabel J. Toennies, A.A., Fla. Valley Coll., 1964; B.S., So. Ill. U., 1966, B.A., 1967, M.A., 1969; m. Ervin Morris Eggers, June 19, 1937; children—Eugene, Bonnie, Paula, Marci. Tchr., Parkway Sch. Dist., St. Louis, 1967-69, Pattonville Sch., 1969—. Mem. Bridgeton (Mo.) Park Bd., 1964-66; vol. probation parole officer State of Mo., 1976-77. Mem. Am., St. Louis personnel guidance assns., Mo. Guidance Assn., Mo. State Tchrs.' Assn. Mem. United Ch. Christ. Co-editor, Bookworm, Bridgeton. Home: 3216 Bristolhall Ct Bridgeton MO 63044 Office: 195 Fee Fee St Maryland Heights MO 63043

EGGERS, WILLIAM THEODORE, social work adminstr., clergyman; b. Tacoma, Apr. 27, 1912; s. William A. and Rosette (Pritzleff) E.; grad. Concordia Sem., 1935, D.D. (hon.), 1977; postgrad. Marquette U., 1935-36; m. Marcella Martha Ella Nohos, Nov. 3, 1938; children—William C., Mary (Mrs. James Wiertzema), Joan (Mrs. Donald C. Wendelburg). Ordained to ministry Luth. Ch.; pastor chs., Ill. and Wis., 1937-53; adminstr. Home for Aged Luths., Wauwatosa, Wis., after 1954, now exec. v.p. Chmn. com. govt. relations Wis. Council Homes for Aging, pres., 1960-67; mem. Wis. Council on Aging; chmn. adv. com. nursing home regulations Wis. Council Nursing Homes; mem. Luth. Radio Com.; cons. on aging to Profl. Nursing Home mag. Pres., chmn. bd. Oconomowoc (Wis.) Meml. Hosp., 1951-55. Mem. Am. Assn. Homes for Aging (past pres.), Am. Hosp. Assn., Milw. Council on Aging (past dir.), Employers Assn. Milw. (past dir.). Author: Space of Joy, 1968. Editor: Affirm, 1971—; chmn. editorial com. Concern. Home: 2510 N Swan Blvd Wauwatosa WI 53226 Office: 7500 W North Ave Wauwatosa WI 53213

EGGERT, JAMES ROBERT, assn. exec.; b. Akron, Ohio, Apr. 22, 1949; s. Dennis Floyd and Martha Louise (Cole) E.; B.A. in Journalism, Ohio State U., 1971; M.B.A., Xavier U., 1976; m. Suellen Vey, Dec. 17, 1948; children—Tamara Ellen, James Bradley. Reporter, Columbus (Ohio) Dispatch, 1970-71; dir. pub. relations Order United Comml. Travelers of Am., Columbus, 1971—. Mem. Westerville (Ohio) Shade Tree Commn., 1976—; vol. worker Citizens

With Celeste campaign, 1977—. Recipient Honor certificate Freedoms Found. at Valley Forge, 1974. Mem. Pub. Relations Soc. Am. (accredited, award of Excellence, East Central dist.), Internat. Assn. Bus. Communicators, United Comml. Travelers, Sigma Nu. Roman Catholic. Editor The Sample Case, mag., 1971—, Leader mag., 1976—. Home: 740 Vancouver Dr Westerville OH 43081 Office: 632 N Park St Columbus OH 43215

EGGSPUEHLER, JACK JAY, educator; b. Des Moines, Mar. 12, 1930; s. Florian Roman and Myrtle Charlotte (Heathman) E.; student Augustana Coll., 1949-51; B.S., U. Ill., 1954, M.S., 1962; m. Joan Bye, Feb. 1, 1956; children—Jay Bernard, Pete Roman, Brad Leslie. Instr., U. Ill., 1955-57; chief flight instr., dept. aviation Ohio State U., Columbus, 1958-59, prof., chmn., dept. aviation, 1959—; dir. Aerosafe, Inc., Traveling Aviation Seminars, Inc., TAS Flight Services, Inc. Recipient Distinguished Service award Flight Safety Found., 1964, Wheatley award Univ. Aviation Assn., 1965, award Air Force Assn. Ohio, 1966. Mem. Nat. (dir., Meritorious Service award 1966), Ohio (sec.-treas.) aviation trades assns., Nat. Assn. Aerial Applicators (dir.), Nat. Assn. Flight Instrs. (pres.), Nat. Assn. Engring. Edn., CAP, Aircraft Owners and Pilots Assn. (Meritorious award for contbns. to flight safety), Nat. Pilots Assn., Quiet Birdmen. Club: Rotary. Home: 6514 Winston Ct E Worthington OH 43085 Office: PO Box 3022 Ohio State U Columbus OH 43210

EGNOR, RONALD WILLIAM, lawyer; b. Lego, W.Va., Aug. 12, 1940; s. Ray Albert and Georgia (Smith) E.; B.A. (Inst. World Affairs fellow), Eastern Mich. U., 1964; J.D., U. Mich., 1967; m. Mary Hunt, June 13, 1964; children—Ronald William, Mary Elizabeth, Tara Michelle. Admitted to Mich. bar, 1968, also U.S. Supreme Ct.; appellate counsel Nat. Labor Relations Bd., Washington, 1967-69; partner firm Egnor & Hamilton & Muth, Ypsilanti, Mich., 1969—; pres. Ypsilanti Leasing Corp.; city atty., Ypsilanti, 1975—; instr. Sch. Indsl. and Labor Relations, U. Mich., 1970-75, Eastern Mich. U., 1965-67. Bd. dirs. United Fund. Served with AUS, 1959-60. Selected as one of five Outstanding Young Men of Mich. Mem. Am., Mich., Washtenaw County bar assns., Mich., Am. trial lawyers assns., Jaycees, ACLU, Pi Kappa Delta, Phi Alpha Delta. Democrat. Lion (pres.). Home: 702 Collegewood St Ypsilanti MI 48197 Office: 33 S Huron St Ypsilanti MI 48197

EHLMANN, CARLTON MELVIN, photographer; b. St. Charles, Mo., Nov. 23, 1936; s. Martin Louis and Clara Catrina (Heitgerd) E.; student Winona Sch. Profl. Photography, 1972-73, 76-77, Lindenwood Coll., 1974; m. Annette Sophia Nolle, Aug. 1, 1959; children—Cynthia, Deborah, Sharon. Auto body repairman, 1959-70; owner Ehlmann Photography, St. Charles, 1970—. Served with USNR, 1956-57. Recipient 3 blue ribbon awards, also best of show trophy pictorial div. Mo. Profl. Photography competition, 1974. Lutheran. Club: St. Louis Bow Hunters. Address: 540 Boonslick St Charles MO 63301

EHRENSAFT, MORRIS, supply co. exec.; b. Chgo., June 18, 1917; s. Joseph and Dora (Karlins) E.; student pub. schs., Chgo.; m. Edith Hoyt, June 15, 1940; children—Philip, Diane, Richard. Purchasing agt. Garden City Plating and Mfg., 1937-43; sales staff Triangle Supply Co., 1943-45; v.p. Marklin Supply Co., Chgo., 1946-71, pres., 1972—. Treas., North Central Homeowners Assn., 1956, v.p., 1957-60; v.p. spl. events Skokie Caucus party, 1958-65, pres., 1965-69. Hon. fellow Truman Meml. Library. Mem. Chgo. Assn. Commerce and Industry, Art Inst. Chgo., Smithsonian Instn., Common Cause, Public Citizens. Clubs: Masons, Fraternal Order Police. Home: 8943 Kilpatrick St Skokie IL 60076 Office: 3060 Elston St N Chicago IL 60618

EHRKE, WALTER LOUIS, wholesale drug co. exec.; b. West Allis, Wis., Sept. 24, 1911; s. Gustav Paul and Mathilda Caroline (Pawelke) E.; student U. Wis., 1929-31; m. Helen Margaret Luettgen, Mar. 30, 1940; children—Lance, Lauren Ehrke Lauritch, Muriel Ehrke Stanton, Eric. Supt. Yahr-Lange Drug Co., Inc., Milw., 1942-46, Milw., Rockford, Ill., and LaCrosse, Wis., 1946-53, gen. ops. mgr., 1953-64, dir., Milw., 1962—, v.p., 1964-72, sr. v.p., 1972—; operation mgr. Crandon Drug Co., Miami, Fla., 1953-62, v.p., 1962-72, pres., 1972—, also dir.; designer, gen. ops. mgr. Crandon Drug Co., Fort Lauderdale, Fla., 1962-70; designer, pres. Crandon Drug Co., Lakeland, Fla., 1976—. Mem. Nat. Wholesale Drug Assn. (mem. systems com. 1973-74, chmn. 1974-75), Travellers of Wis. Roman Catholic. Kiwanian. Home: 2645 Willow Springs Dr Brookfield WI 53005 Office: 800 Wall St Elm Grove WI 53122 also 500 NE 191st St Miami FL 33162

EHRLICH, CLARENCE EUGENE, obstetrician, gynecologist; b. Rosenberg, Tex., Oct. 19, 1938; s. Oscar Lee and Gertrude Gene (Walzel) E.; B.A., U. Tex., 1961; M.D., Baylor Coll., 1965; m. Arlene Anderson, May 18, 1973; children—Tracey, Bradley, Suzanne. Intern Phila. Gen. Hosp., 1965-66; resident Charity Hosp., Tulane U., New Orleans, 1966-69; fellow gynecologic oncology U. Tex. 1971-73; practice medicine specializing in obstetrics and gynecology, 1973—; asst. prof. obstetrics and gynecology, Ind. U., 1973—, chief sect. gynecologic oncology, med. center, 1973—. Served to maj. USAF, 1969-71. Diplomate Am. Bd. Obstetrics and Gynecology. Fellow A.C.S.; mem. Am. Coll. Obstetrics and Gynecology, Am., Ind. State med. assns., Conrad G. Collins Obstetric and Gynecologic Soc. of Tulane U., Felix Rutledge Soc., Central Assn. Obstetricians and Gynecologists, Ind. State Obstetricians and Gynecologists Soc., Am. Soc. Colposcopists and Colpmicroscopists, Gynecologic Oncology Group. Unitarian. Contbr. articles to med. jours. Home: 620 Oakwood Dr Indianapolis IN 46260 Office: 1100 W Michigan St Indianapolis IN 46202

EICHACKER, GEORGE LOUIS DONALD, accountant, savs. and loan exec.; b. Homestead, Iowa, Mar. 9, 1930; s. Charles Alexander and Marie (Geiger) E.; B.A. in Econs., State U. Iowa, 1951, M.A. in Accounting, 1952; m. Lois Ann Harper, Apr. 27, 1969; children—Milton, Lois Ann, Virginia. Accountant McGladrey, Hansen, Dunn & Co., 1955-58; exec. sec. United Fund of Keokuk (Iowa), 1958-65; partner McGaughey & Assos., 1958-60; self employed as C.P.A., Keokuk, 1960—. Sec.-treas. Keokuk Fed. Savs. and Loan (Iowa) 1962—. Chmn. Keokuk Urban Renewal Agy., 1966-69; trustee, sec. Graham Hosp. Assn., Keokuk, 1960—; bd. dirs. United Fund of Keokuk, 1965—. Served with AUS, 1952-54. Named Outstanding Young Man of Iowa Jr. C. of C., 1963. C.P.A., Iowa Mem. Am. Inst. C.P.A.'s, Keokuk Jr. C. of C. (pres. 1957). Episcopalian. Clubs: Keokuk Rotary (pres. 1969). Mem. Phi Beta Kappa. Home: Rural Route 2 Box 44 Fort Madison IA 52627 Office: 20 N 4th St Keokuk IA 52632

EICHENBERGER, WILLIAM AUSTIN, hardware mfg. co. exec.; b. Nampa, Idaho, July 2, 1926; s. William C. and Bertha (Murphy) E.; student Pacific Coll., 1946-48; m. Margie Mittendorf, Sept. 13, 1972; children—Sandra, William B., Celi. Vice pres. Crawford Door Sales Corp. Oreg., Portland, 1948-63; pres. Pacific Spring and Hardware Mfg. Corp., Portland, 1963-66; pres. Am. Power Unit Corp. Ltd., Montreal, Que., Can., 1967-77; pres. APCO Power Unit Corp., Toledo, 1977-78, dir., chmn. bd. Mem. Nat. Assn. Garage Door Mfrs. (past dir., chmn. metric com.), Door and Operator Dealers Am. (dir.). Contbr. Door and Operators Dealers Am. News, 1977-78. Home: 6339 Grandview Dr Erie MI 48133 Office: 1216 Expressway Dr S Toledo OH 43608

EICHER, ALLISON BOYD, TV prodn. co. exec.; b. Detroit, Aug. 1, 1935; s. Boyd E. and Eleanora (Sting) E.; student Bay City Jr. Coll., Delta Coll., Wayne State U.; m. Kathryn E. Braun, July 19, 1958; children—Laurie, David. TV engr., tech. dir. WNEM-TV, 1957-61; owner WMIC, 1961-62; v.p. Campbell Ewald Advt. Agy., 1962-71; dir. communications Teletape Corp., 1971-72; v.p., gen. mgr. Magnetic Video Corp., Farmington, Mich., 1972—. Mem. adv. bd. WBHS; mem. council Am. Luth. Brotherhood; mem. Bloomfield Hills Athletic Commn.; past pres. Bloomfield Hills Sch. PTO. Served with U.S. Army. Mem. Internat. Tape Assn. (adv. bd.), Soc. Motion Picture and TV Engrs., Detroit Council Churches (radio and TV bd.), Acad. Video Communicators (dir.), Mich. Bee Keepers Assn. Home: 1415 Lenox Rd Bloomfield Hills MI 48013 Office: 23434 Industrial Park Ct Farmington Hills MI 48024

EICHHORST, THOMAS EDWARD, lawyer; b. St. Louis, Sept. 4, 1937; s. Edward F. and Mary Adelia (Dulany) E.; A.A., Harris Tchrs. Coll., 1957; B.S. in Pub. Adminstrn., U. Mo. at Columbia, 1960; J.D., Washington U., 1961; M.A., Lincoln U. Mo., Jefferson City, 1968; m. Barbara Jean Johnson, Oct. 17, 1964; children—Christine Elise, James Edward. Admitted to Mo. bar, 1961; mem. staff Com. on Legis. Research, Jefferson City, 1962-64; asst. atty. gen. Mo., Jefferson City, 1964-65; counsel Am. Optometric Assn., St. Louis, 1965—. Instr. polit. sci. U. Mo. at St. Louis, 1965-66; dir. Internat. Library Archives and Mus. Optometry, St. Louis, 1973-77. Pres., Young Democrats Met. St. Louis, 1968. Recipient Merit award mgmt. achievement Am. Soc. Assn. Execs., 1971. Mem. Am. Bar Assn., Coll. Legal Medicine, Mo. Bar, Delta Theta Phi, Pi Sigma Alpha, Mensa. Home: 5228 Creighton Dr St Louis MO 63123 Office: 7000 Chippewa St St Louis MO 63119

EICHNER, EDUARD, obstetrician, gynecologist; b. Cleve., Nov. 11., 1905; s. Nathan Jacob and Dora (Guren) E.; A.B., Case Western Res. U., 1925, M.D., 1929; m. Helen Augusta Short, Sept. 11, 1931; children—William Eduard, Judith Eichner Henderson. Intern, St. Alexis Hosp., Cleve., 1929-30; resident obstetrics St. Ann Hosp., Cleve., 1930-31; proctor-tng., intervals obstetrics and gynecology Mt. Sinai Hosp., Cleve., 1932-36; gen. practice medicine, Cleve., 1931-37; practice medicine specializing in obstetrics and gynecology, Cleve., 1938—; asso. obstetrician, gynecologist, dir. family planning clinic Mt. Sinai Hosp., Cleve., 1954-72, asso. vis. physician, dir. family planning, 1972—. Asso. clin. prof. obstetrics and gynecology Case Western Res. U. Sch. Medicine, Cleve., 1973—; med. dir. preterm, 1974—. Mem. med. adv. bd. Met. Health Planning Com., Cleve. Dist., 1974—; clin. adv. bd. Cuyahoga County Bd. Mental Retardation, Cleve., 1969—; mem. Am. Com. on Maternal Welfare, Chgo., 1947-60. Trustee Circle Workshop, Cleve., Parents Vol. Assn., Cleve., 1972—. Served with USNR, 1942-46. Recipient awards for original investigation Am. Coll. Obstetricians and Gynecologists, 1954, 63, Ohio Med. Assn., 1955, 63, A.C.S., 1955, Modern Medicine, 1956, Diplomate Am. Bd. Obstetrics and Gynecology. Fellow A.C.S., Am. Coll. Obstetrics and Gynecology, Internat. Coll. Surgeons (v.p. sect. obstetrics-gynecology); mem. A.M.A., Central Assn. Obstetricians and Gynecologists, Endocrine Soc., Soc. for Exptl. Biology and Medicine, Am. Fertility Soc., Am. Inst. Biologic Sci., Internat. Soc. for Research in Reproduction, Pan-Pacific Surg. Assn., Pan-Am. Med. Soc., N.Y. Acad. Sci., Med. Alumni Assn. Case Western Res. U. (pres. 1967), Cleve. Soc. Obstetricians and Gynecologists (pres. 1960), Cleve. City Club, Sigma Xi, Kappa Nu, Phi Lambda Kappa. Contbr. numerous articles to profl. jours. Home: 3333 Daleford Rd Shaker Heights OH 44120 Office: 5 Severance Circle Dr Cleveland OH 44118

EIFLER, NORMAN CARL, dentist; b. Berwyn, Ill., Nov. 29, 1932; s. Frederick Charles and Selma Mary (Schwerin) E.; student Albion Coll., 1950-53; B.S., U. Ill., 1954, D.D.S., 1957; m. Ada Jean Muma, Dec. 29, 1956; children—David, Robert, Debra, Kathryn. Pvt. practice dentistry, Mt. Pleasant, Mich., 1960—. Cubmaster, Cub Scouts Am., Mt. Pleasant, 1965-69; treas. Pullen Sch. PTA, 1967. Bd. dirs. YMCA, Mt. Pleasant, 1970-73, chmn. bd., 1972-73; bd. dirs. United Way of Isabella County. Served with AUS, 1958-60. Mem. Am., Mich. dental assns., 9th Dist. Dental Soc. (pres. 1964), Am. Soc. Preventive Dentistry. Methodist. Lion (pres. 1977-78). Home: 1211 E Broadway Mount Pleasant MI 48858 Office: 1114 E Chippewa St Mount Pleasant MI 48858

EIGEL, EDWIN GEORGE, JR., educator; b. St. Louis, June 4, 1932; s. Edwin George and Catherine (Rohan) E.; B.S., Mass. Inst. Tech., 1954; postgrad. U. Marburg (Germany), 1954-55; Ph.D., St. Louis U., 1961; m. Marcia Jeanne Duffy, May 30, 1959; children—Edwin George III, Mary Marcia. Lectr. math. George Washington U., 1961; asst. prof. math. St. Louis U., 1961-64, asso. prof., 1964-69, prof., 1969—, asst. to dean Grad. Sch., 1965-67, dean Grad. Sch., 1968-71, asso. acad. v.p., 1971-72, acad. v.p., 1972—, Danforth asso., 1964—. Commr., McDonnell Planetarium, St. Louis, 1972—. Served to lt. AUS, 1959-61. Mem. Am. Math. Soc., Math. Assn. Am., Mo. Acad. Sci., Sigma Xi, Phi Beta Kappa, Pi Mu Epsilon. Research in math. applications of computers. Home: 10111 Hilltop Dr St Louis MO 63128

EIGER, NORMAN NATHAN, circuit ct. judge; b. Chgo., Aug. 6, 1903; s. Isaac and Rachel (Brender) E.; J.D., DePaul U., 1924; m. Leona Wolan, Dec. 31, 1935; children—Lawrence H., Rodney I. Admitted to Ill. bar, 1924; mem. exec. staff, capital stock tax assessor Ill. Tax Commn., 1932-36; asst. to corp. counsel City of Chgo., 1936-47; chmn. Ill. Bd. Rev., Dept. of Labor, 1948-52; judge Municipal Ct., Chgo., 1952-64; judge Circuit Ct. of Cook County, Ill., Chgo., 1964—; lectr. DePaul U. Coll. Law; mem. arbitration panel Fed. Mediation and Conciliation Service. Past v.p. Coll. Jewish Studies; lectr. various groups; exec. sec. Patriotic Found., Sponsors of Washington, Morris and Solomon monuments, Chgo.; v.p. Adult Edn. Council Met. Chgo. Past chmn. lawyers div. Chgo. Combined Jewish Appeal; former co-chmn. Conciliation Commn., Chgo. Fedn. United Am. Hebrew Congregations; past v.p. Bd. Jewish Edn., now hon. life trustee. Served with USCGR, World War II. Mem. Ill., Chgo. bar assns., Am. Arbitration Assn. (arbitration panel), Decalogue Soc. Lawyers (past fin. sec.), Patriotic Found. Chgo. (exec. sec.), Ill. Judges Assn. (pres., chmn. ann. conv. 1973-77), Nu Beta Epsilon (past grand chancellor), Alpha Epsilon Pi (hon.). Jewish (hon. life trustee temple). Mem. B'nai B'rith (past v.p. Chgo. council, past pres. Jackson Park Lodge, mem. awards com. Youth Orgn.). Home: 505 N Lake Shore Dr Chicago IL 60611

EIKLEBERRY, JANE LEE, lawyer; b. Lincoln, Nebr., Sept. 23, 1951; d. Robert Woodrow and Kara Lee (Coldiron) Eikleberry; B.A., Grinnell Coll., 1973; J.D., U. Iowa, 1976. Admitted to Iowa bar, 1976. Partner firm Oleson & Eikleberry, Iowa City, 1976—. Mem. Iowa Bar Assn., Nat. Women's Polit. Caucus, Phi Delta Phi. Office: Suite 6 Paul-Helen Bldg Iowa City IA 52240

EILAU, LEMBIT, adminstrv. elec. engr.; b. Tartu, Estonia, Dec. 25, 1921; s. Peeter and Mathilde (Porgassaar) E.; B.S. in Elec. Engring., Tech. Sch. Dorpat (Estonia), 1944; M.B.A., Loyola U. Chgo., 1972; m. Luule Paid, Feb. 23, 1952; 1 dau., Ann Marie. Designer, Pioneer Service & Engring. Co., Chgo., 1951-57; group leader V.E. Alden Engrs., Chgo., 1957-59; elec. engr. R.E. Hattis Engrs., Skokie, Ill., 1959-60; head elec. div. Harza Engring Co., Chgo., 1960—, asso., 1970—. Registered profl. engr., Ill., Calif., Colo., other states. Mem. Internat. Conf. Large High Tension Electric Systems, IEEE (internat. practices subcom.). Office: Harza Engineering Co 150 S Wacker Dr Chicago IL 60606

EILBERT, JACQUELYNN JOY, state govt. ofcl.; b. Boone, Iowa, July 24, 1952; d. Raymond Ernest and Wanita Pearl (Lorenzen) E.; B.S., Iowa State U., 1974; M.S., Drake U., 1978. Research asso. Iowa Dept. Pub. Instruction, Des Moines, 1974—. Mem. Career Expo Adv. Com., 1976-77. Mem. Soc. Profl. Journalists, Am., Iowa personnel and guidance assns., Am., Iowa vocat. guidance assns., Iowa Shorthorn Lassies Assn. (pres. 1977—). Lutheran. Home: 1620 Iowanola Ave West Des Moines IA 50265 Office: Grimes State Office Bldg Des Moines IA 50319

EIMERS, HOWARD GORDON, ins. co. exec.; b. Milw., June 28, 1926; s. Edward and Hilda (Brushaber) E.; B.S. in Bus. Adminstrn. with distinction, Northwestern U., 1950; M.A. in Math., U. Mich., 1951; m. Joyce Elsie Taylor, Jan. 14, 1950; children—Dennis John, Paul Timothy, David James. Actuary, Am. Life & Accident Ins. Co. Ky., 1951-53; with Washington Nat. Ins. Co., Evanston, Ill., 1953—, actuary, 1958-62, chief actuary, 1962-63, v.p., actuary, 1963-69, sr. v.p., 1969—, actuary, 1969-71, dir., 1971—; v.p., dir. Washington Nat. Corp., Evanston, Ill., 1970—; chmn. bd. Washington Nat. Life Ins. Co. N.Y., N.Y.C., 1975—. C.L.U. Fellow Soc. Actuaries, Life Mgmt. Inst.; mem. Beta Gamma Sigma, Alpha Tau Omega. Home: 240 Avon St Northfield IL 60093 Office: 1630 Chicago Ave Evanston IL 60201

EINHORN, HILLEL JASON, educator; b. Bklyn., June 12, 1941; s. Sonny T. and Lulu (Perleman) E.; B.A., Bklyn. Coll., 1964, M.A., 1966; Ph.D., Wayne State U., 1969; m. Susan Bernice Michaels, June 16, 1966. Asst. prof. behavior scis. U. Chgo., 1969-71, asso. prof., 1973-76, prof., 1976—; vis. asst. prof. Carnegie Mellon U., Pitts., 1971-72; grantee, NIMH, 1970, Spencer Found., 1972-74; mem. bd. human resources Naval Research Adv. Com. Mem. Am. Psychol. Assn., Soc. Multivariate Exptl. Psychology, Am. Statis. Assn., Sigma Xi, Psi Chi. Contbr. articles to profl. jours. Editorial bd. Organizational Behavior and Human Performance, 1970—. Home: 5217 S University Ave Chicago IL 60615

EINHORN, JAY, cons., psychologist, educator; b. New Haven, Apr. 23, 1949; s. Martin and Jennie (Tuckman) E.; B.A., Goddard Coll., 1972; M.S., So. Conn. State Coll., 1974; m. Ann Rees Williams, Sept. 13, 1968. Staff mem. New Haven Center Human Relations, 1972-74; psychotherapist New Haven, 1972-74; staff psychotherapist Methadone Maintenance Inst., Chgo., 1974-75; instr. psychology, cons. exptl. edn. Coll. DuPage, Glen Ellyn, Ill., 1975-76; instr. psychology Columbia Coll., Chgo., 1976-77; cons. vocat. rehab. Goodwill Rehab. Center, Chgo., 1977—; instr. psychology Oakton Community Coll., Morton Grove, Ill., 1975—; lectr. in field. Mem. Assn. Advancement Human Understanding (pres. 1977—), Am. Personnel and Guidance Assn. Home: 3733 N Wilton St Chicago IL 60613 Office: AAHU Box 6641 Chicago IL 60680

EINHORN, STEPHEN EDWARD, chem. cons.; b. Bklyn., June 25, 1943; s. Benjamin and Rosalyn (Nuss) E.; B.A., Cornell U., 1964; postgrad. Wharton Sch. U. Pa., 1965-66; M. Chem. Engring., Bklyn. Poly. Tech. Inst., 1966; m. Nancy Lore, May 22, 1965; children—David, Daniel. With Adelphi Industries, Carlstadt, N.J., 1964-75, gen. v.p., 1974-75; cons. mergers and acquisitions, chem. fields, Milw., 1975. Real estate broker, Wis. Home and office: 8049 N Links Way Milwaukee WI 53217

EISEMAN, PAUL JAMES, foot care co. exec.; b. Chgo., Dec. 11, 1912; s. Albert and Helene (Hirdes) E.; student U. Ill., 1932-35; J.D., John Marshall Law Sch., 1938; m. Phyllis E. Scholl, Nov. 13, 1948; children—John, Janice. Admitted to Ill. bar, 1939; with Scholl, Inc., Chgo., 1946—, gen. counsel, 1950—, v.p., 1968—; dir. Arno Bldg. Co., Michigan City, Ind.; sec., dir. Dr. Scholl's Shoe Mfg. Co., Jefferson, Wis., 1969—; treas. Dr. Scholl's Foot Comfort Shops, Inc., Chgo., 1961—. Trustee, bd. dirs. William M. Scholl Found., 1960—. Served with AUS, 1943-46. Mem. Am., Chgo. bar assns. Clubs: Union League (Chgo.); Biltmore Country (Barrington, Ill.). Home: Rural Route 2 Bateman Circle Barrington IL 60010 Office: 213 W Schiller St Chicago IL 60610

EISENBEIS, ROLAND, conservationist; b. Ashley, N.D., Jan. 13, 1918; s. John and Mary (Herman) E.; ed. N.D. Sch. Forestry; m. Betty Broman, June 23, 1946; children—Susan, Gail, Scott, John. With U.S. Fish & Wildlife Service, 1937-39; with Forest Preserve Dist., River Forest, Ill., 1947—; cons. in outdoor and conservation edn., fish and lake mgmt., open space and park mgmt. Served with USAAF, 1941-45; CBI. Mem. Assn. Interpretive Naturalists, Friends of Native Landscape, Ill. Nature Preserves Commn. Home: 4208 Oak St Brookfield IL 60513 Office: 536 N Harlem Ave River Forest IL 60305

EISENBERG, RUSSELL ADLAND, lawyer; b. Milw., Feb. 7, 1937; s. Edward and Charlotte (Adland) E.; student U. Wis., 1957-58; LL.B., Marquette U., 1961; m. Marilyn Gecker, Sept. 6, 1959; children—Julie, Joseph, Rebecca. Admitted to Wis. bar, 1961, U.S. Supreme Ct. bar, 1969, D.C. bar, 1976; asso. firm Eisenberg & Kletzke, Milw., 1961-62, Howard & Peterman, Milw., 1962-66; partner firm Howard, Peterman & Eisenberg, Milw., 1966—. Lectr., coordinator adult edn. teaching programs Milw. Sch. Bd., 1961-66. Campaigner United Fund and Milw. Jewish Fedn.; mem. Milw. Jewish Council, 1972—; trustee Congregation Emanu-el, Milw., 1977—. Mem. Milw. Bar Assn. (chmn. bankruptcy and insolvency sect. 1972-73; co-chmn. joint bar and bench com. 1973-76), Am., Waukesha County bar assns., State Bar Wis. (chmn. bankruptcy, insolvency and creditors rights sect. 1975—), Comml. Law League Am., Internat. Assn. Jewish Lawyers and Jurists, Milw. Jr. Bar Assn. (chmn. civic affairs com. 1965-66), Phi Sigma, Sigma Delta Pi. Asso. editor Comml. Law Jour., 1971—. Contbr. articles to profl. jours. Home: 5262 N Diversey Blvd Milwaukee WI 53217 Office: 700 N Water St Milwaukee WI 53202

EISENDRATH, JOHN LOUIS, mktg. and sales co. exec.; b. Chgo., June 18, 1938; s. Joseph Louis and Gladys (Rothafell) E.; student Butler U., 1956-60, Northwestern U., 1959-60, Lake Forest Coll., 1961-62, N.Y. Inst. Photography, 1967-68; m. Linda Jane Pfaelzer, Oct. 8, 1961; children—Steven, Laura, Robert. Asst. sales promotion, advt. mgmt. Banthrico, Inc., Chgo., 1960-61, salesman, 1961-65, regional sales mgr. 1965-67, gen. sales mgr., 1967-69, v.p., 1969—; exec. v.p., dir. Signature Prime Inc., 1973-75; pres. John L. Eisendrath Assos., 1975—; free-lance photographer, 1968—. Served with USMCR. Mem. Bank Pub. Relations and Mktg. Assn., Chgo. Fin. Advertisers, Savs. Instns. Mktg. Soc. Am., Sigma Nu. Republican. Jewish. Home: 997 Ridgewood Dr Highland Park IL 60035 Office: 221 N LaSalle St Chicago IL 60601

EISENDRATH, JOSEPH LOUIS, bank spltys. mfg. co. exec.; b. Chgo., June 12, 1908; s. Joseph L. and Laura (Sloman) E.; Ph.B., U. Chgo., 1929; m. Gladys Rothafel, Apr. 9, 1936; children—John L.,

Peter E. Sec.-treas. Banthrico Inc., Chgo., 1931-55, pres., chmn. bd. dirs., 1955—; pres. Chgo. Archtl. Bronze Co., 1955-71. Mem. nat. council Boy Scouts Am., 1969—, Silver Beaver award, 1957, Silver Antelope award, 1975; dir. Highland Park (Ill.) Community Chest, 1968—; mem. Ill. Bicentennial Commn., 1974-76. Fellow Collectors Club Chgo., Royal Philatelic Soc. London; mem. Cicero Mfrs. Assn. (pres. 1976-77, dir.) Civil War Round Table (pres. 1949-51), Am. Air Mail Soc. (Conrath award 1959, pres. 1963-65), Philatelic Press Club (pres. 1972-74). Club: Northmoor Country. Author: Military Correspondence of Abraham Lincoln, 1947. Editor-in-chief Am. Air Mail Catalogue, 1968-75; editor Airpost Jour., 1955-63. Contbr. articles to profl. jours. Office: 4615 W Roosevelt Rd Chicago IL 60650

EISENHAUER, DONALD LEE, farmers coop. exec.; b. Bloomfield, Nebr., Aug. 30, 1939; s. Arthur Henry and Emma Caroline Marie (Gieselman) E.; student pub. schs., Bloomfield; m. Mary Marie Staples, Dec. 7, 1963; children—Steven, Jon, Anita, Tami, Bradley. Grocery clk. in Bloomfield, 1960-62, 64; milk route, 1962-63; farm hand, 1963; salesman Tankwagon, Farmers Coop. Elevator Co., Bloomfield, 1964-67, asst. mgr., 1967-69, gen. mgr., 1969—. Emergency med. technician Bloomfield Ambulance Squad, 1970—, squad leader, 1974—; mem. City Council, Bloomfield, 1974—, chmn. bd., 1976—; dir. Nebr. Coop. Council for 19th Legislative Dist., 1976—. Mem. U.S., Bloomfield chambers commerce, Nat. Livestock Feeders Assn., Nebr. Coop Council, Nebr. Petroleum Marketers, Inc., Nebr. Grain and Feed Dealers Assn., Nebr. Fertilizer Inst. Home: 301 S 1st St Bloomfield NE 68718 Office: Box 448 Bloomfield NE 68718

EISENMENGER, MICHAEL P., rec. studio exec.; b. Humphrey, Nebr., Sept. 3, 1910; s. Michael and Mary (Pelle) E.; grad. Omaha Bus. Inst., 1928-30; m. Ruth Milck, Dec. 21, 1975; children—Marianne, Richard, Carol (Mrs. Charles Lee), Thomas, Paula, Geri. Page, NBC, Chgo., 1933-34, announcer traffic, 1935-37, sound effects technician, 1937-51, mgr. rec. dept., producer transcriptions, 1951-56; pres. Sound Studios Inc., Chgo., 1956—; pres. sta. WGMI-TV, Gary, Ind., 1969—; mgr. Gen. Media, Chgo., 1971—. Instr., NBC-Northwestern Radio Summer Sch., 1947-48. K.C. Home: 357 Alexander St Elmhurst IL 60126 Office: Sound Studios Inc 230 N Michigan Ave Chicago IL 60601

EITEL, DEAN FRANCIS, govt. ofcl.; b. Chgo., Aug. 30, 1941; s. Cliffe Dean and Mary Elizabeth (Francis) E.; B.S., St. Louis U., 1964, postgrad., 1966-68; postgrad. U. Mo., 1964, U. Md., 1968-69, USDA Grad. Sch., 1971-72; certificate Harvard, 1967, Pa. State U., 1973, U. Ill., 1973; grad. pub. mgmt. U.S. Exec. Seminar Center, 1975; M.P.A., Roosevelt U., 1977; m. Katherine Ann Stelkovics, July 3, 1965; children—Jill, Susan, Steven, Christine. Chief comml. map sect. Rand McNally & Co., Chgo., 1964-66; research cartographer Def. Mapping Agy. Aerospace Center, St. Louis, 1966-68; research environ. scientist adv. devel. group Raytheon Co., Alexandra, Va., 1968-71; environ. specialist engr. Agy. Resources Inventories C.E. Topographic Labs., Washington, 1971-73, environ. resources planner, 1973—, acting chief environ. planning br. North Central Div. C.E., Chgo., 1974-75, chief, 1975—, asst. chief planning div., 1977—; lectr. U. Ill. at Chgo. Circle, 1974; mem. Environ. Impact Study Task Force Fed. Regional Council, Chgo., 1973—, NASA Interagy. Land Use Panel, 1972, environ. health work group Gt. Lakes Basin Commn., 1973. Mem. Am. Soc. Pub. Adminstrn. (governing council Chgo. chpt. 1977—), Am. Soc. Planning Ofcls., Am. Soc. Photogrammetry, Assn. Am. Geographers (placement com. 1968-71). Contbg. editor: Geo-Abstracts, 1970-71; mem. tech. rev. bd. Photogrammetry Engring. and Remote Sensing Jour., 1972-75. Contbr. articles to profl. jours. Home: 1732 N Wilshire Ave Arlington Heights IL 60004 Office: 536 S Clark St Chicago IL 60605

EITER, THOMAS PATRICK, moving co. exec.; b. Chgo., Aug. 4, 1945; B.S. in Accounting St. Joseph's Coll., Rensselaer, Ind., 1967; m. Linda Jo Grassi, July 17, 1971. Sr. accountant Ernst and Ernst, Chgo., 1967-70; supr. profit planning and cash control Allied Van Lines, Inc., Chgo., 1970-72, mgr. accounting, 1972-74, asst. controller, 1974-77, controller, 1977—. Mem. Am. Accounting Assn. Office: Allied Van Lines 25th St and Roosevelt Rd Broadview IL 60153

EKBERG, DAVID JEROME, computer co. exec.; b. Mpls., May 11, 1929; s. Carl E. and Ruth (Olin) E.; B. in Mech. Engring., U. Minn., 1952, B.B.A., 1952; m. Joan McCormack, Nov. 28, 1952; children—Karen, Elizabeth. Sales engr. Gen. Electric Co., Schenectady and Mpls., 1952-64; mgr. European original equipment mfg. sales Control Data, Frankfurt, Germany, 1964-66, gen. sales mgr., 1966-69; v.p. mktg. Data 100 Corp., Mpls., 1969—. Mem. Engrs. Club Mpls., Tau Beta Pi, Pi Tau Sigma, Beta Gamma Sigma. Club: Interlachan Country. Home: 6513 Navaho Trail Edina MN 55435 Office: 7725 Washington Av S Edina MN 55435

EKELOF, JOHN DEAN, ednl. adminstr.; b. Henry County, Ill., Mar. 11, 1925; s. Carl Frederick and Hazel Louella (Brown) E.; B.A., Western Ill. U., 1948, M.A., 1951; postgrad. Central Mich. U., 1969-74, Mich. State U., 1970-74; m. Betty Jean Pogue, Aug. 15, 1948; children—Nan Elise, John Dean II. Tchr., coach, Herrick, Ill., 1948; tchr., prin., Oquawka, Ill., 1949-52; prin. unit dist. 115 High Sch., Gladstone, Ill., 1952-57; tchr., coach high sch., Saginaw, Mich., 1957-61, sr. counsellor, 1962-64, asst. prin. and prin., 1965-68; prin. South Jr. High Sch., Saginaw, 1968—. Served with USMCR, 1943-45. Decorated Air Medal with 3 clusters, D.F.C. Mem. Saginaw Valley Prins. Assn. (past pres.), Saginaw Assn. Secondary Sch. Prins., Mich. Assn. Secondary Prins. (sec. 1973-74), Saginaw, Mich., Nat. assns. secondary schs. prins. Presbyn. Mason (Shriner), Kiwanian. Clubs: Pioneer, Germania, Bridgeport Country. Home: 1038 Passolt St Saginaw MI 48602 Office: 224 N Elm St Saginaw MI 48602

EKISS, JOHN PATTON, sales exec.; b. Akron, Ohio, Mar. 7, 1929; s. John Keith and Beatrice Lillian (Beldon) E.; student Baylor U., 1948-51; m. Muriel Jean Bondurant, Mar. 7, 1977; children by previous marriage—Karen, Patton, Christopher. Zone mgr., Dr Pepper Co., Dallas, 1960-64; dist. franchise mgr., Frostie Co., Camden, N.J., 1964-67, Nesbitt Food Products, Los Angeles, 1967-69; area sales mgr. Chattanooga Glass Co., 1969-76; pres. E & E Sales Co., Grandview, Mo., 1976—. Recipient Manhood award VFW, 1944. Clubs: Advt. and Sales Execs., Toastmasters. Home: 6325 E 127th St Grandview MO 64030 Office: PO Box 409 Grandview MO 64030

EKKEBUS, DANIEL ELOY, mgmt. cons.; b. Chgo., June 24, 1943; s. Eloy Daniel and Catherine Marie (Fuhrmann) E.; B.B.A., U. Notre Dame, 1965; m. Barbara Vandivier, Aug. 12, 1967. Vice pres. sales Laird, Inc., 1967-73; v.p. sales G.H. Walker, Laird, Inc., Chgo., 1973-76; v.p. Rambert & Co., Lake Bluff, Ill., 1976-77; pres. Bardan Group, Inc., Lake Bluff, 1977—. Home: 949 N Sheridan Rd Lake Forest IL 60045 Office: 42 Sherwood Terr Lake Bluff IL 60044

EKLEBERRY, LEVI NEAL, camp adminstr.; b. Sycamore, Ohio, Nov. 2, 1919; s. Orely and Bernice Leona (Shedenhelm) E.; student Northeastern U., 1968; m. Olive Gertrude Larick, May 21, 1943; children—Patricia Jo (Mrs. Gene Manson), Carol Sue (Mrs. Dale Flockerzie). Mill operator Swan Rubber Co., Carey, Ohio, 1945-47; forest ranger Mohican Forest, Perrysville, Ohio, 1947-65; camp adminstr. Wooster Forest, Perrysville, 1965—; security guard Pinkerton Security Inc., Akron, Ohio, 1973—. Served with AUS, 1942-43, USAAF, 1943-45. Recipient Conservation award Richland County, 1969; named Outstanding Ranger, Sohio mag., 1963. Mem. Am. Camping Assn., Am. Forestry Assn., Assn. Camp Adminstrs. U.S.A., Ohio State Patrol Aux., Am. Legion, Aircraft and Pilots Assn., Nat. Rifle Assn. Republican. Presbyn. (elder, commr. to synod). Rotarian (chmn. program com. 1968), Lion, Mason. Home: RFD 2 Perrysville OH 44864 Office: Wooster Outdoor Center Perrysville OH 44864

EKVALL, BERNT, dentist; b. Nora, Sweden, June 25, 1915; s. Johan Alexis and Elin Karolina (Persson) E.; L.D.S., U. Stockholm, 1944; D.D.S., U. Mich., 1951; m. Margit Andersson, June 23, 1940; 1 dau., Lucie Margita. Came to U.S., 1949, naturalized, 1954. With Swedish Govt. Dental Services, 1943-45; pvt. practice dentistry Sweden, 1945-49, Clinton, Mich., 1951-52, Dearborn, 1951-55, 57-58, Detroit, 1958—; mem. staff Alexander Blain Meml. Hosp. Vice pres. Scandinavian Am. Republican Club, 1960-68, pres., 1968-72; treas. Rep. State Nationalities Council, 1971-73; Bd. dirs. Scandinavian Symphony Soc., 1961-72; bd. mgrs. Hannan br. YMCA, 1962—, chmn. Eastside br., 1976. Served to capt. AUS, 1955-57. Fellow Royal Soc. Health; mem. Am., Mich. dental assns., Detroit Dist. Dental Soc., Detroit Dental Clinic Club (membership sec. 1972-73, sec. 1973-74, pres. 1975-76), Bunting Periodontal Study Club, Acad. Gen. Dentistry (sec. 1975-76, v.p. 1976—). Clubs: Economic (Detroit); Grosse Pointe Hunt. Home: 1063 Woodbridge E St Clair Shores MI 48080 Office: 2141 E Jefferson Ave Detroit MI 48207

ELAM, CHARLES HENRY, art historian, museum ofcl.; b. Ashland, Ky., Feb. 13, 1915; s. Charles Milton and Mabel Claire (McNeny) E.; A.B., U. Cin., 1938; A.M., N.Y. U., 1952. Archivist, Peale Mus., Balt., 1954-59; chief curator, editor bull. Dayton Art Inst., 1959-64; curator Am. art Detroit Inst. Arts, 1964-67, art mus. registrar, 1970—; editor Wayne State U. Press, Detroit, 1967-70. Served with AUS, 1941-46, 50-52. Mem. Am. Assn. Museums. Editor: Detroit Inst. Arts Bulletin, 1964-66, 70-71. Home: 25 E Palmer Ave Detroit MI 48202 Office: Detroit Inst Arts Detroit MI 48202

ELAM, WILLIAM WARD, ednl. exec.; b. Greenville, Ill., July 18, 1934; s. William Archer and Georgia Juanita (Grill) E.; B.S. in Edn., No. Ill. U., 1958, M.S. in Edn., 1959; Ph.D. in Geography (Title IV fellow 1968-71), U. Okla., 1973; m. Patsy Larene Bolender, Sept. 19, 1954; children—Cheryl, Bradley, William, Beverly. Tchr. geography Geneva (Ill.) High Sch., 1959-65; instr. social studies, asst. dir. Title III program Ill. Office Supt. Pub. Instruction, Springfield, 1965-68; exec. dir. Nat. Council for Geog. Edn., Oak Park, Ill., 1971-77; asso. editor Kendall/Hunt Pub. Co., 1977—; ednl. cons. Denoyer-Geppert Co., Chgo., 1967-73, Scott, Foresman & Co., 1977-78. Bd. dirs. Alliance for Environ. Edn., Inc., Washington, 1973—, mem. steering com., 1972-73, v.p., 1973-75, pres.-elect, 1976-77. Served with USMCR, 1954-56. Mem. Assn. Am. Geographers, Am., Ill. geog. socs., Nat. Council Social Studies, Council for State Social Studies Specialists, Sigma Xi, Gamma Theta Upsilon. Republican. Methodist. Home: 1229 Rita Ave St Charles IL 60174 Office: 322 W State St Geneva IL 60134

ELBERT, JOHN ALLAN, orthodontist; b. Rice Lake, Wis., Mar. 13, 1924; s. John Walter and Hattie (Pollatz) E.; student St. Olaf Coll., 1941-43; D.D.S., U. Marquette, 1946; postgrad. U. Minn., 1959-61; m. Mary Treat Stebbins, Aug. 10, 1946; children—John Arthur, Stephen Thomas, Bruce William, James Edward. Individual practice gen. dentistry, Rice Lake, 1948-59, practice orthodontics, 1961—. Chmn. Barron County (Wis.) Republican party, 1961-62. Served with Dental Corps, AUS, 1946-48. Mem. ADA, Wis. Dental Assn., Wis. Orthodontic Soc., Am. Assn. Orthodontists, Ducks Unltd. (chpt. chmn.), Delta Sigma Delta. Episcopalian (sr. warden 1964-65). Elk, Kiwanian. Home: 911 W Stout Rice Lake WI 54868 Office: 515 N Main St Rice Lake WI 54868

ELCHINGER, KENNETH JOSEPH, environ. engr., educator; b. Lima, Ohio, June 20, 1947; s. Paul Joseph and Alice Magdaline (Duling) E.; B.S. in Civil Engring. with high honors, Tri-State Coll., 1969; postgrad. Ohio State U., 1972; M.S. in Engring. Sci., U. Toledo, 1973. Jr. engr. Finkbeiner, Pettis & Strout, Ltd., Cons. Engrs., Toledo, 1969-70, project engr., 1971-74; self-employed constrn. industry, 1975-76; asst. prof. dept. indsl. edn. and tech. Bowling Green (Ohio) State U., 1976-78. Registered profl. engr., Ohio. Mem. Am. Water Works Assn., ASCE (asso.), Tau Sigma Eta. Home: Rural Route 1 New Bavaria OH 43548 Office: Bowling Green State Univ Bowling Green OH

ELDER, EDWARD VIRGIL, dentist; b. Heber Springs, Ark., Aug. 6, 1907; s. Isham Davis and Margaret (Orr) E.; student St. Louis U., 1925; D.D.S., Washington U., 1930; m. Loretta C. Newcomb, Feb. 22, 1939; children—Elaine, Glenn. Gen. practice dentistry, St. Louis, 1930—. Served with USNR, 1943-46. Mem. ADA, St. Louis Dental Soc., Delta Sigma Delta. Presbyn. (elder). Mason, Lion. Home: 500 Iron Lantern Dr Ballwin MO 63011 Office: 10449 St Charles Rock Rd St Ann MO 63074

ELDER, LOWELL LEVON, mech. engr.; b. Mark Center, Ohio, Feb. 8, 1926; s. Levon A. and Gladys L. (Worthington) E.; B.S. in Mech. Engring., Ohio State U., 1949; m. Margy Ann Boone, Aug. 22, 1948; children—Debbie Kay, Nancy Ann. Jr. corrosion engr., Atlantic Seaboard Corp., Elkins, W. Va., 1949-50; corrosion engr. Columbia Gas System Service Corp., Columbus, Ohio, 1950-53, asst. sr. transmission engr., 1953-55, sr. transmission engr., 1955-60, supervisory engr., 1960-65, sr. research engr., 1965-74, mgr. research adminstrn., 1974—. Served with USAAF, 1944-46; PTO. Registered profl. engr., Ohio. Mem. ASME (chmn. gas piping standards com. 1970—, mem. policy bd. for codes and standards, mem. safety codes and standards com. 1974—). Republican. Methodist. Clubs: Shriners, Masons, Sports Car of Am. Home: 2187 Glenmere Rd Columbus OH 43220 Office: 1600 Dublin Rd Columbus OH 43215

ELDERKIN, CECIL OLIVER, realtor; b. Akron, Ohio, Dec. 22, 1914; s. Harry Albert and Mildred Blanche (Hupp) E.; student evenings Akron U.; m. Kay Elizabeth McGee, June 5, 1942; 1 dau., Susan L. With various dept. stores, Akron, 1934-46; salesman Stanson & Stroup Realty, Akron, 1946-48; pres., founder Security Realty Co., Akron, 1948-51; founder, pres., owner C.O. Elderkin Realty, Cuyahoga Falls, Ohio, 1951—. Comml. solicator St. Thomas Hosp. bldg. drive, Akron, 1963, Akron Hosp., 1965. Bd. dirs. Summit County Mental Health Clinic, 1966-72; trustee Cuyahoga Falls Music Assn.; trustee Fallsview State Mental Hosp., 1973—, pres., 1975—; v.p. Cuyahoga Falls Civic Music Assn., 1977—. Served with AUS, 1942-45. Named Outstanding Service Man of Year, Council Inter-Service Clubs, Cuyahoga Falls, 1966. Mem. Cuyahoga Falls, Ohio, Nat. real estate bds. Kiwanian (Mr. Kiwanian 1962; pres. 1966), Mason (Shriner, Jester, 32 deg.), Methodist. Club: Silver Lake Country. Address: 2871 Marcia Blvd Cuyahoga Falls OH 44223

ELDREDGE, W. THEODORE, broadcasting exec.; b. Hyannis, Mass., Dec. 31, 1936; s. Walter Joseph and Elizabeth (Blackman) E.; B.S. cum laude, Lincoln (Mo.) U., 1971; M.A., U. Mo., 1972; m. Mary Gail Spinner, May 6, 1966. With Sta. WHB and KUDL, Kansas City, Mo., 1962-65, program dir. Sta. KWOS, Jefferson City, Mo., 1965-70; gen. mgr. Sta. KBIA-FM, U. Mo., Columbia, 1972—, instr. speech, 1974—. Active Central Mo. Humane Soc. Served with U.S. Army, 1961-64. Mem. Mo. Pub. Radio Assn. (pres.), Pub. Radio in Mid-Am. (v.p.), Assn. of Pub. Radio Stas. (past dir.), Nat. Assn. of Ednl. Broadcasters, Mo. Broadcasters Assn., Nat. Assn. of Broadcasters. Episcopalian. Home: Route 5 Columbia MO 65201 Office: 409 Jesse Hall Columbia MO 65201

ELDRIDGE, CARLTON BRADY, educator; b. Auburn, Ind., Apr. 4, 1911; s. Jenkson and Elizabeth E. (Yorty) E.; B.Mus. with high honors, Mich. State U., 1934, M.Mus. with distinction, 1949; postgrad. Eastern Mich. U., 1934, State U. Iowa, 1959-60; m. Blythe Axford, June 23, 1943; children—Daniel, Bonnie Blythe Eldridge Biagioli, David Carlton. Concert, oratorio, radio tenor engagements, 1934-70, including Messiah, Orch. Hall, Chgo., 1953, Western Ont. (Can.) U., London, 1948, 49, So. Oreg. U., 1963, Wis. State U., Eau Claire, 1968; head voice dept., choir dir., opera coach, musicologist Springfield Coll. in Ill., 1949—. Choirmaster, St. Mary's Cathedral, Lansing, Mich., 1940-49; adj. instr. voice Mich. State U., East Lansing, 1945-49; choir dir. Ursuline Acad., Springfield, 1950-73; lectr. music, 1967—; adj. asso. prof. music Sangamon State U., Springfield, 1973—; lectr. role of blind in teaching profession, 1972, 74. Chmn., Boy Scouts Am., Springfield, 1959-62. Bd. dirs. Rees Carillon Soc., Springfield, 1962-72, Te Deum Internat. Forum, 1967-70. Mem. Mich. Fedn. Music Clubs, Am. Guild Organists, Nat. Assn. Tchrs. Singing, Ill. (v.p. 1971-73), Nat. assns. blind tchrs., Nat. Cath., Ill. Jr. Coll. music educators assns., Springfield Coll. Music Guild, Phi Kappa Phi, Phi Mu Alpha. Author published works. Home: 422 W Canedy St Springfield IL 62704

ELDRIDGE, MABEL ELIZABETH, educator; b. Franklin, Ohio, Feb. 7, 1900; d. William Bevan and Winifred (Earhart) E.; B.E., Miami U., Oxford, Ohio, 1922, postgrad., 1944-45, 54, 56, 59; M.Ed., U. Cin., 1943; student McGill U., Montreal, Can., 1926, U. Chgo., 1930, U. Sorbonne, Paris, 1950. Tchr. English and French, Lemon Twp. High Sch., Monroe, Ohio, 1922-23, Middletown (Ohio) High Sch., 1923-55, dean of girls, 1930-62; tchr. creative writing and world lit. Miami U., Middletown (Ohio) Br., 1955-62, lectr. English, tchr. children's lit., 1967-72, staff Internat. Children's Lit. Workshop, European Study Center, Luxembourg, 1974; dealer in out-of-print books Hillside Book Cellar, Franklin, 1975-76; instr. English, Middletown Bus. Coll., Franklin, 1977—; lectr. childrens lit. and local history. Mem. adv. bd. Y-Teens, Middletown, 1930-62; bd. dirs. Middletown Civic Assn., 1936-39, Middletown Girls' Club, 1936-62, Ohio Dist. YWCA, 1941-47; trustee Franklin Pub. Library, 1967-71, v.p., 1970-71; resource cons. in local history Franklin Community Resources Workshop, 1971. Recipient Bishop medal for Meritorious Pub. Service, Miami U., 1955; certificate of appreciation Middletown Sch. Bd., 1962; named Woman of Year, Middletown Bus. and Profl. Women's Club, 1969; many others. Mem. Franklin Area Hist. Soc. (pres. 1974-75), Ohio Assn. Women Deans, Adminstr. and Counselors, Nat., Ohio, Ret. tchrs. assns., Nat. Writers Club, Delta Kappa Gamma, Kappa Delta Pi. Republican. Baptist. Clubs: Ten O'Clock Scholrs, O.M.T. Contbr. articles and book revs. to jours. and newspapers. Home: 215 E 2d St Franklin OH 45004

ELDRIDGE, VERA HAWORTH (MRS. WILLIAM EGBERT ELDRIDGE), journalist; b. Kansas City, Mo., Mar. 25, 1910; d. Vincent Edgar and Grace Stuart (Taylor) Haworth; student pub. schs.; m. William Egbert Eldridge, June 6, 1931; children—Richard Haworth, Margaret Ann Eldridge Fields. Editor, Modern Boxoffice Mag., Asso. Publs., Inc., Kansas City, Mo., 1969-70; indsl. editor Nat. Bellas Hess News, 1962-67; editor McCleary Hosp., Excelsior Springs, Mo., 1967-69; Clay County editor Discover North issue of Suburban Views, 1973—; dir. pub. relations Liberty Hosp., 1973-74. Mem. Landmark Commn., Bicentennial Commn. Bd. dirs., treas. Liberty Park and Recreation, 1950-64; treas. Girl Scouts U.S.A., 1961-65, camping chmn., 1957-61; scenario chmn. Clay County Sesquicentennial, 1972. Mem. Nat., Mo. (contest winner), press women, Nat. Pen Women, D.A.R. (vice regent 1958-60), Mo. Clay County (tour chmn. 1973), Antioch Ch., Smithville, Excelsior Springs, Platte County hist. socs., Friends of Library of Mo., Clay County Mus. Assn. Author: (with W.E. Eldridge) The Golden Anniversary of North Kansas City, 1962; 100 Years of the National Commercial Bank of Liberty, 1967; Index of the Original Land Grants of Clay County—1818-1874, 1967. Home: 832 Hillside Ave Liberty MO 64068

ELDRIDGE, WILLIAM EGBERT, county ofcl.; b. Gainesville, Tex., Nov. 28, 1902; s. John Egbert and Irene (Brady) E.; student U. Tex., 1923-25, Tex. Technol. Coll., 1925-26; m. Vera Marie Haworth, June 6, 1931; children—Richard Haworth, Margaret Ann. Accountant Chevrolet Motor Co., Kansas City, Mo., 1928-31, accountant, purchasing agt. McClure-Norrington Chevrolet, Kansas City, 1931-35; auditor, property accountant Cook Paint & Varnish Co., North Kansas City, Mo., 1935-67; financial adviser McCleary Meml. Hosp., Excelsior Springs, Mo., 1967-69; office mgr. Woodstock-Hoefer Wholesale Jewelry Co., Kansas City, Mo., 1969-70; recorder of deeds Clay County (Mo.), Liberty, 1970—. Hist. cons. Clay County, Mo., 1960—; writer, lectr. Clay County and Mo. history, 1960—. Chmn. com. to establish state park Watkin's Mill, N.E. Clay County, 1964; from scoutmaster to dist. explorer Boy Scouts Am., commr. Clay and Platte Counties, 1957-64. Recipient Order of Merit Kansas City council Boy Scouts Am., 1959, Baden-Powell's Wood badge Philmont Scout Ranch, 1959. Mem. Clay County Mus. Assn. (founding pres. 1961, historian, dir.), Mo., Platte County, Antioch Ch. (dir.), Smithville (hist. adviser) hist. socs., Westerners, Friends of Library U. Mo. Democrat. Methodist. Contbr. numerous hist. articles to newspapers, mags. Home: 832 Hillside Ave Liberty MO 64068 Office: Court House Liberty MO 64068

ELEMA, ORVILLE JAMES, photographer; b. Muskegon, Mich., June 3, 1940; s. Jacob and Jennie (Hopma) E.; student Muskegon Bus. Coll., 1958-60, Winona Sch. Photography, 1966, 67; m. Nelly Katherina Sonnega, Aug. 31, 1962; children—Jon, Eric, Kristin. Pres., Paris Studios, Inc., Muskegon, Profl. Color Service; work represented in permanent loan collection Profl. Photographers Am. Bd. dirs. Youth for Christ. Certified profl. photographer, Mich. Mem. Profl. Photographers Am., Profl. Photographers Mich. (pres.), Profl. Photographers Muskegon. Club: American Business. Home: 1522 W Summit St Muskegon MI 49441 Office: 137 E Laketon Ave Muskegon MI 49442

ELEY, LYNN W., educator; b. Zearing, Iowa, Oct. 23, 1925; s. Wilbur Charles and Myrtle (Wolford) E.; B.A., Harvard, 1949; M.A., U. Ia., 1951, Ph.D., 1952; m. Elizabeth Sherwood Hill, Aug. 25, 1950 (div. 1970); children—Thomas Wendell, David Matthew, Mary Sherwood; m. 2d, Janet Burdy, Aug. 26, 1971; children—Benjamin Charles, Margaret Burdy. Orgn. and methods analyst U.S. Dept. Agr., Washington, 1952-55; research asso., supr. Lansing Office, Inst. Pub. Adminstrn., 1955-58; asso. dir. Extension Service, asso. prof. polit. sci. U. Mich., 1959-64, dir. Peace Corps Tng. Project, 1964; dean Sch. Continuing Edn. and Summer Sch., asso. prof. polit. sci. Washington U., St. Louis, 1964-68; asst. chancellor U. Wis., Milw., 1968-72; prof. polit. sci. dept. govtl. affairs U. Wis. Extension, also sr. research asso. Milw. Urban Obs., 1972—; editorial asst. Com. on Appropriations, U.S. Ho. of Reps., 1953; instr. U.S. Dept. Agr. Grad. Sch., 1954-55.

Sec. Gov.'s Adv. Com. on Reorgn. State Govt. Mich., 1958-62; mem. Mich. YMCA adv. com., 1958-64; mem. Mo. Community Services Adv. Council, 1966-68; mem. planning com. Midwest Fulbright Conf. Higher Edn., 1968-70. City councilman, Ann Arbor, Mich., 1961-63. Served with USNR, 1944-46. Ellis L. Phillips Found. Postdoctoral Internship in Academic Adminstrn., 1963-64. Mem. Am. Soc. Pub. Adminstrn., Am. Assn. for Higher Edn., Nat. Univ. Extension Assn. Democrat. Author: The Executive Reorganization Plan: A Survey of State Experience, 1967; The Regionalization of Business Services in the Agricultural Research Service, 1967; Local Ombudsmen in America, 1973; An Ombudsman for Milwaukee?, 1974; (with others) Representation of the Poor in Milwaukee's War on Poverty, 1977. Sr. editor: The Politics of Fair-Housing Legislation: State and Local Case Studies, 1968. Mem. bd. adv. editors Transaction Mag., 1964-68; mem. editorial bd. Pub. Adminstrn. Rev., 1969-72. Home: 11417 N Spring Ave Mequon WI 53092 Office: Dept of Govtl Affairs U Wis-Milw Milwaukee WI 53201

ELFERS, LAWRENCE ANTHONY, environmental research co. exec.; b. Cin., Dec. 1, 1938; s. Lawrence Herman and Eleanor Louise (Contant) E.; B.S., Xavier U., 1963; m. Melanie Esther Minnich, Jan. 21, 1961; 1 dau., Melanie Mary. Research chemist, div. radiol. health USPHS, Cin., 1961-64; supr. lab. Nat. Air Pollution Control Adminstrn., Cin., 1964-69; sr. chemist Resources Research, Inc., cons. environmental engrs., Cin., 1968-69; dir. field and lab. activities Pedco Environ. Inc., Cin., 1969—, treas., 1969—. Mem. adv. com. for diversified health tng. program Princeton Sch. Dist., Cin., 1973-74; dist. chmn. Xavier U. Living Endowment Fund drive, 1971-72. Recipient Superior Performance award USPHS, 1964. Mem. Air Pollution Control Assn., Am. Chem. Soc., Am. Inst. Chemists. K.C. Club: Cintac. Home: 7200 Woodland Circle West Chester OH 45069 Office: Chester Towers Chester Rd Cincinnati OH 45246

ELIA, ANTHONY STEPHEN, real estate co. exec.; b. Lebanon, Pa., Sept. 21, 1945; s. Charles Joseph and Mary Irene (Gardner) E.; B.S., Franklin U., i970; m. Joyce Ann Rappich, Apr. 17, 1971. With Nationwide Devel. Corp., Columbus, Ohio, 1970-72, property mgr., 1971-72; gen. mgr., promotion dir. Westland Mall, Columbus, 1972-75; regional mgr. N.E. Iowa group Gen. Growth Mgmt. Corp., Des Moines, 1975-76; Midwest regional mgr. Crossroads Center, Inc., Scottsdale, Ariz., 1976-77; asst. dir. constrn. and devel. John W. Galbreath & Co., Columbus, Ohio, 1977—. Served with AUS, 1967-68. Recipient pub. relations, community service awards Big Bros. Club, U.S. Army, Navy, Marine Corp recruiting, Sports Car Concourse, Secret Santa. Mem. Internat. Council Shopping Centers, Waterloo (Iowa) C. of C., Council Bus. Devel., Council State Legislature. Home: 5595 Woodridge Dr Columbus OH 43213 Office: 180 E Broad St Columbus OH 43215

ELICAÑO, RENE VENZON, mgmt. cons. and exec. search co. exec.; b. Manila, Philippines, Jan. 16, 1938; s. Tranquilino E. and Quintina E. (Venzon) E.; B.A., Ateneo U., 1956; M.S. in Indsl. Engring., Stanford, 1957; M.B.A., Marquette U., 1959; Ph.D. in Bus. Adminstrn., Mich. State U., 1967; m. Anita Hansen, May 10, 1969. Came to U.S., 1956, naturalized, 1969. Head operations research Allis-Chalmers Mfg. Co., Milw., 1957-62; mgr. Prodn. Control div. and dir. mgmt. systems. Lear Siegler, Inc., Grand Rapids, Mich., 1962-69; dir. corporate planning and systems Kaiser Jeep Corp., Toledo, 1969-70; owner, pres., dir. Sanford Rose Assos., Toledo, 1970—. Named Outstanding Young Man of Philippines, Jr. C. of C., 1960. Mem. Am. Inst. Indsl. Engrs. (dir. 1956—), Operations Research Soc. Am., Toledo C. of C. Contbr. articles to profl. and trade jours. Home: 5204-C Regency Dr Toledo OH 43615 Office: 420 Madison Ave Suite 721 Toledo OH 43604

ELIEFF, LEWIS STEVEN, stockbroker; b. Sofia, Bulgaria, Aug. 2, 1929; s. Steven and Vera (Svetcoff) E.; B.B.A., U. Mich., 1953, M.B.A., 1954; m. Evanka Brown, May 25, 1958; children—Nancy Ann, Robert and Richard (twins). Statistician, tax accountant Gen. Motors Corp., Flint, Mich., 1954-60; stockbroker William C. Roney & Co., Flint, 1960-73, ltd. partner, 1973—. Tchr. stock market curriculum Flint Pub. Schs., 1960-68, Genesee County Community Coll., 1968-73. Mem. Grand Blanc Twp. Econ. Devel. Commn.; mem. regents-alumni scholarship com. U. Mich., 1977—. Served with AUS, 1954-56. Mem. U. Mich. Alumni Club and Assn. Club: University (Flint). Home: 6612 Kings Pointe Grand Blanc MI 48439 Office: 523 Harrison St Flint MI 48502

ELIJAH, RICHARD ALLEN, agrl. co. exec.; b. Cedar Rapids, Iowa, July 30, 1930; s. David Earl and Martha Murl (Greer) E.; student Iowa State U., 1948-50; m. Norma Phyllis Nelson, Aug. 27, 1950; children—Rebecca Ellen (Mrs. Greg Caldwell), Richard Lee, David Nelson. Farmer, Clarence, Iowa; pres. Elijah Farms, Inc., 1970—; pres., founder Acricpro Inc., Ames, Ia., 1973—; dir. Clarence Savs. Bank. Chmn., Iowa Soybean Promotion Bd., 1972-74. Mem. Clarence Consol. Sch. Dist., 1966-72, pres., 1968-72. Recipient Farm Efficiency award Ford Found., 1968. Mem. Iowa Soybean Assn. (pres. 1971-72, chmn. market devel. found.). Republican. Methodist (trustee). Rotarian, Mason (Shriner). Address: Clarence IA 52216

ELIOT, MARVIN (SONNY), actor, writer; b. Detroit, Dec. 5, 1926; s. Jacob and Jennie (Schlossberg) E.; B.A., Wayne State U., 1959, M.A., 1960; m. Annette Gaertner, May 19, 1962. Performer, program host, weatherman stas. WWJ and WWJ-TV, Detroit, 1950—; commr. Detroit Aviation Commn.; pub. relations dir. WWJ-TV, AM, FM; now v.p. Lindell Aviation Co.; columnist Detroit News, 1967—; part owner restaurant Sonny's Weather Station. Served with USAAF, 1942-47; ETO. Decorated D.F.C., Purple Heart; recipient award Nat. Assn. TV Program Execs., Nat. Safety award, Mich. Sch. Bell award, News Media award Midwestern Aviation Conf. Mem. Am. Meteorol. Soc., A.F.T.R.A., Screen Actors Guild, Actors' Equity, Adcraft Club Mich. (bd. dirs.), Sigma Delta Chi. Author: Eliot's Ark, 1972. Home: 1417 Nicolet St Detroit MI 48207 Office: WWJ-TV 622 W Lafayette St Detroit MI 48231

ELIOT, ROBERT SALIM, cardiologist; b. Oak Park, Ill., Mar. 8, 1929; s. Salim and Ruth (Buffington) Elia; B.S., U. N.Mex., 1952; M.D., U. Colo., 1955; m. Phyllis Allman, June 15, 1957; children—William Robert, Susan Elaine. Intern, Evanston Hosp., 1955-56; resident in medicine U. Colo., 1956-58, fellow in cardiology, 1958-60; trainee cardiovascular pathology U. Minn., Charles T. Miller Hosp., St. Paul-Mpls., 1962-63; practice medicine specializing in cardiology; instr. U. Minn., 1963-65, asst. prof., 1965-67; mem. faculty U. Fla., Gainesville, 1967-72, prof. medicine, 1969-72; chief div. cardiology VA Hosp., Gainesville, Fla., 1970-72; prof. medicine, dir. div. cardiology, dir. cardiovascular center U. Nebr., Omaha, 1972—, Monsour Med. Found. prof. cardiovascular medicine, 1977—; cons. Clearinghouse for Smoking & Heart Disease NIH, 1969—; cardiology cons. Cape Kennedy, 1971—, Medicall, 1972; tchr., lectr. Nebr. Outreach program. Pres. Alachua County Heart div. 1969-70, Internat. Stress Found., 1977—. Served to capt. AUS, 1960-62. USPHS, VA, Fla. Heart Assn. grantee. Fellow A.C.P., Clin. Council Am. Heart Assn., Am. Coll. Cardiology (continuing edn. com. mountain states coordinator for continuing edn., long range planning com., exec. com., gov. for Nebr., vice chmn. bd. govs., 1976-77, chmn. bd. govs., 1977-78, chmn. liaison com. Am. Coll. Cardiology-Am. Acad. Family Physicians), N.Y. Acad. Scis.; mem. AMA, Nebr. Med. Assn., Central Soc. Clin. Investigation, Biophy. Soc., Alpha Omega Alpha, Phi Sigma, Phi Rho Sigma. Contbr. numerous articles to profl. jours.; editor: The Acute Cardiac Emergency, Stress and the Heart, Practical Mmgt. of Hypertension, Cardiac Emergencies; mem. editorial bd. Heart & Lung, 1972—; creator edn. TV series Heartline to Health. Home: 1006 Martin Dr W Bellevue NE 68005 Office: Univ Nebr Med Center 42d and Dewey Sts Omaha NE 68105

ELISEO, THOMAS STEPHAN, psychologist; b. Bklyn., Apr. 9, 1932; s. Frank and Leonarda (Caruso) E.; B.A., Queens Coll., 1953; M.S., Purdue U., 1959, Ph.D., 1960; m. 2d, Marcia A. Donaldson, Aug. 28, 1976. Clin psychologist VA Hosp., Lebanon, Pa., 1960-63, Psychiat. Services, Knoxville, Tenn., 1963-64; pvt. practice clin. psychology, Rockford, Ill., 1964—; lectr. Rockford Coll., 1965-71; cons. Swedish Am. Hosp., Rockford, 1965—. Served with AUS, 1953-55. Diplomate Am. Bd. Profl. Psychology. Mem. Am. Psychol. Assn., AAAS, Soc. Clin. and Exptl. Hypnosis. Democrat. Roman Catholic. Contbr. articles to profl. jours. Office: 1335 Charles St Rockford IL 61108

ELKINS, JAMES PAUL, physician; b. Lincoln, Nebr., Mar. 20, 1924; s. James Hill and Antonia (Wohler) E.; M.D., U. Va., 1947; m. May Hollingsworth Reynolds, June 15, 1946; children—Patricia May, Paulette Frances, James Barrington. Intern DePaul Hosp., Norfolk, Va., 1947-48; resident in obstetrics and gynecology Alexandria (Va.) Hosp., 1948-49, Franklin Sq. Hosp., Balt., 1949-50, St. Rita's Hosp., Lima, Ohio, 1950, Tripler Army Hosp., Honolulu, 1953-54; practice medicine specializing in obstetrics and gynecology, Indpls., 1954-73; chief obstetrics and gynecology St. Francis Hosp., Beech Grove, Ind., 1965-66; mem. teaching staff Gen. Hosp., Indpls., 1954-73. Dep. coroner Marion County, 1965-74; med. cons. disability determination div. Ind. Rehab. Services; med. dir. Phys. Exams. Inc. Served with AUS, 1949-54. Mem. Am. Coll. Obstetrics and Gynecology, A.M.A., Ind. Obstet. and Gynecol. Soc., Ind. State Med. Assn., Marion County Med. Soc., Indpls. Press Club, Police League Ind., Fraternal Order Police, Nat. Sojourners, 500 Festival Assos., U.S. Auto Club (life), Phi Chi. Mason (Shriner). Home: 2045 Lick Creek Dr Indianapolis IN 46203 Office: 801 Illinois Bldg Indianapolis IN 46204

ELLENS, JAY HAROLD, theologian, educator; b. McBain, Mich., July 16, 1932; s. John S. and Grace (Kortmann) E.; A.B., Calvin Coll., 1953, B.D., Calvin Sem., 1956; Th.M., Princeton Sem., 1965; Ph.D., Wayne State U., 1970; m. Mary Jo Lewis, Sept. 7, 1954; children—Debra, Jackie, Dan, Beckie, Rocky, Brenda. Ordained to ministry, Christian Reformed Ch., 1956; pastor Newton (N.J.) Christian Reformed Ch., 1961-65; pastor North Hills Ch., Troy, Mich., 1965-67; pastor Univ. Hills Ch., Farmington Hills, Mich., 1967-77; prof. communication psychology Calvin Sem., 1967-70, Oakland Community Coll., 1970-74, Oakland U., 1974—; pvt. practice psychotherapy, Farmington Hills, Mich., 1967—; religious broadcaster TV, weekly, 1970-74, and periodically to date; lectr. humanities classics Wayne State U., John Wesley Coll., 1970—; vis. fellow Princeton U., 1978—. Served to col. AUS, 1956-61. Created knight by Queen Juliana, 1974. Mem. Christian Assn. Psychol. Studies (exec. sec. 1974—), AAUP, Am. Psychol. Assn., Soc. Bibl. Lit. and Exegesis, Speech Communication Assn., Mil. Chaplain Assn., Reserve Officers Assn., Archaeol. Inst. Am., Am. Personnel and Guidance Assn., Mil. Order World Wars, Am. Sci. Assn., World Assn. Christian Communicators. Republican. Mem. Christian Reformed Ch. Author: History of TV Format Development, 1970; Models of Religious Broadcasting, 1974; (with M.G. Gerhardt and W. Hyatt) An Oral History, 1977. Editor: Ethical Reflections, 1977. Home: 27000 Farmington St Farmington Hills MI 48018

ELLENSON, GERALD MARTIN, psychiat. social worker; b. Monticello, Minn., Jan. 13, 1918; s. Sever Edward and Gladys (Hoblit) E.; B.A., Hamline U., 1946; M.S.W., U. Minn., 1959; m. Phyllis Harriet Storch, Sept. 5, 1958; children—(by previous marriage)—Gerald Seward, Steven Martin, Gordon Eugene; stepchildren—Karen Cecilia (Mrs. John Thomas), James Richard, Linda Louise. With Koochiching County Welfare Dept., International Falls, Minn., 1946-49; field rep. Minn. Dept. Pub. Welfare, 1949-55, caseworker, 1959-60; dir. Cass County Welfare Dept., Walker, Minn., 1955-57; clin. social worker psychiatry Hennepin County Gen. Hosp., Mpls., 1960-63; clin. social worker Hennepin County Mental Health Center, Day Hosp., Mpls., 1963-67, sr. psychiat. social worker, 1967-69, acting dir., 1968, dir., 1969-70, prin. psychiat. social worker, 1969-70; pvt. practice marriage and family counseling, Mpls., 1963—; clin. field instr. U. Minn. Grad. Sch. Social Work, 1964—; pvt. practice Met. Psychiat. Clinic, 1970-71; cons. Met. Mental Health Center, 1970-71; sr. psychiat. social worker Crisis Intervention Center, Hennepin County Med. Center, 1971—. Served with USAAF, 1943-45. Decorated Air medal with five oak leaf clusters. Mem. Nat. Assn. Social Workers (chpt. chmn. mental health council 1966). Acad. Certified Social Workers, Minn. Welfare Assn. Methodist. Home: 3410 Pleasant Ave S Minneapolis MN 55408 Office: Hennepin County Med Center 7th St and Park Ave Minneapolis MN 55404

ELLENSON, PHYLLIS STORCH (MRS. GERALD M. ELLENSON), realtor; b. Willmar, Minn., Sept. 21, 1920; d. Harry Phillip and Jessie Mae (De Camp) Storch; student Hamline U., 1938-39, St. Cloud Tchrs. Coll., 1939-40; grad. Grad. Realtors Inst., 1971; m. Gerald Martin Ellenson, Sept. 5, 1958; children—Karen (Mrs. John Thomas), James Stiebinger, Linda Stiebinger. Saleswoman, Janney, Semple Hill Co., Mpls., 1944-58; agt. Barton Realty Co., Mpls., 1963-67, div. mgr., 1967—, v.p., 1970—. Mem. Nat. Assn. Real Estate Bds. (v.p. women's council 1971-72), Greater Mpls. Area Bd. Realtors (v.p. 1978). Home: 3410 Pleasant Ave S Minneapolis MN 55408 Office: 5516 Lyndale Ave Minneapolis MN 55419

ELLERY, JOHN BLAISE, educator, author; b. N.Y.C., Feb. 3, 1920; s. William Hoyt and Thea (Kavanagh) E.; A.B., Hamilton Coll., 1948; M.A., U. Colo., 1950; Ph.D., U. Wis., 1954; m. Ellen Jane Savacool, Sept. 21, 1946; children—Thea Jane, Martha Ann, Sarah S., John Blaise, Jessica Joyce. Instr., U. Colo., 1948-50; asst. prof. U. Iowa, 1952-56; asso. prof. Wayne State U., 1957-61; prof., chmn. dept. English, East Tenn. State U., Johnson City, 1961-66; on leave, sr. lectr. Njala U. Coll., West Africa, 1966-68; asst. to chancellor U. Wis.-Stevens Point, 1968-74, vice chancellor, 1974—, dean Coll. Natural Resources, 1970-72. Mem. Wis. Gov.'s Commn. on Edn., 1969; pres. Central Wis.-Managua com. Partners of Ams., 1976—. Served to ensign USNR, 1937-41; with inf. AUS, 1941-45. Decorated Conspicuous Service Cross, Silver Star, Bronze Star with oak leaf cluster, Purple Heart with oak leaf cluster (U.S.); Croix de Guerre, Medaille Militaire Fourragere. Mem. Ret. Officers Assn., U.S. Naval Inst., Sigma Phi Epsilon, Sigma Tau Delta, Eta Sigma Phi, Delta Sigma Rho, Alpha Psi Omega. Contbr. author: Introduction to Graduate Study in Speech and Drama, 1961; Essays on Language and Literature, 1969; author: John Stuart Mill, 1964; Linguistic Impedance and Dialect Interference Among Certain African Tribes, 1970, also short stories, articles, poems. Home: 4217 Janick Circle N Stevens Point WI 54481

ELLIOT, WILLARD SOMERS, musician; b. Ft. Worth, July 18, 1926; s. Chester Somers and Grace Roberta (Bruyere) E.; Mus.B., North Tex. State Coll., 1945; Mus.M., Eastman Sch. of Music, 1946; m. Patricia Joan Bills, July 19, 1976. Bassoonist, Houston Symphony Orch., 1946-49, Dallas Symphony Orch., 1951-56, solo bassoonist, 1956-64; solo bassoonist Chgo. Symphony Orch., 1964—; lectr. Northwestern U.; instr. De Paul U.; composer. Served with AUS, 1953-55. Co-winner Koussevitzky Found. award for Elegy for Orch., 1960; recipient 1st prize Nat. Fedn. Music Clubs Contest for Composition, 1947. Home: 9538 Central Park Evanston IL 60203 Office: care Chgo Symphony 220 S Michigan Ave Chicago IL 60604

ELLIOTT, AGNES BARBERRY (MRS. DONALD B. ELLIOTT), librarian; b. Beardsley, Kans.; d. John Stanley and Mary Rose (Chleborad) Skolout; A.B., U. Kans., 1939; M.S., Kan. State Tchrs. Coll., 1961; m. Donald B. Elliott, May 31, 1959. With Boeing Co. Library, Wichita, Kans., 1959-61; sch. librarian Wichita Bd. Edn., 1961—, Horace Mann Sch., 1964—, adviser sch. newspaper. Rose judge, cons. rosarian central dist. Am. Rose Soc., 1965—. Mem. Wichita Rose Soc. (pres. 1967-68), A.L.A., N.E.A., Kans. Assn. Sch. Librarians, Kans. Tchrs. Assn. Club: Wichita Library (pres. 1962). Editor: Alpha Gamma Delta Alumnae News, 1965. Contbr. articles to various publs. Home: 623 N Hampton Rd Wichita KS 67206 Office: 1243 N Market Wichita KS 67214

ELLIOTT, CATHERINE PAULINE, sch. guidance counselor; b. Chgo., Sept. 29, 1950; d. Joseph Marion and Adeline Pauline (Kutz) Swiderski; B.S. in Secondary Edn. and Math., DePaul U., 1972, M.Ed. in Guidance and Counseling, 1976; m. William Paul Elliott, July 23, 1977. Math. tchr. St. Pascal Sch., Chgo., 1972-75; guidance counselor Resurrection High Sch., Chgo., 1975—. Recipient St. Catherine of Alexandria medal for service to DePaul U. and community, 1971; Outstanding Leadership award DePaul U. chpt. Blue Key, 1972. Mem. Nat., Ill. councils of tchrs. of math., Nat. Vocat. Guidance Assn., Am. Personnel and Guidance Assn. Roman Catholic. Author: Counselor Self-Evaluation Criterion. Home: 4908 N Harlem Ave Harwood Heights IL 60656 Office: 7500 W Talcott Ave Chicago IL 60630

ELLIOTT, DONALD BRUCE, elec. engr.; b. Wakeeney, Kans., June 17, 1928; s. William Hugh and Dorthea (Humfeldt) E.; B.S. in Elec. Engring., U. Kans., 1957; m. Agnes Barberry Skolout, May 30, 1959. Engring. publs. writer, editor Boeing Co., Wichita, Kans., 1957—, field service rep., 1960—. Chmn. publicity com. Regional Sci. Fair, Wichita, 1965—. Served with USAF, 1950-54. Mem. I.E.E.E., Nat. Soc. Profl. Engrs., Kans. Engring. Soc. (chmn. publs. com. 1965—, state dir. 1975-77), Wichita Profl. Engring Soc. (past pres.). Home: 623 N Hampton Road Wichita KS 67206 Office: Boeing Co Wichita KS 67210

ELLIOTT, GEORGE HORTON, lawyer; b. Middletown, Ohio, Aug. 21, 1926; s. Clifford Withrow and Anne (Horton) E.; student Miami U., Oxford, Ohio, 1947-48; J.D., U. Cin., 1950; m. Betty Louise Ford, May 2, 1953; children—Elizabeth Anne, Claudia Jean, John Carleton. Admitted to Ohio bar, 1950, U.S. Supreme Ct., 1964; practiced in Middletown, 1950—; partner firm Elliott & Boyd, 1966—; dir. Radio Sta. WPFB, Middletown, Radio Sta. WPAY, Portsmouth, Ohio. Del. Democratic Nat. Conv., 1952. Served to 1st lt. AUS, 1944-46; PTO. Mem. Ohio State, Butler County, Middletown (pres. 1958) bar assns., Am. Soc. Hosp. Attys., Lawyer-Pilots Bar Assn., Order of Quiet Birdmen, Aircraft Owners and Pilots Assn., Nat. Pilots Assn., Am. Legion, Theta Chi, Phi Alpha Delta. Club: Aviation (Middletown). Home: 500 Ken Ridge Dr Middletown OH 45042 Office: 1601 1st Ave Middletown OH 45042

ELLIOTT, JAMES WADE, dentist; b. Eldon, Mo., Sept. 5, 1939; s. Roy Wesley and Thelma Lee (Williams) E.; student Jefferson City Jr. Coll., 1957-58, Lincoln U., 1958-60; B.S., U. Mo., Columbia, 1961, D.D.S., Kansas City, 1966; m. Judith Ann Eads, Aug. 15, 1964; children—Susan Cortney, David James. Pvt. practice dentistry, Columbia, 1968—. Bd. dirs. Boone County Cancer Soc. Served to capt., AUS, 1966-68. Mem. ADA, Columbia (pres. 1971), Central Mo. (pres. 1976), Mo. (pres. elect 1976, sec.-treas. 1977) dental socs. Home: 2702 Bayonne Ct Columbia MO 65201 Office: 201 W Broadway Columbia MO 65201

ELLIOTT, JOHN ANDREW, hotel exec.; b. Bklyn., Nov. 24, 1900; s. Henry Michael and Josephine (Grundy) E.; Ph.B., U. Notre Dame, 1925; m. Virginia Baker, Aug. 24, 1927 (dec. June 1951); m. 2d, Marian Reichert Geyer, Jan. 27, 1959; 1 dau., Alexandra Geyer Elliott (Marston). Asst. mgr. Nelson Hotel, Rockford, Ill., 1925-27; asst. mgr. Hotel Stoddard, LaCrosse, Wis., 1927-28, gen. mgr., pres., 1928-72; pres. No. Hotel Co., LaCrosse, 1951—; owner, mgr. Cass Realty Co., LaCrosse, 1952—; chmn. bd. Stoddard Properties, Inc., LaCrosse, 1972—. Mem. bd. Gateway area Boy Scouts Am., 1976—. Mem. Am. Hotel and Motel Assn. (dir. 1960-70), Wis. Innkeepers Assn. (pres. 1959-60, chmn. bd. 1960-61, dir. 1971—), LaCrosse C. of C. (dir. 1969-71), Notre Dame Alumni Assn. Roman Catholic. K.C., Rotarian (pres. 1967-68), Knight of Malta, Knight of Holy Sepulchre. Club: LaCrosse (Wis.) Country. Home: Hotel Stoddard LaCrosse WI 54601

ELLIOTT, ROBERT ALEXANDER, lawyer; b. Dawson, N.Mex., Apr. 9, 1915; s. Carey Baker and Bess Alma (Durham) E.; student N.Mex. Mil. Inst., 1933-35; B.S., U. Mich., 1938, J.D., 1940; m. Phoebe Marie Hurlbut, Nov. 12, 1948; children—Stephen C., Anne Marie. Admitted to Ill. bar, 1940; practice law Chgo. since 1940; mem. Plunkett, Nisen, Elliott & Meier and predecessor firms, 1951—; dir. Frank A. Edmunds & Co., Welmaid Products, Inc., Hinsdale Clin. Lab., Inc. Trustee Glen Ellyn (Ill.) Pub. Library, 1956-62. Served with USAAF, 1942-46. Mem. Chgo., Ill., Am. bar assns., Phi Gamma Delta, Phi Delta Phi. Episcopalian (vestryman 1957-62). Clubs: Union League, Tower (Chgo.); Glen Oak Country (Glen Ellyn, Ill.). Home: 266 Montclair St Glen Ellyn IL 60137 Office: One N LaSalle St Chicago IL 60602

ELLIOTT, ROBERT BETZEL, physician; b. Ada, Ohio, Dec. 8, 1926; s. Floyd Milton and Rose Marguerite (Betzel) E.; B.A., Ohio No. U., 1949; M.D., U. Cin., 1953; m. Margaret Mary Robichaux, Aug. 26, 1954; children—Howard A., Michael D., Robert Bruce, Douglas J., John C., Joan O. Intern, Charity Hosp., New Orleans, 1953-54; resident pathology Baptist Meml. Hosp., Memphis, 1958-59; practice medicine, specializing in family practice, Ada, 1954—; staff Ohio No. U. Health Service, 1960-70. Mem. Ada Exempted Village Sch. Bd., 1960—, pres., 1966-69, 72—, v.p., 1971—. Coroner Hardin County, 1973. Served with AUS, 1945-46; PTO. Diplomate Am. Bd. Family Practice. Mem. A.M.A., Ohio State Med. Assn., Hardin County Med. Soc. (pres. 1964), Am., Ohio, Lima acads. gen. practice, Am. Coll. Health Assn. Democrat. Presbyn. Mason (Shriner, 32 degree), Elk. Home: Route 1 Box 45 Ada OH 45810 Office: 302 N Main St Ada OH 45810

ELLIOTT, THOMAS ALBERT, physician; b. Elkhart, Ind., Dec. 31, 1920; s. Lloyd Albert and Cora Mae (Keyser) E.; B.S., Northwestern U., M.D., 1946; m. Mary Noble, June 15, 1942; children—Kathryn Alice, David Lloyd, Thomas Noble, Douglas William, Elizabeth Keyser, Cora Juliette. Intern, Cook County Hosp., Chgo., 1946; fellow in internal medicine Oschner Clinic, New Orleans, 1949-51, mem. staff, 1951; practice medicine specializing in internal medicine, Elkhart, Ind., 1952—; mem. staff Elkhart Gen. Hosp., 1952—, chief of staff, 1964—, cons. internal medicine, 1952—, dir. coronary care unit, 1964—; organizer mem. internal med. staff Elkhart Clinic, 1954—; cons. internal medicine Goshen (Ind.) Gen. Hosp.; a founder, pres. FIDE Corp., 1954—; dir. St. Joseph Valley Bank, Elkhart. Mem. community adv. council South Bend br. Ind. U. Sch. Medicine; founder, pres. United Health Found., 1961—; founder, v.p., pres., bd. dirs. Elliott Found. for Med. Edn. and Research, 1960—; founder, 1st pres., bd. dirs. Adult and Child Guidance Clinic; past pres., past bd. dirs. Mental Health Assn.; v.p., bd. dirs. N. Central Ind. Med. Edn. Found.; bd. dir. Elkhart Gen. Hosp. Assn., 1963-67, trustee, bd. dirs. hosp. found.; bd. dirs. South Bend Med. Found., Inc., 1965-70, No. Ind. Health Services Agy.; past bd. dirs. ARC, Retarded Children's Soc. Served to capt. M.C., U.S. Army, 1943-48. Diplomate Nat. Bd. Med. Examiners, Am. Bd. Internal Medicine. Fellow A.C.P. (life); mem. AMA, Internat., Am. Socs. internal medicine, Am., Ind. thoracic socs., Pan Am. Med. Assn., Am., Ind. (dir. 1974—) heart assns., Ind. Med. Assn. (pres. 13th dist. 1960), Elkhart County Med. Soc. (pres. 1976), Am. Legion, Mensa, Beta Theta Pi, Nu Sigma Nu. Unitarian. Clubs: Elks, Elcona Country. Contbr. articles in field to profl. jours. Home: 5 Kim Ct Elkhart IN 46514 Office: 303 S Nappanee St Elkhart IN 46514

ELLIS, A(THAEL) BARRY, food industry cons. co. exec.; b. Wyoming, Ohio, Aug. 4, 1927; s. Athael Barry and Laura Carolyn (Moeller) E.; B.B.A., U. Cin., 1950; m. Patricia Arnold Reece, Sept. 13, 1952; children—Andrew Barry, Anne Kate, Matthew Taylor. Salesman, then sales mgr. Proctor & Gamble Distbg. Co., 1950-59; div. mgr. Hoosier Brokerage Co. subsidiary Seavey & Flarsheim Brokerage Co., 1966-70, dir. marketing services Seavey & Flarsheim, Oak Brook, Ill., 1970-73, dir., 1968-73; pres. Solutions Unltd., Glen Ellyn, Ill., 1973—; v.p. mktg. sales Azteca Corn Products Corp., Chgo., 1973—. Pres. Glen Ellyn Park Dist. Tennis Assn., 1975; bd. dirs. Cathedral Shelter of Chgo. Served with AUS, 1945-46. Mem. Am. Soc. Tng. Dirs., Merchandising Execs. Club Chgo., Grocery Mfrs. Sales Execs. Chgo., Delta Tau Delta. Republican. Episcopalian (former vestryman). Home: 690 Oak St Glen Ellyn IL 60137 Office: Azteca Corn Products Corp 4850 S Austin Blvd Chicago IL 60638

ELLIS, DWIGHT BENJAMIN, resort assn. exec.; b. Columbus, Ohio, May 28, 1918; s. Benjamin Franklin and Edna Forest (Wanless) E.; B.C.S., Benjamin Franklin U., 1941; m. Ruth Elizabeth Lawrence, July 18, 1937; children—Lawrence Dwight, Nancy Lynn (Mrs. Bruce M. Draudt). IBM operator B.F. Goodrich, Akron, Ohio, 1936-38; spl. agt. FBI, U.S. Dept. Justice, Washington, 1938-42, Indpls., 1942-43, Pitts., 1943-44, Phila., 1944-46, Cleve., 1946-49, 63-68, Akron, 1949-63; gen. mgr. Lakeside (Ohio) Assn., religious family resort, 1968—, mgr. Lakeside Summer Symphony, 1968—. Methodist. Kiwanian. Home: 229 Park Row Lakeside OH 43440 Office: 236 Walnut Ave Lakeside OH 43440

ELLIS, FRANCES HANKEMEIER, educator; b. Galena, Ill., Jan. 6, 1892; d. Christopher and Elizabeth (Meyer) Hankemeier; A.B. magna cum laude, Ind. U., 1914, M.A., 1928; Ph.D., U. Wis., 1939; m. Forrest E. Ellis, June 23, 1917 (dec. Dec. 1954). Tchr. Sheridan (Ind.) High Sch., 1914-15, Tech. High Sch., Indpls., 1915-21; instr. German, U. Ind., 1927-39, asst. prof., 1940-50, asso. prof., 1950-57, prof., 1957-62, prof. emeritus German, 1962—. Mem. admissions com., edn. for women com. U. Ind. Participant Washington Conf., 1953; guest of German Fed. Republic, 1955. Recipient Distinguished Alumni Service award Ind. U., 1974. Fulbright Research grantee, Heidelberg, Germany, 1956-57. Mem. Modern Lang. Assn. (sec. sect. II, 1949-50. chmn. sect. 1950-51, nominating com. 1950-54, chmn. nominating com. 1954), Fgn. Lang. Elementary Schs. (state chmn. for German 1955-60), Luth. Acad. for Scholarship (nat. sec.; mem. exec. bd. 1947-54), Assn. Tchrs. German State of Ind. (pres. 1945-46), Renaissance Soc. Am., Modern Humanities Research Assn., A.A.U.W. (local past mem. exec. com., sec.-treas. 1942-46, area rep. internat. relations 1975-77), Am. Assn. Tchrs. German, A.A.U.P. (sect.-treas. 1944-46), Mortar Board (hon.), Delta Zeta, Delta Kappa Gamma, Phi Beta Kappa (local pres. 1954-55, vice chmn. E. Central Dist. 1949-52, 58-61, chmn. 1961-64, exec. com. 1964-67). Republican. Lutheran. Clubs: Ind. University (v.p. 1959-60), Lang. (sec.-treas. 1943-45, pres. 1945-46), Women's Faculty (sec.-treas. 1940-41, pres. 1942-43). Author: Hans Sache Studies I: Das Walt Got, 1941; The Early Meisterlieder of Hans Sachs, 1974. Contbr. to publs. including Dictionary World Literature, Lutheran Scholar, German Quar., Indiana Mag. of History, Publs. Modern Lang. Assn., also book reviews. Home: 522 Ballantine Rd Bloomington IN 47401

ELLIS, HOWARD WOODROW, clergyman, artist; b. Linton, Ind., Feb. 19, 1914; s. Lee and Effie (Walraven) E.; A.B., U. Evansville, 1943, H.H.D. (hon.), 1962; B.D., Garrett Theol. Sem., 1946, Th.M., 1973; student Washington Sch. Art, 1928-29, Am. Art Acad., 1944-45, Chgo. Art Inst., 1945-46, Peabody Coll., 1958-59, U. Tenn., 1960-64; m. Susanna Goldsmith, Aug. 27, 1942; children—Patricia Sue Ellis Beebe, Mary Lou. Ordained to ministry, United Methodist Ch., 1949; nat. staff Gen. Bd. Evang., Meth. Ch., Nashville, 1946-66; minister outreach Central Ave. Meth. Ch., Indpls., 1966-68; pastor Main St. United Meth. Ch., Boonville, Ind., 1968-74, Wall St. United Meth. Ch., Jeffersonville, Ind., 1974—. Condr. missions to Sweden, Norway, Denmark, Finland, 1957-59, Mexico, 1961, 65; mem. evang. team Korea, 1961; exhibited art in one-man shows at Sacred Arts Assos., Mpls., Parthenon Gallery, Nashville, 1960, U. Evansville, 1960, Concordia Sem., St. Louis, 1964, Augustana Coll., Mpls., 1965, Valparaiso (Ind.) U., 1966, Bethany Theol. Sch., 1971, Garrett Theol. Sem., 1972, Evang. Theol. Sem., 1972, others; exhibited in group shows at U. Evansville, 1971, Smithsonian Inst., 1960, Ultimate Concerns Ohio U., 1960, Nashville Fine Arts Festival, 1959, 60, 61, Tenn. State Fair, 1959-66, Ewah Univ., Seoul, Korea, 1962, Nat. Convocation Meth. Youth Purdue U., 1964; represented in numerous permanent collections. Mem. Internat. Transactional Analysis Assn. Author: Sallman Interpretations, 1944; Evangelism for Teen-Agers, rev. edit. 1966; The Witnessing Fellowship, 1961. Author, illustrator: How to Draw and Speak, 1961; He Took the Cup, 1963. Co-Author, editor, illustrator: (with Ted McEachern) Reflections on Youth Evangelism, 1964. Author: (with Kenneth Reed) Encounter Dialog in Art, 1966. Home: 512 Graham St Jeffersonville IN 47130 Office: 240 Wall St at Chestnut Downtown Jeffersonville IN 47130

ELLIS, JOSEPH GILBERT, cardiologist; b. Chgo., Feb. 20, 1935; s. Joseph Gilbert and Ruth Cora (Arenson) E.; student U. Chgo., 1950-53; B.A., U. Calif., 1956; M.D., Stanford, 1962; m. Janet Lynn Connor, Apr. 14, 1976. Intern, U. Ill. Hosp., Chgo., 1962-63; resident in medicine Stanford (Calif.) Hosp., 1963-64; Nat. Heart Inst. trainee in cardiology Scripps Clinic, La Jolla, Calif., 1964-66; mem. med. staff Scripps Clinic, La Jolla, Calif., 1966-67; practice medicine specializing in cardiology, Danville, Ill., 1968-74, Urbana, Ill., 1974—; mem. staff, dir. cardiac catherization and angiography lab. Carle Hosp., 1974—; clin. asso. U. Ill. Basic Scis. Med. Sch.; cons. VA Hosp., Danville; Tb control officer Vermilion and Champaign counties, Ill. Served with USNR, 1956-57. Tex Heart Inst. fellow in cardiology, 1970. Fellow Am. Coll. Physicians, Am. Coll. Angiology; mem. AMA. Developer hemodialysis unit for E. Central Ill., cardiac lab. for Central Ill. Home: 1904 S Vine Urbana IL 61801 Office: 602 W University Ave Urbana IL 61801

ELLIS, JOSEPH HARVELL, county ofcl.; b. Baton Rouge, Feb. 7, 1914; s. John M. and Edna (Easley) E.; student Frank Wiggins Inst., Los Angeles, 1939-40, Lawrence Tech., Detroit, 1947-48; m. Irene E. Boice, Dec. 29, 1936; children—Joanne (Mrs. David Bellmard), Floice (Mrs. Michael Frazer), Joseph W. Elec. contractor Ellis Electric, 1944—. Supr. Brighton Twp., 1959-63; county clk., Livingston County, 1963—. Mem. Brighton Elec. Examining Bd.; dir. elections Livingston County. Chmn. exec. com. Livingston County Republican Party, state del. Bd. dirs. Livingston County Mental Health Clinic. Served with USN, 1934-38. Mem. Mich. County Clks. Assn. (past pres., chmn. legis. forum, v.p.), United County Officers (chmn. bd control edn. div.), SAR. Lutheran. Elk, Lion. Home: 4344 Van 'Amburg Brighton MI 48116 Office: 201 Grand River Howell MI 48843

ELLIS, LUCILLE LORRAINE LAUGHLIN (MRS. WALLACE IVERSON ELLIS), realtor; b. Solsberry, Ind., Sept. 22, 1914; d. Rutherford and Mabel (Ingles) Laughlin; student Ind. U., 1930-31, 60, Danville Central Normal, 1931-32; m. Wallace Iverson Ellis, July 28, 1931; children—Betty Lucille (Mrs. Timothy Wininger), Charles Robert, Mary (Mrs. Hane), Rebecca. Tchr., LaCrosse Sch., Martinsville, Ind., 1932-33; partner Ellis Gen. Store, Springville, Ind., 1933-44; partner, mgr. Ellis Super Market, Bloomington, Ind., 1945-59; founder, owner Ellis Real Estate, Bloomington, 1960—. Den Mother White River council Boy Scouts Am., 1948-50; brownie leader Tulip Trace council Girl Scouts U.S.A., 1954-56. Patron Hoosier Art Salon, Indpls. Mem. Bloomington Bd. Realtors (sec.-treas. 1963-65), Ind. Real Estate Assn., Nat. Assn. Real Estate Bds., Bloomington C. of C. (bd. dirs., sec. exec. com. 1969-70), Ind. U. Alumni Assn. (life), Internat. Platform Assn., Motel Assn. Am., Nat. Brokers Council, Delta Sigma Kappa (life mem.; nat. treas. 1965-67, nat. v.p. 1967-69, nat. pres. 1969-71, chmn. bd. 1971-73). Clubs: Arganaut, Women's Dept. (Bloomington). Republican. Presbyn. Home: 835 Sheridan Rd Bloomington IN 47401 Office: 408 S Walnut St Bloomington IN 47401

ELLIS, WILLIAM DONOHUE, author; b. Riverton, N.J., Sept. 23, 1918; s. William Otterbein and Maude (Donohue) E.; B.A., Wesleyan U. Conn., 1941; m. Dorothy Ann Naiden, June 13, 1942; children—William Naiden, Sarah Elizabeth. Writer, Storycraft, Inc., Cleve., 1947-52; writer, pres. Edit. Services, Inc., Cleve., 1952—; mem. staff Writers Conf., U. N.H., 1958; novels include: The Bounty Lands, 1952, Jonathan Blair, Bounty Lands Lawyer, 1954, The Brooks Legend, 1958; (non-fiction) How to Win the Conference, 1955; The Cuyahoga, 1966, Clarke of St. Vith, 1974, Land of the Inland Seas, 1974. Served with AUS, 1941-46. Decorated Bronze Star, Purple Heart; recipient Ohioana Fiction award, 1952; Western Res. Hist. Soc. award, 1952; Top Fiction of Year award Sat. Rev., 1954; Cleve. Arts Council Lit. award, 1967; nominated for Pulitzer prize, 1954. Mem. Authors Guild. Home: 1060 Richmar Dr Westlake OH 44145 Office: 1276 W 3d St Cleveland OH 44145

ELLISON, ROBERT JAY, civil engr.; b. St. Paul, May 25, 1915; s. Jay Theodore and Emma Sophia (Paulson) E.; B.C.E., U. Minn., 1937; m. Marie Catherine Robinson, Apr. 30, 1938 (dec. Nov. 1972); children—Robert Jay, William Theodore, Barbara Marie. Mgr. field office Hallett Constrn. Co., Ashton, Ia., 1937; field engr. United Constrn. Co., Troy, Mo., 1938; dist. structural engr. Portland Cement Assn., Chgo., 1938, Madisonville, Ky., 1939, St. Louis, 1940-41; sr. engr. Banister Engring. Co., St. Paul, 1946-50; self-employed as cons. engr., St. Paul, 1950-57; pres., Ellison-Pihlstrom, Inc., St. Paul, 1958—. Chmn. troop com. Arrowhead council Boy Scouts Am., 1950-56. Served from 1st lt. to maj., CAC, AUS, 1941-45. Registered profl. engr., Minn., Wis., Ia. Mem. Am. Soc. C.E. (pres. N.W. sect. 1969-70), Am. Water Works Assn., Nat. Soc. Profl. Engrs., Water Pollution Control Fedn., Am. Arbitration Assn., Cons. Engrs. Council Minn. (pres. 1958-59), Beta Theta Pi. Episcopalian (vestryman 1963-65). Home: 2143 Bayard Ave St Paul MN 55116 Office: 2305 Ford Pkwy St Paul MN 55116

ELLOIAN, PETER, artist, engraver, educator; b. Cleve., Apr. 20, 1936; s. Oscar and Haigo (Minasian) E.; B.F.A., Cleve. Inst. Art, 1962; M.F.A., U. Iowa, 1965; m. Carolyn Ann Autry, May 27, 1966; 1 dau., Cybele. Instr. printmaking Toledo Mus. of Art, U. Toledo (Ohio), 1966—; represented in permanent collections Library of Congress, Phila. Mus. Art, Minn. Mus. Art, Okla. Art Center, Albrecht Art Museum, others. Mem. art adv. com. Montessori Acad., Toledo, 1977-78. Served with U.S. Army, 1957-59. Mem. Soc. Am. Graphic Artists, Internat. Platform Assn., Phila. Print Club, Coll. Art Assn. Am. Home: 3348 Indian Rd Toledo OH 43606

ELLZEY, ELIZABETH ANN, broadcasting exec.; b. Chgo., Oct. 23, 1955; d. Marvin Hullon and Oliva (Kersey) E.; A.A., Kennedy King Coll., 1974; B.A., Govs. State U., 1976, M.A., 1977. Testing coordinator Kennedy King Coll., Chgo., 1972-74; audio visual technician Govs. State U., Chgo., 1974-77; researcher, prodn. asst. ABC-TV, Chgo., 1977. Tuition scholar, 1972-77. Mem. Nat. Assn. Ednl. Broadcasters, Assn. Ednl. and Communications Tech., Advs. for Media Awareness (v.p.). Office: ABC TV 190 N State St Chicago IL 60601

ELROD, RICHARD JAY, county ofcl.; b. Chgo., Feb. 17, 1934; s. Arthur X. and Della (Glasser) E.; B.A., Northwestern U., 1955, J.D., 1958; m. Marilyn Arline Mann, June 18, 1955; children—Steven Michael, Audrey Marlene. Admitted to Ill. bar, 1959; asst. corp. counsel City of Chgo., 1958-70, chief city prosecutor, 1965-70; sheriff Cook County, 1970—. Commr., Ill. Law Enforcement Commn. Chmn. Young Democrats of Cook County, 1961-62; del. State Rep. Nominating Conv., 1964; mem. Ill. Ho. of Reps. from 13th Dist., 1969-70. Mem. Am., Chgo., Ill., N. Suburban bar assns., Decalogue Soc. Lawyers, Am. Judicature Soc., Internat. Assn. Chiefs of Police, Nat. (v.p. 1976—), Ill. (v.p. 1977—), No. Ill. sheriffs assns., Ill. Police Assn. Nat. Soc. State Legislators, Amvets. Jewish religion. Mason (Shriner); mem. B'nai B'rith. Home: 6629 Longmeadow Lincolnwood IL 60646 Office: 704 Richard J Daley Center Chicago IL 60602

ELROD, ROBERT GRANT, lawyer; b. Indpls., Feb. 24, 1940; s. French McElroy and B. Burrlene (Holland) E.; B.A. with honors, DePauw U., 1962; J.D. cum laude, Harvard, 1965; m. Beverly Anne Wahl, Aug. 23, 1964; children—Franklin Matthew, Benjamin Grant, Jeremiah French, Jonathan Filar. Admitted to Ind. bar, 1965; since practiced in Indpls.; asso. Elrod, Taylor & Williams, 1965-66; partner Elrod & Elrod, Indpls., 1967—; asst. county atty., Indpls., Marion County, Ind., 1967-68, county atty., 1969, asst. atty., city-county legal div., 1970-71, gen. counsel, city-county council, 1972—; dir. Bel-Mar Products Corp., All-Am. Employment Services, Inc. Treas., Young Republicans Marion County, 1968-69, sr. v.p., 1969-71, pres., 1971-73; 11th dist. chmn. Ind. Young Rep. Fedn., 1971-74, nat. committeeman, 1975-77; del. Rep. State Conv., 1968, 70, 72, 74, 76; precinct committeeman Rep. party, 1970—, ward chmn., 1977. Recipient Ind. Outstanding Male Young Rep. award Ind. Young Rep. Fedn., 1972, Marion County, 1974. Mem. Am., Ind. State, Indpls. bar assns., Am. Judicature Soc., Comm. Law League Am., Lawyers Assn., Indpls. Bar Found. Methodist. Mason. Club: Columbia (Indpls.). Home: 6440 Woodwind Dr Indianapolis IN 46217 Office: 803 First Fed Bldg Indianapolis IN 46204 also 310 Nat Bank of Greenwood Greenwood IN

ELSASSER, EDWARD ORR, historian; b. Oak Park, Ill., Feb. 16, 1918; s. William Everett and Bertha Gertrude (Orr) Kenyon; student U. Mich., 1936-37; B.A., Bethany Coll., 1942; M.A., Clark U., 1948; Ph.D., U. Chgo., 1954; m. Leila Marie Mitchell, Feb. 8, 1975; children—Brian Jensen, Eric Orr. Lectr. history Roosevelt U., Chgo., 1954-55; asst. prof. Western Mich. U., Kalamazoo, 1955-59, asso. prof., 1959-64, prof., 1964—. Mem. Kalamazoo Housing Bd. Appeals, 1971-75, chmn. 1973-75; bd. dirs. Kalamazoo Council on Human Relations, 1959-62. Served with AUS, 1942-44. Decorated Bronze Star. Fulbright grantee, Argentina, 1963. Mem. AAUP (pres. Western Mich. U. chpt. 1965-66), InterAm. Assn. Democracy and Freedom, Am. Hist. Assn., Latin Am. Studies Assn., Conf. Latin Am. History, Midwest Assn. Latin Am. Studies, Soc. History of Edn. Republican. Episcopalian. Contbr. articles to profl. jours. Home: 3124 Winchell St Kalamazoo MI 49008 Office: Western Mich Univ Kalamazoo MI 49008

ELSBACH, HENRY GEORGE, dentist; b. Hamburg, Germany, Dec. 3, 1931; s. Kurt Joe and Hanna (Wolff) E.; came to U.S., 1936, naturalized, 1943; student St. Mary's U., 1951, Trinity U., 1952; B.S., U. So. Calif., 1954; D.D.S., Chgo. Coll. Dental Surgery, 1958; certificate Pedodontics, State U. Iowa, 1960; m. Judith Carole Wehner, Dec. 2, 1967 (dec. Nov. 1972); m. 2d, Mary Janice Rheinlaender, Oct. 20, 1973; 1 dau., Amelia Marie. Practice pedodontics, Alton, Ill., 1960—; asso. prof. clin. pedodontics So. Ill. U. Sch. Dental Medicine. Served with USAF, 1951-52. Mem. Am., Chgo., St. Louis, Madison Dist. (chmn. dental health com. 1965-68, pres. 1976-77), Greater Alton Area (pres. 1968-69) dental socs., Am. Soc. Dentistry for Children, Am. Acad. Pedodontists, Am. Soc. Clin. Hypnosis, Psi Omega. Rotarian (pres. Alton-Godfrey 1974-75). Home: 4308 Briar Cliff Dr Alton IL 62002 Office: 2305 State St Alton IL 62002

ELSEA, RICHARD STAUNTON, realtor; b. Detroit, Dec. 18, 1929; s. Staunton Marion and Marjorie (Booth) E.; B.A., Mich. State U., 1952; m. Patricia Stoll, Jan. 13, 1953; children—Stuart, Daniel. Vice pres., gen. mgr. Elsea Realty & Investment Co., Detroit, 1954-70; pres., chief exec. officer Real Estate One, Inc., 1970—. Served with USAF, 1952-54. Named Realtor of Year, Western Wayne and Oakland County Bd. Realtors, 1967. Mem. Am. Legion, United Northwestern Realtors Assn. (dir., past pres.), Nat. Inst. Real Estate Brokers, Mich. Real Estate Assn., Detroit Real Estate Bd. Home: 30043 Fox Run Birmingham MI 48010 Office: 29630 Orchard Lake Rd Farmington MI 48018

ELSON, JAMES MALCOLM, JR., landscape architect; b. Peoria, Ill., June 5, 1947; s. James Malcolm and Glenola May (Lockhart) E.; B.Landscape Architecture, Kans. State U., 1970; m. Carol Sue Alberts, Aug. 24, 1968. With Scruggs & Hammond, Inc., East Peoria, 1965-71; landscape architect Elson & Assos., Peoria, 1971—. Mem. Pub. Art Com. Peoria, 1974—; mem. outdoor center com. YMCA, Peoria, 1972-74. Bd. dirs. Peoria City Beautiful, 1972—, v.p. 1975-76, pres., 1977—. Recipient Landscape Design award Peoria City Beautiful, 1974. Mem. Am. Soc. Landscape Architects (certificate of merit 1970, sec.-treas. Ill. chpt. 1975-77, now pres. elect), Peoria Assn. Commerce. Kiwanian (bd. dirs. Peoria 1975—, treas. 1977-78). Club: Creve Coeur. Home: 4946 Joos Ct Peoria IL 61614 Office: Jefferson Center Peoria IL 61602

ELVING, PHILIP JULIBER, chemist, educator; b. Bklyn., Mar. 14, 1913; s. Bernard David and Rose (Juliber) E.; A.B., Princeton U., 1934, A.M., 1935, Ph.D., 1937; m. Beulah Londow Round, June 20, 1937; children—Elizabeth R. Elving Bass, Louise Elving Carr. Instr. chemistry Pa. State U., 1937-39, prof., 1949-52; instr. chemistry Purdue U., 1939-41, asst. prof., 1941-43, asso. prof., 1947-49; head analytical, phys. chemistry div. research lab. Publicker Industries, Inc., 1943-45, asst. dir. chem. research, 1945-47; vis. prof. chemistry Harvard U., 1951-52, Hebrew U., 1966, 73; prof. chemistry U. Mich., Ann Arbor, 1952—; mem. Internat. Com. for Electrochem. Thermodynamics and Kinetics, 1960-69, NRC Com. Analytical Chemistry, 1958-61. Recipient Anachem award Detroit sect. Am. Chem. Soc., 1958, Fisher award analytical chemistry Am. Chem. Soc., 1960. Mem. Am. Chem. Soc., Electrochem. Soc. (dir., div. chmn.), Polarographic Soc., Soc. Analytical Chemistry, Brit. Chem. Soc., Phi Beta Kappa, Sigma Xi, Phi Lambda Upsilon. Jewish. Editor: (with I.M. Kolthoff) Treatise on Analytical Chemistry 1959—; (with J.D. Winefordner) Chemical Analysis Series, 1957—; contbr. articles to profl. jours, chpts. to books. Home: 2309 Devonshire Rd Ann Arbor MI 48104 Office: Dept Chemistry U Mich Ann Arbor MI 48109

ELWELL, KENNETH RAY, dentist, educator; b. East Liverpool, Ohio, Jan. 23, 1912; s. Harry Elmer and Grace Emma (Thomas) E.; student Ohio U., 1929-31; B.S.D., Northwestern U., 1937, D.D.S., 1937; M.P.H., U. Mich., 1957; m. Argie Cappelli, Dec. 25, 1933; children—Carole Elwell Parjari, Katherine Elwell Gardner, James T. Resident dentist State Soldiers Home, Sandusky, Ohio, 1937-40; commd. 1st lt., Dental Corps, U.S. Army, 1940, advanced through grades to col. USAF, 1956; asst. dental surgeon, Carlisle Barracks, Pa., 1940; staff dental surgeon 66th Inf. Div., 1943-45; chief dentist 235th Gen. Hosp., France, 1945-46, 113th Evacuation Hosp. and 388th Sta. Hosp., 1946-48; base dental surgeon, Grenier AFB, 1948, Offutt AFB, 1948-52; command dental surgeon SAC, 1948-52; chief preventive dentistry and research div. Office Asst. Surg. Gen. for Dental Services, 1952-56; chief dentist PACAF Base Command, 1957-60; dir. dental services USAF Med. Service Sch., 1960-65; command dental surgeon Air Force Systems Command, 1965-67; ret., 1967; asso. prof. pub. health dentistry, chmn. dept. community dentistry Case Western Res. U., Cleve., 1967-72, prof., chmn. dept. community dentistry, 1972—; mem. dental study sect., div. research grants NIH, USPHS, com. on dentistry, div. med. scis. NRC, Nat. Acad. Scis.; tech. adviser Air Force dental tng. films on preventive dentistry and practice mgmt.; program dir. USPHS grant Tng. a Community-Minded Dentist; program coordinator USPHS and Am. Coll. Dentists 7-11 Ann. Insts. for Advanced Edn. in Dental Research; mem. adv. com. Met. Health Planning Corp., Cleve.; mem. Cleve. Dental Health Task Force, 1968-70; chmn. search com. for dental dir. Met. Hosp., Cleve. trustee, exec. council, adv. com. on alcoholism Cleve. Neighborhood Health Services, Inc.; mem. adv. com. Health Consumer Affairs; mem. adv. group Youngstown Area Health Edn. Network. Diplomate Am. Bd. Dental Pub. Health. Fellow Am. Pub. Health Assn. (vice chmn., acting chmn. dental health sect. 1962-63), Am. Coll. Dentists; mem. Am. Acad. Periodontology, ADA (chmn. pub. health sect. 1970), Ohio Dental Assn., Cleve. Dental Soc., Am. Assn. Dental Schs., Internat. Assn. Dental Research, Am. Assn. Pub. Health Dentists (exec. council 1970-73, sec.-treas. 1973-76, pres. 1977—), Omega Beta Pi, Alpha Chi, Omicron Kappa Upsilon (pres. 1976-77). Clubs: Mason (32 deg.), Shriners. Decorated Legion of Merit, Bronze Star medal with oak leaf cluster, Air Force Commendation medal with oak leaf cluster, U.S. Army Commendation medal, Medaille de la Reconnaissance Française (French). Author: (with Kenneth A. Easlick) Classification and Appraisal of Objections to Fluoridation, 1960; Statistical Methods for Oral Research, 1969; Biostatistics for Dental Students, 1968; Contbr. articles to profl. jours. Home: 4661 W

Farnhurst Rd South Euclid OH 44121 Office: Sch Dentistry Case Western Res U 2123 Abington Rd Cleveland OH 44106

ELWOOD, DAVID LEQUE, psychologist; b. New Castle, Ind., Feb. 14, 1930; s. Marion Lee and Mollie Novella (Boone) Ellwood; m. Ella Mae Anderson, June 23, 1956; children—Michael David, Mark Stephen, John Andrew. B.A. cum laude, Olivet Nazarene Coll., 1955; M.A., So. Ill. U., 1958; Ph.D., Purdue U., 1963. Certified psychologist, Ind. Intern, Anna (Ill.) State Hosp., 1957-58; staff psychologist LaRue D. Carter Memorial Hosp., Indpls., 1958-60; staff psychologist Quinco Consulting Center, Columbus, Ind., 1962-73, prin. investigator research projects NIMH, 1967-76, chief of research, 1973-76, mgr. admission and automated services, 1976—; cons. psychologist Madison (Ind.) State Hosp., 1964-67; adj. asso. prof. psychology U. Louisville, 1972-75. Bd. dirs. Opportunity Center, Inc., Columbus, 1965-73, pres. 1971; v.p., bd. dirs. Region Ten Mental Retardation, Inc., Columbus, 1970-71; trustee, sec. Ch. of the Nazarene, Columbus, 1973-77; dir. Inst. Continuing Edn. in Psychology, 1973-76. Mem. Am., Ind. (pres. 1977—) psychol. assns., Internat. Assn. Applied Psychology, Phi Delta Lambda. Contbr. articles in field to profl. jours. Home: 3422 Grove Pl Columbus IN 47201 Office: 2075 Lincoln Park Dr Columbus IN 47201

ELY, ROBERT LEROY, criminalist; b. Lancaster, Ohio, Sept. 9, 1934; s. Paul Raymond and Marjorie (Davis) E.; student Ohio State U., 1967-69, Ohio U., 1967, Ind. U., 1968, Ohio State Hwy. Patrol Tng. Acad., 1956; m. Lois Ellen Ward, July 20, 1956; children—Sharon, David, Elizabeth, JoAnn, Paula. Patrolman, Ohio State Hwy. Patrol, Mansfield, 1956-59, Circleville, 1959-67, cpl. investigation and identification sect. Cambridge Dist. Hdqrs., 1967-69, mem. sci. staff Crime Lab., Gen. Hdqrs., Columbus, 1967-69, sgt., crime lab. dir., 1969—. Mem. Ohio Assn. Criminalists (chmn. 1975-76), Pickaway County Hist. Soc. (pres. 1976-77), Ohio State Hist. Soc., Nat. Muzzle Loading Rifle Assn. Home: 1117 McGraw Rd Circleville OH 43113 Office: 660 E Main St Columbus OH 43205

ELY, WAYNE HARRISON, broadcast engr.; b. Alliance, Ohio, Aug. 31, 1933; s. Dwight Harrison and Mable Evellen (Jones) E.; student Mount Union Coll., 1955-56, Ohio U., 1956-62; m. Roslyn Rose Ambrose, June 14, 1964; children—Eric, Kevin, Gayle, Mitchell. Transmitter engr. Sta. WOUB-AM-FM, Ohio U., Athens, 1958-62; studio field engr. ABC, N.Y.C., 1962-66, 67-72; studio engr. CBS, N.Y.C., 1966-67; transmitter supr. Sta. WOUC-TV, Ohio U., Quaker City, 1972—; tchr. radio tech. Ohio U., Zanesville. Served with C.E., U.S. Army, 1952-54. Sr. mem. Soc. Broadcast Engrs. Home: 904 Clark St Cambridge OH 43725 Office: WOUC-TV Route 3 Quaker City OH 43773

ELYN, MARK, opera singer, educator; b. Seattle, Feb. 4, 1932; s. Isadore and Goldie E.; student U. Wash., 1948-51, Seattle U., 1951-52; m. Jaclyn Rendall. Debut in opera, New York City Opera, 1956; leading roles in San Francisco Opera, NBC Opera, Phila. Lyric; leading bass Cologne, Munich, Hamburg, Stuttgart, Vienna, Monte Carlo, Geneva, Barcelona; roles include Philip II in Don Carlo, Figaro in Marriage of Figaro, Don Giovanni in Don Giovanni; asso. prof. music U. Ill., Urbana, 1969-77, prof., 1977—. Mem. Am. Guild Musical Artists, Deutsche Buehnengenossenschaft, Nat. Assn. Tchrs. of Singing. Home: 2012 Vawter Urbana IL 61801 Office: 207 Smith Hall Univ Ill Urbana IL 61801

EMENS, JOHN RICHARD, II, lawyer; b. Jackson, Mich., May 3, 1934; s. John Richard and Aline Louise (Brainerd) E.; B.A. magna cum laude, DePauw U., 1956; J.D., U. Mich., 1959; m. Mary Anne Francis, July 27, 1957; children—Anne Francis, John David, Alaine Francis, Elizabeth Francis. Admitted to Mich. bar, 1959, Ohio bar, 1964, U.S. Supreme Ct. bar, 1968; partner firm W. K. McInally, Jackson, 1959-64, Emens & Ashworth, Marion, Ohio, 1964-67, Emens, Hurd, Kegler & Ritter, Columbus, Ohio, 1968—; dir. Patrick Petroleum Co., Standard Savings and Loan Assn.; atty. mem., sec. State Ohio Oil and Gas Bd. Rev., 1965-75; mem. legal com., Ohio reporter Interstate Oil Compact Commn., 1965—. Mem. Ind. Petroleum Assn. Am. (dir. 1970—), Ohio Oil and Gas Assn. (trustee 1966—), Am., Ohio bar assns., State Bar Mich., Phi Beta Kappa, Phi Delta Phi, Beta Theta Pi. Home: 1724 Roxbury Rd Columbus OH 43212 Office: 250 E Broad St Columbus OH 43215

EMERSON, WILLIAM WESLEY, petroleum co. exec.; b. Kansas City, Mo., Apr. 7, 1942; s. Dwight Marvin and Mary Alice (Launder) E.; B.B.A., U. Mo. at Kansas City, 1967; m. Kay Louise Frisby, Oct. 25, 1963; 1 dau., Melissa. Auditor, cons. Peat, Marwick, Mitchell & Co., Kansas City, 1967-71; controller Maurice L. Brown Co., Kansas City, 1971-73, treas., 1973-75, exec. officer, 1975—; dir. Fin. Leasing Inc., Vada Penn Corp. Mem. Mo. Trout Fishermen's Assn. (1st v.p. 1975), (pres. 1976), Am. Inst. C.P.A.'s, Mo. Soc. C.P.A.'s. Home: 9232 Slater St Overland Park KS 66212 Office: 8301 State Line Rd Kansas City MO 64114

EMHARDT, CHARLES DAVID, lawyer; b. Indpls., Feb. 13, 1931; s. John W. and Martha (MacDougall) E.; grad. Culver Mil. Acad., 1948; B.S., Purdue U., 1952, postgrad., 1966; LL.B., Harvard U., 1955; m. Ann Devaney, Nov. 12, 1954; children—John D., Carol A., Frederick D., Martha A., Lucy E. Admitted to D.C. bar, 1955; patent atty. Western Electric Co., Washington and Balt., 1955-57, asso. Harold B. Hood, Indpls., 1957-59, asso. Lockwood, Woodard, Smith & Weikart, Indpls., 1959-64; partner Woodard, Weikart, Emhardt & Naughton, 1965—. Bd. dirs. Jordan YMCA, 1968-73, chmn. bd., 1970—. Served to capt. Ind. N.G., 1961-65. Mem. Am., Ind. (chmn. patent sect. 1967-68), Indpls. bar assns. Presbyterian. Mason. Clubs: Indpls. Athletic, Downtown Optimist (bd. mem. 1968-73), Contemporary, Woodstock. Home: 430 W 93d St Indianapolis IN 46260 Office: One Indiana Sq Suite 2670 Indianapolis IN 46204

EMISON, JAMES WADE, petroleum mktg. co. exec.; b. Indpls., Sept. 21, 1930; s. John Rabb and Catherine (Stanbro) E.; B.A., DePauw U., 1952; m. Cornelia Coyle, July 5, 1952; children—Catherine Emison, Elizabeth Ann, Thomas Weston, William Ash. Sales mgr. Oskey Bros. Petroleum Co., St. Paul, 1960-66; v.p. mktg. Newfoundland Refining Co., Ltd., N.Y.C., 1966-69; v.p. Oskey Gas and Oil Co., Mpls., 1969-77; pres. Western Petroleum Co., Mpls., 1977—; mem. Nat. Petroleum Council, 1970—; founder, dir. Suburban Nat. Bank, Eden Prairie, Minn. Served with USMC, 1952-56. Mem. DePauw U. Alumni Assn. (dir.). Home: 18702 Heathcote Dr Wayzata MN 55391 Office: 2950 Metro Dr Suite 301 Minneapolis MN 55420

EMMERICH, JAMES CHARLES, athletic trainer, coach; b. New Ulm, Minn., Mar. 18, 1911; s. Charles and Bertha (Keckeisen) E.; B.S., S.D. State Coll., 1940. Asso. prof. phys. edn., coach of track and field, also cross country, trainer S.D. State Coll. Brookings, 1940-60; phys. therapist Drs. Dooley Clinic, Pomona, Calif., 1962; vis. lectr. Eastern Mich. U., Ypsilanti, 1966, Calif. Western U., San Diego, 1968. Am. Specialist U.S.A. State Dept., 1961. Coach track and field; trainer, adminstrv. asst. Amateur Athletic Union of U.S.A., U.S. Olympic com., 1956—; state leader Pres.'s Council Phys. Fitness. Served with AUS, 1942-46. Named S.D. Coll. Coach of Year, 1954; elected to Helms Hall Track and Field Coaches Hall Fame, N. Central Collegiate Athletic Hall Fame, S.D. State U. Athletic Hall Fame, S.D. Sports Hall Fame. Mem. Nat. Athletic Trainers Assn., Internat., U.S. track coaches assns., Assn. U.S. Army, Am. Legion, D.A.V., Am. Assn. Ret. Persons, Brookings C. of C., Am. Turners, Blue Key, Phi Kappa Phi, Alpha Zeta, Pi Gamma Mu. Conglist. Elk. Lion. Address: General Delivery Brookings SD 57006

EMMERT, ROBERT EDWARD, tractor co. exec.; b. Ferris, Ill., Nov. 15, 1930; s. Richard Lowell and Lola Ellen (Deitrich) E.; B.S. in Mech. Engring., Bradley U., 1960; m. Joyce Marilyn Glay, Sept. 9, 1953; 1 dau., Kristen Lian. Jr. service engr. Caterpillar Tractor Co., Peoria, Ill., 1960-61, service tng. instr., 1961-63, asst. staff service engr., 1963-65, staff service engr., 1965—. Served with USAF, 1950-56; mem. Res., 1956-75. Mem. Soc. Automotive Engrs., Res. Officers Assn., Air Force Assn. Republican. Clubs: Masons, Shriners. Home: 365 S Mississippi Ave Morton IL 61550 Office: 100 NE Adams St Peoria IL 61602

EMMERT-WADSWORTH-WHITMORE, ALICE ELIZABETH, writer; b. Dixon, Ill., Dec. 8, 1918; d. Howard Elmer and Ruth Ella (McClanahan) E.; student Northwestern U., summer 1966, Rockford Coll., 1963-64, 66; m. R. Wadsworth (dec.); m. 2d, John E. Whitmore; 1 son, Michael R. Wadsworth. Religious chmn. First Meth. Ch., Dixon, Ill., bd. mem. women's club; hon. v.p. Centro Studi E. Scambi Internat., Rome, 1976. Recipient Laureate award, Rome, 1976; Gold Laureate Crown for poetry, Philippines, 1976; winner various short story and art awards. Fellow Internat. Platform Assn.; mem. Nat. League Am. Pen Women, Rockford Art Assn., Glacier Nat. Park Hist. Assn. (life), Smithsonian Instn. Methodist. Author: (poetry) A Garland of Leis, 1971; Our Singing States, 1973; contbr. poems to anthologies. Address: 215 W Morgan St Dixon IL 61021

EMRICH, RICHARD EARL, orthodontist; b. Columbus, Ohio, July 21, 1931; s. George John and Edith Irene (Thompson) E.; B.S., Ohio State U., 1953, D.D.S. cum laude, 1961; M.S. in Orthodontics, U. Ill., 1963; m. Nancy Lee Fisher, June 21, 1961; children—Steven, Michael. Pvt. practice orthodontics, Columbus, 1963—; lectr. orthodontics Ohio State U., Columbus, part-time 1967—. Served with USAF, 1953-55. Mem. Psi Omega, Alpha Kappa Psi, Omicron Kappa Upsilon, Sigma Alpha Epsilon, Beta Gamma Sigma. Mason (32 deg., Shriner), Kiwanian (v.p. 1966). Home: 559 Tucker St Worthington OH 43085 Office: 1495 Morse Rd Columbus OH 43229

EMRICK, DONALD DAY, chemist; b. Waynesfield, Ohio, Apr. 3, 1929; s. Ernest Harold and Nellie (Day) E.; B.S. cum laude, Miami U., Oxford, Ohio, 1951; M.S., Purdue U., 1954, Ph.D., 1956 Grad. teaching asst. Purdue U., Lafayette, Ind., 1951-55; with chem. and phys. research div. Standard Oil Co. Ohio, 1955-64, research asso., 1961-64; cons., sr. research chemist research dept. Nat. Cash Register Co., Dayton, Ohio, 1965-72, chem. cons., 1972—. Mem. Ohio Acad. Sci., A.A.A.S., Am. Chem. Soc., Phi Beta Kappa, Sigma Xi. Patentee in Field. Contbr. articles to profl. jours. Home: 4240 Lesher Dr Kettering OH 45429

EMRICK, RAYMOND TERRY, educator; b. Paris, Ill., Aug. 9, 1915; s. Terry Clifford and Maude Pearl (Hickman) E.; B.S., Ind. State U., 1953, M.S., 1954, postgrad. (teaching fellow), 1962-63, 65-66; Ph.D., Walden U., 1972; postgrad. U. Ill., 1958, Indsl. Coll. Armed Forces, Washington, 1969-72. Tchr. high sch., Peoria, Ill., 1955-57, Proviso West High Sch., Hillside, Ill., 1959-65; research asso. Ind. State U., Terre Haute, 1967; instr. psychology, edn. English, Olney (Ill.) Central Coll., 1957—, mem. merit pay evaluation com., 1974, pres.'s adv. com., 1973. Served with USAAF, 1942-46, 51-52. Mem. Mil. Order World Wars, Students Internat. Meditation Soc., Soc. Commd. Officers, Res. Officers Assn., Ret. Officers Assn., Internat. Platform Assn., Am. Legion, A.A.U.P., Phi Delta Kappa. Home: 108 Dogwood Dr Olney IL 62450

ENARSON, HAROLD L., univ. pres.; b. Villisca, Iowa, May 24, 1919; s. John and Hulda (Thorson) E.; B.A., U. N.Mex., 1940; M.A., Stanford, 1946; Ph.D., Am. U., 1951; L.H.D., Kent State U., 1972, U. Detroit, 1975; D.P.S., Bethany Coll., 1975; m. Audrey Pitt, June 7, 1942; children—Merlyn Pitt Enarson Prentice, Elaine Pitt Enarson Hering, Lisa Pitt. Teaching asst., research asst. Stanford, 1940-41; examiner Bur. Budget, Washington, 1942-43, 46-49; asst. prof. Whittier Coll., 1949, Stanford U., 1949-50; exec. sec. Steel Industry Bd., summer 1949; cons. Nat. Security Resources Bd., summer 1950; spl. asst. The White House, Washington, 1950-52; pub. mem. WSB, 1952-53; asst. dir. commerce City Phila., 1953; exec. sec. mayor Phila., 1954; exec. dir. Western Interstate Commn. Higher Edn., 1954-60, mem. Nat. Model Task Force of Analysis and Planning for Improved Distbn. of Nursing Personnel and Services project, 1975; cons. on utilization coll. teaching resources project Fund for Advancement of Edn., 1957-58; Carnegie Corp. adminstrs. fellowship, 1958; mem. surg. gen.'s cons. group on med. manpower, 1960; cons. Ford Found. in UAR, 1960; adminstrv. v.p. U. N.Mex., 1960-61, acad. v.p., 1961-66, asso. prof., 1964-66, past project dir. U. N.Mex. Internships in Latin Am.; pres. Cleve. State U., 1966-72, Ohio State U., Columbus, 1972—. Cons., AID, 1965, dir. edn. services Office Human Resources and Social Devel., 1963-64; mem. nat. adv. health council USPHS, 1964-68, task force on reorganization USPHS, 1967, mem. com. to evaluate health relationships; mem. W.K. Kellogg Task Force on Centers for Advanced Studies in Health Adminstrn., 1975-77; mem. Rural Area Devel. Com. U.S. Dept. Agr., 1962-63; mem. Edn. Commn. of States' Task Force on State Policy and Pvt. Higher Edn., 1976—; cons. Ford Found., Central Am., summers 1961-63; mem. commn. internat. edn. Am. Council on Edn., 1965-67, bd. dirs., 1970-73; mem. com. internat. edn. Am. Assn. Colls. for Tchr. Edn., 1967-69, Coll. Entrance Exam. Bd., 1967-70, Edn. and World Affairs, N.Y., 1967-68; mem. adv. council on developing instns. Office Edn., HEW, Washington, 1968-71; mem. Nat. Com. on U.S.-China Relations, 1976—; council of Overseas Liaison com., 1977—; bd. dirs. Nat. Health Council, N.Y.C., 1968-71; trustee Nat. Commn. for Coop. Edn., 1968—, Ohio Citizens Council for Health and Welfare, 1975-78; mem. Ohio Council on Econ. Edn., 1968—; mem. internat. affairs com. Nat. Assn. State Univs. and Land Grant Colls., 1973—, chmn., 1977—, mem. com. on financing higher edn., 1975—; bd. dirs. council for Fin. Aid to Edn., 1977—; panelist Nat. Identification Program for Advancement of Women in Higher Edn., 1977; mem. commn. on Arts and Scis., 1978; dir., mem. planning com. Nat. Center for Higher Edn. Mgmt. Systems, 1976—; pres. Assn. Urban Univs., 1971-72; adv. com. U.S. Army Command and Gen. Staff Coll., Ft. Leavenworth, Kan., 1975—. Bd dirs. Nat. Dental Research Council, 1958-62; bd. visitors Air U., 1968-70; trustee Griffith Found. for Ins. Edn., 1973—. Served with inf. AUS, 1943-46. Mem. Am. Polit. Sci. Assn., Newcomen Soc., Am. Soc. Pub. Adminstrn., Indsl. Relations Research Assn., Columbus Area (dir. 1973—), Ohio (dir. 1974—) chambers commerce, Nat. Acad. Pub. Adminstrn., Rotarian. Home: 285 Croswell Rd Columbus OH 43214

ENELOW, GERTRUDE STRASBERG (MRS. BENJAMIN FRANKLIN ENELOW), educator, lectr.; b. Chgo.; d. Benjamin and Stella (Johnson) Strasberg; student St. Xaviers Coll., 1922-24, U. Chgo., 1918-19; m. Benjamin Franklin Enelow, July 27, 1921 (dec. May 1957). Founder, supervising dir. Gertrude Sch. of Body Dynamics, Chgo., 1950—; pres. Body Dynamics Learning Center, Chgo., 1974—; instituted Body Dynamics Programs for Ill. Correctional Instns., Dwight Reformatory, 1967-69, Cook County Jail, 1970; mem. faculty Columbia Coll., Chgo., 1969-71. Pres. Enelow Found., 1957—; chmn. women's adv. com. Chgo. Bd. Health, 1965-66; guarantor Lyric Opera, 1960—. Bd. dirs. Chgo. Community Music Found., 1963-66, Adult Edn. Council Greater Chgo., Fine Arts Quartet, Urban Gateways of Chgo., Hull House for Sr. Citizens of Met. Chgo., 1965-69, The Villages, Topeka, Friends of Chgo. Pub. Library; adv. bd. Inst. Psychiatry Northwestern U. Recipient award for outstanding service to sr. citizens Adult Edn. Council Greater Chgo., 1970; Jewish Community Centers Hall of Fame award, 1975. Mem. Chgo. Drama League, Chgo. Assn. Commerce and Industry, English-Speaking Union, Alliance Francaise, Newberry Library Assn., Art Inst. Chgo. (life), Ill. Opera Guild (charter), Chgo. Symphony Soc. (hon. life), Midland Authors, Assn. Humanistic Psychology. Club: Chicago Press. Author: Body Dynamics, The Zen and Zest of Self-development, 1960; Inner Beauty-Outer Youth, 1970; The Joy of Physical Freedom, 1973. Patentee sleep pillow, Body Dynamics; developer phys. fitness program for sr. citizens. Home: 199 E Lake Shore Dr Chicago IL 60611 Office: 900 N Michigan Ave Chicago IL 60611

ENFIELD, RAYMOND LEE, architect; b. Edon, Ohio, Mar. 16, 1938; s. Herman and Vera Florine (Jack) E.; student Tri-State Coll., 1957-58; B.Arch., U. Ill., 1965; m. Susan Jane McDowell, Aug. 25, 1962; children—Laura Ann, David William. Specification writer K/m Asso., Inc., Elkhart, Ind., 1965-67, The Shaver Partnership, Michigan City, Ind., 1967-68; project architect Birkey & Asso., architects, South Bend, Ind., 1968; owner Enfield & Asso., architects, Elkhart, 1968-71; co-owner, v.p., treas. Enfield-Zentz & Asso., Inc., architects, Elkhart, 1971-73; owner, pres. Architects Inc., Elkhart, 1973—. Mem. Elkhart County Econ. Devel. Council, 1975—. Bd. dirs. H.O.M.E., Inc. Mem. Constrn. Specifications Inst. Methodist. Elk, Lion. Contbr. articles to profl. jours. Office: 363 S Elkhart Ave Elkhart IN 46514

ENGEL, ALBERT JOSEPH, judge; b. Lake City, Mich., Mar. 21, 1924; s. Albert Joseph and Bertha Mae (Bielby) E.; student U. Md., 1941-42; A.B. in Polit. Sci., U. Mich., 1948, J.D., 1950; m. Eloise R. Bull, Oct. 18, 1952; children—Albert Joseph, Katherine Ann, James Robert, Mary Elizabeth. Admitted to Mich. bar; adminstrv. asst. U.S. Rep. Ruth Thompson, 1951; practice law Muskegon, Mich., 1952-67; partner firm Engle & Engel, Muskegon, 1952-67; judge Circuit Ct. Mich., Muskegon, 1967-71, U.S. Dist. Ct. Western Mich. Dist., 1971-74, U.S. Ct. Appeals for 6th Circuit, 1974—; gen. partner Engelwood Plantations, Lake City, 1954-70. Served with U.S. Army, 1943-46; ETO. Mem. Am., Mich. bar assns., Am. Judicature Soc., Phi Sigma Kappa, Phi Delta Phi. Episcopalian. Clubs: Rotary, Torch. Home: 7287 Denison Dr Grand Rapids MI 49506 Office: 482 Federal Bldg Grand Rapids MI 49502

ENGEL, EDGAR L., obstetrician, gynecologist; b. Evansville, Ind., Feb. 19, 1909; s. John N. and Sophia (Meyer) E.; A.B., Wabash Coll., 1932; M.D., Washington U., St. Louis, 1936; m. Mildred Mae Stratman, Sept. 22, 1937; children—Phyllis Ann, Rebecca Jane, Catherine Gail, Edgar Leo. Intern, St. Louis City Hosp., 1936-37, resident obstetrics and gynecology, 1937-40; practice medicine specializing in obstetrics and gynecology, Evansville, Ind., since 1940. Diplomate Am. Bd. Obstetrics and Gynecology. Fellow A.C.S.; mem. Am. Coll. Obstetrics and Gynecology. Served as maj., AUS, 1942-45. Mem. Am., Ind., Vanderburgh County (pres. 1965) med. socs., Am. Soc. Study Sterility, Am. Coll. Abdominal Surgeons, Central Turners, Ind. Obstet. and Gynecol. Soc. (pres. 1963), Phi Gamma Delta. Club: Christmas Lake Country. Author sci. papers. Home: 1103 S Burkhardt Rd Evansville IN 47715 Office: 326 SE 7th St Evansville IN 47713

ENGEL, HAROLD JOSEPH, advt. agy. exec.; b. Chgo., Sept. 30, 1938; s. Harold Arthur and Florence (Pawlak) E.; student U.S. Navy Corr. Schs., 1957-59; m. Sarah Margaret Kloos, Sept. 10, 1958; children—Craig, Caroline, Christine, Catherine. Photog. dir., artist, prodn. asst. BAM Studios, Inc., Chgo., 1959-69; owner, pres. Imperial Color, Inc., Chgo., 1969—. Tchr. Christian doctrine high sch., 1970-73; chmn. community relations commn. Village of Hanover Park (Ill.), 1968-70. Served with USNR, 1956-59. Roman Catholic (lector 1965—). Home: 1271 Bristol Ln Hanover Park IL 60103 Office: 5 E Erie St Chicago IL 60611

ENGEL, JUAN JACOBO, gastroenterologist; b. Bogota, Colombia, Dec. 25, 1940; s. Paul and Josefina (Monath) E.; came to U.S., 1967, naturalized, 1976; B. Degree, Am. Sch. Quito (Ecuador), 1958; M.D., U. Central Ecuador, 1966; m. Ruth M. Schumann, Dec. 26, 1965; children—Miriam, Jessica. Intern, Mt. Sinai Hosp., Chgo., 1967-68; resident in medicine Boston VA Hosp., 1968-70, resident in gastroenterology, 1970-72; research fellow in gastroenterology U. Ill. Hosp., Chgo., 1972-73, attending physician, 1973-74; asso. attending physician Michael Reese Hosp., Chgo., 1974—; cons. in gastroenterology W. Suburban Hosp., Oak Park, Ill., 1976—; teaching fellow Boston U., 1969-72; instr. medicine Abraham Lincoln Sch. Medicine, Chgo., 1972-74; asst. prof. medicine Pritzker Sch. Medicine U. Chgo., 1974—. USIS traveling fellow 1963. Diplomate Am. Bd. Internal Medicine, with subspity. in gastroenterology. Researcher prostaglandins and gastric secretion. Home: 723 William St River Forest IL 60305

ENGEL, RONALD L., lawyer; b. Gary, Ind., Jan. 16, 1938; s. Aaron M. and Anna E.; B.S., U. Ill., 1959; J.D. with honors, U. Chgo., 1962; m. Alix L. Schwartz, Dec. 23, 1962; children—Alison Gayle, Carilyn Joan, Lauren Stacey. Admitted to Ill. bar, 1962, since practiced in Chgo.; partner firm Kirkland & Ellis, 1962—, partner, 1965—. Mem. Am., Ill. State bar assns., Am., Chgo. patent law assns., Order of Coif, Tau Beta Pi, Phi Lambda Upsilon, Phi Delta Phi. Clubs: Mid-America, Standard, Carlton, Saddle and Cycle. Home: 233 E Walton Pl Chicago IL 60611 Office: Standard Oil Bldg 200 E Randolph Dr Chicago IL 60601

ENGEL, THOMAS TOBIAS, former advt. exec.; b. Chgo., July 18, 1902; s. Ignatz and Rose (Newman) E.; student De Paul U., 1933-35, Kent Coll., 1932, Chgo. Acad. Fine Arts, 1945, 50, 51, 52, YMCA Community Coll., 1967-69, Northwestern U., 1970; m. Dorothy Wenger, June 26, 1949; 1 son, William. Advt. mgr. Theodore A. Kochs Co., Chgo., 1928-34; v.p., advt. mgr. West Engel Bros., Inc., Chgo., 1934-52; owner Thomas T. Engel Bldg. Constrn. Chgo., 1952-56; advt. mgr. Chgo. Molded Products Corp., 1956-59; founder, pres. Thomas T. Engel & Assos., Inc., Chgo., 1959-72; owner Engel Art Gallery, Highland Park, Ill., 1967-69. Exec. dir. Bachner Award for Outstanding Achievement in Plastics, 1959—. Mem. Art Inst. Chgo., Chgo. Council Fgn. Relations, North Shore Creative Writers (pres. 1974, 75). Editor: Plastics Progress mag., 1956—. Home: 9670 N Dee Rd Des Plaines IL 60016 Office: 175 Skokie Blvd Northbrook IL 60062

ENGELBERG, MARVIN WOOLF, audiologist, speech pathologist; b. Dallas, Sept. 28, 1930; s. Ben and Felice (Wolfe) E.; B.S., Tex. A. and M. U., 1952; M.A. in Audiology and Speech Pathology, U. Ill., 1954; Ph.D. in Audiology and Speech Pathology, U. Mich., 1958; m. Irene Dorothy Silverman, May 15, 1960; children—Suzanne, David. Audiologist, Portland (Oreg.) Hearing and Speech Center, 1958-61, also speech pathologist; chief audiology and speech pathology service VA Hosp., Cleve., 1961—; adj. prof. U. Akron (Ohio), 1976—; chief cons. in audiology HCI, Inc., Rockford, Ill., 1967—; lectr. audiology

Case Western Res. U., Cleve., 1967—; chmn. audiology and speech pathology VA Med. Dist. 13, 1973—. Pres. B'nai Israel Congregation, Mayfield Hts., Ohio, 1970-71; trustee Akiva Hebrew High Sch., Beachwood, Ohio, 1977—; trustee Mayfield Hillcrest Synagogue, 1971—. Recipient Superior Performance award VA, 1966, 69, 71, Fed. Career Service award, 1974. Mem. Am., Ohio speech and hearing assns., Ohio Council Audiology. Author: Audiological Evaluation for Exaggerated Hearing Level, 1970; contbr. articles to profl. jours. Home: 3906 Meadowbrook Blvd University Heights OH 44118 Office: 10701 East Blvd Cleveland OH 44106

ENGELHARDT, THOMAS ALEXANDER, editorial cartoonist; b. St. Louis, Dec. 29, 1930; s. Alexander Frederick and Gertrude Dolores (Derby) E.; student Denver U., 1950-51, Ruskin Sch. Fine Arts, Oxford (Eng.) U., 1954-56, Sch. Visual Arts, N.Y.C., 1957; m. Katherine Agnes McCue, June 25, 1960; children—Marybeth, Carol Marie, Christine Leigh, Mark Thomas. Free-lance cartoonist and comml. artist, N.Y.C., 1957-60, Cleve., 1961-62; asst. editorial cartoonist Newspaper Enterprise Assn., Cleve., 1960-61; editorial cartoonist St. Louis Post-Dispatch, 1962—. Served with USAF, 1951-53. Office: 900 N 12th Blvd St Louis MO 63101

ENGELMAN, WILLIAM ROBERT, physician, dentist; b. Detroit, Dec. 20, 1932; s. Morton Valentine and Gladys Vivian (Holt) E.; B.S., U. Detroit, 1958, D.D.S., 1962; M.D. (Med. Sch. scholar), Wayne State U., 1966; m. Greta Lorraine Faubert, Sept. 16, 1961; children—William Thomas, Laura Lorraine, David John, Matthew Roland. Rotating intern St. Luke's Hosp., Saginaw, Mich., 1966-67; resident in otolaryngology St. Luke's Hosp., Cleve., 1967-68; resident in gen. surgery U. S.C., Charleston, 1968-69, resident in otolaryngology, 1969-71; chief resident S.C. Med. U. Hosp., Charleston, 1970-71; fellow Armed Forces Inst. Pathology, Washington, spring, 1971; practice medicine specializing in otolaryngology, Saginaw, 1971—; mem. staffs St. Mary's Hosp., Saginaw Gen. Hosp.; mem. sr. staff St. Luke's Hosp., chief of surgery, 1975—. Mem. cons. staff Midland (Mich.) Hosp., 1972—; clin. prof. Mich. State U., Saginaw, 1973—; asst. dir. surg. edn. Saginaw Coop. Hosps., 1974—; physician Saginaw County Hearing Clinic, Saginaw, 1971—. Served with AUS, 1951-53; Korea. Decorated Bronze Star with oak leaf cluster. Recipient Versalius award Wayne State Med. U., 1962, Pres.'s Key U. Detroit, 1962. Fellow A.C.S.; mem. Am. Acad. Opthalmology and Otolaryngology, Centurion Club for Deafness Research, Mich. State, Saginaw County med. socs., A.M.A. (Physicians Recognition awards 1961, 72, 74), Midwest Surg. Assn. Roman Catholic. Contbr. articles to profl. publs. Office: 3160 Christy Way Saginaw MI 48603

ENGEN, EUGENE PAUL, psychologist; b. Yankton, S.D., Mar. 4, 1931; s. Oscar Leonard and Cena Caroline (Paulson) E.; B.A., Yankton Coll., 1952; M.A., Mills Coll., 1955; Ph.D. (USPHS fellow), La. State U., 1959; m. Eunice Lorraine Erickson, June 1, 1957; children—Paul Douglas, Brendan Clark. Psychologist, Yankton (S.D.) State Hosp., 1954-56, chief psychologist, 1959-62, 64-67, dir. adolescent treatment program, 1967-71; cons. clin. psychologist Mt. Marty Coll., 1966-67; lectr. Yankton (S.D.) Coll., 1961-62, 74; dir. Lewis and Clark Mental Health Center, Yankton, 1970—; interim dir. Inter-Agy. Mental Health Services, Sioux Falls, 1973; clin. asso. prof. U. S.D., Vermillion, 1966—, clin. asso. prof. U.S.D. Med. Sch., Sioux Falls, 1975—, mem. Bd. Mental Illness, 1974-76; chmn. S.D. Mental Health Adv. Council, 1976—; v.p. S.D. Bd. Examiners of Psychologists, 1976-77; cons. to various colls. and govt. agys., 1960—. Served with USAF, 1952-54, USPHS, 1963. Diplomate Am. Bd. Profl. Psychology. Mem. Am., S.D. (pres. 1961-62, 72-74, bd. examiners 1974-76) psychol. assns. Rotarian (dir. 1964-66, 70-74, pres. 1975-76). Home: Lewis and Clark Lake Rd Yankton SD 57078 Office: 1028 Walnut St Yankton SD 57078

ENGEN, PHILIP SHERMAN, real estate broker; b. Whitehall, Wis., June 24, 1935; s. Ernest Sherman and Bernice Eva (Albrecht) E.; student U. Wis., 1957-60; m. Carole Rose Becker; children—Karen, Eric, Kristen. Foreman power plant Oscar Mayer & Co., Madison, Wis., 1957-67; salesman Ideal Realty Co., Madison, 1967-70; owner Phil Engen Realty, Madison, 1973—. Pres., Madison Bd. Realtors, 1973, Madison Apartment Assn., 1973-74. Named Madison Realtor of Year, 1973. Mem. Wis. Realtors Assn. (v.p. dist. 1976-77, sec. 1977-78), Nat. Assn. Realtors. Club: Rotary (v.p. 1977). Home: 2906 Pelham Rd Madison WI 53713 Office: 901 S Whitney Way Madison WI 53711 also 2201 Winnebago St Madison WI 53704

ENGER, SHELDON MARTIN, accountant; b. Chgo., July 15, 1936; s. Harry and Ruth Lillian (Brody) E.; B.S. in Bus. Adminstrn., Washington U., St. Louis, 1958, M.B.A., 1961; m. Rochelle Sue Sheinbein, Apr. 7, 1963; children—Cindy Gayle, Marc David, Kevin Todd. Staff auditor Haskins & Sells, C.P.A.'s, St. Louis, 1961-66; partner in charge mgmt. cons. Epstein, Aftergut & Co., C.P.A.'s, St. Louis, 1966-69; partner, account exec. Alexander Grant & Co., St. Louis, 1969-73, mng. partner, St. Louis, 1973—, asst. regional mng. partner, Midwest, 1975—, mem. nat. exec. com., 1976—. Asst. prof. accounting, finance Mo. U., St. Louis, 1964-70; lectr. various profl. and mgmt. seminars. Bd. dirs. Jewish Family Children's Service, Jewish Community Center Assn., St. Louis; trustee Sch. Profl. Accounting, U. Mo. Served with AUS, 1958-59. C.P.A., Mo., Iowa, Mich., La., Ill., Ark. Mem. Am. Inst. C.P.A.'s, Mo. Soc. C.P.A.'s, Nat. Accounting Assn., Danforth Found. St. Louis Leadership Group, Jewish Fedn. St. Louis (mem. leadership council 1970—). Clubs: Clayton, Westwood Country, Mo. Athletic. Home: 830 Blue Spring Ln Frontenac MO 63131 Office: 222 S Central Ave St Louis MO 63105

ENGERAN, WHITNEY JOHN, JR., painter, educator; b. New Orleans, Feb. 1, 1934; s. Whitney John and Nora Marie (Boudreaux) E.; B.A., Spring Hill Coll., Mobile, Ala., 1956, M.A., 1958; S.T.L., St. Louis U., 1966; children—Whitney John, Alyce Renee. One man shows: Orleans Gallery, New Orleans, 1967; Barnwell Art Center, Shreveport, La., 1975; St. Mary of the Woods Gallery, Terre Haute, Ind., 1977; group shows include: Topeka (Kans.) Art Guild Gallery, 1962, Sheldon Swope Art Gallery, Terre Haute, 1972, Mo. State Council on Arts, St. Louis, 1972; represented in permanent collections: Ind. State U., Terre Haute, Harold E. Simon Collection, Birmingham, Ala.; Chmn. dept. visual arts Loyola U., New Orleans, 1966-67; asso. prof. Stephens Coll., Columbia, Mo., 1968-71; chmn. dept. art Ind. State U., 1971—, prof. art theory and criticism, applied aesthetics, 1971—, dir. Turman Gallery, curator permanent collection, 1971-75; lectr.in field. Eli Lilly Grantee, 1973. Mem. Nat. Assn. Art Adminstrs., Coll. Art Assn. Democrat. Roman Catholic. Home: 1509 S Center St Terre Haute IN 47803 Office: Art Dept Ind State U Terre Haute IN 47809

ENGLAND, LAWRENCE RUSSELL, hosp. adminstr.; b. Wheeling, W.Va., May 21, 1936; s. William Worrell and Virginia Clara (Kaltenbach) E.; grad. high sch.; m. Ruth Ann Dabrawsky, Sept. 9, 1967; children—Eric, Marc, Laura, Scott, LeeAnn (dec.). Inventory supr. Wheeling Tile Co., 1953-64; chief accountant City Hosp., Bellaire, Ohio, 1964-66, asst. adminstr., 1966-67, acting adminstr., 1967-68, adminstr., 1968—; dir. Asso. Hosp. Service Inc., W.Va. Hosp. Service, Inc. Sec., No. Panhandle Health Council, 1973-74. Bd. dirs. Southeastern Health Planning Assn., 1973-74, Eastern Ohio Alcoholic Councils Belmont County Heart Assn. Served with USNR, 1954-62. Mem. Am. Pub. Health Assn., Royal Soc. Health, Hosp. Mgmt. Systems Soc., Hosp. Financial Mgmt. Assn., Am., Ohio hosp. assns., C. of C. Home: 4858 Cummins Rd Bellaire OH 43906 Office: 47th and Harrison Sts Bellaire OH 43906

ENGLAND, WALTER BERNARD, chemist; b. Hallettsville, Tex., Aug. 23, 1942; s. Marion Bernard and Helen Genevieve (Meinardus) E.; B.S., Purdue U., 1965; Ph.D., Iowa State U., 1973; m. Barbara Joyce Fronczak, Apr. 11, 1962; children—Douglas, Eugene. Postdoctoral fellow, Colo. State U., 1973-74, Argonne Nat. Lab. (Ill.), 1974-76, research asso., 1976—. Mem. Am. Phys. Socs., Am. Chem. Soc. Contbr. articles, reviewer profl. jours. Home: 1314 E Hyde Park Blvd Chicago IL 60615 Office: Argonne Nat Lab 9700 S Cass Ave Argonne IL 60439

ENGLE, ALBERT LEE, control co. sales exec.; b. Abilene, Kans., Oct. 1, 1938; s. Raymond Earl and Pauline Gertrude (Long) E.; B.S. in E.E., Kans. State U., 1962; m. Elizabeth Ann Miser, Feb. 23, 1963; children—Albert Christopher, Mark Edward, Gregory Michael. Sales engr. Reliance Elec., Co., Lubbock, Tex., 1964-66, Memphis, 1966-69, Milw., 1969-72, Youngstown, Ohio, 1972-74; field sales mgr. Cleve. Machine Controls, Cleve., 1974—. Bd. ministers Christ the Redeemer Lutheran Ch., 1975—, pres. congregation, 1977; pack chmn. Cleve. Boy Scouts Am.; mgr. Nordonia Hills Baseball Program, 1974—; pres. Fairview Elementary Sch. P.T.A., Brookfield, Wis., 1971. Mem. Sales and Marketing Execs. Republican. Home: 343 Skylane Dr Northfield Center OH 44067 Office: 7550 Hub Pkwy Cleveland OH 44125

ENGLE, ARTHUR WILLIAM, assn. exec.; b. Elyria, Ohio Mar. 23, 1935; s. Arthur W. and Mary E. (Ebersole) E.; B.B.A., Northwestern U., 1971; m. Dagny M. Nylen, Aug. 25, 1956; children—Scott, Jeff, Mark. Dir. adminstrv. services Hosp. Financial Mgmt. Assn., Chgo., 1967-71; gen. mgr. Am. Judicature Soc., Chgo., 1971-74; pres. Mgmt. Cons. Assos., also Assn. Mgmt. Center, C-M Bus. Service divs. Engle Corp., Glenview, Ill., 1974—; exec. v.p. Assn. Rehab. Nurses, Chgo., 1974—; exec. dir. Chgo. Assn. Fed. Employees, 1976—, Soc. Gastroent. Assts., 1976—, Internat. Assn. Enterostomal Therapists, 1976—. Named Outstanding Young Man of Year, Lorain, Ohio, 1961, Outstanding Local Pres. Ohio, Jaycees, 1961. Mem. Am., Chgo. socs. assn. execs., Inst. Assn. Mgmt. Cos., Adminstrv. Mgmt. Soc., Acad. Certified Adminstrv. Mgrs. Kiwanian (dir. Chgo.). Editor Jour. Nat. Assn. Ct. Adminstn., 1972-74. Office: 1701 Lake Ave Suite 470 Glenview IL 60025

ENGLE, JOHN DAVID, JR., educator, writer; b. Yocum, Ky., Sept. 29, 1922; s. John David and Mary Angeline (Combs) E.; B.A., U. Ky., 1950, M.A., 1953; m. Anita Marie Jacobs, Aug. 20, 1948 (div. Nov. 1972); children—Mariamne A., Brent Elwin. Tchr. English and creative writing in high schs., Belfry, Ky., 1950, Jenkins, Ky., 1950-51, Athens, Ky., 1951-53, Lafayette High Sch., Lexington, Ky., 1953-56, Princeton High Sch., Cin., 1956—; asso. editor Writer's Digest, 1967—; mem. Ohio Arts Council Poets-in-the-Schs. Program; poet-in-residence various Ohio schs.; lectr.; lit. adviser Ohio Arts Council, 1973-75; poetry books include: Modern Odyssey, 1971; Laugh Lightly, 1974; Sea Songs, 1977; poetry represented in two Japanese coll. anthologies; dramas include: The Opening Door, 1957; The Charm, 1958. Served with USAAF, 1942-45. Recipient poetry awards Ind. U. Writers Conf., Nat. Fedn. State Poetry Socs., Ky. Poetry Soc., Ohio Poetry Day Awards. Mem. Poetry Soc. Am., Nat. Fedn. State Poetry Socs., Verse Writers Guild Ohio, Ky. Poetry Soc., NEA, Ohio Edn. Assn. Home: 1311B Chesterwood Ct Cincinnati OH 45246 Office: 11080 Chester Rd Cincinnati OH 45246

ENGLEHART, THEODORE MCNUTT, mfg. co. exec.; b. Brazil, Ind., May 9, 1920; s. Ira Holland and Virginia (McNutt) E.; student DePauw U., 1938-40; B.A., Butler U., 1947; m. Nancy Campbell, Apr. 22, 1944; children—Nancy Anne, Theodore M. (dec.). With Indiana Gear Works (Buehler Corp. since 1966), Indpls., 1940-66, exec. v.p., 1960-66, sr. v.p. 1966-70, also dir.; with Circle Leasing Corp., Indpls., 1970-72; exec. v.p. J.C. Wilson Engring. Corp., Indpls., 1972-73; pres. Lab. Equipment Corp., Mooresville, Ind., 1973—; dir. J.C. Wilson Engring. Corp., Circle Leasing Corp., Wellman Dynamics Corp.; sec., treas., dir. State Gear Co., Inc. Pres. bd. trustees Winona Meml. Hosp. Served to 1st lt. USAF, WW II. C.P.A.; recipient certificate, Winona Meml. Hosp., 1968. Mem. Am. Gear Mfrs. Assn. (pres. 1968, recipient certificate 1968), Soc. Automotive Engrs., Ind. Mfrs. Assn. (dir.). Republican. Methodist. Clubs: Meridian Hills Country, Am. Legion. Holder 3 patents in field of marine propulsion. Home: 7771 Spring Mill Rd Indianapolis IN 46260 Office: 156 E Harrison St Mooresville IN 46158

ENGLERT, HAMILTON EDWARD, judge; b. Valley City, N.D., Jan. 31, 1909; s. Michael J. and Stella E. (Larssen) E.; standard degree Valley City State Coll., 1932; B.A., N.D. U., 1933; postgrad. Gregg Coll., 1935; m. Harriet Agnes Lowe, Aug. 10, 1935; children—Darlene K. (Mrs. William L. Talbott), Ann L. (Mrs. Dennis O'Neill). Reporter Dist. Ct., 1st Jud. Dist. N.D., 1935-62; judge Dist. Ct. N.D., 1962—; admitted to N.D. bar, 1949, practiced law, Valley City, 1949-62. Mem. com. on electronic rec. State Jud. Council, also chmn. pretrial com.; chmn. Com. Jail Rules N.D. Mem. Nat. Council Juvenile Ct. Judges, Am., N.D., Barnes County bar assns., State Trial Judges Assn. (del to Am. Bar Assn.), Nat. Council State Trial Judges (state del., state rep. Nat. Pretrial Study), Am. Judicature Soc., Six State Trial Judges Assn., Valley City C. of C., Greater N.D. Assn., Sigma Chi. Conglist. Elk, Eagle. Home: 506 4th Ave SW Valley City ND 58072 Office: Barnes County Courthouse Valley City ND 58072

ENGLISH, JOHN CAMMEL, educator; b. Kansas City, Mo., Dec. 4, 1934; s. Jacob Cammel and Grace (Mortenson) E.; B.A., Wash. U., 1955; M.Div., Yale, 1958; Ph.D.,Vanderbilt U., 1965; m. Evonne Kludas, July 29, 1966. Asst. prof. history Stephen F. Austin State U., Nacogdoches, Tex., 1962-65; asst. prof. history Baker U., Baldwin, Kans., 1965-66, asso. prof., 1966-68, prof., 1968—, chmn. dept. history and polit. sci., 1965-73, chmn. social sci. div., 1970-72, dir. history of ideas program, 1977—. Mem. Am. Hist. Assn., Am. Soc. Ch. History, Conf. on Brit. Studies, Am. Soc. 18th Century Studies, Hist. Assn. (Gt. Britain), Phi Beta Kappa, Pi Gamma Mu, Phi Alpha Theta. Methodist. Author: The Heart Renewed: John Wesley's Doctrine of Christian Initiation, 1967. Contbr. articles to profl. jours. Home: 125 Santa Fe Dr Baldwin KS 66006

ENGLISH, MILFORD THOMAS, trust co. exec.; b. St. Louis, July 12, 1917; s. Thomas Jordan and Olinda Louise (Ellerman) E.; J.D., Wash. U., 1940; m. Carolyn S. Goyer, Apr. 30, 1941; children—Michael T., Christopher J., Steven R., Laurie (Mrs. Michael Evans). Admitted to Mo. bar, 1940, Ill. bar, 1966; mem. firm Cook, Murphy, Lance & English, St. Louis, 1940-66; with No. Trust Co., Chgo., 1966—, v.p., 1972—. Mem. Mo. Ho. of Reps., 1953-59. Bd. govs. Mid County YMCA, 1964-66. Recipient Distinguished Service award Brentwood Kiwanis Club, 1951. Mem. Am. Judicature Soc., Am., Mo., St. Louis, Ill., Chgo. bar assns., Phi Delta Phi, Theta Xi (Distinguished Service award 1964). Club: Union (Chgo.). Home: 600 5th St Wilmette IL 60091 Office: 50 S LaSalle St Chicago IL 60690

ENGLISH, WALLACE DAVIS, physician; b. Paris, Mo., Feb. 12, 1908; s. Joseph Shelby and Georgia E. (Davis) E.; A.B., U. Mo., 1929; M.D., Washington U., 1933; m. Frances Sue Hodge, Mar. 10, 1930; children—Frank, Merrill, Ronald, Alan; m. 2d, Frieda M. Lomax, Mar. 9, 1944; children—Joe Shelby, Timothy. Intern, St. Louis City Hosp., 1933-34; practice medicine, specializing in surgery, Cardwell, Mo., 1933—; mem. staff Dunklin County Meml. Hosp., Kennett, Mo., chief of staff, 1953-54, vice chief staff, 1951; surgeon Cotton Belt R.R., St. Louis Southwestern R.R., 1950—. Mem. voting bd. Mo. Blue Shield Ins. Co., 1961—; trustee St. Louis Blue Shield, 1968-77. Mem. finance com. Buffalo Twp. Boy Scouts Am., 1949-51. Served to capt. M.C., AUS, 1942. Hon. mem. Cardwell chpt. Future Farmers Am., 1956. Fellow Am. Soc. Abdominal Surgeons, Am. Acad. Family Physicians; mem. A.M.A., Am. Heart Assn., Mo. Med. Assn. (mem. council 1961—), Dunklin County, Miss. Valley med. socs., Am. Acad. Gen. Practice, Alpha Kappa Alpha. Baptist. Rotarian (past sec., pres.), Mason; mem. Order Eastern Star. Club: Weimaraner (Cardwell). Contbr. articles to profl. jours. Address: PO Box 107 Cardwell MO 63829

ENGLUND, STANLEY MONROE, chem. engr.; b. Coats, Kans., Dec. 2, 1927; s. Arnold Joseph and Millicent Ailene (Lemons) E.; B.S. in Chem. Engring., U. Kans., 1950; M.S., Mass. Inst. Tech., 1951; m. Marjorie Ellen Hasse, June 27, 1953; children—Janet, Robert, Annette, Ronald. With Dow Chem. Co., Midland, Mich., 1951—, sect. mgr. process engring., 1969—, process cons., 1970—; also cons. in plastics mfg., Europe, Japan. Active P.T.A., Boy Scouts Am. Served with USNR, 1945-46. Registered profl. engr., Mich. Mem. Am. Inst. Chem. Engrs. (local chmn. 1961-62), Toastmasters, Tau Beta Pi, Sigma Tau, Phi Lambda Upsilon. Methodist. Club: Kiwanis. Patentee in field. Home: 1206 Bayberry St Midland MI 48640 Office: Dow Chem Co Midland MI 48640

ENRIGHT, JOHN FRANCIS, real estate exec.; b. Chgo., Jan. 8, 1933; s. Harold F. and Eleanor J. (Joyce) E.; B.S., Xavier U., 1954; m. Annette M. Graham, Nov. 29, 1958; children—Susan Ann, John Graham, William Joseph, Amy. With Appraisal Asso., Inc., Chgo., 1957—, pres., 1967—. Instr., Northwestern U., Evanston, Chgo., 1960-63. Served with AUS, 1954-57. Mem. Chgo. Real Estate Bd. (prin.), Am. Inst. Real Estate Appraisers, Lambda Alpha. Home: 401 Burr Ridge Club Dr Burr Ridge IL 60521 Office: 111 W Washington St Chicago IL 60602

ENS, PETER DUERKSEN, physician; b. Fairbury, Nebr., Feb. 15, 1914; s. Gerhard K. and Justina (Duerksen) E.; A.A., Tabor Coll., 1941; A.B., Kans. U., 1947, M.D., 1951; postgrad. Friends U., 1941, Temple U., 1942, 43; m. Irma V. Richert, July 12, 1946; children—Deborah R., Kathleen M., Myron J., Stanley. Tchr. pub. schs., Lehigh, Kans., 1941-42; intern Bethany Hosp., Kansas City, Kans., 1951-52; gen. practice medicine, Wellsville, Kans., 1951, Hillsboro, Kans., 1952—; chief staff Salem Hosp., Hillsboro, 1959-68; staff mem. St. Luke's Hosp., Marion, Kans.; coroner, Marion County, 1954-64, pub. health officer, 1956—. Bd. dirs. Parkside Homes. Mem. A.M.A., Kans., Marion County med. socs., Am. Acad. Family Practice, Hillsboro C. of C., Phi Chi. Mem. Mennonite Ch. (med. adviser missions bd.). Kiwanian. Home: 202 S Wilson St Hillsboro KS 67063 Office: 209 S Main St Hillsboro KS 67068

ENSIGN, DWIGHT CHESTER, physician; b. Iowa City, Iowa, Jan. 15, 1899; s. Forest Chester and Lucie Maria (Smith) E.; A.B., State U. Iowa, 1920, M.D., 1924; m. Ruth Martin, Sept. 28, 1924; m. 2d, Mary Jane Field, Oct. 1, 1940 (dec. Oct. 19[75); children—James Martin, Mary Jane Bednas. Intern Henry Ford Hosp., Detroit, 1924-26, resident in internal medicine, 1926-30, chief resident in medicine, 1930-36, asso. internal medicine, 1936-42, chief div. rhematology, 1942-66, cons. div. rheumatology, 1966—; trustee Center for Health Edn., Detroit, 1965—, chmn., 1975—; mem. Med. adv. bd. SSS, WW II. Mem. Franklin Village Planning Commn. Served as 2d lt. U.S. Army, WW I. Diplomate Am. Bd. Internal Medicine. Fellow A.C.P.; mem. AMA, Am., Mich. (pres. 1957-59), rheumatism socs., Central Soc. Clin. Research, St. Dunstan's Guild Cranbrook, Soc. Mayflower Descs., Phi Beta Kappa, Alpha Omega Alpha, Sigma Xi, Omicron Delta Kappa, Nu Sigma Nu, Phi Kappa Psi. Republican. Episcopalian. Club: Village (Birmingham-Bloomfield). Contbr. articles on rehumatic diseases to med. jours. and books; mem. Barbados-Antigua Expdn., State U. Iowa, 1918. Home: PO Box 652 32945 Franklin Ct Franklin MI 48025 Office: Henry Ford Hosp Detroit MI 48202

ENSIGN, WILLIAM JAMES, polit. scientist, educator; b. Cleve., June 21, 1924; s. Harmon O. and Isabella T. (McKay) E.; A.B., U. Notre Dame, 1950, A.M., 1951; m. Joan Marie Kennedy, Nov. 18, 1950; children—Maria T., Kimberly Anne, Christopher William, Joel Francis, Madonna Maureen, Thomas Shannon. Adult probation officer Common Pleas Ct. Lucas County, Toledo, 1951-60; exec. sec. Ohio Pardon and Parole Commn., Columbus, Ohio, 1960-63; dir. Lucas County Welfare Dept., Toledo, 1963-67; mayor Toledo, 1967-71; dir. Ohio Youth Commn., 1971-74, State Office Vol. Coordination, 1974-75; prof. polit. sci., dir. criminal justice program Ohio Dominican Coll., Columbus, 1975—. Instr. sociology Mary Manse Coll., Toledo, 1954-60, 63-67; adj. prof. Xavier U., Cin.; cons. urban problems, crime and delinquency. Mem. Ursuline Activities Council, 1957-66. Trustee St. Angela Merici Hall. Served with USMCR, 1942-46. Mem. Am. Legion, D.A.V. Democrat. Roman Catholic. K.C. (3 deg.), Eagle. Home: 1900 Northam Rd Columbus OH 43221 Office: 1216 Sunbury Rd Columbus OH 43219

ENSLEY, RODNEY GENE, ins. co. exec.; b. Trinway, Ohio, Oct. 26, 1934; s. Byron King and Elena Bernadine (Howell) E.; B.B.A., Case Western Res. U., 1959; m. Shelva Jean Hudson, June 17, 1962; children—Rodney Gene, David Byron. Vice pres., controller Western Res. Life Ins. Co., Cleve., 1964-68; v.p., treas., controller Montgomery Ward Life Ins. Co., Chgo., 1968-71; v.p., controller Guarantee Res. Life Ins. Co., Hammond, Ind., 1971-73; fin. v.p., treas. Globe Life Ins. Co., Chgo., 1973—. Pres. Casa Montessori Sch., 1972-73; treas., bd. dirs. Laren Montessori Sch., 1973-76. Fellow Life Mgmt. Inst.; mem. Ill. Soc. C.P.A.'s, Am. Inst. C.P.A.'s, Am. Soc. C.L.U., Beta Gamma Sigma, Phi Soc. Republican. Unitarian. Club: Omni Tennis. Home: 9412 Cottonwood Dr Munster IN 46321 Office: 222 N Dearborn Chicago IL 60601

ENSWEILER, RICHARD LAURENCE, assn. exec.; b. Milw., Dec. 1, 1940; s. Donald George and Nancy Ruth (Kulk) E.; B.S., Lakeland Coll., 1963; m. Judith Ann Johnson, Dec. 14, 1973. Mgmt. trainee State Central Credit Union, Milw., 1964-65; mgr. Harley Davidson Credit Union, Milw., 1965-68; league rep. Mich. Credit Union League, Southfield, Mich., 1968-71; asst. mng. dir. Minn. League Credit Unions, St. Paul, 1971, mng. dir., 1971-74; pres. Ill. Credit Union League, Bensenville, 1974—. Pack chmn. Cub Scouts, Addison, Ill., 1974-76. Mem. Internat. Assn. Mng. Dirs. (sec.), Am. Soc. Assn. Execs. (certified), Credit Union Legis. Action Com. (pres. 1975—), Lakeland Coll. Alumni Assn. (dir.), Mu Lambda Sigma. Mason. Home: 1340 Meyer Dr Addison IL 60101 Office: 1035 S York Rd Bensenville IL 60106

EPHRAIM, DONALD MORLEY, lawyer; b. Chgo., Jan. 14, 1932; s. Jacob H. and Belle (Freundlich) E.; B.S.C., DePaul U., 1952; postgrad. Northwestern U.; C.P.A., U. Ill., 1953; J.D., U. Chgo., 1955; m. Sylvia Zupnik, Aug. 13, 1961; children—David Marc, Eliot Scott, Eric Alan. Admitted to Ill. bar, 1955; atty. Ross, McGowan & O'Keefe, Chgo., 1955; C.P.A., Arthur Andersen & Co., Chgo., 1957-60; atty. Pennish, Steel & Rockler, Chgo., 1960-63, Schradzke, Gould & Ratner, Chgo., 1963-65, practice law Chgo., 1965—; pres., dir. Presdl. Properties, Ltd., 1970—; v.p., dir. Continental Marine Corp. Served with AUS, 1956-57. C.P.A., Ill. Mem. Am., Ill., Chgo. bar assns., Am. Assn. Atty.-C.P.A.'s, Am. Inst. C.P.A.'s, Ill. Soc. C.P.A.'s, Chgo. Estate Planning Council, Phi Sigma Delta, Pi Gamma Mu. Jewish religion. Home: 111 Red Oak Lane Highland Park IL 60035 Office: 172 N Franklin St Chicago IL 60606

EPLER, HAROLD BENJAMIN, devel. co. exec.; b. Marietta, Ohio, Dec. 2, 1906; s. George B. and Hulda V. (Ahicht) E.; B.Sc., Ohio State U., 1928; m. Frances M. Blotzer, Jan. 11, 1941; children—Harold Benjamin, Donald Fredrick. With Gen. Clay Products Corp., Columbus, Ohio, 1935—, sales mgr., 1937-40, pres. 1940-72, chmn. bd., 1972—; chmn. bd. Gen. Wadsworth Brick Corp., Jubilee Devel. Co., Oxford Transmission Co. Mem. Am., Ohio ceramic socs., Columbus Bldrs. Exchange. Office: Gen Clay Products Corp 1445 W Goodale Blvd Columbus OH 43212

EPP, ELDON JAY, educator; b. Mountain Lake, Minn., Nov. 1, 1930; s. Jacob Jay and Louise (Kintzi) E.; A.B. magna cum laude, Wheaton Coll., 1952; B.D. magna cum laude, Fuller Theol. Sem., 1955; S.T.M., Harvard, 1956, Ph.D., 1961; m. ElDoris Balzer, June 13, 1951; children—Gregory Thomas, Jennifer Elizabeth. Spl. research asst. Princeton Theol. Sem., 1961-62; vis. instr. Drew U. Theol. Sch., 1962; asst. prof. religion U. So. Calif. Grad. Sch. Religion, 1962-65, asso. prof., 1965-67, asso. prof. classics, 1966-68; asso. prof. religion Case Western Res. U., Cleve., 1968-71, Harkness prof. Bibl. lit., 1971—, dean humanities and social scis., 1977—. Mem. Am. exec. com. Internat. Greek New Testament Project, 1968—. Bd. mgrs. St. Paul's Episcopal Cathedral, Los Angeles, 1964-68; active Boy Scouts Am. Harvard Div. Sch. fellow, 1956-58, Harvard Faculty Arts and Scis. fellow, 1958-59, Rockefeller Doctoral fellow in religion, 1959-60; Guggenheim fellow, 1974-75. Mem. Am. Acad. Religion (sect. pres. 1965-66), Soc. Bibl. Lit. (chmn. textual criticism seminar 1966, 71—), Studiorum Novi Testamenti Societas, Cath. Bibl. Assn., New Testament Colloquium (chmn. 1974), Soc. Mithraic Studies, A.A.U.P. (chpt. exec. com. 1970-72), Inst. Antiquity and Christianity (corr.). Author: The Theological Tendency of Codex Bezae Cantabrigiensis in Acts, 1966. Asso. editor Jour. of Bibl. Lit., 1971—. Mem. editorial bd. Soc. Bibl. Lit. Monograph Series, 1969-72, Soc. Bibl. Lit. Centenniel Publs., 1975—, Studies and Documents, 1971—; exec. sec. Hermeneia: A Critical and Historical Commentary on the Bible, 1962—, mem. editorial bd., 1966—. Contbr. articles, reviews to publs. Home: 19051 Fairmount Blvd Shaker Heights OH 44118 Office: Office Dean Western Res Coll Case Western Res U Cleveland OH 44106

EPPARD, CLYDE MONROE, elec. engr.; b. Redfield, Iowa, Jan. 24, 1903; s. Willard McVern and Jennie A. (Fenimore) E.; B.S., Iowa State U., 1928; m. Frances Helen Middleton, Dec. 24, 1928; children—Joanne Frances (Mrs. John Daniel Prien II), Sandra Jean (Mrs. David Leigh Kagy). Asst. elec. engr. Substa. div. Cahokia Plant Union Elec. Co., St. Louis, 1929-35, asst. elec. supt. Cahokia, Venice Power Plants, 1936-40, elec. supt. Venice No. 2 Power Plant, 1941-46, gen. supt. steam, elec., 1947-55, asst. to v.p., operations exec., 1956-67; cons. engr. C.E. Cons., Fairview Heights, Ill., 1968—; profl. cons. coal handling systems for power plants; dir. Utility Employee's Savs. & Loan Assn. Mem. Community Progress, Inc., East St. Louis, Ill., 1962-64. Registered profl. engr., Mo. Mem. Nat., Ill., St. Clair County profl. engrs. socs., Am. Arbitration Assn. (nat. panel arbitrators), Eta Kappa Nu. Republican. Presbyn. Mason. Patentee in field. Home and office: 8908 Fair Oaks Dr Fairview Heights IL 62208

EPPERSON, WILLIAM THOMAS, news service exec.; b. Galesburg, Ill., Feb. 8, 1926; s. Walter William and Florence Maude (Streeter) E.; student pub. schs.; m. Coilla Linnea Anson, July 20, 1947; 1 dau., Kimberly Ann. Asst. mgr. J.J. Newberry Co., Peoria and Rock Island, Ill., 1946-49, mgr., 1949-59; asst. mgr. Waibel Variety Store, East Peoria, Ill., 1960-65; store mgr. The Book Emporium, Inc., Peoria, 1965-67, v.p., 1968, exec. v.p., 1969—; exec. v.p. Ill. News Service, Inc., Peoria, 1973—, also dir. Served with U.S. Army, 1944-46. Mem. Nat. Pilots Assn., Aircraft Owners and Pilots Assn., Peoria C. of C., Sheridan Village Bus. Men's Assn. Clubs: Elks, Masons, Shriners, Creve Coeur (Peoria), Wee-Ma-Tuk Country (Cuba, Ill.). Home: 4427 W Ducharme Ave Bartonville IL 61607 Office: 1301 SW Washington St Peoria IL 61602

EPSTEIN, DANIEL N., lawyer, real estate co. exec.; b. Chgo., Mar. 14, 1938; s. Julius E. and Dorothy (Brenner) E.; B.A., Cornell U., 1959; J.D., Yale, 1962; m. Gail Margolis, June 18, 1961; children—Abra, Joel. Admitted to Ill. bar, 1962; asso. firm Schradzke, Gould & Rather, Chgo., 1963-68; mem. firm Yacker, Gerson & Epstein, Chgo., 1969-71; chmn. bd. Haven Devel. Corp., Chgo., 1972—; mem. firm Fortes, Eiger, Epstein & Skirnick, Chgo., 1975-77; individual practice, 1977—. Lectr., Ill. Bar Assn., 1970-71, Ill. Housing Devel. Authority, 1972—, U. Ill., Chgo., 1971. Mem. Am. Bar Assn. (spl. com. on housing 1973—). Jewish religion. Home: 2865 Sheridan Pl Evanston IL 60201 Office: 228 N LaSalle St Chicago IL 60601

EPSTEIN, HERBERT MARVIN, physician; b. Newburgh, N.Y., Jan. 21, 1925; s. Charles and Rose (Shafer) E.; student Yale, 1942-43, Princeton, 1943-45; M.D., U. Rochester, 1949; m. Sylvia Eskin Rottman, Sept. 7, 1947; children—Susan Faith, Peter. Intern, Grace-New Haven Hosp., 1949-50; resident anesthesiology Hartford (Conn.) Hosp., 1952-54; practice medicine, specializing in anesthesiology, Evanston, Ill., 1954—; sr. attending physician Evanston Hosp., 1954—, chief div. anesthesia, 1972—; cons. Community Hosp., Evanston, Shriners Hosp., Chgo.; asso. prof. clin. anesthesia Northwestern U. Med. Sch., 1973—, mem. faculty senate, 1971—. Mem. Glencoe Caucus, 1956-60. Served with AUS, 1942-45; to lt., M.C., USNR, 1949-52. Diplomate Am. Bd. Anesthesiology. Fellow Am. Coll. Anesthesiology; mem. A.M.A., Ill., Chgo. med. socs., Am. Soc. Anesthesiology, Am., Ill., Chgo. (v.p.) socs. anesthesiologists, Soc. for Contemporary Art, Art Inst. Chgo. Clubs: Yale (Chgo.); Birchwood Tennis (Highland Park, Ill.). Home: 369 Bluff St Glencoe IL 60022 Office: Evanston Hosp Evanston IL 60201

EPSTEIN, MARVIN MORRIS, internat. marketing exec.; b. Cleve., June 2, 1928; s. Isadore A. and Rose (Gevelber) E.; student Western Res. U., 1947-49; B.A., U. Mich., 1951; m. Lois M. DeSure, June 10, 1956; children—Deborah Leigh, David Alan. Reporter, Cleve. Plain Dealer, 1951-52; editor A.P., Columbus, Ohio, 1952-54; asst. mng. editor Times-Star, 1954-56; internat. editor Milw. Jour., 1956-59; sr. asso. Eden & Assos., Cleve., 1959-61; with Austin Co., Cleve., 1961—, dir. internat. sales and mktg. services, 1968. Served with AUS, 1946-47. Mem. U. Mich. Alumni Assn., Am. Jewish Com., Soc. Profl. Journalists, Greater Cleve. Growth Assn., Kappa Tau Alpha. Democrat. Jewish. Contbr. numerous articles to profl. jours. Home: 4161 Hadleigh Rd University Heights OH 44118 Office: 3650 Mayfield Rd Cleveland OH 44121

EPSTEIN, SHERWIN LEWIS, lawyer; b. N.Y.C., Sept. 29, 1930; s. Theodore Henry and Tillie (Gitelis) E.; A.B., U. Mo., 1955, J.D., 1957; m. Ruby Lee Snider, Apr. 2, 1966 (div. May 1976); 1 son, Mark Harold. Admitted to Mo. bar, 1957, U.S. Supreme Ct. bar, 1975; atty. firm Achtenberg, Sandler & Balkin, Kansas City, Mo., 1957-59; atty. Kansas City Title Ins. Co. (Mo.), 1959-61; atty., asso. city counselor, Kansas City, Mo., 1961-68; practiced in Kansas City, Mo., 1968-70; sr. partner firm Stubbs, Epstein & Mann, Kansas City, Mo., 1970-76; instr. U. Mo., Kansas City. Counsel, City Planning Commn. and Bd. Zoning Adjustment, 1962-68. Bd. dirs. Downtown, Inc., Heart Am. Eye Assn., Temple B'nai Jehudah Brotherhood. Served to 1st lt. USAF, 1952-54. Hon. fellow Harry S Truman Library Inst. Mem. Am. (real estate com.), Mo., Kansas City (chmn. real estate law com.) bar assns., Am. Judicature Soc., Lawyers Assn., Phi Alpha Delta, Alpha Epsilon Pi. Democrat. Jewish. Mem. B'nai B'rith. Home: 11800 Central St Kansas City MO 64114 Office: 1105 Grand Ave Kansas City MO 64106

EPSTEIN, WILLIAM HENRY, educator; b. Easton, Pa., Oct. 31, 1944; s. Benjamin Maurice and Elena Sylvia (Freedman) E.; B.A., Dartmouth Coll., 1966; M.A., Columbia U., 1967, Ph.D., 1972; m. Mildred Ann Rose, June 30, 1968; children—Jessica Irma, Rebecca Elena Madeline. Instr. in English, Purdue U., West Lafayette, Ind., 1970-72, asst. prof., 1972-76, asso. prof., 1976—. Mem. Modern Lang. Assn., Am. Soc. 18th Century Studies. Democrat. Jewish. Author: John Cleland: Images of a Life, 1974. Home: 516 Robinson St West Lafayette IN 47906 Office: Dept English Purdue U West Lafayette IN 47907

ERDMAN, EARL GUSTAV, retail trade exec.; b. Wykoff, Minn., July 3, 1915; s. Emil A. and Alvina (Sturm) E.; grad. high sch.; m. Leone B. Mertz, Sept. 29, 1937; children—Daryl, Dianne. Sec.-treas. Erdman Supermarkets, Inc., Kasson, Minn., 1933-65, pres., 1965—; pres. Erdman's, Inc., 1950—; v.p. Rotab Corp., Rochester, Minn., 1976—; sec.-treas. Aldeens Inc., 1975—. Mem. adv. bd. Minn. Vocat. Sch. Served with USAF, 1945-46. Mem. Rochester C. of C., Am. Legion. Lutheran. Elk. Clubs: Commercial (pres.) (Kasson); St. Croix Yacht. Home: 2210 11th Ave NW Rochester MN 55901 Office: 19 2d Ave NW Kasson MN 55944

ERICKSON, ALCOTT PARNELL, wood fencing mfg. co. exec.; b. Wis., Oct. 16, 1919; s. Harry I. and Ella (Christensen) E.; student U. Minn. Sch. Bus. Adminstrn., 1948-51; m. Dorothy Goodman, July 17, 1948; 1 dau., Deborah Sue. Accountant, Nat. Auto-Owners Inter-Ins. Assn., Gladstone, Mich., 1937-41; with Soo Line R.R., Gladstone, Mpls., Enderlin, N.D., 1941-55; pres. Sterling Bldg. Supplies, Inc., Gladstone, 1955-65; exec. v.p. Early Am. Fence Co., Am. Timber Homes, Inc., Escanaba, Mich., 1965-68; owner Early Am. Industries, Powers, Mich., 1968—. County treas. Republican Party, Escanaba, 1963-65. Served with Transp. Corps AUS, 1942-45. Mem. Gladstone C. of C. (past dir.), Am. Legion. Mem. Evang. Covenant Ch. Mason, Rotarian. Club: Gladstone Yacht. Home: 703 Dakota Ave Gladstone MI 49837 Office: PO Box 166 Powers MI 49874

ERICKSON, ELWYN HOWARD, educator; b. St. Charles, Ill., Nov. 27, 1911; s. Nels Olaf Edwin and Mary Christine (Timm) E.; student U. Ill., 1931; Northwestern U., 1932, U. Calif. at Berkeley, 1942, Cosmopolitan Sch. Music, 1947-51, Sherwood Music Sch., 1948; m. Adelia Howard, May 1, 1961. Show bus., 1926-58; night club soloist piano and organ, Chgo. area, 1946-56; tchr. piano, organ Hiltbrunnen Music Co., Cedar Rapids, Iowa, 1956—. Served with AUS, 1941-46. Home: 1100 18th St NW Cedar Rapids IA 52405 Office: 1100 18th St NW Cedar Rapids IA 52405

ERICKSON, GEORGE EVERETT, JR., lawyer; b. Ft. Scott, Kans., July 20, 1937; s. George Everett and Kathleen Cora (Hayden) E.; B.S., U.S. Naval Acad., 1959; J.D., Washburn U., 1966; m. Carrol Ann Guthridge, Dec. 23, 1966; children—Ingrid Ann, Karin Ruth. Admitted to Okla., Kans. bars, 1966; with legal dept. Amerada Petroleum Corp., Tulsa, 1966-69; partner law firm Cosgrove, Webb & Oman, Topeka, 1969-73; pvt. practice law, Topeka, 1973—; city atty., Auburn, Kans., 1976—. Asst. prof. law Washburn U., Topeka, 1973-74; farmer, Topeka, 1974—; counsel Topeka Fellowship House, 1969-72. Vol. probation officer, Topeka, 1970-72. Served with USN, 1959-63. Mem. Kan., Topeka (com. chmn. 1971—), Am. bar assns., Am. Trial Lawyers Assn., Lawyers Club Topeka, Phi Alpha Delta. Republican. Elk, Lion. Club: Army-Navy (Washington). Asso. editor Washburn Law Jour., 1965-66. Home: 6000 Urish Rd Topeka KS 66604 Office: 420 W 33d St Topeka KS 66611

ERICKSON, GEORGE OLOF, banker; b. Dalbo, Minn., Nov. 8, 1926; s. Elmer V. and Otelia E. (Forslund) E.; student Gustavus Adolphus Coll., 1944-45, U. Minn., 1945-46; m. Roselyn A. Stone, Nov. 29, 1952; children—Kim Marie, Kathy Ann, Kristin Lee. With Cambridge State Bank (Minn.), 1946—, pres., 1967—. Sec.-treas. Cambridge Bus. Devel. Co., Inc. (Minn.), 1967—; mem. council City of Cambridge, 1972-75, mayor, 1976-77. Served with AC, AUS, 1945. Mem. Am. Legion. Club: Minneapolis Athletic. Home: 827 S Birch St Cambridge MN 55008 Office: Box 472 Cambridge MN 55008

ERICKSON, KARLE JOSEPH, condr., educator; b. Braham, Minn., Oct. 11, 1938; s. Marvin Kenneth and Inga (Flaa) E.; B.A. cum laude, St. Olaf Coll., 1960; B.S., U. Ill., 1966; Ed.D., U. Ill., 1970; m. Hannah Marie Troen, Aug. 4, 1962; children—Kristofer, Kari, Kelsey. Dir. choirs St. James (Minn.) High Sch., 1960-62, Sterling (Ill.) Twp. High Sch., 1962-65; grad. asst. music edn. U. Ill., Urbana, 1965-67; dir. choral studies, chmn. dept. music edn. Lawrence U. Conservatory of Music, Appleton, Wis., 1967—. Mem. Am. (pres. N. Central div. 1974-77), Wis. (pres. 1972-74) choral dirs. assns., A.A.U.P., Wis. Sch. Music Assn. (dir. 1969-75), Music Educators Nat. Conf., Am. Choral Found. Contbr. articles to profl. jours. Home: 2837 E Hietpas St Appleton WI 54911 Office: 115 N Park St Appleton WI 54911

ERICKSON, SALLY WISHEK LOVELL, lumber co. exec.; b. Aberdeen, S.D., Sept. 30, 1928; d. Max A. and Viola L. (Hezel) Wishek; B.A., U. Ariz., 1950; M.S. in Guidance and Edn., No. State Coll., Aberdeen, 1970; m. Orrin B. Lovell, June 30, 1951 (div. 1970); children—James, Faith, Kent, Christopher, Gregory; m. 2d, Donavan L. Erickson, May 27, 1973. Elementary tchr., Riverdale, N.D., 1950-51; addiction counselor Jamestown (N.D.) State Hosp., 1971-72; elementary sch. counselor, Belcourt, N.D., 1973-75; sec.-treas. Ashley Lumber Co., 1975—; v.p., dir. Wishek Investment Co., Inc., Ashley; v.p. Union Elevator Co., Ashley, dir. McIntosh County Bank, Ashley, N.D. Mem. Am. Personnel and Guidance Assn., Am. Legion Aux., Alpha Phi. Address: Ashley ND 58413

ERICKSON, SCOTT WILLIAM, cons. firm exec.; b. Brodhead, Wis., Jan. 21, 1948; s. Orville Arnold and Eleanor Mary (Johnson) E.; B.A., U. Minn., Morris, 1970; M.A., U. Minn., Mpls., 1973, Ph.D., 1978. Instr. edn. U. Minn., Mpls., 1973-77; pres., cons. Future Systems, Ins., Mpls., 1977—. Recipient Provost's award U. Minn., Morris, 1970. Mem. Am. Hist. Assn., World Future Soc., Minn. Futurists Assn. Author articles on the future of edn., also exploration and colonization of space; editor Futurics, Quar. Jour. Futures Research, 1977—. Office: PO Box 14067 University Sta Minneapolis MN 55414

ERICKSON, W(ALTER) BRUCE, educator; b. Chgo., Mar. 4, 1938; s. Clifford E. and Mildred B. (Brinkmeier) E.; B.A., Mich. State U., 1959, M.A., 1960, Ph.D. in Econs., 1965. Research asso. Subcom. on Antitrust and Monopoly, U.S. Senate, 1960-61; asst. prof. econs. Bowling Green (Ohio) State U., 1964-66; asst. prof. bus. and govt. Coll. Bus. Adminstrn., U. Minn., Mpls., 1966-70, asso. prof., 1971-75, prof., 1975—, chmn. dept. mgmt., 1977—; cons. rock salt antitrust cases for atty. gens. of Mich., Calif., Ill., Wis. and Minn.; cons. to U.S. Dept. Justice. Mem. Am. Econ. Assn., Royal Econ. Soc. Author: An Introduction to Contemporary Business, 2d edit., 1976; contbr. articles on econs. to profl. jours. Home: 2849 35th Ave S Minneapolis MN 55406 Office: 868 BA Tower Coll Bus Adminstrn Univ Minn Minneapolis MN 55455

ERICKSON, WALTON, supt. schs.; b. Escanaba, Mich., Aug. 17, 1919; s. John E. and Anna (Nicholson) E.; B.S. in Commerce, Ferris Inst., 1948; M.A. in Adminstrn., U. Mich., 1953; m. Marguerite M. Scheppelman, July 19, 1942; children—Glenn, Alan, Linda, Ronald. Tchr., Stanwood (Mich.) Rural Agrl. Sch., 1948-50; prin., 1951-54, supt., 1954-58; comml. tchr. Reed City (Mich.) Pub. Schs., 1950-51; supt. schs. Morley (Mich.) Stanwood Community Schs., 1958—. Fin. auditor Mecosta and Newaygo Counties, 1949-70; mem. budget com. Mecosta County United Fund; mem. Mecosta County Council on Aging; mem. adv. bd. Sch. Assembly Services, Inc.; mem. control br. Mecosta Meml. Hosp., Stanwood; councilman Village of Morley; bd. dirs. Morley Stanwood Pub. Library. Served as pilot USNR, 1941-45. Mem. Am., Mich. assns. sch. adminstrs., Mich. Sch. Bus. Ofcls., Mich. Assn. for Retarded Children, Morley C. of C., Ret. Officers Assn., Am. Legion. Lutheran. Mason, Elk, Lion. Home: 281 N Cass St Morley MI 49336 Office: Morley Stanwood High Sch US 131 Morley MI 49336

ERICKSTAD, RALPH JOHN, state justice; b. Starkweather, N.D., Aug. 15, 1922; s. John T. and Anna L. Erickstad; student U. N.D., 1940-43; B.S. in Law, U. Minn., 1947, LL.B., 1949; m. Lois Katherine Jacobson, July 30, 1949; children—John Albert, Mark Anders. Admitted to N.D. bar, 1949; mem. firm Teigen & Erickstad, Devils Lake; police magistrate, Devils Lake, 1951-53; states atty., Ramsey County, 1953-57; mem. firm Erickstad & Foughty; asso. justice Supreme Ct. of N.D., Bismarck, 1963-73, chief justice, 1973—. Mem. Gov.'s Spl. Com. on Labor, 1960; past commr. Missouri Valley council Boy Scouts Am.; mem. N.D. Senate, 1957-62, asst. majority floor leader; chmn. bd. trustees Missouri Valley Family YMCA, 1966-77. Recipient Silver Beaver award Boy Scouts Am., 1967, Sioux award U. N.D., 1973. Mem. Am., N.D., Burleigh County bar assns., Am. Judicature Soc., Am. Law Inst., Nat. Conf. Chief Justices (exec. council). Republican. Lutheran. Club: Kiwanis. Home: 1266 W Highland Acres Rd Bismarck ND 58501 Office: Supreme Ct ND Capitol Bldg Bismarck ND 58505

ERICSON, EARL DONALD, real estate broker; b. Elsmore, Kans., Apr. 2, 1923; s. Earl and Agnes (Appelquist) E.; student Chanute (Kans.) Jr. Coll., 1941-42, Allen County (Kans.) Jr. Coll., 1974; m. Betty Patricia Edwards, Nov. 9, 1946; 1 dau., Sammie Jo (Mrs. Tom J. Ragonese). Foreman/supt. pipeline constrn. co., 1949-62; farmer/rancher, Hepler, Kans., 1962-69; pres. H&H Agy., Inc., real estate, Chanute, 1969-75, Pittsburg, Fort Scott and Girard (all Kans.), 1975—; chmn. bd. Bank of Bronson (Kans.), 1974-75. Pres., Neosho County Bd. Realtors, 1971-72, dir., 1971-72. Mem. Chanute C. of C. Mason (Shriner), Elk. Republican. Lutheran. Home: 1001 S Tennessee St Chanute KS 66720 Office: 19 N Lincoln Ave Chanute KS 66720

ERIKSEN, CARL AHLERS, hobby wholesaler exec.; b. Lawrence, Kans., May 6, 1909; s. Conrad John and Amanda Josephine (Anderson) E.; B.S., U. Kans., 1930; m. Dorothy Ann Graber, Nov. 27, 1931; 1 son, John Graber. Various positions in Kans., Okla., 1931-37; salesman B.F. Goodrich Co., Joplin, Mo., 1937-42; buyer Boeing Airplane Co., Wichita, Kans., 1942-45; with sales Fisk Tire Co., Hutchinson, Kans., 1945-49; founder Eriksen's Crafts, Hutchinson, 1949, pres., 1959-72, chmn. bd., 1972—. Cons. articles trade mags. Mem. Hobby Industry Assn. Am. (bd. dirs. 1969-75), Sigma Nu. Presbyn. Mason (32 deg.), Lion. Home: 24 Tomahawk Rd Hutchinson KS 67501 Office: 1101 N Halstead St Hutchinson KS 67501

ERLENBORN, JOHN NEAL, congressman; b. Chgo., Feb. 8, 1927; s. John H. and Veronica M. (Moran) E.; student U. Notre Dame, 1944, U. Ill., 1945-46; J.D., Loyola U. (Chgo.), 1949; m. Dorothy C. Fisher, May 10, 1952; children—Debra Lynn, Paul Nelson, David John. Admitted to Ill. bar, 1949; practiced in Wheaton, Ill., 1949-50, mem. firm Erlenborn and Bauer, 1952-63, Erlenborn, Bauer, and Hotte, 1963-71; mem. 88th-95th Congresses 14 dist. Ill. Mem. Ill. Ho. of Reps., 1956-64; assistant States Atty., DuPage County, Ill., 1950-52. Served with USNR, 1944-46. Mem. Am. Legion, C. of C. Republican. Club: Lions (Elmhurst, Ill.). Home: Glen Ellyn IL 60137 Office Rayburn House Office Bldg Room 2236 Washington DC 20515

ERNEST, DAVID JOHN, ednl. adminstr., composer, musician; b. Chgo., May 16, 1929; s. Rudolph James and Sylvia Rose (Travnicek) E.; diploma Wright Jr. Coll., Chgo., 1949; Mus.B. (Rudolph Ganz scholar), Chgo. Mus. Coll., 1951; M.S., U. Ill., 1956; postgrad. (Fulbright scholar), Sorbonne, U. Paris (France), 1958-59; Ed.D., U. Colo., 1961; m. Prudence Ellene Michael, Aug. 30, 1959; children—David, Stephen, Bryan, Christopher. Instr. double reeds and music edn., U. Colo., Boulder, 1956-58, 59-61; chmn. div. Fine and Applied Arts, Glenville (W.Va.) State Coll., 1961-63; chmn. dept. music St. Cloud (Minn.) State U., 1963—. Oboe and English Horn soloist Chgo. Civic Orch., 1949-54, Boulder Symphony, 1956-61, St. Cloud Civic Orch., 1975—, others; chmn. bd. govs. Atwood Meml. Center, St. Cloud, 1971-73; condr. community mus. groups, St. Cloud, 1963—; mem. Nat. Com. on Logistics of Music Edn., 1970-72, Music Educators Nat. Conf., Reston, Va., 1954—. Served with AUS, 1951-54. Mem. Am. Ednl. Research Assn., Nat. Council on Measurement Edn., Minn. Coll. and Univ. Council for Music (pres. 1972-74), Internat. Soc. Harpsichord Builders, Galpin Soc., A.A.U.P. (pres. 1968-69), Nat. Assn. Schs. of Music (rep. region IV 1971—), Phi Delta Kappa (pres. 1975-76), Phi Mu Alpha. Composer: Sonatine for oboe and strings, 1969; (opera) Ten Year Thunder, 1963, numerous smaller compositions. Home: Crest Rd Route 5 St Cloud MN 56301

ERNST, RONALD LEROY, mgmt. cons.; b. Toledo, Ohio, Mar. 15, 1949; s. Richard Harry and Audrey Jayne (Sprengel) E.; B.S., Ind. U., 1971; M.B.A., Ohio State U., 1972; m. Virginia Walters, June 17, 1972. Research and cons. asso. Mgmt. Horizons, Inc., Worthington, Ohio, 1971-75, sr. cons. asso., Columbus, 1976—; project mgr. mktg. research Federated Dept. Stores, Cin., 1975-76; lectr. in bus. adminstrn. Franklin U., 1972-73. Mem. Am. Mktg. Assn., Am. Mgmt. Assn., Assn. of M.B.A. Execs. Democrat. Lutheran. Contbr. articles to profl. jours. Home: 1099 Kirk Ave Worthington OH 43085 Office: 450 W Wilson Bridge Rd Worthington OH 43085

ERNSTING, RICHARD HARVEY, dentist; b. Indpls., Feb. 2, 1925; s. Harry Deitrick and Charlotte (Harvey) E.; student Arsenal Tech. Schs., 1938-42; D.D.S., Ind. U., 1952; m. Anna M. Baxter, Sept. 23, 1967. Pvt. practice dentistry, Indpls., 1952—. Mem. teaching staff Ind. U. Sch. Dentistry, 1952-57; dentist Marion County Home, 1959-73. Elder, Central Christian Ch., 1969—, chmn. bd., 1975-76. Served to 1st lt. AUS, 1943-46. Mem. Am., Ind. dental assns., Indpls. Dist. Dental Soc., Xi Psi Phi. Club: Sertoma (pres. 1968-69) (Indpls.). Home: 3919 E 57th St Indianapolis IN 46220 Office: 6326 Rucker Rd Suite B Indianapolis IN 46220

ERSKINE, ADDINE GRADWOHL (MRS. LUCIAN ERSKINE), scientist, educator; b. Omaha; d. Harry C. and Jennie (Ettman) Gradwohl; grad. Harris Tchrs. Coll., St. Louis; student McGill U., 1932; D.Sc. (hon.), Tech. Coll. Sussex, 1970; D.Lit. (hon.), Internat. Free Protestant Episcopal U., 1968; m. Lucian Erskine, Mar. 26, 1932 (dec. Feb. 1962); step-children—Lucian Jr., Frank S. (dec. 1974). Formerly tchr. St. Louis pub. sch. system med. technologist; med. technologist Gradwohl Lab., St. Louis County Hosp., St. Louis; asst. dir. Gradwohl Sch. Lab. Technique, St. Louis; former asst. editor The Lab. Digest, later asso. editor; former vis. prof. biol. Scis. Lane Coll., Jackson, Tenn. Spl. cons. to med. div. U.S. Dept. State, 1967-68. Pres. bd. dirs. Gradwohl Sch. Lab. Technique. Recipient award Clara Maass Soc. of N.J. Hosp. Assn., 1963; Honor Key award Alumni Assn. of Gradwohl Sch., 1962; Eloy Alfaro Grand Cross and Certificate, Republic of Panama, 1965; Scroll of Appreciation, U.S. Sec. of State, 1968; spl. award for contbns. to sci. edn. Lane Coll., 1969. Fellow Royal Soc. Tropical Medicine and Hygiene (London), AAAS, Royal Micros. Soc. (London), Philos. Soc. Eng. (hon. life); mem. Mo. State Tchrs. Assn., Internat. Coll. Tropical Medicine, N.J. Acad. Sci., St. Louis Acad. Sci., N.Y. Acad. Sci., Nat. Wildlife Preservation Soc., Am. Guild Organists, Internat. Soc. Clin. Lab. Technologists (award for excellence in editorial work 1968, hon. life mem.), Am. Soc. for Microbiology (editor Mo. br. Newsletter). Author: Principles and Practice of Blood Grouping, 1973, (with W.W. Socha) 2d edit., 1978; contbg. author: Clinical Laboratory Methods and Diagnosis; co-author: Laboratory Technique, 1932; Questions in Laboratory Methods, 1967; Blood Types, Transfusions, Rh, and Heredity, 1970. Home: 3721 Clifton St St Louis MO 63109 Office: 3514 Lucas St Louis MO 63103

ERVIN, JOHN BERNARD, found. exec.; b. Birmingham, Ala., July 20, 1916; s. James and Ruby (Browder) E.; B.S., Kent State U., 1938; M.A., Columbia, 1946, Ed.D. (Dean's Scholar), 1950; LL.D. (hon.), Kent State U., 1969; m. Jane Minter, Sept. 14, 1946; 1 dau., Jacquelyn (Mrs. Ladorn Creighton). Tchr. adult edn. dept. Portage County (Ohio) Pub. Schs., 1935-39; tchr. Goshen Twp. Pub. Sch., 1941-42, Akron (Ohio) Pub. Schs., 1943-49; dir. student teaching Stowe Tchrs. Coll., 1949-54; prof. edn. Harris Tchrs. Coll., 1954-62, dean instrn., 1962-65; asso. dean Sch. Continuing Edn., also summer sch. Washington U., St. Louis, 1965-68, dean, 1968-77; v.p. Danforth Found., 1977—; vis. prof. Hampton Inst., Atlanta U., St. Louis U., So. Ill. U.; mem. Nat. Adv. Council on Extension and Continuing Edn., 1976—. Vice chmn. Mo. Commn. Human Rights, 1967-70; mem. Mo. adv. com. U.S. Civil Rights Com., 1965—. Bd. dirs. United Way Greater St. Louis, Municipal Theatre Assn., St. Louis council Boy Scouts Am. Recipient Outstanding Achievement in Tchr. Edn., award Kent State U. Semi-centennial, 1960, Outstanding Alumni award, 1969. Mem. Assn. for Higher Edn., Nat. Univ. Extension Assn., Assn. for Continuing Higher Edn., Kappa Delta Pi, Phi Delta Kappa, Alpha Sigma Lambda, Alpha Phi Alpha, Sigma Pi Phi. Baptist. Home: 8605 Mayflower Ct St Louis MO 63132

ERVIN, PATRICK FRANKLIN, nuclear engr.; b. Kansas City, Kans., Aug. 4, 1946; s. James Franklin and Irma Lee (Arnett) E.; B.S., Kans. State U., 1968, M.S., 1972; m. Rita Jeanne Kimsey, Aug. 12, 1967; 1 son, James Arden. Reactor health physicist Kans. State U. Triga Mark II Nuclear Reactor Facility, Manhattan, 1968-69; research asst. Kans. State U. Neutron Activation Analysis Lab., Manhattan, 1969-70, sr. reactor operator, temporary facility dir., 1970-72; system start-up engr. Commonwealth Edison Co., Zion, Ill., 1972-74, shift foreman, 1974-76, principle engr., 1976-77, tech. staff supr. Byron Nuclear Generating Sta., Byron, Ill., 1977—. Registered profl. engr., Ill. Mem. Am. Nuclear Soc., Phi Kappa Tau. Roman Catholic. Author research papers on neutron activation analysis and counting statistics, 1969-74. Home: 510 Elizabeth St Oregon IL 61061

ESCHBACH, JESSE ERNEST, fed. judge; b. Warsaw, Ind., Oct. 26, 1920; s. Jesse Ernest and Mary W. (Stout) E.; B.S., Ind. U., 1943, J.D. with distinction (Hastings scholar), 1949; m. Sara Ann Walker, Mar. 15, 1947; children—Jesse Ernest III, Virginia. Admitted to Ind. bar, 1949; partner firm Graham, Rasor, Eschbach & Harris, Warsaw, 1949-62; city atty., Warsaw, 1952-53; dep. pros. atty. 54th Jud. Circuit Ct. Ind., 1952-54; judge U.S. Dist. Ct. Ind., 1962-74, chief judge, 1974—. Pres. Endicott Church Furniture, Inc., 1960-62; sec., gen. counsel Dalton Foundries, Inc., 1957-62. Trustee, Ind. U., 1965-70. Served with USNR, 1943-46. Recipient U.S. Law Week award, 1949. Mem. U.S. (labor relations com. 1960-62), Warsaw (pres. 1955-56) chambers commerce, Nat. Assn. Furniture Mfrs. (dir. 1962), Ind. Mfrs. Assn. (dir. 1962), Am., Ind. (bd. mgrs. 1953-54, ho. dels. 1950-60, 7th Circuit Fed. bar assns., Am. Judicature Soc., Order of Coif. Presbyterian. Rotarian (pres. Warsaw 1956-57). Editorial staff Ind. Law Jour., 1947-49. Office: Fed Bldg 1300 S Harrison PO Box 59 Fort Wayne IN 46801*

ESCO, JAMES HOWARD, JR., baking exec.; b. Winder, Ga., June 7, 1920; s. James Howard and Ila I. (Wilbanks) E.; student Ga. Tech., 1958, 59; m. Sara Nell Crowe, Oct. 29, 1940; children—James Richard, William Phillip. Route salesman Colonial Baking Co., Inc., Indpls., 1942-44, route supr., 1944-48, sales mgr., 1948-56, sales service mgr., 1956-59, v.p., asst. gr., 1959-64, pres., 1965—. Active Jr. Achievement, Indpls., 1969-72, Boy Scouts Am., Indpls., 1961-62. Mem. Ind. Grocers Assn. (dir.), Ind. Bakers Assn. (pres. 1973-74). Methodist (mem. ch. bd. 1971-72). Mason (Shriner). Club: Greentree Country. Home: 6828 Balfore Ct Indianapolis IN 46220 Office: 2465 Winthrop Ave Indianapolis IN 46205

ESGUERRA, ANUNSACION C., radiologist; b. Pasig, Rizal, Philippines, Aug. 15, 1935; s. Marcial S. and Felisa R. (Cruz) E.; M.D., U. Santo Tomas (Philippines), 1958; came to U.S., 1958, naturalized, 1972. Staff radiologist West Side VA Hosp., Chgo., 1970-74; staff radiologist Hines (Ill.) VA Hosp., 1974-76, asst. chief, radiology service, 1976—; instr. Loyola U. Med. Sch., Chgo.; ednl. coordinator Trinton Coll. Radiol. Tech. Sch., Ill. Diplomate Am. Bd. Radiology. Home: 2250 S 18th Ave Broadview IL 60153

ESHBAUGH, W(ILLIAM) HARDY, botanist, educator; b. Glen Ridge, N.J., May 1, 1936; s. William H. and Elizabeth (Wakeman) E.; B.A., Cornell U., 1959; M.A., Ind. U., 1961, Ph.D., 1964; m. Barbara Jean Keller, Sept. 6, 1958; children—David, Stephen, Wendy, Jeffrey. Lectr. Ind. U., 1963; spl. asst. to chief ecology and epidemiology br. Dugway (Utah) Proving Ground, 1964-65; asst. prof. botany, curator herbarium So. Ill. U., Carbondale, 1965-67; asst. prof. Miami U., Oxford, Ohio, 1967-72, asso. prof., 1972-77, prof., 1977—; cons. to conservation orgns. Chmn. troop com. Dan Beard council Boy Scouts Am., 1970-75; chmn. Park Adv. Com., Oxford, 1972-75. Trustee Ohio chpt. Nature Conservancy, 1970—, vice chmn., 1973-75; trustee Pomfret (Conn.) Sch., 1976-80. Served with AUS, 1964-65. Am. Philos. Soc. grantee, 1967, 70; Nat. Geog. Soc. grantee, 1970, 72; NSF grantee, 1970, 72, 74. NSF fellow. Mem. Bot. Soc. Am., Am. Inst. Biol. Scis., Assn. for Tropical Biology, AAAS, Internat. Assn. for Plant Taxonomy, Am. Assn. Plant Taxonomists, Soc. for Study of Evolution, Soc. Econ. Botany (sec. 1977-80), Systematics Assn. (Gt. Britain), Sierra Club, Nat. Audubon Soc. Contbr. articles and revs. to profl. jours. Authority on chili peppers (Capsicum). Home: 209 McKee Ave Oxford OH 45056

ESHLEMAN, (JOHN) ROBERT, librarian; b. Myerstown, Pa., Jan. 18, 1909; s. David Shantz and Florence (Doup) E.; Mus.B., Ind. Central Coll., 1929; B.A., Lebanon Valley Coll., 1931; postgrad. Bonebrake Theol. Sem., 1931-32, Columbia, 1932-33; M.A. in L.S., U. Ky., 1952. Mng. dir. Asso. Players, N.Y.C., 1933-43; English tchr. Arcanum (Ohio) pub. sch., 1945-46; head librarian Arcanum Pub. Library, 1946-53; reference librarian, story-telling coach Dayton (Ohio) Pub. Library, 1950-55; head librarian Franklin (Ohio) Pub. Library, 1955-72; librarian Otterbein Home, Lebanon, Ohio, 1972—; organist Otterbein United Meth. Ch., Lebanon, 1975—. Mem. ALA, Am. Guild Organists, Ohio Library Assn., Franklin Area Hist. Soc., Beta Phi Mu. Methodist. Rotarian. Home: 704 Redbud Ct Lebanon OH 45036 Office: Otterbein Home Lebanon OH 45036

ESKEW, WILLIAM CHARLES, planning and devel. analyst; b. Dayton, Ohio, Nov. 13, 1945; s. Charles W. and Nancy L. (Mezger) E.; B.A., Wright State U., 1969; M.A., Ball State U., 1971; m. Barbara Ann Randall, Dec. 21, 1968; 1 son, Jason R. Tchr. English, Northridge Bd. Edn., Dayton, 1969-71; housing and redevel. specialist Miami Valley Regional Planning Commn.—Supportive Council on Preventive Effort, Dayton, 1971-74; dir. for urban renewal, asst. dir. for community devel. City of Xenia (Ohio), 1974-75; prin. partner Hanselman, Eskew & Assos., Dayton, 1975—. Instr., U. Dayton, 1973-74. Mem. Am. Sociol. Assn., Nat. Assn. Housing and Redevel. Ofcls., Am. Soc. Planning Ofcls., Ohio Planning Conf. Home: 201 W 2d St Xenia OH 45385 Office: 201 W 2d St Xenia OH 45385

ESLER, HAROLD DEAN, psychoanalyst; b. Detroit, Oct. 7, 1930; s. Daniel B. and Mary G. (Esler) E.; B.S., Wayne State U., 1957, M.A., 1959; Ph.D., Mich. State U., 1964; m. Nancy L. Valentine, Aug. 12, 1955; children—Pamela M., Laura V., Diana L. Staff psychologist Northville State Hosp., 1959-61; sch. psychologist Lansing Schs., 1961-62; chief psychologist, dir. W.J. Maxey's Boy's Tng. Sch., 1962-64; out-patient child psychologist Plymouth State Home, 1964-66; chief psychologist intense treatment unit Northville State Hosp., 1966-70; pvt. practice psychoanalysis, 1959—; cons. psychoanalyst Mexico Inst. Psychoanalysis. Served with USMC, 1951-53. Mem. Am., Mich. psychol. assns., Mich. Cons. Psychologists Assn., S.W. Assn. Psychoanalysis (v.p.), Nat. Assn. Psychoanalysis (dir.), Internat. Psychoalalytic Fedn. (dir.), Democrat. Roman Catholic. Home: 172 E Hickory Grove St Bloomfield Hills MI 48013 Office: 640 N Woodward St Birmingham MI 48011

ESLINGER, EVERETT WILLIAM, bus. cons. co. exec.; b. Morrison, Ill., Feb. 25, 1915; s. William J. and Emma Elizabeth (Anderson) E.; accounting degree LaSalle U., 1944; m. Lucille Amanda Griswold, Nov. 12, 1937; children—Carla Kay Eslinger Laasch, Carolyn Joy Eslinger Bomberger. Bookkeeper, Badger Lumber Co., Morrison, 1936-41; cost accountant Libby, McNeill & Libby, Chgo., 1941-45; owner E.W. Eslinger, Bus. Cons., Clinton, Iowa, 1945—. Farm owner, Clinton, 1966—; dir., sec. Frontier Motor Inn, Inc., Clinton, 1965—. Pres. bd. dirs. Clinton YMCA, 1972-74; bd. dirs. Scottish Rite Charitable and Ednl. Found. Iowa, Des Moines; bd. dirs., sec. E.C. Armstrong and F.E. Curtis Found., Clinton, 1961—. Mem. Clinton C. of C. (treas. 1954-56), Nat. Soc. Pub. Accountants. Republican. Presbyn. (pres. 1971-73). Mason (33 deg., mem. adv. com. for sovereign grand insp. gen. 1972—). Club: Clinton Country (treas. 1970-72). Home: 400 N 10th St Clinton IA 52732 Office: Exec Plaza Bldg 1127 N 2d St Clinton IA 52732

ESSER, DONALD JOSEPH, engring. co. exec.; b. Madison, Wis., Apr. 25, 1924; s. Raymond Frank and Emma Frances (Gugel) E.; B.M.E., U. Wis., Madison, 1949, postgrad., Milw., 1957-70; m. Virginia Ann Irgens, Aug. 28, 1954; children—Peter, Susan. Engr., Gen. Electric Co., Lynn, Mass., 1949-53; project engr. Allis-Chalmers Corp., Milw., 1953-57; sales engr. George H. Fredricks & Co., Inc., Milw., 1957-62, v.p., 1962-71, prs., 1971—, dir., 1948—; instr. mech. engring. U. Wis.-Madison. Active Boy Scouts Am., 1967-70; ski instr. Chgo. Tribune Free Ski Sch., 1968-72, Blizzard Ski Sch., 1967-76. Served in USAAC, 1943-46; ETO. Registered profl. engr., Wis. Mem. ASME (sec. Milw. sect. 1957, sect. treas. 1958, dir. 1957—), Instrument Soc. Am., Milw. Council Elec. and Sci. Socs. (ASME del. 1978—). Wis. Alumni Assn. (life), Phi Gamma Delta. Club: Western Racquet (charter) (Elm Grove, Wis.). Home: 2037 Sunset Ct Wauwatosa WI 53226 Office: 4524 W Burleigh St Milwaukee WI 53210

ESSER, NICHOLAS M., corp. counsel; b. Aurora, Ill., Feb. 7, 1923; s. Raymond E. and Elizabeth (Steichen) E.; student St. Procopius Coll., 1940-42; diploma meteorology N.Y. U., 1944; J.D., DePaul U., 1948; M.Patent Law, John Marshall Law Sch., 1950; m. Elaine Carlson, Oct. 17, 1945; children—Nicholas M., Dale Leslie. Admitted to Ill. bar, 1949, Fed. bar, 1949; patent atty. Automatic Electric Co., Chgo., 1948-50, Singer, Stern & Carlberg, Chgo., 1950-52; gen. patent counsel Chemetron Corp., Chgo., 1952-74, chief patent counsel, 1974—, mgr. licenses, 1959—; dir. H.A. Schlatter Inc., Rockford; partner Esser Bros. Aviation, Hampshire, 1961—. Trustee Village of Bloomingdale, 1957-61. Mem. DuPage Elementary Dist. 13 Sch. Bd., Bloomingdale, 1957-60; pres. DuPage High Sch. Dist. 108 Sch. Bd., Roselle, Ill., 1965-70. Served to capt. USAAF, 1943-46. Named Alumnus of Year, St. Procopius Coll., 1960. Mem. Am., Ill., Chgo. bar assns., Chgo. Patent Law Assn., U.S. Trademark Assn., Internat. Assn. for Protection Indsl. Property, A.A.A.S., Am. Legion, St. Procopius Coll. Alumni Assn. (pres. 1952-54, dir. 1954-64), Delta Theta Phi. Republican. Home: 6 N 371 Roselle Rd Roselle IL 60172 Office: 111 E Wacker Dr Chicago IL 60601

ESSER, SYLVAN ALOYSIUS, utility co. exec.; b. Earling, Iowa, Aug. 24, 1914; s. Herman Joseph and Kathryn (Bissen) E.; student in diesel engring O.F. Schoeck Sch., 1936-38, in automobile engring. Am. Tech. Sch., 1937-40; m. Jennie Phyllis Brown, July 9, 1938; children—Marcella, Philip, Sharon, Bruce, Annette, Patrick, Pamala. Chief insp. 5th Army Automobile Repair Shops, Omaha, 1942-47; supr. motor equipment Northwestern Bell Telephone Co., Omaha, 1947—, supr. area bldgs., 1951—, energy conservation coordinator, 1973—; mem. speakers bur. U. Nebr. Extension Div., Omaha Safety Council. Dist. camping chmn. Mid Am. council Boy Scouts Am., 1962-67, award of merit, 1966; mem. Omaha Safety Council, 1955-70. Recipient commendation War Dept., 1946. Mem. Soc. Automotive Engrs., Nat. Assn. Fleet Adminstrs. Roman Catholic. Home: 4537 Pine St Omaha NE 68108 Office: 100 S 19th St Omaha NE 68102

ESSEX, MARTIN W., state ofcl.; b. Ray, Ohio, Mar. 25, 1908; s. John S. and Cora (McCormick) E.; B.S., Ohio State U., 1930, M.A., 1934; D.Pd. (hon.), Baldwin-Wallace Coll., 1950; LL.D. (hon.) U. Akron, 1958, Ohio U., 1970; D.Pub. Service (hon.), Miami U.; H.H.D. (hon.), Capital U., 1976; m. Blanche Davis, Aug. 12, 1933. Tchr. Middleport, Ohio, 1930-32, high sch. prin., 1932-35, supt. schs., 1935-41; prin., East Liverpool, Ohio, 1941-43, supt. schs., 1943-45; prin. Ferndale, Mich., 1945-46, supt. schs., 1946-47; supt. schs., Lakewood, Ohio, 1947-55, Akron, Ohio, 1955-66; state supt. pub. instrn., State of Ohio, 1966-77; exec. dir. Ohio Advisory Council Vocat. Edn., 1977—; vis. lectr. univs.; study tour USSR, 1959; dir. 5 yr. comparative study USSR edn., 1964, 74; chmn. adv. council vocational edn. HEW, 1966-68; mem. Nat. Council for Accreditation Tchr. Edn.; chmn. adv. council Nat. Merit Scholarship Corp., 1968-69; adv. council nat. ednl. labs. and research and devel. centers U.S. Office Edn.; U.S. State Dept. cons. to Am. Schs. in Europe, 1970; chmn. 1st Nat. Goverance Study Edn. in U.S., 1972-74. Vice pres. Nat. Congress Parents and Tchrs., 1960-63. Trustee Aerospace Edn. Found. Recipient Freedoms Found. Am. Educators medal, 1969; Ohio B'nai B'rith Human Rights award, 1970; Centennial Achievement award Ohio State U., 1970; named Man of Year, Am. Vocat. Assn., 1968; Martin W. Essex Sch. for Gifted established at Ohio State U., 1977, also Martin W. Essex fellowship. Mem. Joint Council Econ. Edn. (chmn. 1962-68), Council Chief State Sch. Officers U.S. (pres. 1974), Nat. Community Edn. Adv. Council (chmn. 1975—), Am. Assn. Sch. Adminstrs. (pres. 1960), NEA, Phi Alpha Theta, Phi Delta Kappa. Rotarian. Mem. editorial adv. bds. The Nation's Schs. and Colls. Home: 3117 Carisbrook Rd Columbus OH 43221 Office: 5900 Sharon Woods Blvd Columbus OH 43229

ESSEX, WANDA ELIZABETH, speech pathologist; b. Benham, Ky., Jan. 25, 1925; d. Nathaniel Otto and Elizabeth Marie (Ausmus) Irwin; student Cath. U., Washington, 1945-47; B.S., U. Nebr. at Lincoln, 1969, M.A., 1973; m. Earl Woodrow Essex, Nov. 28, 1947; children—Michael, Elane, Christopher. Classifier fingerprints FBI. Washington, 1943-45; sec. Library of Congress, Washington, 1948-49; speech pathologist Edn. Service Unit 6, Milford, Nebr., 1969, Fremont (Nebr.) Pub. Schs., 1969—; pvt. practice speech pathology Meml. Hosp. Dodge County, Fremont, 1975—. Mem. Am. (certified speech pathologist). Nebr. speech and hearing assns., Council Exceptional Children (pres. Mideast Nebr. chpt. 1976-77), NEA, AAUW, Bus. and Profl. Women, Delta Kappa Gamma, Beta Sigma Phi. Home: 1200 N L St Apt 121 Fremont NE 68025 Office: 957 N Pierce St Fremont NE 68025

ESSIG, RICHARD NORMAN, mgmt. exec.; b. Sanborn, Minn., May 28, 1933; s. Joseph J. and Marie D. (Pabst) E.; student Addison State U., 1958-60, U. Mass., 1972-74; m. Corinne J. Skjervold, Dec. 27, 1951; children—Linda J., Michael R. Journeyman maintenance man Interstate Power Co., 1952-60; powerline constrn. Ariz. Pub. Service Co., 1960-67; S.E. regional sales engr. Malleable Iron Products, Birmingham, Ala., 1967-69, N.E. regional sales mgr., Greenfield, Mass., 1969-70; nat. sales and mktg. mgr. Injection Molded Plastics Products, Greenfield, 1970-75; tech. mgr. Reliable Electric, Franklin Park, Ill., 1975—; cons., 1967—. Mem. IEEE, Vt. Elec. Assn., Electric Council New Eng., Am. Mgmt. Assn., Am. Mktg. Assn., Nat. Elec. Mfrs. Assn. Republican. Club: Odd Fellows. Home: 154 Danby St Villa Park IL 60181 Office: PO Box 906 Bensenville IL 60106 also Reliance Electric Co 11333 Addison St Franklin Park IL 60131

ESSMAN, JOHN FREDRICK, screw machine product co. exec.; b. St. Louis, June 22, 1943; s. Orvell Woodrow and Florence Edna (Thornhill) E.; student U. Mo., 1961-69; m. Joyce F. Kassel, May 31, 1969; children—Stephanie, Coleen. Screw machine operator Measuregraph Co., St. Louis, 1963-74, sales engr., 1972-74; plant mgr. Chase Brass & Copper Screw Machine Shop, Pioneer, Ohio, 1974-76; owner, pres. Essman Screw Products Inc., 1976—. Mem. Nat. Screw Machine Products Assn., Soc. Mfg. Engrs., Am. Soc. Metals, Jaycees. Republican. Club: Rotary. Home: Route 5 Bryan OH 43506 Office: 100 S State St Pioneer OH 43506

ESTES, EDWARD RICHARD, JR., cons.; b. Richmond, Va., Mar. 2, 1925; s. Edward Richard and Mamie Cleveland (Bugg) E.; B.Engring., Tulane U., 1945; M.S., Va. Poly. Inst., 1948; m. Elizabeth Hood Lee, Oct. 28, 1950; children—Virginia, Susan, Edward, Elizabeth, William. Asst. prof. Sch. Engring. U. Va., Charlottesville, 1948-55; partner Kinnier & Estes, Charlottesville, 1952-55; research engr. Am. Inst. Steel Constrn., N.Y.C., 1955-60; dir. engring. Fla. Steel Corp., Tampa, 1960-66; M-B Co., Lynchburg, Va., 1966-68; chief research engr. Am. Iron & Steel Inst., N.Y.C., 1968-69; engring. mgr. Republic Steel Corp., Youngstown, Ohio, 1969-72; cons. engr. Estes & Assos., Youngstown, 1972—. Served with Civil Engr. Corps, USNR, 1945-46. Recipient A.F. Davis Silver medal Am. Welding Soc., 1964; Lincoln Arc Welding 3rd award, 1964. Fellow Am. Soc. C.E.; mem. Am. Welding Soc., Am. Soc. for Testing and Materials, Am. Inst. Steel Constrn., Skyline Profl. Engrs. (pres. 1954-55), Research Council on Riveted & Bolted Structural Joints (mem. exec. com. 1969, chmn. 1974—), Sigma Xi, Chi Epsilon, Delta Sigma Phi. Methodist (mem. ofcl. bd. 1969). Clubs: Boardman Swim (trustee 1973-76, pres. 1975) (Youngstown); Tulane (pres. 1959-60) (N.Y.C.). Contbr. articles in field to profl. jours. Home: 910 Westport Dr Youngstown OH 44511 Office: 33 N Hazel St Youngstown OH 44503

ESTES, ELLIOTT MARANTETTE, automobile co. exec.; b. Mendon, Mich., Jan. 7, 1916; student Gen. Motors Inst., 1934-38, U. Cin., 1940. Chief engr. Pontiac Motor div. Gen. Motors Corp., Detroit, 1956-61, gen. mgr., corp. v.p., 1961-65, v.p., gen. mgr. Chevrolet div., 1965-69, group exec. Car and Truck group, 1969-70, v.p. overseas ops., 1970-72, exec. v.p. ops. staff, dir., 1972-74, pres., chief operating officer, dir., 1974—. Mem. vis. com. Harvard U. Bus. Sch. Mem. Soc. Automotive Engrs., Nat. Acad. Engring. Office: 3044 W Grand Blvd Detroit MI 48202

ETCHISON, DON LEE, state ofcl.; b. Oklahoma City, Apr. 12, 1949; s. John Andrew and Ethel Cordell (Bramble) E.; B.S., Eastern Ill. U., 1971; M.A., So. Ill. U., 1974; postgrad. U. Miami (Fla.), 1974-76; m. Christie Anne LeFevre, Jan. 13, 1973. Cons., salesman Etchison Motors Co., Flora, Ill., 1968-71; grad. asst. anthropology U. Miami, 1973-75; self-employed writer, 1975-77; owner Unicorn Enterprises, Flora, Ill., 1976—; legis. asst. Ill. Legislature, Springfield, 1977-78. Grad. grantee U. Miami, 1975-76. Mem. Am. Hist. Assn., Latin Am. Studies Assn., Arms Control Assn., Peace Research Assn., Internat. Studies Assn., North Central Council Latin Americanists, Phi Alpha Theta. Republican. Author: The United States and Militarism in Central America, 1975; also articles. Address: Rural Route 1 Flora IL 62839

ETEROVICH, ALICE MARIE TROYAN, educator; b. Pleasant City, Ohio, Aug. 5, 1923; d. Steve and Marie (Slifko) Troyan; B.S. in Edn., Kent State U., 1945; postgrad. U. Wis., 1947; M.A., Western Res. U., 1960; m. Anthony W. Eterovich, June 22, 1950; 1 dau., Karen Ann. Tchr., Tremont Jr. High Sch., Cleve., 1945-47; tchr. phys. edn. and modern dance Lincoln Jr. High Sch., Cleve. and Lincoln Sr. High Sch., 1947-5-; tchr. phys. edn. and modern dance James Ford Rhodes High Sch., Cleve., 1953-56, head dept., 1953-56; instr. modern dance Oberlin (Ohio) Coll., 1949-50; guidance counselor, vocat. dir. West Tech. High Sch. and Lincoln Jr. High Sch., Cleve., 1962-67; guidance and ednl. counselor John Marshall High Sch., Cleve., 1967—. Hostess, USO, 1943-46; phys. therapist asst. Crile Mil. Hosp., 1945;

instr. Cleve. adult recreation YWCA, 1945-53; supr. Cleve. Summer Recreation, 1948, 49; coach girls basketball Cath. Youth Orgn., 1948, 49. Mem. AAUW (charter mem. Parma br.), Am., Northeastern Ohio personnel and guidance assns., Am. Sch. Counselor Assn., Ohio Counselor Assn., Ohio Assn. Gifted Children, Northeastern Ohio Women Deans, Adminstrs. and Counselors Assn. (sec. 1963-64). Byzantine Catholic. Contbr. to publs. in field. Home: 3223 Somia Dr Parma OH 44134 Office: 3952 W 140th St Cleveland OH 44111

ETEROVICH, ANTHONY WILLIAM, educator, artist; b. Cleve., Apr. 2, 1916; s. George and Ann (Petrovich) E.; art diploma Cleve. Inst. Art, 1938; B.S. in Edn., Western Res. U., 1941, M.A., 1947; postgrad. Ohio U., 1949, N.Y. Art Students League, 1950-51; m. Alice Troyan, June 22, 1950; 1 dau., Karen. Tchr. various schs., Cleve., 1941-62; tchr. James Ford Rhodes High Sch., Cleve., 1962—, head dept. art, 1962—. Art supr. children's classes Cleve. Inst. Art, 1969—; exhibited in group shows Downtown Gallery, N.Y.C., 1951, Cleve. Mus. Art., annually, 1938—, also nat. exhbns., Butler Art Gallery, Youngstown, Ohio, 1951—. Served with AUS, 1943-45. Recipient First prize purchase award Butler Inst. Am. Art, 1951; Union Ind. Colls. Art grantee, 1974. Mem. Am. Soc. Esthetics. Developer exemplary motivational teaching techniques. Home: 3223 Somia Dr Parma OH 44134 Office: 5100 Biddulph Ave Cleveland OH 44109

ETHINGTON, IVAN CLAIRE, ry. exec.; b. Alden, Iowa, Jan. 20, 1922; s. Harold J. and Helen G. (Clute) E.; B.S. in Civil Engring., Iowa State U., 1948; postgrad. exec. mgmt. program Northwestern U., 1961, advanced mgmt. program Harvard, 1967; m. Lois Jean Garner, Oct. 10, 1942; children—Pamela (Mrs. Jay Galligan), Jay, Claire, Steven. With C., B. & Q. R.R. and Burlington No., Inc., 1948—, v.p. operations, Chgo., 1965-70, regional v.p., 1970-71, v.p. ops., St. Paul, 1971-75, sr. v.p. mktg., 1976—; dir. Trailer Train Co., Pullman Co., Western Fruit Express, Duluth Union Depot & Transfer, Burlington Truck Lines, BN Air Freight, Inc. Served to 1st lt. AUS, 1942-45. Mem. Am. Ry. Engring. Assn., Phi Delta Theta. Presbyn. Clubs: Union League (Chgo.), St. Paul Athletic, North Oaks Golf (St. Paul). Home: 4 Meadow Ln North Oaks St Paul MN 55110 Office: 176 E 5th St St Paul MN 55101

ETTER, DAVID PEARSON, poet; b. Huntington Park, Cal., Mar. 18, 1928; s. Harold Pearson and Judith (Goodenow) E.; B.A., U. Ia., 1953; m. Margaret Ann Cochran, Aug. 8, 1959; children—Emily Louise, George Goodenow. Editor Northwestern U. Press, Evanston, Ill., 1961-63; asst. editor Ency. Brit., Chgo., 1964-71; staff editor Compton's Ency., Chgo., 1972-73; free-lance editor, 1972—; manuscript editor No. Ill. U. Press, DeKalb, 1974—. Served with AUS, 1953-55. Author: (poems) Go Read the River, 1966, The Last Train To Prophetstown, 1968, Strawberries, 1970, Voyages to the Inland Sea, 1971, Crabtree's Woman, 1972, Bright Mississippi, 1975, Well You Needn't, 1975; (anthologies) Heartland: Poets of The Midwest, 1967, Where Steel Winds Blow, 1968, 31 New American Poets, 1969, Contemporary American Poetry, 1973, Western Wind, 1974, Pictures That Storm Inside My Head, 1976. Contbr. poems lit. mags. Home: 414 Gates St Elburn IL 60119

ETTER, HOWARD LEE, painter; b. Moberly, Mo., Jan. 22, 1931; s. John Harmon and Mildred Lee (Elsea) E.; student Art League Calif., San Francisco, 1954-55, Acad. Art, San Francisco, 1955-57; m. Martha Lou Klepfer, Jan. 20, 1953; 1 dau., Cynthia Lou. Mem. staff various comml. art studios and advt. agys., 1957-67; free-lance comml. and fine artist, Detroit, 1967—; paintings represented by Collectors Showroom, Chgo., Allen Rubiner Gallery, Royal Oak, Mich., Xochipilli Gallery, Rochester, Mich.; instr. art Lawrence Inst. Tech., Southfield, Mich. 1968-77. Recipient Purchase award Friends Am. Art, 1975, 39th ann. mid-year exhbn. award, Butler Inst. Am. Art, Youngstown, Ohio. Home: 23450 Rensselaer St Oak Park MI 48237

ETTER, PETER ERICH, ednl. adminstr.; b. Lauenstein, Germany, Sept. 11, 1941; s. Friedrich Wilhelm and Luise Emma (Etter) Schnook; came to U.S., 1950, naturalized, 1956; B.S., U. Wis., 1965, M.S., 1969, postgrad. 1970—; m. Sharon Emily Sperle, Aug. 1, 1964; children—Michael Erich, Kristina Elaine. Tchr. pub. schs., Germantown, Wis., 1965-66; tchr. pub. schs. Darien, Wis., 1966-70, prin., dist. adminstr., 1970—. Active Boy Scouts Am., Darien and Delavan, 1966—. Mem. Wis. Elementary Sch. Prins. Assn., Kappa Delta Phi. Kiwanian (sec.-treas. 1974-76), Moose. Home: Route 2 PO Box 33B Delavan WI 53115 Office: 125 S Walworth St Darien WI 53114

EULER, JACK RICHARD, lawyer; b. Wathena, Kans., Apr. 1, 1929; s. Everett J. and Gladys (Wiegant) E.; A.B., LL.B., Washburn U., 1953; children—Jack Richard II, Joel Randall. Admitted to Kans. bar, 1953, Mo. bar, 1954; gen. practice Troy, Kans., 1956—; atty. Doniphan County, Kans., 1956-63; mem. Kans. Legislature, 1963-73; v.p. Farmers Lumber & Supply Co., Inc., Wathena, Kans. Mem. Kan. Jud. Council, 1965-73, Gov.'s Commn. on Criminal Adminstrn., 1966-67, 71-73; mem. Dist. Bd. Wathena Grade Sch., 1963-65. Served with AUS, 1954-56. Mem. Am., Kans., N.E. Kans. (pres. 1965), Doniphan County bar assns., Am. Trial Lawyers Assn., Delta Theta Phi. Methodist. Mason (Shriner), Elk. Home: 102 Mill St Wathena KS 66090 Office: Box 326 Troy KS 66087

EUSEBIO, ERNESTO BAUTISTA, surgeon; b. Manila, Philippines, July 9, 1936; s. David Vitocruz (Bautista) E.; A.A., Far Eastern U., 1957, M.D., 1963; m. Theresita H. Cruz, Apr. 14, 1961; children—Ernesto, Eduardo, Eleanor, Ephraim, Eleazar. Came to U.S., 1964. Intern, St. Barnabas Hosp., Mpls., 1964-65; resident surgery Mt. Sinai Hosp., Mpls., 1965-68, chief surg. resident, 1968, asst. chief surgery, 1970—; fellow colon and rectal surgery U. Minn., Mpls., 1969, instr. surgery, 1970-73, asst. prof., 1973—; clin. asso. So. Ill. U. Med. Sch., 1976—; staff surgeon Springfield (Ill.) Clinic, 1975—. Diplomate Am. Bd. Surgery, Am. Bd. Colon and Rectal Surgery. Fellow A.C.S.; mem. Assn. Acad. Surgery. Researcher intestinal bypass for exogenous obesity, diverticular disease of colon in the young. Home: One Downing Ln Springfield IL 62707 Office: 1025 S 7th St Springfield IL 62703

EUSTIS, WARREN PENHALL, lawyer; b. Fairmont, Minn., Nov. 30, 1927; s. Irving Nelson and Florence (Penhall) E.; B.A., Carleton Coll., 1950; J.D., U. Chgo., 1953; M.A., U. Ark., 1956; m. Doris Anne Grieser, Mar. 1951 (div. Nov. 1968); children—Lillian, Paul; m. 2d, Nancy N. Anderson, Jan. 15, 1971; 1 son, Soren. Admitted to Minn. bar, 1953, since practiced in Rochester and Mpls.; mem. firm Holmes & Eustis. Counsel Upper Midwest Research and Devel. Council; dir. Twin Cities Health Project, 1972—. Adj. prof. Law U. Minn., 1973—. Orgnl. cons. in health and ednl. delivery systems. Mem. Rochester Charter Commn., 1960-70, Minn. Higher Edn. Commn., 1965-67; pres. Rochester Council Chs., 1966; pres. Minn. Chem. Dependency Assn. Chmn., 1st Congl. Dist. Minn. Democratic-Farmer Labor party, 1959-66, state finance chmn., 1962-67. Served with Sci. and Profl. Corps, AUS, 1954-56. Mem. Minn. Trial Lawyers Assn. (bd. govs.), Olmsted County Bar Assn. (past pres.), Delta Upsilon, Phi Alpha Theta. Home: 58 Groveland Terr Minneapolis MN 55403 Office: 1140 Dain Tower Minneapolis MN 55402

EVANS, CHARLES HOWARD, JR., surgeon; b. Syracuse, N.Y., Oct. 1912; s. Charles Howard and May Charlotte (MacKinnon) E.; student Duke U., 1930-33; M.D., C.M., McGill U., 1937; m. Mary Jane Richholt, Sept. 20, 1942; children—Charles Howard III, Madelyn J. Rotating intern Royal Victoria Hosp., Montreal, Que., Can., 1936-37; intern pathology Inst. Pathology, Univ. Lakeside Hosps., Cleve., 1937-38; intern medicine U. Chgo. Clinics, 1938-39; intern surgery Barnes Hosp., Shriners' Hosp. for Crippled Children, Children's Hosp., Bernard Skin and Cancer Hosp., St. Louis, 1938-39; fellow surgery, asst. in orthopedics and surgery, asst. surgeon Mayo Found. and Mayo Clinic, Rochester, Minn., 1940-44; surgeon Blanchard Valley Hosp., Findlay, Ohio, 1944—, Findlay Clinic, 1950—; instr. pathology Western Res. U., Cleve., 1937-38. chief surgeon Northwestern Ohio CD Corps, col., corps surgeon Ohio NG, 1955-61. Recipient Silver Beaver award Boy Scouts Am., 1966, Ohio Commendation Medal Ohio NG O.D.C., 1977. Diplomate Am. Bd. Surgery, Am. Bd. Abdominal Surgery. Mem. Internat. Coll. Surgeons, Am. Soc. Abdominal Surgeons, AMA, AAAS, Northwestern Ohio Med. Assn. (past pres.). Republican. Presbyterian. Club: Kiwanis. Home: 226 W Sandusky St Findlay OH 45840 Office: 1900 S Main St Findlay OH 45840

EVANS, DAVID ALLAN, author, educator; b. Sioux City, Iowa, Apr. 11, 1940; s. Arthur Clarence and Ruth (Lyle) E.; B.A., Morningside Coll., 1962; M.A., U. Iowa, 1964; M.F.A., U. Ark., 1976; m. Janice Kay Johnson, July 4, 1958; children—Shelly, David, Karlin. Mem. faculty Marshalltown Community Coll., 1963-64, Adams State Coll., 1966-68; asso. prof. English, S.D. State U., 1968—; asso. with Poets-in-the-Schools, S.D., 1973—; poet, editor. Grantee Nat. Endowment for Arts, 1974; Breadloaf scholar, 1972. Author: Among Athletes, 1971; Train Windows, 1976. Editor: New Voices in American Poetry, 1973; From Language to Idea, 1971; Means and Ends in Writing, 1972. Home: 1222 3d St Brookings SD 57006

EVANS, DAVID WALTER, Congressman; b. Lafayette, Ind., Aug. 17, 1946; s. Isaac Walter and Margaret Laurine (Reppert) E.; B.A., In Polit. Sci., Ind. U., 1967; postgrad. Butler U., 1970-72; m. Darlene Marie Ginder, Feb. 20, 1975; 1 dau., Jennifer Marie. Tchr., asst. prin. St. Anns Sch., Indpls., 1968-72, St. Andrews Sch., Indpls., 1972-74; mem. 95th Congress from 6th Ind. Dist. Bd. dirs. Ind. Soc. of Washington. Mem. Franklin Jr. C. of C., Kiwanis Club. Recipient Democrat of Year award 19th Dist. Democrat Club, 1974; named Outstanding Young Hoosier, Ind. Jr. C. of C., 1977. Office: 4th Floor Adminstrn Bldg Indpls Internat Airport Indianapolis IN 46241

EVANS, JAMES DAVID, educator; b. Warren, Ohio, Oct. 15, 1946; s. LeRoy Eugene and Charlotte Geraldine (Brooks) E.; B.S., Geneva Coll., 1968; M.S. (research asst.), Iowa State U., 1969, Ph.D., 1974; m. Lois Ann Palyash, Dec. 23, 1967; 1 dau., Laura Lynn. Instr. psychology Geneva Coll., Beaver Falls, Pa., 1969-72; instr. psychology part time Iowa State U., Ames, Iowa, 1972-74; asst. prof. psychology The Lindenwood Colls., St. Charles, Mo., 1974—; cons. in field. NSF fellow. Mem. Am., Midwestern, Mo. psychol. assns., Smithsonian Assn., AAUP, Sigma Xi. Methodist. Author numerous publs. in field. Home: 3043 St Camella St St Charles MO 63301 Office: Watson & Kings Hwy St Charles MO 63301

EVANS, JAMES WILLIAM, mfg. co. exec.; b. Cin., Oct. 8, 1925; s. James Frank and Mary Elizabeth (VanWinkle) E.; B.S., U. Cin., 1951; m. Mary Louise Rempe, Dec. 21, 1946; children—Michael William, Sherry Lynn. Project engr. Cin. Milacron Co., 1947-58; sr. design engr. King Machine Tool Co., Cin., 1958-61; chief engr. Karl Kiefer Machine Co., Cin., 1961-62; with Cherry Burrell Corp., Cedar Rapids, Iowa, 1962—, v.p. engring., 1974—. Mem. tech. adv. com. Kirkwood Community Coll., Cedar Rapids, Iowa, 1974—; pres. N. Coralville Lake Manor Improvement Assn., 1976—. Served with USNR, 1944-46. Mem. Tau Beta Pi, Pi Tau Sigma. Republican. Presbyterian. Home: 130 Thompson Dr SE Cedar Rapids IA 52403 Office: 2400 6th St Cedar Rapids IA 52405

EVANS, JERRY JOE, pediatrician; b. Hammond, Ind., July 23, 1937; s. George Thomas and Marion Ruth (Gruen) E.; B.A., DePauw U., 1959; M.D., Northwestern U., 1963; m. Linda Ann Simmance, Sept. 1, 1962; children—Jeffery Charles, Gregory Gruen, Jennifer Jo. Commd. lt. U.S. Navy, 1963, advanced through grades to lt. comdr., 1968; intern U.S. Naval Hosp., Chelsea, Mass., 1963-64, resident in pediatrics, 1967-69; med. officer U.S.S. Tallahatchie County, 1964-66, U.S. Naval Hosp., Naples, Italy, 1966-67; resident in pediatrics Tufts New Eng. Med. Center, Boston, 1969; chief pediatrics U.S. Naval Hosp., Pensacola, Fla., 1970-71; ret., 1971; pvt. practice pediatrics, Saginaw, Mich., 1971—; mem. staffs St. Luke's Hosp., St. Mary's Hosp., Saginaw Gen. Hosp., Saginaw Osteo. Hosp., St. Joseph Hosp., Tawas, Mich.; pres. bd. dirs. Saginaw County Child Devel. Centers, Inc., 1973-75; trustee East Central Mich. Comprehensive Health Planning Council, Inc., 1974—. Diplomate Am. Bd. Pediatrics. Mem. Am. Acad. Pediatrics, Perintal Assn. Mich. (trustee), Northeastern Pediatric Soc. (treas. 1976-77), Saginaw County, Mich. State med. socs. Methodist. Home: 1754 Brockway St Saginaw MI 48602 Office: 3160 Christy Way Saginaw MI 48603

EVANS, JOHN ALBERT, univ. ofcl.; b. Knoxville, Tenn., Sept. 4, 1924; s. William Ernest and Helen Wilimine (Stewart) E.; B.S., U. Tenn., 1949; postgrad. Central Mo. State U., 1971-72; m. Betty Jane Schureman, Feb. 1, 1965; children—Chandler, Julia, Leslie, Nancy. Radio-TV operator NBC, N.Y.C., 1950-65; TV prodn. trainer, ops. supr. TV of Saudi Arabia, Riyadh, 1965-66; TV prodn. and mgmt. cons. Amman, Jordan, 1967-70; ednl. TV programming mgr. Ednl. TV, New Orleans, 1971-72; TV coach Central Mo. State U., Warrensburg, 1972-73; ednl. radio-TV adminstr. U. Nebr., Omaha, 1973—. Served with USAAC, 1943-46. Decorated Air medal. Mem. Nat. Assn. Ednl. Broadcasters, Met. Omaha Ednl. Broadcasting Assn., Phi Gamma Delta. Republican. Presbyterian. Home: 5102 Franklin St Omaha NE 68104 Office: 65th and Dodge Sts Omaha NE 68101

EVANS, JOHN CLINTON, JR., physicist, lawyer; b. Ottawa, Kans., Jan. 15, 1924; s. John Clinton and Gertrude Sue (Barnes) E.; B.S., Adelbert Coll. Western Res. U., 1948; J.D., Cleve. State U., 1967, LL.M., 1969; D. Jur., York U. (Can.), 1976; m. Kathleen Mae Hoon, May 27, 1952; children—Karyn Ann (Mrs. Richard Proppe), John Clinton III. Asst. chief engr. McGean Chem. Co., Cleve., 1952; plant mgr. Dracco Corp., Cleve., 1952-54; asst. chief engr. Firestone Tire & Rubber Co., Harbel, Liberia, 1954-56; research engr. Atlas ICBM Gen. Cynamics Corp., San Diego, 1957-62; research scientist Lewis Research Center NASA, Cleve., 1962—; admitted to Pa. bar, 1972, U.S. Supreme Ct. bar, 1975; practice law, 1972—. Chief adminstrv. officer Credential Calif. Community Colls. Served with USAAF, 1943-46. Fellow Inst. Physics and Phys. Soc., Royal Microscopical Soc., Royal Astron. Soc.; mem. Am. Bar Assn., A.A.A.S., Am. Vacuum Soc., Am. Judicature Soc., Am. Legion, Delta Theta Phi. Contbr. articles on electron microscopy, solar energy, outer space law, thin film deposition franchising and debenture financing to profl. jours. Patentee in laser and energy fields. Home: PO Box 138 North Olmsted OH 44070 Office: Lewis Research Center NASA 21000 Brookpark Rd Cleveland OH 44135

EVANS, JOHN LLOYD, clergyman; b. Scott, Ohio, May 8, 1899; s. James and Mary Ella (Boyce) E.; student, Ohio State, 1917-18; A.B., Wooster Coll., 1921; B.D., Princeton, 1923, M.Div., 1924; D. Applied Pub. Service Hocking Tech. Coll., 1972—; m. Elizabeth Reese, June 17, 1924; 1 son, John Lloyd. Ordained to ministry of Presbyn. Ch., 1924; pastor First Ch., Nelsonville, Ohio, 1924—; mgr. Athena Brick Corp., 1935-41; supt. and English instr. Murray City High Sch., 1943-46, mgr. Meigs Co. Johnson Estate Farm, 1932-43; mgr. Long Reach (W.Va.) Johnson Homestead Farm, 1944—; mgr. Presbyn. Farm, Union Furnace, Ohio, 1945. Founder Daily Vacation Bible Schs., Southeastern Ohio, 1925; dir. Hocking Valley Miners Relief, Nelsonville, 1926-35; chmn. Indsl. Devel. Assn., 1930-40; chmn. Nat. Missions Athens Presbytery, 1946—. Moderator Synod Ohio Presbyn. Ch., 1950-51. Mem. City Park Commn., City Recreation Com. Mem. Miners Strike Settlement Com., 1927-32; Hocking Valley Reemployment chmn. Reforestation Strip Mine Area, 1932-46; chmn. Selective Service Reemployment. Chmn. Citizens Com., Nelsonville, 1954-56; chmn. City Charter Commn., Athens County Christmas Seal, Athens County Ministerial Program com. Recipient Caritas award outstanding ecumenical spirit, Diocese Steubenville; Citizenship award VFW, 1976. Mem. Am. Legion, State of Ohio Town and Rural Com., City and Immigrant Com. Synod of Ohio. Republican. Mason (32 deg., K.T.). Author: Early Farmers of the Hocking Valley, 1964; Abundant Trees of the Hocking Valley, 1965; The Early Residents in The Hocking Valley, 1966; Tri-County Vocational School, 1967; Nature's 12 Month Calendar, 1968; The Story of Clay in The Hocking Valley, 1969; Tri-County Technical Institute, 1970. Home: 62 E Columbus St Nelsonville OH 45764

EVANS, MERRILL BROWN, assn. exec.; b. Chillicothe, Ohio, June 16, 1922; s. Leon Merrill and Florence Marie (Brown) E.; B.S., Ohio State U., 1947, M.S., 1948, Ph.D., 1951; m. Rowena June Mayhew, Apr. 25, 1944; children—James, David, Michael, Daniel. Asso. prof. marketing Mich. State U., East Lansing; supr. price and volume, tractor and implement div. Ford Motor Detroit; Co., former instr agrl. econs. Ohio State U., Columbus, also asst. prof.; dir. Iowa Marketing Research Corp., Des Moines, 1958; now v.p., dir. marketing research and personnel Iowa Farm Bur. Fedn., Des Moines. Active Boy Scouts Am. Served with AUS, 1943-46; now maj. gen. U.S. Army Res. Decorated Legion Merit. Mem. Am. Marketing Assn., Nat. Assn. Ind. Insurers (chmn. personnel com. 1973), Adminstrv. Mgmt. Soc., Am. Mgmt. Assn., Am. Soc. Personnel Adminstrn., Gamma Sigma Delta. Author govt. research bulletins. Home: Rural Route 1 Prole IA 50229 Office: 507 10th St Des Moines IA 50309

EVANS, ROBERT GRAVES, sculptor, educator; b. Rawlins, Wyo., Nov. 19, 1944; s. Robert Graves and Dorothy Evelyn (Rochelle) E.; B.F.A., Atlanta Sch. of Art, 1969; M.F.A., Tulane U., 1972; m. Mint Kitchens, Feb. 14, 1969; children—Tyler Clifton, Hadley Corinne. Asst. prof. art Terre Haute, Ind., 1972—; one man exhbn. Brenville Gallery, 1972; maj. works include sculpture Ind. State U., Central Mich. U. campus. Recipient 1st. place sculpture award, 1977. Mem. So. Assn. Sculptors. Home: 1500 S 6th St Terre Haute IN 47802 Office: Ind State Univ Terre Haute IN 47809

EVANS, ROBERT LEE, equipment mfg. co. exec.; b. Kansas City, Mo., Mar. 3, 1935; s. Walter Lee and Annabelle (Lee) E.; B.S., Finley Engrng. Coll., 1959; m. Marilyn Mae Keener, Dec. 27, 1953; children—Debra, Dan, David. Salesman, Wearever & Lustre Craft Cookware, Kansas City, Mo., 1952-58; sales engr. Sinclair Refining Co., Kansas City, 1958-59; with Rexnord, Inc., Kansas City, Mo., 1959—, dist. sales mgr., 1966—. Served with AUS, 1953-55. Mem. Kansas City Engrs. Club, Am. Soc. Agrl. Engrs. Club: Toastmasters. Presbyn. Home: 249 E Bridlespur Dr Kansas City MO 64114 Office: 9233 Ward Pkwy Kansas City MO 64114

EVANS, ROBERT LEONARD, physiologist; b. Duluth, Minn., May 30, 1917; s. John Leonard and Amy (Magnusson) E.; student Duluth Jr. Coll., 1934-36; B.Chemistry, U. Minn., 1938, M.S., 1939, Ph.D., 1951; m. Frances J. Bentley, Dec. 21, 1941 (dec.); children—Amy Elizabeth, Thomas Randall, Julia May; m. 2d, Elsie F. Hardy, Jan. 11, 1957. Asso. metallurgist U.S. Bur. Mines, Salt Lake City, 1940-44; research asso. Allegany Ballistics Lab., Cumberland, Md., 1944-45; instr. math. and mechanics U. Minn., Mpls., 1945-54, asst. prof. physiology, 1954-63, asso. prof. biometry and math. biology, 1963-70, lectr. physiology, 1970—. Rockefeller Found. grantee, 1954-59; USPHS grantee, 1958-68, 1966-69. Mem. AAAS, Am. Chem. Soc., Minn. Acad. Sci. (pres.), Wilderness Soc., Nature Conservancy, Sigma Xi. Unitarian. Author: The Fall and Rise of Man, If..., 1973; contbr. articles on chemistry, math. and biomed. research to profl. jours. Patentee in hydrometallurgy. Home: 2500 St Anthony Blvd Minneapolis MN 55418 Office: Dept Physiology U Minn Minneapolis MN 55455

EVANS, TED BEATTY, banker; b. Joplin, Mo., Sept. 15, 1934; s. Ramon Arthur and Louise Dorothy (Beatty) E.; B.A., Westminster Coll., 1956; grad. Grad. Sch. Banking, U. Wis., 1965; m. Helen Daphne Cornell, Aug. 27, 1955; children—Pamella Sue, Carolyn C., Ted Beatty. With Central Nat. Bank, Carthage, Mo., 1958—, asst. trust officer, 1959-63, asst. v.p., 1960-63, v.p., 1963-68, exec. v.p., 1969, pres., 1970—, also dir.; chmn. bd., pres., dir. United Mo. Bank Carthage, 1970—; dir. United Mo. Bancshares Inc., Kansas City; dir. L & P Investment Co., Inc. Instr. econs. Adult Edn. Class, Carthage, 1970—. Pres. United Fund, 1960; mem. Gov.'s Econ. Council on Emergency Planning, also Gov.'s Community Affairs Commn., Mo., 1968-69; pres. Jasper County Devel. Assn., 1971; v.p., treas. Carthage Indsl. Devel. Assn., 1971; pres. Prosperity Dam Assn., 1974; bd. dirs., v.p. Ark. Basin Devel. Assn., Tulsa, 1975—; bd. dirs. St. Luke's Nursing Home, 1973-75; active promotion Youth Center. Mem. City Planning and Zoning Commn., 1967-69. Served to capt., inf. AUS, 1956-58. Named Outstanding Young Man of Year, Carthage Jr. C. of C., 1969. Mem. Carthage C. of C. (pres. 1968), Am. Legion, Sigma Chi. Episcopalian. Rotarian (pres. 1964). Home: 1010 Bellaire St Carthage MO 64836 Office: 300 Grant St Carthage MO 64836

EVANS, THOMAS ARTHUR, physicist; b. Hammond, Ind., Oct. 27, 1943; s. Wilbur Lee and Lois Jean (Klusmeier) E.; B.S., Rose-Hulman Coll., 1965; M.S., Purdue U., 1968, Ph.D., 1970; m. Sharyn Lynn Fagen, Aug. 27, 1966; children—Sean Thomas, Bradford Michael. Research physicist Gen. Electric Co., Cleve., 1970-73, mgr. computer systems lab., 1973-76, mgr. advanced engring., 1976-78, mgr. photoflash engring., 1978—. Sales advisor Jr. Achievement Program, 1976. NASA trainee, 1965-68. Mem. Tau Beta Pi, Sigma Pi Sigma. Home: 8985 Perkins Dr Mentor OH 44060 Office: Bldg 321 Nela Park East Cleveland OH 44112

EVANS, THOMAS PASSMORE, univ. adminstr.; b. West Grove, Pa., Aug. 19, 1921; s. John and Linda (Zeuner) E.; B.S., Swarthmore Coll., 1942; M. Engring., Yale U., 1948; m. Lenore Jane Knuth, June 21, 1947; children—Paula S., Christina L., Bruce A., Carol L. Engr., Atomic Power Div. Westinghouse Electric Corp., 1948-51; dir. research and devel. AMF Inc., N.Y.C., 1951-60; dir. research O.M. Scott & Sons Co., Marysville, Ohio, 1960-62; v.p. research and devel. W.A. Sheaffer Pen Co., Ft. Madison, Iowa, 1962-67; dir. research Mich. Tech. U., Houghton, 1967—. Served to lt. USNR, 1943-46. Mem. Mich. Energy and Resource Research Assn. (trustee), Am. Forestry Assn., Am. Def. Preparedness Assn., Am. Phys. Soc., IEEE,

Soc. Plastics Engrs., Am. Mgmt. Assn., Yale Sci. and Engring. Assn., Sigma Xi, Tau Beta Pi. Club: Rotary. Patentee in field. Office: Mich Tech U Houghton MI 49931

EVANS, WILLIAM G., pub. relations and advertising exec.; b. Mounds, Ill., Aug. 25, 1921; s. William Grant and Isabella Margareta (Frick) E.; student Mo. U., 1940-42; B.S., St. Louis U., 1952; m. Norma Frieda Mueller, Dec. 14, 1946; children—William Grant, Norman Henry, Rebecca Susanne. Tchr., prin. Lutheran Schs., St. Louis area, 1948-60; holder various positions community edn., organization and development with pub. and pvt. agencies, St. Louis area, 1960-67; cons. pub. relations and advt., St. Louis, 1967-68; dir. pub. relations, advt. Blue Cross Hosp. Service, Inc., St. Louis, 1968—; lectr. in pub. relations and communications. Mem. pub. relations com. Heart Assn., St. Louis, 1977—; bd. dirs. Lutheran Mission Assn., St. Louis, 1976—, Humane Soc. of St. Louis, 1974-77, vice chmn., 1974; panel mem. United Way Fund Dr., St. Louis, 1969-74. Served with USMC 1942-45. Mem. Press Club of Greater St. Louis, Internat. Assn. Bus. Communicators, Advt. Club of Greater St. Louis, Media Club. Lutheran. Contbr. numerous articles in fields to various publications. Home: 1760 Parker Rd Florissant MO 63033 Office: 4444 Forest Park St Louis MO 63108

EVARTS, GEORGE WILLIAM, investment banker; b. Newburgh, N.Y., July 18, 1936; s. Morley Kellogg and Jennie Hall (Stone) E.; student Cornell U., Ithaca, N.Y., 1954-57; B.S. in Indsl. Mgmt., Carnegie-Mellon U., Pitts., 1959; m. Marylyn L. Sayle, Apr. 10, 1965; children—Daniel W., L. Paisley, Michael S. Plant location engr. The Austin Co., 1961-62; asso. Case & Co., Inc. Mgmt. Cons.'s, 1962-66; dir. corporate growth Youngstown Steel Door Co., Cleve., 1966-68; v.p. corporate fin. Disbro & Co., Inc., Cleve., 1968-71, Baker & Co., Inc., Cleve., 1971-74; pres. Evarts Capital, Inc., Chagrin Falls, Ohio, 1975—. Coach, Orange Community Athletic Assn.; mem. Cleve. Orch. Chorus; trustee Greater Cleve. Neighborhood Centers, 1968-72; mem. alumni council Phillips Exeter Acad. Served to 1st lt., C.E., AUS, 1960-61. Republican. Methodist. Club: Cleve. Racquet. Office: 70 Meadowhill Ln Chagrin Falls OH 44022

EVAVOLD, DALE EDWARD, lawyer; b. Fergus Falls, Minn., Jan. 13, 1937; s. Ephraim M. and Inez (Olson) E.; B.A., Augsburg Coll., 1958; J.D., U. N.D., 1970; m. Sharon N. Helland, July 22, 1967; children—Robin, Grant. Admitted to Minn. bar, 1970; legal aid asst. Pine Ridge Indian Reservation (S.D.), 1969; Fort Totten, N.D., 1970; asso. mem. firm Darby & Brewer, Rushford, Minn., 1970-72; partner Darby, Brewer and Evavold, Rushford, 1972-74; partner McMahon, Darby, Evavold & Price, 1974—. Lectr. seminar Winona State Coll., 1973; city atty. Rushford, 1972—. Served with AUS, 1960-62. Mem. Am., Minn., Filmore County, Winona County bar assns., Phi Alpha Delta. Lutheran. Lion. Home: Box 478 Rushford MN 55971 Office: Box 39 Rushford MN 55971

EVENS, RONALD GENE, physician; b. St. Louis, Sept. 24, 1939; s. Robert and Dorothy (Lupkey) E.; B.A., Washington U., 1960, M.D., 1964, postgrad. bus. and edn., 1970-71; m. Hanna Blunk, Sept. 3, 1960; children—Ronald Gene, Christine, Amanda. Intern, Barnes Hosp., St. Louis, 1964-65; resident Mallinckrodt Inst. Radiology, 1965-66, 68-70; research asso. Nat. Heart Inst., 1966-68; asst. prof. radiology, v.p. Washington U. Med. Sch., 1970-71, prof., head dept. radiology, dir. Mallinckrodt Inst. Radiology, 1971-72, Elizabeth Mallinckrodt prof., head radiology dept., dir. Mallinckrodt Inst., 1972—; radiologist in chief Barnes and Childrens Hosp., St. Louis, 1971—; mem. adv. com. on specialty and geog. distbn. of physicians Inst. Medicine, Nat. Acad. Scis., 1974-76. Dir. City Bank St. Louis. Lodge adviser, Order of Arrow, Boy Scouts Am., 1975—; elder Glendale Presbyterian Ch., 1971-74; bd. dirs. St. Louis Comprehensive Neighborhood Health Center, OEO, 1970-74. Served with USPHS, 1966-68. James Picker Found. advanced acad. fellow, 1970; Hickey lectr., 1976; recipient Distinguished Service award St. Louis C. of C. 1972; Fellow Am. Coll. Radiology; mem. Mo. Radiol. Soc. (pres. 1977-78), Soc. Nuclear Medicine (trustee 1971-75), AMA, St. Louis Med. Soc., Mo. State Med. Assn., Soc. Chmn. Acad. Radiology Depts., Radiol. Soc. N.Am., Assn. Univ. Radiologists, Am. Roentgen Ray Soc., Phi Beta Kappa, Alpha Omega Alpha (Sheard-Sanford award). Contbr. numerous articles to profl. jours. Office: 510 Kingshwy South St Louis MO 63110

EVENSON, DAVID A., comml. laundry co. exec.; b. St. Paul, Feb. 11, 1935; s. Clifford A. and Thora (Flekke) E.; B.A., U. Minn., 1957; m. Carmen Buckner, Mar. 25, 1966; 1 son, Eric A. Vice-pres. River Falls Launderers & Cleaners (Wis.), 1958-64; mgr. Tumpane Laundry, Ankara, Turkey, 1966-67; pres. Johnson Mankato Laundry, Mankato, Minn., 1968; cons., dir. 3-F Co., Madison, Wis., 1968-70; partner, sec.-treas. Red Wing Laundry, Inc. (Minn.), 1964-65, 70-74, 75-76, 77—; gen. mgr. Combines Services, Inc., Miami, Fla., 1974; mng. dir. Jet Wascherei G.M.B.H., Wurzburg, Fed Republic Germany, 1976-77. Scoutmaster Boy Scouts Am., 1959-64. Mem. Internat. Fabricare Inst., U. Minn. Alumni Club. Republican. Lutheran. Home: RR 4 Red Wing MN 55066 Office: 315 Plum St Red Wing MN 55066

EVERETT, CHARLES ALBERT, dentist; b. Terre Haute, Ind., Aug. 1, 1905; s. Albert Milo and Anna Elizabeth (Stoll) E.; student Ind. State U., 1924-25; D.D.S., Ind. U., 1930; m. Kathryn Pearl Conover, Dec. 19, 1933; children—Katy Ann (Mrs. William Arthur Rose), Charlene (Mrs. Andrew Frank Gleaves III). Gen. practice dentistry, Indpls., 1930—. Served with AUS, 1943-46: ETO. Mem. Am., Ind., Indpls., N. Indpls. (pres. 1948, 52) dental assns., Delta Sigma Delta. Methodist. Mason. Home: 6017 Crittenden Ave Indianapolis IN 46220 Office: 6325 Guilford Ave Indianapolis IN 46220

EVERETT, GORDON G., publishing co. exec.; b. Oakland County, Mich., Apr. 13, 1919; s. Clarence S. and Sarah J. (Gray) E.; student Presbyn. Coll., 1945; m. Marlene J. Blake, Dec. 21, 1960; 1 son, Gary G. Publisher, The No. Star, Gaylord, Mich., 1960—; pres. Central Printing Corp., Gaylord, 1968—; founder Weeklies Inc., Gaylord, 1971, pres., 1971—; founder Advertisers Postal Service Corp., Gaylord, 1970, pres., 1970—; founder Mich. Advt. Inc., Gaylord, 1973, pres., dir., 1973—. Mem. Otsego County Fair Bd., 1963-76, pres., 1973-74; trustee Otsego Meml. Hosp., 1970-72. Served with USAAF, 1941-46; ETO. Mem. Nat. Assn. Advt. Pubs., Shopping Guides Mich. (pres. 1968). Republican. Episcopalian. Designer of mid-America's first pvt. postal system. Home: 618 McCoy Rd Gaylord MI 49735 Office: PO Box 620 Gaylord MI 49735

EVERETT, JAMES ALBERT, advt. and pub. relations co. exec.; b. Alton, Ill., Mar. 20, 1928; s. Jesse James and Lucy Pearl (Eggen) E.; A.A., Graceland Coll., 1948; B.S., Brigham Young U., 1950; M.A., U. Chgo., 1959; m. Marolyn Ardis Briggs, Aug. 17, 1952; children—Mary Lynne, Randi Susan. Mng. dir. Frazar Internat. (Scandinavia), Stockholm, 1960-63; v.p. Robert R. Mullen & Co., Stockholm, 1963-67, Amsterdam, 1968-72, Washington, 1972-74; pres. Everett, Brandt & Bernauer, Inc., Independence, Mo., 1974—; mng. dir. The Brussels Times, 1970-71; bd. govs. Internat. Sch. Amsterdam; mem. Randstad Com. Promotion chmn. Municipal Services Center for City of Independence; chmn. bd. Friends of Kansas City Aquarium. Recipient certificate of appreciation People-to-People, 1966. Mem. Pub. Relations Soc. Am., John Whitmer Hist. Assn., Independence, Greater Kansas City (Mo.), Blue Springs (Mo.) chambers commerce, Friends of Truman Campus. Republican. Mem. Reorganized Ch. Jesus Christ of Latter-Day Saints. Clubs: Rotary (Independence); Pachyderm (Kansas City). Home: 3913 Ponderosa St Lee's Summit MO 64063 Office: 314 W 24 Hwy Independence MO 64050

EVERETT, JAMES BRIAN, mfg. co. exec.; b. Columbus, Ohio, Jan. 2, 1944; s. Dan Kenison and Mary Joan (Coady) E.; student U. Md., 1967-68, Ohio Dominicon Coll., 1968-69; B.S., Ohio State U., 1972; m. Ruth Ann Chorniak, Oct. 11, 1969; 1 son, Geoffrey Kenison. Pres., D.R. & J. Enterprises, Inc., Columbus, 1969-73, mdse. mgr. Gold Circle Discount Stores, Columbus, 1969; mgr. Columbia Mktg. Research, Columbus, 1970; now with Dobson Park Industries, Columbus. Mem. population research com. Citizens Research, 1969-73, capital improvements com., 1969-73; mem. speakers bur. Columbus Devel. Dept., 1969-70, Citizens Com. for Progress, 1970-72; bd. dirs. Columbus Zoo. Served with USAF, 1965-68. Mem. Am. Mktg. Assn. (pres. 1973-74). Home: 580 D'Lyn St Columbus OH 43228 Office: Dobson Park Industries 4041 N High St Columbus OH 43228

EVERHART, DAVID LESLIE, hosp. adminstr.; b. Newark, Ohio, May 24, 1928; s. William Alfred and Mary Elder (Lough) E.; B.A., Denison U., 1950; M.S. in Hosp. Adminstrn., Columbia, 1953; m. Margaret Weber, June 23, 1951; children—John David, Barbara Weber, Margaret Leslie. Adminstrv. intern Ohio State U. Hosp., 1950-51; adminstrv. resident Henry Ford Hosp., Detroit, 1952-53, adminstrv. asst., 1953-55, asst. dir., 1955-61, asso. dir., 1961-63; adminstr., adminstrv. v.p. Johns Hopkins Hosp., Balt., 1963-70; exec. dir. New Eng. Med. Center Hosp., Boston, 1970-75, v.p. bd. govs., 1973; pres. Northwestern Meml. Hosp., Chgo., 1976—; cons. to surgeon gen. USAF; Mem. Am. Hosp. Assn. (mem. council profl. services, council on manpower and edn.), Am. Coll. Hosp. Adminstrs., Assn. Am. Med. Colls. (sec. adminstrv. bd. of coll. teaching hosps. 1973-76, chmn. elect 1976—), Mass. Hosp. Assn. (trustee 1970-76, chmn. bd. trustees 1974-76), Soc. Health Service Adminstrs., Am. Pub. Health Assn., Inst. Medicine, Ill. Hosp. Assn. (trustee 1976—), New Eng. Hosp. Assembly, Phi Gamma Delta, Phi Mu Alpha, Blue Key. Presbyn. Office: 216 E Superior Chicago IL 60611

EVERILL, ROYAL BURDETTE, JR., tool mfg. co. exec.; b. Beloit, Wis., Sept. 4, 1939; s. Royal Burdette and Alice Mildred (Grenawalt) E.; A.B., Harvard, 1961, M.B.A., 1967; m. Sandra Jeanne Solem, Dec. 11, 1961; children—Holly Ann, Jeanne Marie, Susan Elizabeth. Reporter-photographer Beloit (Wis.) Daily News, 1957-61; systems engr., analyst IBM Corp., Madison Wis. and Bethesda, Md., 1961-65; plant mgr. Boise Cascade Corp., Hillside Ill. and La Porte, Ind., 1967-72; pres. Gay-Lee Co., carbide tool mfr., Clawson Mich., 1972—. Pres. Emerson U-U Fellowship, 1975-76; chmn. Clawson Downtown Devel. Authority, 1977-78. Served with U.S. Army, 1962-64. Mem. Detroit Inst. Arts (founders soc.). Cranbrook Inst. Sci., Clawson, Mich. chambers commerce, Soc. Tool, Carbide Engrs., Cutting Tool Mfrs. Assn., Soc. Mfg. Engrs., Harvard Alumni, Bus. Sch. assns.; Mich. United Conservation Club, Detroit Sportsman's Congress. Unitarian. Home: 1290 Greenridge Rd Rochester MI 48063 Office: 71 W Fourteen Mile Rd Clawson MI 48017

EVERS, CHARLES HUBERT, drug treatment adminstr.; b. Harvey, Ill., Aug. 28, 1923; s. Hubert H. and Frances E.H. (Kortz) E.; B.S., U. Ill., 1947; m. Dolores Frances Martozie, Dec. 14, 1963; children—Marian Ruth, Cynthia Jean. Bldg. trade contractor pvt. practice Chgo., 1947-63; salesman real estate McKey & Poague, Chgo., 1964-70. Baird & Warner Inc., Chgo., 1970-75; founder, dir. Project Reconciliation, Chgo., 1963—. Mem. Ill. com. Nat. Council Crime and Delinquency, 1970—; developer correctional programs for drug abusers, addict-felons; established instnl. drug abuse therapy program Ill. Dept. Corrections, 1976. Served with USAF, 1943-45. Mem. Am. Soc. Criminology, Am. Correctional Assn., Correctional Edn. Assn., Am. Acad. Polit. and Social Scis. Presbyterian. Home: PO Box 43 Blue Island IL 60406 Office: 811 W 63d St Chicago IL 60621

EVERS, RUTH HALLA, speech pathologist; b. Chgo., May 26, 1947; d. Richard Charles and Mildred Johanna (Kral) Halla; B.S. magna cum laude, U. Ill., 1969, M.A., 1970; m. Robert Werner Evers, July 22, 1973. Staff speech pathologist Luth. Gen. Hosp., Park Ridge, Ill., 1970-73, acting dir. speech pathology and audiology dept., 1973-74, sr. staff speech pathologist, 1974-75, dir. speech pathology and audiology dept., 1975—. Office of Edn. fellow, 1970; Edmund James scholar, 1967; certified Am. Speech and Hearing Assn. Mem. Am., Ill. (chmn. local arrangements ann. conv. 1977, 78) speech and hearing assns., U. Ill. Alumni Assn., Phi Beta Kappa, Phi Kappa Phi. Republican. Lutheran. Office: Speech Pathology and Audiology Dept Lutheran Gen Hosp 1775 Dempster St Park Ridge IL 60068

EVERT, EDWARD PAUL, JR., r.r. exec.; b. Michigan City, Ind., Apr. 19, 1939; s. Edward Paul and Alice Therese (Sheehan) E.; B.S. in Econs., U. Detroit, 1963, M.A. in Econs., 1964; m. Colleen Finnerty, Apr. 20, 1963; children—Kathleen Marie, Jennifer Erin. Mgr. on-line ops. Chgo. & North Western Transp. Co., Chgo., 1968, dir. data communications, 1969-71, dir. telecommunication and data entry, 1971-75, dir. computer ops., 1975—. Mem. Assn. Am. R.R.'s, Ry. Systems and Mgmt. Assn., Western Ry. Club. Republican. Roman Catholic. Home: 945 Sunset Rd Geneva IL 60134 Office: 4809 N Ravenswood Ave Chicago IL 60640

EVNEN, EVERETT ARNOLD, poultry and egg co. exec.; b. Lincoln, Nebr., Dec. 8, 1927; s. Eli Meyer and Dorothy (Lettween) E.; B.S., U. Nebr., 1950; m. Elaine Rae Sherman, June 24, 1951; children—Robert Barnett, Richard Lewis, Jane Ellen, Judith Ann. Sec., Tri-State Produce Co., Sioux City, Iowa, 1951-56; poultry distrbr. Nat. Poultry Market, Lincoln, 1956-57; pres., owner Lincoln Poultry and Egg Co., 1957—; v.p. Capitol Broadcasting Co., 1966—; sec. Eggs, Inc., 1965—; pres. EPF Enterprises, 1967—; v.p. Brody's Internat. Inc. Trustee, treas. Madonna Home. Served with AUS, 1946-47. Mem. Exec. Club (pres. 1970), Nat. Ind. Poultry and Food Distbrs. Assn. (pres. 1970-73, Man of Year award 1973), Nebr. Alumni Assn., Am. Legion, Zeta Beta Tau Alumni Assn. (pres. 1968-69). Republican. Mason (Shriner), Elk; mem. B'nai B'rith. Jewish (treas. synagogue 1969-73). Home: 3020 O'Reilly Dr Lincoln NE 68502 Office: 20th and M Sts Lincoln NE 68510

EWALD, RICHARD ALEXANDER, dentist, med. service adminstr.; b. LaSalle, Ill., Oct. 1, 1934; s. Edward F. and Josephine L. (Bartoli) E.; student U. Notre Dame, 1952-54; D.D.S., U. St. Louis, 1958; postgrad. U. Ill., 1969-71; m. Joretta Emily Cheli, Aug. 4, 1956; children—Lynne, Gregory, Lisa, Roger II. Practice dentistry specializing in pedodontics, Sunnyvale, Calif., 1963-69, Elmhurst, Ill., 1970-71, Ottawa, Ill., 1971—; mem. staff El Camino Hosp., Mountain View, Calif., 1963-69, vice chief dental dept., 1968-69; resident staff Ill. Research and Edn. Hosp., Chgo., 1969-71; mem. staff Ill. state Pediatric Inst., Chgo., 1969—, asst. dental dir., 1969-71; instr. dept. pedodontics, U. Ill., Chgo., 1970-71, asst. prof., 1971-75; mem. courtesy staff Kaiser Hosp., Santa Clara, Calif., 1963-69, Community Hosp., Ottawa, Ill., 1971—. Guest lectr. dept. dental hygiene San Jose City Coll., San Jose, Calif., 1965-69; del. to Calif. state Dental Conv., San Francisco, 1965, 69; mem. adv. com. dental asst. program, San Jose City Coll., 1964-68; pres. Santa Clara Valley Pedodontic Acad., Santa Clara County, Calif., 1968-69; lectr. to various profl. assns. and socs.; chmn. pedodontic splty. exam. Ill. Dept. Registration and Edn., 1976-77. Mem. Santa Clara County Com. for Mentally Handicapped, 1968-69. Served to capt. Dental Corps, USAF, 1958-62. Mem. Am., Calif. dental assns., Am., Ill. acads. of pedodontics, Ill., LaSalle County, Chgo. dental socs., Acad. of Dentistry for the Handicapped, Am. Soc. of Dentistry for Children, Ill. Soc. of Dentistry for Children (exec. council 1971-72). Clubs: Ottawa Boat, Town Lake Gun. Home: 105 Leland Ln Ottawa IL 61350 Office: 1704 Polaris Circle Ottawa IL 61350

EWALD, ROGER ADOLPH, ophthalmologist; b. LaSalle, Ill., Oct. 1, 1934; s. Edward Francis and Josephine Loretta (Bartoli) E.; student U. Notre Dame, 1952-54; M.D., St. Louis U. 1960; Lancaster Course, Colby Coll., 1965; m. Edith Selena Reinsch, Dec. 22, 1956; children—Edward II, Kurt, Richard II, Stephen, Vincent. Intern Walter Reed Gen. Hosp., Washington, 1960-61, resident pathology, 1961-62, resident ophthalmology, 1964-67, research staff Inst. Research, 1962-64; commd. 1st lt. U.S. Army, 1960, advanced through grades to lt. col., 1969; chief eye, ear, nose throat service U.S. Army Hosp., Ford Ord, Calif., 1967-69; asst. chief ophthalmology service Letterman Gen. Hosp., San Francisco, 1969-70; ret., 1970; practice ophthalmology Carle Clinic Assn., Urbana, Ill., 1970—, bd. govs., 1977—; mem. staff Carle Found Hosp., Urbana, head dept. ophthalmology, 1973-77. Clin. asso. ophthalmology Sch. Basic Med. Scis. U. Ill., Urbana, 1971—. Dir. 1st State Bank of Monticello (Ill.), 1977—. Recipient Beaumont Research prize, 1960; Lederle Research fellow, 1958. Diplomate Am. Bd. Ophthalmology, Nat. Bd. Med. Examiners. Fellow A.C.S., Am. Acad. Ophthalmology and Otolaryngology, Soc. Mil. Ophthalmologists; mem. Am., Ill. (dir. 1976—) assns. ophthalmology, Ill. Soc. Ophthalmology and Otolaryngology, Chgo. Ophthalmologic Soc., A.M.A., Ill. Med. Soc., Champaign County Med. Soc., Alpha Kappa Kappa, Alpha Omega Alpha. Republican. Roman Catholic. Clubs: Decatur (Ill.); Town Lake Gun (Henry, Ill.); Monticello Country. Contbr. profl. jours. Home: 24 Foothill Rd Monticello IL 61856 Office: 602 W University Ave Urbana IL 61801

EWELL, JOHN ALBERT, III, mathematician; b. Newellton, La., Feb. 28, 1928; s. John Albert and Carolyn E. (Fay) E.; B.S., Morehouse Coll., 1948; M.A., U. Calif., Los Angeles, 1955, Ph.D., 1966; postgrad U. Colo., 1949-51; m. Perdy Viola Lavik, Oct. 15, 1960; children—Ginger A., Lars A., Philip A. Instr. math So. U., Baton Rouge, 1955-57; asst. prof. math Calif. State U., Long Beach, 1961-66; postdoctoral fellow U. Man., (Can.), 1966-67; asst. prof. York U., Toronto, Ont., Can., 1967-70; asso. prof. math Calif. State Coll., Somoma, 1970-73; asso. prof. No. Ill. U., DeKalb, 1973—. NRC Canada fellow, 1967; NSF grantee, summer 1971. Mem. Am. Math. Soc., Math. Assn. Am., Sigma Xi. Home: 121 Pooler Ave DeKalb IL 60115 Office: Dept Math Northern Ill Univ DeKalb IL 60115

EWERT, QUENTIN ALBERT, lawyer; b. Griggsville, Ill., Aug. 19, 1915; s. Albert Merrit and Anna Mable (Beard) E.; student Jackson Jr. Coll., 1934-36; A.B., Mich. State U., 1938; J.D., U. Mich., 1946; m. Frances Hiewitt Norfleet; children—David Norfleet, Gregory Albert, Catherine Ann, Mary Frances, Jane Cranton; m. 2d, Arlayne Joy Brown. Admitted to Mich. bar, 1946; practice law, 1947-53; pres. Guardsman Ins. Agy., Pasadena, Calif., 1953-55; partner Loomis, Ewert, Ederer, Parsley, Davis & Gotting, Lansing, Mich., 1955—; city atty., Grand Ledge, Mich., 1948-50; mem. 6th Congl. Dist. State Bar Grievance Panel. Met. area chmn. Republican party, 1952. Served as lt. comdr. Supply Corps, USNR, 1941-45. Mem. Am., Ingham County bar assns., State Bar Mich. (mem. corp. and securities com. 1959—), Am. Judicature Soc., U. Mich. Alumni Club (pres. 1963-64), Mich. State U. Alumni Club, Delta Theta Phi, Kappa Sigma. Episcopalian. Kiwanian. Clubs: Lansing Ski; Walnut Hills Country. Home: 1447 Old Mill Rd East Lansing MI 48823 Office: 1200 Bank of Lansing Bldg Lansing MI 48933

EWING, RAYMOND HOOD, clergyman, educator; b. Richland Center, Wis., Dec. 22, 1890; s. James Harvey and Laura (Barton) E.; A.B., William Jewell Coll., 1916; B.D., U. Chgo., 1921, M.A., 1929; m. Ruth Grimes, Oct. 22, 1921; children—Mary (Mrs. John Roatch), James W. Prof. English, Wayland Acad., Hang Chow, China, 1916-18; ordained to ministry Congl. Ch., Bapt. Ch., 1916; missionary, Tura, Assam, India, 1921-29; state dir. Christian Edn. Wis., Milw., 1929-39; pastor Bluemound Community Ch., Milw. 1939-42; supt. Congl. chs. No. half Minn., Staples, 1945-49; pastor Congl. Ch., Staples, Minn., 1949-54, Circle, Mont., 1954-59; interim pastor Bertha Faith United Ch. of Christ, Bertha, Minn.; now spl. tchr. Model Sch., Staples, Minn. Mem. exec. bd. Central Minn. council Boy Scouts Am., 1959—; chmn. A.R.C., Staples, 1959—. Rep. of Republican Party, Staples, 1959—. Served with AUS, 1918. Recipient Distinguished Service award Staples Jaycees, 1972. Mason (Shriner); mem. Order Eastern Star. Author: India Educational System, 1921; Garo Customs and Folklore, 1929. Home: 218 W Dakota Ave Staples MN 56479

EWING, RAYMOND PEYTON, ins. co. exec., pub. relations dir.; b. Hannibal, Mo., July 31, 1925; s. Larama Angelo and Winona Fern (Adams) E.; A.A., Hannibal La-Grange Coll., 1948; B.A., William Jewell Coll., 1949; M.A. in Humanities, U. Chgo., 1951; m. Audrey Jane Schulze, May 7, 1949; 1 dau., Jane Ann. Marketing mgmt. trainee Montgomery-Wards, Chgo., 1951-52; sr. editor Commerce Clearing House, Chgo., 1952-60; corp. communications dir. Allstate Ins. Cos. & Allstate Enterprises, Northbrook, Ill., 1960—; pub. relations dir. Chicago Mag., 1966-67, book columnist, 1968-70; staff Book News Commentator, Sta. WRSV, Skokie, Ill., 1962-70; lectr. pub. relations. Mem. Winnetka (Ill.) Library Bd., 1969-70; pres. Skokie Valley United Crusade, 1964-65. Bd. dirs. Suburban Community Chest Council, Onward Neighborhood House, Chgo., Kenilworth Inst. Served with AUS, 1943-46; ETO. Mem. Pub. Relations Soc. of Am. (accredited; Silver Anvil awards for pub. service, 1970, 72, for fin. relations 1970, for bus. spl. events 1976), Publicity Club of Chgo. (v.p. 1967, bd. dirs. 1966-68; Golden Trumpet award for pub. affairs, 1969, 70, 72, for financial relations 1970), Mensa, Chgo. Press Club, Chgo. Poets and Writers Found. (pub. relations dir. 1966-67). Editor Publicity Club of Chgo. Jour., 1971—. Contbr. articles to mags. Home: 316 Richmond Rd Kenilworth IL 60043 Office: Allstate Plaza Northbrook IL 60062

EXON, CHARLES STUART, surgeon; b. Wichita, Kans., Nov. 13, 1920; s. George Edward and Carolyn Elizabeth (Stuart) E.; A.B., Kans. U., 1941; M.D., Washington U., St. Louis, 1944; m. Anne Lewis, Apr. 15, 1945; children—Carolan, Charles Stuart, Ellen. Intern, Bapt. Hosp., New Orleans, 1944-45; resident in surgery Vanderbilt Hosp., Nashville, 1947-48, Winter VA Hosp., Leavenworth, Kans., 1949-51; pvt. practice Jefferson City (Mo.) Surgeons, Inc., 1955—; asst. clin. prof. surgery U. Mo. Served with M.C., U.S. Army, 1945-47. Fellow A.C.S.; mem. AMA, Mo. State Med. Assn., Mo. State Surg. Soc., Am. Cancer Soc. (pres.-elect Mo. div.). Methodist. Home: 916 Boonville Rd Jefferson City MO 65101 Office: 1505 SW Blvd Jefferson City MO 65101

EXON, J(OHN) JAMES, gov. Nebr.; b. Geddes, S.D., Aug. 9, 1921; s. John James and Luella (Johns) E.; student U. Omaha, 1939-41; m. Patricia Ann Pros, Sept. 18, 1943; children—Stephen James, Pamela Ann, Candace Lee. Mgr., Universal Finance Corp., Nebr. 1946-53;

pres. Exon's, Inc., Lincoln, Nebr., 1954-71; gov. State of Nebr., 1971—. Mem. Edn. Commn. of States, 1971—; mem. exec. com. Nat. Govs.' Conf., 1971, Democratic Govs.' Conf., 1971, 74; vice chmn. Midwest Govs.' Conf., 1973, chmn., 1974; co-chmn. Old West Reg. Commn., 1974-75. Active state, local, nat. Democratic coms., 1952—; del. Dem. Nat. Conv., 1964; Dem. nat. committeeman, 1968-71. Served with Signal Corps, AUS, 1942-45. Mem. Am. Legion. Mason (32 deg., Shriner), Elk. Club: Lincoln C. of C., Nat. Office Products Dealers Optimists Internat. (past lt. gov. Nebr. dist.). Home: Gov's Mansion 1425 H St Lincoln NE 68508 Office: State Capitol Lincoln NE 68509

EXUM, HERBERT ADOLPH, psychologist; b. Tarboro, N.C., Feb. 13, 1949; s. Savalius Adolph and May Belle (Moten) E.; student Duke U., 1967-69; B.A., Fed. City Coll., 1972; M.A., U. Minn., 1974, Ph.D., 1977; m. Edith Anne Lewis, Mar. 1, 1975; 1 dau., Kalimah Imani Mae-Ann. Mem. Medicaid Task Force HEW, Washington, 1969-70; counselor/intern Counseling Center, Fed. City Coll., Washington, 1970-72; dir. crisis house Wilder Community Group, St. Paul, 1974-75, coordinator research and devel., 1975-76; counselor St. Mary's Jr. Coll., Mpls., 1974-75, developer, coordinator peer tutoring, counseling, 1975-77; asst. prof. div. counselor edn. U. Iowa, Iowa City, 1977—; cons. in field. Active Urban League. Mpls. Ford Found. grantee-in-aid, 1967-69; Edn. Profl. Devel. Act fellow, 1972-74; Urban League fellow, 1973. Mem. Am. Psychol. Assn., Am. Personnel and Guidance Assn., Black Student Psychol. Assn. Home: 716 W Chestnut St Goldsboro NC 27530 Office: 1303 7th St Coralville IA 52241

EYERMAN, THOMAS JUDE, architect; b. Columbus, Ohio, June 11, 1939; s. Raymond Jacob and Lucille (Garno) E.; B.Arch., Ohio State U., 1963; M.B.A., Harvard U., 1965; m. Mary Kay Evans, Nov. 3, 1962; children—Matthew, David, Nicole. With Skidmore, Owings & Merrill, Chgo., 1966—, asso. partner, 1971-74, gen. partner, 1974—. Bd. dirs. Thatcher Woods council Boy Scouts Am. Recipient Texnikoi award as outstanding alumnus Ohio State U. Coll. Engring., 1974. Mem. A.I.A. (Chgo. treas. 1972, chmn. office practices com. 1974); mem. Harvard Bus. Sch. Assn., Chgo. Orch. Assn. (life mem.), Phi Delta Theta. Clubs: Harvard, Arts; Metropolitan, Monroe (Chgo.). Author: Financial Management Concepts and Techniques for the Architect, 1973. Home: 1046 N Grove Ave Oak Park IL 60302 Office: 30 W Monroe St Chicago IL 60603

EYRE, IVAN, artist, educator; b. Tulleymet, Sask., Can., Apr. 15, 1935; s. Thomas and Kay Eyre; m. Brenda Fenske, June 14, 1957; children—Keven, Tyrone. Mem. faculty U. N.D., 1958-59; mem. faculty U. Man., Winnipeg, (Can.), 1959—, prof. drawing and painting, 1975—, head drawing dept., 1974—; one man shows include Montreal Mus. Fine Arts, 1964, Winnipeg Art Gallery, 1964, 66, 74, Fleet Galleries, Winnipeg, 1965, 69, 71, Albert White Galleries, Toronto, 1965, Atelier Vincitore Gallery, Brighton, Eng., 1967, Yellow Door Gallery, Winnipeg, 1966, Jerrold Morris Gallery, Toronto, 1969, 71, 73, Frankfurter Kunst Kabinett, Frankfurt, Ger., 1973, Burnaby Art Gallery, 1973, Siemens Werk, Erlangen, Germany, 1974, New Brunswick Mus., St. John, 1976; group shows include London Art Gallery, 1963, Agnes Lefort Gallery, Montreal, 1964, Nat. Gallery, Ottawa, 1965, 67, 74, Yellow Door Gallery, Winnipeg, 1965, Toronto Gallery, 1968, Montreal Mus. Fine Arts, 1970, 76, Art Gallery Ont., 1970, 76, Winnipeg Art Gallery, 1976, Glenbow-Alta. Inst., Calgary, 1976, Vancouver Art Gallery, 1977, Saskatoon Art Gallery, 1977, Harbourfront Art Gallery, Toronto, 1977; represented in permanent collection at Winnipeg Art Gallery, Nat. Gallery, Ottawa, Vancouver Art Gallery, Montreal Mus. Fine Arts. Can. Council sr. fellow, 1966. Mem. Royal Acad. Arts. Home: 1098 Trappistes St Norbert MB R3V 1B8 Canada Office: Sch Art U Manitoba Winnipeg MB Canada

EZELL, WILLIAM ALEXANDER, veterinarian; b. Kansas City, Mo., Nov. 18, 1922; s. Wayman and Lula (Hynson) E.; student Kans. State Coll., 1940-41, U. Nebr., 1942-43; D.V.M., Mich. State U., 1946; m. Ina Jane Smith, July 15, 1946; children—William Alexander, Ruth E. (Mrs. Francis Byrne), Wayman, Paul. Head dept. physiology Tuskegee Sch. Vet. Medicine, 1946-47; vet. insp. Detroit Dept. Health, 1948-49; pvt. practice vet. medicine, Inkster, Mich., 1949—. Mem. Inkster Library Commn., 1957—; mem. Inkster Bd. Edn., 1955—, pres., 1969—; mem. vet. alumni council Mich. State U.; life mem. N.A.A.C.P. Bd. dirs. United Found., Boys Club, Mich. Humane Soc., African Art Gallery, Detroit Inst. Arts; mem. adv. bd. Family and Neighborhood Services. Recipient Recognition resolution Mich. Legislature, 1972. Mem. Southeastern Mich. Vet. Med. Assn. (pres. 1972-73), Alpha Phi Alpha. Home: 28426 Michigan Ave Inkster MI 48141 Office: 28438 Michigan Ave Inkster MI 48141

FAATZ, MABEL V., mus. adminstr., historian; b. Carlyle, Ill., Feb. 18, 1924; d. John and Anna M. (Poore) Keilbach; grad. high sch.; m. Francis E. Faatz, Oct. 11, 1950; children—William E., Clara A. Ins. underwriter Utilities Ins. Co., St. Louis, 1946-50; with Hazelwood (Mo.) Hist. Soc., 1968—, pres., 1972—. Dir. Little Red Sch. House, Hazelwood, 1970—; historian of Hazelwood, 1969—. Mem. St. Louis Geneal. Soc. (v.p. 1974-75, pres. 1976-77), V.F.W. Aux. (pres. 1967-68), Friends of Old St. Ferdanand's Shrine (life). Research family histories, history of Hazelwood. Home: 8 Bon Vue Dr Hazelwood MO 63042 Office: PO Box 64 Hazelwood MO 63042

FABER, EUGENE JAMES, interior designer, artist, property mgr.; b. Milw., July 13, 1910; s. George Albert and Isabel J. (Roddis) F.; B.E., Milw. State Tchrs. Coll., 1933; postgrad. in edn. U. Wis., 1951—. Free-lance interior designer, Milw., 1945—; property appraiser City Milw., 1958-73; owner, dir., pres., gen. mgr. Woolley Wick Co., Inc., Milw., 1954—, Brayton House Co., Inc., Milw., 1957—; v.p. Lynn Lawn Co., Inc., Milw., 1962-66. Lectr. interior design and decoration Shorewood (Wis.) Opportunity Sch., other adult evening schs., 1951—. Served to 1st lt. AUS, 1942-46. Mem. Am. Fedn. State, County and Municipal Employees (wages and salary negotiating com. Local 40 1961-65, sec. Local 40 1964-65, v.p. 1966, pres. local 40 1971), Wis. Painters and Sculptors Assn. Home: 2823 N Cramer St Milwaukee WI 53211

FABER, JOHNNA LYNN, youth counselor; b. Charleston, W.Va., Mar. 16, 1952; d. John Henry and Nova Jean (Haynes) F.; B.A. in Psychology cum laude, W.Va. U., 1974, M.A. in Counseling, 1975. Elementary sch. counselor, Wilmington, Del., 1975-76; edn. counselor Butterfield Youth Services, Marshall, Mo., 1976-77, counselor, 1977—; family counselor Family Edn. Centers, Morgantown, W.Va. and Wilmington, Del., 1974-76. Certified elementary sch. counselor, Del. Mem. N.Am. Soc. Adlerian Psychology, Am. Personnel and Guidance Assn., Gamma Phi Beta (pres. W.Va. U. chpt. 1974-75). Home: 262 W Washington St Marshall MO 65340 Office: Box 333 Marshall MO 65340

FABIAN, LEONARD WILLIAM, anesthesiologist, educator; b. Little Rock, Nov. 12, 1923; s. Leonard Edward and Susan Ellen (Chitwood) F.; B.S., U. Ark., 1950, M.D., 1951; m. Elizabeth Mardelle Bishop, Jan. 8, 1947; children—Beverly, Susan, Leonard William, Edward, Ronald. Intern, U. Ark. Hosp., 1951-52, resident in anesthesiology, 1952-54; fellow Phila. Children's Hosp., 1954; instr. in anesthesiology U. Ark., 1954-55; asst. prof. anesthesiology Duke, 1955-58; prof., chmn. dept. anesthesiology U. Miss. Med. Center, 1958-71; prof. Washington U., St. Louis, 1971—; mem. staffs Barnes and Associated Hosps., St. Louis, St. Louis Children's Hosp.; nat. cons. emeritus in anesthesiology Surgeon Gen. USAF. Served with USN, 1942-46; PTO. Diplomate Am. Bd. Anesthesiology. Fellow Am. Coll. Anesthesiologists (chmn. bd. govs. 1964-65); mem. Am. Soc. Anesthesiologists, Internat. Anesthesia Research Soc., AMA, St. Louis, Mo. State med. socs., Mo., St. Louis socs. anesthesiologists, Assn. Univ. Anesthetists, Am. Fedn. Clin. Research, Assn. Physician Faculty of Nurse Anesthesia Schs., Mo., St. Louis (chmn. com. on cardiopulmonary resuscitation, comr.) heart assns. Contbr. numerous articles to profl. publs.; editor: Anesthesia and the Circulation, 1964; Clinical Anesthesia: A Decade of Clinical Progress, 1971. asso. editor Clin. Anesthesia, 1965—, Survey Anesthesiology, 1965—. Home: 1570 Foxleigh Ct St Louis MO 63131 Office: 660 S Euclid Ave St Louis MO 63131

FABRIC, FRED, dentist; b. Chgo., July 23, 1920; s. Nathan and Ella (Kowalsky) F.; Ph.B., U. Wis., 1943; D.D.S., at Chgo., 1946; M.S., U. Mich., 1950; m. Vida Rosalee Miller, Dec. 16, 1955; 1 dau., Nancy Ellen. Practice orthodontics, St. Louis, 1952—. Asst. prof. orthodontics Washington U. at St. Louis, 1950-63, asso. prof., 1963-67; cons. orthodontist, So. Ill. U., Alton, 1971—; pres. Central Regional Dental Testing Service, 1973-74. Served to 1st lt. AUS, 1946-48. Named hon. Col. and mem. Gov.'s staff Mo., 1968-72. Fellow Am. Coll. Dentists; mem. Mo. Dental Bd. (pres. 1967-72), Midwestern Soc. Orthodontics (pres. 1966-67), Washington U. Study Group Orthodontics (pres. 1963), Clayton C. of C., Am. Assn. Orthodontists, Am., Mo. dental assns., Am. Assn. Dental Examiners, Greater St. Louis Dental Soc., Am. Soc. Dentistry for Children, Omicron Kappa Upsilon, Alpha Omega. Mason. Clubs: Westwood Country, Clayton.

FABRYCY, MARK ZDZISLAW, economist, educator; b. Sosnoviec, Poland, Nov. 18, 1922; s. Ludomir Adam and Alicia Barbara (Bielska) F.; came to U.S., 1959, naturalized, 1964; B.Commerce with honors, U. London, 1950; M.A., City U. N.Y., 1962, Ph.D., 1967; m. Marie Barbara Fabierkiewicz, Jan. 25, 1949. Overseas contracts engr. Crompton Parkinson, Ltd., elec. mfrs., London, Eng., 1950-53; pres. Mark Z. Fabrycy & Assos., econ. research cons., Montreal, N.Y.C., Dayton, 1953—; asst. prof. econs. N.Y. U., N.Y.C., 1965-67, asso. prof., 1967-72; prof. econs. Wright State U., Dayton, Ohio, 1972—; prin. Urban Research Assos., N.Y.C., 1966-69, Tech-Mark Research Assos., N.Y.C., 1967—. Served with Brit. Army, 1942-45. Decorated Mil. Cross, Army Cross. Mem. Econometric Soc., Am. Econ. Assn., Royal Econ. Soc. Club: Racquet. Contbr. articles to profl. jours. Home: 6710 Carinthia Dr Dayton OH 45459 Office: Wright State U Dept Econs Dayton OH 45431

FACHES, WILLIAM GEORGE, lawyer; b. Cedar Rapids, Iowa, Feb. 15, 1928; s. George Vlasios and Androniki (Panagopoulos) F.; student Coe Coll., 1947-48; B.A., U. Iowa, 1951, J.D., 1955; m. Mary Matzanias, Dec. 6, 1959; children—Andrea Lynn, Allison Lynn. Admitted to Supreme Ct. Iowa, 1955, U.S. Supreme Ct., 1971, U.S. Dist. Ct. No. Dist. Iowa, 1955, U.S. Dist. Ct. So. Dist. Iowa, 1970; mem. firm Reilly & Faches, Cedar Rapids, 1955-67; 1st asst. county atty., Linn County, 1965-67, county atty., 1967-74; sr. mem. firm Faches, Klinger & Gloe (and predecessor firms), Cedar Rapids, 1967-74. Mem. Mayors Ad Hoc Com. on Alcholism, 1967-68, Linn County Crime Commn., 1971—. Pres., Young Democrats, 1960; mem. central com. Linn County Dem. Com., 1956-58, 60-68. Bd. dirs. Linn County Assn. Mentally Retarded, 1968-72, Cedar Rapids Teen Club, 1968-76. Served with Air Corps, AUS, 1946-47. Recipient Civil Libertarian award Ia. Civil Liberties Union, 1974. Mem. Linn County, Ia. bar assns., Ia. County Attys. Assn., Nat. Dist. Atty.'s Assn., Am. Judicature Soc., Phi Alpha Delta. Greek Orthodox. Club: Sertoma. Home: 1901 5th Ave SE Cedar Rapids IA 52403 Office: 318 Paramount Bldg Cedar Rapids IA 52401

FADNESS, PETER ANDREW, employment counselor; b. Portage, Wis., July 30, 1932; s. Andrew C. and Elva F.; B.S., U. Wis., Eau Claire, 1958; M.Ed., U. Mo., 1967; m. Karen LaVon Bowen, Aug. 11, 1973; children—William, Angela. Elec. contractor, Rio, Wis., 1951-53; salesman Group Health Mut. Ins. Co., St. Paul, 1958-60; employment counselor Wis. Job Service, Eau Claire, 1960—; cons. in field. Served with USN, 1953-54. Licensed electrician. Mem. Am., Wis. personnel and guidance assns., Wis. Employment Counselors Assn. (pres. 1970), Am. Guild Organists (dean Chippewa Valley chpt. 1966, 67, 70). Congregationalist. Clubs: Masons, Shriners. Home: 3516 Brian St Eau Claire WI 54701

FAESTEL, DAVID JOEL, investment co. exec.; b. Waukesha, Wis., July 2, 1944; s. Gerald Henry and Harriet (Kubal) F.; B.A., Marguette U., 1968; M.B.A., U. Wis., 1970; m. Catherine Delores McCormick, June 19, 1971; children—Joel, Paul, Todd. Regional mgr. Multicon Properties, Inc., Columbus, Ohio, 1970-72; fin. analyst IC Industries, Chgo., 1972-73; pres. Faestel Investments, Inc., Crystal Lake, Ill., 1973—, dir.; pres. Am. Self Storage Centers, Inc. Mem. Nat. Assn. Home Builders, Urban Land Inst., U.S. C. of C., Nat. Apartment Assn. Am. Simmnetal Assn. Roman Catholic. Club: Kiwanis. Office: 3717 Buck Horn Dr Crystal Lake IL 60014

FAGAN, GEORGE EDWARD, physician; b. Mt. Sterling, Ill., Aug. 10, 1922; s. Frank Glenn and Mary (Shork) F.; student Springfield Jr. Coll., 1940-42, U. Ill., 1942-43; M.D., St. Louis U., 1947; 2 children. Intern, Presbyn. Hosp., Chgo., 1947-48; asst. resident in obstetrics gynecology Grady Meml. Hosp., Atlanta, 1948-49; asst. resident in obstetrics gynecology Presbyn. Hosp., Chgo., 1949-50, sr. resident, 1952-54; practice medicine specializing in obstetrics gynecology, Champaign, Ill., 1959—; mem. staff Burnham City Hosp., Champaign, Mercy Hosp., Urbana, Ill. Served to capt. M.C. U.S. Army, 1950-52; ETO. Diplomate Am. Bd. Obstetrics-Gynecology. Fellow Am. Coll. Obstetrics-Gynecology, A.C.S.; mem. AMA, Am. Soc. Abdominal Surgeons, Internat. Coll. Surgeons, Am. Fertility Soc., Ill. Obstetrics-Gynecology Soc., Alpha Omega Alpha. Republican. Roman Catholic. Elk. Home: 2503 W Springfield St Champaign IL 61820 Office: 302 E Stoughton St Champaign IL 61820

FAGAN, RICHARD DWIGHT, coll. dean, mortgage co. exec.; b. Clinton, Iowa, Mar. 15, 1932; s. Dwight Harry and Mildred (Ward) F.; B.S., Western Ill. U., 1956, M.S., 1957; postgrad. N. Tex. State Coll., 1961, N. Ill. U., 1963, 64, U. Ky., 1965-67; m. Beverly Jean Donahue, Nov. 12, 1955; children—Barbara, Karen, Steven, Diane, Sandra, David. Tchr., Sabula (Ia.) High Sch., 1956-57, Savanna (Ill.) High Sch., 1957-58, Rock Falls (Ill.) High Sch., 1958-60; dean Massey Coll., 1960-62; chmn. div. bus. adminstrn. Freeport Community Coll., 1962-67; dean bus. affairs Highland Community Coll., 1967—; exec. v.p. Unicap Ltd., Freeport, Ill., 1972—; admissions Madison (Wis.) Bus. Coll. Instr., coordinator Am. Inst. Banking, Birmingham, Ala., 1962, Am. Savs. & Loan, Rockford, Ill., 1962-64; tchr. bus. edn. Lakeland High Sch., Minocqua, Wis.; examiner Accrediting Commn. for Bus. Schs. Mem. No. Ill. U. Jr. Coll. Bd. Mem. exec. bd. Blackhawk area council Boy Scouts Am. Served with AUS, 1953-55. Mem. Am. Assn. Jr. Coll., Nat., Ill., Freeport (v.p. 1963-64, auditor 1966) edn. assns., N. Central Bus. Edn. Assn. (exec. bd. mem. 1967-70; pres. 1971), Nat. Bus. Edn. Assn. (exec. bd. 1971-72), Ill. Jr. Coll. Assn., Nat. Assn. Sch. Bus. Ofcls., Ill. Assn. Community and Jr. Colls., Ill. Assn. Sch. Bus. Ofcls., Phi Sigma Epsilon (life), Phi Delta Kappa. Kiwanian (ednl. com. 1965-66). Home: PO Box 486 Lake Tomahawk WI 54539 Office: 671 W Stephenson St Freeport IL 61032 also Madison Business Coll 215 W Washington St Madison WI

FAGAN, STEPHEN JOSEPH, automobile agy. exec.; b. Topeka, Apr. 15, 1939; s. Peter Raymond and Mary Virginia (Etzel) F.; student Washburn U., 1957-61, Clark Sch. Bus., 1960-61; m. Carol Sue Griffin, Oct. 13, 1970; children—Ryan Raymond, Brennan Patrick. With Pat Patterson Motors Co., Inc., Topeka, 1961-75, v.p., 1967-75; owner, operator Steve Fagan Classic Cars, Topeka, 1975—. Served with AUS, 1961-62. Mem. Assn. Fleet and Lease Adminstrs., Nat. Assn. Fleet Adminstrs. Roman Catholic. Moose, K.C. Home: 6711 SW 40th St Topeka KS 66610 Office: 222 W 7th St Topeka KS 66606

FAGER, JOHN FREDERICK, chem. and mech. engr.; b. O'Neill, Nebr., Jan. 21, 1939; s. James Harold and Lillian Anne (Gustavson) Fager; m. Claire Prucha, Dec. 26, 1962; children—Carrie, Christie. B.S., U. Nebr., 1961, M.S., 1969; grad. U.S. Navy Officer Candidate Sch., 1962, engr. in training, 1962-65. Registered profl. engr., Nebr. Chem. engr. Omaha Pub. Power Dist., 1961-62, engr., 1965-73; tech. supr. Ft. Calhoun (Nebr.) Nuclear Power Sta., 1973, mgr. project engring., 1974; div. mgr. projects and constrn. Omaha Pub. Power Dist., 1975—. Mem. Am. Inst. Chem. Engrs., Nat. Soc. Profl. Engrs., Profl. Engrs. Nebr., Am. Nuclear Soc., Am. Soc. Mech. Engrs., Sigma Phi Epsilon. Recipient Outstanding Chmn. award, United Way, Omaha, 1976-77. Home: 117 S 68th Ave Omaha NE 68132 Office: Electric Bldg 1623 Harney St Omaha NE 68102

FAGERBERG, ROGER RICHARD, lawyer; b. Chgo., Dec. 11, 1935; s. Richard Emil and Evelyn (Thor); B.S. in Bus. Adminstrn., Washington U., St. Louis, 1958, J.D., 1961, postgrad. 1961-62; m. Virginia Fuller Vaughan, June 20, 1959; children—Steven Roger, Susan Vaughan, James Thor, Laura Craft. Grad. teaching asst. Washington U., St. Louis, 1961-62; admitted to Mo. bar, 1961, since practiced in St. Louis; asso. firm Rassieur, Long & Yawitz, 1962-64; partner firm Rassieur, Long, Yawitz & Schneider and predecessor firms, 1965—. Mem. exec. com. citizens' adv. council Pkwy. Sch. Dist., 1974—, pres.-elect, 1976-77, pres., 1977-78; bd. dirs. Parkway Residents Orgn., 1969—, v.p., 1970-73, pres., 1973—. Mem. Am., St. Louis bar assns., Mo. Bar, Christian Bus. Men's Com. (dir. 1975—), Full Gospel Bus. Men's Fellowship, Order of Coif, Omicron Delta Kappa, Beta Gamma Sigma, Pi Sigma Alpha, Phi Eta Sigma, Phi Delta Phi, Kappa Sigma. Republican. Presbyn. (elder, congregation pres. 1977—). Kiwanian (bd. dirs. 1972-74, 76—), Mason (Shriner). Home: 13812 Clayton Rd Manchester MO 63011 Office: 100 N Broadway St Louis MO 63102

FAHR, ROBERT EV, beverage distbr.; b. Waterloo, Iowa, Apr. 12, 1952; s. Everett Herman and Helen Elizabeth (Towell) F.; B.S. with honors in Commerce, St. Louis U., 1974. Asst. gen. mgr., v.p. Fahr Beverage Inc., Waterloo, also dir. Vice chmn. Wartburg Design for Tomorrow. Mem. Am. Mktg. Assn., Nat. Beer Distbrs. Assn., Iowa Wholesale Beer Distbrs., Waterloo C. of C., Jr. C. of C., Delta Sigma Phi, Alpha Sigma Nu. Lutheran. Clubs: Elks, Eagles. Home: 1151 Meadowlane St Apt G1 Waterloo IA 50701 Office: 323 W 17th St Box 2155 Waterloo IA 50702

FAHRNBRUCH, DALE EUGENE, judge; b. Lincoln, Nebr., Sept. 13, 1924; s. Henry and Bessie (Osborn) F.; certificate journalism U. Nebr., 1948, B.S., 1950; J.D., Creighton U., 1951; m. Margaret L. Hunt, July 4, 1952; children—Rebecca Kay, Daniel David. Reporter, Lincoln Jour. Newspapers, 1946-51, city editor, 1951-52; admitted to Nebr. bar, 1951; practiced in Nebr., 1952-73; dep. county atty., Lancaster County, 1952-55, chief dep. county atty., 1955-59; partner firm Beynon, Hecht & Fahrnbruch, attys., 1959-73; dist. judge, Lincoln, 1973—. Pres. Child Guidance Clinic. Served with AUS, 1942-46. Mem. Am., Nebr., Lincoln (dir. 1965) bar assns., Am. Legion, Delta Theta Phi, Sigma Delta Chi. Lutheran (past mem. bd.). Elk, Kiwanian. Home: 920 Ferndale Rd Lincoln NE 68510 Office: County-City Bldg 555 S 10th St Lincoln NE 68508

FAHY, EDWARD JOSEPH, lawyer; b. Toluca, Ill., Mar. 26, 1911; s. Michael and Josephine (Luppens) F.; A.B., Georgetown U., 1933, J.D., 1937; m. Helen C. Simmons, Nov. 6, 1937; children—Michael Joseph, Mary Katherine (Mrs. C.W. Norwood), Jean Marie (Mrs. Michael J. Hanley). Admitted to U.S. Dist. Ct. and Ct. of Appeals, 1936, Ill. bar, 1937, U.S. Ct. Appeals, 1949, Supreme Ct. U.S., 1956; practiced in Rockford, Ill., 1939—; partner Shultz, Fahy & Street, Rockford, Ill., 1945—. Mem. Am., Ill. State (chmn. labor law sect. 1951-53), Winnebago County bar assns., Rockford C. of C. (dir. 1963-66), Pi Gamma Mu. K.C. Contbr. articles to profl. jours. Home: 1821 Harlem Blvd Rockford IL 61103 Office: 501 Gas-Electric Bldg Rockford IL 61101

FAIER, MARTIN, patent lawyer; b. Omaha, July 18, 1930; s. John and Goldie (Shapiro) F.; B.S., Northwestern U., 1952, J.D., 1953; student Stanford, 1951; m. Kathleen Gindich, Oct. 25, 1955; children—Melinda Beth, James Michael. Admitted to Ill. bar, 1953; practiced in Chgo., 1954—; mem. firm Kegan and Kipnis, 1954, Martin Faier, 1955—. Sec., dir. Little Giant Products, Inc., Peoria, Ill., 1961—, Toronto, Ont., 1964-75, Beerse, Belgium, 1966—, Mexico, 1970, Fullerton, Calif., 1972—; dir. Fast Heat Europe, Herentals, Belgium, 1977—; sec., dir. Boardwalk, Inc., 1970-72; pres. Chem. Devel. Corp., Chgo., 1964-72; partner Faier Properties, U.S. Supply Stores Co., both of Omaha. Chmn. Young Democrats, 13th Congl. Dist., 1954. Trustee Little Giant Profit-Sharing and Pension Trusts, 1970-74. Mem. Am., Ill. State, Chgo. bar assns., Phi Epsilon Pi, Tau Epsilon Rho. Home: 330 Brookside Ln Glencoe IL 60022 Office: 120 S LaSalle St Chicago IL 60603

FAILLA, PATRICIA MCCLEMENT (MRS. GIOACCHINO FAILLA), research scientist; b. N.Y.C., Dec. 22, 1925; d. Morgan Hall and Louise (Yandell) McClement; A.B., Barnard Coll., 1946; Ph.D., Columbia, 1958; M.B.A., U. Chgo., 1976; m. Gioacchino Failla, Jan. 22, 1949 (dec. Dec. 1961). Asst. physicist physics lab. N.Y.C. Dept. Hosps., 1946-48; AEC predoctoral fellow, 1948-50; research sci. Radiol. Research Lab., Columbia, 1950-60; asso. biophysicist Argonne (Ill.) Nat. Lab., 1960-71, asst. dir. radiol. and environ. research div., 1971-73, program coordinator, office of dir., 1973-74, asst. to lab. dir., office of dir., 1974—. Mem. tech. electronic product radiation safety standards com. HEW, 1973-75. Ill. Republican precinct committeewoman, 1966-70. Mem. Radiation Research Soc. (councilor-at-large 1976—), Health Physics Soc., A.A.A.S., Biophys. Soc., Am. Assn. Physicists in Medicine, Corp. Marine Biol. Lab., Sci. Research Soc. Am., Phi Beta Kappa, Sigma Xi (mem. com. membership-at-large 1970—, qualifications com. 1973—, bd. dirs. 1975—, budget com. 1975), Sigma Pi Sigma. Home: 301 Lake Hinsdale Dr Clarendon Hills IL 60514 Office: 9700 S Cass Ave Argonne IL 60439

FAILOR, HARLAN JOHN, internist; b. Cedar Grove, Wis., Sept. 18, 1926; s. Carlton Braley and Agnes Hilda (Vanderwall) F.; B.S., Hope Coll., 1950; M.D., U. Wis., 1954; M.S., U. Minn., 1958; m. Patricia Jean Flom, June 19, 1954; children—Bruce Harlan, Kathryn Ann. Intern, Detroit Receiving Hosp., 1954-55; fellow in internal medicine Mayo Clinic, Rochester, Minn., 1955-58; bd. govs. Carle Clinic, Urbana, Ill., 1973—, chmn., 1975, 76; dir. Busey 1st Nat. Bank of Urbana. Trustee Carle Found., 1970-73, sec.-treas., 1972, 73; bd. dirs. ARC, 1961-66. Served with USNR, 1944-46. Fellow A.C.P.; mem. AMA, Ill., Champaign County (exec. com. 1964-67) med. socs., Am. Group Practice Assn., Am. Cancer Soc. (pres. 1967-70), Nu Sigma Nu, Am., Ill. (sec.-treas. 1969-71) socs. internal medicine. Republican. Presbyterian. Club: Champaign (Ill.) Country. Home: 9 Litchfield Ln Champaign IL 61820 Office: Carle Clinic 602 W University St Urbana IL 61802

FAIMAN, CHARLES, endocrinologist; b. Winnipeg, Man., Can., Dec. 6, 1939; s. Max and Bessie Freedman) F.; B.Sc. in Medicine (Harry Silverberg, Isbister, Lederle scholar), U. Man., 1962, M.D., 1962, M.Sc., 1966; m. Carol Lee Fien, June 16, 1963; children—Barton Shale, Gregg Howard, Matthew Randall. Intern Winnipeg Gen. Hosp., 1962-63, resident, 1963-64; Med. Research Council Can. fellow, Winnipeg Gen. Hosp., 1964-65, U. Ill. Coll. Medicine, 1965-67, Mayo Clinic, Rochester, Minn., 1967-68; asst. prof. physiology U. Man., 1968-71, asso. prof., 1971-75, prof., 1975—; dir. clin. investigation unit Winnipeg Gen. Hosp., 1971-74, infertility clinic, 1972—; head sect. endocrinology and metabolism dept. medicine U. Man. and Health Scis. Centre, Winnipeg. Bd. dirs. Winnipeg Hebrew Sch., 1969-76, 77—. Med. Research Council Can. scholar, 1968-73; recipient Prowse prize for research, 1966. Fellow Royal Coll. Physicians Canada; mem. Endocrine Soc., Am. Fedn. Clin. Research, Soc. Exptl. Biology and Medicine, Canadian Soc. Clin. Investigation, Canadian Soc. Endocrinology and Metabolism, Central Soc. Clin. Research, N.Y. Acad. Scis., AAAS, Am. Soc. Clin. Investigation, Sigma Xi. Home: 61 Primrose Crescent Winnipeg MB Canada Office: Health Sciences Center 700 William Ave Winnipeg MB Canada

FAIR, JOSEPH JAMES, chem. engr.; b. Dover, Ohio, Mar. 14, 1948; s. James Emerson and Eva Mae (Wagner) F.; student Otterbein Coll., 1966-68; B.S. in Chem. Engring., Ohio State U., 1971, M.S., 1971. Dairy mgr. Big Bear, New Philadelphia, Ohio, 1964-66, summer, 1967; asst. operator Dover Chem. Co. (Ohio), summer 1969; devel. engr. Inland div. Gen. Motors Corp., Dayton, Ohio, 1971—. Registered profl. engr., Ohio. Mem. Soc. Automotive Engrs., Am. Inst. Chem. Engrs., So. Ohio Rubber Group div. Am. Chem. Soc., Order of Engrs. Methodist. Home: 11960 Steck Rd Rural Route 1 Brookville OH 45309 Office: 2727 Inland Ave Dayton OH 45417

FAIRAND, BARRY PHILIP, physicist; b. Watertown, N.Y., May 20. 1934; s. Charles Francis and Dorothy Marie (Piche) F.; B.S., Le Moyne Coll., 1955; M.S., Detroit U., 1957; Ph.D., Ohio State U., 1969; m. Jeanine Fontana, June 13, 1959; children—Mary, Joan, John, Amy, Ann. Physicist, Battelle Meml. Inst., Columbus (Ohio) Labs., 1957—. Mem. Am. Phys. Soc., Photo-optical Instrumentation Engrs. Soc., Sigma Xi, Sigma Pi Sigma. Contbr. articles to profl. jours. Patentee laser shock processing of materials, laser atomization of metals, laser generated X-rays. Home: 1169 Regency Dr Columbus OH 43220 Office: 505 King Ave Columbus OH 43201

FAIRBANKS, RICHARD MONROE, broadcasting co. exec.; b. Indpls., Mar. 27, 1912; s. Richard Monroe and Louise (Hibben) F.; grad. Yale U., 1934; m. Virginia Nicholson Brown, Oct. 26, 1968; children (by previous marriage)—Anthony Caperton, Richard Monroe III, Scott Andrew, Charles Hibben. Reporter, asst. mng. editor Indpls. News, 1932-42; pres. radio sta. WIBC, Indpls., 1947—, radio sta. WNAP, Indpls., 1968—, radio sta. WKOX, Framingham, Mass., 1970—, radio sta. WVBF, Framingham and Boston, 1971—, Fairbanks Broadcasting Co., Inc., 1968—, KVIL AM and FM, Dallas, 1973—, Fairbanks Broadcasting Co. Pa., Inc., also Sta. WIBG, Phila., 1975—; dir. Mchts. Nat. Bank & Trust Co., Indpls. Bd. dirs. Indpls. United Fund, Trinity Episcopal Ch. Meml. Fund, Indpls. Bar Found.; bd. dirs. Cornelia Cole Fairbanks Found., 1958—, pres., 1968—; bd. corporators Crown Hill Cemetery, 1965—; trustee Butler U. Served to lt. comdr. USNR, World War II. Home: 5712 Sunset Ln Indianapolis IN 46208 Office: 2835 N Illinois St Indianapolis IN 46208

FAIRBANKS, VIRGIL FOX, hematologist; b. Ann Arbor, Mich., June 7, 1930; s. Avard Tennyson and Beatrice Maude (Fox) F.; B.A., U. Utah, 1951; M.D., U. Mich., 1954; m. Sheary Jill Eggertsen, Nov. 25, 1955; children—Eric, Julie, Caroline. Intern, Bellevue Hosp., N.Y.C., 1954-55; resident in internal medicine Salt Lake County Hosp., VA Hosp., Salt Lake City, 1957-59; fellow Scripps Clinic, LaJolla, Calif., 1959-60; hematologist City of Hope Med. Center, Duarte, Calif., 1960-63, Los Angeles County Hosp., 1960-63, Permanente Med. Group, Portland, Oreg., 1964-65; cons. in hematology Mayo Clinic and Found., Rochester, Minn., 1965—; mem. faculty U. Calif. Coll. Medicine, Los Angeles, 1963-64, U. Oreg. Med. Sch., 1964-65; asso. prof. medicine Mayo Grad. Sch. Medicine, Rochester, 1974—. Served with USN, 1955-57. Fellow Internat. Soc. Hematology. Mem. Am. Fedn. Clin. Research, Am. Soc. Hematology, Am. Coll. Physicians, Am. Soc. Human Genetics, Academic Clin. Lab. Physics and Scientists, Central Soc. Clin. Research, Zumbro Valley Med. Soc. Democrat. Author: (with E. Beutler and J.L. Fahey) Clinical Disorders of Iron Metabolism, 1963, 1971; contbr. articles to med. jours. and textbooks. Home: 620 Colombia Ct NE Rochester MN 55901 Office: Mayo Clinic 200 1st St SW Rochester MN 55901

FAIRBANKS, WENDELL LEE, physician; b. Hastings, Nebr., Jan. 19, 1938; s. Lyle W. and Myrna (Haskins) F.; A.B., Nebr. Wesleyan U., 1959; M.D., U. Nebr., 1963; m. Sarah Hinds, Aug. 28, 1959; children—Wendelyn Sue, Nancy Jane, Linda Jo. Rotating intern Nebr. Methodist Hosp., Omaha, 1963-64; practice medicine Auburn (Nebr.) Clinic, 1964—; mem. staff Nemaha County Hosp., chief, 1971; clinic asso. gen. practice, mem. Coll. Nebr. Preceptorship program, U. Nebr., 1966—. Bd. dirs. Am. Heart Assn. Served with Nebr. N.G., 1964-70. Recipient Merit award Omaha Midwest Clin. Soc., 1970; merit certificate Am. Acad. Gen. Practice Annual Assembly, San Francisco, 1970. Diplomate Am. Bd. Family Practice. Mem. S.E. Nebr. Med. Soc. (chmn. sci. programs 1968—), Nebr. Acad. Family Practice (bd. dirs. 1969-72), Tau Kappa Epsilon, Alpha Omega Alpha, Phi Chi. Republican. Methodist. Mason (past master). Club: Auburn Kiwanis. Contbr. articles to profl. jours. Home: 1906 23d St Auburn NE 68305 Office: 1202 Central Ave Auburn NE 68305

FAIRCHILD, ROBERT CHARLES, pediatrician; b. Kansas City, Mo., Dec. 22, 1921; s. Charles Clement and Ada Mae (Baker) F.; postgrad. Kansas City Jr. Coll., 1938-40; B.A., U. Kans., 1942, M.D., 1950; m. Patricia Louise Russell, May 28, 1964; children—Robert, Nancy, Rex Hartman, Dan Hartman. Intern, Kansas City Gen. Hosp., 1950-51; resident in pediatrics Univ. Kans. Med. Center, 1951-53; practice medicine specializing in pediatrics, Mission Kans., 1953-70; dir. area clinics Children's Mercy Hosp., Kansas City, Mo., 1970-74, dir. outpatient services, 1974—; asso. prof. pediatrics Univ. Mo.-Kansas City Sch. Medicine, Univ. Kans. Sch. Medicine. Mem. advisory com. Asso. Degree Nursing Program, Johnson County Community Coll., Vis. Nurses Assn., corp. bd. Blue Cross. Served to major U.S. Army, 1942-46. Decorated Bronze Star. Recipient Porter Scholarship award, Univ. Kans. Sch. Medicine, 1950, Physician's Recognition award, AMA, 1976. Diplomate Am. Bd. Pediatrics. Mem. AMA, Mo. State Med. Assn., Jackson County Med. Soc., Kansas City SW Pediatric Soc., Kansas City SW Clin. Soc., Am. Acad. Pediatrics, Alpha Omega Alpha, Nu Sigma Nu, Sigma Nu. Presbyterian. Contbr. articles in field to med. jours. Lectr. in field. Home: 8425 Reinhardt Ln Leawood KS 66206 Office: 24th & Gillham Rd Kansas City MO 64108

FAIRCHILD, THOMAS E., judge; b. Milw., Dec. 25, 1912; s. Edward Thomas and Helen (Edwards) F.; student Princeton, 1931-33; A.B., Cornell U., 1934; LL.B., U. Wis., 1938; m. Eleanor E. Dahl, July 24, 1937; children—Edward, Susan, Jennifer, Andrew. Admitted to Wis. bar, 1938, practiced Portage, Wis., 1938-41, Milw., 1945-48, 53-56; atty. O.P.A., Chgo., Milw., 1941-45, hearing commr., Chgo. Region, 1945; atty. gen., Wis., 1948-51; U.S. Atty. for Western Dist. Wis., 1951-52; asso. justice Supreme Ct. Wis., 1957-66; judge U.S. Ct. Appeals 7th circuit, Chgo., 1966—, chief judge, 1975—. Democratic candidate for senator from Wis. 1950, 52. Mem. council Am. Law Inst. Mem. Am., Wis., Milw. bar assns., Jr. Assn. Milw. Bar, Phi Delta Phi. Democrat. United Ch. of Christ. K.P. Home: 2626 Lakeview Ave Chicago IL 60614 Office: 219 S Dearborn St Chicago IL 60604

FAIRCHILD, WILLIS ARNOLD, dentist; b. Cooper, Ky., Aug. 18, 1929; s. Sam and Florida (Abbott) F.; student Campbellsville Coll., 1950-53; D.M.D., U. Louisville, 1957; m. Ina Carleen Norfleet, Jan. 6, 1951; 1 dau., Valynnda Karon. Gen. practice dentistry, Shelbyville, Ind., 1957—. Farmer, breeder Charolais cattle, 1962—. Mem. Shelby County Republican Club. Served with USNR, 1946-50, 51-52. Mem. Ind. Cattlemens Assn., Indpls. Dist. Dental Soc., Ind., Am. dental assns., Delta Sigma Delta, Beta Delta, Phi Kappa Phi. Baptist. Patentee life saving device for swimming and plant to be used as tobacco substitute with insignificant amount of nicotine and tars, also safety hitch pin for connecting motorized vehicles to farm implements, other trailers. Home: Rural Route 6 Shelbyville IN 46176 Office: 273 W Broadway Shelbyville IN 46176

FAIRES, C(ARL) DICKSON, JR., lawyer; b. Edwardsville, Ill., Dec. 3, 1936; s. Carl Dickson and Lela (Christy) F.; student Trinity Sch., N.Y.C., 1952-54, U. Okla., 1954-57; B.S., Ind. U., 1960, LL.B., 1964; m. Lynda Shytle, Mar. 30, 1968 (div. 1977); children—Kimberly Lynne, Carl Dickson III. Admitted to Ind. bar, 1964; dep. atty. gen. Ind., 1964-65; partner firm White, Raub, Reis & Wick, Indpls., 1965-73; partner firm Buckley, Frost & Faires, Indpls., 1973-74, Frost & Faires, Indpls., 1974—. Asso. mem. '500' Festival Assos., Inc., Indpls., 1970—. Indpls. Mus. Art, 1968—. Served with AUS, 1960-61. Mem. Am., Ind., Indpls. bar assns., Ind. Def. Lawyers Assn., Newcomen Soc. N.Am., U.S. Lawn Tennis Assn., Ducks Unltd., Nat., Ind. skeet shooting assns. Republican. Clubs: Ind. Gun, Sports Car America, Lambs, Racquet, University (Indpls). Home: 7621 Somerset Bay Apt B Indianapolis IN 46240 Office: 3665 N Washington Blvd Indianapolis IN 46205

FAIRMAN, WILLIAM HORACE, ednl. adminstr.; b. Buchanan, Mich., Oct. 3, 1931; s. George W. and Anna M. (Fullhart) F.; B.A., Mich. State U., 1954, M.A., 1958; Ed.D., Walden U., 1972; m. Marilyn Hewitt, Aug. 31, 1952; children—Michele, Sharon, Judith, William, Megan. Tchr., coach Coldwater (Mich.) Pub. Schs., 1954-59; tchr. Buchanan (Mich.) Pub. Schs., 1959-64, asst. supt., 1964-67; tchr. Niles (Mich.) Community Schs., 1967-68, dir., 1968-69, asst. supt., 1969-73, supt., 1973—. Chmn. ednl. div. United Fund, 1970-71; mem. Greater Niles Recreation Bd., 1973—; mem. Lake Mich. Coll. Adv. Bd., 1975—; mem. Niles Sch.-Community Adv. Council, 1973—. Mem. Greater Niles C. of C., Berrien-Cass Counties Adminstrs. Assn., Personnel Roundtable Assn., Mich. State U. Alumni Assn., Mich., Am. assns. sch. adminstrs., Mich. Assn. Sch. Bds. Presbyn. (elder 1963—, sec. 1973-74, trustee 1971-74, mem. choir 1968—). Rotarian. Clubs: Orchard Hills Country, Pickwick. Home: 415 S 4th St Niles MI 49120 Office: 720 E Main St Niles MI 49120

FAIRWEATHER, OWEN, lawyer; b. Chgo., Aug. 18, 1913; s. George O. and Nellie (Dieter) F.; A.B., Dartmouth Coll., 1935; J.D., U. Chgo., 1938; m. Sally Hallberg, May 4, 1940; children—Ellen Vail, Peter Gustav. Admitted to Ill. bar, 1938; practiced in Chgo., 1938—; asso. firm Pope & Ballard, Chgo., 1938-43, partner, 1943-45; partner firm Seyfarth, Shaw, Fairweather & Geraldson, Chgo., 1945—; dir. Danly Machine Corp., Chgo., Self Insurers Service, Inc., Chgo. Mem. Am. (council labor law sect. 1973—), Chgo. (legal ethics com. 1943-44, grievance com. 1955-56), Ill. (labor law com. 1944-45) bar assns. Author: Labor Relations and the Law (studies 6 European countries); Practice and Procedure in Labor Arbitration. Contbr. articles to legal publs. Home: 59 Hawthorne Rd Barrington IL 60010 Office: 55 E Monroe St Chicago IL 60603

FAIST, CLARA ROSE, mathematician, educator; b. Lena, Ill., July 30, 1923; d. Louis Andrew and Helen Frances (Hodapp) Faist; B.A., Rosary Coll., 1945; M.S., Northwestern U., 1958, Ph.D., 1972. Tchr. math. Sacred Heart Acad., Lisle, Ill., 1945-47, Elizabeth (Ill.) High Sch., 1947-49, Orangeville (Ill.) High Sch., 1949-52, Wauconda (Ill.) High Sch., 1952-53, Glenbard High Sch., Glen Ellyn, Ill., 1953-59; tchr. math., dept. chmn. Glenbard East High Sch., Lombard, Ill., 1960—. Mem. Math. Assn. Am., NEA, Nat. Council Supervisors Math., Nat. Council Tchrs. Math., Glenbard Edn. Assn., Ill. Council Tchrs. Math., Met. Math. Club., West Suburban Math. Dept. Chmn., Delta Kappa Gamma. Roman Catholic. Home: 460 Raintree Ct Glen Ellyn IL 60137 Office: 1014 S Main Lombard IL 60148

FAIT, LAWRENCE EDWARD, optometrist; b. Morse, Wis., June 20, 1923; s. Edward C. and Sophia M. (Swetz) F.; student U. Wis., 1941-43, Carleton Coll., 1943-44; B.S., Dr. Optometry cum laude, Ill. Coll. Optometry, 1947; m. Marie R. Richter, Apr. 15, 1944; children—Robert L., James C., Thomas G., William J. (dec.), Gary P., Kathleen M., Joanne M. Pvt. practice optometry, Burlington, Wis., 1947—; instr. Ill. Coll. Optometry, 1946-47; cons. Internat. Corr. Soc. Optometry. Served with USAAF, 1942-44. Mem. South Eastern Wis. Optometric Soc., Burlington Hist. Soc., Accademia di S. Marciano (Italy), U. Wis. Alumni Assn., N.Am. Indian Relic Collectors Assn., Am. Optometry Assn., Am. Legion, Circus Hist. Soc., Arms and Armour Soc. (Eng.), Wis., Balkan and E. European geneal. socs., Augustan Soc., Wis. Hist. Soc., Wis. Optometric Assn., Wis. Geneal. Soc., Internat. Wildlife Fedn., Mzuri Safari Found., Fishing Hall Fame, Tomb and Kev (pres. 1946-47), Internat. Game Fish Assn., Oriental Inst. U. Chgo., Smithsonian Instn., Am. Mus. Natural History, Nat. Audubon Soc., Alpha Kappa Lambda, Omega Delta. K.C. (4 deg.). Clubs: U.S. Broadbill, Safari Internat. Home: 117 Midwood Dr Burlington WI 53105 Office: 309 McHenry St Burlington WI 53105

FAIT, ROBERT LAWRENCE, optometrist; b. Burlington, Wis., Mar. 1, 1945; s. Lawrence Edward and Marie Ruth (Richter) F.; asso. B.S., U. Wis., 1965; B.S., Ill. Coll. Optometry, 1967, Dr. Optometry, 1968; m. Judith Ruth Spriggs, Aug. 9, 1969; m. 2d, Alison Shannon; children—Garrett, Christopher. Practice optometry, Fait Pippin Med. Clinic, Burlington, 1968—. Cons. developmental vision, area schs. Diplomate Nat. Bd. Examiners Optometry. Fellow Coll. Optometric Vision Devel.; mem. Wis. (dir.), Southeastern Wis. (pres. 1969-72, dir. 1969-72) optometric assns., Jr. C. of C. (dir. 1969-72). Club: K.C. Contbr. articles to profl. jours. Home: 148 Kings Ct Burlington WI 53105 Office: 309 McHenry St Burlington WI 53105

FAITHORN, WALTER ERNEST, JR., mfg. co. exec.; b. Chgo., Nov. 1, 1915; s. Walter Ernest and Elsie (Dixon) F.; grad. Phillips Acad., Andover, Mass., 1934; A.B., Harvard U., 1938; m. Eleanor Rand, Feb. 22, 1941 (div.); children—Eleanor Perry, Elizabeth Dixon; m. 2d, Mary Valentine Scott, July 28, 1958; 1 son, Charles Wallace. Able seaman Donnaldson Line, Glasgow, Scotland, 1938; chief factory cost accountant Dorr Pump Co., Whitewater, Wis., 1938-39; machine tool operator to sales engr. Alemite and Instrument div. Stewart-Warner Corp., Chgo., 1939-42; asst. to vice chmn. WPB, Washington, also asst. sec. Combined Brit.-Canadian Am. Prodn. and Resources Bd., Office Pres. U.S., 1942-43; rep. Stewart-Warner Corp., Washington, 1946-53, asst. sec., govt. mgr., 1953-67, export mgr. Chgo., 1967-70, mgr. internat. ops., 1971-76, dir. internat. mktg., asst. gen. mgr. Internat. div., 1976—; v.p. Indsl. Alemex, S.A., Mexico; dir. Stewart Warner Ltd. Eng., Stewart Warner Alemite GmbH, Germany. Dist. dir. Adlai Stevenson for Pres. Campaign, 1952. Bd. govs., chmn. finance com. Key Sch., Annapolis, Md., until 1968; trustee, chmn. fin. com., mem. exec. com., treas., Latin Sch. of Chgo., 1972-74; trustee, mem. exec. com. Roycemore Sch., Evanston, Ill., 1976—. Served to lt. USCGR, 1943-45. Mem. Am. Ordnance Assn. (chmn. fuze sect. 1963-68), Revel Athletic Assn. (past dir.). Democrat. Unitarian. Clubs: Arts (Chgo.); Metropolitan (Washington); Severn Sailing Assn. (Annapolis, Md.); Oconomowoc (Wis.) Lake; Directors (London). Home: 2518 Orrington Ave Evanston IL 60201 also Whitehall Rd St Margarets Annapolis MD 21401 Office: 1826 Diversey Pkwy Chicago IL 60614

FAITZ, EVERETT KARL, JR., city ofcl.; b. Chgo., Aug. 16, 1932; s. Everett Karl and Frances (Stanton) F.; student Wilson Jr. Coll., 1950-51, U. Ill., 1952-54; B.B.A. with Distinction, Northwestern U., 1972; m. Susanne Ewing, July 14, 1956 (div. Feb. 1971). News rep. F.W. Dodge Corp., 1955-60; bldg. insp. Village of Oak Lawn (Ill.), 1960-63, bldg. commr., 1963—, also dir. bldg. and zoning. Mem. faculty U. Ill. Acad. for Code Adminstrn. and Enforcement, 1969—, U. Wis. Extension Div., 1973—; zoning cons., adviser to Oak Lawn Planning and Devel. Commn., 1963—; co-adviser Ill. Contractor License Legislation, 1967—; zoning cons. Village of McCook (Ill.), City of Hickory Hills (Ill.); mem. Ill. Bldg. Code Adv. Commn., 1969—. Chmn. Community Chest, Oak Lawn, 1968, co-chmn., divisional leader, 1965-71 active Boy Scouts Am., Salvation Army; leader YMCA, 1957, 63. Recipient Distinguished Service award Evergreen Park-Oak Lawn Jr. C. of C., 1965. Named one of Outstanding Young Men of Am., Outstanding Young Ams., Inc., 1967. Mem. S. Suburban Bldg. Ofcls. Assn. (pres. 1964-66, exec. bd. 1966—), Suburban Bldg. Ofcls. Conf. (mem. exec. bd. 1966—, chmn. code change com. 1966—, pres. 1971-72), Bldg. Ofcls. and Code Adminstrs. Internat., Am. Soc. Testing Materials, Nat. Fire Prevention Assn., Western Soc. Engrs., Pershing Rifles, Order Arrow, Delta Mu Delta, Alpha Phi Omega. Clubs: Nomads Ski; Oak Lawn Racquet, Chicago Double JJ. Contbr. articles in Boca News, Bldg. Ofcl. mags. Home: 5641 Circle Dr Oak Lawn IL 60453 Office: 5252 W James St Oak Lawn IL 60453

FAJARDO, BEN RONDEZ, physician; b. Cebu, Philippines, May 5, 1943; s. Antonio B. and Marcelina C. (Rondez) F.; came to U.S., 1966, naturalized, 1975; A.A., U. San Carlos, Philippines, 1960; M.D., Cebu Inst. Tech., 1966; m. Pacita Baculad Trasmonte, Aug. 11, 1942; children—Christine, Robert, Marvin. Intern, St. John's Episcopal Hosp., Bklyn., 1967; gen. practice resident St. Joseph Hosp., Flint, Mich., 1968-69, Swedish Covenant Hosp., Chgo., 1970; resident in internal medicine St. John's Hosp., Detroit, 1971-73; practice medicine specializing in internal medicine, Mt. Clemens, Mich., 1974—; asso. attending physician St. Joseph Hosp., Mt. Clemens. Diplomate Am. Bd. Internal Medicine. Mem. AMA, Am. Soc. Internal Medicine, Mich. Med. Soc., Am. Diabetes Assn. Office: 243 S Gratiot Ave Mt Clemens MI 48043

FALETTI, RICHARD JOSEPH, lawyer; b. Spring Valley, Ill., Nov. 15, 1922; s. Micheal Joseph and Alfonsa M. (Delo) F.; B.S., U. Ill., 1947, J.D., 1948; m. Barbara Louise Shaft, Aug. 11, 1947; children—Martha D., Joan D., Carol L., Micheal J., Margaret M. Admitted to Ill. bar, 1949; mem. firm Arrington & Healy, Chgo., 1948-50; asst. prof. law U. Ill., 1950-55; partner Winston & Strawn, Chgo., 1955—. Dir. Wheaton (Ill.) Nat. Bank, Bank of Clarendon Hills; sec. Carus Corp., LaSalle, Ill. Trustee Village of Clarendon Hills, 1960-64. Bd. govs. Hinsdale Community House, 1968-71; governing life mem. Art Inst. Chgo. Served to 1st lt. USAAF, 1943-45. Decorated Air medal with 2 oak leaf clusters. Mem. Am., Ill., Chgo. bar assns., Am. Judicature Soc., Law Club of Chgo., U. Ill. Alumni Assn. (exec. com. 1962-68). Roman Catholic. Clubs: Mid-Day (Chgo.); Hinsdale Golf. Contbr. articles in profl. jours. Home: 1 Hammill Ln Clarendon Hills IL 60514 Office: 1 First National Plaza Chicago IL 60603

FALK, LAWRENCE ADDNESS, JR., virologist, microbiologist; b. Houston, May 5, 1938; s. Lawrence A. and Lorraine Oletha (Wilson) F.; B.A., Centenary Coll. of La., 1962; M.S., U. Houston, 1966; Ph.D. (USPHS fellow), U. Ark., 1970. USPHS postdoctoral fellow dept. microbiology Rush-Presbyterian-St. Luke's Med. Center, Chgo., 1969-71, asst. prof., 1971-75, asso. prof., 1975—; vis. scientist Inst. for Tumorbiologi, Stockholm, 1976-77. Recipient Leukemia Soc. of Am. scholarship award, 1975-80. Mem. AAAS, Am. Soc. for Microbiology, Am. Assn. Immunologists, Soc. Exptl. Biology and Medicine, Am. Assn. for Cancer Research, Soc. for Cryobiology, Tissue Culture Assn., Internat. Assn. for Comparative Research on Leukemia and Related Diseases, Am. Assn. Tissue Banks, Sigma Xi. Office: Dept Microbiology Rush-Presbyterian-St Lukes Med Center 1753 W Congress Pkwy Chicago IL 60612

FALK, MARSHALL ALLEN, physician; b. Chgo., May 23, 1929; s. Ben and Frances (Kamins) F.; B.S., Bradley U., 1950; M.S., U. Ill., 1952; M.D., Chgo. Med. Sch., 1956; m. Marilyn Levoff, June 15, 1952; children—Gayle Debra, Ben Scott. Intern, Cook County Hosp., Chgo., 1956-57; gen. practice medicine, Chgo., 1959-64, specializing in psychiatry, 1964—; mem. staff Edgewater Hosp., Chgo., Louis A. Weiss Meml. Hosp.; prof., dep. chmn. psychiatry Chgo. Med. Sch.; dean Chgo. Med. Sch. U. Health Scis., 1974—. Served to capt. AUS, 1957-59. Recipient Alumnus of Year award Chgo. Med. Sch., 1976. Diplomate Am. Bd. Psychiatry, 1969. Fellow Chgo. Inst. Medicine, Am. Psychiat. Assn., Am. Coll. Psychiatrists; mem. A.M.A., Chgo., Ill. (contbn. to edn. Silver Award 1968, chmn. council mental health) med. socs., Ill. Psychiat. Soc. Author articles on med. econs., research and psychiat. drugs. Home: 226 Kilpatrick St Wilmette IL 60091 Office: 2020 W Ogden Chicago IL 60612

FALK, VICTOR SOFUS, JR., physician; b. Stoughton, Wis., Sept. 10, 1915; s. Victor Sofus and Florence Keiler (Ladd) F.; B.A., U. Wis., 1936, M.D.. 1939; m. Nina Raechel Stare, Nov. 28, 1964; children—Victor Sofus III, Thomas S., Frederick N. Intern, Ancker Hosp., St. Paul, 1939-40; resident Carle Hosp., Urbana, Ill., 1940-41, Augustana Hosp., Chgo., 1947; practice medicine specializing in surgery, Edgerton, Wis., 1948—; chief staff Edgerton Hosp., 1957—; vol. physician for Vietnam, 1966, 67, 70, 72. Trustee Meml. Union Bldg. Assn., U. Wis.; bd. dirs. Wis.-Nicaragua Partner of Americas. Served with USN, 1941-47. Decorated Silver Star. Fellow A.C.S. (pres. Wis. chpt. 1970-72), State Med. Jour. Group (dir. 1972—), Am. Assn. Vol. Physicians (councilor 1974-75), Wis. Surg. Soc. (pres. 1976-77),

Kappa Sigma, Nu Sigma Nu, Phi Kappa Phi. Med. editor Wis. Med. Jour., 1962—, mem. editorial bd., 1952—. Home: Route 4 Box 447 Stoughton WI 53589 Office: 5 W Rollin St Edgerton WI 53534

FALKENHAIN, VERNON EDWARD, optometrist; b. Rosamond, Ill., May 11, 1937; s. Vernon Arthur and Virginia Louise (Davis) F.; student U. Ill., 1955-57, So. Ill. U., 1957-58; D. Optometry, So. Coll. Optometry, 1961; m. Linda Lee Russell, June 4, 1960; children—Dina, Michael, David, Donna. Pvt. practice optometry, Rolla, Mo., 1965—; visual cons. Schwitzer div. Wallace Murry Corp., 1970—; Mo. dir. Vol. Optometric Service for Humanity, 1977—. Central div. U.S. Geol. Survey, 1972—. Bd. dirs. Skills Builder Sch., 1972-73. Served to 1st lt. AUS, 1962-65. Mem. Am. Mo. (trustee) optometric assns., Heart of Am. Contact Lens Soc., C. of C., Beta Sigma Kappa, Sigma Alpha Sigma, Theta Xi, Omega Delta. K.C., Rotarian. Home: Route 2 Rolla MO 65401 Office: 10th and Pine Sts Rolla MO 65401

FALLAH, ABRAHAM, physician; b. Kashan, Iran, Oct. 23, 1942; s. Ali Fard and Aliah Fallah; M.D., Tehran U. Med. Sch., Iran, 1967; m. Fatima Gilack, Sept. 12, 1966; children—Marc Alireza, Melissa Mariam. Intern, Nat. Iranian Oil Co. Hosp., Tehran, 1966, Tehran U. Hosp., 1966-67, Iranian Army Family Health Center, 1967-69, Northern Westchester Hosp., Mt. Kisco, N.Y., 1969-70; resident in internal medicine Grasslands Hosp., Westchester Med. Sch., 1970-71, Bklyn. Cumberland Med. Center, 1971-73, chief resident in internal medicine, 1972-73; fellow in gastroenterology Henry Ford Hosp., Detroit, 1973-75; cons. gastroenterology Ingalls Meml. Hosp., Harvey, Ill., 1975-77; staff internal medicine and gastroenterology St. Francis Hosp., Blue Island, Ill., 1975-77. Diplomate Am. Bd. Internal Medicine. Mem. AMA, Ill. State, Chgo. med. socs., Am. Coll. Physicians, Am. Soc. Gastroenter-intestinal Endoscopy. Contbr. article in field to profl. jours. Home: 1704 Cambridge Flossmoor IL 60422 Office: 2320 W High St Blue Island IL 60406

FALLEY, MARGARET DICKSON (MRS. GEORGE FREDERICK FALLEY), author, genealogist; b. Mpls., Nov. 8, 1898; d. George E. and Edith (Baker) Dickson; B.S., Northwestern U., 1920; m. George Frederick Falley, Mar. 10, 1921 (dec. 1962); children—Katharine (Mrs. Edward H. Bennett, Jr.), Margaret Jane (Mrs. Raymond M. Galt), Carol (Mrs. Warner G. Baird, Jr.), Priscilla (Mrs. Henry W. Apfelbach). Ann. lectr. to Am. Inst. Genealogy at Nat. Archives, Washington, 1955-60, Geneal. Inst. Samford U., Birmingham, Ala., 1967; participant Inst. Humanistic Studies, Aspen, Colo., 1967; geneal. lectr. state, tchr. hist. socs., clubs, orgns. Recipient Merit award Nat. Geneal. Soc., 1963. Fellow Am. Soc. Genealogists (v.p. 1962-63); Am. rep. council Harleian Soc., London; colonial mem. New Eng. Historic Geneal. Soc.; mem. Northwestern U. Alumni Assn. (v.p. 1935-36), Northwestern U. Settlement Sr. Bd. (pres. 1945-46), Colonial Dames Am., DAR, Nat. Soc. Descs. Lords of Md. Manors, Daus. of Barons of Runnymeade, Kappa Kappa Gamma (Outstanding Alumnae award 1970). Methodist. Clubs: Union League (Chgo.); Glen View (Golf, Ill.). Author: Richard Falley and Some of His Descendants Including Grover Cleveland, 1952; Palmer Genealogy, Part I (English and Irish Ancestry of George Palmer), 1957; Irish and Scotch-Irish Ancestral Research, 2 vols., 1962; Baird-Green and Allied Families, Part II, 1976. Contbr. articles to geneal. jours. Address: 1500 Sheridan Rd Wilmette IL 60091

FALLIS, HENRY C, veterinarian; b. Delaware County, Ind., Jan. 27, 1926; s. Mark C. and Veree Lavonne (Baker) F.; B.S., Mich. State U., 1958, D.V.M., 1960; m. Donna Lavonne Hollmeyer, May 22, 1944; children—John, Dean, Henry C II. Practice vet. medicine, Hagerstown, Ind., 1960—. Served with AUS, 1944-46; ETO. Decorated Presdl. citation with two oak leaf clusters. Mem. Am., Ind. pub. health assns., Am. Ind. vet. med. assns., Am. Legion. Address: 560 N Washington St Hagerstown IN 47346

FALLS, OSWALD BENJAMIN, JR., cons. engr.; b. Denison, Tex., Apr. 28, 1913; s. Oswald Benjamin and Glennie (Parker) F.; B.S., U. Richmond, 1934; B.S., Mass. Inst. Tech., 1936, M.S., 1937; LL.D., Spring Arbor Coll., 1976; m. Mary Elizabeth Laird, Dec. 19, 1936; children—Harriet Elizabeth (Mrs. W.H. Burnett), Margaret Parker (Mrs. R.J. DiBianro), Susan Laird (Mrs. Venard Fegley). Test engr. to marketing mgr. Gen. Elec. Co., 1935-63; pres. Commonwealth Assos., Inc., Jackson, Mich., v.p., dir. Commonwealth Services, Inc., Jackson, v.p. Commonwealth Services Internat., Inc., 1963-70; v.p. Ralph M. Parsons Co., N.Y.C., 1970-71; with Internat. Atomic Energy Agy., Vienna, 1972-73; dir. Arabian Devel. Assos., 1963-70; Nat. Bank of Jackson. Vice pres., dir. Boy Scouts Am.; dir. Goodwill Industries, 1st Baptist Ch. of Jackson; v.p., dir. Mich. Bapt. Homes, Inc. Recipient Engr. of Year award, Mich. Soc. Profl. Engrs., 1976. Mem. IEEE, Am. Nuclear Soc., Sigma Pi Sigma, Omicron Delta Kappa, Sigma Alpha Epsilon, Tau Beta Pi. Republican. Clubs: Country of Jackson, Town of Jackson. Contbr. articles profl. jours. Home: 2107 Dale Rd Jackson MI 49203 Office: 728 W Michigan St Jackson MI 49201

FALSTAD, WILLIAM JAMES, bank note co. exec.; b. Superior, Wis., Jan. 5, 1934; s. Ralph Leonard and Patricia Sarah (Calhoun) F.; student Carleton Coll., 1952-53; B.B.A., U. Wis., 1956; m. Diane Margaret Hollis, Apr. 28, 1958 (div. Dec. 1971); children—David, Daniel, Julie, Robert; m. 2d, Jacquelyn Durham, Sept. 1, 1977. Accountant Arthur Andersen & Co., Chgo., 1956-60; pres. Kansas Bank Note Co., Fredonia, 1961—; dir. First Nat. Bank, Fredonia. Mayor, Fredonia, 1969-71, 77—; chmn. Kans. Republican State Com., 1970-73; co-chmn. Pres. Ford Com. Kans., 1975-76; co-chmn. Johnston for Congress Com. (5th Kans. Congl. Dist.), 1977-78. Mem. Kans. C. of C. (bd. dirs. 1969-72), Pi Kappa Alpha, Beta Alpha Psi. Mason (32 deg., Shriner), Elk, Lion. Home: Box 360 Fredonia KS 66736 Office: 301 N 5th St Fredonia KS 66736

FALSTEIN, LAWRENCE L., packaging co. exec.; b. Chgo., July 25, 1925; s. Harry and Fannie (Horwitz) F.; B.S. in Journalism and Advt., Northwestern U., 1948; m. Beverly Winowsky, Oct. 31, 1948; 1 son, Lyndon Harry. With Triangle Container Corp., Chgo., 1948-61, v.p. 1956-61; gen. mgr. Menasha Corp., Chgo., 1961-64; founder, pres. Tri-Pack Corp., Chgo., 1964—; pres. Western Tri-Pack Corp., San Francisco, 1970—. Adviser personnel dept. State of Ill., 1965-69. Group chmn. Jewish United Fund, Chgo., 1968-69. Served with inf. AUS, 1943-45. Decorated Purple Heart with oak leaf cluster. Mem. Am. Vets. Com. (pres. 1946), Nat. Paper Trades Assn., Fibre Box Assn. (chmn. sheet plant group 1976—), Assn. Ind. Corrugated Converters (dir. 1976—), UN Assn., Praetorian Frat. (pres. 1947). Jewish (v.p. congregation 1973-77). Home: 3750 Lake Shore Dr Chicago IL 60613 Office: 2828 S Lock St Chicago IL 60608

FALVEY, JAMES MURRAY, food co. exec.; b. Detroit, Sept. 30, 1933; s. James Patrick and Eleanor Mary (Murray) F.; B.B.A., U. Toledo, 1955; postgrad. Loyola U., Chgo., 1957-58, St. Louis U., 1960-61; m. Martha Ann Moloney, Nov. 24, 1962; children—Mary Eleanor, Kathleen, Maureen, Patricia. Export sales mgr. Owens-Ill., Inc., Toledo, Ohio, 1957-72; pres. Steger-Showel Co., Toledo, 1973—; mng. partner Falvey, Clukey and Assos., Inc. Asso. bd. chmn. St. Vincent Hosp., Toledo; pres. bus. alumni bd. U. Toledo; bd. dirs. Crosby Park Toledo Small Bus. Assn. Served to lt. U.S. Army, 1955-56. Mem. Food Equipment Distbrs. Assn. Republican. Roman Catholic. Clubs: Rotary, Toledo, Toledo Country. Home: 3534 Ridgewood Rd Toledo OH 43606 Office: 421 Main St Toledo OH 43605

FAN, SEN, educator; b. Kiangsu, China, Aug. 17, 1927; s. Chin-Mon Fan and Fong Shih Fan; came to U.S., 1960, naturalized, 1970; B.S., Taiwan Normal U., 1954; M.S., U. Ill., 1961; postgrad. Brown U., 1965-66, U. Calif., Santa Barbara, 1968-71; m. Hsu Ying, Jan. 5, 1958; children—Paul, Grace, Robert. Instr. math. Chia-Kao High Sch., Taiwan, 1953-54, Cheng Kung U., Taiwan, 1954-58, Nanyang U., Singapore, 1958-60; asso. prof. math. Morningside Coll., Sioux City, Iowa, 1966-68; instr. math. U. Minn., Morris, 1961-64, asst. prof., 1964-66, 68-71, asso. prof., 1971—; coordinator, 1975—. NSF fellow, 1965-66, NSF grantee, U. Minn. grantee. Mem. Math. Assn. Am., W. Central Council Tchrs. Math., Kappa Mu Epsilon, Pi Mu Epsilon. Office: U Minn Morris MN 56267

FANDRICH, LLOYD LINCOLN, ednl. adminstr.; b. Jamestown, N.D., Feb. 12, 1934; B.S., Jamestown Coll., 1956; M.S., N.D. State U., 1965; Specialist Degree, U. S.D., 1977; postgrad. U. Minn., 1977; m. Ardith Joanne Schlenker, Aug. 5, 1960; children—Steven Douglas, Daniel Scott, Sue Ann. Supt. several small rural schs. in N.D., Minn., 1956-77. Mem. region I arts task force com. N.W. Regional Devel. Commn., 1977—; water safety instr., swimming pool cons. A.R.C., Jamestown, 1956-76; chmn. Rock County Drug Council, 1972-73; pres. Rock County Town Meeting, 1972, 73; scoutmaster, commr. and mem. exec. com. Pheasant council Boy Scouts Am., 1975. Recipient award for service to schs. No. Interscholastic Press Assn., 1966, 67; Charles F. Kettering Idea fellow, 1969, 70, 74; Sch. Planner of Year award, 1970. Mem. Am. (evaluation com. 1971), Minn. (mem. constn. com. 1977-78, personnel com. 1977-78) assns. sch. adminstrs., Am. Personnel and Guidance Assn. (nat. del. 1969), Council Ednl. Facilities Planners, Upper Midwest Small Schs. Project (charter), Schoolmen's Assn. (past pres.), Phi Delta Kappa. Lutheran (deacon, Sunday sch. tchr., lay reader). Mason, Lion, Elk, Rotarian. Club: Country. Home: Humboldt MN 56731 Office: Independent School Dist 352 Humboldt-St Vincent MN 56731

FARABAUGH, MARLYCE MARIE, utility co. exec.; b. Gary, Ind., Oct. 21, 1953; d. John and Charlotte Claire (Petersen) Bielak; student Ind. U., 1971-73; certificate system design programming IBM, Chgo., 1973; m. Mitchell L. Farabaugh, Sept. 25, 1976. Mgr. data processing Gary-Hobart Water Corp., Gary, Ind., 1973—. Mem. System/3 Forum, Smithsonian Assos. Democrat. Roman Catholic. Home: 2045 Timlin Ct Demotte IN 46310 Office: 650 Madison St Gary IN 46402

FARBER, LESTER JOSEPH, lawyer; b. Cleve., May 17, 1908; s. Samuel J. and Bertha (Ziegler) F.; A.B., Adelbert Coll., Western Res. U., 1929, LL.B., 1931; m. Zelda Hantman, Aug. 5, 1941 (dec. Sept. 1966); children—Stephen E., Jane E.; m. 2d, Ruth Wratslavsky, Oct. 13, 1970. Admitted to Ohio bar, 1931; practiced in Cleve., 1931—; partner Diehm & Farber, 1949—; chief atty., advisor U.S. Navy Family All Act, Cleve., 1975—; dir. Union Gospel Press. Mem. Local Draft Bd., 1948-71. Mem. Am., Ohio, Cleve. (judicial selection com. 1967-71, grievance com. 1971-74), Cuyahoga County (trustee 1963-73) bar assns., Tau Epsilon Rho. Republican. Mem. Jewish religion. Mem. B'nai B'rith. Home: 3715 Warrensville Center Rd Shaker Heights OH 44122 Office: 330 Leader Bldg Cleveland OH 44114

FARBER, MILTON LEWIS, JR., historian; b. Columbus, Ohio, Apr. 4, 1929; s. Milton L. and Freda S. Cohen; B.A., Miami U., Oxford, Ohio, 1950; M.A., Ohio State U., 1951, Ph.D., 1959; m. Rowena Tronnes, June 15, 1952. Instr., Ohio State U., 1959-60; mem. faculty Butler U., Indpls., 1961—, prof. history, 1977—. Served with USAF, 1951-55. Mem. Am. Hist. Assn., Orgn. Am. Historians. Democrat. Home: 5362 N Illinois St Indianapolis IN 46208 Office: Butler Univ Indianapolis IN 46208

FARBER, RUDOLPH EMERSON, banker; b. Dallas, Feb. 7, 1941; s. Arnold and Irene (Williams) F.; B.S. summa cum laude, Northwestern U., 1963; M.B.A. (Arman Erpt fellow), Columbia, 1964; m. Dorothy Lee Wade, Aug. 16, 1967; children—Aaron Wade, Nori Michelle. Exec. v.p. Bank Neosho (Mo.), 1967—; also dir.; pres., dir. Security State Bank, Republic, Mo.; dir. Southwest Lime Co., Neosho, Ozark Terminal, Neosho. Chmn. City Beautification Com., 1969—, Newton County March of Dimes, 1972—; mem. exec. com., treas. Mokan Area council Boy Scouts Am., 1968—. Bd. dirs. Crowder Sheltered Workshop, Neosho, 1968—, Crowder Coll. Found., 1968—. Recipient Outstanding Young Man of Am. award Jaycees, 1968. Served to lt. USNR, 1964-67. Mem. C. of C. (dir., treas. 1970-72), Beta Gamma Sigma. Rotarian (pres. 1971, dir. 1969-71). Office: 100 S Wood St Neosho MO 64850

FARGO, PAUL GENNARO, lawyer; b. Boston, July 20, 1927; s. Anthony Allen and Mary (Zajac) F.; B.S. in Bus. Adminstrn., Boston U., 1950, J.D., 1951; LL.M. in Labor Law, N.Y.U., 1952; LL.M. in Taxation, Northeastern U., 1953; m. Karen Peterson; children—Paul, Carolyn. Admitted to Ill. bar, 1956, Mass. bar, 1952, Mo. bar, 1955, Minn. bar, 1969; asso. firm Avery, Dooley, Post & Avery, Boston, 1953-54, firm Reeder, Griffin & Dvsart, Kansas City, Mo., 1954-55; atty. law dept. Montgomery Ward & Co., Chgo., 1955-56; atty. legal dept. Gen. Finance Corp., Evanston, Ill., 1956-58; asst. gen. counsel Central Standard Indemnity Co., Chgo., 1958-60; legis. atty. Am. Mut. Ins. Alliance, 1960-65; practiced in Chgo., 1956-65; asst. dir. (staff) Am. Bar Assn., 1965-68; sec.-gen. counsel Gamble Alden Life Ins. Co., Chgo., 1968-70; sr. atty., asst. sec. Nat. Homes Corp., Lafayette, Ind., 1970-73; corp. atty. Interco Inc., St. Louis, 1973-74; pvt. practice law, 1974—. Recipient full tuition scholarships, Parshard Holding Corp., Cambridge, Mass., 1945-53. Mem. Mo. Integrated Bar Assn., Am. Ill., Chgo., Boston bar assns., Assn. Trial Lawyers Am., Boston U. Nat. Alumni Council. Methodist. Home: 2740 Orchard Ln Wilmette IL 60091

FARHA, WILLIAM FARAH, food co. exec.; b. Lebanon, Nov. 27, 1908; s. Farah Farris and Nahima (Salamy) F.; grad. Indsl. Coll. Armed Forces, 1948, Brookings Inst., 1968; m. Victoria Barkett, Apr. 15, 1934; 1 son, William George. With F & E Wholesale Grocery Co., 1929-64; pres. River Bend Shopping Center, Wichita, William F. Farha & Son Enterprises. Chmn. Wichita Leadership Prayer Breakfast; invited to attend Presdl. Prayer Breakfast in Eisenhower, Kennedy, Johnson, Nixon and Ford adminstrns.; field adviser nat. bd. Small. Bus. Adminstrn., 14 years; former chmn. Wichita Police and Firemen Pension Plan. Past trustee Wichita Symphony Soc.; former mem. nat. bd. Inst. Logopedicts; former mem. bd. St. Joseph Research Hosp. Center; mem. bd. advisers Salvation Army; bd. dirs. Nat. Conf. Christians and Jews, Kans. Found. for Blind; trustee met. bd. YMCA, Antiochian Greek Orthodox Archdiocese of All N.Am.; mem. internat. bd. YMCA World Service; past mem. bd. govs. St. Jude Research Hosp., Memphis. Hon. col. State of Okla.; named to Wisdom Hall Fame, 1970; recipient Gold Medallion Antiochian Patriarch of Damascus, 1952; Antonian Gold medal of merit Antiochian Orthodox Christian Archdiocese N.Y. and all N.Am., 1972. Mem. Wichita Ind. Bus. Men's Assn. (adv. bd.), Nat. Security Council (adv. bd.), Wichita C. of C. (past dir.). Rotarian. Club: Rolling Hills Country. Home: 8630 Shannon Way Wichita KS 67206 Office: 2220 Somerset Wichita KS 67204

FARHI, VICTOR NISSIM, mfg. co. exec., mech. engr.; b. Istanbul, Turkey, Jan. 13, 1929; s. Nissim J. and Rebecca R. Farhi; came to U.S., 1948, naturalized, 1957; B.S. in Mech. Engring., Robert Coll., Istanbul, 1948; M.S. in Mech. Engring., Case Inst. Tech., 1950. Tool engr. Nat. Acme Co., Cleve., 1951-54; transmission project engr. Towmotor Corp., Cleve., 1954-59; asst. chief engr. J.I. Case Co., Churubusco, Ind., 1959-61; v.p., owner UTEMCO, cons. engrs., Ft. Wayne, Ind., 1961-68; v.p. engring. Mobile Aerial Towers Inc., Ft. Wayne, 1968—; instr., cons. Purdue U., Ft. Wayne. Bd. dirs. Allen County (Ind.) Cancer Soc., 1973-76. Registered profl. engr., Ohio, Ind. Recipient Prize Paper award Hydraulics & Pneumatics, 1969. Mem. Ind. (pres., dir. Anthony Wayne chpt.), Nat. socs. profl. engrs., ASME, Soc. Automotive Engrs., Ft. Wayne C. of C., MENSA. Club: Wildwood Racquet (Ft. Wayne). Patentee in field. Home: 2303 Stonington Rd Fort Wayne IN 46825 Office: 2314 Bowser Ave Fort Wayne IN 46803

FARINA, LOUIS P., city ofcl.; b. New Buffalo, Mich., Apr. 24, 1923; s. Philip and Frances (Colletti) F.; student DePaul U., John Marshall Law Sch., grad. Real Estate Sch. Ill., 1949; m. Rose Taurina, June 16, 1951; children—Phillip, James, Richard, Mark Anthony. Co-owner Farina & Co., Chgo., 1949-51; spl. investigator Dept. Revenue, Ill. 1948-51; city field dir. Mayor Daley's Citizens Com. Cleaner Chgo., 1951-58; supt. parking City of Chgo., 1958-68; dep. commr. Dept. Streets and Sanitation, dir. Bur. Parking, until 1969; head parking devel. dept. Seay & Thomas, Inc., 1971; later exec. dir. Ednl. Service Cook County, Ill.; ward supt. City of Chgo.; asst. commr. Dept. Streets and Sanitation, 1974—, now dep. commr., head city sanitation and health services; dir. City of Chgo. Neighborhood Pride and Beautification Com.; producer, moderator Louis P. Farina Chgo. Happenings Show, WCIV-TV, Chgo. Founder Operation Friendship polit. leaders exchange program, 1959. Pres. Ill. Young Democrats, 1958-60; chmn. Cook County Young Democrats, 1956-58; chmn. subcom. Inter-Am. affairs Young Democrats Am.; pres. 36th ward Regular Dem. Orgn. Served with AUS, World War II. Decorated Purple Heart, Bronze Star, Knights of Malta Cross (King Peter II of Yugoslavia); Star of Solidarity (Italy); Knight of St. John (Franz Joseph) (Austria); named the Outstanding Young Man of Year, Young Democrats of Ill., 1964; recipient Michael Reese Hosp. Cancer Research award, 1964, Spl. Citation award Loyola Univ., 1964; Citizens award Chgo. Police Dept., 1973. Mem. Internat. Municipal Parking Congress (exec. sec. 1962-63), Am. Legion (1st vice comdr. chpt.), Joint Civic Com. Italian-Ams. (past dir.), K.C. (4th deg.). Home: 1744 N Newland Ave Chicago IL 60635 Office: City Hall 54 W Hubbard 6th floor Chicago IL 60610

FARION, DMYTRO, physician; b. Bohatkivci, Ukraine, Oct. 30, 1921; s. Stephen and Anna (Stochanska) F.; M.D., U. Munich, 1950; m. Maria Irena Cybyk, Apr. 24, 1949; children—George Zenon, Roma Maria, Anna Maria, Irene Maria, Marko Oleh. Came to U.S., 1951, naturalized, 1956. Intern St. Peter's Hosp., Bklyn., 1951-53; resident North Community Hosp., Glen Cove, N.Y., 1953-55; practice medicine specializing in gen. practice, Cleve., 1955—; mem. staffs Deaconess Hosp., Cleve., Parma (Ohio) Community Hosp., Luth. Hosp., Cleve. Dir. Parma Savs. Co., 1964-67. Mem. St. Josaphat Sch. Bd., Parma 1971—. Mem. A.M.A., Ohio State Med. Soc., Cleve. Acad. Medicine, Cleve. Health Mus., Cleve. Mus. Natural History, Cleve. Med. Library Assn., Ukrainian Med. Assn. N. Am. Republican. Home: 6305 S Park Blvd Parma OH 44134 Office: 5604 Memphis Ave Cleveland OH 44144

FARKELL, GEORGE DAVID, pub. relations exec.; b. Mpls., Aug. 24, 1927; s. George Lewis and Velma Faith (Thompson) F.; B.A. in Journalism, U. Minn., 1949; m. Jean Audrey Mix, May 20 1950; children—Christine Ann, Kathleen Jo, Jeffrey David, Steven John. Employed with various weekly newspaper, Iowa, Wis., Minn., 1949-54; mgr. corporate communications Minn. Mining & Mfg. Co., St. Paul, 1954-67; dir. pub. relations Stevenson & Assos., Mpls., 1967-69; v.p. Don Braman & Assos., Mpls., 1969-75; v.p. McMarthy Communication Inc., Mpls., 1975-77; sr. pub. relations account mgr. Kerker & Assos. Inc., Mpls., 1977—. Vol. pub. relations dir. Nat. Alliance Businessmen, Mpls., 1969-72; mem. finance com. Hospitality House, Mpls., 1977—. Served with USNR, 1945-58. Mem. Pub. Relations Soc. Am. (accredited), Am. Acad. Polit. Social Sci., Minn. Press Club, Alpha Phi Omega (life). Club: Masons (White Bear Lake, Minn.). Home: 2295 Lakeridge Dr White Bear Lake MN 55110 Office: 1000 Southgate Office Plaza Minneapolis MN 55437

FARLEY, JAMES THOMAS, hosp. adminstr.; b. Chgo., Apr. 12, 1925; s. Thomas Walter and Nona F. (Kelly) F.; B.S.A., Loyola U., Chgo., 1950; M.S. in Hosp. Adminstrn., Northwestern U., 1956; m. Mary Jean Powers, Oct. 4, 1947; children—James Thomas, Mary Margaret, Michael, Thomas, Patricia, Donal Joseph (dec.). Vice pres. Sloan-Kettering Cancer Center, N.Y.C., 1964-68; pres. St. John Hosp., Detroit, 1968—, trustee, 1968—; chmn. bd., dir. Mich. Hosp. Assn. Mut. Ins. Co. Cons. NIH. Trustee St. Vincent's Hosp., N.Y.C. Served with USAF, 1943-46. Fellow Coll. Hosp. Adminstrs.; mem. Am., Mich. hosp. assns., Soc. Hosp. Adminstrv. Assos. Knight of Malta. Contbr. articles to hosp. jours. Home: 26 Colonial Rd Grosse Pointe MI 48236 Office: 22101 Moross Rd Detroit MI 48236

FARLEY, LLOYD EDWARD, educator; b. Milburn, Nebr., June 20, 1915; s. Arthur L. and Effie (Tyson) F.; A.B., Kearney State Coll., 1945; M.A., Stanford, 1947, Ed.D., 1950; postgrad. U. Hawaii, U. Oreg., Princeton U. Tchr. elementary and secondary schs., also adminstr., 1937-41, 47-51; ednl. specialist U.S. Govt., Washington, Anchorage, Edwards, Calif., 1952-60; prof. edn. U. Alaska, Anchorage, 1960-64; Louis D. Beaumont Distinguished prof. edn., head div. social sci., Marshall faculty William Woods Coll., Fulton, Mo.; chmn. dept. edn. Westminster and William Woods Colls., Fulton, 1964—; vis. prof. St. Cloud State U., summers 1968-72. Served to maj. AUS, 1941-46. Named Hon. Tchr. Korea; recipient Centennial medal William Woods Coll. Mem. Mo. Tchrs. Assn., Nat. Assn. Tchr. Educators, Internat. Council on Edn. for Teaching, Phi Delta Kappa. Methodist. Kiwanian. Address: 12 Tucker Ln Fulton MO 65251

FARMAKIS, GEORGE LEONARD, educator, ednl. adminstr.; b. Clarksburg, W.Va., June 30, 1925; s. Michael G. and Pipitsa A. (Roussopoulos) F.; B.A., Wayne State U., 1949, M.S. in Edn., 1950, M.A., Wayne State U., 1966, Ph.D., 1971. Tchr., Roseville (Mich.) pub. schs., 1951-57, also audio-visual dir., 1951-57; tchr. Birmingham (Mich.) pub. schs., 1957-61; resource specialist Highland Park (Mich.) pub. schs., 1961—; founder High Intensity Tutoring Project in Math., Ford Middle Sch., Highland Park, 1970. Mem. Nat. Council Tchrs. Math., Nat. Council Social Studies, Acad. Polit. Sci., Am. Hist. Assn., Am. Philol. Assn., U. Mich. Alumni Assn., Wayne State U. Alumni Assn., Phi Delta Kappa. Home: 752 Trombley Rd Grosse Pointe Park MI 48230 Office: 20 Bartlett St Highland Park MI 48230

FARMER, DAVID JAMES, ops. research analyst; b. Denver, Oct. 2, 1936; s. James Lenard and Clara Agnes (Wellman) F.; B.S. in Physics, Colo. State U., 1960; postgrad. U. Ala., 1966-70; m. Patty Lou Lightsey, Dec. 25, 1960; children—David Stanley, Matthew Jay, Ruth Renee. Physicist, operations research analyst U.S. Army Missile Command, Huntsville, Ala., 1963-72; supervisory operations research analyst U.S. Army Combined Arms Combat Devels. Activity, Ft.

Leavenworth, Kans., 1972—. Served with AUS, 1960-63. Decorated Army Commendation Medal. Mem. Am. Phys. Soc., Assn. U.S. Army, Colo. State U. Alumni Found., Full Gospel Bus. Men's Assn. Internat., Mensa. Republican. Mem. Disciples of Christ Ch. Home: Route 4 Box 358 Leavenworth KS 66048 Office: CACDA ATCA CAT Fort Leavenworth KS 66027

FARMER, EDWARD LEWIS, historian; b. Palo Alto, Calif., May 25, 1935; s. Edward McNeil and Mabel Ferris (McKibbin) F.; A.B., Stanford U., 1957; M.A., Harvard U., 1962, Ph.D., 1968; m. Judith Cleavenger Lehman, 1958; children—Joy Lehman, Edward McNeil. Acting instr. history Yale U., 1967-68; asst. prof. history U. Minn., Mpls., 1968-76, asso. prof., 1976—, chairperson E. Asian studies program, 1976—; cons. in field. Served with U.S. Army, 1957-61. Mem. Assn. Asian Studies, Am. Hist. Assn., Com. Concerned Asian Scholars. Democratic-Farmer-Labor Party. Author: Early Ming Government: The Evolution of Dual Capitals, 1976; co-author: Comparative History of Civilizations in Asia, 1977; editor Ming Studies, 1975—. Home: 147 Cecil St SE Minneapolis MN 55414

FARMER, JIM GUEEN, III, fin. exec.; b. Fort Smith, Ark., Jan. 2, 1949; s. Jim Gueen Jr. and Jane (Woodruff) F.; B.S. in Bus. Adminstrn., U. Ark., 1971; M.B.A. in Fin., St. Louis U., 1974; m. Carol Soult, May 25, 1974. Mgr. trainee Feld Truck Leasing Corp., St. Louis, 1971-72; salesman, adminstr. Manchester Leasing Corp., St. Louis, 1972-74; pres. Pelham Corp., St. Louis, 1974—, also dir.; dir. Fidelity Bank and Trust Co., Landmark Northwest Bank; dir., treas. Ins. Brokers and Cons. Mem. Sigma Alpha Epsilon. Clubs: University (St. Louis); Old Warson Country; La Mirada Country (Geneva, Switzerland). Democrat. Methodist. Home: 11541 Conway St Louis MO 63131 Office: 7751 Carondelet St Louis MO 63105

FARNER, ROBERT LEWIS, physician; b. Streator, Ill., Feb. 4, 1930; s. Lewis Frederick and Marie (Vallazza) F.; student Wartburg Coll., 1948-51; M.D., U. Ill., 1955; m. Kathleen A. Murray, Apr. 6, 1958; children—Robert M., David L., Charles B. Intern Ill. Central Hosp., Chgo., 1955-56; practice medicine, specializing in family medicine, Toluca, Ill., 1958—; mem. staff St. Mary's Hosp., Streator, Ill. Served with USAAF, 1956-58. Fellow Am. Acad. Family Physicians (charter); mem. A.M.A., Ill. Med. Soc., Engle Lane Theatre, Smithsonian Instn., Nat. Hist. Soc., Alpha Kappa Kappa. Lutheran. Home: 403 W Santa Fe Ave Toluca IL 61369 Office: 204 E Santa Fe Ave Toluca IL 61369

FARNHAM, HARRY JUD, lawyer; b. Lincoln, Nebr., Sept. 20, 1925; s. Harry C. and Grace M. (Binfield) F.; LL.D., U. Colo., 1949; m. Sally Link, June 10, 1946; children—Jeff, Dan, Amy. Admitted to Nebr. bar, 1949, since practiced in Omaha. Mem. Nebr. State Racing Commn., 1961—, chmn., 1963—; pres. Nat. Assn. State Racing Commrs., 1969. Mem. legacy com. Morris Animal Found. Served with USMCR, 1943-45. Recipient Racing Man of Year award Jockeys' Guild, 1970; Distinguished Service award Am. Horse Council, 1972; Man of Year award Horseman's Benevolent Protective Assn., 1970; named to Nebr. Racing Hall of Fame, 1971, Gt. Plains Amateur Boxing Assn. Hall of Fame, 1975. Fellow Am. Acad. Matrimonial Lawyers; mem. Am., Nebr., Omaha bar assns. Democrat. Mason (33 deg.). Home: Rural Route 1 Elkhorn NE 68022 Office: 9700 W Dodge Rd Omaha NE 68114

FARQUHAR, ROBERT NICHOLS, lawyer; b. Dayton, Ohio, Apr. 23, 1936; s. Robert Lawrence and Mary Frances (Nichols) F.; A.B., Kenyon Coll., 1958; J.D., Cornell, 1961; m. Elizabeth Lynn Bryan, Aug. 29, 1959 (div. 1971); children—Robert Nichols, Laura Ann; m. 2d, Carol A. Smith, Dec. 27, 1975. Admitted to Ohio bar, 1961, U.S. Dist. Ct., 1962, U.S. Ct. Appeals, 1966; asso. Altick & McDaniel, Dayton, 1961-69; partner Gould, Bailey & Farquhar, and predecessor firms, Dayton, 1969—; dir. Illini Bldg. Systems, Inc., ACB Am., Inc. (all Dayton); mem. adv. bd. Bellbrook Community Bank, 1971—. City atty., Centerville, Ohio, 1969—. Mem. Montgomery County Rep. Central Com., 1965-69, Exec. Com., 1968-69. Bd. dirs. Centerville Hist. Soc., 1971-75, pres., 1973-74; trustee Montgomery Legal Aid Soc., 1972-76; trustee Dayton Law Library Assn., 1972—, sec., 1975—. Mem. Am., Ohio, Dayton (sec., exec. com. 1975-76) bar assns., Delta Phi, Phi Delta Phi. Episcopalian. Clubs: Dayton Bicycle, Dayton Lawyers. Home: 170 Lyons Dr Centerville OH 45459 Office: 226 Talbott Tower Dayton OH 45402

FARRAGE, JAMES ROBERT, orthodontist; b. Riverside, Calif., Mar. 3, 1939; s. James and Esther (Snyder) F.; A.A., San Bernardino Valley Coll., 1961; D.D.S., Loyola U. at Chgo., 1965, certificate orthodontics, 1967; m. Joanna Lynn Plese, Apr. 23, 1960; children—James Robert, Joseph Matthew, Jana Lynn. Practice orthodontics, LaGrange, Ill., 1969-71, Omaha, 1972—; asso. clin. prof. orthodontics Creighton U., Omaha, 1971—, dir. orthodontics, orthodontist on maxio-facial cleft lip and palate team; cons. Med. Center U. Nebr., Omaha, 1972—; pres. dental staff Children's Meml. Hosp., Omaha. Served with USAF, 1967-69. Named Outstanding 1st year tchr. Creighton U. Dental Sch., 1972. Mem. Am. Dental Assn., Nebr. Dental Soc., Omaha Dental Soc., Am. Assn. Orthodontists, Midwestern Soc. Orthodontists, Nebr. Orthodontic Soc., West Omaha Study Club (past pres.), Orthodontic Study Club, Delta Sigma Delta, Omicron Kappa Upsilon. Home: 916 Fawn Pkwy Omaha NE 68154 Office: 9006 Ohio St Omaha NE 68134

FARRAGHER, WILLIAM EDGAR, marketing cons.; b. Youngstown, Ohio, July 22, 1922; s. William Edgar and Jessie Alice (Selby) F.; A.B., Ohio Wesleyan U., 1949; postgrad. Kenyon Coll., U. Wis.; m. Arden Louise Smith, Dec. 29, 1951; children—Kelly Ann, Allison Selby, Mark Douglas, Kate Louise; 1 foster son, Robert Schellenbarger. Copywriter, Arthur Towell Advt. Agy., Madison, Wis., 1950-51; asst. advt. mgr. Magnecord, Inc., Chgo., 1951-52; copywriter Howard Swink Advt. Agy., Marion, Ohio, 1952-53; plant mgr. Instantwhip, Inc., Columbus, Ohio, 1953-54; account exec. Robert Joyce Advt. Agy., Youngstown, 1954-55; pres. Tower Asso., advt. agy., Youngstown, 1955-57; dir. advt. Youngstown Sheet & Tube Co. div. Lykes Corp., 1957-69; exec. v.p. Thomas/Farragher Asso., advt. agy., Youngstown, 1969-71; pres. Farragher Mktg. Services, Canfield, Ohio, 1971—; mng. dir. Bradford Inst., Canfield, 1973—; ltd. duty instr. Youngstown State U., 1956—; chmn. bd. trustees Center for Mktg. Communications, Princeton, N.J., 1968-69. Licensed lay reader Episcopal Ch., Ohio Diocese; mem. vestry St. John's Episc. Ch., Youngstown; mem. bishop's council Ohio Diocese, 1970-71. Served with M.C., U.S. Army, 1942-46. Mem. Pub. Relations Soc. Am., Am. Mktg. Assn., Center for Mktg. Communications, Bus.-Profl. Advt. Assn., Ohio Wesleyan U. Alumni Assn. (dir. 1975—). Home: 275 Bradford Dr Canfield OH 44406 Office: PO Box 39 Old Courthouse Bldg 7 Court St Canfield OH 44406

FARRAN, DON WILSON, author; b. Rowan, Iowa, Mar. 24, 1902; s. John Simon and Charlotte (Duncan) F.; student U. Iowa, 1922-1923, Dartmouth Coll., 1942. Editor, Fed. Writers Project, Des Moines, 1937; state dir. Fed. Hist. Survey, Des Moines, 1937-38; regional dir. Fed. Theatre Service Bur., Chgo., 1938-39; nat. editor Fed. Am. Imprints Inventory, Chgo. and Washington, 1940-41, nat. dir., 1941-42; asst. nat. dir. Hist. Records Survey, 1941-42; commd. lt. U.S. Navy, 1942, advanced through grades to comdr., 1953; writer/dir./producer films U.S. Navy, head worldwide motion picture prodn. Coast Guard, 1958-64; ret., 1964; author books: (with MaMurtrie) Wings for Words, 1940; Ballad of the Silver Ring, 1933; author plays: (with others) Off The Record, 1939; Broadway D., 1940; Pie in the Sky, 1939, Dirt; biographer of actor Richard Bennett, 1936; screenwriter numerous motion pictures for USN, USCG, State Dept., 1942-64; writer screenplay The Seventh Fleet, 1956; contbr. numerous short stories, articles, poems to nat. mags.; cons. Iowa Bicentennial, 1976. Decorated Gen. Alfaro gold medal (Ecuador); recipient awards, including: First prize Liberty Mag. Short Story Contest, 1933, award Edinburgh Film Festival, 1959, Am. Film Festival, 1959, 1960, 1961, 1962, 1963, 1964. Fellow Internat. Soc. Biographers; mem. Gypsey Lore Soc. Gt. Britain, Calif. Writers Club, Iowa Authors Club (pres. 1933, 1934), Screenwriters Guild Am., Am. Poetry Soc. (v.p. 1928-29). Home: Rowan IA 50470

FARRAR, FRANK LEROY, lawyer, past gov. S.D.; b. Britton, S.D., Apr. 2, 1929; s. Virgil William and Venetia Soule (Taylor) F.; B.S., U. S.D., 1951, LL.B., 1953; m. Patricia Jean Henley, June 5, 1953; children—Jeanne Marie, Sally Ann, Robert John, Mary Susan, Anne Marie. Admitted to S.D. bar, 1953; practice in Britton, 1957-63, 71—; internal revenue agt., 1955-57; judge Marshall County, 1958; states atty. Marshall County, 1959-62; atty. gen. S.D., from 1963, then gov. Mem. Retarded Childrens Sch. Bd., 1961; pres. Pheasant council Boy Scouts Am.; active Mental Health Assn.; fund chmn. S.D. Mental Assn.; state chmn. March of Dimes, S.D. chmn. Marshall County Republican Com., 1959; asst. sgt. at arms Rep. Nat. Conv., 1960. Served to capt. U.S. Army; Korea. Mem. Midwest Atty. Gen.'s Assn. (v.p., mem. exec. bd.), S.D., Ind., Wash. bar assns., S.D. States Atty. Assn. (past pres.), Nat. Dist. Attys. Assn., Alpha Tau Omega, Phi Delta Phi. Clubs: Masons, Shriners, Lions, Elks, Sportsman (Britton). Home: Box 190 Britton SD 57430

FARRAR, PATRICIA JEAN HENLEY (MRS. FRANK FARRAR), civic worker; b. Britton, S.D., Aug. 13, 1931; d. Percy D. and Margaret (Schneider) Henley; B.A., U. S.D., 1953; m. Frank L. Farrar, June 5, 1953; children—Jeanne, Sally, Robert, Mary, Anne. Tchr., Summit (S.D.) High Sch., 1953; sec., Britton, 1954-56, part-time 1958-60; dir. Citizens Bank, Enderlin, N.D. Pres., Marshall County chpt. Am. Cancer Soc., 1967, 68, mem. S.D. State bd. advisers for youth, 1973-77; mem. apparel and textile adv. bd. S.D. State U., 1970—; mem. S.D. Commn. on Status Women, 1969—, S.D. Library Week Com., 1969, Dean Colton Fine Arts Scholarship Com. U. S.D., 1969—; mem. adv. com. on arts John F. Kennedy Center for Performing Arts, 1972-77. Named South Dakota Hon. Mother of Year, 1974. Mem. S.D. Edn. Assn., P.E.O., Pi Beta Phi. Republican. Presbyn. Clubs: Britton Study, Britton Garden. Home: 203 9th Ave Britton SD 57430

FARRAR, RICHARD EDWARD, research co. exec. b. Lynchburg, Va., Mar. 13, 1917; s. William Henry and Mary Alice (Bailey) F.; B.S., Va. Poly. Inst., 1938; M.E., Johns Hopkins U., 1950; D.Eng., 1951; m. Marion Frances Bray, Mar. 28, 1946; 1 dau., Martha. Asst. chemist, control div. Mead Corp., Lynchburg, Va., 1938-40; chief chemist Columbia Paper Co., Buena Vista, Va., 1940-41; prodn. supr. U.S. Army Chem. Center, Edgewood, Md., 1941-43, area engr., devel. div., Edgewood, 1945-48; mgr. research and devel. Colgate-Palmolive Co., Jersey City, N.J., 1951-60, research coordinator, household products div., 1960-62, dir. research and devel., European div., London, 1962-65; dir. product devel. Reynolds Industries, Winston-Salem, N.C., 1965-70; v.p. Lane Services, consumer testing, Winston-Salem, 1967-70; exec. v.p., chief operating officer Dairy Research Inc., Rosemont, Ill., 1970—. Served with AUS, 1943-45. Mem. Am. Inst. Chem. Engrs., Am. Chem. Soc., Am. Dairy Sci. Assn., Inst. Food Technologists, Sigma Xi. Patentee in field. Home: 588 N Cumnock Rd Palatine IL 60067 Office: 6300 N River Rd Rosemont IL 60018

FARREHI, CYRUS, cardiologist; b. Malayer, Iran, Jan. 26, 1935; s. Mansoor and Nikzad (Agah) F.; M.D., U. Tehran, 1958; m. Z. Jane Christensen, June 6, 1964; children—Peter M., Paul C., Lisa N., Mary M. Teaching fellow dept. medicine U. Alta. Med. Sch., 1964-66; asst. prof. medicine U. Ore. Med. Sch. also dir. cardiac catheterization lab. VA Hosp., Portland, Ore., 1966-69; chmn. dept. medicine McLaren Gen. Hosp., Flint, Mich., 1971-73, dir. cardiovascular diagnostic service, 1973—; clin. asso. prof. medicine Mich. State U., 1973—. Diplomate Am. Bd. Internal Medicine, Am. Bd. Cardiovascular Diseases. Fellow Am. Coll. Physicians, Royal Coll. Physicians and Surgeons of Can., Am. Coll. Cardiology, Clin. Council Am. Heart Assn.; mem. Detroit Heart Club. Roman Catholic. Contbr. articles to med. jours. Home: 8398 Old Plank Rd Grand Blanc MI 48439 Office: 1071 N Ballenger Hwy Flint MI 48504

FARRELL, EDMUND JAMES, assn. exec., educator, author; b. Butte, Mont., May 17, 1927; s. Bartholomew J. and Lavinia H. (Collins) F.; A.B., Stanford U., 1950; M.A., 1951; Ph.D., U. Calif. at Berkeley, 1969; m. Jo Ann Hayes, Dec. 19, 1964; children—David, Kevin, Sean. Chmn. English dept. James Lick High Sch., San Jose, Calif., 1954-59; supr. secondary English, U. Calif. at Berkeley, 1959-70; field rep. Nat. Council Tchrs. English, 1970-71, asst. exec. sec., 1971-73, asso. exec. sec., 1973—; adj. prof. English U. Ill., Urbana, 1973—. Speaker at local, state and nat. confs. of English tchrs., 1954—; cons. to NDEA Insts., 1965-68; reader compositions for advanced placement program, Rider Coll., Princeton, N.J., 1969, 72-77; participant revision of lit. objectives Nat. Assessment of Ednl. Progress, Denver, 1972-73; chmn. English discipline com. Coll. Entrance Exam. Bd., 1974—. Served with USNR, 1945-46. Mem. Nat. Council Tchrs. of English, Am. Assn. of Higher Edn., Calif. Assn. Tchrs. of English (pres. 1962-63), Phi Delta Kappa. Unitarian. Author: Exploring Life Through Literature, 1964, Counterpoint in Literature, 1967, Projection in Literature, 1967, Outlooks in Literature, 1973; Fantasy: Forms of Things Unknown, 1974; Science Fact/Fiction, 1974; Comment, 1976; Myth, Mind, and Moment, 1976; I/You, We/They, 1976; Traits and Topics, 1976; Up Stage/Down Stage, 1976; To Be, 1976; Conflict in Reality, 1976. Home: 1710 S Pleasant Urbana IL 61801 Office: 1111 Kenyon Rd Urbana IL 61801

FARRELL, JAMES ROBERT, biologist; b. Memphis, Feb. 3, 1949; s. Richard Ashley and Vivian (Hudson) F.; B.S. in Biology, Southwestern U., Memphis, 1971; postgrad. N. Tex. State U., Intermittently, 1971—; m. Linda Kay Carroll, July 20, 1974; 1 son, William Curtis. R.A. Welch Found. research asst. N. Tex. State U., 1971; staff biologist Environment Cons., Inc., Dallas, 1973-74; asso. biologist NALCO Environmental Scis., Lincoln, Nebr., 1974—. NSF grantee, 1970; EPA water quality trainee, 1973. Mem. Am. Water Works Assn., Am. Inst. Biol. Scis., Phycol. Soc. Am., Nat. Geog. Soc. Methodist. Home: 5346 W Zeamer St Lincoln NE 68524 Office: 4010 NW 39th St Lincoln NE 68524

FARRELL, SISTER MARY HOWARD, librarian; b. Cleve., Mar. 24, 1927; d. Howard Joseph and Mary Teresa (Finucan) Farrell; B.S. in Edn., St. John Coll., 1959; M.L.S., Case Western Res. U., 1971. Joined Ursuline Community, 1946; tchr. St. Joseph Sch., Cleve., 1947, St. Clare Sch., Lyndhurst, Ohio, 1948-56, St. Jerome Sch., Cleve., 1956-62, St. Therese Sch., Garfield Heights, Ohio, 1962-64, Immaculate Conception Sch., Willoughby, Ohio, 1964-66, tchr. St. Mary Magdalene Sch., Willowick, Ohio, 1966-69; asst. prin. St. Ann Sch., Cleveland Heights, Ohio, 1969-71; librarian Villa Angela Acad., Cleve., 1971-72; head librarian Ursuline Coll., Cleve., 1972—; bibliographer, research guide World Book Ency. Corp., Chgo., 1972. Mem. Am., Cleve., Cath. library assns., Ednl. Media Council Ohio, Asso. Cath. Colls. Cleve. Home: 2600 Lander Rd Cleveland OH 44124

FARROW, JONELLE MCLEMORE (MRS. BOBBY JAMES FARROW), psychologist; b. Valley Mills, Tex., Feb. 3, 1942; d. Ernest Garth and Evelyn Princella (Carlson) McLemore; B.A., U. Tex., 1964, Ph.D., 1969; m. Bobby James Farrow, Dec. 23, 1965; children—Kathryn Suzanne, Richard John. Lectr. dept psychology Ind. U., South Bend, 1966-69, asst. prof. psychology, 1969-73, acting chmn. dept. psychology, 1970-72, asso. prof., chmn. dept. psychology, 1973—. Vis. prof. psychology Inst. Psychology Pontifica Universidade Catholica, Rio de Janeiro, Brazil, summer, 1967; research cons. and program devel. Planned Parenthood N.W. Ind., 1969—; research asso. Latin Am. Population Research Center, summer 1967. Recipient Ulysses G. Weatherly award Ind. U., 1976. Ind. Com. for the Humanities grantee, 1973, Ind. U. South Bend research grantee, 1973, 75. Mem. Am., Rocky Mountain, Southwestern psychol. assns., Psi Chi. Contbr. articles on exptl. psychology, also on psychol. characteristics of socio-econ. groups and their relationship to family planning to profl. jours. Home: 1508 Hoover Ave South Bend IN 46615 Office: Dept Psychology Ind U South Bend IN 46615

FARSTAD, ELMER KARLEIF, real estate cons., appraiser; b. Trondheim, Norway; Nov. 22, 1921; s. Johan Magnus and Anne Elise (Pedersen) F.; came to Can., 1925, naturalized, 1937; diploma Dominion Bus. Coll., 1940; m. Muriel Kathleen Dracass, Nov. 6, 1948; children—Corinne Savoie, Brenda Hillman, Karla. Mem. staff Farstad Cabinet Shop, Winnipeg, Man., 1946-47; Aronovitch & Leipsic Ltd., Winnipeg, 1947-49, Oldfield Kirby & Gardner Ltd., Winnipeg, 1950-55, L.A. MacDonald Ltd. Winnipeg, 1956, Royal Trust Co., Winnipeg, 1957-62; prin. E. Karl Farstad & Assos. Ltd., Winnipeg, 1962—; lectr. in field. Served with Royal Norwegian Air Force, 1942-45. Mem. Winnipeg Real Estate Bd., Appraisal Inst. Can., Am. Inst. Real Estate Appraisers, Winnipeg C. of C., Viking Club Winnipeg (pres. 1972-73). Mason. Club: Niakwa Country. Home: 98 Duluth Bay Winnipeg MB R2J 1W5 Canada Office: 506 211 Portage Ave Winnipeg MB A3B 2A2 Canada

FARY, JOHN G., Congressman; b. Chgo., Apr. 11, 1911; student Real Estate Sch. Ill., Loyola U., Midwest Inst.; m. Lillian Makowski, 1934; children—James, Marian. Mem. Ill. Gen. Assembly, 1955-75; mem. 94th-95th congresses from 5th Ill. Dist. Mem. Polish Nat. Alliance, Polish Roman Catholic Union, Chgo. C. of C. Clubs: Moose, Eagles, Kiwanis, Lions, K.C. Office: Room 1116 Longworth House Office Bldg Washington DC 20515*

FASKA, ERNEST ODON, mfg. co. exec.; b. Hazelton, Pa., Sept. 27, 1921; s. Paul and Helen (Riczinger) F.; B.B.A., Western Res. U., 1949; m. Edna Mae Gallagher, Sept. 21, 1946; children—Ernest Odon, Paul V., Thomas M., Timothy J. With Master Builders div. Martin-Marietta Corp., Cleveland Heights, Ohio, 1949—, asst. purchasing mgr., 1958-64, asst. dir. purchasing, 1964-67, dir. purchasing, 1967—. Served with USAAF, 1942-46. Mem. Inst. Scrap Iron and Steel. Lutheran. Home: 620 Merrimak Dr Berea OH 44017 Office: 2490 Lee Blvd Cleveland Heights OH 44118

FASNACHT, DANIEL WILLIAM, veterinarian; b. Annville, Pa., Sept. 13, 1928; s. Allen Victor and Myrtle Olive (Trautman) F.; student Lebanon Valley Coll., 1948-50, 51-52; V.M.D., U. Pa., 1956; m. Dorothy Mae Dipper, June 12, 1954; children—Thomas, Cynthia, Timothy, James, Valeria. Head large animal div. Bedford (Pa.) Labs., 1956-60; mgr. Libertyville (Ill.) Animal Hosp., Div. Pet Services, Inc., after 1960; now pres. 4-D Pet Enterprises; owner, operator Lindenhurst Animal Hosp. Pres. P.T.A., Oak Grove, Ill., 1969-70. Bd. dir. Young Republican Club, Libertyville, 1961-64. Served with AUS, 1946-47, 50-51. Mem. Allergic and Immunology Soc., Lake County Vet. Med. Soc. (pres. 1964-66, dir. 1966—), Am. Legion (comdr. 1968-69), Firemen's Assn. Methodist (stewardship chmn. 1969—, pres. congregation, pres. bd. trustees, lay leader). Moose, Lion. Home: Route 4 Box 273 Antioch IL 60002 Office: Linden Plaza Pet Land 2084 E Grand Ave Lindenhurst IL 60046

FASONE, SALVATORE ANTHONY, agri-business co. exec.; b. Kansas City, Mo., Jan. 16, 1940; s. Anthony Frank and Mary Ann (Tumino) F.; B.M.E., Mo. Sch. Mines and Metallurgy, 1961; m. Josephine Lucille Sallee, Feb. 11, 1961; children—Anthony, Jean Marie, Mary Beth. Instrumentation engr. Boeing Co., Aerospace div., Seattle, 1961, machine design engr., Wichita, Kans., 1962; process engr. Remington Arms Co., Lake City Arsenal, Mo., 1962-63, ballistics engr., 1963-64; mech. engr. engine testing Farmland Industries, North Kansas City, Mo., 1964-65, mgr. petroleum testing lab., 1966-72, mgr. fuels and lubricants research, 1972—. Mem. Coordinating Research Council, 1966—. Mem. Soc. Automotive Engrs. (chmn. Kansas City sect. 1975, regional adviser 1977-78). Roman Catholic. Clubs: Am. Sons of Columbus, Civic Italian-Am. Orgn. Home: 404 N Gladstone Blvd Kansas City MO 64123 Office: Farmland Industries Research Center 103 W 26th Ave North Kansas City MO 64116

FAST, DANIEL B., optometrist; b. Milw., Jan. 10, 1911; s. Hans and Emma (Schwerman) F.; D. Optometry, Ill. Coll. Optometry, 1933; postgrad. Ohio State U., 1950-51; m. Dorothy M. Colby, June 29, 1935; children—Judith (Mrs. R.E. Wilson), Susan (Mrs. W.H. Molin), Lynda (Mrs. R.L. Thompson). Pvt. practice optometry, Marinette, Wis., 1933—. Mem. gov.'s com. Spl. Learning, Marinette County, Wis., 1970—; exec. com. Mental Health Assn. Mem. Marinette Sch. Bd., 1957-52. Mem. Wis. Bd. Examiners 1955-60, pres., 1958-59; mem. optometric extension program; bd. dirs. Am. Optometric Found. Named optometrist of the year Northeastern Optometric Soc., 1966, Wis. Optometric Assn., 1971, Am. Optometric Assn., 1971. Mem. Am., Wis. optometric assns., Omega Delta, Beta Sigma Kappa. Methodist. (trustee 1950—). Mason (Shriner), Elk, Lion (pres. 1950). Home: Riverside Blvd Menominee MI 49858 Office: 1554 Main St Marinette WI 54143

FAST, HENRY, mathematician; b. Bochnia, Poland, Oct. 4, 1925; s. Leon and Rena (Stiel) F.; student U. Saratov (USSR), 1945-46; M.Ph., U. Wroclaw (Poland), 1950; D.Math., Math. Inst. Polish Acad., Warsaw, 1958; m. Maria Jolanta Hellwig, Feb. 24, 1968; children—Monica Tamara, Simon Emmanuel Thomas, Sheila Natasha, Jessica Rosemary. Came to U.S., 1962. Asst., sr. asst. U. Wroclaw, 1950-52, adj., 1956-60; sr. research asst., research adj. Math. Inst. Polish Acad., 1954-60; asst. prof. math. U. Notre Dame (Ind.), 1962-66; asso. prof. math. Wayne State U., Detroit, 1966—; vis. scholar Math. Centre, Amsterdam, Netherlands, 1973-74. Mem. Am. Math. Soc., Math. Assn. Am., Sigma Xi. Contbr. papers to profl. jours. Home: 19733 Shrewsbury Rd Detroit MI 48221

FATELEY, WILLIAM GENE, scientist, educator, adminstr.; b. Franklin, Ind., May 17, 1929; s. Nolan William and Georgia (Scott) F.; A.B., Franklin Coll., 1951, D.Sc. (hon.), 1965; postgrad. Northwestern U., 1951-53, U. Minn., 1956-57; Ph.D., Kans. State U.,

1956; m. Wanda Lee Glover, Sept. 1, 1953; children—Leslie Kaye, W. Scott, Kevin L., Jonathan H., Robin Lee. Head, phys. measurement Dow Chem. Co., Williamsburg, Va., 1958-60; fellow Mellon Inst., Pitts., 1960-62, head sci. relations, 1962-64, asst. to pres., 1964-67, sr. fellow in ind. research, 1965-72, asst. to v.p. for research, 1967-72; asso. prof. chemistry, 1967-69, prof., 1969-72; prof., head chemistry dept. Kans. State U., 1972—. Dir. Pitts. Conf. on Analytical Chemistry and Applied Spectroscopy, 1964-65, pres., 1971. Recipient Coblentz award for outstanding contbn. to molecular spectroscopy, 1965; Spectroscopy award, 1976. Fellow Optical Soc.; mem. Am. Chem. Soc. (pres. phys.-inorganic sect. Pitts.), Phi Beta Kappa (hon.), Sigma Xi, Sigma Alpha Epsilon, Phi Lambda Epsilon, Pi Mu Epsilon. Author 2 books. Editor in chief Jour. Applied Spectroscopy, 1974—; editor Raman Newsletters, 1975. Contbr. articles to profl. jours. Home: 203 14th St Manhattan KS 66502

FATZER, HAROLD R., justice; b. Fellsburg, Kans., Aug. 3, 1910; s. John R. and Rella (Shannon) F.; student Kans. State Coll., 1928-30; J.D., Washburn Coll. (now U.), 1933, LL.D. with honors, 1971; m. Frances Josephine Schwaup, Mar. 21, 1936; 1 son, John Richard. Admitted to Kans. bar, 1933, practiced in Kinsley. County atty. Edwards County, 1934-40; chief counsel State Dept. Social Welfare, 1941-43; asst. atty. gen., Kans., 1943, 45-49, atty. gen., 1949-56; justice Supreme Ct. Kans., 1956—, chief justice, 1971—; mem. Appellate Judges' Seminar, N.Y.U., 1959; mem. Inst. Jud. Adminstrn.; exec. council Conf. Chief Justices, 1975. Lectr. on legal ethics Washburn Law Sch., 1964-68. Pres. Kans. County Attys. Assn., 1939-40; mem. exec. council Nat. Conf. Chief Justices. Trustee Kans. Masonic Found., Washburn Coll.; bd. dirs. Santa Fe Trail Found. Recipient Distinguished Service award Washburn U., 1966, Washburn Law Sch. Assn., 1967; award for meritorious achievement Kans. Dist. Ct. Judges Assn., 1973; named hon. asst. atty. gen. Ga., 1954, adm. Great Navy of Nebr. Mem. Nat. Assn. Attys. Gen. (pres. 1952-53), Am. Legion, 40 and 8, Am. Vets., Disabled Amvets, Am. Judicature Soc. (Herbert Lincoln Harley award 1973), Inst. Jud. Adminstrn., Am., Kans. State bar assns., Washburn U. Alumni Assn. (pres. 1966-67), Kans. Hist. Soc. (dir.), Tau Delta Pi, Kappa Sigma, Delta Theta Phi. Republican. Conglist. Mason (Shriner). Home: Kinsley KS 67547 also 1415 Ward Pkwy Topeka KS 66604 Office: Supreme Ct Bldg Topeka KS 66612

FAUCETT, MARY KATHERINE, counselor; b. Parsons, Kans., Nov. 4, 1917; d. Howard Crawford and Rhoda May (Bartlett) Markham; B.M.E., U. Kans., 1939; M.A., U. Minn., 1968; m. Robert Lynn Faucett, June 28, 1941 (dec.); children—Russell Bartlett, Julia Ann. Tchr. music, pub. schs., Kans., 1939-41; counselor Normandale Community Coll., Bloomington, Minn., 1968—. Pres., League Women Voters, Rochester, Minn., 1959-61, treas., chmn. finance Minn. League Women Voters, 1963-64; sec. Friends Mpls. Inst. Arts, 1968. Mem. Am., Minn. (sec.) coll. personnel assns., Am., Minn. personnel guidance assns., Nat. Vocational Guidance Assn., Gertontological Soc., Minn. Gerontological Soc., Am. Retirement Soc., Audubon Soc., PEO. Presbyn. Home: 2400 102d St W #311 Bloomington MN 55431 Office: 9700 France Ave Normandale Community Coll Bloomington MN 55431

FAULKNER, CHARLES BRIXEY, govt. ofcl., lawyer; b. Springfield, Mo., Feb. 11, 1934; s. Charles Franklin and Josephine Frances (Brixey) F.; B.S., U. Ark., 1956; LL.B., U. Mo., 1960; m. Noralee Phariss, Dec. 29, 1956; children—Charlesa, Charles Byron. Admitted to Mo. bar, 1960, Fed. bar, 1962; partner Ratican & Faulkner, Aurora, Mo., 1960-71; legal adviser U.S. Bur. Prisons, U.S. Med. Center, Springfield, Mo., 1972; regional atty U.S. Bur. Prisons, Kansas City, Mo., 1974—; pros. and county atty., Lawrence County, Mo., 1961-70; city atty. Aurora, 1970-72, Marionville, Mo., 1961-72. Chmn. bd. dirs. A.R.C., Lawrence County, 1963-65. Served with 1st div., 26th Ind., AUS, 1956-57. Recipient Kansas City Trust award in estate planning, 1960. Mem. 39th Jud. Circuit Bar Assn. (v.p. 1966-70), Scabbard and Blade, Beta Gamma Sigma. Rotarian (dir. 1961-72). Editorial bd. Mo. Law Rev., 1958-60. Home: 312 S Elliott St Aurora MO 65605 Office: KCI Bank Bldg 8800 NW 112th St Kansas City MO 64153

FAULKNER, FREDERICK LEWIS, JR., computer co. exec.; b. Chgo., June 23, 1925; s. Frederick Lewis and Violet Beatrice (Cooksey) F.; B.S., Ill. Inst. Tech., 1949; m. Helen Anne Enzenberger, Feb. 1, 1947; children—Anne, Frederick Lewis III, Kristin. Gen. mgr. Chief Printing Co., Chgo., 1949-62; mem. sales staff Stewart & Fryer Printing Co., Chgo., 1962-64; exec. v.p., gen. mgr. Edward Keogh, Printing Co., Chgo., 1964-68; founder, pres. Graphic Arts Data Service, Chgo., 1966—. Mem. Cook County Dist. 106 Bd. Edn., 1959-64; bd. trustees Village Western Springs, 1963-67. Served with Signal Corps, AUS, 1943-46. Mem. Printing Industry Am., Lithographers Club Chgo., Chgo. Club Printing House Craftsmen, Alpha Sigma Phi. Club: University Chicago. Home: 309 53d St Western Springs IL 60558 Office: 200 W Monroe St Chicago IL 60606

FAULKNER, JAMES WILLIAM, urologist; b. Joliet, Ill., Mar. 2, 1921; s. Raymond Francis and Lucille Catherine (Norton) F.; B.S., B.M., U. Ill., 1941; M.D., Northwestern U., 1945; M.S., U. Minn., 1951; m. Betty Barbara Bond, June 1, 1946; children—Judith, Sara, James William III, Dan, Thomas. Intern Evanston (Ill.) Hosp., 1944-45; resident Wesley Meml. Hosp., 1945-46; jr. resident Mayo Clinic, Rochester, Minn., 1948-53; practice medicine specializing in urology, Arlington Heights, Ill., 1958—; mem. staff Children's Meml. Hosp., Luth. Gen. Hosp., N.W. Community Hosp. Med. dir. World Wide Ins. Co., 1973-75. Pres., Winnetka Environ. Soc. 1974-75. Served to capt. USAAF, 1946-48. Diplomate Am. Bd. Urology, Am. Bd. Surgery. Mem. Am. Urological Soc., A.C.S., Sigma Xi, Alpha Omega Alpha, Phi Eta Sigma. Club: Skokie Country. Contbr. articles to profl. jours. Home: 875 Sheridan St Winnetka IL 60093 Office: 1430 N Arlington Heights Rd Arlington Heights IL 60004

FAULMANN, ROGER RAY, educator; b. Mt. Clemens, Mich., Jan. 27, 1938; s. Raymond John and Esther Ida (Neiman) F.; student Eastern Mich. U., 1956-57; B.Mus., Baldwin-Wallace Coll., 1960; M.Mus., U. Mich., 1967; postgrad. U. Ill., 1968-72; m. Elizabeth Josephine Dunbar, Dec. 27, 1964; 1 son, Bryan Andrew. Tchr. instrumental and vocal music Fraser (Mich.) Pub. Schs., 1960-63, Port Huron (Mich.) Pub. Schs., 1963-64; dir. bands Lake Orion (Mich.) Community Schs., 1964-67; instr. percussion, asso. dir. bands Ill. State U., 1967—; nat. clinician Ludwig Drum Co. div. Ludwig Industries, Chgo., 1977—; free-lance club drummer, timpanist, percussionist, condr., composer; cons. music educators, drum cos. Mem. Mich. Sch. Band and Orch. Assn. (treas. 1960-61), Percussive Arts Soc. (pres. Ill. chpt. 1973-75), Nat. Assn. Rudimental Drummers, Coll. Band Dirs. Nat. Assn., Pi Kappa Lambda, Delta Omicron, Phi Mu Alpha Sinfonia. Lutheran. Author: The Junior Percussionist. Home: 1300D Kingsridge Ct Normal IL 61761

FAURI, FEDELE FREDERICK, state ofcl.; b. Crystal Falls, Mich., Apr. 28, 1909; s. Joseph and Angela (Chesky) F.; A.B., U. Mich., 1930, J.D., 1933; m. Iris M. Peterson, June 11, 1938; children—David Peter, Eric Joseph, Paul Frederick, Greta Susan. Supr. Mich. State Bur. Social Security, 1941-43; dir. Mich. State Dept. Social Welfare, 1943-47; cons. on pub. assistance, ways and means com. Ho. Reps., 1945-46; social security adviser, 1949; sr. specialist legislative reference service Library Congress, 1947-51; pub. assistance research dir., adv. council social security Senate Com. Finance, 1948, social security adviser, 1950-56; mem. gov. commn. to study problems of aging; dean pub. welfare adminstrn. sch. social work U. Mich., 1951-70, prof., 1951—, v.p. state relations and planning, 1970-75; racing commr. State of Mich., 1975—; v.p., dir. Mich. Welfare League; chmn. council on employment security, U.S. Dept. Labor, 1954-60; chmn. Adv. Council Pub. Welfare, U.S. Dept. Health, Edn. and Welfare, 1964—; mem. nat. com. Citizens Crusade Against Poverty; trustee Nat. Council Crime and Delinquency, 1963-65; pres. Council on Social Work Edn., 1954-56; adv. com. on pub. and pvt. pensions Nat. Bur. Econ. Security; bd. dirs. Mich. United Fund. Recipient award Nat. Conf. Social Work, 1955; W.S. Terry, Jr. Meml. Merit award Am. Public Welfare Assn., 1957; Distinguished Service award Council on Social Work Edn., 1968. Mem. Internat., Nat. confs. social work, Mich. Bar Assn., Am. Pub. Welfare Assn. (dir. pres. 1967—), Mich. Council on Social Work Edn. (dir. 1967—), Nat. Conf. on Social Welfare (pres. 1961-62), Phi Kappa Phi. Author: Study of Employment Security Adminstrative Costs (with J. Borus), 1953; Significant Findings on the Impact of the 1957-58 Recession (with Harber & Cohen), 1959. Chmn. editorial bd. Ency. Social Work, 1963. Contbr. articles profl. jours. Home: 1025 Spruce Dr Ann Arbor MI 48104

FAUSSET, CALVIN BASIL, neurosurgeon; b. Pendleton, Ind., May 26, 1905; s. Calvin H. and Nelle (Richardson) F.; A.B., Ind. U., 1927, M.D., 1930; children—Gloria Gay, Matt Hand. Intern, Indpls. Gen. Hosp., 1930-31, resident surgery, 1931-32; resident neurosurgery N.Y. Hosp., N.Y.C., 1937-40; practice medicine, specializing in neurol. surgery, Indpls., 1940—; active mem. med. staff Meth. Hosp., Indpls., Winona Meml. Hosp., Indpls., Community Hosp., Indpls., St. Vincent's Hosp., Indpls.; cons. mem. med. staff Ind. U. Med. Center, Indpls., St. Francis Hosp., Beech Grove, Ind. Mem. Am. med. polit. action com. Rep. party, 1970-72. Served with USAAF, 1942-43, AUS, 1943-46. Decorated Bronze Star medal. Diplomate Am. Bd. Surgery, Am. Bd. Neurol. Surgery. Mem. Am., Ind., Marion County med. assns., Internat. Coll. Surgeons, Pan Pacific Surg. Assn., Congress Neurol. Surgeons, Interurban Central neurosurg. socs., Am. Assn. Neurol. Surgeons, Ind. Neuropsychiat. Assn., Aerospace Med. Assn., Flying Physicians Assn., Am. Legion, Quiet Birdmen, Sigma Alpha Epsilon, Phi Rho Sigma. Mason (Shriner). Clubs: Indiana Univ; Meridian Hills Country. Home: 3016 Lake Shore Dr Indianapolis IN 46205 Office: 1815 N Capitol Ave Indianapolis IN 46202

FAUVER, STUART LESLIE, lawyer; b. Oberlin, Ohio, Nov. 24, 1940; s. Robert N. and Jane (Herig) F.; B.A., Ohio State U., 1964; J.D., Western Res. U., 1967; m. Gloria Roka, Aug. 25, 1962; children—Pier L., Reed S. Admitted to Ohio bar, 1967; partner Fauver & Fauver, Oberlin, Ohio, 1967—. Chmn. Christmas Seals Lorain County, 1970; v.p. Oberlin Community Welfare Council, 1972. Bd. dirs. Oberlin United Fund, 1970-74, v.p., 1975, 76; bd. dirs. Lorain County Children Services Bd., 1970—, chmn., 1975. Solicitor City Oberlin, 1972—. Mem. Am., Ohio, Lorain County (exec. com. 1975) bar assns. Home: 374 W College St Oberlin OH 44074 Office: 5 W College St Oberlin OH 44074

FAVIS, DIMITRIOS VASILIOS, chemist; b. Sparta, Greece, Sept. 10, 1914; s. Vasilios I. and Elektra (Papadakos) F.; B.S. in Math., U. Athens, 1938, B.S. in Chemistry, 1946; Ph.D. in Phys. Chemistry, McGill U., Montreal, Que., Can., 1951; m. Odette Trepanier, Sept. 27, 1952; children—Basil, Marie. Research chemist Imperial Oil Enterprises Ltd., Sarnia, Ont., Can., 1951—, now research asso. Served to 2d lt. Greek Army, 1938-41. Fellow Chem. Inst. Can.; mem. Am. Chem. Soc., N.Y. Acad. Scis. Patentee in field. Home: 464 Lakeshore Sarnia ON N7V 2S5 Canada Office: Imperial Oil Enterprises Ltd Sarnia ON Canada

FAWCETT, SHERWOOD LUTHER, research lab. exec.; b. Youngstown, Ohio, Dec. 25, 1919; s. Luther and Clara (Sherwood) F.; B.Sc., Ohio State U., 1941; M.S., Case Inst. Tech., 1948, Ph.D., 1950; m. Martha L. Simcox, Feb. 28, 1953; children—Paul, Judith, Tom. Mem. staff Battelle Meml. Inst., Columbus, Ohio, 1950-64, mgr. physics dept., 1959-64, pres., 1968—; dir. Pacific N.W. labs., Richland, Wash., 1964-67. Served with USNR, 1941-46. Decorated Bronze Star medal. Registered profl. engr., Ohio. Mem. Am. Phys. Soc., Am. Nuclear Soc., Nat. Soc. Profl. Engrs., Atlantic Inst. Internat. Affairs, Atlantic Council U.S., Sigma Xi, Delta Chi, Sigma Pi Sigma, Tau Beta Pi. Home: 2820 Margate Rd Columbus OH 43221 Office: 505 King Ave Columbus OH 43201

FAXON, JACK, state senator; b. Detroit, June 9, 1936; s. Morris and Pauline (Krimsky) F.; B.S., Wayne State U., 1956, M.Ed., 1958; M.A., U. Mich., 1962, postgrad., 1961-63. Tchr. pub. schs., Detroit, 1956-64; mem. Mich. Ho. of Reps., 1965-71, mem. Mich. Senate, 1971—. Headmaster City Sch. of Detroit. Del., Constl. Conv., 1961; candidate Mich. State Senate, 1962. Bd. advisers Sch. Theology Diocese Mich. Mem. ACLU, Anti-Defamation League. Home: 15343 Warwick Detroit MI 48223 Office: State Capitol Lansing MI 48902

FAY, LEONARD EDWARD, chiropractor, ednl. adminstr.; b. Chgo., Aug. 23, 1925; s. Leonard Theodore and Marie (Barbian) F.; B. Gen. Edn., Morton Coll., 1945; D. Chiropractic, Nat. Coll. Chiropractic, 1949; m. Angela Mary Marrese, Sept. 9, 1950; children—Marilen (Mrs. Richard F. Reimer), John, Catherine (Mrs. David C. Frost), Richard, Anne, Marianne. Mem. faculty Nat. Coll. of Chiropractic, Lombard, Ill., 1949-51, asst. to pres., 1962-64, v.p., 1964-67, exec. v.p., 1967—; pvt. practice chiropractic medicine, Chgo., 1950-75. Cons. Medicare, Ill. Med. Services, 1973—, CNA Ins. Co., 1973—, Travelers Ins. Co., 1975—; mem. adv. com. Ill. Dept. Pub. Aid. Fellow Internat. Coll. Chiropractors; mem. Am., Ill., Chgo. chiropractic assns., Council on Chiropractic Edn. (v.p. 1972-74, pres. 1974-76), Nat. Chiropractic Assn. (Ill. del. 1961-62), Council on Chiropractic Roentgenology, Council on Chiropractic Neurology (pres. 1971-72), Am. Assn. for Higher Edn., Am. Pub. Health Assn., Am. Assn. Univ. Adminstrs., N.Y. Acad. Scis., Sigma Phi Kappa, Eta Nu, Pi Kappa Alpha (pres. and trustee 1972-74). Roman Catholic. Lion. Home: 22 WO 64 Stratford Pl Glen Ellyn IL 60137 Office: 200 E Roosevelt Rd Lombard IL 60148

FAYE, GERALD EITIG, educator; b. N.Y.C., Jan. 8, 1930; s. Gerald Eitig and Marion (Durkin) F.; A.B., U. Cin., 1956; M.A., U. Mich., 1960, postgrad., 1964-74; m. Edith Skobo, Nov. 27, 1959; children—Jefferson, Kirsten Kjaer. Legislative asst. to speaker Mich. Ho. of Reps., 1965; asso. prof. polit. sci. Oakland Community Coll., 1966-69, provost, prof., 1969-73, chairperson acad. senate, 1974—; research asso. U. Mich., 1973—; cons. Mich. Dept. Pub. Instrn., 1973-74. Co-dir. Mich. Citizens for Johnson-Humphrey, 1964; dir. Mich. 2d Congl. Dist. Robert F. Kennedy campaign, 1968. Served with USAF, 1950-54. Ford Found. grantee, 1963-64. Mem. Am. Polit. Sci. Assn., Phi Delta Kappa, Sigma Phi Epsilon. Episcopalian. Author: History of Political Science at University of Michigan, 1960. Home: 1540 Broadway Ann Arbor MI 48105 Office: Orchard Ridge Campus Oakland Community Coll Farmington MI 48024

FAYED, MUHAMMED EL-SAWI, chem. engr.; b. Sal-Haghar, Egypt, Jan. 18, 1943; s. Al-Sawi Ibrahim and Fathiya Mohamad (Hitata) F.; came to U.S., 1975; B.Sc. with honors, Cairo U., 1964, M.Sc., 1968; Ph.D., U. Waterloo (Ont., Can.), 1972; m. Salwa H. Abou-Omar, Apr. 1, 1971; 1 son, Marwan Muhammad. Plant chem. engr. Abou-Zaabal Fertilizer and Chem. Co., Cairo, 1964-67; NRC of Can. grantee, research asso., process engr. U. Waterloo and Spring Chem. Ltd., Toronto, Ont., 1972-74; process mgr. Peabody Engring. Can., Mississauga, Ont., 1974-75; process and research engr. Pullman Kellog Co., Houston, 1975-77; prof. chem. engring. Institut Algerien de Petrole representing Gas Devel. Corp. and Inst. Gas Tech., Chgo., 1977—; speaker Rotary and Kiwanis clubs. Govt. Can. youth grantee, 1971. Mem. Am. Inst. Chem. Engrs. (organizer and chmn. solids handling sessions 1977 conf.), Inst. Chem. Engrs. (London) (grad.), Fine Particle Soc. U.S.A., Assn. Profl. Engrs. Ont., Egyptian Assn. Profl. Engrs. Contbr. articles to profl. jours. Address: Gas Devel Corp/Inst Gas Tech 3424 S State St Chicago IL 60616 also 29 Hickory St Guelph ON N1G 2X2 Canada

FAYYAZ, MAHMOOD MALKANA, physician; b. Amritsar, India, Apr. 15, 1933; s. Taj Din and Amir Begum (Malkana) Choudhary. B.Sc., U. of the Panjab, Lahore, West Pakistan, 1951; M.B., B.S., King Edward Med. Coll., 1956; L.R.C.P., M.C.R.S., Conjoint Bd., London, Eng., 1969; m. Janet Gradwell, June 16, 1967; children—Sarah Yasmin, Sima Nasreen, Maria Heather. Med. officer various positions Dept. Health Services, Govt. West Pakistan, Lahore, 1956-63; practice medicine specializing in gen. surgery, Eriksdale, Man., Can., 1970—. Fellow Royal Coll. Surgeons (Edinburgh, Scotland); mem. Canadian, Brit. med. assns. Home: 471 Kingston Crescent Winnipeg MB Canada Office: Mall Med Group 280 Memorial Blvd Winnipeg MB Canada

FAZIO, CHARLES RICHARD, ednl. inst. exec.; b. Bklyn., Aug. 5, 1936; s. George D. and Helen T. (Mulcahy) F.; A.B., Georgetown U., 1957; m. Carolyn R. Raffa, June 25, 1973; children—Carla, Teresa, Charles III, Francesca, Victoria. Regional dir. devel. Georgetown U., Washington, D.C., 1963-66; v.p., sr. account exec. C.W. Shaver and Co., Inc., N.Y.C., 1966-74; v.p. St. Mary's Jr. Coll., Mpls., 1975-77; exec. dir. Inst. Devel. Tng. and Advancement div. McManis Assos., Washington, 1977—; sr. cons. Collins Assos., Inc., Mpls.; financial advisor Occupational Training Center, St. Paul. Chmn. bd. Our House of Minn.; bd. dir. Young Adult Centers, Inc. Served with U.S. Army, 1958-63. Recipient Certificate for Fund Raising Techniques U. Chgo., 1974. Mem. Council for Advancement and Support of Edn., Nat. Soc. Fund Raisers, Archdiocesan Devel. Dirs. (Mpls./St. Paul) St. Paul Area C. of C. Roman Catholic. Clubs: Exchange of Southtown Mpls. (bd. dirs.), Lions, Riverview Mpls. Editor manual on fund raising, philanthropic devel. tech., 1977. Home: 8065 Casper Way Inver Grove Heights MN 55075 Office: 1201 Connecticut Ave NW Washington DC 20036

FEAGLES, GERALD FRANKLIN, account mgr.; b. Kansas City, Kans., Dec. 8, 1934; s. George Joseph and Florence Ada (Johnson) F.; student Kansas City Jr. Coll., 1953-55; m. Eleanor Jean Holder, Aug. 31, 1957; 1 son, Gerald Franklin. Various mktg. positions Sears Roebuck & Co., Kansas City, Mo., 1963-70; sales engr. E.F. Hauserman, Lenexa, Kans., 1970-74, br. mgr. Tex., 1974-75, account mgr., 1977—; cons., analyst in field. Active Boy Scouts Am. Mem. Constrn. Specifications Inst., Producers Council, Asso. Gen. Contractors Assn. Baptist. Home: Route 1 Box 36K Basehor KS 66007 Office: 9393 W 110th St Overland Park KS 66210

FEARNEHOUGH, GEORGE SAMUEL, microbiologist; b. Failsworth, Eng., July 14, 1922; s. John and Ida Jane (Buckthought) F.; came to U.S., 1961, naturalized, 1969; grad. Coll. of Tech., Manchester U. (Eng.), 1950; m. Mary Elizabeth Wright, July 25, 1969; stepchildren—David Michael, Robert Alan, Mary Kathleen. Chief technologist N.W. Regional Lab., Pub- Health Lab. Service, Manchester, 1948-57; sr. technologist Provincial Dept. of Health, Ont., Can., 1957-61; instr. microbiology Med. Sch., U. Mich., Ann Arbor, 1961-69; chief microbiologist Peoples Community Hosp. Authority, Wayne, Mich., 1969—. Lectr. bacteriology Inst. of Med. Lab. Tech., Eng., 1954-57; lectr. in microbiology Ont. Dept. of Health, 1957-61; examiner Can. Soc. Lab. Tech., 1958-61; lectr. Eastern Mich. U., 1970; instr. microbiology Washtenaw Community Coll., 1964-69. Pres. Citizens Adv. Council to Washtenaw County Drain Commr., 1973-75. Ordained elder United Presbyn. Ch. of Am., 1973; interim minister First Congl. Ch., Ann Arbor, 1963-64; lay preacher Meth. Ch. of Britain, Manchester, 1941-57. Fellow Royal Microscopical Soc.; mem. Am. Soc. for Microbiology, Am. Pub. Health Assn., Mich. Soc. for Infection Control (editor 1974—), Assn. Practitioners of Infection Control. Author: Elementary Medical Microbiology Manual, 1966. Home: 35 Revere Ct Ann Arbor MI 48104 Office: People's Community Hosp Authority Annapolis Ave Wayne MI 48184

FEARS, GARY R., mgmt. co. exec.; b. Granite City, Ill., June 8, 1946; s. Floyd Ray and Edna Pauline (Brawley) F.; student Western Ill. U., 1964-65; B.A., So. Ill. U., 1971; div.; 1 son, Victor. Nat. mktg. mgr. Sears Tax Service, Chgo., 1970-72; pres. Estar Corp., Colo. Springs, Colo., 1972-73; tng. cons. Ill. Dept. Local Govt. Affairs, Springfield, 1973, chief adminstrv. officer community services, 1973-74; spl. asst. to sec. Ill. Dept. Transp., Springfield, 1974-76; pres. South Western Mgmt. Inc., Granite City, Ill., 1976—. Co-chmn. Madison County Citizens for McCarthy, 1968; state chmn. McCarthy Students for Humphrey, 1968; organizer Dan Walker for Gov., 1972; So. Ill. campaign coordinator Carter for Pres., 1976; mem. exec. com. Democratic Nat. Finance Council. Mem. ACLU, Acad. Polit. Sci., Council State Community Affairs Agys. Democrat. Address: 5 Barbara St Granite City IL 62040

FEASEL, FRED, lawyer; b. nr. Fostoria, Ohio, Aug. 14, 1892; s. John Leroy and Mary Alice (Steward) F.; student U. Colo., 1914-16; B.S., Ohio State U., 1919; M.A., U. Chgo., 1920; LL.B., LaSalle Extension U., 1936; J.D., Blackstone Sch. Law, 1938. Tchr. rural schs., Jackson Twp., Ohio, 1912-14; head dept. econs. and bus. adminstrn. U. N.Mex., 1920-23; accountant State of N.Mex., Albuquerque, 1923-36; admitted to N.Mex. bar, 1936, also Ohio bar; practiced in Albuquerque, 1936-42, Fostoria, 1946—; individual practice, 1946—. Sec. N.Mex. Bd. Accounting, 1930-32. Served with Air Service, U.S. Army, 1917-18; served to col. USAAF, 1943-46. C.P.A., Ohio. Mem. Am. Inst. C.P.A.'s. Ohio Soc. C.P.A.'s, Am., N.Mex., Ohio bar assns. Clubs: Masons (32 deg.), Shriners, Elks. Address: 6511 N County Rd Suite 3 Route 4 Fostoria OH 44830

FEAZELL, ROBERT RAY, accountant; b. Portsmouth, Ohio, Aug. 31, 1940; s. William Franklin and Clara Lee (Hasler) F.; student U. Cin.; m. Glenda Ruth Cantrel, Feb. 27, 1960; children—Kevin, Michael, William, Todd. Clk., Merry Mfg. Co., Cin., 1957-60; bookkeeper Dallas Trucking Co., Cin., 1960-62; controller Mees Distbg. Inc., Cin., 1962-66, Four Seasons Co., Cin., 1966-68; owner, exec. partner Robert R. Feazell & Co., Cin., 1960—; dir. F & N Motor Inc., No. Hills Oil Inc. Adviser, Jr. Achievement, 1960-65; mem. nat. adv. council Nat. Fedn. Ind. Bus., 1972-77; adv. bd. Vocat. Sch., Diamond Oaks, 1976-77. Mem. Nat. Soc. Pub. Accountants (dir. 1972-76, bd. govs. 1977—), Pub. Accountants Soc. Ohio (pres. 1972, chmn. bd. 1973), Mt. Healthy Bus. Assn. (pres. 1977). Republican. Methodist. Clubs: Clovernook Country, Bankers, Masons, Shriners. Home: 1072 Galbraith Rd Cincinnati OH 45231 Office: 9284 Compton Sq Cincinnati OH 45231

FEDDER, NORMAN JOSEPH, theatrical artist, educator; b. N.Y.C., Jan. 26, 1934; s. Abraham Herbert and Harriet Dorothy (Solomon) F.; student Johns Hopkins, 1950-52; B.A., Bklyn. Coll., 1955; M.A., Columbia, 1956; Ph.D., N.Y. U., 1962; m. Deborah Pincus, Nov. 24, 1955; children—Jordan Michael, Tamar Beth. Asst. prof. English, Trenton (N.J.) State Coll., 1960-61; asso. prof. English, Indiana (Pa.) U., 1961-64, Fla. Atlantic U., Boca Raton, 1964-67; asso. prof. drama U. Ariz., Tucson, 1967-70; asso. prof. theater Kans. State U., Manhattan, 1970—. Judge Am. Coll. Theatre Festival, 1972-75; pres. Ecumenical Council for Drama and Other Arts, 1977—. Mem. Kans. Assn. of Arts, Religious Communities and the Am. Revolution (pres. 1975—), Assn. Kans. Theatre (exec. bd. 1974—), Am. Theatre Assn. (chmn. religious theatre project 1974—). Jewish religion. Author: The Influence of D.H. Lawrence on Tennessee Williams, 1966; writer, producer numerous plays. Home: 1309 Nichols St Manhattan KS 66502

FEDOR, GEORGE EDWARD, lawyer; b. Czechoslovakia, Mar. 28, 1909; s. George and Mary (Talas) F.; came to U.S., 1913, naturalized, 1921; B.A., Western Res. U., 1931; LL.B. magna cum laude, Cleve. Law Sch., 1939; m. Helen R. Evansick, Apr. 24, 1934; children—Bruce G., Dennis G., Donna M. Fedor Wimbiscus, Thomas J., Mark Q., Louise A. Fedor Ortiz, Renee M. Fedor Bauchmoyer, Christopher A. Salesman Standard Oil Co., Cleve., 1930-46, bus. devel. specialist, 1945-46; admitted to Ohio bar, 1940, since practiced in Cleve.; asso. firm Fedor & Fedor. Dir. law City of Lakewood. Pres. Lakewood Slovak Civic Club, 1941-42; mem. Lakewood Planning Commn., 1955-57, mem. adv. bd. St. Andrew's Abbey, Cleve., 1967—. Mem. Ohio Ho. of Reps., 1949-52; chmn. speaker's bur. Cuyahoga County Democratic Com., 1947-48. Trustee Citizens League, Cleve., 1955-61, St. Augustine Manor, Cleve., 1971—. Recipient Outstanding Alumni award Cleve. Marshall Law Sch., 1964. Mem. Am. Judicature Soc., Am., Cleve., Cuyahoga County, Ohio bar assns., 1st Catholic Slovak Union. 1st Catholic Slovak Ladies Assn., Nat. Slovak Soc., Catholic Slovak Sokol. Democrat. Roman Catholic. Home: 18603 W Valley Ln Fairview Park OH 44126 Office: 1026 Terminal Tower Cleveland OH 44113

FEENEY, DON JOSEPH, JR., assn. exec.; b. Greenville, N.C., Jan. 17, 1948; s. Don Joseph and Louise Ann (Saieed) F.; B.A. (grantee), Colgate U., 1971; M.A., Governor's State U., 1973; Ph.D. candidate (assistantship) Loyola U. (Chgo.), 1974—; m. Diane Lynn Fetherling, July 23, 1971. Psychologist, tng. coordinator Silvis Grove Alcoholism Treatment Center, Manteno, Ill., 1972-76; clin. coordinator Champaign County (Ill.) Council on Alcoholism, Champaign, 1976—; tchr. St. Mary's Sch., Park Forest, Ill., 1971-72; cons., research advisor Grant Hosp. Alcoholism Program, 1977—; lectr. in field; condr. workshops in alcoholism and group therapy. Mem. Am. Personnel and Guidance Assn., Ill. Group Psychotherapy Soc., Ill. Alcohol and Drug Dependence Assn., Ill. Psychol. Assn., Explorations Inst. Calif., Phi Kappa Psi. Contbr. articles in field to profl. jours. Home: 711 W Vermont Urbana IL 61801 Office: PO Box 1501 Champaign IL 61820

FEENEY, DONALD PETER, physician; b. Bklyn., Aug. 30, 1930; s. Edward A. and Madeline J. (Cusack) F.; B.S., Holy Cross Coll., 1952; M.D., Cornell U., 1956; m. Frances M. Clegg, Apr. 26, 1958; children—Carol, Laura, Douglas, Gregory. Intern in surgery Yale Med. Coll., 1956-57; resident in gynecology N.Y. Hosp. Cornell U., N.Y.C., 1957-58; resident in urology Mayo Clinic, Rochester, Minn., 1960-63; practice medicine specializing in urology, Rockford, Ill., 1964—; clin. asst. prof. urology U. Ill. Med. Coll., 1973—. Served with M.C., USAF, 1958-60. Mem. A.C.S., Am., N. Central urol. assns., Chgo., Urol. Soc. Roman Catholic. Office: 2300 N Rockton Ave Rockford IL 61101

FEGERT, CHARLES DONALD, newspaper exec.; b. Chgo., Nov. 8, 1930; s. Charles Donald and Virginia Louise (Henault) F.; A.A., Morgan Park Jr. Coll., 1950; B.B.A., Loyola U., 1952; m. Patricia S. Althaus, Dec. 15, 1965; children—Michael, Lisa, Charles Donald. With Chgo. Sun-Times-Chgo. Daily News, 1955—, retail supr., 1962-64, retail mgr., 1964-69, advt. mgr., 1969-72, v.p. advt. and mktg., 1972—. Bd. dirs. Better Bus. Bur. Met. Chgo., Chgo. Conv. and Tourism Bur., NCCJ; trustee Brain Research Found., U. Chgo.; v.p. Mentally Retarded Olympian Program. Served with USCGR, 1953-55. Recipient Chgo. Conf. for Brotherhood award, 1975. Mem. Internat. Newspaper Advt. Execs. (mem. plans com. 1973—), Chgo. Advt. Club (dir.). Clubs: Evanston Golf, Mid-Am. Tavern, Metropolitan, Whitehall, Economic of Chgo. (com. econ. devel. 1965—). Home: 6087 Kirkwood St Chicago IL 60645 Office: 401 N Wabash Ave Chicago IL 60611

FEHLHABER, CLINTON LEROY, photographer; b. Gibonsburg, Ohio, Apr. 26, 1920; s. Frank August and Clara Amelia (Henline) F.; student Davis Bus. Coll., Toledo, 1939-40; m. Virginia Clara Tabbert, Apr. 9, 1944; children—David, Sue, Todd. With sales dept. Sun Oil Co., Toledo, 1941-43. Cost accountant tool and die shop Mayle Mfg. Co., Toledo, 1943-44; office mgr. Toledo Camera Shop, 1946-47; owner Fehlhaber Studio, Oak Harbor, Ohio, 1947—; photographer Fehlhaber Paint and Wallpaper, 1950—; with Inter State Studio, Sedalia, Mo., 1955—, state mgr., 1972—. Served with USNR, 1944-46. Mem. C. of C., Am. Legion (past dist. comdr.), Profl. Photographers Am., Photographers Ohio. Lutheran. Home: 370 E Main St Oak Harbor OH 43449 Office: 168 W Water St Oak Harbor OH 43449

FEIEREISEN, JOHN HENRY, educator; b. Mpls., Sept. 9, 1943; s. George A. and Lucille J. (Vos) F.; student U. Minn., 1961-62; A.A. with honors, Southwestern Jr. Coll., 1964; student U. Calif. at Santa Barbara, 1964-65; B.S. with honors, U. Wis., 1967, M.A. (Ford Found. fellow), 1971; m. Wendy Tillman, June 6, 1966 (div. 1976); children—Caleb B., Brook. Teaching asst. U. Wis., Madison, 1967-69; faculty philosophy, chmn. dept. Nicolet Coll., Rhinelander, Wis., 1970—. Pres., Manitowish Waters (Wis.) Skiing Skeeters, 1963, show dir. 1964; v.p. Manitowish Waters Fire Dept., 1972; bd. dirs. Lakeland Council on Alcoholism and Other Drug Abuse, 1976—. Recipient Outstanding Teaching award U. Wis., 1969. Club: Trout Unltd. Founder, pub. monthly paper Nicolet Issues Forum, 1976—. Home: Box 471 Lake Tomahawk WI 54539 Office: Box 581 Rhinelander WI 54501

FEIERMAN, STEVEN, historian; b. N.Y.C., Dec. 12, 1940; s. Alexander and Jeanette (Sobel) F.; B.A., Columbia U., 1961; M.A., Northwestern U., 1962, Ph.D., 1970; D.Phil., Oxford U., 1972; m. Elizabeth Karlin, July 25, 1964; children—Joshua, Jessica. Instr. history U. Wis., Madison, 1969-70, asst. prof., 1970-73, asso. prof., 1973-77, prof., 1977—. Nat. Endowment Humanities fellow, 1973-74; Fgn. Area fellow, 1964-67. Mem. African Studies Assn. Author: The Shambaa Kingdom, 1974; African History (with others), 1977. Office: Dept History Univ Wisconsin Madison WI 53706

FEIGERT, M. WESLEY, surgeon; b. Van Wert, Ohio, June 10, 1920; s. Martin W. and Anna Elma (Thomas) F.; B.A., Ohio State U., 1942, M.D., 1946; m. Ruby Inez Tye, Mar. 20, 1947; children—James, Martin, Karen, Susan. Intern, Christ Hosp., Cin., 1946-47; resident urology St. Vincent Hosp., Toledo, 1949-52; practice medicine specializing in urology Findlay, Ohio, 1952—; active staff Blanchard Valley Hosp., 1952 —. Mem. Findlay Sch. Bd., 1960-62. Served with M.C., AUS, 1947-49. Diplomate Am. Bd. Urology. Mem. Am., Ohio State med. assns., Am. Urol. Assn., A.C.S., Findlay Skeet Club, Phi Delta Theta, Nu Sigma Nu. Methodist. Elk. Clubs: Findlay Country. Home: 2432 S Main St Findlay OH 45840 Office: 1400 S Main St Findlay OH 45840

FEIGHNY, ROBERT EUGENE, physician; b. Delia, Kans., May 30, 1920; s. Thomas Joseph and Catherine Veronica (McDonnell) F.; student Rockhurst Coll., 1939-40; M.D., U. Kans., 1951; m. Helen Louise Glynn, Sept. 21, 1943; children—Julia (Mrs. Richard Wilkinson), Robert, Leo, Dennis, Virginia (Mrs. Larry Coffelt), Rebecca, Patrick. Commd. 2d lt. U.S. Army, 1951, advanced through grades to lt. col., 1965, ret., 1967; intern Brooke Army Hosp., San Antonio, Tex., 1951-52; resident Army-Navy Hosp., Hot Springs, Ark., 1952-53, Letterman Gen. Hosp., San Francisco, 1953-56, Shriners Hosp. Crippled Children, Lexington, Ky., 1957; practice medicine, specializing in orthopedic surgery, Salina, Kans., 1967—; pres. staff Asbury Hosp., Salina, 1975—. Served with USNR, 1940-45. Decorated Bronze Star. Diplomate Am. Bd. Orthopedic Surgery. Mem. Kans. (pres. 1973), Mid-Central orthopedic socs., Kans. Med. Soc., A.M.A., Am. Acad. Orthopedic Surgeons. Home: 2018 Ridglea St Salina KS 67401 Office: 519 S Santa Fe St Salina KS 67401

FEILER, STUART IRWIN, historian; b. Newark, July 5, 41; s. Morris E. and Annette R. (Bleyfeder) F.; A.A., Sper Coll. Judaica and Oakton Community Coll., 1975; B.A., Northeastern Ill. U., 1975, M.A., 1977; m. Arlene Marilyn Dusick Dec. 25, 1959; children—David Dean, Brett Alan. Various te hing positions Jewish history and mysticism High Sch. Jewish Studies, Chgo. Jewish Youth Council Free High Sch., various temples, 1971—; guest lectr. Jewish history Chg. Theol. Sem. 1974, Am. social history Northeastern Ill. U., Chgo., 1976-77; tchr. High Sch. Jewish Studies, Skokie, Ill., 1973—; lectr. in field. Youth dir. Niles Twp. Jewish Congregation, 1972; area chmn. Maine Twp. Republican party, 1969—. Served with USAF, 1958-60. Gen. Assembly Ill. scholar, 1974—. Mem. Am. Hist. Assn., Orgn. Am. Historians, Nat. Trust Historic Preservation, Assn. Nat. Archives, Phi Alpha Theta. Home: 7773 Nordica Ave Niles IL 60648

FEINBERG, BERNARD, banker; b. Chgo., Dec. 4, 1924; s. Joseph and Bessie (Ferdinand) F.; student Ill. Inst. Tech., 1942-45. Real estate broker, Chgo., 1946—; chain operator Currency Exchange, Chgo., 1946-63; dir. Jefferson State Bank, Chgo., 1957—, chmn. bd., pres., 1959-61, pres., 1961—; pres. Jefferson Leasing Co. Chgo., Jefferson Financial Systems, Inc., Chgo.; sr. partner Fleetwood Realty Co., Chgo.; owner Div. Constrn. Co. Chgo., Division Mgmt. Co. Vis. lectr. Roosevelt U., 1966. N.W. Side chmn. Chgo. Real-Estate Bds., Better Neighborhood Crusade, 1958-59. Mem. U.S. C. of C., Ill. C. of C., Chgo., North West real estate bds., Nat. Assn. Real Estate Bds., Jefferson Park C. of C. (dir.), Am., Ill., Ind. bankers assns., Am. Inst. Banking, Art Inst. Chgo. (life), Field Mus. Natural History, ACLU (life), Soc. Paper Money Collectors, Anti-Defamation League, Chgo. Symphony Soc. Jewish (synagogue trustee). B'nai B'rith, Lion (Jefferson Park br. Chgo.). Club: Northside Bankers (past pres.). Home: 1000 Lake Shore Plaza Chicago IL 60611 Office: 5301 W Lawrence Ave Chicago IL 60630 also 5245 W Lawrence Ave Chicago IL 60630 also 200 W Jackson Blvd Chicago IL 60606

FEINBERG, SIDNEY S., lawyer; b. Bklyn., Aug. 30, 1910; s. Samuel and Minnie (Komaroff) F.; student Carleton Coll., 1924-25; B.A., U. Minn., 1928, J.D., 1930; m. Elizabeth Hoffman, Sept. 4, 1931; children—Thomas Davis, Sherry (Mrs. Richard Israel). With Davis & Michel, Mpls., 1926-35; admitted to Minn. bar, 1930; practice law, Worthington, Minn., 1935-43; enforcement atty. OPA, Washington, 1943-47; asso., then partner firm Robins, Davis & Lyons, Mpls., 1948—. Chmn. Minn. Civil Service Bd., 1968-72. Bd. dirs. Legal Aid Soc. Mpls., Legal Rights Center, Sholom Home, Inc.; hon. trustee North Star chpt. Multiple Sclerosis Soc. Fellow Am. Coll. Probate Counsel; mem. Am. (ho. dels. 1968-69), Hennepin County (pres. 1962-63), Minn. (pres. 1967-68) bar assns., Am. Judicature Soc., Motor Carrier Lawyers Assn., Comml. Law League Am. (gov. 1969-72). Republican. Mason (Shriner), Kiwanian (dir.). Clubs: Mpls. Athletic, Oak Ridge Country. Home: 4370 Brookside Ct Edina MN 55436 Office: 33 S 5th St Minneapolis MN 55402

FEINBERG, WALTER, educator; b. Boston, Aug. 22, 1937; s. Nathan and Adeline (Weisberger) F.; A.B., Boston U., 1960, Ph.D., 1966; m. Eleanor Kemler, June 21, 1964; children—Deborah Lee, Jill Suzanne. Asst. prof. edn. Oakland U., 1965-67; asst. prof. philosophy edn. U. Ill., Urbana, 1967-70, asso. prof. ednl. policy studies, 1970-75, prof. ednl. policy studies, 1975—, prof. Bur. Ednl. Research, 1977—. U. Ill. faculty fellow, 1969; Nat. Inst. Edn. grantee, 1976. Mem. Philosophy Edn. Soc., Am. Ednl. Studies Assn. (pres.-elect 1978), Am. Philosophy Assn. Jewish. Author: Reason and Rhetoric, 1975 (One of Outstanding Books in Edn., Choice mag., 1975); co-editor: Work, Technology and Education, 1975; asso. editor Ednl. Theory, 1969—; corr. editor Theory and Society, 1977; editor Equality and Social Policy, 1978. Home: 1704 Henry St Champaign IL 61820 Office: 377 Education Bldg U Ill Urbana IL 61801

FEINGOLD, EUGENE NEIL, educator; b. Bklyn., Mar. 21, 1931; s. Paul and Rose Elaine (Brook) F.; A.B., Cornell U., 1952; postgrad. Syracuse U., 1952-53; M.A., Princeton, 1958, Ph.D., 1960; m. Marcia Louise Goldberg, Mar. 26, 1960; children—Eleanor, Ruth. Research fellow govtl. studies The Brookings Instn., 1959-60; instr. polit. Sci., U. Mich., Ann Arbor, 1960-63, ast. prof., 1963-66, asso. prof. med. care orgn., 1966-71, prof., 1971—, acting chmn. dept. med. care orgn., 1970, chmn., 1971-77, chmn. program dirs. in health adminstrn. Schs. Pub. Health, 1976-77, asso. dean Rackham Sch. Grad. Studies, 1977—; dir. Mich. Blue Shield, 1974-75, Mich. Blue Cross-Blue Shield, 1975—. Research fellow Nat. Center for Health Services Research and Devel., 1970-71. Served with AUS, 1953-55. Mem. Am. Polit. Sci. Assn., Am. Pub. Health Assn. (governing council 1976—), Am. Civil Liberties Union of Mich. (bd. dirs. 1963—). Author: Medicare: Politics and Policy, 1966. Mem. editorial bd. Medical Care Review, 1968—, Poverty and Human Resources, 1966-71, Jour. Health Politics, Policy and Law, 1976—, Internat. Jour. Health Services, 1974-75. Home: 352 Hilldale Dr Ann Arbor MI 48105

FEINSTEIN, MANLEY BURTON, retailer; b. Mitchell, S.D., Apr. 12, 1927; s. Saul and Jean (Coval) F.; B.S., Northwestern U., 1949; m. Carol Feiman, June 19, 1949; children—Barry A., Marc S., Wendy R. Mgr., Feinstein's of Mitchell, 1949-53; mgr.-owner Feinstein's of Aberdeen, S.D., 1953—; dir. Aberdeen Nat. Bank. Mem. Aberdeen Sch. Bd., 1961-70; mem. S.D., Hwy. Commn., 1971—; mem. S.D. Bd. Transp., 1973—. Past trustee Presentation Coll., Aberdeen; trustee St. Luke's Hosp., Aberdeen. Served with USNR, 1945-46. Recipient Jaycees State Silver Key, 1957. Mem. Aberdeen C. of C. (past v.p.), Tau Delta Phi. Jewish religion. Mason (Shriner), Elk. Home: 1314 N 3d St Aberdeen SD 57401 Office: 305 S Main St Aberdeen SD 57401

FEIRICH, JOHN COTTRILL, lawyer; b. Chgo., Jan. 2, 1933; s. John Kenneth and Mary (Roy) F.; student Northwestern U., 1951-53; J.D., U. Ill., 1956; children—John Charles, Elizabeth Suzanne. Admitted to Ill. bar, 1956, U.S. Supreme Ct. bar, 1962; practiced in Carbondale, 1956—; partner firm Schoen, Mager, Green & Assos., 1977—; spl. asst. atty. gen. State of Ill., 1958-62. Founder, pres. Air Ill., Carbondale, 1970—; pres. So. Ill. Sailing Sch., Carbondale, 1968—. Mem. com. pattern jury instrn. Ill. Supreme Ct., 1966-77. Chmn. Carbondale Pub. Bldg. Commn., 1965-67; mem. com. on sch. problems Carbondale Grade Sch., 1968; mem. Carbondale Community High Sch. Bd. Edn., 1969-75. Chmn. bd. dirs. YMCA, Carbondale, 1958-62; bd. dirs. Carbondale chpt. United Fund, 1959-67. Mem. Am. (nat. dir. 1962-63), Ill. (gov.) bar assns., Am. Judicature Soc. (dir.), Am. Coll. Trial Lawyers, U.S. Yacht Racing Union. Elk, Lion. Club: Crab Orchard Sailing (Carbondale). Author: State Conference on Judicial Selection and Court Administration, 1961. Home and office: 2001 W Main St Carbondale IL 62901

FEIT, JEROME ANTHONY, chemist; b. Chgo., Aug. 4, 1922; s. Aloysius J. and Barbara (Piper) F.; Student Northwestern U., 1942, Purdue U., 1943; B.S., Northwestern U., 1949; m. Genevieve Trella, June 14, 1947; children—Jerome Jeffrey, Antonia Camille, Lawrence Anthony. Cons. chemist, 1950: founded Jerome & Co., cosmetics co., 1959-65, pres., chmn. bd. Jerome Labs., Inc., Chgo., 1965—. Served with USAAF, 1942-46; ETO. Fellow Am. Inst. Chemists, Am. Chem. Soc., ASTM, Smithsonian Instn., Audubon Soc.; mem. Chgo. Perfumery, Soap and Extract Assn. (dir.), Soc. Cosmetic Chemists, Ill. Mfrs. Assn., Proprietary Assn., Chgo. Drug and Chem. Assn. Patentee in field. Office: 95 E Bradrock Dr Des Plaines IL 60018

FEIT, MICHAEL, food co. exec.; b. Tarnopol, Poland, Sept. 8, 1928; s. Henry and Anna (Taube) F.; came to U.S., 1949, naturalized, 1953; B.S. cum laude, N.Y. U., 1955; postgrad. Boston U., 1958; m. Irene Mischel, Mar. 17, 1956; children—Elizabeth, Susan, Mgr. cost accounting Raytheon Co., Waltham, Mass., 1957-59; cons. Price Waterhouse Co., Boston, 1959-64; mgr., mgmt. information services Scott Paper Co., Phila., 1964-68; dir. mgmt. information services Admiral Corp., Chgo., 1968-70; controller Superior Tea & Coffee Co., Chgo., 1971-76; controller, chief fin. officer Ride Corp., Chgo., 1977—. C.P.A., Mass., Pa. Recipient Silver medal Mass. Soc. C.P.A.'s, 1961. Mem. Am. Inst. C.P.A.'s, Inst. Mgmt. Sci. Home: 1691 Berkeley Rd Highland Park IL 60035 Office: 6345 W 65th St Chicago IL 60638

FEJER, PAUL HARALYI, design engr.; b. Gyoma, Hungary, Feb. 27, 1921; s. Lajos Haralyi Fejer and Laura (Varasdi) Persaits F.; B.S., Ludovica Academia, Budapest, Hungary, 1944; m. Maria Wasylchenko, Nov. 16, 1946; children—Paul Haralyi, Alexandra Martha, Douglas Kay. Came to U.S., 1949, naturalized, 1955. Sr. product analyst Chrysler Corp., Highland Park, Mich., 1962-68; sr. design engr. Ford Motor Co., Mt. Clemens, Mich., 1968—. Served to 2d lt. Hungarian Army, 1944-45. Mem. Macomb Electronics Assn. (treas. 1958), Indsl. Math. Soc. (treas. 1970-73), Soc. Automotive Engrs., Soc. Plastic Engrs., Soc. Mfg. Engrs., Soc. Exptl. Stress Analysis. Author: The Measuring Numbers System, 1975. Originator measuring numbers system for measuring continuous magnitudes, dynamic geometry. Home: 23 Lodewyck St Mount Clemens MI 48043 Office: 151 Lafayette St Mount Clemens MI 48043

FELBER, RICHARD JAMES, decorative fabrics co. exec.; b. Cleve., Oct. 12, 1928; s. Tobias L. and Mina (Liebenthal) F.; B.S. in Marketing, U. Ill., 1950; m. Ann Wasserman, Dec. 27, 1953 (div. July 1972); children—Andrew T., Carolyn J., Linda D. Sales rep. S.M. Hexter Co., Cleve., 1950-57, v.p., 1957—. Mem. adminstrv. bd. Goodrich/Sterling Center Settlement House; mem. men's com. Cleve. Playhouse, 1971—. Home: 17100 Van Aken Blvd Shaker Heights OH 44120 Office: 2800 Superior Ave Cleveland OH 44114

FELDER, BRUCE BENJAMIN, title ins. co. exec.; b. Cleve., Sept. 27, 1937; s. Emanual H. and Theresa C. (Benjamin) F.; student John Carroll U., 19S5, Cleve. Marshall Law Sch., 1959; m. Linda G. Steinsapir, June 23, 1963; children—Teri, Traci, Todd. Dep. clk. Ct. of Common Pleas, Cuyahoga County, Ohio, 1958, clk., 1959; founder Legal Messenger Service, Inc., (co. name changed to Record Data Internat., Inc. 1972), Cleve., 1959, pres., treas., 1959—. Mem. Nat. Second Mortgage Lenders Assn., Am. Land Title Assn., Ohio Land Title Assn. Democrat. Jewish. Mason. Home: Winding Creek 3200 Som Center Pepper Pike OH 44124 Office: 725 St Clair Ave NW Cleveland OH 44113

FELDMAN, EDGAR ALLAN, surgeon; b. Chgo., Apr. 16, 1936; s. Irving and Beatrice (Berg) F.; B.S., U. Ill., 1956, M.D., 1960; m. Ina Y. Scheckman, June 21, 1959; children—Robert A., Steven I., Susan L., Laura B. Resident in gen. surgery Brooke Gen. Hosp., Ft. Sam Houston, Tex., 1960-65, chief resident, 1964-65; chief of surgery Dewitt Army Hosp., Ft. Belvoir, Va., 1965-66; chief surgeon, army hosp., Ft. Carson Colo., 1966-68; surgeon 5th Inf. Div., Ft. Carson, Colo., 1968-69; attending surgeon Sherman Hosp., and St. Joseph Hosp., Elgin, Ill., 1969—; cons. surgeon Geneva (Ill.) Community Hosp. Pres. Dist. Bd. Edn. Schaumburg (Ill.), 1974—. Served with M.C., U.S. Army, 1960-69. Diplomate Am. Bd. Surgery. Fellow A.C.S., mem. Kane County (Ill.) Med. Soc. (dir. 1975—). Contbr. articles to surg. jours. Office: 1795 Grandstand Pl Elgin IL 60120

FELDMAN, EGAL, historian, univ. adminstr.; b. N.Y.C., Apr. 9, 1925; s. Morris and Chaya Feldman; B.A., Bklyn. Coll., 1950; M.A., N.Y.U., 1954; Ph.D., U. Pa., 1959; m. Mary Kalman, June 28, 1959; children—Tyla, Auora, Naomi. Asst. prof. history U. Tex. at Arlington, 1960-66; asso. prof. history U. Wis.-Superior, 1966-68, prof., 1968—, chmn. dept. history and philosophy, 1973—, dean Coll. Letters and Scis., 1977—. Named Tchr. of Year, U. Wis., 1969, recipient Inst. Jewish Research award, 1954, Max Levine award, 1975. Jewish. Author: Fit for Men: History of New York's Clothing Trade, 1960. Contbg. author books, contbr. articles to profl. pubis. Home: 2019 Weeks Ave Superior WI 54880 Office: 227 Old Main Superior WI 54881

FELDMAN, EUGENE PIETER ROMAYN, mus. ofcl.; b. Sheboygan, Wis., Sept. 14, 1915; s. Sam and Goldie (Zimmerman) F.; B.A., U. Wis., 1949; postgrad. DePaul U., 1966; Editor, So. Newsletter, Winston-Salem, N.C. and Chgo., 1956-61; instr. Ency. Brit. Acad., Chgo., 1961-63; founder, dir. publs. and research DuSable Mus. African Am. History, Chgo., 1961—, adminstrv. asst. for devel., 1971—. Tchr. black studies Pontiac (Ill.) State Prison, 1969-74; history cons. for hist. project Better Boys Found., 1974. Past mem. bd. dirs., v.p. DuSable Mus. African Am. History. Served with USAAF, 1942-45; PTO. Sears grantee, 1971-75. Author: Introduction to Black History, 1968, Black Power in Old Alabama, 1970. Editor: Figures in Black History, 1970. Home: 1923 N Fremont St Chicago IL 60614 Office: 740 E 56th Pl Chicago IL 60637

FELDMAN, HARRIS JOSEPH, radiologist, educator; b. Balt., Mar. 4, 1942; s. Charles William and Ruth (Emanuel) F.; A.B., Western Md. Coll., 1963; M.D., U. Md., 1967. Intern, Mercy Hosp., Balt., 1967-68; resident in radiology George Washington U. Hosp., Washington, 1968-71; staff radiologist U. Ill. Hosp., Chgo., 1973—; cons. radiologist Langley AFB Hosp., 1972-73; asst. prof. Abraham Lincoln Sch. Medicine, Chgo., 1974—. Served with M.C., USN, 1971-73. Diplomate Am. Bd. Radiology. Mem. AMA, Ill., Chgo. med. socs., Am. Coll. Radiology, Ill., Chgo. radiol. socs., Radiol. Soc. N.Am. Home: 1339 N Dearborn St Chicago IL 60610 Office: 840 S Wood St Chicago IL 60612

FELDMAN, HARRY H., city-county ofcl.; b. Indpls., Oct. 17, 1916; s. Louis and Sarah (Green) F.; B.S., Ind. U., 1939, M.S., 1951, Directorate Degree in park and recreation adminstrn., outdoor edn., 1952; m. Emma Jane West, June 10, 1942; children—Steven, David, Jan, Susan. With Indpls. Parks and Recreation Dept., 1935-42, Indpls. Bd. Edn., 1939-42, Normal Coll., 1941-42; dir. youth activities and community service, nat. hdqrs. Am. Legion, Indpls., 1946-48; dir. community services, parks and recreation Lebanon and Boone County (Ind.), 1948-51; supt. municipal Park and recreation City of Port Huron (Mich.), 1952-54; cons., planning dir. United Community Services, Columbus and Franklin County (Ohio), 1954-68; dir., asso. prof. outdoor edn. center Antioch Coll., Yellow Springs, Ohio, 1968-70; supt. outdoor and environ. edn. Dept. Parks and Recreation, Indpls. and Marion County, 1970—; dir., coordinator Mayor's Garden and Canning Program. Faculty Ohio State U., Columbus, 1954-68, Butler U., 1970—; owner, operator Teays-Valley Ranch, camp for boys and girls, Ashville, Ohio, 1952-72. Exec. sec. Youth Services Council, 1954—; chmn. City Beautification Campaign, Columbus, 1956-60, I Am An American Day, Columbus, 1959; chmn. recreation bond issue and park tax levy campaign, Columbus and Franklin County, 1963; chmn. outdoor edn. com. Dayton-Miami Valley Consortium of Colls. and Univs., 1968-73. Mem. Park and Recreation Commn., Greene County, Ohio, 1968-70. Field dir. Area and Neighborhood Councils Met. Columbus, 1958-62. Served from lt. to capt. AUS, 1942-46. Recipient Meritorious Service award Ohio Park and Recreation Assn., 1963, award Neighborhood and Area Councils, Columbus, 1966, recognition award Marion County Soil and Water Conservation Dist., 1972; Mayor's Outstanding Achievement award, 1977. Mem. Nat. Outdoor Edn. Assn. (dir. 1959-60), Nat. Recreation and Parks Assn. (dist. rep.), Am. Park and Recreation Soc. (dir.), Am. Camping Assn. (dist. chmn. 1964-65), Audubon Soc. (chmn. 1957), Assn. Interpretive Naturalists Mason, Lion. Home: E Ringgold-Northern Rd Rural Route 2 Ashville OH 43103 Office: 6515 De Long Rd Indianapolis IN 46254

FELDMAN, JAMES DENNIS, retail camera exec.; b. Cambridge, Mass., June 18, 1945; s. Walter Sidney and Eve Minnie (Cohen) F.; student U. Ill., 1962-63, Kans. State U., 1963-66, Washburn Law Sch., 1966-67, Emporia U., 1967-69; M.B.A., U. Ill., 1977. Pres., Photographs Unlimited, Topeka, Kans. and Champaign, Ill., 1966—; pres., dir. Consol. Camera Centres, Champaign, 1974—, Freelance ADS, Inc., Champaign, 1975—, Advanced Bus. Electronics, Inc., Champaign, 1977—; dir. Asset Mgmt. Corp., Homewood, Ill., 1975—; lectr. U. Ill. Active United Way. Recipient Outstanding Probation Officer award Shawnee County Juvenile Ct., 1967. Certified photo counselor Parkland Coll. Mem. Photo Mktg. Assn., Nat. Assn. Real Estate Brokers, Aircraft Owners and Pilots Assn., Nat. Assn. Ind. Camera Stores, Nat. Assn. Audio-Visual Dealers, Profl. Photographers Assn., Nat. Assn. Bus. Execs., Campus Mchts. Assn. (dir.), Ill. Pilots Assn. (dir.). Jewish. Office: 520 E Green St Champaign IL 61820

FELDMAN, LEON, govt. ofcl.; b. Chgo., Oct. 5, 1929; s. Isadore and Anna (Superstein) F.; B.S., U. Wis., 1955; M.A., U. Chgo., 1961; m. Valerie Berger, Mar. 25, 1956; 1 dau., Suzanne. Dir. community relations Michael Reese Hosp., Chgo., 1964-65; account exec. Cooper & Golin Inc., Chgo., 1965-67; pub. affairs officer Midwest Office of HEW, Chgo., 1967—. Served with USMC, 1951-53. Mem. Publicity Club Chgo. (dir. 1965-68), Pub. Relations Soc. Am., Chgo. Headline Club (dir. 1966-70). Home: 424 Melrose Chicago IL 60657 Office: 300 S Wacker Dr Chicago IL 60606

FELDMAN, WELDON, refining co. exec.; b. Chgo., Sept. 9, 1933; s. Samuel A. and Pearl (Gordon) F.; student Cornell U. With Grobet File Co. Am., 1954-56; with United Am. Metals, Chgo., 1958—, pres., 1964—. Served with AUS, 1956-58. Club: Covenant of Ill. Home: 200 E Delaware Pl Chicago IL 60611 Office: 2246 W Hubbard St Chicago IL 60612

FELDSTEIN, CHARLES ROBERT, pub. relations counsel; b. Chgo., Nov. 9, 1922; s. Herman and Fannie (Frank) F.; student Northwestern U., 1940-42; A.M., U. Chgo., 1944; postgrad. Harvard, 1945-46; m. Janice Ruth Josephson, Sept. 6, 1948; children—James Frank, Frances Emily, Thomas Mark. Asst. dir. Hillel Founds., Harvard, Radcliffe, Mass. Inst. Tech., 1944-45, dir. Tufts and Simmons Colls., 1945-46; dir. advt. Field's Stores, Inc., N.J., 1946-48; exec. asst. to v.p. U. Chgo., 1948-51, dir. devel., 1951-1953; pres. Charles R. Feldstein & Co., Inc., 1953—; dir. Charles Frank & Co. Mem. vis. com. to Sch. Social Service Adminstrn., U. Chgo. Bd. dirs. Center Psychosocial Studies; trustee Inst. Psychoanalysis, Chgo. Mem. Am. Assn. Fund-Raising Counsel, Pub. Relations Soc. Publicity Club. Jewish (bd. dirs. congregation). Clubs: Standard, Quadrangle, Cliff Dwellers, Harvard of N.Y. Home: 932 Edgemere Ct Evanston IL 60202 Office: 221 N LaSalle St Chicago IL 60601

FELKNER, MYRTLE EMILENE, educator; b. Bremer County, Iowa, Apr. 14, 1925; d. Hans Edward and Florence Christina (Fredericksen) Koefoed; grad. Am. Inst. Bus., 1943; m. Paul Eugene Felkner, Aug. 19, 1945; children—Barbara Clarke, Joan William Edward. Auditor, Iowa Dept. Revenue, 1943-44; legal sec., 1945; certified instr. Christian Labs., United Meth. Ch., 1968—; Christian edn. asst. Faith United Parish, Centerville, Iowa, 1972—; mem. nat. bd. discipleship United Meth. Ch., 1977—; mem. Iowa Conf. Bd. Edn., 1972-76; mem. Dist. Bd. Edn. United Meth. Ch., 1976—; bd. dirs. Rathbun Lake Ministry, 1972-76; mem. care rev. bd. Centerville Care Center, 1976—. Mem. Nat. League Am. Penwomen, Christian Educators Fellowship, PEO. Republican. Author plays, articles, verses, childrens stories, with emphasis on religious edn., 1945—. Home: Rt 3 Centerville IA 52544 Office: 410 Main St N Centerville IA 52544

FELLOWS, JOE FRANK, orthopedic surgeon; b. Ames, Iowa, Nov. 17, 1938; s. Joseph Goode and Marjorie Josephine (Reichenbach) F.; student Iowa State U., 1956-59; M.D., State U. Iowa, 1963; children—Joseph Darrell, Christopher John, Nanci Elisabeth. Intern, Los Angeles County Hosp., Los Angeles, 1963-64, resident in orthopedic surgery, 1966-67; resident in orthopedic surgery Mayo Grad. Sch. Medicine, Rochester, Minn., 1967-71; practice medicine specializing in orthopedic surgery, Des Moines, 1971—; mem. staffs Iowa Luth. Hosp., Mercy Med. Center; mem. teaching staffs Iowa Meth. Med. Center, Broadlawns Gen. Hosp., VA Hosp. Served with M.C., U.S. Army, 1964-66. Mem. Am. Acad. Orthopedic Surgeons, Iowa, Polk County (Iowa) med. socs., AMA, Alpha Omega Alpha. Republican. Methodist. Clubs: Des Moines Golf and Country, Embassy. Office: 1515 Linden Des Moines IA 50312

FELT, ALLEN RUDOLPH, land devel. co. exec.; b. Monroeville, Ind., Mar. 3, 1931; s. Herman C. and Lena L. (Ruble) F.; grad. high sch.; m. Evelyn Jane Summers, Mar. 30, 1952; children—Alice (Mrs. Michael Charron), Jeanine (Mrs. Gregory Erpelding), Ray, Bill, Kristine. Owner, Allen R. Felt Co., land devel., Monroeville, 1954—; salesman Ideal Suburban Homes Inc., Decatur, Ind., 1962—; realtor Ideal Realty, Decatur, 1963—. Served with AUS, 1951-53. Madison Twp. (chmn. 1967-69), Allen County farm burs., United Comml. Travelers, Adams-Jay-Wells County Bd. Realtors. Lutheran. (ch. chmn.). Home: Rural Route 2 Figel Rd Monroeville IN 46773 Office: 522 S 13th St Decatur IN 46733

FELT, MICHAEL GENE, communications exec.; b. Phila., Apr. 17, 1947; s. Cornelius Eugene and Marjorie Elaine (Brenner) F.; B.A. in Broadcasting, Marquette U., Milw., 1969, M.A. in Communications, 1971; m. Anne Irene Toedt, June 6, 1971. With Internat. Harvester Co., 1973—, supr. videotape prodn., Sheridan, Ill., 1974—; media cons. Served to 1st lt. AUS, 1971-73. Mem. Nat. Assn. Ednl. Broadcasters, Internat. Indsl. TV Assn., Am. Soc. Tng. and Devel. Home: 417 Mooseheart Rd Morris IL 60450 Office: Internat Harvester Photographic Center Harvester Rd Sheridan IL 60551

FELTES, JOHN, machinery co. exec.; b. Bitburg, Germany, Oct. 21, 1936; s. Matthias and Katharina (Hettinger) F.; student Bus. Coll., Handels Sch., Bitburg, 1950-52; B.B.A., Industrie and Handelskammer, 1955; m. Barbara Lambrecht, Sept. 19, 1964; children—Eric, Robert. Came to U.S., 1958, naturalized, 1966. With banks, Irrel, Germany, 1953-57, Trier, Germany, 1957-58; with Seiwert, Chgo., 1958-59; asst. office mgr., 1961-65; office mgr. Weiler Engrings., Inc., Elk Grove, Ill., 1966-68, asst. sec., treas., 1968—; sec., treas. A.L.P., Inc., Elk Grove, 1968—. Served with AUS, 1959-61. Home: 731 Tarbat Ct Inverness Barrington PO IL 60010 Office: 2445 E Oakton St Elk Grove IL 60005

FELTMAN, ELVIN CRANE, JR., dentist; b. Shiloh, N.J., July 22, 1925; s. Elvin Crane and Ruth Ann (Watson) F.; B.A., Columbia Union Coll., 1948; postgrad. O. State U., 1958-60; D.D.S., Western Res. U., 1962; m. Lillian May Elliott, Sept. 15, 1946; children—David, John, Donald. Adviser, clergy and youth Ohio Conf. Seventh Day Adventists, Defiance, also Newark, Ohio, 1948-55; salesman, then asst. sales mgr. Fuller Brush Co., Millersburg, Ohio, 1955-58; practice dentistry Cleve., 1964-65, Milan, Ohio, 1965—. Chmn. adv. bd. Dental Assisting Dept. Ehove Vocation Sch., Milan, 1968-71. Pres. Erie County Cancer Soc., 1973; parade chmn. Milan Melon Festival, 1965-70. Bd. dirs. Cancer Soc., 1970-72. Fellow Acad. Gen. Dentistry (Ohio dist. dir.), Internat. Coll. Dentists; mem. Am., Ohio, N. Central Ohio Cleve., Toledo dental assns., Milan C. of C. (bd. dirs. 1964-71, pres. 1967). Home: 34 Bank St Milan OH 44846 Office: Public Square Milan OH 44846

FELTON, MARTHA HARRIET, educator; b. Schenectady, May 22, 1925; d. Clinton Forrest Sparta and Harriet (Lendrum) Felton; A.B., Hope Coll., 1951; M.A., Columbia U., 1951, P.D., 1960; postgrad. Mich. U., 1959; Ph.D. in Reading, Mich. State U., 1978; postgrad. U. Hawaii, 1959, State U. N.Y. at Albany, 1968, Aquinas Coll., 1970, U. Albuquerque, 1971, Western Mich. U., 1975. Tchr., Bd. Edn., Kalamazoo, Mich., 1951-56, Grand Rapids, Mich., 1956—. Adminstr. USWAC Sch., Ft. McClellan, Ala., 1960-61; critic tchr. Western Mich. U., 1971. Leader, Campfire Girls, 1971-72; membership com. PTA, 1972-73; pres., Women's Overseas Service League, 1972; pres. Western Mich. Pistol League, 1971-73; alumni class rep. Hope Coll., 1973-77. Del. county conv. Republican party, 1972. Served to capt. U.S. WAC, 1945-49, 60-62; capt. Res. ret. Decorated Army Commendation medal; recipient Service award Grand Rapids Bd. Edn., 1972, Outstanding Service award Keewano Council Campfire Girls, 1972. Mem. Assn. Childhood Edn. Internat. (life), NEA, (life), Mich. Edn. Assn. (life), Nat. Retired Tchrs. Assn. (life), Res. Officers Assn. (life), DAV (life), Women's Army Corps Assn. (life), Nat. Rifle Assn. (life), Grand Rapids Edn. Assn., Christian Bus. and Profl. Women. Mem. Reformed Ch. (lay missionary to Vietnam 1966; Sunday sch. and catechism tchr. 1971—). Home: 8525 Cedarcrest Dr Jenison MI 49428 Office: 143 Bostwick St NE Grand Rapids MI 49502

FENBURR, HERBERT LESTER, chem. coatings co. exec.; b. N.Y.C., Dec. 11, 1913; s. Joseph Henry and Nancy (Levy) F.; B.Chem. Engring., Ohio State U., 1934, M.S., 1935, Ph.D., 1937; m. Dorothy H. Joseph, Sept. 3, 1936; 1 dau., Margaret Jane. Instr. chem. engring. Ohio State U., Columbus, 1935-37; with Hanna Chem. Coatings Co., Columbus, 1937—, chief engr., 1960—; pres. Reed-O-Matic Inc., Columbus, 1957—, also dir. Capt. indsl. div. Community Chest, 1950-56; active Charity Newsies of Columbus, 1950—. Named Distinguished Alumnus, Ohio State U. Coll. Engring., 1967. Mem. Fedn. Socs. for Coating Tech. (pres. 1968; George Baugh Heckel award 1976), Am. Chem. Soc., Paint Research Inst. (pres. 1969-73), Am. Inst. Chemists, Am. Inst. Chem. Engrs., A.A.A.S., N.Y. Acad. Sci., Sigma Xi, Tau Beta Pi, Phi Lambda Upsilon. Jewish religion (past dir. temple). Mason. Clubs: Cincinnati. Winding Hollow Country. Contbr. articles to profl. jours. Patentee in field. Home: 2742 Bryden Rd Columbus OH 43209 Office: 1313 Windsor Ave Columbus OH 43216

FENDER, DOUGLAS HOWARD, assn. exec.; b. Julesburg, Colo., June 18, 1945; s. Lawrence Alton and Ella Lanora (Reed) F.; A.A., N.E. Jr. Coll., Sterling, Colo., 1965; B.S., U. Colo., 1967, M.A., 1970; m. Lynn Homewood, Apr. 26, 1969; children—Erin, Paige. Grad. asst. U. Colo., Boulder, 1969-70; sr. journalism instr. Washburn U., Topeka, Kans., 1970-73; dir. pub. relations Golf Course Supts. Assn. Am., Lawrence, Kans., 1973-76, dir. communications, 1976—. Served with U.S. Army, 1967-69. Recipient 1st place award excellence Ad Club Topeka, 1974; award of Recognition, Consol. Paper Co., 1974. Mem. Golf Writers Assn. Am., Soc. Nat. Assn. Publs., Pub. Relations Soc. Am. Home: 2313 Westchester Rd Lawrence KS 66044 Office: 1617 St Andrews Dr Lawrence KS 66044

FENELON, WILLIAM JOHN, supt. schs.; b. Fond du Lac, Wis., Feb. 21, 1920; s. Edward Cogan and Loretta Marie (Griffin) F.; B.A., Wis. State U., 1950; M.A., Northwestern U., 1951, Ph.D., 1958; m. Anne Nummerdor, Aug. 26, 1946. Tchr. English, Evanston (Ill.) Pub. Schs., 1950-51; prin. Port Washington (Wis.) Pub. Schs., 1951-56; dir. instrn. Whitefish Bay (Wis.) Schs., 1956-61; asso. prof. philosophy, adminstrn. U. Wis., Milw., 1961-62; prof. philosophy, adminstrn.; dean Sch. Edn., De Paul U., Chgo., 1962-66; supt. Deerfield (Ill.) Pub. Schs., 1966—. Tech. adviser edn. Joint Youth Devel. Com., Chgo., 1963-64; cons. Eastern Mich. U., 1972-73; vis. prof. child and adolescent devel. U. Wis., Parkside, 1967—; vis. prof. Marquette U., summers 1954, 56, Mich. State U., summer 1956; condr. surveys elementary and secondary schs. Brit. Isles, 1967-68; cons. to state dept. pub. instrn. on evaluations, Ill., 1974. Mem. exec. bd. No. Suburban Spl. Edn. Dist., Highland Park, Ill., 1966—. Mem. Am., Ill. assns. sch. adminstrs., Phi Delta Kappa. Club: Rotary. Home: 745 Carlisle Ave Deerfield IL 60015 Office: Adminstrv Center 517 Deerfield Rd Deerfield IL 60015

FENG, TSE-YUN, engr., educator; b. Hangchow, China, Feb. 6, 1928; s. Shih-ching and Lin Shao; B.S., Nat. Taiwan U., 1950; M.S., Okla. State U., 1957; Ph.D., U. Mich., 1967. m. Elaine Hu, June 12, 1965; children—Wu-chun, Wu-chi, Wu-chang. Asst. engr. Tawian Power Co., 1950-56; sr. designer Ebasco Services, N.Y.C., 1957-60; teaching fellow U. Mich., 1962-65, research asst., 1965-66, asst. research engr., 1966, research asso., 1967; asst. prof. elec. and computer engring. Syracuse U., 1967-71, asso. prof., 1971-75; prof. elec. and computer engring. Wayne State U., 1975—; cons. Transidyne Gen., Syracuse U., Pattern Analysis and Recognition Corp.; chmn. Internat. Conf. on Parallel Processing, 1975—; dir. N.E. Consortium for Engring. Edn., 1976—; cons. USAF. Mem. IEEE (chmn. computer soc. standards com. 1974—, mem. computer soc. govering bd. 1977—, computer soc. distinguished visitor 1973—), Assn. Computing Machinery, Am. Nat. Standards Inst. (info. systems standards mgmt. bd. 1974—), Sagamore Computer Conf. (chmn., editor proc. 1972-75), Phi Kappa Phi, Tau Beta Pi, Eta Kappa Nu, Sigma Xi, Phi Tau Phi, Hon. Order of Ky. Cols. Contbr. articles to Jour. Franklin Inst., IEEE Transactions on Computers, others. Patentee in field. Home: 4425 Hardwoods Dr West Bloomfield MI 48033 Office: Dept Elec and Computer Engineering Wayne State U Detroit MI 48202

FENNEBERG, HARRY GUSTAVE, theatre exec.; b. Toledo, Aug. 10, 1913; s. Gustave George and Caroline Maud (Wallace) F.; A.B. magna cum laude, U. Toledo, 1934. Adminstrv. asst. research and devel. center Aberdeen (Md.) Proving Ground, 1942-46; exec. sec. Toledo Repertoire Theatre, 1946—. Mem. ANTA, Phi Kappa Phi. Democrat. Unitarian. Home: 302 E 2d St Perrysburg OH 43551 Office: 16 10th St Toledo OH 43624

FENNER, HARWOOD HUSS, roofing and sheet metal co. exec.; b. Rochester, N.Y., Oct. 10, 1933; s. Harwood Clyde and Dorthea Mae (Huss) F.; student Mich. State U., 1952-54; m. Claudette Jean Ballard, Jan. 23, 1960; children—Debra Lynn, Susan Gail, Michael Wayne, Pamela Jean. Accountant, Fabricated Steel Co., South Bend, Ind., 1958-61; mgr. Gen. Roofing & Insulation Co., South Bend, 1961-68; pres., owner Fenner Roofing and Sheet Metal Inc., Sodus, Mich., 1968—. Served with AUS, 1954-57. Mem. South Bend Joint Apprenticeship Roofing Com. (pres.), Associated Roofing Contractors Western Mich. (sec.-treas.), Nat., Mich. roofing contractors assns., Midwest, Mich. roofing assns., Asso. Roofing Contractors Western Mich., Sheet Metal Assn. Michigan. Presbyterian. Club: Rotary. Home: 3030 Dozer Dr St Joseph MI 49085 Office: 3834 Pipestone Rd Sodus MI 49126

FENNESY, THOMAS VINCENT, engr.; b. Kansas City, Mo., Aug. 10, 1931; s. John J. and Charlotte (Maloney) F.; B.S., U. Kans., 1959; m. Marilyn T. (Carrigan) F., Aug. 24, 1957; children—Vincent, Gerard, Jack, Nancy. Licensed profl. engr. Mo., Kans., Tex., Nebr., Colo., Mich., Iowa. Data process engr. McDonnell Aircraft Co., 1959-60; elec. design engr. Lutz & May, Kansas City, Mo., 1960-62; design engr. Lutz, Daily & Brain, Overland Park, Kans., 1962-65, elec. engr., 1965-67, mgr. dept. elec. engring., 1967—. Mem. IEEE, Mo. Soc. Profl. Engrs., Leawood S. Country Club. Home: 909 Tam-o-Shanter St Kansas City MO 64145 Office: 6400 Glenwood St Shawnee Mission KS 66202

FENSTERMANN, DUANE WELLINGTON, librarian; b. Greeley, Iowa, Jan. 25, 1939; s. Wesley Wellington and Berdice Estella (Schwichtenberg) F.; student U. Dubuque, 1956-58; B.A., Morningside Coll., 1961; M.Div., Duke U., 1964; M.S. in L.S., U. N.C., 1968; m. Marlene Kay Fiet, Aug. 25, 1961; 1 son, Mark Wellington. Circulation asst. Med. Center Library, Duke U., Durham, N.C., 1964-65; curator asst. Josiah C. Trent collection, 1965; acquisitions librarian Luther Coll., Decorah, Iowa, 1966— head, tech. services, 1969—. Editor, dir. Northeast Iowa Union List of Serials, 1967—; adviser on title III Interlibrary Coop. Adv. Council, Iowa State Traveling Library, 1970. Mem. ALA (life mem.), Iowa Hist. Materials Preservation Soc. (exec. council 1976—), Iowa Pvt. Acad. Libraries Assn. (steering com. 1977—), Iowa Library Assn., Midwest Archives Conf., Winneshiek County Hist. Soc. Office: Luther Coll Decorah IA 52101

FENTON, JEAN GILTNER, architect; b. Welch, W.Va., Nov. 19, 1921; d. James Bristow and Marian Orna Eloise V. (Bornemann) Giltner; student Wheaton Coll., Norton, Mass., 1940, Boston U., 1941-43; Wyndham Coll., Boston, 1944; B.Arch., Western Res. U., 1949; m. D.G. Fenton, 1943 (dec. 1944); m. 2d, Warren Edward Finkel, Jan. 25, 1954 (div. 1974). Estimator, Roediger Constrn. Co., Cleve., 1947-49; architect Outcalt-Guenther Architects, Cleve., 1949-50, 54; estimator F.E. Young Constrn. Co., San Diego, 1950-51; designer, job coordinator George A. Fuller, San Diego, 1951-52; architect San Diego Unified Sch. Dist., 1952-53; partner Finkel & Finkel, Architects, Lorain, Ohio, 1954-74; prin. Jean Giltner Fenton, Lorain, 1974—; faculty, Lorain County Community Coll., 1975—; mem. adv. bd. WUAB-TV. Schweinfurth scholar, 1949. Mem. AIA, Architects Soc. Ohio. Important works include Lorain Community Hosp., Murray Ridge Sch., Lorain City Hall; (with others) Lorain County Community Coll., addition to Bettcher Industries, Birmingham, Ohio, 1976, Golden Acres-Lorain County Home, addition to YMCA, residences and additions to residences. Home: 2316 Harborview Blvd Lorain OH 44052

FENTON, RUSSELL SANBERG, mfrs. rep.; b. Pitts., June 18, 1917; s. Patrick Henry and Mary Wilhelmina (Yokee) F.; grad. high sch.; m. Eleanor Hope Forbes, Sept. 15, 1941; children—Judith Lynn (Mrs. George Micklos Gomory), Karen Hope, Priscilla Beth (Mrs. James John Siwek). Molder, Universal Steel Co., 1935-37; owner, operator Fenton Radio Co., Bridgeville, Pa., 1937-41; parts mgr. Motor-Radio Distbg. Co., Pitts., 1941-42; quality control mgr. Gen. Electric Co., Bridgeport, Conn., 1942-45, product mgr., sales mgr. component parts div., Syracuse, N.Y., 1945-50, v.p., gen. mgr., dir. Permoflux Corp., Chgo., 1950-56; partner Gianaras Sales Co., Chgo., 1956—; v.p. Transformer Mfrs., Inc., Chgo., 1956—; founder, pres. Fenton Products Co., Chgo., 1976—; dir. Superior Valve & Fitting Co., Pitts. Chmn. Northfield Community League, 1953-56; mem. Northfield Safety Commn., 1959-60, Northfield Adv. Commn., 1965-68, Human Relations Commn., 1966-70; sr. warden St. James The Less, Northfield, Ill., 1972. Mem. Electronic Industries Assn. (chmn. speaker div., mem. exec. bd. parts div.), Radio Old Timers (life). Mason (Shriner). Club: Glenbrook Shrine (dir., past pres.) (Glenview). Patentee in field. Home: 308 Eaton St Northfield IL 60093 Office: 7051 W Wilson St Chicago IL 60656

FENTON, WILLIAM CONNER, music adminstr.; b. Dravosburg, Pa., Dec. 19, 1927; s. Harold Conner and Martha Stevenson F.; B.Mus., Cin. Conservatory Music, 1950; B.S., U. Cin., 1951, Ed.D., 1967; M.Ed., Miami U., Oxford, O., 1956; m. Virginia Rawnsley, Aug. 23, 1951; children—William, Thomas, David, Joan, Julie, Amy. Supr. music Indian Hill Schs., Cin., 1950-61; dean students Ohio Coll. Applied Sci., Cin., 1961-62; dean boys, counselor Oak Hills High Sch., Cin., 1962-65; chmn. dept. music Wright State U., Dayton, 1965—; ch. musician, guest choral condr., clinician, cons., adjudicator; condr. concert tours Wright State U. Chamber Singers, Spain and Portugal, 1973, Germany and Austria, 1974. Active Boy Scouts Am. Bd. dirs. Dayton Philharmonic Orch.; trustee Dayton Ballet Co., pres., 1972. Served with AUS, 1951-53. Teaching fellow U. Cin., 1959-61. Mem. Am. Choral Dirs. Assn., Phi Mu Alpha Sinfonia, Phi Delta Kappa. Recipient hon. citizenship award Valencia, Spain, 1973; named hon. scholar U. Granada, Spain, 1973. Episcopalian (So. Ohio Diocesan Music Commn.). Contbr. chpt. to Ways To Teach about Religion in the Public Schools, 1977. Home: 120 Woodfield Pl Dayton OH 45459

FENWICK, DONALD DEAN, psychologist, educator; b. Grant, Nebr., Apr. 4, 1938; s. Earl William and Fanchon Phyllis (Sexson) F.; B.A., Nebr. State Coll., 1962; M.A., U. Nebr., 1965, Ed.D., 1967; m. Carol Sue Roberts, June 30, 1973. Sch. psychologist Dept. of Def. Overseas Dependents Schs., Pacific Area, Japan, 1967-69; learning disabilities cons., sch. psychologist Dept. Def., European Area, Eng. and Germany, 1969-73; sch. psychologist, coordinator pupil personnel services Mediterranean dist. U.S. Dependents Ednl.

System, European Area, Athens, Greece, 1973-75, Naples, Italy, 1975-76; psychologist, coordinator pupil personnel services dist. 1, Dept. Def. Overseas Dependent Schs., 1976—. Coordinator child study groups and family counseling services Dept. Def., Heidelberg, Germany, 1971-73. Home: 628 Washington Ave Grant NE 69140 Office: Zama High Sch US Army Garrison Honshu APO San Francisco CA 96343

FENYES, IMRE, pathologist, lab. adminstr., educator; b. Budapest, Hungary, Nov. 21, 1926; s. Lajos and Julia (Englerth) F.; came to U.S., 1957, naturalized, 1962; M.D., U. Budapest, 1951; m. Jacqueline M. Walko, Aug. 19, 1962; 1 son, Richard M. Staff pathologist Michael Reese Hosp., Chgo., 1965-67; asso. dir. labs. and pathology dept. Edgewater Hosp., Chgo., 1968—; asst. prof. pathology Chgo. Med. Sch., 1976—. Fellow Coll. Am. Pathologists; mem. AMA (Continuing Med. Edn. award 1976), Chgo. Path. Soc. Roman Catholic. Contbr. articles on pathology to med. jours. Home: 2025 Sherman Ave Evanston IL 60201

FERGUSON, ARDALE WESLEY, indsl. supply exec.; b. Cedar Springs, Mich., Aug. 6, 1908; s. George Ardale and Alice Lucina (Andrus) F.; student pub. schs.; m. Hazel Frances Lokker, Oct. 28, 1931; children—Constance Ann (Mrs. Donald F. Klaasen), Mary Alice (Mrs. Robert A. Ritsema), Judy Kaye (Mrs. Charles Ruffino); m. 2d., G. Dolores Laker, Aug. 1976. Sales exec. John Deere Plow Co., Lansing, Mich., 1935-50; exec.-treas., mgr. Ferguson Welding Supply Co., Benton Harbor, Mich., 1950-76; sec.-treas. Lape Steel Stores, Inc., Benton Harbor, 1976—; dir. Modern Light Metals, Inc. Mem. Benton Twp. Bd. Rev., 1963, Mich. Econ. Advancement Council, 1963-64; chmn. Mich. Hwy. Commn., 1964-68; pres. Twin Cities Community Chest, 1956. Treas. Mich. Republican Central Com., 1957-61; del. to Rep. Nat. Conv., 1960. Recipient award of spl. merit, Twin Cities Community Chest, 1956. Mem. Welding Supply Assn. Methodist. Clubs: St. Joseph-Benton Harbor Rotary (pres. 1960), Berrien Hills Country, Mountain Shadows Country, Peninsular. Office: Benton Harbor MI 49022

FERGUSON, DEE ARNOLD, bus. exec.; b. Hermitage, Mo., Oct. 31, 1906; s. George W. and Tennie (Low) F.; A.A., S.W. Bapt. Coll., 1927; A.B., S.W. Mo. State Coll., 1930; M.Ed., U. Mo., 1941, postgrad., 1942-51; m. Beulah Leona Gillman, May 11, 1930; children—Betty Elaine (Mrs. Richard L. Wilson), John Dee, Linda Ann (Mrs. Dale Vest). Prin., Job High Sch., Pittsburg, Mo., 1928, Stella (Mo.) High Sch., 1929-31; prin. Noel (Mo.) High Sch., 1931-36, supt., 1936-43; supt. Crane (Mo.) Consolidated Sch., 1943-48, Cabool (Mo.) Consol. Sch., 1948-63. Reorganized Sch. R-1, Tarkio, Mo., 1963-72; regional mgr. F.E. Compton Co., 1972-73; sales master field trainer Ency. Brit., 1973-75; instr. grad. div. Drury Coll., summer 1962. Chmn. exec. com. Bi-State Coop. Project in Sci. Edn., 1967-70. Pres. Community Summer Recreation Assn., Crane, Mo., 1946-48; pres., sec. Cabool Civic Park 1958-62. Recipient Spl. Service Award, Tarkio Community Betterment, 1969, hon. certificate Mo. State Bd. and Commr. Edn., 1975; named Man of Year, Cabool, 1960. Mem. Am., Mo. assns. sch. adminstrs., Phi Delta Kappa, Phi Gamma Mu. Kiwanian, Rotarian. Co-author edn. continuous progress program. Contbr. articles in field to profl. jours. Home: 1540 S Delaware Springfield MO 65804

FERGUSON, FRANCIS EUGENE, ins. co. exec.; b. Batavia, N.Y., Feb. 4, 1921; s. Harold M. and Florence (Munger) F.; student Cornell U., 1938-39; B.S., Mich. State U., 1947; m. Patricia J. Reddy, Aug. 11, 1945; children—Susan Lee, Patricia Ann. Asst. sec.-treas. Fed. Land Bank Assn., Lansing, Mich., 1947-48; appraiser Fed. Land Bank, St. Paul, 1948-50; specialist agrl. econs. Mich. State U. Extension, 1951; with Northwestern Mut. Life Ins. Co., Milw., 1951—, specialist, 1951-52, asst. mgr. farm loans, 1952-56, mgr. farm loans, 1956-62, gen. mgr. mortgage loans, 1962-63, v.p. mortgage loans, 1963-67, trustee, pres., 1967—; dir. Cutler-Hammer, Inc., Ralston Purina Co., Wis. Gas Co., Oscar Mayer & Co., Inc., Rexnord, Inc., Green Bay Packaging Inc. Gen. campaign chmn. United Fund, 1965; corp. mem. Milw. Children's Hosp.; bd. dirs. Marquette U., Columbia Hosp.; bd. dirs. Com. for Econ. Devel., Greater Milw. Com.; chmn. Milw. Devel. Group; pres. Milw. Redevel. Corp. Served to capt. USAAF, 1942-45. Decorated Purple Heart. Republican. Methodist. Clubs: Milwaukee, University, Milwaukee Country. Home: 1115 W Green Tree Rd Milwaukee WI 53217 Office: 720 E Wisconsin Ave Milwaukee WI 53202

FERGUSON, HARRY, engring. scientist; b. Dayton, Ohio, May 1, 1914; s. Robert and Isabella (Gamble) F.; B.S., Boston U., 1939; A.M., Harvard U., 1949; Ph.D., U. Pitts., 1958; m. Helen B. Baker, July 7, 1941. Mem. faculty Ohio U., Northeastern U., Tufts U., 1939-50; applied mathematician Wright-Patterson AFB, 1950-56, aero. research engr., 1956-59; asso. prof. math. U. Cin., 1959-66, prof. engring. scis., 1966—; v.p., owner Ferguson Sales, Inc., Alpha, Ohio. Mem. Am. Math. Soc., Math. Assn. Am., Soc. Indsl. and Applied Math., Soc. Natural Philosophy, Am. Soc. Engring. Edn., Alpha Tau Omega. Methodist. Clubs: Harvard (Dayton), Masons, Shriners. Home: 3224 Fairway Dr Dayton OH 45409 Office: Dept of Engineering Science U Cincinnati Cincinnati OH 45221

FERGUSON, HUGH EDWARD, mfg. co. exec.; b. Chgo., May 25, 1932; s. Hugh Edward and Lydia Grace (Loar) F.; student U. Ill., 1953-54, Ill. Benedictine Coll., 1954-55; B.S. in Math., Ill. Inst. Tech., 1965; m. Suzanne Carol McArdle, Nov. 19, 1955; children—Kathleen M., Michael D., Julie Ann, Mary Beth, Corinne C., Susan D., Jeffrey J., Kevin P. Statis. analyst White Cap Co., Chgo., 1956-58; quality control engr. White Cap div. Continental Group, Inc., Chgo., 1958-60, quality control supr., 1960-68, quality control mgr., 1968—. Served with inf. U.S. Army, 1952-54; Korea. Mem. Am. Mgmt. Assn., Am. Soc. Quality Control, Fedn. Socs. Coatings Tech. Republican. Roman Catholic. Home: 832 Linden St Elmhurst IL 60126 Office: 1819 N Major St Chicago IL 60639

FERGUSON, JAMES A., surgeon; b. Grand Rapids, Mich., Aug. 22, 1915; s. Ward Smith and Ethel Ann (Gray) F.; M.D., U. Mich., 1939; m. Margaret Alice Bevan, June 25, 1940; children—Bevany (Mrs. William Farmer), Margaret (Mrs. Nickolas Booras), James A. II. Intern St. Joseph's Hosp., Lexington, Ky., 1939-40; resident Multnomah County Hosp., Portland, Oreg., 1940-41, U. Mich., 1945-48; practice medicine specializing in rectal and colon surgery, Grand Rapids; mem. staff Ferguson Droste Ferguson Hosp., St. Mary's Hosp., Blodgett Hosp., Butterworth Hosp.; sr. cons. Ferguson Clinic, Grand Rapids. Chmn. bd. dirs. Ferguson Droste Ferguson Hosp. Served with USAAF, 1942-45. Diplomate Am. Bd. Surgery (pres.), Am. Bd. Colon and Rectal Surgery. Fellow A.C.S., Am. Soc. Colon and Rectal Surgeons, Frederick A. Coller Surg. Soc., Royal Soc. Medicine (hon.). Mem. Kent County, Mich. med. socs., A.M.A. Lion, Mason (Shriner). Contbr. articles to profl. jours. Home: 30 College Ave SE Grand Rapids MI 49503 Office: 72 Sheldon Ave SE Grand Rapids MI 49503

FERGUSON, JOHN RICHARD, publishing co. exec.; b. Columbus, Ohio, Oct. 23, 1937; s. Charles A. and A. Mildred (Weate) F.; A.A., Graceland Coll., 1957, B.L.S., 1973; student Harbor Coll., 1957, Calif. State Coll., 1965, Rockhurst Coll., 1970-71; m. Carole Mae Sturtevant, Aug. 16, 1957; children—Steven Paul, Connie Marie. Mgr. retail depts. Sears Roebuck and Co., Riverside, Calif., 1959-63, personnel mgr., 1964-66; ordained to ministry Reorganized Ch. of Jesus Christ of Latter-day Saints, 1955; minister Long Beach (Calif.) Ch., 1963-64; dist. pres. Reorganized Ch. of Jesus Christ of Latter Day Saints, Los Angeles, 1966-68; asst. mgr. Herald Pub. House, Independence, Mo., 1968-69, mgr., 1969—; pres. Silver Fox Ltd., realty; dir. Standard State Bank. Pres. Independence Bd. Edn., 1970-76. Bd. dirs. Health Missions Internat., Buckhorn Camp., Met. Kansas City chpt. Leukemia Soc.; vol. parole and probation officer. Mem. Protestant Church-Owned Publs. Assn. (dir. 1970—). Lion (charter pres. Independence 1970). Contbr. articles to religious publs. Home: 14925 33 St Independence MO 64055 Mailing address: 3225 S Noland Rd PO Drawer HH Independence MO 64055

FERGUSON, RICHARD, accountant; b. Mansfield, Ohio, Nov. 2, 1946; s. Walter and Margaret Irene (McDonald) F.; B.B.A., Widener Coll., 1968; m. Dorothy Agnes Cocola, Oct. 19, 1968; children—Christina Maria, Andrea Maria. Accountant Ernst & Ernst Co., Columbus, Ohio, 1968-69, 71-73; div. controller Worthington Industries, Columbus, 1973-77, corp. controller, 1977—. Adviser Jr. Achievement, Columbus, 1973—. Served with U.S. Army, 1969-71. Decorated Silver Star, Bronze Star, Air medal; C.P.A., Ohio. Mem. Nat. Assn. of Accountants, Ohio Soc. of C.P.A.'s, Am. Inst. of C.P.A.'s. Roman Catholic. Home: 6649 Merwin Rd Worthington OH 43085 Office: 1205 Dearborn St Columbus OH 43085

FERGUSON, RICHARD OLIVER, editor; b. Ironton, Mo., Jan. 6, 1941; s. Oliver Baker and Virginia Alice (Ryan) F.; B.J., U. Mo., 1963; m. Emily R. Brennecke, Aug. 17, 1966; children—Kathryn Ryan, Richard. Editor, The Democrat-News, Fredericktown, Mo., 1963—, pub., 1975—; v.p. Mineral Area Pubs., Inc., Farmington, Mo., 1968—; dir. New Era Bank, Fredericktown, 1975—. Served with U.S. Army, 1965-70. Mem. Fredericktown Jaycees (dir.), Fredericktown C. of C. (pres. 1971-72). Democrat. Methodist. Clubs: Rotary (pres. 1975-76), Elks, Masons, Shriners. Home: 10 Head Dr Fredericktown MO 63645 Office: 110 N Mine La Motte Fredericktown MO 63645

FERGUSON, ROBERT WILLIAM, telephone co. exec.; b. Newark, Feb. 1, 1923; s. Elbert W. and Henriette (Schaefer) F.; B.S., Rutgers U., 1947; postgrad. indsl. relations Princeton U., 1952; postgrad. Inst. Humanistic Studies for Execs., U. Pa., 1956; m. Jeanne Kathleen Schroth, Apr. 22, 1950; children—Robert William, John William, Thomas William, Bruce William, Jeanne Marie, Elizabeth Marie, Emily Marie, Kathleen Marie, Frank William, Christine Marie. With N.J. Bell Telephone Co., 1948-50, 50-55; with Bell Telephone Co. Pa., 1955, gen. traffic engr., 1957-59, div. plant supt., 1959-60, gen. comml. mgr., 1960-64, gen. ops. mgr., Pitts., 1964-66, v.p. staff, 1966-67, v.p., gen. mgr. Eastern area, Phila., 1967-68, also v.p., gen. mgr. Diamond State Telephone Co. (Del.), 1967-68; engr. Am. Tel. & Tel. Co., 1955-57, asst. v.p. ops., N.Y.C., 1968-73; v.p. ops. Wis. Telephone Co., Milw., 1973-76; v.p. ops. Southwestern Bell Telephone Co., St. Louis, 1976—, also dir., mem. exec. com.; dir. Mercantile Bancorp., Inc., St. Louis, Mercantile Trust Co., St. Louis, Marine Corp., Milw. Vice chmn. suburban cos., bus. and industry div. United Fund, 1969; chmn. orgn. and extension Gen. Wayne dist., Valley Forge council Boy Scouts Am., troop dir., Newton Square, Pa.; bd. dirs. Ams. Competitive Enterprise System, Delaware Valley Council, Family and Children's Service, Negro Emergency Ednl. Fund, Pa. Council Crime and Delinquency; trustee St. Elizabeth Coll. Served with AUS, World War II; PTO. Recipient Meritorious Service award Bell System; named Businessman of Day. Mem. Pitts. C. of C. (dir.). Rotarian (v.p.). Clubs: Aronimink Golf (Newtown Square); Noonday, Media, Mo. Athletic (St. Louis); Seaview Country (Absecon, N.J.); Canoe Brook Country (Summit, N.J.). Home: #3 Barclay Woods Ladue MO 63124 Office: 1010 Pine St St Louis MO 63101

FERKEL, LOUIS ROBERT, dentist; b. Chgo., Sept. 15, 1915; s. Meyer and Sarah (Berkman) F.; student Lewis Inst., 1937-39; B.S., U. Ill., 1940, D.D.S., 1943; m. Eve Rebecca Borick, July 25, 1943; children—Donna (Mrs. Lawrence Krause), Richard. Practice dentistry, Rockford, Ill., 1945—; mem. staff Swedish Am. Hosp. Examining dentist Rockford Pub. Sch. Systems; participating dentist Rock Valley Coll. Dental Assts. Program. Served with USNR, USAAF. Fellow Royal Soc. Health; mem. Nat. Bd. Am. Dental Assn., Ill. Dental Assn., Winnebago County, Chgo. dental assns., Alpha Omega. Mason (Shriner). Home: 1102 Nassau Pkwy Rockford IL 61107 Office: 115 7th St Rockford IL 61104

FERNBERG, SHIRLEY CARLOTTA WEISSMAN (MRS. LOUIS PROCTOR FERNBERG JR.), counselor, cooking sch. adminstr., mental health adminstr.; b. Cleve., Feb. 15, 1922; d. Joseph and Kate (Randell) Weissman; B.S., Ohio State U., 1944; occupational therapy diploma Phila. Sch. Occupational Therapy, 1945; M.A., Case Western Res. U., 1968, certificate in Bus. Adminstrn., 1976; postgrad. N.Y. U., 1972; certificate Le Cordon Bleu, Paris, France, 1966; diploma Culinary Inst. Am., 1968; primary certificate Inst. Advanced Study in Rational Psychotherapy, 1977; m. Louis Proctor Fernberg, Jr., Feb. 29, 1948; children—Michael Joseph, Kurt Alan, Laurence Seth. Staff occupational therapist Kingsbridge VA Hosp., Bronx, N.Y., 1945-46; asst. chief, acting chief occupational therapy dept. Crile VA Hosp., Parma, Ohio, 1946-48; supr. occupational therapy Vocational Guidance Rehab. Services, Cleve., 1965; instr. foods Cuyahoga Community Coll., Cleve., 1966-68; owner La Cuisinique Sch. Cookery, Cleve., 1968—; pub. relations instr. Copco Sch. Creative Cooking, Copco, Inc., N.Y.C., 1968—; mental health adminstr. Warrensville Center for Retarded, 1975-76; chief occupational therapy dept. Green Cross Gen. Hosp., Cuyahoga Falls, Ohio, 1976-78; pvt. practice counseling, dir. Total Living Concept, Shaker Heights, Ohio, 1977—; occupational therapy cons. Belmore Nursing Home, East Cleveland, Ohio, 1970-73, Western Res. Psychiat. Habilitation Center, Northfield, Ohio, 1975-77, Eliza Jennings, Cleve., 1976-77, Richland Neuropsychiat. Hosp., Mansfield, Ohio, 1976—. Publicity chmn. Cub Scouts, Shaker Heights (Ohio) Boy Scouts Am., 1957-68, P.T.A., 1962-64; mem. benefit planning com., gourmet adviser Shaker Lakes Regional Nature Center, 1970—. Mem. World Fedn. Occupational Therapists, Am., Ohio occupational therapy assns., Sommelier Soc. Am., Am. Fedn. Radio and TV Artists, Le Confrerie de la Chaine des Rotisseurs, Am., Les Amis du Vin, Les Amis de Chartreuse, Phi Delta Gamma. Clubs: Garden Clubs Ohio (life mem. Cleve.); Four Seasons Garden (pres. Shaker Heights 1963-65). Author: (with others) The Party in the Park Cookbook; editor: Phancy Fixin's and Something Special, specialty foods newsletters; also radio scripts on food specialties. Home: 20696 S Woodland Rd Shaker Heights OH 44122

FERNQUIST, CYRIL L., elec. products co. exec.; b. Englevale, N.D., Aug. 6, 1921; s. Charles and Laura (Nygard) F.; B.E.E., U. Minn., 1953; m. Olive M. Abrahamson, Oct. 10, 1946; children—Paul, Mary. Prodn. engr. Univac div. Sperry Rand Co., St. Paul, 1953-58; v.p. engring. Tec, Inc., Eden Prairie, Minn., 1958-72, dir., 1965-72; pres. Data Panel Inc., Edina, Minn., 1972—. Served with AUS, 1941-45. Home: 163 Spring Valley Dr Minneapolis MN 55420 Office: 7313 S Washington Ave Edina MN 55435

FERRARA, RICHARD JOHN, physician, dermatologist; b. Morgantown, W.Va., Aug. 7, 1925; s. Emil and Filomena (Purificato) F.; A.B., W.Va. U., 1946, B.S., 1948; B. Medicine, Northwestern U., 1950, M.D., 1951; M.S., Wayne State U., 1958; m. Joan Elaine Stefani, June 30, 1951; children—Andrea, Virginia, Judith, Linda, Richard John. Intern, Harper Hosp., Detroit, 1950-51, resident in dermatology, 1951-52; resident in dermatology Receiving Hosp., Dermatology, Detroit, 1952-55; individual practice dermatology, Grosse Pointe Woods, Mich., 1958—; clin. instr., also asso. prof. dermatology Wayne State U., Detroit, 1955—. Served to capt., M.C., U.S. Army, 1956-58. Mem. Wayne County, Macomb County, Mich. med. socs., Detroit, Noah Worcester dermatol. socs., Am. Acad. Dermatology, Am. Cutaneous Surgery, Phi Chi. Roman Catholic. Club: Lochmoor. Contb. articles to profl. publs. Home: 1035 Berkshire St Grosse Pointe Park MI 48230 Office: 20045 Mack Ave Grosse Pointe Woods MI 48236

FERRARO, EUGENE, filmmaker; b. Framingham, Mass., July 25, 1946; s. Anthony F. and Dora M. (Leverone) F.; B.A., Bowdoin Coll., 1968; M.F.A., Columbia U., 1970; postgrad. U. Mo., 1974—; m. Jo Ann M. Connell, Sept. 7, 1968; children—Amy E., Christopher Eugene. Free-lance filmmaker, 1968—; film production services coordinator Sta. WGBH-TV, Boston, 1973-74; film maker, grant adminstr. U. Mo., Columbia, 1974—; instr. TV radio film dept. Stephens Coll., Columbia, Mo. Served with U.S. Army, 1970-73. Nat. Endowment Arts pub. media program grantee, 1977. Mem. Am. Film Inst., Nat. Assn. Ednl. Broadcasters, Univ. Film Assn., Info. Film Producers Am., Theater Hist. Soc., Kappa Tau Alpha. Roman Catholic. Producer: Rivers (Gold Plaque, Chgo. Internat. Film Festival, 1976), 1976; Lady on the Lower (Cine Golden Eagle, 1977), 1977; editor Slowly the Singing Began, 1977. Home and office: 1582 Lakewood Dr Columbia MO 65201

FERRARO, JOHN RALPH, chemist; b. Chgo., Jan. 27, 1918; s. Charles and Jennie (Carlotta) F.; B.S., Ill. Inst. Tech., 1941, Ph.D., 1954; M.S., Northwestern U., 1948; m. Mary J. Leo, June 21, 1947; children—Lawrence, Janice, Victoria. Chemist, Kankakee Arsenal (Ill.), 1941-42; with Argonne Nat. Lab., 1948—, sr. chemist, 1968—. Spectroscopy adv. bd. Chem. Rubber Co., Cleve., 1971—; vis. prof. U. Rome (Italy), 1966-67; vis. prof. U. Ariz., 1973-74, adj. prof. planetary scis., 1974—. Served with USAAF, 1942-46. Recipient outstanding achievements in spectroscopy award N.Y. sect. Soc. for Applied Spectroscopy, 1970; Distinguished Scientist award Argonne Univs. Assn., 1973, Meggers award, 1975. Mem. Am. Chem. Soc., Research Soc. Am., Coblentz Soc. (bd. mgrs. 1969-73), Soc. for Applied Spectroscopy (pres. 1965, hon. mem.; Profl. Achievement in Spectroscopy award Chgo. sect. 1975), Am. Inst. Chemists, N.Y., Ill. acads. sci., Sigma Xi, Sigma Pi Sigma. Author: (with J.S. Ziomek) Introductory Group Theory and Its Application to Molecular Structure, 1969, 2d edit., 1976; Low Frequency Vibrations of Inorganic and Coordination Compounds, 1971. Asst. editor Applied Spectroscopy, 1967-68, editor, 1968-74. Home: 568 Saylor Ave Elmhurst IL 60126 Office: 9700 S Cass Argonne IL 60439

FERRELL, ROBERT LEE, surgeon; b. West Union, W.Va., Sept. 8, 1939; s. John Bruce and Hester Isabelle (Hogue) F.; B.S., Fairmont (W.Va.) State Coll., 1961; M.D., W.Va. U., 1965; m. Janet Sue Cusick, Nov. 5, 1965; children—Carolyn Sue, Cynthia Lou, James Bruce, Daniel Tyler. Resident gen. surgery Creighton U., Omaha, 1968-69, resident in otorhinolaryngology U. Nebr., 1969-72; practice medicine specializing in otorhinolaryngology and facial plastic surgery, Rapid City, S.D., 1973—; attending staff Rapid City Regional Hosp.; asso. staff Nebr. Meth. Hosp., Omaha, Children's Meml. Hosp., Omaha; fellow ENT br. Armed Forces Inst. Pathology, 1971; program dir. U. Nebr.-Pine Ridge Oglala Sioux Otitis Media Program; asst. prof. U. Nebr. Coll. Medicine, 1972; asst. clin. prof. U. S.D. Coll. Medicine, 1975. Served with M.C., USAF, 1966-68. Decorated Bronze Star, Air medal with oak leaf cluster; medal of Honor (Viet Nam). Fellow Am. Acad. Otolaryngology, A.C.S.; mem. S.D. Acad. Otolaryngology (sec. 1975-76), Nebr. Acad. Otolaryngology, Ducks Unlimited, Rushmore Retriever Club. Home: 716 San Marco St Rapid City SD 57701 Office: 629 Quincy St Rapid City SD 57701

FERRIS, JAMES DEFOREST, architect; b. Passaic, N.J., June 13, 1925; s. Walla Leon and Harriet Rachael (Stearns) F.; B.S., Ill. Inst. Tech., 1949, M.A., 1951. Draftsman Philip C. Johnson, architect, 1951-52; designer The Austin Co., 1952-54, Skidmore, Owings and Merrill, San Francisco and Chgo., 1955-60; archtl. designer C.F. Murphy, Chgo., 1960-67; architect Bertrand Goldberg Assos., 1967-69; chief architect Graham Anderson, Probst & White, 1969-73; owner J.D. Ferris & Assos., Chgo., 1973—; vis. prof. Grad. Sch. Architecture and Planning, Ill. Inst. Tech., 1976—. Served with AUS, 1943-45. Recipient award Carl Forstman Meml. Found., 1949, 50. Fellow A.I.A.; mem. Ill. Inst. Tech. Alumni Assn., Art Inst. Chgo., Mus. Contemporary Art, Friends of Mies van der Rohe Mus., Modern Art Mus., Chgo. Council Fgn. Relations, Chgo. Assn. Commerce and Industry. Club: Chgo. Athletic Assn. Prin. archtl. works include United Airlines Tng. Sch. and Exec. Office Bldg., Elk Grove Twp., Ill., 1959; Fine Arts Center Grinnel Coll., Iowa, 1959; CNA Ins. Bldg., Chgo., 1960, addition, 1969; First Nat. Bank, Chgo., 1965; YMCA Addition, Des Plaines, Ill., 1976; Gordon Tech. High Sch. addition, Chgo., 1976; Motorola, Inc. Office Bldg. and Warehouse, Schaumburg, Ill., 1977. Home: 2801 N Sheridan Rd Chicago IL 60657 Office: 1 N Wacker Dr Suite 300 Chicago IL 60606

FERRIS, RICHARD J., airline exec.; b. Sacramento, 1936; B.S., Cornell U., 1962; postgrad. U. Wash. Grad. Sch. Bus. Staff analyst and restaurant mgr. Olympic Hotel, to 1971; gen. mgr. Savoy Plaza, Anchorage Westward Hotel, Continental Plaza Hotel, Carlton Hotel; project officer-new constrn. Western Internat. Hotels, to 1971; pres. carrier's food services div. United Air Lines, Chgo., 1971-75, sr. v.p. mktg., 1975-76, pres., 1976, now pres., chief exec. officer, dir.; dir. UAL, Inc., Western Internat. Hotels. Office: PO Box 66100 Chicago IL 60666*

FERTIS, DEMETER GEORGE, educator; b. Athens, Greece, July 25, 1926; s. George P. and Athanasia (Papazachari) F.; B.S., Mich. State U., 1952, M.S., 1955; D.Eng., 1964 diploma Eng. Nat. Tech. U., Athens, Greece 1962; m. Vasilike J. Beltsos, July 26, 1953; children—Athanasia, Evaggelia. Planner-in-charge Ohio, Army C.E., Greece, 1948-50; research engr. Mich. Hwy. Dept., Lansing, 1952-57; asst. prof. mechanics dept. Wayne State U., 1957-63; vis. prof. Nat. Tech. U., Athens, Greece, 1963-64; asso. prof. U. Iowa, 1964-66; prof. civil engring. dept. U. Akron (Ohio), 1966—; cons. in field. Mem. Am. Soc. C.E., Am. Soc. Engring. Edn., Ohio Planners-in-Charge, Am. Concrete Inst., Indsl. Math. Soc., N.Y. Acad. Scis., Contemporary Authors. Mem. Greek Orthodox Ch. Author: Tranverse Vibration Theory, 1961; Deflection and Vibration of Engineering Structures, 1964; Notes on Structural Dynamics, 1966; Dynamics of Structural Systems, Vol. 1, 1971, Vol. 2, 1972; Dynamics and Vibration of Structures, 1973. Contbr. articles to profl. publs. Home: 2961 Chamberlain Rd Akron OH 44313

FESCO, EDWARD JOHN, surgeon; b. Tarrytown, N.Y., July 10, 1930; s. John and Mary (Lantosh) F.; B.S., Villanova (Pa.) U., 1952; M.D., Northwestern U., 1956, M.S., 1955; m. Anne Elizabeth Condron, June 1956; children—Eileen, Mary, John, Nora, Carol,

Beth. Intern, Presbyn.-St. Luke's Hosp., Chgo., 1956-57; resident in surgery VA Hosp., Hines, Ill., 1957-61; practice medicine specializing in gen. surgery, La Salle, Ill., 1963—; pres. med. staff Ill. Valley Hosp., La Salle. Served with M.C., USAF, 1961-63. Diplomate Am. Bd. Surgery. Fellow A.C.S.; mem. AMA, La Salle County Med. Soc. (pres. 1976). Roman Catholic. Home: 709 3d St La Salle IL 61301 Office: 206 Marquette St La Salle IL 61301

FETERL, LEON GEORGE, mfg. co. exec.; b. Salem, S.D., Jan. 28, 1930; s. Louis Edward and Mary (Huls) F.; student pub. schs.; m. Marilyn R. Kass, Nov. 23, 1953; children—David Michael, Mary Louise, Daniel Leon, Douglas Richard, Margery Katherine, Darryl Carl, Marcine Marie, Molly Anne. Owner, mgr. Tony's Welding Shop, Salem, S.D., 1953-62; pres. Feterl Mfg. Co., Inc., Salem, 1962—; pres. F & W Concrete Products, Salem, 1962—, F & W Precast of Iowa, Spencer, 1968—, Maquoketa div. F & W Precasting of Iowa, Inc., 1977—, F & W Precasting of Nebr., Inc., Central City, 1972—; v.p. Jenerl, Inc., Salem, S.D., 1977—; dir. Forward, Inc., Huron, S.D. Mem. S.D. Indsl. Devel. Expansion Agy., 1971—; mem. S.D. Planning Commn., 1971—; mgmt. assistance cons. SBA, 1971-76; bd. dirs. Greater S.D. Assn., 1976—. Served with AUS, 1951-53; Germany. Named South Dakotan of Yr., U. S.D., 1972, Small Businessman of Year in S.D., 1973. Mem. S.D. Mfrs. and Processors Assn. (dir.), Am. Legion, 40 and 8. Roman Catholic. Club: McCook County Country (dir.). Elk, Lion. Patentee in field. Home: 300 E Lightner St Salem SD 57058 Office: 411 W Center St Salem SD 57058

FETRIDGE, BONNIE JEAN CLARK (MRS. WILLIAM HARRISON FETRIDGE), civic worker; b. Chgo., Feb. 3, 1915; d. Sheldon and Bonnie (Carrington) Clark; student Girls Latin Sch., Chgo., The Masters Sch., Dobbs Ferry, N.Y., Finch Coll., N.Y.C.; m. William Harrison Fetridge, June 27, 1941; children—Blakely (Mrs. Harvey H. Bundy III), Clark Worthington. Bd. dirs. region VII com. Girl Scouts U.S.A., 1939-43, mem. nat. program com., 1966-69, mem. nat. adv. council, 1972—, mem. internat. commr.'s adv. panel, 1973-76, mem. Nat. Juliette Low Birthplace Com., 1966-69, region IV selections com., 1968-70; bd. dirs. Girl Scouts Chgo., 1936-51, 59-69, sec., 1936-38, v.p., 1946-49, 61-65, chmn. Juliette Low world friendship com., 1959-67, 71-72; mem. Friends of Our Cabana Com. World Assn. Girl Guides and Girl Scouts, 1969—; bd. dirs. Jr. League of Chgo., 1937-40, Vis. Nurse Assn. of Chgo., 1951-58, 61-63, asst. treas., 1962-63; women's bd. dirs. Children's Meml. Hosp., 1946-50. Staff aide, A.R.C. and Motor Corps, World War II. Vice pres. Latin Sch. Parents Council, 1952-54; bd. dirs. Latin Sch. Alumni Assn. 1964-69; women's bd. U.S.O., 1965-75, treas., 1969-71, v.p., 1971-73; women's service bd. Chgo. Area council Boy Scouts Am., 1964-70, mem.-at-large Nat. council, 1973-76, mem. nat. Exploring com., 1973-76. Mem. Nat. Soc. Colonial Dames Am. (Ill. bd. mgrs. 1962-65, 69-76, v.p. 1970-72, state chmn. geneal. information services com. 1972-76), Youth for Understanding, English-Speaking Union, Chgo. Dobbs Alumnae Assn. (past pres.), Nat. Soc. D.A.R., Conn., Chgo. geneal. socs., New Eng. Historic Geneal. Soc., N.Y. Geneal. and Biog. Soc., Auguan Soc., Newberry Library Assos., Chgo. Hist. Soc. Guild, Antiquarin Soc. Republican. Episcopalian. Clubs: Casino, Saddle and Cycle, Woman's Athletic. Home: 2430 Lakeview Ave Chicago IL 60614

FETRIDGE, WILLIAM HARRISON, publisher; b. Chgo.; s. Matthew and Clara (Hall) F.; B.S., Northwestern U., 1929; LL.D., Central Mich. U., 1954; m. Bonnie Jean Clark, June 27, 1941; children—Blakely (Mrs. Harvey H. Bundy III), Clark Worthington. Asst. to dean Northwestern U., 1929-30; editor Trade Periodical Co., 1930-31; with Chgo. Tribune, 1931-34, H. W. Kastor & Son, 1934-35, Roche, Williams & Cleary, Inc., 1935-42; mng. editor The Republican mag., 1939-42; vice pres. Popular Mechanics mag., 1946-53, exec. v.p., 1953-59; v.p., Diamond T Motor Truck Co., Chgo., 1959-61, exec. v.p. Diamond T div. White Motor Co., 1961-65; pres. Dartnell Corp., Chgo., 1965—; dir. Bank of Ravenswood. Pres. United Rep. Fund of Ill., 1968-73, hon. pres., 1973—; campaign mgr. Merriam for Mayor Chgo., 1955; alternate del.-at-large Republican Nat. Conv., 1956, del.-at-large, Nat. Conv., 1968, hon. del. at large, 1972; chmn. Midwest Vols. for Nixon-Lodge, 1960; chmn. Nixon Recount Com., 1960; chmn. Rep. Forum, 1958-60; mem. Rep. Nat. Finance Com. Trustee Jacques Holinger Meml. Assn.; past pres. bd. trustees Latin Sch. Chgo.; trustee Lake Forest Coll.; nat. v.p., mem. nat. exec. bd. Boy Scouts Am.; pres. U.S. Found. for Internat. Scouting; chmn. Johnston Scout Mus., North Brunswick, N.J.; vice chmn. World Scout Found., Geneva, Switzerland, 1977—. Served as lt. comdr. USNR, 1942-45. Decorated chevalier Grand Priory of Malta; Sovereign Order St. John of Jerusalem; recipient Silver Antelope, Silver Beaver, Silver Buffalo, Distinguished Eagle awards Boy Scouts Am. Bronze Wolf, World Scout Conf., Nairobi, Kenya, 1973. Mem. Navy League U.S. (past regional pres., trustee Chgo. council), Beta Theta Pi. Clubs: Chicago, Union League, Saddle and Cycle, Casino (Chgo.); Capitol Hill (Washington); Chikaming Country (Lakeside, Mich.). Author: The Republican Precinct Worker's Manual, 1942; Abbot Hall U.S.N.R., 1945; With Warm Regards, 1976. Editor: The Navy Reader, 1943; The Second Navy Reader, 1944; American Political Almanac, 1950; The Republican Precinct Worker's Manual, 1968. Home: 2430 Lakeview Ave Chicago IL 60614 Office: 4660 N Ravenswood Ave Chicago IL 60640

FETROW, KENNETH OGDEN, orthopaedic surgeon; b. Peoria, Ill., May 26, 1930; s. Harry M. and Matilda E. (Blab) F.; M.D., U. Ill., 1955. Intern, Cook County Hosp., Chgo., 1955-56, resident St. Francis Hosp., Peoria, 1956-57, U. Ill. Research and Ednl. Hosps., Chgo., 1959-61; clin. asso. prof. orthopaedic surgery U. Ill. Coll. of Medicine, Chgo., 1962—; practice medicine specializing in orthopaedic and hand surgery, Calumet City, Ill., 1962—. Served with USAF, 1957-59. Diplomate Am. Bd. Orthopaedic Surgery. Fellow Am. Acad. Orthopaedic Surgeons, A.C.S., Internat. Coll. Surgeons; mem. Am., Lake County med. assns., Ind., Chgo. med. socs., Hammond Surg. Soc., Ind., Chgo. orthopaedic socs., Am. Soc. Surgery of Hand, Chgo. Com. on Trauma, Clin. Orthopaedic Soc., Internat. Soc. Orthopaedics and Traumatology. Elk. Contbr. articles to profl. jours. Home: 101 Forestdale Pkwy Calumet City IL 60409 Office: 852 State Line Ave Calumet City IL 60409

FETTER, BRUCE SIGMOND, historian; b. Ashland, Ky., June 8, 1938; s. Henry Lewis and Sylvia Sarah (Freedman) F. B.A., Harvard U., 1960; B.Phil., Oxford U., 1962; Ph.D., U. Wis., 1968; m. Victoria Lewin, Aug. 5, 1966; children—David, Emmanuelle. Instr. history U. Wis., Milw., 1967-68, asst. prof., 1968-74, asso. prof., 1974—. Fulbright sr. lectr. Nat. U. Zaire, 1972-73; recipient Kiekhofer Teaching award, 1972. Mem. Am. Hist. Assn., African Studies Assn., Social Sci. Hist. Assn. Democrat. Jewish. Vice pres. Am. Jewish Com., Milw. Author: The Creation of Elisabethville, 1910-40, 1976. Editor: Urbanism Past and Present, 1975—. Home: 2937 Summit Ave N Milwaukee WI 53211 Office: Dept History Univ Wis Milwaukee WI 53201

FETTER, RICHARD ELWOOD, mfg. co. exec.; b. Lewisburg, Pa., Feb. 25, 1923; s. Elwood Merrill and Emily Ruel (Rogers) F.; B.S., Bucknell U., 1947; m. Mary Virginia Gabriel, June 22, 1947; 1 dau., Molly Elizabeth. With Gen. Electric Co., 1947-64, fin. mgr. indsl. heating dept., Shelbyville, Ind., 1954-64; controller F.W. Dodge div. McGraw-Hill, Inc., 1964-65; v.p. Standard & Poor's subsidiary McGraw-Hill, 1965-67, fin. v.p., N.Y.C., 1967-70; v.p. fin. and adminstrn. Research-Cattsell, Inc., Bound Brook, N.J., 1970-75; v.p., fin., sec.-treas. Debron Corp., St. Ann, Mo., 1975—. Bd. dirs. Shelby County United Fund, 1963-64; mem. Chatham Twp. (N.J.) Fin. Adv. Com., 1971-74. Served with USAAF, 1945-47. Decorated Air Medal. Mem. Fin. Execs. Inst., Am. Soc. Corporate Secs., Ind. C. of C. (fed. fin. com. 1962-63), Phi Gamma Delta, Omicron Delta Kappa. Republican. Presbyn. Club: Elks. Home: 253 Litchford Ct Creve Coeur MO 63141 Office: 500 Northwest Plaza St Ann MO 63074

FETTER, WILLIAM ALLAN, computer graphics researcher/designer; b. Independence, Mo., Mar. 14, 1928; s. William Herbert and Edna Katherine (Werner) F.; B.F.A., U. Ill., 1952; student Kansas City U., 1948-49; m. Barbara Ann Shaffer, Dec. 21, 1963; children—Brant Shaffer, Elena Katherine. Designer, press art div. U. Ill. Press, Urbana, 1950-54; art dir. Family Weekly mag., Chgo., 1954-58, John Higgs Studios, Chgo., 1958-59; supr. computer graphics The Boeing Co., Wichita, Kans. and Seattle, 1959-69; cons. Computer Graphis, Inc., Newport Beach, Calif., 1969-70; lectr., researcher So. Ill. U., Carbondale, 1970—; prin. researcher So. Ill. Research Inst., 1977—; vis. and adj. prof. U. Utah, Salt Lake City, 1972-73; cons. Wright State U., Dayton, Ohio, Computer Vision Users Group, Chgo., Am. Oil Co., Tulsa. Served in U.S. Army, 1946-48. NSF grantee, 1974—; recipient award U.S. Art Dirs. Club, 1962, many other awards and medals. Mem. Transp. Research Bd., NRC, Am. Inst. Aeros. and Astronautics (asso. fellow), Counc il on Social Graphics, Indsl. Graphics Internat. (com. chmn.). Author: Computer Graphics in Communication, 1964; also artic les. Home: 402 Walker Dr Carbondale IL 62901 Office: So Ill Research Inst Carbondale IL 62901

FETZER, JOHN EARL, bus., baseball, broadcasting exec.; b. Decatur, Ind., Mar. 25, 1901; s. John Adam and Della Frances (Winger) F.; student Purdue U., 1921; A.B., Andrews U., 1927; student U. Mich., 1929; LL.D., Western Mich. U., 1958; LL.D., Kalamazoo Coll., 1972; Litt.D., Elizabethtown Coll., 1972; m. Rhea Maude Yeager, July 19, 1926. Owner, chmn. bd. Fetzer Broadcasting Co., 1930—, Fetzer TV Corp., Kalamazoo-Grand Rapids, Mich., 1970—, Cornhusker TV Corp., Lincoln, Neb., 1953—; pres., owner Detroit Tigers Am. League Baseball Club, 1956—, Fetzer Music Corp., Fetzer TV, Inc., Cadillac, Mich., 1958—, John E. Fetzer, Inc., 1968—; chmn. Wolverine Cablevision, Inc., 1967—; dir. emeritus Am. Nat. Bank & Trust Co., Kalamazoo. Chmn., Maj. League TV Com., 1963-71. U.S. Censor of radio, 1944-45; reporting to Gen. Eisenhower, engaged in ETO radio studies in Eng., France, Russia, Germany, Italy and other European countries, 1945; fgn. corr. radio-TV-newspaper mission Europe and Middle East, 1952; mem. mission Radio Free Europe, Munich, Germany, and Austrian-Hungarian border, 1956; Broadcasters Mission to Latin-Am., Dept. State, 1962, Detroit Tiger Baseball tour of Japan, Okinawa, Korea, under auspices Dept. State, 1962; mem. A.P. tour Europe, 1966; Dept. State del. Japanese-U.S. TV Treaty, 1972; mem. adv. bd. N.Am. Service, Radio Diffusion Francaise, Paris, 1946-47. Trustee Kalamazoo Coll., 1954—. Recipient Broadcast Pioneers award, 1968; Distinguished service award Nat. Assn. Broadcasters, 1969; Mich. Frontiersman award, 1969; Fourth Estate award Am. Legion, 1972; citation Mich. Legislature, 1972; C. of C. Detroit Tiger 75th Anniversary award, 1976; Mich. Legis. citation, 1976; Nebr. Pub. TV citation, 1976. Fellow Royal Soc. Arts London; mem. Nat. Assn. Broadcasters (chmn. TV bd. 1952), C. of C. (past pres.); Nat. Geneal. Soc., Acad. Polit. Sci., Am. Soc. Mil. Engrs., IEEE (life mem.), Internat. Radio and TV Execs. Soc., Broadcast Pioneers, Alpha Kappa Psi. Presbyn. Mason (33 deg., Shriner), Elk. Clubs: Park, Kalamazoo Country (Kalamazoo); Economic, Detroit Athletic, Press, Detroit (Detroit); Tucson Country. Author: One Man's Family, 1964; The Men from Wengen and America's Agony, 1972. Contbr. Radio and Television Project, Columbia, 1953. Home: 2714 Clovelly Rd Kalamazoo MI 49008 Office: Kalamazoo MI 49008 also Tiger Stadium Detroit MI 48216

FEUDNER, JOHN LLOYD, JR., charitable trust exec.; b. Akron, Ohio, June 20, 1912; s. John Lloyd and Ethel Thay (Harbaugh) F.; B.A., U. Akron, 1934; m. Elsie Barbara Herget, Aug. 22, 1936; children—John Lloyd III, Barbara L. (Mrs. Stephen F. Schaal), Jean E. (Mrs. Gerald F. Ewald). With M. O'Neil Co., Akron, 1935-72, exec. v.p., gen. mgr., 1959-63, pres., gen. mgr., 1963-69, chmn. bd., 1969-72; v.p. May Dept. Stores, 1960-72; exec. dir. Akron Community Trusts, 1971—; dir. Akron Nat. Bank, Ohio Edison Co. Pres. Akron Area C. of C., 1964; trustee Ohio Council Retail Mchts., 1964, v.p., 1969-71, chmn., 1972. Vice pres. Akron area council Boy Scouts Am., 1964, pres., 1966-69, mem. exec. com. region IV, 1969-72, mem. exec. com. East Central region, 1972-77; v.p. Family Service Soc. Akron, 1964; pres. Parents Assn. Wittenberg U., 1964-65; sec. Akron Regional Devel. Bd., 1975-77, exec. dir., 1977—. Trustee Akron Gen. Hosp., 1964—, mem. exec. com., 1973—; trustee Akron Met. Transit Authority, 1969-77, Area Progress Bd., 1968-75, Musical Arts Assn. (Cleve.), 1970—; mem. bus. adv. com. U. Akron, 1964—, Kent State U., 1964—; trustee, vice chmn. N.E. Ohio U. Coll. Medicine, 1974-77, chmn., 1977—. Mem. Lutheran Laymen's Movement, Lone Star Frat. (past pres.), Ohio C. of C. (dir. 1966-68). Clubs: City (past pres.), Fairlawn Country (past pres.), Sharon Golf, Cascade Men's (chmn. 1974-75). Home: 332 Afton Ave Akron OH 44313 Office: 1 Akron Center Bldg Akron OH 44308

FEULING, DANIEL THOMAS, newspaper pub.; b. Ft. Wayne, Ind., Feb. 11, 1948; s. John Eugene and Mary Ann (Fishering) F.; B.A., Drake U., 1970; m. Patricia Dianne Shaw, Aug. 24, 1968; children—John Shaw, Jennifer Dianne. Regional mgr. Maytag Co., S.D., 1970, Colo., 1970-73, Calif., 1973-74; owner, pub. New Hampton Pub. Co. (Iowa), 1974—; partner, dir. Signs by Design of Iowa, 1976—. Sec., New Hampton Indsl. Corp. Mem. Iowa Press Assn., Nat. Newspaper Assn., New Hampton C. of C. (v.p.). Roman Catholic. Clubs: Lions, Elks, New Hampton Golf and Country (v.p.). Home: 814 Sunset St New Hampton IA 50659 Office: 10 N Chestnut St New Hampton IA 50659

FEWELL, BOBBY LEE, civil engr.; b. North Vernon, Ind., Dec. 22, 1927; s. J. Frank and Jessie Mae (Dilk) F.; student Purdue U., 1951-54; m. Helen Mae Bannister, Aug. 10, 1949; 1 son, Lee Scott. Asst. project engr. Ind. Hwy. Commn., Seymour, Ind., 1955-58; cons. engr. C.E. Williams & Assos., Indpls., 1958-61; project engr. Ind. Hwy. Comm., 1961-71; pres. B.L. Fewell & Assos., Inc., North Vernon, Ind., 1971—; dir. Lee's Inns of Am., 1975—. Charter mem. Jennings County Area Planning Commn., 1966-69. Served as sgt. USAF, 1945-48. Mem. Nat. Ind. socs. profl. engrs. Methodist. Mason (Shriner). Home: Box 41 North Vernon IN 47265 Office: Box 41 138 E Walnut St North Vernon IN 47265

FEY, CYRIL JOSEPH, cons. engr.; b. Cin., Oct. 11, 1921; s. John P. and Matilda (Riedinger) F.; Chem. Engr., U. Cin., 1944; student Xavier U., 1945-62, Coffeyville Jr. Coll., 1972; m. Juliana Dillhoff, Feb. 27, 1954; children—Paula, Mary Frances, Monica. Chem. engr. Brighton Corp., Cin., 1944-48; v.p., gen. mgr. Hamilton Copper & Brass Co. (Ohio), 1949; chem. engr. Stacy Bros. Gas Constrn. Co., Cin., 1950-51; project engr. Nat. Lead Co. Ohio, Cin., 1951-71; project mgr. cons. Sherwin Williams Inc., Coffeyville, Kans., 1972; exec. sec. Archdiocesan Council of Laity, Cin., 1973; project mgr. cons. Cin. Milacron Chems., 1974; asst. project mgr. cons. Eli Lilly & Co., Indpls., 1975—; dir. Cumminsville Loan & Bldg. Co., Cin., 1960—. Mem. engring. adv. com. N.W. Sch. Dist. Cin., 1960-64, social planning council, 1967-71. Bd. dirs. Council of Laity, Cin., 1960—; bd. edn. Archdiocese Cin., 1965-70. Recipient St. Thomas More award Nat. Council Catholic Laity, 1971. Mem. Am. Inst. Chem. Engrs., Engring. Soc. Cin., Alpha Chi Sigma (pres. Alpha Delta chpt. 1943-44). K.C. Address: 3643 Hanley Rd Cincinnati OH 45239

FIDELMAN, SELWYN NORMAN, psychologist; b. N.Y.C., Oct. 8, 1929; s. Irving and Irene (Fisch) F.; B.A., N.Y. U., 1952, M.A., 1953; Ph.D., Mich. State U., 1962; m. Terry Klar, May 20, 1972; 1 dau., Amy Lyn Inez. Instr. Mich. State U., East Lansing, 1958-59; staff psychologist Allen Park (Mich.) VA Hosp., 1959-61, 64-66; staff psychologist Wayne County Mental Health Clinic, Detroit, 1961-64; dir. behavioral sci. edn. and research, chief psychologist Clinton Valley Center, Pontiac, Mich., 1966—; pvt. practice psychotherapy, Birmingham, Mich., 1962—; asst. clin. prof. psychiatry Mich. State U. Coll. Human Medicine, East Lansing, 1971—; cons. to Benedictine Sisters Convent, Oxford Mich., 1967-69, Peace Corps, 1971, Kingswood Hosp., 1968—, Springport (Mich.) Pub. Sch. System. Served with AUS, 1953-55; Korea. NIMH grantee, 1971-72. Mem. Am., Mich. psychol. assns., Am. Acad. Psychotherapists, Assn. Humanistic Psychology. Home: 1868 W Square Lake Rd Bloomfield Hills MI 48013 Office: 140 Elizabeth Lake Rd Pontiac MI 48053

FIECHTER, RAY ALLEN, mfg. co. exec.; b. Decatur, Ind., Nov. 20, 1945; s. Homer H. and Clara M. (Schladenhauffen) F.; B.M.E., Purdue U., 1970; m. Carol Payne, July 18, 1965; children—Shantelle Rae, Shurell Alane. Process engr. Corning Glass Co., Bluffton, Ind., 1964-66; research and devel. engr. Detroit Diesel Allison div. Gen. Motors Corp., Indpls., 1970-71; applications engr. Schwitzer div. Wallace Murray Co., Indpls., 1971-72, sales mgr., 1972—. Mem. ASME, Soc. Profl. Engrs. Home: 226 Mill Farm Rd Noblesville IN 46060 Office: 2403 S J St Elwood IN 46036

FIEDLER, VERE LOUIS, civil engr.; b. Oakdale, Wis., Oct. 28, 1903; s. Louis and Louisa (Coplan) F.; B.S., Tri-State Coll., 1925; m. Grace Haase, Dec. 4, 1924; children—Harold L., Ronald Ray, Dean E. With Wis. Div. Hwys., LaCrosse, Green Bay, Madison, 1926-68, sec. Wis. Hwy. Commn., Madison, 1960-68; coordinator transp., heavy constrn. Owen Ayres & Assos., cons., Eau Claire, Wis., 1969—. Served with U.S. Bur. Pub. Rds., World War II. Recipient meritorious service award Am. Assn. State Hwy. Ofcls., 1956. Registered profl. engr., Wis. Mem. Fraternal Aesthetic Cultural Tech. Soc., Wis. Assn. Professions (sec. 1973), Nat. Wis. socs. profl. engrs. Lutheran (ch. council). Mason, Rotarian. Home: 4814 Fond du Lac Trail Madison WI 53705

FIELD, CHARLIE KAY, coll. dean; b. Redkey, Ind., Nov. 8, 1919; s. Charlie Kay and Mary A.R. (Myer) F.; student Purdue U., 1937-38, Ind. Bus. Coll., 1938-40; B.S., Tri-State Coll., 1947; postgrad. Mich. State U., 1971, Western Mich. U., 1970, Wayne State U., 1973; Ph.D., Walden U., 1976; m. Thelma Louise Wright, Feb. 21, 1942; children—Dianne (Mrs. Larry Welchko), Sandra Louise, Susan (Mrs. Glenn Robinson), Barbara Ann (Mrs. R. Freridge). Personnel mgr. Anchor Hocking Corp., Winchester, Ind., 1947-57; indsl. relations dir. Velsicol Chem. Corp., Marshall, Ill., 1957-59; personnel dir. Nat. Standard Co., Niles, Mich., 1959-66; indsl. relations dir. Benton Harbor Malleable Industries, Inc. (Mich.), 1966-71; instr. Lake Michigan Coll., Benton Harbor, 1970-71, prof., 1971—, dean of continuing edn. and community services, also mgmt., personnel and ednl. cons., 1971—. Pres. Field & Asso., St. Joseph, Mich., 1970—. Pres. Jr. Achievement Bd. of Four Flags Area, Niles, 1963. Bd. dirs. Berrien County Cancer Service, 1960-76. Served with USNR, 1941-45. Mem. Am. Soc. for Personnel Adminstrn. (accredited personnel diplomate), Am. Soc. for Tng. and Devel., Assn. Univ. Evening Colls., Am. Assn. for Higher Edn., Mich. Adult Edn. Assn., Mich. Acad. Arts and Sci., Mich. Community Coll. Community Services Assn. (pres. 1977), Southwestern Mich. Personnel Assn. (pres. 1970-71, Am. Soc. Mgmt. Cons. (charter). Mason, Rotarian (pres. 1972-73). Home: 307 S Veronica Ct St Joseph MI 49085 Office: Lake Michigan College 2755 E Napier Ave Benton Harbor MI 49022

FIELD, MARSHALL, V, publisher; b. Charlottesville, Va., May 13, 1941; s. Marshall IV, and Joanne (Bass) F.; grad. Deerfield Acad., 1959; B.A., Harvard, 1963; m. Joan Best Connelly, Sept. 5, 1964 (div. 1969); 1 son, Marshall; m. 2d, Jamee Beckwith Jacobs, Aug. 19, 1972; children—Jamee, Stephanie Caroline. With N.Y. Herald-Tribune, 1964-65; dir. Field Enterprises Inc., Chgo., 1965—, mem. exec. com., 1966—, chmn. bd., 1972—, mem. exec. com. newspaper div., 1965—; pub. Chgo. Daily News and Chgo. Sun-Times, 1969—; dir. Field Enterprises Ednl. Corp., 1965—, pub., 1973—; dir. 1st Nat. Bank Chgo., 1st Chgo. Corp. Mem. adv. bd. Chgo. area council Boy Scouts Am.; mem. nat. com. Am. Land Trust; mem. Chgo. com. Chgo. Council on Fgn. Relations; mem. profl. journalism adv. com. Stanford U.; co-chmn. adv. bd. Broader Urban Involvement and Leadership Devel., Inc.; mem. adv. bd. Presdl. Classroom Young Ams. Trustee Art Inst. Chgo., Field Mus. Natural History, Rush-Presbyn.-St. Luke's Med. Center, Am. Newspaper Pubs. Assn. Found., Mus. Sci. and Industry, U. Chgo., MacMurray Coll., Jacksonville, Ill.; governing mem. Orchestral Assn., Chgo.; bd. dirs. Chgo. Boys Clubs, Salt Water Internat. Fishing Telesis, Internat. Atlantic Salmon Found., McGraw Wildlife Found., Nat. Book Com., Field Found. Ill., Newspaper Advt. Bur., Lincoln Park Zool. Soc., Restoration Atlantic Salmon in Am. Inc., U.S. appeal World Wildlife Fund; hon. bd. dirs. Nat. Commn. Prevention of Child Abuse; adv. bd. Dialogue with the Blind, Fine Arts Com., U.S. Dept. State. Mem. Nat. Com. Newspaper Pubs. Clubs: Casino, Chicago, Commercial, Harvard, Hundred of Cook County, Merchants & Manufacturers, Mid-Am., Tavern, Racquet, Saddle & Cycle (Chgo.); River (N.Y.C.); Owentsia (Lake Forest, Ill.); McGraw Wildlife (Dundee, Ill.). Office: 401 N Wabash Ave Chicago IL 60611

FIELD, SISTER MARY, librarian; b. Wisconsin Dells, Wis., Jan. 17, 1918; d. Henry Augustus and Georgia Berenice (Coakley) Field; B.A., Rosary Coll., 1939, M.A. in L.S., 1960; M.A., U. Wis., 1940. Joined Dominican Religious Order, 1945; tchr., librarian Medford (Wis.) High Sch., 1942-43, Reedsburg (Wis.) High Sch., 1943-44; librarian Sinsinawa Dominican High Sch. libraries, Ill., D.C., Mont., Okla., 1945-60; reference librarian Rosary Coll., River Forest, Ill., 1960-64, chief librarian, 1964—, mem. com. planning new library bldg., 1966-70. Mem. A.L.A., Cath. Library Assn. (sec. local unit 1962-63), Kappa Delta Pi. Home: 1204 Jackson Ave River Forest IL 60305 Office: Rosary College River Forest IL 60305

FIELDING, IVOR RENÉ, chemist; b. Jefferson, Iowa, July 3, 1942; s. Leslie Wayne and Roberta (Oakes) F.; B.A., Simpson Coll., 1964; postgrad. U. Colo., 1964, Kans. State U., 1964-66; M.S., Creighton U., 1970; Ph.D., U. Pitts., 1970; M.S., Midwest Coll. Engring., 1977; m. Anna Theresa Damas, Aug. 10, 1968; children—Maria Ona, Krista Terese. Teaching asst. Kans. State U., Manhattan, 1964-66, Creighton U., Omaha, 1966-68; teaching, research asst. U. Pitts., 1968-70; research chemist Amoco Chems. Corp. div. Standard Oil Ind., Naperville, Ill., 1970—. Class agt. Simpson Coll. Alumni Annual Fund, 1972-73, class coordinator, 1974-75. Simpson Coll. grantee,

1960-64; NSF grantee, 1968-70. Mem. Am. Chem. Soc., Am. Inst. Chemists, Sigma Xi, Sigma Tau Delta, Phi Lambda Upsilon. Patentee in field. Home: 115 N Brainard St Naperville IL 60540 Office: PO Box 400 Naperville IL 60540

FIELDS, ARTHUR DAVID, state ofcl.; b. Florence, Ala., June 29, 1949; s. Arthur Fields and Charlie (Boddie) F.; B.A., Miles Coll., 1972; M.A., Eastern Mich. U., 1976; postgrad. U. Mich., 1976—, U. Notre Dame 23d Ann. Midwest Inst. Alcoholic Studies, summer 1977; m. Clima Ingram, Aug. 29, 1970; 1 son, Khari David. Community assistance Boniface Community Corp., 1972-73; parole officer Mich. Dept. Corrections, Detroit, 1975—. Mem. Am. Personnel and Guidance Assn., Assn. Non White Concerns in Personnel and Guidance, Phi Beta Sigma. Democrat. Methodist. Club: Masons. Home: 14258 Artesian St Detroit MI 48227

FIELDS, DONALD LEE, pediatrician; b. Muncie, Ind., May 3, 1928; s. Ellis Loree and Sarah Isabelle (Moomaw) F.; A.B., Ball State U., 1950; M.D., Ind. U., 1955; m. Elizabeth Ann Jarrett, Aug. 23, 1952; children—Richard, Ann, Barbara, Donald Scott. Intern, Riverside (Calif.) Gen. Hosp., 1955-56; resident in pediatrics Ind. U. Med. Center, 1958-60, asst. in pediatrics, 1977—; practice medicine specializing in pediatrics, Kokomo, Ind., 1960—; mem. staffs Howard Community Hosp., St. Joseph Hosp; cons. Grissom AFB, Ind. Served with USAF, 1956-58. Diplomate Am. Bd. Pediatrics. Fellow Am. Acad. Pediatrics (exec. com. Ind. chpt.); mem. AMA, Ind. State Med. Assn., Howard County Med. Soc. Republican. Methodist. Club: Rotary. Home: 3304 Tallyho Dr Kokomo IN 46901 Office: 3804 Southland Ave Kokomo IN 46901

FIELDS, THEODORE, cons. med. physicist; b. Chgo., Jan. 23, 1922; s. Samuel and Jean (Golber) F.; B.S., U. Chgo., 1942; M.S., 1953, DePaul U.; m. Audrey Helena Engerman, June 24, 1945; children—Brad, Scott, Gary. Pres., Isotope Measurements Lab., Northbrook, Ill., 1969—, Health Physics Assos., Northbrook, 1965—, Fields, Griffith & Assos., Glencoe, Ill., 1974—; clin. asso. prof. radiology Loyola U. Med. Sch., Chgo., 1974—. Served with USAAF, 1945-46. Fellow Am. Coll. Radiology, Am. Pub. Health Soc.; mem. IEEE, Radiol. Soc., N. Am., Radiation Research Soc., Am. Phys. Soc., Health Physics Soc., Am. Assn. Physicists in Medicine, Sigma Xi. Author: Clinical Use of Radioisotopes, 1957, 61; Treatment of Toxic Goiter with Radioactive Iodine, 1953; contbr. articles to profl. jours. Patentee in field. Home: 1141 Hohlfelder Rd Glencoe IL 60022 Office: 3304 Commercial Rd Northbrook IL 60062

FIETSAM, ROBERT CHARLES, accountant; b. Belleville, Ill., Oct. 18, 1927; s. Celsus J. and Viola (Ehret) F.; B.S., U. Ill., 1955; m. Miriam Runkwitz, Apr. 12, 1952; children—Robert C., Guy P., Nancy A., Lisa R. Claims adjuster Ely & Walker Dry Goods, St. Louis, 1947-48; jr. accountant Price Waterhouse & Co., 1949-51; staff accountant J.W. Boyle & Co., East St. Louis, 1955-59; owner R.C. Fietsam, C.P.A., Belleville, Ill., 1960-68, sr. partner R.C. Fietsam & Co. C.P.A.'s, 1969—. Past pres. Signal Hill Improvement Assn. Served with USAF, 1951-53. Recipient Optimist of Year award Optimist Club, Belleville, 1977. C.P.A., Mo., Ill. Mem. Ill. (past pres. So. chpt., Mr. So. Chpt. award 1976), Mo. socs. C.P.A.'s, Am. Inst. C.P.A.'s, U. Ill. Alumni Assn. (life), U. Ill. Greater Belleville Illini Club (past pres.), Belleville C. of C. (past pres.), Belleville Jr. C. of C. (life, Key Man award 1959-60, Outsanding Citizen award 1976), Lambda Chi Alpha Alumnae Assn. Mem. United Ch. of Christ (past pres.). Elk, Moose. Club: St. Clair Country. Home: 9 Gerold Ln Belleville IL 62223 Office: 325 W Main Belleville IL 62220

FIFE, WILLIAM HAROLD, JR., advt. agy. exec.; b. St. Cloud, Minn., Mar. 17, 1928; s. William H. and Gretchen Elise (Thorne) F.; student Columbia Coll., 1947-48, Chgo. Acad. Fine Arts, 1949, Northwestern U., 1949-51; m. Dolores Jeanette Musick, Sept. 22, 1951; children—Michael, Gregory, Patricia, Marybeth, Brian, Elise. Asst. promotions mgr. Montgomery Ward & Co., Chgo., 1950-52; asst. copy chief Motorola, Chgo., 1952-54; copywriter Roy Knipschild Advt. Agy., Chgo., 1954; advt., marketing and sales tng. dir. EKCO Products Co., Chgo., 1954-61; co-founder Mills, Fife & MacDonald, Inc., Chgo., 1961, pres., treas., 1965—, chief exec. officer, 1969—, also dir. Active Little League, Des Plaines, Ill. Served with USNR, 1944-47. Mem. Columbia Coll. Bus. Assn. (pres. 1952), Northshire Civic Assn. (past v.p., Outstanding Achievement award 1959), Jaycees (Des Plaines Key Man of Year 1959, 60, dir. 1960, Spoke of Year 1959), Am. Soc. Bakery Engrs., Allied Trades of The Baking Industry, Internat. Foodservice Mktg. Assn., Chgo. Foodservice Mktg. Club. Alpha Delta Sigma. Clubs: Businessman's Breakfast (v.p. 1971-72); Bakers (Chgo.); Bakers Courtesy (dir.). Home: 1108 Perry Dr Palatine IL 60067 Office: 2340 River Rd Des Plaines IL 60018

FIGHTMASTER, WALTER JOHN, coll. ofcl.; b. Barberton, Ohio, Dec. 14, 1930; s. Verderman Cantrill and Amanda (Stone) F.; B.S., U. Louisville, 1952, M.A., 1954; m. Sue N. Tabler, June 8, 1958. Cons. psychologist Kemper & Assos., Louisville, 1952-54; research psychologist George Washington U., Washington, 1957-58; sr. indsl. psychologist Martin Marietta Corp., Balt., 1958-59, Westinghouse Electric Corp., Balt., 1959-60; staff psychologist Bendix Corp., Ann Arbor, Mich., 1960-63; chief staff psychologist Ling-Temco-Vought, Inc., Warren, Mich., 1963-65; dir. community services Oakland Community Coll., Bloomfield Hills, Mich., 1965-68, exec. dir. of community services, 1968-71, provost Southeast campus, 1971—. Chartered com. mem. Oakland County Police Acad. Served to capt. USAF, 1954-57. Commd. col. Hon. Order Ky. Cols., 1966. Licensed certified psychologist, D.C.; licensed cons. psychologist, Mich. Mem. Am. Assn. Jr. Coll., A.A.A.S., Am., Midwestern, D.C., Eastern, Mich. Ky. psychol. assns., U.S.A., Mich. adult edn. assns., Nat., Mich. assns. for pub. sch. adult edn., N.E.A., Human Factors Soc., Mich Soc. for Instrnl. Tech. (pres.), Am. Assn. Community and Jr. Colls. (past pres., dir.), Nat. Council on Community Services, Psi Chi. Home: 5400 Sunnycrest Rd West Bloomfield MI 48033 Office: Oakland Community Coll Southeast Campus 13200 Oak Park Blvd Oak Park MI 48237

FIKE, ROY F., II, accountant; b. Cheyenne, Wyo., Feb. 7, 1948; s. Roy Kenneth and Doris Ann (Moody) F.; B.S., U. Tulsa, 1970, postgrad., 1970. Part-time accountant George W. Underwood, C.P.A., Tulsa, 1968-70; pres. Roy F. Fike & Assos., Inc., St. Louis, 1970—; dir. Enders Enterprises, Inc., Daniel's Florist, Inc., Larry Reynolds & Assos., Inc., Collins Distbg., Inc., Boyce Assos., Inc., Boyce Scientific, Inc., Ann Boyce Interiors, Inc., Unimed, Inc., Joni's, Inc., Gateway Enterprises, Inc. (all St. Louis). Midwest dir. Mandate-Drug Abuse, Caldwell (N.J.) Edn. Program, 1972-73. Served to 2d lt. USAF, 1968-71. Mem. U. Tulsa Alumni Assn. (pres. 1973—, dir. 1973—), Westerners Bowling League (sec. 1974-75) Am. Bar Assn. (mem. law student div. 1970-76), Nat. Soc. Pub. Accountants (Mo. del. ann. meeting 1974-76), Accreditation Council for Accountancy, Assn. Enrolled Agts (dir.), Ind. Accountants Soc. Mo. Office: 232 S Meramec Clayton MO 63105

FILECCIA, ANTHONY, bldg. supt.; b. Chgo., Apr. 5, 1923; s. Rosairo and Margaretta (Congelose) F.; grad. high sch.; m. Mary Elizabeth Cavoto, Sept. 28, 1946; 1 son, Anthony T. Custodial engr. Nicklas Realty, Chgo., 1947-54, Bd. Edn., Chgo., 1954-56; bldg. supt. Am. Bar Center, Chgo., 1956—. Designer, fabricator, installer numerous exec. offices, security signal systems. Bd. dirs., v.p. A.B.C. Credit Union, Chgo., 1961-64. Served with USAAF, 1942-45. Decorated Bronze Star medal with oak leaf cluster; Air medal with 3 oak clusters. Mem. Nat. Assn. Power Engrs., Soc. for Preservation and Encouragement of Barber Shop Quartet Singing Am. (pres. 1968-70, chorus dir. 1963-68). Roman Catholic. Moose. Home: 15140 Dorchester Dolton IL 60419 Office: 1155 E 60th St Chicago IL 60637

FILECCIA, ANTHONY ADALGISO, ins. co. exec.; b. Detroit, Aug. 14, 1948; s. Frank Francis and Levia (Giannini) F.; B.A., Sophia U., Tokyo, 1969; M.S., U. Detroit, 1975, B.S. in Math. and Ops. Research 1974, B.A. in Exptl. Psychology, 1974; m. Karen Elizabeth Smith, Aug. 1, 1975; stepchildren—Kimberly, Scott, Todd. Vice pres. Fileccia Studios, Sterling Heights, Mich., 1971-74; pres. Systemx and Devel. Corp., Warren, Mich., 1973-75; prin., owner Internat. Trade Cons., Detroit, 1974—; chief analyst, research opns. control div. Blue Cross Blue Shield Mich., Detroit, 1976—. Served with USAF, 1966-69; Vietnam. Decorated Bronze Star, Purple Heart; NSF grantee. Mem. UN Assn., Assn. Am. States, AAAS, Am. Soc. Quality Control Engrs., Am. Mgmt. Assn., Math. Assn. Am., Opns. Research Soc., Am. Psychol. Soc., Psychophysiological Research Soc., Artificial Intelligence and Psychol. Simulation Assn. Home: 1555 Moulin St Madison Heights MI 48071 Office: 600 Lafayette E #0412 Detroit MI 48226

FILING, DAVID PETER, audio-visual technician; b. Medway, Maine, Apr. 12, 1949; s. Peter and Fern (Heilman) F.; A.A. in Indsl. Tech., Akron U., 1972; m. Laura Mae Achberger, Nov. 12, 1976. High Pressure boiler fireman aux. tender Ohio Edison Gorge Power Plant, Akron, 1970-72; banbury operator Goodyear Tire Co., Akron, 1972-76; audio-visual technician Cuyahoga Falls (Ohio) pub. schs., 1976—; v.p., bd. chmn. F-M Prodns., Inc., Cuyahoga Falls, 1975—; lectr., workshop dir. on audio-visual equipment. Club: Lions. Home: 2029 10th St Cuyahoga Falls OH 44221 Office: 431 Stow Ave Cuyahoga Falls OH 44221

FILKINS, JAMES HEASOM, educator; b. Coffeyville, Kans., Dec. 18, 1925; s. James Frederick and Wilma Blanche (Heasom) F.; B.A., Hardin-Simmons U., 1949; M.B.A., U. Dallas, 1968-70; Ph.D., N. Tex. State U., 1973; m. Lois Jean Popp, July 28, 1950; children—Timber Lee, Terence James, Tamara Jean. Chemist, Pure Oil Co., 1949-52; tech. service dir. Comml. Testing & Engring. Co., 1952-53; regional mgr. Indsl. Filter Mfg. Co., 1953-55; dist. mgr. Waukesha Sales & Service, 1955-58; ind. mgr. Sun Oil Co., 1958-69; dir. marketing Freguson Industries, 1969-70; asst. prof., controller, asso. dean U. Dallas, 1970-73; v.p., dir. Mgmt. Labs. Am., 1971-73; asso. prof., chmn. dept. bus. adminstrn., dir. M.B.A. programs Coll. of Racine (Wis.), 1973-74; asso. prof. bus. adminstrn. St. Marys Coll., Notre Dame, Ind., 1974-76; prof., dir. grad. mgmt. programs Aquinas Coll., Grand Rapids, Mich., 1976-77; prof. Coll. of St. Thomas, St. Paul, 1977—; cons. Tex. Instruments, Inc., Campbell Taggart, others. Trustee, chmn. Ursuline Endowment Fund, Dallas, 1967-73. Served with USMCR, 1943-45. Mem. Fin. Mgmt. Assn. (chmn. coll. and univ. div.), Am. Mktg. Assn. Internat. Materials Mgmt. Soc., Sigma Iota Epsilon, Beta Gamma Sigma. Author: (with Donald L. Caruth) Lexicon of American Business Terms, 1973. Home: 10600 Aquila Ave S Bloomington MN 55438 Office: College of St Thomas St Paul MN 55105

FILLER, BERNARD MYRON, lawyer, investment banker; b. Cairo, Ill., Oct. 16, 1935; s. Leon and Jeannette (Sanofsky) F.; B.S. in Accounting, U. Ill., 1957; LL.B., Stanford U., 1962; m. Judith A. Sperling, June 16, 1957; children—Deborah, Mark, Lisa. Admitted to N.Y. bar, 1963, Ill. bar, 1970, Calif. bar, 1975; firm Paul, Weiss, Rifkind, Wharton & Garrison, N.Y.C., 1962-69, v.p., dir. Storm Drilling & Marine, Inc., Chgo., 1969-74; with firm Holleb, Gerstein & Glass, Chgo., 1974-76; pres., dir. Capital B Corp., Chgo., 1977—; law lectr. N.Y. U. Law Sch., Loyola U. Law Sch., DePaul U. Law Sch., Chgo. Served with USNR, 1957-59. C.P.A. Mem. Order Coif. Jewish. Home: 1960 Partridge Ln Highland Park IL 60035 Office: 10 S LaSalle St Suite 707 Chicago IL 60603

FINCH, BARBARA LAKE, pub. relations dir.; b. Charleston, W.Va., Jan. 10, 1938; d. Nelson Smith and Mildred (Pearson) Lake; student Agnes Scott Coll., 1955-57; A.B., U. Ky., 1958; m. John Myler Finch, Oct. 11, 1958; children—Stephen Myler, Sarah Elizabeth. Asst. dir. news bur. St. Louis U., 1965-67; dir. pub. information Jefferson Coll., Hillsboro, Mo., 1972-73; publicity cons. Arts and Ednl. Council Greater St. Louis, 1972-73; dir. pub. relations St. Joseph Hosp., Kirkwood, Mo., 1973—. Mem. Pub. Relations Soc. Am., Hosp. Pub. Relations Soc. Greater St. Louis (pres. 1976-77), Women in Communications (pres. St. Louis profl. chpt. 1970-71). Home: 642 Gaslite Lane Kirkwood MO 63122 Office: 525 Couch Ave Kirkwood MO 63122

FINCH, BERNIE ORDERS, chiropractor, applied kinesiologist; b. Indpls., Dec. 27, 1939; s. Gerald F. and Myra Jean (Morris) F.; A.B., Bob Jones U., 1962; Th.B., Berca Sch. Theology, 1964; postgrad. U. Toronto, 1966; M.A., St. Thomas Coll., London, Eng., 1967; D. Chiropractic, Northwestern Coll. Chiropractic, 1972; m. Helen Louise Wellman, Apr. 3, 1969; children—Lynn Gail, Noel Jean, Bernie Scott, Arne Gerald. Ordained minister Baptist Ch., 1961; pastor Waterman Baptist Ch., Lodi, Ind., 1963-65; ednl. missionary Mid-Liberia Baptist Mission, 1965-69; chiropractor Martin (S.D.) Chiropractic Clinic, 1972-75, pvt. practice, Rapid City, S.D., 1975—. Dean Berea Sch. Theology, Pekin, Ill., 1963-65, Midwest Baptist Coll., Danville, Ill., 1965-66; pres. Suakoko (Liberia) Baptist Bible Inst., 1967-68. Active Boy Scouts Am. Chmn. long distance running Ind. Am. Athletic Union, 1964-66, mem. nat. long distance running com. and walking com. 1964 Olympics. Trustee Hope Baptist Ch., Martin, 1972-75. Mem. Am. Chiropractic Assn., Internat. Karate Fedn., Am. Mountain Men, Profl. Bowhunters Soc., Nat. Rifle Assn., Nat. Muzzle Loading Rifle Assn., Nat. Assn. Primitive Riflemen, Xi Upsilon Psi, Chi Omega Phi. Elk. Home: Route 1 Box 96 Rapid City SD 57701 Office: 115 St Joseph St Rapid City SD 57701

FINCH, DONALD GEORGE, poet; b. Peoria, Ill., June 30, 1937; s. Lloyd Lindo and Jean Alberta Harsy; student Bradley U., 1955—. Works include: On Strawberry Eve, 1972; She Waits for Me, 1972; A Dandelion is Not a Rose, 1973; Georgia, 1976; We Are All the Children of God Through Jesus, 1977. With Peoria Post Office. Served with USAF, 1957-60. Mem. Peoria Poetry Club (v.p.) United Amateur Press, DAV. Methodist. Home: PO Box 1014 Peoria IL 61601

FINCH, EUGENE CLIFFORD, wholesale trade exec.; b. Fosston, Minn., Sept. 11, 1915; s. Henry Kirk and Louise Minnie (Routmann) F.; student pub. schs.; m. Joyce Dorothea Goodchild, Sept. 18, 1947; children—Jeanne, Eugene Clifford, Suzanne, Caroline, Kirk. Vice-pres., gen. mgr. Keegan Farm Equipment Co., Mpls., 1954-59; pres. Finch Distbg. Co., Mpls., 1959-65; pres. Select-O-Rax, Inc., Burnsville, Minn., 1965—, also dir. Served with AUS, World War II. Mem. Babbitt (Minn.) Youth Clubs (hon.), Nat. Assn. Rec. Merchandisers, Nat. Assn. Ind. Record Distbrs., Nat. Assn. Truck Stop Operators, Am. Zool. Soc., Am. Legion. Club: Racquet (Palm Springs, Calif.). Home: 6930 Rosemary Rd Eden Prairie MN 55343

FINCH, F. SINCLAIR, physician; b. Armada, Mich., Aug. 24, 1914; s. Floyd S. and Rosetta May (Sinclair) F.; A.B., Wayne State U., 1936, M.B., 1940, M.D., 1941; m. Marseline A. Metz, Jan. 13, 1942; children—Robert S., Patricia A. Intern Grace Hosp., Detroit, 1940-41; resident Saratoga Gen. Hosp., Detroit, 1941-42, 46-48, mem. staff, 1948—, chief staff, 1963-64; pvt. practice medicine and surgery, East Detroit, 1948—; nat. chief med. officer Unlimited Power Boat Assn. Pres. Armada Oil & Gas Co., Texaco distrbrs., 1966—. Served to maj. M.C., AUS, 1942-46. Mem. Spirit of Detroit Assn., Phi Rho Sigma. Club: Detroit Yacht (fleet surgeon 1964, 68). Home: 894 N Renaud St Grosse Pointe Woods MI 48236 Office: 21325 Gratiot St East Detroit MI 48021

FINCH, JOSEPH WARREN, civil engr., surveyor; b. Youngstown, Ohio, Aug. 7, 1923; s. John P. and Mable A. (Poorman) F.; B.C.E., Cornell U., 1947; m. Norinne A. Lyden, July 25, 1944; children—Madonna, Cathy, Michael. Project engr. Joseph Bucheit Co., 1947-48; chief engr. Edward J. De Bartolo Corp., 1948-52; mgr. sales Webrib div., Copperweld Steel Co., 1952-53; gen. supt. constrn. E.J. DeBartolo Corp., 1953-57, mgr. constrn., 1962-70; pres. J.W. Finch Constrn. Co., 1957-62; v.p., project mgr. Park City Shopping Center, 1970-71; project mgr. Hannon Co., 1971-72; v.p. constrn. Stratford Enterprises, Youngstown, Ohio, 1972—; owner J.W. Finch & Son, contractors and engrs., Youngstown, 1972-75, pres. J.W. Finch & Son, Inc., 1975—. Mem. Mahoning County Planning Commn., 1963-65; mem. Bd. Bldg. Standards State Ohio, 1972-76. Served to capt. AUS, World War II; ETO. Decorated Bronze Star medal. Fellow ASCE; mem. Sigma Phi Epsilon. Elk. Clubs: Chesterton, Cornell (Youngstown). Address: 7427 Westview Dr Youngstown OH 44512

FINCHER, GLEN EUGENE, ednl. adminstr.; b. Oct. 29, 1935; B.S., Ohio U., 1959, M.S., 1961, Ph.D. with highest honors, 1963; m. Sue Ann Lenhart; children—Debra Sue, Glen Eugene. Teaching fellow Ohio U., 1960-63; asst. prof. Kent State U., 1963-67; asso. prof. Arizo State U., 1967-68; prof. Akron State U., part time, 1968-70; dir. research and fed. programs Canton (Ohio) City Sch., 1968—. Vis. lectr. Ariz. U., 1963, Malone Coll., Canton, 1969—; cons. numerous pub. sch. systems, Gen. Learning Corp., Charles Jones Pub. Co.. Mem. Community Coordinated Child Care Program Planning Commn., Canton, 1969-70, Mayor's Tech. Adv. Bd., Canton, Stark County Teen Adv. Com. Treas. Young Republicans Club Tuscarawas County, 1958-60. Mem. Canton, East Central Ohio profl. educators asns., N.E.A., Ohio Edn. Assn., Nat. Council Tchrs. Math., Phi Delta Kappa, Kappa Delta Pi, Phi Kappa Phi. Contbr. articles to profl. publs. Home: 4003 Bellwood Dr NW Canton OH 44708

FINDLEY, JAMES ROBERT, psychologist; b. Terre Haute, Ind., Jan. 4, 1941; s. Okel Francis and Jessie Edna (Mott) F.; B.A., Ind. State U., 1964; M.S., Purdue U., 1968, Ph.D., 1973; m. Mary Alice Comar, July 29, 1967; children—Jack Michael, James Brent. Tchr., Washington Community Schs., 1963-65, Griffith Pub. Schs., 1965-66; sch. counselor Delphi (Ind.) Community Schs., 1968-69; asst. personnel dir. Duncan Electric Co., Lafayette, Ind., 1969; counselor, caseworker Cath. Charities, Kokomo, Ind., 1969-70; clin. social worker/counseling psychologist Mental Health Center, Alpena, Mich., 1970-74; sch. psychologist Alpena (Mich.) Pub. Schs., 1974-76; exec. dir. Community Family and Children Services, Alpena, 1976—. Chmn., Alpena County Community Services Council, 1973; mem. No. Mich. Regional Substance Abuse Adv. Bd., 1975-76; active Civic Theatre, Arts Council. Lilian Berry scholar to Am. Acad. Rome, 1965, NDEA fellow 1966-69; licensed psychologist and marriage counselor, Mich. Mem. ACLU, Am., Mich. psychol. assns., Mich. Assn. Marriage Counselors, Inst. Rational Living. Roman Catholic. Club: Racquet (Alpena, Mich.). Home: 8021 US 23 South Ossineke MI 49766 Office: 614 Oldfield St Alpena MI 49707

FINDLEY, PAUL, congressman; b. Jacksonville, Ill., June 23, 1921; s. Joseph S. and Florence Mary (Nichols) F.; A.B., Ill. Coll., 1943, LL.D. (hon.), 1973; L.H.D. (hon.), Lindenwood Coll., 1969; m. Lucille Gemme, Jan. 8, 1946; children—Craig Jon, Diane Lillian. Pres., pub. Pike Press, Inc., Pittsfield, Ill., 1947—; mem. 87th-95th Congresses from 20th Dist. Ill.; made factfinding mission to Paris, 1965; mem. ho. internat. relations com., ho. com. on agr. Del., del. to NATO Parliamentarians Confs., 1965, 66, 67; del. North Atlantic Assembly, 1968-70, 72-73, 76-77. Bd. dirs. Fed. Union, Inc., Washington, Abraham Lincoln Assn., Springfield, Ill., Lincoln Group of Washington. Trustee Ill. Coll. Served to lt. (j.g.) USNR, World War II. Recipient Outstanding Service award So. Ill. U. Sch. Agr., 1970; Hon. State Farmer degree Ill. Future Farmers Am., 1971; Logan Hay medal Abraham Lincoln Assn., spl. medal S.A.R. Mem. Ill. Press Assn. (past dir.), Am. Legion, V.F.W., Amvets, Am. Soc. Internat. Law, Am. Acad. Polit. and Social Sci., Internat. Movement for Atlantic Union (sec.), Mems. Congress for Peace through Law, Nat. Future Farmers Am. Alumni Assn. Phi Beta Kappa. Republican. Conglist. Lion. Author: Federal Farm Fable, 1968. Home: 115 W Jefferson St Pittsfield IL 62363 Office: House Office Bldg Washington DC 20515

FINDORFF, JOHN REEVE, constrn. co. exec.; b. Madison, Wis., Aug. 7, 1918; s. Milton Bremer and Leona Lovina (Reeve) F.; student U. Wis., 1936-38; B.S., Lehigh U., 1941; m. Carol Flora Kay, June 13, 1945; children—Alicia (Mrs. Orvin Nordness, Jr.), Tecla (Mrs. Kenneth Rowin, Jr.), Claire (Mrs. Franklyn Halverson). Gen. contractor, J.H. Findorff & Son, Inc., Madison, Wis., 1941—, pres., 1971—. Served to lt. (j.g.) USCGR, 1942-46. Bd. dirs. Vilas Park Zool. Soc., 1964—, pres., 1974; bd. dirs. Goodwill Industries. Mem. Asso. Gen. Contractors (state pres. 1974, dir. 1971—). Clubs: Madison, Maple Bluff Country, (Madison); Stevens Point (Wis.) Country. Home: 25 Cambridge Ct Madison WI 53704 also Valhalla Townhouse 5 Cable WI 54821 Office: 601 W Wilson St Madison WI 53701

FINE, DWIGHT LYLE, state ofcl.; b. Taylor County, Iowa, July 18, 1942; s. Orris Leroy and Ardith Claire (Lister) F.; A.A., S.W. Bapt. Coll., 1962; B.A., Ouachita U., 1964; M.S. in Pub. Adminstrn., U. Mo., 1966; m. Eva Louise Hargrove, Apr. 8, 1966; 1 son, Marc Louis. Budget analyst div. of Budget and Comptroller, State of Mo., Jefferson City, 1965-67; exec. asst. dir. Mo. Dept. of Revenue, 1967-69; adminstrv. asst. to Mo. Sec. of State, 1970-72; adminstrv. mgr. Mo. State Auditor's Office, Jefferson City, project dir. for statewide sales-ratio study of Mo. property tax levels of assessment, 1975-77; chief clk. Mo. Ho. of Reps., 1978—. Certified adminstrv. mgr. Mem. Mo. Inst. Pub. Adminstrn., Jefferson City Personnel Mgmt. Assn. Democrat. Baptist. Home: Route 3 PO Box 463 Holts Summit MO 65043 Office: House Post Office Jefferson City MO 65101

FINE, ROBERT, mfg. co. exec.; b. Chgo., June 13, 1927; s. Max and Jeanette (Lurie) F.; Ph.B., Northwestern U., 1950, M.B.A., 1956; m. Beryl Lichtenstein, Oct. 7, 1950; children—Larry Evan, Marla Renee. Owner, mgr. Max Fine & Son, Chgo., 1945-55; asst. sales mgr. Bernard Edward Co., Chgo., 1955-58; with Hamilton of Indiana, Inc., Chgo., 1958—, dir. marketing, 1968—. Tchr. Wilson and Fenger Jr. Coll., Chgo., 1955-57. Mem. parents bd. YMCA High Sch., Chgo., 1970-71; Group leader Recovery, Inc. mental health, Chgo., 1972—. Recipient Silver award Variety and Dept. Store Merchandisers, 1968, 69. Mem. Nat. Housewares Mfg. Assn., Alumni Assn. Northwestern U., Variety Stores Assn. Mason. Clubs: Mather Park Tennis (pres.

1966-67); Edens Tennis. Home: 5041 N Monticello Ave Chicago IL 60625 Office: 3772 W Devon Ave Chicago IL 60659

FINE, SIDNEY, historian; b. Cleve., Oct. 11, 1920; s. Morris Louis and Gussie (Redalia) F.; B.A. with 1st sr. honor, Western Res. U., 1942; M.A., U. Mich., 1942, Ph.D. (Rackham fellow), 1948; m. Jean Schechter, Dec. 5, 1942; children—Gail Judith, Deborah Ann. Instr. history U. Mich., 1948-51, asst. prof., 1951-55, asso. prof., 1955-59, prof., 1959—, Andrew Dickson White prof. history, 1974—, Richard Hudson research prof. history, 1963-64, 76-77, chmn. dept. history, 1969-71; pres. Labor Historians, 1969-71; mem. Nat. Archives Advisory Council, 1969-71. Served with USN, 1942-46. Recipient Alumni Citation award Case-Western Res. U., 1968; Distinguished Faculty Achievement award U. Mich., 1969; award of Merit, Hist. Soc. Mich., 1970; Guggenheim fellow, 1957-58. Mem. Am. Hist. Assn., Orgn. Am. Historians, AAUP, Social Sci. History Assn. Jewish. Author books including: Laissez Faire and the General Welfare State, 1956; The Automobile under the Blue Eagle: Labor, Management and the Automobile Manufacturing Code, 1963 (Assn. State Local History award of Merit 1964, U. Mich. Press award 1965); Sit-Down: The General Motors Strike of 1936-37, 1969 (U. Mich. Press award 1971); Frank Murphy: The Detroit Years, 1975; contbr. numerous articles to profl. jours.; editorial bd. Labor History, 1963—, chmn., 1976—; bd. editors Jours. Am. History, 1964-67, Revs. Am. History, 1973—. Home: 825 Russett Rd Ann Arbor MI 48103 Office: History Dept Univ Michigan Ann Arbor MI 48109

FINESMITH, STEPHEN HARRIS, scientist, state ofcl.; b. N.Y.C., Nov. 7, 1934; s. Murray and Cele (Lerner) F.; B.B.A., Coll. City N.Y., 1955; postgrad. State U. N.Y. at Buffalo, 1955-59, 71-74, U. Wis., 1976-77; m. Barbara Kaden, Aug. 28, 1955 (div. June 1977); children—Terri, Robin. Asso. scientist Systems Devel. Corp., Santa Monica, Cal., 1959-60; asst. prof. Rutgers U., New Brunswick, N.J., 1960-62; systems analyst Internat. Tel. & Tel. Co., Paramus, N.J., 1962-63; prin. systems design engr., head new techniques and systems group Univac div. Sperry Rand Corp., St. Paul, 1963-67; asso. prof. U. So. Miss., Hattiesburg, 1967-68; asso. prof. Mankato (Minn.) State Coll., 1968-71; prof. Governors State U., Park Forest South, Ill., 1971-72; pres., Serendipity Systems, Inc., Janesville, Wis., 1973-75, now chmn. bd.; prof., chmn. psychology dept. Milton (Wis.) Coll., 1972-76; asst. dir. Bur. Systems and Data Processing, Wis. Dept. Revenue, Madison, 1976-77; psychotherapist, communications therapist. Cons. In Mental Health, Janesville, 1973-74. Research scientist, human relations lab. cons., 1960—. Mem. Am. Psychol. Assn. (asso.), A.A.A.S., Assn. Humanistic Psychology, Assn. for Computing Machinery, Wis. Data Processing Mfrs. Assn. Club: Country (Lake Windsor, Wis.). Inventor bionic evolutionary adaptive stock trading system, 1964. Home: 6665 Charlie Grimm Rd Windsor WI 53598 Office: Bur Systems and Data Processing Wis Dept Revenue Madison WI 53705

FINIFTER, ADA WEINTRAUB (MRS. BERNARD M. FINIFTER), polit. scientist, educator; b. N.Y.C., June 6, 1938; d. Isaac and Stella (Colchamiro) Weintraub; B.A., Bklyn. Coll., City U. N.Y., 1959; M.A., U. Mich., 1961; Ph.D., U. Wis., 1967; m. Bernard M. Finifter, June 12, 1960. Asst. prof. polit. sci. Mich. State U., East Lansing, 1967-72, asso. prof., 1972—. Congl. fellow, 1973-74. Mem. Am., So., Midwest polit. sci. assns., World Assn. for Pub. Opinion Research. Editor: Alienation and the Social System, 1972; also articles in profl. jours. Mem. editorial bd. Am. Polit. Sci. Review, Am. Politics Quar., Sex Roles: A Jour. of Research. Home: 1743 Old Mill Rd East Lansing MI 48823

FINK, DENNIS LEE, educator; b. Chicago Heights, Ill., Feb. 26, 1942; s. Reinhardt Henry and Mabel (Emde) F.; B.S. with honors in Edn., Ill. State U., 1965, M.S., 1967; m. Patsy Ann Wilhelmsen, Aug. 29, 1964; children—Melissa Lynn, Greg Robert. Tchr. history Homewood-Flossmoor (Ill.) High Sch., 1966—; supr. student tchrs. No. Ill. U., DeKalb, 1970—, instr. grad. edn., 1974—. Home: 1245 Thomas St Homewood IL 60430 Office: 999 Kedzie St Flossmoor IL 60422

FINKEL, WARREN EDWARD, architect; b. Elyria, Ohio, Nov. 2, 1920; s. Edward Raymond and Hazel (Allen) F.; ed. Western Res. U. (now Case Western Res. U.), 1950; m. Jean Giltner, Jan. 23, 1953. With Dalton-Dalton, Cleve., 1950, R.G. Wheeler, San Diego, 1951-52, Weinberg & Teare, Cleve., 1953-54; partner Jean Fenton Finkel-Warren Edward Finkel, Lorain, Ohio, 1955—; pres. Finkel & Finkel, Inc.; treas. Lorain Community Broadcasting Co.; dir. Central Security Nat. Bank. Mem. Lorain Community Devel. Com.; mem. capital improvement com. Lorain Community United Appeal; mem. Urban Renewal-Community Devel. Com. Served with USN, 1938-45. Registered architect, Ohio, Mich., Fla., Nat. Council Archtl. Registration Bds. Mem. A.I.A. (corporate), Architects Soc. Ohio, Lorain C. of C. (pres. 1967). Rotarian. Prin. works include: Oak Hills Country Club, Lorain, 1960, 1st Ch. of Christ, Scientist, Lorain, 1960, Lorain Community Hosp., 1962, Firelands Retirement Center, Lorain-Oberlin, 1963, Lorain Nat. Bank, 1964, Lorain County Community Coll., 1965, Lorain County Red Cross Hdqrs, 1966, Lorain County Sch. for Retarded Children, 1967, Lorain Family YMCA, 1968, Lorain Community Hosp., 1969, Lorain County Community Coll., 1970, Lorain City Hall, 1971, Learning Resource Center, 1974, Elyria Savs. and Trust Bank, 1976, Fine Arts Center, 1977. Office: Masonic Bldg Lorain OH 44052

FINKELMAN, ROLAND ISRAEL, photog. co. exec.; b. Bklyn., May 3, 1928; s. William Wolf and Matie (Charnes) F.; student Ithaca Coll., 1946-47; A.B., Syracuse U., 1951; m. Iris Tuck, Oct. 27, 1951; children—Daniel Paul, Eve Lynn, Jesse Charles. With publicity dept. N.Y. Times radio sta. WQXR, 1951-52; with Internat. Latex Corp., Dover, Del., 1952-68, dir. manpower planning, 1963-64, dir. indsl. relations, 1965-66, v.p. indsl. relations, 1966-68; dir. orgn. devel. and indsl. relations Bell & Howell Co., Chgo., 1968-69, v.p. orgn. devel., 1969—. Mem. Chgo. Crime Commn., 1971-72, Met. Housing Devel. Corp., 1971-72; mem. bus. adv. com. Oakton Community Coll., 1971-72. Bd. dirs. Chgo. Bus. Opportunity Fair, Bell & Howell Found. Mem. Employers Assn. Greater Chgo. Home: 19 Londonderry Ln Lincolnshire IL 60015 Office: 7100 McCormick Rd Chicago IL 60645

FINLAY, CHARLES WILLIAM, photographer; b. Ashland, Ohio, Jan. 17, 1931; s. Walter Holly and Lois Lucille (Mumaw) F.; student Winona Sch. Profl. Photography; m. Mary Ann Dickman, Sept. 10, 1950; children—Barry Lynn, Terry Renee (Mrs. Randy Stackhouse), Christopher William. With Gerald's Studio & Camera Shop, Inc., Ashland, 1948—, pres., 1949—. Recipient numerous awards for photography. Mem. Profl. Photographers Am., Profl. Photographers Ohio. Mason (Shriner). Home: 863 E Bank St Ashland OH 44805 Office: 136 E Main St Ashland OH 44805

FINLAY, WALTER LEONARD, metal product co. exec.; b. Bklyn., Mar. 20, 1913; s. Thomas John and Bertha Katherine (Heinrichs) F.; B.S., Lehigh U., 1936; M.S., Yale, 1947, D. Engring., 1948; m. Margaret Alverta Palmer, May 1, 1937; children—Diane (Mrs. James Carleton Harrison), Lois Marie (Mrs. George W. Kenzy). Supr. chem. and metallurgical research Remington Arms Co., Bridgeport, Conn., 1936-50; dir. research Rem-Cru Titanium, Inc., Midland, Pa., 1950-58; dir. research Crucible Steel Co. Am., Pitts., 1958-65; v.p. research and devel. Copper Range Co., N.Y.C., and White Pine, Mich., 1965—; pres. Contemporary Research, Inc., Natick, Mass., 1970—; v.p., dir. White Pine Copper Co., (Mich.), 1970—. Bd. dirs. Beaver Valley YMCA, New Brighton, Pa., 1960-65. Recipient Schwab medal Am. Iron and Steel Inst., 1963, award Dept. Def., 1945. Mem. Nat. Acad. Sci. (chmn. materials adv. bd. 1967-68), Nat. Research Council. Clubs: Rotary (pres. 1976) (White Pine); University (N.Y.C.). Author: Silver-Bearing Copper, 1968; Common Sense and Common Science, 1977. Patentee in field. Home: PO Box 97 White Pine MI 49971 Office: White Pine Copper Co White Pine MI 49971

FINLEY, DALE ROY, transit authority exec.; b. Berea, Ohio, Aug. 22, 1935; s. Roy C. and Marie H. (Morton) F.; m. Lee Millsom, July 25, 1959; 1 dau., Kristen Lee; student Wittenberg U. Owner, mgr. Finley Wholesale Egg Distbrs., 1957-74; exec. dir. No. Ohio Urban Systems Research Corp., Cleve., 1974—; pres. Greater Cleve. Regional Transit Authority, 1975—; chmn. Met. Cleve. Hwy. Users Fedn.; state chmn. Legis. Land Use Adv. Council; partner Harvest House Food Distbrs., Skitown, Inc., Social Devel. Corp. Mem. Strongsville (Ohio) City Council, 1965-68, pres., 1967; mayor, Strongsville, 1968-74; mem. Cuyahoga County Republican Exec. Com.; bd. dirs. S.W. Gen. Hosp.; mem. adv. bd. Cuyahoga Community Coll., Dyke Coll.; mem. exec. bd. Luekemia Soc. Am., Greater Cleve. March of Dimes. Mem. Am. Pub. Transit Assn. (dir.), Ohio Planning Conf., U.S. (sen., past dir.), Ohio (past v.p., chmn.), Strongsville (past pres.) jr. chambers commerce. Clubs: Masons (32 deg.), Shriners, Columbia Hills Country Club (dir.), U.S. Ski Assn. Recipient Jaycees Distinguished Service award, 1970; Ohio Commodore. Home: 12220 Woodridge Circle Strongsville OH 44136 Office: 1404 E 9th St Cleveland OH 44114

FINLEY, ELDEN DELOSS, ednl. cons.; b. Blandinsville, Ill., June 18, 1901; s. Joseph Bertram and Carrie Bell (Wright) F.; B.S., Knox Coll., 1923; M.A., Columbia U., 1928; postgrad. Purdue U., U. So. Calif., Ill. U.; m. Ethel Pearl Rulifson, Aug. 14, 1924; 1 son, Jon David. Instr. math., band Keokuk, Iowa, 1923-25; instr. Pekin Community High Sch. (Ill.), 1925-28, edn. counselor, asst. prin., 1928-31; supt. Delavan Community High Sch., 1931-49; asst. supt. pub. instrn. State of Ill., 1949-58; asso. prof. edn. Chgo. Tchrs. Coll., 1958-59; supt. schs., Chicago Ridge, Ill., 1959-73, supt. emeritus, 1973—. State adviser Ill. Assn. Student Councils; chmn. Chgo. Ridge Salvation Army, 1961-73. Exec. bd. Cook County Ednl. Devel. Coop., Cook County Coop. Assn. Spl. Edn. Recipient resolution for service to edn. Ill. Gen. Assembly, 1973; Elden D. Finley Jr. High Sch. named in his honor, Chicago Ridge, Ill., 1970; sch. library named Elden D. Finley Library, Ridge Lawn, Ill., 1965. Mem. Ill. High Sch. Assn. (bd. dirs., v.p.), Nat., Ill. (div. v.p.) edn. assns., Am., Ill. (Presdl. citation 1973), S. Cook County (pres. 1969-70) assns. sch. adminstrs., Assn. Supervision and Curriculum Devel., No. Ill. Supt.'s Round Table, Allerton House Conf. Edn. in Ill., Nat., Ill. sch. pub. relations assns., Phi Sigma Kappa. Rotarian (dist. gov. 1940-41). Home: 408 W 3d St Delavan IL 61734

FINLEY, JOSEPH ROBERT, mental health counselor; b. Morgantown, W.Va., Apr. 11, 1953; s. Cecil Clay and Lucy Louise (King) F.; A.A., Parkersburg Community Coll., 1973; B.A., Ohio State U., 1975; M.Ed., Ohio U., 1978; m. Debra Lynn Minerd, Apr. 10, 1976. Owner, operator Joseph Finley Painting, Belpre, Ohio, 1971-76; counselor Washington County Open Door Home, Marietta, Ohio, 1977—. Bd. dirs. Parkersburg (W.Va.) Big Bros., 1975-76; cons. St. Joseph's Hosp., Parkersburg. Mem. Am. Personnel and Guidance Assn., Am. Mental Health Counselors Assn., Pub. Offenders Counselors Assn., Ohio State, Parkersburg Community Coll. alumni assns. Methodist. Home: 2404 36th St Parkersburg WV 26101 Office: 1608 Colegale Dr Marietta OH 44750

FINLEY, ROBERT MCLAREN, economist, educator; b. Vilas, Colo., May 10, 1927; s. Charles Amos and Lillas Mae (Irwin) F.; B.S., Kans. State U., 1950, M.S., 1953; Ph.D., U. Ill., 1957; m. Gloria Glee Mann, Aug. 1949; 1 dau., Jennifer. Instr. U. Ill., Urbana, 1955-57; asst. prof. U. Nebr., Lincoln, 1957-62, asso. prof., 1962-63; prof. agrl. econs. U. Mo., Columbia, 1963—; cons. U.S. AID, 1974; mem. Mo. Gov.'s Adv. Council on Agr. Served with USN, 1945-46. Mem. Am. Econ. Assn., Am. Agrl. Econ. Assn., Agrl. History Soc. Home: 12 Russell Blvd Columbia MO 65201

FINN, BARBARA JO, counselor; b. St. Louis, Apr. 10, 1942; d. Edward Taylor and Evelyn (Conniff) Eaton; B.A., Washington, 1964, M.A. in Edn., 1974; postgrad. St. Louis U., 1974-76; Ed.D., Am. Internat. Open U., 1977; m. Kenneth Wayne Finn, Oct. 9, 1964. Tchr. Mehlville Sch. Dist., St. Louis, 1964-73, sch. counselor, 1973-74, dir. parent edn., 1974-77; mem. managerial communications program Printing Industries St. Louis, 1976-77; cons. in field, 1974—. Mem. foster parent group St. Louis County Juvenile Ct., 1974-76; mem. parenting task force com. Mo. Gov.'s Conf. Edn., 1976—. Mem. Nat. Council on Family Relations, Am. Personnel and Guidance Assn., Mo., St. Louis guidance assns., Mo. Soc. for Individual Psychology, Gamma Phi Beta, Phi Beta Kappa, Kappa Delta Pi. Contbr. articles to profl. jours. Home: 4658 Trails End Dr House Springs MO 63051 Office: 3120 Lemay Ferry Rd St Louis MO 63125

FINN, CHESTER EVANS, lawyer; b. Dayton, Ohio, July 13, 1918; s. Samuel Lawrence and Lillian Rose (Evans) F.; grad. Phillips Exeter Acad., 1936; B.A., Yale, 1940; LL.B., Harvard, 1946; m. Phyllis M. Kessel, Apr. 29, 1942; children—Chester Evans, Natalie K., Samuel J. Admitted to Ohio bar, 1947; asso. mem. firm Estabrook, Finn & McKee, Dayton, 1947-53, partner, 1953—; dir. 1st Nat. Bank Dayton, Cassano Enterprises, Inc., Dayton, Dimco-Gray Co., Dayton, Edward Rose Homes, Inc., Dayton, others. Bd. dirs. United Fund Dayton, 1965, Community Research, Inc., Dayton, 1970, Dayton-Maimi Valley Consortium, 1970. Served with USNR, 1942-45: PTO. Mem. Dayton (pres., 1968-69), Am., Ohio bar assns. Clubs: Moraine Country, Meadowbrook, Bicycle, City (Dayton); Yale (N.Y.C.). Mason. Home: 514 Valewood Ln Dayton OH 45405 Office: 2100 First National Bank Bldg Dayton OH 45402

FINN, JULIA ELIZABETH, counselor; b. St. Louis, Aug. 10, 1926; d. Carl Jacobs and Pauline Frances (Young) F.; A.B., Washington U., St. Louis, 1947, M.A. in Edn., 1963. Research technician Washington U. Sch. Medicine, St. Louis, 1947-52; tchr. Clopton High Sch., Clarksville, Mo., 1953-54, Hancock High Sch., Lemay, Mo., 1954-60; counselor Sumner High Sch., St. Louis, 1963-65, St. Charles (Mo.) Sr. High Sch., 1965—. Alderman, Portage des Sioux, Mo., 1974—. Mem. Am. Personnel and Guidance Assn., Nat. Vocat. Guidance Assn., Am. Sch. Counselors Assn., Mo. State Tchrs. Assn., AAUW, Kappa Delta Pi. Contbr. articles to med. research jours. Home: 1850 Main St Portage des Sioux MO 63373 Office: St Charles Sr High Sch Kingshwy and Waverly St Saint Charles MO 63301

FINNEBURGH, MORRIS LEWIS, mfg. exec.; b. Ft. Worth, Sept. 3, 1900; s. Lewis Henry and Lillie (Lewis) F.; student pub. schs.; LL.D., Ariz. Tech. Coll., 1975; m. Frieda Fox, Oct. 17, 1920; 1 son, Morris L. Partner, adminstrv. exec. Finney Co., Bedford, Ohio, 1952—, now chmn. exec. com.; chmn. bd. Finney Mfg. Co., 1952—, now chmn. bd.; chmn. bd. Bedford Realty Corp., 1952—. Nat. chmn. All-Industry Electronics Conf. Speakers' Bur., 1961—; chmn. Electronics Industry Council. Trustee, mem. exec. com. Superior Ind. TV Service Fund. Recipient Friends of Service award, 13 consecutive years, Humanitarian award Bernon Industries; named to Electronic Hall of Fame, 1969; recipient Bernon Humanitarian award, 1969. Mem. Nat. Alliance Technicians and Electricians Assn., Nat. Electronics Distbrs.' Assn., Technicians Service Assn., Ind. Electronic Servicemen's Assn., Electronic Technicians Guild, Nat. Alliance Television and Electronic Service Assns. (hon. life, chmn. nat. merger com. with Nat. Electronics Assn.), Nat. (life-time hon. mem.), Kans. (hon. life), La. (hon. life), Calif. (hon. life), Va. (hon. life), Tex. electronics assns., Electronics Industry Assn. (hon. life), Maine Electronics Technicians Assn. (hon. life), Television Reception Industry Program (nat. chmn.). Mason. Clubs: Lake Forest Country, Forest Hills. Public Speaker. Author: The Black Book. Contbr. articles to profl. jours. Home: 3111 Monticello Blvd Cleveland Heights OH 44118 Office: 34 W Interstate St Bedford OH 44014

FINNEGAN, THOMAS JOSEPH, lawyer; b. Chgo., Aug. 18, 1900; s. Thomas Harrison and Marie (Flanagan) F.; J.D., Chgo. Kent Coll. of Law, 1923; m. Hildreth Millslagel, July 1, 1933. Admitted to Ill. bar, 1923, and since practiced in Chicago; mem. firm Fithian, Spengler & Finnegan, 1935-51; mem. firm Korshak, Rothman, Oppenheim & Finnegan, 1951—. Mem. Am., Fed., Ill., Chgo. bar assns., Chgo. Law Inst., Phi Alpha Delta. Home: 5630 Sheridan Rd Chicago IL 60660 Office: 69 W Washington St Chicago IL 60602

FINNEY, DAVID BERTRIC, JR., druggist; b. Petersburg, Ill., June 15, 1919; s. David Bertric and Christine (Lewis) F.; student Ill. Coll., Jacksonville, 1937-38; Pharm.B., U. Ill., 1943; m. Doris Virginia Smith, Nov. 17, 1946; children—Catherine Diane Finney Heiden, Laurie Beth Finney Beard. With Finney Drug Store, Petersburg, Ill., 1946-47, Longs Pharmacy, Jacksonville, Ill., Vedder Drug Store, Rushville, Ill., 1948; owner Finney Drug Store, Virginia, Ill., 1949—; former pres., dir. Va. Bldg. & Savs. Assn.; dir. Petefish, Skiles & Co. Bank. Former sec. bd. trustees Passavant Meml. Area Hosp., Jacksonville; chmn. Ill. Faith at Work Conf., Decatur, 1971, 72. Served to capt. AUS, 1943-46. Recipient Laymans award Ill. Council Chs., 1969. Mem. Virginia C. of C. (sec.), Ill. Pharm. Assn., Nat. Assn. Retail Druggists. Republican. Presbyn. (ruling elder, pres. Virginia council chs. 1967-69). Mason (32 deg., Shriner), Kiwanian. Home: 242 S Stowe St Virginia IL 62691 Office: South Side Sq Virginia IL 62691

FINNEY, JOAN MARIE MCINROY, state ofcl.; b. Topeka, Feb. 11, 1925; d. Leonard L. and Mary M. (Sands) McInroy; B.A., Washburn U., 1974; m. Spencer W. Finney, Jr., July 24, 1957; children—Sally, Dick, Mary. Sec. Washington and Topeka offices U.S. Senator Frank Carlson, 1953-69; commr. elections Shawnee County, Kans., 1970-72; adminstrv. asst. to mayor of Topeka, 1973-74; treas. State of Kans., Topeka, 1974—. Candidate for U.S. Ho. of Reps., 1972. Bd. dirs. Girls Club of Topeka. Mem. Kans. Women's Polit. Caucus, Women Aware, Bus. and Profl. Women's Club, Sigma Alpha Iota. Roman Catholic (bd. dirs. mem. fin. com.). Home: 4600 W 19th St Topeka KS 66604 Office: Office of State Treasurer 535 Kansas Topeka KS 66603

FINSTAD, MARTIN M., ret. educator; b. Winger, Minn., Feb. 11, 1900; s. Martin and Martha (Lutness) F.; B.A., St. Olaf Coll., 1920; postgrad U. Minn., 1921-22; B.D., Chgo. Luth. Theol. Sem., 1934; M.A. in Edn., Northwestern U., 1936, M.A. in History and Social Studies, 1939, postgrad. 1944-45; M. Divinity, Luth. Sch. Theology, Chgo., 1972; m. Gertrude Gilbert, May 29, 1930. Prin. Nelson (Minn.) Consol. Sch., 1920-21; supt. Montrose (Minn.) Pub. Schs., 1922-24; tchr. history Stillwater (Minn.) High Sch., 1924-31; instr. social studies Proviso Twp. High Sch., Maywood, Ill., 1934-65, instr. psychology, evening sch., 1944-55. Pres. Maywood Pub Library Bd., 1955-69; village clk., Maywood, 1961-69; active other civic affairs. Bd. dirs. Chgo. Luth. Theol. Sem., 1954-63. Served with U.S. Army, 1918. Recipient Churchman of Yr. award Ch. Fedn. Greater Chgo., 1958. Mem. Nat. Council for Social Studies, Adult Edn. Assn., A.L.A., Internat. Inst. Municipal Clks., N.E.A., Am. Legion (vice comdr. Ill. 1950-51), Ill. Tchrs. Assn. (dir. 1958-61), Phi Delta Kappa. Republican. Lutheran. Mason (K.T., 32 deg., Shriner), Elk. Contbr. articles to profl. jours. Home: 350 W Schaumburg Rd Schaumburg IL 60194

FIONDO, JOHN PHILLIP, sch. adminstr.; b. Detroit, Apr. 6, 1929; s. Phillip and Rose (Marandola) F.; B.S., Wayne State U., 1962, M.S., 1962, Ph.D., 1967; m. Silvia Gudy Netto, Nov. 30, 1957; children—Stephen, Andrea. Elementary sch. tchr. Detroit Pub. Schs., 1957-62, psychologist, 1962-69, adminstrv. psychologist, 1969—. Adj. prof. U. Mich., Ann Arbor, 1971—, Mercy Coll. Detroit, 1973—, Wayne State U., Detroit, 1968—; cons. psychologist pvt. practice, Grosse Pointe Woods, Mich., 1969—; cons. Mich. Office Vocat. Rehab., 1968—. Mem. Am. Psychol. Assn., Am. Assn. Mental Deficiency, Phi Delta Kappa. Home: 23324 Colonial Ct S St Clair Shores MI 48080 Office: 20323 Mack Grosse Pointe Woods MI 48236

FIRARI, HARVEY, educator; b. Lowell, Wis., Oct. 30, 1921; s. William and Emma (Eskstaedt) F.; B.A. cum laude, Carroll Coll., 1950; M.A., Northwestern U., 1951; postgrad. (Wm. Morris Agy. fellow) Yale Drama Sch., 1959-60; m. Nancy Allen, Mar. 11, 1955; children—Fairlie Allen, Robert Allen. Faculty Culver (Ind.) Mil. Acad., 1952—, tchr. English, speech and history, dir. theatre, 1968—. Cons. on composition Nat. Commn. English, 1966, 67. Served with USAAF, 1942-45. Mem. Assn. Coll. and Univ. and Community Arts Adminstrs., Theta Alpha Phi, Sigma Tau Delta, Lambda Psi. Author: (plays) Philip Sandan, 1960; Yew Trilogy, 1962; Deadlock, 1963; Companion Pieces, 1965; Telamon, 1972; Uncle Jamesie, 1975. Contbr. articles to profl. jours. Home: 196 North Terr Culver IN 46511 Office: Culver Mil Acad Culver IN 46511

FIREOVED, MAVALINE FERRIER, corp. exec.; b. Angola, Ind.; d. Floyd Erwin and Ruth (Cain) Ferrier; student Tri-State Coll., summers 1937-38; B.S. in Bus., Ind. U., 1941; m. George M. Fireoved, Dec. 10, 1942 (div. Sept 1953); children—Gwen Anne, David Mark. Tchr. commerce, English, Lafayette Central High Sch., Ft. Wayne, Ind., 1941-42; with Gen. Electric Co., Ft. Wayne, 1942-43; tchr. commerce New Haven High Sch., Ft. Wayne, 1943-44; sec., v.p. Wayne Fabricating Corp., Ft. Wayne, 1952-53, pres., gen. mgr., 1953—; founder, pres. L.T.L., Inc., 1957—. Mem. AAUW, Fine Arts Found., Ind. U. Found., Ind. U. Alumni Assn. (life), Internat. Platform Assn. Methodist (mem. ofcl. bd.). Mem. Daus. Nile, Internat. Order King's Daus. Home: 319 W Fleming Ave Fort Wayne IN 46807

FIRESTONE, RALPH WAYNE, elec. engr.; b. Salem, Ohio, Feb. 28, 1935; s. Howard Edward and Gertrude Mildred (Carlson) F.; B.S. in Elec. Engring., Ohio U., 1958; m. Shirley June Derr, Aug. 17, 1958; children—Ralph Wayne, Christopher Lee, Howard Edward, Heather Elizabeth. Tchr. elec. night sch. Salem Bd. Edn., 1959-66; engring. cons. on elec., heating, ventilating and air conditioning, 1958-73; now pres. Firestone Electric Co., Salem. Registered profl. engr., Ohio, Pa., W.Va., Ill., Ga., Ala., Fla., Ariz. Mem. Nat., Ohio socs. profl. engrs., I.E.E.E., Am. Soc. Heating, Refrigeration and Air Conditioning Engrs., Columbiana Co. Profl. Engrs. (pres. 1965), Nat. Elec.

Contractors Assn. (bd. dirs., v.p.), Phi Delta Theta. Mason, Rotarian. Home: 435 N Union St Salem OH 44460

FIRESTONE, ROGER MORRIS, computer scientist; b. Washington, Aug. 23, 1945; s. Linn Jacob and Regina Caroline (Steiner) F.; student U. Minn., 1963; A.B. summa cum laude, Brown U., 1967, Sc.M., 1967; M.S., N.Y.U., 1969, Ph.D. (NSF grad. fellow), 1971; M.B.A., Coll. of St. Thomas, 1976. With Sperry Univac div. Sperry Rand Corp., Roseville, Minn., 1970—, prin. programmer, 1971-72, supervising programmer, 1972—; instr. Army Edn. Center, 1977—; mem. standards planning and requirements com. on text processing Am. Nat. Standards Inst., 1976—. Flute and piccolo player St. Paul Center Symphony, 1972—, Mpls. Center Symphony, 1971—; alternate State Dem. Conv., 1972; mem. music com. Mpls. Jewish Community Center, 1973—. Mem. AAAS, Assn. for Computing Machinery, Soc. for Indsl. and Applied Math., Phi Beta Kappa, Sigma Xi. Democrat Farm Labor Party. Jewish. Clubs: St. Paul Athletic, N.Y.U. Club (N.Y.C.), Masons. Contbr. articles to profl. jours. and confs.; leading and supporting roles in many plays, musicals, one feature film, one opera. Home: 1808 Colvin Ave St Paul MN 55116 Office: MS 4953 Sperry Univac PO Box 3942 St Paul MN 55165

FIRNSTAHL, KENNETH PAUL, broadcasting exec.; b. Long Prairie, Minn., Oct. 16, 1924; s. Otto Francis and Cecelia Ann (Holweck) F.; student McPhail Sch. Speech and Drama, 1946-47, Brown Inst. Radio Broadcasting, 1948, U. Minn., 1949; m. Mary Louise Haas, Aug. 20, 1949; children—Renae, Janice, Patricia, Jeffrey, Mary Jo. Advt. salesman WIKB, Iron River, Mich., 1950-52; sales mgr. KEYD, Mpls., 1953-60; gen. sales mgr. KTCR AM and FM, Mpls., 1960—. Chmn. Fridley Chamber Music, 1962-66; chmn. twin city broadcasters Am. Heart Assn., 1970-72. Served with USNR, 1943-46; PTO. Mem. Mpls. Advt. Club, Sports and Health Club, U. Minn. Alumni. Club: Bear Fax. Home: 565 Rice Creek Terr Minneapolis MN 55432 Office: 3701 Winnetka St Minneapolis MN 55427

FISCH, HARRISON CLEVE, county ofcl.; b. Gaza, Iowa, Sept. 23, 1924; s. Cleve Orla and Irene Delores (Webster) F.; B.S., Iowa State U., 1949; M.S., Mich. State U., 1952; m. Marjorie Jean Terrell, Dec. 26, 1948; children—Brian, Jonathan, Mary, Martha. Instr. agrl. engring. Mich. State U., East Lansing, 1949-55, mem. tech. mission to Nat. U. Colombia, 1953-55; farmer, Primghar, Iowa, 1955—; mem. O'Brien County Bd. Suprs., 1966—. Mem. O'Brien County Bd. Edn., 1958-66. Chmn. bd. Northwest Iowa Mental Health Center, 1971—, Upper Des Moines Opportunity, 1972—. Registered profl. engr., Iowa. Mem. Am. Soc. Agrl. Engrs., Iowa Farm Bur., Alpha Zeta, Pi Mu Epsilon. Republican. Conglist. Home: RD 2 Primghar IA 51245

FISCH, ROBERT OTTO, med. educator; b. Budapest, Hungary, June 12, 1925; s. Zoltan and Irene (Manheim) F.; came to U.S., 1957, naturalized, 1965; med. diploma U. Budapest, 1952; study art Acad. Fine Arts, Budapest, 1943, Walker Art Center, Mpls., 1968-69, U. Minn., 1969-70, Mpls. Coll. Arts and Design, 1970-76; m. Joyce D.E. Gulasch, May 30, 1969; 1 dau., Rebecca A. Gen. practice medicine, Hungary, 1951-55, pub. health officer, 1955; pediatrician Hosp. for Premature Children, Budapest, 1956; intern Christ Hosp., Jersey City, 1957-58; intern pediatrics U. Minn. Hosps., 1958-59, resident, 1959-60, research fellow, 1961; instr. U. Minn. Sch. Medicine, 1961-63, asst. prof., 1963-72, asso. prof., 1972—, dir. phonylketonuria clinic, 1961—, dir. child care clinic, 1972—; Minn. dir. child devel. study, collaborative study of 14 med. univs. of U.S., 1963-75. Mem. Am. Acad. Pediatrics, Assn. Ambulatory Pediatric Services. Contbr. to publs. in field. Exhibited art works in various one-man and group shows. Home: 2298 Folwell St Saint Paul MN 55108 Office: Box 487 Mayo Hosp U Minn Minneapolis MN 55455

FISCHBACH, JULIUS, clergyman; b. Huntington, W.Va., Apr. 25, 1894; s. Julius and Mary (Woody) F.; A.B., U. Mich., 1917; Th.M., So. Bapt. Theol. Sem., 1920; D.D., Hillsdale Coll., 1943; m. Mary Mildred Bibb, June 17, 1925; children—David Bibb, Mary Ellen (Mrs. William H. Heater). Ordained to ministry Bapt. Ch., 1918; pastor Mo. Hope Ch., W. Va., 1920-25, Morgantown, W.Va., 1925-28, 1928-36; pastor First Ch., Lansing, Mich., 1936-61, pastor emeritus, 1961—; interim minister, Bapt. chs. Mich., 1962, Madison, Wis., 1963, Providence, R.I. and Clearfield, Utah, 1964, Mpls., Yakima, Wash., 1965 San Bernardino, Cal., 1966, Mich., 1967-71; asso. minister Peoples Ch., East Lansing, Mich., 1972—; guest minister to chs. in Scotland and Eng., 1951; around the world tour of mission fields, preaching in Philippines, Burma, Assam, India, and Eng., 1955. Chmn. Nat. Adv. Com. Juvenile Protection, 1954-56; mem. Nat. Ch. Extension Com., 1952-55, pastoral relations com. Bapt. Ministers Council, 1948-50, gen. council of Am. Bapt. Conv., 1947-53 (mem. exec. com. 1952, 53), mem. commn. on ministry, 1951, dir. Green Lake Assembly, 1952, 53, chmn. com. Children and Church, 1940-44, council on finance and promotion, 1936-39, on Christian Edn., 1942-46, mem. Convocation team, 1942, leader Christian Life Crusade team, 1945. Dir. Lansing YMCA, 1939-54; pres. W.Va. Bapt. Assembly, 1933-36; mem. W.Va. Bapt. Exec. Bd., 1930-36; sec. W.Va. Bapt. Edn. Soc., 1930-36. Trustee Hillsdale Coll., 1945-54, Alderson-Broaddus Coll., 1932-36. Mem. Mich. Bapt. Conv. (exec. com. 1939-59, pres. 1955-58), Mich. Council Chs. (commn. internat. relations), Radio Com. for Chs. (chmn.), Civil Rights Com. Clubs: Kiwanis (pres. 1961; Legion of Honor 1971), Inter-City Wranglers, Friendly Hour, The Club. Author: Squaring Up, 1941; Story Sermons for Boys and Girls, 1947; Sermonettes for Boys and Girls, 1949; Children's Sermons in Stories, 1955; The Juvenile Protection Story, 1955; Talks for Children on Christian Ideals, 1959; The Children's Moment, 1966; Tell Us A Story, 1978; also articles. Contbr. to book: A Treasury of Story Sermons for Children, 1957. Daily radio program, Thought For the Day, 1950-63. Home: 1122 N Genesee Dr Lansing MI 48915 Office: Peoples Church 200 W Grand River East Lansing MI 48823

FISCHER, DELBERT LAWRENCE, orthopaedic surgeon; b. Chgo., July 24, 1923; s. Fred William and Barbara Ceceila (Witzgall) F.; B.A., Hiram Coll., 1944; M.D., Western Res. U., 1948; m. Jean Aileen Reese, May 21, 1949; children—Barbara, Catherine, Brian, Susan, Linda, Frances, Martha, Pamela. Intern Wesley Meml. Hosp., Chgo., 1948-49; resident gen. surgery Cleve. VA Hosp., 1949-50, resident orthopaedic surgery, 1950-52; resident Children's Orthopaedic Gates Hosp., Elyria (Ohio) Hosp., 1955; practice orthopaedic surgery, Lorain, Ohio, 1956—; mem. staff St. Joseph Hosp., Lorain, Elyria Meml. Hosp.; bd. dirs. Lorain Rehab. Center, 1969-71. Served with AUS, 1944; USNR, 1952-54. Diplomate Am. Bd. Orthopedic Surgery. Fellow Am. Acad. Orthopedic Surgery; mem. Am., Ohio med. assns., Lorain County Med. Soc. (pres. 1968), Ohio Orthopedic Soc., Pan Am. Med. Assn., Cleve. Orthopedic Club, Soc. (Latin Am.) Orthopedics and Traumatology, Nat. Assn. Hist. Preservation, Am. Fund Dept. State, Avon Hist. Soc. (pres. 1969-70), Alpha Omega Alpha, Phi Rho Sigma. Home: 2940 Stoney Ridge Rd Avon OH 44011 Office: 125 W 21st St Lorain OH 44052

FISCHER, DONALD ALEXANDER, architect; b. Bklyn., Mar. 14, 1936; s. Murray and Evelyn (Katz) F.; student U. Miami, 1953-55; B.Arch., Pratt Inst., 1959, postgrad., 1959; m. Anita Fractor, Dec. 22, 1957; children—Karen Elizabeth, Jenifer Ruth, Eric Michael. Designer, Morris Ketchum Jr. & Assos., architects, N.Y.C., 1958-62; project architect Edward Durell Stone, architect, N.Y.C., 1962-65; partner Weinberg, Teare, Fischer, architects, Cleve., 1965-67; partner Weinberg, Teare, Fischer & Herman, architects, Cleve., 1967-71; dir. architecture Bldg. Systems Housing Corp., Cleve., 1972-73, builders and developers Welfare Island, N.Y.C., Riverview, Yonkers, N.Y., 1973, Park Centre, Cleve., 1973, Southeast Loop, Rochester, N.Y., 1973, Campus Green, Chgo., 1973, Ivy Hill, Warren, Ohio, 1972; designer Kekst & Assos. Architects; dir. devel. Shannon Constrn. Inc., Cleve.; dir. E. 81st St. Corp.; v.p. Canterbury Corp.; pres. D.A.F. Designs, Inc., Design Internat. Inc.; builder Coll. Jewish Studies, Cleve., 1975, Blue Meadow Apts., Lexington, Ky., 1975. Bd. dirs. Shaker Dad's Club, Park Synagogue Parents League; treas. No. Ohio council Am. Jewish Congress. Registered architect, N.Y., Ohio, Ind., Ill., Mich. Mem. A.I.A. (chpt. com. chmn. 1966-67), Am. Craftsmens Council, Archtl. Soc. Ohio Soc. Archtl. Historians, Nat. Assn. Housing and Redevel. Ofcls., Nat. Council Archtl. Registration Bds., Zeta Beta Tau. Mem. B'nai B'rith. Archtl. works include: Jewish Community Fedn. Hdqrs., 1965; Chesterfield Apts., 1967 (both Cleve.); Chapel Hill Shopping Center, Akron, 1967; Trinity Ch. Home for Aged, Boston, 1968; Parmatown Shopping Center, Cleve., 1968; Vanderbilt Towers, Naples, Fla., 1969; Viewpoint, Sandusky, Ohio, 1969, Conrad House, Erie, Pa., 1971, Sheraton Hopkins Hotel, Cleve., 1971, others. Home: 3575 Lytle Rd Shaker Heights OH 44122 Office: 2800 Euclid Ave Cleveland OH 44115

FISCHER, DONALD EDWARD, JR., psychiatrist; b. Council Bluffs, Iowa, Oct. 1, 1941; s. Donald Edward and Loretta Frances (O'Connell) F.; M.D., Creighton U., 1968; m. Kathleen Frances Collins, June 20, 1970; children—Donald Edward III, David Edward. Intern in medicine Creighton-St. Joseph's Hosp.; intern in psychiatry Nebr. Psychiat. Inst. and affiliates Omaha VA Hosp., U. Nebr. Hosp. and Immanuel Community Mental Health Center, Omaha, 1968-69, resident in psychiatry, 1969-72; staff psychiatrist Douglas County (Nebr.) Community Mental Health Center, Omaha, 1972-73, sr. psychiatrist, chief of ward, 1973-74, chief psychiatry, dir. center, 1974-77, cons., 1977—; med. dir., chief psychiatry Great Plains Mental Health Center, North Platte, Nebr., 1977—; chief psychiatry Great Plains Med. Center, 1977—; asst. prof. psychiatry and neurology Creighton U. Sch. Medicine; active staff St. Joseph's Meml. Hosp., 1972—; family and sex therapist. Mem. policy adv. com. Creighton-St. Joseph's Hosp., 1974-75; mem. exec. com. Douglas County Mental Health Adv. Com., 1973-74. Spl. dep. sheriff, Council Bluffs, 1968-72, Omaha, 1974-75. Bd. dirs. Indian Alcoholism Program, 1972-73; mem. exec. com. Douglas County Hosp., 1973—; sponsor Omaha Civic Opera Co., 1972—. Recipient Physicians's Recognition award A.M.A., 1972. Mem. Am. Psychiat. Assn., Sioux Psychiat. Soc., Nebr. Med. Assn., Douglas County Med. Soc., Assn. Advancement Psychotherapy, Neb. Assn. Alcoholism Counselors, Omaha Area Council Alcoholism, Phi Rho Sigma. Roman Catholic. Contbr. articles to med. jours. Home: 821 Gilman Ave North Platte NE 69101 Office: Dept Psychiatry 3d Floor Faculty Bldg Creighton U-St Joseph's Hosp Omaha NE 68108 also Douglas County Hosp Community Mental Health Center 4102 Woolworth Av Omaha NE 68105

FISCHER, HENRY FRED, pub. affairs counsel; b. Fair Haven, Minn., Nov. 9, 1938; s. Fred Henry and Ann Evelyn (Steenlage) F.; student U. Minn., 1956-57; m. Janet M. Torgerson, Aug. 11, 1963; children—Jennifer, Christopher. Exec. dir. Minn. D.F.L. party, 1968-70; dir. orgn. Wendell Anderson for Gov. Com., 1970; spl. asst. to U.S. Sen. Walter F. Mondale, 1970-72; chmn. Minn. Democratic Party, 1972-75; prin. JMF, Inc., Mpls., 1975—. Bd. dirs. Twin Cities Indsl. Opportunities Center; v.p. Dem. State Chairmen's Assn., 1973-77; sec. Midwest Dem. Conf., 1973-76; mem. Dem. Nat. Com., 1972-76. Mem. Savs. League Minn., Campaign Planners Assn. Lutheran. Author polit. monographs. Home: 4309 Williston Rd Minnetonka MN 55343 Office: Suite 303 625 2d Ave S Minneapolis MN 55402

FISCHER, JEANETTE LUCILLE STOCKETT (MRS. RICHARD ALLEN FISCHER), occupational therapist; b. Albert Lea, Minn., Nov. 13, 1937; d. Stewart Joseph and Bessie Lucille (Junk) Stockett; B.S. in Occupational Therapy, Washington U., St. Louis, 1960; m. Richard Allen Fischer, Oct. 22, 1960; children—Richard Arnold, Robert Andrew. Dir. occupational therapy Alexian Bros. Hosp., St. Louis, 1960-62, Americana Healthcare Center, Florissant, Mo., 1975—; occupational therapy aide St. Louis State Hosp., 1958-59. Clinic vol. aide ARC, 1971-73. Treas., Midland Valley Estates Improvement Assn., 1966-68, 69-70, v.p., 1971-72, pres., 1972-74, bd. dirs., 1974-76; treas., Marion PTA, 1967-68, carnival chmn., 1968-69, v.p., 1969-71, picnic chmn., 1969-73; sch. talent show dir. Boy Scouts Am., 1971-72; mem. St. Louis Civic Ballet, 1973-75; mem. KETC-TV Ednl. TV, 1971-75; sec.-receptionist - Michael Simms Acad. Dance, St. Louis, 1974-75; vacation Bible sch. tchr. Chapel of the Cross Lutheran Ch., 1970, arts and crafts dir., 1971-72, 74—; mem. Friends St. Louis Art Mus., 1976—. Mem. Am., Mo. (pub. relations chmn. 1965, treas. 1963-65), occupational therapy assns., World Fedn. Occupational Therapy, Internat. Platform Assn., Met. Ballet St. Louis, St. Louis Dance Concert Soc., Humane Soc. Mo., Alpha Xi Delta. Home: 10025 Pebble Beach Dr Overland MO 63114 Office: Americana Healthcare Center 1200 Graham Rd Florissant MO 63031

FISCHER, JOHN WESLEY, orthodontist; b. Cin., Sept. 23, 1939; s. Norvin Valentine and Jane Louise (Moore) F.; B.A., Ohio Wesleyan U., 1961; D.D.S. summa cum laude, Ohio State U., 1965; M.S., U. Mich., 1967; m. Carolyn Howell MacFarland, Aug. 12, 1961; 1 son, John Edward. Practice orthodontics, Cin., 1967—; dir. orthodontic program Cin. Children's Hosp., 1968—. Diplomate Am. Bd. Orthodontics. Mem. Am. Soc. Dentistry for Children (pres. 1973), Cin. Dental Soc. (treas. 1975), Western Hills Dental Study Club (pres. 1972), Omicron Kappa Upsilon, Phi Kappa Phi, Chi Gamma Nu, Sigma Phi Epsilon, Delta Sigma Delta. Patentee orthodontic process. Office: 3012 Glenmore Ave Cincinnati OH 45238

FISCHER, ROBBINS WARREN, oilseed industry cons. co. exec.; b. Turin, Iowa Mar. 31, 1919; s. Lewis Warren and Edith (Robbins) F.; B.A., U. Colo., 1942; postgrad. U. Colo. Sch. Law, 1944-45, Rutgers U., 1954; m. Jean Noreen Greenawalt, Apr. 10, 1943; children—Barbara Jean, Martha Lou, Dorothy Ellen. Co-owner, operator Fischer Farms, Turin, 1947-53; sales promotion mgr. Payway Feed Mills, Kansas City, Mo., 1953-55; regional sales mgr. Bristol Myers Co., Kansas City, Mo., 1956-58; campaign dir. Burrell, Inc., Kansas City, Mo., 1958-59; asst. to pres. Soybean Council Am., Waterloo, Iowa, 1960-63; pres. Internat. Bus. Assos., Cedar Falls, Iowa, 1965—, Soypro Internat., Inc., Cedar Falls, 1963—; pres. Soypro of Iowa, Cedar Falls, 1973—; v.p. Continental Soya, Manning, Iowa, 1973—. Mem. adv. bd. Profl. Farmers Am., 1976-77; mem. Dist. Export Council, 1974-77; bd. dirs. Black Hawk County (Iowa) Bicentennial Commn., 1973-76; vice chmn. Iowa Farm Council, 1950-53; mem. Pres. Kennedy's Task Force on Internat. Trade in Agrl. Products, 1962. Mem. Cedar Falls C. of C. (dir.), Inst. Food Technologists, Monona Harrison Flood Control Assn. (pres. 1951-54), Phi Beta Kappa, Delta Sigma Rho, Pi Gamma Mu. Conglist. Rotarian, Mason. Home: 5614 University Ave Cedar Falls IA 50613 Office: 314 Main St Cedar Falls IA 50613

FISCHER, ROBERT CHARLES, coll. adminstr.; b. Cin., June 15, 1937; s. Byron Bracker and Helen Frances (Hofmann) F.; A.B., U. Cin., 1959; M.A., Georgetown U., 1962; postgrad. U. Mich., 1961-64. Spl. research asst. Nat. Commn. on Accrediting, Washington, 1966-67; exec. asso. Am. Assn. State Colls. and Univs., Washington, 1967-69; project devel. officer Univ. Assos., Inc., Washington, 1970-71, cons., 1971—; dir. spl. projects, asst. to pres. and acad. dean Olivet (Mich.) Coll., 1971—. Cons. Alvin M. Bentley Found., Owosso, Mich., 1971—; exec. dir. Mich. Center for Teaching State and Local Govt., 1977—; cons. Murray Seasongood Good Govt. Fund, Cin., Ohio No. U. Mem. Am. Polit. Sci. Assn., Mich. Conf. Polit. Scientists, Am. Assn. Higher Edn., Ripon Soc., Center for Dem. Instns., Alpha Tau Omega, Omicron Delta Kappa, Tau Kappa Alpha, Pi Kappa Delta, Pi Delta Epsilon. Republican. Clubs: Cincinnati; Capitol Hill (Washington); Univ. (Lansing, Mich.). Home: 129 1/2 S Main St Olivet MI 49076 Office: 306 E Mott Center Olivet Coll Olivet MI 49076

FISCHER, WAYNE LOUIS, sales exec.; b. Esterville, Iowa, Sept. 29, 1943; s. Arthur Leonard and Lucille Hazel (Clausen) F.; B.S., U. Minn., 1965; m. Iris Jane Wahl, Mar. 26, 1966; children—Victoria Marie, Waylon Ryan. Territorial salesman Allied Mills, Harlan, Iowa, 1971-72, dist. salesman, Wayne, Nebr., 1972-75, asst. regional sales mgr., St. Louis, 1975, regional sales mgr., Iowa City, 1975—. Served with USMCR, 1966-71. Decorated Air medals (34), Navy Commendation medal. Mem. C. of C. Lutheran (Sunday Sch. supt. 1974-75). Address: 1405 Derwen Dr Iowa City IA 52240

FISCHER, WILLIAM MICHAEL, mfg. co. exec.; b. St. Louis, Feb. 5, 1943; s. John Erwin and Margaret Mary (Kerr) F.; B.S., St. Louis U., 1967; m. Mary Margaret Eck, Nov. 28, 1970; children—William Michael, Alicia Elizabeth; adopted children—Cheri Sue, Gina Lynn, Tracy Lee. Accountant E.J. Fischer Plumbing Co., 1967-69; corp. treas. E.J. Fischer, Inc., St. Louis, 1969-73; comptroller MADECO, Inc., Mascoutah, Ill., 1973-75; data processing mgr. Fritz Electric, Inc., Mascoutah, 1973-75; self-employed in designing and implementing accounting and costing systems for contractors for use on small computer system; comptroller Binkley Co., 1975—. Pres., Catholic Youth Council, 1958-59. Served with USAF, 1967. Mem. Am. Prodn. and Inventory Control Soc., Am. Mgrs. Assn., Assn. Gen. Contractors St. Louis, Aircraft Owners and Pilots Assn., Mo. Air N.G., Am. Contract Bridge League, System 3 Users Group, Alpha Phi Omega, Delta Delta. Home: Route 3 Box 85A Owensville MO 65066 Office: Main and Elm Sts Warrenton MO 63383

FISCHMAN, JOSEPH HERMAN, real estate broker; b. St. Louis, Oct. 6, 1930; s. Arthur and Sarah (Mayer) F.; B.S., Washington U., St. Louis, 1952; m. Elaine Carole Cohen, July 6, 1952; children—Michael, Jeffrey. Salesman, Arthur Fischman Realty Co., Brentwood, Mo., 1952-62, gen. partner, 1962—. Pres., Conway Elementary Sch., 1968-69, East Ladue Jr. High Sch., 1971-72, Horton Watkins High Sch., 1972-73; pres. Ladue Dist. Council, 1974-75. Bd. dirs. Ladue Sch. Dist. Bd. Edn., 1975—, treas., 1977—. Hon. fellow Harry S Truman Library Inst. Mem. Nat. Assn. Real Estate Bds., St. Louis Real Estate Bd., Mo. Assn. Realtors, Zeta Beta Tau. Jewish. Clubs: Normandie Golf, Missouri Athletic. Home: 22 Salem Estates Dr Ladue MO 63124 Office: 1516 S Brentwood Blvd Brentwood MO 63144

FISH, DAVID FREDERICK, counselor; b. Harlingen, Tex., May 1, 1944; s. David Charles and Marjorie Grace (Baker) F.; B.A., U. Iowa, 1966; M.Ed., U. No. Iowa, 1968. Residence hall dir. Ball State U., Muncie, Ind., 1968-72; counselor Hawkeye Inst. Tech., Waterloo, Iowa, 1972—; personal growth cons. Mem. Am. Coll. Personnel Assn., Am., Iowa personnel Guidance assns., Assn. Specialists in Group Work, Assn. Humanistic Edn. Devel. Democrat. Home: 1117 Ravenwood St Apt 1B Waterloo IA 50702 Office: PO Box 8015 Waterloo IA 50704

FISHER, BARBARA ANN, city ofcl.; b. South Bend, Ind., Mar. 30, 1952; d. Verner Jasper and Janet Stowell (Smith) Fisher; B.A., Western Mich. U., 1973, M.A., 1976; 1 son, David James. Veterans coordinator Kalamazoo Valley Community Coll., 1974; sec. Western Mich. U., Kalamazoo, 1974-75, student supr., 1975-77; child guidance worker Kalamazoo County Juvenile Home, 1975; case mgr., community placement program Kalamazoo Dept. Mental Health, 1977—. Volunteer, Kalamazoo County Juvenile Ct., 1975—; mem. Sheriffs Dept. Mounted Aux. Div. Western Mich. U. Bd. trustees scholar, 1973. Mem. Am. Personnel and Guidance Assn., Southwestern Mich. Psychol. Assn. Home: 3651 Kenbrooke Ct Kalamazoo MI 49007 Office: Kalamazoo County Dept Mental Health 230 N Burdick St Kalamazoo MI 49006

FISHER, CHARLES THOMAS, III, banker; b. Detroit, Nov. 22, 1929; s. Charles Thomas, Jr. and Elizabeth Jane (Briggs) F.; A.B. in Econs., Georgetown U., 1951; M.B.A., Harvard, 1953; m. Margaret Elizabeth Keegin, June 18, 1952; children—Margaret Elizabeth, Charles Thomas IV, Curtis William, Lawrence Peter II, Mary Florence. With Touche, Ross, Bailey & Smart, C.P.A.'s, Detroit, 1953-58; asst. v.p. Nat. Bank Detroit, 1958-61, v.p., 1961-66, sr. v.p., 1966-69, exec. v.p., 1969-72, pres., chief adminstrv. officer, 1972—, also dir.; pres., dir. Nat. Detroit Corp., 1973—; dir. Internat. Bank of Detroit, Detroit Edison Co., Prime Securities Corp., Hiram Walker-Gooderham & Worts, Ltd., Gen. Motors Corp., Am. Airlines. Mem. Mackinac Bridge Authority. Bd. dirs. Greater Detroit Area Hosp. Council; trustee Mt. Elliott Cemetery, Detroit; nat. bd. Smithsonian Assos. Named Detroit Young Man of Year, Detroit Jr. Bd. Commerce, 1961. C.P.A., Mich. Mem. Assn. Res. City Bankers, Am. Inst. C.P.A.'s, Mich. Assn. C.P.A.'s. Republican. Roman Cath. Clubs: Bloomfield Hills (Mich.) Country; Country of Detroit (Grosse Pointe); Detroit Athletic, Detroit, Recess, Yondotega (Detroit); Links (N.Y.C.). Office: National Bank Detroit Detroit MI 48232

FISHER, DAN L(EON), banker; b. Tobias, Nebr., May 19, 1935; s. Leon G. and Nina M. (Bergsen) F.; student Nebr. Wesleyan U., 1953-56; B.S., U. Neb., 1963; postgrad. U. Colo., 1964-67; m. Mary Alice Jennings, Aug. 9, 1959; children—D. Jennings, Mary Catherine, Amy Susan. Vice pres. Crawford (Nebr.) State Bank, 1963-69, pres., 1969—, chmn. bd., 1976—; owner Crawford Bank Agy., Ins., 1975—; owner, operator OK Ranch, Crawford, 1972—; chmn. bd. dirs., pres. Crawford State Co., banking, ins. and real estate. Exec. dir. Pan-Handle Health Dist., Crawford, 1970-73, Wyo-braka Boy Scouts Am., 1970-71. Bd. dirs. Crawford Community Hosp., 1968-73. Served to 1st lt. USMCR, 1958-62. Recipient Boss of the Year award Jaycees, 1974. Mem. Crawford Area C. of C. (dir. 1964-67), Am. Legion. Republican. Methodist (trustee 1966-70). Clubs: Eagles, Masons, Shriners, Elks. Home: Box 506 Crawford NE 69339 Office: PO Box 506 Crawford NE 69339

FISHER, DAVIS LEE, clergyman; b. Oak Park, Ill., Apr. 2, 1942; s. Frank Theodore and Helen Anabelle (Davis) F.; certificate Goethe Inst., Berlin, 1963; B.A., Lawrence U., Appleton, Wis., 1964; M.Div., Gen. Theol. Sem., N.Y.C., 1967; M.B.A., U. Chgo., 1972; m. Sandra Rae Lehto, June 19, 1965; children—Elizabeth, Ian, Sarah. Ordained priest Episcopal Ch., 1967; seminarian asst. chs., East Harlem, N.Y., 1964-65, Bronx, N.Y., 1965, N.Y.C., 1965-67; chaplain intern Methodist Hosp., Bklyn., 1966; curate Ch. of Holy Comforter,

Kenilworth, Ill., 1967-69; part-time asst. Ch. of Our Saviour, Chgo., 1969—; participant 1st nat. scholar program 1st Nat. Bank Chgo., 1969-71, trust officer, 1972—; mem. Commn. on Ministry, Episcopal Diocese of Chgo., 1971—. Mem. Wilmette (Ill.) Sch. Bd. Caucus, 1976—. Mem. Nat. Assn. for Self-Supporting Active Ministry (dir. 1972—, past chmn.), Lawrence U. Alumni Assn. (dir. 1972—, treas. 1974-75, v.p. nat. alumni councils 1975-77, assn. pres. 1977—). Home: 719 Park Ave Wilmette IL 60091

FISHER, HARRY NOBLE DE FOLDESSY, lawyer, advt. agency exec.; b. Grand Forks, N.D., June 15, 1931; s. George DeFoldessy and Evelyn Sarah (Korroll) F.; A.B. with honors, U. Chgo., 1950, J.D., 1953; m. Joy Marilyn Waltke, Nov. 12, 1955; children—Hal, Diane. Admitted to Iowa bar, 1953, Mo. bar, 1957; legal clk. Marathon Oil Co., Findlay, Ohio, 1952; asso. firm Stolar, Kuhlmann & Meredith, St. Louis, 1957-59; account exec. Lemoine Skinner, Jr., Pub. Relations, Inc. St. Louis, 1959-63; dir. pub. relations Stemmler, Fisher, Waltke & Hagen, St. Louis, 1963—, pres., 1977—; lectr. bus. law So. Ill. U., 1963; resident scholar Ecumenical Inst. Advanced Theol. Studies, Tantur, Jerusalem, 1977; dir. Archway Publs., Inc., St. Louis. Pub. relations dir. U.S. Youth Games, 1968. Served to capt. USAF, 1953-57. Mem. Hymn Soc. Am., Pub. Relations Soc. Am., Bar Assn. St. Louis. Club: Mo. Athletic. Author: Advice to Divers and other poems, songs and hymns, 1975; North Slope and Other Poems, 1976; Luke-Acts as Legal Brief, 1977. Home: 6 Godwin Ln St Louis MO 63124 Office: 8007 Clayton Rd St Louis MO 63117

FISHER, HEATHER MARIE, graphic arts co. exec.; b. Rockford, Ill., Aug. 1, 1946; d. G. Rogers and Suzanne (Johnson) Livingston; B.A., U. Ill., Champaign-Urbana, 1968; m. Stanley M. Fisher, Jan. 15, 1969. Staff artist I. Hanson Graphics, Inc., Chgo., 1969-70, advt. dir., 1970-73, v.p. production, 1973-75, president, 1975—. Recipient Gold Medal Chgo. Printing Assn., 1970; Outstanding Achievement award Nat. Graphics Assn., 1971; named Advt. Artist of Yr., Midwest Assn. Graphic Arts, 1972. Mem. Graphic Artists Guild, Chgo. Printing Assn., Nat. Graphics Assn., Midwest Assn. Graphic Arts, Soc. Advt. Artists. Democrat. Lutheran. Address: 450 W. Melrose Apt 422 Chicago IL 60657

FISHER, LESTER EMIL, zoo dir.; b. Chgo., Feb. 24, 1921; s. Louis and Elizabeth (Vodicka) F.; V.M.D., Ia. State U., 1943; m. Elizabeth Jane, Oct. 2, 1948; children—Jane Serrita, Katherine Clark. Supr. animal care program Northwestern U. Med. Sch., 1946-47; attending veterinarian Lincoln Park Zoo, Chgo., 1947-62, dir. zoo, 1962—; owner, dir. Berwyn (Ill) Animal Hosp., 1947-63; producer, moderator ednl. closed circuit TV for nat. vet. meetings, 1949-69; mem. staff microbiology dept., Presbyn.-St. Luke Hosp., Chgo., 1963—; vet. cons. Sears Roebuck & Co., 1957-70. Asso. prof. biology dept. DePaul U., Bd. dirs. Lincoln Park Zool. Soc. Inst. for Cultural Devel. Mem. citizens com. U. Ill. Served to maj. Vet. Corps., AUS, 1943-46. Mem. Am. Animal Hosp. Assn. (regional dir.), Am. Vet. Med. Assn., Am. Inst. Park Execs., Am. Assn. Zoo Veterinarians (pres. 1968), Am. Assn. Zool. Parks and Aquariums (exec. bd., pres. 1972-73), Internat. Union Dirs. Zool. Gardens (sec.-treas.), Theta Zi. Clubs: Adventurers (pres. 1969), Tavern, Arts Executives (exec. bd.) (Chgo.). Asso. editor British Small Animal Jour., Small Animal Clinician, 1958-70. Contbr. articles med. and tech. publs. Home: 2242 Lincoln Park W Chicago IL 60614 Office: Lincoln Park Zool Garden Chicago IL 60614

FISHER, MARIAN SUE, social worker; b. Waterloo, Iowa, Apr. 15, 1942; d. Frank Marion and Florence Lucille (Wharton) Greenlee; B.A., No. Iowa U., 1964; M.S.W., Ind. U., 1966; m. Edward Fisher, Sept. 26, 1971. NIMH grantee, 1964-66; psychiat. social worker Ill. Psychiat. Inst., Chgo., 1966-69; social worker Luth. Welfare Services of Ill., Chgo., 1969-71; community counseling services dir. Randolph County Mental Health Services, Chester, Ill., 1972—, cons. to gen. hosp., health facility. Certified social worker, Ill. Mem. Nat. Assn. Social Workers, Acad. Social Workers, Clin. Social Workers, Am. Personnel and Guidance Assn. Methodist. Home: 1158 George St Chester IL 62233

FISHER, MILTON LEONARD, lawyer; b. Pitts., Jan. 17, 1922; s. Jacob M. and Sara (Weiner) F.; A.B., Oberlin Coll., 1943; J.D., Northwestern U., 1949; m. Jean Freiler, Apr. 30, 1950; children—Susan Elizabeth, Janet Sarah, Joseph Freiler. Admitted to Ill. bar, 1949, Ohio bar, 1949; practice law, Chgo.; mem. firm Mayer, Brown & Platt, Chgo., 1950—. Chmn., Highland Park (Ill.) Civil Service Commn., 1963-70; mem. Chgo. exec. com. Anti-Defamation Bd., 1962—; mem. Chgo. Crime Commn. Bd. dirs. Met. Housing Devel. Corp., Better Govt. Assn. Served to lt. (j.g.) USNR, 1943-46. Mem. Northwestern Law Sch. Alumni Assn. (dir.), Law Club, Am., Ill., Chgo. bar assns. Clubs: Cliff Dwellers, Metropolitan (Chgo.); Lake Shore Country (Glencoe, Ill.). Home: 349 Woodland Rd Highland Park IL 60035 Office: 231 S LaSalle St Chicago IL 60604

FISHER, PIERRE JAMES, JR., physician; b. Chgo., Oct. 29, 1931; s. Pierre James and Evelyn (Trevithick) F.; student Ball State U., 1951-52, Taylor U., 1949-51; M.D., Ind. U., 1956; m. Carol Ann Walton, Mar. 16, 1950; children—James Walton, David Alan, Steven Edward, Teresa Ann. Intern, U.S. Naval Hosp., San Diego, 1956-57, resident in surgery, 1957-61; practice medicine specializing in surgery Surgeons Inc., Marion, Ind., 1965—, pres., 1977—; mem. staff Marion Gen. Hosp., also chief staff, 1970. Served with USN, 1956-65. Recipient Physicians Recognition award AMA, 1974; diplomate Am. Bd. Surgery. Fellow A.C.S.; mem. AMA. Methodist. Clubs: Rotary, Exchange, Mecca. Home: 911 Overlook Rd Marion IN 46952 Office: 500 Wabash Ave Surgeons Inc Marion IN 46952

FISHER, ROBERT ERWIN, automotive engr.; b. Lansing, Mich., Aug. 16, 1926; s. Marcus Cecil and Alice Etta (Whelan) F.; B.S., Purdue U., 1953; m. Mary Helen Donaldson, June 24, 1950; children—Bruce Alan, Katharine Sue, Dianne Marie. With Oldsmobile div. Gen. Motors Corp., Lansing, Mich., 1950—, project engr., 1956, sr. project engr., 1959—. Scoutmaster, Boy Scouts Am., Lansing, 1961-74. Served with USAAF, 1945. Mem. Soc. Automotive Engrs. Home: 3319 Sunnylane Lansing MI 48906 Office: 1014 Townsend St Lansing MI 48933

FISHER, ROGER KOCH, lawyer; b. St. Paul, Oct. 29, 1939; s. Herbert William and Evelyn Katherine (Koch) F.; B.S. in Bus. Adminstrn., U. Mo., 1961, J.D., 1964; m. Barbara Stewart Jones, Dec. 27, 1960; children—Nicole Elizabeth, Douglas Stewart. Admitted to Mo. bar, 1964; asso. firm Morrison, Hecker, Cozad, Morrison & Curtis, Kansas City, Mo., 1966-68; partner Warten & Fisher, Joplin, Mo., 1969—. Bd. dirs. Joplin Pub. Library, 1971—, Joplin Hist. Soc., 1972—, Mo. Assn. for Children with Learning Disabilities, 1969—. Served to 1st lt., arty. AUS, 1964-66. Mem. Kappa Sigma. Presbyn. Rotarian (dir., pres. 1975-76). Home: 930 N Sergeant St Joplin MO 64801 Office: 612 1st Nat Bldg Joplin MO 64801

FISHER, STANLEY MORTON, lawyer; b. Dover, Ohio, Feb. 15, 1928; s. Jacob M. and Sara (Weiner) F.; B.A., Oberlin Coll., 1950, J.D., U. Mich., 1953; m. Elaine Rhoda Rosenthal, Feb. 5, 1950; children—Lee, Barbara, Richard, Suzanne. Admitted to Ohio and Mich. bars, 1953; law clk. to chief justice U.S. Ct. Appeals 6th Circuit, 1953-54; asso. firm Ulmer, Berne, Laronge, Glickman & Curtis, Cleve., 1954-55; partner firm Fuerst & Fisher, Cleve., 1955-60, Fuerst, Fisher, Levy & Goulder, 1960-72, Fuerst, Fisher & Levy, 1973-74; of counsel firm Guren, Merritt, Sogg & Cohen, 1974-75, mem. firm, 1975—. Sec., Welcome Radio, Inc., Cleve., 1964—; dir. Cook United, Inc.; spl. counsel Atty. Gen. Ohio, 1972—. Co-chmn. Cleve. Exec. Adv. Program, 1972-74; trustee, v.p. Council Gardens, Cleve., 1974-77. Served with U.S. Army, 1945-46. Mem. Bar Assn. Greater Cleve. (trustee 1975—, chmn. grievance com. 1972-73, chmn. ethics com. 1973-74), Cuyanoga, Fed. (nat. membership chmn., nat. council), Ohio, Am. bar assns., Commerce Club (trustee, pres.), Am. Judicature Soc., Am. Trial Lawyers Assn. Club: Cleve. Racquet. Contbr. articles to profl. jours. Office: 650 Terminal Tower Cleveland OH 44113

FISHLEIGH, CLARENCE TURNER, cons. engr.; b. Chgo., July 31, 1895; s. John A. and Henrietta P. (Turner) F.; B.S.E.E., U. Mich., 1917; J.D., Detroit Coll. Law, 1939; m. Thea Holste, May 16, 1923; children—Elayne (Mrs. M. Russell Bramwell), Marilyn (Mrs. Pierce). Mech. prodn. Ford Motor Co., 1919-22; exptl. motor testing, asst. prodn. mgr. Am. Car and Foundry Co., Chgo., also Rich Tool Co., Detroit, 1923-24; mgr. Clarence T. Fishleigh Co., 1924-30; asso. engr., cons. engr. Walter T. Fishleigh, 1930-47; cons. engr., Detroit, 1947-51, Chgo., 1951—. Splty. automotive engr., patent experting. Served as 2d lt., USAAC, 1917-19. Decorated Croix de Guerre. Registered profl. engr., Ill., Mich., N.Y., Ohio, Fla., Tex. Mem. Soc. Automotive Engrs., Am. Soc. M.E., Western Soc. Engrs., Engring. Soc. Detroit, Am., Mich. patent law assns., Patent Law Assn. of Chgo., Am., Ill., Mich., Chgo. bar assns. Club: Union League (Chgo.). Address: 920 Kenton Rd Deerfield IL 60015

FISHMAN, LESLIE ABRAHAM, psychologist; b. Boston, Jan. 13, 1951; s. Sevek and Lonia (Goldman) F.; B.S., U. Mass., 1972; M.A., State U. N.Y., 1974; M.S., Ind. U., 1975, Ph.D., 1978. Desensitization therapist U. Mass., 1972; diagnostic examiner Belchertown (Mass.) State Hosp., 1972; teaching asst. State U. N.Y. at Oswego, 1973-74; asso. instr. dept. ednl. psychology Ind. U., 1975—; counselor, supr. Center for Human Growth, Bloomington, Ind., 1975; counselor Psychiatric div. Student Health, Ind. U., 1976; counselor Monroe County Community Mental Health Center, Bloomington, 1976; staff counselor Ind. U.-Purdue U., Indpls., 1978. Ford Found. grantee, 1970; U. Mass. Commonwealth scholar, 1970; Ind. U. research grantee, 1978. Mem. Am. Psychol. Assn., Am. Personnel and Guidance Assn., Assn. Counselor Edn. and Supervision. Home: 3209 E 10th St Bloomington IN 47401 Office: Dept Ednl Psychology Sch Edn Room 105 Ind U Bloomington IN 47401

FISK, ROBERT CLARK, lawyer; b. Curlew, Iowa, Apr. 6, 1917; s. Orville B. and Grace (Foster) F.; student Ft. Dodge Jr. Coll., 1933-35; B.A., U. Iowa, 1938, J.D., 1941; m. Ruth A. Gordon, July 20, 1957. Admitted to Nebr. bar, 1941, Ia. bar; practice in Omaha, 1941—; mem. firm Finlayson, McKie & Fisk, 1965—; dir. Central States Health & Life Co., Omaha, Bank of Millard, Omaha. Lectr., Creighton U. Law Sch., Omaha, 1952—. Served with M.I., AUS, 1942-46. Mem. Am., Iowa, Nebr., Omaha bar assns., Omaha C. of C., Ak-Sar-Ben, Am. Legion, Res. Officers Assn. Republican. Methodist. Mason (32 degree), Kiwanian. Home: 2608 N 51st Ave Omaha NE 68104 Office: 1475 One First Nat Center Omaha NE 68102

FISKE, GUY WILBUR, diversified industries exec.; b. Upton, Mass., Sept. 28, 1924; s. Frederick Wilbur and Daisy Mae (Phillips) F.; B.A. in Math., Brown U., 1946; m. Elsie Jacqueline Strachan, Sept. 2, 1949; children—Jacqui Lynne, Melinda, Melissa. Sales agt. Felt & Tarrant Mfg. Co., Providence, 1946-48; with Gen. Electric Co., 1949-68, nat. sales mgr. electronics div., Columbia, S.C., 1960-63, mgr. mktg. capacitor div., Glens Falls, N.Y., 1964-66, gen. mgr. computer support ops., Phoenix, 1966-68; worldwide product line mgr. electronics, indsl. products and automotive products ITT, N.Y.C., 1969-72, corporate v.p., group exec. automotive products, 1972-77; exec. v.p., dir. Gen. Dynamics Corp., St. Louis, 1977—; chmn. bd. Asbestos Corp., Ltd., Montreal, Que., Can.; dir. Stromberg Carlson Corp., Rochester, N.Y., DatagraphiX, San Diego, Gen. Dynamics Communications Corp., St. Louis. Founder, elder Presbyn. Ch., Havenwood, Md. Served with AUS, 1944-46; comdr. USNR, ret. Mem. Soc. Automotive Engrs., ASEE. Presbyterian. Clubs: Old Warson Country, St. Louis (St. Louis); Bloomfield Hills (Mich.) Country; Port Royal Country (Hilton Head Island, S.C.); Internat. Golf (Bolton, Mass.); Metropolitan (N.Y.C.). Office: Gen Dynamics Corp Pierre Laclede Center Saint Louis MO 63105

FISKE, KENNETH VAN DYNE, conservation exec.; b. Oak Park, Ill., Apr. 18, 1925; s. Kenneth Morton and Eunice (Van Dyne) F.; grad. U.S. Mcht. Marine Acad., 1946; B.S. in Agr., U. Wis., 1950; m. Darlene Alma Sharp, Oct. 23, 1954; children—Diana, Jennifer, Nancy. Agrl. engr. Nat. Safety Council, Chgo., 1955-60; dir. field ops. Velsicol Chem. Corp., Chgo., 1960-68; exec. dir. N.E. Ill. Natural Resource Service Center, Lisle, Ill., 1968-71; exec. dir. McHenry County Conservation dist., Woodstock, Ill., 1971—. Dir. Wis. Alpha Corp., Madison. Research asso. Morton Arboretum, Lisle, 1970—; editor Farm Safety Rev. mag. Nat. Safety Council. Chmn. Pres.'s Commn. on Pesticide Safety, 1964; chmn. County Soil and Water Conservation Dist., McHenry County, Ill., 1963—; leader 4-H Club, Woodstock, 1951-65; pres. Ill. chpt. Soil Conservation Soc. Am., 1971; chmn. N.E. Ill. Land Council. Served to lt. (j.g.) UNSR, 1944-46. Recipient conservation awards Goodyear Co., 1963, 66, Theta ecology award McHenry County Defenders, 1971. Mem. Assn. Ill. Soil and Water Conservation Dists., Am. Soc. Agrl. Engring., Am. Soc. Farm Mgrs. and Rural Appraisers, Sigma Alpha Epsilon, Alpha Zeta. Elk. Club: Chicago Press, Union League (both Chgo.). Author: The Fox River Basin, 1971. Home: 9313 Bull Valley Rd Woodstock IL 60098 Office: PO Box 502 Woodstock IL 60098

FITCH, EDWARD HUBBARD, rubber co. exec.; b. Phila., Aug. 9, 1906; s. Edward Hubbard and Bessie (McFarlin) F.; B.A., Williams Coll., 1929, M.B.A., Harvard, 1931; m. Jane Farrell, Oct. 16, 1943; children—Farrell, Edward Hubbard, Jonathan Winchester. With B.F. Goodrich Co., Akron, Ohio, 1931-71, dir. gen. mktg. services, 1968-71; dir. Robin Hill Inc., Hudson, Ohio. Founding pres. Hudson Heritage Assn., 1962-64, pres., 1974-75; campaign vice chmn. United Fund-Red Cross, Summit County, 1970, gen. campaign chmn., 1971; chmn. Akron met. area Nat. Alliance Businessmen, 1972-73; mem. Akron Manpower Area Planning Council, 1972-73; mem. adv. bd. Met. Akron Jobs Council, 1974—. Trustee United Found. Summit County, 1972-76, United Community Council Summit County, 1972-76, Hudson Bicentennial Commn. Mem. Aviation Distbrs. and Mfrs. Assn. (pres. 1961), Episcopalian (sr. warden 1957). Rotarian. Clubs: Wings (N.Y.C.); Carleton, Metropolitan (Washington). Home: 2727 Hudson-Aurora Rd Hudson OH 44236 Office: Robin Hill Inc Box 637 Hudson OH 44236

FITCH, FRANK WESLEY, educator; b. Bushnell, Ill., May 30, 1929; s. Harold Wayne and Mary (Frank) F.; M.D. with honors, U. Chgo., 1953, M.S., 1957 Ph.D., 1960; m. Shirley Dobbins, Dec. 23, 1951; children—Mary Margaret, Mark Howard Wesley. Intern, U. Hosp., Ann Arbor, Mich., 1953-54; USPHS postdoctoral research fellow, 1954-55, 57-58; instr. pathology U. Chgo., 1957-60, asst. prof., 1960-63, asso. prof., 1963-67, prof., 1967—, Albert D. Lasker prof. med. sci., 1976—, asso. dean for med. and grad. edn., 1976—; vis. prof. Swiss Inst. Exptl. Cancer Research, Lausanne, 1974-75. Served to capt. USAF, 1955-57. John and Mary R. Markle Found. scholar, 1961-66; Lederle Med. Faculty award, 1958-61; John Simon Guggenheim Meml. Found. fellow, 1974-75. Mem. Am. Assn. Immunologists, Am. Assn. Med. Colls., Am. Assn. Pathologists and Bacteriologists, Am. Soc. Exptl. Pathology, Radiation Research Soc., Chgo. Pathol. Soc., Reticuloendothelial Soc., Sigma Xi, Alpha Omega Alpha. Home: 5449 S Kenwood Ave Chicago IL 60615

FITCH, JANE FARRELL (MRS. EDWARD HUBBARD FITCH), designer; b. Detroit; d. Benjamin Thomas and Anna Una (Simpson) Farrell; student U. Toledo, 1938-42; B.A., Radcliffe Coll., 1942, postgrad., 1943; m. Edward Hubbard Fitch, Oct. 16, 1943; children—Farrell, Edward Hubbard, Jonathan Winchester. Free lance designer, Hudson, Ohio, 1945-56; designer Rorimer Brooks, Cleve., 1956-59, Robin Hill Interiors, Cin., Hudson, 1960-63; v.p. design, partner, dir. Robin Hill Ltd., Hudson, 1964-66, v.p., treas., dir., 1966—. Mem. Vassar Coll. Symposium on Am. Design. Active Jr. League, Akron, Ohio, 1945—; mem. Govs. Commn. for Day Care for Children, 1956-58; mem. womens bd. Akron Gen. Hosp., 1950-60; jr. council Cleve. Mus. Art, 1960—. Mem. Assn. Interior Design. Episcopalian. Clubs: Intown, Radcliffe (Cleve.). Spl. assignments include Blair House, Pres. Guest House, Washington; exec. offices Walter Gropius Bldg., Cleve., Cleve. Rehab. Center, Gould Internat., Samuel Moore Corp., Republic Steel, Timken Co., others. Home: 2727 Hudson Aurora Rd Hudson OH 44236 Office: Box 637 Hudson OH 44236

FITHIAN, FLOYD, congressman; b. Vesta, Nebr., Nov. 3, 1938; s. James Creston and Eva May (Ballard) F.; B.A., Peru (Nebr.) State Coll., 1951; M.A. in History, U. Nebr., 1955, Ph.D. in Am. history, 1964; m. Marjorie Heim, Nov. 1, 1952; children—Cindy, Judy, John. Former tchr. history and govt. high schs.; now asso. prof. Am. history Purdue U., Lafayette, Ind.; mem. 94th and 95th Congresses from 2d Ind. dist., mem. Coms. on Agr. and Small Bus., also Rural Caucus and House Reform, chm. Subcom. on Jobs. Active Democratic campaigns, Tippecanoe County, Ind.; Served with USN, 1951-54. Mem. Am. Legion, Am. Hist. Assn., Ind. Cattlemen's Assn., Orgn. Am. Historians, Tippecanoe County Hist. Soc., Ind. State Council Social Studies (past pres.). Methodist (tchr., lay speaker). Contbr. articles to profl. jours. Office: Room 1205 Longworth House Office Bldg Washington DC 20515 also 3711 N 500 E Lafayette IN 47901

FITZ, ANNETTE ELAINE, physician; b. Jasper County, Iowa, Mar. 13, 1933; d. Eugene Elmer and Hazel Matilda (Wehrman) Fitz; student Iowa State U., 1950-52; B.A., U. Iowa, 1954, M.D., 1958. Intern, U. Utah Affiliated Hosps., Salt Lake City, 1958-59; resident VA Hosp. and dept. medicine U. Iowa, Iowa City, 1959-62; research fellow hypertension and renal diseases, cardiovascular research lab. Univ. Hosps., Iowa City, 1962-64; NIH spl. research fellow St. Mary's Hosp., London, Eng., 1967-68; staff physician VA Hosp., Iowa City, 1968—, chief hypertension clinic, 1968-73; instr. internal medicine U. Iowa Coll. Medicine, Iowa City, 1963-64, clin. asso., 1964-67, clin. asst. prof., 1967, asst. prof., 1968-72, asso. prof., 1972-76, prof., 1976—; mem. cardio-renal drug adv. com. FDA, 1973-77. Mem. Am., Iowa heart assns., AAAS, AAUP, Am. Soc. Nephrology, Am. Med. Women's Assn., Am. Soc. Artificial Internal Organs, Central Soc. Clin. Research, Midwest Salt and Water Club, Iowa Med. Soc., Iowa Clin. Med. Soc., Soc. Exptl. Biology and Medicine (med. adv. bd. council high blood pressure research), Sigma Xi, Alpha Omega Alpha. Contbr. articles to profl. jours. Home: 1030 River St Iowa City IA 52240 Office: VA Hosp Iowa City IA 52240

FITZGERALD, HAROLD ALVIN, newspaper publisher; b. St. Johns, Mich., Aug. 3, 1896; s. Howard and Zylphia Irene (Shaver) F.; A.B., U. Mich., 1917; LL.D., Oakland U.; m. Elizabeth Millis, June 16, 1923; children—Howard Harold, II, Nancy E. Connolly, Richard Millis. With Pontiac (Mich.) Daily Press, 1919—, telegraph editor, bus. mgr. to 1930, editor and mgr., 1930-44, publisher, chmn. bd., until 1969; 1st v.p. A.P., 1951-54, dir., 1955-64; dir. Fed. Home Loan Bank Ind.-Mich., 1950-59, Community Nat. Bank Pontiac, 1942-68; v.p. Hillsdale (Mich.) News. Former trustee Kingswood Cranbrook, Brookside Schs., Bloomfield Hills. Mem. Mich. Constl. Commn., 1942; vice chmn. Cranbrook Found., Bloomfield Hills, 1935-68; chmn. Mich. State U. Oakland Found., 1960-71; vice chmn. Oakland County Civilian Def., 1939-45; pres. Pontiac United Fund. Served as 2d lt. Air Service, U.S. Army, 1917-18. Mem. Am. Soc. Newspaper Editors, Inter-Am. Press Assn. (dir.), Am. Legion, Alpha Delta Phi, Sigma Delta Chi. Episcopalian (former vestryman). Clubs: Rotary (past pres.); Bloomfield Hills Country (past pres.); Orchard Lake Country; University of Mich. (Ann Arbor); Marco Polo (N.Y.C.). Contbr. to Sat. Eve. Post, Am. Mag., Look, others. Home: 148 Ottawa Dr Pontiac MI 48053

FITZGERALD, JAMES THOMAS, interior architect; b. Dayton, Ohio, Sept. 3, 1934; s. James Leo and Marguerite (Cummins) F.; B.A., Josephinum Coll., Worthington, Ohio, 1956; B.Arch., U. Notre Dame, 1962; m. Leslie Veronica Schmilinski, Apr. 9, 1967; children—James Eduardo, Sean Tomas, Bridgett Patricia. Designer Gartner, Burdick & Bauer-Nilsen, architects, Cin., 1962-66, asso., 1966-68; pres. James T. Fitzgerald, Interior Architecture, Inc., 1968-72; pres. Space Design/Interior Architecture, Inc., 1972—; instr. design Ursuline Tchr. Coll., 1964-65; asst. prof. design U. Cin., 1967-72. Dir. Liturgical Arts Group of Cin., 1967—. Mem. planning bd. Profl. Design Cons.; mem. Contemporary Arts Center, Cin. Art Mus. Mem. Cin. City Mgr.'s Task Force on Culture, Parks and Open Spaces. Recipient Hexter award, 1967, 76. Mem. AIA (corp. mem., mem. nat. com. interior architecture, dir. Cin. chpt., past pres.), Architects Soc. Ohio. (trustee), Merc. Library Assn. Home: 2514 Ritchie Ave Cincinnati OH 45208 Office: 407 Vine St Cincinnati OH 45202

FITZGERALD, JOHN MOONAN, judge; b. Rochester, Minn., Jan. 20, 1923; s. William A. and Rose Mary Kathleen (Moonan) F.; student Rochester Jr. Coll., 1940-41, Mich. State U. Agr. and Applied Sci., 1943; B.S. in Law, U. Minn., 1947, LL.B., 1948; m. Mary Alice Mach, May 5, 1951; children—Maureen, Erin, Brigid, Shelia, Megan, John. Admitted to Minn. bar, 1948, since practiced in New Prague; now judge Dist. Ct. Charter mem. New Prague Library Bd. Mem. 60th-62d session Minn. Ho. of Reps. Trustee Minn. Soldiers Home, 1955-56. Served as 1st lt., USAAF, 1943-45. Decorated Air medal. Mem. Am., Minn. (bd. govs. 1969-70) bar assns. Am. Legion, V.F.W. Clubs: K.C. (4 deg.), Rotary (New Prague). Home: 201 Sun Rise Ave NE New Prague MN 56071 Office: Court House Shakopee MN 55379

FITZGERALD, JOHN WARNER, judge; b. Grand Ledge, Mich., Nov. 14, 1924; s. Frank D. and Queena (Warner) F.; B.S., Mich. State U., 1947; J.D., U. Mich., 1954; m. Lorabeth Moore, June 6, 1953; children—Frank Moore, Eric Stiles, Adam Warner. Mem. pub. relations staff Mich. State U., 1947-52; admitted to Mich. bar, 1954, practiced in Grand Ledge; mem. firm Fitzgerald & Wirbel; legal counsel Mich. Senate, 1955-58; state senator 15th Mich. Dist., 1958-65, chmn. senate bus. com., 1961-65; judge Mich. Ct. Appeals, Lansing, 1965-74, chief judge pro tem, 1965-74; justice Mich. Supreme Ct., 1974-76, dep. chief justice, 1976—. Bd. dirs. Thomas M. Cooley Law Sch., 1975—. Served U.S. Army, 1942-44. Mem. Inst. Jud. Adminstrn., Am., Mich., Eaton County (pres. 1963) bar assns.,

Hist. Soc. Mich. Author: The Land Contract as a Farm Finance Plan, 1973, also articles on agrl. law. Home: 219 W Jefferson St Grand Ledge MI 48837 Office: Law Bldg Lansing MI 48901

FITZGERALD, ROBERT HANNON, orthopaedic surgeon; b. Denver, Colo., June 13, 1904; s. Dennis Lawrence and Mary (Hannon) F.; student Regis Coll., 1921-22; M.D., St. Louis U., 1931; postgrad. Washington U., 1946; m. Gertrude Pauline Willmert, Jan. 15, 1948; children—Mary (Mrs. Gerald Olson), Robert Hannon. Intern St. Louis U. Hosps., 1931-32, resident in gen. surgery, 1932-34; resident orthopaedic surgery Dixon and Dively Group, Kansas City, Mo., 1947-49; pvt. practice orthopaedics, 1949—; chmn. surgery Research Hosp. and Med. Center, Kansas City, Bd. trustees Mo. Valley Coll. Served to comdr. USNR, 1943-46. Diplomate Am. Bd. Orthopaedic Surgery. Mem. Acad. Cerebral Palsy, Am. Acad. Neurology, Mid-Central States Orthopaedic Soc., Mo., (pres. 1971), Kansas City (pres. 1968-69) orthopaedic socs., Kansas City Med. Soc., Am., Mo. med. assns., Am. Acad. Orthopaedic Surgery, Phi Chi. Clubs: Kansas City, 611, Saddle and Sirloin (Kansas City, Mo.); Garden of the Gods (Colorado Springs, Colo.). Home: 8505 Cherokee Place Leawood KS 66206 Office: 6400 Prospect Ave Kansas City MO 64132

FITZ-GERALD, ROGER MILLER, lawyer; b. N.Y.C., July 13, 1935; s. Gerald Hartpence and Rovenia Francis (Miller) F-G; B.S. with honors, U. Ill., 1957, J.D. with honors, 1961; m. Martha Ann Odell, Oct. 28, 1967; children—Kathleen Odell, Maureen Roxanne, Arthur Thomas. Admitted to Ill. bar, 1961, U.S. Dist. Ct. bar, 1961, bar U.S. Patent and Trademark Office, 1965; asso. firm Kirkland, Ellis, Hodson, Chaffetz & Masters, Chgo., 1961-64, Fitch, Even, Tabin & Luedeka, specializing in fgn. patent law, Chgo., 1964-72; patent atty. Bell & Howell Co., Chgo., 1972-74, sr. patent atty., 1974-75, group patent atty., 1975-76, group patent counsel, 1976—. Constl. revision chmn. Ill. Young Republican Orgn., 1968-70. Served with AUS, 1957. Mem. Am., Ill. State, Chgo. bar assns., Patent Law Assn. Chgo., Am. Patent Law Assn., Order of Coif, Phi Beta Kappa, Phi Eta Sigma, Phi Delta Phi, Delta Upsilon (province gov. 1969-75). Republican. Club: Executives (Chgo.). Author: (with Ferdinand J. Zeni) Precinct Captain's Guide, 1968; contbg. author: Materials on Legislation (Read, MacDonald, Fordham and Pierce), 1973. Office: 7100 McCormick Rd Chicago IL 60645

FITZ GERALD, THOMAS JOE, psychologist; b. Wichita, Kans., July 8, 1941; s. Thomas Michael and Pauline Gladys (Zink) F.; B.A., San Francisco State Coll., 1965; M.A., U. Utah, 1969, Ph.D., 1971. Dir. behavioral services programs VA Hosp., Topeka, 1971-73; pvt. practice as psychologist, Topeka, 1973-74, Kansas City, Kans., 1974—; clin. instr. Menninger Sch. Psychiatry, Topeka, 1972-74; sec.-treas. Kans. Bd. Examiners for Psychologists, 1976—; pres. Psychol. Services Corp., Kansas City, Kans., 1974—. Mem. Gov.'s Commn. on Criminal Adminstrn., 1974-76. Served with USMCR, 1958-60. Mem. Am., Kans., Mo., Okla. psychol. assns., Am. Psychology-Law Assn., Assn. for Advancement of Psychology, Office: 2108 W 75th St Suite 400 Prairie Village KS 66208

FITZGERALD, WILLIAM JAMES, banker; b. Kewanee, Ill., Jan. 27, 1924; s. William Murray and Catherine Genivieve (Girvin) F.; B.S., Bradley U., 1949; m. Bernadine J. MacKorosky, Aug. 17, 1947; children—Laurel Anne, Kevin James, Mary Elizabeth, Patrick Terrence. Mgr. Block & Kuhl Dept. Store, Peoria, Ill., 1951-59; mgr. Carson, Pirie, Scott & Co., Chgo., 1959-65, div. v.p., 1964-66; v.p. Champaign County (Ill.) Bank & Trust Co., Urbana, 1966—. Chmn., U. Ill. Grant-In-Aid program; active, Civic Symphony; area chmn. Am. Cancer Soc. Served with USAF, 1943-45. Mem. Am. Mktg. Assn., Bank Mktg. Assn., Urbana C. of C. (pres.). Republican. Roman Catholic. Clubs: Advt., Jaycees, K.C., Elks. Home: 601 Evergreen Ct Urbana IL 61801 Office: 102 E Main St Urbana IL 61801

FITZGIBBON, WILLIAM EDWARD, educator; b. Loogootee, Ind., Apr. 15, 1908; s. Thomas Martin and Amanda (Lents) F.; B.A., Divine Word Sem., 1931; Philosophia Licentiatus, Gregorian U., Rome, 1936, Ph.D., 1963; B.S., DePaul U., 1951, M.S., 1953. Ordained priest Roman Catholic Ch., 1934; faculty Cath. U., Peking, China, 1938-48; prof. philosophy and sci. Divine Word Sem., Techny, Ill., 1956-58; prof. sci. Divine Word Sem., Duxbury, Mass., 1958-66; prof. philosophy Divine Word Coll., Epworth, Iowa, 1966—, dept. chmn. 1971-74, 76—. Dir. scholarship program Soc. Divine Word Cath. U., Chgo., 1950-56. Fulbright grantee, 1969. Mem. Am. Cath. Philos. Assn., Philosophy of Sci. Assn. Address: Divine Word Coll Epworth IA 52045

FITZ GIBBONS, JAMES PATRICK, obstetrician, gynecologist; b. Chgo., Mar. 16, 1908; s. James Joseph and Ellen (O'Brien) FitzG.; B.S.M., Loyola U., Chgo., 1934, M.D., 1936; m. Rita Ann Fisher, Aug. 8, 1950; children—Margaret Ellen, Michael James, Ann, Thomas Patrick, James Jospeh, Robert Emmett. Practice medicine specializing in obstetrics and gynecology, Chgo., sr. attending physician Grant Hosp., Chgo., Swedish Covenant Hosp., Chgo.; clin. asso. prof. dept. obstetrics and gynecology Abraham Lincoln Sch. Medicine U. Ill., Chgo. Served as capt. M.C., U.S. Army, 1941-46. Fellow A.C.S., Am. Coll. Obstetrics and Gynecology; mem. Ill., Chgo. med. socs., AMA. Home: 2944 Grant St Evanston IL 60201 Office: 2073 N Lincoln Ave Chicago IL 60614

FITZPATRICK, JOHN JAMES, III, psychohistorian; b. Plattsburgh, N.Y., Dec. 30, 1941; s. John James and Helen Ransom (Johnson) F.; B.A., Georgetown U., 1966; M.A., U. Calif., Los Angeles, 1967, Ph.D., Berkeley, 1975; m. Gayle Elizabeth Sohigian, Feb. 20, 1965; children—Maia Kathryn, Sarah Elizabeth. Instr., acting asst. prof. Am. studies and history U. Calif., Berkeley, 1970-72; instr. history Phillips Exeter (N.H.) Acad., 1972-73; fellow in interdisciplinary studies program Menninger Found., Topeka, Kans., 1974-77, instr. Menninger Sch. Psychiatry, 1974—; asst. prof. Am. studies U. Kans., Lawrence, 1977—. Grantee Mabelle McLeod Lewis Meml. Fund, 1971-72, U. Calif. Chancellor's Patent Fund., 1971; Spencer Found. fellow, 1976-77. Mem. Mid-Am. Psychosocial Study Group, Group for Use Psychology in History, Am. Hist. Assn., Orgn. Am. Historians, Am. Studies Assn., Council Advancement Psychoanalytic Edn. Author: Psychoanalysis and Crime, 1976; Erik H. Erikson and Psychohistory, 1976; Psychoanalytic Perspectives on the Life Cycle, 1977; co-editor Psychohistory Rev., 1977—; contbg. editor Jours. Psychohistory, 1976—. Home: 124 Greenwood Ave Topeka KS 66606 Office: Menninger Found Topeka KS 66601

FITZPATRICK, THOMAS CHARLES, constrn. co. exec.; b. Wooster, Ohio, Apr. 6, 1921; s. Albert John and Ruth (Shields) F.; B.C.E., Ohio State U., 1943; m. Margaret M. McDonald, Sept. 13, 1943; children—Michael J., Alice Maureen (Mrs. Richard A. Amorose), Thomas J. Waterboy, Elford, Inc., Columbus, Ohio, 1935-42, job foreman, 1946-52, chief engr., 1952-56, exec. v.p., 1956-65, pres., gen. mgr., 1965—. Pres. Franklin County Heart Assn., 1963; vice-chmn. United Appeals, Columbus. 1957-60; mem. adv. bd. Salvation Army, Columbus, 1961—, chmn., 1969, 70; mem. exec. bd. Central Ohio council Boy Scouts Am., 1963—, v.p., 1973; mem. Worthington Planning Commn., 1960-62; mem. Riverfront Devel. Commn., 1964—; mem. Columbus Diocese Bldg. Commn., 1969—; mem. adv. bd. Ohio Dominican Coll., 1962—. Trustee Grant Hosp., 1972—; chmn. bd. Central Ohio Heart Assn., 1975-77. Served to lt. USNR, 1943-46. Named Man of Year, Builders Exchange, 1964; recipient Gold medal Heart Assn., 1967, Silver medal, 1972; Silver Beaver award Boy Scouts Am., 1971. Mem. Asso. Gen. Contractors (pres. Ohio chpt. 1970, nat. dir. 1971—), Ohio (mem. bd. 1973—), Columbus Area (mem. bd. 1972—) chambers commerce, Builders Employers Assn. (pres. 1963-64), Builders Exchange (dir. 1956-62). Republican. Roman Catholic. Rotarian. Club: Athletic of Columbus. Home: 185 Medick Way Worthington OH 43085 Office: 555 S Front St Columbus OH 43215

FITZPATRICK, WILLIAM ALLEN, mcht., pharmacist; b. St. Louis, Jan. 1, 1942; s. Raymond Allen and Irene (Fry) F.; B.S., St. Louis Coll. Pharmacy, 1965; m. S. Elaine Smith, Sept. 24, 1966; children—Julie, Kelly, Debbie and Cheri (twins), Jodi. Retail and hosp. pharmacy work, 1965-70; adminstr. St. Louis Geriatric Center, 1971-72; exec. sec. Kappa Psi, nat. fraternity, St. Louis, 1970-72; owner Fitzpatrick Pharmacy, St. Louis, 1973—. Sec.-treas. fund dr. St. Louis Coll. Pharmacy, 1969-70. Recipient Johnson & Johnson leadership award St. Louis Coll. Pharmacy, 1965; Mo. Pharmacist Man of Yr. award, 1975. Mem. Am., Mo., Ill., St. Louis pharm. assns., Acad. Gen. Practice Pharmacy, St. Louis Hosp. Pharmacy Assn., St. Louis Coll. Pharmacy Alumni Assn. (pres. 1968-69), Kappa Psi (pres. province 7, 1965-69, nat. pres. 1974-79, grand officer). Home: 1034 Terracewood Circle Manchester MO 63011 Office: Fitzpatrick Pharmacy 130 Manchester Rd Ballwin MO 63011

FITZSIMMONS, WILLIAM ALLEN, physicist, educator; b. Canton, Ohio, Feb. 21, 1940; s. Albert William and Mildred (Benson) F.; B.S., U. Mich., 1961, M.S., 1964; M.A., Rice U., 1966, Ph.D., 1968; m. Mary Ann Olsen, Nov. 6, 1939; children—Anne Katherin, Kathleen Marie, William Benson. Mech. engr. Cyclotron project U. Mich., Ann Arbor, 1960-64; postdoctoral asso. physics Rice U., Houston, 1968-69; asst. prof. physics U. Wis., Madison, 1969-73, asso. prof., 1973-75, prof., 1975—; pres. Nat. Research Group Inc., Madison, 1975—, also dir. Recipient award research physics Houston chpt. Sigma Chi, 1968. Fellow Am. Phys. Soc. Home: 1015 Edgehill Dr Madison WI 53705

FIXLER, CARL, shopping center exec.; b. Cleve., Jan. 11, 1943; s. Leo E. and Helen F. (Moskovitz) F.; B.A., Fenn Coll., 1965; student Cleve. Marshall Law Sch., 1971-73; m. Elaine M. Skufca, Feb. 6, 1971; 1 son, Michael. Dep. auditor Cuyahoga County Auditor's Office, Cleve., 1966-70; exec. v.p. Terminal Tax Consultants, Cleve., 1971-72; asst. v.p., gen. mgr. shopping center, Cleve. Mem. Huron Rd. Hosp. Assos. com. 1973—. Home: 3905 Faversham Rd University Heights OH 44118 Office: 320 Williamson Bldg Cleveland OH 44114

FIZZELL, ROBERT BRUCE, lawyer; b. Taylorville, Ill., Sept. 20, 1889; s. James Albert and Martha Catherine (Allen) F.; A.B., U. Ill., 1910; LL.B., Harvard, 1913; m. Florence Edith Hoover, Nov. 27, 1916 (dec.); children—Robert Bruce, Dorothy F.; m. 2d, Vera L. Hagen, July 10, 1965. Admitted to Mo. bar, 1913, since practiced in Kansas City, Mo.; now mem. Stinson, Mag, Thomson, McEvers & Fizzell. Trustee Kansas City Art Inst.; trustee Friends of Art of Kansas City, pres., 1937-39. Fellow Am. Bar Found.; mem. Am., Mo., Kansas City bar assns., Lawyers Assn. of Kansas City (pres. 1947), Soc. of Fellows of Nelson Gallery Found., Phi Beta Kappa, Delta Sigma Rho. Democrat. Clubs: University, Kansas City Country. Home: 1228 W 68th Terr Kansas City MO 64113 Office: 2100 Ten Main Center Kansas City MO 64105

FLADLAND, RAYMOND ARTHUR, real estate exec.; b. Grand Forks, N.D., Oct. 13, 1927; s. Eddie Arthur and Elsie Evelyn (Simmons) F.; B.S., U. N.D., 1950; m. Faye Eleanor Vantine, Sept. 5, 1948; children—Paul Raymond, Peggy Louise, Sally Mace. Owner, pres. Fladland Real Estate and Ins. Co., Grand Forks, 1950—. Bd. dirs. United Hosp., 1969-76, United Way, 1964-67. Served with USNR, 1945-46. Recipient Realtor of Year award for N.D., 1962. Mem. Grand Forks Bd. Realtors (pres. 1959-60), N.D. Assn. Realtors (pres. 1963-64), Grand Forks Ind. Ins. Agts. Assn. (pres. 1970-71), Grand Forks C. of C. (v.p. 1976), Am. Legion. Republican. Lutheran. Mason, Elk, Lion. Home: 2605 Olson Dr Grand Forks ND 58201 Office: 802 DeMers Ave Grand Forks ND 58201

FLAHIFF, GEORGE BERNARD, archbishop; b. Paris, Ont., Can., Oct. 26, 1905; s. John James and Eleanor Rose (Fleming) F.; B.A., St. Michael's Coll., U. Toronto, 1926; student U. Strasbourg (France), 1930-31; Dipl. Archiviste-Paleographe, Ecole Nat. des Chartes, Paris, France, 1935; hon. degree in law U. Seattle, 1965, U. Notre Dame, 1969, U. Man., 1969, U. Windsor, 1970, U. Winnipeg, 1972, U. Toronto, 1972; S.T.D., Université Laval, Quebec, 1974, St. Bonaventure U., 1975, U. St. Thomas, Houston, 1977. Ordained priest Roman Catholic Ch., 1930; prof. medieval history Pontifical Inst. Medieval Studies and U. Toronto, 1935-54, sec. Inst., 1943-51; superior-gen. Basilian Fathers, 1954-61; archbishop of Winnipeg, Can., 1961—; named to Coll. Cardinals, 1969; mem. Sacred Congregation for Religious, Sacred Congregation for Edn. Decorated companion Order Can., 1974. Home: 39 Bishop's Ln Charleswood MB R3R 0A8 Canada Office: 50 Stafford St Winnipeg MB R3M 2V7 Canada

FLANAGAN, EDWARD JOSEPH, chiropractor; b. Cleve., Feb. 13, 1931; s. Edward Joseph and Esther Mary (White) F.; student Kent State U., 1950-52; D. Chiropractic, Great Lake Coll. Chiropractic, 1961; postgrad. roentgenology Lincoln Chiropractic Coll., 1968-70; m. Betty Sue Boone, Apr. 24, 1954; children—Linda, Susan, June, Collette, Lori, Mary Lou, Eddie. Pvt. chiropractic practice, North Olmsted, Ohio, 1961—; lectr.; cons. x-ray specialist Assos. Diagnostic Center, Akron, Ohio; owner Lorain Chiropractic Center, Memphis Chiropractic Center. Served with USNR, 1952-54. Licensed mechanotherapist, Ohio. Diplomate Am. Bd. Chiropractic Roentgenology. Mem. Am., Ohio, Northeastern Ohio chiropractic assns. Contbr. articles to profl. jours. Home: 31686 Lake Rd Avon Lake OH 44012 Office: 27712 Lorain Ave North Olmsted OH 44070

FLANAGAN, GEORGE CLEMENT, physician; b. Chgo., Aug. 24, 1928; s. Charles Larkin and Helen Marie (Sullivan) F.; M.D., U. Chgo., 1953; m. Sarah Stanley Gunn, Apr. 27, 1967; children—George Hunter, Elizabeth Hanford. Intern, U. Chgo. Clinics, 1953-54; resident Presbyn.-St. Luke's Hosp., Chgo., 1957-60; asso. prof. medicine U. Ill. Med. Schs., Chgo., 1967-69; asso. prof. medicine Rush Med. Coll., Chgo., 1971—, asso. dean, 1974—. Served with USNR, 1954-56. Mem. A.C.P., AMA, Assn. Am. Med. Colls. Roman Catholic. Home: 2335 Central Park Evanston IL 60201 Office: 600 S Paulina St Chicago IL 60612

FLANAGAN, HUGH JOSEPH, dentist; b. Chgo., Jan. 17, 1929; s. John Joseph and Mary (Barlow) F.; B.S. in Zoology, De Paul U., 1951; B.S., U. Ill., 1954, D.D.S., 1956; m. Darlene Bernick, June 1, 1957; children—Therese, Denise, Hugh Patrick, Kathleen, Maureen. Practice dentistry, Burbank, Ill., 1959—; clin. instr. dept. crown and bridge dentistry Coll. Dentistry, U. Ill., Chgo., 1958-59. Served with Dental Corps, USNR, 1956-58. Mem. Am. Dental Assn., Ill., Chgo. dental socs., Acad. Gen. Dentistry, Am. Soc. Dentistry for Children. Psi Omega. Roman Catholic. Mem. Independent Order Foresters. Home: 1203 Berry Ln Flossmoor IL 60422 Office: 7902 Narragansett St Burbank IL 60459

FLANAGAN, JOHN KEARNEY, city atty.; b. La Crosse, Wis., May 2, 1928; s. John Edward and Margaret Mary (Kearney) F.; student U. Wis.-La Crosse, 1946-48; B.S., U. Wis., 1951, LL.B., 1952; m. Kathleen A. Holicky, Aug. 16, 1958; children—Diane, Mary Ellen, Michael, Thomas. Admitted to Wis. bar, 1952; asst. city atty., La Crosse, 1955-56, city atty., 1956—. Mem. adv. bd. Catholic Social Services of La Crosse, Inc., 1965-67; mem. La Crosse Co. Indsl. Devel. Council, 1956-70; mem. adv. bd. Manpower Devel. & Tng. Act., 1966; mem. nat. com. on Uniform Traffic Laws and Ordinances, 1968-70. Served with AUS, 1952-54. Mem. Wis., La Crosse County bar assns., Assn. Wis. Planners, Nat. Inst. Municipal Law Officers (state chmn. 1965), League Wis. Municipalities, Am. Legion, Jr. C. of C., La Crosse County Hist. Soc. Elk, Rotarian. Home: 217 N 23d St La Crosse WI 54601 Office: 507 Schneider Bldg La Crosse WI 54601

FLANAGAN, PATRICK MICHAEL, med. engr., educator; b. New Kensington, Pa., Apr. 15, 1950; s. James Russell and Kathryn Elinor (Elliston) F.; B.M.E. (Trustee scholar), Clarkson Coll. Tech., 1972; M.M.E. (Nat. Inst. Gen. Med. Scis. trainee), Mass. Inst. Tech., 1975; postgrad. U. Cin., 1975—. Asst. project coordinator Clarkson Coll. Tech., Potsdam, N.Y., 1971-72; research asst. Mass. Inst. Tech., Cambridge, 1972-75; affiliated personnel Harvard Mass. Inst. Tech. Rehab. Engrng. Center, Cambridge, 1973-75; teaching asst. mech. engrng. U. Cin., 1975-76, acoustic cons., dir. transducer devel. Stroke Research Lab., Coll. Medicine, 1975—, instr. mech. engrng., 1976—. Recipient Norman L. Rea award, 1972. Mem. Acoustical Soc. Am., Sigma Xi, Tau Beta Pi. Researcher detection of cerebral aneurysms and acoustic tissue characterization. Home: 707 Dixmyth Ave Apt 810 Cincinnati OH 45220 Office: U Cin Room 858 Cincinnati OH 45220

FLANAGAN, PAUL KING, owner ins. agy.; b. Huron, S.D., Dec. 30, 1932; s. Earl F. and Ruby T. (Dinkins) F.; B.F.A. cum laude, U. S.D., 1954; m. Laura M. Wickham, Nov. 22, 1951; children—Jeanne, Valerie, Dan, Kathleen, Lisa. Gen. mgr. U. S.D. Book & Supply Inc., 1954-59; exec. dir. U. S.D. Student Union, 1954-59; owner, mgr. Flanagan Agy., ins., Huron, S.D., 1959—. City commr. City of Huron, 1973—. Recipient Huron Distinguished Service award Huron Jaycees, 1970. C.L.U. Mem. Am. Ind. Agts. Assn., Am. Soc. C.L.U. (pres. Eastern S.D. chpts.), Nat. S.D. (pres, nat. committeeman 1972-78), assns. life underwriters, Huron Life Underwriters Assn. (pres. 1960), Huron C. of C. (pres. 1968), Izaak Walton League Am. Democrat. Roman Catholic. Club: Elks. Home: 1478 Utah Ave SE Huron SD 57350 Office: 50 3d St SW Huron SD 57350

FLANDERS, DWIGHT PRESCOTT, economist, educator; b. Rockford, Ill., Mar. 14, 1909; s. Daniel Bailey and Lulu Iona (Nichol) F.; B.A., U. Ill., 1931, M.A., 1937; postgrad. Beloit Coll., 1933-34; Ph.D., Yale, 1939; m. Mildred Margaret Hutchison, Aug. 27, 1939; children—James Prescott, Thomas Addison. Instr. coll. algebra Burr Sch., Beloit (Wis.) Coll., 1933-34; instr. U.S. history secondary schs., Rockford, 1934-36; asst. prof. econs. and statistics Syracuse U., 1939-42; prof. econs. U. Ill., Urbana-Champaign, 1946-77, prof. emeritus, 1977—, chmn. masters research seminar, 1947-74. grad. adviser, 1949-75; cons. in field. Del., Hazen Nat. Conf. Religion and Edn., 1948. Pres. Three Lakes (Wis.) Waterfront Homeowners Assn., 1969-71, mem. ofcl. bd., 1971—. Served with AUS, 1930, 42-46. Recipient Best Grad. Tchr. award Coll. Commerce, U. Ill., 1977. Mem. Am. Econ. Assn., Econometric Soc., Royal Econ. Soc., Phi Beta Kappa, Phi Kappa Phi, Alpha Kappa Psi, Beta Gamma Sigma (pres. U. Ill. chpt. 1959-60, historian 1960-77), Chi Beta, Chi Psi. Club: Yale (Chgo.). Asso. editor Current Econ. Comment, 1946-54. Author monographs, books; contbr. articles to profl. publs. Home: 719 S Foley Ave Champaign IL 61820 Office: Dept Econs U Ill Urbana IL 61801

FLARSHEIM, ALFRED, psychiatrist; b. Cin., June 19, 1921; s. Henry and Miriam (Laub) F.; M.D., U. Cin., 1944; m. Marjorie Marquette, Feb. 19, 1943; children—Donna (Mrs. Albert Parramore), Nancy (Mrs. Roger Hallum). Intern, Boston City Hosp., 1944-45; resident Cin. Gen. Hosp., 1945-49, U. Chgo. Billings Hosp., 1949-50; practice medicine specializing in psychiatry, Chgo., 1950—; mem. staffs Michael Reese Ravenswood hosps., Chgo.; prof. psychiatry Garrett Theol. Sch., Evanston, Ill., 1958—; clin. asso. prof. psychiatry U. Ill., Chgo., 1954—; cons. Sonia Shankman Orthogenic Sch., U. Chgo., 1970—, Family Service Center, Wilmette, Ill., 1960—. Diplomate Am. Bd. Psychiatry and Neurology, Nat. Bd. Med. Examiners. Fellow Am. Psychiat. Assn., Am. Orthopsychiat. Assn.; mem. A.M.A., Am. Psychosomatic Soc., Group for Advancement Psychiatry, Alpha Omega Alpha. Contbr. articles to profl. jours. Home: 729 8th St Wilmette IL 60091 Office: 400 E Randolph St Chicago IL 60601

FLECK, HENRIETTA (HENRIETTA FLECK HOUGHTON), educator; b. Papillion, Nebr., Sept. 22, 1903; d. John Peter and Wilhelmina (Prinz) Fleck; student Peru (Nebr.) Tchrs. Coll., 1921-23; B.S., U. Nebr., 1928, Sc.D. (hon.), 1970; M.S., Columbia U., 1932; Ph.D., Ohio State U., 1944; m. Dale Houghton, June 6, 1956. Home econs. tchr. Nebr. high schs., 1923-27; dietitian in charge metabolic div. Santa Barbara (Calif.) Cottage Hosp., 1928-29; head dept. foods and nutrition U. Del., 1932-42; research asst., bur. ednl. research Ohio State U., 1942-44; chmn. home econs. dept. Ill. State U., Normal, 1944-46, N.Y. U., 1946-71, prof., 1971—; cons. edn. procs. N.Y. Dept. Edn., bus. corps., social orgns., 1946—. Mem. NEA (pres. home econs. dept. 1953-55), Am. Home Econ. Assn., AAAS, Am. Dietetic Assn., Am. Edn. Research Assn., Soc. Nutrition Edn., Nat. Council Family Relations (dir.), AAUP, Nat. Soc. Study Edn., Omicron Nu, Pi Lambda Theta. Author: A Recipe Primer, 1949; How to Evaluate Students, 1953; The Coed Cookbook, 1967; Toward Better Teaching of Home Economics, 2d edit., 1974, Japanese edit., 1974; Introduction to Nutrition, 3d edit., 1976. Co-author: Everybody's Book of Modern Diet and Nutrition, 1955; Exploring Homemaking and Personal Living, 1959, 4th edit., 1977; Living With Your Family, 1965. Editor: Macmillan series coll. home econs. text books, 1957-63; contbg. editor Forecast mag. for home economists, 1949-62, ednl. and curriculum adviser, contbr., 1963-75. Contbr. profl. jours. Home: 6100 Vine St Apt H-45 Lincoln NE 68505 Office: 537 E Bldg Washington Sq New York City NY 10003

FLEENER, GEORGE GORDON, biologist; b. Berlin, N.D., Mar. 25, 1923; s. Merle Carroll and Dorothy May (Gordon) F.; student Bemidji State Coll., 1942-43, North Central Coll., Naperville, Ill., 1943-44; B.S., Utah State U., 1946, M.S., 1950; m. Rosezella Mae Graham, Dec. 27, 1946; children—Theodore George, Timothy William. Fishery biologist, stream investigator Mo. Dept. Conservation, Columbia, 1950—; cons. to state and fed. agys. Served with AUS, 1943-46; ETO. Mem. Am. Inst. Fisheries Research Biologists, Am. Fisheries Soc. (chmn. publicity com. 1966, chmn. awards com. 1970-73), Mo. Acad. Sci., Sigma Xi, Xi Sigma Pi. Baptist. Mason. Contbr. articles to profl. publs. Home: 1411 Richardson St Columbia MO 65201 Office: 1110 College St Columbia MO 65201

FLEISCHAKER, JACK, lawyer; b. Joplin, Mo., Mar. 3, 1912; s. Isadore and Johanna (Erlich) F.; student U. Mo., 1930-36; J.D., Washington U., St. Louis, 1937; m. Elaine Barlow, Apr. 23, 1939; children—James B., Jacelaine (Mrs. Lawrence Horn), William J., Johanna. Admitted to Mo. bar, 1937, since practiced in Joplin; asso. firm Thompson & Roberts, 1937-57; partner firm Roberts & Fleischaker, 1957—; asst. atty. gen. State of Mo., 1948-52. Dir., chmn. trust com. United Mo. Bank of Joplin. Mem. Library Bd. of City of Joplin, 1948-52; mem. Mo-Kan. Area council Boy Scouts Am., 1950-55; v.p. Joplin Community Concert Assn., 1959-60; chmn. Airport Adv. Com., Joplin, 1963—. Mem. Joplin Bd. Edn., 1950-56, pres., 1955-56; chmn. Dem. Com. Jasper County, 1956-62; chmn. Dem. party 7th Congl. Dist., 1960-62. Trustee Freeman Hosp., 1948—; adv. bd. YWCA, 1960-64. Served with AUS, 1941-46. Mem. Am. Bar Assn., Mo. Bar, Jasper County Bar, Am. Trial Lawyers Assn., Am. Legion (post trustee 1948—), Aircraft Owners and Pilots Assn., Mo. Pilots Assn. Mason, Elk, Kiwanian. Home: 320 N Moffet St Joplin MO 64801 Office: 711-19 First National Bldg Joplin MO 64801

FLEMING, BRUCE THOMAS, realtor; b. Watseka, Ill., Apr. 11, 1920; s. Blythe and Mabel (Kirkpatrick) F.; B.S. in Agrl. Econs., Purdue U., 1942; m. Betty Jean Gordon, June 12, 1943; children—Philip J., Anthony P., Thomas J. Loan supr. U.S. Dept. Agr., Crown Point, Ind., 1942-46; owner, operator Fleming & Monroe Realty Co., Crown Point, Ind., 1946—, v.p., treas. Fleming, Corbin & Bates Ins. Inc.; pres. Hermits Lake Inc.; sec., part owner Turnkey Builders Inc.; treas., part owner All Seasons Home Inc.; pres. S. Suburban Multiple Listing Service, 1973-74; past pres. S. Lake County Bd. Realtors, 1960. Past pres. Civic Club, 1955; fin. chmn. Methodist Ch., Crown Point. Named realtor of year, 1974. Mem. Am., Ind., Crown Point real estate assns., Am., No. Ind. assns. home builders, Am. Soc. Farm Mgrs. and Rural Appraisers, Soc. Residential Appraisers, Jaycees (past pres. Crown Point 1950). Clubs: Youche Country, Lakes of Four Seasons Country, Crown Point Bridge League; Masons, Shriners. Home: 4110 Hermits Ln Crown Point IN 46307 Office: 216 E Joliet St Crown Point IN 46307

FLEMING, LOIS FREESH (MRS. CHARLES W. FLEMING), geographer, educator; b. nr. Hammond, Ill., Sept. 9, 1912; d. Russell Parker and Mollie (Price) Freesh; A.A., Blackburn Coll., 1931; B.S. with honors, Eastern Ill. State U., 1957, M.S., 1962; postgrad U. Ill. Extension, 1962-65; Ph.D., Ind. State U., 1972; m. Charles W. Fleming, Dec. 24, 1932; children—Charles William, Harriett (Mrs. Hanson C. Lilly), Russell Ernest, Mary Jane (Mrs. Charles S. Taylor). Tchr. elementary schs., Coles County, Ill., 1931-33, 44-48, Douglas County, 1949-62, Cook County, 1962-63; instr. geography dept. East Tex. State Coll., Commerce, 1963-64, Eastern Ill. State U., Charleston, 1964-65; instr. geography Butler U., Indpls., 1965-66; asst. prof. geography So. State Coll., Magnolia, Ark., 1966-69; postgrad. Ind. State U., Terre Haute, 1969-72; asso. prof. geography Northwestern State U. La., Natchitoches, 1972—. Mem. Assn. Am. Geographers, Nat. Council Geog. Edn., Ill. Geog. Soc., Audubon Soc. (pres. Natchitoches chpt. 1974-75), Gamma Theta Upsilon. Baptist. Home: Rural Route 1 Humbolt IL 61931 Office: Northwestern State Univ Natchitoches LA 71457

FLEMING, MILO JOSEPH, lawyer; b. Roscoe, Ill., Jan. 4, 1911; s. John E. and Elizabeth (Shafer) F.; A.B., U. of Ill., 1933, LL.B., 1936; m. Dorothea H. Kunze, Aug. 15, 1942 (dec. 1944); m. 2d, Lucy Anna Russell, June 30, 1948; step-children—Michael Russell, Jo Ann Russell (Mrs. Clemens); 1 dau., Elizabeth. Pvt. practice law, 1936-42, 58-59; mem. firm Pallissard and Fleming, Watseka, Ill., 1942-46, Pallissard, Fleming & Oram, 1946-58, Fleming & McGrew, 1960-76, Fleming, McGrew and Boyer, 1977, Fleming & Boyer, 1977—; master in chancery, Iroquois County, Ill., 1943-44. City atty., Watseka, Ill., 1949-57, 61—, Gilman, Ill., 1966-69; village atty. Milford, Ill., 1942-70, Wellington, 1962-72, Woodland, Danforth, Crescent City, Martinton, Sheldon, Onarga, Papineau; atty. Lake Iroquois Lot Owners Assn. and Central San. Dist.; asst. atty. gen. Iroquois County, 1964-69; pres. Iroquois County Devel. Corp., 1961-68; bd. dirs. Belmont Water Co. Farmer. Chmn., Iroquois County Universities Bond Issues Campaign, 1960; mem. State Employees Group Ins. Adv. Commn., Ill. Candidate, state rep., Apr. 1940. Mem. Am. (vice chmn. com. ordnances and adminstrv. regulations 1968-69, 73-75, chmn. 1969-72, 75—), Ill., Iroquois County (pres. 1966-67) bar assns., Def. Research Inst., Smithsonian Instn., Phi Eta Sigma, Sigma Delta Kappa. Democrat. Methodist. Mason (Shriner, 32 deg.), Odd Fellow (mem. jud. and appeals com. Ill. 1960-62, grand warden Ill. 1962, dep. grand master 1963, grand master 1964; grand rep. 1966; trustee Old Folks Home, Mattoon, Ill., 1966-71, sec. bd. 1966-68, vice chmn. bd. 1970—, atty. 1966—). Author: One Hundred Twenty-five Years of Odd Fellowship at Watseka, Illinois. Prepared Municipal Code for City of Watseka, 1953, Milford, 1957, Martinton, 1960, Crescent City, 1960, Woodland, 1961, Cissna Park, 1961. Home: 120 W Jefferson St Watseka IL 60970 Office: Fleming & Boyer Odd Fellows Bldg 216 E Walnut St Watseka IL 60970

FLEMING, ROBBEN WRIGHT, univ. pres.; b. Paw Paw, Ill., Dec. 18, 1916; s. Edmund Palmer and Emily Jeanette (Wheeler) F.; B.A., Beloit Coll., 1938; LL.B., U. Wis., 1941; 19 hon. degrees; m. Aldyth Louise Quixley, Apr. 3, 1942; children—Nancy Jo, James Edmund, Carolyn Elizabeth. Admitted to Wis. bar, 1941; a reorgn. div. SEC, Washington, 1941-42, War Labor Bd., Washington, 1942; dir. Indsl. Relations Center, U. Wis., 1947-52; exec. dir. nat. WSB. Washington, 1951; dir. Inst. Labor and Indsl. Relations, U. Ill., 1952-58, prof. law, 1957-64; prof. law, chancellor U. Wis., 1964-67; prof. law, pres. U. Mich, Ann Arbor, 1968—; exchange prof., Germany, summer 1950. Norway and Sweden, winter 1956; arbitrator indsl. disputes; mem. Atomic Energy Labor-Mgmt. Relations Panel, 1958—; exec. dir. Armour Automation Com., 1960-61; dir. Chrysler Corp., 1972—, John Deere & Co., 1975—; chmn. Commn. on Doctoral Edn., N.Y. State Regents, 1972; chmn. bd. Am. Council on Edn., 1976-77; pres. Assn. Am. Univs., 1974; chmn. bd. Carnegie Fund Advancement Teaching, 1978. Served with AUS, 1942-46. Mem. Indsl. Relations Research Assn., Nat. Acad. Arbitrators (past pres.), Order of Coif, Phi Beta Kappa, Beta Theta Phi. Presbyn. Co-editor: Emergency Disputes and National Policy, 1955; The Politics of Wage-Price Decisions, A Four-Country Analysis, 1965; The Labor Arbitration Process, 1966. Contbr. articles on indsl. relations to profl. publs. Home: 815 S University Ann Arbor MI 48109

FLEMING, RODNEY R., assn. exec.; b. Mankato, Minn., Mar. 15, 1923; s. Raymond E. and Mae (Johnson) F.; B.S., Iowa State U., 1947, M.S., 1950; m. Marguerite L. Meurer, Sept. 7, 1946; children—Diane L., Dennis R. City engr., City of North Mankato, 1950-52, City of Mankato, 1952-55; city engr., dir. pub. works City of Owatonna (Minn.), 1955-59; city engr., City of Sioux City (Iowa), 1959-60; pub. works editor Am. City Mag., N.Y.C., 1960-71; asso. exec. dir. Am. Pub. Works Assn., Chgo., 1971—. Commn. Mcpl. Swimming Pool; mem. Bldg. Commn. Metuchen, N.J., 1965-69. Served with AUS, 1943-46. Registered profl. engr., Minn. Mem. Am. Pub. Works Assn., ASCE, Nat. Soc. Profl. Engrs., Inst. Solid Wastes, Pub. Works Hist. Soc. Home: 3121 Stonegate Ct Flossmoor IL 60422 Office: 1313 E 60th St Chicago IL 60637

FLEMING, THOMAS BRACELAND, nuclear instrumentation mfg. co. exec.; b. Pottsville, Pa., Apr. 25, 1931; s. Joseph Leo and Madlyn (Quinn) F.; B.S.Eng., Pa. State U., 1954; m. Cynthia Dale Zulick, Aug. 7, 1954; children—Anne, Barbara. Indsl. engr., Western Electric Co., Allentown, Pa., 1958-60; v.p. mktg. Reuter-Stokes Inc., Cleve., 1960—. Served with USN, 1954-57. Mem. Am. Nuclear Soc., Soc. Exploration Geophysicists. Home: 7755 Holyoke Dr Hudson OH 44236 Office: 18530 Miles Pky S Cleveland OH 44128

FLEMING, WILLIAM JOSEPH, chem. engr.; b. Lima, Ohio, May 10, 1950; s. Joseph Edward and Mary Roesetta (Perrin) F.; B.S. in Chem. Engring., U. Cin., 1973; m. Georgia Jo Battista, Aug. 9, 1975; 1 dau., Josephine Margaret. Process engr. Diamond Shamrock Corp., Ashtabula, Ohio, 1973, Houston, 1973-74, Painesville, Ohio, 1974-76, staff engr., Chgo., 1977—. Research on hot lime-soda-phosphate external treatment facilities. Home: 15021 W Huntington Ct Orland Park IL 60462 Office: 4201 W 69th St Chicago IL 60629

FLEMMA, ROBERT JOHN, cardiovascular surgeon; b. Herkimer, N.Y., Jan. 18, 1935; s. Saverio Michael and Margherita (Ferrari) F.; B.A. cum laude, Amherst Coll., 1956; M.D., U. Rochester, 1960; m. Mary Ann Fariello, June 27, 1959; children—Robert John, Margherita, Saverio Michael, Gerald, Nicholas, Thomas. Intern, resident in cardiovascular surgery Med. Center, Duke U., 1960-67; asst. clin. prof. surgery Med. Coll. Wis., Milw., 1969-72, asso. clin. prof., 1972—; mem. Cardiovascular Surgery Assos., Milw., 1969—; now chief cardiac surgery VA Hosp., Milw.; also chief sect. thoracic and cardiovascular surgery St. Luke's Hosp., Milw.; pvt. practice medicine, specializing in cardiovascular surgery, Milw. Served to maj., M.C., U.S. Army, 1967-69. Diplomate Am. Bd. Surgery, Am. Bd. Thoracic Surgery. Mem. Am. Assn. Thoracic Surgery, Soc. Thoracic Surgeons, Internat. Cardiovascular Soc., A.C.S., Assn. Acad. Surgery, Am. Coll. Chest Physicians, Am., Wis. heart assns., Wis. Surg. Soc., Milw. Acad. Surgery. Roman Catholic. Contbg. author books, contbr. articles to profl. publs. Home: 8315 River Rd River Hills WI 53217 Office: 9800 W Bluemound Rd Milwaukee WI 53226

FLERLAGE, RAEBURN, radio producer, photographer; b. Cin., July 13, 1915; s. William McKinley and Beulah Eldora (Schmid) F.; student Ill. State Normal U., 1936-37, Roosevelt U., 1969-71, Chgo. City Colls., 1963-68, Ill. Inst. Tech., 1962-63; m. Louise Murray, Dec. 28, 1966; children—Kristin, William, Karen, Linda. Free-lance photographer, record-radio producer, 1940—; owner, mgr. Kinnara Record & Tape Distbrs., Inc., Chgo., 1971—; writer music and record rev. columns, 1940—; reporter, music interviewer Cin. Post, 1940; Midwest exec. sec. People's Songs, Inc., 1946-48. Mem. Nat. Assn. Ind. Record Distbrs., Chgo. Vedanta Soc. (chmn. bd. dirs. 1972-73). Home: 6821 S Crandon Ave Chicago IL 60649 Office: 4323 N Elston Ave Chicago IL 60641

FLETCHER, JOHN FRIZELL, dentist; b. Pratt, Kans., Apr. 19, 1936; s. Zell and Beatrice Maxine (Watkins) F.; B.S. in Edn., U. Kans., 1960, M.S. in Edn., 1962; D.D.S., U. Mo. at Kansas City, 1968; m. Janice Joy Cornwell, Dec. 27, 1959 (div. July 1973); children—John Michael, Linda Carol, James Matthew; m. 2d, Jean Marie Vest, Sept., 1973; 1 son, Scott Andrew. Instr. oral diagnosis U. Mo., Kansas City, 1968-69; dentist Osawatomie (Kans.) State Hosp., 1969-70; pvt. practice dentistry, Kansas City, Kans., 1968-74, Leavenworth, Kan., 1970—; courtesy staff Providence-St. Margaret's Health Center, Kansas City, Kans., 1969—. Bd. mgmt. YMCA, 1972. Mem. Am., Kans. dental assns., Kaw Valley Dental Study Club, Leavenworth, Wyandotte County, Northeast Dist., 1st Dist. (peer rev. com. 1972) dental socs., Acad. Gen. Dentistry, Acad. Oral Medicine, Pierre Fauchard Acad., Leavenworth Area C. of C., Fellowship Christian Athletes, Phi Gamma Delta, Phi Epsilon Kappa, Phi Delta Kappa, Xi Xsi Phi. Lion, Elk. Club: Optimist (Kansas City). Presbyn. (elder 1961-63). Home: 901 Halderman Leavenworth KS 66048 Office: 300 Shawnee Leavenworth KS 66048

FLETCHER, RALPH, educator; b. Chgo., Jan. 2, 1932; s. Ralph John and Sylvia (Jones) F.; B.S., Chgo. State U., 1971, M.S., 1977; 1 son, Ralph III. Engr., Gen. Tel. Co., 1963-66, ATT, Ill. Bell Tel. Co., 1966-69; instr. Malcom X Community Coll., Chgo., 1971-73, Chgo State U., 1975-76; tchr. math. disadvantaged students Central YMCA Community Coll., Chgo., 1976—. Served with USAF, 1952-56. Named Educator of Year Malcom X Community Coll., 1972. Mem. Am. Math Soc., Math. Assn. Am., IEEE, Nat. Council Tchrs. Math. Home: 716 E 51st St Chicago IL 60615 Office: Dept Math YMCA Community Coll 211 W Wacker Dr Chicago IL 60606

FLETCHER, RONALD ROBERT, lawyer; b. Des Moines, Nov. 25, 1940; s. Robert V. and Wilma A. (Roberts) F.; B.S., Drake U., 1967, J.D. with honors, 1969; m. Jean Travis, Aug. 21, 1965; children—Jacquelyn, John, David. Admitted to Iowa bar, 1969, Minn. bar, 1969; atty. firm Larkin, Hoffman, Daly & Lindgren, Ltd., Mpls., 1969—; dir. Summit State Bank of Richfield, Sports Films & Talents, Inc., Snow Sports, Inc., Bill Holm Assos., Inc. Served with U.S. N.G., 1960-71. Mem. Am., Minn., Iowa, Hennepin County bar assns. Mem. Democratic-Farm Labor Party. Presbyterian. Home: 5001 Kingsdale St Minneapolis MN 55437

FLICK, PAUL JOHN, artist; b. Rock Island, Ill., Feb. 5, 1943; s. P. J. and Cora Agnus (Burney) F.; B.A., U. Minn., 1970, M.F.A., 1972. One-man shows include: U. Minn. Studio Gallery, Mpls., 1972; C.S.B. St. Louis Park, 1975-76; Northland Gallery, St. Louis Park, 1976; group shows include: U. Minn. Studio Gallery, 1970, 71, 72; Minn. Mus. Art, St. Paul, 1976; represented in permanent collections including: U. Minn., U. Tenn.; also numerous pvt. collections, U.S., Japan; pvt. tchr. art; cons. CSB Gallery, De Novo Mag. Served with USMC, 1962-66. Mem. Artists Equity Assn. Minn. (pres. 1976-77, dir. 1977-78), Twin City Metro Art Alliance, Artists Rights Today. Home: 4032 Lyndale Ave S Minneapolis MN 55409

FLIEGLER, DOROTHY SCHERR (MRS. LOUIS A. FLIEGLER), occupational therapist; b. N.Y.C., June 19, 1921; d. Morris and Rose E. (Marcus) Scherr; B.A., Hunter Coll., 1942; B.A., Columbia, 1945; m. Louis A. Fleigler, June 29, 1945; children—Gail, Susan. Govt. ordnance insp. N.Y. Ordnance Dept., N.Y.C., 1943-45; occupational therapist Army Hosp., Tilton Gen. Hosp., 1945, N.Y.C. Hosp., Welfare Island, N.Y.C., 1945, VA Hosp., Brentwood Gen. Hosp., Letterman Gen. Hosp., Bronx VA Hosp., 1945-47; tchr. physically handicapped, Syracuse, N.Y., 1956-60; tchr. mentally retarded, Denver, 1960-66; tchr. learning disabled, Akron, Ohio, 1966—. Instr. ceramics U. Wyo., Sheridan, 1953. Bd. dirs. sheltered workshop United Cerebral Palsy Center, Denver, 1954. Mem. B'nai B'rith Women, NEA, Am. Occupational Therapy Assn., Ohio, Akron edn. assns., ORT. Home: 1827 Kingsley Ave Akron OH 44313 Office: 55 S Portage Path Akron OH

FLITCRAFT, RICHARD KIRBY, II, chem. co. exec.; b. Woodstown, N.J., Sept. 5, 1920; s. H. Milton and Edna (Crispin) F.; m. Bertha LeSturgeon Hitchner, Nov. 14, 1942; children—Alyce, Anne, Elizabeth, Richard. B.S., Rutgers U., 1942; M.S., Washington U., St. Louis, 1948. With Monsanto Co., St. Louis, 1942—, dir. inorganic research, 1960-65, dir. mgmt. info. and systems dept., 1965-67, asst. to pres., 1967-68, group mgr. Electronics Enterprises, 1968-69, gen. mgr. Electronic Products Div., 1969-71, v.p., dir. Monsanto Research Corp., 1971—, v.p. ops., 1975-76, pres., 1976—. Mem. AAAS, Am. Chem. Soc., Am. Inst. Chem. Engrs., Am. Inst. Chemists, Am. Mgmt. Assn., N.Y. Acad. Scis., Research Soc. Am., Soc. Chem. Industry. Sigma Xi. Home: 6051 Kimway Dr Dayton OH 45459 Office: 1515 Nicholas Rd Dayton OH 45407

FLOCK, ERIC VANCE, nursing home adminstr.; b. Carrolton, Ill., May 14, 1951; s. Paul Ben and Dimple Cuba (Presely) F.; B.S. in Bus. Adminstr., So. Ill. U., Edwardsville, 1973; m. Deborah Ann Lorton, Nov. 20, 1971; children—Stephanie, Jason. Adminstr. Calhoun Care Center, Hardin, Ill., 1974—. Mem. Vol. Fire Dept., Hardin, Lion. Home: Box 84 Hardin IL 62047 Office: Calhoun Care Center South Route 100 Hardin IL 62047

FLOERCHINGER, JAMES SHUBERT, ophthalmologist, clin. adminstr.; b. St. Louis, Aug. 26, 1939; s. Lawrence L. and Esther (Shubert) F.; B.S., Colo. Coll., 1961; M.D., Washington U., St. Louis, 1965, postgrad. law, 1977—; m. Ann Merrill Kraeger, July 12, 1969; children—James Lawrence, Julia Ann. Intern, Presbyn. Med. Center, Denver, 1965-66; resident in ophthalmology Washington U., St. Louis, 1966-68; chief resident in ophthalmology St. Louis City Hosp., 1969-70; fellow in ophthalmology Barnes Hosp., St. Louis, 1969-70; practice medicine specializing in ophthalmology, Denver, 1970-71; asst. chief ophthalmology City and County of Denver, 1971-73; clin. asst. in surgery U. Colo. Med. Sch., Denver, 1971-73; chief dept. ophthalmology St. Charles (Mo.) Clinic, 1974—; pres., dir. W.L.S.S. Health Found., Inc.; clin. researcher drug delivery systems ALZA Corp., 1972-73; dir. Telebeam Corp. Diplomate Am. Bd. Ophthalmology. Fellow Am. Acad. Ophthalmology and Otolaryngology; mem. Contact Lens Assn. Ophthalmologists, Pan Am. Ophthalmol. Assn. Republican. Episcopalian. Author articles on med. economics. Home: 25 Carrswold Dr Clayton MO 63105 Office: 2860 W Clay St Saint Charles MO 63301

FLOETER, ERNST WERNER, photographer; b. Stettin, Germany, Aug. 8, 1925; s. Ernst and Elisabeth (Glasenap) F.; came to U.S., 1957, naturalized, 1962; grad. high sch.; m. Walburg B. Hildebrand, June 12, 1953; children—Dorothea E., Cornelia A., Dietrich G. With Photog. Trade Sch., Berlin, Germany, 1947-50; owner, comml. photographer Ernst Floeter Studio, Grand Ledge, Mich., 1960—. Served with German Army, 1943-46; P.O.W., 1944-46. Mem. Profl. Photographers Mich., Triangle Photographers Assn. (pres. 1973-75, 77-78). Rotarian. Address: 513 S Bridge St Grand Ledge MI 48837

FLOGGE, ALBERT JOSEPH, mcht.; b. Kent, Ohio, Sept. 11, 1934; s. Joseph and Mary (Polite) F.; B.S. in Bus. Adminstrn., Kent State U., 1956. With Allied Stores Corp., Akron, Ohio, 1956-57, 59-60, Muskegon, Mich., 1960-63, divisional merchandising staff asst. Allied Stores, N.Y., Cleve., 1963-67; v.p. Allied Stores Mich., Inc., 1967—; pres., gen. mgr. Hardy Herpolsheimer's subsidiary, Muskegon, 1967—. Vice chmn. drive Muskegon County United Appeal, 1970, chmn. drive, 1971; pres. Muskegon County United Way, 1973; lay chmn. Grand Rapids Diocesan Devel. Fund; mem. promotion com. Muskegon County Community Found. Trustee Greater Muskegon Indsl. Fund.; chmn. Downtown Muskegon Council, 1969, also bd. dirs.; bd. dirs. Miss. Mich. pageant, 1969-73, Muskegon County Cath. Edn. Fund, Inc., Crime Prevention Bur., 1974—, St. Mary's Parish Council, 1974—; divisional bd. dirs. Mercy Hosp., 1974—; bd. dirs. Muskegon Cath. Social Services, pres. 1973, 74. Recipient Distinguished Service award Jaycees, 1971; Outstanding Citizen award United Way, 1975. Served with AUS, 1957-59. Mem. Am. Inst. Mgmt. (mem. pres.'s council). Roman Catholic. (mem. Bishops Penta Council 1969-70). Clubs: Serra (Muskegon). Home: 704 Miller Dr North Muskegon MI 49445 Office: 277 Muskegon Mall Muskegon MI 49440

FLOMENHOFT, HOWARD CHARLES, lawyer; b. Phila., Nov. 29, 1940; s. Jay and Rosalie (Stein) F.; B.A., Cornell, 1962; J.D., U. Chgo., 1965; m. Carol Jacobi, Apr. 16, 1967; children—Michael, Steven, Michelle. Admitted to Ill. bar, 1965, No. Dist. Ill., 1965, U.S. Tax Ct., 1972, U.S. 6th Circuit Ct., 1974; mem. firm Quinn, Jacobs & Barry, Chgo., 1965; atty., estate and gift tax IRS, Chgo., 1965-68; mem. firm Levenfeld, Kanter, Baskes & Lippitz, Chgo., 1968-74, Howard C. Flomenhoft, Ltd., Chgo., 1974—. Bd. dirs. Indian Ridge Homeowners Assn., Northbrook, Ill., 1971—; mem. young leadership cabinet United Jewish Appeal. Mem. Am., Ill., Chgo., Fed. bar assns., Chgo. Council Lawyers. Edit. bd. Taxation for Lawyers, 1972—. Contbr. profl. jours. Home: 3257 Prestwick Ln Northbrook IL 60062 Office: 180 N LaSalle St Suite 1905 Chicago IL 60601

FLORESTANO, DANA JOSEPH, architect; b. Indpls., May 2, 1945; s. Herbert Joseph and Myrtle Mae (Futch) F.; B. Arch., U. Notre Dame, 1968; m. Peggy Joy Larsen, June 6, 1969. Designer, draftsman Kennedy, Brown & Trueblood, architects, Indpls., 1965-69, Evans Woolen Assn., architects, Indpls., 1966; designer, project capt. James Assos., architects and engrs., Indpls., 1969-71; architect, v.p. comml. projects Multi-Planners Inc., architects and engrs., 1972-73; pvt. practice architecture, Indpls., 1973—; pres. Florestano Assos., Inc., constrn. mgrs., Indpls., 1974—; co-founder, pres. Solargenics Natural Energy Corp., Indpls., 1975—; instr. in field. Tech. adviser hist. architecture Indpls. Model Cities program, 1969-70; mem. Hist. Landmarks Found. Ind., 1970-72; chmn. Com. to Save Union Sta., 1970-71, founder, pres. Union Sta. Inc., Indpls., 1971—. Recipient 2d design award Marble Inst. Am., 1967, 1st design award 19th Ann. Progressive Architecture Design awards, 1972; Design award for excellence in devel. Marriott Inn, Indpls., Met. Devel. Commn.-Office of Mayor, 1977. Mem. U. Notre Dame Alumni Assn., Notre Dame Club Indpls., A.I.A. (nat. com. historic resources 1974—, commn. on community services, Speakers Bur. Indpls. chpt. 1976—), Ind. Soc. Architects (chmn. historic architecture com. 1970—), Constrn. Specifications Inst., Constrn. Mgrs. Assn. Ind. (incorporator, dir. 1976—). Home: 5697 N Broadway St Indianapolis IN 46220 Office: 6214 N Carrollton Ave Indianapolis IN 46220

FLORETH, EARL HENRY, welding distbn. co. exec.; b. Jacksonville, Ill., Aug. 18, 1921; s. Dorris Oliver and Ruth F.; B.S., U. Ill., 1942; m. Dolores Taylor, Oct. 1950; children—Sandra Lee, Deborah Gay, Brad Gregory. Sales mgr. Ill. Tire & Battery Co., Jacksonville, 1945-59; v.p., Ill.-Mo. Welding Products Co., Jacksonville, 1959—. Pres. bd. trustees Passavant Area Hosp., Jacksonville, 1970. Served to lt. (s.g.), USNR, 1941-45. Mem. Am. Welding Soc., Am. Assn. Respiratory Therapy, Jacksonville C. of C., Nat. Welding Supply Assn., U. Ill. Alumni Assn. Methodist. Club: Jacksonville Country (pres. 1966-67). Home: 35 Westfair Dr Jacksonville IL 62650 Office: 555 Sandusky St Jacksonville IL 62650

FLORY, CLYDE REUBEN, JR., physician; b. Sellersville, Pa., Oct. 2, 1933; s. Clyde Reuben and Miriam Wagner (Hummel) F.; B.A., Lehigh U., 1955; M.D., Johns Hopkins U., 1959; m. Karen Colleen McComb, Mar. 9, 1963; children—William Brian, Robert Scott, Timothy Allen. Intern, resident in internal medicine and allergy Henry Ford Hosp., Detroit, 1959-64; pvt. practice medicine, specializing in allergy-immunology, Lansing, Mich., 1964—; faculty Mich. State U. Coll. Human Medicine, East Lansing, 1973—, asso. clin. prof. medicine, 1976—; chief, allergy sub-div. Ingham Med. Hosp., Lansing, 1975—; teaching staff E.W. Sparrow Hosp. Pres. ch. council St. Paul Luth. Ch., East Lansing, 1973. Diplomate Am. Bd.

Allergy and Immunology. Fellow Am. Acad. Allergy and Immunology, Am. Coll. Allergists, Am. Assn. Clin. Allergy and Immunology, Am. Coll. Chest Physicians (asso.); mem. AMA, Mich., Ingham County med. socs., Mich. Allergy Soc., Mich. Lung Assn. (dir. Central region 1973—), Mich. Thoracic Soc. Phi Beta Kappa. Clubs: Greater Lansing Racket, Masons. Home: 1022 Whitman Dr East Lansing MI 48823 Office: 201 W Hillsdale St Lansing MI 48933

FLOTO, WILLIAM MATHEW, recreational co. exec.; b. Los Angeles, Dec. 11, 1930; s. Frederick Francis and Adderne Lake (King) F.; A.A., Fullerton Jr. Coll., 1958; certificate in bus. U. Calif. at Los Angeles, 1963; m. Peggy Virginia Pepall, July 7, 1956; children—Cheri Virginia, William Howard, Steven Mathew. Mgr. regional sales office Beckman Instruments, Fullerton, Calif., 1956-62, Toronto, Ont., Can., 1963-65; Chgo., 1965-66; mgr. prodn. planning Bourns, Riverside, Calif., 1966-67; mgr. sales prodn. adminstrn. Amax Aluminum, Riverside, 1967-69; mgr. master scheduling Day Night Payne Co., La Puente, Calif., 1969; pres. Red E Kamp, Mira Luma, Calif., 1970-71; pres. Recreational Industries, Warren, Ohio, 1971—, also dir.; dir., v.p. ops. Toro Enterprises Inc. Bd. dirs. Y Indian Guide Program, Northbrook, Ill., 1965-66. Served with USAF, 1951-55. Mem. Am. Prodn. Control Soc. (pres. Inland Empire chpt. 1966-67). Patentee in field. Home: 1535 Fisher Dr Liberty OH 44425 Office: PO Box 3143 5232 Tod Ave Warren OH 44485

FLOWER, ANDREW ARTHUR, elec. engr.; b. Junction City, Kans., Feb. 5, 1925; s. Andrew A. and Nellie (Pruett) F.; B.S. in Elec. Engring., Kans. State U., 1950; m. Verna E. Beeson, May 1, 1972. Field engr. John C. Leavitt Co., Garden City, Kans., 1950-51; elec. engr. Wheatland Elec. Co-op., Scott City, Kans., 1951—. Pres., City Council, Scott City, 1961; mem. Scott City-Scott County Area Planning and Zoning Commn., 1966-69, chmn., 1969. Served with AUS, 1943-45. Mem. I.E.E.E., Nat. Soc. Profl. Engrs., Kans. Engring. Soc. (dir. S.W. chpt. 1964-65), Soc. Am. Mil. Engrs., V.F.W. (trustee 1963-65, adj., 1969, post comdr. 1971-72), Am. Legion, Am. Rifle Assn. Methodist. Contbr. articles to trade mags. Home: 1308 Elizabeth St Scott City KS 67871 Office: 101 Main St Scott City KS 67871

FLUEGEL, NEAL LALON, musician, assn. exec., educator; b. Freeport, Ill., Mar. 21, 1937; s. Nelson Otto and Elnora (Beine) F.; B.A. in Edn., Ariz. State U., 1960; M.M., So. Ill. U., 1963; postgrad. U. Wis., 1965-66; m. Diane Francis Hanson, Dec. 27, 1957; children—Taunia Suzanne, Kyra Michaelle. Tchr. pub. schs. Ill., 1960-62; instr. music Ariz. State U., Tempe, 1964-65; teaching fellow U. Wis., 1965-66; asso. prof. music Ind. State U., Terre Haute, 1966—, also chmn. Annual Contemporary Music Fest., 1971—. Prin. percussionist Phoenix Symphony Orch., 1964-65, Madison (Wis.) Symphony Orch., 1965-66; now timpanist Terre Haute Symphony Orch.; chmn. Indpls. Symphony-Ind. State U. Contemporary Music Festival; regular appearances About Music TV series, Channel 2, Terre Haute, 1971-72. Mem. Percussive Arts Soc. (internat. exec. sec.; editor Percussionst jour.), Music Tchrs. Nat. Assn. (chmn. brass, woodwind and percussion div., state pres., 2d v.p. East Central region), Mid-East Instrumental Music Conf. (chmn. percussion activities), Music Educators Nat. Conf. (percussion program chmn. 1968), Nat. Assn. Coll. Wind and Percussion Instrs., Am. Musicol. Soc., Am. Bell Assn., Kappa Kappa Psi, Phi Mu Alpha (mem. Sinfonia). Optimist (pres.). Home: 130 Carol Dr Terre Haute IN 47805

FLYNN, DAVID LAMER, environ. engr.; b. Leavenworth, Kans., Sept. 17, 1918; s. David William and Eugenie Angelique (LaMer) F.; B.S. in Mech. Engring., Columbia, 1941; B.S. in C.E., Rensselaer Poly. Inst., 1954; m. Nora Mae Woods, Aug. 26, 1966; children—Stephen LaMer, Cheryl Kealoha. Mfg. engr., Lockheed Aircraft Corp., Burbank, Calif., 1941-46; cost control engr. C.F. Braun Co., Alhambra, Calif., 1946; commd. lt. (j.g.) U.S. Navy, 1947, advanced through grades to lt. comdr., 1957; various duties including pub. works officer, resident in charge constrn. Air Sta., Hutchinson, Kan., 1955-57, exec. officer Naval Mobile Constrn. Battalion No. 10, Calif., Adak, Alaska, Guam, Marianas Islands, Kodiak, Alaska, 1959-61; civil engr. Fleet Marine Force Pacific, 1962-64; project mgmt. engr. Facilities Engring. Command Staff, Seattle, 1964-65; ret., 1965; project mgr. Stanley Cons., Inc., Muscatine, Iowa, 1965-69; asst. mgr. constrn. Havens & Emerson Ltd., Cleve., 1969—. Active Boy Scouts Am., 1959-65. Registered profl. engr., N.Y., Ohio, Wash., Iowa. Fellow ASCE; mem. ASME, Nat., Ohio socs. profl. engrs., Cleve. Soc. Profl. Engrs. (bd. dirs. 1972—), Tau Beta Pi. Projects in Liberia, Hydroelectric Power, 1966, deep water harbor, Antigua, 1967, gas and sewage sludge disposal incinerators Met. San. Dist. Chgo., 1971, Middletown, Ohio, Willoughby, Ohio, Dunkirk, N.Y., Euclid, Ohio, Cin., 1973-75. Home: 411 Sterling Circle Berea OH 44017 Office: 700 Bond Ct Cleveland OH 44114

FLYNN, MICHAEL FRANCIS, priest, psychologist; b. Chgo., Dec. 2, 1935; s. Michael Joseph and Mary Ellen (Lydon) F.; B.A. in Philosophy, St. Bonaventure U., 1958, B.S. in Math., 1960; theology certificate Whitefriars Hall, 1962; M.A., DePaul U., 1966; Ph.D., Loyola U., Chgo., 1974. Ordained priest Roman Catholic Ch., 1961; tchr., counselor DeSales High Sch., Louisville, 1962-63; asst. prin., tchr., counselor Carmel High Sch. for Boys, Mundelein, Ill., 1963-68; dir. Carmelite Inst. Renewal, Mundelein, 1968-70; psychology clk. West Side VA Hosp., Chgo., 1970-71, dir. tng., clin. psychologist, 1974—; clin. intern psychology Ill. Psychiat. Inst., Chgo., 1971-72, research intern psychology, 1972-73; HEW research fellow Ill. Mental Health Insts., Chgo., 1973-74; asst. prof. psychiatry U. Ill., Chgo., 1974—; asst. prof. Ill. Sch. Profl. Psychology, 1977—; psychology cons. Marriage Tribunal, Catholic Archdiocese of Chgo., 1974; diagnostic cons. Chgo. Police Dept., 1977—; pastoral counselor, marital therapist Nativity of Our Lord Parish, Chgo., 1971—. Mem. Am., Ill. psychol. assns., Ill. Group Psychotherapy Soc., Assn. Psychology Internship Centers. Democrat. Home: 653 W 37th St Chicago IL 60609 Office: Psychology Dept 116B PO Box 8195 Chicago IL 60680

FLYNN, NORMAN DAVID, real estate co. exec.; b. La Crosse, Wis., July 19, 1941; s. Percy David and Irene Ann (Polodna) F.; B.S., Wis. State U., 1963, M.S., 1967; postgrad. U. Wis., 1967-70; m. Susan Ann Romanski, June 6, 1964; children—Melanie, Andrea, David. Tchr., Aquinas High Sch., La Crosse, 1963-67, Monona Grove (Wis.) High Sch., 1967-70; exec. v.p. Munz Investment Real Estate, Inc., Madison, 1970—. Pres., Immaculate Heart of Mary Sch. Bd., Monona, Wis., 1971-72. Trustee Greater Wis. Found., Madison, 1972-73; bd. dirs. Wis. Partners of Am., 1972-77, Wis. Jaycees Found., Appleton, 1972-74; bd. govs. Grad. Realtor Inst., 1974-77. Bd. dirs. East Madison YMCA, 1975-77, v.p., 1976. Named Outstanding Young Educator of La Crosse, La Crosse Jaycees, 1966, Outstanding Young Profl., Central States Speech Assn., 1967, Outstanding Young Man in Monona, Monona Jaycees, 1975, Outstanding Young Man in Wis., Wis. Jaycees, 1975, Realtor of Year Madison Bd. Realtors, 1975. Mem. Sales and Mktg. Execs., Wis. High Sch. Forensics Assn. (dir. 1968-70), Great Madison Bd. Realtors (dir., pres. 1976), Nat. Assn. Realtors, Wis. Apt. Assn. (v.p. 1974-75, pres. 1975-76), Wis. Nat. Forensics League (state chmn. 1969-70), Wis. 1974-75, Assn. (dir. 1968-70), Monona (pres. 1969), Wis. (nat. dir. 1971, state pres. 1972) Jaycees. Roman Catholic (parish council 1969-72, v.p., 1971-72, mem. pastoral council Madison diocese 1973-77, pres. 1974-75). Elk. Home: 6209 Winnequah Rd Monona WI 53716 Office: 134 E Johnson St Madison WI 53703

FLYNN, ROBERT JAMES, veterinarian; b. Chgo., Jan. 8, 1923; s. James Robert and Rose (Kunz) F.; student Kennedy-King Coll., 1940-41; D.V.M., Mich. State U., 1944; m. Doris Jean Ashe, Dec. 19, 1942; children—Robert J., Jean B., Susan J., Nancy J., James R., Betty J. With Argonne (Ill.) Nat. Lab., 1948—, successively supr. animal quarters, 1948-55, asso. veterinarian, 1948-66, sr. veterinarian, 1966—, research on care and diseases of lab. animals, 1948-76, asst. dir. for animal facilities, 1962-76, research on biology of aging, 1971-74, on viral carcinogenesis, 1976-77, on environ. impacts, 1977—; vet. insp. state of Ill., 1944-57; veterinarian, Lake County, Ill., 1957-76, rabies insp., 1970-73, animal control adminstr., 1973—; veterinarian Lake County Health Dept., 1976—; mem. NRC, 1967-70, mem. com. vet. med. research and edn., 1968-72. Served with AUS, 1943-44. Diplomate Am. Coll. Lab. Animal Medicine (dir. 1956-64, 73-75, sec.-treas. 1956-62, pres. 1963). Mem. Am. Assn. Lab. Animal Sci. (dir. 1949-65, sec.-treas. 1953-62, pres. 1963-64, Griffin award 1968, R.J. Flynn award 1969). Editor numerous texts, including Laboratory Animal Science; a review of the literature, 1966; also (with W.F. Riley, Jr. and K.W. Smith) The Year Book of Veterinary Medicine, vols. 1, 2 and 3; Parasites of Laboratory Animals, 1973; Laboratory Animal Science, 1976—. Contbr. numerous articles to profl. jours. Organizer, participant in nat. and internat. symposia. Home: 421 E Westleigh Rd Lake Forest IL 60045 Office: 9700 S Cass Ave Argonne IL 60439 also 3010 Grand Ave Waukegan IL 60085

FOBES, VERNON HOMER, brick and tile mfg. co. exec.; b. Moorhead, Minn., Apr. 9, 1920; s. Charles Vernon and Amy Leonne (Swanson) F.; B.S. in Agrl. Engring., U. Minn., 1949; m. Virginia LeClaire Clark, July 8, 1950; children—Clark V., Scott D., Natalie B., Amy L. Salesman Roll Inc. div. Mason City Brick and Tile Co. (merged into Can-Tex Industries 1968), N.D., Minn., 1947-50, engr. Iowa, Minn., Wis., 1950-57, asst. sales mgr., Mason City, Iowa, 1957-59, sales mgr., 1959-66, plant mgr., Ft. Dodge, 1966-67, Ottumwa, Iowa, 1967-72, sales mgr. brick and tile div. Can-Tex Industries, West Des Moines, Iowa, 1972-75, v.p. Can-Tex, 1975—. Mem. Waverly (Iowa) Sch. Bd., 1955-57; mem. Builders Exchange, Mason City, 1959-66, pres., 1963. Bd. dirs. Ottumwa United Fund, 1969-72. Served to lt. USNR, 1941-45. Mem. Iowa Engring. Soc., Agrl. Engring. Soc., Nat. Soc. Profl. Engrs., Am. Soc. Agrl. Engrs., ASTM (chmn. drain tile com. 1967), Brick Inst. Am. (pres. 1977—), Optimist Club. Rotarian. Author: (with others) Tile Drainage, 1957. Home: 322 51st St Des Moines IA 50312 Office: 101 Ashworth Rd West Des Moines IA 50265

FOCKE, ARTHUR ELDRIDGE, metall. engr.; b. Cleve., June 17, 1904; s. Francis Arthur and Mary Worthington (Butts) F.; B.Met.E., Ohio State U., 1925, M.S., 1926, Ph.D., 1928; m. Mona Gale, Oct. 5, 1929 (dec. May 1966); m. 2d, Janis Lyons, Mar. 16, 1968. Spl. metallurgist Cleve. Wire div. Gen. Elec. Co., Cleve., 1927-29; chief engr. P.R. Mallory Co., Indpls., 1929-31; research metallurgist, chief metallurgist Diamond Chain Co., 1931-52; mgr. materials devel. and metall. aircraft nuclear propulsion dept. Gen. Elec. Co., Cin., 1951-61; asso. prof. to prof. metall. engring. U. Cin., 1962-74; pres. A.E. Focke Corp., Cin., 1974—. Fellow Am. Soc. Metals (nat. pres. 1950); mem. ASTM, Am. Nuclear Soc. (charter), Am. Inst. Metall. Engrs., Metals Soc. U.K. Republican. Presbyterian. Club: Masons. Editor: Bridging the Gap, 1976. Patentee in field. Home: 7799 E Galbraith Rd Cincinnati OH 45243 Office: 8041 Hosbrook St Cincinnati OH 45236

FOELL, WESLEY KAY, nuclear engr., environ. scientist, educator; b. Elgin, Ill., May 20, 1935; s. Otto William and Lillian Mae (Hari) F.; B.S.E.E., Stanford U., 1958, Ph.D. in Nuclear Engring., 1964; M.S., Mass. Inst. Tech., 1959; m. Anne C. Schuller, Oct. 6, 1962. Scientist, Phillips Petroleum Co., Idaho Falls, Idaho, 1962-64, Nuclear Research Center, Kablsruhe, Germany, 1965-66; vis. asso. prof. nuclear engring. and environ. studies U. Wis., Madison, 1967-69, asso. prof., 1969-74, prof., 1974—; head, ecology environment dept. Internat. Inst. Applied Systems Analysis, Austria, 1975-76; cons. Argonne (Ill.) Nat. Labs., Ford Found., OECD. NSF fellow, 1959-60; AEC fellow, 1958-59. Mem. AAAS, Am. Nuclear Soc., Phi Beta Kappa, Tau Beta Pi. Author: Small-Sample Reactivity Measurements in Nuclear Reactors, 1972; Resources and Decisions, 1975; (with C. J. Cicchetti) Energy Systems Forecasting, Planning, and Pricing, 1975. Home: 35 Bagley Ct Madison WI 53705 Office: Nuclear Engring U Wis Madison WI 53706

FOGG, DANIEL ANTHONY, mech. engr.; b. Newburyport, Mass., Sept. 9, 1924; s. Charles Phillip and Nora (Murphy) F.; B.M.E., Ill. Inst. Tech., 1949; M.B.A., Western Mich. U., 1972; m. Sylvia Carr, Nov. 21, 1970; 1 dau. by previous marriage, Marcie Fogg Whitherell; 1 stepdau., Nancy Carr Sumner. Project engr. Rapistan Co., Grand Rapids, Mich., 1961-66; design project engr. Gerber Products Co., Fremont, Mich., 1966-68, project engr., 1968-72, mgr. engring. devel., 1972—; vice-chmn. Mich. State Bd. Registration Profl. Engrs., 1976—. Served with U.S. Navy, 1942-46. Recipient Mich. Soc. Profl. Engrs.-Profl. Engrs. in Industry Distinguished Service award, 1976. Mem. Mich. Soc. Profl. Engrs. (pres. 1971-73, state dir. 1974-76) Nat. Soc. Profl. Engrs. (nat. dir. 1971-73) ASME, Nat. Council Engring. Examiners. Clubs: Rotary, Ramshorn Country (Fremont dir. 1976—). Patentee in field. Address: PO Box 55 Fremont MI 49412

FOGO, WILLIAM ROLLIN, chemist; b. Richland County, Wis., Mar. 29, 1938; s. Rollin Franklin and Thelma Lorraine (Stayton) F.; B.S., Wis. State U., Platteville, 1960; Lab. technician Endocrine Labs., Inc., Madison, Wis., 1961-63; supervising technician, 1963-67; lab. supr. FS Services, Inc., Mendota, Ill., 1967-76, area feed quality supr., Tiffin, Iowa, 1976—. Treas., Mendota council Campfire Girls Am., 1968-71; bd. dirs. Triumph Youth League, Mendota, 1972-76. Served with U.S. Army, 1956-60. Mem. Am. Assn. Feed Microscopists. Methodist. Club: Elks, Mendota Community Theatre. Home: PO Box 329 West Branch IA 52358 Office: PO Box 8 Tiffin IA 52340

FOK, THOMAS DSO YUN, civil engr., educator; b. Canton, China, July 1, 1921; s. D.H. and C. (Tse) F.; came to U.S., 1947, naturalized, 1956; B.Eng., Nat. Tung-Chi U., Szechuan, China, 1945; M.S., U. Ill., 1948; M.B.A. (Dr. Nadler Money Markteen scholar), N.Y.U., 1950; Ph.D., Carnegie-Mellon U., 1956; m. Maria M.L. Liang, Sept. 18, 1949. Structural designer Lummus Co., N.Y.C., 1951-53; design engr. Richardson, Gordon & Assos., cons. engrs., Pitts., 1956-58; asso. prof. engring. Youngstown (Ohio) U., 1958-68, dir. Computing Center, 1963-67; partner Cernica, Fok & Assos., cons. engrs., Youngstown, 1958-64; prin. Thomas Fok & Assos., cons. engrs., Youngstown, 1964-65; partner Mosure-Fok & Syrakis Co., Ltd., cons. engrs., Youngstown, 1965-76; cons. engr. Mahoning County Engr., Ohio, 1960-65, engr., 1960—; pres. Computing-Systems & Tech., Youngstown, 1967-72; chmn. Thomas Fok and Assos., Ltd., cons. engrs., Youngstown, 1977—. Trustee Pub. Library of Youngstown and Mahoning County, 1973—, Youngstown State U., 1975—, Youngstown Ednl. Found., 1975—. Recipient Walter E. and Caroline H. Watson Found. Distinguished Prof.'s award Youngstown U., 1966. Registered profl. engr. N.Y., Pa., Ohio, Ill., Ky. W.Va., Ind., Md. Fellow ASCE; mem. Am. Concrete Inst., Internat. Assn. for Bridge and Structural Engring., Am. Soc. Engring. Edn., Nat. Soc. Profl. Engrs., A.A.A.S., Soc. Am. Mil. Engrs., Ohio, N.Y. acads. scis., Sigma Xi, Beta Gamma Sigma, Sigma Tau, Delta Pi Sigma. Rotarian. Contbr. articles to profl. jours. Home: 325 S Canfield-Niles Rd Youngstown OH 44515 Office: 5121 1/2 Mahoning Ave Youngstown OH 44515

FOLAND, DONALD LEROY, adminstrv. and utility engr.; b. Ft. Wayne, Ind., Apr. 8, 1927; s. Virgil Herman and Lela Cleota (Scott) F.; B.S. in Mech. Engring., Ind. Inst. Tech., 1949; m. Ruth Ann Fowler, Nov. 22, 1947; children—Penny Sue, Kimberly Kay. Jr. engr. Ft. Wayne Water Utility, 1949-52, design engr., 1952-67, project engr., 1967-72, chief engr., 1972—, city adminstrv. engr., 1976—; cons. in field. Served with USNR, 1945-46; PTO. Registered profl. engr., Ind. Mem. Am. Water Works Assn. (chmn. Ind. sect. 1975, pres. Northeastern Dist. Ind. sect., 1970-71), Am. Pub. Works Assn., Nat., Ind. socs. profl. engrs. Kiwanian. Home: 429 French Ave Ft Wayne IN 46807 Office: City-County Bldg Ft Wayne IN 46802

FOLDA, RICHARD GERALD, lawyer; b. Schuyler, Nebr., Oct. 9, 1923; s. Kajetan J. and Tillie L. (Pakes) F.; LL.B., U. Nebr., 1949; m. Marianne Srb, July 19, 1949; children—Kathryn J., Gail Ellen. Admitted to Nebr. bar, 1949; pvt. practice Schuyler, 1950—, partner Folda & Co., 1950—; dir. Security Fed. Savs. and Loan Assn.; dir., sec.-treas., mng. officer, 1958-64, pres., dir., mng. officer, 1964—; dir. Standard Reliance Ins. Co., Schuyler State Bank; Nebr. dir. Fed. Home Loan Bank of Topeka, 1976—. Pres. Midwest Savs. Conf., 1963-64. City atty. Schuyler, 1950-58; sec. Schuyler Bd. Edn., 1950-58, pres., 1963—. Served from pvt. to lt. USAAF, 1943-45. Mem. Am., Nebr., Colfax County (pres. 1958) bar assns., Sixth Jud. Dist. Bar (sec. 1957), C. of C., Nebr. State Sch. Bds. Assn. (dir. 1966—, pres. 1970-71), Nebr. League Savs. and Loan Assn. (pres.), U.S. Savs. and Loan League (Nebr. dir. 1970-74), Sigma Phi Epsilon, Phi Delta Phi, Innocents Soc., Am. Legion, 40 and 8. Republican. Roman Catholic. Clubs: Rotary (past pres.), Lions (past pres.), Schuyler Country (past pres.), Kosmet. Home: 1009 Chicago St Schuyler NE 68661 Office: 1103 B St Schuyler NE 68661

FOLEY, ANNA BERNICE WILLIAMS (MRS. WARREN MASSEY FOLEY), exec., librarian; b. Wigginsville, Ohio, Nov. 20, 1902; d. Karl Howland and Bertye (Young) Williams; student U. Cin., 1920-24, Columbia, 1931, Nanking (China) Lang. Coll., 1926; Grad. Sch. certificate Jesus Coll., Oxford U., 1969; m. Warren Massey Foley, Feb. 25, 1924; children—Williams Massey, Karlanne (Mrs. William Scully Hauer). Radio commentator WKRC, Cin., 1934, WSAI, Cin., 1938; commentator WCPO-TV, Cin., 1939-44; lectr. fashions U. Cin. Evening Coll., 1941-44; spl. events coordinator Mabley & Carew Dept. Store, 1951-66; model McCall Patterns-Singer Sewing Machine Co., Moscow, USSR, 1957; dir. The Martha Kinney Cooper Ohioana Library Assn., Columbus, Ohio, 1966-77, also editor Quar. Mag., Yearbook, 1966-77. Lectr. creative writing; book reviewer Sunday Columbus Dispatch, 1967-77, The Asia Mail, 1976-77. Bd. dirs. Ohio Poetry Day, 1968-77. Mem. English Speaking Union (br. pres. 1966-69), World Assn. Women Journalists, Ohio Press Women, Women in Communications (pres. 1973-74), Sigma Delta Chi, Kappa Kappa Gamma (Achievement award 1974). Clubs: Overseas Press of Am., Faculty. Author: (juvenile books) Star Stories, Spaceships of the Ancients. Author weekly column Columbus Scene, 1971-77. Home: 1505 Hammond North 5300 Hamilton Ave Cincinnati OH 43224

FOLEY, DANIEL EMMETT, restaurant chain exec.; b. Ponca City, Okla., Mar. 1, 1932; s. Daniel Emmett and Cecil Ione (Robertson) F.; B.F.A., Wichita State U., 1950-54; m. Betty J. Fellers, Sept. 1, 1951; children—Danelle (Mrs. Timothy Hesse), Robin, Tracy, Erin. Illustrator, Boeing Aircraft Co., Wichita, Kans., 1956-62; partner Taco Tico Inc., Wichita, 1961-67, pres., 1967—. Bd. dirs. Goodwill Industries Wichita. Served to 1st lt. AUS, 1954-56. Mem. Beta Theta Pi. Roman Catholic. Rotarian. Office: 3305 E Douglas Wichita KS 67218

FOLEY, EDMUND FRANCIS, physician; b. Chgo., Aug. 18, 1896; s. John B. and Margaret Francis (Burke) F.; B.S. U. Chgo., 1918, M.D., 1920; m. Ruth Allen Farnham, Oct. 14, 1933; children—Edmund Francis, Jr., Thomas Francis. Intern, Cook County Hosp., Chgo., 1920-21, resident, 1921-23; practice medicine specializing in internal medicine, Chgo., 1928-73; prof. medicine emeritus U. Ill. Coll. Med., Chgo., 1943-65; dean Cook County Grad. Sch., 1961-73; attending physician Cook County Hosp., Columbus Hosp., Research and Ednl. Hosp., U. Ill; chief of staff Cook County Hosp., 1952-62, Columbus Hosp., 1962-65; cons. in field. Recipient E.S. Hamilton Teaching award, 1970, Allen award U. Ill. 1949, 1954, 1960, 1963; trustee Hektorn Inst. Med. Research; Edmund F. Foley professorial chair in internal medicine named for him. Fellow A.C.P.; mem. AMA, Ill., Chgo. med. socs., Am. Heart Assn., Central Soc. Clin. Research, Chgo. Soc. Internal Medicine, Inst. Medicine, Sigma Xi, Alpha Omega Alpha. Contbr. articles in field to profl. jours. Home: 5820 4B Oakwood Dr Lisle IL 60532

FOLEY, EDWARD MINTER, primary metals producing co. exec.; b. Bassett, Va., Dec. 15, 1929; s. Ansley Tinsley and Mildred (Minter) F.; B.S., U. Tenn., 1960; m. Evelyn Jo Cooter, Apr. 28, 1951; children—Mildred Kathleen, Edward Minter. Research physicist, nuclear div. Union Carbide Corp., Oak Ridge, 1955-66; sr. research physicist Union Carbide Corp., Greenville, S.C. and Kokomo, Ind., 1966-69; sr. research engr. stellite div., Cabot Corp., Kokomo, 1970-72, mgr. powder metals parts mfg. stellite div., 1972-74, product mgr. Stellite div., 1974—; dir. Powder Metallurgy Industries Fedn., 1975—. Served with U.S. Army, 1953-55. Recipient IR-100 award Indsl. Research Mag., 1974. Mem. Metal Powder Industries Fedn. (Part of Year award of distinction 1974, mem. pub. relations council 1975—), Am. Powder Metallurgy Inst., Am. Soc. Metals, Nat. Rifle Assn. (life), Nat. Geog. Soc. Methodist. Clubs: Masons, Order Eastern Star. Patentee in field. Home: RR 2 Box 142 Russiaville IN 46979 Office: 1020 W Park Ave Kokomo IN 46901

FOLEY, JOHN JAMES, mfrs. rep.; b. Cleve., May 23, 1923; s. Frank Joseph and Mary Agnes (Mc Gowan) F.; B.B.A. John Carroll U., 1949; student Fenn Coll., 1942, U. Ala., 1943; m. Marita Ann Mullen, July 16, 1949; children—Judith Ann, Gregory Mullen, John David, Terrence George. Sales rep., purchasing agt. Nottingham Steel Co., Cleve., 1949-54; sales rep., partner N.W. Duffin Co., Cleve., 1954-59; partner Foley & Beilstein Co., Westlake, Ohio, 1960-74; pres., founder John J. Foley Co., Westlake, 1975—. Chmn. Citizens for Nixon Com., Rocky River, Ohio, 1972; trustee Beach Cliff, Rocky River, 1965-71, pres., 1971. Served with USAAF, 1942-46. Decorated Air Medal with 2 oak leaf clusters. Mem. East End Purchasing Agts. Assn., Purchasing Mgrs. Assn. Cleve. (asso.), U.S. Power Squadron. Republican. Roman Catholic. Clubs: Cleve. Yachting, Lions (past v.p.). Home: 224 Cornwall Rd Rocky River OH 44116 Office: 26612 Center Ridge Rd Westlake OH 44145

FOLEY, KEVIN MICHAEL, scientist, lawyer; b. Cin., Nov. 22, 1942; s. Matthew Joseph and Mary Alice (Keller) F.; m. Jeanne Ann Westrick, Aug. 21, 1965; children—Tony, Keith, Brian. B.S., Xavier U., 1964; Ph.D., Purdue U., 1970; J.D., Capital U., 1974. Admitted to Ohio bar, 1975; teaching asst. Purdue U., 1964-65, instr., 1965-66; sr. scientist Owens-Corning Fiberglas Corp., Granville, Ohio,

1970-75; research scientist The Andersons, Maumee, Ohio, 1975—. Chmn. Lucas County Med. Malpractice Arbitration Panel, 1976. Mem. Am. Assn. of Cereal Chemists, Inst. Food Techs., Am. Oil Chemists Soc., Inst. for Briquetting and Agglomeration, Am. Chem. Soc., Ohio, Lucas County, Toledo bar assns., Toledo Patent Law Assn. Recipient Order of the Curia, 1975; Stauffer Chem. Co. fellow, 1967; Phillips Petroleum Co. fellow, 1968; Petroleum Research Fund fellow, 1969. Contbr. articles to profl. jours.; holder numerous patents. Home: 633 Dussel Dr Maumee OH 43537 Office: 126 E Dudley St Maumee OH 43537

FOLEY, PHILIP SEATON, lumber co. exec.; b. Piggott, Ark., Sept. 25, 1923; s. Albert Clarence and Gertrude Dorothea (Seaton) F.; B.S., U. Mich., 1949; m. Margarethe Streschniak, Aug. 15, 1946; children—Linda S., Stephen A.T., Albert J. Supr. cabinet div. RCA, Pulaski, Va., 1949-51; sec., treas., plant supt. Pennington-Foley Furniture Co., Inc., Martinsville, Ind., 1951-53; sec., mill supt. T.A. Foley Lumber Co., Inc., Paris, Ill., 1953—; v.p., dir. Edgar County Savs. & Loan Assn. Treas. Edgar County and Paris Sesquicentennial Commn., 1972—; mem. Paris Bicentennial Commn., 1975-76. Mem. Paris Park Bd., 1967-74; commr. Pub. Property Paris, 1967-71. Served with 1st inf. div. AUS, 1944-46. Decorated Purple Heart, Bronze Star medal. Mem. U.S., Ill. (econ. devel. com. 1969-73), Paris (pres. 1965) chambers commerce, Forest Products Research Soc. (trustee Midwest sect. 1967-68), Soc. Wood Sci. and Tech., Ill. Tech. Forestry Assn., Ill. C. of C., Soc. 1st Div., Am. Legion, Beta Phi Sigma. Elk, Kiwanian (sec. Paris, past pres.). Episcopalian. Club: Society Les Voyageurs (U. Mich.). Home: East Twin Lakes PO Box 336 Paris IL 61944 Office: 1800 S Jefferson St Paris IL 61944

FOLKERT, JAY ERNEST, educator; b. Holland, Mich., Dec. 16, 1916; s. Mannes and Mabel H. (Koopman) F.; A.B., Hope Coll., 1939; M.A. (State scholar), U. Mich., 1940; Ph.D., Mich. State U., 1955; m. Marian Slag, Apr. 5, 1946; children—Elaine Rose Folkert Heneveld, Victor Jay, Calvin Wayne. Tchr., Hamilton, Mich., 1940-42; tchr. Holland Christian High Sch., 1946; mem. faculty math. dept. Hope Coll., Holland, 1946—, prof. math., 1957—; dir. NSF Summer Insts. for High Sch. Tchrs., Hope Coll., 1960-74. Served with USAAF, 1942-45. Decorated Bronze Star medal. Mem. Am. Math. Soc., Math. Assn. Am., Nat. Council Tchrs. of Math., Am. Sci. Affiliation, Sigma Xi. Mem. Reformed Ch. in Am. Home: 148 W 22d St Holland MI 49423 Office: Hope Coll Holland MI 49423

FOLKMAN, JEROME DANIEL, clergyman; b. Cleve., Sept. 25, 1907; s. Ben and Rose (Tronstein) F.; A.B., U. Cin., 1928; B.H.L., Hebrew Union Coll., 1928, rabbi, 1931, D.D., 1957; student U. Mich., 1934-36; Ph.D., Ohio State U., 1953; m. Bessie Schomer, Dec. 14, 1930 children—Moses Judah, David Hillel, Joy (Mrs. Arthur J. Moss). Rabbi, Temple Beth Israel, Jackson, Mich., 1931-36, Temple Emanuel, Grand Rapids, Mich., 1937-47; rabbi Temple Israel, Columbus, Ohio, 1947-73, rabbi emeritus, 1973—; adj. prof. sociology Ohio State U., 1963—; Englander Meml. lectr. Hebrew Union Coll., 1957; McKinley Vis. scholar Walsh, Malone and Mt. Union colls., 1976; Benjamin Tintner Meml. lectr. N.Y. Assn. Reform Rabbis, 1976; vis. prof. Otterbein Coll., Westerville, Ohio, 1977. Founder, 1st pres. Kent County (Mich.) Council Social Agys., 1939-42; dir. Family and Children's Service Bur. of Franklin County, 1948-56, chmn. case com., 1950-51; mem. penal study com. Ohio State Post-War Commn., 1948-49; mem. Mayor's Adv. Com. on Pub. Relations, 1952-53, Columbus Commn. on Pub. Relations, 1953-56; pres. Ohio Conf. on Family Relations, 1955-57; mem. Ohio State Mental Health Survey, 1955-57; mem. bd. govs. Hebrew Union Coll., Jewish Inst. Religion, 1952-56; bd. dirs. Community Chest of Columbus and Franklin County, 1955-56, Am. Cancer Soc., Franklin County unit, 1966-73, Ministers Life and Casualty Union, 1966-71, Ohio Citizens Council Health and Welfare, 1966-69; trustee Columbus Hosp. Fedn., 1956-71; bd. dirs. Grant Hosp., 1960—; trustee Union of Am. Hebrew Congregations, 1960-64; mem. Columbus Adv. Council on Naval Affairs, 1958-73; bd. dirs. Franklin County chpt. Nat. Found., 1958-59; mem. bd. Franklin County Heart Assn., 1959-73; mem.-at-large, exec. com. Nat. Council Family Relations, 1961-63; mem. adminstrv. com., v.p. United Community Council; bd. dirs. Columbus Urban League, 1962-65, Better Bus. Bur. Central Ohio, 1977—; cons. religious resources to President's spl. asst. for mental retardation, 1963-65; mem. Ohio Comprehensive Mental Health Planning Project, 1963-65; mem. Ohio Commn. on Nursing, 1973-75; fin. sec. Central Conf. Am. Rabbis, 1969-71; alumni overseers Hebrew Union Coll., Jewish Inst. Religion, 1966-70. Recipient Forney W. Clement Meml. award Mich. Dist. Kiwanis, 1944. Gold Key of Jr. C. of C., Grand Rapids, as Outstanding Citizen under 35 yrs. of age, 1939, named one of ten outstanding citizens of Columbus, by Columbus Citizen, 1954; B'nai B'rith Sanford Lakin award, 1961; Citizen of Year award Frontiers Internat., 1967; Gov. Ohio's award, 1968; Distinguished Contbn. to Edn. award Central Ohio chpt. Pi Lambda Theta, 1965; Outstanding Citizenship award Central Ohio chpt. Pub. Relations Soc. Am., 1974; Excellence in Teaching citation Student Council Coll. Arts and Scis., Ohio State U., 1976. Fellow Am. Sociol. Assn.; mem. Soc. Sci. Study Religion, Synagogue Council Am. (commn. family life), Family Service Assn. Am. (dir. 1965-68), Jewish Family Service Assn. Columbus (v.p. 1966-68), Columbus Bd. Rabbis (chmn. 1967, 72-73), Central Conf. on Am. Rabbis (chmn. com. on marriage home and family 1950-58, mem. exec. bd. 1957-59, chmn. com. on Judaism and medicine 1963-65), Internat. Council Christians and Jews (gov. body 1948-50), Soc. Study Social Problems, Alpha Kappa Delta. Mem. B'nai B'rith. Kiwanian. Clubs: Torch (pres. 1976-77), Faculty (Ohio State Univ.). Author: The Cup of Life, 1955; Design for Jewish Living, 1955; (with Nancy M. Clatworthy) Marriage Has Many Faces, 1970. Mem. editorial adv. bd. Highlights for Children, 1953—. Home: 2538 Maryland Ave Columbus OH 43209

FOLLETT, MARY VIERLING, artist, art conservator; b. Chgo., Feb. 9, 1917; d. Arthur Garfield and Grace May (Cummings) Vierling; student U. Southern Calif., 1932-34, grad. Acad. Profl. Art Conservators, 1975; m. Garth Benepe Follett, Feb. 16, 1945; 1 dau., Dawn Goshorn; 3 stepchildren. Exhibited in group shows Palette and Chisel Acad. Fine Arts, 1975, 76, 77, Municipal Art League, 1972-77, others; represented in permanent collection Fla., Calif., Italy, others; owner, mgr. Paintin' Place, gallery, Oak Park, Ill., 1973—; dir. Palette and Chisel Acad. Fine Arts, Chgo. Vice pres. Oak Park League Women Voters, 1952-54, welfare chmn. 1956-58; treas. Oak Park Council Internat. Affairs, 1962-74. Recipient Gold medal Palette and Chisel Acad. Fine Arts, 1976-77, 1st award Civics and Art Found. Union League Chgo., 1977. Mem. Oak Park River Forest Art League (dir.), Pen Women Am., Municipal Art League Chgo., Am. Soc. Artists, Art Inst. Assos. of Oak Park and River Forest (womens bd. 1967—), Oak Park River Forest Hist. Soc. Club: 19th Century Womens. Home: 1440 Park Ave River Forest IL 60305 Office: 181 Oak Park Ave S Oak Park IL 60302

FOLLIS, THOMAS BURTON, veterinarian; b. Bowling Green, Ky., Mar. 26, 1927; s. William Blackburn and Grace Neel (Russell) F.; B.S., Western Ky. State Coll., 1950; D.V.M., Ohio State U., 1954; Ph.D., Utah State U., 1972; m. Nancy Louise Sisson, June 12, 1954; children—Karen Wright, David Sisson. Diagnostician, Reynoldsburg (Ohio) Diagnostic Lab., 1954-55; practice veterinary medicine, Taylorsville, Ky., 1954-69; head veterinary medicine and research World Wildlife Safari, Winston, Oreg., 1972-73; mgr. veterinary services Ralston Purina Co., St. Louis, 1973-76, asst. dir. corp. regulatory compliance, 1976—; dir. World Wildlife Safari, Winston. Mem. Sch. Bd. Spencer County, Ky., 1969; mem. Library Bd., Spencer County; chmn. Infantile Paralysis Found., Spencer County. Served with USAC, 1945-47. Utah Dept. Natural Resources fellow, 1969-72. Mem. F-2 Wildlife Assos. (co-founder), AVMA, Am. Animal Hosp. Assn., Nat. Wildlife Found., Ky. Vet. Med. Assn., Fine Arts Assn. Lindenwood Coll., Assn. St. Louis Art Museum, Am. Assn. Indsl. Veterinarians. Methodist. Club: Masons. Editor: The Morphology of Canine and Feline Blood Cells (R.R. Rich), 1974; Allergic Inhalant Dermatitis (Anderson), 1975. Contbr. articles to profl. jours. Home: 6 Weldon Spring Heights St Charles MO 63301 Office: Ralston Purina Co Checkerboard Sq St Louis MO 63188

FOLLMAR, JEROME ALBERT, dentist; b. Hammond, Ind., Dec. 19, 1929; s. John Joseph and Marie Bertha (Retzloff) F.; student Butler U., 1960-61; D.D.S., Ind. U., 1966; m. Jacqueline Frances Wyld, Dec. 11, 1971; children—Frederick Johnones, Nancy Sue, Allison Leigh, Jerome Albert II, Amy Lynn, Jack David. Gen. practice dentistry, Indpls., Anderson, Ind.; chief dental service Central State Hosp., Indpls., 1967-73, chief med. staff, 1972-73. Asst. clin. instr. James W. Riley Children Hosp. Dental Clinic, 1968-73. Served with AUS, 1952-54. Mem. Am. Soc. Dentistry for Children (mem. exec. com. Ind. unit 1968-73, sec.-treas. 1973-75, v.p. 1975-77, pres. 1977—), Am. Soc. Forensic Odontology, Am., Ind. dental assns., Ind. Pub. Health Dentists Orgn. (pres. 1970), Indpls. Dist. Dental Soc., Westside Dental Group (pres. 1968). Home: 2316 Wildwood Dr Anderson IN 46011 Office: 123 W 12th St Anderson IN 46016

FOLTZ, RICHARD GERALD, cons. engr.; b. Indpls., Aug. 24, 1944; s. Gerald James and Alice Barbara (Dickey) F.; B.S.E.E., Rose-Hulman Inst. Tech., 1966; M.B.A., U. Mo., 1972; m. Dava Mae Sue Emery, Aug. 28, 1976; children—Brian H., Jason D., Sharon S. Cons. engr. Burns & McDonnell Engring. Co., Kansas City, Mo., 1970—. Served with C.E., U.S. Army, 1967-69. Registered profl. engr., Ind., Mo., Kans., Ark., Nebr., Minn., Calif., Md. Mem. IEEE, Power Engring. Soc., Nat., Mo. socs. profl. engrs., Am. Nuclear Soc., Am. Pub. Power Assn. Baptist. Home: 9606 W 92nd Terr Overland Park KS 66212 Office: PO Box 173 Kansas City MO 64141

FOLZ, SYLVESTER DEL (BUD), research scientist; b. Marshfield, Wis., Feb. 26, 1941; s. Joseph Mathew and Isabella (Brost) F.; B.S., U. Wis., 1964, M.S., 1966, Ph.D., 1968; m. Judith E. Harter, Nov. 24, 1962; children—Susan, Steven, Brian. Research asst. U. Wis., Madison, 1965-66, research and tng. asst., 1966-68; research asso. Upjohn Co., Kalamazoo, 1968-69, sr. research scientist, 1969-75, research head, 1975—; cons. to practicing veterinarians, Kalamazoo, Kalamazoo Mfg. Co. Pres. schs. supt's. adv. council, 1975, 76, 77, 78; v.p. Comstock N. PTA, 1973, pres., 1974; v.p. Comstock Citizens Adv. Council, 1976. Recipient Masters Certificate, Center for Mgmt. Studies, Kalamazoo Coll., 1975. Mem. Am., Australian socs. parasitologists, Am. Assn. Veterinary Parasitologists, Soc. Protozoology, Am. Inst. Biol. Scis., Soc. Tropical Medicine and Hygiene, Helminthal. Soc. Washington, Animal Health Inst., Sigma Xi. Contbr. sci. writings to publs.; patentee in field of chemotherapy; mem. editorial bd. Jour. Veterinary Parasitology. Home: 6209 Enola St Kalamazoo MI 49004 Office: Upjohn Co 9680-190-1 Kalamazoo MI 49001

FONDA, JOHN REAGAN, engr., mfg. co. exec.; b. Knoxville, Tenn., Aug. 25, 1917; s. Howard E. and Mabel (Reagan) F.; student Wayne State U., Mich. State U.; m. Joyce May Rupprecht, Feb. 21, 1949. With Dihydrol Co., 1946—, sec.-treas., 1950-60, pres., Highland Park, Mich., 1960—. Registered profl. engr., Mich. Mem. Nat. Assn. Corrosion Engrs., Am. Water Works Assn., Am. Soc. San. Engrs. (pres.). Baptist. Mason (32 deg., Shriner). Research in water chemistry. Patentee on equipment for chem. treatment water. Home: 30815 Billington Ct Birmingham MI 48010 Office: 150 Victor Ave Detroit MI 48203

FONDER, AELRED CHARLES, dentist; b. Sisseton, S.D., Nov. 11, 1916; s. John Joseph and Albertina (Nigg) F.; student Huron Coll., 1936, St. Henry's Coll., 1938-39, St. Paul Sem., 1940; B.A. in Philosophy and Chemistry, St. John's U., 1943; postgrad. Sch. Dentistry, No. Pacific Coll., 1943-44; D.D.S., Northwestern U., 1946; postgrad. U. Ill., 1946; m. Jane Marie Schoenberg, May 13, 1944; children—Nancy (Mrs. Randolph Wayne Osborn), Thomas, Robert, John, James. Practice dentistry, Hubbard Woods, Ill., 1946-49, Winnetka, Ill., 1949-53; founder Rehab. Inst. Chgo., 1952, Am. Acad. Maxillofacial Prosthetics, 1953; established maxillofacial prosthetics program U.S. Army and Air Force, Brooke Army Hosp., Tex., 1955; practice dentistry specializing in temporo mandibular joint problems, Rock Falls, Ill., 1955—; staff U. Ill. Coll. Dentistry, 1946-47, now asst. prof.; staff Northwestern U. Dental Sch., 1947-49; dir. Dental Research Found., Rock Falls. Research Maxillofacial prosthetics U. Chgo., 1964-65; lectr. Michael Reese Hosp., Chgo., 1967-68; developer Sterling Profl. Bldg. (Ill.), 1967-68. Co-Founder Self-Help Enterprises, Sterling-Rock Falls, Ill., 1959. Bd. dirs. Found. Internat. Coop. Served with USNR, 1943-45, to capt. AUS, 1953-55. Fellow Ill. Dental Soc., Royal Soc. Health (Eng.); mem. Am. Acad. Maxillofacial Prosthetics (founder), Christian (bd. dirs.), Internat., Am., Ill. dental socs., Am. Acad. Physiol. Dentistry, Am. Acad. Functional Prosthodontics, Am. Assn. for Advancement Tension Control, Internat. Assn. Preventive Medicine, Psi Omega. Roman Catholic. Author: The Dental Physician; Goodbye Headaches. Editor: Basal Facts. Contbr. articles to profl. jours. Inventor functional artificial hand for amputees, 1952, artificial skin-like materials, 1953. Home: 1512 1st Ave Sterling IL 61081 Office: 303 W 2d St Rock Falls IL 61071

FONOW, JAMES THOMAS, beer distbg. co. exec.; b. Steubenville, Ohio, July 11, 1950; s. James Robert and Mary Ann (Villies) F.; B.S., Coll. Steubenville, 1973; m. Karen Louise Lucke, Sept. 27, 1974. With Ft. Steuben Distbg. Co., Inc., Steubenville, 1972—, sec., 1975—, treas., 1975—. Mem. Ohio Beer Wholesale Assn. (chmn. planning com. 1976—), Steubenville C. of C. Roman Catholic. Moose. Home: 824 Oakmont Ave Steubenville OH 43952 Office: 1031 Kingsdale Rd Pottery Addition Steubenville OH 43952

FOOTE, JOEL LINDSLEY, biochemist; b. Cleve., Jan. 11, 1928; s. Joel Lindsley and Beth Eliza (Brainard) F.; B.S. in Edn., Miami U., 1952; postgrad. Ohio State U., 1955; Ph.D., Case Inst. Tech., 1960; m. Alice Lydia Tanner, June 16, 1951; children—Robert Lindsley, Karen Ann. Tchr. sci., Wilmington (Ohio) pub. schs., 1952-53; tchr. sci. and mathematics, Springfield (Ohio) pub. schs., 1953-56; NSF postdoctoral fellow, U. Mich., Ann Arbor, 1960-62, instr. and asst. research biochemist, 1962-65; asst. prof., asso. prof., Western Mich. U., Kalamazoo, 1965—. Originator, founding chmn. City of Kalamazoo Environ. Concerns Com., 1970-72; Kalamazoo County Democratic exec. com., 1968—; candidate for county commr., 1968, 70. Served with USN, 1946-48. NIH research grantee, 1966-70. Mem. Am. Soc. Biol. Chemists, Am. Chem. Soc., AAAS, AAUP, Phi Beta Kappa, Sigma Xi. Unitarian. Contbr. articles in field to sci. publs. Home: 3623 Lancaster Dr Kalamazoo MI 49007 Office: Dept Chemistry Western Mich Univ Kalamazoo MI 49008

FOOTLIK, IRVING MELVIN, cons. engr.; b. Chgo., Feb. 7, 1918; s. Louis and Rose (Elman) F.; B.S., Ill. Inst. Tech., 1939; m. Sylvia Gollay, Mar. 10, 1940 children—Janice B., Robert B. Jr. engr. U.S. Air Corps, Dayton, O., 1939-41; chief perishable tool sect. U.S. Army Ordnance, Chgo., 1941-45; asst. to v.p. Ekco Products Co., Chgo., 1946-48; gen. plant mgr. Galter Products, 1948-50; cons. engr. Footlik and Assos., Evanston, Ill., 1950—, pres., 1950—; dir. Met. Bank; lectr. Mem. Skokie Traffic Safety Commn., 1971-74. Recipient Am. Material Handling Soc. honors award, U.S. Army Ordnance Civilian meritorious service award, Internat. Materials Mgmt. Soc. Ten Year Presdl. award. Mem. Assn. Profl. Material Handling Cons. (sec.), ASME, Internat. Material Mgmt. Soc., Ill. C. of C., Ill. Soc. Profl. Engrs. Material handling editor: Supply House Times mag. Contbr. to publs. in field. Address: 1548 Tower Rd Sylvia Ln Winnetka IL 60093 Office: 2530 Crawford Ave Evanston IL 60201

FOOTLIK, ROBERT BARRY, engr.; b. Chgo., Oct. 29, 1946; s. Irving M. and Sylvia (Gollay) F.; B.S.I.E., Ill. Inst. Tech., 1968; m. Beth Ann Iglitzen, Dec. 16, 1969; children—Jennifer, Ari. Exec. v.p. Footlik and Assos., Evanston, Ill., 1971—; mem. adv. bd. Met. Bank & Trust Co., Addison, Ill. Bd. dirs. Skokie Valley Symphony Orch. Assn.; lectr. in field; cons. in field. Licensed profl. engr., Ill., 1972. Mem. Nat., Ill. (Young Engr. of Year 1972) socs. profl. engrs.; Internat. Materials Mgmt. Soc. (pres. Chgo. chpt. 1976-77), Assn. Profl. Material Handling Cons., Midwest Indsl. Mgmt. Assn. Contbr. articles in field to profl. jours. Home: 236 Wentworth Ave Glencoe IL 60022 Office: 2530 Crawford Ave Evanston IL 60201

FORAKER, ROBERT ALLEN, banker; b. Canton, Ohio, Dec. 1, 1944; s. Robert E. and Ester (Freudeman) F.; student Akron U., 1968-69, Fla. Tech. Coll., 1976; m. Mary F. Mucci, Sept. 10, 1966; children—Robert Anthony, Robynn Marie. With Central Trust, Canton, Ohio 1962-69, sr. programmer, 1965-69, sales rep., 1967-69; with Citizens Savs. of Canton, 1969—, officer, asst. treas., 1971—, service mgr., 1973-77, sales and service mgr., 1975-77; owner, dir. Ohio Microfilm, Inc., 1975-76. Served with Ohio N.G., 1965-71. Mem. Savs. and Loan Inst., Savs. Assn. Pub. Affairs Com. Ohio. Democrat. Roman Catholic. Patentee 24 hour home bank. Home: 3600 21st St NW Canton OH 44708 Office: 100 Central Plaza S Canton OH 44708

FORBES, FRED W., architect, engr.; b. Aug. 21, 1936. Pres., Fred W. Forbes & Assos., Inc., Xenia, Ohio. Recipient Exceptional Civilian Service award USAF; Young Engr. of Yr. award Ohio Soc. Profl. Engrs., 1970; One of 5 Young Engrs. award Nat. Soc. Profl. Engrs., 1973; Victor A. Prather award Am. Astron. Soc., 1969; Archtl. Excellence award Dayton Area Masonry Inst., 1976. Fellow Brit. Interplanetary Soc. Contbr. articles to profl. publs. Patentee in field. Office: 158 E Main St PO Box 443 Xenia OH 45385

FORBES, GORDON WILLIAM, ins. co. exec.; b. Akron, Ohio, May 17, 1920; s. James Robert and Mae Elizabeth (Dye) F.; LL.B., Atlanta Law Sch., 1947, LL.M., 1949; m. Frances Clare Moore, Aug. 3, 1943; 1 dau., Frances Dianne Forbes Gaines. With Hartford Ins. Group, 1946—, bond underwriter, Atlanta, 1945-50, mktg. rep., Birmingham, Ala., Greensboro, N.C., Tampa, Fla., 1950-66, mktg. mgr., Charlotte, N.C., 1967-68, asst. gen. mgr., St. Louis, 1968-71, gen. mgr., 1971—; instr. ins. adult edn. U. Tampa, 1958-66; adv. com. Mo. Ins. Info. Inst., Ins. Service Office; past mem. governing exec. coms. Mo. Ins. Placement Facility. Deacon, past ch. bd. Parkway Baptist Ch., Creve Coeur, Mo. Served with USAF, 1942-45. Republican. Mem. Sigma Delta Kappa. Home: 612 Thunderbird Ct Chesterfield MO 63017 Office: 795 Office Pkwy Creve Coeur MO 63141

FORBES, KENNETH ALBERT FAUCHER, urol. surgeon; b. Waterford, N.Y., Apr. 28, 1922; s. Joseph Frederick and Adelle Frances (Robitaille) Faucher; B.S. cum laude, U. Notre Dame, 1943; M.D., St. Louis U., 1947; m. Eileen Ruth Gibbons, Aug. 4, 1956; children—Michael, Diane, Kenneth E., Thomas, Maureen, Daniel. Rotating intern St. Louis U. Hosps., 1947-48; resident urol. surgery, Dean's com., VA Hosp., Washington U., St. Louis U. schs. medicine, 1949-52; asst. chief urology Letterman Army Hosp., San Francisco, 1952-54; postgrad. West Roxbury VA Hosp., Harvard Teaching Unit, Boston, 1955; asst. chief urology VA Hosp., East Orange, N.J., 1955-58; attending urologist St. Mary's, St. Vincent, Bellin Meml. hosps., Green Bay, Wis., 1958—; cons. in field, lectr.; pvt. practice urology, Green Bay, 1958—; dir. Urol. Surgeons Ltd., Green Bay, 1969—, sec., 1969. Health officer DePere, Wis., 1973-74. Dir. fund raising program Fox River Valley area St. Louis U., 1959-63, Green Bay area U. Notre Dame Summa Campaign, 1969. Served with USNR, 1944-46, AUS, 1952-54. Diplomate Am. Bd. Urology. Fellow A.C.S. (founder Wis. chpt. 1969, councillor 1977), Internat. Coll. Surgeons (credentials com. 1970—), Boston Med. Library; mem. A.M.A., Brown County (legislator contact com. 1973—), Wis. (chmn. med. def. com., physicians alliance commn.) med. socs., Am. Urol. Assn. (exec. com. N. Central sect., Wis. rep. 1972-75), Wis. Urol. Soc. (pres. 1977), Urologists Corr. Club, A.A.A.S. (life), N.Y. Acad. Scis., Royal Soc. Medicine (London), Green Bay Area C. of C., U. Notre Dame Acad. Sci., Notre Dame Club Green Bay and Fox River Valley (Man of Year 1965), Phi Beta Pi (pres. Lambda chpt. 1945). Republican. Roman Catholic. Clubs: Gt. Lakes Cruising, Sturgeon Bay Yacht, Oneida Golf and Riding. Contbr. articles to profl. jours. Home: 414 Randall Ave DePere WI 54115 Office: 2021 S Webster Ave Green Bay WI 54301

FORBES, LYMAN MILTON, JR., automotive co. exec.; b. Harvey, Ill., May 6, 1931; s. Lyman M. and Myrtle Viola (Harwood) F.; B.S., Northwestern U., 1953; M.S., U. Wis., 1955; m. Gwendolyn MacKenzie, Aug. 22, 1953; children—Anne, Kenneth, Christine. With Ford Engring. div. Ford Motor Co., Dearborn, Mich., 1957—, operational factors mgr. environ. and safety engring., 1968—. Served with AUS, 1955-57. Mem. Soc. Automotive Engrs. (chmn. driver vision research com. 1969-74), Northwestern U. Alumni Assn. (pres. Detroit chpt. 1971-73), Human Factors Soc. (A.R. Lauer award 1974), Am. Psychol. Assn. Home: 963 Warwick Rd Birmingham MI 48008 Office: Automotive Safety Center PO Box 2053 Dearborn MI 48121

FORBES, RAYMOND HORACE, educator; b. Omaha, Oct. 9, 1923; s. Conrad Raymond and Lillian (Bilder) F.; B.A., Pomona Coll., 1946; postgrad. U. Ala., 1946-47, Middlebury Coll., 1946, 47; M.A., U. Ill., 1948; postgrad. U. Minn., certificate Ph.D., 1956; certificate Bestätigung für Germanisten, Goethe Inst. (Munich, Germany), 1958; m. Ethel Asserina Nelson, Aug. 26, 1955; children—Jennifer, Jane, Heather, Cynthia, Pamela, Geoffrey and Catherine (twins). Instr. German, U. Ala., 1946-47; asst. prof. dept. German, W.Va. U., Morgantown, 1950-51, U. of South, Sewanee, Tenn., 1951-52; asst. prof. German and English, Jamestown (N.D.) Coll., 1952-53; instr. Pensacola (Fla.) Jr. Coll., 1956-62; asst. prof. German Ripon (Wis.) Coll., 1962-63; asst. prof. German St. Cloud (Minn.) State Coll., 1963-70, chmn. fgn. lang. dept., 1964-65; prin. Holy Innocents High Sch., St. Cloud, 1971-72; dir. Metaphys. Research Inst., 1972—; painter in oils. Served with AAC, 1942-43. Fulbright fellow, 1958. Mem. Modern Lang. Assn. Am., Internat. Platform Assn., Smithsonian Instn., Am. Metaphys. Assn., Internat. New Thought Alliance, Am. Legion, Delta Phi Alpha, Epsilon Delta Chi.

Republican. Episcopalian. Home: 808 Washington Meml Dr St Cloud MN 56301 Office: PO Box 981 Saint Cloud MN 56301

FORCE, RONALD CLARENCE, psychologist, ret. air force officer; b. Toledo, Apr. 10, 1917; s. Rockwell and Anna (Briner) F.; B.A., Heidelberg Coll., 1940; M.A., Miami U., Oxford, Ohio, 1941; postgrad. U. Cal. at Berkeley, 1948-50; m. Winifred A. Schnatz, Dec. 15, 1942; children—Eric, Hugh, Bryan, Gregory. Instr., Miami U., 1945-47; commd. 2d lt. U.S. Air Force, 1942, advanced through grades to lt. col., 1962; psychologist USAF, ret.; clin. coordinator/psychologist St. Francis Boys' Homes, Salina, Kans., 1966—; instr. Amarillo Coll., 1958-60, West Tex. State U., 1961-63, Marymount Coll., 1967-69, Bethany Coll., 1970-71. Bd. dirs. Test Systems, Inc., Wichita. Adviser, Big Bros. Amarillo, 1962-65. Bd. dirs. Amarillo-Potter County Child Welfare Agy., 1954-56, 61-64. Served with USMCR, 1942, AUS, 1943-48. Fellow A.A.A.S.; mem. Am. Psychol. Assn., Am. Correction Assn., Nat. Council Crime and Delinquency, Am. Orthopsychiat. Assn., Am. Assn. Children's Residential Centers. Presbyn. (elder). Contbr. articles to profl. jours. Home: 2811 Melanie Ln Salina KS 67401 Office: St Francis Boys' Homes PO Box 1348 Salina KS 67401

FORD, GERALD R., JR., former President of U.S.; b. Omaha, July 14, 1913; s. Gerald R. and Dorothy (Gardner) F.; A.B., U. Mich., 1935; LL.B., Yale U., 1941; LL.D. (hon.), Mich. State U., Aquinas Coll., Spring Arbor Coll., Albion Coll., Grand Valley State Coll., Belmont Abby Coll., Western Mich. U.; m. Elizabeth Bloomer, Oct. 15, 1948; children—Michael Gerald, John G., Steven M., Susan Elizabeth. Admitted to Mich. bar, 1941, practiced in Grand Rapids, 1941-49; asso. firm Butterfield, Amberg, Law & Buchen, Grand Rapids, 1946-51; mem. firm Amberg, Law, Buchen & Fallon, 1951-59, Buchen & Ford, after 1960; mem. 81st to 93d congresses from 5th Mich. Dist., mem. appropriations com., minority leader, 1965-73; vice pres. U.S., 1973-74, Pres. U.S., 1974-77. Served to lt. comdr. USN, 1942-46. Recipient 1948 Grand Rapids Jr. C. of C. Distinguished Service award; Distinguished Service award as one of ten outstanding young men in U.S., U.S. Jr. C. of C., 1950, Sports Illus. Silver Anniversary All-Am. award, 1959, Congl. Distinguished Service award Am. Polit. Sci. Assn., 1961; George Washington award Am. Good Govt. Soc., 1966; Gold Medal award Nat. Football Found., 1972. Mem. Am., Mich., Grand Rapids bar assns., Delta Kappa Epsilon, Phi Delta Phi. Republican. Episcopalian. Mason. Clubs: University, Peninsular (Kent County). Co-author: Portrait of the Assassin. Home: 1624 Sherman St SE Grand Rapids MI 49506

FORD, GORDON BUELL, JR., educator, author; b. Louisville, Sept. 22, 1937; s. Gordon Buell and Rubye (Allen) F.; A.B., Princeton, 1959; M.A., Harvard, 1962, Ph.D., 1965; postgrad. U. Oslo (Norway), 1963-64, U. Sofia (Bulgaria), 1963, U. Uppsala, 1963-64, U. Stockholm, 1963-64, U. Madrid, 1963. Asst. prof. Indo-European and Baltic linguistics Northwestern U., 1965-72; asso. prof. English and linguistics U. No. Iowa, Cedar Falls, 1972-74, prof. English, linguistics and teaching English as fgn. lang., 1974-76; research prof. gen. linguistics, hist. and comparative linguistics, Slavic and Baltic linguistics Gorgay Corp., Louisville, Chgo., and Palm Beach, Fla., 1973—; vis. asst. prof. medieval Latin U. Chgo., 1966-67, lectr. linguistics U. Chgo. extension, 1966-67, 70-72; asst. prof. anthropology Northwestern U. Evening Divs., 1971-72. Mem. Linguistic Soc. Am., Internat. Linguistic Assn., Modern Lang. Assn. Am., Am. Philol. Assn., Am. Assn. Tchrs. Slavic and East European Langs., Mediaeval Acad. Am., Societas Linguistica Europaea, Assn. for Advancement Baltic Studies, S.A.R., Phi Beta Kappa. Baptist. Clubs: Harvard, Louisville Country, Princeton. Author: The Ruodlieb: The First Medieval Epic of Chivalry from Eleventh-Century Germany, 1965; The Ruodlieb: Linguistic Introduction, Latin Text, and Glossary, 1966; The Ruodlieb: Facsimile Edition, 1967; Old Lithuanian Texts of the Sixteenth and Seventeenth Centuries with a Glossary, 1969; The Old Lithuanian Catechism of Baltramiejus Vilentas (1579): A Phonological, Morphological, and Syntactical Investigation, 1969; Isidore of Seville's History of the Goths, Vandals, and Suevi, 1970; The Letters of St. Isidore of Seville, 1970; The Old Lithuanian Catechism of Martynas Mazvydas (1547), 1971; Isidore of Seville: On Grammar, 1978; Readings in Comparative Linguistic Methodology, 1978, others. Translator: A Concise Elementary Grammar of the Sanskrit Language with Exercises, Reading Selections, and a Glossary (Jan Gonda), 1966; The Comparative Method in Historical Linguistics (Antoine Meillet), 1967; A Sanskrit Grammar (Manfred Mayrhofer), 1972: Home: 126 N Peterson Ave Louisville KY 40206

FORD, HENRY, II, automobile mfr.; b. Detroit, Sept. 4, 1917; s. Edsel B. and Eleanor (Clay) F.; grad. Hotchkiss Sch., 1936; student Yale, 1936-40; m. Anne McDonnell, July, 1940 (div.); children—Charlotte, Anne, Edsel Bryant II; m. 2d, Maria Cristina Vettore Austin, Feb. 1965. Dir., Ford Motor Co., 1938—, with co., 1940—, v.p., 1943, exec. v.p., 1944-45, pres., 1945, chmn. bd., 1960—. Co-chmn. Detroit Renaissance; mem. Bus. Council; bd. govs. UN Assn. U.S.A.; trustee The Ford Found., 1943-76. Home: Grosse Pointe Farms MI Office: Ford Motor Co Dearborn MI 48121

FORD, HOMER DONNOLLY, photographer; b. Titusville, Fla., July 10, 1918; s. Homer C. and Margaret H. (Hastings) F.; student U. San Diego, 1959, La Salle Extension U., 1956-60; m. Hazel June Boyette, June 9, 1939; 1 dau., Margaret Augusta. Enlisted U.S. Navy, 1936; photographers mate served Torpedo Squadron Five, U.S. Naval Air Sta., Jacksonville, Fla.; U.S.S. Franklin, PTO, 1943-44; chief warrant officer U.S. Naval Photog. Center, Washington, 1945-46, Naval Antarctic Expdns., 1946-47, Naval Proving Grounds, Dahlgren, Va., 1948-50, U.S.S. Essex, 1951-52, Naval Sta., Norfolk, Va., 1952-54, Photog. Reconnaissance Squadron 61, 1954-56, U.S. Fleet Camera Group, Pacific, 1956-57, U.S. Midway CVA-41, 1957-58; ret., 1958; spl. field rep. Bank of Am. Trust & Savs. Assn., San Diego, 1958-62; mem. tech. staff N.Am. Aviation Corp., Columbus, Ohio, 1962-69; chief photographer Riverside Methodist Hosp., Columbus, 1970—. Certified, registered biol. photographer. Mem. Profl. Photographers of Central Ohio, Biol. Photog. Assn. Episcopalian. Clubs: Toastmasters (pres. 1973-74). Home: 4786 Colonel Perry Dr Columbus OH 43229 Office: 3535 Olentangy River Rd Columbus OH 43214

FORD, JOHN BATTICE, III, import-export co. exec.; b. Detroit, July 3, 1924; s. John Battice and Katharine (Tanner) F.; B.S., Yale, 1949; m. Mary Louise McDonald, June 21, 1946; 1 son, John Battice IV. Adminstrv. asst. Nat. Bank of Detroit, 1950-53; asst. treas. Huron Portland Cement Co., Detroit, 1953-58, treas., 1958-59; owner, pres. TRADCO/DETROIT, Inc., 1960-69; pres. H.M. Robins Co., 1961-67; pres. Gentrex, Inc., 1969—. Bd. dirs. U.S. Com. for Refugees, Leader Dogs, United Found., Boys Republic, Detroit Macomb Hosp. Assn. Mem. Founders Soc. Detroit Inst. Arts. Episcopalian. Clubs: Detroit, Country of Detroit; Grosse Pointe (Mich.); Yale (N.Y.C.); Anglers (Key Largo, Fla.); Bath and Tennis (Delray, Fla.). Home: 431 Lakeshore Rd Grosse Pointe Farms MI 48236 Office: Ford Bldg Detroit MI 48226

FORD, JOHN RICHARD, employment bur. exec.; b. LaGrange, Ill., Nov. 1, 1920; s. August W. and Dorothy E. (Toole) F.; B.S. in Commerce, Northwestern U., 1951; m. Grace M. Doyle, Apr. 18, 1942; children—Margaret J., James R., Kevin R., Dorothy H., Mary T., Kathleen, Brian, Virginia M. Pres. Oak Brook Employment Bur., Edgewood Employment Bureau, 1967—. Cons. to pvt. employment agys., 1953—. Chmn. La Grange Park Village Caucus, 1963-65. Served to lt. USCGR, 1941-45. Mem. Nat. (past area dir.), Ill. (past pres.) employment assns., Oak Brook Assn. Commerce and Industry (pres. 1972—), Holy Name Soc. Roman Catholic. K.C., Rotarian. Author: Your New Life, 1953. Home: 429 N Dover Ave La Grange Park IL 60528 Office: 900 Jorie Blvd Oak Brook IL 60521

FORD, JON ALLAN, psychologist; b. Iowa Falls, Iowa, July 17, 1943; s. Verner Allen and Edna Marie (Huse) F.; B.A. in Math., U. No. Iowa, 1966, M.A. in Psychology, 1968; doctoral candidate Ind. U.; m. Vicki Lea Hoogestraat, Sept. 5, 1966; children—Jon, Sara. Tchr. math. and sci., Iowa, 1967-69; teaching asst. U. No. Iowa, 1969-70; psychol. intern Area Edn. Agy. 7, Cedar Falls, Iowa, 1970-71; psychologist Joint County Sch. Dist., Cedar Falls, 1971-72; asso. instr. Ind. U., 1972-73, psychotherapist univ. developmental tng. center, 1972-73; supr. severe emotional disabilities program Area Edn. Agy. 7, Cedar Falls, 1973—; pvt. practice, 1972—; adj. asst. prof. U. No. Iowa, 1975; cons., workshop leader in field. Mem. Am., Iowa psychol. assns., Nat., Iowa edn. assns., Iowa Sch. Psychologists Assn., Council Exceptional Children, Assn. for Gifted. Contbr. articles to profl. publs. Home: 215 Midlothian Blvd Waterloo IA 50701 Office: 416 Lincoln St Waterloo IA 50703

FORD, LEE, scientist, educator, lawyer; b. Auburn, Ind., June 16, 1917; d. Arthur W. and Geneva (Muhn) Ford; B.A., Wittenberg Coll., 1947; M.S., U. Minn., 1949; Ph.D., Iowa State Coll., 1952; J.D. U. Notre Dame, 1972. CPA auditing, 1934-44; asso. prof. biology Gustavus Adolphus Coll., 1950-51. Anderson (Ind.) Coll., 1952-55; vis. prof. biology U. Alta. (Can.), Calgary, 1955-56; asso. prof. biology Pacific Luth. U., Parkland, Wash., 1956-62; prof. biology and cytogenetics Miss. State Coll. for Women, 1962-64; chief cytogeneticist Pacific N.W. Research Found., Seattle, 1964-65; dir. Canine Genetics Cons. Service, Parkland, Wash., 1963-69. Sponsor Companion Collies for the Adult, Jr. Blind, 1955-65; dir. Genetics Research Lab., Butler, Ind., 1955—, cons. cytogenetics, 1969—; legis. cons., 1970—; dir. chromosone lab. Inst. Basic Research in Mental Retardation, Staten Island, 1968-69; exec. dir. Legislative Bur. U. Notre Dame Law Sch., also editor New Dimensions in Legislation, 1969; exec. asst. to Gov. Otis R. Bowen, Ind., 1973-75; dir. Ind. Commn. on Status Women, 1973-74; editor Ford Assos. Inc., pubs.; mem. Pres.'s Adv. Council on Drug Abuse, 1976-77. Admitted to Ind. bar, 1972. Adult counselor Girl Scouts; mem. exec. bd. Ind.-Ky. Synod Lutheran Ch. Am. Mem. or ex-mem. A.A.U.W., A.A.A.S., Genetics Soc. Am., Am. Human Genetics Soc., Am. Genetic Assn., Am. Inst. Biol. Scis., Am. Soc. Zoologists, La., Miss., Ind., Iowa acads. sci., Bot. Soc. Am., Ecol. Soc. Am., Am., Ind. bar assns., Nat. Assn. Women Lawyers, Bus. and Profl. Women's Club. Assn. So. Biologists, Phi Kappa Phi. Club: Altrusa. Editor: Breeder's Jour., 1958-63; also numerous vols. dog genetics and breeding, and guide dogs for the blind. Contbr. articles cytogenetics to jours. in field; active contbr. Am. Kennel Club Gazette, others. Researcher in field. Home: 336 Hickory St Butler IN 46721 Office: 701 S Federal Ave Butler IN 46721

FORD, RUTH VAN SICKLE (MRS. ALBERT G. FORD), artist, educator; b. Aurora, Ill., Aug. 8, 1897; d. Charles P. and Anna (Miller) Van Sickle; student Chgo. Acad. Fine Arts, 1915-18, Art Students League, summers 1916-17; D.F.A., Aurora Coll., 1974; m. Albert G. Ford, Feb. 7, 1917; 1 dau., Barbara (Mrs. Rodman Turner). Exhibited in one man shows, Chgo. Art Inst., Grand Central Galleries, N.Y.C., 1947, Mexico City Country Club, Oklahoma City Art Center, 1948, Pomona Coll., Claremont, Calif., Hickory Mus. Art, N.C., 1948, Laguna Beach (Calif.) Art Assn., Centre D'Art, Port-au-Prince, Haiti, 1949, Palmer House Galleries, Chgo., 1949; exhibited in group shows at N.A.D., N.Y.C., Chgo. and Vicinity Artists Show at Chgo. Art Inst., Internat. Water Color Shows, Am. Artists Show at Art Inst., Pa. Acad. Ann. Water Color Show, Nat. Assn. Women Artists, 1949, Traveling Water Color Show, Oakland (Calif.) Art Gallery, 1949, Argent Gallery, N.Y.C., 1949, Miami Beach (Fla.) Art Center, Chgo. Painter and Sculptors Shows, Am. Water Color Soc., N.Y.C., Water Color, U.S.A.; pres. bd. dirs., owner, operator Chgo. Acad. Fine Arts, 1937-60; instr. art Aurora (Ill.) Coll., 1964-72; tchr. pvt. classes, Aurora, 1973—. Recipient numerous art awards. Mem. Conn. Acad., Grand Central Galleries, Chgo. Painters and Sculptors Assn., Salon Women Painters, Nat. Assn. Women Artists N.Y., Artists Guild Chgo. (hon.), Palette and Chisel Acad., Am. Artist Prof. League, Am. Watercolor Soc., Rockport Artists (asso.), Clinton Art Assn. (asso), Palette and Chisel (hon.). Home and studio: 69 Central St Aurora IL 60506

FORD, WILLIAM CLAY, automotive mfg. exec., profl. football team exec.; b. Detroit, Mar. 14, 1925; s. Edsel Bryant and Eleanor (Clay) F.; B.S., Yale, 1949; m. Martha Firestone, June 21, 1947; children—Martha, Sheila, William Clay, Elizabeth. Sales and advt. staff Ford Motor Co., 1949, indsl. relations, labor negotiations with U.A.W., 1949, quality control mgr. gas turbine engines Lincoln-Mercury div., Dearborn, Mich., 1951, mgr. spl. product operations, 1952, v.p., 1953, gen. mgr. Continental div., 1954, group v.p. Lincoln and Continental divs., 1955, v.p. product planning and design, 1956—, dir., 1948—. Pres., owner Det. Lions Profl. Football Club; chmn. Edison Inst., Edsel B. Ford Inst. for Med. Research; trustee Thomas A. Edison Found.; sec.-treas. Henry Ford Hosp.; dir. Dearborn Y.M.C.A.; mem. bd. Girl Scouts Am. Mem. Soc. Automotive Engrs. (asso.), Automobile Old Timers, Phelps Assn., Psi Upsilon. Mason (K.T.). Home: Grosse Pointe MI 48236 Office: Ford Motor Co Dearborn MI 48121 also 1200 Featherstone Rd Box 4200 Pontiac MI 48057

FORD, WILLIAM D., congressman; b. Detroit, Aug. 6, 1927; s. Robert H. and Jean B. Ford; student Wayne U.; B.S., J.D., U. Denver; children—William D., Margaret Helene, John Phillip. Practice law, 1952—; justice of peace Taylor Twp., Mich., 1955-57; city atty., Melvindale, Mich., 1957-59; twp. atty. Taylor, 1957-64; Mich. senator, 1963-64; mem. 89th-95th congresses from 15th Mich. Dist., mem. Edn. and Labor Com., chmn. post-secondary edn. subcom.; mem. post office and civil service com., Nat. Democratic whip-at-large, 1975—; house rep. to White House Library Conf.; vice-chmn. Conf. Gt. Lakes Congressmen. Del., Mich. Constl. conv., 1961-62. Served with USNR, 1944-46. Named Outstanding Young Man of Taylor, 1962. Mem. Downriver (pres. 1961-62), Mich., Am. bar assns., Taylor Jr. C. of C. (charter mem.), Phi Delta Phi. Mem. United Ch. of Christ. Mason (32 deg., Shriner), Moose, Eagle, Rotarian. Home: Taylor MI 48180 Office: Rayburn House Office Bldg Washington DC 20515

FORD, WILLIAM ELLIS, psychologist; b. Sewickley, Pa., July 6, 1945; s. Robert William and Theresa Louise (Weber) F.; B.S., U. Pitts., 1967; M.S., U. Mass., 1970, Ph.D., 1973; m. Maria Jane Fradel, July 29, 1967. Trainee, VA Hosp., Northampton, Mass., 1967-71; intern Norfolk (Nebr.) Regional Center, 1971-72, staff psychologist, 1973; dir. data systems div. Nebr. Dept. Pub. Instns., Lincoln, 1973-75; dir. Nebr. Div. on Alcoholism, Lincoln, 1975—; clin. asso. prof. U. Nebr., Lincoln, 1976—; instr. med. psychology Nebr. Psychiat. Inst., Omaha, 1976—; chmn. adv. council Midwestern Area Alcohol Edn. and Tng. Program. Mem. Am., Nebr. psychol. assns., Am. Pub. Health Assn., Nebr. Pub. Health Assn., Council State and Territorial Alcoholism Authorities, Phi Beta Kappa, Phi Eta Sigma, Psi Chi. Home: 7544 South St Lincoln NE 68520 Office: Box 94728 Lincoln NE 68520

FORDONSKI, PAUL LEO, pub. accountant, state ofcl.; b. Chgo., July 19, 1941; s. Leo Peter and Helen A. Guzik F.; student U. Ill., Chgo., 1959-60, Ill. Inst. Tech., 1960-69, Internat. Accountants Soc., Chgo., 1970-73, Lincoln Land Community Coll., Springfield, Ill., 1975-77; m. Carol F. Rose, June 25, 1966. Specification writer Western Electric Co. Inc., Chgo., 1960-65, cost accountant, 1967-69; v.p. Rodor Co. Inc., Palisades Park, N.J., 1969-70; tax preparer File Rite Tax Aid Inc., Chicago Heights, Ill., 1970; self-employed pub. accountant, Chgo., 1970-74; fiscal officer Ill. Dept. Vets. Affairs, Springfield, 1974—. Pres., Oakview Homeowners Assn., 1972-73. Served with AUS, 1965-67. Decorated Purple Heart. Mem. Am. Mgmt. Assn., Ind. Accountants Assn. Ill., Ill. Assn. Enrolled Fed. Tax Accountants (dir. 1973-74), Nat. Soc. Pub. Accountants. Home: 2650 Cooper Ave Apt 207 Springfield IL 62704 Office: 126 W Jefferson St Springfield IL 62701

FORDYCE, HOMER EDMUND, civil engr.; b. Ridgeway, Mo., Aug. 1, 1916; s. Orey Francis and Mabel Edna (Baxter) F.; B.C.E., U. Wyo., 1941; m. Mary Louise Gilbert, Mar. 25, 1948; 1 son, Jerry Edmund; 1 stepdau., Mary Lee Sooter Phillips. Cons. in gen. design Marley Co., Mission, Kans., 1945—. Mem. Mo. Republican Com., Clay County. Served with USAF, 1942-45. Mem. ASCE, Am. Concrete Inst. (v.p. Kans. chpt. 1977-78, pres. Kans. chpt. 1978). Patentee in cooling tower designs. Home: 811 NE 83d St Kansas City MO 64118 Office: 5800 Foxridge Dr Mission KS 66202

FORMAN, DONALD, hosp. exec.; b. N.Y.C., Feb. 27, 1932; s. Jack and Fannie (Jaffe) F.; B.S., Bklyn. Coll., 1953; M.S., Wayne State U., 1957, Ph.D., 1959; m. Florence Sporn, Aug. 22, 1953; children—Joan, Debra, Steven. Biochemist, Hazelton Research Lab., Falls Church, Va., 1959-60; clin. biochemist Mercy Med. Center, Chgo., 1960-63; with Evanston (Ill.) Hosp., 1963—, dir. clin. chemistry 1963—; asso. prof. biochemistry and pathology Northwestern U. Med. Sch., Chgo., 1961—. Served with AUS, 1953-55. Am. Heart Assn. grantee, 1964-68. Mem. Am. Assn. Clin. Chemistry, Am. Chem. Soc., Assn. Clin. Scientists, Am. Inst. Chemists, Sigma Xi. Home: 4954 Morse St Skokie IL 60076 Office: Evanston Hosp 2650 Ridge Ave Evanston IL 60201

FORMANEK, LUELLA HELEN, govt. staff mem., civic worker; b. Mpls., Aug. 11, 1924; d. Peter Paul and Mary Ann (Stepanek) Formanek; student U. Minn., 1957. Model, N.Y.C., 1946-55; traffic expert Illinios Central R.R. Co., Mpls., 1957-64; govt. employee, clk. XIV Army Corps, Vets. Ins., U.S. Post Office. Vol. Semper Fidelis, 1943, USO, 1943, Community Chest, 1945-46; chmn. Merry-Go-Round Gold Ring Club for Aged, Greenwich, Conn., 1950-53; vol. Greenwich Hosp., 1952-54; mem. aux. St. Mary's Hosp., Mpls., 1963; active Nat. Council Cath. Women, 1950—, Women in Service to Edn. Orgn., 1974—, Trust, 1975—, March of Dimes, 1976—, Am. Heart Assn., 1977—. Mem. Cath. Jr. League. Home: 4452 Portland Ave S Minneapolis MN 55407

FORNELLI, JOE PETE, civil engr.; b. Roseland, Kans., Dec. 8, 1915; s. Michele and Margherita (Marietta) F.; B.S. in Civil Engring., U. Kans., 1939; m. Mary Kathryn Watson, June 30, 1961; 1 son, Mike Amos. Insp. U.S. Engrs., St. Joseph, Mo., 1939-40; civil engr., Carter Oil Co., St. Elmo, Ill., 1939, 40; insp. Navy Dept., Parris Island, S.C., 1940-41; instrument man Consoer, Townsend & Quinlan, Parsons, Kans., 1941-42; party chief William S. Lozier, Inc., DeSoto, Kans., 1942-43; airways engr. C.A.A. 1943-45, 46-47; resident engr. Wilson Engrs., Salina, Kans., 1948; owner Fornelli Constrn. Co., Atwood, Kans., 1949-56; area supt. Girdler Co., Lawrence, Kans., 1953-54; civil engr. CAA, Kansas City, Mo., 1956-58; civil engr. FAA, Kansas City, 1959—. Served with AUS, 1945-46. Mem. ASCE, Am. Legion, Sigma Tau. Home: 16601 E 31st St Independence MO 64055 Office: 2300 E Devon Des Plaines IL 60018

FORNSHELL, DAVE LEE, ednl. broadcasting exec.; b. Bluffton, July 9, 1937; s. Harold Christman and Mary Ann Elizabeth (Fox) F.; B.A., Ohio State U., 1959; m. Ann Blanche Komminsk, June 7, 1969; 1 son, John David. Continuity dir. WTVN-TV, Columbus, O., 1959-61; traffic dir., asst. program, mgr. WOSU-TV, Columbus, 1961-69; ops. mgr. Md. Center for Pub. Broadcasting, Balt., 1969-70; exec. dir. Ohio Ednl. TV Network Commn., Columbus, 1970—; dir. Central Ednl. Network. Pres. Landings Residents Assn., 1973; active March of Dimes, 4-H. Served with USAF, 1961-62. Recipient award Dayton Fedn. Women's Clubs, 1974. Mem. N.G. Assn., Ohio State U. Alumni Assn., Nat. Acad. TV Arts and Scis. (2d. v.p. Columbus 1968-69, gov. 1970—), Nat. Assn. Ednl. Broadcasters, Health Scis. Communications Assn., Alpha Epsilon Rho, Alpha Delta Sigma, Sigma Delta Chi. Club: Kiwanis. Home: 2861 Chateau Circle Columbus OH 43221 Office: 2470 N Star Rd Columbus OH 43221

FORSHEE, F. LAMAR, assn. exec., lawyer; b. Ann Arbor, Mich., Oct. 17, 1912; s. Dewey M. and Lulu Mary (Nanry) F.; A.B., U. Mich., 1935, J.D., 1937; M.A. in Govt., Boston, 1962; m. Mary Annelle Smith, Mar. 15, 1946; 1 dau., Claudia N. Admitted to Calif. bar, 1938, U.S. Supreme Ct. bar, 1955; asso. firm Swaffield & Swaffield, Long Beach, Calif., also Los Angeles, 1938-41; labor relations counsel Vultee Aircraft Co., Downey, Calif., 1941-43; commd. ensign USN, 1943, advanced through grades to comdr., 1953, asst. staff legal officer, comdr. U.S. Forces Eastern Atlantic and Mediterranean, 1955-57; ret., 1964; gen. counsel State Bar Calif., San Francisco, 1964-73; exec. dir. Center for Profl. Discipline, Am. Bar Assn., Chgo., 1973—. Mem. Nat. Orgn. Bar Counsel (pres. 1971-72), State Bar Calif., Am. Bar Assn., Fed. Bar Assn., Am. Judicature Soc. Roman Catholic. Clubs: Army-Navy Country, Pickwick Golf. Home: 1475 Scott St Winnetka IL 60093 Office: 1155 E 60th St Chicago IL 60637

FORSLEFF, LOUISE STEWART PETERSON, cons. psychologist; b. Portland, Maine, Oct. 7, 1933; d. Roland Elliott and Gertrude May (More) Peterson; A.B., Lake Erie Coll., Painesville, Ohio, 1959; M.A., Western Mich. U., Kalamazoo, 1962; Ph.D., Mich. State U., E. Lansing, 1967; m. Elmer Andrew Forsleff, Dec. 24, 1965; children—Mary Anne Chahbazi, John Clark Chahbazi. Mem. faculty Western Mich. U., 1962—, prof. counseling, 1969—, dir. Counseling Center, 1968-73; pvt. practice cons. psychology, 1976—; bd. dirs., coordinator profl. exchange clearinghouse Internat. Assn. Counseling Services; cons. in field. Mem. Am. Personnel Guidance Assn., Am. Coll. Personnel Assn., Am. Assn. Sex Educators Counselors Therapists, Mich. Soc. Cons. Psychologists, Mortar Bd. (hon.). Quaker. Home: 1421 W Lovell St Kalamazoo MI 49007 Office: Counseling Center Western Mich Univ Kalamazoo MI 49008

FORSTER, KENNETH ELWYN, cons., cattle breeder; b. Glen Elder, Kans., June 26, 1918; s. Franklin Thomas and Agnes (Gaston) F.; student Wichita U., 1936-38, U. Chgo., 1944, U. Tex., 1961; m. Nancy L. Gothberg, Feb. 1, 1957; children—Deborah Lee, Nancy Kaye. Blockman, Internat. Harvester Co., St. Louis, also Quincy, Ill., 1944-47; dist. mgr. Midwest ty. Macmillan Petroleum Co., St. Louis, 1947-50; self employed, Memphis, 1950-54; gen. sales mgr. Saft

Corp., Lodi, N.J., 1954-56; gen. sales mgr. Barrett Cravens Co., Northbrook, Ill., 1956-61; v.p. sales M-D Blowers, Inc. (now MD Pneumatics, Inc.), 1961-74; cons. in field, 1974—; now engaged in cattle breeding. Mem. Water Pollution Control Fedn. Republican. Presbyn. Mason (Shriner). Home: 309 N Hersey Beloit KS 67420

FORSYTHE, JAMES LEE, historian; b. Bransford, Tex., Dec. 18, 1934; s. Roy Theodore and Irma May (Smith) F.; B.S., N. Tex. State U., 1960, M.A., 1962; Ph.D. (fellow), U. N.Mex., 1971; m. Sherrill Kay Zartman, Aug. 10, 1956; children—James Lee, Garen David, Dana Sean. Transp. agt. Delta Air Lines, Dallas, 1952-62; asst. prof. history Ft. Hays (Kans.) State Coll. (now Ft. Hays State U.), 1963-68, asso. prof. history, 1968-71, prof., 1971—, chmn. dept. history, 1975—; mem. Kans. Hist. Records Adv. Bd., 1976—; dir. Western Kans. Regional Oral History Project, 1969—. Treas., Ellis County Young Democrats, 1966-70; precinct committeeman, 1974—. Served with Air N.G., 1953-55; U.S. Army, 1955-57. Recipient Distinguished Alumni award Grapevine (Tex.) High Sch., 1970; Harry S. Truman Library Inst. Nat. and Internat. Affairs grantee, 1967, 72. Mem. Rocky Mountain Social Sci. Assn. (exec. council), Western Social Sci. Assn. (pres. 1976-77), AAUP (pres. Kans. 1972-73), Kans. State Hist. Soc. (dir. 1977—), Kans. Com. for Humanities (exec. com.), Agrl. History Assn., Orgn. Am. Historians, So., N.Mex., Kans., Western hist. assns., Phi Alpha Theta, Pi Sigma Alpha, Phi Kappa Phi. Baptist. Author: The First 75 Years: A History of Fort Hays State University, 1909-1977, 1977; contbr. articles in field to profl. jours. Home: 2927 Walnut St Hays KS 67601 Office: Dept History Fort Hays State U Hays KS 67601

FORTIN, CLIFFORD CHARLES, educator; b. Hamel, Minn., Apr. 7, 1922; s. Philip P. and Mary (Schultz) F.; B.S., U. Minn., 1943, M.A., 1951, Ph.D., 1970. Acquisitions librarian Kans. State Coll., Manhattan, 1951-55; asst. librarian, librarian Wis. State U. Lab. Sch., River Falls, 1955-63, asso. prof. library sci., 1963—. Served with USAAF, 1943-46. Mem. ALA, Wis. Library Assn., AAUP, NW Wis. Edn. Assn., Phi Delta Kappa. Home: 195 Hamel Rd Hamel MN 55340 Office: 53 Davee Library U Wis River Falls WI 54022

FORTIN, PHILIP PAUL, mfg. exec.; b. Hamel, Minn., Aug. 6, 1924; s. Philip P. and Mary C. (Schultz) F.; B.S., U. Minn., 1948; m. Betty J. Rubert, Sept. 12, 1946; children—Pamela, Paula, Philip, Robb, Jana, Tim. Shop supt. Bauer Welding and Metal Fabricators, Mpls., 1951-62; dir. mfg. Metal Matic, Inc., Mpls., 1962-76; pres. Progressive Assembly Machine Co., Inc., Plymouth, Minn., 1977—; mgmt. cons. Served with C.E., AUS, 1945-46, 50-51. Mem. Minn. Soc. Indsl. Engrs., Indsl. Mgmt. Soc. Methodist. Club: Appollo of Mpls. (past pres.). Home: 4300 Niagara Ln N Wayzata MN 55391 Office: 2010 E Center Circle Plymouth MN 55441

FORTINO, ALFRED JULIO, lawyer; b. Pontiac, Mich., Nov. 16, 1914; s. Michele and Giovannina (Scarcello) F.; A.B., Alma Coll., 1937; M.A. in Econs., U. Mich., 1938, J.D., 1940; m. Mary Alice Damon, Feb. 15, 1941; children—Charles M., Richard D., Thomas A. Admitted to Mich. bar, 1940; practice law. St. Louis, Mich., 1940-59, Alma, Mich., 1959—; partner Fortino, Plaxton & Moskal, Alma, Simon & Fortino, Alma; pres. Pine River Plaza, Alma, 1961—; treas. Bobenal Investments, Inc., Alma, 1962—; dir. Pine River Motel Co., Alma, Mid-State Properties, Alma; partner various other bus. Bd. trustees Central Mich. U., 1968—, chmn., 1969, 77. Served with AUS, World War II. Decorated Bronze Star medal. Mem. Am. Judicature Soc., Am. Bar Assn., State Bar Mich. Republican. Home: 303 E Saginaw St St Louis MI 48880 Office: 175 Warwick Dr Alma MI 48801

FORTNEY, ROGER DAVID, veterinarian; b. Prairie du Chein, Wis., Sept. 15, 1930; s. Harry Melvin and Ella Leona (Root) F.; student U. Wis., 1948-51, 56; B.S. in Vet. Sci., U. Minn., 1958, D.V.M., 1960; m. Carol Celeste Koester, Sept. 14, 1957; children—Roberta Lee, Rebecca Ann, David Roger, Karen Louise. Individual practice vet. medicine, Farmington, Minn., 1960-61; veterinarian Dept. Agr., Madison, Wis., 1961-62; individual practice vet. medicine, Madison, 1962-66; dir. animal prodn. ARS/Sprague-Dawley div. Mogul Corp., Wis., 1966-74, v.p. ops., 1974—; pilot North Central Airlines, 1960-67. Served with USAF, 1951-55. Mem. Am., Wis., Dane County vet. med. assns., Air Line Pilots Assn., Phi Alpha Theta, Pi Sigma Alpha, Phi Zeta. Patentee safety light switch, 1967. Home: 6421 Keelson Dr Madison WI 53705 Office: 2826 Latham Dr Madison WI 53713

FORTUNSKI, ANTHONY CASMER, metal products mfg. co. exec.; b. Detroit, June 13, 1917; s. John and Stella (Rutkowski) F.; B.S. in Chem. Engring., Lawrence Inst. Tech., 1939; m. Bernice Radziszewski, Sept. 28, 1940; children—Mary Jane, Mary Margaret, Alan A. Engr., Udylite Corp., Detroit, 1941-43; pres. Fargo Machine & Tool Co., Detroit, 1943—, Brown-Hutchinson, Inc., 1964—; dir. Liberty State Bank. Mem. adv. council Mich. Dept. Commerce. Served to lt. (j.g.)) USNR, 1944-46. Recipient Achievement award Lawrence Inst. Tech.; named Profl. Engr. Year Detroit, 1975. Fellow Engring. Soc. Detroit; mem. Mich. Assn. Professions, Nat., Mich. (pres. Detroit 1962-63, pres. soc. 1970-71), nat. dir. 1975-76), socs. profl. engrs., Am. Soc. Tool and Mfg. Engrs., Engring. Soc. Detroit, Am. Vets. Clubs: Detroit Yacht, Detroit Athletic. Patentee in field. Home: 1207 Berkshire Rd Grosse Pointe Park MI 48230 Office: 1801 Caniff Ave Hamtramck MI 48212

FORTY, ROBERT JOHN, air conditioning and heating co. exec.; b. Chgo., May 5, 1940; s. Robert A. and Gwendolyn (Kretsinger) F.; B.S., Kans. State Coll., Emporia, 1965; m. Sandra Lea Leino, Aug. 21, 1965; children—Eric, Tara. West Central dist. mgr. Century Creations, Venice, Calif., 1969-72; sales mgr. Comfortlease, Inc., Glen Ellyn, Ill., 1972-74; pres. Calcorp Inc., North Aurora, Ill., 1974-76; owner, pres. Energy Services Air Conditioning and Heating Co., Lisle, Ill., 1976—, also dir. Mem. Naperville C. of C., Refrigeration Service Engrs. Soc. DuPage County. Republican. Club: Kiwanis. Home: 1536 North Columbia St Naperville IL 60540 Office: 4659 Old Tavern Rd Lisle IL 60532

FOSNIGHT, WALLACE JAY, banker; b. Ft. Wayne, Ind., Nov. 8, 1938; s. Howard J. and Edna Mae (Paff) F.; B.S. in Bus. Adminstrn., Ind. U., 1963; postgrad. U. Colo., 1973-74; m. Joan L. Moore, Aug. 30, 1958; children—Wendy Jo, Jonell Marie. Product mgr. Pittsburgh Nat. Bank, 1963-68, investment officer, 1968-69; dir. mktg. Lincoln Nat. Bank, Ft. Wayne, 1969-75; dir. advt. Peoples Trust Bank, Ft. Wayne, 1975—. Chmn. bd. dirs. Ft. Wayne Pub. TV, 1970-76; bd. dirs. Ft. Wayne Urban League, 1975—, 2d v.p., 1978-79; bd. dirs. Mental Health Assn. Allen County (Ind.), 1978—, 2d v.p., 1978-79. Served with U.S. Army, 1956-57. Mem. Am. Inst. Banking, Am. Mktg. Assn., Bank Mktg. Assn., Ind. Cactus and Succulent Soc. Home: 6031 Red Oak Dr Ft Wayne IN 46815 Office: 913 S Calhoun Ft Wayne IN 46802

FOSS, KARL ROBERT, income tax auditor; b. Madison, Wis., Aug. 26, 1938; s. Robert Henry and Ethel Caroline (Huston) F.; student U. Wis., 1956-59, 62; B.S., Madison Bus. Coll., 1961. Auditor income tax Wis. Dept. Revenue, Madison, 1962—; owner, mgr. LIST, Middleton, Wis., 1968-76. Bd. dirs. Middleton Hist. Soc., 1976-78; legis. adv. Old Car Hobby, 1971-78. Co-recipient Spl. Interest Autos Appreciation award, 1971. Mem. Wis. Automobile Clubs in Assn. Inc. (co-founder 1971, pres. 1972-74, 77, v.p. 1975-76), Oldsmobile Club Am. (nat. dir. 1973—), Accounting and Mgmt. Assn., Contemporary Hist. Vehicle Assn., Studebaker Drivers Club, Nash Car Club Am., Crosley Car Club, Antique Automobile Club Am., Model T Ford Am. Publisher: Suppliers List, 1968, Suppliers List Directory, 1969. Home: 7324 South Ave Middleton WI 53562

FOSSATI, CHARLES GLEN, inventor; b. Buenos Aires, Argentina, Mar. 6, 1926; s. Carlos Luis and Glenys Jane (Gould) F.; came to U.S., 1928; naturalized, 1946; B.A., U. Mich., 1949, M.A., 1952; m. Rosamonde Davis, June 11, 1949; children—Linda, Carlos, Lee, Catherine. Instr. in Romance Languages U. Mich., Ann Arbor, 1951-52; founder Service Tectonics, Inc., Adrian, Mich., 1962; founder, pres. Maskote Corp., Detroit, 1972. Served in USN, 1943-46. Patentee in indsl. processes, machinery, vacuum metalizing. Mem. Soc. Plastic Engrs., Cousteau Soc., Econ. Club Detroit. Clubs: Masons, Windsor Yacht, Grosse Pointe Sail, Great Lakes Cruising, Grosse Pointe Boat. Home: 39 Lakecrest Ln Grosse Pointe Farms MI 48236 Office: 17168 E Warren St Detroit MI 48224

FOSSEN, LESLIE JULIAN, structural engr.; b. Sauk Centre, Minn., Aug. 23, 1938; s. Leslie Judean and Alice Theodora (Ranten) F.; B.S. in Civil Engring., U. Miss., 1963; m. Harriet Violet Rosen, July 3, 1958. Hwy. and railroad bridge designer Howard, Needles, Tammen & Bergendoff, Kansas City, Mo., 1963-65, project engr., 1965-72, structures dept. head, Chgo., 1972—. Served with U.S. Army, 1956-59. Registered profl. engr., Mo.; registered profl. structural engr., Ill. Mem. ASCE, Prestressed Concrete Inst. Lutheran. Designer I-435 bridge over Mo. River at Kansas City, Willow Springs Rd. bridge over DesPlaines River. Home: 429 North Ave Naperville IL 60540 Office: 221 N LaSalle St Room 638 Chicago IL 60601

FOSTER, CLIFTON NEAL, supt. schs.; b. Benedict, Nebr., Feb. 27, 1934; s. John Wesley and Gertrude Natalie (Fredeen) F.; B.A., Nebr. Wesleyan U., 1957; M.Ed., U. Neb., 1963, Ed.D., 1966; m. Marilyn Marie Jensen, Aug. 24, 1962; children—John Wesley, Matthew Jay, Natalie Anne, Halcyon Jean. Tchr., Stromsburg (Nebr.) pub. schs., 1957-59; lectr. Oak Ridge Inst. Nuclear Studies, 1959-60; asso. prof. Eastern Ill. U., Charleston, 1966-70; supt. schs. Woodland Park, Colo., 1970-72, Broken Bow, Nebr., 1972-74, Seward (Nebr.) Pub. Schs., 1974—. Cons. Title I, Sch. Surveys, Nat. Council Accreditation Tchr. Edn. Evaluation Teams, 1970-71; dir. Sandhills Spl. Edn. Coop., 1973-74. Mem. Nebr. Legislature, 1963-65. Served with AUS, 1953-55; Korea. Mem. NEA, Am., Nebr. assns. sch. adminstrs., Assn. for Supervision and Curriculum Devel., Nebr. Council Tchr. Edn. (dir. 1963-65), Neb. Council for Ednl. TV, C. of C. Republican. Methodist (steward 1966-70). Rotarian, Elk. Home: 620 Circle Dr Seward NE 68434 Office: 803 Seward St Seward NE 68434

FOSTER, DOUGLAS L., physician; b. Mar. 3, 1931; B.S., Coll. City N.Y., 1953; M.D., Meharry Med. Coll., 1957; postgrad. Cook County Grad. Sch. Medicine, 1972; married; 3 children. Intern St. Margaret Hosp., Hammond, Ind., 1957-58, asso. attending physician, 1958-61; resident, fellow Menninger Sch. Psychiatry, 1961-64; resident Topeka VA Hosp., 1961-64, Vocat. Rehab. Project Menninger Found., 1962-64; acting dir. Mental Health Center Stone-Brandel Center, Chgo., 1966; practice medicine specializing in psychiatry, Gary, Ind., 1966-67; attending psychiatrist St. Catherine Hosp., East Chicago, Ind., 1966-68; dir. mental health and day hosp. programs Methodist Hosp. Gary, 1968-69; asst. supt. Tinley Park (Ill.) Mental Health Center, 1969-71; clin. dir. Tinley Park Mental Health Center, 1971; individual practice medicine specializing in psychiatry, Chgo., 1971—; chmn. dept. psychiatry Jackson Park Hosp. and Med. Center, Chgo., 1971—; prin. investigator, med. dir. West Side Orgn. Drug Abuse and Rehab. Project, 1971-72; cons. psychiatrist Tabernacle Hosp., Chgo., Palos Heights Community Heights, South Suburban Hosp., Hazel Crest, Ill., South Chgo. Community Hosp.; instr. psychiatry Jefferson Med. Coll., Phila., 1965-66; asst. clin. prof. psychiatry Abraham Lincoln Med. Sch. U. Ill., Chgo., 1966-67, asst. prof., 1967-68, asst. dir. med. sch. tng. program, 1966-68; community prof. Governor State U., 1973—; cons. in field. Mem. Med. Center Complex U. Ill. Med. Center, 1966-68; mem. Gary Mayor's Model Cities Tech.-Adv. Com., 1968-69; chmn. comprehensive research and devel. corp. Mental Health Task Force, 1971-75; mem. Ill. Gov.'s Commn. Revision Mental Code, 1973. Guest speaker Black on Black TV show, 1973. Trustee Jackson Park Hosp. Found. Served to lt. comdr. USNR, 1964-66; lt. Res. Mem. Am. (task force delivery psychiat. services in poverty area 1971—), Ill. psychiat. assns., Am. Ortho-Psychiat. Assn., Ill. A.M.A., Lake County Med. Assn., A.A.U.P., A.A.A.S., Meharry Med. Sch., Menninger Sch. Psychiatry alumni assns., Nat. Med. Assn. Contbr. numerous articles to profl. jours. Home: 134 Graymoor Ln Olympia Fields IL 60461 Office: 7531 Stony Island Ave Chicago IL 60649

FOSTER, EDGAR MURRAY, assn. exec.; b. Grand Rapids, Mich., Aug. 14, 1920; s. Edgar Burral and Anna (Druse) F.; m. Elinor Marianna Spiess, June 29, 1946; children—Laura (Mrs. Dee J. DeLong), Edgar Murray Jr. Exec. dir. United Fund, Indpls., 1950-53, Pitts., 1953-61, Miami, Fla., 1961-63, Boston, 1965-68, Grand Rapids, 1968—; nat. dir. program devel. United Health Founds. Inc., N.Y.C., 1963-64. Served to 1st lt., inf., AUS, 1940-45. Decorated D.S.C., Purple Heart; recipient several civic awards. Mem. Grand Rapids C. of C. Rotarian. Club: Peninsular, University (Grand Rapids); Kent Country. Home: 7750 Leonard St NE Ada MI 49301 Office: 500 Commerce Bldg Grand Rapids MI 49502

FOSTER, EDWIN THOMAS, JR., mfg. co. exec.; b. Benton Harbor, Mich., Dec. 17, 1923; s. Edwin Thomas and Caroline (Klenk) F.; B.S., Mich. State U., 1950; m. Jean Auer, June 26, 1948; children—Judith, Edwin Thomas III. Purchasing mgr. Whirlpool Corp., St. Joseph, Mich., 1950-60; pvt. practice as cons. engr., St. Joseph, 1961-62; with DuWel Metal Products, Inc., Bangor, Mich., 1962—, v.p. mfg., 1969—, also dir. Chmn. fund-raising drives various local charitable orgns. Served with USAAF, 1943-45. Mem. Am. Soc. Agrl. Engrs., Am. Electroplaters Soc., Soc. Die Cast Engrs., Am. Die Casting Inst., Mich. Water Pollution Control Assn., Am. Legion. Mason. Club: Mich. State University Alumni. Contbr. articles, patentee in field. Home: Box 441 Route 3 South Haven MI 49090 Office: Box 160 Bangor MI 49013

FOSTER, F. BLANCHE, librarian; b. Centerville, Tenn., Jan. 6, 1919; d. George and F. Blanche (Nunnelly) Foster; B.S., Tenn. State U., 1940; B.L.S., Atlanta U., 1947; A.M. in Library Sci., U. Mich., 1953. Librarian, prof. Sam Huston Coll., Austin, Tex., 1947-50; librarian, lectr. Detroit Pub. Schs., 1951-70; lectr. U. Ibadan (Nigeria), 1971-73; librarian South Vigo High Sch., Terre Haute, Ind., 1974—. Chmn., Martin Luther King Jr. Day, Terre Haute, 1975—. Mem. ALA, Am. Fedn. Tchrs., YWCA, NAACP. Author: Kenya, 1969; Dahomey, 1971; The West Indies, 1976. Home: 2239 Spruce St Terre Haute IN 47807 Office: 3737 7th St S Terre Haute IN 47802

FOSTER, GERALD A., psychologist; b. Aug. 31, 1928; B.S. in History, U. Wis., Stevens Point, 1955; M.A. in Guidance Counseling, U. Mich., 1960; Ed.D., Ariz. State U., 1963. Secondary sch. tchr. Oconto (Wis.) Bd. Edn., 1955-59; asso. prof. psychology and edn. Ind. State U., Terre Haute, 1962-65; mgr. guidance, counseling and psychol. services Job Corps Center, Westinghouse Mgmt. Services, Inc., Edinburg, Ind., 1965-66; program dir. for adult basic edn. U.S. Office Edn., Nat. U. Extension Assn., Washington, 1966-68; asso. dir., div. edn. and tng. Avco Econ. Systems Corp., Washington, 1968-69; psychol. cons. to mgmt. Rohrer, Hibler & Replogle, Boston, 1969-70; psychologist, E.E.O. officer C.N. Flagg & Co., Inc., Meriden, Conn., 1970-76; self employed cons. in counseling and psychology, 1976—. Served with U.S. Army, 1946-48, 50-51. Address: U Mich 3200 Student Activities Bldg Ann Arbor MI 48109

FOSTER, JAMES HADLEI, clergyman, educator; b. Valdosta, Ga., Apr. 29, 1938; s. Arthur and Willie Mae (Wright) F.; B.A., Morris Brown Coll., 1960; postgrad. Boston U., 1961-62, Carnegie-Mellon U., summer 1965, Chgo. Grad. Sch. Theology, summers 1964, 65, Tulane U., summer 1966, Pitts. Theol. Sem., 1969-70, Vanderbilt U.; M.Div., United Theol. Sem., 1974; L.H.D. (hon.), Union Bapt. Coll., 1971; m. Bessie Mae Johnson, Aug. 5, 1962; 1 son, James II. Chaplain to migrants Mass. Council Chs., Boston, summers 1962, 63; chaplain Albany (Ga.) State Coll., 1962-66; chaplain Alcorn A. and M. Coll., Lorman, Miss., 1966-67; asst. to vis. tchr., dir. social services Head Start Program, Valdosta City Sch. System, 1967-69; asst. to pastor St. James African M.E. Ch., Pitts., 1969-71; asso. dir. Christian Assos. Met. Erie (Pa.), 1970-72; chaplain, instr. philosophy Wilberforce (Ohio) U., 1972—. Adviser, Conf. com. Ind. Newman Found., 1974—. Mem. Community Hosp. Found., Springfield, Ohio, 1974—. Mem. Am., Ohio philos. assns., Ministry to Blacks in Higher Edn., Commn. on Higher Edn. Religion Studies Ohio. Home: 1848 Commonwealth Dr Xenia OH 45385 Office: Office of Chaplain Wilberforce U Wilberforce OH 45384

FOSTER, JOHN WILLARD, optometrist; b. Black River Falls, Wis., Sept. 5, 1925; s. Leo W. and Martha (Dietsche) F.; student U. Minn., 1943-48; B.S., Pacific U., 1951, Dr. Optometry, 1953; m. Dolores Schlaeger, Sept. 3, 1949; children—John, Jeffrey, Gregory, Gary, Mark. Practice optometry, Thorp, Wis., 1953—, Owen, Wis., 1957—, also Neillsville, Wis., Mem. Am. Optometric Found., Optometric Extension program. Mem. Am., Wis. optometric assns., Illuminiating Engring. Soc. (asso. mem.) Minn. Fedn. Engring. Socs., Blue Key, Omega Delta. K.C., Lion (pres., dir., chmn. visually handicapped childrens com.). Address: Box 31 Neillsville WI 54456

FOSTER, LOUIE J., optometrist; b. Williamston, Mich., Jan. 30, 1926; s. Louie J. and Lula Marguerite (Peacock) F.; student Hillsdale Coll., 1949-50; O.D., So. Coll. Optometry, 1954; m. Lois Faye Cayce, Nov. 27, 1959; children—Bradley Brian, Barbara Faye. Practice optometry, Jonesville, Mich., 1955—. Mem. City Council, 1961-65. Served with USAF, 1944-46. Mem. Omega Delta. Mason (master 1964-66), Rotarian (pres., 1971- 72). Home: 494 Parkwood St Jonesville MI 49250 Office: 211 Harley St Jonesville MI 49250

FOSTER, LOWELL WALTER, elec. co. exec.; b. Mpls., Oct. 22, 1919; s. Walter James and Ferne Constance (Edmunds) F.; grad. USCG Acad., 1944; student U. Minn., 1950, Mpls. Inst. Arts, 1953; m. Marion Jane Bjorklund, Feb. 5, 1944; children—Michael Lowell, Janette Marie, John Edward. With Honeywell, Inc., Mpls., 1946-77, successively tool designer, lead tool designer, asst. supr. tool design., lead standardization engr., sr. standardization engr., prin. standardization engr., project adminstr., sr. project adminstr., dir. corporate standardization services, dir. corp. standardization, 1974-77, dir. industry standards, 1977; pres. Tech. Concepts and Engring. Internat., 1977—; adviser drafting curriculum Mpls. Pub. Schs., 1973—; engring. cons.; tech. adviser Ferris State Coll., Big Rapids, Mich., 1970—. Active Viking council Boy Scouts Am., 1956-59, 73-77; v.p. John Ericsson Sch. P.T.A., 1971—. Bd. dirs. Am. Nat. Standards Inst. Served with USCG, 1941-46; PTO. Fellow Standards Engrs. Soc. (Leo B. Moore award 1973, Distinguished Service award Minn. sect. 1970); mem. Internat. Standards Orgn., Soc. Mfg. Engrs., Air Conditioning and Refrigeration Inst., Soc. for Advancement Mgmt., Honeywell Engrs. Club (past pres.), Am. Legion, Author 12 books, numerous articles. Home: 3120 E 45th St Minneapolis MN 55406 Office: Tech Concepts and Engring Internat Minneapolis MN 55406

FOUNTAIN, DONALD REX, farm equipment co. exec.; b. Sioux City, Iowa, Feb. 6, 1926; s. Rex Ira and Doris Giehm Fountain; B.S., Morningside Coll., Sioux City, 1948; m. Carol Jean Corrie, June 5, 1948; children—Nancy Ann, Dee, Julia, Rex. Partsman, salesman Rex Fountain, Sloan, Iowa, 1948-59; mgr., pres. Fountain's Inc., Beresford, S.D., 1959—; pres. DCR Leasing Co. Inc., Beresford; dir. Beresford Devel. Corp. Served with U.S. Navy, 1944-46. Mem. U.S., Beresford Chambers Commerce, U.S. Livestock Feeders Assn., Am. Legion, Retail Farm Equipment Assn. of S.D. and Minn. Congregationalist. Clubs: Lions, Shriners. Home: 400 S 13th St Beresford SD 57004 Office: W Hwy 46 Beresford SD 57004

FOURIE, LOUIS V., dentist; b. Molteno, Republic of South Africa, Nov. 13, 1923; s. Louis P. and Gertruida (Vanderwalt) F.; student U. Witwatersrand, 1941-42; D.D.S., U. Mich., 1949; m. Margaret S. More, Sept. 17, 1949; children—Jaime Margaret, Leslie Ann. Came to U.S., 1945, naturalized, 1954. Gen. practice dentistry, Ann Arbor, Mich., 1949-50, Park Ridge, Ill., 1950-52, Cape Town, South Africa, 1952-53, Rockford, Ill., 1955—. Bd. counselors Rockford Coll. Served with Dental Corps, AUS, 1953-55. Fellow Internat. Coll. Dentists; mem. Acad. Gen. Dentistry, ADA (ho. of dels.), Ill. (exec. council, pres.), Winnebago County (pres. 1966) dental socs., Pierre Fauchard Acad., Federation Dentaire Internationale, Delta Sigma Delta. Rotarian (Rockford). Home: 4544 Georgian Trail Rockford IL 61103 Office: 2623 Charles St Rockford IL 61108

FOURNIER, SERGE RAYMOND-JEAN, orch. condr.; b. Mayet, France, Sept. 28, 1931; s. Raymond and Genevieve (Brisset) F.; came to U.S., 1961, naturalized, 1969; grad. Conservatoire Nat. Superieur de Musique, Paris, 1956; student Berkshire Music Center, 1961-62, Friedelind Wagner's Master Class, Beyreuth, Ger., 1963; D.F.A., U. Toledo, 1974. Flutist, Lamoureux Orch., France, 1958-60; condr. Compagnie Madeleine Renaud and Jean Louis Barrault, Theatre de France, 1960; asst. to Leonard Bernstein, condr. N.Y. Philharmonic Orch., 1962, 63; music dir., condr. Toledo Symphony Orch., 1964—; guest appearances Radio Diffusion and Television Française, Paris, 1963, Orch. Grand Casino de Vichy, 1957, 58, Berkshire Music Festival, 1961; guest condr. in Europe, U.S., Mexico City, Japan and Can. Served in French Army, 1952-54. Recipient Première Medaille de Solfège, 1948, Premier Prix de Flute, 1949, Premier Prix d'Histoire de la Musique, 1951, Premier Prix d'Ensemble Instrumental, 1952, Premier Prix de Direction d'Orchestre, 1956, Deuxième accessit de Contrepoint, 1956, Koussevitzky Meml. Conducting prize, 1961; named One of Ten Outstanding Young Men, Toledo C. of C., 1965. Licensed comml. pilot FAA. Club: Rotary. Home: 640 N Lallendorf Rd Oregon OH 43616 Office: Toledo Symphony Orch One Stranahan Sq Toledo OH 43604

FOUST, PAUL JOHN, clergyman; b. Hillsdale, Mich., June 16, 1920; s. Ray A. and Louise (Baerlin) F.; student Hillsdale Coll., 1938-39; B.D., Concordia Sem., 1945; m. Virginia M. Mahrley, Feb. 3, 1945; children—Paul, Caroline Foust Jakubcin, Susan, Gretchen Foust Beattie. Ordained to ministry Lutheran Ch., Seattle, 1945; minister chs., Seattle, 1945-46, Milan, Mich., 1946-54, Albion, Mich., 1954-61, Detroit, 1961-66; minister Greenfield Ch., Peace Ch., Battle

Creek, Mich., 1966-69; exec. sec. stewardship and evangelism Mich. dist. Luth. Ch. Mo. Synod, Ann Arbor, 1969—. Home: 1807 Huron River Dr Ypsilanti MI 48197 Office: 3773 Geddes Rd Ann Arbor MI 48105

FOWLER, DONN NORMAN, dentist; b. Denver, June 7, 1922; s. Roy Eugene and Vera Louise (Alderson) F.; B.S., Northwestern U., 1945, D.D.S., 1953; m. Charlotte Jean Goff, Mar. 18, 1944; children—Donna Jean (Mrs. Donald J. McLoughlin), Linda (Mrs. Malcolm Cardy), Charles R., Peter N., Paul R. Gen. practice dentistry, Glenview, Ill., 1953—; instr. Coll. Dentistry, Northwestern U., Chgo., 1953-55. Trustee, Kendall Coll., Evanston, Ill. Served to lt. (j.g.) USNR, 1943-46; PTO. Mem. Pierre Fauchard Acad., Acad. Gen. Dentistry, Am. Dental Assn., Chgo. Dental Soc., North Suburban Acad. Dental Research (past pres.), Glenview C. of C., Pi Kappa Alpha. Methodist (lay del. to ann. conf.). Kiwanian. Home: 1548 Maple Ave Northbrook IL 60062 Office: 1761 River Dr Glenview IL 60025

FOWLER, LUCY BARR (MRS. CHARLES WORTHINGTON FOWLER II), occupational therapist; b. Allentown, Pa., Feb. 19, 1932; d. William Bryce and Lucy Agnes (Chaundy) Barr; B.S. in Phys. Edn., Pa. State U., 1953; certificate occupational therapy U. Pa., 1956; m. Charles Worthington Fowler II, July 21, 1956; children—Charles Worthington III, Ellen Bryce, Timothy Neville. Staff occupational therapist, recreation dir. Palo Verde Psychiat. Hosp., Tucson, 1965-66; staff occupational therapist Neb. Psychiat. Inst.-U. Nebr. Med. Center, Omaha, 1970-72; dir. occupational therapy Island of Hope Alcoholic Rehab. and Research Center, Omaha, 1973-76, Douglas County (Nebr.) Community Mental Health Center, Omaha, 1977—; mental retardation and nursing home cons. Costume chmn., designer Omaha Ballet Soc.; costumer Creighton U. Dance Co., 1971-75; active (dir.) Omaha Ballet Guild. Omaha Symphony Guild, Omaha Symphonic Chorus, Opera Angels, Omaha Assistance League (charter mem.). Certified profl. alcoholism counselor, Nebr. Mem. Am., Nebr. (treas., finance chmn. 1972-74, editor newsletter 1978) occupational therapy assns., World Fedn. Occupational Therapists, Nat. Rehab. Assn., Nat. Assn. Alcoholism Counselors, Nebr. Assn. Alcoholism Counselors, Alcohol and Drug Problems Assn. Am., DAR, St. Andrews Scottish Soc., Audubon Soc., (rec. sec.), Chi Omega (alumnae v.p. 1973-74). Republican. Epsicopalian. Clubs: Regency Lake and Tennis (Omaha); Gavin's Point Yacht (Yankton, S.D.). Home: 1329 S 93d St Omaha NE 68124 Office: 711 N 21st St Omaha NE 68102

FOWLER, WILLIAM EDWARD, JR., lawyer; b. Pitts., April 20, 1919; s. William Edward and Helen (Kerr) F.; grad. Phillips Exeter Acad., 1938; B.S., Yale, 1942; J.D., U. Mich., 1948; m. Jean Louise Moore, Apr. 24, 1943; children—Mary Jane, John Moore, William Edward III, James Kerr. Admitted to Ohio bar, 1948; asso. firm Harrington, Huxley & Smith, Youngstown, Ohio, 1948-55, partner, 1956—. Mem. Ohio Bd. Bar Examiners, 1965-70. Active Youngstown Community Chest and other fund drives. Mem. Boardman Local Sch. Dist. Bd. Edn., 1960-76. Mem. Yale Alumni Bd., 1958-71. Served as lt. (s.g.), USNR, World War II. Mem. Am., Ohio (council of dels.; mem. exec. com. 1963-66), Mahoning County (sec.-treas. 1956-58) bar assns. Pa.-Ohio Yale Alumni Assn. (pres.). Home: 50 Forest Hill Youngstown OH 44512 Office: Mahoning Bank Bldg Youngstown OH 44503

FOX, ALAN HUGO, woodwind instruments mfg. co. exec.; b. Chgo., Apr. 1, 1934; s. Hugo E. and Mary M. (Richter) F.; B.S. in Chem. Engring., Purdue U., 1955; m. Pamela Michue, June 13, 1964; 1 dau., Karen Ann. Sales coordinator Procon, Inc., Des Plaines, Ill., 1957-60; v.p., gen. mgr. Fox Products Corp., designer profl. bassoons and contrabassoons, South Whitley, Ind., 1960-69, pres., 1970—. Served to 1st lt. AUS, 1955-57. Club: Wawasee Sailing (commodore 1972) (Lake Wawasee, Ind.). Home: Rural Route 1 South Whitley IN 46787 Office: RFD 1 South Whitley IN 46787

FOX, BARRY LEE, electronics co. exec.; b. Youngstown, Ohio, Sept. 7, 1945; s. Melvin R. and Barbara Z. (Levy) F.; B.S., U. Ill., 1970; postgrad. No. Ill. U., 1977; m. Joyce P. Fosco, Apr. 18, 1971; 1 son, Edward Frank. Quality control engr. Cinch Connectors div. TRW, Elk Grove Village, Ill., 1976-77, quality control mgr. Lunt facility, 1977—. Served to lt. j.g. USN, 1970-76. Mem. Am. Soc. Quality Control. Jewish. Club: Lions. Home: 795 Brandywine Dr Roselle IL 60172 Office: 1501 Morse Ave Elk Grove Village IL 60007

FOX, BYRON LESTER, health orgn. exec.; b. Toledo, Jan. 7, 1906; s. Ammon Lester and Josephine (Krieghaum) F.; B.A., B.S., Ohio State U., 1928, M.A., 1930, Ph.D., 1947; m. Nancy Littell, Dec. 5, 1966; 1 dau. by previous marriage, Caroline Jo (Mrs. Jack E. Heck). Tchr. English, Berea (Ohio) High Sch., 1928-29; asst. prof. sociology and econs. Bethany (W.Va.) Coll., 1932-36; asst. prof. sociology and anthropology Ohio Wesleyan U., Delaware, 1936-40; field supr. Nat. Youth Adminstrn., Cleve., 1940-42; personnel and adminstrv. officer Office for Emergency Mgmt., Cleve., 1942-44, U.S. Dept. State, Washington, 1944-46; adviser on social sci. Div. Internat. Exchange of Persons, Washington, 1946-47; asso. prof. sociology Syracuse (N.Y.) U., 1947-65; prof. sociology No. Ariz. U., Flagstaff, 1965-67; prof., chmn. dept. sociology and anthropology Carleton Coll., Northfield, Minn., 1967-71; regional dir. S.W. Nebr. Health Edn. Services, Inc., McCook, 1973—. Pres. Onondaga Consumers Coop., Inc., Syracuse, 1949-52. Fellow Am. Sociol. Assn.; mem. A.A.U.P., Am. Assn. Ret. Persons, Midwest, Eastern sociol. socs., Soc. for the Study of Social Problems (pres. 1957-58). Democrat. Episcopalian. Contbr. articles to profl. jours. Home: 907 2d E McCook NE 69001 Office: 1205 3rd E McCook NE 69001

FOX, CAROL, opera producer; b. Chgo., June 15, 1926; d. George Edward and Virginia (Scott) Fox; grad Girls Latin Sch., Chgo.; pvt. voice studies with Giovanni Martinelli, Edith Mason, Vittorio Trevisan, Virgilio Lazzari, also studies in Italy; Mus D. (hon.) Chgo. Conservatory, 1955; LL.D., Rosary Coll., 1958; m. C. Larkin Flanagan, June 22, 1957; 1 dau., Victoria. Founder Lyric Theatre of Chgo. (became Lyric Opera of Chgo.), 1952, pres., gen. mgr., 1952-56, gen. mgr., 1956—. Decorated Cavaliere al Merito della Repubblica Italiana, 1956; 1st season presented 1954. Mem. Chgo. Jr. League. Home: 220 E Walton Pl Chicago IL 60611 Office: 20 N Wacker Dr Chicago IL 60601

FOX, CHARLES EPHRAIM, bus. exec.; b. Bronxville, N.Y., Aug. 22, 1922; s. Charles E. and Kathryn (Umstad) F.; B.A., Dartmouth, 1946; M.B.A., Stanford, 1948; m. Rosemary Quinn, 1959; children—Elizabeth, Charles Ephraim. Govt. relations specialist Arabian Am. Oil Co., Dhahran, Saudi Arabia, 1946-48; gen. asst. to pres. Winchester Electronics, Inc., Norwalk, Conn., 1948-57; internat. exec. recruitment cons. Booz, Allen & Hamilton, Inc., Chgo., 1957-64; pres. Billington, Fox & Ellis, Inc., Chgo., 1964—. Trustee Jane Adams Hull House, Chgo. Presbyn. Clubs: Bath and Tennis (Lake Bluff, Ill.); Union League, Stanford and Dartmouth Alumni, Metropolitan (Chgo.). Home: 1467 Conway St Lake Forest IL 60045

FOX, GERALD EDWIN, surgeon; b. Watseka, Ill., Jan. 22, 1941; s. Willis Orville and Hazel Amelia (Bowen) F.; B.S., Bradley U., 1964; M.D., U. Ill., 1966; m. Juline Carol Duis, Sept. 6, 1964; children—Charlene Deanne, Bryan Joseph, Cynthia Marie. Intern, St. Francis Hosp., Peoria, Ill., 1966-67; resident in gen. surgery William Beaumont Hosp., Royal Oak, Mich., 1969-73, chief surg. resident, 1972-73; attending surgeon Good Samaritain Hosp., So. Ill. Clinic, Mt. Vernon, Ill., 1973—. Served with USAF, 1967-69. Mem. AMA, A.C.S., Am. Trauma Soc., Am. Soc. Abdominal Surgeons. Lutheran. Office: 1 Doctors Park Rd Mt Vernon IL 62864

FOX, HENRY RONALD, librarian; b. Valentine, Nebr., Apr. 12, 1938; s. U. Wesley and Margaret Z. (Manifold) F.; B.A., Nebr. Wesleyan U., 1962; postgrad. Kearney State Coll., 1965-67; M.L.S., U. Okla., 1967-68. Reference librarian Wayne (Nebr.) State Coll., 1968-71; chief librarian VA Hosp., Grand Island, Nebr., 1971—. Mem. Am., Nebr. Med., library assns., Employees Assn. VA Hosp., YMCA. Republican. United Methodist. Mason (Shriner); mem. Order Eastern Star. Club: Kiwanis (dir.). Home: 112 W 16th St Grand Island NE 68801 Office: Library VA Hosp Grand Island NE 68801

FOX, JOHN JAY, JR., architect, engr.; b. Chgo., June 21, 1919; s. John Jay and Ellen Sarah (McCotter) F.; B.S. in Architecture, Armour Inst. Tech., 1940; m. Lorraine Whalen, Feb. 5, 1949; children—John Jay, Michael, James, Marguerite, Colleen, Daniel. Partner firm Fox and Fox, Chgo., 1946—; mem. com. on standards and tests, City of Chgo., 1964—. Trustee Bros. of the Good Shepherd, Inc., 1971—; mem. alumni bd. Ill. Inst. Tech., 1973-75; mem. bd. dirs. (hon.) Cardinal Stritch Found., 1967—. Registered architect, Ill., Wis., Ind., N.Y., Minn.; profl. engr., Ill. Mem. Ill. Soc. Architects (dir. 1972-75; v.p., 1976—), Delta Tau Delta. Clubs: Beverly Country, Grand Beach, K.C. Recipient award of Merit, Triton Coll., 1969. Home: 9900 S Longwood Dr Chicago IL 60643 Office: 11 S LaSalle St Chicago IL 60603

FOX, LARRY EUGENE, computer specialist; b. Columbus, Ohio, Jan. 6, 1942; s. Donald Norman and Frances (Grile) F.; student Capital U., 1971—; m. Ellen Catherine Spires, Nov. 28, 1963; children—Christopher Allen, Jeffrey Michael, Karen Michelle, Kathleen Elizabeth. With Rockwell Internat. Corp., Columbus, 1961-69, 70—, computer programmer, 1965-69, sr. programmer, analyst, 1970—; cons. programmer, analyst E. Ralph Sims Jr. & Assos., Lancaster, Ohio, 1969-70. Instr. data processing concepts Automation Inst., Columbus, 1966. Mem. Am. Mgmt. Assn., Data Processing Mgmt. Assn., Assn. Systems Mgmt. Home: 2048 Wadsworth Dr Columbus OH 43227 Office: Rockwell Internat Corp Columbus Aircraft Div 4300 E 5th Ave D-92 B-6 Columbus OH 43216

FOX, LAWRENCE MARTIN, veterinarian; b. Chgo., Feb. 26, 1946; s. Alexander Louis and Annette (Singer) F.; B.S., U. Ill., 1966, D.V.M., 1968; m. Carlina Mary Renzy, Mar. 18, 1967; children—Kevin Lawrence, Brandon Douglas, Robin Christopher. Practice vet. medicine, Chgo., 1970-72, River Grove Ill., 1972—; dir. Elmwood-Grove Animal Hosp., Ltd., River Grove, 1972—; treas., dir. Oak Park (Ill.) Village Humane Soc., 1974-76. Served as capt. Vet. Corps, U.S. Army, 1968-70. Mem. Am., Ill. State, Chgo. vet. med. assns., Am. Animal Hosp. Assn., Chgo. Zool. Soc., Mensa. Unitarian. Club: River Grove Lions (lion tamer, tail twister, dir. 1972—). Contbr. articles to profl. jours., 1968—. Home: 1200 Franklin Ave River Forest IL 60305 Office: 8035 Grand Ave River Grove IL 60171

FOX, LILBORN LOWELL, JR., veterinarian; b. Albuquerque, July 2, 1945; s. Lilborn Lowell and Imogene Harriet (Diedrich) F.; B.S. in Agr., U. Mo., 1967, D.V.M., 1969; m. Janice Carole Pederson, Mar. 31, 1977. Foreman, Platte County (Mo.) Weed Control, 1965, 66, 67; vet. trainee U.S. Dept. Agr., Jefferson City, Mo., 1968; resident vet. intern U. Mo., Columbia, 1968-69; Mo. dist. veterinarian Animal Health div. U.S. Dept. Agr., Parkville, 1969-73; pvt. practice vet. medicine Kansas City (Mo.) Stockyards, 1973-74, Parkville, Mo., 1974—; operator small livestock farm, Parkville, 1969—; owner Platte County Livestock Auction, Platte City, Mo., 1977—. Mem. adv. bd. Platte County Citizens Against Annexation, 1970. Mem. Am., Mo. vet. med. assns., Am., Mo. (sec.-treas. 1975—) simmental assns. Home: RFD 27 Parkville MO 64153

FOX, NOEL PETER, fed. judge; b. Kalamazoo, Aug. 30, 1910; s. Charles K. and Caroline C. (Kokx) F.; Ph.B., Marquette U., 1933, J.D., 1935; m. Dorothy Ann McCormick, Aug. 1, 1934; children—Maureen, Noel Joseph, Virginia Lynn. Admitted to Wis. bar, 1935, Mich. bar, 1935, also U.S. Supreme Ct.; asso. firm Bunker & Rogoski, 1935-39, Fox & Beers, 1945-49; pvt. practice, 1935-44, 46-51; asst. pros. atty., Muskegon County, 1937-39; circuit judge 14th Jud. Circuit of Mich., 1951-62; U.S. dist. judge Western Dist. Mich., 1962—, chief U.S. dist. judge, 1971—. Mem. faculty Fed. Jud. Center for Seminars for Newly Apptd. Dist. Judges, 1970-72. Served with USNR, World War II. Mem. Mich. Judges Assn. (past pres.), State Bar Mich. (past chmn. ct. adminstrn. com.), Nat. Jesuit Scholastic and Hon. Soc., Fed., Am., Muskegon, Grand Rapids bar assns., Jud. Conf. Com. Trial Practice and Techniques. Am. Judicature Soc. Office: 416 Federal Bldg 110 Michigan St NW Grand Rapids MI 49503

FOX, PAUL FABIAN, surgeon; b. Chilton, Wis., Jan. 28, 1911; s. Leo Patrick and Pauline Adelaide (Hanert) F.; B.S., U. Notre Dame, 1931; M.D., Loyola U., Chgo., 1934; m. Mardie Elizabeth Stevens, Nov. 28, 1936; children—Elizabeth, Paul, Alice, James Sheila (Mrs. William McLaughlin), Lawrence. Intern, Cook County Hosp., Chgo., 1934-36; resident surgery Children's Meml. Hosp., Chgo., 1951-52; practice medicine, specializing in surgery Chgo., 1937—; attending staff Cook County hosp., Chgo., Loyola Med. Center, Chgo., 1937—; dir. surgery St. Anne's Children's Meml. hosp.; clin. prof. surgery Loyola U. Med. Sch., Chgo., 1969—, acting chmn. dept. surgery, 1969-70. Bd. dirs. Suburban Cook County Tb Dist., 1965-68. Diplomate Am. Bd. Surgery. Fellow A.C.S.; mem. Chgo. (pres. Aux Plaines br. 1952), Ill. med. socs., Chgo. (pres. 1966), Ill., surg. socs., AMA, Central, Western surg. assns., Inst. Medicine Chgo., Soc. Surgery Gastrointestinal Tract, Alpha Omega Alpha. Roman Catholic. Contbr. articles profl. publs. Home: 1046 Monroe Ave River Forest IL 60305 Office: 6710 W North Ave Chicago IL 60635

FOX, PETER, legislator; b. Yugoslavia, May 31, 1921; s. George and Marie (Moldovan) F.; student United Coll., 1948-49, U. Man., 1949-51; m. Nancy Grant, May 28, 1948; children—Donald Peter, Kenneth George, Elaine Marie. Stationary engr. Can. Packers, Winnipeg, Man., 1942—; 1st v.p. Winnipeg and Dist. Labour Council, 1964-69; dir. Man. Hydro Co., 1969-71; v.p. Local 216, Canadian Food and Allied Workers, 1960-69; dir. Indsl. Devel. Bd. Greater Winnipeg, 1965-71; mem. Man. Legis. Assembly, 1966—, speaker, 1971—. Mem. adv. bd. Nat. Employment Service for Prairie Region. Served with Royal Winnipeg Rifles, 1943-46. Decorated Can. medal; France-Germany star; 1939-45 medal; Can. Centennial medal, Canadian Vol. medal and clasp, Canadian Commonwealth medal. Mem. Canadian Food and Allied Workers Assn., Royal Canadian Legion, Army, Navy, Air Force Vets. Assn., Commonwealth Parliamentary Assn. (pres. Man. div.). Club: Canadian German. Home: 116 Pike Crescent Winnipeg MB Canada Office: 244 Legislative Bldg Winnipeg MB Canada

FOX, RONALD BOWEN, dentist; b. nr. Binghamton, N.Y., Jan. 15, 1909; s. Edwin Charles and Cecelia (Cooley) F.; A.B., Hope Coll., 1932; D.D.S., U. Mich., 1935, M.S. in Pub. Health, 1939, M.S. in Prosthodontics, 1956; m. Marion Gertrude Katte, Sept. 16, 1936; children—John Peter, James Edwin, Robert Cooley, Mary Vyn, William Evans. Practice dentistry, specializing in restorative dentistry, Ann Arbor, Mich., 1940—; mem. staff St. Joseph's Mercy Hosp., Ann Arbor. Cons. Mich. Crippled Childrens Commn., 1958—. Inst. rep. Portage Trails council Boy Scouts Am., 1946-50; mem. scout com. P.T.A., Ann Arbor, 1946-50. Mem. Am. Dental Assn., Am. Prosthodontic Soc., Francis B. Vedder Soc., Richard H. Kingery Prosthetic Club, Russell W. Bunting Periodontic Study Club. Republican. Episcopalian. Club: Ann Arbor Garden. Address: 400 Maynard St Ann Arbor MI 48108

FOX, RONALD ERNEST, clin. psychologist; b. Conover, N.C., May 11, 1936; s. Fred Yount and Carolyn Victoria (Weeks) F.; A.B., U. N.C., 1958, M.A., 1961, Ph.D., 1962; m. Margaret Elizabeth Smith, Dec. 27, 1956; children—Kelley Victoria, Brett Anthony, Jonathan Eric. Asst. prof. dept. psychiatry and psychology U. N.C., 1963-68; asso. prof. dept. psychiatry and psychology Ohio State U., 1968-74, prof., 1974—, coordinator edn. and tng. dept. psychiatry, 1968—, dir. Family Therapy Clinic, Ohio State U. Med. Sch., 1970—; dean Sch. Profl. Psychology, Wright State U., 1977—; cons. Midwest Career Devel. Center, Columbus. Diplomate Am. Bd. Profl. Psychology. Fellow Am. Psychol. Assn.; mem. Ohio Psychol. Assn., Am. Acad. Psychotherapists, Am. Soc. Psychologists in Pvt. Practice, Assn. Psychology Internship Centers. Club: Worthington Community Theater. Author: (with others) Patients View Their Psychotherapy, 1968; (with others) Abnormal Psychology, 1972; contbr. articles to sci., profl. jours. Home: 572 Lambourne Ave Worthington OH 43085 Office: Dept Psychiatry Ohio State U Med Sch Columbus OH 43210

FOX, SHAYLE PHILLIP, lawyer; b. Chgo., July 20, 1934; s. Charles and Beatrice (Chazin) F.; B.S. with high honors, U. Ill., 1954; J.D., DePaul U., 1957; m. Deanna Fingersh, May 30, 1959; children—Sara, Leslie, Anthony. Admitted to Ill. bar, 1957; since practiced in Chgo.; partner firm Fox & Grove, Chgo., 1965—. Vice pres., dir. Young Peoples div. Jewish United Fund Chgo., 1965-74. Bd. dirs. Schwab Rehab. Hosp., Chgo.; bd. dirs. Jewish Community Center Chgo., 1977—. Served with AUS, 1958. C.P.A., Ill. Mem. Ill. C. of C., Chgo. Assn. Commerce and Industry, Chgo., Ill., Am. bar assns., Am. Judicature Soc., Ill. Soc. C.P.A.'s. Home: One Rockgate Ln Glencoe IL 60022 Office: Suite 7818 Sears Tower 233 S Wacker Dr Chicago IL 60606

FOX, THEODORE ALBERT, orthopaedic surgeon; b. Chgo., Feb. 16, 1913; s. Albert and Jennie (Friedman) F.; B.S., U. Chgo., 1933, M.D., 1937; m. Marcella Schaeffer, June 14, 1936; children—Susan, Nancy. Intern, Cook County Hosp., 1937-39, fellow in pathology, 1939, resident in fractures, 1939-40; in gen. surgery Mt. Sinai Hosp., N.Y.C., 1940-41; in orthopaedic surgery U. Ill., 1945-47; practice medicine specializing in orthopaedic surgery, 1947—; asso. prof. orthopaedic surgery U. Ill., 1950—; attending orthopaedic surgeon Ill. Masonic Med. Center, 1949—, chmn. orthopaedic sect., 1970—. med. dir. Center for Sports Medicine, 1975—; orthopaedic surgeon Chgo. Bears Football Club, 1947—; chmn. subcom. on athletic injuries of Chgo. Com. on Trauma, A.C.S., 1970-75. Served with USNR, 1941-46. Fellow A.C.S., Am. Acad. Orthopaedic Surgeon; mem AMA, Chgo. Med. Soc., AAAS, Assn. Am. Med. Colls., Clin. Orthopaedic Soc., Am. Med. Writers Assn., Latin Am. Soc. Orthopaedic and Traumatology, Interstate Orthopaedic Soc., MW Orthopaedic Soc., Am. Geriatric Soc., Pan Am. Med. Assn., Ill. Soc. Med. Research. Club: Briarwood Country (Deerfield, Ill.). Contbr. articles, chpts. to med. jours. and texts. Home: 1170 Oak St Winnetka IL 60093 Office: 836 Wellington Chicago IL 60657

FOY, DONALD FRANCIS, med. assn. exec.; b. N.Y.C., Apr. 11, 1932; s. John Aloysius and Margaret Teresa (Thompson) F.; B.S., Loyola U. at Los Angeles, 1956; M.S., U. So. Calif., 1962; M.P.H. (USPHS fellow), U. Calif. at Los Angeles, 1967; m. Frances Mary O'Donnell, Aug. 13, 1960; children—Brian, Anne Marie, John, Donald Francis. Mgmt. trainee Western Electric Co., Los Angeles, 1957-59; tchr. Los Angeles City Schs., 1960-64; asso. dir. Lawton Sch. Med. and Dental Assts., Beverly Hills, Calif., 1967-71; dir. dept. health manpower A.M.A., Chgo., 1971-72, dir. mgmt. services div., 1972-75; exec. dir. Ind. State Med. Assn., Indpls., 1976—. Pres. Westlake Town Home Owners Assn., 1973-74; commr. Bloomingdale (Ill.) Bd. Fire and Police Commrs., 1973-74. Served with USAF, 1951-52, USPHS, 1967-71. Fellow Am. Pub. Health Assn.; mem. Am. Soc. Assn. Execs., Am. Assn. Med. Soc. Execs., Loyola U. Alumni Assn., U. So. Cal. Alumni Assn., Republican. Clubs: Woodland Country, Royal Dublin Golf, Columbia. Coordinator medicare study requested by U.S. Senate Finance Com. Author: A Textbook for Medical Assistants, 1967; A Comprehensive Review for the Medical Assistant, 1971. Home: 5242 Rucker Circle Indianapolis IN 46250 Office: 3935 N Meridian St Indianapolis IN 46208

FOYE, THOMAS HAROLD, lawyer; b. Rapid City, S.D., Nov. 23, 1930; s. Harold Herbert and Jean (McCormick) F.; B.S., Creighton U., 1952; LL.B., Georgetown U., 1955; m. Laurene, Aug. 7, 1972. Admitted to Fed. bar, 1956, S.D. bar, 1955; trial atty. U.S. Dept. of Justice, tax div., Washington, 1955-58; practiced in Rapid City, S.D., 1958—; mem. firm Bangs, McCullen, Butler, 1958-59, Bangs, McCullen, Butler, Foye, & Simmons and predecessor firm, 1960—. Lectr. Continuing Legal Edn. Programs, State Bar S.D., Heart of Am. Tax Inst., Kansas City, Mo. Fund dir. chmn. Am. Cancer Soc., Rapid City, S.D., 1959-61, dir., 1961-68; mem. adv. group to Commr. Internal Revenue, 1973-74. Sec., dir. Black Hills Sports, Inc., 1960-69. Mem. Am., S.D., Pennington County (pres. 1962) bar assns., Delta Sigma Pi, Phi Delta Phi, Alpha Sigma Nu. Home: Canyon Lake Heights Route 4 Box 1026 Rapid City SD 57701 Office: PO Box 2670 818 St Joseph St Rapid City SD 57709

FRACKELTON, WILLIAM HAMILTON, surgeon, educator; b. Milw., Apr. 5, 1911; s. Albert Goodrich and Grace Lancing (Hamilton) F.; M.D., Harvard U., 1936; m. Jane Rohn Love, June 18, 1938 (dec. 1971); children—William Hamilton (dec.), William Hamilton II, Susan Love; m. 2d, Jane McMillan Kinzer, Apr., 1972. Intern, Columbia Hosp., Milw., 1937-38; resident in surgery Passavant Meml. Hosp., Chgo., 1938-40; practice medicine specializing in plastic surgery, Milw., 1946—; faculty mem. Wis. Coll. Medicine, Milw., 1941-58, clin. prof. plastic surgery, chmn. dept., 1958-70; staff physician Columbia Hosp., Deaconess Hosp., Luth. Hosp., Milw. Children's Hosp., Milw. County Instns., St. Joseph's Hosp., St. Mary's Hosp., VA Hosp. (all Milw.); vis. prof. plastic surgery various univs. Active, Boys Club Milw.; corporate mem. Milw. Symphony Orch., Chgo. Symphony Orch. Assn. Served to col. M.C., U.S. Army, 1941-46. Decorated Legion of Merit; diplomate Am. Bd. Surgery, Am. Bd. Plastic Surgery. Mem. A.C.S., AMA, Am. Soc. Aesthetic Plastic Surgery, Am. Acad. Orthopaedic Surgeons (hon.), Am. Assn. Plastic Surgeons (pres. 1961-62), Am. Cleft Palate Assn., Am. Soc. Plastic Reconstructive Surgery, Am. Soc. Surgery of Hand (pres. 1952), Internat. Soc. Burn Injuries, Midwestern Assn. Plastic Surgeons (pres. 1969-70), Milw. Acad. Surgery, Nat. Rehab. Assn., Pan-Pacific Surg. Assn., Wis. Soc. Plastic Surgeons (pres. 1964), Wis. Surg. Soc., Am. Burn Assn. Club: Harvard. Home: 929 N

Astor St Milwaukee WI 53202 Office: 2266 N Prospect Ave Suite 608 Milwaukee WI 53202

FRAME, VELMA ANITA, counselor; b. Decatur County, Ind.; d. Frederick Virgil and Emma Flora (Robbins) Williams; B.S., Ball State U., 1935, M.A., 1949, postgrad. 1973; m. David C. Frame, June 29, 1946; Tchr. high sch., Yorktown, Ind., 1935-42, Daleville, Ind., 1951-59; counselor Central High Sch., Marion, Ind. 1959-62; Muncie (Ind.) Southside High Sch., 1962-71; counselor, dir. guidance high sch., Daleville, Ind., 1971—. Mem. Am., Ind. (pres.) sch. counselors assns., Am., Ind., E. Central (pres.) personnel and guidance assns., Nat. Vocat. Guidance Assn. Democrat. Home: 307 Arch St Yorktown IN 47396 Office: PO Box 525 Daleville IN 47334

FRANCE, WALTER DEWAYNE, JR., automotive co. exec.; b. New Haven, Nov. 9, 1940; s. Walter DeWayne and Ellen Hall (Grant) F.; B.E., Yale U., 1962; Ph.D., Rensselaer Poly. Inst., 1966; m. Margit Elisabeth Geering, Aug. 24, 1963; children—Wayne, Douglas, Elisabeth. Asso. sr. research chemist Gen. Motors Research Labs., Warren, Mich., 1966-69, sr. research chemist, 1969-73, asst. dept. head, 1973—. Chmn. bd. trustees Congl. Ch. of Birmingham (Mich.), 1974, moderator, 1975. Registered profl. engr., Mich. Mem. Am. Chem. Soc., Am. Soc. Metals, ASTM (award of appreciation for outstanding services as com. chmn. 1976), Nat. Assn. Corrosion Engrs. (A.B. Campbell award 1971, citation of recognition for outstanding contbns. 1974), Am. Inst. Chemists, Assn. Analytical Chemists, Sigma Xi. Co-editor: Galvanic and Pitting Corrosion, 1976; contbr. tech. articles to profl. jours. Home: 6455 Bloomfield Glens West Bloomfield MI 48033 Office: Research Labs Gen Motors Tech Center Warren MI 48090

FRANCIOSI, RALPH ANTHONY, physician; b. Montclair, N.J., July 3, 1937; s. Joseph Vincent and Grace Marie (de Stefano) F.; grad. Seton Hall Prep. Sch., 1955; B.A., Seton Hall U., 1958, M.D., 1962; m. Leona Patt Rodgers, Apr. 4, 1964; children—Michael Joseph, Patricia Quinn, James Paul. Intern, Jersey City Med. Center, 1962-63; resident Columbia-Presbyn. Med. Center, N.Y.C., 1963-67; instr. Columbia U. Coll. Phys. and Surg., N.Y.C., 1966-67; staff pathologist U.S. Naval Med. Sch., Nat. Naval Med. Center, Bethesda, Md., 1967-69; pathologist Children's Hosp., Denver, 1969-72; pathologist, also dir. labs. Children's Health Center, Mpls., 1972—; project dir. Minn. Sudden Infant Death Syndrome Program. Trustee Nat. Sudden Infant Death Syndrome Found.; chmn. profl. adv. com. Metro chpt. March of Dimes. Served with USNR, 1967-69. Mem. Pediatric Pathology Club. Contbr. articles on pediatrics and pathology to med. jours. Home: 4501 Drexel Ave Edina MN 55424 Office: Children's Health Center and Hospital 2525 Chicago Ave Minneapolis MN 55404

FRANCIS, CLARA A(VONELLE) HARE (MRS. RICHARD J. FRANCIS), plastics mfg. co. exec.; b. Harrod, Ohio, Mar. 7, 1914; d. William E. and Margret (Thomas) H.; student Bliss Coll., 1947-49; m. Richard J. Francis, Feb. 4, 1953. Dept. mgr. Walgreen Drugs, Columbus, Ohio, 1945-54; sec., treas., dir. Francis Industries, Pataskala, Ohio, 1956—; sec., treas. Richard J. Francis Asso., 1954—; pres. Francis Electronics, Pataskala. Lectr. Ohio State U., Columbus, 1948; bd. cons. Basic and Applied Sci. Lab., U. Cin., 1972—. Active Civil Def., Lima, Ohio, 1942-44; pres., founder Children's Hosp. Twig, Columbus, 1950-52. Named hon. distinguished alumna U. Cin., 1972; named admiral Neb. Navy, also Ky. col. Mem. Bus. and Profl. Womens Club. Baptist. Mem. Order Eastern Star. Clubs: Pataskala Archery (co-founder, v.p. 1957-59), Zonta (dir. Columbus 1964-66). Patentee. Home: 21 Edgewood Dr Granville OH 43023 Office: 431 W Broad St Pataskala OH 43062

FRANCIS, ERLE WILLIAM, lawyer; b. Westmoreland, Kans., Aug. 31, 1909; s. Erle Seth and Margaret (Hesse) F.; J.D., Washburn U., 1933; m. Marie Margaret Price, Sept. 2, 1939; children—Sarah (Mrs. Charles N. Henson), Mary Louise (Mrs. Gerald L. Counter), Michael Erle. Admitted to Kans. bar, 1933; atty. Kan. Vehicle Dept., 1938; asso. firm Crane & Crane, 1933-37; partner firm Francis & Francis, 1937-57; practice law, Topeka, 1957—; asst. atty. gen. for Kans. Bd. Edn., 1969-75, atty., 1976—. Bd. dirs., past pres. Kans. Children's Service League. Served with USNR, 1943-47. Mem. Kans., Topeka (pres. 1971) bar assns., Native Sons Kans. (pres. 1939), SAR (pres. Kans. 1965), Kappa Sigma. Republican. Congregationalist. Clubs: Masons (grand high priest Kans. 1977), Elks, Topeka High Twelve (pres. 1950), Topeka Knife and Fork (pres. 1964-65), Shawnee Country (Topeka). Home: 1608 High St Topeka KS 66604 Office: 700 Kansas Ave Topeka KS 66603

FRANCIS, JOHN GEORGE, dentist; b. Chgo., Oct. 28, 1918; s. Charles Karl and Mary Eleanor (Ruzic) F.; D.D.S., Loyola U., 1940; postgrad. Cook County Sch. Medicine, 1954; m. Winifred Susan Kent, Jan. 16, 1943; children—John Kent, Roger Glenn, Joanne Susan, Pvt. practice dentistry, Chgo., 1940—. Fellow Internat. Assn. Anesthesiology; mem. Am. Dental Assn., Ill., Chgo. dental socs., Royal Soc. Health, Blue Key. K.C. (4 deg.). Club: Beverly Country (Chgo.). Home: 10029 S Claremont Ave Chicago IL 60643 Office: 9101 S Western Ave Chicago IL 60620

FRANCIS, JOHN KENT, dentist; b. Chgo., Apr. 12, 1944; s. John George and Winifred Susan (Kent) F.; student Notre Dame U., 1962-64; D.D.S., Loyola U., Chgo., 1968; certificate periodontology U. Ill., 1970; m. Antoinette Celeste Piet, June 2, 1968; children—Jennifer Norine, Debborah Joy. Pvt. practice dentistry, Oak Brook, Ill., 1968-70; pvt. practice periodontology, Oak Brook, Ill., 1970—; asso. prof. Loyola U. Dental Sch., Chgo., 1970—; Sec., chmn. bd. dirs. Hinsdale Hosp.; mem. bd. dirs. Avery Coonley Sch. Diplomate Am. Bd. Periodontics; Fellow Am. Coll. Stomatologic Surgeons; mem. Ill., Chgo. dental socs., Am. Dental Assn., Am. Assn. Periodontists, Ill., Midwest socs. periodontists. Home: 338 N Quincy St Hinsdale IL 60521 Office: 120 Center Mall Oak Brook IL 60521

FRANCIS, JOSEPH SNELSON, cons. engr.; b. Canton, N.C., Jan. 13, 1914; s. William Lee and Iva (Snelson) F; student Berea (Ky.) Coll. and Ia. State Coll.; B.S. in Mech. Engring., U. N.C., 1938; m. Gertrude R. Cherry Withers; children—Joseph Gregory, Roger. Successively design engr. for J.V. Deloi Engring. Co., Durham, N.C.; Mojonnier Bros. Co., Chgo., Consol. Aircraft Corp., San Diego, Internat. Harvester Co., Chgo.; pres. Francis Co., 1940—; owner Western Research & Engring. Co. Registered profl. engr. Ill., Okla., Ga., Tex., Colo. Mem. Soc. Automotive Engrs., Am. Soc. M.E., Army Ordnance Assn. Mason (32 deg., Shriner). Home: 1057 E 161st St South Holland IL 60473 Office: 3200 E 87th St Chicago IL 60617

FRANCIS, LEROY ANDREW, lawyer; b. Terre Haute, Ind., June 14, 1910; s. Nathan I. and Flora I. (Campbell) F.; B.S., Ind. U., 1948, J.D., 1949; m. Mary Kathryn Reveal, Oct. 4, 1935; children—Richard L., Mary Kay, William Jay, Sharon Rose. Admitted to Ind. bar, 1949; since practiced in Terre Haute; mem. firms Hilleary, Shafer & Francis, 1949-73, Francis, Brames & Cook, 1973—. Pres., Sunset Harbor, Inc., 1965-73; judge Superior Ct., Vigo County, Ind., 1958. Served to lt. col. AUS, 1941-45. Decorated Bronze Star medal. Mem. Am., Ind., Terre Haute bar assns., C. of C., Ind. U. Alumni Assn., Delta Tau Delta, Sigma Delta Kappa, Delta Sigma Pi. Mason (33 deg., Shriner), Elk. Home: 2220 N 10th St Terre Haute IN 47804 Office: 101 Sycamore Bldg Terre Haute IN 47807

FRANCIS, MARY FRANCIS VAN DYKE, real estate exec., editor; b. Sedalia, Mo., Nov. 17, 1925; d. Frank B. and Mary Irene (Sims) Van Dyke; student Central Mo. State Coll.; children—David Eugene, Lois Irene (Mrs. Edward Elbert Smith), Roland Wayne, Eric Brian. Tchr. grade sch. Pettis County, Mo., 1943-44; timekeeper Montgomery Ward & Co., Kansas City, Mo., 1944-45; instr. new operators Southwestern Bell Telephone Co., Independence, Mo., 1945-47; real estate salesman Russell Realtors, Independence, 1958-66; owner Mary Francis, Realtor, Independence, 1967—; exec. sec., editor Eastern Jackson County Bd. Realtors, 1962-68; exec. asst., pub. relations dir., editor Kansas City Realtor, 1968-71; mktg. asst., regional office Chgo. Title Co., Kansas City, Mo., 1971-75; chmn. bd., pres. Muranco, Inc., Kansas City, Mo., 1975—. Cub Scout den mother Boy Scouts Am. Recipient Outstanding Service award Eastern Jackson County Bd. Realtors, 1964, Salesmanship award, 1965. Mem. Nat. Assn. Real Estate Bds. (charter pres. Greater Kansas City chpt., gov. Mo. Womens Council, mem. editorial adv. com., exec. officers council), Mo. Real Estate Assn. (mem. Speakers Bur.), Kansas City Indsl. Editors, Internat. Council Indsl. Editors. Club: Soroptimist (past pres., Independence). Address: PO Box 1158 Independence MO 64051

FRANCIS, WILLIAM CHARLES, educator; b. Chgo., Nov. 25, 1937; s. Joseph George and Catherine (Crnich) F.; B.S., Western Mich. U., 1961; M.A., Central Mich. U., 1965; Ph.D., Ohio U., 1973; m. Nancy Lee Snakenberg, July 1, 1967; children—Michael Joseph, Andrea Lee. Pub. sch. speech clinician Tuscola Intermediate Sch. Dist., Caro, Mich., 1961-66; dir. speech and hearing div. McDonald Training Center for Mentally Retarded, Tampa, Fla., 1966-67; vis. lectr. U. South Fla., Tampa, 1966-67, instr., 1967-69; grad. teaching asst. Ohio U., Athens, 1969-72; asso. prof. speech pathology and audiology Western Ill. U., Macomb, 1972—; speech clinician Central Mich. U. Remedial Clinics, Cleft Palate div., Mt. Pleasant, summers 1962-64; faculty adviser Glass Menagerie Corvette Club, Macomb, Ill., 1973-76. Mem. Macomb Bd. Park Commrs., 1977—. Served with USMCR, 1956-58. Recipient Certificate of Clinical Competence, Am. Speech and Hearing Assn., 1969. Mem. Am., Ill. speech and hearing assns., Am. Fedn. Tchrs. Mason, Elk. Contbr. articles to profl. jours. Home: 1137 Debbie Ln Macomb IL 61455

FRANCK, ARDATH AMOND, ednl. adminstr.; b. Wehrum, Pa., May 5, 1925; d. Arthur and Helen Lucille (Sharp) Amond; B.S. in Edn., Kent State U., 1947, M.A., 1948; Ph.D., Western Res. U., 1956; m. Fred Mack Franck, Mar. 18, 1945; children—Sheldon Mack, Candace Lucille. Instr., U. Akron, 1947-50; sch. psychologist Summit County (Ohio) Schs., 1950-60; dir. Akron (Ohio) Speech and Reading Center, 1950—; coordinator spl. academic class, Wadsworth; cons. Pre-Sch. program Richfield United Ch. Christ. Founder, current dir. 4-U Baton Twirling Assn. Mem. Am. Speech and Hearing Assn. (clin. certification), Internat. Reading Assn., Ohio Edn. Assn. Author: Your Child Learns, 1974; weekly ednl. column Wodsworth News Banner, 1970-76. Home: 631 Ghent Rd Akron OH 44313 Office: 700 Ghent Rd Akron OH 44313

FRANCONA, NICHOLAS TORRESSO, JR., dentist; b. Chgo., June 15, 1949; s. Nicholas Torresso and Jessie J. (Paulson) F.; B.S., Loyola U., Chgo., 1971, postgrad. in biology, 1972, D.D.S., 1976. Faculty, Loyola U., Chgo., 1972; pvt. practice dentistry, Lincolnshire, Ill. 1977—. Mem. Am. Dental Assn. Home: 428 W Russell Barrington IL 60010 Office: 430 N Milwaukee Ave Lincolnshire IL 60069

FRANCOUR, HUGH WILLIAM, dentist; b. Green Bay, Wis., Mar. 21, 1918; s. Joseph and Agnes (Christech) F.; B.S. in Commerce, U. Notre Dame, 1949; student Ind. U., 1949-51; D.D.S., Northwestern U., 1954; m. Evelyn B. Anderson, June 3, 1942; children—Sandra, Charles, Robert. Builder Thompson Bros. Boat Mfg. Co., Peshtigo, Wis., 1937-41; research lab. technician Mastic Asphalt Corp., South Bend, Ind., 1947-51; practice of dentistry, South Bend, 1954—. Served with AUS, 1941-46; lt. comdr. USN Res. Ky. Col. Mem. Am. Dental Assn., Dental Assn. St. Joseph County (Ind.), Michiana Acad. Practice Adminstrn., U. Notre Dame, Ind. U., Northwestern U. alumni assns., Ind. Conservation Council, Izaac Walton League, Ind. Polit. Actions Assn., Delta Sigma Delta. Methodist. Elk. Home: 507 Monterey Ct South Bend IN 46637 Office: 801 N Michigan St South Bend IN 46601

FRANK, CHARLES EDWARD, educator; b. Phila., May 5, 1911; s. Harry Jacob and Carrie (Miller) F.; B.A., Haverford Coll., 1933; M.A., Princeton, 1938, Ph.D., 1939; m. Dorothy Almira Berry, June 7, 1941; children—Charles W., Geoffrey A., Constance (Mrs. John C. Ronald), Barbara E., David A. Asst. in English, Haverford (Pa.) Coll., 1933-35, instr. English, 1935-37; asst. prof. English, Ill. Coll., Jacksonville, 1939-42, prof., 1945-55, 57-73, Dunbaugh Distinguished prof., 1973—, Pixley prof. humanities, 1977—, chmn. dept. English, 1957—; asso prof. U. Nev., Reno, 1955-57. Research cons. Ill. Legis. Council, 1959-61. Alderman 6th ward, Jacksonville, 1973—. Bd. dirs. Am. Field Service, Big Bro.-Big Sister, Jacksonville Symphony Soc., World Service Com., YMCA. Served to lt.-comdr. USNR, 1942-45, 50. Faculty fellow Fund for Advancement of Edn., Ford Found., 1953-54. Mem. Jacksonville-MacMurray Music Assn. (bd. dirs. 1970-73), Am. Soc. for 18th Century Studies, Charles Lamb Soc., English Inst., English-Speaking Union, Literary Union, Phi Beta Kappa. Author: Six Franks Abroad: One Man's Sabbatical, 1967. Book reviewer, So. Humanities Review, 1968—. Home: 236 Park St Jacksonville IL 62650

FRANK, CLINTON EDWARD, advt. agy. exec.; b. St. Louis, Sept. 13, 1915; s. Arthur A. and Daisy Marian (Irwin) F.; grad. Lawrenceville Acad., 1934; A.B., Yale, 1938; m. Frances Calhoun Price, July 25, 1941 (div. 1967); children—Marcia Case, Clinton Edward, Laurie Anne, Cynthia Calhoun, Arthur A. III; m. 2d, Margaret Rathje Mullins, May 24, 1967. Account exec. Blackett-Sample-Hummert, 1938-41, Dancer-Fitzgerald-Sample, 1947-48; sales promotion mgr. E.J. Brach & Sons, Chgo., 1948-49; v.p., treas., partner Price-Robinson & Frank, Inc., 1949-53; pres. Clinton E. Frank Inc., Chgo., 1954-67, chmn. exec. com., dir., 1967-76, hon. chmn., 1977—; dir. Stanray Corp. Bd. dirs. Passavant Meml. Hosp. Served with USAAF, 1941-45. Clubs: Chicago, University, Commonwealth, Glen View, Indian Hill. Home: 28 Bridlewood Rd Northbrook IL 60062 Office: 120 S Riverside Plaza Chicago IL 60606

FRANK, DAVID SCOTT, psychologist, educator; b. Chambersburg, Pa., Mar. 2, 1930; s. George A. and Elizabeth A. (Feldman) Trail; B.S., Shippensburg State Coll., 1954; M.Ed., Western Md. Coll., 1958; postgrad. U. Mo., Temple U.; Ed.D., W.Va. U., 1972; m. Doris Jean Witmer, Sept. 12, 1954 (div.); children—Kimberley Michelle, David Scott III; m. 2d, Luz Maria Latoni, June 24, 1968; stepchildren—James Brian, Edward Scott, Karen Irene. Tchr. area schs., Carlisle, Pa., 1954-58; guidance counselor, sch. psychologist No. Joint Schs., Dillsburg, Pa., 1958-64; pvt. practice as psychologist and counselor, 1958-68; asso. prof. Shippensburg (Pa.) State Coll., 1965-67; asst. prof. edn. Purdue U., Westville, Ind., 1967-72; pres. David S. Frank Psychol. Services Inc., Michigan City, Ind., 1972—. Cons. Pa. Dept. Vocational Rehab., 1958-68; vocational expert Social Security Adminstrn., Bur. Hearings and Appeals, HEW, 1964—; psychologist LaPorte County Superior and Circuit Cts. 1970—; psychologist drug abuse treatment program Ind. State Prison, 1975—, clin. dir. therapeutic community tomorrows aspirations, 1976—. Active LaPorte County Youth Service Bur., 1972—, Meals on Wheels, 1973—; mem. admission com. United Fund, 1972—. Bd. dirs. Family and Children's Service, Michigan City, Ind., 1968—, No. Ind. Council Children with Learning Disabilities. Served with USMC, 1949-52. Mem. Am. Personnel and Guidance Assn., Nat. Vocat. Guidance Assn. (profl. mem.), Nat. Rehab. Assn., Nat. Rehab. Counseling Assn. (profl. mem.), Ind. Corrections Assn. (certificate of merit 1971), A.A.U.P. (pres. local chpt. 1969-71), Pa. Sch. Counselors Assn., Internat. Bd. on Counseling Services, Internat. Transactional Analysis Assn., Assn. Counselor Educators and Suprs., Wrestling Referees Assn. (pres. 1964-65), Phi Delta Kappa. Presbyn. (deacon). Contbg. author: New Developments In Educating the Able, 1966. Home: 3207 Cleveland Ave Michigan City IN 46320 Office: David S Frank Psychol Services Inc 1101 E Coolspring Ave Michigan City IN 46320

FRANK, JOHN ELLSWORTH, educator; b. Union Furnace, Ohio, Feb. 8, 1918; s. Charles Homer and Nellie Theoptra (Shaw) F.; student Western Ky. U., 1943-44; D.D.S., U. Minn., 1948; M.P.H., Johns Hopkins, 1961; m. Josephine Ellen Leighton, Sept. 18, 1948; children—John Leighton, Melanie Ann and Victoria Rose (twins). Commd. asst. dental surgeon USPHS, 1948, advanced through grades to dental dir., 1969, ret. 1969; hon. asso. prof. S.D. State U. Coll. Nursing, Health Scis., S.D. State U. Brookings, 1969—. Fellow Am. Pub. Health Assn.; mem. ADA, Am. Soc. Dentistry for Children, Commd. Officers Assn., Delta Sigma Delta (life mem.). Home: 929 4th St Brookings SD 57006 Office: SD State U HN 217 Brookings SD 57006

FRANK, ROBERT EDWIN, hosp. adminstr.; b. St. Louis, Nov. 30, 1926; s. Edwin J. and Genevieve Ernestine (Graeff) F.; m. Mary Catherine Porter, Sept. 10, 1949; children—Michael, Nancy Frank Vahldieck; B.S., St. Louis U., 1950; M.H.A., Washington U., 1962. Asst. personnel dir. Gen. Cable Co., 1950-53; personnel dir. DePaul Hosp., St. Louis, 1953-61; intern hosp. adminstrn. Barnes Hosp., St. Louis, 1961, asst. dir., 1961-64, asso. dir., 1964-65, acting dir., 1965-66, dir., 1966—, pres., 1973—; asst. prof. program in health care adminstrn. Washington U. Sch. Medicine. Bd. dirs. Vis. Nurse Assn. Mem. Am. Coll. Hosp. Adminstrs., Mo. Hosp. Assn., Hosp. Assn. Met. St. Louis, Greater St. Louis Health Systems Agy. Club: Forest Hills. Home: 1525 Hampton Hall Dr Chesterfield MO 63017 Office: Barnes Hosp Plaza Saint Louis MO 63110

FRANK, ROBERT LEE, educator; b. Lincoln, Nebr., Sept. 29, 1931; s. Henry and Elizabeth (Younker) F.; B.S., U. Nebr., 1953, M.E., 1957, Ed.D., 1964; m. Dorothy Rasmusen, Aug. 11, 1956; children—Kent Robert, Jeffrey Allen. Counselor, tchr., Scottsbluff, Nebr., 1955-58; county guidance cons. Shelby Iowa County Sch. System, Harlan, 1958-59; prof. No. State Coll., Aberdeen, S.D., 1960-62; prof. U. No. Iowa, Cedar Falls, 1962—. Served with USAF, 1953-55. NDEA fellow, 1959-60. Mem. Am. (bd. dirs. 1972-75), Iowa (past pres.) personnel guidance assns., Iowa Vocat. Assn. (past pres.), Adults Edn. Assn., Assn. Counselor Edn. Supervision (exec. council 1977). Democrat. Lutheran. Club: Lions. Dir. Project Pace (personalized adult counseling experiences), 1976—. Home: 108 Summit Dr Cedar Falls IA 50613 Office: 510 Edn Center Univ Northern Iowa Cedar Falls IA 50613

FRANK, ROBERT LEE, clergyman, educator; b. Lake City, Iowa, Sept. 22, 1938; s. Carl W. and Janna (Gerdes) F.; B.A., Buena Vista Coll., 1962; M.Div., U. Dubuque, 1966; Ph.D., Hastings Seminary, Chgo., 1972; m. Carol Jane Kubasiewitz, July 30, 1961 (div. 1973); children—Robert L., Carl B. Ordained to ministry Congregational Ch., 1966; pastor Atkinson (Ill.) Congregational Ch., 1962-66; pastor Huntley (Ill.) First Congregational Ch., 1966-77; pastor McHenry County (Ill.) County Coll., Crystal Lake, 1973—, chmn. div. humanities and communication, 1977—. Trustee Huntley Community Credit Union, 1967-68, bd. dirs., 1969; chmn. Huntley Planning Commn., 1972-73; trustee Village of Huntley, 1973—. Named Tchr. of Year, McHenry County Coll., 1976-77. Mem. No. Assn. United Church of Christ (chmn. evangelism com. 1966-70), Ill. Conf. United Ch. Christ. Home: 11602 2d St Huntley IL 60142 Office: McHenry County College Route 14 and Lucas Rd Crystal Lake IL 60014

FRANK, ROCHELLE SHIRLEY, speech and lang. pathologist; b. Chgo., June 15, 1925; d. Meyer and Kate Fay (Cooper) Fine; B.S., Northwestern U., 1946; postgrad. U. Chgo., 1947, Nat. Coll. Edn., Evanston, Ill., 1975-76; m. Julian S. Frank, Dec. 25, 1945; children—Ellen, Susan. Individual practice speech therapy, Chgo., 1947-51; audiologist Chgo. Bd. Edn., 1950-51; speech therapist Oak Grove Sch., Libertyville, Ill. and Rondout (Ill.) Sch., 1962-68; speech and lang. pathologist Glencoe (Ill.) Pub. Schs., 1968—; lectr. in field. Co-chmn. edn. com. PTA, 1960-61. Mem. Lake County Speech Therapists Assn. (pres. 1966-67), Am. Speech Hearing Assn. (certified), N. Suburban Speech Lang. Assn., Internat. Transactional Analysis Assn., Sigma Delta Tau. Home: 3108 University Ave Highland Park IL 60035 Office: South Sch Glencoe IL 60022

FRANK, WILFRED ROBERT, JR., motion picture producer; b. Mpls., Nov. 14, 1930; s. Wilfred Robert and Lucile (Boffenmyer) F.; student U. Minn., 1948-49, Harvard, 1953; m. Shirley Ann Latin, Aug. 30, 1952; 1 son, Wilfred Robert III. With W.R. Frank Assos., Mpls., 1946—, v.p., 1953—; pres. Avalon Amusement Co., Boulevard Restaurants, Inc., W.R. Frank Prodns., Inc. Calif., Fair Oaks Hotels, Inc., Boulevard Confectioners, Inc. Aurora Prodns., Inc., v.p. Boulevard Amusement Co. Mem. Young Republican League, Bloomington, Minn., 1962-63. Patron mem. Mpls. Inst. Art. Served with AUS, 1953. Mem. Mpls. C. of C., Minn. Motel Assn. (pres.), Motel Assn. Am (pres.), Am., Minn. hotel assns., Pi Eta. Lutheran. Club: Minikahda. Home: 4300 Sunnyside Rd Edina MN 55424 Office: 1420 Zarthan St Minneapolis MN 55416

FRANKE, ARNOLD GENE, real estate devel. exec.; b. Mt. Olive, Ill., Nov. 3, 1932; s. Bernard G. and Hannah (Scheiter) F.; B.S., Eastern Ill. U., 1955; M.S., Purdue U., 1960; postgrad. St. Louis U., 1961-68; m. Roseanne Moruskey, June 19, 1954; children—Cara, Lisa, Jenny, Susan. Indsl. relations analyst Shell Oil Co., Wood River, Ill., 1960-65; dir. personnel Catalytic Constrn. Co., Phila., 1966; mem. faculty So. Ill. U., Edwardsville, 1965—, lectr. bus., 1968—, adminstr. bus. affairs, 1976—; pres. Franke & Assos. Inc., 1976—. Pres., Judevine Center for Autistic Children; bd. dirs. YMCA, Edwardsville; mem. dist. council Boy Scouts Am. Served to lt. USN, 1955-60. Mem. Naval Res. Assn. (v.p.), Indsl. Relations Research Assn., Am. Soc. Personnel Adminstrs., Nat. Assn. Coll. and Univ. Bus. Officers, Midwest Bus. Adminstrn. Assn., Res. Officers Assn., Navy League, Am. Legion. Mem. United Ch. Christ. Clubs: Moose, Faculty. Home: 730 St Louis St Edwardsville IL 62025 Office: Sch Bus So Ill U Edwardsville IL 62026

FRANKEL, PENINA, univ. counseling psychologist; b. Jersey City, N.J., June 3, 1933; d. Harry and Masha (Resnik) Ducoff; student Bklyn. Coll., 1950-53; B.A. summa cum laude, Wayne State U., Detroit, 1959; M.S., State U. N.Y., Albany, 1969; postgrad. Northwestern U., 1976-77; m. Reuven Frankel, Aug. 31, 1953; children—Hillel, Aaron, Noam. Employment advisor Oakland U., Rochester, Mich., 1969-70; ednl. and vocational counselor Jewish Vocational Service, Chgo., 1971-76, also coordinator, dir. Career Devel. Workshops Women, Chgo., 1971-77; counseling psychologist Roosevelt U., Chgo., 1976—. Certified counselor Inst. for Psychoanalysis, Chgo., 1975. Mem. Am. Personnel and Guidance Assn. (certified rehab. counselor), Assn. Rehab. Counselors, Am. Psychol. Assn., Ams. for Mental Health in Israel. Jewish. Author: Women: a Study of Vocationally-Relevant Needs, 1976-77; author multi-media cantatas: (with Reuven Frankel) Jerusalem, Echo of Eternity, 19—, From Minsk to Manhattan, 1975. Home: 1360 Linden St Highland Park IL 60035 Office: Roosevelt University 430 S Michigan Ave Chicago IL 60035

FRANKEN, EDMUND ANTHONY, JR., pediatric radiologist, educator; b. Springfield, Mo., Oct. 28, 1936; s. Edmund Anthony and Eloise (Appleby) F.; student St. Louis U., 1954-57; M.D., U. Okla., 1961; m. Penelope Ann Vanderhook, Nov. 25, 1960; children—Kenneth, Katherine (dec.), Michael, Jennifer. Intern, St. Johns Hosp., Tulsa, 1961-62; resident in radiology Ind. U. Med. Center, Indpls., 1964-67; asst. prof. radiology, 1967-71, asso. prof., 1971-75, prof., 1975—; fellow in neuroradiology Mallinckrodt Inst. Radiology, St. Louis, 1967; dir. radiology James Whitcomb Riley Hosp. for Children, 1967—; academic practice medicine specializing in pediatric radiology; mem. staffs J.W. Riley Univ., Wishard hosps. Served with USPHS, 1962-64. Fellow Am. Coll. Radiology; mem. Marion County (Ind.) Med. Soc., Ind. State, Am. med. assns., Ind. (treas.), Am. Roentgen ray Socs., Radiol. Soc. N.Am., Assn. Univ. Radiologists, Soc. Pediatric Radiology, European Soc. Pediatric Radiology (asso.). Roman Catholic. Author: Gastrointestinal Radiology in Pediatrics, 1975; contbr. articles to med. jours. Home: 3801 Springfield Ovlk Indianapolis IN 46234 Office: 1100 W Michigan St Indianapolis IN 46202

FRANKLE, ALLAN HENRY, psychologist; b. Des Moines, Nov. 5, 1921; s. Harry Raymond and Ruth (Cohen) F.; student U. Chgo., 1939, Ph.D., 1953; student U. Minn., 1943; m. Esther Alpern, June 22, 1947; children—Katherine, Jonathan. Dir. Des Moines Child Guidance Center, 1947-52; pvt. practice clin. psychology, Des Moines, 1952—; Univ. fellow Drake U., 1970—; vis. clin. asso. prof. psychology U. Iowa, 1969-70; cons. clin. psychology Broadlawns Polk County Hosp., 1967—; cons. VA Hosp., Knoxville, Iowa, 1976—; supervising psychologist N.Am. Mensa, 1966—. Served with U.S. Army, 1943-45. Decorated Bronze Star. Diplomate Am. Bd. Profl. Psychology. Mem. Am., Iowa (pres. 1960-61, Distinguished Service award 1973) psychol. assns., Am. Acad. Psychotherapists, Am. Orthopsychiat. Assn., Internat. Neuropsychology Soc., Sigma Xi, Psi Chi, Mensa. Democrat. Jewish. Home: 717 54th St Des Moines IA 50312 Office: 550 39th St Des Moines IA 50312

FRANKLIN, BENJAMIN EDWARD, bankruptcy judge; b. Mobile, Ala., Sept. 5, 1922; s. James Alexander and Dora Alice (Cochraham) F.; Ph.B., Xavier U. of La., 1947; LL.B., U. Detroit, 1952; m. Pauline Buckner Brooks, Nov. 8, 1952; children—Alicmarie Cornelia, Benjamin Edward Jr. Admitted to Kans. bar, 1954; practiced in Kansas City, also Topeka, 1954, Kansas City, Kans., 1969—; asst. counselor Wyandotte County, Kans., 1957-61; asst. U.S. Atty. Dist. of Kans., 1961-68, U.S. Dist. Atty, Kans., 1968-69; atty. for Bd. Pub. Utilities, Kansas City, Kans., 1969; mem. firm Harding & Franklin, Kansas City, 1969—; bankruptcy judge Dist. Kans., 1976—. Asst. vice chmn. United Fund, Kansas City, 1971-73. Mem. Catholic Diocese Sch. Bd. Eastern Kans., 1970—. Bd. dirs. Mental Health Assn., Kansas City YMCA. Served with AUS, 1943-45; ETO. Decorated Bronze Star medal with three oak leaf clusters. Recipient John Marshall award U.S. Dept. Justice, 1968, Award of Excellence Kansas City, Kans. Bar Assn., 1969, B'nai B'rith Brotherhood award, 1969, C. Francis Strandford award Nat. Bar Assn., 1969. Mem. Nat., Am., Fed., Kansas City, Kans., Wyandotte County bar assns., Bar Assn. State of Kans., N.A.A.C.P., Alpha Phi Alpha, Sigma Pi Phi. Democrat. Roman Catholic. Home: 1044 Grandview Bldg Kansas City KS 66102 Office: 454 New Brotherhood Bldg 8th and State Ave Kansas City KS 66101

FRANKLIN, CARTHEL FLOYD, realty exec.; b. Rittman, Ohio, Aug. 26, 1920; s. William Frederick and Queen Rebecca (Dickerson) F.; student Purdue U., 1939-40; 1 dau., Catherine F. Real estate broker, Chgo., 1946-54; gen. sales mgr. Swift Homes, Inc., Pitts., 1954-62; v.p. sales Gen. Homes subsidiary Koppers Co., Ft. Wayne, Ind., 1962-64; pres. C.F. Franklin & Co., Inc., Ft. Wayne, 1964—. Pres., Allied Real Estate Bd., Chgo., 1954. Served with USCGR, 1942-45. Mem. Ft. Wayne Bd. Realtors, Nat. Assn. Flight Instrs., Am. Legion, Soaring Soc. Am., Quiet Birdmen, Aircraft Owners and Pilots Assn. Mason (Shriner, K.T.), Elk, Kiwanian. Address: 9622 Aboite Center Rd Ft Wayne IN 46802

FRANKLIN, FREDERICK RUSSELL, assn. exec.; b. Berlin, Germany, Mar. 20, 1929; s. Ernest James and Frances (Price) F.; A.B., Ind. U., 1951, J.D. with high distinction, 1956; m. Barbara Ann Donovan, Jan. 26, 1952; children—Katherine Elizabeth, Frederick Russell. Admitted to Ind. bar, 1956; trial atty. criminal div. and ct. of claims sect., civil div. U.S. Dept. Justice, Washington, 1956-60; gen. counsel Ind. State Bar Assn., Indpls., 1960-67; dir. continuing legal edn. for Ind., adj. prof. law Ind. U., Indpls., 1965-68; staff dir. profl. standards Am. Bar Assn., Chgo., 1968-70; exec. v.p. Nat. Attys. Title Assurance Fund, Inc., Indpls., 1970-72; asst. dir. legal practice Am. Bar Assn., Chgo., 1972—. Served to capt. USAF, 1951-53. Mem. Am., Ind., Ill. bar assns., Fed. Bar Assn. (officer, found. bd. dirs. 1974—, nat. council 1965—, nat. v.p. 1967-69, chpt. pres. 1965-66), Nat. Orgn. Bar Counsel (pres. 1967), Order of Coif, Phi Delta Phi. Kiwanian, Elk. Home: 3617 Parthenon Way Olympia Fields IL 60461 Office: 1155 E 60th St Chicago IL 60637

FRANKLIN, GREGORY COVAL, psychologist, coll. adminstr.; b. Aurora, Ill., Apr. 27, 1939; s. Harvey A. and Emalee (Voltman) F.; B.Ed., No. Ill. U., 1961; M.Ed., Ph.D. (Fellow), U. Ill., 1969; m. Susan Marie Tesch, Sept. 7, 1963; children—Jeffrey Scott, Stephanie. Instr. biology U. Chgo., 1961-63; counselor U. Ill., Urbana, 1964-66, Glenbrook High Sch., Glenview, Ill., 1966-68, William Rainey Harper Coll., Palatine, Ill., 1968-72; asso. dean student devel. Muskegon (Mich.) Community Coll., 1972—. Mem. W. Mich. Health Planning Unit. Mem. Phi Sigma, Phi Delta Kappa. Lutheran. Contbr. articles to profl. jours. and encys. Home: 2066 Hillside St Muskegon MI 49441

FRANKLIN, JAMES ELLIOTT, elec. engr.; b. Sedalia, Mo., Nov. 14, 1944; s. Amos Elliott and Dorothy Mae (Shelley) F.; B.S., U. Mo., 1966, M.S. in Elec. Engring., 1975; m. Suzanne Frances Sims, Aug. 20, 1966; children—Amy Nicole, Emily Thea. Asst. dist. engr. Mo. Pub. Service Co., Lee's Summit, 1966-68, substa. engr., 1968-72, ops. engr., 1972-73, distbn. design and planning engr., 1973—. Registered profl. engr., Mo. Mem. Am. Pub. Works Assn., Kansas City Engrs. Club, Pi Mu Epsilon, Eta Kappa Nu. Home: 1110 Walnut Lee's Summit MO 64063 Office: 10700 E 50 Hwy Kansas City MO 64138

FRANKLIN, MARGARET LAVONA BARNUM (MRS. C. BENJAMIN FRANKLIN), civic leader; b. Caldwell, Kans., June 19, 1905; d. LeGrand Husted and Elva (Biddinger) Barnum; B.A., Washburn U., 1952; student Iowa State Tchrs. Coll., 1923-25, U. Iowa, 1937-38; m. C. Benjamin Franklin, Jan. 20, 1940; children—Margaret Lee (Mrs. Michael J. Felso), Benjamin Barnum. Tchr. pub. schs., Union, Iowa, 1925-27, Kearney, Nebr., 1927-28, Marshalltown, Iowa, 1928-40; advance rep. Chautauqua, summers 1926-30. Mem. Citizens Adv. Com., 1965-69; mem. Topeka Hosp. Aux. Recipient Waldo B. Heywood award Topeka Civic Theatre, 1967; named Outstanding Alpha Delta Pi Mother of Kans., 1971. Mem. DAR (state chmn. Museum 1968-71), AAUW, Topeka Art Guild, Topeka Civic Symphony Soc. (dir. 1952-57, Service Honor citation 1960), Doll Collectors Am., Marshalltown Community Theatre (pres. 1938-40), Topeka Pub. Library Bd. (trustee 1961-70, treas., 1962-65, chmn. 1965-67), Kans. Library Assn., Shawnee County Hist. Soc. (dir. 1963-75, sec. 1964-66), Nat. Multiple Sclerosis Soc., (dir. Kans. chpt. 1963-66), Stevengraph Collectors Assn., Friends of Library (dir. 1970—), P.E.O., Alpha Beta Gamma, Nonoso. Republican. Mem. Christian Ch. Clubs: Western Sorosis (pres. 1960-61), Minerva, Woman's (1st v.p. 1952-54). Home: 4808 W Hills Dr Topeka KS 66606

FRANKLIN, MAX SCHWAB, physician, educator; b. St. Louis, June 13, 1907; s. Morris N. and Celia (Lovett) F.; B.S., Harvard U., 1928, also postgrad.; M.D., St. Louis U., 1933; postgrad. Emery U., Wayne U., N.Y. U., U. Colo.; m. Gertrude Cohen, Apr. 11, 1936; 1 dau., Dale Helaine. Intern, Jewish Hosp., St. Louis, 1933-34; practice medicine specializing in internal medicine and cardiology, St. Louis, 1936—; mem. staff Faith Hosp., St. Louis, 1937—, pres. staff, 1977—, chief medicine and cardiology, 1937—; asst. instr. St. Louis U. Sch. Medicine, 1948 and after, later instr. and sr. instr., asso. prof. clin. medicine, 1977—; chmn. Med. Div. St. Louis Mayor's Commn. Aging 1970-73. Served with USAF, 1942-46. Diplomate Am. Bd. Internal Medicine. Fellow A.C.P., Am. Coll. Cardiology, Am. Geriatrics Soc.; mem. Mo. Med. Assn. (pres. 1977), St. Louis Med. Soc. (pres. 1967), Phi Delta Epsilon. Republican. Jewish. Club: Westwood Country, Masons. Home: 585 Coeur Royale Apt 401 Creve Coeur MO 63141 Office: 1040 N Mason Rd St Louis MO 63141

FRANKLIN-WHITE, PETER, artist, educator; b. Shoreham, Kent, Eng., Jan. 27, 1924; s. Charles and Olga (Hart) F.; came to U.S., 1969; 1 son, Michael Carol. Mem. Ballet Rambert, London, 1939-42; mem. Royal Ballet, 1942-66, prin. dancer, 1955-66; trainer, dir. operas and opera tng. program Vancouver, B.C., Can., 1967-69; mem. faculty theatre dept. U. B.C., 1968-69; faculty U. Ill., Urbana, 1969-77, prof. theatre arts, 1970-77; lectr. in field; instr., choreographer Nat. Acad. Arts, Champaign, Ill., 1972-77; free lance choreographer, dir., instr. in opera dance and drama Grand Valley State Coll., Western Mich. U., Kalamazoo Coll., others; dir. opera Camilla; dir. Absurd Person Singular, Kalamazoo Civic Theatre, 1977-78. Mem. Ill. Arts Council (dance adv. panel 1972-75), Soc. Stage Dirs. and Choreographers, Am. Guild Musical Artists, Am. Guild Film Artists, Brit. Actors Equity. Author: Sadler's Wells Ballet Goes Abroad, 1951. Choreographer numerous ballets including Exuberance, El Salon Mexico, Peter and the Wolf, Facade, musicals Oliver, Fantastiks, Man of La Mancha, Cabaret, Oh, What a Lovely War, Indians. Home: 126 Prospect SE Grand Rapids MI 49503

FRANKOVELGIA, NICHOLAS RICHARD, physician; b. Willisville, Ill., Aug. 14, 1919; s. Joseph and Felicia (Cuccia) F.; student Lewis Inst. of Chgo., 1936-39; B.S., U. Ill., 1940, M.D., 1943; M.P.H., U. Mich. Sch. Pub. Health, 1951; m. Angela Carmelita Orvino, Oct. 11, 1952; children—Valerie, Jen, Kimberly, Candice, Nikki, Lisa Marie, Joella S. Intern, Grant Hosp., Chgo., 1944; indsl. surgeon, 1944; pub. health adminstr. Stickeey Pub. Health Dist., Berwyn, Ill., 1946-59; also health officer Berwyn Pub. Health Dist., 1953-57; preventive medicine cons. MacNeal Meml. Hosp., Berwyn, 1955-62; attending physician Christ Community Hosp., Oak Lawn, Ill.; asst. prof. family practice Rush Med. Sch., Chgo. Served as lt., Sixth Div., USMC, 1944-46, exec. officer med. unit Marshall Islands, also in Guadalcanal and Hawaii. Diplomate Am. Bd. Preventive Medicine. Fellow Am. Pub. Health Assn., Sch. Health Assn., A.M.A. Office: 6360 W 79th St Burbank IL 60459

FRANSWAY, ROBERT LEROI, psychiatrist; b. Green Bay, Wis., July 2, 1922; s. Oliver Francis and Otilia (McCloskey) F.; B.S. cum laude, U. Wis., 1948, M.D., 1951; M.S. in Psychiatry, U. Mich., 1968; m. Claire Sandra Giancola, May 19, 1947; children—Paul R., Renee T. (Mrs. Lowell R. Spotts), Lynn M., Anthony F. Intern, Mercy Hosp., Des Moines, 1951-52; resident psychiatry Northville (Mich.) State Hosp., 1964-67; resident pathology St. Joseph Hosp., Milw., 1956-57; asst. med. dir. Continental Assurance Co., Chgo., 1952-53; gen. practice Fond du Lac, 1953-56; plant physician Ford Motor Co., Wayne, Mich., 1957-59; clin. investigator, coordinator Parke Davis & Co., Ann Arbor, Mich., 1959-64, 67-69; practice medicine specializing in psychiatry, Ann Arbor, 1967—. Cons. psychiatry Washtenaw Community Coll., Ann Arbor, 1968-69; cons. alcoholism therapy St. Joseph Mercy Hosp., Ann Arbor, 1972-76; chief of staff Mercywood Hosp., Ann Arbor, 1975. Served to 1st. lt. USAAF, 1942-44, AUS, 1944-46. Diplomate Am. Bd. Psychiatry. Mem. AMA, Am. Psychiat. Assn., N.Y. Acad. Sci., Mich. Med. Soc. Roman Catholic. K.C. Research drugs for cardiovascular, renal, allergy treatment, 1959-64, psychiat. and neurol. applications, 1967-69. Home: 2785 Park Ridge Dr Ann Arbor MI 48103 Office: 343 S Main St Ann Arbor MI 48108

FRANTTI, GORDON EARL, geophysicist, educator; b. Palmer, Mich., July 28, 1928; s. Leonard I. and Alice H. (Antilla) F.; B.S., Mich. Tech. U., 1953, M.S., 1954; postgrad. in Seismology, U. Mich., 1960-64; m. Ruth M. Mukka, Mar. 22, 1952; children—Sara E., Bruce G., Donald A., Michael E., Margaret R., Kalle P., Ross T. Mining engr., geologist Copper Range Co., Painesdale, Mich., 1954-55; geologist/geophysicist Cleveland-Cliffs Iron Co., Ishpeming, Mich., 1955-56; research geophysicist U.S. Bur. Mines, Mpls., 1956-59; asst. prof. physics Mich. Tech. U., Houghton, 1959-60; asso. research geophysicist U. Mich., Ann Arbor, 1960-65; asso. prof. geophysics Mich. Tech. U., 1965—; cons. in field. Served with USNR, 1946-48. C.I. Indsl. Research fellow, 1953-54; Mich. Tech. U. faculty research fellow, 1966-77; Shell Found. grantee, 1976-77; Nuclear Regulatory Commn. grantee, 1977-78. Mem. Seismol. Soc. Am., Soc. Exploration Geophysicists, Am. Geophys. Union, Soc. Explosives Engrs., Tau Beta Pi. Lutheran. Prin. investigator contract research projects seismology; contbr. articles to profl. publs. geophysics. Home: 134 S Pewabic St Laurium MI 49913 Office: Mich Tech U Dept Geology Houghton MI 49931

FRANZ, WILLIAM JOHN, accountant; b. Cleve., July 24, 1903; s. John and Katherine (Henry) F.; B.B.A., Cleve. State U., 1927; m. Louise Rose Schall, June 6, 1931; children—Douglas W.J., Patricia Louise (Mrs. A. Mancuso). Founder, prin. firm W.J. Franz & Co., Cleve., 1931-38, sr. partner, 1958—; dir. Monroe, Inc., Duplicator Sales, Hoffman Foundry, Advance Art Studios, Gier Devel. Corp., Plotz Machine. Pres. Ohio Accountancy Bd., 1972—; mem. bd. nat. field advisers SBA, 1953—. Pres. Cleve. Crime Commn., 1949; mem. pub. affairs com. Greater Cleve. Growth Assn., 1954—; sec.-treas. Nat. Council Philanthropy, 1954; mem. central com., exec. com. Cleve. Republican Com. Recipient Selective Service medal Pres. Truman, 1945. Mem. Smaller Businesses Am. Inc. (founder 1937, nat. pres. 1966—), Pub. Accountants Soc. Ohio, Cleve. State U. Alumni Assn. (pres. bd. govs.). Republican. Lutheran. Mason (32). Clubs: City, Athletic, Ad (Cleve.). Home: 3414 Euclid Heights Blvd Cleveland Heights OH 44118 Office: 430 Chester St Cleveland OH 44114

FRASER, DONALD MACKAY, congressman; b. Mpls., Feb. 20, 1924; s. Everett and Lois (MacKay) F.; B.A. cum laude, U. Minn., 1944, LL.B., 1948; m. Arvonne Skelton, June 30, 1950; children—Thomas Skelton, Mary MacKay, John DuFrene, Lois MacKay, Anne Tallman (dec.), Jean S. Admitted to Minn. bar, 1948; practice in Mpls., 1948-62; partner firm Lindquist, Fraser & Magnuson, and predecessors, 1950-62; mem. Minn. Senate, 1954-62, sec. Senate Liberal Caucus, 1955-62; mem. 88th-95th Congresses from 5th Dist. Minn., mem. internat. relations com., budget com., sec., whip, chmn. Dem. study group; mem. study and rev. com. Dem. Caucus; congl. adviser U.S. del. to Law of Seas Conf., 1972-77, to UN Conf. on Disarmament, 1968-73, to UN Commn. on Human Rights, 1974; U.S. del. to 30th session UN Gen. Assembly, 1975, organizer regional presdl. candidate forums, 1975; mem. Commn. on Role and Future of Presdl. Primaries, 1976—. Vice chmn., mem. bd. Mpls. Citizens Com. on Pub. Edn., 1950-54. Sec. Minn. del. Democratic Nat. Conv., 1960, mem. rules com., 1972, 76; chmn. Minn. Citizens for Kennedy, 1960; mem. platform com. Dem. Nat. Conv., 1964; chmn. commn. on party structure and del. selection Nat. Dem. Com., 1971-72, chmn. subcom. on internat. orgns.; nat. chmn. Dem. Conf., 1976—. Served as lt. (j.g.) USNR, 1944-46. Mem. Mpls. Fgn. Policy Assn. (pres. 1952-53), Citizens League Greater Mpls. (sec. 1951-54), Minn., Hennepin County bar assns., U. Minn. Law Alumni Assn. (dir. 1958-61), Ams. for Dem. Action (nat. pres. 1973-75, nat. chmn.). University Dist. Improvement Assn. (pres.). Address: 817 7th St SE Minneapolis MN 55414

FRASER, JAMES EARL, mfrs. rep.; b. Mpls., July 28, 1917; s. Clyde Elwood and Pearle (Dunklee) F.; student U. Wis., 1935, 36, U. Idaho, 1936, 37; m. Alma Sophia Bleicher, Nov. 29, 1941; children—James Earl, Joanne Alma, Mary Elizabeth. Pres., J. Earl Fraser Co., Inc., Detroit, 1969—, Jefair Co. of Detroit, 1975—; v.p. Dorrie Process Co., Inc., Norwalk, Conn., Monroe City Diecasting Co., Kuhlman Diecasting Co., Diemakers, Inc., Monroe City, Mo. Mem. Soc. Automotive Engrs., Soc. Body Engrs. Republican. Methodist. Clubs: Grosse Pointe Yacht (commodore 1963), Country of Detroit, Detroit Golf, Detroit Athletic, Bermuda Dunes Country (Calif.), Recess, Otsego Ski. Home: 80 S Deeplands Rd Grosse Pointe Shores MI 48236 Office: 21040 Kelly Rd East Detroit MI 48021

FRASER, (WILLIAM) DEAN, educator; b. Wells River, Vt., Oct. 3, 1916; s. Donald and Barbara (Dean) F.; B.S., Harvard, 1938; M.S., U. Ill., 1939, Ph.D., 1941; m. Rosemary Buehler Bayles, Mar. 5, 1965; children by previous marriage—John D., John L., Barbara Dallas Fraser Baird. Chemist, Monsanto Chem. Co., St. Louis, 1941-45; research fellow Calif. Inst. Tech., 1946-47; asst. research prof. Princeton, 1947-48; research fellow U. Calif. at Berkeley, 1948-50, asst. research biochemist, 1950-52, asso. research biochemist, 1952-55; mem. faculty Ind. U., Bloomington, 1955—, prof. microbiology, 1960—, chmn. dept., 1970-77. Bd. dirs. Planned Parenthood Assn., 1966-67; pres. Planned Parenthood South Central Ind., 1976. NRC cancer fellow, 1948-50; research fellow Calif. Inst. Tech., 1946-47; NIH fellow, 1961; Nat. Inst. Allergy and Infectious Diseases grantee, 1956-71. Mem. Am. Soc. Microbiology, Ind. Acad. Sci., N.Y. Acad. Sci., Sigma Xi, Alpha Chi Sigma. Author: Viruses and Molecular Biology, 1967; The People Problem, 1970. Contbr. articles to profl. jours. Home: 310 Gilbert Ave Bloomington IN 47401

FRAZE, JAMES EUGENE, accountant; b. Union City, Ind., Mar. 4, 1943; s. Charles Eugene and Doris Irene (Ketring) F.; B.S., Tri State U., 1966; m. Sue Ann Fennig, June 12, 1966; children—Larry Eugene, Aaron Eugene. Accounting mgr. Bloomington (Ind.) Hosp., 1966-71; partner J.F. Long and Co., Muncie, Ind., 1971—. Bd. dirs. Delaware County Assn. for Retarded Citizens. C.P.A., Ind. Mem. Nat. Assn. Accountants, Hosp. Fin. Mgmt. Assn., Ind. Assn. C.P.A.'s. Clubs: Moose, Elks, Sertoma. Home: Rural Route 12 28 Lone Beach Dr Muncie IN 47302 Office: PO Box 508 4021 Rosewood Ave Muncie IN 47305

FRAZEE, P.C., lawyer; b. Mt. Hope, Kans., Sept. 10, 1905; s. Charles and Lula (Martin) F.; LL.B., U. Kans., 1931; m. Catherine McAdam, Jan. 13, 1936. Admitted to Kans. bar 1931, since practiced in Syracuse; also abstracter real estate. Mem. Am., Kans., S.W. Kans. bar assns., Kans. Abstract Assn., V.F.W. Am. Legion, C. of C., Sigma Nu. Presbyn. Elk, Rotarian. Home: 701 Sumner St Syracuse KS 67878 Office: 301 N Main St Syracuse KS 67878

FRAZER, RICHARD SYMONS, assn. mgmt. exec.; b. Evanston, Ill., Nov. 10, 1920; s. George E. and Helen J. (James) F.; B.A., U. Wis., Wis., 1942; M.A., Roosevelt U., 1967; Ph.D., Neotarian Coll., 1967; LL.D., Far East Theol. Sem., 1968; H.L.D., Far East U., 1968; Litt. D., Hwa Kiu U., 1969; m. Mardean Hole, Feb. 14, 1948; children—Richard Symons, Georgette, Pamela, Laurie Helen, Marion, Eddie Jane. Jr. accountant, Frazer and Torbet, Chgo., 1942, mng. accountant, 1946-49; sec. Nat. Transitads, Inc., 1949-54, dir., 1949-54; pres., dir. Christy Trades Sch., Inc., 1949—; asst. to pres. Motorola, Inc., 1956-59; pres. Richard S. Frazer & Co., 1959—; pres. Assn. Mgmt. Co., 1968—. Pres. Assn. Home Study Schs., 1962-67, exec. dir., 1968-69; exec. dir. Ambulance Assn. Am., 1969-70; pres. Am. Soc. Bldg. & Constrn. Insps., 1971-76, Winnetka Village Caucus, 1961-62; pres. Forty Plus, Chgo., 1969-71. Served from pvt. to capt., finance dept., AUS, 1943-46; PTO. Mem. Wis. Soc. of Chgo. (pres. 1955), S.A.R., Alpha Delta Phi (pres. Wis. soc. 1955-57). Episcopalian. Republican. Clubs: University, Executives, Union League, City. Home: 225 Linden St Winnetka IL 60093 Office: Suite 500 625 N Michigan Ave Chicago IL 60611

FRAZIER, CHET JUNE, advt. co. exec.; b. Wynona, Okla., May 17, 1924; s. R.C. and Alice (Terry) F.; B.S., Okla. State U., 1949, M.S., 1950; m. Lucille Whetzel, Nov. 17, 1942; children—John, Lynette, Terry, Luanna. Editor, Okla. News Service, Stillwater, 1949-50; product sales mgr. Ralston Purina, St. Louis, 1951-58, advt. mgr., 1958-63; v.p. Bozell & Jacobs, N.Y.C., 1964-68, sr. v.p., 1968-71, exec. v.p., 1971—, also dir. Served with AUS, 1943-46; PTO. Named Advt. Man of Year, Advt. Fedn. Am., 1968. Mem. Nat. Agrl. Advt. and Marketing Assn. (pres. 1967-68, mem. bd. 1967-70), Am. Feed Mfg. Assn., Farm Equipment Mfg. Assn., Agrl. Pubs. Assn. Methodist (trustee). Kiwanian. Contbr. numerous articles on agrl. advt. Home: 901 Dillon Dr Omaha NE 68132 Office: One Dag Hammarskjold Plaza New York City NY 10017 also 10250 Regency Circle Omaha NE 68114

FRAZIER, GLENN GREVE, architect; b. Centralia, Ill., Oct. 23, 1925; s. Roy E. and Mildred (Greve) F.; student Centralia Jr. Coll., 1943; B.Arch., U. Ill., 1948. With H. Samuel Kruse, architect, 1942-43; partner S.A. Clausen & Assos., Decatur, Ill., 1948-52; pres.

firm Glenn G. Frazier & Assos., Urbana, 1961; mem. exec. com. Am. Comml. Investment Corp., 1965—; bd. dirs. Christian Universal Life Ins. Co. Mem. Ill. Gov.'s Rev. Bd. for Archtl. Exams., 1960. Pres., United Community Council, 1964-65; mem. United Fund Board, 1964-65. Bd. dirs. Family Service, 1958-65, pres., 1961, 62. Registered architect, Ill., Ia., Ind., Fla., Ky. Mem. Nat. Council Archtl. Registration Bds., A.I.A., Gargoyle Soc., Constrn. Specifications Inst. (v.p. 1964-67, nat. del. 1959-75, chmn. Chgo. chpt. delegation 1965-67, bd. tech. rev. 1964-67, pres. Chgo. chpt. 1968-69, pres. central Ill. chpt. 1971-73, nat. dir. 1975—) Am. Registered Architects, U.S. C. of C., Urbana Assn. Commerce, Ill. Assn. Sch. Bds., Alpha Delta Phi. Mason (Shriner), Elk. Designer nat. hdqrs. Nat. Council Tchrs. of English, Southern Hills bldgs. at So. Ill. U., Burnsides Research Lab., U. Ill., Research Hosp. for Mentally Retarded, Harrisburg, Ill., 1000 units pub. housing, Burnsides Nursing Home, Marshall, Ill. Home: 111 W Park Ave Urbana IL 61801 Office: 104 W University Ave Urbana IL 61801

FRAZIER, JOHN HOWIE, JR., steel co. exec.; b. Pitts., Mar. 5, 1921; s. John H. and Bertha (Allison) F.; student Coll. of Wooster, 1939-40; B.A., U. Mich., 1942; m. Virginia Lindenmuth, Jan. 25, 1944; children—Dianne (Mrs. Robert Lytle), Jeffrey, Deborah. Office mgr. Sennett Steel Corp., Detroit, 1946-52; partner Tartan Steel Co., Detroit, 1952-57; v.p. Mich. Metal Processing Corp., Detroit, 1957-69, pres., 1969—; pres. M&F Cartage Co., Detroit, 1959—. Exec. adv. bd. Fla. Atlanta U. Served to 1st lt. USAAF, 1942-45. Decorated Air medal, Purple Heart. Mem. USCG Aux. Presbyn. Clubs: Kiwanis, Detroit Yacht; Mackinac Island (Mich.) Yacht. Home: 144 Claremont Dr Dearborn MI 48124 also 2871 N Ocean Blvd Boca Raton FL 33432 Office: 6650 Mt Elliott Ave Detroit MI 48211

FRAZIER, JOHN HUGH, JR., grain co. exec.; b. Toledo, Sept. 27, 1917; s. John Hugh and Minnie Alice (Smith) F.; B.S., U. Pa., 1939; m. Dolores Thornhill, June 14, 1941; children—John Hugh III, Richard Thornhill. Warehouse examiner U.S. Dept. Agr., Indpls., 1940-42; v.p. P.R. Markley, Inc., Phila., 1946-52, pres., 1952—; pres. Tarheel Grain Co., Inc., Morehead City, N.C., 1952-62, Beam & Co., 1964—, Am. Mining & Exploration Co., 1965—; partner Hennessy & Assos., 1969-76; v.p. Bunge Corp., Phila., 1962-69; v.p. Tiger Tails Farms, Inc., Dyersburg, Tenn.; dir. Frazier div. Clayton Brokerage Co.; dir. Comml. Exchange of Phila., 1953-56, v.p., 1956-68. Mem. Comml. Exchange Phila., 1953-56, v.p., 1956-58; mem. Chgo. Bd. Trade, 1968—, dir., 1974—, vice chmn., chmn. fin. com., 1977—; mem. agrl. adv. com. Fed. Energy Office, 1974—; chmn. Feed Grain Contract Com., 1976-77. Sec. Troop Com., Troop 19, Boy Scouts Am., Bryn Mawr, 1961-64. Trustee P.W. Markley Trust, Nat. Grain and Feed Found. Served to 1st lt., USNR, 1943-46. Mem. Nat. Assn. Grain and Feed Assn. (dir., mem. exec. com. 1960-64, pres. 1971-74, chmn. exec. com. 1974-76), Internat. Platform Assn. Presbyn. (deacon, elder, trustee). Mason. Clubs: Union League, Downtown (Phila.); Overbrook Golf (Radnor, Pa.); Capitol Hill (Washington); Monroe (Chgo.). Home: 400 E Outer Dr Apt 2719 Chicago IL 60601 also 204 Buck Ln Haverford PA 19041 Office: Bd Trade Chicago IL 60604

FRAZIER, ROBERT GREGORY, pediatrician, assn. exec.; b. Oak Park, Ill., Apr. 16, 1923; s. Cecil Austin and Harriet DeGolyer (Greenleaf) F.; Ph.B., U. Chgo., 1943, B.S., 1944, M.D., 1947; m. Ruth Ann Johnson, Nov. 25, 1950; children—Stephen, Thomas, Carolyn. Intern, Grace New Haven (Conn.) Community Hosp., 1947-48; resident U. Chgo. Clinics, Bobs Roberts Hosp., 1948-50; instr. pediatrics U. Colo., 1952; asst. prof. pediatrics State U. Iowa, 1954-58; asst. prof., Northwestern U., 1962—; asso. attending physician Children's Meml. Hosp., Chgo., 1960—; asst. sec. Am. Acad. Pediatrics, Evanston, Ill., 1958-60, sec., 1960-67, exec. dir., 1967—. Served to 1st lt. U.S. Army, 1952-54. Mem. AMA, Am. Pediatric Soc. Home: 1226 Ashland Ave Wilmette IL 60091 Office: 1801 Hinman Ave Evanston IL 60204

FRAZIER, STERLING REGINALD, health services exec.; b. Troy, Ala., Mar. 18, 1936; s. James Gilbert and Ella Mae (Flowers) F.; student U. Ill., 1962-64, U. Md., 1968-69; children—Sterling, Aaron, Kevin, Clifford. Dir. Woodlawn Orgn., Chgo., 1968-71; dir. health planning and community programs-health and hosps. Governing Commn. Cook County, Chgo., 1971—, mem. sci. research com., chmn. lay com. on human experimentation, 1972—, mem. com. on bio-ethics, 1973—. Instr. community relations Cook County Sheriff's Acad., 1971-72; instr. community health services, grad. nurses program U. Ill. Med. Sch., 1971-72. Pres., Charles Kozminski Sch. P.T.A., 1970-73; corporate sec. Merit Real Estate Investment Trust, 1971—. Bd. dirs. Hyde Park-Kenwood Community Orgn., 1973-76. Served with USAF, 1952-56. Robert F. Kennedy Meml. fellow, 1969-70. Mem. Nat. Assn. Health Service Execs. (pres. Midwest chpt. 1974-76). Home: 1520 W Birchwood Chicago IL 60626 Office: 1900 W Polk St Chicago IL 60612

FRAZIER, THOMAS PAUL, dentist; b. Portsmouth, Ohio, Aug. 21, 1933; s. James Hamilton and Louise Marian (Kreger) F.; student Wilmington Coll., 1951-53; D.D.S., Ohio State U., 1958; m. Martha Jane Farry, Sept. 27, 1958; children—Diane, Paula, David. Pvt. practice dentistry, Centerville, Ohio, 1963—. Mem. Centerville Charter Commn., 1968; mem. bd. mgmt. YMCA, Centerville, 1970—. Served with USAF, 1958-63. Mem. Am., Ohio (chmn. council on membership 1973—) dental assns., Dayton Dental Soc., Am. Soc. Preventive Dentistry, Am. Soc. Dentistry for Children, Delta Tau Delta, Psi Omega, Tau Kappa Beta. Presbyn. (deacon 1964-67, elder 1968-71). Club: Optimist (pres. 1970, dist. lt. gov. 1971, dist. gov., mem. leadership and devel. com. 1977, Key Man award 1970, Outstanding Pres. award 1970, Outstanding and Distinguished Gov. award 1976). Home: 5540 Woodbridge Ln Dayton OH 45429 Office: 26 E Franklin St Centerville OH 45459

FRECKMAN, HERMAN ALBERT, physician; b. Cin., Sept. 2, 1911; s. Otto Louis and Sophia (Shapoff) F.; B.S., U. Cin., 1935, M.B., 1937, M.D., 1938; m. Eunice Marie Katterheinrich, June 5, 1937; children—Janice Dian (Mrs. Stephen R. Gooder), Sheryl Ann (Mrs. Wayne B. Shephard II). Intern Conemaugh Meml., Johnstown, Pa., 1937-38; practice medicine, specializing in clin. oncology, Cin., 1938—; mem. staff Christ, Bethesda, Deaconess hosps. Recipient Hull award, 1960. Mem. Am. Soc. Clin. Oncology. James Ewing Soc., N.Y. Acad. Scis., Cin. Acad. Medicine, Ohio Med. Assn. (Gold medal 1960), A.M.A., European, Am. assns. for cancer research, Internat. Coll. Angiology, A.A.A.S., Societa Italiana di Terapia dei Tumori. Contbr. articles on cancer chemotherapy to med. jours. Address: 994 W Galbraith Rd Cincinnati OH 45231

FREDERICK, GEORGE ANGELO, pipeline co. exec.; b. Chgo., May 14, 1922; s. Modesto and Emilia (Teglia) F.; B.S. Ill. Wesleyan, 1951; postgrad. U. Ill. Inst. Tech., 1957; m. Mary Jane Theivagt, Sept. 3, 1950; children—James Michael, Steven George. With Natural Gas Pipeline Co., Chgo., 1951-60, 61—, devel. engr., 1961-67, supr. controls dept., 1967—; sr. research engr. Gen. Dynamics Co., Chgo., 1960-61; owner, mgr. Crooked Creek Farm, Versailles, Ill., 1953—. Served with USAAF, 1941-45; ETO, PTO. Decorated Bronze Star medal (U.S.); Croix De Guerre Avec Palm (France). Mem. Assn. Computing Machinery, Am., So. gas assns., Instrument Soc. Am., Theta Chi. Patentee in field. Home: 207 N Beverly St Wheaton IL 60187 Office: 122 S Michigan Ave Chicago IL 60603

FREDERICKS, HENRY JACOB, lawyer, counselor; b. St. Louis, Dec. 1, 1925; s. Henry Jacob III and Mary Elizabeth (Pieron) F.; J.D., St. Louis U., 1950, postgrad. Sch. Commerce and Finance, 1945-47; m. Marjorie Helen Kiely, 1951 (div. 1962); children—Joseph Henry, James Andrew, Elizabeth Ann; m. 2d, Jeannette Elizabeth Wetteroth, 1965 (div. 1968); m. 3d, Joan Louise Marciak, 1970; (div. 1971); m. 4th, Susan Kay Brennecke, 1971; 1 son, William Michael. Admitted to Mo. bar, 1950, U.S. Dist. Ct., 1951, Mo. Supreme Ct., 1954; practice law, St. Louis County, 1950—; with firm Mark D. Eagleton, 1960, Goldenhersh, Fredericks & Newman, 1961-69; now partner firm Friedman and Fredericks; chief trial atty. for circuit atty. St. Louis, 1955; 1st asst. to circuit atty., 1957; spl. asst. to circuit attys., 1960—; lectr. in field. Judge boxing Mo. Athletic Commn. 1974-76; boxing chmn. Ozark AAU, 1977; mem. law and legis. com., jr. Olympic boxing judge Nat. AAU, 1977—. Served with USAAF, 1943-46; ETO. Decorated Air Medal. Mem. Am., Mo., St. Louis County bar assns., Am. Trial Lawyers Assn., Internat. Platform Assn., Delta Theta Phi. Home: 2243 Whitby Rd Clarkson Valley MO 63017 Office: 7730 Carondelet Ave Clayton MO 63105

FREDERICKS, MARSHALL MAYNARD, sculptor; b. Rock Island, Ill., Jan. 31, 1908; s. Frank A. and Frances Margaret (Bragg) F.; student John Huntington Poly. Inst., Cleve.; grad. Cleve. Sch. Art, 1930; student Heimann Schule, Schwegerle Schule, Munich, Germany, Academie Scandinav, Paris, France, pvt. studios Rome and London, Carl Milles' Studio, Stockholm, Sweden, Cranbrook Acad. Art Bloomfield Hills, Mich.; m. Rosalind Bell Cooke, Sept. 9, 1943; children—Carl Marshall and Christopher Matzen (twins), Frances Karen Bell, Rosalind Cooke, Suzanne Pelletreau. Faculty Cleve. Sch. Art, 1931, Cranbrook Acad. Art, Kingswood Sch., Cranbrook, 1932-42; Royal Danish consul Mich.; local, nat., internat. exhbns. art since 1928 include: Carnegie Inst., Cleve. Mus., Pa. Acad., Chgo. Art Inst., Whitney Mus., Detroit Art Inst., Denver Mus., Phila. Internat. Invitational, N.Y. World's Fair Am. art exhbn., Modern Sculpture Internat. Exhbn. Detroit, Internat. Sculpture Show Cranbrook Mus., A.I.A., Nat. Sculpture Soc., Architectural League of N.Y., Mich. Acad., Brussels, Belgium, others; commn. includes: New York World's Fair Baboon Fountain; Levi Barbour Meml. Fountain, Rackham Meml. Bldg., Fort Street Sta., Vets. Meml. Bldg., Detroit; adminstrn. bldg., war meml. U. Mich.; Louisville Courier-Jour. Bldg., Jefferson Sch.; Wyandotte, Mich., Holy Ghost Sem., Ann Arbor, Mich., union bldg. Ohio State U., Ford Rotunda, Marc Joslyn Meml., Alvan Macauley Meml. City-County Bldg., Ford Auditorium, Detroit Zoological Garden, also the Indian River Shrine, State Dept. Fountain, Washington; Cleve. War Meml. Fountain, Milw. Pub. Mus. Sculpture, N.Y. World's Fair permanent sculpture, Fed. Bldg. sculpture, Cin., Community Nat. Bank, Pontiac, Mich., Sir Winston Churchill Meml., Freeport, Bahamas, Two Sister fountain, Cranbrook, Michigan, Dallas Library sculpture, Henry Ford Meml., Dearborn, Mich., fountain Oakland U., Rochester, Mich., Midland (Mich.) Center Arts, Crittenton Hosp., Rochester, Mich., many others; portrait comms. include Senator Arthur Vandenburg, Willard Dow, Midland, Mich., George G. Booth Meml., Cranbrook, Mrs. Horace Rackham Meml., Yoshita, Pres. John F. Kennedy, others; works included numerous museums, pvt., civic collections. Co-founder, dir. DIADEM Program for Internat. Exchange of Handicapped; trustee Am. Scandinavian Found., People-to-People Program. Served with C.E., AUS, 1942-44, lt. col. 20th bomber command; 8th Air Force, Okinawa, 1944-45. Decorated knight Order of Dannebrog, 1963, officer, 1971; knight cross 1st class order St. Olav (Norway); recipient of 1st prize Cleve. Mus. Art, 1931; Anna Scripps Whitcomb prize Detroit Inst. Arts, 1938; 1st prize internat. exhbn. Dance Internat., Rockfeller Center, N.Y.C., 1st prize Barbour Meml. nat. competition, medal Mich. Inst. Architects, fine arts gold medal A.I.A., 1952, gold medal honor Mich. Acad. Arts, Letters, Sci., 1953; Achtl. League of New York; Golden Plate award Am. Acad. Achievement; citation Am. Inst. Decorators, Nat. Soc. Crippled Children and Adults, State of Mich., U. Detroit, others; Henry Hering medal Nat. Sculpture Soc., 1972. N.A. Fellow Internat. Inst. of Arts and Letters: mem. Michigan Soc. Architects, AIA, St. Dunstans Dramatic Guild, Mich. Acad. Sci., Arts, Letters, C. of C., Nat. Acad. Design, Am. Inst. Decorators, Nat. Soc. Interior Designers, Beta Sigma Phi, Alpha Beta Delta. Clubs: Royal Sedish Yacht; Orchard Lake Country; Architectural League N.Y. (N.Y.C.) Prismatic (Detroit); Royal Norwegian Yacht; Royal Danish Yacht. Home: 440 Lake Park Dr Birmingham MI 48009 Studio: 4113 N Woodward Ave Royal Oak MI 48072 also East Long Lake Rd Bloomfield Hills MI 48072

FREDERICKS, WARD ARTHUR, mfg. co. exec.; b. Tarrytown, N.Y., Dec. 24, 1939; s. Arthur George and Evelyn (Smith) F.; B.A. cum laude, Mich. State U., 1962, M.B.A., 1963; m. Patricia A. Sexton, June 7, 1960; children—Corrine E., Lorrine L., Ward A. Asso. dir. Technics Group, Grand Rapids, Mich., 1964-68; gen. mgr. logistics systems Massey-Ferguson Inc., Des Moines, 1968-69, v.p. mgmt. services, comptroller, 1969-73, sr. v.p. fin., dir. fin. Americas, 1975—; comptroller Massey-Ferguson Ltd., Toronto, Ont., Can., 1973-75; cons. W.B. Saunders & Co., Washington, 1962—; dir. Harry Ferguson Inc., M.F. Credit Corp., M.F. Credit Co. Can. Ltd. Am. Transp. Assn. fellow, 1962-63; Ramlose fellow, 1962-63. Mem. Am. Mktg. Assn., Nat. Council Phys. Distbn. Mgmt. (exec. com. 1974), Toronto Bd. Trade, Beta Gamma Sigma. Rotarian. Author: (with Edward W. Smykay) Physical Distribution Management, 1974. Contbr. articles to profl. jours. Home: 141 37th St Des Moines IA 50312 Office: 1901 Bell Ave Des Moines IA 50315

FREDERICKSON, PAUL DONALD, psychologist; b. Winnipeg, Man., Can., Nov. 26, 1937; s. Cyrus and Glendor E. (Anderson) F.; came to U.S., naturalized, 1937; B.A., DePauw U., 1959; M.A., Ariz. State U., 1961, Ph.D., 1973; m. Suzanne Wedeking, June 21, 1959; children—Andrew, Kristen, Jill. Psychologist Ariz. State Hosp., Phoenix, 1960-63, Child Guidance Clinic of Marion County, Indpls., 1963-74, chief psychologist, co-dir., 1974—. Cons. Ind. United Meth. Children's Home, Lebanon, 1967—; pvt. practice clin. psychology, Indpls., 1964—. Mem. Am., Ind. psychol. assns., Ind. Civil Liberties Union. Home: 319 Ridgeview Dr Indianapolis IN 46219 Office: 6640 E Washington St Indianapolis IN 46219

FREDMAN, DORRIS JUNE, artist; b. Poplar Bluff, Mo., Feb. 4, 1935; d. Bert A. and Gracie (Frank) Brannon; student Washington U., St. Louis, 1952-55; B.A., U. Ariz., 1959, postgrad. Coll. Law, 1957-58; M.A. in English, Southeast Mo. State U., 1973, M.A. in Counseling, 1977; m. Sanford Harvey Fredman; children—Charles, Daniel; 1 son by previous marriage—Bruce Schulman. Costume designer, Stephen Foster Drama Assn., Bardstown, Ky., 1959; tchr. English, Oak Ridge (Mo.) High Sch., 1969-71; instr. English, Southeast Mo. State U., Cape Girardeau; one woman shows Jackson (Mo.) Pub. Library, 1973, Howard Johnson's, Cape Girardeau, Mo., 1975; exhibited in group shows Reflections Gallery, 1973, Art-in-the-Park, Cape Girardeau, 1973-75. Recipient 1st prize acrylics Festival Mo. Women in Arts, 1974. AAUW grantee, 1975. Mem. Creative Arts Guild (pres. 1974-76), Am. Personnel and Guidance Assn., AAUW (state bd. Mo. div., area rep. for cultural interests 1974-76). Author play: Noah Built an Ark, 1977; also poetry in anthologies. Home: Route 1 Box 77 Millersville MO 63766

FREDRICKS, EDGAR JOHN, state legislator; b. Holland, Mich., June 27, 1942; s. Russel John and Audrey Kathryn (Beckman) F.; A.B., Calvin Coll., 1964; M.A., Western Mich. U., 1967, M.A., 1968. Mem. staff U.S. Congressman Guy VanderJagt, 1967; exec. dir. Mich. Citizens for Nixon, 1968; with Fgn. Service Inst., Dept. State, Washington, 1969; vice consul Am. Embassy, Seoul, Korea, 1970-72; fgn. service res. officer Dept. State, polit. officer Bur. Internat. Orgn. Affairs, Washington, 1972-74; mem. Mich. Ho. of Reps. from 54th Dist., 1975—, vice chmn. labor com. Mem. U.S. del. UN Trusteeship Council, N.Y.C., 1972, 73; vice chmn. Mich. Conservative Union, 1977—. Recipient award Mayor of Seoul, Korea, 1972. Mem. Christian Reformed Ch. Author: MacArthur: His Mission and Meaning, 1968. Home: 392 W 35th St Holland MI 49423 Office: Ho of Reps The Capitol Lansing MI 48901

FREE, ALFRED HENRY, chem. co. exec.; b. Bainbridge, Ohio, Apr. 11, 1913; s. Alfred H. and Alice (Clymer) F.; B.A., magna cum laude, Miami U., Ohio, 1934; M.S., Western Res. U., 1936, Ph.D., 1939; m. Helen Mae Murray, Oct. 18, 1947; children—Charles Alfred, Jane, Barbara, Eric Scot, Penny Alene, Kurt Allen, James Jacob, Bonnie Anne, Nina Joann. Mem. faculty Western Res. U., Cleve., 1935-46; cons. Ben Venue Labs. Bedford, Ohio, 1943-46; with Miles Labs. Inc. Elkhart, Ind., 1959—, head biochem. sect. Miles Ames Research Labs., 1946-59, dir. Ames Research Labs., 1959-64, dir. tech. services Ames Co. div., 1964-72, v.p. tech. services, sci. relations, 1972-76, v.p. sci. relations, 1976—. Diplomate Am. Bd. Clin. Chemistry. Fellow Am. Inst. Chemists (Chgo. chpt. hon. scroll award 1967); mem. Am. Assn. Clin. Chemists, Am. Chem. Soc., AAAS, Am. Inst. Nutrition, Inst. Vitamin Chemists, Am. Soc. Biol. Chem., Am. Diabetes Assn., Assn. Clin. Scientists (diploma of honor 1973), N.Y. Acad. Scis., Soc. Exptl. Biology and Medicine, Am. Pub. Health Assn., Am. Soc. Med. Tech., Sigma Xi, Phi Beta Kappa. Co-author (with Helen M. Free) Urinalysis in Clinical Laboratory Practice, 1975; contbr. numerous articles to profl. jours. Home: 3764 E Jackson Blvd Elkhart IN 46514 Office: 1127 Myrtle St Elkhart IN 46514

FREE, DOYLE HENDERSON, poultry orgn. exec.; b. Blue Springs, Nebr., Sept. 1, 1920; s. Harry Walker and Minnie Mae (McPheron) F.; B.S., U. Nebr., 1943, postgrad., 1949-51; m. Edna Louise Gill, Dec. 27, 1942; children—James Doyle, Russel Kenan, Bette Louise, Wayne Henderson. Prof. mil. sci. Colo. State U., Ft. Collins, 1948-49; exec. sec. Nebr. Poultry Improvement Assn., 1950-69; gen. mgr. Nebr. Poultry Industries, Inc., 1969—; chief div. poultry and egg devel. utilization and mktg. Nebr. Dept. Agr., 1976—. Bd. dirs. Nebr. Agrl. Council, 1971—, pres., 1974, chmn. legis. com., 1975—; Nebr. state coordinator Nat. Poultry Improvement Plan, 1953—; mem., gen. conf. com., nat. poultry improvement plan U.S. Dept. Agr., 1954-56; legis. rep. Nat. Turkey Fedn., 1973; bd. dirs. Midwest Poultry Fedn., 1974—, mem. pullorum com., north central states disease conf., 1966-70; pres. Nat. Good Egg Club, 1956-58. Mem. com., troop 50 Boy Scouts Am., 1954—. Served to capt. AUS, 1943-49. Recipient Blue Rooster award Poultry and Egg Nat. Bd., 1959, Scouting award Troop 50, Boy Scouts Am., 1958; named Nebr. Poultryman of Yr., Nebr. Poultry Industries, Inc., 1975. Mem. Poultry Sci. Assn., Am. Soc. Assn. Execs., Res. Officers Assn. U.S., Am. Legion, Sigma Xi, Gamma Sigma Delta (award of merit Nebr. chpt. 1976). Republican. Methodist (chmn. ofcl. bd. 1973—). Club: Kiwanis. Home: 4146 Y St Lincoln NE 68503 Office: Poultry and Wildlife Sci Bldg U Nebr Lincoln NE 68503

FREE, HELEN MAE, chemist; b. Pitts., Feb. 20, 1923; d. James Summerville and Daisy (Piper) Murray; grad. Coll. Wooster, 1944; m. Alfred H. Free, Oct. 18, 1947; children—Eric Scot, Penny Alene, Kurt Allen, James Jacob, Bonnie Anne, Nina Joann. Chemist, Ames Co. div. Miles Labs., Elkhart, Ind., 1946-60, group leader Ames Research Lab., 1960-64, Ames Product Devel. Lab., 1964-66, Ames Tech. Services, 1966-68, mgr. new products, clin. test systems, 1968-73, sr. new products mgr. microbiology test systems, 1974-76, dir. specialty systems, 1976—. Mem. Womens Pub. Affairs Com.; inspector election bd.; elder Presbyn. Ch. Recipient (with Alfred Free) Honor Scroll award Am. Inst. Chemists, Chgo., 1967. Mem. Am. Chem. Soc., Am. Soc. Med. Technologists, Ind. Soc. Med. Technologists, Am. Assn. Clin. Chemistry, Assn. Clin. Scientists, Chemists Club, NOW, AAUW, Alpha Mu Tau, Iota Sigma Pi (hon.), Kappa Kappa Kappa. Fellow Am. Inst. Chemists, AAAS. Republican. Clubs: Elks, Elkhart Concert, Altrusa. Author 2 books. Contbr. articles to profl. jours. Patentee in field. Home: 3764 Jackson Blvd E Elkhart IN 46514 Office: 1127 Myrtle St Elkhart IN 46514

FREEBAIRN, ALONZO GEORGE, educator; b. Pitts., Jan. 9, 1922; s. Thomas and Margret (Montooth) F.; B.A., Earlham Coll., 1943; M.A., Concordia Tchrs. Coll., 1971; m. Bettie Ruth Hargrave, Apr. 1, 1944; children—Judith Lynn, Donald Scott, Bruce Douglas. Sec., YMCA, Detroit, 1945-50, Chgo., 1950-60; social worker Cook County Office Equal Opportunity Settlement Houses, Chgo., 1960-69; tchr. Dist. 25 schs., Arlington Heights, Ill., 1970—. Served with AUS, 1943-45. Certified social worker; certified YMCA sec. Mem. Am. Personnel and Guidance Assn., Nat. Vocat. and Guidance Assn., NEA, Am. Legion. Presbyterian. Clubs: Moose, Lions (sec. 1964-67). Home: 730 E 164th St South Holland IL 60473

FREED, CATHERINE CAROL MOORE (MRS. DEBOW FREED), educator; b. Omaha, Dec. 27, 1925; d. Prentice Lauri and Henryetta (Banker) Moore; B.A., B.F.A., U. Tex., 1948; M.A., U. Kans., 1961; m. DeBow Freed, Sept. 10, 1949; 1 son, DeBow II. Mem. Faculty St. Mary's Coll., Xavier, Kans., 1958-59, U. Kans., Lawrence, 1959-61, U. N.Mex., Albuquerque, 1961-65, Huntingdon Coll., Montgomery, Ala., 1965-67; lectr. in English, Ladycliff Coll., Highland Falls, N.Y., 1967-69. Adviser, Albuquerque Sch. System on Gifted Child Edn., 1962-64; speaker and subject of film on purposes and objectives of PTA, 1964; pres. Alliance Community Concert Assn., 1970-74. Mem. Speech Assn. Am., Nat. Council Tchrs. English, Daus. of U.S. Army (pres. chpt. Ft. Benning, Ga. 1954-55), Mortar Bd., Phi Beta Kappa, Delta Sigma Rho, Pi Kappa Delta, Alpha Psi Omega, Alpha Delta Pi. Home: 605 N 6th St Monmouth IL 61462 Office: Office of Pres Monmouth College Monmouth IL 61462

FREEDMAN, ARTHUR MICHAEL, psychologist; b. Boston, Nov. 14, 1937; s. Jacob Solomon and Mollie (Weinstein) F.; B.S., Boston U., 1960, M.B.A., 1963; Ph.D., U. Chgo., 1971. Pvt. practice psychotherapy and organizational consultation Bellefontaine Psychol. Inst., Houston, 1969-71; asst. adminstr. tng. and devel. Region 2, Ill. Dept. Mental Health, Chgo., 1971-75; chief psychologist, dir. tng. Tinley Park (Ill.) Mental Health Center, 1975-76; pvt. practice psychology, Chgo., 1969—. vis. asso. prof. Coll. Edn. Roosevelt U., 1976-77. Served with U.S. Army, 1960-61. Registered psychologist, Ill. Fellow Nat. Tng. Labs. Inst. for Applied Behavioral Sci.; mem. Am., Ill. psychol. assns., Soc. Psychol. Study Social Issues, Ill. Group Psychotherapy Soc., Orgn. Devel. Network, Am. Mgmt. Assn., Am. Soc. Tng. and Devel., Am. Group Psychotherapy Assn. (asso.). Contbr. articles to profl. jours. Home and Office: 700 W Aldine Ave Chicago IL 60657

FREEDMAN, MARVIN, psychoanalyst; b. Chgo., June 16, 1932; s. Morris and Tillie (Samuels) F.; B.S., U. Ill., 1954, M.D., 1957; postgrad. Inst. for Juvenile Research Chgo., 1962-64, Ill. Neuropsychiat. Inst., 1957-58, 61-62; grad. in adult and child psychoanalysis Chgo. Inst. Psychoanalysis, 1977; m. Beverley Ruth Schiffman, Dec. 24, 1955; children—Lee, Keith, Lisa. Intern Michael Reese Hosp., Chgo., 1957-58; resident Ill. Neuropsychiat. Inst., 1957-58, 61-62, Inst. for Juvenile Research, Chgo., 1962-64; practice psychoanalysis, Highland Park, Ill., 1966-70, Old Orchard, Skokie, Ill., 1962-66, Glencoe, Ill., 1970—. Clin. asst. prof. psychiatry U. Ill. Coll. Medicine, 1967—; cons. Edison Park Home, Niles, Ill., 1972-74, Niles E. High Sch., 1972-76, Irene Josselyn Clinic, Winnetka, Ill., Glencoe Family Service. Served with USAF, 1958-60. Mem. A.M.A., Am., Ill. psychiat. assns., Am. Acad. Child Psychiatry, Chgo. Council for Child Psychiatry, Am., Ill. socs. adolescent psychiatry, Am., Chgo. psychoanalytic socs. Address: 277 Sylvan Rd Glencoe IL 60022

FREEMAN, WILLIAM JOSEPH, optometrist; b. Detroit, July 12, 1914; s. Harry and Bertha (Gleisner) F.; D. Optometry cum laude, No. Ill. Coll. Optometry, 1937; m. M. Patricia Frazis, May 28, 1967; children—Roger, Fred; stepchildren—Mary Rosin (Mrs. Stephen Keys), Joseph Rosin, James Rosin. Pvt. practice optometry, Jackson, Mich., 1940, Wyandotte and Melvindale, Mich., 1941-42, Wyandotte and Southgate, Mich., 1944-67, Ypsilanti, Mich., 1967—; contact lens tng. Obrig Labs., N.Y.C., 1944. Served with M.C., AUS, 1942-43. Mem. Am., Mich. optometric assns., Nat. Eye Research Found., Wayne County Soc. Optometrists, U.S. Power Squadron, Tomb and Key, Mu Sigma Pi. Rotarian. Home: 545 Marion St Ypsilanti MI 48197 Office: 1715 Washtenaw St Ypsilanti MI 48197

FREEL, STEVEN KIM, dairy farm exec.; b. Washington, Iowa, Aug. 12, 1953; s. Herbert Lyle and Darlene Virginia (Dickson) F.; student U. No. Iowa, 1971-73; B.S., U. Colo., 1976; m. Marilyn Louise Berry, Aug. 4, 1973. Mgr. dairy ops. Modern Dairy Farms, Fort Madison, Iowa, 1974—, v.p., 1977—, v.p. Castle View Dairy Farms, Inc., New Castle, Ky., 1976—, Modern Dairy-Oklawaha (Fla.), 1977—. Home: Route 1 Box 41A Montrose IA 52639 Office: Box 21 Route 2 Fort Madison IA 52627

FREEMAN, BARBARA JOSEPH, psychologist; b. Trenton, N.J., Jan. 5, 1945; d. Gerhard H. and Miriam (Selden) Joseph; B.A./B.Sc., Ohio State U., 1966; M.A., U. Cin., 1968; m. Marc Alan Freeman, June 26, 1966; children—Lee Aaron, Michael Elliot. Staff psychologist Marion County Child Guidance Clinic, Indpls., 1968—; lectr. Butler U., Indpls., 1971—; cons. Hebrew Acad. Indpls., 1971—. Bd. dirs. Womens Services League, 1975—; group treas. Hadassah-Hasachar, 1971-73. Mem. Am., Ind. psychol. assns., AAUP. Home: 100 W 54th St Indianapolis IN 46208 Office: 1949 E 11th St Indianapolis IN 46201

FREEMAN, DONALD HALSTED, metal products mfg. co. exec.; b. N.Y.C., Aug. 11, 1920; s. John Milton and Helen Elizabeth (Halsted) F.; B.A., Wesleyan U., Middletown, Conn., 1942; M.B.A., Harvard, 1948; m. Harriette Leonard Judd, June 22, 1946; children—Judd, Mark Carr. Vice pres. Mich. Brass Co., Grand Haven, 1948-52; pres. AGM Industries Inc., Grand Rapids, Mich., 1953—, also dir.; dir. Union Bank & Trust Co., Aves Advt. Agy., Mansco Inc., Heckethorn Mfg. Co., Gt. Lakes Financial Co., A.F. Holden Co. Trustee Aquinas Coll., Blodgett Meml. Med. Center. Served with AUS, 1943-46. Mem. Chevaliers du Taste Vin, Phi Beta Kappa, Chi Psi. Clubs: Kent Country, Peninsular, Kinne Creek, Athletic. Office: 450 Union Bank Bldg Grand Rapids MI 49502

FREEMAN, FLAVIUS BENNETT, lawyer; b. Elwood, Mo., May 30, 1911; s. Samuel Flavius and Leila Jessie (Bennett) F.; B.A., Drury Coll., 1932; LL.B., U. Mo., 1935; m. Frances Louise Ferguson, Apr. 18, 1936; children—Mercedes (Mrs. Ted A. Smith), Martha (Mrs. John C. Collet), Samuel Flavius II. Admitted to Mo. bar, 1935; since practiced in Springfield; mem. firms Neale & Newman, 1935-40, Neale, Newman, Neale & Freeman, 1940-46, Neale, Newman, Neale, Freeman & Wampler, 1946-51, Neale, Newman, Bradshaw, Freeman & Neale, 1951-68; sr. partner Neale, Newman, Bradshaw & Freeman, 1968—; dir. Commerce Bank, Springfield, Southwest Mfg. Co., Aurora, Mo., Concrete Co. of Springfield. Mem. Mo. Trade Mission to Europe, 1964. Chmn. Springfield United Fund, 1958; gen. chmn. Springfield Community Chest, 1957; Chmn. Greene County (Mo.) Democratic Com., 1958-60. Trustee Drury Coll., 1954—, chmn., 1965-70; trustee U. Mo. Law Sch. Found., 1952-64, chmn., 1959. Served with AUS, 1944-46. Recipient Citation of Merit U. Mo. Law Sch., 1969, Presdl. Achievement medal Drury Coll., 1974; named Springfieldian of the Year Springfield C. of C., 1968; Hon. Col. gov. Mo. 1960-68. Fellow Am. Bar Found.; mem. Am., Greene County (pres. 1975) bar assns., The Missouri Bar (chmn. trustees 1960—), Internat. Assn. Ins. Counsel, Springfield C. of C. (dir. 1962-64), U. Mo. Gen. Alumni Assn. (nat. pres. 1958), Sigma Nu (nat. pres. 1966-68, trustee 1970—, hall of honor, U. Mo. Faculty-Alumni Gold medal 1975), Phi Alpha Theta (hon.). Presbyn. (ruling elder 1951—). Mason (Shriner), Kiwanian (pres. Downtown club 1957). Club: Hickory Hills Country (pres. 1950-51). Home: 1303 E Loren St Springfield MO 65804 Office: 705 Woodruff Bldg 331 St Louis St Springfield MO 65806

FREEMAN, FREDERICK ROE, lawyer, mut. fund co. exec.; b. Arkansas City, Kans., July 11, 1914; s. Claude Kenneth and Agnes (Roe) F.; A.B., Southwestern Coll., 1952; J.D., U. Mo. at Kansas City, 1954; m. Joy Parman, May 1, 1936; children—Sheryl Ann (Mrs. Heath B. Matthews), Frederick William. Owner, mgr. ins. and real estate co., 1936-40; sec.-treas., sales mgr. Ark. Transp. Lines, Inc., 1940-45; owner, mgr. income tax service, real estate, ins. agy., 1945-54; admitted to Mo. bar, 1954, U.S. Supreme Ct. bar, 1965; practice law, Kansas City, 1954—; trust officer, pension and profit sharing plan specialist, 1954-59; sec.-treas. David L. Babson Investment Fund, Inc., Kansas City, 1959-76, v.p., treas., 1976—; sec.-treas. Jones & Babson, Inc., Kansas City, 1959-65, v.p., dir., 1965—; pres., dir. Income and Retirement Security Corp., Kansas City, 1975—. Mem. Am., Kansas City bar assns., Mo. Bar (taxation com.), Lawyers Assn. of Kansas City, Nat., Mo., Kansas City life underwriters, S.R., Phi Alpha Delta. Presbyn. Club: Kansas City Athletic. Home: 6023 Wyandotte St Kansas City MO 64113 Office: Crown Center G-15 2440 Pershing Rd Kansas City MO 64108

FREEMAN, HARRY WILLIAM, home constrn. co. exec.; b. St. Louis, Nov. 10, 1930; s. Thomas and Louise (Roberts) F.; ed. high sch.; m. Jeanne M. McLaughlin, Apr. 11, 1953; children—Patti, Dennis, Kym, Karen, Harry William. Salesman, Harry Vatteratt Real Estate, St. Louis, 1953-56, L. J. McNeary Real Estate, St. Louis, 1956-60; owner, operator H.W. Freeman Constrn. Co., Fenton, Mo., 1960—; dir. Hampton Bank St. Louis. Recipient Homer awards, 1971, 72, 74. Mem. Nat. Assn. Home Builders (nat. dir. 1969—), Home Builders Assn. Greater St. Louis (pres. 1969-70). Home: 9882 N Bridge Rd Ladue MO 63124 Office: 2071 Hwy 141 Fenton MO 63026

FREEMAN, JOHN JAMES, ednl. exec.; b. New Haven, Mar. 11, 1921; s. John James and Emily (Welch) F.; B.S., Yale, 1948; M.B.A., Harvard, 1951; m. Joan Russell, Apr. 11, 1955; children—John James, Melissa Reed, Russell Thomas, Julia May. Jr. elec. engr. United Illuminating Co., New Haven, 1941-43, 48-49; new bus. dept. Lee Higginson Corp., N.Y.C., 1951-53; asst. factory mgr. Internat. Register Co., Chgo., 1953-59; v.p., gen. mgr., dir. Magnetrol, Inc., Downers Grove, Ill., 1959-67; pres. U.S. Perlite Sales Corp., Chgo., 1967-71; pres. Am. Inst. Engring. and Tech., Inc., Chgo., 1971—; pres. Coyne Am. Inst. Served as 1st lt. USAAF, 1943-45; PTO. Decorated D.F.C. Mem. Am. Soc. M.E., Instrument Soc. Am. Clubs: Skokie Country; Economic (Chgo.). Home: 337 Melrose Ave Kenilworth IL 60043 Office: 1235 W Fullerton Ave Chicago IL 60614

FREEMAN, LEE ALLEN, JR., lawyer; b. Chgo., July 31, 1940; s. Lee Allen and Brena (Dietz) F.; A.B. magna cum laude, Harvard, 1962, J.D. magna cum laude, 1965; m. Glynna Gene Weger, June 8, 1968; children—Crispin McDougal, Clark Dietz. Admitted to Ill., D.C. bars, 1966, U.S. Supreme Ct. bar, 1969; practiced in Washington, 1965-68, Chgo., 1968—; law clk. to Justice Tom C. Clark, Washington, 1965-66, asst. U.S. atty., 1966-68; partner firm Freeman, Rothe, Freeman & Salzman, 1970—; spl. asst. atty. gen. Ill., W.Va., 1969—, Wis., Mich., Minn., Colo., Pa., Ky., Ind., 1973—; spl. asst. corp. counsel City of Chgo., 1971-76. Pres., Chgo. Lyric Opera Guild, Fine Arts Music Found., Chgo.; governing life mem. Chgo. Art Inst.; mem. vis. com. dept. humanities U. Chgo. Mem. Am., Ill., Chgo. bar assns. Clubs: Standard, Arts, Tavern. Home: 232 E Walton St Chicago IL 60611 Office: 1 IBM Plaza Chicago IL 60611

FREEMAN, M(AX) JAMES, immunologist, educator; b. Columbus, Ohio, Aug. 28, 1934; s. Harry Jennings and Neva M. (Akers) F.; student U. Fla., 1952-54; D.V.M., Auburn U., 1958; M.S., U. Wis., 1960; Ph.D., 1961; m. Doris Ann Johnson, Aug. 29, 1959; children—Louise Ann, James David, William Philip. Research asst. U. Wis., Madison, 1958-59, project asst., 1959-61; asst. prof. Ohio Agrl. Exptl. Sta., Wooster, 1961-62; postdoctoral fellow Case Western Reserve U., Cleve., 1962-64; asst. prof. microbiology U. Kans., Lawrence, 1964-67, asso. prof., 1967; asso. prof. vet. microbiology Purdue U., Lafayette, Ind., 1967-70, prof., 1970—. NIH postdoctoral fellow, 1963-64. Mem. AVMA, A.A.A.S., Am. Assn. Immunologists, Am. Soc. Exptl. Pathology. Contbr. articles to sci. jours. Home: 5634 N 225 W West Lafayette IN 47906

FREEMAN, PAUL DOUGLAS, orch. conductor; b. Richmond, Va., Jan. 2, 1936; s. L.H. F.; B.Music, Eastman Sch. Music, 1956, M. Music, 1957, Ph.D. in Theory, 1963; m. Cornelia Perry; 1 son, Douglas Cornel. Dir. Hochstein Music Sch., Rochester, N.Y., 1960-66; music dir. Opera Theatre of Rochester, 1961-66; dir. San Francisco Community Music Center, 1966-68; condr. San Francisco Conservatory Orch., 1966-67; music dir. San Francisco Little Symphony, 1967-68; asso. condr. Dallas Symphony, 1968-69, 69-70; condr.-in-residence Detroit Symphony Orch., 1970—; guest condr. Minn. Symphony, 1965-68, San Francisco Symphony, 1967, New Orleans Philharmonic, 1967, Oklahoma City Symphony, 1968, 72, Atlanta Symphony, 1968, Balt. Symphony, 1968, 69, 73, 74, Chgo. Symphony Ravinia Festival, 1969, 70, Birmingham (Ala.) Symphony, 1968, 69, Symphony of New World, Philharmonic Hall of Lincoln Center, N.Y.C., 1969, 74, Denver Symphony, 1970, 74, Grant Park Summer Festival, Chgo., 1970, Buffalo Philharmonic, 1970, Richmond Symphony, 1971, Cleve. Orch., 1972, St. Louis Symphony, 1973; prin. guest condr. Helsinki (Finland) Philharmonic Orch., 1974—; also numerous guest appearances, Europe. Recipient prize Dimitri Mitropolous Internat. Condrs. Competition, 1967, Spoleto award, 1968. Recording artist Columbia Records, Vox, Orion. Address: Ford Auditorium 20 E Jefferson St Detroit MI 48226

FREEMAN, RAYMOND SAVAGEAU, pediatrician, hosp. adminstr.; b. Denver, Nov. 17, 1920; s. William Bradly and Gertrude Eda (Savageau) F.; B.A., Yale, 1943; M.D., U. Colo., 1950; m. Babette Hartzell Stiefel, Apr. 20, 1961; children—William B., Gary Stiefel, Raymond S., Scott Dana, Peter Alexis. Practice medicine specializing in pediatrics, Denver, 1953-59; pediatrician Mowery Clinic, Salina, Kans., 1959—; pres. med. staff Asbury Hosp., Salina, 1968—; health officer, Saline County, Kans., 1965-70. Diplomate Am. Bd. Pediatrics. Fellow Am. Acad. Pediatrics; mem. Saline County Med. Soc. (pres. 1976). Republican. Episcopalian. Office: 737 E Crawford Ave Salina KS 67401

FREEMAN, RICHARD MYRON, physician; b. Merced, Calif., Aug. 19, 1933; s. Myron Jay and Louise Irene (Devaurs) F.; B.S., U. Redlands (Calif.), 1955; M.D., Stanford U., 1959; m. Barbara Griffith, Aug. 31, 1957; children—Richard Griffith, Amy, Catherine, Ann. Resident in internal medicine Stanford U. Med. Center, 1959-62; fellow in nephrology N.C. Meml. Hosp., Chapel Hill, 1962-63; asst. dir., staff physician, hemodialysis unit VA Hosp., Iowa City, Iowa, 1966-68; asst. prof. medicine and urology, dir. clin. nephrology Vanderbilt U., Nashville, 1968-69; prof. medicine, dir. hemodialysis, asso. chmn. ednl. programs dept. internal medicine U. Iowa, Iowa City, 1969—; mem. Iowa Renal Disease Adv. Com., Des Moines, 1972-76. Served to capt., M.C., U.S. Army, 1964-66. Recipient C.V. Mosby honor award, 1959; Nat. Found. fellow, 1962. Fellow A.C.P. (dir.), Am. Coll. Nutrition; mem. Nat. Kidney Found. (chmn. nat. med. adv. bd. 1977-78). Contbr. articles to med. jours. Home: 248 Hutchinson St Iowa City IA 52240

FREEMAN, ROSS ROBERT, lawyer; b. Ellsworth, Kans., Apr. 28, 1939; s. Robert Ralph and Mildred Lillian (Hand) F.; B.S., Kans. State U., 1961; J.D., Washburn U., 1967; postgrad. Harvard Bus. Sch., 1975; m. Fern Louise Jahnke, June 4, 1961; children—Debra Lynn, Nanette Dawn, Amy Louise, Sara Jo. Numerical analyst Pratt & Whitney Aircraft, Fla. Research and Devel. Center, West Palm Beach, 1961-64; admitted to Kans. bar, 1967; asst. sec. Security Benefit Life Ins. Co., Topeka, Kans., 1968-71, asst. counsel, 1968-73, sec., 1971—, gen. counsel, 1973—, v.p., 1976—; dir. SBL Service Corp., Nat. Asst. Actuaries & Cons., Inc., (both Topeka). Lectr., Benedictine Coll. Forum, Kansas City, Mo., 1975. Chmn., Mo. Valley Amateur Athletic Union Basketball Tournament, Topeka, 1972. Republican precinct committeeman, 1968-75; Rep. nominee U.S. Congress, 1976. Bd. dirs. Kans. Assn. Mental Health, 1972-75, pres., 1973-74; bd. dirs. Security Benefit Clinic and Hosp., Topeka, 1973-77; sec.-treas. Ballet Midwest; treas. Kaw Valley council Girl Scouts U.S.A. Recipient Outstanding Young Topekan award Active 20-30 Club, 1972; Boss of Year award Am. Bus. Women's Assn., 1973. Mem. Am., Kans., Topeka bar assns., Assn. Life Ins. Counsel, Delta Upsilon, Phi Alpha Delta. Presbyn. (clk. session 1974-76). Clubs: Topeka (dir. 1975—), Topeka 20-30 Club (pres. 1971-72), Topeka Knife and Fork, West Topeka Rotary. Home: 232 Fairlawn Topeka KS 66606 Office: 700 Harrison St Topeka KS 66636

FREEMAN, RUGES RICHMOND, JR., educator; b. St. Louis, Feb. 25, 1917; s. Ruges Richmond and Willie Cortez (Barr) F.; student Stowe (Mo.) Tchrs. Coll., 1931-32; B.E., So. Ill. U., 1935; M.A., U. Ill., 1936; postgrad. U. Chgo., 1939-40, St. Louis U., 1947-49; Ph.D., Washington U., St. Louis, 1972; m. Maxine Carter, May 21, 1936; 1 dau., Wilatrel (Mrs. Clyde Stockton). Tchr. Dunbar High Sch., Metropolis, Ill., 1936-38; caseworker Chgo. Relief Adminstrn., 1938-40; tchr. Vashon High Sch., St. Louis, 1940-50, Dunbar elementary sch., 1950-51; prin. Dumas elementary sch., St. Louis, 1952-55, Carver elementary sch., St. Louis, 1955-56, Cote Brilliante elementary sch., St. Louis, 1956-64, Harrison elementary sch., St. Louis, 1968-73; asst. prin., Sumner High Sch., St. Louis, 1964-68; asso. prof., coordinator secondary student teaching So. Ill. U., Edwardsville, 1973—. Treas. Soc. Health Assn. Greater St. Louis, 1970—; sec.-treas. Princess Pat Children's Center, 1971—. Served with AUS, 1944. Mem. N.E.A., Nat. Assn. Elementary Sch. Prins., Mo. State Tchrs. Assn. (pres. St. Louis dist. 1971-72, mem. State exec. com., 1972), Nat. Soc. for the Study of Edn., Secondary Sch. Adminstrs. Assn. (pres. 1965-66), Sch. Adminstrs. Club (pres. 1970-71), St. Louis Elementary Prins. Assn. (pres. 1972-73), Am. Ednl. Research Assn., Assn. for Supervision and Curriculum Devel., Phi Delta Kappa, Alpha Phi Alpha. Clubs: Gaylords, Gnashers. Home: 8027 Bennett Ave Richmond Heights MO 63117 Office: Box 49 So Ill U Edwardsville IL 62025

FREEMAN, SANDI, TV personality. Co-host A.M. Chicago, WLS-TV. Winner, Chgo. Area Emmy award, 1976. Office: WLS-TV 190 N State St Chicago IL 60601*

FREEMAN, THOMAS MASON, univ. ofcl.; b. Oak Hill, W.Va., May 22, 1938; s. Carbett Crockett and Sarah Elizabeth (Mason) F.; B.A., W.Va. U., 1960, M.B.A., 1962; Ph.D., Mich. State U., 1967; m. Florence Ellen Henkle, June 7, 1963; children—Mark, Kevin. Instr. Coll. Commerce, W.Va. U., Morgantown, 1961-62; adminstrv. intern to v.p. bus. and finance Mich. State U., East Lansing, 1963-64, asso. dir. Office Instl. Research and Acad. Planning, 1972-75, dir., 1975—, also asso. prof. adminstrn. and higher edn.; research asso. Mich. Council of State Coll. Presidents, Lansing, 1964-65; ops. research analyst Office of the Chief of Staff, U.S. Army, Washington, 1968-70; moblzn. designee, staff officer Office Dep. Chief Staff for Research, Devel. and Acquisition, Washington, 1971-76; asst. professorial lectr. George Washington U., part time, 1968-70; econ. cons. Econ. Edn. Workshops, 1962—. Served to maj. AUS, 1962-76. Decorated Army commendation medal. Mem. Am. Econ. Assn., Am. Ednl. Research Assn., Assn. Instl. Research, Am. Acad. Polit. Social Scis., Beta Gamma Sigma, Pi Sigma Alpha, Pi Kappa Alpha. Contbr. articles to profl. pubs. Home: 4557 Arrowhead Rd Okemos MI 48864 Office: 320 Administration Bldg Mich State U East Lansing MI 48823

FREESE, MARCUS JAMES, gastroenterologist; b. Steubenville, Ohio, July 15, 1931; s. Marcus Stenger and Alice Marie (Thompson) F.; B.S., Ohio State U., 1953, M.D., 1957; m. Gwen Stingley, Dec. 22, 1956; children—Marc, David, Michael. Intern, Miami Valley Hosp., Dayton, Ohio, 1957-58; resident in medicine Dayton VA Center, 1961-63, fellow in gastroenterology, 1963-64, cons. gastroenterology, 1977—; practice medicine specializing in internal medicine and gastroenterology, Dayton, 1964—; chief of staff Kettering Meml. Hosp., 1977—; clin. asso. prof. medicine Wright State U., Dayton, 1976-77. Served with M.C., USNR, 1959-61. Diplomate Am. Bd. Internal Medicine, Mem. AMA, Ohio, Montgomery County med. socs., Am. Soc. Internal Medicine, Dayton Soc. Internal Medicine (pres. 1970). Republican. Episcopalian. Panelist and guest speaker med. socs. Office: 2033 E Stroop Rd Kettering OH 45429

FREGA, JOHN VICTOR, architect, planner; b. Saracena, Italy, Mar. 13, 1931; s. Gennaro and Antoinette M. (Scillone) F.; came to U.S., 1934; B.Arch., Ill. Inst. Tech., 1954, M.S. in City and Regional Planning, 1957; m. Eileen M. Fitzpatrick, Sept. 5, 1959; children—Therese Anne, Annamarie. Designer, Pace Assn., Inc., Chgo., 1956-59; designer, project mgr. Bertrand Goldberg Assos., Chgo., 1959-63; participating asso., asst. to dir. Crosstown project Skidmore, Owings & Merrill, Chgo., 1963-69; asso. partner, project mgr. Metz Train Olson & Youngren, Inc., Chgo., 1969-72; design prin., pres. John Victor Frega Assos., Ltd., Architects-Planners, 1972—. Mem. Mayor's Indsl. Adv. Com. on Drafting Skills, Chgo., 1970—; village architect Village of Alsip and Village of Bridgeview, Ill. Bd. dirs. Misericorida Home. Served to lt. (j.g.) USNR, 1954-56. Mem. AIA (corp.), Am. Inst. Planners, Navy League, Am. Legion, Naval Res. Assn., Chgo. Assn. Commerce and Industry. Roman Catholic (planning bd. 1969-71). Architect, Tol Road Plazas and Restaurants, Marina City Project, others. Home: 55 Kimbark Rd Riverside IL 60546 Office: One N Wacker Dr Chicago IL 60606

FREIDMAN, STANFORD JOSEPH, steel co. exec.; b. Cleve., June 27, 1927; s. Sol H. and Cele (Akers) F.; B.S., M.E., I.E., U. Mich., 1949; m. Louise Glatt, July 19, 1949; children—Steven James, Jonathan Richard, Sally D. Pres., dir. Solar Mid-Con, Inc. (formerly Solar Steel Corp.), Cleve., 1961—, Danstan Realty Corp., Cleve.; dir. Phillip's Syrup Corp., Rolltech Corp., Universal Container Corp. Trustee Solar Found. Mem. ASME, Soc. Automotive Engrs., Am. Iron and Steel Inst. Clubs: Oakwood Country (Cleve.); Standard (Chgo.). Home: 52 Wychwood Dr Moreland Hills OH 44022 Office: 24200 Chagrin Blvd Beachwood OH 44122

FREILINGER, JOHN JOSEPH, speech and lang. pathology cons.; b. Denver, Apr. 21, 1933; s. Joseph Peter and Ann Isabel (Harnby) F.; B.A., U. No. Colo., 1955, M.A., 1960; postgrad. U. No. Colo., 1961, Pa. State U., 1963; Ph.D., U. Kans., 1973. Head speech and hearing clinician Weld County (Colo.) Crippled Children and Adults Speech and Hearing Clinic, Greeley, 1959-60; speech clinician Scott County (Iowa) Bd. Edn., 1960-62, hearing clinician, 1962-65; cons. clin. speech and lang. services Iowa Dept. Pub. Instrn., Des Moines, 1965-68, 72—; supr. speech and hearing clinic, instr. U. Kans., 1968-69; mem. council on speech, hearing and lang. disorder Iowa Dept. Health. Mem. West Des Moines Vol. Fire Dept. Served with USAF, 1955-59. Pa. Bur. Vocat. Rehab. fellow, Pa. State U., 1964; U.S. Bur. Edn. for Handicapped fellow, 1969-72. U.S. Rehab. Service Adminstrn. traineeship, 1971-72. Fellow Am. Speech and Hearing Assn.; mem. Am., Iowa speech and hearing assns., Council Exceptional Children, Council for Langs, Speech and Hearing Cons. in State Edn. Agys. (pres.). Author: (with R.E. Shine) Practical Methods of Speech Correction for the Classroom Teacher, 1962. Asso. editor Asha, 1967-71. Home: 8924 Buena Vista Ct Des Moines IA 50322 Office: Grimes State Office Bldg Des Moines IA 50319

FREIMAN, MARSHALL, dentist; b. Appleton, Wis., Apr. 14, 1941; s. Edward A. and Mildred (Weitzman) F.; student St. Norbert Coll., 1959-60; D.D.S., Marquette U., 1965; m. Donna M. Pack, June 7, 1964; children—Karen Ann, Debbie Kim. Pvt. practice dentistry, Milw., 1967—. Tchr. Marquette U. Sch. Dentistry, 1967-72; cons. Blue Cross-Blue Shield Wis. Served to capt. USAF, 1965-67. Mem. Am. Dental Assn., Alpha Omega. Home: 9439 N Broadmoor Rd Bayside WI 53217 Office: 10031 W Lisbon Ave Milwaukee WI 53222 also 5325 W Villard Ave Milwaukee WI 53218

FREINKEL, NORBERT, physician, educator; b. Mannheim, Germany, Jan. 26, 1926; s. Adolf and Veronika (Kahn) F.; A.B., Princeton, 1945; M.D., N.Y. U., 1949; m. Ruth Kimmelstiel, June 19, 1955; children—Susan Elizabeth, Andrew Jonathan, Lisa Ann. Intern, asst. resident medicine Bellevue Hosp., N.Y., 1949-50; from research fellow to asst. prof. medicine Harvard Med. Sch. and Thorndike Meml. Lab., Boston City Hosp., 1952-66; chief metabolism div. Thorndike Meml. Lab., 1957-66; Kettering prof. medicine, chief sect. endocrinology, metabolism and nutrition, dir. endocrine clinics Northwestern U. Med. Sch., Chgo., 1966—, prof. biochemistry, 1969—, dir. Center for Endocrinology, Metabolism and Nutrition, 1973—. Mem. metabolism study sect. NIH, 1967-69, chmn. designate, 1970; mem. adv. com. on alcoholism NIMH, 1967-70; mem. subcom. on diabetes Fogarty Internat. Center, NIH, 1972-75; mem. com. on renal and metabolic effects space flight Space Sci. Bd., Nat. Acad. Sci., 1973-74; cons. surgeon gen. U.S. Army, 1962—; mem. endocrinology and metabolism adv. com. Bur. Drugs, FDA, 1973-76, cons., 1976—; mem. career devel. com. VA, Washington, 1975-77; mem. Orgn. Commn. IVth Internat. Symposium Early

Diabetes, 1976—; mem. sci. advisory com. Solomon A. Berson Fund Med. Research, Inc., 1976—; mem. Orgn. Commn. Biomed. and Behavioral Research in Nutrition, 1977. Served with USNR, 1943-45, AUS, 1950-52. Am. Cancer Soc. fellow, 1953-55, Nat. Found. fellow, 1955-56. Fellow A.C.P.; mem. Assn. Am. Physicians, Am. Soc. Clin. Investigation, Am. Physiol. Soc., Endocrine Soc. (mem. council 1969-72), Am. Thyroid Assn. (chmn. Van Meter prize com. Am. 1977—), Diabetes Assn. (Lilly award and medal 1966, bd. dirs. 1968-74, chmn. com. sci. programs 1971-75, pres. 1977-78), Soc. Exptl. Biology and Medicine, Alpha Omega Alpha, Phi Beta Kappa, Sigma Xi; hon. mem. High Table, King's Coll., Cambridge, Eng. Editorial bd. Jour. Clin. Endocrinology and Medicine, Jour. Clin. Investigation, Endocrinology, Jour. Developmental Physiology, Internat. Diabetes Fedn. Bull., Jour. Lab. and Clin. Medicine, Ann. Rev. Medicine. Co-editor vol. on The Endocrine Pancreas, Handbook of Physiology Series, Am. Physiol. Soc. Editor-in-chief The Year in Metabolism, 1975—. Contbr. articles in field to profl. jours., chpts. in textbooks. Home: 938 Edgemere Ct Evanston IL 60201 Office: 303 E Chicago Ave Chicago IL 60611

FREISER, LEONARD H., librarian; b. N.Y.C., Feb. 9, 1925; s. Abraham and Henrietta (Graubard) F.; Mus. B., Manhattan Sch. Music, 1948; M.A., Columbia, 1948, M.L.S., 1955; m. Helen Hammer, Dec. 13, 1950; children—Leslie, Erik. Instr. music U. Sask., Can., 1948, Hunter Coll., N.Y.C., 1949, Evansville (Ind.) Coll., 1950; asst. prof. music San Jose (Calif.) State Coll., 1951; trainee, br. librarian Bklyn. Pub. Library, 1954-57; chief librarian Glens Falls (N.Y.) City Library, 1957-60; vis. asso. prof. library sci. State U. N.Y., Albany, 1959-60; chief librarian Toronto (Ont., Can.) Bd. Edn., 1960-68; exec. dir. L.I. Library Resources Council, 1968-70; dep. chief librarian Chgo. Pub. Library, 1970-72; dir. Wilmette (Ill.) Pub. Library, 1972-73; with Nat. Coll. Edn., Evanston, Ill., 1972—, dir. libraries, 1973—, dir. grad. program in library sci. and media, 1975—, dir. performing arts, 1976—. Cons. Fed. City Coll., Washington, U.S. Office Edn., Calgary (Alta.) Sch. Bd., Montreal Protestant Sch. Bd., Toronto Pub. Library, U. Pres.'s of Ontario, Centre for Culture and Tech. Pres., World Affairs Council, Glens Falls, 1959-60. Trustee Glens Falls Bd. Adult Edn. Pres.'s scholar Columbia U., 1949. Mem. A.L.A. (councillor 1963-68), Ont. Library Assn. (pres. 1965-66), Ont. Assn. for Curriculum Devel. (councillor 1964-67). Contbr. articles to mags. and newspapers. Home: 530 Washington Ave Wilmette IL 60091 Office: 2840 Sheridan Rd Evanston IL 60201

FRELS, LOIS MARIAN PARNELL (MRS. CALVIN EDWIN FRELS), educator; b. Geneseo, Ill., Nov. 20, 1929; d. Floyd Vinton and Mary Jane (Davis) Parnell; R.N., Moline (Ill.) Pub. Hosp., 1950; student Pub. Health U. Minn., Loyola U., Chgo., 1951-54; B.S., Augustana Coll., Rock Island, Ill., 1959; M.A., U. Iowa, 1964; diploma for testing, Marianne Frostic Center Ednl. Therapy, Los Angeles, 1969; Ph.D., U. Minn., 1977; m. Calvin Edwin Frels, Oct. 28, 1950; children—Mark Edwin, Arlan James. Sch. nurse East Moline Elementary Schs., 1951-54; pub. health work East Moline Vis. Nurses Assn., 1955-57; sch. nurse, project dir., nurse cons. United Twp. High Sch., East Moline, 1957-67; instr. psychology Blackhawk Jr. Coll., Moline, part time 1966-68; tchr., dir. gifted program Silvis (Ill.) Elementary Schs., 1968; counselor Pleasant Valley (Iowa) High Sch., 1969-70, asst. prof. Marycrest Coll., Davenport, Iowa, 1970-73; chmn. div. nursing Iowa Wesleyan Coll., Mt. Pleasant, 1973-76; dir. div. nursing Bradley U., Peoria, Ill., 1976—. Sec., East Moline Community Resource Council, 1965-67; mem. Riverdale Unit 100 Bd. Edn., Port Byron, Ill., 1964-67, 68-74; chmn. Rock Island County Fact Finding Com. White House Conf. Children and Youth, 1970, del. to conf., 1970; organizer Little White House Conf. Children and Youth, Rock Island County, 1969; 2d v.p. Rock Island County Welfare Council, 1968-70; mem. ednl. task force Rock Island Model Cities Project, 1969-70. Bd. dirs. Opportunity Mentally Handicapped. Ill. Dept. Pub. Instrn. grantee Western Ill. U., 1968; grantee div. nursing U. Minn., 1972-73. Fellow Am. Sch. Health Assn. (chmn. sch. nurse study com. 1973-77), mem. Am., Ill. nurses assns., Am. Pub. Health Assn., Am. Edn. Research Assn., NEA, Iowa League for Nursing (pres. 1976, 77), Royal Soc. Health (London, Eng.), Pi Lambda Theta. Home: 25329-1 Ave N Hillsdale IL 61257 Office: Bradley Univ Peoria IL 61625

FRENCH, ALFRED WILLARD, III, architect; b. Piqua, Ohio, Feb. 5, 1935; s. Alfred Willard and Marjorie (Phelps) F.; B.S.E., Princeton U., 1957, Columbia U., 1959; B.Arch., Mass. Inst. Tech., 1963; m. Allyn Blackwood Robinson, June 28, 1958; children—Allison, Caroline, Alfred. Draftsman I.M. Pei & Assos., Inc., N.Y.C., 1960; designer, job capt. J. Timothy Anderson & Assos., Inc., Boston, 1962-64; staff designer, job capt. Cambridge Seven Assos., Inc. (Mass.), 1964-66; project architect, job capt. Hammel Green & Abrahamson, Inc., St. Paul, 1966-68; co-founder, prin. InterDesign, Inc., Mpls., 1968-72; founder, prin. Alfred French & Assos., Mpls., 1972-74; dir. urban planning and design, asso. Cerny Assos., Inc., Mpls., 1974-77; founder, prin. Alfred French & Assos., Mpls., 1972-74, 77—; critic, lectr. Sch. Architecture, U. Minn., 1976—. Co-founder, pres. Community Design Center Minn., 1969, 70, 71, 74; mem. Princeton Univ. Sch.'s Com., 1968—. Bd. dirs. Antioch-Mpls. Communiversity and Extraordinary Learning and Ednl. Complex, 1970-73. Mem. AIA (urban design com. 1977—), Am. Soc. Landscape Architects (affiliate), Am. Inst. Planners (asso.), Minn. Soc. Architects. Episcopalian. Club: N.W. Tennis. Home: 1961 Kenwood Pkwy Minneapolis MN 55405 Office: 314 Clifton Ave Minneapolis MN 55403

FRENCH, DENNEY GERALD, ednl. adminstr.; b. Winchester, Ind., July 14, 1939; s. Gerald Garver and Letha Bernace (Denney) F.; B.S., Ball State U., 1961; A.M., Ind. U., 1964; postgrad. U. Americas, 1966; Ph.D., Purdue U., 1971; children—Deborah Elaine, Michael Gerald. Social studies tchr. Portland (Ind.) High Sch., 1961-64, Richmond (Ind.) Sr. High Sch., 1964-67; adminstrv. intern Test Jr. High Sch., Richmond, 1967-68; grad. asst. Purdue U., West Lafayette, Ind., 1968-69; exec. vice prin. Richmond Sr. High Sch., 1969-72, prin., 1972—. Instr. Ind. U. East, Richmond, 1974. Chmn. Randolph County (Ind.) Civil War Centennial Commn., 1960-61; sec. Art Assn. Richmond, 1972—. Chmn. Randolph County (Ind.) Young Republicans, 1958-61, Jay County Young Reps., 1962-64. Bd. dirs. Jr. Achievement Wayne County (Ind.), 1974—. Eli Lilly fellow, 1962-64; Fulbright fellow, 1966; David Ross Research fellow, 1969. Mem. Nat. Assn. Secondary Sch. Prins., Randolph County Hist. Soc., Phi Delta Kappa. Episcopalian. Odd Fellow, Kiwanian, Mason (Shriner). Home: PO Box 163 Richmond IN 47374

FRENCH, IVAN MERWYN, physician; b. Ewing, Nebr., Jan. 23, 1920; s. Oscar William and Iona Geraldyne (Hart) F.; A.B., U. Nebr., 1941, M.D., 1943; m. Muriel Oris Johnson, Oct. 4, 1947; children—William, Richard, James, Marcia. Intern Immanuel Hosp., 1944; practice medicine Wahoo (Nebr.) Clinic, 1947—; mem. staff Saunders County Meml. Hosp., Wahoo; courtesy staff Lincoln (Nebr.) Gen. Hosp., Clarkson Meml. Hosp., Omaha, Nebr. Meth. Hosp., Omaha; clin. asso. gen. practice U. Nebr. Coll. Medicine, 1959—; instr. physiology Luther Coll., 1948. Mem. Bd. Edn. Dist. 39, Wahoo, 1964-70, pres., 1967. Served to capt. M.C., AUS, 1945-46. Diplomate Am. Bd. Family Practice (charter mem.). Fellow Am. Acad. Family Practice (charter, del.); mem. Am., Nebr., Saunders County, Sixth Councilor Dist. med. assns., Am., Nebr. (pres. 1961) acads. Family practice, Phi Chi. Republican. Presbyn. (trustee 1964-70). Mason (32 deg. Shriner). Clubs: Wahoo Country, University (Lincoln). Home: 410 W 10th St Wahoo NE 68066 Office: 964 N Laurel St Wahoo NE 68066

FRENCH, MARCUS EMMETT, mfg. co. exec.; b. Worcester, Mass., Jan. 21, 1929; s. Emmett A. and Marion A. (Brady) F.; B.S. in Chemistry, Holy Cross Coll., 1952, M.S. in Chemistry, 1953; m. Mary M. Nugent, Sept. 25, 1954; children—Carol E., Margaret A., Marci M. Sect. leader Allied Chem. Corp., Buffalo, 1953-59; devel. chemist Hewitt Robbins Corp., Franklin, N.J., 1959-60; v.p. Gen. Foam div. Tenneco Chems., Inc., Hazleton, Pa., 1960-70; pres. Janesville Products div. Amtel Inc., Norwalk, Ohio, 1970—. Served with U.S. Army, 1946-48. Mem. ASTM, Soc. Automotive Engrs., Soc. Plastics Engrs. Club: K.C. Patentee on methods of urethane foam in U.S. and fgn. countries. Home: 6 Hillcrest Ct Milan OH 44846 Office: PO Box 349 Norwalk OH 44857

FRENCH, RAY H., artist, educator; b. Terre Haute, Ind., May 16, 1919; s. Edgar and Radie (Miller) F.; student John Herron Art Sch., 1939-42, Ind. State U., 1942, U. Colo., 1943; B.F.A., State U. Iowa, 1947, M.F.A., 1948; m. Martha Ann Simons, June 21, 1952; 1 son, Thomas Ray. Numerous one-man shows 1943—; represented in permanent collections, Mus. of Modern Art, Library of Congress, Bibliotique Nationale in Paris, Victoria and Albert Mus. in London, Denver Art Mus., Pasadena Art Mus., Brooks Meml. Mus., Evansville Mus., Boston Pub. Library, Phila. Museum, Swope Art Gallery, Bklyn. Mus., Peabody Mus., Wayne Art Found., Sheldon Meml. Art Gallery, Columbia U., N.Y. Pub. Library, others; prof. art DePauw U., 1948—, also head art dept., dir. Art Center. Served with AC, AUS, 1942-45. Mem. Iowa Print Group, Am. Soc. Graphic Artists, Mid Am. Coll. Art Assn. Home: 106 E Seminary St Greencastle IN 46135

FRENKEL, MARVIN ALLEN, glove co. exec.; b. Detroit, May 3, 1926; J.D., U. Miami, 1950; postgrad. Ind. U., Mich. State U., Wayne State U., 1966, 74-76. Pres., Advance Glove Mfg. Co., Detroit; mem. industry sector adv. com. on leather and leather products Nat. Def. Exec. Res. Trustee, Temple Beth El, Sr. Center, Inc., Mich. Cancer Found.; trustee, mem. exec. com. Detroit Inst. Tech.; mem. exec. com. Detroit Round Table, NCCJ, Inc.; mem. adv. bd. Music Hall Center for Performing Arts. Mem. Am. Def. Preparedness Assn. (pres. Mich. chpt.), Am. Logistics Assn. (dir., pres. 1971-72 Mich. chpt.), U. Miami Nat. Corps. and Founds. Com., Detroit Com. on Fgn. Relations, Econ. Club Detroit, Engring. Soc. Detroit. Clubs: Detroit Rotary, One Hundred, Standard, Great Lakes, Franklin Hills Country. Author: Slave Trade-U.S.A. and the Looting of America Including Your Food, Wages and Savings, 1973; The Abridging of our Freedom of the Press-Without Really Trying. Patentee in varied fields. Office: 901 W Lafayette Blvd Detroit MI 48226

FRENTZ, LEROY BRAND, author, real estate appraiser; b. Mankato, Minn., Mar. 20, 1915; s. LeRoy and Mabel Gerthe (Knoff) F.; B.S., Northwestern U., 1936; m. Jean Thro, Aug. 19, 1937; children—Brand, John. Newspaper reporter various Ill., Ind. newspapers, 1936-38; mgr. How Service, Lafayette, Ind., 1939-46; asst. editor Purdue (Univ.) Alumnus, West Lafayette, Ind., 1939-46; writer articles, short stories, novelettes pub. in various nat. mags., including True, Argosy, Detective; real estate appraiser, 1958—. Chmn. Blue Earth County Republican Com., 1959-68; mem. Minn. Rep. Central Com., 1959-68; bd. dirs. Nat. Assn. Rep. County Chairmen, 1964-66. Bd. dirs. Minn. Respiratory Health Assn., 1964-74. Mem. Am. Inst. Real Estate Appraisers, Am. Right of Way Assn., Nat. Assn. Realtors, Sigma Delta Chi, Phi Delta Theta. Elk. Club: Mankato Golf. Home: 520 Van Brunt St Mankato MN 56001 Office: 104 E Liberty St Mankato MN 56001

FRENZEL, BILL, congressman; b. St. Paul, July 31, 1928; s. Paul William and Paula (Schlegel) F.; B.A., Dartmouth, 1950, M.B.A., 1951; m. Ruth Purdy, June 9, 1951; children—Deborah Anne, Pamela Ruth, Melissa Lee. With Mpls. Terminal Warehouse Co., 1954-69, mgr., 1957-60, pres., dir., 1960-69; mem. Minn. Legislature, 1962-70; mem. 92d-95th congresses from 3d Minn. Dist. Mem. adv. com. Nat. Rivers and Harbors Congress; former mem. adv. council Minn. Dept. Employment Security. Served with USNR, 1951-54; Korea. Named One of Outstanding Young Men in Am., U.S. Jr. C. of C., 1964. Mem. Am. Legion, C. of C., Citizens League. Home: Golden Valley MN Office: 1026 Longworth House Office Bldg Washington DC 20515

FRERKING, ROBERT GEORGE, agri-bus. coop. co. exec.; b. St. Louis, Aug. 16, 1931; s. Roland Franklin and Clara Martha (Kienzle) F.; B.S. in Bus. Adminstrn., U. Tenn., 1957; m. Carzell Thurman, Dec. 19, 1956; children—Katherine, Mary, William, John, James. Systems programmer U.S. Steel Corp., Birmingham, Ala., 1957-62, systems analyst Computer Center, Pittsburgh, 1962-63; sr. systems analyst Alcoa Corp., Alcoa, Tenn., 1963-65; mgr. programming and ops. FS Services, Inc., Bloomington, Ill., 1965-70; dir. data processing MFA, Inc., Columbia, Mo., 1970—. Chmn. United Fund, Empire Twp., Ill., 1967; mem. LeRoy (Ill.) Sch. Bd., 1969-70; pres. Daniel Boone Little League, Columbia, 1975. Served with USAF, 1950-54. Mem. Beta Alpha Psi. Lutheran. Home: 901 Cowan Dr Columbia MO 65201 Office: 201 S 7th St Columbia MO 65201

FREY, H. GARRETT, stock broker; b. Cin., Dec. 2, 1938; s. John H. and Mary G. (Grever) F.; student U. Detroit, 1956-57, U. Cin., 1957-59, U. Miami, 1960-61; m. Mary Knollman, July 23, 1960; children—John, Robert, Meg, Amy, Brad, Julie. Salesman, Verkamp Corp., Cin., 1958-60, Formica Corp., Cin., Miami, Fla., and Hartford, Conn., 1960-62; stockbroker Westheimer & Hayden Stone, Cin., 1962-64; stockbroker Harrison & Co., 1964-66, gen. partner, 1966-73, mng. partner, 1972-77; v.p. Bache Halsey Stuart Shields Inc., Cin., 1977—; dir. Rembrandt Enterprises, Edina, Minn. Mem. investment com. Sisters of Charity, Cin., 1970. Trustee, treas. St. Joseph Cemetery, Cin. Served with AUS, 1959. Named Big Brother of the Year, 1968. Mem. Cin. (v.p. 1970-72), N.Y., Am. stock exchange, Purcell High Sch. Alumni (pres. 1972-73), Chgo. Bd. Options Exchange, Cath. Big Bros. Cin. (pres. 1966-67). Roman Catholic (council pres. 1971-72). Clubs: Cincinnati Stock and Bond (pres. 1969), Buckeye (pres. 1968-69). Home: 3660 Kroger Ave Cincinnati OH 45226 Office: 400 Formica Bldg Cincinnati OH 45226

FREY, JAMES LEONARD, ophthalmologist; b. Detroit, Mar. 15, 1920; s. J. Leonard and Jemima Ruth (Goudie) F.; B.S., U. Chgo., 1942, M.D., 1944; m. Natalie Elizabeth Mattern, May 20, 1950; children—Kirk A., Eric D. Intern, U. Chgo. Clinics, 1944-45; resident Harper Hosp., Detroit, 1948-51; pvt. practice ophthalmology, Detroit, 1953-76; ophthalmologist Fairlane Center, Henry Ford Hosp., Dearborn, Mich., 1976—; asst. clin. prof. Wayne State U. Med. Sch. Served with USNR, 1945-46, 52-53. Diplomate Am. Bd. Ophthalmology. Fellow A.C.S.; mem. Am. Acad. Ophthalmology, Pan Am. Soc. Ophthalmology, Mich. Ophthal. Soc. (pres. 1977—), Detroit Ophthal. Club (past pres. Eye Study Club), AMA, Mich., Oakland County (treas, 1975—) med. socs. Home: 4316 Echo Rd Bloomfield Hills MI 48013 Office: 19401 Hubbard Dr Dearborn MI 48126

FREY, JOHN MC CORMICK, copper co. exec.; b. Sterling, Ill., Feb. 8, 1921; s. John Kreider and Lucille (McCormick) F.; student pub. schs., Sterling, Ill.; m. Harriette Beryl Cady, Feb. 14, 1942; children—Patricia, John, Robert. Sales rep. Parker Hannefin Co., Otsego, Mich., 1946-59; pres., chief exec. officer John M. Frey Co., Moline, Ill., 1959—. Served with USAF, 1942-46. Republican. Congregationalist. Clubs: Union League, Chgo., Masons. Home: 5340 36th Ave Ct Moline IL 61265 Office: 530 34th St Moline IL 61265

FREY, MARSHA LEE, historian, educator; b. Toledo, Ohio, Feb. 21, 1947; d. Henry H. and Dolores A. (Saionz) Frey; B.A. summa cum laude, B.S. summa cum laude, Ohio State U., 1967, M.A., 1968, Ph.D., 1971. Asst. prof. early modern European history Kans. State U., 1973—; vis. asst. prof. history U. Oreg., Eugene, 1972-73; lectr. history Ohio State U., 1971-72. Recipient Great Ideas nat. award, 1964; NDEA fellow, 1967-70; Stradley scholar, 1964-67; Folger Shakespeare Library fellow, 1974. Author: The Gods Are Athirst, 1977; The View from the Hague, 1978; The Letters of William Harrison, 1978. Contbr. articles to profl. jours. Office: Kansas State Univ History Dept Manhattan KS 66506

FREYMAN, LEONARD, educator; b. Cleve., May 9, 1912; s. Henry Louis and Eva Evelyn (Krohn) F.; B.A., Case Western Res. U., 1939, M.A., 1940, Ph.D., 1955; postgrad. Mich. State U., 1943, Royal Acad. Dramatic Arts U. London, 1945; m. June Delories Snyder, May 24, 1944. Instr. Edmonton (Alta., Can.) Dept. Edn., summers 1940-41; with Cleveland Heights-University Heights (Ohio) City Sch. Dist., 1942, 46—, successively tchr. English, chmn. dept., English coordinator, now dir. edn. elementary and secondary curricula; instr. speech Shrivenham (Eng.) Am. U., 1945, Fenn Coll., Cleve., 1946-48; instr., trainer, cons. Dale Carnegie & Assos., Inc., 1947—; cons. Silver-Burdett Pubs., Morristown, N.J., 1965, Houghton Mifflin Pub., 1966-69. Dir. speech tng., tours, speakers and films div. United Appeal Greater Cleve., 1962-69; chmn. youth adv. com. Greater Cleve. chpt. A.R.C., 1965-67; life mem. Family Service Assn. Greater Cleve.; co-chmn. temples and schs. div. Jewish Welfare Fund Greater Cleve., 1976-77; bd. govs. Western Res. U., 1957-61; bd. overseers Case Western Res. U., 1972-75, vis. com., 1972-76. Served with AUS, 1942-45; ETO Named Alumnus of Year Cleve. Coll. Western Res. U., 1962. Fellow Royal Soc. Arts; mem. No. Ohio Drama Tchrs. Assn. (pres. 1952-54), Greater Cleve. Council Tchrs. English (pres. 1956-58), Nat. Council Tchrs. English (co-chmn. Cleve. conv. 1964). Jewish. Club: Fairmount Temple Brotherhood. Contbg. author: Books for You, 1964; Improving English Composition, 1965. also lang. arts tests. Contbr. articles to profl. jours. Home: 1002 Quarry Dr Cleveland Heights OH 44121 Office: 2155 Miramar Blvd Cleveland OH 44118

FRICKE, GORDON HUGH, chemist; b. Buffalo, Apr. 18, 1937; s. John Carl and Mildred Joanne (Hughes) F.; A.B., Goshen Coll., 1964; M.A., State U. N.Y. at Binghamton, 1966; Ph.D., Clarkson Coll. Tech., 1971; m. Sharon Lee Roesch, July 2, 1960; children—Gretchen Anne, Jason Scott. Teaching, research asso. State U. N.Y. at Buffalo, 1970-71, summer 1971; postdoctoral research fellow Wright State U., 1971-72; asst. prof. chemistry Ind. U.-Purdue U., Indpls., 1972-75, asso. prof., 1975—. AEC-Health and Safety Lab. fellow, 1966-70; Ind. U. Found. grantee 1973, 75, 77; Eli Lilly & Co., grantee, 1973; Purdue U. X-L grantee, 1977; recipient L.T. Jones award for outstanding sci. tchr. Ind. U.-Purdue U., 1977. Mem. Am. Chem. Soc. (sec. Ind. sect. 1977, chmn. elect Ind. sect. 1978), Am. Sci. Affiliation, Sigma Xi. Baptist. Home: 1925 N Mitthoefer Rd Indianapolis IN 46229 Office: Dept Chemistry 1201 E 38th St Indianapolis IN 46205

FRICKE, LOUIS HENRY, JR., elec. engr.; b. St. Louis, Dec. 22, 1928; s. Louis Henry and Violet Loretta (Fightmaster) F.; B.S.E.E., St. Louis U., 1951, M.S.(R), 1957; With Monsanto Co., St. Louis and St. Peters, Mo., 1957—, sr. research specialist, St. Peters, 1971-75, prin. engr., St. Louis, 1975--. Mem. IEEE, Instrument Soc. Am., Am. Inst. Chem. Engrs., Horseless Carriage Club Am./Mo., Kaiser-Frazer Owners, Reo of Am. Sigma Xi. Democrat. Episcopalian. Patentee in process dynamics identification and control instrumentation. Home: 7421 Zephyr Pl Maplewood MO 63143 Office: 800 N Lindbergh Blvd Saint Louis MO 63166

FRICKE, VERNON STANLEY, dentist, educator; b. Berger, Mo., Sept. 24, 1921; s. Frank Oscar and Martha Dina (Wattenberg) F.; student Central Mo. State Tchrs. Coll., 1939-42; D.D.S., Washington U., St. Louis, 1945, fellow pathology, 1945-46; m. Mary Louise Oliver, June 17, 1945; children—John, Kathryn, James, Robert, David. Instr. Washington U., 1946; commd. 2d lt., AUS, 1946, advanced through grades to col. USAF, 1961; ret., 1969; prof. dentistry, dir. dental support services program U. Mo., Kansas City, 1969—. Bd. dirs. Kansas City Heart Assn., 1971—, mem. exec. com., 1973, pres., 1974-75; bd. dirs. Mo. Heart Assn., 1972—, mem. exec. com., 1974—, chmn. cardiopulmonary resuscitation com., 1977—. Decorated Air Force Commendation medal with 2 oak leaf clusters; recipient Heart of Yr. award Kansas City Heart Assn., 1976. Fellow Am. Coll. Dentists (chmn. Kansas City Midwest sect. 1971-72, sec.-treas. 1972-73); mem. Am., Mo. dental assns., Greater Kansas City Dental Soc., Am. Assn. Dental Schs., Delta Sigma Delta, Omicron Kappa Upsilon. Mem. United Ch. of Christ (chmn. bd. Christian edn. 1975-76). Home: 10925 Campbell St Kansas City MO 65131 Office: 650 E 25th St Kansas City MO 64108

FRICKER, DONALD EDWARD, pub. relations exec.; b. Milw., May 4, 1916; s. William Gustave and May Tekla (Christianson) F.; B.A., U. Wis., 1938; m. Beatrice J. Elliott, Sept. 20, 1941; children—Jon Douglas, Sue Ellen, Ann Lynn. With advt. dept. Quality Biscuit Co., Milw., 1938-40; asst. advt. mgr. LeRoi Co., West Allis, Wis., 1940-47; advt. mgr. The Heil Co., West Allis, 1947-56; account exec. Western Advt. Agy., Racine, Wis., 1956-57; gen. supr. advt. and sales promotion, indsl. div. J.I. Case Co., Racine, 1957-60, advt. mgr., 1960-63, pub. relations mgr., 1963—. Pub. relations chmn. Racine United Way, 1965, 76. Served with U.S. Army, 1943-46. Recipient Distinguished Service award Future Farmers of Am., 1965; Distinguished Service award Racine United Way, 1966. Mem. Pub. Relations Soc. Am., Racine Mfrs. and Employers Assn., Racine C. of C., Farm and Indsl. Equipment Inst. Home: 11943 Indian Trail Hales Corners WI 53130 Office: 700 State St Racine WI 53404

FRICS, LASZLO AGOSTON, veterinarian; b. Hungary, Feb. 17, 1941; s. Laszlo and Margaret (Szokolay) F.; came to U.S., 1951, naturalized, 1956; B.S., D.V.M., U. Minn., 1966; m. Lucila Rios, Jan. 19, 1974. Commd. capt. U.S. Army, 1966, advanced through grades to maj.; various research, surgery, teaching and clin. veterinary assignments, 1966-77, ret. 1977; practice veterinary medicine, Emery, S.D., 1977—. Licensed veterinarian 7 states. Mem. Am., Brit. Minn., So. Calif. veterinary med. assns., Am. Animal Hosp. Assn. Roman Catholic. Home: Emery SD 57332

FRIDLEY, RUSSELL WILLIAM, historian; b. Oelwein, Iowa, Mar. 21, 1928; s. Lloyd and Laura (Tift) F.; B.A., Grinnell Coll., 1950; M.A., Columbia, 1953; m. Metta Holtkamp, Feb. 26, 1954; children—Scott, Nancy, Jane, Susan, Elizabeth, Jennifer. Asst. dir. Minn. Hist. Soc., St. Paul, 1953-54, dir., 1954—; v.p. Grinnell (Iowa) Coll., 1966; vice chmn. Nat. Advisory Council on Hist. Preservation, 1967-70; dir. div. edn. and pub. program Nat. Endowment for Humanities, 1968-69; chmn. Minn. Humanities Com., 1970—. Served with U.S. Army, 1946-48; PTO. Mem. Am. Assn. Museums (dir. 1969-73), Am. Assn. State and Local History (pres. 1966-68), Nat. Conf. State Historic Preservation Officers (v.p. 1977—). Author: Minnesota: A Students Guide to Localized History; The Uses of State and Local History; Historic Sites of North Dakota; Minnesota: A State That Works. Home: 740 Amber Dr St Paul MN 55112 Office: 690 Cedar St St Paul MN 55101

FRIED, PAUL GEORGE, educator; b. Leipzig, Germany, Apr. 4, 1919; s. Paul Markus and Emilie J. (Grunhaut) F.; came to U.S., 1939, naturalized, 1943; B.A., Hope Coll., 1946; M.A., Harvard U., 1947; Dr.Phil., U. Erlangen, Germany, 1949. Investigator gen. U.S. Air Force Hist. Div., Germany, 1951-53; instr. history European program U. Md., Hof, Germany, 1951-52; faculty Hope Coll., Holland, Mich., 1953—, prof. history, 1963—, dir. internat. edn., 1964—. Vis. prof. Mexico City Coll., 1954-55. Trustee Assn. Internat. Relations Clubs, 1960-64. Served with AUS, 1942-45. Decorated Bronze Star. Recipient gold medal of merit Republic of Austria, 1968. Mem. Am. Hist. Assn., Mich. Acad. Sci., Arts and Letters (chmn. sect. Russian and E. European history 1967-68), Phi Alpha Theta. Rotarian. Club: Harvard. Editor: Die Welt des Rolf Italiaander (Christian Verlag), 1973. Home: 18 W 12th St Holland MI 49423

FRIED, RICHARD MAYER, historian; b. Milw., Apr. 14, 1941; s. Richard G. and Betty (Mayer) F.; B.A., Amherst (Mass.) Coll., 1963; M.A., Columbia U., 1965, Ph.D., 1972; m. Barbara Brachman, Aug. 1, 1964; children—Richard B., Gail Lynne. Instr., Bowling Green (Ohio) State U., 1967-70; asst. prof. Indiana (Pa.) U., 1970-71, Fairmont (W.Va.) State Coll., 1971-72; mem. faculty U. Ill., Chgo. Circle, 1972—, asso. prof. history, 1977—. Mem. Glendale Heights (Ill.) Plan Commn., 1975-77. Edward John Noble fellow, 1963-66; Herbert H. Lehman fellow, 1966-67; Nat. Endowment Humanities-Rockefeller Found. fellow, Newberry Library, 1977; grantee Harry S. Truman Library Inst., 1967, 77, Eleanor Roosevelt Found., 1977. Mem. Am. Hist. Assn., Orgn. Am. Historians, State Hist. Soc. Wis. Author: Men Against McCarthy, 1976. Home: 255 Forest Ave Glen Ellyn IL 60137 Office: Univ Illinois Chicago Circle Chicago IL 60680

FRIEDBERG, GERALD, ednl. adminstr.; b. Bklyn., June 16, 1946; s. Herbert and Jean Miller; B.E., U. Akron, 1972; postgrad. in Edn., U. Toledo, 1976—; m. Christine Rachel Morehouse, Aug. 3, 1973; 1 dau., Meredith Ann. Copywriter, Norman Malone & Assos., Akron, Ohio, 1971-72; instr. radio broadcasting arts Streetsboro (Ohio) City Schs., 1972-73; dir. radio and TV broadcasting art Toledo Pub. Schs., 1973-77; dir. radio and TV Fahlgren & Ferris/Phillips & Harrington, Sylvania, Ohio, 1977—; cons. U.S. Office of Edn., Ohio State Dept. Vocat. Edn. Served with USCG, 1970-71. Mem. NEA, Nat. Assn. Ednl. Broadcasters, Am. Fedn. Tchrs., Sigma Pi. Jewish. Home: 609 W Poinsetta St Toledo OH 43612 Office: 7654 W Bancroft St Sylvania OH 43617

FRIEDBERG, MAURICE, educator; b. Rzeszow, Poland, Dec. 3, 1929; s. Isaac and Ida (Jam) F.; came to U.S., 1948, naturalized, 1954; B.S., Bklyn. Coll., 1951; A.M., Columbia, 1953; certificate Russian Inst., 1953; Ph.D., Columbia, 1958; m. Barbara Bisguier, Mar. 18, 1956; children—Rachel Miriam, Edna Sarah. Lectr. in Russian, Bklyn. Coll., 1952, Middlebury Coll., 1960-61; asso. Russian Research Center, Harvard, 1953; asso. prof., charge Russian div. Hunter Coll., N.Y.C., 1955-65; prof. Slavic langs. and lits. Ind. U., 1966-75, dir. Russian and East European Inst., 1967-71; prof. Russian lit. and head dept. Slavic lang. and lit. U. Ill. at Urbana, 1975—; vis. asst. prof. Russian lit. Columbia, 1961-62; lectr. Russian lit., N.Y.U., 1965; Fulbright vis. prof. Russian lit., Hebrew U., Jerusalem, Israel, 1965-66. Cons. on Russian lit. and Soviet affairs to pub., radio, etc.; juror Nat. Book Award, 1973. Guggenheim fellow, 1971. Mem. Polish Inst. Arts and Scis. in U.S. (corr.), Am. Assn. Advancement Slavic Studies (dir.), Am. Assn. Tchrs. Slavic Langs., Modern Lang. Assn. (dir. internat. research and exchanges bd.). Jewish. Author: Russian Classics in Soviet Jackets, 1962; The Party and the Poet in the USSR, 1963 (also Spanish edit.); A Bilingual Edition of Russian Short Stories, Vol. I, 1964, Vol. II, 1965; The Jew in Post-Stalin Soviet Literature, 1970 (also Portuguese edit.); A Decade of Euphoria: Western Literature in Post-Stalin Russia, 1977. Editor: The Young Lenin (Leon Trotsky), 1972; deptl. editor Ency. Judaica, 16 vols., 1971-72. Contbr. to scholarly jours. and popular mags. Home: 3001 Meadowbrook Ct Champaign IL 61820 Office: Dept Slavic Lang and Lit U Ill Urbana IL 61801

FRIEDBURG, KLAUS MARTIN, veterinarian; b. Holstein, Germany, Feb. 26, 1917; s. Martin Theodor and Anna Louise (Feddersen) F.; came to U.S., 1937, naturalized, 1947; D.V.M., Ohio State U., 1942; m. Donna Rae Booth, Oct. 22, 1945; children—Martin Lloyd, Paul Eugene. Asst. vetrinarian Beverly Veterinary Hosp., Chgo., 1943-47; owner, mgr. Three Oaks Veterinary Hosp. (Mich.), 1947—; owner, dir. Michigan City (Ind.) Small Animal Hosp., 1949—. Trustee United Methodist Ch., Three Oaks, 1972—. Fellow Royal Soc. Health (London); mem. Three Oaks C. of C., Mich. Veterinary Med. Assn., AVMA, Community Concert Assn., Twin City Symphony Assn. Patentee surgical clamp Faultless Ear Patterns; research, publs. Anesthesia of Parakeets and Canaries, Diseases of Budgerigars. Home: 708 S Elm St Three Oaks MI 49128 Office: Three Oaks Veterinary Hospital Three Oaks MI 49128

FRIEDENBERG, WALTER DREW, editor; b. Meriden, Conn., Dec. 22, 1928; s. Gustav Edward and Adela (Drews) F.; B.A., Wake Forest U., 1949; A.M., Harvard U., 1956; postgrad. U. Chgo., summer 1959; m. Ramona Avila, May 29, 1965; children—Christopher Drew, Eric Avila, Karina Della. Reporter, Rocky Mount (N.C.) Evening Telegram, 1949-50, Winston-Salem Jour., 1950, Richmond (Va.) Times-Dispatch, 1954, Buffalo Evening News, summer 1956; fellow Inst. Current World Affairs, N.Y. in Indian subcontinent, 1956-60; stringer Chgo. Daily News, Fgn. News Service, 1960; reporter Pitts. Press, 1960-61; fgn. corr. in Europe, Africa and Asia, Scripps-Howard Newspaper Alliance, Washington, 1961-66, editorial writer, 1966-69; editor Cin. Post and Times-Star, 1969—. Served to 2d lt. U.S. Army, 1951-53. Mem. Nat. Press Club Washington, Phi Beta Kappa, Omicron Delta Kappa. Club: Queen City (Cin.). Home: 3475 Vista Ave Cincinnati OH 45208 Office: 800 Broadway Cincinnati OH 45202

FRIEDERICH, RAY R., dist. judge; b. Fredonia, N.D., Sept. 20, 1921; s. Jacob and Pauline (Bueber) F.; B.S., U. N.D., 1943; LL.B., U. Minn., 1948; m. Irene C. Kruger, Nov. 7, 1948; children—Kurt M., Kent E. Admitted to N.D. bar, 1948; practiced in Rugby, N.D., 1948-60; states atty. Pierce County, N.D., 1951-56; dist. judge 2d Jud. Dist., Rugby, 1960—. Sec. bd. dirs. Rugby Broadcaster, Inc. Mem. adv. council N.D. Pub. Welfare Bd. Bd. dirs. Crippled Children's Sch., Jamestown, N.D. Served with U.S. Army, 1943-46. Decorated Bronze Star medal, Purple Heart. Mem. Am. Radio Relay League, D.A.V. (past state comdr.), N.D. Peace Officers Assn. (past state pres.). Republican. Lutheran. Club: Lions. Home: 313 3d Ave SW Rugby ND 58368 Office: PO Box 72 Courthouse Rugby ND 58368

FRIEDERSDORF, BURK, coll. adminstr.; b. Madison, Ind., Feb. 28, 1915; s. Carl Barber and Mary Berenice (Knoebel) F.; A.B., Hanover (Ind.) Coll., 1936; M.A. in Journalism, Ball State U., Muncie, Ind., 1975; m. Betty Hayes Henninger, June 15, 1940; children—Christopher B., Anne H. Friedersdorf Vetters. Advt. mgr. Madison (Ind.) Courier, 1936-39; theatre mgr. Madison Theatre Corp., 1939-43; editor Franklin (Ind.) Evening Star, 1946-49; reporter Indpls. Star, 1949-55; v.p. Bozell & Jacobs, Inc., Indpls., 1955-65; dir. information Stephens Coll., Columbia, Mo., 1965-72; editor Greenfield (Ind.) Reporter, 1972-73; dir. devel. and coll. relations Marian Coll., Indpls., 1973—, also adj. prof. Served with AUS, 1943-46. Mem. Pub. Relations Soc. Am. (accredited, v.p. Hoosier chpt. 1977), Council Advancement and Support of Edn. Presbyterian (elder). Clubs: Greenfield Kiwanis (pres. 1977), Masons, Indpls. Press. Author: From Crystal to Color, 1964. Home: Rt 9 Box 209 Greenfield IN 46140 Office: 3200 Cold Spring Rd Indianapolis IN 46222

FRIEDLANDER, DANIEL SIMON, communications co. exec.; b. Chgo., Apr. 11, 1933; s. Leo and Ann (Simon) F.; B.J., U. Colo., 1955; m. Shirley Tishcoff, Sept. 6, 1959; children—Janet, Alan, Robert. Asst. editor City News Bur. Chgo., 1955-57; editor AP, Chgo., 1958; editor Chgo. Am., 1959-61; pub. Warren-Newport News, Gurnee, Ill., 1960-63; co-founder, regional editor Metalworking News, Chgo. and N.Y.C., 1961-69; pres. Universal Communications, Chgo., 1969—, Simon & Friedlander Ltd., Chgo., 1976. Wenzel Trucking Co., Chgo., 1974—, Friedlander Communications, Ltd., Chgo., 1977—; dir. Tra Mor Corp. Chmn. Waukegan Twp. (Ill.) Democrats, 1967-68; chmn. numerous presidential, senatorial, gubernatorial and congl. campaigns; bd. dirs. Citizen's Com. for Battered Children, Chgo. Mem. Assn. Corp. Growth (v.p.), Soc. Profl. Journalists. Jewish. Clubs: Chgo. Press (editor newspaper 1970-76), Chgo. Headline (editor newspaper 1975-76), Execs. of Chgo., Rotary, B'nai B'rith. Home: 2014 N Jackson St Waukegan IL 60085 Office: 9400 W Foster St Chicago IL 60656

FRIEDLANDER, JOANNE KOHN, realtor; b. Chgo., Aug. 22, 1930; d. Isidore E. and Carolyn Dolly (Newman) Kohn; B.A., Northwestern U., 1954; m. Stanley Friedlander, Sept. 10, 1955; children—Mark, Sue. Reporter, Chgo. Sun-Times, 1951-54; free lance writer, 1956-66; tchr. primary grades Chgo. Pub. Schs., 1968-70; realtor J.H. Kahn Realty Co., Glencoe, Ill., 1970—. Vol. worker Jewish United Fund, Chgo., 1975. Mem. Million Dollar Club, Nat. Assn. Realtors, Nat. Marketing Inst., Evanston-N. Shore Bd. Realtors. Jewish. Author: Stock Market ABC, 1969. Home: 1300 Rosemary Ln Northbrook IL 60062 Office: 640 Vernon St Glencoe IL 60022

FRIEDMAN, BYRON, ednl. adminstr.; b. Chgo., Feb. 9, 1916; s. Morris L. and Lillian (Distenfeld) F.; B.S., Roosevelt Coll., 1938; postgrad. Northwestern U. Grad. Sch. Social Work, 1939; m. Sulie Harand, June 7, 1942; children—Jacquelyn, Judith. Field dir. 6th Marine Div., A.R.C., 1943-45; v.p. S. Bloom, Inc. Chgo., 1941-55; founder, pres. Harand Camp of Theatre Arts, Elkhart Lake, Wis., 1955—; dir. Harand Theatre Studios, Chgo. Speaker on theatre, 1958—. Mem. Am. Ednl. Theatre Assn., Am. Camping Assn., Am. Nat. Theatre and Acad. (chmn. bd. dirs. Chgo. chpt. 1960-62). Home: 828 Oakton St Evanston IL 60202 Office: 410 S Michigan Ave Chicago IL 60605

FRIEDMAN, CHARLES MARSHALL, lawyer; b. St. Louis, Sept. 28, 1940; s. Simon and Celia (Filirent) F.; A.B., Washington U., St. Louis, 1963, J.D., 1965; m. Carol Sue Ross, Dec. 25, 1973; children—Scott Andrew, Mark Aaron. Admitted to Mo. bar, 1965; since practiced in St. Louis; with Gray & Sommers, 1965-67; mem. firm Gray & Friedman, 1968-70; partner Gray, Friedman & Ritter, 1968-75, Friedman, Weitzman & Friedman, 1975—. Served with USCGR, 1958-63. Recipient Trial Lawyer award Mo. Bar Found., 1970. Mem. Am. Bar Assn., Am. Trial Lawyers Assn., Mo. Assn. Trial Attys., Bar Assn. of St. Louis, Lawyers Assn. Jewish. Editor: The Missouri Bar Handbook on Evidence Law, 1968. Home: 10505 Frontenac Woods Ln Frontenac MO 63131 Office: 4th Floor Paul Brown Bldg 818 Olive St St Louis MO 63101

FRIEDMAN, GLENN R., rehab. psychologist; b. Cleve., Apr. 9, 1948; s. Glenn Emmerson and Emma Rae (Morehart) F.; M.A. in Clin. Psychology magna cum laude, Cleve. State U., 1974, B.A., 1970. Intern vocat. development center, Cleve., 1973-74; substitute tchr., special edn., Cleve. Bd. Edn., 1971-72; tchr. Learning Community Free Sch., Cleveland Heights, Ohio, 1971-72; asst. psychologist I, Vocat. Devel. Center, Ohio, 1974, asst. psychologist, supr. work adjustment services, 1975-76, psychologist, 1976—; vocat. rehab. specialist Warrensville (Ohio) Center, 1976-78. Mem. ACLU, Am. Psychol. Assn., Nat. Rehab. Assn., Nat. Rehab. Counselors Assn., Vocat. Evaluation and Work Adjustment Assn., Cousteau Soc., Western Pa. Conservancy. Recipient Self Realization fellowship; Certified rehab. counselor, Ohio, 1975, emergency med. technician, Ohio, 1977. Developer evaluation, meditation, vocat. rehab. programs; establishment pre-vocat. workshop and Evaluation and Adjustment Program, Warrensville Center, 1976. Home: 25400 Rockside Rd Bedford Hts OH 44146 Office: 4325 Green Rd Warrensville Twp OH 44146

FRIEDMAN, HARRY SAMUEL, physician; b. Mpls., Sept. 13, 1915; s. Samuel and Mary (Gellerman) F.; B.S., U. Minn., 1937, M.B., 1939, M.D., 1940; m. Gertrude Rotenberg, Aug. 29, 1948; children—Sharon, Rohn, Jeffrey. Intern, Trinity Hosp., Minot, N.D., 1938-40; preceptorship with Dr. I.A. Abrahamson, Cin., 1946-47; resident in ophthalmology Hines (Ill.) VA Hosp., 1947-49; practice medicine specializing in ophthalmology, Mpls., 1949—; asst. chief ophthalmology Hennepin County Gen. Hosp., Mpls., 1960—; chief of staff Mt. Sinai Hosp., Mpls., 1971-73; mem. staff No. Meml., Methodist hosps., (both Mpls.). Clin. asso. prof. ophthalmology U. Minn., Mpls., 1970—. Served with M.C., AUS, 1940-45; ETO. Diplomate Am. Bd. Ophthalmology. Mem. Am., Minn., Hennepin County med. socs., Am., Minn. (council 1973—) acads. ophthalmology and otolaryngology, Minn. Ophthal. Soc. (pres. 1958-59), Assn. for Ophthalmology, Am. Assn. Contemporary Ophthalmology, Am. Intraocular Lens Soc., Contact Lens Assn., Am. Physicians Fellowship, Phi Delta Epsilon. Jewish (dir. synagogue). Club: Rolling Green Country. Home: 4230 Basswood Rd Minneapolis MN 55416 Office: 318 Doctors Bldg 90 S 9th St Minneapolis MN 55402 also Meadowbrook Medical Bldg Minneapolis MN 55426

FRIEDMAN, HOWARD, photo chem. machining co. exec.; b. Chgo., Apr. 27, 1932; s. Max and Rose Ann (Zwick) F.; B.S. in Metall. Engring., U. Ill., 1955; m. Kay Arlene Levinson, June 26, 1955; children—Beth Janet, David Bruce, Richard Neil. Research engr. Armour Research Found., Chgo., 1955-58; pres. Champion Laundry Co., Chgo., 1958-67; founder, pres. Foto Fabrication Corp., Chgo., 1967—. Mem. Am. Soc. Metals, Ill. Mfg. Assn. Jewish. One-man show of photographs Skokie (Ill.) Fine Arts Center, 1976. Home: 9321 Menard St Morton Grove IL 60053 Office: 3758 Belmont St Chicago IL 60618

FRIEDMAN, JEROME JAY, lawyer; b. Cory, Pa., Apr. 5, 1906; s. Simon Friedman and Bertha (Brodsy) F.; A.B., U. Mich., 1927, L.L.B., J.D., 1929; m. Margaret Byfield, Oct. 17, 1942; children—Mary Lee, James Alexander. Admitted to Ill. bar, 1930, and since practiced in Chgo. Chmn. law and order com., city commn. on Human Relations, 1949-57; mem. Mayor's Commn. on Human Relations, 1948-69, temp. acting chmn., 1968, hon. appointee spl. housing and pub. accomodation matters; chmn. exec. com. Joint Def. Appeal of Chgo., 1952-53; chmn. Bishop Shiel Youth of Year award, Chgo., 1951; pres. Chgo. B'nai B'rith Council, 1939; mem. Civil Rights Com., Chgo., also chmn.; mem. exec. com. Chgo. Fedn. U.A.H.C., 1960-63; chmn. lawyers div. Jewish Fedn. Met. Chgo., 1965. Pres. Sinai Temple, Chgo. Served as capt. USAAF, 1942-46. Recipient citations for civic contbns. Mem. Am., Ill., Chgo. bar assns., Anti Defamation League (chmn. Chgo. exec. com. 1949-51, mem. nat. commn. 1954-55). Jewish. Clubs: Standard, Lake Shore Country, Executives. Home: 1000 Lake Shore Plaza Chicago IL 60611 Office: 33 N LaSalle St Chicago IL 60602

FRIEDMAN, MARTIN BURTON, chem. co. exec.; b. N.Y.C., June 21, 1927; s. William L. and Ella (Holstein) F.; student Mt. St. Mary's Coll., 1943-44, Cornell U., 1944-45; B.A., Pa. State U., 1949; m. Rita Fleischman, Mar. 19, 1950; children—Jay Edward, Ellen Jane. Mgr. advt. and promotion chems. group Sun Chem. Corp., N.Y.C., 1949-54; mgr. advt. and promotion textile chems. dept. Am. Cyanamid Co., N.Y.C., 1954-58, mgr. advt. and promotion Organic Chems. div., 1958-60, gen. merchandising mgr. Fibers div., 1961-64, director of sales Fibers div., 1964-65, dir. mktg. Fibers div., 1965-69, asst. gen. mgr. Fibers div., 1969-72; v.p. I.R.C. Fibers Co. subsidiary Am. Cyanamid Co., 1969-72; exec. v.p. Formica Corp., Cin., 1972-73, pres., 1973—; dir. Cin. br. Fed. Res. Bank, Cleve. Served with USNR, 1945-46. Named to Textile Hall of Fame, 1958. Mem. Am. Chem. Soc., Am. Assn. Textile Chemists and Colorists. Club: Chemists (N.Y.C.). Contbr. articles to textile and tech. publs. Home: 7395 Algonquin Dr Cincinnati OH 45243 Office: Formica Corp Cincinnati OH

FRIEDMAN, MIRIAM ZAVELSON, social worker; b. Cleve.; d. Abraham Philip and Sophie (Miller) Z.; B.A., Flora Stone Mather Coll., Western Res. U., 1935; m. Harry Martin Friedman (dec.); 1 son, Richard Everett. Welding insp. Republic Steel, Cleve., 1942-45; occupational therapist aide Cleve. Met. Gen. Hosp., Brecksville VA Hosp., Mt. Sinai Hosp., Cleve., 1946-47; founder, exec. dir. Red Wing Day Camp, Inc., Hinckley, Ohio, 1947-74; ct. liaison officer/intake social worker Cuyahoga County (Ohio) Youth Devel. Center, Hudson, 1975—. Trustee Salzedo Sch. of Harp. Mem. Am. Camping Assn. (pres. Lake Erie sect. 1958-59, chmn. Region 3, mem. nat. bd. 1961-69, past v.p., sec., gen. chmn. central regions conv. 1971), Mt. Sinai Hosp. Aux. (life), Flora Stone Mather Coll. Alumni Assn. (life), Lake Forest Country Club Women's Assn. (bd. mem. 1952-53), United Order True Sisters, Women's City Club Cleve., Nat. Conf. Social Welfare, Cleve. Mus. Art (spl. life), Met. Mus. Art. Home: 24104 Wimbledon Rd Shaker Heights OH 44122 Office: 996 Hines Hill Rd Hudson OH 44236

FRIEDMAN, NAOMI MERRIAM, vocat. service exec.; b. Kansas City, Mo., Feb. 25, 1922; d. Jack N. and May H. (Seliger) Balkin; B.S. in Edn., U. Okla., 1943; M.A. in Edn., U. Mo., Kansas City, 1967; m. Sidney J. Friedman, Nov. 4, 1945; children—Jack Eric Friedman, Diana Gail Friedman Price. Tchr. Welborn (Kans.) Pub. Schs., 1943-44; asso. dir. community relations bur. Greater Kans. City, Mo., 1944-48; subs. tchr. Kansas City (Mo.) Sch. Dist., 1958-65; supr. counseling dept. Jewish Vocat. Service, Kansas City, Mo., 1967—; cons., lectr. in field. Mem. Am. Personnel and Guidance Assn., Nat. Vocat. Guidance Assn., Am. Rehab. Counseling Assn., Nat. Rehab. Counseling Assn., Nat. Assn. Coll. Admissions Counselors. Jewish. Author column: Ask the Counselor Kansas City Chronicle, 1970—. Home: 2300 W 79th St Terr Prairie Village KS 66208

FRIEDMAN, ROBERT LLOYD, radiologist; b. Bklyn., Sept. 20, 1913; s. Samuel and Sadie (Reich) F.; B.S., N.Y. U., 1934; M.D., Royal Colls. Edinburgh, 1940; m. Elsie Korzenik, Jan. 11, 1942; 1 son, Michael Jon. Intern, Newark Beth Israel Hosp., Newark, 1941-42; resident Bklyn. Jewish Hosp., 1947-50; asst. chief dept. radiology VA Hosp., Richmond, Va., 1950-53; asst. clin. prof. radiology Coll. Medicine, Richmond, 1950-53; staff dept. radiology Grant Hosp., Columbus, Ohio, 1953-66, chief dept., 1966—; asst. clin. prof. radiology Sch. Medicine Ohio State U., 1953—. Trustee Temple Tifereth Israel, 1966-68, Columbus Jewish Fedn., 1970-72. Served with M.C., U.S. Army, 1942-46. Decorated Purple Heart. Fellow Am. Coll. Radiology; mem. AMA, Am. Coll. Radiology, Radiol. Soc. N.Am., Roentgen Ray Soc., Acad. Medicine Franklin County, Central Ohio Radiol. Soc. (pres. 1962-63), Ohio State Radiol. Soc. (exec. com.). Jewish. Clubs: Winding Hollow Country, B'nai B'rith, Am. Jewish Congress. Contbr. articles to radiol. jours. Home: 81 S Stanwood Rd Bexley OH 43209 Office: 3341 E Livingston Ave Columbus OH 43227

FRIEDMAN, SONYA, psychologist; b. Bklyn., Mar. 27, 1936; d. Joseph B. Kiel and Frieda (Beekman) Goldman; B.A., Bklyn. Coll., 1956; M.Ed., Wayne State U., 1963, Ph.D., 1967; m. Stephen Friedman, Aug. 5, 1956; children—Sharon, Scott. Speech and hearing therapist Des Moines Pub. Schs., 1956-59; speech therapist Pontiac (Mich.) Pub. Schs., 1959-62; cons. psychologist Rochester (Mich.) Community Schs., 1963-76, Bloomfield Hills (Mich.) Schs., 1977—; pvt. practice Psychol. Resources, Inc., Bloomfield Hills, 1967—. Bd. dirs. Nat. Orgn. to Insure Support Enforcement, Nat. Orgn. Non-Parents. Mem. Am., Mich. psychol. assns., Am. Assn. Marriage Counselors, World Future Soc., Am. Orthopsychiat. assn. Recipient Headliner award Wayne State U. Alumnae Assn., 1974; certified cons. psychologist; certified marriage counselor. Columnist, Birmingham (Mich.) Eccentric, 1970-74. Author: I've Had It, You've Had It, 1974. Resident psychologist AM-Am., AM-N.Y., AM-Detroit, Morning Exchange, Cleve.; syndicated TV series: For A Better Life; spl. correspondent ABC-TV News, 1976—. Home: 2960 Middlebelt Rd Orchard Lake MI 48033 Office: Psychological Resources 1575 Woodward Ave Bloomfield Hills MI 48013

FRIEDMAN, STANFORD JOSEPH, steel co. exec.; b. Cleve., June 27, 1927; s. Sol H. and Cele (Akers) F.; B.S., M.E., I.E., U. Mich., 1949; m. Louise Glatt, July 19, 1949; children—Steven James, Jonathan Richard, Sally D. Pres., dir. Solar Mid-Con, Inc. (formerly Solar Steel Corp.), Cleve., 1961—, Danstan Realty Corp., Cleve.; dir. Phillip's Syrup Corp., Rolltech Corp., Universal Container Corp. Trustee Solar Found. Mem. ASME, Soc. Automotive Engrs., Am. Iron and Steel Inst. Clubs: Oakwood Country (Cleve.); Standard (Chgo.). Home: 52 Wychwood Dr Moreland Hills OH 44022 Office: 24200 Chagrin Blvd Beachwood OH 44122

FRIEDMAN-AXIER, MARJORIE, electronics engr.; b. N.Y.C.; d. Philip and Sophie Charlotte (Friedman) Friedman; B.S. in Physics, Queens Coll.; M.S. in Physics, N.Y. U., 1961; postgrad. in engring. U. Calif., Los Angeles, 1976—. Research physicist, unit leader electron tube techniques lab. U.S. Naval Applied Sci. Lab., Bklyn., 1956-60; sr. engr. research dept. PRD Electronics Co., N.Y.C., 1960-61; research engr. Gen. Telephone and Electronics Labs., N.Y.C., 1961-66; sr. engr. sci. and tech. dept. def. and space div. Westinghouse Electric Co., Balt., 1966-68; mem. tech. staff TRW Systems Group, Los Angeles and Hughes Aircraft Co., Los Angeles, 1969-74; design electronics engr. Gen. Dynamics Corp., Pomona, Calif., 1975-76; staff electronics engr. advanced engring. dept. A-T-O Co., Anaheim, Calif., 1976—; adj. instr. physics and electronics N.Y. Inst. Tech., 1969, El Camino Coll., Torrance, Calif., 1969-75, Los Angeles Trade-Tech.

Coll., 1969-71; asso. mem. adv. group on electron tubes Office Dir. Def., Research and Engring., 1957-60. Mem. IEEE (sr.), Am. Phys. Soc., Sci. Research Soc. Am. Contbr. articles to profl. publs. Home: 21 Kristin Dr Schaumburg IL 60195

FRIEDMANN, IRA JEROME, pediatrician; b. N.Y.C., Feb. 19, 1933; s. Eli B. and Rose (Goldstein) F.; B.S., U. Ark., 1955, M.D., 1960; m. Geraldine Bensky, June 5, 1960; children—Dana, Jill, Miriam. Successively intern, resident in pediatrics, chief resident Jackson Meml. Hosp., Miami, Fla., 1960-63; pediatrician Overland (Mo.) Med. Center, 1965—, med. dir., since 1970; adv. bd. Barnes Hosp., St. Louis; asst. prof. Washington U. Med. Sch., St. Louis. Served with M.C., USNR, 1963-65. Mem. Am. Acad. Pediatrics, Mo., St. Louis pediatric socs. Address: 2428 Woodson Rd Overland MO 63114

FRIEDRICH, CHARLES WILLIAM, indsl. relations exec.; b. Elgin, Ill., Aug. 30, 1943; s. Charles Kenneth and Veronica Elizabeth (Sharpe) F.; B.A., Parsons Coll., 1967; student Loras Coll., 1961-63; m. Janet Lee West, June 20, 1970; children—Joan Elizabeth, Charles Kenneth II. Salesman Bendix Corp., South Bend, Ind., 1967; safety dir., asst. personnel mgr. Nat. Castings div. Midland Ross, Cicero, Ill., 1968-69; personnel mgr. Continental Tube Co. div. Hofmann Industries, Bellwood, Ill., 1969, asst. indsl. relations mgr., 1970, Midwest dir. indsl. relations Hofmann Industries, 1971-73; dir. indsl. relations, gen. mgr. Lemont Shipbuilding and Repair Co. (Ill.), 1973-75; indsl. relations exec. Modern Mgmt. Methods, Inc., Deerfield, Ill., 1975-77, O'Connor & Assos., Palatine, Ill., 1977—; v.p. Standard Cons. Services, Hinsdale, Ill., 1977—. Pres., Burr Ridge (Ill.) Park Dist. Bd. Mem. Packard Automobile Classics Club (regional dir.), Alpha Phi Omega. Home: 10S431 Glenn Dr Hinsdale IL 60521 Office: 835 Sterling St Palatine IL 60067 also 450 S Vine St Hinsdale IL 60521

FRIEDRICHS, NIELS GEORG, bus. exec.; b. Luebeck, West Germany, Dec. 22, 1929; s. Peter H. and Gertrud (Hahn) F.; came to U.S., 1958; ed. Katharineum, Luebeck, 1949; m. Ilona Grund, Dec. 18, 1957; children—Kirsten, Dirk. Printer, Flint, Mich., 1959-61; salesman Lufthansa Airlines, Chgo., 1961-63; mng. dir. German Am. C. of C., Chgo., 1963—; lectr. in field. Mem. Internat. Trade Club (Chgo.), Chgo. Assn. Commerce and Industry, Assn. German Foreign Chamber Mgrs. (Bonn Germany). Lutheran. Club: Ill. Athletic (Chgo.). Home: 515 Linden Ave Wilmette IL 60091 Office: 77 E Monroe St Chicago IL 60603

FRIEHE, ROBERT DEAN, farmer; b. McCook, Nebr., Jan. 26, 1946; s. Ervain John and Nadine June (Klein) F.; B.S. in Agrl. Mechanization, U. Nebr., 1969; m. Mary Louise Pankonin, Aug. 24, 1968; children—Jennifer Marie, Laura Michelle. Vice-pres., mgr. Friehe Farms Inc., McCook, 1969—. Mem. Middle Republic River Natural Resource Dist., 1973-75. Sec. Red Willow County (Nebr.) Democratic Com., 1972—. Named Outstanding Young Farm Family Nebr., 1974. Mem. Am. Soc. Agrl. Engrs., Red Willow County Wheat Growers Assn. (treas. 1969-71, sec. 1972-74), Red Willow County Farm Bur. (dir. 1976—), Alpha Phi Omega. Lutheran. Address: Route 4 McCook NE 69001

FRIEND, JOHN ALVA, JR., farmer, polit. worker; b. Dade County, Mo., July 29, 1920; s. John Alva and Willa (Davis) F.; student pub. schs.; m. Dorothy Jean Cates, Mar. 9, 1946; children—Jennifer Friend Cummings, Johnna Friend Wilson, John Alva Cates. Farmer nr. Greenfield, Mo., 1940—. Mem. adv. com. Prodn. Credit Assn., 1952-72; sec., treas., dir. Producers Grocery Co., Springfield, 1964—. Mem. South Twp. Democratic Com., 1968—. Served with AUS, 1942-46; PTO. Mem. Mo. Farmers Assn. (sec.-treas. 1960-73, dir. 1960-73), Am. Legion. Mem. Disciples of Christ (chmn. unity bd. 1963-73). Address: RFD 1 S Greenfield MO 65752

FRIEND, ROBERT NATHAN, fin. counselor; b. Chgo., Feb. 2, 1930; s. Karl D. and Marion (Wollenberger) F.; A.B., Grinnell Coll., 1951; M.S., Ill. Inst. Tech., 1953; m. Lorraine Pearlman, Apr. 7, 1968; children—Karen, Alan. With K. Friend & Co., Chgo., 1953—, v.p., early 1960's, 1st v.p., 1964—, dir. merger activities with Standard Oil Co. (Ind.), trustee employees' benefit trust, 1958—; active R. Friend Investments, registered investment counselors. Chmn. petroleum div. Combined Jewish Appeal, 1966, 67, Jewish Fedn. Chgo., 1964-66; admissions cons. Grinnell Coll., Ill. Inst. Tech., 1968-70; alumni career counselor Ill. Inst. Tech. Fellow Econ. Edn. and Research Forum; mem. Greater Chgo. Gasoline Marketers Assn. (v.p., dir.), Am. Finance Assn., Execs. Club Chgo., Am. Acad. Polit. and Social Sci., Indsl. Relations Research Assn., Newcomen Soc. N. Am., Chgo. Council Fgn. Relations, Am. Econ. Assn., Acad. Polit. Sci. Home: 2801 Sheridan Rd Chicago IL 60657 Office: 222 W Adams St Chicago IL 60606

FRIEND, WILLIAM JOE, dentist; b. Ft. Scott, Kans., July 29, 1933; s. Joseph Stanley and Gladys Pearl (Griffith) F.; student Kansas City Jr. Coll., 1951-52; D.D.S., U. Mo., 1962; m. Bonnie Jean Barritt, Mar. 1, 1958; children—William Kirk, Olen Kent. Individual practice dentistry, Raytown, Mo., 1962—. Owner, developer Alpine Village Apts., Raytown, Glen Lake Subdiv., Kansas City, Mo.; pres. Walnut Ridge Devel. Corp., Raytown, 1972—, chmn. bd., 1972—. Served with USNR, 1953-57. Mem. Am., Mo., Greater Kansas City dental assns., Southeastern Jackson County Mental Health Assn., Friends of Art, Friends of Zoo, Smithsonian Assos., Internat. Oceanographic Assn., Raytown C. of C. (council of clubs 1972-73), Xi Psi Phi. Methodist (mem. bd. 1968—). Club: Raytown Exchange (pres. 1972-73). Home: Glen Lake Farm 5751 McCoy Kansas City MO 64133 Office: 10301 E 61st St Raytown MO 64133

FRIESENHENGST, ALFRED RUDOLF, retail store exec.; b. Lorain, Ohio, Aug. 27, 1910; s. Rudolf Karl and Wilhelmina Marie (Duldner) F.; A.B. (Ohio scholar), Western Reserve U., 1932; m. Helen Marie Horrall, June 6, 1937; children—Mary Jeanette Friesenhengst Rhoads, Nancy Marie Friesenhengst Briggs. Mgr., F.W. Woolworth Co., Washington, Inc., 1934-41, Libertyville, Ill., 1940-41; owner, operator A.R. Friesenhengst Variety and Clothing Stores, Shoals, Ind., 1941-62, Loogootee, Ind., 1944-62, Crane, Ind., 1946-58, Mitchell, Ind., 1956-58, French Lick, Ind., 1958-62, Huntingburg, Ind., 1948-51; owner, operator Alco Dime Stores, Shoals, Loogootee, French Lick, 1962—, Shoals Discount Mart, 1958—, A.R. Friesenhengst Wholesale Co., Shoals, 1948—; pres., chmn. bd. A.R. Friesenhengst, Inc., Shoals, 1962—; advisory com. John Wesley Ins. Co., Ind., 1974—; advisory bd. Vincennes (Ind.) U., 1975—. Chmn., Martin County Sch. Reorganization Com., 1958-62, Martin County Overall Economic Devel. Com., 1962-63, Tri-County Anti-Poverty Program, 1962-63. Mem. Ind. Retail Assn., C. of C., Nat. Ind. Bus. Methodist. Clubs: Lions, Kiwanis, Masons, Shriners, Alpha Nu Zeta, Lambda Chi Alpha. Home: Rural Route 2 Hwy 50 Shoals IN 47581 Office: Box 10 623 Main St Shoals IN 47581

FRIGERIO, NORMAN ALFRED, scientist, educator; b. Rochester, N.Y., Sept. 4, 1929; s. Karl Alfred and Mathilde (Comi) F.; B.S., Mass. Inst. Tech., 1953; Ph.D., Yale, 1957; D.Sc., Nat. Coll., 1975; m. JoAnn A. Seiler, Dec. 17, 1968; m. 2d, Betty L. Frazier, Aug. 10, 1963; children—Mary, Elias, Nathan, Jude, Raphael, Joshua, Joseph, Caleb, Tobias, Maria, Brenda, Dondi. Chief engr. Usher Aviation Radio Co., New Haven, 1953-57; research scientist Argonne (Ill.) Nat. Lab., 1956—; prof. chemistry, chmn. dept. St. Procopius Coll., Lisle, Ill., 1957-65; vis. lectr. U. Chgo., 1957—; asst. instr. Yale, 1953-55; prof. chemistry Joliet Jr. Coll., 1966-67; prof. oncology Nat. Coll., 1968-73, dir. research, 1973—; prof. biology Am. U., Beirut, 1970-71, 74-75; cons. various firms. Ordained to ministry Greek Catholic Ch., 1968. Decorated Croix de Gallilee, 1968. Served with USAF, 1946-49. Fellow Am. Inst. Chemists; mem. N.Y. Acad. Sci., Am. Chem. Soc., I.E.E.E., Research Soc. Am., Radiation Research Soc., Ill. Acad. Sci. Author: Teachers Guide to Chemistry, 1964; Your Body and Radiation, 1966, 3d edit., 1969; Neutrons in Radiation Biology and Medicine, 1971; Nuclear Medicine in Diagnosis, 1971. Contbr. articles to profl. jours. Patentee in field. Home: 25 W 582 Warrenville Rd Naperville IL 60540 Office: ESP/D-11 Argonne Nat Lab Argonne IL 60439

FRISCHENMEYER, EDWIN F., real estate broker; b. Piqua, Kans., Mar. 23, 1926; s. Henry Charles and Mary Mildred (Fleiss) F.; student Iola (Kans.) Jr. Coll., 1949-50, Ottawa (Kans.) U., 1952; wife dec. Nov. 1974; children—Michael Leo, Suzanne. Real estate sales agt., loan officer Regional Investment Co., Kansas City, Mo., 1957-64; broker, mgr. Woods & Co., Kansas City, Mo., 1967—. Sec.-treas. S. br. Real Estate Bd. Kansas City, 1971, vice-chmn., 1972, chmn. 1973. Served with USNR, 1944-46; PTO. Mem. V.F.W., Mo. Real Estate Assn., Nat. Assn. Realtors. Home: 4110 E 107th Terr Kansas City MO 64137 Office: 8800 Blue Ridge St Kansas City MO 64138

FRITSCH, JAMES RUSSELL, sch. supt.; b. Spencer, Wis., Feb. 18, 1926; s. John Florian and Anna Lucy (Younker) F.; B.Edn., U. Wis., 1952, M.A., 1961; m. Joyce L. West, June 14, 1952; children—John, Joseph, Anna Marie. Tchr. Mineral Point (Wis.) Pub. Schs., 1952-54, Sauk City (Wis.) Pub. Schs., 1954-55; elementary prin., fed. program adminstr. Stevens Point (Wis.) Pub. Schs., 1955-72; supt. Highland (Wis.) Pub. Schs., 1972—. Pres., treas. Community Child Care Center, Stevens Point, 1967-72. Served with USNR, 1943-45. Mem. N.E.A., Wis. Elementary Prin. Assn., Wis. Assn. Sch. Dist. Adminstrs., Am. Assn. Sch. Adminstrs., Big Bros. Am. (pres. 1971-72). Elk, Lion (pres. 1969-70). Home: 511 Dodgeville St Highland WI 53543 Office: PO Box 285 Highland WI 53543

FRITZ, TERRENCE LEE, state govt. ofcl., indsl. engr.; b. Fort Dodge, Iowa, Mar. 10, 1943; s. George and Julia E. (Katnik) F.; B.S. in Indsl. Engring., Iowa State U., 1967; m. Hedy Jean Helsell, Aug. 23, 1966; children—Erich George, Kevin Terrence, Tanya Jean. Project mgr. Martin Marietta Corp., Denver, 1967-69; systems analyst N.Am. Phillips Corp., Denver, 1969; mgmt. cons. Data Methods Corp., Denver, 1969-70, Colo. State U., Fort Collins, 1970-73; pres. T.L. Fritz & Associates, Ft. Collins, 1973-74; exec. dir. Des Moines Metro Transit Authority, 1974-75; transit dir. Iowa Dept. Transp., Des Moines, 1975—; guest lectr. Iowa State U., 1975—; cons. in field. Democratic precinct chmn., Des Moines, 1972—. Named Transit Person of Year, Iowa Transit Assn., 1976; registered profl. engr., Iowa, Colo. Mem. Am. Inst. Indsl. Engrs., Nat. Soc. Profl. Engrs., Sigma Chi (pres. 1965-66). Home: 4805 Western Hills Dr West Des Moines IA 50265 Office: Iowa Dept Transportation Public Transit Div Municipal Airport Office Des Moines IA 50321

FRITZE, EDWIN JACOB WILLIAM, church adminstr.; b. Topeka, Oct. 18, 1914; s. Martin Herman Edwin and Mary (Staerkel) F.; diploma Concordia Seminary, St. Louis; M.Ed., Ind. Univ., 1947; Ed.Sp., So. Ill. Univ., Edwardsville, 1972; m. Loretta Clara Bertha Hackman, Aug. 20, 1940; children—Kathryn Joane Hinz, Carol Elaine Kettner, Marilyn Elizabeth Vogel; m. 2d, Joyce Emily Radcliffe, May 25, 1974. Pastor chs., David City, Nebr., 1940, Bakersfield, Calif., 1941, Merced, Calif., 1942, St. Louis, 1948-70; tchr. Lutheran High Sch., Ft. Wayne, Ind., 1943-48; dir. pastoral trng. in counseling Lutheran Church, Missouri Synod, 1970—; private practice in counseling. Dir. Normandy Osteopathic Hosp., 1966-70. Mem. Am. Assn. Marriage and Family Counselors (approved supvr.), Am. Assn. Pastoral Counselors, Nat. Alliance for Family Life (supr. counseling), Am. Personnel and Guidance Assn., Nat. Council Family Relations. Lutheran. Club: Kiwanis. Contbr. articles to profl. jours. Home: 229 Hunters Ridge St Charles MO 63301 Office: 3558 South Jefferson Ave St Louis MO 63118

FRIZZELL, DENNIS PAUL, univ. adminstr.; b. Canton, Ohio, Aug. 20, 1950; s. Robert William and Barbara Dean (Craven) F.; B.S. in Mathematics, Ohio U., 1972, M.Ed., 1974; m. Colleen Williams, Aug. 24, 1974. Engineer draftsman Enterprise Aluminum Co., Massillon, Ohio, 1968-72; resident dir. Ohio U., 1972-74, area dir. residence halls, 1974-75; asst. dean student affairs Malone Coll., Canton, Ohio, 1975—. Mem. Assn. Christian Deans and Advisors, Nat. Assn. Student Personnel Adminstrs., Am. Personnel and Guidance Assns., Am. Coll. Personnel Assns. Home and office: 515 25th St NW Canton OH 44709

FRIZZELL, ROBERT WAYNE, librarian; b. Marshall, Mo., June 26, 1947; s. Lloyd Dorsey and Lulu Mae (Meyer) F.; student Mo. Valley Coll., 1965-67; A.B., U. Mo., Columbia, 1969; M.A., U. Ill., 1973, M.S., 1975; m. Sue Ann Hamiter, May 25, 1974. Teaching asst. history U. Ill., 1972-74; librarian Ill. Wesleyan U., 1975—. Sec. bd. Unitarian Ch., Bloomington, Ill., 1977—. Served with U.S. Army, 1969-71. Mem. Am. Hist. Assn., Am. Library Assn., Phi Beta Kappa, Phi Alpha Theta, Beta Phi Mu, Pi Kappa Delta. Home: 103 S Towanda St Normal IL 61761 Office: Library Illinois Wesleyan University Bloomington IL 61701

FROEHLICH, ADELE, editor; b. Chgo., July 8, 1918; d. A.I. and Frances Elizabeth (Welch) F. Vocal instr. McHenry (Ill.) Community High Sch., 1944-68; with McHenry Plaindealer, 1941—, mng. editor, 1947—; voice tchr., McHenry, 1951-75. Founder, dir. McHenry Choral Club, 1940—; dir. St. Patrick's Ch. Choir, 1960—, McHenry County Vocal Festival, 1972. Recipient Service award C. of C., 1972; Woman of Year award Bus. and Profl. Women's Club, 1976; 1st place editorial award Ill. Agrl. Assn., 1954; hon. mention Ill. Press Assn., 1973, 74, 1st place editorial award, 1973. Republican. Roman Catholic. Club: McHenry County Tennis (past v.p., Women's Tennis Title holder). Office: 3812 W Elm St McHenry IL 60050

FROELICH, WOLFGANG ANDREAS, neurologist; b. Berlin, Apr. 8, 1927; s. Andreas Ferdinand and Ilsa Gertraud Schultz (Engelhard) F.; came to U.S., 1955; naturalized 1960; M.D., Free U., Berlin, 1955; m. Jean Small, Nov. 28, 1959; children—Morna, Leslie, Mark, Stefan, Andrew. Intern, Huron Rd. Hosp., Cleve., 1955-56, resident in surgery, 1956-57; asst. resident in neurology Barnes Hosp., St. Louis, 1957-58, resident, in neurology, 1958-59, chief resident, instr. neurology, 1959-60; practice medicine specializing in neurology, psychiatry and encephalography, 1961—; instr. neurology Washington U., St. Louis, 1959-60; chief div. neurology Huron Rd. Hosp., Cleve., 1967—; pres. med. staff Windsor Hosp., Cleve., 1971-73; mem. active staff St. Luke's, Windsor hosps.; cons. staff Geauga Community, Marymount, Shaker Med. Center hosps. Served with German Army, 1944-45. Diplomate Am. Bd. Psychiatry and Neurology, Pan. Am. Med. Assn. Fellow Am. Acad. Neurology; mem. Cleve. Acad. Medicine, Cleve. Soc. Neurology and Psychiatry, Ohio State Med. Assn., Am. Electroencephalographic Soc., Am., Ohio psychiat. assns., No. Ohio Neurol. Soc., Epilepsy Found. Am. Club: Cleve. Racquet. Contbr. articles to med. jours. Home: 14807 Shaker Blvd Shaker Heights OH 44120 Office: 3609 Park E #304-N Beachwood OH 44122

FROHMADER, MARY ELLIN, assn. exec.; b. Chgo., May 9, 1917; d. John VanEman and Ellinor (Lewis) Berger; B.A., Carroll Coll., 1938; M.A., U. Wis., 1939; m. Stanley Harrison Frohmader, June 20, 1941; children—John Lawrence, Margaret Jane, Richard Lewis, Elizabeth Ellin. Tchr., Wayland Acad., Beaver Dam, Wis., 1939-41; mem. staff Presbyn. Student Center, U. Wis., 1941-43; 2d v.p. Phi Beta Fraternity, 1959-65, nat. pres., 1965-74; nat. pres. Profl. Panhellic Assn., 1973-77; nat. pres. Profl. Frat. Assn., 1977—. Elder, Presbyn. Ch., 1975—; active Civic Music Assn., Civic Opera Guild; bd. dirs. Presbyn. Student Found., Nat. Interfrat. Found., YWCA. Mem. AAUW, Phi Beta. Home: 514 LeRoy Rd Madison WI 53704

FROHRIB, DARRELL ALBERT, educator; b. Oshkosh, Wis., June 25, 1930; s. Albert August and Caroline Irene (Yorty) F.; B.S., Mass. Inst. Tech., 1952, M.S., 1953; Ph.D., U. Minn., 1966; m. Betty Jane Eserhut, Sept. 12, 1955; children—Ellen Marie, Sandra Jean, Paul Darrell. Engr., Sperry Gyroscope Co., Great Neck, N.Y., 1953-59; lectr. in mech. engring. U. Minn., Mpls., 1959-66, asst. prof., 1966-68, asso. prof., 1968-74, prof., dir. design center in mech. engring., 1974—, grad. faculty in bio-engring., 1968—; cons. in field. Mem. Gov.'s Commn. on Handicapped, State of Minn., 1974-75; v.p. Pilgrim Luth. Ch., St. Paul, 1975. Fulbright fellow, 1970; NIH grantee, 1973-77. Mem. ASME, Sigma Xi, Tau Beta Pi, Pi Tau Sigma. Lutheran. Patentee in field; contbr. articles to profl. jours. Home: 2144 Princeton Ave Saint Paul MN 55105 Office: Room 325 The Design Center Mech Engring Dept U of Minn Minneapolis MN 55455

FROISTAD, MELVIN ANDREAS, accountant; b. Newman Grove, Nebr., Aug. 4, 1905; s. Ole Mathias and Tilda Christina (Tisthammer) F.; student pub. accounting Internat. Accountants Soc., Chgo.; m. Frances Florence Billerbeck, Nov. 27, 1938; children—Barbara Froistad Sienknecht, Melvin Richard, Carol Ann, David. Bookkeeper Farmers Coop. Assn., Newman Grove, Neb., 1924-28; auditor Commer-Audit Co., Omaha, 1928-32; bookkeeper Nash-Finch Co., Davenport, Iowa, 1932-33; office mgr., credit mgr. various brs. Nash-Finch Co., Mpls., 1933-55; auditor, 1956-61; auditor county div. State of Iowa, Des Moines, 1962-65; pvt. practice accounting, Green Bay, Wis., 1965-76; tax cons., Gladbrook, Iowa, 1976—; cons. in accounting; del. Nat. Accountants Conv., 1972-75. Mem. Wis. Accountants Assn. (dir. 1973—), Am. Bookkeeping Assn., Nat. Soc. Pub. Accountants. Republican. Lutheran (pres. 1947-55). Home: Gladbrook IA 50635

FROM, MELVIN DEAN, banker; b. David City, Nebr., Aug. 31, 1943; s. Gene H. and Eloine A. (Bock) F.; B.S., U. Nebr., 1965, M.S. (grad. fellow), 1968; m. Margaret M. Yindrick, Sept. 2, 1967; children—Lisa Victoria, Kevin John. Market research analyst Omaha Nat. Bank, 1968-70, mgr. mktg. research dept., 1970-72, internat. officer, 1972-73, v.p., 1974—; v.p. Travel & Transport Inc., Omaha, 1973-74. Omaha nat. dir. Youth Emergency Services, Inc. Served with USNR, 1965-67. Mem. Am. Mktg. Assn. (chmn. membership com. Lincoln-Omaha chpt. 1970-71), Midwest Internat. Trade Assn., Nebr. Econs. and Bus. Assn. Democrat. Roman Catholic. Contbr. articles to profl. publs. Home: 4506 Morningside Dr Omaha NE 68134 Office: 17th & Farnam Sts Omaha NE 68102

FROMBERG, LA VERNE CHARLOTTE RAY, artist; b. Duvall, Wash., May 6, 1930; d. Verne Federich and Julia Cora (Wright) Ray; B.F.A., U. Wash., 1951, M.F.A., 1953; student Art Students League, N.Y.C., 1951-52, 63-64, Bradley U., 1969-70, U. N.Mex., 1949-50; m. Gerald Fromberg, Sept. 13, 1952; children—Paul Ray, Robert Mathew, Steven Bruce. Instr. art Bradley U., Peoria, Ill., 1954-57; lectr. Ill. State U., Normal, 1969-71; dir. edn. and extension Lakview Center for Arts and Scis., Peoria, 1973-77; instr. Lakeview Center; one- woman shows: Fulton Gallery, N.Y.C., 1964, 65, 66, 69, Contemporary Gallery, Dallas, 1968; group shows: 20th and 24th Ill. Invitational, 1967, 71, Peoria Art Guild, 1977, Ill. Arts Council traveling exhbn., Ill., 1967-68, Mo., 1968-69, Washington, 1969-70; represented in permanent collections: Library Congress, U. Wash., New Orleans Art Mus., Bradley U. Recipient Best of Show award New Orleans Art Museum Annual, 1954, award Carnegie Hall, N.Y.C., 1952, Mem. Midwest Museum Assn., Phi Beta Kappa, Lambda Rho. Democrat. Home and studio: 1205 Glenwood Ave N Peoria IL 61606

FROMMERT, BEVERLEY JEAN, veterinarian; b. Detroit, June 15, 1938; d. Arthur Emil John and Vera Vivian (Helzerman) F.; B.S., Mich. State U., 1962, D.V.M., 1964; m. Henry Abraham Kallet, July 22, 1967. Asso. veterinarian Allen Park (Mich.) Veterinary Hosp., 1964-67; owner Brookeside Veterinary Hosp., Ann Arbor, 1972—; mem. Mich. Bd. Veterinarian Examiners, 1978—. Bd. dirs. Mich. Vet-Pac, 1978—. Mem. AVMA, Am. Animal Hosp. Assn., Mich. Veterinary Med. Assn. (alt. dir.), Washtenaw Acad. Veterinary Medicine. Home: 3324 Bluett Dr Ann Arbor MI 48105 Office: 3010 Warren Rd Ann Arbor MI 48105

FROOM, WILLIAM PETER, pub. relations cons.; b. Chgo., Feb. 27, 1913; s. William Elijah and Eva Victoria McNeill F.; B.S., Northwestern U., 1935, M.S., 1940; Ed.D., Ind. U., 1956; m. Catherine Maxine Wilson, Aug. 9, 1941; children—William Wilson, Richard Thomas, John Donald, Carol Susan. Tchr. English and journalism Monmouth (Ill.) High Sch., 1936-40, Thornton High Sch. and Jr. Coll., Harvey, Ill., 1940-43; photographer Gen. Electric Co., Chgo., summer 1943; asso. dir. pub. relations No. Ill. U., DeKalb, 1947-55, dir. univ. relations, 1956-72, dir. pub. relations coll. edn., 1972-77; pub. relations cons., 1977—. Served with AUS, 1943-46; MTO. Evans scholar 1932-35, Ind. U. fellow, 1952-53. Mem. DeKalb C. of C. (v.p. 1958-59), No. Ill. U. Found., Council for Advance and Support of Edn. (dist. dir. Gt. Lakes dist. V 1972-73), Pub. Relations Soc. Am., Phi Delta Kappa. Methodist (trustee). Home: 618 Russell Rd DeKalb IL 60115

FROOM, WILLIAM WATKINS, corp. exec.; b. Chgo., Nov. 21, 1915; s. Edgar Albright and Gladys (Watkins) F.; student Northwestern U. Sch. Commerce, 1933-37; m. Anne Celich, Apr. 20, 1940; children—Pamela (Mrs. Philip Siegent), Gail (Mrs. Kenneth MacKenzie), Joan Elizabeth (Mrs. Kenneth Sensenbrenner). Sales mgr. Soybean div. Swift & Co., Champaign, Ill., 1937-47; partner I.H. French & Co., Champaign, 1947-64, pres., 1965—, chmn. bd., 1974-75; v.p. Commodity Investment Fund Mgmt. Corp., Cable Communications, Inc., Champaign; pres., chmn. bd. Champaign-Urbana Communications, Inc.; pres., chmn. bd. City Bank, Champaign; dir. F & T Bldg. Corp., Champaign, Champaign Nat. Bank. Presbyn. (elder). Club: Champaign Country (dir. 1965). Home: 1402 Waverly Dr Champaign IL 61820 Office: 502 W Clark St Champaign IL 61820

FROST, RUBEN EWING, ball bearing mfg. exec.; b. Grand Rapids, Mich., Dec. 7, 1918; s. Horace E. and Lotta (Rubens) F.; B.S. in Aero. Engring., U. Mich., 1941; m. Barbara Clarke, June 9, 1940 (dec. Sept. 1967); children—Barbara (Mrs. Mel Hering), Charles, Sandra Kay, Thomas; m. 2d, Doris Bourdelais, May 3, 1969. Asst. gen. mgr. C.L. Frost & Son, Inc., Grand Rapids, 1946-50, gen. mgr., 1950-59, pres.,

1959—. Served to lt. comdr. USNR, 1941-46. Elk. Clubs: Cascade Hills (Grand Rapids) Country, Peninsular (Grand Rapids); Red Run Country (Detroit). Home: 4216 Baywood St Grand Rapids MI 49506 Office: 2020 Bristol St Grand Rapids MI 49504

FRUCHTMAN, MARTIN ZOLLE, allergist; b. Mpls., June 19, 1931; s. Henry and Ann (Gitelman) F.; B.A., U. Minn., 1953, B.S., 1954, M.D., 1956; m. Dolores Samosky, May 19, 1957; children—Cynthia, Susan, Gail. Med. resident Henry Ford Hosp., Detroit, 1959-62; pvt. practice medicine specializing in internal medicine and allergy, Waukesha, Wis., 1962-70, specializing in allergy, 1970—; clin. instr. medicine allergy Marquette U. Med. Sch., Milw., 1964-67; sec. Comprehensive Health Planning Agency SE Wis., 1970-72. Mem. Waukesha County Med. Soc. (sec. 1968-70), AMA (Physicians Recognition award 1974, 77). Jewish. Home: 1215 Downing Dr Waukesha WI 53186

FRUECHTENICHT, BARBARA GOETTE, travel agy. exec.; b. Ft. Wayne, Ind., July 26, 1926; d. Fred Henry and Beulah Marie (Baker) Goette; student Valparaiso U., 1944-47; B.A., Ind. U., 1954; postgrad. Purdue U., 1955-56; R.N., Parkview Meml. Hosp., Ft. Wayne, 1961; children—Kip, Carla Marie, Brent. Nurse, Parkview Hosp., Ft. Wayne, 1961-63; women's editor Jour. Gazette, Ft. Wayne, 1963-71, free lance news reporter, 1971—; mgr. Air Holiday Travel Club, Ft. Wayne, 1971—; pres. Bobbie's Fun Times, 1974—. Sec. Kirkwood Park Assn., 1966-72; mem. Philharmonic Women, Women of Philharmonic-Civic Theatre Guild. Bd. dirs. Allen County Mental Health, 1966-70, Am. Cancer Soc., 1968-74; pub. affairs coordinator congressional campaign, 1977. Named Mother of Yr., March of Dimes, 1972; recipient Woman of Yr. award. Mem. Ft. Wayne C. of C., Ft. Wayne Women's Bur., Valparaiso U. Alumnae Assn. Republican. Lutheran. Clubs: Summit, Olympia, Pine Valley Country, Pres, Fort Wayne Woman's. Home: 2136 Springfield Ave Fort Wayne IN 46805 Office: 3402 N Anthony Blvd Fort Wayne IN 46805

FRUEH, BARTLEY RICHARD, ophthalmologist, ophthalmic plastic surgeon; b. Cleve., Sept. 1, 1937; s. Lloyd Walter and Elizabeth Virginia (Scott) F.; B. Chem. Engring., Cornell U., 1960; M.D. (Internat. fellow), Columbia U., 1964; M.Sc. in Ophthalmology, U. Mich., 1970; m. Frances Mallet-Prevost Gaston, Dec. 31, 1976; children—Bartley, Dylan, Walter; step-children—Eric, Laura. Intern, N.C. Meml. Hosp., Chapel Hill, 1964-65; resident in ophthalmology U. Mich. Hosp., Ann Arbor, 1967-70; preceptor in ophthalmic plastic surgery with Alston Callahan, M.D., Birmingham, Ala., 1970; practice medicine specializing in ophthalmology, Columbia, Mo., 1971—; dir. ophthalmic plastic surgery U. Mo. Med. Center, Columbia, 1971—; active staff mem. Boone County Hosp., Columbia Regional Hosp., Columbia; cons. staff mem. St. Mary's Health Center, Jefferson City, Mo.; cons. in ophthalmic plastic surgery to Eye Research Found., Columbia; asst. clin. prof. ophthalmology U. Mo., Columbia, 1971-75, asso. clin. prof., 1975—. Vice pres. Park Hill (Civic) Assn., 1975. Served with M.C., USAF, 1965-67. Smith, Kline and French Fgn. fellow, 1963; diplomate Am. Bd. Ophthalmology. Fellow A.C.S.; mem. AMA, Mo. State Med. Assn., Boone County Med. Soc., Mo. Ophthal. Soc. (sec.-treas. 1976-78), Am. Acad. Ophthalmology and Otolaryngology, Am. Assn. Ophthalmology, Am. Soc. Ophthalmic Plastic and Reconstructive Surgery (past pres., chmn. bd. advisors). Contbr. articles in field to profl. jours. Home: 606 W Stewart Rd Columbia MO 65201 Office: 909 University Ave Columbia MO 65201

FRY, DAVID LLOYD-GEORGE, physicist; b. Detroit, Sept. 22, 1918; s. Fred and Linda Irene (Fry) F.; B.A., Kalamazoo Coll., 1940; M.S. (Kettering Found. fellow), Ohio State U., 1942; m. Alma Loriene Jones, Mar. 21, 1942; children—David, Lawrence, Randall. Research physicist research labs. Gen. Motors Corp., Warren, Mich., 1942-47, sr. research physicist, 1947-53, supr. chem. physics and magnetics, 1953-76, departmental research scientist, 1976—. Leader, Boy Scouts Am., 1948-58; chmn. bd. trustees First Unitarian Universalist Ch., Detroit, 1958-60; trustee Unitarian Universalist Assn., 1975—. Fellow AAAS, Optical Soc. Am.; mem. Am. Phys. Soc., Engring. Soc. Detroit. Editor: Methods for Spectrochem. Analysis, ASTM, 1960; contbr. articles in field to profl. jours. Home: 685 Princeton Rd Berkley MI 48072 Office: Physics Dept Research Lab Gen Motors Corp Warren MI 48090

FRYDA, CLIFFORD GEORGE, bus. services co. exec.; b. Fond du Lac, Wis., Oct, 3, 1935; s. Alfred W. and Winifred A. (Schraven) F.; certificate data processing Duluth Area Inst. Tech., 1969; m. Rosemary Ann Ruzynski, Nov. 10, 1958; children—Daniel, Nadine, Diane, David, Dean, Darrel, Michele, Debra, Candice. Various trucking positions, Floodwood, Minn., 1963-67; programmer, analyst Midland Nat. Life Ins. Co., Watertown, S.D., 1969-70; mgr. systems Cook's Inc., Watertown S.D., 1970—; lectr. in field. Served with USAF, 1953-63; Korea. Democrat. Roman Catholic. Office: 807 S Broadway St Watertown SD 57201

FRYDENLUND, ARTHUR JORGEN, motel exec.; b. nr. Buffalo, S.D., Aug. 16, 1907; s. Olaf and Ella (Halvorson) F.; student pub. schs.; m. Elaine A. Eyler, June 25, 1934; children—Gerald, John, Karen (Mrs. Gerald Bouzek), Jane (Mrs. Elliott Moore), Eric. Barber, Prairie du Chien, Wis., 1932-51; owner Motel Brisbois, Prairie du Chien, 1951—, Moto-Miter Co., Prairie de Chien, 1959—. City chmn. Heart Fund, Prairie du Chien, 1962—; mem. local adv. bd. Campion Jesuit High Sch., after 1970; pres. Blackhawk Country Tourism Council. Mem. Crawford County (Wis.) Bd. Suprs., 1970—; mem. Mississippi River Pkwy. Commn., 1977—. Bd. dirs. Indsl. Devel., 1952-63, pres., 1963—; trustee Meml. Hosp., Prairie du Chien, 1957—. Mem. Wis. Motel Assn. (dir. 1959-60, 70—), Wis. Innkeepers Assn. (v.p. 1973—), Internat. Platform Assn., Sons Norway, Wis. Hist. Soc. Prairie du Chien C. of C. (pres. 1959, dir. 1952—). Methodist. Patentee bldg. tools, archery equipment. Home: 533 N Marquette Rd Prairie du Chien WI 53821

FRYE, HAROLD FREDERICK, ednl. adminstr.; b. Columbus, Wis., Mar. 22, 1943; s. Harold L. and Esther M. (Johnstone) F.; B.S., Olivet Nazarene Coll., 1967; m. Janice Irene Toone, Jan. 11, 1964; children—Scott, Todd, Michelle. Bookkeeper, teller First Trust and Savs. Bank, Kankakee, Ill., 1963-64; office and pub. relations worker Kankakee Fed. Savs. and Loan Assn., 1965-66; hosp. adminstr. Dept. World Missions, Papua, New Guinea. 1968-74; hosp. cons. Blue Cross of N.E. Ohio, Cleve., 1975; asst. adminstr. Ashtabula (Ohio) Gen. Hosp., 1975-76; adminstrv. asst. and spl. projects dir. Acad. of Medicine, Cleve., 1976—; resident in hosp. adminstrn. Research Hosp. and Med. Center, Kansas City, Mo., 1967-68. Mem. Am. Assn. Med. Soc. Execs., Am. Coll. Hosp. Adminstrs., Health Care Adminstrs. Assn. of N.E. Ohio. Home: 3721 Stoer Rd Shaker Heights OH 44122 Office: Academy of Medicine 10525 Carnegie Ave Cleveland OH 44106

FRYER, EDWARD ROY, automotive engr.; b. Detroit, May 16, 1923; s. Edward Roy and Jewel (Steensma) F.; student Gen. Motors Inst., 1941-43; B.M.E., Mass. Inst. Tech., 1945; commd. U.S. Naval Res. Midshipman's Sch. Columbia U., 1945; m. Audrey Marie Osmon, July 5, 1945; children—Jeffrey, Susanne, Debra-Ellen, Kevin, Tammy. Jr. engr. Nat. Acme Co., Cleve., 1946-47; with Euclid Rd. Machinery Co. (became Terex div. Gen. Motors Co. 1969), 1947—, product engr., Euclid, Ohio, 1953-69, asst. chief engr., Hudson, Ohio, 1969—, div. metric coordinator, 1973—. Served with USNR, 1943-46. Mem. Soc. Automotive Engrs. Contbr. numerous articles to profl. jours.; patentee in field. Home: 966 Oakview Dr Highland Heights OH 44143 Office: 5405 Darrow Rd Hudson OH 44236

FUELLING, JAMES LOUIS, physician; b. Ft. Wayne, Ind., July 16, 1913; s. H.F. Louis and Frances Matilda (Hartzell) F.; B.S., Ind. U., 1935, M.D., 1937; postgrad. U.S. Naval Sch. Aviation Medicine, 1942; grad. Sch. Ophthalmology U. Pa., 1946-47; m. Ruth Elsie Askine, June 22, 1935; children—Elaine (Mrs. Wm. Z. Roper), June (Mrs. Frederick R. Verner). Intern, St. Vincent's Hosp., Indpls., 1937-38; commd. lt. (j.g.) USN, 1940, advanced through grades to capt., 1955; served as flight surgeon, 1942-45; resident in ophthalmology U.S. Naval Hosp., Bethesda, Md., 1951-53; ret. 1960; practice medicine specializing in ophthalmology, Montgomery, Ala., 1961, Marion, Ind., 1962—; mem. staff Davis Clinic, 1962-70; mem. staff Marion Gen. Hosp. Part-time tchr., cons. Ind. U. Med. Center, Indpls., 1962-71. Decorated Navy Cross, Purple Heart. Diplomate Am. Bd. Ophthalmology. Fellow Am. Acad. Ophthalmology and Otolaryngology, Soc. Mil. Ophthalmologists (pres. 1960-61); mem. Am., Ind State Med. assns., Pan Am. Opthal. Assn. Contbr. chpts. to books. Home: 4285 N Rd 210 E Marion IN 46952 Office: 217 E Grant St Marion IN 46952

FUHRER, LARRY, investment banker; b. Ft. Wayne, Ind., Sept. 23, 1939; s. Henry Roland and Wilhelmine Ellen (Kopp) F.; A.B., Taylor U., 1961; postgrad. No. Ill. U., 1965—; m. Linda Larsen, Dec. 31, 1962; 1 son, Lance. Exec. club dir. Youth for Christ, Miami, Fla., 1961; publs. mgr. Campus Life mag. Wheaton, Ill., 1962-65; asst. to pres. Youth for Christ Internat., Wheaton, 1965-66; asso. dir. devel. Ill. Inst. Tech., 1966-68; exec. asst. to pres. The Robert Johnston Corp., Los Angeles, Chgo., N.Y.C., 1968-69; pres. Compro, Inc., Glen Ellyn, Ill., 1969-72; pres. Killian Assos. Inc., Wheaton, 1973-75; chmn. Equibanque Ltd. and its subsidiaries, Fin. Services Group Ltd., Equity Realty Group Inc., Presdl. Services Inc., 1975—; ednl. mgmt. cons. numerous pvt. colls. and sems. Bd. dirs. Chicagoland Youth for Christ. Mem. Am. Mgmt. Assn., Am. Inst. Mgmt. Consultants, DuPage Bd. Realtors, Nat. Ill. assns. realtors, Am. Mktg. Assn., Mortgage Bankers Assn. Presbyterian. Club: Union League (Chgo.). Home: 125 W Seminary St Wheaton IL 60187 Office: 600 Enterprise Dr Oak Brook IL 60521

FUHRER, WILHELMINE ELLEN, accountant; b. Defiance, Ohio, Jan. 12, 1914; d. Herman C. and Rose Amelia (Wandt) Kopp; ed bus. coll., m. Henry R. Fuhrer, June 25, 1936; children—Larry Rolland, Eugene Leo, Beverly Wilhelmine. Circulation mgr. Nat. Stock Dog mag., Butler, Ind., 1960—; individual practice tax computation and accounting, Auburn, Ind., 1940—. Mem. Nat., Ind. socs. pub. accountants, Am. Bus. Womens Assn. Home: Rural Route 2 Rd 35 Auburn IN 46706

FUJISHIRO, SHIRO, metallurgist; b. Kakogawa, Hyogo Prefecture, Japan, Oct. 18, 1930; s. Manji and Shizue (Yumoto) F.; came to U.S., 1956, naturalized, 1972; B.S. in Phys. Chemistry, Tohoku U., Japan, 1953; postgrad. in metall. engring. U. Pa., 1957-60; Ph.D. in Phys. Chemistry, Kyoto U., Japan, 1962; m. Tomoko Takahashi, Oct. 28, 1959; children—Felix, Charlotte. Research chemist Inst. Indsl. Sci., Kyoto (Japan) U., 1953-57; research asst. U. Pa., Phila., 1957-60; chief heat treatment br. Research Lab., Nippon Steel Co., Sagamihara, Japan, 1960-63; research metallurgist USAF Materials Lab., Wright Patterson AFB, Dayton, Ohio, 1963—; vis. scholar Cambridge (Eng.) U., 1968-69. Named Materials Man of Month USAF Materials Lab, 1966; recipient Sci. Achievement award Air Force System Command, 1970. Mem. Am. Inst. Metall. Engrs., Electron Microscope Soc. Am., Phys. Soc. Japan, Sci. Research Soc. Am. Contbr. articles to profl. jours. Home: 1640 Spillan Rd Yellow Springs OH 45387 Office: AFML/LLS Wright Patterson AFB Dayton OH 45433

FUKUSHIMA, MASAYA, computer services exec.; b. Wakayama, Japan, May 25, 1939 (parents Am. citizens); s. Shozo Frank and Miyoko June (Kuwahara) F.; B.A. in Math. and Zoology, U. Calif., 1963; m. Donna Jo McKinsey, Sept. 20, 1963; children—Karen Mika, Melissa Miya. Product mgr. clin. data systems Control Data Corp., La Jolla, Calif., 1963-71; adminstr. Medlab Computer Services, Inc. div. Control Data Corp., Salt Lake City, 1971-73; mgr. health care systems Xerox Corp., El Segundo, Calif., 1973-75; sr. mgr. Internat. Devel. Comshare, Inc., Ann Arbor, Mich., 1975—; bd. dirs. Miroku-Comshare, Inc., Tokyo. Republican. Shinto. Designer on-line data acquisition and large data base mgmt. systems for clin. labs. and hosps. Home: 8614 Meadowland Saline MI 48176 Office: PO Box 1588 Ann Arbor MI 48106

FULK, ROSCOE NEAL, accountant; b. Lebo, Kans., June 23, 1916; s. Roscoe Lloyd and Maude (Calvert) F.; B.S., U. Ill., 1940; m. Marie Therese Rabbitt, June 15, 1946; children—Thomas, Janet, David, Robert, Kenneth, Howard. With Ernst & Ernst, C.P.A.'s, Chgo., 1940-76, partner, 1957-76. Treas. Winnetka (Ill.) Caucus Com., 1956, vice chmn., 1962; chmn. accountants group United Republican Fund Ill., 1958. Met. Crusade of Mercy, 1970; pres. Civic Fedn. Chgo., 1968-70. Pres. New Trier Twp. Citizens League, 1961-65, now dir.; pres. Juvenile Protective Assn., 1970-73, now dir.; v.p. Chgo. Met. Housing and Planning Council, 1970-76; chmn. Winnetka Zoning Commn., 1968-71; chmn. Pres.'s Council Bus. Assos. Elmhurst Coll., 1969-70; mem. adv. com. Coll. Commerce and Bus. Adminstrn., U. Ill., 1970-76; mem. Chgo. Parking Adv. Council, 1970-74, Chgo. Better Schs. Com., 1969-70, Ill. Commn. Urban Area Govt., 1968-72, Ill. Gov.'s Adv. Council, 1969-72; v.p. Catholic Charities Chgo., 1974-76; pres. United Charities Chgo., 1973-75; chmn. grand council Am. Indian Center, 1974-76; mem. citizens bd. U. Chgo.; exec. v.p. Met. Easter Seal Soc. Chgo. Bd. dirs. Chgo. Symphony Orch., Midwest region ARC, Ill. Drug Abuse Council. Served to lt. USNR, 1942-46. Mem. Am. Inst. C.P.A.'s (council 1968-72), Ill. Soc. C.P.A.'s (dir. 1963-64, v.p. 1964-65, sr. v.p. 1968-69, pres. 1969-70, Chgo. Assn. Commerce and Industry (dir.). Roman Catholic. Clubs: Sunset Ridge Country (dir. 1961-65, treas. 1965-66) (Winnetka); Executives, Mid-American, Chicago, Economic (dir.), Commercial (Chgo.). Home: 227 Church Rd Winnetka IL 60093 Office: 150 S Wacker Dr Chicago IL 60606

FULL, RAY HENRY, food products co. exec.; b. Vermilion, Ohio, Mar. 11, 1918; s. Otto Fred and Gertrude (Nau) F.; grad. St. Petersburgh Jr. Coll., 1939; student Fenn Coll., 1950-51, Baldwin Wallace Coll., 1951-52; m. Dawn N. Malson, Nov. 28, 1947; foster children—Carol Skiles, Barbara Ivey. Dir., Kishman Fish Co., Vermilion, Ohio, 1951—, pres., 1960—; pres. So. Lake Erie Inc., 1956-66, R & D Enterprises, 1963—, Conneaut Fisheries, 1972—, Shoreline Fisheries, 1977—; dir. Erie County Bank, 1972—, Lorain (Ohio) Community Hosp., 1976—; adviser Great Lakes Fisheries Commn., 1963—, Great Lakes Commn., 1963-70; mem. Am. Fisheries Advisory Com., 1959-67, 1970-71, Marine Fisheries Advisory Com., 1971-75. Chmn. Festival of the Fish, 1967, 68, 69; sec. Vermilion Planning Commn., 1951-60, Vermilion, Ohio; chmn. Flood Control Com., Vermilion, 1970—, Vermilion United Fund, 1971-74, Vermilion Port Authority, 1975-76, Lorain County (Ohio) Home Town Careers, 1968—; mem. Gov. Gilligan Conservation Task Force, 1973-74; mem. Erie County Republican Central Com., 1968—; bd. dirs. Lorain County United Community Services, 1971-76, Lorain County United Health Found., 1972-76; trustee Wilbur Meml. Fund, 1961—. Recipient Distinguished Service award City of Vermilion, 1966. Mem. Lake Erie Resources Council (pres. 1964-65), Am. Fisheries Soc., Internat. Oceanographic Found., Animal Protection League, Vermilion C. of C. (dir. 1966—, pres. 1969), Ohio Comml. Fisherman's Assn. (pres. 1958-66, sec. 1970-74). Clubs: South Shore Cruising (hon. mem.), Vermilion Boat (dir. 19—, commodore 1951), Rotary (dir. 19—, pres. 1954—). Mem. United Ch. of Christ. Home: 5419 Willow Ln Vermilion OH 44089 Office: Dept Natural Resources Shoreline Mgmt Commn PO Box 22 Vermilion OH 44089

FULLEN, JAMES ROBERT, pub. relations co. exec.; b. Chgo., Oct. 7, 1946; s. William Raymond and Jane Marion (Eiden) F.; student U. Ill., Chgo., 1964-66; m. Anita Janice Holda, June 7, 1969; children—Nicole Diane, Erin Kathleen. Advt. coordinator, asst. mgr. pub. relations Symons Corp., Des Plaines, Ill., 1969-71; account exec. Burson-Marsteller Co., Chgo., 1971-73; pres., chmn. J.R. Fullen Assos. Inc., Park Ridge, Ill., 1973—. Dep. committeeman pub. relations Palatine Twp. Regular Rep. Orgn., 1971-73; mem. pub. relations com. NW Suburban (Chgo.) Boy Scouts Am., 1974—. Served to 1st. lt., C.E., U.S. Army, 1966-69. Mem. Pub. Relations Soc. Am., Constrn. Writers Assn. Club: Publicity Chgo. Home: 33 Heatherlea Dr W Palatine IL 60067 Office: 1400 Renaissance Dr Park Ridge IL 60068

FULLER, BENJAMIN FRANKLIN, physician; b. St. Paul, Aug. 7, 1922; s. Benjamin Franklin and Luella Amelia (Pfaff) F.; B.A., U. Minn., 1942, B.S., 1943, M.D., 1946, M.S. in Internal Medicine, 1950; m. Carol Marie Myre, Sept. 24, 1945; children—Constance J., Benjamin F., Geraldine A., Lynn M. Intern, U. Minn. Hosp., Mpls., 1945-46, resident in medicine; fellow in internal medicine Mayo Found., 1947-50; practice medicine specializing in internal medicine, St. Paul, 1951-66; prof. head dept. family practice and community health U. Minn., Mpls., 1968-71, prof. dept. internal medicine, head sect. primary care, 1972—. Served with USAF, 1946-47, 53. Fellow A.C.P., Am. Coll. Angiology; mem. Ramsey County Med. Soc., Minn. Med. Assn., AMA, Assn. Minn. Internists (pres.), St. Paul Soc. Internal Medicine (pres.), Sigma Xi, Alpha Omega Alpha. Methodist. Home: 2641 S Shore Blvd White Bear Lake MN 55110 Office: 3615 Grand Ave White Bear Lake MN 55110

FULLER, DON, mgmt. cons.; b. San Francisco, Nov. 27, 1905; s. John Wilbert and Alice (McGuire) Fuller-Moye; student Sacred Heart Coll., Fordham U., U. Chgo., U. Calif. at Berkeley; B.A. St. Ignatius Coll., 1925; B.S., Columbia, 1928, M.A., 1931; m. Rose Brough, Oct. 12, 1926 (dec. Dec. 1930); children—Wayne, Robert; m. 2d, Gertrude Scheyer, June 22, 1952. With H.K. Ferguson Co., Cleve., 1950-57; dir. engring., engring. mgmt. Indsl. Edn. Inst., Boston, 1957-70; prin. Don Fuller Assos., Photo Graphics; dir. mgmt. devel. Edn. for Bus. and Industry, Boston, 1970—; pres., dir. Gallery Photog. Arts, Inc., North Olmsted, Ohio, 1974—. Chmn., Nat. Council on Mgmt. Devel. Served with USN, 1929-32. Author: Organizing, Planning and Scheduling for Engineering Operations, 1962; Manage Or Be Managed, 1963; Getting Top Mileage from Your Drafting and Design Operations, 1965; Functional Drafting for Today, 1966; Project Content Analysis and Estimating, 1969; Papers on Management, 1970; Focusing on the World, 1972. Home: 26219 Cranage Rd Olmsted Falls OH 44138

FULLER, GILBERT WESLEY, utility co. exec.; b. Glasco, Kans., Dec. 28, 1924; s. Wesley Newell and Cora A. (Forkner) F.; B.S. in Elec. Engring., Kans. U., 1950; M.S. in Engring. Mgmt., Mo. U., 1974; m. Carolyn Jean Knapp, July 21, 1946; children—Christine Anne, Stephen James, David Gilbert. Elec. design engr. Black & Veatch Cons. Engrs., Kansas City, Mo., 1950-52; plant engr. and constrn. elec. resident Empire Dist. Electric Co., Joplin, Mo., 1952-56, chief engr., 1956-63, plant supt., 1963-67, constrn. elec. cons., 1967-74, supt. prodn. adminstrn., 1974—. Mem. Joplin Bd. of Realtors. Served with USNR, 1943-46; PTO. Registered profl. engr., Kans. Mem. IEEE, Central Engring. Soc., Christian Bus. Mens Com., Power Engring. Soc. Republican. Presbyterian. Clubs: Masons, Shriners, Optimists. Home: 3007 Silver Creek Dr Joplin MO 64801 Office: 602 Joplin St Joplin MO 64801

FULLER, IVAN RICHARD, navy chaplain; b. Lafayette, Ind., Feb. 7, 1936; s. Ivan Walter and Norma Frances (Foppe) F.; B.A., Butler U., 1958; M.Div., Christian Theol. Sem., 1961; m. Yvonne Louise Stiles, June 17, 1962; children—Ivan Walter, II, Michal-Lynn Elizabeth, Patricia Ruth, Stephen Bo Yung, Kimberly Su. Ordained to ministry Christian Ch., 1959; minister Champion Christian Ch., Warren, Ohio, 1961-66; served as chaplain USN, 1966—; squadron chaplain Destroyer Squadron 16, 1966-68; base chaplain, Clarksville Tenn., 1968-69; chaplain USS Sanctuary, Vietnam, 1969-70; depot pastor, regtl. chaplain Marine Corps Recruit Depot, Parris Island, S.C., 1970-73; staff chaplain 3d Marine Div., Okinawa, 1973-74, Naval Tng. Center, Gt. Lakes, Ill., 1974—; Navy liaison officer North Chgo. Sch. Bd.; asst. treas. North Chgo. Clergy Council. Mem. Disciples of Christ Chaplains Assn., Phi Delta Theta. Contbr. articles to internat. religious periodicals, devotional mags. Home: 1944-A Lexington Great Lakes IL 60088 Office: Chaplain Dept Naval Tng Center Great Lakes IL 60088

FULLER, PERRY LUCIAN, lawyer; b. Central City, Nebr., Oct. 26, 1922; s. Perry L. and Ruth (Howorth) F.; A.B., U. Nebr., 1947, J.D., 1949; postgrad. U Chgo. Law Sch., 1946-47; m. Alice Moorman, Mar. 6, 1948; 1 dau., Leslie. Admitted to Ill. bar, 1950, U.S. Supreme Ct. bar, 1966; mem. staff Chgo. Crime Commn., 1949; sr. partner firm Hinshaw, Culbertson, Moelmann, Hoban & Fuller, and predecessors, Chgo., 1956—; dir. Allstate Enterprises Stock Fund, Inc.; lectr. law U. Chgo., 1970-76; vice chmn. exec. com. Law in Am. Soc., 1966, chmn., 1967-69; pres. Law In Am. Soc. Found., 1968—. Chmn. Cook County Civil Service Commn., 1967-69; exec. com. Ill. Law Enforcement Commn., 1972-73. Bd. dirs. Winnetka Community Chest, 1966-69; trustee Fed. Defender Program, Inc.; mem. Chgo. steering com. NAACP Legal Def. Fund, 1970—, vice chmn., 1977—. Served to capt. USMCR, 1944-46, 52-53. Decorated Air medal. Fellow Am. Coll. Trial Lawyers, Am. Bar Found.; mem. Fed., Am. (chmn. pub. relations com. 1968-69, mem. gavel awards com. 1974—, chmn. 1976—), Ill. (family law study com., long range planning com.), Chgo. (bd. mgrs. 1967-69, pub. relations adv. com. 1973—; vice chmn. 1975—) bar assns., Am. Law Inst., Soc. Trial Lawyers Ill. (dir. 1963, 67-68, 73-74, treas. 1974, sec. 1975-76, pres. 1977-78), Am. Judicature Soc., Am. Acad. Polit. and Social Sci., Internat. Assn. Ins. Counsel (profl. liability and malpractice com., vice chmn. advocacy com.), Def. Research Inst. (vice chmn ins. info. com.), Scribes. Republican. Clubs: Executives, Legal, Law (mem. exec. com. 1969—) (Chgo.). Home: 255 Poplar St Winnetka IL 60093 Office: 69 W Washington St Chicago IL 60602

FULLER, RAY WARD, biochem. pharmacologist; b. Dongola, Ill., Dec. 16, 1935; s. Lloyd Myron and Wanda (Keller) F.; B.A., So. Ill. U., 1957, M.A., 1958; Ph.D., Purdue U., 1961; m. Bonnie Sue Brown, Dec. 22, 1956; children—Ray Ward II, Angela Lea. NSF fellow, 1960-61; dir. biochemistry research lab. Ft. Wayne (Ind.) State Hosp., 1961-63; sr. pharmacologist Eli Lilly & Co., Indpls., 1963-66, research scientist, 1967-68, head dept. metabolic research, 1968-71, research asso., 1971-75, research advisor, 1976—; adj. asso. prof. biochemistry Ind. U. Med. Sch., 1974—; vis. lectr. Mass. Inst. Tech., 1976—. Mem. Am. Soc. Pharmacology and Exptl. Therapeutics, Am. Soc. Biol. Chemists, Soc. Neurosci. (past pres. Indpls. chpt.), Endocrine Soc., Am., Internat. socs. neurochemistry, Am. Chem. Soc., N.Y. Acad. Scis., A.A.A.S. Mem. editorial bd. Circulation Research, 1974—, Life Scis., 1975—, Jour. Neural Transmission, 1976—. Contbr. numerous articles on psychopharmacology, neurochemistry, endocrinology, medicinal chemistry, chronobiology, pharmacokinetics, and enzymology to sci. jours., also referee. Patentee in field. Home: 7844 Singleton Dr Indianapolis IN 46227 Office: Lilly Research Labs Eli Lilly & Co Indianapolis IN 46206

FULLER, RAYMOND EVERETT, physician; b. Dennison, Ohio, Nov. 3, 1927; s. Otis Everett and Irene (Zimmerman) F.; B.S., Capitol U., 1949; M.D., Ohio State U., 1954; m. Lillian Louise Martin, Mar. 19, 1951; children—Steven, Timothy, James, Sharon, Charles. Intern, Blodgett Meml. Hosp., Grand Rapids, Mich., 1954-55, resident, 1955-56; resident in internal medicine Henry Ford Hosp., Detroit, 1958-60; practice medicine specializing in internal medicine, Grand Rapids, 1961—; dir. cardiovascular lab. Blodgett Meml. Med. Center, Grand Rapids, 1961—, also cons; cons. Butterworth Hosp., St. Mary's Hosp., Grand Rapids; asso. clin. prof. Mich. State U., 1973—. Served with M.C., U.S. Army, 1956-58. Mich. Heart Assn. grantee, 1963-64, 74-75. Diplomate Am. Bd. Internal Medicine. Fellow A.C.P.; mem. Am. Soc. Internal Medicine, AMA, Mich. State, Kent County med. socs., Am., Mich. (pres. 1974) heart assns. Republican. Contbr. articles to profl. jours. Home: 2249 Shawnee SE Grand Rapids MI 49506 Office: 1900 Wealthy St Grand Rapids MI 49506

FULLER, RAYMOND HAROLD, civil engr.; b. New Plymouth, Ohio, Jan. 12, 1910; s. Charles C. and Chloie Ellen (Meyers) F.; B.S., Ohio U., 1932; m. Rhoda M. Hewitt, Dec. 17, 1938; children—Robert, Mary Ellen (Mrs. Joseph Van Buskirk), Ronald. State and county hwy. engr., Ohio, 1933-35; asso. engr. Burgess & Niple, cons. engr., Columbus, Ohio, 1935-42; chief sna. facilities sect. 5th Service Command Hdqrs. Army Service Forces, Columbus, Ohio, 1942-45; mem. Burgess & Niple, Ltd., cons. engr., specializing in waterworks, wastewater control design and mgmt., Columbus, 1946—, exec. dir., 1960-75, chmn. bd., 1976—; pres., dir. 2015 W. Fifth, Inc., Columbus; dir. Gammatronix Corp., Columbus. Commr. Ohio River Valley Sanitation Commn., 1966-72, chmn., 1971-72; mem. Ohio River Basin Planning Commn., 1970-72. Recipient Meritorious Service award Dept. Army, 1946, Fuller award Am. Water Works Assn., 1958, Distinguished Cons. award Cons. Engrs. Ohio, 1975. Registered profl. engr., Ohio. Mem. ASCE, Am. Water Works Assn., Nat., Ohio socs. profl. engrs., Water Mgmt. Assn. Ohio (trustee 1972-78, treas. 1977). Methodist. Mason. Clubs: Columbus Engineers, University (Columbus). Contbr. articles to profl. and tech. jours. Home: 4321 Olentangy Blvd Columbus OH 43214 Office: 5085 Reed Rd Columbus OH 43220

FULLER, S. B., cosmetic mfg.; b. Monroe, La., 1905. Chmn., pres., treas., dir. Fuller Products Co., Chgo.; pres., treas., dir. Boyer Internat. Labs., Inc. Home: 13500 S Kedzie Ave Robbins IL 60472 Office: 50 E 26th St Chicago IL 60616*

FULLER, STEPHEN HERBERT, automotive co. exec.; b. Columbus, Ohio, Feb. 4, 1920; s. Josiah Allen and Mary Ellen (Quinn) F.; A.B., Ohio U., 1941; student Harvard Law Sch., 1941-42, I.A., Harvard, 1943, M.B.A., 1947, D.C.S., 1958; Ph.D. (hon.), Ateneo de Manila U., 1964, De La Salle Coll., 1971, Ohio U., 1977; m. Frances Gertrude Mulhearn, June 23, 1951; children—Teofilo M. (adopted), Mark Benton, Joseph Barry. Instr. econ. and labor relations Ohio U., 1947; asso. prof. Harvard, 1947-61, prof., 1961-71, dir. internat. tchrs. program, 1959-60, asso. dean external affairs, 1964-71; on leave to serve as pres. Asian Inst. Mgmt., Manila, Philippines, 1969-71, now mem. bd. govs.; v.p. personnel adminstrn. and devel. staff Gen. Motors Corp., Detroit, 1971—; mem. tech. adv. com. Detroit Inst. Tech. Mem. corp. Babson Coll.; trustee Ohio Univ. Fund; mem. vis. com. adminstrn. Harvard; trustee Loyola U., Chgo., 1971-74; mem. Trustees Acad., Ohio U. Served to capt. AUS, 1943-46. Recipient Presdl. Merit medal Republic of Philippines, 1971. Mem. Am. Arbitration Assn., Nat. Mgmt. Assn., James Garfield Soc., Detroit Soc. Internat. Affairs, Philippine-Am. Soc., Phi Beta Kappa, Phi Eta Sigma, Omicron Delta Kappa, Beta Gamma Sigma, Delta Tau Delta. Author: (with others) Problems in Labor Relations, rev. edit., 1958. Home: 1869 Chippingway Bloomfield Hills MI 48013 Office: Gen Motors Corp Detroit MI 48202

FULLER, TERRY ALAN, biophysicist, biomed. engr.; b. Phila., May 2, 1948; s. Jay Ned and Adele F.; M.S., Worcester Poly. Inst. and Clark U., 1972, Ph.D., 1975. Research asso., cons. exptl. psychology Clark U., Worcester, Mass., 1970-71; instr., cons. electro-physiology Worcester Poly. Inst., 1972-75; cons. U. Mass. Med. Sch., Worcester, 1973-75; adj. asst. prof. physics U. Mich., Dearborn, 1975—; adj. asso. clin. instr. Wayne State U. Sch. Medicine, Detroit, 1976—; asso. dir. laser surgery labs. Sinai Hosp. Detroit, 1975—; cons. in field. Active Boy Scouts Am. Mem. AAAS, IEEE, Assn. Advancement Med. Instrumentation, N.Y. Acad. Scis., Laser Inst. Am., Detroit Physiol. Soc. Jewish. Designer, developer glass laser opthalmic system. Home: 25008 Chambley Dr Southfield MI 48034 Office: Dept Laser Surgery Sinai Hosp Detroit 6767 W Outer Dr Detroit MI 48235

FULLERTON, FRANK REEVES, dentist; b. Princeton, Mo., Sept. 14, 1908; s. Frank R. and Cora M. (Malone) F.; D.D.S., U. Mo., 1931; m. Naomi Larie White, May 16, 1936; 1 dau., Frances Anne (Mrs. Larry L. Heck). Pvt. practice dentistry, Kansas City, Mo., 1931—. Served to lt., Dental Corps, USNR, 1944-45. Mem. Am., Mo., Greater Kansas City dental assns., Xi Psi Phi. Methodist (mem. ofcl. bd.). Club: Blue Hills Country (Kansas City). Home: 1219 W 68th Terr Kansas City MO 64113 Office: 3715 E Gregory St Kansas City MO 64132

FULLWOOD, NANCY YVONNE, guidance counselor; b. Dayton, Ohio, May 14, 1940; d. Elwood Mumford and Eve Gertrude (Jennings) Parsons; B.A., Ohio U., 1962; M.S., Wright State U., 1971; m. Ralph Larry Fullwood; 1 son, David. Guidance counselor John H. Linton Intermediate High Sch., Pitts., 1971, Mt. Healthy High Sch., Cin., 1972, Washingtonville (N.Y.) High Sch., 1973, Tulsa Area Vocat. Tech. Sch., 1974, Papillion-LaVista High Sch., Papillion, Nebr., 1976-77, Comprehensive Study Center, Omaha Pub. Schs., 1977—. Co-pres. George W. Norris Sch. PTA, 1976-77. Mem. NEA, Nebr., Omaha edn. assns., Am. Personnel and Guidance Assn., Assn. Non-White Concerns, Nat. Sch. Counselors Assn. Democrat. Roman Catholic. Club: Omaha Disco Dance. Office: 5703 Military St Omaha NE 68114

FULTON, GERE BURKE, educator; b. Harrisburg, Pa., Jan. 11, 1939; s. Graydon Burke and Odella Mae F.; B.S., East Stroudsburg State Coll., 1960; M.A., U. Md., 1962, Ph.D., 1967; m. Marie E. Kmetz, June 4, 1960; children—Douglas, David. Instr., Temple U., 1965-67; asso. prof. Trenton State Coll., 1967-69, prof., 1969-71; prof. health edn. U. Toledo, 1971—, chmn. dept. health edn., 1971-75. Pres. bd. dirs. Planned Parenthood of Greater Toledo, 1975-77. Mem. AAHPER, Assn. Advancement Health Edn., Am. Assn. Sex Educators, Counselors, Therapists. Author: (with W. V. Fassbender) Health Education in the Elementary School: Guidelines and Program Suggestions, 1972; Sexual Awareness, 1974. Home: 7658 Bridgeway Rd Temperance MI 48182 Office: Dept Health Edn U Toledo Toledo OH 43606

FULTON, PAUL ROGER, dentist; b. Cleve., June 9, 1919; s. LeRoy and Ida Catherine (Lang) F.; B.S., Western Mich. U., 1947, B.A., 1948; postgrad., Wayne U., 1949; D.D.S., U. Detroit, 1953; m. Pearl Juanita Harrison, Oct. 12, 1957; children—Pamela Sue, Patrice Corinne, Paul Robert. Practice dentistry, Schoolcraft, Mich., 1953—; mem. med. staff Bronson Meth. Hosp., Kalamazoo, Franklin Meml. Hosp., Vicksburg, Mich.; constable Schoolcraft Twp., Kalamazoo County; spl. dep. for forensic odontology Kalamazoo County Sheriff's Dept.; cons. forensic odontology Cass and Barry County sheriffs depts., East Lansing, Holland and Plymouth (Mich.) state police sci. crime labs.; forensic dental cons. Office Chief Med. Examiners, St. Joseph and Kalamazoo Counties. Active A.R.C., Community Chest; coordinator Kalamazoo County Sheriff, Aux. Police, U.S. Army Def. field exercises, 1959-71; dep. sheriff St. Joseph County. Served from pvt. to col., AUS, 1941-46; ETO. Diplomate Am. Bd. Forensic Odontology. Fellow Royal Soc. Health (Eng.), Am., Mich. dental assns., Kalamazoo Valley Dental Soc., Mich. Assn. Professions, Fedn. Dentaire Internat., Assn. Mil. Surgeons, V.F.W., Am. Legion, Am. Rifle Assn. (life), Res. Officers Assn., Assn. U.S.Army, Fraternal Order Police, Soc. Philatelic Ams., Am. Acad. Forensic Scis., Canadian Soc. Forensic, Sci., Am. Soc. Forensic Odontology, Internat. Soc. for Forensic Odonto-Stomatology, Psi Omega, Theta Chi Delta, Tau Kappa Epsilon. Republican. Presbyn. Mason (Shriner), Elk, Lion. Contbr. articles to profl. jours. Home: 200 W Cass St Schoolcraft MI 49087 Office: 232 N Grand Schoolcraft MI 49087

FUNDERBURG, WILLIAM RUSSELL, surgeon; b. New Carlisle, Ohio, Sept. 24, 1910; s. Herbert D. and Glenna D. (Dredge) F.; A.B., Miami U., Oxford, Ohio, 1932; M.D., Western Res. U., 1935; m. Anna Marie Couch, Sept. 10, 1938; children—Judith Ann, Dr. James C., Betty Jane. Intern, Cleve. Met. Hosp., 1935-36, resident in surgery, 1936-39; practice medicine specializing in surgery, Tiffin, Ohio, 1940—; surg. staff Mercy, Fostoria (Ohio) City, Willard (Ohio) City hosps.; chief of surgery Wyandot Meml. Hosp., Upper Sandusky, Ohio. Diplomate Am. Bd. Surgery. Fellow A.C.S., Internat. Coll. Surgeons, Pan Pacific Surg. Assn., Pan Am. Med. Assn.; mem. AMA. Republican. Club: Elks. Home: Negrotown Rd Tiffin OH 44883 Office: 6 Main St Tiffin OH 44883

FUNK, ARVILLE LYNN, lawyer; b. Corydon, Ind., Dec. 11, 1929; s. Herman E. and Elsie (McMonigle) F.; B.A. in History, Ind. Central Coll., 1955; M.S. in Edn., Butler U.; LL.B., Ind. U., 1963, J.D., 1967; ; m. Rosemary E. Springer, Aug. 25, 1956; children—Cynthia Lynn, Mark Andrew (dec.). Head history dept. Perry Central Jr. High Sch., 1955-61, Perry E. Jr. High Sch., Indpls., 1961-65; admitted to Ind. bar, 1963; partner law firm Hays, O'Bannon & Funk, Corydon, Ind., 1965—; atty. Crawford County, City of Corydon; gen. counsel Ind. Toll Bridge Commn., 1969—. Instr. history Purdue U. extension. Hist. advisor Ind. Dept. Conservation, 1961—; publs. chmn. Marion County Civil War Centennial Commn., 1961-65; chmn. Harrison County Bicentennial Commn. Del., Ind. Republican State Conv., 1966, 68, 70, 72, 74. Pres., dir. North Am. Indian Found., 1966-67. Served to capt. AUS, 1947-48, 50-52. Recipient Nat. Classroom Tchrs. medal Freedom Found., 1962. Mem. Am., Ind., Harrison County (pres.) bar assns., Ind., Harrison County (dir.) hist. socs., C. of C. (dir.), Ind. Central Coll. Alumni (dir.), Phi Delta Phi. Methodist (pres. bd. trustees). Rotarian (dir.). Author: Tales of Our Hoosier Heritage, 1965; 1966; Harrison County In Sesquicentennials Year, Indiana's Birthplace, 1966; Our Historic Corydon, 1967; Pioneers of Harrison County, 1967; Hoosiers in the Civil War, 1968; A Sketchbook of Indiana History, 1969; The Morgan Raid in Indiana and Ohio, 1971; Squire Boone in Indiana, 1973; Historical Almanac of Harrison County, 1974; Revolutionary War Era in Indiana, 1975; Revolutionary War Soldiers in Harrison County, 1975; A Hoosier Regiment in Dixie, 1977. Contbr. articles to profl. jours. Editor Teaching Ind. History, 1962-64. Home: Rural Route 5 PO Box 66 Corydon IN 47112 Office: 303 N Capitol Ave Corydon IN 47112

FUNK, WILLIS LLOYD, dentist; b. Abilene, Kans., Oct. 2, 1928; s. Adolph Willis and Olga Frieda (Weinbrenner) F.; B.S. in Sci., Kans. Wesleyan U., 1952; D.D.S., U. Mo. at Kansas City, 1956; m. Shirley Lee Davis, June 20, 1954; children—Douglas Lloyd, Terri Lynne, Susan Louise, Kathleen Lisa. Practice dentistry, Oakley, Kans., 1956—. Cubmaster Coronado Council Boy Scouts Am., 1966-68, bd. of review 1964-69; master instr. Kans. Hunter Safety Program. Served with AUS, 1946-48. Mem. Am., Kans. dental assns., Northwest Dist. Dental Soc. (sec.-treas. 1968-69,) v.p. 1969-70, pres. 1970-71). Republican. Mem. Christian Ch. (deacon, Sunday sch. supr., chmn. ch. bd. 1974-75). Home: 412 S Smokyhill St Oakley KS 67748 Office: 418 Hudson St Oakley KS 67748 also Box 145 Oakley KS 67748

FUNKHOUSER, JAMES CLAGGETT, hornist, condr., educator; b. Portsmouth, N.H., Sept. 14, 1933; s. James Alexander and Helen (Claggett) F.; student U. N.H., Durham, 1950-51; B.S. in Composition, Juilliard Sch. Music, 1956; postgrad. U. Mo. at Kansas City, 1972; m. Nancy Kaye Crawford, July 23, 1973. Profl. French hornist Calgary (Alta., Can.), Philharmonic, 1958-59, Va. Symphony Orch., Richmond, 1959-60, St. Joseph (Mo.) Symphony Orch., 1962-64, Kansas City (Mo.) Philharmonic Orch., 1960-70, Wichita (Kans.) Symphony Orch., 1972-73; tchr. French horn U. N.H. Summer Youth Music Sch., 1951-56, New Eng. Music Camp, Oakland, Maine, 1960-64, Stephens Coll., Columbia, Mo., 1967-71; asst. condr. Youth Symphony, also Jr. Youth Symphony, Kansas City, Mo., 1963; co-founder, asst. dir., asst. condr. Assn. Creative Study Arts, Inc., Kansas City, Mo., 1966-70. Pvt. tchr. French horn, Kansas City area. Served with AUS, 1956-58. Composer: Concerto for Oboe, Concertine for Clarinet and Strings, Chamber Concerto for Flute and String Quartet, Concertante for Four Winds and Strings, Triptich for Contrabass and Piano, Two Pieces for Brass Septet, other chamber music. Performer own compositions numerous appearances. Home: 7735 Colonial Dr Prairie Village KS 66208

FURCON, JOHN EDWARD, psychologist; b. Chgo., Mar. 17, 1942; s. John F. and Lottie (Janik) F.; B.A., DePaul U., 1963, M.A., 1965; M.B.A., U. Chgo., 1970; m. Carolyn Ann Warden, Aug. 15, 1964; children—Juliana, Annalisa, Diana. With Indsl. Relations Center, U. Chgo., 1963—, project dir., 1966—, research psychologist, 1970—. Mem. faculty DePaul U., 1966-67, Traffic Inst., Northwestern U., 1969—, Sch. for New Learning, 1974—; cons. U.S. Justice Dept., bus., ednl. and govt. orgns. Mem. Gov.'s Adv. Com. on Pvt. Security, 1974—; mem. profl. adv. com. Bur. Testing Services, 1973—. Served to lt. AUS, 1963-65. Mem. Am., Ill. psychol. assns., Chgo. Psychol. Club, Indsl. Psychology Assn. Chgo. (chmn. 1973-75). Contbr. articles to profl. jours. Home: 109 53d St Western Springs IL 60558 Office: Industrial Relations Center Univ Chicago Chicago IL 60637

FURGISON, CLIFFORD FREDRIC, psychotherapist; b. Chgo., Dec. 4, 1948; s. Jack Warren and Vernie Florence (Snyder) F.; B.A., Eastern Mich. U., 1971, M.A., 1975; m. Carolyn Stephanie Albrecht, June 27, 1970; 1 dau., Tracie Michelle. Tchr. Manchester (Mich.) Pub. Schs., 1971-73, staff therapist, dept. substance abuse Providence Hosp., Southfield, Mich., 1975-76, dir. dept. substance abuse, 1976—; guest lectr. Wayne State U., 1976-77, U. Detroit, 1976; cons. in field. Certified alcoholism counselor; certified social worker, Mich. Mem. Am. Personnel and Guidance Assn., Mich. Assn. Alcoholism Counselors, Mich. Alcohol and Addiction Assn., Alcohol and Drug Problem Assn. N. Am. Contbr. articles to profl. jours. Home: 5754 Kilbrennan Birmingham MI 48010 Office: 16001 W 9 Mile Rd Southfield MI 48075

FURLIN, JAMES RODNEY, therapist; b. Centerville, Iowa, Aug. 19, 1947; s. John Leo and Mary Madelyne (Shankster) F.; A.A., Indian Hills Community Coll., 1972; B.S. in Psychology, U. Nebr., Omaha, 1974, M.S. in Counseling, 1976; m. Mildred Frances Stajcar, Mar. 23, 1968; children—Angela Renee, Alana Yvonne and Andrea Marie (triplets). Joined U.S. Army, 1966, entrance examiner, Pitts., 1966-69; USAF, 1971—, mental health therapist, La Vista, Nebr., 1971-77. Mem. Am. Personnel and Guidance Assn., Assn. for Specialists in Group Work, Am. Mental Health Counselors Assn. Democrat. Roman Catholic. Clubs: Masons, Shriners, K.C. Home: 8106 Valley Rd LaVista NE 68128 Office: Mental Health Services Erhling Bergquist Hosp Offutt AFB NE 68113

FURNESS, TERRANCE DANIEL, urologist; b. Pitts., Aug. 7, 1923; s. Thomas Richard and Delia Agnes (Boyle) F.; B.S., U. Pitts., 1948; M.D., Hahnemann Med. Sch., 1952; m. Anita Ellen Boorse, Dec. 29, 1951; children—Susan, Tracy, Terrance (dec.), Jill (dec.), Patrick. Intern, St. Vincent's Hosp., Bridgeport, Conn., 1952-53; resident in urology Huron Rd. Hosp., Cleve., 1953-56; practice medicine specializing in urology, Canton, Ohio, 1956—; tchr., cons. residency program Mercy-Timken-Mercy Hosp., Canton, 1956-70. Served with U.S. Army, 1943-46. Fellow A.C.S.; mem. AMA, Urol. Assn., Royal Soc. Medicine, Ohio Coll. Surgeons. Presbyterian (trustee). Club: Brookside Country. Home: 6522 Danforth Circle NW Canton OH 44718 Office: 211 15th St NW Canton OH 44703

FURNEY, PAUL K., engring. assn. exec.; b. Columbus, Ohio, Dec. 29, 1920; s. Ray Hanlon and Clara B. (Butts) F.; B.S. in Journalism, Ohio State U., 1951; m. Mildred Florence Wright, Mar. 15, 1947; 1 dau., Pamela Kay. Indsl. engr. N.Am. Aviation, Columbus, 1951-59; asst. exec. sec. Ohio Soc. Profl. Engrs., Columbus, 1959-70; exec. dir. Cons. Engrs. Ohio, Columbus, 1970—. Guest lectr. Ohio State U., Case Western Res. U., Ohio No. U. Ad hoc mem. numerous coms. on specialized programs, dedications, community celebrations, Columbus, 1952—. Served with USAAF, 1942-45. Mem. Exptl. Aircraft Assn., Model T Ford Club Central Ohio (sec. 1970-75), other antique car assns. Club: Columbus Athletic. Mason. Republican. Presbyn. Home: 1818 Merriweather Dr Columbus OH 43221 Office: 445 King Ave Columbus OH 43201

FURNEY, THOMAS ALBERT, info. systems dir.; b. Ft. Wayne, Ind., June 23, 1940; s. Kenneth Albert and Beda E.; B.S. in Indsl. Mgmt., Purdue U., 1964; m. Sally Joann Beaver, Nov. 20, 1965; children—Christopher George, Jeffrey John. Systems mgr. Gen. Tire and Rubber Co., Wabash, Ind., 1965-69; systems analyst Univac div. Sperry Rand Co., Ft. Wayne, Ind., 1969-70; data center mgr. Compumatics, Inc., Ft. Wayne, 1970-74, dir. info. systems, 1974—. Vice-pres. Westlawn Civic Assn.; pres. Anthony Wayne Ch. of God. Mem. Data Processing Mgmt. Assn. Home: 611 Nordale Dr Fort Wayne IN 46804 Office: 1619 Magnavox Way Fort Wayne IN 46804

FURRER, JOHN RUDOLF, mfg. co. exec.; b. Milw., Dec. 2, 1927; s. Rudolph and Leona (Peters) F.; grad. Phillips Exeter Acad., 1945; B.A., Harvard, 1949; m. Annie Louise Waldo, Apr. 24, 1954; children—Blake Waldo, Kimberly Louise. Spl. rep. ACF Industries, Madrid, Spain, 1949-51; asst. supr. Thermonuclear Devel. & Test-Los Alamos, Eniwetok Atoll, 1952-53; dir. product devel. dept. Am. Car & Foundry Div., N.Y.C., 1954-58 dir. machinery/systems group FMC Corp., San Jose, Calif., 1959-67, gen. mgr. Engineered Systems div., 1967-69, v.p. in charge planning dept. Central Engring. Labs. and Engineered Systems div., Chgo., 1970, group v.p. in charge Material Handling, Mining and Environ. Equipment Group, 1971-77, v.p. corp. devel., 1977—. Pres., bd. dirs. Santa Clara County Vol. Bur.; v.p., bd. dirs. Childrens Home Soc. Calif.; bd. dirs. Ming Quong Childrens Center; bd. govs. San Francisco Bay Area Council. Served with USNR, 1945-46. Mem. ASME. Clubs: Harvard (N.Y.C. and Chgo.); Glen View Country (Golf, Ill.); Economic, Mid-Am. (Chgo.). Patentee in field. Home: 62 Woodley Rd Winnetka IL 60093 Office: 200 E Randolph Dr Chicago IL 60601

FURSTE, WESLEY LEONARD, II, surgeon; b. Cin., Apr. 19, 1915; s. Wesley Leonard and Alma (Deckebach) F.; A.B. cum laude, Harvard, 1937, M.D., 1941; m. Leone James, Mar. 28, 1942; children—Nancy Dianne, Susan Deanne, Wesley Leonard III. Intern, Ohio State U. Hosp., Columbus, 1941-42; fellow surgery U. Cin., 1945-46; asst. surg. resident Cin. Gen. Hospital, 1946-49; sr. asst. surg. resident Ohio State U. Hosps., 1949-50, chief surg. resident, 1950-51; practice medicine specializing in surgery, Columbus, 1951—; instr. Ohio State U., 1951-54, clin. asst. prof. surgery, 1954-66, clin. asso. prof., 1969-74, clin. prof. surgery, 1974—. mem. surg. staffs Mt. Carmel, Children's, Grant, University, St. Anthony, Riverside Meth. hosps. (all Columbus); surg. cons. Dayton (Ohio) VA Hosp., Columbus State Sch., Ohio State Penitentiary, Mercy Hosp., Columbus; regional adv. com. nat. blood program ARC, 1951-68. chmn., 1958-68; invited participant 2d Internat. Conf. on Tetanus, WHO, Bern, Switzerland, 1966, 3d Internat. Conf., São Paulo, Brazil, 1970, invited rapporteur 4th Internat. Conf., Dakar, Senegal, 1975; mem. med. adv. com. Medic Alert Found. Internat., 1971-73, 76—, bd. dirs., 1973-76; founder Digestive Disease Found. Mem. Ohio Motor Vehicle Med. Rev. Bd., 1965-67; bd. dirs. Am. Cancer Soc. Franklin County, pres., 1964-66. Served from 1st lt. to maj. M.C., AUS, 1942-46; CBI. Diplomate Am. Bd. Surgery. Mem. Central Surg. Assn., Soc. Surgery of Alimentary Tract, A.A.A.S., A.C.S. (chmn. Ohio com. trauma; mem. subcom. prophylaxis against tetanus in wound mgmt.), Am. Assn. Surgery of Trauma, Ohio State, Columbus surg. assns., A.M.A., Am. Trauma Soc. (founding mem., dir.), Ohio State Med. Assn., Columbus Acad. Medicine, Acad. Medicine Cin., Am. Pub. Health Assn., Am. Med. Writers Assn., Robert M. Zollinger Club, Mont Reid Surg. Soc., Am. Geriatrics Soc., N.Y. Acad. Scis., Assn. Physicians of State of Ohio, Collegium Internationale Chirurgiae Digestivae, Assn. Am. Med. Colls., Internat. Brotherhood Magicians, Soc. Am. Magicians. Presbyn. Clubs: Scioto Country, Ohio State University Golf, Ohio State Faculty (Columbus); University (Cin.); Harvard (Boston). Prime author: Tetanos. Contbr. to (book) Advances in Military Medicine, 1948; Management of the Injured Patient, also articles in profl. jours. Home: 3125 Bembridge Rd Columbus OH 43221 Office: 3545 Olentangy River Rd Columbus OH 43214

FURTON, CHARLES KENNETH, fiberglass co. exec.; b. Detroit, Feb. 1, 1937; s. Harry Andrew and Marie (Goosen) F.; student Eastern Mich. U., 1955-56, 58-59; B.B.A., U. Detroit, 1965; m. Elizabeth Freeman, July 6, 1963; children—John, Sheila, Matthew. Credit supr. Gen. Motors Acceptance Corp., Detroit, 1959-66; indsl. relations staff Ford Motor Co., Detroit, 1966; estimator sales John H. Freeman Co., Detroit, 1966-68, also dir.; transp., appliance dist. sales mgr. Owens Corning Fiberglas, Toledo, 1968-76, dist. sales mgr., Detroit, 1976—. Served with USNR, 1956-58. Mem. Producers

Council (pres. 1972), Constrn. Specifications Inst. (1st v.p. 1974), Home Builders Assn., Am. Soc. Heating, Refrigeration and Air Conditioning Engrs., Soc. Automotive Engrs. Kiwanian. Clubs: Maumee River Yacht, Bay View Yacht, Pine Lake Country. Home: 4100 Old Dominion Dr West Bloomfield MI 48033 Office: Owens Corning Fiberglas 15300 W Eight Mile Rd Oak Park MI 48237

FUSARO, JANIECE ELAINE BARRE, librarian; b. Detroit, Feb. 7, 1925; d. William and Augusta Rose (Siebenbrunner) Barre; adopted d. Elizabeth Marie (Siebenbrunner) Moses; B.A., U. Minn., 1946, M.A., 1949, B.S. in L.S., 1953, Ph.D., 1968; postgrad. Middlebury Coll., 1949, Stephens Coll., 1968; m. Ramon M. Fusaro, Aug. 4, 1951; children—Lisa Ann, Toni Ann. Teaching asst. German dept. U. Minn., Mpls., 1947-50, acquisitions librarian U. Minn. Library, 1951-53; prof. German, Coll. St. Catherine, St. Paul, 1964-65; librarian Anoka-Ramsey Community Coll., Coon Rapids, Minn., 1965-69, 70-71; program dir. Minn. Higher Edn. Coordinating Commn., St. Paul, 1969-70; mem. community faculty Met. State U., St. Paul, 1971—; library cons. Golden Valley Luth. Coll., Minn., 1968, writers conf. U. Wis.-River Falls, 1976. Dir. statewide library survey Minn. Higher Edn. Coordinating Commn., 1970; mem. Minn. Planning Com. on Library Automation, 1971, Minn. Adv. Com. on Inter-library Cooperation, 1971. Bd. dirs. Riverside Center, Mpls., 1970-74. Named Minn. Librarian of Year, Minn. Library Assn., 1969; Teaching Excellence award Met. State U., 1977. Mem. Minn. Library Assn. (life), ALA (life), Alpha Lambda Psi. Contbr. articles to profl. jours. Home: 3108 36th Ave NE Minneapolis MN 55418 Office: Metro State U 7th and Robert St St Paul MN 55101

FUSON, DONNA BELLE CARTER, ednl. adminstr.; b. Canton, Ill., Dec. 22, 1935; d. Paul Clayton and Elnora Ellen (Kramer) Carter; B.S., Ill. State U., 1957; M.S., No. Ill. U., 1968; m. William Jean Fuson, Aug. 6, 1960; children—Kathryn Suzanne, David William. Primary tchr. Dennis Sch., Decatur, Ill., 1957-59; stewardess, United Air Lines, Chgo., 1959-60; primary tchr. Ogden Ave. Sch., Dist. 102, LaGrange, Ill., 1960-63; elementary sch. counselor Sch. Dist. 103, Lyons, Ill., 1968-69; coordinator Project EVE, Northwest Ednl. Coop., Arlington Heights, Ill., 1972-75; dir. Career Edn. Service Center, Arlington Heights, 1975—. Mem. Christian edn. commn., Sunday sch. tchr., tchr. trainer First Presbyterian Ch., Western Springs, Ill.; bd. dirs., pres. Western Springs, PTA; mem. Western Springs sch. bd.; mem. caucus com. Cook County High Sch. Dist. 204. Mem. Am., Ill. (v.p. for elementary) sch. counselor assns., Am. Personnel and Guidance Assn., Ill. Guidance and Personnel Assn. (govt. relations chmn.). Republican. Home: 4234 Franklin Ave Western Springs IL 60558

GAASEDELEN, NEWELL ORVILLE, investment assn. exec.; b. Mpls., Sept. 5, 1915; s. Nels O. and Isabel (Naeseth) G.; B.B.A., U. Minn., 1938; Indsl. Adminstr., Harvard U., 1943, M.B.A., 1946; m. Jane Ann Lobstein, Nov. 22, 1950; children—James Robert, Barbara Lynn, Jon Richard. Lectr. econs. U. Minn., Mpls., 1946-56; securities analyst Mpls. Tchrs. Retirement Fund Assn., 1950-67, exec. sec., 1967—; pres. Kans Okla. Cons. Oil Co., Mpls., 1951—, also dir.; pres. Search Investments Corp. Mpls., 1960-63, also dir.; chmn. bd. Waters Instruments Inc., Rochester, Minn., 1959—, dir. 1965-67; incorporator Edina (Minn.) State Bank, also dir.; pres. Berkshire Investment Co., Mpls., also dir.; dir. Employers Overload Co., Served to comdr. Supply Corps, USNR, 1943-46, 50-52. Mem. Fin. Analysts Fedn., Naval Res. Assn., Harvard Bus. Alumni Assn., Twin City Soc. Security Analysts, Torske Klubben, Sons Norway, Nordsmans Ferbundet, Aircraft Owners and Pilots Assn., Am. Legion, Beta Gamma Sigma. Lutheran. Clubs: Six O'Clock, Edina Country, Mpls. Athletic. Home: 4818 Golf Terr Edina MN 55424 Office: 1670 NW Bank Bldg Minneapolis MN 55402

GABBARD, AVERY DALE, ret. ednl. adminstr.; b. Jasonville, Ind., Jan. 24, 1912; s. Cleve H. and Pansy Fay (Beckwith) G.; B.S. in Elementary Edn., Ind. State U., 1941, B.S. in Secondary Edn., 1942, M.S., 1952; m. Juanita Weaver, Apr. 29, 1933; 1 son, L. Joe. Adminstr., basketball coach, tchr., Greene County, Ind., 1933-40; tchr., coach, Vigo County, Ind., 1940-42; asst. prin. high sch. Greene County, 1942-50; prin. West Washington Elementary Sch., Campbellsburg, Ind., 1964-75; tchr. psychology and social studies All Saints Episcopal Pvt. High Sch., Vicksburg, Miss., 1976-77. Mem. Ind. Tchrs. Assn. (chmn. legis. com. 1952-64), N.E.A., Ind. (exec. bd. 1974-75), Nat. elementary prins. assns., Campbellsburg Tchrs. Assn. (pres.). Scoutmaster, Boy Scouts Am., 1952-55. Mem. Pi Gamma Mu, Phi Delta Kappa. Democrat. Baptist (licensed minister, deacon). Mason, Lion, Fraternal Order Police (asso.). Home: 170 Laura Ln Bloomfield IN 47424

GABBERT, ROY ELLIS, lawyer; b. Portsmouth, Ohio, Apr. 4, 1925; s. George Gilbert and Lena (Rider) G.; B.A., Ohio State U., 1949, LL.B., 1951, J.D., 1967; m. Virginia Faye King, Apr. 28, 1946; children—Robin, Terri; m. 2d, Betty Miller, Dec. 29, 1962; children—Gay, Roy Ellis. Admitted to Ohio bar, 1952, since practiced in West Union; gen. counsel World's Plowing Matches, 1957; asst. atty. gen. Ohio, 1959-63; pres. Reggo Builders. Dir. Credit Bur. Adams County, Inc.; sec. Adams County Devel. Corp. Chmn. Adams County chpt. A.R.C. Mayor West Union, 1953; dep. dir. Adams County Civil Def. Served with AUS, 1943-46: PTO. Decorated Bronze Star, medal. Mem. Nat. Council Juvenile Ct. Judges (asso.), Am., Ohio, Adams County (sec. 1953-69, 71—, pres. 1970) bar assns., Nat., Ohio, Shawnee home builders assns., 741st Vets. Assn. (pres.). Presbyn. Home: RFD 1 West Union OH 45693 Office: 301 N Market St West Union OH 45693

GABEL, DUANE ROBERT, constrn. co. exec.; b. Fremont, Wis., May 17, 1928; s. Edward John and Luella Gladys (Thomas) G.; Heating, Ventilating and Air Conditioning Technician, Milw. Sch. Engring., 1946; m. Corinne Joyce Black, Jan. 29, 1949; children—Steven D., Barbara D., Brian D. Sales engr. Trane Co., LaCross, Wis., 1947-48, Appleton, Wis., 1948-52; project engr. August Winter & Sons Inc., Appleton, 1952—, sec., 1953-67, v.p., 1967-70, pres., 1970—; dir. Valley No. Bank. Mem. Appleton Bd. Heating Examiners, 1970—; mem. Wis. State Sheetmetal Apprenticeship Com., 1965—. Registered profl. engr., Wis., Mich., Minn. Mem. Fox Cities Chamber Commerce and Industry (formerly Appleton Area C. of C.) (pres. 1976), Wis., Nat. socs. profl. engrs., Am. Soc. Heating, Ventilating and Refrigeration Engrs., Nat. Assn. Power Engrs. Republican. Methodist. Club: Riverview Country. Home: 2900 E Crestview Dr Appleton WI 54911 Office: 2323 N Roemer Rd Appleton WI 54911

GABER, GEORGE JOSEPH, music educator; b. N.Y.C., Feb. 24, 1916; s. Robert and Dora (Wexler) G.; student Cooper Union, 1931-34, Juilliard Sch. Music, 1937, Manhattan Sch. Music, 1957, Queens Coll., 1955; m. Esther Feinberg, Dec. 8, 1940; children—Robert, Deborah. Mem. faculty Sch. Music, Ind. U., Bloomington, 1960—, prof. music, 1962—. Solo percussionist, concert and jazz, N.Y.C., Colo., Minn., Japan, Brazil, other locations; condr. Ind. U. Percussion Ensemble; rec. artist on RCA, MGM, Columbia, Decca. Music asso. Aspen Festival, 1957-72; adviser, participant Shiraz/Persepolis Festival, 1969. Mem. A.A.U.P., Phi Mu Alpha. Mason. Club: Bohemians. Composer: Salute; Song of a Goat, Carioca Carnival, others. Home: 1909 Arden Dr Bloomington IN 47401

GABER, MARTIN, electronics co. exec.; b. Chgo., Sept. 24, 1917; s. Jacob Leon and Bertha (Berman) G.; S.B., Northwestern U., 1939; m. Lita Leance, Apr. 20, 1941; children—Richard, Susan Gaber Lazar, Pamela, Debra. Project engr. Bell and Howell Co., Lincolnwood, Ill., 1942-45; pres. Continental Corp., Chgo., 1945-54; chmn. bd., pres. Chgo. Switch, Inc., 1954—; cons. mgmt.; broker electronics and carbon industries. Chmn. Am. Assn. for UN of the North Shore, 1953. Mem. Electronics Industries Assn., Chgo. Symphony Orchestral Assn., Newberry Library Assn., Northwestern U. Library Assn., Chgo. Commons Assn., Common Cause, Bus. and Profl. People for Pub. Interest, Chgo. Lit. Club. Club: Cliffdwellers. Patentee self mailers, elec. switch structures. Home: 2301 Greenwood Ave Wilmette IL 60091 Office: 1714 N Damen Ave Chicago IL 60647

GABLE, TOM SCHULTE, san. engr.; b. Allegan, Mich., Feb. 13, 1924; s. Hartley Howland and Estelle (Schulte) G.; B.S. in Civil Engring., Mich. State Coll., 1947; M.P.H., U. Mich., 1951; m. Jeanne M. Greenawalt, Mar. 17, 1947; children—Margaret, Laurence. San. engr. Allegan County Health Dept., 1947-48; chief environ. health Flint (Mich.) Health Dept., 1949-53; pub. health engr., lectr. U. Nebr., 1953-57; dist. engr., tng. officer Allegheny County Health Dept., Pitts., 1957-58; pub. health engr., v.p. customer services Nat. Sanitation Found., Ann Arbor, Mich., 1958—. Resident lectr. U. Mich. Sch. Pub. Health, 1958—. Served with USNR, 1942-46. Fellow Am. Pub. Health Assn. (chmn. sect. on environment); mem. Conf. Local Environ. Health Adminstrs. (past chmn., editor newsletter 1955-65), Nat. Environ. Health Assn., Internat. Assn. Milk and Food Sanitarians, Delta Omega. Home: 957 Greenhills Dr Ann Arbor MI 48105 Office: Nat Sanitation Found 3475 Plymouth Rd Ann Arbor MI 48105

GABRIEL, ARTHUR WILFRED, banker; b. Eudora, Kans., May 13, 1910; s. Samuel J. and Sophia (Brown) G.; student pub. schs., Eudora; m. Alberta Bell Rohe, June 4, 1937; children—Belva Arlee, Arlen Arthur. With DeSoto (Kans.) State Bank, 1933—, successively asst. cashier, cashier, exec. v.p., pres., 1963-77, chmn. bd., 1977—; dir. Centennial State Bank, Mission, Kans., Lenexa State Bank and Trust Co. (Kans.); Councilman, DeSoto, 1938-42; mem. Sch. Bd., 1938-42; mem. Kans. Ho. of Reps., 1966-74; state bank commr. Kans., 1975-76. Served with AUS, 1942-45. Decorated Bronze Star medal. Mem. Kans. Bankers Assn., Kans. C. of C. Republican. Methodist. Mason (32 deg.). Home: 3d Kickapoo St DeSoto KS 66018 Office: 2d St DeSoto KS 66018

GABRIEL, HENRY ROBERT, architect; b. Granite City, Ill., Jan, 30, 1926; s. Henry Joseph and Elizabeth Bernadette (Koehler) G.; B.S. in Architecture, U. Ill., 1950; m. Rosalee Schepers, Sept. 4, 1948; children—Elizabeth Ann, Jane Marie, Karen Sue. With various archtl. firms, 1951-56; pres. Gabriel & Dulgeroff, architects (inc., 1967), Granite City, 1956-73; owner, pres. Henry R. Gabriel & Assos., Inc., 1973—. Pres. Family Thoughtfulness Centers, Inc., Granite City, 1968—. Pres. Granite City Park Dist., 1969-76; mem. Granite City Park Bd. Commrs., 1969-76, City Plan Commn., 1958—. Bd. dirs., pres. St. Elizabeth's Parish Credit Union, 1953—. Served with USNR, 1944-46. Mem. A.I.A. (chpt. pres. 1965-66), Architects Assn. Ill., C. of C. (bd. dirs.). K.C. Clubs: Optimists, Elks. Home: 3656 Terrace Lane Granite City IL 62040 Office: 1930 Cleveland Blvd Granite City IL 62040

GACKLE, DONALD C., publisher; b. Kulm, N.D., Apr. 12, 1929; s. Otto and Alice Irene (Higdem) G.; Ph.B., U. N.D., 1951; m. Phyllis Darlene King, Jan. 28, 1951; children—Michael William, Cynthia Alice. Dir. pub. relations Greater N.D. Assn., Fargo, 1953-63; editor-pub., McLean County Ind., Garrison, N.D., 1963—; pres. BHG Inc., Garrison, 1970—, Sun Enterprises Inc., Garrison, 1976—, Garrison Enterprises, 1976—. Pres. Garrison Civic Club, 1973; state chmn. U. N.D. Devel. Fund, 1977; vice-chmn. journalism adv. council U. N.D., 1976—. Served with U.S. Army, 1951-53. Named Garrison Boss of Yr., 1971. Mem. N.D. (pres. 1974), Nat. newspaper assns., Sigma Delta Chi. Clubs: Masons, Garrison Golf. Home: 103 S 1st St NE Garrison ND 58540 Office: 59 N Main St Garrison ND 58540

GADD, HERMAN PRESTON, data co., bus. forms exec.; b. Wildie, Ky., Aug. 14, 1921; s. Henry P. and Eila P. (Dotson) G.; B.A., Ohio State U., 1950; m. Betty Jean Ullmer, Aug. 22, 1947; children—Kenneth, E. Christine Gadd Minneman, Darcia, John. Staff writer Dayton (Ohio) Daily News, 1950-62; editor News Tribune, Dayton, 1962-63; asst. mgr. advt. and sales promotion Reynolds & Reynolds Co., Dayton, 1964-66, mgr. pub. relations, 1966-69, dir. pub. relations, 1969—. Mem. Trotwood (Ohio) City Planning Commn., 1957-62. Mem. bus. adv. bd. Dayton Opportunities Industrialization Center, 1973—; chmn. pub. relations adv. bd. Wright State U., Dayton; mem. pub. relations com. Dayton Human Relations Com. Served with USMCR, 1942-46. Mem. Pub. Relations Soc. Am. Lion (dir. 1974-76), Kiwanian (pres. 1966). Club: Miami Valley Golf. Home: 106 Sparks St Trotwood OH 45426 Office: 800 Germantown St Dayton OH 45401

GADDY, OSCAR LEE, elec. engr., educator; b. Republic, Mo., July 18, 1932; s. Oscar Franklin and Ruth (Cowart) G.; B.S., U. Kans., 1957, M.S., 1959; Ph.D., U. Ill., 1962; m. Mary Margaret Vaeth, Aug. 8, 1953; children—Oscar Franklin, John Antone, William Lee. Research asst., instr. elec. engring. U. Kans., 1957-59; research asst. dept. elec. engring. U. Ill., Urbana, 1959-62, asst. prof. elec. engring., 1962-65, asso. prof., 1965-69, prof., 1969—, asso. head dept. elec. engring., 1971—; cons. electronics cos.; trustee Nat. Electronics Conf., 1969-71. Fellow IEEE; mem. Am. Phys. Soc., Sigma Xi, Eta Kappa Nu, Tau Beta Pi, Phi Kappa Phi. Contbr. numerous articles to profl. jours. Home: 9 Carriage Way Champaign IL 61820 Office: 155 Elec Engring Bldg U of Ill Urbana IL 61802

GADE, ELDON MERLE, educator; b. Clinton, Iowa, Apr. 5, 1929; s. Edward Ferdinand and Mary Katherine (Geheman) G.; B.A., Iowa State Teachers Coll., 1952, M.A., 1954; Ph.D., U. Wyo., 1961; m. Marlo Ann Powers, Sept. 1, 1962; children—Vicki, Ann. Teacher, Lost Nation (Iowa) Pub. Schs., 1952-53, Clinton (Iowa) Pub. Schs., 1954-56; with U. N.D., 1961—, prof., 1969—. Served with AUS, 1956-59. Mem. Am. Psychol. Assn., Am. Personnel Guidance Assn. Methodist. Home: 2123 5th Av N Grand Forks ND 58201 Office: Dept Counseling Guidance U ND Grand Forks ND 58201

GADES, ROBERT ELLARD, educator; b. Danvers, Minn., Jan. 31, 1931; s. Robert O. and Helen V. (Senholtz) G.; B.S., St. Cloud State Coll., 1956; M.A., Sul Ross State Coll., 1961; Ed.D., N. Tex. State U., 1967; m. Joyce E. Loper, Dec. 21, 1954; 1 son, James W. Bus. tchr. Holloway (Minn.) High Sch., 1956-57; bus. tchr., coach Christoval (Tex.) High Sch., 1957-59; coach, prin. Wall (Tex.) High Sch., 1959-62; prin. Port Isabel (Tex.) High Sch., 1962-65; teaching fellow N. Tex. State U., Denton, 1965-67; asso. prof. bus. edn. U. Nebr., Lincoln, 1967—. Served with USAF, 1950-53. Mem. Nat. Bus. Edn. Assn., Delta Pi Epsilon. Lutheran (pres. 1972-74). Contbr. articles to profl. jours. Home: 1501 N 76th St Lincoln NE 68505

GAEBLER, ROBERT (ADAMS), psychologist; b. Cleve., Jan. 4, 1932; s. Herman Ernest and Ruth (Adams) G.; B.A. with honors, Ohio U., 1955; M.S. in Clin. Psychology (USPHS fellow), Northwestern U., 1959; m. Carol Rose Armin, Mar. 26, 1961; children—David, Kenneth, Michael. Trainee clin. psychology VA Mental Hygiene Clinic, Chgo., 1958-60; USPHS health service fellow Conn. State Hosp., Middletown, 1957-58; clin. psychologist Inst. Juvenile Research, Chgo., 1960-63; sch. psychologist Proviso Spl. Edn., Maywood, Ill., 1963-65, Niles West High Sch., Skokie, Ill., 1965-67; state psychology supr. No. Ill., Ill. Office. Supt. Pub. Instrn., Chgo., 1967-71; individual practice psychology, specializing in services to orgns., Chgo., 1971—. Diagnostic cons. Head Start, various locations, 1965-67. Nat. sec. SCI Internat. Voluntary Service, 1962-63, 69-71, also mem. nat. com., 1961—. Mem. Am. (chmn. com. ethical practices div. sch. psychology 1969-70), Midwest, Ill. (treas. sect. 1969-71, mem. council 1974-76) psychol. assns., Chgo. Psychol. Club (mem. council 1970-72; pres. 1974-75), Nat. Assn. Sch. Psychologists (sec. Ill. 1968-69; Ill. del. 1969-71). Contbr. to profl. jours.

GAENG, PAUL AMI, educator; b. Budapest, Hungary, Aug. 17, 1924; s. Hans Peter and Thérèse ((Brulé) G.; came to U.S., 1948, naturalized, 1955; grad. U. Geneva, Switzerland, 1948; M.A., Columbia, 1950, Ph.D. (Woodbridge hon. fellow), 1965; m. Joan Elisabeth Gallagher, Apr. 6, 1967. Fgn. editorial asst. McGraw-Hill Book Co., N.Y.C., 1951-54; translator-interpreter Guaranty Trust, N.Y.C., 1954-56; fgn. lang. tchr. Montclair (N.J.) Acad., 1957-63; asst., asso. then full prof., dept. chmn. fgn. langs. Montclair State Coll., Upper Montclair, N.J., 1964-69; asso. prof. Romance philology U. Va., Charlottesville, 1969-72; head dept. Romance lang. and lit. U. Cin., 1972-76; head dept. French, U. Ill., Urbana-Champaign, 1976—; vis. lectr. Hofstra Coll., Hempstead, N.Y., 1963, Queens Coll., N.Y.C., 1966, Columbia, 1967-69. Decorated chevalier dans l'ordre des Palmes Academiques. Mem. AAUP, Modern Lang. Assn., Société de linguistique romane, Am. Soc. Geolinguistics (treas. 1965-68). Author: An Inquiry into Local Variations in Vulgar Latin, 1968; Introduction to the Principles of Language, 1971; Studies in Honor of Mario Pei, 1972; A Study of Nominal Inflection in Latin Inscriptions, 1977; (with Mario Pei) The Story of Latin and the Romance Languages, 1976. Contbr. articles on lang. teaching and philology to various jours. Home: #2 Colony West Dr Champaign IL 61820

GAENSLEN, FREDERICK GUSTAV, orthopaedic surgeon; b. Milw., Apr. 24, 1914; s. Frederick Julius and Clara Fredricka (Schock) G.; B.S., Ripon Coll., 1937; M.D., U. Wis., 1940; m. Jeanne Elizabeth Sweet, Nov. 3, 1945; children—Frederick R., Christine Gail, Heidi Ellen, Eric Steven. Intern, Grad. Hosp. U. Pa., Phila., 1940-42; resident orthopedic surgery Univ. Hosp., Madison, Wis., 1942-44; pvt. practice orthopaedic surgery, Milw., 1946—; asst. clin. prof. orthopaedic surgery Med. Coll. Wis., Milw., 1950-74. Teaching mission to Jordan under Medico, 1960. Bd. dirs. Easter Seal Soc. Milwaukee County, 1969-74, pres., 1974—. Served with M.C., USNR, 1944-46; PTO. Mem. Wis. (pres. 1972-73), Milw. (pres. 1949-51) orthopaedic socs., Am. Acad. Orthopaedic Surgery, Clin. Orthopaedic Soc., Wis. State, Milwaukee County med. socs., Milw. Acad. Medicine. Clubs: University (Milw.); Town. Home: 6367 N Berkeley Blvd Milwaukee WI 53217 Office: 1031 N Astor St Milwaukee WI 53202

GAFFNEY, JOHN LEONARD, assn. exec.; b. Manistique, Mich., Mar. 21, 1926; s. Bernard Farrell and Lora (Leonard) G.; B.S., No. Mich. U., 1948; M.A., U. Mich., 1952; Ed.S., Mich. State U., 1962; LL.D., Nazareth Coll., 1974, Northwood Inst., 1975; Ph.D., Lawrence Inst. Tech., 1975; m. Helen Marie Miller, June 21, 1949; children—David, Kathleen, James. Coach, tchr., Portage Twp. pub. schs., Houghton, Mich., 1949-61; dir. guidance Haslett (Mich.) Pub. Schs., 1961-63; dir. Job Tng. Center, Lansing, 1963-65; dir. edn. Mich. Cath. Conf., Lansing, 1965-71; pres. Assn. Ind. Colls. and Univs. Mich., Lansing, 1971—. Vice pres. Diocesan Bd. Edn. Lansing, 1971-75. Cons. Mich. Adv. Council on Post-Secondary Edn., 1971—. Served with USNR, 1944-46. Named Mich. Upper Peninsula Basketball Coach of Year, 1955. Mem. Exec. Dirs. State Assns. Ind. Colls. (exec. com.), Nat. Assn. Ind. Colls. and Univs. (dir. 1976-77), Nat. Assn. Bds. Edn. (exec. com. 1972-75), Am. Soc. Assn. Execs. Roman Catholic. Home: 824 Locher Rd DeWitt MI 48820 Office: 830 Michigan National Tower Lansing MI 48901

GAGE, DONALD PAUL, ednl. adminstr.; b. Cambridge, Mass., Nov. 21, 1947; s. Paul Sumner and Beatrice Louise (Seaver) G.; student U. Tubingen, Germany, 1968-69; B.S., Antioch Coll., 1970; clin. pastoral edn. certificate, Iowa State Mental Hosp. at Cherokee, 1971; M.A. in Theology, Meadville Theol. Sch./U. Chgo., 1973, Dr. Ministry, 1974; certificate advanced grad. study in higher edn. adminstrn., Northeastern U., 1977; m. Ursula Janet Wolf, July 2, 1977. Grad. adminstrv. asst., mem. Ednl. Adminstrn. Student Adv. Council, Northeastern U., Boston, 1976-77; dir. program devel. Suomi Coll., Hancock, Mich., 1977—. Acting coordinator Common Cause, 6th Ill. Congl. Dist., 1974. Rotary Club scholar, 1966-67. Mem. Nat. Assn. Student Personnel Adminstrs., Am. Personnel and Guidance Assn., Am. Coll. Personnel Assn. Democrat. Unitarian Universalist. Office: Suomi Coll Quincy St Hancock MI 49930

GAGE, EDWIN CUTTING, III, mktg. exec.; b. Evanston, Ill., Nov. 1, 1940; s. Edwin Cutting and Margaret (Stackhouse) G.; B.S., Northwestern U., 1963, M.S. in Journalism, 1965; postgrad U. Minn., 1973; m. Barbara Ann Carlson, June 26, 1965; children—Geoff, Scott, Christine, Richard. Account exec. Foote, Cone & Belding, Chgo., 1965-68; dir. marketing devel. Premium Corp. Am., Mpls., 1968-69; dir. mail mktg. and John Plain mail mktg. Premium Corp. Am., Inc., Mpls., 1970-72, v.p., 1973-75, exec. v.p. premium group, 1975—; v.p., mem. mgmt. com. Carlson Cos., Inc., Mpls., 1973—; v.p. Gift Stars, Inc., 1973—, Red Scissors, Inc., 1973—; pres. Southdale Sq. Corp., 1975—, Carlson Mktg. and Motivation, 1977—; chmn. bd. Windosor Group, Inc.; dir. K-Promotions, Inc., Kramer Products, Inc., Herbill, Inc.; partner Major Media of Midwest, Mpls., 1973—, Major Media of S.W. Mpls., 1973—. Vice pres. Minnetonka Montessori, Inc., Wayzata, Minn., 1972-75. Bd. dirs. Outward Bound Minn., 1972-73. Chgo. Federated Advt. Assn. scholar, 1964-65. Mem. Nat. Premium Sales Execs., Midwest Mktg. Assn., Midwest Mail Mktg. Assn., Direct Mail Assn. Am. Club: Wayzata Country. Home: 460 Tonkawa Rd Long Lake MN 55356 Office: 12755 State Hwy 55 Minneapolis MN 55441

GAGE, FRED KELTON, lawyer; b. Mpls., June 20, 1925; s. Fred Kelton and Vivian Luverna (Johnson) G.; B.S., U. Minn., 1948, LL.B., 1950; m. Audrie White, June 12, 1949 (div. Jan. 1972); children—Deborah, Penelope, Fred, Amy, Laurence; m. 2d, Dorothy Almlie, 1974. Admitted to Minn. bar, 1950; practiced in Mankato, 1950—; mem. firm Blethen, Gage & Krause, Mankato, 1950—; dir. Advt. Unltd., Inc. Mem. Minn. State Coll. Bd., 1960-64. Mem. sch. bd., Mankato, 1959-66; mem. Minn. Senate, 1966-72. Served with USNR, 1943-46. Named Outstanding Young Man Minn. Jr. C. of C., 1958-59. Mem. Am., Minn. (pres. tax sect. 1965-66, bd. govs. 1975—, pres.-elect 1976) bar assns. Methodist. Lutheran. Home: 133 Belmont Dr Mankato MN 56001 Office: PO Box 3049 Mankato MN 56001

GAGE, JOHN CUTTER, lawyer, farmer; b. Kansas City, July 4, 1923; s. John Bailey and Marjorie (Hires) G.; student U. Kans., 1940-42, LL.B., 1952; B.S., U.S. Mil. Acad., 1945; m. Eleanor Jane Pack, June 16, 1950; children—John Bailey II, Claudia Anne, David Frank. Admitted to bars Mo., 1952, Kans., 1952; asso. firm Gage, Hillix, Moore & Park, Kansas City, 1952-55; pvt. practice, Lawrence, Kans., 1955-57; partner firm James B. Pearson & John C. Gage, Mission, Kans., 1957-58; partner Gage & Tucker, Kansas City, 1958—; dir. Safety Fed. Savs. & Loan Assn., Kansas City, 1966-77, Am. Royal Arena Corp. Farmer, Eudora, Kans.; dir. Am. Royal Livestock and Horse Show, 1967—, v.p., 1970-72, pres., 1972-73, chmn. exec. com., 1973-75. Served as 1st lt. AUS, 1945-49. Recipient Distinguished Service award Future Farmers Am., 1968, Hon. Am. Farmers degree, 1974. Mem. Am. Milking Shorthorn Soc. (pres. 1960-62), Kans. Holstein-Friesian Assn. (dir. 1972-74), Red and White Dairy Cattle Assn. (sec., treas. 1964-67), Sigma Alpha Epsilon. Contbr. to profl. jours. Home: Route 1 Box 23A Eudora KS 66025 Office: 2345 Grand Ave Kansas City MO 64108

GAGNON, RICHARD IRWIN, constrn. co. exec.; b. Mpls., Feb. 8, 1920; s. Harris P. and Katherine F. (Irwin) G.; Ph.B., U. Wis., 1942; J.D., U. Notre Dame, 1950; m. Gwen C. Sollitt, Sept. 7, 1946; children—Sharon (Mrs. Thomas Schatz), Richard Sollitt, Gwen Ellan. Admitted to Ind. bar, 1950; asso. atty. Jones, Obenchain & Butler, South Bend, 1950-51; with Sollitt Constrn. Co., Inc., South Bend, 1946—, pres., 1970—, also dir.; chmn. bd. Semiconductor Specialists, Inc., Chgo., 1959—; pres. Indsl. Land-Leasing Corp., South Bend, 1959—, also dir.; v.p. Sollitt Found. Inc., South Bend, 1970—, also dir.; dir. Wells Electronics, Inc., South Bend, Benicia Industries Inc. (Calif.). Pres. Com. of 100 of South Bend and Mishawaka, 1963-64; mem. Mayor's Com. Community Action, South Bend, 1964-66. Bd. dirs. Indsl. Found., Inc. of South Bend, pres., 1963-72. Served to lt. USNR, 1941-46. Mem. South Bend Assn. Commerce, Nat. Conf. Christians and Jews (co-chmn. 1963-65), Psi Upsilon. Roman Catholic (trustee). Clubs: Indiana, Summit, South Bend Country; Pickwick (Niles, Mich.); Point O'Woods Country (Benton Harbor, Mich.); Quail Ridge Country (Delray Beach, Fla.). Home: 1522 E Washington Ave South Bend IN 46617 Office: 833 E Northside Dr PO Box 87 South Bend IN 46624

GAIER, GARY BERNARD, publishing co. exec.; b. Chippewa Falls, Wis., Sept. 19, 1937; s. Bernard M. and Ida (Abel) G.; B.S., Wis. State U., 1960; m. Judith Horvatin, Apr. 8, 1961; children—Mary Kathryn, William John, Elizabeth Ann, Paul Christofer, Patricia Jean. Advt. salesman Chippewa Herald-Telegram, Chippewa Falls, 1960-63, advt. mgr., 1963-65, bus. mgr., 1965-68, gen. mgr., 1968—; pres. News Publs. Inc., Chippewa Falls; v.p. Chippewa Pub. Co., Inc., Register Pub. Co., Portage, Wis., Baraboo Pub. Co. (Wis.), Shawano Evening Leader Co. (Wis.), Lavine Media, Chippewa Falls. Mem. Inland Daily Press, Wis. Newspaper Assn. Roman Catholic. Home: Rural Route 5 Box 5 F Chippewa Falls WI 54729 Office: 20-22 W Central St Chippewa Falls WI 54729

GAIHA, VISHNU DAS, cardiologist; b. New Delhi, India, May 2, 1945; s. P.D. and Bhagwati Devi (Johri) G.; came to U.S., 1969; M.B., B.S., All India Inst. Med. Scis., 1969; m. Purnima Saxena, Nov. 11, 1973. Intern Albert Einstein Med. Center, Phil., 1969-70; resident in internal medicine Northwestern U. Hosp., Chgo., 1970-72; fellow in cardiology U. Mich. Hosp., Ann Arbor, 1972-74; practice medicine specializing in internal medicine and cardiology, Evanston, Ill., 1974—; mem. staff St. Francis, Swedish Covenant hosps.; clin. asst. prof. Loyola U. Med. Sch. Diplomate Am. Bd. Internal Medicine. Fellow Am. Coll. Internat. Physicians; mem. A.C.P., Am. Heart Assn., Heart Assn. N. Cook County (dir.). Home: 2940 Moonhill Dr Northbrook IL 60062 Office: 800 Austin St Suite 207 Evanston IL 60202

GAINER, CAROLINE JOSEPHINE, mng. editor newspaper; b. Harwick, Pa., Sept. 18, 1929; d. Joseph and Anna (Kolvek) Kretoski; student Fairmont W.Va. Business Coll., 1947-48, Morgantown W.Va. Cosmetology Coll., 1948; m. Gordon Gainer, Nov. 11, 1950; children—Margaret, Gordon, Patty, Vicki. Owner beauty salon Fairmont, W.Va., 1953; secy. Owens Fiberglass, Newark, 1954-59; deputy registrar Licking County (Ohio) Bureau Motor Vehicles, Newark, 1959-63; editor, owner Ace News, Heath, Ohio, 1963—, corp. sec. treas., 1963—. Mem. advisory com. Licking County Joint Vocat. Sch. Graphic Arts, Newark, 1975—; mem. Licking County Democratic Central Com., 1960; bd. dirs. Licking County YWCA, 1965-67. Mem. League Women Voters (Newark). Democrat. Methodist. Clubs: Business & Profl. Women, Lioness (pres. 1964), Am. Legion Auxiliary, Ohio News Photographers. Ohio editor Ohio Businesswoman, 1976-77. Home: 132 Claren Dr Heath OH 43055 Office: Mid Ohio Indsl Pk Heath OH 43055

GAINES, CHRISTOPHER CLEMENS, nuclear maintenance adminstr.; b. Balt., Mar. 13, 1947; s. Clemens Weaver and Barbara Harris (Riley) G.; B.B.A., U. Wis., Mil., 1975. Prodn. line worker A. O. Smith Co., Milw., 1972-73; instrument maintenance foreman Commonwealth Edison, LaSalle County Nuclear Sta., Seneca, Ill., 1976—. Served with USN, 1966-72. Mem. Am. Nuclear Soc., U. Wis. Alumni Assn. Presbyterian. Home: 231 Ottawa Bend Dr Apt 106D Morris IL 60450 Office: LaSalle County Nuclear Sta Rural Route 1 Box 220 Marseilles IL 61341

GAINES, ERVIN JAMES, librarian; b. N.Y.C., Dec. 8, 1916; s. Ervin J. and Helen (Hennessy) G.; B.S., Columbia, 1942, A.M., 1947, Ph.D., 1952; m. Martha Zirbel, Feb. 11, 1938; children—Colleen Joy (Mrs. John Clark), Sanford Ervin. Instr., Columbia, 1946-53; chief tng. Radio Liberation, 1953-56, Teleregister Corp., 1956-57; free-lance cons., 1957-58; asst. dir. Boston Pub. Library, 1958-64; dir. Mpls. Pub. Library, 1964-74; dir. Cleve. Pub. Library, 1974—. Mem. A.L.A. Home: 1700-H E 13th St Cleveland OH 44114 Office: Cleve Pub Library 325 Superior Ave Cleveland OH 44114

GAINES, HENRY PEDEN, JR., mech. engr.; b. Milledgeville, Ga., Dec. 16, 1952; s. Henry Peden and Olive Lorrene (Weatherspoon) G.; B.S.M.E., Clemson U., 1975; m. Mary Elizabeth Mann, Dec. 16, 1973. Prodn. devel. engr. Dow Chem. U.S.A., Mich. Div., Midland, 1975—. Lic. engr. in tng., S.C., Mich. Mem. ASME (asso.), U.S. Jaycees. Baptist. Inventor in field. Home: 2118 Lambros Dr Midland MI 48640 Office: Dow Chem Co Mich Div 564 Door 5 Midland MI 48640

GAINES, JAMES FRAZIER, veterinarian, air force officer; b. Washington, May 4, 1938; s. Stanley Harry and Versie Fay (Frazier) G.; D.V.M., U. Ga., 1962; M.S., Tex. A. and M. U., 1971; m. Jo Ellen Johnson, Aug. 5, 1967; children—Nance D., Jill A. Pvt. practice veterinary medicine Biscayne Animal Hosp., North Miami, Fla., 1962; commd. 1st lt. USAF, 1962, advanced through grades to maj., 1970; resident in lab. animal medicine Brooks AFB, Tex., 1971-72; staff veterinarian Naval Med. Research Unit Great Lakes, Ill., 1972-74; chief veterinary scis. div., Naval Dental Research Inst., Great Lakes, 1974—. Decorated Bronze Star. Mem. Am. Assn. Lab. Animal Sci., Am. Assn. Zoo Veterinarians, Nat. Rifle Assn. Club: Great Lakes Yacht. Contbr. articles to profl. jours. Home: 1609 Frazier St Waukegan IL 60085 Office: Naval Dental Research Inst Great Lakes IL 60088

GAINEY, DANIEL CHARLES, jewelry mfg. exec.; b. Winona, Minn., Nov. 28, 1897; s. Daniel and Ella (Leach) G.; A.B., Hamline U., 1921, D.B.A., 1948; D. Letters, Coll. St. Thomas, 1974; m. Harriette Swearingen, July 17, 1924; 1 son, Daniel James; m. 2d, Elaine Frock, May 1962. Sports writer Mpls. and St. Paul papers, 1920-21; instr. and athletic coach Hancock, Minn., 1921-22; with Josten's, Owatonna, Minn., 1922—, chmn. bd., 1933-68, chmn. emeritus, 1968—; v.p. Danco Fund, Inc.; pres. Charles Rochester Co., Owatonna, 1950—. Rancher, Scottsdale, Ariz. and Santa Ynez, Calif. Mem. Selective Service Bd., vice chmn. Minn. War Relief, World War II. Del. to Republican Nat. Conv., 1948, 52, 56, 60, 64; floor leader for Stassen, 1952; Minn. finance chmn. Citizens for Eisenhower, 1954; mem. finance com. Nat. Rep. Com., 1956, treas., 1958-60; Goldwater nat. finance chmn., 1964. Bd. govs. Arabian Horse Club Registry of Am., 1942-73, pres., 1958-72, dir., 1948-73, pres. emeritus, 1973—; regent U. Minn., 1939-73; trustee emeritus Am. Grad. Sch. Internat. Mgmt.; trustee Hamline U., Minn. Community Research Council, Inc.; mem. Mayo Sponsors, Rochester, Minn.; chmn. bd. Gainey Found. Mem. N.A.M. (past dir.), Ednl. Jewelry Mfrs. Assn. (past pres., dir.), Minn. Employers Assn. (past dir.), C. of C., Am. Legion. Delta Sigma Phi. Clubs: Minneapolis. Minikahda (Mpls.); Paradise Valley Country (Scottsdale, Ariz.). Home: Route 2 Box 1 Owatonna MN 55060 Office: 154 E Broadway Owatonna MN 55060

GAISANO, JOSEPH SY, mech. engr.; b. Cebu, P.I., Oct. 28, 1940; s. David Sy and Leng Gee (Lee) G.; student Mapua Inst. Tech.; M.S. in M.E., U. Colo., 1967; m. Gloria Chan, Apr. 16, 1961; children—Jade, Janel, Joanne. Instr., Mapua Inst. Tech., P.I., 1964-65; asst. mgr. Rep. Steel Tube, Inc., P.I., 1963-65; prodn. engr., lab. supr. Dow U.S.A., 1967-72; mfg. rep. Dow Chem. Pacific, Ltd., 1973-76; sr. project engr. Dow Chem. U.S.A., Midland, Mich., 1976—. Mem. Am. Soc. M.E., Soc. Mfg. Engrs., Jaycees. Baptist. Club: Red Carpet. Home: 5408 Fairway Pl Midland MI 48640 Office: 433 Bldg Dow Chemical Co Midland MI 48640

GAITHER, JOHN FRANCIS, accountant; b. Louisville, Oct. 26, 1918; s. Thomas R. and Marice F. Gaither; B.C.S., U. Notre Dame, 1941; postgrad. U. Louisville; m. Marjilee Schaeffer, Nov. 26, 1942; children—John Francis, James M. Controller, Evansville (Ind.) div. Whirlpool Corp., 1946-54; asso. prof. fin. U. Evansville, part-time 1946-56; sr. partner Gaither, Hortin & Koewler, C.P.A.'s, pub. accountants, 1954—; city controller, dep. mayor City of Evansville, 1972-76. Past pres. Buffalo Trace council Boy Scouts Am.; past co-chmn. Summa Fund drive U. Notre Dame; adv. com. Ind. Vocat. Rehab.; fin. com. Roman Cath. Diocese Evansville; trustee Brescia Coll., Owensboro, Ky., mem. regional community adv. council Ind. U. Med. Sch.; community adv. council Evansville Center Med. Edn.; chmn. Gov. Ind. Select Com. Ednl. Fin., Gov. Ind. Commn. Energy and Utility Regulation Adv. Com.; Gov.'s rep. Ind. Hosp. Rate Rev. Commn.; active local YMCA, Cancer Soc., Serra Club. Served as officer USNR, 1941-46. Recipient various awards Boy Scouts Am.; C.P.A., Ind. Mem. Am. Inst. C.P.A.'s, Evansville, Ind., Ill. assns. C.P.A.'s, Nat. Assn. Accountants (past pres. Evansville), Ind. Assn. Cities and Towns Controllers Assn. (past pres.), Ind. Soc. Chgo. (v.p. 1977-78), SAR, Evansville C. of C. Republican. Clubs: Evansville Country (past pres.), Kennel, Petroleum, Press (Evansville); Oak Meadow; Columbia (Indpls.). Contbr. articles to profl. jours. Home: 730 Colony Rd Evansville IN 47714 Office: 1500 Old National Bank Bldg Evansville IN 47708

GAJL-PECZALSKA, KAZIMIERA JANINA, pathologist; b. Warsaw, Poland, Nov. 15, 1931, came to U.S., 1970, naturalized, 1977; d. Kazimierz Emil and Anna (Gervais) Gajl; M.D., U. Warsaw, 1955, Ph.D. in Immunopathology, 1964; m. 1949 (div. 1969); children—Kazimierz, Andrzei. Intern, U. Warsaw Hosps., 1953-55, resident in pathology, 1955-58; asst. pediatrician Warsaw Children's Hosp., 1955-58, head dept. pediatric pathology, 1958-65; adj. prof. dept. pathology Postgrad. Med. Sch., Warsaw, 1965-70; resident in pathology U. Minn., 1970-72, asst. prof., 1972-75, asso. prof., 1975—. NIH postdoctoral fellow in immunopathology, Mpls., 1968-69; WHO fellow in immunofluorescence, Paris, 1967, WHO fellow in pediatric pathology, London, 1962; NIH research grantee 1975—. Diplomate Am. Bd. Pathology, Polish Bd. Pediatrics, Polish Bd. Pathology. Mem. Am. Soc. Exptl. Pathology, Am. Soc. Cytology, Brit. Soc. Pediatric Pathology, Minn. Soc. Pathologists, Polish Soc. Pediatrics, Polish Soc. Pathology. Contbr. articles, papers to profl. jours, meetings. Home: 1700 W 90th St Minneapolis MN 55431 Office: 446 Jackson Hall U Minn Minneapolis MN 55455

GALAINENA, MARIANO LUIS, physician; b. Havana, Cuba, Aug. 27, 1922; s. Mariano Jose and Belen (Ugarte) G.; M.D., U. Havana, 1948; m. Dorothy M. Schuman, June 30, 1952; 1 son, David Mariano. Came to U.S., 1959, naturalized, 1963. Intern Deaconess Hosp., Cleve., 1951-52; resident Cleve. Clinic, 1952-54, retina service Mass. Eye and Ear Infirmary, 1957-58; practice medicine specializing in ophthalmology, Havana, 1955-57, 58-59; chief dept. ophthalmology Brocksville (Ohio) VA Hosp., 1962—. Diplomate Am. Bd. Ophthalmology. Fellow Am. Acad. Ophthalmology and Otolaryngology, A.C.S.; mem. Cuban Polit. Refugees Assn., Cuban Med. Assn. in Exile. Home: 12000 Padua Dr E North Royalton OH 44133 Office: 10000 Brecksville Rd Brecksville OH 44141

GALAMBOS, ROBERT HENRY, chem. co. exec.; b. Cleve., Aug. 25, 1926; s. Henry J. and Julia J. (Turvey) G.; student Western Res. U., 1946-47; m. Ruth E. Heck, May 7, 1948; children—William H., Janet L. Sales to asst. sales mgr. Am. Mineral Spirits Co., N.Y.C., Phila., 1949-54; salesman to dist. mgr. Bronoco Solvents & Chems. div. Ashland Oil & Refining Co., Detroit, also Lansing, Mich., 1954-70; pres. Americhem Corp., Mason and Grand Rapids, Mich., 1970—. Served with U.S. Maritime Service, 1944-48. Mem. Lansing C. of C. Mason (Shriner). Club: Chief Okemos Sportsman's. Home: 2909 Boston Blvd Lansing MI 48910 Office: 340 North St Mason MI 48854

GALASINSKI, ROMAN EDWARD, surgeon; b. Milw., Jan. 1, 1906; s. Maxmillian and Anastasia (Kruczynski) G.; B.A. cum laude, Marquette U., 1927, M.D., 1931; m. Florence Stamm, 1933; children—Phyllis (Mrs. Robert Reimer), Charles. Intern, Milw. County Gen. Hosp., 1931-32, resident in surgery, 1932-33; resident in surgery Johnston Emergency Hosp., 1933-35; practice medicine specializing in gen. surgery, Milw., 1935—; pres. Galasinski and Assos. Service Corp., 1960-71; chief surgery St. Luke Hosp., 1942, chief of staff, 1948-51; chief of surgery St. Francis Hosp., 1955-59, chief staff, 1960-61; instr. anatomy Marquette U., 1933-39; chmn. bd., dir. Lincoln Savs. and Loan Assn. Corporate organizer, dir. Hosp. Area Planning Commn., Milw., 1966—; mem. adv. com. Sacred Heart Rehab. Hosp., 1969; gen. chmn. rehab. study Met. Milw., 1966; mem. Com. of 200 Presdl. Conf. Medicare, 1966; chmn. Title XIX Med. Adv. Com. for Wis., 1975—. Initiator Cath. chaplaincy Milw. Cath. and non-sectarian hosps., 1948; mem. Citizens' Adv. Com. Edn., 1966, Gov.'s Conf. Home and Family, 1966, Citizens Adv. Com. Social Service, 1970-71; mem. Archbishop's Adv. Bd., 1971—; dir. adv. bd. Xavierian Missionary Fathers, 1969—. Trustee St. Francis Hosp., 1971—, chmn., 1971—; bd. dirs. United Community Service, Milw., 1960-74, chmn. med. prof. div., 1958, chmn. profl. div., 1961. Served to lt. comdr. USNR, 1942-46. Mem. A.C.S., Pan-Pacific Surg. Soc., A.M.A., Cath. Physicians Guild (pres. 1958), Milwaukee County Med. Soc. (pres. 1962, dir. 1963-67), Wis. Surg. Soc., Med. Soc. Wis. (del., councillor). K.C. Home: 3371 S Princeton Ave Milwaukee WI 53215

GALBRAITH, DONALD ANGUS, psychiatrist; b. Sue Ste. Marie, Ont., Can., Jan. 4, 1937; s. Angus and Helen Gertrude (Case) G.; M.D., U. Western Ont., 1961; m. Cynthia Margaret Ann Rickard, Sept. 28, 1957; children—Cynthia Louise, Gregory Donald, Catherine Susan. Intern Victoria Hosp., London, Ont., 1961-62; psychiat. resident U. Western Ont., 1962-66; dir. profl. edn. Children's Psychiat. Research Inst., London, 1967—. Clin. lectr. psychiatry U. Western Ont., London, 1967, clin. asst. prof., 1970, dir. postgrad. psychiatry, 1970-72; guest lectr. Fanshaw Coll. Applied Arts and Tech., London, 1967—, mem. health and welfare adv. com., 1971-76; cons. Lambton County Centre for Children and Youth, Sarnia, Ont., 1971—, Ont. Hosp. Sch., Cedar Springs, 1971—, edn. clin. Oxford Mental Health Center, Woodstock, Ont., 1972—, Roberts Sch. for Deaf, 1974—. Bd. dirs. Mission Services London, 1972-76. Fellow Royal Coll. Physicians and Surgeons Can.; mem. Ont. (chmn. sect. on psychiat. hosps. and hosp. schs.), Canadian med. assns., Ont. Psychiat. Assn., Coll. Physicians and Surgeons Ont., Canadian Psychiat. Assn., Am. Assn. Mental Deficiency, Canadian Mental Health Assn. Contbr. articles to profl. jours. Home: 1051 Kingston Ave London ON Canada Office: PO Box 2460 Terminal A London N6A 4G6 Canada

GALBRAITH, FRANCIS OMER, photographer; b. Indpls., Jan. 19, 1918; s. Cassius Omer and Melinda Catherine (Franklin) G.; student Winona Sch. Photography, 1940; m. Ruth Schnorenberg, July 10, 1941; children—Terry, Gregg. With Krueger Studio, Hartford, Wis., 1940-42; with Hartup Tool & Die, Columbus, Ind., 1945-50; owner, photographer F.O. Galbraith, Photographer, Columbus, 1950—. Vice pres. Grandview Lot Owners Assn., Columbus, 1975—. Served with Signal Corps, AUS, 1942-45. Decorated Bronze Star medal, Purple Heart. Mem. Profl. Photographers Am., Profl. Photographers Ind., Columbus Exchange Club (pres. 1965), Grandview Conservation Club (v.p. 1974-75). Mason. Club: Daguerre (Ind.) Home: Grandview Lake Columbus IN 47201 Office: 1690 National Rd Columbus IN 47201

GALBREATH, JOHN WILMER, realtor; b. Derby, Ohio, Aug. 10, 1897; s. Francis Hill and Belle (Mitchell) G.; A.B., Ohio U., 1920; LL.D., Athens Coll. (Ala.), 1956, Ohio U., 1957, Ohio State U., 1971; D.B.A., Ohio No. U., 1960; D. Hum., Springfield Coll., 1975; m. Helen Mauck, Sept. 14, 1921; children—Joan Hill, Daniel Mauck; m. 2d, Dorothy Bryan Firestone, Feb. 17, 1955. Organizer, owner John W. Galbreath & Co., Columbus, Ohio, 1924—; dir. Buckeye Fed. Savs. & Loan Assn., 1st Banc Group of Ohio; chmn. Pitts. Pirates Baseball Club. Past pres. Columbus Real Estate Bd., Ohio Real Estate Assn., Nat. Assn. Real Estate Bds. Trustee Ohio U.; bd. dirs. Buckeye Internat. Served as 2d lt., F.A., U.S. Army, World War I. Mem. Am. Inst. Real Estate Appraisers, Soc. Indsl. Realtors, Delta Tau Delta. Mason (33 deg., Shriner). Club: The Jockey. Address: 180 E Broad St Columbus OH 43215 also 150 E 42d St New York City NY 10017 also 600 Grant St Pittsburgh PA 15230

GALE, DANIEL BAILEY, architect; b. St. Louis, Nov. 6, 1933; s. Leone Caryll and Gladys (Wotowa) G.; student Brown U., 1951-53, Ecole Des Beaux Arts, Paris, France, 1954-55; B.Arch., Washington U., 1957; m. Nancy Susan Miller, June 15, 1957; children—Caroline Hamilton, Rebecca Fletcher, Daniel Bailey. Staff mem. Daniel B. Gale Architect, 1959-61, Gale & Cannon, Architects and Planners, 1961-63; asso. dir. mgmt. Hellmuth, Obata & Kassabaum, Inc., Architects, St. Louis, 1962-67; partner Heneghan and Gale, architects and planners, Aspen, Colo., 1967-69; pres. Hellmuth, Obata & Kassabaum, Inc., San Francisco, 1969; exec. v.p. corporate devel., dir. HOK, Inc., St. Louis, 1976; v.p., dir. C.C.C./H.O.K., Anchorage, 1969—. Recipient Henry Adams prize Washington U., 1957, also sophmore and final honors. Mem. AIA, Singapore Inst. Architects, S.A.R., Mo. Assn. Registered Architects, Beta Theta Pi. Home: 35 Glen Eagles Dr Ladue MO 63124 Office: 100 N Broadway St Louis MO 63102

GALEF, VICTOR RAY, drug co. exec.; b. N.Y.C., Mar. 5, 1943; s. Gabriel and Mildred (Rome) G.; B.S., Washington and Lee U., 1965; M.B.A., Pace U., 1967; m. Mary Croft, Oct. 18, 1969; children—Jennifer, Grant, Wendy. Vice-pres., account supr. Ted Bates & Co., N.Y.C., 1966-72; v.p. mktg. Stellar Industries, Buena Park, Calif., 1973-74; brand mgr. Calgon Consumer Products, Pitts., 1974-75; dir. mktg. Wyler Foods/Borden, Northbrook, Ill., 1976-78; group product mgr. Miles Labs., Elkhart, Ind., 1978—. Served with AUS, 1965-72. Mem. Am. Mktg. Assn. Republican. Presbyterian. Home: 1512 Greenbrier Dr Elkhart IN 46514 Office: 1127 Myrtle St Elkhart IN 46514

GALEJS, AINA, physician; b. Riga, Latvia, Apr. 14, 1925; d. Julijs and Erna Marija (Jukevics) Galejs; came to U.S., 1951, naturalized, 1956; M.D., U. Hamburg, Germany, 1950; m. Fricis Dravnieks, July 19, 1952. Intern, Mpls. Gen. Hosp., 1951-52; resident in pathology Hennepin County Gen. Hosp., U. Minn. Hosp., Mpls., 1952-56; pathologist Eitel Hosp., Mpls., 1956-59; pathologist Midway Hosp., St. Paul, 1970-76, locum tenens, 1976—; clin. instr. dept. pathology, lab. medicine U. Minn., 1960—; sec. Latvian Pubs. AkademiskaDzive, 1969—. Mem. Coll. Am. Pathologists, Am., Minn. socs. clin. pathologists, AMA, Minn. Med. Assn., Ramsey County Med. Soc., Latvian Med. Dental Assn. Club: Zonta. Office: 1 Vincent Ave S Minneapolis MN 55405

GALENS, GILBERT J., rheumatologist; b. Detroit, Mar. 7, 1933; s. Harry and Grace (Sweet) G.; B.S. with high distinction, Wayne State U., Detroit, 1954, M.D., 1957; m. Jane Odell Herriman, Aug. 12, 1962; children—David Matthew, Stephen Andrew, Judith Ellen, Daniel Keith. Intern, Mt. Zion Hosp., San Francisco, 1957-58; asst. resident, then resident in medicine U. Mich. Hosp., 1960-62, jr. clin. instr., 1962-63, fellow rheumatology Rackham Arthritis Research Unit, also teaching asso., 1963-64; practice medicine specializing in rheumatology, Birmingham, Mich., 1964—; mem. attending staff, chief div. rheumatology St. Joseph Mercy Hosp., Pontiac, Mich., William Beaumont Hosp., Royal Oak, Mich.; asst. staff Sinai Hosp., Detroit; clin. asst. prof. Wayne State U. Med. Sch. Bd. dirs. Wing Lake Farms Assn., 1972. Served to lt. M.C., USNR, 1958-60. Diplomate Am. Bd. Internal Medicine. Mem. AMA, Mich., Oakland County med. assns., Am., Mich. (pres. 1972) rheumatism assns., Phi Beta Kappa. Jewish. Clubs: Men's Health of Jewish Community Center, Men's. Contbr. articles to profl. jours. Home: 6765 Orinoco Circle Birmingham MI 48010 Office: 31815 Southfield Rd Birmingham MI 48009

GALICHIA, JOSEPH PAUL, cardiologist; b. Pittsburg, Kans., June 3, 1942; s. Joe P. and Natalie (Viano) G.; B.S., Kans. State U., 1964; exchange fellow in philosophy and agr. Justus Liebig U. (Giessen, Germany), 1964-65; M.D., Kans. U. Med. Sch., 1969; m. Kathryn A. Boxberger, June 22, 1968; children—Stephanie, Paul. Intern, St. Francis Hosp., Tulsa, 1969-70; internal medicine and cardiology fellow U. Minn., 1970-73, cardiology fellow, 1975-76; instr. dept. medicine, 1975-76; dir. Riverside Free Clinic, Mpls., 1973-74; asst. clin. prof. medicine U. Kans., 1976—; cardiology cons. St. Francis Hosp., Wichita, Kans., 1976—; mem. staff Mt. Carmel Hosp.,

Pittsburgh, Kans., Labette County Med. Center, Parsons, Kans. Served with MC AUS, 1973-75. Mem. Care Com., Crawford County, 1961-63. Recipient VA Hosp. Research grant, 1972-73. Mem. A.C.P., Am. Coll. Chest Physicians, Am., Sedgwick County med. assns., Kans. Heart Assn. Republican. Methodist. Home: 4 Peach Tree Ln Wichita KS 67207 Office: 1035 N Emporia St Suite 130 Wichita KS 67214

GALITZ, ROBERT FREDERICK, clergyman; b. Chgo., May 24, 1931; s. Raymond Frederick and Edna (Poltrock) G.; B.A., Grinnell Coll., 1953; B.D., U. Chgo., Chgo. Theol. Sem., 1956; postgrad. Garrett Bibl. Inst., 1959; M.A., Western Mich. U., 1966; m. Ramona Austin, June 27, 1955; children—Deborah Rae, Rebecca Ann, Robert Austin. Ordained to ministry Congl. Ch., 1956; minister Denmark, Iowa, 1956-60; asso. minister 1st Congl. Ch., Kalamazoo, 1960-66; campus minister Western Mich. U., Kalamazoo, 1960-65; minister 1st Conglist. Ch., Waukesha, Wis., 1966—. Mem. exec. bd. Kalamazoo County Council of Chs., 1962-65; mem. div. Christian edn. Mich. Conf., United Ch. Christ, 1964-66; mem. exec. bd. Waukesha Council Chs., 1967—, pres., 1967-71; mem. div. ministry Southeast Wis. Assn. United Ch. Christ, 1968—, chmn., 1969—; pres. Waukesha Pastors Assn., 1968-70; exchange pastor Evang. Ch. Union, Germany, 1969; moderator Cooperating Chs. of Greater Waukesha, 1976—. Mem. Kalamazoo Community Relations Bd., 1966; mem. exec. bd. Kalamazoo Human Relations Council, 1966. Republican. Club: Rotary (pres. Waukesha 1978—). Home: 726 Tenny Ave Waukesha WI 53186 Office: 701 N East Ave Waukesha WI 53186

GALL, EDWARD ALFRED, pathologist, educator; b. N.Y.C., June 10, 1906; s. Julius E. and Eva (Fleisch) G.; student Coll. City N.Y., 1923-27; M.D. (Isador Dyer medal), Tulane U., 1931; m. Phyllis H. Rivard, Sept. 17, 1933; children—Eric Papineau, Thomas Monroe. Resident in medicine Boston Dispensary, 1933-35; resident and asst. pathologist Mass. Gen. Hosp., 1935-40; instr. pathology Harvard Med. Sch., Boston, 1940-41; dir. labs. Bethesda Hosp., Cin., 1941-48; asst. then asso. prof. pathology U. Cin., 1941-48, Mary M. Emory prof., chmn. dept. pathology, 1948-71, v.p. and dir. med. center, 1971-74, distinguished service prof., 1974, emeritus, 1976—; cons. in pathology Mass. Eye Ear Infirmary, 1937-40, VA, 1947-72, Armed Forces Inst. Pathology, 1952-62, surgeon gen. Dept. Army, 1962-64. Served to lt. col. M.C., AUS, 1942-46. Diplomate Am. Bd. Pathology; recipient Townsend Harris medal, City Coll. N.Y., 1968; commendation VA Central Office, 1970; E.T. Bell Meml. medal, U. Minn., 1975; Ward Burdick medal, Am. Soc. Clin. Pathologists, 1976. Mem. Ohio Soc. Pathologists (past pres.), Cin. Pathology Soc. (past pres.), Internat. Acad. Pathology (pres. 1969-70), Am. Assn. Pathologists Bacteriologists (pres. 1963-64), Am. Soc. Clin. Pathologists (dir. 1962-68), Pan-Am. Med. Assn. (past pres. sect. pathology), Am. Assn. Cancer Edn. (pres. 1971-72), Am. Fedn. Clin. Oncolgic Socs. (pres. 1973-74), Sigma Xi, Alpha Omega Alpha. Clubs: Univ., Faculty (Cin.). Asso. editor Am. Jour. Clin. Pathology, 1949-54; editor-in-chief Am. Jour. Pathology, 1957-66; co-author: Concepts of Disease, 1971; editor The Liver, 1973. Home: 101 Lafayette Circle Cincinnati OH 45220 Office: University Cincinnati Medical Center 231 Bethesda Ave Cincinnati OH 45267

GALLAGHER, CHARLES VINCENT, assn. exec.; b. Palmer, Mass., Sept. 19, 1934; s. Darius Matthew and Anne Elizabeth (Hinchey) G.; B.A., Wesleyan U., Middletown, Conn., 1962; children from previous marriage—Kevin, Michael, Sean, Matthew. Reporter, Hartford (Conn.) Courant, 1959-62; mgmt. trainee KFBB-TV, Great Falls, Mont., 1962-63; mem. pub. relations dept. Southwestern Bell Telephone Co., St. Louis, 1963-68; exec. dir. Ind. Colls. and Univs. Mo., St. Louis, 1968—. Dir. Richard F. Long, Inc. Pres., North Side Youth Assn., St. Louis, 1965-66; pres. parents council Valley Winds Sch., St. Louis, 1964-65; vol. coordinator, tchr. adult edn. program Human Devel. Corp., 1965-68; mem. selection com., assignment supr. CORO Found., 1974. Served with USMCR, 1955-57. Recipient awards Freedoms Found., 1956, St. Louis Soc. Indsl. Editors, 1963, United Fund Greater St. Louis, 1963, Human Devel. Corp., 1968. Mem. Advt. Club Greater St. Louis, Am. Soc. Assn. Execs., St. Louis Regional Commerce and Growth Assn., Am. Assn. Higher Edn., Nat. Council Ind. Colls. and Univs. (dir. 1972-74), Nat. Assn. Ind. Colls. and Univs. (dir.). Home: 791-B Wiggens Ferry St Louis MO 63141 Office: 607 N Grand Ave Suite 405 St Louis MO 63103

GALLAGHER, FULTON DENT, educator; b. Windber, Pa., Dec. 3, 1934; s. Gilbert Grover and Lillian Helena (Merriman) G.; B.S., Indiana (Pa.) U., 1957, M.S., 1962; D. Music Edn., Ind. U., Bloomington, 1971; m. Nancy Pearl Frederick, Dec. 23, 1957; children—Benjamin Fulton, Julia Ellen. Instr. vocal music high sch. Apollo, Pa., 1957-59; supr. vocal music high sch. Clarion, Pa., 1959-62; mem. faculty Bemidji (Minn.) State Coll., 1963—, prof. music, 1971—, chmn. dept., 1971—, acting head div. fine arts, 1975-76, head div., 1976—; exec. dir. Paul Bunyan Playhouse, 1976—; adjudicator, clinician, guest condr. music festivals; soloist Pitts Grand Opera Co., 1957-59, St Louis August Festival Opera Co., 1963, Ind. U. Opera Theater, 1962-63. Mem. Minn. North Country Steering Com., 1974-75. Mem. mus. adv. panel Minn. Arts Council, 1971—. Danforth asso., 1968—; faculty research grants, 1973, 74. Mem. Minn. Music Edn. Assn. (pres.), AAUP, Music Educators Nat. Conf., Minn. Music Educators Assn., Bemidji C. of C. Home: 1023 Beltrami Ave Bemidji MN 56601 Office: Dept Music State Coll Bemidji MN 56601

GALLAGHER, IDELLA JANE SMITH (MRS. DONALD A. GALLAGHER), found. ofcl., author; b. Union City, N.J., Jan. 1, 1917; d. Fred J. and Louise (Stewart) S.; Ph.B., Marquette U., 1941, M.A., 1943, Ph.D., 1963; postgrad. U. Louvain, Belgium, U. Paris; m. Donald A. Gallagher, June 29, 1938; children—Paul B., Maria Noel. Lectr. philosophy Marquette U., 1943-52, 54-56; instr. philosophy Alverno Coll., Milw., 1956-58; asst. prof. philosophy Villanova U., 1958-62; asst. prof. philosophy Boston Coll., 1962-68, asso. prof., 1968-69; asso. prof. philosophy U. Ottawa, 1969-71, prof., 1971-73; projects adminstr. DeRance Found., Milw., 1973—; vis. prof. philosophy Niagara U., 1976-78. Mem. Sudbury (Mass.) Com. for Human Rights, 1963-69; trustee Mt. Senario Coll., Ladysmith, Wis., 1976—. Recipient Sword and Shield award St. Louis U., Baguio City, Philippines, 1975. Mem. Metaphys. Soc. Am., Am. Cath. Philos. Assn. (exec. council 1967-69), Am. Soc. Aesthetics, Assn. Realistic Philosophy, AAUP, Brit. Soc. Aesthetics, Canadian Philos. Assn., Canadian Assn. U. Tchrs., Phi Alpha Theta, Phi Delta Gamma. Author: (with D. A. Gallagher) The Achievement of Jacques and Raissa Maritain, 1962; The Education of Man, 1962; (with D. A. Gallagher) A Maritain Reader, 1966; (with D.A. Gallagher) St. Augustine—The Catholic and Maniehaean Ways of Life, 1966. Morality in Evolution: The Moral Philosophy of Henri Bergson, 1970. Gen. editor: Christian Culture and Philosophy Series, Bruce Pub. Co., 1965—. Contbr. to New Cath. Ency., also articles to profl. jours. Home: 7714 W Wisconsin Ave Wauwatosa WI 53213 Office: DeRance Found 7700 W Bluemound Rd Milwaukee WI 53213

GALLAGHER, JAMES MILLER, govt. ofcl.; b. Ft. Wayne, Ind., June 22, 1935; s. Edward Francis and Helen Lambert (Miller) G.; B.S., U.S. Naval Acad., 1957; M.Pub. Adminstrn., U. Dayton, 1969; m. Nancy Jo Kuhbander, June 8, 1957; children—Timothy Michael, Mary Jean. Regional rep. Autonetics div. Rockwell Internat., Dayton, 1960-61; with Aero. Systems div. Wright-Patterson AFB, Ohio, 1961—, asst. program dir. F-4 program, 1973-75, asst. dep. airlift/tanker aircraft, 1975-76, asst. program dir., dep. for F-16, 1976—; mem. aero. systems div. Civilian Policy Bd., 1974—. Mem. Ohio 3d Congl. dist. Naval Acad. Screening Com., 1965—, chmn., 1974—; mem. Centerville (Ohio) Bd. Archtl. Rev., 1974—, chmn., 1975—. Served with USAF, 1957-60. Named Greater Dayton Area Supr. Year, 1972, Supr. Year Miami Valley chpt. Federally Employed Women, 1975; recipient Exceptional Civil Service award USAF, 1977. Mem. Am. Def. Preparedness Assn., Leadership Dayton, U.S. Naval Acad. Alumni Assn. Roman Catholic. Home: 294 Cherry Dr Centerville OH 45459 Office: Dep for F-16 (ASD/YP) Wright-Patterson AFB OH 45433

GALLAGHER, JEROME JAY, clin. psychologist; b. Traverse City, Mich., Nov. 13, 1943; s. William Hanna and Hannah Ethyl (Rosen) G.; B.S., Mich. State U., East Lansing, 1967, Ph.D., 1973; m. Sherwood Hughes Hardwick, Oct. 24, 1970; children—Emily Suzanne, William Hanna. Dir. guidance and counseling St. Francis Sch. System, Traverse City, 1968-69; chief clin. psychologist Lansing (Mich.) Mental Health Clinic, 1971-72; clin. dir. drug abuse programs Community Mental Health Bd., Lansing, 1972—; mem. faculty Coll. Osteopathic Medicine, Mich. State U.; cons. U.S. Dept. Social Services, Va. Dept. Substance Abuse. HEW fellow, 1969; HEW grantee, 1971; certified cons. psychologist. Mem. Am. Assn. Advancement Psychology, Am., Mich. psychol. assns., AAAS, Am. Personnel and Guiadance Assn., Am. Amateur Photographers Assn., Ingham County Conservation League, Mich. United Conservation Club, Am. Wildlife Fedn. Clubs: Elks, Masons. (32 deg.). Home: 1888 Linden St East Lansing MI 48823 Office: Ingham County Sherriff's Dept Mason MI 48854

GALLAGHER, JOYCE EILEEN, educator; b. Ironton, Ohio, Sept. 3, 1937; d. Lawrence James and Frances Irene (Wilson) G.; B.S. in Elementary Edn., Coll. St. Teresa, Winona, Minn., 1967; M.Ed. in Guidance Counseling in Elementary Sch., Ohio U., Athens, 1970; Ph.D., Loyola U., Chgo., 1975. Elementary sch. tchr., then jr. high sch. tchr., Ill., Ohio and Minn., 1958-68; instr. psychology Coll. St. Teresa, 1969-72, v.p. student affairs, dean students, 1975-76; dir. instl. research St. Mary's Coll., Winona, 1976-77, asso. prof. psychology, asst. dean academic advising, 1977—. NDEA fellow, 1968-69. Mem. Am., Minn. personnel and guidance assns., Nat. Assn. Women Deans, Adminstrs. and Counselors, Phi Delta Kappa, Psi Chi. Roman Catholic. Home: 1370 C McNally Dr Winona MN 55987 Office: St Mary's Coll Winona MN 55987

GALLAGHER, LIONEL MILTON, physician; b. California, Mo., Dec. 14, 1924; s. Jesse Bernard and Lenora (Burford) G.; B.S., U. Mo., 1950; M.D., U. Cin., 1952; m. Elizabeth J. Steiner, Aug. 22, 1953; children—Michael S., Mark P. Intern Meth. Hosp. Ind., Indpls.; practice of medicine, California, 1953—; mem. staffs Meml. Community Hosp., St. Mary's Hosp., both Jefferson City, Mo.; mem. faculty in community health U. Mo. Sch. Medicine, Columbia, 1969—; city physician, California, 1958—. Trustee Meml. Hosp., Jefferson City. Served with AUS, 1943-46. Mem. Am. Acad. Gen. Practice, A.M.A., Mo. State Med. Assn., So. Med. Assn., Southwest Clin. Soc., Moniteau County Med. Soc. (sec.-treas. 1953—), V.F.W., Am. Legion. Kiwanian. Home: Hwy 87 N California MO 65018 Office: Commons California MO 65018

GALLANIS, THOMAS CONSTANTINE, obstetrician and gynecologist; b. Chgo., Mar. 6, 1927; s. Constantine A. and Kathryn (Koclanes) G.; student U. Ill., 1945-48; B.S., Northwestern U., 1949, M.D., 1952; m. Helen Karkazis, Jan. 30, 1955; children—Kathryn Ann, Craig. Intern, Passavant Meml. Hosp., Chgo., 1952-53, resident in obstetrics and gynecology, 1953-56; practice medicine specializing in obstetrics and gynecology, Evanston, Ill., 1956—; mem. staff Evanston Hosp., Glenbrook Hosp.; faculty dept. obstetrics and gynecology Northwestern U. Med. Sch., 1956—. Diplomate Am. Bd. Obstetrics and Gynecology. Fellow Am. Coll. Obstetricians and Gynecologists; mem. AMA, Ill., Chgo. med. socs., Chgo. Gynecologic Soc., Phi Rho Sigma. Greek Orthodox. Home: 136 Melrose Ave Kenilworth IL 60043 Office: 2500 Ridge Ave Evanston IL 60201

GALLAUGHER, JAMES RANKIN, engr.; b. East Moline, Ill., July 27, 1935; s. Elbert Roy and Myrtis (Dykes) G.; B.S. in Gen. Engring., U. Ill., 1957; m. Joan Ellen Getty, Sept. 1, 1957; children—Kathryn, Jeffrey, Cynthia, Joel. Small arms project engr. Army Weapons Command, Rock Island, Ill., 1962-65, chief, tech. mgmt. div., project mgr. rifles, 1965-71, project engr. cannon launched guided projectile, project mgr. arty., 1971-73, army small arms program coordinator Army Armament Command, 1972-74, dir. indsl. base engring. activity, Rock Island, 1974—; v.p. Gallaugher, Inc., 1962—. Served with USN, 1957-62; served to comdr., Civil Engr. Corps, USNR, 1962—. Recipient various Performance awards U.S. Army, 1962—, Outstanding Res. Seabee Detachment award USN, 1970. Mem. Nat. Rifle Assn., Am. Def. Preparedness Assn. (sec.-treas. Iowa-Ill. chpt. 1976—), Delta Phi. Clubs: Willow Springs Swim; East Moline Masons. Home: 2375 5th St East Moline IL 61244 Office: US Army Indsl Base Engring Activity Rock Island IL 61201

GALLAWAY, LOWELL EUGENE, educator; b. Toledo, Jan. 9, 1930; s. Leroy and Bessie Marguerite (Hiteshew) G.; B.S., Northwestern U., 1951; M.A., Ohio State U., 1955, Ph.D., 1959; m. Gladys Elinor McGhee, Dec. 19, 1953; children—Kathleen Elizabeth, Michael Scott, Ellen Jane. Asst. prof. Colo. State U., Ft. Collins, 1957-59; asst. prof. San Fernando Valley State Coll., Northridge, Calif., 1959-62; vis. asso. prof. U. Minn., Mpls., 1962-63; chief analytic studies sect. Social Security Adminstrn., Balt., 1963-64; asso. prof. U. Pa., Phila., 1964-67; prof. dept. econs. Ohio U., Athens, 1967-74, distinguished prof., 1974—. Served with USN, 1951-54. Ford Found. faculty fellow, 1960, Gen. Electric Found. fellow, 1962, Ford-Rockefeller Population policy research grantee, 1974-75. Author: The Retirement Decision, 1965; Interindustry Labor Mobility in the United States, 1957-1960, 1967; Geographic Labor Mobility in the United States, 1957-1960, 1969; Manpower Economics, 1971; Poverty in America, 1973. Contbr. articles to profl. jours. Home: 33 Longview Heights Rd Athens OH 45701

GALLE, OSWIN KARMIE, JR., chemist; b. Valley Center, Kans., Feb. 11, 1932; s. Oswin K. and Sarah (Schmidt) G.; B.S., Bethel Coll., 1957; postgrad. U. Kans., 1958-65; m. Edna Marie Thieszen, June 1, 1957; children—Michael Lee, Suzanne Marie. Analytical chemist Kans. Geol. Survey, Lawrence, 1957—, chief chemist geochemistry sect., 1968-72, research asso., 1975—, chief chemist, 1972—. Chmn. credit com. Kans. U. Fed. Credit Union, 1970—. Mem. Assn. Ofcl. Analytical Chemists, ASTM, Soc. Applied Spectroscopy (program chmn. Kansas City sect. 1973-74, chmn. 1976, chmn. publs. com. 1973-74), Sigma Xi. Contbr. articles in analytical chemistry to profl. jours.; editorial bd. Applied Spectroscopy, 1976. Home: R R 4 PO Box 69 Lawrence KS 66044 Office: Kans Geol Survey 1930 Ave A Campus West Lawrence KS 66044

GALLEN, EDUARD D., clergyman, ret. educator; b. Libau, Russia, Oct. 21, 1906; s. Julius Eduard and Natalie (Mielentz) G.; came to U.S., 1939, naturalized, 1943; Diploma in Theology, Riga (Latvia) Missionary Bible Inst., 1929; student Lockport Inst. Tech. and Aeros., 1945; M.A. in Guidance, Bradley U., 1960; Ed.D., U. Tulsa, 1969; postgrad. Northwestern U., 1959, U. Iowa, 1963-64, Leipzig (Germany) U., 1932; m. Dorothy E. Busch, May 29, 1941. Ordained to ministry Baptist Ch., 1928; pastor Cesu Bapt. Ch., Cesis, Latvia, 1928-29, Rucava (Latvia) Bapt. Ch., 1932-35, Zion Bapt. Ch., Riga, 1935-39; hon. field supt. Russian Missionary Soc., hdqrs. in London, Eng., 1936-39; hon. chaplain Mil. Forces of Latvia, 1931-39; instr. So. Bapt. Theol. Sem., Louisville, 1939-40; pastor Latvian Bapt. Ch. of Chgo., 1940-46; cons. mgmt. and edn., various bus. firms, schs., churches and welfare orgns., U.S., Can., 1946-59; instr. dept. sociology and psychology Black Hawk Coll., Moline, Ill., 1960-62, asst. prof., 1962-67, asso. prof., 1967-71, prof., 1971-76, prof. emeritus, 1976—; vis. prof. sociology psychology Palmer Jr. Coll., Davenport, Iowa, 1966-72; lectr. to various radio and TV programs, 1976—, various civic orgns. and religious groups, 1976—. Chmn. Greater Chgo. Bilingual Representative Assembly for Polit. Action, 1946-53; v.p. Latvian Relief Inc., N.Y.C., 1947-52; capt. Civilian Defense, Chgo., 1942-45. Served to res. lt. Latvian Army, 1929-39. Recipient Key of Merit award Indsl. Engring. Coll. of Chgo., 1946. Mem. Am. Personnel and Guidance Assn., Ministers Council Am. Bapt. Churches, U. Tulsa Alumni Assn., Phi Delta Kappa. Contbr. articles on indsl. engring., social problems to mags. and newspapers. Address: 2509 30th Ave Court Moline IL 61265

GALLIENNE, WILLIAM FREDERICK, accountant; b. Dayton, Ohio, July 7, 1927; s. Charles Matthew and Helen Emily (Ellis) G.; A.B., U. Ga., 1951; postgrad. U. Dayton, 1951-53; m. Jane Ann Leary, Aug. 14, 1954; children—Paul, Mark, John, Jean. Sr. staff auditor Ernst and Ernst, 1954-60; controller Restaurant Service Corp., Dayton, 1960-63; sr. staff accountant Mitchell, Lloyd and Darner, Dayton, 1963-70; prin. William F. Gallienne, C.P.A., Dayton, 1970—; adj. instr. Wright State U. Served with U.S. Army, 1945-46. Mem. Am. Inst. C.P.A.'s, Ohio Soc. C.P.A.'s, Nat. Assn. Accountants (dir. Dayton chpt.), Am. Accounting Assn. Republican. Episcopalian. Club: Optimists Internat. Home: 3501 Pobst St Dayton OH 45420 Office: 440 3d Nat Bldg Dayton OH 45402

GALLOP, DOUGLAS JAMES, bank exec.; b. Cumberland, Wis., Aug. 29, 1931; s. Albert James and Colista Bertha (Arnes) G.; B.A. in Bus. Adminstrn., Hamline U., 1958; m. Shirley Hawkinson, Mar. 31, 1956; children—Robyn, Brian, Bradley. Trainee, NW Nat. Bank, Mpls., 1958-60; various positions with Camden NW Bank, Mpls., 1960-72; v.p. bank relations NW Bancorp., Mpls., 1972-73; pres. 1st NW Nat. Bank, Grand Rapids, Minn., 1973—. Pres. Itasca Community Coll. Found., Sports Boosters. Served with USAF, 1951-53. Decorated Air Medal. Mem. Minn. Bankers Assn., C. of C. (dir.). Republican. Lutheran. Clubs: Lions (dir.), Masons (Shriner). Home: Rt 5 Box 339 Grand Rapids MN 55744 Office: 220 1st Ave NW Grand Rapids MN 55744

GALLOWAY, ROBERT EDWARD, counselor, educator; b. Fountain County, Ind., Mar. 12, 1931; s. Robert William and Nina DeEtte (Pratt) G.; B.S., Purdue U., 1953, M.S., 1958, Ph.D., 1960; m. Beverly Jean Ricketts, Sept. 6, 1952; children—Cathy Anne, Michael Lynn, Matthew Alan. Tchr. Burlington (Ind.) High Sch., 1955-57; grad. asst. in edn. Purdue U., Lafayette, Ind., 1957-60; prof. psychology and counselor edn., counselor Pittsburg (Kans.) State U., 1960—, coordinator testing, 1975—; cons. in field. Served with M.C., U.S. Army, 1953-55. Grantee Purdue Research Found., 1958, Law Enforcement Assistance Adminstrn. and Kans. Gov.'s Com. Crime Delinquency, 1972. Mem. Am. Personnel Guidance Assn. (chmn. Midwestern region human rights commn. 1972-74), Kans. Personnel Guidance Assn. (pres. 1966), Am. Psychol. Assn., NEA, Phi Delta Kappa. Republican. Methodist. Home: 1915 S Elm St Pittsburg KS 66762

GALLUCCI, JOANNE (PEENIE) MARIE, counselor, educator; b. Bremerton, Wash., Mar. 20, 1952; d. Vincent Anthony and Virginia Angelina (Righi) Gallucci; B.A. magna cum laude in English and Psychology, Gonzaga U., 1973; M.S. in Counseling and Human Systems, Fla. State U., 1976. Tchr. secondary grades St. Rose Acad., San Francisco, 1973-74; intern counseling psychology, spl. lectr. Counseling Testing Center, Boise (Idaho) State U., 1975-76; counselor, instr. Counseling Testing Center, Coll. St Catherine, St. Paul, 1976—; vol. counselor Walk-In Counseling Clinic, Mpls., 1976; vol. therapist Child Guidance Clinic, Wilder Found., St. Paul, 1977; mental health intern Albany Med. Coll., Union U., Albany, N.Y., 1975. Recipient Tchr.'s Spirit award St. Rose Acad., 1974. Mem. Am., Minn. personnel guidance assns., Am., Minn. coll. personnel assns., AAUP, Nat. Assn. Women Deans, Adminstrs. Counselors, Alpha Sigma Nu, Kappa Gamma Pi, Kappa Delta Pi. Democrat. Roman Catholic. Office: Coll St Catherine PO Box 4077 2004 Randolph Ave St Paul MN 55105

GALOWICH, RONALD HOWARD, lawyer; b. Peoria, Ill., Feb. 18, 1936; s. Louis J. and Leah (Kahn) G.; B.S. in Commerce and Law, U. Ill., 1957, J.D., 1959; m. Eleanor Audrey Bernstein, June 16, 1957; children—Jeffrey, Robert, Pamela. Admitted to Ill. bar, 1959, U.S. Supreme Ct. bar; asso. firm John G. Boyle, DeKalb, Ill., 1959-60; partner firm Galowich, Galowich, McSteen & Phelan and predecessor firms, Joliet, Ill., 1960—. Dir., pres. Community Electronics Systems Cable TV, Inc., 1966-72; v.p. Teleprompter Community Electronics Systems, 1972-73; dir., pres. Ronjer, Inc., R J G Inc., 1968—, Ronald H. Galowich Assos. Inc., 1970—, Air Wich Airlines, Inc.; mng. partner Lakeland Investment Co., 1968— (all Joliet); commr. Ill. Supreme Ct. Grievance Com., 1968-70. Bd. dirs., v.p. Joliet YMCA, 1976—; v.p. Joliet Jr. Coll. Found. Served to capt. Ordnance Corps, AUS, 1959-60; Judge Adv. Gen. Corps, 1960-68. Fellow Am. Bar Found.; mem. Am., Ill. (real estate law council, 1976—, lectr., author Ill. Inst. Continuing Legal Edn.), Chgo. bar assns., Am. Judicature Soc., Am. Trial Lawyers Assn., Nat. Assn. Home Builders, Urban Land Inst., Am. Right of Way Assn., Voice Ill. Aviation. Elk, Kiwanian; mem. B'nai B'rith. Home: 3110 Deer Path Dr Joliet IL 60435 Office: 57 N Ottawa St Joliet IL 60431

GALT, RAYMOND MASSON, physician; b. Evanston, Ill., May 28, 1914; s. Arthur Thomas and Ida May (Cook) G.; B.A., Williams Coll., 1935; M.D., Northwestern U., 1940; m. Jane Falley, May 1, 1943; 1 dau., Katharine Hughes. Intern Evanston Hosp., 1939-40; resident in pathology Passavant Hosp., Chgo., 1940-41; resident in internal medicine Cook County Hosp., Chgo., 1942, attending physician, 1947-72; practice medicine specializing in internal medicine, Chgo., 1943—; mem. staff Rush Presbyn.-St. Luke's, Augustana hosps.; asst. prof. medicine U. Ill. Med. Sch., Chgo., 1949—. Trustee, Village of Golf (Ill.), 1952-56. Served to capt. M.C., AUS, 1943-46. Decorated Bronze Star, Silver Star; Croix de Guerre with étoile d'argent (France). Fellow A.C.P.; mem. AMA, Ill., Chgo. med. socs. Republican. Mem. Winnetka (Ill.) Bible Ch. Club: Glen View. Home: 56 Overlook Dr Golf IL 60029 Office: 2155 N Cleveland St Chicago IL 60614

GAMBLE, DANIEL JEFFERSON, lawyer; b. Dothan, Ala., Nov. 15, 1931; s. William Samuel and Anne (King) G.; B.S. in Bus., Ind. U., 1959, J.D., 1962; m. Rita Suzane McCoy, June 9, 1962; children—Daniel Jefferson Jr., Laura Ann, Kristian Jane. Admitted to Ind. bar, 1962; mem. legal dept. State Automobile Ins. Assn., Indpls., 1961-62; partner firm Ellis, Gamble & Nolan and predecessor firms,

Kokomo, Ind., 1962—; dep. pros. atty. Howard County, 1964-69, county atty., 1969-76; dir. Sack It To Me of Marion, Inc., Kokomo, Ind. Chmn. Howard County Legal Aid Soc., 1967—; chmn. sub-com. United Fund., Kokomo, 1966-70, capital fund YMCA, Kokomo, 1963. Chmn. Young Republicans Club, Kokomo, 1964; del. Ind. Rep. Conv., 1966. Served with AUS, 1950-53; Korea. Mem. Am., Ind., Howard County (pres. 1977—) bar assns., Ind. Trial Lawyers Assn., Kokomo C. of C. (head consolidation of contract agreements for city, county govts. task force), Phi Delta Phi, Pi Kappa Phi. Presbyn. (elder). Mason, Elk. Clubs: Y Health, Kokomo Country. Home: 15O2 Arundel St Kokomo IN 46901 Office: 421 W Sycamore St Kokomo IN 46901

GAMBOA, LUCITO GAMBOA, pathologist; b. Pampanga, Philippines, Jan. 7, 1929; s. Serapion Maniago and Jacinta (Lapuz) G.; came to U.S., 1952, naturalized, 1959; M.D., U. Santo Tomas, Philippines, 1952; M.S., U. Colo., 1955; m. Sylvia Roque, Sept. 18, 1953; children—Richard R., Virginia L., Debra Lynn. Intern, Mercy Hosp., Denver, 1952-53; resident in pathology Gen. Rose Meml. Hosp., Denver, 1953-58; chmn. dept. pathology, dir. Labs. Edgewater Hosp., Chgo., 1958-68; pathologist, dir. blood bank Little Co. of Mary Hosp., Evergreen Park, Ill., 1969—; instr. Med. Sch. Northwestern U., Chgo., 1958-60. Recipient Distinguished Physician award Philippine Med. Assn. Chgo., 1966. Mem. Coll. Am. Pathologists, AMA, Internat. Acad. Pathology, Am. Assn. Blood Banks, Am. Soc. Cytology, Am. Soc. Clin. Pathologists, Soc. Nuclear Medicine, Assn. Philippine Practicing Physicians Am. (pres. 1972-74). Roman Catholic. Home: 35 Bradford Ln Oak Brook IL 60521 Office: 2800 W 95th St Evergreen Park IL 60642

GAMERTSFELDER, ROBERT HEHN, architect; b. Geneva, N.Y., Sept. 19, 1920; s. Walter Sylvester and Pearl Agnes May (Hehn) G.; student Ohio U., 1939-40; B.Arch., Ohio State U., 1949; m. Frances Carolyn Zimmerman, Feb. 25, 1946; 1 son, John Walter. Dir. research and design Nationwide Devel. Co., Columbus, Ohio, 1948-66, dir. planning, 1966-71, v.p. planning, 1971—. Mem. Upper Arlington (Ohio) Planning Commn., 1967-71. Served with USAAF, 1943-46. Mem. A.I.A., Architects Soc. Ohio. Republican. Presbyn. Club: Executive's (Columbus). Prin. works include WRFD radio Studio, Worthington, Ohio Credit Union League Hdqrs. Bldg., Columbus, Ohio Central Credit Union Bldg., Columbus. Home: 2691 York Rd Upper Arlington OH 43221 Office: One Nationwide Plaza Columbus OH 43216

GÁMEZ, JOSÉ PAZ, urban orgn. adminstr.; b. Laredo, Tex., Dec. 25, 1944; s. Pedro Tomas and Amelia (Rodriguez) G.; B.A., Tex. A. and I. U., 1969; postgrad. (Ednl. Profl. Devel. Act fellow) Mich. State U., 1970-75; m. Mary Christine Krug, Jan. 29, 1972; children—Fernando Jose, Janaina Cristina. Asst. dir. admissions and scholarships Mich. State U., E. Lansing, 1970-75; v.p. Chicano affairs St. Paul Urban Coalition, 1975-76, exec. dir., 1976—; mem. La Raza Citizens Adv. Com. to Mich. State Bd. Edn., chmn. 1973-75. Bd. dirs. St. Paul Arts and Sci. Council, St. Paul United Way. Served with USAR, 1964. Assn. Chicanos for Coll. Admissions, Serra Internat. Democrat Farmer Labor Party. Co-author: Quality of Educational Services to Michigan's Spanish Speaking Community, 1974. Home: 190 W Isabel St Saint Paul MN 55107 Office: 200 Bremer Bldg Saint Paul MN 55101

GAMMON, JUANITA LAVERNE, artist, educator; b. McLeansboro, Ill.; d. Lloyd W. and Grace F. (Munsell) Gammon; B.F.A., M.F.A., U. Ill. Exhibited N.Y. Acad. Design, U. Ill., Parkland Coll., others; represented in numerous collections; head art program Parkland Coll., Champaign, Ill., 1967—; free lance illustrator, copywriter, guest lectr., art show judge, condr. workshops; dir. Corn Country Graphics; supr. Champaign County Art Show, 1973—; bd. dirs. East Central Ill. Cultural Affairs Consortium, 1973—; chmn. Urbana Art Fair. Mem. NEA, Ill. Art Edn. Assn., Assn. Jr. Colls., Ill. Hist. Soc., U. Ill. Alumni Assn., Art Alumni Assn., Parkland Art Assn. (sponsor), Champaign-Urbana Advt.-Art Club (past treas., dir.). Home: 711 W Healey St Champaign IL 61820

GAMMUTO, JOHN JOSEPH, SR., utility co. exec.; b. Chgo., Jan. 7, 1925; s. Philip D. and Mary (Elia) G.; B.S. in Elementary Edn., 1974, M.A. in Curriculum and Adminstrn., 1976; postgrad. U. Chgo., 1977; m. Catherine H. Maher, Dec. 22, 1945; children—John Joseph, Catherine, James, Andrew. With Commonwealth Edison Co., 1955—, staff asst. gen. office, Chgo., 1970-76, supr. tng. generating stas., prodn. dept., 1977—. Commr., counselor W. Suburban council Boy Scouts Am., 1965-77. Served with USN, 1943-46, 50-51; PTO; Korea. Certified tchr., ednl. adminstr., Ill. Mem. Coll. DePage, DePaul U. alumni assns., Am. Nuclear Soc., ASME, Adult Edn. Assn., Ill. Tng. Dirs. Assn., Am. Soc. tng. and Devel., DePaul Geog. Soc., VFW, Kappa Delta Pi. Roman Catholic. Home: 4804 Oakwood Ave Downers Grove IL 60515 Office: 72 W Adams St Chicago IL 60690

GAMON, ADAM EDWARD, II, internist, chem. co. exec.; b. Hillside, N.J., Sept. 6, 1918; s. Adam Edward and Mary (Yanick) G.; B.S., Alfred U., 1939; M.D., Temple U., 1943; m. Lottie Irene Snyder, Sept. 8, 1939; children—Judith Diane, Robert Edward. Intern, N.Y.C. Hosp., 1944, resident in pathology 1946, asst. med. resident, 1947-48, chief med. resident, 1948-49; resident internal medicine Saginaw (Mich.) Gen. Hosp., 1946-47; pvt. practice internal medicine, Englewood, N.J., 1949-50; practice medicine specializing in internal medicine, Saginaw, 1950-69; with Mich. State Disability Determination Service, Lansing, 1969-71; med. dir. Malleable Iron div. Gen. Motors Corp., Saginaw, 1971-73; med. dir. Dow Corning Corp., Midland, Mich., 1973—; chief of medicine St. Luke's Hosp., Saginaw, 1953-67; cons. St. Mary's Hosp., Gen. Hosp., St. Luke's Hosp., Saginaw, Midland Hosp.; dep. coroner Saginaw County (Mich.) 1973—; cons. physician Social Security Adminstrn., HEW, Saginaw, 1973-77. Served to capt., M.C., U.S. Army, 1944-46. Diplomate Am. Bd. Internal Medicine. Fellow A.C.P. (life), Am. Coll. Angiology, Am. Soc. Internal Medicine, Mich., Midland County med. socs., AMA, Mich. Soc. Internal Medicine, Indsl. Med. Assn., Pan Am. Med. Assn., Am. Radio Relay League. Inventor Disposable tracheotomy set, portable bed chair. Home: 15317 W Brant Rd PO Box 57 Brant MI 48614 Office: Dow Corning Corp S Saginaw Rd Midland MI 48640

GAMSKY, NEAL RICHARD, univ. adminstr.; b. Menasha, Wis., Feb. 17, 1931; s. Andrew and Lillian Gamsky; B.S., U. Wis., 1954, M.S., 1959, Ph.D., 1965; m. Irene Janet Jimos, Aug. 16, 1956; children—Elizabeth, Patricia. Counselor, Appleton (Wis.) Pub. Schs., 1959-62; dir. edn. Wis. Diagnostic Center, Madison, 1962-67; dir. research and pupil services Coop. Edn. Service Agy., Waupun, Wis., 1967-70; dir. student counseling center Ill. State U., Normal, 1970-73, v.p., dean student affairs, 1973—; ednl. and counseling cons. Wis. Div. Mental Hygiene, 1967. Served with AUS, 1954-56; ETO. Profl. Rehab. fellow, 1968. Mem. Am. Psychol. Assn., Am. Personnel and Guidance Assn., Nat. Assn. Student Personnel Adminstrs., Am. Assn. Higher Edn., Am. Council Edn. Author: (with others) The Counselor's Handbook, 1974; also articles, monograph. Home: 114 Cheltenham Dr Normal IL 61761 Office: 506 DeGarmo Hall Ill State U Normal IL 61761

GANDAL, ROBERT, lawyer; b. Cleve., Feb. 9, 1928; s. Henry and Gertrude (Weiss) G.; B.B.A., Case Western Res. U., 1950; J.D., Cleve. State U., 1954; children—Neil, Keith, Gail. Admitted to Ohio bar, 1955; sales mgr. residential lighting fixture div. Midland Elec. Co., Cleve., 1950-65; gen. mgr. Citrus Fruit Juice, Cleve., 1965-67; v.p., sec., corporate counsel Mgmt. Recruiters Internat., Inc., Cleve., 1967—, dir., 1967-72. Active Big Bros. Am. Served with AUS, 1946-47. Mem. Am., Ohio, Cleve. bar assns., Nat. Employment Assn., Internat. Francise Assn. Home: 6805 Mayfield Rd Apt 1217A Mayfield Heights OH 44124 Office: 1015 Euclid Ave Suite 600 Cleveland OH 44115

GANDHI, HAREN SAKARLAL, chem. engr.; b. Calcutta, India, May 2, 1941; s. Sakarlal C. and Ichhaben (Kadakia) G.; B.Chem. Engring., U. Bombay, 1963; M.S., U. Detroit, 1966; De. Enring., 1971; m. Yellow Sheth, Sept. 6, 1966; children—Sangeeta, Anand. Came to U.S., 1963, naturalized, 1967. Prin. research engr. Ford Motor Co., Dearborn, Mich., 1967—. Mem. Am. Inst. Chem. Engrs. Patentee field of pollution, catalysts, reactor design. Home: 7464 Amboy St Dearborn Heights MI 48127 Office: PO Box 2053 Ford Motor Co Dearborn MI 48121

GANDRUD, EBENHARD STEWART, mfg. co. exec.; b. Detroit Lakes, Minn., Oct. 19, 1902; s. Albert E. and Kari (Dahlen) G.; B.S., U. Minn., 1934; m. Edith M. Christensen, July 16, 1935; children—Linda (Mrs. H.L. Stoddard), Dale E. Agrl. extension agt., Pipestone Minn., 1934-37; founder, pres. Gandy Co., Owatonna, Minn., 1936—. Owner, Ramada Inn, Owatonna, 1975—. Mem. exec. bd. Gamehaven council Boy Scouts Am., 1945-75; pres. Gandrud Found., 1940—. Served with War Manpower Commn., World War II. Recipient award for outstanding contbn. to Am. Agr. Congress of U.S., 1967; Silver Beaver award Boy Scouts Am., 1971. Mem. Am. Soc. Agrl. Engrs., N.A.M., Minn. C. of C. (past dir.), Sons of Norway. Lutheran. Elk, Rotarian. Club: Mpls. Athletic. Patentee in field. Home: 517 E School St Owatonna MN 55060 Office: Box 528 Owatonna MN 55060

GANDT, JEROME OTTO, dentist; b. Appleton, Wis., Aug. 28, 1930; s. Otto Anthony and Hedwig (Hoppe) G.; student Lawrence U., 1948-49; B.S., Marquette U., 1952, D.D.S., 1955; children—Brian, Kathleen, Caroline. Gen. practice dentistry, Green Bay, Wis., 1958—; instr. N.E. Wis. Tech. Inst. Inst.; guest instr. U. Wis.-Green Bay, 1968-69; instr. Donovan Acad., Steamboat Springs, Colo. Adviser, N.E. Wis. Dental Assts. Assn. Founder, pres. Wilderness Watch, Inc., Green Bay; mem. citizens adv. council Upper Mississippi River Basin Commn. Served to capt. USAAF, 1955-57. Fellow Acad. Gen. Dentistry, Am. Endodontic Soc.; mem. Am., Canadian dental assns., Wis. (chmn. ins. program), Chgo. dental socs., Internat. Acad. Orthodontics, Am. Acad. Orthodontic for Gen. Practitioner, Nat. Parks and Recreation Soc., Psi Omega. Home: 916 Cedarview Ct Green Bay WI 54301 Office: 1745 Dousman St Green Bay WI 54303

GANGE, JOSEPH GEORGE, JR., mfg. co. exec.; b. Salt Lake City, Apr. 13, 1936; s. Joseph George and Edith Georgia (Farnsworth) G.; student Brown U., 1954-57, Bentley Coll., 1958-59; m. Susan Ginsberg, Dec. 21, 1964; children—Jeffrey Hamilton, Joseph George. Sales expediter Nat. Lead Co., Boston, 1961-65; trade sales rep. Nat. Lead Co., Chgo., 1965-68; mgr. metal sales UV Industries, N.Y.C., 1968-72; v.p. mktg. USS Lead Refinery, Inc. div. UV Industries, East Chicago, Ind., 1973—. Mem. Lead Industries Assn. (dir.), Zinc Industries Assn. (dir. 1970-74), Am. Inst. Mining, Metall. and Petroleum Engrs., Copper Club. Club: Elks. Home: 416 Strieff Ln Glenwood IL 60425 Office: 5300 Kennedy Ave East Chicago IN 46312

GANGWARE, EDGAR BRAND, JR., educator; b. Sandusky, Ohio, May 17, 1922; s. Edgar Brand and Louise Wilhelmina (Schoeneman) G.; B.S., Wittenberg U., 1943, Mus.B., 1947; Mus.M., Northwestern U., 1948, Ph.D., 1959; m. Dorcas Euana Biniores, Sept. 3, 1949; children—Edgar Brand III, Frank Roy, Robert William. Asst. band dir. Northwestern U., Evanston, 1947-49; dir. bands, instr. theory Boston U., 1949-50; dir. bands, dir. summer music clinic Bemidji (Minn.) State Coll., 1952-66; prof. music N.E. Ill. U., Chgo., 1966—. Clinician, condr. Chmn., Civic Music Assn. Bemidji, 1964-65; mem. Northbrook Caucus, 1973-74. Mem. Civil Youth Bd., Northbrook, 1970-72. Served to 1st lt. AUS, 1942-46; PTO. Mem. Am. Bandmasters Assn. (dir. 1973-75), Coll. Band Dirs. Nat. Assn., Music Educators Nat. Conf., Ill. Music Edn. Assn., A.A.U.P. Lion. Compositions for concert band, brass choir, others. Home: 1225 Candlewood Hill Rd Northbrook IL 60062 Office: 5500 N St Louis St Chicago IL 60625

GANNAWAY, STEPHEN DALE, audiologist; b. Mattoon, Ill., May 29, 1947; s. Edward Dale and Evelyn Darlene (Tull) G.; B.S. in Edn. (Scholar), Eastern Ill. U., 1969; M.A. in Audiology, U. Ill., 1971; m. Kathryn Lynn Karloski, July 29, 1972; children—Amy Johanna, Zachary Stephen. Clin. asst. U. Ill., 1970-71; sr. trainee Eastern Ill. U., 1968-69; speech pathologist Decatur (Ill.) Sch. Dist. 61, 1969-70; audiologist Title VI project E. Central Counties of Ill., 1971-72; audiologist John F. Kennedy Diagnostic Center, Joliet, Ill., 1972-73; pres. Joliet Audio Vestibular Labs., Inc., 1973—; chmn. bd., cons. audiologist ENT Surg. Assos. Ltd.; Former chmn. regional hearing conservation com. Ill. Dept. Pub. Health; instr. audiology Coll. St. Francis. Pres. bd. dirs. Big Bros. of Will County; elder St. Peter's Lutheran Ch., also mem. ch. council; cons. Joliet Easter Seal Soc. Certified course dir. Council for Accreditation in Occupational Hearing Conservation. Mem. Am. (certificate of clin. competence in audiology), Ill., Chgo., Will-Grundy speech and hearing assns., Alexander Graham Bell Assn. Soc. Med. Audiology, Nat. Assn. Hearing Speech Action, Am. Audiological Soc., Centurion Club (asso.). Club: Lions (Joliet). Contbr. articles to profl. jours. Home: 1101 Taylor St Joliet IL 60435 Office: 3077 W Jefferson St Joliet IL 60435

GANNON, SISTER ANN IDA, educator; b. Chgo., 1915; d. George and Hanna (Murphy) Gannon; A.B., Clarke Coll., 1941; A.M., Loyola U., Chgo., 1948, LL.D., 1969; Ph.D., St. Louis U., 1952; L.H.D. (hon.), Lincoln (Ill.) Coll., 1965, Luther Coll., 1968, Augustana Coll., 1969, Columbia Coll., 1969, Marycrest Coll., 1972, Ursuline Coll., 1972, Spertus Coll. Judaica, 1974, Coll. Holy Cross, 1974, Rosary Coll., 1975, St. Ambrose Coll., 1975, Stonehill Coll., 1976, Elmhurst Coll., 1977, Manchester Coll., 1977, Marymount-Manhattan Coll., 1977, others. Mem. Sisters of Charity; tchr. English, St. Mary's High Sch., Chgo., 1941-47; residence, study abroad, 1951; chmn. philosophy dept. Mundelein Coll., 1951-57, pres. coll., Chgo., 1957-75, prof. philosophy, 1975—. Dir. No. Ill. Gas Co., Sta. WTTW, Scott Foresman & Co. Mem. com. on planning and devel. Coll. Entrance Exam. Bd., 1971. Mem. Ill. Commn. on Status of Women, 1965-70, chmn. edn. com., 1966-67; nat. bd. dirs. Girl Scouts Am., 1966-74, mem. nat. adv. bd., 1977—; mem. women's com. Nat. Conf. Christians and Jews 1967-69; mem. Pres.'s Task Force on Women, 1969; mem. panel for vol. action by women White House Conf. on Food, Nutrition and Health, 1969; mem. adv. com. AID, 1969-70 mem. Ill. Humanities Council, 1973—, Ill. Bd. Banks and Trusts, 1975-77. Trustee Lincoln Acad. Ill. Millikin U., St. Louis U., Emmanuel Coll., St. Michael Coll.; bd. dirs. Newberry Library, Sears Roebuck Found. Recipient Loyola Alumni citation, 1969, Latere Medal U. Notre Dame, 1975, Aquinas award, 1976; Danforth Found. grantee. Mem. Asso. Colls. Ill. (exec. com. 1957-75), Am. Cath. Philos. Assn. (exec. council 1953-56), Religious Edn. Assn. Am. (dir. 1963-75, pres. 1972-74, chmn. bd., 1974-77), Fedn. Ind. Ill. Colls. (exec. com. 1965-69), Nat. Cath. Edn. Assn. (com. on pub. affairs 1976—), Am. Council on Edn. (dir. 1971-75, mem. exec. com. 1973, chmn. 1973-74), A.A.U.W., Metaphys. Soc. Am., Assn. Am. Colls. (dir. 1965-71, vice chmn. 1968, chmn. 1969), Central States Coll. Assn. (dir. 1965—, sec. 1970, vice chmn. 1971), Nat. Council Ind. Colls. and Univs. (task force financing), N. Central Assn. Colls. and Secondary Schs. (chmn. exec. com. 1976-78, dir. 1973—), Assn. Higher Edn. Contbr. articles to philos. jours. Address: 6363 Sheridan Rd Chicago IL 60660

GANNON, PAUL GABRIEL, surgeon; b. Jersey City, June 2, 1928; s. James J. and Mary (Hurley) G.; B.A. cum laude, Holy Cross Coll., 1950; M.D., Marquette U., 1954; M.S., U. Minn., 1961, Ph.D., 1973; m. Rozalija Mavric, June 14, 1954; children—Barbara, Paul Gabriel, James, Mary Ann. Intern, Madigan Army Hosp., Tacoma; fellow gen. surgery Mayo Clinic, Rochester, Minn., 1957-61; practice medicine specializing in gen. surgery, San Diego, 1961-63; resident cardiovascular and thoracic surgery U. Minn., Mpls., 1963-67, clin. asso. prof. surgery, 1975—; practice medicine specializing in thoracic and cardiovascular surgery, Mpls., 1967—. Served to capt. USAF, 1955-57. Mem. A.C.S., AMA, Soc. Thoracic Surgeons, Minn. State Med. Assn. (Best Sci. award 1974), Minn., Mpls. surg. socs., Minn. Thoracic Soc., Twin City Thoracic and Cardiovascular Surg. Soc., Hennepin County Med. Soc., Hennepin County Med. Soc., Mayo Clinic Med. Found. Alumni. Editorial bd. Minn. Medicine, 1971—. Home: 508 Westwood Dr S Minneapolis MN 55416 Office: 2545 Chicago Ave Suite 111 Minneapolis MN 55404

GANNON, WALTER, sch. adminstr.; b. Detroit, Sept. 12, 1930; s. John and Sadie (Martin) G.; student Highland Park Jr. Coll., 1948-50; B.S., Wayne State U., 1952, M.Ed., 1958; postgrad. Mich. State U., 1962-67, U. Okla., 1965, Bowling Green State U., 1966, Purdue U., 1972; m. Jean Lambie Chanay, Mar. 7, 1951; children—Michael, Kathlyn, Jill, Jennifer. Elementary, secondary tchr. Pontiac, Mich., 1952-59; secondary tchr., chmn. dept. math., Oak Park, Mich., 1960-68; secondary sch. adminstr., Albion, Mich., 1968-69; prin. Engleman Middle Sch., 1969-72, Miller Elementary Sch., Center Line, Mich., 1972—. Officer Troy (Mich.) Library Commn., 1972—. Republican del. to state and county convs., 1974, 75; pres. choir Clawson United Meth. Ch., 1976-77. NSF grantee, 1960-66. Mem. Oak Park Edn. Assn. (dir. 1961-68, pres. 1965-67), Center Line Adminstrv. Assn. (pres. 1974-75), Friends of Troy Library, Mich. Fencers League (finance officer 1954-56), NEA, Mich. Edn. Assn., Assn. for Supervision and Curriculum Devel., Mich. Library Assn., Nat., Mich. councils tchrs. math., AAUP, Nat. Ret. Tchrs. Assn., Kappa Mu Epsilon. Home: 1925 Alexander Dr Troy MI 48084 Office: 23855 Lawrence St Center Line MI 48015

GANOCY, STEPHEN JAMES, indsl. safety health systems analyst; b. Uniontown, Pa., June 17, 1943; s. Louis Emil and Mary Ann (Salansky) G.; B.S. in Math., U. Akron, 1971, M.S. in Math., 1976. Lab. technician Goodyear Tire & Rubber Co., Akron, Ohio, 1967-73, devel. engr., 1973-76, safety health systems analyst, 1976—. Served with USAF, 1963-67. Mem. Am. Statis. Assn., Soc. Indsl. Applied Math., Biometric Soc., Pi Mu Epsilon. Roman Catholic. Home: 769 Anderson Ave Apt 12 Akron OH 44306 Office: 1144 E Market St Dept 108H Akron OH 44316

GANOS, THOMAS, physician; b. Detroit, Sept. 4, 1924; s. John George and Bertha Ann (Gulbronsen) G.; B.S., Wayne State U., 1948, M.D., 1952; m. Gaye Hoag, Nov. 28, 1942; children—Judith (Mrs. Chester Budziak), Beverly (Mrs. Lewis Sinclair), Linda (Mrs. William Hammond), Thomas, Lisa, Doreen. Intern, Detroit Meml. Hosp., 1952-53; resident Wyandotte (Mich.) Hosp., 1953-54, now mem. staff; gen. practice medicine and surgery, Allen Park, Mich., 1953—; pres. staff Outer Drive Hosp., Lincoln Park, Mich., 1968-70; mem. staff Oakwood-Dearborn Seaway Hosp., Trenton, Mich.; pres. Park Ave. Med. Group, Allen Park, Mich., 1969—; pres. Tomco Corp., Lincoln Park, 1960-70; pres. Trenton Chateau Co., Allen Park, 1968—; clin. prof. Medicine Wayne State Med. Sch., 1976-77. Pres. Down River Cancer Found., 1966-68. Bd. dirs. Mich. Cancer Found., Mich. Arthritis Found., Mich. Tb Soc. Served with AUS, 1942-45. Diplomate Am. Bd. Family Practice, Pan Am. Bd. Medicine. Mem. Am. (pres. Wayne County 1968, dir. 1968-70), Mich. (alt. del.) acads. gen. practice, Mich. Assn. Professions (charter mem.), Am Geriatrics Soc., Royal Soc. Health (Eng.), Civil Aviation Med. Assn., Psychosomatic Med. Assn., V.F.W., Mich. (del.), Wayne County (sec. gen. practice sect. 1967-68, chief gen. practice sect. 1968) med. socs., Wayne State U. Sch. Medicine Alumni Assn. (sec. 1977). Episcopalian (jr. warden 1970). Home: 10100 North Way Ct Allen Park MI 48101 Office: 6742 Park Ave Allen Park MI 48101

GANSEN, ADRIAN PETER, JR., dentist; b. Shawano, Wis., July 11, 1924; s. Adrian Peter and Eva Emma (Cattau) G.; D.D.S., Marquette U., 1951; m. Janalee Gay Fellenz, June 16, 1962; children—Patricia (dec.), Adrian III, Steven. Practice dentistry, Shawano, Wis., 1951—. Served with USAAF, 1943-45. Fellow Internat. Coll. Dentists; mem. Wis. Dental Service (trustee 1963-75, pres. 1965-67), Wis. Dental Soc. (chmn. dental ecns. com. 1971-75), Shawano County Dental Soc. (pres. 1955, 57, 65, 72), Am. Acad. Orthodontics for Gen. Practitioner (dir. 1969-74, v.p. 1974-75, pres. 1976-77), C. of C. (dir. 1968-71), Am. Legion, Pierre Fouchard Acad., ADA, Omicron Kappa Upsilon. Mem. United Ch. Christ. Home: 136 Circle Dr Shawano WI 54166 Office: 312 W Green Bay St Box 7 Shawano WI 54166

GANSER, CARL JOSEPH, educator; b. Watertown, Wis., Jan. 1, 1936; s. Ervin R. and Dorothy (Klitzkie) G.; B.Ed., Wis. State Coll., 1961; M.B.A., Ind. U., 1963; Ph.D., U. Wis., 1969; certificate Zanerian Coll. Penmanship, 1970. Grad. asst. Ind. U., Bloomington, 1961-63; faculty U. Wis., Whitewater, 1963—, prof. bus. edn., 1976—; cons. to secondary schs. for basic bus.-econ. edn.; edn. adviser to Mil. Adminstrv. Mgmt. Soc., 1972—; bus. mgr. Wis. Bus. Edn. Assn. pubs. News and Views, Madison, 1970-74. Mem. Wis. Dept. Agr. consumer adv. com. to trade div., 1970-73; mem. Wis. Dept. Pub. Instrn. Consumer Econ. Edn. Com., 1972—. Served with AUS, 1955-58, Wis. N.G., 1958-61. Mem. Am., Nat., Wis., Milw. Area bus. edn. assns., Phi Delta Kappa, Delta Pi Epsilon, Pi Omega Pi. Author: Lettering Freehand Simplified, 1975, 2d edit., 1978. Office: Coll Business and Econs U Wis Whitewater WI 53190

GANSER, RALPH VINCENT, physician; b. Mishawaka, Ind., Oct. 5, 1923; s. Aloysius Martin and Mary Louise (Bosworth) G.; B.S. cum laude, Purdue U., 1949; M.D., U. Chgo., 1952; m. Lila Mae Smith, June 17, 1951; children—Stephanie, Jacqueline, Elizabeth, David. Intern State U. Ia. Hosps., Iowa City, 1952-53, resident, 1954-56; resident Harper Hosp., Detroit, 1953-54; practice medicine specializing in otolaryngology, South Bend, Ind., 1956—; mem. staff Meml. Hosp., St. Joseph's Hosp., South Bend, Elkhart (Ind.) Gen. Hosp. Mem. South Bend Med. Found., 1971-72. Served with AUS, 1943-46. Fellow clin. otology Baylor U., Houston, 1962-63. Diplomate Am. Bd. Otolaryngology. Fellow A.C.S.; mem. St. Joseph County Med. Soc., Ind. Med. Assn., A.M.A., Pan Am. Assn.

Oto-Rhino-Laryngology and Broncho Esophagology, Ind. Acad. Ophatholmology and Otolaryngology, Am. Acad. Opthalmology and Otolaryngology. Club: South Bend Country. Home: 101 N Conestoga Ln South Bend IN 46617 Office: 810 E Colfax St South Bend IN 46617

GANT, BOBBY LEE, psychologist; b. Dallas, Jan. 2, 1951; s. George and Nellie Jane (Gilstrap) G.; B.J., U. Tex., 1972; M.S., Tex. Christian U., 1974; Ph.D., U. Mo., 1977; m. Deborah Ann Gant, Sept. 18, 1971; children—Christopher George, Hillary Tyler. Research fellow Tex. Christian U., Fort Worth, 1974, U. Mo. Family Study Center, Kansas City, 1974-75; intern U. Kans. and Kans. U. Med. Center, Kansas City, 1976, research asso. U. Kans. Bur. Child Research, 1977; clin. psychologist Lincoln (Nebr.) Child Guidance Center, 1977—; lectr. U. Mo., U. Kans.; adj. asst. prof. U. Nebr., 1977. NIMH research fellow, 1974. Mem. Am., Midwestern psychol. assns., Acad. Psychologists in Martial and Family Therapy, Am. Assn. Marriage and Family Counselors, Am. Personnel and Guidance Assn., Soc. Pediatric Psychology, Psi Chi, Alpha Kappa Delta. Home: 3020 R St Lincoln NE 68503 Office: 215 S Centennial Mall Room 312 Lincoln NE 68508

GANT, GEORGE ARLINGTON LEE, chemist; b. Wilson, N.C., Dec. 5, 1941; s. George William and Georgia Eugenia (Cooke) G.; B.S., N.C. Agrl. and Tech. State U., 1962, M.S., 1965; M.B.A., Central Mich. U., 1973; m. Ruth Jacqueline Jeffers, Dec. 5, 1964 (div.); children—Jon Patrick, Jeannine Patricia. Chemist, Dow Corning Corp., Midland, Mich., 1965-66, research chemist, 1966-72, research group leader, 1972-75, sr. supr. tech. service and devel., 1975-77, sect. mgr. tech. service and devel., 1977—; instr., lectr. in field. Mem. Mich. Multiple Sclerosis Soc., 1974—; v.p., 1977-78; mem. adv. bd. Lake Huron Area Council Boy Scouts Am., 1970-73, Salvation Army, 1973-77. Mem. Am. Chem. Soc., Wire Assn., Sigma Xi, Sigma Iota Epsilon (past pres. Central Mich. U. chpt.), Alpha Phi Alpha. Mem. Ch. of God. Clubs: Kiwanis, KiWassee Midland (pres.). Contbr. articles to profl. jours; patentee in field. Home: 2509 Wood St Midland MI 48640 Office: Dow Corning Corp S Saginaw Midland MI 48640

GANZARAIN, RAMON CAJIAO, psychiatrist, psychoanalyst; b. Iquique, Chile, Apr. 18, 1923; s. Eusebio Gastanaga and Maria Gonzalez (Cajiao) G.; came to U.S., 1968; Science Bachellor, Colegio San Ignacio, Santiago, Chile, 1939; M.D., U. Chile, 1947; postgrad. Chilean Psychoanalytic Inst., Santiago, 1947-50; m. Matilde Soto, Oct. 10, 1953; children—Ramon, Mirentxu, Alejandro. Intern, Hosp. Salvador, Santiago, 1946-47; resident C.F. Menninger Meml. Hosp., Topeka, 1972-73; asso. prof. psychiatry U. Chile, 1955-68, dir. dept. med. edn., 1962-68; dir. Chilean Psychoanalytic Inst., 1967-68; tng. analyst Topeka Inst. Psychoanalysis, 1968—; practice medicine specializing in psychiatry and psychoanalysis, Topeka, 1968—; mem. staff C.F. Menninger Meml. Hosp. Fellow Nat. Tng. Labs. Inst. for Group Devel., Washington, 1966—. WHO fellow med. edn., 1961. Diplomate Am. Bd. Psychiatry and Neurology. Fellow Am. Group Psychotherapy Assn.; mem. AMA, Kans. Med. Soc., Internat., Am. psychoanalytic assns., Internat. Assn. Applied Social Scientists, Chilean Psychoanalytic Soc. (pres. 1958-59), Friends of Arts. Contbr. articles to profl. jours. Research in sensitivity tng., using group psychotherapy for tng. med. students, and group psychotherapy. Office: PO Box 829 Topeka KS 66601

GAPLES, HARRY SERAPHIN, telecommunications co. exec.; b. St. Cloud, Minn., Feb. 11, 1935; s. Harry K. and Kalleope (Zafiraki) G.; B.A., U. Minn., 1957, M.A., 1960; M.B.A., U. Chgo., 1974; m. Rita Jean Klingbeil, June 3, 1961; children—Anthony Alexander, Rebecca Lee. Instr. St. Thomas Coll., St. Paul, 1959-60; pres. Croname, Inc., subsidiary Control Data Corp., Chgo., 1968-70; pres. Melabs, Inc. subsidiary SCM Corp., Palo Alto, Calif., 1970; pres. Kleinschmidt div. SCM Corp., Deerfield, Ill., 1970—. Home: 960 North Ave Deerfield IL 60015 Office: 450 Lake-Cook Rd Deerfield IL 60015

GAPP, PAUL JOHN, journalist; b. Cleve., June 26, 1928; s. Bernard Leonard and Florence (Ganley) G.; B.S., Ohio U., 1950; m. Mary Joan Finch, May 16, 1970. Reporter, editor Columbus (Ohio) Dispatch, 1950-56; reporter, editorial page writer, feature editor Chgo. Daily News, 1956-66; exec. dir. Chgo. chpt. and Ill. council A.I.A., 1967; account exec. Dale O'Brien & Co., Chgo., 1968-69; dir. spl. projects, office of v.p. pub. affairs U. Chgo., 1969-72; architecture critic Chgo. Tribune, 1972—. Mem. communications com. Met. Housing and Planning Council, 1968-70. Co-recipient Ill. Asso. Press award for best news reporting, 1965, 77. Mem. Am. Philatelic Soc., South African Philatelic Fraternity (hon. mem.), S. Allan Taylor Soc. (founder 1963, pres. 1963-76), Architects Club Chgo. (hon.), Pi Kappa Alpha. Contbr. articles to U.S. and fgn. newspapers, mags., profl. publs. Home: 2500 N Lakeview Ave Chicago IL 60614 Office: 435 N Michigan Ave Chicago IL 60611

GARANCIS, JOHN CIPRIJANS, pathologist; b. Latvia, May 14, 1924; s. Dominik and Virginia (Pleis) G.; came to U.S., 1950, naturalized, 1955; M.D., U. Heidelberg (Germany), 1949; m. Rita Belkovskis, May 1, 1965; children—Paul, Peter, Virginia. Intern, St. Mary's Hosp., Passaic, N.J., 1950-51; resident St. Luke's Hosp. and Western Res. U. Cleve., 1951-55; postgrad. trainee in electron microscopy U. Cin., 1958, Armed Forces Inst. Pathology, Washington, 1959-60, RCA, Camden, N.J., 1961; asst. prof. pathology U. Miss., 1957-58, U. Cin., 1959-65; asst. prof. Med. Coll. Wis., 1966-68, asso. prof. 1968-73, prof., 1973—; mem. staff Milwaukee County Hosp., 1965—. Served to maj. U.S. Army, 1955-57. USPHS grantee, 1962-65, 66-68, 74—; Wis. Heart Assn. grantee, 1966-67, 73-74; Am. Cancer Soc. grantee, 1967-68, 68-70, 71-72. Diplomate Am. Bd. Pathology. Mem. Am. Soc. Clin. Pathologists, Coll. Am. Pathologists, Am. Assn. Pathologists, Internat. Acad. Pathology, Wis. Soc. Pathologists, Milw. Acad. Medicine, Electron Microscopy Soc. Am., Am. Soc. Nephrology. Republican. Roman Catholic. Contbr. numerous articles to profl. jours. Home: 1545 Spring Dr Brookfield WI 53005 Office: 8700 W Wisconsin Ave Milwaukee WI 53226

GARBER, JOSEPH MAX, fin. co. exec.; b. Dayton, Ohio, May 22, 1920; s. Harry and Ida (Applebaum) G.; B.S. in Bus. Adminstrn., Ohio State U., 1949; student U. Cin., 1940-42; m. Carole Schneider, May 17, 1942; 1 son, Richard. Communications specialist Air Force Nat. Airport, Washington, 1947-48; mgmt. trainee Credit Bur. of Cin., Inc., 1949-50, dept. mgr., 1950-59, treas., 1959-69, v.p., 1969-76, exec. v.p., 1976-77, pres., 1977—, also dir.; dir. Associated Credit Bureaus, 1967—; instr. in mgmt. Bus. Insts. at Kansas U., 1968-70, Ind. U., 1972-73, U. N.C., 1971. Bd. dirs. Pub. Dental Service Soc., 1973—. Served with USAF, 1942-47; ETO. Recipient Paul Bunyan award, 1975-76, Internat. Leadership award, 1973. Mem. Am. Mgmt. Assn., Am. Soc. Assn. Execs., Ohio Collectors Assn., Associated Credit Burs. Ohio, Cin. C. of C., Air Force Assn., Am. Meteorol. Assn. Clubs: Racquet, Cincinnati, Bankers. Contbr. numerous articles on industry and fin. to profl. publs.; instrumental in developing fed. debt collection legislation. Home: 5657 Kugler Mill Rd Cincinnati OH 45236 Office: 309 Vine St Cincinnati OH 45202

GARBER, KEITH ALAN, physician; b. Anderson, Iowa, Feb. 6,, 1933; s. Chester Christopher and Mable Ione (Chambers) G.; student Drake U., 1950-51; B.A., U. Nebr., 1954; M.D., U. Iowa, 1958; m. Ann Carolyn Risk, July 11, 1959; children—Valerie Jeanne, George Andrew, Jennifer Joan, Matthew Risk. Rotating intern Akron (Ohio) Gen. Hosp., 1958-59; practice of medicine, Corydon, Iowa, 1961—; chief of staff Wayne County Hosp., Corydon, 1968-71. Served with USNR, 1959-61. Named Man of Year, Corydon C. of C., 1970. Diplomate Am. Bd. Family Practice. Mem. Am. Acad. Gen. Practice, Iowa (exec. council 1971-76), Wayne County (pres. 1965-71) med. socs., Iowa Acad. Family Practice (dir. 1972, pres. 1976-77), Corydon C. of C. (dir.). Republican. Presbyn. (ruling elder). Mason. Home: 300 W Marion St Corydon IA 50060 Office: 100 E South St Corydon IA 50060

GARBER, SHELDON, hosp. exec.; b. Mpls., July 21, 1920; s. Mitchell and Esther (Amdur) G.; B.A., U. Minn., 1942; postgrad. U. Chgo., 1952-53; m. Elizabeth Sargent Mason, May 16, 1949; children—Robert Michael, Daniel Mason, Sarah Sargent. Reporter, editor U.P.I., Mpls., Chgo., Springfield, Ill., 1938-58; dir. media services U. Chgo., 1958-64; asso. dir. communication Blue Cross Assn., Chgo., 1964-69; exec. v.p. Charles R. Feldstein & Co., 1969-73; v.p. philanthropy and communication Rush-Presbyn.-St. Luke's Med. Center, Chgo., 1973—, sec. bd. trustees, 1976—. Cons. Commn. on Drug Safety, Great Books Found., Am. Assn. U. Programs in Hosp. Adminstrn.; mem. faculty Inst. on Indsl. and Tech. Communications, Colo. State U., Fort Collins, 1970. Adv. bd. Internat. Inst. Edn.; trustee Citizens Information Service; bd. dirs. Urban Gateways. Served to 1st lt. C.E., AUS, 1942-46, 50-52. Mem. Pub. Relations Soc. Am., Publicity Club Chgo., Am. Soc. Hosp. Pub. Relations Dirs., Am. Pub. Health Assn., Royal Soc. Health, A.A.A.S., Nat. Assn. Sci. Writers, Am. Med. Writers Assn., Sigma Delta Chi. Clubs: Quadrangle, Cliff Dwellers (Chgo.). Home: 1030 Michigan Ave Evanston IL 60202 Office: 1725 W Harrison St Chicago IL 60612

GARCIA, CASIMIRO CRISOSTOMO, JR., obstetrician, gynecologist; b. Manila, Feb. 5, 1940; s. Casimiro Almonte and Nelly Cosme (Crisostomo) G.; came to U.S., 1964, naturalized, 1973; B.S., U. Philippines, 1960, M.D., 1964; m. Theresa Ann Jenks, Sept. 24, 1966; children—Kristine Marie, Anthony Casimir, Rotating intern St Vincent's Hosp. and Med. Center, Toledo, 1964-65; resident in obstetrics and gynecology Michael Reese Hosp. and Med. Center, Chgo., 1966-69; clin. fellow gynecol. oncology U. Miss., Jackson, also clin. instr., 1969-70; individual practice medicine, specializing in obstetrics, gynecology, Belleville, Ill., 1971—. Diplomate Am. Bd. Obstetrics and Gynecology. Fellow Am. Coll. Obstetricians and Gynecologists, A.C.S., Internat. Coll. Surgeons, Am. Soc. Abdominal Surgeons; mem. Am. Fertility Soc., St. Louis Gynecol. Soc., AMA, Ill., St. Clair County med. socs., Am. Assn. Gynecol. Laparoscopists, Am. Assn. Pro-Life Obstetricians and Gynecologists, So. Med. Assn. Roman Catholic. Home: 18 Gerold Ln Belleville IL 62223 Office: 8601 W Main St Belleville IL 62223

GARCIA, VINCENT LOPEZ, JR., mental health bd. adminstr.; b. Phila., Oct. 13, 1944; s. Vincent L. and Mary A. (Riley) G.; grad. Peirce Jr. Coll., 1964; B.A., Cath. U., Washington, 1970; postgrad. Fordham U., 1968, 69; M.A., Loyola U., Chgo., 1972; postgrad. No. Ill. U., DeKalb, 1976—. Lectr. psychology Trinity High Sch., River Forest, Ill., 1971-72, Loyola U., Chgo., 1972-74; mem. clin. staff Family Service and Mental Health Center of Oak Park/River Forest, (Ill.), 1972-74; exec. dir. Community Mental Health Bd. Town of Oak Park, 1974—; adminstr. River Forest Mental Health Com., 1975—. Trainer, Hotline vols., 1975—; bd. mem. Oak Park Housing Center, 1975-76; mem. Gov.'s Comm. for Revision Mental Health Code Ill., 1976-77. Mem. Am. Psychol. Assn., Nat. Assn. Social Workers, Assn. Mental Health Adminstrs., Ill. Assn. Community Mental Health Agys., Twp. Ofcls. Ill., Assn. Community Mental Health Authorities Ill., Twp. Ofcls. Cook County, Psi Chi. Home: 333 S East Ave Oak Park IL 60302 Office: 105 S Oak Park Ave Oak Park IL 60302

GARDIPEE, LOUIS JOSEPH, ret. merchant; b. Oconto, Wis., June 25, 1909; s. Louis and Tillie (Zipper) G.; grad. Wis. Tchrs. Coll., Oshkosh, 1933, m. Inez C. Roix, June 21, 1935; children—Judy, Joan, Gaye, Richard, George, Suzie. Mgr., Gamble Dealer Store, Black River Falls, Wis., 1934-42, owner, operator, 1942-73; ret., 1973; owner, dir. Gamble Store, Sparta, Wis., 1966—; pres., chmn. bd. First Fed. Savs. & Loan Assn.; pres., dir. L & A Corp., Jackson County Fed. Savs. & Loan Assn.; dir. D & S Mfg. Co., Thriftway Lumber Co.; chmn. adv. bd. First Fin. Savs. & Loan Assn. Trustee, St. Joseph's Cath. Ch.; past pres. Little League Baseball; past sec.-treas. Black River Falls Vol. Fire Dept.; county chmn. ARC; bldg. chmn. Home for Aged, Jackson County; past pres. Girl Scouts; past mem. Jackson County Bd. Suprs.; bd. dirs. Black River Falls Meml. Hosp., Rye Bluff Corp.; trustee Pine View Home; mem. exec. bd. Gateway council Boy Scouts Am. Mem. Black River Falls C. of C. (dir., past pres., named Outstanding Citizen Black River Falls Community). Clubs: K.C., Lions (past pres., past dist. gov. Wis.). Home: 1235 Harrison St Black River Falls WI 54615

GARDNER, DON CHARLES, dentist; b. Kempton, Ill., Mar. 22, 1931; s. Charles H. and Ila (Malone) G.; B.S., U. Ill., 1953, D.D.S., 1955. Practice gen. dentistry, Mason City, Ill., 1962—; vol. dentist AID, Yucatan, Mexico, 1972, 73, 74. Pres. bd. dirs. Mason City Pub. Library. Served with AUS, 1955-61. Mem. Nature Conservancy, Springfield Audubon Soc., Springfield YMCA. Home: 116 N Perry St Mason City IL 62664 Office: 110 A W Elm St Mason City IL 62664

GARDNER, HOWARD GARRY, pediatrician; b. Gary, Ind., Oct. 5, 1943; s. Oscar and Anita (Arenson) G.; B.A., Ind. U., 1965; M.D., 1968. Intern, then resident in pediatrics Cardinal Glennon Hosp., St. Louis, 1968-73; practice medicine specializing in pediatrics, Hinsdale, Ill., 1973—; mem. attending staff Hinsdale Sanitarium and Hosp.; courtesy staff Loyola McGaw Hosp., Maywood, Ill.; clin. asst. prof. Loyola U. Med. Sch.; med. adv. bd. Des Plaines Valley Health Center, Parent and Childbirth Edn. Soc., Easter Seal Soc., Villa Park, Ill. Served with USNR, 1969-71; Vietnam. Diplomate Am. Bd. Pediatrics. Mem. Am. Acad. Pediatrics, Chgo. Pediatric Soc. Home: 103 W 65th Lake Dr Westmont IL 60559 Office: 550 N Monroe St Hinsdale IL 60521

GARDNER, JAMES RAYMOND, county ofcl.; b. Indpls., Dec. 24, 1924; s. Raymond and Flora (Eberhardt) G.; B.S., Purdue U., 1950; m. Viola M. Chandler, Sept. 7, 1952; 1 son, John S. Personnel rep., labor relations rep. Western Electric Co., 1952-64; clk.-treas. City of Lawrence, Ind., 1956-60; dep. commr. Ind. Revenue Dept., Indpls., 1964-68; pres. G & H Enterprises, Inc., Indpls., 1957—, Gardner & Guidone, Inc., Indpls., 1965—; adminstr. Gov.'s Wage Stblzn. Bd.; treas., controller Marion County Health and Hosp. Corp., 1970—. Pres. Lawrence Twp. Civic Assn., 1955-56; dist. commr. Boy Scouts Am., 1951-54; pres. Marion County Fair, 1976—. Mem. Ind. Soc. Pub. Accountants, Pi Kappa Alpha Home Assn. (pres. 1964-69, dir. 1960-75), Sagamore of Wabash, Pi Kappa Alpha, Alpha Phi Omega. Methodist (chmn. ofcl. bd.). Mason. Home: 7625 E 51st St Indianapolis IN 46226 Office: 1941 City-County Bldg Indianapolis IN 46204

GARDNER, JAMES SPRAY, ednl. adminstr.; b. Greeley, Colo., June 25, 1922; s. Spray Lafayette and Mildred Faye (Simon) G.; B.A., Grinnell Coll., 1944; B.S., U.S. Naval Acad., 1946; postgrad. U.S. Naval Postgrad. Sch., Armed Forces Staff Coll.; m. Nina Scott, Aug. 30, 1947; children—Victoria Gardner Cavaleri, May T., Allen S. Commd. ensign USN, 1946, advanced through grades to capt., 1970; Russian lang. interpreter/translator, 1951-52; asst. naval attache U.S. Embassy, Moscow, 1953-54; comdg. officer destroyer escort, 1960-61, and destroyer, 1965-66; dir. personnel and indsl. relations Beefland Internat., Inc., Council Bluffs, Iowa, 1970-71; exec. v.p. Met. Omaha Builders, Nebr. State Home Builders Assn., Omaha, 1972-75; dir. devel. Park-Tudor Sch., Indpls., 1976—. Lay reader Episcopal Ch., 1955—; lobbyist homebldg. industry Nebr. Unicameral Legislature, 1972-75. Mem. Am. Legion, Navy League, U.S. Naval Inst., Ret. Officers Assn., U.S. Naval Acad. Alumni Assn. Clubs: Masons, Columbia (Indpls.). Home: 815 E 58th St Indianapolis IN 46220 Office: 7200 N College Ave Indianapolis IN 46240

GARDNER, JOHN CRAWFORD, journalist; b. Emory University, Ga., Apr. 19, 1935; s. James Watts and Mary Jane (McCoy) G.; B.J., Northwestern U., 1956; student Columbia, 1956-57; m. Ann S. Lindsay, Mar. 24, 1956; children—Ellen, Elizabeth, Paul, John, Matthew. Writer A.P., N.Y.C., 1956-57; reporter Charlotte (N.C.) Observer, 1957-59; reporter So. Illinoisan, Carbondale, 1959-61, city editor, 1961-62, mgn. editor, 1962-64, editor, gen. mgr., 1964-76, pub., 1977—; pres. So. Illinoisan, Inc., 1966—; dir. Lindsay-Schaub Newspapers, Inc. Lectr. Medill Sch. Journalism, Northwestern U., Evanston, Ill., 1972—; vis. lectr. So. Ill. U., Carbondale, 1977—. Mem. Am. Soc. Newspaper Editors, So. Ill. Editorial Assn., Ill. A.P. Editors Assn., (pres. 1975), Sigma Delta Chi. Episcopalian (vestryman). Home: 2708 Sunset Dr Carbondale IL 62901

GARDNER, JOHN NEWTON, coffee co. exec.; b. Chgo., June 15, 1920; s. Edward T. and Gertrude (Newton) G.; B.A., U. Ill., 1942; m. Dorothy V. Withey, May 22, 1946 (dec. July 1971); 1 son, John A. With Gardner Bros., Inc., Chgo., 1946—, pres. 1956—; gen. mgr. Raymond Downing Assos., Inc., Arlington Heights, 1972—. Pres., Nat. Home Service Assn., Cleve., 1969—. Served with USNR, 1942-46. Mem. Delta Phi. Presbyterian. Home: 5200 Carriageway Dr Rolling Meadows IL 60008 Office: Suite 7 5050 Newport Dr Rolling Meadows IL 60008

GARDNER, JOHN STEPHEN, dentist; b. Steubenville, Ohio, Nov. 14, 1937; s. Stephen Beckwith and Edna Mae (Green) G.; B.A., W. Va. U., 1959; D.D.S., 1963; m. Ila Rae Cobb, June 12, 1960; children—Deborah Rae, Eric Stephen, Keith Usher. Pvt. practice dentistry, Madison, Wis., 1966—. Clin. instr. Sch. Medicine U. Wis., 1972. Served to capt., Dental Corps, AUS, 1963-66. Fellow Acad. Gen. Dentistry; mem. Am. Dental Assn., Am. Acad. Orthodontics for the Gen. Practitioner, Am. Analgesia Soc., Acad. Gen. Dentistry, Greater Milw., Dane County dental assns., Internat. Assn. Orthodontists, Fedn. Dentaire Internationale, Dane County Analgesia Study Club (pres., 1970-71), Psi Omega. Home: 4714 Deerpath Rd Middleton WI 53562 Office: 1050 Regent St Madison WI 53715

GARDNER, JUNIUS RAYMOND, engring. firm cons.; b. Winnebago, Ill., Mar. 12, 1900; s. Junius Slyter and Ella (Phelps) G.; B.C.E., U., Ill., 1923; m. Norene Mary Moore, Aug. 20, 1927 (dec. May 1972); children—Mary Ann, Margaret June (Mrs. Roy Oth). With Warren & Van Praag Inc., Decatur, Ill., 1937-42, 46—, mng. agt., 1946-70, cons., 1970-76; cons. Bainbridge, Gee, Milanski & Assos., Decatur, 1976—. Served with USNR, 1918-21, to capt. San. Corps, AUS, 1943-45; ETO. Registered profl. engr., Ill. Fellow Am. Soc. Civil Engring. (pres. Central Ill. chpt. 1957-58), mem. Coms. Engrs. Council Ill. (pres. 1959-60), Ill. (past chmn.), Nat. socs. profl. engrs., Am. Water Works Assn., Nat. Water Well Assn. Clubs: Masons, K.T., Shriners. Contbr. profl. jours. Home: 145 N Taylor Ave Decatur IL 62522 Office: 1999 W Grand Ave Decatur IL 62522

GARDNER, LARRY DALE, accountant; b. Kirksville, Mo., Nov. 9, 1936; s. Leonard Dale and Wanda (Widner) G.; B.S. in Bus. Adminstrn. N.E. Mo. State U., 1958; m. Nina Jeannine Hays, Aug. 24, 1958; children—Kevin Michael, David Todd. Sr. accountant Dale P. Craven, C.P.A., Kansas City, Mo., 1958-69, partner, Kirksville, 1969—. Dir., mem. exec. com. Kirkville Savs. & Loan Assn. Committeeman, United Fund, 1962; committeeman Cub Scouts 1000 Hills council Boy Scouts Am., 1971, treas. and committeeman Boy Scouts, 1972—; treas. Kirksville Baseball Assn., 1973—, Little League Football, Kirksville, 1973—, N. Central Mo. Youth Football Conf., 1974; mem. Kirksville High Sch. Booster Club, 1973-74. Mem. Nat., Kansas City (treas. 1963, 64, 65) socs. pub. accountants, Nat., Midwest socs. coop. accountants, Mo. Soc. Tax Practitioners (dir. 1959, 60, 61), Pub. Accountants Assn. Kans., Mid-Mo. Soc. C.P.A.'s. Baptist. Rotarian, Mason (Shriner, Outstanding Merit award 1971). Club: Optimist (Kansas City, Mo.). Home: 2 Fairlane Kirksville MO 63501 Office: 407 S Elson Kirksville MO 63501

GARDNER, MAX LEWIS, psychoanalyst; b. Tupelo, Ark., Dec. 14, 1923; s. Lewis Albert and Byrd (Hutchens) G.; student Little Rock Jr. Coll., 1939-41; B.S., U. Ark., 1943, M.D., 1946; M.S., U. Mich., 1951; grad. Inst. for Psychoanalysis, Chgo., 1956-60; m. Doris June Doughty, July 6, 1947; children—Cheryl Lynn, Max Lewis, Gail Elizabeth. Intern Univ. Hosp., Ann Arbor, Mich., 1946-47, asst. resident, 1947-48, jr. clin. instr. Neuropsychiat. Inst., 1950-51; practice psychiatry and psychoanalysis Detroit and Grosse Pointe, Mich., 1951—; clin. asst. prof. psychiatry Wayne U. Sch. Medicine, Detroit, 1957—. Psychoanalytic cons. Northville (Mich.) State Hosp., Wayne County Gen. Hosp., Eloise, Mich., Dearborn (Mich.) VA Hosp., 1964—; lectr. Mich. Psychoanalytic Inst., Detroit, 1968—; mem. Wayne County Bd. Health, 1974—. Mem. exec. com. Grosse Pointe Citizens for Edn.; pres. Family Life Edn. Council, Grosse Pointe, 1970-71. Bd. dirs. Children's Center Wayne County, 1964—. Served with AUS, 1943-46; to capt. M.C., 1948-50. Fellow Am. Psychiat. Assn. (sec. Mich. dist. br. 1960-62, pres. 1964-65); mem. Am. Psychoanalytic Assn., Mich. Psychoanalytic Soc. (pres. 1972-73), Mich. Assn. Psychoanalysis (v.p. 1968), AMA, Phi Chi. Rotarian (treas. 1968-69, pres. 1971-72). Home: 435 Barclay Rd Grosse Pointe Farms MI 48236 Office: 18080 Mack Ave Grosse Pointe MI 48224

GARDNER, MICHAEL DAVID, veterinarian; b. Gary, Ind., Sept. 12, 1942; s. Harold D. and Carolyne Ann (Sinclair) G.; D.V.M., Purdue U., 1966; student Am. Breeders Service Technicians Sch., 1965; children—Michelle, Monica. Practice vet. medicine, Buda, Ill., 1966-68; asst. to chief veterinarian Ill. Div. Meat Inspection, 1968-70; pres. Shannon Animal Health, Inc. (Ill.), 1970—; owner Shannon Nutritional Service, Stephenson Animal Hosp., Freeport, Ill.; cons. in field. Am. Vet. Med. Assn. research grantee, 1964-65. Mem. Am., Ind., Ill. vet. med. assns., Jr. C. of C., Phi Zeta. Roman Catholic. Elk, Lion. Home: 110 S Chestnut St Shannon IL 61078 Office: 21 E Market St Shannon IL 61078 also Stephenson Animal Hosp Rowe 20W Freeport IL 61032

GARDNER, PAUL JAY, educator; b. Wichita, Kans., May 25, 1929; s. Walter Elias and Ethel Dolly (Rogers) G.; A.B., U. Wichita, 1951, M.S., 1955; postgrad. U. Kans., 1955-56; Ph.D., U. Nebr., 1963; m.

Garnet Ann Wannow, Oct. 28, 1949; children—Walter E., Paul J., Michael C., Richard D. Prof., head dept. biology Vincennes U., 1956-60; asst. prof. biology U. Omaha, 1960-63; instr. anatomy U. Nebr. Coll. Medicine, Omaha, 1964-65, asst. prof., 1965-70, asso. prof., 1970-77, prof., 1977—, vice chmn. dept. anatomy, 1977—. U. Nebr. fellow, 1961-64; U. Nebr. research grantee, 1975—; NIH research grantee, 1976—. Mem. Am. Assn. Anatomists, Electron Microscope Soc. Am., Am. Soc. Cell Biology, Sigma Xi, Phi Sigma. Republican. Mem. Christian Ch. Club: Optimist (lt. gov. 1959-60). Contbr. articles to profl. jours. Home: 3611 S 105th St Omaha NE 68124 Office: 42d and Dewey Sts Omaha NE 68105

GARDNER, ROBERT MEADE, bldg. contractor; b. Portsmouth, Ohio, Aug. 12, 1927; s. David Edward and Mary (Gableman) G.; B.S., Ohio Wesleyan U., 1951; m. Ruth Sieker, Aug. 8, 1952; children—Leslie Paula, Robert Meade, Stephen J., Lorianne. With J.A. Jones Constrn. Co., 1944, Struck Constrn. Co., 1945, Wigton-Abbott Constrn. Co., 1945; with D.E. Gardner Co. (co. name changed to The Gardner Co. 1972), Columbus, Ohio, 1946—, supt., 1951-54, gen. supt., 1954, pres., 1955—. Mem. Bldg. Code Commn., Columbus, 1967-77; dir. Builders Exchange Columbus, 1959-61. Trustee Bricklayers Health, Welfare and Pension, Columbus; mem. alumni bd. Ohio Wesleyan U.; bd. dirs. Greater Columbus Tennis Assn.; bd. dirs. Ohio Valley Tennis Assn., pres., 1977. Served with USNR, 1945-46. Recipient Distinguished award, Phi Gamma Delta, 1965; award appreciation Upper Arlington, Ohio, 1970; named to Ohio Wesleyan U. Athletic Hall Fame, 1970. Mem. Young Pres. Orgn., Asso. Gen. Contractors (pres. Central Ohio chpt. 1966), C. of C., Navy League, Phi Gamma Delta, Metal Builders Assn. Kiwanian. Clubs: Scioto Country, Athletic, Olentangy Indoor Tennis, Racquet (Columbus). Home: 2008 Arlington Ave Columbus OH 43212 Office: 4588 Kenny Rd Columbus OH 43220

GARDNER, ROBERT SCOTT, lawyer; b. Oak Park, Ill., Oct. 8, 1931; s. Theodore and Emma (Kane) G.; A.B., U. Mo., 1953, J.D., 1955; m. Susan Jane Mitchell, June 30, 1956; children—Robert Scott, Anne Collins. Admitted to Mo. bar, 1955, to U.S. Supreme Ct. bar, 1969; practiced in Joplin, 1957-58, Sedalia, 1958—; mem. firm Martin, Gibson & Gardner, 1960-73, 75—; sr. v.p., trust officer Third Nat. Bank, Sedalia, 1973-75. City counsellor Sedalia, 1967-68. Bd. dirs. Sedalia Sch. Dist., 1966-69; counsellor Bd. Pub. Works, Sedalia, 1963-67. Precinct committeeman Republican party, 1959-61. Bd. dirs. Sedalia United Fund; bd. dirs. Bothwell Hosp., pres., 1972—; pres. Sedalia Symphony Soc., 1959-61. Served with USAF, 1955-57. Mem. Am., Mo., Sedalia (pres. 1960, 72) bar assns., Phi Gamma Delta, Phi Delta Phi. Episcopalian. Kiwanian. Home: 2606 Plaza Ave Sedalia MO 65301 Office: 320 S Ohio St Sedalia MO 65301

GARDNER, RUSSELL, JR., psychiatrist, educator; b. Granton, Wis., Mar. 19. 1938; s. Russell Robert and Ella Amelia (Haines) G.; B.S., Wis. State Coll., Stevens Point, 1958; M.D., U. Chgo., 1962; m. Mary Louise Braatz, June, 1960; children—Rebecca Claire, Martha Naomi, Benjamin Glenn. Rotating intern Henry Ford Hosp., Detroit, 1962-63; resident in psychiatry Albert Einstein Coll. Medicine, 1963-66, instr., then asst. prof. psychiatry, 1968-74; clin. research fellow Montefiore Hosp. Med. Center, N.Y.C., 1968-70, research psychiatrist, 1970-74; candidate N.Y. Psychoanalytic Inst., 1968-74, grad., 1974; prof. psychiatry, chmn. div. psychiatry-behavioral sci. U. N.D. Med. Sch., Fargo, 1974—; surgeon grants program specialist, clin. reresearch br. NIMH, USPHS, 1966-68, cons. psychiatry edn. br., 1976—. Undergrad. research fellow USPHS, 1959-60; Interdeptl. research fellow Albert Einstein Coll. medicine, 1964-66; recipient Research Scientist Devel. award Montefiore Hosp. Med. Center, 1970-74. Mem. Am. Aging Assn., AAAS, Am. Assn. Chmns. Dept. Psychiatry, AMA, N.D. Med. Assn., Am. Psychiat. Assn., Am. Psychoanalytic Assn., Am. Psychosomatic Soc., Assn. Dirs. Undergrad. Psychiat. Edn., Assn. Psychophysiol. Study Sleep, N.D. Acad. Sci., Internat. Neuropsychology Soc., Geront. Soc. Co-editor: Psychotropic Drugs and Dysfunctions of the Basic Ganglia. Contbr. to profl. jours. Home: 1301 1st St N Fargo ND 58102 Office: 700 1st Ave S Fargo ND 58102

GARDNER, WILLIAM EARL, univ. adminstr.; b. Hopkins, Minn., Oct. 11, 1928; s. William Henry and Ida (Swenson) G.; B.S., U. Minn., 1950, M.A., 1959, Ph.D., 1961; m. Marcia Frances Anderson, Nov. 4, 1950; children—Mary Gardner Fenwick, Bret, Anne, Eric. Tchr. pub. schs. Balaton, Rockford, New Ulm, Minn., 1950-54; instr. Univ. High Sch., U. Minn., Mpls., 1954-61; prof. edn. U. Minn., 1961—, asso. dean Coll. Edn., 1970-77, dean, 1977—, dir. Minn. Curriculum Lab., 1965-67; vis. prof. U. York (Eng.), 1967-68. Mem. Bd. Edn., St. Louis Park, Minn., 1972—; mem. Tchr. Standards and Certification Commn., 1973—. Mem. Nat. Council Social Studies, Am. Ednl. Research Assn., Assn. Supervision and Curriculum Devel., Luth. Human Relations Assn., Phi Delta Kappa. Lutheran. Author: (with others) Education and Social Crisis, 1967; Social Studies in Secondary Schools, 1970; Selected Case Studies in Am. History, 1971. Home: 2631 Burd Pl St Louis Park MN 55426 Office: 104 Burton Hall U Minn Minneapolis MN 55455

GAREK, MORRIS DANIEL, mgmt. cons.; b. Columbus, Ohio, Jan. 25, 1913; s. Louis and Ida (Bloom) G.; grad. high sch.; m. Rose Lee Cohen, June 17, 1934; children—Lois (Mrs. David Madison), Robert, Diane (Mrs. David Romanoff). With Montgomery Ward, Columbus, 1930-35; with F.& R. Lazarus Co., Columbus, 1935-73, exec. v.p., 1966-73, vice chmn. bd., 1970-73; pres., chief exec. M. Garek & Assos. mgmt. cons., Columbus, 1973—. Trustee Better Bus. Bur. Columbus, 1957-73; bd. dirs. Goodwill Industries, 1956-73, Heritage House for Aged, 1963-73. Mem. A.I.M., Columbus C. of C., Nat. Retail Mchts. Assn. Jewish. Club: Winding Hollow Country. Home: 2721 Bryden Rd Columbus OH 43209 Office: 88 E Broad St Columbus OH 43215

GAREY, URIEL ELBERT, mfg. co. exec.; b. Jacksonville, Ill., June 3, 1926; s. Elmer A. and Alma (Fee) G.; B.B.A., U. Wis., 1949; m. Edith Orr, Nov. 25, 1944; children—Michael, Candy (Mrs. Jerome Meyer), Christopher. With Mirro Aluminum Co., Manitowoc, Wis., 1949—, asst. treas., 1959-70, sec.-treas., 1970—. Bd. dirs. Meml. Hosp., Manitowoc, 1970-73, Manitowoc Taxpayers Assn., 1969-73. Served with USAAF, 1944-45. Mem. Am. Mgmt. Assn., Finacial Execs. Inst., Nat. Investors Relations Inst. Club: Branch River Country. Home: 1007 Orchard Dr Manitowoc WI 54220 Office: 1512 Washington St Manitowoc WI 54220

GARFIELD, ROBERT, educator; b. Bronx, N.Y., Feb. 15, 1943; s. Louis and Ruth (Spigelman) G.; B.A., City U. N.Y., 1964; M.A., Northwestern U., 1967, Ph.D., 1971; m. Mary Denise LeCocq, June 21, 1975. Asst. prof. history DePaul U., 1969—. Recipient Council for Inter-Societal Studies Research award, 1967. Mem. Am. Hist. Assn., African Studies Assn., Nat. Geographic Soc., Haklyut Soc., AAUP. Office: 2323 N Seminary Ave Chicago IL 60614

GARFIELD, SOL LOUIS, psychologist, educator; b. Chgo., Jan. 8, 1918; s. Julius and Rebecca (Friedman) G.; B.S., Northwestern U., 1938, M.A., 1939, Ph.D., 1942; m. Amy Nusbaum, Dec. 25, 1945; children—Ann, Joan, Stanley, David. Teaching fellow Northwestern U., 1941-42; chief clin. psychology VA Hosp., Mendota, Wis., 1946-47; chief clin. psychol. VA Mental Hygiene Clinic, Milw. 1949-51; chief clin. psychol. tng. unit, VA Hosp., Downey, Ill., 1951-57; chief clin. psychology div., asso. prof. Nebr. Psychiat. Inst., U. Nebr. Med. Coll., Omaha, 1957-59, prof., 1959-63; prin. research scientist Mo. Inst. Psychiatry, research prof. Washington U., St. Louis, 1963-64; prof. psychology, dir. clin. psychology program Columbia, 1964-70; prof. psychology, dir. clin. psychology, Washington U., 1970—; dir. tng., cons. clin. psychology VA, State of Wis.; asso. prof. psychology U. Conn., 1947-49. Clin. psychologist U.S. Army, 1943-46; cons. VA, 1958—; cons. com. clin. drug evaluation Psycho-pharmacology Service Center, NIMH, 1960-63, Peace Corps, 1964-70; mem. Suicide Prevention Center Rev. Com.; 1967-68. Diplomate in clin. psychology Am. Bd. Examiners in Profl. Psychology. Fellow A.A.A.S., Am. Psychol. Assn. (mem. program com. clin. div., 1953, 54; mem. council of reps. 1955-58, 60-63, 65-67, 72-75, sec.-treas. div. clin. psychology 1960-63, pres. div. clin. psychology, 1964-65, Distinguished Contbn. to Clin. Psychology award 1976); mem. Ill. (pres. elect 1957), Midwestern Psychol. Assn., A.A.U.P., Sigma Xi. Author: Introductory Clinical Psychology, 1957; Clinical Psychology, 1974. Editor: (with A.E. Bergin) Handbook of Psychotherapy and Behavior Change, 1971. Cons. editor Am. Jour. Mental Deficiency, 1964-66, Jour. Abnormal Psychology, 1964-70, 73—; adv. editor Jour. Cons. and Clin. Psychology, 1964-73, now editor-elect. Contbr. numerous articles and chpts. to profl. publs. Home: 419 Polo Dr Clayton MO 63105 Office: Dept Psychology Washington U St Louis MO

GARFIN, LAURENCE ARLEN, dentist; b. Mason City, Iowa, Dec. 5, 1934; s. William and Doris (Teplin) G.; D.D.S., U. Iowa, 1958; certificate in pedodontics Marquette U., 1962; m. Norma Eleanor Bromberg, Aug. 26, 1956; children—Roberta, Jeffrey. Pvt. practice pedodontics, Mpls., 1962—; cons. Minn. Crippled Childrens Services, 1964-76; clin. asso. prof. U. Minn. Sch. Dentistry, 1962-74. Mem. citizens adv. com. St. Louis Park, 1964-66; v.p. P.T.A., St. Louis Park, 1967. Served with USAF, 1960-62. Recipient certificate of appreciation 2d Air Force, 1960; Outstanding Community Service commendation Hennepin County Bd. Commrs., 1975; certificate of appreciation Suburban Hennepin County Area Vo-Tech Centers, 1976. Mem. Mpls. Dist. Dental Soc. (chmn. dental health edn. com., 1971-73, chmn. welfare com. 1974-76, mem. exec. com. 1976-77), Am. Acad. Pedodontics, Am. Dental Assn., Am. Soc. Dentistry for Children (pres. Minn. unit 1969), Min. Soc. Pedodontists (pres., 1966). Mason (Shriner). Contbr. articles to profl. jours. Office: 5851 Duluth St Golden Valley MN 55422

GARFINKLE, RONALD GEORGE, accountant; b. Chgo., June 14, 1938; s. Philip G. and Pearl (Wasserman) G.; B.S., Washington U., St. Louis, 1960, M.B.A., 1961; m. Jill Komiss, June 26, 1960; children—Robert, Richard, Judith, Lauren. Pvt. practice accounting, Chgo., 1966—. Served with USNR, 1962-65. C.P.A., Ill. Mem. Am. Inst. C.P.A.'s, Ill. Soc. C.P.A.'s. Club: Brairwood Country. Home: 225 Old Post Rd Northbrook IL 60062 Office: 1737 W Howard St Chicago IL 60626

GARGIULO, RICHARD MICHAEL, educator; b. S.I., N.Y., Oct. 1, 1947; s. Michael Joseph and Lilliam Elizabeth (Hoffman) G.; B.A., Hiram Scott Coll., 1968; M.S., U. Wis., 1971, Ph.D., 1974; m. Elizabeth Koth, May 18, 1974; 1 dau., Christina. Tchr., Milw. Pub. Schs., 1968-72; research asst. Wis. Research and Devel. Center for Cognitive Learning, Madison, 1972-74; asso. prof. spl. edn. Bowling Green State U., 1974—. Mem. Am., Midwest psychol. assns., Council for Exceptional Children, Am. Assn. Mental Deficiency, Assn. Children with Learning Disabilities, Phi Delta Kappa. Contbr. articles in field to profl. jours. Home: 542 Monroe Ct Bowling Green OH 43402 Office: Dept Spl Edn Bowling Green State U Bowling Green OH 43403

GARLAND, DONALD MERRILL, physician; b. St. Paul, Oct. 7, 1935; s. Donald Field and Anne Clara (Merrill) G.; B.A., U. Minn., 1957; M.D., U. Rochester (N.Y.), 1961; M.P.H., U. Mich., 1964; m. Diane Marie Seymour, Nov. 4, 1961; children—Lorraine Anne, Tracy Marie, Karen Elizabeth. Intern, Highland Hosp., Rochester, 1961-62, resident, 1962-63; resident U. Mich. Hosp., Ann Arbor, 1963-65; asso. med. dir. Pontiac Motor div. Gen. Motors Corp., Pontiac, Mich., 1965-74; med. dir. Mpls. area Honeywell Inc., Mpls., 1974—. Diplomate Am. Bd. Preventive Medicine. Mem. AMA, Minn. State, Hennepin County med. socs., Am., North Central occupational med. assns. Office: Honeywell Inc Honeywell Plaza Minneapolis MN 55408

GARLAND, WILLIAM, educator; b. Vernon, Tex., May 3, 1931; s. Milburn Tower and Rachael Evelyn (Garland) Lemons; B.A., U. Tex., 1953; Ph.D., U. Minn., 1962; m. Elizabeth Ellen Baldwin, May 31, 1968; children—Meghan Elizabeth, Alexander Warner. Faculty Western Mich. U., Kalamazoo, 1962—, prof. anthropology, 1971—. Served with AUS, 1953-55. USPHS fellow, 1960-62, 63-65; USPHS grantee, 1963, 64, 65; Western Mich. U. fellow, 1966. Fellow Am. Anthropol. Assn., African Studies Assn., Royal Anthropol. Soc.; mem. Internat. African Inst., Central States Anthropol. Soc. Contbr. articles to profl. jours. Home: 5174 S 6th St Kalamazoo MI 49009 Office: Dept Anthropology Western Mich U Kalamazoo MI 49008

GARLINGHOUSE, RICHARD EARL, obstetrician, gynecologist; b. Iola, Kans., Mar. 5, 1910; s. Orestes L. and Pearl Amy (Clark) G.; A.B., U. Kans., 1930; M.D., U. Pa., 1934; m. Miriam E. Thoroman, June 17, 1934; children—Richard E., Gretchen Ann. Intern, St. Louis City Hosp., 1934-35, resident in obstetrics and gynecology, 1935-37; obstetrician, gynecologist Lincoln (Nebr.) Clinic, 1937-42; practice medicine specializing in obstetrics and gynecology, Lincoln; active mem. staff Lincoln Gen. Hosp.; hon. mem. staff Bryan Meml. Hosp., Lincoln; mem. courtesy staff St. Elizabeth's Hosp., Lincoln; mem. cons. staff Lincoln VA Hosp.; sr. cons. staff U. Nebr. Sch. Medicine; dir. Nebr. Blue Cross-Blue Shield. Chmn. med. advisory com. Nebr. Selective Service; past mem. Nebr. Bd. Health. Served to comdr. USN, 1942-46. Fellow A.C.S., Am. Coll. Obstetricians Gynecologists; mem. AMA, Nebr. (past pres.), Lancaster County med. socs., Central Assn. Obstetricians Gynecologists, Am. Legion. Republican. Presbyn. Clubs: Lincoln Country, Red Deer Hunting. Home: 3500 S 28th St Lincoln NE 68502 Office: 5440 South St Suite 1100 Lincoln NE 68506

GARMEZY, NORMAN, psychologist; b. N.Y.C., June 18, 1918; s. Isadore and Laura (Weiss) G.; B.B.A. in Econs., Coll. City N.Y., 1939; M.A. in Guidance and Counseling, Columbia U., 1940; Ph.D. in Clin. Psychology, State U. Iowa, 1950; m. Edith Limick, Aug. 8, 1945; children—Kathy, Andrew, Lawrence. USPHS fellow in clin. psychology Worcester (Mass.) State Hosp., 1947-48; asst. prof. to prof. psychology Duke U., Durham, N.C., 1950-61, dir. undergrad. studies, 1951-56, dir. clin. psychology tng. program, 1957-60; tng. specialist in psychology NIMH, Bethesda, Md., 1956-57; sr. research psychologist Worcester State Hosp.; prof. U. Minn., Mpls., 1961—, dir. Center for Personality Research, 1962-67; clin. prof. psychiatry dept. U. Rochester (N.Y.) Sch. Medicine, 1969—; vis. prof. U. Copenhagen, 1965-66, U. P.R., 1969, Cornell U., 1969-70; vis. colleague Inst. Psychiatry, Maudsley Hosp., London, 1975-76; Lasker lectr. Michael Reese Hosp. & Med. Center, Chgo., 1971; Phillips lectr. Haverford (Pa.) Coll., 1973; mem. com. on research in schizophrenia Scottish Rite, Boston, 1968—; cons. NIMH, past mem. grants coms.; spl. rev. cons. Nat. Inst. Drug Abuse, 1974—; mem. task force on research Presdl. Commn. on Mental Health, 1977-78; dir. Founds. Fund for Research in Psychiatry, 1976—. Served with U.S. Army, 1943-45. Recipient Lifetime Research Career award NIMH, 1962—; co-recipient Stanley Dean award for basic behavioral research in schizophrenia, 1967. Fellow Am. Psychol. Assn. (Distinguished Scientist award sect. 3, 1974, Master lectr. 1975, pres. div. clin. psychology 1977-78), Am. Psychopath. Assn.; mem. AAUP, AAAS, Psychonomic Soc., Soc. Research in Child Devel., Assn. Child Psychology and Psychiatry, Assn. Advancement Psychology (chmn. bd. trustees 1977-78), Sigma Xi. Club: Cosmos (Washington). Contbr. numerous articles in field to books and profl. jours.; author (with G. Kimble and E. Zigler) Principles of General Psychology, 4th edit., 1974; mem. internat. adv. editorial bd. Schizophrenia Bull., 1974—, Psychol. Medicine, 1976—; corr. editor Jour. Child Psychology and Psychiatry, 1975—. Home: 5115 Lake Ridge Rd Edina MN 55436 Office: N419 Elliott Hall U Minn Minneapolis MN 55455

GARNER, JAMES PARENT, lawyer; b. Madison, Wis., Jan. 22, 1923; s. Harrison L. and Mary (Parent) G.; B.A., U. Wis., 1947; LL.B. cum laude, Harvard, 1949; m. Georgia Trebilcock, Oct. 12, 1946; children—Gail E., Ann H., Thomas W., Mary F. Admitted to Wis. bar, 1949, Ohio bar, 1950; asso. firm Baker, Hostetler & Paterson, Cleve., 1949-58, partner, 1959—. Served to capt. AUS, 1943-46. Mem. Selden Soc. Republican. Conglist. Club: Union. Home: 2679 Inverness Rd Shaker Heights OH 44122 Office: Union Commerce Bldg Cleveland OH 44115

GARNESS, ARNE HARTWICK, systems analyst; b. Borup, Minn., Feb. 6, 1928; s. Svale Andrew and Christiana IngaMarie (Jacobson) G.; B.A., Concordia Coll. at Moorhead, Minn., 1955; M.S., U. Wis., 1959; m. Murreen Angeline Jensen, May 13, 1949; children—Carolyn, Rochelle, Marilee. Tchr. math. Elbow Lake (Minn.) High Sch., 1955-57, Appleton (Minn.) High Sch., 1957-58; asso. prof. Concordia Coll. at Moorhead, 1959-77, also dir. acad. computing, 1965-77; systems analyst Am. Crystal Sugar Co., Moorhead, 1977—. Served with AUS, 1946-47. NSF fellow 1958, 60, 61, 64. Home: 1401 6th St S Moorhead MN 56560

GARNETT, DIANNE KAY WAMPLER, univ. adminstr.; b. Vincennes, Ind., Apr. 6, 1948; d. Wendell A. and Doris E. (Richter) Wampler; B.A. in Mathematics, U. Evansville (Ind.), 1969, M.A. in Edn., 1973; m. Robert F. Garnett, Sr., July 24, 1976. System analyst, programmer U. Evansville, 1969-74, dir. project computerized vocat. info. system, 1974-76, coordinator academic computing, 1975—, asst. dir. Computer Center, 1976—, instr. computing sci. and edn., 1974—; bd. dirs. Nat. Computerized Vocational Information System Consortium, Inc., 1972—, pres., 1975-77. Mem. Assn. Ednl. Data Systems, Am., Ind. personnel guidance assns., Assn. Devel. Computer-Based Instrnl. Systems, Chi Omega (corr. sec. Evansville Alumni chpt. 1976-77). Methodist. Home: 1635 Brookside Dr Evansville IN 47714 Office: Univ Evansville PO Box 329 Evansville IN 47702

GARNETT, GORDON MARTIN, physician; b. Adelaide, Australia, Feb. 4, 1923; s. Arthur Campbell and Margaret Elsie (Martin) G.; B.A., U. Wis., 1943, M.D., 1946; m. Jeanne Marie Swan, July 7, 1945; children—Gregory, Barbara, James, Harold, Elizabeth, Virginia, Charles, John. Intern Calif. Luth. Hosp., Los Angeles; resident Univ. Hosps., U. Wis., Madison; practice of medicine specializing in anesthesiology, Madison; 1951—; mem. staffs Methodist Hosp., Madison Gen. Hosp., St. Mary's Hosp., all Madison. Asst. clin. prof. anesthesiology U. Wis., Madison, 1962—. Treas. Founds. for Friendship, Inc., Madison, 1969—. Served to capt. AUS, 1943-49. Diplomate Am. Bd. Anesthesiology. Mem. A.M.A., State Med. Soc. Wis., Am., Wis. (pres. 1959, del. 1960-71) socs. anesthesiologists. Mem. United Ch. of Christ. Home: 5310 Loruth Terrace Madison WI 53711 Office: PO Box 4256 Madison WI 53711

GARNIER, JACK WILLIAM, clergyman; b. Windsor, Ont., Can., Jan. 14, 1926; s. William George and Yolah May (Porter) G.; came to U.S., 1950, naturalized, 1952; grad. Meinziners Found. Coll. Comml. Art and Design, Detroit, 1945; m. Fay Dorothy Burger, June 25, 1949; children—Susan Lee (Mrs. Richard G. Benton), David William. Comml. artist Greenhow & Webster Advt., Windsor, Ont., 1946-50; designer Ford Motor Corp., Dearborn, Mich., 1950-52; account exec. George Walker Indsl. Design, Detroit, 1952-54; mgr. Lincoln-Mercury interior design Ford Motor Corp., Dearborn, 1954-55; mgr. Nash styling studio Am. Motors Corp., Detroit, 1955-56; free-lance artist, advt. art and indsl. design, Detroit, 1956-58; engaged in advt. J.L. Hudson Co., Detroit, 1958-62; ordained to ministry Reorganized Ch. of Jesus Christ of Latter-Day Saints, 1962; audio-visual dir. Reorganized Ch. of Jesus Christ of Latter-day Saints World Hdqrs., Independence, Mo., 1962—. Cons., Restoration Trail Found., Independence, 1973—; guest tchr., lectr. Graceland Coll., Lamoni, Iowa, Central Mo. State U., 1971-75; free-lance cons. Calvin Communications, Kansas City, Mo., 1972—; exhibited in several one-man shows, including Graceland Coll., Lamoni, Heritage Hall, Independence, Mo., Independence Community Art Assn.; asso. cinematographer for movie A Smile or A Tear, filmed in Haiti, 1971. Bd. dirs. Outreach Found., Independence. Mem. Kansas City (Mo.) Art Dirs.' Club. Home: 16304 E 31st St Independence MO 64055 Office: RLDS Auditorium 1001 W Walnut Independence MO 64051

GARREN, MORTON ALAN, electronics co. exec.; b. Mpls., Nov. 3, 1930; s. Nathan Oscar and Jennie (Schusterman) Gurewitz; student U. Minn., 1954-55, Am. Inst. of the Air, 1955-56; m. Marilyn Anita Blinder, June 7, 1953; children—Howard Mark, Steven Richard. Announcer, TV weatherman KMSP TV, Mpls., 1960-66; liquor salesman, tng. supr. Old Peoria, Co., Mpls., 1966-73; sales mgr. Dial Communications, Mpls., 1973-74; exec. v.p., gen. mgr. Audio-Sine, Inc., Mpls., 1974—, also dir. mktg., also corporate dir. Hon. guardian City of Hope. Served with USAF, 1951-54. Mem. Assn. Multi Image, AFTRA. Author, narrator, researcher, producer UFO Fact or Fiction syndicated radio series, 1972-75. Home: 1644 Texas Ave S Minneapolis MN 55426 Office: 3415 48th Ave N Minneapolis MN 55429

GARRETT, LILYAN DARLEEN, retail trade exec.; b. Sharon, Pa., Mar. 14, 1950; d. Maurice Edwin and Mary Jane (Vaughn) Garrett; B.S., Youngstown State U., 1972. Inventory clk., Helen Freed's Sharon, Pa., 1971-73; mgr. soft lines mdse. Zayre Dept. Store, Sharon, Pa., 1973-76, group ops. mgr., Niles, Ohio, 1976—. Mem. Am. Mktg. Assn., Alpha Mu. Democrat. Presbyterian. Home: Route 1 Orchard Rd Mercer PA 16137 Office: 5185 Youngstown Warren Rd Niles OH 44446

GARRETT, PATRICK HENRY, II, elec. engr., educator; b. Charleston, W.Va., June 6, 1939; s. Paul Thomas and Mary Catherine (Donahoe) G.; A. in Sci., Capitol Radio Engring. Inst., Washington, 1961; B.S. in E.E., W.Va. U., 1965; M.S., O. U., 1967, Ph.D., 1970; m. Helen Lenore Robinson, Sept. 17, 1965; 1 son, Patrick Henry III. Elec. engr. Wheeling Pittsburgh Steel Corp., Wheeling, W.Va., 1965-66; sr. research asso. Ohio U., Athens, 1969-71, asst. prof. elec. engring., 1971-73; head dept. elec. engring. tech. U. Cin., 1973—. Cons., Tracor, Inc., Austin, Tex., 1972, Wilcox Electric Co., Kansas

City, Mo., 1972, U.S. Army Missile Command Redstone Arsenal, 1973; mem. curriculum adv. com. Tri-County Tech. Coll., Nelsonville, Ohio, 1972. Chmn., Sphinx Talent Show, 1965. Served with USAF, 1957-61. Registered profl. engr., Ohio. Mem. I.E.E.E., Ohio Soc. Profl. Engrs. (award for creating 1 of 7 engring. wonders of Ohio 1972), Blue Key, Sigma Xi, Tau Beta Pi, Eta Kappa Nu. Contbr. articles to profl. jours. Patentee aircraft guidance. Research on radio navigation methods. Home: 5402 Kingsway W Cincinnati OH 45215

GARRETT, SHIRLEY ANN, guidance counselor; b. Trenton, N.J., Oct. 24, 1937; d. Earl Arthur and Adaline Francis (Krouskoupf) Baesel; B.S., Ohio U., 1972; M.Ed., Xavier U., 1974; children by former marriage—Jeffrey, Charles, Becky Ann. Tchr., St. Nicholas Sch., Zanesville, Ohio, 1969-72; tchr. Zanesville City Schs., 1972-75, counselor jr. high sch., 1975—. Mem. Am., Ohio personnel and guidance assns., Ohio Sch. Counselors Assn., Phi Delta Kappa, Delta Kappa Gamma. Methodist. Club: Order Eastern Star. Home: 3250 Maysville Pike Zanesville OH 43701 Office: 714 Pershing Rd Zanesville OH 43701

GARRINGER, ROBERT STEPHEN, heating and air conditioning contractor; b. Anderson, Ind., Mar. 9, 1954; s. Jimmie and Betty Jean (Wood) G.; B.S., Ball State U., 1976; m. Janet Lene Shull, Aug. 16, 1975; 1 son, James Arrick. Vice pres. Jim's Lake, Inc., Gaston, Ind., 1976—. Mem. Muncie-Delaware County Heating and Air Conditioning Contractors Assn. (v.p. 1977—), Goulds Profl. Dealers Assn., Nat. Small Bus. Assn., Ball State U. Alumni Assn. Research in home heating and refrigeration processes. Home: 103 S Sycamore St Gaston IN 47342 Office: 116 W Elm St Gaston IN 47342

GARRISON, DELMER EUGENE, physician; b. Hudson, Mich., Aug. 1, 1935; s. Delmer George and Ethel Roberta (Townsend) G.; student Ohio Wesleyan U., 1953-56, U. Mich. Sch. Dentistry, 1956-58; M.D., Wayne State U., 1962; m. Ruth Ellen Garn, June 10, 1957; children—Christina Ruth, Elisabeth Ann, Robert Eugene. Intern, Grace Hosp., Detroit, 1962-63; gen. practice of medicine, Saline, Mich., 1963—; mem. staff St. Joseph Hosp., Ann Arbor; mem. staff Community Hosp., chief staff, 1968-70; county med. examiner Washtenaw County, 1963-75; sports physician Saline Area Schs., 1963—; mem. exec. bd. Saline Hosp., 1968—. Health officer City of Saline, 1972—; co-chmn. Health Careers Commn., 1974—. Past bd. dirs. Saline Area United Fund; bd. dirs. Saline Community Hosp. Served with USNR, 1966-67, Mem. A.M.A., Mich., Washtenaw County med. socs., Am. Acad. Family Physicians, Delta Tau Delta. Methodist (mem. adminstrv. bd. 1967-73, trustee). Home: 300 E Henry St Saline MI 48176 Office: 205 S Davenport St Saline MI 48176

GARRISON, RAY HARLAN, lawyer; b. Allen County, Ky., Aug. 6, 1922; s. Emmett Washington and Ollie Irene (Keen) G.; B.A., Western Ky. U., 1942; M.A. (fellow), U. Ky., 1944; postgrad. Northwestern U., 1945-46; J.D., U. Chgo., 1949; m. Eunice Anne Bolz, Oct. 7, 1961. Tax accountant Ky. Dept. Revenue, Frankfort, 1943, supr. escheats, 1944-45, fiscal analyst, 1945; research asst. Bur. Bus. Research, U. Ky., Lexington, 1943-44; admitted to Ky. bar, 1951, Ill. bar, 1962, Tax Ct. U.S., 1962, U.S. Customs Ct., 1968, U.S. Ct. Appeals, 1962; research asso. Fedn. Tax Adminstrs., Chgo., 1946-52; spl. atty. U.S. Treasury Dept., St. Louis, 1952-57, spl. asst., 1957-59, asst. regional counsel, 1959-61; sr. atty. Internat. Harvester Co., Chgo., 1961—. Lectr. Loyola U., Chgo., 1949-51. Del. Ill. Constnl. Conv., 1969-70. Mem. Ill. Racing Bd., 1975—; mem. adv. bd. Ill. Thoroughbred Breeders Fund, 1976—. Mem. N.A.M. (mem. taxation com. 1969—), Ill. Mfrs. Assn. (mem. taxation com. 1969—), Motor Vehicle Mfrs. Assn. (mem. taxation com. 1963—), Nat. Tax Assn., Am., Ill., Ky., Chgo. bar assns., Chgo. Tax Club, Beta Gamma Sigma, Ill. Hist. Soc., South Suburban Geneal. and Hist. Soc. (dir. 1973-77), Ky. Hist. Soc., Mecklenburg Hist. Assn. Contbr. articles to various publs. Home: 2625-F Hawthorne Ln Flossmoor IL 60422 Office: 401 N Michigan Ave Chicago IL 60611

GARRY, GERALD FRANCIS, clergyman, coll. ofcl.; b. Schenectady, Jan. 1, 1928; s. William Joseph and Margaret Theresa (Murphy) G.; B.A., Divine Word Seminary, 1955; S.T.L., Pontifical Gregorian U., Rome, Italy, 1961; M.A., Cath. U. Am., 1970. Ordained priest Roman Catholic Ch., 1959; asst. rector Divine Word Sem., Conesus, N.Y., 1963-65; rector Divine Word Coll., Epworth, Iowa, 1970-75, chmn. dept., 1965-68, 70-73. Mem. A.A.A.S., Am. Acad. Polit. and Social Sci., Am. Sociol. Assn., Am. Anthropol. Assn., Rural Sociol. Assn., Am. Soc. for Study of Religion. Address: Divine Word Coll Epworth IA 52045

GARSON, WILLIAM, banker, writer; b. Hammond, Ind., May 1, 1917; s. John Soterus and Helen Glenn (McKennan) G.; B.A., Milton Coll., 1939; m. Florence Rebecca Penstone, Sept. 21, 1974; children (by previous marriage)—Geneva (Mrs. Robert LaMay), Gary William. Mng. editor Rockford (Ill.) Register-Republic, 1952-55; pub. relations dir. Sundstrand Corp., Rockford, 1956-65; mktg. officer City Nat. Bank & Trust Co Rockford, 1966—; pub. relations cons. Imagination Plus, Rockford 1955-66; co-author Polit. Primer, 1960—. Bd. dirs. Tb Assn., Heart Assn., A.R.C., 1952-54; Recipient George Washington Honor medal Freedoms Found., 1966. Mem. Am. Inter-Profl. Inst., Rockford C. of C. (Community Service award 1952), Am. Inst. Banking, Bank Mktg. Assn., Internat. Assn. Bus. Communicators. Conglist. Author: Daddy Wore An Apron, 1974; Brother Earth, 1975; co-author: We The People..., 1976. Home: 3516 Meadow Ln Rockford IL 61107 Office: Box 3126 Rockford IL 61106

GARTEN, SAMUEL, pharmacologist, univ. adminstr.; b. Buffalo, Mar. 2, 1944; s. Charles and Clara (Snitzer) G.; B.S., Morehead Coll., 1965; M.S., U. Mo., 1969, Ph.D., 1971; m. Harriet Joy Singer, Oct. 17, 1968; children—Amy Louise, Alison Elke Jane. Research asso. Nebr. Psychiat. Inst., Omaha, 1970-71; postdoctoral fellow med. computer center and info. sci. group U. Mo., Columbia, 1971-72, asst. prof. pharmacology Sch. Medicine, 1972-77, dir. computer based drug info. system, 1972-77; dir. data processing dept. pharmacology Baxter-Travenol Labs., Chgo., 1977—; dir. Tng. Program for Severely Handicapped in Computer Programming; dir. State Cancer Info. Dial Access Program; adv. mem. Mo. Area II Health System Agy. Bd. dirs. Boone County (Mo.) unit Am. Cancer Soc. Served with U.S. Army, 1959-61. Gov. of Mo. grantee, 1975-76. Mem. Assn. Advancement Computer Machinery, AAAS, Assn. Devel. Computer-Based Instructional Systems, Sigma Xi. Republican. Jewish. Home: 345 Fairview Ave Deerfield IL 60015 Office: Baxter-Travenol Labs 6301 Lincoln Ave Morton Grove IL 60053

GARTON, ROBERT DEAN, state senator; b. Chariton, Iowa, Aug. 18, 1933; s. Jesse Glenn and Ruth Irene (Wright) G.; B.S., Iowa State U., 1955; M.S., Cornell U., 1959; m. Barbara Hicks, June 17, 1955; children—Bradford, Brenda. Personnel rep. Cummins Engine Co., Columbus, Ind., 1959-61; owner Garton Assos., exec. search, Columbus, 1961—, Careers Center Employment Agy., 1973—; mem. Ind. Senate, 1970—, minority caucus chmn., 1976—. Pres. Ind. Pub. Health Found., 1976—; chmn. Ind. Civil Rights Commn., 1969-70; mem. exec. com. Nat. Fedn. Young Republicans, 1966; mem. adv. bd. Ind. Assn. Indsl. Nurses, 1972—; bd. dirs. Rural Water System, Columbus, 1969—, Ind. Outdoor Edn., Inc.; hon. bd. mem. Five-County Big Bros. and Sisters, Inc.; mem. Ind. Community Edn. Council, 1976—. Served with USMCR, 1955-57. Named Hon. Citizen Iowa, 1962; winner internat. speech contest Toastmasters, 1962; recipient Distinguished Service award Jr. C. of C. Columbus, 1968, One of 5 Outstanding Young Men in Ind., 1968. Mem. Beta Theta Pi. Rotarian. Home: RD 9 Wood Lake Columbus IN 47201 Office: 606 Franklin St Columbus IN 47201

GARVEN, DAVID HAROLD, mktg. cons.; b. Mpls.; Oct. 19, 1944; s. Harold Edward and Thelma (Eddy) G.; B.S. in Bus. Edn., Mankato State U., 1969; m. Gayle P. Arnzen, Sept. 25, 1971; children—Jennifer Lynn, Jeffrey David. Sales rep. Scott Paper Co., Mpls., 1969-71; mktg. mgr. Disston, Inc., Pitts., 1971-74; owner, chief exec. officer, pres. Project Mktg. Inc., Mpls., 1974—, Garven Assos. Inc., Mpls., 1976—. Named Dist. Salesman of the Yr., Scott Paper Co., 1970. Mem. Small Bus. Assn., Am. Mgmt. Assn., Am. Mktg. Assn. Presbyterian. Contbr. articles in field to trade jours. Home: 8033 Pennsylvania Rd Minneapolis MN 55438 Office: 7300 France Ave S Edina MN 55435

GARVIN, CHARLES DAVID, social worker, educator; b. Chgo., June 17, 1929; s. Hyman and Etta (Raphaelson) G.; student Wright Jr. Coll., 1946-48; A.M., U. Chgo., 1951, Ph.D., 1968; m. Janet Louise Tuft, Jan. 27, 1957; children—David, Amy, Anthony. Social worker Henry Booth House, Chgo., 1954-56, Jewish Community Centers, Chgo., 1956-63; program dir. U. Chgo., 1964-65; mem. faculty U. Mich., Ann Arbor, 1965—, asso. prof. social work, 1969-72, prof., 1972—. Mem. Model Cities Policy Bd., Ann Arbor, 1970-73. Served with AUS, 1952-54. HEW fellow, Pakistan, 1975, 76. Mem. Nat. Assn. Social Workers, Council Social Work Edn., AAUP, Am. Sociol. Assn., Am. Orthopsychiat. Assn., British Assn. Social Workers. Jewish. Home: 2925 Park Ridge Dr Ann Arbor MI 48103 Office: 1065 Frieze Bldg Univ Mich Ann Arbor MI 48109

GARVIN, DANIAL FRANCIS, ins. agy. exec.; b. Kearney, Nebr., Apr. 26, 1928; s. Milton Francis and Naomi Elizabeth (Cogswell) G.; student Morton Jr. Coll., 1947-48, Northwestern U., 1949-50; m. Carma Lee Johnson, Nov. 29, 1952; children—Danial Francis, Edward Patrick. Factory rep. Armstrong Paints, Chgo., 1957-65; sales mgr. MFA Ins. Co., Columbia, Mo., 1965-72; owner Dan Garvin Ins. Agy., St. Joseph, Mo., 1972—. Bus. sales cons.; guest lectr. area colls., high schs. Buchanan County (Mo.) Republican chmn., 1970-72, committeeman, 1972—. Served with USAF, 1950-54. Mem. Life Underwriters Assn., Christian Businessmen (v.p. 1973), Sertoma Club (sargent at arms 1969). Baptist. (Sunday sch. dir. 1974). Mason (Shriner). Home: 1906 Safari Dr St Joseph MO 64506 Office: 5101 King Hill Ave St Joseph MO 64504

GARZA-GONZALEZ, MARIO, radiologist; b. Piedras Negras, Mex., July 29, 1929; s. Daniel and Aurelia (Gonzalez) G.; M.D., Nuevo Leon U., Monterrey, Mex., 1951; m. Margaret Hillegass, Sept. 10, 1954; children—Mario, Rafael, Reon. Intern, DePaul Hosp., Norfolk, Va., 1953-54; resident in radiology DePaul Hosp., St. Louis, 1955-58; chief radiologist Johnson County Meml. Hosp., Warrensburg, Mo., 1958—; staff physician Whiteman (Mo.) AFB Hosp., Carroll County Meml. Hosp., Carrollton, Mo., Windsor (Mo.) City Hosp. Mem. AMA, Mo. Med. Assn., Am. Coll. Radiology., Am. Bd. Radiology. Club: Elks. Home: 508 Jefferson St Warrensburg MO 64093 Office: Box 317 Warrensburg MO 64093

GARZIA, RICARDO FRANCISCO, computer co. exec.; b. Buenos Aires, Argentina, Sept. 19, 1926; s. Mario Francisco and Zulema Maria (Alvarez) G.; came to U.S., 1967, naturalized, 1975; B.S. in Elec. Engring., Otto Krause Sch., 1945; M.S. in Elec. Engring., La Plata U., 1950; m. Julia Elisa Berrud, Oct. 2, 1948; children—Liliana Julia, Silvia Cristina, Mario Ricardo, Fernando Marcelo. Prof. Nat. Indsl. Sch., Buenos Aires, 1951-53; prof., Nat. Tech. U., Buenos Aires, 1954-67, chmn. elec. dept., 1964-67, dir. computer center, 1964-67; prin. engr. Gen. Dynamics/Electronics, Rochester, N.Y., 1967-69; computer scientist Computer Scis. Corp., Huntsville, Ala., 1969-71; mgr. tech. applications The Babcock & Wilcox Co., Barberton, Ohio, 1971—. Consejo Nacional de Investigaciones Cientificas y Tecnicas grantee Mass. Inst. Tech., 1960-61. Mem. IEEE, Instrument Soc. Am., Ops. Research Soc. Am. Author: Transformada Z, 1966; Introducion a la Computation Digital, 1968; contbg. author: Large-Scale Dynamical Systems, 1976, Rational Fault Analysis, 1977. Home: 509 Vosello Ave Akron OH 44313 Office: 20 S Van Buren St Barberton OH 44203

GASIORKIEWICZ, EUGENE CONSTANTINE, plant pathologist, educator; b. Grabiszew, Poland, Mar. 11, 1920; s. Anthony and Amalja Maryanna Drynkowska G.; came to U.S., 1926, naturalized, 1933; A.B., Marquette U., 1947, M.S., 1948; Ph.D., U. Wis., 1951; m. Loretta A. Kasprzak, Aug. 10, 1946; children—Susan Gene (Mrs. John Zippel), Eugene Anthony. Research plant pathologist U. Mass. Agrl. Experiment Sta., Waltham, 1952-61; horticulturist, plant pathologist S.C. Johnson & Son Inc., Racine, Wis., 1961-66; asst. prof. U. Wis.-Center, Racine, 1966-67; dir. research and devel. Can-Am Plant Co., Burlington, Ont., Can., 1967-68; prof. life scis. U. Wis.-Parkside, Kenosha, 1968—, chmn. div. scis., 1970-73; cons. in field. Dist. commr. Boy Scouts Am., 1961-66. Served with AUS, 1942-46. Mem. Racine Agrl. Soc. (dir. 1962-66), Am. Carnation Soc. (research encouragement award 1954), New Eng. Carnation Growers Assn., Am. Phytopathol. Soc., Am. Inst. Biol. Sci., AAAS. Contbr. articles to profl. publs. Home: 236 Old Pine Circle Racine WI 53402 Office: Wood Rd Kenosha WI 53140

GASKELL, CHARLES THOMAS, bishop; b. St. Paul, Oct. 23, 1919; s. Chester Welles and Gertrude Pauline (Michaud) G.; B.A., U. Minn., 1940; B.D., Seabury-Western Theol. Sem., 1944, D.D. (hon.), 1967; m. Mabel Harriet Armitage, June 1, 1944; 3 children. Ordained priest Episcopal Ch., 1944; priest-in-charge Holy Trinity Ch., International Falls, Minn. and St. Peter Ch., Warroad, Minn., 1944-48; curate St. Matthew Ch., Evanston, Ill., 1948-49; rector Trinity Ch., Rock Island, Ill., 1949-57, St. Mark Ch., Milw., 1958-66; St. Luke Ch., Evanston, 1966-70; dean St. Luke Cathedral, Orlando, Fla., 1971-74; bishop of Milw., 1974—. Office: 804 E Juneau Ave Milwaukee WI 53202*

GASKILL, REX WILLIAM, ednl. adminstr.; b. Hutchinson, Kans., Dec. 21, 1942; s. Floyd Curtis and Nona Faye (Clemons) G.; A.A., Hutchinson Jr. Coll., 1962; B.A., Ft. Hays (Kans.) State Coll., 1964; M.A., U. Nebr., 1969; postgrad. U. Minn., 1970-74; postgrad. Oxford (Eng.) U., 1976. Tchr., Omaha Pub. Schs., 1964-69, chmn. English dept. Burke High Sch., 1966-69; instr. speech Midland Luth. Coll., Fremont, Nebr., 1969-70, Ind. State U., Terre Haute, 1970-72, Wagner Coll., S.I., N.Y., 1972-73; dir. speech activities Normandale Community Coll., Bloomington, Minn., 1973—, discipline coordinator, 1973—. Mem. com. St. Mark's Fine Arts Festival, 1977; dir. ushers Cathedral Ch. of St. Mark, Mpls., 1976—. Mem. Am. Hist. Assn., Speech Communication Assn., Speech Assn. Minn. (gov. 1977—), English Speaking Union (dir. 1976—). Democrat. Episcopalian. Home: 2515 Emerson Ave S Minneapolis MN 55405 Office: 97000 France Ave South Bloomington MN 55431

GASKINS, WILLIAM GEORGE, supt. schs.; b. Morgansville, W.Va., Feb. 8, 1930; s. Kenneth Willard and Elsie Alice (Hurst) G.; student Potomac State Coll., 1949-51; B.A., Glenville State Coll., 1957; M.Ed., U. S.D., 1961; m. Shirley Ann Horlocker, Sept. 19, 1953; children—Sherree Lee, William James. Tchr. high sch., Centerville, S.D., 1957-59, teaching prin., 1959-64; supt. schs. Custer (S.D.) Ind. Sch. Dist. 1, 1964—. Scoutmaster, Sioux council Boy Scouts Am., 1961-62; chmn. emergency com. Custer County Salvation Army, 1970—. Mem. Custer City Planning Commn., 1969-71. Served with USAF, 1951-55. Mem. S.D. Edn. Assn. Conglist. (trustee). Home: Rural Route 1 Custer SD 57730 Office: 527 Montgomery St Custer SD 57730

GASPER, JOHN EDWARD, sch. adminstr.; b. Wellington, Kans., Oct. 17, 1929; s. Linus N. and Katherine (Kay) G.; B.S., Kans. State U., 1952; M.Ed., Wichita State U., 1956; Ed.D., U. Wyo., 1967; m. Margaret Helen Linn, Dec. 26, 1950; children—Steven B., Kerry M., John K. Sch. tchr., Sedgwick County, Kans., 1952-53; prin., supt. Sch. Dist. 120, Sedgwick County, 1953-59; asst. prin. S.E. High Sch., Wichita, 1959-67; prin. Mayberry Jr. High, Wichita, 1967-68, North High Sch., Wichita, 1968-77, N.W. High Sch., Wichita, 1977—; vis. lectr. U. Wyo., 1967, Wichita State U., 1968, 72, 74, 75. Served with AUS, 1947-48. Mem. Sedgwick County Tchrs. Assn. (pres. 1958), Nat., Kans. assns. secondary prins., Phi Kappa Tau, Phi Delta Kappa, Kappa Delta Pi. Home: 9300 Briarwood Wichita KS 67212 Office: 1220 N Tyler Rd Wichita KS 67212

GASSMAN, MAX PAUL, mech. engr.; b. Bonesteel, S.D., Sept. 1, 1930; s. Walter Ernest and Elizabeth (Schibli) G.; B.S. in Mech. Engring., S.D. Sch. Mines and Tech., 1956; M. Mech. Engring., Iowa State U., 1963; m. Gail Elizabeth Evans, Aug. 5, 1955; children—Paul Michael, Philip Walter. With John Deere Co., Waterloo, Iowa, 1956—, sr. design engr., 1965-68, sr. design analyst, 1968—; sec., dir. John C. Rider & Assos., Inc. Cubmaster, Winnebago Council Boy Scouts Am., 1967-70, scoutmaster, 1970-74. Pres. bd. dirs. Splash Inc., 1970. Served with USAF, 1948-52. Registered profl. engr., Iowa. Mem. Nat. Soc. Profl. Engrs. (chmn. Iowa sect. profl. engrs. in industry group), Iowa Engring. Soc. (pres. bd. dirs. N.E. Iowa 1971-72, Anson Marston award 1972), ASME (dir. 1971-72), Waterloo Tech. Soc. (chmn. tech. student activity com. 1970-71), Am. Soc. Agrl. Engrs. (chmn. T-5 computer com. 1975-76), Soc. Automotive Engrs. Club: John Deere Supervisors (Waterloo). Patentee in field. Home: 551 Alpine St Waterloo IA 50702 Office: Product Engring Center Waterloo IA 50704

GASSMANN, ZEAN, banker; b. Olney, Ill., Feb. 17, 1896; s. Henry and Carrie (Goudy) G.; student U. Ill., 1913-14, 16-17, Wharton Sch. U. Pa., 1914-16, John Marshall Law Sch., 1941-42; m. Gertrude Weber, June 25, 1919; children—Mary (Mrs. Ross I. Stonecipher), Katherine (Mrs. W.K. Schaub), Elizabeth (Mrs. C.R. Vaughn), Barbara (Mrs. V.E. Harris), George W., Henry, Martha (Mrs. John F. Kraeger), Gertrude (Mrs. Richard W. Reynolds), Frank C. Pres. Gassman Ice Cream Co., Olney and Flora, Ill., 1919-27; mgr. Midwest Dairy Products Co., 1927-31; pres. Zean Gassmann, Inc., Olney, 1931—; dir. Olney Trust and Banking Co., 1934—, v.p., 1960-67, chmn. bd., 1967—. Supt. food and dairies Ill. Dept. Agr., 1941-49; chmn. Olney Zoning Commn., 1950-58, Central Com. 54th Dist., Republican Com., 1952—. Served to ensign USNR, 1917-19. Mem. Ill. (pres. 1926-28), Nat. (pres. 1926-28) assns. ice cream mfrs., Assn. Food and Drug Ofcls. of U.S. (pres. 1948-49), Am. Legion, V.F.W., Chi Psi, Sigma Delta Chi. Presbyn. Mason, Elk. Home: 409 N Boone St Olney IL 62450 Office: 313 Whittle Ave Olney IL 62450

GASTON, ALONZO DUBOIS, psychologist, educator; b. Gilbertsville, Ky., June 27, 1940; s. Thomas Leon and Minnie (Auto) G.; B.S., Ky. State Coll., 1958; M.Ed., Xavier U., 1968; Ed.D., U. Cin., 1974; m. Marilym LuAnn Hughes, Dec. 2, 1967; children—Amy Marie, Damon Alan. Dir. Upward Bound program Xavier U., also U. Cin., 1970-72; dir. Neighborhood Youth Corps, Cin., 1974-75; asst. to dean U. Cin. Eve. Coll., 1975-76; asst. prof. dept. community health Howard U. Coll. Medicine, Washington, 1976—; cons. in field. NSF fellow, 1965. Mem. Am. Soc. Engring. Edn., AAUP, Am. Personnel and Guidance Assn., Am. Assn. Black Psychologists, Alpha Sigma Kappa, Phi Delta Kappa, Alpha Sigma Lambda. Address: 1314 Waycross Rd Cincinnati OH 45240

GASTON, HUGH PHILIP, marriage counselor, educator; b. St. Paul, Sept. 12, 1910; s. Hugh Philander and Gertrude (Heine) G.; B.A., U. Mich., 1937, M.A., 1941; postgrad. summers Northwestern U., 1938, Yale, 1959; m. Charlotte E. Clarke, Oct. 1, 1945 (dec. 1960); children—Gertrude E. Gaston Crippen, George Hugh. Tchr., counselor U. Mich., Ann Arbor, 1936, W. K. Kellogg Found., Battle Creek, Mich., 1937-41; tchr. spl. edn., Detroit, 1941; instr. airplane wing constrn. Briggs Mfrs. Co., Detroit, 1942; psychologist VA, Ann Arbor, Mich., 1946-51; sr. staff asso. Sci. Research Asso., Chgo., 1951-55; marriage counselor Circuit Ct., Ann Arbor, 1955-60; marriage counselor, Ann Arbor, 1960—; lectr., Eastern Mich. U., Upsilanti, 1964-67, asst. prof., 1967—. Acting postmaster, Ann Arbor, 1960-61. Chmn. com. on marriage Presbytery So. Mich., 1963-68; mem. exec. com., legis. agt., chmn. legis. com. Mich. Council Family Relations, 1972-74. Bd. dirs. Internat. Parents Without Partners, 1968-69, pres. Mich. chpt., 1961. Served with U.S. Army, 1943-46. Decorated Purple Heart, Bronze Star; Medallion of Nice (France); named Citizen of Year, Am. Legion, 1968. Mem. Am. Assn. Marriage Counselors, Am. Personnel and Guidance Assn., Nat. Vocational and Guidance Assn., D.A.V. (past comdr.), Am. Soc. Tng. Dirs., S.A.R. (past pres.), U. Mich. Band Alumni Assn. (pres. 1957-58), Mil. Order Purple Heart (nat. exec. com. 1977-78), Phi Delta Kappa (past pres.). Rotarian. Address: 1404 Cambridge Rd Ann Arbor MI 48104

GASTON, THOMAS LEON, JR., manpower devel. agy. exec.; b. Sheffield, Ala., May 6, 1934; s. Thomas Leon and Minnie Alto (Watson) G.; B.S. in Secondary Edn., Ala. A. and M. U., 1961; M.Ed. in Sch. Adminstrn., Xavier U., Cin., 1967; postgrad. in Community Planning U. Cin., 1968; m. Norma Jean Goodwin, May 29, 1960; children—Sharon, Jocelyn. Instr. in aerospace tech. Ft. Gordon, Ga., 1957; instr. Marshall Space Flight Center, Huntsville, Ala., 1958; tchr. Cin. Pub. Schs., 1961-67; br. mgr. Opportunities Industrialization Center, Cin., 1967-70, exec. dir., Dayton, Ohio, 1970-74; exec. dir. Miami Valley Manpower Consortium, Dayton, 1974—; pres. Techni-Write, Inc. Mem. Dayton Mayor's Council on Econ. Devel.; mem. nat. adv. bd. Nat. Legal Services Fund. Pres. Belle Haven Parent-Tchr. Orgn., Dayton, 1976-78; mem. adminstrv. com. Dayton Sch. Bd., 1975—. Served as cpl. U.S. Army, 1956-58. Recipient certificate of appreciation City of Dayton, 1975, Ta-Wa-Si Club of Dayton, 1976. Mem. Adminstrv. Mgmt. Soc., Nat. Assn. County Manpower Ofcls. (pres. Region V), Nat. Bus. League (v.p. Dayton chpt.), Alpha Phi Alpha. Baptist. Home: 2604 Greenbrier Dr Dayton OH 45406 Office: 40 S Main St Suite 740 Dayton OH 45402

GATES, ARTHUR ROLAND, II, plastics and chem. co. exec.; b. Akron, Ohio, Mar. 30, 1941; s. Arthur Roland and Rita (Murphy) G.; B.S., U. Calif. at Los Angeles, 1964; M.B.A., Kent State U., 1968; grad. Tuck Exec. Program, Dartmouth Coll., 1976; m. Elizabeth Karlene Trenchard, Apr. 24, 1971; children—Amanda, Margaret. Accountant firm Schultz, Krahe, Martin & Long, Cleve., 1965-66; mgr. data processing Burton Rubber Co. (Ohio), 1966-67, U.S. Stoneware Co. Inc., Akron, 1967-68; controller, dir. adminstrn. chem. process products, plastics, synthetics div. Norton Co., Tallmadge, Ohio, 1968—. Bd. dirs., pres. Vis. Nurse Service, Summit County, Ohio. C.P.A., Ohio. Mem. Ohio Soc. C.P.A.'s, Fin. Execs. Inst., Beta

Alpha Psi. Club: Rotary. Home: 3083 Orchard Rd Silver Lake OH 44224 Office: 12 East Ave Tallmadge OH 44278

GATES, CLIFTON WADELL, banker; b. Pine Bluff, Ark., Aug. 13, 1923; s. Lance and Mattie (Berry) G.; student Stowe Tchrs. Coll., 1942-43, Washington U., 1962-64; m. Harriet Cecile Craddock, June 14, 1947; children—Mark Darrell, Lisa Babbette. Pres., C. W. Gates Realty Co., St. Louis, 1959—, Gateway Nat. Bank St. Louis, 1964—; v.p. Mid-Central Mortgage Co., 1963—. Treas., Urban League, St. Louis, 1964—, now pres.; pres. bd. Cath. Charities; exec. com. United Fund; bd. dirs. Boy Scouts Am., Jr. Achievement, St. Louis Municipal Opera; trustee YWCA. Mem. Gov.'s Crime Commn.; v.p. Bd. Police Commrs. Bd. dirs. Ferrier Harris Home for Aged. Served with AUS, 1943-45. Mem. United Mortgage Bankers Am. (dir.), Mo. C. of C. (bd. dirs.), Nat. Soc. Real Estate Appraisers, N.A.A.C.P. (2d v.p. 1965—, dir.), Frontiers. Roman Catholic. Home: 5249 Lindell Blvd St Louis MO 63108 Office: 2921 Union Blvd St Louis MO 63115

GATES, CRAWFORD MARION, condr., composer; b. San Francisco, Dec. 29, 1921; s. Gilbert Marion and Leila (Adair) G.; B.A., San Jose State Coll., 1944; M.A., Brigham Young U., 1948; Ph.D., Eastman Sch. Music, 1954; m. Georgia Lauper, Dec. 19, 1952; children—Stephen Randall, Kathryn, Elizabeth, David Wendell. Orchestrator radio sta. KSL, Salt Lake City, 1946-47; grad. asst. music theory Eastman Sch. Music, 1948-50; mem. faculty Brigham Young U., 1950-66, prof. music, chmn. dept., 1960-66; artist-in-residence Beloit (Wis.) Coll., 1966—; music dir., condr. Beloit Symphony Orch., 1963-64, 66—; music dir. Quincy Symphony Orch., 1969-70, Rockford (Ill.) Symphony Orch., 1970—. Asst. to music dir. Broadway prodn., Redhead, 1958; owner Pacific Publs., music pubs., Beloit, 1948—; free-lance orchestrator, 1946—; guest condr. Utah Symphony, 1948—, Jackson Hole Festival Orch., Quincy Symphony, others. Mem. gen. bd. Mut. Improvement Assn., Ch. Jesus Christ of Latter-day Saints, 1949-66, mem. gen. music com., 1960—; mem. Utah State Inst. Fine Arts, 1964-66. Served with USNR, World War II: PTO. Recipient Max Wald Meml. Fund award, N.Y.C., 1955, Standard award A.S.C.A.P., annually 1965—. Mem. Nat. Fedn. Music Clubs (nat. choral chmn. 1951-55, 69—, adviser, 1968—), A.S.C.A.P. Club: Timpanogos (Salt Lake City). Composer Utah Centennial mus. play, Promised Valley, 1947, Hill Cumorah Pageant, Palmyra, N.Y., 1957—, mus. play, Sand in Their Shoes, 1959, also commns. for religious ednl. films and Utah Symphony, U. Utah, Ball State U., Am. Bicentennial coms. in Ill., Wis. and Utah. Home: 911 Park Ave Beloit WI 53511 Office: Rockford Symphony Orch 415 N Church St Rockford IL 61103

GATES, DAVID MURRAY, scientist, educator; b. Manhattan, Kans., May 27, 1921; s. Frank C. and Margaret (Thompson) G.; student Kans. State U., 1939-40; B.S., U. Mich., 1942, M.S., 1944, Ph.D., 1948; m. Marian Frances Penley, June 4, 1944; children—Murray P., Julie M., Heather M., Marilyn J. Asst. Prof., asso. prof. U. Denver, 1947-55; sci. dir. Office Naval Research, Am. embassy, London, Eng., 1955-57; cons. to dir. Nat. Bur. Standards, Boulder, Colo., 1957-64; prof. natural history U. Colo., 1964-65; dir. Mo. Bot. Gardens, St. Louis, 1965-71; prof. botany Washington U., 1965-71; prof. botany U. Mich., 1971—; dir. U. Mich. Biol. Sta., 1971—. Dir. Harland Bartholomew & Assos., 1971—. Mem. bd. Arapahoe council Boy Scouts Am., Boulder, Colo., 1963-65; mem. Nat. Sci. Bd., 1970—; chmn. Environ. Studies Bd., Nat. Acad. Scis. Nat. Acad. Engring., 1970-73; mem. panel sci. and tech. com. on Sci. and Astronautics U.S. Ho. Reps., 1970-73. Bd. dirs. Cranbrook Inst. Sci., Conservation Found., 1971—. Fellow A.A.A.S., Am. Optical Soc.; mem. Royal Meterol. Soc., Am. Meteorol. Soc., Am. Inst. Biol. Scis. (mem.-at-large governing bd. 1970—, pres. 1975), Am. Geophys. Union, Bot. Soc. Am., Nat. Audubon Soc. (dir. 1972—), Sigma Pi Sigma, Phi Kappa Phi, Kappa Psi, Sigma Xi (pres. Denver chpt.). Clubs: Garden (hon.), University, Round Table (St. Louis); Cosmos (Washington). Author: Energy Exchange in Biosphere, 1962; Man and His Environment: Climate, 1972; Atlas of Energy Budgets of Plant Leaves, 1971. Research in energy exchange of plants and animals, photosynthesis, atmospheric physics, geophysics, optics. Mem. editorial bd. Oecologia Plantarum (France), 1965—, Oecologia (Germany), 1969—, BioScience, 1971—. Address: U Mich Biol Station Ann Arbor MI 48109

GATES, RAYMOND DEE, chemist; b. Akron, Ohio, Oct. 10, 1925; s. David Albert and Florence (Stranahan) G.; B.S., U. Akron, 1949, M.S., 1951, Ph.D., 1961; m. Betty J. Becker, Mar. 27, 1954; children—David Francis, Barbara Louise. Research chemist Firestone Tire & Rubber Co., Akron, 1951-58, Inst. Rubber Research, U. Akron, 1958-60; mgr. applied polymer research Internat. Latex & Chem. Corp., Dover, Del., 1960-66; research supr. PPG Industries, Inc., Barberton, Ohio, 1966-71; mgr. chem. services The Oak Rubber Co., Ravenna, 1971-72; mgr. SBR-Adhesives lab. Morgan Adhesives Co., Stow, 1972—. Served with AUS, 1943-46. Decorated Bronze Star. Mem. A.A.A.S., Am. Chem. Soc., Alpha Chi Sigma. Club: Akron Torch. Home: 3183 Silver Lake Blvd Cuyahoga Falls OH 44224 Office: 4560 Darrow Rd Stow OH 44224

GATTO, LOUIS CONSTANTINE, coll. pres.; b. Chgo., July 4, 1927; s. Louis S. and Marie (Bacigalupo) G.; student Amherst Coll., 1945-46; B.A., St. Mary's Coll. (Minn.), 1950; postgrad. U. Minn., 1950-51; M.A., De Paul U., 1956; Ph.D., Loyola U., Chgo., 1965; m. Kathleen M. Paquette, July 7, 1951; children—Christine, Beth, Mark, Gregory, Janine, Sandra. Speech asst. St. Mary's Coll., 1949-50; staff artist TV Times, Mpls., 1950-51; chmn. English dept. Zion (Ill.)-Benton High Sch., 1951-56; tchr. New Trier High Sch., Winnetka, Ill., 1956-57; instr. English, St. Joseph's Coll., Rensselaer, Ind., 1957-58, asst. prof., 1958-63, asso. prof. Medieval and Renaissance lit., 1963-66, prof., 1966-71, asst. acad. dean, dir. summer session, 1967, acad. dean 1968, v.p. for acad. affairs 1969-71; pres., prof. English, Marian Coll., Indpls., 1971—. Adviser to pres. Lawrence U., and Am. Council Edn. fellow, 1966-67; mem. Ind. Northwest Consortium Private and Pub. Instns., 1968-71; mem. Ind. Fulbright Found. selection com., 1968-70; mem. community adv. council Indpls. Pub. Schs.; mem. policy adv. council parent/child devel. project Bank Street Coll. Edn.; mem. Hist. Landmarks Found. Ind., 1973—; mem. adv. com. Alcohol Safety Action Project, 1972-75; mem. exec. com. Ind. Conf. on Higher Edn., 1973-75; chmn. council of presidents Consortium for Urban Edn., 1974-75, pres., 1975—. Bd. dirs. Greater Indpls. Progress Com., Cath. Social Services, WYFI-TV, Ind. Health Careers, Inc., Asso. Colls. Ind. Hosp. Audiences, Indpls., 1974-76. Served with AUS, 1945-46. Mem. Am., Ind. confs. on higher edn., Nat. Cath. Edn. Assn. (coll. relations com.), Independent Colls. and Univs. Ind. (dir.), Asso. Colls. Ind. (treas.), Modern Lang. Assn., Renaissance Soc. Am., Medieval Acad. Am., Ind. Coll. English Assn. (bus. mgr. Associator, 1965-66), Indpls. C. of C. Club: Indianapolis Athletic. Contbr. articles to profl. jours. Home: 3024 Cold Spring Rd Indianapolis IN 46222

GATTOZZI, ANGELO LUCIANO, engr.; b. Matrice, Campobasso, Italy, Dec. 12, 1947; s. Domenico Germano and Angiolina (Appugliese) G.; B.S., Case Western Res. U., 1971, M.S., 1975; accounting certificate John Carroll U., 1976. Grad. asst. Case Western Res. U., 1971-74; engr. Reliance Electric Co., Cleve., 1974-77, project mgr., 1977—. Mem. IEEE, Am. Inst. C.P.A.'s, Am. Mgmt. Assn. Home: 2023 Natona Rd Euclid OH 44117 Office: 24800 Tungsten Rd Euclid OH 44117

GAUEN, MARY JANE ADSIT (MRS. RICHARD E. GAUEN), writer, photographer; b. Hoopeston, Ill.; d. Joseph Sherman and Eliza Jane (Hickman) Adsit; B.A., U. Ill.; M.A., U. Mich., 1941; m. Richard E. Gauen, July 5, 1940; 1 dau., Susan Carol. Detroit corr. Fairchild Publs., 1942-43; day wire filer, writer weekly drama columns Asso. Press, Detroit, 1943-44; fashion editor, columnist-womens features writer Detroit Free Press, 1944-49; pub. relations dir. of park, recreation and forestry depts. City of Evanston, Ill., 1967—. Mem. Ill. Park and Recreation Assn., DAR, Women in Communications (v.p. N. Shore chpt. 1973-74), N. Shore Pub. Relations Club (pres. 1971-72), Zeta Phi Eta, Alpha Gamma Delta. Presbyn. Home: 42 Williamsburg Rd Evanston IL 60203 Office: 1802 Maple Ave Evanston IL 60201

GAUL, WILLIAM MARTIN, architect; b. Belleville, Ill., Aug. 23, 1933; s. William Henry and Catherine Mary (Lang) G.; B.Arch., U. Ill., 1957; m. Mary Patricia Murphy, Dec. 28, 1963; children—William Louis, Lisa Marie. Draftsman Weisenstein, Rogers & Hausmann Architects, Belleville, 1960-62; project architect Childs & Smith, Inc., architects, Chgo., 1962-64; with Hague-Richards Assos. Ltd., Chgo., 1964-76, sr. v.p., 1974-76; organizer Gaul-Tater Assos., Chgo., 1976—. Served to lt. comdr. USNR, 1957-60; comdg. officer Res. Engring. Co. 9-1, 1969-72, comdr., 1975—. Mem. A.I.A., Nat. Council Archtl. Registration Bds., Naval Res. Assn., Res. Officers Assn., Alpha Rho Chi. Clubs: University, Economic (Chgo.). Home: 2111 Lincolnwood St Evanston IL 60201 Office: 11 E Hubbard St Chicago IL 60611

GAULT, SIDNEY DAVID, dentist; b. Chgo., Apr. 21, 1927; s. Joseph T. and Jessie (Koenigsberg) G.; student U. Ill., 1945; Ph.B., U. Chgo., 1949, B.S., 1951; postgrad. State U. Ia., 1953-55, U. Buffalo, 1955-57; D.D.S., U. Buffalo, 1961; m. Hanne Wustrow Hansen, Oct. 29, 1960; children—Karin, Adam, Eric. Intern Sinai Hosp., Detroit, 1961-62; practice gen. dentistry, Mt. Prospect, Ill., 1961—; research asso. dept. oral surgery U. Ill., Chgo., 1965-68, dental cons. Ill. Dental Soc., 1973; v.p. Transdevel., Inc., Denver, 1973—. Mem. Glencoe (Ill.) Human Relations Com., 1971—, Glencoe Caucus. Am. Cancer Soc. research fellow, 1960. Mem. Am. Dental Assn., N.W. Dental Study Club, Sigma Xi, Gamma Alpha. Contbr. articles to profl. jours. Patentee in field. Home: 574 Drexel Ave Glencoe IL 60022 Office: 1100 W Northwest Hwy Mount Prospect IL 60056

GAUSS, CECELIA ELAINE SNEYD, broadcasting exec.; b. Adrian, Mich., Oct. 26, 1923; d. Seth and Anna (Dart) Sneyd; student Adrian Coll., 1944-45; m. Duane Dale Guass, Jan. 3, 1946 (div. Oct. 1972); 1 son, Gordon Dale. With Gerity Mich. Corp., 1945-56, sec., dir. purchases, 1948-54, buyer, 1954-56; copywriter Gerity Broadcasting Co., Adrian, 1958-62, sec. to pres., 1962-63, asst. to pres., from 1963, now v.p. corporate affairs and finance WABJ, Adrian; officer Lee Travel Burs., Midland-Bay City, Gerity Products, Toledo, WGER-FM, Bay City, Mich., WABJ, Adrian, Gerity Cablevision, Bay City. Bd. dirs. Howe Mil. Sch. Mothers Assn., 1966—; bd. dirs. Goodwill Industries Southeastern Mich., 1967-71, sec., 1969-71; adv. bd. athletics dept. Siena Hts. Coll., Adrian. Recipient Detroit Advt. Woman of Year award, 1969. Mem. Adrian Area, Am. Women in Radio and TV, Lenawee County Hist. Soc., Womens Advt. Club Detroit, Detroit Press Club, Adrian Bus. and Profl. Women, Clubs: Lenawee Country, Adrian Women's, Zonta. Republican. Episcopalian. Mem. Order Eastern Star. Home: 445 College Park Dr Adrian MI 49221 Office: 121 W Maumee St Adrian MI 49221

GAUSTAD, HARLEY ERWYN, dentist; b. East Grand Forks, Minn., Jan. 8, 1914; s. Hans Martinus and Anna Matilda (Erickson) G.; student pub. schs. Europe; m. Vernette Johnson, Aug. 5, 1939; children—Anna (Mrs. James Motzko), Richard, Karn (Mrs. Matthew Rounds). Shipping clk. Internat. Harvester Co., 1933-36; pvt. practice dentistry, Cokato, Minn., 1936—; dir., v.p. First Nat. Bank. Mem. State Ednl. Com., 1963-64; dist. chmn. Viking council Boy Scouts Am., 1958-61. Chmn. sch. bd., Cokato, 1953-65, mem. city council, 1942-51. Recipient Silver Beaver award Boy Scouts Am., 1960, Lamb award Nat. Youth Agy. Relationships, 1972. Mem. Prosthetic Soc., Children's Dental Soc., Acad. Gen. Practice, Am., Minn., Tri-County, Mpls. Dist. dental assns. Mason (Shriner), Rotarian. Clubs: Town and Country (Cokato, Minn.); Mpls. Athletic. Home: 510 Swanson Ave Cokato MN 55321 Office: 145 3d St E Cokato MN 55321

GAUTHIER, CLARENCE JOSEPH, utility exec.; b. Houghton, Mich., Mar. 16, 1922; s. Clarence A. and Muriel V. (Beesley) G.; B.S.M.E., U. Ill., 1943; M.B.A., U. Chgo., 1960; m. Grayce N. Wicall, July 25, 1941; children—Joseph H., Nancy M. With Pub. Service Co. No. Ill., 1945-54; with No. Ill. Gas. Co., 1954—, v.p. fin., 1960-62, v.p. ops., 1962-64, exec. v.p., 1965-69, pres., 1969-76, chmn., chief exec. officer, 1971—, dir., 1965—; chmn., pres., chief exec. officer, dir. NICOR Inc., 1976—; chmn. pres., dir. NICOR Belize Inc., NICOR Exploration Co., NICOR Transp. Co., NICOR Resources Ltd., 1976—; chmn., dir. Mid-Continent Gas Storage Co., 1975—; dir. Mid-Continent Gasification Co., 1975—, chmn., 1976—; v.p. NI-Gas Supply, Inc., 1960-64, exec. v.p., 1970-71, pres., 1971-76, chmn., 1976—, dir., 1960-64, 70—; pres. NI-Gas Exploration, Inc., 1973-76, dir., 1973—, chmn., 1976—; pres., dir. Midwest Nitrogen, Inc., 1968-70, GRG Liquidation Co., 1976—; exec. v.p. Gt. River Gas Co., 1966-71, pres., 1971-76, dir., 1966-76; dir. GATX Corp., Advance Ross Corp., Gas Devels. Corp., Bank of Yorktown, Lombard, Ill., TARGET, Naperville Nat. Bank and Trust Co. (Ill.), Chemetron Corp., GAS, Ltd.; mem. natural gas advisory com. Fed. Energy Adminstrn., 1974—; mem. roster of cons. to adminstr. ERDA, 1976-77; mem. pres.'s council of bus. assos. Elmhurst (Ill.) Coll., 1965-69; mem. businessmen's advisory council Coll. Bus. Adminstrn., U. Ill. at Chgo. Campus, 1971-76, Northwestern U. Assos., 1977—; advisory council Grad. Sch. Mgmt., Northwestern U., 1972—; bd. sponsors Evang. Hosp. Assn., Oak Brook, Ill., 1977—; chmn. devel. campaign Good Samaritan Hosp., Downers Grove, Ill., 1974-77; bd. dirs. Gas Research Inst., 1977—. Trustee George Williams Coll., Downers Grove, 1968-77, Ill. Inst. Tech., 1976—, Ill. Inst. Tech. Research Inst., 1976—, Council Energy Studies, 1977—; trustee Inst. Gas Tech., 1964-70, 71—, chmn. bd. trustees, 1976—; bd. dirs. Mid-Am. chpt. ARC, 1962—; trustee Met. Crusade of Mercy, Chgo., 1965—; citizens bd. U. Chgo., 1972—; bd. govs. Soc. Environ. Awareness, George Williams Coll., 1973—; mem. bus. advisory bd. Nat. Alliance Businessmen, 1976—. Served to capt. C.E., U.S. Army World War II; PTO. Decorated Silver Star, Bronze Star with V; recipient Distinguished Alumnus award U. Ill., 1971, Alumni Honor award, 1974, Loyalty award, 1977; registered profl. engr., Ill. Mem. Am. (dir. 1970-76, chmn. bd. 1974-75, Distinguished Service award 1976), Midwest (dir. 1964-67), So. (dir. 1966-69) gas assns., Ind. Natural Gas Assn. Am. (dir. 1972-73), Chgo. Assn. Commerce and Industry (dir. 1966-71, 73—), Ill. C. of C., Internat. Gas Union (council 1970-73, 74-75, chmn. com. gas utilization 1970-73), Nat. Petroleum Council, AAAS, Am. Fin. Assn., Am. Mgmt. Assn., Pres.'s Assn., Newcomen Soc. N.Am., U. Chgo. Grad. Sch. Bus. Alumni Assn. (pres. 1964-65), U. Ill. Found., ME-IE Alumni Assn. (dir. 1973—, pres. 1976-77), Sigma Pi, Beta Gamma Sigma, Tau Nu Tau. Clubs: Econ., Chgo., Comml., Met., Mid-Am. (Chgo.); Butler Nat. Golf. Contbr. articles to profl. jours. Home: 15 Lochinvar Ln Oak Brook IL 60521 Office: PO Box 200 Naperville IL 60540

GAUTHIER, T(HEOPHILE) EMIL, med. equipment co. exec.; b. Warroad, Minn., Dec. 11, 1910; s. Odilon and Mathilda (Gauthier) G.; grad. Coyne Coll., 1932; student Rochester Community Coll., 1942, U. Minn. 1943; m. Dorothy Ranney, Sept. 11, 1941; children—Janice (Mrs. Arthur Ley), Thomas, Lawrence. Gen. service worker Mayo Clinic, Rochester, Minn., 1934-37; service mgr. Sears Roebuck & Co., Rochester, Minn., 1937-40; asst. prodn. mgr. Waters-Conley Co., Rochester, 1940-46, Kepp Co., Rochester, 1946-47; organizer Rochester Products Co., 1947, mgr., 1947-66; organizer, mgr. Rochester Med. Equipment Co. (Minn.), 1966-72; organizer Gauthier Industries, Inc., sec.-treas., dir., 1974—; dir. Pine Plating Co., Pine Island, Minn., 1962-70, Ability Bldg. Center, Rochester, 1972—. Mem. Rochester (Minn.) Utility Bd., 1956-66, pres., 1956-65; chmn. com. on urban environment City of Rochester, 1974; active Boy Scouts Am., 1924-65; pres. St. Francis P.T.A., 1953; mem. Service Corps of Ret. Execs., 1976—. Recipient Pres.'s award Soc. Mfg. Engrs., 1966, 71, 73. Registered mfg. engr. Mem. Soc. Mfg. Engrs., Am. Mgmt. Assn., Rochester C. of C. (chmn. indsl. com. 1953-58), Coast Guard Aux. (flotilla vice-comdr. 1971-72). Roman Catholic. K.C., Elk. Developed plastic needle for prolonged intravenous therapy, artificial kidney machine for home patients. Home: 1210 4th St NW Rochester MN 55901 Office: Gauthier Industries Inc 300 1st St NE Rochester MN 55901

GAWRONSKI, DANIEL ANTHONY, educator; b. East Chicago, Ind., Dec. 4, 1930; s. Anthony Stephen and Pauline Veronica (Sobieralski) G.; B.S., Northwestern U., 1953, M.A., 1958, Ph.D., 1963; M.Div., N. Park Theol. Sem., 1958; m. Wilma Carlene North, June 17, 1961; children—Anthony, Stephen, Peter, Laura. Ordained minister Evang. Covenant Ch. Am., 1959; pastor Mission Covenant Ch., East Chicago, Ind., 1958-61, 72—; state supr., chief psychologist Vocat. Rehab. Div. Ind., 1962-69; sch. dir. Jeanine Schultz Meml. Sch., Skokie, Ill., 1969-70; asso. prof. psychology and edn., chmn. psychology dept. Calumet Coll., Hammond, Ind., 1970—; pvt. practice psychology, Hammond, 1963—; lectr. Butler U., Indpls., 1968-69. Bd. dirs. Tri City Comprehensive Community Mental Health Center, 1972—. Recipient Merit award N.W. Ind. Spl. Edn. Coop. 1971, AFL-CIO, 1969. Mem. A.A.U.P. (pres. 1971—), Nat. Rehab. Counseling Assn. (nat. certification com. 1968-69), Ind. Rehab. Counceling Assn. (v.p. 1966-67, editor bull. 1966-69), Am. Psychol. Assn., Am. Ednl. Research Assn., Am. Personnel and Guidance Assn., Nat. Rehab. Assn., Christian Assn. for Psychol. Studies. Lion (pres. 1977-78). Club: Hammond Evening. Home: 330 Friar Tuck Dr Schererville IN 46375 Office: Calumet Coll 2400 New York Ave Hammond IN 46394

GAY, ALFONSO YOUNG, surgeon; b. Negros Occ., Philippines, Aug. 17, 1935; s. Antonio G. and Mary (Young) G.; M.D. cum laude, U. Santo Tomas, 1960; m. Lilia Gomez, May 13, 1961; children—Shirley Ann, Alfonso Young, Catherine, Christine. Surg. resident Negros Occ. Provincial Hosp., Philippines, 1961-65; intern Drs. Hosp., Seattle, 1966-67, resident in surg. pathology, 1967; resident in gen. surgery Good Samaritan Hosp., Cin., 1967-71, fellow in peripheral vascular disease, 1971-73; chief of surgery Hocking Valley Community Hosp., Logan, Ohio, 1973—; pres. Gay and Labrador M.D.'s, Inc., Logan. Diplomate Am. Bd. Surgery. Fellow A.C.S.; mem. AMA, Ohio State Med. Assn. Contbr. research article to med. publ. Home: 728 Glenwood Dr Logan OH 43138 Office: Route 5 Box 305 664 N Logan OH 43138

GAYFER, JAMES MCDONALD, musician, educator; b. Toronto, Ont., Can., Mar. 26, 1916; s. Arthur Erskine and Beatrice Annie (McKenzie) G.; MusB., U. Toronto, 1941, MusD., 1950; postgrad. Royal Mil. Sch. Music, Kneller Hall, Eng., 1945-47; m. Sheila Victoria Gardner Rickard, Apr. 10, 1974; children by previous marriage—James Stewart, John Kelvin; stepchildren—Scott Alan Rickard, Patti Lin Rickard. Actuarial clk. N.Am. Life Assurance Co., Toronto, 1934-42; enlisted Canadian Army, 1942, advanced through grades to capt., 1951; various assignments as bandmaster, insp. bands, 1942-51; dir. music 1st Inf. Battalion Band, 1951-53, Canadian Guards Band, 1954-61; music tng. officer Canadian Forces Sch. Music, Esquimalt, B.C., 1961-66, ret., 1967; instrumental music head Southwood Secondary Sch., Cambridge, Ont., 1966-72; asso. prof. instrumental music edn. Dalhousie U., Halifax, N.S., Can., 1972-74; head music Champlain High Sch., Pembroke, Ont., 1975—; organist, choir master various chs., 1940-69; dir. Pembroke Community Choir, 1958-61, Gayfer Singers, Victoria, B.C., 1962-66, Galt (Ont.) Community Choir and Orch., 1968-71. Decorated various medals for service in France, Germany, Korea; recipient prize for composition Canadian Performing Rights Soc., 1943, Composers, Authors and Pubs. Assn. Can., 1947. Mem. Am. Bandmasters Assn., Canadian Band Dirs. Assn., Nat. Band Assn., Canadian Music Educators Assn., Kodaly Inst., Atlantic Fedn. Musicians. Mem. United Ch. of Can. Author works for band, woodwind and string quartet, voice, orch., and piano. Home: 66 Doran St Petawawa ON K8H 1R2 Canada Office: 360 Carmody St Pembroke ON K8A 4G2 Canada

GAYLORD, SANFORD FRED, physician; b. Cleve. May 18, 1923; s. Samuel Goldberg and Eva Neidus; student, John Carroll U., 1945-47; M.D., Chgo. Sch. Medicine, 1951, M.B., 1951; m. Sarah Leslie Hoffman, Jan. 1, 1944; children—Scott, Randy, Gregg, Shelley, Wendy, Judd, Brett, Glenn. Intern, Ill. Central Hosp., Chgo., 1951-52; resident Dearborn VA Hosp., 1952-53, Mt. Sinai Hosp., Cleve., 1953-54; practice medicine specializing in internal medicine, gastroenterology, Youngstown, Ohio, 1954—; chief of medicine, chief gastroenterology St. Elizabeth Med. Center, Youngstown; cons. gastroenterology Northeastern Ohio Coll. Medicine, 1976—; asst. prof. medicine Northeastern Ohio U. Coll. Medicine. Vice pres. Youngstown Symphony Soc., 1965-70. Served with USAAF, 1942-45; ETO. Decorated D.F.C. with 3 oak leaf clusters. Diplomate Am. Bd. Internal Medicine. Fellow A.C.P., Am. Coll. Gastroenterology; mem. AMA, Am. Soc. Internal Medicine, Am. Soc. Gastrointestinal Endoscopy, Ohio State, Mahanies County med. socs., Ohio Soc. Internal Medicine, Flying Physician's Assn., Aircraft Owners and Pilots Assn. Jewish. Clubs: local swim and tennis, B'nai Brith, Mahaniag Lodge. Former piano student of Boris Goldovsky, 1st place winner piano Nat. Solo Contest, 1939, 1940, 1941; Vitamin B12 therapy in multiple sclerosis, tetracycline flourescence in stomach cancers. Home: 5670 Lamplighter Dr Girard OH 44420 Office: 1005 Belmont Ave Youngstown OH 44504

GEAKE, CAROL LYNNE, veterinarian; b. Grand Rapids, Mich., Feb. 19, 1941; d. John Edward and Alice Geraldine (Bussler) Rens; B.S. in Zoology, U. Mich., 1961, M.S. in Parasitology, 1963; D.V.M., Mich. State U., 1968; m. R. Robert Geake, June 9, 1962; children—Roger Rens, Tamara Lynne, William Rens. Research asst. Mollusk div. Museum of Zoology, U. Mich., Ann Arbor, 1960-63, research asst., dept. indsl. toxicology Sch. Pub. Health, U. Mich., 1963-66; asso. veterinarian Plymouth (Mich.) Veterinary Hosp., 1969-70; pvt. practice, Northville, Mich., 1971—; cons. in field. Project leader Wayne County 4-H Veterinary Sci., 1968-72. Mem. Am., Mich., Southeastern Mich., Women's veterinary med. assns., Am. Assn. Equine Practitioners, Northville Bus. and Profl. Women's

Club, Phi Sigma, Phi Zeta. Contbr. articles to profl. jours. Home and Office: 48525 W Eight Mile Rd Northville MI 48167

GEARHART, LOUIS OSSMAN, assn. exec.; b. Ashland, Pa., June 2, 1918; s. Daniel Louis and Florence Helen (Ossman) G.; D.Chiropractic, U. Natural Healing Arts, 1949; m. Dorothy Eleanor Evers, Dec. 13, 1941; 1 dau., Gerry Edwina (Mrs. John Lester Rutherford). Pvt. profl. musician, Ashland, Pa., 1936-49; pvt. chiropractic practice, Denver, 1950-56; pres. Denver U. Natural Healing Arts, 1956-64; exec. sec. Colo. Chiropractic Assn., 1956-64; dir. profl. affairs Am. Chiropractic Assn., Des Moines, 1964-69, exec. dir., 1969—. Mem. Colo. Bd. Basic Sci. Examiners, 1956-64. Mayor, Buckley Veterans Village, Denver, 1947; pres. Arapahoe County (Colo.) Young Democrats, 1950-52. Trustee Springwall Edn. and Research Trust; bd. dirs. U. Natural Healing Arts (Colo.), 1953-56. Served with AUS, 1941-45. Mem. Am. Chiropractic Assn., Am. Soc. Assn. Execs., A.A.A.S., Wilderness Soc., Des Moines C. of C., Am. Forestry Assn. Democrat. Mason. Home: 1133-23d St West Des Moines IA 50265 Office: 2200 Grand Ave Des Moines IA 50312

GEBHART, DAVID LEE, engr.; b. Cleve., June 9, 1928; s. David William and Vista Lee (Glaser) G.; B.S. in Elec. Engring., Ohio U., 1953; children—David Howard, Eric William, Susan Ruth, Diane Lee. Design engr. Delco Products, Dayton, Ohio, 1953-58; planning engr. Boeing Airplane Co., Seattle, 1958-59; design engr. Howell Electric Motors Co., (Mich.) 1959-64; staff engr. Elec. Apparatus Service Assn., St. Louis, 1964—; lectr. in field. Elder, clk. of session Richmond Hts. Presbyterian Ch., 1971—. Served with U.S. Army, 1946-48. Licensed profl. engr., Ohio, Mo. Mem. IEEE. Contbr. articles to Plant Engring. Mag., Elec. Apparatus Mag., author Question and Answer column Elec. Apparatus Mag., 1966—. Home: 9001 N Swan Circle St St Louis MO 63144 Office: 1331 Baur Blvd St Louis MO 63132

GEE, ALBERT GEORGE, grading contractor; b. Mondamin, Iowa, Jan. 8, 1922; s. George Pearl and Delphia (Fosdick) G.; student Omaha U., 1941. East Tenn. State Coll., 1943, Iowa State Coll., 1946-47, Pepperdine Coll., 1947-48; m. Dorothy Jean Teagarden, Aug. 17, 1947; children—Aleta M., David A., Jean A., Daniel D., Stephen P. Foreman, Glen L. Martin Co., Balt. and Omaha, 1941-43; farmer Modamin and Jewell, Iowa, 1948-49 pres. Gee Grading & Excavating Inc. Cedar Rapids, Iowa, 1950—, Gee Asphalt Systems, Inc., 1977—; v.p., sec., treas. Asphalt Systems of Tex. Adv. bd. York Coll., 1960—; chmn. bd. trustees Ch. of Christ Cedar Rapids, 1959—; active Boy Scouts Am. Served with USAAF, 1943-46. Mem. Am. Rd. Transp. Builders Iowa, Small Bus. Assn., Nat. Fedn. Ind. Businessmen, Allied Constrn. Interests, Nat. Assn. Demolition Contractors, Cedar Rapids C. of C. Clubs: Kiwanis, Gideons. Home: Rural Route 3 Cedar Rapids IA 52401 Office: PO Box 1462 Cedar Rapids IA 52406

GEER, EDWARD DOUGLAS, constrn. co. exec.; b. Portland, Oreg., June 9, 1929; s. Lester John and Evelyn Bernice (Olson) G.; B.S., Oreg. State U., 1952; postgrad. U. So. Calif., 1956-61; m. Marylou Damewood, Mar. 15, 1951; children—Steven Douglas, Lynda Diane, Tricia Ellen. Field engr. Bethlehem Steel Co., Los Angeles, 1954-58; sales engr., mgr. H.E. Robertson Co., Los Angeles, 1958-61; mgr., exec. v.p. So. Calif. Erectors Inc., Los Angeles, 1963-65; steel constrn. mgr. Allied Structural Steel Co., Mpls., 1972-74, Murphy Pac Corp., San Francisco, 1966-71; co-owner, v.p. Sehlins & Geer Constrn. Co., Mpls., 1974—; v.p., mgr. European ops., dir. Tokola Offshore, Internat.; offshore constrn. mgr. Burmah Thistle Platform, North Sea Scotland, 1974—. Served to lt. col., U.S. Army, 1952-54; Korea; 1961-62; Berlin. Mem. Nat. Erectors Assn., Am. Welding Soc., ASCE, Am. Mil. Engrs. Republican. Presbyterian. Home: 3564 Shady Oak Rd Minnetonka MN 55343

GEER, EMILY APT, historian; b. West Unity, Ohio, July 28, 1912; d. Norman J. and Pearl W. (Bayes) Apt; B.S., Bowling Green U., 1936, M.A., 1952; Ph.D., Case Western Res. U., 1962; m. Stanley L. Fisher, Mar. 17, 1934 (dec. 1945); children—Constance (dec.), Norman; m. 2d, Ralph H. Geer, Nov. 1, 1947. Tchr. elementary pub. schs., West Unity, 1932-35; staff asst. R.H. Macy & Co., N.Y.C., 1937-42; propr., mgr. Fisher-Smith Archery Co., Bryan, Ohio, 1945-48; instr. history Bowling Green Ohio State U., 1952-62; mem. faculty Findlay (Ohio) Coll., 1964-77, prof. history, 1968-77, chmn. div. social scis., 1966-77, prof. emeritus, 1977—. Pres. N.Y.C. Archers, 1941-42. Mem. Am. Hist. Assn., Orgn. Am. Historians, Ohio Acad. History (exec. council 1971-74, chmn. com. status of women historians 1974-76), AAUW (br. chmn. of coms. 1962-64), Am. Studies Assn., Phi Delta Kappa, Phi Alpha Theta, Pi Kappa Delta, Chi Omega. Methodist. Editorial bd. Hayes Hist. Jour., 1976-. Contbr. articles to hist. jours. Home: 4 Parkwood Dr Bowling Green OH 43402

GEERDES, HAROLD PAUL, writer, acoustical cons., educator; b. Chgo., Sept. 5, 1916; s. Lubbertus K. and Kathrine (Dering) G.; A.B., Calvin Coll., 1937; M.Ed., Chgo. Tchrs. Coll., 1940; studied conducting Nicolai Malko, Chgo., 1942-46; postgrad. Mich. State U., 1943-45, U. Mich., 1956; m. Gladys Van Haitsma, Nov. 22, 1939; children—Paul H., Richard M., Judith A. Music tchr. high schs., Wyoming and Zeeland, Mich., 1937-38, 40-46; organizer, dir. city-wide program instrumental music Grand Rapids (Mich.) Christian Schs., 1947-55; asso. prof. music Calvin Coll., Grand Rapids, 1955—, condr. concert band, 1955-69, symphony orch., 1955-77, oratorio soc., 1967—, mgr. Fine Arts Center, 1966—. Condr., Zeeland Civic Chorus, 1942-46; active as guest condr., adjudicator, 1950—, also as lectr. and cons. on acoustics Olivet Coll. Conservatory, Forest Hills Pub. Schs., numerous others; mem. long-range planning com. Mich. Council for Arts; mem. design com. for new Grand Rapids music hall. Mem. Mich. Sch. Band and Orch. Assn. (hon.), Am. Symphony Orch. League, Acoustical Soc. Am., Music Educators Nat. Conf. (Mich. Bicentennial chmn.), Mich. Music Edn. Assn., Am. String Tchrs. Assn., Nat. Orch. Assn., Mich. Orch. Assn., Grand Rapids Symphony Soc. (trustee), Am. Choral Condrs., Audio Engrs. Soc., Am. Fedn. Musicians, Nat. Assn. Lit. and Arts. Author: Planning and Equipping Educational Music Facilities, 1975; also many mag. articles on music and acoustics. Editor: Bicentennial Music Handbook for Michigan Teachers, 1975. Home: 2210 Woodlawn Ave SE Grand Rapids MI 49506

GEHL, CHARLES HERMAN, gen. contracting co. exec.; b. Hanover, N.H., June 6, 1947; s. Wilbur William and Elizebeth Patricia (O'Neill) G.; B.S., U. Wyo., 1969; m. Barbara Louise Herndon, Aug. 30, 1974;. Mem. staff application tech. Permastone NW, Gering, Nebr., 1969-74; v.p. fin., dir. El-Con Corp., Scottsbluff, Nebr., 1974-77; dir. Monument Homes, Inc., Gering, Nebr., 1977—; owner Tri-State Sporting Goods, Gering, 1976—. Served with Army NG, 1969-75, 77—. Democrat. Home: 1440 P St Gering NE 69341 Office: Box 626 Gering NE 69341

GEHL, EUGENE OTHMAR, lawyer; b. Kohler, Wis., Sept. 6, 1923; s. Math Nicholas and Mamie Mary (Gall) G.; B.B.A., U. Wis., 1949, J.D., 1951; m. Barbara J. Bendinger, June 25, 1949; children—Kathleen Helen, Sally Jean, Timothy Eugene. Admitted to Wis. bar, 1951; mem. firm Axley, Brynelson Herrick & Gehl, Madison, 1951—, partner, 1960—; corporate counsel Wis. Power and Light Co., 1968—, also dir. Tchr., lectr. law U. Wis., 1960—. Served to lt. (j.g.) USNR, 1942-46. Mem. Am. Coll. Trial Lawyers, Am. Trial Lawyers Assn., Internat. Assn. Ins. Counsel, Edison Electric Inst. Legal Com., Assn. Ins. Attys., Soc. Hosp. Attys., State Bar Wis., Am., Dane County bar assns., Order of Coif. Clubs: Madison, Nakoma. Asst. editor: Thayer Legal Control of the Press, 6th edit., 1967. Home: 4102 Chippewa Dr Madison WI 53711 Office: 122 W Washington Ave Madison WI 53703

GEHLHAUSEN, PAUL EDWARD, mgmt. psychol. cons.; b. Marion, Ind., Jan. 17, 1939; s. Hubert Gerard and Alberta Mary (Peter) G.; B.Phys. Edn., Purdue U., 1961, Ph.D., 1969; M.A., Ball State U., 1965; m. Joan Denise Huguelet, July 6, 1974. Tchr., Pomona, Calif., 1961-62, Marion, Ind., 1962-65; psychol. research, counselor Tri State Coll., Angola, Ind., 1968-69; psychol. cons. Rohrer, Hibler & Replogle, Chgo., 1969-71; psychol. cons. to mgmt. Medina & Thompson, Inc., Chgo., 1971—. Mem. Am., Ill. psychol. assns. Office: 100 S Wacker Dr Chicago IL 60606

GEHRING, FREDERICK WILLIAM, mathematician, educator; b. Ann Arbor, Mich., Aug. 7, 1925; s. Carl E. and Hester MacNeal (Reed) G.; B.S.E. in Math., U. Mich., 1946, M.A. in Math., 1949; Ph.D. (Fulbright fellow) in Math., Cambridge U., Eng., 1952, Sc.D., 1976; Ph.D. (hon.) U. Helsinki (Finland), 1977; m. Lois Caroline Bigger, Aug. 29, 1953; children—Kalle Burgess, Peter Motz, Benjamin Peirce. Instr., Harvard U., 1952-55; instr. math. U. Mich., Ann Arbor, 1955-56, asst. prof., 1956-59, asso. prof., 1959-62, prof., 1962—, chmn. dept. math., 1973-75, 77—; vis. prof. Harvard U., 1964-65, Stanford U., 1964, U. Minn., 1971, Inst. Mittag-Leffler, Sweden, 1972. Served with USNR, 1943-46. NSF fellow, 1959-60; Fulbright fellow, 1958-59; Guggenheim fellow, 1953-59. Mem. Math. Assn. Am., Am., Swiss, Finnish, London math. socs., Finnish Acad. Sci. Editor Duke Math. Jour., 1963—, D. Van Nostrand Pub. Co., 1963-69, North Holland Pub. Co., 1970—, Springer-Verlag, 1974—; editorial bd. Procs. Am. Math. Soc., 1962-65, Ind. U. Math. Jour., 1967-75, Math. Revs., 1969-75; contbr. articles on research in pure math. to sci. jours. Home: 2139 Melrose Ave Ann Arbor MI 48104

GEHRKE, CHARLES WILLIAM, biochemist; b. N.Y.C., July 18, 1917; s. Henry Edward and Louise (Mader) G.; B.A. in Edn., Ohio State U., 1939, B.S. in Biochemistry, 1941, M.S. in Biochemistry and Bacteriology, 1941; Ph.D. in Agrl. Biochemistry, Ohio State U., 1947; m. Virginia Dorothy Horcher, Dec. 25, 1941; children—Charles William, Jon Craig, Susan Gay. Prof., head dept. chemistry Missouri Valley Coll., Marshall, Mo., 1942-49; instr. agrl. chemistry Ohio State U., Columbus, 1945-46; asso. prof. agrl. chemistry U. Mo., Columbia, 1949-54, prof. biochemistry, 1954—, also mgr. Expt. Sta. Chem. Labs., 1954—; co-investigator lunar samples NASA, 1969-75. Recipient Faculty Alumni Gold Medal award U. Mo., 1975. Fellow Am. Inst. Chemists. Assn. Ofcl. Analytical Chemists (Harvey W. Wiley award 1971, chmn. Magruder standard sample subcom. 1958-72); mem. N.Y. Acad. Scis., Am. Soc. Biol. Chemists, Am. Chem. Soc. (pres. Mo. sect. 1958-59), Am. Dairy Sci. Assn. (chmn. com. on protein nomenclature 1961-62), Fedn. Am. Socs. Exptl. Biology, AAAS, Internat. Soc. Study of Origin of Life, N.Y. Acad. Sci., Sigma Xi. Club: Cosmopolitan Luncheon. Contbr. articles on agrl. biochemistry to sci. jours.; editorial bd. Jour. Chromatography, 1971—, AutoAnalysis, 1976-77. Home: 708 Edgewood Ave Columbia MO 65201 Office: Agr Bldg U MO Columbia MO 65201

GEHRT, EARL BENJAMIN, physician; b. Manhattan, Kans., July 12, 1932; s. John Henry and Helen (Wahl) G.; B.S., Kans. State U., 1954, M.D., 1962; m. Joanne Ruby Robbins, Dec. 22, 1957; children—Stanley Dean, Susan Kay, Julie Lynn, Dian Marie. Intern, Broadlawn Polk County Hosp., Des Moines, 1962-63; practice medicine specializing in family practice, Chanute, Kans., 1963—; affiliate Ashley Clinic; partner, staff Neosho Meml. Hosp.; preceptor Kans. U. Med. Center. Mem. S.E. Sch. Bd., 1969—, pres., 1975—; mem. Unified Dist. 413 Sch. Bd., 1969-77, pres., 1975, 76, 77. Served as pilot SAC, 1955-57. Diplomate Am. Bd. Family Practice. Mem. Am. Acad. Family Practice, S.E. Kans. Med. Soc. (past pres.), Kans. Med. Soc., AMA, Chanute C. of C. (named Progress Partner of Year 1976). Republican. Lutheran. Home: 1101 S Larson St Chanute KS 66720 Office: 505 S Plummer St Chanute KS 66720

GEIER, PHILIP HENRY, bus. and benefit plans cons.; b. Cleve., Oct. 9, 1912; s. Philip A. and Mary (Wernie) G.; student U. Sch., 1925-31; B.S. in Mech. Engring., U. Mich., 1935; m. Jane M. Gillen, June 2, 1934; children—Philip Henry Jr., James B., Richard R., Peter D., Michael J., Timothy G. Vice pres., dir. P.A Geier Co., Cleve.; 1935-50; pres., dir. Welfare & Pension Planning Co., Cleve., 1950—; sec.-treas., dir. WDBN, Inc., Medina, 1967—; mng. partner Geier Investments, 1959—; dir. Prodn. Machinery Corp., Mentor, Ohio, Cecil Equipment Co., Medina, Ohio; trustee Health Ins. Trust Ohio. Bd. dirs. N.E. YMCA, Cleve., 1945—; trustee Met. budget com., 1966—. Mem. Alpha Delta Phi. Home: 1 Bratenahl Pl Bratenahl OH 44108 Office: Union Commerce Bldg Cleveland OH 44115

GEIGER, DAVID SCOTT, mathematician; b. N.Y.C., Jan. 3, 1928; s. Earl Russel and Margaret Rose (Scott) G.; student U. So. Calif., 1948-51; B.S., U. Ill., 1954, Ph.D., 1961. Computer programmer U. Ill., Urbana, 1960-64; engaged in math. research. Served with U.S. Army, 1946-47. Mem. Am. Math. Soc., Huxley Inst., Soc. to Conquer Mental Illness. Home: 3432 W 66th St Chicago IL 60629

GEIGER, HANS FREDERICH, engr., mfg. co. exec.; b. Indpls., Apr. 12, 1900; s. John George and Lena Barbara (Schmidt) G.; B.S. in Civil Engring., Purdue U., 1923; m. Florence T. Donovan, Nov. 2, 1929. Supr. constrn. Conder & Culdbertson Co., Indpls., 1923-25; supt., constrn. Colven Constn. Co., Indpls., 1925-26; chief engr. Geiger & Peters Inc., Indpls., 1926-30, self employed constrn. engr., 1930-47; salesmgr. Geilo Products, Indpls., 1950—. Served with N.G., 1940-45. Mem. Profl. Engrs. Assn., Purdue U. Alumni Assn., U.S. Power Squadron. Republican. Clubs: Mercator (past pres.), North Side Optimist (past pres.), Masons. Shriners, Elks. Patentee in field. Home and Office: 5845 N New Jersey St Indianapolis IN 46220

GEIGLE, RICHARD DAMON, real estate broker; b. Jamestown, N.D., June 20, 1941; s. Fred G. and Ella (Geidt) G.; grad. Realtors Inst., 1973; m. Lynda R. Herring, Aug. 4, 1961; children—Teresa Kay, Ryan Scott. Dept. mgr. commissary Grand Forks (N.D.) AFB, 1961-63, warehouseman, 1963-66; salesman Severson Real Estate Co., Grand Forks, 1966-72; owner, broker Severson Real Estate Co., Grand Forks, 1972—; v.p. Sweeney Co., Inc., Fargo, N.D., 1973-74; pres. Dakota Properties Ltd., Grand Forks, 1974—, Poly Pak, Inc., Grand Forks, 1974—. Mem. Grand Forks Police Res. 1966-68; com. chmn. Boy Scouts Am., Grand Forks, 1968-69; dir. Sr. Citizens, Grand Forks, 1975—; sponsor United Hosp. Bldg. Fund, Grand Forks, 1975—. Recipient Distinguished Service award Grand Forks Jr. C. of C., 1974. Mem. Nat. Inst. Real Estate Brokers, Grand Forks Bd. Realtors (pres. 1975), N.D. Assn. Real Estate Brokers (dir. 1975—), United Comml. Travelers, Jr. C. of C., Sertoma Club (dir. 1974—). Lutheran (del. to bd. Valley Meml. Home 1975). Elk, Eagle. Home: 418 Campbell Dr Grand Forks ND 58201 Office: 402 University Ave PO Box 637 Grand Forks ND 58201

GEINERT, ROY MICHAEL, farmer; b. nr. Nortonville, N.D., Jan. 8, 1922; s. Michael and Wilhelmena (Entzminger) G.; student pub. schs.; m. Helen Pratschner, June 6, 1944; children—Marcene (Mrs. Gene Klosterman), Julie (Mrs. Tyrone Albertson), Michael, Charlotte, Jeffrey, Jean, Timothy, Barbara, Stephanie. Pres., Kennison Sch. Bd., 1962—; clk. Mikkelson Twp. Bd., 1949—, chmn., treas., city jubilee, 1962; mem. LaMoure County Crops Improvement Assn.; sec. Farmer's Union Local, county del., Nat. Farmers Orgn. Conv., 1967, del., state conv., 1972. 1st pl. winner, county soil conservation contest, 1958. Roman Catholic. Elk, Eagle, K.C. Home: Nortonville ND 58473 Office: Kennison Elementary Sch Dist Nortonville ND 58473

GEIS, GORDON GEORGE, cons. planner; b. Northampton, Mass., Sept. 15, 1923; s. George Fallsington and Ruby Adeleta (Tyler) G.; B.S., U. Mass., 1949, B. Land Architecture, 1950; M.City Planning, U. Mich., 1952; m. Elizabeth Tucker Dame, June 16, 1951; children—Gordon George, David T. Exec. dir. Herbert H. Smith Assos., West Trenton, N.J., 1958-64; regional dir. community and regional planning Metcalf & Eddy, Inc., N.Y.C., 1964-71; dir. planning Floyd G. Browne & Assos., Ltd., Canton, Ohio, 1971—. Adviser, Hunterdon County (N.J.) 4-H Club, 1963-65; chmn. West Amwell Twp. Planning Commn., 1970-71. Served with USAAF, 1943-46. Mem. Am. Soc. Planning Ofcls., Am. Inst. Planners, Ohio Soc. Cons. Planners, Ohio Water Mgmt. Assn. (mem. State tech. advisory com. 208 Water mgmt. plan). Home: 5737 East Blvd Canton OH 44718 Office: 5276 Fulton Dr Canton OH 44718

GEISEN, KRIS ODEAN, educator; b. Devils Lake, N.D., Jan. 22, 1943; s. James Valentine and Leola Ann (Wallnofer) G.; B.S., Bemidji State Coll., 1965, M.S., 1970; m. Sharon Ann Cullen, Mar. 16, 1968; children—Shannon Marie, Brandon James. Self-employed as electronics and constrn. cons., Bemidji, 1961-63; electronics technician Minuteman 11 Missile Systems, Meva Corp., Grand Forks, 1964-65; electronic constrn. Midland Constrn. Co., Grand Forks, 1966; grad. asst. ednl. media and indsl. technology Bemidji State Coll., 1967, asst. instr. ednl. media, 1968, acting dir. ednl. media, 1969, dir. radio broadcasting, 1970-75, stringer, news reporter KDAL-TV, KNMT/KCMT-TV, 1971-73, dir. radio broadcasting, coordinator cable TV, 1975—, coordinator radio and TV broadcasting, instr. communications, 1976-77, acting chmn. dept. mass communications, summers 1972-74; dir. Bunyanland Ednl. TV Corp.; engring. cons. No. Minn. Pub. TV, 1976-77. Mem. advisory com. on Ednl. Radio Broadcasting, 1970-73, mem. Radio Emergency Action Citizens Team, Bemidji, 1966-70; Minn. Higher Edn. Coordinating Comm.; staff sgt. CAP, 1966-70; info. officer Project Pride, Bemidji, 1973. Mem. Nat. Assn. Broadcasters, Nat. Assn. Ednl. Broadcasters, Northwestern Broadcasters News Assn., assn. Minn. Pub. Ednl. Radio stations, Intercollegiate Broadcasting system Audiovisual coordinating assn., Minn., Pi Delta Epsilon. Inventor compreturbine rotary engine; producer of Aspects (pub. radio program series). Home: Rural Route 7 Box 291 Bemidji MN 56601

GEISLER, HANS EMANUEL, physician; b. Ratibor, Germany, Apr. 5, 1935; s. Harry and Marianne (Barthel) G.; A.B., Xavier U., 1955; M.D., Loyola U., 1959; m. Margaret Ann Colglazier, Dec. 28, 1957; children—Dorothy, Kathleen, Stephen, Suzanne, John. Intern, St. Joseph Hosp., South Bend, Ind., 1959-60; resident in obstetrics gynecology Meth. Hosp., Indpls., 1960-63; fellow Meml. Hosp., N.Y.C., 1963-65; practice medicine specializing in gynecol. oncology, Indpls., 1965—; asst. prof. obstetrics and gynecology, Ind. U., Indpls., 1966—; dir. gynecologic oncology St. Vincent Hosp., Indpls., 1972—; chmn. com. cancer Regional Med. Program for Heart, Cancer, Stroke, 1968-69. Bd. Dirs. Little Red Door, Indpls., 1970-75. Diplomate Am. Bd. Obstetrics and Gynecology. Fellow Am. Coll. Obstetricians Gynecologists; mem. AMA, Ind., Marion County med. socs., Continental Gynecologic Soc., Central Assn. Obstetricians Gynecologists, Soc. Gynecologic Oncologists (founding mem.), Ind. Obstetrics Gynecology Soc., Phi Chi. Republican. Roman Catholic. Clubs: Riviera, Meridian Hills. Contbr. articles to profl. jours. Home: 8258 Conarroe Rd Indianapolis IN 46278 Office: 5470 E 16th St Indianapolis IN 46218

GEISLER, JAMES CHARLES, extension forester; b. Owensville, Mo., Feb. 27, 1940; s. Charles Waldo and Faye Effie (Matthews) G.; B.S., U. Mo., 1964; M.S., Kans. State U., 1975; m. Ella May Juedemann, Sept. 2, 1961; children—Deborah Lynn, Pamela Dawn. Research asst. U. Ark., Batesville, 1964-66; dist. extension forester Kans. State U., Hiawatha, 1966-72, area extension forester, Manhattan, 1972—. Mem. middle mgmt. team, rural devel. Kans. Econ. Devel., 1972—; dir. forestry summer camp N.E. Kans., 1969—. Program dir. Kans. dist. Conserama, Boy Scouts Am., 1970—. Recipient Conservation award Project SOAR, 1971. Mem. Soc. Am. Foresters (editor Ozark Reporter 1976—). Republican. Methodist. Elk. Home: 1826 Cedar Crest Dr Manhattan KS 66502 Office: 1515 College Ave Manhattan KS 66502

GEISS, DOROTHY ELIZABETH, retail trade exec.; b. Youngstown, Ohio, Nov. 18, 1918; d. Jacob D. and Elizabeth (Wilson) Geiss; student pub. schs. Sec. Gen. Fireproofing Co., Youngstown, 1937-45; traffic clk. Strouss, Youngstown, 1945-47, traffic mgr., 1947—. Mem. bus. tech. adv. com. Ohio Bd. Regents, 1973—; mem. transp. adv. bd. Youngstown State U., 1977—. Mem. Nat. Retail Merchants Assn. (chmn. traffic group 1977—, dir. 1956—), C. of C. Traffic Group, Delta Nu Alpha. Author: A Mini Traffic Course, 1969. Home: 650 Niles-Cortland Rd NE Warren OH 44484 Office: 20 W Federal St Youngstown OH 44503

GEIST, GLENN WILLIAM, TV service co. exec.; b. Topeka, Jan. 29, 1921; s. William F. and Myrtle Mae (Hardisty) G.; student pub. schs.; m. Jane R. Mol, Apr. 6, 1961; children—Daniel W., Steven W. With Am. Inst. Tech., 1945-47; v.p. TV Engrs. Inc., 1947-51, pres., 1951-57; pres. Certified TV Service Inc., 1957—, Certified Computer Services, Inc., 1972—, Certified Electronic Distbrs., Inc., 1959—; chmn. bd. Andre & Co. Inc., Universal Lamp Co., Inc. (all Chgo.). Served with AUS, 1942-45. Decorated Purple Heart, Bronze Star medal; Crois de Guerre with palm (France). Lion. Home: 6846 N Mendota Ave Chicago IL 60646 Office: 5044 W Fullerton Ave Chicago IL 60639

GEIST, PAUL DEAN, utility co. exec.; b. Topeka, Kans., Nov. 22, 1923; s. William F. and Myrtle M. (Hardisty) G.; student Hutchinson Jr. Coll., 1941-42, Adela Hale Bus. Coll., 1948-51; m. Elnora Gwendolyn Gibbs, Nov. 24, 1948; children—Peggy Evelyn, Steven Paul. With Kans. Power & Light Co., 1946—, div. auditor, Hiawatha, 1953-58, Topeka, 1958-62, regional auditor, Hutchinson region, 1962—. Bd. dirs. ARC, Reno County, Kans., 1973—, first aid instr., 1954—. Served with U.S. Army, 1943-46. Mem. Hutchinson C. of C. Clubs: Moose, Carey Park Country. Home: 1204 W 31st St Hutchinson KS 67501 Office: 20 W 2nd St Hutchinson KS 67501

GEISTFELD, RONALD ELWOOD, educator; b. St. James, Minn., Nov. 9, 1933; s. Victor E. and Viola D. (Becker) G.; student Bethany Jr. Coll., 1950-52; B.S., U. Minn., 1954, D.D.S., 1957; m. Annette Swenson; children—Sharilyn, Mark, Steven, Ann. Gen. pvt. practice dentistry, Northfield, Minn., 1959-72; part-time clin. asst. prof. U. Minn. Sch. Dentistry, Mpls., 1969-72, asso. prof. dept. operative dentistry, 1973—, acting chmn. dept. operative dentistry, 1977—;

dental cons. VA Hosp., St. Paul, 1977—; mem. dental staff Hennepin County gen. Hosp., 1975—. Bd. dirs. Dist. 659 Northfield Bd. Edn., 1969-74; bd. dirs. Rice County Health and Sanitation Bd., 1966-74, chmn., 1972-74. Served to capt. AUS, 1957-59. Fellow Am. Coll. Dentists; mem. Minn. Acad. Restorative Dentistry, Minn. Acad. Gnathological Research, Am. Acad. Operative Dentistry, Am. Acad. Gold Foil Operators, Minn. Prosthodontic Soc., Minn. Dental Assn. (ethics com. 1969-74, univ. relations com. 1975—), Northfield C. of C. (bd. dirs., treas. 1968-70), Omicron Kappa Upsilon, Delta Sigma Delta. Lutheran (elder 1962-67, sec. 1960-62, mem. parish bd. edn. 1968-71). Rotarian (pres. 1972-73). Home: 2173 Folwell St St Paul MN 55108 Office: 8-450 HS Unit A Univ Minn Sch Dentistry Minneapolis MN 55455

GELADAS, JAMES, newspaper editor; b. Kane, Pa., Sept. 1, 1924; s. Constantine and Rose (Soloniuk) G.; B.A., Muskingum Coll., 1948; m. Shirley LeVonne Wood, Apr. 18, 1967. With Zanesville (Ohio) News, 1946-48; editor Danville (Pa.) Morning News, 1948-49, Worthington (Minn.) Globe, 1949-56, Dubuque (Iowa) Telegraph-Herald, 1956—; frequent lectr. photography and newspaper design. Mem. lay adv. bd. Clarke Coll.; trustee Mercy Hosp. Sch. Nursing. Served with USMCR, 1943-46. Mem. Nat. Press Photographers Assn. (named Editor of Year 1963, Picture Editor of Year 1968), Iowa Press Photographers Assn., Nat. Conf. Editorial Writers, Dubuque Hist. Soc. (dir. 1964-66). Dubuque C. of C. (v.p. 1965), Sigma Delta Chi. Home: 2375 Knob Hill Dubuque IA 52001 Office: Telegraph Herald W 8th and Bluff Sts Dubuque IA 52001

GELBACH, JOHN A., banker; b. Ellwood City, Pa., Oct. 22, 1917; s. Loring Lusk and Stella (Fisher) G.; A.B., George Washington U., 1938; M.B.A., Harvard, 1940; m. Marion Soerens, Oct 16, 1941;children—John Loring, Robert Walter. Clk. 1st Wis. Nat. Bank, Milw., 1940-41; v.p., treas., dir. Stock Equipment Co., Cleve., 1941-56; with Central Nat. Bank, Cleve., 1956—, sr. v.p., then pres. and dir., 1969-71, pres., chief exec. officer, 1971-72, chmn. bd., pres., dir., 1972-75, chmn. bd., chief exec. officer, 1975—; chmn. bd., pres., dir. Centran Corp.; dir. Premier Indsl. Corp., Basic, Inc. Chmn. No. Ohio Blood Program, ARC. Trustee, treas. United Torch Greater Cleve., Cleve. Found. Mem, Assn. Res. City Bankers, Newcomen Soc. N.Am., Greater Cleve. Growth Assn. (v.p. adminstrn., dir.), Cleve. Council World Affairs (trustee), Bluecoats, Inc. Clubs: Country, Pepper Pike, Union, Tavern (Cleve.); Bankers (San Francisco); Union League (N.Y.C.); Duquesne (Pitts.). Home: 31615 Creekside Dr Cleveland OH 44124 Office: 800 Superior Ave Cleveland OH 44114

GELBAND, ALAN BRUCE, stockbroker, movie producer; b. N.Y.C., Nov. 15, 1944; s. Harry and Evelyn (Simon) G.; B.B.A., U. Mich., 1966, M.B.A., 1967, Ph.D., 1970. Registered rep. Smith Hague & Co., 1967-69; dir. research and institutional sales Morrison McKeown & Young, Inc., 1969-71; v.p., dir. Walton-Vairex Corp., Ann Arbor, Mich., 1969-71, pres., chmn. bd., dir., 1971-72; pres., chmn. bd. Merger Corp. Am., 1973—; pres. Alan Gelband & Co., stockbrokers, Chgo., 1976—. Mem. Beta Gamma Sigma, Beta Alpha Psi, Phi Kappa Phi. Home: 175 E Delaware Pl Chicago IL 60611 Office: John Hancock Center Chicago IL 60611

GELFAND, IVAN, investment adviser; b. Cleve., Mar. 29, 1927; s. Samuel and Sarah (Kruglin) G.; B.S., Miami U., 1950; postgrad Case-Western Res. U., 1951; grad. Columbia U. Bank Mgmt. Program, 1968; certificates Am. Inst. Banking; m. Suzanne Frank, Sept. 23, 1956; children—Dennis Scott, Andrew Steven. Accountant Central Nat. Bank of Cleve., 1950-53, v.p., mgr. bank and corp. investments, 1957-75; pres. Gelfand, Quinn & Assos. Inc., 1975—, Lindow, Gelfand & Quinn, Inc., 1976—; chief accountant Stars & Stripes newspaper, Darmstadt, Germany, 1953-55; account exec. Merrill Lynch, Pierce, Fenner & Smith, Inc., Cleve., 1955-57. Instr. in investments, Cleve. Bd. Edn. adult div., 1956-58, Am. Inst. Banking 1958-68; lectr. econs., bank portfolio mgmt., 1972—; money market columnist Nat. Thrift News. Mem. Greater Cleve. Growth Assn., 1968—; mem. investment com. United Torch of Cleve., 1972-74; study-rev. team Lake Erie Regional Transp. Assn., 1973—. Mem. exec. bd. Cleve. chpt. Am. Men's Orgn. for Rehab. and Tng., 1968-76, asst. sec., 1970-72. Served with AUS, 1945-47. Mem. Cleve. Soc. Security Analysts, Internat. Platform Assn., Les Politiques, Republican. Mason. Jewish. Clubs: Mid-day, Commerce, (Cleve.); Oakwood Country. Home: 2900 Alvord Pl Pepper Pike OH 44124 Office: 3645 Warrensville Center Rd Shaker Heights OH 44122

GELINAS, JEAN PAUL, photographer; b. LaSarre, Que., Can., Mar. 22, 1922; s. J. Omer and Antoinette (Bedard) G.; student U. Ottawa, 1938-41; diploma N.Y. Inst. Photography, 1948; m. Jeanne Blain, Aug. 18, 1942. Owner, operator Paul Studio, Iroquois Falls A, Ont., Can., 1947—, Timmins, Ont., 1970—. Municipal chmn. Com. for Protection Persons and Property, 1951-56; councillor Twp. of Calvert (Ont.), 1951-56; mem. Ansonville Retarded Children Assn. Bd. Edn., 1962-69; founding pres. Calvert Hist. Bd., Iroquois Falls A, 1965-68. Served with Canadian Mcht. Navy, 1942-45. Recipient recognition certificate Ansonville and Dist. C. of C., 1962; certificate of merit Profl. Photographers Am., 1970, certificate of appreciation, 1968; numerous blue and red ribbons for prints Profl. Photographers Ont., 1957—. Mem. Ansonville C. of C., Royal Canadian Legion (br. v.p. 1970), profl. photographers Am., Can., Ont., Societe St. Jean Baptiste (pres. 1964-66), La Caisse Populaire Ste. Jeanne d'Arc, L'Amie Co-op, Le Centre Culturel Les Copains, Le Centre Culturel La Ronde, Timmins Porcupine C. of C., Canadian Fedn. Independant Bus. Lion. Club: Richelieu. Founding bus. mgr. North Star, Weekly, 1951. Home and office: 167 Pine St Timmins ON Canada

GELLEIN, RAYMOND LANGE, constrn. co. exec., mayor; b. San Diego, Oct. 14, 1920; s. Iver and Eldrid (Lange) G.; B.A., San Diego State Coll., 1943; m. Gladys Catherine Callender, Dec. 19, 1945; children—Raymond Lange, Catherine Gellein Male. Sec.-treas. Marysville Improvement Co. (Mich.), 1946-53; pres. Mobile Trailer Co. of Tex., Terrell, 1953-58; v.p. Marysville Improvement Co., 1958-67, pres., 1973—; exec. dir. St. Clair Progress Corp. (Mich.), 1967-73; mayor City of St. Clair, 1976-77; dir. Algonac Area Devel. Corp. (Mich.). Mem. Bd. Edn., Marysville, 1951-53; first ward alderman St. Clair, 1965-67; chmn. citizens study com. E. China Twp. (Mich.) Sch. Dist., 1965-66. City chmn. Rep. Party, St. Clair, Mich., 1969-73. Served to lt. (j.g.) USNR, 1943-46; ETO. Conglist. (trustee 1967-73, chmn. 1971-73, moderator 1973—). Rotarian (pres. 1971-72). Home: 547 N Riverside St Clair MI 48079 Office: 1320 Michigan Ave Marysville MI 48040

GELPERIN, JULES, psychoanalyst; b. Cin., Jan. 15, 1914; s. Israel and Rose (Levine) G.; B.Sc., U. Cin., 1933, B.M., 1935, M.D., 1937, M.Sc., 1938; grad. Chgo. Inst. Psychoanalysis, 1958; m. Gladys Mae Nabe, July 5, 1939; children—Jack, Ellen Gelperin Bebee, Sally Gelperin Light. Intern, Cin. Gen. Hosp., 1935-36, resident psychiatry, 1936-38, resident neurology, 1938-39; practice medicine, specializing in psychiatry and psychoanalysis, Highland Park, Ill., 1948—; clin. asst. prof. psychiatry Chgo. Med. Sch., 1952-56, U. Ill. Med. Sch., Chgo., 1968-72; cons. Evanston (Ill.) Family Service, 1960—. Served with AUS, 1942-46. Diplomate Am. Bd. Psychiatry. Mem. Am. Psychiat. Assn. (life), Am. Psychoanalytic Assn., Chgo. Psychoanalytic Soc. Club: North Moor Country. Home: 2370 Woodpath St Highland Park IL 60035 Office: 1893 Sheridan St Highland Park IL 60035

GELVIN, JOHN TIETGE, psychotherapist; b. Kansas City, Kans., Nov. 15, 1937; s. Lloyd Jay and Fon Bernice (Tietge) G.; A.A., Trenton Jr. Coll., 1973; B.S., N.E. Mo. State U., 1976, M.A., 1976; m. Ruth Ann Schreiner, Apr. 23, 1960; children—Geni Maria, Matthew Rome, Christine Louise. Mgr., Vumore Co., Brookfield, Mo., 1967, Trenton (Mo.) Cable TV, 1968-71; psychotherapist Kirksville (Mo.) Osteo. Hosp., 1976—. Campaign chmn. Linn County (Mo.) March of Dimes, 1966-68; dir. Adair County (Mo.) Civil Def., 1968-69; scout master Boy Scouts Am., 1976—. Served in USN, 1956-59. Mem. Am. Coll. Neuropsychiatry, Am. Personel and Guidance Assn., Assn. to Advance Ethical Hypnosis. Clubs: Lions, Elks. Home: Rural Route 2 Box 595 Kirksville MO 63501 Office: 800 W Jefferson St Kirksville MO 63501

GENALO, LAWRENCE JAMES, mathematician, educator; b. Bklyn., Oct. 30, 1946; s. Joseph Francis, Jr. and Lorraine May (Mandella) G.; B.A. in Math. magna cum laude (N.Y. State Regents scholar 1969-71, Univ. scholar 1970-71), Hofstra Coll., Hempstead, N.Y., 1971; M.S. (Thielman award), Iowa State U., 1974, Ph.D., 1977; m. Mary A. Mancina, Dec. 17, 1966; children—Lawrence James, Francis Patrick. Actuarial trainee Royal Globe Ins. Cos., N.Y.C., 1971; teaching asst. Iowa State U., 1971-73, instr. math., 1973-76, asst. prof. freshman engring. dept., 1976—. Dep. sheriff Story County (Iowa), 1972-73. Research grantee Iowa State U., 1974. Mem. Am. Math. Soc., Kappa Mu Epsilon, Sigma Alpha Kappa. Roman Catholic. Club: Palmas Softball. Home: 2221 Storm St Ames IA 50010 Office: 407 Marston Hall Iowa State Ames IA 50011

GENGLER, JEANNE (DOROTHY), hosp. pres.; b. Mackville, Wis., Feb. 10, 1912; d. Jacob Joseph and Jeanette (Mullen) Gengler; R.N., Marquette U., 1937, B.S., 1957. Joined Franciscan Sisters, 1932; staff nurse, St. Louis, 1937-40; supr., instr. nursing St. Mary Hosp., Racine, Wis., 1940-50; supr., dir. nursing and personnel, disaster program dir., Waterloo, Iowa, 1950-53; dir. Family and Alcoholic Clinic, St. Michael Hosp., Milw., 1953-58, adminstr., 1958-64, pres., bd. dirs., 1965—; asst. adminstr., project dir., Cape Girardeau, Mo., 1964-65; pres., bd. dirs. St. Josephs Hosp., Milw., 1965—; cons. Rehab. Hosp., Marianjoy Hosp., 1974; vice chmn. Regional Hosp. Council, Milw., 1970-72. Mem. Cath. Family Life Bd., Milw., 1973-75; sec. Ednl. TV Network, Milw.; hon. mem. Fire Dept. Fellow Am. Coll. Hosp. Adminstrs.; mem. Wis. Nurses Assn., Am. Pub. Health Assn., Milw. Council on Alcoholism, Milw. Mental Health Assn., Am. Cancer Assn., Am. and Wis. Hosp. Assn., Wis. Cath. Hosp. Assn. (dir. 1968-74), Concerned Citizens for Life (life). Author: Guide to Executive Selection, 1969. Home and Office: 5000 W Chambers St Milwaukee WI 53210

GENNARO, JACK RUDOLPH, broadcasting exec.; b. Rockford, Ill., Aug. 23, 1926; s. Charles and Mary Anne (Domkoski) G.; B.A., Lake Forest Coll., 1949; m. Joanne Mary Trapani, June 28, 1958; children—Charles, Mary Anne. Sales mgr. WREX-TV, Rockford, 1953-54; free-lance advt. and sales promotions, Rockford, 1955-56; regional sales mgr., sta. mgr. WFRV-TV, Green Bay, Wis., 1957-60, v.p., gen. mgr., 1960-61; v.p., gen. mgr. WOBT Radio, Rhinelander, Wis., 1961-64; v.p., gen. mgr. Radio Stas. WFHR/WWRW, Wisconsin Rapids, Wis., 1964—; sec., gen. mgr. Wis. Network, Inc., Wisconsin Rapids, 1965—; bd. dirs., Community Video, Inc., Wisconsin Rapids, 1968-76. Served with AUS, 1945-46. Mem. Wis. Broadcasters Assn. (dir. 1969-73, 76—), Wis. A.P. Broadcasters Assn. (pres. 1966), Nat. Assn. FM Broadcasters (dir. 1973-75), Nat. Radio Broadcasters Assn. (dir. 1976—), AP Broadcasters (dir. 1976—), Rhinelander (dir. 1960-61), Wisconsin Rapids (dir. 1967-68, pres. 1970) chambers commerce. Elk. Home: 1331 18th St S Wisconsin Rapids WI 54494 Office: 220 1st Ave S Wisconsin Rapids WI 54494

GENO, PHILLIP JOSEPH, ins. co. exec.; b. St. Louis, Oct. 30, 1925; s. Charles A. and Gertrude E. (Geiss) G.; B.S., St. Louis U., 1951; m. Dolores J. Mouldon, Aug. 18, 1951; children—Renee C., Donna M., Colette. Treas. Vico Corp., St. Louis, 1969—, Vico County Mutual Ins. Co., St. Louis, 1965—, Harris Securities Co., St. Louis, 1965—, Vico Leasing Corp., St. Louis, 1971—, Countrywide Services Corp., St. Louis, 1971—, Worldwide Underwriters Ins. Co., St. Louis, 1971—; treas., dir. Volkswagen Ins. Co., St. Louis, 1965—, Vico Life Ins. Co., St. Louis, 1969—; dir. Worldwide Underwriters Ins. Co. Mem. Alumni council St. Louis U., 1955. Served with AUS, 1946-47. Mem. Nat. Assn. Accountants, Am. Mgmt. Assn., Ins. Accounting and Statis. Assn. Home: 15580 Clover Ridge Ct St Louis MO 63017 Office: 11975 Westline Dr St Louis MO 63141

GENSKOW, JACK KUENNE, psychologist; b. Milw., Mar. 19, 1936; s. Harvey M. and Marie (Kuenne) G.; student Yale, 1954-55; B.S., U. Wis., Milw., 1961; postgrad George Peabody Coll., 1961; A.M., U. Ill., 1962, Ph.D., 1967; m. Lillian Margret Jendresen, Jan. 28, 1961; children—Karen, Kenneth. Psychologist, dir. evaluation center Ill. Div. Vocational Rehab., Decatur, 1965-77, resources specialist, 1977—. Adj. asst. prof. So. Ill. U., 1975; adj. asso. prof. Sangamon State U., 1977; mem. adv. council Research and Tng. Center, U. Wis.-Stout, 1976—. Bd. dirs. Decatur Council Community Services, 1967-77. Recipient Boss of Year award Decatur chpt. Am. Bus. Women's Assn., 1971—; Harold Scharper Achievement award U. Ill., 1967. Mem. Nat., Ill. (pres.) rehab. assns., Am., Ill. (chmn. ethics com. 1976-77) psychol. assns., Am. Rehab. Counseling Assn., Am. Personnel and Guidance Assn., Vocational Evaluation and Work Adjustment Assn. (exec. council 1973—), Phi Delta Kappa, Kappa Delta Pi. Home: 1916 Claremont Springfield IL 62703 Office: 623 E Adams Springfield IL 62706

GENTHE, WALTER ALFRED, mfg. co. exec.; b. Ludwigshafen, Germany, Mar. 20, 1926; s. Max Ferdinand and Hildegard (Ebbecks) G.; came to U.S., 1953; naturalized, 1958; Baccalaureat, Heidelberg (Germany) U., 1948; student Wayne State U., 1960; m. Marga Schimmer, July 24, 1945; children—George, Peter J., Michael W. Prodn. engr. Fisher Body div. Gen. Motors Corp., 1953; mgr. Meldrum Tool & Mfg. Co., Ferndale, Mich., 1953-59; v.p., gen. mgr. Worman Pilliant Co., Warren, Mich., 1959-63; gen. mgr. mfg. Paramount Fabricatings Co., automobile parts, Detroit, 1963-67; v.p. Sparton Corp. auto components, Flora, Ill., 1967—, also dir.; v.p., gen. mgr. Spartan Mfg. Co. Mem. Flora High Sch. Bd. Edn., 1971-73; mem. vocat. tech. occupations adv. com. Ill. Eastern Jr. Colls., 1973—. Mem. Ill. Mfrs. Assn., Automobile Service Industry Assn., Flora C. of C., Clay County Arts Guild (pres. 1975-76). Republican. Lutheran. Elk. Clubs: Clay County Country; Fairlane (Dearborn, Mich.). Patentee automotive luggage carrier. Home: RFD 2 Flora IL 62839 Office: Box 399 Flora IL 62839

GENTILE, ANTHONY, coal co. exec.; b. Aquila, Italy, Nov. 1, 1920; s. Gregorio and Antonietta (Duronio) G.; student Youngstown Coll., 1939-42; m. Nina Angela DiScipio, Mar. 4, 1943; children—Robert Henry, Anita Marie, Rita Ann, Thomas Gregory. Co-owner Pike Inn-Restaurant, Bloomingdale, Ohio, 1946-52; asst. to owner Huberta Coal Co., Steubenville, Ohio, 1952-55; gen. mgr. Half Moon Coal Co., Weirton, W.Va., 1955-57; gen. mgr. Ohio River Collieries Co., Columbus, Ohio, 1957-59, pres., 1959—; pres. Lafferty Coal Mining Co., Duke Coal Co., 1959—; v.p. Big Mountain Coals, Inc., Prenter, W.Va., 1962—, chmn. bd., 1962—; v.p. Twin Seam Mining Co., W.Va., 1968—; v.p. N & G Constrn., Bannock Land Co.; dir. Union Bank, Steubenville. Mem. 1st Ohio Trade Commn. to Europe, 1965; mem. Cleve. dist. advt. council Small Bus. Adminstrn. Mem. adv. bd. Coll. of Steubenville; trustee Ohio Valley Hosp., Steubenville; mem. exec. bd. Ft. Steuben council Boy Scouts Am. Served to 1st lt AUS, 1942-45. Decorated Purple Heart, Silver Star. Mem. Am. Inst. Mining, Metall. and Petroleum Engrs., Am. Mining Congress (mem. adv. council coal div. 1965). Home: 4 Normandy Dr Wintersville OH 43952 Office: Ohio River Collieries Co PO Box 128 Bannock OH 43972

GENTLING, PHILLIP HENRY, dentist; b. New Orleans, Jan. 19, 1918; s. Gregory Phillip and Agnes Priscilla (Postier) G.; B.S., Tulane U., 1941; D.D.S., Northwestern U., 1944; m. Mary Jane Holmes, Sept. 9, 1942; children—Kirk, Colin, Linda, Nancy. Pvt. dental practice, Rochester, Minn.; pres. Doctors Gentling Ltd., 1946—; pres., dir. Rochester Mustang Hockey Assn., 1947-52. Bd. dirs. Rochester Softball Assn., 1948; bd. dirs. pres. Bethany Lutheran Home, 1968—; bd. dirs. and planning bd. United Fund, 1962-70; bd. dirs. Samaritan-Bethany Nursing Home, 1975—, Rochester YMCA, 1976—; bd. dirs., mem. personnel com. YMCA Camp Olson, 1977—. Served with USNR, 1942-46. Mem. S.E. Minn. Dist. Dental Soc. (pres. 1974-75, del. to state dental assn. 1973-76), Zumbro Valley Dental Assn. (dir. 1975—), Am. Legion. Mason, Eagle. Lutheran (trustee 1956-62, pres. trustees 1961). Club: Exchange (bd. dirs. 1949-51, pres. 1950), Olmsted County Toastmasters (bd. dirs. 1963-68, pres. 1968). Home: 1615 10th St NE Rochester MN 55901 Office: 2210 N Broadway Rochester MN 55901

GENUNG, THOMAS LIMES, accountant; b. Omaha, Oct. 2, 1943; s. L. T. and Lynndal (Limes) G.; B.B.A., U. Iowa, 1965; m. Janet Arlene Henderson, June 19, 1965; children—Elizabeth Arlene, Lynn Thomas. Staff accountant Peat, Marwick, Mitchell & Co. C.P.A.'s, Cedar Rapids, Iowa, 1966-71; controller Toy Nat. Bank, Sioux City, Iowa, 1971-73; staff accountant Broker Hendrickson & Co., C.P.A.'s, Fargo, N.D., 1973-74; office mgr. Woodbury & Co. C.P.A.'s, Sidney, Iowa, 1974-75; prin. Thomas L. Genung C.P.A., Glenwood, Iowa, 1975—. Adviser, Jr. Achievement, Cedar Rapids, 1968-69, Sioux City, 1971-72; bd. dirs. Glen Haven Home, Glenwood, Iowa, 1976-77. C.P.A. Iowa. Mem. Iowa Soc. C.P.A.'s (chpt. pres. 1977—), Am. Inst. C.P.A.'s, Nebr. Soc. C.P.A.'s, Nat. Assn. Accountants, Glenwood Community C. of C., Greater Omaha Soc. Model Engrs. Methodist. Home: 510 6th St Glenwood IA 51534 Office: 7 N Vine St Glenwood IA 51534

GEORGE, EMERY EDWARD, educator, poet; b. Budapest, Hungary, May 8, 1933; s. Larry Hofbauer and Julianna (Deutsch) G.; came to U.S., 1946, naturalized, 1954; A.B., U. Mich., 1955, M.A., 1959, Ph.D. Ottendorfer Meml. fellow, 1964; m. Mary Gertrude Wiedenbeck, May 9, 1969. Instr., U. Ill., Urbana, 1964-65, asst. prof., 1965-66; asst. prof. U. Mich., Ann Arbor, 1966-69, asso. prof., 1969-75, prof. Germanic langs. and lit., 1975—, faculty research fellow, grantee, 1969. Served with U.S. Army, 1955-58. Recipient Avery Hopwood Award in Poetry, 1960. Fellow Internat. Acad. Poets (founder, Cambridge, Eng.); mem. Modern Lang. Assn. Am., Holderlin-Gesellschaft (Tubingen, Ger.), Poetry Soc. Am., Internat. P.E.N., Internat. Poetry Soc., Shelley Soc. N.Y. (hon.), Spoon River Poetry Soc., U. Mich. Research Club. Author: Holderlin's Ars Poetica, 1973; Mountainwild: Poems, 1974; Black Jesus, 1974; A Gift of Nerve: Poems, 1977; editor: Friedrich Holderlin, 1972; Husbanding the Golden Grain, 1973; translator: Subway Stops (Miklos Radnoti), 1977; founding editor Mich. Germanic Studies, 1975—; asso. editor Russian Lit. Triquarterly, 1973—; editorial bd. Germano-Slavica, 1973—; editor, pub. Kylix Press, 1974—; contbr. poems, articles, translations, revs. Home: 1485 Maywood St Ann Arbor MI 48103 Office: Univ Michigan 3142 Modern Langs Bldg Ann Arbor MI 48109

GEORGE, HAROLD EUGENE, osteopath; b. Lancaster, Mo., Jan. 25, 1923; s. Frederick Milton and Opal (Darby) G.; B.S., Kirksville State Tchrs. Coll., 1949; D.O., Kirksville Coll. Osteopathy and Surgery, 1951; children by previous marriage—Frederick Maurice, Robert Eugene, Jane Ann; m. 2d, Betty Doss Power; children—John Scott, Susan Virginia, Mary Evelyn, Carol Anne. Gen. practice osteo. medicine and surgery, Mt. Vernon, Mo., 1951—; health officer Lawrence County, Mo., 1953—; staff Jane Chinn Meml. Hosp., Webb City, Mo., 1951—, Springfield Gen. Osteo. Hosp., 1951—; chmn. profl. staff Springfield Gen. Osteo. Hosp., 1962-65; owner, dir. Mt. Vernon Clinic, 1957—. Mem. med. care adv. com. Mo. Div. Welfare, 1963—; v.p. George & Harding, Inc., Joplin, Mo. Bd. dirs. Mo. Health Care Found., 1972-73. Served with USAAF, 1943-46. Fellow Am. Clin. Soc. Arthritis; mem. Am., Mo., Ozark Mo. osteo. assns., Am. Soc. Sclerotherapy, Mo. Assn. Osteo. Physicians and Surgeons (mem. pub. relations com. 1965—, mem. com. pub. health del.), Mo. Heart Assn. (dir.), Am. Coll. Gen. Practicioners (pres. Mo. chpt. 1972-73), Am. Coll. Preventive Medicine. Mason (Shriner). Home: Honeysuckle Hill Farms Route 1 Box 98 Mount Vernon MO 65712 Office: Mt Vernon Clinic East Ave and Hwy 166 Mount Vernon MO 65712 also H & B Import Bus Loop I-44 Route 1 Box 3H Mount Vernon MO 65712

GEORGE, JAMES EARL, implement co. exec.; b. Carrollton, Mo., May 13, 1940; s. Edwin Earl and Elizabeth M. (Willis) G.; grad. high sch.; m. Donna Sue Stevens, May 27, 1963; children—James Brian, Elizabeth Bernetta. Partsman, Wolf Implement Co., Carrollton, 1958-64; mechanic Heins Implement Co., Carrollton, 1964-74; parts mgr. Swift Implement Co., Carrollton, 1966—. Twp. committeeman Republican party, 1958—. Served with AUS, 1962-63. Mem. Christian Ch. (deacon 1965—). Mason (Shriner). Home: Route 1 Carrollton MO 64633 Office: Hwy 24-65 S Carrollton MO 64633

GEORGE, JERRY VANCE, petroleum co. exec.; b. Hillsboro, Tex., July 18, 1927; s. Van Theodore and Mayna (Weir) G.; B.S., Tex. A. and M. Coll., 1948; m. Joan Daisy Stoney, Apr. 29, 1960; children—Allen Van, Eric Van. Petroleum engr. Magnolia Petroleum Co., Lake Charles, La., 1949-53, Carmi, Ill., 1953-55; dist. supt. Tex.-Canadian Oil Corp., Paintsville, Ky., 1955-63, R. C. Davoust Co., Paintsville, 1964—; petroleum engr. Quasar, Inc., 1964-66; petroleum cons., Paintsville, Ky., 1967-70; now mgr. operations Guernsey Petroleum Corp., Claysville, Ohio. Served with USNR, 1945-46. Registered profl. engr., Ky. Mem. Am. Inst. Mining, Metall. and Petroleum Engrs. (chmn. East Ky. sect. 1964), Soc. Petroleum Engrs. Republican. Methodist. Home: 943 Somers St Zanesville OH 43701 Office: PO Box 35 Claysville OH 43729

GEORGE, JOHN ARNOLD, educator; b. Wyandotte, Mich., Aug. 8, 1932; s. Arnold John and Elizabeth Henrietta (Hess) G.; B.A., Sacred Heart Sem., 1954; S.T.L. (Detroit archdiocese scholar), Gregorian U., Rome, Italy, 1958; M.A., St. Louis U., 1962, Ph.D., 1966; m. Christina Anne Lovio, June 27, 1970; 1 son, John Joseph. Ordained priest Roman Catholic Ch., 1957; asst. pastor St. Rita parish, Detroit, 1958-60; asst. supt. spl. edn. Archdiocese Detroit, 1962-69; asso. dir., urban program in edn. U. Mich., Ann Arbor, 1969-70; ret. from priesthood, 1969; asst. prof. clin. and ednl. psychology Wayne State U., Detroit, 1970-75, asso. prof., 1975—. Cons. child appraisal center Wyandotte (Mich.) Gen. Hosp., 1970—;

cons. psychologist children and adults S. Bazini Psychiat. Clinic, Dearborn, Mich., 1974—. Mem. Mayor's Com. on Mental Retardation Detroit, 1965-69; exec. mem. United Community Services Mich., 1968-69; mem. Wayne County Center for Retarded, 1973—. Bd. dirs. Mich. Soc. Mental Health, 1967-69, Detroit-Wayne County Mental Health Bd., 1967-69. Mem. Am. Psychol. Assn., Internat. Assn. Pupil Personnel Workers, Council Exceptional Children. Roman Catholic. Designer, Santa Maria Exptl. Sch. for Children with Learning Problems, 1968-70. Home: 2555 Coldspring Dr Bloomfield Hills MI 48013 Office: Coll Education Wayne State Univ Detroit MI 48202

GEORGE, JOHN EDWIN, educator, publisher; b. Ashtabula, Ohio, June 26, 1936; s. John and Sigrid Johanna (Hakkarainen) G.; B.A., Waynesburg Coll., 1958; M.A., Rutgers U., 1962; Ph.D. (Stoddard fellow), U. S.C., 1969; m. Margaret Jeffries, Nov. 9, 1961; children—Cynthia Victoria, Stephanie Elizabeth, Mary Jennifer. Adj. prof. English, Jersey City State Coll., 1965-66; instr. U. S.C., Columbia, 1966-67; asst. prof. reading edn. U. Mo., Kansas City, 1969-71, asso. prof., 1971-75, prof., 1975—, chmn. div. reading edn., 1975-76, chmn. div. reading and spl. edn., 1976—; dir. Reading Acad., 1976—; vis. prof. U. Pitts., 1968, No. Ill. U., 1971, No. Iowa U., 1973; profl. cons. McGraw-Hill Book Co., 1973-75, Scholastic Books, Inc., 1973-75. Mem. Am. Psychol. Assn., Am. Ednl. Research Assn., Internat. Reading Assn., Coll. Reading Assn., Nat. Reading Conf., Nat. Soc. for Study of Edn., Am. Orthopsychiat. Assn., AAUP, Phi Delta Kappa, Pi Lambda Theta. Presbyn. Author books, including: Great Essays: From the 16th Century to the Present, 1969; Tutor-Student System in Beginning Reading, 1971; (with Anne Bengfort and Linda Prugh) Tutor-Student System in Reading Comprehension, 1974, Programmed Reading Comprehension, 1975. Contbr. to publs. in field. Home: 5911 W 94th Terr Overland Park KS 66207 Office: Reading Center U Mo-Kansas City 5100 Rockhill Rd Kansas City MO 64110

GEORGESON, MENAS E., osteo. physician; b. Webb City, Mo., Sept. 29, 1920; s. Emmanuel M. and Mary (Galactos) Georgopulos; B.S., Wayne State U., 1943; D.O., Coll. Osteo. Medicine and Surgery, 1948; children—Christopher, Maria. Pharmacist, 1943-45; osteo. physician, individual practice, Detroit, 1950—. Trustee NW Gen. Hosp., Detroit, 1966—. Served with USNR, 1943-44. Fellow Hypnosis Found. (life); mem. Am., Mich., Wayne County osteo. assns., Am. Soc. Bariatric Physicians. Greek Orthodox. Clubs: Masons, Shriners. Home: 28235 Forestbrook Ct Farmington Hills MI 48018 Office: 19621 W 7 Mile Rd Detroit MI 48219

GEORGEVICH, MIODRAG, educator; b. Belgrade, Yugoslavia, May 6, 1922; s. Joseph and Zorka (Maksic) G. came to U.S., 1949, naturalized, 1955; student U. Dijon (France), 1938-39, U. Belgrade, 1940-41, U. Paris, 1947-48; M.A., U. Wis., 1952; Ph.D., U. Mich., 1970; m. Militza Stojadinovich, Sept. 7, 1950; children—Joseph, Denise. Mem. youth council Yugoslav Royal Govt., Germany, France, 1945-47; accountant Standard Accident Ins. Co., Detroit, 1952-57; with No. Mich. U., Marquette, 1958—. Prof. internat. relations, 1962-75, head dept. polit. sci., 1962-75. Adviser, Young Republicans, No. Mich. U., 1958—; Rep. candidate for state senator. Served as 2d lt. Yugoslav Royal Army, 1941-45. Mem. Am. Polit. Sci. Assn., AAUP. Home: 2 Marquette Dr Marquette MI 49855

GEORGIS, WERNER FELIX, educator; b. Braunschweig, Germany, Feb. 14, 1938; s. George L. and Ingeborg (Koerner) G.; came to U.S., 1948, naturalized, 1961; student Joliet Jr. Coll., 1957-59; B.A. in History, Lewis Coll., 1962; M.A. in History, De Paul U., 1964; postgrad. U. Iowa, 1964-65, No. Ill. U., 1967-69, 76—; div.; 1 dau., Jennifer Lynn. Teaching asst. dept. history U. Iowa, 1964-65; tchr. elementary sch., Joliet, Ill., 1965-66; tchr. history high schs., Lockport, Ill., 1966-71, Romeoville, Ill., 1971-74, Bolingbrook, Ill., 1974—; cons.-trainee grantee for drug abuse prevention programs Region V, U.S. Office Edn., HEW, 1971; cons. Romeo-Brook Drug Abuse Prevention Program, 1971-72. Mem. Am. Hist. Assn., Am. Fedn. Tchrs. (conv. del. 1976, del. to Ill. Fedn. Tchrs. conv. 1976). Lutheran. Home: 1704 Campbell St Joliet IL 60435 Office: 350 W Blair Ln Bolingbrook IL 60441

GEPHARDT, RICHARD ANDREW, congressman; b. St. Louis, Jan. 31, 1941; s. Louis Andrew and Loreen Estelle (Cassell) G.; B.S., Northwestern U., 1962; J.D., U. Mich., 1965; m. Jane Ann Byrnes, Aug. 13, 1966; children—Matthew, Christine. Admitted to Mo. bar, 1965; partner firm Thompson & Mitchell, St. Louis, 1965-76; alderman 14th ward, St. Louis, 1971-76; mem. 95th Congress from 3d Dist. Mo., 1977—. Pres., Children's United Research Effort, Inc., St. Louis Children's Hosp., 1973-76. Democratic committeeman 14th ward St. Louis, 1968-71. Mem. Mo., St. Louis bar assns., Am. Legion, Young Lawyer's Soc. (chmn. 1972-73). Clubs: Kiwanis, Mid-Town (St. Louis). Home: 4121 Fairview St Saint Louis MO 63116 Office: Cannon Bldg Room 509 Washington DC

GEPHART, WILLIAM JAY, assn. exec.; b. Uniontown, Pa., Dec. 26, 1928; s. Everett William and Ruth Josephine (Gladden) G.; student Adrian Coll., 1949-52; B.S., Wayne State U., 1953, M.Ed., 1958; Ph.D., Ohio State U., 1965; m. Mary Joan Curry, June 9, 1951; children—Jeffrey Lee, Brian William. Tchr. Harper Woods (Mich.) Sch. Dist., 1953-58, Orange Sch. Dist., Cleve., 1958-61; faculty Ohio State U., Columbus, 1961-63, U. Wis., Milw., 1963-66; dir. Center on Evaluation, Devel. and Research, Phi Delta Kappa, Inc., Bloomington, Ind., 1966—. Mem. Bloomington Human Rights Commn., 1974-76. Served with USAF, 1946-49. NSF fellow, 1959; NDEA fellow, 1960. Mem. Am., Ind. (co-founder) ednl. research assns., Nat. Symposium for Profs. Ednl. Research (co-founder), Evaluation Network (co-founder), Design Methods Group, Phi Delta Kappa. Unitarian Universalist. Contbr. articles to profl. jours. Editor Center on Evaluation, Devel. and Research Quar., 1967—; watercolor artist, exhibited in numerous galleries, one-man shows and collections. Home: 3500 Morningside Dr Bloomington IN 47401 Office: PO Box 789 Bloomington IN 47401

GERARD, DONALD EDWARD, civil engr.; b. Salina, Kans., Feb. 10, 1923; s. Elmer Evert and Effie (McFarlane) G.; B.S. in Civil Engring., Kans. State U., 1948; m. Helen Lorraine Gans, Sept. 3, 1948; children—Mark Edward, Guy Rondell. Designer bridges U.S. Bur. Reclamation, Denver, 1948-49; constrn. supt. L.W. Rexroad, Salina, 1949-52; civil engr. Kans. Hwy. Commn., Salina, 1953-58, resident engr., 1958-69; asst., gen. mgr. Kans. Bd. Pub. Utilities, McPherson, 1969—. Mem. Sch. Bd. Dist. 7, 1952-55, Sch. Bd. Consol. N.W. Saline County, 1962-65, Unified Sch. Dist. 307, 1965-66. Bd. dirs. Meml. Hosp., McPherson, 1974—, Quivira council Boy Scouts Am., Wichita, 1972—. Served with USMCR, 1942-45. Decorated Air medal with 11 clusters, D.F.C. Registered profl. engr., Kans. Mem. Kans. Engring. Soc. (sec.-treas. 1974-75), South Central Council Chambers (chmn. energy com. 1974-75), Equus Beds Water Mgmt. Dist. 2 (sec. 1975—), V.F.W., Am. Legion. Elk. Home: 1462 Ranch Rd McPherson KS 67460 Office: 400 E Kansas Ave McPherson KS 67460

GERARD, STEPHEN CHENOWETH, lawyer; b. Sigourney, Iowa, Apr. 12, 1923; s. Russell Sage and Mary (Chenoweth) G.; B.S., U. Iowa, 1949, J.D., 1952; m. Helen Jeanette Frank, June 19, 1948; children—Stephen Chenoweth II, Timothy Frank, Karen Mary. Admitted to Iowa bar, 1952, since practiced in Sigourney; mem. firm Stephen C. Gerard, 1952-53, Baumert & Gerard, 1953—; city atty. Sigourney, 1952-56, 62-66, 70—, mayor, 1956-62. Mem. bd. Edn. Sigourney Ind. Sch. Dist., past pres.; pres. Area XV Community Coll. Bd. Edn., 1967-75; pres. Iowa Council Area Sch. Bds., 1973-75; v.p. S. Ia. Council Boy Scouts Am., 1961-64; mem. exec. com., 1961-66. Chmn. Keokuk Co. Dem. central com., 1954-56. Served with USMCR, 1943-46. Decorated Air medal. Mem. Am., Iowa State, Keokuk County (pres.) bar assns., Vets. Fgn. Wars, Am. Legion, Phi Alpha Delta. Mason, Odd Fellow. Home: 714 W Spring St Sigourney IA 52591 Office: Professional Bldg Sigourney IA 52591

GERBER, AARON BERNARD, surgeon, hosp. adminstr.; b. Chgo., Dec. 8, 1919; s. Morris and Fannie Lillian (Senator) G.; A.B., U. Ill., 1941, B.S., 1942, M.D., 1943; m. Vivian Noskin, June 20, 1943; children—B. Thomas, Diane L. Practice medicine specializing in surgery, Park Forest, Ill., 1951—; chmn. dept. surgery Ingalls Meml. Hosp., Harvey, Ill.; chmn. dept. surgery St. James Hosp., Chicago Heights, Ill., pres. med. staff, 1977—. Served with M.C. AUS, 1944-46. Diplomate Am. Bd. Surgery. Fellow Am. Coll. Surgeons; mem. Chgo. Med. Soc. (br. pres.). Jewish. Office: 2605 W Lincoln Hwy Olympia Fields IL 60461

GERBER, BERNARD CHARLES, surgeon; b. Aberdeen, S.D., Nov. 25, 1926; s. Henry P. and Agnes M. (Egan) G.; B.S., No. State Coll., 1949; B.S. in Medicine, U. S.D., 1951; M.D., Northwestern U., 1953; m. Marcella A. Aslesen, Sept. 15, 1951; children—Karen, Jean, Charles, Martin, Lawrence, Christopher. Intern, Passavant Meml. Hosp., & Chgo., 1953-54; resident in surgery Northwestern U., Chgo., 1954-58, Kanavel Meml. fellow in surgery, 1957-58; asso. chief surgery Meml. Med. Center, Williamson, W.Va., 1958-60; practice medicine specializing in surgery, Aberdeen, S.D., 1960—; mem. staff St. Luke's Hosp., 1960—, pres. staff, 1975; mem. staff Dakota Midland Hosp.; preceptor U. S.D. Sch. Medicine, 1972-75, clin. instr. surgery, 1976—; pres. bd. dirs. N.E. Mental Health Center, 1975, 76; mem. S.D. Bd. Examiners Basic Scis., 1975-78. Bd. dirs. Aberdeen Area United Way, 1974-76. Served with U.S. Army, 1945-46. Diplomate Am. Bd. Surgery. Fellow A.C.S. (pres. S.D. chpt. 1975-76, gov. 1977—); mem. AMA, S.D. Med. Assn., Western Surg. Assn., Aberdeen Dist. Med. Soc., S.D. Mental Health Assn. (dir. 1977—). Roman Catholic. Home: 1821 Eisenhower Circle Aberdeen SD 57401 Office: 201 S Lloyd St Aberdeen SD 57401

GERBER, RICHARD WAYNE, electronic lock co. exec., inventor; b. Webster City, Iowa, July 10, 1942; s. Walter H. and Ruth H. (Humphrey) G.; A.A., Webster City Jr. Coll., 1961; student U. Iowa, 1962-63. Owner, operator Gerber Lock & Safe, Webster City, 1968-74; founder Gerber Electronic Lock, Inc., Hugo, Minn., 1974—. Served with Army N.G., 1965-71. Mem. Associated Locksmiths Am., Nat. Locksmiths Assn., Am. Legion. Methodist. Clubs: Elks, Moose. Patentee in field (56). Home: 9517 University St Des Moines IA 50322 Office: 414 9th St Des Moines IA 50309

GERBERDING, MILES CARSTON, lawyer; b. Decatur, Ind., Oct. 25, 1930; s. Arnold Herman and Luella Edith (Lapp) G.; B.S., Ind. U., 1953, J.D., 1956; m. Ruth Hostrup, Aug. 20, 1955; children—Karla M., Greta E., Kent E., Brian K. Admitted to Ind. bar; asso. Nieter & Smith, Ft. Wayne, 1956-57, partner, 1957-58; asso. Barrett, Barrett & McNagny, Ft. Wayne, 1958-61, partner, 1962—. Bd. dirs. Concordia Ednl. Found., 1968—, pres., 1972-74; bd. dirs. Jr. Achievement Ft. Wayne, Big Bros. Greater Ft. Wayne; treas. Luth. Camp Assn., 1976—. Served with USMCR, 1950-52. Fellow Am. Bar Found.; mem. Am. Judicature Soc., Am. (exempt orgns. com. taxation sect.), Ind. (chmn. corp. banking and bus. law sect. 1966-67, dir. taxation sect. 1971-76, chmn. 1975-76, dir. probate sect. 1972-74; bd. mgrs. 1973-75, v.p. 1977-78), Allen County (dir. 1971-73) bar assns., Ft. Wayne Aviation Assn. (dir. 1976—), Ft. Wayne C. of C. (aviation com. 1976—), Ft. Wayne Estate Planning Council (past dir., v.p.), Ft. Wayne Tax Club, Luth. Assn. for Elementary Edn. (pres. 1967-68), Greater Ft. Wayne Assn. Luth. Chs. (v.p. 1964-65), Luth. Laymen's League (pres. Ft. Wayne 1961-62), Blue Key, Beta Gamma Sigma, Delta Sigma Pi, Phi Delta Phi, Kappa Delta Rho. Clubs: Fort Wayne Country, Summit. Home: 3908 Spanish Trail Fort Wayne IN 46815 Office: 3d Floor Lincoln Tower Fort Wayne IN 46802

GERBERICH, WILLIAM WARREN, educator; b. Wooster, Ohio, Dec. 30, 1935; s. Harold Robert and Clarissa Thelma (Ross) G.; B.S. in Engring. Adminstrn., Case Inst. Tech., 1957; M.S. in Indsl. Engring., Syracuse U., 1959; Ph.D. in Materials Sci. and Engring., U. Calif. at Berkeley, 1971; m. Susan Elizabeth Goodwin, Aug. 15, 1959; children—Bradley Kent, Brian Keith, Beth Clarice. Research engr. Jet Propulsion Lab., Calif. Inst. Tech., Pasadena, Calif., 1959-61; research scientist Aeronutronic, Newport Beach, Calif., 1961-64; engring. research specialist Aerojet Gen., Sacramento, 1964-67; lectr., research metallurgist U. Calif. and Lawrence Radiation Lab., Berkeley, 1967-71; dir. materials sci. U. Minn., Mpls., 1972—, asso. prof. dept. chem. engring. and materials sci., 1971-75, prof., 1975—. Cons. accident prevention div. Minn. Dept. Labor and Industry, also steel, constrn. and aerospace cos. Recipient Teleen English prize Case Inst. Tech., 1959; William Spraragen award Welding Jour. for best research paper, 1968. Registered profl. engr., Calif. Mem. ASME, (Metall. Soc.), Am. Soc. Metals, Sigma Xi, Tau Beta Pi, Pi Delta Epsilon, Phi Delta Theta. Republican. Contbr. articles to tech. jours., to internat. symposia. Home: 8016 Ridgeway Rd Golden Valley MN 55426 Office: Chem Engring and Materials Sci Bldg U Minn Minneapolis MN 55455

GERBIE, ALBERT BERNARD, physician; b. Toledo, 1927; M.D., George Washington U., 1951. Intern, Michael Reese Hosp., Chgo., 1951-52; preceptorship with Drs. Baer, Reis and De Costa, 1952-55; attending physician obstetrics and gynecology Prentice Pavillion, Northwestern Meml. Hosp., Chgo.; chief div. obstetrics and gynecology Children's Meml. Hosp.; prof. obstetrics and gynecology, dir. grad. and continuing edn. Northwestern U. Diplomate, examiner, dir. Am. Bd. Obstetrics and Gynecology. Fellow Am. Coll. Obstetricians and Gynecologists, Central Assn. Obstetricians and Gynecologists, A.C.S., Am. Assn. Obstetricians and Gynecologists, Am. Gynecol. Soc.; mem. AMA, Chgo. Gynecol. Soc. (pres. 1977-78). Asso. editor Surgery, Gynecology and Obstetrics, Am. Jour. Obstetrics and Gynecology. Home: 56 Coventry Rd Northfield IL 60093 Office: 707 Fairbanks Ct Chicago IL 60611

GERBIG, CLIFFORD GEORGE, toxicologist/veterinarian; b. Morgantown, Ind., Aug. 9, 1932; s. Eugene Edgar and Evangeline (Foster) G.; B.S. in Agr., Purdue U., 1959, M.S. in Dairy Microbiology, 1960, D.V.M., 1964; m. Georgianne Boxell, Jan. 25, 1959; children—Ruth, Lydia. Dist. veterinarian U.S. Dept. Agr., Mattoon, Ill., 1964-66, head Pharmacology-Toxicology Lab., Pesticide Regulation div., Washington, 1966-67; practice vet. medicine, Effingham, Ill., 1967-69; toxicologist/veterinarian Dow Chem. Co. Indpls., 1969—. Mem. found. com. Heritage Christian Sch., Indpls., 1975—; curator Alumni Museum, Ind. Soldier and Sailors Children's Home, Knightstown, Ind., 1969—, bd. dirs., 1969—. Mem. AVMA, Ind., Central Ind. vet. med. assns., Am. Assn. Lab. Animal Sci. (chpt. exam. bd. 1974—, dir. 1976—), Am. Soc. Lab. Animal Practitioners, Indsl. Vet. Assn., Soc. Comparative Ophthalmology, Ind. Acad. Vet. Medicine, Soc. Primatologists, Ceres, Phi Eta Sigma, Alpha Zeta. Author numerous co. reports. Contbr. articles to profl. jours. Home: 3011 W 96th St Indianapolis IN 46268 Office: PO Box 68511 Indianapolis IN 46268

GERBING, FRANK, JR., accountant; b. Chgo., Sept. 24, 1911; s. Frank and Hattie (Siebold) G.; diploma in commerce Northwestern U., 1935; m. Arlie O. Collins, Apr. 9, 1939. Accountant Transo Envelope Co., Chgo., 1930-34; supervising accountant U.S. Dept. Agr., 1939-44; gen. practice mgr. Coopers & Lybrand, C.P.A.'s, Chgo., 1945-75; chmn. bd., pres. ARL, Ltd., 1976—. Mem. Am. Inst. C.P.A.'s, Ill. Soc. C.P.A.'s, Steuben Soc. Am. Club: Bavarian. Home and Office: 6160 N Damen Ave Chicago IL 60659

GERDES, LOUIS GEORGE, editor; b. Hamlin, Iowa, Jan. 14, 1919; s. Louis George and Mable (Hunt) G.; B.J., U. Mo., 1941; m. Helen M. Swank, July 9, 1941; 1 son, Stephen Lee. Sports editor Grand Island (Nebr.) Herald, 1937; reporter Grand Island Bulletin, summers, 1938, 39; editor Jefferson County (Wis.) Union, 1941; sports copy writer Omaha World-Herald, 1941-43, govtl. and polit. reporter, 1943-51, city editor, 1951-66, exec. editor, dir., 1966—; v.p. World Pub. Co., 1970—. Past bd. dirs. Nebr. Crippled Childrens Soc. Mem. Am. Soc. Newspaper Editors (mem. Pulitzer jury com.). Mem. United Ch. Christ (deacon). Author booklets on municipal govt., parking. Home: 1326 S 91st Ave Omaha NE 68124 Office: Omaha World Herald Omaha NE 68102

GERHARDT, MARTIN, JR., ins. co. exec.; b. Chgo., Apr. 25, 1927; s. Martin and Elizabeth (Kunz) G.; student U. Ill., Chgo., 1948-50; m. Charlotte Ann Lawless, June 21, 1952. With Lumbermen's Mut. Casualty Co., Long Grove, Ill., 1950—, jr. exec., 1963-67, sr. exec., asst. mgr. systems and programming, 1967-72, asso. computer ops. officer, 1972—. Served with USAAF, 1945-46. Certified data processor Data Processing Mgmt. Assn. Roman Catholic. Home: 5039 Menard St Chicago IL 60630 Office: Long Grove IL 60047

GERIG, REGINALD ROTH, musician, educator; b. Grabill, Ind., Apr. 20, 1919; s. Safara Samuel and Sarah (Roth) G.; B. Music, Wheaton Coll., 1942; M.S., Juilliard Sch. Music, 1949; m. Irene Conrad, June 17, 1944; children—Sarah Elizabeth Gerig Campbell, Reginald R. Mem. piano faculty Nyack (N.Y.) Coll., 1946-50, Eastman Sch. Music, U. Rochester, N.Y., 1950-52; asst. prof. music Wheaton (Ill.) Coll., 1952-57, asso. prof., 1957-62, prof., 1962—, chmn. dept. piano, 1969—; organist Coll. Ch. Wheaton, 1953—. Served with USNR, 1942-45. Mem. Music Tchrs. Nat. Assn., Ill. Music Tchrs. Assn., Coll. Music Soc., Nat. Guild Piano Tchrs., Am. Liszt Soc., Soc. Am. Musicians, Wheaton Coll. Scholastic Honor Soc. (pres. 1974-75). Author: Famous Pianists and Their Technique, 1974, 76. Compiler: Piano Preludes on Hymns and Chorales, 1959. Home: 1328 Naperville Rd Wheaton IL 60187 Office: Conservatory Music Wheaton College Wheaton IL 60187

GERLA, MORTON, mech. engr., bus. exec.; b. Bklyn., July 11, 1916; s. Harry and Jennie (Levy) G.; B.Mech.Engring., City U. N.Y., 1937; postgrad. George Washington U., 1940-41, Calif. Inst. Tech., 1944, N.Y. U., 1953, New Sch. Social Research, 1953-57; m. Miriam Kleeger, Oct. 14, 1939; children—Harry Seymour, Lisa Joy. Asst. to Arnold Weisselberg, M.E., cons. engr., N.Y.C., 1937-38; ordnance engr. U.S. Naval Gun Factory, Washington, 1938-45; asst. chief engr. Industro-Matic Corp., cons. engrs., N.Y.C., 1945-47; v.p. Superior Devel. Corp., N.Y.C., 1947-50; mgr. electro-mech. design engring. W.L. Maxson Corp., N.Y.C., 1950-55; v.p. Lalin Constrn. Corp., Nassau County, N.Y., 1955-65; mgr. machine design Anaconda Wire & Cable Co., N.Y.C., 1965-71; mgr. systems and standards Addressograph-Multigraph Corp., Cleve., 1972-76; corp. staff cons. in engring. and mfg. Scott and Fetzer Co., Macedonia, Ohio, 1976-77; project leader, cons. Ocean Systems div. Gould, Inc., Cleve., 1977—; cons. Maschinenfabrik Herborn, Herborn, Dillkreis, W.Ger., 1968-71. Sec. Hillside Civic Assn., New Hyde Park, N.Y., 1948-50. Bd. dirs. New Sch. Assos., N.Y.C., 1954-57, Jamaica Estates Assn., N.Y.C., 1968-72. Recipient Civilian Commendation, Navy Dept., 1945. Registered profl. engr., N.Y., Ohio. Mem. ASME (dir. D.C. sect. 1943-45), Am. Rocket Soc. (pres., dir. N.Y. sect. 1948-50), Am. Nat. Standards Inst. (exec. standards council 1974-75), Am. Soc. Metals, Tau Beta Pi. Jewish (mem. adult edn. commn. United Synagogue 1958-60). Mason. Home: 764 Pipe's Ct Northfield OH 44067 Office: 631 E Aurora Rd Macedonia OH 44056

GERLACH, HANS WERNER, machinery mfg. co. exec.; b. Riddorf, Nordfriesland, Germany, July 4, 1931; s. Christian Bernard and Christine Magdaline (Ingwersen) G.; came to U.S., 1953, naturalized, 1955; student U. Wis., 1956-58; m. Florence Lois Brandmeier, June 21, 1958; children—Christian, Carl. With Rexnord, Milw., 1953-63; founder, pres., gen. mgr., chief exec. officer Summit Metal Fabricating, Inc., Cudahy, Wis., 1965—. Served with U.S. Army, 1954-56. Mem. Am. Welding Soc., Cudahy C. of C. Club: Masons. Home: 4920 S Root River Pkwy Greenfield WI 53228 Office: 5707 S Pennsylvania Ave Cudahy WI 53110

GERLACH, LUTHER PAUL, educator; b. Oct. 25, 1930; B.A., U. Minn., 1952; Ph.D., U. London (Eng.), 1961; m. 1958; 3 children. Vis. lectr. anthropology U. Minn., 1961-71, anthropologist, 1963-65, asst. prof., 1963-65, asso. prof., 1965-71, prof., 1971—; asst. prof. anthropology and sociology Lafayette Coll., 1961-63. Served with AUS, 1952-54. Fulbright Jr. fellow, 1958-60; Hill Family Found. (now Northwest Area Found.), 1967—; Rockefeller Found. research grantee, 1969-70; OWRR grantee, 1969-72, 75-78. Mem. Am. Anthrop. Assn., Soc. Applied Anthropology, African Studies Assn., Internat. African Law Assn. Author: (with Virginia H. Hine) People, Power, Change: Movements of Social Transformation, 1970, Lifeway Leap: The Dynamics of Change in America, 1973. Contbr. articles to profl. jours. Producer films and filmstrips including Zanj-Africa, 1970, People Eco-Action, 1970, Systemic Thinking, 1973; TV series Lifeway Leap. Address: 1879 Cloud Dr Blaine MN 55433

GERLER, EDWIN ROLAND, JR., educator; b. Pueblo, Colo., Dec. 26, 1945; s. Edwin Roland and Agnes Harvey (McMeekan) G.; B.S., Concordia Coll., 1967; M.S. (Fellow), Bucknell U., 1972; Ed.D., Pa. State U., 1975; m. Diane Lynn Alexander, June 5, 1972; 1 son, Jonathan Michael. Math tchr. Heaton Jr. High Sch., Pueblo, 1968-72; counselor, cons. Central Susquehanna Intermediate Unit, Lewisburg, Pa., 1972-74; asst. prof. U. Wis., Whitewater, 1975-77, N.C. State U., Raleigh, 1977—. Bd. dirs. Columbia-Montour Mental Health Assn., Bloomsburg, Pa., 1973-74. Mem. Am. Personnel Guidance Assn., Am. Sch. Counselor Assn., Nat. Vocat. Guidance Assn., Am. Assn. Counselor Edn. Supervision. Lutheran. Contbr. articles in field to profl. jours.; editorial bd. Sch. Counselor, 1975-78. Home: 2502 New Hope Church Rd Raleigh NC 27604

GERLITZ, FRANK EDWARD, biomed. engr.; b. Phila., May 31, 1948; s. Frank Edward and LaNieta Vivian (Souden) G.; B.S., Bucknell U., 1970; B.S., U. Wis., Madison, 1973, M.S., 1977. Biomed. engr. Madison Area Tech. Coll., 1975-76, Otto Hiller Co., Madison, 1973—, U. Wis., Madison, 1973—. Mem. ASCE, ASME, Am. Engring. Model Soc., Biomed. Engring. Soc. Home: 1625 Madison St Madison WI 53711

GERMON, WESLEY MARION, JR., chemist; b. Wellsburg, W.Va., July 29, 1927; s. Wesley Marion and Bertha (Croston) G.; B.S., Bethany Coll., 1953; M.S., U. Akron, 1961; m. June Elizabeth McMillan, June 19, 1954; children—Elizabeth Ann, Wesley Marion III. Jr. chemist Koppers Co., Inc., Monaca, Pa., 1953-54; devel. engr., research chemist Goodyear Tire & Rubber Co., Akron, Ohio, 1954-59, sec. mgr., prin. chemist, 1963—; research chemist Internat. Latex Corp., Dover, Del., 1959-63. Scoutmaster, committeeman Boy Scouts Am., 1966-69. Served with USNR, 1945-46. Mem. Am. Chem. Soc. Republican. Clubs: Wingfoot Fliers, Masons. Patentee in field. Home: 1119 Chestnut Blvd Cuyahoga Falls OH 44223 Office: 1485 E Archwood Ave Akron OH 44316

GERMOVNIK, FRANCIS I., librarian, educator; b. Vodice, Slovenia, Sept. 27, 1915; s. Joseph I. and Frances I. (Kosec) G.; came to U.S., 1946, naturalized, 1952; Juris Canonici Doctor Angelicum, Rome, 1945; Baccalaureate, Our Lady of the Lake Coll., San Antonio, Tex., 1948-50; M.A. in L.S., Rosary Coll., River Forest, Ill., 1967. Prof. librarian St. John's Sem., San Antonio, Tex., 1946-52, Assumption Seminary, San Antonio, 1952-54, St. Mary's Sem., Perryville, Mo., 1954-64, DeAndreis Sem., Lemont, Ill., 1964—. Mem. Canon Law Soc. of Am., ALA, Am. Catholic library assns. Address: DeAndreis Seminary 511 E 127th St Lemont IL 60439

GEROFF, STEVE KURSTO, dentist; b. Madison, Ill., June 3, 1920; s. Christ A. and Helen K. (Engelcoff) G.; student So. Ill. U., 1938-39; B.S., St. Louis U., 1943, D.D.S., 1948; m. Helen Mae Worthen, Sept. 17, 1943; children—Stephen Craig, Robert Kursto, Mary Helen. Pvt. practice dentistry, Madison, Ill., 1948-72, Granite City, Ill., 1972—. Head med. br. Madison Civil Def., 1950-60. Mem. Madison Planning Commn., 1954; bd. mem. Madison Sch. Dist. 12, 1954-66, sec., 1958-59, 62-63. Served with M.C., AUS, 1943-44. Recipient Lion of Yr. award, Madison, Ill., 1961. Mem. Am., Ill., Madison Dist. dental assns., Delta Sigma Delta, Amvets, Am. Legion. Rotarian, Lion. Home: 3322 Princeton Dr Granite City IL 62040 Office: 1420 20th St Granite City IL 62040

GERSON, MYLES ZACHARY, steel co. exec.; b. N.Y.C., Aug. 15, 1925; s. Samuel and Pauline (Farber) G.; student Bordentown (N.J.) Mil. Inst., 1940; grad. Tilton Sch., 1942; m. Albine Roberta Gutterman, Dec. 19, 1948; children—Roger, David, Elizabeth. Mgr., Smith Transport, Ltd., N.Y.C., 1946-48; regional mgr. B & E. Transp., Secaucus, N.J., 1948-51; v.p. Hayes Freight Lines, Springfield, Ill., 1951-56; gen. mgr. Gen. Expressways, Chgo., 1956-63; v.p., gen. mgr. Spl. Commodity div. Navajo Freight Lines, Chgo., 1964—, v.p., Gary, Ind., 1965—, also dir.; now v.p. Allied Tube & Conduit Corp., Harvey, Ill. Mem. com. hwys., N.Y., 1951-53, Ill., 1961-69. Bd. dirs. P.Hs. Symphony, 1954-55. Chmn. transp. com. Prairie State Coll. Served with AUS, 1943-46; PTO. Decorated Purple Heart, Bronze Star medal. Mem. N.Y., Chgo. traffic clubs. Jewish (v.p. local temple). Home: 630 Argyle Rd Flossmoor IL 60422 Office: 16100 Lathrop Harvey IL 60426

GERSPACHER, FREDERICK ANTHONY, govt. ofcl.; b. Dayton, Ohio, Dec. 18, 1915; s. Fred and Mary Elisabeth (Bader) G.; B.A., U. Dayton, 1956; M.A., Indsl. Coll. Armed Forces, 1963; m. Carolyn Eudell Warner, Oct. 1, 1938; children—Frederick Church, Anthony Keith, Timothy Michael. Research scientist, coordinator project devel. Air Force Materials Lab., Wright Patterson AFB, Ohio, 1946-56, negotiator, adminstr. govt. research and devel., 1956—; dir. Centennial Furniture Co., Inc., Xenia, Ohio. Chmn. bd. dirs. Green County community action com. div. SCOPE, also trustee; bd. dirs. Greene County Mental Health Assn., 1973-77; mem. exec. council Mental Health Assns. Miami Valley, 1973-77; mem. adv. bd., human resources div. Dayton Dept. Parks and Recreation; mem. explorer div. service team Tecumseh council Boy Scouts Am., recipient Dist. Merit award, 1976. Served with USAF, 1943-46. Recipient St. George medal and Bronze Pelican award Cin. Archdiocese Council on Cath. Scouting, 1976, 77. Mem. Foremans Club Dayton, Am. Def. Preparedness Assn., Presidents Club, Air Force Assn., Aviation Hall of Fame, Am. Mgmt. Assn., VFW. Roman Catholic. Club: Kiwanis (past pres.). Home: 2364 Gerspacher Dayton OH 45431 Office: USAF ASD/AEAKI Wight Patterson AFB OH 45431

GERSTACKER, ROBERT WILLIAM, govt. ofcl.; b. Lakewood, Ohio, Nov. 10, 1920; s. Edwin Henry and Zouri Frances (Colahan) G.; student Ohio Wesleyan U., Delaware, 1940-42; B.Sc., Northwestern U., 1947; m. Margaret Ann VanHook, Dec. 27, 1946; children—Ann Gerstacker Poole, Lee, Lyn Gerstacker Turner, Beth; Supr., instr. Joseph E. Seagram & Sons, Inc., Lawrenceburg, Ind., 1947-49, Louisville, 1949-51; editor publs. Hiram Walker & Sons, Inc., Peoria, Ill., 1951-60; dir. communications Spectro Freight System, Inc., Chgo., 1960-67; account exec. Beveridge Orgn., Chgo., 1967-69; mgr. pub. relations Trailmobile div. Pullman, Inc., Chgo., 1970-75; gen. mgr. Canpol, Inc., Glendale Heights, Ill., 1975-76; pub. info. officer village of Hoffman Estates (Ill.), 1977—; tchr. pub. speaking Extension div. Purdue U., 1948. Dir. play Peoria Players, 1954; chmn. Community Com. to incorporate Marquette Heights (Ill.) as a city, 1956; founder, pres. U.S. Truck Hist. Soc., 1970-72; v.p. Am. Truck Hist. Soc., Dearborn Heights, Mich., 1972—; mem. alumni steering com. Sch. of Speech, Northwestern U., 1974—, program co-chmn., 1975-76; precinct election judge Republican Party, 1976. Mem. Pub. Relations Soc. Am., Soc. Profl. Journalists, Sigma Delta Chi. Recipient George Washington medal Freedom Found. at Valley Forge, 1954. Home: 362 Elm St Glen Ellyn IL 60137 Office: 1200 N Gannon Dr Hoffman Estates IL 60196

GERSTENMAIER, JOHN HERBERT, rubber co. exec.; b. St. Paul, Aug. 24, 1916; s. Walter and Alma (Lindenberg) G.; B.M.E., U. Minn., 1938; M.Indsl. Mgmt., Mass. Inst. Tech., 1952; m. Lois Rolfing, Dec. 28, 1939; children—John Herbert, Jan Lee McClennan, JoEllen. With Goodyear Tire & Rubber Co., 1938-63, 67—, plant mgr., Logan, Ohio, 1963, exec. v.p., dir., Akron Ohio, 1971-74, pres., chief operating officer, 1974—; pres. Motor Wheel Corp., Lansing, Mich., 1964-67. Mem. Soc. Automotive Engrs., Sigma Nu. Lutheran. Club: Portage Country (Akron). Home: 431 St Andrews Dr Akron OH 44303 Office: 1144 E Market St Akron OH 44316

GERSTMAN, DANIEL ROBERT, educator; b. Champaign, Ill., Apr. 14, 1943; s. Robert Frank and Anna Margaret (Fisher) G.; A.B., U. Ill., 1966; B.S., Ind. U., 1968, D.Optometry, 1969, M.Sc., 1971; m. Vivien Marie Taylor, Jan. 23, 1966; children—Heidi Ann, Matthew Tyler. Practice optometry Rantoul, Ill., 1969—; asso. prof. optometry Ind. U., Bloomington, 1975—, mem. physiol. optics dept., 1972—, dir. Geriatric Clinic, 1972—, dir. Low Vision Clinic, 1971-72, 73. Mem. Bd. Examiners for Low Vision Certification, 1972-73; cons. Nat. Bd. Examiners in Optometry, 1973-74. NSF fellow, 1970-71. Fellow Am. Acad. Optometry, Royal Microscopical Soc.; mem. Ill., Am. optometric assns., Sigma Xi. Author: Optometry Examination Review Book, Vol. II, Clinical Optometry, 1975. Home: 245 James Rd Rantoul IL 61866 Office: Dept Physiol Optics Indiana Univ Bloomington IN 47401

GERSTMAN, GEORGE HENRY, patent lawyer; b. N.Y.C., July 25, 1939; s. Mortimer Zacharias and Adelaide Bernice (Koteen) G.; B.S. in Elec. Engring., U. Ill., 1960; J.D. with honors (Mary Covington Meml. scholar) George Washington Law Sch., 1963; m. Rozanne Millman, Dec. 24, 1960; children—Heidi Ann, Gary Daniel. Patent examiner U.S. Patent Office, Washington, D.C., 1960-63; admitted to Ill. bar, 1964, U.S. Patent Office, 1964, U.S. Customs Ct., 1971, U.S. Supreme Ct., 1971; asso. firm Dressler, Goldsmith, Clement & Gordon, Chgo., 1963-70; mem. firm Pigott & Gerstman, Chgo., 1970—. Govt. appeal agt. SSS, 1964-74. Mem. Northbrook Bd. Zoning Appeals, 1971—. Mem. Am., Chgo. bar assns., Chgo. Patent Law Assn., Bar Assn. 7th Jud. Circuit, Nat. Patent Council, Patent Office Soc., Order of Coif. Asst. patent editor George Washington Law Rev., 1962-63. Contbr. articles to profl. jours. Home: 4041 Picardy Dr Northbrook IL 60062 Office: 105 W Adams St Chicago IL 60603

GERTLER, ALFRED MARTIN, pub. relations exec.; b. N.Y.C., Nov. 15, 1922; s. Harry and Peggy L (Weinberg) G.; B.S. in Journalism, U. Ill., 1947; m. Claire O. Gruenberg, Oct. 19, 1951; children—Eric, Jonathan, Richard. Reporter, editor Peoria (Ill.) Star, 1947; account exec. Ridings & Ferris, Inc., Chgo., 1948; with Harshe-Rotman & Druck, Inc., Chgo., 1948—, sr. exec. v.p., 1973—, chief operating officer, 1977—; counselor U. Ill., 1974-75, lectr., 1975— counselor No. Ill. U., 1974-75, U. Ill. Athletic Assn., 1976-77, Dept. State, 1974. Served with USAAF, 1942-45. Decorated D.F.C., Air medal with five oak leaf clusters. Mem. Pub. Relations Soc. Am. (accredited), Publicity Club Chgo., Sigma Delta Chi. Democrat, Jewish. Contbr. articles to profl. jours. Home: 1450 Ridge Rd Highland Park IL 60035 Office: 444 N Michigan Ave Chicago IL 60611

GERTZ, THOMAS ERWIN, orgn. exec.; b. Chgo., Dec. 4, 1944; s. Erwin August Henry and Camille Bertha (Eschenbach) G.; M. of Human Sexuality, Inst. Advanced Study of Human Sexuality, 1976. Adminstrv. asst. Midwest Population Center, Chgo., 1972-73; adminstrv. asst. Richard L. Bennett, M.D., Akron, Ohio, 1973—; adminstrv. dir., sex educator Akron Forum, Inc., 1973—; mem. faculty Inst. Advanced Study of Human Sexuality, San Francisco, 1976—; past pres., Mattachine Midwest, Inc., Chgo. Bd. dirs. Met. Community Ch. of Akron. Mem. Am. Assn. Sex Educators, Counselors and Therapists, Sex. Info. and Edn. Council of U.S., Soc. for Sci. Study of Sex, Inc., Am. Assn. Sex Educators, Counselors and Therapists (certified). Home: PO Box 1803 Akron OH 44309 Office: Suite 516 111 Cascade Plaza Akron OH 44308

GESELL, MARVIN HOMER, lawyer; b. Bloomington, Ill., Feb. 20, 1929; s. Homer Alfred and Clara Louise (Bird) G.; A.B., U. Ill., 1953; J.D., John Marshall Law Sch., 1958; m. Susan K. Riley, Feb. 19, 1966; children—Tracy Lynn, Gretchen Louise. Admitted to Ill. bar, 1958; asst. states atty., McLean County, Ill., 1958-62; individual practice law, Bloomington, 1962-65; partner firm Arnold, Gesell and Schwulst, Bloomington, 1965—; pub. defender McLean County, 1970—. Mem. steering com. Jr. Coll. Adv. Group McLean County, 1973. Trustee Brokaw Hosp., Normal, 1963-65, 76—. Served with USN, 1946-49. Recipient Key Man of Year award Bloomington-Normal Jr. C. of C., 1964. Fellow Am. Acad. Matrimonial Lawyers; mem. Am. Judicature Soc., Am., Ill., McLean County (treas. 1959-60) bar assns., Ill. Trial Lawyers Assn., Nat. Assn. Criminal Def. Lawyers, Assn. Trial Lawyers of Am., Ill. Pub. Defenders Assn. (commr. Ill. defender project 1972-75), Nat. Legal Aid and Defenders Assn., Assn. Commerce and Industry McLean County, Am. Heritage Soc., McClean County Livestock Assn., Am., Ill. Shorthorn assns. Chi Psi, Phi Delta Phi. Republican. Mem. United Ch. Christ (pres. 1965, mem. bd. 1972—). Mason (Shriner), Elk. Club: Bloomington Country. Home: 906 S Mercer St Bloomington IL 61701 Office: 303 Livingston Bldg Bloomington IL 61701

GESTERFIELD, KATHRYN JENSEN, librarian; b. Minatare, Nebr., Apr. 3, 1915; student Nebr. State Coll., Chadron, 1933-35, Kearney, 1937-38; A.B., U. Denver, 1939; M.L.S., U. Ill., 1961; m. Arnold D. Gesterfield. Br. asst. Denver Pub. Library, 1939-42; librarian Scottsbluff (Nebr.) Pub. Library, 1946-60; asst. reference librarian U. Ill., 1960-61; librarian Champaign (Ill.) Pub. Library, 1962-69; with Ill. State Library, Springfield, 1970—, cons. library devel. br., now dir. Served with WAC, 1942-45. Mem. ALA, Ill. (2d v.p. 1968-69, chmn. pub. library sect. 1963-64), Nebr. (pres. 1951-52) library assns. Office: Ill State Library Centennial Bldg Springfield IL 62706*

GETMAN, CLYDE JAY, clergyman, educator; b. Binghamton, N.Y., Aug. 3, 1940; s. Clyde J. and Ruth I. (Wagner) G.; A.A.S., Broome Tech. Community Coll., 1961; diploma Practical Bible Tng. Sch., 1964; B.A., Barrington Coll., 1965; M.Div., Gordon-Conwell Theol. Sem., 1970; D.Min., Andover Newton Theol. Sch., 1972; m. Suzanne Marie Randall, June 3, 1967; children—Karen Elizabeth, Kristen Ruth, Kimberly Sue. Ordained to ministry Baptist Ch., 1970; dir. Youth for Christ, Newport, R.I., 1965-67; pastor First Bapt. Ch., Mendon, Mass., 1969-73; chaplain St. Louis State Hosp., 1974—; counselor, Care and Counseling, Inc., St. Louis, 1974-75; pvt. practice pastoral psychotherapy, St. Louis, 1974—. Counselor Boy Scouts Am. Fellow Am. Assn. Pastoral Counselors, Am. Protestant Hosp. Assn. Coll. Chaplains; mem. Assn. Clin. Pastoral Edn., Assn. Mental Health Clergy, Am. Assn. Marriage Family Counselors, Soc. Bib. Lit., Assn. Humanistic Psychology, Mo. Chaplains Assn., St. Louis Fedn. Instl. Ministries. Republican. Home: 850 Warder Ave University City MO 63130 Office: 5400 Arsenal St St Louis MO 63139

GETTER, RUSSELL WALLACE, educator; b. Viroqua, Wis., Sept. 22, 1935; s. Jess Wallace and Mildred Fay (Jennings) G.; B.S. magna cum laude, Wis. State U. at LaCrosse, 1967; M.S. (NSF fellow), U. Wis. at Milw., 1968, Ph.D., 1973; m. Mary Jean Mundsack, Dec. 18, 1954; children—Barbara, Roxanne, Denise, Scott, Laurie, Robert. Dairy and tobacco farmer, Vernon County, Wis., 1953-65; retail dairy equipment salesman, Viroqua, 1963-67; asso. prof. polit. sci. U. Kans., Lawrence, 1971—. Commentator election night coverage Sunflower Cablevision, 1974; faculty forum mem. Phillips Petroleum Co., 1972, 73. Mem. exec. com. Vernon County Democratic Com., 1957-64. Named Hillteacher of year U. Kans., 1973, Outstanding Educator, 1977. LaCrosse Community scholar, 1966; NSF grantee, 1970-71. Mem. Am., S.W., Midwest polit. sci. assns., Author: Contemporary Issues in American Politics, 1975. Editor: The Adminstration of Justice: Point, Counterpoint, 1974; The Organization of Congress: Point, Counterpoint, 1974; Electing Public Officials: Point, Counterpoint, 1974. Contbr. articles to profl. jours. Home: RD 4 Box 62 Lawrence KS 66044 Office: Dept Polit Science Univ Kans Lawrence KS 66045

GETTLER, BENJAMIN, lawyer, mfg. co. exec.; b. Louisville, Ky., Sept. 16, 1927; s. Herbert and Gertrude (Cohen) G.; B.A. with high honors, U. Cin., 1945; J.D. (Felix Frankfurter scholar), Harvard U., 1948; m. Deliaan A. Gabriel, Apr., 1972; children—Jorian, Thomas, Gail, Benjamin. Admitted to Ohio bar, 1949; partner firm Brown & Gettler, Cin., 1951-73, Gettler & Katz, Cin., 1973—; chmn. bd. Am. Controlled Industries Inc., Cin., 1973—, Colorpac Inc., Cin., 1973—; chmn. exec. com. Valley Industries Inc., Cin., 1973—, Vulcan Corp., Cin., 1976—; chmn. bd. Cin. Transit, Inc., 1971-73. Served as capt., U.S. Army, 1955-56. Mem. Am., Cin. bar assns., Phi Beta Kappa, Omicron Delta Kappa. Clubs: Harvard, Coldstream Country. Office: 6 E 4th St Suite 1300 Cincinnati OH 45202

GETZ, BERT ATWATER, banker; b. Chgo., May 7, 1937; s. George Fulmer and Olive (Atwater) G.; grad. Lawrenceville (N.J.) Sch., 1955; B.B.A., U. Mich., 1959; m. Sandra L. Maclean, July 17, 1958; children—Lynn, George Fulmer, Bert Atwater. Pres., dir. Globe Corp., 1959—; dir. Upper Av. Nat. Bank Chgo., 1st Nat. Bank, Winnetka, Ill., Ariz. Bank; pres., dir. Ariz. Equities, Inc. Sec.-treas., Metz Found.; sec. Getz Found. Mem. Chgo. Farmers, Sigma Chi. Clubs: Chicago; Glen View (Ill.) Golf; Paradise Valley Country (Scottsdale, Ariz.). Home: Box 224 Route 1 Belvidere Rd Libertyville IL 60048 Office: 3634 Civic Center Plaza Scottsdale AZ 85251 Chicago IL 60611

GEZON, HOWARD JAMES, automotive engr.; b. Seattle, Apr. 25, 1919; s. Martin L. and Mina Willamina (Roesink) G.; B.S. in Indsl. Engring., Mich. State U., 1955; M.B.A., Western Mich. U., 1967; m. Dorothy Smitter, Aug. 7, 1943; children—Lyndel, Kathleen, Vicki, Judy, Mary Ann, Debra. Tool and die maker Fisher One, Grand Rapids, Mich., 1937-41, 52-55; store mgr. Good Housekeeping Shop, Grand Rapids, 1946-52; sr. process engr. div. diesel equipment Gen. Motors Co., Grand Rapids, 1955-71, 73—; engring. mgr. Anchor Fasteners, Cleve., 1971-73. Served with U.S. Army, 1941-46. Mem. Soc. Automotive Engrs. (dir. 1968—). Home: 2037 Osceola St Grand Rapids MI 49506 Office: 2100 Burlingame St Grand Rapids MI 49501

GHANTOUS, ROBERT NICHOLAS, chem. engring. co. exec.; b. Marj'oyoun, Lebanon, Mar. 23, 1939; s. Nicholas Simon and Saida (Basset) G.; came to U.S., 1956, naturalized, 1964; student Toledo U., 1957-62; m. Patricia Ann Langer, Sept. 4, 1957; children—Robert Nicholas, Michael Eric. Lab. technician Maumer Chem. Co., Toledo, 1959, process engr., Cin., to 1965; instrument engr. Chem. & Indsl. Corp., Cin., 1965; with Devel. Cons.'s, Cin., 1965-69; sr. systems engr. Foxboro Co. (Mass.), 1969-70; engr., pres. Ghantous Corp., Cin., 1970—. Registered profl. engr. Ohio. Mem. Instrument Soc. Am., Nat. Soc. Profl. Engrs. Home: 767 Cedarhill Dr Cincinnati OH 45240 Office: AG McKee 6200 Oaktree Blvd Cleveland OH 44131

GHAZARIAN, JACOB GARABED, educator; b. Baghdad, Iraq, Nov. 28, 1937; s. Garabed H. and Victoria (Boyajian) G.; came to U.S., 1958, naturalized, 1972; B.S., Murray State U., 1963; M.S., Memphis State U., 1967; Ph.D., U. Nebr., 1971; m. Charlotte James, Sept. 5, 1965; 1 dau., Kelly Michelle. Instr. chemistry LeMoyne Coll., Memphis, 1965-67; vis. scientist U. Tenn., Memphis, 1970-71; NIH fellow dept. biochemistry U. Wis., Madison, 1971-74, project asso., 1974-75, asst. prof. biochemistry Med. Coll. Wis., Milw., 1975—. Recipient Career Devel. awards NIH, 1976-81; NIH grantee, 1976-79; NSF grantee, 1976-78, 66-68; NIH fellow, 1971-74; NSF fellow, summer 1962, 66, 67. Mem. AAAS, Am. Chem. Soc., Nutrition Today Soc., Sigma Xi, Phi Sigma Kappa. Contbr. articles to profl. jours. Home: 7270 N Range Line Rd Glendale WI 53209 Office: 8701 W Watertown Plank Rd Milwaukee WI 53226

GHERING, MARY VIRGIL, inst. librarian, nun; b. Grand Rapids, Mich., July 18, 1910; d. Henry Christian and Frances Emily (Sharp) Ghering; student Marywood Coll. (now Aquinas Coll.), 1928-32; A.B., Central Mich. U., 1935; M.S., Marquette U., 1948; postgrad. (NSF faculty fellow), Fordham U., 1957-60; Ph.D. (Univ. fellow), Institutum Divi Thomae (now St. Thomas Inst.), 1968. Joined Sisters of St. Dominic, 1929; tchr. high schs., 1931-49, Cath. Central, Grand Rapids, Mich., 1936-38; asst. prof. chemistry Aquinas Coll., Grand Rapids, 1949-57, asso. prof., 1957-61, prof., 1961-68, chmn. dept. phys. scis., 1959-63; librarian St. Thomas Inst., Cin., 1968—. Common Cause telephone coordinator Congl. Dist. 2, Cin., 1973—. Fellow Am. Inst. Chemists; mem. Am. Chem. Soc., D.A.R. Democrat. Home: 2335 Grandview Ave Cincinnati OH 45206 Office: 1842 Madison Rd Cincinnati OH 45206

GHERSI, JUAN CARLOS, psychiatrist; b. Buenos Aires, Argentina, Mar. 12, 1916; s. Leopoldo Juan and Enriqueta (San Roman) G.; B.S., D.F. Sarmiento Coll., Argentina, 1938; M.D., Cordoba (Argentina) U., 1949; m. Clelia Urquijo, Dec. 21, 1946; children—John Charles, Maria Teresa. Came to U.S., 1952, naturalized, 1962. Intern, Truesdale Hosp., Fall River, Mass., 1952; resident pathology St. Luke's Hosp., New Bedford, Mass., 1953; physician Northampton (Mass.) State Hosp., 1953-56; clin. dir. Huntington (W.Va.) State Hosp., 1956-63; clin. dir., supt. Athens (Ohio) State Hosp., 1963-64; resident psychiatry Columbus (Ohio), State Hosp., 1964-66; supt. Springview Hosp., Springfield, Ohio, 1966-72; supt. Nelsonville (Ohio) Tb Center, 1972-73; med. dir. Massillon (Ohio) State Hosp., 1973—; psychiat. cons. Central Stark County Mental Health Center, Canton, Ohio, Hanover House, Massillon. Mem. Am., Ohio, N.E. Ohio psychiat. assns., Ohio Med. Assn., Stark County Med. Soc., Ohio Gun Collectors Assn. Home: 3000 Erie S St Massillon OH 44646 Office: PO Box 540 Massillon OH 44646

GHIA, KIRTI N., aerospace engr.; b. Bombay, India, Feb. 20, 1939; s. Narottamdas K. and Prankaur N. (Parekh) G.; came to U.S., 1961, naturalized, 1978; B.S. with distinction, U. Gujarat, Bombay, 1960; M.S., Ill. Inst. Tech., 1965, Ph.D., 1969; m. Urmila Agarwal, Aug. 30, 1970; 1 dau., Kasturi. Research and devel. engr. Premier Automobiles, Ltd., India, 1960-61; instr., research and teaching asst. Ill. Inst. Tech., Chgo., 1961-64, research asst. Aerospace Research Labs. project., 1964-66, NASA project, 1966-69; asst. prof. aerospace engring. and applied mechanics U. Cin., 1969-74, asso. prof., 1974—; vis. scientist Flight Dynamics Lab., Wright-Patterson AFB, Ohio, 1976, 77; cons. in field. Recipient numerous sci. grants, 1970—. Mem. Am. Inst. Aeros. and Astronautics, ASME, Am. Soc. Engring. Edn. Club: Cin. Faculty. Contbr. articles to profl. jours. Office: Mail Loc #70 U Cin Cincinnati OH 45221

GHIGLIERI, BERNARD JAMES, JR., lawyer; b. Toluca, Ill., Sept. 25, 1922; s. Barney J. and Marie B. (Supan) G.; A.B., U. Notre Dame, 1944; J.D., Georgetown U., 1949; m. Anne Bush, June 23, 1948; children—Bernard J. III, Jane A. Asso. with Travelers Ins. Co., Peoria, Ill., 1949-51; admitted to Ill. bar, 1950; individual practice law, Peoria, Ill., 1951—; asst. states atty. Peoria County, 1954-58; U.S. commr., 1965-70; U.S. magistrate, 1970—; pres. Sandy's of Evansville, Inc., drive-in restaurants, Evansville, Ind., and Paducah, Ky., 1963—; sec., dir. W.L. Bush Co.; dir. Copy Products Co., August H. Schmitz Co., Citizens Nat. Bank, Toluca, Ill., Standard Indsl. Products Co. of Ill., Peoria. Treas. Peoria County Rep. Central Com., 1962-66, vice chmn., 1966-74. Bd. dirs. Exposition Gardens, Peoria, 1950-56. Served as lt. (j.g.) USNR, 1942-46. Named Notre Dame Man of Yr., 1966. Mem. Am., Ill. trial lawyers assns., Am., Ill., Peoria County bar assns., Am. Judicature Soc. K.C., Rotarian. Clubs: Notre Dame (pres. 1954), Creve Coeur, Willow Knolls Country (all Peoria). Home: 4117 N Ashton Ave Peoria IL 61614 Office: 615 First Nat Bank Bldg Peoria IL 61602

GHOLSON, SAMUEL CREED, artist, educator; b. Holly Springs, Miss., July 15, 1919; s. Norman Glasgow and Eliza McNeel (Penick) G.; B.F.A., Pa. Acad. Fine Arts, 1944; student Wayman Adams Sch., summer 1943; M.F.A., Md. Inst., 1960; m. Shirley Elaine Paisley, Aug. 24, 1964; children—Norman William, Eliza Anne. Instr. Md. Inst., Balt., 1960-61, St. Timothy's Sch., Stevenson, Md., 1956-57, Monmouth (Ill.) Coll., 1957-59; asso. prof., head dept. Amarillo (Tex.) Coll., 1963-64; head art dept. Lees Coll., Jackson, Ky., 1965-66; tchr. summer art classes Gholson Studio, Washington, 1960-65; asst. prof.

humanities Ga. Southwestern Coll., Americus, 1966-67; prof. Heidelberg Coll., Tiffin, Ohio, 1967—, head dept., 1967-72. Represented in permanent collections N.Y. Law Sch., U. Pa., U. Tex., Baylor U., U.S. Capitol (House Banking Com.), W.Va. State Capitol, Presidents Mansion, Monrovia, Liberia, numerous others. Mem. Coll. Art Assn. Club: Toledo Artists. Presbyn. Home: 472 E Perry St Tiffin OH 44883

GHOLSTON, ROBERT MICHAEL, lawyer; b. Amarillo, Tex., May 17, 1936; s. John Edward Thurman and Lora (Hodges) G.; student Amarillo Jr. Coll., 1954-56; B.A., North Tex. State U., 1958; postgrad. U. Tex., 1958-59; J.D., Ind. U., 1964; m. Sharon Elaine Crull, July 4, 1958; children—Kevin Michael, Curtis Matthew, Deborah Ann. Admitted to Ind. bar, 1965, Fed. Dist. Ct. Ind., 1965, 7th Circuit Ct. Appeals, 1972, Supreme Ct. U.S., 1972, Ind. Supreme Ct., 1965, Ind. Ct. Appeals, 1965; asso. Acher & Young, Franklin, 1965-67; partner Acher & Gholston, Franklin, 1967—; dep. pros. atty. 8th Jud. Circuit, Ind., 1967; atty. Johnson County Plan Commn. and Bd. Zoning Appeals, 1967-70; town atty. Town of Prince's Lakes, 1967—; city atty. City of Greenwood, 1968-75. Mem. Am., Ind., Johnson County, Indpls., bar assns., 8th Jud. Bar Assn. Ind. (sec.-treas. 1967-68), Am., Ind. trial lawyers assns., Am. Judicature Soc., Ind. U. Indpls. Law Sch. Alumni Assn. (pres. 1972-73), Lambda Chi Alpha, Phi Delta Phi. Republican. Lutheran (pres. ch. council 1972-75). Elk. Clubs: Hillview Country (Franklin, Ind.); Columbia (Indpls.). Home: 470 Valley Ln Greenwood IN 46142 Office: 199 N Main St Franklin IN 46131

GIAMBELLUCA, SAMUEL LEO, retail store shoe exec.; b. Poplar Bluff, Mo., June 28, 1928; s. Charles Vincent and Frances (Frie) G.; grad. high sch.; m. Jewell Perry, Feb. 2, 1954; children—Joan, Teresa, Judith, Mary, Angela. Mgr. Connie Shop, Poplar Bluff, 1952-53, Evans & Six Shoe Co., Poplar Bluff, 1953-55; mgr. Bob Evans Shoes, Poplar Bluff, 1955-74, owner, 1975—; owner Sam's Shoes; cons. in field. Pres. Poplar Bluff Park Bd., 1965-66, 74-75; sec., treas. Poplar Bluff Downtown Assn., 1960-75; mem. Poplar Bluff Job Corps Community Relations Council, 1964-67, mayor's com. for workable programs, 1964-66; v.p. Ozark Assn. Amateur Athletic Union, 1970-71, nat. chmn. Jr. Olympics Girls Track and Field Com., 1966—. Named Man of Year, Poplar Bluff C. of C., 1966, Elk of Year, Poplar Bluff, 1971-72. Roman Catholic. Condr. 1st. Amateur Athletic Union Jr. Olympic nat. basketball championships 1972. Home: 1020 Kendall Dr Poplar Bluff MO 63901 Office: 109 S Main St Poplar Bluff MO 63901

GIANAN, ROGELIO VILLANUEVA, chem. engr.; b. Virac, Philippines, Sept. 20, 1939; s. Jose A. and Isabel (Villanueva) G.; B.Ch. E., Nat. U., 1961; M.S., Kans. U., 1965; m. Estrella F. Amper, Sept. 25, 1965; children—Karen Lee, Jennifer. Design engr. Diamond Corp., Oklahoma City, Okla., 1961-63; research scientist Center for Research and Engring., Lawrence, Kans., 1963-65; process engr. Allied Chem. Corp., Morristown, N.J., 1965-69; sr. process engr., corp. materials engr. Armak Co., Chgo., 1969—; chem. engring. cons. Sec., bd. dirs. Westgate Terrace Community Assn., Chgo., 1971-76. Mem. Am. Inst. Chem. Engrs., Nat., Ill. socs. profl. engrs. Roman Catholic. Clubs: Fil-American Council Chgo., Bisaya Circle of Am., Inc. (sec. 1976-78). Home: 1430 Parrish Ct Downers Grove IL 60515 Office: Armak Co 300 S Wacker Dr Chicago IL 60606

GIANDOMENICO, ADAM MICHAEL, educator; b. Steubenville, Ohio, May 30, 1933; s. Adam and Mary (Puzzuole) G.; B.A., Ohio State U., 1959; M.Ed., Duquesne U., 1963; Ph.D., Case Western Reserve U., 1970; m. Sylvia Margaret Harding, Dec., 22, 1958; children—Carol, George, Daryl, Lisa. Employment counselor Ohio Bur. Employment Security, Steubenville, 1960-63; instr. communication Coll. Steubenville, 1963-66; asso. prof. hearing speech scis. Ohio U., 1967—; speech pathologist Eastern Ohio Speech Hearing Center, Steubenville, 1969-73; dir., cons. Psychol. Services Inst., Steubenville, 1970—. Mem. Mingo Junction (Ohio) Zoning Appeals Bd., 1972-75; Bd. trustees Upper Ohio Valley Kidney Found., Ming Jct., 1974—, pres., 1976-77; mem. Mingo Junction Health Bd., 1975—. Served with USAF, 1951-55. NIH grantee, 1966. Mem. Am. (certificate clin. competence), Ohio speech hearing assns., Ohio Psychol. Assn., Inst. Soc. Gen. Semanics. Democrat. Roman Catholic. Home: 121 Montgomery Ln Mingo Junction OH 43938 Office: Ohio University Belmont Campus St Clairsville OH 43950

GIANNANGELO, EMIL FRANK, dentist; b. Monongahela, Pa., Oct. 5, 1918; s. Frank Fernado and Maria Mary (Schenna) G.; student Bethany Coll., 1939-40, U. Pitts., 1940; D.D.S., U. Mo., Kansas City, 1944; m. Dorotha Jean Gray, Jan. 27, 1947; 1 dau., Maria Letetia. Gen. practice dentistry, Pratt, Kan., 1944—. Vol. dentist CARE, Vols. in Mission, Layman Overseas, and others, 1970-73; mem. staff Pratt County Hosp., 1945-73. Bd. dirs. Pratt County Mental Health Assn. Recipient distinguished service award Pratt Jaycees, 1949; Boss of Yr. award, 1968. Mem. Am. Dental Assn., Kans., Central Kans., Pratt County dental Socs., Acad. Gen. Dentistry, Methodist (adminstrv. bd. 1963-73). Elk, Rotarian (pres. chpt. 1975-76). Home: 205 Stout St Pratt KS 67124 Office: 610 E 2d St Pratt KS 67124

GIANNESTRAS, NICHOLAS JAMES, orthopedic surgeon; b. Macedonia, Greece, May 19, 1909; s. James George and Aspasia (Matis) G.; brought to U.S., 1912, naturalized, 1942; student Tufts, 1927-29, M.D., 1933; m. Gloria Potter Iden, Jan. 18, 1954; children—James Duncan, Lynne Snowden, Peter P., Susan Araminta. Intern Cambridge (Mass.) City Hosp., 1934-35; resident Boston City Hosp., 1933, Mattapan Tb Sanitarium, Boston, 1933-34, Charles V. Chapin Hosp., Providence, 1936, N.Y.C. Orthopaedic Dispensary and Hosp., 1936-38; pvt. practice in orthopaedic surgery, Cin., 1938—; clin. prof. dept. orthopaedics U. Cin. Med. Sch., 1976—; dir. Greater Cin. Spinal Deformity Center; chmn. dept. orthopaedics dept. Good Samaritan Hosp., Cin., 1955-75, dir. orthopaedic edn., 1975—; dir. foot clinic U. Cin. Med. Center. Vis. prof. orthopaedics U. Calif., Los Angeles, 1963, U. Athens (Greece), 1975, U. Hong Kong, 1975, U. Capetown, 1975, Yale U., 1976, U. Oreg., 1976, U. Pretoria, 1975, U. Miami, 1976, U. Philippines, 1977, Tulane U., 1977; med. adviser Liberty Mut. Ins. Co., Cin., 1955-70; vis. lectr. Akron Gen. Hosp., 1976, Cleve. Clinic, 1977; mem. Com. for Advisement Automobile Safety, 1960-70; chmn. med. review bd. Ohio Bur. Motor Vehicles, Dept. Hwy. Safety, Cin. dist., 1964-72; orthopedic cons. Wright-Patterson AFB, Dayton; pres. Cinor, Inc., Cin. Orthopedic Inst., Inc., Giannestras, Schmerge and Assos., also pres. Found. Mem. bd. Holy Trinity-St. Nicholas Greek Orthodox Ch., 1976—. Served with USAAF, 1942-45. Recipient Gold Cross St. Marc, Patriarch of Alexandria. Fellow A.C.S. (gov., mem. com. trauma 1960-69, chmn. subcom. sports injuries 1966-71, cons. 1971-77); mem. Ohio Med. Assn., Cin. Acad. Medicine, U. Cin. Athletic Com. (pres. 1958), Philhellenic Soc. Cin. (pres.), Ohio (pres. 1969). Cin. (pres. 1969), Tri-State (pres. 1956) clin. orthopaedic socs., Am. Acad. Orthopaedic Surgeons, Am. Orthopedic Foot Soc. (founder mem., pres. 1970-71, dir. 1971—), Am. Orthopaedic Assn., Societe Internationale de Chirugie Orthopedique et de Traumatologie, Sociedad Latino Americana de Orthopedia y Traumatologia, Russell A. Hibbs Soc. (founder mem. pres. 1952), South African Orthopaedic Soc. (hon.). Clubs: Queen City, Indoor Tennis, Cincinnati Tennis (Cin.); Bankers. Author: Foot Disorders, Medical and Surgical Management, 2d edit., 1973. Editorial bd. Cin. Jour. Medicine, 1955-76, Orthopaedic Rev., 1977—. Contbr. articles to profl. jours., to textbook Fractures, textbook Orthopaedic Complications. Home: 1707 E McMillian St Cincinnati OH 45206 Office: 2415 Auburn Ave Cincinnati OH 45219

GIARDINO, JOHN RICHARD, geographer, educator; b. Pueblo, Colo., Oct. 21, 1946; s. John Anthony and Margaret Jane (Brothers) G.; B.S., So. Colo. State Coll., 1969; M.A. (univ. fellow), Ariz. State U., 1971; m. Mary F. Boltezar, Jan. 4, 1969. Instr. So. Colo. State Coll., Pueblo, 1971-72; lectr. U. Zambia, Lusaka, 1972-74; vis. distinguished prof. Calif. State U. at Chico, 1974; instr. U. Nebr., Lincoln, 1975—; cons. Livingstone (Zambia) Mus., 1972-74, Nat. Parks Dept. Zambia for South Luangwa Nat. Park, 1972-74. Active Boy Scouts Am. Recipient award for excellence of scholarship Nat. Council for Geographic Edn., 1968; Pres.'s award, So. Colo. State Coll., 1968. NSF trainee, 1971; U. Zambia research grantee, 1973-74; Maude-Fling dissertation grantee, 1976; Sigma Xi grantee, 1977. Fellow Royal Geog. Soc. (London); mem. Zambia Geog. Assn. (pres. 1973), Geol. Soc. Am., Assn. Am. Geographers, Ariz. Acad. Sci., Nat. Council for Geog. Edn., Wilderness Soc., Nat. Parks Assn., Sierra Club, Sigma Xi. Author: Studies of Zambian Landscape, 1974; Regional Geomorphology of Zambia, 1975. Editor newsletter Inst. for Tertiary-Quaternary Studies, 1977. Home: 2321 Sheffield Pl Lincoln NE 68512

GIBAS, ANDREW C., cosmetic co. exec., publisher; b. Walsenburg, Colo., Sept. 26, 1913; s. Albert Joseph and Mary (Gebczynski) G.; B.S., Northwestern U., 1937; postgrad., U. Chgo., 1940-44; m. Grace Braden, June 11, 1939; children—Murray Albert, Allen Henry, Barbara Jane, Rebecca. Ink chemist Poole Bros., Chgo., 1937-38; asst. supt. operations Cities Service Oil Co., Chgo., 1938-44; draftee Civilian Pub. Service, 1944-46; chemist Grace-Lee Products, Inc., Mpls., 1946-56; with LaMaur Inc., Mpls., 1956-72, dir. research, 1968-72; pres. Circle Pioneers, Inc.; founder Circulating Pines, newspaper, Circle Pines, Minn., 1950, publisher, 1956—, co-editor, 1959—. Chmn. Circle Pines Utilities Commn., 1961—; village clk., Circle Pines, 1950-54. Mem. Am. Chem. Soc., Soc. Cosmetic Chemists, Am. Pub. Gas Assn. (dir. 1968—, treas. 1973—). Democrat. Mem. Religious Soc. Friends. Home: 9 West Rd Circle Pines MN 55014 Office: 9201 Lexington Ave Circle Pines MN 55014

GIBAS, GRACE BRADEN, editor, publisher; b. Santiago, Chile, Aug. 14, 1916; d. Charles Samuel and Grace (McMurray) Braden (parents Am. citizens); B.A., Northwestern U., 1939; m. Andrew C. Gibas, June 11, 1939; children—Murray Albert, Allen Henry, Barbara Jane, Rebecca Gibas Gepner. Mem. staff World Christianity, Chgo., 1938-39; co-pub., co-editor Circulating Pines, Circle Pines, Minn., 1959—. Mem. exec. com. Minn. Am. Friends Service Com., 1972—, bd. dirs. N. Central region, 1976—. Recipient 2d pl. best feature story Nat. Editorial Assn. newspaper contest, 1963; 1st pl. excellence in investigative reporting Minn. Newspaper Assn. Better Newspaper Contest, 1968, in sports reporting, govtl. reporting, women's reporting, 1973, govtl. reporting, 1974; 1st pl. for interview Minn. Press Women Contest, 1975. Office: 9201 Lexington Ave Circle Pines MN 55014

GIBB, CLARK RAYMOND, mfrs. rep. co. exec.; b. Cottonwood, Minn., Sept. 5, 1914; s. Raymond J. and Huldah (Pettersen) G.; B.B.A., U. Minn., 1940; m. Margaret L. Foucault, June 30, 1954. Sales engr. Despatch Oven Co., Mpls., 1941; mem. prodn. control staff Gen. Mills, Mpls., 1941-42; owner Aurex Minn. Co., Mpls., 1946-51; partner A & G Chip Steak Co., Mankato, Minn., 1947-61; v.p. Chip Steak & Provision Co., Mankato, 1961-65, pres., owner, 1965—; pres., owner Clark R. Gibb Co., Mpls., 1952—; sec.-treas. Lowry Finance Co., Mpls., 1953—; owner Wooddale Farms, Yellow Medicine County, Minn. Served with AUS, 1942-46, 51-52. Mem. U. Minn. Alumni Assn., Electronic Reps. Assn. (chmn. bd.), Am. Legion. Republican. Presbyn. Elk. Clubs: Mankato (Minn.) Golf; Minneapolis Athletic. Home: 2020 Cedar Lake Blvd Minneapolis MN 55416 Office: 1311 W 25th St Minneapolis MN 55405

GIBB, WILLIAM STEWART, lawyer; b. Des Moines, Nov. 6, 1939; s. Thomas Stewart and Lucille Margaret (Scholty) . G.; B.S. in Indsl. Adminstrn., Iowa State U., 1962; J.D. with honors, Drake U., 1968; m. Nancy Nordland, Oct. 9, 1976; children—Carolin, John. Admitted to Iowa bar, 1968; asso. Betty, Neuman, McMahon, Hellstrom & Bittner, Davenport, 1968-69, Johnson, Burnquist & Erb, Ft. Dodge, 1969-71; partner Johnson, Burnquist, Erb, Latham & Gibb, Ft. Dodge, 1971—. Vice pres. Ft. Dodge Bd. Edn.; bd. dirs. Ft. Dodge Devel. Corp., United Fund; bd. counselors Drake Law Sch. Served as lt. USNR, 1962-65. Mem. Ft. Dodge C. of C. (mem. downtown devel. com. 1969-73, dir. 1969-73), Omicron Delta Kappa, Phi Alpha Delta, Phi Delta Theta. Republican. Congregationalist. Elk, Rotarian. Club: Ft. Dodge Country (pres.). Home: 1320 10th Ave N Fort Dodge IA 50501 Office: 6th Floor Snell Bldg Fort Dodge IA 50501

GIBBONS, EVERETT DURWARD, banker; b. Onaway, Mich., Aug. 19, 1921; s. William R. and Maude (Bryce) G.; student Sch. Consumer Banking, U. Va., 1958-60; grad. Sch. Banking, U. Wis., 1972-74; m. Doris Lorraine Miller, Feb. 12, 1944; children—Gregory Dennis, Pamela Kay. With Saginaw Lumber Co., 1940-41; with Second Nat. Bank, Saginaw, Mich., 1941—; asst. cashier, 1956-59, asst. v.p., 1959, v.p., 1968-72, mgr. loan dept., 1970—, sr. v.p., mgr. retail banking, 1972-76, exec. v.p., 1976—, also dir. Treas. bd. dirs. Child and Family Services, 1965-66, v.p., 1967-68; bd. dirs. St. Lukes Hosp., 1962—, v.p., 1969—. Served with AUS, 1943. Mem. Am. Bankers Assn. (adv. bd. instalment credit div.), Saginaw C. of C. (bd. dirs. 1957-58). Author: Floor Planning The Dealer, 1960. Home: 718 Somerset Rd Saginaw MI 48603 Office: 101 N Washington Ave Saginaw MI 48607

GIBBONS, MRS. JOHN SHELDON (CELIA VICTORIA TOWNSEND), editor, publisher; b. Fargo, N.D.; d. Harry Alton and Helen (Haag) Townsend; student U. Minn., 1930-33; m. John Sheldon Gibbons, May 1, 1935; children—Mary Vee, John Townsend. Advt. mgr. Hotel Nicollet, Mpls., 1933-37; contbg. editor children's mags., 1935—; partner Youth Assos. Co., Mpls., 1942-65; pub. art dir. Mines and Escholier mags., 1954-65; founder Bull. Bd. Pictures, Inc., Mpls., 1954, pres., 1954—; founder Periodical Litho Art Co., Mpls., 1962, pres., 1962-65; artist Cath. Boy mag., 1938; chief photographer Cath. Miss mag., 1955. Mem. Women's aux. Mpls. Symphony Orch.; mem. Fort Lauderdale (Fla.) Art. Mus. Republican chairwoman Golden Valley, Minn., 1950; alternate del. Hennepin County Rep. Conv., 1962. Mem. Mpls. Inst. Arts, Internat. Inst., St. Paul Arts and Sci., Art Guild Boca Raton, Delta Zeta. Club: Woman's, Minikahda; Deerfield Beach Women's. Home: 1416 Alpine Pass Tyrol Hills Minneapolis MN 55416 Office: 1057 A-1-A Hillsboro Beach FL

GIBBS, G. EDWARD, advt. agy. exec.; b. Columbus, Ohio, May 25, 1943; s. George Edward and Hattie (Gable) G.; B.F.A., Columbus Coll. Art and Design, 1963; B.S., U. Cin., 1968; M.F.A., Syracuse U., 1975; m. Deborah Lee Wrigley, Aug. 31, 1967. Partner, v.p. Sontag-Bottoni-Gibbs Design, Cin., 1968-70; pres. E. Gibbs Asso., Toledo, 1968-72; pres. E. Gibbs Design; with Widerschein/Strandberg Asso. Advt. Agy., Toledo, 1972—, designer, exec. creative dir., v.p., partner, 1972—; design cons. major corps., State of Ohio; prints and paintings in museums, galleries and stores in U.S., London, Middle East, Western Europe, Japan. Served with AUS, 1967-73. Recipient over 500 regional, nat. and internat. art awards. Mem. Soc. Illustrators N.Y., N.Y. Art Dirs. Club, Delta Phi Delta, Beta Theta Pi. Home: 3638 Brunswick Rd Toledo OH 43606 Office: 3035 Moffat Dr Toledo OH 43615

GIBBS, P. LAIRD, physician; b. Toronto, Ont., Can., May 3, 1917; s. William Ray King and Eva Grace (Laird) G.; B.A., U. Western Ont., 1948, M.D., 1952; m. Marguerite Helena Hook, Jan. 23, 1941. With Robert Simpson Co., Ltd., advt., Toronto, Ont., 1935-40; served with Royal Canadian Air Force, 1940-46, 51-58, advanced through grades to squadron leader, 1956, retired, 1958; intern Toronto Gen. Hosp., 1952-53; gen. practice medicine, Dresden, Ont., 1958—; mem. med. staff Pub. Gen. Hosp., Chatham, Ont., St. Joseph's Hosp., Chatham; coroner Essex, Elgin, Lambton and Kent counties, 1959; aero-med. examiner Canadian Dept. Transport. Recipient Canadian Forces decoration. Mayor, Corp. Town of Dresden, 1963-65; mem. Kent County Bd. Edn., 1968-70. Bd. dirs. Sydenham Dist. Hosp., 1961-65. Fellow Am. Geriatrics Soc., Royal Soc. Health (London); mem. Coroners' Assn., Ont., Aerospace Med. Assn., Kent County Med. Soc. Home: 571 Hughes St Dresden ON N0P 1M0 Canada Office: 603 St George St S Dresden ON N0P 1M0 Canada

GIBBS, REESE LEONARD, ednl. exec.; b. Strawberry Point, Iowa, Aug. 2, 1930; s. Rae Henry and Erma (Pilgrim) G.; B.A., Upper Iowa U., 1951; M.A., State U. Iowa, 1953; m. Marian Martha Buhr, Aug. 12, 1956; children—Reese Kevin, Kimberly Kay. Civilian Ct. reporter U.S. Govt., Ft. Leonard Wood, Mo., 1955; instr. bus. edn. Strawberry Point Community Schs., 1955-58; instr. bus. edn. and sr. social studies Waverly (Iowa) Community Schs., 1958-60; sec. bd. edn., dir. bus. affairs Waverly-Shell Rock Community Schs., 1960-67; dist. sec., bus. mgr. Marshalltown (Iowa) Community Sch. Dist., 1967—. Bd. dirs. United Way, 1972—, pres., 1975. Served with AUS, 1953-55. Mem. Iowa State Edn. Assn. (treas. NE dist. 1959-67), NEA, Iowa Assn. Sch. Bds. (v.p. 1964, pres. 1965), Assn. Sch. Bus. Ofcls. (v.p. 1973-74, pres. 1974-75), Iowa Assn. Sch. Bus. Ofcls., Marshalltown Area C. of C. (dir. 1972-75, treas. 1975—). Club: Rotary (treas. 1972—). Home: 108 Bohen St Marshalltown IA 50158 Office: 317 Columbus Dr Marshalltown IA 50158

GIBBS, WALTER MANNING, JR., aluminum co. exec.; b. Chgo., Nov. 22, 1923; s. Walter Manning and Josephine (Pickens) G.; B.S. in Bus. Adminstrn., Northwestern U., 1947; m. Jeanne Marjorie Becker, June 18, 1947; children—Susan Jeanne, Carolyn Jo, David Wesley; m. 2d, Margaret Muir Pinkerton, Sept. 23, 1972. Salesman, Winchester Repeating Arms Co., New Haven, 1947-49; salesman Kaiser Aluminum & Chem. Corp., Chgo., 1949-50, br. mgr., Wichita, Kans., 1951, product mgr., Chgo., 1952-57, asst. to v.p., Oakland, Calif., 1958-59, asst. gen. sales mgr., 1960, mktg. mgr., 1961, gen. mgr. sheet and plate div., 1963-65, v.p. industry and product sales, 1965-68, v.p. bus. planning, 1968-70; v.p. mill products and reduction ops. Martin Marietta Aluminum, Torrance, Calif., 1970-74; dir. corporate planning CONALCO, Inc. (name now Consol. Aluminum Corp.), St. Louis, 1974-76, v.p. ops., 1976—. Served lt. (j.g.) USNR, 1944-46. Mem. Acacia. Republican. Presbyn. (elder, trustee). Home: 998 Claygate Ct Manchester MO 63011 Office: PO Box 14448 St Louis MO 63178

GIBBS, WILLIAM CULLEN, JR., govt. ofcl.; b. Chgo., Apr. 30, 1925; s. William Cullen and Minnie Clyde (Harris) G.; student Thornton Jr. Coll., Wilson Jr. Coll., Roosevelt U., U. Chgo.; B.A., 1957; m. Eththelle Faye Byoune, June 29, 1946; children—Spencer Craig, Marvin Kent, William Cullen III. With U.S. Postal Service, 1947—, clk., Chgo., 1947-48, letter carrier, 1948-59, letter carrier, Harvey, Ill., 1959-63, civil service examiner, 1963-64, hearing officer-investigator, 1964-65, asst. br. supt., Markham, Ill., 1965-66, contract compliance examiner, Chgo., 1966, postal service officer, 1966-67, employee relations officer, Chgo., 1967-68, mgr. employee relations br., 1968-71, dist. dir. support, Springfield, Ill., 1971-75, dir. fin., Chgo., 1975—. Chmn. supt. adv. com. Sch. Dist. 205, 1969; pres. Harvey Civic Improvement Assn., 1959-61. Mem. Democratic Nat. Com., 1968-74. Methodist Episcopal. Home: 16139 S Wolcott Ave Markham IL 60426 Office: 433 W Van Buren St Chicago IL 60607

GIBSON, BENJAMIN FRANKLIN, lawyer; b. Safford, Ala., July 13, 1931; s. Eddie and Pearl Ethel (Richardson) G.; B.S., Wayne State U., 1955; J.D. with distinction, Detroit Coll. Law, 1960; m. Lucille Nelson, June 23, 1951; children—Charlotte, Linda, Gerald, Gail, Carol, Laura. Accountant, City of Detroit, 1955-56, Detroit Edison Co., 1956-61; admitted to Mich. bar, 1960; asst. atty. gen., State Mich., 1961-63; asst. pros. atty., County of Ingham, Mich., 1963-64; pvt. practice law, Lansing, Mich., 1964—. Hearing officer City of East Lansing, 1972—. Bd. dirs. Lansing Jr. Achievement, Greater Lansing Legal Aid Bur. Mem. Am. Trial Lawyers Assn., Am. Bar Assn., Ingham County Bar Assn., State Bar Mich. (mem. grievance bd. hearing panel 1971), Sigma Pi Phi. Rotarian. Clubs: University, City, Lansing Ski, Torch, Canadian Lakes. Home: 1505 Stonegate Ln East Lansing MI 48823 Office: 309 N Washington St Lansing MI 48933

GIBSON, CURTIS A., life support systems engr.; b. Springfield, Ohio, Nov. 5, 1929; s. Frank Z. and Helen W. (Cox) G.; Chem.E., U. Cin., 1952. Chem. engr. Sylvania Elec. Products Co., Emporium, Pa., 1952-54; chem. engr. U.S. Air Force, Wright-Paterson AFB, Ohio, 1956-59, mech. engr., 1959-70, life support systems engr., 1970—. Active Boy Scouts Am. Recipient Silver Beaver award Boy Scouts Am., 1973. Mem. Am. Def. Preparedness Assn., Air Force Assn., Internat. Acad. Profl. Bus. Execs. Home: 2806 Oxford Dr Springfield OH 45506

GIBSON, EDWIN CHARLES, dentist; b. Eau Claire, Wis., Feb. 12, 1929; s. John Orr and Esther Ethyl (Svengaard) G.; student Eau Claire State Coll., 1946-49; D.D.S., Marquette U., 1953; m. Dorothy Jean Rowe, Dec. 15, 1951; children—Sandra and Linda (twins), Julie, Lisa. Part time lab. technician Eau Claire E.C. Chem., Inc., 1942-49; individual practice dentistry Midel Fort Clinic, 1955-69; group dental practice Hillside Dental, Ltd., Eau Claire, 1969—, pres., 1969—. Mem. Eau Claire Police and Fire Commn., 1960—, pres., 1969-73; state ins. chmn. Dental Ins. State Wis., 1960-73. Served with USAF, 1952-55. Mem. Nat. Acad. Dentistry, Am. Dental Assn., Eau Claire County Dental Soc. (pres. 1960), Northwest Dist. Dental Soc. (pres. 1973). Clubs: Eau Claire Rod and Gun (pres. 1956-60), Eau Claire Exchange (pres. 1965-66). Home: 3258 Fern Court Eau Claire WI 54701 Office: 507 Main St Eau Claire WI 54701

GIBSON, FLOYD ROBERT, judge; b. Prescott, Ariz., Mar. 3, 1910; s. Van Robert and Katheryn Ida (Weitzel) G.; A.B., U. Mo., 1931, J.D., 1933; m. Gertrude Lee Walker, Apr. 23, 1935; children—Charles R., John M., Catherine L. Admitted to Mo. bar, 1932; partner firm Gibson & Kirtley, Independence, Mo., 1933-37; county counselor Jackson County (Mo.), 1942-44; partner firm Cloud, Loomis & Gibson, Kansas City, Mo., 1937-52, Stubbs, McKenzie, Williams & Gibson, Kansas City, 1952-54, Johnson, Lucas, Bush & Gibson, Kansas City, 1954-61; judge U.S. Dist. Ct., Kansas City, 1961-62, chief judge, 1962-65; judge U.S. Circuit Ct. of Appeals, Kansas City, 1965-74, chief judge, 1974—; pres. Nat. Legis. Conf., 1960; mem. Mo. Ho. of Reps., 1940-46; mem. Mo. Senate, 1946-61, majority leader, 1952-56, pres. pro tem 1956-60; bd. dirs. Jacob L. and Ella C. Loose Found.; trustee U. Kansas City; bd. mgrs. Council State

Govts. Fellow Am. Bar Assn.; mem. Appellate Judges Conf. (chmn. 1973-74), Nat. Conf. Commrs. on Uniform State Laws (commr.), Fed., Kansas City bar assns., Lawyers Assn. Kansas City (v.p.), Inst. Jud Adminstrn., Mo. Law Sch. Alumni Assn. (citation of merit 1975), Mo. Acad. Squires, Phi Delta Phi, Phi Kappa Psi (Man of Year 1974). Clubs: Univ., Carriage, Mercury of Kansas City. Recipient Faculty-Alumni award U. Mo., 1968; named 2d Most Valuable Mem. Mo. Legislature; Globe-Democrat award, 1958, Most Valuable Mem., 1960. Home: 11521 Winner Rd Independence MO 64052 Office: 837 US Courthouse 811 Grand St Kansas City MO 64106

GIBSON, MILTON EUGENE, cardiologist; b. Laporte, Ind., July 11, 1939; s. Maurice Wayne and Mary Leola (Reinhardt) G.; B.A., Valparaiso U., 1961; M.D., Ind. U., 1965; m. Gloria Jean Birky, Aug. 12, 1961; children—Kevin Scott, Bradley Mark. Resident in internal medicine Methodist Hosp., Indpls., 1968-70, fellow in cardiology, 1970-72; practice medicine specializing in cardiology Cardiology Assos., Inc., S. Bend, Ind., 1972—; dir. Cardiac Catheterization Lab., Meml. Hosp., S. Bend, 1975—, dir. Cardiology Services, 1976—, chmn. dept. medicine, 1977—; instr. Ind. U. at Meml. Hosp. Served to capt. U.S. Army, 1966-68. Decorated Bronze Star medal. Asso. fellow Am. Coll. of Cardiology; mem. A.C.P., Am. Heart Assn. (v.p., chmn. med. and sci. programs Ind. affiliate). Contbr. articles in field to med. jours. Home: 5640 Danbury Dr South Bend IN 46614 Office: 919 E Jefferson Blvd South Bend IN 46622

GIBSON, RALPH KENNETH, supt. schs.; b. Mediapolis, Iowa, Apr. 19, 1923; s. Orville Leroy and Ethel Vivian (Ping) G.; student Burlington Jr. Coll., 1940, 54-55; B.A., Iowa State Tchrs. Coll., 1957, M.A., 1961; edn. specialist Iowa State U., 1968; m. Inger Eleanor Barrick, Nov. 23, 1944; children—Kenneth, Karen (Mrs. Larry Cibert), Kathryn, Karla, Kevin. Tchr., Brandon (Iowa) Consolidated Sch., 1957-59; high sch. prin. Marcus (Iowa) Community Sch., 1960-69; supt. schs., Waco Community Sch., Wayland, Iowa, 1969—. Served with USAF, 1942-45. Decorated Air medal with four clusters, D.F.C. Mem. Am., Iowa assns. sch. adminstrs. Methodist (mem. bd. 1974). Lion. Home: Box 294 Wayland IA 52654 Office: Box 158 Wayland IA 52654

GIBSON, RALPH MILTON, educator; b. Cleve., Oct. 5, 1923; s. Samuel Milton and Audrey Ethel (Day) G.; B.S., U. Mich., 1945, M.S., 1947, Ph.D. (USPHS fellow), 1959; m. Rose Cleland Campbell, Dec. 31, 1947; children—Ralph Milton, John Samuel. Counselor, Cuyahoga County Child Welfare Bd., Cleve., 1947; psychologist Cleve. Guidance Center, 1947-49, chief psychologist, 1949-51; instr. dept. pediatrics U. Mich. Med. Sch., Ann Arbor, 1953-63, asst. prof., 1963-66, asso. prof., 1966-70, prof., 1970—, dir. counseling, 1972—, asst. dean student affairs, 1975—; asso. staff mem. Wayne County Gen. Hosp., Eloise, Mich., 1963—. Mem. Human Relations Commn., Ann Arbor, 1957-58; mem. Mich. Adv. Commn. on Certification of Psychologists, 1962-64. Trustee Greenhills Sch., Ann Arbor, 1966—, pres. bd. trustees, 1973-74. Fellow Am. Orthopsychiatric Assn., mem. Am., Mich. psychol. assns., A.A.A.S., Alpha Kappa Delta, Phi Sigma, Psi Chi, Phi Delta Kappa, Alpha Phi Alpha. Author: The Role of Audition in the Development of the Object Concept in the Congenitally Blind Infant, 1966; Trauma in Early Infancy and Later Personality Development, 1965. Home: 321 Riverview Dr Ann Arbor MI 48104

GIBSON, ROBERT LESLIE, lawyer; b. Mattoon, Ill., July 30, 1920; s. Leslie Bayard and Rebecca (Westermeier) G.; A.B., DePauw U., 1942; J.D., U. Mich., 1948; m. Pat Thompson, Jan. 3, 1968; children—Emily G. Soelter, Virginia G. Mason. With Houston & Assos., C.P.A.'s, Paris, Ill., 1948-49; admitted to Ill. bar, 1949; asso. firm Cotton & Massey, Paris, 1949-51; partner firm Massey, Anderson & Gibson, Paris, 1951—; sec., dir. Ill. Cereal Mills, Inc., Meco, Inc., Como Oil Co. Sec., bd. dirs. Hosp. and Med. Found. Paris, Inc., 1958—; mem. Edgar County (ill.) Bd. Suprs., 1959-65; sec. Paris Bd. Fire and Police Commrs., 1958-65; chmn. Edgar County Sheriff Merit Commn., 1971—; elder, trustee Paris Presbyterian Ch., 1949-73. Served with USMC, 1942-46. Decorated Purple Heart. Mem. Nat. Acad. Arbitrators, Am., Ill., Edgar County bar assns., Am. Judicature Soc., Am. Arbitration Assn., Paris C. of C. (pres. 1958-59, 61), Ill. State C. of C. (chmn. labor relations com. 1964-66, dir. 1966-72), Phi Gamma Delta, Sigma Delta Chi. Democrat. Clubs: Rotary, Syacmore Hills Country, Quail Creek Country, Wilderness Country, Elks, Masons. Contbr. articles to legal jours. Home: Rural Route 4 PO Box 298 Paris IL 61944 Office: 908 N Main St Paris IL 61944

GIBSON, THOMAS MARSHALL, elec. co. exec.; b. Chgo., Jan. 20, 1927; s. Humphrey M. and Ethel (Stirdevant) G.; student U. Ill., 1945-46, U. Ariz., 1946-47; m. Betty Lou Bean, June 10, 1950; children—Linda, Terry, Carol; m. 2d, I. Cymala Nitschmann, June 15, 1974. Sec. Gibson Electric Co., Inc., Chgo., 1947-54, now pres.; pres. Thomas Gibson Inc., Glen Ellyn, Ill., 1954—, Gibson Heating & Air Conditioning Inc., Glen Ellyn; formerly sr. v.p. Corplex Internat. Corp. Mem. Electric Assn., Nat. Elec. Contractors Assn. (pres. Ill.), Ill. Mech. Specialty Contractors Assn. (dir.), Phi Kappa Psi. Clubs: Chicago Athletic Assn., Chicago Golf. Home: Oak Brook Club Oak Brook IL 60521 Office: 240 Fencl Ln Hillside IL 60162

GIBSON, WILLIAM HERBERT, optometrist; b. Georgetown, Britsh Guiana, Apr. 24, 1921; came to U.S., 1937, naturalized, 1944; student Bob Jones U., 1937-39; B.S., Ill. Coll. Optometry, 1942, O.D., 1943; m. Bonnie June Nessel, Nov. 16, 1943; children—Kenneth, Keith, Bryan, Brent, Robin. Asso. with Dr. Riorden, Oak Park, Ill., 1943; pvt. practice optometry, Appleton, Wis., 1946—. Spl. guest lectr. vision and traffic safety U. Wis., U. Ill., various state, bus. and civic orgns. Chmn. fund raising Mental Health, 1966, Christian Businessmen's Com. Internat.; mem. adv. com. Project Headstart, Appleton, 1967; active YMCA, Girl Scouts U.S.; mem. gov.'s adv. com. Wis. Motor Vehicle Dept., 1967—. Served with USNR, 1943-45. Recipient 1st Wis. Optometrist of the Year award, 1966. Fellow Am. Assn. Optometry; mem. Wis. (pres. 1969-70), Am. optometric assns., Appleton C. of C., Wis. Council Safety, Internat. Contact Lens Soc. (London), European, Fox Cities optometric socs., Nat. Eye Research Found. Designer prototype red, green, amber tailight assembly, placed bill in Wis. legislature for its use. Home: 2324 W Charles St Appleton WI 54911 Office: 433 N Oneida St Appleton WI 54911

GIEBELHAUSEN, GUSTAV WILLIAM, surgeon; b. Peoria, Ill., Sept. 27, 1918; s. Jacob and Martha (Rosinski) G.; B.S., U. Ill., 1942, M.D., 1944; m. Martha H. Mugrage, June 13, 1943; children—Jane, Richard, Dean. Intern, St. Francis Hosp., 1944-45, resident, 1945-46; practice medicine specializing in surgery, Peoria, 1948—; asst. clin. prof. surgery U. Ill. Sch. Medicine in Peoria. Served with U.S. Army, 1946-48. Fellow ACS; mem. AMA, Peoria Med. Soc., Ill. Med. Soc., Ill., Midwest surg. assns., Mid-State Med. Found. Home: 5826 N Briarwood Ln Peoria IL 61614 Office: 1101 Main St Peoria IL 61606

GIERING, RICHARD HERBERT, computerized infor. systems co. exec.; b. Emmaus, Pa., Nov. 27, 1929; s. Harold Augustus and Marguerite (Bruder) G.; B.S. in Engring. and Math., U. Ariz., 1962; m. Carol Alice Scott, Aug. 16, 1959; children—Richard Herbert, Scott K. Joined U.S. Army, 1947, commd. 2d lt., 1963, advanced through grades to capt., 1965; sect. chief data processing Def. Intelligence Agy., Washington, 1965-67; ret., 1967; with Data Corp. (name changed to Mead Tech. Labs. 1968), Dayton, Ohio, 1967—, v.p. tech. ops., 1970-71, dir. info. systems, 1971—; instr. data processing U. Ariz., Tucson, 1962-63. Mem. Assn. Computing Machinery, Am. Soc. Info. Scis. Inventor data/central (used to establish electronic newspaper libraries). Home: 5460 Royalwood St Dayton OH 45429 Office: Research Park Dayton OH 45432

GIERTZ, ROBERT WILLIAM, heavy equipment mfg. co. exec.; b. Clifton, Ill., Mar. 24, 1925; s. William Chris and Emma Louise (Meyer) G.; B.S., U. Ill., 1950; postgrad. Mass. Inst. Tech., 1964; m. Vera Rosalie Herrmann, Nov. 30, 1946; children—Deborah (Mrs. Thomas Staack), Nancy (Mrs. Scott Natvig), Norman, James, Julie. Mechanical engr. John Deere Waterloo Tractor Works of Deere & Co., Waterloo, Iowa, 1950-64, chief engr., 1964-67, gen. mgr., 1967-74, dir. mfg., Moline, Ill., 1974—; dir. Iowa Pub. Service Co., Nat. Bank of Waterloo. Mem. Dist. Judicial Nominating Commn., 1969-75; mem. Waterloo Indsl. Devel. Assn., 1968-75; past mem. United Services of Black Hawk County. Trustee, Schoitz Meml. Hosp., 1968-74; bd. govs. Iowa Coll. Found., vice chmn., 1976, chmn., 1977; bd. govs. U. No. Iowa Found., pres. 1973-75; past dir. Waterloo Civic Found. Served with USAF, 1946-47. Registered profl. engr., Ill. Mem. Soc. Automotive Engrs., Am. Soc. Agrl. Engrs., Am. Mgmt. Assn. Republican. Lutheran. Clubs: Sunnyside Country, Crow Valley Golf, Symposium. Home: 2410 Eagle Circle Bettendorf IA 52722 Office: Deere & Co John Deere Rd Moline IL

GIESBRECHT, HARRY JOHN, constrn. co. exec.; b. Lichtewau, Russia, Oct. 1, 1928; s. John George and Anna (Goosen) G.; came to Can., 1948, naturalized, 1953; B.S., Mil. Acad., Lotz, Germany, 1944; m. Mary Tamar Doerksen, Sept. 20, 1952; children—Edith, Harold, Louise. With Man. (Can.) Hydro-Engring. Dept., Winnipeg, 1952-56; pres. Central Can. Structures, Ltd., Winnipeg, 1957—, Altra Enterprises, Ltd., Winnipeg, 1968—. Div. mgr. Maple Leaf Constrn., Winnipeg, 1956-57. Pres., Crosstown Credit Union, Winnipeg, 1964-69. Mem. Am. Assn. Agrl. Engrs. (regional vice chmn.). Home: 59 Shier Blvd Winnipeg MB Canada Office: 2245 McGillivary Blvd Winnipeg MB Canada

GIESEN, RICHARD ALLYN, pub. co. exec.; b. Evanston, Ill., Oct. 7, 1929; s. Elmer J. and Ethyl (Lillig) G.; B.S., Northwestern U., 1951; m. Jeannine St. Bernard, Jan. 31, 1953; children—Richard Allyn, Laurie J., Mark St. B. Research analyst new bus. and research depts. Glore, Forgan & Co., Chgo., 1951-57; asst. to pres. Gen. Dynamics Corp., N.Y.C., 1957-60, asst. treas., 1960-61, asst. v.p. ops. and contracts, 1961-63; financial cons. IBM Corp., 1963, exec. asst. to sr. v.p. 1964-65, treas. subsidiary Sci. Research Assos., Inc., Chgo., 1965-66, v.p. finance and adminstrn., 1966-67, exec. v.p., chief operating officer, 1967-68, pres. chief exec. officer, 1968—, also dir.; dir. Sci. Research Assos. (Can.) Ltd., Sci. Research Assos., Ltd. (U.K.), Sci. Research Assos. (Pty), Ltd. (Australia), Société de Recherche Appliquée à l'Education (France), Sci. Research Assos. GmbH (Germany); Stone Container Corp. Mem. pres.'s council Nat. Coll. Edn., Evanston; bus. adv. council Chgo. Urban League. Trustee Roosevelt U. Mem. Young Presidents Orgn., Alpha Tau Omega, Beta Gamma Sigma. Clubs: Chicago; Glen View (Golf, Ill.). Home: 301 N Sheridan Rd Lake Forest IL 60045 Office: 259 E Erie St Chicago IL 60611

GIFFEN, DANIEL H., lawyer; b. Zanesville, Ohio, Feb. 11, 1938; s. Harris MacArtor and Louise (Crawford) G.; A.B., Coll. William and Mary, 1960; M.A. in History of Art, U. Pa., 1963; Ph.D. in Am. Civilization, 1967; 1967; J.D., Case Western Res. U., 1973; m. Jane Louise Cayford, Nov. 23, 1963 (div. 1970); children—Sarah Louise, Thomas Harris; m. 2d, Linda S. Eastin, Aug. 19, 1972. Corp. asst. Lippincott Library, U. Pa., Phila., 1961-63; asso. curator La. State Mus., 1963-64; dir. N.H. Hist. Soc., Concord, 1964-69, also sec.; asst. dir. Arents Research Library, State U. N.Y., Syracuse, 1969-70; v.p. Village Press Publs., Inc., Concord, 1969-74; editor Walter H. Drane Co., Cleve., 1974-76; individual practice law, Cleve. and asst. prof. Cleve. State U., 1976—. Vice pres. N.H. Antiquarian Soc. 1966-68, lectr. 1968; dir. Assn. Hist. Socs. N.H. 1967; mem. faculty Monadock (N.H.) Community Coll., 1968-69. Mem. Ohio, Cleve. bar assns., Cleve. Restoration Soc. (sec.), Am. Assn. Museums, Am. Assn. State and Local Historians, Nat. Trust, Soc. Am. Archivists, Soc. Archtl. Historians, Rushlight Club, Pewter Collectors Club. Author: Adventures in Vermont, 1969; Adventures in Maine, 1970; The New Hampshire Colony, 1970. Editor: Hist. N.H. mag. Contbr. profl. jours. Home: 292 Corning Dr Bratenahl OH 44108 Office: Cleve State U Cleveland OH 44115

GIFFEN, LAWRENCE EVERETT, SR., physician; b. Jefferson City, Mo., Jan. 30, 1923; s. Fred Lee and Angela Henrietta (Patterson) G.; B.S., Lincoln U., Mo., 1960; M.D., Kirksville (Mo.) Coll. Osteo. Medicine, 1945; M.S. in Criminal Justice, Central Mo. State U., 1977; m. Jerena East, June 1955; children—Michael Gregory, Jerena Ann, Lawrence Everett. Intern, Osteo. Hosp. Maine, Portland, 1945-46; resident in anesthesiology Art Center Hosp., Detroit, 1950-51; practice family medicine, Jefferson City, 195; mem. staff St. Mary's Health Center, Meml. Community Hosp.; med. examiner Cole County (Mo.), 1968—; cons. Mo. State Penitentiary, 1971—; med. dir. Renz Correctional Center Women, 1976—; clin. prof. family medicine Kirksville Coll. Osteo. Medicine, 1971-76, clin. prof. anesthesiology, 1968-71. Diplomate Am. Bd. Family Practice. Charter fellow Am. Acad. Family Practice; mem. AMA, So., Mo. med. assns., Am. Acad. Forensic Sci., Am. Correctional Assn., Am. Acad. Dermatology, Am. Coll. Allergy, Am. Acad. Allergy, Cole County Med. Soc. Democrat. Presbyterian. Club: Shriners. Home: 1915 Hayselton St Jefferson City MO 65101 Office: 420 E High St Jefferson City MO 65101

GIFFORD, EDGAR DEMAREST, dentist; b. Chgo., July 24, 1918; s. Edgar and Reta (Demarest) G.; B.A., DePauw U., 1940; D.D.S., U. Ill., 1949; m. Caroline Louise Wilcox, Dec. 24, 1950; children—Anne Louise, Blair Demarest. Gen. practice dentistry, LaGrange, Ill., 1949—. Instr., U. Ill. Coll. Dentistry, 1949-51. Pres., Young Men's Bus. Club LaGrange, 1956-57; pres. Goodman Sch. P.T.A., LaGrange, 1959-60; active various charity drive chairmanships. Mem. LaGrange-LaGrange Park Pub. Sch. Bd., 1960-69; active Boy Scouts Am., 1966-70. Bd. govs. Community Meml. Hosp., LaGrange, 1975—; bd. dirs. Plus Community Beautification Corp., 1975—. Served with AUS, 1942-45. Mem. S.A.R., Am. Legion, West Suburban C. of C. (dir. 1968-71), LaGrange Area Hist. Soc. (dir. 1972—, pres. 1976—), Alpha Tau Omega, Delta Sigma Delta. Conglist. (chmn. bd. deacons 1969-71, chmn. parish life bd. 1971-72, mem. ch. council 1970-72). Rotarian (dist. gov. 1964-65). Club: LaGrange Field (exec. v.p. 1969-70). Home: 415 S Edgewood Ave LaGrange IL 60525 Office: 810 Arlington Ave LaGrange IL 60525

GIFFORD, WINSTON CHARLES, food mfg. co. exec.; b. Belleville, Ill., Nov. 23, 1941; s. George Lawrence and Martha Ann (Schmidt) G.; B. Journalism, U. Mo., 1963; m. Elaine Kay Weltner, Dec. 26, 1975; 1 dau., Stephanie Anne. Tech. writer McDonnell-Douglas Co., St. Louis, 1965-67; adminstrv. asst., also pub. info. officer St. Louis Housing and Redevel. Authorities, 1967-68; dir. pub. relations Bank Bldg. Corp., St. Louis, 1968-70; mgr. employee communications Ralston-Purina Co., St. Louis, 1970—, mgr. urban program, 1974—. Bd. dirs. St. Louis Bus. Resource Center, Met. St. Louis YMCA. Served with USNR, 1963-65. Mem. Pub. Relations Soc. Am. (accredited), Internat. Assn. Bus. Communicators. Winner Silver Screen award U.S. Indsl. Film Festival, 1974. Home: 1717 June Dr St Louis MO 63138 Office: Ralston Purina Co Checkerboard Sq St Louis MO 63188

GIGAX, RICHARD, employment agy. exec.; b. Chgo., Aug. 10, 1918; s. Frederick and Ruby Maude (Brockway) G.; B.B.A., U. Toledo, 1941; m. Rosemarie Gravlin, Sept. 20, 1942; children—Cynthia, Sandra. Personnel asst. Spicer div. Dana Corp., Toledo, 1945-48; labor relations rep. Ford Motor Co., Dearborn, Mich., 1948-50; dir. indsl. relations No. Engraving & Mfg. Co., La Crosse, Wis., 1950-52; asst. to dir. indsl. relations Hughes Aircraft Co., Tucson, 1952-54; asst. v.p. charge personnel Nat. City Bank of Cleve., 1954-63; pres., treas. Westgate Personnel, Inc., Cleve., 1963—. Served with USNR, 1942-45. Mem. Nat. Employment Assn., Am. Soc. Personnel Adminstrn., Am. Inst. Banking (past pres. Cleve. chpt.), Ohio Pvt. Employment Assn., U.S. Power Squadron. Clubs: Cleve. Yachting; Catawba Island. Home: Townhome 112 2000 King James Pkwy Westlake OH 44145 Office: 20325 Center Ridge Rd Cleveland OH 44116

GILBERT, ANNE WIELAND, journalist; b. Chgo., May 1, 1927; d. David and Joy (Arnold) Wieland; B.S., Northwestern U., 1949; m. George Gale Gilbert III, Apr. 7, 1953; children—Douglas, Christopher. Columnist, Chgo. Daily News, 1971-76, also syndicated in N.Y. News, 1973—, San Francisco Chronicle, 1973—; reporter NBC-TV Sunday in Chgo., 1973; guest expert NBC-TV, N.Y.C. Today, 1974—; producer WSNS-TV spl. Collectors World, 1971; performer TV programs KETC-TV, St. Louis; owner syndicated radio spot The Antique Detective. Mem. Chgo. Press Club, Alpha Gamma Delta. Presbyterian. Author: Antique Hunters Guide: For Freaks and Fanciers, 1974; "Collectibles" or Kitsch, 1975; Collecting the New Antiques, 1977. Address: 932-15th St Wilmette IL 60091

GILBERT, BENTLEY BRINKERHOFF, educator; b. Mansfield, Ohio, Apr. 5, 1924; s. John Hopkinson and Mary Bentley (Brinkerhoff) G.; B.A., Miami U., 1949; M.A., U. Cin., 1950; Ph.D., U. Wis., 1954; m. Ellen Margaretta MacVeagh, June 2, 1968; children—Bentley, Margaret, Louis, Francis. Instr. history U. Cin., 1954-55; asst. prof. Colo. Coll., 1955-57; prof. U. Ill., 1967—. Mem. exec. com. Young Democrats Colo.; vestryman St. Elizabeth's Ch., Glencoe, Ill. Served with USAAF, 1942-46. Guggenheim fellow, 1973. Fellow Royal Hist. Soc.; mem. Am. Hist. Assn., Conf. British Studies. Democrat. Episcopalian. Club: Westbook Country. Author: Evolution of National Insurance in Great Britain, 1966; British Social Policy, 1972; Britain Since 1918, 1970; editor: The Heart of the Empire, 1974; editorial bd. Journal History Medicine, 1973-77, Albion, 1975—. Home: 950 Eastwood Rd Glencoe IL 60022 Office: University Illinois Box 4348 Chicago IL 60680

GILBERT, BRUCE FREDERIC, business exec.; b. Whitehall, Wis., Dec. 23, 1932; s. Frederic B. and Louise E. (Hahn) G.; B.S., Marquette U., 1958; m. Ellen F. Strachan, June 28, 1968; children—Susan, James, Eric, Heidi, Sarah. Salesman, Tews Lime & Cement Co., Milw., 1958-64, mgr., 1962-64; pres., sec., dir. Cedar Lake Sand & Gravel Co., Inc., Hartford, Wis., 1962—; sec., dir. Pioneer Materials Inc., Fond Du Lac, Wis., 1975—, Cedar Lake Constrn. Co. Inc., Hartford, 1970—; dir. Jebs Farms Ltd., Cedar Lake Co. Inc. Mem. Asso. Builders and Contractors of Wis. (dir.). Republican. Lutheran. Clubs: Mid-Am. Ski, Moraine Alpine Ski. Home: Route 2 Hartford WI 53027 Office: Cedar Lake Sand & Gravel Co Hwy 41 and Aurora Blvd Hartford WI 53027

GILBERT, CHARLES WALTER, orgn. exec.; b. Wheaton, Ill., Feb. 23, 1924; s. John A. and Jeanette (Wheeler) G.; A.B., DePauw U., 1947; M.S., George Williams Coll., 1975; m. Betty Gunn, Dec. 19, 1945; children—Martha Elizabeth, Jeffry Gunn. With Bus. Press Internat. pubs. Bus. Automation, Office Design, Internat. Bus. Automation, Office Appliances mags., also textbooks, reference services, Elmhurst, Ill., 1948-70, circulation mgr., 1948-50, bus. mgr., 1950-61, exec. v.p., 1961-65, pres., 1965-70; exec. v.p. Hitchcock Pub. Co., Wheaton, 1970-71, dir., 1971—; prof. bus. adminstrn. Elmhurst Coll., now dir. Center Bus. and Econs. Dir. devel. Community Renewal Soc., Chgo., 1971-73; cons. organizational devel. Republican precinct committman DuPage County, Ill., 1947-60. Served to lt. USNR, 1943-46, 50-52. Mem. Advt. Fedn. Am., Data Processing Mgmt. Assn., Soc. for Mgmt. Info. Systems, Internat. Advt. Assn., Am. Bus. Press (dir.), Acad. Mgmt., Nat. Inst. Applied Behavioral Sci., Am. Soc. Tng. Dirs., Am. Acad. Higher Edn., Assn. Computing Machinery, Inst. Bus. Designers, Chgo. Council Fgn. Relations, Carl Duisberg Soc. U.S. (pres.), Community Renewal Soc. (dir.), Sigma Delta Chi, Alpha Delta Sigma. Presbyn. (Elder). Clubs: Economic, Press, Chicago Executives (Chgo.); Club Bahia de Santiago (Manzanillo, Mexico). Home: Nepenthe Spring Green WI 53588 Office: 1 S 95th Spring Rd Elmhurst IL 60126 also Elmhurst College Elmhurst IL 60126

GILBERT, EDWARD GEORGE, ins. agy. exec.; b. Kansas City, Mo., Jan. 11, 1923; s. Edward H. and Camille S. G.; A.B., Grinnell Coll., 1942; M.B.A., U. Chgo., 1943; m. Marilyn G. Rothschild, Mar. 7, 1977; children—Richard, Robert, Charles, Katherine. Research asst. Sch. of Bus., U. Chgo., 1943; with personnel dept. Walgreen Drugs, Chgo., 1943-44; with Uhlmann Grain Co., Kansas City, Mo., 1944-47; with Edgar J. Stern/Assos. Thomas McGee & Sons, Kansas City, 1947-61, partner, 1956-61; pres. Edward G. Gilbert Agy., Kansas City, 1961—, Gilbert-Magill Co., Kansas City, 1961—. Bd. dirs. NCCJ, 1950-53, 57-60; bd. overseers Grinnel Coll., 1964-69; bd. councillors Menorah Med. Center; v.p. Urban League, Kansas City, 1960. C.P.C.U., C.L.U. Mem. Ind. Ins. Agts. Am., Assn. Internat. Ins. Agts. (dir.), Assurex Internat., Million Dollar Round Table, Casualty and Surety Assn., Mo. Ins. Agts. Assn. (treas. 1973), Kansas City Assn. Ind. Ins. Agts. (pres. 1973), Kansas City Chartered Property Casualty Underwriters (treas. 1960), Phi Beta Kappa. Office: Commerce Tower PO Box 13265 Kansas City MO 64199

GILBERT, HERMAN CROMWELL, state ofcl.; b. Mariana, Ark., Feb. 23, 1923; s. Van Luther and Cora (Allen) G.; student LaSalle Extension U., 1940-41, Internat. Bus. Machines Ednl. Center, 1957-72; m. Ivy McAlpine, July 19, 1949; children—Dorthea Ruth, Vincent Newton. Program coordinator AFL-CIO, United Packinghouse Workers Am., Chgo., 1955-57; with Ill. Dept. Labor, Bur. Employment Security, 1957—, chief data processing adminstr., 1971-73, dep. adminstr., 1973—; exec. v.p. Path Press, 1968—; mng. editor Westside Booster, Chgo., 1959-60, Citizen Newspapers, Chgo., 1965-67. Publicity dir. Chgo. League Negro Voters, 1958-65, Protest at the Polls, 1965-68; mem. Joint Fed.-State Com. Automated Systems, Interstate Conf. Employment Security Agencies, 1969-73; chmn. task force data elements standardization Interstate Conf. Employment Security Agencies, 1970-73. Served with USAAF, 1943-46. Author: The Uncertain Sound, 1969. Home: 11539 S Justine St Chicago IL 60643 Office: 910 S Michigan Ave Chicago IL 60605

GILBERT, HOWARD ALDEN, econ Central Bible Inst., Springfield, Mo., 1957; postgrad. Everett (Wash.) Jr. Coll., 1959; B.S. (Danforth fellow), Wash. State U., 1961, M.A., 1962; Ph.D., Oreg.

State U., 1967; postgrad. S.D. State U., 1969-70, Vanderbilt U., 1971; m.; four children. Research asst. dept. agrl. econs. Wash. State U., 1961-62; research asst. dept. agrl. econs. Oreg. State U., 1962-65, grad. asst., 1963-64, asst. in agrl. econs., 1965-66; asst. prof. dept. econs. S.D. State U., Brookings, 1966-73, asso. prof., 1973-76, prof., 1976—, chmn. campus ednl. aids com., 1969-72, student affairs sub-com. on orgns., 1970-72, goals and objectives com., 1973-74, faculty welfare com., 1974-75, citizens high sch. curriculum evaluation com., 1974-75; co-dir. econs. dept. internship program, 1974—, chmn. econs. dept. teaching and curriculum com., 1974—, acad. senate ad hoc com. on univ. core in social sci., 1976. Named Outstanding Tchr. of Year, S.D. State U., 1969-70; NSF grantee Vanderbilt U., summer 1971, Clark Coll., 1976-77. Mem. Am., Western agrl. econs. assns., Am., Western econ. assns., Am. Sci. Affiliation, Phi Kappa Phi, Pi Gamma Mu, Gamma Sigma Delta, Alpha Zeta. Contbr. articles on econs. to profl. publs. Home: 605 9th St Brookings SD 57006 Office: Dept Econs SD State U Brookings SD 57007

GILBERT, JOHN ROBERT, utility exec.; b. Long Beach, Calif., July 17, 1946; s. Walton E. and Marian (Farris) G.; B.A., Washington U., St. Louis, 1969; m. Patricia Rector Gilbert, Apr. 20, 1974; 1 son, Kent Edward. Program dir. Sta. KSHE, St. Louis, 1968-69; broadcaster Sta. KUDL, Kansas City, 1972-73; mgr. nat. pub. relations C. of C. Greater Kansas City, 1973-75; mgr. pub. relations info. and advt. Mo. Pub. Serivce Co., Kansas City, 1975—. Served with U.S. Army, 1969-72. Mem. Pub. Relations Soc. Am. (dir.), Mo. Valley Electric Assn., Smithsonian Assos., Friends of Art. Presbyn. Contbr. articles to popular mags. Home: 5225 Reinhardt St Shawnee Mission KS 66205 Office: 10700 East Hwy 50 Kansas City MO 64138

GILBERT, SIDNEY, dentist; b. Westfield, N.J., Apr. 15, 1917; s. Alexander and Bessie (Sobel) G.; D.D.S., Ohio State U., 1942; m. Shirlee Fae Volk, June 14, 1942; children—Stephen Lee, Donald Bernard, Marilyn Sue, Dorothy Audrey. Gen. practice dentistry, Akron, Ohio, 1946-63, Mogadore, 1963—; owner horse breeding farm, Alliance Ohio, 1973—. Served to maj. USAAF, 1942-46; CBI. Decorated Presdl. citation. Mem. Am., Ohio dental assns., Am. Inst. Orthodontics, Stark County Dental Soc., Am. Endodontic Soc., Am. Morgan Horse Assn., Buckeye Saddlebred Futurity (trustee 1973—), Ohio Saddlebred Horse Assn. (bd. dirs. 1972-74), Alpha Omega, Am. Legion. Mason (Shriner), Elk. Home: 11225 Freshley Ave Alliance OH 44601 Office: 60 S Cleveland Ave Mogadore OH 44260

GILBERT, THOMAS IRVINE, chemist; b. South Williamson, Ky., Oct. 24, 1932; s. Thomas and Mexie (Caines) G.; B.A. in Chemistry cum laude, Inter-Am. U., 1961; m. Lirio Irizarry, Mar. 26, 1955; children—Angeli, Linda, Greer. Research chemist Elco Corp., Cleve., 1961-65, supr. lubricant devel., 1965-67; chief chemist Brooks Oil Co., Cleve., 1967-71; tech. dir. indsl. lubricants Pillsbury Chem. Co., Detroit, 1971; sr. lubrication engr. Climax Molybdenum Co., Ann Arbor, Mich., 1972-75; tech. dir. indsl. lubricants Dri-Slide, Inc., Fremont, Mich., 1975; pres. Native Supply Co., Sidney, Ky., 1976—; propr. T.I. Gilbert & Co., Lubrication Cons., Lorain, Ohio, 1971; lectr. Nat. Lubricating Grease Inst., 1973. Served with AUS, 1951-58. Fellow Am. Inst. Chemists; mem. Am. Chem. Soc., Am. Soc. Lubrication Engrs., ASTM. Patentee in field. Home: 102 Arkansas Ave Lorain OH 44052 Office: PO Box 89 Sidney KY 41564

GILBERT, WILLIAM FREDERICK, elec. engr.; b. South Haven, Mich., Mar. 9, 1924; s. Angus and Alice Marie (Rohloff) G.; B.E.E., Mich. Tech. U., 1945, M.E.E., 1950; m. Elaine Montgomery, May 6, 1944; children—Sandra, Richard, Barbara, Patricia, Susan, Russell. Mem. faculty Mich. Tech. U. at Houghton, 1945-60, asso. prof. physics, 1955-60; asso. elec. engr., mgr. ednl. nuclear reactors labs. Argonne (Ill.) Nat. Lab., 1960-72; tng. coordinator Cooper Nuclear Station, Nebr. Pub. Power Dist., Brownville, 1972—. Mem. Am. Nuclear Soc., Am. Soc. Engring. Edn. Methodist. Clubs: Auburn Country, Elks. Home: 2315 Lynch Ave Auburn NE 68305 Office: PO Box 98 Brownville NE 68321

GILBERTSON, CARLYLE WARREN, educator; b. Winona, Minn., May 31, 1930; s. Nels and Luella Emeline (Solie) G.; B.A., Luther Coll., Decorah, Iowa, 1957; M.S., U. Wis. at Madison, 1960, Ph.D., 1966; m. Ruth Elaine Grotjahn, Aug. 30, 1951; children—Larry, Kara, Heidi, Michael. Tchr., sr. high sch. Viroqua, Wis., 1957-59; sch. counselor, high sch., Oconomowoc, Wis., 1960-64; counseling psychologist U. Wis. at Oshkosh, 1966-69; prof., chmn. dept. counseling U. Wis. at Stout, Menomonie, 1969—. Cons. schs. dists., univs., vocat. and pvt. schs. Served with USN, 1951-54; Korea. Recipient fed. and state grants. Mem. Am. Personnel and Guidance Assn., Am. Psychol. Assn., Wis. Assn. Counselor Edn. and Supervision (pres., 1970-71), Wis. Career Guidance Assn. (pres. 1976-78), Assn. U. Wis. Faculties, Phi Delta Kappa. Contbr. articles to profl. jours. Home: 1208 River Heights Rd Menomonie WI 54751 Office: Univ Wis Stout Menomonie WI 54751

GILBERTSON, CONRAD BRIAN, govt. ofcl.; b. Aneta, N.D., Apr. 11, 1938; s. Ralph and Catherine Josephine (Leon) G.; B.S., N.D. State U., 1961; M.S., S.D. State U., 1963; m. Carolyn Mitchell; children—Taunja Faye, Tausha Jo, Melissa, Suzanne, Cheryl. Extension agrl. engr. N.D. State U., Fargo, 1963-67; devel. engr. U.S. Meat Animal Research Center, Clay Center, Nebr., 1967-68; project leader Agrl. Research Service, U.S. Dept. Agr., U. Nebr., Lincoln., 1968—. Served with USMCR, 1956. Named outstanding young engr. of year, S.E. chpt. Profl. Engrs. Nebr., 1972, Outstanding Young Engr., various orgns., 1967, 73. Registered profl. engr. Nebr. Mem. Am. Soc. Agrl. Engrs. (region vice chmn. 1972-73, Nebr. sect. chmn. 1971-72, Midcentral Region Engr. of Year 1973), Profl. Engrs. Nebr. (sec. 1972-73, Engr. of Year 1973), Gamma Sigma Delta, Sigma Xi, Alpha Epsilon. Presbyterian. Elk. Contbr. articles to profl. publs. Home: 9001 Panama Rd Holland NE 68372 Office: Agrl Engring Dept U Nebr USDA-ARS Lincoln NE 68583

GILBERTSON, HAROLD KENNETH, SR., chiropractor; b. Jackson County, Wis., May 24, 1917; s. Albert Martin and Matilda (Overlien) G.; D.Chiropractic, Palmer Coll. Chiropractic, 1942; H.H.D., Logan Coll., 1972; m. Bernice Clara Gradl, Dec. 1, 1945; children—Deborah Lee (Mrs. Dale E. Shannon), Harold Kenneth II. Pvt. practice chiropractry, University City, Mo., 1944-45, St. Louis, 1945-55, St. Johns, Mo., 1955-74, Bridgeton, Mo., 1974—. Dir., Unity Christ Ch., St. Louis, 1971-72. Mem. Am. (del. 1964-65), Mo. State (pres. 1956-59) chiropractors assns. Clubs: Masons, Shriners. Home: 3744 McKelvey Rd Bridgeton MO 63044 Office: 11901 St Charles Rd Bridgeton MO 63044

GILBERTSON, KRIS KENSON, editor; b. Conde, S.D., Aug. 2, 1911; s. Krist and Gladys L. (Burge) G.; B.S., S.D. State U., 1933; m. Ethel F. Bowe, June 22, 1936; 1 dau., Kay (Mrs. Robert A. Pohnl). With Rhinelander (Wis.) Daily News, 1937-41, 46—, editor, 1968—. Sec., Nicolet Coll. Found. Served to lt. col., AUS, 1941-46. Decorated Bronze Star medal. Purple Heart. Lion. Home: 513 Pelican St Rhinelander WI 54501 Office: 314 Courtney St Rhinelander WI 54501

GILBOE, DAVID DOUGHERTY, educator; b. Richland Center, Wis., July 13, 1929; s. Harvey Bernard and Margaret Lucille (Dougherty) G.; B.A., Miami U., 1951; M.S., U. Wis., 1955, Ph.D., 1958; m. Myrtle Marie Kroll, Aug. 18, 1951; children—Andrew J., Sarah A. Instr. surgery and physiol. chemistry U. Wis., Madison, 1959-61, asst. prof., 1961-67, asso. prof., 1967-73, prof. surgery and physiology, 1973—; ad hoc referee Am. Jour. Physiology. Served with USN, 1951-54. NIH grantee, 1965—; Wis. Alumni Research Found. fellow in surgery, 1958-59; Fulbright lectr. in Med. Sci., U. Chile, Santiago, 1970. Mem. Am. Physiol. Soc., Am. Soc. Biol. Chemists, Am. Soc. for Neurochemistry, Internat. Soc. for Neurochemistry, Soc. for Neuroscience, AAUP, Sigma Xi. Roman Catholic. Clubs: Rotary. Contbr. articles and book chpts. in field of metabolism and physiology of isolated canine brain preparation. Home: 409 Blue Ridge Pkwy Madison WI 53705 Office: Dept of Surgery University Hospitals Madison WI 53706

GILBORNE, JEAN ELIZABETH, librarian; b. Bonfield, Ill., June 21, 1910; d. John V. and Anna Belle (Stroud) Gilborne; B.E., Ill. State Normal U., 1937; M.A. in English, U. Ill., 1944, M.S. in L.S., 1951. Tchr. rural schs., Kankakee County, Ill., 1928-37; tchr. high sch., LaSalle, Montgomery, Coles, Clark and Piat counties, Ill., 1938-50; asst. librarian Univ. High Sch., Urbana, 1950-51; librarian Geneseo (Ill.) High Sch., 1951-54; unit sch. librarian, Geneseo, 1954-75; instr. extension course library sci. U. Ill., 1971-72. Mem. bd. global ministries Central Ill. Conf., United Meth. Ch., 1973—. Mem. Geneseo Bus. and Profl. Women's Club (pres. 1959-61), Ill. Fedn. Bus. and Profl. Women's Club (dist. chmn. 1962-64, mem. Celia Howard scholarship com.), A.L.A., Ill. Library Assn., N.E.A., Ill. Edn. Assn., A.A.U.W., Beta Sigma Phi, Beta Phi Mu. Methodist (chmn. Christian social relations Galesburg dist. 1960-64, chmn. spiritual life cultivation 1964, certified lay speaker 1967—; chmn. Wesleyan Service Guild Galesburg dist. 1968-72). Rebekah. Home: 607 1/2 S Center St Geneseo IL 61254

GILBRIDE, THOMAS LEO, shopping center mgr.; b. Cleve., Sept. 2, 1947; s. John Nelson and Lois Blanch (Dailey) G.; student U. Toledo, 1966-68, Lorain Coll., 1973-74, Baldwin-Wallace Coll., 1974-75; m. Stasia E. Suchora, July 10, 1976. Watchman, Kinsman Marine Transit, Gt. Lakes, 1966-68; with advt. dept. Cleve. Plain Dealer, 1972-74, editorial city room, 1974-75; mall mgr., Jacobs, Visconsi and Jacobs, Cleve., 1975—. Scoutmaster, Canal Zone council Boy Scouts Am., 1970-73; football, baseball coach., 1970-73. Served with U.S. Army, 1969-72. Mem. Internat. Council of Shopping Centers, Smithsonian Inst. Roman Catholic. Contbr. writings to Cleve. Plain Dealer, Milw. Jour., Columbus Messenger. Home: 147 Tarryton Ct W Columbus OH 42228 Office: 4273 Westland Mall Columbus OH 43228

GILBRIDE, WILLIAM DONALD, lawyer; b. Detroit, July 31, 1924; s. William Andrew and Kathryne Agnes (Donnelly) G.; LL.B., U. Detroit, 1950; m. Helen Posselius, May 1, 1954; 1 son, William Donald. Admitted to Mich. bar, 1950; asso. Fildew, Degree & Fleming, Detroit, 1951-53; mem. firm Fildew, Degree, Fleming & Gilbride, Detroit, 1953-65, Fildew, Degree, Gilbride & Smith, 1965-72, Fildew, Gilbride, Miller & Todd, 1972—. Dir. Detroit Marine Terminals. Mem. State Bd. Law Examiners, 1973—; pres. Friends Detroit Pub. Library, 1968-70. Pres. bd. trustees Liggett Sch., 1964-66. Served with Signal Corps, AUS, 1943-46. Fellow Am. Bar Found.; mem. State Bar Mich. (assemblyman 1972-73), Am., Detroit (pres. 1972—) bar assns., Am. Judicature Soc., Engring. Soc. Detroit, Am. Legion, Alpha Kappa Psi, Delta Theta Phi. Clubs: Detroit, Detroit Press, Racquet, University; Grosse Pointe (Mich.). Home: 18 Radnor Circle Grosse Pointe MI 48236 Office: City National Bank Bldg Detroit MI 48226

GILDEA, JOHN RILEY, lawyer, pharm. co. exec.; b. Elkhart, Ind., Dec. 29, 1939; s. Austin Cornelius and Margueritte Louise (Clair) G.; A.B. cum laude, U. Notre Dame, 1961, J.D., 1963; m. Gwendolyn Louise Robinson; children—Tamara Lynn, Christopher Thomas, Sara Marguerite, Brian Clair. Admitted to Ind. bar, 1963; atty. Miles Labs., Inc., Elkhart, 1963-66, sr. atty., 1966-69, asst. sec., 1967-75, asso. counsel, 1969-75, sec., asso. gen. counsel, 1975—. Dir., sec. DGM Corp.; partner Midtown Estate. Mem. Elkhart Econ. Devel. Commn. Bd. dirs. Elkhart Urban League, 1963-69, United Way Elkhart County, 1971—, Elkhart YMCA, 1970—; trustee, sec. Miles Labs. Found. Mem. Am., Ind., Elkhart bar assns., Elkhart C. of C. (1st v.p., dir.). Roman Catholic. Clubs: Elks, Elcona Country, Summit. Home: 811 Strong Ave Elkhart IN 46514 Office: 1127 Myrtle St Elkhart IN 46514

GILDEA, ROBERT LEE, pub. relations exec.; b. Bloomington, Ind., Oct. 21, 1931; s. Ralph Louis and Ruth Lee (Weaver) G.; A.B., Ind. U., 1954, M.A., 1964; m. Margaret Hoadley, 1953 (div. 1972); children—Sarah Lee, Jeffrey Robert, Bradley H.; m. 2d, Mary L. Kirkman, May 5, 1972. City editor, mng. editor Bloomington (Ind.) Herald-Telephone, 1956-57; pub. relations dir. Ind. Area of Meth. Ch., 1957-61; v.p. Howard S. Wilcox, Inc., Indpls., 1971—. Served with U.S. Army, 1954-56. Mem. Pub. Relations Soc. Am. (pres. Hoosier chpt. 1974), Sigma Delta Chi (pres. Ind. chpt. 1963-65). Methodist. Club: Indpls. Literary. Home: 26 N Sheridan St Indianapolis IN 46219 Office: 300 Board Trade Bldg Indianapolis IN 46204

GILDERSLEEVE, HARRY DALE, JR., optometrist; b. Wayne, Nebr., Jan. 28, 1922; s. Harry Dale and Violet Elna (Olson) G.; student Compton Coll., 1941-43, U. Calif. at Los Angeles, 1943-44, Cornell U., 1944; D. Optometry, Los Angeles Coll. Optometry, 1949; m. Helen Margaret Gaylord, Sept. 20, 1944; children—Linda, Kathy, Philip, Donna. Pvt. practice optometry, O'Neill, Nebr., 1949—. Active Boy Scouts Am.; dist. commr. Nebr. Softball Assn., 1976-77. Served to lt. (j.g.) USNR, 1943-46. Mem. Am., Nebr. optometric assns., Am. Legion (post comdr. 1955). Republican. Methodist. Mason (32 deg.), Lion (pres. 1954). Home: 709 E Londonderry Dr O'Neill NE 68763 Office: 128 S 4th St O'Neill NE 68763

GILDZEN, ALEX JOHN, librarian, poet; b. Monterey, Calif., Apr. 25, 1943; s. Alex and Helen (Kovach) G.; B.A., Kent State U., 1965, M.A., 1966. Staff writer Univ. News Service, Kent State U., 1967-70, lectr. dept. English, 1967-70, librarian univ. libraries, 1970—, asst. prof. library adminstrn., 1970-77, asso. prof., 1977—; books include: Into the Sea, 1969; Funny Ducks, 1973; The Year Book, 1974; author pamphlets, broadsides; contbr. numerous poems to lit. jours., U.S., Can., Gt. Britain, 1963—, also to anthologies. Recipient Poetry award Ind. U. Writers Conf., 1967. Mem. Soc. Cinephiles. Editor Toucan, 1967-73, Momentum, 1970-71, Occasional Papers, Kent State U. Libraries, 1971-72. Home: 1520 South Blvd Kent OH 44240 Office: Kent State Univ Libraries Kent OH 44242

GILES, CONRAD LESLIE, physician; b. N.Y.C., July 14, 1934; s. Irving Samuel and Victoria (Ampole) G.; student U. Mich., 1951-53, M.D., 1957, M.S., 1961; m. Marilyn Toby Schwartz, June 20, 1955; children—Keith, Suzanne, Kevin, Brian. Intern U. Mich. Med. Center, 1957-58, resident, 1958-61; clin. asso. NIH, Bethesda, Md., 1961-63, practice medicine, specializing in ophthalmic surgery and pediatric ophthalmology, Detroit, 1963—; mem. staff Detroit Gen. Hosp., Childrens Hosp. Mich., Sinai Hosp.; cons. Wayne County Gen. Hosp.; instr. ophthalmology Wayne State U., 1963-69, asst. clin. prof., 1969-72, asso. clin. prof., 1972—; instr. ophthalmology U. Mich., 1966-72, asst. clin. prof., 1973-77. Trustee, Jewish Family and Childrens Service, Detroit; v.p. O.R.T., Fresh Air Soc.; cabinet mem. Young Leadership Allied Jewish Campaign, 1970-73; bd. govs., exec. com. Jewish Welfare Fedn., Detroit. Mem. Am. Acad. Ophthalmology and Otolarynology, A.M.A., Mich. Ophthalmology Soc., Phi Delta Epsilon. Club: Franklin Hills Country. Asso. editor Am. Jour. Med. Scis., 1964-68, Jour. Pediatric Ophthalmology, 1969—. Contbr. articles to profl. jours. Home: 27260 Willow Green Ct Franklin MI 48025 Office: Northland Med Bldg Southfield MI 48075

GILES, HOMER WAYNE, lawyer; b. Noble, Ohio, Nov. 9, 1919; s. Edwin Jay and Nola Blanche (Tillison) G.; A.B., Adelbert Coll., 1940; LL.B., Western Res. Law Sch., 1943, LL.M., 1959; m. Zola Ione Parke, Sept. 8, 1948; children—Jay, Janice, Keith, Tim, Gregory. Admitted to Ohio bar, 1943; mem. firm Davis & Young, Cleve., 1942-43, William I. Moon, Port Clinton, 1946-48; pres. Strabley Baking Co., Cleve., 1948-53; v.p. French Baking Co., Cleve., 1953-55; law clk. 8th Dist. Court Appeals, Cleve., 1955-58; partner Kuth & Giles, law firm 1958-68, Walter, Haverfield, Buescher & Chockley, 1968—; pres. Clinton Franklin Realty Co., Cleve., 1958—; sec. Holiday Designs, Inc., Sebring, Ohio, 1964—. Trustee, Teamster Local 52 Health and Welfare Fund, 1950-53; mem. Bakers Negotiating Exec. Com., 1951-53; troop com. chmn. Skyline council Boy Scouts Am., 1961-63. Trustee, Hiram House Camp, Florence Crittenton Home, 1965; chmn. bd. trustees Am. Econ. Found. Served with AUS, 1943-46; ETO. Mem. Am. Bar Assn., World Law Assn. (founding), Am. Arbitration Assn. (nat. panel arbitrators), Com. on Econ. Reform and Edn. (life mem.), Speakers Bur. Cleve. Sch. Levy, Citizens League (nationalities service com. 1965), Cleve. Hist. Soc., Delta Tau Delta, Delta Theta Phi. Unitarian (trustee 1965-68). Clubs: Cleveland Skating, Harvard Business. Editor: Banks Baldwin Ohio Legal Forms, 1962. Contbr. articles to profl. publs. Home: 2588 S Green Rd University Heights OH 44122 Office: 1215 Terminal Tower Cleveland OH 44113

GILES, WILLIAM MITCHELL, apparel co. exec.; b. Charlotte, N.C., Apr. 8, 1943; s. Olin Sylvester and Evelyn Jane (Love) G.; student U. N.C., Charlotte, 1961-63; B.S., Clemson U., 1965; m. Janice Elaine Alexander, June 1, 1963; children—Ashley Lynn, Mary Elaine, Amanda Nicole. Project engr., indsl. engr., methods engr. Beaunit Corp., Gastonia, N.C., 1965-69; plant mgr., chief indsl. engr. Alamo Mfg. Co., Florence, S.C., 1969-74; gen. mgr., dir. mfg. Youngwear Products Inc., Smoaks, S.C., 1974-77; dir. corporate planning Wolverine Knitting, Inc., Bay City, Mich., 1977—; owner W.M. Giles and Assos., Mgmt. Consultants, 1970—. Recipient Certificate of Merit, Am. Cancer Soc., 1975, 76, 77. Mem. Am. Inst. Indsl. Engrs., Soc. Mfg. Engrs. Clubs: Oakdale Country, Florence Country, Elks, Rotary (v.p. 1974), Lions, Kiwanis, Toastmasters, U.S. Jaycees. Author: Yield Book of Mathematical Progressions for the Textile Industry, 1967. Patentee Vertical Roving Guide for Paralofler, 1969. Home: 210 Pine St Essexville MI 48732 Office: 1400 S Lincoln Bay City MI 48706

GILL, LYLE BENNETT, lawyer; b. Lincoln, Nebr., May 11, 1916; s. George Orville and Ruth (Bennett) G.; B.A., Swarthmore Coll., 1937; LL.B., Nebr. Coll. Law, 1940; m. Rita M. Cronin, Aug. 28, 1975; children by previous marriage—George, Valerie, Marguerite. Admitted to Nebr. bar, 1940; practice law, Fremont, 1945—; city atty. Fremont, 1959-62, 67—. Vice chmn. A.R.C., Dodge County, 1953-59. Chmn., Dodge County Republican Com., 1945-51. Served with USNR, 1942-45, 1951-52; lt. comdr. (ret.). Mem. Am., Nebr., Dodge County (pres. 1962) bar assns., Trial Lawyers Assn., V.F.W., Am. Legion. Episcopalian. Home: 524 E Linden Ave Fremont NE 68025 Office: First Nat Bank Bldg Fremont NE 68025

GILL, NEAL FASSIG, mech. engr.; b. Columbus, Ohio, May 19, 1904; s. Charles Ambrose and Ida Louise (Fassig) G.; B.M.E., Ohio State U., 1929; m. Ruth Elvere McMillin, Aug. 31, 1929; 1 dau., Constance McMillin Gill Badger. Jr. engr. Cleve. Elec. Illuminating Co., 1929-42, mgr. mech. engring. dept., 1942-61, prin. mech. engr., 1961-69; profl. engr. Pub. Utility Commn. Ohio, Columbus, 1969—; bd. dirs. Atomic Power Devel. Assocs., Detroit, 1962-67, mem. tech. com., 1955-69, econs. com., 1962-69; dep. nuclear specialist Taiwan Economy-Energy Study, U.S. Dept. State, 1965. Mem. ASME (exec. com. Cleve. chpt. 1959-64, chmn. 1962-63), Cleve. Engring. and Sci. Center. Presbyterian. Club: Cleve. City. Office: 180 E Broad St Columbus OH 43215

GILL, PAUL SINGH, coll. adminstr.; b. Sudhar-Punjab, India, Apr. 27, 1936; s. Bhagwan Singh and Gurdev Kaur (Dhaliwal) G.; came to U.S., 1961, naturalized, 1968; B.A., Punjab U., 1959; B.S., Black Hill State Coll., 1963; M.S., S.D. State U., 1965; m. Myrna A. Johnson, July 3, 1964; 1 dau., Manjit Kaur. Tire builder Goodyear Tire & Rubber Co., England, 1959-61; tchr. Custer (S.D.) Pub. Schs., 1963-64; guidance dir. St. Charles (Mich.) Pub. Schs., 1965-68; admissions counselor Saginaw Valley State Coll., Mich., 1968-69, dir. admissions, 1969-73, dir. scholarships and fin. aids, 1973—. Served with Indian Army, 1955-59. Mem. Nat. Assn. Fgn. Student Affairs (panelist), Nat. Assn. Fin. Aid Assns., Mich. Assn. Coll. Registrars Admissions, S.D. Edn. Assn., Am. Personnel Guidance Assn., Midwestern Fin. Aid Assn., Mich. Assn. Fin. Aid. Adminstrs., Coll. Personnel Assn. Democrat. Sikh. Club: Germania (Saginaw). Home: 3530 Hickory Ln Saginaw MI 48603 Office: 2250 Pierce Rd University Center MI 48710

GILLEN, GREGORY RONALD, dentist; b. Portsmouth, Ohio, Dec. 13, 1942; s. Charles Richard and Mildred A. (Guilkey) G.; student Miami U., 1960-63; D.D.S., Ohio State U., 1967; m. Diane M. Butler, Nov. 2, 1968; 1 son, Christian Todd. Pvt. practice dentistry, Portsmouth, Ohio, 1969—. Tchr. dental hygiene Scioto Tech. Coll., 1970—. Adviser on profl. edn. Ohio div. Am. Cancer Soc., 1970-72. Served with AUS, 1967-69. Recipient Carl O. Boucher award Ohio State U., 1967. Mem. Am., Ohio, So. Ohio (sec. 1970, pres. 1974) dental socs., Ohio State Alumni Assn. (pres. Scioto County chpt.). Elk, Rotarian. Home: Route 2 McDermott OH 45652 Office: 1613 Kinneys Ln Portsmouth OH 45662

GILLEN, JAMES P., ins. agent; b. Michigan City, Ind., Sept. 5, 1944; s. Robert M. and Alice M. (Setlak) G.; B.S., Ind. U., 1971; m. Rosemary N. Nimon, June 8, 1968; 1 son, James P. Aircraft data organizer Bendix Corp., 1966; mktg. data supr. Standard Oil Corp., Granger, Ind., 1966-68; mktg. rep. Addressograph-Multigraph Corp., South Bend, Ind., 1968-71; owner James P. Gillen, Ins., South Bend, Ind., Michigan City, Ind., 1971-77; pres. Terrey & Gillen Ins., Inc., Michigan City, Ind., 1977; city controller, Michigan City, 1977. Served with U.S. Army, 1963-66. Mem. Nat. Assn. Ins. Agents, Ind. Ins. Agents Ind. (Young Agt. of Year award 1977). Democrat. Roman Catholic. Clubs: Pottawattomie Country, Knollwood Country. Home: 226 E Coolspring Ave Michigan City IN 46360 Office: 912 S Franklin St Michigan City IN 46360

GILLES, KENNETH ALBERT, educator; b. Mpls., Mar. 6, 1922; s. Albert Peter and Alma (Stodghill) G.; student Augsburg Coll., 1940-42; B.S., U. Minn., 1944, Ph.D., 1952; postgrad. Columbia,

1944; m. Beverly Elaine Barrows, July 1, 1944; children—Jeffrey Alan, Diane Elaine. Research engr. Pillsbury Co., Mpls., 1946-49; instr., research fellow U. Minn., St. Paul, 1949-52; project leader Gen. Mills, Inc., 1952-61; prof. cereal chemistry, chmn. cereal chemistry and tech. dept. N.D. State U., Fargo, 1961-69, v.p. agr., 1969—. Chmn. City Planning Commn., Roseville, Minn., 1955-60, Park Bd., 1960-61; bd. dirs. Fargo Indsl. Devel. Corp., 1977—. Served to lt. (j.g.) USNR, 1944-46. Named Man of Year Roseville C. of C., 1961. Fellow A.A.A.S.; mem. Am. Assn. Cereal Chemists (pres. 1971-72, Geddes award 1976), Am. Chem. Soc., Inst. Food Tech., Assn. Operative Millers, Fargo C. of C. (mem. agrl. com. 1968—, dir. 1974—), Sigma Xi. Mason (Shriner). Editor-in-chief Cereal Chemistry, 1961-68. Contbr. chpts. to books, articles to publs. Home: 925 Park Dr Fargo ND 58102

GILLESPIE, JAMES LAURENCE, historian; b. Cleve., Apr. 5, 1946; s. James Joseph and Elizabeth A. M. (Koch) G.; A.B., Kenyon Coll., 1968; B.S. in Edn., Kent State U., 1973; M.A. (fellow), Princeton U., 1970, Ph.D. (fellow), 1973. Lectr., St. Mary's Coll. of Queen's U., Belfast, No. Ireland, 1971-72; asst. prof. Appalachian State U., Boone, N.C. 1974-75, Lakeland Community Coll., Mentor, Ohio, 1975-76, U. Minn., Duluth, 1976-77, Catawba Coll., Salisbury, N.C., 1977—; reader on medieval English history for Albion publ., 1975—; mem. organizing com. Ohio Conf. Medieval Studies, 1975-76. Vestryman St. Paul's Episcopal Ch., Cleve., 1976—. Mem. Am., So. hist. assns., Cleve. Medieval Soc., Phi Beta Kappa, Kappa Delta Pi, Phi Alpha Theta. Author: Free Speech at St. Joseph's College, 1972; Richard II's Cheshire Archers, 1975; Thomas Mortimer and Thomas Molineux, 1975; A Series of Commentaries on the Sacraments, 1977; Medieval English Multiple Biography, 1978. Home: 956 Roanoke Rd Cleveland Heights OH 44121 Office: Catawba Coll Salisbury NC 28144

GILLESPIE, KENNETH IRA, real estate broker; b. Akron, Ohio, Nov. 9, 1920; s. Marlin Judson and Willodene (Turk) G.; student Hammel Bus. U., 1947; m. Harriett Josephine Hartigan, Sept. 28, 1946; children—Kenneth P., James M., Donna Gillespie Stalnaker, Margaret Gillespie Manson, Robert. With Crawford Realty Co., Akron, 1949-53, Rust Engring. Co., Fla., Ohio, Mass., 1948-49; pres. Gillespie-Pilcher Realty Co., Cuyahoga Falls, Ohio, 1953-70, Gillespie-Pilcher Bldg. and Investment Co., Cuyahoga Falls, 1958-70, Gillespie Pilcher Ins. Agy., Cuyahoga Falls, 1954-71; owner Ken Gillespie Realty Co., Akron, 1970—, Ken Gillespie Bldg. and Investment Co., Inc., Akron, 1970—, Capital Growth and Investment Co., Akron, 1970—; pres. K.G.R. Securities & Investments, Inc., 1974—; sec.-treas. Merit Investment Co., Akron, 1967-74, Tradewind's Inc., Akron, 1966-74; owner Certified Mortgage Corp., 1970—; partner Willows Co., 1977—; investment counsel real estate. Served with AUS, 1940-45. Mem. Akron Area Bd. Realtors (mem. arbitration and ethics com. 1966-72), VFW, Nat., Ohio, Akron home builders assns. Club: Silver Lake Country. Home: PO Box 5345 Akron OH 44313 Office: 2187 Akron-Peninsula Rd PO Box 5345 Akron OH 44313

GILLESPIE, THOMAS, educator; b. Winnipeg, Man., Can., Apr. 16, 1924; s. William John and Margaret (Johnston) G.; came to U.S., 1957, naturalized, 1963; B.Sc., U. Man., 1945; M.Sc., U. Alta., 1947; Ph.D., U. London (Eng.), 1955, D.Sc., 1963; m. Victoria Hrynchuk, May 4, 1945; children—Terrance William Paul, Peter Kelvin. Faculty physics dept. U. Alta., Edmonton and Calgary, 1946-48; with Canadian Def. Research Bd., Suffield, Alta., 1948-51, 55-57; with Ministry of Supply, Salisbury, Eng., 1951-53; dir. plastics fundamental research Dow Chem. Co., Midland, Mich., 1957-68; research mgr. Forest Products Lab., Dept. Forestry, Ottawa, Ont., Can., 1968-69; faculty Saginaw Valley Coll., Univ. Center, Mich., 1969—, dir. engring. tech., prof. engring. and tech., 1972—. Cons., Dow Chem. Co. Contbr. articles to profl. jours. Home: 2510 Manor Dr Midland MI 48640 Office: Saginaw Valley Coll University Center MI 48710

GILLETTE, HALBERT SCRANTON, publisher; b. Chgo., June 29, 1922; s. Edward Scranton and Clarebel (Thornton) G.; student Chgo. Latin Sch. for Boys, 1931-38; grad. Phillips Exeter Acad., 1941; B.S., Mass. Inst. Tech., 1944; m. Mary Livingston, Feb. 12, 1949 (dec.); children—Anne Livingston, Susan L; m. 2d, Karla Spiel, June 8, 1963; children—James McCall, Halbert George, Edward Scranton II. Space buyer for Andrews Agy., 1946-48; advt. mgr. Good Roads Machinery Co., Minerva, Ohio, 1948; exec. v.p. Gillette Pub. Co., Chgo., 1949-60; pub. The Reuben H. Donnelley Corp., 1960-70, Trade Periodicals, 1970-72; exec. v.p. Scranton Pub. Co., Inc., Chgo., 1972—; chmn. bd. Occidental Ins. Co. N.C., 1973-74, McMillen Corp., Peninsula Life Ins. Co., 1974-77; chmn. bd., dir., pres. The Doctor's Tax Letter, Inc., Publisher's Paper Co., Inc., Ednl. Screen Inc., The Diapason, Inc., Piano Trade Pub. Co., Inc., Florist & Nursery Exchange. Served with USNR, 1943-46. Mem. Phi Gamma Delta. Episcopalian. Club: Onwentsia. Home: 255 Foster Pl Lake Forest IL 60045 Office: 435 S Wabash Ave Chicago IL 60605

GILLICK, FRED IRVING, real estate broker; b. Chgo., Jan. 22, 1939; s. John F. and Harriet (Bjorn) G.; B.S., U. Denver, 1961; m. Nancy Ruth Ramsland, Aug. 7, 1965; children—Linda Joanne, Patricia Ann. With Park Ridge Fed. Savs. & Loan Assn. (Ill.), 1964-68; owner, broker Fred I. Gillick Co., Realtors, Park Ridge, 1968—; adv. bd. Park Ridge div. Bell Fed. Savs. & Loan Assn., 1974—. Co-chmn. Park Ridge United Fund, 1965-66. Served to lt. (j.g.), USNR, 1961-64. Mem. Am. Inst. Real Estate Appraisers, Park Ridge Jr. C. of C. (sec. 1966). Lion. Home: 305 East Ave Park Ridge IL 60068 Office: 122 Main St Park Ridge IL 60068

GILLIHAN, JAMES EDWARD, state ofcl.; b. Wabash County, Ill., May 22, 1935; s. James Monroe and Mary Elizabeth (Robinson) G.; B.A., So. Ill. U., 1957, postgrad., 1957-59; postgrad. Evansville U., 1959-63; L.H.D., Sussex Coll., 1971. Mus. lab. asst. So. Ill. U., Carbondale, 1955-57; salvage archaeologist State Ill., Carbondale, 1957-59; curator Evansville (Ind.) Mus. Arts and Scis., 1959-64; dir. Lakeview Center for Arts and Scis., Peoria, Ill., 1964-68, Forest Park Nature Center, Peoria, Ill., 1964-68, S.E. Ark. Arts and Sci. Center, Pine Bluff, 1968-70, W.H. Over Dakota Mus., U. S.D., Vermillion, 1970-73; cultural preservation dir. State of S.D., Pierre, 1973—; gov. of S.D.'s ofcl. rep. to Sioux Indians; lectr. So. Ill. U., 1957-59, Evansville U., 1960-64, Bradley U., 1964-68, Ark. AM&N Coll., 1968-70, U. S.D., 1970-73; dir. art sch. Evansville Mus. Arts and Scis., 1959-64, Lakeview Center for Arts and Scis., Peoria, Ill., 1964-68, Little Firehouse Art Sch., S.E. Ark. Arts and Sci. Center, Pine Bluff, 1968-70; dir. music, art and drama camp Ark. State U., 1970; art lectr. Eden Isle Art Colony, Heber Springs, S.D., 1970; condr. numerous workshops; one man shows Neuman Center, U. S.D., 1971, Western Mall Center, Sioux Falls, 1972, Nat. Bank of S.D., Vermillion, 1972, State Capitol, Pierre, 1972; exhibited group shows Ark. Arts Center, S.E. Ark. Arts and Sci. Center, Pine Bluff, 1968-70, Lakeview Center for Arts and Scis., Peoria, Ark. State Capitol, Little Rock; represented in permanent collections Ark. Arts Center, Worthen Nat. Bank, Little Rock, Lakeview Center for Arts and Scis., Peoria, Ill.; also numerous pvt. collections; organizer various workshops, confs. on arts. Founder, chmn. White Buffalo Corp., Pierre, 1974; mem. State Capitol Restoration Commn.; mem. S.D. Arts Works Com., 1971-77; dept. rep. S.D. Remote Sensing Users Council, 1974-77; mem. council S.D. Com. on Humanities, 1969-77; historic preservation officer Nat. Register Historic Places, 1969-76; state liaison officer Nat. Heritage Trust; bd. advisers Nat. Trust for Hist. Preservation, mem. exec. com., 1977; bd. dirs. Planetarium at Evansville Mus. Arts and Scis., 1959-64. Recipient Outstanding Achievement in Arts award S. and W. Literary Soc., 1969; recipient first prize Grand Prairie Festival Arts, 1969, Ark. Festival Arts, 1969. Mem. Nat. Hist. Soc., Nat. Soc. Lit. and Arts, Assn. S.D. Museums, Am. Assn. Museums. Rotarian. Contbr. articles to profl. jours. Office: State Capitol Pierre SD 57501

GILLIM, PARVIN DOUGLAS, physician; b. Owensboro, Ky., Apr. 12, 1929; s. Parvin Douglas and Marion (Reid) G.; A.B., Dartmouth, 1951; M.D., George Washington U., 1955; m. Mary Dickson Varian, Dec. 30, 1950; children—Mary Augusta, Sarah Ellen, Parvin Douglas, Alice Elizabeth, Claire Varian, Anna Marion. Intern, Edward J. Meyer Meml. Hosp., Buffalo, 1955-56, resident, 1956-57; resident Ind. Univ. Med. Center, Indpls., 1959-62; lectr. ophthalmology Sch. Medicine, Ind. U., 1962-63, instr., 1963-66; practice medicine, specializing in ophthalmology, diseases and surgery of retina, Indpls., 1966—; mem. staff Community, Meth., St. Vincent hosps. (all Indpls.). Served as capt. M.C., AUS, 1957-59. Diplomate Nat. Bd. Med. Examiners, Am. Bd. Ophthalmology. Fellow Am. Acad. Ophthalmology and Otolaryngology; mem. Nu Sigma Nu, Sigma Phi Epsilon. Home: 765 Bloor Ln Zionsville IN 46077 Office: Suite 210 St Vincent Profl Bldg 8402 Harcourt Rd Indianapolis IN 46260

GILLIS, DAVID WESLEY, III, real estate co. exec.; b. St. Clair, Mich., Mar. 20, 1943; s. David Wesley Gillis and Grace Mary (Fernandez) Gillis Hart; diploma in real estate Oakland U., 1973; grad. Realtors Inst., 1973; m. 2d, Carol L. F. Saccoman, June 13, 1974; children—Jamie, Shelley, Leslie; stepchildren—David, Michael, Mark, Lawrence, John. Sales rep. Western-So. Life Ins. Co., Port Huron, Mich., 1965-68; asst. dist. mgr. Chamberlain Real Estate Co., New Baltimore, Mich., 1968-70; gen. sales mgr. Bon Real Estate Corp., Roseville, Mich., 1970-74; gen. mgr. Royale Real Estate Co., Sterling Heights, Mich., 1974—; cons. in mgrt., 1975—; instr. North Central Real Estate Inst., 1976—. Chmn. South St. Clair County March of Dimes, 1970. Served with USAF, 1961-65. Recipient Charles E. Grimm Meml. award Algonac Jaycees, 1969, David M. Green Meml. award Mich. Jaycees, 1970. Mem. Nat., Mich. assns. realtors, Realtors Nat. Mktg. Inst., Women's Council of Realtors (governing bd.), Macomb County (Mich.) Bd. Realtors (Asso. of Year 1977, dir.), Mich. Assn. Sales Trainers. Democrat. Methodist. Contbr. articles to Mich. Realtor, Real Estate Today. Home: 37518 Charter Oaks Blvd Mount Clemens MI 48043 Office: 35135 Dodge Park Sterling Heights MI 48077

GILLIS, FRANK JAMES, librarian; b. Toronto, Ont., Can., Aug. 22, 1914; s. Frank and Marcella (Krokonas) G.; brought to U.S., 1921, naturalized, 1942; B.A. with honors, Wayne State U., 1953; M.A. in L.S., U. Minn., 1958; postgrad. Columbia, 1953-55; m. Ruth Jeanette Kathan, Sept. 13, 1943; 1 son, Christopher Jay. Profl. jazz pianist, Detroit, 1938-53, N.Y.C., 1953-55, Mpls., 1955-64, Bloomington, Ind., 1964—; librarian U. Minn., 1958-64; asso. dir. Archives Traditional Music, Ind. U., Bloomington, 1964-77, dir., 1977—. Served with AUS, 1942-45. Mem. Soc. Ethnomusicology (2d v.p. 1970-71, pres. 1973-75), Am. Folklore Soc., Music Librarians Assn., Assn. Recorded Sound Collections, New Orleans Jazz Soc. Editor: Ethnomusicology, 1966-70, Ethnomusicology and Folk Music: An International Bibliography of Dissertations and Theses, 1966; Oh, Didn't He Ramble, 1974; African Music and Oral Data, 1976. Home: 3508 Morningside Dr Bloomington IN 47401

GILLIS, JOHN HERBERT, judge; b. Detroit, Feb. 2, 1923; s. Joseph A. and Lila M. (Aman) G.; student Spring Hill Coll., 1941-42; J.D., U. Detroit, 1951; m. Joan Murray, June 25, 1949; children—Julie, Jack, Jim, Joseph, Jane. Admitted to Mich. bar, 1952; mem. firm DeBaeke, Ellis, Frohlich & Gillis, 1953-64; justice of peace Grosse Pointe Twp., Mich., 1954-64; judge Mich. Ct. Appeals, Detroit, 1965—. Instr. Law Sch. U. Detroit, 1970, 74. Chmn. Mich. Jud. Tenure Commn., 1969-75, vice chmn., 1977—. Served with USAF, 1943-46; ETO. Mem. State Bar Mich., Am., Detroit bar assns., U. Detroit Law Alumni Assn., Am. Judicature Soc., D.A.V., Gamma Eta Gamma. Home: 9 Colonial Rd Grosse Pointe MI 48236 Office: 900 1st Federal Bldg Detroit MI 48226

GILLIS, RUTH JEANETTE KATHAN, librarian; b. Tulsa, July 26, 1921; d. William Wallace and Edith Viola (Parrish) Kathan; student Wayne State U., 1948-52, Barnard Coll., 1953; B.A., U. Minn., 1960, M.A., 1964; m. Frank James Gillis, Sept. 13, 1943; 1 son, Christopher Jay. Librarian, Univ. Elementary Sch., U. Minn., Mpls., 1962-64; librarian Univ. Elementary Sch., Ind. U., Bloomington, 1964—, univ. vis. lectr., 1969—. Served with WAC, 1943-45. Mem. ALA, Nat. Council Tchrs. English, NEA, Ind. Tchrs. Assn., Ind. Sch. Librarians Assn., Beta Phi Mu, Pi Lambda Theta, Phi Delta Kappa. Democrat. Contbr. articles to profl. jours. Home: 3508 Morningside Dr Bloomington IN 47401 Office: University Elementary School Highway 46 Bypass Bloomington IN 47401

GILLMAN, RAY WALLACE, appliance mfg. co. exec.; b. Smithville, Ohio, Mar. 17, 1922; s. John B. and Jennie May (Smith) G.; B.A., Coll. Wooster, 1948; postgrad. U. Md., 1948, Washington Sch. Protocol, 1969; m. Virginia E. Ritter, Jan. 19, 1946; children—Jeffrey Paul, Janet Louise. Methods analyst Hoover Co., N. Canton, Ohio, 1948-53, gen. office mgr., 1953-54, asso. to pres., 1954-64; v.p. pub. affairs Hoover Worldwide Corp., N. Canton, 1964—; owner, operator Holiday Valley Farm, Millersburg, Ohio, 1965—. Mayor, Canal Fulton (Ohio), 1950-51; mem. adv. bd. Malone Coll., 1969—, chmn., 1977—; mem. adv. bd. Akron U. Center for Econ. Edn., 1975—; trustee Canton Symphony Orch., 1964—; mem. devel. bd. Otterbein Coll. Served to capt. U.S. Army, 1942-46. Mem. Internat. Pub. Relations Assn., Pub. Relations Soc. Am., Nat. Press Club, Am. Legion, Ohio Found. Ind. Colls. (Stark County chmn.), C. of C. Clubs: Rotary, Masons, Canton, Oakwood Country. Office: The Hoover Co North Canton OH 44720

GILLOGLY, CHARLES OWEN, motor carrier co. exec.; b. White Sulphur Springs, Mont., Jan. 15, 1919; s. Hugh Frederick and Bessie Albert (Rader) G.; student Mont. State Coll., 1935-36; B.A., U. Mont., 1941; postgrad. U. Md., 1948-49; m. Emma Laura Rush, Apr. 22, 1941; children—Hugh James, Brian Francis, Margaret Jo (Mrs. Jerry L. Bishop), Laura Teresa (Mrs. Dan J. Brothers), Kevin Rush. Salesman, S.W. Sales Service, Gallup, N.M., 1941; traffic clk. Wingate Ordnance Depot, Gallup, N.M., 1942-44; br. chief Bur. Ordnance, Navy Dept., Washington, 1945-52; exec. v.p. C.I. Whitten Transfer Co., Washington, 1952-68; pres. USAC Transport, Inc., Joplin, Mo., 1969-70; exec. v.p. Tri State Motor Transit Co., Joplin, Mo., 1970—; pres. Huntington Assos. Am., Inc., 1953-64; exec. v.p. Hughes Transp., Inc., 1968-70. Practitioner, ICC, 1949—. Served with USNR, 1944-46. Recipient Certificates of Appreciation, Nat. Defense Transp. Assn., 1955, 68, Delta Nu Alpha, 1956, Traffic Club Washington, 1963. Mem. Munitions Carriers Conf., Inc. (mem. exec. com. 1952-72), Am. Ordnance Assn., Am. Legion, Assn. ICC Practitioners, Sigma Phi Epsilon. Republican. Elk, K.C. (4 deg.), Rotarian. Clubs: Touchdown (Washington); Columbia Country (Chevy Chase, Md.); Twin Hills Country (Joplin, Mo.). Home: 3219 Moorhead Dr Joplin MO 64801 Office: PO Box 113 Joplin MO 64801

GILLUM, JACK DEAN, cons. structural engr.; b. Salina, Kans., Nov. 21, 1928; s. Charles Z. and Lillian D. (Mulnix) G.; student Wichita U., 1946-47; B.S., U. Kans., 1950; m. Alice A. Reese, Dec. 1, 1951 (dec. July 1971); children—Jack A., Timothy, Richard, Traci, Charles; m. 2d, Judith L. Hoffmann, June 1, 1973. Designer, Stearn Roger, Denver, 1952-55; cons. engr. Jack D. Gillum & Assos., Denver, 1955-69, Chgo., 1969-72, St. Louis, 1972—. Served to lt. C.E., AUS, 1951-52; Korea. Registered profl. engr., Colo., Calif., N.Y., Wyo., Mo., Ill., Kans. Mem. Nat. Soc. Profl. Engrs., ASCE, Prestressed Concrete Inst., Am. Concrete Inst. Mason (Shriner). Home: 13682 Peacock Farm Rd St Louis MO 63131 Office: 100 N Broadway St Louis MO 63102

GILMAN, DAVID ALAN, educator; b. Terre Haute, Ind., Sept. 26, 1933; s. Albert Maynard and Ruth Edna (Parsons) G.; B.S., Ind. State Tchrs. Coll., 1955; M.A., Mich. State U., 1962; Ph.D. (NSF fellow), Pa. State U., 1967; m. Elizabeth Ann Barlow, Oct. 7, 1956; children—Ruth Ann, Thomas Alan, William Michael. Tchr. Flint (Mich.) Community Schs., 1955-56, Utica (Mich.) Community Schs., 1957-62; grad. fellow Pa. State U., University Park, 1962-63, research prof., 1965-67; prof. Shippensburg (Pa.) State Coll., 1963-65; prof. edn. Ind. State U., Terre Haute, 1967—; cons. Gen. Learning Corp., 1964-66, Didactics Corp., 1968-73, NSF, 1974-75. Served with CIC, AUS, 1956-58. Recipient Caleb Mills Distinguished Teaching award Ind. State U., 1973. Mem. Internat. Audiovisual Soc., Am. Ednl. Research Assn., Blue Key, Kappa Delta Pi, Phi Delta Kappa. Author: A Course-writer Guide for Teacher-Authors of Materials for Computer-Assisted Insruction, 1967; Alternatives to Tests, Marks, and Class Ranks, 1974. Contbr. articles to profl. jours. Home: 500 Gardendale Rd Terre Haute IN 47803 Office: Indiana State U Terre Haute IN 47809

GILMAN, DONALD EUGENE, assn. exec.; b. Beach, N.D., July 27, 1918; s. Thomas A. and Pearl (Logan) G.; student N.D. State Sch. Sci., 1957-59; m. Loma Clark, Nov. 22, 1942; children—Robert E., Rita Lynne. Chief, Beach Fire Dept., 1948—; pres. N.D. Firemen's Assn., 1957-58, exec. sec., 1962—; state v.p. Internat. Assn. Fire Chiefs, 1965—; instr. N.D. Fire Service Tng., 1959—, N.D. Civil Def. Program, 1962—. Mem. state platform com. Republican Party, 1952. Active Shrine Burn Hosps. and Children's Village, Fargo, N.D. Served with AUS, 1942-46. Mem. Am. Legion. Mason (Shriner). Contbr. articles to profl. jours. Address: 176 1st St NE Beach ND 58621

GILMAN, HENRY, educator; b. Boston, May 9, 1893; s. David and Jane (Gordon) G.; B.S., Harvard U., 1915, A.M., 1917, Ph.D., 1918; postgrad. Zurich Polytechnikum and Oxford, 1916; m. Ruth V. Shaw, July 20, 1929; children—Jane Gordon, Henry Shaw. Instr. chemistry Harvard U., 1918-19; asso. in chemistry. U. Ill., 1919; prof. organic chemistry Iowa State U. 1919—. Cons. AEC; Chem. Corps research project leader; Air Force research dir.; plenary lectr. Internat. Symposia Organometallic and Organometalloidal Chemistry; mem. internat. organizing com., lectr. Internat. Organmetallic Conf., Moscow, USSR, 1971, Internat. Organosilicon Symposium, 1972. Holder of various lectureships and mem. awards coms.; recipient Mid-West Gold medal; Iowa-Am. Chem. Soc. Medal award; Frederic Stanley Kipping award Am. Chem. Soc.; First Firestone Internat. Lectures award in organometallic chemistry; Distinguished Prof. in Sci. and Humanities, 1962; Merit award Iowa Acad. Scis., 1973; Ia. State U. chemistry bldg. named in his honor, 1973. With C.W.S., World War I; Nat. Def. research work (Manhattan Project). Trustee Carver Research Found. Recipient 100th Anniversary Distinguished Fellow award Ia. Acad. Scis., 1975. Fellow AAAS (v.p. chem. sect. 1930), Chem. Soc. London (hon.), Phi Lambda Upsilon (hon.; award merit); mem. Royal Soc. London, Am. Chem. Soc. (councillor at large 1939-41, 42-44; chmn. organic div., Priestley medal), Nat. Acad. Scis. (ofcl. del., lectr. in USSR 1963), N.Y. Acad. Scis. (hon., life), Phi Beta Kappa, Sigma Xi, Phi Kappa Phi. Author: (with C. J. West) Organomagnesium Compounds in Synthetic Chemistry, 1922; (with R.G. Jones) Organo-lithium compounds in Organic Reactions; Metalation in Organic Reactions (with J.W. Morton Jr.); (with D. Wittenberg) Silylmetallic Compounds; (with F.K. Cartledge) Characterization of Organometallics, 1968; More Than One-half Century of Organometallic Chemistry, published in 1968. Editor: Organic Syntheses, Vol. VI, and Collective Vol. I; Organic Chemistry (2 vols.), 1943; Vol. III, IV Organic Chemistry: Organometallic Compounds in Encyclopedia of Chem Tech. (with Benkeser); (with R. K. Ingham) Organopolymers of Silicon, Germanium, Tin, and Lead; (with W. H. Atwell and F. K. Cartledge) Catenated Organic Compounds of Group IV-B; (with G. L. Schwebke) Organic Substituted Cyclosilanes. Mem. editorial bd.; Advances in Organo-Metallic Chemistry, Current Contents—Chemical Sciences, Acta Chimica Inorganica Rev; Organic Preparations and Procedures Internat. Contbg. editor ann. Survey Am. Chemistry, 1928, 1929-30. Organometallic Syntheses, Sci. Citation Index, Organometallic Reactions: asso. editor, Chem. Reviews, 1936, Jour. Organometallic Chemistry; editorial bd., exec. com. Jour. Organic Chemistry; asso. editor Jour. of Am. Chem. Soc. Contbr. to ency.; also co-author monographs; contbr. several hundred articles in field to sci. periodicals. Home: 3221 Oakland St Ames IA 50010

GILMARTIN, GENE FOLEY, yachting club mgr.; b. N.Y.C., Sept. 24 1914; s. Thomas Patrick and Sarah Frances (McNulty) F.; student Lewis Hotel Sch., 1946, Cornell U., 1956; m. Jane Stuart Bickers, Jan. 14, 1956; 1 dau., Page. Gen. mgr. Columbia Yacht Club, Port Washington, N.Y., 1937-42, pub. North Hempstead Beacon, Port Washington, 1946-47; asso. mgr. Army Navy Country Club, Arlington, Va., 1947-52; gen. mgr. The Rotunda Club, Richmond, Va., 1952-57, Cleve. Yachting Club, Rocky River, Ohio, 1957—; mem. faculty Cuyahoga Community Coll.; lectr. Cornell U. Served to capt. U.S. Army, 1942-46. Chmn. water safety com. Cleve. ARC, 1970—. Certified club. mgr. Mem. Greater Cleve. Club Mgrs. Assn. (pres. 1962-63, 70-71), Club Mgrs. Assn. Am. (bd. dirs. 1973—), Rocky River C. of C. (pres. 1966, bd. dirs.). Republican. Episcopalian. Clubs: Cleve. Rotary, Rotunda. Contbr. articles to trade jours.; mem. editorial bd. Club Mgmt., chmn., 1973—. Home: 19334 Frazier Dr Rocky River OH 44116 Office: Cleve Yachting Club Rocky River Island Rocky River OH 44116

GILMORE, HORACE WELDON, judge; b. Columbus, Ohio, Apr. 4, 1918; s. Charles T. and Lucile (Weldon) G.; A.B., U. Mich., 1939, LL.B., 1942; m. Mary Talbot Hays, June 20, 1942; children—Lindsay, Frances. Law clk. U.S. Ct. Appeals, 1946-47; spl. asst. U.S. Atty., 1952; mem. State Bd. Tax Appeals, Mich., 1954; dep. atty. gen. Mich., 1955-56; judge 3d Jud. Circuit Mich., 1957—; lectr. procedure sect. Young Lawyer's Inst. of Inst. Continuing Legal Edn., U. Mich.; part-time faculty Wayne State Univ.; faculty Nat. Coll. State Trial Judges, 1966—; lectr. law Mich. Law Sch. Mem. Mich. Jud. Tenure Commn.; program chmn. Nat. Conf. State Trial Judges, 1969; chmn. Joint Com. Revision Mich. Criminal Law. Served from ensign to lt. USNR, 1942-46. Mem. Am., Mich., Detroit bar assns., Am. Law Inst., Am. Judicature Soc., V.F.W., Am. Legion, Am. Vets., N.A.A.C.P., Alpha Delta Phi, Phi Delta Phi. Mason. Clubs: Detroit Torch, Detroit Press. Author: Michigan Civil Procedure Before Trial, 1964, 1966 Supplement; also chpts. in legal publs. Home: 1113 Harvard Grosse Pointe Park MI 48236 Office: City County Bldg Detroit MI 48226

GILMORE, JAMES STANLEY, JR., advt. agy. exec.; b. Kalamazoo, June 14, 1926; s. James Stanley and Ruth (McNair) G.; student Culver Mil. Acad., Western Mich. U., Kalamazoo Coll., 1945; Litt.D. (hon.), Nazareth Coll.; m. Diana Holdenreide Fell, May 21, 1949; children—Bethany, Sydney, James Stanley III, Elizabeth, Ruth. Owner, pres. Jim Gilmore Enterprises; pres. Gilmore Broadcasting Corp., partner Shamrock Broadcasting Corp.; pres. Jim Gilmore Cadillac-Pontiac Datsun Inc.; mem. Gilmore-Foyt Racing Team, Inc.; dir., v.p. Holiday Inn-Continental Corp. Mich., pres., chmn. bd. Gilmore Advt., Inc.; dir., asst. sec. Fabri-kal Plastics Corp., Kalamazoo; dir., mem. trust com. 1st Nat. Bank & Trust Co. of Kalamazoo; dir. 1st Nat. Bank Financial Corp., Mich. Carton div. St. Regis Paper Co., Shakespeare Co., Columbia, S.C., Continental Lanes, Kalamazoo; partner Hotel Investment Realty Corp., Greater Kalamazoo Sports, Inc. hockey franchise, Kalamazoo Stadium Co.; dir. Fed. Home Loan Bank Indpls.; presdl. adviser North Central Airlines. Former chmn. Mich. Water Resources Commn.; mem. Nat. Adv. Cancer Council, HEW: mem. Citizen's Adv. Com. on Environ. Quality; mem. Nat. Assn. Broadcasters' adv. com. to Corp. for Pub. Broadcasting; mem. Mich. Gov.'s Forum. Mem. Mich. Republican Finance Com.; past chmn. Kalamazoo County Rep. Exec. Com.; mayor of Kalamzoo, 1959-61; former mem. Kalamazoo County Bd. Suprs. Bd. dirs. Martin Luther King Meml. Fund (founder), Mich. bd. Radio Free Europe, Econ. Devel. Commn., Kalamazoo chpt. A.R.C.; hon. trustee Mich. Alvin Bentley Charitable Found.; asso. dir. Boys Clubs Am.; life mem. March of Dimes; nat. sponsor Ducks Unlimited; trustee Greater Mich. Devel. Found., Kalamazoo Nature Center, Children's Home, Family Service Center Kalamazoo. Named Kalamazoo Young Man of 1960, One of Mich.'s 5 Young Men of 1960; Man of Yr., Auto Racing Found. Frat., Mich. Auto Racing Fan Club; Car Owner Sponsor award Milw. Speedway Scholarship Commn. Mem. N.A.M., Mich. Acad. Sci., Arts and Letters, Mich. (law and order com.), Kalamazoo County (mem. indsl. devel., exec. coms.; past pres., dir.) chambers commerce. Served with USAAF 1943-46; ETO. Episcopalian (mem. bd. Western Mich. diocese). Clubs: Park (past dir.); Kalamazoo Country; Gull Lake Country (Richland, Mich.); Mid-America (Chgo.); Otsego Ski (Gaylord, Mich.); Capitol Hill (Washington). Home: 1550 Long Rd Kalamazoo MI 49001 also 5040 Woodlawn Beach Gull Lake Hickory Corners MI Office: Jim Gilmore Enterprises Michigan Bldg Kalamazoo MI 49006

GILMORE, ROBERT WITTER, charitable assn. exec.; b. Hamilton, Ohio, Sept. 6, 1933; s. Robert Foster and Frances Elizabeth (Witter) G.; B.S., Miami U., Oxford, Ohio, 1955; M.S.W., Ohio State U., 1957; m. Sara Louise McIntosh, Dec. 23, 1956; children—Susan Lynne, Robert Riley, Christopher Edwin. Asso. exec. United Fund, Wheeling, W.Va., 1960-61; exec. dir Community Chest and Council, Massillon, Ohio, 1961-64; exec. dir. United Fund and Community Council, St. Joseph, Mo., 1964-68; asso. dir. United Way, Dayton (Ohio) area, 1969-72, exec. dir., 1972—. Served to 1st lt. Med. Services, U.S. Army, 1957-60. Named Outstanding Man of Year, St. Joseph Jr. C. of C., 1967. Mem. Sigma Chi. Presbyterian. Clubs: Masons, Rotary, Engrs. Home: 1408 Streamside Dr Centerville OH 45459 Office: 184 Salem Ave Dayton OH 45406

GILMOUR, C(HARLES) EDWIN, polit. scientist, educator; b. Blairsville, Pa., Sept. 15, 1918; s. John Knox and Harriet Dove (Torrance) G.; B.A., Westminster Coll., 1940; M.B.A., U. Pa., 1942, M.Govt. Adminstrn., 1946, Ph.D., 1951; m. Elizabeth Crosman, Sept. 27, 1947; children—Tori, Betsy, Keith. Research asst. Pa. State Legislature, Harrisburg, 1941-42, Inst. State and Local Govt., U. Pa., Phila., 1946-47, instr. polit. sci., 1947-49; from instr. to prof. polit. sci. Grinnell (Iowa) Coll., 1949—; vis. prof. U. Bombay (India), 1970, 74-75, Iowa State U., summers 1962-64, 66, 76; cons. in field; mem. Iowa Senate, 1959-63. Democratic candidate U.S. Congress, 1959, 60; mem. Dem. State Central Com., 1964-65, 72-74. Iowa dir. War on Poverty, 1965-66. Served to sgt. USAAF, 1942-46. Recipient Rural Service award OEO, 1966. Fulbright-Hayes grantee India 1970, 74-75. Mem. Iowa Conf. Polit. Scientists (pres. 1962), Nat. Assn. Community Devel. (exec. com. 1965-66), Am., Midwest polit. sci. assns., AAUP. Home: 531 9th Ave Grinnell IA 50112

GILPIN, JOHN STEPHEN, veterinarian; b. Kalamazoo, Aug. 30, 1941; s. Gerald Merle and Mildred Elaine (Davidson) G.; D.V.M., Purdue U., 1966. Veterinarian, Gateway Animal Hosp., Glendale, Calif., 1966-67. County Line Animal Hosp., La Habra, Calif., 1970-71, specializing in small animal practice, Highland (Ind.) Animal Hosp., 1971—. Served to capt. U.S. Army, 1967-69; Vietnam. Decorated Bronze Star. Mem. Am., Calumet (Ind.) Area veterinary med. assns. Republican. Episcopalian. Home: 1114 Reyome Apt I Griffith IN 46319 Office: 9308 Indianapolis Blvd Highland IN 46322

GILSON, RICHARD DONALD, educator; b. Lancaster, Pa., Nov. 8, 1943; s. Donald Harry and Doris Margaret (Wright) G.; B.S., U. Conn., 1965; M.A., Princeton, 1967, Ph.D., 1968; m. Elizabeth Weston Lines, Jan. 26, 1965. Asso. prof. dept. aviation and psychology Ohio State U., Columbus, 1971—. Served to lt. USNR, 1968-71. Mem. Aerospace Med. Assn., Psychonomic Soc., Am. Psychol. Assn., Nat. Assn. Flight Instrs., Sigma Xi. Contbr. articles to profl. jours. Office: Box 3022 Columbus OH 43210

GILSTER, PETER STUART, lawyer; b. Carbondale, Ill., Dec. 10, 1939; s. John Sprigg and Ruth E. (Robinson) G.; B.S., U. Ill., 1962, J.D., 1965; m. Carol Clevenger, June 29, 1968; children—John, Thomas. Admitted to Ill. bar, 1965, Mo. bar, 1968, since practiced in St. Louis; mem. firm Koenig, Senniger, Powers & Leavitt, St. Louis, 1967-72, partner, 1971-72; atty. Monsanto Co., St. Louis, 1972-77; partner firm Kalish & Gilster, 1977—. Served to capt. AUS, 1965-67. Mem. IEEE, Mo., Ill. bar assns., Am. Patent Law Assn., Bar Assn. Met. St. Louis (sec.-treas. patent sect. 1972-74, chmn. 1975-76), Asso. Pilots of St. Louis (dir., v.p.), Phi Delta Phi. Mem. Apostolic Ch. (dir., sec.-treas. 1971—). Contbr. articles to profl. jours. Home: 16 Garden Ln Kirkwood MO 63122 Office: 800 N Lindberg Blvd St Louis MO 63166

GILTNER, SISTER ANDREA, counselor; b. Kewanee, Ill., Aug. 8, 1928; d. Horace and Winifred Agnes (Maupin) Giltner; B.A., St. Ambrose Coll., 1964; M.Ed., U. Ill., 1969. Joined Order St. Benedict, Roman Catholic Ch., 1946; tchr., St. Marys Sch., Moline, Ill., 1948-50, St. Anthony Sch., Atkinson, Ill., 1950-52, St. Roch Sch., LaSalle, Ill., 1953-55, St. Columbia Sch., Chgo., 1955-57, St. Boniface Sch., Peoria, Ill., 1957-59, Holy Family Sch., Peoria, 1960-62, St. Thomas More Sch., Muncie, Ind., 1963-64, 67-69, Immaculate Conception Sch., Monmouth, Ill., 1964-65, 69-72; counselor Assumption High Sch., Davenport, Iowa, 1971—. Corr. sec. Sisters Council, Davenport, 1972-75, pres., 1975-77. Mem. Am. Personnel and Guidance Assn., Am. Vocat. Guidance Assn., Am. Sch. Counselor Assn., Adminstrv. Mgmt. Soc., Nat. Cath. Guidance Assn., Nat. Assembly Womens Religious, AAUW, Phi Delta Kappa. Contbr. articles to religious ednl. jours. Home: St Mary Priory Nauvoo IL 62354 Office: 1020 West Central Park Davenport IA 52804

GIMBEL, FRANKLYN MELROYE, lawyer; b. Milw., Mar. 18, 1936; s. Harold J. and Virginia P. (Pivar) G.; B.B.A., U. Wis., 1958; J.D., Marquette U., 1960; m. Barbara Posner, Aug. 3, 1958 (div.); children—Tod I., Joshua Lee. Admitted to Wis. bar, 1960; since practiced in Milw.; mem. firms Gimbel, Gimbel & Boyle, 1969-73, Gimbel, Gimbel & Reilly, 1973—; asst. U.S. atty., Milw., 1963-68. Atty. Milw. Dep. Sheriff's Assn., Milw., 1971; instr. police sci. courses Milw. Tech. Coll., 1967—. Chmn, N. Shore Democratic Com., 1962-63; chmn., toastmaster Jefferson-Jackson Dinner, 1963. Recipient Superior Performance award U.S. Dept. Justice, 1967. Mem. Fed. (chpt. pres. 1967-69), Milw. (pres. 1976-77), bar assns., Wis. Bar Assn. Jewish. Club: Ville du Parc Country (Mequon, Wis.). Home: 1626 W Prospect Ave Milwaukee WI 53202 Office: 900 MGIC Plaza 270 E Kilbourn Ave Milwaukee WI 53202

GIN, JACKSON, architect; b. Chgo., June 11, 1934; s. Frank Tsue and Jennie Shee (Pang) G.; B.S., U. Ill., 1958; m. Jayne Ping Kan, Oct. 5, 1963; children—Paul L., Michael F., Daniel. Designer, Milton M. Schwartz, architect, Chgo., 1958-60; project architect Greenberg & Finfer, architect, Chgo., 1960-62, Hausner & Macsai, architects, Chgo., 1962-70; project architect, partner Dubin, Dubin, Black & Moutoussamy, architects, Chgo., 1967-77; partner Mann, Gin, Ebel & Frazier, architects-engrs., Chgo., 1977—. Bd. dirs. Neighborhood Redevel. Assistance, 1972-74, Chinese Am. Civic Fedn.; trustee Chinese Christian Union Ch., 1968-70. Mem. AIA, Builders Club Chgo. Home: 1332 Peachtree Ln Mount Prospect IL 60056 Office: 8 S Michigan Ave Chicago IL 60603

GINGISS, BENJAMIN JACK, formal clothing stores exec.; b. St. Paul, Feb. 27, 1911; s. Samuel and Betty (Illiewitz) G.; student U. Ill., 1929-32, Northwestern U., 1934, Ill. Inst. Tech., 1941; m. Rosalie Eisenschiml, Apr. 20, 1940; children—Peter, Joel, Randall. Co-founder Gingiss Bros., Inc., Chgo., 1936 (name later changed to Gingiss Formalwear, Inc.), now chmn. Gingiss Formalwear, Inc.; chmn. Gingiss Internat., Inc. Chmn., Fedn. for an Open Lakefront, Chgo., 1967; pres. Ill. Humane Soc., 1960, U.S.O. of Chgo., 1969, 73-74; v.p. Welfare Council Met. Chgo., 1968; commr. Lake Mich. and Adjoining Lands Study Commn., 1969—; mem. Urban Action Commn. YMCA, 1969; city commr. Commn. on Youth Welfare, 1966; chmn. men's clothing div. Combined Jewish Appeal, 1959. Bd. dirs. Big Bros., Goodwill Industries, Union Am. Hebrew Congregations, Chgo. Better Bus. Bur., Lyric Opera of Chgo., 1977; chmn. bd. dirs. U.S.O. Chgo.; bd. dirs., sec. Ill. Humane Soc., pres., 1977; trustee Rosary Coll.; bd. assos. DePaul U. Recipient Phoenix award DePaul U., 1969, Prime Ministers medal State of Israel, 1968, Navy Certificate Merit, 1969, also commendations and awards from U.S. Army, U.S. Navy, USCG, U.S. Air Force, USO. Mem. C. of C. Rotarian. Clubs: City (pres., dir.), Tavern, Standard, Executives (Chgo.). Home: 175 E Delaware St Chicago IL 60611 Office: 180 N LaSalle St Chicago IL 60601

GINLEY, THOMAS JOHN, assn. exec.; b. Chgo., Jan. 25, 1938; s. Harold Francis and Nora C. (Mahoney) G.; B.S., Loyola U., Chgo., 1960, M.A., 1963, Ph.D., 1967; m. Joanne Collins, Aug. 20, 1960; children—Kathleen, Susan, Elizabeth, Matthew, John. Test devel. specialist Chgo. CSC, 1960-63; dir. div. ednl. measurements ADA, Chgo., 1963-70, acting dir. Health Found., 1970-72, sec. Commn. on Accreditation, 1975—, asst. sec. Council on Dental Edn., 1965-70, asso. sec., 1970-73, sec., 1973—. Cons. Vietnam dental edn. project U.S. AID, 1969-74; commn. Nat. Commn. on Accrediting, 1973-74; chmn. Council Specialized Accrediting Agys., 1972—. Chmn. sch. bd., Chgo., 1973-75. Mem. Am. Assn. Higher Edn., Am. Coll. Dentists, Am. Assn. Dental Schs., Assn. Am. Med. Colls., Am. Psychol. Assns., Am. Ednl. Research Assn., Nat. Council Measurement in Edn., Ill. Psychol. Assn., Indsl. Psychology Assn. Chgo. Home: 6710 N LaPorte Lincolnwood IL 60646 Office: 211 E Chicago St Chicago IL 60611

GINN, ALEXANDER, lawyer; b. Cleve., Jan 2, 1913; s. Frank Hadley and Cornelia (Root) G.; B.A., Princeton U., 1934; postgrad. Oxford U., 1934-35; LL.B., Yale U., 1938; m. Helen Marie Vilas, June 28, 1938; children—Frank Hadley, Mary Cornelia, Patricia (Mrs. Michael J. Feeney), Walter Pope. Admitted to Ohio bar, 1939; partner Jones, Day, Reavis & Pogue, Cleve., 1953-77. Trustee Univ. Sch., Cleve. Served to lt. USNR, 1942-45. Republican. Episcopalian (former vestryman). Home: SOM Center Rd Chagrin Falls OH 44022 Office: Union Commerce Bldg Cleveland OH 44115

GINN, H(ORACE) MARVIN, publishing co. exec.; b. Miller, Mo., Jan. 17, 1914; s. Horace Maynard and Jurley (Ward) G.; student S.W. Mo. State Coll., 1934-35, Northwestern U., 1947; m. Laura Marie Birzele, Apr. 16, 1942; children—Marcia Eleanor, Sheila Margaret, Sandra. Tchr., Union Hall Sch., Halltown, Mo., 1936-38; salesman Crowell-Collier Pub. Co., N.Y.C., 1939-42; promotion mgr. Opportunity Mag., Chgo., 1946-50, Irving-Cloud Pub. Co., Chgo., 1950-55; sales mgr. Pubs. Devel. Corp., Skokie, Ill., 1955-61; chmn., pres. H. Marvin Ginn Corp., Chgo., 1961—. Served with inf. AUS, 1942-46; PTO. Decorated Bronze star medal. Mem. Chgo. Assn. Bus. Pubs., Internat. Assn. Fire Chiefs, Fire Equipment Mfrs. and Services Assn. (dir.). Clubs: Chicago Advertising. Author: How to Be An Executive Salesman, 1953. Home: 1959 W Hood St Chicago IL 60660 Office: 625 N Michigan Ave Chicago IL 60611

GINN, MILTON STANLEY, lawyer; b. Miller, Mo., Apr. 3, 1911; s. Milton S. and Sallie (Wright) G.; J.D., U. Mo., 1934; m. Rosemary Lucas, June 21, 1934; children—Nancy (Mrs. Carl H. Almond), Sally (Mrs. Mike Hood). Admitted to Mo. bar, 1934; practice law and prosecuting atty., Lawrence County, Mo., 1934-40; supt. Mo. State Hwy. Patrol, 1941-43; practice law, Columbia, Mo., 1946—. Chmn. bd. Mo. Stores Co., Columbia; vice-chmn. bd. Columbia Nat. Bank; dir. South County Bank, Ashland, Mo., Boone County Abstract Co., Columbia. Mem. Mo. Defense Council, 1942-44. Chmn. Lawrence County Republican Com., 1936-40, Boone County Rep. Com., 1950-64, Mo. Rep. Com., 1948-70; nat. committeeman Young Republicans, 1938-42. Served to lt. USNR, 1945-46. Mem. Mo. Bar Assn. (regional dir. 1938), Am. Legion (judge advocate Mo. dept. 1946), V.F.W., Delta Theta Phi. Mason, Rotarian, Elk. Club: Columbia Country (pres. 1967-68). Home: 303 West Blvd S Columbia MO 65201 Office: 11 N 8th St Columbia MO 65201

GINSBURG, SHELDON HARVEY, accountant; b. Chgo., Mar. 22, 1938; s. Max L. and Sophie L. (Schwimmer) G.; B.S., DePaul U., 1959; children—Howard, Linda, Steven. Prin. Sheldon H. Ginsburg, C.P.A., Skokie, Ill., 1961—; propr. Shell Devel. Corp., 1969—; chmn. bd. Pick Fisheries, Inc.; trustee Food Handlers Local 55 Health and Welfare Fund. C.P.A., Ill. Mem. Am. Inst. C.P.A.'s, Ill. Soc. C.P.A.'s, Beta Gamma Sigma, Pi Gamma Mu, Beta Alpha Psi. Office: 4849 W Golf Rd Skokie IL 60077

GIOIOSO, JOSEPH VINCENT, psychologist; b. Chgo., Mar. 6, 1939; s. Vincent James and Mary (Bonadonna) G.; B.A., DePaul U., 1962, M.A., 1963; Ph.D., summa cum laude, Ill. Inst. Tech., 1971; m. Gay Powers, Dec. 28, 1963; children—Joseph, Randy Marie, Danielle. Psychologist, Sch. Assn. for Spl. Edn. in DuPage County, Wheaton, Ill., 1964-67; pvt. practice as clin. psychologist, Chgo. and Downers Grove, Ill., 1966—; clin. psychologist J.J. McLaughlin, M.D., Profl. Corp., Chgo., 1970—. Founder dept. psychology Ill. Benedictine Coll., Lisle, Ill., 1968, chmn. dept. psychology, prof., dir. testing, 1968-71; cons. psychologist Chicago Ridge (Ill.) Sch. Dist. 127 1/2, 1973-76, Cath. Charities Counseling Service, Chgo., 1963-66, St. Laurence High Sch., Oak Lawn, Ill., 1963-64, Oak Lawn-Hometown Sch. Dist. No. 123, 1967-68, Addison (Ill.) Sch. Dist. 4, 1969-72; vis. prof. psychology Inst. Mgmt., Lisle, 1968-69, George Williams Coll., Downers Grove, 1970-71; chief psychologist Valley View Sch. Dist. 365U, Bolingbrook, Ill., 1971-73; dir. Pub. Program for Exceptional Children, Lisle, 1969-71; mem. Nat. Register Health Service Providers in Psychology, 1975—. Bd. dirs. Ray Graham Assn. for Handicapped, DuPage County, Ill., 1970-73. DePaul U. publ. grantee, 1959-61, Fitzgerald Bros. Found. grantee, 1969-71. Mem. Am., Midwestern psychol. assns., Soc. Pediatric Psychology, Alpha Phi Delta. Clubs: Lakeside Country (Downers Grove); Racquet (Willowbrook, Ill.). Author: Completion Intelligence Test, 1963. Contbr. articles to profl. jours. Office: 6800 S Main St Downers Grove IL 60515

GIORGI, AMEDEO ANDREW, labor union ofcl.; b. Rockford, Ill., Apr. 5, 1926; s. Gabriele and Louise (Di Marco) G.; grad. Rock Valley Jr. Coll.; student Rockford Sch. Bus.; m. Marilyn V. Wardecker, Nov. 19, 1945; children—Nancy Lee, Kimberly Sue. Fin. sec. Rockford United Labor Union, Rockford, 1951-68, pres., 1968—; bus. rep. Retail Clk. Local Union, Rockford, 1968—; pres. Alliance of Labor, 1970—; mem. Winnibago County Bd. Fin. sec. Winnebago Democratic Central Com., 1968; pres. 5th Ward Dem. Club. Served with USAAF, 1944-46. Mem. Am. Legion, VFW. Democrat. Roman Catholic. Club: K.C. Home: 1529 Victoria Ave Rockford IL 61102 Office: 115 7th St Rockford IL 61104

GIRGASH, WILLIAM JOHN, parking service co. exec.; b. Ambridge, Pa., Mar. 9, 1926; s. John R. and Elizabeth Frances (Semega) G.; B.A., Kent State U., 1949; m. Kathryn Viola Mohler, June 18, 1949; children—Mark, John, Rebecca, Judith, Matthew, Paul, Thomas, Patricia. Asst. sports editor Ambridge Daily Citizen, 1944; with Akron (Ohio) Beacon Jour., 1949-56; mgr. pub. relations services, editor news C.&O./B. &O. Rwy. System, Cleve., 1956-67; exec. v.p. Ostrow Pub. Relations, Cleve., 1967-69; v.p., dir. pub. relations Internat. Tel.&Tel. Service Industries, Cleve., 1969-75; v.p., dir. corp. relations APCOA, Inc., Cleve., 1975—. Served with USNR, 1944-46. Mem. Pub. Relations Soc. Am., Soc. Journalists-Sigma Delta Chi, Internat. Council Indsl. Editors (pres. 1963), Northeastern Council Indsl. Editors (pres. 1962), Am. Ry. Editors Assn., Better Service Conf. (pres. 1965), Cleve. Parking Assn. (pres. 1974-76). Rotarian. Home: 1199 Belle Ave Lakewood OH 44107 Office: 1919 E 13th St Cleveland OH 44114

GIROU, MICHAEL LLOYD, computer systems exec.; b. St. Louis, July 2, 1947; s. Jack and Patricia Girou; student U. Mo., 1963-69, Washington U., St. Louis, 1966-67; m. Teddy Dygert, 1974; children—Beverly, James. Computer programmer McDonnell Douglas Co., St. Louis, 1964-66; computer research U. Mo., Columbia, 1967-69; pres. Systems Programming Inc., Columbia, 1967-69; mgr. tech. devel. Honeywell Co., Mpls., 1970-73; chmn., chief exec. officer SSM, Inc., Plymouth, Minn., 1973—, also dir.; dir. Tonka Tackle Inc.; exec. dir. Minn. BPA. Co-chmn. publicity com. Am. Contract Bridge League Gopher Regional, 1977; celebrity auctioneer St. KTCA-TV, 1976, 77. Mem. Assn. Computing Machinery, Am. Math. Soc., Pi Mu Epsilon. Republican. Clubs: Hazeltine Country, Lafayette Country, Minnetonka Country. Contbr. articles on math. and computer sci. to profl. jours. Home: 26600 Smithtown Rd Excelsior MN 55331 Office: 3131 Fernbrook Ln N Plymouth MN 55441

GIRTON, LARRY LEE, wholesale co. exec.; b. Union City, Ind., May 6, 1935; s. Charles Irvin and Catherine May (Wise) G.; student Earlham Coll., 1959—; m. Naoma E Short, June 30, 1956; children—Charles Brent, Renee Lynn. With Girton's, Winchester, Ind., 1953-72, gen. sales mgr., 1963-67, v.p. marketing, 1968-72; founder, pres. Systems Engring. & Supply, Inc., Lynn, 1972—; dir. Union City Mgmt. Club tng. program, Ball State U., 1968-69. Mem. Nat. Mgmt. Assn. (chpt. pres. 1968-69, dir. 1965-70), Fluid Power Soc. Mem. Soc. Friends. Republican. Home: Rural Route 1 Lynn IN 47355 Office: 310 W Sherman St Lynn IN 47355

GIRVIN, JOHN PATTERSON, educator; b. Detroit, Feb. 5, 1934; s. Patterson and Sally Olive (Hawkins) G.; M.D., U. Western Ont., 1958; Ph.D., McGill U., 1965; m. Bettye Ruth Parker, Sept. 13, 1959; children—Douglas Craig, Michael Patterson, Jane Elizabeth. Lectr. dept. physiology McGill U., 1963-64; asst. prof. dept. clin. neurol. scis. U. Western Ont., London, Can., 1968-75, asso. prof., 1975—; bd. trust Victoria Hosp., London, 1971-72, sec. med. staff, 1971. Bd. dirs. Physicians' Services Inc. Found., 1976—. Continual Med. Research Council Can. grantee, 1968-74. Fellow Royal Coll. Physicians and Surgeons Can., Royal Coll. Surgeons; mem. London Acad. Medicine, Canadian, Ont. med. assns., Research Soc. Neurol. Surgeons, South Western Ont. Surg. Assn., Soc. for Neurosci., Am. Assn. Neurol. Surgeons, Am. Epilepsy Assn., Neurosurg. Forum. Club: London Tennis and Badminton (pres. 1975-76). Contbr. articles to profl. publs. Home: 4 Linksgate Rd London ON N6G 2A8 Canada Office: 111 Waterloo St Suite 211 London ON N6B 2M4 Canada

GIRVIN, RICHARD ALLEN, cinema service co. exec.; b. Chgo., Feb. 10, 1926; s. Harry J. and Esther (Easter) G.; Mus.B., Chgo. Mus. Coll., 1950, Mus.M., 1954; D.F.A., Ga. State Tchrs. Coll., 1954; m. Sharon Hillertz, June 9, 1968; children—Gregory, Kimberly, Scott. Instr. music Bob Jones U., 1950-52; tchr. high sch., Chgo., 1954-56; dir. radio and TV, NBC, Chgo., 1956-57; prodn. dir. Coronet Inst. Films, Chgo., 1957-62; producer Gilbert Altschul Prodns., Chgo., 1962-64; freelance producer, writer, Chgo. and Hollywood, Calif., 1964-65; v.p. Zenith Cinema Service, Inc., Chgo., 1965-73, owner, 1973—; pres. Dick Girvin Prodns., Chgo., 1967—; owner, operator Typing Unltd., Chgo., Timbrewood Prodn. Music Co., Chgo., Sharilda Pub. Co., Chgo., Phas 5 Prodns., Chgo., Studio Electronics Co., Chgo., 1967—; instr. film sound Columbia Coll., Chgo., 1973—. Served to 1st lt. USAAF, 1943-45. Recipient Cannes Film Festival award for writing Wine of Morning, 1957, Freedom Found. award, 1961, Cine Golden Eagle award 1964-67, Indsl. Arts award, 1964-74, Atlanta Silver award, 1971, Internat. Film Festival silver award, 1971-74. Fellow Brit. Internat. Audio Soc. mem. Nat. Assn. TV Arts and Scis., Soc. Motion Picture Engrs. and Technicians, Audio Engring. Soc., Aircraft Owners and Pilots Assn., Internat. Brotherhood Magicians, Broadcast Music Inc. Composer: The Seventh Psalm, 1953; film scores for Macbeth, 1951, Pound of Flesh, 1952, numerous films, TV programs. Office: 3252 Foster Ave Chicago IL 60625

GIRZ, ALBERT OSCAR, physician; b. Tiffin, Ohio, Apr. 29, 1937; s. Adolph and Anna Maria (Rueckert) G.; student Western Res. U., 1956-58, U. Heidelberg, 1958-60; M.D., U. Erlangen, Nurnberg, Erlangen, Germany, 1964; m. Joyce Aletha Compomizzo, Aug. 18, 1968. Intern Harper Hosp., Detroit, 1965; med. officer Nuclear Polaris Submarine, 1966-67; med. officer Naval Dispensary, Stockton, Calif., 1967-68; physician U. Mich. Health Service, 1968-70; asst. dir. Med. Clinic, U. Mich. Health Service, Ann Arbor, 1970—; med. adv. YMCA phys. fitness program, Ann Arbor, 1969—; team physician U. Mich. Hockey Team, 1970—. Served with M.C., USNR, 1966-68. Mem. Am. Coll. Health Assn. Unitarian. Office: 207 Fletcher St Ann Arbor MI 48104

GISH, EDWARD RUTLEDGE, physician; b. St. Louis, Sept. 5, 1908; s. Edward C. and Bessie (Rutledge) G.; A.B., Westminster Coll., 1930; M.D., St. Louis U., 1935, M.S., 1939; m. Miriam Schlicker, July

8, 1938; children—Ann Rutledge, Mary Priscilla. Intern, St. Louis U. Hosps., 1935-36; resident in surgery St. Mary's Group Hosps., St. Louis, 1936-39; pvt. practice medicine specializing in surgery, Fulton, Mo., 1946—; staff mem. Callaway Meml. Hosp., Fulton. Served from maj. to lt. col., AUS, 1943-46. Hon. col. Governor's Staff Missouri. Fellow A.C.S.; mem. Internat. Coll. Surgeons, A.M.A., Mo., Callaway County med. socs., Mo. Red Poll Breeders Assn. (pres.), Delta Tau Delta, Alpha Omega Alpha. Contbr. articles to profl. jours. Home: 7 W 10th St Fulton MO 65251 Office: 5 E 5th St Fulton MO 65251

GISLER, GEORGE LOUIS, lawyer; b. Indpls., Aug. 28, 1909; s. Benjamin Harrison and Anna Marie (Twente) G.; A.B., Butler U., 1930; J.D., U. Mich., 1933; m. Georgia Helenanna Umscheid, Apr. 21, 1946; children—John Case, James Robert. Admitted to Ind. bar, 1933, Mo. bar, 1934; asso. Michaels, Blackmar, Newkirk, Eager & Swanson, Kansas City, Mo., 1933-39, Sebree, Shook & Gisler, 1939-42; regional atty. WPB, 1942-43; mem. firm Reeder, Gisler, Griffin & Dysart, 1947-58; individual practice law, 1958-76; dir. Dean Research Corp., Kansas City, 1969—; asst. prof. bus. law Rockhurst Coll., Kansas City, 1939-41. Vice pres. Kansas City Philharmonic Assn., 1960-65; pres. Kansas City Careers Found., 1955-59; chmn. Ind. Voters Assn., 1959; chmn. bd. trustees St. John's Methodist Ch., 1964-66; bd. dirs. Don Bosco Community Center, 1965—, pres., 1973-77; bd. dirs., counsel Consumer Credit Counseling Service of Greater Kansas City, 1969-76; counsel Better Bus. Bur. of Greater Kansas City; bd. dirs. Kansas City Lyric Theater; trustee Kansas City Conservatory Music. Served to lt. USNR, 1943-46. Mem. Am., Mo., Kansas City bar assns., Lawyers Assn. Kansas City (chmn. various coms.). Clubs: Arrowhead Yacht (Lake Winnebago, Mo.); Carriage (pres. 1961-62; bd. dirs. 1959-62) (Kansas City). Contbr. articles to profl. jours. Home: 420 Winnebago Dr Lake Winnebago MO 64034 Office: 9229 Ward Pkwy Suite 229 Kansas City MO 64105

GIUFFRE, ANTHONY ANGELO, business exec.; b. Milw., Apr. 18, 1923; s. Frank and Nancy (Germanotta) G.; heating, refrigeration, air conditioning technician, Milw. Sch. Engring., 1947; m. Rosalie A. Navarra, Aug. 24, 1946; children—Anthony F., Mary Beth. Owner, operator T.A.G. Heating & Refrigeration, Milw., 1947-67; v.p. Nino's, Inc., Milw., 1967-75; pres. T.A.G. Inc., temperature controls, waste heat recovery systems, grease collecting ventilators, Milw., 1975—. Served to sgt. USAAF, 1943-45. Mem. Refrigeration Engrs. Soc. (pres. 1964-65). Patentee in field. Home: 4344 N 70th St Milwaukee WI 53216 Office: 4344 N 70th St Milwaukee WI 53216

GIVAN, RICHARD MARTIN, chief justice Ind. Supreme Ct.; b. Indpls., June 7, 1921; s. Clinton Hodell and Glee (Bowen) G.; LL.B., Ind. U., 1951; m. Pauline Marie Haggart, Feb. 28, 1945; children—Madalyn (Mrs. Larry Hesson), Sandra, Patricia, Elizabeth. Partner firm Givan & Givan, 1952-59, Bowen, Myers, Northam & Givan, 1959-69; pub. defender, Ind., 1952-54; dep. atty. gen. State of Ind., 1954-65; dep. pros. atty., Marion County, Ind., 1965-67; mem. Ind. Ho. of Reps., 1967-68; judge Ind. Supreme Ct., 1969—. Served with USAAF, 1942-45. Mem. Am., Indpls., Ind. bar assns., Ind. Trial Lawyers Assn., Ind. Judges Assn., Ind. Soc. Chgo., Newcomen Soc. N.Am., Sigma Delta Kappa. Mem. Soc. of Friends. Clubs: Arabian Horse; Indianapolis Press. Office: Office of the Chief Justice Indiana Supreme Ct Indianapolis IN 46204 Address: Rural Route 2 PO Box 376 Indianapolis IN 46231

GLADDERS, THOMAS LUKE, shipping co. exec.; b. Carbondale, Ill., Sept. 4, 1941; s. Glen Warren and Emily Jean (Martin) G.; A.B., Dartmouth Coll., 1963; M.B.A., Stanford U., 1965; m. Ann Watkins Buettner, Aug. 28, 1964; children—Arden Brigham, Julia Martin, Thomas Luke. Asst. cashier First Nat. Bank of Chgo., 1965-68; v.p. G.W. Gladders Towing Co., Inc., St. Louis, 1968-73, pres., 1973—, also dir.; dir. Clayton Bank (Mo.). Mem. Nat. Def. Transp. Assn., Water Resources Asso., Am. Waterways Operators (dir.). Republican. Presbyn. Clubs: Dartmouth (v.p. 1970—), Propellor, Knights of Cauliflower Ear, Mo. Athletic (St. Louis); Clayton. Home: 323 Conway Hill Rd St Louis MO 63141 Office: 11 S Meramec Ave St Louis MO 63105

GLADISH, DAVID FRANCIS, writer; b. Chgo., Mar. 18, 1928; s. David Francis and Eleanor (Lindrooth) G.; B.A., Lake Forest Coll., 1950; M.A., U. Ill., 1954, Ph.D., 1961; m. Shirley Glebe, May 17, 1951; children—Frances, Frea, Andrew. Teaching asst. English U. Ill., 1954-61; prof. English, Franklin (Ind.) Coll., 1961-72. Sec., Peaine Twp. Planning Commn., 1973—. Served with AUS, 1950-51. Mem. Modern Lang. Assn. Am., Renaissance Soc. Am. Mem. Ch. of New Jerusalem. Editor: Sir William Davenant's Gondibert, 1971. Home: St James MI 49782

GLADSTONE, WILLIAM SHELDON, JR., radiologist; b. Des Moines, Dec. 19, 1923; s. William Sheldon and Wanda (Rees) G.; B.A., State U. Iowa, 1954, M.D., 1947; m. Ruth Alice Jensen, June 19, 1944; children—Denise Ann, William Sheldon, Stephen Rees. Intern. Hurley Hosp., Flint, Mich., 1947-48; gen. practice medicine, Iowa Falls, Iowa, 1948-49; asst. dept. pathology State U. Iowa Coll. Medicine, Iowa City, 1949-50; resident in radiology Univ. Hosp., Iowa City, 1950-51, 53-54; practice medicine specializing in radiology, Kalamazoo, 1954—; pres. Kalamazoo Radiology; clin. asst. prof. radiology Mich. State U. Coll. Human Medicine; chief radiology Bronson Meth. Hosp., Kalamazoo. Bd. dirs. Kalamazoo County Tb Soc., 1955-59, Mich. Children's Aid, 1960-62, Am. Cancer Soc., Kalamazoo, 1964-66. Served with AUS, 1943-46; served to capt. USAF, 1951-53. Diplomate Am. Bd. Radiology. Fellow Am. Coll. Radiology; mem. Kalamazoo Acad. Medicine, AMA, Mich. Radiologic Soc. (pres. W. Mich. sect. 1976), Mich. State Med. Soc., SW Mich. Surg. Soc., Am. Roentgen Ray Soc., Phi Beta Kappa (pres. SW Mich. chpt. 1963). Republican. Episcopalian. Clubs: Kalamazoo Country, Gull Lake Country, Rotary, Masons, Shriners. Home: 702 E Gull Lake Dr Augusta MI 49012 Office: 524 S Park St Kalamazoo MI 49007

GLAESS, HERMAN LEWIS, educator; b. Harbor Beach, Mich., July 18, 1926; s. Arnold John and Vicenta Rosemary (Sandman) G.; B.S., Concordia Tchrs. Coll., 1948; postgrad. Valparaiso U., 1948; M.Ed., Wayne State U., 1955; Ed.D., U. Neb., 1966; m. Ruth Bruckner, Aug. 5, 1950; children—Anita, Mark, Marian, Lori. Tchr. Immanuel Luth. Sch., The Grove, Tex., 1945-46, Resurrection Luth. Sch., Detroit, 1948-50; prin. Immanuel Luth. Sch., Sebewaing, Mich., 1950-54, St. Peter's Luth. Sch., East Detroit, Mich., 1954-62; asst. prof. Concordia Tchrs. Coll., Seward, Nebr., 1962-66, asso. prof., 1966-73, prof. edn., 1973—, dir. counseling and testing, 1965-68, chmn. dept. edn., 1968-77; guest instr. U. Nebr., Lincoln, 1969—. Coordinator Luth. Schs. Greater Detroit TV Program, 1960-62; cons. Beatrice (Nebr.) State Home, 1966-67, York Pub. Schs., 1968-69, Geneva Girls Tng. Sch., 1969-71, Selection Research, Inc., 1968-71, York Reformatory for Women, 1971—; spl. projects dir. State Dept. Econ. Devel., Lincoln, 1972-73. Mem. edn. div. Nebr. Human Relations Found., 1967—. Mem. S.E. Mich. Tchrs. Conf., Luth. Laymen League Seminar Speakers Bur., Luth. Edn. Assn. (pres. 1970-72). Contbr. articles to profl. jours. Editor: Primary Grades, 1956; Teaching Middle and Upper Grades, 1958; Manual of Orientation of Lutheran Teachers, 1960. Home: 237 Northern Heights Seward NE 68434

GLAMAN, PAUL THOMPSON, mag. editor; b. Jewell, Iowa, July 4, 1926; s. Charles Eli and Lillian (Thompson) G.; B.A., Grinnell Coll., 1950; M.A., Duke, 1951. Asso. editor Instns. Mag., Chgo., 1958-61; mng. editor Profl. Builder, Chgo., 1961-62; editor U.S. Gypsum Co., Chgo., 1962-66, Am. Drycleaner mag., Chgo., 1966—. Served with USNR, 1944-46. Recipient Jesse H. Neal award for editorial excellence, 1973. Contbr. articles to profl. jours. Home: 33 E Cedar St Chicago IL 60611 Office: 500 N Dearborn St Chicago IL 60610

GLAMAN, RICHARD WILLIAM, county ofcl.; b. Portage County, Wis., Nov. 24, 1929; s. Arthur Richard William and Gladys Evelyn (Smith) G.; B.A., U. Wis., 1956, postgrad., 1967-68; m. Dolores Jane Newhall, July 10, 1954; children—Lynn Marie, Richard Newhall, Lauren Jane, Roderick Arthur, Ronald William. Reporter, Appleton (Wis.) Post Crescent, 1956-58; editor Plainfield (Wis.) Sun, 1958-60, Tri-Town News, Hales Corners, Wis., 1960-61; reporter Milw. Sentinel, 1961-66; asst. dir. Dept. Fiscal Liaison, City of Milw., 1966-77; dir. intergovtl. relations Milwaukee County, 1977—. Mem. Wis. Council on Criminal Justice, 1970-77; chmn. Milw. Met. Criminal Justice Council, 1973-77; mem. Council on Local Affairs and Devel., State of Wis. Served with AUS, 1948-52. Decorated Bronze Star medal. Mem. Municipal Intergovtl. Coordinators Assn. (nat. pres. 1972), Municipal Fin. Officers of U.S. and Can. Home: 10072 W Tower Ave Milwaukee WI 53224 Office: 901 N 9th St Milwaukee WI 53233

GLANCY, THOMAS JAMES, investment exec.; b. Hammond, Ind., July 21, 1936; s. Everett Harry and Luella Helen (Daumer) G.; B.S., Ind. U., 1958; m. Carol Francis Krause, June 14, 1958; children—Lora Marie, Lesley Ann, Lisa Ann. Sr. cost clk. Budd Co., Gary, Ind., 1958-61; self-employed in pvt. accounting and tax bus., 1961-64; field auditor Consol. Papers, Inc., Timberlands div., Rhinelander, Wis., 1961-64; gen. mgr., dir. Calumet Propane Gas Co., Inc., Gary, Ind., 1965; pres., treas. Hoosier Publs., Inc., Chesterton, Ind., 1968—; v.p., gen. mgr., treas. Panax Pub. Co., Lansing, Ill., 1966-76; investment exec. A.G. Edwards, 1977—; dir. Krause Corp. Treas. Young Republicans Porter County, 1958-60; clk., Town of Lake Tomahawk, Wis., 1962-64; bd. dirs. Westchester YMCA, 1977—. Mem. Outdoor Writers Assn. Am., Inst. Newspaper Controllers and Fin. Officers, Assn. Great Lakes Outdoor Writers, Hoosier Outdoor Writers Assn. (dir. 1970—, chmn. craft improvement com. 1974-76, pres. 1976—), Ind. State Rifle and Pistol Assn. (dir., sec. 1973—), Ind. Field Trial Assn. (dir. 1974-76, sec.-treas. 1974-76). Lutheran (deacon 1971-72, dir. 1971-76, chmn. bd. evangelism 1974-76). Club: Hoosier Coho (Michigan City, Ind.). Home: PO Box 552 Chesterton IN 46304 Office: 8300 Mississippi St Merrillville IN 46410

GLANDER, KARL WILLIAM, orthodontist; b. Riverside, N.J., June 26, 1932; s. Karl Ernst and Elisabeth (Lusch) G.; B.S., Butler U., 1953; D.D.S., Ind. U., 1956; M.S.D., Fairleigh Dickinson U., 1964; m. Evelyne Maria Werz, Mar. 10, 1956; children—Karl William, Laura Maria, Steven Frederick, David Arnold. Practice dentistry, Red Bank, N.J., 1959-62, specializing in orthodontics, Indpls., 1964—; instr. orthodontics Ind. U. Sch. Dentistry, 1964-66; mem. staff Monmouth Meml. Hosp., 1959-62. Bd. dirs. Baxter YMCA. Served to capt. Dental Corps, USAF, 1956-58. Mem. Am. Ind. dental assns., Am., Ind. orthodontists assns., Izaak Walton League, Nat. Wildlife Soc., Ind. U., Butler U. alumni assns., Fedn. Fly Fishermen (sec.), Indpls. Fly Casters (sr. dir.), Kappa Sigma, Delta Sigma Delta. Presbyn. Club: Indiana U. Hoosier Hundred (Indpls.). Home: 6040 Bryan Dr Indianapolis IN 46227 Office: 7750 Madison Ave Indianapolis IN 46227

GLASCOE, MILTON MARCELLUS, physician; b. Washington, May 26, 1899; s. David Brooks and Carrie Lee (Belt) G.; B.S., Howard U., 1922; M.D., Chgo. Med. Sch., 1926; m. Gloria Carpenter, Mar. 25, 1972; 1 dau. by previous marriage, Barbara Glascoe Matthews. Intern, Wilson Hosp., Chgo., 1926-27; resident Dailey Hosp., Chgo., 1927-29; gen. practice internal medicine, Ill., 1929—; hon. staff Provident Hosp., Chgo. Served with U.S. Army, 1918. Mem. Cook County Physicians Assn., Prairie (pres. 1966-75), Nat. med. assns., Phi Beta Sigma. Elk (grand med. examiner). Author: Man Born of a Dark Woman, 1971; Dawn of Democracy, 1976. Home: 7018 Vernon Ave Chicago IL 60637

GLASER, KURT, educator; b. Ann Arbor, Mich., Aug. 19, 1914; s. Otto Charles and Dorothy Gibbs (Merrylees) G.; A.B., Harvard, 1935, A.M., 1938, Ph.D., 1941; m. Florence W. Riddle, Aug. 11, 1939 (div. Aug. 1948); children—Jeffrey, Kristin; m. 2d, Ingeburg Elfriede Halle, Mar. 8, 1950 (div. Mar. 1976); children—Robin, Angela. With Social Security Bd., U.S. Dept. Agr., Washington, 1938-46; with Mil. Govt. Germany, 1946-49; govt. affairs officer Office of U.S. High Commn., Frankfurt, Germany, 1949-50; curriculum cons. and journalist Munich, Germany, 1950-52; exchange officer, project dir. Govt. Affairs Inst., Washington, 1952-54; office and mgmt. analyst Records Mgmt. Inc., Washington, 1954-55; asst. prof. U. Md. in Germany, 1956-59; lectr. So. Ill. U., Edwardsville, 1959-60, asso. prof., 1960-65, prof. govt., 1965—, project dir. African Exchange and Lang. and grad. devel. studies, 1973—. Dir. spl. projects Found. Fgn. Affairs, Chgo., 1973—; Fulbright lectr. U. Kiel (Germany), 1966-67. Coordinator St. Louis YMCA Dynamic Citizenship Forum, 1961-63. Bd. dirs. Found. for Study of Plural Socs., 1974—. Hoover Inst. grantee, 1968-69. Mem. Univ. Profs. for Acad. Order (dir. 1975—). Asso. editor Modern Age, 1973—, Plural Societies, 1975—. Author: Czecho-Slovakia: A Critical History, 1961; Der zweite Weltkrieg und die Kriegsschuldfrage, 1964. Editor (with David S. Collier) Found. for Fgn. Affairs series on East-West relations, 1962-69; (with J. Barratt, S. Brand and D.S. Collier) Accelerated Devel. in South Africa, 1974; (with J. Barratt, D.S. Collier and Herman Mönnig) Strategy for Development, 1976. Home: 7354 Tulane Ave University City MO 63130

GLASER, ROBERT STANLEY, travel agt.; b. St. Paul, Dec. 22, 1933; s. George Granville and Alice Lucille (Lathrop) G.; A.A., U. Minn., 1958; m. Jane Ehrenberg, Jan. 29, 1965; children—Stephen L., Robert M. Regional sales staff Alitalia Airlines, Mpls., 1963-65; pres. Travel Advisors, Inc., Mpls., 1965—. Bd. dirs. Opportunity Workshop for mentally handicapped, 1970—. Served with U.S. Army, 1953-57; Korea. Mem. Am. Assn. Travel Agts. (pres.). Republican. Clubs: Kiwanis (past pres.), Mason, Shriners, Decathlon Athletic, Minnesota Valley Country, (Mpls.). Home: 1533 Clare Ln Wayzata MN 55391 Office: Southgate Office Plaza 525 Minneapolis MN 55437

GLASGOW, CHARLES CURTIS, JR., assn. exec.; b. Jackson, Tenn., Jan. 11, 1921; s. Charles Curtis and Myrtle Marion (Bates) G.; B.S., U. Tenn., 1949, M.S., 1950; m. Mary Elizabeth Stallcup, Dec. 30, 1940; children—Charles Curtis III, Marion Ellen. Joined AUS, 1940, discharged, 1945, commd. 2d lt. U.S. Army, 1951, advanced through grades to lt. col., 1966, ret. 1968; exec. dir. Am. Soc. Traffic & Transp., Chgo., 1969—. Decorated Legion of Merit, Army Commendation medal with 6 clusters. Mem. Nat. Def. Transp. Assn., Soc. Logistical Engrs., Phi Kappa Phi, Delta Nu Alpha. Methodist. Mason. Office: 547 W Jackson Blvd Chicago IL 60606

GLASS, CLARENCE EDWARD, cons. engr.; b. Nicholasville, Ky., June 27, 1914; s. Edward Joseph and Harriet Lucretia (Wood) G.; M.E., U. Cin., 1936; m. Lucille Garrison, June 4, 1938; children—Kenneth E., Donna L. (Mrs. James Robert Heindl). Draftsman, designer Tool Steel Gear & Pinion Co., Cin., 1936-38; power sales engr. Cin. Gas & Electric Co., 1938-42; with Fosdick & Hilmer, Inc., Cin., 1942—, v.p., 1973—. Instr. elec. engring. Ohio Coll. Applied Sci., 1946-50. Mem. Planning and Zoning Commn., Fort Thomas, Ky., 1954-75, chmn., 1964-74. Recipient Distinguished Alumnus award U. Cin., 1974. Mem. Cons. Engring. Council Ohio (treas. Ohio chpt. 1971), Cin. Engring. Club (life), Amateur Radio Assn., Tau Beta Pi, Pi Tau Sigma. Methodist (trustee 1970-75). Home: 123 Riverside Pkwy Fort Thomas KY 41075 Office: 320 4th and Walnut Bldg Cincinnati OH 45202

GLASS, JAMES WILLIAM, theatre pipe organ installer; b. Oak Park, Ill., Dec. 13, 1946; s. Louis James and Grace Marie (Whaples) G.; B.S. in Elec. Engring., Ill. Inst. Tech., 1968. Electronic design engr. in data communications Gen. Telephone & Electronic Automatic Electric Labs., Inc., Northlake, Ill., 1968-72; self-employed as theatre pipe organ installer, Hinsdale, Ill., 1972—. Mem. Audio Engring. Soc., Am. Theatre Organ Soc., Owl Cinema Organ Guild (pres., chmn. bd. 1971—), Eta Kappa Nu. Home: 806 N Kenilworth St Oak Park IL 60302 Office: 29 E 1st St Hinsdale IL 60521

GLASSCOCK, TERRANCE LYNN, lumber co. exec.; b. Clinton, Mo., Mar. 26, 1948; s. William Robert and Frances Geraldine (Sperry) G.; B.S., Kans. State U., 1971; m. Marlene K. Moyer, May 30, 1970; 1 dau., Cori Ashley. Owner, operator, dir. Kans. Lumber Co., Manhattan, 1971—, Manhattan Developers Inc., 1972—, O'Brien Lumber Co. Inc., Camdenton, Mo., 1972—, 1st. State Bank Elwood (Kans.), 1974—; owner, operator Ridgeview Farms, Clinton, Mo., 1971—; sec., dir. Stagg Hill Enterprises Inc., Manhattan, 1973—; owner, operator Truman Devel. Properties, Clinton, 1975—; owner, developer Knollwood Shopping Center, Manhattan, 1977—. Adviser, Kans. State U. chpt. Mortar Bd., 1976—; mem. Manhattan City Commn., 1977—; bd. dirs. United Way Manhattan, Manhattan chpt. ARC, Women's Center Inc., 1977—. Named by Gov. Kans. to Kans. Cavalry, 1977. Served to 1st lt., inf., U.S. Army, 1971-72. Mem. Mid Am., Kans. lumberman's assns., Kans. Bankers Assn. Republican. Club: Rotary (dir. 1977-78 Manhattan). Home: 3308 Frontier Circle Manhattan KS 66502 Office: 431 S 5th St Manhattan KS 66502

GLASSER, PAUL HAROLD, educator; b. N.Y.C., Aug. 21, 1929; s. David and Rae (Startz) G.; B.S., City Coll. N.Y., 1949; M.S., Columbia U., 1951; Ph.D., U. N.C., 1961; m. Lois Hannah Naefach, Nov. 25, 1954; children—Heather Denys, Frederick Naefach. Chief psychiatric social work section Mental Hygiene Clinic, Camp Chaffee Army Hosp., Ark., 1952-53; asst. dir. residence Child Guidance Home, Cin., instr. psychiatric group work, dept. psychiatry U. Cin. Med. Sch., 1953-55; asst. prof. U. Mich., Ann Arbor, 1958-63, asso. prof., 1963-65, prof. Sch. Social Work, 1965—. Fulbright Hays lectr. social work, Italy, 1971, sociology U. of Philippines, Quezon City, 1966-67, social work, Australia, 1973-74; cons. Mich. Dept. Mental Health, Mich. Dept. Social Services, Office Econ. Opportunity, Children's Bur. and others. Bd. dirs. Washtenaw County Family Service, 1964-66, 69-70. Served to 1st lt. AUS, 1952-53. Mem. Nat. Assn. Social Workers (active various coms., chpt. chmn. 1962-63), Am. Sociol. Soc. Mason. Author: Small Groups in the Hospital Community, 1967, Families in Crisis, 1970; Social Work Education for Family and Population Planning, 1973; Individual Change Through Small Groups, 1974; Social Work Roles and Functions in Family and Population Planning, 1974. Sr. editor Ency. of Social Work, 1971, LaRicerca Valuatative, 1972; editor Jour. Health and Social Behavior, 1970-73, Jour. Social Work, Jour. Family and Marriage Counseling. Home: 4141 Woodland Dr Ann Arbor MI 48103 Office: 1065 Frieze Bldg Univ Mich Ann Arbor MI 48104

GLASSMAN, JAMES HENDRIX, clergyman; b. Seattle, Dec. 5, 1925; s. Ike Willard and Myra Fran (Hendrix) G.; B.A., U. Wash., 1949; Th.M., Dallas Theol. Sem., 1953; Ph.D., U. Edinburgh, 1958; m. Beth June Upham, Sept. 10, 1954; children—James Francis, Anne Cathleen. Intern, United Presbyterian Ch., Ontario, Oreg., 1950-51; staff Inter-Varsity Christian Fellowship, Dallas, 1950-53; ordained to ministry United Presbyn. Ch., 1958; minister of youth West Side Presbyn. Ch., Seattle, 1953-55; asst. pastor Larbert-Dunipace Ch. of Scotland, Stirlingshire, 1956-57; sr. pastor Trinity U.P. Ch., Seattle, 1958-64, Univ. Presbyn. Ch., Laramie, Wyo., 1964-69, Valley Community Presbyn. Ch., Mpls., 1969—. Instr., Sch. Religion, U. Wyo., Laramie, 1965-69; instr. continuing edn. Pub. Sch. Dist. 281, Mpls., 1972—. Served with C.I.C., AUS, 1946-47; Japan. Named Man of Yr., Northgate Rotary, Seattle, 1964. Mem. Am. Soc. Ch. History (reviewer), Scottish Ch. History Soc. Rotarian. Contbr. to publs. in field. Travel and research in Europe and Middle East, 1952—. Home: 3805 Saratoga Ln N Minneapolis MN 55441 Office: 3100 N Lilac Dr Minneapolis MN 55422

GLASSNER, ALVIN, chemist, govt. ofcl.; b. N.Y.C., Nov. 20, 1913; s. James and Elizabeth (Traub) G.; B.S., Coll. City N.Y., 1935; Ph.D., Columbia, 1940; m. Adele Glick, Dec. 22, 1940; children—Geoffrey, Edward, Lisa. Chemist, Signal Corps Lab., Ft. Monmouth, N.J., 1942-46, Argonne (Ill.) Nat. Lab., 1951—; instr. Trinity Coll., Hartford, Conn., 1946-49; physicist Reaction Motors, Inc., Dover, N.J., 1949-51. Pres., Sec. Park Forest Sch. Dist. 163 Bd. Edn., 1952-61, sec. Sch. Dist. 227, 1961-71; trustee Village of Park Forest, 1972-75. Bd. dirs. Dr. Charles Gavin Meml. Found. Mem. Am. Chem. Soc., Am. Phys. Soc., Am. Nat. Standards Inst. (com. chmn.), A.A.A.S. Author: Introduction to Nuclear Science, 1961. Contbr. articles on thermodynamics and electrochemistry to profl. publs. Home: 206 Fir St Park Forest IL 60466 Office: 9700 S Cass Ave Argonne IL 60439

GLAUBER, ROBERT HASKELL, writer, editor; b. N.Y.C., July 28, 1920; s. Lester and Lillian (Green) G.; student pub. schs. Editor, Alfred A. Knopf, Inc., N.Y.C., 1946-49, Decker Press, Prairie City, Ill., 1949-50; dir. pub. relations Nat. Assn. Bedding Mfrs., Chgo., 1951-58; writer pub. relations dept. Ill. Bell Telephone Co., Chgo., 1958—; curator Am. Tel. & Tel. Co., 1972-77; editor Beloit (Wis.) Poetry Jour., 1953—; writer art lit., lang. China and Japan, Ency. Bit. Jr., Chgo., 1965—; art critic Skyline, Art Scene, Chgo., 1967—; instr. lit. Columbia Coll., Chgo., 1967-70. Guest dir. Violence in Recent Am. Art, Mus. Contemporary Art, Chgo., 1968. Served with AUS, 1942-45. Recipient Chris award for documentary films Film Council Columbus (Ohio), 1962; writer Emmy award-winning TV spls. Giants and the Common Man, 1968, From the Ashes, 1976. Contbr. articles to newspapers, lit. mags. Home: 2017 N Cleveland Ave Chicago IL 60614 Office: 225 W Randolph St Chicago IL 60606

GLAVIANO, VINCENT VALENTINO, physiologist, educator; b. Frankfort, N.Y., July 19, 1920; s. Salvatore and Josephine (Manzo) G.; B.S., Coll. City N.Y., 1950; Ph.D., Columbia Coll. Phys. and Surg., 1954; m. Eleanor Spargimino, July 18, 1943; children—Joan J., Vincent S. Research asst. in physiology Columbia, N.Y.C., 1950-53, instr., 1953-54, fellow in medicine dept. medicine, 1954-56; asst. prof. physiology U. Ill. Med. Sch., Chgo., 1956-60; asso. prof. physiology Loyola U. Stritch Sch. Medicine, Chgo., 1960-64, prof., 1964-70;

prof., chmn. dept. physiology and biophysics Chgo. Med. Sch. U. Health Scis., 1970—; cons. physicist in therapeutic radiology Hines (Ill.) VA Hosp. Served with USAAF, 1942-45. Fellow AAAS, N.Y. Acad. Scis., Inst. of Medicine of Chgo.; mem. Am. Physiol. Soc., Am. Heart Assn., Soc. Exptl. Biology and Medicine, Harvey Soc., Faculty Collegium Stritch Sch. Medicine (pres. 1964-65), Am. Soc. for Pharmacology and Exptl. Therapeutics, Sigma Xi (sec.-treas. 1967-69), Alpha Omega Alpha. Contbr. numerous articles on blood and lymphatics, shock, cardiovascular physiology to sci. publs., also chpts. to books. Home: 517 Carlisle Ct Glen Ellyn IL 60137 Office: Chgo Med Sch U Health Scis 2020 W Ogden Av Chicago IL 60612

GLAZE, BERT THEODORE, educator; b. Akron, Ohio, Aug. 1, 1922; s. Bert Leslie and Mabel Marie (Grudier) G.; B.A., U. Akron, 1951; M.A., Ohio State U., 1953, Ph.D., 1962; m. Emma Gene Fish, Aug. 21, 1948; children—Linda Sue, Connie Jean. Teaching asst. Ohio State U., Columbus, 1952-56, instr., 1956-58; asst. prof., chmn. dept. econs. Otterbein Coll., Westerville, Ohio, 1958-63; asso. prof. San Jose (Calif.) State Coll., 1963-66; prof., chmn. dept. econs., mgmt. and accounting Marietta (Ohio) Coll., 1966—, dir. Evening Sch., 1976—. Served with USNR, 1942-46. Mem. Am. Econ. Assn., A.A.U.P., Ohio Assn. Economists and Polit. Scientists, Common Cause, Omicron Delta Epsilon, Beta Gamma Sigma, Tau Pi Phi. Democrat. Author: (with Alvin E. Coons) Housing Market Analysis and the Growth of Non-Farm Home Ownership, 1964. Contbr. articles to profl. jour. Home: 118 Janet Rd Marietta OH 45750

GLAZER, SIDNEY, educator; b. Quincy, Mich., Nov. 1, 1905; s. Max and Mildred (Thal) G.; A.B., Wayne U., 1927; M.A., U. Mich., 1929, Ph.D., 1932. Asst. dept. history U. Mich., 1928-30; instr. Wayne State U., Detroit, 1930-37, asst. prof., 1937-48, asso. prof., 1948-55, prof. 1955—. Mem. Orgn. Am. Historians, Am., Mich. hist. socs., Econ. History Assn., A.A.U.P., Phi Beta Kappa. Author: (with M. M. Quaife) From Primitive Wilderness to Industrial Commonwealth, 1948; Industrial Detroit, 1951; The Middle West, 1962; Detroit: A Study in Urban Development, 1965. Contbr. articles to hist. revs. and mags. Home: Sheraton-Cadillac Hotel Detroit MI 48231

GLAZZARD, CHARLES DONALDSON, psychiatrist; b. Cleve., Apr. 10, 1928; s. Charles Earl and Kathleen Hazel (Donaldson) G.; student U. Miami, 1946-48; A.B., U. Mich., 1951, postgrad. 1951-52; M.D., Wayne State U., 1956; m. Margaret Hughes Leoni, Aug. 2, 1974; children by previous marriage—Charles F., Eric D., Kim E., Teri L.; stepchildren—Dan, Linda and Bill Leoni. Intern, St. Vincents Hosp., Toledo, 1956-57; gen. practice medicine, El Cajon, Calif., 1960-61; resident Menninger Sch. Psychiatry, Topeka, 1961-64; practice medicine, specializing in psychiatry, Kansas City, Mo., 1971-72, Olathe, Kans., 1974—; med. dir. Midcontinent Psychiat. Hosp., 1972-74; mem. staffs various hosps.; asst. sect. chief VA Hosp., Topeka, 1964-67; psychiatrist Forbes AFB, Topeka, 1967-71; acting med. dir. Johnson County Mental Health Center, Olathe, 1974-75, now bd. dirs.; dir. Psychiat. and Edn. Center of Olathe; mem. adv. com. Family Ct. of Johnson County. Mem. Olathe Human Relations Commn., 1974-77; bd. dirs. Cedar House. Served with USNR, 1958-60; qualified submarine med. officer. Diplomate Am. Bd. Psychiatry and Neurology. Comml. pilot. Mem. AMA, Am., Kans. Dist., Mid Continent psychiat. assns., Pan Am. Med. Assn., AAAS, Royal Soc. Health, Johnson County Med. Soc., Flying Physicians Assn., Airplane Owners and Pilots Assn. Rotarian. Home: 14301 Locust St Olathe KS 66061 Office: 407 Clairborne St Olathe KS 66061

GLEASON, DONALD WILLIAM, judge; b. Wrightstown, Wis., Dec. 6, 1907; s. Thomas Emmett and Mary Jane (Egan) G.; B.E., Oshkosh State Tchrs. Coll., 1928; J.D. magna cum laude, Marquette U., 1934; m. Geraldine Wetli, Nov. 24, 1938; children—Kelly, Connie, Nancy, Casey. Tchr. Lincoln High Sch., Manitowoc, Wis., 1928-30, Marquette Univ. High Sch., Milw., 1930-31, West High Sch., Green Bay, Wis., 1934-35; admitted to Wis. bar, 1934; spl. agt. FBI, U.S. Dept. Justice, 1935-36; mem. firm Classon, Colignon and Gleason, 1936-40; pvt. practice law, 1938-40; dist. atty., Brown County, Wis., 1940-44, municipal judge, 1944-61, judge juvenile ct., 1944-61; circuit ct. judge Brown, Door and Kewaunee Counties, 1962-77. Mem. Gov.'s Commn. Human Rights, 1954-56; mem. jud. planning com. Wis. Supreme Ct., 1976—. Mem. Juvenile Ct. Judges Wis. (pres. bd. 1949), Criminal Ct. Judges Wis. (pres. bd. 1954), Brown County, 14th Jud. Circuit, Wis. bar assns. K.C. (state adv. 1950-54; state dep. 1954-56), Rotarian (past pres.). Home: 2636 Beaumont St Green Bay WI 54301 Office: Ct House Green Bay WI 54301

GLEEKMAN, LEWIS WOLFE, cons.; b. Lynn, Mass., June 10, 1920; s. Morris B. and Etta M. (Wolfe) G.; B.Chem. Engring., Cooper Union Inst. Tech., 1942; M.S., State U. Iowa, 1947, Ph.D. (W.A. Schaeffer Pen Co. fellow), 1948; m. Helen Wilensky, Mar. 25, 1945; children—Barbara Share, Anne Etta, David. With Mathieson Alkali Works, Lake Charles, La., 1942-43, Sam Tour & Co., N.Y.C., 1943-45; asst. prof. chem. engring. U. Del., Newark, 1948-52; with Sherritt Gordon Mines Ltd., Ottawa, Ont., Can., 1952-53; chief materials engr. Wyandotte Chems. Corp. (Mich.), 1953-68; adj. prof. Lawrence Inst. Tech., Southfield, Mich., 1964-70; ind. engring. cons., Southfield, 1968—. Served with AUS, 1945-46. Registered profl. engr., Mich., Calif., Ont., La. Fellow Am. Soc. Metals; mem. Am. Inst. Chem. Engrs., Soc. Plastics Industry, ASTM, TAPPI, Nat. Assn. Corrosion Engrs. (dir. 1964-67). Editor: Corrosion Data Survey, 1968-73. Contbr. articles to profl. jours. Home and office: 25667 Friar Ln Southfield MI 48034

GLENDENING, EVERETT AUSTIN, architect; b. White Plains, N.Y., May 20, 1929; s. Gilbert Leslie and Elsie Jane (Fanjoy) G.; B.Arch., U. Cin., 1953; M.Arch., Mass. Inst. Tech., 1954; m. Wilhelmina Louise Hanley, Nov. 26, 1949; children—Nancy, James, Thomas, Terry, Susan. With Duffy Constrn. Co., Cleve., 1951-53, SIS Architects, Cin., 1956-58, T.J. Moore, architect, Denver, 1959; prof. architecture U. Cin., 1960-67; pvt. practice architecture, Cin., 1959—. Served to 1st lt. USAF, 1954-56. Recipient first honor awards Ohio chpt. A.I.A., 1967, 68, 69, 70, 71, honor awards Cin. chpt. A.I.A., 1966, 67, 68, 70, 76, bronze medal, 1969. Mem. A.I.A., Architect's Soc. Ohio, Scarab. Methodist. Mason. Home: 5425 Drake Rd Cincinnati OH 45243 Office: 8050 Montgomery Rd Cincinnati OH 45236

GLENN, JERRY HOSMER, JR., educator; b. Little Rock, Sept. 5, 1938; s. Jerry Hosmer and Anne (Matthews) G.; B.A., Yale, 1960; postgrad. Freie Universität Berlin, 1962-63; M.A., U. Tex., 1962, Ph.D., 1964; m. Sheila Scarlett Griffin, June 9, 1970. Asst. prof. German, U. Wis., Milw., 1964-67; asst. prof. German, U. Cin., 1967-69, asso. prof., 1969-72, prof., 1972—, dir. honors program, 1977—. Mem. Am. Lessing Soc. (sec., treas. 1968-74), Modern Lang. Assn., Midwest Modern Lang. Assn., Am. Assn. Tchrs. German. Republican. Author: Deutsches Schrifttum der Gegenwart (ab 1945), 1971; Paul Celan, 1973. Mng. editor: Lessing Yearbook, 1969-74. Home: 854 Rue de la Paix B-5 Cincinnati OH 45220

GLENN, JOHN HERSCHEL, JR., U.S. senator, former astronaut; b. Cambridge, Ohio, July 18, 1921; s. John Herschel and Clara (Sproat) G.; student Muskingum Coll., 1939, D.Sc., 1961; naval aviation cadet U. Iowa, 1942; grad. flight sch. Naval Air Tng. Center, Corpus Christi, Tex., 1943, Navy Test Pilot Tng. Sch., Patuxent River, Md., 1954; m. Anna Margaret Castor, Apr. 1943; children—Carolyn Ann, John David. Commd. 2d lt. U.S. Marine Corps, 1943, advanced through grades to lt. col.; assigned 4th Marine Aircraft Wing, Marshall Islands campaign, 1944, 9th Marine Aircraft Wing, 1945-46; with 1st Marine Aircraft Wing, 1947-48; flight instr., Corpus Christi, 1949-51; asst. amphibious warfare sch., Quantico, Va., 1951; served as pilot, Korea, 1951-53; project officer flight design Navy Bur. Aeros., Washington, 1959-64; astronaut NASA Project Mercury, Manned Spacecraft Center, 1959-64; pilot Mercury-Atlas 6, orbital space flight, 1962; v.p. corporate devel. and dir. Royal Crown Cola Co., after 1962; U.S. senator from Ohio, 1975—. Decorated D.F.C. (5), Air medal (18), Astronaut medal USMC, Navy commendation; Korean Presdl. citation; Distinguished Merit award Muskingum Coll., Medal Honor N.Y.C. Mem. Soc. Exptl. Test Pilots, Internat. Acad. Astronautics (hon.). Presbyn. Co-author: We Seven, 1962; author: P.S., I Listened to Your Heart Beat. Address: US Senate Washington DC 20510

GLENNER, RICHARD ALLEN, dentist, dental historian; b. Chgo., Apr. 14, 1934; s. Robert Joseph and Vivian (Prosk) G.; B.S., Roosevelt U., 1955; B.S. in Dentistry, U. Ill., 1958, D.D.S., 1959; m. Dorothy Chapman, July 13, 1957; children—Mark Steven, Alison. Gen. practice dentistry, Chgo., 1962—. Served to capt. AUS, 1960-62. Mem. Am., Ill. dental assns., Chgo. Dental Soc., Assn. Mil. Surgeons U.S., Am. Acad. Dental History, Fed. Dentaire Internationale, Alpha Omega. Contbr. articles on dental history to profl. jours. Home: 6715 N Lawndale Ave Lincolnwood IL 60645 Office: 3414 W Peterson Ave Chicago IL 60659

GLENNIE, DONALD MORGAN, seed co. exec.; b. Missouri Valley, Iowa, Mar. 23, 1923; s. James and Anne McPherson (Morgan) G.; B.A., U. Iowa, 1949; m. Gloria Agnes Satterlee, Sept. 1, 1946; children—Elizabeth Ann (Mrs. Terrel Brown), Donald Lachlan, Mary Irene, James M. Retail sales mgr. Am. Field Seed Co., Chgo., 1949-56; regional sales mgr. Berry Seed Co., Clarinda, Iowa, 1956-62; v.p. sales Lowe Seed Co., Kankakee, Ill., 1962-71; v.p. mktg. Jacques Seed Co., Prescott, Wis., 1971—. Served with USNR, 1942-46. Mem. Am. Seed Trade Assn., Sales and Market Execs. Assn. Chgo., Nat. Agrl. and Mktg. Assn., Internat. Platform Assn. Presbyn. (elder). Home: 407 Lake St Prescott WI 54021 Office: 720 St Croix Prescott WI 54021

GLICKMAN, DANIEL R. (DAN), Congressman; b. Wichita, Kans., Nov. 24, 1944; B.A., U. Mich., 1966; J.D., George Washington U., 1969; m. Rhoda Yura, 1966; children—Jonathan, Amy. Practiced law, Washington; trial atty. SEC, 1969-70; partner firm Sargent, Kienda & Glickman, 1973-76; mem. 95th Congress from 4th Kans. Dist. Mem. Wichita Sch. Bd., 1973-76, pres., 1975-76; active Arthritis Found., Big Bros. Mem. NCCJ, Am. Bar Assn. Democrat. Office: Room 1128 Longworth House Office Bldg Washington DC 20515

GLICKMAN, PAUL BERNARD, rheumatologist, educator; b. Birmingham, Ala., Feb. 14, 1929; s. Efraim Elias and Lillian (Rachman) G.; Ph.B., U. Chgo., 1948, S.B., 1950, M.D., 1953; m. Sarita Mae Rubinsky, Feb. 10, 1957; children—Martin Eliot, Judith Tamarah, Joan Annette. Practice medicine, specializing in rheumatology, Chgo., 1962—; asst. prof. medicine U. Chgo., 1960-62; asso. prof. medicine Rush Med. Sch., Chgo., 1972—. Served to maj. M.C. USAF, 1955-57. Fellow Am. Coll. Physicians; mem. Chgo. Rheumatism Soc. (pres.), Am. Rheumatism Assn., Alpha Omega Alpha, Sigma Xi; Contbr. articles to med. jours., 1957—. Office: 55 E Washington St Chicago IL 60602

GLIDDEN, IRIS OLSEN (MRS. JOHN MOULTON GLIDDEN), librarian; b. Winchester, Wis., Dec. 4, 1917; d. Oscar Wilhelm and Violet Sarah (Rammel) Olsen; B.A., Northland Coll., Ashland, Wis., 1962; M.A., U. Wis.-Milw., 1971; m. John Moulton Glidden, Apr. 16, 1938 (dec.); children—Bonnie (Mrs. Robert C. Buchanan), Janice (Mrs. Patrick Scanlon), Marcia (Mrs. Thomas D. Parker), John Moulton. Acting instr. Kenwood Library, U. Wis. Milw., 1961-62; head librarian West Bend (Wis.) High Sch., 1962-70; dir. library services West Bend Pub. Schs., 1970—. Bd. dirs. West Bend Community Meml. Library, 1970—; mem. Council Wis. Libraries. Mem. Am., Wis. library assns., Wis. Assn. Sch. Librarians (chmn. 1971-72), AAUW, Wis. Acad. Scis., Arts and Letters, Wis. Audiovisual Assn. (dir.), League Women Voters, Library Council Met. Milw. (mem. bd.), U. Wis.-Milw. Alumni Assn., Delta Kappa Gamma. Episcopalian. Club: West Bend Country. Home: Big Cedar Lake Slinger WI 53086 Office: 697 S 5th Ave West Bend WI 53095

GLIDDEN, JOHN REDMOND, lawyer; b. Sanford, Maine, July 24, 1936; s. Kenneth Eugene and Kathryn (Gilpatrick) G.; student U. Wis., 1954-55; B.S., Coe Coll., 1958; LL.B., U. Iowa, 1961; m. Jacqueline R. Scales, Aug. 6, 1964; children—Ian, Claire, Jason. Admitted to Iowa bar, 1961, Ill. bar, 1965; asso. firm Williams & Hartzell, Carthage, Ill., 1965-67; partner firm Hartzell & Glidden, 1967-72, Hartzell, Glidden & Tucker, 1972-77, Hartzell, Glidden, Tucker & Neff, 1977—; city atty., City of Carthage, 1969—. Bd. dirs. Carthage Indsl. Devel. Corp. Served with USAF, 1961-65. Mem. Fed., Am., Ill., Iowa, Hancock County bar assns., Am., Ill. (governing bd. 1973—) trial lawyers assns., Am. Legion, Phi Delta Phi, Sigma Nu. Clubs: Kiwanis (dir. 1969-72), Keokuk Country, Carthage Golf (dir. 1967—). Home: Rural Route 3 Carthage IL 62321 Office: PO Box 70 Carthage IL 62321

GLIEBERMAN, HERBERT ALLEN, lawyer; b. Chgo., Dec. 6, 1930; s. Elmer and Jean (Gerber) G.; student U. Ill., 1947, Roosevelt U., 1948-50; J.D., Chgo. Kent Coll. Law, 1953; m. Evelyn Eraci, Nov. 26, 1936; children—Ronald, Gale, Joel. Admitted to Ill. bar, 1954; pvt. practice law, Chgo., 1954—. Trustee Chgo. Kent Coll. Law; bd. dirs. Chgo. Council on Alcoholism. Recipient certificates of appreciation Am. Acad. Matrimonial Lawyers, Ill. Bar Assn., 1967, Assn. Trial Lawyers Am., 1973, Ill. Trial Lawyers Assn., 1974, Decologue Soc., 1965, 66, 68. Mem. Am. Acad. Matrimonial Lawyers, Decologue Soc. Lawyers, Am., Ill., Los Angeles trial lawyers assns., Am., Ill., Chgo. bar assns. Jewish (dir. temple). Author: Some Syndromes of Love, 1965; Know Your Legal Rights, 1974; Confessions of A Divorce Lawyer, 1975. Home: 180 E Pearson St Chicago IL 60611 Office: 69 W Washington St Chicago IL 60602

GLIME, RAYMOND GEORGE, lawyer; b. Highland Park, Mich., Feb. 15, 1931; s. George Henry and Edna Grace (Yutzy) G.; B.S., Wayne State U., 1954, J.D., 1957; M.B.A., U. Mich., 1958; m. Gretchen Ross, Apr. 3, 1954; children—Elizabeth Rae, Rebecca Lee. Admitted to Mich. bar, 1957; asst. pros. atty. Macomb County, Mich., 1958-59; mem. firm. Mather & Glime, Mount Clemens, Mich., 1959-68, Mather, Glime & Daoust, Mount Clemens, 1969-75, Glime, Daoust & Wilds, 1975—. Mem. State Bar Mich., Am., Macomb County (dir. 1970—, pres. 1975-76) bar assns., Nat. Sch. Bd. Attys.' Assn., Nat. Orgn. Legal Problems in Edn., Wayne State U. Law Alumni Assn. (dir. 1965— pres. 1972). Contbr. articles to profl. jours. Home: 37119 Tall Oak Dr Fraser MI 48026 Office: 25 N Gratiot Ave Mount Clemens MI 48043

GLISSON, SILAS NEASE, III, biomed. researcher, educator; b. Springfield, Ill., May 8, 1941; s. Silas Nease and Dorothy Lucille (Reed) G.; student Ill. Coll., 1959-61; B.A., So. Ill. U., 1964; Ph.D., Loyola U., Chgo., 1972; m. Mary Louise Mosimann, Feb. 10, 1968; children—Silas Nease IV, Andrew Edward. Med. research asso. Thudichum Lab., Galesburg, (Ill.) State Research Hosp., 1965-67; instr. dept. pharmacology U. Conn. Sch. Medicine, Farmington, 1971-72; asst. prof. depts. anesthesiology and pharmacology and exptl. therapeutics Stritch Sch. Medicine, Loyola U., Maywood, Ill., 1972—; cons. Hines (Ill.) VA Hosp., 1975—. HEW predoctoral fellow in pharmacology, 1970-71. Mem. AAUP, Am., Ill. socs. anesthesiologists, Internat. Anesthesia Research Soc., Sigma Xi. Contbr. articles to profl. jours. Home: 546 N Stewart Ave Lombard IL 60148 Office: 2160 S 1st Ave Maywood IL 60153

GLOE, DONNA SUE OSBORN, histotechnologist; b. Moberly, Mo., Apr. 24, 1951; d. James Frederick and E. Emogene (Semones) Osborn; B.A., U. Mo., 1973; M.Ed., Lincoln U., 1977; m. Lloyd R. Gloe, Feb. 14, 1975; 1 son, Darin Robert. Lab. technician, dept. pathology U. Mo., Columbia, 1974-75, dept. opthalmology sr. research technician, 1975-76; dept. head histology and cytology lab. Lester E. Cox Med. Center, Springfield, Mo., 1976-77. Nat. Merit scholar, 1969; Regents scholar, 1969. Mem. Am. Personnel and Guidance Assn., Nat. Soc. Histotechnologists, Am. Soc. Clin. Pathologists, AAUW. Baptist. Home: Route 2 Box 171 Marshfield MO 65706

GLOMMEN, HARVEY HAMILTON, social work cons., counselor; b. Suttons Bay, Mich., Mar. 25, 1928; s. Lars Louis and Serena Sadie (Rorem) G.; B.A., Concordia Coll., 1953; postgrad. U. Minn., 1953-54, 60, 61, 62, U. Chgo., summer 1959; M.S.W., U. Mich., 1964; m. Ina Mae Wollertson, June 24, 1951; children—Brent, Barbara, Beth, Brenda. Social worker Hennepin and Anoka counties (Minn.) Welfare Bds., 1954-58; county welfare dir. Cottonwood County (Minn.) Welfare Dept., Windom, 1959-60; dir. Aitkin County (Minn.) Welfare Dept., Aitkin, 1960-63; tng. cons. for exec., supervisory tng. Minn. Dept. Pub. Welfare, St. Paul, 1964-65, supr. adoptions, 1965-66; dir. foster grandparents program Adminstrn. Aging, HEW, Washington, 1966-67; exec. dir. Minn. Assn. Retarded Citizens, Mpls., 1967-69; practice marriage and family counseling, cons. in human service, Mpls., 1972—; incorporator, pres. Our Place, emotionally disturbed facility, Blaine, 1977—; owner, operator Circus Candy Co., Mpls., 1972—, 1048 Residence, Blaine, Minn., 1975—. Mem. city charter commn., Blaine, 1974—; chmn. Blaine City Charter Commn., 1976—; mem. constn. commn. Minn. Dem.-Farmer-Labor Party, 1976—; fin. dir. Minn. Senate Dist. 47, 1975—; treas. Anoka County Assn. for Retarded Citizens, 1949-51, bd. dirs., 1969-72; bd. dirs., incorporator Anoka County Family Service Assn., 1970-72. Served to 2nd lt., AUS, 1946-50; Germany. Minn. Tng. fellow, 1963. Mem. Minn., Nat. pub. health assns., Minn., Nat. vocat. rehab. assns., Phi Kappa Phi. Democrat. Lutheran (youth bd. 1970-73, ch. council 1970-73). Home and office: 1048 87th Ave NE Blaine MN 55434

GLOOR, WILBUR TELL, cons. mech. engr.; b. Cleve., July 27, 1918; s. Walter Tell and Louisa Hedwig (Walther) G.; B.M.E., Case Sch. Applied Sci., 1940, M.M.E., 1947; m. Dorothy Duane Sandridge, Jan. 17, 1948; 1 dau., Catherine Duane. Lab. engr. Hoffman Specialty Co., Stamford, Conn., 1940; jr. mech. engr. A. H. Emery Co., Stamford, 1940-45, supervisory engr., New Canaan, Conn., 1950-56; chief research engr. Motch & Merryweather Machinery Co., Cleve., 1945-46, mgr. div. cutting tools, 1947-49, mgr. tech. promotion, 1949-50; product engr. Baldwin Testing Equipment Co., Waltham, Mass., 1956-60, King of Prussia, Pa., 1960-66; sr. mech. cons. Gilmore Industries, Beachwood, Ohio, 1966-72; pres. Gloor Inc., Aurora, Ohio, 1972—; lectr. in machine design. Advanced gifts chmn. ARC, Norwalk, Conn., 1953-54; chmn. plant com. Sudbury (Mass.) Sch. Survey, 1958-60. Registered profl. engr., Conn., Mass. Mem. ASME, ASTM, Cleve. Engring. Soc., Case Alumni Assn., Sigma Xi. Republican. Congregationalist. Patentee materials testing equipment; inventor three thread weaver. Home and Office: 257 Aurora Hudson Rd Aurora OH 44202

GLOSSBERG, JOSEPH BERKSON, investment counsellor; b. Chgo., Apr. 2, 1941; s. J. William Pearl (Berkson) G.; B.S. in Econs., Wharton Sch., U. Pa., 1963, M.B.A. in Fin., 1965; m. Trudy Sammet, Oct. 1, 1967; 2 sons, Jonathan William, David Louis, Gen. partner, Gofen and Glossberg, Chgo., 1965—. Pres. Med. Research Inst. Council, 1972-74, bd. dirs., 1977—; bd. dirs. U. Pa. Alumni Council on Admission, 1977-78. Served with USCG, 1965. Recipient Alumni award of merit, U. Pa., 1977. Chartered fin. analyst; chartered investment counsellor. Mem. Investment Analysts Soc. Chgo., Fin. Analysts Fedn. Am., Investment Counsel Assn. Am. Republican. Clubs: Standard (Chgo.), City (Chgo.), U. Pa. Alumni Assn. Chgo. (pres. 1974—). Home: 1310 N Sandburg Ter Chicago IL 60610 Office: One IBM Plaza Chicago IL 60611

GLOTFELTY, CLARENCE ALVAH, lawyer; b. Batavia, Iowa, Mar. 6, 1929; s. Vernon Hope and Esther Ellen (Workman) G.; B.S., State U. Iowa, 1952; LL.B., Drake U., 1958; m. Lavina Catherine Eckmann, Aug. 29, 1954; 1 dau., Jane Ann. Admitted to Ia. bar, 1958; practice in Davenport, 1958—; mem. firm Stevens, Glotfelty & Roeder & Sissel, Davenport; legal counsel Iowa Jr. C. of C., 1965; v.p. help thru edn. and law program Scott County Legal Aid Soc., 1972-73. Bd. govs. Nat. Council Chs., 1972-75, Council Chs., Scott and Rock Island Counties, 1969-72. Served with USMCR, 1946-48, AUS, 1953-56. Mem. Am., Fed., Iowa, Scott County (treas. 1964-74) bar assns., Am. Trial Lawyers Assn., Am. Judicature Soc., Iowa Assn. Trial Lawyers (dir. 1976—), Internat. Lawyers Assn., ACLU, Delta Chi, Delta Theta Phi. Home: 2615 Fairhaven Rd Davenport IA 52803 Office: 3127 Brady St Davenport IA 52803

GLOVER, DONALD MITCHELL, surgeon, educator; b. Urbana, Ill., Aug. 2, 1895; s. John Adams and Clara Lobdell (Wood) G.; A.B., U. Ill., 1916; postgrad. U. Wis., 1916; M.D., Harvard U., 1920; m. Leona Van Gorder, July 8, 1924; children—Mary W. (Mrs. Craig R. Smith), Albert V., Donald Mitchell, Leona B. (Mrs. J.C. Champeny). Intern, Boston City Hosp., 1919-20; resident in surgery Boston Children's Hosp., 1920-21, Mass. Gen. Hosp., Boston, 1921-23, St. Luke's Hosp., Cleve., 1923-24; practice medicine, specializing in pediatric and plastic surgery, Cleve., 1924-69; surgeon Univ. Hosp., Cleve., Cleve. Met. Gen. Hosp.; dir. surgery, sr. surgeon St. Luke's Hosp., Cleve., 1969—; demonstrator Case Western Res. U., Cleve., 1924-28, asst. prof. surgery, 1928-42, asso. clin. prof., 1942-51, clin. prof. 1952-69, clin. prof. emeritus, 1969—; cons. to Surgeon Gen., Washington, 1945-46, VA, Cleve., 1946-72; coordinator, N.E. Ohio Regional Med. Program, 1969-72; mem. joint exec. council Cleve. Health Scis. Libraries, 1969-75; chmn. med. adv. bd. Service for Crippled Children of Ohio. Pres. Brittingham Meml. Library, Cleve., 1975—. Bd. govs. Cancer Center, 1972—; trustee Health Fund, 1965-70. Served from maj. to col. M.C., AUS, 1942-46; PTO. Decorated Legion of Merit. Recipient Gov.'s Distinguished Citizen award State of Ohio. Diplomate Am. Bd. Surgery, Am. Bd. Plastic Surgery. Fellow A.C.S.; mem. Am. (v.p. 1949-50), Central, North Pacific (hon.), Cleve. (pres.) surg. assns., Am. Assn. for Surgery of Trauma, Am. Assn. Plastic Surgeons, Am. Soc. Plastic and Reconstructive Surgery, Am. Assn. Med. Colls., Am. Med. Writers Assn., Cleve. Plastic Surgery Assn. (pres.), Ohio Valley Plastic

Surgery Soc., Am. Cleft Palate Assn., Biol. Photog. Assn., Cleve. Med. Library Assn. (pres. 1969), Med. Arts Club Cleve., Assn. Residents Judson Park (pres. 1978). Clubs: Pasteur, Rowfant (Cleve.); Harvard, Aesculapian (Boston). Contbr. numerous chpts. to books, articles to profl. jours. Address: 2181 Ambleside Rd Apt 712 Cleveland OH 44106

GLOVER, REX BURR, real estate exec.; b. Conneaut, Ohio, Jan. 16, 1921; s. James N. and Anna (Frazier) G.; certificate real estate U. Mich., 1968; m. Georgia Lee Richardson, June 29, 1970. Supt., Gerity Mich. Corp., Adrian, Mich., 1951-54; founder, pres., chmn. bd. Glover Real Estate, Inc., Adrian, 1954—, Trade-A-Plan, Inc., Adrian, 1966—; founder, partner Glover Woods Assos., Alma, Mich., 1969—, West Terrace Apts., Adrian, 1970—; pres. Felonoff Industries, Inc., Adrian. Served with M.P., AUS, 1943-46; PTO. Decorated Bronze Star. Mem. Nat. Assn. Realtors, Mich. Assn. Farm and Land Inst. (pres. 1970), Mich. Assn. Realtors (dir.), Real Estate Polit. Edn. Com. (life mem.), Lenawee Realtors Assn. (pres. 1961, 62, 68-70), Real Estate Alumni Mich. (dir.), Am. Legion. Republican. Presbyterian. Clubs: Elks, Rotary. Home: 4383 Evergreen Dr Adrian MI 49221 Office: 203 N Broad St Adrian MI 49221

GLOVER, RICHARD BATES, mech. engr.; b. Chgo., Aug. 16, 1946; s. George W. and Ila C.; B.S., S.D. Sch. Mines and Tech., 1973; m. Marcia A. McColley, May 8, 1968; children—Shannon Lee, Patricia Elizabeth. Prodn. engr. Inland div. Gen. Motors Corp., Dayton, Ohio, 1973, project coordinator, 1974-75, supr. prodn. engring. vinyl compounding, coextrusion, automatic thermoforming of instrument panel vinyl coverings, 1976—. Served with AUS, 1967-69; Viet Nam. Decorated Silver Star with 2 oak leaf clusters, Purple Heart, Bronze Star. Mem. DAV, ASME (asso.), Am. Soc. Plastics Engrs. (asso.), Am. Contract Bridge Assn. Republican. Roman Catholic. Club: Elks. Home: 288 Allanhurst Ave Vandalia OH 45377 Office: PO Box 1224 V 20 Dayton OH 45401

GLOVER, ROBERT EDWARD, ice cream mfg. co. exec.; b. Frankfort, Ind., Nov. 13, 1930; s. Foster Robert and Virginia Mary (Oldshoes) G.; B.S., U. Ark., 1952; m. Virginia M. Mann, Oct. 3, 1954; children—Robert Stephen, Thom Scott, Beth Marie. Pres., Glover's Ice Cream, Frankfort, Ind. Served with AUS, 1952-53. Mem. Sigma Chi. Clubs: Jesters, Masons, Shriners, Elks, Rotary, Moose, Symposiarchs, Country (Frankfort). Home: 609 Harvard Terr Frankfort IN 46041 Office: 705 W Clinton St Frankfort IN 46041

GLUCKSMAN, MONA STEPHAINE, retail co. exec.; b. Phila., May 19, 1947; d. Joseph and Ruth (Rosoff) Morrison; certificate Charles Morris Price Sch. Advt. and Journalism, 1966; m. David Lawrence Glucksman, Feb. 14, 1970. Advt. prodn. mgr. Sale Meeting Mag., Phila., 1966-68; asst. advt. mgr. Phila. Mag., 1968-69; traffic mgr. Weightman Advt. Agency, Phila., 1969-70; advt. mgr. K Mart Corp., Steven Point, Wis., 1973-75, Duluth, Minn., 1975—. Mem. Duluth Newcomers Club, Duluth Club Advt., Phila. Club Advt. Women, Charles Morris Price Sch. Alumni. Jewish. Clubs: Arrowhead Sports Car, Newcomer Gourmet. Home: 1378 Highland Village 18 Duluth MN 55811 Office: 1734 Mall Dr Duluth MN 55811

GLUECK, SIDNEY JOHN, ophthalmologist; b. Phila., Apr. 16, 1914; s. Samuel Jonathan and Anna (Fox) G.; B.A., U. Pa., 1936; M.D., Sch. Medicine of Royal Colls., Edinburgh, Scotland, 1947; m. Charlotte Ornsten, Nov. 8, 1959; children—David, Suzan. Intern, Stobhill Hosp., Glasgow, Scotland, 1946-47; resident Grad. Sch. Medicine U. Pa., 1951-52, D.C. Gen. Hosp., 1953-55; gen. practice, Springfield, Ohio, 1947-51; practice medicine specializing in ophthalmology, Springfield, 1955—; chmn. dept. ophthalmology Community Hosp., Springfield, 1963-76; cons. ophthalmology Mercy Med. Center, Springfield, Mercy Meml. Hosp., Urbana, Ohio, Greene Meml. Hosp., Xenia, Ohio; mem. Oxford Ophthalmological Congress, 1959. Pres., bd. trustees Ridgewood Sch., 1969-74; trustee Springfield Urban League, 1960-63. Diplomate Am. Bd. Ophthalmology. Fellow Am. Acad. Ophthalmology and Otolaryngology, A.C.S., Am. Acad. Facial Plastic and Reconstructive Surgery. Lion. Contbr. articles to profl. publs. Office: 1525 Xenia Ave Yellow Springs OH 45387

GLUYS, CHARLES BYRON, indsl. marketing cons.; b. Richmond, Ind., Apr. 16, 1928; s. J. Howard and Reba Anna (Macy) G.; B.S., Purdue U., 1952, postgrad., 1954-55; m. Patricia Wheeler, July 25, 1953; children—Gary, Robert, Marcia, James. Sales mgr. Carlyle Constrn. Co., Columbus, Ohio, 1958; asst. specialty product mgr. Palmer Donavin Mfg. Co., 1958-61; product mgr. KCL Corp., Shelbyville, Ind., 1963-64; prin. Gluys & Assos., marketing cons., Greenfield, 1964—. Active Boy Scouts Am., 1953-61, chmn. orgn. and extension com. S.E. Dist., Central Ohio, 1960-61. Served with USN, 1946-48. Mem. Assn. Indsl. Advertisers (treas. 1969-70), Am. Marketing Assn. (bd. dirs. 1970-73), Nat. Rifle Assn. Mason (32 deg. K.T.). Home: 221 E McKenzie Rd Greenfield IN 46140 Office: Box 399 Greenfield IN 46140

GNAEDINGER, JOHN PHILLIP, civil engr.; b. Oak Park, Ill., Jan. 11, 1926; s. Robert Joseph and Edna (Metz) G.; B.S., Cornell U., 1946; M.S., Northwestern U., 1947; m. Elizabeth Williams, March 15, 1956; children—John Phillip, Sarah Elizabeth. Structural designer Shaw Metz & Dolio, 1946-48; founder, 1948, since pres. Soil Testing Services, Inc., Chgo. Past chmn. bldg. research adv. bd. Nat. Acad. Sci.-NRC; mem. senate Monmouth Coll. Registered structural engr., Ill., profl. engr., Ind., N.Y. Iowa, Wis., Conn., Calif., Va., Ky. Mem. Western Soc. Engrs. (past pres.), ASCE, Young Pres.'s Orgn., ASTM, Ill. Engring. Council (past pres.), Asso. Soil and Found. Engrs. Inc. (past pres.), Hwy. Research Bd., Cornell Soc. Engrs. Chgo. (past pres.), Nat. Small Bus. Assn., Fed. Constrn. Council (past chmn.), Sigma Xi, Tau Beta Pi, Sigma Chi. Clubs: Cornell (past pres.), University (Chgo.); Exmoor Country. Home: 160 Sheridan Rd Kenilworth IL 60043 Office: PO Box 266 Northbrook IL 60026

GNAT, RAYMOND EARL, librarian; b. Milw., Jan. 15, 1932; s. John and Emily (Syperko) G.; B.B.A., U. Wis., 1954, postgrad. 1959; M.S., U. Ill., 1958; m. Jean Helen Monday, June 19, 1954; children—Cynthia, Barbara, Richard. Page, Milw. Pub. Library, 1950-53, jr. librarian, 1954, librarian, 1958-63; circulation asst. U. Ill., 1956-57, serials cataloger, 1957-58; asst. dir. Indpls.-Marion County Pub. Library, 1963-71, dir., 1972—. Exec. dir. Ind. Nat. Library Week, 1965. Served with AUS, 1954-56. Mem. Am., Ind. library assns., Bibliog. Soc. Am., Greater Indpls. Info., Inc., Indpls. Adult Edn. Council. Club: Literary. Home: 8246 Shadow Circle Indianapolis IN 46260 Office: 40 E St Clair St Indianapolis IN 46204

GNEZDA, MARY ANTONIA MERULLO (MRS. WALTER F. GNEZDA), educator; b. Columbus, Ohio, Sept. 5, 1926; d. Fortunato and Susie (Verrilli) Merullo; B.A., Ohio Wesleyan U., 1948; M.A., Ohio State U., 1966, Ph.D. in Edn., 1972; m. Walter F. Gnezda, Mar. 29, 1951; children—Nicole Marie, M. Therese, Eric Walter. Sec. to jr. dean Ohio State U. Coll. Commerce, 1948-50; tchr. Columbus Acad. for Boys, 1950-51; remedial reading tchr. Benjamin Center, 1956-57; head tchr. four year kindergarten N. Broadway Meth. Ch., 1960-62; librarian Columbus Sch. for Girls, 1962-63, tchr., guidance counselor, 1963-66; guidance counselor Manpower Devel. Tng. Act, 1966-67; teaching asso. humanities edn. Ohio State U., Columbus, 1967-73, asst. prof. Coll. Dentistry, 1973-76, asso. prof., 1976—, asst dean and dir. ednl. services and research, 1976—. Mem. Worthington (Ohio) Kindergarten Study Group, 1957; mem. parent council U. Sch., 1956-67, chmn., program chmn., 1961-62; mem. P.T.A., 1965—, v.p. Worthington High Sch., 1968-69, chmn. welfare and legislation Worthington Middle Sch., 1969-70. Mem. Multiple Sclerosis Key, 1959-61, Child Conservation League, 1957-65. Mem. Am. Personnel and Guidance Assn., Am. Sch. Counselors Assn., Am. Assn. Dental Schs., Nat. Council Tchrs. English, Pi Lambda Theta, Phi Delta Kappa. Home: 218 Longfellow Ave Worthington OH 43085

GOBRECHT, HARRY DANA, mfg. co. exec.; b. Waukegan, Ill., Sept. 25, 1924; s. Edwin R. and Ruth (Parmenter) G.; A.A., Pasadena Jr. Coll., 1946; B.S., U. So. Calif., 1948; m. Barbara Jean Goertz, June 13, 1948; children—Thomas D., Sandra J., Richard K., Debra J. Asst. Western traffic mgr. U.S. Gypsum Co., Los Angeles, 1948-57, asst. to v.p., Chgo., 1957-63, asst. gen. traffic mgr., 1963-66, gen. traffic mgr., 1966, gen. mgr. transp. and phys. distbn., 1966-73, dir. transp. and phys. distbn., 1973-77, v.p. transp. and phys. distbn., 1977—. Dist. chmn. Boy Scouts Am., 1967—. Served with USAAF, 1942-46. Recipient Silver Beaver award Boy Scouts Am. Mem. Nat. Indsl. Traffic League, Am. Soc. Traffic and Transp. (Ill. pres. 1965), Assn. I.C.C. Practitioners, Nat. Freight Traffic Assn. Republican. Presbyterian. Clubs: Union League, Traffic (Chgo). Home: 704 N Russel St Mount Prospect IL 60054 Office: 101 S Wacker Dr Chicago IL 60606

GODING, CHARLES ARTHUR, chem. co. exec.; b. Aurora, Ill., Aug. 13, 1934; s. Arthur Walter and Lillian (Berg) G.; B.A., U. Ill., 1956; grad. with honors Inst. Advanced Advt. Studies, 1965; m. Corrine Doris Dau, Aug. 31, 1957; children—Charles Arthur, Craig Jon, Cynthia Lynn. Copywriter J. Walter Thompson Co., Chgo., 1956-61, Campbell-Mithun Inc., Chgo., 1961-64; account exec., supr. Marsteller Inc., Chgo., 1964-70; dir. advt. Nalco Chem. Co., Chgo./Oak Brook, Ill., 1970—. Task force com. Sch. Dist. 205, 1975—; active Jr. Achievement, Boy Scouts Am. Mem. Bus. Profl. Advt. Assn. (life, pres. Chgo. chpt. 1975-76), Delta Upsilon. Republican. Lutheran. Home: 259 Cottage Hill Elmhurst IL 60126

GODLEWSKI, MICHAEL PATRICK, physicist; b. Detroit, Oct. 9, 1938; s. Michael Stephen and Anna Katherine (Bush) G.; B.S., U. Detroit, 1960, M.S., 1964; m. Carol Anne Sowa, July 20, 1963; children—Kathleen, Jennifer, Michael. Aerospace technologist NASA, Lewis Research Center, Cleve., 1962-64, nuclear engr., 1964-68, physicist, 1968—. Recipient Cleve. Fed. Exec. Bd. Personal Merit award, 1974. Mem. Am. Phys. Soc., IEEE (sr. mem.), AAAS, Sigma Pi Sigma. Contbr. articles to profl. jours., co-editor IEEE-Electron Devices spl. pub., 1977. Home: 337 Kraft St Berea OH 44017 Office: 21000 Brookpark Rd Cleveland OH 44135

GODWIN, WILLIAM COLIN, dentist, educator; b. Welland, Ont., Can., Jan. 28, 1922; s. Lloyd Stafford and Effie (Milloy) G.; came to U.S., 1924, naturalized, 1942; student Wayne State U., 1940-42; D.D.S., U. Mich., 1951, M.S., 1954; m. Lois Elizabeth Walker, Feb. 14, 1944; children—David, Robert, Carl, Christopher. Pvt. practice dentistry, Ann Arbor, Mich., 1951—; clin. instr. U. Mich., Ann Arbor, 1951-55, asso. prof. dentistry, 1955-63, asso. prof., 1963-71, prof., 1971—, chmn. athletic dentistry, 1962—. Mem. Am., Med. Com. on Athletic Medicine for Washtenaw County, Ann Arbor, Mich., 1970—; mem. curriculum com. Washtenaw Community Coll., Ann Arbor, 1970—. Bd. dir. Ann Arbor (Mich.) Amateur Hockey Assn., 1967-69. Served to 1st lt. USAAC, 1942-45. Decorated Purple Heart, Air medal. Recipient Govs. trophy for med. scis. State of Mich., 1962. Mem. Am., Mich. (mem. mouth guard com. 1964-67) dental assns., Washtenaw Dist. Dental Soc., Richard H. Kingery Prosthetic Group, Omicron Kappa Upsilon. Cons. editor: Jour. Am. Dental Assn., 1965—. Home: 1205 Country Club Rd Ann Arbor MI 48105 Office: 1110 Henry St Ann Arbor MI 48104

GOEBEL, MARISTELLA, educator; b. Racine, Wis., Sept. 10, 1915; d. James Nicholas and Henrietta Marie (Rademacher) Goebel; B.S., Edgewood Coll., 1944; M.A., Cath. U. Am., 1947, Ph.D., 1966. Entered Order Dominican Sisters, Roman Catholic Ch., 1933; tchr. English, Cathedral High Sch., Sioux Falls, S.D., 1946-47, Heart of Mary High Sch., Mobile, Ala., 1947-49; asso. prof. Rosary Coll., River Forest, Ill., 1949—, chmn. dept. psychology, 1968—. Psychol. cons. Dominican Motherhouse, Sinsinawa, Wis., 1966—; clin. psychologist, researcher on biofeedback and relaxation Hines (Ill.) VA Hosp., 1970—. NIMH grantee, 1962-63, 66; Cath. U. Am. scholar, 1962. Mem. Am., Wis. psychol. assns., AAAS, Ill. Psychol. Assn. (sec.-treas. 1973-75), Ill. Assn. for Student Teaching (pres. 1960-61), Psychologists Interested in Religious Issues, Am. Assn. Biofeedback Clinicians, Biofeedback Soc. Ill. Editor Teacher's Guides, 9 vols., 1948-51. Home: 7900 W Division St River Forest IL 60305

GOELLER, CARL GILBERT, JR., greeting card co. exec.; b. Wichita, Kans., May 20, 1930; s. Carl Gilbert and Sarah Elizabeth (Nothstine) G.; A.B., U. Wichita, 1951, postgrad., 1960-61; m. Kay Branson, June 9, 1951; children—Sheila (Mrs. Richard Engelhardt), Ben D. Mng. editor Hallmark Cards, Kansas City, Mo., 1953-61; editor in chief Rust Craft Cards, Dedham, Mass., 1961-64, research dir., 1962-66, market devel. mgr., 1964-66, dir. advt. and sales promotion, 1966-68; pres. SPV & P, Inc., Tauton, Mass., 1964-71; editorial dir, research dir. Am. Greetings Corp., Bay Village, Ohio, 1968—; editorial cons. Paramount Cards, 1968. Served to 1st lt., AUS, 1951-53. Recipient Mens Honor Five, U. Wichita, 1951. Author: Selling Poetry, Verse & Prose, 1962; You're a Once in a Lifetime Friend, 1970; A Dynamic Personality, 1971; Writing to Communicate, 1972. Home: 30200 Ashton Ln Bay Village OH 44140 Office: 1300 W 78th St Cleveland OH 44102

GOERGEN, DONALD JOSEPH, priest, educator; b. Remsen, Iowa, Aug. 16, 1943; s. Julius Frank and Sylvia Madelaine (Wilhelmi) G.; B.A., Loras Coll., 1965; M.A., Aquinas Inst., 1965, Ph.D., 1972. Ordained priest, Roman Catholic Ch., 1975; researcher dept. religion and psychiatry Menninger Found., Topeka, 1969-70; chaplain Kans. Neurol. Inst., Topeka, 1969-70; prof. systematic theology Aquinas Inst., Dubuque, Iowa, 1971—, dir. M.A. program, 1973—, acting dir. Ph.D. programs, 1975-76; regent of studies Dominican Province of St. Albert the Great, Roman Cath. Ch., 1975—. Mem. Am. Teilhard Assn., Am. Acad. Religion, Cath. Theol. Soc. Am. Author: The Sexual Celibate, 1975. Address: 2570 Asbury St Dubuque IA 52001

GOERING, JOSEPH WILSON, banker; b. Galva, Kans., Sept. 22, 1916; s. Jacob M. and Anna J. (Graber) G.; A.B., Bethel Coll., 1939; postgrad. U. Kans., 1939-40; m. Lovella June Schneider, Nov. 16, 1940; children—Patricia (Mrs. Bill D. Smith), Joseph Ward, Joyce Eileen (Mrs. Christopher Saricks). Pres. Moundridge Motors (Kans.), 1940-49; owner Joe Goering Chevrolet Co., Moundridge, 1949-62; pres., chmn. bd. Citizen State Bank, Moundridge, 1962—; farmer, Moundridge, 1939-69; pres. Moundridge Telephone Co., Ami, Inc., Citizens Enterprise, Inc., Gringoe, Inc. (all Moundridge). Mem. Moundridge High Sch. Bd. Edn., 1958-65, chmn., 1959-65; bd. dirs. Moundridge Indsl. Devel.; chmn. bldg. com. Mercy Hosp., 1967-68. Served to ensign USNR, 1944-45. Named McPherson County Agrl. Key Banker, Kans. Bankers Assn., 1970, 73. Mem. Kans. Bankers Assn. (mem. agrl. com. 1970-71), Am. Legion. Democrat. Methodist (Kans. West conf. bd. trustees 1968—, local finance chmn. 1969-72). Elk, Lion. Home: Box 470 Moundridge KS 67107 Office: Citizens State Bank Box 110 Moundridge KS 67107

GOETTIG, RAYMOND JOHN, accountant; b. Fulda, Minn., Mar. 9, 1927; s. John Henry and Marie Agnes (Brown) G.; Accountant, LaSalle Extension U., 1963; m. Doris Catherine Platz, Oct. 29, 1947; children—Gwyn (Mrs. Scott Erickson), Mary (Mrs. John Murphy), Ruth. Master mechanic, custom flooring, design and installation Rehkamp Furniture, Marshall, Minn., 1947-52; self-employed as pub. and tax accountant, Sleepy Eye, Minn., 1957—. City treas. Sleepy Eye, Minn., 1961-71. Served with AUS, 1946-47. Mem. Nat. Assn. Enrolled Agts. (nat. treas. 1973-75, dir. 1976-78), Nat. Soc. Pub. Accountants, Nat. Fedn. Ind. Bus., Nat. Adv. Council, Am. Legion, Minn. Assn. Pub. Accountants. K.C., Eagle, Lion. Home: 628 2d Ave NE Sleepy Eye MN 56085 Office: 104 W Main St Sleepy Eye MN 56085

GOETZ, LARRY WILLIAM, physician; b. Mayview, Mo., Feb 3, 1936; s. Leander Daniel and Minnie Evaline (Starke) G.; B.A., Mo. U., 1958; M.D., Kans. U., 1962; m. Patricia Louise Vahrenberg, June 6, 1959; children—Devon Daniel, Dana Cecile, Lauren Elizabeth, Lance Leander. Intern Martin Army Hosp., Fort Benning, Ga., 1962-63; practice medicine, Creston, Iowa, 1965—; v.p. Creston Med. Clinic, P.C., 1973—; mem. staff Greater Community Hosp., Creston. Dir. Blue Shield Bd. Iowa Med. explorer adviser Boy Scouts Am., Creston, 1965-67; mem. Union County Bd. Health, 1968-77. Bd. dirs. Creston Community Sch. Dist., 1969-75, Crossroads Mental Health Clinic, Union County, Rural Health Services, Bloomfield, Iowa. Served to capt. AUS, 1962-65. Diplomate Am. Bd. Family Practice. Mem. AMA, Iowa Acad. Family Practice (mem. cancer com. 1969—), Union County Med. Soc., Creston C. of C., Sigma Chi. Mem. United Ch. of Christ. Clubs: Crestmoor Golf (pres. 1968-69), Elk's, Union Investment. Home: Rural Route 3 Creston IA 50801 Office: 526 New York Ave Creston IA 50801

GOETZ, PETER HENRY, artist; b. Slavgorod, Siberia, Sept. 8, 1917; s. Henry Peter and Justina Yvonovna (Friesen) G.; Fine Art Degree, Waterloo Coll., 1943; postgrad. Doon Sch. Fine Art, 1944-46; m. Helena Warkentin, Aug. 9, 1941; children—Jean Margot Hoover, Peter Andrew, Exhibited in one-man shows: Kitchener-Waterloo Gallery, 1946—, Shaw-Rimmington Gallery, Toronto, Ont., Can., Hamilton Art Gallery, London (Ont., Can.) Gallery, Windsor Art Gallery, Sarnia Art Gallery; group shows: Royal Canadian Acad., Ont. Soc. Artists, Canadian Soc. Painters in Water Colour, Soc. Canadian Artists; lectr. fine art, Ont. Mem. Ont. Soc. Artists, Can. Soc. Painters Water Colours, Soc. Can. Artists, Internat. Platform Assn., Am. Fedn. Art, Centro Studi E Scambi Internazionali. Fellow Internat. Inst. Arts Letters. Home, office: 784 Avondale Ave Kitchener ON N2M 2W8 Canada

GOETZ, ROBERT EUGENE, landscape architect; b. St. Louis, Sept. 10, 1922; s. Otto Emil and Alice (Stone) G.; B.S., U. Ill., 1947; m. Pauline Edwards, Nov. 23, 1944; children—Gail (Mrs. Ted Meiling), Gary, Ronald. Landscape architect O.E. Goetz Nursery, Crestwood, Mo., 1947-56; owner, prin. Robert F. Goetz & Assos., Webster Groves, Mo., 1956—. Chmn. planning com. Coalition for the Environment, St. Louis region, 1970—; pres. Open Space Council, St. Louis region, 1973-75; mem. tech. adv. and rev. com. St. Louis County Planning Commn., 1975—. Served with AUS, 1943-46. Recipient award for excellence Nat. Swimming Pool Assn., 1969, Commendation award Am. Soc. Landscape Architects, 1969; Citizen Conservationist award Ozark chpt. Sierra Club, 1974. Mem. Am. Soc. Landscape Architects (pres. St. Louis sect. 1965-66), Mo. Assn. Landscape Architects, Phi Beta Kappa. Home: 909 S Gore St Webster Groves MO 63119 Office: 34 N Gore St Webster Groves MO 63119

GOETZMAN, BRUCE EDGAR, architect; b. Rochester, N.Y., June 6, 1931; s. Benjamin Byron and Ila Belle (Flowers) G.; B.Arch., Carnegie Mellon U., 1954; M.S., Columbia, 1956; M.Community Planning, U. Cin., 1965; m. June Grady McRae, June 25, 1955; children—Adam Britt, Ben Evan. Asso. prof. architecture U. Cin., 1959—; prin. architect Goetzman & Follmer, architects and planners, Cin., 1965—. Vice-chmn. Cin. Archtl. Rev. Bd., 1967—; chmn. Ohio Historic Site Preservation Adv. Bd., 1972-77; chmn. environ. design panel Ohio Arts Council, 1969-73; v.p. Better Housing League Cin., 1975—; mem. exec. com. Miami Purchase Assn., 1973—. Served with AUS, 1956-58. Mem. AIA, Architects Soc. Ohio (dir. 1974—). Home: 187 Greendale Ave Cincinnati OH 45219 Office: 2606 Vine St Cincinnati OH 45219

GOFF, STEPHEN CHARLES, retail trade exec.; b. St. Paul, Sept. 21, 1945; s. Stillman Reese and Marion Emma (Zinsmeister) F.; B.S., Bradley U., 1967; M.S., No. Ill. U., 1967-69; m. Donna Jean Domnick, Mar. 9, 1969; children—Dale, Donald. Grad. resident adv. No. Ill. U., DeKalb, 1968-69; cons. Thorolf Gregerson A/S, Oslo, Norway, 1968; market research dir., planner Nash Finch Co., retail trade, St. Louis Park, Minn., 1969—; guest lectr. U. Minn., Ohio State U. Adv. HELP, minority bus. cons., St. Paul Model Cities, 1971-73; faculty Met. State U., 1975. Pres., Social Innovations, Golden Valley, Minn., 1971—; pres. Bldg. Block Nursery Sch. and Day Care Center, Mpls., 1971—. Del. local precinct Republican Party, 1972. Mem. Am. Mktg. Assn. (nat. minority bus. assistance com.), North Central Corp. Planning Soc., Nat. Assn. Edn. Young Children, Minn. Minority Bus. Cons., Food Mktg. Inst. (adv. bd.), Food Distbn. Research Soc., Day Care and Child Devel. Council Am., Greater Mpls. Day Care Assn., Greater St. Paul Council Coordinated Child Care, Minn. Assn. Edn. Young Children, Minn. Jr. C. of C. (state dir. drug edn. 1971-72), Golden Valley Jr. C. of C., Minn. Wine Tasting Soc. (pres. 1973), Sigma Chi. Author: Computerized Food Shopping, 1974; Super Marketing in Japan, 1977. Home: 1820 Du Pont Ave S Minneapolis MN 55403 Office: 3381 Gorham Ave St Louis Park MN 55426

GOGATE, ANAND BALKRISHNA, cons. engr.; b. Rangoon, Burma, Jan. 28, 1935; s. B.S. and Sushila B. (Phadke) G.; came to U.S., 1962, naturalized, 1970; B.E., U. Poona, 1958; M.S., U. Iowa, 1963; Ph.D., Ohio State U., 1977; m. Shashi Gogate, June 20, 1962; children—Gita, Soniya, Sanjay. Engr., Koyna project, Hindustan Contrn. Co., India, 1958-59; asst. engr. Municipal Corp. of Delhi, India, 1959-62; design engr. Peterson & Appel Engrs., Des Moines, 1963-65; chief structural engr. A.E. Stilson & Assos., Columbus, Ohio, 1967-72, Elgar Brown Engrs., Worthington, Ohio, 1972—. Fellow ASCE (State of the Art award 1974, Raymond C. Reese award 1976); mem. Am. Concrete Inst. Hindu. Home: 6112 Sedgewick Rd Worthington OH 43085

GOGATE, SHASHIKALA A., pathologist, lab. dir., educator; b. Indore, India, July 9, 1938; d. Kashinath M. and Manorama K. Ranade; came to U.S., 1963, naturalized, 1973; M.B.B.S., M.D., Mahtma Gandhi Med. Coll., Indore, 1962; M.S. in Pathology, Ohio State U., 1969; m. Anand B. Gogate, June 20, 1962; children—Sangita, Soniya, Sanjay. Resident in pathology Ohio State U. Hosp., Columbus, 1967-69, instr., research asso. dept. pathology, 1971-72, asst. prof. dept. pathology Ohio State U., 1972-75, clin. asst. prof., 1975—; dir. Columbus (Ohio) Pathology Labs., 1975—; chief pathologist Lancaster-Fairfield County (Ohio) Hosp., 1976—. Mem. local adv. bd. Internat. Meditation Soc. Center, 1976—, recipient award, 1976. Fellow Coll. Am. Pathologists. Hindu religion. Contbr.

articles to med. jours. Home: 6112 Sedgwick Rd Worthington OH 43085 Office: 5212 W Broad St Columbus OH 43228

GOGGIN, JOHN EDWARD, county ofcl.; b. Chgo., Oct. 20, 1923; s. John Patrick and Sara (McCabe) G.; student U. Ill., 1941-42, DePaul U., 1946-47; B.S.C., Chgo. Kent Coll. Law, 1953; m. Helen Marie McSweeney, Dec. 29, 1945; children—John, Michael, Terrence, Brian, Kevin, Trudi, Daniel. Personal bailiff to judge municipal ct., 1946-53; ins. broker, Chgo., 1950—; pub. relations mgr. Gen. Outdoor Advt., Chgo., 1953-56, regional dir., 1956-64; asso. clk. law div. Circuit Ct. Cook County, Ill., 1965—; sec. GHJ Transport Co., 1956-60. Cons. advt. and pub. relations Cook County Democratic Central Com., 1965-72. Mem. pres. council St. Xavier's Coll. Trustee Ill. Benedictine Coll. Served to capt., AUS, 1943-46; CBI. Decorated Bronze Star with cluster Combat Infantry Badge; comdr. Order St. Lazarus. Mem. Inf. Assn., Mil. Order World Wars, Ill. Mfrs. Assn., Ill. Assn. Commerce, Chgo. Assn. Commerce and Industry (com. chmn. 1956-61), Chgo. Athletic Assn., Am. Legion, Alpha Delta Phi, Phi Delta Theta. Clubs: K.C., Federated Advertising (Chgo). Home: 7700 Augusta St River Forest IL 60305 Office: Daley Center Chicago IL 60602

GOHIL, JIVANLAL, psychiatrist; b. Khambhalia, India, July 9, 1934; s. Pushottam R. and Jivibai P. (Parmar) G.; came to U.S., 1963, naturalized, 1976; B.Sc., Elphinstone Coll., Bombay U., 1956; M.D., Topiwala Nat. Med. Coll., Bombay U., 1963; m. Kusum N. Shah, Aug. 28, 1960. Rotating intern Meml. Hosp., Pawtucket, R.I., 1964; resident in psychiatry Inst. Mental Health, Howard, R.I., 1965-66; practice medicine specializing in psychiatry, Marion, Ind., 1976—; staff psychiatrist S.C. State Hosp., Columbia, 1970-73; clinic dir. Mid-Mo. Mental Health Center, Columbia, 1973-76; asst. prof. psychiatry U. Mo., Columbia, 1974-76; exec. dir., med. dir. G.B. Mental Health Center, Marion, 1976-77; cons. psychiatry Regional Mental Health Center, Kokomo, Ind., 1977—. Mem. Am. Psychiat. Assn., Am. Acad. Psychiatry and Law, AMA, Howard County Med. Soc., Ind. State Med. Assn. Home: 1909 Hawthorne Rd Marion IN 46952 Office: 505 Wabash Ave Marion IN 46952

GOLD, IKE, internat. union ofcl.; b. Russia, Apr. 25, 1912 (parents Am. citizens); s. Louis and Rose (Shainsky) G.; student U. Akron; m. Gertrude Glass, Aug. 1, 1937; children—Larry, Harvey. Propr. used-automobile firm to 1942; maintenance, constrn. welder Firestone Tire & Rubber Co., Akron, Ohio, 1942; with United Rubber Workers Am., 1942—, successively union committeeman, divisional chmn., v.p., pres. local union, 1942-60, internat. sec.-treas., 1960—; sec.-treas. Rubber, Cork, Linoleum and Plastic Workers Am. Sec. treas., com. Nat. AFL-CIO; operating com. Com. on Polit. Edn., administrv. com. Mem. exec. bd. Akron Area exec. council Boy Scouts Am.; mem. exec. bd. Akron Jewish Center; bd. dirs. U. Akron, Mental Retardation; trustee, mem. labor ops. com. United Fund; trustee, mem. exec. com. Akron NAACP; trustee United Community Council. Mem. Nat. Planning Assn. (nat. council), Nat. Trade Union Council for Human Rights, Nat. Platform Assn. Mem. B'nai B'rith. Home: 350 Crestview Ave Akron OH 44320 Office: 87 S High St Akron OH 44308

GOLDBERG, A. STUART, real estate broker; b. Lincoln, Nebr., Oct. 29, 1924; s. Harry and Rose (Gordon) G.; A.B., U. Nebr., 1946, M.A., 1947; m. Marilyn Adler, Aug. 20, 1946; 1 dau., Linda L. Instr. Bradley U., Peoria, Ill., 1947-48; owner Univ. Drug Sundries, Lincoln, 1951-54; realtor Loomis & Hoyt, Lincoln, 1955-65, Anderson, Goldberg, Hein & Pershing, Lincoln, 1965-68; real estate broker Gateway Realty, Inc., Lincoln, 1968—; real estate appraiser State of Nebr., 1974—. Class agt. U. Nebr. Found., 1948—; mem. U. Nebr. Alumni Council, 1975—. Served with AUS, 1943. Mem. Lincoln Bd. Realtors (dir. 1965-67), Nebr. Real Estate Assn., Nat. Assn. Real Estate Bds., Am. Legion, Nebr. Art Assn., Zeta Beta Tau. Elk; mem. B'nai B'rith. Jewish. Clubs: Cornhusker Kennel (dir. 1964), University. Author: Augustus Ford Harvey, 1856-1871, 1947. Home: 2814 Winthrop Rd Lincoln NE 68502 Office: 6211 O St Lincoln NE 68510

GOLDBERG, ARNOLD IRVING, psychoanalyst; b. Chgo., May 21, 1929; s. Morris Henry and Rose (Auerbach) G.; B.S., U. Ill., 1949, M.D., 1953; m. Constance Pendleton Obenhaus, Apr. 22, 1972; 1 son, Andrew. Intern, Cin. Gen. Hosp., 1953-54; resident psychiatry Michael Reese Hosp., Chgo., 1957-59; pvt. practice psychoanalysis Chgo., 1959—; asso. Northwestern U. Med. Sch., Chgo., 1961-65; clin. asso. prof. U. Chgo., 1971—; faculty Chgo. Inst. Psychoanalysis, 1963—; cons. in field. Served to capt. AUS, 1957-59. Recipient Fleming award teaching excellence, 1973. Fellow Am. Psychiat. Assn.; mem. Chgo. Soc. Adolescent Psychiatry (pres. 1973-74), Am. Psychoanalytic Assn., Am. Soc. Adolescent Psychiatry, Phi Beta Kappa, Phi Kappa Phi, Alpha Omega Alpha. Author: Models of the Mind. Contbr. articles and book revs. to profl. publs. Home: 844 Chalmers Chicago IL 60614 Office: 180 N Michigan Ave Chicago IL 60602

GOLDBERG, DAVID JAIME, psychiatrist, educator; b. Buenos Aires, Argentina, Mar. 8, 1941; s. Herschel and Maria H. (Fizbin) G.; came to U.S., 1968; B.S., Esteban Etcheverria (Argentina), 1959; M.D., U. Buenos Aires, 1966; m. Martha Haydee Kagel, Oct. 18, 1968; children—Corinne Leilani, Nisse Aloma. Pvt. practice medicine, Buenos Aires, Argentina, 1966-68; intern, Kuakini Hosp., Honolulu, 1969; resident in psychiatry U. Hawaii, Honolulu, 1970-72, chief resident, 1971; staff psychiatrist Aiea Clinic, Hawaii Dept. Health, 1973-74; clin. teaching asst. psychiatry U. Hawaii Sch. Medicine, Honolulu, 1971-73; psychiatric cons. Leeward and Wahiawa Gen. Hosps., Aiea, 1973-74; asst. prof. psychiatry U. Nebr. Coll. Medicine, Omaha, 1974—. Recipient Physician's Recognition award Am. Med. Assn., 1972. Mem. Am. Psychiat. Assn., Sioux Psychiat. Soc., Assn. for Acad. Psychiatry, Omaha Mid-West Clin. Soc. Home: 2410 S 102nd St Omaha NE 68124 Office: 8300 Dodge St Omaha NE 68114

GOLDBERG, DAVID PHILLIP, physician; b. Chgo., Nov. 16, 1939; s. David Charles and Hazel Esther (Gottstein) G.; B.A., Northwestern U., 1961; M.D., Chgo. Med. Sch., 1965; m. Patricia Ann Full, Sept. 23, 1972; children—Robert Jay, Cary Trent. Intern, Michael Reese Hosp., Chgo., 1965-66, fellow in nuclear medicine, 1967-68, resident in radiology, 1968-71; staff radiologist Englewood Hosp., Chgo., 1971—, dir. nuclear medicine, 1971—; staff radiology, dir. med. ednl. Palos Community Hosp., Palos Heights, Ill., 1972—, dir. nuclear medicine, 1972—; asso. prof., med. dir. radiologic technology program Moraine Valley Community Coll., Palos Hills, 1973—. Mem. Chgo., Ill. med. socs., AMA, Inst. Medicine, Am. Coll. Radiology, Am. Coll. Nuclear Medicine, Soc. Nuclear Medicine, Phi Delta Epsilon, Palos C. of C. (v.p. 1975-77). Home: 16201 S 118th Ave Orland Park IL 60462 Office: 123d & 80th Ave Palos Heights IL 60463

GOLDBERG, ELLIOTT MARSHALL, physician; b. N. Adams, Mass., Dec. 18, 1930; s. Jack and Ida (Lenhoff) G.; A.B. with high honors, U. Rochester (N.Y.), 1952; M.D., Tufts U., Medford, Mass., 1956; m. Darlis Nell Ray, Apr. 17, 1966; children—Brett, Carey, Sandra, Jeffrey, Dara. Intern, D.C. Gen. Hosp., 1956-57; resident in internal medicine Meml. Worcester, Mass., 1960-61, Univ. Hosps., Madison, Wis., 1962-63; practice medicine specializing in internal medicine, Flint, Mich., 1965—; mem. staff, chief medicine Hurley Hosp; chief medicine Hurley Hosp.; prof. medicine Mich. State Coll. Human Medicine. Bd. dirs: Medgar Evers Found. Served to capt. M.C., AUS, 1957-59. Endocrine fellow U. Wis., 1961-62; NIH fellow, 1963-64; recipient Outstanding Tchr. award Mich. State U., 1972-73; Humanitarian award NAACP, 1974. Diplomate Am. Bd. Internal Medicine. Fellow A.C.P.; asso. Royal Coll. Surgeons; mem. Endocrine Soc., Am. Fed. Clin. Research, Am. Diabetes Assn., Mass., Mich., Genesee County med. socs., Mich. Assn. Med. Edn. (pres. 1972-75). Author: (novels) The Karamanov Equations, 1972; The Anatomy Lesson, 1974; also med. papers. Book editor Physicians Radio Network, 1972—. Home: 2151 Crestline Dr Burton MI 48509 Office: Hurley Medical Center Flint MI 48502

GOLDBERG, HENRY MORRIS, physician, surgeon; b. Milw., July 7, 1936; s. Nat J. and Shirley B. (Rozran) G.; B.S., Marquette U., Milw., 1958, M.D., 1962; m. Iris Greenberg, June 23, 1963; children—Kenneth, Peter. Intern, Kings County Hosp., Bklyn.; resident in combined surg. residency program Marquette U., 1963-64; gen. practice family medicine and surgery, Milw., 1964-67, 70—; bd. dirs. Med. Coll. Wis. Served to maj. M.C. U.S. Army, 1967-69. Fellow Royal Soc. Health; mem. Wis. Acad. Family Practice (pres. SE chpt.), AMA (Continuing Edn. award). Home: 3405 N Lake Dr Milwaukee WI 53211

GOLDBERG, ISADORE EDWARD, physician; b. N.Y.C., Sept. 8, 1905; s. Julius and Reva Rose (Duscoff) G.; student N.Y. U., 1924-26, Columbia, 1926; M.D., U. Kans., 1930. Intern, Jewish Hosp. of St. Louis, 1930-31; dispensary resident U. Kans. Med. Center, Kansas City, 1931; practice of medicine, Polo, Mo., 1931-41, Braymer, Mo., 1947—; mem. staffs Menorah Med. Center, Kansas City, Mo. Served to maj. M.C., AUS, 1941-46. Decorated Silver Star medal, Bronze Star medal, Purple Heart with two oak leaf clusters. Mem. A.M.A., Mo. Med. Assn., A.A.A.S., So. Med. Assn., Am. Acad. Family Practice, Alpha Omega Alpha. Mason, Rotarian. Home: Braymer MO 64624 Office: Braymer Clinic Braymer MO 64624

GOLDBERG, SAMUEL IRVING, educator; b. Toronto, Ont., Can., Aug. 15, 1923; s. Jacob L. and Rachel (Berkovitz) G.; B.A., U. Toronto, 1948, M.A., 1949, Ph.D., 1951; student Cambridge (Eng.) U., 1945-46; m. Sheila Richmond, Nov. 11, 1951; children—Julia Anna, Barry Howard, Jay Michael. Research officer Def. Research Bd., Valcartier, Que., Can., 1951-52; asst. prof. math. Lehigh U., Bethlehem, Pa., 1952-55; asso. prof. Wayne State U., Detroit, 1955-61; asso. prof. U. Ill., Urbana, 1960-65, prof., 1965—. Served with Canadian Army, 1943-46. Sci. Research Council vis. fgn. scientist U. Liverpool (Eng.), 1973; Harvard research fellow, 1959-60. Mem. Am. Math. Soc. Jewish. Club: B'nai B'rith. Author: Curvature and Homology, 1962; (with R.L. Bishop), Tensor Analysis on Manifolds, 1968; (with W.C. Weber) Conformal Deformations of Riemannian Manifolds, 1969. Home: 24 Greencroft Dr Champaign IL 61820 Office: Dept Math U Ill Urbana IL 61801

GOLDBERGER, ARTHUR EARL, JR., indsl. engr.; b. El Paso, Tex., Sept. 2, 1950; s. Arthur Earl and Mary Ann (Hobbs) G.; B.S. in Systems Engring., U. Ariz., 1974, B.S. in Indsl. Engring., 1974; M.S. in Indsl. Engring., Tex. A. and M. U., 1977. Gen. engr., researcher Intern Tng. Center, Red River Army Depot, Devel. and Readiness Command, U.S. Army, Texarkana, Tex., 1975-76, gen. engr. Aviation Systems Command, St. Louis, 1976—. Chmn., Jr. Republican Club, Tucson, 1969, active in campaigns, 1969, 72. Recipient Service award Ariz. Student Union Assn., 1971. Mem. Nat., Tex., Mo. socs. profl. engrs., Am. Inst. Indsl. Engrs., Am. Soc. Quality Control, Engrs. Club St. Louis, Jr. C. of C., Alpha Pi Mu, Theta Tau. Lutheran. Home: 334 Avant Dr Hazelwood MO 63042 Office: USA AVSCOM DRSAV-PUEB PO Box 209 St Louis MO 63166

GOLDBERGER, ARTHUR STANLEY, educator; b. N.Y.C., Nov. 20, 1930; s. David M. and Martha (Greenwald) G.; B.S., N.Y. U., 1951; M.A., U. Mich., 1952, Ph.D, 1958; m. Iefke Engelsman, Aug. 19, 1957; children—Nina Judith, Nicholas Bernard. Acting asst. prof. econs. Stanford, 1956-59; asso. prof. econs. U. Wis., 1960-63, prof., 1963-70, H.M. Groves prof., 1970—; vis. prof. Center Planning and Econ. Research, Athens, Greece, 1964-65; Keynes vis. prof. U. Essex, 1968-69. Fulbright fellow Netherlands Sch. Econs., 1955-56, 59-60; vis. prof. U. Hawaii, 1969, 71. Guggenheim fellow Stanford U., 1972-73; Center for Advanced Study in Behavioral Scis. fellow, 1976-77. Fellow Am. Statis. Assn., Econometric Soc. (council 1975—), Am. Acad. Arts and Scis.; mem. Am. Econ. Assn. Author: (with L. R. Klein) An Econometric Model of the United States, 1929-52, 1955; Impact Multipliers and Dynamic Properties, 1959; Econometric Theory, 1964; Topics in Regression Analysis, 1968. Editor: (with O.D. Duncan) Structural Equation Models in the Social Sciences, 1973; (with D.J. Aigner) Latent Variables in Socio-economic Models, 1977. Asso. editor Jour. Econometrics, 1973-77; bd. editors Jour. Econ. Lit., 1975—. Home: 2828 Sylvan Ave Madison WI 53705 Office: U Wis Dept Econs Madison WI 53706

GOLDBERGER, DAVID ALAN, lawyer; b. Chgo., July 13, 1941; s. Melvin A. and Sarah (Hazan) G.; student U. Ill., 1959-60; A.B., U. Chgo., 1963, J.D., 1967; postgrad. Columbia, 1963-64; m. Judith Mathews, June 10, 1972. Admitted to Ill. bar, 1968, U.S. Supreme Ct. bar, 1972; practiced in Chgo., 1967; legal and legislative dir. Ill. div. A.C.L.U., Chgo., 1967-73, dir. Ill. div., 1975—; atty. Legal Assistance Found., 1973-75, legal dir., 1975—. Lectr. Ill. Inst. Tech., Chgo. Kent Coll. Law, 1972—; instr. dept. polit. sci. Roosevelt U., 1975-76. Bd. dirs. Midwest Central Com. for Conscientious Objectors, 1970-73. Mem. Amnesty Internat., John Howard Assn. (dir. 1974—), Chgo. Council Lawyers (bd. govs. 1970-73). Office: 5 S Wabash Chicago IL 60604

GOLDBLATT, PHILIP HENRY, chem. engr.; b. Bklyn., Feb. 13, 1946; s. Harry and Lillian (Greenhut) G.; B.Ch.E., Rensselaer Poly. Inst., 1967; M.S.E., U. Mich., 1968; Ph.D., U. Tenn., 1972; postgrad. U. Mass., 1973. Research chemist DeSoto, Inc., Des Plaines, Ill., 1974-75; process engr. Sherwin-Williams Co., Chgo., 1976—. Mem. Am. Inst. Chem. Engrs., Chgo. Soc. Coatings Tech., Soc. Rheology. Home: 18164 Kedzie Ave Hazel Crest IL 60429 Office: 11541 S Champlain Ave Chicago IL 60628

GOLDBLATT, STANFORD JAY, dept. store exec.; b. Chgo., Feb. 25, 1939; s. Maurice and Bernice (Mendelson) G.; B.A. magna cum laude, Harvard, 1960, LL.B. magna cum laude, 1963; m. Ann Dudley Cronkhite, June 17, 1968; children—Alexandra, Nathaniel, Jeremy. Admitted to Ill. bar, 1963; law clk. U.S. Ct. Appeals, Fifth Judicial Circuit, New Orleans, 1963-64; atty. firm Winston & Strawn, Chgo., 1964-67; v.p. Goldblatt Bros., Inc., Chgo., 1967-76, pres., chief exec. officer, 1976—; dir. MacLean Fogg Lock Nut Co., Mundelein, Ill., 1973—. Trustee U. Chgo., U. Chgo. Cancer Research Found., Newberry Library; bd. dirs. Chgo. Youth Centers; bd. govs. Orchestral Assn., Chgo. Clubs: Economic, Standard (Chgo.). Office: 333 S State St Chicago IL 60604

GOLDEN, FREDERIC, clin. psychologist, educator; b. Bklyn., Apr. 21, 1947; s. Solomon and Julie (Hoffman) G.; B.S., Bklyn. Coll., 1967; M.A., W.Va. U., 1970, Ph.D., 1972. Clin. practicum, staff psychologist Western State Sch. and Hosp., Cannonsburg, Pa., 1968; clin. practicum W.Va. U. Student Counseling Service, 1969, dept. behavioral medicine and psychiatry, 1969; staff psychologist Human Resources Assn. Counseling Center, Fairmont, W.Va., 1970-71; intern Malcolm Bliss Mental Health Center, St. Louis, 1971-72; staff psychologist, coordinator community programming Children's Center for Behavioral Devel. E. St. Louis, Ill., 1972-74, clin. dir., 1975—; cons. St. Clair County Parochial Schs., 1972—, Call for Help Crisis Center, Belleville, Ill., 1973-75; asst. prof. St. Louis Community Coll., at Forest Park, 1972—; adj. asst. prof., vis. lectr. So. Ill. U., Edwardsville, 1974—. Certified psychologist, Mo., Ill. Mem. Am., Mo., So. Ill. psychol. assns., St. Clair County Child Advocacy Council (dir. 1975—). Contbr. articles in field to Behavior Therapy, Corrective and Social Psychiatry and others. Home: 1621 Red Bud Dr Collinsville IL 62234 Office: 353 N 88th St East Saint Louis IL 62203

GOLDENBERG, GERALD JOSEPH, educator; b. Brandon, Man., Can., Nov. 27, 1933; s. Jacob and Fanny (Walker) G.; M.D., U. Man., 1957; Ph.D., U. Minn., 1965; m. Sheila Claire Melmed, Jan. 4, 1959; children—Lesley Peace, Jacob Alan, Suzanne Elise, Ellen Rachel. Intern, Winnipeg Gen. Hosp., 1957-58; resident U. Minn. hosps., Mpls., 1958-62; lectr. dept. medicine U. Man., Winnipeg, 1964-66, asst. prof., 1966-70, asso. prof., 1970-75, prof., 1975—; clin. research asso. Nat. Cancer Inst. Can., 1967; research dir. Man. Inst. Cell Biology, 1973-74; dir. Man. Inst. Cell Biology, 1974—. Cons. oncology Winnipeg Children's Hosp. Recipient gold medal U. Man., 1957. Fellow Royal Coll. Physicians (Can.); mem. Am. Soc. Exptl. Pathology, Am. Assn. Cancer Research, Canadian Soc. Clin. Investigation. Club: Masons. Office: 700 Bannatyne Ave Winnipeg R3E 0V9 MB Canada

GOLDFARB, BERNARD SANFORD, lawyer; b. Cleve., Apr. 15, 1917; s. Harry and Esther (Lenson) G.; A.B., Adelbert Coll., Case Western Res. U., 1938, J.D., 1940; m. Barbara E. Brofman, Jan. 4, 1966; children—Meredith Stacy, Lauren Beth. Admitted to Ohio bar, 1940; practice law, Cleve., 1940—; partner firm Goldfarb & Reznick; spl. counsel to atty. gen. Ohio, 1950, 71-74. Mem. Ohio Commn. for Uniform Traffic Rules, 1973—. Served with USAAF, 1942-45. Mem. Am., Ohio, Cleve. bar assns. Contbr. articles to profl. jours. Home: 39 Pepper Creek Dr Pepper Pike OH 44124 Office: 1825 Illuminating Bldg 55 Public Sq Cleveland OH 44113

GOLDFLIES, JEROME WOLF, physician; b. Chgo., Jan. 28, 1919; s. Herman M. and Rose (Weiss) G.; B.A., U. Cin., 1942; M.B., Chgo. Med. Sch., 1945, M.D., 1946; m. Elaine C. Tenenbaum, Mar. 23, 1947; children—Mitchell, Lonny, Myles. Intern Edgewater Hosp., Chgo., 1945-46, gen. med. resident, 1946-47; practice of medicine, Chgo., 1947—; attending staff Edgewater Hosp., Chgo., 1947—, asso. dept. obstetrics and gynecology, 1954—, sec. med. staff, 1977—; active staff Walther Meml. Hosp., Chgo., chief of staff, 1971-73; courtesy staff Columbus Hosp., Chgo. Served with AUS, 1951-53. Recipient recognition award A.M.A., 1972, 74. Charter fellow Am. Acad. Family Physicians; mem. A.M.A., Am. Acad. Gen. Practice (chpt. pres. 1964, 70, 72-76), Pan Am. Med. Assn., Ill., Chgo. med. socs., Phi Lambda Kappa. Home: 4601 W Touhy Ave Lincolnwood IL 60646 Office: 2015 W Armitage Ave Chicago IL 60647

GOLDING, BRAGE, univ. pres.; b. Chgo., Apr. 28, 1920; s. Leon M. and Viola B. (Brage) G.; B.S., Purdue U., 1941, Ph.D., 1948; LL.D., Wright State U., 1975; m. Hinda F. Wolf, Dec. 21, 1941; children—Brage, Susan, Julie. Asso. dir. research Lilly Varnish Co., Indpls., 1948-57, dir. research, 1957-59; research asso. Purdue U., 1948-57, vis. prof. engring., 1957-59, head Sch. Chem. Engring., 1959-66; v.p. Ohio State U. also Miami U., 1966; pres. Wright State U., Dayton, Ohio, 1966-72; pres. San Diego State U., 1972-77; pres. Kent (Ohio) State U., 1977—. Cons. to industry. Mem. Am. Chem. Soc., Am. Inst. Chem. Engrs., Soc. Plastic Engrs., Am. Soc. Engring. Edn., AAUP, AAAS, Phi Beta Kappa. Club: Rotary. Author: Polymers and Resins, 1959; also articles. Home: 1100 E Main St Kent OH 44240

GOLDISH, ROBERT JOSEPH, physician; b. Duluth, Minn., Jan. 21, 1924; s. Samuel L. and Hattie (Kenner) G.; diploma Duluth Jr. Coll., 1942; B.A., U. Minn., 1943, B.S., 1944, M.B., 1946, M.D., 1946; m. Selma Senior, Mar. 18, 1951; children—Lisa H., Susan R., Melanie T., Bruce B. Intern St. Luke's Hosp., Duluth, 1946-47; resident VA Hosp., Mpls., 1949-52, mem. staff and chief hematology dept. and blood bank, 1952-53; practice of medicine, Duluth, 1953—; chief staff Miller Meml. Hosp., Duluth, 1970-71; mem. staffs St. Luke's, St. Mary's hosps., Duluth; clin. asso. prof. medicine U. Minn., Duluth, 1973—. Dir. No. City Nat. Bank, Duluth. Mem. Mental Health Med. Policy Com., State of Minn., 1967-73. Pres. Jewish Fedn. and Community Council, Duluth, 1974-76. Former mem. bd. dirs. Guthrie Theatre Found., Mpls.; trustee Minn. Med. Found., 1976—. Served from lt. to capt. USAF, 1947-49. Diplomate Am. Bd. Internal Medicine. Mem. AMA, Minn. Soc. Internal Medicine, Assn. Minn. Internists, St. Louis County Med. Soc. (v.p. 1965), Duluth C. of C., Phi Theta Kappa, Phi Delta Epsilon. Clubs: Masons, B'nai B'rith, Optimist. Home: 1520 Vermilion Rd Duluth MN 55812 Office: 220 Medical Arts Bldg Duluth MN 55802

GOLDMAN, DOUGLAS, psychiatrist; b. N.Y.C., Jan. 22, 1906; s. Bernard and Gisela (Goldstein) G.; B.S., U. Cin., 1926, M.B., 1928, M.S. in Pathology, M.D., 1929; m. Natalie Dreyfoos, 1927; children—Susan Abel, Douglas Samuel, Grace Angela Goldman Mesel, John Nicholas; m. 2d, Evelyn Kerchner, 1948; children—Donald Edward, Constance Pamela. Intern, Cin. Gen. Hosp., 1928-29; resident in medicine C. P. Huntington Meml. Hosp., Boston, 1930-32; practice medicine specializing in psychiatry and internal medicine, Cin., 1932—; mem. staff Jewish Hosp., Good Samaritan Hosp.; clin. dir. Longview State Hosp., Cin., 1937-62; asst. clin prof. psychiatry U. Cin. Coll. Medicine, 1950—; cons. Exec. Com. Collaborative Studies VA, 1960-73, rev. com. Psychopharmacology Service Center, NIMH, 1961-62. Life fellow Am. Psychiat. Assn.; mem. Cin. Acad. Medicine, Internat., Am. colls. neuropsychopharmacology, Assn. Research Nervous Mental Disease, Am. Acad. Neurology, Sigma Xi, Alpha Omega Alpha. Author: (with George Ulett) Practical Psychiatry for the Internist, 1968; contbr. articles on psychiatry and internal medicine to profl. jours. Home: 7000 Fair Oaks Dr Amberley Village Cincinnati OH 45237 Office: 179 E McMillan St Cincinnati OH 45219

GOLDMAN, FRANK LYLE, motion picture co. exec.; b. St. Louis, Aug. 9, 1893; s. Louis Sworn and Edda (Leventhal) G.; B.S., U. Ill., 1917; m. Anne Elizabeth Champagne, Aug. 10, 1919; children—Donna (Mrs. Raoul Weisman), Robert Donald. Founder, Carpenter Goldman Laboratories, N.Y., 1922, sec.-treas., 1922-33; with Jam Handy Orgn., Detroit, 1935—, mgr. animation dept. and special effects, 1970—. Lectr. on animated cartoons, midwest advt. clubs, 1936-38. Recipient best picture sci. research award, Internat. Film Festival, 1961, Gold Medal award for pharmacy field, 1961. Mason. Inventor in field. Home: 1050 Wall St Ann Arbor MI 48105 Office: 2821 E Grand Blvd Detroit MI 48211

GOLDMAN, JOSEPH RICHARD, polit. scientist, historian; b. Bogota, Colombia, May 24, 1943; s. Israel and Bina (Brannover) G.; came to U.S., 1946, naturalized, 1951; B.A., U. Minn., 1965, M.A.

1967, Ph.D., 1971; postgrad. U. Kans., 1976. Vis. asst. prof. history U. Minn., Mpls., 1972-74; instr. mil. history U.S. Army Command and Gen. Staff Coll., Ft. Leavenworth, Kans., 1974-76; asst. instr. polit. sci. U. Kans., Lawrence, 1976—; asst. prof. polit. sci., Park Coll., Kansas City, Mo., 1977—; vis. prof. Jewish history Jewish Community Center Mpls., 1973-74; lay tchr. Jewish studies Jewish chapel, Ft. Leavenworth, Kans., 1974-76. McMillan fellow to Austria, U. Minn., 1969. Recipient Distinguished Civil Service award U.S. Civil Service Commn., 1976; named outstanding young man of yr. Kansas City Jaycees, 1977. Mem. Am. Hist. Assn., Am. Polit. Sci. Assn., Midwest Polit. Sci. Assn., Democrat. Mem. B'nai B'rith, Mason, Shriner. Lectr. profl. orgns. Home: 2834 Raleigh Ave S Minneapolis MN 55416 Office: Dept Polit Sci Park Coll Kansas City MO 64152

GOLDNER, ARTHUR PAUL, lawyer; b. Cleve., Nov. 27, 1923; s. Michael and Ethel (Wilson) G.; B.S., Miami U., Oxford, Ohio, 1948; J.D., Salmon P. Chase Sch. Law, Cin., 1959; m. June Elaine Royer, Aug. 17, 1944; 1 son, Timothy S. Broker, Oxford Real Estate Sales, 1950—; admitted to Ohio bar, 1959, since practiced in Oxford; solicitor Oxford Village, Oxford, 1960-64; pres. Cogo Co., Oxford, 1964—; dir. 1st. Nat. Bank & Trust Co. Hamilton, Ohio. Regional chmn. Butler County Republican Central Com., 1965-69; mem. exec. com. Butler County, 1960—. Bd. dirs. Wesley Found., Oxford Community Improvement Corp.; pres. bd. trustees Talawanda Recreation Inc., 1966-70. Served to lt. (j.g.), A.C., USNR, 1942-45. Named Oxford Citizen of Year 1967. Mem. Ohio, Butler County bar assns., Phi Alpha Delta, Sigma Chi (chmn. founding site com. 1974—). Mason (32 deg.). Club: Oxford Country. Office: 5995 Fairfield Rd Oxford OH 45056

GOLDNER, LEO, steel co. exec.; b. Toledo, July 3, 1923; s. Herman and Margaret (Fleishacker) G.; student U. Toledo, 1942; m. Marian R. Baron, July 6, 1944; children—Paul, Marcia, Janet, Camryn. Vice pres. Baron Steel Co., Toledo, 1947-53; pres. Tyler Steel Co., Toledo, 1953-55, Parker Steel Co., Toledo, 1955—; hypnotist. Bd. dirs. Myasthenia Gravis Found., N.Y.C., Collingwood Temple, Toledo. Served with inf. U.S. Army, 1942-46; Philippines. Mem. Assn. Steel Distbrs. (pres. 1965-66, Steel Man of Year 1968, dir. 1960—), Internat. Brotherhood of Magicians (pres. 1963-66). Clubs: Elks, Kiwanis, Masons. Office: 4239-41 Monroe St Toledo OH 43606

GOLDNER, LOUIS B., retail and service co. exec.; b. Akron, Ohio, July 27, 1924; s. Ben and Goldie (Weisman) G.; student U. Akron, 1942, 46. m. Rosalie Baskin, July 18, 1948; children—Gary, Mark, Bruce, Laura Beth. Partner, Sun Formal Wear, Akron, 1950-56; owner, founder Cleveland Tux and parent co. Tuxamerica, Inc., Macedonia, Ohio, 1956—. Served with U.S. Army, 1942-46. Mem. Black Tie Hall Fame, 1975. Mem. Am. Formalwear Assn. (founding pres. 1974). Democrat. Jewish. Club: Masons. Office: 440 E Highland Rd Macedonia OH 44056

GOLDNER, RICHARD DAN, psychiatrist; b. Decatur, Ind., Jan. 4, 1924; s. Dallas Benjamin Edward and Emma Louise (Weidler) G.; student Heidelberg Coll., 1941-43; B.S., Wayne State U., 1947, M.D., 1948; m. Elizabeth Ann Collier, Feb. 27, 1952; children—Karen Anne, Raymond Dan, Donald Henry, Gayle Louise. Intern, Detroit Receiving Hosp., 1948-49; resident psychiatry Ypsilanti (Mich.) State Hosp., 1949-52; practice medicine, specializing in psychiatry, Saginaw, Mich., 1955—; mem. staffs Saginaw Gen. Hosp.; cons. physician St. Luke's Hosp., St. Mary's Hosp., V.A. Hosp.; instr. pub. health U. Mich., Saginaw, 1959-61; founder Saginaw Valley Nut Nursery, 1976. Served with AUS, 1942-44. Diplomate Am. Bd. Psychiatry and Neurology. Mem. A.M.A., Am. Psychiat. Assn., Saginaw County Med. Soc., Soc. Biol. Psychiatry, Mich. Soc. Psychiatry, Am. Rose Soc. (chpt. pres. 1968), Mich., No. nut growers assns., Alpha Omega Alpha, Phi Rho Sigma. Research in psychiat. somatic therapies. Home: 8285 Dixie Hwy Birch Run MI 48415 Office: 705 Adams St Saginaw MI 48602

GOLDSMITH, DALE PRESTON JOEL, educator; b. Catasauqua, Pa., Oct. 30, 1916; s. Wayne A.E. and Ruth (Seyfried) G.; B.S., Lehigh U., 1938; M.S., Harvard, 1940; Ph.D., Pa. State U., 1942; m. Marjorie Martin, Nov. 25, 1972. Sr. chemist Merck & Co., Rahway, N.J., 1942-55; instr. dept. physiology U. Rochester (N.Y.) Sch. Medicine, 1957-63, asst. prof., 1963-64; asso. prof. biochemistry U. Nebr. Coll. Medicine, Omaha, 1964—. Vis. scientist, Saigon, 1970. Mem. Am. Chem. Soc., A.A.A.S., Am. Phys. Soc., Am. Inst. Chemists, Nebr. Acad. Sci., Tau Beta Pi, Alpha Chi Sigma, Phi Delta Epsilon, Phi Lambda Upsilon. Home: 11716 Mayberry St Omaha NE 68154

GOLDSTEIN, NATHAN LAWRENCE, beauty supply co. exec.; b. Chgo., Aug. 20, 1913; s. Morris Louis and Frieda Reva (Weiss) G.; student pub. schs.; m. Shirley Lila Kaplan, May 31, 1936; children—Leonard, Phyllis. With Chgo. Hair Goods Co., 1929—, pres., 1958—; wig expert, cons. to industry. Active City of Hope; mem. Greater Chgo. com. State of Israel Bonds; bd. dirs. Nat. Jewish Hosp., Denver. Mem. Ill. Pharm. Travellers Assn. Jewish (exec. council synagogue). Mason (32 deg., Shriner); mem. B'nai B'rith. Clubs: Pharmacos Mens (treas. 1969—), Chgo. Drug, Variety, Covenant. Patentee Royal Manicure Bowl, Roto-Beauti-File. Home: 2925 Rascher Ave Chicago IL 60625 Office: 428 S Wabash Ave Chicago IL 60605

GOLDSTEIN, PAUL H., ophthalmologist; b. Chgo., May 20, 1936; s. Alex and Leah (Swabsky) G.; B.S., U. Ill., 1958, M.D., 1960; m. Marilyn Gail Holtzman, Sept. 4, 1960; children—Todd, Jordan, Karen, Ross. Intern, Cook County Hosp., Chgo., 1960-61; resident, 1962-64; practice medicine specializing in ophthalmology, Milw., 1965—; mem. staffs Mt. Sinai, Deconess, Milw. County hosps.; chief dept. ophthalmology Milw. Children's Hosp., 1973—; clin. asst. prof., dept. ophthalmology Med. Coll. Wis., 1965—. Mem. Am., Wis., Milwaukee County med. assns., Am. Acad. Ophthalmology and Otolaryngology, Wis. Soc. Prevention Blindness, Milw. Ophthal. Soc. (pres. 1975-76), Alpha Omega Alpha. Home: 4848 N Ardmore Ave Whitefish Bay WI 53217 Office: 2040 W Wisconsin Ave Milwaukee WI 53233

GOLDSTEIN, STANTON LOUIS, neurosurgeon; b. Chgo., Oct. 3, 1917; s. Louis E. and Estelle (Herzberger) G.; B.S., U. Chgo., 1938, M.D., 1941; M.S., Northwestern U., 1952. Intern, Cedars Lebanon Hosp., Los Angeles, 1941-42; asst. resident in neurosurgery Boston City Hosp., 1942-43, resident in neurosurgery, 1943-44; resident in neurosurgery VA Hosp., Hines, Ill., 1946-51; practice medicine specializing in neurosurgery, Moline, Ill., 1952—; mem. staff, lectr. sch. nursing Moline Pub. Hosp., Luth. Hosp., St. Anthony's Hosp., St. Luke's Hosp., Mercy Hosp.; instr. surgery Northwestern U., 1951-52; clin. asso. neuroscience Peoria (Ill.) Sch. Medicine, 1977; cons. neurosurgery Galesburg (Ill.) State Research Hosp., East Moline (Ill.) State Hosp. Served to capt. M.C. U.S. Army, 1944-46. Diplomate Am. Bd. Neurol. Surgery. Fellow Am. Coll. Surgeons; mem. AMA, Congress Neurol. Surgeons, Iowa Clin. Surg. Soc., Am. Assn. Neurol. Surgeons, Iowa-Midwest Neurosurgical Soc., Rock Island County, Scott County (courtesy) med. socs. Contbr. articles to med. jours. Home: 2508 37th Ave Rock Island IL 61201 Office: 1504 7th St Moline IL 61265

GOLDSTONE, SIDNEY RICHARD, physician, surgeon; b. Rock Island, Ill., Nov. 28, 1924; s. Morris and Fannie (Borenstein) G.; B.S., U. Ill., 1945; M.D. with honors, 1947; m. Muriel Glabman, Dec. 22, 1946; children—James R., Rande Goldstone Shapiro, Meri Ellen. Intern, Cook County Hosp., Chgo., 1948, preceptor in surgery, 1948-50; pvt. practice surgery, Gary, Ind., 1952—; chief of surgery MacDill USAF Hosp., Tampa, Fla., 1950-52; pres. Physicians and Surgeons Liability Ins. Co., Munster, Ind., 1976—. Pres. Civil Aviation Med. Examiners; commr. Gary Airport bd., 1964-70, pres., 1966-67. Served with AUS, 1944-46, to capt. USAF, 1950-52. Diplomate Am. Acad. Family Practice. Fellow Am. Geriat. Soc.; mem. Flying Physicians Assn. (dir. 1974), Am. Soc. Abdominal Surgeons, Aerospace, Civil Aviation med. socs. Clubs: Masons, Shriners. Home: 9129 Elmwood Dr Munster IN 46321 Office: 535 W 35th Ave Gary IN 46408

GOLLNICK, WALTER OTTO, JR., banker; b. South Bend, Ind., Nov. 25, 1943; s. Walter Otto and Ruth Elizabeth (Starkey) G.; B.S., Purdue U., 1966; 1 dau., Michele. With First Bank & Trust Co., South Bend, 1966—, asst. treas., 1973—, customer service officer, 1974—, asst. v.p., 1976—. Mem. Portage Trails Dist. com. Boy Scouts Am., South Bend, 1970—; dist. chmn. YMCA Community Service Div. Adv. Com., 1973-74; mem. adv. bd. Nat. Alliance Businessmen, 1972-74. Mem. Purdue U. Alumni Assn., Culver Legion, Jr. C. of C. (Oldston Crane Meml. award 1971, state dir. 1970-71, pres. 1971-72), Am. Inst. Banking (chpt. dir. 1974), Sigma Pi. Mem. United Ch. Christ (mem. ch. bd. 1971-75, bd. deacons 1971-75, vice chmn. 1971-72). Home: 204 Ct of Royal Arms South Bend IN 46637 Office: 133 S Main St South Bend IN 46601

GOMBIS, LEON GEORGE, dentist; b. Chgo., Nov. 21, 1939; s. George and Dorothy Diane (Ayanoglou) G.; D.D.S., U. Ill., 1963; m. Kathryn Ann Kristak, Nov. 25, 1967; children—Cassandra Joy, Timothy George, Alison Kaye, Gillian Ruth. Pvt. practice dentistry, Oak Lawn, Ill., 1966—. Bd. dir. Internat. Christian Fellowship Mission, 1971. Served to lt. USNR, 1963-66. Mem. Am., Chgo. dental assns., Psi Omega, Delta Delta Sigma. Republican. Baptist. Home: 9740 S Kenneth Ave Oaklawn IL 60453 Office: 9101 S Cicero Ave Oak Lawn IL 60453

GOMER, LEWIS EUGENE, supt. schs.; b. Brooten, Minn., Aug. 26, 1934; s. August Otto and Henrietta (DeVries) G.; B.A., Wartburg Coll., 1957; M.A., S.D. State U., 1960; m. Mary Ann Biel, Aug. 11, 1957; children—Gregory, Gary, Sandra, Julie Ann. Sci. tchr., athletic coach, White, S.D., 1957-59, Centerville, S.D., 1959-62; high sch. prin., Ellsworth, Minn., 1962-64; supt. schs., Bristol, S.D., 1964-68, Garretson, S.D., 1968-77, Faulkton, S.D., 1977—. League chmn. Big Sioux Conf., 1974-75. Club: Commercial (dir. 1970—) (Garretson). Home: 404 Dows St Garretson SD 57030 Office: 500 Main Ave Garretson SD 57030

GONG, MERY LEE, data processor; b. Cleve., June 14, 1931; d. Wing and Shee (Woo) Gong; B.S., Ohio State U., 1954. With Ohio State U. Instruction and Research Computer Center, Columbus, 1954—, computer operator, 1954-56, programmer, cons., 1956-61, ops. supr., 1961-65, adminstrv. asst., 1965-72, asst. dir., 1972—. Computer cons. Cole-Layer-Trumble Co.; instr. Ohio State U. continuing edn. Children's Hosp., Columbus, 1969. Mem. Ohio Commn. on Status of Women. Mem. Am. Mgmt. Assn., Assn. Computing Machinery, Data Processing Mgmt. Assn., Air Force Assn., Assn. Systems Mgmt., Ohio State U. Alumni Assn., Northwest Area Council for Human Relations, LWV, Upper Arlington Civic Assn., Columbus Area Civil Rights Council. Club: Quota (Columbus). Home: 1776 Ridgecliff Rd Columbus OH 43221 Office: 1971 Neil Ave Columbus OH 43210

GONGE, JOHN FOSTER, air force officer; b. Ansley, Nebr., Nov. 5, 1921; s. Maxwell John and Ruby Mae (Foster) G.; m. Marilyn Jean Martin, May 11, 1944; children—Jon Lynn Gonge Kerchner, John Craig, Jorja Martin Gonge Carr; student USAAF Flying Sch., Lubbock, Tex., 1943, Nat. War Coll., 1965-66. Commd. 2d lt. USAAF, 1943, advanced through grades to maj. gen. USAF; spl. projects officer, later adminstrv. asst. to comdr. Office Dept. Chief of Staff for Ops., Pacific Div., MATS, Hickam AFB, Hawaii, 1953-56, Parks AFB, Calif., 1956-58; comdr. 1506th Support Squadron, Clark Air Base, P.I., 1958-60; chief Program Div., later asst. dep. chief of staff for plans and manpower Hdqrs. Western Transport Air Force, Travis AFB, Calif., 1960-63; dep. asst. chief of staff Mil. Air Transport Service, Scott AFB, Ill., 1963-65; chief Resources Capability br. Office Spl. Asst. for Strategic Mobility, then chief Short and Mid-Range br., later chief Policy br. Plans Div., Orgn. Joint Chiefs of Staff, Washington, 1966-69; vice comdr. 60th Mil. Airlift Wing, Travis AFB, 1969-70; comdr. 63d Mil. Airlift Wing, Norton AFB, Calif., 1970-71; vice comdr. 21st Air Force, McGuire AFB, N.J., 1971-72; comdr. 22d Air Force, Travis AFB, 1972-75; vice comdr. Mil. Airlift Command, Scott AFB, 1975-77, vice comdr. in chief, 1977—. Mem. Air Force Assn., Order of Daedalians, Masons. Decorated D.S.M. Legion of Merit, D.F.C., Meritorious Service medal, Air medal, Air Force Commendation medal with oak leaf cluster, Army Commendation medal. Home: 200 9th St Scott Air Force Base IL 62225 Office: Mil Airlift Command Scott Air Force Base IL 62225

GONSER, DAVID EARL, co. exec.; b. Detroit, Feb. 14, 1936; s. Kenneth Earl and Beatrice Mary (Martin) G.; student Wayne State U., 1954-55; B.A., Bob Jones U., 1960, M.A., 1962; m. Constance M. Good, Aug. 27, 1960; children—Jill, Kimberly. Asst. mgr. Bob Jones U., food services program, Greenville, S.C., 1962-64; ordained to ministry Ch. of God, 1968; clergyman Evanswood Ch. of God, Troy, Mich., 1964-69; pres. Tri Royal Industries, Inc., injection molding of plastics, Madison Heights, Mich., 1969-75; pres. Dyadic Assos., Inc. (Dunkin Donuts of Grand Blanc and Saginaw, Mich.), 1975—. Baptist (trustee 1971-72, deacon 1972—). Home: 4228 Rosewold Royal Oak MI 48073 Office: 12500 S Saginaw Grand Blanc MI

GONZALEZ-MENOCAL, PABLO, hosp. exec.; b. Havana, Cuba, May 7, 1939; s. Eulogio Fernando and Maria Josefa (Menocal) Gonzalez; came to U.S., 1957, naturalized, 1972; B. Indsl. Engring., Ga. Inst. Tech., 1963; postgrad. U. Mich., 1968; m. Ilse Ursula Steinbrecher, June 9, 1960; children—Sylvia Maria, Evelyn Ruth, Helen Louise. Materials handling engr. Constrn. Machinery div. Allis Chalmers, Springfield, Ill., 1963-66, Consol. Packaging Corp., Monroe, Mich., 1967-68; mng. dir. Community Systems Found., cons., Ann Arbor, Mich., 1968-72; v.p. Community Mgmt. Service, Denver, 1972-73; cons. Chi Systems Inc., Ann Arbor, 1973-76; asst. exec. dir. Health and Hosp. Corp. of Marion County, Indpls., 1976—; instr. Iowa Western Community Coll., Council Bluffs, 1973; lectr. in field. Recipient Key Man award Springfield Jaycees, 1965, Spoke award, 1966. Fellow Royal Soc. Health; mem. Am. Inst. Indsl. Engrs. (sr.), Hosp. Mgmt. Systems Soc. Contbr. articles to nat. and internat. profl. jours. Home: 4570 Buckingham Ct Carmel IN 46032 Office: Adminstrn Wishard Meml Hosp 1001 W 10th St Indianapolis IN 46202

GOOCH, DONALD BURNETTE, artist, educator; b. Bloomingdale, Mich., Oct. 17, 1907; s. Milford Henry and Nina Pearl (Burnette) G.; student Western Mich. U., 1923-25; B.S., U. Mich., 1935, M. Design, 1939; postgrad. Am. Sch. Painting (France), 1937; m. Marjorie Gilchrist, June 26, 1937; children—Nancy Jane, Peter Gilchrist. Tchr. pub. schs., Bloomingdale, 1925-27; instr. Detroit Sch. Lettering, 1928-32; instr. Detroit Art Acad., 1933-35; art tchr. pub. schs., Washington, 1936; instr. U. Mich., Ann Arbor, 1936-45, asst. prof., 1945-52, asso. prof., 1952-59, prof. design, 1959-73, prof. emeritus, 1974—. Advt. design cons.; exhibited paintings Detroit Inst. Arts, 1936-48, San Francisco Cow Palace, 1940, Am. Fedn. Arts, 1941, Pepsi Cola Paintings of Year, 1947, Pa. Acad., 1947. Recipient Alumni prize Am. Acad. Rome, 1935; Founders prize Detroit Inst. Arts, 1947. Horace H. Rackham grantee, 1960, 65. Mem. Mich. Watercolor Soc., Mich. Acad. Arts, Sci. and Letters, Internat. Inst. Arts and Letters, Nat. Soc. Lit. and Arts, Phi Kappa Phi, Alpha Rho Chi, Tau Sigma Delta. Editor: American Taste in Advertising, 1956; Search for Certainty in Advertising, 1959; Research in Pictographic Communication for Non-Literates in Nepal, 1961, 67; Theatre and Main Street, 1964. Address: 1633 Leaird St Ann Arbor MI 48105

GOOD, JOHN EHRMIN, cons. mining engring. co. exec.; b. Lykens, Pa., Dec. 29, 1911; s. Luther Milton and Amy (John) G.; B.S. Va. Poly Inst., 1934; m. Margaret Grant, June 8, 1935; 1 dau., Linda Jane. Engr., Rochester & Pitts. Coal Co., Indiana, Pa., 1934-38; engr., mine foreman Cerro de Pasco Copper Corp., Goyllarisquisga, Peru, 1940-42; adviser Brazilian Nat. Dept. Mineral Prodn., WPB and U.S. Bur. Mines, Brazil, 1942-47; cons. to industry, U.S.A., S.Am., 1948-50, U.S. Bur. Mines, Washington, 1948-50; resident chief engr. Paul Weir Co., Zonguldak, Turkey, 1950-58; v.p., Chgo., 1958-70, sr. v.p. 1970—, also dir. Tchr. mining Pa. State U. Extension Div., Indiana, Pa., 1935-37. Recipient citation for important contbns. to geol. knowledge, mineral devel. Brazil, Brazilian Geol. Soc., 1963. Registered profl. engr., Alta., Can. Mem. Am. Inst. Mining, Metall. and Petroleum Engrs., Am. Inst. Cons. Engrs., Turkish Mining Engrs. Soc. (hon.), Tau Beta Pi, Omicron Delta Kappa. Home: 720 Oakton St Evanston IL 60202 Office: 20 N Wacker Dr Chicago IL 60606

GOOD, LARRY DAVID, civil engr.; b. Indpls., July 20, 1945; s. Donald Robert and Mildred (Stanley) G.; B.S., Purdue U., 1967, M.S., 1971; m. Patricia L. Jessup. Asst. county supr. FHA, U.S. Dept. Agr., North Vernon, Ind., 1971; engr., Sieco, Inc., Columbus, Ind., 1972-77, v.p. environ. engring., 1975—. Bd. dirs. Mental Health Assn. Bartholomew County. Served with AUS, 1968-69. Registered profl. engr., Ind. Mem. Nat. Soc. Profl. Engrs., Am. Soc. Agrl. Engring., Columbus Jr. C. of C., Alpha Zeta, Alpha Epsilon, Tau Beta Pi. Home: 3515 Autumn Ct Columbus IN 47201 Office: 309 Washington St Columbus IN 47201

GOOD, LARRY RALPH, dentist; b. Hutchinson, Kans., Dec. 6, 1940; s. Chester Ralph and Vera Ellen (Fast) G.; B.S., Ft. Hays (Kans.) State U., 1962; D.D.S., U. Mo., 1967; m. Suzanne Doris Soard, June 23, 1967; children—Jeffrey Lawrence, Gretchen Suzanne, Heather Ellen. Individual practice dentistry, Hays, Kans., 1970—; mem. med.-dental staff Hadley Regional Med. Center, Hays, St. Anthony Hosp., Hays, 1970-77. Mem. Hays Arts Council, 1972-77; v.p., bd. dirs. Hays Baseball Assn., 1975-77. Served with USNR, 1967-69. Mem. Am., Kans. dental assns., Am. Legion, VFW, Golden Belt Dist. Dental Soc., Oil Belt Dental Study Club (pres. 1972), Hays C. of C., Hays Jaycees (dir. 1974-75), Fort Hays Kans. State U. Alumni Assn. (life, dir. 1976-77). Seventh Cavalry, Nat., Kans. rifle assns., Ellis County Hist. Soc., Kans. Wildlife Fedn., Nat. Audubon Soc., Early Am. Soc., Nat. Parks and Recreation Assn., Acad. Gen. Dentistry, Ft. Hays Kans. State U. Tiger Club (pres. 1975), Beta Beta Beta, Phi Kappa Phi, Xi Psi Phi. Methodist (adminstrv. bd.). Club: Optimist (dir. 1976-77). Home: 2707 Cottonwood Ln Hays KS 67601 Office: 3005 Hall St Hays KS 67601

GOOD, SHELDON FRED, realtor; b. Chgo., June 4, 1933; s. Joseph and Sylvia (Schwartz) G.; student Drake U., 1951; B.B.A., U. Ill., 1955; m. Lois Kroll; children—Steven, Todd. Sales mgr. Baird & Warner Real Estate, Chgo., 1957-65; pres. Sheldon F. Good & Co. Realtors, Chgo., 1965—; guest lectr. Northwestern U., U. Chgo., Vanderbilt U., U. Ill.; staff instr. Central YMCA City Coll., Chgo.; cons. in field. Chmn. real estate divs. Chgo. Crusade Mercy, United Settlement Appeal, Chgo., YMCA Edn. Library Drive, Chgo., Chgo. Jewish United Fund. Bd. dirs. Child, Inc. Served with AUS, 1955-57. Recipient Levi Eshkol Premier medal State Israel, 1967, Crown of A Good Name award Jewish Nat. Fund, 1972; named one of 10 outstanding young men Chgo., 1968. Mem. Chgo. Real Estate Bd., Nat. Assn. Real Estate Bds., Chgo. Better Bus. Bur., Chgo. Assn. Commerce and Industry, Alpha Epsilon Pi, Lambda Alpha, Omega Tau Rho. Author: How to Sell Apartment Buildings; Techniques of Investment Property Exchanging; How to Lease Suburban Office Buildings; The Real Estate Auction as a Marketing Tool. Home: 1100 Sheridan Rd Evanston IL 60202 Office: 11 N Wacker Dr Chicago IL 60606

GOODALL, PENDLETON, JR., lawyer; b. St. Louis, Mar. 11, 1925; s. Pendleton and Margaret S. (Olsen) G.; student Washington U., St. Louis, 1941-43, J.D., St. Louis U., 1956; m. Mary E. Neher, Nov. 8, 1963; children—Mary M., Pendleton III. With Wabash Railroad, St. Louis, 1942-51, Ocean Accident & Guarantee Corp., Ltd., St. Louis, 1951-52; adjuster Fidelity & Casualty Co., St. Louis, 1952-56; admitted to Mo. bar, 1956; practiced in St. Louis, 1956—; mem. firms Rassieur, Kammerer Rassieur & Erker, 1956-58, Lashly & Goodall, 1966-77, Sweet & Goodall, 1977—; asst. Atty gen. Mo., St. Louis, 1961-63. Bd. dir. Catholic Youth Council, 1971—. Mem. Mo. Bar, St. Louis, St. Louis County, Lawyers bar assns. Mason. Home: Route 1 78 Vixen Dr Pacific MO 63069 Office: 1750 Brentwood Blvd Brentwood MO 63144

GOODE, IRVING HOWARD, real estate broker; b. Chgo., Oct. 7, 1916; s. Samuel and Esther (Rubenstein) G.; A.A., YMCA Coll., 1935; LL.B., DePaul U., 1939; postgrad. Northwestern U., 1939-41, Am. U., 1941-42; m. Lorraine Wolper, July 7, 1948; children—Mark Bernard, Steven Jay. Admitted to Ill. bar, 1939; practiced law, Chgo., 1939-40; atty. Social Security Bd., Washington, 1940-42; salesman real estate, Chgo., 1946-49; v.p. Lustig Goode & Co., Chgo., 1950-59; pres. I.H. Goode & Co., Chgo., 1960-67; pres. Kaplan, Goode & Co., Chgo., 1967—. Served to capt. inf. AUS, 1942-46. Decorated Purple Heart. Mem. Soc. Indsl. Realtors (pres. 1977), Assn. Indsl. Real Estate Brokers, Chgo. Real Estate Bd., Nat. Assn. Real Estate Bds., Assn. Commerce and Industry. Jewish. Rotarian. Clubs: Covenant; South Shore Fellowship (pres. 1964). Home: 2883 Arlington Ave Highland Park IL 60035 Office: 2 N Riverside Plaza Chicago IL 60606

GOODIN, CARL VINCENT, police chief Cin.; b. Louisville, Mar. 21, 1933; B.S. in Commerce, Salmon P. Chase Coll., 1961; M.S. in Pub. Safety, Mich. State U., 1968; With Cin. Policy Dept., 1956—, now police chief. Adj. instr. Xavier U. Served with USAF. Mem. Assn. Internat. Assn. Chiefs Police (cons.). Office: 310 Lincoln Park Dr Cincinnati OH 45203

GOODKIN, MICHAEL, pub. co. exec.; b. N.Y.C., June 10, 1941; s. Harold and Rose (Mostkoff) G.; B.A., Harvard U., 1963; postgrad. U. Chgo. Bus. Sch., 1964; m. Helen Graham Fairbank, Oct. 1, 1971; children—Graham Laird, Nathalie Fairbank. Trainee, Random House, 1964-65; asst. dir. Simulmatics, N.Y.C., 1966-67; account exec. World Book Ency., Inc., Chgo., 1967-70, research dir., 1970-73, v.p. mktg., 1973-76, v.p., gen. mgr. mail order div., 1976—. Trustee

Art Inst. Chgo., 1975—, pres. aux. bd., 1975-77; bd. dirs. Urban Gateways, Chgo. Area Project. Served with Army N.G., 1963-69. Mem. Direct Mail Advt. Assn., Modern Poetry Assn. (trustee). Clubs: Racquet, Harvard (N.Y.C.); Harvard (Boston). Office: Room 446 Merchandise Mart Plaza Chicago IL 60654

GOODMAN, DAVID LAWRENCE, dentist; b. Findlay, Ohio, Sept. 13, 1939; s. Lawrence Hayse and Beatrice Ann (Fromm) G.; student U. Mich., 1957-60, D.D.S., 1964; m. Joan Elizabeth Gray, Aug. 3, 1963; children—Christine Hayse, John David. Pvt. practice dentistry, Findlay, 1964—; mem. adv. com. Sch. Dental Hygiene, Ohio State U., Lima, 1972-74. Chmn. profl. div. United Way, 1974; bd. dirs. Hancock County Cancer Soc., Hancock County chpt. ARC. Mem. ADA, Acad. Gen. Dentistry, Ohio Dental Assn. (chmn. membership com., del.), Northwestern Ohio (chmn. nat. children's dental health week 1969-70, v.p.), Hancock County (pres. 1969-70) dental socs., Findlay Tennis Assn., U. Mich. Alumni Assn. (gov.), C. of C., Chi Psi, Delta Sigma Delta. Methodist (mem. ofcl. bd. 1965-69). Club: Findlay Country. Home: 510 Churchill Dr Findlay OH 45840 Office: 309 E St Findlay OH 45840

GOODMAN, DAVID S., pub. relations exec.; b. Racine, Wis., Feb. 28, 1917; s. Julius and Esther (Sanderson) G.; B.S. in Journalism, Northwestern U., 1937; m. Phyllis F. Steinberg, Apr. 6, 1941; children—Jeffrey, Kathy (Mrs. Charles Aller), Laurie (Mrs. Steven Horowitz), Theodore. Real estate editor Waukegan Post, 1939-41; reporter Wall St. Jour., Chgo., 1941-43; asso. editor Flying Mag., Chgo., 1943-45; pub. relations supr., med. systems dept. Gen. Electric Co., Milw., 1945-58; account supr. Barkin, Herman, Solochek & Paulsen (and predecessor firms), Milw., 1958—; v.p., dir. Darrs Realty Co., Milw., 1940—. Author: President's Letter Book, 1970; Emotional Well-Being through Rational Behavior Training, 1974. Contbg. editor Pub. Relations Jour., 1960-63. Home: 8915 N Bayside Dr Milwaukee WI 53217 Office: Barkin Herman Solochek & Paulsen 777 E Wisconsin Ave Milwaukee WI 53202

GOODMAN, DONALD JOSEPH, dentist; b. Cleve., Aug. 14, 1922; s. Joseph Henry and Henrietta Inez (Mandel) G.; D.D.S., Case-Western Reserve U., 1945; m. Dora May Hirsh, Sept. 18, 1947; children—Lynda (Mrs. Barry Allen Levin), Keith, Bruce; m. 2d, Ruth Jeanette Weber, May 1, 1974. Pvt. practice dentistry, Cleve., 1949—; v.p. Holiday Inns Trav-l-Park, Sandusky, Ohio, 1971—. Served with Dental Corps, USNR, 1946-48. Mem. Am. Acad. Gen. Dentistry, Am., Ohio State dental assns., Cleve. Dental Soc., Fedn. Dentaire Internationale, Cleve. Council on World Affairs, Phi Sigma Delta, Zeta Beta Tau, Alpha Omega. Clubs: Masons (32 deg.), Shriners, Lake Forest Country (Hudson, Ohio). Home: 29099 Shaker Blvd Pepper Pike OH 44124 Office: 2031 W 25th St Cleveland OH 44113

GOODMAN, LOWELL IRVIN, psychiatrist; b. Chrisney, Ind., Nov. 2, 1924; s. Elza Ira and Lona Katheryn (Cox) G.; student La. State U., 1943, U. Okla., 1944; B.S., Yale, 1948, M.D., 1951; m. Ione Mae Thompson, Apr. 24, 1954; 1 son, Christopher Marshall. Intern, Percy Jones Army Hosp., Battle Creek, Mich., 1951-52; resident adult and child psychiatry Carter Hosp., Indpls., U. Ill., Inst. Juvenile Research, Chgo., 1953-58; faculty U. Ill. Med. Sch., Chgo., 1958-63; practice medicine, specializing in psychiatry, Chgo., 1956-63, Michigan City, Ind., 1963-70; clin. research dir. Parke, Davis & Co., Ann Arbor, Mich., 1970—; faculty U. Mich. Med. Sch., Ann Arbor, 1971—. Served with AUS, 1943-46, 51-53. Fellow Am. Psychiat. Assn.; mem. Am. Coll. Neuropsychopharmacology, Mich. Psychiat. Soc., Mich., Washtenaw County med. socs. Home: 959 Greenhills Dr Ann Arbor MI 48105 Office: 2800 Plymouth Rd Ann Arbor MI 48106

GOODMAN, NORTON VICTOR, lawyer; b. Columbus, Ohio, June 15, 1936; s. William L. and Min H. (Hemmelstein) G.; B.A. magna cum laude, Yale U., 1957; J.D., Harvard, 1961; m. Elaine G. Goldstein, Aug. 11, 1957; children—Jeffrey, Arlyn, Julie, David. Admitted to Ohio bar, 1961; mem. firm. Topper and Alloway, Columbus, 1961— (name is now Topper, Alloway, Goodman, DeLeone and Duffey). Mem. Commn. Vocational and Tech. Edn., State of Ohio, 1970-71; mem. Ohio Bd. Regents, 1976—; mem. Central Ohio Bicentennial Observance Com. Mem. exec. com. Franklin County Republicans, 1970—. Trustee, United Jewish Fund and Council, Heritage House, Jewish Center, Columbus Torah Acad.; mem. Ohio Bd. Regents, 1976—; bd. dirs. Columbus Children's Mental Health Center, 1973-76. Recipient Therese Stern Kahn leadership award United Jewish Fund and Council, 1969. Mem. Am. (active coms), Ohio, Columbus bar assns. Republican. Mem. Jewish (synagogue trustee 1969—, chmn. bd. 1976—). Mem. B'nai B'rith (dist. bd. govs. 1967-68). Clubs: University (Columbus). Asso. editor The Developing Labor Law, Bur. Nat. Affairs, Inc. Home: 2667 Sherwood Rd Columbus OH 43209 Office: 17 S High St Columbus OH 43215

GOODMAN, RONALD, pub. relations counsel; b. Chgo., June 3, 1920; s. Morris Goodman and Anna (Mautner) G.; diploma Univ. Coll. Northwestern U. Coll., 1941; m. Ethel A. Weiss, Oct. 8, 1949; children—Anne Margaret, Victoria, Amy, Peter Kirk, Ellen. Sr. mem. The Mitchell Mc Keown Orgn., Chgo., 1947-54; pres. Ronald Goodman Pub. Relations Counsel, Inc., Chgo., 1954-67, The Pub. Relations Consortium, Chgo., 1967-75; pres., mgr. partner Ronald Goodman & Co., Inc., pub. relations counseling mgmt. and cons. firm, Des Moines, 1975—. Dir. Gateway House Found. Inc., Chgo., 1967-74; trustee N. Shore Unitarian Ch., Deerfield, Ill. Served with USAF, 1942-46. Mem. Pub. Relations Soc. Am. (Silver Anvil 1963, dir., accredited pub. relations counselor), Internat. Pub. Relations Assns. Club: Tower of Chgo. Author publs. in field. Home: 3505 SW 27th St Des Moines IA 50321 Office: 800 2d Ave PO Box 1712 Des Moines IA 50306

GOODMAN, SIDNEY RICHARD, computer service co. exec.; b. Cleve., June 29, 1940; s. David H. and Rose W. (Woolman) G.; B.S., Miami U., 1962; m. Diane Susan Katz, Aug. 12, 1962; children—Martin, Wendy, Tracey. Accountant Ernst & Ernst, 1962-65; exec. v.p. Becker C.P.A. Review Course, 1965; asst. to controller Foseco, Inc., Cleve., 1966-68; controller Arby's Northfield Systems, Cleve., 1968-69; pres. Datassistance Corp., Cleve., 1969-71; pres. Mgmt. Reports, Inc., Beachwood, Ohio, 1971—; pres. Watersavers, Inc., 1976—; Niagara Computer Pl., Niagara Falls, Ont., Can., 1977—; dir. Leasepac Corp. Bd. govs. Temple Emanuel, 1973—, treas., 1975, v.p., 1976. Mem. Ohio Soc. C.P.A.'s, Am. Inst. C.P.A.'s. Jewish. Patentee in field. Home: 25515 Halburton Rd Beachwood OH 44122 Office: 23945 Mercantile Rd Beachwood OH 44122

GOODNER, JACK WAYNE, cons. psychologist; b. Oklahoma City, May 13, 1931; s. Otis H. and Effie Mae (Foster) G.; B.A., U. N.Mex., 1953, M.A., 1960; Ed.D. (grad. fellow), Ariz. State U., 1964; m. Frieda Marie Flook, Sept. 1, 1951; children—Jack Wayne, Steven C., Stuart R., Lanette L. Tchr., counselor, adminstr. Albuquerque Pub. Schs., 1955-63; dir. sales and mgmt. tng. Sci. Research Assos. div. IBM, Chgo., 1963-69, dir. Am. Coll. Testing Programs in Midwest, 1969-71; asso. Thomas and Assos., psychol. cons. services to mgmt., Liberty, Mo., 1974—; lectr., trainer, cons. on mgmt. and bus. devel., 1971—. Mem. Am. Personnel and Guidance Assn., Am. Psychol. Assn., Fellowship Christian Athletes (former nat. v.p.), Phi Delta Kappa. Baptist. Contbr. articles to profl. jours. Address: 216 N Water St Liberty MO 64068

GOODRICH, ELIZABETH ANNE, educator; b. Seattle; d. Frank Allen and Hildegarde Anne (Hoffman) Goodrich; secretarial certificate Western Mich. U., 1961, B.B.A., 1963; M.A., Mich. State U., 1968; Ph.D., U. Colo., 1975. Secretarial position Inst. for Social Research, U. Mich., Ann Arbor, 1963-64, Downtown Kalamazoo Assn., 1964-66; instr. Lansing (Mich.) Community Coll., 1967; grad. asst., instr. bus. law and office adminstrn. dept. Mich. State U., E. Lansing, 1966-68; tchr., chmn. bus. dept. Grand Ledge (Mich.) High Sch., 1968-72; instr., coordinator student tchrs., officer adminstr. dept. U. Colo., Boulder, 1972-75; asso. prof. bus. edn. and adminstrv. services dept. Central Mich. U., Mt. Pleasant, 1975—. Certified profl. sec. Inst. for Certifying Secs.; permanent secondary teaching certificate in bus. edn. Mich. Dept. Edn.; vocat. edn. permanent teaching certificate Mich. Bd. Edn. Mem. AAUW, NEA, Nat., N. Central bus. edn. assns., Nat. Secs. Assn., Adminstrv. Mgmt. Soc. Internat., Mich. Bus. Edn. Assn., Mich. Edn. Assn., Delta Pi Epsilon. Office: Sch Bus Adminstrn Central Mich U Mount Pleasant MI 48859

GOODRICH, JAMES WERNER, pub. affairs exec.; b. Hamilton, Ohio, Aug. 7, 1932; s. James Carlyle and Ellen Elsie (Schneider) G.; A.B., Miami U., Oxford, Ohio, 1954; postgrad. Ohio State U., 1956; m. Saundra Sue Glass, May 23, 1954; children—Malinda, James D., David L. Reporter, editor Internat. News Service, Columbus, Ohio, 1956-57; chief pub. information officer Ohio Dept. Hwys., 1957-59; with Lazarus, Columbus, 1959-70; dir. pub. relations, urban affairs, 1966-70; pres. James Goodrich Assos., Columbus, 1971—. Mem. exec. com. Columbus Met. Community Action Orgn.; mem. nat. emergency com. Nat. Council Crime and Delinquency; mem. Mid-Ohio Regional Planning Commn., Pres.'s Council on Youth Opportunity; bd. mem. United Community Council; 1st chmn. Mayor's Council Youth Opportunity, Columbus; mem. bus. adv. com. U.S. Office Econ. Opportunity. Democratic candidate U.S. Congress, 1970, 72. Served with U.S. Army Security Agy., 1954-56. Recipient United Appeal award, 1967, others; named one of Ten Outstanding Young Men of Year Columbus Jr. C. of C., 1967; Ford Found. grantee 1956. Mem. Pub. Relations Soc. Am., Nat. Alliance Businessmen, Am. Retail Fedn., Columbus Area C. of C., Columbus Urban League. Presbyterian (bd. deacons). Club: Press (Ohio). Home: 2232 Bryden Rd Columbus OH 43221 Office: 407 E Livingston Ave Columbus OH 43215

GOODRICH, PHILIP RICHARD, agrl. engr., educator; b. Lockport, N.Y., Oct. 11, 1940; s. John Gardner and Marion Francis (Downes) G.; B. Agrl. Engring., Cornell U., 1963; M.S., Purdue U., 1968, Ph.D., 1970; m. Helen Dorothy Facer, Sept. 4, 1965; children—Peter Alan, Wendy Lynn. Vol., team leader Algeria for Internat. Vol. Services Inc., Washington, 1963-65; research asst. Dept. Agrl. Engring. Purdue U., Lafayette, Ind., 1965-70; asst. prof., extension agrl. engr. U. Minn., St. Paul, 1970-75, asso. prof., extension agrl. engr., 1975—; cons. animal waste problems. Mem. Am. Soc. Agrl. Engrs., Water Pollution Control Fedn., Nat. Soc. Profl. Engrs., Aircraft Owners and Pilots Assn., Sigma Xi, Alpha Epsilon, Gamma Sigma Delta. Methodist (trustee). Home: 1129 Pike Lake Dr New Brighton MN 55112 Office: Agrl Engring Bldg U Minn St Paul MN 55108

GOODRICH, ROBERT EDWARD, JR., clergyman; b. Cleburne, Tex., June 9, 1909; s. Robert Edward and Moye (Wilson) G.; B.A., Birmingham-So. U., 1931; M.A., Perkins Theol. Sch., 1940; D.D., Centenary Coll., 1950; LL.D., Central Meth. Coll., 1973; m. Thelma Quillian, June 5, 1939; children—Thelma Jean (Mrs. James Skinner), Lucy (Mrs. James Caswell), Robert Edward III, Paul Quillian. Ordained to ministry Methodist Ch., 1933; pastor in Port Arthur, Tex., 1935-37, Houston, 1937-44, El Paso, Tex. 1944-46, First Meth. Ch., Dallas, 1946—; bishop United Meth. Ch., 1972—, now presiding bishop Mo. area. Past chmn. jurisdictional council So. Central Jurisdiction Meth. Ch., also past chmn. jurisdictional TV, radio and film commn.; del. World Meth. Conf., 1966, Gen. Conf., 1952, 60, 64, 66, 68, 70. Chmn. bd. trustees St. Paul Sch. Theology, Kansas City, Mo., 1972—; trustee Southwestern U., So. Meth. U., Meth. Home for Children. Mem. Kappa Alpha. Author: What's It All About, 1955; Reach for the Sky, 1960; Lift Up Your Heart, 1961; On the Other Side of Sorrow, 1962, 70; Dear God Where Are You?, 1969. Created 1st dramatic religious TV show, 1949; preacher on radio. Address: 4625 Lindell Blvd Suite 420 St Louis MO 63108

GOODSMITH, DALE HAROLD, mech. engr.; b. Detroit, July 27, 1929; s. Harold Carl and Eva Elizabeth (Jones) G.; B.S., Lawrence Inst. Tech., 1971; m. Mavis Ruth Macomber, July 8, 1950; children—Mark Dale, Paul Alan, Glenn Richard. With Diversified Products, Detroit, 1949-51; aircraft technician Mich. N.G., Romulus, 1952-56; lab. technician Vickers, Inc., Troy, Mich., 1956-64, project engr., Troy, 1964-71; project engr. Multifastener Corp., Detroit, 1971-76, asst. chief engr., 1976—. Served to capt. USAF, 1951-52. Mem. Soc. Automotive Engrs., Nat. Geographic Soc. Republican. Lutheran. Patentee in field. Home: 31743 Middleboro St Livonia MI 48154 Office: 12668 Arnold St Detroit MI 48239

GOODSON, LEROY BEVERLY, physician; b. Elyria, Ohio, Feb. 11, 1933; s. Franklin Beverly and Inez Marie (Leach) G.; student Kenyon Coll., 1951-53; B.A., U. Mich., 1955, M.D., 1959; m. Evelyn Rae Wimmer, Aug. 27, 1965; 1 son, Parker Brook. Intern St. Rita's Hosp., Lima, Ohio, 1959-60; staff physician Lima State Mental Hosp., 1959-60; practice of medicine, Springfield, 1960-61, 63—; v.p. staff Community Hosp., 1973—, med. dir. alcohol chem. detoxication unit, 1975—; mem. staff Mercy Med. Center, Springfield; asso. clin. prof. family practice Wright State U., 1975—; med. dir. Clark County Drug Control, 1974—; dir. Med. Econs., Dayton; mem. adv. bd. Financial Enterprises, Cleve., 1969. Pres. Operation Big Sister, Springfield, 1968; mem. exec. com. A.R.C., 1966—; bd. dirs. Clark County Council Drug Abuse, 1970—. Mem. exec. com. bd. trustees Community Hosp., Springfield, 1966-68. Served to capt. AUS, 1961-63. Recipient Rackham Arthritic grant U. Mich., 1956. Recipient Community Service award Frontiers Internat., 1973. Mem. Ohio Assn. Gen. Practice (Mem. Hosp. com. 1971), Clark County Med. Soc. (pres. 1971). Democrat. Methodist (trustee). Home: 3152 Sherwood Park Dr Springfield OH 45505 Office: 2615 E High St Springfield OH 45505

GOODSTEIN, SANDERS ABRAHAM, scrap iron co. exec.; b. N.Y.C., Oct. 3, 1918; s. Samuel G. and Katie (Lipson) G.; student Wayne State U., 1934-36; A.B., U. Mich., 1938, M.B.A., 1939, J.D., 1946; postgrad. Harvard, 1943; m. Rose Laro, June 29, 1942; children—Peter, Esther, Jack, Rachel. Admitted to Mich. bar, 1946; sec., Laro Coal & Iron Co., Flint, Mich., 1946-60, pres. 1960—; owner, operator Paterson Mfg. Co., Flint, 1953—; gen. partner Indianhead Co., Pontiac, Mich., 1955-70, pres., 1965-70; sec. Amatac Corp., Erie, Pa., until 1969; chmn bd. Gen. Foundry & Mfg. Co., Flint, Mich., 1968— pres., 1970—; pres. Lacron Steel Co., Providence, 1975—; mem. corp. body Mich. Blue Shield, 1970-76. Served to lt. comdr. USNR, 1942-46. Mem. Fed. Bar Assn., Am. Bar Assn., Bar Mich., Am. Pub. Works Assn., Am. Foundrymen's Soc., Order of Coif, Beta Gamma Sigma, Phi Kappa Phi. Jewish. Home: 2602 Parkside Dr Flint MI 48503 Office: 6301 Dort Hwy Flint MI 48507

GOODWIN, ANDREW JACKSON, III, aquarium mfg. co. exec.; b. Washington, Oct. 22, 1943; s. Andrew Jackson Goodwin, Jr. and Charlotte Head Goodwin Simmons; A.B., Princeton U., 1966; M.B.A., Northwestern U., 1968; m. Janet Wilkinson, Jan. 31, 1963; children—Elizabeth, Andrew. Registered rep. Smith Barney & Co., Chgo., 1968-73; v.p. mktg. O'Dell Mfg. Inc., Saginaw, Mich., 1973-76; pres. C & A Mfg. Co., Bensenville, Ill., 1976—; dir. Equity Pet, Inc. Trustee Home for Destitute and Crippled Children, Chgo., 1972—. Recipient Achievement certificate U. Calif. at Los Angeles Grad. Bus. Sch. Mktg. Conf., 1975. Mem. Am. Pet Products Mfrs. Assn. (dir.), Pet Industry Distbrs. Assn., Pet Industry Joint Adv. Council. Episcopalian. Clubs: Univ. (Chgo.); Winter (Lake Forest, Ill.). Home: 1421 Conway Rd Lake Forest IL 60045 Office: 210 W Gateway Rd Bensenville IL 60106

GOODWIN, GLENN LAVERN, accountant; b. Hayward, Wis., Oct. 2, 1931; s. Vernon Willis and Violet Helen (Markstedt) G.; B.S., Brigham Young U., 1956; m. Rosemary Badger, Aug. 29, 1955; children—Mark, Catherine, Ruth, Alysha, Christine, Accountant, Arthur Young & Co., Los Angeles, 1956-62; partner Seidman & Seidman, Grand Rapids, Mich., 1963—. Mem. nat. scouting com. Boy Scouts Am., 1976—, scout chmn. State Mich., 1976—; stake pres. Ch. Jesus Christ of Latter-day Saints, 1975—. Served withy USAF, 1957-59. C.P.A. Mem. Am. Inst. C.P.A.'s, Mich. Soc. C.P.A.'s, Nat. Assn. Accountants, Municipal Fin. Officers Assn., Assn. Govtl. Accountants. Home: 2510 Lake Dr SE Grand Rapids MI 49506 Office: 700 Union Bank Plaza Grand Rapids MI 49502

GOODWIN, JESSE FRANCIS, clin. chemist, city ofcl.; b. Greenville, S.C., Feb. 7, 1929; s. Jesse and Francis (Byrd) G.; B.S. in Pharmacy cum laude, Xavier U., 1951; M.S., Wayne State U., 1953, Ph.D., 1957; m. Della M. McGraw, Dec. 26, 1959; children—Gordon Francis, Paula Therese, Jesse Stephen. Research asso. Detroit Receiving Hosp., Wayne State U. Coll. Medicine, Detroit, 1958-59; biochemist Wayne County Gen. Hosp., Eloise, Mich., 1959-63; staff biochemist Children's Hosp. Mich., Detroit, 1963-73, also dir. Core Lab. Clin. Research Center for Children, Wayne State U. Sch. Medicine, Children's Hosp. Mich., 1963-73; dir. clin. labs. Detroit Dept. Health, 1973—. Instr. Wayne State U. Sch. Medicine, 1964-66, asst. prof., 1966-73. Co-founder Meyers-7-Schaefer Community Council, v.p. 1964-74, pres., 1974—; mem. edn. com. New Detroit Com. Inc., 1971—. Fellow Am. Inst. Chemists; mem. N.A.A.C.P. (chmn. edn. com. Detroit br., dir. 1968—, 3d v.p. 1976—), Am. Assn. Clin. Chemists (Mich. sect. chmn. 1967), Am. Chem. Soc., A.A.A.S., N.Y. Acad. Sci., Assn. Analytical Chemists, Engring. Soc. Detroit, Detroit Physiol. Soc., Sigma Xi, Phi Lambda Upsilon, Rho Chi, Alpha Kappa Mu, Alpha Phi Alpha (pres. chpt. 1972-75). Roman Catholic. Club: Detroit Renaissance Lions (charter). Contbr. articles to profl. jours. Home: 19214 Appoline St Detroit MI 48235 Office: Detroit Health Dept 1151 Taylor St Detroit MI 48202

GOODYEAR, ARTHUR NELSON, TV broadcasting adminstr.; b. Sunderland, Mass., July 4, 1922; s. Robert Nelson and Elsie (Dexter) G.; grad. Leland Powers Sch. Radio Theatre TV, 1948; m. Cynthia Dorothy Haydock; children—Diana, Lois, Kathleen, Roberta. Announcer, writer Sta. WSYB, Rutland, Vt., 1948, Keene, N.H., 1948-50, Sta. WFBM-TV and Sta. WIBC, Indpls., 1961-65; pub. info. officer Ft. Benjamin Harrison, Indpls., 1966-69, chief of ednl. TV, U.S. Army Adminstrn. Center, 1969-77, tng. aids and audio-visual officer, 1977—. Served with U.S. Army, 1941-45, 50-61; ETO, Korea. Mem. Nat. Assn. Ednl. Broadcasters, Ind. Artists Craftsmen, Ind. Potters Guild, VFW, Tau Kappa Epsilon. Home: 2929 Boehning Ave Indianapolis IN 46219 Office: Training Aid Service Office Ft Benjamin Harrison IN 46216

GOOGASIAN, GEORGE ARA, lawyer; b. Pontiac, Mich., Feb. 22, 1936; s. Peter and Lucy (Chobanian) G.; B.A., U. Mich., 1958; J.D., Northwestern U., 1961; m. Phyllis Elaine Law, June 27, 1959; children—Karen Ann, Steven George, Dean Michael. Admitted to Mich. bar, 1961; atty. Marentay, Rouse, Selby, Fischer & Webber, Detroit, 1961-62; asst. U.S. atty., Detroit, 1962-64; mem. firm Beier, Howlett, McConnell, Googasian & McCann, Bloomfield Hills, Mich., 1964—. Chmn. Oakland County Democratic Com., Pontiac, 1964-70; state campaign chmn. Sen. Philip A. Hart, 1970. Bd. dirs. Big Bros. Oakland County, 1968-73. Fellow Am. Coll. Trial Lawyers; mem. State Bar Mich., Am., Oakland County (dir.) bar assns., Am. Judicature Soc. Presbyterian. Home: 3750 Orion Rd Rochester MI 48063 Office: 74 W Long Lake Bloomfield Hills MI 48013

GOPPERS, MANEKS VELTA, chemist; b. Gostini, Latvia, Feb. 28, 1915; came to U.S., 1949, naturalized, 1954; d. Karlis and Milda Maneks; m. Sergejs Goppers, 1941 (div. 1947); 1 dau., Ilze. M.S., U. Riga, Latvia, 1944. Asst. U. Riga, Latvia, 1940-44; analytical chemist Farben Industries, Germany, 1944-45; instr. tech. sch. Stuttgart, Germany, 1945-47; mgr. pharmacy and chem. preparation lab. Esslingen, N. Germany, 1947-49; analytical chemist Twin City Testing and Engring Lab., St. Paul, 1949-52; chem. U. Minn., 1952-53, jr. scientist, 1953-59, sr. scientist Sch. Pub. Health, 1959-68, sr. scientist Space Sci. Center, 1968-70, sr. scientist Sch. Pub. Health Environ. Health, 1970—. Fellow Am. Inst. Chemists, AAAS; mem. Am. Indsl. Hygiene (asso.), Am. Chem. Soc., Am. Inst. Physicis, Sigma Xi, Iota Sigma Pi, Sigma Delta Epsilon. Recipient research award Iota Sigma Pi, 1976; contbr. articles to profl. jours. Home: 5164 Abercrombie Dr Minneapolis MN 55435 Office: U Minn Sch Pub Health Environmental Health Minneapolis MN 55455

GOR, VISHNU JETHALAL, chem. engr.; b. Malpur, India, Oct. 21, 1940; s. Jethalal V. and Maniben G. (Pandya) G.; B.S. in Chemistry, St. Xavier's Coll., 1961; B.S. in Chem. Engring., U. Mo., Rolla; m. Surya D. Pandya, June 20, 1960; children—Kanak V., Niraj V. Research chemist Burgess Cellulose Co., Freeport, Ill., 1965-66; sr. polymer chemist Paint Research Assos. Lab., Chgo., 1966-68; research engr. Continental Can Co., Chgo., 1968-74, supr., 1974—. Mem. Am. Inst. Chem. Engrs., Fedn. Paint Tech., Am. Soc. Lubrication Engrs. Hindu. Club: Toastmasters (Able Toastmasters award 1975). Patentee in field. Home: 17543 S Anthony Ave Country Club Hills IL 60477 Office: 1350 W 76th St Chicago IL 60620

GORALNIK, OLIVER AARON, chain store exec.; b. Newark, June 13, 1907; s. Abe and Anna (Krugman) G.; B.S., Washington U., 1930; m. Alma Hirsch, Oct. 27, 1935; children—Barbara (Mrs. Bernard G. Kohm), Jane Ellen (Mrs. Hans Levi), Mary Beth (Mrs. Joseph H. Mohrman, Jr.). Accountant, C. B. Adams, C.P.A.'s, St. Louis, 1930-31; asst. sales mgr. Weilkalter Mfg. Co., St. Louis, 1931-36; store mgr. P.N. Hirsch & Co., Retail Jr. Dept. Stores, St. Louis, 1936-44, div. merchandise mgr., 1944-46, treas., 1946—, also dir. Bd. dirs. Jewish Employment and Vocational Service. Mem. Beta Gamma Sigma, Omicron Delta Gamma. Jewish. Home: 14 Lake Forest St St Louis MO 63117 Office: 2001 Walton Rd St Louis MO 63114

GORALSKI, CHRISTIAN THOMAS, chemist; b. Cleve., Jan. 6, 1942; s. Walter Thomas and Emma Catherine (Binder) G.; B.S., Case Inst. Tech., 1964; Ph.D., Purdue U., 1968; m. Carol Lee Thompson, June 22, 1968; children—Anna Katherine, Christian Thomas, Timothy Mark, Leah Kuenzel. With Dow Chem. Co., Midland, Mich., 1968—, research chemist, 1968-71, research specialist, organic chem. research dept., 1975—. Mem. Midland Case Alumni Club (pres.

1974-76). Am. Chem. Soc. (chmn. elect. Midland 1977), Sigma Xi, Tau Beta Pi, Alpha Chi Sigma, Pi Delta Epsilon, Sigma Chi, Methodist. Patentee in chem. compositions and processes. Contbr. articles to profl. jours. Home: 2715 Georgetown Dr Midland MI 48640 Office: Dow Chemical Co 438 Bldg Midland MI 48640

GORDILLO, MANUEL E., psychiatrist; b. Lima, Peru, Aug. 29, 1930; s. Manuel E. and Lidia A. (Vasquez) G.; came to U.S., 1958, naturalized, 1963; M.D., San Marcos U., Lima, 1957; m. Ruth Ann Smith, Aug. 18, 1959; children—Gregory, Gayle, Christine, Nancy, Daniel, Mathew, Michael. Psychiat. resident U. Minn., 1963-66; practice medicine, specializing in psychiatry, Cleve., 1966—; chief staff Woodruff Hosp., Cleve., 1973-74, also trustee. Diplomate Am. Bd. Psychiatry and Neurology. Fellow Am. Psychiat. Assn.; mem. Ohio Psychiat. Assn. (chmn. peer rev. com. 1973—), Am., Ohio med. assns., Cleve. Acad. Medicine, Cleve. Soc. Psychiatry and Neurology (pres. 1973-74). Home: 17810 Lake St Cleveland OH 44107 Office: 15644 Madison Ave Lakewood OH 44107

GORDIN, RICHARD DAVIS, univ. athletic dir.; b. South Charleston, Ohio, July 16, 1928; s. Edwin Ray and Mildred (Davis) G.; B.A., Ohio Wesleyan U., 1952; M.A., Ohio State U., 1954, Ph.D., 1967; m. Paula Alice Egan, July 23, 1949; children—Richard D. Jr., Robert H., Douglas P. Grad. asst. phys. edn. Ohio State U., 1953; dir. recreation United Cerebral Palsy, Columbus, Ohio, 1954; instr. phys. edn. Ohio Wesleyan U., Delaware, 1954-59, asst. prof., 1959-67, asso. prof., 1967-71, prof., 1971—, dir. athletics, 1977—; ednl. cons. Nat. Golf Found., 1966—; mem. parks recreation bd. City of Delaware, 1970-77, chmn., 1974. Recipient citation Delaware City Council, 1977. Co-author: Golf Fundamentals, 1973. Editor: The Golf Coach's Guide, 1975. Home: 80 Hillside Dr Delaware OH 43015 Office: Ohio Wesleyan Univ Delaware OH 43015

GORDON, CHARLES OTTO, coll. dean; b. Peoria, Ill., May 4, 1928; s. Russell Milton and Florence Marie (Stults) G.; B.A., Blackburn Coll., 1950; M.Ed., U. Ill., 1952; m. Mary Frances Norton, Mar. 24, 1951; children—Russell Arthur, David Charles. Coach, tchr., prin. elementary sch. Girard (Ill.) Community Unit Sch. Dist., 1952-55; asst. supt. schs. Carlinville (Ill.) Community Unit Sch. Dist., 1955-57; dean students Blackburn Coll., Carlinville, 1957—, registrar, financial aids officer, 1957-68. Mem. Am., Ill. personnel guidance assns., Am. (pres. 1973-74), Ill. coll. personnel assns., Nat. Assn. Student Personnel Adminstrs., Ill. Assn. Collegiate Registrars Admissions Officers (hon., pres. 1967-68), Phi Delta Kappa. Methodist. Club: Rotary (Carlinville). Editor: (with C. R. Hughes and R. L. Underbrink) Collective Negotiations in Higher Education—A Reader, 1973. Home: 410 Hillcrest Dr Carlinville IL 62626 Office: 700 College Ave Carlinville IL 62626

GORDON, EDGAR GEORGE, lawyer, bus. exec.; b. Detroit, Feb. 27, 1924; s. Edgar George and Verna (Hay) G.; A.B., Princeton U., 1947; postgrad. Harvard Bus. Sch., 1945; J.D., Harvard, 1950; m. Alice J. Irwin, Feb. 4, 1967; children—David, Scott. Admitted to Mich. bar, 1951, U.S. Supreme Ct. bar; asso. firm Poole, Warren & Littell, 1950-54; partner firm Poole, Warren, Littell & Gordon, Detroit, 1954-63; corporate counsel Hygrade Food Products Corp. 1963-69, asst. sec., 1965-66, sec., 1966-69, v.p., counsel 1968-69; v.p., sec., counsel City Nat. Bank of Detroit, 1969—; v.p., sec., counsel No. States Bancorp., 1971—; dir. Kelly Mortgage and Investment Co. Mem. Founders Soc. Detroit Inst. Arts. Bd. dirs. Inner-City Community Clinic, 1961-69. Served to lt. (j.g.) USNR, 1943-46. Mem. Am. Judicature Soc., Am. Soc. Corp. Secs., Detroit Hist. Soc., Am., Detroit, Mich. bar assns. Presbyn. Clubs: Detroit, Detroit Country, Economic (Detroit). Home: 210 Lothrop Rd Grosse Pointe Farms MI 48236 Office: Suite 3900 Tower 400 Renaissance Center Detroit MI 48243

GORDON, EDWIN FREDERICK ROBERT, metal fabricating co. exec.; b. Oak Park, Ill., Jan. 4, 1921; s. Edwin C. and Alice (Heller) G.; B.S., Concordia Coll., 1942; M.A., Northwestern U., 1945; Ph.D., Purdue U., 1951; m. Jennifer Adams, Oct. 31, 1941 (div.); children—Dawn Alice, Denise Ann, E. Robert F., Allen D., Roger M., James Adams; m. 2d, Jeri Walker, Jan. 4, 1973 (div.); 1 son, John Robin. Pres., dir. Geuder, Paeschke & Frey Co., metal fabricating co., Milw., after 1955, now chmn. bd., dir.; dir. Gordon-Hoover & Assos., Inc., mgmt. consultants, Chgo., Capital Investments, Inc., Milw.; chmn. bd. Boyer-Rosene Moving & Storage Co., Inc., Arlington Heights, Ill.; pres. Hillsboro Land Mark, Inc., Hillsboro Beach, Fla., Gordon Studios Inc., Davie, Fla. Mem. Am. Psychol. Assn., Sigma Xi. Home: 1021 Hillsboro Mile Hillsboro Beach FL 33062 Office: 324 N 15th St Milwaukee WI 53201

GORDON, GILBERT, chemist, ednl. adminstr.; b. Chgo., Nov. 11, 1933; s. Catherine and Walter G.; B.S., Bradley U., 1955; Ph.D. in Chemistry, Mich. State U., 1959; m. Joyce Elaine Masura; children—Thomas, Susan. Postdoctoral research asso. chemistry U. Chgo., 1959-60; asst. prof. chemistry U. Md., College Park, 1960-64, asso. prof., 1964-67, prof., 1967; prof. chemistry U. Iowa, Iowa City, 1967-73; prof., chmn. dept. chemistry Miami U., Oxford Ohio 1973—; vis. prof. Japanese Soc. Promotion Sci., Japan, 1969; cons. Nat. Bur. Standards, Internat. Dioxide Corp., Olin Corp. Mem. Am. Chem. Soc., Chem. Soc. London, Faraday Soc., Sigma Xi, Phi Kappa Phi. Editor catalysis kinetics sect. Chem. Abstracts, 1970—; editorial bd. synthesis inorganic metalorganic chemistry Ohio Jour. Sci., 1971—; contbr. articles to chem. jours. Address: 190 Shadowy Hills Dr Oxford OH 45056

GORDON, HOWARD AARON, electric supply co. exec.; b. Danville, Ill., Mar. 15, 1922; s. Harold and Irene (Seifer) G.; B.S. in Gen. Engring., U. Ill., 1943; m. Vivian Miller, June 22, 1947; children—Nancy Cara, James Miller. Plant engr. Diamond Wire & Cable Co., Sycamore, Ill., 1947-50; dist. mgr. Western Tire & Auto Stores, Chgo., 1950-52; with Gordon Electric Supply, Inc., Kankakee, Ill., 1952—, pres., 1958—; dir. City Nat. Bank, Kankakee. Bd. dirs. Riverside Hosp., 1971-77, YMCA; adv. bd. St. Mary's Hosp., Kankakee; adv. bd. Kankakee Bd. Edn., 1955-57. Served as lt. s.g. USNR, 1943-47. Mem. Kankakee C. of C. (dir. 1970-73), Nat. Assn. Elec. Distbrs. (bd. govs.). Jewish. Clubs: B'nai B'rith, Kankakee Country, Rotary, Ravisloe Country, Elks. Home: 1006 Gardner Rd Flossmoor IL 60422 Office: Route 50 N Kankakee IL 60201

GORDON, HOWARD LYON, advt. and mktg. exec.; b. Chgo., Oct. 8, 1930; s. Milton Arthur and Betty Z. (Ginsburg) G.; B.S., U. Ill., 1952; M.S., Northwestern U., 1954, M.B.A., 1962; m. Lois Jean Kaufman, Aug. 21, 1955; children—Carolyn Ann, Leslie Meredith. Mktg. research mgr. Marsteller Inc., advt., Chgo., 1960-68, v.p. mktg. services, 1969-76; dir. client service Britt and Frerichs Inc., mktg. research and advt. cons., Chgo., 1977—; lectr. advt. and mktg. Northwestern U., 1963—. Regional chmn. Crusade of Mercy, Evanston, Ill., 1969. Served with AUS, 1954-56. Recipient award Dept. Def., 1956. Mem. Am. Mktg. Assn. (dir., v.p. mktg. mgmt.), Sigma Delta Chi. Contbr. articles to profl. publs. and mktg. texts. Home: 2025 Sherman Ave Evanston IL 60201 Office: Wrigley Bldg 410 N Michigan Ave Chicago IL 60611

GORDON, JAMES WILLIAM, hosp. adminstr.; b. Jackson, Mich., Apr. 16, 1921; s. George Edward and Anna (Housman) G.; B.B.A., St. Marys U., 1964; postgrad; m. Jeanne Helene Teller, Apr. 23, 1946; children—Olivia (Mrs. W. Stewart), Michelle (Mrs. C. Thoman), Dolores (Mrs. C. Gardiner), Jaqueline, James William III, Mark L. Inducted U.S. Army, 1942, advanced through grades to lt. col., 1961, ret. 1962; exec. dir. planning Hosp. and Related Facilities Planning Unit, Grand Rapids, Mich., 1967-69; adminstr. Starke Meml. Hosp., Knox, Ind., 1969—. Mem. Am. Coll. Hosp. Adminstrs., Am., Ind. (dir.), No. Ind. (dir.) hosp. assns., Am. Acad. Med. Adminstrn., V.F.W., Am. Legion, Ret. Officers Assn., Nat. Rifle Assn. (life), others. Mason (Shriner). Home: Box 314 Rural Route 5 Knox IN 46534 Office: Starke Memorial Hospital 102 E Culver Rd Knox IN 46534

GORDON, LEWIS ALEXANDER, electronics exec.; b. Milw., Oct. 4, 1937; s. Lewis Alexander and Verna Alma (Stocker) G.; B.S. in Mech. Engring., Purdue U., 1959; postgrad. RCA Insts., 1962; postgrad. No. Ill. U., 1967-68; m. Frances Rita Dziadzio, June 4, 1960; children—Robert Alan, Richard Alan, Pamela Ann. Process engr. Ill. Tool Works, Elgin, 1959-63; chief engr. Norcon Electronics, Elgin, 1963-65; v.p. Midland Standard, Inc., Elgin, 1964—, chmn. bd., 1967—. Del. Joint Electronics Industry Conf.; mem. adv. bd. Electronics mag., 1976—. Vice pres. bd. trustees Gail Borden Pub. Library Dist., 1971—, rep. North Suburban Library System, 1971—. Bd. advisers Easter Seal Assn., Elgin, 1971-74. Registered profl. engr., Ill., Mich. Mem. Ill. C. of C., Elgin Assn. Commerce, A.L.A., Ill. Library Assn. (automation com. 1975—), Ill. Soc. Profl. Engrs., Nat. Brit. Horological Inst., So. Calif. Computer Soc., Ill. Mfrs. Assn., Assn. Watch and Clock Collectors, Agent-Aeronca Champion Club, Pi Tau Sigma. Lutheran. Contbr. articles to profl. jours. Patentee in field. Home: 705 Diane Ave Elgin IL 60120 Office: 603 E Chicago St Elgin IL 60120

GORDON, ROBERT STANLEY, archivist; b. Tokyo, Apr. 18, 1923; s. Joseph and Olga (Kniaz) G.; B.A., McGill U., 1952; M.A., Carleton U.; m. F.M. Jacqueline Wilson, Sept. 2, 1963; children—Stephanie, Drew, Alexandra. Staff archivist, Anglican Diocesan Archives, Montreal, Que., Can., 1951-52; staff archivist Pub. Archives Canada, Ottawa, Ont., 1956-64, head, post confederation sect., 1964-65, chief of manuscript div., 1965—; chmn. Nat. Archival Appraisal Bd., 1971—. Served with British Army, World War II. Fellow Soc. Am. Archivists (chmn. internat. archival affairs com.); mem. Canadian Hist. Assn. (dir., treas., 1956—). Contbr. articles to profl. jours. Home: 244 Clemow Ave Ottawa ON K1S 2B6 Canada Office: 395 Wellington St Ottawa ON K1A 0N3 Canada

GORDON, ROBERT THOMAS, surgeon; b. Chgo., Feb. 13, 1950; s. David and Eunice (Wienshienk) G.; B.S. with highest distinction in Medicine, Northwestern U., 1971, M.D. with highest distinction, 1972. Resident dept. surgery Wesley, Passavant, Evanston, VA, Children's Meml. hosps., 1972-76, chief resident gen. surgery, 1976-77; chief resident cardio-thoracic surgery Northwestern U. Med. Sch., Northwestern U. Hosps., 1977—; instr. gen. surgery Northwestern U. Med. Sch., 1976-77, instr. cardio-thoracic surgery, 1977—; cons., researcher in field; staff asso. Nat. Inst. Health HEW, 1974. Recipient Hoffman LaRoche award, 1971-72; Macy Found. Research fellow, 1967; G.D. Searle scholar and fellow, 1967-73; Med. Scientist Life Ins. fellow, 1969; Northwestern U. Med. Research fellow, 1968; Phi Beta Pi scholar, 1970; Frederick K. Rawson, Jr. scholar, 1972; diplomate Nat. Bd. Med. Examiners. Mem. AMA (Physician's Recognition award 1975—), Chgo. Med. Assn., Ill. State Med. Soc., Flying Physicians Assn., Northwestern U., Northwestern U. Med. Sch. alumni assns., Ill. Jr. Acad. Scis. (hon.), U.S., Chgo. Dist. tennis assns., Alpha Omega Alpha, Phi Eta Sigma. Contbr. numerous articles to profl. jours. Home and Office: 4936 W Estes Skokie IL 60077

GORDON, STEVEN STANLEY, automotive parts co. exec.; b. Detroit, Aug. 29, 1919; s. Andrew C. and Mary (Matlak) G.; B.B.A., Detroit Inst. Tech., 1954; m. Eleanore Clare Pazgrat, Apr. 27, 1946; 1 dau., Kathleen Anne. With Republic Automotive Parts, Inc., St. Clair Shores, Mich., 1941—, office mgr., 1946-49, asst. to pres., 1949-54, v.p. sales, 1954-58, gen. mgr., 1957—, pres., 1958—, dir., 1957—; chmn. bd. Parts Warehouse, Anchorage, Republic Parts, Inc., St Clair Shores, Mich.; dir. Hayes-Albion Corp., Hayden Trans Cooler, Inc.; chmn. joint operating com. Internat. Automotive Service Industries Show, 1977, chmn. Eastern Automotive Show, 1973. Served to capt. AUS, 1942-46. Mem. Motor and Equipment Mfrs. Assn. (pres., dir. 1963-64, 1965-70, treas. 1971-73, adv. bd. 1974—), Automotive Sales Council (dir., pres. 1966-67), Automotive Presidents Council (founder, pres. 1972-73), Newcomen Soc. Roman Catholic. Club: Lochmoor Country. Home: 818 Sunningdale Dr Grosse Pointe MI 48236 Office: 20200 E Nine Mile Rd St Clair Shores MI 48080

GORDON, THEODORE, dentist; b. Chgo., July 22, 1923; s. Harry and Anne (Glickman) G.; D.D.S., Loyola U. at Chgo., 1946; m. Lorraine Maltz, June 11, 1944; children—Jeffry Gordon, Stephen, Robert. Practice dentistry Chgo., 1946-51, 53—. Asso. prof. Sch. Dentistry, Northwestern U., Chgo., 1972—. Served to capt. USAF, 1951-53. Mem. Pierre Fauchard Acad., Fedn. Dentaire Internationale, Chgo. Acad. Dental Research (pres. 1956-58), Am. Dental Assn., Ill., Chgo. dental socs., Am. Acad. Periodontology, Dental Technicians Soc. Chgo. Office: 111 N Wabash Ave Chicago IL 60602

GORDON, VIRGINIA NISWONGER, coll. adminstr.; b. Dayton, Ohio, Dec. 13, 1927; d. Milo E. and Irma (Kupf) Niswonger; B.S., Ohio State U., 1949, M.A., 1972, Ph.D., 1977; m. George D. Gordon, July 21, 1950; children—David, Catherine, Robert. Instr. dental hygiene Coll. Dentistry Ohio State U., Columbus, 1949-52, academic advisor, 1972-73, coordinator career devel., acad. advisement, 1973—, also adj. asst. prof. Coll. Edn.; cons. in field. Mem. Am. Personnel and Guidance Assn., Am. Coll. Personnel Assn., Nat. Vocat. Guidance Assn., Mortar Bd. (nat. council 1964-73), Phi Delta Kappa. Author numerous publs. in field. Home: 3160 Kioka Ave Columbus OH 43221 Office: 025 W Hall Univ Coll Ohio State Univ Columbus OH 43210

GORECKI, JAN, educator; b. Warsaw, Poland, Apr. 10, 1926; s. Jozef Hilary and Jadwiga Barbara (Frendzel) G.; came to U.S. 1969, naturalized, 1974; Magister Juris, Cracow (Poland) U., 1947, D.Sc. Juridicarum, 1958; Dr. Jur., Wroclaw (Poland) U., 1949; m. Danuta M. Wojnar, Dec. 26, 1954; children—Piotr S., Marie J. Asst. to asso. prof. Law U. Cracow 1947-68; fellow Center for Advanced Study in Behavioral Scis., Stanford, Calif., 1969-70, research asso. Stanford Law Sch., 1970; prof. sociology U. Ill., Urbana, 1970—, exec. com. Russian and East European Center, 1971—, asso. Center for Advanced Study, 1976-77; fgn. Univs. Exchange Scheme visitor U. London, 1963; Brit. Council scholar London Sch. Econs. 1959-60; Rockefeller fellow in humanities, 1976-77. Mem. Am., Internat. sociol. assns. (sociology law research com.), Internat. Soc. Family Law, Am. Assn. for Advancement Slavic Studies, A.A.U.P. Author: Divorce in Poland, A Contribution to Sociology of Law, 1970. Editor, contbr. Sociology and Jurisprudence of Leon Petrazycki, 1975. Contbr. articles to profl. jours. Home: 510 W Washington St Urbana IL 61801

GOREN, HERSHEL, physician; b. Detroit, Oct. 9, 1938; s. Phillip and Sylvia (Demb) G.; B.S. with high honors, Mich. State U., 1960; M.D., Wayne State U., 1964. Intern, Cleve. Met. Gen. Hosp., 1964-65; resident neurology Mayo Grad. Sch. Medicine, Rochester, Minn., 1965-68; practice medicine specializing in neurology, Cleve., 1970—; mem. staff Cleve. Clinic, 1970—; clin. instr. neurology La. State U. Sch. Medicine also vis. physician Charity Hosp. La., New Orleans, 1970. Served with USAF, 1968-70. Diplomate Am. Bd. Psychiatry and Neurology. Mem. Am. Acad. Neurology, Am. Electroencephalographic Soc. (asso. mem.), Am. Heart Assn. (fellow stroke council), Am. Epilepsy Soc., Alpha Omega Alpha. Home: 17100 Van Aken Blvd Shaker Heights OH 44120 Office: 9500 Euclid Ave Cleveland OH 44106

GOREN, SEYMOUR BERNARD, ophthalmologist; b. Bklyn., Apr. 8, 1934; s. Benjamin and Mollie (Greenberg) G.; B.A. with distinction, U. Rochester, 1955; M.D., U. Chgo., 1958; m. Cynthia Sara Levin, June 10, 1958; children—William, Matthew, Nancy. Intern, Phila. Gen. Hosp., 1958-59; resident U. Chgo. Clinics, 1959-63; instr. ophthalmology U. Chgo., 1962-63; practice medicine specializing in ophthalmology, Chgo., 1965—; sr. attending physician Northwestern Meml. Hosp., 1965—; asst. prof. ophthalmology Northwestern U., 1965—. Mem. Bd. edn., Lincolnwood, Ill., 1968-75, pres., 1970-73. Served as capt. AUS, 1963-65. Recipient several fed. and pvt. research grants. Mem. A.M.A., Ill., Chgo. med. socs., Chgo. Ophthalmology Soc. (v.p. 1975), Am. Acad. Ophthalmology and Otolaryngology, Am. Coll. Surgeons, Assn. Research in Vision, Assn. Research to Prevent Blindness, Pan Am. Assn. Ophthalmology, Sigma Xi, Sigma Nu. Mem. Jewish. Mem. B'nai B'rith (bd. dirs. 1968). Contbr. articles to profl. publs. Home: 6503 Navajo Lincolnwood IL 60646 Office: 2419 Prudential Plaza Chicago IL 60601

GOREN, SIMON LESLIE, librarian, educator; b. Gencs, Hungary, Nov. 9, 1913; s. Ignac and Elizabeth (Klein) Grossman; came to U.S., 1959, naturalized, 1965; Matriculation certificate, Realgimnasium, Debrecen, Hungary, 1923-31; diploma of law, British Mandatory Govt. Law Sch., 1948; M.L.S., Columbia U., 1960; m. Hilda Feuerstein, Aug. 11, 1943; children—Daphne Judith, Michael. Practice of law, Haifa, Israel, 1951-59; librarian Cleary, Gottlieb, Steen & Hamilton, N.Y.C., 1960-63; asst. law librarian Cornell U. Sch. of Law, 1964-67; law librarian Case Western Reserve U., Cleve., 1967—, prof. law, 1970—. Mem. Internat. Assn. Law Libraries, Am. Library Assn., Am. Assn. Law Libraries, Order of Coif. Home: 3380 Ingleside Rd Shaker Heights OH 44122 Office: 11075 East Blvd Cleveland OH 44106

GORHAM, EUGENE TIMOTHY, conveyor co. exec.; b. Chgo., May 2, 1935; s. Sidney Smith and Corinne (McVoy) G.; B.M.E., Stanford, 1957; m. Barbara Francis Steinke, Nov. 26, 1966; children—Jonathon Lewis, Eugene Timothy, Brooke Lee, Whitney Ann. Indsl. engr. U.S. Rubber Co., Chgo., 1959-60, Oscar Mayer Co., Chgo., 1960-61; sales engr. Olson Conveyor Co. (now div. ACCO), Franklin Park, Ill., 1962-67; v.p. sales Automotion, Inc. (Ill. Corp.), Alsip, Ill., 1967-73, pres. Automotion Inc. (Del. Corp.), Alsip, 1973—, also dir.; partner AW & H Leasing Corp.; dir. A.W. & H. Corp., Alsip. Served with AUS, 1957. Mem. Internat. Material Mgmt. Soc., Material Handling Equipment Distbrs. Assn. (chmn. engineered products com. 1971-75), Chi Psi. Clubs: Pentwater (Mich.) Yacht; Saddle and Cycle, Tavern (Chgo.). Home: 445 Briar Pl Chicago IL 60657 Office: 11743 S Mayfield Ave Alsip IL 60482

GORHAM, SIDNEY SMITH, JR., , lawyer; b. LaGrange, Ill., Dec. 23, 1906; s. Sidney Smith and Myrtle (Willett) G.; grad. Phillip Exeter Acad., 1924; student Princeton, 1928; Ph.B., U. Chgo., 1928, J.D., 1930; m. Corinne McVoy, Sept. 22, 1928; children—Sidney Smith III, E. Timothy, Jeffrey H. Admitted to Ill. bar, 1930, since practiced in Chgo.; partner Miller, Gorham, Wescott & Adams Chgo., 1932-75, Gorham, Metge, Bowman & Hourigan, 1976—. Mem. Am., Ill., Chgo. (treas. 1952-54) bar assns. Clubs: Law, Legal, Tavern, Saddle and Cycle, Mid-day (Chgo.). Home: 1242 Lake Shore Dr Chicago IL 60610 Office: 33 N LaSalle St Chicago IL 60602

GORI, LEE LOUIS, chemist; b. Litchfield, Ill., Jan. 10, 1946; s. Earl Louis and Edith B. (Giuliani) G.; m. Judith A. Perkins, Feb. 20, 1969; children—Randy, Tracy. B.S. in Chemistry, U. Mo., 1969; postgrad Washington U., 1974-75. Engr. quality control N.L. Industries, St. Louis, 1969-72; chief shift chemist research and devel., match div. U.M.C. Industries, Ferguson, Mo., 1972-74, dir. quality control, plant chemist, 1974—. Vol. sci. instr. State Mental Hosp., St. Louis. Mem. Am. Chem. Soc., Am. Soc. for Quality Control, U. Mo. St. Louis Alumni Assn. Home: 1901 Elkins Dr St Louis MO 63136 Office: 400 Paul Ave Ferguson MO 63135

GORMAN, GERALD WARNER, lawyer; b. North Kansas City, Mo., May 30, 1933; s. William Shelton and Bessie (Warner) G.; A.B. cum laude, Harvard Coll., 1954; LL.B. magna cum laude, Harvard, 1956; m. Anita Belle McPike, June 26, 1954; children—Guinevere Eve, Victoria Rose. Admitted to Mo. bar, 1956, since practiced in Kansas City; asso. firm Dietrich, Tyler, Davis, Burrell & Dicus, 1956-62, partner, 1963—; dir. North Kansas City State Bank. Bd. govs. Citizens Assn. Kansas City, 1962—; trustee Kansas City Mus., 1967—, Citizens Bond Com. of Kansas City, 1973—; bd. dirs. Spofford Home for Children, 1972—. Served with AUS, 1956-58. Mem. Lawyers Assn. Kansas City (exec. com. 1968-71), Am., Mo., Kansas City, Clay County bar assns., Harvard Law Sch. Assn. Mo. (pres. 1973). Republican. Methodist. Clubs: Harvard (pres. 1966), University, Kansas City, Old Pike Country. Home: 917 E Vivion Rd Kansas City MO 64118 Office: Dwight Bldg Kansas City MO 64105

GORMAN, ROBERT JAMES, lawyer; b. Chgo., Apr. 22, 1915; s. James E. and Isabel M. (O'Brien) G.; student Northwestern U., 1934-37; J.D., Chgo. Kent Coll. Law, 1940; children—Robert C., Gregory X., Candace. Admitted to Ill. bar, 1940; practice law, Chgo., 1945—; mem. firm Gorman & Gorman; atty. Roosevelt U. Served to 1st lt. C.E., AUS, 1941-45. Mem. Am., Ill., Chgo. bar assns., Nat. Assn. Coll. and Univ. Attys., Phi Alpha Delta. Democrat. Unitarian. Club: So. Shore Yacht. Home: 3734 N Wilton St Chicago IL 60613 Office: 10 S LaSalle St Chicago IL 60603

GORNICK, ALAN LEWIS, lawyer, tax counsel; b. Leadville, Colo.; s. Mark and Anne (Grayhack) G.; A.B., Columbia U., 1935, LL.B., 1937; m. Ruth L. Willcockson, 1940 (dec.); children—Alan Lewis, Diana (Mrs. Lawrence J. Richard), Keith Hardin; m. Pauline Martoi, 1972. Admitted to N.Y. State bar, 1937, practiced with firm Baldwin, Todd & Young, N.Y.C., 1937-41; practiced with firm Milbank, Tweed, Hope & Hadley, 1941-47, mem. firm, 1947; asso. counsel charge tax matters Ford Motor Co., Dearborn, Mich., 1947-49, dir. tax affairs, tax counsel, 1949-64; lectr. tax matters N.Y.U. Inst. on Fed. Taxation, 1947—, Am. Bar Assn. and Practising Law Inst. courses on fundamentals in fed. taxation, 1946—, Am. Law Inst. courses in continuing legal edn., 1950—; spl. lectr. sch. bus. adminstrn. U. Mich., 1949, 53; pres. Otsego Ski Club-Hidden Valley, Inc., Gaylord, Mich., Perry-Davis, Inc.; v.p. Meadowbrook Park Devel. Co., Bloomfield Center, Inc., Bloomfield Hills, Mich., Seagate

Hotel, Inc., Delray Beach, Fla.; dir. Castleton Industries, Inc., N.Y.C., Brooks & Perkins, Inc. Chmn. state and fed. tax coms.; mem. Mayor's Detroit Tomorrow Com., Citizens Adv. Com. on Taxation to Mich. Senate, Detroit Bd. Commerce; chmn. Mich. tax survey adv. com. Legis. Interim Tax and Revenue Study Com., 1951-53; chmn. Mich. State Aid Survey Com.; pres. Mich. Assn. Emotionally Disturbed Children, 1962; mem. exec. bd. of adv. council Detroit area council Boy Scouts Am.; v.p., trustee Detroit chpt. Archives of Am. Art; mem. fin. com. Mich. Heart Assn. Recipient Gov.'s Spl. Award State of Colo., 1952; Distinguished Alumni Accomplishment medal Columbia, 1947. Mem. Fed., Am. (mem. fed. tax com. 1954-56; chmn. subcom. on health and welfare plans, com. pension and profit sharing trusts, sect. taxation 1950—, com. extra-territorial application of taxes 1951—), Mich. Detroit, N.Y.C. (chmn. subcom. estate and gift taxes, 1943(47) bar assns., Am. Law Inst., Tax Inst. Inc. (pres. 1954-55, dir. 1951—), Nat. Tax Assn. (exec. com. 1954-56), Internat. Fiscal Assn. (council mem.; nat. reporter 6th Internat. Congress Fiscal Law, Brussels 1952), Internat. Law Assn., World Assn. Lawyers, U.S. C. of C. (mem. taxation com.), Assn. Ex-Mems. Squadron A., Nat. Fgn. Trade Council (mem. com. taxes 1950—), Automobile Mfrs. Assn. (chmn. com. taxation 1961-63), Tax Exec. Inst. (pres. 1956-57), Fedn. Alumni Columbia (dir. 1946), Class of 1935, Columbia Coll. (permanent pres.), Supreme Ct. Hist. Soc. (founder), N.Y. Adult Edn. Council, Inc. (dir. 1939-45), Detroit Racing Assn. (v.p.), Phi Delta Phi. Clubs: Bloomfield Hills Country; Detroit, Detroit Athletic; University (Washington); Columbia University, Church (N.Y.C.); Lawyers (Univ. Mich.); Little (Gulfstream, Fla.); Columbia University Alumni of Mich. (pres. 1950—). Episcopalian. Author: Divorce, Separation and Estate Taxes, Estate Tax Handbook, 1952; Arrangements for Separation or Divorce, Handbook of Tax Techniques, 1952; Taxation of Partnerships, Estates and Trusts, rev. edit., 1952. Adv. editor Nat. Tax Jour., 1952—. Contbr. articles tax matters to various law revs., profl. publs. Home: 150 Lowell Ct Bloomfield Hills MI 48013 Office: PO Box J 1565 Woodward Ave Suite 8 Bloomfield Hills MI 48013

GORNY, JOHN LOUIS, printing co. exec.; b. Toledo, Oct. 14, 1914; s. John Louis and Pauline (Kinest) G.; grad. high sch.; m. Lorraine Norma Thorp, July 24, 1942; children—David, Shelley (Mrs. John Hickey Schoenherr). Partner, Gorny-Winzeler, Inc., Bryan, Ohio, 1934-42, owner, 1942—; owner, Surrey Shop, Gaylord, Mich., 1960, Four Seasons Gifts, Gaylord, 1975—. Served with USAAF, 1942-45. Mem. Nat. Office Products Assn., Nat. Office Machine Dealers Assn., Nat. Assn. Printers and Lithographers, Ohio Retail Dealers Assn., Mich. Retailers Assn. (dir. gift div. 1972-76), Bryan C. of C. (dir. 1949-57, pres. 1956). Moose, K.C., Eagle. Clubs: Otsego Ski, Hidden Valley (Gaylord); Orchard Hill Country (Bryan). Home: Route 4 3548 Nowak Rd Gaylord MI 49735 Office: 110-120 S Lynn St Bryan OH 43506

GORRELL, DAVID PAUL, ednl. adminstr.; b. Ft. Wayne, Ind., Sept. 6, 1939; s. Paul Clifford and Marcelene Theresa (Koch) G.; B.S., Taylor U., 1963; M.S., St. Francis Coll., 1968; adminstrn. certificate Ball State U., 1974; m. Judy Kaye Liechty, June 21, 1964; children—Lori, Ricky, Randy. Tchr., Harlan (Ind.) Elementary Sch., 1963-64, South Adams Sch., Berne, Ind., 1964-67, Adams Central Schs., Monroe, Ind., 1968-70; prin. Adams Central Elementary Sch., Monroe, 1970—. Treas., Berne Recreational Swim Team, 1974. Mem. Nat., Ind. assns. elementary sch. prins., Ind. State Tchrs. Assn. Mem. Missionary Ch. (mem. ch. bd. 1973-75). Home: 318 Parkway St Berne IN 46711 Office: 222 W Washington St Monroe IN 46772

GORSUCH, JOHN WILBERT, pub. co. exec.; b. Bloomingdale, Ohio, Apr. 6, 1930; s. John Simpson and Susanna Mae (Poe) G.; student Ohio State U., 1948-50; B.A., U. N.M., 1956; m. Georgia Anne Batting, Sept. 26, 1953; children—Neil Justin, Greta Jean. Field rep., acquisition editor John Wiley & Sons, N.Y.C., 1957-60; regional sales mgr. coll. dept. The Macmillan Co., 1960-65; market mgr., 1965-67; v.p., dir. coll. dept. William C. Brown Co., pubs., Dubuque, Iowa, 1967-75; pres. Gorsuch Scarisbrick, pubs. 1975—. Bd. dirs. Dubuque Indsl. Bur., 1971—. Served with AUS, 1952-54. Mem. Dubuque C. of C. (dir.), Rotarian. Club: Dubuque Golf and Country. Home: 495 W 5th St Dubuque IA 52001 Office: 185 Main St Dubuque IA 52001

GORTMAKER, DENNIS LEE, systems engr., farmer; b. Monroe, S.D., Aug. 7, 1940; s. Leonard and Ramona Maxine (Newlon) G.; B.M.E., S.D. State U., 1963; postgrad. LaSalle Extension U., 1970-75. Farmer with father nr. Monroe, 1958; systems analyst Boeing Airplane Co., Seattle, 1963-66; pvt. practice systems engring., 1967—; farmer nr. Canistota, 1967—. Ch. youth dir. United Methodist Ch., 1969-70, tchr. Sunday sch., ch. youth counsellor, state ch. camp counsellor, ann. state ch. del. Briggs scholar, 1960-63; NSF trainee, 1966—. Mem. ASME, Farmers Union. Republican. Home and Office: Rural Route 1 Box 220A Canistota SD 57012

GORTON, WILLIAM FRANK, banker; b. Flint, Mich., Mar. 30, 1938; s. Gernsey Frank and Lilye Corrine (Campbell) G.; student U. Mich., 1956-60; B.S., Eastern Mich. U., 1961, postgrad., 1961-63. Tchr., Saginaw, Oxford (both Mich.), also Babbitt, Minn., 1961-66; mgr. indsl. research dept. C.&O./B.&O. R.R., Detroit, 1966-68; real estate rep. Burger King Corp., Detroit, 1968-69; area devel. officer Continental Ill. Nat. Bank, Chgo., 1969-77, investment officer real estate fund No. 1, 1977—. Mem. Am. Indsl. Devel. Council, Am. Assn. Geographers, Assn. Indsl. Real Estate Brokers Chgo., Gt. Lakes Area, Ill. (pres. 1975) devel. councils, Chgo. Assn. Commerce and Industry (chmn. industry com. 1977), Mortgage Bankers Assn. Clubs: Demolay, Masons. Home: 1039 S Oak Park Ave Oak Park IL 60304 Office: 231 S LaSalle St Chicago IL 60693

GOSMAN, JAMES HUBERT, dermatologist; b. Jasper, Ind., Aug. 10, 1915; s. William and Emily (Dittmer) G.; B.S., Ind. U., 1936, M.D., 1938; m. Margaret Lynn Donnelly, Dec. 27, 1941; 1 dau., Linda Ann. Intern, Marion County Gen. Hosp., 1938-39, resident, 1939-41; fellow dermatology U. Pa. Hosp., Phila., 1947-49; practice medicine specializing in dermatology, Indpls., 1949—; asso. prof. Ind. U. Med. Center, 1949—. Cons. VA; chmn. edn. com. Methodist Hosp., Indpls. Served with USAAF, 1941-46. Decorated Legion of Merit. Fellow Am. Acad. Dermatology; mem. A.C.P., Ind. State Med. Assn. (past pres.). Home: 8235 Washington Blvd Indianapolis IN 46240 Office: 1815 N Capitol St Indianapolis IN 46202

GOSSER, JON WALTER, educator; b. Seattle, May 15, 1941; s. Lawrence and Ellinore (Jones) G.; B.S. cum laude, U. Wash., 1962, M.S., 1964, postgrad., 1964-65; postgrad. U. Kans., 1965-67; m. Christina Mathew, Jan. 29, 1973. Reader in statistics U. Wash., Seattle, 1962, research asst. in psychology, 1962-63, USPHS predoctoral research fellow, NIMH, 1963-65; predoctoral trainee in ednl. research Bur. Child Research, U. Kans., Kansas City, 1965-66; tchr. psychology, logic and marriage and family relations Kansas City (Kans.) Community Jr. Coll., 1966-67; instr. psychology Delta Coll., University Center, Mich., 1967-69, asst. prof., 1970-75, asso. prof., 1975—, dir., Mid-Mich. Psychologist, Inc., 1973-76. Mem. Data Processing Mgmt. Assn. (dir. 1971-73), Am., Mich. psychol. assns., Assn. Computing Machines, Am. Assn. Community and Jr. Colls., A.A.A.S., A.A.U.P. (corr. sec. Delta chpt. 1969), Am. Ednl. Research Assn., Midwestern Assn. Behavior Analysis, Mich. Acad. Sci., Arts and Letters, Sigma Xi. Author: (with Harbans Lal) Research on Teaching Pharmacy: The Role of Student Ratings, 1968; A Computerized Method of Longitudinal Evaluation of Student Performance, 1969; Computerized Test Library, 1974; Longitudinal Evaluation and Improvement of Teaching: An Empirical Approach Based on Analysis of Student Behaviors, 1975. Home: 3200 Noeske St Midland MI 48640 Office: Delta Coll University Center MI 48710

GOSSETT, ELIZABETH HUGHES (MRS. WILLIAM THOMAS GOSSETT), civic worker; b. Albany, N.Y., Aug. 19, 1907; d. Charles Evans and Antoinette (Carter) Hughes; student Brearley Sch., N.Y.C., 1917-19, Miss Madeira's Sch., Washington, 1923-25; A.B., Barnard Coll., Columbia, 1929; LL.D. (hon.), N.Y. Law Sch., 1977; m. William Thomas Gossett, Dec. 19, 1930; children—Antoinette Carter (Mrs. A.G. Denning), William Thomas, Elizabeth G. Karaman. Former bd. dirs. Detroit Urban League; v.p. found. trustees Mich. State U., Oakland 1957-67; trustee Barnard Coll., 1953-70, Merrill-Palmer Inst., Detroit, 1957-71; former bd. dirs. Kingswood Sch., Cranbrook, Brookside Sch. Cranbrook, Bloomfield Hills, Mich.; former nat. bd. dirs. NCCJ; bd. dirs. Cranbrook Acad. Art and Cranbrook Ednl. Community, Bloomfield Hills, Mich. Mem. UN Assn. (past pres. Detroit), Supreme Ct. Hist. Soc. (pres.), Jr. League. Republican. Episcopalian. Clubs: Barnard College of Detroit; Sulgrave (Washington). Home: 420 Goodline Rd Bloomfield Hills MI 48013

GOSSMAN, NORBERT JOSEPH, historian; b. Ridgeway, Iowa, Feb. 21, 1924; s. Leo Patrick and Anastasia (McCabe) G.; B.A., U. Iowa, 1947, M.A., 1948, Ph.D., 1952; m. Martha Jane Dawson, Dec. 29, 1949; children—Susan, Christopher, Patricia, Mary Elizabeth. Instr. history Coe Coll., 1952-53, Whitman Coll., Walla Walla, Wash., 1953-54; asst. prof. history Wis. State U., Eau Claire, 1954-55; asso. prof. history U. Detroit, 1955-69, prof., 1969—. Served with USAAF, 1943-46. Grantee Social Sci. Research Council, 1958, Nat. Endowment for Humanities, 1976. Mem. AAUP, Am. Hist. Assn., Conf. Brit. Studies. Democrat. Roman Catholic. Editor: (with J. M. Hayden) Readings in Western Civilization, 1963; (with Joseph O. Baylon) Biographical Dictionary of Modern British Radicals, 1977. Contbr. articles to profl. publs. Home: 12654 Beaverland St Detroit MI 48223 Office: 4001 W McNichols St Detroit MI 48221

GOSWAMI, SANTOSH RANJAN, educator; b. India, Jan. 11, 1935; s. Brojaraj Goswami and Hiran Bala Devi; G.; student Calcutta U., 1950-53; I. Sc., B.Sc., Indian Inst. Tech., Kharagpur, 1957; M. Engring., McGill U., Montreal, 1962; M.S. in San. Engring., U. Ill., Urbana, 1964; Ph.D., Okla. State U., 1969; m. Manju Bhattacharjee, Jan. 18, 1970; children—Pulak, Alak. Came to U.S., 1962, naturalized, 1967. Asst. engr. Durgapur Steel Project, India, 1958-60; research asst. Gault Research Sta., McGill U., 1962, civil engring. dept. U. Ill., Urbana, 1962-64; teaching asst. Okla. State U., Stillwater, 1965, research asst., 1965-69; san. engr. Ill. Dept. Pub. Health, Springfield, 1969-70; environ. protection engr. State Ill. EPA, Springfield, from 1970—, then supr.; now asso. prof. Cleve. State U. Demonstrator, McGill U., part-time 1960-62; del., speaker 4th Mid-Atlantic Indsl. Waste Conf., 2d Iranian Congress Civil Engrs., Shiraz. Bd. dirs. Pub. Instrn., West Bengal, Nopany Edn. Trust, R.C. Mitra, 1953-55, West Bengal Refugee, Relief and Rehab., 1953-57, Canadian Commonwealth, 1960, Tech. Student Gymkhana, 1955-56. Recipient Okiepin, Gov. Okla. Watmull Found. grantee (Hawaii), 1969. Registered profl. engr., Iowa, Ill., Okla., Ohio, Pa. Diplomate Am. Acad. Environ. Engrs. Mem. ASCE, Inst. Civil Engrs., Am. Water Works Assn., Inst. Civil Engrs. France (asso.), Sigma Xi, Omicron Delta Kappa, Chi Epsilon, Tau Beta Pi. Home: 515 Karl Dr Cleveland OH 44143

GOTSHALL, WILLIAM WEIR, research co. exec.; b. Cleve., May 1, 1920; s. Glenn Harold and Blanche Low (Hayward) G.; B.S. in Chem. Engring., Mich. State U., 1943; m. Jeanne Margaret Moffett, Aug. 12, 1944; children—Lynn (Mrs. Randall Allison), Susan (Mrs. Brian Quinlan), William (dec.), Glenn. Research engr. Sharples Chems., Wyandotte, Mich., 1943-47; gen. mgr. B.K. Pancoast Co., Jersey City, 1947-48; partner G.H. Gotshall Co., Detroit, 1948-56; mgr. tech. services Marathon Oil Co., Detroit, 1956-73; pres. Carbon Devel. Corp., Walled Lake, Mich., 1973—. Mem. natural resources com. Greater Detroit Bd. Commerce, 1958-64; pres. Orchard Lake Level Control Com., 1956-60. Mem. Oakland County Republican Com., 1960-72. Mem. Am. Inst. Chem. Engrs. (chmn. Detroit sect. 1957), Am. Chem. Soc., Akron Rubber Group, Mich. State C. of C. (mem. natural resources com. 1957-64). Patentee in field. Home: 3081 Walma Dr Orchard Lake MI 48033 Office: 2891 Haggerty Rd Walled Lake MI 48088

GOTTESMAN, KAREN LESLIE, counselor; b. N.Y.C., Mar. 21, 1952; d. Herbert Charles and Selma (Wollenberg) G.; A.B., Boston U., 1973; M.Ed., Washington U., St. Louis, 1974; postgrad. U. Va., 1974; doctoral candidate Ill. Sch. Profl. Psychology. Dorm counselor Washington U., 1973-74; counselor Moraine Valley Community Coll., Palos Hills, Ill., 1975—; now tchr. psychology. Mem. Ill. Psychol. Assn., Am. Personnel and Guidance Assn., Am. Coll. Personnel Assn., Psi Chi. Home: 2317 N Commonwealth Ave Chicago IL 60614 Office: Moraine Valley Community Coll 10900 S 88th Ave Palos Hills IL 60465

GOTTFRIED, MAX, med. equipment mfg. co. exec.; b. Toledo, Aug. 27, 1921; s. Morris and Gussie (Yerzy) G.; student Toledo U., 1939-40, 46-48; m. Caroline Gladstone Briggs, Sept. 18, 1959; children—Brent Morris, Mark Ellis. Sales mgr. Columbus Hosp. Supply Co., Toledo, 1951-60; v.p. Jobst Inst., Toledo, 1960—; v.p. Gottfried Hosiery Mills Inc., Hildebran, N.C. Trustee Conrad Jobst Found. for Vascular Research. Served with AUS, 1940-45. Mem. Aerospace Med. Assn., Assn. for Advancement Med. Instrumentation, Health Care Exhibitors Assn. (dir.). Patentee med. products. Home: 418 Riverside Dr Rossford OH 43460 Office: 653 Miami St Toledo OH 43694

GOTTLIEB, REYNOLD JAMES, radiologist; b. N.Y.C., Jan. 16, 1922; s. B. J. and Irene (Mollin) G.; B.A., N.Y. U., 1943; M.D., Chgo. Med. Sch., 1950; m. Ellen Jennette Frame, Sept. 18, 1949; children—Elizabeth, John, Margaret, Laurie. Intern, U. Ill. Hosps., Chgo., 1950-51; resident in radiology St. Luke's Hosp., Chgo., 1951-53, Cook County Hosp., Chgo., 1953-54; chmn. dept. radiology Oak Forest (Ill.) Hosp., 1954—; chief radiologist Suburban Hosp., Hinsdale, Ill., 1955—; cons. in radiology Armed Forces Induction Center, Western Electric Co.; clin. asso. Loyola U. Stritch Sch. Medicine, Chgo., 1970-76; dir. Heritage Bank Oakwood, Westmont, Ill. Served with U.S. Army, 1943-46, to col. USAR, 1946—. Diplomate Am. Bd. Radiology. Mem. AMA, Am. Coll. Radiology, Am. Coll. Chest Physicians. Republican. Presbyterian. Clubs: Itasca Country, Oak Brook Polo, Execs. of Oak Brook (pres., founder). Home: 27 Brighton Ln Oak Brook IL 60521 Office: 120 Professional Bldg Oak Brook IL 60521

GOTTSCHALK, ROBERT, lawyer, cons.; b. N.Y.C., Jan. 10, 1911; B.S. in Elec. Engring., McGill U., 1931; LL.B. cum laude, Bklyn. Law Sch., 1934; m. Elizabeth von Papen, 1934; 1 son, William P. Admitted to N.Y. bar, 1935, Ill. bar, 1946, D.C. bar, 1973, U.S. Supreme Ct. bar, 1974; mem. firm von Briesen and Schrenk, N.Y.C., 1934-41; patent and trademark counsel Corn Products Co., Chgo., 1941-46; asst. dir. devel. and patent dept., dir. of contracts and legal matters standard Oil Co. of Ind., Chgo., 1946-61; gen. patent counsel Canteen Corp., Chgo., 1961-65; dir. patents Gen. Aniline & Film Corp., N.Y.C., 1965-70; dep. commr. of patents U.S. Patent Office, Washington, 1970-71, commr. of patents, 1971-73; cons. to Govt. Patents Bd., 1950-55, White House Office of Telecommunications Policy, 1976, Iranian Nat. Petrochem. Co., 1976, lectr. in law U. Chgo., 1957; chmn. Commn. Patent Policy Nat. Acad. Sci., 1962-67; mem. advisory bd. Patent Trademark and Copyright Jour., 1975—; legal and tech. cons., 1973—. Head U.S. Delegation to Vienna (Austria) Diplomatic Conf., 1973; mem. U.S. Signatory to Trademark Registration Treaty, 1973. Mem. Fed., Am. (chmn. com. on atomic energy 1947-48, com. on govt. patent policy 1955-56), Am., N.Y., Chgo. patent law assns. Clubs: Nat. Lawyers (Washington); Chemists (N.Y.C.); Internat. Trade (Chgo.). Home: 183 Dickens Rd Northfield IL 60093 Office: 150 S Wacker Dr Chicago IL 60606

GOTTSCHALK, ROBERT OWEN, real estate broker; b. Rochester, Ind., Nov. 4, 1927; s. Frederick Omer and Helen (Shuman) G.; student Ind. Tech. Coll., 1948; grad. Ind. Realtors Inst., 1973; m. Marde Elaine Weller, Aug. 26, 1948; children—David, Steven, Richard, Connie. Winding dept. supr. Joyner Corp., Bourbon, Ind., 1948; with Studebaker Corp., South Bend, Ind., 1949-51, Fuller Brush Co., Rochester, 1951; salesman United Home Life Ins. Co., Rochester, 1952, Midwestern United Life Ins. Co., Rochester, 1953, Armour & Co., Benton Harbor, Mich., 1954; farmer, Rochester, 1955-65; with Gt. Fidelity Life Ins. Co., Rochester, 1966-67, Phila. Life Ins. Co., Rochester, 1968, Lancaster-Deamer Casualty Ins. Co., Rochester, 1969, Deamer & Deamer Realtors, Rochester, 1969-71; owner, mgr. Gottschalk Realty, Rochester, 1972—; dir. 1st Nat. Bank of Rochester. Trustee Rochester Twp., 1971-74, adv. bd., 1975—; mem. Rochester Community Sch. Bd., 1970-74; mem. Rochester Vocat. Bdg. Trades Co., 1971—. Chmn. bd. dirs. Fulton County Family YMCA, 1974—. Served with AUS, 1945-47; ETO. Mem. Fulton County Bd. Realtors (chmn. 1972-73, Realtor of Yr. award 1976), Ind. Assn. Realtors (dir. 1974—), Rochester C. of C. (v.p. 1975, pres. 1976, dir. 1974—). Mem. Christian Ch. (elder 1955—, deacon 1953-55). Clubs: Masons (32 deg.), Shriners. Home: Route 6 Rochester IN 46975 Office: 122 E 8th St Rochester IN 46975

GOUGIS, BRYAN PATRICK, nursing home adminstr.; b. Chgo., Feb. 23, 1950; s. Henry and Nannie (Hopkins) G.; B.A. in Biology, U. Dubuque, 1972; M.A. in Ednl. Adminstrn., U. Ia., 1973. Meter reader People Gas Light & Coke Co., Chgo., 1970-71; bus operator Chgo. Transit Authority, 1971-72; mem. staff Starnes Nursing Home, Dixmoor, Ill., 1972—, 1973—. Nursing home cons., 1971-72. Mem. N.A.A.C.P., PUSH (People United to Save Humanity, Am. Coll. Nursing Home Adminstrs., Am. Nursing Home Assn. Home: 14537 S Vincennes Harvey IL 60426 Office: 14434 S Hoyre St Dixmoor IL 60426

GOULD, ALBERT OREN, educator; b. Chatham, Ill., Nov. 11, 1912; s. Franklin Lewis and Harriet Amelia (White) G.; B.A., Carthage Coll., 1934, Mus.M., Northwestern U., 1944; Mus.D., U. Ill., 1961; m. Dorothy Edna Ziegler, Dec. 27, 1934; children—Ruth Anne (Mrs. Charles Bruce Krider), Kenneth David, Robert Marshall, Dorothy Kay (Mrs. James E. Robinson), Charles Franklin. Sch. music tchr., Vandalia, Ill., Exline and Moravia, Ia., 1934-38; dir. recreation U.S.O., McCoy Wis., 1943-44; dir. music pub. schs., Lake Forest, Ill., 1938-47; dir. music Western Ill. U. Lab. Sch., Macomb, 1948-67, prof. music, 1965-74, prof. emeritus, 1974—. Dir. music research project U.S. Office Edn., Macomb, 1965-68; music cons. Cultural Enrichment Project Hancock County, Carthage, Ill., 1967-68; clinician, lectr., festival condr., 1958—; originator Your Mus. Classroom, Macomb, 1948-58; developer films, video tapes for music instrn., 1958—; mem. music adv. bd. Ill. High Sch. Assn., 1958-65. Mem. Ill. Music Educators Assn. (exec. bd. 1963-67, dist. pres. 1963-67, chmn. com. research in music edn. 1966-70, v.p. for higher edn. 1970-74, historian 1975—), Music Educators Nat. Conf. (leadership commn. 1959—, research council 1974—), Nat., Ill. edn. assns., Ill. Assn. for Higher Edn., AAUP, Nat. Jazz Educators Assn., Pi Kappa Lambda, Phi Delta Kappa. Presbyn. Rotarian, Kiwanian. Author: Finding and Learning to Use the Singing Voice, 1968; Developing Specialized Programs for Singing, 1969; (with Edith Savage) Teaching Children to Sing, 1972. Contbr. articles to profl. jours. Home: 120 Richmond Rd Macomb IL 61455

GOULD, ARLEN STUART, candy co. exec.; b. Bklyn., Feb. 12, 1945; s. Daniel D. and Evelyn G.; B.S., U. Ill., 1966; m. Josephine H. Boelen, Nov. 12, 1976. Tchr. handicapped children, Chgo., 1967-70; spl. edn. coordinator Gov.'s Office Human Resources Ill., 1970-71, asst. to dir., dir. state developmental disabilities program, 1971-72; pres. Lanzi Candy Co., Chgo., 1972—. Bd. dirs. Chgo. Assn. Children with Learning Disabilities, 1971-73, Broader Urban Involvement and Leadership Devel.; alumni adv. council U. Ill., 1970-73. Recipient Outstanding Achievement award Ill. Assn. Children with Learning Disabilities, 1972; U.S. Office Edn. Bur. Handicapped Children grantee. Mem. Nat. Confectioners Assn., Nat. Food Distbrs. Assn., Nat. Assn. Splty. Foods and Candy, Nat. Candy Wholesalers. Assn. Office: 1135 Chicago Ave W Chicago IL 60622

GOULD, BENJAMIN Z., lawyer; b. Chgo., July 27, 1913; s. Samuel and Fanny (Tendrich) G.; A.B., U. Chgo., 1935, J.D. cum laude, 1937; m. Shirley Handleman, Nov. 22, 1942; children—Fredrick G., Edward S., Barbara F. Admitted to Ill. bar, 1937, since practiced in Chgo.; asso. firm Gould & Ratner (and predecessors), 1937-49, sr. partner, 1949—. Sec., gen. counsel Material Service Corp. subsidiary Gen. Dynamics Corp., Marblehead Lime Co.; sec., gen. counsel Freeman United Coal Mining Co. div. Material Service Corp., sec., gen. counsel Lemont Shipbldg. and Repair Co., Sioux City and New Orleans Terminal Corp., Sioux City and New Orleans Barge Lines, Utah Marblehead Lime Co.; v.p., sec., gen. counsel, dir. Standard Forgings Corp.; sec., gen. counsel, dir. Century-Am. Corp., Follansbee Metals Co.; sec., gen. counsel Thomas B. Bishop Co. div. Univ. Exchange Corp.; San Francisco, sec., gen. counsel, dir. Monticello Realty Corp., Stickney Terminal Corp., Oils, Inc., Producers Supply Co., Mascar Corp.; sec., gen. counsel Santa Barbara Research Park div. Univ. Exchange Corp.; sec., gen. counsel, dir. Burton-Dixie Corp., Henry Crown (Ill.) and Co., U. Exchange Corp.; gen. counsel, sec., dir., mem. exec. com. Central Enterprises, Inc.; v.p., sec., gen. counsel, dir. Exchange Bldg. Corp. Bd. dirs. Hebrew Theol. Coll.; sec., gen. counsel Arie and Ida Crown Meml. Served with USCGR, World War II. Mem. Am. Arbitration Assn. (mem. nat. panel), Chgo. Council Fgn. Relations, Am. Soc. Corp. Secs., AIM (asso.), Internat., Am. Ill., Chgo. bar assns., Navy League U.S., Am. Judicature Soc., Phi Beta Kappa. Jewish (dir. congregations). Clubs: Executive, Standard, One Hundred (Chgo.). Home: 1170 Michigan Ave Wilmette IL 60091 Office: 300 W Washington St Chicago IL 60606

GOULD, BETTY LOUISE KOONTZ, educator; b. Atwood, Ind., Mar. 3, 1935; d. Donald H. and Opal Lee (Stidham) Koontz; B.A., Simpson Coll., 1957; postgrad. U. Iowa, Iowa State U., Drake U., U. No. Iowa, Okla. State U.; m. James J. Gould, Dec. 22, 1957 (div. Oct., 1970); 1 son, John Prescott. Tchr., Moravia (Iowa) Community Schs., 1963-64, 66-67; tchr. English and speech, coach forensics Lake City (Iowa) Community Schs., Westview High Sch., 1967-76; tchr. Interstate 35 Jr. High Sch., New Virginia, Iowa, 1976—. Vol. worker

Pied Piper Day Care, Indianola, Iowa, 1969—; dir. live nativity scene, Lake City, 1970-72. Mem. Speech Communication Assn., Central State Speech Assn., Iowa Communication Assn., Lake City Ednl. Assn., Interstate 35 Edn. Assn., Blackfriars, Alpha Delta Kappa, Pi Beta Phi. Home: Apt 8 501 W Clinton Ave Indianola IA 50125

GOULD, JAMES JOHN, tech. cons.; b. Harlan, Iowa, Nov. 8, 1933; s. Russell T. and Florence C. (Holmquest) G.; B.S. in Bus. Adminstrn., Simpson Coll., 1957; M.A. in Guidance and Counseling, U. No. Iowa, 1971; postgrad. in counselor edn. U. Iowa, 1971-74; m. Jean L. Letch, June 5, 1971; 1 son, John P. Insp., Retail Credit Co., Centerville, Iowa, 1962-65; tchr. Lake City (Iowa) High Sch., 1967-70; grad. asst. U. No. Iowa, Cedar Falls, 1970-71, Am. Coll. Testing Program, Iowa City, 1972-73; tech. cons. Iowa Dept. Pub. Instrn., Des Moines, 1974—. Served with U.S. Army, 1957-59. Mem. Am. Personnel and Guidance Assn., Iowa State Edn. Assn., NEA, Nat. Assn. Users of Computer Assisted Learning, Phi Delta Kappa. Democrat. Methodist. Club: Masons. Home: 1332 Broad St Grinnell IA 50112 Office: Grimes State Office Bldg Des Moines IA 50319

GOULD, WILLIAM ALLEN, planner, architect; b. Lakewood, Ohio, Mar. 8, 1930; s. Daniel and Esther (Itlaner) G.; B.Arch., U. Mich., 1952; M.Arch., Cranbrook Acad. Art, 1956; diploma Fountainbleau (France) Acad. of Art, 1957; m. Harriet Rosenthal, June 23, 1959; children—Philip, David, Rebecca. Sr. planner City of Cleve. Planning Commn., 1953-59; prin. William A. Gould & Assos., Cleve., 1961—; asst. prof. architecture Western Res. U., 1958-61; lectr. Case Inst. Tech., 1960-61; vis. asst. prof. architecture and environ. design Kent State U., 1972-73. Mem. City Cleveland Heights Planning Commn. Served to 1st lt. USAF, 1952. Mem. A.I.A. (dir. Cleve. chpt. 1967—), Am. Inst. Planners (pres. No. Ohio chpt. 1967-69, nat. urban design com.). Works include Cascade Plaza, Akron, Ohio, Hillel Center Case Western Res. U., Wayne Gen. and Tech. Coll. U. Akron, Univ. Circle Research Center; planner Blossom Music Center, Cleve.; executed capital improvement program analysis Ohio Bd. Regents, new city plans for Barberton, Shaker Heights and Youngstown, Ohio; master plan update NASA Lewis Research Center, Cleve.; planned communities Greenwood Village, Sagamore Hills, Ohio, Riverbend East, Athens, Ga.; renovation and expansion plans Masillon (Ohio) State Hosp.; Cleve. Warehouse Dist. study; Ohio City master plan; socio-econ. study Ashtabula County. Home: 2722 Scarborough Rd Cleveland Heights OH 44106 Office: 1404 E 9th St Cleveland OH 44114

GOULDING, ROBERT CHARLES, optometrist; b. Toledo, Sept. 23, 1935; s. Carl C. and Helen (Bennett) G.; B.S., U. Toledo, 1957, postgrad. 1960-62; postgrad. U. Louisville, 1958-59; O.D., Ill. Coll. Optometry, 1965; m. Patricia Fischer, June 3, 1961; children—Michael R., Mark C. Practice optometry, Rossford, Ohio, 1965—, also Morenci, Mich., 1971—; mem. staff Med. Coll. Ohio at Toledo. Rep. Peter Navarre Dist. council Boy Scouts Am., 1967-71. Trustee Health Planning Assn. N.W. Ohio, 1973—. Recipient Ill. Coll. Optometry Faculty Meml. Research award, 1965, Scouting commendation City Rossford, 1970. Fellow Am. Acad. Optometry; mem. Maumee Valley (pres.), Ohio (chmn. Pub. Information com. 1971-72, trustee 1976—) optometric assns., Rossford Businessmen and Assos., Jr. C. of C. (1st v.p. 1969-70), Beta Sigma Kappa. K.C. (4 deg.). Club: Exchange (pres. 1969-70). Served to 1st lt. AUS, 1957-60. Home: 3119 Haughton Dr Toledo OH 43606 Office: 849 Dixie Hwy Rossford OH 43460

GOVE, JAMES ROBERT, ednl. adminstr.; b. Paris, Ill., Feb. 24, 1938; s. Robert B. and Edith (Stoddard) G.; B.S., Ind. State U., 1960, M.S., 1964; m. Gay Lynn Garver, Nov. 12, 1960; 1 dau., Jane Renee. Speech correctionist Joliet (Ill.) Pub. Schs., 1960-62; adminstrv. aid Valley View Schs., Romeoville, Ill., 1964-65, dir. gifted program, 1965-66, dir. multi-media service, 1966-68, asst. supt. schs., 1968—. Mem. Nat. Council Year Round Schs., Nat. Rifle Assn. Co-author: The Year Round School. Developer 45-15 yr. round sch. plan. Home: 2406 Eastline Dr Joliet IL 60435 Office: 636 Dalhart Ave Romeoville IL 60441

GOWDEY, MARILYN PATRICIA, educator; b. Burlington, Vt., Oct. 6, 1944; d. Philip Edwin and Barbara (West) Gowdey; student Middlebury Coll., 1962-64; A.B., Cornell U., 1966; M.A. in English and Edn., U. Chgo., 1969. Tchr. English and performing arts Central YMCA High Sch., Chgo., 1967—, co-chmn. English dept., 1968-72, chmn., 1974—, co-developer humanities program in fine and performing arts, 1971, developer team teaching program, 1972, coordinator reading program, 1975-76, in-service tng., 1976, curriculm, 1976; cons. R.S. McLary & Assos., Ltd., 1975—. Mem. Internat. Platform Assn., Smithsonian Assos., Phi Beta Kappa, Phi Kappa Phi. Home: 415 W Rosalyn Pl Chicago IL 60614 Office: Central YMCA High Sch 29 W Randolph St Chicago IL 60603

GOWELL, RONDA SUE, veterinarian; b. Breckenridge, Mich., June 19, 1948; d. Samuel B. and Bessie Mae (Kellogg) Cole; D.V.M., Mich. State U., 1972; m. Elmer Burton Gowell, Mar. 22, 1974. Veterinarian, Hart, Mich., 1972-75, Rothbury, Mich., 1975—. Mem. Mich., Am., Women's veterinary med. assns. New Testament Baptist. Home and Office: 475 E Cleveland St Rothbury MI 49452

GOWIN, RICHARD DALE, dentist; b. Rochester, N.Y., Sept. 5, 1931; s. Lloyd Francis and Flossie Elizabeth (Hixson) G.; student Kent State U., 1950, Wooster Coll., 1954, 55, 56; D.D.S., Ohio State U., 1960; m. Joyce Delores Grogne, Nov. 8, 1963; children—Stanley, Peggy, Laura, Richard, Kenny, Joyce, David. Pvt. practice dentistry, Cuyahoga Falls, Ohio, 1960—; pub. sch. dentist, Akron, Ohio, 1965-66. Served with USMCR, 1951-53. Mem. Am., Ohio dental assns., Akron Dental Soc. Mason. Home: 1939 Chestnut Blvd Cuyahoga Falls OH 44223 Office: 2810 Cedar Hill Rd Cuyahoga Falls OH 44223

GOYAL, RAGHBIR CHAND, mech. engr.; b. Khai Kalota, India, Aug. 14, 1942; s. Ramji Dass and Jamuna Devi G.; came to U.S., 1962, naturalized, 1973; B.S., Punjab U., Chandigarh, India, 1962; student mech. engring. Ind. Inst. Tech., 1963-64; postgrad. U. Notre Dame, 1970-71; m. Dianne Mary Procissi, Aug. 14, 1965; children—Rani, Anissa M. Successively draftsman, project engr., mgr. value engring. ILG Industries, Chgo., 1964-68; devel. engr., now engring. mgr. Kawneer Co., Franklin, Ind., 1968—; cons. in field. Mem. ASME, Nat. Mgmt. Assn., Soc. Am. Value Engrs. Hindu. Clubs: Valle Vista Golf and Country, Eldorado Golf and Country. Patentee automatic entrance device. Home: 3117 Greensview Dr Greenwood IN 46142 Office: Kawneer Co PO Box 302 Franklin IN 46131

GRABAU, GENE HENRY, pediatrician, pediatric allergist; b. St. Louis, May 8, 1915; s. John Henry and Gertrude (Wittich) G.; P.H.G., St. Louis Coll. Pharmacy, 1937; M.D., Washington U., 1942; m. Vera Mae Dyer, July 2, 1947; children—Gary, Karen, Linda, Deborah. Intern, St. Louis City Hosp., 1942-43; resident in pediatrics St. Louis Children's Hosp., 1946-47, asso. prof. clin. pediatrics, mem. staff, 1947—; dir. allergy clinic H.G. Phillips Hosp., St. Louis, 1947—. Served to capt. M.C., U.S. Army, 1943-46. Decorated Bronze Star. Diplomate Am. Bd. Pediatrics. Mem. Am. Acad. Allery (cerf.), Audubon Soc., Mo. Conservancy, NAACP, Sierra Club, Com. for Environ. Info. Contbr. article to med. jour. Home: 1342 Belgrove St Saint Louis MO 63137 Office: 8036 N Broadway Saint Louis MO 63147

GRABEK, FREDERICK MARCEL, air conditioning co. exec.; b. Niagara Falls, N.Y., Jan. 21, 1943; s. Alfred Harry and Irene (Kajda) G.; B.S. in Elec. Engring., Purdue U., 1967; m. Marilyn Ann Vaccarella, Aug. 28, 1965; children—Eric Marcel, Stephanie Irene. Quality control engr. Union Carbide Corp., Niagara Falls, N.Y., 1963-66; project engr. Frigidaire div. Gen. Motors Corp., Dayton, Ohio, 1967-72, sr. project engr., 1972-74; sr. project engr. Delco Air Conditioning div. Gen. Motors Corp., Dayton, 1975-76, supr. performance testing engring. dept., 1976—. Mem. Dayton Chpt. Soc. Automotive Engrs. Patentee in field. Home: 4412 Paletz Ct Dayton OH 45424 Office: PO Box 824 Dayton OH 45401

GRABER, DWIGHT EVERETT, real estate broker; b. Allen County, Ind., Sept. 29, 1935; s. Francis S. and Verda (Liechty) G.; B.S., Goshen Coll., 1957; M.S., Ind. U., 1966; m. Marla Grove Palmatier, May 8, 1975; children—Sandra Graber McComb, Jody, Debra, Jill, Sally, Jon, Julie. Tchr., coach North Vernon, Ind., 1963-67; partner Graber Homes, Inc., Ft. Wayne, Ind., 1968—; owner Graber Realty, Inc., Ft. Wayne, 1968—, pres., 1973—; pres. Realty Cons., Inc., Ft. Wayne, 1973—; owner Pine Canyons Inc., Woodmont, Inc., Village II, Inc. (all Ft. Wayne), 1974—. Named Cross Country Coach of Year, Ind. Coaches Assn., 1963, S.E. Regional Basketball Coach of Year, 1966. Mem. Ind. Bd. Realtors (dir. 1974—), Fort Wayne Bd. Realtors (dir. 1973-75), Ind. Homebuilders Assn. (dir. 1974—), Ft. Wayne Homebuilders (1st v.p. 1975-76, pres. 1976), Ft. Wayne Community Land Developers, Homebuilders and Realtors (dir., mem. polit. action com. 1974—), Ind. Homebuilders (area v.p. 1977). Mem. United Ch. of Christ. Home: 1032 Oak Branch Ct Fort Wayne IN 46825 Office: 6002 E State St Fort Wayne IN 46825

GRABER, VIRGIL RICH, obstetrician, gynecologist; b. Wayland, Iowa, Jan. 15, 1921; s. Joseph and Barbara (Rich) G.; B.A., State U. Iowa, 1946, M.D., 1949; m. Evelyn Louise Scarff, Aug. 13, 1944; children—Donald, Thomas, Robert, Joan. Intern, Sparrow Hosp., Lansing, Mich., 1949-50; gen. practice medicine, St. Johns, Mich., 1950-52; resident in obstetrics and gynecology Akron (Ohio) City Hosp., 1953-56; practice medicine specializing in obstetrics and gynecology, Elkhart, Ind., 1956—; mem. active staff and bd. dirs. Elkhart Gen. Hosp.; mem. cons. staff Goshen Gen. Hosp. Diplomate Am. Bd. Obstetrics and Gynecology. Mem. Ind. Obstetrics Gynecology Council, Elkhart County (Ind.) Med. Soc. (pres.), Mennonite Med. Soc. Contbr. articles to obstet. jours. Office: 1400 Hudson St Elkhart IN 46514

GRABILL, WILSON FLETCHER, JR., cons.; b. Shreveport, La., Nov. 19, 1935; s. Wilson Fletcher and Margaret Harriet (Haynes) G.; B.A., Ohio State U., 1960; m. Joyce Ellen Naftzger, Dec. 28, 1957; children—Wilson Fletcher III, Julia Ellen, Paul John. Sales rep. Gen. Foods Co., Denver, 1961-62; with Ency. Brit., Columbus, Ohio, 1962-64; with IBM, Columbus, Ohio, 1964-66; cons. Computer Applications Center, Columbus, 1966-67, Honeywell Corp., Detroit, 1967-68; mgr. Hamilton (Ohio) Tool Co., 1968-72; pvt. data processing and computer systems cons., Cin., 1973-75; pres. Integrity Systems, Inc., Cin., 1975—; chmn. Indepent Honeywell Group, 1977; instr. disk concepts course Cin. Tech. Inst., 1971. Treas. Wesley Found., Miami U., Oxford, Ohio, 1971-73. Served with USAF, 1954-57. Mem. Honeywell Computer Users Assn. (dir. 1969-72). Home: 210 Beechpoint Dr Oxford OH 45056 Office: 4812 Interstate Dr Cincinnati OH 45246

GRABLE, EDWARD E., obstetrician, gynecologist; b. Canton, Ohio, Aug. 22, 1926; s. Hugh R. and Daisy M. (Myers) G.; B.S., Western Res. U., 1946, M.D., 1950. Intern, Mercy Hosp., Canton, 1950-51, resident, 1951-53, 55; resident U.S. Naval Hosp., Bremerton, Wash., 1954, Cleve. City Hosp., 1955-56; practice medicine specializing in obstetrics and gynecology, Canton, 1956—; active staff Timken Mercy Hosp.; cons. staff Molly Stark Hosp., Louisville, Ohio; courtesy staff Aultman Hosp., Canton; instr. obstetrics and gynecology Western Res. U., 1956-59; mem. council of chiefs Northeastern Ohio U. Sch. Medicine, 1975, clin. asst. prof., 1977—; dir. Stencil-Art Co., Inc., Trustee Health Planning and Devel. council, Wooster, Ohio, 1965—, Timken Mercy Hosp., 1977—. Served to lt., M.C., USNR, 1944-45, 53-54. Diplomate Am. Bd. Obstetrics and Gynecology. Fellow A.C.S., Am. Coll. Obstetricians and Gynecologists; mem. Central Assn. Obstetrics and Gynecology, Cleve. Soc. Obstetrics and Gynecology, AMA, Ohio State Stark County med. socs., Catnon Acad. Medicine, Am. Fertility Soc., N.Y. Acad. Sci. Club: Congress Lake (Hartville, Ohio). Contbr. article to med. jour. Home: 351 17th St NW Canton OH 44703 Office: 2525 13th St NW Canton OH 44708

GRABLE, REGINALD HAROLD, psychologist; b. Putnam County, Ind., Sept. 22, 1917; s. Reginald R. and Cecil Ruth (Jones) G.; A.B., U. Kans., 1938, tchrs. diploma, 1940; M.A., U. Minn., 1949; m. Elizabeth Hannah Baird, Aug. 17, 1946; children—Celia, Nancy, Daniel. Group leader occupational coders Nat. Roster Sci. and Specialized Personnel, Washington, 1940-42; vocational counselor U. Minn., Mpls., 1947; clin. psychologist trainee VA Hosp., St. Paul, 1947-49; clin. psychologist, chief Willmar (Minn.) State Hosp., 1949-51, Winnebago (Wis.) State Hosp., 1951-61; clin. psychologist Hackley Adult Mental Health Clinic (name changed to West Shore Mental Health Clinic), Muskegon, Mich., 1961—. Tchr. extension div. U. Wis., 1956-61; mem. profl. adv. bd. Wis. Council Mentally Retarded Children, 1956-61; pvt. practice as psychologist, Willmar, Minn., 1949-51, Oshkosh, Wis., 1951-61, Spring Lake, Mich., 1961—. First aid instr. ARC, 1963—; mem. exec. bd. Grand Valley council Boy Scouts Am., 1966—, dist. chmn., 1968-70; pres. PTA, 1959; active Vols. in Probation. Served with AUS, 1942-46. Certified consulting psychologist, Mich. Mem. Am. Psychol. Assn., Mich. Assn. Children with Learning Disabilities. Mem. Christian Ch. (Disciples) (chmn. bd. 1970-73). Home: 717 Summer St Spring Lake MI 49456 Office: 2525 Hall Rd Muskegon MI 49442

GRABOW, WESLEY JOHN FRED, educator; b. Morgan, Minn., Aug. 23, 1921; s. Emil Paul and Alma Louise (Hecker) G.; B.B.A., U. Minn., 1944, M.A., 1950, certificate in Philosophy, 1968, Ph.D., 1970; teaching certificate Minn. Dept. Edn., 1967. Asst. sta. agt. Mpls. & St. Louis R.R., 1939-40; communication technician U. Minn., Mpls., 1946-50, audio visual materials adviser, 1951-59, dir. audio visual edn. service, 1960-70, prof. info. agrl. journalism, dir. Instructional Devel. Center, 1970—. Cons. Ency. Brit., 1970, Head Start, 1971, 4-H Exhibit Program, 1970—. Chmn., Info. Center, Twin City Film Council, 1951-59, pres., 1955, 56; bd. dirs. Film Council Am., 1956-59; chmn. adv. com. Minn. Bd. Edn., 1964-67; mem. Gov.'s Pub. Relations Commn. on Hwy. Safety, 1965. Recipient Golden Reel award, 1954; Screen Producers Guild Silver medallion 1955; certificate of acceptance Am. Film Festival, 1956; Best Film award Marching Band Assn., 1961. Flaherty Film Study grantee, 1966. Mem. Audio Visual Communications Assn. Minn. (chmn. awards and scholarship 1958-64, pres. 1963, 64, chmn. bd. 1965, chmn. comml. liaison 1973—), Univ. Film Producers Assn., Assn. for Ednl. Communications and Tech. (nat. newsletter chmn. 1964-67, affiliate relations council 1964-67, affiliate pres. chmn. 1974, nat. confs. steering com. 1958, 72), Phi Delta Kappa, Gamma Sigma Delta. Author: Flannelgraph, 1955; Your Audio-Visual Handbook, 1958; Candence West, 1960; News Letter Editors Handbook, 1966; Development of Audio-Visual Education at University of Minnesota, 1970. Resources editor NACTA Jour., 1976—. Home: 3100 Wendhurst Ave NE Minneapolis MN 55418 Office: Instructional Devel Center U Minn St Paul MN 55108

GRACE, OLIVER DAVIES, veterinarian; b. Washington, Dec. 21, 1914; s. Oliver Joseph and Gladys Susannah (Davies) G.; D.V.M., Colo. State U., 1940; M.S., U. Ill., 1952; m. Vera Hanawalt, July 14, 1948; children—Kerstin Elaine, Edward Oliver. With U.S. Dept. Agr., N.D., Va., N.H., 1940-45; research investigator FDA, Urbana, Ill., 1946-53; head dept. veterinary medicine Baxter Labs., Morton Grove, Ill., 1953-55; mem. faculty U. Nebr., Lincoln, 1955—, prof. veterinary sci., 1964—, acting chmn dept., 1976-77. Recipient grants NIH, U.S. Dept. Agr. Mem. AVMA, Nebr. Veterinary Med. Assn. (spl. service award 1977), Am. Assn. Avian Pathologists, Conf. Research Workers in Animal Diseases, Conf. Veterinary Lab. Diagnosticians. Democrat. Methodist. Club: Kiwanis. Contbr. articles to Nat. Hog Farmer. Home: 1720 Donald Circle Lincoln NE 68505 Office: 149 Veterinary Diagnostic Center Nebr Lincoln NE 68583

GRACE, RICHARD MILTON, educator; b. Albany, N.Y., Jan. 25, 1928; s. Charles Jay and Lucille (Walters) G.; Mus.B., U. Cin., 1950, Mus.M., 1952; Ph.D., U. Iowa, 1967; m. Loretta Jeanne Glenn, May 30, 1956; children—Gary Steven, Christopher Herald. Asst. prof. music Western Carolina Coll., 1954-58; prof. voice U. Nebr., Lincoln, 1961—, music dir., condr. univ. opera, 1963—. Minister music chs. Ohio, N.C., Iowa, Nebr., 1963—. Mem. Nat. Assn. Tchrs. Singing, Central Opera Service (mem. central com. 1968—), Pi Kappa Lambda. Methodist. Music reviewer Lincoln Star newspaper. Home: 1815 Connie Rd Lincoln NE 68502

GRADEN, MAYNARD A., III, electronics engr.; b. Norwich, Conn., May 23, 1945; s. Maynard A., Jr. and Jacqueline Yvette (Cote) G.; Asso. Sci. in Electronics Engring., Mitchell Coll., 1968; B.S., Ohio Inst. Tech., 1973. Design engr. Am. Computer Communications Co., Columbus, Ohio, 1973-76, North Electric Co. Research Lab., Delaware, Ohio, 1976—; tech. writer Popular Electronics mag., 1977—. Rec. sec. Plantation Lakes Condominium Bd. Mgrs. Mem. IEEE. Finalist, Nat. Design Contest sponsored by Intersil Corp., 1976. Home: 2441 Natchez Dr Columbus OH 43209 Office: PO Box 20345 Columbus OH 43220

GRADISON, WILLIS DAVID, JR., congressman; b. Cin., Dec. 28, 1928; s. Willis David and Dorothy (Benas) G.; A.B., Yale, 1948; M.B.A., Harvard, 1951, D.C.S., 1954; m. Helen Ann Martin, June 25, 1950 (div. 1975); children—Ellen, Anne, Margaret, Robin, Beth. With W.D. Gradison & Co., Cin., 1949, gen. partner, 1958—; asst. to under sec. Treasury, Washington, 1953-55; asst. to sec. HEW, Washington, 1955-57; mem. 94th-95th Congresses from 1st Ohio dist. Mem. Cin. City Council, 1961-74, mayor, 1971. Home: 2200 Victory Pkwy Cincinnati OH 45206 Office: 1519 Longworth House Office Bldg Washington DC 20515

GRADOLPH, DAVID, petroleum and mfg. cos. exec.; b. Akron, Ohio, May 25, 1930; s. Alfred Peter and Marion Esther (Boerstler) G.; A.B., Harvard U., 1952; B.S., Akron U., 1954; postgrad. Ohio State U., 1962-63, Kent State U., 1958-59; m. Kathleen J. Pattison, Apr. 27, 1957; children—Richard S., Stephen O., Carl W. Pres., Akron Petroleum Co., 1955—; chmn. Bremen Mfg. Co. Inc. (Ohio), 1962—. Served with U.S. Army, 1956-57. Mem. ASME, Am. Inst. Indsl. Engrs. Republican. Clubs: Marina Bay; Le Club Internat. (Ft. Lauderdale). Home: 2625 Wheeling Rd Lancaster OH 43130 Office: 245 N Broad St Bremen OH 43107

GRADY, JOHN DONOVAN, nuclear engr.; b. N.Y.C., Dec. 28, 1940; s. John Donovan and Estelle Sylvia (Rough) G.; B.S. in Marine Engring., U.S. Merchant Marine Acad., 1963; m. Eileen Marie Byard, Feb. 27, 1965; children—John Donovan III, Robert James. Marine engr. MSTS Lines, Bklyn., 1963-65; shift supr., project engr. DIG Nuclear Plant, Gen. Electric Co., West Milton, N.Y., 1965-69; nuclear engr. Bechtel Corp., San Francisco, 1969-70; sr. tng. engr. Westinghouse Electric Corp., Pitts., 1970-72, mgr. site and specialty tng., 1972-75, mgr. Westinghouse Nuclear Tng. Center, Zion, Ill., 1975—; guest lectr. U. Calif., Los Angeles, 1975. Extraordinary minister Roman Catholic Ch., 1972—. Mem. Am. Nuclear Soc. (exec. com. reactor ops. div.). Kiwanian. Home: 1141 Magnolia Ln Libertyville IL 60048 Office: 505 Shiloh Blvd Zion IL 60099

GRAEF, LUTHER WILLIAM, cons. civil engr.; b. Milw., Aug. 14, 1931; s. John and Pearl (Luther) G.; B.C.E., Marquette U., 1952; M.C.E., U. Wis., 1961; m. Lorraine Linnerud, Sept. 18, 1954; children—Ronald, Sharon, Gerald. Engr., C.W. Yoder & Assos., cons. engrs., Milw., 1956-61; partner Graef-Anhalt-Schloemer, cons. engrs., Milw., 1961—. Sec., v.p. Graef Anhalt Schloemer Assos., Inc., Milw., 1967—; chmn. engr. adv. com. U. Wis., Milw., also U. Wis. extensions. Active Boy Scouts Am. Chmn. bd. assessment, City of Milw., 1962—. Served to 1st lt. AUS, 1953-56. Mem. ASCE (sect. pres. 1968), Nat., Wis. socs. profl. engrs., Cons. Engrs. Council Wis. (pres. 1973-75), Engrs. Scientists Milw. (pres. 1975), Am. Legion, Marquette U. Alumni Assn., Tau Beta Pi, Pi Mu Epsilon, Chi Epsilon. Lutheran (pres. ch. council 1969). Home: 3788 S Massachusetts St Milwaukee WI 53220 Office: 6415 W Capitol Dr Milwaukee WI 53216

GRAETTINGER, JOHN SELLS, physician, educator; b. Ontario, Calif., June 24, 1921; s. Rupert Frederick and Alice (Sells) G.; candidate A.B., Harvard, 1943, M.D., 1945; m. Elizabeth Dun Shorey, June 29, 1946; children—John Sells, William Frederick, Alan Mitchell, Robert Shorey, George Douglass. Intern Harvard med. service Boston City Hosp., 1945-46, asst. resident, 1946, 48-49; research asst. cardiology and internal medicine U.S. Naval Sch. Aviation Medicine, Pensacola, Fla., 1949-53; dir. sect. cardio-respiratory diseases, dept. medicine Presbyn. Hosp., also Presbyn.-St. Luke's Hosp., Chgo., 1953-68, chmn. div. medicine Presbyn-St. Luke's Hosp., Chgo., 1966-70; asst. prof. U. Ill. Coll. Medicine, 1953-58, asso prof., 1958-64, prof. medicine, 1964-70; asso. dean student and faculty affairs Rush Med. Coll., 1970-72, prof. medicine, 1970—; dean Rush U., 1972—; exec. v.p. Nat. Intern-Resident Matching Program, 1975—. Pres., Bishop Anderson Found., 1960-62, bd. dirs, 1954—; bd. dirs. Chgo. Heart Assn. Served to lt. USNR, 1946-53. Diplomate Am. Bd. Internal Medicine. Fellow A.C.P.; mem. Am. Soc. Clin. Investigation, Central Soc. Clin. Research, Assn. U. Cardiologists (councillor 1964-69, pres. 1969-70), Chgo. Soc. Internal Medicine (pres. 1971-72), Inst. Medicine Chgo., N.Y. Acad. Sci. Club: Harvard of Chicago (chmn. schlorship com. 1962-64, dir. 1968—), University, Chicago Yacht. Publs. and monographs on the heart and circulation. Home: 999 Lake Shore Dr Chicago IL 60611 Office: 1753 W Congress Pkwy Chicago IL 60612

GRAF, EDWIN XAVIER, mech. engr.; b. N.Y.C., Oct. 29, 1949; s. Alfons and Anna (Tillmann) G.; B.M.E., U. Detroit, 1971; M.M.E., U. Wis., 1977. Design engr. Warner Electric Brake & Clutch Co., S. Beloit, Ill., 1972; cons. mech. engring., Rockton, Ill., 1972—; devel. engr. Beloit Corp. Research, Rockton, Ill., 1973—; cons. product liability; expert witness. Mem. ASME, Soc. Mfg. Engrs., Am. Soc. Metals, Flying Engrs. Internat. (treas. 1973). Home: PO Box 335 Rockton IL 61072

GRAF, TRUMAN FREDERICK, agrl. economist, educator; b. New Holstein, Wis., Sept. 18, 1922; s. Herbert and Rose (Sell) G.; B.S., U. Wis., 1947, M.S., 1949, Ph.D., 1953; m. Sylvia Ann Thompson, Sept. 6, 1947; children—Eric Kindley, Siri Lynne, Peter Truman. Marketing specialist, coop. agt. U.S. Dept. of Agr. and U. Wis., 1948-50; instr. agrl. econs. U. Wis., 1951-53, asst. prof., 1953-56, asso. prof., 1956-61, prof., 1961—. Mem. Gov.'s Com. on Wis. Dairy Marketing; mem. 3 man team to make marketing analysis in Nigeria for U.S. Dept. Agr., 1962, made marketing analyses in 13 Caribbean countries, 1964, also for U. Wis. in Mexico, 1965; made analysis U.S. agrl. policy for U.S. Senate, 1965-68; made marketing analysis for U.S. Ednl. Found., Finland, 1970, for Rumanian Ministry Edn., U.S. Dept. State, Rumania, 1976; made U.S. milk mktg. study for U.S. Dept. Agr., 1971; research for internat. agrl. marketing agys., 1963—. Active Cub Scouts. Bd. dirs. Univ. Houses Assn., 1955-56, Univ. Hill Farm Assn., 1958-59, Univ. Hill Farm Swim Club, 1959-60. Served with USNR, 1942-45; comdr. Res. Recipient Uhlman award Chgo. Bd. Trade, 1952. Mem. Am. Farm Econs. Assn., Am. Marketing Assn., Madison Naval Res. Assn. (pres. 1968—), Am. Econ. Assn., Hist. Soc., Civil War Club. Lutheran. Kiwanian (chmn. internat. relations com.). Contbr. articles to profl. jours. Applied research study for dairy firms, agrl. orgns., state and Fed. regulatory agys. and agrl. bus. firms. Home: 5022 LaCrosse Ln Madison WI 57305

GRAHAM, BARNEY DAN, dentist; b. Lincoln, Neb., Sept. 18, 1928; s. Maurice Daniel and Margret Pearl (Barney) G.; B.S., U. Kan., 1949; D.D.S., U. Mo., 1953; m. Carol Ann Hastings, Jan. 29, 1950; children—Barney Scott, Christopher Hastings, Janice Ann. Practice dentistry, Olathe, Kan., 1956—; dir. 1st Nat. Bank, Olathe. Pres. Carham, Inc. real estate, Olathe, Kan., 1963—, Robar Farms, 1970—. Mem. Olathe Sch. Bd., 1960-66, pres., 1963, Johnson County Sch. Unification Bd., 1964-65. Bd. dirs. Midwest Christian Counseling Center, Kansas City, Mo., 1972—. Served to lt. USNR, 1953-55. Mem. Am. Dental Assn., Am. Acad. Gen. Practice, Am. Acad. Orthodontics for Gen. Practice, Xi Psi Phi, Aircraft Owners and Pilots Assn., Delta Chi. Presbyn. (elder). Mason, Rotarian. Home: RD 1 Paola KS 66071 Office: 234 S Cherry St Olathe KS 66061

GRAHAM, BRUCE DOUGLAS, pediatrician; b. Roberts, Wis., Dec. 15, 1915; s. Francis J. and Mary (Turner) G.; A.B., U. Ala., 1939; M.D., Vanderbilt U., 1942; m. Louise Alice Rowekamp, Jan. 21, 1946; children—John Gardiner, Mary Augusta, Anne Louise. Intern U. Mich. Hosp., 1942-43, resident dept. pediatrics, 1946-48, dir. pediatric labs., 1949-59; faculty pediatric dept. U. Mich., 1948-59, asso. prof., 1954-59, prof., 1959; prof., head dept. pediatrics U. B.C., 1959-63; pediatrician-in-chief Vancouver Gen. Hosp., Can., 1959-63; chief pediatrics Children's Hosp., Vancouver, 1961-63; prof. pediatrics Ohio State U. Coll. Medicine, 1964—, chmn. dept., 1964-76; chief staff Children's Hosp., Columbus, Ohio, 1964-70, med. dir., 1970-74, chief pediatrics, 1974-76, chief ambulatory services, 1976—; chief pediatric div. U. Hosp., Ohio State U., 1964-76; med. dir. Children's Hosp. Research Found., Columbus, 1966-76. Mem. med. adv. com. State Crippled Children's Bur.; mem. Greater Dublin Community Council. Bd. dirs. Franklin County Health Planning Council; trustee Mid-Ohio Health Planning Fedn. Served to maj. M.C., AUS, 1943-46. Diplomate Am. Bd. Pediatrics. Mem. Soc. Pediatric Research, Am. Pediatric Soc., Ambulatory Pediatric Assn., AMA, Am. Acad. Pediatrics (dist. chmn.), AAAS, Assn. Am. Med. Colls., Midwest, Western socs. pediatric research, Ohio State Med. Assn., Central Ohio Pediatric Soc., Acad. Medicine Columbus and Franklin County, Am. Pub. Health Assn., Am. Assn. Maternal and Child Health, Sigma Xi, Alpha Omega Alpha. Home: 4915 Brand Rd Dublin OH 43017 Office: 700 Children's Dr Columbus OH 43205

GRAHAM, BRUCE EDWARD, ins. agy. exec.; b. Hannibal, Mo., Mar. 15, 1953; s. Roy Gene and Anna Elizabeth (Raybourn) G.; student N.E. Mo. State U., 1971-72, Mo. U., 1973. Gen. mgr. Modular Housing plant Universal Homes, Auxvasse, Mo., 1973-74; partner, mgr. Graham Mobile Home Sales, Auxvasse, 1974-77; partner, broker Graham Real Estate, Auxvasse, 1974—; v.p., dir. Universal Homes Corp., Auxvasse, 1973—; partner Graham Ins. Agy., 1976—; auctioneer Graham Auction Service, 1976—; dir. Universal Industries, Auxvasse. Mem. Jackson Twp. com. Callaway County Central Republican Com., 1972—. Mem. Audrain County Bd. Realtors (sec.-treas. 1975-76). Address: PO Box 67 Auxvasse MO 65231

GRAHAM, CARL FRANCIS, chem. products co. exec., chemist; b. Limon, Colo., Jan. 2, 1915; s. Karl and Edith (Nesselrode) G.; B.S., Baker U., 1938; postgrad. U. Kansas City, 1938-39; m. Marjorie Ruth Killebrew, Apr. 27, 1941; children—David Carl, Nancy Lou (Mrs. J.R. Flink), Carol Ann. Head of lab. Procter and Gamble Mfg. Co., Kansas City, Kans., 1938-41; sect. head research dept., J.B. Ford Co., Wyandotte, Mich., 1941-43; supr. analytical research Wyandotte Chems. Corp. (Mich.), 1943-56, mgr. analytical research, 1956-57; dir. research and devel. Turco Products Inc., Wilmington, Calif., 1957-65; adminstrv. asst. to v.p. chem. research Purex Corp., Ltd., Wilmington, 1964-66; mgr. research and devel. Amway Corp., Ada, Mich., 1967-70, mgr. industry and govt. tech. relations, 1970-72, sr. adviser legis. and regulatory standards, 1970-76, mgr. govt. affairs, 1976—; cons. to Chem. Corps., U.S. Army, 1952-62, Chem-Biol.-Radio. Agy., Edgewood (Md.) Arsenal, 1962-63. Fellow Am. Inst. Chemists; mem. Am. Chem. Soc. (com. on nat. defense 1963-70), ASTM (councilor Detroit dist. 1955-57, councilor So. Cal. dist. 1962-66), Soap and Detergent Assn. (legal com. tech. and materials div. 1970-74), Cosmetic, Toiletry and Fragrance Assn. (govt. relations com. 1972—), Chem. Specialties Mfrs. Assn. (chmn. div. com. legis. standards 1971—, bd. govs. 1976-78), Am. Def. Preparedness Assn. (tech. com. on surface preservation 1958-66), Chemists Club of N.Y. Home: 2648 Berwyck Rd SE Grand Rapids MI 49506 Office: 7575 E Fulton Rd Ada MI 49355

GRAHAM, CHARLES PATTISON, JR., surgeon; b. Wilmington, N.C., June 24, 1940; s. Charles Pattison and Jean Victor (McKoy) G.; A.B. in History, U. N.C., 1961, M.D., 1965; m. Vera Ann Mingos, Dec. 30, 1967; children—Vera Michelle, Katie McKoy, Caroline Pattison and Morey McLean (twins). Intern, then resident in surgery Vanderbilt U. Hosp., 1965-71; practice medicine specializing in surgery, Decatur, Ala., 1973-74, Topeka, 1974—; mem. staff St. Francis, Stormont-Vail, Meml. hosps.; surg. cons. Menninger Found., Topeka, 1976—, Topeka State Hosp., 1976—. Served to maj. M.C., AUS, 1971-73. Decorated Army Commendation medal; John M. Morehead scholar, 1957-61. Mem. A.C.S., Kans. Med. Soc., H.W. Scott Soc. Episcopalian. Contbr. articles to med. jours. Home: 117 Greenwood St Topeka KS 66606 Office: Continental Med Bldg 7th and Horne Sts Topeka KS 66606

GRAHAM, CLAYTON JAMES, metal finishing co. exec.; b. Oak Park, Ill., Oct. 31, 1942; s. Barclay M. and Olive W. (Carlstrom) G.; B.S., Purdue U., 1964; M.B.A., Northwestern U., 1968; M.A., Roosevelt U., 1968; m. Margaret Ann Dewenter, June 26, 1965; children—Candace, Ashley. Asso., A. T. Kearney Inc., Chgo., 1969-73; partner Graham Plating Works, Chgo., 1973—, Graham Leasing Co., Barrington, Ill., 1974—. Leaseco Internat., Barrington, 1976—; pres. TWR Service Corp., Rosemont, Ill., 1975—; speaker at profl. meetings. Mem. pres's. council Purdue U.; mem. dean's council Northwestern U. Grad. Sch. Mgmt.; pollution control and econ. adviser to Congress and the White House, 1974-76. Mem. Inst. Mgmt. Sci., Chgo. Electro Platers Inst. (dir.), Nat. Assn. Metal Finishers. Clubs: Barrington Hills Country; Met., Carlton (Chgo.); Meadow (Rolling Meadows, Ill.); Marco Island (Fla.) Country. Home: 1104 North Shore Ct Barrington IL 60010 Office: 4500 W North Ave Chicago IL 60639

GRAHAM, DOUGLAS LYNN, agrl. engr.; b. Fort Wayne, Ind., July 29, 1938; s. Earl Donovan and Verda May (Anglemeyer) G.; B.S. in Agrl. Engring., Purdue U.; m. Judy Ann Overmyer, Aug. 27, 1960; children—Andrew, Blake, Corey. Product engr., mgr. M & W Gear Co., Gibson City, Ill.; now pres. Graham Enterprises, Inc., Auburn, Ind., Solarcrete Corp., Auburn. Mem. Am. Soc. Agrl. Engrs. Presbyn. Research and devel. numerous grain processing equipment, solar heated constrn. Patentee grain dryers. Home: Route 2 Auburn IN 46706 Office: Commerce Bldg PO Box 543 Auburn IL 46706

GRAHAM, GEORGE WESLEY, engr.; b. Utica, N.Y., Sept. 27, 1932; s. Leon Erastus and Marion (Babcock) G.; B.M.E., Purdue U., 1959; M.S., No. Ill. U., 1971; Ph.D., Kans. State U., 1976; m. Marelu Satterley, Sept. 7, 1957; 1 dau., Rebeca. Materials engr. Micro Switch div. Honeywell Internat., Freeport, Ill., 1959-71; prof. engring. Pittsburg (Kans.) State U., 1971-77; cons. in field; chmn. vocat. edn. Plastics Ednl. Found. U.S.A., 1975-77. Precinct committeeman Republican party, Freeport, 1966-70. Served with U.S. Army, 1954-56. Mem. Nat., Kans. socs. profl. engrs., ASME, Am. Soc. Engring. Educators, Soc. Plastics Engrs., Rock Valley Soc. Plastics Engrs. (past pres.), Kansas City Plastics Engrs. (Plastics Educator of Year 1976, dir. 1973—). Republican. Presbyterian. Clubs: Masons, Shriners, Eastern Star. Home: 520 Utah St Pittsburg KS 66762 Office: Dept Technology Pittsburg State U Pittsburg KS 66762

GRAHAM, JAMES WALLACE, credit reporting agy. exec.; b. Greensburg, Pa., Feb. 7, 1926; s. Archibald Wallace and Dolta Lavonia (Shriver) G.; student U. N.C., Ga. State Coll. Bus. Adminstrn.; m. Mildred Jean Clarke, Oct. 11, 1947; children—James Wallace, Douglas Sheldon, Charlene Yvonne. Asst. credit sales mgr. Rich's, Inc., Atlanta, 1953-62; operations mgr. Credit Bur. of Atlanta, 1962-65; treas., sec. Frederick Atkins, Inc., N.Y.C., 1965-73; pres., sec. Credit Bur. of Cleve., Inc., 1973—; vice chmn., dir. Greater Cleve. Consumer Credit Counselling Service. Trustee City Mission, Cleve. Served with USNR, 1944-46; PTO. Mem. Am. Mgmt. Assn., Christian Businessmen's Com. U.S.A., Am. Retail Assn. Execs., Cleve. Soc. Assn. Execs., Asso. Credit Burs. Ohio (dir.), Asso. Credit Burs., Cleve. Advt. Club. Republican. Clubs: Cleve. Athletic, Rotary (Cleve.); Acacia Country. Home: 1042 Professor Rd South Euclid OH 44124 Office: 666 Euclid Ave Cleveland OH 44114

GRAHAM, JAMES WILLIS, assn. exec.; b. Madison, Wis., May 9, 1930; s. Willis Alexander and Anna Caroline (Pankratz) G.; B.A., New Melleray Sem., 1954; S.T.L., Angelicum U., Rome, Italy, 1959; Ph.D., Loyola U., Chgo., 1972; m. Linda Louise Pote, June 3, 1972. Dean students, prof. religion New Melleray Sem., Dubuque, Iowa, 1959-68; dir. rehab. Good-Will Rehab. Center, Chgo., 1970-72; dir. div. ednl. measurements Am. Dental Assn., Chgo., 1972—. Pvt. cons. Good-Will Rehab. Center, 1970—. Arthur Schmidt scholar, 1969-70. Mem. Am. Psychol. Assn., Am. Ednl. Research Assn., Am. Assn. Dental Schs., Assn. Am. Med. Colls., Nat. Council Measurements in Edn., Phi Delta Kappa. Home: 42 Abbotsford Rd Winnetka IL 60093 Office: 211 E Chicago Ave Chicago IL 60611

GRAHAM, JANICE ELIZABETH, counselor; b. Wyandotte, Mich., Oct. 31, 1948; d. Robert Lewis and Wanda Elizabeth (Janice) Rutt; B.A., Eastern Mich. U., 1971, M.S., 1973; Ph.D., Kent State U., 1977. Counselor, Drug Help, Ann Arbor, Mich., 1972-73; staging psychologist, coordinator, ACTION, Peace Corps, Washington, D.C., 1973-74; tchg. fellow, grad. asst., Kent (Ohio) State U., 1974-77, instr., Dept. Counseling & Personnel Services, 1977; counselor Akron U. Counseling Center, 1977—; cons. drug edn., crisis intervention; cons. death edn., sensitivity tng.; co-founder, chmn. Oncology Support Group, Summit (Ohio) County, 1977—. Recipient Organization Development of Merit, Kent (Ohio) State U., 1976, David J. Bowers research support award, Phi Delta Kappa, 1977. Mem. Kent State U. Grad. Student Senate (exec. bd., chmn. selection com. for grad. student teaching awards 1975-76), Am. Personnel Guidance Assn., Assn. Humanistic Psychology, Assn. for Women in Psychology, Forum for Death Edn. and Counseling, Omicron Delta Kappa, Phi Delta Kappa. Home: 3006 Prior Dr Cuyahoga Falls OH 44223 Office: Counseling & Testing Bureau U Akron Akron OH 44325

GRAHAM, JARLATH JOHN, magazine exec.; b. Chgo., Dec. 18, 1919; s. Jarlath John and Isabelle Marie (Corboy) G.; B.A., U. Chgo., 1949; m. Elizabeth Grace Carlson, Aug. 23, 1958; children by previous marriage—Carol, Karen. With Advt. Age, weekly bus. publ., Chgo., 1950—, editor, 1969-75; v.p. Crain Communications Inc., Chgo., 1963—; dir. editorial devel., pub. Crain Books, 1975—, v.p. communications and editorial devel., 1977—. dirs. Bateman Sch., Chgo. Served to capt. AUS, World War II. Mem. Sigma Delta Chi. Contbr. Ency. Brit., 1966—. Home: 322 Belden Ave Chicago IL 60614 Office: Crain Communications Inc 740 N Rush St Chicago IL 60611

GRAHAM, JOHN DALBY, pub. relations exec.; b. Maryville, Mo., Aug. 24, 1937; s. Kyle T. and Irma Irene (Dalby) G.; student U. Mo., 1955-59; m. Jean Elizabeth Landon, Aug. 30, 1958; children—Katherine Elizabeth, David Landon. Editor, Hallmark Cards, Inc., Kansas City, Mo., 1959-62; dir. pub. relations St. Louis Met. YMCA, 1962-66; with Fleishman-Hillard, Inc., St. Louis, 1966—, v.p., dir., sr. partner, 1970-74, pres., 1974—. Served as lt. U.S. Army, 1959-60. Mem. Pub. Relations Soc. Am. (accredited), Nat. Investor Relations Inst. Clubs: Univ., Noonday, Bermuda Bath Tennis, Frontenac Tennis. Home: 83 Bellerive Acres Saint Louis MO 63121 Office: 1 Memorial Dr Saint Louis MO 63102

GRAHAM, M(ARIE) FRANCES, educator; b. Sioux City, Iowa, Feb. 11, 1930; d. James Perry and Anna Hedvig (Holm) Gibson; R.N., St. Joseph Mercy Sch. Nursing, Sioux City, 1951; certificate Briar Cliff Coll., 1961; B.S., U. Minn., 1957; S.S., U. S.D., 1963, M.A., 1966; postgrad. Ind. U., 1969; m. Hewitt K. Graham, Aug. 6, 1977. Instr. orthopedic nursing St. Joseph Mercy Sch. Nursing, 1951-55; inst. St. Mary's Sch. Nursing, Rochester, Minn., 1957-59; asst. exec. dir. Iowa Nurses Assn., Des Moines, 1959-60; tchr. Sioux City Community Dist., 1961-67, jr. high sch. counselor, 1967-68; dean women Briar Cliff Coll., Sioux City, 1968-70; instr., coordinator asso. degree nursing Western Iowa Tech. Merged Area XII, Sioux City, 1970-77; supr. health occupations div. Iowa Tech. Community Coll., Sioux City, 1977—; cons. in field. Active Sioux City Community Theater, 1961—; vol. ARC, Sioux City, 1952—; mem. Luth. Hosp. Assn. St. Luke's Med. Center. Mem. Nat., Iowa assns. women deans and counselors, AAUW, Iowa, Sioux City, Nat. edn. assns., Am., Iowa personnel and guidance assns., Am., Iowa vocat. assns., Alpha Tau Delta. Lutheran (mem. choir). Club: Zonta (Sioux City). Home: 19 McCook Lake Jefferson SD 57038

GRAHAM, MARJORIE RUTH KILLEBREW, ednl. adminstr.; b. Kansas City, Mo., Sept. 25, 1915; s. Robert Herman and Edith Cruce (Tyler) Killebrew; B.A., U. Okla., 1936; M.A., U. Mich., 1969; m. Carl Francis Graham, Apr. 27, 1941; children—David Carl, Nancy Graham Flink, Carol Ann. Reference librarian Kansas City (Kans.) Pub. Library, 1936-40; librarian LaQuinta High Sch., Garden Grove, Calif., 1963-67, Central High Sch., 1967-71, Ottawa High Sch., Grand Rapids, Mich., 1971-73; supr. instructional media, Grand Rapids, 1973—. Lectr. library sci. U. Mich., 1970—. Pres., Garden Grove P.T.A. council, 1963-65. Mem. ALA, Am. Assn. Sch. Librarians, Mich. Assn. for Media in Edn. (v.p. 1976), Mich. Assn. Sch. Curriculum Devel., Assn. for Ednl. Communications and Tech., Phi Beta Kappa, Beta Phi Mu, Delta Kappa Gamma, Gamma Phi Beta. Republican. Methodist (trustee 1965-66). Club: U. Mich. Alumnae (group pres. Grand Rapids 1973-74). Home: 2648 Berwyck Rd SE East Grand Rapids MI 49506 Office: 143 Bostwick NE Grand Rapids MI 49502

GRAHAM, RICHARD MARSTON, sculptor; b. Lynn, Mass., July 29, 1939; s. Stuart Webster and Ellen Marston (Connor) G.; B.F.A., Boston U., 1962; M.F.A., R.I. Sch. Design, 1964. Instr., Va. Commonwealth U., 1966-68; asst. prof. art Ithaca Coll., 1968-69, Old Dominion U., 1969-70; asst. prof. Mpls. Coll. Art, 1970—, chmn. div. basic studies, 1973—; one-man exhbns. include: Albany (N.Y.) Inst. Art, 1967, Paul Schuster Gallery, Cambridge, Mass., 1971-75, J. Hunt Gallery, Mpls., 1977; group shows include: So. Assn. Sculptors traveling exhbns., 1971-75, Sculptors Guild ann. exhbns., N.Y.C., 1973-76, Minn. Sculpture, Mpls., 1977; represented in permanent collections, including: Minn. Mus. Art, St. Paul, Carleton Coll., U. Tenn., Chattanooga, Ark. Art Center, Little Rock, 1st Nat. Bank, Altanta; fellow Macdowell Colony, 1971, 75, Yaddo, 1971, Va. Center for Arts, 1973-75. Recipient 1st prize in sculpture Festival of Sculpture, Atlanta, 1970, Carleton Coll. Invitational, 1975; citation of excellence for design in steel Am. Inst. Iron and Steel, 1973; 1st prize toys designed by artists Ark. Art Center, 1975; purchase prize Minn. Mus. Art, 1976; Blanche E. Colman Found. grantee, Boston, 1970; Am. the Beautiful grantee, 1971-73; Union Ind. Colls. Art faculty research grantee, 1972; Minn. Arts Bd. artist-in-residence program grantee Nancy Hauser Dance Co., 1972. Mem. AAUP, Art Educators Minn., Artists Equity Assn., Am. Crafts Council. Coll. Art Assn., Minn. Craftsman's Council, Nat. Art Edn. Assn., Sculptors Guild N.Y. Home: 2446 Harriet Ave S Minneapolis MN 55405 Office: 200 E 25th St Minneapolis MN 55404

GRAHAM, RUTH VOGEL, TV broadcaster, communications cons.; b. Milw., Sept. 30, 1945; d. Richard Hermann and Hannah (Nachman) Vogel; B.A., Northwestern U., 1967; m. Stephen Shafton Graham, Sept. 17, 1967; children—Justin Vogel, Charles Spencer. Intern, U.S. Dept. State, Washington, 1965, 66; asst. dir. pub. relations Mundelein Coll., Chgo., 1967; dir. pub. info. Cook. County Hwy. Dept., Chgo., 1969-71; account supr. Janet Diederichs and Assos., Chgo., 1972-77; trading mem. Mid-Am. Commodity Exchange, Chgo., 1976—; anchorperson, interviewer, newscaster, producer and host Market Basket program Sta. WCIU-TV, Chgo., 1976—. Mem. governing bd. Chgo. Internat. Film Festival. Mem. Pub. Relations Soc. Am., Nat. Acad. TV Arts and Scis. Clubs: Arts Club of Chgo. Home: 144 Oak Knoll Terr Highland Park IL 60035 Office: 141 W Jackson Blvd Chicago IL 60604

GRAHAM, STEPHEN SHAFTON, lawyer, securities trader; b. Chgo., July 10, 1938; s. Sidney G. and Phyllis (Shafton) G.; A.B. cum laude, Harvard, 1960, J.D., 1963; m. Ruth I. Vogel, Sept. 17, 1967. Admitted to Ill. bar, 1964; exec. trainee Office of Sec. Def., Washington, 1963-65; v.p., sec. dir. Nat. Soda Straw Co., Chgo., 1966-75; mem., market-maker Chgo. Bd. Options Exchange, 1975—, mem. securities com., 1975—; pres., dir. Pacesetter Industries, Inc. Chgo., 1968—, Optec Investments Ltd., 1974—. Mem. Com. on Ill. Govt. 1966-74, mem. edn. and housing task forces, 1966-67, bd. dirs., 1970-72; mem. exec. bd. Expt. in Internat. Living, Chgo. Council, 1966-70. Mem. central com. Cook County Young Democrats, 1966-70; exec. bd. Ill. State Young Dems., 1966-70. Mem. Fed., Ill., Chgo. bar assns., Council Fgn. Relations (com. on fgn. affairs), Chgo. Assn. Commerce and Industry, Assn. for Corporate Growth, Harvard Law Sch. Assn. Club: Harvard (Chgo.). Home: 144 Oak Knoll Terr Highland Park IL 60035 Office: 141 W Jackson 7th Floor Box 253 Chicago IL 60604

GRAHAM, WILLIAM ALEXANDER, JR., pathologist; b. Chgo., Oct. 12, 1936; s. William Alexander and Helen Jeanette (Bury) G.; B.S., U.S. Naval Acad., 1958; M.D., Creighton U., 1967; children—Sandra Lynne, Richard Brian, David Jeffrey. Intern, Orange County (Calif.) Med. Center, 1967-68; resident in pathology Los Angeles County/U. So. Calif. Med. Center, 1968-72; asso. pathologist San Clemente Gen. Hosp. (Calif.), 1972-73; dir. labs. and pathology East Liverpool (Ohio) City Hosp., 1973—; instr. U. So. Calif., 1970—. Served to lt. USN, 1958-63. Diplomate Am. Bd. Pathology. Fellow Coll. Am. Pathology, Am. Soc. Clin. Pathologists; mem. Ohio Assn. Blood Banks (trustee 1977—), AMA. Club: Rotary. Home: 48660 Lakeview Circle East Liverpool OH 43920 Office: 425 W 5th St East Liverpool OH 43920

GRAHAM, WILLIAM QUENTIN, used computer dealer; b. Ann Arbor, Mich., Jan. 17, 1944; s. William and Marie (MacGregor) G.; B.B.A., Eastern Mich. U., Ypsilanti, 1969; m. Susan H. Scheinker, Sept. 10, 1967; 1 son, David Aaron. Research asst. TRW, Los Angeles, 1965; field engr. IBM, Ann Arbor, 1966-69, salesman, Detroit, 1969-73; salesman Cambridge Memories, Inc., 1973-76; account rep. CMI Corp., Birmingham, Mich., 1976—; data processing cons. and advisor. Jewish. Clubs: AAU, Motor City Striders, B'nai B'rith. Home: 5693 Warrenshire Dr West Bloomfield MI 48033 Office: 1500 N Woodward Ave Birmingham MI 48011

GRAINGER, DAVID WILLIAM, elec. equipment distbn. co. exec.; b. Chgo., Oct. 23, 1927; s. William Wallace and Hally (Ward) G.; grad. Phillips Exeter Acad., 1945; B.S. in Elec. Engring., U. Wis., 1950; m. Juli Ann Plant, June 15, 1949; children—Susan, Thomas, Nancy. With Franklin Electric Corp., Bluffton, Ind., 1950-52; with W. W. Grainger, Inc., Chgo., 1952—, v.p., sec., dir., 1958-68, chmn. bd. dirs., 1968-73, chmn. bd., pres., 1974—. Treas., Grainger Found. Served with USAAF, 1946-47. Mem. I.E.E.E., Delta Tau Delta, Tau Beta Pi. Office: 5959 Howard St Chicago IL 60648

GRAJEWSKI, MARION JOHN, utility exec.; b. N.Y.C., Sept. 23, 1922; s. Ignatius and Sophie (Gryglewicz) G.; Certificate engring. N.C. State Coll., 1944; B.S., N.Y. U., 1948, M.A., 1952; m. Florence Blejwas, Aug. 26, 1950; children—Marion John, Richard, Barbara Ann. With Kings County Lighting Co., Bklyn., 1941-55, chief accountant, 1954-55; spl. agt. intelligence div. IRS, 1955-59; with Mich. Gas Utilities Co., Monroe, 1960—, asst. treas., 1960-76, controller, 1968-76, asst. sec., 1970-76, v.p., 1972—, sec., 1976—. Bd. dirs. United Fund, 1968-76, Mich. Cancer Soc., 1963-74, Jr. Achievement, 1963-77, Mercy Meml. Hosp., 1972-74. Mem. Am. Gas Assn., Am. Legion (comdr. post 1951-77). Home: 161 Cranbrook Blvd Monroe MI 48161 Office: 889 S Telegraph St Monroe MI 48161

GRAM, CHRISTINE ELISE GROEFSEMA HARRIS (MRS. HENRY H. GRAM), educator; b. Detroit, Dec. 29, 1924; d. Elmer H. and Mary Blanche (Gibbons) Groefsema; A.B. with distinction and honors, U. Mich., 1948, A.M., 1963, Ph.D. 1971; m. Henry H. Gram, June 13, 1970; children by previous marriage—Robert, Jeanne (Mrs. James Reyer), John, James, David, Gregory. Owner, Farmington Automatic Laundry (Mich.), 1952-54; research asst. Mich. Osteo. Assn., 1963-64; instr. Lawrence Inst. Tech., Southfield, Mich., 1964, Oakland Community Coll., Union Lake, Mich., 1965-67; prof. econs., dept. chmn. Oakland Community Coll., Farmington, 1968—; cons., examiner North Central Assn., Higher Edn. Commn. A.A.U.W., U. Mich. Alumnae Assn., Phi Kappa Phi. Home: 26090 Pleasant Valley St Farmington MI 48024

GRAMCZAK, MARY EULODIA, ednl. adminstr., nun; b. Chgo., July 28, 1928; d. Andrew and Catherine (Kucharczyk) Gramczak; Ph.B., DePaul U., 1957, M.Ed., 1963. Joined Congregation of Sisters of St. Felix (Felician Sisters), 1947; tchr. parochial schs., Chgo., 1949-56, math., sci. tchr. St. Joseph High Sch., 1957-62, math. tchr., counselor Good Counsel High Sch., 1962-71; guidance dir. Providence High Sch., New Lenox, Ill., 1971-75; dean students, fin. aid dir. Felician Coll., Chgo., 1975—. NSF grantee De Paul U., 1960-62; NDEA grantee, Counseling Inst. Loyola U., 1964, Vocat. Guidance Inst., Ill. Inst. Tech., 1968, 70. Mem. Am., Ill. personnel guidance assns., Am., Ill. sch. counselor assns., Nat. Vocat. Guidance Assn., Am., Ill. coll. personnel assns. Home and office: 3800 W Peterson Ave Chicago IL 60659

GRANAT, BRUCE ARNOLD, librarian; b. Chgo., July 21, 1939; s. Harry Jeremiah and Nettie (Small) G.; B.S. in Psychology, Roosevelt U., 1961; M.A., U. Chgo., 1964; m. Jacqueline Eliane Kraft, Aug. 26, 1962; children—Deborah Kathryn, Rebecca Jean. Librarian trainee applied sci. and tech. dept., Chgo. Pub. Library, 1961-62; reference librarian John Crerar Library, Chgo., 1962-64; head librarian bus. information service, Abbott Labs., North Chicago, 1964-65; mgr. and head librarian Continental Ill. Nat. Bank & Trust Co. of Chgo. Library, 1965-73; dir. corp. libraries and communications services G.D. Searle & Co., Skokie, Ill., 1973—; vis. lectr. Rosary Coll.; library cons. and adv. work to various orgns., 1967—; mem. governing bd. Library of Internat. Relations. NATO Advanced Study Inst. grantee on evaluation libraries and info. centers, 1975; mem. automation com. Ill. State Library, 1975—. Mem. A.L.A., Spl. Libraries Assn. (chmn. nat. consultation com. 1976—, officer nat. documentation div. 1976—), Med. Library Assn., Am. Soc. for Info. Sci., Pharm. Mfrs. Assn. (sci. info. subcom. 1975—), U. Chgo. Alumni Assn., Beta Phi Mu. Contbr. articles to profl. publs. Home: 1401 Dempster St Evanston IL 60201 Office: GD Searle & Co Box 1045 Skokie IL 60076

GRANDSTAFF, CHARLES HARRY, oral surgeon; b. Mounds, Ill., Nov. 1, 1904; s. Charles Lester and Golda Pearl (Auganbright) G.; student Knox Coll., 1929; D.D.S., Loyola U. Chgo., 1933, M.Dental Surgery, 1935; m. Virginia Kathleen Dursch, Nov. 26, 1949; children—Craig, Carol, Tom, Catherine, Christine. Individual practice oral surgery, Rockford, Ill., 1936—. Served to lt. col. Dental Corps, AUS, 1942-45. Diplomate Am. Bd. Oral Surgery. Mem. Assn. Mil. Surgeons, Am., Brit. socs. oral surgeons, Phi Delta Theta. Mason (Shriner). Home: 1816 Parkview Ave Rockford IL 61107 Office: 1108 Talcott Bldg Rockford IL 61101

GRANGAARD, B. C., banker; b. Rogers, N.D., Apr. 5, 1911; s. M. O. and Agnes (Brusegaard) G.; J.D., U. Minn., 1933; pre-standard and standard certificates Am. Inst. Banking; grad. Pacific Coast Banking Sch., 1949; m. Mary Pettit, June 13, 1936; children—Robert P., Richard C., Carol Ruth. Credit investigator Fed. Res. Bank of Mpls., 1933-40; cashier First Nat. Bank, Windom, Minn., 1941-42; asst. cashier Nat. Bank of S.D., Sioux Falls, 1943-44; cashier First Nat. Bank, Grand Forks, N.D., 1944-45; v.p. Seattle-First Nat. Bank, 1946-62; pres., dir. Central Nat. Bank & Trust Co., Des Moines, 1962-67, chmn., dir., 1967—. Bd. dirs. Greater Des Moines Com. Mem. Des Moines C. of C., Assn. Res. City Bankers, Am. Bankers Assn., Phi Delta Theta, Phi Alpha Delta. Lutheran. Rotarian. Clubs: Des Moines, Wakonda. Home: 3663 Grand Ave Des Moines IA 50312 also 9453 110th Ave Sun City AZ 85351 Office: Central Nat Bank & Trust Co Locust at 6th Des Moines IA 50304

GRANT, BARRY MARVIN, judge; b. Detroit, Jan. 16, 1936; s. Daniel and Pauline (Dantzig) G.; B.A., Mich. State U., 1957; J.D., Wayne State U., 1960; postgrad. Northwestern U., 1964; m. Lisa Geffen, Jan. 31, 1960; children—James D., Nanci J., L. Scott. Admitted to Mich. bar, 1961, U.S. Ct. Appeals, U.S. Supreme Ct. bar, 1966; probate clk. Oakland County, Mich., 1960; legal investigator Mental Health Div., asst. pros. atty. Oakland County, 1961—; judge Oakland County Probate Ct.; probate ct. referee Oakland County, 1962, 63, 71; chmn. Oakland County Condemnation Commn., 1964-72; trial atty. Oakland County, Southfield, 1961—; mem. Oakland County Criminal Jurisprudence Comm., 1977—; lectr. estate planning, juvenile problems, 1961-72. Traffic safety commr. Mich., 1964; mem. Parent-Youth Guidance Commn., 1963-64; chmn. Oakland County Lawyers United Found. Torch Drive, 1968, 71; exec. sec. Southfield Beautification Com., 1963. Mem. Nat. Congl. Republican Adv. Com., 1966-70; 67th Legis. Rep. chmn., 1966; Rep. del. State Rep. Conv., 1964-70; pres. Oakland County Rep. Lincoln Orgn., 1970; trustee Southfield Bd. Edn., 1964, treas. 1968. Mem. State Bar Mich., Am. (dir.), Oakland County bar assns., Am. Trial Lawyers Assn., Oakland County Law Enforcement Assn., Blue Key Honor Soc. Mason (Shriner). Clubs: Michigan State University Alumni. Home: 20975 Potomac Southfield MI 48076 Office: 21751 W Eleven Mile Rd Southfield MI 48075

GRANT, BRIAN WILLIAM, clergyman, pastoral counseling dir.; b. Kansas City, Mo., Nov. 13, 1939; s. Fred W. and Winifred Ruth (Phillips) G.; B.S.J., Northwestern U., 1961; B.D., Lexington Theol. Sem., 1964; M.A., U. Chgo., 1966, Ph.D., 1971; m. Claudia Katherine Ewing, June 3, 1972; children—Donna Jo, Mary Carol, Helen Ann. Ordained to ministry Disciples of Christ Ch., 1966; interim pastor, asso. minister, youth minister Univ. Disciples Christ Ch., Chgo., 1964-68; chaplain U. Chgo. Hosps., 1965-68; instr. religion and personality U. Chgo. Div. Sch., 1968-69; asso. dir. continuing edn. mental health Christian Theol. Sem., Indpls., 1969-76, affiliate prof., 1969—; acting dir. Ind. Counseling Pastoral Care Center, Indpls., 1976-77, tng. dir., 1977—; cons., supr. Inst. Pastoral Counseling, Indpls., Buchanan Counseling Center, Indpls. Diplomate Am. Assn. Pastoral Counselors (nat. chmn. centers and tng. com.); mem. Am. Assn. Marriage Family Counselors (approved supr.). Author: Schizophrenia: A Source of Social Insight, 1975 (Hon. Mention, Am. Med. Writers). Home: 5168 N Kenwood St Indianapolis IN 46208 Office: 1717 W 86th St Indianapolis IN

GRANT, CHARLES HENRY, energy scis. co. exec.; b. Chgo., July 8, 1927; s. Alexander Richardson and Eleanor Farrel (Riley) G.; diploma mining engring. Wis. Inst. Tech., 1950; m. Catherine Veronica Fitzpatrick, Dec. 29, 1948; children—Deborah Ann, Charles H. From asst. to chief mining engr. Minn. ore div., Jones & Laughlin Steel Corp., 1950-60; mgr. sales dir. research, mgr. mfg. ops., New explosives Dow Chem. Co., Virginia, Minn., 1960-65, gen. mgr. explosives, Midland, Mich., 1976—; pres. treas. dir. E.S.&C. Inc., 1976—; bd. govs. Inst. Makers Explosives. Mem. Am. Inst. Mining Metall. Petroleum Engrs. (sec. to vice chmn. Minn. sect. 1963-65, Peele award 1964). Contbr. articles in field to trade jours.; patentee in field. Home: Star RT Box 3290 Tower MN 55790 Office: Box B Biwabik MN 55708

GRANT, CLIFFORD DEWEY, dentist; b. Clinton, Iowa, June 1, 1893; s. Frank D. and Clara Louise (Burghardt) G.; D.D.S., U. Iowa, 1918; m. Hulda Louise Claussen, July 10, 1919 (dec. Apr. 1947); 2d. m. Katherine C. Hemmett, Aug. 13, 1951; 1 son, Lawrence Hemmett. Pvt. practice dentistry, Clinton, 1919—. Served with U.S. Army, 1917-18. Pres. Clinton County Study Club 1927-28. Mem. Am., Clinton County dental assns., Iowa, Chgo. dental socs., Sigma Chi. Republican. Presbyn. Kiwanian (charter mem.), Mason (Shriner), Elk, Blue Lodge. Clubs: Clinton Country. Home: 919 1st St Camanche IA 52730 Office: 206 Wilson Bldg Clinton IA 52732

GRANT, EVVA H., writer, editor; b. Rock Island, Ill., Feb. 22; d. Morris and Ida (Learner) Handelman; A.B., Augustana Coll., 1934, A.M., State U. Iowa, 1937; m. Herman Grant, June 5, 1934; 1 son, David. Tchr. pre-sch. and parent edn., St. Louis, 1936-37; editor P.T.A. mag., 1940-77, editor-in-chief Nat. Congress Parents-Tchr., 1940-72; asso. Boutwell, Crane & Moseley Asso., 1972-77; interpreter (voice P.T.A.) on Baxters radio program sponsored by P.T.A. and NBC. Vis. lectr. Northwestern U., summers 1945, 46; mem. edn. faculty Lincoln Acad. Ill. Cons. pub. advisory bd. FOA, 1954; lectr. child devel. and parent edn. Sec. U.S. nat. Com. Internat. Union Family Orgns., 1963-65. Mem. bd. visitors Singer Learning Centers for Early Childhood Edn. Mem. Ednl. Press Assn. Am. (pres. 1941-43, exec. com. 1943-45), Edn. Writers Assn., Am. Child Guidance Found. (advisory bd.), N.E.A., Sigma Xi (asso.), Delta Kappa Gamma. Cons. editor: Community Life in a Democracy (Nat. Congress Parents and Teachers), 1942; editor: Guilding Children as They Grow, 1959, P.T.A. Guide to What's Happening in Education, 1965. Author: Parents and Teachers as Partners, 1952, rev. edit., 1971. Contbr. to ednl. jours. Home: 2600 N Lakeview Chicago IL 60614 Office: 52 Vanderbilt Ave New York City NY 10017 Deceased Oct. 3, 1977.

GRANT, FREDERICH DOUGLAS, advt./pub. relations agy. exec.; b. Chgo., Aug. 25, 1932; s. Roy Everett and Rebecca (McNair) G.; A.B., Roosevelt U., 1962; certificate Boston Coll. Franchise Inst., 1968; m. Elizabeth Anne Rankin, Jan. 28, 1965; children—George Frederich, Rebecca Margaret, John David, Cory McNair. Sr. editor Cahner's Pub., Chgo., 1968; account coordinator Vince Cullers Advt., Chgo., 1968-70; exec. v.p., Communicon, Inc., Chgo., 1970-74, pres., 1975—; dir. Ehr-Grant Corp. Cons. food service edn. curricula Chgo. Bd. Edn., 1969-71; tchr. contemporary Black Am. history Chgo. YMCA, 1968. Bd. dirs. Midwest Assn. Sickle Cell Anemia, Clarence Darrow Community Center; mem. exec. com. Operation Push Expo, 1972-73. Served with USAF, 1950-56. Recipient 2 CLIO awards for radio writing, 1975. Mem. Inst. for Religion in Age of Sci. Office: 333 N Michigan Ave Chicago IL 60601

GRANT, KINGSLEY B., pathologist; b. Belize, Brit. Honduras, Feb. 13, 1931; s. Ezekiel A. and Wilhelmina E. (Morter) G.; B.S. summa cum laude, Howard U., Washington, 1955, M.D., 1959; m. Margaret Ward; children—Ward, Conrad, Maxwell. Intern, St. Luke's Methodist Hosp., Cedar Rapids, Iowa, 1959-60, resident in pathology, 1960-62, asso. pathologist, 1964-70, co-dir. pathology labs., 1970-75, dir. pathology labs., 1975—, exec. com. med. staff, 1975; resident Los Angeles County Harbor Gen. Hosp., Torrance, Calif., 1962-64; clin. asst. prof. pathology U. Iowa. Bd. dirs. United Way, 1966-71; mem. commn. race and religion Iowa conf. United Meth. Ch.; chmn. Cedar Rapids Human Rights Commn., 1969-71, Cedar Rapids chpt. NCCJ, 1969. Recipient Community Builder award B'nai B'rith, 1970, certificate of appreciation City of Cedar Rapids, 1974. Mem. Iowa Assn. Pathologists (exec. com.), Am. Soc. Clin. Pathologists, Coll. Am. Pathologists, AMA, Nat. Med. Assn., Linn County Med. Soc., Phi Beta Kappa. Clubs: Rotary, Met., Pickwick. Contbr. articles to profl. jours. Office: 1026 A Ave NE Cedar Rapids IA 52402

GRANT, MICHAEL PETER, elec. engr.; b. Oshkosh, Wis., Feb. 26, 1936; s. Robert J. and Ione (Michelson) G.; B.S., Purdue U., 1957, M.S., 1958, Ph.D., 1964; m. Mary Susan Corcoran, September 2, 1961; children—James, Steven, Laura. With Westinghouse Research Labs., Pitts., summers 1953-57; mem. tech. staff Aerospace Corp., El Segundo, Calif., 1961; instr. elec. engring. Purdue U., 1958-64; sr. engr. Indsl. Nucleonics Corp., Columbus, Ohio, 1964-67, mgr. advanced devel. and control systems, 1967-72, mgr. control and info. scis. div., 1972-74, asst. gen. mgr. indsl. systems div., 1974-76, mgr. system design, 1976—. Mem. IEEE, Sigma Xi. Eta Kappa Nu, Pi Mu Epsilon, Tau Beta Pi. Contbr. articles to profl. jours. Patentee in field of automation. Home: 4461 Sussex Dr Columbus OH 43220 Office: 650 Ackerman Rd Columbus OH 43202

GRANT, PAUL ROGER, utility co. exec.; b. Logansport, Ind., Aug. 18, 1947; s. Paul Arthur and Ruby Virginia (Gooch) G.; B.S., Purdue U., 1969, M.S., 1975; m. Jane Kathryn Knoy, June 8, 1968; children—Timothy Mark, Stephanie Jane. Engr., Pub. Service Ind., Plainfield, Ind., 1969-74, sr. tech. analyst, 1974—. Mem. Assn. Computing Machinery (pres. Central Ind. chpt. 1975-76), Central Ind. OS/VS Users Group (sec. 1975). Club: Optimist. Home: Route 2 Box 608 Plainfield IN 46168 Office: 1000 E Main St Plainfield IN 46168

GRANT, ROBERT BYRON, business exec.; b. St. Louis, Jan. 15, 1922; s. Gordon Gilbert and Mary (Byron) G.; B.S. in Chem. Engring., Washington U., St. Louis, 1943, M.S., 1948, Sc.D., 1951; m. Mary Bell Greenwell, June 5, 1948; children—Martin Vincent, Victoria Mary, Gertrude Ann, Alexander Joseph. Lectr., Washington U., 1946-51; research mgr. S.W. Research Inst., San Antonio, 1951-55; tech. cons. Philippis Petroleum Co., Bartlesville, Okla., 1955-57; mgr. engring. and operations analysis div., 1957-64; dir. mgmt. services Celanese Corp. Am., N.Y.C., 1964-68; v.p. N.Y. Stock Exchange, N.Y.C., 1968-69; chief exec. officer Computer Utilization, Inc., 1969-70; pres. Alpha Omega Assos., St. Louis, 1970—. Lectr. mgmt. devel. and systems design to indsl. seminars. Pres. St. John's Sch. Bd. Served to capt. AUS, 1943-46; PTO. Fellow A.A.A.S.; mem. Operations Research Soc. Am., Inst. Mgmt. Scis., Assn. Computing Machinery, Soc., Indsl. and Applied Math., Econometric Soc., Am. Mgmt. Assn., Sigma Xi, Tau Beta Pi. Contbg. author: Analog Computers, Their Industrial Applications, 1956; Systems Approach to Integrated Management Operating Controls, 1962. Reviewer, Applied Mechanics Revs. Home: 601 Meadowbrook Dr 204 Warrensburg MO 64093 Office: PO Box 534 Warrensburg MO 64093

GRANT, ROSS ALLAN, physician; b. St. Marys, Ont., Can., Feb. 15, 1927; s. Albert William and Jean Jardine (Stewart) G.; student St. Marys Collegiate Inst., 1940-46; M.D., U. Western Ont., 1952; m. Ena Doreen Victoria Randall, June 2, 1951; children—David Ross, Stephen Randall, Cythia Jean, Robert Allan, Elizabeth Doreen. Intern, Kitchener-Waterloo Hosp., Kitchener, Ont., 1952-53; gen. practice of medicine, Kitchener, Ont., Can., 1953—; mem. staffs St. Mary's Gen., Kitchener-Waterloo hosps. Mem. Coll. Family Practice Can., Canadian, Ont. med. assns. Clubs: Westmount Golf and Country (Kitchener, Ont., Can.). Home: 323 Longfellow Dr Waterloo ON Canada Office: 765 King St W Kitchener ON Canada

GRANT, STANLEY CAMERON, geologist; b. Cedar Rapids, Iowa, Apr. 21, 1931; s. Hobart McKinley and Elizabeth (Cameron) G.; student Cornell Coll., 1949-51; B.A., Coe Coll., 1953; M.A., U. Wyo., 1954; Ph.D., U. Idaho, 1971; m. Jeanne Stevens, June 26, 1954; children—Laura Lynn, Stuart Cameron, Douglas Stevens. Petroleum geologist Calif. Co., Casper, Wyo., 1955; chief geologist Gas Hills Uranium, Am. Nuclear, Riverton, Wyo., 1955-56; prof. geology U. No. Iowa, Cedar Falls, 1970-75; state geologist, dir. Iowa Geol. Survey, Iowa City, 1975—; pres. Grant Stevens Geol. Services, Inc.; mem. Iowa Energy Policy Council; mem. exec. com. Iowa Dept. Environ. Quality; chmn. Iowa Interagy. Resources Council; vice-chmn. Nat. Gov.'s Council on Sci. and Tech.; geol. cons.; adj. prof. geology U. Iowa, Iowa State U., U. No. Iowa. Served to maj. USAF, 1956-59. Decorated AF Commendation medal; Danforth grad. fellow, 1953-71. Fellow Iowa Acad. Sci.; mem. Am. Inst. Mining, Metall. and Petroleum Engrs., Geol. Soc. Am., Am. Soc. Photogrammetry, Wyo. Geol. Assn., Geol. Soc. Iowa (dir.), Sigma Xi. Episcopalian. Club: Rotary (Distinguished Served award). Office: 123 N Capitol St Iowa City IA 52242

GRANT, WILLIAM ROBERT, advt. agy. exec., commodity trader; b. Evanston, Ill., Aug. 11, 1943; s. Will C. and Mary Julia (Waller) G.; B.A., Duke, 1965; M.B.A., Am. Grad. Sch. Internat. Mgmt., 1967; m. Carol E. McGregor, Apr. 10, 1971. Account supr. Grant Advt., Inc., N.Y.C., 1965-66; pres., Grant Advt. Panama, S.Am., 1968-69; exec. v.p. Grant Advt., Inc., Chgo., 1969-71; exec. v.p. Grant Advt. Internat., Inc., Chgo., 1972—, also dir.; pres., dir. W.R. Grant, Inc., 1974—; mem., commodity floor trader Mid Am. Commodity Exchange. Bd. dirs. Travelers Aid Soc., Midwest chpt., 1974—. Mem. Internat. Advt. Assn. (dir. Midwest chpt. 1973-76), Advt. Assn. Panama (v.p. 1967-68), Northbrook Sport Club. Clubs: Indian Hill Country, University (Chgo.). Home: 2148 Beechwood S Wilmette IL 60091 Office: 400 N Michigan Ave Chicago IL 60611

GRAPER, HENRY ELBERT, JR., city ofcl.; b. Memphis, Sept. 23, 1940; s. Henry Elbert and Alice Stratton (Jones) G.; B.S., Lambuth Coll., 1963; m. Leanne Townsend, Apr. 4, 1964; children—Henry Elbert III, Howard Townsend. Account exec. Stratton Assos., Inc., Southfield, Mich., 1963-69, v.p., 1966-69, pres. 1969-71; city mgr. Dowagiac, Mich., 1971—. Fed. programs coordinator, urban renewal dir. Garden City, Mich., 1962-71; disposition coordinator, Inkster, Mich., 1963-71; urban renewal coordinator, financial adviser, disposition coordinator City of Riverview (Mich.), City of Rochester (Mich.), City of Centerline (Mich.), City of Bellville (Mich.), 1963-71. Exec. dir., sec. City of Garden City (Mich.) Housing Commn., 1969-71, City of Dowagiac Housing Commn., 1971—; mem. exec. bd. Cass County Planning Commn., Cassapolis, Mich., 1971—; v.p. exec. bd. Potawatomi council Boy Scouts Am., Cass County, Mich., 1972—. Bd. dirs., pres. Jack and Jill Day Care Center. Mem. Internat. City Mgrs. Assn., Municipal Finance Officers Assn., Mich. Municipal League. Rotarian, Elk. Home: 206 Green St Dowagiac MI 49047 Office: Park Pl Dowagiac MI 49047

GRASSE, JAMES MARTIN, accountant; b. Chgo., Dec. 17, 1941; s. Jerome F. and Kathryn J. (Crapser) G.; B.S., Olivet Nazarene Coll., 1963; M.Ed., U. Ill., 1967; m. Rebecca L. Fralin, Aug. 25, 1962; children—Suzanne, David. Tchr. history Herscher (Ill.) High Sch., 1963-68; accountant Vernon D. Corzine, accountants, Bradley, Ill., 1969-70; self-employed as accountant James M. Grasse & Assos., Bourbonnais, Ill., 1970—. Tax instr. Marycrest Bus. Coll., Kankakee, Ill., 1971, 72. Village treas. Village of Bourbonnais, 1973-77. Mem. Ch. of Nazarene (treas. 1972—). Home: 460 S Cleveland St Bourbonnais IL 60914 Office: 397 S Main St Bourbonnais IL 60914

GRASSLEY, CHARLES E., congressman; b. New Hartford, Iowa, Sept. 17, 1933; s. Louis Arthur and Ruth (Corwin); B.A., U. No. Iowa, 1955, M.A., 1956; postgrad. U. Iowa, 1957-58; m. Barbara Ann Speicher, Aug. 22, 1954; children—Wendy, Lee, Jay, Robin, Michele. Farmer, New Hartford, 1959—; mem. Iowa Legislature, 1959-74; mem. 94th and 95th Congresses from 3d Dist. Iowa. Mem. Iowa, Butler County hist. socs., Farm Bur. Baptist. Mason. Home: Route 1 New Hartford IA 50660 Office: 1227 Longworth House Office Bldg Washington DC 20515

GRATT, STANLEY HOWARD, graphite co. exec.; b. East Chicago, Ind., Dec. 16, 1937; s. Stanley Alex and Jean (Napierkowski) Grotkiewicz; B.S. in Mech. Engring., Chgo. Tech. Coll., 1959; m. Judith Ethel Austin, Jan. 23, 1960; children—Jill Renee, Stanley Theodore. Product designer Muffler Corp., Chgo., 1959-61; plant engr. Central Comml. Co., Chgo., 1961-62; machine designer Charles Bruning Co., Chgo., 1962-63; plant engr. Ford Motor Co., Chgo., 1963-67; plant mgr. Superior Graphite Co., Chgo., 1967—. Served with AUS, 1960-66. Mem. P.N.A. Mem. Ch. of Messiah (vestry 1966—). Club: Jackson Park Yacht. Office: 6540S Laramie St Chicago IL 60638

GRAUEL, TRUMAN WILLARD, obstetrician, gynecologist; b. Denver, Feb. 8, 1941; s. Elmer Willard and Alice Florence (Butz) G.; student U. Wichita (Kans.), 1959-62; M.D., U. Wis., 1966; m. Mildred Elaine Gates, Aug. 31, 1963; children—Vincent Charles, Timm Carlton. Intern, Parkland Meml. Hosp., Dallas, 1966-67; resident in obstetrics gynecology U. Kans., Kansas City, 1967-70, clin. asso., Sch. Medicine, Wichita, 1973—; practice medicine specializing in obstetrics gynecology, Wichita, 1973—. Served with M.C. USAF, 1970-73. Diplomate Am. Bd. Obstetrics Gynecology. Mem. Am. Coll. Obstetricians Gynecologists, Kans. Obstet. Gynecol. Soc. Office: Suite 301 3333 E Central St Wichita KS 67208

GRAVA, ALFRED HERBERT, transp. co. exec.; b. Detroit, Sept. 21, 1935; s. Alphonse and Margaret (Decker) G.; B.S., Gen. Motors Inst., 1958; postgrad. U. Detroit, 1963-65, Harvard U., 1977—; m. Phyllis Rose Wolnoy, Dec. 3, 1963; children—Mark, Scott, Brad. Foreman maintenance Detroit gear and axle plant Chevrolet div. Gen. Motors Corp., 1958-62, gen. foreman, 1962-63, div. supt., 1964-66, supt. mfg., 1966-68, gen. supt. mfg., 1968-72, asst. mgr. mfg. research and devel. Chevrolet Motor div., 1972-73; v.p., gen. plants mgr., truck axle div. Rockwell Internat. Corp., Troy, Mich., 1973-76, v.p., gen. mgr., 1976-77, pres. Off-Hwy. and Supply Group, 1977—. Served with U.S. Army, 1958-59. Mem. Soc. Automotive Engrs., Engring. Soc. Detroit. Club: Pine Lake Country. Home: 7255 Edinborough St West Bloomfield MI 48033 Office: 2135 W Maple Rd Troy MI 48084

GRAVEN, NORMAN REUBEN, lawyer; b. Charles City, Iowa, June 2, 1938; s. James Howard and Florence Ethel (Feuerhelm) G.; student Cornell Coll., 1955-56, U. Oslo, 1956; B.A., Wartburg Coll., 1962; J.D., U. Iowa, 1964; m. M. Ann Benz, July 11, 1964; children—Kristin Elise, Kurt Norman, Mara Ann. Admitted to Iowa bar, 1964; mem. firm Graven & Graven, Greene, Iowa, 1964—; atty. City of Greene, 1965—. Mem. cultural com. North Iowa Area Devel., Mason City, 1968-70, mem. exec. com., 1970-72; sec. Greene Housing Devel. Corp., 1972—. County chmn. Young Republicans, 1965-66; orgn. chmn. County Rep. Central Com., 1968-71, precinct committeeman, 1971-74; mem. exec. bd. Winnebago Council, Boy Scouts Am., 1967-76; pres. bd. trustees Albrecht Bldg., 1972—. Mem. Am., Iowa (county membership chmn. 1966-72, county chmn. young lawyers sect. 1965-72, mem. com. on legal aid 1972—), Butler County bar assns., Am. Judicature Soc., U. Iowa Alumni Council (Butler county rep. 1966), Jr. C. of C. (pres. 1966-67), Delta Theta Phi. Lutheran. Elk. Home: 324 S Main Greene IA 50636 Office: 107 S 2nd St Greene IA 50636

GRAVENS, DANIEL LEE, microbiologist; b. Latonia, Ky., Feb. 6, 1937; s. Charles Leavy and Georgia Cason Eubanks G.; A.B., Thomas More Coll., 1960; M.A., So. Ill. U., 1969; m. Carol Jean Klosterkemper, June 16, 1962; children—Christopher, Laura, David. Research asst. U. Cin., Cin. Gen. Hosp., 1960-62; lab. supr. Hartford Found. Research Labs., burn research, Barnes Hosp., St. Louis, 1962-69; sr. microbiologist Vestal Labs. div. Chemed Corp., St. Louis, 1969—; lectr. in field. Vice chmn. bd. mgrs. YMCA. Mem. Am. Soc. Microbiology (pres. Mo. br. 1977-78), Am. Acad. Microbiology. Contbr. articles to profl. publs. Home: 28 Parkland Ave St Louis MO 63122 Office: 5035 Manchester Ave St Louis MO 63110

GRAVEREAU, VICTOR P., marketing cons., ret. educator; b. Thunder Bay, Ont., Can., Mar. 20, 1909; s. James and Malvina (Lemieux) G.; came to U.S., 1910, naturalized, 1934; B.A., Ohio Wesleyan U., 1936; M.A., Kent State U., 1943; M.B.A., Case Western Res. U., 1951; m. Mildred Irene Snyder, Aug. 11, 1934. Salesman, Motorists Mutual Ins. Co., Wooster, Ohio, 1936-37; tchr. of commerce Rittman (Ohio) High Sch., 1937-46; accountant Gerstenslager Co., Wooster, Ohio, 1944; asst. prof. commerce Kent State U., Kent, Ohio, 1946-49, asso. prof. commerce, 1949-51, prof. marketing, 1951-76, prof. marketing emeritus, 1976—, coordinator coll. grad. program, 1957-60, asst. dean, 1960-61; partner Pfeiffer, Gravereau & Associates, Kent, Ohio, 1954-63; dir. and v.p. Clark Zimmerman & Associates, Inc., Cleve., 1971—. Recipient Pres.'s. medal Kent State U., 1977; Republic Steel Corp. Economics-in-Action fellow Case Western Res. U., 1964. Mem. Am. Mktg. Assn., Am. Acad. Advt., Nat. Assn. of Purchasing Mgmt. (faculty intern fellow 1962), Bus. Profl. Advt. Assn., Beta Gamma Sigma, Delta Sigma Pi, Delta Tau Delta, Kappa Delta Pi. Clubs: Masons, Kiwanis, Akron City. Author: Purchasing Management: Selected Readings, 1973; contbr. articles in field to profl. publs.; mktg. scholarship Kent State U. established in his name, 1977. Home: 212 Elmwood Dr Kent OH 44240

GRAVES, HARRIS BREINER, physician; b. Lincoln, Nebr., Apr. 29, 1928; s. Fred T. and Anna Marie (Breiner) G.; A.B., U. Nebr., 1948, M.D., 1952; m. Marilyn Jane Eidam, Apr. 6, 1950; children—John W., Stephen B. Intern, Kansas City (Mo.) Gen. Hosp., 1952-53; practice medicine specializing in emergency medicine, Omaha, 1953—; dir. emergency services Neb. Meth. Hosp., Omaha, 1967—; mem. staffs Lincoln Gen. Hosp., U. Nebr. Hosp., Omaha; pres. Midwest Physicians Services, Inc., 1971—; clin. asso. U. Nebr. Coll. Medicine, 1953—. Mem. emergency services council Health Planning Council Midlands; mem. Nebr. Emergency Services Adv. Council; pres. Waterloo (Nebr.) Booster Club, 1970—. Pres. Waterloo Sch. Bd., 1972—. Served to capt. USAF, 1954-56. Mem. Am. Coll. Emergency Physicians (bd. dirs., pres. 1975), Am. Acad. Family Physicians (mem. health care services commn.), Am., Nebr. State (emergency services com. 1968—) med. assns., Am., Nebr. (pres. 1962) acads. gen. practice, Omaha-Douglas County Med. Soc., Omaha-Midwest Clin. soc., Am. Hosp. Assn. (community emergency services com.), Phi Rho Sigma, Sigma Alpha Epsilon. Republican. Methodist (ofcl. ch. bd. 1959-60). Club: Fremont Golf (Fremont, Nebr.). Home: 619 Shorewood Ln Waterloo NE 68069 Office: 8303 Dodge St Omaha NE 68114

GRAVES, JACK RUSSELL, city ofcl.; b. Berwyn, Ill., Aug. 26, 1937; s. George Pawnell and Pearl Delores (Lahomey) G.; student U. Mo. at St. Louis, 1968-69, Northwestern U., 1969, Triton Coll., 1969, Coll. Dupage, 1970; m. Brenda Kay Bottoms, Dec. 23, 1971; children—Michael, Mark, Michelle. Test engr. Internat. Harvester, Braodview, Ill., 1957-60; maintenance supt. Burlington Truck Lines, Berwyn, Ill., 1960-67; supt. motor equipment City of Elmhurst (Ill.), 1967-71, Kansas City, Mo., 1971—; dir. equipment and maintenance Inst. Pub. Safety, U. Pa., 1971—; pres. Graves-Jensen & Assocs., consultants, 1977—; mem. exec. com. Nat. Safety Council, 1976—, mem. edn. tng. com. pub. employee sect., 1976—; chmn. heavy equipment adv. com. Kansas City Community Coll., 1975—; sr. faculty Am. Pub. Works Assn. Edn. Found. Workshop Series, 1974—; faculty NSF-Pub. Tech. Energy Conservation Workshop Series, 1975—. Mem. Mo. Gov.'s Task Force 1990, 1976—. Served with USMC, 1954-57. Registered profl. engr., Kans. Mem. Inst. Equipment Services (exec. council 1973—, v.p. 1974-75, pres. 1975—), Am. Pub. Works Assn. (coordination council 1974—), Soc. Automotive Engrs., Soc. Safety Engrs., Nat. Safety Council. Moose, Karate Club (green belt). Contbr. articles to profl. jours. Home: 4858 N Kansas St Kansas City MO 64119 Office: 4105 Waddell Bldg D Kansas City MO 64111

GRAVES, JOHN PAUL, JR., lawyer; b. Chgo., Feb. 20, 1936; s. John Paul and Ethel (Milhouse) G.; B.B.A., Lake Forest Coll., 1959; J.D., Kent Coll. Law, 1961; m. Gail M. Peterson, Nov. 12, 1965; children—Kevin Eric, Kristen Erica, Karron Elizabeth, Kia Elise. Admitted to Ill. bar, 1961, Feb. bar, 1961, Wis. bar, 1971; asst. house counsel Gen. Accident Ins. Co., Chgo., 1961; asso. mem. firm Hinshaw, Culbertson, Muelmann, & Hoban, Chgo., 1962-67; partner firm Gilbert, Powers & Graves, Rockford, Ill., 1967-71; partner Korf, Pfeil & Graves, Elkhorn, Wis., 1971-76; sr. partner Graves, Greenway, Maier and Miner, East Troy, Wis., Rockford, 1976—; chmn. bd. Sunstone Corp. Bd. dirs. YMCA, Lake Geneva, 1972—; charter mem., past officer Eagle Scout Assn., Chgo., past dist. vice chmn. Boy Scouts Am. Rockford. Served with AUS, 1955-57; Korea. Mem. Am., Ill., Wis., Lawyer-Pilots bar assns., Wis. Acad. Trial Lawyers, Nat. Assn. Municipal Law Officers, Ill. Def. Counsel, Chgo. Trial Lawyers, Am. Judicature Soc., Fedn. Ins. Counsel, Aircraft Owners and Pilots Assn., Nat. Pilots Assn. Lion. Home: North Lake Shore Dr Williams Bay WI 43191 Office: Church St East Troy WI 53120 also 321 W State St Rockford IL 61101

GRAY, ALLEN GIBBS, metallurgist, editor, assn. exec.; b. Birmingham, Ala., July 28, 1915; s. Crawford H. and Marie (Gibbs) G; M.S., Vanderbilt U., 1938; Ph.D., U. Wis., 1940; m. Jean Breckenridge, Apr. 5, 1948; children—Alice, James. Chemist, metallurgist E. I. du Pont de Nemours & Co., 1940-52; tech. work Manhattan Atomic Bomb Project, 1943-45; tech. editor Steel mag., 1952-58; editor Metal Progress mag., Am. Soc. for Metals, 1958-72, pub., 1972—, dir. periodical publs., 1963—, tech. dir. of soc., 1974—. Adv. com. on indsl. info. AEC, 1952—; mem. spl. com. tech. aspects critical and strategic materials Nat. Materials Bd., 1969—; gen. chmn., organizer 1st Nat. Conf. on Materials Availability and Utilization, 1975. Mem. Ohio Gov.'s Council on Atomic Energy, 1956-58. Mem. Inst. Metals, Brit., ASTM, Sigma Xi, Sigma Delta Chi. Author: Modern Electroplating, 1953. Contbr. sect. steel tech. Ency. Americana, sect. alloy steels Ency. Brit. Patentee in field. Home: 2741 Belvoir Blvd Shaker Heights OH 44122 Office: Metals Park Novelty OH 44072

GRAY, AVRUM, auto parts mfg. exec.; b. Chgo., Sept. 13, 1935; s. Joseph J. and Mae (Kalis) G.; B.S. in Mech. Engring., Purdue U., 1956; postgrad. Northwestern U., Ill. Inst. Tech.; m. Joyce Taymor, Aug. 10, 1962; children—Lori, James Avrum, Matthew Issac. Engr., Alloy Mfg. Co., Chgo., 1956-57, plant supt., 1957-60, v.p., 1960—, also dir.; pres. Croy Mfg. Co.; v.p. Automotive Filter, Inc., Alloy Automotive Corp.; pres., dir. Automotive Internat. Corp. Bd. dirs. Joseph J. Gray Found.; trustee Spertus Coll. of Judaica. Served to 1st lt. Ordnance Corps, U.S. Army, 1956-58. Mem. ASME, Soc. Automotive Engrs., Young Pres.'s Orgn., Sigma Delta Chi, Alpha Epsilon Pi. Jewish (dir. temple). Mem. B'nai B'rith (v.p.). Designer electronic safety devices. Home: 1077 Elm Ridge Dr Glencoe IL 60022 Office: 3207 S Shields St Chicago IL 60616

GRAY, BYRON EVERETT, indsl. engr.; b. St. Louis, Mar. 14, 1918; s. Bryon A. and Edna (Brueggemann) G.; B.S. in Engring. Adminstrn., Washington U. 1941; m. Marguerite Jane Westphalen, Aug. 6, 1940; children—Byron Everett, Robert W., Richard T. Field engr. Sverdrup & Parcel, St. Louis, 1940-42; materials rev. engring. supr. airframe div. Curtiss Wright Corp., St. Louis, 1942-45; engr. tanning div. Interco, St. Louis, 1945-48, chief engr. tanning div., 1948-52, mgr. product and process devel. div., 1952-58, mgr. research and devel. div., 1958-64; pvt. practice engring., St. Louis, 1964—; tech. cons. Nat. Shoe Mfrs. Assn., 1964-72, editor Tech. JOur., 1965-68; chmn. safety footwear com. Am. Nat. Standards Inst., 1969—. Bd. dirs. YMCA Greater St. Louis, 1953—, mgr. Downtown br. bd., 1963-64; pres. Village Lutheran Ch., Ladue, Mo., 1976. Registered profl. engr., Mo. Mem. ASME, Brit. Boot and Shoe Inst., Soc. Plastics Industry (chmn. shoe div. 1961-65), ASTM, Nat. Safety Council, Am. Footwear Industries Assn., Rotary. Lutheran. Club: Mo. Athletic. Patentee metatarsal hinge for safety shoes, safety shoe toe box design. Home: 6 Treebrook Ln St Louis MO 63124 Office: 7701 Forsyth Blvd St Louis MO 63105

GRAY, CHARLES ELMER, lawyer; b. Elvins, Mo., July 23, 1919; s. Grover P. and Martha Elizabeth (Sullivan) G.; student Flat River Jr. Coll., 1937-38, U. Hawaii, 1940-41; LL.B, Washington U., 1947; m. Beulah Hennrich Gray, July 4, 1942; children—Karen Lee, Cecilia Jean, Bette Sue, Marsha Dawn. Admitted to Mo. bar, 1947; since practiced in St. Louis; partner Schoenbeck & Gray, 1954; partner firm Gray & Ritter; sec., gen. counsel Don V. Davis Co.; pres. Don-Ite Corp. Mem. Mo. Appellate Judicial Commn.; mem. rules com. Supreme Ct. Mo., 1970—. Served sgt. to capt. USAF, 1939-45. Fellow Internat. Acad. Trial Lawyers (dir.), Am. Coll. Trial Lawyers, Internat. Soc. Barristers (state chmn., dir.); mem. Am., Mo., St. Louis bar assns. Lawyers Assn. of St. Louis (v.p. 1954, mem. bd. govs.), Phi Delta Phi. Home: 12 Cliff Side Dr Glendale MO 63122 Office: 900 Locust Bldg 1015 Locust St St Louis MO 63101

GRAY, CHARLES LUCIEN, physician; b. McPherson, Kans., Nov. 11, 1921; s. Charles Lucien and Betty Marie (Chamberlain) G.; A.B., U. Kans., 1943, M.D., 1945; m. Betty Marie Arnold Berger, Mar. 27, 1971; children by previous marriage—Charles Lucien, Dorothy Louise Nixon, Mark Morrell, John Thomas; 1 stepson Mark Allen Arnold. Intern, Syracuse U., N.Y., 1945; resident gen. surgery VA Hosp., Wadsworth, Kans., 1948-49; resident otolaryngology State U. Iowa Univ. Hosps., Iowa City, 1949-52; practice medicine specializing in otolaryngology, Wichita, Kans., 1952—; mem. staffs Wesley, St. Joseph hosps.; pres., Wesley Med. Staff, Wichita, 1963. Served to capt. M.C., AUS, 1946-48. Diplomate Am. Bd. Otolaryngology. Fellow Am. Acad. Ophthalmology and Otolaryngology; mem. A.M.A., Kans., Sedgwick County med. socs., Kansas City Soc. Ophthalmology and Otolaryngology, Pan Am. Assn. Otorhinolaryngology and Bronchoesophagy, Am. Council Otolaryngology, Phi Gamma Delta, Nu Sigma Nu. Republican. Methodist. Home: 7333 N Sheridan Rural Route 2 Valley Center KS 67147 Office: 4821 E Central Wichita KS 67208

GRAY, CHARLES WEBSTER, civil and mech. engr.; b. nr. Clinton, Mo., Sept. 9, 1914; s. Harvey Gant and Mary (Lay) G.; student Central Coll., 1931-33, U. Mo., 1933-36, Pittsburg (Kans.) State Coll., 1949-50; m. Frances Louise Thomas, Sept. 6, 1936; children—Mary Elizabeth (Mrs. James E. Bolin, Jr.), Charles Webster. Started as jr. engr., supr., asst. state planning engr. WPA, Jefferson City, Mo., 1936-40; design engr., field engr., asst. maintenance supt. Hercules Powder Co., Radford, Va., Wilmington, Del., 1940-46; maintenance and engring. cons., Carthage, Mo., 1946; engr., sr. engr., projects supt. Spencer Chem. Co., Quaker Valley Constructors, Inc. subs., Pittsburg, Kans. and Kansas City, Mo., 1947-53; sr. maintenance engr., maintenance supt. Am. Cyanamid Co., New Orleans, 1953-59; maintenance cons., pres. Gray Equipment, Inc., Metairie, La., 1959-61, chmn. bd., 1959—; resident engr. Barnard and Burk, Baton Rouge, Seneca, S.C., 1961-62; chief planner, project supt., project mgr. cons. Catalytic Inc., Orange, Tex., Toledo, Phila., 1962—. Mgmt. and engring. cons., 1961—. Recipient numerous commendations and certificates from industry, govt. agys. Registered profl. engr., Mo., Kans., La. Mem. Nat., Mo. socs. profl. engrs., Am. Welding Soc. (dir. 1954-55), Internat. Platform Assn., Am. Mgmt. Asso., La. Engring. Soc. Democrat. Methodist (ofcl. bd.). Elk. Home: 121 N Livingston Pl Metairie LA 70005 Office: care George Butler Assos 15 W 10th St Hanover Bldg Kansas City MO 64105 also 1908 Dana Dr Adelphi MO 20783 also 613 S Patterson St Gibsonburg OH 43431 also Centre-Sq West Catalytic Inc 1500 Market St Philadelphia PA 19102

GRAY, GEORGIA NEESE, banker; b. Richland, Kans.; d. Albert and Ellen (O'Sullivan) Neese; A.B., Washburn Coll., 1921; D.B.A. (hon.), 1966; student Sargent's, 1921-22; L.H.D., Russell Sage Coll., 1950; m. George M. Clark, Jan. 21, 1929; m. 2d, Andrew J. Gray, 1953. Began as actress, 1923; asst. cashier Richland State Bank, 1935-37, pres., 1937—; pres. Capital City State Bank & Trust Co., Topeka, now vice-chmn.; treas. of U.S., 1949-53. Del.-at-large nat. adv. com. SBA; treas. Girls Club Topeka. Democratic nat. committeewoman, 1936-64; hon. chmn. Villages project C. of C. Bd. dirs. Kans. A.A.A., 1950—; bd. dirs., former chmn. Kans. div. Am. Cancer Soc.; mem. bd. exec. campaign and maj. gifts com. Georgetown U.; bd. dirs. Seven Steps Found., Harry S. Truman Library; chmn. Alpha Phi Found., 1962-63; mem. nat. bd. Womens Med. Coll. Pa.; chmn. bd. regents Washburn U., 1975—; mem. bd., treas. Sex Information and Edn. Council U.S. Recipient Distinguished Alumni award Washburn U., 1950. Mem. Am. Bus. Women's Assn., Topeka C. of C., Met. Bus. and Profl. Womens Club, Women in Communications, Alpha Phi (nat. trustee), Alpha Phi Upsilon. Clubs: Soroptomist (hon. life), Met. Zonta, Topeka Country. Address: Box 1433 Topeka KS 66601

GRAY, GRATTAN, editor; b. Adrian, Mich., Aug. 24, 1925; s. JS Ralph and Harriett Kimball (Taylor) G.; B.S., Northwestern U., 1947; postgrad. Fred Archer Sch. Photography, 1953; m. Amy Louise Thomas, Oct. 23, 1948; children—Stephen Thomas, Matthew Harris. Copy boy San Francisco Chronicle, 1946; reporter Monroe (Mich.) Evening News, 1947-48, city editor, 1948-49, acting mng. editor, 1949-50, editorial page editor, 1948-50, circulation mgr., 1953-58, asso. editor, 1958-72, editor, 1972—, gen. mgr., 1977—; pres. Monroe Pub. Co., 1977—. Mem. Amateur Radio Emergency Corps, 1960—. Bd. dirs. United Fund, 1956-62, YMCA, 1956-59, Jr. Achievement, 1960-64. Served with USNR, 1943-46, 50-51. Mem. Am. Newspaper Pubs. Assn., Am. Soc. Newspaper Editors, Internat. Press Writers Inst., Inter Am. Press Assn., Nat. Conf. Editorial Writers, Central States Circulation Mgrs. Assn. (dir. 1957-59), Mich. Press Assn. (pres. 1973), Inland Daily Press Assn. (dir. 1973-76), Mich. Asso. Press Assn. (dir. 1975—), Univ. Press Club Mich., Monroe County Radio Communications Assn. (pres. 1966-67). Home: 1929 W Hurd Rd Monroe MI 48161 Office: 20 W 1st St Monroe MI 48161

GRAY, MERLE, educator, author; b. Portersville, Ind., June 21, 1897; d. John D. and Emma (Rudolph) Gray; Ph.B., U. Chgo., 1934; M.A., Columbia 1939; Ph.D. (hon.), Oakland City College, 1967. Tchr. rural schs. Pike County Ind. 1918-19; tchr. Petersburg, Ind., 1919-21, Hammond, Ind., 1921-28, dir. elementary edn., 1928-58; editor, author textbooks Silver Burdett Co., Morristown, N.J. 1958-62, textbook author, 1963—. Chmn. mayor's com. for care of children in war time, 1941-43, Ind. Council for Children and Youth, 1953-55. Mem. Assn. for Childhood Edn. Internat. (pres., mem. U.S. com. on childhood edn. 1955—), N.E.A., A.A.U.W., League Women Voters, Delta Kappa Gamma, P.E.O. Presbyn. Author: (with others) Making Sure of Arithmetic, 1947, rev. edit., 1958, Modern Arithmetic Through Discovery, 1962, rev. edit., 1965, Modern Mathematics Through Discovery, grades 3-6, 1966, grades 1-2, 1967, grades 1-6, rev. edit., 1970. Home: 1308 Southdowns Dr Bloomington IN 47401

GRAY, RICHARD ALAN, film dir., photographer; b. Kansas City, Mo., Jan. 17, 1938; s. William Clinton and Geneva Nordica (Durham) G.; B.A. in Speech, U. Kansas City, 1959; M.A. in Theatre Arts, U. Calif., Los Angeles, 1962; m. Kathleen Coel Murdock, Jan. 15, 1977. Film editor Calvin Prodns., Kansas City, Mo., 1960, service dir., 1961-63, film dir., 1964-70; film editor John Lamb Prodns., Beverly Hills, Calif., 1960, Healthway Corp., Los Angeles, 1960; film dir. and still photographer Capricorn Prodns., Kansas City, 1971—; instr. film aesthetics and prodn. Kansas City Art Inst.; photographer Newsweek Mag. Chmn. membership com. 2d Presbyterian Ch., Kansas City, 1969-70. Democrat. Producer ofcl. U.S. film entry, Cannes, Lebanon, and Vienna festivals, 1962; films include: Image of the Sea, 1962, For All the People, The Harry S. Truman Library, 1969, Patients Need You, 1969, Land of the Chinook, 1970, A World of Concern, 1974; one-man photography show Mo. State Library, Jefferson City, 1976. Home and Office: 7340 Harrison St Kansas City MO 64131

GRAY, SANFORD DURHAM, educator; b. Kansas City, Mo., Mar. 3, 1929; s. William Clinton and Geneva (Durham) G.; B.A., U. Mo., 1951, M.A., 1954; m. Marie Isabel Correll, June 9, 1959 (div.); children—Sharon Marie, Martin Sanford, Clinton Bruce; m. 2d, Joan Frances McConville, June 27, 1970; children—Angela Nordica, Christopher Hansford. Rec. engr. Artist Rec. Studios, Kansas City, Mo., 1954; grad. asst. U. Mo., 1956-58; instr. U. Calif. at Los Angeles, 1958-59; recording engr. Calvin Prodns., Inc., 1960; asst. prof. communication U. S.D., Vermillion, 1960—, also dir. film prodn.; owner Orpheus Records, Vermillion, 1957—. Recipient Calvin Notable film award, 1965; CINE Golden Eagle award, 1968; honors certificate Am. Film Festival, 1969. Mem. Internat. Platform Assn., Speech Communication Assn., Univ. Film Assn. (dir.), Soc. Motion Picture and TV Engrs., AAUP, Sigma Phi Epsilon. Presbyn. Mason (Shriner). Author mystery novels. Designer electronic devices. Home: 425 Adams St Apt 68 Vermillion SD 57069

GRAY, SHELDON, automotive co. exec.; b. Chgo., Oct. 7, 1938; s. Joseph J. and Mae (Kalis) G.; B.A., Brandeis U., 1960; postgrad. Ill. Inst. Tech., 1961. With Alloy Mfg. Co., Chgo., 1960—, v.p., 1964—; exec. v.p. Alco Automotive Products Co., 1963—; v.p. Alloy Automotive Co., 1969—, Alloy Internat. Corp., 1973—; pres. Automotive Filters, Inc., 1973—, also dir. Mem. marketing com. Motor Equipment Mfrs. Assn.; mem. Automotive Sales Council, 1973—. Mem. automotive div. com. Combined Jewish Appeal, 1964. Bd. dirs. Joseph J. Gray Family Found; Fellow pres.'s council Brandeis U. Served with USAF, 1960-61. Mem. Automotive Service Industry Assn., Young Execs. Forum, Brandeis U. Alumni Assn. Clubs: Brandeis U. Club Chgo. (pres. 1970-73), Young Executives, Standard. Pioneer universal joint-drive shaft testing drive systems on motor vehicles. Home: 30 E Elm St Chicago IL 60611 Office: 3207 S Shields St Chicago IL 60616

GRAY, WILLIAM OXLEY, lawyer; b. Iowa Falls, Iowa, Nov. 23, 1914; s. Clarence Otis and Hazel (Oxley) G.; B.A., Coe Coll., 1936; J.D., U. Iowa, 1938; m. Mary F. Comstock, Oct. 19, 1940; children—William Scott, J. Steven, Mary Ellen, James C. Admitted to bar, 1938; mem. firm Silliman Gray & Stapleton, Cedar Rapids, Iowa, 1938-42, 46—; spl. agt. FBI, Washington, 1942-46. Chmn. Iowa Hwy. Commn., 1969-73. Trustee Coe Coll., Cedar Rapids, 1950—. Mem. Linn County (pres. 1952-53), Iowa Am. bar assns., Soc. Former Spl. Agts. FBI (pres. 1970-71), Phi Delta Phi. Republican. Conglist. Elk, Mason (Jester, Shriner). Clubs: Cedar Rapids Country; Union League (Chgo.). Home: 509 Knollwood Dr SE Cedar Rapids IA 52401 Office: 807 American Bldg Cedar Rapids IA 52401

GRAY, WILLIAM PHILIP, lawyer; b. Chgo., May 12, 1938; s. William Edward and Marjorie H. (Moulton) G.; B.A., DePauw U., 1959; LL.B., U. Mich., 1962; LL.M., Georgetown U., 1967; m. Martha Alice Cotton, July 27, 1968; 1 dau., Anne Elizabeth. Admitted to Ill. bar, 1962; partner Eckhart, McSwain, Hassell & Silliman, Chgo., 1967—. Served to capt. AUS, 1963-67. Decorated Bronze Star. Mem. Am., Ill., Chgo. (mem. exec. com. young lawyers sect. 1971, membership chmn. 1972) bar assns., Sigma Alpha Epsilon, Delta Theta Phi. Republican. Methodist (trustee 1972-75). Club: Legal (Chgo.). Home: 1650 Plum Ct Downers Grove IL 60515 Office: Room 3160 One First National Plaza Chicago IL 60603

GRAYBILL, ROBERT VANN, dentist; b. Little Rock, Oct. 1, 1947; s. Virgil James and Rose Marie (Koch) G.; B.A., U. Ark., 1970, B.S., 1972; D.D.S., U. Mo., 1976. Pvt. practice dentistry, Kansas City, Kans., 1976—; instr. dept. oral surgery U. Mo., Kansas City, 1976—. Mem. Am., Kans., Wyandotte County dental assns., Theta Nu Epsilon, Zi Phi Psi, Alpha Kappa Lambda. Home: 1715 S 31st St Kansas City KS 66106 Office: 3500 Strong Ave Kansas City KS 66106

GRAYSON, LEONARD DAVID, physician; b. Bklyn., Aug. 20, 1921; s. Irving Al and Elizabeth Pearl (Maller) G.; B.S., L.I. U., 1943; M.B., Chgo. Med. Sch., 1950, M.D., 1951; postgrad. N.Y. U., 1952-53; m. Rosalin Esther Berman, Dec. 25, 1946; children—Laura (Mrs. Gerald Timmerwilke), Elizabeth, Gail, Mitchell. Intern U.S. Marine Hosp., S.I., N.Y., 1950-51; resident VA Hosp., Bklyn., 1951-52; preceptee Dr. M. Sulzberger, N.Y.C., 1953-55; clin. asst. in dermatology N.Y. State U., Bklyn., 1954-55; practice medicine specializing in allergy, immunology and dermatology, Quincy, Ill., 1955—; mem. staff Blessing Hosp.; staff St. Mary's Hosp., Quincy, v.p. med. staff, 1977; mem. staff Physicians and Surgeons Clinic, Quincy, 1955—, treas. exec. bd., 1960-70, chmn., pres. exec. bd., 1973—. Asst. in clin. medicine Washington U., St. Louis, 1963-70; cons. McDonough Dist. Hosp., Macon Dist. Hosp., Meml. Hosp. Mem. exec. bd. Adams County (Ill.) chpt. Am. Cancer Soc., 1967-74; sec. Western Ill. Found. for Med. Care, 1973-74. Served with AUS, 1943-46; PTO. Diplomate Am. Bd. Dermatology, Am. Bd. Allergy and Immunology. Fellow Am. Acad. Dermatology, Am. Acad. Allergy, Am. Geriatric Soc., Am. Med. Writers Assn., Am. Assn. Clin. Immunology and Allergy; mem. A.M.A., Ill. State, Adams County (pres. 1975) med. socs., Pan Am. Med. Assn. (life), Am. Dermatology Soc. for Allergy and Immunology, Ill. Dermatol. Soc., Mo. Allergy Assn., Quincy C. of C. (chmn. community affairs 1966-69). Editor: Quincy Med. Bull., 1959-68, Adams County Mental Health Assn. Bull., 1962. Contbr. articles to profl. jours. Home: 2109 N Wilmar Dr Quincy IL 62301 Office: 1101 Maine St Quincy IL 62301

GRAZIANO, CHARLES DOMINIC, pharmacist; b. Cariati, Italy, June 28, 1920; s. Frank Dominic and Marianna (Bambace) G.; student Dowling Jr. Coll., 1939, 40; B.S. in Pharmacy, Drake U., 1943; m. Corrine Rose Comito, Feb. 5, 1950; children—Craig Frank, Charles Dominic II, Marianne, Kimberly Rose, Mark, Suzanne. Pharamacist Kings Pharmacy, Des Moines, 1946-47; partner Bauder Pharmacy, Des Moines, 1948-61, owner, 1962—. Mem. Des Moines Art Center. Served with AUS, 1943-45; ETO. Decorated Bronze Star. Mem. Des Moines C. of C., Nat. Assn. Retail Druggists, Iowa, Polk County pharm. assns., St. Vincent de Paul Soc., Am. Pharm. Assn., Phi Delta Chi. Roman Catholic. Home: 1302 Cummins Pkwy Des Moines IA 50311 Office: 3802 Ingersoll Ave Des Moines IA 50312

GRAZIANO, SALVATORE JOSEPH, elec. equipment mfg. co. exec.; b. Chgo., Mar. 25, 1944; s. Sam Joseph and Angela Marie (Bruno) G.; student St. Procopius Coll., 1961-63; B.S., U. Ill., 1965; m. Marijo Halm, July 4, 1964; children—Peter Andrew, Robert Sean, Elizabeth Anne, Megan Marie. Engr. statis. quality control Western Electric Corp., 1964-67; systems analyst Motorola, Inc., 1967-69; sr. design engr. Victor Comptometer Co., Chgo., 1969-71, project mgr., 1971-75; applications engr. Intel Corp., Oak Brook, Ill., 1975-77; regional sales mgr. Monolithic Memories, Inc., Naperville, Ill., 1977—. Home: 981 W Bauer St Naperville IL 60540

GREDESKY, JOSEPH NOLAN, publisher; b. Washington, Pa., Nov. 17, 1948; s. Joseph Nolan and Leona Jane (Dixon) G.; student Kent State U., 1966-70; m. Mary Ann Siers, Nov. 23, 1974. Advt. account exec., reporter Record Pub. Co., Ravenna, Ohio, 1970-72; pub. Tribune-Gazette, Brimfield, Ohio, 1972—, also dir.; gen. partner Ben Franklin's Printers and Pubs. Co. Active Portage County Republican Party, 1969-73; del. Ohio State Rep. Conv., 1970; sec. Brimfield Twp. Zoning Bd. of Appeals, 1974, Brimfield Zoning Commn., 1974; mem. Jetport Study Commn. for Portage County, 1975. Served with Ohio N.G., 1971-77. Recipient Osmond C. Hooper award, 1976; Pub. Service award Brimfield Jaycees, 1974. Mem. Ohio Newspaper Assn., Buckeye Press Assn., Brimfield C. of C. (charter mem.). Methodist. Club: Brimfield Kiwanis (dir. 1976-77). Home: 4190 Hattick Rd Rootstown OH 44272 Office: 3982 State Route 43 Brimfield OH 44240

GREELEY, JOSEPH MAY, ret. advt. agy. exec.; b. Winnetka, Ill., Sept. 13, 1902; s. Morris Larned and Anne (Foote) G.; student Phillips Exeter Acad.; B.S., Harvard U., 1925, M.B.A., 1927; m. Margery Gerould, Dec. 18, 1928 (div. June 1958); children—Margery (Mrs. Forrest I. Watson) Samuel Joseph May; m. 2d, Elizabeth Knode Conrad, Apr. 8, 1961. Advt. mgr. Quaker Oats, Ltd., London, 1930-39; asst. gen. mgr. Hecker Products Corp., N.Y.C., 1939-41; account exec. Pedlar & Ryan, N.Y.C., 1941-42; v.p. Dancer, Fitzgerald, Sample, Chgo., 1942-48; v.p. Leo Burnett, Chgo., 1948-55, v.p. charge mktg., 1955-58, exec. v.p. mktg. services, 1958-70, agy. cons., 1971-77. Mem. Asso. Harvard Alumni (regional dir. 1972-75). Clubs: University, Harvard (dir.), Mid-America (Chgo.); Indian Hill; Royal Poinciana, Hole-in-the-Wall Golf, Port Royal, Naples Yacht. Home: 966 Fisher Ln Winnetka IL 60093 also 600 Galleon Dr Naples FL 33940 Office: Prudential Bldg Chicago IL 60601

GREEN, DAVID, editor; b. Saskatoon, Sask., Can., Dec. 6, 1930; s. Joel and Lillian Marian G.; student U. N.M., 1947-49; B.A., Wayne State U., 1970; postgrad. U. Windsor, 1971-72; m. Muriel C. Snider, Feb. 19, 1955; children—Catharine E., Margaret C., James D., Eric K. Music critic Montreal (Que., Can.) Gazette, U.P.I., 1951-52; city editor Stratford (Ont., Can.) Beacon-Herald, 1952-55; book and travel editor Kitchener-Waterloo (Ont.) Record, 1955-67; with fin. dept. Detroit News, 1967—; pres. Clover Press, Detroit, 1974—, Green's Mag., Inc., Detroit, 1972—; dir. Clover Holdings (Calgary), Ltd. Adj. lectr. Oakland U., 1970—, Wayne State U., 1975—. Served to maj. Canadian Army, 1952-72. Mem. Detroit Press Club, Sigma Delta Chi. Home: 361 Betty Dr Windsor ON N8S 3W9 Canada Office: Box 313 Detroit MI 48231

GREEN, EDWARD JAMES, dentist; b. Cleve., May 29, 1915; s. Arthur and Gertrude (Herman) G.; B.A., Ohio State U., 1937; D.D.S., Case Western Reserve U., 1941, M.A., 1962; m. Eleanor C. Martin, Dec. 22, 1974. Pvt. practice dentistry, Cleve., 1941—; asst. prof. dentistry Case Western Reserve U. Sch. Dentistry, Cleve., 1971-77; research asso. Cuyahoga Community Coll., Cleve., 1969-70; pres. Profl. Ednl. and Devel. Co., Cleve., 1972-77, Dentasyst Corp., Cleve., 1970-77; mem. health adv. bd. Cuyahoga Community Coll., Cleve., 1969-77, mem. dental hygiene adv. bd., 1969-77; mem. adv. bd. Cleveland Hgts. Dental Assts. Tng. Program; intern Nat. Tng. Labs.; grad. trainer Gestalt Inst.; postgrad. lectr. univs. in U.S., Europe, Africa, Asia. Fellow Am. Coll. Dentists; mem. Am. (sect. chmn.) Ohio dental assns., Ohio Acad. Dental Practice Adminstrn. (founder), Am. Acad. Dental Adminstrn. (founder), Cleve. Dental Soc. Author: (with Nathan Kohn) Selection-Hiring and Training of Dental Auxiliaries, 1970; Work Simplification in Dentistry. Cons. editor: Dental Clinics of N. Am., 1972; editor Clin. Dentistry, 1975-77. Contbr. articles to profl. publs. Patentee in field. Home: 18975 Van Aken Blvd Shaker Heights OH 44122 Office: 20119 Van Aken Shaker Heights OH 44122

GREEN, ENID MARGARET, lawyer, cons. and devel. co. exec.; b. Cambridge, Eng., July 31, 1941; d. William Henry and Lily Cordelia G.; came to U.S., 1967; B.A., U. B.C., Can., 1961; LL.B., Dalhousie U., N.S., Can., 1965. Admitted to Ill. bar, 1976; intergovtl. coordinator urban renewal, Calgary, Alta., Can., 1965-66; research officer Ford Found., Brit. Inst. Internat. and Comparative Law, London, 1966-67; researcher Larry Smith & Co., Chgo., 1967-68; v.p. Palmer, France, Green & King, Ltd., Chgo., 1968—; pvt. sector advisor Northeastern Ill. Planning Commn., 1976—. Author: Housing and Housing Resources, 1976; Housing Laws: Basic Provisions, 1968; Statutes of Limitation in the British Commonwealth, 1967; editor pub. Deadline, Community Devel. & Housing, and Deadline, Housing & Devel. Home: 624 W Briar Pl Chicago IL 60657 Office: 1 E Wacker Dr Chicago IL 60601

GREEN, FARNO LOUIS, exec. engr.; b. Memphis, Nov. 29, 1919; s. Everett F. and Eva (Smith) G.; B.A., Miss. Coll., 1941; M.S., La. State U., 1949; m. Ruth Cole, Dec. 21, 1944; children—Franklin F., Walter L. Asso. prof., head dept. physics Wayland Coll., Plainview, Tex., 1948-49; head dept. physics Howard Coll. (now Stamford U.), Birmingham, Ala., 1949-51; physicist Oak Ridge (Tenn.) Nat. Lab., 1951-55; sr. research physicist, group leader GM Research Labs., GM Tech. Center, Gen. Motor Corp., Warren, Mich., 1956-63, exec. engr. GM Mfg. Devel., 1966—; v.p., gen. mgr. Viso Corp. subs. Ex-Cello Corp., Detroit, 1963-66; cons. materials conservation Office of Tech. Assessment, U.S. Congress, Washington, 1977—. Served with U.S. Army, 1940-42, with USAAC, 1942-45, to maj. with Ala. Nat. Guard, 1950-51. Decorated 2 presdl. unit citations; Croix de Guerre avec palm; co-recipient Silver medal Am. Roentgen Ray Soc., 1962. Mem. Soc. of Mfg. Engrs., Am. Soc. Nondestructive Testing, Engring. Soc. of Detroit, Am. Nuclear Soc., Am. Def. Preparedness Assn. Presbyterian. Holder 4 patents in field; contbr. over 35 papers in field to profl. jours. Home: 5934 Blandford Rd Bloomfield Hills MI 48013 Office: GM Mfg Development GM Tech Center Warren MI 48090

GREEN, FRANK EARL, civil engr.; b. Joplin, Mo., Nov. 24, 1931; s. Lloyd Cuthberson and Gladys Alberta (Kennedy) G.; B.S. in Math., Southwest Mo. State U., 1953; B.S. in Civil Engring., Kans. State U., 1958; m. Joan Imogene Wheeler, July 25, 1953; children—Kevin Joe, Keely Sue. With Mo. State Hwy. Dept., 1958—, hwy. designer, 1959-65, dist. hwy. design engr., 1965—. Trustee Grandview (Mo.) United Methodist Ch. Served with U.S. Army, 1953-55. Registered profl. engr., Mo.; registered land surveyor, Mo. Mem. Nat., Mo. socs. profl. engrs., ASCE. Republican. Home: 5608 E 100th Terr Kansas City MO 64137 Office: 5117 E 31st St Kansas City MO 64128

GREEN, FREDERICK SHEPHERD, judge; b. Urbana, Ill., Nov. 23, 1923; s. Frederick and Lois (Shepherd) G.; B.S., U. Ill., 1949, LL.B., 1951; m. Carolyn Wildman, Dec. 23, 1949; children—Louis Mandeville, Frederick S., James Durell. Admitted to Ill. bar, 1951, practiced law in Urbana, 1951-56; asso. Henry I. Green law offices, 1951-54; partner Green Law Offices, 1954-56; county judge Champaign County, Ill., 1956-64, circuit judge 6th Jud. Circuit, 1964-74; appellate judge 4th Jud. Dist., 1974—. Pres., Frances Nelson Home for Dependent Children, 1955-56. Mem. Ill. Commn. on Human Relations, 1955-57. Served with 6th F.A. Bn., 37th Inf. Div., U.S. Army, 1943-45; PTO. Mem. Am., Ill., Champaign County bar assns., Phi Delta Phi, Sigma Alpha Epsilon. Presbyterian (past pres. bd. trustees, elder). Club: Rotary. Home: 1806 Pleasant St Urbana IL 61801 Office: 201 Lincoln Sq Urbana IL 61801

GREEN, H(AROLD) DANIEL, dentist; b. Scranton, Pa., Feb. 4, 1934; s. Harold Charles and Viola M. (Brown) G.; B.A., Beloit Coll., 1956; D.D.S., Northwestern U., 1960; m. Cornelia Ann Ellis, Aug. 1, 1959; children—Scott Alan, Mary Ann. Dental intern VA Research Hosp., Chgo., 1960-61; practice dentistry, Beloit, Wis., 1964—; chief of dental staff, Beloit Meml. Hosp., 1970-72, now sec. dental staff. Bd. corporators Beloit Savs. Bank. City chmn. Nat. Children's Dental Health, 1966-69, 70-71; commr. Boy Scouts Am., Beloit, 1965-69. Sec., bd. dirs. Beloit (Wis.) YMCA, 1967-69, gen. chmn., membership campaign, 1968; 2d v.p. Am. Cancer Soc., Rock County, Wis., 1971—; chmn. Am. Cancer Soc., Beloit, 1971—; adv. bd. Salvation Army, 1970-73; mem. Art League Beloit, 1971; div. chmn. Stateline United Givers, 1971—; chmn. Citizen's Sch. Com., 1971; corp. mem. Health Planning Council, 1972; Horizons '76 chmn. Greater Beloit Bicentennial Commn.; trustee Beloit Coll., 1976—. Served with AUS, 1961-64. Recipient Johnson and Johnson Creativity award, 1970, Ambassador Club Alumni award Beloit Coll., 1972, award Beloit Boosters, 1972; named Young Man of Yr., Beloit Jr. C. of C., 1969. Mem. Wis. Dental Assn. (exec. council 1968—, mem. exec. com. 1970-73, sec. 1974-75, 1st v.p. 1977-78), Rock County Dental Soc. (program chmn. 1967—, pres. 1976), Christian, Chgo. (asso., pres. 1976) Greater Milw. Dental Assn., Rock County Dental Study Club (chmn. 1968-70), Acad. Gen. Dentistry, Am. Soc. Preventive Dentistry, ADA (del. 1977), Beloit Coll. Alumni Assn. (pres. 1970-72), Internat. Dental Fedn. (life), Greater Beloit Assn. Commerce (dir. 1972-73, pres. 1976, past pres., Distinguished Service citation 1977), Wis. Health Council, Wis. Assn. of Professions (dir. 1971—, sec. 1972, pres. 1974-75), Nat. Eagle Scout Assn. (chmn. Eagle recognition Sinissippi council 1976-77), Delta Sigma Delta (chpt. pres. 1960), Omicron Delta Kappa, Tau Kappa Epsilon (chpt. v.p. 1956). Methodist (pres. Men's Club 1965-67, commn. chmn. membership and evangelism 1967—, mem. ofcl. bd. 1966—). Lion (v.p. 1972-73), DeMolay (pres. 1953). Author booklet: Your Dental Health. Home: 2207 W Collingswood Dr Beloit WI 53511 Office: 419 Pleasant St Beloit WI 53511

GREEN, ISAAC, state ofcl.; b. Detroit, Dec. 2, 1924; s. Abe and Freda (Grinker) G.; B.S. in Engring., U. Mich., 1945; postgrad. Columbia, 1948; B.Arch., Ill. Inst. Tech., 1952; m. Barbara Stutman Cohen, May 15, 1965; children—Simon, Samuel, David. Asst. prof. urban planning U. Chgo., 1954-56; dir. housing research and devel. Republic Devel. Co., Detroit, 1956-58; prin. Green & Savin, Architects, Detroit, 1958-69; dep. exec. dir. Mich. Housing Devel. Authority, Lansing, 1970—. Served with USNR, 1943-46. Mem. A.I.A. (housing com.). Author: (with others) Townhouse Development Process, 1970; (with others) Housing for the Elderly: The Development and Design Process, 1975. Home: 500 Northlawn St East Lansing MI 48823 Office: 401 S Washington St Lansing MI 48909

GREEN, JERRY HOWARD, banker; b. Kansas City, Mo., June 10, 1930; s. Howard Jay and Selma (Stein) G.; B.A., Yale U., 1952; m. Ann Buzard Atha, Mar. 14, 1966; children—Donald Joseph Atha, Alan Paul Atha. Pres., Union Chevrolet, 1955-69, Union Securities, Inc., Kansas City, Mo., 1969—; chmn. Stadium Bank, Kansas City, 1976—, Budget Rent-A-Car of Mo., Inc., 1961—; dir. Aiken Engring., Inc., Kansas City, Stadium Bank, Kansas City. Bd. dirs. Boys' Clubs Kansas City. Served to 1st lt. USAF, 1952-55. Mem. Am. Bankers Assn., Nat. Automobile Dealers Assn., Advt. and Sales Execs. Club. Republican. Clubs: Woodside Racquet, Kansas City, Oakwood Country; LaJolla Beach. Home: 2302 West 69th Terr Shawnee Mission KS 66208 Office: 8959 East New Hwy 40 Kansas City MO 64129

GREEN, LARRY EDWARD, chiropractor; b. Greenville, Mich., Aug. 31, 1934; s. Norman Milton and Merle Elizabeth (Blanding) G.; student U. Mich., 1952-54; D.C., Nat. Coll. Chiropractic, 1958; m. Betty May Cooper, June 18, 1955; children—Jennifer, Julia. Practice chiropractic, Greenville, 1958—, specializing in orthopedics, 1964—. Mem. faculty Nat. Coll. Chiropractic, 1965-74; lectr. throughout U.S. and Can.; appt. to Am. Bd. Chiropractic Orthopedists, 1971—. Recipient Chiropractic award for highest achievement as undergrad. in chiropractic profession Chi Rho Sigma, 1958. Diplomate Chiropractic Orthopedics. Mem. Mich. State (dist. certificate of appreciation 1973), Am. chiropractic assns., Am. Council on Chiropractic Orthopedics, Mich. Soc. Chiropractic Orthopedists (pres. 1969), Methodist (chmn. edn. 1974-75, lay speaker). Lion. Contbr. articles to profl. jours. Licensed private pilot. Home: PO Box 126 Greenville MI 48838 Office: 823 W Washington St Greenville MI 48838

GREEN, LEONARD NATHAN, neurologist; b. N.Y.C., Mar. 29, 1935; s. Louis J. and Lillian B. (Scheinfeld) G.; B.A., Yeshiva U., 1955; M.D., Albert Einstein Coll. Medicine, 1959; m. Adele Cohen, June 25, 1960; children—Lawrence J., Stuart A., Joshua. Intern, Boston (Mass.) City Hosp., 1959-60; resident neurology Bronx (N.Y.) Municipal Hosp., 1960-63, chief resident, 1962-63; practice medicine specializing in neurology, Youngstown, Ohio, 1963—; mem. staffs St. Elizabeth, Trumbull Meml. hosps.; pres. Computerized Cerebral Scanning, 1974—. Pres. med. adv. bd. Easter Seal, Youngstown, 1971—. Served to capt. M.C., AUS, 1966-68. Recipient fellowship Am. Physicians, 1970—. Fellow Am. Acad. Neurology; mem. No. Ohio Neurol. Soc. (pres. 1971-73). Asso. editor: Computerized Tomography, 1977. Home: 2515 5th Ave Youngstown OH 44505 Office: 510 Gypsy Ln Youngstown OH 44504

GREEN, MANUEL SANFORD, printing plate mfg. co. owner; b. Indpls., Feb. 7, 1916; s. John Edgar and Lola Delpha (True) G.; grad. high sch.; m. Susan Miranda Conner, July 28, 1934; children—James A., Lawrence R., Donna J. Green Moeller. Engraver, Bemis Bag Co., Indpls., 1932-38; owner Precision Rubber Plate Co., Beech Grove, Ind., 1938—; pres. Hand M Devel. Corp., Southport, Ind., 1966—. Trustee, John J. Easley Trust. Mason (Shriner). Home: 4750 Carson Ave Indianapolis IN 46227 Office: PO Box 159 Beech Grove IN 46107

GREEN, MARTIN WILSON, physician and surgeon; b. Chgo., June 30, 1915; s. Solomon R. and Anna T. (Metrekich) G.; B.S., Northwestern U., 1936; M.D., Chgo. Med. Sch., 1940; m. Rita Marie Roberty, Sept. 20, 1941 (div. Feb. 1961); children—Richard Martin, Randal Arthur, Timothy Everett; m. 2d, Jean Poe, Dec. 1961; children—Martin Wilson, Jr., Lisa Ann. Intern, St. Joseph Hosp., Mishawaka, Ind., 1940, obstet. and gynecol. resident, 1941; sr. staff Westlake Hospital, 1945—, exec. staff, chief obstetrician and gynecologist, 1950, co-chief 1950-56; staff Oak Park (Ill.) Hosp., 1954-72, chief dept. obstetrics and gynecology, 1965-68; practice of medicine specializing in obstetrics and gynecology, River Forest, Ill., 1942—. Med. adviser to SSS, 1941-73; med. dir. Civilian def. Proviso Twp.; chmn. 1st Ill. Congress on Maternal Care. Served as lt. col. M.C., AUS, World War II. Decorated Congl. Medal of Merit, Bronze Star medal; recipient Dir.'s Honor award U.S. Secret Service, 1970. Fellow A.C.S., Am. Acad. Psychosomatic Medicine, Pan Am. Cytology Cancer Society, Internat. Coll. Surgeons, Am. Coll. Obstetrics and Gynecology, Am. Assn. Abdominal Surgeons, Internat. Obstetrics and Gynecology Assn.; mem. A.A.A.S., Am. Med. Edn. Found., A.M.A., Am. Acad. Obstetrics and Gynecology, Ill. Med. Soc., Ill. Obstet. and Gynecol. Soc. (chmn. council), Assn. Mil. Surgeons, Am. Com. Maternal Welfare, Ill. Soc. Med. Research, Am. Geriatrics Soc., St. Luke's Holy Name Soc. (past dir.), Res. Officers Assn., V.F.W., Am. Legion. Clubs: Oak Park; Proviso Township (Ill.) Physicians (past pres.). Contbr. profl. jours. Home: 1124 N Linden Ave Oak Park IL 60302 Office: 7579 W Lake St River Forest IL 60305

GREEN, MEYER H., dentist; b. Kolno, Poland, Mar. 22, 1917; brought to U.S., 1928, naturalized, 1929; s. Louis A. and Bessie (Fellander) G.; student Wayne U., 1935-40; D.D.S., U. Detroit, 1943; m. Hilda Rosenberg, Sept. 30, 1944; children—Marc Stephen (dec.), Janice Beth. Gen. practice dentistry Detroit, 1946-51, 51—; sr. asso. attending staff, mem. med. staff teaching dental interns Sinai Hosp. Detroit, 1962—. Bd. dirs., past v.p. Young Israel of Oak Woods (Mich.). Served to capt. AUS, 1943-46. Diplomate Am. Bd. Oral Medicine, Am. Bd. Clin. Hypnosis in Dentistry. Fellow Royal Soc. Health, Am. Acad. Oral Medicine (hon. and acad. fellow; nat. rec. sec., trustee 1958—, nat. pres. 1978—, gen. chmn. ann. meeting 1977); mem. Mich. Soc. Oral Medicine (past pres. Mich. sect.), Mich. Soc. Psychosomatic Dentistry (past pres.), Am. Med. Writers Assn., Am. Soc. Preventive Dentistry, Acad. Gen. Dentistry, Internat. Acad. Orthodontics, Bunting Periodontal Study Club. Club: Century Univ. of Detroit. Home: 24331 Eastwood Oak Park MI 48237 Office: 14110 Gratiot Ave Detroit MI 48205

GREEN, NETTIE LUTHER CLECKLER (MRS. CLATIS GREEN), univ. adminstr.; b. Arab, Ala.; d. Gordon and Evie (Story) Clecker; B.S., U. Ala., 1957, M.A., 1961; m. Clatis Green, May 31, 1924 (dec. June 1954). Classroom tchr., Ala., 1932-50; asso. resident dir. YWCA, Birmingham, 1955; residence dir. U. Ala., 1956-59; dean girls Menand Sch., Albuquerque, 1959-60; resident counselor Sch. Nursing, U. Ala., 1960-61; asst. to dean of women, instr. Shepherd Coll., Shepherdstown, W.Va., 1961-63; resident counselor Stephens Coll., Columbia, Mo., 1963-64, Wis. State U., Eau Claire, 1964-66, Troy (Ala.) State U., 1966-69, U. Wis., Eau Claire, 1969—. Mem. Nat., Wis. assns. women deans and counselors, Assn. Wis. State U. Faculties, Ala. Alumni Assn., N.E.A., A.A.U.W., Women's Soc. Christian Service (life mem., pres. 1940-43). Methodist. Address: Putman Hall Wis State U Eau Claire WI 54701

GREEN, PAUL CONRAD, mfg. co. exec.; b. Aberdeen, S.D., Nov. 2, 1899; s. Ansel Theodore and Mary Delphina (Conrad) G.; student pub. schs., S.D.; D.Bus. Adminstrn., Dakota Wesleyan U., 1970; m. Mayme Carolyn Spiel, June 15, 1935; children—Paul Theodore, Elizabeth Jane. Mgr., Hub City Iron Co., Aberdeen, 1920-65, pres., owner 1933-65; pres., owner Hub City Iron Store, 1932-69, chmn. emeritus, 1969—; pres. P.T. Green Co., 1968—. Exec. reservist Commerce Dept., 1965—. Pres. YMCA, 1941-43, 52-53, 65-66, mem. nat. council, 1955-58, mem. internat. com., 1959-62, mem. N. Central area bd., 1958-61, mem. area council, 1958-64; pres. Aberdeen Community Chest, 1949-50; mem. Aberdeen Planning Commn., 1960-62; chmn. Urban Center, 1965; active U.S. Savs. Bond Campaign. Bd. dirs. Dakota Wesleyan U., Dakota Midland Hosp.; trustee Bethesda Home Aberdeen, 1969. Recipient Free Enterprise award, 1965. Mem. Am. Inst. Mgmt. (pres.'s council), Kiwanian. Home: 1741 S Main St Aberdeen SD 57401 Office: 105 S 3d St Aberdeen SD 57401

GREEN, RICE ANDREW, restoration co. exec.; b. Hot Springs, Ark., July 15, 1928; s. Horace Jewel and Winona (Suddeth) G.; B.S. in B.A., U. Ark., 1950; m. Irene Lowe Abbay, Mar. 27, 1951; children—Linda Abbay, Robert Andrew, Russell Alan. Salesman Union Carbide Consumer Products, Little Rock, 1953-54, Oklahoma City, 1957-60, St. Louis, 1960-62, div. mgr., Dallas, 1962-69; v.p. devel. Breckenridge Hotels Corp., St. Louis, 1969-76; sec., dir. Rudder Rd. Constrn. Co., Fenton, Mo., 1970-76: pres. G&M Constrn., Inc., 1976—, Green & McGuire Investment Co., 1976—. Mem. planning com. Y Webster Teen Center, 1972-73. Chmn. Jefferson Twp., Webster Groves, 1962, Gravois Twp., 1970; mem. Webster Groves Bd. Police Commrs. Served with USAF, 1954-56. Mem. U. Ark. Alumni Assn. (dir. 1970-73), Webster Groves Hist. Soc., Tenn. Soc. of St. Louis, Sigma Chi. Republican. Presbyn. Rotarian. Home: 238 Park Rd Webster Groves MO 63119 Office: 2819 Breckenridge Industrial Ct St Louis MO 63144

GREEN, ROBERT GLENN, psychologist; b. Bellevue, Ohio, Jan. 28, 1927; s. Taylor Joseph and Margaret Ann (Reinhart) G.; B.S., Bowling Green State U., 1950; M.Ed., Toledo U., 1961, postgrad., 1963; m. Suzette Marie Lepley, June 18, 1949; children—Linda, Barbara (Mrs. Richard McCauley), James, Michael, Susan, Timothy, Thomas, John, Joseph, Edward. Tchr., coach Port Clinton (Ohio) City Schs., 1953-60; guidance counselor Maumee (Ohio) City Schs., 1960-63; psychologist, dir. pupil personnel Port Clinton Schs., 1963-66; psychologist, Sandusky (Ohio) City Schs., 1966—. Cons. psychologist Erie-Ottowa Guidance Center, 1965—. Mem. adv. bd. Sandusky Sch. Practical Nursing, 1970-75, Help Our Youth, Bellevue, 1972-75; mem. Youth Services Com. Erie County, 1969-75; mem. adv. bd. Prisoner Helper, Inc., 1971-73; mem. Erie County Citizens Com. on Adult and Juvenile Detention Services, 1972-73. Bd. dirs. Family Services Assn. Erie County. Served with USMCR, 1946-47. Mem. Am., Ohio psychol. assns., Ohio Ednl. Assn., Ohio Sch. Psychologists Assn. (tng. and certification com. 1973-75), Phi Delta Kappa. Rotarian, K.C. Home: 419 Euclid Ave Bellevue OH 44811 Office: 407 Decatur St Sandusky OH 44870

GREEN, ROBERT LEE, steel co. exec.; b. Coshocton, Ohio, Sept. 10, 1937; s. William H. and Audrey D. (Simmons) G.; student Muskingum Coll., 1955-56; grad. Columbus Bus. U., 1962; m. Bertha Ruth Gress, Sept. 18, 1965; 1 son, Robert Lee. Accountant, Sokol Bros. Ins. Co., Columbus, Ohio, 1961-62; cost clk. Universal Cyclops Steel div. Cyclops Corp., Coshocton, 1963-65, cost analyst, 1965-70, plant controller, 1971—. Served with USN, 1956-60. Mem. Ohio Archeol. Soc. Mem. Christian Ch. Club: Masons. Home: 46594-TR285 Coshocton OH 43812 Office: PO Box 548 Universal Cyclops Co Coshocton OH 43812

GREEN, THOMAS HARRISON, lawyer; b. Milw., Mar. 26, 1922; s. James R. and Anna M. (Sieben) G.; A.B., U. Mich., 1946, M.B.A., 1949, J.D., 1950; m. Patricia R. Robertson, May 26, 1946 (dec.); children—John P., Richard T., Kathleen A., Barbara M., Brian M. Admitted to Mich. bar, 1950; with legal dept. Ford Motor Co., Dearborn, Mich., 1950-52; mgr. Washtenaw County Office, Burton Abstract & Title Co., Ann Arbor, Mich., 1952-57; mem. firms Forsythe, Campbell & Green, Ann Arbor, 1962-66, Conlin, Kenney & Green, Ann Arbor, 1967—. Pres. Washtenau County Tb and Health Assn., 1973-75. Served with USAAF, 1943-46. Fellow Acad. Matrimonial Lawyers; mem. State Bar Mich., Am., Washtenaw County bar assns., Mich. Trial Lawyers Assn. Clubs: Ann Arbor (Mich.) Golf and Outing; Optimist (gov. Mich. dist. 1957-58) (Ann Arbor, Mich.). Home: 2318 Buckingham Rd Ann Arbor MI 48104 Office: 210 E Huron St Ann Arbor MI 48108

GREEN, WARREN HAROLD, publisher; b. Auburn, Ill., July 25, 1915; s. John Anderson Logan and Clara Christina (Wortman) G.; student Presbyn. Theol. Sem., 1933-34, Ill. Wesleyan U., 1934-36; B.M., Southwestern Conservatory, Dallas, 1938; M.M., St. Louis Conservatory, 1940, Ph.D., 1942; m. Joyce Reinerd, Oct. 8, 1960. Prof. voice, composition and aural theory St. Louis Conservatory,1938-44; program dir. USO, Highland Park, Ill., Brownwood, Tex., Orange, Tex., Waukegan, Ill., 1944-46; community service specialist Rotary Internat., Chgo., 1946-47; editor in chief Charles C. Thomas, Pub., Springfield, Ill., 1947-66; pub., pres. Warren H. Green, Inc., St. Louis, 1966—; sec. John R. Davis Assos., Chgo., 1955—; exec. v.p. Visioneering Advt., St. Louis, 1966—; mng. dir. Publishers Service Center, St. Louis, Mo., and Longview, Tex., 1967—. Cons. to U.S. and European publishers, profl. socs.; lectr. med. pub. and Civil War. Mem. Mayor's Com. on Water Safety; mem. Met. St. Louis Art Mus., Mo. Bot. Gardens. Recipient Presdl. citation outstanding contbn. export expansion program U.S., 1973. Mem. Civil War Round Table (v.p. 1969—), Am. Acad. Criminology, Am. Acad. Polit. and Social Sci., Am. Assn. Med. Book Pubs., Am. Judicature Soc., Great Plains Hist. Soc., Co. Mil. Historians, Am. Soc. Personnel Adminstrn., Mktg. Club St. Louis. Clubs: Mo. Athletic, World Trade, Elks (St. Louis). Contbr. articles and books on Civil War history, writing and editing to profl. jours. Home: 12120 Hibler Dr Creve Coeur MO 63141 Office: 8356 Olive Blvd St Louis MO 63132

GREEN, WILLIAM RALPH, constn. co. exec.; b. O'Brien County, Iowa, Mar. 7, 1900; s. John Henry and Emily Minerva (Gallup) G.; student Iowa State U., 1921-26; m. Sylvia Groesbeck, Nov. 19, 1930; 1 dau., Anna Elizabeth (Mrs. Sigund Einer Anderson). Founder, pres.-treas. Green Constn. Co., Des Moines, 1929-69, chmn. bd., 1970—. Registered profl. engr., Iowa. Mem. Asso. Gen. Contractors Iowa (pres. 1937). Mason (Shriner). Clubs: Des Moines, Wakonda Golf and Country. Home: 6018 N Waterbury Rd Des Moines IA 50312 Office: 2015 Grand Ave Des Moines IA 50312

GREEN, WILLIAM WHITNEY, real estate broker; b. Kansas City, Mo., Mar. 6, 1947; s. William and Georgia Sisson (Whitford) G.; B.B.A., Washburn U., 1970; m. Evelyn Kelley Haydon, June 15, 1968; children—Kelley Whitford, Whitney Haydon. Real estate broker, Topeka, 1969—; owner, broker Bill Green Realtors, Topeka, 1972—. Dean Kans. Grad. Realtors Inst., 1975-76, bd. govs., 1975—. Served with AUS, 1968. Mem. Nat., Kans. assns. realtors, Topeka Bd. Realtors (dir. 1974—, treas. 1974, pres. 1976, Realtor of Yr. 1976), Phi Delta Theta (dir.). Club: 20-30 (v.p. 1974). Home: 3441 Randolph St Topeka KS 66611 Office: 3100 W 10th St Topeka KS 66604

GREENBERG, FRANK, lawyer; b. Chgo., July 21, 1910; s. Samuel and Sophie (Nowosenitz) G.; Ph.B., U. Chgo., 1930, J.D. cum laude, 1932; m. Bernice Jenks, Nov. 12, 1938. Admitted to Ill. bar, 1932, practiced in Chgo.; partner firm Greenberg, Keele, Lunn & Aronberg, and predecessors, 1938—. Dir. Oppenheimer United Co. and subsidiaries. Gen. counsel Nat. PTA, Ill. 1949—; mem. Ill. Jud. Inquiry Bd., 1971—; chmn. spl. inquiry com. Ill. Supreme Ct., 1969. Served to lt. comdr. USNR, 1942-45. Mem. Am., Ill., Chgo. (chmn. grievance com. 1963, inquiry com. 1959-60, bd. mgrs. 1964-66, 1967-71, pres. 1969-70) bar assns., Am. Judicature Soc., U. Chgo. Law Sch. Alumni Assn. (pres. 1976—). Club: Standard (Chgo.). Home: 320 W Oakdale Ave Chicago IL 60657 Office: 1 IBM Plaza Chicago IL 60611

GREENBERG, GLENN RICHARD, mfg. co. exec.; b. Rockford, Ill., July 14, 1938; s. Stanley Theodore and June Evelyn (Quincy) G.; grad. high sch.; m. Carole Elizabeth Tierney, Feb. 18, 1961; children—Glenn Michael, Todd Theodore, Kevin William, Darla Elizabeth, Sarah Jane. Computer operator Kabel News, Mt. Morris, Ill., 1962; programmer Rockford Screw Co., 1963-65; system analyst, program supr. Besley Wells, Beloit, Wis., 1966-69; pres. CV Products, Rockford, 1968—; v.p. Midwest Credit Assn., Rockford. Pres., St. Francis Sch. Parent Tchr. Orgn. Mem. Ill. C. of C., Photog. Finishers Assn., Golfers League, Harmony Sportsman Club, Harmony Singing Soc., Hobby Assn. Clubs: World Trade, Eagles (auditor). Home: 3108 Springlake Dr Rockford IL 61111 Office: 5026 27th Ave Rockford IL 61125

GREENBERG, JOSEPH HERMAN, engring. co. exec.; b. Chgo., June 7, 1918; s. Charles and Bertha (Lesser) G.; B.S., Mass. Inst. Tech., 1940; postgrad. Ill. Inst. Tech., 1945-50; m. Edith Betty Winter, Feb. 23, 1941; children—Charles Robert, Richard Lee. Plant metall. engr. Perfection Gear Co., Harvey, Ill., 1940-45; evening instr. metallurgy Ill. Inst. Tech., Chgo., 1941-58; with Boynton Engrs., Chgo., 1945-64, v.p., 1961-64; with A.J. Kearney, Inc., Chgo., 1964—, v.p., 1972—. Fellow Am. Soc. Metals; mem. Am. Inst. Mining and Metall. Engrs., Assn. Iron and Steel Engrs., Am. Foundrymen's Soc. Club: Covenant (Chgo.). Contbr. articles to trade jours. Patentee in field. Home: 6833 N Kedzie Ave Chicago IL 60645 Office: 100 S Wacker Dr Chicago IL 60606

GREENBERG, MILTON, educator; b. Bklyn., Feb. 20, 1927; s. Samuel and Fannie (Schnell) G.; B.A., Bklyn. Coll., 1949; M.A., U. Wis., 1950, Ph.D. (Univ. scholar), 1955; m. Sonia B. Brown, June 20, 1948; children—Anne S., Nancy R.; Instr. polit. sci. U. Tenn., Knoxville, 1952-55; asst. prof. Western Mich. U., Kalamazoo, 1955-59, asso. prof., 1959-64, prof., 1964, chmn. polit. sci. dept., 1965-69; dean Coll. Arts and Scis., Ill. State U., Normal, 1969-72; v.p. acad. affairs, dean faculties Roosevelt U., Chgo., 1972—; research asso. Cleve. Met. Services Commn., 1957; cons. Citizens for Mich. (Constl. Reform Movement), 1960. Mem. Mich. Gov.'s Commn. on Legis. Apportionment, 1962, Kalamazoo Community Relations Bd., 1964-65. Social Sci. Research Council grantee, 1959, 61. Mem. Am., Midwest (exec. council 1972-75) polit. sci. assns., Law and Soc. Assn., AAUP, Am. Assn. Higher Edn., N.Central Assn. Colls. and Schs. (commn. on instns. higher edn. 1975—, cons.-evaluator 1975—). Author: (with J.C. Plano). The American Political Dictionary, 1962, 4th edit., 1976; (with others) The Political Science Dictionary, 1973; contbr. to Colliers Yearbook, 1959—. Home: 175 E Delaware Pl Chicago IL 60611 Office: 430 S Michigan Ave Chicago IL 60605

GREENBERG, MILTON EDWARD, dentist; b. Youngstown, Ohio, Jan. 8, 1919; s. Max and Rebecca (Fertman) G.; student Washington U., St. Louis, 1936-38; D.D.S., Ohio State U., 1943; m. Frances Jane Yoffee, Nov. 24, 1955; children—Bruce Loren, Debra Ann, Karen Maxine. Individual practice dentistry, Youngstown, 1947—. Lectr. Choffin Vo-Tech Sch., 1967-71, 75—, U. Pitts. Sch. Dentistry, 1975—; staff periodontist and endodontist Youngstown Hosp. Assn., 1960—; dental cons. Heritage Manor, 1967—. Co-pres. Youngstown Playhouse, 1956-57. Bd. dirs. Heritage Manor, 1965—, Jewish Fedn. Youngstown, 1955—. Served with AUS, 1943-46. Diplomate Am. Bd. Endodontics. Mem. Am., Ohio dental assns., Am. Acad. Periodontology, Am. Assn. Endodontists, Corydon Palmer Dental Soc. (pres. 1963), Jewish War Vets., Ohio Periodontists Study Club, Ohio Endodontists Study Club. Alpha Omega. Mem. B'nai B'rith. Club: Squaw Creek Country (Youngstown). Editor: Corydon Palmer Dental Soc. Bull., 1964-67. Home: 2477 Barth Dr Youngstown OH 44505 Office: 1350 5th Ave Youngstown OH 44504

GREENBERG, PAUL, publ. co. exec.; b. Indpls., Aug. 4, 1921; s. Louis and Ida (Schwartz) G.; B.S., Purdue U., 1949; m. Janet Sussman, May 5, 1957; children—Beth, Amy. Research and devel. engr. Reilly Tar & Chem. Co., Indpls., 1949-51; with RCA, Indpls., 1951-75, gen. plant mgr., 1970-73, ops. mgr., 1973-75; dir. quality control Revlon, Inc., N.Y.C., 1958-59. group dir. ops. ITT Publ. Co., Indpls., 1976—. Served with USAF, 1942-46. Home: 211 Pine Dr Indianapolis IN 46260 Office: 4300 62d St W Indianapolis IN 46268

GREENBERG, RONALD K., art gallery adminstr.; b. St. Louis, July 17, 1937; s. John and Faye (Kaiserman) G.; student Washington U., St. Louis, 1955-59, Mo. U., 1956-57; m. Jan Clare Schonwald, Aug. 24, 1963; children—Lynn, Jeanne, Jackie. Partner Greenberg Devel. Co., Clayton, Mo., 1965-72; dir. Greenberg Gallery, St. Louis, 1972—; dir. New Music Circle, St. Louis, 1971—. Served with AUS, 1962-63. Mason (Shriner). Club: Westwood Country. Home: 3 Brentmoor Park Clayton MO 63105 Office: 7526 Forsyth Ave Clayton MO 63105

GREENBERT, HAROLD C., dentist; b. Detroit, Jan. 25, 1922; s. Max and Clara (Katz) G.; student Wayne U., 1939-43; B.S., U. N.D., 1943; D.D.S., U. Mich., 1950; m. Gloria Mae Fox, Aug. 19, 1947; children—Gail Susan, Marcy Ann, Alan Jay. Pvt. practice dentistry, Royal Oak, Mich., 1950—. Served with AUS, 1942-45. Decorated Bronze Star. Mem. Am. Dental Assn., Mich., Detroit Dist., Oakland County dental socs., U. Mich., Alumni Assn., Alpha Omega. Clubs: Tam O'Shanter Country (Orchard Lake, Mich.). Home: 28090 Tavistock Trail Southfield MI 48076 Office: 603 W Eleven Mile Rd Royal Oak MI 48067

GREENBLATT, DEANA CHARLENE, educator; b. Chgo., Mar. 13, 1948; d. Walter and Betty (Lamasky) Beisel; B.S. in Edn., Chgo. State U., 1969; M.A. in Guidance and Counselling, Roosevelt U., 1973; m. Mark Greenblatt, June 22, 1975. Tchr., counselor Chgo. Pub. Schs., 1969-75, City Colls. of Chgo. GED-TV, 1976; tchr. Columbus (Ohio) Pub. Schs., 1976—; participant learning exchange, Chgo. Active B'nai B'rith; vol. Right-to-Read, Columbus. Certified tchr. K-9, Ill., Ohio; certified personnel guidance, Ill., Ohio; certified Chgo. Bd. Edn. Mem. Am. Personnel and Guidance Assn. Democrat. Home: 500 S Hamilton Rd Columbus OH 43213

GREENE, CHARLES LEONARD, realtor, real estate co. ofcl.; b. Cleve., May 31, 1921; s. Charles H. and Grace E. (Chappell) G.; student Cleve. State U., 1940-42, 50-52; m. Geraldine A. Wettrick, May 30, 1942; children—Judith Ann (Mrs. C. David Aufderhaar), Cheryl Lynn (Mrs. A. L. Burwell), Betty Jeanne (Mrs. R.H. Shoemaker). Resident mgr. Universal Investment Co., Cleve., 1948-49; asst. v.p., leasing coordinator Ostendorf-Morris Co., Cleve., 1949-55, v.p., 1955-58; pres., treas., dir. Charles L. Greene & Co., Cleve., 1958—; pres., dir. Greene, Jordan, Newell & Co., Cleve., 1959-64; pres., treas., dir. Granger Holding, Inc., Cleve., 1962—; sr. v.p., dir. Cragin, Lang, Free & Smythe, Inc., Cleve., 1974—; dir. 1st Fed. Savs. and Loan Assn. of Willoughby; dir., mem. audit com. Euclid Nat. Bank, Cleve., 1967-72. Instr. indsl. real estate seminar, John Carroll U., Cleve., 1970; cons. to various comml. firms and mfg. cos., 1958—. Served with AUS, 1943-45; ETO. Decorated Bronze Star medal. Mem. Soc. of Indsl. Realtors (sec. Ohio chpt. 1967, treas. Ohio chpt. 1968, v.p. 1969, pres. 1970), Nat. (dir. 1973-75), Ohio assns. of real estate bds., Cleve. Area Bd. of Realtors (trustee 1972-74, bldg. awards com. 1963, 73, govtl. affairs com. 1966-67, memberships com. 1966-67, pub. relations com. 1968-69), Ohio Econ. Devel. Council. Rotarian, Mason. Clubs: Cleveland Athletic, Hillbrook Club, Chagrin Valley Racquet Club, Pine Ridge Country, Mid-day Club of Cleveland. Home: 2250 Parlane Dr Willoughby Hills OH 44094 Office: 1200 Investment Plaza Cleveland OH 44114

GREENE, EARL GEORGE, JR., pathologist; b. Salmon, Idaho, Aug. 22, 1924; s. Earl George and Vera M. (Harrison) G.; B.S., U. Nebr., Lincoln, 1952, M.D., 1952; m. Mary Frances Janulewicz, Sept. 4, 1950; children—Mary E., William H., Earl G., Margaret M., Phillip F., Anne M. Intern, Charles t T. Miller Hosp., St. Paul, 1952-53; resident in pathology Bishop Clarkson Meml. Hosp., Omaha, 1953-55, asso. pathologist, 1957-67, chmn. dept. pathology, dir. labs., 1967—; resident in clin. pathology Indpls. Gen. Hosp., 1955-56; resident in pathological anatomy Armed Forces Inst. Pathology, Washington, 1956-57; asst. prof. pathology U. Nebr. Coll. Medicine; dir. Med. Labs., Inc., Omaha, 1960—; dir. sch. med. tech. Bishop Clarkson Meml. Hosp. Served with U.S. Army, 1943-46. Diplomate Am. Bd. Pathology. Fellow Coll. Am. Pathologists, Am. Soc. Clin. Pathologists; mem. Am., Nebr., Douglas County med. socs., Nebr. Assn. Pathologists, Internat. Acad. Pathology, Omaha Midwest Clin. Soc. Contbr. articles exhibits in field. Home: 3703 Mormon St Omaha NE 68112 Office: Bishop Clarkson Meml Hosp 44th & Dewey Sts Omaha NE 68105

GREENE, GEORGE ELSWORTH, accountant; b. Shelburn, Ind., May 8, 1916; s. Ray Elsworth and Bonnie (Chastain) G.; B.S., Ind. U., 1937; m. Vera Mae Wampler, Nov. 22, 1939; children—David Elsworth, James Kent. Accountant, Owens-Ill. Glass Co., Terre Haute, Ind., 1937; jr. accountant Price Waterhouse & Co., Chgo., 1938; accountant Ind. U., 1938-39; field examiner Ind. Bd. Accountants, Indpls., 1939-42, 45-49; self-employed accountant, Linton, Ind., 1948-66; partner George E. Greene & Co., Linton, 1966—. Mem. Ind. State Bd. Pub. Accountancy, 1969-72, pres. 1970-71. Treas., Linton-Stockton Sch. Bd., 1953-58, Linton-Stockton United Fund, 1963-70. Served from ensign to lt. (j.g.) USNR, 1943-45. Mem. Nat. Assn. Accountants, Am. Inst. C.P.A.'s (mem. council 1961-64, 67-68, 70-73, mem. trial bd. 1970-76), Ind. Assn. C.P.A.'s (pres. 1968-69), So. Ind. Estate Planning Council (pres. 1975-76), Am. Accounting Assn., Linton C. of C. (past v.p., dir.), Sigma Alpha Epsilon. Methodist (ofcl. bd.). Mason, Rotarian (past pres.). Contbg. editor Jour. Accountancy, 1964—; mem. editorial bd. Practical Accountant, 1967—. Contbr. articles to profl. jours. Home: 3501 Homestead Dr Bloomington IN 47401 Office: 1111 N Walnut Bloomington IN 47401 also 77 A St NE Linton IN 47441

GREENE, GEORGE WILLIAM, lawyer; b. Mpls., Oct. 17, 1938; s. George William and Verla (Clausen) G.; B.A., U. Minn., 1960, LL.B., 1965; postgrad. U. Tex., 1962-63; m. Suzanne Elizabeth Selover, Aug. 5, 1961; children—Alison Jay, Robert Clausen, Andrew McKinnon. Admitted to Wis. bar, 1965, U.S. Supreme Ct., 1972; atty. Wickham, Borgelt, Skogstad & Powell, Milw., 1965-70; trial atty. Prosser, Wiedabach & Quale S.C., Milw., 1970—. Mem. Wis. Lawyers for Nixon, 1972; mem., clk., pres. Mapledale-Indian Hill Sch. Bd., 1975—. Served to capt. AUS, 1960-62. Mem. Am., Wis., Milw. Jr. bar assns., Internat. Assn. Ins. Counsel, Am. Philatelic Soc., Wis. Postal History Soc., U.S. Philatelic Classics Soc., Milw. Zool. Soc., Sigma Chi, Phi Delta Phi. Episcopalian (vestry sec. 1972-75). Clubs: Milw. Winter, Gyro Internat. (Milw.); Ozaukee Country. Home: 505 W Dean Ct Milwaukee WI 53217 Office: 626 E Wisconsin Ave Milwaukee WI 53202

GREENE, GERALD MICHAEL, clin. psychologist; b. Chgo., May 7, 1940; s. Albert and Ruth (Kaplan) G.; B.A., Carleton Coll., 1961; Candidate I Diplomate Rijksuniversiteit Te Leiden (Netherlands), 1963; M.S., U. Okla., 1966, Ph.D., 1971; m. Janice Briece, Jan. 28, 1967; children—Erin Kylie, Kegan Ellery, Gavin Gregory. Asst. instr. U. Kans., Lawrence, 1966-68; chief psychologist Head Start Program of East Central Kans., Ottawa, 1967-68; asso. dir. East Central Kans. Supplementary Tng. Program, adj. instr. Emporia State Tchr's. Coll., 1967-68; instr. Rockhurst Coll., 1968-69; staff psychologist Osawatomie (Kans.) State Hosp., 1968-69; coordinator program, asst. prof. edn. and psychology Central State U., Edmond, Okla., 1969-71; mem. staff Okla. Psychol. and Ednl. Center, Oklahoma City, 1970-71; instr. phys. therapy Northwestern U. Med. Sch., 1971-72, postdoctoral fellow and intern in clin. psychology, 1971-72, project coordinator Rehab. services, 1972-73, asso. dept. psychiatry, 1972—, dept. community health and preventive medicine, 1973—, Sch. Dentistry depts. pedodontics and orthodontics, 1972—, intervention dir. Multiple Risk Factor Intervention Trial, 1973—; pvt. practice clin. psychology, Chgo., 1972—; cons. Chgo. Bd. Mental Health, 1972—; field supr. U. Ill. Jane Adams Sch. Social Work, 1976—. OEO grantee, 1967-68; Office Edn. tng. grantee, 1969-71; social and Rehab. Services grantee, 1972-76; City of Chgo. Head Start-Model Cities grantee, 1972-76; licensed clin. psychologist, Ill. Mem. Am., Ill., Midwestern psychol. assns., Council Exceptional Children, AAUP, NEA, Assn. Tchr. Educators Emotionally Disturbed Children, Council Children with Behavior Disorders, Assn. Children with Learning Disabilities, Assn. Advancement Behavior Therapy, Midwestern Assn. Advancement Behavior Therapy, Chgo. Psychol. Club, Acad. Psychologists in Marital and Family Counseling, Ill. Biofeedback Soc., Psychol. Soc. (Republic of Panama; hon. diplomate), Sigma Xi, Psi Chi, Phi Delta Kappa, Kappa Delta Pi. Home: 2327 Castilian Circle Northbrook IL 60062 Office: 500 N Michigan Ave Suite 542 Chicago IL 60611

GREENE, JAMES ALEXANDER, III, nephrologist; b. Indpls., June 17, 1930; s. James Alexander and Selina Margaret (Nystrom) G.; B.A., State U. Iowa, 1953; M.D., Harvard U., 1955; m. Doris Jeannette Hoffmann, June 23, 1973. Rotating intern U. Mich. Med. Center, Ann Arbor, 1955-56, asst. resident internal medicine, 1956-57, 59, resident internal medicine, 1959-60; USPHS postdoctoral fellow in physiology, dept. physiology U. Mich., Ann Arbor, 1961-63, jr. clin. instr. internal medicine Med. Sch., 1960-61, instr., 1961-64, asst. prof., 1964-67, asso. prof., 1967-71, prof., 1971; prof. med. sci., clin. dir. physicians asst. program Western Mich. U., Kalamazoo, 1973-75; practice medicine specializing in nephrology, Kalamazoo, 1971—; co-dir. Mich. Nephrology Center, Kalamazoo, 1971-73, dir., 1973—; mem. active staff dept. internal medicine Borgess Hosp., Kalamazoo, 1971—, Bronson Meth. Hosp., Kalamazoo, 1971—, Mercy Hosp., Benton Harbor, 1975—; cons. Ann Arbor (Mich.) VA Hosp., 1966-71. Mem. sci. adv. bd. Kidney Found. Mich., 1968-72, mem. exec. com., 1972—, chmn., 1976; vice-chmn. adv. and review bd. Southwestern Mich. Area Health Edn. Center, 1973-75; mem. tech. com. on hemodialysis training Mich. Dept. Pub. Health, 1969—. Served to capt. M.C., AUS, 1957-59. Recipient Distinguished Service award U. Mich., 1967. Mem. Am. Fedn. Clin. Research (mem. exec. council Ann Arbor-Detroit-Toledo chpt., 1964-65), A.M.A., Internat. Soc. Nephrology, Renal Soc. of Fedn. Am. Socs. Exptl. Biology, Am. Soc. Artifical Internal Organs, Am. Soc. Nephrology, Am. Physiologic Soc., Am., Mich. heart assns., Central Soc. Clin. Research, Central Clin. Research Club, Midwest Salt and Water Club, Mich. State Med. Soc., Kalamazoo Acad. Medicine. Club: Harvard. Author: Examination of the Urine: A Programmed Text, 1966. Contbr. articles to profl. jours. Home: 2134 Sheffield St Kalamazoo MI 49008 Office: 1521 Gull Rd Kalamazoo MI 49001

GREENE, RALPH VERNON, lawyer; b. Cleve., Apr. 5, 1910; s. Charles Roscoe and Pauline Johanna (Desch) G.; student Cleve. Coll. of Western Reserve U., 1938-42; J.D., Cleve. Marshall Law Sch., 1946; m. Martha Florence Burwell, Aug. 12, 1939; 1 dau., Betsy (Mrs. Betsy Buzek). Various positions Cleve. Trust Co., 1930-43; admitted to Ohio bar, 1946; practiced in Willoughby, Ohio, 1946—; mem. firm Greene and Tulley, Willoughby, 1962-66, 77—; dir. Feedall, Inc., Osborne Concrete & Stone Co., Osborne Excavating Co., Fairport Trucking Co. Mem. Willoughby Hills (Ohio) Charter Commn., 1970-71; mem. Lake County Bd. Mental Retardation, 1971-73; mem. bd. mgrs. YMCA, 1968-77, trustee, 1975-77; trustee Willoughby Sch. Fine Arts, 1967-75. Served with AUS, 1943-45. Mem. Am., Ohio, Lake County (pres. 1956) bar assns. Methodist (pres. bd. trustees 1966-77). Home: 36951 Riviera Ridge Willoughby Hills OH 44094 Office: 38052 Euclid Ave Willoughby OH 44094

GREENE, ROBERT BERNARD, JR., journalist; b. Columbus, Ohio, Mar. 10, 1947; s. Robert Bernard and Phyllis Ann (Harmon) G.; m. Susan Bonnet Koebel, Feb. 13, 1971; B.J., Northwestern U., 1969. Reporter, Chgo. Sun-Times, 1969-71, columnist, 1971-78; syndicated columnist Field Newspaper Syndicate, 1976-78; columnist Chgo. Tribune, 1978—; commentator CBS TV and radio. Recipient award for best newspaper column in Ill., AP, 1975, award for best sustaining feature in Chgo., Chgo. Newspaper Guild, 1976; Nat. Headliner award for best newspaper column in U.S., 1977. Author: We Didn't Have None of Them Fat Funky Angels on the Wall of Heartbreak Hotel, 1971; Running: A Nixon-McGovern Campaign Journal, 1973; Billion Dollar Baby, 1974; Johnny Deadline, Reporter: The Best of Bob Greene, 1976. Office; 435 N Michigan Ave Chicago IL 60611

GREENE, ROBERT LEROY, railroad exec.; b. Muskegon, Mich., June 29, 1947; s. Raymond A. and Alma A. (Hoekenga) G.; B.S., U. Mich., 1972; M.B.A., Tulane U., 1976. Indsl. engr. Sealed Power Corp., Muskegon, 1973; estimator Dresser Industries, Muskegon, 1973-74; mktg. research mgr. Interstate System, Grand Rapids, Mich., 1976-77; competitive research analyst Union Pacific R.R., Omaha, Nebr., 1977—. Served with U.S. Army, 1966-69. Mem. Am. Marketing Assn., Am. Mensa Assn. Republican. Mem. Reformed Ch. in Am. Home: 5411 Hascall St Omaha NE 68106 Office: 1416 Dodge St Omaha NE 68102

GREENEBAUM, JAMES EUGENE, II, aerosol valve mfg. co. exec.; b. Chgo., Aug. 16, 1927; s. Frederic J. and Julie (Friedman) G.; student gen. engring. Purdue U., 1945-48; B.S. in Bus. Adm., Northwestern U., 1950; m. Lilli Beatrice Meyer, Apr. 25, 1954; children—David Roy, Robert Frederic. Indsl. engr. Ohmite Mfg. Co., 1950-52; bakery engr. Ekco Products Co., Chgo., 1952-58; tech. dir. Aero-Valve Co., Cary, Ill., 1958-64; exec. v.p. Seaquist Valve Co. div.

Pittway Corp., Cary, 1964—; v.p. Seaquist Valve Co. Can., Ltd., Downsview, Ont. Active Boy Scouts Am. Served with AUS, 1945-47. Mem. Chem. Spltys. Mfrs. Assn., Chgo. Perfumers Assn., Soc. Cosmetic Chemists, Nat. Rifle Assn. (life). Clubs: Elms; Sheridan Rifle and Pistol (dir.) (Highland Park, Ill.). Home: 1755 Sunnyside Ave Highland Park IL 60035 Office: 1160 N Silver Lake Rd Cary IL 60013

GREENEISEN, DAVID PAUL, marine engr., automotive components mfg. co. exec.; b. Fayetteville, N.C., June 6, 1941; s. Franklin Robert and Mildred Alida (Cassidy) G.; B.S., U.S. Naval Acad., 1963; M.S., Mass. Inst. Tech., 1968; M.B.A., St. John's U., 1970; m. Susan Dee Besgrove, June 5, 1963; children—David Geoffrey, Kirsten Lynn. Commd. ensign U.S. Navy, 1963, advanced through grades to lt. comdr., 1971; sta. USS Wm. V. Pratt, then various shipbldg. and design activities; res., 1973; research mgr. Kelsey Hayes, Ann Arbor, Mich., 1973-75, dir. quality assurance Romulus, Mich., 1975—. Mem. IEEE, Soc. Naval Architects and Marine Engrs., Soc. Automotive Engrs., Am. Soc. Quality Control, Tau Beta Pi, Sigma Xi, Beta Gamma Sigma. Republican. Methodist. Club: Bruin Lake. Home: 1230 Barrister Rd Ann Arbor MI 48105 Office: 38481 Huron River Dr Romulus MI 48174

GREENFIELD, JOHN CHARLES, bio-organic chemist; b. Dayton, Ohio, Apr. 10, 1945; s. Ivan Ralph and Mildred Louis (House) G.; B.S. cum laude, Ohio U., 1967; Ph.D., U. Ill., 1974. High sch. sci. instr., Dayton, 1968-71; grad. research asst. U. Ill., 1971-74; post-doctoral research fellow Swiss Fed. Inst. Tech., Zurich, 1975-76; research chemist infectious diseases research Upjohn Co., Kalamazoo, 1976—. Am.-Swiss Found. for Sci. Exchange fellow, 1975; NSF-NATO postdoctoral fellow, 1975-76. Mem. Am. Chem. Soc., AAAS, Am. Soc. Microbiology, Sigma Xi. Home: 231D Braemar Ln Kalamazoo MI 49007 Office: The Upjohn Co Infectious Diseases Research Kalamazoo MI 49001

GREENLEE, EVERETT EUGENE, retail co. exec.; b. Danville, Ind., May 11, 1932; s. James Howard and Mildred Pearl (Hughes) G.; student Ind. U., 1958; m. Lois Ann Hester, June 22, 1956; children—Larry Wayne, Jon David. Clerk Pub. Service Co. Ind., Plainfield, 1950-52, tab operator, 1954-56; tab operator Kroger Co., Indpls., 1956-59; tab supr. Stop & Shop Supermarket, Indpls., 1959-62; with Hook Drugs, Inc., Indpls., 1962—, data processing mgr., 1962—. Served with AUS, 1952-54. Decorated Purple Heart. Mem. Data Processing Mgmt. Assn. (exec. v.p. 1972-73; chpt. mem. bd. dirs. 1972-74). Home: 1716 Arlene Dr Indianapolis IN 46219 Office: 2800 Enterprise St Indianapolis IN 46226

GREENLEE, HERBERT BRECKENRIDGE, surgeon; b. Rockford, Ill., Sept. 6, 1927; s. Harvey James and Abbie (McCathran) G.; A.B., Beloit Coll., 1951; M.D., U. Chgo., 1955; m. Shirley Claire Rurik, June 12, 1955; children—Herbert, William, Kenneth, Anne. Intern, U. Chgo. Clinics, 1956, resident in surgery, 1956-62; practice medicine specializing in surgery, Chgo., 1964-66; staff surgeon VA Hosp., Madison, Wis., 1966-67; asst. prof. surgery U. Wis., Madison, 1966-67; asst. chief surg. service VA Hosp., Hines, Ill., 1967-72, chief surg. service, 1972—; asso. prof. surgery Stritch Sch. Medicine, Loyola U., Maywood, Ill., 1967-72, prof. surgery, 1972—. Served with M.C., U.S. Army, 1962-64. Recipient Raymond W. McNealy award Chgo. Surg. Soc., 1956. Diplomate Am. Bd. Surgery. Fellow Am. Cancer Soc., A.C.S. (med. motion pictures com. 1975, coordinator gen. surgery film sessions 1976—), Inst. Medicine Chgo.; mem. Am. Gastroenterology Assn., AMA, Soc. Surgery of Alimentary Tract, Midwest Gut Club, Chgo. Soc. Gastroenterology (pres. 1973-74, counselor 1974-75), Ill. (pres. 1975-76, trustee 1976—), Chgo. (sec. 1974-77), Charles B. Puestow surg. socs., Assn. VA Surgeons, Assn. Acad. Surgery, Collegium Internat. Chirurgiae Digestivae, Western Midwest, Central surg. assns., Internat. Soc. Surgery, Pancreas Club, Phi Beta Kappa, Sigma Xi, Alpha Omega Alpha. Author: Surgery of the Small and Large Intestine, 1973, Spanish edit. 1976; contbr. articles to sci. publs. Home: 807 Keystone St River Forest IL 6030S Office: VA Hosp 112 Hines IL 60141

GREENLEE, ROBERT LEONARD, psychiatrist; b. Akron, Ohio, Mar. 23, 1922; s. Albert Robert and Bessie Mae (Atkinson) G.; student Ind. U., 1941-42, U. Cin., 1943-44, U. Miss., 1944-45; M.D., George Washington U., 1949; m. Louise Jean Toombs, Dec. 22, 1946; children—Kent, Mark, Allen. Intern Brooke Army Med. Center, San Antonio, 1950; resident Traverse City (Mich.) Hosp., 1950-52, U. Louisville, 1952-54; dir. Fort Wayne (Ind.) Child Guidance Center, 1954-67, Mental Health Center, Fort Wayne, 1967—. Cons. Fort Wayne State Hosp. and Tng. Center, 1956; lectr. program mental health tech. Purdue U., Ft. Wayne, 1970. Served with AUS, 1942-45, with USAF, 1949-50. Diplomate Am. Bd. Psychiatry and Neurology. Mem. Ind., Fort Wayne med. socs., Am. Psychiat. Assn., Am. Group Psychotheropy Assn., Orthopsychiat. Assn. Home: 3344 Sanibel Dr Fort Wayne IN 46805 Office: 909 E State Blvd Fort Wayne IN 46805

GREENSLIT, JOHN F., recreation assn. adminstr.; b. Morton, Minn., July 3, 1937; s. John H. and Grace M. G.; B.S. in Phys. Edn. and Gen. Sci., N.D. State Coll., 1960; postgrad. (NSF scholar) Carleton Coll., 1962; M.A. in Recreation Adminstrn., Central Mich. U., 1974. Tchr., coach St. Leo's Sch., Minot, N.D., 1959-60; tchr. St. James (Minn.) pub. schs., 1961-63; instr. sci. N.D. State Coll., Minot, 1963-65, intramural dir. dept. of health, phys. edn. and recreation, 1963-65, also head coach, 1963-65; dir., state liaison officer N.D. State Outdoor Recreation Agy., Bismarck, 1966-72; pub. relations exec. Great-West Life Assurance of Can., Minot, N.D., 1971-72; exec. dir. Mich. Recreation and Park Assn., Lansing, 1972—. Sports writer Minot Daily News, 1974; lectr. radio sta. KLPM, Minot, 1966-72; N.D. State High Sch. Tournament announcer radio sta. KFYR, Bismarck, 1969-72; guest lectr. Wayne State U., Detroit, 1974, Ohio State U., 1975, Eastern Mich. U., 1975; vis. instr. Central Mich. U., Mt. Pleasant, 1972-75; asst. instr. Mich. State U., Lansing, 1972-75; mem. Delta Twp. Parks and Recreation Commn., Lansing, Mich., 1974-75; speaker Ill. Park and Recreation Conf., Arlington Heights, 1973; mem. Mich. Dept. Edn. Phys. Edn. Referent Com., 1975—; mem. Delta/Lansing Twps./Waverly Schs. Community Services Commn., Lansing, 1975—; World Recreation and Leisure Assn. del. to Soviet Union, 1975. Exec. sec. Gov.'s Council on Phys. Fitness, State of N.D., 1968-72; mem. Nat. Gov.'s Conf., Lake of Ozarks, Mo., 1970; staff dir. com. on natural resources and environment, 1970. Recipient Appreciation award Edison Found., 1975, N.D. Commodore-Gov.'s award, 1970. Mem. Mich. Amateur Athletic Union (bd. govs. 1973—), Nat. Recreation and Park Assn. (conf. speaker Midwest dist. 1973), Am. Soc. of Assn. Execs., Mich. Community Sch. Edn. Assn., Mich. Soc. of Gerontology, Orgn. Execs. of Mich. (dir. 1974-77), Nat. Assn. of State Outdoor Recreation Liaison Officers (exec. dir. 1969-73). Lutheran (mem. youth activities com. 1973-75). Home: 1127 E Arlington Dr Lansing MI 48917 Office: Michigan Recreation and Park Association 6425 S Pennsylvania Ave Lansing MI 48910

GREENSTEIN, CHARLES ALLAN, banker; b. Evanston, Ill., Feb. 5, 1927; s. Max H. and Esther (Messer) G.; B.S., Loyola U., Chgo., 1950, J.D., 1953; m. Lenore Gould, June 21, 1953; children—Marla, Caryn, Vicki. Admitted to Ill. bar, 1953; asso. Sidney J. Goldstein, Chgo., 1953-61; gen. counsel, v.p. Mfrs. & Comml. Factors Corp., Chgo., 1961-62; counsel v.p. A.I.C. Financial Corp., A.I.C. Leasing Corp., 1962-68; v.p. Lawndale Nat. Bank of Chgo., 1968-71; sr. v.p. Lawndale Trust & Savs. Bank, 1971-77; v.p. 1st Nat. Bank of Lincolnwood (Ill.), 1977—. Mem. athletic staff Loyola U. Founder, adviser Midwest Inter-Collegiate Bowling Conf. Legislative adviser to state rep. Ill. 8th Dist., 1957-66; campaign and legislative adviser to state rep. Ill. 10th Dist., 1966-70; mem. Com. on Ill. Govt., 1959—. Served with USNR, 1945-46, Named to Athletic Hall of Fame, Loyola U. C.P.A., Ill. Mem. Am., Ill., Chgo. bar assns., UN Assn. U.S.A., Am. Inst. Parliamentarians (2d v.p., dir. 1959-73), Loyola U. Law Alumni Assn. (treas. 1959-60), Ill. Soc. C.P.A.'s, Tau Delta Phi, Phi Alpha Delta. Mem. B'nai B'rith (pres. lodge 1959-60). Clubs: Lincoln Park Golf of Chicago (pres. 1959). Home: 7525 N Claremont Ave Chicago IL 60645 Office: 6401 N Lincoln Ave Lincolnwood IL 60645

GREENSTEIN, MELVIN, mental health center adminstr.; b. Chgo., Feb. 28, 1920; s. David and Sarah Bella (Green) G.; B.A., U. Chgo., 1939, M.B.A., 1940, m. Pearl Barach, Dec. 28, 1940; children—Judith Carol Greenstein Sloss, Barbara Phyllis, Robert Jonathan. Vocat. counselor Jewish Vocat. Service, Chgo., 1959-61; exec. dir. Kennedy Job Tng. Center, Palos Park, Ill., 1962-70, Orchard Center for Mental Health, Skokie, Ill., 1971—. Mem. Nat. Rehab. Assn., Am. Assn. Mental Deficiency, Ill. Assn. Community Mental Health Agys. Home: 3001 S Martin Luther King Dr Chicago IL 60616 Office: 8600 Gross Point Rd Skokie IL 60076

GREENWOLD, WARREN ELDON, physician; b. Chgo., Mar. 11, 1923; s. Charles Lauritz and Leona Clare (Alexander) G.; B.S., U. Chgo., 1944, M.D., 1946; M.S., U. Minn., 1956; m. Dorothy Marie O'Neil, Sept. 28, 1946; children—Marcia, Warren Eldon, Charles L., Gail Ann. Intern, Presbyterian Hosp., Chgo., 1946-47; gen. practice medicine, Cissna Park, Ill., 1949-52; pediatric fellow Mayo Clinic, 1953-56; practice medicine specializing in pediatrics Carle Clinic Assn., Urbana, Ill., 1956—; clin. asso. Sch. Basic Med. Scis., U. Ill., 1972—. Mem. regional bd. Ill. Childrens Home and Aid Soc.; trustee, past pres. Carle Found. Served with AUS, 1947-49. Diplomate Am. Bd. Pediatrics. Mem. Champaign County, Ill., Iroquois County (past pres.) med. socs., AMA, Am. Diabetes Assn., Am. Acad. Pediatrics, Central Ill. Pediatric Soc. Asso. editor Exceptional Children, 1976—. Home: 2502 Melrose Dr Champaign IL 61820 Office: 602 W University Ave Urbana IL 61801

GREENWOOD, GWENDOLYN YVONNE, counselor, educator; b. Chgo., Feb. 1, 1935; d. Mack and Alberta (Thomas) Springer; student U. Ill., 1951-53; B.S., George Williams Coll., 1956; M.S., Chgo. State U., 1968; m. George Greenwood, Jr., Apr. 23, 1961; 1 dau., Gina Rebecca. Jr. sec. YMCA, Chgo., 1954-58; tchr., counselor pub. schs., Chgo., 1959—. Mem. advisory council for minorities Ill. Coll. Optometry, 1972; advisory council for nursing Chgo. State U., 1976-77; counselors advisory council ACT Am. Coll. Testing Co., 1977; counselor advisor Principal Scholar Program, 1975—; counselor advisor Greater Chgo. Area Program, 1976—. Gen. Elec. fellow for counselors U. Louisville, 1972. Mem. Am. Personnel and Guidance Assn., Ill., Chgo. guidance and personnel assns., Ill. Counselor Educators and Suprs., Ill. Vocat. Guidance Assn., Ill. Sch. Counselors Assn., Ill. Coll. Personnel Assn., Ill. Assn. Non-White Concerns, Am. Sch. Counseling Assn., Assn. Non-White Concerns, Council for Coll. Attendance, Delta Sigma Theta. Home: 9852 S King Dr Chicago IL 60628 Office: 821 E 103rd St Chicago IL 60628

GREENWOOD, HERMAN EDWARD, lawyer; b. Indpls., July 21, 1942; s. Herman Otto and Kathlyne ELizabeth (Fougerousse) G.; B.S., Ind. U., 1965, J.D., 1968; m. Yolanda Smriga, Aug. 27, 1966; children—Matthew Scott, Mark Edward, Jason Nathaniel. Admitted to Ind. bar, 1968; individual practice law, Speedway, Ind., 1968—; chief counsel Ben Daris Cadet Football Assn., 1975—; Speedway Little League Football, Inc., 1976—. Ind. bus. chmn. fund dr. Speedway area Am. Cancer Soc., 1975; Dem. mem. Speedway Election Bd., 1975. Recipient Citation for Service, Town of Speedway, 1975. Mem. Am., Ind., Indpls. bar assns., Phi Alpha Delta, Kappa Kappa Phi. Roman Catholic. Club: Optimist (past pres. Indpls. chpt., named Optimist of Year 1972). Home: 1102 N Lyndhurst Dr Speedway IN 46224 Office: 5135 W 10th St Speedway IN 46224

GREENWOOD, JANET KAE DALY, psychologist, ednl. adminstr.; b. Goldsboro, N.C., Dec. 9, 1943; d. Fulton Benton and Kelminy Ethel Esther (Ball) Daly; A.A., Peace Coll., 1963; B.S. in English and Psychology, E. Carolina U., 1965, Ed.M. in Counseling, 1967; postgrad. N.C. State U., 1967-69, U. London (Eng.), 1969; Ph.D. in Counseling and Higher Ednl. Adminstrn., Fla. State U., 1972; m. Thompson Hollowell Greenwood, Feb. 22, 1970; 1 son, Gerald Thompson. Tchr. English, Kinston City (N.C.) Schs., 1965-66, Goldsboro City schs., 1966-67; counselor and psychometrist primary and secondary schs. of Wake County, N.C., 1967-69; coordinator for Am. Inst. for Fgn. Study, 1969, supr. of student tours in Eng., France, Switzerland, Italy and Capri, 1969; counselor Fla. State U., Tallahassee, 1969-72; asst. dir. counseling Rutgers U., New Brunswick, N.J., 1972-73, cons. to v.p. for student services, 1973-74, lectr. in counseling psychology, 1972-74; coordinator and asso. prof. counselor edn. U. Cin., 1974-77, adviser to grad. students, 1974—, vice provost student affairs, 1977—; cons. guidance S. Plainfield Pub. Schs., 1973-76; adviser Parents Without Partners, 1976—. Mem. Gov.'s Ad Hoc Edn. Com. on Tchr. Edn. and Counselor Edn., State of Ohio, 1975; chairwoman of Twin Rivers Tenants Rights Assn., 1972-74. Recipient Teacher We Honor award Goldsboro City Schs., 1967, Stunt Night Dedication award, 1967. Mem. Am. Coll. Personnel Assn. (editor chairperson media bd. 1975—), Am., Cin. personnel and guidance assns., Ohio, Cin. psychol. assns., Organizational Behavior Assn., AAUP, Am., Ohio sch. counselors assns., Assn. for Women Faculty, NOW, Ohio Counselor Edn. and Supervision Assn., Kappa Delta Pi. Contbr. articles on higher ednl. adminstrn. and counseling to profl. publs. Home: 10133 Leacrest Rd Lakeshore Estates Cincinnati OH 45215 Office: Vice Provost Student Affairs TUC 350 Univ Cincinnati Cincinnati OH 45221

GREER, WILLIAM LEWIS, educator; b. Gladwin, Mich., Sept. 22, 1919; s. James and Eva (Edick) G.; B.S., Western Mich. U., 1949; M.A., Stetson U., 1955; postgrad U. Mich., 1956; Ed.D., Colo. State Coll., 1964; m. Josephine Hildebrand, June 6, 1943; children—James L., Lowell D. Ordained to ministry Methodist Ch., minister, 1944-56; mem. faculty Fla. So. Coll., 1956-61; asst. prof. U. Wis. at Eau Claire, 1961-63; asst. prof., asso. prof. Westminster Coll., New Wilmington, Pa., 1964-66; mem. faculty U. Wis. at Whitewater, 1966—, prof. sociology, 1968—. Grad. Council scholar Stetson U., 1954-55; faculty scholar Fla. So. Coll., 1960—. Mem. Kappa Delta Pi, Alpha Kappa Delta. Home: Shereda Rd Whitewater WI 53190 Office: 800 Main St Whitewater WI 53190

GREESON, BERNARD DAYTON, sch. adminstr.; b. Fairfield, Iowa, Mar. 25, 1911; s. C. Bertram and Fannie M. (McKee) G.; B.S., Parsons Coll., 1933; M.A., Northwestern U., 1939; m. Shirley Maxine Hayward, Dec. 22, 1940; children—Bernard Dandridge, Shirley Suzanne. Dir. pub. relations Parsons Coll., Fairfield, 1933-35; tchr. speech-drama Missouri Valley (Iowa) High Sch., 1935-39; head drama and speech dept. Centerville (Iowa) High Sch. and Jr. Coll., 1939-42; dir. Moline (Ill.) Inst. Commerce, 1945-48; tech. dir. Shorewood High Sch. and Adult Evening Sch., Milw., 1948-67; dir. Shorewood Opportunity Sch., Milw., 1967-70; dist. coordinator Milw. Area Tech. Coll. Evening Schs., 1970-72; dean career edn. Milw. Area Tech. Coll., 1972—. Mem. Shorewood (Wis.) Village Traffic Safety Commn., 1964—; mem. career edn. com. Milw. Sch. Bd. Bd. dirs. Shorewood Travel and Adventure Film Lecture Series, 1967—. Served to lt. (s.g.) USNR, 1942-45. Mem. Milw. Suburban Council Edn. Assn. (pres. 1968-69), Nat. Thespian Assn. (state dir. 1964—), N.E.A., Wis. Edn. Assn., Milw. County Suburban Council (past pres.), Wis. Speech Assn., Am. Ednl. Theatre Assn., Nat. Assn. Pub. Sch. Adult Educators, Milw. Council Adult Learning, Wis. Assn. Vocat. and Adult Edn., Am. Vocat. Assn., Wis. Adult Edn. Assn. (sec. 1975-76), Profl. Travel Film Dirs. Assn., Geog. Soc. Chgo., Nat. Assn. Career Edn. Republican. Methodist. Rotarian. Club: Shorewood Men's (past pres.). Home: 3548 N Cramer St Shorewood WI 53211 Office: 1015 N 6th St Milwaukee WI 53203

GREETHAM, JAMES SIDNEY, ret. physician; b. Fremont, Ohio, Jan. 19, 1915; s. Sydney and Elsie (Shreffler) G.; A.B., Bowling Green U., 1936; M.D., Western Res. U., 1940; postgrad. ophthalmology U. Pa., 1941; m. Mary Gray, June 13, 1940; children—Lynn Krigbaum, James Sidney. Intern Lucas County Hosp., Toledo, 1940; resident Univ. Hosp., Cleve., 1941-44; practice medicine specializing in ophthalmology, Marion, Ohio, 1947—; mem. staff Marion Gen. Hosp. Asst. clin. prof. ophthalmology Ohio State U., Columbus, 1960—. Pres., operating officer Home Federal Savs. & Loan, Marion, 1971—. Mem. Marion Bd. Edn., 1953-70. Bd. dirs. YMCA, 1965—; Boy Scouts Am., 1948-72, United Community Service, 1955-65. Served to maj., M.C., AUS, 1943-47. Diplomate Am. Bd. Ophthalmology. Mem. A.C.S., Am. Acad. Ophthalmology and Otolaryngology, Columbus Opthalmol. Soc., A.M.A., Ohio Med. Assn., Marion Acad. Medicine. Rotarian (dir. 1950-55, pres. 1953). Club: Marion Country (dir. 1964-67, pres. 1966). Home: 328 S Seffner St PO Box 613 Marion OH 43302 also 685 15th Ave South Naples FL 33940

GREGG, FRANKLIN, accountant; b. Cadillac, Mich., Feb. 2, 1923; s. Franklin George and Ruth Mary (Fortiage) G.; B.A., Mich State U., 1945; m. Marjorie Lillian Karmenzind, June 26, 1949; 1 dau., Sandra Alice. Accountant, Price, Waterhouse & Co., Detroit, 1945-48, Bernstein, Bernstein, & Wile, Detroit, 1948-49, Floyd Livermore, Dearborn, Mich., 1949-50; prin. Franklin Gregg, C.P.A., East Lansing, Mich., 1950—; asst. auditor gen. State of Mich., Lansing, 1964—; dir., sec., treas. LGL Asso., Inc., C.P.A., Mich. Mem. Am. Inst. C.P.A.'s, Mich. Assn. C.P.A.'s, Nat. Assn. Accountants, State Govt. Accountants Assn. (past pres.), Municipal Fin. Officers Assn. of U.S. and Can., Lansing Accountants Assn., Mich. State Employees Assn. (past chpt. pres.), Mich. Assn. Professions, Mich. State U. Alumni Assn. (past pres.), East Lansing C. of C. (past pres.), Sigma Epsilon. Republican. Clubs: Kiwanis, Walnut Hills Country. Home: 1654 Walnut Heights Dr East Lansing MI 48823 Office: 567 Hollister Bldg Lansing MI 48933

GREGG, FREDERICK W., real estate broker; b. Charity, Mo., July 20, 1926; s. George Wallace and Floy Mable (McGee) G.; student S.W. Bapt. Coll., 1943-44; m. Kenneth Bell Powell, Mar. 1, 1946 (div.); children—Jeanette, Frederick W., Terry Lee, Kathy Lynn. Farmer, Charity, 1939-52, 54-56, Fair Grove, Mo., 1970—; mechanic St. Louis Pub. Service, 1952-54; milker Verkaik Dairy, Corona, Calif., 1956-64; carpenter Larwin Co., Simi Valley, Calif., 1964-70; owner Gregg Realty, Fair Grove, 1970—; mgr. McCurry Service Center, Fair Grove, 1974—. Address: Route 1 PO Box 113 Fair Grove MO 65648

GREGG, LUCIUS PERRY, banker; b. Henderson, N.C., Jan. 16, 1933; s. Lucius Perry and Rachel Rose (Jackson) G.; B.S. with distinction in Elec. Engring., U.S. Naval Acad., 1955; M.S. in Aeros. and Astronautics, Mass. Inst. Tech., 1961; postgrad. Cath. U. Am., 1961-63; grad. Advanced Mgmt. Program, Harvard U., 1975; m. Doris Marie Jefferson, May 30, 1959; 1 son, Lucius Perry III. Commd. 2d lt. USAF, 1955, advanced through grades to maj., 1965; research scientist space systems div. contract USAF instrumentation lab. Mass. Inst. Tech., 1960-61; research adminstr. Hdqrs. Aerospace Research, Washington, 1961-62; project scientist Air Force Office Sci. Research, Washington, 1962-65, also sr. pilot, mission comdr. VIP flights, 1962-65; maj. USAF Res., 1965—; dir. Office Research Coordination, Northwestern U., Evanston, Ill., 1965-69, instr. mech. engring. and astro scis., 1965-69, asso. dean scis., 1966-69; program officer Alfred P. Sloan Found., N.Y.C., 1969-72; now v.p. First Nat. Bank of Chgo.; pres. First Chgo. Univ. Finance Corp. Mem. adv. council Ill. Tech. Services Act, 1967-69; chmn. edn. com. Evanston Anti-Poverty Council, OEO, 1967-69; mem. Evanston Citizens Com. Human Relations, 1968-69; mem. univs. organizing com. for space research Nat. Acad. Scis., 1968-69, mem. com. on role of U.S. engring. schs. in fgn. tech. assistance, 1971—; mem. Ill. Commn. Urban Area Govt., 1968-69; mem. panel on support for maritime research and edn. U.S. Maritime Transp. Research Bd., 1971—; adviser to Chief of Naval Personnel, 1972—; mem. panel for research mgmt. improvement program NSF, 1973. Bd. govs. Lunar Sci. Inst.; trustee Rust Coll., Holly Springs, Miss., 1973, Univs. Research Assn. (Weston Accelerator); bd. dirs. United Community Services, Evanston, 1967-69, Chgo. Commons Assn., 1973, Community Hosp. Evanston, 1973, Ill. Better Govt. Assn., 1973, Corp. Pub. Broadcasting, 1974—, Garrett Theol. Sem., Roosevelt U., Chgo. Council Fgn. Relations; bd. acad. advisers U.S. Naval Acad., Annapolis, Md., 1971—; bd. dirs., mem. exec. com. NCCJ, 1970-72; adv. bd. Student Nat. Med. Assn., Washington, 1971—; mem. vis. coms. Harvard U., Mass. Inst. Tech., Tulane U. Recipient Bausch & Lomb Math. and Sci. award, 1950, certificate of Recognition for outstanding young engr. Washington Acad. Scis., 1964; named 1 of 10 Outstanding Young Men, Chgo. Jr. Assn. Commerce and Industry, 1966, Man of Year award Servi Guild of Evanston, 1966. Mem. AAAS, Sigma Psi, Sigma Gamma Tau (hon.). Clubs: University, Economic (Chgo.). Home: 812 Monticello Pl Evanston IL 60201 Office: One First Nat Plaza Chicago IL 60670

GREGOR, HAROLD LAURENCE, painter, educator; b. Detroit, Sept. 10, 1929; s. Robert McKay and Annie Malcolm (Cameron) G.; B.S. in Edn., Wayne State U., 1951; M.S., Mich. State U., 1953; Ph.D., Ohio State U., 1960; children—Kathy Lynn, Matissa Suzanne. One-man shows: Calif. Coll. Arts Crafts, Oakland, 1968, Met. State Coll., Denver, 1973, Va. Commonwealth U., 1973, Nancy Lurie Gallery, Chgo., 1974, 77, Tibor De Nagy Gallery, N.Y.C., 1977; group shows include: Expo 74, Spokane, 1974, Imagist Realism, Norton Mus. Art, W. Palm Beach, Fla., 1974, New Realism, Auckland, New Zealand, 1975, Bloomington Group Show, Calif. State U., 1976, Chgo. Connection Exhibition Crocker Gallery, Sacramento, Calif., 1976-77; represented in permanent collections: Am. Telephone and Telegraph, N.J., Kemper Ins. Co., Long Grove, Ill., Owens-Corning Corp., N.Y.C., Filipacci Collection, Paris, Govett-Brewster Mus., New Plymouth, New Zealand; asst. prof. San Diego State U., 1960-62, Purdue U., 1963-66; asso. prof., head of dept. Chapman Coll., 1966-70; prof. Ill. State U., Normal, 1970—. Served with U.S. Army, 1953-55. Nat. Endowment Arts grantee, 1973. Mem. San Diego Art Guild. Home: 1116 E Jefferson St Bloomington IL 61701 Office: Art Department Illinois State Univ Normal IL 61761

GREGORCY, JOHN RAYMOND, controls engr.; b. Rockford, Ill., Dec. 3, 1929; s. Stanley and Evelyn Alice; student in Indsl. Electronics, Memphis State U., 1948-52; m. Willie May, Aug. 12,

1950; children—Perry, Paul, Patricia, Pamela, Philip. Design engr. W.F. and John Barnes Co., Rockford, 1952-56; chief elec. engr. Ill. Water Treatment Co., Rockford, 1956-72; chief controls engr. Techni-Chem, Inc., Cherry Valley, Ill., 1972—. Trustee, Techni-Chem, Inc. Pension Fund. Served with U.S. Navy, 1948-52. Recipient award Foxboro Instrument Sch., 1966. Mem. IEEE, Instrument Soc. Am., Rockford Engring. Soc. Republican. Lutheran. Club: Rockford Hockey. Designer cobolt unit treatment, solid state ion exchange unit. Home: 912 Starview Dr Rockford IL 61108 Office: 205 E State St Cherry Valley IL 61016

GREGORY, CLAIRE DISTELHORST, TV producer; b. Chgo., Mar. 6, 1926; d. Robert Henry and Genevieve (McCall) Distelhorst; A.B., Ind. U., 1947, M.S., 1954, postgrad. 1959; children—Charles, Martha. Tchr., pub. schs., Bismarck and Rossville, Ill., 1947-50, Helmsburg Ind., 1950-51; grad. asst. Audio Visual Center, Ind. U., Bloomington, Ind., 1953-55, lectr., dir. Women's, Children's and Social Service Programs, Radio and TV, 1956-59; exec. dir. Community Service Council, Inc., Bloomington, 1971-75; producer, asst. supr. Instructional TV Program Devel., Ind. U. Radio and TV Services, Bloomington, 1975—. Chmn., Telecommunications Council of Bloomington, 1975—. Mem. Women in Communications. Producer: Russian Revolution and the Arts, parts I and II, 1976; Teleconference on Mass Transp., 1976; Total Teach, 1977; video taped programs developmental skills Internat. Devel. Inst., 1976, 77; Transportation Briefing, 1977. Home: 2949 Ramble Rd E Bloomington IN 47401 Office: Radio and TV Bldg Ind Univ Bloomington IN 47401

GREGORY, FRANCIS ARNOLD, JR., advt. agy. exec.; b. Lynchburg, Va., Oct. 24, 1926; s. Francis Arnold and Cecile (Grasty) G.; student Cleve. Coll., 1946-48; m. Janet Fay House, July 1, 1950. Circulation promotion writer Nat. Petroleum Pub. Co., Cleve., 1949-52; advt. exec. Warner & Swasey Co., Cleve., 1952-55; v.p. The Wellman Co., advt. agy., Cleve., 1955-64; pres. Northlich, Stolley, Gregory, advt. agy., Cleve., 1964-66; pres. Gregory, Inc., advt. agy., Cleve., 1966—; vice chmn. Mktg. Communications Research Center, Princeton, N.J., 1969-70. Bd. dirs. Cleve. council Camp Fire Girls, Inc., v.p., 1970-72. Served as sgt., F.A., AUS, 1944-46. Mem. Assn. Indsl. Advertisers (regional v.p. 1971-73), Indsl. Marketers Cleve. (pres. 1961-62), Am. Inst. Mgmt. (mem. pres.'s council 1967—), Cleve. Advt. Club. Mem. United Ch. of Christ. Rotarian. Club: Cleveland Racquet. Author: Advertising Agency Selection, 1969. Home: 1701 E 12th St Apt 22 T West Cleveland OH 44114 Office: Gregory Inc 1375 Euclid Ave Cleveland OH 44115

GREGORY, KARL DWIGHT, educator, mgmt. and econ. cons.; b. Detroit, Mar. 26, 1931; s. Bertram Vincent and Sybil Louise (Wynter) G.; B.A., Wayne State U., 1952; M.A., 1957; Ph.D., U. Mich., 1962; m. Tenicia Ann Banks, June 7, 1959; children—Karin, Sheila, Kurt. Fiscal economist Bur. Budget, Exec. Office Pres., Washington, 1961-64; asst. prof. econs. Wayne State U., 1964-68; chief organizer, chmn. bd. First Independence Nat. Bank of Detroit, 1968-71, now dir.; chmn. bd., pres. Accord Inc., constrn. co., Detroit, 1969-71; pres. Karl D. Gregory & Assos., 1968—; prof. econs. and mgmt. Oakland U., Rochester, Mich., 1968—, asst. to chancellor for urban affairs, 1968-69; on leave as vis. scholar Congl. Budget Office, Washington, 1975-76; vis. prof. State U. N.Y. at Buffalo, 1975. Mem. Detroit Mayor's Adv. Com. Small Bus. Devel., 1960-61; chmn. Washington chpt. CORE, 1963-64; exec. dir. Fedn. for Self-Determination, 1967-68; adviser Bur. Census; bd. dirs., v.p. Black Econ. Research Center, N.Y.C.; bd. dirs. Independence Capital Formation, Inner City Bus. Improvement Forum; former trustee Episcopal Diocese Mich.; mem. NAACP Task Force Africa; resource person Congl. Black Caucus; advisory task force for Africa Interreligious Found. Community Orgn. Served to 1st lt. AUS, 1953-56. Carnegie fellow in higher edn., 1960-61. Mem. Nat. Econ. Assn. (past chmn.), Am. Econ. Assn., Am. Soc. Pub. Adminstrs., Fin. Mgmt. Assn., Am. Mgmt. Assn., AAUP, Phi Kappa Phi. Contbr. articles to profl. jours. Home: 18495 Adrian Southfield MI 48075 Office: Oakland U Rochester MI 48063

GREGORY, RICHARD ROBIN, dentist; b. Peoria, Ill., Mar. 11, 1942; s. Victor Robin and Pauline Bernice (Kinkade) G.; student U. Wis., 1960-62; B.A., U. Hawaii, 1965; B.S., U. Ill., 1967, D.D.S., 1969; m. Barbara Jean Cheval, June 22, 1968; 1 son, Richard Robin, II. Dentist, Barry, Ill., 1969—, Quincy, Ill., 1972—; dental cons. Barry Community Care Center. Bd. dirs. Pike County Pub. Health, Pittsfield, Ill., 1970-73, Pike County Head Start, Pittsfield, 1970-73. Recipient Fellowship Ill. State Dept. Pub. Health, 1969. Mem. Am. Soc. Preventive Dentistry (mem. chpt. bd. dirs. 1971-72), T L Gilmer (sec., treas. 1972, pres. 1978), Adams County (pres. 1976), Chgo. dental socs., Acad. Gen. Dentistry, Delta Sigma Delta. Mason, Kiwanian. Home and office: 110 S 20th St Quincy IL 62301

GREIG, JACK CATTON, assn. exec.; b. Bedford, Ind., Nov. 15, 1904; s. James Andrew and Marie (Catton) G.; student pub. schs.; m. Dorothy Norinne Stewart, July 9, 1930; children—Donna (Mrs. Theodore A. Braun), Jacquelyn (Mrs. Billy J. Kahler). With A.P. 1920-32, night wire mgr. to staff writer/legislative, Des Moines, 1927-29, wire editor to night bur. supr., Cleve., 1930-32; with U.S. Rubber Co., 1932-38; asst. pub. relations dir. Ind. Employment Security, 1938-42; mgr. South Bend Safety Council, 1942-44; dir. Henry County Intergovtl. Study, 1944-48; research dir. Ind. Econ. Council, 1948-50; copy, research dir. Curtiss, Quinlan, Keene & Peck, Advt., 1950-53; asst. dir. traffic safety Ind., 1953-55; dir. pub. traffic safety edn. Nat. Safety Council, Chgo., 1955-58; account exec. Gardner-Jones-Cowell, Inc., Chgo., 1958-59, Beveridge Orgn., Chgo., 1959-60; pub. relations dir. Sitefinders, Inc., 1960-62; adminstrv. dir., co-founder, editor Jour. The Organ Tchr., Nat. Assn. Organ Tchrs., Hammand, Ind., 1962—. Bd. dirs. Hammond Community Concert Assn., Northwest Ind. Symphony Orch. Mem. Am. Mktg. Assn. (chpt. pres. 1952), Nat. Indsl. Advertisers Assn. (chpt. pres. 1951), Indpls. Press Club (founding, life). Address: 7938 Bertram Ave Hammond IN 46324

GREIG, WALTER, lawyer, ret. coll. pres.; b. Austin, Tex., Nov. 16, 1906; s. Walter and Elizabeth (Kopperl) G.; student U. Tex., 1924-30; B.S. (hon.), Cleary Coll., 1949, B.B.A., 1960, M.B.A., 1961, Sc.D., 1962; D.C.S., Drake Coll. Fla., 1964; m. Shirley Jean Coker, Dec. 7, 1946; children—Carol Ann, Walter C. Admitted to Tex. bar, 1931, Mich. bar, 1946, U.S. Supreme Ct. bar, 1942; practice of law, Austin, Tex., 1931-41, Detroit, 1946; sec. bd. trustees Cleary Coll., 1950-70, treas. bd. trustees, 1970-74, exec. v.p., 1951-70, pres., 1970-74, pres. emeritus, 1974—, also trustee. Pres. Ypsilanti Area Indsl. Devel. Corp., 1973-74. Exec. sec. Mich. Liquor Control Commn., 1947-48; Mich. indsl. ambassador, 1962-63; pres. Estabrook P.T.A., 1960-61; mem. Ypsilanti Bd. Commerce; chmn. Ypsilanti City Compensation Comm., 1973—, City Tax Bd. Rev., 1977. Served with M.I., AUS, 1941-46; lt. col. Res. ret. Recipient honors Mich. Legislature, 1974, Mayor Ypsilanti, 1974. Mem. Res. Officers Assn. (past chpt. pres.), Am. Legion, Internat. Platform Assn., Am. Bus. Law Assn., Mil. Order Fgn. Wars (past comdr. Mich.), Nat., Mich. edn. assns., Nat. Bus. Tchrs. Assn., Mich. Secondary Sch. Assn., State Bar Mich., State Bar Tex., Royal Order Scotland, U. Tex. Ex-Students Assn. (pres. Detroit-Toledo chpt. 1976-77). Republican. Mason (33 deg., Shriner, Jester), Kiwanian. Clubs: Economic (Detroit); Washtenaw High Twelve (pres. 1975-76). Author: History of Austin, Texas, 1936. Home: 1223 Washtenaw St Ypsilanti MI 48197

GREIMEL, KARL HANS, architect, educator, univ. dean; b. Detroit, July 21, 1930; s. Karl Borromeo and Martha Elizabeth (Ide) G.; A.S., Jackson Jr. Coll., 1951; B.S. in Archtl. Engring., U. Detroit, 1954, M.B.A., 1957; m. Jill Tozer, June 21, 1969; children—Karl Hans II, Timothy Albert. Project designer Giffels & Assos., 1954; project dir. Minoru Yamasaki, 1956; prin. William Kessler Assos., 1957-59; pres. Greimel-Malcomson & Assos., Inc., 1959—, Hammond Fowler Inc., Detroit, 1962-68, Bruno Leon Assos. Inc., Detroit, 1969-72; prof. architecture U. Detroit, 1963-72, asst. dean Sch. Architecture, 1968-72, acting dean, 1970; Louis Sullivan chair of architecture Lawrence Inst. Tech., 1972-73, prof., dean Sch. Architecture, 1973—; guest lectr. U. Wis.; guest critic U. Mich. dir. Urban Am., Inc. Bd. dirs. Archtl. Barriers Soc., Lake Orion Devel. Corp.; chmn. bd. Profl. Skills Alliance; pres. Clawson Center Inc.; sec. Devel. Cons. Inc.; trustee Donna Vitale Found. Named Distinguished Alumnus Jackson Jr. Coll. Mem. Mich. Soc. Architects (dir. 1974), Urban Land Inst., Soc. Am. Value Engrs., Engring. Soc. Detroit, Constrn. Specifications Inst. (dir.), A.I.A. (dir. Detroit chpt., pres. 1973), Blue Key (life). Clubs: Rotary (Detroit); President's (Lawrence Inst. Tech.). Contbr. numerous articles to profl. jours. Home: 5719 Lost Ln PO Box 408 Rochester MI 48063 Office: 3000 Town Center Southfield MI 48075 also 21000 W Ten Mile Rd Southfield MI 48075

GREIVE, WILLIAM HENRY, chemist; b. Bowling Green, Ohio, Dec. 30, 1933; s. Henry Fredrick and Bernadine (Hagemeyer) G.; B.A., U. Toledo, 1976; m. Teresa Mae Pierce, Nov. 16, 1957; children—Roger F., Susan L. Technician, Toledo Edison Co., 1952-59; chemist Continental Aviation & Engring. Corp., Toledo, 1959-60; chemist Owens-Ill. Inc., Toledo, 1960—; cons. Analytical Chemistry Lab.; lectr. instrumental chemistry U. Toledo; substitute instr. analytical chemistry Community Tech. Coll., Toledo. Mem. Parks Com. Maumee (Ohio), 1975—. Mem. Am. Chem. Soc., Soc. Plastics Engrs., ASTM, Sigma Xi. Episcopalian. Contbr. articles in field to profl. jours. Home: 1441 Bradshaw Ct Maumee OH 43537 Office: 1700 N Westwood Ave Box 1035 Toledo OH 43666

GREM, FRANCIS MATTHEW, physician; b. Phila., June 29, 1915; s. Martin E. and Catherine (Bausch) G.; B.S., St. Joseph's Coll., 1936; M.D., Jefferson Med. Coll., 1940; m. June Olson, Apr. 3, 1943; children—Ann, Marsha, Philip, Joan, Jean. Resident in anesthesiology U. Ill., 1946, asst. prof., 1946-47; prof. anesthesiology Cook County Grad. Sch. Medicine, Chgo., 1947-49, chmn. dept. anesthesiology, 1947-49; asso. prof. anesthesiology Loyola U. Sch. Dentistry, Chgo., 1954-63, prof. anesthesiology, 1963-67; attending anesthesiologist Oak Park (Ill.) Hosp., 1950-71, 76—, dir. anesthesia service, 1971-76. Served from 1st lt. to capt. M.C., AUS, 1941-46, ETO. Fellow Am. Coll. Anesthesiologists; mem. Am. (editor Newsletter 1962-68), Ill., Chgo. socs. anesthesiologists. Club: Chgo. Press. Home: 546 N Elmwood Ave Oak Park IL 60302 Office: 460 S Northwest Hwy Park Ridge IL 60068

GREM, JUNE OLSON, pub. co. exec.; b. Chgo., Sept. 14 1920; d. David G. and Ebba (Sandberg) Olson; B.A., Stanford U., 1940; m. Frank M. Grem, Apr. 3, 1943; children—Ann Grem Bregent, Marsha Grem Lopez, Philip C., Joan Grem Porschakin, Jean Linette. Underwriting trainee Johnson & Higgins, Chgo., 1941-42; research worker Coronet-Esquire mag., Chgo., 1942-46; pres. Enterprise Publs., Inc., Oak Park, Ill., 1971—. Leader, Girl Scouts U.S.A., 1956-60. Recipient Congress of Freedom award, 1974. Mem. AAUW. Mem. Libertarian Party. Author: The Money Manipulators, 1971; Karl Marx, Capitalist, 1972. Home: 546 N Elmwood Ave Oak Park IL 60302 Office: PO Box 448 Oak Park IL 60303

GRESCHAW, CHARLES RANDOLPH, orthodontist, educator; b. Detroit, Jan. 5, 1941; s. Charles Louis and Dolores (Teasdale) G.; student Wayne State U., 1958-61; D.D.S. (scholar), U. Mich., 1965, M.S., 1970; m. Cynthia Lee Slocum, Aug. 15, 1964; children—Mark Andrew, Pamela Jean. Pvt. practice orthodontics, Ypsilanti, Mich., 1970—; asst. prof. orthodontic dept. U. Mich. Sch. Dentistry, Ann Arbor, 1970—. Served to capt. USAF, 1965-68. Recipient Internat. Coll. Dentists award U. Mich., 1965. Mem. Mich., Washtenaw Dist. dental socs., Am. Dental Assn., Am. Assn. Orthodontists, Gt. Lakes Soc. Orthodontists, Delta Chi, Psi Omega, Omicron Kappa Upsilon. Home: 3430 Wexford Ct Ann Arbor MI 48104 Office: 3020 Packard St Ypsilanti MI 48197

GRETHER, CARL FREDERICK, artist; b. New Bremen, Ohio, Apr. 15, 1911; s. Alfred and Mary (Sprow) G.; student Heidelberg Coll., Tiffin, Ohio, Art Inst. Pitts., Art Inst. Chgo.; m. Ruth Irene Scherry, Mar. 24, 1940; children—Sherry, Mary, Tim. Engr., Defiance Pressed Steel Co. (Ohio); artist Woodward and Lothrop, Washington; illustrator Bielefeld Studio, Chgo.; art dir. Leo Burnett Co., Chgo.; v.p., exec. art dir. Shaw-LeVally, Inc., Chgo.; owner Carl Grether Studio, Chgo., 1950—; watercolors exhibited in one-man shows, also group shows Artists Guild Galleries, Chgo.; represented in pvt. collections. Recipient Design awards Art Dirs. Club Chgo., 1957, 63; Fine Arts awards Artists Guild Chgo., 1965, 66, 67. Mem. Chgo. Soc. Communicating Arts, Artists Guild Chgo. (dir. 1966-68), Art Inst. Chgo., Chgo. Art Inst. Alumni Assn. dir.; pres.). Republican. Presbyn. (elder). Home: 529 Blackstone Ave LaGrange IL 60525 Office: 222 W Adams St Chicago IL 60606

GREVE, JOHN HENRY, educator; b. Pitts., Aug. 11, 1934; s. John Welch and Edna Viola (Thuenen) G.; B.S., Mich. State U., 1956, D.V.M., 1958, M.S., 1959; Ph.D., Purdue U., 1963; m. Sally Jeanette Doane, June 21, 1956; children—John Haven, Suzanne Carol, Pamela Jean. Asso. instr. Mich. State U., East Lansing, 1958-59; instr. Purdue U., Lafayette, Ind., 1959-62; mem. faculty Iowa State U., Ames, 1963—, prof. vet. parasitology, 1968—. Mem. adv. bd. Des Moines Children's Zoo, 1970—; cons. parasitic diseases to various zoos. Dist. chmn. Boy Scouts Am., 1975-76. Recipient Norden Distinguished Tchr. award Norden Labs., Inc., Lincoln, Nebr., 1965, Outstanding Tchr. award Standard Oil, 1972. Mem. Am., Iowa vet. med. assns., Washington Helminthological Soc., Am. Assn. Vet. Parasitologists, World Assn. Advancement Vet. Parasitology, Iowa Wildlife Fedn., Annual Mid-western Conf. Parasitologists (pres. 1976), Am. Soc. Parasitologists, Am. Assn. Vet. Med. Colls. (council edn.), Sigma Xi, Omega Tau Sigma (asso.), Gamma Sigma Delta, Phi Eta Sigma, Phi Kappa Phi, Phi Zeta. Kiwanian (dist. lt. gov. 1972-73). Home: 334 24th St Ames IA 50010

GREWAL, MANOHAR SINGH, microbiologist; b. Belgaum, India, Apr. 15, 1927; s. Mahman Singh and Basant Kaur (Mann) G.; came to U.S., 1972; B.S., Govt. Coll. Ludhiana, Punjab, 1947; B.Sc. with honors U. Coll., Hoshiarpur, Punjab, 1949, M.Sc. with honors, 1951; Ph.D., Sch. Hygiene and Tropical Medicine, London, Eng., 1956; D.Sc., U. London, 1973; m. Ranjit Mann, Mar. 4, 1962; children—Sangeeta, Aashuwinder S. Lectr. biology Govt. Coll., Rupar, Punjab, India, 1951-53; research scholar Sch. Hygiene and Tropical Medicine, London, 1953-56; sr. lectr. Govt. Coll., Chandigarh, Coll. Edn. and Kurukshetra U., Govt. Ranbir Coll., Sangrur, Punjab, 1956-64; lectr., asst. prof. Postgrad. Inst. Med. Edn. and Research, Chandigarh, India, 1964-72; microbiologist Dearborn Med. Center and Hosp., Highland Park Gen. Hosp., Detroit, 1973; microbiologist, immunologist Pontiac (Mich.) Osteo. Hosp., 1973-75; asso. dir., dir. microbiology, immunology and serology Clinton Valley Splty. Lab. Inc., Pontiac, 1974-77; microbiologist, asso. dir. Sci. Med. Labs. of Detroit, 1975—. Vis. prof. Meml. U. Nfld. (Can.), St. John's, 1968; spl. invitee Jansen Pharmaceutica Beerse, Belgium, 1970. Mem. Am. Soc. Microbiology, Internat. Soc. Parasitologists, Mich. Pub. Health Assn. Contbr. numerous articles to profl. publs. Home: 722 Sheryl Dr Pontiac MI 48054 Office: Sci Med Labs of Detroit 14745 W Eight Mile Rd Detroit MI 48235

GRICE, ALFRED BERNARD, assn. exec.; b. Omaha, Mar. 22, 1923; s. Paul General and Rebecca (Oliver) G.; B.S., U. Nebr., 1950; m. Beulah Fields, Mar. 22, 1953 (dec. Oct. 1977); children—Carolyn Louise, Beverly Ann. Self-employed trucker, 1950-52; mgr. housing authority City of Omaha, 1952-65; owner, mgr. Grice & Co., Realtors, Omaha, 1965-74; exec. dir. Mid-City Bus. and Profl. Assn., Omaha, 1974—. Exec. com. Presbyn. Econ. Devel. Corp., N.Y.C., 1973—; mem. nat. council YMCA's 1969-75. Served with AUS, 1943-46. Mem. Greater Omaha C. of C. (mem. North Council exec. com. 1973-77), Nat. Bus. League, Frontiers Internat. (chpt. pres. 1975—), Alpha Phi Alpha. Democrat. Presbyterian (ruling elder 1950—, vice moderator Presbytery 1977, moderator 1978). Club: F16 Bridge. Home: 5520 N 49th St Omaha NE 68104 Office: 3222 N 24th St Omaha NE 68110

GRIDER, JOSEPH ALLEN, dental surgeon; b. New Castle, Ind., Feb. 22, 1936; s. Oliver Gordon and Golcie Mae (Conner) G.; B.S., Ball State U., 1960; D.D.S., Ind. U. Sch. Dentistry, 1968; m. Greta Anne Wiggins, June 1, 1963; children—Lisa Anne, Christopher, Kelly Kristina. Tchr. chemistry high schs., New Castle, 1963-64; dental surgeon, New Castle, 1968—; chief dental div. Henry County Meml. Hosp., New Castle; dental cons. Heritage House Convalescent Center, New Castle, 1971—, mem. utlization review com. Mem. Ind. U. Hoosier 100; pres. Henry County Meml. Hosp. Found.; mem. New Castle Community Sch. Corp. Served with AUS, 1954-56; maj. USAF Res. Mem. Am., Ind., Eastern Ind. dental assns., Amigos de La Americas, Direct Relief Found., Federation Dentaire Internationale, Ind. U. Alumni Assn., Delta Sigma Delta (student pres. 1967-68; sec. 1966-67), Theta Chi. Presbyterian (trustee). Rotarian (bd. dirs. 1972—). Home: 610 Riley Rd New Castle IN 47362 Office: 540 D St Main New Castle IN 47362

GRIDER, JOSEPH KENNETH, clergyman, educator; b. Madison, Ill., Oct. 22, 1921; s. William S. and Elizabeth (Krone) G.; Th.B., Olivet Nazarene Coll., 1944, A.B., 1945; B.D., Nazarene Theol. Seminary, 1947; M.Div. Summa cum laude, Drew U., 1948, M.A., 1950; Ph.D., Glasgow U., 1952; postgrad Oxford (Eng.) U., 1964; m. Virginia Florence Ballard, July 4, 1942; children—Jennifer Elizabeth, Joseph Kenneth, Carol Christine. Ordained to ministry Church of the Nazarene, 1944; pastor chs., Ill., Mo., N.J., 1943-50, Glasgow, Scotland, 1950-51; tutor Hurlet Nazarene Coll., Glasgow, Scotland, 1950-52; asso. prof. philosophy and theology Pasadena (Calif.) Coll., 1952-53; asso. prof. theology Nazarene Theol. Seminary, Kansas City, Mo., 1953-64, prof., 1964—. Mem. Am., Wesleyan theol. socs. Author: Repentance unto Life, 1964; Taller My Soul, 1965; author numerous poems; contbr. articles to encyclopedias, dictionaries, Bible commentaries. Office: 1700 E Meyer St Kansas City MO 64131

GRIER, BARBARA G. (GENE DAMON), editor, lectr., author; b. Cin., Nov. 4, 1933; d. Phillip Strang and Dorothy Vernon (Black) Grier; grad. high sch. Author: The Lesbian in Literature, 1967, (with others) 2d edit., 1975; The Least of These (in Sisterhood is Powerful), 1970; The Index, 1974; Lesbiana, 1976; The Lesbian Home Jour., 1976; The Lavender Herring, 1976; Lesbian Lives, 1976; pub. The Ladder mag., 1970-72, fiction and poetry editor, 1966-67, editor, 1968-72; dir. promotion Naiad Press, Reno, Nev., 1973—, treas., 1976—. Republican. Home: Rural Route 1 Box 16522 Bates City MO 64011 Office: 20 Rue Jacob Acres Bates City MO 64011

GRIER, DAVID CHARLES, lawyer; b. Albion, Mich., Jan. 27, 1928; s. Kenneth Charles and Mary Elizabeth (Hoag) G.; B.A., Albion Coll., 1954; LL.B., U. Mich., 1957; m. Betty Noble, Aug. 17, 1957; children—Judith Elizabeth, Kathleen Ann, Elizabeth Kay. Admitted to Mich. bar, 1957; mem. firm Jones & Grier, Marcellus, Mich., 1957-61, Neal, Grier, Schutt, Hanson & Hanson, South Haven, Mich., 1962—; counsel Peoples Savs. Assn., Benton Harbor, Mich., 1961-62; city atty., South Haven, 1964-66; asst. state pub. adminstr. for Van Buren County, 1968—. Chmn., South Haven Redevel. Com., 1963-64; councilman South Haven City Council, 1964-66. Served with Security Agy., AUS, 1946-49, Armed Forced Security Agy., 1950-52. Mem. State Bar Mich. (rep. assembly 1972—), Am., Van Buren County bar assns., Phi Beta Kappa. Home: 316 Clinton St South Haven MI 49090 Office: 401 Center St South Haven MI 49090

GRIESHEIMER, RONALD EDWARD, state legislator, lawyer; b. Chgo., Jan. 25, 1936; s. Edward Ray and Carolyn (Knapp) G.; student U. Ill., 1954-57, Bradley U., 1957-58; LL.B., So. Meth. U., 1961; m. Jean Christie Harris, Aug. 6, 1977; children—Amy Lynne, David Edward. Admitted to Ill. bar, 1961, Ill. Supreme Ct., 1961, Tex. Supreme Ct., 1961, Fed. Dist. Ct. for No. Ill., 1965, U.S. Supreme Ct. bar, 1970; asso. firm Hall, Meyer, Fisher, Holmberg, Snook & May, Waukegan, Ill., 1965-68; founder firm Griesheimer & Thompson, Waukegan, 1968—; mem. Ill. House of Reps., 1972—. Vice chmn. North dist. Northeast-Ill. Council Boy Scouts Am., 1968-70; membership chmn. YMCA, Waukegan, 1969-70; chmn. March of Dimes, Waukegan, 1970-71, Lake County Heart Fund, 1977; campaign chmn. Con-Con Del. John Wenum, 1968; pres. Waukegan Young Reps., 1968-70, Lake County Young Reps. Fedn., 1971-72; 12th dist. Congl. Dist. Gov. Ill. State Young Rep. Orgn., 1968-71. Mem. bd. Lake County Music Center, 1967-69; legal counsel Waukegan Hist. Soc., 1967—. Served to maj. USAF, 1961-65; judge adv. Ill. Air N.G., 1976-77. Named Outstanding Young Rep. Man in U.S. Nat. Young Rep. Fedn., 1970-71. Mem. Waukegan-North Chicago C. of C. (chmn. com. 1969-70), Am. Trial Lawyers Assn., Am., Ill., Lake County (mem. bd. govs. 1969—) bar assns. Elk. Home: 2105 Lorraine Ave Waukegan IL 60085 Office: 216 Madison St Waukegan IL 60085

GRIEVES, JOHN WILLIS, lawyer; b. Winner, S.D., July 27, 1930; s. Donald Gardner and Eugenia Ruth (Sewell) G.; B.S., U. S.D., 1952; J.D., 1954; m. Mary Lou Nielsen, Jan. 12, 1952; children—Holly Cheryl, Heather Lynn. Admitted to S.D. bar, 1954; partner with Donald G. Grieves, Winner, 1957-58; individual practice, Winner, 1958—. Pres., Winner Camp Fire Girls, 1966-69; mem. Winner Ind. Sch. Dist. Bd. Edn., 1965—; mem. S.D. Arts Council, 1970-71. Chmn. Tripp County, Todd County and Mellette County (S.D.) Bds. Mental Illness, 1975—; trustee Tripp County Library Bd., 1976—; bd. dirs., mem. exec. bd. Rosebud Area Guidance Center, 1974—, pres.-elect, 1977—. Served with Chem. Corps AUS, 1955-57. Mem. S.D. (commr. 1965-68), Am. bar assns., Am. Trial Lawyers Assn., Am. Choral Dirs. Assn., Phi Delta Phi, Phi Mu Alpha. Christian Scientist. Rotarian (pres. 1969-70), Mason (Shriner), Elk. Home: 590 W 10th St Winner SD 57580 Office: 337 Main St Winner SD 57580

GRIFFIN, BENJAMIN LEE, JR., mgmt. cons.; b. Dayton, Ohio, Sept. 23, 1946; s. Benjamin Lee and Marian Jean (Nighbert) G.; B.A., Rollins Coll., 1968, M.B.A., 1969; m. Virginia Ann Paese, Oct. 4,

1969. Venture devel. mgr. Internat. Paper Co., N.Y.C., 1969-71; group product mgr. Progressive Casualty Ins. Co., Cleve., 1971-75; mng. partner Griffin, Marsh & Assocs., Inc., Cleve., 1975-77, Griffin, Hodgson & Co., Inc., Cleve., 1977—. Mem. Soc. Ins. Research, Am. Mktg. Assn. Home: 1029 Hillstone Rd Cleveland Heights OH 44121 Office: 24200 Chagrin Blvd Cleveland OH 44122

GRIFFIN, DONALD JOHN, trust co. exec.; b. Anamosa, Iowa, Sept. 11, 1917; s. John George and Cecelia Catherine (Kelly) G.; student Columbia U., 1935-36, U. Chgo., 1957; m. Maureen Margaret Moes, Sept. 11, 1940; children—Michael John, Kathleen Ann (Mrs. Dennis M. Sampson). Mgr. automotive advt. Rockford (Ill.) Newspapers Inc., 1940-48; exec. v.p. Rockford Real Estate Bd., Inc. (Ill.), 1948-53; with Chgo. Title & Trust Co., 1953—, v.p. customer relations, 1963—. Chmn. finance sect. Mayor's Summer Jobs for Youth, Chgo., 1968-70; chmn. real estate sect. Crusade of Mercy, Chgo., 1964. Bd. dirs. Booth Meml. Hosp., Chgo.; bd. chmn. Mercy Halfway House Inc., Chgo., 1970—. Served with AUS, 1945-46. Mem. Pub. Relations Soc. Am., Chgo. Real Estate Bd., Chgo. Assn. Commerce and Industry (chmn. govtl. affairs council 1971—), Rockford Bd. Realtors (hon. life), Chgo. Mortgage Bankers, Ill. State C. of C., Chgo. Athletic Assn. (pres. 1978). Roman Catholic. Clubs: Executives (hon. life, pres. 1969-70, chmn. exec. com. 1970-71), Chicago Yacht (Chgo.). Home: 1350 Buttonwood Ln Glenview IL 60025 Office: 111 W Washington St Chicago IL 60602

GRIFFIN, GEORGE ANN, computer systems analyst; b. Evansville, Ind., Nov. 12, 1950; d. George Theophilus and Laura Evelyn (Burke) Griffin; B.A., U. Evansville, 1971; M. Ed., U. Louisville, 1976. Tchr. Cath. Diocese Evansville, 1971-73; computer programer/analyst Sears, Roebuck & Co., Louisville, 1973-75; counselor/tchr. Jefferson County Schs., Louisville, 1975-76; computer systems analyst Credithrift Financial Inc., Evansville, 1976—. Vol., Southwestern Indian Mental Health Assn., Evansville Psychiat. Children's Center. Membership chmn. Wessleman Park Nature Center Soc., 1977—. Certified sch. guidance counselor, Ky.; certified tchr. Ind. Mem. Am. Personnel and Guidance Assn., Assn. Specialists in Group Work, Alpha Omicron Pi. Clubs: Jr. League, Evansville Country, Evansville Petroleum, Order Eastern Star, Order of Amaranth, Order White Shrine Jerusalem, Daus. Nile. Home: 2700 Wayside Dr Evansville IN 47711 Office: 601 NW 2d St Evansville IN 47708

GRIFFIN, MARY VELMA SHOTWELL (MRS. JAMES LEONARD GRIFFIN), author; b. nr. Carrollton, O., Aug. 11, 1904; d. Winfield Scott and Eva Anaz (Smith) Shotwell; certificate elementary edn., Kent State U., 1925; m. James Leonard Griffin, Oct. 2, 1929. Accordionist, Radio Sta. WTAM, Cleve., 1926, Chatuauqua and Lyceum circuits, 1927-28, Accordion Gypsies, 1931-48, Ringling Bros.-Barnum and Bailey Circus, 1935-36; tchr. pub. schs., Ohio, 1922-65; ret., 1965; now free lance writer. Gray lady, ARC, 1967—; bd. dirs. Bell-Herron Scholarship Found., 1965—; pres. Carroll County Hist. Soc., 1965-67, dir., 1963—, curator, 1967—. Mem. NEA, Carroll County Ret. Tchrs. Assn., Ohio, Carroll County (pres. 1964-65) edn. assns., Ohio Hist. Soc., Ohio, Carroll County geneal. socs., Ohioana Library Assn. (county chmn. 1958—). Republican. Methodist. Rebekah; mem. Order Eastern Star. Author: Fair Prize, 1956; Circus Daze, 1957; Mystery Mansion, 1958; numerous short stories pub. in popular mags. Home: 6 Arch St Dellroy OH 44620

GRIFFIN, ROBERT P., U.S. senator; b. Mich., Nov. 6, 1923; s. J. A. and Beulah M. Griffin; A.B., B.S., Central Mich. U., LL.D. (hon.), 1963; J.D., U. Mich.; LL.D., Eastern Mich. U., Albion Coll., U. Mich., Detroit Coll. Law, Detroit Coll. Bus.; L.H.D., Hillsdale Coll.; J.C.D., Rollins Coll.; D.Ed., No. Mich. U.; m. Marjorie J. Anderson; 4 children. Admitted to Mich. bar; practiced in Traverse City, Mich., 1950-56; mem. 85th-89th Congresses, 9th Mich. Dist.; mem. U.S. Senate from Mich., 1966—, minority whip, 1966-77. Served with 71st Inf. Div., AUS, World War II; overseas. Named 1 of 10 Outstanding Young Men in Am., U.S. Jaycees, 1959. Mem. Am., Mich. bar assns., Am. Legion. Republican. Clubs: Elks, Kiwanis. Co-author: Landrum-Griffin Labor-Mgmt. Reform Act, 1959. Home: Traverse City MI Office: Senate Office Bldg Washington DC 20510

GRIFFIN, WALTER ROLAND, historian; b. Carbondale, Pa., Nov. 20, 1942; s. Walter Joseph and Maud Loftus (Boland) G.; B.A., Loyola Coll., Balt., 1963; M.A., U. Cin., 1964; m. Mary Eleanor Armstrong, Aug. 16, 1961; children—Becky, Kathy, Shawn. Lectr. in history Xavier U., Cin., 1965-66; asst. prof. history Mt. St. Mary's Coll., Emmitsburg, Md., 1967-68; asst. prof. history Upper Iowa U., Fayette, Iowa, 1966-67, 68—, chairperson div. of social scis. and bus. adminstrn., also chairperson history dept., 1969—, asso. acad. dean, 1977—. Mem. City Council City of Fayette, 1971-76; chairperson Fayette County Democratic Com., 1972-77, 2d. Iowa Congl. Dist. Campaign Com., 1974-77; mem. Iowa Dem. Central Com., 1974—. Md. State scholar, 1959-63; Taft Teaching fellow U. Cin., 1963-64; research grantee Colo., N.J. hist. socs. 1971-72. Recipient Voter Identification Program award Iowa Democratic party, 1974. Mem. Am. Hist. Assn., Orgn. Am. Historians, Soc. Historians Am. Fgn. Relations, Iowa State Hist. Soc., Iowa Higher Edn. Assn., Phi Alpha Theta, Pi Gamma Mu. Democrat. Unitarian. Contbr. articles to profl. publs. Home: PO Box 384 105 Alexander St Fayette IA 52142 Office: Upper Iowa Univ History Dept Fayette IA 52142

GRIFFIN, WILLIAM EDWARD, constrn. co. exec.; b. Nashville, May 4, 1915; s. Ollie Franklin and Monnie Zell (West) G.; B.S. in C.E., Tenn. Poly. Inst., 1939; m. Elizabeth Freed, Mar. 2, 1940; children—William Edward, Elizabeth (Mrs. Robert Allen Jett). Constrn. engr. TVA, Ft. Loudoun Dam, Lenoir City, Tenn., 1940-43, J.A. Jones Constrn. Co., Oak Ridge, 1943-45, Buggs Island Dam, Va., 1948-51; constrn. engr. Carbide & Carbon Chem. Co., Oak Ridge, 1945-48, asst. plant engr., Paducah, Ky., 1951-55; chief engr. to exec. v.p., dir. and pres. subsidiary Hoffman Rosner Corp., Hoffman Estates, Ill., 1955—; pres. Du-Co Constrn. & Engring. Co., Tri-County Builders Supply Co., North States Constrn. Co. Pres. Ky. Lake chpt. Ky. Soc. Profl. Engrs., 1954-55. Registered profl. engr., Ill., Pa., N.J., Ariz., Tenn., Wis. Mem. Water Pollution Control Assn., Nat., Ill. socs. profl. engrs. Mem. Ch. of Christ. Mason (32 deg., Shriner). Home: 520 S Martha St Lombard IL 60148 Office: PO Box 10 Hoffman Estates IL 60195

GRIFFIN, WILLIAM JULIAN, II, machinery mfg. co. exec.; b. Indpls., Feb. 10, 1925; s. Frank Julian Cox and Mary (Williams) G.; student Butler U., 1942-43, Citadel, 1943-44; grad. Ind. Bus. Coll., 1948; m. Mary Jane Noel, Apr. 24, 1953; children—William Julian III, Kevin L., Kirk E., Kerry J. Buyer, Griffin Realty Corp., 1946-47; prodn. mgr. Griffin Engring. Co., Worthington, Inc., 1949-51; sec.-treas., gen. mgr. Imperial Machine & Tool Corp., Worthington, 1952-53; v.p., gen. mgr., dir. So. Ind. Machine Co., Inc., Worthington, 1954-60, pres., gen. mgr., dir. Griffin Engring. div., 1961—; pres., dir. GBF Dodge, Inc., Casa Grande, Ariz., 1964—; owner, mgr. Griffin Audit Service, 1965—. Bd. dirs. Hulen Meml. Youth Center. Served with AUS, 1943-46, 50. Mem. Am. Ordnance Assn., Am. Legion (past local comdr.), D.A.V. (life), V.F.W. Mem. Disciples of Christ Ch. Mason (Shriner). Elk. Home: Extension St Worthington IN 47471 Office: Southern Ind Machine Co Inc 3d and Williams Sts Worthington IN 47471 also Gila Bend Hwy Casa Grande AZ 85222

GRIFFITH, ALAN LEE, counselor; b. Rochelle, Ill., Dec. 26, 1951; s. Stanwood Charters and Frances Jane (Spangler) G.; A.B., Knox Coll., 1973; M.S., Western Ill. U., 1976; m. Janet Eileen Corney, July 24, 1976. Instr. extension course Kirkwood Community Coll., Cedar Rapids, Iowa, 1977; guidance counselor, tchr. social studies Clarence-Lowden Pub. High Sch., Clarence, Iowa, 1976-77; guidance dir. Clarence-Lowden Community Schs., 1977—, mem. adminstrv. advisory com.; cons. career info. system Dept. Pub. Instruction, State of Iowa. Active Iowa City Chamber Singers. Mem. Am., Iowa personnel and guidance assns., Am. Sch. Counselor Assn., Ill. Guidance and Personnel Assn., Iowa Vocat. Assn. (secondary edn. rep. to legis. com.), Nat. Hist. Soc., Grant Wood Area Edn. Agency Counselor's Roundtable, Assn. for Human Devel. (ex-officio), Internat. Plastic Modelers Soc., Les Amis du Vin, Iowa Assn. Counselors, Educators and Suprs., Confluent Edn. Devel. and Research Center, Phi Delta Kappa, Phi Delta Theta, Phi Mu Alpha. Methodist. Home: 724 8th Ave N Mount Vernon IA 52314 Office: Clarence-Lowden High School Clarence IA 52216

GRIFFITH, B(EZALEEL) HEROLD, physician, educator; b. N.Y.C., Aug. 24, 1925; s. Bezaleel Davies and Henrietta (Herold) G.; student Johns Hopkins U., 1943-44; M.D., Yale U., 1948. Intern, Grace-New Haven Community Hosp., Yale U., 1948-49; resident surgery VA Hosp., Newington, Conn., 1949-50; asst. resident in surgery 2d Cornell Surg. Div., Bellevue Hosp., N.Y.C., 1952-53; resident plastic surgery VA Hosp., Bronx, N.Y., 1953-55, U. Glasgow (Scotland), 1955, N.Y. Hosp.-Cornell Med. Center, N.Y.C., 1956; research fellow plastic surgery Cornell U. Med. Coll., 1956-57; practice medicine specializing in plastic surgery, Chgo., 1957—; attending plastic surgeon Northwestern Meml. Hosp., Childrens Meml., VA Lakeside hosps., Rehab. Inst. Chgo.; asst. in surgery Yale, 1948-49; instr. surgery Cornell U., 1955-56; instr. surgery Northwestern U., 1957-59, asso. in surgery, 1959-62, asst. prof. surgery, 1962-67, asso. prof. surgery, 1967-71, prof., 1971—, chief div. plastic surgery, 1970—. Trustee Roycemore Sch., Evanston, Ill. Served to lt. M.C., USNR, 1950-52. Diplomate Am. Bd. Plastic Surgery (bd. dirs. 1976—). Fellow A.C.S., Am. Assn. Plastic Surgeons, Chgo. Surg. Soc., Royal Soc. Medicine; mem. Am. Soc. Plastic and Reconstructive Surgeons (sec. 1972-74), Brit. Assn. Plastic Surgeons, Plastic Surgery Research Council (chmn. 1969), Am. Cleft Palate Assn., N.Y. Acad. Scis., Nat. Paraplegia Found. (med. adv. com.), AAAS, AMA, Ill., Chgo. med. socs., Assn. Am. Med. Colls., Midwestern Assn. Plastic Surgeons, Ill., Chgo., hist. socs., Civil War Round Table, Evanston Hist. Soc. (trustee), Sigma Xi. Clubs: Univ. (Evanston); Faculty (Northwestern U.); Masons. Contbr. articles to profl. jours. Research in transplantation, skin tumors, cleft palate, paraplegia. Office: 251 E Chicago Ave Chicago IL 60611

GRIFFITH, CALVIN ROBERTSON, baseball club exec.; b. Montreal, Que., Can., Dec. 1, 1911; s. James and Jane (Davies) Robertson; adopted by Clark C. Griffith, 1923; brought to U.S., 1921; ed. Staunton Mil. Acad., 1928-32, George Washington U., 1932-35; m. Natalie N. Niven, Feb. 1, 1940; children—Clark C., N. Corinne, Clare. Sec. Chattanooga Baseball Club, 1935-37, pres., 1937, mgr., 1937; pres., mgr., treas. Charlotte Club, 1938-41; v.p. Washington, Am. League Baseball Club, 1943-55, pres., 1955-61; pres. Minn. Twins, Am. League, 1961—; v.p. Am. League Profl. Baseball; mem. planning com. Profl. Baseball, also rules com. Named Baseball exec. of Year, 1965. Mem. Am. Legion (v.p.). Presbyterian. Address: Metropolitan Stadium Bloomington MN 55420

GRIFFITH, DAVID WILLIAM, library dir.; b. Johnstown, Pa., Mar. 10, 1922; s. William and Pearl (Swank) G.; B.A. in Edn., U. Pitts., 1948; M.L.S., Carnegie Inst. Tech., 1950; m. Doris Marie Wilson, May 1, 1948; children—Debra Ann, Bruce Michael. Reference librarian Cambria Free Library, Johnstown, Pa., 1948-49; library dir. Pub. Library, Steubenville, Ohio, 1950-64, Youngstown (Ohio) Pub. Library, 1965—. Trustee Butler Art Inst., Youngstown, 1967—; bd. dirs. Mahoning chpt. ARC, 1976—. Served with USAAF, 1943-45. Mem. Ohio Library Assn. (pres. 1961, chmn. legis. com. 1966-68). Rotarian (chmn. mag. com. 1966-67; editor The Clatter 1967-68). Club: Youngstown. Home: 2530 Timothy Knoll Dr Poland OH 44514 Office: 305 Wick Ave Youngstown OH 44503

GRIFFITH, JAMES DAVID, lawyer; b. Evanston, Ill., Aug. 28, 1929; s. Wendell Crabtree and Mary Irma (Griffith) G.; B.A., DePauw U., 1951; J.D., Northwestern U., 1953; m. Elizabeth Meyer, Sept. 21, 1957; children—Ian Hunt, Alison Gail. Admitted to Ill. bar, 1953, since practiced in Chgo.; asso. firm Campbell, Clithero, Fischer & Guy, 1956-63; partner Graham, Stevenson & Griffith, 1963-67; pvt. practice 1967-69; partner Pauker & Griffith, Ltd., 1969—. Magistrate, Village of Glenview, Ill., 1961-65; chmn. Def. of Prisoners Com., 1962-63. Founder, Com. on Lake Mich. Pollution, pres., 1967-69, 73-74, treas., 74—; chmn. Lake Mich. Fedn., 1975-76; mem. Chgo. Crime Com., 1965-76. Served with AUS, 1954-56. Mem. Chgo. Council Lawyers, Phi Alpha Delta. Club: Sheridan Shore Yacht (commodore 1970), Wilmette Harbor Assn. (dir. 1964—). Contbr. articles to legal jours. Home: 636 Hunter Rd Glenview IL 60025 Office: 111 W Washington Chicago IL 60602

GRIFFITH, JAMES HOMER, chemist; b. Chgo., Feb. 8, 1936; s. Homer Franklin and Dora (Bauman) G.; B.S., U. Ill., 1959; Ph.D., Cornell, 1962; M.B.A., U. Chgo., 1975; m. Elizabeth Louise Caldwell, Nov. 28, 1959; children—Eric David, Valerie Ann, Alona Diane. Research asso. dept. chemistry U. Ariz., 1962-64; research chemist E. I. duPont de Nemours & Co. Research and Devel. Lab., Circleville, Ohio, 1964-67; sr. scientist Sherwin-Williams Co. Research Center, Chgo., 1967-69, group supr., 1969, sect. supr., 1969-75, supt. varnish prodn. Sherwin-Williams Co., 1975-76, mgr. Chgo. resin mfg., 1976—. Chmn. mgmt. info. system policy adv. com. Ill. Community Coll. Bd., 1973—; dir. Ill. Community Coll. Trustees Assn., 1974—. Chmn. labor com. N.Y. Young Republicans, 1960-62, chmn. platform com., 1962; Co-chmn. precinct orgn. com. South Suburban Com. Calling Constl. Conv., 1968; pres. Vol. Orgn. to Encourage Republicanism, 1969-73; v.p., area coordinator Bremen Twp. Rep. Orgn., 1970-75. Bd. dirs. University YMCA, 1958-59; trustee Prairie State Coll., 1970—, chmn. bd. trustees, 1971-73, vice-chmn. bd., 1973-74, 75—, sec. bd., 1974-76. Served with AUS, 1954-56. Mem. Am. Chem. Soc. (co-chmn. polymer group Chgo. sect. 1968-70), Am. Assn. Textile Chemists and Colorists, Chgo. Soc. for Paint Tech., Chgo. Paint, Varnish and Laquer Assn., A.A.A.S., N.Y. Acad. Sci., Chgo. South C. of C. (mem. edn. com.), Alpha Chi Sigma, Phi Lambda Upsilon. Contbr. articles in field to sci. jours. Home: 17812 S Turtle Creek Dr Homewood IL 60430 Office: 11541 Champlain Ave Chicago IL 60628

GRIFFITH, JAMES MARK, radio sta. exec.; b. Ardmore, Okla., July 23, 1910; s. Mark Mason and Nina Ethel (Smith) G.; A.B., Baylor U., 1930; m. Christeen Whitley, Mar. 7, 1942; 1 dau., Nina (Mrs. J.H. Latimer, Jr.). News writer, reporter, sports editor Daily Ardmoreite, Ardmore, 1930-36; mgr. KVSO radio, Ardmore, 1936-40; gen. mgr. radio sta. KADA, Ada, Okla., 1940-42, 45-47; gen. mgr. radio sta. KSEK, Pittsburg, Kans., 1947-50; owner, pres., gen. mgr. KARE, Atchison, Kans., 1950—. Sec.-treas. Okla. Network, Inc., Ada, 1945-47. Chmn. adv. bd. Salvation Army, Atchison, 1957-58, 72-73. Bd. govs. Benedictine Coll., Atchison, 1972—. Served with USNR, 1942-45. Mem. C. of C. (dir. 1952-58), Sigma Delta Chi. Presbyterian (elder). Clubs: Kiwanis (past pres.), Masons, Elks. Home: 503 N 2d St Atchison KS 66002 Office: 200 N 5th St Atchison KS 66002

GRIFFITH, JOHN FRANCIS, chem. engr.; b. San Juan, Tex., May 8, 1922; s. Francis Marion and Anna Margret (Walker) G.; grad. Edinburg Jr. Coll., 1941; B.S. in Chem. Engring., U. Tex. at Austin, 1943; postgrad. Villanova U., 1953-56; m. Lee Ann Ruff, Aug. 22, 1947; children—Lynn Ann Griffith Staton, Kimberly Suzanne Griffith Peters. Startup engr., Rubber Reserve Co., Port Neches, Tex., 1943-47; with Firestone Plastics Co., Pottstown, Pa., 1947-67, tech. mgr. chem. div., 1956-63, coordinator research and devel. plastics and fibers, 1964-67; asst. dir. research Firestone Tire & Rubber, Akron, 1967-69, sr. research engr., cast tire process devel., 1969—. Dir., v.p. South Coventry Twp. (Pa.) Sch., 1961-64. Bd. dirs. No. Chester County Pa. Adult Sch., 1959-67. Mem. Am. Inst. Chem. Engrs., Am. Assn. Cost Engrs., Nat., Pa., Ohio (dir., 1974—) socs. profl. engrs. Republican. Mem. Christian Ch. (deacon, elder). Rotarian. Patentee in field. Home: 812 Spring Water Dr Route 7 Akron OH 44313 Office: 1200 Firestone Pkwy Akron OH 44317

GRIFFITH, RICHARD EUGENE, controller; b. Utica, N.Y., Aug. 6, 1934; s. Raymond Frank and Ethel Margaret (Edwards) G.; B.S. in Accounting, Utica Coll., 1959; student law Syracuse U., 1960; m. Marilyn Catherine Maronde, Nov. 9, 1962; children—Richard, Reade. Financial mgmt. trainee Gen. Elec. Co., Syracuse, N.Y., 1960-62; budgets and mfg. cost control adminstr. RCA, Cambridge, Ohio and Camden, N.J., 1962-66; mgr. forecasts and budgets Continental Motor Corp., Muskegon, Mich., 1966-68; asst. controller FMC Corp., South Charleston, W.Va., 1968-70, program fin. mgr., Mpls., 1970-71, accounting and auditing mgr., Mpls., 1971-73, controller, Mpls., 1973—; cons. Active Minn. Taxpayers Assn., Central Minn. council Boy Scouts Am., Jr. Achievement. Served with USAF, 1952-56. Mem. Nat. Assn. Accountants, Nat. Contract Mgmt. Assn., Fed. Govt. Accountants Assn. Republican. Roman Catholic. Home: 1025 River Pkwy Champlin MN 55316 Office: Columbia Heights PO Minneapolis MN 55421

GRIFFITH, RUSSELL EVAN, JR., educator; b. Akron, Ohio, Sept. 15, 1923; s. Russell Evan and Mary Kathryn (Mummart) G.; B.S., Huntington Coll., 1947; B.S. in Edn., Miami U., 1949, M.A., 1950; H.S.D., Ind. U., 1958; m. Marilyn Marie Kauff, Sept. 28, 1946; children—Sondra, Judith, Barbara, David, Russell Evan III. Tchr. Ossian (Ind.) High Sch. 1947-48; mem. faculty Miami U., Oxford, Ohio, 1950—, prof. dept. zoology and physiology, 1970—; part-time prof. dept. anatomy Wright State U. Sch. Medicine, Dayton, Ohio, 1974—. Pres. Federated Clubs, Oxford, 1965-67; mem. Oxford Welfare Com., 1968-71. Served with USNR, 1943-46, 50-70. Recipient Outstanding Tchr. award Miami U., 1971, Alumnus of Year award Huntington Coll., 1971; named Oxford Area Citizen of Year, 1965. Mem. Kappa Phi Kappa (nat. sec. treas. 1960—), Omicron Delta Kappa, Phi Sigma, Kappa Delta Pi, Phi Delta Kappa, Phi Kappa Tau. Kiwanian (pres. 1965; chmn. com. 1971—, chmn. Scout troop 1970—, lt. gov. Ohio dist. 1975—). Home: 213 McKee Ave Oxford OH 45056

GRIFFITHS, JOHN DAVID, constrn. co. exec.; b. Washington, July 8, 1909; s. David and Emmigene (Lilley) G.; C.E., U. Cin., 1933; m. Grace Fels, Dec. 7, 1934; children—Sally (Mrs. Kenneth Olsen), Jane. Structural designer U.S. Corps Engrs., Washington, 1937-41; dist. engr. Am. Inst. Steel Constrn., various locations, 1945-54; chief engr. Gate City Steel Co., Boise, Idaho, 1954-60; v.p. engring. Paxton & Vierling Steel Co., Omaha, 1960—. Chmn. research com. Am. Inst. Steel Constrn., 1970—. Served to comdr. C.E., USNR, 1941-45. Registered profl. engr., Nebr., Iowa, Idaho. Mem. ASCE (pres. Idaho sect. 1959), Nebr. Soc. Profl. Engrs. (pres. 1955), Omaha Engrs. Club (pres. 1951). Author pamphlets: Single Span Rigid Frames in Steel, 1949; Multiple Span Gabled Frames, 1954. Home: 1510 S 90th St Omaha NE 68124 Office: PO Box 1085 Omaha NE 68101

GRIFFITHS, LARRY, clergyman, educator; b. Milw., Oct. 24, 1931; s. Ernest and Effie Catherine (Rowland) G.; postgrad. Moody Bible Inst., 1950-52; grad. U. Wis., Platteville, 1959; postgrad. U. Wis., Eau Claire and River Falls, 1963-70, U. Mo., 1976; m. Marlys Siemens, Dec. 31, 1954; children—Terri Sue, Patti Jeanne. Ordained to the ministry Baptist Ch., 1955; pastor Mt. Ida (Wis.) Bapt. Ch., 1954-58; tchr. Chetek (Wis.) Jr. High Sch., 1959-63, Eau Claire Jr. High Sch., 1963—; clergyman Amy Chapel, Elk Mound, Wis., 1970-74; owner, pres. Strum (Wis.) Nursing Home, Inc., 1970—, owner Golden Age Nursing Home, Inc., Whitehall, Wis., 1970—. Mem. Eau Claire County Council Alcoholism, 1970-76; mem. Wis. Educators for Polit. Action, 1969-73; mem. Protect Our Pub. Schools, 1969-73. Mem. Eau Claire Edn. Assn. (pres. 1969-71), Wis. Edn. Assn. (governance task force 1968-72), N.E.A., Internat. Platform Assn., Nat. Fed. Tchrs., U. Wis. Platteville Alumni Assn., Wis. Heart Assn. Club: Optimist. Address: 221 Elm St Strum WI 54770

GRIGG, JOHN WARREN, otolaryngologist; b. nr. Munger, Mich., Mar. 7, 1927; s. Roy and Marie A. (Rudell) G.; student Bay City Jr. Coll., 1948-50, U. Mich., 1950-51; M.D., Wayne State U., 1955; m. Marilyn Janet Cochrun, June 19, 1955; children—Scott Allen, Lisa Ann, Judith Lynn, Christopher Lee. Intern St. Luke's Hosp., Saginaw, Mich., 1955-56; resident Wayne State U. Hosp., Detroit, 1960-63; practice medicine specializing in otolaryngology, Bay City, 1963—; mem. staffs Bay Med. Center, Inc., Bay City, Bay City Hosp., St. Mary's Hosp., Saginaw, Midland Community Hosp.; asst. clin. prof. otolaryngology Wayne State U. Coll. Medicine, Detroit, 1976—. Trustee bd. Essexville Hampton Sch. dist., 1972—. Served with USN, 1945-48. Diplomate Am. Bd. Otolaryngology. Fellow A.C.S., Am. Acad. Facial Plastic and Reconstructive Surgery, Acad. Ophthalmology and Otolaryngology, Am. Soc. for Head and Neck Surgery; mem. Mich. (chmn. state sect. 1971; del. sect. otolaryngology 1971—; mem. jud. commn. 4th dist. 1972—, chmn. jud. commn. 1974-75), Bay County (pres. 1972) med. socs., Mich. Otolaryngol. Soc., Am. Council Otolaryngology (chmn. Mich. soc. 1974—, chmn. profl. liability com. 1975—). Clubs: Elks, Country (Bay City). Home: 106 Birney St Essexville MI 48732 Office: 515 Mulholland St Bay City MI 48706

GRIGG, VIOLA E. WIITALA (MRS. PAUL GRIGG), educator, social worker; b. Marquette, Mich., Mar. 7, 1913; d. Axel and Maria (Michelson) Wiitala; B.S., No. Mich. U., 1934; M.Ed., Wayne State U., 1958, M.S.W., 1963; m. Paul Grigg, Sept. 1, 1937; children—Lyn A. (dec.), Nancy J., Edward P. Tchr., Morgan Heights Preventorium (Mich.), 1934-36, Trenary (Mich.) High Sch., 1936-37, Brown City (Mich.) Sch., 1937-38; substitute tchr., Dearborn, Mich., 1953-56, tchr., 1956-58, sch. social worker, 1958—; now coordinator spl. edn. Dearborn Pub. Schs. Mem. Civic Center Planning Commn., Dearborn, 1951-53. Mem. Mich. Sch. Social Work Assn. (pres. 1964, 68, exec. bd. 1959-69), Am. Orthopsychiat. Assn., Mich. Guidance and Personnel Assn., Nat. Assn. Social Workers, Acad. Certified Social Workers, Midwest Sch. Social Work Conf., Pi Lambda Theta. Home: 20775 Audette St Dearborn MI 48124 Office: 4824 Lois St Dearborn MI 48126

GRIGGS, DOUGLAS MERIWETHER, JR., physiologist; b. Portland, Maine, Aug. 14, 1928; s. Douglas Meriwether and Mackye Garwood (Reed) G.; B.A., Harvard, 1949; M.D., U. Va., 1953; m.

Anne Lee Hager, May 26, 1956; children—Douglas III, Stephen. Intern St. Lukes Hosp., N.Y.C., 1953-54, resident, 1954-58; asst. prof. internal medicine Hahnemann Med. Coll., Phila., 1962-66, asso. prof., 1966-67; asso. prof. physiology U. Mo. Med. Sch., Columbia, 1967-70, prof., 1970—; research com. Mo. Heart Assn., 1972; study sect. cardiovascular and pulmonary NIH. USPHS Research Career Devel. grantee, 1963-72. Mem. Am. Physiol. Soc., Am. Fedn. Clin. Research. Contbr. articles in field cardiovascular research to profl. jours. Address: 1016 Yale St Columbia MO 65201

GRIGGS, IONE QUINBY, newspaper columnist; b. Salina, Kans.; d. William Paine and Laura (Peck) Quinby; student Northwestern U.; m. Bruce Eggleston Griggs, Nov. 19, 1932 (dec. Dec. 1933). Reporter Evening Post, Chgo., 1926-32; corr. Consol. Press and Central Press Assn., 1928-33; columnist Milw. Jour., 1934—. Named Newspaperwoman of Yr., Theta Sigma Phi, 1970. Mem. Milw. County Western Springs (Ill.) hist. socs. Author: Murder for Love, 1931; Growing Up with Jim and Jean, 1936. Contbr. numerous articles to mags. Club: Milw. Press. Home: 720 N 3d St Milwaukee WI 53203 Office: 333 W State St Milwaukee WI 53201

GRIGGS, JOHN BRADFORD, librarian, mus. curator; b. Lincoln, Nebr., Sept. 4, 1935; s. Roger and Alice (Waters) G.; B.A., U. Wis., 1957; M.L.S., U. Ky., 1961; m. Lorinda Mae Jhoslien, July 16, 1960; children—Susan Ann, Paul Edward. Reference librarian Milw. Pub. Library, 1960-63; engring. librarian Purdue U., 1963-65; sci. librarian Cin. Pub. Library, 1965-72; dir. Lloyd Library and Mus., Cin., 1972—. Co-pub. Lloydia, The Jour. of Natural Products, 1972—; vis. faculty U. Ky., 1973. Mem. Ohio, Spl. library assns., Cin. Area Health Scis. Library Assn. Home: 2714 Pineview Dr Villa Hills KY 41016 Office: 917 Plum St Cincinnati OH 45202

GRIGSBY, LEWIS MATTHEWS, SR., lawyer; b. Pittsfield, Ill., Aug. 7, 1921; s. Earl S. and Helen Matthews (Lewis) G.; B.A., U. Ill., 1943, J.D., 1948; m. Juanita Vey Zimmerman, Dec. 20, 1942; children—Lewis M., Jr., Gloria Grigsby Carrell, Juanita K. Admitted to Ill. bar, 1948; since practiced in Pittsfield; mem. firms Weaver & Jenkins, 1948-50, Weaver & Grigsby, 1951-57, Grigsby & Irving, 1958—. Pres. Farmers State Bank, Pittsfield, Ill., 1964—; asst. atty. gen., 1952-60. Dir. U. Ill. Alumni Assn., 1964-70. Served with USAAF, 1943-45; ETO. Mem. Am., Ill. bar assns., Phi Delta Theta, Phi Delta Phi. Republican. Conglist. Lion. Home: 830 E Washington St Pittsfield IL 62363 Office: 118 E Adams St Pittsfield IL 62363

GRILLOT, FRANCIS ALBERT, JR., mfg. co. exec.; b. Parsons, Kans., Feb. 3, 1935; s. Francis Albert and Eleanor Francis (Hillegas) G.; B.S. in Chem. Engring., Kans. State U., 1958; M.S. in Bus. Adminstrn., Wichita State U., 1965; m. Mary Ellen Haley, July 20, 1958; children—Timothy, Tammy, Jackie, Janetta. Mgr. prodn. and maintenance Vulcan Materials Co., Wichita, Kans., 1960-70; v.p., dir. FC Schaffer & Assos., Baton Rouge, 1970-74; v.p. mktg. devel. Peabody TecTank Inc., Parsons, 1974—, dir., 1974—; owner, pres. GHD Corp., 1972—. Mem. County Republican Com., 1975-76. Served with AUS, 1954-62. Registered profl. engr. Kans., Fla., Tex., La., Va. Mem. Nat. Soc. Profl. Engrs., Am. Inst. Chem. Engrs., Am. Legion, Kans. Engring. Soc., Water Pollution Control Fedn. Home: 625 S 35th St Parsons KS 67357 Office: South Industrial Park Parsons KS 67357

GRIMES, ALAN PENDLETON, educator; b. S.I., N.Y., Feb. 3, 1919; s. Willard Mudgette and Mildred Blanchard (Staples) G.; B.A., U. N.C., 1941, M.A., 1946, Ph.D., 1948; m. Margaret Edna Whitehurst, May 16, 1942; children—Margaret, Alan, Katherine, Peter. Asst. prof. polit. sci. U. N.C., Chapel Hill, 1948-49; asst. prof. Mich. State U., E. Lansing, 1949-51, asso. prof., 1951-57, prof., 1957—. Served to lt. USNR, 1942-45. Mem. Am., Midwest polit. sci. assns. Democrat. Author: The Political Liberalism of the New York Nation, 1953; American Political Thought, 1960; Equality in America, 1964; The Puritan Ethic and Woman Suffrage, 1967. Home: 728 Lantern Hill Dr East Lansing MI 48823 Office: Political Science Dept Michigan State University East Lansing MI 48824

GRIMES, HUGH GAVIN, physician; b. Chgo., Aug. 19, 1929; s. Andrew Thomas and Anna (Gavin) G.; student Loyola Acad., 1943-47, Loyola U., 1947-50; B.S., U. Ill., 1952, M.D., 1954; m. Rose Anne Leahy, Aug. 21, 1954; children—Hugh Gavin, Paula Anne, Daniel Joseph, Sarah Louise, Nancy Marie, Jennifer Diane. Intern St. Joseph Hosp., Chgo., 1954-55, resident obstetrics and gynecology, 1955-58; pvt. practice obstetrics and gynecology Chgo., 1960—; asso. prof. obstetrics and gynecology Stritch Sch. Medicine Loyola U., Chgo.; active staff St. Joseph Hosp., Chgo., also mem. exec. adv. bd., v.p. med. staff, 1977-78; asso. staff St. Francis Hosp., Evanston, Ill. Mem. lay adv. bd. Regina Dominican High Sch. Served to capt. M.C., AUS, 1958-60. Diplomate Am. Bd. Obstetrics and Gynecology. Fellow Am. Coll. Obstetrics and Gynecology; res. asso. fellow Chgo. Gynecol. Soc.; mem. Am. Assn. Maternal and Infant Health, Am. Cancer Soc. (mem. profl. edn. com. Chgo. unit), Am. Fertility Soc., A.M.A., Ill., Chgo. med. socs., Cath. Physicians Guild, Assn. Am. Physicians and Surgeons, Am. Soc. for Colposcopy and Colpomicroscopy, Am. Assn. Gynecologic Laparoscopists, Assn. Art Inst. Chgo., Assn. Field Mus., Assn. Smithsonian Instn., Pi Kappa Epsilon. Contbr. articles to profl. jours. Home: 1003 Romona Rd Wilmette IL 60091 Office: 5214 N Western Ave Chicago IL 60625

GRIMES, JOHN EDWARD, JR., psychologist; b. Murphysboro, Ill., July 16, 1933; s. John Edward and Lorene Anna (Vaughn) G.; B.A., So. Ill. U., 1955, M.A., 1962; Ph.D., U. Ariz., 1974; m. Nancy Lynn Wickiser, June 15, 1961; children—John Michael, Kathlyn Elene, Karen Elizabeth. Rehab. counselor Tex. Rehab. Commn., Houston, 1961-66; psychologist Ariz. Tng. Center, Tucson, 1966-68; psychologist Counseling Center Eastern Ill. U., Charleston, Ill., 1968—; chief examiner G.E.D. Test, Charleston, 1969—; cons. psychologist Shelby County Mental Health Center, Shelbyville, Ill., 1970-71, Moultrie County Mental Health Center, Sullivan, Ill., 1975-77; psychologist Fed. Disability Program, Charleston, 1971—. Bd. dirs. Coles County Mental Health Assn., v.p., 1972, 76, pres., 1973, treas., 1975. Served to sgt. AUS, 1955-58. Mem. Am., Ill. psychol. assns., Acad. Psychologists in Marriage and Family Therapy, Am. Assn. Sex Educators, Counselors and Therapists, Am. Assn. on Mental Deficiency, Am. Assn. on Suicidology, Am. Personnel and Guidance Assn., Nat., Ill. rehab. assns., Nat., Ill. rehab. counseling assns., Coles County Mental Health Assn., Coles County Assn. for Retarded. Home: 723 Olean Pl Charleston IL 61920 Office: Counseling Testing Center Eastern Ill U Charleston IL 61920

GRIMLEY, LIAM KELLY, educator; b. Dublin, Ireland, Apr. 4, 1936; s. William and Eileen (Kelly) G.; came to U.S., 1970; B.A., Nat. U. Ireland, 1960; L.Ph., Faculté Libre, Paris, 1963; H.D.Ed., Clongowes Wood Coll., Ireland, 1964; Th.B., Inst. Philosophy and Theology, Dublin, 1968, S.T.L., 1970; M.Ed., Kent State U., 1971, Ph.D., 1973; m. Marie Sadon, Aug. 26, 1973; 1 son, Kevin. English teacher Lycée Moderne, Le Puy, France, 1961-62; asst. dir. Summer Sch. English, Observatorio del Ebro, Tortosa, Spain, 1961-62; tchr. math. and modern langs. Clongowes Wood High Sch., Ireland, 1963-64; tchr. math. and classical langs. St. Ignatius Elementary and Secondary Sch., Galway, Ireland, 1964-66; instr. statistics and probability theory Univ. Coll., Galway, Ireland, 1965-66; prof. theology Conf. Major Religious Superiors, Dublin, 1969-70; counselor Newman Center, Syracuse U., 1970; social studies tchr. Walsh Jesuit High Sch., Cuyahoga Falls, Ohio, 1971; asst. dir. Ohio Soc. Crippled Children and Adults, Tiffin, summer 1971; intern sch. psychologist Field Local Sch. Dist., Ohio, 1972-73; research and devel. dir. lab. sch. Kent State U., 1972-73; prof. spl. edn., Ind. State U., Terre Haute, 1973—, chmn. dept., 1975—, dir. Inst. Continuing Edn. in Psychology, 1976—; cons. Joseph P. Kennedy Found., 1973—; mem. State Adv. Com., Div. Pupil Personnel, 1975—. Mem. Ind. State Manpower Steering Com., 1977—. Mem. Am., Ind. psychol. assns., Nat. Assn. Sch. Psychologists. Roman Catholic. Club: Rotary. Contbr. articles to profl. jours.; editor The Sch. Psychology Digest, 1976—. Home: 43 Allendale Terre Haute IN 47802 Office: Spl Edn Dept Ind State U Terre Haute IN 47809

GRIMM, DANIEL FREDERICK, veterinarian; b. Evansville, Ind., Nov. 14, 1941; s. Stanley G. and Ruth Marie (Bumb) G.; D.V.M., Purdue U., 1965; m. Virginia Ann Dawson, June 27, 1964; children—Daniel Frederick, Elizabeth Lynn, Matthew Edward. Asso. veterinarian Parkdale Animal Hosp., Newburgh, Ind., 1965-68; self employed Greenbrier Animal Hosp., Evansville, 1968—. Mem. Evansville Animal Nuisance Commn., 1969-77, pres., 1972-73, 74-77; dir. Vanderburgh County Humane Soc., 1970-76. Mem. Am., Ind. (dir.), S.W. Ind. (pres. 1969) vet. med. assns., Am. Assn. Equine Practitioners, Purdue Univ. Agr. Alumni Assn. (sec., treas 1969-70), Evansville Purdue U. Alumni Assn. (pres. 1972—), Am. Animal Hosp. Assn. (asso. mem.), Theta Xi, Phi Zeta, Alpha Zeta. Methodist (mem. commn. edn. 1969—, mem. finance com., mem. nominating com., co-chmn. family life, pres. trustees 1974-76). Clubs: John Purdue, Kiwanis (dir. 1970—, sec. 1972-73) (Green River); Purdue (pres. 1972-73), Quarterback (dir.) (Evansville). Home and Office: 4307 N Green River Rd Evansville IN 47715

GRIMM, OLIVER GILBERT, dentist; b. Aurora, Ill., Aug. 31, 1932; s. Ivan Sylvester and Dorothy (Pritchard) G.; student Beloit Coll., 1950-53; D.D.S., Northwestern U., 1957; M.S., Loyola U. (Chgo.), 1963; m. Judith Ann Albers, Aug. 17, 1955; children—Dana Lee, Kurt Andrew, Eric Jon. Practice dentistry, specializing in orthodontics, Peoria, Ill., 1963—. Pres. Peoria Civic Ballet, 1971. Capt. Dental Corps, USNR, 1957—. Diplomate Am. Bd. Orthodontics. Mem. Peoria Dist. (pres.-elect.), Am. dental assns., Am. Assn. Orthodontists, Tau Kappa Epsilon, Delta Sigma Delta. Republican. Mason (Shriner, Jester). Home: 5014 Prospect Rd Peoria Heights IL 61614 Office: 6901 N Knoxville Peoria IL 61614

GRIMSON, LYNN GUDMUNDUR, lawyer; b. Langdon, N.D., May 28, 1912; s. Gudmundur and Ina Viola (Sanford) G.; B.A., U. N.D., 1933; LL.B., U. Minn., 1935; m. Mary Ann Divine, May 1, 1937; children—Janet (Mrs. James S. Loos), Judy (Mrs. Judy M. Smith). Admitted to N.D. bar, 1935; ct. reporter Second Jud. dist., Rugby, N.D., 1937-40; asst. atty. gen., Bismarck, N.D., 1940-41; practice law, Grafton, N.D., 1945—. Clk. Grafton (N.D.) Pub. Sch. Dist., 1955-76; city atty., Grafton, 1951-53; municipal judge, Grafton, 1971-73. Pres. Kopperud Found., Grafton, 1963. Served with AUS, 1942-45. Decorated Bronze Star. Mem. Am., N.D. (exec. dir. 1954-59), Minn. bar assns., Am. Coll. Probate Counsel, Am. Counsel Assn., Am. Judicature Assn., VFW, Am. Legion. Mason (Shriner), Elk, Eagle, Kiwanian. Home: 615 Birch Ct Grafton ND 58237 Office: 640 Hill Ave Grafton ND 58237

GRINSTEAD, LEONARD SYLVESTER, elec. and electronics engr.; b. East Palestine, Ohio, Dec. 27, 1939; s. Sylvester Leonard and Dorothy Catherine (McClellan) G.; student pub. schs., Youngstown, Ohio; m. Patricia Ann Jacobson, Aug. 22, 1961; children—Leonard Mark, Mary Patricia. Systems analyst Newark (Ohio) Air Force Sta., 1962-64; electronics technician instr. Youngstown AFB, Vienna, Ohio, 1964-65; electronics instr. A.T.E.S. Tech. Sch., Niles, Ohio, 1965-66; sr. electronics design engr. Automatic Sprinkler Corp., Cleve., 1966-68; quality control engr. Economy Engine Co., Girard, Ohio, 1968-72; sr. electronics design engr. Fox Industries, Inc., Youngstown, 1972-74; elec./electronics engr. Trumbull Cons., Inc., Canfield, Ohio, 1974—. Served with USN, 1957-60. Roman Catholic. Home: 706 E Philadelphia St Youngstown OH 44502 Office: 73 N Broad St Canfield OH 44406

GRISWOLD, PAUL MICHAEL, clin., cons. psychologist; b. Milw., Sept. 26, 1945; s. Willard Matthew and Evelyn (Haerle) G.; B.A., Marquette U., 1967, M.S., 1969; Ph.D., Kent State U., 1972; m. Ann Mari Gerardine LaValle, Aug. 2, 1969; 1 son, Matthew Paul. Sr. staff psychologist Wis. Div. of Corrections, 1972—; pvt. practice clin., cons. psychology, Milw., 1973—; lectr. dept. behavioral scis. Mt. Mary Coll., Milw., 1973—. Mem. Am., Wis., Milw. County Psychological assns., Assn. of Correctional Psychologists, Wis. Assn. for Behavior Therapy (dir. 1973-74). Home: 1366 County Hwy J Hubertus WI 53033 Office: 6914 W Appleton Ave Milwaukee WI 53216

GROENING, WILLIAM ANDREW, JR., lawyer, ret. chem. co. exec.; b. Saginaw, Mich., Nov. 20, 1912; s. William Andrew and Rose (Egloff) C.; B.A., U. Mich., 1934, J.D., 1936; LL.D., Saginaw Valley State Coll., 1974; m. Virginia Jane Gann, July 27, 1940; children—Mary R. (Mrs. George H. Flores), William Andrew III, Janet R. (Mrs. James G. Marsh), Phyllis L. (Mrs. Richard A. Beehr), Theodore J. Admitted to Mich. bar, 1936; with legal dept. Dow Chem. Co., Midland, Mich., 1937-51, asst. gen. counsel, 1951-67, gen. counsel, 1968-77, asst. sec., 1955-71, v.p., 1971-77, mem. fin. com., 1972-77; sec., dir. Dow Corning Corp., 1961-77, Kartridge Pak Co., 1966-77; v.p., dir. Dow Chem. Inter-Am., Ltd., Dow Chem. Internat., 1952-77. Mem. Regina High Sch. Bd., 1963-67; bd. arbitrators Roman Catholic Province of Mich., 1970-71; chmn. pension com. Mich. Cath. Conf., chmn. bd. Saginaw Valley Coll., 1963-73. Charter commr. City of Midland, 1944, city councilman, 1946-52. Trustee Willard and Martha Dow Meml. Ednl. Fund, 1949-75, pres., 1951-75. Mem. State Bar Mich. (chmn. anti-trust law sect. 1967-68), Mich. Conf. Bar Presidents (chmn. 1952-53), Am., Midland County (past. pres.) bar assns., Am. Judicature Soc. (dir., sec., mem. exec. com.). Republican. Roman Catholic. K.C., Clubs: Midland Country, Saginaw Valley Torch, Rotary. Home and Office: 4204 Arbor Dr Midland MI 48640

GROFF, RICHARD LAMARR, retail splty. co. exec.; b. Lancaster, Pa., Aug. 6, 1925; s. Frank L. and Martha E. G.; B.S., Franklin and Marshall U., 1950; M.B.A., U. Pitts., 1951; m. Betty Mastrocola, May 25, 1974. Mgmt. trainee Higbee Co., Cleve., 1951-53, buyer, 1953-58, mdse. mgr. sportswear, 1958-61, fashion, 1961-66, gen. mgr. suburban store, 1966-72, gen. mgr. Loft div., 1972—. Served with USAAF, 1944-46. Mem. Am. Mgmt. Assn., Nat. Retailer Mgmt. Assn. Clubs: Rotary, Masons. Home: 624-6 Fairington Oval Aurora OH 44202 Office: Higbee Co 100 Public Sq Cleveland OH 44113

GROMACKI, ROBERT GLENN, clergyman, theologian; b. Erie, Pa., Sept. 20, 1933; s. Sylvester Theodore and Thelma Evelyn (Woodell) G.; Th.B., Baptist Bible Sem., 1956; Th.M., Dallas Theol. Sem., 1960; Th.D., Grace Theol. Sem., 1966; m. Gloria Gay Julyan, June 4, 1954; children—Gary Robert, Gail Lynn. Ordained minister Baptist Ch., 1960; faculty, Cedarville (Ohio) Coll., 1960—, prof. Bible and Greek, 1960—, chmn. Bibl. Edn. dept., 1960—. Mem. Evangelical Theol. Soc., Soc. Bibl. Lit., Creation Research Soc., Near East Archeol. Soc. Author: The Modern Tongues Movement, 1967; Are These The Last Days?, 1970; Salvation Is Forever, 1973; The Virgin Birth: Doctrine of Deity, 1974; New Testament Survey, 1974; Called to be Saints, 1977. Home: 178 Palmer Dr PO Box 601 Cedarville OH 45314

GRONEK, STANLEY ANTHONY, banker; b. Chgo., July 29, 1951; s. Walter and Chesterine (Leos) G.; B.A., U. Wis., Madison, 1974; postgrad. Jagiellonian U., Cracow, Poland, 1973; now postgrad. in pub. adminstrn., Roosevelt U., Chgo., DePaul U. Law Sch. Trust adminstr. Sears Bank & Trust Co., Chgo., 1976—. Served with USNR, 1969-71. Kosciuszko Found. fellow, 1973. Mem. Internat. Pub. Personnel Assn., Am. Soc. Pub. Adminstrn., Ill. Paralegal Assn., Am. Bankers Assns., Christian Youth Orgn., Nat. Trust Historic Preservation, Phi Alpha Theta. Club: Kiwanis Key. Home: 3412 S Grove St Berwyn IL 60402 Office: Sears Bank & Trust Co Sears Tower Chicago IL 60606

GRONINGER, JAMES GRANT, investment banking co. exec.; b. Chgo., Mar. 25, 1944; s. Jack Miller and Nelda Jean (Roth) G.; B.S., Yale U., 1966; M.B.A., Harvard U., 1968; m. Elisabeth Rogers Jackson, June 20, 1969; 1 son, James Hunter. Staff mgmt. cons. Donald R. Booz & Assos., Chgo., 1968-71; corporate fin. partner William Blair & Chgo., 1971—; dir. Sabre Farms, Inc., Boardman, Oreg., Safeguard Bus. Systems, Inc., Ft. Washington, Pa. Bd. dirs. Bensenville (Ill.) Nursing Home. Clubs: Yale (treas.), Univ. (Chgo.). Home: 775 Lincoln Ave Winnetka IL 60093 Office: 135 S LaSalle St Chicago IL 60603

GRONKIEWICZ, EDMUND, lawyer; b. Chgo., Feb. 4, 1939; s. Edmund J. and Mary Ann (Balonek-Klimek) G.; A.B. summa cum laude, Loyola U. of Chgo., 1961, M.A. magna cum laude, 1963, J.D. cum laude, 1965. Admitted to Ill. bar, 1965; partner firm Morgan, Lanoff, Denniston & Madigan, Ltd., Chgo., 1969—. Pres. Chgo. Intercollegiate Council, 1965-66. Adv. bd. mem. St. Mary of Nazareth Hosp., 1971—, sec., 1976—. Recipient pub. service award St. Mary of Nazareth Hosp., 1972. Mem. Am., Ill., Chgo., West Suburban bar assns., Advocates Soc., Am. Soc. Hosp. Attys., Am. Coll. Legal Medicine (law affiliate), Blue Key, Phi Sigma Tau. Club: Chgo. Soc. of Polish Nat. Alliance. Contbr. articles to profl. jours. Home: 2346 Wesley Ave Berwyn IL 60402 Office: 1 First National Plaza Chicago IL 60670

GRONLI, JOHN VICTOR, coll. adminstr.; b. Eshowe, S. Africa, Sept. 12, 1932; s. John Einar and Marjorie Gellet (Hawker) G.; came to U.S., 1934; naturalized, 1937; B.A., U. Minn., 1953; M.Div., Luther Theol. Sem., 1958, D.Min., 1978; M.A., Pacific Luth. U., 1975; m. Jeanne Louise Ellertson, Sept. 15, 1952; children—Cheryl Marie Gronli Mundt, Deborah Raechel, John Timothy, Peter Jonas, Daniel Reuben. Ordained to ministry, 1958; pastor Brocket-Lawton Luth. Parish, Brocket, N.D., 1958-61; Harlowton (Mont.) Luth. Parish, 1961-66; sr. pastor St. Luke's Luth. Ch., Shelby, Mont., 1966-75; missionary Paulinum Sem., Otjimbingwe, Namibia, 1975-76; dean, chmn. dept. philosophy and humanities Golden Valley Luth. Coll., Mpls., 1976—; bd. dirs. Mont. Assn. Chs., 1973-75; sec. bd. for communications and mission support Am. Luth. Ch., 1973-75; mem. dist. council Rocky Mountain Dist., 1963-75, sec., 1963-70. Mem. personnel and guidance assns., Am., Minn. coll. personnel assns. Editor: Rocky Mountain Dist. Yearbook, 1963-70; Rocky Mountain Views, 1973-75; contbr. to Lutheran Standard, 1973-77; contbr. articles to religious jours. Home: 1321 Orkla Dr Minneapolis MN 55427 Office: 6125 Olson Minneapolis MN 55422

GRONLUND, ARTHUR CLARENCE, real estate broker; b. Fargo, N.D., Apr. 7, 1916; s. Olaf Anderson and Selina Marie (Samuelson) G.; student Interstate Bus. Coll., 1937; m. P. Virginia Eide, Aug. 24, 1956; 1 son, Robert David. Accountant, Internat. Harvester Co., Fargo, N.D., 1937-40, Bearson Motor Co., Fargo, 1944-50; auto dealer Clay Motors, Inc., Moorhead, Minn., 1950-55; real estate broker Universal Realty Co., Fargo, 1956—. Adv. bd. dirs. Fargo YMCA, 1947-50. Mem. Fargo-Moorhead Bd. Realtors (pres. 1975), N.D. Assn. Realtors, Minn. Assn. Realtors, Nat. Assn. Realtors, Realtors Nat. Mktg. Inst., Fargo C. of C., Sons of Norway. Republican. Lutheran. Elk. Home: 1418 S 8th St Fargo ND 58102 Office: PO Box 2265 510 4th Ave N Fargo ND 58102

GROPPI, JAMES E., clergyman, civic leader; b. Milw., 1930; m. Margaret Rozga, Apr. 22, 1976. Ordained priest Roman Cath. Ch.; asst. pastor St. Boniface Ch., Milw.; now mem. pastoral team St. Michael's Parish, Milw.; mem. Fellowship of Christian Ministries; lectr. on sexism in the Church, the Church and human rights. Active promotion civil rights legislation including open-housing ordinance Milw. Home: 1302 N 26th St Milwaukee WI 53205

GROSBERG, HERBERT LYNN, accountant; b. Detroit, Dec. 28, 1921; s. Benjamin and Hattie Ethel (Rhinowitz) G.; student U. Mich., 1940-43; certificate in accounting U. Detroit, 1947; m. Claire Yavitz, July 10, 1966; children—Pamela, Ilene, Richard, Linda. Pvt. practice accounting, Detroit, 1952—; partner Getto, Grosberg & Assos., Southfield, Mich., 1975—; chief exec. officer Bakrite Enameling Co., Ferndale, Mich., 1966-69; partner B&G Groves & Devel. Co., Homestead, Fla., 1954-74. Mem. Citizens Tax Advisory Com., State of Mich., 1957-58; past trustee Optometric Inst. of Detroit, McNamara Hosp., Warren, Mich. C.P.A., Mich. Mem. Internat. Assn. Fin. Planners, Am. Arbitration Assn., Am. Soc. Bus. and Mgmt. Cons., Engring. Soc. Detroit, Republican. Jewish. Clubs: Lions, Masons, Shriners. Home: 4011 Moselle Dr West Bloomfield MI 48033 Office: 501 Northland Towers E Southfield MI 48075

GROSBY, HERBERT LEON, investment co. exec.; b. St. Louis, June 22, 1919; s. Herman Garzell and Sarah (Zemansky) G.; student U. Ill. at Chgo., 1940-46, N.Y. Inst. Finance, 1947; m. Audrey Elaine Spiro, Aug. 20, 1950; children—Steven E., Sara Ann. Securities agt. Credit Thrift, Evansville, Ind., 1951-54; broker Merrill Lynch Pierce Fenner & Smith, Chgo., 1946-50, Bache & Co., Chgo., 1950-55; with Firstmark Corp. (formerly CIC Corp.), also Indpls. Morris Plan, 1955—, v.p. both firms, 1968—. Past pres. IHC Brotherhood; active United Fund, Jewish Welfare Fedn., Ind. Interreligious Commn. Human Equality. Bd. dirs. Anti- Defamation League, 1955-73, Jewish Community Center Indpls., Marion County Mental Health, Jewish Edn. Assn. Mem. Mental Health Bd., 1972-73. Mem. Indpls. C. of C., Indpls. Mus. Art Mason (Shriner), Elk, Lion (dir. Northside club 1973, now v.p.). Clubs: Columbia, Economic, Executive. Home: 8225 Windcombe Blvd Indianapolis IN 46240 Office: 110 E Washington St Indianapolis IN 46204

GROSKI, DONALD S., advt. agy. exec.; b. Johnston City, Ill., May 11, 1924; s. Stanley and Edith (Hoffman) G.; student DePaul U. Sch. Commerce, 1946-50; m. Helen Bazela, May 20, 1945; children—Donald S., Robert J. Staff accountant Wolf & Co., C.P.A.'s, Chgo., 1950-55; with Tatham-Laird & Kudner, Inc., Chgo., 1955-70, controller, 1965-70; v.p. finance I/MAC, Inc., 1970-73; treas. Marvin Advt. Co., 1973—, Prime Time Mktg., Inc., 1973-74; controller Kelly Scott & Madison, Inc., 1973—. Served with AUS, 1943-46. C.P.A., Ill. Mem. Ill. Soc. C.P.A.'s. Home: 501 Deborah Ln Mount Prospect IL 60056 Office: 1 IBM Plaza Chicago IL 60611

GROSS, ALLEN EUGENE, sch. adminstr.; b. Sidney, Nebr., Mar. 8, 1923; s. Frank and Lena Anna (Fastenau) G.; B.A., Midland Coll., 1949; M.A., Colo. State Coll., 1958; m. Mildred Anne Thomas, May 20, 1956; children—Arden Dale, Alison Anne. Asst. mgr. Farmers Elevator Co., Cozad, Nebr., 1950-51; tchr., coach, prin. Ericson (Nebr.) High Sch., 1951-58; tchr., prin. Albin (Wyo.) Pub. Sch., 1958-59; supt. Peetz (Colo.) Plateau Sch., 1959-61; Page (Nebr.) Pub. Schs., 1961-64, Glendo (Wyo.) Pub. Schs., 1964-65; prin. Plainview (Nebr.) Pub. Schs., 1965-67; supt. Meridian Reorganized Pub. Sch., Daykin, Nebr., 1967-77, Wheeler Central Schs., Bartlett, Nebr., 1977—. Served with AUS, 1943-45; ETO. Mem. Nebr. Council Sch. Adminstrs., Nebr. Edn. Assn., Am. Legion, VFW, Phi Delta Kappa. Republican. Lutheran (edn. com. 1968—). Lion, Odd Fellow. Home: PO Box 36 Bartlett NE 68622 Office: PO Box 68 Bartlett NE 68622

GROSS, BETHUEL (B.G.), educator, musician, composer, orgn. exec., columnist; b. Leavenworth, Kans., Mar. 7, 1910; s. Robert and Carrie (Hoefflin) G.; A.B., Mus.B., Washburn U., 1928; Mus.B., Mus.M., Northwestern U., 1930, B.Mus.Edn., 1932, Ph.D., 1941; M.A., Loyola U., 1965; pvt. study Am. Conservatory, 1931-36; postgrad. Eastman Sch. Music, 1939-40, U. Chgo., 1942-44; m. Doris Johnson, Aug. 26, 1949; children—Brent, Dean. Prof. music Tulsa U., 1929-30; dir. music George Williams Coll., 1939-41; head dept. music U. Akron, 1941-45; dir. grad. div. Ill. Wesleyan U., 1945-46; dean students, dir. music Shurtleff Coll., 1946-48; dir. tests and measurements DePaul U., 1948-50, Chgo. Conservatory, 1950-55, also dir. choral music; dir. collegium musicum, univ. organist Loyola U. Organist, dir. St. James Choir Sch., Meth. Ch., Chgo., 1937-50; minister music Buena Meml. Presbyn. Ch., Chgo., 1950-56; organist-dir. Baker Meml. United Meth. Ch., St. Charles, Ill., 1956—; minister edn. Peoples Ch. Chgo.; founder, gen. dir. South Shore Music Festival, Gary, Nat. Composers Clinic; condr. several sch., civic orchs. Bd. dirs. indsl. relations YMCA, Chgo., 1960; bd. dirs. Indsl. Services Center, Leaning Tower YMCA. Columnist, Adminstrn., Forum, Lerner and Chronicle Newspapers, Liberalists; mem. faculty Nat. Restaurant Assn. Exec. Seminars; commd. composer Nat. Fedn. Music Clubs, also WIND radio sta.; exec. sec. Northtown Indsl. Mgmt. Council, Northtown Vocational Council; moderator WGSB Town Hall of Air. Bd. dirs. Northwest Sch. Fine Arts, Suburban Mental Health Referral Center. Mem. A.S.C.A.P., Am. Psychol. Assn., Phi Delta Theta, Pi Kappa Lambda. Composer 6 organ symphonies, 11 oratorios, 2 symphonic poems, 20 anthems, 14 art songs, 10 piano works. Home: 45 Warwick Rd Winnetka IL 60093 Office: 6300 W Touhy Ave Chicago IL 60648

GROSS, GORDON E(DWARD), physicist, mech. engr.; b. Plattner, Colo., July 29, 1925; s. Ben and Edna Pearl (Nelson) G.; B.S., Central Mo. U., 1947; A.M., U. Mo., 1949; postgrad. U. Kans., 1950-52, Rheinische-Westfalische Technische, Germany 1963-64, U. Mo., 1974-75; m. Shirley Savage, Mar. 7, 1947; children—Gordon Edward, Allen Wallace, Gilbert Lee. Asst. prof. physics Northwestern Mo. U., Maryville, 1949-50; physicist Libby, Owens Ford Glass Co., Ottawa, Ill., 1952-53; physicist Midwest Research Inst., Kansas City, Mo., 1953-56, head physics sect., 1956-70, mgr. materials scis., 1970-73, prin. engr., 1973—; lectr. in physics U. Mo., Kansas City, 1973-74, Longview Community Coll., Kansas City, 1971-73. Served with USNR, 1944-46. Registered profl. engr., Mo., Kans., Colo. Mem. Am. Phys. Soc., Am. Inst. Energy Resource Mgmt., Am. Soc. Heating, Refrigeration and Air Conditioning Engrs., Nat. Soc. Profl. Engrs., Sci. Research Soc. N.Am., AAAS, Sigma Xi, Sigma Pi Sigma, Am. Radio League. Presbyterian. Contbr. articles in physics to sci. jours. Home: 11108 Kensington St Kansas City MO 64137 Office: 425 Volker Blvd Kansas City MO 64110

GROSS, HENRY EMMETT, petroleum engr., cartographer; b. Glendale, Mo., Aug. 8, 1906; s. Hugo Carl and Frieda (Bruno) G.; B.S., Mining Engr., Mo. Sch. Mines, 1928, E.M., 1934; M.S. in Mining Engring., U. Ill., 1933; m. Margrete Wilhelmine Brauer, Sept. 6, 1941. Mem. oil well drilling crew Shell Oil Co., Santa Fe Springs, Calif., 1928-29; engr. Pacific Western Oil Co., Los Angeles, 1929-31; research grad. asst. mining engr. U. Ill., 1931-33; petroleum engr. Shell Petroleum Corp., Tulsa, Okla., 1933-36; asst. prof. petroleum engring. U. Okla., 1936-38; asso. prof. petroleum engring. Tex. A. & M. Coll., 1938-42; chief reservoir engring. sec. Petroleum Adminstrn. for War Dist. 2. Chgo., 1942-45; chief petroleum engr. Kingwood Oil Co., Effingham, Ill., 1945-46; cons. engr., cartographer pub. maps, Webster Groves, Mo., 1946-72; owner H.E. Gross Maps, Webster Groves, 1946-72. Registered profl. engr., Ill., Mo., Tex. Mem. Am. Inst. Mining, Metall. and Petroleum Engrs. (sr., Legion of Honor 50-Year mem.), Am. Assn. Petroleum Geologists (emeritus), Tau Beta Pi. Lutheran. Invented marine foundation that was instrumental in exploiting continental shelves for petroleum, U. Okla., 1937; set forth drilling method for deep ocean floor that foretold Glomar Challenger operations. Patentee deep ocean salvage apparatus. Home and office: 1141 S Elm Ave Webster Groves MO 63119

GROSS, JAMES DEHNERT, pathologist; b. Harvey, Ill., Nov. 15, 1929; s. Max A. and Marian (Dehnert) G.; B.S. in Biology, U. Chattanooga, 1951; M.D., Vanderbilt U., 1955; m. Marilyn Agnes Robertson, Jan. 9, 1960; children—Kathleen Anne, Terrence Michael, Brian Andrew, Kevin Matthew. Rotating intern U.S. Naval Hosp., St. Albans, N.Y., 1955-56; resident in anatomic and clin. pathology Nat. Naval Med. Center, Bethesda, Md., 1956-59; dir. labs. St. Mary's Hosp., Streator, Ill., 1962—, pres. med. staff, 1972-73; instr. pathology and microbiology U. Tenn. Med. Sch., 1960-62; bd. dirs. La Salle County br. Am. Cancer Soc., 1966-68. Mem. parish council St. Anthony's Roman Cath. Ch., Streator, 1969-72. Served to lt. comdr. M.C., USNR, 1955-68. Diplomate Am. Bd. Pathology. Fellow Am. Soc. Clin. Pathologists, Coll. Am. Pathologists, Assn. Clin. Scientists (founder); mem. AMA, Ill. Med. Soc., Am. Assn. Blood Banks, Catholic Hosp. Assn., N.Y. Acad. Scis., Sigma Chi, Alpha Kappa Kappa. Republican. Clubs: K.C., Rotary (past dir.) (Streator). Home: 54 Sunset Dr Streator IL 61364 Office: 111 Spring St St Mary's Hosp Streator IL 61364

GROSS, JOHN DONALD, project engr.; b. Evansville, Ind., Sept. 28, 1951; s. Donald Robert and Sylvia Estelle (Whobrey) G.; B.S., U. Evansville, 1973; m. Donna Rae Reuter, June 21, 1975. Engr., Ashdee div. George Koch Sons, Inc., Evansville, Ind., 1973-75, project engr., 1975—. Mem. Soc. Automotive Engrs., ASME. Republican. Mem. United Ch. Christ. Home: 3512 Ridgeway Ave Evansville IN 47715 Office: 10 S 10th Ave Evansville IN 47702

GROSS, MILTON EUGENE, univ. dean; b. Pacific, Mo., Aug. 1, 1916; s. Eugene William and Florence Edna (Mayle) G.; B.J., U. Mo., 1939, M.A. in Journalism, 1941; m. Juliet Ixora Mayfield, June 1, 1940; children—Stephen, Philip, Kendal. With advt. dept. Vick Chem. Co., N.Y.C., 1940-41, Jefferson City (Mo.) News and Tribune, 1941; instr. Tex. Coll. of Mines, El Paso, 1941-42; from instr. to prof. U. Mo. Sch. Journalism, Columbia, 1942—, asst. dean, 1963-70, acting dean, 1970-71, asso. dean, 1971—; cons., U. Nebr., 1974—. Served with USNR, 1943-46. Recipient Faculty Alumni award U. Mo., 1973. Mem. Am. Assn. for Edn. in Journalism (accrediting com.), Am. Council on Edn. for Journalism (sec., treas. 1968—), Common Cause, Advt. Club St. Louis, Advt. Club Kansas City. Democrat. Home: 2100 Woodlea Dr Columbia MO 65201

GROSS, MORTIMER DAVID, psychiatrist; b. Newark, Sept. 22, 1921; s. Joseph and Rosalie (Kerner) G.; B.S., Poly. Inst. Bklyn., 1942; M.S., U. Akron, 1947; M.D., U. Chgo., 1950; m. JoAnn Brabenec, Oct. 10, 1952; children—David Joseph, Jonathan Paul. Intern, U. Ill. Hosps., Chgo., 1951; resident in psychiatry Elgin (Ill.) State Hosp., 1952, U. Ill., Chgo., 1953, Michael Reese Hosp., Chgo., 1954; practice medicine, specializing in psychiatry, Highland Park, Ill., 1955—; chmn. sect. on psychiatry Highland Park (Ill.) Hosp., 1960—; cons. Ill. State Psychiat. Inst., Chgo., 1956-74; clin. asso. prof. psychiatry, U. Ill. Med. Center at Chgo., 1962—; dean Forest Hosp. Postgrad. Center, Des Plaines, Ill., 1962-76. Chmn. Highland Park (Ill.) Lakefront Commn., 1974—. Fellow Am. Psychiat. Assn., Am. Soc. Social Psychiatry; mem. Am. Med. Assn. Rotarian. Author: (with W. C. Wilson) Minimal Brain Dysfunction, 1974. Home: 205 Sheridan Rd Highland Park IL 60035 Office: 1893 Sheridan Rd Highland Park IL 60035

GROSS, PHILLIP WILLIAM, JR., educator; b. Milw., Oct. 20, 1927; s. Phillip William and Mildred (Gregg) G.; B.S. in Chem. Engring., U. Wis., 1952; postgrad. Capitol U., 1966; Am. U., 1967, Ripon Coll., 1968; m. Mary Anne Suetholz, Oct. 9, 1954; children—Anne, Mary, Phillip T. Chem. engr. A.P. Controls, Milw., 1952, Pabst Brewing, Milw., 1954, Globe Union, Milw., 1954-62; tchr. Milw. Pub. Schs., 1963—. Mem. Shorewood (Wis.) Sch. Bd., 1969—, dist. clk., 1973-76, pres., 1977—. Chmn., Milw. County Young Republicans, 1956-58; state treas. Wis. Fedn. Young Reps., 1957-58. Served with AUS, 1946-47. NSF grantee, 1966-68. Mem. N.E.A. (life), U. Wis. Alumni Assn. (life), Milw. Tchrs. Edn. Assn. (exec. bd. 1967-73), Co-op. Ednl. Service Agy. (v.p. 1974-76), Nat. Assn. Parliamentarians, Am. Legion. Club: Shorewood Men's. Home: 4421 N Murray Ave Shorewood WI 53211 Office: 2751 S Lenox St Milwaukee WI 53207

GROSS, STUART DIEHL, coll. adminstr.; b. Vincennes, Ind., Feb. 2, 1914; s. Charles Adam and Winnie Amanda (McGillivary) G.; B.A., Hope Coll., Holland, Mich., 1936; m. Vernice Marian Lee, Aug. 5, 1939; children—Amy Kathleen Gross Grzesiak, Mary Alice Gross Daenzer. Reporter, Saginaw (Mich.) News, 1936-65, city editor, 1965-67; dir. community affairs Saginaw Valley State Coll,, Saginaw, Mich., 1967-76, asst. to pres., 1976—; cons., dir. Youth for Understanding, 1963-73; mem. Mich. Com. Financing Equitable Edn., 1975-77. Recipient Mich. Sch. Bell award Edn. Reporting, 1961. Author publs. in local history and edn. Home: 315 Kennely Rd Saginaw MI 48603 Office: 2250 Pierce Rd University Center MI 48710

GROSS, WILLIAM CHARLES, savs. and loan exec.; b. Elmhurst, Ill., Jan. 7, 1942; s. Leon August and Esther Marie (Ortenstone) G.; student No. Ill. U., 1959-60; B.S. in Accounting, Walton Sch., Chgo., 1963; m. Linda Sue Mansfield, June 1, 1963; children—Michelle Lynn, D'Anne Marie, Heather Sue. Sr. auditor Crofford H. Buckles & Co., C.P.A.'s, Chgo., 1963-66; mgr. financial div. Wolf & Co., C.P.A.'s, Chgo., 1966-67; chief internal auditor Hoyne Savs. & Loan Assn., Chgo., 1967-73; v.p. Marshalltown Savs. & Loan (Iowa), 1973— C.P.A., Ill., Iowa. Mem. Ill., Iowa socs. C.P.A.'s, Am. Inst. C.P.A.'s, Accounting Research Assn., Nat. Soc. Savs. and Loan Financial Officers, Marshalltown C. of C. (dir.). Republican. Lutheran. Clubs: Elmwood Country (sec.-treas., dir.), Rotary (Marshalltown). Home: 517 Eastview Rd Marshalltown IA 50158 Office: 303 W Main St Marshalltown IA 50158

GROSS, WILLIAM JOSEPH, city ofcl.; ; b. Toledo, Apr. 27, 1926; s. Clarence W. and Olive (Smith) G.; B.S., U. Toledo, 1950; m. Donna J. Munson, June 28, 1947; children—Marcia, Jeffery, James, Jacqueline. Asst. to city mgr. City Toledo, 1954-56, dir. pub. service, 1956-59; dep. dir. Ohio Hwy. Dept., Columbus, 1959-63; adminstr. Lucas County, Toledo, 1963-66; cons. civil engr., Toledo, 1966-68; safety service dir. City of Oregon (Ohio), 1967-68, safety service dir., chief adminstrv. officer, 1971—; city mgr. City Toledo, 1968-71. Served with USNR, 1944-46. Recipient merit award Toledo Area San. Dist., 1959. Registered profl. engr. and surveyor, Ohio, Mich. Mem. Am. Soc. C.E. (past pres. Toledo), Am. Right-of-Way Assn. (past regional dir.), Nat. Soc. Profl. Engrs., City Mgrs. Assn. Ohio, Internat. City Mgrs. Assn., Nat. League Cities, Am. Pub. Works Assn., Ohio Water Pollution Control Bd. Contbr. articles to tech. jours. Home: 3243 Shakespeare Lane Toledo OH 43615 Office: 5330 Seaman Rd Oregon OH 43616

GROSS, WILLIS CHARLES, JR., dentist; b. St. Louis, June 3, 1924; s. Willis Charles and Mary Ida (Kelly) G.; A.A., Harris Jr. Coll., 1943; D.D.S., St. Louis U., 1946; postgrad. U. Detroit, 1952-53; m. Rosemarie Dorothy Horak, Feb. 14, 1948; 1 son, Alan Charles. Commd. 1st lt. Dental Corps, U.S. Army and USAF, 1946, advanced through grades to maj., 1952; ret., 1953; pvt. practice dentistry, Affton, Mo., 1954—; pres. Willis C. Gross Dental Assos.; v.p. C & W Gross Corp.; dir. Washington Commerce Bank (Mo.). Served with AUS, 1942-44. Fellow Acad. Gen. Dentistry, Royal Soc. Health (Eng.); mem. Am., Mo. dental assns., St. Louis Dental Soc., Concord Village Bus. Men's Assn., Am. Legion, V.F.W., Alpha Sigma Nu, Omicron Kappa Upsilon, Delta Sigma Delta (pres., sec.-treas. St. Louis chpt.), Alpha Phi Omega. Republican. Mason (Shriner, 32 deg.), Lion (pres. Concord Village 1965-66). Clubs: Liberty Country (dir.) (Horine, Mo.); Big Game Hunters (St. Louis). Home: 20 Dorclin Ln St Louis MO 63128 Office: 7 Concord Center Dr Affton MO 63123

GROSSA, DOUGLAS Q., psychologist; b. Detroit, Nov. 6, 1942; s. Elvio Q. and Carmine (Falcone) G.; B.A., No. Mich. U., 1968; M.A., Central Mich. U., 1970, specialist in psychol. services, 1974. Clin. sch. psychologist Center for Human Devel., Mt. Pleasant, Mich., 1969-76, sr. staff psychologist, 1976-77; resource devel. and tng. specialist Dept. Mental Health, Mt. Pleasant, 1977—; psychol. examiner Vocat. Rehab. Services, Mt. Pleasant, 1972—; instr. in psychology Central Mich. U., 1974—. Served with USN, 1960-63. Certified psychol. examiner, Mich.; certified sch. psychologist, Mich. Mem. Am. Psychol. Assn., Am. Assn. Mental Deficiency, Mich. Assn. Profl. Psychologists. Home: 1512 W Broadway Mount Pleasant MI 48858 Office: PO Box 448 Mount Pleasant MI 48858

GROSSGUT, PAUL JOHN, financial cons.; b. Chgo., Jan. 30, 1943; s. Paul and Eleanor (Gracyas) G.; Ph.D. (Univ. fellow, Robert A. Welch Found. fellow), Tex. Christian U., 1971; M.B.A., U. Chgo., 1977; m. Gail Ann Glatzhofer, Sept. 2, 1967; children—Julie, Aaron, Heather. Asso. dir. research CNA, Ins., Chgo., 1971-76; cons. Am. Valuation Cons., Des Plaines, Ill., 1976—. Mem. Am. Statis. Assn., Am. Phys. Soc., Sigma Xi, Sigma Pi Sigma. Home: 1540 N Columbia St Naperville IL 60540 Office: 2200 E Devon St Des Plaines IL 60018

GROSSMAN, EDWIN, lawyer; b. St. Louis, Jan. 6, 1912; s. Morris and Sara (Sachs) G.; A.B., Washington U., St. Louis, 1931; J.D., Harvard U., 1934; m. Betty Greenfield, Sept. 29, 1940. Admitted to Mo. bar, 1934, U.S. Supreme Ct. bar, 1944; asso. firm Burnett, Stern and Liberman, St. Louis, 1934-42; with legal div. St. Louis Ordnance Dist., U.S. Army Ordnance Dept., 1942-46, chief, 1946—; dir. numerous corps. Pres., Planned Parenthood Assn. St. Louis; nat. v.p. Am. Council for Judaism, 1960-70, pres. St. Louis chpt., 1943—; treas. St. Louis Artists Guild; sec. Mycenaean Found.; mem. citizens adv. com. Homer Phillips Hosp.; bd. dirs St. Louis Inst. Music. Community Music Sch., Community Assn. Schs. for Arts, St. Louis Opera Theatre. Recipient commendation for Meritorious Civilian Service Army Services Forces, World War II. Mem. Mo., St. Louis bar assns., Am. Judicature Soc. Clubs: Westwood Country Noonday, Washington U. Faculty. Home: 4605 Lindell Blvd St Louis MO 63108 Office: 319 N 4th St St Louis MO 63102

GROSSMAN, HOWARD FORD, publisher; b. Plymouth, Ind., Oct. 22, 1903; s. Stacey Frederick and Cora May (Myers) G.; student Ind. U., Northwestern U.; m. Beulah Rhinehart, Jan. 9, 1924; children—Phyllis Elaine Massey, Rodger J.; m. 2d., Lois I. Morris, Nov. 27, 1971. Bookkeeper, H.J. Heinz Co., Kewanna, Ind., 1926; mng. editor, advt. mgr. Plymouth (Ind.) Daily Pilot, 1927-49; owner, pub. Salem Leader (Ind.), 1949-73, pub., 1973—, pres., mgr., 1965-73. Recipient Nat. Award Merit, Nat. Newspaper Assn. Republican. Methodist. Mason. Home: 100 Virginia Ave Salem IN 47167 Office: 117 E Walnut St Salem IN 47167

GROSSMAN, MORRIS M., accountant; b. Stropkov, Czechoslovakia, Apr. 26, 1918; s. Harry and Matilda (Goldberger) G.; certificate bus. adminstrn. Fenn Coll., 1947; student Western Res. U., 1948-53; m. Idelle Bialosky, Jan. 26, 1947; children—Richard, Debra, Marc. Office mgr. Am. Greetings Co., Cleve., 1937-41; examiner income, other taxes IRS, U.S. Govt. Treasury Dept., Cleve., 1944-53; pvt. practice as pub. accountant, tax cons., Cleve., 1973—; dir. Meyers Corrugated Box Co., Am. Internat. Funding Co., Taylor Elevator Co., Cedar Grandview Co., Exact Mold & Die Inc. Served with M.C., AUS, USAAF, 1942-44. Mem. Nat. Soc. Pub. Accountants, Am. Legion. Mason (32 deg.). Home: 2910 Washington Blvd Cleveland Heights OH 44118 Office: Hanna Bldg Cleveland OH 44115

GROT, JAMES STEPHEN, psychologist, educator, cons.; b. Ottawa, Ill., Apr. 26, 1943; s. Wilbur Walter and Eleanor Dorothy (Wruck) G.; B.S., Loyola U., Chgo., 1966; M.A., No. Ill. U., 1970, Ph.D., 1973; m. Sharon Pavett, Jan. 21, 1967; children—Jonathan, Kristin, Jennifer, James. Clin. psychology intern Galesburg State Research Hosp. (Ill.), 1970-71; staff psychologist Dixon (Ill.) Developmental Center, 1972-74, supervising psychologist, 1974—; asso. prof. Sauk Valley Coll., 1973—; psychol. cons. Midwest Speech and Hearing Assos., Ill., 1976—. Registered psychologist, Ill. Mem. Am., Midwestern psychol. assns., Am. Assn. Mental Deficiency, Lost Nation Lakes Assn., Sigma Xi. Contbr. articles in field to profl. jours. Home: Rural Route 4 Dixon IL 61020 Office: Dixon Developmental Center 2600 N Brinton St Dixon IL 61021

GROTE, MANFRED WILHELM, educator; b. Sulingen, Germany, Sept. 3, 1938; s. Ferdinand and Elisabeth (de Bruycker) G.; came to U.S., 1963, naturalized, 1969; student McPherson Coll., 1956-59; B.A., U. Kans., 1960, M.A., 1962; postgrad. Hamburg U., 1962-63; Ph.D., U. Md., 1967; m. Susanne Relyea Wilson, Sept. 26, 1966; 1 son, Manfred. Instr. polit. sci. U. Md., 1965-67; head polit. sci. dept. Calumet Campus, Purdue U., Hammond, Ind., 1968-74, asso. prof. polit. sci., 1974—. Mem. Am. Polit. Sci. Assn., Pi Sigma Alpha. Address: 7339 Van Buren Ave Hammond IN 46324

GROTH, BETTY, conservationist, author; b. Oak Park, Ill.; d. Herman A. and Bertha L. (Luepke) Groth; grad. Vassar Coll., 1932. Sec., Oak Park YMCA, 1935-42; sec. Ill. Commn. for Handicapped Children, 1943-46; pvt. sec. Chgo. Assn. Commerce and Industry, 1947-53, Chgo. Heart Assn., 1953-75. Mem. Save-The Dunes Council. Bd. dirs., v.p. Du Page County Clean Streams, 1967-69; bd. dirs., sec. Natural Resources Council Ill., 1967-69, vice chmn., 1970-71; v.p. conservation and dir. Ill. Audubon Soc., 1962-73, sec. bd. dirs., 1973-74; founder, chmn. No. Conservation Cabinet, 1970-75. Mem. Nat. Audubon Soc., North Central Audubon Council, The Morton Arboretum, Nat. Wildlife Fedn., Am. Bald Eagle Club, Conservation Explorers Club, (pres. 1975-77). Baptist. Club: Chgo. Vassar. Author: Open Spaces in Illinois, 1962; Surprise In The North Woods, 1966; Wildlife By John Burroughs Cabin, 1967; King's Ransom to Save a Prairie, 1968; Ivory Bills in Texas Big Thicket, 1969; Great Swamp Wildlife Refuge vs Jetport, 1970; The Fate of Thorn Creek Woods, 1971; Man's Dominion of the Green Earth, 1972; King of Sky, Land and Water, 1973; Country Estate, 1973; Ted's North Woods Shoreline, 1975. Contbr. articles to profl. jours. Home: Ten-0-Seven Front St Lisle IL 60532

GROTZINGER, LAUREL ANN, educator; b. Truman, Minn., Apr. 15, 1935; d. Edward F. and Marian Gertrude (Greeley) Grotzinger; A.B., Carleton Coll., 1957; M.S., U. Ill., 1958, Ph.D., 1964. Instr. asst. librarian Ill. State U., 1958-62; asst. prof. Western Mich. U., Kalamazoo, 1964-66, asso. prof., 1966-68, prof., 1968—, asst. dir. Sch. Librarianship, 1965-72. Mem. ALA, (sec.-treas. Library History Roundtable 1973-74), Assn. Am. Library Schs., Am. Assn. Higher Edn., Am. Soc. Info. Sci., Mich. Library Assn., AAUP (sec. W.M. chpt. 1968-70), Phi Beta Kappa (pres. Southwestern Mich. Assn. 1977-78), Beta Phi Mu (v.p., pres. Kappa chpt.), Pi Delta Epsilon, Alpha Beta Alpha. Author: The Power and the Dignity, Scarecrow, 1966; mem. editorial bd. Jour. Edn. for Librarianship, 1973-77, Dictionary Am. Library Biography, 1975-77; contbr. articles to profl. jours. Home: 313 Solon Ave Kalamazoo MI 49007

GROUNDS, PHILIP CLAYTON, profl. engr.; b. nr. St. Francisville, Ill., Aug. 8, 1936; s. George Carl and Mary Evelyn (Ramsey) G.; A.S., Vincennes U., 1957; B.S., U. Evansville, 1960; m. Linda Jo O'Haver, Oct. 31, 1960; 1 dau., Kelly Lynn. Project engr. Lester W. Routt & Assos., Vincennes, Ind., 1960-66, v.p., 1966-69; owner Philip C. Grounds, P.E., Vincennes, 1969—, also staff engr. Vincennes U., 1969—; pres. CCI Corp.; city engr. City of Vincennes, 1976—; instr. Vincennes U.; instr. refrigeration service Engrs. Soc. Mem. Nat. Soc. Profl. Engrs., ASME, Refrigeration Service Engrs. Soc., Wabash Valley Elec. Soc. (pres. 1971-72), Wabash Valley Engring. and Mfg. Soc. (sec. 1976-77). Elk. Club: Harmony Soc. (Vincennes). Home and Office: 803 Seminary St Vincennes IN 47581

GROVE, EWART LESTER, chemist; b. Greensburgh, Kans., May 31, 1913; s. William Ewart and Theo Etha (Grove) G.; B.Ed., St. Cloud State Coll., 1934-38; M.A., Ohio State U., 1945; Ph.D., Western U., 1951; m. Ethel Lucille Metcalf, June 12, 1944; children—Edward Lester, Ernest William. Tchr., Tyler (Minn.) High Sch., 1938-40, Cuyahoga Heights High Sch., Cleve., 1940-47; instr. Fenn Coll., 1942-44, Minn. State Tchrs. Coll., St. Cloud, 1947-48; research participant Oak Ridge Nat. Lab., summers 1953-54; asso. prof. U. Ala., 1951-59; research chemist, sr. scientist, mgr. analytical chemistry research Ill. Inst. Tech. Research Inst., Chgo., 1960-70; v.p. Freeman Labs., Inc., Rosemont, Ill., 1970-75; sr. scientist Ill. Inst. Tech. Research Inst., Chgo., 1976—. Mem. Am. Chem. Soc., Soc. Applied Spectroscopy, Am. Inst. Chemists, AAAS, AAUP, Sigma Xi. Methodist. Co-author math. textbooks. Editor: Developments in Applied Spectroscopy. Editor, contbr. Analytical Emission Spectroscopy, Vols. I-II, Applied Atomic Spectroscopy, Vols. I-II. Contbr. numerous articles to profl. jours. Home: 166 Lawler Ave Lombard IL 60148 Office: Ill Inst Tech Research Inst Chicago IL 60616

GROVE, HELEN HARRIET, historian, artist; b. South Bend, Ind.; d. Samuel Harold and LaVerne Mae (Drescher) Grove; grad. Bayle Sch. Design, Meinzinger Found., 1937-39, Washington U., 1940-42;

spl. studies, Paris, France. Owner studios of historic research and illustration, St. Louis, Chgo., 1943—; dir. archives, bus. history research Sears, Roebuck & Co., 1951-67; com. missions art and research for Northwestern U., Chgo.-Sears Roebuck & Co. Home: 6326 N Clark St Chicago IL 60626 Studio: 6328 N Clark St Chicago IL 60626

GROVE, KALVIN M., lawyer; b. Chgo., Aug. 27, 1937; s. Jacob S. and Hazel (Levitetz) G.; B.A., U. Mich., 1958; J.D., DePaul U., 1961; m. Eileen Dobbs, June 22, 1965; children—Pamela Joy, Jonathan. Admitted to Ill. bar, 1961; trial atty. NLRB, Tampa, Fla. and Chgo., 1962-65; pvt. practice law, Chgo., 1965—. Guest lectr. labor law DePaul U.; arbitrator Am. Arbitration Assn., Fed. Mediation and Conciliation Service. Mem. Gov. Kerner's Com. on Manpower, 1966-68. Served with AUS, 1962. Mem. Am., Ill., Fla. bar assns., Am. Judicature Soc. Contbr. articles to profl. jours. Office: Suite 7818 Sears Tower 233 S Wacker Dr Chicago IL 60602

GROVER, RICHARD KINSEL, dentist; b. Carson City, Mich., Oct. 7, 1921; s. Fred Otis and Lulu (Kinsel) G.; B.S., Mich. State U., 1943; D.D.S., U. Mich., 1954; m. Carolyn Rose Rourke, Oct. 9, 1954; children—Patricia Lou, Robert Rourke, Richard Kinsel, Michael David. Research chem. engr. Standard Oil N.J., Elizabeth, 1946-50; pvt. practice dentistry, Grandville, Mich., 1954—. Pres., dir. GGM Co.; dir. Croton Devel. Co. Served with AUS, 1943-46; PTO. Mem. W. Mich. Dental Soc. (past dir.), Am., Mich. dental assns., Tau Beta Pi, Omicron Kappa Upsilon, Grandville C. of C. (pres., dir. 1970), Phi Kappa Phi, Sigma Alpha Epsilon, Delta Sigma Delta. Clubs: Grandville Rotary (dir.); Sunnybrook Country; Innis Brook (Tarpon Springs, Fla.); Tamarron (Durango, Colo.). Mem. editorial bd. of Jour. Cryobiology, 1964-65. Contbr. articles to profl. jours. Patentee in field. Home: 3628 Chickasaw Ct Grandville MI 49418 Office: 3460 Wilson St SW Grandville MI 49418

GROVES, ANN BLAKESLEY, psychologist, educator; b. Houston, Sept. 6, 1934; d. Ralph C. and Mildred L. (James) Blakesley; B.A. in Psychology, Rice U., 1956; M.A. in Social Sci., U. Chgo., 1957; Ph.D. in Psychology, Ill. Inst. Tech., 1968; m. Marion H. Groves, June 1, 1963; children—Mariann Jama, Montgomery St. Clair. Caseworker children's div. Cook County Dept. Welfare, Chgo., 1958-59; instr. Thornton Community Coll., Harvey, Ill., 1959-62; intern Inst. Juvenile Research, Chgo., 1965-66; prof. psychology Chgo. State U., 1968—, chmn. dept., 1973-78, Recipient grants HEW, 1973, 76, Bd. Higher Edn., 1976, Dangerous Drugs Commn., 1975, 76. Mem. Am. Psychol. Assn., Am. Personnel and Guidance Assn., Chgo. Psychol. Club (pres. 1973-74). Home: 72 Shore Dr Ogden Dunes IL 46368 Office: 9500 S King Dr Chicago IL 60628

GROVES, DAVID UPDEGRAFF, mgmt. cons. co. exec.; b. Lexington, Mo., Nov. 10, 1926; s. William Lester and Adelaide Rebecca (Updegraff) G.; B.A., U. Md., 1950; M.A., Johns Hopkins, 1951; m. Nancy Jane Bustamante, June 23, 1951; children—Nancy Alice, Patricia Rebecca. Cartoonist, Stars & Stripes, 1946, Washington Post, 1947-48; artist, researcher syndicated newspaper feature Spotlight on Bus., 1949-51; cons. mgmt., pub. relations and indsl. relations Washington, 1951-54, Guatemala City, Guatemala, 1954-58, Havana, Cuba, 1958-60; gen. mgr. pub. and indsl. relations Relaciones Publicas Interamericanas S.A., Mexico City, Mexico, 1960-72; Midwest regional dir. Internat. Mgmt. Center, Cleve., 1973—; pres. David U. Groves and Assos., Cleve., 1977—; Mex. rep., Klein & Saks, mgmt. cons., Washington, 1967-72. Bd. dirs. Mexican Devel. Found., 1969-72, Fomento Educacional Found., Mexico City, 1971-72. Served with AUS, 1944-46. Mem. Am. C. of C. of Mexico (chmn. communication adv. com. 1971-72), Pub. Relations Soc. Am., Internat. Communication Assn., Shaker Heights (pres., dir. 1973—), Am. philatelic socs., Soc. Intercultural Edn., Greater Cleve. Growth Assn., Am. Acad. Polit. and Social Sci., Cleve. Council World Affairs. Roman Catholic. Clubs: University (Mexico City); Mid-Day (Cleve.). Home: 2648 Berkshire Rd Cleveland Heights OH 44106 Office: PO Box 22022 Cleveland OH 44122

GROVES, FRANKLIN NELSON, constrn. co. exec.; b. Mpls., Dec. 28, 1930; s. Frank M. and Hazel (Nelson) G.; B.B.A., U. Minn., 1954; m. Carolyn Mary Thomas, July 31, 1954; children—Catherine Mary, Franklin Nelson, Elizabeth Ann. Asst. sec., treas. S.J. Groves & Sons Co., Mpls., 1956-57, treas., 1957-64, v.p., treas., 1964-69, pres., 1969-71, chmn. bd., 1971—, also dir., pres. subsidiary corps., 1964—. Trustee Mpls. Soc. Fine Arts, Groves Found.; founder, officer, mem. bd. dirs. Groves Learning Center for Children with Learning Disabilities, 1971. Served to 1st lt. USAF, 1954-56. Mem. Beavers, Moles, Beta Gamma Sigma, Phi Beta Kappa. Congregationalist. Club: Minneapolis Athletic. Home: 1482 Hunter Rd Wayzata MN 55391 Office: 10000 Hwy 55 Minneapolis MN 55441

GRUBB, MERRITT BYRON, physician; b. Indpls., Oct. 31, 1941; s. Charles William and Phyllis Jean (Bailey) G.; student Wabash Coll., 1960-61, Ind. U., 1961-62, U. Stockholm (Sweden), 1962-63; M.D., Ind. U., 1967; m. Nancy Ann Seddelmeyer, Nov. 27, 1968; 1 son, Erik Byron. Intern, Bethesda Luth. Hosp., St. Paul, 1967-68; resident in dermatology, Ind. U., Indpls., 1970-73; practice medicine specializing in dermatology Med. Arts Clinic, Minot, N.D., 1973; instr. U.N.D., also asso. in medicine, 1973—. Served with USPHS, 1968-70. Bd. dirs. Med. Arts Clinic, 1976-77. Diplomate Am. Bd. Dermatology. Fellow Am. Acad. Dermatology, Soc. Investigative Dermatology; mem. AMA, N.D. Med. Assn., N.D. Dermatol. Soc., Minn. Dermatol. Soc., Nat. Muzzleloading Rifle Assn., Nat. Assn. Promitive Riflemen, Am. Legion, Nat. Wildlife Fedn. Clubs: Ducks Unlimited, Minot Gun. Home: Rt 1 Burlington ND 58722 Office: 120 4th Ave SE Minot ND 58701

GRUBER, CHARLES A., city ofcl.; b. Chgo., Mar. 24, 1947; s. Florian Charles and Millicent Vivian G.; B.A., Elmhurst Coll., 1972; student So. Police Inst., 1974; m. Linda Marie Stark, Feb. 7, 1970; children—Daniel, Gini, Kenneth. With Adison (Ill.) Police Dept., 1968-76, watch comdr., ops. comdr., to 1976; police chief Quincy, Ill., 1976—; mem. Ill. Law Enforcement Commn., 1977—. Served as sgt. USMC, 1964-68; Vietnam. Mem. Addison Jaycees (v.p. 1974, Outstanding Law Enforcement Officer 1974), Ill. Jaycees (state program chmn. 1974), Central Ill. Police Chiefs Assn., Internat., Ill. assns. chiefs of police, Fraternal Order Police. Clubs: Exchange, Quincy Country, K.C. Home: 610 Kimberly Ct Quincy IL 62301 Office: 507 Vermont St Quincy IL 62301

GRUBER, CHARLES LAMAR, corp. dir.; b. Elkhart, Ind., 1937; s. George Marlin and Lillie Ellen (Rowe) G.; B.S. in Accounting, Ball State U., 1959; m. Paula Francis Bolerjack, Aug. 22, 1959; children—Darcy, Dexter, Barton. Accountant General Motors Corp., Muncie, Ind., 1959; divisional staff accountant Kroger Co., Cin., 1960-62, plant controller, 1962-63, corp. programmer analyst, 1963-64; field auditor Montgomery Ward Co., Cin., 1964-65, met. sr. auditor, Chgo., 1965-66, supervising sr. auditor, St. Paul, 1966-68; divisional controller Sta-Rite Industries, Inc., Delavan, Wis., 1968-71, corp. dir. data processing, 1971—; police officer City of Delavan, 1975—. Pres., Walworth County Assn. for Retarded Citizens, 1974—, Boy Scouts of Am. Served with AUS, 1960. Mem. Soc. Certified Data Processors, Blue Key Nat. Honor Soc., K.C., Lion. Home: 708 Tyrell Ave Delavan WI 53115 Office: 234 E 8th St Delavan WI 53115

GRUENSFELDER, ROBERT CHARLES, govt. ofcl.; b. St. Louis, Mar. 24, 1938; s. Roland and Florence R. (Mueller) G.; B.S., St. Louis U., 1960, M.S.W., 1967; m. Joan Gertrude Wetstein, Jan. 23, 1960; children—Susan, Joanne, Mary, Robert, Valerie, Anita, Carolyn. Probation officer St. Louis County (Mo.), 1963-68, chief probation officer, 1968-69, dir. div. of adult correctional instn., 1969-73; exec. dir. Mo. Council on Criminal Justice, Jefferson City, 1973-75; dir. ops. Region V Law Enforcement Assistance Adminstrn., Chgo., 1975-77, area dir., 1977—. Mem. Nat. Conf. State Criminal Justice Planning Adminstrn., 1973-75; instr. criminal justice St. Louis U., 1967-71, U. Mo., St. Louis, 1971-73; nat. correctional cons., 1967-75. Chmn. Sch. Bd. St. Andrews Elementary Sch., St. Louis, 1970-71; mem. Mo. Law Enforcement Assistance Council, 1973. Mem. adv. bd. St. Louis U., 1972-75; trustee Notre Dame Coll., St. Louis. Served with USAF, 1960-63. Recipient Achievement award Air Def. Command, 1963. Mem. Am. Correctional Assn., Mo. Corrections Assn. (pres. 1970), Greater St. Louis Probation and Parole Assn. (v.p. 1969-71), Acad. Certified Social Workers, Am. Soc. Crime, Internat. Assn. Chiefs of Police, Nat. Jail Assn. (v.p. 1971-72), Nat. Council Crime and Delinquency, St. Louis U. Alumni Assn. (pres. 1968-70), Alpha Sigma Nu. Home: 1561 Henry Ave Des Plaines IL 60016 Office: 3166 Des Plaines Ave Des Plaines IL 60018

GRUENWALD, GEORGE HENRY, advt. and mktg. co. exec.; b. Chgo., Apr. 23, 1922; s. Arthur Frank and Helen (Duke) G.; B.S., Northwestern U., 1947; student Evanston Acad. Fine Arts, 1937-38, Chgo. Acad. Fine Arts, 1938-39, Grinnell Coll., 1940-41, U. Florence (Italy), 1945; m. Corrine Rae Linn, Aug. 16, 1947; children—Helen Marie (Mrs. M.T. Orlando, Jr.), Paul Arthur. Ednl. dir. Uarco Inc., 1947, asst. to pres., 1947-49; mdse. mgr., creative dir. Willys-Overland Motors Co., 1949-51; brand, advt. mgr. Toni Co., 1951-53; creative dir., account exec. Edward H. Weiss Co., 1953-55; v.p., accounts supr. North Advt., Inc., Chgo., 1955-65, sr. v.p., mgmt. supr., dir. planning and devel., 1965-67, exec. v.p., 1967-71; pres. Pilot Products Industries, Inc., Chgo., 1964-71, Advance Brands, Inc., Chgo., 1966-71; exec. v.p. Campbell-Mithun, Inc., Mpls., 1971, pres., 1972—. Chmn., Twin Cities Ednl. TV; vice chmn. Minn. Pub. Radio. Trustee Chgo. Pub. TV, Mpls. Soc. Fine Arts. Served with USAAF, 1943-45; MTO. Mem. Art Inst. Chgo., Am. Assn. Advt. Agys. (mgmt. com.), Am. Mktg. Assn., Deru, Sigma Delta Chi, Phi Gamma Delta. Methodist. Clubs: Tavern (Chgo.); Wayzata (Minn.) Country; Minneapolis. Editor-in-chief Oldsmobile Rocket Circle mag., 1956-65. Hudson Family Mag., 1955-56. Creator numerous packaged consumer products. Home: 1725 Hunter Dr Wayzata MN 55391 Office: Illinois Center Bldg 111 E Wacker Dr Chicago IL 60601 also 1000 Northstar Center Minneapolis MN 55402

GRUMBLES, CARL EDWIN, educator; b. Hammond, Ind., Dec. 20, 1941; s. Edward Eugene and Frances Harriet (Moore) Grumbles; B.A., Purdue U., 1965; M.A., Northeastern Ill. U., 1976; m. Donnejean Ferner, Sept. 2, 1966; children—Jack, Dan, Scot, Chris. Asst. editor Leader, mag. Christian Service Brigade, Wheaton, Ill., 1966-68; tchr., prin. Open Door Children's Home, Hazard, Ky., 1968-69; tchr. Lombard (Ill.) Sch. Dist. 44, 1969—. Vol. counselor Christ Ch. Oak Brook Counseling Center, 1976—, Lafayette Juvenile Delinquents, 1963-64, Bethany Children's Home, 1962-64; counselor, program dir., camp dir. Camp Kaskitowa, 1966-74; mem. precinct com. Republican party, 1976—; bd. dirs. Lombard YMCA, 1976—. Recipient award Outstanding Merit Christian Camping, Central Camping Assn., 1972, Outstanding Young Educator award Lombard Jaycees, 1972. Mem. Lombard, Nat. (life), Ill. edn. assns., Am. Personnel and Guidance Assn., Am. Sch. Counseling Assn. Home: 5709 Essex St Lisle IL 60532 Office: Sch Dist 44 Lombard IL 60148

GRUNDMAN, ROSE ANN, educator; b. Chgo., Oct. 30, 1926; d. Paul Albert and Rose (McGilvray) Grundman; B.S., Northwestern U., 1947, M.S., 1948. Instr. math. U. Ariz., 1948-49, U. Ill. Med. Center, Chgo., 1949-57, asst. prof. math. and statistics, 1957-72, asso. prof., 1972—. Mem. Am. Math. Soc., Math. Assn. Am., A.A.A.S., Am. Statis. Assn., A.A.U.P. (sec.-treas. chpt. 1960—), Acad. Pharm. Scis., Phi Beta Kappa, Sigma Xi, Chi Omega. Methodist. Contbr. numerous articles to profl. jours. Home: 2626 Lakeview St Chicago IL 60614

GRUNDMANIS, JOHN VISVALDIS, architect; b. Liepaja, Latavia, Aug. 9, 1926; s. Christopher and Luise (Dobele) G.; came to U.S., 1950, naturlized, 1955; student Munich (Germany) Inst. Tech., 1949; B.Arch., U. Minn., 1954, postgrad., 1968; postgrad. U. Calif. at Berkeley, 1969, U. Wis., 1970, Mpls. Coll. Art and Design, 1971; m. Ieva Metra, June 21, 1975; children from previous marriage—Ava Biminita, Marcis Visvaldis, Lauris Janis. Draftsman-architect-designer Hills, Gilbertson & Fisher, architects, Mpls., 1954-66; sr. architect for maj. projects Minn. Mining & Mfg. Co., St. Paul, 1966-71; profl. asso. Ellerbe Architects-Engrs.-Planners, Bloomington, Minn., 1971—. Licensed architect, Ala., Calif., Fla., Ill., Ind., Iowa, Mass., Mich., Minn., Mo., Nebr., N.Y., Okla., Pa., S.D., Tex., Wis. Mem. AIA, Minn. Soc. Architects, Lettonia. Lutheran (deacon 1964—). Prin. archtl. works include: Decorative Products Plant, Nevada, Mo., lab. and office bldg. Chemolite, Minn., Med. Products Plant, Brookings, S.D., Rochester (Minn.) Meth. Hosp., Irvin Army Hosp., Ft. Riley, Kans., St. Paul Ramsey Med. Center, Gillette Children's Hosp., St. Paul, St. Luke Hosp., Cedar Rapids, Iowa, St. Raphael Hosp., New Haven, Mother Frances Hosp., Tyler, Tex. Home: 185 NE Hartman Circle Fridley MN 55432 Office: 1 Appletree Sq Bloomington MN 55420

GRUNDSTROM, DONALD WILLIAM, mfg. co. exec.; b. Taylor Ridge, Ill., Jan. 12, 1923; s. Gust Gunnar and Harriet (Carothers) G.; student Wheaton Coll., 1943; m. Betty Mae Keuter, July 26, 1956; 1 stepdau., Judith Ann. With John Deere Co., 1941—, supt. foundry, Dubuque, 1951-71, supt. foundry, Tractor Works div., Waterloo, 1971-77, works mgr., 1977—. Served with U.S. Army, 1943-46. Mem. Am. Foundrymens Soc., Waterloo C. of C. Republican. Clubs: US Power Squadron, Julien Dubuque Yacht, Elks, Rotary. Home: 3384 Monticello Ave Waterloo IA 50701 Office: 400 Westfield Ave Waterloo IA 50704

GRUNEWALD, ALVIN HERBERT, dentist; b. Athens, Wis., Sept., 20, 1906; s. Gustav G. and Alvina (Koepp) G.; B.S., Marquette U., 1930, D.D.S., 1931; M.S., Georgetown U., 1949; m. Gertrude Eleanor Welsch, July 22, 1945; children—Ann Louise, Mary Margaret (Mrs. Paul Counsell). Practice dentistry, Milw., 1931-34; commd. lt. (j.g.) U.S. Navy, 1931, advanced through grades to capt., 1950; research asso. U.S. Bur. Standards, 1947-49; ret., 1957; prof., chmn. dept. prosthetics Dental Sch. Northwestern U., Chgo., 1957-70; pvt. prosthodontic practice, Mayville, Wis., 1970—. Fellow Am. Coll. Dentists, Acad. Denture Prosthetics, Am. Coll. Prosthodontists; mem. Am. Dental Assn., Am. Legion, Acad. Denture Prosthetics (pres. 1972, sec.-treas. 1973—), Am. Prosthodontic Soc., Internat. Assn. Dental Research, Tau Epsilon Delta (pres. 1944, sec.-treas. 1957), Omicron Kappa Upsilon. Rotarian. Home and office: 5 Cottonwood Ln Mayville WI 53050

GRUNSFELD, ERNEST ALTON, III, architect; b. Chgo., June 5, 1929; s. Ernest Alton and Mary Jane (Loeb) G.; student Art Inst. Chgo., 1947; B.Arch., Mass. Inst. Tech., 1952; m. Sally Riblett, July 10, 1954; children—Marcia, John Mace. Pvt. practice as architect, Chgo., 1954-56; partner Yerkes & Grunsfeld, Chgo., 1956-65; owner Grunsfeld & Assos., architects, Chgo., 1965-75, sr. partner, 1975—. Vice-pres. Urban Gateways, 1969—, dir., 1968—; mem. Highland Park Plan Commn., 1969-75. Bd. dirs., chmn. Grunsfeld Fund, 1965—; mem. council for arts Mass. Inst. Tech., 1977—. Served to 1st lt. USAF, 1952-53. Recipient First Honor award Burlington Mills, 1968. Mem. AIA (corp. mem., Distinguished Bldg. award 1962, 69), Art Inst. Chgo. (life), Field Mus. Natural History (life), Oriental Inst. Chgo., Chgo. Symphony Soc. (hon. life). Clubs: City (dir.), Tavern, Mass. Inst. Tech. (Chgo.); Lakeshore Country (Highland Park, Ill.). Contbr. articles to profl. jours. Office: 520 N Michigan St Chicago IL 60611

GRUNWALD, MARY ELLEN, lawyer, plastic mfg. co. exec.; b. Bklyn.; d. Edwin J. and Helen M. (Brzezinska) Grunwald; B.S., Bklyn. Coll.; LL.B., N.Y. Law Sch.; postgrad. No. Ill. U. Admitted to N.Y. bar; law clk. Hays St. John Abramson and Heilbron, N.Y.C.; reading specialist Dist. 300, Ednl. Bd., Carpentersville, Ill., 1970-75; v.p. adminstrn. Plas-Met. Corp., Schaumburg, Ill., 1975—, dir., 1976—; legal cons., 1975—. Mem. Soc. of Plastic Engrs., Arista Soc., Phi Beta. Contbr. articles on a state's legal responsibilities for pub. safety to newspapers. Office: 1380 Mithcell Blvd Schaumburg IL 60193

GUARNIERI, DONALD LEWIS, lawyer; b. Warren, Ohio, May 8, 1934; s. Albert A. and Elsie C. (McKay) G.; A.B., Hiram Coll., 1956; LL.B., Cleve. State U., 1960, LL.M., 1963, J.D., 1964; m., July 11, 1970; 1 son, Lewis Donald. Admitted to Ohio bar, 1960; pvt. practice law, Warren, 1960—; land developer; pres. Champion Mall Corp., Parkhurst Mall Corp., Norwalk Mall Corp. Commr. Little All Am. Football; bd. dirs. A.R.C., Family Service Assn., Civic Music Assn., Warren Symphony, Youngstown Symphony. Served with AUS, 1957. Elk, Moose, Eagle, Kiwanian, K.C. Clubs: Mosquito Yacht (Cortland, Ohio); Olympic, Trumbull (Warren). Author: 8th Day of May, 1968. Contbr. articles to profl. jours. Home: 399 Golf Dr Warren OH 44481 Office: 151 E Market St Warren OH 44481

GUBBINS, JOAN MARGARET (MRS. DALE GEORGE GUBBINS), state senator; b. N.Y.C., July 2, 1929; d. Arthur L. and Margaret (Hedge) Barton; student U. Ill., 1947-49; m. Dale George Gubbins, May 6, 1949; children—Gregory Dale, Carol Jane. Mem. Ind. Senate, 1969—. Vice pres. Nat. Commn. on Status of Women. Research chmn. Ind. Goldwater for Pres. Com., 1964; del. Ind. Republican State Conv., 1966, 68, 70, 74; Rep. precinct committeewoman, Indpls., 1966-70. Mem. Nat. Fedn. Rep. Women, Ind. State Legislators Club, Citizens Forum, Pro America, Poet's Corner (hon.), Am. Contract Bridge League, Central Ind. Bridge Assn., Alpha Chi Omega. Mem. Missionary Alliance Ch. Home: 1000 E 81st St Indianapolis IN 46240

GUDENAS, JOHN WAYNE, computer scientist; b. Chgo., Aug. 5, 1946; s. Andrew J. and Irene E. (Rakauskas) G.; B.S. in Physics, Ill. Benedictine Coll., 1968; M.S. in Info. Sci., Ill. Inst. Tech., 1971; m. Patricia Barlett, July 11, 1970; 1 dau., Juliet. Computer scientist Argonne (Ill.) Nat. Lab., 1968-73; sr. analyst Standard Oil Co. Ind., Chgo., 1973-77; pres., dir. Valentine Equipment Co., Inc., Bridgeview, Ill., 1977—. Mem. Assn. Computing Machinery. Contbr. articles on air quality to profl. jours. Home: 215 S Edgewood St LaGrange IL 60525

GUDERLEY, GEORGE WARREN, JR., hwy. engr.; b. Chgo., Oct. 12, 1922; s. George W. and Alma (Matthies) G.; student Ill. Inst. Tech., 1940-49; m. Lois R. Christell, Sept. 3, 1949; children—Susan Gail, George W. III. Chief engr. adminstrn. Cook County Hwy. Dept., Chgo., 1946-68; exec. dir. Ill. Toll Hwy. Authority, Oakbrook, Ill., 1969-72; asso. Brighton Engring. Co., Frankfort, Ky., 1972—. Mem. Ill. Hwy. Research Council, 1962-72, chmn. sub-com. for research mgmt., 1969-72. Trustee, Village of Inverness, Ill., 1969—; mem. exec. bd. Northwest Suburban council Boy Scouts Am., 1969—. Served with USAAF, 1942-45, USAF, 1951-53, 62; maj. Ret. Decorated Air Medal with oak leaf cluster, Purple Heart. Mem. Chgo. Assn. Commerce and Industry, Res. Officers Assn. (pres. 1963), Computer User's Exchange Orgn. (chmn. hwy. design com. 1961), Am. Pub. Works Assn., Ill. Transp. Council (pres.), N.W. Municipal Conf. Home: 1482 W Banbury Rd Inverness PO Palatine IL 60067 Office: 830 E Higgins Rd Schaumburg IL 60195

GUELKER, FRANCIS THEODORE, mfg. co. exec.; b. St. Louis, Feb. 3, 1922; s. Theodore Henry and Anna Marie (Schlangen) G.; B.S., Washington U., 1954; M.B.A., St. Louis U., 1962; m. Catherine Marie Purdum, Dec. 29, 1945; children—Anne Catherine, Catherine Lucille, Thomas Francis. Adminstr., Laclede Christy Co., St. Louis, 1946-50; with White Rodgers div. Emerson Electric Co., St. Louis, 1950-72, v.p., dir., 1969-72, corporate group v.p., 1972—; vice chmn. Emerson P.R., Inc., 1969—; instr. bus. adminstrn. St. Louis Jr. Coll. Dist., 1964-66. Pres. Flora Place Assn., 1966-67. Bd. dirs. Assos. St. Louis U. Libraries. Served with Signal Corps AUS, 1941-45, ETO. Recipient Language award St. Louis German Club, 1940. Mem. Pvt. Libraries Assn. (Eng.), Am. Printing History Assn., Am. Mgmt. Assn., Franklin Library. Clubs: Media, Benton Dramatic (St. Louis). Home: 4052 Flora Pl St Louis MO 63110 Office: 8100 Florissant St Louis MO 63136

GUENDLING, JOHN EDWARD, author; b. Buffalo, N.Y., Jan. 8, 1928; s. John Edmund and Edna Catherine (Datzman) G.; student U. Notre Dame, 1948-49; B.S., Columbia, 1952, M.A., 1953, postgrad., 1960-63. Fgn. service officer U.S. Dept. State, 1955-60, vice consul, Munich, Frankfurt, Warsaw; mem. faculty philosophy Columbia, 1961-63, Purdue U., 1963-64, Ark. Tech. Coll., 1964-70. Served with AUS, 1945-46. Mem. Am. Catholic Philos. Assn., Am. Polit. Sci. Assn., Am. Hist. Assn. Author: America: The Dream As Nightmare, 1970; Value Systems, 1973. Editor: Values In Crisis, 1969. Contbr. articles on philosophy and history to profl. jours. Address: 806 E 5th St Fowler IN 47944

GUENTHER, DENNIS ALFRED, mech. engr., educator; b. Cleve., Sept. 29, 1946; s. Alfred Edward and Ellen (Manuel) G.; B.M.E., Purdue U., 1968; postgrad. (fellow), Princeton U., 1968-69; M.Sc., Ohio State U., 1971, Ph.D., 1974; m. Judith Ann Hawley, Mar. 20, 1971; children—Dax Alexander, Derek Allan. Asst. prof. mech. engring. Ohio State U., Columbus, 1974—; dir. engring. Systems Engring. Assos., Atlanta and Tampa, Fla., 1974—. Registered profl. engr., Ohio, W.Va., Ind., Mich., Ky., Ga., N.C., S.C., Md., Pa., Tenn. Mem. Nat. Soc. Profl. Engrs., Nat. Safety Council, ASME, Am. Soc. Safety Engring., Edn., Am. Soc. Engring. Edn., ASTM, AAUP, Acoustical Soc. Am., Soc. Automotive Engring. Presbyterian. Contbr. articles in field to profl. jours. Home: 1951 Glenn Ave Columbus OH 43212 Office: 7349 Worthington Galena Rd Columbus OH 43085

GUENTHER, FRANCIS HARVEY, banker; b. Sheboygan Falls, Wis., May 19, 1915; s. Frank and Margaret Olga (Erbach) G.; student U. Wis., 1954; m. Etta Freyberg, Aug. 20, 1938; children—Marilyn, William, Carol, Joyce. Asst. v.p. Citizens Bank Sheboygan (Wis.), office mgr., Sheboygan Falls, 1952—; v.p., dir. Sheboygan Falls Mut. Ins. Co., 1973—. Bd. dirs. Mobile Meals Sheboygan County, Community Service Council Sheboygan County. Served with USN, 1945-46. Mem. Fox River Valley Safe Deposit Assn. (past pres.), Sheboygan Falls C. of C. (pres.). Club: Lions. Supt., treas. Sunday Sch., tchr. at camp, Bethel Baptist Ch. Home: 216 Crestwood Dr

Sheboygan Falls WI 53085 Office: 806 Monroe St Sheboygan Falls WI 53085

GUENTZEL, RICHARD DALE, historian; b. Mankato, Minn., Jan. 1, 1934; s. Edgar Theodore and Harriet Louise (Dimmel) G.; B.S., Mankato State U., 1955, M.S., 1964; Ph.D. (Heitzmann fellow), U. Nebr., 1976; m. Evelyn Carol Nelson, Aug. 7, 1965; children—Melanie Jane, Heather Lynn. History tchr. Litchfield (Minn.) High Sch., 1955-57, Mound (Minn.) High Sch., 1960-64, John Marshall High Sch., Rochester, Minn., 1965-66; instr. history Austin (Minn.) Community Coll., 1967—. Served with U.S. Army, 1957-59, 60-61. Named Outstanding Social Studies Grad. Mankato State U., 1955. Mem. Minn. Community Coll. Faculty Assn., Am. Hist. Assn., Nebr., Minn. hist. socs., Phi Alpha Theta. Democrat. Lutheran. Contbr. articles to profl. jours. Home: 1104 6th Ave NW Austin MN 55912

GUENTZLER, RONALD EDWARD, educator; b. Cleve., May 17, 1934; s. Edward Frederick and Mary (Prochaska) G.; B.S. in Elec. Engring., Case Inst. Tech., 1956, M.S. in Elec. Engring., 1963; children—Judy Louise, Gretchen Suzanne. Asst. engr. transmission and protection sect., gen. engring. dept. Ohio Bell Telephone Co., Cleve., 1956-60; lectr., instr. Tech. Inst., dept. elec. engring. Fenn Coll., Cleve., 1956-67; asso. prof. dept. elec. engring. Ohio No. U., Ada, 1967—. Emergency communications coordinator A.R.C., Ada, 1973—. Mem. I.E.E.E. (sr.), Am. Radio Relay League, Tau Beta Pi, Eta Kappa Nu. VHF editor RTTY Jour., 1967—. Contbr. articles to profl. jours. Home: 212 Grandview Blvd Ada OH 45810

GUERNSEY, PATRICIA JANE, hotel exec.; b. Salina, Kans., Oct. 12, 1921; d. William Russell and Beulah Louise (Allen) Royse; ed. Edler Ballet Sch.; m. Russell Lund Guernsey, July 12, 1945; children—Jeffrey Russell, Michael Royse. With Rathburn Sch. Dance, 1936-41, Nat. Cath. Community Service Women's Div., USO, 1943-44; sec. to dir. Salina YMCA, 1946-47; social dir. St. John's Sch., Salina, 1949-61; office mgr. Salina Community Inns Am., Inc., 1962-68; dir. sales Salina Hilton Inn, 1968-70, pres., gen. mgr., 1975—; sec.-treas. Salina Community Inns of Am., 1968-75. Former v.p. Salina County Republican Women; former pres. 20th Century Forum, Salina P.T.A., Christ Episcopal Women; precinct committeewoman, 1974—. Named Kans. hotel/motel person of year, 1975. Mem. Am. (bd. dirs.), Kans. (past pres.) hotel and motel assns., Kans. Restaurant Assn., Kans. Assn. Commerce Industry, Salina Area C. of C. (bd. dirs.), Kans. Food Lodging Adv. Com. (chmn.). Home: 112 Overhill Rd Salina KS 67401 Office: PO Box 1363 Salina KS 67401

GUERTAL, ROCHELLE, religious order adminstr.; b. Canton, Ohio, June 11, 1946; d. John Norman and Nadyne Veronica (Leahy) Guertal; B.S.E., St. John Coll., 1974; postgrad. John Carroll U., 1976—. Joined Order Sisters of Most Holy Trinity, Roman Catholic Ch., 1964; tchr. St. John Vianney Sch., Bronx, 1967-68, St. Rocoo Sch., Cleve., 1968-70, 72-75, St. Ann Sch., Bristol, Pa., 1970-71, Nativity Sch., Brandon, Fla., 1971-72; formation directress Sisters of Most Holy Trinity, Euclid, Ohio, 1975—. Mem. exec. bd. Sisters Senate, Diocesan Pastoral Council, Diocesan Liturgy Commn., Nat. Sister Vocation Conf. Mem. Am. Personnel and Guidance Assn., Am. Sch. Counselor Assn. Home: 21320 Euclid St Euclid OH 44117

GUEST, M. I., educator; b. New Smyrna Beach, Fla., Jan. 6, 1921; s. Marion Ashby and Hattie (Rawls) G.; student N.Y. U., 1956-57; B.Arch., U. Fla., 1948; M.Pub. Adminstrn., City U. N.Y., 1963; m. Louise Marie Blake, Aug. 5, 1961; children—Matthew Blake, Laura Louise. Design draftsman Loyd Frank Vann, A.I.A., Miami, Fla., 1948-49; joined U.S. Army C.E., 1950, advanced through grades to lt. col., 1962; dep. dir. U.S. Army Engr. Waterways Expt. Sta., Vicksburg, Miss., 1963-66; ret., 1966; prof., chmn. constrn. dept. Bradley U., Peoria, Ill., 1966—. Pres. Asso. Schs. Constrn., 1970-72. Served to capt., inf. AUS, 1942-46. Decorated Bronze Star medal. Recipient Faculty Service award Coll. City N.Y., 1961. Mem. Am. Inst. Constructors (dir.), AIA (profl. affiliate), Am. Mgmt. Assn. Phi Kappa Phi. Presbyterian. Mason (32 deg.). Office: 117 Morgan Hall Bradley U Peoria IL 61625

GUETH, THOMAS FRANKLIN, elec. engr.; b. Columbus, Ohio, Jan. 18, 1950; s. Clarence Francis and Jacqueline (Cummins) G.; B.S. in Elec. Engring., Ohio State U., 1973. Elec. engr. Warrick operations Alcoa, Newburgh, Ind., 1974-77, sr. elec. engr., 1978—. Mem. Tau Beta Pi. Home: 358 Kimber Ln Evansville IN 47715 Office: Warrick Operations Newburgh IN 47630

GUHL, LOUISE ELEANOR, educator; b. Lovell, Wyo., Feb. 1, 1908; d. Carl Joshua and Olga Maria (Lindquist) Peterson; B.A., St. Olaf Coll., 1929; m. Franz Otto Guhl, Mar. 5, 1937; 1 son, John Alfred. Tchr. pub. schs. Cooperstown, N.D., 1929-30; instr. piano St. Olaf Coll., 1930-32; tchr. pub. schs., Kasson, Minn., 1932-35, Cokato, Minn., 1935-36; pvt. instr. piano, Dassel, Cokato, Minn., 1938-67; asst. prof. music U. Minn., Mpls., 1967-77; vis. tchr. piano Concordia Coll., St. Paul, U. Minn., Morris, 1976; instr. U. Minn. Continuing Edn. Extension, 1977—. Mem. Music Tchrs. Nat. Assn. (nat. exec. bd. 1968-73), Nat. Guild Piano Tchrs. (Hall of Fame), Minn. Music Tchrs. Assn. (hon. life, pres. 1971-73, exec. bd. 1969-75), Mpls. Music Tchrs. Forum (hon. life), Thursday Musical Mpls. (artist life mem.), Sigma Alpha Iota (patroness). Lutheran. Author: Keyboard Proficiency. Home: Box 179 Dassel MN 55325

GUIBOR, GEORGE PIRTLE, ophthalmologist; b. St. Louis, June 13, 1895; D.D.S., Washington U., St. Louis, 1918; M.D., Rush Med. Coll., 1929; m. Helen Hecathorn, Mar. 3, 1928; children—George, Pierre. Fellow in ophthalmology and otolaryngology Rush Med. Coll., Chgo., 1930-31; practice medicine specializing in ophthalmology and otolaryngology, Ottawa, Ill., 1933—. Fellow Am. Acad. Ophthalmology; mem. AMA, Am. Soc. Contemporary Ophthalmology, Acad. Cerebral Palsy. Author text on strabismus; contbr. articles on motor anomalies of eye to profl. jours. Home: 225 E Prospect Ave Ottawa IL 61350

GUICE, C. NORMAN, historian, univ. adminstr.; b. Summit, Miss., Feb. 2, 1911; s. C. Norman and Erma (Tucker) G.; B.A., Hendrix Coll., 1931; M.A., Duke U., 1937; Ph.D., U. Calif., Berkeley, 1952; m. Elizabeth Lillian Eichbauer, Feb. 27, 1940; children—Tucker, Frances, Norman F., John A., Matthew C., Stephen A. Teaching fellow in history U. Calif., Berkeley, 1940-41, 1946; instr. social sci. Stephens (Mo.) Coll., 1942-43; lectr. history U. Mich., Ann Arbor, 1947; asst. prof. history, Wayne State U., Detroit, 1947, asso. prof. history, 1957—, asst. dean and grad. officer Coll. Liberal Arts, 1964—; spl. cons. Com. on Accreditation of Service Experiences, Am. Council Edn., 1954-56; cons. Inter-Am. Adult Edn. Sem., 1961. Served with USN, 1943-46. W.H. Mills fellow, 1941-42; Fulbright sr. lectr., Peru, 1959-60; Rockefeller Found. grantee, 1960. Mem. Am. Hist. Assn., Conf. Latin Am. History, Latin Am. Research Assn., Midwest Assn. Latin Am. Studies. Episcopalian. Contbr. articles in field to hist. jours. Home: 1022 Bedford Rd Grosse Pointe Park MI 48230 Office: 545 Mackenzie Hall Wayne State U Detroit MI 48202

GUIDA, EDWARD ARTHUR, environ. engr.; b. Dec. 14, 1946; s. Edward S. and Mary P. (Guilding) G.; B.S., N.J. Inst. Tech., 1968; m. Judy R. Gentry, Dec. 14, 1970. Commd. 2d lt. U.S. Air Force, 1968, advanced through grades to capt., 1971; bioenviron. engr. Little Rock AFB, 1968-72, Ching Chuan Kang AFB, Taiwan, 1972-73; bio environ. engr. Scott AFB, Ill., 1973—, officer in charge Environ. Health Service, 1973—. Registered profl. engr., Ill. Mem. Nat., Ill. socs. profl. engrs., Soc. Am. Mil. Engrs. Home: 7 Roclare Dr Belleville IL 62221 Office: USAF Med Center/SGPM Scott AFB IL 62225

GUIKEMA, DALE JOHN, electric co. fin. exec.; b. Grand Rapids, Mich., Dec. 29, 1940; s. Siebrand and Gertrude Esther (Brinks) G.; student Calvin Coll., 1958-60; B.B.A., U. Mich., 1963, M.B.A., 1964; m. Joan Ellen Korschot, Sept. 2, 1961; children—Susan Elizabeth, Beth Ellen, Nancy Esther. Auditor, Arthur Young & Co., Chgo., 1964-68, mgmt. cons., 1968-71, mgr., 1970-71; controller Chain div. Borg Warner Corp., Ithaca, N.Y., 1971-74; sec.-treas. Koontz-Wagner Electric Co., Inc., South Bend, Ind., 1974—; instr. Ind. U., South Bend, 1975-76. Active United Way. C.P.A., Ill. Mem. South Bend Area C. of C., Am. Inst. C.P.A.'s., Fin. Execs. Inst., Ind. Soc. C.P.A.'s. Republican. Mem. Christian Ref. Ch. Home: 53266 Bonvale Dr South Bend IN 46635 Office: 3801 Voorde Dr South Bend IN 46628

GUILD, RONALD JOHN, lawyer; b. Geneva, Ill., Dec. 24, 1928; s. John William and Helen Jean (Earle) G.; B.S., U. Ill., 1950, LL.B., 1955; m. Marilyn Stephens, Mar. 23, 1956; children—John S., Susan E. Admitted to Ill. bar, 1956, Fed. bar, 1956; mem. firm Hubbard, Hubbard & Dorgan, Chgo., 1955-59, McDermott, Will & Emery, 1960-68, partner, 1966-68; partner Teitelbaum, Wolfberg, Guild & Toback and predecessor firms, Chgo., 1968—; dir. First Comml. Bank, Chgo., Rancho LaCosta and La Costa Land Co., Carlsbad, Calif. Mem. sch. bd. Wheaton-Warrenville Elementary Schs., 1969-72; active Wheaton Community Assn., 1971—, pres., 1975-76. Served to 1st lt. arty. AUS, 1951-52. Mem. Am., Chgo. (exec. com. 1963-68), Ill. bar assns., Am. Arbitration Assn. (panel), Delta Sigma Phi, Alpha Delta Sigma, Phi Alpha Delta. Democrat. Presbyterian. Club: Glen Oak Country (Glen Ellyn, Ill.). Contbg. author books pub. Ill. Inst. Continuing Legal Edn. Home: 186 W Elm St Wheaton IL 60187 Office: 39 S LaSalle St Chicago IL 60603

GUIN, JERE DONALD, dermatologist; b. Russellville, Ala., Feb. 5, 1931; s. Junius Foy and Ruby (Pace) G.; student U. Ala., 1947-51, Vanderbilt U., 1950; B.M.S., Northwestern U., 1952, M.D., 1955; m. Diane Jeanne Tarter, June 29, 1956; children—Jere Donald, Jamie Diane, Jason William. Intern, Baylor U. Coll. Medicine, Houston, 1955-56, resident, 1956-59; practice medicine specializing in dermatology; mem. staff Howard Community Hosp., Kokomo, Ind., 1963-74, chief of medicine, 1967; mem. staff St. Joseph Hosp., Kokomo, 1963—, chief of medicine, 1969, 76; cons. staff Marion County Gen. Hosp., Indpls.; clin. asst. rpof. dermatology Ind. U. Sch. Medicine, Indpls., 1965—. Bd. dirs. ARC, Kokomo, 1973-75; del. Ind. Republican Conv., 1972. Served with USAF, 1956-63. Diplomate Am. Bd. Dermatology. Fellow Am. Acad. Dermatology; mem. Soc. Investigative Dermatology, AMA, Ind. Med. Assn., Ala., Tenn., Chgo. dermatol. socs., Soc. Dermatologic Surgery, Am. Acad. Psychosomatic Diseases, Am. Dermatol. Soc. for Allergy and Immunology, Howard County Med. Soc., Howard County C. of C. (dir. 1975-77). Mem. Ch. of Christ. Club: Rotary (Kokomo). Home: 4401 North Pkwy Kokomo IN 46901 Office: 804 S Berkley Rd Kokomo IN 46901

GUJU, JOHN G., physician; b. Youngstown, Ohio, June 13, 1924; s. George and Frances (Ratz) G.; B.A., Youngstown State U., 1944; M.D., Marquette U., 1947; m. Margaret Ann Poole, May 11, 1952; children—John Howard, Paula Jean, Nancy Elissa. Rotating intern Youngstown Hosp., 1947-48, asst. resident in surgery, 1948-49, later vice chief obstetrics and gynecology, now chief. Resident in obstetrics and gynecology Cleve. City Hosp., 1949-50, U. Hosps., 1950-52; practice medicine specializing in obstetrics and gynecology, Youngstown, 1955—; med. dir. Planned Parenthood Fedn., Youngstown, 1960—; clin. prof. in obstetrics and gynecology Northeastern Ohio Univs. Coll. Medicine, 1975—. Mem. youth com. YMCA, 1965—. Bd. dirs. Ohio div. Am. Assn. for Maternal and Child Health. Served from 1st lt. to capt., USAF, 1953-55. Recipient Alan F. Gutmacher award for service and dedication to Planned Parenthood of Mahoning Valley, 1976. Diplomate Am. Bd. Obstetrics and Gynecology. Fellow A.C.S., Am. Coll. Obstetricians and Gynecologists; mem. A.M.A., Am. Soc. Abdominal Surgeons, Am. Assn. Planned Parenthood Physicians, Am. Fertility Soc. Club: Youngstown Country. Home: 1350 Virginia Trail Youngstown OH 44505 Office: 435 Gypsy Ln Youngstown OH 44504

GULLEKSON, EDWIN HENRY, JR., physician; b. Flint, Mich., May 14, 1935; s. Edwin Henry and Amy Marcella (Graves) G.; student Flint Community Coll., 1953-56; M.D., U. Mich., 1961; m. Rosemary Evelyn Leppien, May 5, 1968; children—Kathryn Dawn, Hans Edwin, Heidi M. Intern McLaren Gen. Hsop., Flint, 1961-62, resident, 1962-63; gen. practice medicine, Flint, 1963—; mem. staffs McLaren Gen., Hurley, St. Joseph, Genesee Meml. hosps. (all Flint). Served to capt. M.C., AUS, 1966-67. Upjohn Research grantee, 1958, 59, 60. Diplomate Am. Bd. Family Practice. Mem. Mich., Genesee County med. socs., A.M.A., Am. Acad. Family Practice, Mich. Acad. Gen. Practice. Patentee surg. instrument. Home: 1721 Laurel Oak Dr Flint MI 48507 Office: 2765 Flushing Rd Flint MI 48504

GULLEN, GEORGE EDGAR, JR., univ. pres.; b. Detroit, Mar. 6, 1914; s. George Edgar and Alice Maud (Scruton) G.; J.D., Wayne State U., 1936; LL.D., U. Mich., 1972; L.H.D., Olivet Coll., 1972; m. Mary Ruth Gullen, Jan. 9, 1937; children—Nancy (Mrs. Gerald Scheffler), George Edgar III, Gail (Mrs. Paul Fitzsimmons), Kathryn Frederick, John. Admitted to Mich. bar, 1936; asst. sec. Detroit Motors Corp., 1940-45; dir. labor relations Am. Motors Corp., Detroit, 1955-63, v.p. indsl. relations, 1963-66; v.p. univ. relations Wayne State U., Detroit, 1966-71, acting pres., 1971-72, pres., 1972—. Commr. Mich. Civil Rights Commn., 1967-71. Vice pres. exec. com. Mich. United Fund. Bd. dirs. YMCAs N.Am.; pres. Nat. Council YMCAs. Recipient Alumni award Wayne State U., 1962. Mem. Indsl. Relations Research Assn., Am. Arbitration Assn. Conglist. Mason. Home: 441 W Ferry St Detroit MI 48202 Office: McKenzie Hall Detroit MI 48202

GULLICKSON, GARY RICHARD, educator; b. Downing, Wis., Aug. 25, 1937; s. Richard Grant and Margel Margaret (Smith) G.; B.A., Westmont Coll., 1960; M.A., U. Hawaii, 1963; postgrad. U. Ia., 1963-65; Ph.D., Ill. Inst. Tech., 1970. Research asst. infant and child psychophysiology U. Hawaii, 1961-63; research asst. devel. psychophysiology U. Ia., 1963-65; med. research asso. to dir. div. psychophysiology Inst. Juvenile Research, Chgo., 1965-71; instr. psychology Roosevelt U., 1969-72; asso. dept. psychiatry Northwestern U. Med. Sch., Chgo., 1971—. Pre-doctoral fellow NIMH, 1965. Mem. A.A.A.S., Am. Electroencephalog. Soc., Am. Psychol. Assn., Central Assn. Electroencephalographers, Contingent Negative Variation Group, Internat. Soc. Devel. Psychobiology, Midwest Psychol. Assn., Soc. Neursci., Soc. Psychophysiol. Research, Soc. Research Child Devel., Sigma Xi. Editor: The Psychophysiology of Darrow, 1973; mem. bd. cons. editors of Psychophysiology, 1970. Contbr. articles to profl. jours. Home and office: 2630 N Dayton St Chicago IL 60614

GULLICKSON, MILES JUSTIN, surgeon; b. Fertile, Minn., Apr. 29, 1910; s. Albert O. and Sophia J. (Sletto) G.; A.B., Macalester Coll., 1931; M.D., U. Minn., 1934; m. Pauline Lillian Silas, Apr. 6, 1939; children—Ann Marget, Charles Justin. Intern, Detroit Receiving Hosp., 1934-35, resident, 1935-37; resident Wayne County Gen. Hosp., Detroit, 1946-48; gen. practice medicine and surgery, Ironwood, Mich., 1938-42; practice medicine specializing in gen. surgery, Rockford, Ill., 1950—; acting chmn. dept. surgery Rockford Sch. Medicine, U. Ill., 1972—; pres. Rockford Surg. Service. Served with M.C. U.S. Army, 1942-46. Mem. A.C.S., Am. Coll. Chest Physicians, Am. Thoracic Soc., AMA. Home: 1927 Boscobel Ct Rockford IL 61107 Office: 1221 E State St Rockford IL 61108

GULLY, HAROLD WAYNE, pub. relations exec.; b. Winnsboro, Tex., Oct. 19, 1917; s. Holly Walton and Erma (Sheppeard) G.; student U. Tex., 1936-39, U. Md., 1951-52; m. Jean Grace Edwards, May 17, 1964; 1 son, David Neal. Reporter-photographer Austin (Tex.) Am.-Statesman, 1939-41; with NEA Service, Inc., Dallas, 1941-42; mgr. southwestern div. Acme Newspictures, Dallas, 1946-51; mgr. central div. newspictures United Press, Chgo., 1953-58; gen. European newspictures mgr. U.P.I., London, Eng., 1958-60; mgr. pub. relations Leo Burnett Co., Inc., N.Y.C., 1960, mgr. pub. relations dept., Chgo., 1961—, v.p. pub. relations, 1974—. Bd. dirs. Pub. Service Communications Council Met. Chgo., 1971—, mem. exec. com., 1974—; mem. asso. bd. Community Meml. Gen. Hosp. of La Grange, 1972—; bd. dirs. Chgo. Lung Assn., 1973—. Served with USAAF, 1942-45; served to maj. USAF, 1951-53. Decorated Air medal with cluster. Mem. Pub. Relations Soc. Am. (accrediated mem.; chpt. pres. 1973), Chgo. Headline Club, Nat. Acad. TV Arts and Scis. (dir. Chgo. chpt. 1974—), Sigma Delta Chi. Home: 645 S Waiola Ave La Grange IL 60525 Office: Leo Burnett Co Inc Prudential Plaza Chicago IL 60601

GUM, CARL DEWITT, JR., lawyer; b. Nevada, Mo., July 30, 1932; s. Carl DeWitt and Maryana (Burford) G.; B.A., U. Mo., 1954, LL.B., 1960; m. Elaine J. Bailey, Nov. 25, 1971; children—Cary Maryana, Carl DeWitt III, William Warren. Admitted to Mo. bar, 1960; partner Thayer, Gum, Ernst & Wickert, Grandview and Belton, Mo., 1960—; dir. Belton Star Herald. City atty. Belton, 1960-64; pros. atty. Cass County, 1964-70. Chmn. Region I, Mo. Council Criminal Justice; pres. Richards-Gebaurer Base Community Council. Adv. trustee Research Hosp., Kansas City, Mo. Served with USAF, 1954-57; now maj. JAG, Res. Mem. Am., Kansas City, Mo., Cass County bar assns., Am., Mo. trial lawyers assns., Belton C. of C. (pres.). Methodist (chmn. bd. trustees). Mason (Shriner), Optimist. Home: 408 Westover Circle Belton MO 64012 Office: Main St at Walnut St Belton MO 64012

GUMBERT, E(DGAR) THOMAS, consulting co. exec.; b. St. Joseph, Mo., Apr. 3, 1924; s. Edgar Albert and Winifred B. (Estes) G.; B.A. in Econs., Westminster Coll., 1947; M.B.A. in Marketing, U. Chgo., 1949; m. Carol Baisden, Feb., 1952 (div. 1961); children—Suzanne, Cynthia, Shirley; m. 2nd. Geraldine Gipe, Oct., 1968 (div. 1975). Mgr. Cargill, Inc., Tampa, Fla., 1951-53, Dannen Mills, Omaha, 1951-56; owner, mgr. A Plus Employment, Omaha, 1956-73; pres. Gumbert Exec. Exchange, Omaha, 1961—. Chmn. Republican ward, Omaha, 1964; dist. chmn. to Rep. Neb. Conv., 1964. Served to ensign USNR, 1943-47. Mem. Midwest Employers Council (asst. treas. Omaha chpt. 1967-68, dir. 1966-69), Nat. Employment Assn. (dir. 1962-65), Nat. Personnel Assn. (v.p. 1963-65), Nebr. Placement Services Assn. (pres. 1964-66, v.p. 1977-78), Nebr. Soc. Mayflower Descs. (gov. 1969-71), Midland Winemakers Soc. (pres. 1972, 73, 75), Porsche Club Am., U. Chgo. Alumni Assn., Phi Delta Theta. Episcopalian. Clubs: Masons, Shriners, Order Eastern Star (past patron). Home: 9218 V Plaza Omaha NE 68127 Office: 1000 Omaha Tower Omaha NE 68124

GUMBERT, JACK LEE, surgeon; b. Ft. Wayne, Ind., July 14, 1934; s. Martin Fredrick and Beulah Faye (McClain) G.; B.A., Cin. U., 1957, M.D., 1961; m. Lois Irene Scheimann, June 15, 1957; children—Jack, Lori, Brad, Grant, Joseph. Intern, Marion County Gen. Hosp., Indpls., 1961-62, resident 1962-66; practice medicine specializing in surgery, Ft. Wayne, Ind., 1968—; staff surgeon Parkview, Luth., St. Joseph hosps., Ft. Wayne, 1968—; chmn. surgery service Parkview Hosp., 1977; asso. faculty mem. Ind. U. Sch. Medicine. Bd. dirs. Ft. Wayne YMCA, UPD Inc., Dukes Day Inc. Served to capt. M.C., U.S. Army, 1966-68. Decorated Bronze Star, Air medal (Vietnam); Army Commendation medal with oak leaf cluster. Diplomate Am. Bd. Surgery. Fellow A.C.S., mem. AMA, Ind. State, Ft. Wayne med. socs., Ind. State, Ft. Wayne surg. assns. Lutheran. Club: Pine Valley Country (pres. 1976-77). Contbr. articles to med. jours. Home: 10810 Old Colony Rd Fort Wayne IN 46825 Office: 5010 Riviera Ct Fort Wayne IN 46825

GUND, GEORGE, III, chmn. bd. Cleve. Barons Hockey Team. Office: Cleve Barons 2923 Stretboro Rd Richfield OH 44286

GUNDERSEN, GUNNAR ADOLF, physician; b. La Crosse, Wis., June 12, 1924; s. Gunnar and Mary C. (Baldwin) G.; student Yale U., 1942-43, U. N.H., 1944; M.D., Harvard U., 1948; m. Elizabeth Hanmer, Mar. 29, 1952; children—Gunnar, Lincoln, Ralph, Sven, Per. Intern in internal medicine Mass. Meml. Hosp., Boston, 1948-49; intern in surgery N.Y. Hosp., N.Y.C., 1949-50; fellow in radiology U. Minn., Mpls., 1951, 53-56; radiologist La Crosse (Wis.) Luth. Hosp. and Gundersen Clinic, La Crosse, 1956—; mem. State Bd. Med. Examiners, 1959-63. Campaign chmn. Community Chest, 1962; candidate for Congress, 1968; mem. La Crosse Bd. Edn., 1968-71. Served with U.S. Army, 1943-46; served to capt., M.C., USAF, 1951-53. Diplomate Am. Bd. Radiology, Am. Bd. Nuclear Medicine. Mem. La Crosse County, Wis. State med. socs., AMA, Wis., N.Am. radiol. socs., Am. Coll. Radiology, Soc. Nuclear Medicine. Democrat. Unitarian-Universalist. Home: Arbor Hills Route 1 La Crosse WI 54601 Office: 1836 South Ave La Crosse WI 54601

GUNDERSON, GEORGE BRUCE, food machinery co. exec.; b. Berlin, Wis., Mar. 15, 1926; s. George B. and Eva Louise (Doty) G.; Ph.B., U. Wis., 1947; m. Marjorie D. Kettelhon, Aug. 14, 1948; children—Richard, Thomas, Stuart. Salesman, sales mgr. Swift & Co., Minn., Wis., 1947-54; owner, operator Gunderson Ford & Mercury, Inc., Columbus, Wis., 1954-61; exec. v.p. Hughes Co., Inc., Columbus, 1961-69; founder, pres. Badger Food Machinery Corp., Fall River, Wis., 1970—; dir. Farmers & Mchts. Bank, Columbus, Forty-Niners. Mem. Forty Niners, Young and Old Guard. Republican. Club: Maple Bluff Country (Madison, Wis.). Home: Route 1 Columbus WI 53935 Office: Fall River WI 53932

GUNDERSON, HARVEY SAMUEL, educator; b. Eau Claire, Wis., Nov. 25, 1944; s. Samuel O. and Sophie N. (Nelson) G.; B.S., U. Wis., Eau Claire, 1966; M.A., U. Kans., 1968; Ph.D., U. Wis., Madison, 1974; m. Carol Susan Schuyler, Aug. 24, 1967; Instr., U. Wis., Oshkosh, 1968-71; lectr. U. Wis., Madison, 1971-74; ops. research analyst Forest Products Lab., Madison, 1973; instr. U. Wis., Eau Claire, 1974-75, asst. prof., 1975-76; asso. prof. U. Wis., Madison, 1976; asso. prof. U. Wis., Eau Claire, 1976—, asst. to dean Sch. Bus.,

1977—; bus. cons., 1974—. NDEA fellow, 1966-68. Mem. Am. Inst. Decision Scis., Math. Assn. Am., Inst. Mgmt. Sci., Pi Mu Epsilon, Phi Kappa Phi. Home: 1111 Graham Ave Eau Claire WI 54701 Office: U Wis Eau Claire WI 54701

GUNDERSON, THOMAS EDWARD, residential home mfr., builder; b. Cottonwood, Minn., June 10, 1924; s. Thomas Arnold and Bertha W. (Wastun) G.; student U. Minn., 1946-49; m. Wanda E. Swennes, June 22, 1947; children—Jill Elaine, Jane Ellen, Thomas Lee. Domestic sales mgr. Telex, Inc., St. Paul, 1949-62; sales mgr. Capp Homes, Mpls., 1962-70; pres., chmn. bd. Waconia (Minn.) Homes, Inc., 1970-78; pres. Gunderson Homes, Inc., Waconia, 1978—. Served with U.S. Army, 1942-46. Mem. Waconia C. of C. (dir.). Republican. Lutheran. Home: 504 Janalyn Circle Golden Valley MN 55416 Office: Box 266 Waconia MN 55387

GUNDLACH, NORMAN JOSEPH, lawyer; b. Belleville, Ill., May 23, 1907; s. Joseph E. and Bertha (Steudle) G.; B.S., U. Ill., 1928, LL.B., 1931; m. Maxine Rain, Jan. 26, 1935; children—Gayle (Mrs. Donald McLean), Frank N. Admitted to Ill., Mo. bars, 1931; partner firm Gundlach, Lee, Eggmann, Boyle & Roessler, and predecessor firms, Belleville, 1931—; dir. Bankers Trust Co., Belleville, Belleville Bancshares, Inc. Mem. citizens com. U. Ill. Served with USNR, 1943-45. Fellow Am. Coll. Trial Lawyers, Am. Bar Found.; mem. Am., Ill. (pres. 1st dist. 1955), Mo., St. Clair County (pres. 1969-70), East St. Louis (pres. 1948) bar assns., Nat. Assn. R.R. Trial Counsel, Ill. Def. Counsel, U. Ill. I Men's Assn. (past pres.), Phi Delta Phi. Home: 19 S 78th St Belleville IL 62223 Office: 5000 W Main St Belleville IL 62223

GUNGOR, BAHRI ORHAN, physician; b. Russe, Bulgaria, July 6, 1928; s. Orhan Semsi and Ayse Hasim (Bingor) G.; Middle Edn. degree, Hristo Botef, Russe, 1942-46; M.D., Istanbul (Turkey) U., 1954; m. Lilly Robles, Sept. 29, 1958; children—Steven, Mark, Edwin, Leyla, Erol, Semra; came to U.S., 1956, naturalized, 1963. Rotating intern, obstetrics resident Lincoln Hosp., Bronx, N.Y., 1956-58; house physician Dover Gen. Hosp., Dover, N.J., 1958-59; surg. staff physician Lynchburg (Va.) Tng. Sch., also pvt. practice, Vienna, Va., 1959-60; practice medicine DeWitt Army Hosp., Fort Belvoir, Med. Dispensary, Fort Myer, 1960-62; gen. practice medicine, Loyal and Neillsville, Wis., 1962—; mem. staff Meml. Hosp., Neillsville, chief staff, 1968; med. adviser Clark County Health Com., Clark County Hwy. Safety Com.; mem. profl. edn. chmn. Am. Cancer Soc., 1965-67. Diplomate Am. Bd. Family Practice. Mem. A.M.A., Wis., Clark County (pres. 1968-70) med. socs., Acad. Gen. Practice. Lion. Home: 101 Clay St Neillsville WI 54456 Office: Neillsville Clinic Neillsville WI 54456

GUNNINGS, THOMAS SYLVESTER, psychologist, med. adminstr.; b. Gastonia, N.C., Feb. 8, 1935; s. Garfield and Marie (Webb) G.; B.S. in Edn., Winston-Salem Tchrs. Coll., 1958; M.A. in Guidance, Psychology, Oreg. State U., 1967, Ph.D. in Counseling Psychology, 1969; m. Barbara Ann Byrd, June 28, 1959; 1 dau. Sonya Renita. Asso. prof. Mich. State U., East Lansing, Mich., 1969-72, prof. psychiatry Coll. Human Medicine, prof. Coll. Urban Devel., exec. dir. urban counseling program; nat. cons. to fed., state, local agencies. Active local, state, nat. politics. NIMH grantee, 1972-78. Mem. Am. Psychol. Assn. (scientist, vis. psychologist, 1969-72), Assn. Black Psychologists (bd. dir., mid-west coordinator, 1972), Am. Personnel and Guidance Assn. (nat. awards 1974—) Kappa Delta Pi. Cons., editor Jour. of Non-White Concerns, 1974-78. Home: 1000 Blanchette East Lansing MI 48823 Office: Mich State Univ East Lansing MI 48824

GUNTER, FRANK DELANO, retail store exec.; b. McLeansboro, Ill., July 25, 1933; s. Ernest George and Velma (Veach) G.; B.S., So. Ill. U., Edwardsville, 1963; m. Dolores A. Schmulbach, Mar. 19, 1955; children—Tracy Ann, Kreg Franklin. Tax agt. Phillips Petroleum Co., St. Louis, 1954-60; tax accountant Peabody Coal Co., St. Louis, 1960-66; v.p. taxes Continental Telephone Co., Merrifield, Va., 1966-73; v.p. taxes May Dept. Stores Co., St. Louis, 1973—; owner accounting practice, Belleville, Ill., 1959-70. Served with USN, 1951-54. Mem. Tax Execs. Inst., Internat. Assn. Assessing Officers, Nat. Tax Assn., U.S. Independent Telephone Assn. (chmn. tax com.). Mem. Ch. of Christ (elder). Mason (32 deg.). Home: 36 Clover Dr Belleville IL 62221 Office: 6th and Olive Sts St Louis MO 63012

GUNTER, FRANK ELLIOTT, artist; b. Jasper, Ala., May 8, 1934; s. Frank Marion and Lucy Ellen (Butler) G.; B.F.A., U. Ala., 1956; M.A., Fla. State U., 1960; m. Dora Carolyn Carlton, Aug. 9, 1958; 1 dau., Lisa Cameron. Tchr. art Birmingham (Ala.) Pub. Schs., 1956-58; asst. prof. art Murray State U., 1960-62; prof. U. Ill., 1962—; numerous one-man shows, 1957—, including: Cultural Center for Am. Embassy, Paris, 1971, Am. Library, Brussels, 1972, Maison Descarte, Amsterdam, 1973, Ill. Arts Council, Chgo., 1970; group shows include: No. Ariz. U. Art Gallery, Flagstaff, 1975; Madison (Wis.) Art Center, 1977; represented in permanent collections: Birmingham Museum Art, Evansville (Ind.) Mus., Swope Gallery, Terre Haute, Ind., Ill. State Mus., Springfield, Bank of Ind., Merrillville, Purdue U., St. Paul Art Center, U. N.D.; asso., U. Ill. Center Advanced Study, 1974-75. U. Ill. travel fellow, 1964, 66, 68, 74, 77. Episcopalian. Home: 806 S Elm Blvd Champaign IL 61820 Office: 134 Fine Arts Bldg Univ Ill Urbana IL 61820

GUNTERMANN, ALFRED ERNEST, cons. engr.; b. Chgo., June 25, 1943; s. Alfred Ernest and Elizabeth Margaret (Erhart) G.; B.M.E., U. Wis., 1967; m. Elizabeth Jane Tucker, Feb. 25, 1968; children—Daniel Scott, Katharine Marie. In charge Ft. Wayne (Ind.) office Trane Co., 1967-74; pres. Energy Econs., Ft. Wayne, 1974—; lectr. in field. Co-chmn. Bowl Down Cancer dr. Am. Cancer Soc., Ft. Wayne, 1977. Mem. Am. Soc. Heating, Refrigeration and Air Conditioning Engrs. (pres. 1974-75, Ind. moderator 1976), Nat. Soc. Profl. Engrs. (sec. 1977-78), C. of C. Congregationalist. Club: Kiwanis. Contbr. articles in field to profl. jours. Home: 1007 Nuttman Ave Fort Wayne IN 46807 Office: 2420 US 30 Bypass N Fort Wayne IN 46805

GUPTA, PARKASH DEV, cardiologist; b. Fazilka, India, Mar. 7, 1936; s. Gursharan Dass and Dharam Vati (Aggarwal) G.; came to U.S., 1964, M.B. B.S., Govt. Med. Coll., Patiala, India, 1958, M.B.B.S., 1958; m. Kamlesh Aggarwal, Sept. 12, 1970; children—Malini, Vikas, Vishal. Asst. registrar medicine Govt. Med. Coll., Patiala, 1960-64; resident internal medicine Louisville (Ky.) Gen. Hosp., 1965-66; fellow in cardiology Mt. Sinai Hosp., 1965-66, Hines VA Hosp., Chgo., 1966-68; fellow in pediatric cardiology Cook County Hosp., Chgo., 1968-70, resident in internal medicine, 1970-71; mem. staff MacNeal Meml. Hosp., Berwyn, Ill., 1971—; clin. asst. prof. medicine Abraham Lincoln Sch. Medicine, U. Ill., Chgo. Fellow Council Clin. Cardiology Am. Heart Assn., Royal Coll. Physicians Can., Am. Coll. Cardiology, A.C.P.; mem. AMA, Ill., Chgo. med. socs. Hindu. Contbr. articles to med. jours. Home: 3684 Downers Dr Downers Grove IL 60515 Office: 3249 S Oak Park Ave Berwyn IL 60402

GUPTA, PARSHOTAM DASS, educator; b. Ambala City, India, Feb. 5, 1936; s. Jugal Kishore and Maya (Vati) G.; M.S., Panjab U., India, 1959; M.S., Carnegie Inst. Tech., 1963; Ph.D., Carnegie Mellon U., 1968; m. Kamesh Goyal, Aug. 2, 1969; children—Raymond, Sandhya. Instr. physics dept. Panjab U., India, 1959-60; project physicist, Carnegie-Mellon U., Pitts., 1963-68; asst. prof. Purdue U. Calumet Campus, Hammond, Ind., 1968-77, asso. prof., 1977—. Mem. Am. Phys. Soc., Am. Assn. Physics Tchrs., AAUP, Sigma Xi. Condr. research, contbr. articles in nuclear and particle physics; reviewer Study Guide in Physics (V. Namias), 1974, 76. Home: 613 Jackson Ave Dyer IN 46311 Office: Purdue Univ Calumet Campus 2233 171st St Hammond IN 46323

GUREVITCH, RUSS, veterinarian; b. Berkeley, Calif., Nov. 28, 1945; s. Leo and Evelyn (Schneider) G.; B.A., U. Calif. at Berkeley, 1967; D.V.M., U. Calif. at Davis, 1974; postgrad. Calif. State Coll., 1967-68; m. Cecilia Marie Klein, June 22, 1969. Biology, chemistry tchr. Los Gatos Joint Union High Sch. Dist., Saratoga, Calif., 1968-70; tchr. vet. technicians Mt. Diablo Unified Sch. Dist., Concord, Calif., 1972; intern, clin. instr. dept. small animal clinics Purdue U., W. Lafayette, Ind., 1974-75; resident, clin. instr. surgery small animal clinics Ohio State U. Coll. Vet. Medicine, Columbus, 1975—. Mem. Am., Calif. vet. med. assns., Am. Animal Hosp. Assn., Vet. Orthopedic Soc. Phi Zeta. Home: 2898 Howey Rd Columbus OH 43224 Office: 1935 Coffey Rd Columbus OH 43210

GUSMER, JOHN H., paper co. exec.; b. Plainfield, N.J., Sept. 7, 1932; s. Henry Svend and Hildegarde (Wallich) G.; B.S., Mass. Inst. Tech., 1954; m. Carolyn Keene, Oct. 6, 1956. Design engr. IBM, Endicott, N.Y., 1954-55; with Filter Materials, Inc., Waupaca, Wis., 1957—, pres., gen. mgr., 1962—; pres., dir. Cellulo Co., Sandusky, Ohio, 1964—, Fresno, Calif., 1970—; dir. A. Gusmer, Inc., Hoboken, N.J. Mem. Spl. Taxpayers Com. on State Budget, Wis., 1962-75. Bd. dirs. Waupaca Community Chest, Inc., 1961-70, pres., 1962-64. Mem. Bd. Edn., Waupaca Unified Sch. Dist., 1970—, chmn. personnel com., 1971—. Served with AUS, 1955-57. Mem. Paper Industry Mgmt. Assn., Am. Inst. Chem. Engrs., TAPPI, ASTM (com. on filtration standards), Soc. Preservation Encouragement Barber Shop Quartet Singing Am., Tau Beta Pi, Pi Tau Sigma, Sigma Xi. Lion. Office: PO Box 329 Waupaca WI 54981

GUSTAFSON, GLADYS IRENE, speech pathologist; b. Polk County, Wis., Oct. 25, 1912; d. Lewis W. and Sena (Hansen) Nielsen; B.S., U. Minn., 1962; M.A., George Peabody Coll., 1971; children—Bonnie Gustafson Beaver, Nyla Gustafson Rayburn. Tchr. elementary sch. Polk County, Wis., 1930-34, Hennepin County, Minn., 1939-44; tchr. kindergarten Orono Sch. Dist., Long Lake, Minn., 1954-60, speech pathologist, 1961-77. Mem. Minn., Nat. edn. assns., Am. Speech and Hearing Assn., Nat., Minn. Assn. Children With Learning Differences, Orton Soc. Presbyterian. Home: 240 N Central St Wayzata MN 55391 Office: Orono School District Schumann Elementary Bldg Long Lake MN 55356

GUSTAFSON, PETER ALAN, univ. adminstr.; b. Ashtabula, Ohio, Oct. 1, 1951; s. Gunnard L. and Leona I. (Bell) G.; B.S., Bowling Green U., 1974, M.A., 1975; m. Donna Jeanne Lucha, July 25, 1975. Head resident and dir. student activities Urbana (Ohio) Coll., 1974-75; residence hall dir. Ind. State U., Terre Haute, 1975-77; asst. dean student affairs Rose Hulman Inst. Tech., Terre Haute, Ind., 1977—. Recipient Pres.'s Award Distinguished Service, Bowling Green State U., 1974; Outstanding Service award, Urbana Coll., 1975. Mem. Am., Ind. coll. personnel assns., Am. Personnel Guidance Assn. Lutheran. Home and office: 5500 Wabash Ave Terre Haute IN 47803

GUSTAFSON, ROY DAVID, educator; b. Rockford, Ill., Dec. 12, 1936; s. Roy H. and Lois M. Gustafson; B.A., Beloit Coll., 1958; M.S., No. Ill. U., 1962; M.A. Teaching (NSF scholar), Rockford Coll., 1965; m. Carol Ann Groves, June 11, 1960; children—Kristy Lynn, Steven Roy. Tchr. math. Rockford West High Sch., 1958-65; prof. Rock Valley Coll., 1965-67, chmn. div. math. and humanities, 1967—; lectr. math. Rockford Coll., 1965—; mem. North Central Evaluation Teams for Sch. Accreditation. Mem. Rockford Bd. Edn., 1971-74, sec., 1974. Named Outstanding Young Educator, Jr. C. of C., 1965. Mem. Nat., Ill. councils tchrs. of math., Math. Assn. Am. Presbyterian. Author: (with Frisk) Elementary Plane Geometry, 1973. Home: 6580 Glen Devon Rd Rockford IL 61111 Office: 3301 N Mulford Rd Rockford IL 61101

GUSTAVSON, ERICK BRANDT, broadcasting and publishing exec.; b. Rockford, Ill., June 2, 1936; s. Sven Ragner and Ruth E. (Johnson) G.; student Northwestern Coll., 1954-56, Cuyahoga Community Coll., 1963-64, Loyola U., Chgo., 1969-70; m. Mary Janet; children—Ruth, Timothy. Announcer WBEL, Beloit, Wis., 1953-54; announcer KTIS, Mpls., 1954-58, asst. to mgr., 1957-58; v.p. Better Choir Publs., Mpls., 1958-59; announcer, asst. mgr. WCBC, Anderson, Ind., 1959-60; announcer WCRF, Cleve., 1960-67, sta. mgr., 1961-67; gen. mgr. KAIM, Honolulu, 1967-68; dir. broadcasting Moody Bible Inst., Chgo., 1968-74, v.p., adminstr. devel., 1974—; v.p. Evang. Christian Pubs. Assn. Mem. exec. com., finance com. Moody Meml. Ch. Mem. Nat. Assn. Broadcasters, Nat. Religious Broadcasters (v.p. 1970—). Home: 110 Columbia Ave Park Ridge IL 60068 Office: 820 N LaSalle St Chicago IL 60610

GUSTIN, RALPH LEON, postmaster; b. Madison County, Ind., Apr. 21, 1925; s. Vance and Georgia (Ball) G.; student pub. schs.; m. Sally Ann Caudell, Oct. 20, 1948; children—Ralph M., Richard L., Debbie A., Dianna L., Darlene K. With Delco Remy div. Gen. Motors Corp., 1950-56; postmaster City of Markleville, Ind., 1956—; dir. Hancock Rural Telephone Corp., also pres. bd. Mem. South Madison Sch. Bd., 1968. Served with AUS, 1943-46. Club: Masons. Home: PO Box 121 Markleville IN 46056 Office: U S Post Office Markleville IN 46056

GUTH, HARRY EARL, JR., journalist; b. Perryville, Mo., Sept. 30, 1924; s. Harry E. and Grace M. (O'Mara) G.; B.J., U. Mo., 1949; student Cape Girardeau U., 1942-43; m. Barbara Jean Seitz, July 28, 1950; children—Vicki, Marlene, Mark. Editor, Perry County (Mo.) Republic. Served with U.S. Army, 1942-46. Mem. Perryville C. of C. (pres. 1970), Perryville Jaycees (pres. 1958-59), VFW, Am. Legion. Republican. Presbyterian. Big 8 track champion, 1947, 48; Kans. relays champion, 1946-48. Home: 124 S Spring St Perryville MO 63775 Office: 7 N Main Perryville MO 63775

GUTH, RICHARD RALPH, lighting co. ofcl.; b. St. Louis, Jan. 11, 1945; s. James Walter and Joann Busch (Gildehaus) G.; B.A., Tulane U., 1967; postgrad. St. Louis U., 1972—; m. Mary Wilson Skinner, Aug. 1, 1970. Shipping supr. Guth Lighting Co., St. Louis, 1967-68, head cost accounting, pricing and quotation dept., 1968-72, materials mgr., purchasing agt., 1972—. Mem. Nat. Assn. Purchasing Mgrs., St. Louis Jr. C. of C., Illuminating Engrng. Soc., Internat. Material Mgmt. Soc., Phi Delta Theta (pres. Mo. Gamma house bd.). Home: 7025 Northmoor Dr St Louis MO 63105 Office: 2615 Washington Blvd St Louis MO 63103

GUTHEIL, ROBERT WILLOUGHBY, mktg. exec.; b. N.Y.C., Dec. 11, 1924; s. Rudolph W. and Emma (Hauck) G.; A.B., Princeton U., 1949; m. Helen Frain, Apr. 3, 1954; 1 dau., Kate Louise. Mgr. rendering dept. Baugh Chem. Co., Phila., 1949-50, gen. mgr. adhesive dept., 1950-52, gen. mgr. Phila. plant, 1952-54; gen. mgr. adhesive div. Armour & Co., Chgo., 1954-59, gen. mgr. Am. Tape div., 1966—; pres. Standard Insulation Co., 1959-64; gen. mgr. Armour Coated Products & Adhesives Co., Chgo., 1964-69; pres. Armour Indsl. Products Co., 1969-71; group v.p. Borden Chem. div. Borden & Co., Columbus, Ohio, 1971—. Fin. chmn. Ill. Sch. Dist. 67. Served with USMC, 1942-45. Mem. Nat. Assn. Glue Mfrs. (dir.), Pressure Sensitive Tape Council (dir., pres. 1971), Adhesive Mfrs. Assn. (regional v.p. 1966), Coated Abrasive Mfrs. Inst. (dir.), Drug, Chem. and Allied Trades Assn. (dir.), Mfg. Chemists Assn., Chemists Club. Clubs: Lake Forest (bd. dirs.); Worthington Hills Country; Columbus Athletic. Home: 1260 Clubview Blvd S Worthington OH 43085 Office: 50 W Broad St Columbus OH 43215

GUTHIER, LLOYD CHARLES, real estate and ins. broker; b. Elysian, Minn., Sept. 10, 1918; s. Charles Edward and Alice Eliza (Jones) G.; student No. State Coll., Aberdeen, S.D., 1939; m. Pearl Elizabeth Andersen, Apr. 2, 1942; children—Michele E. (Mrs. David E. Peterson), Michael L. Owner gen. ins. agy., Owatonna, Minn., 1948—, real estate broker, 1963—. Vice chmn. S.E. Minn. Area Health Planning Council, 1970-72, chmn., 1973; sec.-treas. Luther N. Youndahl Human Relations Center. Bd. dirs. Owatonna City Hosp., 1962-70. Served with AUS, 1941-47, 50-52. Mem. Minn. Assn. Mut. Agts. (nat. dir., past pres.), Minn. Bd. Realtors (state sec., pres. local bd.), Am. Legion, V.F.W. Mason (Shriner), Elk, Eagle. Home: 410 Havana Rd Owatonna MN 55060 Office: 325 N Cedar St Owatonna MN 55060

GUTHMANN, HOWARD MILTON, accounting co. exec.; b. Duluth, Minn., Nov. 30, 1922; s. Milton Emil and Ruth Sophia (Freimuth) G.; B.B.A., U. Minn., 1943; m. Elizabeth Diane Heimann, Apr. 5, 1952; children—Susan Lee, John Howard, Debra Sue, Patricia Ann. With Hines & Wilkerson (name now Wilkerson, Guthmann & Johnson Ltd.), St. Paul, 1943—, sr. officer, 1973—. Lectr. accounting U. Minn., 1947-52. Treas., mem. exec. com. Community Planning Orgn., Inc., St. Paul; bd. dirs., treas. Better Bus. Bur. Minn., 1975—; chmn. St. Paul Open Golf Tournament, 1957; mem. St. Paul Charter Commn., 1960-68; mem. exec. bd. Indianhead council Boy Scouts Am., 1977—; mem. St. Paul Bd. Edn., 1968-76, treas., 1968-75, vice chmn., 1968-75, chmn., 1975-76. Bd. dirs. St. Paul Area United Way, 1970-76. Recipient Silver Beaver award Boy Scouts Am., 1959; named Outstanding Young Man St. Paul, 1958, Marks and Howard award Jaycees, 1959. C.P.A., Minn. Mem. Am. Inst. C.P.A.'s (council 1975-76), Minn. Soc. C.P.A.'s (pres. 1975-76), Am. Arbitration Assn. (panel arbitrators 1972—), St. Paul Jaycees (life mem.), Minn. Transp. Mus., Minn. Landscape Arboretum, St. Paul Audubon Soc., Ft. Snelling State Park Assn., Minn. Hist. Soc., Twin City Inst. Talented Youth (pres. 1969-71, dir. 1967-72), Voyageurs Nat. Park Assn., Nature Conservancy, St. Paul Urban League, Nat. Audubon Soc., Wilderness Soc., Minn. Zool. Soc., St. Paul C. of C., U. Minn. Alumni Assn., Citizens League. Unitarian Universalist (chmn. bd. trustees local ch. 1963-65, 75-76, treas. dist. 1970—). Rotarian. Clubs: Mendakota Country, Innijiska, St. Paul Athletic (dir. 1968-71). Home: 815 S Fairview Ave St Paul MN 55116 Office: 1300 NW National Bank Bldg St Paul MN 55101

GUTHRIE, ELEANOR Y., lawyer; b. Annawan, Ill., Aug. 12, 1915; d. James M. and Nell (Stevenson) Young; B.A., U. Ill., 1937; LL.B., Chgo.-Kent Coll. Law, 1940; m. George B. Guthrie, Dec. 26, 1941; 1 son, Richard Y. Editor, Commerce Clearing House, Inc., 1940-42; lawyer Defrees & Fiske, Chgo., 1942-52, partner, 1952—; mem. hearing bd. for atty. registration and disciplinary commn. Ill. Supreme Ct. Pres. Joint Com. on Woman's Ct. and Detention Home, Chgo., 1957-58; vol. worker teen-age program Erie Neighborhood House, 1954-62; mem. com. on social security Ill. C. of C.; bd. dirs., mem. loop center com. YWCA, v.p., 1974-77; bd. dirs. Community Fund of Chgo.; asst. sec. U.S.O. Chgo., 1969-73. Del., Women's Share in Pub. Service, also Ill. Women's Conf. on Legislation. Mem. Women's Bar Assn. Ill. (pres. 1950-51), Nat. Assn. Women Lawyers (state del. 1952, labor law com.), Am. (vice.chmn. com. on occupational health and safety 1972-73, labor law sect.; mem. fed. labor standards legislative com.), Chgo. (mem. labor law, house, grievance coms., chmn. ho. com. 1970-72) bar assns., Central Bus. and Profl. Women, Alliance Bus. and Profl. Women Chgo. (pres. 1964-65), Nat. (parliamentarian 1973-74), Ill. (parliamentarian 1958—) fedns. bus. and profl. women's clubs, AAUW, Internat. Platform Assn., Zeta Phi Eta. Congregationalist. Clubs: Pilot (pres. 1955-56), Execs. of Chgo. Home: 547 Belleforte Ave Oak Park IL 60302 Office: 72 W Adams St Chicago IL 60603

GUTHRIE, MYRNA JEAN, educator; b. Newton, Iowa, June 30, 1929; d. Frank Andrew and Hazel (Dolph) Guthrie; student Central Coll., 1947-49; B.A., Drake U., 1951, M.S., 1963. Child Welfare worker State of Iowa, 1951-60; guidance counselor Newton Community Schs., 1960—, counselor Upward Bound, Central Coll., Pella, Iowa, 1967; cons. Jasper County Headstart program, 1968; coordinator Newton Achievement Motivation Project, 1971-72, Futures project Newton Community Sch., 1975. Past bd. dirs. Jasper County Community Action; past pres. RMR Soc.; bd. dirs. Newton Community Orch. Recipient Maytag Found. Conv. award, 1965. Mem. Internat. Platform Assn., Nat., Newton edn. assns., Am., Iowa personnel and guidance assns., Newton Bus. and Profl. Womens Club (past pres.), Jasper County Hist. Soc., Iowa Woman's Polit. Caucus, Newton Community Theater, Questers (pres.), Alpha Xi Delta, Alpha Kappa Delta, Beta Sigma Phi. Republican. Methodist. Clubs: Soroptimist (past pres.) (Newton); Hazel Dell Acad. Home: 326 E 4th St S Newton IA 50208

GUTHRIE, RICHARD ALAN, physician; b. Nov. 13, 1935; s. Merle Pruitt and Cleona Marie (Weaver) G.; A.A., Graceland Coll., 1955; M.D., U. Mo., 1960; m. Diana Fern Worthington, Aug. 17, 1957; children—Laura, Joyce, Tamara. Intern, U.S. Naval Hosp., Camp Pendleton, Calif., 1960-61; dir. dependent services U.S. Naval Hosp., Sangley Point, Philippines, 1961-63; asst. instr., resident in pediatrics U. Mo., 1963-65, NIH fellow in endocrinology and metabolism, 1965-68, asst. prof., dir. newborn services, 1968-71, asso. prof. pediatrics, 1971-73; prof., chmn. dept. pediatrics U. Kans. Med. Sch., Wichita, 1973—. Served with USN, 1960-63. Recipient NIH grants, 1968—; Outstanding Faculty award U. Kans. Wichita, 1976. Diplomate Am. Bd. Pediatrics. Fellow Am. Acad. Pediatrics; mem. Am. (dir. 1972-77), Kans. (pres. 1975, chmn. bd. 1976-78) diabetes assn., Kans., Sedgewick County med. socs., Soc. Med. Sch. Pediatric Dept. Chmn., Soc. Pediatric Research, Lawson Wilkins Pediatric Endocrinology Soc., Midwest Soc. Pediatric Research, Lambda Delta Sigma, Sigma Xi. Mem. health commn. bd. Reorganized Ch. Jesus Christ Latter-day Saints. Co-author: Nursing Management in Diabetes Mellitus; contbr. articles to profl. jours. Home: 4961 Hillcrest St N Wichita KS 27220 Office: 2221 Hillside St N Wichita KS 67219

GUTHRIE, WILBUR DEAN, entomologist; b. Woodward, Okla., Mar. 3, 1924; s. Ivens and Francis (Moser) G.; B.S., Okla. State U., 1950, M.S., 1951; Ph.D., Ohio State U., 1958; m. Mary E. Peters, Sept. 9, 1946; children—Justina (Mrs. Richard Gordon), Yvonne, Larry, Gary, Scott. Research entomologist Agrl. Research Service, U.S. Dept. Agr. Ankeny, Iowa, 1964—; research leader Corn Insect Research, Ankeny, 1973—. Served with USNR, 1944-46. Mem. Sigma Xi, Phi Sigma, Phi Kappa Phi, Alpha Zeta, Gamma Sigma Delta. Contbr. articles to profl. jours. Home: RFD 2 Nevada IA 50201 Office: Corn Insect Research Unit RD2 Box B Ankeny IA 50021

GUTMANN, JOSEPH, art historian; b. Würzburg, Germany, Aug. 17, 1923; s. Henry and Selma (Eisemann) G.; B.S., Temple U., 1949; M.A., N.Y. U., 1952; Ph.D., Hebrew Union Coll., 1960; m. Marilyn Tuckman, Oct. 8, 1953; children—David H., Sharon D. Prof. art history Hebrew Union Coll., Cin., 1960-69, Wayne State U., Detroit, 1969—; vis. prof. Antioch Coll., 1964. Served with USAAF, 1943-46; ETO. Morgenthau Traveling fellow, 1957-58; recipient grants Wayne State U., Am. Philos. Soc., Am. Council Learned Socs., Meml. Found. Jewish Culture. Mem. Coll. Art Assn. Am., Soc. Bibl. Lit., Central Conf. Am. Rabbis, World Congress Jewish Studies, Soc. Bibl. Lit. Reform rabbi, 1957—. Author: Jewish Ceremonial Art, 1964; Beauty in Holiness, 1970; No Graven Images, 1971; Moses Jacob Ezekiel, 1975; The Temple of Solomon, 1976; The Image and the Word, 1977; The Dura-Europos Synagogue, 1973; co-editor religion and arts Scholars Press; editor Library Jewish Art, Ktav Publ. House; editorial bd. Wayne State U. Press, 1973—. Contbr. articles to profl. jours. Home: 14651 Ludlow Oak Park MI 48237 Office: Dept Art History Wayne State Univ Detroit MI 48202

GUTTERMAN, MILTON M., operations research analyst; b. N.Y.C., Nov. 5, 1927; s. Benjamin and Gussie (Rothchild) G.; B.S., Coll. City N.Y., 1948; M.S., U. Chgo., 1949; m. Joan Helen Levey, Nov. 30, 1952; children—Gail Rosemary, Allen Bernard. Researcher, Inst. Air Weapons, 1952-54, Ill. Inst. Tech. Research Inst., Chgo., 1954-66; sr. operations research cons. Standard Oil Co. Ind., Chgo., 1966—. Served with AUS, 1946-47. Mem. Operations Research Soc., Assn. Computing Machinery, Math. Programming Soc., Spl. Interest Group for Math. Programming, SHARE, Chgo. Hort. Soc., Am. Contract Bridge League (life master), Am. (cons. rosarian Ill.-Ind. dist.), Chgo. Regional, Northeastern Ill. rose socs. Jewish. Editor: Computer Applications 1962, 1964; asso. editor ACM Transactions Math. Software, 1975—. Home: 5049 Lee St Skokie IL 60076 Office: 200 E Randolph Dr Chicago IL 60601

GUTTMAN, RALPH MYRON, immunologist; b. Orange, N.J., June 29, 1946; s. Herbert J. and Constance R. (Roth) G.; B.S., Morris Harvey Coll., 1968; M.S., Marquette U., 1972; m. Loretta M. Payne, Dec. 18, 1967; 1 son, David E. Teaching asst. Med. Coll. Wis., 1970-72; research immunologist Burn Research Lab. St. Mary's Hosp., Milw., 1972—, lectr. in-service edn. St. Mary's Hosp., 1972—, dir. Skin Bank, 1976—. Bd. dirs. Les Mariners St. Mary's Hosp. NIH trainee, 1968-72. Mem. Am. Soc. Microbiology, Am. Assn. Tissue Banks (charter mem., chmn. skin banking standards com.), Soc. for Cryobiology, Milw. Tissue Culture Assn., Milw. Immunology Club, Sigma Xi, Chi Beta Phi. Contbr. articles to profl. jours. Home: 5956 N Bay Ridge Ave Whitefish Bay WI 53217 Office: St Mary's Hosp PO Box 503 Milwaukee WI 53201

GUTZLER, BRETT MELVIN, mech. design engr.; b. Centralia, Ill., Mar. 9, 1948; s. Harlan Edward and Norma Linda (Kline) G.; A.A., Kaskaskia Jr. Coll., 1968; B.S.M.E., U. Mo., Rolla, 1971; M.B.A., Lindenwood Coll., 1981; m. Cynthia Lou Rowekamp, May 4, 1974; 1 son, Chad Harlan. Project engr. Blaise Mech. Contractors, 1971-74; design engr. Nat. Mine Service Co., 1974; mech. design engr. Monsanto Corp., St. Louis, 1974-76, sr. mech. design engr., 1977—. Registered profl. engr., Mo., Ill. Mem. ASME, Am. Soc. Heating, Refrigeration and Air Conditioning Engrs., Ill. Soc. Profl. Engrs., U. Mo. Rolla Alumni Assn. Democrat. Lutheran. Home: 22 Millbrooke Dr Saint Charles MO 63301 Office: 800 N Lindbergh Blvd Saint Louis MO 63166

GUY, CARVIN HARRY, farmer, ednl. adminstr.; b. Hillhead, S.D., Apr. 19, 1920; s. Harvey Harry and Lena (Ives) G.; grad. high sch., 1940; m. Anita Maud Nelson, Feb. 27, 1942; children—Karen (Mrs. Wayne Buss), Arlyce (Mrs. Harley Oland), Gerald, Rita (Mrs. Dan Fish). Owner and mgr. registered Shorthorn ranch, 1952—; dir. Grain Terminal Assn.; chmn. meat bd., Nat. Farmers Orgn.; Township bd. dir.; pres. Veblen sch. bd., 1973-74. Active 4-H, leader, 1957-70. Democratic committeeman. Recipient County Farmer of the Year award Soil Conservation Service Dept. Agr., 1962, 2d top recorder of registered Shorthorns, 1974; won sire of yr. award for Shorthorns, 1976. Lutheran (Sunday sch. tchr., officer). Club: Ruritan (dir.). Address: Route 2 Box 120 Veblen SD 57270

GUY, ERNEST THOMAS, assn. exec.; b. Detroit, May 12, 1921; s. William G. and Anna (Utas) G.; B.A., Mich. State U., 1943; postgrad. U. Ga., 1946, U. Mich., 1948; m. Bernice Louise Smith, Mar. 8, 1945 (dec.); children—E. Timothy, Cynthia Louise. State coordinator vets. tng. Ga. Dept. Edn., Atlanta, 1946-47; mgr. sta. WATL, Atlanta, 1947-48; program dir. sta. WKNX, Saginaw, Mich., 1948-50; pub. relations dir. Mich. Heart Assn., Detroit, 1950-53, exec. dir., 1953-58; exec. dir. Tex. Heart Assn., Houston, 1958-68, Chgo. Med. Soc., 1968-69, Cal. Dental Assn., San Francisco, 1969-73, So. Calif. Dental Assn., Los Angeles, 1972-73, Unified Calif. Dental Assn., 1973-74, Am. Soc. Clin. Hypnosis, Des Plaines, Ill., 1974-75; dir. meetings Am. Bar Assn., Chgo., 1975—; mem. industry adv. bd. Meeting World, 1978. Mem. adv. com. Tex. Rehab. Assn. Faculty pub. health classes U. Mich., Ann Arbor, 1953-58; del. White House Conf. Edn., 1956; vice chmn. Fed. Service Campaign for Health Agys. in Tex., 1961-62; mem. governing council Soc. Heart Assns. Profl. Staff, 1959-62. Mem. Pres.'s Bicentennial Commn. Precinct worker Houston Republican Com. Served to capt. AUS, 1943-46. Co-recipient Blakeslee award, 1953; recipient award of merit Mich. Heart Assn., 1958, Merit award Tex. Heart Assn., 1968, commendation award Calif. Dental Assn. Certified assn. exec. Mem. Am. Soc. Assn. Execs. Am. Pub. Relations Soc., Nat. Assn. Parliamentarians, Profl. Conv. Mgmt. Assn., Internat. Platform Assn., Am. Assn. Dental Editors, Nat. Pub. Relations Council, Nat. Assn. Exhibit Mgrs. Republican. Episcopalian (lay reader). Contbr. numerous articles to profl. publs. Home: 930 N Northwest Hwy Unit 202 Park Ridge IL 60068 Office: 1155 E 60th St Chicago IL 60637

GUY, JOHN MARTIN, lawyer, state senator; b. Detroit, July 16, 1929; s. Alvin W. and Ann G. (Martin) G.; B.S., Butler U., 1958; J.D., Ind. U., 1961; m. Norma J. Puterbaugh, Aug. 13, 1950; children—Janice Lynn, Robert John. Admitted to Ind. bar, 1962, since practiced in Monticello; atty. firm Siferd, Roth, Christopher and Guy, 1962—; mem. Ind. Ho. of Reps., 1971-74, house majority leader, 1973-74; mem. Ind. Senate, 1977—. Dir. State and Savs. Bank, Hively's Pharmacy. Pros. atty. 39th Jud. Circuit, 1963-67. Pres. White County Mental Health Assn., 1965-68. Trustee Monticello-Union Twp. Library Bd., pres., 1970-71. Served with USAF, 1951-55. Named Outstanding Republican Freshman Ind. Ho. of Reps., 1971, Ind. Senate, 1977. Mem. Am., Ind., Monticello bar assns., Am. Judicature Soc., Am. Trial Lawyers Assn., Monticello C. of C. (pres. 1975—), Am. Legion. Clubs: Masons, Shriners, Elks, Moose. Home: 200 Western Heights Dr Monticello IN 47960 Office: 115 W Broadway Monticello IN 47960

GUYER, TENNYSON, congressman; b. Findlay, Ohio, Nov. 29, 1913; s. William H. and Myrtle (Hartsock) G.; B.S., Findlay Coll., 1934; m. Edith Mae Reuter, June 10, 1944; children—Sharon Mae, Rosetta Kae. Ordained minister Chs. of God of N. Am., 1936; mayor, Celina, Ohio, 1940-44; pub. affairs dir. Cooper Tire & Rubber Co., Findlay, 1950-72; mem. Ohio Senate, 1959-72; mem. 93d-95th Congresses from 4th Ohio dist. Mem. Ohio Republican Central Com., 1954-66. Mem. Internat. Platform Assn. Mason (Shriner), Rotarian, Elk, Lion. Author: The Church-Institution or Destitution: Blueprints for Youth, 1955. Home: Findlay OH Office: 114 Cannon House Office Bldg Washington DC 20515

GUZIEC, ROBERT ALAN, physician; b. Chgo., Dec. 18, 1938; s. Philip Edward and Dorothy May (Zimmer) G.; M.D., U. Ill., 1963; m. Anita Francis Peklo, June 18, 1970; 1 son, Philip Robert, Intern, Cook County Hosp., Chgo., 1963-64; gen. surgery resident Ill. Masonic Hosp., 1966-67; otolaryngology resident U. Ill. Hosp., 1967-70; attending physician, chmn. sect. otolaryngology and maxillofacial surgery Ill. Masonic Hosp., 1975—; attending physician, cons. Walther Meml., Sydney Forkosh, Martha Washington hosps. Served with USPHS, 1964-66. Diplomate Am. Bd. Otolaryngology. Mem. A.C.S., Am. Acad. Otolaryngology, AMA, Am. Council Otolaryngology, Internat. Soc. Aquatic Medicine, Ill. State, Cook County, Chgo. med. socs., Chgo. Laryngol. and Otological Soc., Alpha Omega Alpha. Office: Suite 1107 30 N Michigan Ave Chicago IL 60602

GUZZETTA, DOMINIC JAMES, univ. pres.; b. Fredonia, N.Y., July 21, 1919; s. James and Josephine (Giordano) G.; student U. Alfred, 1937-38; B.A. cum laude, U. Buffalo, 1948, M.Ed., 1951, Ed.D., 1953; student U. Rochester, 1950-51, Syracuse U., 1951-52; LL.D., Akron U., 1968, Kent State U., 1971; D.Sc., Marian Coll., 1971; L.H.D., Walsh Coll., 1972; m. Marilynn Butler, Feb. 17, 1977; children by previous marriage—JoAnne Nola, Elaine Marie. Tchr. pub. schs., 1948-51; asst. dean Millard Filmore Coll., 1951-53; supr. productivity program FOA, Washington, 1953-54; asst. dean evening and adult edn. div. U. Akron, 1954-56, dean, 1956-59, prof. edn., 1960-68, dir. summer session, 1956-59, acting dean Coll. Edn., 1958-59, dean gen. coll., 1959-62, v.p., dean adminstrn., 1962-66, sr. v.p., provost, 1966-68, coordinator research, 1959-62; pres., prof. history Marian Coll., 1968-71; pres. U. Akron (Ohio), 1971—, prof. higher edn., 1971—. Cons. evaluator higher edn. North Central Assn. Pres. Cuyahoga Falls City Bd. Edn.; trustee Akron Children's Hosp., Akron City Hosp., Walsh Coll., Canton, Ohio. Served from pvt. to capt. AUS, 1940-46; lt. col. Ohio N.G. Mem. Ohio Coll. Assn. (pres. adult edn. sect.), Am. Soc. Tng. Dirs. (pres. N.E. Ohio chpt.), Assn. Univs. Evening Colls., Adult Edn. Assn., Internat. Inst. Akron (pres.), Am. Assn. Sch. Adminstrs., Nat. Council on Ednl. Research, Am. Assn. State Colls. and Univs. (chmn. com. on urban affairs), Ohio Coll. Assn. (mem. exec. com.), Phi Sigma Kappa, Delta Sigma Pi, Kappa Delta Pi, Alpha Sigma Lambda, Phi Delta Kappa, Chi Sigma Nu, Omicron Delta Kappa. Clubs: Cascade, Indpls. Literary, Rotary. Home: 856 Mayfair Rd Akron OH 44303 Office: U Akron Akron OH 44304

GWINN, CECIL WILLIAM, physicist; b. Wheeling, W.Va., Mar. 29, 1921; s. William J.B. and Mildred (Hale) G.; student Ohio State U., 1946-49; m. Geneva Evaline Absalom, Aug. 25, 1956. Physicist, Nat. Bur. Standards, Washington, 1950-53; asst. chemist Goodyear Atomic Corp., Waverly, Ohio, 1954-55; physicist in electromagnetics Wright Patterson AFB, Ohio, 1955-60, research physicist cybernetics, 1960—; vis. lectr. cybernetics U. Nottingham (Eng.), 1966, U. Naples (Italy), 1967, U. Ariz., Tempe, 1968, U. Tenn. Space Inst., 1972. Recipient Achievement awards USAF, 1957, 62, 64, 66, 68. Mem. AAAS, Am. Math Assn., Soc. Gen. Systems Theory, Am. Cybernetics Soc., C.G. Jung Found. for Analytic Psychology, ASCAP. Contbr. articles to profl. jours. Home: 401 Kenilworth Ave Dayton OH 45405 Office: Wright Patterson AFB OH 45433

GYURO, STEVEN JOHN, ednl. instn. exec.; b. Flint, Mich., June 3, 1934; s. Steven John and Helen Marie (Zsigray) G.; B.S., Ohio State U., 1957, M.A., 1964, Ph.D., 1969; m. Jane Ellen Harmon, July 10, 1958; children—Steven Thomas, Carolyn Jane, Robert Michael, Susan Marie. Tchr. Columbus (Ohio) Pub. Schs., 1957-67; asst. prof. edn. U. Ky., Lexington, 1969-71; coordinator product design and devel. Research for Better Schs., Inc., Phila., 1971-72; asst. dir. Comprehensive Career Edn. Model Center for Vocat. Edn., Ohio State U., Columbus, 1972-74, mgmt. analyst Center for Vocat. Edn., 1974-76, asst. to dir., 1976—; cons. in ednl. mgmt.; guest lectr. Temple U., 1971-72. Vice pres. St. Andrew's Bd. Edn., 1967-69. Served with inf. AUS, 1958-59. Mem. Am. Ednl. Research Assn., Nat. Soc. Study Edn., Project Mgmt. Inst., Am. Vocat. Assn., Phi Delta Kappa. Editor: Educational Research Manager, 1972—. Office: 1960 Kenny Rd Columbus OH 43210

HAAKE, JOHN JAY, cons. archtl. woodwork; b. Waukegan, Ill., Nov. 28, 1923; s. Walter Gerhardt and Nena Mae (Falkner) H.; student U. Ill., 1947-48, 67-69; B. Gen. Studies, Roosevelt U., 1973, postgrad., 1973—; m. Mary Joan DeVol, Dec. 24, 1948. Apprentice, Waukegan Sash & Door Co., 1945-49, v.p., plant mgr., 1953-57, pres., 1957-67; archtl. relations rep. Chgo. chpt. Archtl. Woodwork Inst., 1968-71, archtl. woodwork cons., 1971—. Vice-pres. Waukegan Import and Export Corp., 1955-57, pres. 1957-67; v.p. Haake Inc., Waukegan, 1963-67. Adviser constrn. Triton Coll., River Grove, Ill., 1975. Mem. adv. bd. Salvation Army Waukegan, 1957-67, v.p. 1963, pres. 1964. Mem. Ill. Woodwork Assn. (sec. 1965), Am. Legion, Forest Products Research Soc., Constrn. Specifications Inst. (dir. Chgo. chpt. 1976, 77), Lake Michigan Yachting Assn. Presbyn. (deacon). Elk, Kiwanian (dir. 1958 Waukegan). Club: Waukegan Yacht (rear commodore 1957). Address: 1905 N Bonnie Brook Ln Waukegan IL 60085

HAAKER, LESTER WALTER, mech. engr.; b. Chgo., Oct. 24, 1923; s. Lester Walter and Lillian Marie (Tess) H.; B.S., Ill. Inst. Tech., Chgo., 1955; m. Margaret Theresa Wisnewski, June 25, 1949; 1 son, Kevin Lester. Engr., Argonne (Ill.) Nat. Lab., 1950-56; sr. engr. Cook Elec. Co., Chgo., 1956-59; research engr. Central Research Labs., Inc., Red Wing, Minn., 1959—. Mem. Red Wing Harbor Commn., 1972—. Served with AUS, 1943-46; ETO. Mem. Am. Nuclear Soc. (exec. com. remote systems tech. div.), ASME, VFW. Roman Catholic. Clubs: K.C., Elks. Patentee U.S. and abroad. Home: 1000 Hallstrom Dr Red Wing MN 55066 Office: PO Box 75 Red Wing MN 55066

HAAS, EDWARD LEE, accounting firm exec.; b. Camden, N.J., Nov. 9, 1935; s. Edward David and Mildred (Wynne) H.; B.A., LaSalle Coll., 1958; postgrad. Temple U., 1960-62; m. Mary Ann Lind, Dec. 27, 1958; children—John Eric, Gretchen Lind. Mgr. systems devel. RCA Corp., Cherry Hill, N.J., 1966-71; mgr. computer tech. services The Gen. Tire & Rubber Co., Akron, Ohio, 1971-74; mgr. computer applications research and devel. Ernst & Ernst, Cleve., 1974-76, dir. nat. systems group, 1976—. Served with arty., U.S. Army, 1958-59. Mem. Soc. of Certified Data Processors, Data Processing Mgmt. Assn., Assn. for Systems Mgmt., Assn. for Computing Machinery. Republican. Roman Catholic. Clubs: Cleve. Athletic, Hudson Country, Western Reserve Racquet. Home: 312 Aurora St Hudson OH 44236 Office: 1300 Union Commerce Bldg Cleveland OH 44115

HAAS, ERIC RICHARD, bus. exec.; b. Fremont, Ohio, Aug. 24, 1945; s. Ted Joseph and Evelyn L. (Wheeler) H.; m. Cheryl Lyn Tucker, Jan. 29, 1946; 1 son, Derek Jerome; student Capitol U., 1966; B.A., Bowling Green State U., 1967, M.B.A., 1968. Pres., Step-Craft Mfg. Co., Fremont, 1968-70, Poly-Foam Internat., Inc., Fremont, 1971-72, AML Plan, Inc., Indpls., 1972-76, Datappraise, Inc., Indpls., 1976—; cons. Foremost Ins. Co.; cons. editor NADA Appraisal Guides. Mem. Ind. Mobile Home Assn., Mfd. Housing Inst. Author: A Plus for Profits Via Northwest Ohio, 1967; Evaluating the True Worth of Mobile Homes, 1975; How to Appraise a Mobile Home, 1976; Mobile Home Appraisal Guide, 1977. Home: 10146 Osceola Dr Indianapolis IN 46234 Office: PO Box 34072 Indianapolis IN 46234

HAAS, ERWIN, med. scientist; b. Budapest, Hungary, Sept. 11, 1906; s. Jaques and Hedwig (Bass) H.; came to U.S., 1938, naturalized, 1945; Ph.D., U. Chgo., 1942, postgrad., 1942-44; m. Elisabeth Tysper, Feb. 6, 1932; children—Wolfgang, Robert. Research asso. Kaiser Wilhelm Inst., Berlin, 1928-39; asst. prof. chemistry U. Chgo., 1938-44; sr. mem. Worcester Found., Shrewsbury, Mass., 1944-45; asst. prof. exptl. pathology Western Res. U., 1945-46; asst. dir. Cedars of Lebanon Hosp., Hollywood, Calif., 1946-53; dir. L. D. Beaumont Meml. Lab., Mt. Sinai Hosp., Cleve., 1953—. Recipient Goodman award Mt. Sinai Hosp., 1965; USPHS NIH grantee, 1954-77. Mem. Am. Heart Assn. (council high blood pressure research), Internat. Soc. Cardiology (sci. council hypertension), Nat. Soc. Med. Research Am. Soc. Biol. Chemists, Am. Chem. Soc. Research and numerous publs. in medicine, biochemistry. Home: 1081 Carver Rd Cleveland Heights OH 44112 Office: 1800 E 105th St Cleveland OH 44106

HAAS, JAMES WAYNE, accountant; b. Merrill, Wis., Sept. 27, 1944; s. Frank Joseph and Verna Antoinette (Beilke) H.; Asso. in Accounting, North Central Tech. Inst., 1968; m. Patrice Marie Will, June 2, 1973; children—Christopher Jon, Scott James. Controller, asst. treas. House of Merrill Inc., Merrill, 1968-72; controller Semling Menke Co., Inc., Merrill, 1968-72; treas., dir. North Star Communications, Ltd., Gleason, Wis., 1971-72; v.p., sec., dir. Profl. Accounting Systems, Inc., Merrill, 1975—; pres., dir. Haas Enterprises, Inc., 1971—; pres., sec., dir. Haas Millwork Corp., Merrill, 1975—; v.p., treas. ops. mgr. Accounting Bookkeeping Inc., Wauwatosa, Wis., 1975-76; v.p. Marathan Mining & Mfg. Corp., Wausau, Wis., 1976, pres., 1977—; treas., controller, prodn. mgr. Moduline Windows, Inc., Wausau, 1977—. Active Affiliated Merrill Area United Way; treas. com. To Save Pine Crest, 1975. Mem. Nat. Soc. Pub. Accountants, Adminstrv. Mgmt. Soc., Inst. Internal Auditors, Wis. Assn. Accounts, Inst. Record Mgrs. and Adminstrs., Merrill Area C. of C., Am. Soc. Notaries, Am. Inst. Profl. Numismatists (charter mem.), Brookfield Jaycees, Merrill Jaycees. Democrat. Roman Catholic. Clubs: K.C., Kiwanis (New Club Bldg. award), Optomists. Home: 206 John St Merrill WI 54452 Office: PO Box 393 Merrill WI 54452

HAAS, KENNETH BROOKS, JR., veterinarian; b. Pitts., Jan. 14, 1928; s. Kenneth Brooks and Verna Viola (Hoffman) H.; M.A., Western Mich. U., 1961; D.V.M., Ohio State U., 1949; m. Rae Marie Hardy, Feb. 14, 1953; children—Kenneth, Patricia, Jeffrey, Susan. Veterinarian in charge Christensen Animal Hosp., Chgo., 1949-53; asst. editor Vet. Medicine, Kansas City, Mo., 1953; staff veterinarian The Upjohn Co., Kalamazoo, Mich., 1953—; clin. prof. medicine, physicians' assts. program Western Mich. U., 1975—; instr. Kalamazoo Valley Community Coll., 1977—. Mem. AVMA. Club: Elks. Home: 2722 Carlyle Dr Kalamazoo MI 49008 Office: Upjohn Co Kalamazoo MI 49001

HAAS, LARRY ALFRED, chemist; b. Zeeland, N.D., Nov. 28, 1935; s. August and Martha (Wagemann) H.; B.A., U. S.D., 1957; M.S., U. Minn., 1964; m. Eleanor Louise Allen, Sept. 4, 1959; children—David Larry, Douglas Allen. Chemist, Honeywell, Mpls., 1957-62; research chemist U.S. Bur. Mines, Mpls., 1962-69, project leader, 1969—. Chmn. Mpls. Area Boys Brigade, 1968-72; bd. dirs. Minn. Camping Assn., 1972—. Served with USAR, 1959-67. Mem. Am. Inst. Mining, Metal. and Petroleum Engrs., Am. Inst. Chem. Engrs., Am. Chem. Soc., Catalysis Soc. Am. Clubs: Berea Volley Ball, Christian Service Brigade, Camp Nathanael. Contbr. articles to profl. jours. Patentee in catalysis, plasma discharges and metal extraction. Home: 2606 River Hills Dr Burnsville MN 55337 Office: PO Box 1660 Twin Cities MN 55111

HAAS, LEONARD CLARENCE, univ. chancellor; b. Eau Claire, Wis., Feb. 17, 1915; s. Lee Leon and Laura (Brown) H.; B.E., Wis. State Coll., Eau Claire, 1935; M. Philosophy, U. Wis., 1938; student Columbia, 1939, U. So. Calif., 1940; Ph.D., U. Minn., 1954; LL.D. (hon.), St. Olaf Coll., 1968; m. Dorellen Marie Lambert, May 31, 1941; children—Karen Marie, Kristine Kay. Elementary sch. tchr., Watertown, S.D., 1935-37; grad. asst. history U. Wis., 1937-38; dir. guidance, faculty Wausau (Wis.) Sr. High Sch., 1938-41; faculty Inst. History and Polit. Sci., Wis. State U., Eau Claire, 1941-44, 46-48, dir. tchr. tng. and placement, 1944-46, dean instrn., registrar, 1948-59, pres., 1959-71; exec. v.p. U. Wis. system, 1971-73; chancellor U. Wis. at Eau Claire, 1973—; exec. dir. Wis. State Univs., 1971—. Chmn. council of chancellors U. Wis. System, 1974-75. Mem. div. ednl. services Luth Ch. U.S.A., Bd. Coll. Edn., Am. Luth. Ch., 1954-70; v.p. Eau Claire City Council, 1949-55, pres., 1955-57. Bd. dirs. Eau Claire United Fund, Luther Hosp.; trustee Eau Claire Pub. Library; pres. Grace Luth. Found. Recipient Luth. layman's award, 1957; Kiwanis achievement award for civic service, 1957. Mem. Wis. League Municipalities (dist. v.p. 1954), N.E.A., Wis. Edn. Assn., Wis. Com. Gen. Edn. (chmn. 1956), Am. Assn. Coll. Registrars (Wis. pres. 1952), Hesperia Lit. Soc., Eau Claire C. of C.

HABAK, PHILIP A., cardiologist; b. Cairo, Egypt, Sept. 24, 1937; s. Antoine and Jeanette Habak; came to U.S., 1965; naturalized, 1969; student St. Joseph Coll., Cairo, 1952-56; M.B., B.Ch., Ainshams Faculty Medicine, 1963, m. Hermina Geels, Feb. 7, 1970; children—Patricia Jane, Glenn Eric. Intern Cook County (Ill.) Hosp., 1965-66; resident Univ. Hosps., Iowa City, Iowa, 1966-69, fellow in cardiology, 1971-73; practice medicine specializing in cardiology, 1974—; asso. cardiovascular div. dept. internal medicine U. Iowa, 1973-74. Served to maj. M.C., U.S. Army, 1969-71. NIH grantee, 1971-73; diplomate Am. Bd. Internal Medicine. Fellow A.C.P., Am. Coll. Cardiology, Council on Clin. Cardiology, Am. Heart Assn.; mem. AMA, Iowa State Med. Soc. Research coronary primary prevention trial, Lipid Research Clin., U. Iowa, 1973-74. Office: 1706 Brady Suite 309 Davenport IA 52803

HABAYEB, KELLY MOHAMMED, engr.; b. Tulkarm, Palestine, Nov. 2, 1942; s. Mohammed Mustfa and Salima (Salem) H.; came to U.S., 1963, naturalized, 1975; B.M.E., Ind. Inst. Tech., 1968; 1 son, Omar K. Product engr. Gen. Tire & Rubber Co., Wabash, Ind., 1968-69; project engr. Wabash Alloys, Inc., 1969-70, maintenance supt., 1970-72, chief project engr., 1972-74, chief engr., 1974—, also corp. subsidiaries. Recipient certificate of appreciation Rotary Club of Wabash, 1969. Mem. Am. Metal Soc., Aluminum Recycling Assn. (chmn. energy conservation com.) Republican. Moslem. Club: Elks. Patentee Wabash System. Home: 56 W Sinclair St Wabash IN 46992 Office: Wabash Alloys US 24 W Wabash IN 46992

HABLE, EDWARD GERARD, metal bldg. designer; b. Maple Heights, Ohio, Oct. 16, 1919; s. John and Mary Theresa (Vanek) H.; B. Structural Engring., Fenn Coll., 1949; hon. degree Cleve. State U., 1967; m. Joanna Marguerite Zahnke, Apr. 24, 1948; children—William, Louise, James, Michael, Paul, Steven. Engr. Cleve. Transit System, 1950; plant engr. Cadillac Tank Plant, Brook Park, Ohio, 1951; design engr., Richard Hawley Cutting & Assos.,

1952; design engr. H. Fischer & Assos., Cleve., 1953; project engr. Steel Craft Mfg. Co., Cin., 1954-58; chief engr. Inland Steel Products Co., Milw., 1959-63; v.p. engring. Closing Offices of Am., Elkhart, Ind., 1964-65; registered chief engr. Designed Facilities, Inc., El Monte, Calif., 1966-67; chief engr. Sommer Steel Bldg. Fabricating Inc., Waukesha, Wis., 1967-76; chief engr. Sonoco bldgs. Sonoco Products Co., 1976—; dir. Hilton Spacemaster Corp., Continental Spacemaster Corp. Fallout shelter analyst Office of Civil Def., 1970; multi-disaster design analyst Def. Civil Preparedness Agy., 1973. Served with USAAF, 1941-45. Decorated Bronze Star medal. Registered profl. engr., Wis., Ill., Ind., Ohio, Mich., Iowa, W.Va., Ky. Mem. Wis. (past sec., treas., past pres. Milw. No. chpt.), Nat. socs. profl. engrs., D.A.V., Veritas Forum, Lambda Tau Delta, Alpha Phi Omega. K.C. (past grand knight), Elk. Club: Royal Oks (Cleveland). Home: 8504 W Holly Rd 115N Mequon WI 53092 Office: 19775 Sommer Dr Waukesha WI 53186

HABRYL, EDMUND JOHN, machinery mfg. co. exec.; b. Chgo., May 6, 1935; s. Edward John and Martha Sylvia (Schroeder) H.; B.A. in Math., Roosevelt U., 1962; m. Marilyn Ann Sowa, Jan. 28, 1961; children—Carolyn, Diane. Staff asst. communications cons. Ill. Bell Telephone Co., Chgo., 1958-65; asst. data processing mgr. Toni div. Gillette Co., Chgo., 1965-68; project mgr. G.D. Searle Co., Skokie, Ill., 1968-69; systems mgr. Leo Burnett Co., Chgo., 1969-72; project devel. mgr. Kraftco Corp., Glenview, Ill., 1972-74; project mgr., marketing information systems mgr. A.B. Dick Co., Niles, Ill., 1974—. Mem. Ill. N.G., 1958-64. Served with AUS, 1958-59. Mem. Am. Statis. Assn., Assn. Systems Mgmt. (div. dir. 1968-69, dir. at large 1969-70), Inst. Mgmt. Scis., Am. Mktg. Assn., Operations Research Soc., Smithsonian Inst., Art Inst. Chgo., Holy Name Soc. Roman Catholic (parish council). Home: 5713 W Patterson St Chicago IL 60634 Office: AB Dick Co Niles IL

HABRYL, JOY, psychologist; b. Chgo., July 30, 1937; d. Fred F. and Claire (Gard) Habryl; B.S., Northwestern U., 1958, Ph.D., 1971; M.A., Radcliffe Coll., 1960. Tchr., Evanston Twp. (Ill.) High Sch., 1959-67; asst. prof. student affairs Wis. State U., LaCrosse, 1969-71; clin. psychologist VA, Downey, Ill., 1971—. Reading cons. Sci. Research Assos., Chgo., 1963-64. Mem. Human Relations Council LaCrosse, 1969—, Cath. Interracial Council, 1969—. Bd. dirs. Jr. Governing Bd. Chgo. Symphony Orch., 1968—. Mem. Nat. Assn. Women Deans and Counselors, Am. Personnel and Guidance Assn., Ill. Acad. Criminology, Am., Nat., Ill. psychol. assns. Home: 4943 N Francisco St Chicago IL 60625 Office: Psychology Service VA Hospital 183 Downey IL 60064

HACHMEISTER, ALBERT W., pub., editor; b. Chgo., June 1, 1919; s. Walter Christian and Phoebe (Thompson) H.; student Northwestern, U., 1937-38; m. Muriel Jean Marx, Sept. 7, 1946; children—Ann, David, Peter. Asso. editor Smith Publs., 1938, advt. mgr., 1939, editor, 1939-40; pub., editor Marking Devices Pub. Co., 1941—, pres., chmn. bd., 1942—; pres. Plymouth Agy., Inc.; pres. Mktg. Decision Data, Inc. Mem. 68th-74th Ill. Gen. Assemblies, 10th Dist.; minority leader 74th Ill. Gen. Assembly; chmn. Great Lakes Commn., 1955-61. Pres. 44th Ward Rep. Orgn., 1956-64. Exec. officer C.E. chief of engrs., 1943-45. Vice chmn. Intergovtl. Coop. Commn., 1963-66; chmn. Worlds Fair Commn. 1976; chmn. Ill.-Ind. Port Study Commn., 1957-61. Asso. mem. bd. trustees Shimer Coll. Mem. Art Inst. Chgo. (life), Am. Forestry Assn., Greater Chgo. Churchmen, Am. Mktg. Assn., Am. Inst. Mgmt. (asso.), Council State Govts., Better Govt. Assn. (dir.), Salvation Army Assn., Sigma Delta Chi. Clubs: Headline, Marking Device, Press. Home: 339 Barry Ave Chicago IL 60657 Office: 18 E Huron St Chicago IL 60611

HACHMEISTER, ROBERT JOHN, restaurant exec.; b. Chgo., Aug. 8, 1943; s. Marvin Robert and Marcella Anna (Kosinski) H.; student Our Lady of Benburb Priory, Benburb, No. Ireland, 1962-64, Stonebridge Priory, 1964-65; Mus.B., Roosevelt U., 1968; m. Mary Claire Carey, Oct. 5, 1968; children—Michael Robert, Matthew Joseph, Patricia Anne. Organist, choir dir. St. Luke Ch., River Forest, Ill., 1966-68, St. Teresa Ch., Belleville, Ill., 1968-73, Blessed Sacrament Ch., Belleville, 1973-74; mgr. Jacks or Better Restaurant, Fairview Heights, Ill., 1974—; organist United Methodist Ch., Belleville, 1977—. Dir. Belleville Philharmonic Chorale, 1969—, Belleville Diocesan Chorale, 1972-74, 76-77; chmn., instr. organist tng. program Belleville Diocese, 1969-71, mem. liturgy and music commn., 1973—; pvt. tchr. piano and organ, 1969—; condr. Belleville Philharmonic Orch., 1974-75. Bd. dirs. Belleville Philharmonic Soc., 1970—, chmn. music com., 1973-76. Mem. Travelers Protective Assn. Am., Roosevelt U. Alumni Assn. Roman Catholic. Author: Helpful Hints for Church Organists, 1970. Composer numerous choral compositions. Home: 122 N Missouri Ave Belleville IL 62221 Office: Jacks or Better Restaurant Fairview Heights IL 62208

HACHTMAN, SAMUEL JOSEPH, food co. exec.; b. Chgo., Apr. 25, 1910; s. Isaac and Molly (Burr) H.; J.D., Northwestern U., 1922; emeritus degree, U. Chgo., 1971; m. Rose Cohn, Dec. 16, 1923; 1 dau., Harriet Hachtman Wallen. Admitted to Ill. bar, 1922; corporate and gen. practice law; pres. Sugarless Candy Corp. Am., Chgo., 1964—, Health Snacks, Ltd., Chgo., 1973—, Mem. Am., Ill. (sr. counsellor), Chgo. bar assns., Decalogue Soc., Am. Judicature Soc. Clubs: Masons, Shriners, Ill. Athletic. Patentee in field. Home: 1108 N Harlem Ave River Forest IL 60305 Office: 3537 W North Ave Chicago IL 60647

HACK, RAYMOND CHARLES, hotel exec.; b. Chgo., Feb. 23, 1942; s. Conrad and Mary (Heizman) H.; B.S., Christian Bros. Coll., 1965; m. Carin Primozic, Nov. 20, 1971. Supr., Campbell Soup Co., Chgo., 1965-66; programmer Household Finance Corp., Chgo., 1966-68; data center mgr. Hilton Hotels Corp., Chgo., 1968-76, Hyatt Corp., Rosemont, Ill., 1976—. Mem. Assn. Systems Mgmt. Home: 909 71st St Darien IL 60559 Office: 9300 W Bryn Mawr St Rosemont IL 60018

HACKBARTH, CLARENCE WALTER, educator; b. West Allis, Wis., Dec. 12, 1927; s. Clarence Walter and Norma (Keikbush) H.; B.A., Elmhurst Coll., 1954; postgrad. Eden Theol. Sem., 1954-56; M.S., U. Wis., 1958; postgrad. U. Colo., 1963, Fla. State U., 1972, U. Belgrade (Yugoslavia), 1972; m. June Ellen Splittstoesser, Aug. 17, 1957; children—Richard, Scott, Mark. Counselor, Ill. State Tng. Sch. for Boys, St. Charles, 1953-54; instr. sociology Florence (Ala.) State Coll., 1958-61, Wis. State U., Superior, 1961-64; supply analyst systems mgmt. USN Electronics Supply Office, Gt. Lakes, Ill., 1964-65; asso. prof. sociology Delta Coll., University Center, Mich., 1965-76, chmn. social sci. div., 1976—. On-site asst. dir. Yugoslavia project League of Innovation in Community Colls., 1972. Mem. com. Boy Scouts Am., 1972-73, Little League, 1974—; county chmn. Mich. Internat. Week, 1972. Served with USNR, 1945-46. Fellow League for Innovation in Community Colls.; mem. Am., Mich. sociol. assns., A.A.U.P. (chpt. sec. 1968-69, mem. state com. on student rights and responsibilities 1967-69), A.C.L.U., Common Cause. Home: 1205 Scott St Midland MI 48640 Office: Delta Coll University Center MI 48710

HACKER, DONALD WILBUR, mail advt. exec.; b. Ionia, Mich., June 18, 1914; s. Herman F. and Helena (Steinke) H.; grad., Chgo. Acad. Fine Arts, 1937, U. Ga., 1942-43; m. Ruby Elaine Simonson, Sept. 28, 1943; children—Eve Rulaine, David Kent, Donna Kathleen. Asst. advt. mgr. Gen. Furniture Co., Inc., Chgo., 1937-39; advt. merchandising mgr. Franc's, Davenport, Ia., 1939-42; owner Lettercraft Co., Detroit, 1946—; pres. D.W. Hacker Co., Detroit, 1950, University Type, Inc., 1965—, Hacker-Stutz Corp., 1963—. Bd. dirs. Detroit Cerebral Center; active community drs.; bd. dirs., pres. United Cerebral Palsy Found.; pres. Living Opportunities, Inc., 1969; vice pres. United Cerebral Palsy Assn. Mich. Served as dir. pub. relations U.S.A. C.E., AUS, 1944-46. Mem. Mail Advt. Service Assn. Internat. (pres. 1954-57), Detroit Chpt. Mail Advt. Service Assn. (pres. 1947-52), Advt. Fedn. Am. (dir. 1954-57). Lutheran. Clubs: Forest Lake Country (Bloomfield Hills); Detroit Executive's Assn. (sec., dir. 1955—), Recess (Detroit); Innisbrook Golf and Country (Tarpon Springs, Fla.); Rolls Royce Owners; The Club at Crayton Cove (Naples, Fla.). Home: 4778 Lahser Rd Bloomfield Hills MI 48013 also 1817 Cliff Rd Point Aux Barques MI 48467 Office: 2180 E Milwaukee Ave Detroit MI 48211

HACKER, EDWARD GEORGE, real estate co. exec.; b. Rochester, Mich., May 30, 1893; s. Thomas William and Hattie Celiste (Coulton) H.; grad. high sch.; m. Della Barbara Guenther, Aug. 26, 1919; children—Barbara (Mrs. William W. Baldwin), Edward Thomas, Richard Christian. Partner, T.W. Hacker & Son, 1919-22; pres. Edward G. Hacker Co., Lansing, Mich., 1922-63; chmn. Edward G. Hacker Co., Hacker Land Co. Mem. Bd. Water and Light Commrs. Lansing, 1946-50; pres. Community Chest, Lansing; v.p. mem. exec. and chmn. finance coms. Mich. United Fund, 1949-56. Bd. dirs. YMCA. Served with U.S. Army, 1918-19. Recipient Centennial award Mich. State Coll., 1955; Distinguished Citizen's citation, Distinguished Citizen award City of Lansing, 1959; Community Service award C. of C. Greater Lansing, 1962; Realtor of Year award Lansing Bd. Realtors and Mich. Real Estate Assn., 1967; Paul Harris fellow Rotary Found., 1972. Mem. Nat. Assn. Realtors (gov. soc. real estate counselors 1965-67), Mich. Real Estate Assn. (chmn. Russel A. Pointer Scholarship Fund 1973, 74-75), Lansing Bd. Realtors (chmn. ednl. com. 1944-45), Lansing C. of C. Conglist. Mason, Rotarian. Clubs: Country, City (Lansing). Home: 3301 Moores River Dr Lansing MI 48910 Office: 225 W Washtenaw St Lansing MI 48933

HACKETT, JOHN THOMAS, economist; b. Ft. Wayne, Ind., Oct. 10, 1932; s. Harry H. and Ruth (Greer) H.; B.S., Ind. U., 1954, M.B.A., 1958; Ph.D., Ohio State U., 1961; m. Ann E. Thompson, July 24, 1954; children—Jane, David, Sarah, Peter. Instr. Ohio State U., 1958-61; asst. v.p., economist Fed. Res. Bank, Cleve., 1961-64; dir. planning Cummins Engine Co., Columbus, Ind., 1965—, v.p. finance, 1966-71, exec. v.p., 1971—, also chief fin. officer, dir.; dir. Fed. Res. Bank Chgo. Bd. dirs. Cummins Engine Co. Found.; trustee Camping and Edn. Found. Served to 1st lt. AUS, 1954-56. Mem. Am. Econ. Assn., Am. Fin. Assn., Fin. Mgmt. Assn., Fin. Execs. Inst., Bus. Economists Assn., Conf. Bd. (fin. execs. council), Beta Gamma Sigma. Home: 1005 Hawthorne Dr Columbus IN 47201 Office: 1000 5th St Columbus IN 47201

HACKETT, MARY MILAM (MRS. RALPH C. HACKETT), banker, farmer; b. Chelsea, Okla., May 16, 1916; d. Jesse Bartley and Elizabeth (McSpadden) Milam; B.A., U. Okla., 1937; m. George Joseph Stevenson, Jr., Nov. 5, 1938 (dec. Apr. 1962); children—George Joseph III, Gelvin Lee, Mark Milam, Elizabeth Ellen; m. 2d, Ralph C. Hackett, Mar. 22, 1970. Bookkeeper, Phillips & Milam, 1937-38; mgr. grain and livestock farm, Tarkio, Mo., 1962—; former v.p., now chmn. bd. Farmers & Valley Bank; pres. Water Supply Co., Inc., Chelsea, Okla; partner Phillips & Milam Oil Co., Chelsea, 1949-74, Miller & Stevenson Ins. Co., Tarkio, Mo., 1962-74, M. & S. Trailer Rental Co., Harlingen, Tex., 1962-67. Mem. children and youth com. N.W. div. Mo. Assn. Social Welfare; chmn. ways and means com. Fairfax Hosp. Aux.; bd. dirs. Midland Empire Council Girl Scouts U.S.A., 1959-68, dist. chmn., 1960-65; bd. dirs. Atchison County chpt. A.R.C., 1957—, water safety chmn., 1955-60; mem. finance com. Tarkio Coll.-Community Farm Project; mem. Tarkio Bicentennial Com. Bd. dirs. Mo. Soc. Crippled Children and Adults; bd. dirs. Tarkio Coll., 1962-75, sec., 1962-68, asst. treas., 1969-75, exec. bd., 1965-68, 1970-75. Mem. Nat. Assn. Bank Women, Am. Assn. U. Women (mem. exec. bd.), Okla. Hist. Soc., Cherokee Nat. Hist. Soc., League Democratic Women Voters, Am. Legion Aux., P.E.O. (past pres.), Atchison County Hist. Soc., Mule Barn Theater Guild, Kappa Alpha Theta. Presbyn. (trustee ch. 1973-76, elder 1977—, past pres. Presbyn. Women's Assn.). Home: 902 Park St Tarkio MO 64491 Office: 302 Main St Tarkio MO 64491

HACKL, DONALD JOHN, architect; b. Chgo., May 11, 1934; s. John Frank and Frieda Marie (Weichmann) H.; B.Arch., U. Ill., 1957, M.S. in Architecture, 1958; m. Bernadine Marie Becker, Sept. 29, 1962; children—Jeffrey Scott, Craig Michael, Cristina Lynn. Mem. staff Comm, Comm & Moses architects, Chgo., 1959-60; mem. mechanics research div. Am. Machinery and Foundry, Niles, Ill., 1960-62; project architect Loebl Schlossman & Bennett, Architects-Engrs., Chgo., 1962-64; asso. Loebl, Schlossman Bennett & Dart, Chgo., 1967—, partner, 1970—, exec. v.p., 1974—; also dir.; pres., dir. Loebl Schlossman & Hackl, 1975—, Dart-Hackl Internat., Ltd., 1975—. Mem. com. to draft minimum design standards for design of dentention facilities Ill. Dept. Pub. Safety, 1971. Mem. Ill. Right to Life Com., 1973; mem. Chgo. Met. Cancer Crusade, 1973; chmn. architects and engrs. subcom., 1974. Mem. AIA (mem. documents bd.; treas., dir. Chgo. chpt. 1976-77), Chgo. Bldg. Congress, Chgo. Council on Fgn. Relations. Roman Catholic. Clubs: Tavern, Carlton, Economic. Prin. works include: Samsonite Corp. Hdqrs., Denver, 1968, Water Tower Place, Chgo., 1974, HFC World Hdqrs., Northbrook, Ill., 1978, Square D Internat. Hdqrs., Palatine, Ill., 1978, Cancer Research Inst., King Faisal Specialist Hosp., Riyadh, Saudi Arabia, 1978. Contbr. articles to profl. jours. and trade publs. Home: 1534 Walnut St Wilmette IL 60091 Office: 845 N Michigan Ave Chicago IL 60611

HACKMAN, DONALD JON, mech. engr.; b. Youngsville, Pa., July 24, 1936; s. William and Catherine (Morgach) H.; B.S., Cleve. State Coll., 1962; M.S., Ohio State U., 1969; m. Christine Joan Barclay, Oct. 6, 1962. Engr. asst. Sylvania Elec. Co., Warren, Pa., 1957-62, design engr., 1962-64; research engr. Battelle Inst., Columbus, Ohio, 1964-74, sr. engr., 1974—; cons. on ocean engring. to USN, Recipient award for Excellence in Machine Design, Machinery Mag., 1962. Mem. ASME, Sigma Xi. Patents, publs. on underwater tools. Home: 3499 Kirkham Rd Columbus OH 43221 Office: 505 King Ave Columbus OH 43201

HACKMAN, HELEN ANNA HENRIETTE, home economist; b. New Melle, Mo., Oct. 8, 1908; d. John Henry and Lydia Eliza (Meier) Hackman; A.B., Central Wesleyan Coll., Warrenton, Mo., 1929; B.S., U. Mo., 1942, postgrad., 1942; postgrad. U. Wis., 1934, U. Colo., 1953, 75, U. Ariz., 1975, 77. Prin., Wright City High Sch., 1929; home econs. tchr., Cape Girardeau, Mo., 1930-42; sr. extension adviser home econs. U. Ill., Pittsfield, 1942—. Dietitian, buyer Oshkosh Wis. Camp Fire Girls Camp, summers 1935, 36, 37; sec.-treas. Western Ill. 4-H Camp Assn., 1952-54; mem. Western Ill. Fair Bd. Com., Griggsville, 1946—; v.p. Tri-county Assn. for Crippled, 1960—; tech. cons. White House Conf., 1960, 70; pres. Pike County Heart Assn., 1969, organizer Family Planning Centers, Diabetic and Blood Pressure Clinics, Pike County Health Dept., 1971. Bd. dirs. Pike County Mental Health. Recipient Distinguished Service award Nat. Home Demonstration Agts. Assn., 1952; Meritorious Service award Heart Assn., 1960, 61. Mem. Ill. Home Adviser's Assn. (sec. 1948), Nat. Assn. Extension Home Economists (3d v.p. 1951-53, pub. relations chmn. 1951-53), Am. Home Econs. Assn. (sec. Ill. nutrition com. 1967-69), Epsilon Sigma Phi (chief 1962), Gamma Sigma Delta. Home: 230 S Illinois St Pittsfield IL 62363 Office: PO Box 227 Hwy 36 and 54th St E Pittsfield IL 62363

HACKMANN, EMIL EDWARD, educator; b. Concordia, Mo., Jan. 14, 1923; s. Edward H.F. and Emma (Krueger) H.; A.B., Concordia Sem., 1944, M.Div., 1947; M.A., Washington U., 1953; Ph.D., U. Nebr., 1963; m. Gladys Pauline Roseman, Aug. 16, 1947; children—P. Edward, J. David, G. Gloria, K. Kristian, Lisa, E. Kurt. Instr. Concordia Sem., Springfield, Ill., 1947-49, asst. prof., 1949-53; asso. prof. Concordia Tchrs. Coll., Seward, Nebr., 1957-66, chmn. philosophy, religion and social scis. div., 1963-66; prof. Capital U., Columbus, Ohio, 1966—, chmn. dept. philosophy, 1966—; part-time instr. U. Nebr., Lincoln, 1960-66; prof. Ohio U., Athens, 1966-73. Ordained to ministry, Lutheran Ch., 1953; pastor Holy Cross Luth. Ch., Anita, Iowa, 1953-55, Immanuel Luth. Ch., Eagle, Nebr., 1955-57; European tour dir., chmn. Ohio So. Pastor-Tchr. Conf., 1973-75. Aid Assn. for Lutherans faculty fellow, 1961-62. Mem. Am., Ohio philos. assns., Am. Acad. Religion. Lutheran (chmn. bd. edn. 1972-74). Home: 1733 Baltimore Rd Lancaster OH 43130 Office: Philosophy Dept Capital U Columbus OH 43209

HACQUEBORD, DAVID GEORGE, elec. engr.; b. Berwyn, Ill., Sept. 7, 1940; s. George Andrew and Carol Elizabeth (Rowe) Hacquebord; m. Joan Kullberg, Dec. 21, 1968; children—Jodi, Daniel. B.S., U. Ill. at Chgo. Circle, 1974. Elec. engr. Tri-Tronics Co., Oakbrook, Ill., 1968-74, gen. mgr., 1974, v.p., gen. mgr., 1977—. Mem. Western Springs (Ill.) Fire Dept., 1963-71; mem. LaGrange (Ill.) Civil Defense Police, 1972-76, capt., 1976—; trustee Western Springs Baptist Ch., 1972-74. Asso. mem. Ill. Police Assn. Home: 414 S Ashland Ave LaGrange IL 60525 Office: 619 Enterprise Dr Oak Brook IL 60521

HADDAD, DELORRE SALEM, orthodontist; b. Canton, Ohio, Jan. 22, 1935; s. Tofy S. and Sumia (Rahal) H.; student Kent State U., 1953-56; D.D.S., Ohio State U., 1960, M.S. in Orthodontics, 1969; m. Lily Jean Baker, Mar. 18, 1956; children—Ellen Sue, David DeLorre. Individual practice dentistry, Brunswick, Ohio, 1962-67; individual practice orthodontics, Medina, Ohio, 1969—; mem. staff Medina Community Hosp. Pres. Medina County Heart Assn., 1965-67, med. del., 1969; bd. dirs., chmn. benefit Medina County Charities, 1974, 75; bd. dirs. Medina YMCA, 1972-73, sec., 1973-75, chmn. YM-YWCA Joint Bldg. Fund Campaign, Medina County, 1971; trustee N.E. Ohio chpt. Am. Heart Assn. Served with USAF, 1960-62. Mem. Am., Ohio dental assns., Cleve., Akron dental socs., Gt. Lakes, Cleve. orthodontic socs., Eico Orthodontic Study Group, Am. Assn. Orthodontists, Brunswick C. of C. (chmn. membership com. 1965-66, recipient achievement award 1966), Medina C. of C. (chmn. parks and recreation com., dir. 1972-73, v.p. 1973-74, pres. 1974-75, Outstanding Achievement award 1974), Delta Upsilon. Methodist (dir., mem. finance com. 1972-74). Home: 835 Weymouth Rd Medina OH 44256 Office: 257 S Court St Medina OH 44256

HADDAD, GEORGE RICHARD, musician, educator; b. East End, Sask., Can., May 11, 1918; s. Richard and Labeeby (Salloum) H.; asso. Toronto Conservatory Music, 1931, licentiate, 1941; Mus.B., U. Toronto, 1940; M.A., Ohio State U., 1954; student Royal Conservatory Music Toronto, 1936-40, Juilliard Grad. Sch., N.Y.C., 1940-43, Paris (France) Conservatoire, 1950-52; m. Lilyan Aboud, May 20, 1949; children—Constance, Diane, Carolyn. Appeared in various recitals, guest appearances throughout U.S., Can., Europe, 1944—; tchr. piano Bay View Summer Coll. Music, summers, 1948-51; prof. Sch. Music, Ohio State U., Columbus, 1952—; guest artist leading symphony orchs. in U.S., Can. and Europe including Detroit Symphony, Toronto Symphony, Luxembourg Symphony. , Mem. Music Tchrs. Nat. Assn., Nat. Music Guild Piano Tchrs., Ohio Music Tchrs. Assn., Musicians Union, Pi Kappa Lambda. Clubs: Faculty; Kinsmen of Can.; Torch. Home: 2689 River Park Dr Columbus OH 43220

HADDAD, JOSEPH NICHOLAS, travel agency exec.; b. Chgo., Aug. 31, 1931; s. Fadlallah and Hannie (Bitar) H.; B.S., U. Ill., 1957; postgrad Mich. State U., 1969-71. Loan analyst Fed. Reserve Bank Chgo., 1949-53; regional credit mgr. CIT Corp., Chgo., 1957-62, v.p., gen. mgr. Transcontinental Credit Corp., Chgo., 1962-67; chmn., pres. Diners Fugazy Travel and Incentive Ltd., Chgo., 1967—; guest lectr. Internat. Travel and Tng. Sch.; dir. N. Point State Bank, Arlington Heights, Ill., Garfield Ridge Trust & Savs. Bank. Served with U.S. Army, 1952-53; Korea. Mem. Mid-America Arab C. of C. (dir.), Am. Soc. Travel Agents, Inst. Certified Travel Agts. (life), Pacific Area Travel Assn., Chinese Passenger Traffic Club (v.p.). Roman Catholic. Home: 6473 N Leoti Ave Chicago IL 60646 Office: 105 W Adams St Chicago IL 60603

HADDEN, STUART TRACEY, thermodynamicist; b. Grand Rapids, Mich., Aug. 13, 1911; s. H. Tracey and Lilo (Sharpe) H.; student Mich. State U., 1929-31; B.S.Engring. in Math., U. Mich., 1934, B.S. in Chem. Engring., 1935; M.A., Temple U., 1951; D.Engring. Sci., N.Y. U., 1965; m. Kathryn Kirkwood Martin, Nov. 2, 1940; 1 dau., Sharon (Mrs. Michael James Tannler). Chem. engr. Calco Chem. Co., Bound Brook, N.J., 1935-37; technologist Mobil Oil Corp., Paulsboro, N.J., 1937-53, cons., N.Y.C., 1958-59, sr. engr., 1959-60; cons. React Motors, Inc., Denville, N.J., 1954-56; systems engr. Dow Chem. Co., Midland, Mich., 1960-63; sr. project engr. Gulf Research; Devel. Co., Pitts., 1963-67; mathematician specialist Monsanto Co., St. Louis, 1967-70; staff cons. Altek Engring. Ltd., St. Louis, 1971-73; cons. Mobil Research and Devel. Corp., Princeton, 1973-77; cons. Ortloff Corp., Midland, Tex., 1977—. Instr. extension div. U. Mich., 1935, Rutgers U., 1946; instr., Fairleigh Dickinson U., 1956-58; instr., engring. scientist N.Y. U., 1953-57. Recipient Founders Day award N.Y. U., 1966. Petroleum Research Fund scholar, 1954-57. Mem. Assn. Cons. Chemists and Chem. Engrs., Am. Chem. Soc., Am. Inst. Chem. Engrs., Sigma Xi, Alpha Chi Sigma. Contbr. articles to profl. jours. Patentee in field. Address: 36 Tealwood Dr Creve Coeur MO 63141

HADEN, JACK LEE, dentist; b. Springfield, Mo., Oct. 28, 1932; s. James Clifford and M. Marie (Walsworth) H.; grad. Kansas City (Kans.) Jr. Coll., 1952; D.D.S., U. Mo., 1959; m. Norma Jeanne Moore, Mar. 1, 1952; children—Kim Leigh, Shauna Beth, Jamie Brent, Kyle Edward, Kristin Marie. Gen. practice dentistry, Kansas City, Kans., 1964—; mem. staff Bethany, Providence hosps.; part-time instr. U. Mo., 1964—; internat. lectr., tchr. seminar for occlusal studies. Mem. Kansas City (Kans.) Pub. Bldg. Commn.; mem. Turner Unified Sch. Bd., 1969-72; bd. dirs. YMCA, Family and Childrens Service. Served with Dental Corps, AUS, 1959-64. Mem. Am. Dental Assn., Kans. (pres. 1st dist.), Wyandotte dental socs., Pierre Fauchard Soc., Am. Equilibration Soc., Am. Prosthodontist Soc., Kaw Valley Study Club, Omicron Kappa Upsilon, Xi Psi Phi. Republican. Methodist. Clubs: Kaw Valley Dental Study, Terrace (past pres.), Optimist (lt. gov. Kan. dist.), Kansas City Racket, Woodside Racket. Contbr. articles to profl. jours. Home: 6826 Garfield St Kansas City KS 66102 Office: 659 New Brotherhood Bldg Kansas City KS 66101

HADLEY, PAUL ROBERT, JR., assn. exec.; b. Woodstock, Ont., Can., May 9, 1920 (parents Am. citizens); s. Paul Robert and Isabelle (Montgomery) H.; B.S., Ithaca Coll., 1948, B.F.A., 1948; M.B.A., U. Ky., 1953; grad. Inst. Orgn. Mgmt. U. Colo., 1973, Acad. Orgn. Mgmt., 1977; m. Alice Churchill, Nov. 25, 1942; children—Alice Anne, Paul Robert III, Patricia E., Sandra Kim. Prodn. supr. Rural Radio Network, Ithaca, N.Y., 1948-49; v.p., gen. mgr., dir. Churchill Weaver, Berea, Ky., 1949-60; dir. arts, crafts div. Dept. Econ. Devel., State Ky., 1960; v.p., dir. Ky. Metalcrafters, Inez, 1961; pres., dir. Pink Pig, Inc., Frankfort, Ky., 1961-63; v.p., dir. Tradewater Craft Center, Providence, Ky.; sec. JADA Corp.; dir. mktg. services marine group Am. Comml. Lines, Inc., 1965-68; v.p., gen. mgr. marine div. Kayot, Inc., Mankato, Minn., 1969-70; exec. v.p. Mankato C. of C., 1970—; exec. v.p., dir. Region 9 Chamber Assn., 1974—; instr. Mankota State U., 1976—. Mem. Pres. Com. Crime Prevention; sec. ManKato Airport Adv. Commn., Clark County Airport Commn.; dir. Ky. Mountain Crafts, Jackson; tourist, travel cons. Gov's. Tourist Commn.; bd. dirs. Madison County Air Bd., 1961-63; sec. Berea Planning, Zoning Commn., 1958-61; bd. dirs. So. Highlands Handcraft Guide, Asheville, N.C., Region 9 Devel. Council, Hwy. 14 Assn.; exec. sec., dir. Ky. Guild Artists, Craftsmen; chmn. houseboat standards com. BIA, 1968; mem. Region 9 Indsl. Safety Council. Served with USNR, 1941-45. Named Man of Yr. C. of C., 1960; Ky. Col. Mem. Soc. Safety Engrs., Louisville Personnel Assn., Am. Craftsmen Council, Ky., Berea, Clark County (exec. v.p., exec. dir.) chambers commerce, Internat. Houseboat Assn. (pres. 1966-70, regatta sec. 1966-70), Boat Mfrs. Assn. (dir. 1967-69), Pub. Relations Soc. Am., Am. Indsl. Devel. Council, Am., Minn. (dir.) chamber commerce execs. Elk, Rotarian. Club: Lake Washington (pres.). Contbg. editor Houseboating mag., 1969-75; houseboating editor Motorboat Mag., 1975—; contbr. articles to boating mags. Home: 1501 LarRay Dr North Mankato MN 56001

HAECKER, GEORGE WOODS, JR., architect; b. Lincoln, Nebr., Oct. 28, 1939; s. George Woods and Letitia (Foster) H.; B.Arch., U. Nebr., 1963; m. Judith Marian Adams, 1960; children—Audrey, Adam, Alexander. Designer, Vladimir, Ossipoff & Assos., Honolulu, 1960-61; designer Sargent, Webster, Crenshaw & Folly, San Juan, P.R., 1963-65, Syracuse, N.Y. 1965-68; architect Dana, Larson, Roubal & Assos., Omaha, 1968-71; prin., v.p. Bahr, Vermeer & Haecker, Omaha, 1971—. Instr., U. Nebr., Coll. Architecture, 1970; pres. Landmarks Inc., 1977—; dir. State Securities Co., Lincoln. Mem. Omaha Symphony Council. Mem. AIA (mem. nat. urban planning and design com.), Phi Kappa Psi, Sigma Tau. Club: Omaha. Co-author: Omaha City Architecture. Home: 716 N 57th Ave Omaha NE 68132 Office: 1623 Farnam St Omaha NE 68102

HAEFNER, LONNIE EDWARD, transp. engr.; b. Webster Groves, Mo., July 7, 1941; s. Lawrence E. and Pearl (Norton) H.; A.B. in Geography, Northwestern U., 1963; M.C.E., U. Ill., 1967; Ph.D., in Civil Engring. (Automotive Safety Found. fellow, Dissertation fellow) Northwestern U., 1970; m. Vera Jean Martin, Feb. 3, 1966; children—Erica Lynn, Bradley Martin. Constrn. engr. Mo. State Hwy. Dept., 1963-64; traffic planning engr. St. Louis County (Mo.), 1965-66; planning engr. St. Louis County Urban Rds. Office, Clayton, 1967; asst. project dir. of state traffic records system project Northwestern U. Traffic Inst., Evanston, Ill., 1968; sr. research engr. Gen. Motors Research Labs., Warren, Mich., 1970; asst. prof. dept. civil and environ. engring. U. Md., College Park, 1971-73; asso. prof. dept. civil and environ. engring. Washington U., St. Louis, 1973—; cons. in transp. and urban systems engring. to various pvt., local, state and fed. pub. works programs, 1970—; mem. Mo. Air Conservation Traffic Adv. Com., 1972-74, Transp. Research Bd. Com. on Transp. Systems Design, 1970-74, nat. chmn. Transp. Research Bd. Com. on Inland Water Transp., 1973—; real estate broker Mo., 1973—. Mem. St. Louis Bi-state chpt. ARC, 1955—; mem. St. Louis council Boy Scouts Am., 1949—, vice commodore St. Louis council, sea scout commodore exec. com., Boy Scouts Am., 1971—; adviser Sea Scout Ship 352, Boy Scouts Am., 1974-76; dir. Civic Systems, Inc., 1973—, v.p., 1973—. Mem. Inst. Traffic Engrs., Inst. Mgmt. Scis., Am. Rd. Builders Assn. (adv. council on urban pub. transp. 1972—), Traffic Engring. Assn. Met. St. Louis, Ops. Research Soc. Am. (nat. sec. transp. sci. sect. 1973-74, nat. vice-chmn. 1974-75, chmn. 1975-76), Assn. Am. Geographers, Severn, Carlyle Sailing assns. Contbr. articles on transp. systems and urban planning to profl. jours. Home: 10 Finlay Rd Kirkwood MO 63122 Office: 218 Urbauer Hall Washington U Saint Louis MO 63130

HAEGERT, DARYL LEE, ednl. adminstr.; b. Esbon, Kans., Nov. 7, 1934; s. Alonzo Otto and Ethel Norine (Sloan) H.; B.S., Kans. State U., 1956, M.S. 1963, Ed.D., 1972; m. Jo Anne Rundell, Sept. 3, 1955; children—Dirk Lynn, Darin Scott, Jody. Tchr. vocat. agr., Harper, Kans., 1959-65; high sch. prin., Harper, 1965-69; asst. in edn. placement U. Kans., Lawrence, 1969-70; adminstr. Community Unit Sch. Dist. 325, Peoria Heights, Ill., 1970-73; supt. Unified Sch. Dist. 507, Satanta, Kans., 1973—. Mem. C. of C., Am., Kans. assns. sch. adminstrs., Phi Delta Kappa. Methodist. Lion. Home: 402 Pubelo St Satanta KS 67870 Office: Modoc Caddo Satanta KS 67870

HAEHNLE, CLYDE GEORGE, media brokerage co. exec.; b. Cin., Oct. 6, 1922; s. Stanley John and Lily (Hafner) H.; E.E., U. Cin., 1944; m. Ethel Ann Mohr, Apr. 19, 1948; children—Theresa, Donna, Garry, Cathy, Allen. With Avco Broadcasting Corp., Cin., 1942-76, v.p., engring., 1966-76; v.p. R.C. Crisler & Co., Inc., Cin., 1976—. Mem. Mayor's Task Force on Cable TV, 1972-73. Bd. dirs. Community Improvement Corp., 1971-77; bd. dirs. Greater Cin. Ednl. TV Found., 1972-77, vice chmn., 1977—. Mem. IEEE (sr.), Cin. Engring. Soc., Delta Tau Delta. Clubs: Bankers, Maketewah Country. Home: 6728 Sandalwood Ln Cincinnati OH 45224 Office: Suite 801 580 Bldg Cincinnati OH 45202

HAENICKE, DIETHER HANS, coll. adminstr.; b. Hagen, Germany, May 19, 1935; s. Erwin Otto and Helene (Wildfang) H.; came to U.S., 1963, naturalized, 1971; student U. Goettingen (Germany), 1955-56, U. Marburg (Germany), 1957-59; Ph.D., U. Munich (Germany), 1962; m. Carol Ann Colditz, Sept. 30, 1962; children—Jennifer Ruth, Kurt Robert. Faculty, Wayne State U., Detroit, 1963—, prof. German, 1972—, chmn. Romance and Germanic lang., lit., 1971-72, asso. dean Coll. Liberal Arts, 1972-75, univ. provost, 1975—, v.p., 1977—. Fulbright scholar, 1963-65. Mem. Modern Lang. Assn. Am., Am. Assn. Tchrs. German, Hoelderlin Gesellschaft, Engring. Soc. Detroit. Author: The Challenge of German Literature, 1970; Ludwig Tieck's Works, 3 vols., 1968-71; Versepos d. 20. Jahrhunderts, 1962. Contbr. articles, revs. to U.S., Canadian, German profl. jours. Home: 215 Mt Vernon Blvd Royal Oak MI 48073 Office: Office of Provost Wayne State U Detroit MI 48202

HAERER, DEANE NORMAN, pub. relations exec.; b. N.Y.C., Feb. 14, 1935; s. Frederick Sidney and Florence Agnes (Jackson) H.; A.A., Boston U., 1955, B.S., 1957; postgrad. N.Y. U. Grad. Sch. Bus. and Finance, 1958-60, Drake U. Grad Sch. Sociology, 1965-67; m. Polly Ann Dunn, Feb. 24, 1961; children—Jennifer A., Heather J. Account exec. pub. relations and advt. Charles Abbott Assos., Inc., N.Y.C., 1957-60; dir. alumni, community and ch. relations Iowa Wesleyan Coll., 1960-61; tech. writer J.I. Case Co., Burlington, Iowa, 1961-64; dir. publs., asst. dir. pub. relations Drake U., 1964-68; pub. relations account supr. Thomas Wolff Assos., Des Moines, 1968; dir. sch.-community relations Des Moines Pub. Sch. System, 1968-74; mktg. communications and corp. pub. relations coordinator Stanley Consultants, Inc., Muscatine, Iowa, 1974—. Guest lectr. Sch. Journalism Drake U., 1970-74. Bd. dirs. Heart of the Hawkeye council Camp Fire Girls, Des Moines, 1969-72. Recipient 1st place publ. award University Div. Mid-Am. Conf. Am. Coll. Pub. Relations Assn., 1965, 66, nat. awards outstanding ednl. publs. Nations Schs. and Sch. Mgmt. mags., 1972, 73. Mem. Pub. Relations Soc. Am. (accredited, charter mem., pres. 1976, bd. dirs. Iowa chpt.), Nat. Sch. Pub. Relations Assn., Acad. Am. Educators. Contbr. articles profl. publs. Home: Rural Route 6 PO Box 70D-3 Muscatine IA 52761 Office: Stanley Consultants Inc Stanley Bldg Muscatine IA 52761

HAFFER, GLORIA SCHOTTENSTEIN, advt. agy. exec.; b. Cin., Jan. 28, 1941; d. Benjamin and Dorothy (Signer) Schottenstein; student Sophie Newcomb Coll., 1958-60; B.A., U. Cin., 1962; J.D., Chase Coll. Law, 1977; m. Myles Haffer, Jan. 28, 1962; children—Beth, Stephen. Caseworker, Hamilton County (Ohio) Welfare Dept., 1962-64; buyer, Ben's Dept. Store, Cin., after 1964; sec. Haffer Advt., Inc., after 1968, now pres.; asst. sec. White Oak Shopping Center, Inc., Cin., 1960—. Bd. dirs. Bonds for Israel, 1968-72, Jewish Fedn. of Cin., 1968-71, Jewish Family Service, 1972, Council of Jewish Women, 1965-71, United Appeal, 1968-71. Mem. Student Bar Assn. div. Am. Bar Assn., Alpha Epsilon Phi. Clubs: Cincinnati, Crest Hills Country (Cin.). Home: 8300 Arborcrest Dr Cincinnati OH 45236 Office: 721 Central Ave Cincinnati OH 45202

HAFIZ, ABDUL, radiologist; b. Dacca, Bangladesh, Feb. 19, 1930; s. Abul Maqsood and Shahzadi Khanum; student Dacca Coll., 1948-50; M.B., B.S., Dacca Med. Coll., 1956; m. Rawnaq Ara Khanum, Mar. 24, 1957; children—Ishraq, Tanvir. Intern, Elyria (Ohio) Meml. Hosp., 1957-58, resident, 1958-59; resident Mercy Hosp., Denver, 1962-63, Youngstown (Ohio) Hosp., 1963-67; gen. practice medicine, Dacca, 1959-62; asso. radiologist Regina (Sask., Can.) Gen. Hosp., 1968-72; radiologist, also dir. Assos. in Radiology, Inc., Youngstown, 1972—. Fellow Royal Coll. Physicians Can.; mem. Ohio, Mahoning County med. socs., A.M.A., Am. Coll. Radiology, Canadian Assn. Radiologists. Contbr. articles to med. jours. Home: 7993 Hitchcock Rd Youngstown OH 44512 Office: 1027 Boardman-Canfield Rd Youngstown OH 44512

HAFLING, ELMER ROLAND, mech. engr.; b. Greeley, Colo., Nov. 2, 1921; s. Ernst Lawrence and Mable Marie (Roche) H.; B.S. in Mech. Engring., U. Colo., 1949; m. Lona May Erich, Mar. 18, 1947; children—Larry, Michael. With A.T. & S.F. Ry. Co., Topeka, 1949—, asst. shop extension engr., 1968-69, asst. mech. engr., 1969—. Served with USNR, 1942-51; PTO. Mem. ASME, Kans. Engring. Soc., Local Home Assn. (pres. 1974), Locomotive Maintenance Officers Assn. (chmn. com. shop 1975-77). Presbyterian (deacon, pres. ch. 1974—, chmn. 1977). Mason. Home: 2711 James St Topeka KS 66616 Office: 1001 NE Atchison St Topeka KS 66616

HAGAN, DONALD VERNON, orthodontist; b. Atkins, Iowa, July 2, 1930; s. Chester Beatty and Mabel (Risdale) H.; student Coe Coll., 1947-48, U. Md., 1953-54; B.S., Iowa State U., 1957; D.D.S., U. Iowa, 1964, M.S., 1969; m. Dorothy Lea Meek, Sept. 11, 1960; children—Douglas, Jeffrey, Cynthia, Christy. Farmer, Atkins, 1958-59; pvt. practice orthodontics, Des Moines, 1969—. Served with USAF, 1951-54, USPHS, 1964-67. Mem. Midwest, Iowa socs. orthodontists, Iowa Dental Assn., Iowa Dental Study Club, Central Iowa Orthodontic Study Club, Phi Kappa Phi, Omicron Kappa Upsilon, Gamma Sigma Delta. Mason. Club: Wakonda Country (Des Moines). Home: 5020 Harwood Dr Des Moines IA 50312 Office: 530 39th St Des Moines IA 50312

HAGAN, ROBERT CARL, nuclear engr.; b. Newton, Kans., Apr. 8, 1939; s. Theodore Carl and Patience (Williams) H.; B.S., U. Kans., 1962; M. Nuclear Engring., U. Va., 1970, Ph.D., 1974; m. Lois Ann Potzler, Aug. 28, 1962; children—Daniel Robert, David Lee. Nuclear engr. Babcock & Wilcox, Lynchburg, Va., 1967-71, mgr. nuclear and fuels, 1971-74; dir. plant services Kans. Gas & Electric Co., Wichita, 1972—; v.p. Utility Fuel Co. subs. Kans. Gas & Electric Co., Wichita, 1976—. Served with USN, 1963-67. AEC trainee, 1969-70. Mem. Am. Nuclear Soc. (sect. pres.), Edison Electric Inst. (nuclear fuel com.), Electric Power Research Inst. (adj. mem. fusion program com.). Lutheran. Office: PO Box 208 Wichita KS 67201

HAGBERG, RALPH ALBERT, chem. co. exec.; b. Boston, Sept. 3, 1915; s. Fred Axel and Gerda (Oberg) H.; B.S. in Chem. Engring. (cum laude), Tufts U., 1936; m. Mary Louise Pownall, May 13, 1939; 1 son—Lawrence Christian. Dist. mgr. chem. div. Westvaco Corp., Cleve., 1937-54; tech. dir., S.S. Skelton Co., Cleve., 1954-60; chem. div. mgr. Capital City Products div., Stokely VanCamp, Columbus, Ohio, 1960-63; v.p. Ziegler Chem. and Mineral Corp., Chgo., 1963-68, SuCrest Corp., Dolton, Ill., 1968—. Cons. on air/water pollution, Village of Dolton. Chmn. bd. dirs. Provincetown Homeowners Assn. Served as maj. AUS, 1943-46; PTO. Decorated Bronze Star medal. Mem. Am. Oil Chemists Soc., Cereal Chemists, Bakery Engrs. Alpha Tau Omega. Episcopalian (vestryman). Club: Calumet Country (Homewood, Ill.). Contbr. profl. jours. Home: 1115 Williamsburg Rd Country Club Hills IL 60477 Office: Dolton Div SuCrest Corp 14622 Lakeside Ave Dolton IL 60419

HAGE, GUNNAR HARALD, hosp. adminstr.; b. Thomasville, Ga., Feb. 10, 1909; s. Alfred and Agnete (Quedens) H.; B.S., U. Md., 1963; M.B.A., Xavier U., 1976; m. Sallie Payne, Dec. 16, 1941. Commd. 2d lt. U.S. Army, 1942, advanced through grades to col., 1956; personnel comdr. Walter Reed Army Med. Center, Washington, 1954-58; chief Med. Service Corps, career assignments Army Surgeon Gen. Office, Washington, 1958-59; exec. officer 9th Hosp. Center, Landstuhl, Germany, 1960-62, 97th Gen. Hosp., Frankfurt, Germany, 1962-64; asst. adminstr. Booth Meml. Hosp., Covington, Ky., 1964-66; adminstr. Holmes Hosp., U. Cin., 1966—. Chmn. common contract com. Greater Cin. Hosp. Council, 1970—. Decorated Legion of Merit, Bronze Star medal, Army Commendation medal. Fellow Royal Soc. Health, Am. Coll. Hosp. Adminstrs.; mem. Am., Ohio hosp. assns., Word of Life Fellowship Internat. Office: Eden and Bethesda Aves Cincinnati OH 45219

HAGE, ROLF BORRESEN, banker; b. Madelia, Minn., Jan. 14, 1904; s. George S. and Hanna (Borresen) H.; B.A., Carleton Coll., 1927; m. Irma Delores Breening, June 29, 1939; children—Ingrid Lynn (Mrs. Charles Patric Doom), Fredrick Rolf. With First State Bank, Storden, Minn., 1927-37; asst. examiner banking dept. State of Minn., 1939-45; pres. Westbrook (Minn.) State Bank, 1946—; chmn. Currie State Bank (Minn.), 1958-78; dir. Ind. State Bank of Minn., Mpls. Bd. dirs. Minn. Valley council Boy Scouts Am., 1960-65, SW Found.-SW Univ., Marshall, Minn., 1976—. Mem. Ind. Bankers Minn. (treas. 1973—), Minn. Bankers Assn. (council adminstr. 1957-60). Mason (32 deg., Shriner). Clubs: Golf, Commercial (Westbrook); Athletic (Mpls.). Address: Westbrook MN 56183

HAGEDORN, THOMAS M., congressman. Mem. 94th and 95th congresses from 2d Minn. dist. Office: Room 325 Cannon House Office Bldg Washington DC 20515*

HAGELIN, DANIEL WARN, librarian; b. Jamestown, N.Y., Sept. 11, 1916; s. Charles August and Pearl Sunbeam (Warn) H.; B.A., Fenn Coll. (now Cleve. State), 1941; B.L.S., Western Res. U., 1946; M.A., 1952; m. Virginia Louise Morgan, Apr. 21, 1945; children—Patricia Marie, David Morgan. Profl. asst. history div. Cleve. Pub. Library, Cleve., 1946-52; first asst. reference dept. Lakewood (Ohio) Pub. Library, 1953-56, head reference dept., 1956—. Mem. com. Cleve. Area Information Network; chmn. reference adv. com. Cleve. Area Met. Library System, 1976—. Mem. Lakewood Fire Prevention Com., 1955-60; mem. Lakewood Safety Council, 1960-63; bd. dirs. Lakewood YMCA, 1975—. Served with AUS, 1941-45. Decorated Purple Heart. Mem. Ohio Library Assn. (sec.-treas. jr. mems. sect. 1949-50, chmn. 1950-51; vice chmn. reference services round table 1968-69, chmn. 1969-70; mem. library devel. com. 1970-71), A.L.A. (v.p. jr. mems. round table 1950-51, pres. 1951-52 mem. library jr. list reference books com., reference and adult services div. 1974—), Cleve. State U. Alumni Assn., Case Western Res. Sch. Library Sci. Alumni Assn. (v.p. 1972-73, pres. 1973-74), Case Western Res. Grad. Sch. Alumni Assn. Democrat. Methodist. Home: 4818 W 19th St Cleveland OH 44109 Office: 15425 Detroit Ave Lakewood OH 44107

HAGELMAN, RONALD RUDOLPH, ins. co. exec.; b. Houston, June 23, 1926; s. Charles W. and Anna Marie (Griffin) H.; B.A., M.A., U. Tex., 1948; m. Rebecca O'Bannon, Nov. 25, 1953; children—Ronald Rudolph, Carl Frederick, Curt Rudolph, Christa Marie, Claus Edward. Agt. New Eng. Mut. Life Ins. Co., Houston, 1952-54; asst. to v.p. Am. Gen. Life Ins. Co., Houston, 1954-56; asst. dir. agys. Union Nat. Life Ins. Co., Lincoln, Nebr., 1956-57; pres. So. Heritage Life Ins. Co., Charlotte, N.C., 1957-59; chief exec. officer, v.p. Zurich Life Ins. Co., Chgo., 1959-60; pres., dir. Inland Life Ins. Co., 1960-62; pres. Guardsman Life Ins. Co., West Des Moines, Iowa, 1962—; dir. Guardsman Equity Corp, Engring. Enterprises, Houston, Nat. Life and Accident Ins. Co., Nashville, Nored Corp., Adair, Iowa. Served with USNR, 1944-45; served to 1st lt. AUS, 1950-52. Episcopalian. Clubs: University, Mid-America (Chgo.). Home: 6843 Trail Ridge Dr Des Moines IA 50323 Office: 1025 Ashworth Rd West Des Moines IA 50265

HAGEN, DUANE QUENTIN, psychiatrist; b. Hardin, Ill., Nov. 27, 1935; s. Manuel G. and Beatrice Mary (Pregaldin) H.; B.S. cum laude, St. Louis U., 1956, M.D., 1960; m. Catherine Conway, Jan. 2, 1965; children—Holly, John, Todd. Intern, Mpls. Gen. Hosp., 1960-61; resident psychiatry Mass. Mental Health Center, Boston, 1963-64, Mass. Gen. Hosp., Boston, 1964-66; staff Harvard U. Health Services, Cambridge, 1966; NIMH career tchr. psychiatry dept. psychiatry, St. Louis U., 1968-70; staff psychiatrist St. Louis U. Hosps., 1968-71; chmn. dept. psychiatry, St. John's Mercy Med. Center, St. Louis, 1971—; clin. asst. prof. psychiatry St. Louis U. Sch. Medicine, 1971—; clin. asso. prof. psychiatry Mo. Inst. Psychiatry U. Mo. at Columbia, 1975—. Bd. dirs. Suicide Prevention, Inc., St. Louis, 1969—. Served with USPHS, 1966-68. Recipient Borden award St. Louis U. Sch. Medicine, 1960; NIMH Career Tchr. award, 1968-70. Mem. Eastern Mo. Psychiat. Soc., Am. Psychiat. Assn., Group for Advancement Psychiatry, Am. Assn. Acad. Psychiatry, A.M.A., Eastern Mo. Psychiat. Soc. (sec.-treas. 1973, pres. 1977-78), Mo. Psychiat. Assn. (sec.-treas. 1973), Jersey Calhoun Med. Soc. (pres. 1963), Alpha Omega Alpha. Home: 20 Willow Hill Rd St Louis MO 63124 Office: 621 S New Ballas Rd St Louis MO 63141

HAGEN, ELDON BRUCE, state ofcl.; b. Devils Lake, N.D., June 21, 1930; s. Ernest W. and Mildred (Bryn) H.; student Devils Lake Jr. Coll., 1948-49; Ph.B. in Social Studies, U. N.D., 1953, M.A. in Govt. and Econs., 1955; postgrad. U. Wis., 1955-56; m.; children—Jennifer, Marin. Farmer, Benson and Ramsey Counties, 1956—; N.D. dep. motor vehicle registrar, 1961; N.D. pub. service commr., Bismarck, 1961—. Faculty, Bismarck Jr. Coll.; mem. Twelve State Govs.' Transp. Com., 1965—, U.S. Dept. Agr. Mktg. Research Adv. Com., 1965-68, Northwest Shipper's Adv. Com., 1961-70, personnel policy and procedures subcoms. Gov.'s Com., 1961-68, N.D. Safety Com., 1967—, Gov.'s Personnel Appeal Bd., 1974—; chmn. Gov.'s Com. Dual Inspection N.D. Grain by Minn., 1962-64, Gov.'s Adv. Com. grain Hold Points, 1962-64; joint bd. substitute mem. ICC, 1961, 65—; pres. N.D. Pub. Service Commn., 1969-70; chmn. Pub. Relations and Inter-agy. Planning Com. for Vocat. Rehab., 1968; v.p. Upper Gt. Plains Transp. Adv. Council, 1968; exec. com. N.W. Shippers Adv. Bd., 1969; mem. Field Bd. for Fuel, Energy and Transp., 1971—; mem. State Planning Adv. Council in charge Bus. Regulation and Consumer Protection, 1971; N.D. rep. Midwestern Govs.' Com. on Midwest Energy Requirements and Environ. Protection, 1972—; mem. resources research com. Commn. Comml. Air Transp., 1972. Adviser on transp. legisl. council Democratic-Non Partisan League, 1966, mem. exec. com., 1966—, dist. dir., 1964; candidate for U.S. Congress, 1968. Served with AUS, 1950-52. Named One of Outstanding Young Men of Am., 1965. Mem. Nat. (mem. com. rates pub. utilities 1962—), Midwest (1st v.p. 1967-68, pres. 1968-69) assns. railroad and utilities commrs., N.W. Weights and Measures Assn., U.S. Durum Growers Assn., Am. Acad. Polit. and Social Sci., Am. Assn. UN, N.D. Water Users Assn., U. N.D. Alumni (mem. adv. com. 1966-70), Farmers Union, Am. Legion, State Hist. Soc. N.D., Nat. Assn. Regulatory-Utility Commrs. (mem. ad hoc com. U.S.-Can. energy supply), Phi Delta Theta, Phi Alpha Theta. Lutheran. Toastmaster. Sec., Leader Dem. newspaper, 1961-64, mem. bd., 1961—. Home: 902 3d St NW Mandan ND 58554 Office: Pub Service Commn State Capitol Bldg Bismarck ND 58501*

HAGEN, JEANNE LYNN CLEGG, info. systems exec.; b. Joliet, Ill., Apr. 10, 1944; d. Samuel Emery and Alice Verne (Parsons) Clegg; M.B.A., U. Ill., 1978. Programmer Lewis U., 1965-66; project mgr. U. Ill., Urbana, 1966—. Mem. Data Processing Mgmt. Assn. (pres. 1971-72, 73-74, Individual Performance award 1974, Individual Performance Silver award 1976). Office: 54 Adminstration Bldg U Ill Urbana IL 61801

HAGEN, JOHN WILLIAM, educator; b. Mpls., May 11, 1940; s. Wayne Sigvart and Elfie Marie (Erickson) H.; B.A., U. Minn., 1962; Ph.D., Stanford U., 1965; adopted children—Darus Gene, Lonny John. Asst. prof. psychology U. Mich., Ann Arbor, 1965-69, asso. prof., 1969-73, prof. psychology, 1973—, chmn. developmental program, 1971—. Mem. Mich. Gov.'s spl. commn. on age of majority, 1970-71; mem. adv. council Mich. Dept. Edn., 1972-74. Bd. dirs. Guild House Campus Ministry, Ann Arbor, 1972—. Recipient Standard Oil Found. award, 1967. USPHS traineeship, 1963-65; Woodrow Wilson fellow, 1962-63. Mem. Am., Midwestern psychol. assns., Soc. Research in Child Devel., Internat. Soc. for Study of Behavioral Devel., Phi Beta Kappa. Unitarian Universalist. Clubs: University; Alumni (Ann Arbor, Mich.). Contbr. articles to profl. jours. Co-author: Perspectives on the Development of Memory and Cognition, 1977. Cons. editor Merrill Palmer Quarterly, 1968—, Child Devel., 1972—. Home: 3421 Burbank Dr Ann Arbor MI 48105

HAGEN, KEITH ARNOLD, savings and loan exec.; b. Spring Valley, Minn., Dec. 27, 1923; s. Rolf Donald and Edna Agnes (Howe) H.; student Rochester Jr. Coll., 1942-43; C.L.U., Am. Coll. Life Underwriters, 1947; C.P.C.U., Am. Inst. Property and Liability Underwriters, 1952; m. Kathryn Jean Lindsay, May 29, 1950; children—Sally, Lindsay, Lisa, Amy. With Osterud Agy., Inc., Spring Valley, Minn., 1944—, exec. v.p., also dir., 1968—; with Home Fed.

Savs. and Loan Assn., Spring Valley, 1944—, pres., 1977—, also dir., 1973—; dir., sec. New Industries, Inc., 1960—. Bd. dirs. Community Meml. Hosp., 1962-67, United Fund of Spring Valley, S.E. Minn. Chpt. A.R.C. Methodist. (chmn. bldg. and planning com. 1971-73). Mason. Club: Root River Country. Home: 1121 S Broadway Spring Valley MN 55975

HAGENMEYER, WILLARD HARVEY, flour milling co. exec.; b. Cleve., July 11, 1907; s. William F. and Carrie V. (Peters) H.; B.A., Baldwin-Wallace Coll., 1928; M.A., Oberlin Coll., 1929; m. Gladys M. Hamilton, Oct. 28, 1939; 1 son, Willard Harvey. Div. sales mgr. Pillsbury Flour Mills, Cleve., 1930-32; v.p. Comml. Milling Co., 1932-43, Internat. Milling Co., Detroit, 1952—; pres. Hagenmeyer Enterprises, Inc. Organizer, head food sect. Community Chest, Detroit, 1944-45, chmn. food industry com. 1963—; pres. Culver Fathers Assn., 1948-52; past pres. Annapolis Fathers Assn. Bd. dirs. Culver Mil. Acad., 1950-52, now mem. long-range planning con.; trustee Baldwin Wallace Coll. Mem. Mich. Bakers Assn., Mich. Millers Assn., Mich. Bakers Allied Trades Assn., Board of Commerce (bd. dirs., pres. food council), Pi Kappa Delta, Alpha Phi Gamma, Lambda Chi Alpha, Theta Alpha Chi. Republican. Methodist. Mason (K.T.). Clubs: Detroit Production Mens, Detroit Athletic, Bayview Yacht, Economic (Detroit); Grosse Pointe (Mich.) Hunt; Grayling (Mich.) Game; Shikar Safari; Circumnavigators; Polar Equator. Home: 54 N Deeplands Grosse Pointe MI 48236 Office: Hagenmeyer Enterprises Inc 929 Penobscot Bldg Detroit MI 48226

HAGER, JOHN, purchasing exec.; b. Chgo., Sept. 1, 1927; s. Johann and Katarina (Kray) H.; student pub. schs. Receiving clk. Chgo. Printed String, 1943-45; dock handler Well Pump Co., Chgo., 1948-49, order picker, 1950, assembler, 1950-51, receiving clk., 1951, shipping floor, 1951, stock room foreman, 1951-52, with service dept., 1952-53, prodn. mgr., 1953-66, dir. purchasing, 1966—. Served with AUS, 1946-47. Roman Catholic. Home: 3725 N Christiana St Chicago IL 60618 Office: 1530 N Fremont St Chicago IL 60622

HAGER, MARY VIRGINIA, educator; b. Chgo., July 2, 1931; d. Harry James and Jeannette (Vander Werp) Hager; B.A., Wheaton Coll., 1952; M.A., Western Mich. U., 1957; Ed.S., Mich. State U., 1968. Tchr. commence girls' phys. edn. Frenchburg (Ky.) schs., 1952-54; tchr. commence girls' phys. edn. Zeeland (Mich.), pub. schs., 1954-57, chmn. guidance dept. Zeeland High Sch., 1957-72, registrar, 1972—. Mem. ad hoc adv. com. follow-up survey Mich. Dept. Edn., 1975—. NDEA guidance scholar, summer 1961, Herman Miller Travel Scholar, 1963. Mem. W. Mich. Personnel and Guidance Assn., Mich. Vocat. Guidance Assn., Assn. Measurement and Evaluation in Guidance, Mich. Assn. Measurement and Evaluation in Guidance, NEA, Mich., Zeeland (pres. 1971-72) edn. assns., Nat. Vocat. Guidance Assn. Mem. Ref. Ch. Am.

HAGERTY, ROBERT LEWIS, city engr.; b. St. Louis, Aug. 15, 1935; s. Virgil L. and Ethel (Aliff) H.; student Sch. Mines, Rolla, Mo., 1955-57; certificate bus. mgmt. Whitcomb Sch., Los Angeles, 1962; m. Betty Lou Beyreis, July 6, 1957; children—Christy, Robin, Gregg, Todd. Engring. insp. Kirkwood Mo. Hwy. Dept., 1958-61; head drafting dept. Dresser Electric, Northridge, Calif., 1961-64; mgr. Father Motels, Muskogee and Oklahoma City, 1964-68; asst. city engr. Muskogee, 1968-69; city engr. Centralia, Mo., 1969-76; dir. pub. work City of Boonville (Mo.), 1976—. Pres., Centralia Indsl. Devel., 1970—; chmn. youth div. Community Betterment, 1970-72; asst. troop cubmaster 1972—; mem. exec. bd. United Fund, 1970-76, co-chmn., 1971; sec. Centralia Planning and Zoning, 1974—. Trustee, vice chmn. Boone County Sewer Dist., 1973-76. Registered land surveyor. Mem. Am. Pub. Works Assn. (sec.-treas. Mo. chpt. 1974-75), Water Pollution Control Assn., Mo. Water and Sewerage Conf., Am. Soc. Planning Ofcls., Mo. Planner Assn., Inst. Solid Waste, Mo. River Pub. Water Supplies Assn. (dir. 1977—), Am. Water Works Assn., Mo. Assn. Registered Land Surveyors, Inst. for Certification Engring. Technicians (sr. engr.). Methodist. Mason (Shriner, 32 deg.). Club: N.E. Dist. Mo. Square Dancer Assn. (pres.). Home: 620 Weyland Rd Boonville MO 65233 Office: 920 4th St Boonville MO 65233

HAGGERTY, BRIDGET NANCY, advt. mgr.; b. Surrey, Eng., June 14, 1946; d. Edward and Helena Bridget (Kenny) O'Flaherty; came to U.S., 1963, naturalized, 1976; ed. Ursuline Convent, 1957-62; m. Russell Owen Haggerty, Oct. 5, 1963; children—Catherine, Scott, Benjamin. Typesetter, Shillito's Budget Store, Cin., 1973-74, coordinator mdse., 1974, copywriter, 1974-76, asst. mgr. advt., 1976—. Active women's com. Cin. Symphony Orch.; chmn. face-painting Septemberfest, Cin., 1975—. Club: Advertisers Cin. (sec. bd. dirs. 1977—, fin. sec. Advance mag. 1977—). Home: 5670 Meryton Pl Cincinnati OH 45224

HAGGLUND, CLARANCE EDWARD, lawyer; b. Omaha, Feb. 17, 1927; s. Clarence Andrew and Esther (Kelle) H.; student Augustana Coll., 1946-47; B.A., U.S.D., 1949; LL.B., St. Paul Coll. Law, 1953; m. Dorothy Souser, Mar. 27, 1953; children—Laura, Bret; m. 2d, Merle Peterson, Oct. 28, 1972. Admitted to Minn. bar, 1955, since practiced in Mpls.; partner firm Mordaunt, Walstad, Cousineau & Hagglund, 1960-63, Wiese, Cox & Hagglund, 1964-66, Hagglund & Johnson (all Mpls.), 1966-73, Clarance E. Hagglund P.A. and predecessor firm, 1973—. Sec., Southwest, Inc., 1961-68. Served with USNR, 1945-46. Mem. Am., Minn. bar assns., Fedn. Ins. Counsel, Am. Judicature Soc., Res. Officers Assn., Toastmaster's Internat. (past chpt. pres.), Lawyer Pilots Bar Assn., U.S. Maritime Law Assn., Trial Attys. Am., Delta Theta Phi, Beta Theta Phi, Pi Kappa Delta. Club: Mpls. Athletic. Contbr. articles to profl. jours. Home: 3719 Xerxes Ave S Minneapolis MN 55410 Office: Midwest Plaza Bldg Minneapolis MN 55402

HAGLUND, DONN KEITH, educator; b. Kenosha, Wis., Dec. 10, 1926; s. Leonard Edwinn and Ann Martha (Harwood) H.; B.A., Drake U., 1948; M.A., U. Pa., 1950, Ph.D., 1958; m. Alma B. Hebel, Sept. 3, 1949; 1 son, Erik. Faculty geography U. Wis., Milw., 1958—, asso. dean, 1969-72. Vis. prof. McGill U., Can., 1964, U. Alaska, 1966, Stockholm (Sweden) Sch. Econs., 1970, Carleton U., Can., 1976, U. Sask. (Can.), 1977. Dist. commr. Boy Scouts Am., 1962-65, dist. advancement chmn., 1971—. Served with AUS, 1945-46. Recipient Silver Beaver award Boy Scouts Am., 1977. Fellow Arctic Inst. N.Am., Explorers Club; mem. Assn. Am. Geographers (nat. council 1962-63, 67-70), Canadian Assn. Geographers, Am. Polar Soc., Wis. Council for Geog. Edn. (pres. 1966-67), Phi Beta Kappa, Sigma Xi, Beta Gamma Sigma, Pi Gamma Mu, Tau Kappa Epsilon, Phi Sigma Iota. Author: (with Harkin, MacDonald, Lord, others) Federal Land Laws and Policies in Alaska, 1969. Contbr. articles to profl. jours. Home: 4925 N Bartlett Ave Whitefish Bay WI 53217 Office: Dept Geography U Wis Milwaukee WI 53201

HAGLUND, E(DWARD) JAMES, retail exec.; b. Muskegon, Mich., Apr. 8, 1913; s. Andrew William and Cora (Champoux) H.; student Muskegon Jr. Coll., 1931-33; m. Margaret Hetzner, June 27, 1936; 1 son, Robert James. With S.S. Kresge Co., various locations, 1934—, buyer S.S. Kresge Hardware, Detroit, 1964-68, pres. K. Mart Enterprises S.S. Kresge subsidiary, Royal Oak, Mich., 1968—. Home: 3995 Oakland Dr Birmingham MI 48010 Office: 3000 W 14 Mile Rd Royal Oak MI 48068

HAGUE, RICHARD NORRIS, architect; b. Chgo., Aug. 4, 1934; s. Howard B. and Harriette (Jones) H.; B.A. in Architecture, U. Ill., 1959; m. Gail L. Elwell, Mar. 24, 1960; children—Jeffrey Scott, Jonathan Norris, Mark Richard. Prin. firm Richard N. Hague, River Forest, Ill., 1961-63; with firm Hague-Richards Assos., Ltd., (formerly Harper-Richards Assos., Ltd.), Chgo., 1964—, v.p., 1966-69, pres., 1969—, also dir. Mem. A.I.A. (recipient fall-out shelter design award 1964), Nat. Council Archtl. Registration Bds., Alpha Rho Chi, Scarab. Clubs: Tavern, University, Mid-America, Arts, (Chgo.); River Forest (Ill.) Tennis. Home: 1240 William St River Forest IL 60305 Office: 153 W Ohio St Chicago IL 60610

HAHN, CHARLESS, pub., author; b. San Antonio, Feb. 13, 1919; s. Mannel and Nancy (Coonsman) H.; student U. Wis., 1936-38; B.A., U. Chgo., 1940; m. Harriet Abercrombie Paine, Dec. 27, 1940; 1 dau., Padraig deNormandie (Mrs. Brennen). Editor, Postal Markings, 1940-42, Weekly Philatelic Gossip, 1943-44, Am. Philatelist, 1956-57, Bebidas, 1947-57, Beverages, 1947-57, La Framacia Moderna, 1948-57, Radio Y Articulos Electricos, 1948-57, Elaboraciones Y Envases, 1947-57, La Tienda, 1948-57; stamp columnist Chgo. Sun-Times, 1944—. Pub. Bebidas, Beverages, Chgo., 1961—. Contbr. articles to profl. jours. Home: 370 Walnut St Winnetka IL 60093 Office: 222 W Adams St Chicago IL 60606

HAHN, JACK ALBERT LOUIS, hosp. adminstr.; b. Evansville, Ind., Apr. 24, 1922; s. Albert George and Grace (Osborn) H.; B.A., U. Evansville, 1943, LL.D., 1958; M.H.A., Northwestern U., 1948; LL.D., DePauw U., 1970; m. Lois A. Walther, June 13, 1946; children—Susan Louise, Louis Albert, Joan Katheryn. Adminstrv. asst. Chgo. Wesley Meml. Hosp., 1946-47; adminstr. Meml. Hosp., Fremont, O., 1948-52; asst. supt. Meth. Hosp. Ind., Inc., Indpls., 1952-53, exec. dir., 1954-69, pres., 1969—; vis. lectr., also residency preceptor George Washington U., 1959—, Washington U., 1959—, Xavier U., 1966—, Trinity U., 1970—, Columbia U. Internat. program, 1963-69. Cons. U.S. State Dept., Alliance for Progress, 1962, 67. Mem. Surgeon Gen.'s Com. Emergency Planning, 1963-69; mem. research study sect. Nat. Center Health Services Research and Delivery, 1970-74; commr. Joint Commn. on Accreditation Hosps., 1974—, chmn. bd., 1976; trustee Tri-State Hosp. Assembly, 1975—, treas., 1976—; mem. Ind. Statewide Healthcare Coordinating Council, 1977—. Served as lt. (j.g.) USNR, 1943-46. Fellow Am. Coll. Hosp. Adminstrs. (regent 1964-65); mem. Nat. Health Council (del. 1963-69, trustee 1967-69), Am. (Ind. del. 1955-60, vice chmn. council adminstrv. practice 1960-63, chmn. council asso. services 1962-65, chmn. ethics com. 1962-65, trustee 1965-68, mem. coordinating council 1962-65, pres. 1971, chmn. gen. council 1970, chmn. house dels. 1972, distinguished service award 1973, chmn. com. commrs. 1975—), Ind. (pres. 1962-63) hosp. assns., Nat. Assn. Practical Nurse Edn. and Service (dir. 1956-62, chmn. hosp. adv. council 1955-60), Am. Protestant Hosp. Assn. (pres. 1966, dir., Distinguished Service award 1977), Nat. Assn. Methodist Hosps. and Homes (pres. 1975), Ind. (trustee, mem. exec. com.), Nat. (bd. govs. 1970-71) Blue Cross assns. Methodist (mem. gen. bd. hosps. and homes 1965-72, treas. 1968-72, mem. certification council 1965-72, chmn. 1968-70, pres. nat. assn. health and welfare ministries 1975). Club: Rotary. Contbr. articles to hosp. and nursing jours. Home: 4716 Laurel Circle N Dr Indianapolis IN 46226 Office: Meth Hosp 1604 N Capitol Ave Indianapolis IN 46202

HAHN, JACK DEAN, banker; b. Alliance, Ohio, June 2, 1927; s. Ray Hiram and Mildred Tyrone (Felgar) H.; student Ohio Sch. Banking, 1958-59, Mellon Sch. Banking, 1960; m. Evelyn Lucille Jacobs, Sept. 26, 1948; children—Jeffery, Scott, Leslie Sue. With First Nat. City Bank, Alliance, 1948—, v.p., cashier, 1966-73, exec. v.p., cashier, 1973—. Instr. Am. Inst. Banking, Canton, Ohio, 1966—. Treas. Citizens Hosp. Assn., Alliance, 1968—. Served with AUS, 1945-46. Mem. Am., Ohio bankers assns., Am. Inst. Banking. Mem. United Ch. of Christ (deacon 1969—). Mason (Shriner, 32 deg.). Club: Alliance Country. Home: 10859 Clapsaddle Ave Alliance OH 44601 Office: 504 E Main St Alliance OH 44602

HAHN, LEWIS EDWIN, educator; b. Swenson, Tex., Sept. 26, 1908; s. Edwin D. and Ione (Brewster) H.; B.A., U. Tex., 1929, M.A., 1929; Ph.D., U. Calif., 1939; m. Elizabeth Herring, June 30, 1932; children—Helen E., Mary L., Sharon K. Teaching fellow U. Calif., 1931-34; instr. philosophy U. Mo., 1936-39, asst. prof., 1939-46, asso. prof., 1946-49; vis. lectr. Princeton U., 1947; prof. philosophy, chmn. dept. Washington U., 1949-63, asso. dean grad. sch. arts and scis., 1953, dean grad. sch. arts and scis., 1954-63; research prof. philosophy So. Ill. U., 1963-77, emeritus, 1977—; distinguished vis. prof. Baylor U., 1977. Mem. U.S. Nat. Commn. for UNESCO, 1965-67. Fellow AAAS; mem. Am. Philos. Assn. (exec. bd. 1950-54, 70-73, chmn. com. placement, available personnel 1951-54, past sec., treas. Western div.; sec.-treas. 1960-66, com. on internat. cooperation 1967—), AAUP, Am. Soc. Aesthetics, S.W. Philos. Conf. (pres. 1955), Mo. Philosophy Assn. (pres. 1949-50), Western Conf. on Teaching Philosophy (chmn. 1958-60), So. Soc. for Philosophy and Psychology (pres. 1958-59), Ill. Philos. Conf. (pres. 1969-71), Phi Beta Kappa. Author: A Contextualistic Theory of Perception, 1942; Value: A Cooperative Inquiry, (with others), 1949; co-author Guide to the Works of John Dewey, 1970; contbr. articles to profl. jours. Home: Reed Station Rd Route 2 Carbondale IL 62901

HAHN, RAYMOND MARTIN, tree harvesting equipment mfg. co. exec.; b. Hines, Minn., Feb. 16, 1923; s. Lowell Otis and Zella Mae (Lingenfelter) H.; student pub. schs. Mizpah, Minn.; m. Carolyn June Bursack, Aug. 30, 1945; children—Carole, Nancy Hahn Olsen, Beverly Hahn Bright, Sharon. Owner, operator Raymond Hahn Co., Schroeder, Minn., 1945-75; owner Hahn Machinery, Inc., Two Harbors, Minn., 1972—. Patentee in field. Home: PO Box 244 Two Harbors MN 55616 Office: PO Box 299 Two Harbors MN 55616

HAHN, ROBERT OTTO, distbg. co. exec.; b. St. Louis, Jan. 7, 1926; s. Otto Joseph and Margaret (Hasey) H.; ed. pub. schs.; m. Marie Helen Robertson, June 28, 1948; children—Marsha Lynn, Robert Steven, Alan Gregory. Salesman, buyer Beaver Home and Auto Supply, St. Louis, 1946-49; salesman, buyer Kiefer's Jewelers, St. Louis, 1949-64; buyer, merchandise dir., v.p. merchandise Maritz Motivation, St. Louis, 1964-76; founder, partner Tyme Shoppe, Hahn Distributors, H & M Assos., Fenton, Mo., 1976—. Served with USAAF, 1944-45. Mem. United Ch. of Christ. Clubs: Masons, Shriners. Home: 720 Shallowford Dr Manchester MO 63011 Office: 519 B Rudder Rd Fenton MO 63026

HAHN, WENDELL WAYNE, bus. exec.; b. Springfield, Ill., Aug. 2, 1930; s. Chester E. and Edna G. (Wheeler) H.; B.S., U. Ill., 1956; m. Ruth Eleanor Mittler, Apr. 18, 1954; children—Steven, Nancy. Personnel and mgmt. devel. specialist RCA, 1956-59; v.p., sec. Federated Funeral Dirs. Am., Springfield, Ill., 1960-74, pres., 1974—. Chmn., Ill. Gov.'s Prayer Breakfast Com., 1968; pres. Abraham Lincoln council Boy Scouts Am., 1970-72, recipient Silver Beaver award, 1967. Served with USNR, 1950-54. Mem. Internat. Platform Assn. Lutheran (ch. pres. 1965-67). Home: 1030 Bedford Rd Springfield IL 62704 Office: 1622 S MacArthur Blvd Springfield IL 62708

HAIDET, BUDDY KEITH, univ. ofcl.; b. Akron, Ohio, June 1, 1935; s. Sherwood A. and Pearl (Fisk) H.; B.S., Miami U., 1957, M.Ed., 1963; m. Patricia Margaret Schehl, Dec. 28, 1957; children—Jeffrey Keith, James Scott, Laura Lee, Mark Edward. Instr. phys. edn. Miami U., 1961, asst. dir. purchases and central services, 1964-69, dir. athletic ticket sales and promotion, 1969—, dir. summer sports sch., 1976-77; tchr., coach Eaton (Ohio) High Sch., 1962; dir. recreation, coach Talawanda Sch. Dist., Oxford, Ohio, 1963-64. Cons., bd. rep. Oxford United Appeal, 1965—; mem. Oxford-Milford Water Assn., 1970—; v.p. Oxford Recreation Bd., 1968-71; pres. Talawanda Sch. Dist. Bd. Edn., 1976-77. Served to capt. USMCR, 1957-61. Recipient Spl. recognition award Oxford United Appeal, 1971-72. Mem. Mid-Am. Athletic Promotion and Sales Com., Ohio Citizens Council Health and Welfare, Izaak Walton League Am., Miami Alumni Assn. (Distinguished Service award 1970-71, sec.-treas., dir.), Delta Kappa Epsilon. Lion. Club: Tomahawk. Home: 6525 Morning Sun Rd Oxford OH 45056

HAIMAN, FRANKLYN SAUL, author, educator; b. Cleve., June 23, 1921; s. Alfred Wilfred and Stella (Weiss) Haiman; m. Louise Goble, June 11, 1955; children—Mark David, Eric Saul. B.A., Case Western Res. U., 1942; M.A., Northwestern U., 1945, Ph.D., 1946. Faculty mem. Northwestern U., Evanston, Ill., 1948—, chmn. dept. communication studies, 1964-75, prof. communication studies and urban affairs, 1970—. Pres., Ill. div. ACLU, 1964-75, nat. corp. sec., 1976—. Mem. Speech Communication Assn., Am. Psychol. Assn., AAUP, Phi Beta Kappa. Author: Group Leadership and Democratic Action, 1951; The Dynamics of Discussion, 1960; Freedom of Speech: Issues and Cases, 1965; Freedom of Speech, 1976; editor book series To Protect These Rights, 1976-77; contbr. articles to profl. jours. Home: 824 Ingleside Pl Evanston IL 60201 Office: 1822 Sheridan Rd Evanston IL 60201

HAINES, NANCY ANN STUTLER, librarian; b. Akron, Ohio, Aug. 25, 1934; d. Ernest Lynn and Sophrona Rebecca (Pepper) Stutler; student U. Akron, 1952-54; B.A., Kent State U., 1956; m. Clifford Frank Haines, Aug. 20, 1960 (div.). Jr. asst. librarian E. Br. Library Akron, 1956-59; hosp. librarian VA Hosp., Northampton, Mass., 1959-61; med. librarian VA Hosp., Brecksville, Ohio, 1961-65; chief librarian, 1965-75; chief librarian Cleve. VA Hosp., 1975—. Mem. Med. Library Assn., N.E. Ohio Med. Library Assn., Zeta Tau Alpha. Home: 7035 Carriage Hill Brecksville OH 44141 Office: 10701 East Blvd Cleveland OH 44106

HAINING, JAMES HOWARD, JR., publishing co. exec.; b. Dallas, Feb. 5, 1950; s. James Howard and Gladine (Watson) H.; student Quincy Coll., 1968-71; B.A., Antioch Coll., 1973; m. Michaela Moore, 1976. Partner, Gem City Printery, Quincy, Ill., 1977; owner Salt Lick Press, Quincy, 1969—. Lectr. Bradley U., Drake U., Earlham Coll., Trinity U., Stephens Coll., Culver-Stockton U., Marshall U., Antioch Coll., Ill. Central Coll., 1970-75. Mem. lit. panel Ill. Arts Council. Coordinating Council Lit. Mags. grantee, 1970, 72, 74; Quincy Found. grantee, 1971; Nat. Endowment Arts grantee, 1975; Ill. Arts Council grantee, 1975, 77. Mem. Com. Small Mag. Editors and Pubs., Coordinating Council Lit. Mags., Print Center. Contbr. articles to profl. jours. Home: 337 Chestnut St Quincy IL 62301 Office: PO Box 1064 Quincy IL 62301

HAISLET, EDWIN L., educator, assn. exec.; b. Utica, Mont., Oct. 2, 1908; s. Sam S. and Stella (D'autremont) H.; B.S., U. Minn., 1931; A.M., N.Y. U., 1933, Ed.D., 1938; m. Mary Margaret McNally, June 12, 1935; children—Marcia Anne, Charles Arthur. Asst. dir. intramural athletics U. Minn., 1933-35; mgr., dir. Haislet Health System, Mpls., 1935-37; instr. edn. N.Y. U., 1937-38; asst. prof. recreation, dir. recreation leadership tng., maj. advisor U. Minn., 1938-42, asso. prof., dir. recreation tng., 1945-47, dir. div. prevention, youth conservation commn., 1947-48, dir. alumni relations, prof., exec. sec. Minn. Alumni Assn., 1948-62, exec. dir., 1962-76; dir. U. Minn. Alumni Fund, 1963-72. Dir. N.W. Golden Glove Tournaments, 1936-42, 45-47; chmn. Minn. Gov.'s adv. com. recreation; mem. U.S. Olympic Com.; mem. Mpls. Bd. Park Commrs., 1951-57, pres. bd., 1953; mem. Mpls. Planning Commn., 1953; mem. mayor's adv. com., 1958-61, mayor's law enforcement com., 1958-61, mayor's Com. White House Conf. for Children City Mpls., 1959; Minn. co-chmn. Crusade for Freedom, 1954-55; chmn. gen. services div. United Hosp. Fund, 1956-57; pres. Council House for Sr. Citizens, 1955-56. Served as lt. comdr. USNR, World War II. Mem. Sigma Nu, Alpha Sigma Pi, Phi Epsilon Kappa. Author: Boxing in Education, 1939; Boxing, 1940; Boxing, The Naval Aviation Physical Training Manual, 1943. Home: 3724 W 22d St Minneapolis MN 55416 Office: Southgate Office Plaza Minneapolis MN 55437

HAITH, EDWARD EARL, surgeon; b. Kansas City, Mo., Dec. 2, 1932; s. William and Ruth (Stein) H.; A.B., Washington U., St. Louis, 1954; M.D., U. Kans., 1959; m. Rickie Arlene Schere, June 8, 1958; children—Elisa Kim, Dion Patrice, Brian Kent. Intern U. Kans. Med. Center, 1959-60, resident gen. surgery, 1960-64; pvt. practice medicine, specializing in gen. surgery, Kansas City, Mo., 1965—; instr. gen. surgery U. Kans. Med. Center, 1964—; lectr. medicine U. Mo. Med. Sch. at Kansas City, 1972—; head sect. gen. surgery Menorah Med. Center, also coordinator surg. gen. edn. program, 1974—, mem. exec. com., 1977—, head dept. surgery, 1977—; mem. staff Bapt. Meml. Hosp., med. staff sec., 1971-72, coordinator residency in surgery program, 1973—, sec. dept. gen. surgery, 1970-71, chmn. dept. surgery, 1974—; mem. staff Jackson County Hosp., chief surgery, 1969—; mem. staff St. Josephs Hosp., 1976—. Mem. exec. bd. Hebrew Acad. Greater Kansas City, pres. P.T.A., 1970-72; bd. dirs. Mid-Am. Comprehensive Health Planning Agy., Chabad House, Kansas City, Mo.; mem. Mo. Gov.'s Adv. Com., 1977, County Execs. Council, 1977. Diplomate Am. Bd. Surgery (mem. splty. bd.). Fellow A.C.S., Am. Coll. Angiology; mem. Kansas City Surg. Soc., Mo. State Med. Assn. (del. 1973—), A.M.A., Jackson County Med. Soc., Internat. Platform Assn. Contbr. papers, articles to profl. jours. Home: 836 Huntington Rd Kansas City MO 64113 Office: 751 E 63d St Kansas City MO 64110

HAJJAR, WALEED MOHAMMED, biomed. engr.; b. Damascus, Syria, May 2, 1947; s. Sharif and Wafeka (Nouri) H.; came to U.S., 1967; B.S.M.E. (Univ. scholar), U. Ill., Chgo. Circle, 1972; M.S.M.E., U. Ky., 1975; m. Linda Forbush, July 24, 1976. Mech. engr. Elcen Co., Chgo., 1972-73; grad. research asst. in biomed. engring. U. Ky., 1973-75; research asso. dept. surgery So. Ill. U. Sch. Medicine, Springfield, 1976—. Mem. ASME (asso.), IEEE, Assn. Advancement Med. Instrumentation. Moslem. Research on noninvasive techniques in diagnostic medicine; introduced compression-free photoplethysmography for evaluation of extracranial circulation, 1977. Home: 1023 S College St Springfield IL 62704 Office: Saint John's Hosp Room 380 SW Springfield IL 62702

HAKANSON, RICHARD COLLAR, photographer; b. Conneaut, Ohio, May 25, 1906; s. Oliver Justus and Maude Myrtle (Collar) H.; student U. Pitts., 1923-24; m. Elarka Marie Towne, Dec. 30, 1933; children—Richard Harwood, Elarka Sarah Hakanson Yuen. Owner, photographer R.C. Hakanson Forensic Photographer, Cleve., 1946—. Chief instr. evidence photography Winona Sch. Profl. Photography, Winona Lake, Ind., 1966; instr. Cleve. Coll., 1945, Ga. Police Acad., Atlanta, 1972; incorporator Evidence Photographers Internat.

Council, 1968, sec.-gen., 1968—. Speaker trainer United Appeal, Cleve., 1965-70. Recipient Service award, Photog. Soc. Am., 1955; Honors award, Profl. Photographers Am., 1966, 1973; Service award Soc. Photog. Scientists and Engrs., 1972. Fellow Evidence Photographers Internat. Council, Nat. Photog. Art Soc. Sri Lanka, Inst. Inc. Photographers (Gt. Britain); mem. Profl. Photographers Am., Photog. Soc. Am. (pres. Cleve. chpt. 1945-47), Internat. Assn. for Identification, Soc. Photog. Scientists and Engrs., Soc. Photo-Optical Scientists and Engrs., Crime Clinic Cleve., Royal Photog. Soc. Gt. Britain (asso.), Western Res. Soc. Sons Am. Revolution (pres. 1971), Cleve. Colony Soc. Mayflower Descs. (lt. gov. 1972), Greater Books Group Bratenahl, Western Res. Hist. Soc. Christian Scientist. Clubs: Rotary, Cheshire Cheese (Cleve.); Hermit Club; Rolls-Royce Owners. Contbr. articles to profl. jours. Editor Photographic Soc. Am. Newsletter, 1952-55; Jour. Evidence Photography, 1969-77. Home: 10322 Lake Shore Blvd Bratenahl Cleveland OH 44108

HAKARINE, DUANE DENNIS, engineer; b. Virginia, Minn., Feb. 11, 1939; s. Wayne and Alice Clara (Bruneau) H.; A.S., Va. (Minn.) Jr. Coll., 1959; B. Chemistry, U. Minn., 1964; m. Connie Hatfield, Aug. 30, 1964; children—Kevin James, Kerrie Lynn. Test tech. Gould, Inc., Mendota Heights, Minn., 1964-65, materials tech., 1965-66, materials engr., 1966-67, sr. materials engr., 1967-70, sr. product design engr., 1970-74, mgr. product engring., 1974-77, mgr. original equipment sales engring., 1977—. Treas. Bklyn. Park Snowmobile Safety Patrol, 1975-76. Mem. Soc. Automotive Engrs., Battery Council Internat. Republican. Methodist. Patent Battery safety vent, side terminal battery. Home: 7119 Newton Ave N Minneapolis MN 55430 Office: PO Box 3140 St Paul MN 55165

HAKEL, EDWIN HENRY, clergyman; b. Silver Lake, Minn., June 2, 1909; s. Stephen and Emily (Zbitovsky) H.; student Macalester Coll., 1929, McPhail Sch. Music, Mpls., 1930-32, Mpls. Sch. Music, 1934-35, U. Minn., 1949, Western Pastor's Sch., 1956; m. Alice Vera Svihel, Aug. 16, 1946; adopted children—Pollyann, Richard. Ordained to ministry Congl. Ch., 1954; minister, St. Paul, 1945-54, Staples, Minn., 1954-60, 1st Congl. Ch., Sherburn, Minn., 1960-73, St. Matthew's United Ch. of Christ, Litchfield, Minn., 1973—. Tchr. Leadership Tng. Inst., 1961; registrar No. Pacific Assn. Congl. Chs., 1955-60, scribe Minn. Conf., 1961, youth adviser Southwestern Assn., 1962-63, registrar, 1962-63; registrar Southwestern Assn. United Ch. Christ, 1964, 65, 69, 70, 71; condr. Vesper Hour TV program, 1973-74; past pres. Litchfield Area Ministerial Assn.; United Ch. of Christ rep. region Minn. Council Chs., 1976, 77. Vice pres. Sherburn-Dunnell PTA, 1970, pres., 1971—; mem. Meeker County Community Adv. Council, 1976—; tenor Litchfield Male Chorus, v.p., 1976-77, pres., 1977—. Bd. dirs. Sherburn Civic and Commerce Assn., 1972-73; bd. dirs. Meeker County Concert Assn., 1976, 77; v.p. Meeker County unit Am. Cancer Soc., 1977—, pres.-elect 1978; pres.-elect Meeker County Music and Arts Assn., 1978. Served with AUS, 1942-45. Recipient Good Neighbor to NW award Radio Sta. WCCO, 1977; Certificate of Recognition for Bicentennial contbns. from Gov. Minn., 1977. Mem. Litchfield Area Ministerial Assn. (v.p. 1974-75, pres. 1975—), Am. Legion (chaplain 4th dist. 1953-54, 71, chaplain 2d dist. 1972-73, chaplain 7th dist. 1976, 77), N. Central Camera Club Council. Kiwanian (pres. elect Sherburn 1964, lt. gov. div. 2 Minn.-Dakotas dist. 1965, div. 5, 1977-78, v.p. Sherburn 1970, pres. 1971, dir. Litchfield 1974—, pub. relations chmn. 1975—). Club: Fairmont Camera (pres. 1966-67, 70-71; Gold Cup Trophy for color slide competition 1964-66, 70). Address: St Matthew's United Church of Christ Rural Federal Delivery 3 Litchfield MN 55355

HAKKINEN, RAIMO JAAKKO, aero. scientist; b. Helsinki, Finland, Feb. 26, 1926; s. Jalmari and Lyyli (Mattila) H.; diploma aero. engring., Finland Inst. Tech., 1948; M.S., Calif. Inst. Tech., 1950, Ph.D. cum laude, 1954; m. Pirkko Loyttyniemi, July 16, 1949; children—Bert, Mark. Came to U.S., 1949, naturalized, 1960. Head tech. office Finnish Aero. Assn., Helsinki, 1948; instr. engring Tampere Tech. Coll., 1949; design engr., aircraft div. Valmet Corp., Tampere, Finland, 1949; research asst. Calif. Inst. Tech., 1950-53; mem. research staff Mass. Inst. Tech., 1953-56; with Western div. McDonnell Douglas Astronautics Co., Santa Monica, Calif., 1956—, chief scientist phys. scis. dept., 1964-70, chief scientist flight scis. McDonnell Douglas Research Labs., St. Louis, 1970—. Lectr. engring. U. Calif. at Los Angeles, 1957-59; vis. asso. prof. aeros and astronautics Mass. Inst. Tech., 1963-64. Served with Finnish Air Force, 1944. Asso. fellow Am. Inst. Aeros. and Astronautics (mem. fluid dynamics com. 1969-71, honors and awards com. 1975—, tech. activities com. 1975—, dir. at large 1977—); mem. Am. Phys. Soc., Assn. Finnish Engrs., Caltech Alumni Assn., Sigma Xi. Lutheran. Contbr. articles to profl. jours. Home: 5 Old Colony Ln St Louis MO 63131 Office: PO Box 516 St Louis MO 63166

HALAS, GEORGE STANLEY, JR., profl. football exec.; b. Chgo., Sept. 4, 1925; s. George Stanley and Minnie (Bushing) H.; B.S. in Commerce, Loyola U., Chgo., 1950; m. Therese Leona Martin, Apr. 20, 1963; children—Christine, Stephen. Gen. mgr. May-Halas, mail order house, Chgo., 1955-60; treas. Chgo. Bears Football Club, 1953-55, gen. mgr., 1960-63, pres., 1963—. Fellow St. Josephs Coll., Rensselaer, Ind., 1964—. Clubs: Chgo. Athletic Assn., Ridgemoor Country (Chgo.). Office: Chicago Bears 55 E Jackson Blvd Chicago IL 60604

HALBE, DONALD JAMES, housewares mfg. co. exec.; b. Evanston, Ill., Jan. 18, 1944; s. William George and Margaret Barbara (May) H.; student fin. Roosevelt U., 1965-68, indsl. engring. Internat. Corr. Schs., 1968-69; m. Doris Joan Roeske, Mar. 24, 1964; children—David James, Douglas Jay. Insp., data processor, accountant Conal Pharms., Chgo., 1962-64; cost accountant EKCO Products Co., Chgo., 1964-65, cost accounting supr., 1966-67, asst. plant controller, 1967-68, plant controller, 1968-69, asst. plant mgr., 1969-72, div. controller, 1972-74, treas., 1975—; gen. accounting supr. Victon Golf Co., 1965-66. Mem. Am. Inst. Corporate Comptrollers. Home: 59 N Spring Ave Glen Ellyn IL 60137 Office: 9234 W Belmont Ave Franklin Park IL 60131

HALBE, THOMAS GRAY, optometrist; b. Oak Park, Ill., Jan. 18, 1926; s. Earl Oscar and Pearl (Fisk) H.; D. Optometry, Monroe Coll. Optometry, 1948; certificate in children's vision Ill. Coll. Optometry, 1972, certificate in gen. and ocular pharmacology, 1975; m. Patricia Whitney, Oct. 7, 1950; children—Kathleen Annette, Earl Oscar II. Clk., U.S. Post Office, 1949-51; machinist, various cos., Chgo. and Aurora, Ill., 1951-64; pvt. practice optometry, specializing in child vision, Chgo., 1952-55, 1964—, Aurora, 1955-64. Clin. asso. Optometric Extension Program, 1971—. Del., N.W. Community Orgn., Chgo., 1968-71; optometric coordinator Rogers Park Save Our Sight, 1966-68. Served with AUS, 1944-46. Recipient Humanitarian award Chgo. North Side Optometric Soc., 1967. Mem. Am., Ill. (mem. exec. council 1968-69, 74-76) optometric assns., Chgo. North Side Optometric Soc. (pres. 1968-69, 74-76, dir. 1967—). Congregationalist. Lion. Home: 2728 N Hampden Ct Chicago IL 60614 Office: 2202 N Lincoln Ave Chicago IL 60614

HALBERT, FREDERIC LESLIE, farmer, agrl. engring. cons.; b. Battle Creek, Mich., Mar. 14, 1945; s. Frederick P. and Esther Evelyn (Page) H.; B.S., Mich. State U., 1967, M.S., 1968; m. Sandra Edith Huhtala, Feb. 24, 1968; children—Stephanie, Kristen, Lisa. Research engr. Eastman Kodak, Rochester, N.Y., 1967-68, Dow Chem. Co., Midland, Mich., 1968-71; propr., mgr. dairy farm, Barry County, Mich., 1971—; cons. in animal nutrition, 1971—. Recipient Roy Manty award for Distinguished Service to Health of People of Mich., 1977. Mem. Am. Inst. Chem. Engrs., Am. Radio Relay League. Instrumental in discovery of a massive chem. contamination of food chain, 1974. Address: 12150 Banfield Rd Route 2 Delton MI 49046

HALCOMB, ROBERT WESLEY, investment and ins. exec.; b. Cin., Sept. 20, 1930; s. Glenn I. and Cynthia L. (Ellis) H.; certificate in bus. adminstrn. U. Cin., 1956; m. Vivian Thompson, Dec. 31, 1949; children—Darlene Gail, Deborah Vivena, Sharon Gay, Robert Wesley, Robin Leslie, John William. Zone bus. mgmt. mgr. Buick Motor div. Gen. Motors Corp., 1956-58; v.p., gen. mgr. Monarch Buick Co., Inc., 1958-60; gen. mgr., regional v.p., agy. dir. Gt. No. Life Ins. Co., 1960-65; pres. Robert W. Halcomb & Asso., 1963—, Union Securities Corp., 1965—, P.S.I. Enterprises, Inc., Mobile Home Estates, Inc., Presidential Mobile Homes, Inc. Served with inf. AUS, 1951-52. Recipient Nat. Quality award. C.L.U. Mem. Ind. Manufactured Housing Assn. (Citizen of Year award 1974; pres. Capitol City chpt.), Million Dollar Round Table, Ind. Life Ins. Leaders Club, Alpha Sigma Lambda. Mason (Shriner). Home: 6147 E 65th Pl Indianapolis IN 46220 Office: 4020 S High School Rd Indianapolis IN 46241

HALE, ALLAN MCKEAG, bot. ecologist; b. Chgo., Nov. 20, 1946; s. Harold Walton and Lucille Marie (McKeag) H.; B.A., Monmouth Coll., 1968; M.A., U. Colo., 19—, Ph.D., 1971; m. Jean Marie Didier, Aug. 22, 1970; children—David, Thomas. Greenhouse supr. U. Colo., Boulder, 1969-70, teaching asst. botany, 1969-70, lab. supr. cellular and human physiology, 1970-71; bot. ecologist Dames & Moore Co., Cin., 1972—, project mgr., 1973—. Served with Med. Service Corps. U.S. Army, 1971-72. Sigma Xi research grantee, 1969. Mem. Ohio Acad. Sci., Bot. Soc. Am., Am. Soc. Photogrammetry (pres.-elect Soc. Range Mgmt. 1978), Greater Cin. Amateur Radio Assn., Amateur Radio Emergency Corps., Am. Radio Relay League, Amateur Radio Satellite Corp., Nat. Collegiate Players, Pi Kappa Delta, Phi Sigma. Presbyterian. Home: 1337 Leders Ln Cincinnati OH 45238 Office: 1150 W 8th St Cincinnati OH 45203

HALE, CLAYTON GOULD, ret. business exec.; b. Cleve., Mar. 27, 1902; s. Jesse G. and Edith M. (Clayton) H.; A.B., U. Mich., 1924; B.B.A., Fenn Coll. (now Cleve. State U.), 1932, LL.D., 1956; student econs., 1946; LL.D., Baldwin-Wallace Coll., 1975; m. Laura Bartlett, Oct. 8, 1927; children—Sally L. (Mrs. Thales Bowen, Jr.), William C. Property ins. agt. and broker, 1924; licensed in eleven states and Province of Ont.; mng. partner Hale & Hale Co., Cleve., 1939-63, pres., 1962-67, chmn. bd., 1967-76; pres. Basic Investments, Inc., 1961—; prof. ins. Grad. Sch. Bus. Adminstrn., U. Mich., 1949-56, lectr., 1935-49; editorial cons. for interpretation ins. statistics and trends, on staff The Spectator, 1948-52; asst. chief ins. div. Navy Dept., 1942-43; ins. cons. office sec. def., 1950-62; mem. bd. ins. advisers Munitions Bd., 1950-53; ins. cons. to Ohio Turnpike Commn., 1953-58; dir. 2 corps. Invited del. White House Com. Hwy. Safety, 1954-58. Life Trustee Cleve Met. YMCA; chmn. bd. trustees Fenn Ednl. Found., 1967-69; mem. vis. com. U. Mich. Grad. Sch. Bus. Adminstrn.; trustee Western Res. Hist. Soc. Fellow Ins. Inst. Am.; mem. Ins. Soc. N.Y., Am. Risk and Ins. Assn. (com. on gen. ins. terminology), Order Founders and Patriots Am., S.A.R., Chi Phi. Republican. Conglist. Clubs: Clifton (Lakewood, O.); Westwood Country (Rocky River, O.); Union (Cleve.); University (Chgo. and Ann Arbor, Mich.). Author: An Approach to Fire Insurance, 1933. Contbr. tech. articles to various jours. Cons. editor Property and Casualty Ins. Handbook, 1962-70. Home: 1056 Kirtland Ln Lakewood OH 44107 Office: The Arcade Cleveland OH 44114

HALE, FLOYD EUGENE, dentist; b. Hymera, Ind., Feb. 22, 1922; s. William Glessie and Emma Katherine (Craig) H.; student Marquette U., 1945-48; D.D.S., Ind. U., 1955, postgrad., 1955-59; m. Dorothy Ann Duckworth, June 20, 1948; children—Anna Marie, Alan Eugene. Practice dentistry, Indpls., 1955—; asso. prof. prosthetic dentistry Ind. U., 1955—. Pres., 6116 Corp., 1965—. Mem. exec. com. Explorer Post, Boy Scouts Am., 1965—; mem. Freedom Found. Com., 1966-68. Served to lt. USN, 1941-49; ETO. Mem. Am. Dental Assn., Am. Prosthodontic Soc., Internat. Coll. Dentists, Acad. for Plastics Research in Dentistry, Chgo. Dental Soc., Am. Acad. Internal Medicine (hon.), Ind. U. Sch. Dentistry Alumni Assn. (dir.), Am. Legion (past post comdr.), Omicron Kappa Upsilon (Mosby award in prosthetic dentistry 1955), Delta Sigma Delta (Scholastic and Achievement awards 1955). Mason (Shriner), Elk. Club: Hillcrest Country (Indpls.). Home: 5430 Hedgerow Dr Indianapolis IN 46226 Office: 6116 N College Ave Indianapolis IN 46220

HALES, LOYDE WESLEY, educator; b. Kansas City, Mo., Mar. 9, 1933; s. Thomas Wesley and Lola Alice (Bretches) H.; B.S., U. Kans., 1956, M.S., 1960, Ed.D., 1964; m. Annie King Loudon, Mar. 21, 1961; 3 children. Research asso. Harvard U., Cambridge, Mass., 1964-66; asst. prof. ednl. psychology Wichita (Kans.) State U., 1966-67; prof. ednl. research and evaluation Ohio U., Athens, 1967—. U. Aberdeen (Scotland) exchange scholar, 1960-61; Ohio U. Research Inst. fellow, 1972-73, Fulbright sr. research scholar, 1974-75. Mem. Am. Ednl. Research Assn., Am., Ohio personnel and guidance assns., AAUP, Assn. for Measurement and Evaluation in Guidance, Nat. Council on Measurement in Edn., Nat. Vocat. Guidance Assn., Phi Delta Kappa. Author: (with J. C. Marshall) Classroom Test Construction, 1971, Essentials of Testing, 1972; (with B. J. Fenner) Ohio Work Values Inventory, 1971, 73; Inventaire des Valeurs Relatives au Travail, 1975; contbr. articles to profl. jours. Home: 180 Park Lane Dr Athens OH 45701 Office: Coll Edn Ohio U Athens OH 45701

HALEY, JOHNETTA RANDOLPH, musician, educator; b. Alton, Ill., Mar. 19, 1923; d. John A. and Willye E. (Smith) Randolph; Mus.B. in Edn., Lincoln U., 1945; Mus.M., So. Ill. U., 1972; m. David Haley, Apr. 6, 1947; children—Karen, Michael. Vocal and gen. music tchr. Lincoln High Sch., E. St. Louis, Ill., 1945-48; vocal music tchr., choral dir. Turner Sch., Kirkwood, Mo., 1950-55; vocal and gen. music tchr. Nipher Jr. High Sch., Kirkwood, 1955-71; asst. prof. music Sch. Fine Arts, So. Ill. U. at Edwardsville, 1972—; adjudicator music festivals; area music cons. Ill. Office Edn., 1977-78; program specialist St. Louis Human Devel. Corp., 1968; interim exec. dir. St. Louis Council Black People, summer 1970. Bd. dirs. YWCA, 1975-78, Artist Presentation Soc., St. Louis, 1975, United Negro Coll. Fund, 1976-78; bd. curators Lincoln U., Jefferson City, Mo., 1974—, pres., 1978—; mem. Nat. Ministry on Urban Edn., Lutheran Ch.-Mo. Synod, 1975-78; nat. chmn. Cleve. Job Corps, 1976-78. Recipient Cotillion de Leon award for Outstanding Community Service, 1977; Distinguished Alumnae award Lincoln U., 1977; Distinguished Citizen award St. Louis Argus Newspaper, 1970; named Duchess of Paducah, 1973; received Key to City, Gary, Ind., 1973. Mem. Council Luth. Chs., AAUP, Coll. Music Soc., Music Educators Nat. Conf., Ill. Music Educators Assn., Nat. Choral Dirs. Assn., Assn. Tchr. Educators, Midwest Kodaly Music Educators, Nat. Assn. Negro Musicians, Jack and Jill Inc., Friends of St. Louis Art Mus., Alpha Kappa Alpha, Mu Phi Epsilon, Pi Kappa Lambda. Clubs: Las Amigas Social. Home: 7326 Stanford Ave Saint Louis MO 63130 Office: Box 71 So Ill U Edwardsville IL 62026

HALFPOP, ROGER LEWIS, distbg. co. exec.; b. Goodell, Iowa, Jan. 20, 1934; s. Edward Lewis and Fanny Christina (Landon) H.; student pub. schs. Kanawha, Iowa; m. Carole Ann Holecek, Apr. 2, 1953; children—Christine, Connie, Cary. Mgr. feed div. Minn. Farm Bur., St. Paul, 1950-65; sales mgr. Mix Mill Inc., Bluffton, Ind., 1966-71; pres. Pro Mark Inc., Alexander, Iowa, 1971—; chmn. bd. Mem. Central Iowa Mktg. Execs. Republican. Methodist. Club: Belmond Country. Home: Route 1 Belmond IA 50421 Office: 200 County Rd Alexander IA 50420

HALIKAS, JAMES ANASTASIO, med. educator, psychiatrist; b. Bklyn., Nov. 26, 1941; s. Peter Simon and Olga Peter (Vavayanni) H.; B.S. (N.Y. State Regents scholar), Bklyn. Coll., 1962; M.D., Duke, 1966; m. Anna May Van Der Meulen, Aug. 20, 1967; children—Peter Christopher, Anna Catherine. Intern, Barnes Hosp., St. Louis, 1966-67; resident psychiatry Barnes/Renard hosps., Sch. Medicine, Wash. U., St. Louis, 1967-70; research fellow alcoholism and drug abuse Sch. Medicine, Washington U., St. Louis, 1969-70, instr. psychiatry, 1970-72, asst. prof., 1972—, mem. com. on admissions, 1975—; asst. psychiatrist Barnes, Renard and Affiliated hosps., 1970—; cons. Malcolm Bliss Mental Health Center, St. Louis, 1970—; dir. psychiat. div. Webster Coll. Student Health Service, Webster Groves, Mo., 1973-75; dir. Grace Hill Settlement House Psychiatry Clinic, St. Louis, 1973—; clin. instr. psychiatry dept. psychiatry Mo. Inst. Psychiatry, U. Mo., St. Louis, 1972-74; mem. profl. adv. com. Judevine Center for Autistic Children, St. Louis, 1975—; psychiat. research cons. Reproductive Biology Research Found., St. Louis, 1975—. Mem. Mo. Gov.'s Adv. Council on Alcoholism and Drug Abuse, 1974-75; exec. com. Drug and Substance Abuse Council Met. St. Louis, 1973—, pres., 1971-72; chmn. Children's Mental Health Services Council Met. St. Louis, 1973-74; host KMOX-TV weekly TV series Trips — the Teenage Point of View about Drugs, spring-summer 1971; adviser on drug abuse St. Louis County Juvenile Ct., 1970-72; mem. adv. bd. Drug Crisis Intervention Unit, St. Louis, 1971—; adviser on drug abuse Drug Info. Center, St. Louis, 1970-74, Human Devel. Corp., St. Louis, 1970-73, Alliance for Regional Community Health, 1972-74. Bd. dirs. Mental Health Assn. Metropolitan St. Louis, 1973—. Recipient NIMH Psychiatry Career Tchr. award in narcotics, drug abuse and alcoholism, 1972-75. Mem. Am. Psychiat. Assn., Eastern Mo. Psychiat. Soc., Am. Med. Soc. on Alcoholism, Am. Psycho-Pathol. Assn., Acad. Med. Educators and Researchers in Substance Abuse, N.Y. Acad. Scis., AAAS, Kappa Nu. Greek Orthodox. Contbr. numerous articles to profl. jours. Office: Dept Psychiatry Sch Medicine Washington U 4940 Audubon Ave St Louis MO 63110

HALL, BARNARD, physician; b. Roswell, N.Mex., Jan. 4, 1916; s. William Oscar and Margaret (Barnard) H.; B.A., U. Oreg., 1938, M.D., 1942; m. Margaret Blanche Chaney, Apr. 10, 1943; children—Edmund Barnard, Margaret Susan, John William. Intern U. Wis., 1942-43; resident U. Minn., 1946-50; radiologist St. John's Hosp., St. Paul, 1949—; asst. clin. prof. U. Minn. Med. Sch., 1950—; faculty mediclinics, St. Paul, 1970; sec. Minn. State Med. Assn., St. Paul, 1960-66, councillor, 1966-72, pres., 1967-68; chief of staff, bd. dir. St. John's Hosp., St. Paul, 1957-58. Served to capt., USAAF Med. Corps., 1943-46. Recipient 4-H alumni recognition award, 1972. Am. Coll. Radiol. fellow, 1968—. Mem. Twin Cities Radiol. Soc. (pres., 1958), Northlands Regional Med. Program (bd. dir., 1969—), Radiol. Soc. N.Am., Am. Roentgen Ray Soc., A.M.A. Club: St. Paul Athletic, Minnesota, White Bear Yacht, Minn. Home: 2440 Arona N St Paul MN 55113 Office: 572 Lowry Medical Arts Bldg St Paul MN 55102

HALL, BARRÉ WILLIAM, lawyer; b. Winnipeg, Man., Can., Apr. 25, 1942; s. Clair William and Isabelle Maude (Pennock) H.; B.S., U. Man., 1963, LL.B. with honors, 1967; LL.M., Northwestern U., 1968; m. Kathleen Pascoe, May 27, 1967; children—Jeffrey Jay, Jonathan William. Called to Man. bar, 1967; partner firm Thompson, Dorfman, Sweatman and predecessor firm, Winnipeg, 1968—; dir. Burlington No. (Man.) Ltd.; sec. Inter-City Gas Ltd., Fortin Electronics Corp., Inter-City Mfg. Ltd.; asst. sec. Safeguard Bus. Systems, Ltd. subsidiary Safeguard Industries, Inc., Canadian Soc. Cardiology Technicians, D.R. Milne & Co., Ltd., Shino Internat. Cycle, Ltd. Mem. Isaac Pitblado Lectures Com., 1974. Asst. legal counsel Progressive Conservative party Man., 1973, 77; v.p. Winnipeg S. Progressive Conservative Assn., 1973-75; asso. legal counsel Progressive Conservative party Can., 1974; pres. Ft. Garry Progressive Conservative Assn., 1974-77. Mem. Canadian Bar Assn., Law Soc. Man., League Am. Wheelmen. Club: Winnipeg Bicycling (asst. sec. 1974-77). Home: 16 Bromley Pl Winnipeg MB R3T 3S5 Canada Office: Thompson Dorfman Sweatman 500 3 Lombard Pl Winnipeg MB R3B 1N4 Canada

HALL, CLIFTON AYRES, II, photographer; b. Kansas City, Mo., Oct. 22, 1951; s. Clifton Ayres and Virginia (Gray) H.; B.A., U. Mo., 1975. Salesman, photographer Metro Photo, Overland Park, Kans., 1968-74; photographer Clifton Hall, Photography, Kansas City, Mo., 1967-74; owner Photog. Creations & Illustrations, Kansas City, Mo., 1974—. Cinematography cons., psychology dept. U. Mo., Kansas City, 1974; exhibited 20th Century Am. Photography, Nelson-Atkins Sales and Rental Gallery, Kansas City, 1974. Address: 3828 Harrison Blvd Kansas City MO 64109

HALL, DAVID MCKENZIE, air force officer; b. Gary, Ind., June 21, 1928; s. Alfred McKenzie and Grace Elizabeth (Crimiel) H.; B.A., Howard U., 1951; M.S., Agrl. and Tech. State U. N.C., 1966; m. Jacqueline Virginia Branch, Apr. 30, 1960; children—Glen David, Gary Duane. Commd. 2d lt. U.S. Air Force, 1953, advanced through grades to col., 1974; chief computer ops. Air Force Accounting and Fin. Center, Denver, 1967-71, Mil. Aircraft Command, Scott Air Force Base, Ill., 1971-72, asst. for social actions, 1972-74, base commdr., 1974-76; asst. comptroller Wright Patterson AFB, Ohio, 1976-77; comptroller, 1977—. Chmn. troup com. Denver Area council Boy Scouts Am., 1969-71. Decorated Legion of Merit; recipient Dist. award of Merit, St. Clair Dist. Okaw Valley Council Boy Scouts Am., Belleville, Ill., 1976; Merit award, Citizens of E. St. Louis, Ill., 1976. Citation of Recognition, Dept. Ill. Am. Legion, 1976. Mem. Air Force Assn., Data Processing Mgmt. Assn., Assn. for Computing Machinery, Kappa Alpha Psi. Home: 513 Johnson Dr Wright Patterson AFB OH 45433

HALL, DEE MOREY (MRS. HARRY F. HALL), psychologist; b. Pa., Aug. 19, 1914; d. Benjamen H. and Belva (Holt) Morey; B.S., State U. N.Y., 1951; M.S., Westminster Coll., 1953; postgrad. Kent State U., 1953-56, Ohio State U., 1957, Washington U., St. Louis, 1963; Ph.D., St. Louis U., 1968; m. Harry F. Hall, May 19, 1934; 1 son, David H. Tchr. elementary sch. McDonald O., 1950-56; guidance dir. Struthers (Ohio) High Sch., 1956-58; supr. test scoring and reporting Psychol. Corp., N.Y.C., 1958-60; sch. psychologist Boardman (Ohio) Schs., 1960-62, Spl. Dist., St. Louis County, Mo., 1962-63; staff psychologist St. Louis City Child Guidance, 1963-68, sr. staff psychologist, 1968-69; pvt. practice clin., sch. and cons. psychology, Clayton, Mo., 1969—. Cons. to Parent Child Center, 1969-71. St. Louis (Mo.) Soc. for Crippled Children, 1967—, Shaare Emeth Nursery Sch., St. Louis, 1969—. Diplomate Am. Bd. Profl.

Psychology. Mem. Am., Mo. psychol. assns., Psi Chi, Delta Kappa Gamma, Kappa Delta Pi. Home: 114 Francis Ct St Charles MO 63301 Office: Meramec Bldg 111 S Meramec Ave Clayton MO 63105

HALL, EDWARD SHOCK, architect; b. Dallas, Tex., Oct. 18, 1935; s. William Arthur and Mary Frances (Shock) H.; student Purdue U.; B.S. in Architecture, U. Ill., 1959. Designer, George Fred Keck, Architect, Chgo., 1963-64; partner Norton and Hall, Architects, Chgo., 1964-72; v.p. Mittelbusher, Tourtleot, Norton and Hall, Architects, Chgo., 1972-75; pres. Enterprise Real Estate Co., 1970—, Hall Assos., archtl mktg. cons., Chgo., 1975—. Served with U.S. Army, 1959-62. Registered architect, Ill., Ind.; certified Nat. Council Archtl. Registration Bds.; licensed real estate broker, Ill.; recipient Distinguished Building award for Park Forest (Ill.) Pub. Library, AIA, 1970. Mem. AIA, Am. Soc. Planning Ofcls., Home Builders Assn., Am. Mktg. Assn., Chgo. Real Estate Bd., Phi Eta Sigma. Presbyterian. Author: The Architects' Mktg. Manual, Vol. I and II, 1976. Office: 235 W Eugenie St Chicago IL 60614

HALL, EMMA HENRIETTA LEAKE, civic worker; b. Aurora, Mo., Jan. 23, 1904; d. John Wesley and Lottie C. (Henderson) Leake; A.B., U. Mo., 1922, M.Ed., 1949; m. Noel Maxwell Hall, Mar. 7, 1923; children—Jacqueline Hall Durante, Noel Maxwell. Piano tchr., 1945; instr. U. Mo., 1945-49; pub. sch. music tchr., guidance counselor, S.W. Mo. pub. schs., 1950-72; tchr. career devel., counselor Sch. of Ozarks, 1972-74; vol. worker OEO, S.W. Mo. Area Agy. Aging; chmn. Christian county Council on Aging, 1973—; bd. dirs. Mo. chpt. Easter Seals Soc. Crippled Children and Adults, 1974, chmn. Christian County chpt., 1956—; past pres. 6th dist. Mo. Fedn. Women's Clubs; mem. Silver Haired Legis. Mo., 1975-77. Mem. Am. Personnel and Guidance Assn., Nat. Vocat. Guidance Assn. Democrat. Presbyterian. Clubs: Springfield Music; Ladies Lit. (pres. 1977-78) (Ozark); Order Eastern Star (past worthy matron). Address: PO Box 237 301 W Jackson St Ozark MO 65721

HALL, EVELYN LOUISE LONG (MRS. RICHARD MALCOLM HALL), govt. ofcl.; b. Hillsboro, Ind., Nov. 8, 1921; d. David Paul and Lelah (Hershberger) Long; student pub. schs.; m. Richard Malcolm Hall, Sept. 11, 1942; 1 son, Robert Malcolm. Clerical worker Indiana Farmers Mutual Ins. Co., Indpls., 1939-42, Fountain County Assessor's Office, Covington, Ind., 1951-56; county assessor Fountain County, 1956—. Past pres. Attica Women's Republican Club; sec. Fountain County Women's Republican Club, 1969-71, v.p., 1974-76, pres., 1976—; bd. dirs. Fountain County Tb Assn., 1955—, exec. v.p., 1969-73, West Central Ind. chpt. Am. Lung Assn., 1973—. Mem. Ind. County Assessor's Assn., Attica Bus. and Profl. Women's Club (pres. 1977—). Home: Route 4 Box 238 Veedersburg IN 47987 Office: Court House Covington IN 47918

HALL, FRANCIS LINDLEY, tire valve mfg. co. exec.; b. Damascus, Ohio, Oct. 14, 1915; s. Barclay Stratton and Mary Elizabeth (Cameron) H.; student Pasadena Bus. Coll., 1934-35, Goodyear Indsl. U., 1942-43; m. Rachel Elizabeth Stratton, July 27, 1935; children—Larry, John, Janice. Devel. engr. Goodyear Tire & Rubber Co., Akron, 1944-52; dist. sales mgr. M.R.S. Mfg. Co., Los Angeles, 1952-55; account exec. Goodyear Tire & Rubber Co., Milw., 1955-70; pres. Haltec Corp., Winona, Ohio, 1970—. Pres., United Local Sch. Dist., Hanoverton, Ohio, 1948-50. Mem. Soc. Automotive Engrs. Republican. Mem. Soc. of Friends. Club: Masons (Shriners). Home: 31778 Winona Rd Winona OH 44493 Office: 32123 Winona Rd Winona OH 44493

HALL, FRANK BRADEN, lawyer; b. Chgo., Jan. 24, 1917; s. Thrasher and Amalia (Linda) H.; B.Sc. in E.E., Ill. Inst. Tech., 1947; J.D., DePaul U., 1956; m. Joan Brockhoff, May 11, 1957; children—Braden Brock, Scott Frank. Admitted to Ill. bar, 1956, U.S. Patent Office, 1972; instr. and tech. cons. Indsl. Tng. Inst., 1948-49; engr. Beardsley & Piper Div. Pettibone Corp., 1950-52, chief engr. elec. engring. 1952-59; sr. engr. Three E Co., 1959-60; asso. elec. engr. Argonne Nat. Lab., 1960-64; chief control engr. Beardsley and Piper, 1965-72, patent atty., 1972—. Served with USAAF, 1942-44. Registered profl. engr., Ill. Sr. mem. I.E.E.E.; mem. Am. Foundrymen's Soc., Chgo. Bar Assn., Patent Law Assn. Chgo., Fluid Power Soc., Nat. Soc. Profl. Engrs., S.A.R., Soc. Am. Magicians. Contbr. articles to tech. jours. Cons. editor Foundry Mag. Home: 855 N Northwest Hwy Park Ridge IL 60068

HALL, FRED HAMNER, dentist; b. Columbus, Ohio, Mar. 22, 1921; s. Fred Ellis and Xenna Lee (Hamner) H.; B.A., Ohio State U., 1948, D.D.S., 1950; m. Josephine Sharp, Mar. 18, 1944 (dec. 1965) children—Jacklyn Mohney, Linda, Nancy, Steven; m. 2d, Lillian Huddy Wilson, Apr. 24, 1970. Instr., Ohio State U. Coll. Dentistry, 1950-53; pvt. practice dentistry, Columbus, 1950—. Mem. Upper Arlington Civic Assn., 1953—; sec. Ohio Lions Blind Welfare, 1966-70. Bd. dirs. Upper Arlington Booster Club, 1967-70, Pilot Dogs. Served with M.C., AUS, 1943-46. Mem. Central Ohio Acad. Dental Practice, Am., Ohio dental assns., Columbus Dental Soc. (past editor, council), Ohio Forestry Assn., Psi Omega. Republican. Methodist. Mason (Shriner; pres., chmn. Past Shrine Club Presidents), Lion. Clubs: Swiss, Germania, Columbus Maennerchor, Cotillion of Columbus (pres. 1974-75). Home: 3391 Stonehenge Ct Columbus OH 43221 Office: 3250 Northwest Blvd Columbus OH 43221

HALL, FREDERICK LEONARD, writer, lectr., conservationist; b. Seneca, Mo., Oct. 30, 1899; s. Frederick Bagby and Corinne (Steele) H.; student Washington U., St. Louis, 1920, LL.D., 1970; student U. Wis., 1921-22; LL.D., Westminster Coll., Fulton, Mo., 1950, Washington U., St. Louis, 1970; m. Virginia Watson, May 28, 1942; 1 son, Frederick Leonard. With Nat. Oats Co., 1926-30, R.R. Donnelley & Sons Co., 1930-45; columnist St. Louis Post Dispatch, 1943-59, St. Louis Globe Democrat, 1959—; conservation lectr. Nat. Audubon Soc., others, 1944—. Chmn. adv. commn. Ozark Nat. Scenic Riverways, 1965-69. Served with USNR, 1917-19. Named Master Conservationist in Mo., 1948; recipient Thomas Stokes award Nieman Fellows of Harvard, 1959; named State Conservationist by Gov. Mo., 1966, appointed to Govs. Acad. Mo. Squires, 1967. Mem. Wilderness Soc., Nat. Audubon Soc., Nat. Parks Assn., (trustee), Am. Forestry Assn., Defenders of Wildlife (dir.), Humane Soc. U.S., Mo. Conservation Fedn., Sierra Club, Sigma Delta Chi. Author: Possum Trot Farm, 1948; Country Year, 1958; Stars Upstream, 1962; Ozark Wildflowers, 1969; also numerous articles in nat. mags. Wildlife films: An Ozark Anthology, 1960; Audubon's Wilderness, 1962; Forever Yours, 1966; Birds Over Florida, 1967; Country Year, 1971. Address: Possum Trot Farm Caledonia MO 63631

HALL, HARBER HOMER, state senator; b. Chgo., Sept. 24, 1920; s. Harry H. and Dorothy (Harber) H.; student U. Miami, 1939-40; m. Jeanette Buttell; children—Heather, John S. Joined USAF, 1942; advanced through grades to maj., 1955; ret. lt. col. res., 1972; farm mgr., 1956-60; personnel dir. Union Ins. Group, 1960-62; treas. McLean County (Ill.), 1962-66; mem. Ill. Ho. of Reps., 1966-72; mem. Ill. Senate, 1973—; owner H.H. Hall Real Estate Investment and Devels. Del. 17th Ill. Congl. Dist. Republican Conv., 1972. Decorated D.F.C. with oak leaf cluster. Mem. Res. Officers Assn., County Treas.'s Assn. Ill. (pres. 1966-67), Am. Legion. Presbyn. Mason (Shriner). Home: 1202 E Jefferson Bloomington IL 61701 Office: 1523 W Market Bloomington IL 61701

HALL, HAROLD CLIFFORD, cons. geotech. engr.; b. Springfield, Mo., Nov. 17, 1927; s. Lawrence Emanuel and Mary Avilla (Abel) H.; B.S. in Civil Engring. with honors, Iowa State U., 1953; M.S. in Civil Engring., Northwestern U., 1970; m. Elaine Audrey Hanson, Nov. 25, 1948; children—Daniel Lee, Susan Elaine, David Eugene, Nancy Corrine, Jennifer Gail, Curtis Edward. Engr., Surveyor Howard Needles Tammen Bergendoff, Kansas City, Mo., 1953-54; draftsman Pfuhl & Shideler, Kansas City, 1954-55; design engr. Black and Veatch, Kansas City, 1955-57; structural engr. Tinsley, Higgins, Lighter & Lyon, Des Moines, Iowa, 1957-58; chief structural engr. Powers & Assos., Iowa City, 1957-59; pres. Hall Engr. Services, Inc., Iowa City, 1959-62; v.p. Shive-Hall-Hattery Engr. Services, Inc., Iowa City, 1962-67; pres. Soil Testing Services of Iowa, Inc., Iowa City, 1965-67; v.p. Soil Testing Services, Inc., Northbrook, Ill., 1967-73; owner H. C. Hall, cons. Civil Engr., Hart, Mich., 1973—. Chmn., Soil Mechanics Lecture Series, Am. Soc. of Civil Engrs., Chgo., 1973. Pres., Silver Lake Dunes Corp., 1975-77; mem. Oceana County Zoning Bd.; chmn. bd. Christian edn. Congregational United Ch. of Christ, Hart, Mich., 1973—. Served with U.S.N., 1944-48. Registered profl. engr., Iowa, Minn., N.D., Mich.; registered structural engr., Ill. Mem. Am. Cons. Engrs. Council, ASTM, ASCE, Cons. Engrs. Council Mich., Nat. Soc. Profl. Engrs., Tau Beta Pi. Republican. Club: Rotary. Contbr. articles to profl. jours. Home: Route 1 Mears MI 49436 Office: 49 State St Hart MI 49420

HALL, HUBERT RAY, land surveyor; b. Parke County, Ind., Aug. 5, 1935; s. Fred S. and Sylvia Jane (King) H.; B.S., Ind. State U., 1957; postgrad. Ark. Poly., 1963, U. Ill., 1969-70, U. Wis., 1975; m. Ramona Mae Watson, Aug. 6, 1960; children—Ann Michele, Fred Charles, William Joseph, Deborah Renee, Elizabeth Rae. Jr. engr. N.Y. Central R.R., Indpls., 1957-58; instrumentman Mo. Pacific R.R., Osawatomie, Kans., 1958, maintenance of way trainee, 1959, asst. roadmaster, construction insp., asst. office engr., Mo., Ark., La., Tex., Kans., 1960-68; designer, estimator Am. Water Works Service Co., Belleville, Ill., 1968-75; prodn. supt. Peoria Water Co. (Ill.), 1975—. Registered land surveyor, Ill., Ky., Ohio. Mem. Ill. Potable Water Treatment Operators Assn., Am. Water Works Assn., Am. Congress Surveying and Mapping, Chem. Engring. Product Research Panel. Baptist. Clubs: Masons. Home: 237 N Illinois Ave Peoria Heights IL 61614 Office: 129 SW Monroe St Peoria IL 61654

HALL, JERRY RAY, data processing exec.; b. Denver, Aug. 9, 1951; s. Jessie Ray and Vivian Genevieve (King) H.; student U. Mo., Kansas City, 1969, Penn Valley Jr. Coll., 1971-72. Computer operator Colony Paints, Kansas City, Mo., 1969-71, Continental Grain, Kansas City, 1971-72; tech. cons., ops. mgr. Asso. Credit, Houston, 1972-75; v.p., ops. mgr., dir. operations, sec.-treas., dir. Credit Bur. Ft. Wayne (Ind.), 1975—; cons. credit and computers; tchr. Ivy Tech. Sch. Mem. Personnel Assn., UN Assn., Ft. Wayne Jaycees, Ft. Wayne Scholarship Assn., Sport Car Club Am. Baptist. Clubs: Percolator, Ski. Home: 3231 Oxford Ln South Bend IN 46615

HALL, JOHN LEROY, real estate co. exec.; b. Paxton, Ill., Jan. 31, 1907; s. Frank LeRoy and Eva Hester (Flora) H.; student Knox Coll., 1931; m. Geraldine L. Myrda, Jan. 26, 1963; 1 dau., Kendall Kostek. Sales mgr. Baird & Warner, Inc., Park Ridge, Ill., 1954-59, sr. v.p., gen. sales mgr., 1959-73; sr. v.p., gen. sales mgr. Ira E. Berry, Inc. Realtors, St. Louis, 1973—. Mem. Nat. Assn. Real Estate Bds. (past dir.), Chgo. (pres. 1970-72), Northside (pres. 1953-54) real estate bds., Lambda Alpha, Omega Tau Rho. Mason (Shriner). Clubs: St. Louis, Castle Oak Figure Skating (pres. 1975-77). Home: 18 W Brentmoor Park Clayton MO 63105 Office: 7701 Clayton Rd St Louis MO 63117

HALL, JOSEPH BATES, fin. exec., civic worker; b. Harvey, Ill., July 13, 1899; s. Joseph B. and Harriet Holzman (Kurtz) H.; Ph.B., U. Chgo., 1921; B.S.C. (hon.), U. Cin., 1959; D.H.L. (hon.), Ohio U., Athens, 1970; m. Mildred Eastburn Wessel, Oct. 20, 1924: children—Joseph Parker, Janice Gail, Wayne. Bookkeeper, Morris & Co., Chgo., 1921-22; with Gordon Strong & Co., Chgo., 1923-25; pres. Hamilton Bond and Mortgage Co., Chgo., 1925-27; exec. sec. Chgo. Mortgage Bankers Assn., 1928-29; asst. mgr. real estate dept. Continental Ill. Bank & Trust Co., Chgo., 1929-30; with Kroger Co., Cin., 1931-64, pres., 1946-62, chmn. bd., 1962-64; chmn. exec. com., dir. Access Corp., Cin., 1965—; past dir. Armco Steel Co., Goodyear Tire & Rubber Co., Tenneco Inc., Cin. Bell Telephone Co.; past chmn. bd. govs. 4th dist. Fed. Res. Bd.; pres. Cin. Redevl. Corp., 1966-71. Trustee Christ Hosp., Cin.; trustee, v.p. Cin. Inst. Fine Arts; past bd. dirs. Ohio U.; hon. mem. exec. bd. Dan Beard area council Boy Scouts Am.; past chmn. bd. Cin. Symphony. Named Gt. Living Cincinnatian, Cin. C. of C., 1971. Mem. Am. Inst. Real Estate Appraisers (past pres.), Bus. Council (hon.), Order of C, Phi Beta Kappa. Clubs: Hundred (treas.), Bankers (chmn. bd.), Queen City (govs. bd.). Home: 3 Grandin Terr Cincinnati OH 45208 Office: Room 2620 DuBois Tower Cincinnati OH 45202

HALL, JUDY ANN, charitable orgn. exec.; b. St. Louis, Oct. 1, 1938; d. Roy Miller and Margaret Estelle (Scheybal) Ragan; B.A., Washington U., St. Louis, 1959, M.S.W., 1969; postgrad. St. Louis U.; m. Robert E. Hall, Nov. 9, 1968; children by previous marriage—Keith J. Bennett, Kristin D. Bennett. Tchr., Orange County (Fla.) Schs., 1962-63, 66-67; tchr., dir. Webster Groves (Mo.) Schs. Adjustment Center, 1967-68, sch. social worker Webster Groves Schs., 1969-72; dep. juvenile officer St. Louis County Juvenile Ct., 1968-69; counselor Melville Sch. Dist., St. Louis, 1974-75, dir. pupil personnel services, 1975-78; regional dir. Ill. Children's Home and Aid Soc., Alton, 1978—; pvt. practice social work; tchr., group leader Bapt. Mission Bd.; workshop leader; social service dir. Schall-Douglass Summer Insts. Mem. Nat. Assn. Social Workers, Am. Coll. Social Workers, Clin. Register Social Workers, Am., St. Louis personnel guidance assns., Mo. Suburban guidance assns., Mensa, Angel Flight, Phi Beta Kappa, Alpha Lambda Delta. Baptist. Author: Elementary Counselor, 1973. Home: 12231 Mentz Hill Rd St Louis MO 63128 Office: 1002 College St Alton IL 60002

HALL, KENNETH FRANKLIN, author, editor; b. Columbiana, Ohio, Dec. 13, 1926; s. Herbert David and Martha (Starbuck) H.; A.B., Anderson (Ind.) Coll., 1948, B.D., Butler U., 1954; D.Ministry, Christian Theol. Sem., 1973; m. Arlene Stevens, Sept. 18, 1949; children—David Eric, Kenneth Douglas. With Warner Press, Inc., Anderson, Ind., 1948—, news editor Vital Christianity mag., 1948-67, youth editor, 1951-56, book editor, 1956-67, dir. curriculum, 1967—; ordained clergyman Ch. of God, 1951. Recipient Distinguished Alumnus award Anderson Coll., 1975. Mem. Coop. Publ. Assn., Theta Phi, Alpha Chi, Alpha Psi Omega, Alpha Phi Gamma, Sigma Tau Delta. Kiwanian (pres. Anderson). Author: They Stand Tall, 1954; What Do You Believe, 1955; So You Work with Senior Highs, 1959; On the Trail of a Twin, 1961; (with Charles Schulz) Two-by-Fours, 1965; On Bumping Into God, 1972; co-author: Basics for Teaching in the Church, 1968; How I Became the World's Strongest 96 1/2 Pound Weakling, 1968; also several vols. ch. curriculum. Contbr. articles to mags. Home: 712 Maplewood Ave Anderson IN 46012 Office: Warner Press Inc PO Box 2499 Anderson IN 46011

HALL, LLOYD LEONARD, lawyer, assn. exec.; b. Waco, Nebr., Feb. 21, 1920; s. David Leonard and Ethel Bell (Van Hooser) H.; A.B., U. Nebr., 1942, LL.B., 1948; m. Dorothy Ford, July 26, 1966; children—Constance (Mrs. Patrick Hubbell), Cynthia, Linda, Leonard. Admitted to Kans. bar, 1948; prof. Washburn U., Topeka, 1948-51; instr. Sch. of Law Topeka, 1951-60; exec. sec. Kansas Assn. Osteo. Medicine, Topeka, 1951—; exec. v.p. Kansas Osteo. Found., Topeka, 1968—; pres. Calif. Acres Inc., Topeka, 1962—; exec. dir. Kans. Assn. Life Underwriters, 1963-70. Pres., ARC, 1968-70; city atty. Topeka, 1951-53; bd. dirs. Osteo. Hosp. Wichita, 1960—. Served with USAF, 1941-46. Mem. Assn. Osteo. State Exec. Dirs., Assn. Osteo. Publs., Kansas Health Manpower Ofcls., Kansas Health Careers Conf. Home: 5127 Brentwood Rd Topeka KS 66606 Office: 835 Western Ave Topeka KS 66606

HALL, NORMAN WILLIAM, real estate co. exec.; b. Fond du Lac, Wis., Oct. 10, 1904; s. William and Anna G. (Hitzler) H.; student Walton Sch. Commerce, Chgo., 1925-26, Loyola U., Chgo., 1927; m. Erla Hannah Campbell, Mar. 3, 1924; children—Earl C., Erlamarie Hall Noffke. With Crane Co., Chgo., 1924-33; real estate broker, Fon du Lac, Wis., property mgmt. rep. Home Owner Loan Corp., 1935-39; owner, mgr. Norman W. Hall Co., Inc., Appleton, Wis., 1939—. Named Wis. Realtor of Year, 1961. Mem. Wis. Realtors Assn. (pres. 1957, dir. 1950—), Nat. Mktg. Inst., Nat. Bd. Realtors. Clubs: Elks, K.C. Home: 719 S Summit St Appleton WI 54911 Office: 103 W College Ave Appleton WI 54911

HALL, OWEN EDWARD, real estate co. exec.; b. Benton Harbor, Mich., Feb. 4, 1923; s. Frank Loomis and Anna Elizabeth (Anderson) H.; certificate in real estate, U. Mich., 1950; grad. Realtor's Inst. Mich., 1968; m. Betty Charlyne Wroughton, May 12, 1945; children—Frank Loomis II, Letha Lynn. Active in real estate, Birmingham, Bloomfield Hills, Farmington, Mich., 1946-77; pres. Hall & Hall, Inc., Realtors, West Bloomfield, Mich., 1963—; pres. Condo-Mart, Inc., Realtors, Farmington Hills, Mich., 1974—. Served with USNR, USCG, 1943-45. Named Realtor of Year, Bd. Realtors, Birmingham, Mich., 1967. Mem. Nat. Realtors Nat. Mktg. Inst. (pres. 1969), Birmingham-Bloomfield Bd. Realtors (pres. 1960), Nat., (dir. 1969), Mich. (dir. 1960) assns. realtors, Detroit Bd. Realtors (dir. 1969), Inter-City Relocation Service Inc. (pres. 1972), Am. chpt. Internat. Real Estate Fedn., Omega Tau Rho. Club: Plum Hollow Golf (Southfield, Mich.). Contbr. articles to trade jours. Home: 4344 Knightsbridge Ln Orchard Lake MI 48033 Office: 27888 Orchard Lake Rd Farmington Hills MI 48018

HALL, RALPH CHARLES, architect, mech. engr.; b. Lowell, Ohio, June 9, 1925; s. Joseph Ralph and Florence (Misel) H.; B.Mech. Engring., Ohio State U., 1948; M.Div., Grace Theol. Sem., 1951; m. Elizabeth Ruth Lenox, June 28, 1947; children—Nancy Elaine (Mrs. Richard Eugene Bell), Stephen Mark. Ordained to ministry Brethern Ch., 1952; pastor Riverside Brethren Ch., Johnstown, Pa., 1951-56, Meyersdale Brethren Ch. (Pa.), 1957-60; profl. engr. Brethren Archtl. Service, Winona Lake, Ind., 1960—. Instr., Ohio State U., Columbus, 1957; sec. bldg. ministries Brethern Home Missions Council. Chmn. plan commn., Winona Lake, 1972—. Registered profl. engr., Ind.; registered architect, Ohio. Mem. Nat. Fellowship Brethren Ministers, Nat., Ind. socs. profl. engrs., A.I.A., Am. Soc. Heating, Refrigerating and Air Conditioning Engrs. Author: Let Us Rise Up and Build, 1966; Custom Designed Churches, 1968. Home: Route 8 Warsaw IN 46580 Office: Box 587 Winona Lake IN 46590

HALL, RAYMOND JOSEPH, trade assn. exec.; b. Boston, Mar. 2, 1938; s. Gordon Bradford and Mary Agnes (Dodge) H.; grad. U. Ill., 1959; m. Anita E. Lapinskas, Aug. 20, 1960; children—Katherine, Raymond Joseph, Tracey. Accounting analyst Ceco Steel, Cicero, Ill., 1959; gen. mgr. Bur. Assn. Services, Chgo., 1960; owner Raymond Hall Assos., Chgo., 1963-70; chief exec., gen. mgr. Elec. Reps. Assn., Chgo., 1970—. Precinct chmn. Republican party, 1959-62. Trustee, chmn. Soc. Assn. Execs. Ins. Trust. Served with USMCR, 1954-57. Mem. Am. Mktg. Assn., Hotel Sales Mgrs. Assn., Assn. Execs. Club, Am., Chgo. socs. assns. execs., Sales Mgrs. Execs. Home: 531 Roscoe St Chicago IL 60657 Office: 233 E Erie St Chicago IL 60611

HALL, RICHARD ALEXANDER, advt. agy. exec.; b. Nacogdoches, Tex., Mar. 11, 1925; s. William Burke and Gertrude (Manchester) H.; B.J., U. Mo., 1948; postgrad. Rollins Coll., Fla., Stetson Coll.; m. Lela Orilla Arnett, June 26, 1950; children—Patricia Lynn, Richard Harrison, David Manchester, Andrew Smith. Sales mgr. Blooming Offset Process, Inc., Bloomington, Ill., 1949-50; v.p. Don Heinrich Advt., Peoria. Ill., 1950-52; v.p. Jackson, Haer, Peterson & Hall, Peoria, 1952-57; pres. Hall, Haerr, Peterson & Harney, Peoria, Ill., Jefferson City, Mo., N.Y.C., 1957—; dir. Family Benefit Life Ins. Co. Jefferson City, Family Benefit Investment Co., Jefferson City, Tune Inn, Dallas. Bd. dirs. United Methodist Ch.; bd. govs. Meml. Community Hosp., Jefferson City; v.p. aquatics Mo. Valley AAU. Served with AUS, 1942-46. Decorated Purple Heart, Bronze Star medal with oak leaf cluster; Arms of Colemar (France). Mem. C. of C., Alpha Delta Sigma, Phi Kappa Psi. Methodist. Club: Mo. Athletic (St. Louis); Jefferson City Country. Home: 1518 Calvin Ln Jefferson City MO 65101 Office: Lehman Bldg Peoria IL also 312 E Capitol Ave Jefferson City MO

HALL, ROBERT MALCOLM, judge; b. Danville, Ill., Jan. 14, 1944; s. Richard Malcolm and Evelyn Louise (Long) H.; A.B., Ind. U., 1966, J.D., 1969; m. Jeanette Kemp Tracy, Jan. 21, 1967; children—Richard Mahlon, Kevin Michael. Admitted to Ind. bar, 1969; practiced in Covington, Ind., 1969-74; mem. firms Rex V. Keller, 1969-70, Keller & Hall, 1971-74; judge Warren Circuit Ct., Williamsport, Ind., 1974—; bd. dirs. Region III Ind. Criminal Justice Planning Agy. Legacy chmn. Am. Cancer Soc., Fountain County, 1970-71, v.p., 1971-72. Treas., Fountain County Young Republicans, 1970-71. Mem. Am. Judicature Soc., Am., Ind., Warren County, Fountain County (pres. 1972-73) bar assns., Ind. Judges Assn., Nat., Ind. councils juvenile ct. judges, Covington Jaycees (pres. 1971-72). Lion (pres. 1973-74). Home: 520 N Monroe St Williamsport IN 47993 Office: Courthouse Williamsport IN 47993

HALL, STUART PHELPS, pub. relations exec.; b. Cortland, N.Y., Nov. 29, 1919; s. Glenn Schermerhorn and Helen Winifred (Phelps) H.; B.S. in M.E., Rensselaer Poly. Inst., 1940; m. Maxine Margaret McCloy, Sept. 19, 1942; children—Philip McCloy, Allan Glenn. Engr., Buick Motor div., 1940-47; asso. editor Product Engring. Mag., McGraw Hill Pub. Co., 1947-48; editor Design News Mag., Rogers Publ. Co., 1948-52; founder, pres. Hall Indsl. Publicity Inc., Troy, Mich., 1953—. Mem. applied sci. adv. council Miami U. (Ohio), 1972-76. Recipient Indsl. Advt. Service award Till Forbid Club Detroit, 1976. Mem. ASME, Soc. Automotive Engrs., Soc. Mfg. Engrs., Engring. Soc. Detroit, Sigma Xi, Pi Tau Sigma, Sigma Chi. Republican. Mem. United Ch. of Christ. Clubs: Detroit Athletic, Miami U. Presidents, Elks. Home: 1060 Hall Ln Lake Orion MI 48035 Office: 2855 Coolidge Rd Suite 105 Troy MI 48084

HALL, THOMAS LYNN, assn. exec.; b. Decatur, Ill., June 15, 1943; s. Donald W. and Wilma L. (Padgett) H.; student Ariz. State U., 1961-62; B.S., Eastern Ill. U., 1965; M.S., Millikin U., 1969; m. Sonia L. Strohl, Aug. 18, 1961; children—Amy Lee, Craig Thomas. Cost accountant Firestone Tire Co., Decatur, 1965-66; tchr., coach Clinton

(Ill.) Sch. Dist., 1966-72; jr. high prin. Tolono (Ill.) Sch. Dist., 1972-73; exec. v.p. DeWitt County Fed. Savs. & Loan Assn., Clinton, 1973—; county adviser Roosevelt Nat. Ins. Co., Springfield, Ill., 1973—. Pres. DeWitt County United Fund, 1974-75. Bd. dirs. Clinton YMCA, 1973—. Mem. Clinton C. of C. (pres. 1974-75). Methodist. Mason (Shriner), Elk. Club: Clinton Country (dir. 1970—). Home: 24 Beech Dr Clinton IL 61727 Office: 302 W Main St Clinton IL 61727

HALL, WARREN EDWARD, JR., printing co. exec.; b. Weston, Mo., Jan. 18, 1921; s. Warren E. and Rosalie (Scott) H.; B.S. in Gen. Bus., U. Kans., 1948; m. Mary Elizabeth Dunden, June 13, 1946; children—Stephen E., Barbara Ann. Accountant, Lawrence Paper Co., 1947-50; sec.-treas. Merritt Foods Co., 1950-64; v.p., treas. Bus. Data Corp., Kansas City, Mo., 1965-66; pres., gen. mgr. Boecte-Hall Litho Inc., Shawnee Mission, Kans., 1967—. Bd. govs. John County YMCA, 1961-74; elder, deacon Presbyterian Ch. Home: 8025 Tomahawk Rd Prairie Village KS 66208 Office: 4700 W 52d St Shawnee Mission KS 66205

HALL, WILBUR ALONZO, writer, speech pathologist; b. Canton, Ohio, June 14, 1919; s. Walton Thomas and Esther Viola (Rowly) H.; B.S. in Edn., Kent State U., 1951; M.A., U. Ala., 1953; m. Marguerite L. Beem, July 13, 1941 (div. Feb. 1961); children—Sharon L., Margo Mae; m. 2d, Phyllis Rose Piccolantonio, June 11, 1965; children—Joanne, Marcia, Denise. Speech therapist Del. Dept. of Pub. Instrn., Kent County, 1954-59; head speech dept. Hamarville Rehab. Center, Pitts., 1959-60; head speech clinic Goodwill Industries Rehab. Clinic, Canton, 1963-70; pvt. practice speech therapy, Canton, 1960-63; writer, 1970—; counselor Crisis Intervention Center Stark County, 1977—. Mem. adv. bd. Am. Security Council. Served to capt. AUS, 1941-46. Mem. Canton Council United Comml. Travelers (exec. com.). Presbyterian (deacon 1963-66, elder 1969—). Author: Faith at Work, Journey Toward Wholeness, 1965. Contbr. articles to profl. jours. Address: 3024 16th St NW Canton OH 44708

HALLAN, JAMES ARTHUR, soft drink co. exec.; b. Mabel, Minn., July 9, 1917; s. Arthur M. and Inez M. (Gilbert) H.; B.A., Hope Coll., 1939; postgrad. Naval Supply Corps Sch. Harvard U., 1943; m. Frances M. Price, Sept. 12, 1941; children—Roberta, Sally Jo, James P. Salesman, Gerber Products Co., 1939-41; personnel-purchasing positions Baker Furniture Inc., Holland, Mich., 1945-54; vending positions Brooks Products Inc., Holland, Mich., 1954-57, sales mgr., 1957-63, v.p. sales, 1963-70, exec. v.p., 1970-72, pres., 1972—. Bd. dirs. Holland Sch. Bd., 1946-57, pres., 1956; active Keep Mich. Beautiful. Served with Supply Corp, USNR, 1941-45. Mem. Holland C. of C. (pres. 1968-69), Mich., U.S. chambers commerce, W. Mich. Purchasing Agts. Assn. (pres. 1952), Am. Mgmt. Assn., Mich. Mfrs. Assn., Nat., Mich. soft drink assns. Republican. Clubs: Am. Legion, Peninsular, Rotary, Elks. Home: 185 Sorrento Dr Holland MI 49423 Office: 777 Brooks Ave Holland MI 49423

HALLAUER, ARNEL ROY, geneticist; b. Netawaka, Kans., May 4, 1932; s. Roy Virgil and Mabel Fern (Bohnenkemper) H.; B.S. with honors, Kans. State U., 1954; M.S., Iowa State U., 1958, Ph.D., 1960; m. Janet Yvonne Goodmanson, Aug. 29, 1964; children—Elizabeth, Paul. Agronomist Agrl. Research Service, U.S. Dept. Agr., Ames, Iowa, 1958-60, geneticist, Raleigh, N.C., 1960-62, research geneticist, Ames, 1962—; adv. bd. Egyptian Jour. Genetics and Cytology, 1971—; faculty Iowa State U., Ames, 1962—. Served with AUS, 1954-56. Recipient Milling award, Kans. State U., 1954. Mem. Am. Soc. Agronomy (Iowa chpt. pres. 1973-74), Crop Sci. Soc. Am., Am. Genetic Assn., Iowa Acad. Sci., Orgn. Profl. Employees U.S. Dept Agr., Sigma Xi, Phi Kappa Phi, Gamma Sigma Delta. Asso. editor Crop Sci., 1977—, Maydica, 1977—. Home: 516 Luther Dr Ames IA 50010 Office: Room 101B Dept Agronomy Iowa State U Ames IA 50011

HALLENBECK, JAN TRAVER, historian, educator; b. N.Y.C., Apr. 13, 1940; s. Chester Traver and Marian (Lyston) Jones H.; B.A., Kenyon Coll., 1961; M.A., N.Y. U., 1962; Ph.D., 1966; m. Carol Ann George, Sept. 7, 1963; children—Thomas Traver, Michael Stuart. Instr., Queens Coll., N.Y.C., 1962-63; asst. prof. history Ind. U., Fort Wayne, 1966-69; asst. prof. Ohio Wesleyan U., Delaware, 1969-72, asso. prof., 1972-77, prof., 1977—, chmn. dept. history, 1976—. Recipient Sherwood Dodge Shankland Teaching award Ohio Wesleyan, 1975. Mem. Am. Hist. Assn., Mediaeval Acad. Am., Am. Catholic Hist. Assn., Ohio Acad. History, AAUP. Democrat. Episcopalian. Contbr. articles to profl. jours. Home: 130 Griswold St Delaware OH 43015 Office: Dept History Ohio Wesleyan Univ Delaware OH 43015

HALLENE, ALAN MONTGOMERY, elevator, escalator co. exec.; b. Moline, Ill., Mar. 12, 1929; s. Maurice Mitchell and Ruth (Montgomery) H.; B.S., U. Ill., 1951; postgrad. Oak Ridge Sch. Reactor Tech., 1951-52; m. Phyllis Dorene Welsh, June 16, 1951; children—Alan, Carol Louise, Janet Lee, James Norman. Reactor engr. U.S. AEC, Oak Ridge and Chgo., 1951-53; sales engr. Montgomery Elevator Co., Moline, Ill., 1953-54, mgr. accessories div., 1954-57, br. mgr. Jacksonville, Fla. office, 1957-58, chief engr., Moline, 1958-60, v.p., dir., 1960-64, exec. v.p., dir., 1964-68, pres., dir., 1968—; dir. Moline Nat. Bank. Bd. mem. Moline Dist. 40 Bd. Edn., 1966-70; mem. Tchr. Corps adv. com. Dept. Edn.-Health, Edn. and Welfare, 1970-73; mem. Gov.'s Adv. Council Ill., Ill. Commn. on Atomic Energy, 1968-73. Bd. dirs. Moline Luth. Hosp., Augustana Coll.; trustee Moline Found., Butterworth Meml. Trust, bd. dirs. Moline YMCA, 1959-66, Am. Coll. Testing Program, U. Ill. Found. Named Outstanding Young Man of Moline, 1963. Mem. U. Ill. Alumni Assn. (pres. 1973-75), Western Golf Assn. (dir.), Acacia (pres. 1950). Republican. Congregationalist (trustee). Club: Rotary (pres. Moline 1961). Home: 1885 24th Ave A Moline IL 61265 Office: 30 20th St Moline IL 61265

HALLER, JOHN SAMUEL, JR., historian; b. Pitts., July 22, 1940; s. John Samuel and Katherine (Nolan) H.; B.A., Georgetown U., Washington, 1962; M.A., John Carroll U., 1964; Ph.D., U. Md., 1968; m. Robin M. Gillespie, Feb. 3, 1968; 1 son, Peter Nolan. Asst. prof. history Ind. U. NW, Gary, Ind., 1969-72, asso. prof., 1972-76, prof., 1976—, asso. dean faculties, 1977—; lectr., cons. in field. Mem. Orgn. Am. Historians, Am. Inst. History Pharmacy, Assn. History Medicine, Assn. History Anthropology. Author: Outcasts from Evolution: Scientific Attitudes of Racial Inferiority, 1859-1900, 1971 (Anisfield-Wolf prize in race relations, 1971); (with Robin Haller) The Physician and Sexuality in Victorian America, 1974. Contbr. articles to profl. publs. anthropology, ethnology, history, medicine, pharmacy, sexuality. Home: 1127 Ripley St Gary IN 46403 Office: 3400 Broadway St Gary IN 46408

HALLIDAY, HERBERT EDWIN, pharm. co. exec.; b. Pleasantville, N.Y., Feb. 25, 1917; s. Arthur S. and Gertrude Adele (Myers) H.; student Harvard, 1938, 68, Mass. Inst. Tech., 1948; m. Allena Wiggins, Nov. 27, 1942; 1 son, Geoffrey H. Asst. to pres. Tailby-Nason Co., Cambridge, Mass., 1946-53, asst. gen. mgr., 1946-53; exec. v.p., also gen. mgr. Martin H. Smith Co., N.Y.C., 1954-58; gen. sales mgr., also dir. marketing Conal Pharms., Inc., Chgo., 1959-70; exec. v.p., also gen. mgr. Cole Pharm. Co., St. Louis, 1970-76; v.p., nat. sales coordinator O'Neal, Jones & Feldman, Inc., Maryland Heights, Mo., 1976—. Mem. long range planning bd., Natick, Mass., 1948-50; chmn. Parks and Recreation Bd., 1949-51. Served to maj. AUS, 1941-45. Decorated 2 Bronze Stars. Republican. Presbyn. (pres. men's club 1964-65, deacon 1975—). Mason. Home: 101 High Valley Dr Chesterfield MO 63017 Office: 2510 Metro Blvd Maryland Heights MO 63043

HALLIDAY, STEPHEN MILLS, lubrication engring. exec.; b. Columbus, Ohio, Mar. 6, 1927; s. Earnest Raymond and Violet Jean (Mills) H.; B.A., Princeton U., 1950; m. Elizabeth Reynolds, May 21, 1955; children—Lisa, Tracy, Stephanie. Successively sales engr., sales v.p., exec. v.p., pres. Renite Co., Columbus, 1957—. Trustee Center of Sci. and Industry, 1973-76; com. chmn. Auction Fund, 1971-73; trustee Columbus Sch. for Girls, 1975—. Served with USNR, 1945-46; PTO. Republican. Presbyterian. Clubs: Rocky Fork Country, Columbus, Princeton (N.Y.C.), Rotary. Home: 193 Stanbery Ave Columbus Bexley OH 43209 Office: 2500 E 5th Ave Columbus OH 43219

HALLOWELL, ROBERT EDWARD, educator; b. Charleston, Ill., Aug. 30, 1918; s. Edward Everett and Elizabeth (Stockover) H.; B.S., Eastern Ill., U., 1939, Ped.D. (hon.), 1965; M.A., U. Ill., 1940, Ph.D., 1942; postgrad. U. Geneva (Switzerland), 1946-47; m. Mirzl Mueller, Aug. 11, 1949; 1 son, Eric Edward. Spl. investigator War Dept., Ger., 1945-46; instr., then asst. prof. French, U. Ill., 1948-60; asso. prof. French and Italian, U. Wis. at Milw., 1961-63, prof., 1963-68, chmn. dept., 1964-68; prof. French U. Ill. at Chgo. Circle, 1968—, acting head dept., 1970; lectr. Centre d'Etudes Superieures de la Renaissance, Tours, France, summer 1964; Fulbright sr. research fellow, France, 1966-67. Mem. Modern Lang. Assn. (chmn. French Renaissance lit. sect. 1968, mem. Del. Assembly 1974-76), Am. Assn. Tchrs. French, Renaissance Soc. Am., Assn. Internat. des Etudes Francaises, Phi Kappa Phi, Kappa Delta Pi, Pi Delta Phi. Club: Cliff Dwellers (Chgo.). Author: Ronard and the Conventional Roman Elegy, 1954; articles and revs. in periodicals U.S. and France. French Editor: Modern Lang. Jour., 1960-64. Home: 1564 Bowling Green Dr Lake Forest IL 60045 Office: Univ Hall Univ Illinois Chicago IL 60680

HALLQUIST, ROY STUART, electronics mfg. co. exec.; b. Omaha, Sept. 28, 1940; s. Carl Oscar and Kathryn A. (Stuart) H.; B.S., So. Methodist U., 1963; M.S., U. Nebr., 1968, Ph.D., 1973; m. Nancy Kay Parks, Nov. 24, 1964; children—Roy, David. Asst. dir. U. Nebr. Computing 1969-71; asst. prof. computer sci., 1970-73, tech. dir., 1971-73; v.p. TransAmerica Data Systems, Lincoln, Nebr., 1973—, also dir. Mem. Assn. Computing Machinery. Home: 5430 Fairdale Rd Lincoln NE 68510 Office: 640 N 48th St Lincoln NE 68504

HALPERIN, PHILLIP HAROLD, surgeon, educator; b. Madison, Wis., Sept. 28, 1909; s. Charles H. and Anna (Wigonetz) H.; B.S., U. Wis., 1931, M.D., 1933; M.Med.Sci. in Surgery, U. Pa., 1939; m. Dorothy Milgram, Apr. 9, 1940; children—Janice Milgram Earle, Alan Keith. Intern, Mt. Sinai Hosp., Milw., 1933-34; resident in surgery Mt. Sinai Hosp., Milw., 1934-35, Albert Einstein Hosp., Phila., 1936-37; practice medicine specializing in gen. surgery, Madison, Wis., 1937-40, Kansas City, Mo., 1940—; former chmn. dept. surgery Manorah Med. Center, Kansas City; clin. prof. surgery U. Mo., Kansas City; clin. asso. in surgery U. Kans., Kansas City. Served with M.C., U.S. Army, 1942-46. Diplomate Am. Bd. Surgery. Mem. A.C.S., Internat. Coll. Surgeons, Pan-Pacific Surg. Assn., AMA, Kansas City SW Clin. Soc., Mo., Southwestern, Kansas City (pres. 1959-60) surg. socs., Mo., Jackson County med. socs. Jewish. Club: Oakwood Country. Contbr. articles in field to profl. jours. Home: 8348 Somerset St Prairie Village KS 66207 Office: 601 E 63d St Kansas City MO 64110

HALSEY, JIM, theatrical producer, talent mgr.; b. Independence, Kans., Oct. 7, 1930; s. Harry Edward and Carrie Lee (Messick) H.; student Independence Community Coll., 1948-50; m. Jo Ann Sherman, Oct. 3, 1953; children—Sherman Brooks, Gina Halsey. Producer shows for auditoriums, fairs, rodeos, celebrations various cities U.S., Can., 1950—; pres. Thunderbird Artists, Inc., Independence, 1952—, Jim Halsey Co., Inc., Jim Halsey Agy., James Halsey Property Mgmt., Jim Halsey Radio Mgmt. (KTOW and KGOW Tulsa), Pencil Music, Quill Music, Palo Duro Music, Brazos Valley Music, Parker Lane Music, Otter Creek Music, Open Air Music, Town Crier Music, Fish Music, Palo Mesa Music; gen. partner Circle R Ranch, Tulsa; producer Kans. Celebration Neewollah, Independence, 1958—; v.p. country and Western div. Gen. Artists Corp., Beverly Hills, Calif., 1966-67, Singin' T Prodns., NERECO Prodns.; dir. Farmers & Mchts. Bank, Mound City, Kans.; personal mgr. various entertainment personalities. Commr., Kans. Centennial Commn., 1960-61; mem. Independence Park Bd., 1969-72. Served with AUS, 1954-56. Recipient Distinguished Service award U.S. Jr. C. of C., 1959. Mem. Independence C. of C. (dir. 1958-61), Country Music Assn. (dir. 1963-64, 70-71), Acad. Country Music (dir. 1969-70, 73-74, v.p. 1975-76). Episcopalian. Rotarian, Elk (trustee). Home: 801 W Beech St Independence KS 67301 Office: 3225 S Norwood St Tulsa OK 74135

HALSTEAD, JAMES ALLEN, bus. cons., accountant; b. Mt. Pulaski, Ill., June 29, 1940; s. Roland Peter and Bonnie Elizabeth (Stopner) H.; m. Mary Ellen Cowan, June 13, 1963. Tchr. math. Balt. city high schs., 1966; programmer, systems analyst Revere Copper & Brass Co., Scottsboro, Ala., 1967-70; project leader Cabot Corp., Kokomo, Ind., 1970-71; systems analyst State Farm Ins. Co., Bloominton, Ill., 1971-77; founder, owner Gen. Bus. Services, Joliet, Ill., 1972-77; mng. partner James Halstead & Assos., Joliet, 1977—; mem. faculty Joliet Jr. Coll. Served with U.S. Army, 1963-66. Mem. Joliet Region C. of C. Club: Lions (Joliet). Home: 904 Westshire St Joliet IL 60435 Office: 1551 Plainfield Rd Joliet IL 60435

HALVORSEN, DANIEL KASBERG, physician; b. Duluth, Minn., Mar. 15, 1922; s. Daniel and Christine (Kasberg) H.; B.A., St. Olaf Coll., 1946; M.D., Yale, 1949; m. Maxine Schult, July 8, 1945; children—Daniel Kasberg II, Mari Joycelyn, Lionel Craig. Intern U. Minn. Hosps., 1949-50, residency in surgery, 1950-51; practice medicine, specializing in gen. practice, Owatonna, Minn., 1950—; chief staff Owatonna City Hosp.; med. examiner FAA, Nat. Guard; med. adv. Selective Service, Steele County Red Cross; coroner Steel Co., 1956-66. Pres. Kraig, Inc., Owatonna, Minn. Served with AUS, 1942-46. Fellow Am. Acad. Family Physicians; mem. Am., Minn. (gen. practice com. 1959—) med. assns., Am. Acad. Family Practice, S. Minn. Acad. Gen. Practice (pres. 1959-60), Steele County Med. Soc. (pres. 1962—), Aerospace Med. Assn., St. Olaf Coll. Alumni Council, St. Olaf Coll. Alumni Assn. (class agent), Yale U. Alumni Assn., Flying Physicians Assn. (v.p.), Gt. Lakes Flying Physicians Assn. (pres.). Lutheran (pres. 1966, 71). Home: 605 S Cedar St Owatonna MN 55060 Office: 111 W Main St Owatonna MN 55060

HALVORSON, WILLIAM ARTHUR, cons. actuary; b. Menomonie, Wis., June 26, 1928; s. George Henry and Katherine Eileen (Dietsche) H.; student Stout Inst., 1945-46, U. Mich., 1948; B.B.A., U. Wis., 1950, M.B.A., 1951; m. Patricia Janet von Trebra, Dec. 27, 1951; children—Robert, James, Janet, Audrey, Katherine. Asst. group actuary N.Y. Life Ins. Co., N.Y.C., 1951-56; cons. actuary Milliman & Robertson, Inc., San Francisco, 1956-61, Milw., 1961—, exec. v.p., 1972—. Served with AUS, 1946-47. Recipient Alumni award Menomonie High Sch., 1945. Fellow Soc. Actuaries (v.p. 1973-75, pres. 1977-78); mem. Wis. Actuarial Club (pres. 1964-65), Am. Acad. Actuaries (sec. 1971-73, v.p. 1973-74), Milw. Assn. Commerce, Midwest Pension Conf., Wis. Retirement Plan Profls. Ltd., Beta Gamma Sigma, Phi Kappa Phi, Chi Phi. Roman Catholic. Clubs: Union League (Chgo.); Oconomowoc Golf. Contbg. author: Group Insurance Handbook, 1965. Home: 34430 Valley Rd Oconomowoc WI 53066 Office: 200 Executive Dr Brookfield WI 53005

HAMACHEK, DON E., psychologist, educator; b. Milw., May 6, 1933; s. Evans O. and Marvis (Borgeson) H.; A.B., U. Mich., 1955, M.S.W., 1957, Ph.D., 1960; m. Alice; children—Deborah, Daniel. Teaching fellow U. Mich., 1959-60; prof. ednl. psychology and child devel. Mich. State U., East Lansing, 1960—; pvt. practice individual and group psychotherapy, 1960—. Producer-moderator weekly TV show over CBS-affiliate sta. WJIM-TV, Lansing, 1963-67. Mem. Am., Mich. psychol. assns., Am. Personnel and Guidance Assn., Am. Ednl. Research Assn. Author: Encounters with the Self, 1971. Editor: The Self in Growth, Teaching and Learning, 1965; Human Dynamics in Psychology and Education, 1968, 3d edit., 1977; Behavior Dynamics in Teaching, Learning, and Growth, 1975. Contbr. articles to profl. jours. Office: 463 Erickson Hall Mich State U East Lansing MI 48823

HAMADY, MARY LAIRD, publisher, author; b. Milw., Jan. 19, 1948; d. Harold Remington and Clarice (Shawver) Laird; B.A., U. Wis., 1970; m. Walter Samuel Hamady, July 27, 1969; 1 dau., Laura Evans. Partner, chief compositer, distbr. Perishable Press Ltd., Mt. Horeb, Wis.; poet, illustrator: This Gentle Strength, 1969; An Everyday Celebration, 1972; Eggplant Skin Pants, 1973. Home: Box 7 Mt Horeb WI 53572

HAMANN, DERYL FREDERICK, lawyer; b. Lehigh, Iowa, Dec. 8, 1932; s. Frederick Carl and Ada (Hollingsworth) H.; A.A., Ft. Dodge Community Coll., 1953; B.S., U. Nebr., 1956, LL.B. cum laude, 1958; m. Carrie S. Rosen, Aug. 29, 1954; children—Karl E., Daniel A., Esther E., Julie K. Admitted to Nebr. bar, 1958; partner Baird, Holm, McEachen, Pedersen, Hamann & Haggart, Omaha, 1959—; chmn. Farmers & Mchts. Bank & Trust, Watertown, S.D., Fremont County State Bank, Sidney, Iowa, Decatur Co. State Bank, Leon, Iowa, Citizen's State Bank, Corydon, Iowa; dir. Great Plains Fed. Tax Inst., Inc.; sec., dir. Hawkeye Bancorp., Des Moines. Mem. exec. com. Luth. Ch. in Am. Found., N.Y.C.; trustee Midland Luth. Coll., Fremont, Nebr. Mem. Am., Nebr. bar assns., Order of Coif, Phi Delta Phi. Lutheran. Optimist (pres. breakfast 1972-73). Club: Omaha. Home: 600 Loveland Dr Omaha NE 68114 Office: 1500 Woodmen Tower Omaha NE 68102

HAMANN, JOHN BERNARD, psychologist; b. Milw., Sept. 19, 1941; s. James Francis and Isabelle Mary (Cawley) H.; B.E., U. Wis., Whitewater, 1963; M.A., U. No. Colo., 1964, Ed.D., 1968; m. Stephanie Marie Land, Nov. 24, 1968; 1 son, Chad Michael. Tchr. Watson Jr. High, Security, Colo., 1964-65, head, dept. English, 1965-66; instr. U. No. Colo., summer 1968; dir. counseling and testing U. Wis., River Falls, 1968—. Counseling psychologist partner St. Croix Psychol. Service, River Falls, 1971—; cons., Totem Town, St. Paul, fall 1972, Miss. Valley Clinic, Hastings, Minn., 1972-73, Zeller Inst. for Living, St. Paul, 1973—, Vollrath Refrigeration, River Falls, 1974—; group therapy leader, cons. St. Croix Dale Hosp., Prescott, Wis., 1972-73; exchange prof. Taiwan Provincial Coll. Edn., Changhua City, 1975-76. Alternate rep. Democratic State Conv., 1969. Mem. Am., Wis. psychol. assns., Am. Soc. Clin. Hypnosis, Wis. Coll. Personnel Assn., Phi Delta Kappa. Roman Catholic. Home: Route 3 Box 88 River Falls WI 54022

HAMANN, JOHN RIAL, utilities exec.; b. Chgo., Jan. 1, 1915; s. Louis and Zoe (Rial) H.; B.S., Mich. State U., 1937, D.Sc. (hon.), 1977; m. Lois Agnes Sherman, Aug. 6, 1938; children—Joan (Mrs. Terry Mountford), Rial, John, Steven. With Detroit Edison Co., 1937—, v.p., 1971-73, exec. v.p. ops., 1973-74, sr. exec. v.p. ops., 1974-75, pres., chief operating officer, 1975—; pres., dir. Midwest Energy Resources Co.; dir. Nat. Detroit Corp., Nat. Bank Detroit. Councilman, City of Grosse Pointe, 1967-71. Mem. Lawrence Inst. Tech.; bd. dirs. Mich. Com. Jobs and Energy; trustee Bon Secours Hosp. Served to lt. col. AUS, 1940-45. Registered profl. engr., Mich. Fellow ASME, Engring. Soc. Detroit; mem. Assn. Edison Illuminating Cos., Nat. Assn. Electric Cos. (dir.), Greater Detroit C. of C. (vice chmn., dir.), Mich. State U. Engring. Alumni Assn. (dir.). Clubs: Economic of Detroit (dir.), Detroit, Detroit Athletic; Lochmoor. Home: 441 Rivard Blvd Grosse Pointe MI 48230 Office: 2000 2d Ave Detroit MI 48226

HAMBLEN, JOHN WESLEY, computer scientist, educator; b. Story, Ind., Sept. 25, 1924; s. James William and Mary Etta (Morrison) H.; A.B. in Math., Ind. U., 1947; M.S., Purdue U., 1952, Ph.D. in Math. and Statistics, 1955. Tchr. math. and sci. Kingsbury (Ind.) High Sch., 1946-48, Bluffton (Ind.) High Sch., 1948-51; asst. prof. math. Okla. State U., Stillwater, 1955-57, cons. in statis. methods for research staff Agrl. Experiment Sta., 1955-56, asso. prof. math., 1957-58, dir. Computing Center, 1957-58, asso. prof. statistics, dir. Computing Center, U. Ky., Lexington, 1958-61; prof. math. and tech. So. Ill. U., Carbondale, 1961-65, dir. Data Processing and Computing Center, 1961-65; project dir. computer scis. So. Regional Edn. Bd., Atlanta, 1965-72; prof. U. Mo., Rolla, 1972—, also chmn. dept. computer sci., 1972—. Cons. to research staff D-X Sunray Oil Co., Tulsa, 1957-58, Systems Devel. Corp., Santa Monica, Cal., 1965-67; mem. tech. adv. com. Creative Application of Tech. to Edn., Tex. A. and M. U., 1966-68; mem. tech. adv. panel, Western Interstate Commn. for Higher Edn., 1969-70. Purdue Research Found. fellow, 1954-55. NSF grantee, 1966—; Esso Edn. Found. grantee, 1966, IBM grantee, 1966. Fellow AAAS; mem. Am. Math. Soc., Assn. for Computing Machinery (chmn. edn. com. 1964-66, reviewer for computing revs. 1968, sec. 1972-76, chmn. curriculum com. on computer sci. 1976-78), Inst. Math. Statistics (mem. subcom. on math. tables 1958—), Nat. Council Tchrs. Math., Assn. for Ednl. Data Systems (pres. 1968-69, award 1971, sec. 1976-77, dir. 1975-79), Am. Fedn. Info. Processing Socs. (mem. edn. com. 1965—, chmn. edn. com. 1971-72), Soc. for Indsl. and Applied Math., Am. Statis. Assn., Math. Assn. Am., Am. Assn. Higher Edn., Sigma Xi, Pi Mu Epsilon, Upsilon Pi Epsilon, Alpha Chi Sigma. Editor Ednl. Data Processing Newsletter, 1964-65; asso. editor Jour. Ednl. Data Processing, 1965-67; editor Jour. of Assn. Ednl. Data Systems, 1967-68. Contbr. articles to profl. publs. Home: Route 1 Box 256A St James MO 65559 Office: Dept Computer Sci U Mo Rolla MO 65401

HAMBLETON, CHALKLEY JAY, ret. banker; b. Chgo., June 22, 1912; s. Chalkley Jay and Elizabeth (McMurray) H.; student Princeton, 1930-33; A.B., U. Chgo., 1934; m. Betty Moore Davis, Feb. 16, 1952; children—Chalkley Jay, Douglas McMurray. With Harris Trust & Savs. Bank, Chgo., 1935-77, v.p., 1960-65, sr. v.p., 1965-71, sec., 1962-71, head trust dept., 1963-71, pres., 1971-76, vice chmn. bd., 1976-77, also dir.; pres. Harris Bankcorp, Inc., until 1977. Bd. mgrs. Graceland Cemetery Co., 1965-74; trustee Orchestral Assn. Chgo., 1963—, v.p., 1977-78; trustee Berkshire Sch., Sheffield, Mass., 1968-72, Old Peoples Home City of Chgo.; alternate mem. trustees com. Chgo. Community Trust, 1963-77; governing mem. Glenwood Sch. for Boys, 1966-77; trustee Latin Sch., Chgo., 1961-70, pres.,

1967-70; trustee Newberry Library, 1974—; bd. dirs. Mid-Am. chpt. A.R.C., 1972—. Served to lt. comdr. USNR, 1942-46. Mem. Am. (pres. trust div. 1973-74), Ill. (pres. trust div. 1968-69) bankers assns., Corp. Fiduciaries Assn. Ill. (pres. 1967-68, exec. com. 1963-72), Shedd Aquarium Soc. (treas. 1966—, trustee), Northwestern U. Assos. Clubs: Commercial, Economic, Univ., Casino, Princeton, Commonwealth (treas., dir. 1971—), Tavern (Chgo.). Home: 70 E Cedar St Chicago IL 60611 Office: 111 W Monroe St Chicago IL 60690

HAMBLIN, HENRY SAILOR, supply co. exec.; b. Bedford, Iowa, July 28, 1922; s. Allen W. and Grace (Sailor) H.; B.A., Coe Coll., 1948; M.S. with highest distinction in Journalism, Northwestern U., 1950; m. Barbara Jean McCready, Aug. 7, 1948; children—Nancy, Kathlyn, Allen, Paul, Daniel. Printer, Bedford Times-Press, 1939-41; advt. copywriter Gen. Electric Co., Schenectady, 1950-51, account supr. indsl. advt., mgr. press relations aviation def. systems and services, mgr. indsl. products advt., 1953-59; asso. Russell-Hampton Co., Chgo., 1959—, v.p., 1960-67, pres., 1967—, chmn. bd., 1975—; v.p., dir. Russell-Hampton Can., Ltd., Toronto, Ont., 1963—; mem. faculty Northwestern U. Evanston, 1951-53. Mem. PTA Bd., Western Springs, Ill., 1960-62; co-pres. Coe Coll. Chgo. area Alumni Assn., 1966-70; active mem. Theatre Western Springs, 1969—. Served to sgt., AUS, 1943-46; ETO. Recipient mgmt. award Gen. Electric Co., 1955. Paul Harris fellow, 1976. Mem. Sigma Delta Chi. Republican. Conglist. Rotarian (bd. dirs. Chgo.). Club: Illinois Athletic (Chgo.). Home: 11223 Timberview Ln LaGrange IL 60525 Office: 2550 Wisconsin Ave Downers Grove IL 60515

HAMBRIGHT, ALFRED GALE, metal finishing machine co. exec.; b. Sturgis, Mich., Aug. 12, 1933; s. Alfred E. and Dorcas N. (Bupp) H.; ed. pub. schs.; m. LaVonda Lee Gouker, Jan. 19, 1963; children—Brenda, Bryan, Brandie. Apprentice welder Mecha Finish Corp., 1953-55, process and lab. technician, 1955-57, sales trainee, also field service mgr., 1957-61; asst. sales mgr., 1961-65, gen. mgr., 1965-68, pres., 1968—. Bd. dirs. Green Valley Campground, Inc. Elk, Lion. Home: Rural Route 4 Diana Dr Sturgis MI 49091 Office: 304 W South St Sturgis MI 49091

HAMBURGER, JOEL IVAN, physician, author; b. Detroit, May 22, 1924; s. Isadore and Henrietta (Harris) H.; B.A., U. Mich., 1951, M.D., 1954; m. Hilda Fishman, June 16, 1953; children—Sheldon, Paul, Daniel, Aaron. Intern, Ohio State U. Hosp., Columbus, 1954-55; resident Sinai Hosp., Detroit, 1958-60; fellow in endocrinology Henry Ford Hosp., Detroit, 1960-61; practice medicine specializing in thyroid diseases, Southfield, Mich., 1961—; clin. instr. medicine Wayne State U. Coll. Medicine, Detroit, 1961-65, adj. asst. prof. medicine, 1965-71; cons. endocrinology and nuclear medicine Crittenton Gen. Hosp., Detroit, 1961-74, Park Community Hosp., Detroit, 1965—, N. Detroit Gen. Hosp., 1965—; mem. staff Highland Park (Mich.) Gen. Hosp., 1961-72, chmn. dept. medicine, 1971-72; cons. thyroidologist U. Hosp., Ann Arbor, Mich., 1977—. Served with USAF, 1955-57. Diplomate Am. Bd. Internal Medicine. Fellow A.C.P.; mem. Soc. Nuclear Medicine, Mich., Oakland County (editor bull. 1972-73, pres. 1975-76) med. socs., Am. Fedn. Clin. Research, Am. Coll. Nuclear Physicians, Am. Thyroid Assn., Endocrine Soc., AMA. Jewish. Author: Diagnosis and Management of Common Thyroid Problems, 1969; Your Thyroid Gland-Fact and Fiction, 1970; Hyperthyroidism, Concept and Controversy, 1972; Nontoxic Goiter, 1973; Clinical Thyroidology, 1974; Problems in Clinical Thyroidology, 1977; contbr. numerous articles on endocrinology to profl. jours. Home: 23511 Sussex St Oak Park MI 48237 Office: 20905 Greenfield St Southfield MI 48075

HAMBURGER, RICHARD JAMES, physician; b. Phila., Feb. 2, 1937; s. W. Charles and Margaretha Gertrude (Schwab) H.; student Villanova U., 1954-58; M.D., Jefferson Med. Coll., 1962; m. Mary Jane Murphy, Jan. 25, 1964; children—Ellen, Joan, Mary Lou, Richard, Maureen, James. Intern, Jefferson Med. Coll., Phila., 1962-63, resident in medicine, 1963-65, fellow in nephrology, 1965-66; practice medicine specializing in nephrology, Indpls., 1968—; mem. staff Ind. U. Hosp., Wishland Meml. Hosp., VA Hosp.; asst. prof. Ind. U. Med. Sch., 1968-72, asso. prof., 1972-77, prof., 1977—. Trustee Kidney Found. Ind., 1970-74, mem. med. adv. bd., 1969—. Served with AUS, 1966-68. Diplomate Am. Bd. Internal Medicine. Fellow A.C.P.; mem. Ind. Soc. Internal Medicine (trustee 1975-77), N. Central Dialysis and Transplant Soc. (dir. 1972-75), Am. Soc. Nephrology, Internat. Soc. Nephrology, Am. Soc. Artificial Internal Organs, Am. Fedn. Clin. Research, Nat. Kidney Found., Am. Soc. Internal Medicine. Roman Catholic Club: Indpls. Racquet. Contbr. articles to profl. jours. Home: 1215 Chessington Rd Indianapolis IN 46260 Office: 1100 Michigan St W Indianapolis IN 46202

HAMBY, ALONZO LEE, historian, educator; b. Humansville, Mo., Jan. 13, 1940; s. David Alonzo and Lila Lolita (Summers) H.; student S.W. Mo. State Coll., 1956-57; B.A., S.E. Mo. State Coll., 1960; M.A., Columbia, 1961; Ph.D. (NDEA fellow, Wilson fellow), U. Mo., 1965; m. Joyce Ann Litton, June 6, 1967. Asst. prof. history Ohio U., Athens, 1965-69, asso. prof., 1969-75, prof., 1975—. Woodrow Wilson fellow, 1960-61; John C. Baker fellow, 1969; Nat. Endowment for Humanities fellow, 1972-73; Evans Research fellow, Truman Inst., 1973-74; recipient David D. Lloyd prize, 1972-73, Phi Alpha Theta 1st Book Award, 1975. Mem. Ohio Acad. History (publ. award 1974, chmn. publ. award com. 1976-77), Am. Hist. Assn., Orgn. Am. Historians (joint com. historians and archives), So. Hist. Assn., Soc. for History Am. Fgn. Relations. Author: Beyond the New Deal: Harry S. Truman and American Liberalism, 1973; The Imperial Years: The United States Since 1939, 1976. Editor: The New Deal, 1969; Harry S. Truman and the Fair Deal, 1974; Historians, Archivists and Access to the Papers of Recent Public Figures, 1977. Contbr. articles to profl. publs. Home: 16 Euclid Dr Athens OH 45701

HAMDY, AZIZ (HAMED), scientist; b. Cairo, Egypt, Dec. 7, 1929; s. Hamed and Nefisa (Sultan) H.; D.V.M., Cairo U., 1953; M.S., Ohio State U., 1956, Ph.D., 1958; m. Heidi H. Mawardi, Dec. 14, 1960. Instr. Ohio Agrl. Exp., Sta. Dept. Vet. Sci., 1954-58; research asso. U.S. Naval Med. Research Unit, NAMRU-3, 1958-60, asso. prof. vet. preventive medicine Ohio Agr. Research and Devel. Center and Ohio State U., 1960-66; sci. animal health research and devel. Upjohn Co., 1966—, currently sr. scientist. Diplomate Am. Coll. Vet. Microbiology. Mem. AVMA, Am. Soc. Microbiology, Conf. Research Workers, AAAS, Phi Zeta. Rotarian. Research on bovine respiratory diseases, swine diseases, poultry diseases and mycoplasma. Home: 1781 Greenbriar St Kalamazoo MI 49008 Office: Upjohn Co Kalamazoo MI 49001

HAMEISTER, LAVON LOUETTA, social worker; b. Blairstown, Iowa, Nov. 27, 1922; d. George Frederick and Bertha (Anderson) Hameister; B.A., U. Iowa, 1944; postgrad. N.Y. Sch. Social Work, Columbia, 1945-46, U. Minn. Sch. Social Work, summer 1952; M.A., U. Chgo., 1959. Child welfare practitioner Fayette County Dept. Social Welfare, West Union, Iowa, 1946-56; dist. cons. services in child welfare and pub. assistance Iowa Dept. Social Welfare, Des Moines, 1956-58, dist. field rep., 1959-64, regional supr., 1964-65, supr., specialist supervision, adminstrn. Bur. Staff Devel., 1965-66, chief Bur. Staff Devel., 1966-68; chief div. staff devel. and tng. Office Dep. Commr., Iowa Dept. Social Services, 1968-72, asst. dir. Office Staff Devel., 1972—. Active in drive to remodel, enlarge Oelwein (Iowa) Mercy Hosp., 1952. Mem. Bus. and Profl. Women's Club (chpt. sec. 1950-52), Am. Assn. U. Women, Nat. Assn. Social Workers (chpt. sec.-elect 1958-59), Am. Pub. Welfare Assn., Iowa Welfare Assn., Acad. Certified Social Workers. Lutheran. Home: 3440 Grand Ave Des Moines IA 50312 Office: State Office Bldg Des Moines IA 50319

HAMERSKI, HENRYK WINCENTY, physician; b. Nowemiasto, Poland, Feb. 22, 1915; s. Cyryl Metody and Franciszka Elzbieta (Ostrowski) H.; M.B., Ch.B., Polish Sch. Medicine, Edinburgh, Scotland, 1947; certificant, C.C.F.P.(C), Coll. Family Physicians of Can., 1972; D.V.M., Veterinary Coll., Edinburgh, Scotland, 1944; m. Virginia Rosetta Davis, Jan. 19, 1949; children—Cyryl James, Renata Ellen, Franciszka Lucinda, Marek Anthony. Resident house physician Roundway Hosp., Devizes, Wilts, Eng., 1948; house surgeon Willsborough Hosp., Kent, Eng., 1948-49; practice medicine specializing in family practice, 1950—; staff Kingston Gen. Hosp., Kingston, Ont., Can., 1950, Porcupine Gen. Hosp., South Porcupine, Ont., 1950—; chief dept. anesthesia St. Mary's Gen. Hosp., Timmins, Ont., 1950—. Dir. St. Mary's Gen. Hosp. Cons. in Anesthesia; regional pathologist for S. Cochrane, lectr. in obstetrics St. Mary's Hosp. Sch. Nursing, 1952-65. Served with Polish Army, 1940-43. Mem. Ont., (dir. 1965-73), Canadian med. assns., Coll. Family Physicians Can., Ont. Med. Found. Home: Gryf House 510 Patricia Blvd Timmins ON Canada Office: 14 Pine St S Timmins ON Canada

HAMILTON, CALVIN KENNETH, U.S. magistrate; b. Caplinger Mills, Mo., Sept. 28, 1924; s. Len and Neva (Bland) H.; A.B. in Econs., Drury Coll., 1949; LL.B., U. Mo. at Kansas City, 1956; m. A. Geraldine Chadwick, Jan. 8, 1946; children—Celia Lynn, Sabina Joy. Admitted to Mo. and Kans. bars, 1956; atty. criminal div. Dept. Justice, Washington, 1956-57; practiced in Springfield, Mo., 1957-59; asst. atty. gen. State Mo., Jefferson City, 1959-61; 1st asst. U.S. atty. Western Dist. Mo., Kansas City, 1961-67, U.S. atty., 1967-70; 1st asst. U.S. atty. Western Dist. Mo., Kansas City, 1970-71; chief U.S. magistrate Western Dist. Mo., 1971—. Served with AC, USNR, 1943, USAAF, 1943-46, USAF, 1950-51. Mem. Fed., Am., Mo., Platt County bar assns., Am. Judicature Assn., Nat. Council U.S. Magistrates, Sigma Phi Epsilon, Phi Alpha Delta. Democrat. Club: Masons. Home: 9807 NW 82 Terr Parkville MO 64152 Office: 811 Grand Ave Kansas City MO 64106

HAMILTON, CARL PORTER, dentist; b. Trenton, Mo., May 30, 1940; s. Ralph Howard and Lora Lou (Laughlin) H.; B.A., U. Iowa, 1962. D.D.S., 1965; m. Danielle Dee Davis, Apr. 23, 1960; children—Kristin Heather, Randall Howard, Rebecca Rae. Pvt. practice dentistry, Newton, Iowa, 1967—; faculty U. Iowa, 1971-72; Jasper County dental health chmn., 1968-73. Bd. dirs. Newton Community Theatre. Served to lt. Dental Corps, USNR, 1965-67. Recipient Sci. award Bausch-Lomb, 1958. USPHS grantee, 1966. Mem. Am. Acad. Gen. Dentistry, Am., Iowa dental assns., Am. Soc. Dentistry for Children, Jasper County Dental Soc. (pres. 1969-70), Newton C. of C. (dir. 1974—), U. Iowa Alumni Assn., Phi Delta Theta, Omicron Kappa Upsilon, Psi Omega. Republican. Episcopalian. Rotarian (dir. Newton). Club: Country (Newton). Home: 703 S 6th Ave W Newton IA 50208 Office: Newton Shopping Center Newton IA 50208 also 2525 E Euclid Ave Des Moines IA 50317

HAMILTON, JAN MICHAEL, lawyer; b. Miami, Okla., Apr. 2, 1948; s. Alexander George and June Elizabeth (Tuggle) H.; student Kans. State Tchrs. Coll., Emporia, 1966-67, Kans. State Coll., Pittsburg, 1967-68; B.A., Washburn U., Topeka, 1970, J.D., 1973; m. Joan Marlene Mattingly, Jan. 18, 1970. Announcer, radio Sta. KSEK, Pittsburg, 1967-68; air personality, producer Radio Sta. KEWI, Topeka, 1968-72; program dir. radio stas. KEWI, KSWT, 1972-73; admitted to Kans. bar; ops. mgr., house counsel Midland Broadcasters, Inc., Topeka, 1973-75; partner firm Hamilton & Hausheer, Topeka, 1974—; adj. instr. Washburn U., 1973—. Bd. dirs. Help Unite Human Relations. Recipient Order of Barristers award, 1972. Mem. Kans., Topeka bar assns., Kans. Trial Lawyers Assn. Republican. Home: 2032 Washburn St Topeka KS 66604 Office: 820 Quincy St Topeka KS 66612

HAMILTON, JOHN ALBERT, dentist; b. Detroit, Jan. 18, 1921; s. Merlin Coe and Mable Dyme (Bodenstab) H.; student U. of South, 1938-39; D.D.S., U. Detroit, 1946; m. Harriet Jane Taylor, Nov. 30, 1946; children—Susan (Mrs. John Roy Penberthy), Jacqueline, John Douglas, Thomas Michael. Salesman, J.L. Hudson Co., Detroit, 1937-39; salesman, sales mgr., photog. co., 1940; factory worker Cadillac Motor Car Co., also Allison Aircraft Engine, 1940; practice dentistry, essentially full mouth reconstrn., Detroit, 1948-70, Petoskey, Mich., 1971—. Founder, pres. Herr Bodenstab Kennel, Inc., 1963; developer Hamilton Estates East, West, North, 1972—. Active Boy Scouts Am. Served to lt. jg., USNR, 1943-48. Mem. Detroit Dental Clinic Club, Am., Mich. dental assns., Vacationland Dist. Dental Soc., Phi Gamma Delta, Delta Sigma Delta. Episcopalian (vestryman 1949-62, sr. warden 1962). Home: Country Club Rd Petoskey MI 49770 Office: 3141/2 Howard St Petoskey MI 49770

HAMILTON, JOHN HANDLEY, machinery mfg. co. exec.; b. Streator, Ill., Sept. 1, 1925; s. James J. and Arlene M. (Diest) H.; B.S., U. Ill., 1949; m. Catherine J. Chambers, Oct. 22, 1949; children—Jeffrey, David, Susan. With Internat. Harvester Corp., now mktg. planning mgr., Chgo. Agrl. engring. adviser Pa. State U., 1973-79. Served with USAAF, 1943-45; PTO. Recipient agrl. medal and diplome of distinction, French Govt., 1969. Mem. Am. Forage and Grassland Council (dir.), Am., India (U.S. dir.) socs. agrl. engrs., Delta Tau Delta. Home: 1105 Summit Hills Ln Naperville IL 60540 Office: 401 N Michigan Ave Chicago IL 60611

HAMILTON, LEE H., congressman; b. Daytona Beach, Fla., Apr. 20, 1931; s. Frank and Myra (Jones) H.; A.B. cum laude, DePauw U., 1952; postgrad. Goethe U., Frankfurt au Main, Germany, 1952-53; J.D., Ind. U., 1956; m. Nancy Ann Nelson, Aug. 21, 1954; children—Tracy Lynn, Deborah Lee, Douglas Nelson. Mem. firm Wilkinson, Witwer & Moran, Chgo., 1956-57; partner firm Sharpnack & Bigley, Columbus, Ind,; mem. 89th to 95th congresses from 9th Congl. Dist. Ind., mem. Fgn. Affairs Com., also mem. Post Office and Civil Service Com. Chmn. Bayh for Senator com., 1962, Citizens for Kennedy Com., 1960; treas. Bartholomew County Young Democrats, 1960-63, pres., 1963-64. Chmn., Mayor's Commn. on Human Relations, 1962-63; sec. Columbus Growth, Inc., 1961-64; mem. DePauw U. Nat. Requests Com. Recipient Distinguished Service award, Jr. C. of C., 1962. Mem. Ind. Bar Assn. Methodist. Clubs: Rotary, 89th Congress (pres, 1965—). Home: 4216 Peachtree Pl Alexandria VA 22304 Office: Cannon House Office Bldg Washington DC 20515

HAMILTON, RICHARD ALFRED, univ. adminstr., educator; b. Pitts., Dec. 22, 1941; s. Robert Curtis and Dorothy Katherine (Sexauer) H.; B.A., Otterbein Coll., 1965; M.B.A., Bowling Green State U., 1968; D.Bus. Adminstrn. (Univ. fellow 1968-71, Marathon Oil Co. dissertation fellow 1972), Kent State U., 1973. Production rate analyst dept. indsl. engring. RCA, Findlay, Ohio, 1966-67; computer systems analyst dept. market research Marathon Oil Co., Findlay, 1967-68; teaching fellow Coll. Bus. Adminstrn. Kent State U., 1968-71; asso. dean, asso. prof. mktg. U. Mo., Kansas City, 1971—; pres. Mission Woods Cons., Inc.; univ. asso. Lawrence Leiter and Co.; bd. dirs. Survey Unit for Mo. Mgrs., Academicians; cons. U.S. Senate Permanent Subcom. on Investigations, 1973-74, Midwest Research Inst. and Office of Tech. Assessment of U.S. Congress, 1974-75; speaker to profl. orgns. Mem. Am. Acad. Advt., Am. Inst. Decision Scis., Am. Mktg. Assn., Assn. M.B.A. Execs., Sales, Mktg. Execs., Beta Gamma Sigma. Methodist. Author: (with David R. Bywaters) How to Conduct Association Surveys, 1976; rev. editor Akron Bus. and Econ. Rev., 1977. Home: 5306 Mission Woods Rd Mission Woods KS 66205 Office: Sch of Adminstrn U of Mo Kansas City MO 64110

HAMILTON, RICHARD HUGH, dentist; b. Ft. Scott, Kans., Jan. 13, 1920; s. John V. and Ruth (McElroy) H.; B.S., U. Mo., 19—, D.D.S., 1943; m. Lorene Edna Miller, Oct. 30, 1954; children—Douglas Hugh Hamilton, Brad Hugh, Scott D'Arcy. Practice gen. dentistry, Topeka, 1946-51, practice orthodontics, 1951—; dir., also sec. KABODI, Inc.; dir., also pres. Delta Dental Plan of Kans. Served with Dental Corps, AUS, 1943-46. Fellow Am. Internat. colls. dentists; mem. Royal Soc. Health, First Dist. Dental Soc. (pres. 1956-66), Kans. Orthodontic Soc. (pres. 1965-66), Kans. Dental Assn. (pres. 1971-72). Mason (shriner). Clubs: Topeka Country, Topeka Town. Home: 5000 Redbud Ct Topeka KS 66606 Office: 4301 Huntoon St Topeka KS 66604

HAMILTON, ROBERT CHARLTON, physician; b. Evanston, Ill., May 14, 1933; s. Cloyce Charlton and Gladys Goodwin (Pratt) H.; B.S., U. Ill., 1955, M.D., 1957. Intern U. Ill., 1957-58, resident 1958-62; practice of medicine specializing in orthopaedic surgery, Chgo., 1962—, practice limited to athletic injuries, 1969—; mem. staffs Augustana Hosp., Ravenswood Hosp.; chief orthopedic surgery St. Joseph Hosp., Chgo.; asso. chief U. Ill. Amputee Clinic, 1963—; clin. asst. prof. U. Ill. Coll. Medicine, 1962—; lectr. Northwestern U. Med. Sch., 1965—. Served to comdr. USNR, 1967-69; capt. Res. Decorated Bronze Star medal. Diplomate Am. Bd. Orthopaedic Surgery. Fellow Am. Acad. Orthopaedic Surgeons, A.C.S.; mem. Am. Coll. Sports Medicine, AMA, Ill., Chgo. (vice chmn. council) med. socs., Ill., Chgo. orthopaedic socs. Home: 1032 W Loyola Ave Chicago IL 60626 Office: 25 E Washington St Chicago IL 60602

HAMILTON, WILMER LEE, agrl. engr.; b. Shattuck, Okla., Mar. 5, 1943; s. John and Bertha May (Getz) H.; B.S., Okla. State U., 1968; m. Susan Gay Cooper, May 30, 1969; children—John Cooper, Andrew Guthrie. Systems test engr. Boeing Co., Wichita, Kans., 1968-69; design engr. Precision Contours, Inc., 1969-71; design engr. Star Agri Products (formerly Starcraft Co.), agrl. products div., Goshen, Ind., 1971-72, chief design engr., 1972-74, mgr. engring., 1974-75, plant mgr., 1975-76; supt. engring. and planning Central Soya Co., Decatur, Ind., 1977—. Mem. Am. Soc. Agrl. Engrs. (student honor award Okla. State U. student br. 1967). Presbyn. (deacon 1975—). Kiwanian (treas. 1972-73). Home: Route 5 Box 60 Decatur IN 46733 Office: 1200 N 2d St Decatur IN 46733

HAMLAR, DAVID DUFFIELD, dentist; b. Roanoke, Va., Sept. 27, 1924; s. Robert Alfred and Maude (Smith) H.; student Hampton Inst., 1941-43; B.E., Toledo U., 1948; D.D.S., Howard U., 1952; m. Maxine Eloise Harbour, Apr. 16, 1945; children—Jocelyn, David Duffield, Deidre. Gen. practice dentistry with spl. attention to surgery and orthodontics, Columbus, Ohio, 1953—. Mem. Children's Dental Health Week Com.; state chmn. nat. black caucus Nat. Sch. Bds., 1971; exec. bd. Urban Edn. Coalition. Mem. Columbus Bd. Edn., 1966—, pres., 1975—. Trustee Central Community House. Served with USNR, 1943-45. Named Man of Yr., Columbus Urban League, 1976, Columbus Tomorrow Edn. Now. Mem. Columbus Dental Soc. (co-chmn. health information com. 1972), Ohio Sch. Bd. Assn. (trustee), Nat. Dental Soc. (state rep. 1972), Columbus C. of C. (mem. downtown area com. 1972), Cavaliers (pres. 1967), Omega Psi Phi (Omega Man of Yr. 1976). Home: 2626 Kenview Rd S Columbus OH 43209 Office: 705 Bryden Rd Columbus OH 43205

HAMLIN, GRIFFITH ASKEW, clergyman; b. Richmond, Va., Feb. 24, 1919; s. Charles Hunter and Mary Virginia (Griffith) H.; B.A., Atlantic Christian Coll., 1939; B.D., Duke U., 1946; Th.D., Iliff Sch. Theology, 1953; m. Margaret Geneva Cook, June 1, 1943; children—Griffith Askew, John Charles. Ordained to ministry Christian Ch., 1939; asso. prof. religion and philosophy Atlantic Christian Coll., 1948-50, trustee coll., 1959-60; pastor First Christian Chs., Hampton, Va., 1951-57, Goldsboro, N.C., 1957-61; chmn. div. humanities, prof. religion William Woods Coll., Fulton, Mo., 1961—, registrar, 1969-73. Active, Kingdom of Callaway Hist. Assn.; county rep. Mo. Symphony Soc., 1974; bd. dirs. Disciples of Christ Hist. Soc., 1970-71. Recipient Distinguished Prof. award, 1968, Centennial award, 1970, Alumni Appreciation award, 1971 (all William Woods Coll.); Monticello Coll. Found. award for research and writing, 1973-75. N.Y. U. fellow, summer 1965. Mem. Am. Acad. Religion, Mo. Philos. Soc., Smithsonian Assos., Internat. Council on Edn. for Teaching, Early Am. Soc. Democrat. Clubs: Masons; Internat. Sporting and Leisure; Fulton Flying. Author: The Old Testament: Its Intent and Content, 1959; In Faith and History: The Story of William Woods College, 1965; Monticello: The Biography of a College, 1976. Home: 201 Lynn Ave Fulton MO 65251 Office: William Woods Coll Fulton MO 65251

HAMLIN, RICHARD EUGENE, coll. pres.; b. Royal, Iowa, June 2, 1925; s. Fred E. and Nancy Jane (Schuetz) H.; student Drury Coll., 1943; B.S., George Williams Coll., 1949; M.A., U. Omaha, 1952; Ph.D., U. Nebr., 1956; m. C. Joan Dahl, Aug. 14, 1949; children—Robert E., Elizabeth Ann. Asst. camp dir., camp counselor, asst. youth sec. YMCA, 1946-49, exec. sec. South Omaha (Nebr.) YMCA, 1949-51, program sec., adult edn. dir., Omaha, 1951-53, asso. dir. research nat. bd., 1953-61; pres. George Williams Coll., 1961—; tchr. summer confs. Am. Youth Found., summer sch. U. Omaha. Dir. Bank Yorktown, Lombard Ill. Mem. Am. Psychol. Assn., Downers Grove C. of C. (chmn. bd.), Alpha Omicron Alpha (past pres.). Conglist. (lay moderator). Clubs: Economic, University (Chgo.). Author: Hi-Y Today, 1955; A New Look at YMCA Physical Education, 1957. Co-editor: YMCA Yearbook, 1958-61. Home: 3908 Forest Dr Downers Grove IL 60515

HAMM, FRANKLIN ALBERT, physicist; b. New Tripoli, Pa., Feb. 23, 1918; s. Mahlon Albert and Helen Ruth (Reimert) H.; B.S., Muhlenberg Coll., 1939; M.S., Cornell U., 1941, Ph.D. (Nat. Def. Research Com. grantee), 1943; m. Frances Melba Wertz, Sept. 9, 1941; children—Michael F., Terry F. Group leader Gen. Aniline & Film Corp., Easton, Pa., 1943-52; asst. dir. research Burroughs Corp., Phila., 1952-53; group leader research labs. Eastman Kodak, Rochester, N.Y., 1953-58; sect. leader 3M Co., St. Paul, 1958-63, lab. mgr., 1964-73, sr. research specialist, 1974—. Chmn. commuter com. St. Croix (Minn.) Area United Fund, 1961-62; active Boy Scouts Am., Paoli, Pa., 1952-53, Rochester, N.Y., 1954-58. Recipient Am. Chem. Soc. award Muhlenberg Coll., 1939; 1st prize Am. Soc. Testing and Materials Photog. Contest, 1946. Mem. Electron Microscope Soc. Am. (dir. exec. council 1947-50), Am. Phys. Soc. Presbyn. (elder 1963-66). Patentee in field. Contbr. articles to profl. jours. Home: 1505

N 2d St Stillwater MN 55082 Office: 3M Center PO Box 33221 St Paul MN 55133

HAMM, JOHN EDWARD, mfg. co. exec.; b. Ft. Wayne, Ind., May 19, 1950; s. Arthur Edsel and Marjorie Ellen (Larimore) H.; B.M.E., Purdue U., 1972. Research and devel. test engr. H.K. Porter, Inc., Huntington, Ind., 1972-74; product engr. Zimmer U.S.A., Warsaw, Ind., 1974-75, mgr. surg. products devel., 1975—. Chmn. Am. Lung Assn. walk-a-thon, Kosciusko County, Ind., 1976. Mem. ASME, Soc. Automotive Engrs., Purdue Alumni Assn., Warsaw Jaycees (sec. 1977—). Home: Route 3 Box 172 Warsaw IN 46580 Office: 727 N Detroit St Warsaw IN 46580

HAMM, RUSSELL LEROY, educator; b. nr. Quincy, Ind., Sept. 6, 1926; s. Bert and Ruby (Sutherlin) H.; B.S., Ind. U., 1950, M.S., 1952, Ed.D., 1960; m. Jean Robinson, Sept. 10, 1953 (div. Nov. 1956); 1 dau., Rebecca Anne. Tchr., Cloverdale, Ind., 1950-53, Bloomington (Ind.) High Sch., 1953-56; grad. asst. Ind. U., Bloomington, 1957; coll. supr. student tchrs. St. Cloud (Minn.) State Coll., 1957-60; coordinator curriculum, instr. Roseville (Minn.) Schs., 1960-65; asso. prof. edn. Ind. State U., Terre Haute, now prof. edn., coordinator founds. Sch. Edn. Guest tchr. Macalaster Coll., St. Paul, 1964. Pres., Minn. Core Conf., 1959-60, Bloomington Citizenship Council, 1956-57. Served with AUS, 1945-47. Recipient poetry awards Poets' Corner, 1952, Knox Coll., 1956. Mem. NEA, Internat. Platform Assn., Assn. for Supervision and Curriculum (pres. Minn. chpt. 1964), Ind. Assn. for Supervision and Curriculum Devel. (exec. sec. 1967-71), Phi Delta Kappa. Republican. Author: Genamica, 1950; On the Bridge, 1960; Minnesota-A Teaching Guide, 1962; As Sounding Brass, 1963; An Ecological Approach to Conservation, 1964; Conservation Education in Indiana, 1967; Hooks For the Darkness, 1971; Intraclass Grouping in the Secondary Schools, 1971; Philosophy and Education: Alternatives in Theory and Practice, 1974. Co-author: Role and Status of Curriculum Workers in Indiana, 2 vols., 1969-70; co-author: The Arenas of Power: Focus on Schooling, 1977; Environmental Education in Indiana Public Schools, 1975; 101 Old Recipes, 1976. Co-editor: Ind. Yearbook of Edn., 1970, 71; Innovations in Indiana Schools, 1971; The American Intermediate School, 1974; contbr. articles to profl. jours., poetry to mags. Home: 213 Elm St Rosedale IN 47874 Office: Ind State U Terre Haute IN 47809

HAMMAN, ROBERT JOHN, mgmt. cons.; b. Rochester, N.Y., Feb. 21, 1914; s. Arthur William and Florence (Mathis) H.; B.S., U. Mich., 1938; m. Leah Collins, June 10, 1939; children—Robert John, David A., Thomas C. Indsl. engr. Owens Ill. Glass Co., Toledo, O., 1938-41; prodn. supt. Murray Corp., Detroit, 1941-45; asso., partner, dir. A. T. Kearney, Inc., Chgo., 1945-75, cons., 1975—; dir. Portec, Inc., B-W Steel, Tuthill Pump, Prab Conveyors, Ircon, Timet, Inc., Valley Pattern. Mem. adv. com. U. Ill., 1970-75. Bd. dirs. Salvation Army. Mem. Ill. C. of C. Clubs: Glen View, University (Chgo.). Home: 140 DeWindt Rd Winnetka IL 60093 Office: 100 S Wacker Dr Chicago IL 60606

HAMMEL, ROBERT DALE, sports writer; b. Huntington, Ind., Oct. 6, 1936; s. Dale T. and Beautrice Mae (Davis) H.; Ind. U., 1953-54; m. Julie Ann Sowerwine, June 22, 1958; children—Richard Robert, Jane Ann. Sports editor-reporter Herald-Press, Huntington, 1954-63; copy editor Ft. Wayne News-Sentinel, 1963-64; sports editor Kokomo (Ind.) Morning Times, 1964-65; sports writer Indpls. News, 1965-66; sports editor Bloomington (Ind.) Herald-Telephone, 1966—. Recipient Chris Savage award journalism dept. Ind. U., 1973; named Ind. Sportswriter of Year, 1971, 74, 75, 76. Mem. Football Writers Assn., U.S. Basketball Writers Assn., Nat. Sportswriters and Broadcasters Assn. Author: Knight with the Hoosiers, 1975; NCAA, Indiana all the Way, 1976. Home: 213 Sheffield Dr Bloomington IN 47401 Office: 1900 S Walnut Bloomington IN 47401

HAMMER, OLIVER STARR, ednl. adminstr.; b. New Albany, Ind., July 23, 1917; s. James Frederick and May (Starr) H.; student U. Tenn., 1945-46, Ind. U., 1947-48; m. Helen Shaw, Mar. 20, 1941; children—Sue Hammer Rexrote, Helen Hammer Brown, Dorothy. Chief instr. FM sch., Lexington Signal Depot, Avon, Ky., 1942-43; gen. elec. supr. AEC, Oak Ridge, 1943-47; faculty United Electronics Inst., Louisville, 1947-49, dir. tng., 1949-52, v.p., dir. edn., 1952-65, exec. v.p., 1965—. Bd. dirs. Inst. for Certification of Engring. Tech., Washington, 1958-61. Registered profl. engr., Ky. Mem. Nat. Soc. Profl. Engrs. (award 1964), Am. Soc. Engring. Edn., Am. Tech. Edn. Assn., Am. Vocat. Assn., Toastmasters. Author numerous tng. manuals in electronics. Home: 1316 Ridgeway Ave New Albany IN 47150 Office: 3947 Park Dr Louisville KY 40216

HAMMERSLEY, WILLIAM LAMOINE, dentist; b. Frankfort, Ind., Mar. 5, 1905; s. William L. and Mable F. (Kingsburry) H.; A.B., Ind. Central Coll., 1931; D.D.S., Ind. U., 1936; m. Georgia LaVinia Jackson, Aug. 18, 1937; children—Richard William, Diana S. Gen. practice dentistry, Frankfort, 1936—; mem. staff Clinton County Hosp., Ind. Meth. Home for Elderly, Home Hosp., Lafayette, Ind. Asst. commr. Clinton dist. Boy Scouts Am., 1965-66, adviser med. post, 1965—; mem. City Area Planning Commn. Served with AUS, 1942-46. Recipient Silver Beaver award Boy Scouts Am., 1968. Mem. Am. Dental Assn. (life), W. Central (life mem., pres. 1948-49), Clinton County (pres. 1946) dental socs., Pierre Fauchard Acad., Am. Soc. Dentistry for Children, Royal Soc. Health (London, Eng.), Indpls. Dental Soc., Fedn. Dentaire Internationale, Am. Acad. Gen. Practice, Ind. Dental Assn. (life), Frankfort C. of C. (dir. 1971-73), Zi Psi Phi (life). Methodist. Mason (32 deg., Shriner). Home: 1500 S Williams St Frankfort IN 46041 Office: 53 E Walnut St Frankfort IN 46041

HAMMES, RICHARD GEORGE, psychologist; b. Sheboygan, Wis., Feb. 13, 1941; s. Sherman George and Kristine Therese (Mliner) H.; B.S., U. Wis., 1965; M.A., U. Chgo., 1968; Ed.D., No. Ill. U., 1972. Mental health adminstr. Elgin (Ill.) State Hosp., 1968-74; subregional coordinator developmental disabilities Ill. Dept. Mental Health and Developmental Disabilities, Elgin, 1974—. Part-time instr. psychology Elgin Community Coll., 1971—, Waubonsee Community Coll., Sugar Grove, Ill., 1972—. Served with AUS, 1959, 61-62. Mem. Am., Midwest, Ill. psychol. assns., Nat. Assn. Social Workers, Acad. Certified Social Workers. Author: The Myth of Education in the University, 1976. Home: 667 Grand Ave Elgin IL 60120 Office: 750 S State St Elgin IL 60120

HAMMING, KENNETH WAYNE, engring. co. exec.; b. Chgo., Sept. 22, 1918; s. Joseph George and Esther (Farley) H.; student North Park Jr. Coll., 1935-37; B.S. in Gen. Engring., U. Ill., 1940; m. Joyce Onalee Thom, Feb. 2, 1952; children—Stephen, Nancy, Gregory. With Sargent & Lundy, Chgo., 1940-44, 1945—, partner, 1956—, mgr. mech. and nuclear dept., 1964, dir. engring., 1965—, sr. partner, 1966—; weight control engr. Consol.-Vultee Aircraft Co., San Diego, 1944-45. Bd. dirs. Ill. Inst. Tech., 1976—. Registered profl. engr., Ill., Ind., Ky., Wis., Minn., La., Iowa. Fellow ASME; mem. Am. Nuclear Soc., Western Soc. Engrs. (trustee 1968-74), Atomic Indsl. Forum, Inc., Nat. Acad. Engring., Chgo. Assn. Commerce and Industry (dir. 1971-76), Air Pollution Control Assn., Nat. Soc. Profl. Engrs. Clubs: Chicago, Chicago Athletic Assn., Chicago Yacht; Westmoreland Country. Home: 527 Meadow Dr W Wilmette IL 60091 Office: 55 E Monroe St Chicago IL 60603

HAMMITT, COURTNEY CLARK, retail co. exec.; b. McKeesport, Pa., Feb. 5, 1915; s. Courtney Clark and Catherine Agnes (Brannan) H.; B.S., Ohio State U., 1939; student Northwestern U., 1942; m. Hannah Marie Reese, Sept. 7, 1947; 1 dau., Mary. Retail and wholesale salesman C.G. Conn Co., Elkhart, Ind., Boston and Chgo., 1939-42; dept. mgr., buyer Strouss Dept. Store div. May Co., New Castle, Pa., 1946-50, divisional mdse. mgr., Warren, Ohio, 1950-51, Youngstown, Ohio, 1951-70, 71-75, v.p. br. stores, gen. mgr. So. Park Mall, Boardman, Ohio, 1946—; dir. Met. Savs. & Loan Co., Youngstown, 1968-75. Chmn. retail and gen. bus. div., chmn. exec. com. United Appeal, 1973-77. Bd. dirs. Goodwill Industries, pres., 1976-77. Served to lt. USNR, 1942-46; PTO. Mem. Westminster Coll. Parents' Assn. (past pres.), Ohio State Alumni Assn. (pres. Mahoning County 1975-76), So. Park Mall Mchts. Assn. (dir., pres. 1976), Phi Kappa Psi. Baptist. Clubs: Youngstown, Youngstown Country. Home: 173 Alburn Dr Youngstown OH 44512 Office: 7401 Market St Youngstown OH 44512

HAMMITT, FREDERICK GNICHTEL, engr., educator; b. Trenton, N.J., Sept. 25, 1923; s. Andrew Baker and Julia Stevenson (Gnichtel) H.; B.S. in Mech. Engring., Princeton U., 1944; M.S. in Mech. Engring., U. Pa., 1949; M.S. in Applied Mechanics, Stevens Inst., 1956; Ph.D. in Nuclear Engring., U. Mich., 1958; m. Barbara Ann Hill, June 11, 1949; children—Frederick, Harry, Jane. Engr., John A. Roebling Sons Co., Trenton, 1946-48, Power Generators, Ltd., Trenton, 1948-50; project engr. Reaction Motors, Inc., Rockaway, N.J., 1950-53, Worthington Corp., Harrison, N.J., 1953-55; research asso. U. Mich., Ann Arbor, 1955-57, asso. research engr., 1957-59, asso. prof., 1959-61, prof. nuclear engring., 1961-65, mech. engring. dept., 1965—, also prof. in charge Cavitation and Multiphase Flow Lab., 1967—; cons. numerous govtl. and indsl. concerns; vis. scholar Electricite de France, Paris, 1967, Société Grenobloise Hydrauliques, Grenoble, France, 1971; Fulbright sr. lectr. French Nuclear Lab., Grenoble, 1974. Served with USNR, 1943-46. Registered profl. engr., N.J., Mich. Fellow ASME, Inst. Mech. Engrs. (U.K.) (past chmn. cavitation com. fluids div.); mem. ASTM (past chmn. com. cavitation and liquid impingement), Am. Nuclear Soc. (past chmn. Mich. sect.) Internat. Assn. for Hydraulic Research, Phi Beta Kappa, Sigma Xi, Tau Beta Pi. Republican. Presbyterian (elder 1965—, deacon 1961-63). Author: (with R.T. Knapp, J.W. Daily) Cavitation, 1970; Cavitation and Multiphase Flow Phenomena, 1978. Contbr. about 200 articles, papers to profl. jours. Patentee in field. Home: 1306 Olivia St Ann Arbor MI 48104

HAMMITT, JACKSON LEWIS, III, musician, educator; b. McKeesport, Pa., Feb. 22, 1938; s. Jackson Lewis and Helen Louise (Johnston) H.; Mus.B., Ohio Wesleyan U., 1959; Mus.M., U. Mich., 1961, Ph.D., 1970; m. Margaret Anne Read, June 24, 1961. Dir. music 1st Meth. Ch., Pitts., 1961-62; teaching fellow, asst. condr. univ. choirs U. Mich., 1962-67; lectr. music history U. Mo. at Columbia, 1967; prof. music Chadron (Nebr.) State Coll., 1967—; music dir. Platte Valley Oratorio Soc., Scottsbluff, 1971-76; performer. Mem. liturg. commn. and commn. on ministry Episcopal Diocese of Nebr., 1973—. Bd. dirs. Am. Youth Symphony and Chorus. Andrew Mellon fellow, 1961-62. Mem. Am. Musicological Soc., Am. Guild Organists, Music Tchrs. Nat. Assn., Music Educators Nat. Conf., Am. Choral Dirs. Assn., NEA, Phi Mu Alpha, Pi Kappa Lambda, Kappa Delta Pi, Phi Kappa Phi, Phi Kappa Tau, Phi Delta Kappa. Club: Kiwanis (pres. local club 1975-76, dist. adminstr. 1974—, lt. gov. 1977-78). Home: 630 Pine Crest Dr Chadron NE 69337 Office: Chadron State Coll Chadron NE 69337

HAMMITT, JOHN MICHAEL, data processing mgr.; b. Chgo., Sept. 21, 1943; s. John Melvin and Catherine (Ivanuski) H.; B.S. in Chem. Engring., Ill. Inst. Tech., 1970; M.B.A., U. Chgo., 1976; m. Kathryn Logan, Sept. 9. 1972. Engring. and research technician Moffett Research Lab., CPC Internat., 1962-67, mgr. process control computer Argo plant, 1968-70; sr. systems analyst Morton-Norwich Products, Inc., Chgo., 1970-72, mgr. corporate info. services, 1972—; cons. use of computers in lab. automation, 1968-71. Mem. Am. Inst. Chem. Engrs., Soc. Mgmt. Info. Systems, Chgo. Council Fgn. Relations, Chgo. Geog. Soc., Phi Theta Kappa. Club: Young Execs. (Chgo.). Home: 10 Valdon Rd Rural Route 1 Mundelein IL 60060 Office: 110 N Wacker Dr Chicago IL 60606

HAMMOND, DARRELL DEAN, civil engr.; b. Wesley, Iowa, July 20, 1935; s. Oscar and Pearl (Rosetta) H.; Engr., Iowa State U., 1957; m. Mary Jean Kahler, Sept. 18, 1956; children—Darrell Dean, Lori M., Deann M. Designer Iowa Hwy. Commn., Ames, 1957-65; sr. engr. firm Van Doren-Hazard-Stallings-Schnacke, Topeka, Kans., 1965-73; county engr. Jackson County (Mo.) Dept. Pub. Works, Independence, 1973-76; asso. Van Doren-Hazard-Stallings, Mpls., 1976—. Commr. Jayhawk Council Boy Scouts Am., 1965-73, adviser Heart of Am. Council, 1975—. Registered profl. engr., Iowa, Kans., Mo. Mem. Iowa Employees Assn. (pres. hwy. br. 1957). K.C., Moose. Home: 6075 Goldenrod Osseo MN 55369 Office: 3025 Harbor Ln Minneapolis MN 55441

HAMMOND, JOHN FARNSWORTH, III, mfg. co. exec.; b. New Orleans, Apr. 27, 1927; s. John Farnsworth and Elizabeth (Raub) H.; student U. Va., 1947-48; B.S., Purdue U., 1960; postgrad. Goshen Coll., 1961; m. Iola Ann Atterberry, Nov. 23, 1957; children—Jacqueline Ann, William Claude. Expediter, Inland Steel Co., Indiana Harbor, Ind., 1948-58; asso. pharmacologist Miles Labs., Elkhart, Ind., 1960-62; pharm. med. rep. Abbott Labs., Oak Park, Ill., 1962-75; lab. med. sales rep. Lancet Med. Industries, Inc., Des Plaines, Ill., 1975-76; lab. med. sales rep. Brown Clin. Labs., Inc., Mt. Prospect, Ill., 1976—. Pres. Washington Irving Sch. P.T.A., Oak Park, Ill., 1969-71; mem. Indian Guide program YMCA, 1972—; mem. Oak Park Twp. Revenue Sharing Adv. Com., 1973-75; chmn. Oak Park Twp. Revenue Sharing Adv. Task Force, 1973. Served with USNR, 1945-47. Mem. A.A.A.S., Am. Soc. for Microbiology, Purdue U. Alumni Assn. Democrat. Presbyterian (deacon 1968-74). Moose. Club: Purdue. Home: 1163 S Ridgeland Ave Oak Park IL 60304 Office: 530 W Northwest Hwy Mt Prospect IL 60056

HAMMONS, JOSEPH ERNEST, restaurant chain exec.; b. Leeper, Mo., May 17, 1913; s. William Edmund and Lida (Dunn) H.; student pub. schs., Mo.; m. Dorothy Mae Hogg, July 10, 1938; children—Margaret Grace, Linda Sue, Joseph Lee, Sally Anne. Partner, Jim Hogg's Super Market, Poplar Bluff, Mo., 1946-72, land devel. co., Poplar Bluff, 1967—, Skate City, Poplar Bluff, 1972-76, Burger Chef, Poplar Bluff, 1968—; dir. Trico Devel. Corp., Skate City. Deacon, tchr. men's Bible class So. Baptist Ch. Republican. Clubs: Optimist, Rotary. Home: Box 143B Route 6 Poplar Bluff MO 63901 Office: Highway 67 and Vine St Poplar Bluff MO 63901

HAMMONTREE, ROBERT JAMES, civil engr.; b. Akron, Ohio, Dec. 16, 1933; s. Robert James and Helen Martha (Cully) H.; B.C.E., U. Akron, 1957; m. Irene F. Marcinkoski, Sept. 14, 1957; children—Robert J., Charles F., Hope M., Barbara H. Design engr. Howard Needles, Tammen & Bergendoff, Cleve., 1959-64; engr. City of N. Canton, Ohio, 1964-66; pres. Hammontree & Friedl, Consulting Engrs., Canton, 1966-71; chmn. Hammontree & Assos. Ltd., Canton, 1971—. Served with U.S. Army, 1957-59. Mem. Nat. Soc. Profl. Engrs., Profl. Land Surveyors Ohio, Ohio Assn. Consulting Engrs., Am. Congree on Surveying and Mapping, ASCE. Roman Catholic. Clubs: Brookside Country, Rotary, K. of C. Home: 2824 Brentwood Close NW Canton OH 44708 Office: 5233 Stoneham Rd North Canton OH 44720

HAMPARIAN, ARTHUR MANOUG, dentist; b. Detroit, Sept. 29, 1934; s. Mihran and Dorothy (Benian) H.; B.S., U. Detroit, 1957, tchr.'s certificate, 1958, D.D.S., 1952; M.S., Wayne State U., 1971. Tchr. math. Tappan Jr. High Sch. Dist., Detroit, 1957-58; dental intern VA Hosp., Allen Park, Mich., 1962-63; staff dentist Fort Custer State Hosp., Augusta, Mich., 1963-64; gen. practice dentistry Garrison Pl. Med. Center, Dearborn, Mich., 1964—; mem. med. staff Oakwood Hosp., Dearborn, Mich., Bon Secur Hosp., Grosse Pointe, Mich.; cons. vocat. tng. program Dearborn Bd. Edn. Instr. Wayne State U. Med. Sch., 1964-71, asst. prof., 1971—; asst. prof. anatomy Detroit Dental Sch. Mem. Am. Dental Assn., Am. Acad. Oral Medicine, Am. Acad. Dentistry for Handicapped, Mich. Dental Soc., Detroit Dist. Dental Soc. (council 1977-80), Am. Assn. Anatomists, Dearborn C. of C., Armenian Revolutionary Fedn. (chmn. chpt. 1967-69). Home: 35625 Oakdale Dr Livonia MI 48154 Office: 19855 W Outer Dr Dearborn MI 48124

HAMPEL, ROBERT EDWARD, advt. agy. exec.; b. Cin., Apr. 29, 1941; s. John Edward and Ruth Elizabeth (Pister) H.; B.B.A., U. Cin., 1964; m. Nanci Jean Nau, Aug. 24, 1963; children—Jeffrey, Finance trainee Proctor & Gamble Co., Cin., 1964-65, asst. accounting mgr. Balt. plant, 1965-66, corporate forecaster, Cin., 1966-68; asst. controller Keller-Crescent Co. subsidiary Am. Standard Co., Evansville, Ind., 1968-69, dir. financial planning and mgmt. info. services, 1969-72, v.p. finance, 1973—; pres., bd. mem. Rustic Lakeside Corp. Pres. bd. dirs. Jr. Achievement S.W. Ind., Ind. State U., Evansville Found. Mem. Nat. Assn. Accountants (v.p. Evansville chpt., nat. certificate of merit 1977), Evansville, Evansville Jr. chambers commerce, Alpha Kappa Psi, Beta Alpha Psi, Phi Delta Theta. Clubs: Tri-State Flying (sec. 1974, treas. 1975—); Toastmasters (pres. Evansville 1971). Home: Rural Route 1 15 Old Stone House Rd Newburgh IN 47630 Office: 1100 E Louisiana St Evansville IN 47711

HAMPTON, CHARLES STUART, physician; b. Oslo, Norway, June 19, 1936; s. Charles Stuart and Barbara Lesley (McEwan) H.; student Trinity Coll., Glenalmond, Scotland, 1949-54; M.B.Ch.B., St. Andrews U., Scotland, 1960; m. Michaela Vasiliu Cristea Boaden, June 2, 1962; children—Catherine Mary Jane, Abigail Xenia. Intern, Dundee (Scotland) Royal Infirmary, 1960-61; med. officer Kuwait Oil Co., Kuwait, 1961-62; med. officer, Alice Springs, Australia, 1962-63; demonstrator anatomy St. Andrews U., Scotland, 1963-64; resident Dorset County (Eng.) Hosp., 1965-67; registrar renal research unit Leeds, Eng., 1967-69; med. dir., pres. med. staff Brandon Gen. Hosp., 1973—. Fellow Royal Coll. Physicians (Can.); mem. Royal Coll. Physicians (Edinburgh), Royal Hort. Soc., Folio Soc. Club: Special Forces (London, U.K.). Home: 9 Grant Blvd Brandon MB R7B 2L4 Canada Office: Brandon Gen Hosp Brandon MB Canada

HAMPTON, JAMES ELWIN, engring. co. exec.; b. Steubenville, Ohio, Oct. 23, 1921; s. William B. and Sylvia A. (Hupp) H.; student U. Ky., 1943; B.C.E., U. Detroit, 1949; m. Elizabeth A. Kalahar, Nov. 11, 1950; children—Robert, Michael, Patricia, David, John, William. Civil engr. C.E., Detroit, 1949-58; tech. dir. Am. Aggregates Corp., Detroit, 1958-62; pres. Mich. Testing Engrs., Inc., Detroit, 1960—. Served to 1st lt. AUS, 1943-46. Decorated Bronze Star with oak leaf cluster. Registered profl. engr., Mich., Ohio, Ind., Ky., Fla. Ill. Mem. Nat., Mich. socs. profl. engrs., Am. Soc. C.E., Am. Soc. for Testing Materials, Engring. Soc. Detroit, Am. Concrete Inst., Assn. Asphalt Paving Technologists. Rotarian. Clubs: Oakland Hills Country; Detroit Athletic. Office: 24355 Capitol Ave Detroit MI 48239

HAMPTON, JOHN WILLIAM, educator; b. Coshocton, Ohio, July 2, 1939; s. Boyce and Pearl (Watson) H.; B.S., Kent State U., 1964; M.S., U. Akron, 1968. Tchr., librarian Twinsburg (Ohio) Local Schs., 1964-69; tchr. Ridgewood Local Schs., West Lafayette, Ohio, 1969—. Mem. Nat., Ohio, Ridgewood edn. assns., Internat. Platform Assn. Baptist. Home: Route 4 Coshocton OH 43812 Office: PO Box 68 Fresno OH 43824

HAMPTON, PHILIP MICHAEL, cons. engring. firm exec.; b. Asheville, N.C., Sept. 5, 1932; s. Boyd Walker and Helen Reba (Smith) H.; A.B. in Geology, Berea Coll., 1954; m. Wilma Christine Gross, July 7, 1951; children—Philip Michael, Deborah Lynn, Gregg Ashley. Draftsman-designer Johnson & Anderson, Inc., Pontiac, Mich., 1955-57, designer, also project mgr., 1955-59, dir. bus. devel., 1962-76, v.p., 1966-74, exec. v.p., 1974-76; v.p. Spalding G. DeDecker & Assos. Inc., Madison Heights, Mich., 1976—. Vice pres. JAVLEN Internat., 1971-73; co-founder, owner My World Shops and Hampton Galleries, Ltd., 1976—; mem. pub. adv. panel GSA, 1977—; chmn. task force of com. fed. procurement of architect/engr. services Am. Bar Assn., 1977—. Pres., Waterford Bd. Edn., 1969-71; 19th dist. coordinator George S. McGovern for Pres., 1972; mem. state resolution com. Democratic Conv., 1972; exec. com. Oakland County Dem. Com., 1973-74; precinct del., 1972-74. Trustee Environ. Research Assos., sec.-treas., 1969-71, pres., 1971-73. Fellow Am. Cons. Engrs. Council (internat. engring. com. 1971—, vice chmn. pub. relations com. 1970-72, chmn. publs. com. 1972-74, chmn. Am. Bar Assn. model procurement code com. 1977—); mem. Nat. Water Well Assn. (chmn. tech. div. 1969-71), ASCE, AAAS, Cons. Engrs. Council Mich. (awards com. 1970-74), Am. Arbitration Assn. (comml. panel 1977—). Presbyterian. Clubs: Pontiac Exchange, Pontiac-Detroit Lions Quarterback. Editor: Total Scope, 1963-71. Home and office: 2440 Ostrum Pontiac MI 48055

HAMPTON, PHILLIP JEWELL, artist, educator; b. Kansas City, Mo., Apr. 23, 1922; s. Cordell Daniels and Goldie (Kelly) H.; student Kans. State Coll., 1947-48, Drake U., 1948-49, Kansas City U., 1949-52; B.F.A., Kansas City Art Inst., 1951, M.F.A., 1952; m. Dorothy Louise Smith, Sept. 27, 1946; children—Harry J., Robert Keith. Staff artist Kansas City (Mo.) Call Newspaper, 1951; faculty, dir. art Savannah (Ga.) State Coll., 1952-69, asso. prof. art, 1966-69; asso. prof. art So. Ill. U., Edwardsville, 1969—; exhibited group shows Nelson Gallery Art, Kansas City, Mo., Mid-Am. Gallery, Kansas City, Telfair Acad. Arts and Scis., Savannah, Dulin Gallery, Knoxville, Atlanta U., Tuskegee (Ala.) Inst., Coastal Empire Arts Festival, Savannah, Jesup (Ga.) Arts Festival; represented in permanent collections Lincoln U., Jefferson City, Mo., Tuskegee Inst. Mem. com. Gov.'s Honors Program, mem. adv. bd., 1964—. Bd. Honors Program, 1964—. Bd. dirs., mem. adv. bd., YMCA, Savannah, 1965—; mem. Com. planning com. Coastal Empire Art Festival, Savannah, 1965-67. Served with AUS, 1943-46. Recipient awards Greenbriar Children's Center, 1961, Savannah chpt. Links, 1966, Nat. Conf. Artists, 1966; named Outstanding Tchr., N.E.A., 1964. Mem. Savannah Art Assn. (dir. 1967—, chmn. edn. com. 1967), Coll. Art Assn. Am., AAUP, Nat. Conf. Artists, Nat. Art Edn. Assn., Telfair Acad. Arts and Scis. Presbyn. Executed mural Hammond Hall, Savannah State Coll., 1958. Home: 832 Holyoake Rd Edwardsville IL 62025

HAMRA, DONALD EDD, dentist; b. Memphis, Nov. 26, 1931; s. Richard Albert and Nellie (Hodge) H.; A.B., Central Methodist Coll., 1954; D.D.S., U. Tenn., 1962; m. Shirley Louise George, Nov. 22, 1962; 1 dau., Olivia Carole. Practice gen. dentistry, Malden, Mo., 1962—. Mem. Malden Zoning Commn.; adminstrv. adviser Boy Scouts Am., 1965-66. Served with Dental Corps, AUS, 1955-58. Mem. Malden Inner City Bus. Assn. (pres. 1972), Am., S.E. Mo. (bd. of censures 1977—) dental assns., Malden C. of C. (pres. 1977-78), Xi Psi Phi, Sigma Alpha Chi. Democrat. Methodist (vice chmn. trustees). Lion (pres. Malden 1966-67, zone chmn. 1968-69). Researcher in thrombocellulitis and herpes simplex. Home: 907 Park St Malden MO 63863 Office: Box 252 110 W Howard St Malden MO 63863

HAMRICK, RUFFNER GERALD, supt. schs.; b. Orma, W. Va., Apr. 1, 1927; s. John K. and Zana B. (Parsons) H.; student Mason Sch. Music and Fine Arts, 1950-51; M.E., Kent State U., 1958, postgrad. 1958-66; A.B., Salem Coll., 1953; postgrad. Akron U., 1967— Ed.D., Heed Univ., 1972; m. Jane L. O'Brien, Aug. 24, 1952; children—Debra Sue, David Alan. Tchr., W. Va., 1948-52, Akron, Ohio, 1953-60; prin. Field Local schs., 1960-65; supt. Southeast local schs., Portage County, 1965-67; supt. schs., Alliance, Ohio, 1967—; ednl. cons., 1969—. Bd. trustees United Fund, 1968—; bd. dirs. YMCA, 1968—; adv. bd. Stark County Mental Health, 1969—; mem. mayor's community relations com., 1967-71. Vice-pres. Alliance Ednl. Found. Served with USN, 1945-48. Named Gold Medal educator Project Edn's Hall Fame, 1970; recipient Distinguished Service award Alliance Jaycees, 1972. Mem. Am. Assn. Sch. Adminstrs., Nat., Ohio edn. assns., Buckeye Assn. Sch. Adminstrs., Nat. Sch. Bds. Assn., Nat. Assn. Behavioral Arts and Scis. (dir.), Portage County Prins. Assn. (pres. 1963-65), Internat. Platform Assn., Phi Delta Kappa, V.F.W. Mason, Rotarian, Elk. Editorial bd. Edn. Jour. Home: 860 W Milton St Alliance OH 44601 Office: 200 Glamorgan St Alliance OH 44601

HAMRICK, WILLIAM JEAN, ednl. adminstr.; b. Vigo County, Ind., Nov. 27, 1924; s. Floyd James and Kathryn Amy (Russell) H.; student Rose-Hulman Inst., 1943, 1946, Iowa Wesleyan Coll., 1944; B.S., Ind. State U., 1948, M.S., 1951; postgrad. Ind. U., 1960; m. Mary Claire Thomas, June 30, 1956; children—Charles Robert, Sally Antoinette. Tchr., counselor pub. schs., Terre Haute, Ind., 1950-60, asst. principal, 1960-61; asst. state dir. pupil services Ind. State Dept. Instns., Indpls., 1968-69; coordinator guidance and special edn. Vigo County Sch. Corp., Terre Haute, 1961-68, dir. pupil services, 1969-71, asst. supt. sch., 1971—, acting supt. sch., 1974-75; chmn. Region 7 Planning Com. Mental Retardation; mem. State Adv. Council Title IV-C. Bd. dirs. Katherine Hamilton Mental Health Center, 1965—, Vigo County Assn. Retarded Children, 1968-71, United Fund, 1967-69, Vigo County United Cerebral Palsy, 1966-69, Vigo County Hist. Soc., 1968-72. Served with USAAF, 1943-45. Recipient Acad. Fellows Distinguished Edn. award Charles F. Kettering Found., 1976-77; Human Devel. award Ind. Psychol. Assn., 1975; Outstanding Merit award State Supt. Pub. Instruction, 1974. Mem. NEA, Am., Ind. personnel and guidance assns., Am. Counselor Educators and Suprs., Nat. Assn. Pupil Personnel Adminstrs., Council for Exceptional Children, Ind. Sch. Adminstrs. Assn., Nat. Assn. Supervision and Curriculum Devel., Phi Delta Kappa, Lambda Psi Sigma. Methodist. Clubs: Kiwanis, Ind. Schoolmen's, Elks. Author: Psychological Evaluation and Prescription Development Handbook, 1971; contbr. articles in field to profl. jours. Home: 6 Monroe Blvd Terre Haute IN 47803 Office: 961 Lafayette Ave Terre Haute IN 47807

HAN, LIT SIEN, mech. engr., educator; b. Shanghai, China, May 5, 1923; s. Zenphu and Yuchen (Hsia) H.; B.S., Chiao-Tung U., Shanghai, 1945; M.Sc., Ohio State U., 1948, Ph.D., 1954; m. Tsung-men Shen, Sept. 6, 1953; children—Barbara, Derek, Byron. With Shanghai Ry. Adminstrn., 1947-48, Ohio Research Found., 1948-54; engring. cons. Janitrol Aero div. Midland-Ross Corp., 1955-70; prof. mech. engring. Ohio State U., Columbus, 1960—. Cons., Battelle Meml. Inst., Columbus, 1960—, Air Force Flight Dynamics Lab., 1970, Bell Telephone Labs., 1974; vis. prof. U. Göttingen (Germany), 1961-62. NSF sr. postdoctoral fellow. Mem. ASME, Soc. Automotive Engrs., Am. Inst. Aeros. and Astronautics, Sigma Xi, Tau Beta Pi, Phi Tau Phi. Contbr. articles on solid and fluid mechanics and heat transfer to profl. jours., also book revs. Home: 4280 Camborne Rd Columbus OH 43220

HANBACK, JACQUELINE TANKERSLEY (MRS. WILLIAM F. HANBACK), rehab. counselor; b. Jacksonville, Ill., Nov. 18, 1926; d. James H. and Mary E. (Hamilton) Tankersley; grad. MacMurray Coll., Jacksonville, 1948; M.A., U. Ill., 1965, postgrad., 1966; m. William F. Hanback, Apr. 9, 1950 (div. 1977); 1 dau., Mary Murla. Tchr., Jacksonville, 1948-60; program dir. Elm City Rehab. Center, Jacksonville, 1960-63, profl. adv. com., 1967-76; rehab. counselor for psychiatrically disabled Div. Vocat. Rehab., Jacksonville, 1963—; mem. Scott County Sch. Unit 1 Bd. Edn., 1967—, Interagy. of Morgan County, 1967-74; mem. Four Rivers Operating Bd. Spl. Edn., 1972-75, chmn., 1973-75; mem. Gov.'s Adv. Council on Mental Health, 1975-76. Mem. Am. Personnel and Guidance Assn., Am. Rehab. Counselors Assn. (nat. awards com. 1972), Nat. (pres.'s council 1969-71, del. 1967-70, pres. Ill. Welfare Assn. dist. 6, 1972-74, membership chmn. 1971-72, sec.-treas. 1973-74), Ill. (pres. 1969-70) rehab. counseling assns., Nat. (nat. membership chmn. 1970-71, sec.-treas. 1972-73, dir. 1974-76, chm. operating council 1977-78, program chmn. 1975), Ill. (dir. 1967-69) rehab. assns., Ill. Alcoholism and Drug Dependence Assn. (task force on certification mems. 1977—), Ill. Assn. Sch. Bds. (vice chmn. Two Rivers dist. 1973-77). Club: Soroptimist (vice chmn. 1971-72, 75, chmn. 1976). Home: Rural Route 1 Winchester IL 62694 Office: 1440 W Walnut St Jacksonville IL 62650

HANCE, KENNETH G., educator; B.A., Olivet Coll., 1924, M.A. 1926, L.H.D., 1961; student Harvard U., 1928-30, Columbia U., 1932; Ph.D., U. Mich., 1937. Instr. Olivet Coll., from 1924, later asst. prof., asso. prof.; asst. prof. Albion Coll., 1930-37, prof., 1937-40; asso. prof. U. Mich., 1940-45, prof., asst. dean Sch. Speech, Northwestern U., 1945-56; prof., dir. grad studies in speech Mich. State U., 1956-71, prof. emeritus, 1971—; provost Olivet Coll., 1968-71, acting acad. v.p., asst. v.p., 1971-73, asst. pres., dir. ch. relations, 1973-74, emeritus adminstr., 1974—; adj. prof. Garrett Theol. Sem., 1945-56, Seabury Western Theol. Sem., 1945-56, Andrews U. and Theol. Sem., 1962-70; vis. prof. Calif. State U. at Los Angeles, 1966; distinguished vis. prof. Central Mich. U., 1970-72. Recipient Distinguished Alumni award Pi Kappa Delta, 1963, Delta Sigma Rho-Tau Kappa Alpha, 1964, Mich. Speech Assn., 1964; Distinguished Service award Interstate Oratorical Assn., 1973; Distinguished Alumni award Olivet Coll., 1975. Mem. Speech Assn. Am. (exec. v.p., 1955-57, pres. 1960), Mich., Ill., Central States speech assns., Nat. Mich., edn. assns., Am. Assn. Higher Edn., Interstate Oratorical Assn. (exec. sec. 1939-60), Delta Sigma Rho (nat. sec. 1939-50, nat. treas. 1939-72). Co-author Principles and Methods of Discussion, 1938; Discussion In Human Affairs, 1950; Public Speaking and Discussion for Religious Leaders; sr. author Principles of Speaking, 1962, Principles of Speaking, 2d edit., 1969; Principles of Speaking, 3d edit., 1974. Editor The Illinois Speech Journal, 1946-50; The Gavel, 1939-50. Editor-author History of Speech Education in Michigan. Contbr. articles to profl. jours. Home: 509 Ship St Saint Joseph MI 49085

HANCOCK, DAVID ELWOOD, test, reliability and quality control engr., fin. cons.; b. Holden, Mo., Apr. 12, 1935; s. Willis Elwood and Olan Amber (Shimel) H.; B.S., Central Mo. State U., 1956, postgrad, 1962-64; m. Mavis Lee Shatwell, June 2, 1960; children—Charles Dewayne, Paula Jean, Cheryl Lynn, Paul David, Scott Allen. Engr., McDonnell Douglas Co., St. Louis, 1955-58, Bendix Corp., Kansas City, Mo., 1958-65; test engr., statistician Brown Engring. Co., Huntsville, Ala., 1965-66; engr. Sperry Rand Co., Huntsville, 1966-70; engr. Fed. Electric Co., Huntsville, 1970-71; test engr. Certain-Teed Products Co., Kansas City, Kans., 1972—; dist. mgr. Vanguard Security Life, Huntsville, 1968-70; chmn. bd., mgr. Holden Investments, Inc. (Mo.), 1971-77. Mem. Reorganized Ch. Jesus Christ Latter-day Saints. Home: 705 W 3d St Holden MO 64040 Office: 2920 Fairfax Rd Kansas City KS 64115

HANDAHL, DONALD HERMAN, food products co. exec.; b. Mpls., Apr. 17, 1924; s. Herman C. and Gertrude Marie (Kallestad) H.; grad. Mankato Comml. Coll., 1942; B.A. in Econs., St. Olaf Coll., 1949; m. R. Joann Estrem, June 24, 1950; children—Mark, Ross, Heidi, Holly. Office mgr. Farmers Produce Co., Willmar, Minn., 1949-52; controller First Fed. Savs. & Loan Assn., Willmar, 1952-53; with Jennie-O Foods, Inc., Willmar, 1953—, v.p. adminstrn., 1971—, also dir.; dir. Earl B. Olson Farms, Willmar; partner, sec.-treas. HAP Realty Co., Willmar. Bd. dirs. Rice Meml. Hosp., sec., 1969, v.p., 1971, pres., 1972. Served with USNR, 1942-46; PTO. Mem. Minn. Turkey Growers Assn. (dir. 1975—). Republican. Lutheran (council 1956-62). Club: Willmar Golf. Home: 921 Meadow Ln Willmar MN 56201 Office: 2505 Willmar Ave SW Willmar MN 56201

HANDEL, CHARLES HAROLD, clin. psychologist; b. Cin., Jan. 2, 1947; s. Charles H. and Helen Audrey (Schlosser) H.; m. Mary Patricia Harmeier, June 15, 1973; B.S., Xavier U., Cin., 1969; M.A., U. Dayton, 1972; postgrad. U. Cin., 1973—. Clin. psychology trainee Dayton Mental Health Center, 1970-72; intern clin. psychologist Dayton Children's Psy. Hosp. and Child Guidance Center, 1972-74; intern clin. psychologist Mental Health Services-East, Cin., 1974-76, clin. psychologist, 1976—; cons. psychologist St. Ursula Acad., Cin., 1976—. Licensed psychologist. Mem. Am., Ohio, Cin. psychol. assns., Am. Assn. Orthopsychiatry. Home: 706 Tweed Ave Cincinnati OH 45226 Office: 3322 Erie Ave Cincinnati OH 45208

HANDEL, MILTON RICHARD, county ofcl., civic worker; b. Menno, S.D., Mar. 8, 1927; s. Richard and Ella (Heckenliable) H.; B.S., U. S.D., 1951; m. Rita M. Hein, Sept. 7, 1958; children—Tarrel, Deono, Teresa, Rena. Engr., S.D. Dept. Transp., Tyndall, 1951-53; engr. Hutchinson County Hwy. Dept., Olivet, S.D., 1953—. Cons. drainage and asphalt surfacing to various cities Hutchinson County, 1954—. Mem. bd. edn. Menno Sch. Dist. 111, 1957-58, pres. bd. edn., 1968-77. Served with AUS, 1945-46. Mem. S.D. Hwy. Supts. Assn. (mem. exec. bd. 1972—), Am. Legion (post comdr. 1955). Mem. United Ch. of Christ (sec. 1960—). Elk. Home: Box 131 Olivet SD 57052 Office: Box 134 Olivet SD 57052

HANDLEY, ROBERT EUGENE, photographer; b. Bloomington, Ill., May 23, 1945; s. Bernard A. and Edna Margarete (Manahan) H.; student So. Ill. U., 1966-67, Ill. State U., 1967-68; grad. N.Y. Inst. Photography, 1972, Winona Sch. Profl. Photography, 1974. Formerly publicity photographer Ringling Bros. and Barnum & Bailey Circus; owner Robert E. Handley, Photography, Bloomington, 1969—. Lectr. photography for nat., state, regional confs., high schs. Mem., chmn. Bloomington Down Town Council, 1976—. Served with AUS, 1962. Recipient Excellence award Profl. Photographers Am., 1973; Ct. of Honor trophy State of Ill.; numerous other awards. Mem. Profl. Photographers Am. (Photog. Craftsman degree 1976; asst. nat. conv. mgr. 1976), Assn. Commerce and Industry Mclean County, Asso. Profl. Photographers Ill., Profl. Photographers No. Ill. (dir. 1976—), Profl. Photographers So. Ill., Profl. Photographers Calif., Profl. Photographers West, Inst. Inc. Photographers (Gt. Britain), Soc. Photographers in Communications, Am. Soc. Photographers, Photog. Soc. Am., Wedding Photographers Am., Asso. Photographers Internat. (life), So. Ill. Art League, Winona Sch. Alumni Assn. Moose. Contbr. articles to profl. jours. Home: 710 N Lee St Bloomington IL 61701

HANDWERKER, SY, pub. relations exec.; b. Chgo., Apr. 5, 1933; s. Alex and Bella (Schwartzberg) H.; B.S., U. Ill., 1954; postgrad. DePaul U. Coll. Law, 1954-56; m. Marilyn Iris Parker, Aug. 6, 1961; children—Jaye, Dana, Steven. Reporter, asst. radio news editor City News Bur. Chgo., 1951-54; asst. dir. pub. information U. Ill., Chgo., 1954-59; owner Sy Handwerker Pub. Relations, Chgo., 1959-61; pub. relations account exec. Aaron D. Cushman Assos., Inc., Chgo., 1961-64, Cooper & Golin. Inc., Chgo., 1964-67; v.p. Bernard E. Ury Assos., Inc., Chgo., 1967-69; v.p. pub. relations Data Transformation, Inc., Skokie, Ill., 1969-70; pres. Hanlen Orgn., Inc., Chgo., 1970—. Served with AUS 1956-58. Recipient Publicity Club Chgo. Honor award, 1962, 63. Home: 1637 Sherwood Rd Highland Park IL 60035 Office: 401 N Michigan Ave Chicago IL 60611

HANDY, DRUCILLA, pub. relations counsel; b. Lynchburg, Va., Aug. 21, 1924; d. John Bryant and Allen (Steele) Handy; student Swarthmore (Pa.) Coll., 1942-45; m. Robert M. Redinger, Oct. 30, 1954. Mem. publicity dept. Metro-Goldwyn-Mayer Studios, 1945-46; editor E.I. du Pont de Nemours & Co., 1947-48; with Rosemary Sheehan Publicity, 1948-50; account group supr. Mayer & O'Brien Pub. Relations, 1950-53; pub. relations dir. Helene Curtis Industries, 1953-54; account group supr. Gardner & Jones, Inc., 1954-56; pres. Drucilla Handy Co., Chgo., 1956—. Mem. Pub. Relations Soc. Am., Fashion Group, Art Inst., Lyric Opera of Chgo. Clubs: Arts, Metropolitan, Barclay, Publicity (Chgo.). Contbr. articles to pub. relations, home furnishings and bus. publs. Office: 813 Merchandise Mart Chicago IL 60654 also 654 Madison Ave New York City NY 60621

HANDY, RICHARD LINCOLN, civil engr., educator; b. Chariton, Ia., Feb. 12, 1929; s. Walter Newton and Florence Elizabeth (Shoemaker) H.; B.S. in Geology, Iowa State U., 1951, M.S., 1953, Ph.D., 1956; m. Charlsee Avonne Pitt, Apr. 18, 1964; 1 dau., Beth Susan. Asst. prof. civil engring. Ia. State U., Ames, 1956-59, asso. prof., 1959-63, prof., also dir. Soil Research Lab., 1963—; cons. in soil engring., soil and rock testing, landslide stabilization; v.p. research W.N. Handy Co., 1958-76. Recipient faculty citation Ia. State U., 1976. Fellow AAAS, Geol. Soc. Am., Ia. Acad. Sci.; mem. ASCE, ASTM, Soil Sci. Soc. Am., Clay Minerals Soc., Internat. Soc. Soil Mech. and Found Engrs. Author: (with M.G. Spangler) Soil Engineering, 1973, also numerous articles; patentee in soils field. Home: Rural Route 4 Ames IA 50010 Office: Dept Civil Engring Iowa State U Ames IA 50011

HANEBUTT, RALPH LOUIS, social worker, govt. ofcl.; b. Evansville, Ill., Apr. 3, 1927; s. Louis H. and Clara (Wolter) H.; B.A., So. Ill. U., 1950; M.S.W., Washington U., 1953; m. Erline Lauterjung, Sept. 2, 1950; children—Brian Jay, Gordon Ray. Caseworker Luth. Welfare Soc., Fargo, N.D., 1951-52; supr. Ill. Dept. Pub. Welfare, Bloomington, Ill., 1953-57; regional dir. Ill. Dept. Children and Family Services, Champaign, Ill., 1957-64, adminstrv. supr. regional offices, Springfield, 1964-69, chief downstate ops., 1969-73, asst. dep. dir. program services, 1973-74, area adminstr., Decatur, 1974—. Served with USCGR, 1945-46. Mem. Ill. Welfare Assn. (past dist. chmn.), Nat. Assn. Social Workers (past chpt. chmn.), Am. Pub. Welfare Assn., Nat. Conf. Social Welfare, Ill. Assn. Maternal and Child Health (dir. 1971-75), Acad. Certified Social Workers, Child Care Assn. Ill. Lutheran. Home: 259 S Austin Ave Decatur IL 62522 Office: 119 W William St Decatur IL 62523

HANGEN, WILLIAM J., elec. products mfg. co. exec.; b. St. Louis, Mar. 28, 1931; s. William M. and Mabel Josephine (Jinkerson) H.; student Washington U., St. Louis, 1948-51; B.S., U. Mo., 1953; postgrad. Wayne State U., 1957-62; m. Shirley Mae Diebal, June 13, 1953; children—William Eric, Lori Jean, Jill Marie, Kurt David. Chemist, pigments dept. E. I. duPont de Nemours & Co., Newark, 1955-56; materials engr. missile div. Chrysler Corp., Detroit, 1956-64; engring. and mgmt. positions, elec. products and advanced products divs. G. T. Schjeldahl Co. (name now Sheldahl, Inc.), Northfield, Minn., 1964—, v.p., gen. mgr. elec. products div., 1970-76, sr. v.p., gen. mgr. indsls. group, 1976—; corp. rep. Inst. Printed Circuits, 1970—, bd. dirs., 1974—, treas., 1976—, mem. program com., 1975—. Served with Ordnance Corps, AUS, 1953-55. Mem. Am. Chem. Soc., Walter's Lake Property Owners Assn. (pres. 1962-64), Alpha Chi Sigma. Republican. Lutheran (past trustee, past sponsor Luther League). Clubs: Optimist (v.p. Waterford, Mich. 1963-67); Northfield Golf, Northfield Hockey Assn. Contbr. articles to profl. jours. Home: Old Dutch Rd Rural Route 5 Northfield MN 55057 Office: Box 170 Northfield MN 55057

HANKINS, ROBERT ECKES, physician; b. Parshall, N.D., Jan. 22, 1927; s. Frederick H. and Emma (Eckes) H.; student Marquette U., 1944-46; B.S., U. N.D., 1948; M.D., Loyola U., Chgo., 1950; m. Florita Clare Thielen, Sept. 16, 1950; children—Kathryn, Fred, Jeanette, Carol, James, Nancy. Intern, Milw. County Hosp., 1950-51; practice medicine, Mott, N.D., 1953-75; dir. family practice residency program U. N.D. Family Practice Center, Minot, 1975—; chmn. bd. Blue Shield of N.D., 1973-74; asso. clin. prof. U. N.D., 1975—. Mem. Merit System Council of N.D., 1963-68; exec. com. S.W. Areawide Health Planning Council, 1969-75. Served with M.C., USNR, 1951-53. Mem. AMA, N.D. Med. Assn., Am., N.D. acads. family practice, Soc. Tchrs. Family Medicine, Am. Cancer Soc., Am. Diabetes Assn. Republican. Roman Catholic. Clubs: Lions, Minot Country, Elks. Home: 4 Country Club Acres Minot ND 58701 Office: 307 5th Ave SE Minot ND 58701

HANKINS, VAUGHAN LEE, collection agy. exec.; b. Libertyville, Ill., Apr. 29, 1943; s. Kenneth O. and Ethel M. (Ray) H.; B.S. in Mgmt. and Adminstrn., Ind. U., 1965; m. Donna Faye Gerlach, Aug. 22, 1965; children—Bryan Christopher, Jason Benjamin. Vice pres. Credit Bur. So. Ind., New Albany, 1965-74; owner Credit & Collection Enterprises, New Albany, 1974—. Served with AUS, 1960-61. Recipient State Leadership award, Asso. Credit Bur., Inc., 1973. Mem. Asso. Credit Bur. (dir. 1973—), Ind. Collectors Assn. (treas. 1969-77, v.p. 1977—, legis. commn. 1972—), Asso. Credit Bur. of Ind. (pres. 1971-73). Mem. Ch. of Christ (treas. 1977—). Kiwanian. Home: 26 Hilltop Rd New Albany IN 47150 Office: 1417 State St New Albany IN 47150

HANKLA, WALFRID BYRON, lawyer; b. Minot, N.D., Sept. 29, 1930; s. Walter Brown and Alice Marie (Samuelson) H.; B.S., U. N.D., 1956, LL.B., 1958, J.D., 1969; m. Winifred Ann Bergem, Aug. 18, 1957; children—Barbara Jean, Brian Walter, Peter Bergem. Admitted to N.D. bar, 1958; asst. counsel N.D. Legislative Research Com., 1958-60; partner McGee, Hankla, Backes & Wheeler, Minot, 1960—. Mem. Souris River Flood Control-Planning Com., 1972—; dir. Minot United Fund, 1964—, Ward County A.R.C., 1961-64; mem. Minot Mayor's Airport Study Commn., 1971—. Sec. 1st Luth. Found., 1965—. Served with USAF, 1951-55. Fellow Am. Coll. Probate Counsel; mem. Am., Ward County (past pres.) bar assns., State Bar Assn. N.D., Am. Legion, Phi Alpha Delta. Lutheran. Elk. Clubs: Rotary, Minot Country (Minot). Home: 1405 4th Ave SW Minot ND 58701 Office: First Nat Bank Bldg Minot ND 58701

HANLON, C. ROLLINS, physician; b. Balt., Feb. 8, 1915; s. Bernard and Harriet (Rollins) H.; A.B., Loyola Coll., Balt., 1934; M.D., Johns Hopkins, 1938; m. Margaret M. Hammond, May 28, 1949; children—Philip, Paul, Richard, Christine, Thomas, Mary, Martha, Sarah. Intern, John Hopkins Hosp., 1939-40, W.S. Halsted fellow in surgery, 1939-40, instr. surgery, 1946-48, asst. prof., 1948-50; asst. resident, resident in surgery Cin. Gen. Hosp., 1940-41, 43-44; exchange fellow surgery U. Calif., 1941-42; prof. surgery, chmn. dept. St. Louis U., 1950-69; prof. surgery Northwestern U. Med. Sch., 1969—; Chmn. surgery study sect. NIH, 1965-66; pres. Council Med. Speciality Socs., 1974-75; chmn. Coordinating Council on Med. Edn., 1976-77. Served to lt. (j.g.) M.C., USNR, 1944-46; CBI. Recipient Fleur-de-lis award St. Louis U., 1968; Statesmen in Medicine award Airlie Found., 1974. Diplomate Am. Bd. Surgery, (chmn. 1966-67); founder group Am. Bd. Thoracic Surgery, 1949, Fellow A.C.S. (gov., regent 1967-69, dir. 1969—), Royal Australian Coll. Surgeons (hon.), Royal Coll. Surgeons Ireland (hon.); mem. Am. Heart Assn. (surgery research study com. 1966-68), Internat. Cardiovascular Soc. (pres. N.Am. chpt., 1963-64), Soc. Vascular Surgery (pres. 1968), So., Central, Am. (sec. 1968-69) Western surg. assns., Am. Assn. Thoracic Surgery (treas. 1962-68), Soc. Clin. Surgery (pres. 1968-70), Soc. Univ. Surgeons (pres. 1968), Johns Hopkins Med. and Surg. Assn. (v.p. 1975-77); St. Louis Surg. Soc., Alpha Omega Alpha. Roman Catholic. Club: Serra (1st v.p.) (St. Louis). Bd. dirs. Surgery, Gynecology and Obstetrics, yec obsttr 1973-74. Contbr. articles to profl. jours. Address: 55 E Erie St Chicago IL 60611

HANN, CHARLES STEPHEN, paint mfg. co. exec.; b. Kansas City, Mo., July 11, 1917; s. Claire Stephen and Bertha M. (Smith) H.; B.S. in Chem. Engring., U. Mich., 1941; m. Virginia M. Sands, Oct. 5, 1940; children—Stephen S., Charles Sandford. Chemist, E.I. du Pont de Nemours & Co., Inc., 1941-46; tech. dir. Great Western Paint Mfg. Corp., Kansas City, Mo., 1946-54; pres. Douglas Paint Co., Kansas City, 1954—, Mem. Acacia. Lutheran. Club: Brookridge Country. Home: 9608 W 105th Terr Overland Park KS 66212 Office: 1300 W 8th St Kansas City MO 64101

HANNA, CHARLES ROY, city ofcl.; b. Boonville, Mo., Dec. 1, 1930; s. Charles W. and Opal A.M. (Klinksick) H.; B.A., U. Mo., 1957; postgrad. U. Minn., 1969-72; m. Elaine G. Michaud, June 4, 1955; children—Michelle Ann, Charles B. Editor, Sedalia (Mo.) Capital, 1948-50; staff writer Columbia (Mo.) Daily Tribune, 1955-57, Mpls. Tribune, 1957-63; pub. information dir. City of Mpls., 1963-70, exec. sec. Capital Long-Range Improvements Com., City of Mpls., 1970—. Served with USAF, 1951-55. Recipient Nat. Award for municipal pub. relations program Am. Municipal Assn., 1964. Episcopalian. Home: 4332 Dupont Ave S Minneapolis MN 55409 Office: 302 City Hall Minneapolis MN 55415

HANNA, GEORGE LEWIS, lawyer; b. Centralia, Ill., Feb. 3, 1927; s. Leroy Wayne and Georgia (Lewis) H.; B.S., Purdue U., 1949; J.D., Ind. U., 1953; m. Mary A. Gilmor, Nov. 3, 1951; children—Stephen Paul, Charles David, Susan Elizabeth. Admitted to Ind. bar, 1953; practice law, Lafayette, 1953—; dep. pros. atty. Tippencanoe County, 1954-58, pros. atty., 1959-68; mem. firm Hanna & Gerde, 1972—; spl. pros. atty., Lafayette, 1975—; lectr. bus. law Purdue U., 1965—.

Served with USNR, 1945-46, 51-52. Recipient Distinguished Service award Lafayette Jr. C. of C., 1956. Am., Ind., Tippencanoe County (pres. 1973-74) bar assns., Nat. Assn. Criminal Def. Lawyers, Assn. Trial Lawyers Am. Home: 2305 Bennett Rd Lafayette IN 47905 Office: Fifth Floor Bank and Trust Bldg PO Box 1098 Lafayette IN 47902

HANNA, MARTIN SHAD, lawyer; b. Bowling Green, Ohio, Aug. 4, 1940; s. Martin Lester and Julia Loyal (Moor) H.; student Bowling Green State U.; B.S., Purdue U., 1962; J.D., Am. U., 1965; m. Sharon Ann Higgins, Feb. 10, 1969; children—Jennifer Lynn, Jonathan Moor, Katharine Anne. Admitted to Ohio bar, 1965, D.C. bar, 1967, U.S. Supreme Ct. bar, 1969; partner law firm Hanna, Middleton & Roebke, 1965-70, Hanna & Hanna, Bowling Green, 1971—; spl. counsel for atty. gen. Ohio, 1969-71, Ohio Bd. Regents, 1974. Instr., Bowling Green State U., 1970, Ohio Div. Vocational Edn., 1970—, Ohio Peace Officer Tng. Council, 1968. Legal adviser N.W. Ohio Vol. Firemen's Assn., 1970—. State chmn. Ohio League Young Republican Clubs, 1972-73; nat. vice-chmn. Young Rep. Nat. Fedn., 1973-75, counselor to chmn., 1975-77; vice-chmn. Wood County (Ohio) Rep. Exec. Com., 1972—, precinct committeeman, 1968—; trustee Bowling Green State U., 1976—. Recipient George Washington honor medal award Freedoms Founds. at Valley Forge, 1969, award of merit Ohio Legal Center Inst., 1973, Robert A. Taft Distinguished Service award, 1974, James A. Rhodes Leadership award, 1975. Named One of Ten Outstanding Young Men, Ohio Jr. C. of C., 1968. Mem. Am., Ohio, N.W. Ohio, Wood County, D.C. bar assns., Phi Delta Phi. Presbyterian (elder, lay minister). Kiwanian. Contbr. articles to profl. publs. Home: 506 Knollwood Dr Bowling Green OH 43402 Office: 700 N Main St Bowling Green OH 43402

HANNA, MARY MARGARET MELSON (MRS. JOHN ALDEN HANNA) librarian; b. nr. Rolfe, Iowa, Oct. 17, 1913; d. Randall and Fern Sigourney (Beers) Melson; B.A., Morningside Coll., 1934; postgrad. U. Iowa, 1936, Iowa State U., 1937, U. No. Iowa, 1956; M.A., U. Wis., 1966; m. John Alden Hanna, Aug. 17, 1938 (dec. 1963); children—Carolyn (Mrs. Gary Clinton Snell), Frank Richard, Cynthia (dec. 1947). Tchr. English, Milford (Iowa) High Sch., 1934-37; prin. Ankeny (Iowa) High Sch., 1937-38; tchr. English, Blairsburg (Iowa) High Sch., 1957-59; tchr. Am. lit. Webster City (Iowa) High Sch., 1959-64; dir: Kendall Young Library, Webster City, 1966—. Asst. sec. Kendall Young Library and Trust Estate, 1966—. Mem. Iowa Library Assn., Bus. and Profl. Women, P.E.O. Republican. Methodist. Club: Women's (Webster City). Home: 1404 Grove St Webster City IA 50595 Office: 1201 Willson Ave Webster City IA 50595

HANNA, NESSIM, educator, mktg. cons.; b. Assiut, Egypt, Apr. 30, 1938; s. Yanni and Lulu (Shehata) H.; came to U.S., 1961, naturalized, 1973; B.S. in Commerce, Cairo U., 1958; M.S. in Mktg., U. Ill., 1964, Ph.D. in Mktg., 1969; m. Gretchen Lelia Wright, Aug. 18, 1968. Asst. prof., chmn. dept. mktg. W.Va. Inst. Tech., Montgomery, 1968-69; asso. prof. bus. adminstrn. Middle Tenn. State U., Murfreesboro, 1969-70; asso. prof. mktg. No. Ill. U., DeKalb, 1970—; mktg. cons. Arab Research and Adminstrn. Center, 1975—, Investments Consultants Internat., 1974-77. Named Outstanding Citizen, Citzenship Council of Met. Chgo., 1974. Mem. Southwestern Social Sci. Assn., Am. Mktg. Assn., Midwest Bus. Adminstrn. Assn., Assn. Egyptian-Am. Scholars, Phi Beta Lambda, Beta Gamma Sigma. Mem. Congregational Ch. Author: Marketing Opportunities in Egypt: A Business Guide, 1974. Contbr. articles to profl. publs. Home: 580 Normal Rd DeKalb IL 60115 Office: Dept Marketing Northern Illinois Univ DeKalb IL 60115

HANNA, RICHARD DENNIS, farmer; b. nr. Forest City, Iowa, June 23, 1934; s. Dewey Raymond Grant and Ruby Olive (Kittleson) H.; grad. high sch.; m. Deloris Georgann Dahl, Sept. 18, 1955; children—Cynthia Lou, Mark Dennis, Randall Dean. Farm hand, 1952-54; farmer, Joice, Iowa, 1956, owner, 1966—; chmn. bd. dirs. Joice Co-op Elevator, 1966—; chmn. bd. Joice Devel. Corp., 1970-71. Leader 4-H, 1964-74. Mem. agr. edn. adv. council N. Iowa Area Community Coll., 1971—; mem. People to People Internat. Goodwill Tour East and West Europe, 1972; mem. Iowa farm del. People's Republic of China, 1977. Served with USMC, 1954-56. Named Outstanding Young Farmer by Jr. C. of C., Northwood, Iowa, 1969. Mem. Farm Bureau (bd. dirs. 1964-65, pres. Worth County 1974-75), Future Farmers Am. (Iowa farm degree 1952, Am. farm degree 1953), Minn. Valley Breeders Assn. (bd. dirs., 1958-59), Worth County Pork Producers (founders com. 1970, bd. dirs. 1971), Worth County Beef Producers (sec.-treas., bd. dirs. 1970-71). Lutheran (council 1968-70, v.p. 1969, chmn. bd. edn. 1970). Club: Community (one of founders, sec.-treas. 1969) (Joice). Home: Rural Route Joice IA 50446

HANNAFORD, FRANK JOHN, systems analyst; b. Vallejo, Calif., Dec. 28, 1947; s. Charles Gerard and Helen Elizabeth (Wiser) H.; B.A. in History, U. Nebr. at Omaha, 1971; m. Linda Kay Wilds, Aug. 30, 1969; 1 dau., Heather Elizabeth. Research asso., programmer analyst Planning Research Corp., Omaha, 1974-76, asso., systems analyst, 1976—. Served with USAF, 1967-74. Mem. Air Force Assn. Republican. Roman Catholic. Home: 7318 S 33rd St Omaha NE 68147 Office: 1502 Kennedy Dr Bellevue NE 68005

HANNAFORD, JULE MURAT, III, lawyer; b. St. Paul, Nov. 4, 1912; s. Jule M. and Caroline (Schurmeier) H.; B.A., Yale U., 1935, LL.B., 1938; m. Barbara Battin, Feb. 2, 1952; children—Caroline (Mrs. Philip W. Pillsbury, Jr.), Barbara (Mrs. Robin R. Steiner), Elizabeth, Jule Murat IV. Admitted to Minn. bar, 1938; mem. firm Dorsey, Windhorst, Hannaford, Whitney & Halladay, Mpls., 1938—. Dir. Rosemount Inc., Downtown Auto Park, Inc.; mem. adv. com. to dir. NIH, 1976—. Mem. Fgn. Policy Assn. Minn., (pres. 1946-50), St. Paul-Mpls. Com. on Fgn. Relations (chmn. 1965-71), Minn. UN Assn. (pres. 1953-55. Episcopalian. Clubs: White Bear Yacht, Mpls., Inland Lakes Yachting Assn. (commodore 1952-53); University (St. Paul); Birnham Wood Country (Santa Barbara, Calif.); Yale (N.Y.C.). Contbr. articles to profl. jours. Home: 9 Manitou Island White Bear Lake MN 55110 Office: 2300 1st Nat Bank Bldg Minneapolis MN 55402

HANNAH, FRANKLIN (JESSE), religious adminstr.; b. White County, Ark., Apr. 30, 1945; s. Charley Edward and Zoria Rosia (Brooks) H.; Grad. Bus. Adminstrn., Ark. State U., 1972; m. Gloria Kay Howard, Mar. 21, 1969; children—Kenneth Edward, Kevin Dewayne, Kimberley Michelle. Tchr. 5th grade Cotton Plant (Ark.) Pub. Sch., 1968-69; mgr. Butler Shoes Co., Indian Mill, Jonesboro, Ark., 1969-71; salesman, supr. ABC Termite and Pest Control Co., Searcy, Ark., 1971-72; unit mgr. Union Life Ins. Co., Wynne, Ark., 1972-74; fin. sec. div. fgn. missions Gen. Council Assemblies God, Springfield, Mo., 1974—, outpost comdr. Central Assembly God Royal Rangers, 1976—. Mem. Adminstrv. Mgmt. Soc. (v.p. Springfield 1977). Licensed minister Gen. Council Assemblies God, 1969. Kiwanian (chmn. membership com. Wynne, Ark., 1973-74). Home: 303 E Whiteside St Springfield MO 65807 Office: 1445 Boonville Ave Springfield MO 65802

HANNER, RODNEY CARTER, engr.; b. Hillsboro, Ill., Sept. 2, 1949; s. Carter Barry and Ruth Elenor (Dahlberg) H.; B.S., Elmhurst (Ill.) Coll., 1974. m. Sharon K. Uchitjil, Feb. 21, 1971; children—Julie, Mathew. Authorized nuclear insp., Ill., Pa., Ohio, Ind., Iowa, Nebr., Colo. Planned maintenance coordinator U.S. Navy, 1969-73; nuclear insp. factory Mut. Engrng. Corp., Chgo., 1973-76; chief application engr. nuclear power mktg. div. Magnetrol Internat. Co., Downers Grove, Ill., 1976-77, mgr. nuclear div. Indsl. Engrng. & Equipment Co., St. Louis, 1977—. Mem. Am. Nuclear Soc., ASME, Am. Soc. Quality Control, Nat. Bd. Boilers and Pressure Vessels Insps. Home: 3836 LeMay Ferry Village St Louis MO 63125 Office: 425 Hanley Industrial Ct St Louis MO 63144

HANNEWYK, CORNELIUS MARVIN, paint co. exec.; b. Grand Rapids, Mich., Mar. 11, 1908; s. Cornelius Marvin and Mary Catherine (Koekkock) H.; B.S., U. Mich., 1928; m. Armella Catherine Buechler, Oct. 15, 1937; 1 son, Cornelius Marvin III. Salesman, Jones Dabney Co., Louisville, 1930-45; with Niles Paint Co., (Mich.), 1945—, pres. 1946—; pres. Kordell Industries, Mishawaka, Ind., 1967—, Knox Grey Iron Service (Ind.), 1974—. Home: Hedgecroft Farms New Carlisle IN 46552 Office: Box 626 Niles MI 49120

HANNON, DONALD WILLIAM, surgeon; b. St. Paul, Dec. 28, 1924; s. Patrick William and Mary Ellen (Diehl) H.; M.D., U. Minn., 1947; m. Marjoriey Welling, Aug. 4, 1951; children—Robert, Kathleen, William, James, Donald, Paul, David, Margaret. Intern, Ramsey Hosp., St. Paul, 1947, resident in surgery, 1950-52; resident in surgery U. Minn., 1954-56; gen. practice surgery, 1957—; prof. surgery U. Minn., St. Paul, 1974—. Served to lt. USN, 1952-54. Nat. Heart trainee, USPHS, 1955-56. Fellow A.C.S.; mem. St. Paul, Minn. surg. socs., Minn. Acad. Medicine, Am. Bd. Surgery, Am. Legion. Home: 784 WCO Rd I Saint Paul MN 55112 Office: 625 Lowry Med Arts Bldg Saint Paul MN 55102

HANNON, JOSEPH P., ednl. adminstr.; b. Fitchburg, Mass.; B.A., Fitchburg State Coll., 1959; M.A. in Sch. Adminstrn., Stanford U., 1968; Ed.D., U. No. Colo., 1970; married, 1 dau., Kelley. Elementary, secondary tchr., then asst. principal Nantucket (Mass.) Pub. Schs., 1959-64; asst. prin. Am. Community Schs., Athens, Greece, 1964-65; asst. supt. schs. facilities planning City of Chgo., 1970-75, supt. schs., 1975—; ednl. cons. Davis, Mac Connell and Ralston, Palo Alto, Calif., Westinghouse Learning Corp., Alexandria, Va. Roman Catholic. Office: 228 N LaSalle St Chicago IL 60601

HANRAHAN, ROBERT PAUL, assn. exec.; b. Chicago Heights, Ill., Feb. 25, 1934; s. William Joseph and Ida Frances (Koenig) H.; B.S., Bowling Green State U., 1956, M.Ed., 1959, Ph.D. (hon.), 1971, 75; m. Barbara Ann Golletz, Aug. 31, 1957; children—Kevin R., Brian P., Greg C. Tchr. social sci. Thornton Twp. High Sch., Harvey, Ill., 1957-60; dean of boys, guidance counselor Thornridge High Sch., Dolton, Ill., 1960-64; asst. supt. Thornton Twp. High Sch. and Jr. Coll., Harvey, Ill., 1964-67; supt. schs., Cook County, Chgo., 1967-71; midwest commr. edn., 1971; mem. 93d Congress from 3d Ill. dist.; dep. asst. sec. for edn. HEW, 1975-77; exec. dir. Nat. Assn. Coll. Admissions Counselors, 1977—. Pres. Young Republicans, Thornton Twp., Cook County, Ill., 1957-58, gov., 4th Congl. Dist., 1958-59; Republican auditor Bloom Twp., Cook County, Ill., 1965-67. Trustee Chgo. Adler Planetarium. Recipient Institutional award, Coll. and U. Personnel Assn., 1967; Outstanding Educator award Chgo. Little Flower Soc., 1970; Supt.'s award Ill. Am. Legion, 1970; Chmn.'s award Better Bus. Bur., Chgo.; Nat. Knights of Lithuania award, 1975. Woodrow Wilson Teaching fellow. Mem. Am. Assn. Sch. Adminstrs., Nat. Assn. Secondary Sch. Prins., Assn. for Sch., Coll. and Univ. Staffing, Am. Soc. Pub. Adminstrs., Assn. Sch. Personnel Adminstrs., N.E.A., Ill. Edn. Assn., Ill. C. of C., Chgo. Assn. Commerce and Industry, Chgo. Jr. C. of C., Ill. Assn. Sch. Adminstrs., Internat. Platform Assn., Bowling Green Alumni (trustee 1971), Phi Alpha Theta, Phi Delta Kappa. Club: Executives (Chgo.). Author several ednl. articles. Home: 1101 Valley Rd Homewood IL 60430 Office: 9933 Lawler Ave Suite 500 Skokie IL 60076

HANS, ROBERT LYLE, banker; b. Lincoln, Nebr., Apr. 21, 1936; s. Lyle C. and Betty L. (Friesen) H.; B.S. U. Nebr., 1958, M.A., 1965; m. Lily Marian Greve, July 7, 1962; children—Bryce Aaron, Monica Sue. With Pacific Nat. Bank, San Francisco, 1961; with Nat. Bank of Commerce Trust & Savings Assn., Lincoln, Nebr., 1962—, asst. cashier, 1964-66, asst. v.p., 1966-68, v.p., 1968-75, sr. v.p., 1975—, trust investment com., 1968—. Mem. City-County Health Adv. Bd., 1965-66; mem. Capital Improvements Fin. Adv. Com., 1969-71, City St. Adv. Com., 1974-75, City-County Planning Commn., 1977—; mem. City-County Planning Goals and Policies Com., 1971-77, chmn., 1973-76; mem. City-County Tech. Com. Transp., 1973-76; mem. planning bd. United Community Services, 1972-75; trustee YWCA, 1971-77, vice chmn., 1972-74; bd. dirs. Youth Employment Service, Inc., 1967-70; treas. Malone Community Center, 1968-69, trustee, 1967-70; mem. community adv. com. East High Sch., 1975—, chmn., 1977—. Served with USMC, 1959. Mem. Omaha-Lincoln Soc. Fin. Analysts, Nebr. Art Assn., Lincoln Symphony Assn., Lincoln C. of C., Theta Xi. Democrat. Unitarian (trustee 1967-72, pres. 1970-72). Clubs: Sertoma, (dir. 1968-70), University, Hillcrest Country. Home: One Camden Pl Lincoln NE 68506 Office: PO Box 82408 Lincoln NE 68508

HANSEN, ALLEN J., machinery co. exec.; b. Menasha, Wis., Apr. 18, 1930; s. Edward J. and Laura (Larsen) H.; M.E., U. Miami, 1957; m. Stephanie A. Mack, Aug. 21, 1954; children—Bradford, Lisa. Engr., Wis. Mich. Power Co., Appleton, Wis., 1957-58; salesman Equitable Reserve Assn., Neenah, Wis., 1958-59; sales engr. Sinclair Refining Co., Wis. area, 1959-61; sales engr. Overly, Inc., Neenah, 1961-68, sales mgr., 1968-74; gen. mgr. Appleton Mfg., Menasha, 1974—. Served with AUS, 1951-53. Mem. TAPPI, Pulp and Paper Machinery Mfrs.' Assn., Can. Pulp and Paper Assn., Paper Industry Mgmt. Assn., Graphic Arts Tech. Found., Sigma Alpha Epsilon. Clubs: Buttes Des Morts Golf (Appleton), Rotary. Home: 362 River Dr Appleton WI 54911 Office: PO Box 329 Menasha WI 54952

HANSEN, ARTHUR GENE, univ. pres.; b. Sturgeon Bay, Wis., Feb. 28, 1925; s. Henry A. and Ruth (Anderson) H.; B.S. in Elec. Engrng., Purdue U., 1946, M.S. in Math., 1948, D.Eng., 1970; Ph.D. in Math., Case Inst. Tech., 1958; D.Sc., Tri-State Coll., 1972; m., 5 children. Research scientist NASA, 1948-49, 50-58; tchr. U. Md., 1949-50; sect. head Cornell Aero. Lab., Buffalo, 1958-59; mem. faculty mech. engrng. U. Mich., 1959-66; dean Ga. Inst. Tech., 1966-69, pres., 1969-71; pres. Purdue U., 1971—; prof. mech. engrng. Tuskegee Inst., 1965; sr. research engr. Douglas Aircraft Co., 1964; curriculum cons. Gen. Motors Inst., 1965; cons. to industry, 1961-70. Dir. Internat. Paper Co., Internat. Harvester Co., Cutler/Hammer Inc., ROVAC Corp. Chmn. Atlanta Civic Design Commn., 1967-69; mem. Ga. Sci. and Tech. Commn., 1968-71, Ga. Ocean Sci. Center of Atlantic Commn., Atlanta, 1968-71; mem. adv. council Skidaway Oceanographic Inst. for Univ. System Ga., 1968-71; vice chmn. adv. council Electric Power Research Inst.; chmn. adv. council Gas Research Inst., Nat. Acad. Engring.; mem. gen. adv. com. ERDA, 1975-76; mem. acad. adv. bd. U.S. Naval Acad.; pres. Ind. Conf. Higher Edn., 1975; chmn. com. on minorities in engring. NRC, 1974-76; chmn. bd. visitors Air U., 1974-77; trustee Nat. Fund for Minority Engrng. Students. Served with USMCR, 1943-46. Registered profl. engr., Ga. Mem. Nat. Soc. Profl. Engrs., AAAS, Am. Soc. Engrng. Edn. Sigma Xi, Eta Kappa Nu, Pi Tau Sigma, Tau Beta Pi, Phi Kappa Phi, Omicron Delta Kappa, Phi Eta Sigma, Kappa Kappa Psi, Sigma Delta Chi (Leather medal). Author: Similarity Analyses of Boundary Layer Problems in Engineering, 1964; Fluid Mechanics, 1967. Office: Purdue U West Lafayette IN 47907

HANSEN, BRUCE WINSTON, educator; b. Chgo., Aug. 12, 1938; s. Carl Robert and Mary Ethel (McClun) H.; B.S., Monmouth Coll., 1952; M.S., U. Wis., 1955; postgrad. (USPHS fellow) U. Ill., 1955-57, Ohio State U., 1967-68. Various bus. positions, 1957-61; asso. prof. biology Union Coll., Barbourville, Ky., 1961-64; asst. prof. Emory and Henry Coll., 1964-66, Slippery Rock (Pa.) State Coll., 1966-67, Mars Hill (N.C.) Coll., 1968-70; cons. Biol. Sci. Curriculum Study Bellaire (Ohio) City Schs., 1970-71; bookkeeper John M. McClun Real Estate Co., 1971-73; instr. sci. Villa Sch., Toltec, Ariz., 1973-75; spl. tchr. sci. children with learning disabilities New Community Sch., Richmond, Va., 1975-76. Mem. Am. Inst. Biol. Scis. Club: Civitan. Home and office: 10301 S Christiana St Chicago IL 60655

HANSEN, CARL R., mgmt. cons.; b. Chgo., May 2, 1926; s. Carl M. and Anna C. (Roge) H.; M.B.A., U. Chgo., 1954; m. Christa Marie Rosa Franziska Hilda Loeser, Dec. 31, 1952; 1 son, Lothar. Dir. market research Kitchen of Sara Lee, Deerfield, Ill.; dir. market research Earle Ludgin & Co., Chgo., service v.p. Market Research Corp. Am., 1956-67; pres. Chgo. Assos., Inc., mgmt. cons., 1967—. Chmn. Ill. adv. council SBA, 1973-74; mem. exec. com. Ill. Gov.'s Adv. Council, 1969-72; resident officer U.S. High Commn. for Germany, 1949-52. Vice-chmn. Republican Central Com. Cook County, 1964-66, 68—; chmn. Young Rep. Orgn. Cook County, 1957-58, 12th Congl. Dist. Rep. Orgn., 1971-74, Suburban Rep. Orgn., 1974—; del. Rep. Nat. Conv., 1968; chmn. 3d Legislative Dist. Ill., 1964—; del. Rep. State Conv., 1962-76; bd. dirs. United Rep. Fund, Ill., 1958—; Elk Grove Twp. Rep. Committeeman, 1962—; pres. John Ericsson Rep. League of Ill., 1975-76; Rep. presdl. elector Ill., 1972; mem. Cook County Bd. Commrs., 1970, 74—. Served to 1st lt. AUS, 1944-48; now maj. Res. Mem. Am. Mktg. Assn., Am. Statis. Assn., Res. Officers Assn., Chgo. Assn. Commerce and Industry, U. Chgo. Alumni Assn., Chgo. Hist. Soc., Am. Scandinavian Found., Am. Legion. Clubs: Masons, Shriners, Lions, Danish, Norwegian, Swedish (Chgo.). Home: 110 S Edward St Mount Prospect IL 60056 Office: 75 E Wacker Dr Chicago IL 60601

HANSEN, CHARLOTTE LORRAINE HELGESON (MRS. GORDON H. (HANSEN) editor; b. Jamestown, N.D., June 1, 1922; d. Louis Sebern and Ida Ethelyne (Clough) Helgeson; student Jamestown Coll., 1940-41; B.S., U. Minn., 1944; m. Gordon H. Hansen, Oct. 31, 1945; 1 dau., Jo-Ida Charlotte. Hematologist, Hanford Engrng. Co., Richland, Wash., 1944-45; serologist Tex. Dept. Health, Wichita Falls, 1945-46; instr. microbiology Jamestown Coll., 1951-61; food editor Jamestown Sun, 1949—; sec.-treas., v.p. Hansen Bros., Inc.; dir. Jamestown Indsl. Devel. Corp., Jamestown Nat. Bank, First Bank System, Mpls. Mother adviser Rainbow Girls, 1964-73. Pres., United Fund, Jamestown council Girl Scouts U.S.A.; bd. dirs. Camp Rokiwan, James River Sr. Citizens; trustee first United Methodist Ch. Recipient Grand Cross of Color, Rainbow Girls, 1940, Thanks badge Girl Scouts U.S.A., 1964; named Merit Mother of N.D., 1969; named Outstanding Woman of N.D. in Civics and Community Services, 1974, Outstanding Citizen of Jamestown, 1978. Mem. AAUW, Nat. Fedn. Press Women, N.D. Press Women, Am. Legion Aux., P.E.O., Zonta, Theta Tau Sigma, Delta Kappa Gamma, Sigma Delta Chi. Mem. Order Eastern Star. Clubs: Wednesday, Civic Music. Author: Kitchen Magic, 1964; Favorites of My Family, 1972. Home: 309 11th Ave NE Jamestown ND 58401 Office: 121 2d St NW Jamestown ND 58401

HANSEN, GERALD RICHARD, banker; b. Toledo, Aug. 25, 1938; s. Louis Richard and Kathryn Julia (Rohr) H.; B.S., Wayne State U., 1960; m. Maureen McDonald Craigie, Apr. 15, 1961; children—Scott, Lynn. Sr. v.p. Nat. Lumberman's Bank, Muskegon, Mich., 1974—. Faculty bus. adminstrn. Am. Inst. Banking. Trustee, Greater Muskegon Indsl. Fund. Recipient Gold Key award Pub. Relations News, 1971. Mem. Am., Bank marketing assns., Am. Inst. Banking, Muskegon Area C. of C. Presbyn. (elder). Clubs: Muskegon Country, Century. Home: 227 Pennsylvania Ave North Muskegon MI 49445 Office: PO Box 87 1st and Webster Sts Muskegon MI 49443

HANSEN, GERALDINE MARIE, rehab. researcher; b. Tracy, Minn., Aug. 24, 1947; d. Edward Nicholas and Theresa Josephine (Silver) H.; student Coll. St. Teresa, Winona, Minn., 1965-66; B.S., Mankato (Minn.) State Coll., 1969, M.S., 1972; postgrad. U. No. Colo., 1975-77. Vocat. rehab. counselor Multi Resource Centers Inc., Mpls., 1971-74, supr. profl. services, 1974-75; community faculty Met. State U., St. Paul, 1972-75; research asso. Met. State Coll., Denver, 1977—; research specialist U. Wis., Menomonie, 1977-78; cons. in field. Certified rehab. counselor, Minn. Mem. Minn. (pres. 1974—), Am. rehab. counseling assns., Nat., Minn. rehab. assns., Am., Minn. personnel and guidance assns. Democrat. Roman Catholic. Office: Research and Tng Center U Wis-Stout Menomonie WI 54751

HANSEN, HAROLD CLEMENT, photographer; b. Benton Harbor, Mich., Apr. 1, 1918; s. Joseph Bartholmew and Frances Agnes (Denner) H.; grad. high sch., 1936; m. Dorothy Lindemann, Nov. 29, 1941; children—Judith Ann (Mrs. Donald Marshall), Stephen, Richard, Patricia James. Machinist Nineteen Hundred Corp. (now Whirlpool Corp.), St. Joseph, Mich., 1937-47; field rep. Hoover Vacuum Cleaner Co., North Canton, Ohio, 1947-55; asst. prodn. mgr. Kaywood Venetian Blind Co., Benton Harbor, 1955-57; chief photographer Heath Co., 1957—. Founder The West Central Neighborhood Orgn., Benton Harbor, 1967, chmn. polit. action com., 1967-68, pres., 1969-75; parliamentarian officer Benton Harbor Mich. Citizens advisory bd., 1974—; co-chmn. Benton Harbor Clean-Up Drives, 1968-70. Catholic (asst. choir dir., 1973-75, chmn., christian services com. 1974—). Address: 129 Apple St Benton Harbor MI 49022

HANSEN, H(ARVEY) KENNETH, diversified mfg. co. exec.; b. St. Paul, Dec. 27, 1924; s. Harvey Arthur and Lillian (Lindquist) H.; B.A. in Journalism, U. Minn., 1950; diploma Northwestern Electronics Inst., Mpls., 1942; m. Marlys Maxine Huseth, Aug. 30, 1947; children—Stephen Jay, Cheryl Jean, Kay Louise. Reporter, news editor Rose Tribune, St. Paul, 1949-51; news editor, advt. mgr. Sauk Centre (Minn.) Herald, 1951-52; copy editor Duluth (Minn.) News-Tribune, 1952-53; advt. mgr., feature writer, news editor Hutchinson (Minn.) Leader, 1953-59; sr. tech. writer No. Ordnance div. FMC Corp., Mpls., 1959—. Served with USMCR, 1942-46. Decorated Bronze Star medal. Mem. Soc. Tech. Communication (nat. chmn.), Nat. Def. Preparedness Assn., U.S. Metric Assn., Indsl. Graphics Internat., Soc. Wireless Pioneers (life), Assn. Tchrs. Tech. Writing, Twin Cities Media Project, Inc., U. Minn. Journalism Alumni Assn., Am. Legion. Unitarian. Mng. editor Tech. Talk (Soc. Tech. Communication newsletter), 1967-72, recipient 2 Excellence awards; abstract writer, referee Tech. Communication Jour., 1976-77; contbr. tech. articles to govt. publs. Home: 9500 N Oliver Ave Minneapolis MN 55444

HANSEN, KENNETH MARTIN, dentist; b. Beloit, Kans., Dec. 14, 1922; s. Martin and Ruth Marea (Johnson) H.; Asso. Sci., El Dorado (Kans.) Jr. Coll., 1958; D.D.S., U. Kansas City, 1963; m. Jean Claire Bourbon, Feb. 1, 1942; children—Ruth Ann (Mrs. David A. Hanson),

Janet Jean. Parts and service mgr. Fuller Motor Co., Beloit, Kans., 1951-58, McClure Motor Co., El Dorado, Kans., 1963—; pvt. practice dentistry, Parkville, Mo., 1964—. Cons. dentist N. Kansas City Hosp., 1969—. Bd. dirs. Emergency Relief Assn. Clay County Health Dept., 1969—. Served with AUS, 1943-44. Mem. Greater Kansas City Dental Soc., Clay Platte County Dental Soc. (pres. 1969-71), Am. Legion, Beloit C. of C., Am. Legion. Methodist. Optimist, Elk. Club: Dental Study. Home: 4023 Main St Kansas City MO 64116 Office: 2906 W Vivion Rd Parkville MO 64150

HANSEN, NILES M., JR., dentist; b. Holland, Mich., Sept. 21, 1922; s. Niles M. and Emily J. (Constantine) H.; student Hope Coll., 1940-42; B.S., Creighton U., 1953, D.D.S., 1957; M.Sc. in Dentistry, Ind. U., 1960; m. Carmen Dolores Rivera Maldonado, June 24, 1944; children—Niles M., Joseph R., Carmen M., Jerilyn Marie. Salesman Donnelly-Kelley Glass Co., Holland, Mich., 1946-50; practice dentistry, specializing in periodontia, Indpls., 1958—; asso. prof. dentistry Ind. U. Sch. Dentistry, 1958—. Cons. Wood High Sch. dental assistance program; mem. Cons. Nutrition Council of Community Service Council Met. Indpls., Inc., 1966—. Served with AUS, 1942-46. Fellow Am. Coll. Dentists; Am., Ind. dental assns., Indpls. Dist. dental soc., Am. Acad. Periodontists, Midwest Soc. Periodontists, Ind. State Assn. Periodontists (pres. 1971), Omicron Kappa Upsilon. K.C. Researcher on the histologic effects of high frequency sound waves on the oral tissues of rats. Home: 5101 Knoll Crest Ct Indianapolis IN 46208 Office: 1265 W 86th St Indianapolis IN 46260

HANSEN, NORMAN ARDEN, SR., utility co. exec.; b. Duluth, Minn., Sept. 21, 1917; s. John Christian and Anna Bergitte (Fossen) H.; grad. Duluth Bus. U., 1947; student U. Minn. Extension, 1938, Internat. Accountants Soc., 1948-49, IBM Sch., 1960, m. Mary Jane Dunne, Aug. 15, 1942; children—Norman Arden, Judith (Mrs. Gerald A. Broman), Darrell T., Ronald C. With Minn. Power & Light Co., Duluth, 1937—, supr. customer accounting, 1961-63, customer accounting mgr., 1963-65, asst. treas., 1965-67, treas., 1967—. Mem. local bd. SSS, 1972—; mem. phys. improvement panel Rehab. Bd. Rev., Model Cities Adminstrn., 1971—. Served with AUS, 1942-45. Decorated Purple Heart. Mem. Nat. Machine Accountants Soc., Adminstr. Mgmt. Soc. (pres. 1970-71), V.F.W., Duluth C. of C. Lutheran. Mason (Shriner). Clubs: Central Hillside Community, Duluth Athletic. Home: 14 E 7th St Duluth MN 55805 Office: 30 W Superior St Duluth MN 55802

HANSEN, ROBERT WAYNE, ret. state justice; b. Milw., Apr. 29, 1911; s. Edwin A. and Martha (Siggelkow) H.; J.D., Marquette U., 1933; m. Dorothea Belle Angus, Feb. 14, 1941; children—Karen (Mrs. Robert Schaf), John, Susan, James. Admitted to Wis. bar, 1933; practiced in Milw., 1933-54; judge Milw. Dist. Ct., 1954-60; circuit judge, Milw., 1960-68; chief judge Milw. County, 1967-68; justice Wis. Supreme Ct., 1968-78; instr. family law Nat. Coll. State Trial Judges, 1964-71. Eagle (pres. 1943-44, 53-54). Home: Route 1 Box 325 Nashotah WI 53058

HANSEN, THOMAS LOUIS, ednl. adminstr.; b. Des Plaines, Ill., June 29, 1940; s. Louis W. and Marion R. (Ryan) H.; B.F.A., Notre Dame U., 1962; M.Ed., Loyola U. (Chgo.), 1965; m. Maureen E. Curtin, June 5, 1965; children—Thomas, Kathryn, Matthew. Tchr., coach, counselor St. Viator High Sch., Arlington Heights, Ill., 1962-65, vocational counselor Forest View High Sch., 1965-71; dir. pupil services Elk Grove (Ill.) High Sch., 1971—; counselor Mental Health Clinic, Wheeling, Ill., 1965-73. Bd. dirs. Elk Grove-Schumberg Mental Health Clinic. NDEA grantee U. Rochester (N.Y.), 1967. Mem. Am. Personnel and Guidance Assn., Counsel Exceptional Children, Ill. Personnel and Guidance Assn., Ill. Council Exceptional Children, Suburban Dirs. Pupil Services (pres. 1977-78). Roman Catholic. Club: Elk Grove Village Rotary (sec. 1977-78). Home: 1224 Borders Dr Palatine IL 60067 Office: 500 Elk Grove Blvd Elk Grove IL 60007

HANSEN, VERNE JOHN, accountant, ins. broker; b. Gettysburg, S.D., Apr. 19, 1932; s. Leonard Dale and Mary Ann (McLean) H.; degree Aberdeen Sch. Commerce, 1953; m. Mickie L. Bierman, Sept. 9, 1956; children—Wade, Ward, Jess. Bookkeeper, Nicodemus Auto Electric, Pierre, S.D., 1953-54; office mgr. J.H. Brashear, D.V.M., Faulkton, S.D., 1954-60; pub. accountant, ins. broker, Faulkton, 1960—; sec.-treas. Faulkton Developers, Inc.; financial officer Faulkton I.O.O.F. Office Bldg.; vice-pres. Faulk County Health Services, Inc.; treas. City of Faulkton, 1961-66, now mayor. Bd. dirs. Pickler Hist. Site Corp., Faulk County Water Users, Faulk County Law Enforcement Com., Faulk County Sr. Citizens Adv. Bd.; sec.-treas. Parkview Devel. Corp. Mem. Profl. Ins. Agts. of S.D. (dir.), Faulk County Hist. Soc. (charter pres.), S.D. Assn. Mut. Ins. Agts. (pres. 1974-75). Clubs: Faulkton Community, Lions (charter sec.-treas. Faulkton area). Address: Box 514 Faulkton SD 57438

HANSEN, WALDEMAR CONRAD, chemist; b. Sturgis, S.D., Feb. 9, 1896; s. Hans and Anine (Iversen) H.; B.S. in Chemistry, Mont. State Coll., 1917; postgrad. U. Iowa, 1919-20; Ph.D., Columbia U., 1922; m. Muriel Anna Bruggman, May 21, 1924; children—Donald Waldemar, Edward Andrew. Plant chemist Three Forks Portland Cement Co., Trident, Mont., 1917; food and drug insp. Mont. Bd. Health, Helena, 1919; teaching asst. U. Iowa, 1919-20, Columbia U., 1920-22; instr. Mont. State Coll., 1922-23; research chemist Midwest Refining Co. (Wyo.), 1923-24; Portland Cement Assn. fellow Bur. Standards, Washington, 1924-29; research chemist Am. Cyanamid Co. (name changed to Am. Cyanamid & Chem. Corp. 1934), Linden, N.J., 1929-34, plant mgr., 1934-38; research chemist Portland Cement Assn., Chgo., 1938-45; dir. research Universal Atlas Cement dvi. U.S. Steel Corp., Gary, Ind., 1945-61; cons. chemistry, Valparaiso, Ind., 1961—; chmn. advisory com. to bldg. div. Nat. Bur. Standards, 1959-62. Served with U.S. Army, 1917-19. Fellow ASTM (hon. mem., award of Merit 1963), AAAS, Am. Concrete Inst.; mem. Hwy. Research Bd.; emeritus mem. Am. Chem. Soc., Am. Ceramic Soc., Sigma Xi, Gamma Alpha, Phi Lambda Epsilon, Sigma Alpha Epsilon. Methodist. Clubs: Columbia U of Chgo.; Mathesis of Valparaiso (pres. 1954-55). Author: (with J.S. Offutt) Gypsum and Anhydrite in Portland Cement, 1969; contbr. numerous articles to profl. jours.; patentee in gypsum and portland cement. Home and Office: 155 Maple St Valparaiso IN 46383

HANSEN, WILLIAM FREEMAN, classical scholar, educator; b. Fresno, Calif., June 22, 1941; s. William Freeman and Helen Marian (Jensen) H.; student Reed Coll., 1959, Bakersfield (Calif.) Coll., 1960-61; A.B., U. Calif., Berkeley, 1965, Ph.D., 1970; m. Marcia Jean Cebulski, Aug. 14, 1972; 1 dau., Inge Margrethe. Asst. prof. classical studies Ind. U., Bloomington, 1970-77, fellow Folklore Inst., 1970—, asso. prof., 1977—. Nat. Endowment Humanities fellow, 1972-73; Am. Council Learned Socs. fellow, 1977-78. Author scholarly publ. in field. Home: 804 S Lincoln St Bloomington IN 47401 Office: Univ Indiana Classical Studies BH547 Bloomington IN 47401

HANSEN, WILLIAM JAMES, ins. co. exec.; b. Rhinelander, Wis., Jan. 5, 1928; s. Sophus William and Martha LaBarr (Dunning) H.; B.S. in Fire Protection Engring., Ill. Inst. Tech., 1952; C.P.C.U., Am. Inst. for Property and Liability Ins., 1973; m. Dorothy Mildred Anderson, July 31, 1954; 1 son, David Arthur. Engr., Factory Ins. Assn., Mnpls., 1952-54; mgr. engring. dept. Charles W. Sexton Co., Mnpls., 1954-62; dist. mgr. Protection Mut. Ins. Co., Mnpls., 1962-66, regional v.p., Milw., 1966-69, v.p. mktg., Park Ridge, Ill., 1969—. Served with U.S. Army, 1946-48. Mem. Soc. Fire Protection Engrs., Newcomen Soc. N.Am., Soc. C.P.C.U. Clubs: Metropolitan, Chgo. Athletic, Toastmasters Internat. Home: 1031 Woodland Ave Barrington IL 60010 Office: 300 S Northwest Hwy Park Ridge IL 60068

HANSER, CAROLYN JEAN, ednl. adminstr.; b. Cleve., Dec. 2, 1935; d. Oscar Otto and Gertrude (Gross) Hanser; B.S. in Bus. Edn., Bowling Green State U., 1957; M.Ed., Kent State U., 1964, postgrad., 1965—. Personnel work Educators Assn., Inc., Cleve., summer 1953; office work Producers Milk Co., summers 1953-57; dormitory counselor Kent (Ohio) State U., 1954-55; tchr. Parma (O.) Sr. High, 1957-62, adult edn. classes 1957-61; counselor Valley Forge High Sch., Parma Heights, 1962-66, adminstrv. asst. for guidance, 1966—; tchr. playground instr., Parma, 1957-58, also Saturday morning recreation leader. Vol., Red Cross, Cleve., 1961; rec. sec., v.p. Parma Schaaf High Sch. Alumni Council, 1958-61; mem. Parma Youth Commn. on Juvenile Delinquency, 1968-70, Parma Sch. Community Relations Com., 1973-74, Parma City Schs. Curriculum Council, 1975-76; mem. alumni adv. com. in counseling Kent State U., 1971-72. Mem. Nat., Ohio, Parma (pub. relations com., newspaper staff) edn. assns., Am. Sch. Counselors Assn., Nat. Vocat. Guidance Assn., Am., Ohio (chmn. new mems. brs. com.), Northeastern Ohio personnel and guidance assns., Lake Erie League Assn. Counselors (chmn. progress report evaluation com. Parma city schs. 1969—), Parma Assn. Secondary Sch. Adminstrs. (sec., treas. 1971-74), Nat., Ohio assns. secondary sch. prins., Cleve. Area Prins. Discussion Group, Assn. Parma Adminstrs. (sec. 1975-76), Gamma Delta (program chmn., v.p. 1953-57), Phi Gamma Nu (v.p. 1954-57), Pi Omega Pi (sec., v.p. 1954-57), Kappa Delta Pi, Quill Type (program chmn. 1955-57), Cardinal Key, Alpha Chi Omega. Lutheran (ch. organist 1955—, choir 1967—, stewardship com. 1967-68, bd. Christian Edn., 1972-74, nominating com. 1977—). Club: Altrusa (Cleve.). Home: 6488 State Rd B-10 Parma OH 44134 Office: 9999 Independence Blvd Parma Heights OH 44130

HANSER, THEODORE HENRY, ret. surgeon; b. St. Louis, July 29, 1896; s. Rudolph and Marie Margaret (Schenkel) H.; grad. St. Paul's Coll., Mo., 1916; B.S., Washington U., St. Louis, 1920, M.D., 1922; LL.D., Concordia Theol. Sem., 1977; m. Edna A. Ulrich, Feb. 3, 1932; children—Naomi Hanser McCann, Mary Beth Hanser Neiger, David T. House officer Mass. Gen. Hosp., Boston, 1922-25; practice medicine specializing in surgery, St. Louis, 1925-65; mem. staff Lutheran Med. Center, St. Louis; med. dir. Anheuser-Busch Inc., St. Louis, 1925-65, med. cons., 1965-77; pres. emeritus Grandel Med. Group, St. Louis, 1925—; physician and surgeon Washington U. Sch. Medicine, St. Louis, 1925-27. Bd. dirs. Blue Shield, 1952-61; with SSS, 1939-43. Served to 2d lt. U.S. Army, 1918. Recipient Certificate of Appreciation, Pres. Franklin D. Roosevelt, 1943, Apostle Paul award St. Paul's Coll., 1966. Diplomate Nat. Bd. Med. Examiners. Fellow A.C.S. (med. record honor certificate 1933); mem. St. Louis Surg. Soc., St. Louis City Med. Soc., AMA. Republican. Evang. Lutheran. Clubs: Mo. Athletic, Racquet, Knights of the Cauliflower Ear. Home: 18 Old Westbury Ln Saint Louis MO 63119 Office: 3555 Sunset Office Dr Saint Louis MO 63127

HANSON, ARLEE C., county ofcl.; b. Denton, Mont., Feb. 20, 1911; s. Fred Oscar and Minnie (Johnson) H.; B.S., N.D. State U., 1934; m. Helen M. Brunner, Oct. 28, 1932; children—Kathleen (Mrs. James Potts), Barbara (Mrs. Gerald Person), Constance (Mrs. Ronald Larson), Mary Jane (Mrs. Ralph Kennedy), Thomas, William, Leon. Agronomist, area conservationist U.S. Dept. Agr., Whitehall, Ill., 1934-46; farmer, Garrison and Litchville, N.D., 1946—; chmn. West McLean County Soil Conservation Dist., 1949-51; chmn. La Moure County (N.D.) Water Mgmt. Bd., 1964-76; commr. La Moure County, 1965-77; chmn. La Moure County Planning Bd. Pres. Dickey-LaMoure County Farmers Union Youth Found., 1970-73; chmn. LaMoure County Summer Mus. Theatre, 1972—; chmn. Tri-County Quality of Life Orgn., 1974-76. Mem. N.D. Crop Improvement Assn. (dir.), S.E., N.D. County Commrs. Assn. (chmn. 1968-69), La Moure County Farmers Union (dir. 1968-73), Gradstone Farmers Union Local (pres. 1966-73). Chmn. 27th Legislative Dist. Democratic Resolutions Com., 1968. Roman Catholic. Home: Marion ND 58466 Office: Court House La Moure ND 58458

HANSON, CHARLES EASTON, JR., mus. ofcl.; b. Holdrege, Nebr., Apr. 4, 1917; s. Charles Easton and Irene Hazel (Adkins) H.; student Kearney State Coll., 1934-35, U. Colo., 1949-50; m. Eva Marie Phillips, Apr. 18, 1936; children—Charles Easton, William Raymond, James Austin. Adminstrv. engr. 7th Service Command, Sioux City, Iowa, 1942-43, Bur. Reclamation, McCook, Nebr., 1946-51, USAF, Wiesbaden, Germany, 1952, Dept. Agr., Casper, Wyo. and Washington, 1954-69; dir. Mus. Fur Trade, Chadron, Nebr., 1955-58, 69-72, 74—, cons. dir., 1960-68, editor mus. quar., 1965—. Spl. lectr. various colls., hist. confs.; cons. antique weapons various mus. Hon. chmn. Alexander Culbertson Meml. Com., Orleans, Nebr., 1951. Bd. dirs. Mus. Assn. Am. Frontier, Chadron. Recipient Post Comdr. citation Liberal Army Airfield for exceptional civilian service, 1943. Fellow Co. Mil. Historians; mem. Nebr. Gun and Cartridge Collectors Assn. (pres. 1958), Potomac Westerners (sheriff 1965), Md. Arms Collectors, Am. Soc. Arms Collectors, Phi Tau Gamma. Republican. Methodist. Author: The Northwest Gun, 1955; The Plains Rifle, 1960. Contbr. articles to profl. jours. Home: Route 2 PO Box 18 Chadron NE 69337

HANSON, FRED T., lawyer; b. Wakefield, Nebr., Feb. 25, 1902; s. Peter H. and Hannah Ulrika (Anderson) H.; LL.B., U. Nebr., 1925; m. Helen Elizabeth Haddock, Nov. 12, 1928; 1 son John Fredrik. Admitted to Nebr. bar, 1925, since in pvt. practice; probate judge, 1931-42, pros. atty., 1927-30, 51-54; spl. asst. to U.S. atty. gen., 1954-62. Life mem. Nat. Conf. Commrs. Uniform State Laws from Nebr., com. on uniform probate code. Served as capt. AUS, 1942-46. Mem. Am. Judicature Soc., Am. Coll. Probate Counsel (regent), Am., Nebr., local bar assns., Am. Legion. Office: 316 Norris Ave Mc Cook NE 69001

HANSON, GLEVA MARIE, educator; b. Tulare, S.D., Jan. 8, 1913; d. Herman Henry and Emma Dorothea (Roeber) Binger; B.A., Morningside Coll., 1934; M.A., Northwestern U., 1963; postgrad. Iowa State U., 1951-56, State U. N.Y., 1970, (Tessie Agan scholar), Trinity U., 1971, U. Graz, Austria, 1972, Denver U., 1974-75. Head speech dept., instr. English Oto (Ia.) High Sch., 1934-37, Onawa (Ia.) High Sch., 1937-41; instr. English, Gustavus Adolphus Coll., St. Peter, Minn., 1946-48; asso. prof. speech Southwestern Coll., Winfield, Kans., 1964—, trustee coll. Assn. Colls. and Univs. for Internat.-Intercultural Study faculty travel-study grantee, 1972, 76. Mem. Speech Communication Assn., Am. Theatre Assn., Kans. Speech Assn., Wichita Amateur Camera Club (pres. 1975-76), P.E.O. (local pres. 1958), Delta Kappa Gamma. Methodist (mem. ofcl. bd. 1968). Home: 905 E 9th St Winfield KS 67156

HANSON, HOWARD HENRY, assn. exec.; b. White River, S.D., May 4, 1924; s. Otto Theodore and Margaret (Bramer) H.; diploma S.D. Sch. for Blind, 1942; B.S., S.D. State Coll., 1947, M.S., 1948; postgrad. U. Mich., 1949; m. Phyllis Marie Geis, Apr. 23, 1954; 1 son, Phillip Gerald. Owner, operator Coffee Shop, Brookings, S.D., 1948-49; counsellor, home tchr. S.D. Service to Blind, Pierre, 1949-52, dir. agy., 1952-77; exec. dir. Ark. Enterprises for Blind, Little Rock, 1978—. Adviser, N.W. Rehab. Center for Blind, Mpls.; teaching cons. Inst. for Home Tchrs., Little Rock, Ark. Cons., founder S.D. Lions Sight and Service Found.; U.S. del. to World Council on Welfare Blind, New Delhi, India; mem. Nat. Task Force Geriatric Blindness, 1969—; chmn. first session on blindness, World Congress Rehab. Internat., Sidney, Australia, 1972; v.p. Nat. Accreditation Council Agys. Serving the Blind and Visually Handicapped, 1973—, also mem. nat. accreditation commn. Trustee Am. Found. for Blind (mem. service com. on geriatric blindness); chmn. subcom. capital fund drive YMCA, 1976-77. Named Outstanding Handicapped Citizen of S.D., 1963; recipient Distinguished Alumnus award S.D. State U., 1972. Mem. Am. Assn. Workers for Blind (pres. 1968-69), Nat. Council Execs. Agys. for Blind (pres. 1972-73), S.D. Assn. for Blind (Gus Zachte award 1974; treas.), S.D. Social Welfare Conf. (pres. 1964), S.D. Rehab. Assn. (pres. 1967), Council State Adminstrs. Vocational Rehab. (pres. 1967), Dirs. Vocational Rehab. (pres. region 6 1967), Nat. Planning Commn. Rehab. Blind, Nat. Rehab. Assn. (pres. 1970), Phi Kappa Delta. Lutheran. Mason, Elk, Lion (internat. counsellor, life mem. Pierre, dist. gov. 1957-58, state chmn. capital fund dr. to expand workshop for blind 1977). Home: 417 W 2d Pierre SD 57501 Office: State Capitol Pierre SD 57501

HANSON, J. ROBERT, symphony condr.; b. Osakis, Minn., Oct. 24, 1929; s. John R. and Alpha E. (Halstenson) H.; m. Lois Shirleen Beckstrom, Aug. 28, 1951; children—John, George, James, Thomas. B.A., Concordia Coll., 1951; M.A., U. Iowa, 1952, M.F.A., 1953, Ph.D., 1958. Instr. trumpet U. Iowa, 1956-59; music tchr. U. Wis., Milw.; trumpet player Milw. Symphony, 1959-66; music tchr. Concordia Coll., Moorhead, Minn., 1966—; condr. Fargo-Moorhead Symphony, 1974—. Mem. Music Educators Nat. Conf., Minn. Music Educators Assn., Phi Beta Mu, Phi Mu Alpha Sinfonia. Composer: Fanfare Prelude-O How Shall I Recieve Thee, 1974; Reflections for Orchestra, 1976. Home: Route 3 Box 29 Moorhead MN 56560

HANSON, JOHN FREDRIK, lawyer; b. McCook, Nebr., Apr. 21, 1940; s. Fredrik Theodor and Helen Elizabeth (Haddock) H.; student Am. U., 1959; B.A. magna cum laude, Doane Coll., 1961; J.D. with distinction, U. Mich., 1964; m. Mary Lou Harris, June 27, 1964; children—Thomas Robert, Andrew Lynn. Admitted to Neb. bar, 1964; practiced in Indianola, Nebr., 1964-67; partner Hanson & Hanson, attys., McCook, 1967—. Mem. Nat. Conf. Commrs. on Uniform State Laws, 1967-71. County atty., Hayes County, Nebr., 1969-71, 72—; city atty., Indianola, 1964—; village atty., Hayes Center, 1972—. Mem. Am., Nebr., Western Nebr. (pres. 1972-73), 14th Jud. Dist. (pres. 1974-75) bar assns., Am., Nebr. land title assns., Am. Legion (adj. 1972—, dist. comdr. 1969-71), Phi Eta Sigma, Pi Kappa Delta, Phi Alpha Theta. Republican. Lutheran. Rotarian (sec. 1972—). Club: Indianola Commercial (sec. 1964-73). Home: Indianola NE 69034 Office: 316 Norris Ave McCook NE 69001

HANSON, JUNE P. JENSEN, banker; b. Mpls.; d. Arthur P. and Ebba (Fredericks) Jensen; grad. Mpls. Bus. Coll., 1940; m. Burton H. Hanson, Aug. 22, 1942 (div. Dec. 1959); children—Gary Paul, Richard A., Joyce Arlene (Mrs. Terry Crow), Robert Burton, James Arthur. Secretarial work Physicians & Hosp. Supply Co., Mpls., 1940-43, G. E. Mack Co., Mpls., 1956-59; asst. cashier 2d Northwestern Nat. Bank, Mpls., 1965-73, asst. v.p., 1973—. Mem. Am. Inst. Banking Nat. Secs. Assn. (pres. 1969-70), Nat. Assn. Bank Women (sec. 1968-69, chmn. Minn. group 1972-73), regional v.p. 1976—, nat. dir. 1976—), Mpls. C. of C. Home: 5740 14th Ave S Minneapolis MN 55417 Office: 3430 University Ave SE Minneapolis MN 55414

HANSON, KENNETH HAMILTON, lawyer; b. Chgo., Sept. 10, 1919; s. Clinton H. and Della (Bonson) H.; student North Park Coll., 1939-40; B.S., Northwestern U., 1943, J.D., 1949; m. Elaine F. Bleck, May 19, 1951; children—Christine E., Karen D., Kenneth Hamilton. Admitted to Ill. bar, 1949; practiced law, Chgo., 1949-53; atty. bus. devel. dept. First Nat. Bank Chgo., 1953-61; trial atty. Antitrust div. U.S. Dept. Justice, Chgo., 1961—. Served to lt. (j.g.) USNR, 1943-46. Mem. Am., Fed., Chgo. bar assns., Beta Theta Pi, Phi Delta Phi. Republican. Presbyn. Home: 955 Melody Rd Lake Forest IL 60045 Office: 219 S Dearborn St Chicago IL 60604

HANSON, KENNETH HAROLD, ins. co. exec.; b. Hayward, Wis., Oct. 18, 1922; s. Bernard John and Ruth Bergetta (Jorgenson) H.; J.D., U. Wis., 1948; m. Carol Barbara Davis, July 3, 1947; children—Andrea, Eric, Jeffrey. Adjuster Ohio Casualty Ins. Co., Hamilton, Ohio, 1948-49, 51-54, supr., 1954-57, mgr., 1957-63, v.p., 1963-72; exec. v.p., dir. Bellefonte Ins. Co., Middletown, Ohio, 1973-77; exec. v.p. Proprietors Ins. Co., Delaware, Ohio, 1977—. Admitted to Wis. bar, 1949; atty. Langer & Cross, Baraboo, Wis., 1949-51. Served with AUS, 1943-45. Mem. C.P.C.U., Fed. Ins. Counsel, Internat. Assn. Ins. Counsel, Phi Alpha Delta. Presbyterian (elder 1970—). Clubs: Masons, Elks. Home: 113 St Julien Worthington OH 43085 Office: 7991 Columbus Pike Delaware OH 43015

HANSON, LLOYD CLARENCE, assn. exec.; b. Willmar, Minn., Nov. 30, 1913; s. Edwin William and Esther Dorthea (Lundquist) H.; B.S. (Caleb-Door scholar), U. Minn., 1939; M.B.A., Fla. Atlantic U., 1972; m. Wilva Mae Woodworth, Apr. 29, 1939; children—Stephen, Kathleen (Mrs. James Noel), Claudia (Mrs. Michael Brown). Dep. seed commr., state seed dept. N.D. State U., Fargo, 1939-45; asst. dept. head seed div. Cargill, Inc., Mpls., 1946-53; regional rep. Nat. Hwy. Users Conf., Washington, 1954-58; with Crown Life Ins., Mpls., 1958-59; exec. v.p. N.D. Grain Dealers Assn., Fargo, 1959—. Certified assn. exec. Mem. Am., N.D. (pres. 1964-65) socs. assn. execs., Nat. Secs. Circle (pres. 1966-67), Agrl. Assn. Execs. Council. Lutheran (trustee 1968-70). Mason (32 deg., Shriner), Elk. Established scholarship fund at N.D. State U., 1974. Home: 2525 W Country Club Dr Fargo ND 58102 Office: 212 Black Bldg Fargo ND 58102

HANSON, MYRLE GEORGE, coll. ofcl.; b. Sioux Falls, S.D., Aug. 12, 1931; s. Myrle George and Georgia Gertrude (Peters) H.; B.S. in Edn., Black Hills State Coll., 1953; M.A. in Adminstrn., U. No. Colo., 1960; M.S. in Sci. Edn., U. Utah, 1964; m. Shirley Ann Doutt, Aug. 4, 1956; children—Mark, Lisa, Erik, Dane. Tchr., coach Harlowton (Mont.) Pub. Sch., 1958-59, Powell (Wyo.) Pub. Sch., 1959-65; faculty No. State Coll., Aberdeen, S.D., 1965—, dir. extension, continuing edn., 1972—, asst. to v.p., 1972—; info. officer S.D. for U.S. Naval Acad., 1967—. Served with USNR, 1953-58. NSF grantee, summers 1961-64. Mem. Aberdeen C. of C., Phi Delta Kappa. Episcopalian. Elk, Rotarian. Home: 1804 S Lincoln St Aberdeen SD 57401

HANSON, PAUL ERNEST, lumber co. exec.; b. Geneva, Minn., Nov. 11, 1923; s. Richard Chris and Christine Louise (Christensen) H.; student U. Minn., 1955; m. Phyllis Pauline Petersen, Jan. 23, 1946; children—James, Susan, Richard, DeLoyce, Robert, Teresa. Farmer, Ellendale, Minn., 1946-51; constrn. worker Wayne Constrn. Co., Geneva, Minn., 1951-54; truck driver Clarks Grove Lumber Co., Clarks Grove, Minn., 1954-57, mgr., 1957-77, dir., 1960-77, gen.

mgr., treas., 1957—. Mayor city Clarks Grove, 1967-77, vol. fireman, 1957-77. Mem. Minn. Flying Farmers, Freeborn County League Cities (sec. treas. 1970-76). Baptist. Clubs: Elks, Albert Lea Country. Home: 202 2d Ave N E Clarks Grove MN 56016 Office: 201 W Main St Clarks Grove MN 56016

HANSON, PHYLLIS MARIE GEIS (MRS. HOWARD H. HANSON), realtor; b. Sioux Falls, S.D.; d. William H. and Jane Irene (Manley) Geis; student Nettleton Bus. Coll., 1943; grad. Realtors Inst. S.D., 1972; m. H.S. Eidy, Mar. 8, 1942 (div. 1947); m. 2d, Howard H. Hanson, Apr. 23, 1954; 1 son, Phillip G. Co-owner, mgr. hotel, 1942-43; asst. mgr. State Theatre, asst. to dir. for Eastern S.D., Minn. Amusement Co., 1943-45; owner, operator Brunch House Cafe, 1947; founder home econs. dept. L.C. Lippert Co., Sioux Falls, 1948, dir., 1949-54; salesman Dorothy Poulos, Real Estate, Pierre, S.D., 1959; partner Poulos & Hanson, Real Estate, Pierre, 1961—. Mem. Central S.D. Bd. Realtors, 1959—, sec., 1961, treas., 1962, pres., 1963, chmn. state real estate conv., 1963, named Realtor of Year, 1963, 73; mem. S.D. Bd. Realtors, 1959—, state bd. dirs., 1971—. Mem. S.D. Assn. for Blind, 1954—. Recipient Outstanding Service award S.D. Lions Internat., 1970. Mem. Nat. Assn. Real Estate Bds. (mem. Women's Council), Nat. Brokers Inst., S.D. Realtors Assn. (dir. 1971-75), Pierre C. of C. (dir. 1966-69, treas. 1967-69, exec. bd. 1967-69, dir. 1973-76, pres. 1976-77), U.S. C. of C. (mem. tourist and conv. com. 1964-65), Beta Sigma Phi (host pres. state conv. 1966, 1st pres. Pierre City council 1968). Roman Catholic (pres. band 1963). Club: Pierre Lioness (charter mem.). Home: 417 W 2d St Pierre SD 57501 Office: 302 Coteau St Pierre SD 57501

HANSON, ROBERT LEONARD, office supply co. exec.; b. Chgo., May 19, 1937; s. James Levoid and Thyra Hildegard (Johnson) H.; A.A., Northwestern Mich. Coll., 1956; B.S., Ferris State Coll., 1958; m. Mary Frances Filomeno, Nov. 18, 1961; children—Linda, Michael, Jeffrey, Karyn, Tracy. Sr. accountant Arthur Andersen & Co., 1958-66; controller ACCO div. Gary Industries, Chgo., 1966-69; v.p., gen. mgr. ACCO Canadian, Toronto, Ont., 1969-72; v.p. ACCO Internat., Wheeling, Ill., 1972—. Mem. Wheeling Indsl. Devel. Bd.; chmn. scouting Skokie Valley dist. Boy Scouts Am.; coach Northbrook Bantam Hockey Club, 1977. Served with U.S. Army, 1961. Mem. Assn. Internal Mgmt. Cons., Assn. for Systems Mgmt., Data Processing Mgmt. Assn., Wheeling C. of C. (pres.). Clubs: Rotary (dir.) (Wheeling); Northbrook (Ill.) Hockey. Home: 3010 Margo Ln Northbrook IL 60062 Office: 770 S Acco Plaza Wheeling IL 60090

HANSON, WALTER EDMUND, cons. engr.; b. Lyndon, Kans., July 14, 1916; s. Andrew C. and Laura (Mickelson) H.; B.S., Kans. State U., 1939; M.S., U. Ill., 1947; m. Sue Roling, Sept. 14, 1940; 1 dau., Karen Sue. Draftsman computer, Petty Geophys. Engring. Co., San Antonio, 1939-40; bridge detailer and designer, Howard, Needles, Tammen & Bergendoff, Kansas City, Mo., 1940-42; instr. civil engring. U. Ill., 1942-43; asst., asso. prof. civil engring. U. Ill., 1946-51; engr. bridges Ill. Div. of Hwys., 1951-54; cons., practice Springfield, 1954—. Served to lt. (j.g.) USNR, 1943-46. Mem. Am. Soc. C.E., Ill. Engring. Council, Nat., Ill. socs. profl. engrs., Am. Cons. Engrs. Council, Am. Concrete Inst., Am. Railway Engr. Assn., Am. Soc. Testing Materials, Sigma Tau, Chi Epsilon. Republican. Presbyn. Co-author: Foundation Engineering (textbook). Contbr. articles to profl. jours. Home: 81 Linden Ln Springfield IL 62707 Office: 1525 S 6th St Springfield IL 62703

HANSON, WILLIAM C., fed. judge; b. Green County, Iowa, May 14, 1909; s. Willis and Pearl (Cook) H.; B.A., Iowa State U., 1933, J.D., 1935; m. Ruth Hastings. Admitted to Iowa bar, 1935; county atty., 1938-46; judge 16th Dist. Iowa, 1955; U.S. dist. ct. judge No. Dist. Iowa, 1962—, U.S. dist. ct. judge So. Dist. Iowa, 1962, now chief judge. Mem. Iowa C. of C. Republican. Methodist. Clubs: Rotary, Masons. Office: US Dist Ct PO Box 1157 Fort Dodge IA 50501

HANTEN, ROBERT LEE, biologist; b. Sioux City, Iowa, Dec. 12, 1934; s. Albert Alexander and Margaret Rose (Tholl) H.; B.S., S.D. State U., 1960, postgrad., 1960-61; postgrad. Pa. State U., 1969; m. Carroll Jana Eggee, June 13, 1970; 1 son, Robert Peter. Survey entomologist S.D. State U., Brookings, 1961; fisheries mgmt. biologist S.D. Dept. Game, Fish and Parks, Webster, S.D., 1962-65; asst. supt. fisheries, 1965-67, supt. fisheries, 1967-70, staff fisheries specialist, 1970—. Mem. State S.D. Perimeter Rds. Com. 1969-71. Recipient Isaak Walton scholastic Achievement award, 1960. Tng. grantee Sport Fishing Inst., 1969. Mem. Am. Fisheries Soc. (chpt. chmn. ad hoc com. water level mgmt. for fisheries propagation 1972-74), Gt. Plains Fisheries Workers Assn., Ducks Unlimited, Gamma Sigma Delta. Republican. Roman Catholic. Home: Star Route 3 Pierre SD 57501 Office: Dept Game Fish and Parks SD Pierre SD 57501

HAPAK, FRANCIS MICHAEL, orthodontist; b. Whiting, Ind., Sept. 10, 1925; s. Valentine and Caroline (Maslach) H.; student Valparaiso U., 1946; D.D.S., Ind. U., 1951, M.S., 1953; m. Charlotte Simms Haydon, Sept. 10, 1949; children—Charlotte H., Mark, Susan, F. Haydon, Tracy Ann, Madeline, Holly. Pvt. practice dentistry specializing in orthodontics, Indpls., 1953—. Cons., mem. Ind. U. Sch. Medicine Cleft Palate Clinic, 1953-63; dir. Unified Underwriters, Inc., 1956-68, Unified Mut. Shares, Inc., 1959-68. Mem. adv. council Small Bus. Adminstrn. Ind., 1970—. Served with USNR, 1943-46. Diplomate Am. Bd. Orthodontics. Mem. Am. Assn. Orthodontists, Edward H. Angle Soc. Orthodontists, Tweed Found. for Orthodontic Research. Club: Meridian Hills Country. Contbr. articles to profl. publs. Home: 729 Round Hill Rd Indianapolis IN 46260 Office: 1810 Broad Ripple Ave Indianapolis IN 46220

HAPP, LAWRENCE RAYMOND, metal engr.; b. Mendota, Ill., Mar. 11, 1945; s. Albert William and Mary (Becker) H.; B.S. in Metall. Engring., U. Ill., 1968; m. Susan Jean Beste, Mar. 4, 1971; children—Brian, Donald, Debra, Gregory. Supr. welding devel. labs. Caterpillar Tractor Co., Peoria, Ill., 1968-69; welding engr. Trane Co., LaCrosse, Wis., 1969-73, sr. welding engr., quality control mgr., Burlington, Iowa, 1973-74; welding and materials engr. Paul Mueller Co., Springfield, Mo., 1974—. Mem. Cursillo Movement, Birthright, Right to Life; active Scripture Study groups. Registered profl. engr., Mo. Mem. Mo. Solar Energy Assn., Am. Welding Soc., Am. Soc. Metals, Nat., Mo. socs. profl. engrs., ASME, ASTM. Roman Catholic. Home: 3428 Westwood St S Springfield MO 65807 Office: 1600 Phelps St W Springfield MO 65801

HARASYMIW, STEFAN J., educator; B.A., U. Conn., 1961, M.S. in Sch. Psychology, 1963; Ph.D. in Rehab. Research, 1971; m. Roxolana Irene Harasymiw; 1 son, Lew Jaroslaw. Sr. programmer United Aircraft Corp., East Hartford, Conn., 1963-66; sr. research asst. ednl. tech. group devel. research div. Ednl. Testing Service, Princeton, N.J., 1966-68; asst. prof. spl. edn. Boston U., asst. prof. rehab. medicine Northwestern U., Chgo., 1975—; mem. Nat. Task Force on Mgmt. Info. Systems, 1972, Nat. Task Force on Materials and Methods Evaluation, 1972; mem. staff New Eng. Med. Center Hosp., Boston, 1975. Licensed psychologist, Mass. Mem. AAAS, Am. Congress Rehab. Medicine, Am. Ednl. Research Assn., Am. Psychol. Assn., Assn. for Computing Machinery, Council for Exceptional Children, IEEE, Nat. Rehab. Assn., Sigma Xi, Phi Kappa Phi. Contbr. articles to profl. jours. Office: Medical School Dept Rehab Med 345 E Superior St Chicago IL 60611

HARBESON, JOHN WILLIS, polit. scientist; b. New Brunswick, N.J., Sept. 14, 1938; s. Robert Willis and Gladys Irene (Evans) H.; B.A., Swarthmore Coll., 1960; M.A., U. Chgo., 1962; Ph.D., U. Wis., 1970; m. Ann Elizabeth Warmoth, Aug. 25, 1963; children—Eric John, Kristen Lynne. Lectr., fellow Inst. Devel. Studies, U. Nairobi, 1965-67; asst. prof. polit. sci. U. Wis., Parkside, 1967-72, asso. prof., 1972—, chmn. div. social scis., 1976—; vis. asso. prof. Haile Sellassie I U., Ethiopia, 1973-75. Mem. exec. bd. Racine (Wis.) Urban League, 1971-73; sec. Wis. Civil Liberties Union, Kenosha, 1972-74; chmn. congl. campaign Rep. Les Aspin, 1970, 72; chmn. Udall for Pres., Racine County, 1976. Recipient grants U. Wis., 1967, 68, 71, 76, 77; NDEA fellow, 1965-67. Mem. Am. Polit. Sci. Assn., African Studies Assn. Democrat. Conglist. Author: Nation Building in Kenya: The Role of Land Reform, 1973; Ethiopian Transformation: Revolution in a Traditional Polity. Home: 1020 Park Ave Racine WI 53403 Office: Div Social Sciences Univ Wisconsin Kenosha WI 53140

HARBIN, CALVIN EDWARD, coll. ofcl.; b. Puxico, Mo., Mar. 26, 1916; s. Samuel Wesley and Ada Maria (Shelton) H.; B.S., S.E. Mo. State U., 1949; M.A., George Peabody Coll. Tchrs., 1949; Ed.D., U. Mo., 1952; postgrad. U. Chgo., 1953, Harvard, 1963-64, Coll. Law, Western State U., 1975-76; m. Dorothy Comoh, June 26, 1947; children—Maria Catherine, Ruth Ella, Charles Edward. Prof. edn. Ft. Hays State Coll., Hays, Kans., 1952—, dean edn., 1972-77, spl. asst. to pres., 1977—; cons. faculty Army Command and Gen. Staff Coll., Ft. Leavenworth, Kans., 1968-74. Served to capt. AUS, 1941-46; Col. Res. Mem. NEA, Phi Delta Kappa. Republican. Presbyn. (elder 1960—). Kiwanian. Author: Teaching Power, 1967. Home: 303 W 19th St Hays KS 67601

HARBINSON, BROTHER CAMILLUS, retarded adults home adminstr.; b. Belfast, No. Ireland, Apr. 18, 1924; s. William Edward and Elizabeth (Thompson) H.; L.P.N., St. Joseph Hosp., Albuquerque, 1953. Came to U.S., 1951. Joined Bros. of the Good Shepherd, asst. superior gen., 1969; dir. Ozanam Inn., New Orleans, 1954-57; adminstr. St. Martin Home, Columbus, Ohio, 1957-63, Good Shepherd Manor, Wakefield, Ohio, 1963-71, Momence, Ill., 1971—. Address: PO Box 260 Momence IL 60954

HARBOR, WILLIAM HENRY, state ofcl.; b. Henderson, Iowa, Oct. 28, 1920; s. Ora L. and Pearl (Wilkerson) H.; B.A., U. Iowa, 1943. Tchr., coach Afton (Iowa) Community Sch., 1945-46; mgr. grain elevator, Henderson, 1947-52; owner, operator Harbor Feed & Grain Co., Henderson, 1952—; mem. Iowa Ho. of Reps., 1955-57, 67-73, 77—, speaker, 1969-73, chief clk., 1973-75; mem. Iowa senate, 1957-61. Pres. Henderson Vol. Firemen's Assn.; mem. Nat. Legis. Conf. Intergovtl. Relations Com. Bd. dirs. Iowa Housing Devel. Corp., Iowa Right to Work Com.; chmn. Iowa Heart Fund. Served to lt. (j.g.) USNR, World War II. Mem. Iowa Grain and Feed Assn. (dir. 1960-63), Am. Legion (post comdr. 1948-49, county comdr. 1952-53). Methodist (trustee). Clubs: Masons, Elks. Home: Henderson IA 51541 Office: State Capitol Bldg Des Moines IA 50319

HARBOUR, JEANNE DULAS, child psychiatrist; b. Labatut, France, Feb. 9, 1921; d. Pierre and Dorothy (Stafas) Dulas; M.D., Sch. Medicine, Paris, France, 1947; M.D., Wis. U., 1968; m. Howard Harbour, June 15, 1962. Came to U.S., 1958, naturalized, 1967. Sch. pub. health med. insp., France, 1948-58; intern Presbyn.-St. Luke's Hosp., Chgo., 1958-59, resident, 1959-61; clin. asst. psychiatry Ill. U., 1959-61; fellow psychiatry McGill U., 1962, Toronto U., 1963; fellow child psychiatry Chapel Hill Meml. Hosp., N.C. U., 1964-65; cons. child psychiatry North Shore Hosp., Winnetka, Ill., 1966-67, Mendota State Hosp., Madison, Wis., 1968-71; now child psychiatrist, mem. med. staff Children's Meml. Hosp., Chgo.; asst. prof. psychiatry Rush Med. Coll., Chgo. Diplomate Am. Bd. Psychiatry and Neurology, Am. Bd. Child Psychiatry. Fellow Am. Orthopsychiat. Assn.; mem. AMA, Am. Psychiat. Assn., Ill. Med. Soc., Am. Med. Womens Assn., Chgo. Council Child Psychiatry. Research on color blindness of sch. children. Home: 535 N Michigan Ave Chicago IL 60611 Office: 2400 W 95th St Evergreen Park IL 60642

HARD, ARNE MAYNARD, savs. and loan exec.; b. Kiron, Iowa, Jan. 21, 1921; s. Perry A. and Hannah E. (Carlson) H.; student Am. Inst. Bus., 1937-40; m. Shirley C. Eckman, Apr. 22, 1944. With Am. Fed. Savs. & Loan Assn., 1946-61; with Hawkeye Savs. and Loan Assn., Boone, Iowa, 1961—, pres., 1971—; chmn. First Central Service Corp., Des Moines 1973-74; dir. Mid Iowa Security Corp.; dir., pres. Mid Central Service Corp. Pres. Boone County YMCA, 1971-73; past dir., chmn. Boone County chpt. ARC; past dir., chmn. fund drive United Fund; trustee Mamie Eisenhower Birth Place Restoration Com. Served with USAAF, 1942-46. Named Boss of Year Jr. C. of C., 1965, Ames chpt. Am. Bus. Women's Assn., 1975. Mem. Am. Inst. Bus. (trustee), C. of C. (pres. 1965). Lutheran (bd. 1963-69, treas. 1963-69). Lion. Home: 1128 Country Club Dr Boone IA 50036 Office: 8th and Arden Sts Boone IA 50036

HARDEN, OLETA ELIZABETH (MRS. DENNIS CLARENCE HARDEN), educator; b. Jamestown, Ky., Nov. 22, 1935; d. Stanley Virgil and Myrtie Alice (Stearns) Mc Whorter; B.A., Western Ky. U., 1956; M.A. in English, U. Ark., 1958, Ph.D. in English, 1965; m. Dennis Clarence Harden, July 23, 1966. Teaching asst. U. Ark., Fayetteville, 1956-57, 58-59, 61-63; instr. S.W. Mo. State Coll., Springfield, 1957-58, Murray (Ky.) U., 1959-61; asst. prof. English, Northeastern State Coll., Tahlequah, Okla., 1963-65; asst. prof. Wichita (Kans.) State U., 1965-66; asst. prof. English Wright State U., Dayton, Ohio, 1966-68, asso. prof., 1968-72, prof., 1972—, asst. chmn. English dept., 1967-70, asst. dean coll. liberal arts, 1971-73, asso. dean, 1973-74, exec. dir. Gen. Univ. Services, 1974-76. Wright State U. Research and Devel. grantee, 1969, Found. grantee, 1971; Nat. Endowment for Humanities nominee, 1977. Mem. Modern Lang. Assn., Coll. English Assn., AAUP. Author: Maria Edgeworth's Art of Prose Fiction, 1971. Home: 2618 Big Woods Trail Fairborn OH 45324 Office: Dept English Wright State U 7751 Colonel Glenn Hwy Dayton OH 45431

HARDESTY, DONALD LEE, research co. exec.; b. Mulberry, Kans., Dec. 10, 1936; s. Glen Leroy and Winnie Edith (Radford) H.; B.S., Wichita U., 1960; M.S. (Dunlap fellow Indsl. Psychology), Kans. State U., 1963, Ph.D., 1964; m. Marilyn Rae Dondlinger, Sept. 2, 1961; children—Jeff, Jennifer, Julie, Elizabeth. Staff psychologist Standard Oil Co. Ohio, Cleve., 1964-66; chmn. psychology dept. Washburn U., Topeka, 1966-70; indsl. research cons. Menninger Found., Topeka, 1966-68; pres. Central Research Corp., Topeka, 1970—. Cons. in field. Chmn., Shawnee County Mental Health Adv. Bd., 1967, Topeka Human Relations Commn., 1968-70, Goals for Topeka, 1971-73. Recipient Exceptional Service award City of Topeka, 1971. Mem. Am., Kan. psychol. assns., Psi Chi. Rotarian. Home: 1615 W 27th St Topeka KS 66611 Office: Suite 900 1st Nat Bank Tower Topeka KS 66603

HARDIN, PAUL FRANKLIN, realtor, appraiser; b. Indpls., Aug. 25, 1914; s. Joseph Charles and Ethel May (Chastain) H.; student Ind. U., 1958-62, Purdue U., 1944; m. Helen Marie Simpson, Aug. 18, 1936; children—Rita (Mrs. John A. Swift), Paul T. Dist. office clk. Goodyear Tire & Rubber Co., Indpls., 1940-43; supr. maintenance, mgr. subcontracting Adams Rd. Machinery, Indpls., 1943-58; owner, mgr. real estate and ins. agy. Paul Hardin Agy., Plainfield, Ind., 1958—; fee appraiser, property mgr. VA, Plainfield, 1967—; pres., resident mgr. Eldinwood Devel. Corp., Plainfield, 1959-64. Exec. com. Guilford Twp. Civic Council, 1953. Del., Ind. Republican Conv., 1952. Mem. Hendricks County Bd. Realtors (pres. 1961, 70), Ind. State Bd. Realtors. Mem. Soc. Friends (trustee). Clubs: Masons, Rotary (pres. Plainfield 1965), Elks. Home: 16 Crest Ct Plainfield IN 46168 Office: 10 S East St Plainfield IN 46168

HARDING, THOMAS S(PENCER), librarian; b. Gaines, N.Y., Feb. 24, 1910; s. Harrison Herbert and Jessie Louise (Call) H.; B.A. summa cum laude, U. Buffalo, 1933, B.S. in L.S., 1937; M.A., U. Chgo., 1939, Ph.D., 1957. Library asst. U. Buffalo, 1930-36; librarian Univ. Coll., Northwestern U., 1937-42, Mo. Valley Coll., 1946-48, Evansville (Ind.) Coll., 1948-66, Washburn U. of Topeka, 1966-75, librarian emeritus, 1975—. Served with USNR, 1942-45. Mem. ALA, AAUP, Phi Kappa Phi, Pi Gamma Mu. Unitarian. Mason. Author: College Literary Societies: Their Contribution to Higher Education in the United States, 1815-1876. Contbr. articles to publs. Home: 2120 High St Topeka KS 66611

HARDISON, LESLIE CLAIRE, air pollution engring. co. exec.; b. Chgo., Feb. 16, 1929; s. William Leland and Lyda Sue (Sims) H.; B.S. in M.E., Ill. Inst. Tech., Chgo., 1950; m. Dolores Elanor Wachdorf, June 14, 1952; children—William, John, Patricia, Susan, Janet, James, Paul. Project engr. Ill. Inst. Tech. Research Inst., Chgo., 1950-53; bldg. and grounds supt. Universal Oil Products, Des Plaines, Ill., 1953-55, petroleum process design engr., 1955-58, chief pilot plant design engr., 1959-61, supr. operations process devel. div., 1961, asst. mgr. process devel. div., 1961-63; dir. research and devel. Catalytic Combustion Co., 1963-66; tech. dir. Air Correction div. Universal Oil Products, 1966-70, v.p. air resources, 1970—. Registered profl. engr., Ill., Colo., Pa. Mem. ASME, Am. Inst. Chem. Engrs., Am. Chem. Soc., Air Pollution Control Assn. Republican. Contbr. articles on pollution control to profl. jours. Patentee in field. Home: 233 Apple Tree Ln Barrington IL 60010

HARDY, GEORGE, diagnostic radiologist; b. Winnipeg, Man., Can., Aug. 17, 1924; s. William and Mary (Piseski) H.; M.D., U. Man., 1952; m. Nel Salome, July 17, 1948; 1 son, Brian. Apprentice, C.P. Ry., Winnipeg, 1941-43; intern St. Boniface, Winnipeg, 1951-53; gen. practice medicine, Winnipeg, 1953-63; resident Winnipeg Gen. Hosp., 1963-66; practice medicine specializing in diagnostic radiology, Winnipeg, 1963—; mem. staffs Health Scis. Centre; asst. prof. diagnostic radiology U. Man., 1970; pres. Coll. Gen. Practice Man., 1960-61. Served with Canadian Army M.C., 1941-43. Home: 427 Bower Blvd Winnipeg MB R3P 0L6 Canada Office: Med Arts Bldg 233 Kennedy St Winnipeg MB R3C 3J5 Canada

HARDY, H. GUY, lawyer; b. Bloomfield, Iowa, July 18, 1918; s. Rufus Guy and Mabel (Kenworthy) H.; student Bloomfield Jr. Coll., 1936-38, B.A., State U. Iowa, 1940, J.D. 1942; LL.M., Harvard, 1947; m. Dorothy Rice, Apr. 22, 1949; children—Susan (Mrs. Michael Doland), Barbara (Mrs. Samuel Maihack), Beverly (Mrs. Scott Montgomery), Richard, Nancy. Admitted to Iowa bar, 1942, Ohio bar, 1948; practiced in Cleve., 1947—; mem. firm McDonald, Hopkins & Hardy Co., Cleve., 1947—. Dir., sec. Am. Handling Equipment Co., Harvest Life Ins. Co., Daniels Funeral Home, Inc., Jaquay Lake Park, Inc.; dir. Harvest Pub. Co., Harvest Ins. Agy., Inc., Lakewood Furnace Co. Asst. area chmn. United Appeal, Cleve., 1966-67; bd. mgrs. West Shore YMCA, 1963—; trustee Combined Health Fund Drive, Bay Village, Ohio, 1964-68; trustee Bay Village Swimming Pool Inc.; councilman Bay Village, O., 1956-61, pres., 1960-61; mem. bd. edn., Bay Village, 1964-73, pres., 1968-70. Served to capt. CIC, AUS, 1942-46, 51. Recipient Extension award Lions Club, 1953. Mem. Am. Judicature Soc., Am., Ohio State, Cleve. bar assns., Order of Coif. Episcopalian (vestryman 1963-66). Lion. Home: 28334 Osborn Rd Bay Village OH 44140 Office: East Ohio Bldg Cleveland OH 44114

HARDY, JAMES EUGENE, utility co. exec.; b. Pontiac, Mich., June 10, 1929; s. Kenneth and Eva Juanita (Poling) H.; B.S. in Indsl. Mgmt., Purdue U., 1951; m. Jerry J. Humbert, June 9, 1951; children—Julie Diane, Jay Douglas. With Continental Steel Corp., Kokomo, Ind., 1951-71, asst. treas., 1968, v.p. corp. devel., 1969), v.p., also treas., 1970, dir., also mem. exec. com., 1970-71; exec. v.p. Kokomo Gas and Fuel Co., 1971-76, pres., chief exec. officer, 1976—. Bd. dirs. United Fund; trustee YWCA. Served to 1st lt. AUS, 1951-53. Mem. C. of C. (dir.). Alpha Tau Omega. Congregationalist (ch. treas.). Clubs: Columbian (Indpls.), Kokomo Country (dir. 1970-72), Elks. Home: 4697 S Dixon Rd Kokomo IN 46901 Office: 900 E Blvd Kokomo IN 46901

HARDY, RICHARD EARL, physicist; b. Mpls., Mar. 31, 1933; s. Richard Earl and Minola (Jensen) H.; B.Physics, U. Minn., 1958; m. Bette A. Williams, Dec. 5, 1954; children—Richard Earl Hardy, Susan Mae. Physicist, Lawrence Radiation Lab., Livermore, Calif., 1958-61; sr. systems engr. FMC Corp., San Jose, Calif., 1961-64; project dir., sr. analyst Data Dynamics Inc., Tampa, Fla., 1964-72; dir. computer ops., project dir. efficacy study of diagnostic radiologic procedures Am. Coll. Radiology, Chgo., 1972—. Served with USNR, 1952-53. Mem. Am. Mgmt. Assn., Conf. Med. Soc. Execs. Greater Chgo. Home: 252 Strathmore St Bloomingdale IL 60108 Office: 20 N Wacker Dr Chicago IL 60606

HARDY, ROBERT EARL, psychologist; b. Flint, Mich., May 23, 1941; s. Melvin Bryant and Pearl Eugenia (Dunbar) H.; B.S., Western Mich. U., 1964; M.Ed., No. Ill. U., 1967; Ed.D., Western Mich. U., 1971; m. Jacqueline Phairas, Dec. 24, 1965; 1 dau., Tasha Pearl. Mott fellow Mott Found., Flint, Mich., 1968-69; counselor Comstock (Mich.) Pub. Schs., 1969-72; dir. Richfield (Minn.) Pub. Schs., 1972—; founder Self-Defeating Behavior Inst., St. Louis Park, Minn., 1975—. Bd. dirs. Gestalt Therapy Inst. Minn. Mem. Am. Psychol. Assn., Am. Personnel and Guidance Assn. Home: 4321 Brook Ln St Louis Park MN 55416

HARDY, WALTER LINCOLN, chem. co. exec.; b. Chgo., Feb. 28, 1916; s. Thomas Jefferson and Nellie J. (Collins) H.; B. Chemistry, Cornell U., 1937, M. Chem. Engring., 1938; M.B.A., U. Chgo., 1969; m. Ruth Elizabeth Heinig, Nov. 10, 1944; children—Meredith Lynn, Thomas George, Elizabeth Ellen. Devel. engr. and tech. asst. to research dir. Tide Water Oil Co., Bayonne, N.J., 1938-41; gen. mgr. Protective Coatings Corp., Nutley, N.J., 1945-48; v.p. and gen. mgr. Leed Pak, Inc., N.Y.C., 1948-52; dir. engring. client relations Foster D. Snell Inc., N.Y.C., 1952-59; mgr. chem. research Internat. Minerals & Chem. Corp., Skokie, Ill., 1959-62; v.p. research and devel. Simoniz Co., Chgo., 1962-65; dir. research and devel. The Richardson Co., Melrose Park, Ill., 1965—. Mem. Army-Navy patent adv. bd., 1942-46, Nat. Prodn. Authority, 1950-52. Mem. Ill. Sch. Bd. Dist. 110, Deerfield, Ill., 1961-67, v.p., 1965-66, pres., 1967; village trustee, 1973—; mem. Cornell U. Council, Ithaca, N.Y., 1965—. Served from lt. to lt. col. Engring. Div., USAAF, 1941-46. Registered profl. engr., N.Y. Fellow Am. Inst. Chemists; mem. Indsl. Research Inst., T.A.P.P.I., Reseach Dirs. Assn. Chgo. (pres. 1971—), Am. Assn. Cost Engrs. (charter), Am. Mgmt. Assn., Alpha Chi Sigma. Roman Catholic. Clubs: Cornell Club Chgo. (pres. 1966-68); Anchor and

Saber of N.Y.C. (pres. 1957-58); Suburban (Glenview, Ill.); Tennaqua (Deerfield, Ill.). Home: 3065 Blackthorn Rd Deerfield IL 60015 Office: 2700 Lake St Melrose Park IL 60160

HARE, ROBERT Y., educator; b. McGrann, Pa., June 14, 1921; s. Robert Deemar and Beulah (Yates) H.; student Carnegie-Mellon U., 1939-41; Mus.B., U. Detroit and Detroit Inst. Musical Art, 1948; M.A., Wayne State U., 1950; Ph.D., U. Iowa, 1959; m. Constance Rutherford, Mar. 31, 1948; children—Stephen, Beverly, Madeleine. French hornist Pitts. Symphony Orch., 1941-43, 44-45, Buffalo Philharmonic, 1943-44, Cin. Summer Opera Co., 1945, Indpls. Symphony Orch., 1945-46, San Antonio Symphony Orch., 1947-49; instr. Marietta (Ohio) Coll., 1949-51, Del Mar Coll., Corpus Christi, Tex., 1951-55; prof., chmn. grad. studies San Jose (Calif.) State Coll., 1956-65, condr. Coll. Symphonic Band, 1956-63; prof., dean Eastern Ill. U. Sch. Music, Charleston, 1965-74; prof., dir. Sch. Music Ohio State U., Columbus, 1974—. Condr. U. Symphony, 1968-71; mus. arranger San Antonio Symphony; condr. San Jose Youth Symphony, 1957-59. Mem. com. for grad. and profl. edn. Ill. Bd. Higher Edn.; mem. performing arts com. Ill. Sesquicentennial, 1967; trustee Columbus Symphony Orch., 1975—. Mem. Am. Musicol. Soc., Music Educators Nat. Conf. (publs. planning com. 1970-74), Music Tchrs. Nat. Assn., Ill. Music Educators Assn. (council music edn. in higher edn. 1969—), Coll. Music Soc., Phi Mu Alpha Sinfonia (hon.). Mason (Shriner). Contbr. articles to profl. jours. Office: Sch Music Ohio State U Columbus OH 43210

HARE, RONALD CHARLES, photographer; b. Niagara Falls, N.Y., May 17, 1933; s. Charles Henry and Ida May (Myers) H.; grad. Whitney Ave. Sch., 1952, N.Y. Inst. Photography, 1955, Am. Sch. Photography, 1957, Nat. Camera Repair Sch., 1963; m. Barbara Fay, Sept. 29, 1961; children—Christopher, Stacey. Darkroom tech. photographer photog. dept. Uhl-Hall-Rich Constrn. Engrs., N.Y. State Power Authority, Niagara Falls, 1960-61; photographer Leep Zelones Photography Studio, Niagara Falls, 1955-59, 61-63; sr. photographer corp. communications, audio visual dept. Addressograph-Multigraph Corp., Cleve., 1966-77; prin. Ronald C. Hare Photography, Parma, Ohio, 1977—. Photographs exhibited Mus. Modern Art, N.Y.C. Mem. Profl. Photographers Am. (Merit awards 1970-71), Profl. Photographers Ohio. Contbr. photographs to profl. jours. Address: 5944 Twin Lakes Dr Parma OH 44129

HARE, WILLIAM RUSSELL, veterinarian; b. Detroit, June 17, 1943; s. William R. and Thelma E. (Hennessy) H.; A.S. with honors, Macomb County Community Coll., Warren, Mich., 1967; B.S., D.V.M. with honors, Mich. State U., 1970; m. Jeannette C. Rinke, Nov. 2, 1963; children—Deborah, William Russell III, Wendy, Rebecca. Asso. veterinarian Vetter's Vet. Clinic, Raymond, Wash., 1970-71; owner Hare Vet. Clinic, Romeo, Mich., 1971—; founder Milk Well Dairy Farm, 1975—. Mem. North Macomb Vocational Edn. Adv. Bd., 1975—. Recipient Pfizer vet. student award, 1970. Mem. AMVA, Mich., Wash., Thumb (sec., treas.), Macomb County vet. med. assns., Bovine, Equine, Swine practitioners assns., Am. Vet. Soc. Study of Breeding Soundness, Am. Soc. Vet. Anesthesiology, Am. Animal Hosp. Assn., A.A.A.S., Mich. Assn. of Professions, Mich. Farm Bur., Mich. State U. Alumni Assn. Lutheran. Club: Shriners. Office: 149 W St Clair St Romeo MI 48065

HAREL, ZEV, gerontologist; b. Baia Mare, Roumania, Jan. 27, 1930; s. Joseph and Berta (Grossfeld) Herskovits; came to U.S., 1965, naturalized, 1973; B.S.W., Hebrew U., Jerusalem, 1963; M.S.W., U. Mich., 1967; Ph.D., Washington U., St. Louis, 1971; m. Bernice E. Benjamin, Oct. 16, 1966; children—Hadas, Naomi. Sr. research asso. Applied Gerontology Research Center, Benjamin Rose Inst., Cleve., 1972-76; asso. prof. social service dept. Cleve. State U., 1976—; psychiat. social worker U. Mich. Hosp., Ann Arbor, 1967-69; cons. Elderly Research Center, Wayne State U., Detroit, 1972—. Bd. dirs. Youth Village Gallim, Israel, 1963-65; mem. cultural com. Kibbutz Sdeh Nachum, Israel, 1952-53. Served with Israel Army, 1948-49. Recipient Segal award Hebrew U., 1962; Nat. Council Jewish Women fellow, 1965-67, U. Mich. Internat. Center fellow, 1967. Fellow Gerontol. Soc. (research com. 1973-76, chmn. sect. research com. 1977—); mem. Am. Orthopsychiat. Assn. (program com. 1973-76, chmn. aging task force, 1976—), Nat. Assn. Social Workers, Council Social Work Edn. Home: 2563 Channing Rd University Heights OH 44118 Office: 314 Mather Hall Cleveland OH 44115

HARFST, ERNEST DENNIS, coll. adminstr.; b. Havana, Ill., Nov. 8, 1926; s. Eilert E. and Eva W. (Thomason) H.; B.S., U. Ill., 1950; M.S., No. Ill. U., 1974; m. Betsy C. Perteit, Aug. 29, 1948; children—Sue Ann, Michael D., Patrick L. Indsl. mgmt. trainee various cos., Ill., 1950-54; design engr. Ideal Industries, Sycamore, Ill., 1954-62, lab. mgr., 1962-68; instr. electronics Kishwaukee Coll., Malta, Ill., 1968-72, chmn. indsl. tech. and pub. service occupations, 1972—; cons. in field. Active Boy Scouts Am., 1964-72. Served with USAF, 1945-46. Mem. Nat. Fire Protection Assn., Water Pollution Control Fedn., Ill. Assn. Electrical-Electronic Educators, Kishwaukee Amateur Radio Club, Nat. Rifle Assn., Am. Legion. Republican. Home: 825 Meadow Ln Sycamore IL 60178 Office: Kishwaukee Coll Malta IL 60150

HARGETT, HERBERT PECKOVER, ophthalmologist; b. Augusta, Ky., Oct. 5, 1918; s. Marmaduke and Susan Oridge (Barnhard) H.; A.B., U. Ky., 1940; M.D., U. Louisville, 1943; postgrad. in opthalmology, N.Y. U., 1947-48; m. Marion Hurlbut, June 9, 1945 (dec.); children—William Hurlbut, Kathryn (Mrs. Steven Webb), Pamela (Mrs. John W. Wheeler); m. 2d, S. June Cleveland, Aug. 3, 1974. Intern, Springfield (Ohio) City Hosp., 1943; resident ophthalmology Nichols VA Hosp., Louisville, 1948-50; practice medicine specializing in ophthalmology, Springfield, 1950-61, Jeffersonville, Ind., 1962—; head dept. ophthalmology Clark County Meml. Hosp., 1962—; pres. Clark County Optical Service, Inc., 1962—. Instr. ophthalmology U. Louisville, 1948-50. Pres. Clark County Chpt. Am. Cancer Soc., 1964. Served to capt. M.C., AUS, 1944-46. Diplomate Am. Bd. Ophthalmology. Mem. Clark County, Ind. State med. socs., AMA, Pan-Am. Ophthal. Soc., Barraquer Inst., Barcelona, Spain, Am. Acad. Ophthalmology, Internat. Eye Found., Soc. Eye Surgeons. Clubs: Elks, Lions. Home: 2304 St Andrews Rd Jeffersonville IN 47130 Office: 100 E 12th St Jeffersonville IN 47130

HARGRAVE, HAROLD, ret. educator; b. Boonville, Ind., June 10, 1908; s. Jacob Thurman and Dora (West) H.; B.S. in Edn., Oakland City Coll., 1930, LL.D., 1971; M.S. in Edn., Ind. U., 1936; m. Rowena Hullett, June 4, 1935; 1 dau., Ruth Ann. Began career as tchr. Crowe Sch., Ind., 1926-27, Kings (Ill.) Sch., 1930-31; tchr., guidance dir. pub. schs., LaPorte, Ind., 1931-56, prin., 1956-58, supt. schs., 1958-72; mem. faculty N.Y. U., 1947-49, Peabody Tchrs. Coll., 1948, Butler U., 1946-55. Pres. elect Ind. Pub. Sch. Study Council, 1971; spl. asst. to mayor 1972—; sec. LaPorte Econ. Devel. Commn., 1972—; exec. com. Fairview Youth Treatment Center, 1973—. Trustee Community Hosp., Roger Williams Found.; bd. dirs. Haven Hubbard Home for Ret., 1974-77. Mem. Am. Assn. Sch. Adminstrs., N.E.A., Ind. Assn. Pub. Sch. Supts. (v.p. 1967-68, pres. 1969-70), C. of C. (v.p. 1974-75), Phi Delta Kappa. Mason, Elk, Kiwanian (pres. 1945, lt. gov. 1947). Home: 1808 Monroe St LaPorte IN 46350

HARGRAVE, SARAH QUESENBERRY, corporate found. exec.; b. Mt. Airy, N.C., Dec. 11, 1944; d. Teddie W. and Lois Knight (Slusher) Quesenberry; student Radford Coll., 1963-64, Va. Poly. Inst. State U., 1964-67. Mgmt. trainee Thalhimer Bros. Dept. Store, Richmond, Va., 1967-68; Central Va. fashion and publicity dir. Sears Roebuck & Co., Richmond, 1968-74, nat. decorating sch. coordinator, Chgo., 1973-74, nat. dir. bus. and profl. women's programs, Chgo., 1974-76, v.p., treas., program dir. Sears-Roebuck Found., Chgo., 1976—; mem. com. on equal opportunity for women Am. Assembly Collegiate Schs. Bus., 1977—, donors' forum women's issues group, 1974—. Co-dir. Ill. Internat. Women's Year Center, 1975; mem. pastor-parish com. Broadway United Methodist Ch., Chgo., 1974-76. Named Outstanding Young Woman of Year, Ill., 1976; Woman of Achievement, State St. Bus. and Profl. Womans Club, 1978. Mem. Assn. Humanistic Psychology, Am. Home Econs. Assn., Am. Personnel and Guidance Assn., Nat. Fedn. Bus. and Profl. Women's Clubs, Women and Founds./Corporate Philanthropy. Home: 421 W Melrose St Chicago IL 60657 Office: Sears-Roebuck Found Sears Tower Chicago IL 60684

HARGRAVE, VICTORIA E(LIZABETH), librarian; b. Ripon, Wis., Aug. 22, 1913; d. Alexander Walter and Estelle Winifred (Swanson) Hargrave; A.B., Ripon Coll., 1934; library diploma U. Wis., 1938; M.A., U. Chgo., 1947; postgrad. U. Calif. at Los Angeles, 1970. Tchr. Brandon (Wis.) High Sch., 1934-37; extension librarian Iowa State Coll. Library, 1938-44; librarian Ripon Coll., 1944-46, MacMurray Coll., Jacksonville, Ill., 1947—. Mem. adv. council librarians U. Ill. Grad. Sch. Library Service, 1962-64. Mem. ALA, AAUW, League Women Voters. Home: 141 Caldwell St Jacksonville IL 62650

HARGREAVES, GEORGE MACDONALD, advt., pub. relations co. exec.; b. Highland Park, Mich., Sept. 6, 1927; s. George Wellock and Florence (Macdonald) H.; B.S. in Physics, Hillsdale Coll., 1951; m. Catherine Armstrong, Sept. 1, 1951; children—Amy, George, Jane. Engr. Chrysler Corp., Highland Park, Mich., 1951-54; editor Soc. Mfg. Engrs., Detroit, 1954-59; advt. mgr. Detroit Stamping Co., 1959-60, Indsl. Controls div. Bendix Corp., Detroit, 1960-61; tech. dir. Parker Willox Fairchild & Campbell Inc., Saginaw, Mich., 1961—, v.p., 1972—; dir. Techniques Co., 1968—. Mem. Saginaw Valley Rehab. Center, 1973—. Served with USNR, 1945-46. Mem. Indsl. Marketers Detroit, Bus., Profl. Advertisers Assn. Presbyn. (ruling elder, trustee). Kiwanian (pres. Saginaw 1971). Author: Bench Saw Techniques, 1968. Patentee disposable cartop carrier. Home: 124 Larch St Saginaw MI 48602 Office: Parker Willox Fairchild & Campbell Inc 808 N Michigan Ave Saginaw MI 48602

HARGROVE, RICHARD JOHN, historian; b. N.Y.C., May 29, 1941; s. Richard Joseph and Grace Agnes (Weibel) H.; B.A., Adelphi Coll., Garden City, N.Y., 1965; M.A. (scholar), Duke U., 1968, Ph.D. (Woodrow Wilson fellow), 1971; m. Anne Elizabeth Chard, June 6, 1970; 1 son, Andrew Wilson. Temp. instr. history Central Mich. U., 1969-70; asst. prof. history Western Ill. U., Macomb, 1970—. Mem. Am. Hist. Assn., Orgn. Am. Historians, Phi Alpha Theta. Episcopalian. Club: Philosophy (Macomb). Home: 1131 Bobby Ave Macomb IL 61455 Office: Dept History Western Ill Univ Macomb IL 61455

HARHAY, WARREN CHARLES, electric vehicle mfg. co. exec.; b. Cleve., Aug. 3, 1943; s. Joseph Stephen and Hedwig (Krucke) H.; student Kent State U., 1962-66; B.A., Cleve. State U., 1969; m. Marcie Lee Gibson, June 10, 1967; children—Matthew, Marshall, Mitchell. Field service engr., Ohio Sound Systems, Northeast Ohio, 1964-67; broadcast studio and transmitter engr., Stas. WERE, WJW, WMMS, Cleve., 1967-69; sr. instr. electronics, Normandy High Sch., Parma, Ohio, 1969-73; pres. Electric Vehicle Assos., Inc., Cleve., 1973—; pres. EVA/Chloride Corp.; dir. EVA/Chloride Electrobus EVA/Chloride Electrovan. Ordained deacon, ruling elder, chmn. stewardship com. United Presbyterian Church. Mem. IEEE, Soc. Automotove Engrs. Expert witness, U.S. Congress, 1974, Dept. Transp., 1977; contbr. tech. papers to confs. Home: 6374 Fry Rd Brook Park OH 44142 Office: 9100 Bank St Cleveland OH 44125

HARIMAN, DONALD GEORGE, chiropractor; b. Grand Forks, N.D., Feb. 4, 1925; s. George E. and Emma Lou (Cowger) H.; B.S., U. N.D., 1947; D.C., Nat. Coll. Chiropractic, 1950; m. Darlyne Lee Hamilton, Aug. 17, 1947; children—Robert Donald, Ann Maria, Jean Louise. Practice chiropractic medicine, Grand Forks, N.D.; mem. postgrad. faculty in roentgenology Can. Meml. Chiropractic Coll. Served with USNR, 1943-46. Diplomate Am. Chiropractic Bd. Roentgenology. Fellow Can. Chiropractic Coll. Roentgenology, Internat. Coll. Chiropractors; mem. Am. Chiropractic Coll. Roentgenologists, Am. Chiropractic Bd. Roentgenology (sec. 1970—), Am., N.D. (sec.-treas. 1954-66, pres. 1970-71) chiropractic assns., N.D. Bd. Chiropractic Examiners (sec. 1969—), Grand Forks C. of C. (chmn. capital funds review bd. 1970—), Sigma Alpha Epsilon, Lambda Phi Delta. Democrat. Presbyn. (elder). Mason. Club: Grand Forks Country. Home: 1616 Riverside Dr Grand Forks ND 58201 Office: 1610 S Washington St Grand Forks ND 58201

HARING, DAVID ALVIN, food co. exec.; b. Akron, Ohio, Feb. 10, 1945; s. Stanley Alvin and Harriet Marie (Stark) H.; B.S., Baldwin-Wallace Coll., 1967; M.B.A., Ohio State U., 1973; m. Luella Mae Wiley, June 10, 1967; children—Douglas, Brian, Bradford. Porgrammer, systems analyst Chem. Abstracts Service, Columbus, Ohio, 1967-71; mgr. systems and programming Borden, Inc., Columbus, 1971-75; dir. mgmt. info. services Tremco, Inc., Cleve., 1975-77; dir. systems and data processing The Stouffer Corp.; Cleve., 1977—. Recipient Theodore O. Hoffman edn. grant Borden, Inc., 1973. Lutheran. Home: 6713 Duneden Ave Solon OH 44139 Office: 1375 Euclid Ave Cleveland OH 44115

HARKER, JACK VINCENT, packing co. exec.; b. Le Mars, Iowa, Sept. 23, 1925; s. John Vincent and Eleanor Joan (Carlton) H.; B.B.A., Bradley U., 1950; m. Dorothy Ross, July 21, 1950; children—Susan, Vicki, Jim. Partner, Harkers Wholesale Meat Co., Inc., Le Mars, 1950-62, pres., 1962—; dir. Le Mars Savs. Bank. Trustee Floyd Valley Hosp. Served with Constrn. Bn., USNR, 1943-45. Mem. Nat. Assn. Meat Purveyors (dir.), C. of C. (dir.), Am. Mgmt. Assn. Republican. Methodist. Clubs: Lions, Elks. Home: 624 4th Ave SE Le Mars IA 51031 Office: 527 8th Ave SW Le Mars IA 51031

HARKEY, WILLIAM GEORGE, research exec.; b. Chgo., Aug. 27, 1914; s. William George and Leona Caroline (Tetzke) H.; Asso. Bus. Adminstrn., Central YMCA Coll. Chgo., 1936; postgrad. U. Chgo., 1938; Advanced Mgmt. Program Harvard, 1946; m. Naomi Jean McDermott, Oct. 12, 1947. Copywriter, research asst. Marsteller Advt. Agy., Sears Roebuck, Chgo., 1937-47; account exec. Price, Hedrick & Tanner, advt. agy., Saginaw, Mich., 1947-54, Parker Ad Agy., Saginaw, 1954-56; prin. Whipple & Black Advt. Agy., Saginaw, 1956-59; mktg. mgr. Ultra Carbon Corp., Bay City, Mich., 1959-64; founder, dir. Northwood Inst. Research Center, Midland, Mich., 1964-76, Northwood Inst. Press, 1976—. dir. Gen. Graphites Corp., Bay City. Pub. relations chmn. Saginaw chpt. ARC, 1950-52, Midland chpt., 1973-76; with pub. relations Family Soc. Saginaw, 1952-54; adminstrv. bd. mem. Northwood Inst., 1964-76. Served to capt. USAAF, 1942-46. Recipient Idea Man award Indsl. Marketing Publ., 1960; letter of commendation Pres. Nixon, 1958. Mem. Am. Assn. Higher Edn. Presbyterian (elder). Club: Tri-City Advertising. Author: The Expense Account, 1968; Speak Out, 1976; Appreciating the Nine Fine, 1977. Editorial bd. Community Edn. Jour. Home: 2200 Wingate Village Midland MI 48640 Office: Northwood Inst Press Midland MI 48640

HARKIN, THOMAS RICHARD, congressman; b. Cumming, Iowa, Nov. 19, 1939; s. Patrick and Frances Harkin; B.S., Iowa State U., 1962; J.D., Catholic U. Am., 1972; m. Ruth Raduenz, July 6, 1968; 1 dau., Amy. Staff aide to Congressman Neal Smith, 1969-70; mem. staff U.S. House Select Com. on U.S. Involvement in S.E. Asia, 1970; admitted to Iowa bar, 1972; mem. 94th-95th Congresses from 5th Iowa dist., mem. sci. and tech. com., agr. com.; atty. Polk County (Iowa) Legal Aid Soc., 1973. Bd. dirs. SANE, Iowa Consumers League. Served as lt. USN, 1962-67. Named Outstanding Young Alumnus, Iowa State U., 1974. Mem. Iowa Bar Assn. Democrat. Home: 3412 Ontario Ames IA 50010 Office: 324 Cannon House Office Bldg Washington DC 20515

HARKINS, DAVY JOE, veterinarian; b. Paola, Kans., July 21, 1948; s. Dennis Max and Harriet Ilo (Carter) H.; student Kans. State Tchrs. Coll., 1965-66; B.S. in Biology, Kans. State U., 1967, D.V.M., 1971; m. Mary Gail Klemm, May 15, 1972; children—Amanda Jo, Jamie Michelle, Joseph Andrew. Veterinarian, El Dorado (Kans.) Animal Clinic, 1971-76, owner, 1976—. Mem. Am., Kans. veterinary med. assns. Roman Catholic. Club: K.C. Home: 1349 W Olive St El Dorado KS 67042 Office: 111 E Locust St El Dorado KS 67042

HARKINS, MICHAEL JOSEPH, ednl. adminstr.; b. Omaha, Mar. 24, 1949; s. Leonard Joseph and Virginia Marie (Saitta) H.; B.S., in Edn., U. Nebr., 1970, M.A. in History, 1973; M.A. in Ednl. Adminstrn., Concordia Coll., River Forest, Ill., 1976. Faculty asso., English, history, U. Nebr., Omaha, 1969-73; evaluation specialist Ill. Office Edn., Springfield, 1974-75; tchr. pub. schs., Glenview, Ill., 1973-76; prin. Pius X High Sch., Lincoln, Nebr., 1976—. Mem. Omaha Mayor's Com. for Establishment Urban History Archives and Mus., 1973. Colonial Williamsburg fellow, hist. adminstrn., 1973; Fulbright-Hayes scholar, 1976. Mem. Nebr. Hist. Soc., Nat. Assn. Secondary Sch. Prins., Phi Alpha Theta. Democrat. Roman Catholic. Club: Optimists. Contbr. articles in field to profl. jours. Home: 5521 Woolworth Ave Omaha NE 68106 Office: 6000 A St Lincoln NE 68510

HARKNESS, KENNETH ALFRED, mfg. co. exec.; b. Scott City, Kans., Jan. 5, 1930; s. Charles E. and Delia (Deng) H.; B.S. in Engring., Kans. State U., 1951, M.S. in Engring., 1955; postgrad. (NSF Faculty Sci fellow), Ohio State U., 1963-65; m. Vada Viola Wright, Aug. 27, 1948; children—Diane Lynn, Brian Kent, Jane Ella. Faculty Kans. State U., Manhattan, 1952-55; faculty dept. agrl. engring., Ohio State U., Columbus, 1956-73; owner IDEAnamics, Auto Pac Systems, Inc., Visual Communication Systems and Slow Vehicle Emblem Cos., Columbus, 1963—. Pres. Whetstone Sr. High Sch. PTA, 1971-72, Cranbrook Elementary Sch. P.T.A., 1965-66. Chmn. adv. bd. Ohio State U. br. YMCA, 1960-61. NSF Faculty Sci. fellow, 1963-64; Danforth Found. grantee, 1964-65; recipient Resolution of Commendation, 105th Ohio Gen. Assembly, 1963; Certificate of Commendation, Nat. Safety Council, 1964. Mem. Am. Soc. Agrl. Engrs., Am. Soc. Engring. Edn., AAAS, Am. Inst. Biol. Scientists, Phi Kappa Phi, Sigma Tau, Gamma Sigma Delta, Blue Key, Tau Beta Pi. Inventor Slow Vehicle emblem, automatic grocery bundler for checkout counters in supermarkets. Home: 1533 Rayne Ln Columbus OH 43220

HARL, NEIL EUGENE, economist, lawyer, educator; b. Appanoose County, Iowa, Oct. 9, 1933; s. Herbert Peter and Bertha Catherine (Bonner) H.; B.S., Iowa State U., 1955, Ph.D., 1965; J.D., U. Iowa, 1961; m. Darlene Ramona Harris, Sept. 7, 1952; children—James Brent, Rodney Scott. Field editor Wallace's Farmer, 1957-58; research asso. U.S. Dept. Agr., Iowa City and Ames, Iowa, 1958-64; asso. prof. econs. Iowa State U., Ames, 1964-67, prof., 1967—, Charles F. Curtiss Distinguished prof., 1976—. admitted to Iowa bar, 1961. Trustee Iowa State U. Agrl. Found., 1969—. Served to 1st lt., AUS, 1955-57; capt. USAR. Recipient outstanding tchr. award Iowa State U., 1973; outstanding extension program award Am. Agrl. Econ. Assn., 1970, award excellence in communicating research results, 1975, distinguished undergrad. tchr. award, 1976. Mem. Iowa State Bar, Am. Bar Assn., Am. Agrl. Econ. Assn. Author: Farm Estate and Business Planning, 1973, 2d edit., 1974, 3 edit., 1977. Contbr. articles to profl. publs. Producer ednl. films, audio and videotape programs. Home: 2821 Duff Ave Ames IA 50010

HARLAN, JACK RODNEY, geneticist; b. Washington, June 7, 1917; s. Harry Vaughn and Augusta (Griffing) H.; B.S. in Botany with distinction, George Washington U., 1938; Ph.D. in Genetics, U. Calif. at Berkeley, 1942; m. Jean Yocum, Aug. 4, 1939; children—Sue (Mrs. Robert Hughes), Harry, Sherry (Mrs. Mark Wilson), Richard Edwin. Research asst. Tela R.R. Co., Honduras, 1942; geneticist Dept. Agr., Woodward, Okla., 1942-51, Stillwater Okla., 1951-61; prof. agronomy Okla. State U., 1951-66; prof. plantgenetics U. Ill. at Urbana, 1966—; botanist Dept. of Agr. plant exploration and introduction, Turkey, Syria and Iraq, 1948, Iran, Afghanistan, Pakistan, India and Ethiopia, 1960; sr. staff mem. Iranian prehistoric project Oriental Inst. of U. Chgo., 1960, also Turkish prehistoric project, 1964. Fellow A.A.A.S., Am. Soc. Agronomy; mem. Crop Sci. Soc. Am. (pres. 1966), Am. Inst. Biol. Scientists, Bot. Soc. Am., Am. Soc. Agronomy, Nat. Acad. Scis., Phi Beta Kappa, Sigma Xi. Presbyn. (elder). Contbr. articles to profl. jours. Home: 1822 Crescent Dr Champaign IL 61820 Office: Crop Evolution Lab Agronomy Dept U Ill Urbana IL 61801

HARLAN, NORMAN RALPH, builder; b. Dayton, Ohio, Dec. 21, 1914; s. Joseph and Anna (Kaplan) H.; Indsl. Engring. degree U. Cin., 1937; m. Thelma Katz, Sept. 4, 1955; children—Leslie, Todd. Pres. Am. Constrn. Corp., Dayton, 1949—, Mainline Investment Corp., 1951—, Harlan, Inc., realtors; treas. Norman Estates, Inc. Mem. Dayton Real Estate Bd., Ohio Real Estate Assn., Nat. Assn. Real Estate Bds., C. of C., Pi Lambda Phi. Home: 303 Glenridge Rd Kettering OH 45429 Office: 2451 S Dixie Hwy Dayton OH 45409

HARLEY, JAMES PRESTON, educator; b. Junction City, Kans., Jan. 20, 1943; s. James O. and Betty (Woodward) Harley; B.A., Washburn U., 1965; M.A., Bowling Green State U., 1968, Ph.D., 1971; 1 dau., Jennifer Paige. Licensed psychologist, Wis. Research asso. dept. psychiatry U. Mich. Med. Sch., Ann Arbor, 1971-73; asst. prof. dept. neurology U. Wis. Med. Center for Health Scis., Madison, 1973—. Mem. Am., Wis. psychol. assns., AAAS, Internat. Neuropsychology Soc., Soc. for Psychophysiol. Research. Contbr. articles in field to profl. jours. Home: 4118 Sunset Ct Madison WI 53705 Office: 1954 E Washington Ave Madison WI 53704

HARLEY, RICHARD ARLEN, hosp. adminstr.; b. Portsmouth, Ohio, Feb. 18, 1931; s. William Paul and Martha Jane (Daniels) H.; ed. Ohio U.; m. Jean Papillon, May 20, 1951; children—Richard Arlen, William Henry. Loan mgr. Comml. Credit Corp., Huntington, W.Va., 1952-58; terminal mgr. Keystone Motor Express, Portsmouth, 1958-62; asst. adminstr. Scioto Meml. Hosp., Portsmouth, 1964-68; adminstr. So. Hills Hosp., Portsmouth, 1968-69, Madison County Hosp., London, Ohio, 1969—. Del. to Mid-Ohio Health Planning

Fedn., 1969—; mem. Madison County Health Planning Council, 1969—. Trustee Scioto Hills Baptist Youth Camp. Mem. Ohio Hosp. Fedn. Home: 77 Chrisman Ave London OH 43140 Office: 210 N Main St London OH 43140

HARLEY, ROBERT ELDEN, lawyer; b. Springfield, Ohio, Mar. 21, 1931; s. Charles William and Susie Ethel (Bayes) H.; student Bowling Green State U., 1950-51, 51-52; B.S., Ohio State U., 1955; LL.B., 1956; LL.M., N.Y.U., 1963; m. Martha Louise Thompson, June 26, 1964. Admitted to Ohio bar, 1957; asso. Arthur Young and Co., N.Y.C., 1957-58; asso. Arthur Andersen and Co., N.Y.C., 1958-60; asso. Peat Marwick Mitchell and Co., Cin., 1960-62; asso. firm Martin, Browne, Hull and Harper, Springfield, Ohio, 1963—, partner, 1971. Trustee Springfield Bar and Law Library Assn. Served with AUS, 1957. Mem. Am., Ohio bar assns., Dayton Estate Planning Council, Cowan Lake Sailing Assn. Mason (master 1970). Club: Dayton Cycling. Home: 2870 Ironwood Dr Springfield OH 45504 Office: 203 First National Bank Bldg Springfield OH 45501

HARLOW, BARBARA ANN, hotel pub. relations dir.; b. Kansas City, Kans.; d. James Vernon and Jennie Alice (Flint) Bigler; B.A., U. Nebr., 1970; children—Ronald Eric Harlow, Gregory Brent Harlow. Exec. dir. March of Dimes, Omaha, 1970-71, regional cons., Kansas City, Mo., 1971-73, nat. cons., 1973-74; pub. relations dir. Crown Center Hotel, Kansas City, 1974—; cons. women in mgmt. Active pub. relations Clark Welfare Council, Clark AFB, P.I.; counselor Neighborhood Youth Corps, Kansas City; mem. women's div. Kansas City Philharmonic Orch. Mem. Pub. Relations Soc. Am., Kansas City C. of C. Club: Kansas City Ski. Home: 7615 E Gregory Blvd Kansas City MO 64133 Office: 1 Pershing Rd Kansas City MO 64108

HARLOW, CHARLES ALTON, educator; b. New Boston, Tex., Mar. 14, 1940; s. Aubrey and Geneva (Perry) H.; B.S. in Elec. Engring., U. Tex., 1963, Ph.D., 1967; m. Elaine Kenas, Aug. 19, 1961; children—Raelon Jil, Janda Lea. Asso. prof. elec. engring. U. Mo., 1970-72, prof., 1972—; vis. prof. U. Calif. at Berkeley, 1974. Mem. IEEE, Assn. for Computing Machinery, Sigma Xi, Tau Beta Pi, Eta Kappa Nu. Contbr. articles to profl. jours. Home: 3613 Southland Dr Columbia MO 65201

HARM, PAUL FREDRICK, city ofcl.; b. Elwood, Nebr., Dec. 28, 1915; s. Fred Herman and Rose Augusta (Berndt) H.; student Nebr. Coll. Commerce, Hastings, 1937, Mont. State U., 1953-55, U. Colo., 1956-63; m. Marie Kathryn Snyder, Mar. 13, 1939; 1 dau., Merleglea (Mrs. Victor Olsen). Implement dealer John Deere, Elwood, 1946-52; mgr. Broken Bow (Nebr.) C. of C., 1953-55, Alliance, 1955-58; gen. mgr. C. of C. Scottsbluff, 1958-64; with Nebr. State C. of C., 1965; city adminstr., Norfolk, 1966—. Legislative chmn. Nebr. Environmental Control Council, 1972-73, chmn., 1974-76. Mem. Nebr. City Mgmt. Assn. (pres. 1972-73), League Nebr. Municipalities (pres. 1973-74), Nat. League Cities (state chmn. revenue finance com. 1972—), C. of C. Execs. Assn. Elk, Lion. Home: 2206 Hardison Dr Norfolk NE 68701 Office: PO Box 209 Norfolk NE 68701

HARMAN, ROBERT MALEY, real estate, ins. broker; b. New Albany, Ind., Dec. 20, 1928; s. Robert Chris and Mary Bunelle (Maley) H.; student Lincoln Meml. U., 1947; m. Helen Marie Ulrey, Sept. 14, 1952; children—Janet Lynn (Mrs. Daniel L. Threlkeld), Kathleen Sue. Broker, Harman Agy., Inc., Lebanon, Ind., 1950—, v.p., 1950-65, pres., 1965—. Drive chmn. bd. dirs. Boone United Fund, 1957-58, treas., 1958-59, pres., 1959-60; chmn. Boone County Ind. Heart Assn., 1955-56; city chmn. Crossroads Rehab. Center Indpls., 1954-55. Served with USNR, 1948-50. Recipient Distinguished Service award Lebanon Jaycees, 1960. Mem. Boone County Bd. Realtors (pres. 1953). Baptist (past deacon, trustee). Clubs: Kiwanis (charter mem. Lebanon, pres. 1961, lt. gov. 1977-78, Key Club chmn. founder club Lebanon High Sch. 1971), Masons, Shriners, Elks. Home: 1304 N East St Lebanon IN 46052 Office: 212 W Main St Lebanon IN 46052

HARMET, A(RNOLD) RICHARD, editor; b. Chgo., Nov. 13, 1932; s. Alfred Aloysius and Evelyn Amelia (Riesche) H.; A.B., Ripon Coll., 1954; M.J.S., Northwestern U., 1958; m. Joan Harriet Morris, Dec. 28, 1957; children—Lynn Anne, Andrew Morris. Mng. editor Popular Mechanic Press, Chgo., 1958-61; dir. publs. Armour Research Found., Chgo., 1961-63; dir. lit. counseling A.M.A., Chgo., 1963-65; with Field Enterprises Ednl. Corp., Chgo., 1965—, v.p., exec. editor World Book Ency., 1969—. Served to 1st lt. AUS, 1954-56. Mem. A.A.A.S., Nat. Assn. Sci. Writers, Sigma Delta Chi, Chgo. Headline Club. Home: 635 Lake Rd Glen Ellyn IL 60137 Office: Merchandise Mart Room 262 Chicago IL 60654

HARMISON, CHARLES RICE, biochemist, educator; b. Lewistown, Mont., Feb. 28, 1916; s. Charles Rice and Frances (Bays) H.; student Mont. State U., 1933-35, Intermountain Union Coll., 1935-36; B.A., Mont. State U., 1937; Ph.D., U. Ill., 1941; m. Helen Buker, Jan. 3, 1944; children—Mary, Bette, Nancy. Postdoctorate fellow Harvard Med. Sch., 1940-42; chemist Prolamine Products Co., Columbus, Ohio, 1942-43; biochemist Armour Labs., Chgo., 1943-45, Ortho Pharm. Corp., Rariton, N.J., 1945-51; asso. Coll. Physicians and Surgeons, Columbia U., 1951-58; asst. prof. Sch. Medicine Wayne State U., Detroit, 1958-73, asso. prof., 1973—, biophysicist dept. psychiatry, 1969—. Fellow AAAS, Council on Arteriosclerosis of Am. Heart Assn., Gerontol. Soc., Am. Inst. Chemists; mem. Am. Chem. Soc. (sect. chmn. 1967-68), Biophys. Soc., Am. Soc. Biol. Chemists, Internat. Soc. Quantum Biology, AAUP (chpt. pres. 1967-68), N.Y. Acad. Scis., Sigma Xi. Home: 663 Barrington St Grosse Pointe MI 48230 Office: Lafayette Clinic 951 E Lafayette St Detroit MI 48207

HARMON, DENVER CHARLES, dentist; b. Camden, Mich., Feb. 19, 1929; s. Fred C. and Ilah Bird (Woodring) H.; B.A., Western Mich. U., 1950; D.D.S., U. Detroit, 1954; m. Caroline Louise Stiefel, Aug. 2, 1958; children—Steven, Michael, Anne. Dentist Receiving Hosp.-Dental Clinic, Detroit, 1954; practice gen. dentistry, Big Rapids, Mich., 1957—; pres. profl. corp., 1972—. Mem. Big Rapids Civic Council, 1964-67; pres. Riverview P.T.A., 1965-67. Served to capt., Dental Corp., USAF, 1954-56. Mem. Am., Mich. dental assns., W. Mich. Dental Soc., Episcopalian (vestryman 1961-64, 71-74, sr. warden 1964, 72, recipient Bishops Service Cross, 1965). Home: 707 Cypress St Big Rapids MI 49307 Office: 229 S Warren Ave Big Rapids MI 49307

HARMON, JAN MARY, guidance counselor; b. Portland, Oreg., Dec. 6, 1942; d. Dave D. and Bernice W. (Classen) H.; B.A., Cardinal Stritch Coll., Milw., 1967; M.Ed., Loyola U., Chgo., 1974. Joined Sisters St. Francis Assisi, Roman Catholic Ch.; spl. edn. tchr. Lt. J.P. Kennedy Sch., Palos Park, Ill., 1967-74; elementary sch. counselor St. Veronica Sch., Milw., 1974—, St. Gregory the Great Sch., Milw., 1974—, Immaculate Conception Sch., 1977—, coordinator elementary sch. counseling services Archdiocese Milw., 1977—; instr. Cardinal Stritch Coll., Milw., 1975—. Mem. Am., Wis. (treas. 1977-79) personnel and guidance assns., Am. Sch. Counselor Assn., Wis. Sch. Counselor Assn., Milw. Archdiocesan Catholic Guidance Council (sec. 1974-75, pres. 1975-76), Psychol. Assn. Cardinal Stritch Coll. Contbr. articles to profl. jours. Home: 353 E Norwich St Milwaukee WI 53207

HARMON, VERNA LEOLA CLAY (MRS. FLOYD HARMON), ret. med. assistance cons.; b. Roselm, Ohio; d. William Oliver and Minnie (Jackson) Clay; R.N., W.A. Foote Hosp. Tng. Sch., 1925; student Cin. Coll. Embalming, 1950; m. Floyd Harmon, May 8, 1926 (dec. 1971); 1 dau., Geraldine (Mrs. Jack Schaweker) (dec. 1966). Pvt. duty nurse, Albion, Mich., Jackson, Mich., Ann Arbor, Mich., Niles, Mich., Ft. Wayne, Ind., Dayton, Ohio, Findlay, McComb, Ohio, 1925-48; office nurse, Dayton, 1927-28; adminstrv. asst. Miller-McComb Hosp., 1948-50; exec. sec., nurse cons. Am. Cancer Soc. of Hancock County, Ohio, 1951-59; co-owner, Asst. Harmon Funeral Home, McComb, 1930-66; med. assistance cons. Toledo dist. Ohio Dept. Pub. Welfare, 1966-69, adminstrv. specialist, utilization rev. Bur. Med. Assistance, 1969-71; field rep. Ohio Soc. for Crippled Children and Adults, Columbus, 1962-65. Instr. classes home nursing ARC, 1942-43, mem. adv. com. Home Health Nursing Service Hancock County, 1967-74; sec. to adv. council Home Health Agency of Findlay-Hancock County, 1969-70, 77—; sec. Adv. Council for Home Health Care Services Hancock County, 1973-74; pres. Hancock County Cancer Soc., 1973-75. Dist. religion Gen. Fedn. Women's Clubs, 1960-62; mem. Nat. Council on Aging; former coordinator aging Hancock County for Ohio Commn. on Aging; charter pres. McComb Community Garden Club. Trustee Blanchard Valley Hosp., Findlay; life bd. dirs. Hancock County unit Am. Cancer Soc. Recipient citation Am. Cancer Soc., 1958, meritorious service citation Ohio Pub. Health Dept., 1961. Mem. Ohio Funeral Dirs. Assn., Bus. and Profl. Women's Club, Progress Study Club McComb (pres. 1955-56), Nat., Ohio Rep. women's assns., Ohio Pub. Health Assn. (life), Am., Ohio nurses assns., Bus. and Profl. Women's Club, Blanchard Valley Hosp. Guild. Methodist. Mem. Order Eastern Star. Clubs: Nat. Travel; Zonta (charter Findlay). Author: Some of Verna's Verses, 1977. Home: 201 E Pearl St Findlay OH 45840

HARMS, WILMER ALLEN, physician; b. Hillsboro, Kans., July 2, 1922; s. William W. and Anna C. (Thiessen) H.; student Tabor Coll., 1941-42, 48-50; A.B., Kans. U., 1952, M.D., 1956; certificate in basic scis. ophthalmology Harvard, 1968; m. Esther M. Ediger, Oct. 21, 1946; children—Willard Keith, Kevin Lynn. Intern, Bethany Hosp., Kansas City, Kans., 1956-57; practice gen. medicine, Hesston, Kan., 1957-68; fellow clin. ophthalmology Johns Hopkins, 1969; resident ophthalmology Okla. U. Med. Center, 1969-72; asso. Hertzler Clinic, Halstead, Kans., 1972—; pres. med. staff Bethel Deaconess Hosp., Newton, Kans., Halstead Hosp., 1975—; pres. Hesston Assos., 1962-68, Hertzler Clin. Assos., 1975—; clin. instr. ophthalmology Med. Sch., Okla. U., 1972-76, asst. clin. prof., 1976—. Vice pres. Hesston Builders, Inc., 1965—. Pres. Hesston Credit Union, 1961-68, 76—. Diplomate Am. Bd. Ophthalmology and Otolaryngology. Fellow Am. Acad. Family Physicians; mem. A.M.A., Kan., Harvey County (pres. 1967), Christian med. socs. Home: 205 E 8th St Halstead KS 67056

HARNAR, ROBERT HIRAM, JR., pub. relations ofcl., automobile co. exec.; b. Lawrence, Kans., Dec. 26, 1926; s. Robert Hiram and Lenore Genevieve (Cashion) H.; B.S. in Bus., U. So. Calif., 1951; m. Marilyn Hodges, Aug. 17, 1952; children—Ronald Scott, Lori Ann, Jeffrey Dean. Bur. mgr. Copley Newspapers, Los Angeles, 1952-57; with Ford Motor Co., Los Angeles, 1957-60, Dearborn, Mich., 1961-63, N.Y.C., 1964-68, Midwest pub. relations, Chgo., 1969—. Mem. pub. relations com. Chgo. Crusade of Mercy, 1975. Bd. dirs., v.p. Cosmopolitan C. of C., 1974—. Served with paratroops, AUS, 1945-47. Mem. Nat. Alliance of Businessmen (pub. relations adv. com. 1973—), Pub. Relations Soc. Am. Presbyn. (ruling elder). Club: Chgo. Athletic Assn. Office: 1 E Wacker Dr Chicago IL 60601

HARNESS, EDWARD GRANVILLE, soap products mfr.; b. Marietta, Ohio, Dec. 17, 1918; s. Lewis Nye and Mary (McKinney) H.; A.B., Marietta Coll., 1940; m. Mary McCrady Chaney, Aug. 7, 1943; children—Frances Ann (Mrs. Daniel J. Jones), Edward Granville, Robert R. With Proctor & Gamble Co., Cin., 1940—, v.p. paper products div., 1963-66, v.p.-group exec., dir., 1966-70, exec. v.p., 1970-71, pres., 1971—, chmn. bd., 1974—; dir. Exxon Corp. Chmn. bd. trustees Marietta Coll., Ohio Found. Ind. Colls., Cin. Children's Home. Served with USAAF, 1942-46. Mem. Grocery Mfrs. Am., Conf. Bd., Bus. Council. Clubs: Commercial, Carmargo, Queen City, Commonwealth (Cin.). Office: 301 E 6th St Cincinnati OH 45202

HARPER, CHARLES LITTLE, steel co. exec.; b. Evanston, Ill., Mar. 23, 1930; s. H. Mitchell and Margaret (Little) H.; B.S., Princeton U., 1952; m. Alice Patterson Fall, Oct. 19, 1955; children—Charles, Margaret, Greta, Alice, and Serena Harper. Various positions with The H.M. Harper Co., now pres., dir. ITT-Harper, Morton Grove, Ill. Served to lt. USNR, 1952-54. Mem. Am. Soc. Metals, Am. Inst. Mining Engrs., Am. Iron and Steel Inst., Midwest Indsl. Mgmt. Assn. (dir.), Newcomen Soc. Clubs: Economic of Chicago, Executive, Glen View. Home: 644 Pine Ln Winnetka IL 60093 Office: 8200 Lehigh Ave Morton Grove IL 60053

HARPER, DONALD DEAN, educator; b. Zanesville, Ohio, Feb. 8, 1950; s. William Everett and Marie (Wilson) H.; B.S., Ohio State U., 1972; student Xavier U., 1973—; m. Patricia Jean Abele, Oct. 5, 1971; children—Douglas William, Jill Christine. Tchr. Eng., 8th and 9th grades, Milford Jr. High Sch., Cin., 1972-75, Sandy Ln. Jr. High Sch., Duncan Falls, Ohio, 1975—; cons. sch. dropouts Muskingum (Ohio) County Schs., 1975-77; participant writing clinic, Duncan Falls, 1975-77. Coach, Little League Baseball, Duncan Falls, 1975—. Recipient Curtis award for contbns. to sch. and community, Philo, Ohio, 1968. Mem. Poetry Pen Pals, NEA, Nat. Council Tchrs. of English, Ohio Assn. English Tchrs., Ohio Edn. Assn., Am. Profl. Guidance Assn. Contbr. poetry to New Voices For 1978. Home: 5690 Adamsville Rd Zanesville OH 43701 Office: Mill St Duncan Falls OH 44734

HARPER, LEO MERLE, sch. adminstr.; b. Vinton County, Ohio, Apr. 4, 1918; s. Lewis Edgar and Cora Edna (Dye) H.; student Rio Grande Coll., 1939-40; B.S., Butler U., 1948, M.S., 1949; Ed.D., Ind. U., 1960; m. Rita Marie Hill, Feb. 25, 1941; children—Betty Marie (Mrs. John Dell), Edgar Lee. R.R. brakeman B. & O. R.R., Indpls., 1942-49; tchr. Indpls. Pub. Schs., 1948-57, prin., 1957-70; prin. M.S.D. Lawrence Twp. Sch., Indpls., 1970—. Lectr., Butler U., 1962, 68, Ind. U.-Purdue U. at Indpls., 1974-75; pres. Avon Schs. Holding Corp., 1968-69. Served with AUS, 1943-46, PTO, 50-52, Korea. Mem. Ind. Elementary Prins., Am. Legion, Phi Delta Kappa. Home: Route 2 Box 211 I Zionsville IN 46077

HARPER, RAMEY WILSON, railroad exec.; b. Muskogee, Okla., Apr. 15, 1920; s. Edgar Batte and Eva (Stephens) H.; student Westminster Coll., 1938-40; B.S., U. Ariz., 1942; m. Elizabeth Martha Smith, July 9, 1966; children—Elizabeth Martha, Dorothea Louise. Sr. accountant Arthur Andersen & Co., Chgo., 1946-49; gen. auditor Midland Valley R.R. Co. and affiliated cos., Muskogee, 1949-64; spl. asst. staff studies A.T. & S.F. Ry. Co., Chgo., 1964-67, exec. asst. finance, 1967-70, v.p. finance, 1970—; treas. Santa Fe Industries, Inc., Chgo., 1967—; v.p. Gulf Central Pipeline Co., Chgo., 1969—; v.p. finance, dir. Santa Fe Pipeline, Inc., 1971—; dir. Trailer Train Co., Am. Rail Box Car Co. Served to comdr. USNR, 1942-46. Mem. Financial Mgrs. Assn., Chgo. Assn. Commerce and Industry, Phi Delta Theta. Presbyn. Club: Chicago Athletic Assn. Home: 399 Fullerton Pkwy Chicago IL 60614 Office: 80 E Jackson Blvd Chicago IL 60604

HARPER, RICHARD ALLEN, veterinarian; b. West Frankfort, Ill., May 4, 1939; s. Leonard and Agnes Marjorie (Throgmorton) H.; B.S., So. Ill. U., 1962; B.S., D.V.M., U. Ill., 1973; m. Janet Kay Hubbard, Oct. 7, 1960; children—Bradley Scott, Lisa Kay. Spl. agt. Office of Spl. Investigation, Tinker AFB, Oklahoma City, 1962-66; computer programmer Nat. Cash Register Co., Carbondale, Ill., 1966-68; pvt. practice veterinary medicine, Johnston City, Ill., 1973—. Served with USAF, 1962-66. Mem. Am., Ill., So. Ill. veterinary med. assns., Nat. Heartworm Soc. So. Bapt. Home: Rural Route 1 Johnston City IL 62951 Office: Rural Route 1 West Frankfort IL 62896

HARPER, ROGER WESLEY, consumer products co. exec.; b. Youngstown, Ohio, July 11, 1933; s. Harry Edward and Helen Marjorie (Young) H.; B.A., Wittenberg U., 1956. Sales rep. Shell Oil Co., Cleve., 1958-62, Chicopee Mills, Inc., N.Y.C., 1962-64; sales rep. H.H. Cutler Co., Grand Rapids, Mich., 1964-68; exec. v.p. Scharp Contemporary, Inc., Columbus, Ohio, 1968—, also dir.; dir. Am. Colortype Distbrs. of Mich., Inc., Livonia, Am. Leather Village, Inc., Columbus. Served with U.S. Army, 1956-58. Lutheran. Home: 1084 Iron Gate Lane Columbus OH 43213 Office: 3551 E Fulton St Columbus OH 43227

HARRAH, BETTY LOUISE, ednl. adminstr.; b. Bloomington, Ind., Mar. 2, 1926; d. Herbert S. and Elsie Zola (Whaley) H.; A.B., Ind. U., 1948; M.A., Roosevelt U., 1963, Ed.D., 1969. Commd. ensign U.S. Navy, 1950, advanced through grades to comdr., 1964; staff, comdr. Western Sea Frontier, San Francisco, 1954-56; staff Naval Air Tech. Tng. Center, Memphis, 1959-61; staff adminstrv. command, Great Lakes, Ill., 1961; with reserves, 1961-73, ret., 1973; residence counselor U. Fla., Gainesville, 1964-66; head counselor Ind. U., Bloomington, 1967-69; dir. residence hall personnel and programs Ball State U., Muncie, 1969—. Mem. Am. Assn. for Higher Edn., Am. Coll. Personnel Assn., Am. Personnel and Guidance Assn., Nat. Assn. Student Personnel Adminstrs., Nat. Assn. Women Deans Adminstrs. and Counselors. Club: Altrusa. Home: 1001 Alden Rd Muncie IN 47304 Office: Lucina Hall Ball State U Muncie IN 47304

HARRELL, JOHN LIMPUS, charitable inst. exec.; b. Frankfort, Ind., May 9, 1918; s. Jesse Albert and Mildred Vale (Limpus) H.; A.B., Franklin Coll., 1940; M.A., Ohio State U., 1941; m. Helen Vernon Schumacher, Nov. 23, 1943; 1 dau., Helen F. Asst. dir. Duluth (Minn.) Community Fund, 1941-43; exec. sec. Community Chest and War Chest, Green Bay, Wis., 1943-46; exec. dir. Community Chest, Watertown, N.Y., 1946-50, Cedar Rapids, Iowa, 1950-54; exec. dir. United Way of Wyandotte County, Kans., 1954—. Med. field agt. SSS, 1943-46; mem. Human Relations Commn., Kansas City, 1966-75, vice chmn., 1970-71; mem. Manpower Planning Bd., City-County Consortia, 1975—; mem. citizens adv. com. Kans. Dept. Social Rehab. Services, 1976—; bd. dirs., Cons. Econ. Opportunity Found., Inc., 1965—, recipient Service Appreciation award, 1974, Founder's award, 1976. Recipient Silver Bow award, Boy Scouts Am., 1972, Com. award, YMCA, 1972, Service award United Way of Am., 1972. Mem. C. of C., Nat., Kans. confs. social welfare, Kappa Delta Rho. Republican. Baptist. Rotarian. Home: 8135 Greeley Ave Kansas City KS 66109 Office: PO Box 2391 710 Minnesota Ave Kansas City KS 66110

HARRELL, SAMUEL RUNNELS, business exec.; b. Noblesville, Ind., Nov. 25, 1897; s. Samuel and Vivian (Voss) H.; B.S. in Econs., U. Pa., 1919; LL.B., Yale, 1924; m. Mary Robertson Evans, Oct. 10, 1925 (div. Mar. 1972); children—Evans Malott, Mary Eleanor, Samuel Macy. First employed, Land Title & Trust Co., Phila.; admitted to Ind. bar, 1922; former chmn. bd., chmn. exec. com. Gen. Grain, Inc., now hon. chmn., adviser; pres. Acme Evans Co., Inc. 1945-59, chmn. bd., 1954—; pres. Acme Goodrich, Inc., 1947-52, chmn. bd., chmn. exec. com., 1952—; pres., chmn. bd. Tidewater Grain Co., Phila.; chmn. exec. com., chmn. bd., dir. The Early & Daniel Co., Cin., from 1946, now hon. chmn., adviser; dir. Cleve. Grain Co., 1950-58, pres., chmn. bd., 1955-58; pres. Harrell & Co.; dir. Terminal Elevator Grain Mchts. Assn., N.Am. Export Grain Assn., Indpls. Union Ry. Co.; Chmn. bd. dirs. Indpls. Bd. Trade; mem. Chgo. Bd. Trade. Co-chmn. Ind. adv. com. on commerce, industry, agr., pub. relations. Served with Naval Aviation Pilot Div. of Naval Res., 1918. Chmn., trustee Nat. Found. for Edn. in Am. Citizenship, trustee U. Pa., 1940-50, Wharton Sch. Finance and Commerce, 1950-54; mem. vis. com. Harvard Grad. Sch. Edn., 1941-56; mem. adv. com. U.S. Banking and Currency Com.; del. Am. Legion to Paris, 1937. Mem. exec. council, nat. treas. Am. Heart Assn., 1947-48; founder Ind. Heart Found., Sagamores of Wabash; founder, charter mem. Acropolitan Research and Cultural Center. Mem. Ind. Millers Assn., (pres.), Am. Bar Assn., Am. Econ. Assn., Am. Polit. Sci. Assn., Acad. Polit. Sci., Am. Acad. Polit. and Social Sci. Am. Soc. for Pub. Adminstrn., Citizens Com. Hoover Commn., S.R., S.A.R., Delta Tau Delta, Phi Delta Phi. Presbyn. Mason (32 deg.). Clubs: Racquet, Sharswood Law (Phila.); Harvard Faculty (Cambridge); University (Chgo., N.Y.); Contemporary, Athletic, Lawyers, Literary, Pioneer, Pennsylvania, Yale (Indpls.); Queen City (Cin.); Pendennis (Louisville). Chmn. and editor Nat. Found. Press. Publisher: Fundamental American Principles. Home: care Valley Forge Farms Route 4 Noblesville IN 46060 Office: 902 Washington Ave Indianapolis IN 46204

HARRIMAN, RICHARD LEE, educator; b. Independence, Mo., Sept. 10, 1932; s. Walter S. and M. Eloise (Faulkner) H.; A.B., William Jewell Coll., 1953; M.A., Stanford U., 1959. Instr., asst. prof. English U. Dubuque, Iowa, 1960-62; asst. prof. English William Jewell College, Liberty, Missouri, 1962, acting head English dept., 1965-69, dir. fine arts program, 1965—, asso. prof., 1966—. Served from pvt. to cpl., AUS, 1953-55. Recipient Woodrow Wilson fellowship from Woodrow Wilson Fellowship Found., 1957. Mem. Shakespeare Assn. Am., Modern Language Assn., Assn. Coll. Univ. and Community Arts Adminstrs. (nat. exec. bd.), Nat. Council Tchrs. English, Am. Assn. U. Profs., Lambda Chi Alpha, Sigma Tau Delta, Alpha Psi Omega. Meth. Home: Route 5 Box 6 Liberty MO 64068

HARRINGTON, CATHRYN L., judge; b. Alexandria, Ky., May 1, 1917; d. William Courtney and Myrtle (Poe) Lamb; student U. Ky., 1937; A.B., Western Coll., 1938; J.D., U. Cin., 1941; m. Robert L. Harrington, Jan. 1, 1944; children—Ruth Angeline, Susan Dale. Admitted to Ky., Ohio bars, 1941; asso. Ebert, Cook & Burke, attys., Newport, Ky., 1941-44; mem. firm Harrington & Harrington, Van Wert, Ohio, 1944-58; spl. counsel for atty. gen. State of Ohio, 1957-58, probate-juvenile judge, Van Wert County, Ohio, 1958—, Mem. AAUW (pres. 1957-59), Nat. Council Juvenile Ct. Judges, Nat. Juvenile Ct. Found., Ohio Assn. of Juvenile Ct. Judges, Am., Ohio, Ky., Northwestern Ohio, Van Wert County (pres. 1955-57) bar assns., Assn. Ohio Probate Ct. of Judges, Phi Delta Delta (Cin. pres. 1940-41). Republican. Episcopalian. Home: 239 N Jefferson St Van Wert OH 45891 Office: Van Wert County Court House Van Wert OH 45891

HARRINGTON, DORIS VIRGINIA, educator, counselor; b. St. Louis, July 3; d. Ophelia Virginia (Mullins) Harrington; B.A., Harris Tchrs. Coll., 1961; M.Ed., St. Louis U., 1966, Ph.D., 1972. Tchr.

Mason Elementary Sch., St. Louis, 1961-66, counselor St. Louis Bd. Edn., 1966-68, coordinator Diagnostic Center, 1968-69, cons., 1969-70, counselor Lincoln High Sch., St. Louis, 1970-76; instructional coordinator Ames Magnet Sch., St. Louis, 1976—; counselor, cons. Met. Coll. St. Louis U., 1973-76. Bd. dirs. St. Louis Tchrs. Credit Union, 1977—. Mem. Assn. Non-White Concerns in Personnel and Guidance (editor nat. newsletter 1974-76), Am., Mo. personnel and guidance assns., St. Louis Assn. Black Psychologists, Mo. Assn. Non-White in Personnel and Guidance, Alpha Delta Kappa, Sigma Tau Delta. Methodist. Home: 4400 Lindell Blvd St Louis MO 63108 Office: 2900 Hadley St St Louis MO 63107

HARRINGTON, HARVEY DANIEL, II, design engr.; b. St. Paul, Sept. 26, 1941; s. Harvey Daniel and Marjorie Mary (Cusick) H.; A.A., U. Minn., 1961, A.Lang. Arts, 1977; diploma in bldg. constrn. Dunwoody Inst., 1964; m. Kathleen Joyce McIalwain, Nov. 11, 1967. Draftsman, Farmers Union Central Exchange, Inc., South St. Paul, Minn., 1965-67, design draftsman, 1967-70, chief draftsman, 1970-74; mgr. design engring. Cenex Co., St. Paul, 1974—; cons. Harrington Inc., Harrington Heating. Coach surburban woman's softball teams, summers 1970—. Served with USAR, 1961-67. Recipient award for engring. excellence Cons. Engrs. Council of Minn., 1976; certified bldg. ofcl., Minn. Mem. Smithsonian Assos., Irish-Am. Cultural Inst. Home: 1576 Merrill St St Paul MN 55108 Office: 1185 N Concord St S St Paul MN 55075

HARRINGTON, LOUIS ROBERT, lawyer; b. Detroit, Nov. 30, 1904; s. Lewis E. and Josephine (Lucas) H.; B.S., U. Detroit, 1926, LL.B., 1929 J.D,, 1968; m. Madeleine Emmerich, Apr. 5, 1970. Admitted to Mich. bar, 1929, since practiced in Detroit; sec., dir., gen. counsel Commando Tool Co., 1946—, Hamco Products Co., 1960—, Pasco Corp., 1964—. MacDonald Tube Products, 1963—, Piecemaker Corp., 1965—, Patton Bldg. Corp., 1964—, Sailmasters of Mich. Chmn. Mich. Conf. Bar Officers, 1970-72. Fellow Am. Coll. Probate Counsel; mem. Fed., Am., Mich., Detroit bar assns., Detroit Hist. Soc., Detroit Mus. Arts Founders Soc., Acad. Polit. Scis., Alpha Kappa Psi. K.C., Kiwanian, Elk. Clubs: Detroit Yacht; Lake Shore (Chgo.); Lost Lake Woods, National Lawyers of Washington. Home: 494 N Fox Hills Bloomfield Hills MI 48013 Office: First National Bldg Detroit MI 48226

HARRINGTON, RICHARD STANHOPE, community devel. cons. co. exec.; b. Wellington, Ohio, May 2, 1935; s. Frank Minor and Marie Eugene (LeGault) H.; M. in Broadcast Journalism, Northwestern U., 1965; m. Velma Jean Staley, Sept. 8, 1973; children—Pamela Diane, Daniel Mark, Melissa Anne. Commd. officer U.S. Marine Corp, advanced through grades to capt., 1969; assigned Armed Forces Radio, Korea, 1953-55; with NCOIC Radio-TV, Cherry Point, N.C., 1955-60; radio-TV dir. Marine Air Res., 1960-63; broadcaster, WGN-Radio-TV News, Chgo., 1962-68; CO-PR cons., 1969-75; v.p. Urban Data Systems, Columbus, Ohio, 1971-75; pres. Tekton, Inc., Columbus, 1976—; v.p. McClendon Enterprises, Inc., Columbus, 1975—. Housing adminstr. Mid-Ohio Regional Planning Commn., Columbus, 1976—. Recipient Gold Mike award, Armed Forces Radio, 1955; Freedom Found. Television Documentary award, 1969. Mem. Bldg. Ofcls. And Codes Adminstrs. Internat., Nat. Assn. Housing and Redevel. Ofcls., Ohio Conf. of Community Devel., Canadian Assn. Redevel. Ofcls., Am. Soc. Bldg. and Construction Inspectors. Episcopalian. Clubs: Past Master Councilor, Chevalier, Order of DeMolay. Home: 1841 Willoway Circle N Columbus OH 43220 Office: 1030 Dublin Rd Columbus OH 43215

HARRINGTON, ROBERT LEVANT, judge; b. Lima, Ohio, Jan. 13, 1914; s. Fred William and Grace M. (Biner) H.; cadet U.S. Mil. Acad., 1934-35; J.D., Ohio No. U., 1941; grad. Command and Gen. Staff Sch., 1945; m. Cathryn Dale Lamb, Jan. 1, 1944; children—Ruth Angeline, Susan Dale. Admitted to Ohio bar, 1941; pvt. practice Alger, Ohio, 1941-42, Van Wert, Ohio, 1946-58, sr. mem. Harrington and Harrington, 1946-58; jurist, 1958—. Served from pvt. to capt. AUS, 1942-46. Admitted to all Fed. Cts. Mem. Am., Northwestern Ohio, Ohio, Van Wert County (pres. 1960-62) bar assns., Am. Legion (commr. Buckeye Boys State 1965—), V.F.W., Am. Judicature Soc., Am. Judges Assn., Ohio Municipal Judges Assn., West Point Soc. Northwestern Ohio (pres.), Assn. Graduates U.S. Mil. Acad. Republican. Mason (K.T., 32 deg., Shriner) (pres. 1964-65), Elk (past exalted ruler, hon. life mem.), Odd Fellow (past noble grand). Home: 1007 Oak Ln Van Wert OH 45891 Office: County Ct House Van Wert OH 45891

HARRINGTON, WILLIAM CHARLES, sculptor, educator; b. Chgo., June 20, 1942; s. William J. and Rose M. (Cogilanese) H.; B.F.A. in Sculpture, U. Ill., 1964; M.F.A. in Sculpture (Chi Psi Nat. Grad. fellow), U. Hartford (Conn.), 1966; m. Diana Rae Becker, Oct. 14, 1967. Asst. prof. sculpture, design, drawing, Ind. State U., Terre Haute, 1970-72; asst. prof. design and sculpture Iowa State U., Ames, 1974—; workshop asst. to George Rickey, E. Chatham, N.Y., 1965. Served with U.S. Army, 1968-69; combat artist, Vietnam. Recipient Beech Grad. Honors award, 1966. Commd. artist, various sculptures. Home: 1019 Grand St Ames IA 50010 summer: Rural Route 1 Box 128 A Bent Mountain VA 24059

HARRINGTON, WILLIAM GENE, county ofcl.; b. Davenport, Iowa, July 5, 1923; s. Frank Marion and Martha (Jost) H.; B.S., Iowa State U., 1949; children—Debra Jo, Mark Joseph, James Alan. Asst. county engr. County of Marion, Knoxville, Iowa, 1950-52; county engr., Cedar County, Iowa, 1953-54, Scott County, 1955-57; dist. secondary roads engr. Iowa Hwy. Commn., Cedar Rapids, 1957-59; county engr. Linn County, Cedar Rapids, Iowa, 1959—. Active civic work. Served with AUS, 1943-46. Named hon. soils engr. soils research dept. Iowa State U., 1970. Mem. Nat. Assn. County Engrs. (pres. 1966-67), ASCE, Transp. Research Bd., Am. Road Builders Assn. (dir. county div. 1963-66, 72-76), Tau Lambda Rho. Mason (Shriner). Editorial cons. Better Roads mag., 1972—. Home: 956 Center Point Rd NE Cedar Rapids IA 52402 Office: Court House Cedar Rapids IA 52401

HARRIS, BEVERLY HOWARD, educator; b. Lee's Summit, Mo., Aug. 22, 1927; s. Howard K. and Mattie (Beggs) H.; A.A., SW Bapt. Coll., 1947; B.S., SW Mo. State U., 1949; M.A., U. Mo., 1953, Ed.D. (Curators scholar), 1963; m. Zorene Pruitt, May 21, 1950; children—Susan Annette, Steven Howard, Joy Aileen. Instr. mathematics U. Mo., Columbia, 1951-52; instr. SW Bapt. Coll., Bolivar, Mo., 1952-64, prof., chmn. dept., 1964—, scholarship coordinator, 1973—. Co-organizer, Mo. Tng. Center for Mentally Retarded Children, Bolivar, 1964; organizing com. Day Care Center So. Hills Bapt. Ch., Bolivar, 1972. Served with U.S. Army, 1946-47. Mem. Math. Assn. Am., Phi Delta Kappa. Baptist (deacon, dir. Sunday Sch.). Club: Bolivar Tennis (pres. 1975-77). Home: 910 E Division St Bolivar MO 65613 Office: 623 S Pike St Bolivar MO 65613

HARRIS, BOYD THOMSON, real estate and ins. agt.; b. Williamsfield, Ill., Sept. 18, 1912; s. Arthur LeRoy and Mabel (Cornwell) H.; A.B., Knox Coll., 1934; m. Jane Ellen McCanna, June 15, 1940; children—Lois, Boyd, Arthur, Amy, Moira. Coll. rep. Appleton-Century Co., 1934-40; coll. rep. Macmillan Co., N.Y.C., 1940-45, editor coll. and trade depts., 1945-51, acting asst. to pres., 1951-52; owner, mgr. The Harris Agy., Pontiac, Ill., 1953—. Pres. Credit Bur. of Pontiac, 1956-58, Alderman City of Pontiac, 1956-65; chmn. Pontiac Plan Commn., 1965-69. Mem. Bloomington-Normal Bd. Realtors, Nat. Assn. Real Estate Bds., Nat. Inst. Real Estate Brokers. Republican. Methodist. Mason. Elk. Rotarian. Club: Union League (Chgo.). Home: 8 Crystal Ct Pontiac IL 61764 Office: 101 N Mill St Pontiac IL 61764

HARRIS, CHARLES BURT, educator; b. LaGrange, Tex., Nov. 2, 1940; s. Gus B. and Ruth L. (Hess) H.; B.S., Tex. Luth. Coll., 1963; M.A., So. Ill. U., Carbondale, 1965, Ph.D., 1968; m. Victoria Frenkel, Mar. 16, 1968; children—Kimberly Lynne, Gregory Paul. Inst. in English, So. Ill. U., 1966-68; asst. prof. English, Ill. State U., Normal, 1968-72, asso. prof., 1972—, grantee, 1974, 75, 76, 77. Mem. Modern Lang. Assn., Midwest Modern Lang. Assn., AAUP, Popular Culture Assn., Coll. English Assn., Nat. Council Tchrs. of English, Common Cause, Ind. Voters of Ill. Author: Contemporary American Novelists of the Absurd, 1971; contbr. articles revs. to profl. publs. Home: 218 Riss Dr Normal IL 61761 Office: English Dept Ill State U Normal IL 61761

HARRIS, CHAUNCY DENNISON, geographer; b. Logan, Utah, Jan. 31, 1914; s. Franklin Stewart and Estella (Spilsbury) H.; A.B., Brigham Young U., 1933; B.A., Oxford U. (Rhodes scholar, 1934-36), 1936, M.A., 1943 D.Litt., 1973; student London Sch. Econs., 1936-37; Ph.D., U. Chgo., 1940; D.Econ. (honoris causa) Catholic U., Chile, 1956; m. Edith Young, Sept. 5, 1940; 1 dau., Margaret. Instr. geography Ind. U., 1939-41; asst. prof. geography U. Nebr., 1941-43; asst. prof. geography U. Chgo., 1943-46, asso. prof., 1946-47, prof., 1947—, dean social scis., 1955-60, dir. Center Internat. Studies, 1966—, chmn. dept. geography, 1967-69, Samuel N. Harper distinguished service prof., 1969—, spl. asst. to the pres., 1973-75, v.p. for acad. resources, 1975—. Del. Internat. Geog. Congress, Lisbon, 1949, Washington, 1952, Rio de Janeiro, 1956, Stockholm, 1960, London, 1964, New Delhi, 1968 Montreal, 1972, Moscow, 1976; U.S. del. 17th Gen. Conf. of UNESCO, Paris 1972; v.p. Internat. Geog. Union, 1956-64, sec.-treas., 1968-76, mem. U.S. Com., 1949-76. Mem. Exec. com. div. behavioral sci. NRC, 1967-70; mem. Joint Com. on Slavic Studies, 1954-65, Inter-Univ. Com. on Travel Grants, 1956-65, Joint Com. on Fgn. Area Fellowship Program 1962-70; mem. exec. com. Internat. Research and Exchanges Bd., 1968-71; mem. adv. com. internat. orgns. and programs. Nat. Acad. Scis., 1969-73, mem. bd., 1973-76. Recipient Distinguished Service award Geog. Soc. Chgo., 1965; Alexander Csoma de Korosi Mem. medal Hungarian Geog. Soc., 1971; named Laureat d'Honneur, Internat. Geog. Union, 1976. Mem. Assn. Am. Geographers (sec. 1946-48, v.p. 1956, pres. 1957, Honors award 1976), Am. Geog. Soc. (council 1962-74, v.p. 1969-74), Am. Assn. Advancement Slavic Studies (pres. 1962), Regional Sci. Assn. (v.p. 1963-64), Social Sci. Research Council (bd. dirs. 1959-70, vice chmn. 1963-65, com. programs and policy 1959-67, exec. com. 1967-70), Internat. Council Sci. Unions (exec. com. 1969-72); hon. mem. Royal Geog. Soc., geog. societies of Berlin, Frankfurt, Rome, Florence, Paris, Warsaw. Clubs: Univ., Quadrangle (Chgo.). Author: Cities of the Soviet, 1970; Guide to Geographical Bibliographies and Reference Works in Russian or on The Soviet Union, 1975; Bibliography of Geography: Part I, Introduction to General Aids, 1976. Editor: Economic Geography of the U.S.S.R., 1949, Internat. List of Geog. Serials, 1960, 1971; Soviet Geography: Accomplishments and Tasks, 1962; contbg. editor The Geog. Rev., 1960-73. Contbr. articles to profl. jours. Home: 5649 S Blackstone Ave Chicago IL 60637 Office: Center for Internat Studies U of Chgo 5828 University Ave Chicago IL 60637

HARRIS, DANIEL KEATING, med. assn. exec.; b. Chgo., Oct. 1, 1943; s. Daniel Phillip and Helen Margaret (Schillo) H.; B.S.B.A., Marquette U., 1965; M.B.A. in Personnel Adminstrn., Indsl. Mgmt., DePaul U., 1968; m. Karen Anne Stroup, Oct. 17, 1970. Systems analyst Eaton Yale & Towne, Chgo., 1965-69; cons., Booz Allen & Hamilton, Chgo., 1969-71; project mgr. Blue Cross & Blue Shield Nat. Assn., Chgo., 1971-73; dir. computer systems in medicine Am. Med. Assn., Chgo., 1973—; ind. cons. organizational and systems analysis, free-lance med. writer. Served with USMCR, 1962-65. Mem. Soc. for Advanced Med. Systems, Am. Assn. of Med. Soc. Execs. Clubs: Chgo. Athletic Assn. Editor-in-chief Computers and Medicine, 1974—; contbg. editor Jour. of Med. Systems, 1977—. Home: 603 N Park Blvd Glen Ellyn IL 60137 Office: 535 N Dearborn St Chicago IL 60610

HARRIS, DAVID JAMES, oral and maxillo-facial surgeon; b. LaPorte, Ind., June 3, 1937; s. James Milo and Dorothy Phyllis (Wyczawski) H.; student U. Notre Dame, 1955-57; B.S., Ind. U., 1958, D.D.S., 1962; m. Jean Ann Mertins, Nov. 26, 1960; children—Catherine Jean, David James, Pamela Jean. Intern (NIH fellow), U. Okla. Med. Center, 1963-64, resident oral surgery, 1964-66; practice dentistry specializing in oral and maxillo-facial surgery, South Bend, Ind., 1967—. Cons. VA Hosp., Oklahoma City, 1966-67; chmn. div. oral and dental surgery Meml. Hosp., South Bend, 1977—; instr. oral surgery U. Okla. Med. Center, 1966-67; instr. pharmacology and anesthesia Ind. U. at South Bend, 1969-74, lectr. oral pathology, 1973—. Bd. dirs. St. Joseph County Cancer Soc. Diplomate Am. Bd. Oral Surgeons. Fellow Am. Dental Soc. Anesthesiology; mem. Am., Ind. dental assns., North Central (pres. 1977-78), St. Joseph County (pres. 1977-78, dir.) dental socs., Internat. Assn. Oral Surgeons, Am., Ind. (dir. 1976—), Gt. Lakes socs. oral surgeons, Delta Sigma Delta. Clubs: Elks, Kiwanis. Home: 22621 State Rd 4 Lakeville IN 46536 Office: 211 N Eddy St South Bend IN 46617

HARRIS, DONALD, optometrist; b. Cleve., Aug. 25, 1930; s. Louis and Sarah (Young) H.; student Western Res. U., 1948-50; B.Sc., Ohio State U., 1953; m. Ellen Harriet Sacharow, Sept. 1, 1963; children—Lawrence Jeffery, Kenneth Alan (dec.). Pvt. practice optometry, Cleve., 1957-59; optometrist Union Eye Care Center, Euclid, Ohio, 1959—. Served with AUS, 1954-56. Mem. V.F.W. Mason. Home: 23902 E Groveland St Beachwood OH 44122 Office: 1353 E 260th St Euclid OH 44132

HARRIS, DONALD LEE, vet. pathologist, toxicologist; b. Girard, Kans., Aug. 20, 1940; s. Bud L. and Florence Ellen (Westhoff) H.; student Kans. State Tchrs. Coll. Pittsburg, 1958-61; B.S., Kans. State U., Manhattan, 1964, D.V.M., 1966; M.S., U. Wis., Madison, 1970; m. Penny Lee Corbin, Dec. 20, 1969; children—Jonathan Christopher, James Clayton. Postdoctoral trainee Dept. Vet. Sci., U. Wis., Madison, 1968-70; chief pathologist/toxicologist, head pathology/clin. pathology sect. biology dept. Warf Inst., Madison, 1970-77; head pathology and clin. pathology section indsl. bio-test Wedge's Creek Research Farm, Neillsville, Wis., 1977—. Chmn. Dane County Bicentennial wagon train, 1976. Served with Vet. Corps, U.S. Army, 1966-68. Mem. Am. Coll. Vet. Toxicologists, Dane County, Am. vet. med. assns., Am. Acad. Clin. Toxicology, Am. Assn. Lab. Animal Sci., Oreg. Horse Assn. (pres. 1974—). Roman Catholic. K.C. Home: 6027 Sun Valley Pkwy Oregon WI 53575 Office: Box 26 Neillsville WI 54456

HARRIS, E. EDWARD, educator; b. West Burlington, Iowa, Nov. 15, 1931; s. Earl and Anne M. (Mollen) Harris; B.A., U. No. Iowa, 1953; M.A., U. Minn., 1959; Ed.D., No. Ill. U., 1965; m. Evonne L. Meier, May 29, 1954; children—Julie Anne, James Edward. Tchr.-coordinator office and distributive edn. Davenport (Iowa) Community Schs. 1955-63, head bus. edn. dept. West High Sch., 1960-63; asst. prof. edn. No. Ill. U., DeKalb, 1963-64, asso. prof., 1965-67, prof., 1968—, coordinator profl. devel. in occupational edn., 1970-72, chmn. bus. edn. and adminstrv. services dept., 1973—. Cons. in field. Chmn., U.S. Office Edn. Region V Planning Com. Distributive Edn., 1966-69. Mem. DeKalb County Devel. Corp., 1974—. Bd. dirs. United Campus Ministry, Ill. Found Distributive Edn. Served with AUS, 1953-55. Recipient Outstanding Service award Distributive Clubs Am., 1963, Ill. chpt., 1967; Excellence in Teaching award No. Ill. U., 1969; Man of Year award Distributive Edn. Clubs Ill., 1972. Mem. Am. Vocat. Assn. (life, chmn. distributive edn. publs. com. 1966-74), Nat. Bus. Edn. Assn., Council Distributive Tchr. Educators, Ill. Co-op. Vocat. Edn. Coordinators Assn. (dir.), Ill. Secondary Mktg. and Distributive Edn. Coordinators Assn. (dir.), Delta Pi Epsilon, Pi Omega Pi. Presbyn. (ruling elder). Author: An Articulated Guide for Cooperative Occupational Education, 1971; Marketing Research, 1971; Employer Preferences and Teacher Coordinator Practices, 1971; Methods of Teaching Business and Distributive Education, 3d. edit., 1972; Principles of Retailing, 6th edit., 1974; Handbook for Cooperative Vocational Education in Illinois, 1977; Annotated Bibliography of Instructional Materials in Cooperative Vocational Education, 1977. Editor: Nat. Bus. Edn. Yearbook, 1976; editor mktg. and distbn. sect. Nat. Bus. Forum, 1976-77. Home: 802 Sunnymeade Trail DeKalb IL 60115

HARRIS, EDWARD EUGENE, educator; b. Topeka, Feb. 27, 1933; s. Frank Edward and Portia Verlea (Payne) H.; A.B., Lincoln U., 1954; A.M., U. Iowa, 1958, Ph.D., 1963; postgrad. Wis. U., 1972. Faculty, Prairie View (Tex.) A. and M. Coll., 1963-64; asst. prof. California (Pa.) State Coll., 1965-68; asso. prof. sociology Ind. U.-Purdue U., Indpls., 1968—, chmn. dept., 1969-74. Served with AUS, 1956-58. Mem. Am., N. Central sociol. assns. Editorial bd. Coll. Student Jour., 1971—. Contbr. articles to profl. jours. Home: 3470 N Meridian St Indianapolis IN 46208

HARRIS, FRANCES ALVORD, ret. broadcasting and advt. exec.; b. Detroit, Apr. 19, 1909; d. William Roy and Edith (Vosburgh) Alvord; A.B., Grinnell Coll., 1929; m. Hugh William Harris, Sept. 24, 1932; children—Patricia Anne (Mrs. Floyd A. Metz), Hugh William, Robert Alvord. Staff advt. dept. Himelhoch Bros. & Co., Detroit, 1929-31; broadcaster as Julia Hayes, Robert P. Gust Co., 1931-34; with tng. and personnel dept. Ernst Kern Co., 1935-36; broadcaster as Nancy Dixon, Young & Rubicam, Inc., 1939-42; women's editor Sta. WWJ, 1943-64, WWJ-TV, 1947-64, spl. features coordinator WWJ Stas., 1964-74; owner Fran Harris & Assos., Detroit. Del., chmn. Asia-Am. Women Broadcasters Conf., Hawaii, 1966; del. III World Conf. Women Journalists, Israel, 1973. Exec. bd. Wayne County Dept. Mich. Soc. for Mental Health, 1953-63; chmn. Mental Health Week, 1958-59; publicity com. YWCA, 1945, chmn., 1961-67; publicity com. Tri-County League for Nursing, 1956-62; campaign dist. chmn. United Found., 1959-61, chmn. Speakers' Bur., 1974; mem. governing bd. Women's com. United Community Services; mem. Mayor's Com. Freedom Festival, 1959-63, UN Week, 1959-62; mem. Mich. Gov.'s Commn. Status Women, 1963-69, Mich. Women's Commn., 1970-76; mem. Wayne County Commn. Aging, 1974—, chmn., 1976—; pres. bd. dirs. Homemaker Service Met. Detroit, 1967-68, Met. YWCA, 1968, Mich. State U. Consumer Adv. Council, 1967; pres. bd. Vis. Nurse Assn., 1974-76; mem. nat. council Camp Fire Girls, 1970-73, nat. cons., 1975—, also mem. bd.; bd. control Ferris State Coll., 1968—; bd. dirs. Travelers' Aid, Detroit; past bd., radio-TV div. Met. Detroit Council Churches; mem. def. adv. com. Women in Service, 1970-73, chmn., 1973; bd. dirs. Det. Met. YMCA, Friends of Det. Pub. Library, Children's Museum Friends, 1972-74, Sr. Center, Inc. Adv. com. to trustees Grinnell Coll.; mem. Mich. coordinating com. Internat. Women's Year, 1976-77. Recipient Mental-Health Soc. Mich. award, 1958, Grinnell Coll. Alumni award, 1959, Theta Sigma Phi Headliner award for Mich. 1951, nat., 1952; Women's Advt. Club of Detroit Civic award, 1957; AWRT Outstanding Community Service, 1972; named Advt. Woman of Year, Detroit, 1958, 73, Soroptimist Woman of Yr., 1965, Mich. Vol. of Year, 1974, Heart of Gold, 1976. Mem. Am. Women in Radio-TV (pres. Detroit chpts. 1957-58; chmn. nat. conv. 1966), Women's Advt. Club Detroit (past pres.), Advt. Fedn. Am. (dist. lt. gov., v.p. and exec. bd. 1966-67, nat. bd. 1963-67). Mich. Assn. UN (past exec. board), Conf. of the Americas (chmn. 1968), Nat. Fedn. Press Women (hon.), Women in Communications (pres. Detroit 1950-51, nat. pres. 1971-73), Pi Epsilon Delta. Episcopalian (communications com. local congregation and Diocese of Mich.). Club. Press (Detroit). Author: Focus: Michigan Women 1701-1977, 1977. Address: 8120 E Jefferson Detroit MI 48214

HARRIS, FRED MILO, bus. exec.; b. Ottawa, Kans., Nov. 26, 1915; s. Fred Milo and Helen (Janes) H.; B.A., U. Kans., 1936; m. Josephine Elizabeth Burrow, Nov. 21, 1936; children—Fred Milo III, Nancy (Mrs. Ronald Lee Chandler), Cynthia Ann, David Christopher. With Chanute (Kans.) Tribune, 1936-52, asso. editor, 1942-48, pub., 1948-52, 73—; promotion-publicity dir. KMBC-TV and Radio, Kansas City, Mo., 1955-59; mgr. S.E. Kan. Westam. Securities, Inc., Chanute, 1959-71; div. mgr. Internat Securities Corp., 1971-75; resident mgr. Weinrich, Zitzmann, Whitehead, Inc., Investment Securities, 1975—; pres., dir. Chanute Pub. Co.; pres. Mid-Am., Inc., 1967-68, chmn., 1968-69. Bd. advisers Gladys Kelse Sch. Bus. and Econ. Devel., Kans. State Coll., Pittsburg, 1974—; chmn. Neosho Meml. Hosp. Endowment Found., Chanute; chmn. Kans. Adv. Commn. on Alcoholism; mem. Kans. Adv. Com. on Drug Abuse. Mem. Chanute City Commn., 1964-67; mayor Chanute, 1966-67; mem. Kan. Ho. of Reps., 1968-76, chmn. House Transp. and Utilities Com., 1973-76. Trustee William Allen White Found., Sch. Journalism, U. Kans., 1974—. Served to lt. (j.g.) USNR, 1943-46. Mem. Chanute C. of C. (past dir., pres.), Am. Legion (past comdr.), Kans. Assn. Commerce and Industry (past dir.), V.F.W., Nat. Council Alcoholism. Sigma Delta Chi, Phi Kappa Psi. Republican. Episcopalian. Home: 1202 W 2d St Chanute KS 66720 Office: 4 W Main St Chanute KS 66720

HARRIS, GALE ION, physicist; b. Arlington, Calif., Aug. 7, 1935; s. Albert Ion and Carmen Angeline (Waters) H.; B.S., U. Kans., 1957, M.S., 1959, Ph.D., 1962; S.M. (Sloan fellow), Mass. Inst. Tech., 1973; m. Bonnie Jean Hazlett, Mar. 31, 1956; children—Gayla Jean, Nathan Ward. With Aerospace Research Lab. USAF, Wright-Patterson AFB, Dayton, Ohio, 1965-74, project leader nuclear physics, 1962-72, dep. dir., sr. scientist solid state physics lab., 1973-74; dir. Office Mgmt. Research, Johns Hopkins Med. Sch., Balt., 1974-75, also adminstr. dept. radiology and asst. prof. radiology; asso. prof. radiology and physics Mich. State U., East Lansing, 1975—; pres. Mich. Research Center, 1975—. Served with USAF, 1962-65. Fellow Am. Phys. Soc., Soc. Nuclear Medicine, AAAS, Am. Assn. Physicists in Medicine, New Eng., Md. hist. socs., Sigma Xi, Sigma Pi Sigma, Sigma Tau, Tau Beta Pi. Contbr. articles to profl. jours. Home: 1312 Basswood Circle East Lansing MI 48823 Office: Dept Radiology Mich State Univ East Lansing MI 48824

HARRIS, IRVING BROOKS, bus. and broadcasting exec.; b. St. Paul, Aug. 4, 1910; s. William and Mildred (Brooks) H.; A.B., Yale, 1931; m. Joan Frank, June 19, 1974; children from earlier marriage—Roxanne, Virginia, William. Exec. in finance business, 1931-42, aircraft part bus., 1944-46; exec. Toni Home Permanent Co., 1946—; sold stockholdings in Toni Co. to Gillette Safety Razor Co., 1948; dir. Gillette Safety Razor Co. 1948-60; exec. v.p. Toni Co., 1946-52; chmn. bd. Sci. Research Assos., 1953-58; pres. Michael Reese Hosp. and Med. Center, Chgo., 1958-61; pres., dir. Standard Shares; chmn. bd. Pittway Corp. Served with Bd. Econ. Warfare, OPA, 1942-44. Trustee U. Chgo., Bush Found.; chmn. Harris Found.; pres. Erikson Inst. Early Edn., Chgo. Inst. Psychoanalysis, 1969-75; chmn. WTTW, ednl. TV sta., Chgo. Clubs: Standard, Lake Shore Country, Midday (Chgo.). Home: 209 E Lake Shore Dr Chicago IL 60611 Office: Suite 2576 1 First National Plaza Chicago IL 60603

HARRIS, JANE MCCANNA, social work adminstr.; b. Chillicothe, Ill., Sept. 7, 1916; d. Walter Thomas and Ella (Dougherty) McCanna; B.A., Knox Coll., 1938; M.A., Fordham U., 1940; m. Boyd T. Harris, June 15, 1940; children—Lois Ellen, Boyd McCanna, Arthur Russell, Amy Jane and Moira Jane (twins). Counselor, Bowen County Club, Waukegan, Ill., 1937, Chgo. Commons Settlement House, Chgo., 1938, Christodora Settlement House, N.Y.C., 1939; social worker Children's Bur., Phila., 1940-41, Ill. Children and Family Services, Bloomington, 1956-58, supr., 1958-59; sch. social worker Pontiac (Ill.) elementary schs., 1959-64; supt. Livingston County Dept. Pub. Aid, Pontiac, 1964—. Mem., sec., Livingston County Bd. Health, 1966—; mem. Nat. Conf. Social Welfare, 1972. Mem. Nat. Assn. Social workers, Ill. Assn. Pub. Welfare Adminstrs., Ill. Welfare Assn., (dist. IV chmn. 1972-73), Mortar Board, Pi Beta Phi.

HARRIS, JASPER WILLIAM, psychologist, educator; b. Kansas City, Mo., Dec. 10, 1935; s. Jasper and Mary Pearl (Smith) H.; B.S. with honors, Rockhurst Coll., 1958; M.A., U. Mo., 1961; Ph.D. (Univ. Edn.'s Professions Devel. Act fellow), U. Kans., 1971; m. Joann Sadie Harper, Aug. 23, 1969; 1 son, Jasper William. Secondary tchr. Kansas City (Mo.) Sch. Dist., 1963-65; counselor, project dir. Neighborhood Youth Corps, Kansas City, Mo., 1965-67; adminstr. Kansas City (Mo.) Sch. Dist., 1968-69; research asst. U. Kans. Bur. Child Research, Kansas City, 1969-71; research asso., prof. U. Kans., Kansas City, 1971—; cons., vis. prof. U. Vt., Norfolk State Coll., U. Nebr., U. Calif. at Santa Barbara, Minot (Minn.) State Coll., Kansas City (Kans.) Sch. Dist., Kansas City (Mo.) Sch. Dist., U. Mo., others. Recipient Spoke award, U.S. Jr. C. of C., 1967; named Outstanding Young Educator Greater Kansas City, Jr. C. of C., 1968-69, Outstanding Young Man Am., 1970. Sci-Edn. and Adminstrn. fellow, 1961-62. Mem. Am. Psychol. Assn., Council for Exceptional Children, Kaw Valley Med. Soc., Council on Minority Programs Phi Delta Kappa (award in recognition community service 1974), Alpha Phi Alpha, Sigma Pi Phi. Contbr. articles to profl. jours. Home: 11945 Pennsylvania Ave Kansas City MO 64145 Office: 2021 N 3d St Kansas City KS 66101

HARRIS, JOSEPH BENJAMIN, dentist; b. Richmond, Va., June 8, 1920; s. Joseph Brown and Alice (Burrell) H.; B.S. summa cum laude, Va. Union U., 1949; D.D.S., Howard U., 1953; m. Pauline Elizabeth McKinney, June 19, 1955; children—Paula Jo, Joseph Carter, Joya Renee. Pvt. practice dentistry, Detroit, 1953—; dir. C.A. Howell & Co., mfr. and distbr. beauty supplies, 1967—, pres., chmn. bd., 1972—. Served with AUS, 1943-46. Recipient award Am. Soc. Dentistry for Children, 1953. Mem. Am., Nat., Wolverine, Mich., Detroit dental socs., Mich. Assn. Professions, Omicron Kappa Upsilon, Alpha Kappa Mu. Home: 1190 W Boston Blvd Detroit MI 48202 Office: 2431 W Grand Blvd Detroit MI 48208

HARRIS, LAUREN JULIUS, educator; b. Chgo., July 9, 1940; s. Julius Norman and Belle (Saplitzky) H.; B.S., U. Ill., Chgo.-Urbana-Champaign, 1961; M.A., U. Minn., 1963, Ph.D., 1965; Asst. prof. psychology Mich. State U., East Lansing, 1965-69, asso. profl, 1969-75, prof., 1975—; vis. prof. psychology dept. McGill U., Montreal, Que., Can., 1971-72; NSF/Am. Psychol. Assn. vis. sci. lectr. Albion (Mich.) Coll., 1974, Spring Arbor (Mich.) Coll., 1975. Fellow Am. Psychol. Assn.; mem. Soc. Research in Child Devel., Psychonomic Soc., AAS, Internat. Neuropsychology Soc., Midwest Psychol. Assn., Sigma Xi. Jewish. Masthead cons. editor Devel. Psychology, 1973—; editorial bd. Child Devel. Abstracts and Bibliography, 1974-77; contbr. articles to books and profl. jours. Home: 704-104 Cherry Ln East Lansing MI 48824 Office: Dept Psychology Mich State U East Lansing MI 48824

HARRIS, LEWIS ELDON, research adminstr.; b. Cedar, Kans., Dec. 3, 1910; s. Homer E. and Kathryn (Ashbaugh) H.; B.S., U. Nebr., 1932, M.S., 1933, Sc.D., 1970;; m. Antonia E. Synovec, June 15, 1935; children—Ronald L., Robert B. Pres. Harris Labs., Inc., Lincoln, Nebr., 1933—; chmn. bd. Sci. Devel. Corp., 1958—; dir. Smith Kline Corp., Nat. Bank of Commerce; spl. lectr. U. Nebr., 1940-65. Fellow Am. Inst. Chemists; mem. Am. Chem. Soc., Am. Pharm. Assn., Am. Assn. Cereal Chemists, Lincoln C. of C., Asso. Industries of Nebr. Contbr. articles to profl. jours. Patentee in pharmaceuticals and food processing. Home: 1414 Ridgeway Rd Lincoln NE 68506 Office: 624 Peach St Lincoln NE 68501

HARRIS, MICHAEL TYRRELL, photographer; b. Licking County, Newark, Ohio, Mar. 2, 1939; s. James Dennie and Laura Ludana H.; student Beaver Falls (Pa.) Community Coll., 1969-77; m. Linda Sue Hopkins, Jan. 11, 1957; children—Coby Lynn, Michael Bryan. Owner, photographer Portrait Palace, Galion, Ohio, 1968—; lectr. in field. Pres., United Ch. Dirs. Galion, 1964-68; Mem. Internat. Brotherhood Magicians (territorial rep. 1968—), Profl. Photographers Central Ohio (treas.), Profl. Photographers Am., Profl. Photographers Ohio, Triangle Assn. Photographers. Mason. Office: 251 Portland Way N Galion OH 44833

HARRIS, MORRAN DENVER, state legislator, lawyer; b. nr. Wisdom, Mo., Oct. 17, 1921; s. Pressa Denver and Elberta May (Breshears) H.; A.B., Central Mo. State Coll. 1946; J.D., U. Mo., 1949, M.A., 1956; m. Artalee Wheeler, June 4, 1949; children—Sheryl Lee, Lila Gayl (dec.), Denver Wesley, Julie Kay, Marita Ann, Mark Wheeler. Admitted to Mo. bar, 1949; gen. practice Osceola, 1949—; pros. atty. St. Clair County, 1951-52, 55-63; state rep. from St. Clair County, 1963—. Active Boy Scouts. Served with U.S. Army, 1942-45; ETO. Mem. Am. Bar Assn., Mo. Bar, State Hist. Soc. of Mo., Phi Kappa Phi. Democrat. Baptist. Author: Political Trends in Missouri, 1900-54, 1956. Home: PO Box 330 Osceola MO 64776 Office: Osceola MO 64776

HARRIS, OWEN LESLIE, microbiologist; b. Chgo., July 15, 1942; s. Robert and Beatrice (Marcus) H.; B.A., So. Ill. U., 1965; M.S., U. Okla, 1968; Ph.D., U. Mo., 1971; m. Nancy Tuckman, Oct. 30, 1976. Food technologist Sara Lee, Deerfield, Ill., 1971-72; quality control scientist Ovaltine, U.S.A., Villa Park, Ill., 1972-73, sr. scientist, 1978—; pres. Harris Cons., Inc., Chgo., 1973-76; dir. tech. services Grafs Beverages, Inc., Milw., 1976-78. NIH fellow, 1970. Mem. Am. Soc. Microbiology, Inst. Food Technologists, Soc. Indsl. Microbiology, Am. Soc. Quality Control, Chgo. Dairy Tech. Soc., Sigma Xi. Author 2 books; contbr. articles to profl. jours. Home: 6437 N Kedzie Ave Chicago IL 60645 Office: 1 Ovaltine Ct Villa Park IL 60181

HARRIS, PERCY GENE, physician; b. Durant, Miss., Sept. 4, 1927; s. Norman Henry and Glendora (Roundtree) H.; B.S., Howard U., 1953: B.A., 1953, M.D., 1957; student Iowa State Tchrs. Coll., 1948-50; m. Evelyn Lileah Furgerson, July 8, 1950; children—Bruce A., David P., Lileah F., Peter C., Philip L., Paul N., Mark S., Anne C., Sarah B., Matthew C., Grant A., Rebecca R. Intern St. Luke's Hosp., Cedar Rapids, Iowa, 1957-58; practice medicine specializing in family practice Cedar Rapids, 1958—; asst. med. dir., 1958-59, dir. out-patient clinic, 1959-62; mem. staff Mercy Hosp., v.p. med. and dental staff St. Luke's Hosp., 1973-76, pres., 1976; asst. coroner Linn County, 1958-59, coroner, 1959-60; Linn County med. examiner, 1961—; mem. Linn County Psychiat. Bd., 1974—; mem. Iowa Found. for Med. Care, 1977—; chmn. bd. Oakhill Engring., Inc.; founder, pres. Community Cable Co., Cedar Rapids, 1973. Pres. bd. Cedar Rapids Edn. Assos. Mem. Black Culture Adv. bd. Coe Coll., 1968—; mem. Cedar Rapids-Marion Human Relations Council, Mayor's Commn. on low-cost housing, 1967—; v.p. Cedar Rapids Non-Profit Housing Corp.; bd. dirs. United Community Services, Cedar Rapids, 1969— (chmn. nominating com. 1972), Cedar Rapids non-profit housing corp., 1968—; bd. dirs. Jane Boyd Community House, Cedar Rapids, 1959-69, pres. bd., 1966-69; bd. mem. Oakhill-Jackson Econ. Devel. Corp. 1972-75; bd. regents State of Iowa, 1977—. Mem. Linn County Med. Soc., Cedar Rapids Negro Civic Orgn. (charter), N.A.A.C.P. (life; past pres. Cedar Rapids chpt.), Democrat. Club: Indian Creek Nature. Home: 3626 Bever Ave SE Cedar Rapids IA 52403 Office: 119 3d St NE Cedar Rapids IA 52401

HARRIS, PHILIP BREWER, ret. banker; b. Mpls., June 28, 1911; s. Walter Stewart and Jeannette (Brewer) H.; student U. Minn., 1930-34; m. Marian Ardene Berg, Nov. 9, 1940 (dec. Sept. 1976); children—Philip Brewer, Daniel Stewart, Timothy Jenkins, Thomas Vincent; m. 2d, Shirley L. Fisher, Apr. 1977. Vice pres. Charles W. Sexton Co., Mpls., 1934-42, 45-52; civilian chief USAAF Material Command Ins. Div., Dayton, Ohio, 1942-45; exec. v.p., dir. Northwestern Nat. Bank, Mpls., 1952-69, pres., 1969-73, chmn., chief exec. officer, 1974-76, now dir.; Belgian consul for Upper Midwest, 1973—; dir. Gen. Mills, Inc., Gt. No. Ins. Co. Chmn. bd. Mpls. Soc. Fine Arts; trustee Mpls. Found., bd. dirs. Midwest Research Inst., War Meml. Blood Bank, Cargill Found., Abbott-Northwestern Hosp.; chmn. bd. Nat. Solar Energy Research Inst. Mem. Mpls. C. of C. (past pres.). Presbyn. (trustee). Clubs: Minneapolis, Woodhill, Minikahda; Royal Poinciana Golf (Fla.). Home: 985 Edgewood Hill Rd Wayzata MN 55391 also 1275 Gulf Shore Blvd N Naples FL 33940 Office: 1150 Northwestern Bank Bldg 7th at Marquette Ave Minneapolis MN 55480

HARRIS, ROBERT ARCH, musician; b. Rich Hill, Mo., May 8, 1928; s. Archie Lester and Edith Jeannette (Bailey) H.; Mus. B., Pittsburg (Kans.) State U., 1950, M.S., 1953; postgrad. Aspen Music Sch., 1958, 65-70; student Rosina Lhevinne, 1958, 65-70. Instr. piano, 1949—; instr. of music Our Lady of the Ozarks Coll., 1949-53, 55-57; asst. prof. piano and music history Mo. So. State Coll., 1971—; organist First United Meth. Ch., Carthage, Mo., 1955—; counselor Nat. Fedn. Jr. Music Clubs, Carthage; bd. dirs. Joplin (Mo.) Community Concerts Assn., 1971-76, chmn. artists com., 1975-76. Served with U.S. Army, 1953-55. Mem. Am. Music Scholarship Assn., Music Tchrs. Nat. Assn. (certified), Mo. Music Tchrs. Assn., Fellowship United Meth. Musicians, Nat. Fedn. Music, Clubs, Carthage Music Club. Methodist. Home: 1344 S Main St Carthage MO 64836 Office: Mo So State Coll Joplin MO 64801

HARRIS, ROBERT BRUCE, lab. exec.; b. Lincoln, Nebr., Feb. 8, 1945; s. Lewis Elden and Antonietta E. (Synovac) H.; B.S., U. Nebr., 1968, postgrad., 1968-70; m. Diana Rae Heckman, June 11, 1976; children—Stephanie, Matthew, Sean, Theodore. With Harris Labs., Inc., Lincoln, 1960—, v.p., 1970-76, chmn. bd., 1977—; founder, prin. R.B. Harris Co., Lincoln, 1975—; founder, pres. Harris Sci., Inc., Lincoln, 1973—; dir. PSA, Inc., Sci. Devel. Corp. Mem. Assn. Systems Mgmt., Nebr. Assn. Commerce and Industry, Fertilizer Inst., Nat. Fertilizer Solutions Assn., Am. Council Ind. Labs., Council Soil Testing and Plant Analysis, Am. Advt. Fedn., Am. Soc. Agrl. Engrs., Council Agrl. Sci. and Tech., others. Republican. Presbyterian. Contbr. articles to profl. jours. Home: 2829 S 31st St Lincoln NE 68501 Office: 624 Peach St Lincoln NE 68501

HARRIS, ROBERT EDWIN, oil co. cons.; b. Massillon, Ohio, Dec. 24, 1940; s. Leland Leslie and Ruth Meriam (Reinochl) H.; B.S. in Chem. Engring., Ohio State U., 1962; M.S. in Chem. Engring., Northeastern U., 1965, Ph.D., 1968; m. Beverly Anne Fagone, Jan. 24, 1965; 1 dau., Amy Anne. Process engr. Exxon Corp., Bayonne, N.J., 1962-63; instr. Northeastern U., 1965-66; tech. service mgr. Monsanto Co., St. Louis, 1968-70, product mgr., 1970-73; cons. Standard Oil Co. Ohio, Cleve., 1973—; adj. asso. prof. Case Western Res. U., 1974—. NDEA fellow, 1966-68. Mem. Am. Chem. Soc., Am. Inst. Chem. Engrs., Sigma Xi, Phi Kappa Phi, Omega Chi Epsilon. Author: Flowtran: an Approach to a Computer Aided Process Analysis and Design Tool, 1971; Distillation Designs Using Flowtran, 1972. Office: 205CB Midland Bldg Standard Oil Co Cleveland OH 44115

HARRIS, ROBERT LAIRD, clergyman; b. Brownsburg, Pa., Mar. 10, 1911; s. Walter William and Ella Pearl (Graves) H.; B.S. in Chem. Engring., U. Del., 1931; postgrad. Washington U., St. Louis, 1931-32; Th.B., Westminster Theol. Sem., 1935, Th.M., 1937; M.A. in Oriental Studies, U. Pa., 1941; Ph.D., Dropsie U., 1947; m. Elizabeth Krugar Nelson, Sept. 11, 1937; children—Grace (Mrs. Richard Duane Sears), Allegra (Mrs. Peter Laird Smick), Robert Laird. Ordained minister Reformed Presbyn. Ch., 1936; instr. Faith Theol. Sem., Phila., 1937-43, asst. prof., 1943-47, prof. Bibl. Exegesis, 1947-56; prof. O.T. Covenant Theol. Sem., St. Louis, 1956—, dean, 1964-71; vis. lectr. Wheaton (Ill.) Coll., 1957-61; prof. Winona (Ind.) Summer Sch. Theology, 1964, 66, 67; prof. Near East Sch. Archaeology and Bible, Jerusalem, 1962; lectr. Japan, Korea, 1965. Recipient 1st. prize Zondervan Textbook Contest, 1955; E.I. DuPont de Nemours fellow, 1930-31. Mem. Soc. Bibl. Lit. and Exegesis, Am. Schs. Oriental Research, Am. Inst. Archaeology (sec. St. Louis chpt. 1971-73), Evang. Theol. Soc. (pres. 1961), Nat. Assn. Profs. Hebrew, Tau Beta Pi, Phi Kappa Phi. Author: Introductory Hebrew Grammar, 1950; Inspiration and Canonicity of the Bible, 1957; Your Bible, 1960; Man—God's Eternal Creation, 1971; contbg. author books. Chmn. editorial bd. New Internat. Version of Bible, 1970-74. Home: 12304 Conway Rd St Louis MO 63141 Office: Covenant Theol Sem 12330 Conway Rd St Louis MO 63141

HARRIS, ROBERT MILTON, lawyer; b. Amherst, Nebr., Apr. 27, 1924; s. Oliver Dell and Ada Blanche (King) H.; A.B., Nebr. State Tchrs. Coll. at Kearney, 1947; J.D., U. Mich., 1950; m. Jean Frances Pierson, June 4, 1954; children—Karl R., Judith A. Admitted to Nebr. bar, 1950, U.S. Dist. Ct. Neb. bar, 1955; law librarian, asst. prof. law Stanford, 1950-51; practiced in Gering, Nebr., 1951-54, Scottsbluff, Nebr., 1955—; mem. firm Holtorf & Harris, Gering, 1951-54, Wright, Simmons & Harris and predecessor, Scottsbluff, 1955-60; dep. county atty. Scotts Bluff County, 1952-54, 61-62; Police magistrate, Gering, 1951-54, 65-73. Trustee West Nebr. Gen. Hosp., 1954-60; lay del. to Gen. Conf., United Meth. Ch., Portland, Oreg., 1976, to South Central Jurisdictional Conf., Lincoln, Nebr., 1976; mem. Nebr. Library Commn., 1977—. Served as sgt. USAAF, 1943-45. Mem. Am., Nebr. bar assns. Republican. Methodist (del. ann. conf. 1961—). Home: 2020 14th St Box 54 Gering NE 69341 Office: 212 W 27th St Scottsbluff NE 69361

HARRIS, ROBERT NORMAN, marketing exec.; b. St. Paul, Feb. 11,, 1920; s. Nathan and Esther (Roberts) H.; B.A., U. Minn., 1940; m. Mildred Burton, June 21, 1941; children—Claudia, Robert Norman, Randolph B. With Toni Co. div. Gillette Co., Chgo., 1944-55, v.p., 1954-55; v.p., account supr. Lee King & Co., Chgo., 1955-60; exec. v.p. Wrisley co. div. Purex Corp. Ltd., Chgo., 1960-62; exec. v.p. North Advt. Inc., Chgo., 1962-71, partner 1962-71, mgmt. supr., 1963-71, dir. client services, 1964-71, also dir.; pres., dir. Mktg. Behavior, 1971-77, Harco Enterprises, 1972-76; exec. v.p. Advance Cablevision, 1971—; pres. Robert Piguet, Ltd., Harris Creative Group, 1972-77; corp. exec. v.p., pres. Creamer Lois FSR, Chgo., 1977—; dir. Advance Corp., Los Angeles. Served with USNR, 1941-44. Mem. Am. Assn. Advt. Agys., Community Antenna TV Assn., Execs. Club Chgo. Contbg. author: A Handbook for the Advertising Agency Account Executive, 1969. Home: 475 Laurel St Highland Park IL 60035 Office: 410 N Michigan Ave Chicago IL 60611

HARRIS, RONALD LEE, research lab. co. exec.; b. Lincoln, Nebr., Aug. 1, 1942; s. Lewis E. and Antonia (Synovec) H.; B.S., U. Nebr., 1965, M.B.A., 1968; m. Christine Marie Olson, June 19, 1965; children—Bretton Charles, Jennifer Ann. Lab. technician Harris Labs. Inc., Lincoln, Nebr., 1956-66, v.p. adminstrn., 1967-74, pres., 1974—; dir. Scientific Devel. Corp., Prescription Soil Analysis Co., Harris Scientific Inc. Pres. Asso. Industries of Lincoln, 1974. Mem. Am. Pharm. Assn., Adminstrv. Mgmt. Soc. (chpt. pres. 1975), Am. Mgmt. Assn., Am. Council Ind. Lab. Republican. Methodist. Club: Lion. Home: 2501 County Down Court Lincoln NE 68512 Office: 624 Peach St Box 80837 Lincoln NE 68501

HARRIS, SAMUEL DAVID, orthodontist; b. Romney, Russia, Apr. 23, 1903; s. Harry and Fannie (Mirvis) H.; brought to U.S., 1910, naturalized, 1935; D.D.S., U. Mich., 1924; m. Ethel Gibbing, Feb. 6, 1932; children—John Gibbing, David Blaine, Paul Austin. With Forsyth Dental Infirmary for Children, 1924-25; pvt. practice ltd. to orthodontics, Detroit, 1925—. Diplomate Am. Bd. Pedodontics. Mem. Am. Coll. Dentistry, Am. (founder, past pres.), Mich. (past pres.) socs. dentistry for Children, A.A.A.S., Pan Am. Council Dentistry for Children (past pres., past chmn. bd.), Am., Mich., Detroit dental assns., Am. Acad. Pedodontics (past pres.), Am. Assn. Dental Editors, Detroit Dental Clinic Club, Detroit Pedodontic Study Club (past pres.). Republican. Clubs: Kiwanis (dir.), Inter Collegiate (Detroit). Author: A Digest of Pedodontic Practice, 1938; History of the American Society of Dentistry for Children, 1970. Contbr. articles profl. jours.; founder, past editor Jour. Dentistry for Children. Home: 1407 Nicolet St Detroit MI 48207 Office: Broderick Tower Detroit MI 48226

HARRIS, STANLEY GALE, JR., banker; b. Chgo., June 19, 1918; s. Stanley Gale and Muriel (Bent) H.; student Yale U., 1936-38; certificate in indsl. adminstrn. Harvard Grad. Sch. Bus. Adminstrn., 1943; children—John Trumbull, Thomas Bartlett; m. 2, Alice Harwood, Nov. 4, 1972. With Nat. Bank Commerce, Seattle, 1939-42, Carnegie-Ill. Steel Corp., 1943-44; with Harris Trust & Savs. Bank, Chgo., 1944—, now chmn. bd., dir.; chmn. bd., dir. Harris Bankcorp Inc.; dir. Snap-On Tools Corp., Kenosha, Wis. Hon. trustee Ill. Children's Home and Aid Soc., U. Chgo., Rush-Presbyn.-St Luke's Med. Center. Mem. Res. City Bankers Assn. Clubs: Chicago, Commercial, Casino, Tavern, Attic, Economic, Bankers (Chgo.); Little Wheels, Skokie Country. Home: 180 E Pearson St Apt 4704 Chicago IL 60611 Office: Harris Trust & Savs Bank 111 W Monroe St Chicago IL 60690

HARRIS, STEVEN HESSE, geologist, oil co. exec.; b. Cin., Nov. 18, 1924; s. Ira and Eugenia Claire (Hesse) H.; B.A., U. Cin., 1948, M.S., 1950; m. Mary Kathleen Broderick, Oct. 6, 1955; children—Steven, Bruce, Terry, Wayne, Diane. Exploration geologist Shell Oil Co., Tulsa, 1950-52; cons. geologist Harris, Brown & Klemer, Bismarck, N.D., 1952—; pres. Camargo Corp., Bismarck, N.D., 1965—. Served with AUS, 1942-46. Fellow Geol. Soc. Am.; mem. Ind. Petroleum Assn. Am. (dir.), N.D. Geol. Soc. (pres. 1965, 72), Am. Inst. Profl. Geologists (sect. pres. 1973-75), Am. Assn. Petroleum Geologists, Soc. Econ. Paleontologists and Mineralogists, Am. Legion, Dakota Petroleum Club (pres. 1960, 65), Sigma Xi, Sigma Gamma Epsilon, Kappa Kappa Psi. Clubs: Masons, Elks, Shriners. Contbr. articles to various publs. Home: 1120 N 1st St Bismarck ND 58501 Office: 222 W Bowen St Bismarck ND 58501

HARRIS, THOMAS LORBER, advt. co. exec.; b. Dayton, Ohio, Apr. 18, 1931; s. James and Leona (Blum) H.; B.A., U. Mich., 1953; M.A., U. Chgo., 1956; m. Jo Ann Karch, Apr. 14, 1957; children—James Howard, Theodore Robert. Exec. v.p. Daniel J. Edelman, Inc., Chgo., 1957-63, North Advt. Inc., Chgo., 1966-68; v.p., dir. pub. relations, advt. accounts supr. Needham, Harper & Steers, Inc., Chgo., 1963-65, 1969-73; v.p., dir. Foote, Cone & Belding Pub. Relations, 1973-77, pres., 1977—. Bd. dirs. Off the Street Club, 1966—. Dir. advt. for candidates for gov., 1968, 1972, lt. gov., 1968, and supt. pub. instrn., 1970. Bd. dirs. Pub. Service Communications Council Chgo. Served with AUS, 1953-55. Mem. Pub. Relations Soc. Am. (chpt. bd. dirs. 1966—), Zeta Beta Tau. Contbr. articles to profl. jours. Home: 556 Cherokee St Highland Park IL 60035 Office: 401 N Michigan St Chicago IL 60601

HARRIS, WILLIAM PAGE, lumber co. exec.; b. Alpena, Mich., Dec. 29, 1920; s. Clinton P. and Norma (Richardson) H.; B.A., Dartmouth Coll., 1942; postgrad. George Washington U., 1949; m. Dewilda E. Naramore, July 14, 1956; children by previous marriage—Clinton P., Nancy E. Fgn. service officer, vice-consul sec. embassy, Germany, Switzerland, 1950-54; dir. Allison Lumber Co., Bellamy, Ala., 1954-60; pres. Harris Concrete & Supply Co., Taylor, Mich., 1956-63; v.p. Detroit office Tex. Industries, Inc., 1963-64; pres., dir. Mohawk Lumber & Hardware Co., Detroit, 1965—. Served to lt. USNR, 1942-45. Recipient Sec. of State commendation Geneva Conf. Fgn. Ministers, 1954. Club: Detroit. Home: 626 Yarboro Dr Bloomfield Hills MI 48013 Office: 14525 W Chicago Ave Detroit MI 48228

HARRISON, E. FRANK, coll. dean; b. Seattle, July 1, 1929; s. Ernest and Ethel (Stutler) H.; B.A. magna cum laude, U. Wash., 1956, M.B.A., 1961, Ph.D., 1970; m. Monique Adrienne Pelletier. With Shell Oil Co., Seattle, 1956-58; mgmt. positions Boeing Co., Seattle, 1958-70; lectr. Grad. Sch. Bus. Adminstrn., U. Wash., 1968-71, Sch. Bus. Adminstrn., Seattle U., 1968-74; dir. Sch. Bus. and Pub. Adminstrn., dir. grad. programs, prof. mgmt. U. Puget Sound, Tacoma, Wash., 1970-74; dean Coll. Bus., prof. mgmt. Ill. State U., Normal, 1974—, also dean Fin. Dept. Served with USMC, 1946-49. Recipient Wall St. Jour. Student Achievement award, 1956. Mem. Acad. Mgmt., Internat. Biog. Assn., Am. Acad. Polit. and Social Sci., Am. Inst. Decision Sci., Am. Sociol. Assn., Phi Beta Kappa, Beta Gamma Sigma. Author: The Management Decision Making Process, 1975; Management and Organizations, 1978; numerous articles. Home: 1009 Barton Dr Normal IL 61761

HARRISON, EARLE, dept. store exec.; b. Rainsville, Ala., May 20, 1905; s. Robert Lee and Sarepta Ophelia (Hansard) H.; A.B., Northwestern U., 1929, grad. student bus. adminstrn., 1942, LL.B., Chgo.-Kent Coll. Law, 1935; m. Joan Mary Jackson, Jan. 24, 1942. With Marshall Field & Co., Chgo., 1929—, div. operating mgr., 1958-60, v.p. ops., 1960-64, v.p., treas,, 1964-69. Pres., dir. Family Financial Counseling Service of Greater Chgo., 1966-69; cons., adminstr. Lake County Nursing Home, 1973—; adminstr. Condell Meml. Hosp., Libertyville, 1973—, pres., bd. dirs., 1975-77, chmn. bd., 1977—. Mem. bd. dirs. Credit Bur. Cook County, 1949-69, pres., 1958—; mem. Lake Bd. Suprs.; chmn. Lake County Planning and Zoning Com.; pres. Northeastern Ill. Planning Commn., 1973, mem. exec. com., 1975—. Mem. Phi Delta Phi. Episcopalian. Club: Chgo. Athletic Assn. Home: 501 Oakwood Lake Forest IL 60045

HARRISON, FRANK JOSEPH, lawyer; b. Streator, Ill., Dec. 5, 1919; s. Frank Joseph and Nell (Webb) H.; A.B., U. Chgo., 1941, J.D., 1947; LL.M., Harvard, 1947; m. Shirley Anne Summerhays, Dec. 30, 1950; children—Ellen, Paul, Janice, Mark. Admitted to Ill. bar, 1942; atty. Chicago Title and Trust Co., 1948-51, Pub. Housing Adminstrn., Chgo., 1951-53; practice gen. law, Streator, Ill., 1953—; sr. law clk. Third Dist. Ill. Appellate Ct., 1971-74, 2d Dist. Ill. Appellate Ct., 1974-76. City atty. City of Streator, Ill., 1965-71, 73—. Served with AUS, 1942-46. Mem. Am., Ill., Chgo., La Salle County, Streator bar assns., Beta Theta Pi, Phi Delta Phi. Presbyn. Contbr. articles to profl. jours. Home: 135 W First St Streator IL 61364 Office: 114 N Bloomington St Streator IL 61364

HARRISON, GEORGE LOUIS, clergyman, social worker; b. Moorhead, Iowa, Oct. 24, 1928; s. Hugh and Beth (Whitehead) H.; A.B., Minn. Bible Coll., 1951; B.D., Lincoln (Ill.) Christian Sem., 1962; M.S., Ft. Hays (Kans.) State Coll., 1971; m. Francel Oliver, May 14, 1950 (dec.); children—Wayne, Emily. Ordained to ministry, Disciples of Christ Ch., 1950; pastor Christian Churches, Iowa, Ill., Tenn., 1950-62, supply minister, Disciples of Christ and Ch. of Christ, United Ch. of Christ chs., Minn., 1963—; sr. caseworker, Minn. State Dept. Corrections, Lino Lakes, 1963—; career counselor for released inmates, 1976—. Grantee, Law Enforcement Ednl. Program, 1968-72. Mem. Am. Personnel and Guidance Assn., Am. Rehab. Counseling Assn., Minn. Corrections Assn., Minn. Bible Coll. Alumni (area pres., 1966-67). Contbr. articles to Christian Standard mag. Home: 7661 Lake Dr Circle Pines MN 55014 Office: Box L Circle Pines MN 55014

HARRISON, HAROLD DUANE, advt. exec.; b. Detroit, Mar. 9, 1930; s. Hartley Curtis and Helen Magdalen (Bailey) H.; B.S. in Speech, Northwestern U., 1951; M.A., Ball State U., 1972; m. Joyce Irene Rohde, Feb. 19, 1955; children—Cheryl Jean, David Keith. Staff announcer, news dir. WBIW, Bedford, Ind., 1952; reporter, feature writer, columist Bedford Daily Times Mail, 1953-60; staff corr. Indpls. News, 1953-60; owner, pub. Star Jour., Hope, Ind., 1960-67; asst. dir. pub. relations Ball Corp., Muncie, Ind., 1967-72; v.p., Grove & Assos. Inc., Muncie, 1972—, lectr. in field; part-time instr. dept. journalism Ball State U., 1975—; advisor Ball State chpt. Pub. Relations Student Soc. Am., 1977. Founding dir. Eastern Ind. Community TV Inc., 1971-72; pub. relations chmn. Delaware County United Way, 1976. Mem. Pub. Relations Soc. Am. (accredited, v.p., dir. Hoosier chpt. 1975-76, counselor's sect. 1974). Democrat. Lutheran. Clubs: Kiwanis (Muncie), Muncie Advt. (past pres.). Author articles in field. Home: 3501 N Vienna Woods Dr Muncie IN 47304 Office: 105 N Ridge Rd Muncie IN 47304

HARRISON, HENRY STUART, iron ore co. exec.; b. Cleve., Nov. 25, 1909; s. Henry Thomas and Regina (Troler) H.; A.B., Yale, 1932; LL.D., Mich. Tech., 1964; LL.D., No. Mich. U., 1967; m. Suzanne Brookhart, Oct. 30, 1943; children—Mary Suzanne (Mrs. John T. Lansing), Henry Stuart, Virginia (Mrs. Kirk Knight). With Corrigan McKinney Steel Co., Cleve., 1932-33; mem. trust dept. Central Hanover Bank and Trust Co., N.Y.C., 1933-36; investment counsel Lionel D. Edie and Co., N.Y.C., 1936-37; with Cleve.-Cliffs Iron Co., 1937—, exec. v.p., 1958-60, pres. 1960—, chief exec. officer, 1971—, chmn. bd., 1974—, also dir.; dir. Cleve. Trust Co., Northwestern Mut. Life Ins. Co., Republic Steel Corp., Medusa Corp., Midland-Ross Corp. Chmn. distbn. com. Cleve.-Found.; trustee Cleve. Council on World Affairs; trustee, mem. finance com. Cleve. Inst. Art, Univ. Hosps., Univ. Sch., No. Mich. U. Devel. Fund. Mem. Am. Inst. Mining and Metall. Engrs., Newcomen Soc. Clubs: Union, Tavern, Chagrin Valley Hunt, Kirtland Country, Pepper Pike (Cleve.); Duquesne (Pitts.); Ottawa (Fremont, Ohio). Home: 22089 Shaker Blvd Shaker Heights OH 44122 Office: 1460 Union Commerce Bldg Cleveland OH 44115

HARRISON, JOSEPH HEAVRIN, lawyer; b. Evansville, Ind., July 23, 1929; s. Homer William and Lillie Isabelle (Heavrin) H.; A.B., U. Notre Dame, 1952, J.D., 1953; m. Julie Anne Gerard, Dec. 10, 1976; children—Joseph Heavrin, Sara Ann. Admitted to Ind. bar, 1953, since practiced in Evansville; asso. firm Buthod and Barnett, 1955-57; partner firm Bowers, Harrison and Kent, predecessor firms, 1957—; v.p. Sandys of Evansville, 1963—, also dir.; asst. sec. Wichita Industries, Inc., 1965—; dir. Developmental Assocs., Inc. Served with AUS, 1953-55. Mem. Ind., Evansville, Am. bar assns., Vanderburgh County Legal Aid Soc. (pres. 1965-67), Petroleum Club. Club: Evansville Country (pres. 1976). Home: 509 Martin's Ln Evansville IN 47715 Office: Suite 49 Permanent Savings Bldg Evansville IN 47708

HARRISON, MICHAEL (MICK) BRENT, artist; b. Mobridge, S.D., Oct. 2, 1945; s. Kenneth Eklund and Lucille Edith (Newton) H.; student pub. schs., Mobridge; m. Noreen Margaret Sessions, Sept. 13, 1974; 1 dau., Jaime Lynn. Rancher, Mobridge, 1958-63; draftsman aid S.D. Hwy. dept., 1963-65; collections dept. Universal CIT Corp., Burbank, Calif., 1968-69; house painter Custom Painting Co., Santa Ana, Calif., 1969-70; interior decorator, Portland, Oreg., 1970-72; comml. artist Collins Radio Group, Rockwell Internat. Corp., Cedar Rapids, Iowa, 1973-75; freelance Western artist, Mobridge, 1973—. Treas., Klein Mus., Mobridge, 1977—. Served with U.S. Army, 1965-68; Viet-Nam. Recipient First Prize award George Phippen Meml. Western Outside Art Show, 1977. Mem. S.D. Western Artists Assn. (founding mem.), Mobridge Arts Council. Republican. Congregationalist. Home and Office: 709 E 4th Ave Mobridge SD 57601

HARRISON, ROBERT STATLER, mech. engr.; b. Rochester, N.Y., Sept. 10, 1941; s. Robert P. and Clara S. (Statler) H.; asso. degree in applied sci., State U. N.Y., 1961; m. Susan Della Brown, Feb. 22, 1964; children—Todd, Jon, Kristen. Lab. technician Gen. Motors Co., Rochester, 1961-64; carburetor design engr. Ford Motor Co., Dearborn, Mich., 1964-71, sect. supr. advanced carburetor applications, 1971-73, supr. solid and fluid mechanics, 1973-76, systems engr. engine certification strategy, 1976—. Mem. Soc. Automotive Engrs. Holder 19 patents in field automotive engring. Home: 27792 Johnson St Grosse Ile MI 48138 Office: Ford Motor Co PO Box 2053 Dearborn MI 48124

HARROD, JOHN PRICE, JR., physician; b. Savannah, Ga., Apr. 18, 1923; s. John Price and Gladys (Still) H.; student Emory U., 1943; M.D., U. Ga., 1946; m. Kathleen L. Sheedy, Nov. 13, 1948; children—John Price III, William Joseph, Laurence Lee, Susan Byron. Intern, Gorgas Hosp., Panama, C.Z., 1946-47; resident in obstetrics and gynecology U. Hosp., Augusta, Ga., 1947, 49, Duval County Hosp., Jacksonville, Fla., 1949-50, Chgo. Lying-In Hosp., 1951-52; asst. prof. obstetrics and gynecology, 1963—; practice medicine specializinig in obstetrics and gynecology, Chgo., 1958—; mem. active staff S. Chgo. Community Hosp., 1958—, chmn. dept. obstetrics and gynecology, 1963—, bd. dirs., 1977—, pres. staff, 1972, pres. elect 1973; cons. staff Chgo. Lying-In Hosp., 1963—; asso. staff Cook County Hosp., Chgo., 1959-61. Bd. dirs. chmn. med. adv. com. Chgo. Area Planned Parenthood Association; Served to capt. M.C., AUS, 1947-49. Diplomate Am. Bd. Obstetrics and Gynecology. Mem. AMA, Chgo. Gynecol. Soc. (sec. 1970-73, pres. 1974-75), Central Assn. Obstetrics and Gynecology. (exec. com. 1971-75), South Chgo. C. of C., Association Am., Med. Colls., Pan Am. Med. Soc., Am. Coll. Obstetricians and Gynecologists (vice chmn. Ill. sect. 1969-72, chmn., 1972-75, dist. vice-chmn. 1977—), Chgo. Med. Soc. (trustee 1975—), Ill. Soc. Obstetrics & Gynecology. Clubs: Mid-Am. Confreire de la Chaine des Rotisseurs (vice chancelier Chgo.), Connoisseurs Internat. Home: 10014 S Seeley Ave Chicago IL 60643 Office: 2315 E 93d St Chicago IL 60617

HARRY, ORMSBY L., univ. adminstr.; b. Richmond, Ind., Aug. 28, 1918; s. Fern Cullers and Bess (Keselring) H.; student Kendall Coll., 1938-39; B.S., Ohio U., 1942, M.S., 1947; Ed.D., Mich. State U., 1960; m. Helen Louise Barklow, June 26, 1943; children—Howard David, Kathryn S., Anne L. Overlien, Rachel Lynne. Head resident Ohio U., Athens, 1946-47; asso. dean students U. Omaha, 1947-52; grad. asst. Mich. State U., East Lansing, 1952-53; asso. dean students, asso. prof. edn. Mich. Tech. U., Houghton, 1953-59; dean students, prof. edn. Shepherd Coll., Shepherdstown, W.Va., 1959-63, asst. chancellor student affairs, prof. psychology U. Wis.-Eau Claire, 1963—. Leadership tng. chmn. Winchester (Va.) Boy Scouts Am., 1961-63, Chippewa Valley (Wis.) Council, 1964-69. Served with USAAF, 1942-46. Mem. Danzarine Dance Club, Phi Kappa Phi, Phi Eta Sigma (nat. exec. com. 1976—), Omicron Delta Kappa, Delta Tau Delta, Alpha Phi Omega. Presbyn. (elder). Kiwanian (dir. Houghton, Mich., 1955-58, Eau Claire, 1963—). Home: 1515 E Webster St Eau Claire WI 54701

HARSH, LESTER, state legislator; b. Bartley, Nebr., Mar. 13, 1910; s. J.A. and Anna (Brahmer) H.; student U. Nebr., 1928-31; m. Elizabeth Mills, Apr. 27, 1932; children—Del, Stephen, Philip. Farmer, Bartley, 1931—; mem. Nebr. Legislature, Lincoln, 1965—. Mem. schs. redistricting group Edn. Com. Nebr., 1956-64; mem. Nebr. Commn. Higher Ed., Nebr. Assn. Resource Dists.; pres. bd. Hester Homes, Binkleman, Nebr.; founder Heritage Days Celebration. Mem. Am. Hist. Soc. Germans from Russia (dir.). Methodist. Home: 2205 Norris St McCook NE 69001 Office: 1201 J Lincoln NE 68508

HARSHA, WILLIAM HOWARD, congressman; b. Portsmouth, Ohio, Jan. 1, 1921; s. William Howard and Imogene (Matthews) H.; A.B., Kenyon Coll., 1943, LL.D. (hon.), 1975; LL.B., Western Res. U., 1947; m. Rosemary Spellerberg, Sept. 23, 1946; children—Bill, Mark, Bruce, Brian. Admitted to Ohio bar, 1947; asst. city solicitor, Portsmouth, 1947-51; prosecutor Scioto County, 1951-55, practice Portsmouth, 1947-61; mem. 87th-95th Congresses from 6th Dist. Ohio, mem. pub. works com. Chmn. Scioto County Tb and Health Assn., 1948-49; bd. dirs. Scioto County Cancer Soc., 1958-59, Portsmouth chpt. ARC, 1956—. Served with USMCR, World War II. Recipient Outstanding Citizenship award, award of Life, Internat. Road Safety award (1st Am.). Mem. Grange, Scioto County Agrl. Assn., Portsmouth Bar Assn., Amateur Trapshooting Assn. (life), Bus. and Profl. Mens Club Portsmouth, Am. Legion, 40 and 8, DAV. Republican. Clubs: Masons (33 deg.), Odd Fellows, Elks, Portsmouth Exchange. Home: 2021 Suprise Ave Portsmouth OH 45662 also 1102 Delf Dr McLean VA 22101 Office: House Office Bldg Washington DC 20515

HARSHAW, JACK RAYMOND, newspaperman; b. Creston, Iowa, Oct. 23, 1927; s. John Winter and Mary Margaretha (Schwalbe) H.; student Creston Jr. Coll., 1948-49; B.J., U. Mo., 1953; m. Betty Doris Matthews, Aug. 21, 1954. Sports editor Carthage (Mo.) Press, 1953-69, farm editor, 1953-75, wire editor, 1958-59, city editor, 1970—; cons., lectr. in field. Active United Fund campaign, ARC dr. Bd. dirs. Carthage YMCA. Served with AUS, 1946-47, 50-51; PTO, Korea. Mem. Soc. Profl. Journalists, Athletic Booster Club Carthage, A.P. Mng. Editors Assn., Sigma Delta Chi. Rotarian. Home: 951 Wendy Ln Carthage MO 64836 Office: 527 Main St Carthage MO 64836

HARSHBARGER, KENNETH E., dairy scientist; b. Arcola, Ill., Nov. 12, 1914; s. Harry H. and Maude Ethel H.; B.S., U. Ill., 1937, M.S., 1939, Ph.D., 1960; m. Elsie Joan Brown, Aug. 31, 1957; children—Kenneth Lee, Keven E., Kent E., Karen E. Vocational-agr. instr. LaRose (Ill.) High Sch., 1937-38; asst. dairy production U. Ill., Urbana, 1938-41, instr. dairy production, 1946, asst. prof. dairy science 1946-60, asso. prof., 1960-62, prof., 1962-63, prof. nutrition in dairy science, 1963—; asso. head dept., 1963-69, head dept. dairy science, 1969—; cons. in field. Served with U.S. Army, 1941-46. Mem. Am. Inst. Nutrition, Am. Soc. Animal Science, Am. Dairy Science Assn., Alpha Zeta, Sigma Xi, Phi Kappa Phi, Gamma Sigma Delta. Office: Dept Dairy Science Univ Ill Urbana IL 61801

HARSHMAN, MORTON LEONARD, physician; b. Youngstown, Ohio, Apr. 21, 1932, s. Ben and Lillian (Malkoff) H.; B.S., Ohio State U., 1953, M.D., 1957; m. Barbara Elmore, June 21, 1957; children—Beth, Melissa. Intern Grant Hosp., Columbus, Ohio, 1957-58; practice medicine specializing in family practice, Cin., 1960—; v.p. med. staff Bethesda Hosp., 1974-75, pres., 1975—; mem. staff Christ Hosp., Children's Hosp., Deaconess Hosp., Providence Hosp. (all Cin.). Pres., bd. dirs. Morton Harshman Inc., 880 Real Estate Co. Served with USNR, 1958-60. Fellow Am. Acad. Family Practice (charter); mem. Am. Bd. Family Practice (charter), A.M.A., Ohio Med. Assn. Cin. Acad. Medicine, Ohio, Southwestern Ohio acads. family practice, Kentucky Col. Assn., Phi Beta Kappa, Alpha Epsilon Delta, Club: Phi Delta Epsilon Grad. (Cin.). Home: 630 Flagstaff Dr Cincinnati OH 45215 Office: 880 Reynard Dr Cincinnati OH 45231

HART, DONALD LEROY, bearing co. exec.; b. Mansfield, Ohio, Feb. 1, 1933; s. George W. and Martha (Main) H.; B.S., Ohio U., 1956; postgrad. Harvard, 1973; m. Rhoda Hoffman, Aug. 18, 1956; children—Douglas George and David William (twins). Sales engr. trainee Timken Co., Canton, Ohio, 1956-58, sales engr., dist. mgr. indsl. div., Los Angeles, 1959-62, sales engr. internat. div., Canton, 1962-64, advt. mgr., 1964-68, dir. sales Europe div., 1968-70, group mgr. sales, automotive service sales internat., Canton, 1970-77, group mgr. sales, indsl., railroad and steel, 1977—. Capt., Q.M.C., AUS Res., 1956-63, Mem. ASME, Assn. Iron and Steel Engrs., Soc. Automotive Engrs., Delta Tau Delta, Clubs: Canton, Brookside Country. Home: 3704 Parkhill Circle NW Canton OH 44718 Office: 1835 Dueber Ave SW Canton OH 44706

HART, DONN VORHIS, univ. adminstr.; b. Anaheim, Calif., Feb. 15, 1918; s. Edgar Manton and Iva (Vorhis) H.; A.B., U. Calif. at Berkeley, 1941; M.A., Harvard, 1942; Ph.D., Syracuse U., 1954; m. Harriett Elizabeth Colegrove, May 31, 1954; 1 dau., Susan Elizabeth. Asst. prof. anthropology U. Denver, 1951-54; vis. prof. anthropology U. Philippines, Quezon City, 1956-57; research asso. Yale, 1956-57, Syracuse (N.Y.) U., 1957-71; prof. anthropology, dir. Center S.E. Asian Studies, No. Ill. U., DeKalb, 1971—; Fulbright fellow research Philippines, 1950-51, 54-56, 64-65; cons. in field. Chmn. Com. Research Materials S.E. Asia, 1971-74; exec. sec. Philippine Study Com., 1975—; mem. S.E. Asia Region Council, 1970-72. Served with USAAF, 1942-46. Mem. Assn. Asian Studies, Am. Anthropology Assn., Am. Folklore Assn., Sigma Nu. Author: (with H.E. Wilson) The Philippines, 1946; Riddles in Philippine Folklore: An Anthropological Analysis, 1965; Compadrinazgo: Ritual Kinship in the Philippines, 1977. Home: 430 Hillcrest Dr DeKalb IL 60115

HART, HARRY JAMES, paper co. exec.; b. Chgo., June 17, 1918; s. Robert J. and Peggy (Slutzker) H.; B.S., Northwestern U., 1939. Br. mgr. Nat. Bond & Investment Co., Evanston, Ill., 1939-41; with Schwarz Paper Co., Chgo., 1946—, dir., 1960—, v.p., 1967—. Bd. dirs., v.p. Sr. Centers Met. Chgo., 1974—; trustee Harry J. Hart Found. Served to capt. AUS, 1941-46. Mem. Cercle Universitaire Franco Americaine, Alliance Francaise, Paper Club of Chgo. (pres. 1965-66). Clubs: Lake Shore Country (Glencoe, Ill.); Downtown, Executives (Chgo.). Home: 2321C N Geneva Terr Chicago IL 60614 Office: Schwarz Paper Co 8338 N Austin Ave Morton Grove IL 60053

HART, JAY ALBERT CHARLES, realtor; b. Rockford, Ill., Apr. 16, 1923; s. Jabez Waterman and Monty Evangeline (Burgin) H.; student U. Ill., 1941-42, U. Mo., 1942-43, U. Miami (Fla.), 1952-56, Rockford Coll., 1961-62; m. Marie D. Goetz, July 16, 1976; children—Dale M. (Mrs. Richard Peel Jr.), Jay C.H. Exec. v.p. Hart Oil Co., Rockford, 1947—; pres. Internat. Service Co., Pompano Beach, Fla., 1952-58; v.p. Ipsen Industries Inc., Rockford, 1958-61; owner Hart Realtors, Rockford, 1961—. Lectr. in field; trustee, sr. analyst Anchor Real Estate Investment Trust, Chgo., 1971—. Dir. Winnebago County (Ill.) CD, 1975. Chmn. Rock River chpt. A.R.C., 1973, nat. nominating com., 1971, disaster chmn. Illiana div., 1972—; bd. counselors Rockford Coll., 1974—; emergency coordinator 9th Naval dist. M.A.R.S., USN, 1960-68, civilian adv. council, 1968—. Office mgr. Citizens for Eisenhower, Chgo., 1952. Served with USAAF, 1943-46. Mem. Rockford Art Guild (pres. 1974, 76), Tamaroa Watercolor Soc. (v.p. 1974—), Rockford Boys Club Assn. (dir.), Exptl. Amateur Radio Soc. (pres. 1960—), Internat. Council Shopping Centers, Nat. Assn. Real Estate Appraisers, Soc. Indsl. Realtors, Nat. Assn. Realtors, Phi Eta Sigma. Mason (Shriner). Clubs: Rockford Country, Mid-Day, Gaslight. Author: Real Estate Buyers and Sellers Guide, 1961. Paintings in pvt., pub. collections; illustrations in numerous publs. Home: 2406 E Lane Rockford IL 61107 Office: 3623 E State St Rockford IL 61108

HART, JOHN BIRDSALL, physicist, educator; b. Hamilton, Ohio, Aug. 24, 1924; s. John Wilson and Elizabeth (Birdsall) H.; B.S., Xavier U., 1948, M.S., 1950; m. Agnes Marie Roegner, June 17, 1948; 1 dau., Mary Agnes. Instr., Xavier U., Cin., 1950-56, asst. prof., 1956-62, asso. prof., 1962-68, prof., 1968—, chmn. physics dept., 1958-71, dir. internat. conf. on quantum mechanics, 1962. Vis. prof. Fla. State U., 1967-68, Miami U., Oxford, Ohio, 1974; cons. prof. Ohio U., 1970-71; lectr. numerous sci. confs., Ednl. TV. Served with USNR, 1943-46. Mem. Am. Assn. Physics Tchrs., Nat. Sci. Tchrs. Assn., Am. Physical Soc. (Ohio sect.), Ohio Acad. Sci., Sigma Xi, Sigma Pi Sigma. Author: Lectures on Atomic Physics, 1957. Patentee in field. Home: 3836 Ledgewood Dr Cincinnati OH 45207

HART, JOSEPH MONTRAVILLE, JR., banker; b. Davenport, Nebr., Aug. 24, 1921; s. Joseph Montraville and Bessie Ann (Sien) H.; student U. Nebr., 1939, Banking Sch., U. Wis., 1960; m. Wilma Harriet Stutt, June 9, 1946; children—Charles M., Robert J., Jeannine A. Bookkeeper, Farmers & Traders Bank, Waco, Nebr., 1941-42; with North Side Bank, Omaha, 1945—, dir., 1955—, exec. v.p., 1967, pres. 1967—. Chmn. Mayor's Econ. Devel. Com., Omaha, 1970-71; chmn. mgmt. com. Miller Park YMCA, 1963-64; mem. Omaha Charter Rev. Com., 1965; co-chmn. supt.'s adv. com. Omaha Sch. Dist., 1967; mayor's adv. com., Omaha, 1966-67; pres. Florence Hist. Found. Vice pres. Bd. Edn., Omaha, 1969-70, pres., 1971-73. Bd. dirs. Dist. 7 Nebr. State Sch. Bd. Assn., South Omaha Indsl. Park, 1972-73; trustee Omaha Tchrs. Retirement System, 1971-73, Nebr. Ind. Coll. Found., 1977—; pres., mem. bd. Met. Tech. Community Coll. Found., 1976—; bd. dirs. Florence Home for Aged, Landmarks, Inc. Served with USAAF, 1942-45. Recipient of Sch. Bell award Omaha Edn. Assn. 1972. Certified comml. lender Am. Bankers Assn. Mem. Nat. Assn. Bank Auditors and Controllers (chpt. pres. 1954-55), C. of C. (bd. dirs. 1971-73), Nebr. PTA (life mem.), Nebr. Hist. Found. (trustee 1969—), Nat. Congress P.T.A.'s (life), Nebr. (exec. bd. 1974—), Douglas County (bd. dirs. 1962—, treas. 1977) hist. socs., Nebr. (legis. com.), Omaha bankers assns. (pres. 1973), Omaha-Lincoln Fin. Analysts, Robert Morris Assos. (gov.), Am. Legion, VFW. Clubs: Commercial (pres. 1965-66), Kiwanis (pres. 1959-60) (Omaha). Home: 7815 Fairway Dr Omaha NE 68152 Office: 31st St and Ames Ave Omaha NE 68111

HART, MARY MARGARET, elementary sch. counselor; b. Mpls., Sept. 8, 1946; d. Thomas Mathew and Margaret Ann (Mc Govern) H.; A.B., Coll. Mt. St. Joseph-on-the-Ohio, Cin., 1968; M.Ed., Miami U., Oxford, Ohio, 1969. Elementary sch. counselor Columbus (Ohio) Pub. Schs., 1969—. Mem. Am. Personnel and Guidance Assn., Am. Sch. Counselors Assn., Columbus Elementary Sch. Counselors. Assn. (exec. bd., chmn. social com. 1976—). Roman Cahtolic. Address: 2550 Dover Rd Columbus OH 43209

HART, RICHARD HOWE, gen. surgeon; b. Battle Creek, Mich., Feb. 15, 1923; s. William Lafayette and Rose Marie (Ainsworth) H.; B.S., U. Ill., 1944, M.D., 1946; m. Jeredith L. White, June 21, 1969; children—Richard Howe, Steven, Linda. Intern U. Mich., Ann Arbor, 1946-47, resident in gen. surgery, 1947-53; sr. surgeon Akron (Ohio) City Hosp., 1970—; privileged surgeon Akron Children's Hosp., 1970-75; chief of staff, exec. com. Akron City Hosp., 1970-75, chief, 1974-75; individual practice medicine, specializing in gen. surgery Akron, 1953—; asso. clin. prof. surgery Ohio State U. Coll. Medicine, Columbus, 1974—; Served to capt., M.C., AUS, 1948-50. Diplomate Am. Bd. Surgery. Fellow A.C.S.; mem. AMA, Ohio, Summit County med. assns., Coller Surg. Soc., Sigma Chi, Alpha Omega Alpha, Phi Kappa Phi, Phi Eta Sigma. Republican. Mem. United Ch. Christ. Club: Fairlawn Country. Home: 624 Fairhill Dr Akron OH 44313 Office: 159 S Main St Akron OH 44308

HART, ROBERT GORDON, ret. constrn. co. exec.; b. Rockford, Ill., Sept. 11, 1907; s. Eugene Earl and Nettie (Smith) H.; B.S. in Civil Engring., U. Ill., 1928; m. Rita Marie Sullivan, June 1, 1940 (dec. Jan. 1973); children—John, Anita (Mrs. Joseph Balliro, III), William, Mary. Field engr. B. &O. C.T. R.R., Chgo., 1928-32; constrn. supt. Nat. Park Service, Marseilles, Ill., 1933-40; project engr. U.S. Corps Engrs., Baraboo, Wis., 1940-45; constrn. supt. Siesel Constrn. Co., Milw., 1946-60, v.p., treas., 1960-74, ret., 1974; part time instr. Marquette U., Milw., 1974-75; part-time cons., constrn. mgmt.

services, 1975—. Bd. dirs., pres. Allied Constrn. Employment Assn., Milw., 1963-67; dir. Builders Exchange Milw., 1964-72, pres., 1970-71. mem. adv. com. Milw. Equal Econ. Opportunity Com., 1968-71. Named Milw. Constrn. Man of Year Allied Constrn. Employees Assn., 1973. Mem. Am. Soc. Civil Engrs. (sect. dir., pres. 1960-65), Assn. Gen. Contractors Milw. (dir. 1959-63, S.I.R. award 1973). Home: 8505 W Hadley St Milwaukee WI 53222

HART, RONALD CARY, ops. research analyst; b. Norfolk, Va., Feb. 25, 1949; s. Robert Clyde and Mary Julia (Scott) H.; B.S., Va. Poly. Inst. and State U., 1971; M.S., U. Notre Dame, 1977; m. Deborah Woodruff Froehlich, Aug. 21, 1971; children—Michelle Naomi, Ronald Cary. Analyst, Computing and Software, Inc., Hampton, Va., 1971-72; systems analyst Space Radiation Effects Lab., NASA, Newport News, Va., 1972; sr. analyst Gen. Electric Co., Beltsville, Md., 1972-74; sr. ops. research analyst Miles Labs., Inc., Elkhart, Ind., 1974—; fin. cons., systems cons. Pledge chmn. Unitarian Universalists, 1976—; vol. leader No. Ind. council Boy Scouts Am., 1967—. Mem. Am. Chem. Soc., Soc. Research Adminstrs., Am. Mgmt. Assn., Phi Kappa Phi, Sigma Pi Sigma. Contbr. articles to tech. jours. Home: 137 Bank St Elkhart IN 46514 Office: 1127 Myrtle St Elkhart IN 46514

HART, RUTH ALICIA, mktg. exec.; b. Portsmouth, Va., Sept. 20, 1944; d. Chester Eustice and Dorothy (Dunbar) Hart; B.S. in Edn., Central Conn. State Coll., 1968, M.S., 1973; postgrad. Roosevelt U., 1977—. Tchr., West Hartford (Conn.) Pub. Schs., 1968-73; sales promotion asst. in mktg. communications dept. Aetna Life & Casualty Co., Hartford, Conn., 1973-74, supr. advt. dept., 1974-76; mktg. asst. Allstate Ins. Co., Northbrook, Ill., 1976-77; mktg. list mgr. Aldens, Inc., Chgo., 1977—. Mem. Chgo. Direct Mktg. Assn. Home: 929 Washington St Evanston IL 60202 Office: Aldens Inc 5000 W Roosevelt Rd Chicago IL 60607

HART, WILLIAM THOMAS, lawyer; b. Joliet, Ill., Feb. 4, 1929; s. William M. and Geraldine (Archambeault) H.; J.D., Loyola U., 1951; m. Catherine M. Motta, Nov. 27, 1954; children—Catherine, Susan, Julie, Sally, Nancy. Admitted to Ill. bar, 1951, U.S. Dist. Ct., 1951, U.S. Ct. Appeals 7th Circuit, 1954, U.S. Ct. Appeals D.C., 1977; asst. U.S. atty. No. Dist. of Ill., 1954-56, atty. DeFrees, Fiske, O'Brien & Thompson, Chgo., 1956-59; atty., partner, Schiff, Hardin, Waite, Dorschel & Britton, Chgo., 1959—. Special asst. atty. gen. Ill., Hodge Investigation and Litigation, 1957-58; spl. asst. states atty. Cook County, Chgo. Police Dept. Grand Jury Investigation, 1960. Bd. dirs., exec. com. Aurora Area Blood Bank; v.p. adv. bd. Mercy Center for Health Care Service; bd. dirs. Chgo. Legal Assistance Found. Served with AUS, 1951-53; Korea. Decorated Bronze Star. Mem. Am., Ill., Chgo. (vice chmn. div. II inquiry com.), 7th Circuit bar assns., Soc. Trial Lawyers, Phi Alpha Delta. Republican. Roman Catholic. Clubs: Metropolitan, Union League (Chgo.); Aurora Country. Home: 123 S Evanslawn Aurora IL 60506 Office: 233 S Wacker Dr Chicago IL 60606

HARTDAGEN, GERALD EUGENE, coll. ofcl.; b. Thurmont, Md., June 25, 1931; s. Francis Stone and Frances (Blickenstaff) Orendorff; B.A., U. Md., 1957; M.A., Northwestern U., 1959, Ph.D., 1965; m. Doris N. Perrie, Aug. 3, 1957; children—Sandra Elaine, Diane Carol. Instr. history Ill. State U., Normal, 1959-61, U. Ill., Chgo., 1964; asst. prof. history Lycoming Coll., Williamsport, Pa., 1964-68; vis. prof. history Long Beach (Calif.) State Coll., summer 1967; asso. prof. history Ind. U.-Purdue U., Indpls., 1968-74, prof., 1974-75; v.p. for acad. affairs, dean Concordia Coll., Moorhead, Minn., 1975—. Served with USN, 1948-52. Danforth fellow, 1957-64. Mem. Am. Hist. Assn., Orgn. Am. Historians, Md. Hist. Soc. Soc. for Religion in Higher Edn. Contbr. articles to profl. jours. Home: 1411 23d Ave S Moorhead MN 56560

HARTE, J. RICHARD, psychiatrist; b. St. Louis, May 23, 1928; s. William J. and Mary A. (Cashman) H.; B.S., Central Mo. State Coll., 1951; M.D., Washington U., 1954; m. Corrine A. Lemire, Aug. 6, 1965; children—Jim, Jean, Paul, Chris. Intern, Kansas City (Kans.) Gen. Hosp., 1954-55; resident gen. psychiatry Menninger Clinic, Topeka, 1955-58; fellow child psychiatry Washington U., 1960-62; dir. St. Clair County (Ill.) Mental Health Center, 1958-60, Madison County (Ill.) Mental Health Center, 1959-65; dir. child psychiatry Jewish Hosp., St. Louis, 1963-65; practice, specializing in child psychiatry, Kansas City, Mo., 1965—; dir. child guidance program, dir. tng. in child psychiatry Greater Kansas City Mental Health Found., 1965—. Served with AUS, 1946-47. Fellow Am. Psychiat. Assn.; mem. Am. Orthopsychiat. Assn., Am. Acad. Child Psychiatry, Am. Soc. Autistic Children, Mo. Assn. Children with Learning Disabilities. Office: 600 E 22d St Kansas City MO 64108 also Suite 202 4400 Broadway Kansas City MO 64111

HARTER, DONALD HARRY, med. educator; b. Breslau, Germany, May 16, 1933; s. Harry Morton and Leonor Evelyn (Goldmann) H.; m. Lee Grossman, Dec. 18, 1960 (div. 1976); children—Kathryne, Jennifer, Amy, David; came to U.S., 1940, naturalized, 1945; A.B., U. Pa., 1953; M.D., Columbia, 1957; intern medicine Yale-New Haven Med. Center, 1957-58; asst. resident, then resident neurology N.Y. Neurol. Inst., 1958-61; guest investigator Rockefeller U., 1963-66; mem. faculty Columbia Coll. Phys. and Surg., 1960-75, prof. neurology and microbiology, 1973-75; attending neurologist N.Y. Neurol. Inst., Presbyn. Hosp., 1973-75; Charles L. Mix prof., chmn. dept. neurology Med. Sch., Northwestern U., Chgo., 1975—; chmn. dept. neurology Northwestern Meml. Hosp., Chgo., 1975—. Mem. adv. com. on fellowships Nat. Multiple Sclerosis Soc., 1976—, chmn., 1977; mem. Nat. Commn. on Venereal Disease, HEW, 1970-72; med. adv. bd. Am. Parkinson's Disease Assn., 1976—. Diplomate Am. Bd. Psychiatry and Neurology. Mem. Am. Soc. Clin. Investigation, Am. Neurol. Assn., Am. Assn. Neuropathologists, Soc. Exptl. Biology and Medicine, Assn. U. Profs. Neurology, Infectious Disease Soc. Am. Tissue Culture Assn., Am. Acad. Neurology, Am. Assn. Immunologists, Am. Soc. Microbiology, Harvey Soc., Phi Beta Kappa, Sigma Xi. Spl. fellow USPHS, 1963-66; Am. Cancer Soc. scholar, 1973-74; Guggenheim fellow, 1973. Home: 900 Lake Shore Dr Chicago IL 60611 Office: Dept Neurology Northwestern U Med Sch 303 E Chicago Ave Chicago IL 60611

HARTER, HUGH ANTHONY, educator; b. Columbus, Ohio, Dec. 13, 1922; s. Anthony H. and Georgiana (Hayes) H.; student Ohio Wesleyan U., 1940-41; B.A., Ohio State U., 1947, Ph.D., 1958; M.A., U. Americas (Mexico), 1951; m. Francis D. Reichman, Oct. 7, 1970. Instr., asst. prof. romance langs. Wesleyan U., Conn., 1953-59; asso. prof. Elmira Coll., 1959-60; postdoctoral Mellon fellow U. Pitts., 1960-61; asso. prof. Chatham Coll., Pitts., 1961-64; asso. prof. Loyola U., Chgo., 1964-66; prof., chmn. dept. Ohio Wesleyan U., Delaware, 1966—, dir. Ohio Wesleyan U.-Otterbein Coll. jr. year abroad program Spain, 1968—. Vice pres. Alliance Francaise, Columbus, 1969-75, life pres. Fundacion Juan-Ruiz, Segovia, Spain, 1971—; pres. Horizons for Learning, 1974—; v.p. Delaware Heritage, 1974-76, bd. dirs., 1976—. Served with M.I., Air Transport Command, AUS, World War II ETO. Editor: (with Willis Barnstone) Cervantes' Rinconete y Cortadillo, 1960; (with R. C. Allen) A First Spanish Handbook For Teachers in Elementary Schools, 1961; (with R. C. Allen) A Second Spanish Handbook, 1963. Transl. A History of Spanish Literature (G. Diaz-Plaja), 1971. Contbr. articles to profl. jours. Home: 52 W Winter St Delaware OH 43015 Office: Ohio Wesleyan U Delware OH 43015 also 25 Central Park W New York City NY

HARTER, JOHN J., state ofcl.; b. nr. New Castle, Ind., Dec. 25, 1922; s. Claude and Arnetta (Miller) H.; student agrl. econs. Purdue, 1940-42; m. Norma Wantz, July 24, 1942; children—Nancy Ellen (Mrs. Ronald Futrell), Zeta Kay (Mrs. George Carter), Barry Merrill. Dairy farmer, New Castle, 1942-60; commr. Henry County, New Castle, 1960-64, 64—, planning commr., 1965-66, recorder, 1967-73; dir. Ind. Sch. Food and Nutrition Programs, 1973—. Leader Community Fund, 1966, Heart Fund. 1956. Recipient of Golden Ruler award for Co. Officials 1971. Mem. Ind. Assn. Counties (bd. dirs.), Northeastern Dist. County Ofcls., Ind. Recorders Assn., Ind. Commrs. Assn. (sec. 1963-64), Ind. (sec. 1960-66, recipient distinguished service award 1966), Am. (recipient secretarial award 1965) Jersey cattle clubs, Henry County Purdue U. Alumni Assn. Mem. Disciples of Christ Ch. Optimist (pres. 1968-69). Home: 425 Cedar Dr New Castle IN 47362 Office: 120 W Market Indianapolis IN 46204

HARTIGAN, NEIL F., former lt. gov. Ill., banker; b. Chgo.; grad. social scis. Georgetown U.; LL.B., Loyola U., Chgo.; m. Marge Hartigan; children—John, Elizabeth, Laura, Bridget. Admitted to Ill. bar; formerly adminstrv. asst. to Chgo. Mayor Richard J. Daley; legislative counsel City Chgo. in Ill. 75th Gen. Assembly; then chief legal counsel Chgo. Park Dist.; lt. gov. Ill., 1972-77; v.p. 1st Nat. Bank of Chgo., 1977—; pres. Real Estate Research Corp., 1977—, lectr. Active Am. Cancer Soc. drives. Democratic committeeman 49th ward Chgo., 1968-72. Bd. regents Georgetown U. Named among Ten Outstanding Young Men Yr. Chgo. Jr. C. of C., 1967, among Zoo Future Leaders Am., Time mag.; hon. pres. Spanish-speaking div. Jr. C. of C., Chgo.; hon. citizen several Latin Am. countries; recipient award Ill. Assn. Park Dists., 1972. Mem. Nat. Conf. Lt. Govs. (regional vice chmn.), Dem. Adv. Council Elected Ofcls. Home: 1120 W Albion St Chicago IL 60626 Office: 1st Nat Bank of Chgo One 1st Nat Plaza Chicago IL 60670*

HARTLAUB, LAWRENCE PHILIP, bakery exec.; b. Cin., Aug. 3, 1913; s. Sylvester Leo and Loretta (Gerver) H.; student Central YMCA Coll.; J.D., John Marshall Law Sch., 1939; m. Helen E. Bruhn, Oct. 12, 1940; children—Lawrence Philip, Mary Loretto, Anne Elizabeth. Admitted to Ill. bar, 1939; with firm Bennett & Colbach, Chgo., 1929-38, Furst & Furst Collection Agy., Chgo., 1938-42; finance dept. Jewel Cos., Barrington, Ill. and Melrose Park, Ill., 1942-61; v.p.-treas., counsel Salerno-Megowen Biscuit Co., Chgo., 1961—, also trustee employees profit sharing plan and pension plan; partner firm Hartlaub & Hartlaub, Barrington, 1969—; sec.-treas., dir. Salerno Machinery Corp., Niles, Ill., 1970—; dir. Repro Supply Co., Chgo. Chmn., Barrington Planning Commn., 1959-74, village trustee, 1975—; mem. Barrington Area Devel. Council, 1966-74. Served with USNR, 1944-46. Mem. Am. Legion. Roman Catholic. K.C. (4 deg.). Club: Lake Geneva (Wis.) Yacht. Home: 113 Elm Rd Barrington IL 60010 Office: 7777 N Caldwell St Niles IL 60648

HARTLE, RICHARD EUGENE, physician; b. nr. Kenton, Hardin County, Ohio, Nov. 15, 1932; s. Clair K. and Gladys Irene (Benge) H.; B.S., Ohio State U., 1954, M.D., 1958; m. Myrna Mae Knight, Sept. 19, 1954; children—Michael, Cheryl, Susan, Andrew. Intern Brooke Army Hosp., San Antonio, 1958-59; resident Riverside Meth. Hosp., Columbus, Ohio, 1963-64; pvt. practice medicine specializing in gen. practice, Lancaster, Ohio, 1964—; attending physician Lancaster Fairfield County Hosp., 1964—, chief dept. gen. practice, 1968-70, pres. med. staff, 1977—; mem. Lancaster City Bd. Health, 1967—, pres. pro tem, 1970-76. Served to capt. AUS, 1959-63. Mem. Am., Ohio, Fairfield County (pres. 1969-70) acads. gen. practice, Fairfield County Med. Soc. (v.p. 1968, 73, pres. 1974), AMA, Ohio Med. Assn. (8th dist. councilor), Assn. Am. Physicians and Surgeons, Lancaster Area C. of C. (dir.), Phi Beta Kappa, Alpha Epsilon Delta. Presbyn. Mason; mem. Order Eastern Star. Home: 1788 Baltimore Rd Lancaster OH 43130 Office: 600 Pleasantville Rd Lancaster OH 43130

HARTLEY, WYNONA SMUTZ (MRS. RICHARD GLENDALE HARTLEY), sociologist; b. Iowa City, Iowa, Aug. 6, 1927; d. Ralph H. and Margaret (Conard) Smutz; A.A., Stephens Coll., Columbia, 1946; B.A., State U. Iowa, 1948; certificate, Stephens Coll., 1949; M.A., State U. Iowa, 1951; Ph.D., 1961; m. Charles O. Garretson, Oct. 9, 1952, (div. June 1961); m. 2d, Richard Glendale Hartley, Oct. 27, 1962; 1 stepdau., Patricia Hartley Young. Asst. residence hall counselor Stephens Coll., 1947-48; instr. sociology Iowa Wesleyan Coll., Mt. Pleasant, Iowa, 1952-55; asst. prof., 1955-58, asso. prof., 1959-61, head dept. 1955-61; leave of absence to Danforth Tchrs. Grant, 1958-59; research specialist Div. Spl. Services, State U. Iowa, 1961-62; continuing research and writing, 1962—; sr. research asso. epidemiol. field sta. Greater Kansas City (Mo.) Mental Health Found., 1967-70; asso. prof. dept. psychiatry U., Mo. Sch. Medicine, 1968—; asst. prof. dept. community health U. Kans. Sch. Medicine, 1970—. Mem. Am. Midwest, Iowa (past sec.-treas.) sociol. assns., Am. Pub. Health Assn., Delta Gamma. Republican. Episcopalian. Home: 8704 Lafayette Ct Kansas City KS 66109

HARTMAN, GEORGE EDWARD, educator, mktg. scientist; b. Newton, Kans., Oct. 20, 1926; s. Albert J. and Ellen Pawlick H.; B.S., Kans. U., 1950; M.B.A., Ind. U., 1951; Ph.D., U. Ill., 1958; J.D., U. Cin., 1964. Instr. mktg. Tex. A. and M. U., 1951-52; asst. prof. U. N.D., Grand Forks, 1952-55; instr. mktg. U. Ill., Urbana, 1955-58; prof. mktg. U. Cin., 1958—; admitted to Ohio bar, 1964, practice law, Cin., 1964—; cons. mktg. Mem. regional export council Dept. Commerce, 1969-74; bd. mgrs. U. Cin. YMCA; bd. dirs. U. Cin., SW Ohio Consumer Assn. Served with Adj.-Gen.'s Office, AUS, 1945-46. Mem. World Trade Club (chmn. edn. com. 1974-75), Cin. C. of C., Am. Mktg. Assn., Am., Ohio bar assns., Acad. Internat. Bus., Am. Council Consumer Interests, AAUP, Beta Gamma Sigma, Delta Sigma Pi, Phi Delta Phi, Lambda Chi Alpha. Democrat. Presbyterian. Mason (32 deg.). Contbg. author Handbook of Modern Marketing, 1970. Bd. editors legal devel. sect. Jour. Mktg. 1965—; columnist Mktg. News, 1965—. Home: 310 Bryant St Cincinnati OH 45220

HARTMAN, MARTHA ELIZABETH (MRS. WILLIAM HARTMAN), artist; b. Ashland, Ala., May 11, 1922; d. Charles Marion and Lela (Braswell) Dye; student Ringling Sch. Art, 1945-46, Manatee Jr. Coll., 1966, U. So. Fla., 1967; m. William Hartman, June 2, 1946; children—William Benton, Carol Marie (Mrs. Philippe J. Salazar). Exhibited in one man shows at Hackley Mus. Muskegon, Mich., 1956, Parthenon, Nashville, 1956, Sarasota Art Assn., 1953, U. Fla., 1958; exhibited in group shows at Fountainbleau Gallery, Miami and Ft. Lauderdale, Fla., 1966. Tadlow Galleries, White Hall, Mich., 1967-68, Traveling Show and Ann. Exhibit Petticoat Painters, 1953—. Southeastern Show and Soc. Four Arts, Palm Beach, Atlanta, 1959; operator Hartman Gallery, Sarasota, 1952-60, co-dir., instr. Hartman Studio, Sarasota, 1952—, Silver Lake, Mich., 1967—; organizer, dir. Petticoat Painters, 1952—; mem. staff Ringling Mus., 1966-68. Co-dir. Art Workshops for Sarasota's First Summer Festival, 1953. Recipient awards Fla. Artist Group, 1962-64, Internat. Show So. Coll., Lakeland, 1953, Sarasota Art Assn., 1962, 63, 65, 66, 72, 75, Manatee Art League, 1960, 65, Sun Festival El Paso (Tex.) Mus., 1963. Mem. Nat. Assn. Penwomen, Petticoat Painters, Sarasota Art Assn. (com. chmn. dir.), Ringling Sch. Art Alumni Assn. (pres. 1977). Address: 1393 40th St Sarasota FL 33580 also Silver Lake MI 48760

HARTMAN, WILLIAM, artist, educator; b. Muskegon, Mich., Mar. 8, 1906; s. Thomas and Kate (Karel) H.; studied painting with Harold Anthony DeYoung, Art Inst. Chgo., Dan Lutz, Oxbow Sch., Saugatuck, Mich.; Ringling Sch. Art, Sarasota, Fla.; Jerry Farnsworth Sch., Sarasota; m. Mar Fla.; Jerry Farnsworth Sch., Sarasota; m. Martha Elizabeth Dye, June 2, 1946; children—Carol Marie Hartman Salazar, William Benton. Artist Hartman Gallery and Studio Classes, 1952-68; instr. Ringling Sch. Art, 1969—; instr. summer classes Hackley Gallery, Muskegon, Mich., Tadlow Gallery, Whitehall, Nashville Art Assn.; exhibited in one-man shows Hackley Gallery, Muskegon, Vose Gallery, Boston, Fitchburg (Mass.) Art Center, Children's Art Mus., Boston, Parthenon, Nashville, Loch Haven Art Center, Orlando, Fla., Tadlow Galleries, Whitehall and Holland, Mich., U. Fla. at Gainesville, Stetson U., Deland, Fla.; exhibited in group shows at Southeastern Show, Atlanta, Four Arts, Palm Beach, Arvida, Ringling Mus., Sarasota. Served with M.C., U.S. Army, 1942-45. Home: Route 1 Silver Lake Mears MI 49436

HARTNETT, JOSEPH FRANCIS, mfg. co. exec.; b. St. Louis, Dec. 30, 1947; s. William and Kathleen H. (Hannefin) H.; M.A. in Psychology, N.Mex. State U., 1972; M.B.A., U. Mo., 1975. Asst. to pres. Weather Corp. Am., St. Louis, 1972-73, exec. v.p., 1974-75; pres. Weather Guard, Inc., Earth City, Mo., 1975—, also dir. Served with U.S. Army, 1970-72. Mem. Fin. Mgmt. Assn., Home Builders Assn., World Future Soc., Am. Gas Assn., ACLU. Democrat. Home: 12758 Parkway Estates Dr Saint Louis MO 63141 Office: 4308 Riverline Dr Earth City MO 63045

HARTOCOLLIS, PETER, psychiatrist, hosp. dir.; b. Greece, Nov. 29, 1922; s. Thomas and Mary (Mandrapelias) H.; came to U.S., 1923, naturalized, 1956; student Athens (Greece) U., 1946; B.A., Clark U., 1949; M.A., Mich. State U., 1951, Ph.D., 1954; M.D., Lausanne U., 1955; postgrad. Menninger Sch. Psychiatry, Topeka Inst. Psychoanalysis; m. Pitsa Palli, Apr. 8, 1953; children—Anemona, Lina, Thomas. Intern, St. Mary's Hosp., Waterbury, Conn., 1956; resident in psychiatry Kans. U. Med. Center, 1957, Topeka VA Hosp., 1957-60; staff psychiatrist C.F. Menninger Meml. Hosp., Topeka, 1960-66, sect. chief, 1966-69, research dir., 1969—, hosp. dir., 1973—; cons. Topeka State Hosp., 1964-69, alcoholism program VA Hosp., Topeka, 1966—; tng. and supervising analyst Topeka Inst. Psychoanalysis, 1973—. Diplomate Am. Bd. Psychiatry and Neurology. Fellow Am. Psychiat. Assn., A.C.P.; mem. Am. Psychoanalytic Assn., Internat. Psychoanalytic Assn., AMA, Am. Psychol. Assn., AAAS, N.Y. Acad. Scis. Club: Order of Ahepa. Contbr. articles to profl. jours. Home: 134 Woodlawn St Topeka KS 66606 Office: Menninger Foundation Topeka KS 66601

HARTUNG, DONALD NORMAN, mfg. co. exec.; b. Lima, Ohio, Dec. 31, 1915; s. Glen J. and Amelia (Dune) H.; student U. Akron, 1934-36; m. Hazel Jane Springer, July 18, 1937; children—Donald Glenn, Daniel Richard, James Lee. Various mgmt.-engring. positions Goodyear Aerospace Corp., Akron, Ohio, Brunswick Corp., Muskegon, Mich., 1953-55; factory mgr. Kaydon Engring. Corp., Muskegon, 1955-65; chief tool engr. Reliance Electric and Engring. Co., Ashtabula, Ohio, 1965; gen. mgr. Centerline, Inc., Euclid, Ohio, 1965-66; mgr. mfg. Marquardt Corp., Ogden, Utah, 1967-69; v.p. mfg. United Aircraft Products, Inc., Forest, Ohio, 1969-71; plant mgr. Unverferth Mfg. Co., Inc., Kalida, Ohio, 1971—. Mem. Aircraft Owners and Pilots Assn. Clubs: Kiwanis, Elks, Optimists. Home: 3138 Clifford Dr Lima OH 45805

HARTUNG, HAZEL JANE SPRINGER (MRS. DONALD NORMAN HARTUNG), advt. agy. exec.; b. Youngstown, Ohio, Feb. 19, 1918; d. Homer Edward and Cora (Nichols) Springer; student pub. scis., Akron, Ohio; m. Donald Norman Hartung, July 18, 1937; children—Donald Glenn, Daniel Richard, James Lee. Newspaperwoman, Muskegon (Mich.) Chronicle, 1953-56; indsl. editor Muskegon Piston Ring Co., 1956-57; account exec. Studio 5 Advt. Agy., 1957-59; personnel and pub. relations dir. Hardy-Herpolsheimer's Dept. Store, 1959-61; dir. advt. and pub. relations Nat. Lumberman's Bank, 1961-65; advt., pub. relations dir. Farmers Nat. Bank & Trust Co., 1965-66; mgr. advt. and promotion Fasson Products Corp., 1966-67; pub. service dir. David O. McKay and Thomas D. Dee Meml. Hosps., Ogden, Utah, 1967-69; pub. relations dir. Lima (Ohio) Meml. Hosp., 1969—; mem. adv. bd. Allen Inn; free-lance writer for trade and religious mags., 1953—, editor hosp. publs. Advt. and pub. relations dir. Greater Muskegon's Seaway Festival, 1963; mem. Juvenile Writer's Workshop. Dir., bd. mem. Child and Family Service, Marimor Workshop, v.p. Child and Family Agy.; chmn. pub. relations com. United Fund. Recipient Outdoor Advt. award for creation and execution bill-boards, 1963. Advt. Woman of Year award Advt. and Sales Club Western Mich., 1964. Best Publ. Layout award, Intermountain Council Indsl. Editors, 1969. Mem. Greater Muskegon C. of C. (dir. women's div. 1901-64), Lima Advt. Club, internat. Platform Assn. Mem. Reorganized Ch. of Jesus Christ of Latter-day Saints (women's leader 1961-63, 73-74). Clubs: Zonta (dir. 1962-63, treas. 1963-64), West State Press. (charter; dir. 1963-64), Soroptimist. Home: 3138 Clifford Dr Lima OH 45805 Office: Linden and Mobel Sts Lima OH 45804

HARTUNG, KARL LEA, extension agt.; b. Macon, Mo., Mar. 10, 1936; s. Charley and Lena Berniece (Davis) H.; B.S., U. Mo., 1957, M.S., 1969; m. Elizabeth Coleen Clemmons, Nov. 16, 1969; children—Jeaneeta Clemmons, Janie Lea. Staff extension div. U. Mo., 1958—, asst. agt. Monroe County, 1958-59, balanced farming agt. Montgomery County, 1959-61, agrl. agt. and area livestock specialist Lake of Ozarks Area, Lebanon, 1961-70, area livestock specialist Green Hills Area, Linneus, 1970—. Recipient Dow Study Tour, 1965; Meritorious Service award U. Mo., 1974, Distinguished Service award, 1975; Distinguished Service award Nat. Assn. County Agts., 1976. Mem. U. Mo. Extension Assn. (personnel com. 1973—), Am. Soc. Animal Sci., Alpha Gamma Sigma. Mem. Christian Ch. Home: Box 303 Brookfield MO 64628 Office: Courthouse Linneus MO 64653

HARTUNG, RICHARD PENN, museum exec.; b. Columbus, Ohio, Jan. 31, 1938; s. Maurice Leslie and Gertrude Lillian (Penn) H.; m. Ilah Bjorklund, Aug. 27, 1960; children—Daniel, Gregor. Adminstrv. asst. Philip Koenig Architect, Chgo., 1956-61; dir. Rock County Hist. Soc., Janesville, Wis., 1964—; instr. local history series U. Wis., 1976—; appointee Wis. Hist. Preservation Review Bd., 1972—; active Janesville Area Human Rights Council, 1965-70; sec. Rock Praire Arts Council, 1975-77. Recipient scholarships Am. Bar Assn., Am. Law Inst., 1975. Mem. Am. Assn. State and Local History (scholar 1967), Nat., Chgo., Wis. socs. archtl. historians, Am. Hist. Assn., Nat. Trust for Hist. Preservation (scholar 1970), Am. Assn. Museums (scholar 1973), Midwest Museums Conf. Congregationalist. Co-author, editor (with Nancy S. Douglas) Rock County Historic Sites and Buildings, 1976; editor: Joseph Russell Jones, 1965. Home: 121 S Academy St Janesville WI 53545 Office: PO Box 896 Janesville WI 53545

HARTZELL, ROBERT LEROY, food co. exec.; b. Barron, Wis., June 23, 1941; s. Ray A. and Ruth (Schrader) H.; B.S., U. Wis., 1959-63; m. Mary C. Ladlie, Sept. 5, 1964; children—Christopher Lee, Elizabeth Ann. Mgr. sales and merchandising Wilson & Co. Inc., Albert Lea, Minn. 1963-65, mgr. merchandising, Salt Lake City, 1965-66, Denver, 1966-67, Chgo., 1967-69, product mgr. Domain, Ind., 1969-71; owner North Star Foods Inc., St. Charles, Minn., 1971—. Mem. St. Charles C. of C. Home: 849 Church Ave St Charles MN 55972 Office: North Star Foods Inc PO Box 587 St Charles MN 55972

HARTZLER, HARROD HAROLD, educator; b. Ft. Wayne, Ind., Apr. 7, 1908; s. John Marion and Anna Mary (King) H.; A.B., Juniata Coll., 1930; Ph.D., Rutgers U., 1934; m. Dorothy Baker, Sept. 1, 1933; children—Harold E., Theodosia R. (Mrs. Elvin D. Yoder), Jonathan E. Prof. math and physics Elizabethtown (Pa.) Coll., 1935-37; prof. math. Goshen (Ind.) Coll., 1937-58; prof. math. Mankato (Minn.) State Coll., 1958-76, prof. emeritus, 1976—. Exec. sec. Am. Sci. Affiliation, 1961-72. Bd. dirs. Minn. Acad. Sci. Mem. A.A.A.S., Am. Astron. Soc., Am. Math. Soc., N. Am. Phys. Soc., Sigma Xi, Tau Kappa Alpha. Home: 1311 Warren St Mankato MN 56001

HARVEY, CHARLES HANCOCK, devel. and mgmt. co. exec.; b. Indpls., Sept. 26, 1939; s. Charles H. and Lorene Caroline (Bastin) H.; A.B., Ind. Central U., 1961; M.B.A., Butler U., 1969; m. Patricia Ann Wantland, Aug. 26, 1961; 1 dau., Natalie Ann. Asst. br. mgr. Am. Fletcher Nat. Bank, Indpls., 1960-65; regional appraiser Prudential Co. Am., Indpls., 1965-70; gen. mgr. Indpls. ops. Edward Rose & Sons, Inc., 1970; pres. Deci-Ma Corp., also Deci-Ma Constrn. Co., Indpls., 1971—. Home: 8000 N Illinois St Indianapolis IN 46260 Office: 2441 Production Dr Indianapolis IN 46241

HARVEY, CLYDE FRANCIS, real estate exec.; b. Port of Spain, Trinidad, W.I., Jan. 29, 1925; s. Norman and Henrietta (Harvey) Telemaque; m. Frances Hosanna Chow Yuk, Mar. 15, 1960; children—Diane, Allison. Customs officer Trinidad Civil Service, 1943-49; cook Chgo. YMCA, 1949-50, Spiegel Inc., Chgo., 1950; salesman Englewood Realty, Chgo., 1955-60, Peterson Real Estate, Chgo., 1960-67; with Lamplighter Real Estate, 1967—, gen. sales mgr. for several co. offices, 1974—. Mem. Chgo. Real Estate Bd., 1968—. Mem. Ill. Assn. Real Estate Bds., Million Dollar Club. Home: 1858 W 82d St Chicago IL 60670 Office: 7017 S Ashland Ave Chicago IL 60636

HARVEY, DONALD ANDREW, physician; b. Fremont, Nebr., Feb. 28, 1925; s. Andrew and Mabel Isabel (Thom) H.; B.A., Carleton Coll., 1948; M.A., U. Nebr., 1950, M.D. (Lederle fellow), 1957; Ph.D., Ohio State U., 1953; m. Joan Neuenswander, Aug. 19, 1949; children—Jennifer Ruth, Patricia Ann. Intern St. Joseph Mercy Hosp., Ann Arbor, 1963-64; dept. head, biological control The Upjohn Co., Kalazazoo, Mich., 1957-60, sci. mgr., 1960-63; practice medicine, specializing in internal medicine, Immanuel Med. Center, Omaha, 1964-69, med. officer div. Fed. employee health, Omaha, 1968—; emergency medicine, 1969—; clin. asso. internal medicine U. Nebr. Coll. Medicine, 1965—, dir. medicine clinics, 1966-67, Arthritis Clinic, 1966—; mem. staff Clarkson Meml. Hosp. Pres. Arthritis Found. Served with USN, 1942-45. Mem. A.M.A., Soc. Indsl. Microbiology, Am. Coll. Emergency Physicians (sec.-treas., past pres. state chpt.). Home: 10346 Fieldcrest Ct Omaha NE 68114 Office: Immanuel Med Center Omaha NE 68122

HARVEY, ERIC ROBINSON, psychologist; b. Phila., Nov. 10, 1944; s. Cyrus Robinson and Marcia (Minor) H.; B.S. cum laude, Central Mich. U., 1969; M.A., Miami U., Oxford, Ohio, 1971, Ph.D., 1972; m. Janet Lee Richardson, Oct. 2, 1965; 1 dau., Rachel Kathryn. Research asst. Center for Human Devel., Mt. Pleasant, Mich., 1969, dir. behavior services, 1972-74; teaching fellow Miami U., Oxford, Ohio, 1970-72; program dir., sr. psychologist Muskegon (Mich.) Developmental Center, 1975—. Council mem. Timberline Troop, Boy Scouts Am., Muskegon, 1975-77. Served with USAF, 1963-67. Mem. Am., Midwestern psychol. assns., Am. Assn. Mental Deficiency, AAUP, Soc. Pediatric Psychologist, Sigma Xi. Contbr. articles to profl. jours. Home: 135 Prospect St Grand Haven MI 49417 Office: 1903 Marquette Ave Muskegon MI 49442

HARVEY, LYNNE COOPER (MRS. PAUL HARVEY), broadcasting exec., civic worker; b. nr. St. Louis; d. William A. and Margaret (Kehr) Cooper; A.B., Washington U., St. Louis, 1939, M.A., 1940; m. Paul Harvey, June 4, 1940; 1 son, Paul Harvey. Broadcaster ednl. program KXOK, St. Louis, 1940; broadcaster-writer women's news WAC Variety Show, Fort Custer, Mich., 1941-43; gen. mgr. Paul Harvey News, ABC, 1944—; pres. Paulynne Prodns., Ltd., Chgo., 1968—, exec. producer Paul Harvey Comments, 1968—. Pres. woman's bd. Mental Health Assn. Greater Chgo., 1967-71, v.p. bd. dirs., 1966—; pres. woman's aux. Infant Welfare Soc. Chgo., 1969-71, bd. dirs., 1969—; nominating chmn. Salvation Army Woman's Adv. Bd., 1967-69; reception chmn. Community Lectures; Woman's com. Chgo. Symphony, 1972—. Bd., Oak Park-River Forest, Ill., 1963-69; pres. Mothers Council, River Forest, 1961-62; charter bd. mem. Gottlieb Meml. Hosp., Melrose Park, Ill.; mem. adv. bd. Nat. Christian Heritage Found., 1964—; mem. woman's bd. Ravinia Festival, 1972—. Recipient Religious Heritage of Am. award, 1974. Mem. McGraw's Wildlife Found., Phi Beta Kappa, Kappa Delta Pi, Phi Sigma Iota, Eta Sigma Phi. Clubs: Chicago Golf, Woman's Athletic, Nineteenth Century Woman's, Press (Chgo.); Oak Park Country. Home: 1035 Park Ave River Forest IL 60305 Office: Box 77 River Forest IL 60305

HARVEY, MICHAEL KENT, hydraulics co. exec.; b. Chgo., Aug. 21, 1934; s. Charles Donald and Emily Jane (Lambert) H.; B.B.A., U. Wis., 1959; m. Adele Ann Rosplock, Aug. 18, 1956; children—Jacqueline, Michael Kent, Charles, Colleen, Suzanne. Salesman Ryerson Steel Co., Chgo., 1960-63; v.p. Wis. Steel & Tube Co., Milw., 1963-66, Valley Steel Co., St. Louis, 1966-67; pres. Husky Hydraulics, Two Harbors, Minn., 1967—. Bd. dirs. Two Harbors Civic Assn., 1971—, Two Harbors Youth Center, 1974—. Served with AUS, 1954-56. Named employer of year Two Harbors Jaycees, 1973. Moose, Rotarian. Home: Box 480 Mounted Route Two Harbors MN 55606 Office: Box K Two Harbors MN 55606

HARVEY, VIRGINIA PEASELEY, educator; b. Richmond, Va.; d. Gabriel B. and Florence V. (White) Peaseley; B.S., in Chemistry, U. Md., 1929; M.S. in Phy. Edn., U. Wis., 1932; Ed.D. in Ednl. Psychology, Western Res. U., 1963; postgrad. Temple U., 1966-67; m. E. W. Harvey, Apr. 8, 1939 (div. 1958); 1 dau., Virginia Lynn. Instr. U. Mich., 1932-38; asst. prof. Kent (Ohio) State U., 1938-42, 44-46-54, asso. prof., 1954-64, prof., 1964-76, prof. emeritus, 1975—, faculty senate vice chairperson, 1973-74. Vis. prof. group dynamics Temple U., summer 1967; mem. Nat. Tng. Lab. Inst. Applied Behavioral Sci.; pres. Cons. for Organizational and Personal Effectiveness. Recipient Distinguished Tchr. award Kent State U., 1971, Service award Phi Delta Kappa, 1972. Amy Morris Homans fellow, 1962-63; licensed psychologist, Ohio. Mem. AAUP, Am. Soc. Tng. and Devel., Am. Assn. Higher Edn., Am. Personnel and Guidance Assn., Assn. Counselors Educators, Kappa Kappa Gamma, Alpha Psi Omega, Delta Psi Kappa, Phi Delta Kappa, Omicron Delta Kappa. Mem. Disciples of Christ Ch. Home: 1315 Greenwood Ave Kent OH 44240

HARVEY, WILLIAM EUGENE, food co. exec.; b. Denver, July 27, 1914; s. Harry S. and Ruth (Watson) H.; student Northeastern Coll., 1934, Advanced Traffic Mgmt. Inst., 1939, Stanford, 1965; m. Margaret G. Falls, Sept. 16, 1937; children—John W., Joanne Kann. Salesman, P. Lorrilard Tobacco Co., Denver, 1936-38; statistician U.P. R.R., Denver, 1938-43; mgr. purchasing-transp. Swift & Co., Denver, 1943-55, purchasing agt., 1955-65, gen. mgr. transp., 1965—. Fund dir. Girl Scouts U.S.A., Chgo., 1973-74. Mem. Am. Meat Inst. (chmn. traffic com. 1974-75), Nat. Indsl. Traffic League (regional v.p. 1973-75), Pvt. Truck Council, Nat. Freight Traffic Assn., Nat. Perishable Traffic Assn. (pres. 1976), Chgo. Traffic Club (pres. 1977), Denver Traffic Club (pres. 1953), Denver C. of C., Chgo. Assn. Commerce and Industry. Episcopalian. Mason. Club: Raquet (Hinsdale, Ill.). Home: 4248 Franklin St Western Springs IL 60558 Office: 115 W Jackson St Chicago IL 60604

HARWICK, JOHN WILLIAM, med. clinic adminstr.; b. Rochester, Minn., Dec. 22, 1912; s. Harry John and Margaret (Graham) H.; student Phillips Exeter Acad., 1929-31; A.B., Dartmouth, 1935; m. Linda Rollins, Aug. 27, 1935; children—Hannah, Elizabeth, Prudence, Harry John II, Peter R. Chmn. dept. adminstrn. Mayo Clinic, also vice chmn. bd. trustees Mayo Found.; dir. Kahler Corp., 1st Nat. Bank Mpls., Rochester Airport Co., Northwestern Nat. Life Ins. Co. Trustee, chmn. bd. Rochester Found. Mem. Dragon, Psi Upsilon. Conglist. Clubs: University (Rochester); Minneapolis. Home: 1021 10th St SW Rochester MN 55901 Office: 200 1st St SW Rochester MN 55901

HASBARGEN, ARTHUR, educator; b. Kankakee, Ill., Apr. 20, 1925; s. Arthur and Zelpha (Spence) H.; B.S., No. Ill. U., 1949; M.A., Mich. State U., 1950; Ed.D., U. Ill., 1969; m. Lorayne Raguse, Aug. 24, 1946; children—James, Janet, Karen, Nancy. Dir. student personnel N.D. State U., Fargo, 1950-52; head guidance Kankakee Sch. Dist. Ill., 1952-64; tchr., counselor Am. Dependents Sch., Stuttgart, Germany, 1959-60; dir. spl. edn. Kankakee State Hosp., 1964-66, dir. mental retardation div., 1968-71; dir. programs, Coldwater (Mich.) State Home and Tng. Sch., 1971-74; chmn. spl. edn. dept. Western Ill. U., Macomb, 1974—, asso. prof.; cons. in field. Served with USAAF, 1943-46; ATO. U.S. Office Edn. fellow, 1966-68; Ill. Dept. Mental Health Employment Edn. grantee, 1966-68. Mem. Nat. Vocat. Guidance Assn., Am. Personnel and Guidance Assn., Council for Exceptional Children, Am. Assn. Mental Deficiency, Western Ill. Adminstrs. Round Table, Kappa Delta Pi, Phi Delta Kappa. Lutheran. Club: Kiwanis. Contbr. articles in field to profl. jours. Home: 813 Orchard Dr Macomb IL 61455 Office: 25C Horrabin Hall Western Ill Univ Macomb IL 61455

HASBROUCK, WILBERT ROLAND, architect; b. Mapleton, Iowa, Dec. 17, 1931; s. Russell M. and Hazel Elizabeth (Hornby) H.; B.S. in Archtl. Engring., Ia. State Coll., 1954; m. Marilyn Jean Whittlesey, Aug. 31, 1958; children—Charles Russell, John Whittlesey. Archtl. engr. Ill. Central R.R., Chgo., 1954-67; exec. dir. A.I.A., Chgo., 1968-75; Practice architecture as Office of Wilbert R. Hasbrouck, Historic Rousources, 1970—. Life trustee Chgo. Sch. Architecture Found., mem. exec. com., 1966-75. Served to 1st lt. C.E., AUS, 1955-57. Recipient citation Nat. Trust for Historic Preservation, 1974. Fellow A.I.A.; mem. Soc. Archtl. Historians (past nat. dir.) Presbyn. Mason. Club: Cliff Dwellers. Author: Architectural Essays from the Chicago School, others, also articles.; editor, pub. Prairie Sch. Rev., 1964—. Home: 12509 S 89th Ave Palos Park IL 60464 Office: 1900 S Prairie Chicago IL 60616

HASCALL, JEAN MARY TEAGUE (MRS. CARLETON CHANDLER HASCALL, JR.), artist; b. Shepherd, Mich.; d. Cassius Homer and Helen (Winegar) Teague; A.B., Wayne State U., 1940; m. Carleton Chandler Hascall, Jr., Jan. 23, 1943; children—Carleton Chandler III, John T., Mary Elizabeth. Indsl. designer George W. Walker Co., 1940; fashion illustrator Detroit Newspaper, 1941; engring. draftsman Chrysler Corp., 1942; exhibited one-man shows Wayne State U., Women's City Club Gallery, Grosse Ile Gallery, Lee Gallery, also others; exhibited in group shows Detroit Mus. Arts, Scarab Club Gallery, Detroit Artists' Market; represented in permanent collections Ann Arbor Mus. Arts, Marquette Library, Grosse Ile Schs., several hosps.; also pvt. collections. Vol., Rec. for Blind. Bd. dirs., pres. Community Theatre Grosse Ile (Mich.); mem. St. James Adoremus Bell Choir; bd. dirs. Archives of Am. Art. Mem. Detroit Soc. Women Painters and Sculptors (pres. 1950), Down River Guitar Club. Clubs: Grosse Ile Book (pres. 1963-64, 77-78, dir. 1975-77), Grosse Ile Golf and Country, Grosse Ile Friday Musicale (dir. 1975-77). Home: 28273 Elba Dr Grosse Ile MI 48138

HASELHORST, DONALD DUANE, digital electronic equipment mfg. co. exec.; b. Northville, S.D., May 21, 1930; B.E.E., S.D. State U., 1956; m. Nancy G. Wilz, Aug. 29, 1953; children—Stephen, Linda, Lynn. Engr., Univac div. Sperry Rand Corp., St. Paul, 1956-59; v.p. Fabri-Tek Inc., Amery, Wis., 1959-67, pres. Nicolet Instrument Corp. (name changed from Fabri-Tek Instruments 1971), Madison, Wis., 1967—; dir. Affiliated Bank Madison, Viking Ins. Co., Demco Ednl. Corp., Union State Bank, Amery, Famous Footwear, Inc., Wis. Life Ins. Co. Served with USAF, 1948-52. Mem. IEEE, Am. Mgmt. Assn. (pres.'s council). Lutheran. Clubs: Nakoma Golf; Kiwanis of Madison. Home: 4106 Saint Clair St Madison WI 53711 Office: 5225 Verona Rd Madison WI 53711

HASH, LESTER JACKSON, JR., civil engr.; b. Corwith, Iowa, Apr. 29, 1928; s. Lester J. and Flora M. (Bosworth) H.; B.S., Sioux Falls Coll., 1953; B.S. in Civil Engring., S.D. Sch. Mines and Tech., 1958; m. Mercedes M. Bertsch, July 20, 1952; children—Terese, Mark, David. Gen. sci. tchr., basketball and football coach Washington Sr. High Sch., Sioux Falls, S.D., 1953-56; design engr. Minn. State Hwy. Dept., Mankato, 1958; project engr., estimator Al Johnson Constrn. Co., Mpls., 1958-61; gen. supt. City Water Dept., Sioux Falls, S.D., 1961—. Tchr. adult edn. courses Southeastern Vocat. Tech. Sch., 1962-67. Served with USMCR, 1946-48. Recipient certificate Meritorious Service, U.S. Dept. Labor, 1965; named Outstanding Water Works Operator in S.D., S.D. Water and Waste Water Conf., 1969. Mem. Am. Water Works Assn. (Utility Man of Year 1970), Am. Pub. Works Assn., Fellowship Christian Athletes, C. of C., Geol. Soc. Baptist. (chmn. trustees 1968-69, vice-chmn. deacons 1964-65). Rotarian (pres. 1975). Home: 2901 S Jefferson St Sioux Falls SD 57105 Office: 224 W 9th St Sioux Falls SD 57102

HASKELL, CHARLES LEONARD, restaurant chain exec.; b. Bklyn., Mar. 28, 1944; s. Daniel Joseph and Muriel (Fink) H.; B.S. in Econs., U. Pa., 1965; M.B.A., U. Chgo., 1967; m. Elona Sophia Vebras, May 24, 1974. Budget analyst Humble Oil & Refining Co., Houston, 1967-69; sr. asso. William M. Kordsiemon & Assos., mgmt. cons., Chgo., 1969-71; dir. Sanderhoff & Assos., mgmt. cons., Chgo., 1971—; dir. Sunway Fruit Products; v.p. Lettuce Entertain You Enterprises, 1975—. Cons. Native Am. Organized Tng. Center, Chgo., 1973—; guest lectr. U. Chgo., Ill. Inst. Tech., Chgo., 1973—. C.P.A., Tex., Ill. Mem. Am. Inst. C.P.A.'s, Ill., Tex., Houston socs. C.P.A.'s, Chgo. Assn. Commerce and Industry. Home: 1430 N Astor St Chicago IL 60610 Office: 860 DeWitt Pl Chicago IL 60611

HASKELL, SAUL SIMON, physician; b. Newark, July 17, 1930; s.; Isadore David and Elena B. (Greenbaum) H.; B.A., Vanderbilt U., 1952, M.D., 1955; m. Roselyne Levine, Apr. 27, 1957; children—Sharon Ann, Ian David. Intern Michael Reese Hosp., Chgo., 1955-56, resident gen. surgery, 1956-57; resident Children's Orthopedics Hosp. for Crippled Children, Newark, 1959-60, orthopedic program Northwestern Med. Sch., 1960-63; attending orthopedic surgeon Michael Reese Hosp., 1964—; clin. instr. orthopedic surgery; dir. Crisis Ministry Chgo., pres., 1972. Mem. Chgo. Com. on Trauma. Served with USAF, 1957-59. Diplomate Am. Bd. Orthopedic Surgeons. Fellow Am. Acad. Orthopedic Surgeons; mem. A.M.A., Clin. Orthopaedic Soc., Ill., Chgo. med. socs., Ill., Chgo. orthopedic socs., Société Internationale de Chirurgie Orthopédique et de Traumatologie, Alpha Epsilon Pi. Mem. B'nai B'rith. Home: 3419 Pratt St Lincolnwood IL 60645 Office: 2320 Peterson Ave Chicago IL 60645

HASKELL, THEODORE JAMES, educator, former city ofcl.; b. Chgo., Oct. 11, 1926; s. Ted James and Grace (Hasenstab) H.; student St. Norbert's Coll., 1944; B.S., Mich. State U., 1949, M.S., 1966; m. Barbara Mae Bible, Sept. 16, 1950; children—Judith Lee, Bruce James, Rebecca Lynn. Ranger, Huron-Clinton Met. Authority, Milford, Mich., 1949; forestry foreman City of Lansing, Mich., 1949-55, asst. forester, 1955-59, forester, 1959-64, asst. dir. dept. parks and recreation, 1962-72, dir., 1973-76; asso. prof., extension specialist park and recreation resources Mich. State U., East Lansing, 1976—; cons. forestry 1956—; tchr. adult edn. Lansing sch. Dist., 1961-65; lectr. Mich. State U., 1960-72. Mem. (Lansing) Mayor's Com. River Improvement, 1963-72; chmn. com. adminstrv. control Mich. Grand River Watershed, 1967—, vice chmn. exec. bd., 1972-76, chmn., 1976—; del. to White House Conf. on Aging 1971. Mem. bd. Michigan Shade Tree Research Found., also pres., 1969—. Served with AUS, 1945-46. Named Forest and Park Conservationist of 1972, Mich. United Conservation Clubs; recipient Fellowship award Mich. Recreation and Park Assn., 1975. Registered forester, Michigan. Mem. Am. Inst. Park Execs. (Distinguished Service award 1965), Am. Mgmt. Assn., Internat. Shade Tree Conf. (bd. govs.), Nat. Recreation and Park Assn., Mich. Forestry and Park Assn. (pres.) Mich. Acad. Sci., Arts and Letters, Scabbard and Blade, Xi Sigma Pi, Phi Kappa Phi. Conglist. (trustee). Club: Torch (Lansing). Author (with others) Basic Ground Maintenance, 1971. Contbr. to profl. manuals. Home: 1801 Harding St Lansing MI 48910 Office: Dept Park and Recreation Resources Mich State U East Lansing MI 48824

HASKINS, ERNEST BLAINE, state ofcl.; b. Crown City, Ohio, July 20, 1922; s. Stanley Henry and Laura (Sheets) H.; student Ohio State U., 1939-41, 1967; m. Wanda L. Thomas, Jan. 24, 1947; children—Thomas B., John G., William D., Elaine B., James P., Richard C., Philip S. Bus. mgr. London (Ohio) Correctional Instn., 1947-53, warden, 1962-75; asst. chief Ohio Div. Correction, Columbus, 1953-62; asst. dir. Ohio Dept. Rehab. and Correction, 1975—. Served to 1st lt. AUS, 1942-46. Mem. Am. Correctional Assn., Nat. Warden's Assn. Baptist. Home: 173 S Chester St West Jefferson OH 43162 Office: 1050 Freeway Dr N Columbus OH 43229

HASLER, JAMES BURTON, optometrist; b. Hancock, Mich., Mar. 25, 1925; s. Joseph Charles and Maude Marie (Beaulieu) H.; D. Optometry, No. Ill. Coll. Optometry, 1949; m. Elizabeth Gutschenritter, Oct. 7, 1950; children—Joseph, Mary, Barbara, Sarah, Philip, Kathryn. Practice optometry, Hartford, Wis., 1949-54, Reedsburg, Wis., 1954—; mem. staff Sauk County Health Care Center; indsl. vision cons. Hankscraft Co., chmn. optometry examining bd. State of Wis., 1973; mem. com. on continuing edn. Nat. Health Council, 1976-77. Vice chmn. Reedsburg Pub. Housing Authority. Del. Wis. Republican Conv., 1971; bd. dirs. Dist. 4 Vocat. and Tech. Sch. Served with AUS, 1943-46. Named Optometrist of Year, Wis. Optometric Assn., 1972. Mem. North Central States Optometric Council (pres. 1976), Am. (chmn. commn. on continuing edn. 1975-77), Wis. (2d v.p. 1977-78) optometric assns., Ill. Coll. Optometry Alumni Assn. (dir.), Reedsburg C. of C. (dir. 1963-67). Club: Lions. Home: 615 N Walnut St Reedsburg WI 53959 Office: 211 2nd St Reedsburg WI 53959

HASLER, JAMES LOUIS, co-op. exec.; b. Hamilton, Ohio, Apr. 4, 1933; s. John Ralph and Louise (Prentise) H.; B.S., Ohio State U., 1955; m. Barbara Ann Richardson, Aug. 29, 1959; children—Leesa Jean, Jeffrey James. Commodity fieldman Clinton County Farm Bureau Co-op., Wilmington, Ohio, 1956-59, br. mgr. Sabina, 1959-65, asst. gen. mgr., Wilmington, 1965-71, gen. mgr., 1971—, asst. treas., 1968—. Chmn. Clinton County Council of Farmer Coops., pres. Tri-County Grain Dealers. Bd. dirs. Clinton County Extension Adv. Council, Miss Southwestern Ohio Pageant, 1960-61. Mem. Jaycees (past pres.), C. of C. (pres. 1973-74), Farm Bur. Ohio, Alpha Gamma Rho. Republican. Presbyterian (trustee 1968-71, pres. bd. trustees 1973-74, 75—, elder 1977—). Rotarian (sec. 1973-74, pres. 1974-75), Elks. Club: Saddle and Sirloin (v.p. 1954) (Columbus, Ohio). Home: 542 N South St Wilmington OH 45177 Office: PO Box 512 Wilmington OH 45177

HASLING, ROBERT JOHN, lawyer, ins. co. exec.; b. Aitkin, Minn., Oct. 28, 1929; s. Robert Nicholas and Elsie (Spalding) H.; student St. John's U., 1947-49; B.S., St. Paul Coll. Law, 1953, LL.B., 1954; m. Fern Ellen Pearson, Dec. 26, 1953; children—Joseph R., Thomas J., Lori A., James A., Sara K. Admitted to Minn. bar, 1954; with Minn. Mut. Life Co., St. Paul, 1949—, v.p., sec., gen. counsel, 1968—; dir. Financial Life Ins. Co., Armonk, N.Y. Served with AUS, 1951-52. Mem. Am., Minn., Ramsey County bar assns., Assn. Life Ins. Counsel, Am. Council Life Ins. (del. conv.). Home: 3327 Churchill St St Paul MN 55112 Office: Minn Mut Life Ins Co 345 Cedar St St Paul MN 55101

HASPESLAGH, JEAN ANNE, educator; b. Columbus, Ohio, May 26, 1940; d. Robert Louis and Lydia (Sheets) Haspeslagh; B.S. in Nursing, U. Akron (Ohio), 1969, M.S. in Edn., 1974; diploma nursing Akron City Hosp., 1961. Staff nurse Vis. Nurse Service Summit County (Ohio), 1961-69, instr., 1967-69; staff nurse Barberton (Ohio) Citizens Hosp., 1968-70, instr. Akron Sch. Practical Nursing-Barberton Citizens Hosp., 1970-73; instr. U. Akron Coll. Nursing, 1973-76, asst. prof. nursing, 1976—; instr. basic life support A.R.C., Am. Heart Assn. Pres. Little Lake in the Woods Assn., 1976-77. Mem. Am. Nurses Assn., Nat. League Nursing, Am. Personnel and Guidance Assn., Canal Fulton Hist. Soc. Roman Catholic. Home: 423 Colony Rd Canal Fulton OH 44614 Office: Univ Akron Sch Nursing Akron OH 44325

HASS, BRUCE STUART, biophysicist; b. Chgo., Oct. 5, 1938; s. Wilmon Heinrich Adolf and Nona Leonora (Morse) H.; A.B., Tex. A. and M. U., 1961, Ph.D., 1974; m. Sally Floyd Vierling, May 1, 1965; children—Carl R., Charlotte A., Heidi S., Samuel M., Jennilyn F., Joel H. Research technician Argonne (Ill.) Nat. Lab., 1963-65, research asso., 1975—; research technician U. Tex., Austin, 1965-67; veterinary toxicology lab. postdoctoral appointee U.S. Dept. Agr., College Station Tex., 1974-75. Served with USMCR, 1956-64. USPHS fellow, 1970-72; Robert E. Welch fellow, 1972—. Mem. Internat. Soc. Stereology, Internat. Soc. Quantum Biologists, Electron Microscopy Soc. Am., Radiation Research Soc., Am. Soc. Photobiology, Sigma Xi, Phi Eta Sigma, Phi Lambda Upsilon.

Mormon. Contbr. articles to sci. jours, hist. paper to Louisiana History. Home: 210 N Julian St Naperville IL 60540 Office: 9700 S Cass Ave Argonne IL 60439

HASSAN, MOHAMMAD ZIA, educator; b. Gurgaon, Brit. India, Apr. 2, 1933; s. Mohammad Izhar-Ul and Wilayat (Begum) H.; B.S., U. Punjab, Lahore, Pakistan, 1954; M.S., Ill. Inst. Tech., 1958, Ph.D., 1965; m. Shakeela Hamiduddin, Dec. 18, 1959; children—Rubeena, Ayesha, Isra. Came to U.S., 1955, naturalized, 1967. Indsl. engr. Dukane Corp., St. Charles, Ill., 1956-58; mfg. analyst Webcor, Inc., Chgo., 1958-60, mgmt. cons., 1960-62; instr. dept. indsl. engring. Ill. Inst. Tech., Chgo., 1960-65, asst. prof., 1965-69; asso. prof., 1969—, chmn. dept. mgmt. scis., 1977—; mgmt. cons. Warwick Electronics, Inc., Chgo., 1962—, H.K. Porter & Co., Delta Star Elec. div., Chgo., 1965-67, Standard Kollsman Industries, Inc., Melrose Park, Ill., 1967, Hamilton Industries, Chgo., 1969-71, GRI Inc., Chgo., 1974-75. Mem. Am. Inst. Indsl. Engrs., Am. Soc. Quality Control, Inst. Mgmt. Scis., Ops. Research Soc. Am., Sigma Xi, Tau Beta Pi, Alpha Pi Mu, Sigma Iota Epsilon. Home: 5633 S Woodlawn Ave Chicago IL 60637 Office: 3300 S Federal St Chicago IL 60616

HASSEL, CHARLES EDWARD, dentist; b. Mishawaka, Ind., Sept. 11, 1929; s. Edward George and Elsie Elizabeth (Hiatt) H.; B.S., Ball State U., 1953; D.D.S., Ind. U., 1967; widower; children—Jill, Michael, Mathew. Tchr., Knox (Ind.) High Sch., 1956-57; packaging mgr. Whitehall Labs., Elkhart, Ind., 1957-61; pvt. practice dentistry, Bremen, Ind., 1967—. Instr. pedodontics Ind. U. Med. Center, Indpls., 1967-68; instr. radiology Ind. U., South Bend, 1968-69; med. missionary Grace Children's Hosp., Port au Prince, Haiti, 1977. Served to 1st lt. USAF, 1953-56; capt. Res. ret. Recipient Outstanding Alumni award Ball State U., Muncie, Ind., 1976. Fellow Royal Soc. Health; mem. Kosciusko County Dental Soc. (pres. 1972-73), Bremen C. of C. (sec.-treas. 1973). Kiwanian (lt. gov. div. 1977). Contbr. feature articles to Bremen Enquirer, 1955-56. Home: 122 N Maryland St Bremen IN 46506 Office: 125 S Stewart St Bremen IN 46506

HASSELL, GORDON ELMER, personnel cons. exec.; b. Sharon, Pa., Jan. 13, 1929; s. Elmer Harry and Margaret (Weller) H.; B.S., Colgate U., 1951; student U. Pitts. Law Sch., 1951-52; m. Jean Treverton Hays, Sept. 8, 1951; children—Karen Lynne, Megan Ann. Mgr. staff employment Trane Co., LaCrosse, Wis., 1956-60; v.p. Longberry Employment Service, Inc., Niles, Ohio, 1960—. Vice pres. Trumbull County YMCA. Served to lt. (j.g.) USNR, 1952-56. Mem. Nat. Personnel Cons. (past pres., dir.), Nat. Employment Assn., Am. Soc. Personnel Adminstrn., Niles C. of C., Theta Chi. Republican. Presbyn. Home: 7401 Mines Rd SE Warren OH 44484 Office: Niles Bank Bldg Niles OH 44446

HASSELQUIST, MAYNARD BURTON, lawyer; b. Amador, Minn., July 1, 1919; s. Harry and Anna M. (Froberg) H.; B.S. in Law, U. Minn., 1941, LL.B., 1947; m. Nov. 20, 1948; children—Mark D., Peter L. Admitted to Minn. bar, 1947; mem. tax dept. Gen. Mills, Inc., Mpls., 1946-53; sr. partner firm Dorsey, Windhorst, Hannaford, Whitney & Halladay, Mpls., 1953—; dir. Graco Inc., Mpls., Magnetic Controls Co., Mpls., Fogautolube, France, Food Producers of Japan, McLaughlin Gormley King Co., Mpls. Served with U.S. Navy, 1941-46. Mem. Am., Minn., Hennepin County, Internat. bar assns., Am. Soc. Internat. Law, Japan-Am. Soc. Minn. (pres.), Swedish Council Am. (dir.), Am. Swedish Inst. (dir.). Lutheran. Club: Mpls. Home: 6712 Arrowhead Pass Edina MN 55435 Office: 2100 First National Bank Bldg Minneapolis MN 55402

HASSLER, DONALD MACKEY, II, educator; b. Akron, Ohio, Jan. 3, 1937; s. Donald Mackey and Frances Elizabeth (Parsons) H.; B.A. (Alfred P. Sloan scholar), Williams Coll., 1959; M.A. (Woodrow Wilson fellow), Columbia, 1960, Ph.D., 1967; m. Diana Cain, Oct. 8, 1960 (dec. Sept. 19, 1976); children—Donald, David; m. 2d, Sue Smith, Sept. 13, 1977. Instr., U. Montreal, 1961-65; instr. English dept. Kent (Ohio) State U., 1965-67, asst. prof., 1967-71, asso. prof., 1971-76, prof., 1977—, dir. honors and exptl. coll., 1973—. Co-chmn. Kent Am. Revolution Bicentennial Commn., 1974—. Mem. Phi Beta Kappa. Presbyterian. (deacon 1971-74, elder 1974—). Club: Kiwanis (dir.). Author: Erasmus Darwin, 1974; The Comedian as the Letter D: Erasmus Darwin's Comic Materialism, 1973; Asimov's Golden Age: The Ordering of an Art, 1977. Home: 1226 Woodhill Dr Kent OH 44240

HASSMAN, PAUL LAVERNE, bank exec.; b. Canal Fulton, O., May 23, 1937; s. Walter Joseph and Violet Dorothy (Rohr) H.; B.B.A., Kent State U., 1959; m. Thelma Mae Gantz, June 13, 1964; children—Diane, David, Deane. Accountant, Ernst & Ernst, Canton, Ohio, 1963-68; asst. comptroller Peoples-Merchants Trust Co., Canton, 1968-72, comptroller, 1972-76, v.p., controller, 1976—. Served with AUS, 1960-62. C.P.A., Ohio. Mem. Louisville Jaycees (pres. 1970-71, treas. 1969-70, sec. 1968-69), Nat. Assn. Accountants, Am. Inst. C.P.A.'s, Ohio Soc. C.P.A.'s, (dir. 1973-74). Roman Catholic. Club: K.C. Home: 8840 Ontario St NW Massillon OH 44646 Office: 237 W Tuscarawas St Canton OH 44702

HASTINGS, JAY BRADLEY, ednl. adminstr.; b. Connersville, Ind., Aug. 15, 1939; s. C. Frederick and Lorraine W. (Canaday) H.; B.A., Ball State U., 1962, M.A., 1964; Ed.D., U. Ill., 1971; m. Jonell Jarrett, July 20, 1960; children—Laura Korrine, Jay Bradley, Stacia C. Tchr. English, Selma (Ind.) High Sch., 1962-64, Muncie (Ind.) Central High Sch., 1964-66; tchr. English and reading Muncie Trade Sch., 1964-66, Ind. Reformatory, Pendleton, 1966; placement counselor U. Ill., Urbana, 1966-69, dean's asst. Coll. of Edn., 1969-71; counselor Parkland Coll., Champaign, Ill., 1971-73, counselor and coordinator of services to disabled students, 1973—. Vis. lectr. U. Ill., 1973-74; mem. Ill. Sch. Bd. Task Force on Elementary Schs., 1973. Mem. Am. Psychol. Assn., Am., Ill., East Central Ill. (pres. 1973-74) personnel and guidance assns., Am. Coll., Am. Sch. personnel assns., Assn. Humanistic Edn. and Devel. (treas. 1975), Ill. Sch. Counselor Assn. (v.p. 1973, gov. 1974, pres. 1975), Phi Delta Kappa (pres. chpt. 1975). Home: 2507 Pond St Urbana IL 61801 Office: 2400 W Bradley Champaign IL 61820

HASTINGS, WILLIAM CHARLES, judge; b. Newman Grove, Nebr., Jan. 31, 1921; s. William C. and Margaret (Hansen) H.; B.Sc., U. Nebr., 1942, J.D., 1948; m. Julie Ann Simonson, Dec. 29, 1946; children—Pamela, Charles, Steven. Admitted to Nebr. bar, 1948; with FBI, 1942-43; mem. firm Chambers, Holland, Dudgeon & Hastings, Lincoln, 1948-65; judge 3d judicial dist. Nebr., Lincoln, 1965—. Pres. Child Guidance Center, Lincoln, 1962, 63; v.p. Lincoln Community Council, 1968, 69; vice chmn. Antelope Valley Boy Scouts Am., Lincoln, 1968, 69. Pres. First Presbyn. Ch. Found., Lincoln, 1968—. Served with AUS, 1943-46. Mem. Am., Nebr., Lincoln bar assns., Neb. Dist. Judges Assn., Lincoln Jr. C. of C. (pres. 1954-55), Phi Delta Phi. Republican. Presbyn. (deacon, elder, trustee). Club: East Hills Country (pres. 1959-60). Home: 1544 S 58th St Lincoln NE 68506 Office: County Ct House 555 S 10th St Lincoln NE 68508

HATCH, ALBERT JEROLD, physicist; b. Little Rock, Ill., Apr. 23, 1916; s. Paul Winfield and Salisbury Augusta (Lower) H.; B.S. in Elec. Engring., U. Ill., 1939, M.S. in Physics, 1947; m. Helen Cecile Glenn, Feb. 2, 1946; children—Cecilia L. Hatch Kobliska, Rebecca J., David A. (dec.). Instr., asst. physicist N.Mex. State U., Las Cruces, 1947-49, asst. prof., asso. physicist, 1949-56; asso. physicist Argonne (Ill.) Nat. Lab., 1956-72, physicist, 1972-73, asst. dir. physics div., 1973—; lectr. Ill. Inst. Tech., 1963-71; cons. Ultek Corp., 1963-64. Fellow Am. Phys. Soc.; mem. Am. Nuclear Soc., Sigma Xi. Home: 5460 S Cornell Ave Chicago IL 60615 Office: 9700 S Cass Ave Argonne IL 60439

HATCH, ELIZABETH DAWN, psychologist; b. Amarillo, Tex., Jan. 9, 1937; d. Augustus Barnett and Velma (Bourland) Dawn; B.S. with honors (Ford Found. fellow), U. Utah, 1955; M.Ed., U. Wyo., 1967, Ph.D., 1969; m. John A. Hatch, June 13, 1954 (div.); children—Carol Dawn, Susan Vanet. Tchr. elementary schs., Smyrna, Tenn., 1958-59, Abilene, Tex., 1964, Cheyenne, Wyo., 1965-66; high sch. counselor, Cheyenne, 1966-67; guidance dir. Lab. Sch., U. Wyo., instr. staff dept. counselor edn. and supervision, 1967-69; sch. psychologist Cedar Rapids (Iowa) Pub. Schs.; instr. psychology Coe Coll., 1969-72; evaluation cons. Title III Fed. Programs; coordinator of evaluation Cedar Rapids Pub. Schs., 1973-77, adminstrv. asst.-instruction, 1977—. Mem. St. John's Episcopal Sch. Bd., Abilene, 1962; mem. adv. bd. Linn County Day Care Center, 1969-70; bd. dirs. Linn County Day Care Services, 1970-73, Y Crest Services, 1974-77. Mem. Am. Psychol. Assn., Am. Ednl. Research Assn. Spurs, P.E.O., Phi Delta Kappa, Alpha Delta Pi. Republican. Episcopalian. Home: 4521 Rushmore Dr NE Cedar Rapids IA 52402 Office: 346 2d Ave SW Cedar Rapids IA 52404

HATCH, HENRY CLIFFORD, beverage co. exec.; b. Toronto, Ont., Can., Apr. 30, 1916; s. Harry C. and Elizabeth (Carr) H.; student St. Michael's Coll. Sch., Toronto; m. Joan Ferriss, May 1, 1940; children—Henry Clifford, Gail Elizabeth Todgham, Sheila Mary McNamara, Richard Ferriss. Salesman, T.G. Bright & Co., Ltd., Niagara Falls, Ont., 1933-37, now dir.; merchandising staff Hiram Walker, Inc., Walkerville, Ont., 1937; dir. Hiram Walker & Sons., Ltd., 1938—, asst. to v.p. in charge sales, 1946—, v.p., 1946—; v.p., dir. Hiram Walker-Gooderham & Worts, Ltd., Walkerville, 1955-61, exec. v.p., 1961-64, pres., 1964—; dir. Toronto-Dominion Bank, Bell Can., Montreal, Que., Curtis Co. Ltd., Windsor, Ont. Served as comdr. Royal Canadian Navy, 1940-45, in command HMCS Drummondville, Ville de Que. Clubs: Rosedale Golf (Toronto); Essex Golf; Detroit Athletic. Home: 7130 Riverside Dr E Windsor ON N8S 1C3 Canada Office: 2072 Riverside Dr E Walkerville ON N8Y 4S5 Canada

HATCH, LOREN LORENZO, govt. ofcl., physician; b. Spencer, Iowa, Feb. 27, 1923; s. Otto Leon and Alta May (Elwood) H.; B.S., U.S. Maritime Acad., 1944; D.O., Chgo. Osteo. Coll., 1951; Ph.D. in Higher Med. Ed., Mich. State U., 1975; m. Elizabeth Louise Chard, June 1, 1946; children—April, Mark, Loren C. Intern, Flint (Mich.) Osteo. Hosp. 1951-52; practice osteo. medicine, specializing in anesthesia, Erie, Pa., 1952-57; adminstr., med. dir. Dallas (Ga.) Hosp., 1957-61; med. adminstr. Drs. Hosp., Buffalo, 1961-63; adminstr., med. dir. Lancaster (Pa.) Osteo. Hosp., 1963-66; med. dir. Mt. Clements Gen. Hosp. (Mich.), 1966-69; asst. clin. prof. family and community medicine Coll. Osteo. Medicine, Mich. State U., 1969-75, physician Coll. Human Medicine Health Center, 1969-75; med. officer (occupational medicine) Nat. Inst. Occupational Safety and Health, Pub. Health Service, HEW, Cin., 1975—. Cons. on Medicare, Social Security Adminstrn.; mem. Corp. Mich. Coll. Osteo. Medicine. Served to lt. comdr. USNR, 1944-64. Named Young Man of Yr., Jr. C. of C., 1956. Fellow Am. Occupational Med. Assn., Am. Acad. Med. Adminstrs., Osteo. Coll. Hosp. Adminstrs.; mem. Pa. Osteo. Hosp. Assn. (pres.), Lancaster County Hosp. Council (pres. 1965-66). Methodist. Mason (32 deg., K.T.); mem. Order Eastern Star, Moose. Clubs: Lions (Dallas, Ga.), University (pres.) (Lancaster, Pa.). Author: Hospital Personnel, 1964; Hospital Cost Reduction, 1965; Arts of Communication, 1966; Relationship of Education, Director and Administrator, 1966; Systems Analysis for Medical Curricula, 1975. Home: 5012 David Ct Cincinnati OH 45215

HATCH, W.A.S. (WENDY ANN SWANSON), artist, printmaker; b. Bridgeport, Conn., Mar. 19, 1948; d. William E. and Irene Aini (Ahonen) Swanson; B.F.A., Syracuse U., 1970; M.F.A., Pratt Inst., 1972; m. Denison H. Hatch, Sept. 4, 1971. Asst. prof art Bradley U., Peoria, Ill., 1973—; chairperson Bradley Nat. Print and Drawing Exhbn., 1975, 77; one-woman shows of prints include: Silvermine Guide of Art, 1974; Wallnuts, Phila., 1975, 77; Monmouth (Ill.) Coll., 1976; Peoria (Ill.) Art Guild, 1977; Anna Gardner Gallery, Stinson, Calif., 1977; group shows include: Associated Am. Artists, N.Y.C., 1977; World Print Competition, San Francisco, 1977; Am. Printmakers in Venice (Italy), City Mus., 1977; represented in permanent collections: U. Leeds (Eng.), City Coll. N.Y., San Diego U., U.S.I.A., Ill. State Mus. Bradley U. Research grantee, 1974, 75, 76, 77. Mem. Coll. Art Assn. Home: 110 W Grand Ave Chicago IL 60610 Office: Bradley Univ School Art Peoria IL 61606

HATCHER, CHARLES WESLEY, rubber co. exec.; b. Ft. Worth, Jan. 23, 1920; s. Charles Wesley and Ruth Corinne (McNorton) H.; student U. Cin., 1937-42; M.B.A., Harvard, 1947; m. Elizabeth Turner Oxley, June 14, 1941; children—Charles Oxley, Laura. Asst. to pres. Cin. Transit Co., 1947-55; personnel mgr. Vernay Labs., Inc., Yellow Springs, Ohio, 1955-70; treas., 1970—, v.p., 1973—. Vice pres. Cin. Pub. Recreation Commn., 1950-55. Trustee Antioch Coll., 1971-76, Children's Med. Center, Dayton, Ohio, 1969—. Served with USMC, 1943-46. Home: 1832 US 68 North Xenia OH 45385 Office: Vernay Laboratories Inc Yellow Springs OH 45387

HATCHER, HERBERT JOHN, research co. exec.; b. Mpls., Dec. 18, 1926; s. Herbert Edmund and Florence Elizabeth (Larson) H.; student Ill. Inst. Tech., 1947-50; B.A., U. Minn., 1953, M.S. (Walter G. Karr fellow), 1963, Ph.D. (W.G. Karr fellow), 1965; m. Beverly Jean Johnson, Mar. 28, 1953; children—Dennis M., Steven C., Roger D., Mark A., Susan D., Laura J. Asst. bacteriologist Glen Lake Sanatorium, Tb Hosp., Oak Terrace, Minn., 1953-56; bacteriologist VA Hosp., Wilmington, Del., 1956-57; microbiologist Smith, Kline & French Labs., Phila., 1957-61; research asso. soil dept. U. Minn., St. Paul, 1965; microbiologist Clinton Corn Processing Co., Clinton, Iowa, 1966-67; scientist Econs. Lab. Inc., St. Paul, 1967—. Served with USNR, 1945-46. Mem. Am. Soc. Microbiology, Am. Soc. Brewing Chemists. Contbr. articles to profl. jours. Patentee in field. Home: 12756 Monroe St NE Blaine MN 55434 Office: Osborn Bldg St Paul MN 55102

HATCHER, MILLARD GENE, chiropractor; b. Auburn, Ill., Jan. 24, 1929; s. Ralph Gardner and Pearl Louise (Martin) H.; student Bradley U., 1947-48; D. Chiropractic, Lincoln Chiropractic Coll., 1957; m. Ellen Joann Gudgel, May 2, 1954; children—Gregory Gene, Gayle Lynn, Michael Dean. Pvt. practice as chiropractor, Fort Wayne, Ind., 1957—. State mem. Peer Rev. Com., 1974-76. Served with USN, 1948-52. Mem. Ind. Chiropractic Assn. (pres. N.E. dist. 1958-62). Methodist (music dir. 1970-71). Mason (Shriner). Home: 7823 Delcon Dr Fort Wayne IN 46809 Office: 3210 S Calhoun St Fort Wayne IN 46807

HATHAWAY, ALAN DEAN, dentist; b. Conesville, Iowa, Apr. 22, 1929; s. Seward Theodore and Georgia Lorraine (Gamble) H.; student Muscatine Jr. Coll., 1948; D.D.S., State U. Iowa, 1953; m. Margaret Genevieve Fuller, Dec. 27, 1950; children—Gregg, Jeffrey, Charles, Theodore, Anne, Anthony. Practice dentistry, Davenport, Iowa, 1955—; mem. State Health Facilities Council, 1968-72; trombonist, leader Dixiecat Band. Pres. Hist. Lincoln Hwy. Bur., 1975—; chmn. Davenport Democratic Com., 1967-72; mem. Davenport Levee Commn., 1976—. Served with AUS, 1953-55. Mem. Davenport Dist. Dental Assn. (pres.-elect 1977), Scott County Dental Soc. (pres. 1959-61), U.S. (mem. governing bd. 1971-73, dist. comdr. 1973—, asst. chmn. nat. fin. 1977—), Quad City (comdr. 1968-70) power squadrons. K.C., Lion. Home: 2503 Gaines St Davenport IA 52804 Office: 1333 W Lombard Davenport IA 52804

HATTER, EDWARD, cons. services co. exec.; b. Chgo., Oct. 11, 1929; s. Edward Ferdinand and Mildred Mary (Mach) Kloboucnik; certificate Bus. Adminstrn., Herzl Jr. Coll., Chgo., 1949; B.S., Northwestern U., 1951; M.S., Roosevelt U., 1960; m. Patricia Frances Connell, May 6, 1961; children—Wendy Ann, Gregg Edward, Brian James. Corp. statistical and budget mgr. Fansteel Metal Corp., North Chgo., Ill., 1956-61; sr. financial analyst Brunswick Internat. C.A., Chgo., 1961-62; asst. controller Advance Transformer Co., 1963-67; controller Booz Allen Applied Research Inc., 1968-70, group controller Booz Allen & Hamilton, Inc., 1971-74; treas.-asst. sec. Middle West Service Co., Chgo., 1975—. Served with AUS, 1953-55. Mem. Planning Execs. Inst. (chpt. pres. 1969, regional dir. 1971—), Corporate Planning Council, Planning Execs. Inst., Midwest Planning Assn., Plum Grove Manor Homeowners Assn. (pres. 1975). Home: 114 Imperial Ct Palatine IL 60067 Office: 55 E Monroe St Chicago IL 60603

HAUCH, JOHN WALTER, financial consultant; b. Oak Park, Ill., May 7, 1933; s. Walter John and Agnes Marie (Mayer) H.; B.S. in Bus. Adminstrn., Syracuse U., 1954; m. Marlene Ann Hauptmann, June 18, 1960; children—Linda Sue, Robert Dean. Mgr., Touche, Ross & Co., Chgo., 1956-66; mgmt. cons., Chgo., 1966-69; partner Main Lafrentz & Co., Chgo., 1969-72; pres. J.W. Hauch, Ltd., fin. consultants, Oak Brook, Ill., 1972—. Bd. dirs. Helping Hand Sch., LaGrange, Ill., 1962-68; treas., bd. govs. Community Meml. Hosp., LaGrange, 1970—. Served with U.S. Army, 1954-56. C.P.A., Ill. Mem. Am. Inst. C.P.A.'s, Ill. Soc. C.P.A.'s. Republican. Office: 1200 Harger Rd Oak Brook IL 60521

HAUCK, ALLAN, educator, clergyman; b. Springfield, Ohio, May 19, 1925; s. George and Alma Marie (Blinn) H.; A.B., Kenyon Coll., 1945; Th.M., Hamma Sch. Theology, 1947; Th.D., Hartford Sem. Found., 1950; m. Shirley Myers, July 12, 1947; children—Deborah, Tamara. Ordained to ministry Lutheran Ch., 1947; pastor Hope Lutheran Ch., Detroit, 1947-48; prof. Roanoke Coll., Salem, Va., 1950-51; pastor St. Mark's Ch., Newport, Ky., 1951-54, Auburn, Ind., 1954-58; prof. Midland Coll., Fremont, Nebr., 1958-68; prof. religion Carthage Coll., Kenosha, Wis., 1968—. Mem. Internat. Soc. Reply Coupon Collectors (pres. 1949—). Author: Calendar of Christianity, 1961; also specialized catalogues of reply coupons. Home: PO Box 176 Kenosha WI 53140 Office: Carthage Coll Kenosha WI 53140

HAUERWAS, STANLEY MARTIN, theologian, educator; b. Dallas, July 24, 1940; s. Coffee Martin and Joanna Gertrude (Berry) H.; B.A. cum laude in Philosophy, Southwestern U., Georgetown, Tex., 1962; B.D. cum laude, Yale U., 1965, M.A. in Christian Ethics, 1967, Ph.D. in Christian Ethics (Rockefeller fellow), 1968; m. Elizabeth Anne Harley, Dec. 29, 1962; 1 son, Adam John. Grad. asst. religion in western culture, Yale Coll., 1967-68, systematic theology, Yale Div. Sch., 1968; asst. prof. theol. ethics Augustana Coll., Rock Island, Ill., 1968-70; asst. prof. theol. ethics U. Notre Dame (Ind.), 1970-73, dir. grad. studies, 1973—, asso. prof., 1974—; sr. research fellow Kennedy Center Bioethics Georgetown U., 1973; prof. med. ethics U. Tex. Med. Sch., Galveston, 1975; prof. Christian ethics U. San Francisco, 1976. Recipient Tew prize Yale Div. Sch., 1963, Hooker prize, 1965. Author: Vision and Virtue: Essays in Christian Ethical Reflection, 1974; Character and the Christian Life: A Study in Theological Ethics, 1975; Truthfulness and Tragedy: Further Investigations in Christian Ethics, 1977; editorial bd. Am. Soc. Christian Ethics; asso. editor Ency. Bioethics; contbr. articles and revs. to profl. jours. Home: 210 E Pokagon St South Bend IN 46617 Office: Univ Notre Dame Dept Theology Notre Dame IN 46556

HAUGAN, HAROLD WALTER, plastics engr.; b. Stoughton, Wis., June 17, 1902; s. Paul Julius and Emma (Kildahl) H.; B.S., U. N.D., 1925, M.S., 1927; Ph.D., St. Andrews U., 1959. Adminstr. chemistry physics dept. York (Nebr.) Coll., 1939-41; instr. Eau Claire (Wis.) State Tchrs. Coll., 1941-43; research supr. U.S. ammunition plant, 1943-45; mem. research devel. staff Curtiss-Wright Research Lab., Cheektowage, N.Y., 1945-47, Cornell U. Aero. Lab., 1947-49; devel. engr. Bell Aircraft Corp., 1949-54; prin. Harold Haugan Assos., Devel. Engrs., 1954-56; supr. plastics Mich. ordinance missile plant missile div. Chrysler Corp., 1956-63; plastics engr. space div. Chrysler Corp., New Orleans, 1963-68; promoter plastics edn. in schs. and libraries throughout U.S., 1968—; pioneer developer plastics for missiles and Saturn space boosters, 1947-68. Author tech. publs. in plastics engring. Home: 1396 Smith St Birmingham MI 48009

HAUGAN, ROBERT ELLSWORTH, pub. co. exec.; b. New Richland, Minn., Mar. 21, 1917; s. Henry Albert and Ella (Gardson) H.; B.B.A., U. Minn., 1942; m. Clyde Johnson, Jan. 2, 1946; children—Eric A., Robert R., Caryle C. With Ernst & Ernst, C.P.A.'s, Mpls., 1942, 1946-51; controller Corn Belt Hatcheries, Joliet, Ill., 1951-54; controller Webb Pub. Co., St. Paul, 1954-59, treas., 1959-61, sec., 1961-64, v.p., 1964-67, exec. v.p., 1967-69, pres., 1969—, also dir.; dir. First Nat. Bank, St. Paul, No. States Power Co., Printing Industries Twin Cities, St. Paul; trustee Minn. Mut. Life Ins. Co., St. Paul. Treas. St. Paul Rehab. Center, 1965-66, pres., 1967. Served with USNR, 1942-46. C.P.A., Minn. Mem. St. Paul C. of C. (dir. 1970), St. Paul Employers Assn. (bd. dirs., mem. exec. com. 1971, pres. 1977), Twin City Financial Execs. Assn., Minn. Soc. C.P.A.'s, Am. Legion. Lutheran (treas. 1958-63; 1966-69). Rotarian (pres. 1968-69),Mason (Shriner). Clubs: St Paul Athletic; Minneapolis; Minnesota (dir. 1968-70) Town and Country (dir. 1968-71). Home: 407 Mount Curve Blvd St Paul MN 55105 Office: 1999 Shepard Rd St Paul MN 55116

HAUGEN, ORRIN MILLARD, lawyer; b. Mpls., Aug. 1, 1927; s. Oscar M. and Emma (Moe) H.; B.S. in Chem. Engring., U. Minn., 1948, LL.B., 1951; m. Marilyn Dixon, June 17, 1950; children—Melissa, Kristen, Eric, Kimberly. Admitted to Minn. bar, 1951; patent lawyer Honewell, Inc., Mpls., 1951-59, Univac div. Sperry Rand, 1959-63; pvt. practice specializing in patent law, Mpls., 1963—. Pres. Arrowhead Lake Improvement Assn., Inc., Mpls., 1958—. Served with USNR, 1945-46. Mem. Am., Minn. bar assns., Minn. Patent Law Assn., Minn. Acacia Alumni Assn., Inc. (pres. 1961-63), Acacia. Methodist. Kiwanian. Home: 6612 Indian Hills Rd Edina MN 55435 Office: Midwest Plaza Bldg Minneapolis MN 55402

HAUKEDAHL, OREL ELDEN, ret. govt. ofcl.; b. Madison, Wis., May 12, 1907; s. Louis A. and Mina E. (Andrus) H.; B.S. in Elec. Engring., U. Wis., 1932; m. Ellen Sorensen, Sept. 1, 1951; children—Jane E., Brian L. Engr., Civil Works Adminstrn., Madison, 1933-34; works sec. Wis. Emergency Relief Adminstrn., 1934-35; area engr. Works Progress Adminstrn., 1935-41; asst. engr. Fed. Power Commn., Washington, 1941-42, asso. engr., Atlanta, 1942-46, supervising hydraulic engr. Chgo. Regional Office, 1946-53; engr. charge River Basin work Chgo. Fed. Power Commn., 1953-57, dep.

regional engr., 1957-77; alternate Souris-Red-Rainy Basin Commn., 1967-73, Great Lakes Basin Commn., 1967-77, Mo. River Basin Commn. 1972-77, Upper Miss. River Basin Commn. 1972-77. Mem. coordinating com. on The Missouri River main stem reservoir operations, 1954-77. Served from lt. (j.g.) to lt. (s.g.), USNR, 1943-46. Mem. U. Wis. Alumni Assn., Am. Soc. Pub. Adminstrn. Lutheran. Mason, Moose. Home: 360 Neola Park Forest IL 60466

HAUKEDAHL, STANLEY GEORGE, holding co. exec.; b. Madison, Wis., June 24, 1913; s. Lois Anton and Mina (Andrus) H.; student U. Wis., 1931-37, Northwestern U. Traffic Inst., 1945, FBI Nat. Acad., Washington, 1953; m. Helen Anna Landis, Mar. 2, 1935 (dec. Apr. 1970); children—Sharon Lee Rumachik, Blane Leroy, Mark Steven, Reed Allen; m. 2d, Ruth E. Mace, May 27, 1972. Policeman, Dane County (Wis.) Police, Madison, 1938-42, Wis. State Patrol, 1942-48; chief of police, Kenosha, Wis., 1948-64; agy. v.p. 20th Century Guardian Life Ins. Co., Battle Creek, Mich.; former chmn. bd. Forum Internat. Inc.; sales adminstrn. Am. Diversified Holding Corp., Columbus, Ohio; pres. Am-Diversified Securities Co., Columbus; now v.p. First Ohio Investment Group. Co-ordinator police agys. Mobile Bn. 2, Wis. Civil Def., 1948-64; rep. police Govs. Civil Def. Hwy. Commn., 1948-64; mem. Kenosha Traffic Study Com., 1948-64. Mem. bd. Voters for Community Action, Calhoun County, Mich. Mem. Internat. Assn. Chiefs Police, Inc. (sgt.-at-arms 1960-63), Nat. Acad. Assos., Internat. Platform Assn., Am. Life Underwriters, Wis. F.B.I., Nat. Acad. Assn., U. Wis. Alumni Assn. Methodist. Mason (32 deg., Shriner), Kiwanian, Eagle. Club: National W. Home: 1483 Bradshire Dr Columbus OH 43220 Office: 1810 Mackenzie Dr Columbus OH

HAUN, RICHARD MELVIN, dentist; b. nr. Galatia, Kans., Nov. 11, 1917; s. John and Pauline Elizabeth (Strecker) H.; student U. Kans., 1935-39; D.D.S., U. Mo., Kansas City, 1943; m. Marian Jane Sphar, Feb. 9, 1947; 1 son, Ronald Melvin. Pvt. practice dentistry, Ottawa, Kans., 1946-47, Lawrence, Kans., 1947—. Served from 1st lt. to capt. Dental Corps, AUS, 1943-46; PTO. Mem. Am., Kans., 1st Dist. (pres. 1967), Douglas County dental assns., Vets. Dental Clinic Club, Xi Psi Phi. Republican. Lutheran (v.p. council 1962). Club: Sertoma (life, pres. Lawrence 1952-53). Home: 1027 Avalon Rd Lawrence KS 66044 Office: 645 1/2 Massachusetts St Lawrence KS 66044

HAUPTMAN, HERBERT MORRIS, accountant, lawyer; b. Chgo., May 26, 1907; s. Philip and Carrie (Singer) H.; diploma in commerce Northwestern U., 1931; LL.B., John Marshall Law Sch., 1934, J.D., 1970; C.P.A., Ill., 1953; m. Rhoda J. Jacobs, Jan. 1, 1929; children—Margaret S. (Mrs. Barnard Klein), Philip C. Office mgr. Lyons and Kennelly, Inc., 1926-33; salesman Morris Fisheries, Inc., 1933-34; comptroller Meadowmoor Dairies, Inc., 1934-36; admitted to Ill. bar, 1936, since in pvt. practice law and accounting, Chgo.; sr. partner Schur. Hauptman & Co., C.P.A.'s. Jewish (pres. temple mens club 1955-57, mem. temple bd. dirs. 1955-57, mem. exec. bd. nat. fedn. temple mens club 1960, v.p. and bd. mem. nat. fedn. temple brotherhoods 1966-72; hon. nat. bd. mem. 1972—; exec. bd. Jewish Chautauqua Soc., 1962; v.p. and bd. mem. 1966-72; hon. nat. bd. mem. 1972—; temple pres. 1974-76, bd. dirs. temple 1976—). Home: 5000 S Cornell Ave Chicago IL 60615 Office: 20 N Wacker Dr Chicago IL 60606

HAUPTMAN, RHODA JOY JACOBS (MRS. HERBERT MORRIS HAUPTMAN), civic worker; b. Chgo., Apr. 25, 1908; d. Alexander and Margaret (Spare) Jacobs; student U. Chgo., 1925-27; m. Herbert Morris Hauptman, Jan. 1, 1929; children—Margaret Spare (Mrs. Barnard F. Klein), Philip Carl. Librarian, Chgo. Pub. Library, 1927-29; profl. book reviewer, 1960—; columnist Nat. Jewish Post and Opinion, 1964—. pres. Sarah Greenebaum lodge 16, United Order True Sisters, 1942-44, mem. nat. exec. bd., 1963—; pres. sisterhood Temple K.A.M., 1948-51, dir. temple, 1948-56, sec. congregation, 1954-56, v.p. congregation, 1972-74; exec. com. Chgo. Fedn. Reform Synagogues; chmn. welfare bd. Chgo. Woman's Aid, 1953-55, Chgo. Presidents' Council, 1949; mem. Chgo. Conf. Religion and Race; 1st v.p. Chgo. Armed Services Council; asst. treas. Midwest sect. Nat. Jewish Welfare Bd., vice chmn. women's orgn. services, 1967—; mem. nat. council U.S.O., 1966—; v.p. Conf. Jewish Women's Orgns., 1960-62, bd. dirs., 1959—; v.p. Union Inst. Camp, 1955-57. Bd. dirs. women's div. Jewish Fedn. Chgo., 1948-53; bd. dirs. Chgo. sect. Nat. Women's Com. Brandeis U.; trustee Chgo. U.S.O. Mem. Nat. (exec. bd. 1953-57), Midwest (founding pres. 1956-59), Ill. (pres. 1955-56, hon. pres. 1976—) fedns. temple sisterhoods. Address: 5000 Cornell Ave Chicago IL 60615

HAUSBERG, WILLIAM, toiletry and soap co. exec.; b. Charles City, Iowa, Oct. 25, 1912; s. Ernest and Margaret Frothingham (Shivler) H.; grad. Phillips Andover Acad., 1932; B.A., Yale, 1936; grad. Advanced Mgmt. Program, Harvard, 1967; m. Marian Collester, May 8, 1943; children—Peter, Mark. With Lehn & Fink Products Corp., N.Y.C., 1936-56, advt. dir., 1948-56; v.p. advt. Andrew Jergens Co., Cin., 1956-67, v.p. marketing, 1967-70, exec. v.p., 1970-71, pres., dir. 1971—; pres., dir. Andrew Jergens Co., Ltd., Perth, Ont., Can., Sugar Beet Products Co., Saginaw, Mich., Chem. By-Products, Ltd., Toronto, Can.; dir. Albert Verley & Co., South Plainfield, N.J. Served with USNR, 1942-45; PTO. Clubs: Queen City (Cin.); Yale (N.Y.C.). Home: 2600 Willowbrook Dr Cincinnati OH 45237 Office: 2535 Spring Grove Ave Cincinnati OH 45214

HAUSER, JAMES EDWARD, stained glass window mfg. and restoration co. exec.; b. White Bear Lake, Minn., Aug. 30, 1916; s. Albert Earl and Josephine Grace (Czapiewski) H.; grad. high sch.; m. Genevieve Agnes Wicka, May 12, 1938; children—James A., Thomas P., Patricia J., Michael F., Susan M., Debra A., Jone M. Founder, Hauser Art Glass Co., Inc., Winona, Minn., 1946, chmn. bd., pres., 1964—; chmn. bd. Willet Stained Glass Studios, Inc., Phila. Mem. pres.'s adv. council St. Teresa Coll., Winona. Served with AUS, 1944-46; PTO. Mem. NAM, Minn. Taxpayers Assn., Minn. Assn. Commerce and Industry, Nat. Fedn. Ind. Bus., Winona, Nat. chambers commerce. Democrat. Roman Catholic. Home: 217 W 4th St Winona MN 55987 Office: 177 Lafayette St Winona MN 55987 also 1171 Mankato Ave Winona MN 55987

HAUSER, JON WILLIAM, indsl. designer; b. Sault Ste. Marie, Mich., June 8, 1916; s. Kenneth and Arlie (Hershey) H.; m. Jean MacCallum, Aug. 30, 1939; 1 son, Jon William II. With United Motors Co., 1936; stylist Gen. Motors Corp., 1936-41, Chrysler Corp., 1941-43, Budd Mfg. Co., 1939; dir. design Sears, Roebuck & Co., 1943-45; designer Dave Chapman, Chgo., 1945-46, Barnes & Reinecke, 1946-49, Reinecke Asso., 1949-52; pres. Jon W. Hauser, Inc., St. Charles, Ill., 1952—; dir. State Bank St. Charles. Del., Internat. Council Socs. Indsl. Design, 1963-65, 67; chmn. judging com. Design in Housewares awards, 1966; chmn. judging com. Wescon Indsl. Design Awards, 1968, 69; lectr. indsl. design. Bd. dirs. Delnor Hosp. Men's Found., v.p. bd. trustees. Furnished two designs named in Best 100 Designs History, 1959. Mem. Indsl. Designers Soc. Am. (chmn. bd. 1968), Indsl. Designers Inst. (award 1956, pres. 1962-64, chmn. bd., fellow, mem. nat. exec. com., trustee Chgo. chpt.); Quiet Birdmen. Mason (32 deg. Shriner). Clubs: St. Charles Country, Fox Valley Shrine. Home: 3N981 Route 31 St Charles IL 60174 Office: 10 State Ave St Charles IL 60174

HAUSER, WILLARD ALLEN, physician; b. Cleve., Mar. 6, 1937; s. Willard Ephriam and Annabelle (Garnett) H.; A.B., Western Res. U., 1958; M.D., St. Louis U., 1962; postgrad. Northwestern U., 1963-66, U. Minn., 1968-70; m. Leeana Belle Gregory, June 13, 1964; children—Bernard, Rachel, Michel. Intern, St. Louis U., 1962-63; resident neurology Northwestern U., 1963-66; teaching asso. neurology Walter Reed Army Hosp., 1967-68; research asst. sect. med. statistics epidemiology and population genetics Mayo Clinic, Rochester, Minn., 1968-69, research asso. sect. med. statistics, epidemiology and population genetics, 1969-70, asso. in epidemiology, 1970—; asst prof. dept. neurology U. Minn., 1970-75, asso. prof., 1975—; staff neurologist, dir. EEG Lab., Mpls. VA Hosp., 1970-73; dir. EEG Lab., St. Paul Ramsey Hosp., 1973—. Diplomate Am. Bd. Qualification in Electroencephalography, Am. Bd. Neurology and Psychiatry. Mem. A.M.A., Central Soc. for Neurologic Research, Am. Acad. Neurology, Soc. for Epidemiologic Research, Am. Electro-encephalographic Soc., Central Electro-encephalographic Soc., Am. Epilepsy Soc. Contbr. articles to tech. jours. Home: 4400 Fremont Ave S Minneapolis MN 55409 Office: 640 Jackson St St Paul MN 55101

HAUSKEN, SALLY ANN, ednl. counselor; b. Wahpeton, N.D., Aug. 10, 1934; d. Clyde Olaf and Lois Beatrice (Mc Michael) H.; B.S., Northwestern U., 1956; M.S., U. Colo., 1967; Sec. to pres. North Central Airlines, Mpls., 1958-59; service club dir. U.S. Army, Germany, 1959-61; tchr. bus., counselor Littleton (Colo.) High Sch., 1962-66; secondary counselor Detroit Lakes (Minn.) High Sch., 1967-68; secondary counselor Minnetonka West Jr. High Sch., Excelsior, Minn., 1968—. Mem. Northwestern U. Alumni Admissions Council, 1972—. Mem. Am., Minn. personnel and guidance assns., Lake Area Counselors Assn., NEA, Minn. Edn. Assn., Minnetonka Tchrs. Assn. Episcopalian. Home: 1540 Skyview Dr Chaska MN 55318 Office: 6421 Hazeltine Blvd Excelsior MN 55331

HAUSMAN, WILLIAM WALKER, mfg. co. exec.; b. St. Louis, Nov. 4, 1937; s. Russell Joseph and Elizabeth Dorothy (Walker) H.; A.B., Washington U., 1959, M.B.A., 1967. Asst. brand mgr. Pet, Inc., St. Louis, 1967; asst. product mgr. Ralston Purina, 1967-68; mgr. market research Gen. Steel Industries, Inc., 1969-71; mgr. market research Central States Diversified, Inc., 1971—; pres. Columbia Maintenance Co., 1972—. Served with AUS, 1962-65. Mem. Beta Gamma Sigma, Sigma Chi. Democrat. Presbyn. Clubs: Noonday, Bath and Tennis (St. Louis). Home: 400 N Price Rd St Louis MO 63132 Office: 1170 S Big Bend Ave St Louis MO 63117

HAUSMANN, EUGENE ROBERT, architect; b. Belleville, Ill., Feb. 3, 1932; s. Edwin Lawrence and Clotilda Catherine (Fellner) H.; B.Arch., U. Notre Dame, 1954; m. Mary Ann Bedel, July 6, 1957. With Lyman Weisenstein, architect, Belleville, 1956-61, Weisenstein, Rogers & Hausmann, 1961-72, Weisenstein, Hausmann, Ganschinietz & Klingel, Inc., 1972—. Pres., Belleville Philharmonic Soc., 1973—; mem. City Plan Commn., 1974—, City Hist. Preservation Commn., 1974—. Served with AUS, 1954-56. Recipient Distinguished Service award Jr. C. of C., 1967. Mem. A.I.A. (past pres. So. Ill. chpt.), St. Louis Theatre Organ Soc. Elk, Rotarian. Club: Serra of St. Clair County (pres. 1975). Archtl. works include St. Augustine of Canterbury Ch., Belleville, Ill., St. Clair County Jail. Home: 38 N Pennsylvania Belleville IL 62221 Office: 3201 W Main Belleville IL 62221

HAUWILLER, ROBERT PAUL, univ. adminstr.; b. St. Paul, June 24, 1934; s. Paul Helidore and Bertha Elizabeth (Sherman) H.; B.S., St. Mary's Coll., Minn., 1956; M.S., U. Notre Dame, 1962; m. Mary Agnes Walsh, Aug. 15, 1970. High sch. tchr., Ill., 1956-63; asst. prof. math., registrar Lewis U., Lockport, Ill., 1963-68; asst. registrar Chgo. State U., 1968-70, dir. instl. research, 1976—; dir. admissions and records, prof. math. Governors State U., Park Forest, Ill., 1968-76. NSF grantee, 1960-61. Mem. Am. Assn. Collegiate Registrars and Admissions Officers, Am. Math. Assn., Phi Delta Kappa. Roman Catholic. Club: K.C. (4 deg.). Home: 661 Sullivan Land Park Forest South IL 60466 Office: Chicago State Univ 95th St and King Dr Chicago IL 60628

HAVEL, JEAN EUGÈNE MARTIAL, educator; b. Le Havre, France, June 16, 1928; came to Can., 1959, naturalized, 1966; Licence en Droit (LL.B.), Université de Paris (France), 1950; Diplôme de l'Institut des Etudes Politiques, 1952, postgrad. Institut des Etudes Scandinaves, 1952-53, Doctorat ès Lettres, 1956; postgrad. in law (Norwegian Govt. scholar), U. Oslo (Norway), 1953-54; m. Anne Marie Luhr, Aug. 22, 1955 (dec. Jan. 1977); children—Jean Guillaume, Frédérik, Sophie Mathilde, Ingrid Lucie. Part-time tchr. extension div. U. Stockholm (Sweden), 1956-59; asst. prof. polit. sci. U. Montreal (Que., Can.), 1959-62; asst. prof. polit. sci. Laurentian U., Sudbury, Ont., Can., 1962-64, asso. prof., 1964-69, prof., 1969—. Guest speaker U. New Brunswick, 1968, U. London (Eng.), 1969, U. Helsinki/Helsingfors (Finland), 1969, U. Padova (Italy), 1969, U. Rouen (France), 1969, U. Caen (France), 1969, U. Ottowa (Ont., Can.), 1974. Recipient Centennial medal Govt. Can., 1967; award European Center of Carnegie Endowment for Internat. Peace, 1958; Swedish Inst. Cultural Relations with Foreign Countries scholar, 1954-55, Council of Europe research scholar, 1957-58, Can. Council Leave fellow, 1968-69, 75-76. Mem. Am., Can. polit. sci. assns. Author: Cours de Journalisme: La Rédaction, 1956; La Fabrication du Journal, 1957; La Politique Suédoise du Logement de 1940 à 1957, 1957; Le Mouvement Socialiste Norvégien, 1958; Le Socialisme Danois, 1958; Le Socialisme Réformiste Modéré en Suède, 2 vols., 1958; La Condition de la Femme, 1961, Italian transl., 1962, Spanish transl., 1965, Japanese transl., 1970; Politics in Sudbury: A Survey of Mass Communications, Political Behavior, and Political Parties in Sudbury, 1966, French transl., 1966; Les Etats Scandinaves et l'Intégration Européenne, 2d edit., 1970; Habitat et Logement, 4th edit., 1974, Spanish transl., 1961; La Finlande et la Suède, 1978. Contbr. articles to profl. jours. Office: Dept of Political Science Laurentian Univ Sudbury ON Canada

HAVENER, WILLIAM HENRY, ophthalmologist; b. Portsmouth, Ohio, June 2, 1924; s. Gilbert and Laura (Braunlin) H.; B.A., Wooster Coll., 1944; M.D., Western Res. U., 1948; postgrad. Harvard, 1950-51; M.S., U. Mich., 1953; m. Phyllis Ann Johnson, Jan. 26, 1946; children—Michael, Mark, Ann, Gail, John, Amy, Neal. Intern Univ. Hosps. of Cleve., 1948-50; resident neuropsychiatry Cleve. Receiving Hosp., 1950; resident ophthalmology U. Mich., 1951-53; practice medicine, specializing in ophthalmology, Columbus, Ohio, 1954—; mem. staff Univ., Mt. Carmel, Children's hosps., Columbus; asst. prof. ophthalmology Ohio State U., Columbus, 1954-56, asso. prof., chmn. dept. ophthalmology, 1956-61, 72—, prof., 1961—. Author: Atlas of Diagnostic Techniques and Treatment of Retinal Detachment, 1967; Atlas of Diagnostic Techniques and Treatment of Intraocular Foreign Bodies, 1969; Nursing Care in Eye, Ear, Nose and Throat Disorders, 1968, 3d edit., 1974; (with others) Ocular Pharmacology, 3d edit., 1974; Synopsis of Ophthalmology, 4th edit., 1974; Atlas of Perimetric Technique, 1972; Atlas of Cataract Surgery, 1972. Contbr. articles to profl. publs. Home: 1859 Bedford Rd Columbus OH 43212 Office: 456 Clinic Dr Columbus OH 43210

HAVENS, DWIGHT BOWLES, orgn. exec.; b. Sac City, Iowa, May 31, 1913; s. Lucian Emmett and Ella (Bowles) H.; student Drake U., 1931-32; B.A., U. Nebr., 1936; postgrad. Mich. State U., 1961; m. Roma Erleen Harrington, Nov. 15, 1934; children—Ralph E., Daniel B., Michael D. Staff exec. Lincoln (Nebr.) C. of C., 1936-41; mgr. Norfolk (Nebr.) C. of C., 1941-46; mgr. Hastings (Nebr.) C. of C., 1946-48; exec. v.p. Rochester (Minn.) C. of C., 1948-51; mgr. C. of C. dept. U.S. C. of C., Washington, 1951-64; pres. Greater Detroit C. of C., 1964—; instr. insts. for orgn. mgmt. Mich. State U., 1953-63, U. Santa Clara, 1960-65, U. Colo., 1953-63, U. Houston, 1960-64, U. Ga., 1960-64, U. Syracuse U., 1960-63. Vice pres. Met. Detroit YMCA, 1967—; mem. Gov.'s Commn. on Urban Problems, 1966—; bd. dirs. S.E. Mich. Transp. Authority, 1976—; trustee Met. Meth. Ch., 1974—. Served with USNR, 1944-45. Named Nebr.'s Outstanding Young Man, Nebr. Jr. C. of C., 1948. Mem. Am. C. of C. Execs. (pres. 1967-68). Home: 541 Robert John Rd Grosse Pointe Woods MI 48236 Office: 150 Michigan Ave Detroit MI 48226

HAVERDINK, VIRGIL DEAN, farm equipment co. designer; b. Le Mars, Iowa, June 27, 1942; s. Gillis and Wilhelmina (Korver) H.; student Northwestern Coll., 1960-61; B.S. in Agrl. Engring., Iowa State U., 1964; M.S., 1967; m. Audrey Ann Verdoorn, June 5, 1964; children—Michael Dean, Michelle Ann, Marlon Dale. Engring. researcher Deere & Co., Moline, Ill., 1964-65; farm equipment designer John Deere Co., Des Moines, 1967—. Registered profl. engr., Ia. Mem. Am. Soc. Agrl. Engrs., Phi Kappa Phi. Mem. Reformed ch. (deacon 1969-75, elder 1977—). Patentee on tillage equipment. Home: 210 SE Wanda Dr Ankeny IA 50021 Office: PO Box 1595 Des Moines IA 50306

HAVERFIELD, BETTY LUKER (MRS. ROBERT W. HAVERFIELD), sorority exec.; b. Chgo.; d. George House and Florence (O'Conner) Luker; student Rockford Coll., 1937-38; B.J., U. Mo., 1942, postgrad., 1963-64; m. Robert Walter Haverfield, Sept. 14, 1944; children—Judith Ann Beaupre, Robert David. Asso. editor Indsl. Med. Mag., Chgo., 1942-44, Pioneer Publs., Chgo., 1944-46; editor Crescent, Gamma Phi Beta, Columbia, Mo., 1964-74, internat. grand pres., 1974-78. Pub. relations chmn. Girl Scouts U.S.A., Jefferson City, Mo., 1946-50, Camp Fire Girls, 1953-55; publicity chmn. United Fund, Columbia, 1956; pres. Mothers Forum, Columbia, 1948-49. Bd. dirs. Columbia Mental Health. Mem. City (pres.), Nat. (chmn. editors conf. 1973) panhellenic assns., P.E.O., Mid Mo. Press Club, U. Mo. Alumnae assns., U. Journalism Women, Gamma Phi Beta, Theta Sigma Phi, Gamma Alpha Chi. Republican. Mem. Christian Ch. Home: 507 Medavista Dr Columbia MO 65201

HAVERFIELD, ROBERT WALTER, educator; b. Kansas City, Mo., June 28, 1919; s. Walter Wildey and Mabel (Leach) H.; B.J., U. Mo., 1941, M.A., 1957; m. Betty Ann Luker, Sept. 14, 1944; children—Judith Ann, Robert David. Advt. mgr. Mo. Power & Light Co., Jefferson City, 1945-48; faculty U. Mo., Columbia, 1948—, asst. prof. journalism, placement dir., 1963-72, prof. 1972—, mem. bd. student publs., 1966-73, chmn., 1971-73; cons. Leo Burnett Advt., London, Eng., 1973—. Vice pres. bd. dirs. Daniel Boone Regional Library, Columbia; bd. dirs. Columbia Library. Served with USNR, 1941-45; PTO. Internat. Harvester fellow, summer 1954; Am. Assn. Advt. Agys. fellow, 1961; Pub. Relations Soc. Am. fellow, 1963. Mem. Direct Mail Advt. Assn. (ednl. adviser), Am. Assn. Advt. Agys. (Mo. educator chmn. 1961—, central U.S. educator chmn. 1975—), Am. Acad. Advt., Am. Library Trustees Assn. (midwestern v.p. 1964-66, designer ofcl. emblem, chmn. 50th anniversary Freedom of Press, U.S. Postage Stamp 1968), Midwest Coll. Placement Assn., Alpha Delta Sigma (editor Linage 1950-63), Pi Kappa Alpha, Kappa Tau Alpha. Republican. Club: Kiwanis. Author: 100 Books on Advertising, 1961, 10th edit., 1976. Home: 507 Medavista Dr Columbia MO 65201

HAVILAND, CAMILLA KLEIN, judge; b. Dodge City, Kans., Sept. 13, 1926; d. Robert Godfrey and Lelah (Luther) Klein; A.A., Monticello Coll., 1946; B.A., Radcliffe Coll., 1948; J.D., Kans. U., 1958; m. John Bodman Haviland, Sept. 7, 1957. Admitted to Kans. bar, 1955; practice law, Wichita, Kans., 1955-56, Dodge City, 1956—; judge Probate County and Juvenile Cts. of Ford County, Dodge City, 1957-77, Municipal Ct. of Dodge City, 1971—. Mem. Met. Area Planning Commn., 1958-61, Atty. Gen.'s Youth Com., 1962-66, Kans. Jud. Council Spl. Com. to Study Revision of Probate Code, 1972-76; mem. probate forms com. Jud. Council, 1975—. Mem. pres.'s council St. Mary of the Plains Coll., 1961-67; mem. adv. com. Kans. U. Sch. Religion, 1968—, Sch. Social Welfare, 1972—; mem. adv. bd. Salvation Army, 1956—; mem. exec. com. Ford County Red Cross, 1956-62. Nat. committeewoman Young Democrats of Kans., 1948-54; v.p. Young Dems. of Am., 1953-55. Recipient Nathan Burkan Meml. award A.S.C.A.P., 1954. Mem. Am. (ins. and probate com. 1967—), Kans., S.W. Kans. (pres. 1967-68), Ford-Gray County bar assns., Kans. Probate Judges Assn. (pres. 1963-64), Dodge City Women's C. of C. Episcopalian. Mem. P.E.O. Clubs: Broadmoor Golf, Garden of Gods (Colorado Springs, Colo.). Author: Poems by Camilla, 1948. Contbr. articles to legal jours. Home: 2006 Eastlane Dodge City KS 67801 Office: Box 17 Dodge City KS 67801

HAVLAS, MIKE VACLAV, physician; b. Pisek, Czechoslovakia, Oct. 27, 1914; s. Joseph and Svatava (Moravcova) H.; student Charles U., Prague, Czechoslovakia, 1933-39, grad. in medicine, 1945; m. Vivian Bozena Myskova, Sept. 27, 1941; children—Daana, Tom. Chief med. rep. Fr. Schnöbling Pharms., Prague, 1939-45; staff physician univ. clinics, pub. hosps., Czechoslovakia, 1945-48; family physician, dir. county health unit, Doksy, 1948-56; family physician, supervising physician, Liberec, Czechoslovakia, 1956-68; dir. med. counceling Center for Smokers, Liberec, 1960-68; staff physician Ont. Hosp. Sch., Cedar Springs, Ont., Can., 1969—. Asso. mem. Canadian Psychiat. Assn. Baptist. Home: PO Box 54 Chatham ON N7M5KI Canada Office: Rural Route 1 Cedar Springs ON Canada

HAWES, JOSEPH MILTON, historian; b. Ft. Davis, Tex., May 9, 1938; s. Milton Doe and Jessie Emily (Weatherby) H.; B.A., Rice U., 1960; M.A., Okla. State U., 1962; Ph.D., U. Tex., 1969; m. Kathryn Schnell, Dec. 22, 1962; children—Lyda Kathryn, John Irl. Tchr. social studies Ysleta (Tex.) Pub. Schs., 1960-61, Ensworth Sch., Nashville, 1962-64; asst. prof. history Ind. U. SE, Jeffersonville, 1969-71; asst. prof. history Kans. State U., Manhattan, 1971-73, asso. prof., also head dept. 1973—. Field humanist Kans. Com. for Humanities, 1974—; bd. dirs. Manhattan House, 1975. U. Tex. grad. fellow, 1967-69. Mem. Am. Hist. Assn., Orgn. Am. Historians, AAUP, So. Hist. Assn., Phi Alpha Theta. Author: Children in Urban Society: Juvenile Delinquency in the Nineteenth Century, 1971. Home: 729 Elling Dr Manhattan KS 66502

HAWES, NANCYE ELIZABETH (MRS. GEORGE JASON HAWES), newspaperwoman; b. Somerset, Ky., Mar. 10, 1932; d. William Henderson and Ava Agnes (Foster) Smith; grad. high sch.; m. George Jason Hawes, Feb. 11, 1950; children—George Kelly, William Kevin, Kimberly Ellen. With Anderson (Ind.) Herald, 1965—, bridal editor, 1967-68, women's editor, 1968-72, editor Accent on Living, 1972-74, asst. news editor, 1974-75, city editor 1976-77, area news editor, 1977—. Chmn., Mental Health Blue Bell Ball Com., 1965; asst. leader Wapehani council Girl Scouts U.S.A., 1971; pub. relations dir. Kikthawenund council Boy Scouts Am., 1966-70. Del., Republican State Conv., 1970, 72; dir. Madison County Women's Rep. Club,

1970-72; mem. Hoosiers for Equal Rights Amendment. Bd. dirs. Madison County Assn. for Mental Health, 1965-73, Planned Parenthood Madison County, A.R.C. Recipient Unknown Scout award, 1957; award AP; certificate of merit Heart Fund Ind., 1971. Mem. Women's Orch. Guild, YWCA, N.A.A.C.P., Urban League, Indpls., Press Club, Lady Elks, Women of Moose, Women in Communications, Women's Press Club Ind. (editor state newsletter, 1st v.p. 1978—), Nat. Fedn. Press Women, Sigma Delta Chi (pres. 1977—), Beta Sigma Phi (Girl of Year award 1964). Mem. Christian Ch. Clubs: Exchangettes (v.p. 1970-72) Soroptomist (pres. 1970-72). Home: 5122 Pearl St Anderson IN 46014 Office: PO Box 1090 Anderson IN 46015

HAWK, GERALD WAYNE, elec. engr.; b. Montpelier, Ind., Feb. 20, 1928; s. Orval William and Grace Ellen (Fetty) H.; student U. Ill., Urbana, 1955-56; B.E.E., Ind. Inst. Tech., 1960; m. Patricia Jo Ann Wakeland, Apr. 1, 1967; children—Connie Lynn, Carla Jo, Sally Jo, Carol Joyce, Cindy Joy, Susan Diane. Design engr. to supr. D.C. press drives design Hurletron, Inc., Danville, Ill., 1960-66; sr. equipment engr. to sr. control engr. Corning Glass Works, Bluffton, Ind., 1966—. Served with AUS, 1946-47, 51-53; col. Res. Decorated Bronze Star (3), Purple Heart (3). Mem. Res. Officers Assn., Am. Legion. Baptist. Clubs: Moose, Elks. Home: 517 S Poplar St Hartford City IN 47348 Office: Corning Glass Works Corning Rd Bluffton IN 46714

HAWK, JEFFERY LEE, mil. adminstrn. analyst; b. Chillicothe, Ohio, Jan. 4, 1946; s. Donald Lee and Regina Ann (Breen) H.; B.A., John Carroll U., 1968; M.A., Miami U., Oxford, Ohio, 1969; postgrad. Ind. U., 1974—; m. Margaret Jennifer Schuer, Aug. 31, 1968; children—Donald Lee, Jeanne Marie. Dir. Speaker Bur., instr. speech Miami U. Oxford, 1969-70; asso. instr. speech, dir. speakers bur., dept. speech Ind. U., Bloomington, 1972-74; mil. adminstrn. analyst, orgn. materiel evaulation div., combat devel. directorate U.S. Army, Adminstrn. Center, Ft. Benjamin Harrison, Ind., 1974—. Volunteer, Cleve. Welfare Fedn., 1965-67. Served as info. officer, speech writer AUS, 1970-72. Mem. John Carroll U., Miami U. alumni assns., VFW. Republican. Roman Catholic. Home: 2644 Sheffield Dr Indianapolis IN 46229

HAWK, MARION EARL, structural engr.; b. Stone Creek, Ohio, Oct. 13, 1899; s. Francis and Alizuma Harriet (Wherley) H.; B.S., Tri-State Coll. Engring., 1946; postgrad. Purdue U., 1966, U. Wis., 1968; m. Della Mae Frutiger, Nov. 26, 1925. Apprentice plasterer Melbourne Constrn. Co., Canton, Ohio, 1920-25; design and constrn. bridges Melvin E. Lutz, Cons. Engr., 1925-35; project engr. large dams George M. Brewster & Son, Bogota, N.J., 1935-40; gen. supt. Hunkin-Conkey Constrn. Co., Cleve., 1940-44; structural engr. cons., Canton, 1950—, pres. M.E. Hawk, Inc., cons. engr., 1951-66; engr., cons. Mellett Homes, Inc. Shopping Mall, Canton, 1966—, Universal Engring. & Testing Labs., Canton, 1970-75; pvt. design practice structural steel, soils, foundations and reinforced concrete, Canton, 1975—. Life mem. ASCE. Mason (32 deg.). Address: 508 Bedford Ave NW Canton OH 44708

HAWKINS, ARNOT ROY, physician; b. Saskatoon, Sask., Can., Dec. 10, 1932; s. Roy Arnot and Winnifred Eda (Haffenden) H.; B.A., U. Sask., 1953, M.A., 1956, M.D., 1960; m. Lenore Edith Seed, June 16, 1956; children—Patricia Anne Lenore, Clare Arnot, David Harold. Intern Univ. Hosp., Saskatoon, 1960-62; gen. practice medicine Port Arthur Clinic, Thunder Bay, Ont., 1962—; mem. staff Port Arthur Gen. Hosp., St. Joseph's Gen. Hosp. Bd. dirs. Inter-Varsity Christian Fellowship Can. Recipient Vanier award Jr. C. of C. of Can., 1972. Mem. Canadian Diabetic Assn. (nat. dir. 1975-77). Christian Brethren (elder 1972—). Home: 123 Cottonwood Crescent Thunder Bay ON Canada Office: 194 N Court St Thunder Bay ON Canada

HAWKINS, BRETT WILLIAM, social scientist; b. Buffalo, N.Y., Sept. 15, 1937; s. Ralph C. and Irma A. (Rowley) H.; A.B., U. Rochester, 1959; M.A., Vanderbilt U., 1962, Ph.D., 1964; m. Linda L. Knuth, Oct. 31, 1974; 1 son, Brett William. Instr. polit. sci. Vanderbilt U., Nashville, 1963; instr. polit. sci. Washington and Lee U., Lexington, Va., 1963-64, asst. prof., 1964-65; asst. prof. polit. sci. U. Ga. at Athens, 1965-68, asso. prof., 1968-70; asso. prof. polit. sci. U. Wis.-Milw., 1970-71, prof., 1971—. Mem. Phi Beta Kappa, Iota of N.Y. Author: Nashville Metro, 1964, The Ethnic Factor in American Politics, 1970, Politics in the Metropolis, 2d edit., 1971, Politics and Urban Policies, 1971. Contbr. articles in field to profl. jours. Home: 3909 N Murray Ave Shorewood WI 53211 Office: Dept of Political Science Univ of Wisconsin Milwaukee WI 53201

HAWKINS, HAL WOODBRIDGE, architect; b. Springfield, Mo., Dec. 12, 1920; s. Earl and Grace Winthrop (Anable) H.; student S.W. Mo. State U., 1946; B.S. in Architecture, Kans. State U., 1950; m. Jean Marie Donnell, May 30, 1949; children—Sandra Marie, Mary Kathryn. With Hawkins & Esterly, Architects, Springfield, Mo., 1950-52; with architect's office St.L.&S.F.R.R., 1952-56; prin. Hal Hawkins AIA, Architect & Assos., 1956—. Mem. planning tech. adv. com. Mo. Dept. Community Affairs, 1971-72. Served with USMC, 1939-46; PTO. Mem. AIA (chpt. bd. dirs., v.p., pres. 1969—, mem. nat. urban planning com., 1971), Mo. Assn. Registered Architects (bd. dirs. 1968—, v.p. 1969), S.W. Mo. Assn. Architects (dir., pres. 1962—) Mo. Council Architects (pres. 1970-71, dir. 1977—), Springfield C. of C. (chmn. hwys. com. 1971-72), Am. Ex-Prisoners War (life), DAV, Sigma Nu, Kappa Beta Phi. Presbyterian (trustee 1965, 75—, deacon 1966-69, elder 1975-77, elder-commr. to John Calvin Union Presbytery 1975-77). Clubs: University (pres. 1970, 2d v.p. 1978) (Springfield), Masons, K.T., Shriners, Elks. Editor Missouri Architect, 1968-69. Office: 1516 S Glenstone Springfield MO 65804

HAWKINS, HAROLD ELMER, ret. automotive engr., artist; b. Perry, Mich., Aug. 13, 1914; s. Marvil Perry and Nellie (Butler) H.; student Mich. State U., 1944-46, Lansing (Mich.) Community Coll., 1977—; m. Bonnie Emmaline Lockwood, Nov. 19, 1937; 1 son, Robert Joel. Barnstormer for short flights and country fairs, 1933-36; design engr. Oldsmobile div. Gen. Motors Corp., Lansing, Mich., 1936-73, design group supr., 1965-73; propr., mgr. Custom Printing Co., Lansing, 1973-77; instr. art, Arts Crafts Soc., Lansing,; one man shows of paintings include: Henry Ford Centennial Library, Dearborn, Mich., 1974, Sloan Mus., Flint, Mich., 1975, Mich. State U., E. Lansing, 1975; represented in permanent collections; artist pictorial history of aviation World of Wings. Mem. Soc. of Automotive Engrs., Mich. Aerospace Edn. Assn., OX-5, Nat. Aviation Pioneers, Silver Wings Fraternity, Oldsmobile Quarter-Century Club. Methodist. Home: 2023 Byrnes Rd Lansing MI 48906

HAWKINS, ROBERT LYON, JR., chem. co. exec.; b. Cleve., Apr. 22, 1922; s. Robert Lyon and Catherine (Hanselman) H.; B.S. in Chem. Engring., Case Inst. Tech., 1947, M.S. in Indsl. Chemistry, 1956; m. Patricia O'Callaghan Boswell, Nov. 9, 1968; children—Robert Lyon III, Anne S., John W.; stepchildren—William O. Boswell, James T. Boswell. Paint chemist Empire Varnish Co. (name changed to Waterlox Chem. & Coatings Corp., 1967), Cleve., 1947-50, asso. tech. dir., 1950-56, corp. sec., 1950-60, exec. v.p., 1956-61, chmn. bd., chief exec. officer, 1961—. Bd. dirs. Cleve. Paint-Up Clean-Up Fix-Up Campaign, 1961-62. Served to 1st lt., USAF, 1942-46. Fellow Am. Inst. Chemists; mem. A.A.A.S., Am. Chem. Soc., Am. Mgmt. Assn., Cleve. Paint Varnish and Lacquer Assn. (pres. 1961-62, exec. bd. 1970-71), Cleve. Soc. Paint Tech. (exec. com. 1968-71), Citizens League Cleve., Cleve. Art Mus., Mus. Natural Hist., Alpha Chi Sigma, Beta Theta Pi. Clubs: Hermit (dir. 1976—) (Cleve.), Mayfield Country; Mentor Harbor Yachting (Ohio). Patentee in field. Home: 10000 Lake Shore Blvd Bratenahl Cleveland OH 44108 Office: 9808 Meech Ave Cleveland OH 44105

HAWKINS, WILLIAM SHELDON, accountant; b. Marengo, Ind., July 18, 1938; s. Sheldon James and Effie Fern (Hollis) H.; B.S., U. Louisville, 1963. Accountant, auditor Imhof, Veatch & Wilcoxson, C.P.A.'s, Louisville, 1963-66, Arthur E. Sallee, Bedford, Ind., 1966-70; self-employed as accountant, Paoli, Ind., 1970—. Named Ky. Col. Mem. Nat., Ind. socs. accountants, Ind. Sheriff's Assn., Paoli C. of C. Mem. Christian Ch. Mason (Shriner), Elk, Lion. Club: Green Acres Country. Home: Marengo IN 47140 Office: 4-A Kimball Plaza Paoli IN 47454

HAWKINSON, JAMES R., bus. cons.; B.A., Carleton U.; M.B.A., Northwestern U. Past sales supr. Procter and Gamble Co.; past mem. staff Booz, Allen and Hamilton, Marsteller Co., advt. agy.; past prof. mktg. asst. dean Grad. Sch. Mgmt., acting dean, chmn. dept. mktg. Northwestern U., Evanston, Ill., now prof. emeritus mktg.; cons. mktg. mgmt., Evanston; lectr. exec. devel. program, seminars at univs.; lectr. colls., univs., including Eton (Eng.) Coll., 1970; dir. mktg. mgmt. confs. in Europe, Mgmt. Center, Europe, Brussels, 1962-72. Mgmt. personnel devel. specialist for fed. war agencies, then dir. fed. work improvement program for govt. agencies, 1941-44. Mem. AAUP, Am. Mktg. Assn., Am. Mgmt. Assn., Beta Gamma Sigma, Delta Pi, Sigma Chi. Address: 1600 Hinman Ave Evanston IL 60201

HAWKINSON, JOHN, investment mgmt. co. exec.; b. Walker, Iowa, May 26, 1912; s. Theodore W. and Gertrude (Nietert) H.; A.B., U. Iowa, 1936; m. Florence Mallaire, Oct. 12, 1946; children—Diane, Judith. With Halsey, Stuart & Co., Inc., Chgo., 1936-41, 46-49; v.p., treas., dir. Central Life Assurance Co., Des Moines, 1950-62; pres., dir. Kemper Fin. Services, Inc., Chgo., 1962—; pres., dir. Tech. Fund, Inc., 1963—, Kemper Income & Capital Preservation Fund, Inc., Kemper Money Market Fund, Inc., Kemper Growth Fund, Inc., Kemper Total Return Fund, Inc., Kemper Summit Fund, Inc., Kemper Municipal Bond Fund; dir. Am. Fed. Savs. & Loan Assn. Central Iowa, Iowa-Kemper Ins. Co., Mapco, Inc., Kemper Corp., Kansas City So. Industries, Kansas City So. R.R., Louisian & Ark. R.R., Am. Motorists Ins. Co., Berkley & Co., Gen. Growth Properties, Studebaker-Worthington, UMC Industries, Inc. Mem. Securities Adv. Com. to Sec. State Ill. Bd. dirs. U. Iowa Found.; bd. govs., also mem. divisional com., investment adviser div. Investment Co. Inst., Washington. Served with AUS, 1942-46; col. Res., ret. Decorated Legion Merit. Mem. Nat. Fedn. Fin. Analysts. Clubs: Glen View (Golf, Ill.); Chicago, Attic (Chgo.). Home: 10 Rolling Ridge Rd Northfield IL 60093 Office: 120 S LaSalle St Chicago IL 60603

HAWKS, KEITH MERWIN, utilities co. exec.; b. Marengo, Wis., Oct. 3, 1922; s. Merwin Nelson and Margaret Lindsey (Mallory) H.; student U. Wis., 1941-42, B.S. in Soils and Agr. Edn., 1952; m. Ruth Fay Edie, Aug. 3, 1958; children—Wendy Kay, Kim Laureen, Mark Winton. Vocational agr. tchr. Wausau (Wis.) Vocational Sch., 1952-54; farm electrification adviser Wis. Pub. Service Corp., Green Bay, Wis., 1954-60, farm sales supr., 1960-72, rural devel. supr., 1972—. Mem. research farm planning and devel. com. U. Wis., 1965—, agr. engring. adv. com., 1974—; mem. Brown County Coordinating Council, 1970—, visitors com. Green Bay Area Visitor and Conv. Bur., 1972—; mem. Brown County Planning Adv. Council, 1974; mem. Brown County Bi-Centennial Commn., 1974-75; mem. exec. com. Brown County Overall Econ. Devel. Program, 1975—; mem. citizens com. Bay Lake region Wis. Coastal Zone Mgmt. Program, 1975—. Bd. dirs. N.E. Wis. Recreation Industries; bd. dirs. Wis. Agrl. Bus. Council, sec., 1976—. Recipient Hon. Chpt. Farmer Degree, De Pere chpt., Future Farmers Am., 1969; Community Service award Fed. Land Bank, 1966. Mem. Edison Electric Inst. (chmn. farm devel. and research com. 1969), Wis. Utilities Assn. (chmn. exec. marketing sect. 1961, 64, 73), Wis. Farm Electrification Council (dir.), Green Bay Area C. of C., Wis. Alumni Assn. (pres. bd. dirs. Green Bay chpt. 1971-72), Agrl. and Life Scis. Alumni Assn. U. Wis. (organizer 1972, dir.; v.p. 1973-74, pres. 1974-75, 77), Am. Soc. Agrl. Engrs., Alpha Gamma Rho. Clubs: Investment, Men's. Contbr. articles to profl. jours. Home: Route 5 Anston Rd Green Bay WI 54303 Office: 700 N Adams St Green Bay WI 54305

HAWLEY, HELEN MARY CULP (MRS. ARCHIE HAWLEY), nurse; b. nr. Sinking Spring, Pa., Feb. 19, 1917; d. Allen M. and Bessie M. (Cutler) Culp; R.N., Homeopathic Hosp. Chs. of Nursing, Reading, Pa., 1938; certificate in pub. health nursing, Simmons Coll., Boston, 1940; B.S., Millikin U., Decatur, Ill., 1965; M.B.A., Sangamon State U.; m. Archie Hawley, Sept. 16, 1944; 1 dau., Margaret Louise. Staff nurse Pottstown Homeopathic Hosp., Pottstown, Pa., 1938-38, Vis. Nurse Assn., Reading, Pa., 1940-41, Vis. Nurse Assn., Wilmington, Del., 1940-41; pub. health nurse USPHS, 1941-46; supr. Vis. Nurse Assn., Decatur, Ill., 1949-56; pub. health instr. Sch. Nursing, Decatur Macon County Hosp., 1957-62; instr. Decatur Sch. Practical Nursing, 1962-65; med.-surg. coordinator sch. nursing Mennonite Hosp., Bloomington, Ill., 1965; formerly curriculum coordinator, now cons. hosp. div. Ill. Dept. Pub. Health, Springfield, Ill. Active A.R.C. Bd. dirs. region IX, Ill. Heart Assn., 1949—, now vice chmn.; bd. dirs. Sangamon County Vis. Nurse Assn., Springfield; mem. Macon County Mental Health Assn. Mem. Am. Nurses Assn., Am., Ill. pub. health assns., Internat. Platform Assn. Methodist. Club: Ill. Fedn. Bus. and Profl. Women's (dist. chmn. 1964-65, parliamentarian). Home: PO Box 771 Decatur IL 60525 Office: 525 Jefferson St Springfield IL 62702

HAWLEY, JOHN BABCOCK, educator; b. Nutley, N.J., May 8, 1918; s. Dewey Tanner and Cecile Ruth (Colvin) H.; grad. Mount Hermon Sch. Boys (Mass.), 1935; student U. Buffalo, 1935-36; A.B., Hamilton Coll., 1939; M.A., Columbia U. Tchrs. Coll., 1948; Ph.D., U. Mich., 1957; m. Irene Julia Borchardt, May 2, 1957. Tchr. English, Mount Berry Sch. for Boys, Rome, Ga., 1940-41; adult edn. specialist N.Y. State Bur. Adult Edn., Albany, 1945-52; asso. prof. sociology Chico (Calif.) State U., 1956-58; community devel. adviser Govt. of Iran, Tehran, 1958-61; researcher Inst. Community Studies, U. Sask., Saskatoon, Can., 1961-64; program analyst HEW, Washington, 1964-65; dir. community devel. services So. Ill. U., Carbondale, 1965-68, prof. higher edn., 1968—, pres. univ. senate, 1972-74, pres. adv. com. univ. goals and objectives, 1974. Served to 1st lt. USAAF, 1941-45. Recipient Sepah medal of Honor 2d class for service to edn. in Iran, Govt. Iran, 1960. Smith-Mundt grantee, Germany, 1951. Mem. Assn. for Study Higher Edn., Am. Ednl. Research Assn., So. Ill. U. Employees Credit Union (dir., chmn. credit com. 1970-71). Unitarian. Author: (with Buckley & Kew) The Indians and Metis of Northern Saskatchewan, 1963. Home: 402 Orchard Dr Carbondale IL 62901

HAWTHORN, HORACE B(OLES), sociologist; b. Castana, Iowa, Dec. 4, 1889; s. William Franklin and Annie (Masters) H.; student State U. Iowa, 1907; B.S., Iowa State Coll., 1914, M.S., 1915; Ph.D., U. Wis. (fellow in economics, 1920), 1922; m. Hazel Waples, Sept. 21, 1916; children—Miriam (Mrs. Carl Baker), Clarice (Mrs. Donald Watson), Horace Duane. Asst. prof. sociology Iowa State Coll. 1921-26; asso. prof. sociology Municipal U. of Akron, 1926-30; prof. sociology Morningside Coll., Sioux City, Iowa, 1931-58, prof. emeritus, 1958—; research sociologist Morningside Social Research and Publs. Service, 1959; rural sociologist Iowa Agrl. Expt. Sta., 1925-26; research sociologist Better Akron Fedn., 1926-30; lectr. Civic and Welfare Assn., 1928. Mem. Am. Sociol. Soc., Am. Assn. U. Profs., National Writers Club, Alpha Kappa Delta, Phi Kappa Phi, Delta Sigma Rho, Gamma Sigma Delta, Pi Gamma Mu. Methodist. Author: Outlines of Sociology, 1923; Sociology of Rural Life, 1926; Sociology of the World Crisis, 1947; Efficiency of Akron Welfare Agencies Bd., 1928; Sociology of the United Nations World, 1952; Culture of Sioux City Youth, bulletin, 1936; Sociology of Personality Functioning, 1954; Immortal Survival of the Human Personality, 1959, rev. edition, 1967. Case Study of Iowa School Reorganization, 1966; Case Study in Sociology of Creative Scholarship, 1969; Case Study of Social Innovation, 1971. Research in personality adjustment in rural and urban communities. Home: 901 S Mulberry Sioux City IA 51106

HAWTHORNE, JOHN BOONE, fin. cons.; b. Arcadia, Nebr., June 18, 1921; s. Cecil Clyde and Augusta Doris (Peters) H.; B.A., U. Mich., 1950; m. Marjie Phyllis Horner, Sept. 27, 1943; children—S. Lynn, John C., Timothy R., Peter C., Mathew J. Mem. corporate finance dept. Kidder, Peabody & Co., Chgo., 1950-55; sr. securities analyst Investors Diversified Services, Inc., Mpls., 1955-60; pres. Midwest Tech. Devel. Corp., Mpls., 1960-62; mgr. corporate finance dept. Paine, Webber, Jackson & Curtis, Mpls., 1962-66; owner, operator John Hawthorne Co., Mpls., 1966—; lectr. in field. Active United Fund, YMCA; mem. Wayzata Ind. Sch. Dist. 284 Bd. Edn., Minn., 1970—. Served with Coast Arty., U.S. Army, 1942-46; PTO. Mem. Nat. Small Bus. Assn., Internat. Assn. Fin. Planners. Republican. Mem. United Ch. of Christ. Home: 3015 Urbandale Ln Wayzata MN 55391 Office: 1st Nat Bank Bldg Wayzata MN 55391

HAWTREY, CHARLES EDWARD, urologist; b. Burlington, Wis., July 9, 1935; s. William Charles Tate and Ora Hulda (Longley) H.; B.A., Grinnell Coll., 1957; M.D., U. Iowa, 1961; m. Elizabeth Roberts Patterson, Aug. 29, 1959; children—Catherine, Elizabeth, Martha, Thomas. Intern, Presbyterian-St. Luke's Hosp., Chgo., 1961-62; resident U. Iowa Hosps., Iowa City, 1962-67; asst. prof. urology U. Iowa, 1969-72, asso. prof. urology, 1972-77, prof. urology, 1977—; cons. urology Iowa City VA Hosp.; asso. editor Yearbook of Cancer, 1974, Human Sexuality, 1976. Served with USN, 1967-69. Am. Cancer Soc. Clin. fellow, 1964-65; USPHS fellow in oncology, 1965-66. Fellow A.C.S.; mem. Am. Assn. Med. Colls., Soc. Univ. Urologists, AMA, Johnson County Med. Soc., Iowa Urol. Soc. (v.p. 1970-71), Am. Urol. Assn. (N. Central sect.), Am. Assn. of Clin. Urologists, Soc. for Pediatric Urology, Assn. U. Urologists, Assn. for Acad. Surgery, Am. Fedn. for Clin. Research, Iowa Clin. Surg. Soc., Sigma Xi. Republican. Episcopalian. Contbr. numerous articles to profl. jours. Home: 715 S Summit St Iowa City IA 52240 Office: Dept Urology Univ Iowa Hosps and Clinics Iowa City IA 52242

HAY, JAMES GORDON, educator; b. Waipukurau, New Zealand, Nov. 5, 1936; s. Franklin George and Irene Muriel Nora (Smith) H.; came to U.S., 1964; diploma in phys. edn. U. Otago, New Zealand, 1956; M.A. U. Iowa, 1965, Ph.D., 1967; m. Hilary Williamson, May 17, 1958; children—Linda Irene, Karen June. Tchr. phys. edn. and mathematics Hawera Tech. High Sch., New Zealand, 1958-64; vis. prof. State U. N.Y., 1966; sr. lectr. U. Otago, 1967-71; asso. prof. biomechanics, U. Iowa, 1971—; cons. New Zealand Amateur Rowing Assn., Nissen Corp. Fellow Am. Acad. Phys. Edn.; mem. Internat. (exec. council 1977—), Am. socs. biomechanics, Am. Coll. Sports Medicine, Am. Alliance of Health, Phys. Edn. and Recreation. Club: Rotary. Author: The Biomechanics of Sports Techniques, 1973; A Bibliography of Biomechanics Literature, 1977; editor: Olympic Track & Field Techniques, 1976; editor New Zealand Jour. of Health Physical Education and Recreation, 1968-70; contbr. articles in field to profl. jours. Home: 3056 American Legion Rd Iowa City IA 52240 Office: Department Physical Education University Iowa Iowa City IA 52242

HAYASHI, TETSUMARO, author, editor, educator; b. Sakaide, Japan, Mar. 22, 1929; s. Tetsuro and Shieko (Honjo) H.; came to U.S., 1954, naturalized, 1969; B.A., Okayama U., 1953; M.A., U. Fla., 1957; M.A. in Library Sci., Kent State U., 1959; Ph.D. in English, 1968; m. Akiko Sakuratani, Apr. 14, 1960; 1 son, Richard Hideki. Asst. prof. English, asso. dir. Culver-Stockton Coll. library, 1959-63; instr. English, Kent State U., 1965-68; asst. prof. English, Ball State U., 1968-72, asso. prof. English, 1972—, also asso. chmn. Midwest English Conf., 1974-75. Dir. John Steinbeck Soc. Am., 1966—, pres., 1977—, editor Steinbeck Quar., 1968—, gen. editor Steinbeck Monograph Series, 1970—; chmn. Tudor lit. sect. Medieval Conf., Western Mich. U., 1973. Rotary Internat. Jr. fellow, 1955-56; Folger Shakespeare Library fellow summer, 1972; Am. Council Learned Socs. fellow, 1976. Fellow Am. Philos. Soc.; mem. Modern Language Assn. Am., Midwest Modern Lang. Assn. Am., Am. Studies Assn., Shakespeare Assn. Am. Author: Sketches of American Culture, 1960; John Steinbeck: A Concise Bibliography, 1967; Arthur Miller Criticism, 1969; Robert Greene Criticism, 1971; Shakespeare's Sonnets: A Record of 20th Century Criticism, 1972; (monographs) A Textual Study of A Looking Glasse for London and England, 1969, Steinbeck: A Guide to Doctoral Dissertations, 1971, Steinbeck Criticism, 1974; A Textual Study of Robert Greene's Orlando Furioso, 1973. Editor: A Looking Glasse for London and England: An Elizabethan Text, 1970; (with Richard Astro) Steinbeck: The Man and His Work, 1971; Steinbeck's Literary Dimension, 1973; A Study Guide to Steinbeck, 1974; Steinbeck and the Arthurian Theme, 1975; John Steinbeck: A Dictionary of His Fictional Characters, 1976; A Study Guide to Steinbeck's The Long Valley, 1976; Steinbeck's Prophetic Vision of America, 1976. Home: 1405 N Kimberly Ln Muncie IN 47304

HAYCRAFT, REXFORD GORDON, internist, ret. air force officer; b. Snap, Ky., July 14, 1916; s. Joe Allen and Della Lee (Reeves) H.; student U. Denver, 1946-48, B.S., 1950; M.D., U. Colo., 1952; m. Juanda Elaine Cameron, June 19, 1944; children—Barbara Lee, Gordon Lowell, Linda Lou. Commd. 1st lt. USAF, 1952, advanced through grades to col., 1968; intern Denver Gen. Hosp., 1952-53; resident in internal medicine Brooke Army Hosp., San Antonio, 1955-58; dir. hosp. services Scott AFB, Ill., 1970-76, ret., 1976; internist USAF Med. Center, Scott AFB, 1976—. Served to 1st lt. USAAF, 1941-44. Decorated Air medal with 3 oak leaf clusters, D.F.C., Legion of Merit; diplomate Am. Bd. Internal Medicine. Fellow A.C.P. Club: Officers (Scott AFB). Contbr. articles to med. jours. Home: 807 Meadowlark Dr O'Fallon IL 62269

HAYDEN, ALBERT A., educator; b. Cape Girardeau County, Mo., Sept. 18, 1923; s. Howard E. and Clara A. (Rust) H.; student Chgo. City Jr. Coll., 1946-48; B.A., U. Ill., 1950; M.A., Bucknell U., 1952; Ph.D., U. Wis., 1959; m. Priscilla Anne Redin, Sept. 11, 1954; children—Keith Alan, Anne Marie. With Swift & Co., 1941-43; faculty Wittenberg U., Springfield, Ohio, 1959—, prof. history, 1970—. Vis. prof. history Kent State U., summer 1964. Served with USAAF, 1943-46. Mem. Ohio Acad History, Am. Hist. Assn.,

AAUP, Conf. on Brit. Studies. Author: New South Wales Immigration Policy, 1856-1900, 1971; contbg. author: Australian Dictionary of Biography. Mng. editor Studies in British History and Culture. Office: Dept History Wittenberg U Springfield OH 45501

HAYDON, ROBERT RODNEY, rehab. officer; b. Dows, Iowa, Nov. 9, 1924; s. Howard Julius and Alice Mary (Perry) H.; B.A., Luther Coll., 1965; postgrad. in counseling Ind. U., 1971—, Gestalt Inst. Chgo., 1975—; m. A. Louise, July 24, 1946; children—David L., Daniel E. Chief probation officer Elkhart (Ind.) Probation Office, 1968-72; chief rehab. officer Elkhart County (Ind.) Sheriff's Dept., 1972—. Served with U.S. Army, 1943-45. Decorated Purple Heart, Bronze Star; certified probation officer, Ind. Mem. Am. Personnel and Guidance Assn., Ind. Correctional Assn., Nat. Council on Crime and Delinquency, Nat., Ind. sheriff's assns. Lutheran. Clubs: Mishawaka Pilot's (Elkhart), Moose, Elkhart Little Theatre, Elkhart Racquet, Kiwanis. Initiator inmate treatment and work release program. Home: 1606 Frances Ave Elkhart IN 46514 Office: 111 N 3d St Goshen IN 46526

HAYEK, ALLEN JAMES, sch. adminstr.; b. Clarkson, Nebr., Jan. 29, 1921; s. Emil and Bessie (Podany) H.; B.A., Wayne State Coll., 1945; M.S., Gallaudet Coll., 1960; M.A., Calif. State U., 1963; m. Virginia I. Scheidel, Oct. 27, 1945; children—Daniel Allen, Dean Kent, Sally Beth. Tchr., coach Cheroke (Iowa) Pub. Sch., 1946-49, Oreg. Sch. for the Deaf, Salem, 1949-54, Ark. Sch. for the Deaf, Little Rock, 1955-56; prin. Idaho Sch. for the Deaf, Gooding, 1956-63; prin. N.D. Sch. for the Deaf, Devils Lake, 1963-68, supt., 1968—. Served with inf. AUS, 1943-45. Decorated Purple Heart, Bronze Star, Silver Star. Mem. Nat., N.D. (pres. 1963-65) edn. assns., Council for Exceptional Children (dir. 1965-67, com. for deaf-blind children 1969—), C. of C. (chmn. heritage program 1972-75, regional adv. com. for vocat. edn. 1972—). Baptist (deacon 1964-72). Lion (pres. 1973-74), Rotarian. Address: Sch for the Deaf Devils Lake ND 58301

HAYES, ALVA ALLEN, seed co. exec.; b. Coon Rapids, Iowa, Oct. 20, 1920; s. Leonard Leroy and Violet Daisy (Wright) H.; B.S., Iowa State U., 1943, M.S., 1948; m. Carol Jean Remus, May 22, 1949; children—Susan, Jeannine, Scott. Publicity mgr. Iowa Crop Improvement Assn., Ames, 1947-48, indsl. editor, advt. asst., 1948-58; asst. sales mgr. Pioneer Seed Co., Des Moines, 1958-65, sales dir., 1971—. Bd. dirs. Des Moines Better Bus. Bur. Served to lt. USNR, 1943-46. Mem. Des Moines Advt. Club (pres. 1959-60), Sales and Marketing Execs. Central Iowa (pres.). Republican. Mem. Christian Ch. (elder). Club: Wahkonda (Des Moines). Home: 4021 45th St Des Moines IA 50310 Office: 1206 Mulberry St Des Moines IA 50308

HAYES, ARTHUR CHESTER, safety cons., state legislator; b. Ft. Wayne, Ind., Aug. 24, 1918; s. Walter F. and Marie P. (Hardesty) H.; B.S., Ind. U., 1948; m. Miriam E. Peck, Feb. 1, 1946 (dec. Nov. 1968); children—Arthur C., Bethany M., Gayle W. Crosby. Sales corr. Magnavox Corporation, 1948-54; supr. Budget State Hwy. Dept., 1954-58; owner Vernors Bottling Co., Ft. Wayne, 1959-63; became dist. mgr. Colonial Life & Accident Ins. Co., 1963; mem. Ind. Ho. of Reps., 1963-72, 77—, ho. mem. Ind. Statutory com. on Commn. on Protection and Advocacy for Developmentally Disabled; safety cons. Chmn. Interstate Cooperation Com., Recodification of Cities and Towns Commn.; mem. Sesquicentennial Commn.; chmn. speakers bur. Ind. Am. Revolution Bicentennial Commn.; mem. Ind. Am. Negro Emancipation Centennial Commn. Served with AUS, 1941-45. Mem. Ft. Wayne C. of C., Am. Legion. Clubs: Ft. Wayne Civitan (pres. 1963-68; lt. gov. Midwest 1967). Home: 2001 Oakland St Fort Wayne IN 46808 Office: State House Bldg Indianapolis IN 46204

HAYES, CHARLES EDWARD, newspaper editor; b. Evanston, Ill., Mar. 13, 1931; s. Chester K. and Dorothy (Wilger) H.; B.S., Wittenberg U., 1953; M.S. in Journalism, Northwestern U., 1955. With Paddock Publs., Inc., Arlington Heights, Ill., 1954-75, newspaper series on social problems, 1958-75, exec. editor, 1960-68, editor in chief, 1968-75, v.p., 1970-75, publisher, 1971-75, also chmn. and trustee profit sharing and trust, 1967-75; v.p., editor Area Publs. Corp., Hinsdale, Ill., 1975—. Mem. adv. com. Suburban Press Found., Inc., Chgo., 1967-69; v.p. Opportunity Council Inc., 1958-59, pres., 1959-60; sec. Helene Bristol Meml. Scholarship Program, 1965-75. Chmn. bd. dirs., Salvation Army Community Counselling Center, 1971-75, mem. 1968—; mem. Ill. Health Facilities Authority, 1973—. mem. consumer adv. bd. Northwest Surgicare; community leadership tng. bd. Harper Coll. Recipient Instrument Peace award Christian Family Movement, 1960; named Arlington Heights Jr. C. of C. Man of Year, 1964. Mem. Chgo. Press Club, Chgo. Headline Club (pres. 1969-70), Soc. Profl. Journalists-Sigma Delta Chi, Chgo. Press Veterans Assn., League United Latin Am. Citizens (hon.), Blue Key, Kappa Phi Kappa, Pi Delta Epsilon, Phi Kappa Psi. Democrat. Lutheran. Contbr. monographs and articles to various publs. Home: 2307 Bel Aire Dr Arlington Heights IL 60004 Office: 765 N York Rd Hinsdale IL 60521

HAYES, CHARLES SHERMAN, educator; b. Davenport, Iowa, Mar. 16, 1945; s. Charles Richard and Dorothy Darleen (Folsom) H.; B.A., Augustana Coll., 1967; M.A., U. Iowa, 1969, Ph.D., 1970; m. Marcia Valerie Lynch, Aug. 27, 1966; children—Charles, Jeffrey. Asst. prof. pediatrics (psychology), child devel. clinic U. Iowa, Iowa City, 1971—. Cons. Iowa Braille and Sight Sav. Sch., 1971—, Skyline, Inc., Clinton, 1974-75; mem. local adv. com. Nat. Inst. on Recreation for Deaf Blind, 1973-74. USPHS grantee, 1972-74. Mem. Am. Psychol. Assn., Am. Assn. Mental Deficiency, Phi Beta Kappa, Sigma Xi. Home: 1512 Tracy Ln Iowa City IA 52240

HAYES, DAVID JOHN ARTHUR, JR., lawyer; b. Chgo., July 30, 1929; s. David J.A. and Lucille M. (Johnson) H.; A.B., Harvard, 1952; LL.B., Chgo.-Kent Coll. Law, 1961; m. Anne Huston, Feb. 23, 1963; children—David J.A. III, Cary H. Admitted to Ill. bar, 1961; asst. sec., trust officer First Nat. Bank of Evanston (Ill.), 1962-63; gen. counsel Ill. State Bar Assn., 1963-66; asst. dir. Am. Bar Assn., 1966-68, div. dir., 1968-69, asst. exec. dir., 1969—; exec. dir. Naval Res. Lawyers Assn., 1971—. Dist. capt. United Fund Drive, Wilmette, 1969; chmn. U.S.O. Lawyers Fund Drive Com., 1968. Served as capt. USNR. Mem. Ill. State Bar Assn. (mem. various coms., assembly rep., 1972—), Nat. Orgn. Bar Counsel (pres. 1967), Phi Alpha Delta. Roman Cath. Contbr. to profl. jours. Home: 1233 Sixteenth St Wilmette IL 60091 Office: 1155 E 60th St Chicago IL 60637

HAYES, DAVID THOMAS, educator; b. Gallia County, Ohio, June 12, 1939; s. Buell D. and Ada I. (Harding) H.; B.S., Ohio U., 1961; M.A. in Teaching, Duke, 1965; Ph.D., Ohio State U., 1972; m. Nancy V. Clark, Aug. 19, 1961; children—Kari, John. Tchr. math. Lincoln High Sch., Cleve., 1961-65; instr. Riverside Sch. of Nursing, 1966-69; teaching asso. in math. Ohio State U., Columbus, 1965-69, asst. prof., coordinator of math. Lima campus, 1969-76; asst. prof. ednl. curriculum and instrn. and math. Bowling Green Ohio State U., 1976—. Recipient Outstanding Teaching award Lima campus Ohio State U., 1973. Mem. Nat. Council Tchrs. Math., Sch. Sci. and Math. Assn., Math. Assn. Two Yr. Colls., Ohio Assn. Two Yr. Colls., Nat. Council Suprs. of Math., Ohio Council Tchrs. Math., Phi Delta Kappa. Club: Exchange. Baptist. Home: 613 Pasteur Ave Bowling Green OH 43402 Office: Edn Bldg S College Dr Bowling Green OH 43403

HAYES, DONALD BLAIR, banker; b. Western Springs, Ill., June 4, 1931; s. John L. and Aleece I. (Stanley) H.; B.A., Butler U., 1957; m. Mary Anita Carter, Aug. 30, 1953; children—Laurinda Anne, Donald Blair, Delos A. Trust officer Granite City Trust & Savs. Bank, Granite City, Ill., 1960-64; exec. v.p., trust officer, dir. Met. Bank of Lima (Ohio), 1964—. Mem. exec. bd., treas. Shawnee council Boy Scouts Am., 1965-72, Lima Symphony Orch., 1970-72; trustee, treas. Lima Community Found., 1967—; bd. dirs. Better Bus. Bur. Served with USMCR, 1950-53. Mem. Ohio Bankers Assn. (exec. bd. trust div. 1969-72, 74—). Methodist. Mason, Rotarian, Elk. Club: Shawnee Country, Lima (pres. 1968). Home: 2509 Struthmore Dr Lima OH 45805 Office: Met Bank of Lima Drawer M Lima OH 45802

HAYES, ELIZABETH ANN, counselor, spl. educator; b. Albuquerque, Jan. 28, 1950; d. Lawrence Elmer and Gail Virginia (Whitlow) H.; B.A. with distinction, U. N.Mex., 1972; M.S. in Edn., Eastern Ill. U., Charleston, 1976. Legal sec., bookkeeper, Albuquerque, 1969-72; spl. edn. tchr. disturbed children, Selma, Ala., 1972-74, Rantoul, Ill., 1975-76; counselor, learning disabilities tchr. Downers Grove (Ill.) High Sch., 1976—; writer, advt. agt. mags. Tennis Everyone, Racquetball Everyone; cons. in field. Sr. fellow spl. edn. U. N.Mex., 1971-72. Mem. Council Exceptional Children, Nat., Ill., Downers Grove edn. assns., Am. Ill. personnel and guidance assns., Assn. Sch. Counselors, Humanistic Psychology Assn., Animal Protection Inst., Mortar Bd., Phi Kappa Phi. Democrat. Address: 6017 Forest View Rd Lisle IL 60532

HAYES, ERNEST A., ins., investment sales; b. New London, Iowa, Jan. 20, 1904; s. Alonzo D. and Margaret E. (Ferrell) H.; student Iowa Wesleyan Coll., 1921-24, H.H.D. (hon.), 1964; A.B., Washington Univ., 1924, M.S., 1926; m. Ruth Anita Irons, Feb. 13, 1937; children—Ruth Jo Ann (Mrs. Edmund J. Farrell), Janet Elizabeth (Mrs. Richard A. Dougherty). President of Central States Mutual Insurance, Assn., 1929-59; chmn. bd. Capitol Savs. & Loan Assn., 1937-77; pres. Hillsboro Savs. Bank (Iowa), 1950-76, Henry County Indsl. Devel. Corp.; chmn. bd. New London State Bank, 1945-76, Town & Country Bank, Quincy, Ill., 1974-76; dir. Burlington Bank & Trust Co. (Iowa), Hawkeye Ban Corp., Des Moines; pres. Hawkeye Nat. Investment Co., Hawkeye Nat. Life Ins. Co. (both Des Moines); dir. Henry Co. Savs. Bank (Mt. Pleasant), Iowa Bus. Devel. Credit Corp.; vice chmn. bd., sec. Iowa Blue Cross. Mem. exec. com. S.E. Iowa council Boy Scouts Am.; mem. Burlington (Iowa) Youth Resources Bd.; vice chmn. Iowa Hosp. Found., Des Moines; mem. U.S. Hist. Adv. Com., Washington, Hoover Found.; chmn. Iowa Devel. Commn.; regional Dir. U.S. Savs. Bond Div.; Republican State Finance Chmn., 1961-69; mem. Nat. Rep. Finance Com., 1961-69; chmn. bd. dirs. Henry County Meml. Hosp., Iowa Wesleyan College; trustee Midwest Research Inst., Kansas City. Recipient S.E. Iowa Man of Yr., 1961. Mem. Iowa Assn. Ind. Ins. Agts., Navy League, Sigma Phi Epsilon, Delta Sigma Pi, Omicron Delta Gamma. Methodist. Mason (Shriner). Moose, Elk. Clubs: Kiwanis, Des Moines, Lincoln, Bohemian (Des Moines). Home: 400 Broadway Mount Pleasant IA 52641 Office: Hayes Bldg Mount Pleasant IA 52641

HAYES, JOHN FRANCIS, lawyer, state legislator; b. Salina, Kans., Dec. 11, 1919; s. John Francis and Helen (Dye) H.; A.B., Washburn Coll., 1941; LL.B., Washburn U., 1946; m. Elizabeth Ann Ireton, Aug. 10, 1950; children—Carl Ireton, Ann Chandler. Admitted to Kans. bar, 1946; practice law, Hutchinson, Kans., 1946—; partner Gilliland, Hayes & Goering, and predecessor firm, 1959—; dir. Central State Bank, Hutchinson. Mem. Kans. Ho. of Reps., 1953-55, 67—, majority leader, 1975-77. Served as capt. AUS, 1942-46. Fellow Am. Coll. Trial Lawyers; mem. Hutchinson C. of C. (pres 1961), Kans. Assn. Def. Counsel (pres. 1972-73), Internat. Assn. Ins. Counsel. Republican. Home: 106 Crescent Blvd Hutchinson KS 67501 Office: 330 W 1st St Hutchinson KS 67501

HAYES, JOHN MARION, structural engr.; b. Wingate, Ind., May 18, 1909; s. William Lucas and Margaret Elize (Gallaher) H.; B.S., Purdue U., 1931, C.E., 1946; M.S., U. Tenn., 1944; m. Coye Matilda Cunningham, June 22, 1935; children—Marian (Mrs. George William Jernigan), Julia (Mrs. Robert Harold Casey). Miscellaneous engring. experience, 1931-35; structural engr. TVA, Knoxville and Chattanooga, 1935-46; bridge engr. U.S. Bur. Pub. Rds., Little Rock, 1946-48; asso. prof. structural engring. Purdue U., West Lafayette, Ind., 1948-58, prof., 1958-75, emeritus, 1975—; pvt. practice cons. structural engr., 1948—. Recipient spl. citation award Am. Inst. Steel Constrn., 1971, juror for nat. prize bridge constrn., 1975; Outstanding Engring. Alumnus award U. Tenn., Knoxville, 1975. Mem. ASCE (sect. pres. 1961-62, dist. bd. dirs. 1963-66, zone v.p. 1968-70, chmn. exec. com. edn. div. 1970-75), Nat. Soc. Profl. Engrs., Am. Concrete Inst., Am. Welding Soc., Internat. Assn. Bridge and Structural Engring., AAAS, Soc. Exptl. Stress Analysis (active various coms.), Am. Soc. Engring. Edn. (chpt. pres. 1954-55, sect. rep. 1955-56), Indpls. Sci. and Engring. Found., Am. Ry. Engring. Assn. (com. sec. 1961—), Am. Soc. for Testing and Materials, Sigma Xi, Chi Epsilon. Methodist. (adminstrv. bd. 1971-75). Lion. Home: 312 Highland Dr West Lafayette IN 47906

HAYES, K. MICHAEL, orthodontist; b. Wareham, Mass., Aug. 20, 1950; s. Kenneth O. and Doris H.; student Ind. U., 1969-71, D.D.S., 1975; m. Sandra Jeanne Martin, Apr. 3, 1971; children—Amy Marie, Andrew Michael. Practice dentistry specializing in orthodontics, Auburn, Ind., 1976—. Mem. ADA, Ind. Dental Assn., Am. Assn. Orthodontists (asso.), Great Lakes Soc. Orthodontists (asso.), Ind. Soc. Orthodontists (asso.). Roman Catholic. Home: 1308 Culbertson St Auburn IN 46706 Office: 107 N Cedar St Auburn IN 46706

HAYES, PAUL WESLEY, psychiatrist, neurologist; b. Bigelow, Mo., Jan. 27, 1911; s. Oren Wesley and Jennie Maye (Parks) H.; student Central Meth. Coll., Fayette, Mo., 1928-31; B.S., U. Nebr., 1933, M.D., 1936; certificate Am. Bd. Psychiatry, 1953; m. Dorothy Elizabeth Neal, June 2, 1935; children—Karen Lea, Phillip Scott Morgan. Intern, U. Nebr. Hosp., Omaha, 1936-37; asso. physician gen. medicine Black Hills Clinic, Hot Springs, S.D., 1937-41; served to col. M.C., cons. psychiatry U.S. Army, 1941-61; resident psychiatry John Sealy Hosp., U. Tex., Galveston, 1948-51; sr. partner, sr. neuropsychiatrist Thompson, Brumm, Knepper Clinic, St. Joseph, Mo., 1961-76; sr. neuropsychiatrist Mo. Meth. Med. Center, St. Joseph, 1961—; sr. neuropsychiatrist St. Joseph Hosp., 1961—; clin. dir. staff St. Joseph State Hosp. 2, 1976—. Decorated certificate of Achievement, Commendation medal. Recipient certificate of appreciation Nat. Police Officers Assn. Am., 1973. Mem. Nat., Mo., St. Joseph mental health assns., Mo. Acad. Psychiatry, Am., Mid-Continent psychiat. assns., Buchanan County (Mo.), Titus Harris med. socs., Am., Mo. State med. assns., Western Mo. Dist. br. Neuropsychiat. Assn., Am. Legion, Alpha Kappa Kappa; profl. asso. Mo. Assn. Mental Health. Methodist (dir.). Mason (Shriner). Author: Psychological Factors in Repeated Motor Vehicle Accidents, 1954. Home: 610 N Noyes Blvd St Joseph MO 64506 Office: 3400 Frederick Ave St Joseph MO 64506

HAYES, RICHARD JOHNSON, assn. exec.; b. Chgo., May 25, 1933; s. David John Arthur and Lucille Margaret (Johnson) H.; B.A., Colo. Coll., 1955; J.D., Georgetown U., 1961; m. Mary R. Lynch, Dec. 2, 1961; children—Susan, Richard, John, Edward. Admitted to Ill. bar, 1961; with Sears & Streit, Chgo., 1961-63, Peterson, Lowry, Rall, Barber & Ross, Chgo., 1963-65; staff dir. Am. Bar Assn., Chgo., 1965-70; exec. dir. Internat. Assn. Ins. Counsel, Chgo., 1970—. Served to 1st lt. U.S. Army Res., 1955-57. Mem. Am., Ill. (chmn. jr. bar 1964—), Chgo. (mem. com. devel. law 1973—) bar assns., Beta Theta Pi. Roman Catholic. Club: Rotary/One of Chgo. Contbr. articles to legal jours. Home: 1920 Thornwood Ave Wilmette IL 60091 Office: 20 N Wacker Dr Chicago IL 60606

HAYES, ROBERT STANLEY, retail grocery store exec.; b. Marshalltown, Iowa, May 17, 1930; s. Joseph Eckle and Anna Marie (Anderson) H.; B.S., Kans. State U., 1952; postgrad. U. Tulsa, 1956-58; m. Billie Kathleen Rickard, Aug. 20, 1950; children—Kathy, Steven R., Robert A. Mgr. trainee Shell Oil Co., Gainesville, Tex., 1954-55, Great Bend, Kans., 1955-56, Tulsa, 1956-58; asst. mgr. Leekers Supermarket, Wichita, Kans., 1958-59; mgr. R & G Supermarket, Inc., Manhattan, Kans., 1959-63, pres., chief exec. officer, 1963—; pres., chief exec. officer R. & H. Enterprises, Inc., Manhattan, 1963—, Stan Hayes, Inc., Manhattan, 1969—, P.A.P., Inc., Manhattan, 1969—, R & G Market Inc., Manhattan, 1963—. Dir. First Nat. Bank Manhattan, 1966, Blue Shield, Topeka, 1969—. Mem. Manhattan Environ. Bd., 1972-74. Served to 1st lt. USAF, 1954-56. Mem. Kans. Assn. Commerce and Industry (pres. retail council 1975, dir.), Manhattan C. of C. (chmn. 1973-75), Kans. Food Dealers (dir. 1965—, v.p.), Alpha Kappa Psi, Sigma Alpha Epsilon. Republican. Episcopalian. Clubs: Manhattan Country, Elks, Kiwanis. Home: 1920 Grandview St Manhattan KS 66502 Office: 1522 Poyntz Ave Manhattan KS 66502

HAYFORD, JOHN SARGENT, accountant; b. Balt., Mar. 23, 1940; s. John Enoch and Anne Margaret (Weniger) H.; B.B.A., U. Notre Dame, 1962; m. Barbara Jean McGann, Oct. 10, 1964; children—Kathryn Chase, John Enoch, Patrick McGann. Partner, Ernst & Ernst, C.P.A.'s, Chgo. Served with USCGR, 1963-64. Recipient Elijah Watt Sells gold medal Nat. Uniform C.P.A. exam, 1966. C.P.A., Ill. Mem. Am. Inst. C.P.A.'s, Ill. Soc. C.P.A.'s. Clubs: Tavern, Chicago Literary, Notre Dame (Chgo.). Home: 1110 Lake St Evanston IL 60201 Office: 150 S Wacker Dr Chicago IL 60606

HAYMAKER, RANDY LEE, newspaper editor; b. Franklin, Ind., Dec. 7, 1948; s. Robert Norman and Mary Lousie H.; B.A. in Humanities, Purdue U., 1971; m. Joan Ellen Carter, Sept. 12, 1970. Intern, Mooresville (Ind.) Times, 1969, news editor, 1971—; intern Indpls. News, 1970. Mem. Mooresville Town Bd., 1973-75; chmn. Morgan County (Ind.) Democratic Com., 1976, del. Ind. Dem. Conv., 1973. Home: Rural Route 1 Box 168 Bargersville IN 46106 Office: 23 E Main St Mooresville IN 46158

HAYNES, FRANK MAURICE, profl. adminstrn. co. exec.; b. Kansas City, Mo., June 1, 1935; s. William John and Marguerite Ida (Brown) H.; B.B.A., U. Colo., 1958; M.B.A. with honors, Roosevelt U., 1974; postgrad. Sch. Mgmt. Northwestern U., 1974-75; m. Arlene Claire Kidd, June 25, 1966. Owner, operator Frank M. Haynes Ins. Agy., Chgo., 1960-65; pres. Employees Union Health & Welfare Agy., Inc., Chgo., 1965-72; cons. pension, health and welfare plans, Chgo., 1972-75; exec. v.p. W. J. Haynes & Co., Inc., Chgo., 1975—. Served with U.S. Army, 1958-59. Recipient Wall St. Jour. award, 1974; certificate of merit Prudential Ins. Co., 1964; C.L.U. Mem. Am. Risk and Ins. Assn., Am. Soc. C.L.U.'s, Internat. Found. Employee Benefit Plans, Nat. Assn. Life Underwriters, Chgo. Assn. Life Underwriters, Am. Fin. Assn., Beta Gamma Sigma. Home: 2408 Birchwood Ln Wilmette IL 60091 Office: 3525 W Peterson Ave Chicago IL 60659

HAYNES, HOWARD DOME, sch. adminstr.; b. Kansas City, Mo., Sept. 22, 1935; s. Howard Brawford and Evelyn (Dome) H.; B.A. in Econs., Baker U., 1957; postgrad. Washington U., St. Louis, 1957, DePauw U., 1958, Harvard, 1963; m. Faith Marise Newton, Nov. 2, 1957; children—Valerie Faith, H. Lee, Sarah-Elizabeth. Asst. dir. admissions Baker U., Baldwin, Kans., 1956-58; dir. admissions Tarkio (Mo.) Coll., 1958-61; dir. admissions U. Akron (Ohio), 1961-68, dir. housing, 1964-66; exec. dir. Grafton Sch., Berryville, Va., 1968-71; founder, dir. Questover and High Hope, homes retarded children, Kansas City, Mo., 1971—; chmn. bd. Haynes Investment Corp., Akron and Kansas City, 1963—; pres. N.Am. Riding for the Handicapped. Bd. dirs. Kansas City Philharmonic, Lyric Theatre, Kansas City U. Conservatory, Genesis Sch., Prime Health, Historic Kansas City Found. Mem. Council for Exceptional Children, Am. Personnel and Guidance Assn., Coll. Admission Officers, Assn. Ind. Schs., Westport Hist. Soc., Nat. Trust, Friends of Art, Delta Tau Delta. Clubs: Millwood Country, University, Blue Ridge Hunt, Mission Valley Hunt. Home: Questover 3530 Charlotte St Kansas City MO 64109

HAYNES, JOHN THOMAS, physician; b. Indpls., June 28, 1931; s. Edgar T. and Della Barker H.; student Northwestern U., 1949-50; A.B., Ind. U., 1953, M.D., 1956; m. Helen Smith, May 12, 1956; children—Thomas Edgar, Robert William. Intern, Methodist Hosp., Indpls., 1956-57, resident internal medicine, 1957-59, resident in allergy, 1962-63; practice gen. medicine, Indpls., 1959-62, practice allergy, 1963—; asso. dir. allergy clinic Methodist Hosp., 1963-72, Riley Hosp., 1963-74; asso. prof. Ind. U. Sch. Medicine, Indpls., 1973—. Diplomate Am. Bd. Immunology and Allergy. Fellow Am. Acad. Allergy, Am. Coll. Allergists, Am. Assn. Clin. Immunology and Allergy. Rotarian. Contbr. articles to profl. publs. Home: 4139 Juniper Ct Indianapolis IN 46250 Office: 1815 N Capitol St Indianapolis IN 46202

HAYS, WILLARD CARL, mfg. co. exec.; b. Cleve., Jan. 6, 1921; s. Willard J. and Edna J. (Issel) H.; B.S. in Mech. Engring., Case Inst. Tech., 1942; m. Mary Elizabeth Hamner, Feb. 19, 1949; children—Willard, Susan, James, Robert. Asst. to gen. mgr. Gramm Trailer Corp., Lima, Ohio, 1951-53; became v.p. mktg. Indsl. Nucleonics Corp., Columbus, Ohio, 1965, group v.p., until 1977; pres. Medron, Inc., Columbus, 1977—. Pres. Upper Arlington (Ohio) Civic Assn., 1969—. Served to 1st lt. USAAF, 1943-45. Decorated DFC, Air medal. Mem. Soc. Plastics Engrs., Instrument Soc. Am., Am. Mgmt. Assn., Columbus Sales Execs. Club (dir. 1967-68), Alumni Council Case Inst. Tech. Methodist. Mason. Patentee in field. Home: 2460 Abington Rd Columbus OH 43221 Office: 650 Ackerman Rd Columbus OH 43202

HAYWARD, GEORGE CURTIS, city ofcl.; b. Richmond, Ind., June 6, 1909; s. George H. H. and Mae (Horner) H.; A.B., U. Mich., 1933, M.L.D., 1936; children—George Joel, Gregory Todd; m. Nancy Hamilton, June 6, 1976; children—Lincoln H. O'Brien, David E. O'Brien. City planner for City Planning Commn. Bay City, Mich., 1938-40, Flint, Mich., 1940-45; prin. planner master plan div. City Planning Commn., Cin., 1945-46; planning dir. City Plan Commn., Ft. Wayne, Ind., 1947-48; exec. sec. Citizens Development Com., Cin., 1948-67; dir. planning and devel. Greater Cin. C. of C., 1967-74; exec. dir. greater Cin. Bicentennial Commn., 1974-76; hearing examiner, Xenia, Ohio, 1974-76; fin. programs coordinator City of Cleveland Heights (Ohio), 1976—. Mem. Am. Inst. Planners, Am. Soc. Planning

Ofcls. Am. Planning and Civic Assn., Engring. Soc. Cin. (dir.), Ohio Planning Conf. (dir.), Cincinnatus Assn., Queen City Assn., Tau Sigma Delta, Lambda Chi Alpha. Episcopalian (warden). Clubs: Cincinnati, Exchange (pres., dist. gov.). Home: 3105 Warrington Rd Shaker Heights OH 44120 Office: City Hall 2953 Mayfield Rd Cleveland Heights OH 44118

HAYWOOD, CHARLES RICHARD, food co. exec.; b. St. Louis, May 8, 1940; s. Charles Richard and Doris Louise (Korhammer) H.; B.S., Southeast Mo. State U., 1963; M.B.A., U. Mo., 1972; m. Judith Ann Vaccaro, Aug. 17, 1963; children—Cheryl Lynn, Susan Marie. With Anheuser-Busch, St. Louis, 1963—, mgr. operations research corporate planning div., 1972-74, exec. asst. to pres., 1974—. Mem. Inst. for Mgmt. Sci., Operations Research Soc. Am., Assn. for Computer Machinery, Data Processing Mgmt. Assn. Home: 12931 Dunstone Dr Florissant MO 63033 Office: 2800 S 9th St St Louis MO 63118

HAZARD, WILLIS GILPIN, bus. and indsl. hygiene cons.; b. West Chester, Pa., Apr. 27, 1907; s. Willis Hatfield and Mary D. (Creigh) H.; A.B., Harvard, 1929, M.A., 1930; m. Elizabeth Anne Ericson, Sept. 20, 1941; children—Willis Gilpin, Samuel Garth, David Creigh, Barbara Anne. Instr. indsl. hygiene Harvard Sch. Pub. Health, 1930-34; with Personnel Relations Dept., Owens-Ill. Glass Co. (co. name changed to Owens-Ill. Inc.), Toledo, 1934-72, various personnel and occupational health assignments, dir. indsl. hygiene; cons. indsl. hygiene, Toledo, 1972—; cons. indsl. hygiene Commn. Nat. Corps. and Indsl. Devel. Bur., Taiwan, 1975. Mem. indsl. hygiene Fellowship Bd., Oak Ridge Inst. Nuclear Studies, 1960-63. Trustee Indsl. Health Found., Pitts. Served as maj. USPHS, 1941-46. Diplomate Am. Bd. Indsl. Hygiene (mem. bd. 1964—, pres. 1966—). Registered profl. engr., Ohio. Mem. Am. Indsl. Hygiene Assn. (pres. 1961-62, dir. 1951-54, Cummings award 1968), Acoustical Soc. Am., Am. Soc. Heating, Refrigerating and Air Conditioning Engrs., Am. Pub. Health Assn. Episcopalian. Contbr. articles to profl. jours. Patentee in field. Home: 3609 Mapleway Dr Toledo OH 43614 Office: 3609 Mapleway Dr Toledo OH 43614

HAZEL, ERIK RICHARD, market researcher; b. Jamestown, N.Y., Dec. 16, 1944; s. George Arthur and Marthanne; A.B., Wittenberg U., 1970; M.A., Case Western Reserve U., Ph.D. (Newbell Niles Puckett award) 1974; m. Cheryl Anne Sponsel, Sept. 2, 1972; 1 dau., Sara Anne. Instr. Am. studies, social scis. and humanities Case Western Reserve U., Cleve., 1971-75; coordinator assessment center Cuyahoga Community Coll., Cleve., 1975-76; mktg. researcher Southwestern Bell Telephone Co., St. Louis, Mo., 1976—; cons. Cleve. community colls. Served with U.S. Army, 1964-67. Mem. Am. Mktg. Assn., Am. Film Inst., Am. Studies Assn., Am. Philatelic Assn., Phi Alpha Theta, Democrat. Clubs: Phi Gamma Delta. Editor: Connections, 1971-73; author: The Hollywood Image: An Examination of the Literary Perspective, 1978. Home: 11945 Red Barn Ct Florissant MO 63033 Office: 1010 Pine St St Louis MO 63102

HAZEL, GERALD VERNON, banker; b. nr. Toledo, Feb. 26, 1931; s. Wayne Willard and Clarice Eloise (Bihn) H.; B.B.A., U. Toledo, 1952; postgrad. Northwestern U., 1960-61, Rutgers U., 1962-64; m. Loujean Marie Metzger, June 7, 1952; children—Elizabeth, Katherine. Trust adminstr. The Ohio Citizens Trust Co., Toledo, 1956-64, asst. v.p., 1964-68; v.p. and dir. mktg., 1968-75, v.p., trust officer, 1975—. Mem. Toledo Convention Assn., Community Planning Council of N.W. Ohio; chmn. dental com. Lucas County Health Study Commn., 1967; pres. Toledo Dental Dispensary Assn., 1965-75. Bd. dirs. Lutheran Social Services of N.W. Ohio, 1971—, treas., 1971-76, pres., 1977—. Served with USNR, 1952-56; capt. Res. (ret.). Mem. Toledo Sales and Mktg. Execs. Assn., Am. Inst. Banking, Toledo C. of C. (chmn. mil. affairs com. 1973). Lutheran (pres. council 1971-72). Mason, Kiwanian (pres. 1977). Home: 407 W Front St Perrysburg OH 43551 Office: One Levis Square Toledo OH 43603

HAZELTINE, ROBERT EARL, librarian; b. Fremont, Ohio, May 30, 1916; s. Nick A. and Catherine Henrietta (Keefer) H.; B.A., U. Akron, 1949; M.S. in L.S., Case-Western Res. U., 1950; m. Anna Theis, Sept. 6, 1947; children—Robert T., Catherine Ann, Amy Elizabeth. Asst. cataloger Bowling Green (Ohio) State U. Library, 1950-54, cataloger, 1954-55; head tech. processes Canton (Ohio) Library, 1955-60; head librarian Portsmouth (Ohio) Pub. Library, 1960-66; dir. Ashtabula County (Ohio) Dist. Library, 1966—; part-time instr. Ashtabula area campus Kent State U., 1968—; chmn. Council of Ashtabula County Libraries, 1973; pres. Northeastern Ohio Library Assn., 1973-75. Pres. Roosevelt Sch. PTA, Portsmouth, 1964-65; pres. Portsmouth PTA Council, 1965-66; mem. bd. trustees, exec. com. Ashtabula Area Devel. Assn., 1969—. Served with USAAF, 1942-45. Mem. No. Ohio Catalogers (chmn. 1955-56), Am. (state rep. recruitment com. 1964-69), Ohio (chmn. recruitment com. 1964-66) library assns. Lutheran (trustee 1964-65; sec. 1966). Kiwanian. Club: North End (Ashtabula). Home: 811 Myrtle Ave Ashtabula OH 44004 Office: 335 W 44th St Ashtabula OH 44004

HAZELTON, LUCY REED, advt. exec., writer; b. St. Louis, Sept. 9, 1929; d. Ferdinand Maximillian and Elizabeth Emily (Benson) Schaeffer; student Washington U., St. Louis, 1947-48, St. Louis U., 1954-56, U. Colo., summer, 1968, U. Houston, summer, 1971; m. Burton W. Hazelton, Feb. 15, 1958; children—Terence G. Reed, Deborah Lucy Reed, Ellen Frisch. Writer and artist for ednl. programming Webster Pub. Co., Crestwood, Mo., 1962-63, Scharr Printers, St. Louis, 1966-67; advt. writer Christian Bd. Publs., St. Louis, 1967-69; mgr. advt. and pub. relations A.G. Edwards & Sons, Inc., St. Louis, 1969—. Bd. dirs. Poetry Center Inc. of St. Louis, v.p., 1975-78. Recipient Marianne Moore award, 1977, Merit award Fin. World Mag., 1973-77. Mem. Acad. Am. Poets, St. Louis Writers Guild (treas. 1975), Advt. Prodn. Club of St. Louis. Author: (book of poetry) Three Circles and the Princess, 1976; (verse plays) The Still Point (E. Oscar Thalinger award), 1965, The River Laughs, 1966. Contbr. poetry to various lit. mags. Home: 668 Kirkshire Dr Kirkwood MO 63122 Office: 1 N Jefferson St Louis MO 63103

H'DOUBLER, FRANCIS TODD, JR., physician; b. Springfield, Mo., June 18, 1925; s. Francis Todd and Alice Louise (Bemis) H'D.; student Washington U., St. Louis, 1943, Miami U., Oxford, Ohio, 1943-44; B.S., U. Wis., 1946, M.D., 1948; m. Joan Louise Huber, Dec. 20, 1951; children—Julie and Sarah (twins), Kurt, Scott. Intern, Milw. Hosp., 1948-49; resident in surgery U.S. Naval Hosp., Oakland, Calif., 1950-51; pvt. practice medicine specializing in thyroid surgery, Springfield, 1952—. Active YMCA; mem. Commn. to Reapportion Mo. State Senate, 1971; chmn. Sch. Bond and Tax Levy Com., 1958. County chmn. Republican party, 1974-75; mem. Rep. state finance com., 1972-75. Bd. dirs. Shrine Galveston Burns Inst.; bd. dirs. St. Louis Shrine Hosp. for Crippled Children, chmn. long-range planning com., 1975—; mem. steering com. Wilson's Creek Battlefield Nat. Park, 1951-61; mem. pres.'s adv. council Sch. Ozarks, Point Lookout, Mo., 1975—. Served with USNR, 1943-46, 49-51, Fleet Marines, 1950. Recipient Humanitarian award S.W. Mo. Drug Travelers Assn., 1971; Distinguished Service award Mo. Jaycees, 1959. Fellow Am. Coll. Nuclear Medicine (founder's group); mem. AMA, Greene County Med. Assn., Mo. med. soc., Southwestern Surg. Congress, Mo. Surg. Assn., Soc. Nuclear Medicine, Am. Thyroid Assn., Order DeMolay Legion Honor (hon.), Springfield Jr. C. of C. (past pres.), Springfield C. of C., Sigma Nu, Nu Sigma Nu. Mason (Shriner). Home: 2445 Melbourne Rd Springfield MO 65804 Office: 1443 N Robberson St Med Tower Springfield MO 65802

HEAD, HENRY BUCHEN, physician; b. Evanston, Ill., Nov. 24, 1933; s. Jerome Reed and Jean Helen (Milne) H.; B.A., Amherst Coll., 1955; M.D., Northwestern U., 1959; M.S. in Medicine, U. Minn., 1964; m. Suzanne Elizabeth Spletzer, Feb. 15, 1961; children—Elizabeth, Catherine, Heather, Henry, Alexander. Intern, Phila. Gen. Hosp., 1959-60; fellow in medicine Mayo Clinic, Rochester, Minn., 1960-63; fellow in gastroenterology Northwestern U., Evanston, 1963-65; instr. medicine, 1965-70, asso. medicine, 1970—; practice medicine specializing in internal medicine and gastroenterology, Chgo.; mem. attending staff Northwestern Meml. Hosp., Chgo. Served to maj. U.S. Army, 1967-69. Diplomate Am. Bd. Internal Medicine. Fellow A.C.P.; mem. AMA (Physician's Recognition award 1969), Ill. State, Chgo. med. socs., Inst. of Medicine of Chgo., Northwestern Med. Clin. Faculty Assn. (chmn. 1977). Presbyterian. Clubs: Tavern (Chgo.). Contbr. articles to profl. jours. Home: 1145 Sheridan Rd Evanston IL 60202 Office: 251 E Chicago Ave Chicago IL 60611

HEAD, JAMES S., publisher; b. Tuscumbia, Ala., Dec. 7, 1934; s. Doyal and Ida (Mitchell) H.; B.A., U. Ala., 1957; m. Clara Jane Stanley, Mar. 10, 1963; children—James, Jon, Jeffery, Jennifer. Pub. Cushing (Okla.) Citizen, 1965-69; gen. mgr. Florence (Ala.) Times, 1969-72; pub. S.W. Daily Times, Liberal, Kans., 1972—; owner Head Newspapers, Liberal, 1974—, Bonham (Tex.) Newspapers, Inc., Drumright (Okla.) Newspapers, Inc.; pres. Florence (Ala.) Newspapers Inc., 1973—; pres. Liberal Newspapers Inc., 1972—, also dir. Pres. MacArthur P.T.A., 1973-75. Trustee Seward County Community Coll. Found. Served with USNR, 1956-70. Mem. Liberal C. of C. (dir.-sponsor econ. devel. 1973—). Republican. Baptist. Elk, Rotarian. Home: 640 Lilac St Liberal KS 67901 Office: Liberal SW Daily Times 16 S Kansas St Liberal KS 67901

HEADE, JOAN TERESE, educator; b. St. Louis, July 6, 1930; d. Joseph Daniel and Henrietta Marie (Wurdack) Heade; A.B., Harris Tchrs. Coll., 1969; M.A., U. Mo., 1973. Clk., Metropolitan Life Ins. Co., Clayton, Mo., 1949; with Aero Chart & Info. Center, St. Louis, 1950-53, Lynch & Hart Advt., 1954, Mc Donnell Aircraft, St. Louis, 1955; tchr., Archdiocesan Schs., St. Louis, 1958-69, St. Louis Pub. Schs., 1969-72; tchr., guidance counselor Pattonville Sch. Dist., Maryland Heights, Mo., 1973—. Mem. Am., Mo. personnel and guidance assns., St. Louis Personnel and Guidance Assn., Cousteau Soc., Smithsonian Instn., Phi Delta Kappa. Roman Catholic. Office: 115 Harding St Maryland Heights MO 63043

HEADLEE, RAYMOND, psychoanalyst, educator; b. Shelby County, Ind., July 27, 1917; s. Ortis Verl and Mary Mae (Wright) H.; A.B. in Psychology, Ind. U., 1939, A.M. in Exptl. Psychology, 1941, M.D., 1944; grad. Chgo. Inst. Psychoanalysis, 1959; m. Eleanor Case Benton, Aug. 24, 1941; children—Sue, Mark, Ann. Intern St. Elizabeth's Hosp., Washington, 1944-45, resident psychiatry, 1945-46; resident psychiatry Milw. Psychiat. Hosp., 1947-48, pres. staff, 1965-70; practice medicine specializing in psychiatry and psychoanalysis, Elm Grove, Wis., 1949—. Clin. asst. prof. psychiatry Med. Coll. Wis., Milw., 1958-59, clin. asso. prof. psychiatry, 1959-62, clin. prof. psychiatry 1962—, chmn. dept., 1963-70; prof. psychology Marquette U., Milw., 1966-76. Bd. dirs. Elm Brook (Wis.) Meml. Hosp., 1969-71. Served to 1st lt. Fort Knox Armored Med. Research Lab., AUS, 1945; to maj. at NIH, USPHS, Bethesda, Md., 1953. Diplomate Am. Bd. Psychiatry and Neurology (examiner 1964—). Fellow Am. Psychiat. Assn. (life), Am. Coll. Psychiatry; mem. State Med. Soc. Wis. (editorial dir. 1971-77), Wis. Psychiat. Assn. (pres. 1971-72). Clubs: Beefeater (upper warder 1972—) (London); Milwaukee. Author: (with Bonnie Corey) Psychiatry in Nursing, 1949. Contbr. numerous articles to profl. jours. Home: 12505 Gremoor St Elm Grove WI 53122 Office: 1055 Legion St Box 207 Elm Grove WI 53122

HEADLEE, RICHARD HAROLD, ins. co. exec.; b. Ft. Dodge, Iowa, May 6, 1930; s. William Clarke and Violet Rebecca (Lunn) H.; B.A., Utah State U., 1953; m. Mary E. Mendenhall, Oct. 21, 1948; children—Mike, Douglas, Kathy, Bruce, Natalie, Carolyn, Laura, Howard, Elaine. Account exec. Burroughs Corp., Salt Lake City, 1957-66; cons., field dir. Romney Assos., 1966-68; pres., dir. Morbark Industries, Inc., 1968-69; pres., chief exec. officer Hamilton Internat. Devel. Corp., Farmington, Mich, 1970-72; v.p. Alexander Hamilton Life Ins. Co. of Am., 1970-72, pres., chief exec. officer, 1973—; dir. West Oakland Bank. Mem. dist. adv. bd. SBA, 1970—; del. Pres.'s Econ. Summit, 1974. Mem. steering com. Am. Landmarks assn., 1963-66; a founder S. Davis Welfare assn., 1960, Davis County Community Concerts Assn., 1961. Nat. chmn. Young Bus. Leaders For Nixon, 1968; mem. exec. com., United Republican Fund, 1970. Bd. dirs. Nat. Multiple Sclerosis Soc., 1963-65; mem. Nat. Mental Health Adv. Bd., 1963-64, Project Concern, 1971—; trustee Oakland U. Served to 1st lt. AUS, 1953-56. Recipient Outstanding Alumnus award Utah State U., 1964. Distinguished Service award Bountiful, 1960. Mem. U.S. (pres. 1963-64, nat. chmn. golden anniversary 1970), Utah (pres. 1961-62) junior chambers commerce, U.S. (dir. 1964-65), Mich. (bd. dirs., vice chmn.) chambers commerce, Utah State U. Round Table, Blue Key, Sigma Nu. Mem. Ch. of Jesus Christ of Latter-day Saints (bishop 1972-74, state pres. 1975). Bd. editors Outstanding Young Men Am., 1964-71. Home: 26129 Hidden Valley Farmington MI 48024 Office: 33045 Hamilton Blvd Village of Quakertown Farmington MI 48024

HEADLEE, WILLIAM HUGH, emeritus educator; b. Morristown, Ind., June 15, 1907; s. Walter C. and Nellie Ann (Adams) H.; A.B., Earlham Coll., 1929; M.S. (Rockefeller Found. fellow), U. Ill., 1933; Ph.D. (Rockefeller Found. fellow), Tulane U., 1935; m. Gabrielle Mills, Aug. 4, 1937; children—Joan (Mrs. Charles Barrett Bowden), Anne. Instr. biology Am. U., Cairo, Egypt, 1929-31; research asst. internat. health div. Rockefeller Found., Cairo, 1930-32; asst. prin. Friendsville Acad., Tenn., 1933-34; instr. biology Purdue U., 1935-42, asst. prof. zoology, 1942-43; asst. prof. parasitic diseases Ind. U. Sch. Medicine, Indpls., 1943-46, asso. prof., 1946-53, prof., 1953-77, prof. emeritus, 1977—. Chmn. dept. biology Nat. Pedagogic Inst., Caracas, Venezuela, 1937-38; coordinator, dir. Ind. U.-AID, Pakistan Project to develop Jinnah Postgrad. Med. Center, 1957-66; asso. dir. Div. Allied Health Scis., Ind. U. Sch. Medicine, 1968; cons. epidemiologist Ind. Regional Med. Program, 1969-77. John and Mary Markle Found. fellow, 1943, 44. Fellow AAAS (council 1957-62), Ind. Acad. Sci.; mem. AAUP (pres. Ind. Conf. 1975), Am. Soc. Parasitologists, Am. Soc. Tropical Medicine and Hygiene, Assn. Am. Med. Colls., Royal Soc. Tropical Medicine and Hygiene, Soc. Internat. Devel., Internat. Coll. Tropical Medicine, Sigma Xi, Phi Sigma. Unitarian (bd. trustees 1953, 70-73, chmn. nominating com. 1970-71). Contbr. articles to profl. jours., including 49 publs. on epidemiology of parasite infections. Home: 762 N Riley Ave Indianapolis IN 46201

HEALEY, ROBERT MATHIEU, theologian; b. N.Y.C., June 1, 1921; s. James Christopher and Catherine (Mathieu) H.; A.B., Princeton U., 1942; M.F.A., Yale U., 1947, B.D., 1955, M.A., 1956, Ph.D., 1959; m. Edith Louise Welle, June 20, 1953; children—Christopher Leon (dec.), Paul David. Instr. English, Mercersburg (Pa.) Acad., 1942-44, Rensselaer Poly. Inst., Troy, N.Y., 1948-52, New Haven Coll., 1954-56; ordained to ministry Presbyterian Ch. U.S.A., 1956; mem. faculty Dubuque (Iowa) Theol. Sem., 1956—, prof. Am. ch. history, 1966-74, prof. ch. history, 1974—, head div. history and theology, 1968-70, interim acad. dean, acting dir. acad. program, 1970-71; theologian in residence Am. Ch., Paris, 1965-66; bd. dirs. Assn. Theol. Sems. Iowa, 1967-71, 76—; adminstrv. council. Sch. Theology, Dubuque, 1968-71; mem. council theol. edn. United Presbyn. Ch., 1966-69, cons. gen. council of gen. assembly, 1972; cons. Am.-Holyland project Hebrew U., Jerusalem, 1973-74; resident scholar Ecumenical Inst. Advanced Theol Studies, Jerusalem, 1973-74; guest mem. Ecumenical Theol. Research Fraternity, Jerusalem, 1973-74; mem. Assn. Faculty Theol. Edn. Profls., Theol. Sem. U. Dubuque, 1973—, pres., 1973, 75-77. Advisory bd. Dubuque Area Sheltered Workshop, 1971; mem. Dubuque County Com. Handicapped Persons, 1977, named Handicapped Employee of Yr., 1977; mem. Iowa govs. com. on employment of the handicapped Iowan, 1978. Faculty fellow Am. Assn. Theol. Schs., 1957-58, 65-66; Mem. Am. Acad. Religion, Am. Soc. Ch. History, Dubuque County, Presbyn. hist. socs., Religious Edn. Assn., Soc. Sci. Study Religion. Democrat. Author: Jefferson on Religion in Public Education, 1962; The French Achievement: Private School Aid, A Lesson for America, 1974. Office: 2570 Asbury Rd Dubuque IA 52001

HEALY, DANIEL JOSEPH, labor union ofcl.; b. Ireland, Aug. 8, 1908; s. John and Mary Josephine H.; grad high sch., Ireland; m. Rose, 1933; 2 children. Staff rep. for New Eng., AFL, 1943-53, regional dir., New Eng., 1954-55; with AFL-CIO, 1956—, asst. regional dir. New Eng., 1956-57, regional dir. Ill. and Ind., 1957-74, regional dir. Region 1 (Ill., Ind., Iowa, Minn., Mich., Wis.), Rosemont, Ill., 1974—. Office: 6300 River Rd Rosemont IL 60018*

HEALY, DAVID FRANK, educator; b. River Falls, Wis., Oct. 21, 1926; s. Manley Burdette and Florence (Moll) H.; B.A., U. Wis., 1951, M.A., 1957, Ph.D., 1960; m. Ann Karen Erickson, Oct. 17, 1959; children—Matthew, Ellen, Jonathan. Asst. prof. history Ill. Coll., Jacksonville, 1960-64, U. Del., Newark, 1964-66; asso. prof. U. Wis., Milw., 1966-71, prof., 1971—. Served with USN, 1951-55. Recipient grant-in-aid Am. Council Learned Socs., 1971. Mem. Am. Hist. Assn., Orgn. Am. Historians, Phi Beta Kappa. Author: The United States in Cuba, 1963; U.S. Expansionism: The Imperialist Urge in the 1890's, 1970; Gunboat Diplomacy in the Wilson Era: The U.S. Navy in Haiti, 1915-1916, 1976. Home: 2515 E Menlo Blvd Milwaukee WI 53211

HEALY, JAMES THOMAS, vocat. rehab. counselor; b. Detroit, Oct. 29, 1946; s. John H. and Gladys N. (Bartle) H.; B.S. in Bus. Adminstrn., Wayne State U., 1968, M.A. in Vocat. Rehab. Counseling, 1975; m. Donna Marie Allen, May 19, 1971. Vocat. rehab. specialist, veterans benefit counselor VA, Detroit, 1971-77; vocat. rehab. counselor Dept. of Ednl.-Vocat. Rehab. Service, State of Mich., Warren, 1977—. Mem. Mich. Rehab. Counselors Assn. (bd. dirs.), Mich. Rehab. Assn., Am. Personnel and Guidance Assn. Baptist. Home: 35955 Jeffrey Dr Sterling Heights MI 48077

HEALY, JOHN CORNELIUS, exploration geophysicist; b. Fairbury, Ill., Sept. 26, 1921; s. James Patrick and Rose (Rusterholtz) H.; B.S., U. Houston, 1951. Instr. physics U. Houston, 1947-51; jr. operator Tex. Rogers Explorations Inc., 1951, jr. seismologist Colo., Mont., Wyo., 1952-54, seismologist Wyo., Mont., 1955-57, geophysicist Venezuela, Libya, 1957-63, geophysicist W. Tex., S.E. N.Mex., Ohio, Mich., Wyo., Okla., 1964—. Served with USAF, 1940-45; PTO. Mem. Soc. Exploration Geophysicists. Roman Catholic. Home: PO Box 65 Chatsworth IL 60921 Office: PO Box 1325 Midland TX 79702

HEALY, LAURIN HALL, pub. relations exec.; b. Chgo., Sept. 22, 1913; s. John J. and Katharine (Andrews) H.; A.B., Williams Coll., 1935; M.B.A., U. Chgo., 1964; m. Patricia Kelly, Apr. 8, 1939; children—Laurin Hall, Deirdre Dow (Mrs. Henderson), John Duncan. Tchr., Thacher Sch., Ojai, Calif., 1935-36; writer Chgo. Daily News, 1936-42; dir. advt. pub. relations Ency. Brit. Films, 1946-52, mem. bd. editors, 1946-52; owner Laurin Hall Healy Co., 1952—; partner Healy, Baker & Bowden, 1967-74, Gardner, Jones & Co., 1974—. Consul gen. Thailand, at Chicago, 1964—. Bd. mem. Library Internat. Relations, Chgo., pres., 1948-50; pres. Ill. Soc. for Prevention of Blindness, Citizens Honest Elections Found., Chgo., Goodwill Industries. Served to lt. USNR, 1942-46. Mem. Chgo. Council of Fgn. Relations (bd. mem.), Sigma Phi, Sigma Delta Chi. Clubs: University of Chicago; Indian Hill (Winnetka, Ill.). Headline of Chicago. Author: The Admiral, biography of Admiral George Dewey, U.S.N., 1944; You and Your Ballot, 1962. Editor: Illinois Almanac, pub. biennially, 1967—. Home: 874 Hill Rd Winnetka IL 60093 Office: 111 E Wacker Dr Chicago IL 60601

HEAP, JAMES CLARENCE, mech. engr.; b. Trinidad, Colo.; s. James and Elsie Mae (Brobst) H.; B.S. in Mech. Engring., Ill. Inst. Tech., 1944, M.S., 1960; m. Alma Mae Swartzendruber. Sr. mech. engr. Cook Electric Research Lab., Morton Grove, Ill., 1955-56; asso. mech. engr. Argonne (Ill.) Nat. Lab., 1956-66; sr. project engr. Union Tank Car Co., East Chicago, Ind., 1966-71; sr. engr. Thrall Car Mfg. Co., Chicago Heights, Ill., 1971—; cons. in mech. design and stress analysis, 1965—. Served with USAF, 1946-47. Registered profl. engr., Wis. Mem. ASME. Club: Masons. Author: Formulas for Circular Plates Subjected to Symmetrical Loads and Temperatures, 1966; also tech. papers. Patentee in field. Home: 1913 Lambert Ln Munster IN 46321 Office: 26th and State Sts Chicago Heights IL 60411

HEARN, RICHARD STEVEN, lawyer; b. Wabash, Ind., July 30, 1937; s. Emera Wilson and Isabel (Harrop) H.; B.B.A., So. Methodist U., 1961; J.D., Ind. U., 1966; m. Delores M. Jones, June 19, 1965; children—Edward Wilson, Richard Steven II, Elizabeth Anne. Sheriff, Ind. Supreme Ct., 1963-65; admitted to Ind. bar, 1966; law clk. Ind. Supreme Ct. 1965-66; partner Reed & Hearn, Syracuse, Ind., 1966—; pros. atty. Kosciusko County, Ind., 1969—; mem. jud. study commn. Juvenile Justice div. State of Ind., 1976—. Pres., Kosciusko County Soc. for Crippled Children and Adults, 1972. chmn., Kosciusko County Young Republicans, 1969-73. Mem. Ind. State Bar Assn., Ind. Pros. Attys. (dir. 1974-76), Assn. Republican. Methodist. Clubs: Masons, Elks. Home: Box 63 Leesburg IN 46538 Office: 122 W Main St Syracuse IN 46567

HEARST, BELLA RACHAEL, physician, artist; b. Pitts.; d. Aba and Bertha (Alpern) Hearst; B.M., Chgo. Med. Sch., 1949, M.D., 1950; postgrad. Johns Hopkins, 1952-53, Art Inst. Chgo., 1958-68. Rotating intern Norwegian Am. Hosp., Chgo., 1949-50; jr. asst. pathologist Cook County Hosp., Chgo., 1950-52; fellow med. legal pathology U. Md., 1953-54; sr. pathology resident Charity Hosp., New Orleans, 1955-56; spl. cardiac research Armed Forces Inst. Pathology, Washington, 1956-57; dir., coordinator pathology dept. Hosp. O'Rearon, Merida, Yucatan, Mexico, 1957-58; founder Bertha Hearst Found., Inc., 1958, exec. dir., 1958-63; founder Diabetic Inst. Am., Inc., Chgo., 1959, exec. dir., 1959-63; founder Internat. Diabetic Inst., Inc., Chgo., 1963, exec. dir., 1963-72; staff physician, asso. prof. health scis. Western Ill. U., Macomb, 1972—, dir. cardiac and exercise research project. research asso. microbiology Stritch Sch. Medicine, Loyola U., Chgo. Art exhibit Shuster Art Gallery, N.Y., 1966,

Internat. Dermatology Congress, Munich, 1967. Dist. med. dir. Bur. Employees Compensation, U.S. Dept. Labor, Chgo., 1968—; research dir. Safety and Fire Council Chgo. developed health fair concept. Recipient 3d prize for art exhibit AMA Conv., Chgo., 1962. Fellow Am. Geriatric Soc., Am. Coll. Angiology, Royal Soc. Pub. Health, Am. Soc. Angiology; mem. Internat. Acad. Pathology, Am. Women's Med. Assn., Am. Soc. Microbiology, Am. Assn. for Study Neoplastic Diseases, Reticulo-Endothelial Soc. Author: Diabetes and Juvenile Delinquency, 1964; Diabetes, Early Detection, Prevention and Eradication, 1964; Diabetes and Fitness, 1964; Diabetic Statistical Research Survey, 1961-65; Diabetes and Blood Groups, 1965; Diabetes and Aging, 1965; Sex 'n Things on the Campus, 1973; Diabetes and Newborns; Your Heart, 1974. Contbr. articles related to diabetes, tumors, reticuloendothelioses, ABO blood groups preventive cardiac rehab., aging to med. publs. Editor: Archives of Diabetes, 1963—. Pioneer in early mass detection, cure, prevention, eradication of diabetes; also pioneer geriatric medicine in Chgo. Home: 514 W Jefferson Macomb IL 61455 Office: Willoughby Towers 8 S Michigan Ave Chicago IL 60603 also PO Box 8-3579 Chicago Loop Post Office Chicago IL 60690

HEARST, GLADYS WHITLEY HENDERSON (MRS. CHARLES JOSEPH HEARST), writer; b. Wolfe City, Tex.; d. William Henry and Helen (Butler) Whitley; student Trinity U., 1924-26; B.A., U. Tex., 1928, m. Journalism, 1928, postgrad., 1938-40; m. Robert David Henderson, May 17, 1933 (dec. 1941); m. 2d, Charles Joseph Hearst, Oct. 30, 1943. Editor, Future Farmer News, Austin, Tex., 1930-33; dir. Service Bur., Tex. Congress Parents and Tchrs., Austin, 1933-36; dir. Student Union, U. Tex., 1939-42; free lance writer, 1945—. Instr. writing Waterloo YWCA, 1966-69. Vice chmn. Black Hawk County Democratic party, 1945-57. Mem. County Extension Program Planning Com., 1965-68. Served as lt. WAVES, 1942-45. Recipient Des Moines Register Press award. Mem. AAUW (Iowa chmn. Status of Women 1954-56, past pres. Cedar Falls br.), Iowa (life), Cedar Falls (life) hist. socs., Rural Readers Club, P.E.O., Women in Communications, Inc. (formerly Theta Sigma Phi) (nat. pres., Distinguished Service award 1962, 73, chmn. by-laws com. 1969-74, mem. nat. task force 1973-74, Iowa, nat. awards, 1969, historian Cedar Falls 1976—), Zeta Tau Alpha (life), Kappa Tau Alpha. Mem. United Ch. Christ (long-term planning com. 1975—). Club: Capital Gains Investment (past pres. Cedar Falls, treas. 1971-73); Wednesday. A writer Cedar Falls Centennial Pageant, 1952; writer, editor hist. book Cedar Falls Naval Station, 1942-45. Address: 2511 Ashland Ave Cedar Falls IA 50613

HEASLEY, BERNICE ELIZABETH, speech pathologist; b. Kent, Ohio, Aug. 12, 1919; d. Cary D. and Hattie M. (Garber) Derry; B.A. cum laude, Kent State U., 1962, M.Ed., 1964; m. William H. Heasley, May 24, 1940; children—Dennis G., W. Derry. Speech pathologist Rehab. Center, Akron, Ohio, 1963-64; coordinator Canton (Ohio) City Deaf Program, 1964-68; supr. speech and hearing therapy Stark County Schs., Louisville, Ohio, 1968-73; dir. speech, hearing and language services Human Devel. and Counseling Assos., N. Canton, Ohio, 1973—. Mem. Am., Ohio speech and hearing assns., Am. Mortar Bd. Author: Auditory Perceptual Disorders, 1974; Listeneers and others, 1977; (with J. R. Grosklos) Programmed Lessons for Young Language-Disabled Children, 1976; (with K. K. Ward) The Ward-Heasley Evaluation of Expressive Language, 1977, Receptive Word Order Jest, 1977. Home: 226 Howe Rd Kent OH 44240 Office: 1421 Portage Rd North Canton OH 44720

HEASLEY, ROBERT KENNETH, TV exec.; b. Natrona Heights, Pa., May 15, 1948; s. Robert W. and Bette M. (Connolly) H.; B.F.A., U. Cin., 1971; children—Jill Suzanne, Robert Scott. Program coordinator Scenes, Inc., Cin., 1968-69; asst. to chief engr. U. Cin., 1968-69, instr., summer 1968; audio engr., technician Sta. WKRC-TV, Cin., 1969-70; audio engr., tech. dir. Sta. WCPO-TV, Cin., 1970—. Mem. Nat. Assn. Broadcast Employees and Technicians (pres. local 44 1973—). Roman Catholic. Home: 404 Mohican Dr Loveland OH 45140 Office: 500 Central Ave Cincinnati OH 45202

HEATH, FRANK CRONMILLER, lawyer; b. Weston, W.Va., Aug. 30, 1913; s. Frank Cronmiller and Amanda (Carper) H.; A.B. cum laude, Dartmouth, 1934; LL.B., Cornell U., 1937; m. Constance Allen, Nov. 4, 1939 (div. June 1951); children—Barbara B., Beverly B. 2d, Laura Russell Lincoln, Feb. 4, 1952; stepchildren—Lucy P. Lincoln, James F. Lincoln, III, George Russell Lincoln. Admitted to Ohio bar, 1938; asso. firm Tolles, Hogsett, Ginn, Cleve., 1937-38; asso. firm Jones, Day, Reavis and Pogue, Cleve., 1939-47, partner, 1948—. Dir. Lord Corp., Erie, Pa., Erico Products, Inc., Cleve. Mem. adv. council Cornell Law Sch., 1958—, chmn., 1975—; pres. Cornell Law Assn., 1969-71. Sec. Inner City Protestant Parish, 1954-58, chmn. bd. trustees, 1958-61, trustee, 1954—; trustee Cuyahoga unit Am. Cancer Soc., 1968—, sec., 1968-73, pres., 1973-75, trustee Ohio div., 1976—. Mem. Am., Ohio, Cleve. bar assns., Cleve. C. of C. Order of Coif, Beta Theta Pi, Delta Theta Phi. Presbyn. Republican. Clubs: Clevelander, Union (Cleve.); Mayfield Country (dir. 1960-63), Court of Nisi Prius. Home: 22770 Canterbury Ln Shaker Heights OH 44122 Office: Union Commerce Bldg Cleveland OH 44115

HEATH, GEORGE FREMONT, sales exec., rancher; b. St. Louis, Aug. 15, 1907; s. George Baldwin and Jennie Bell (Jones) H.; B.S. in Civil Engring., Mo. Sch. Mines, 1930; LL.B., Benton Coll. Law, 1936; m. Frances Jackson; children—Susan, Sarah, George Fremont. Engr., James A. Hooke & Assos., St. Louis, 1930-34; sales engr., asst. sales mgr. Laclede Steel Co., St. Louis, 1934-40; sales mgr. Cleve. Worm & Gear Corp., Farval Corp., Cleve., 1940-46; owner Geo. F. Heath Co., Inc., St. Louis, 1946—; pres. Continental Pump Co., Lancer Equipment Co., Heartland, Inc., House of Heath, Inc., Vari-Master, Inc., Fremont Investments, Inc. Mem. St. Louis C. of C., Theta Tau, Sigma Nu. Republican. Clubs: Engineers, World Trade (St. Louis). Home: Route 3 Box 103 Warrenton MO 63383 Office: 11811 Westline Industrial Dr St Louis MO 63141

HEATH, JOHN LAWRENCE, candy co. exec.; b. Robinson, Ill., Dec. 30, 1935; s. Vernon Lawrence and Beatrice (Kane) H.; student U. Ill., 1953-55; B.S. in Social Sci., Eastern Ill. U., 1958; m. Sheila Carole Owens, June 8, 1958; children—Lawrence A., Kerry L., April J., David O. Program dir., sta. mgr. Sta. WEIC, Charleston, Ill., 1960-62; advt. merchandising and promotions mgr. L.S. Heath & Sons, Inc., Robinson, 1962-64, gen. mgr. fund raising div., 1964-69, sr. v.p., 1969-71, chmn., pres., chief exec officer, 1971—; v.p., dir. 2d Nat. Bank of Robinson; dir. Central Ill. Pub. Service Co., Springfield. Mem. State of Ill. Bldg. Authority, 1971-74; chmn. fund raising Blackhawk dist. Wabash Valley council Boy Scouts Am., 1970-71; chmn. Embarras Regional Health Planning Council, Olney, Ill., 1975-76; bd. dirs. Crawford County council Camp Fire Girls, 1968-74, 1st v.p., 1970-71; trustee U. Ill. YMCA, Champaign, 1970-75; bd. dirs. Ill. 4-H Found., Champaign, 1973-75; bd. dirs. Crawford County Hosp. Dist., 1974—, 1st vice chmn., 1975-76, chmn., 1977—. Served with AUS, 1958-60. Mem. Nat. Confectioners Assn. (pub. relations and sugar adv. coms. 1970— co-chmn. program com. 1974, dir. 1974—), Chocolate Mfrs. Assn. U.S. (dir. 1977—), Robinson (dir. 1968-71), U.S., Ill. (dir. 1976—), chambers commerce, Alpha Tau Omega. Methodist (adminstr. bd. 1968—, lay leader 1972-75). Elk, Moose, Kiwanian (pres. 1967). Clubs: Quail Creek Country (trustee 1974—) (Robinson); Columbia (Indpls.); Union League (Chgo.). Home: 804 Scott Dr Robinson IL 62454 Office: 206 S Jackson St Robinson IL 62454

HEATON, PATRICK JAMES, ret. judge; b. Central City, Nebr., Mar. 17, 1904; s. Patrick Sarsfield and Ada Vivian (Kombrink) H.; A.B., Nebr. Central Coll., 1929; J.D., Creighton U., 1929; LL.M., Cath. U. Am., 1930; m. Katharine Gutting, Oct. 7, 1930; children—Patrick J., Catherine A. (Mrs. Oakley E. Osborn), James (dec.), Margaret M. (Mrs. Margaret M. Powers), Michael P. Admitted to Nebr. bar, 1929; practiced in Sidney, 1930-73; mem. firm Heaton & Heaton; pros. atty. Cheyenne County, Nebr., 1932-36; city atty., Sidney, Nebr., 1940-49; dist. county judge 19th Dist., Sidney, Nebr., 1973-77. Vice chmn. Nebr. Democratic Party, 1950-60. Home: 805 Maple St Sidney NE 69162 Office: PO Box 274 Sidney NE 69162

HEBEN, GERMAINE FOX, educator; b. Cleve., Mar. 3, 1923; d. Edward and Clara Fritch (Spitzig) Fox; B.S., Ursuline Coll., Cleve., 1944; postgrad. St. Louis U., 1944-45; M.A., Western Res. U., 1965, Ph.D., Case-Western Res. U., 1975; m. Edward J. Heben, June 18, 1949; children—Edward J., Mary Ellen, Elizabeth, Laura, Carol, Michael. Dietitian, City of Cleve., 1945-47, Berea (Ohio) City Hosp., 1947-49; tchr. Cleve. Bd. Edn., 1963-65, guidance counselor, 1965—; lectr. in field. Mem. exec. com. Democratic party Cuyahoga County, 1976—; active Common Cause. Grad. fellow St. Louis U., 1944-45; Martha Holden Jennings grantee, 1972. Certified tchr. and guidance counselor, Ohio. Ohio Assn. Gifted Children (chmn. membership 1976—), Am., Northeastern Ohio, Ohio personnel and guidance assns., Am. Sch. Counselors Assn., Am. Assn. for Measurement and Evalution in Guidance, Terminal Tower Tennis Club. Roman Catholic. Home and office: 11001 Edgewater Dr Cleveland OH 44102

HEBENSTREIT, JEAN ESTILL STARK, Christian Sci. tchr. and practitioner; d. Charles Dickey and Blanche (Hervey) Stark; student Conservatory of Music, U. Mo. at Kansas City, 1933-34; A.B., U. Kans., 1936; C.S.B., Mass. Metaphys. Coll., 1964; m. William J. Hebenstreit, Sept. 4, 1942; children—James B., Mark W. Authorized C.S. practitioner, Kansas City, 1955—; chmn. bd., pres. 3d Ch., Kansas City, 1953-54, reader, 1959-62; authorized C.S. tchr., Kansas City, 1964—. Bd. dirs. Principle Found., Religions and Cultures United for Peace, Inc. Mem. Art of Assembly Parliamentarians (charter, 1st pres.), Internat. Platform Assn., Pi Epsilon Delta, Alpha Chi Omega (past pres.). Clubs: Carriage, Kansas City Athletic. Contbr. articles to C.S. lit. Home: Wornall Plaza Kansas City MO 64112 Office: Skelly Bldg 605 W 47th St Kansas City MO 64112

HEBL, HAROLD JOSEPH, sch. counselor; b. Iosco Twp., Minn., Aug. 4, 1922; s. Joseph Francis and Albina Theresa (Stangler) H.; B.S., Mankato (Minn.) State U., 1943, M.S., 1954; counselor certificate Coll. St. Thomas, St. Paul, 1967; m. Agatha Louise Kucera, June 17, 1946; children—Karol, Adele, Kevin, Paula, Steven, Rita. Music tchr., Waterville and Forest Lake, Minn., 1943-57; vocal music tchr. Como Park Jr. High Sch., St. Paul, 1957-68, counselor, 1968—; counselor St. Paul Evening High Sch., 1970-75, dir., 1975-76. Lectr., minister extraordinary Maternity of Mary Roman Catholic Ch., St. Paul, 1974—; area chmn. United Way, 1976, 77; vice chmn. bd. Maternity of Mary Sch., 1962-66; bd. dirs. Minn. chpt. Citizens Scholarship Fund. Mem. Nat., Minn. edn. assns., Am., Minn. personnel and guidance assns., Am. (del. assembly 1975—), Minn. (pres. 1976-78) sch. counselors assns., St. Paul Counselors Assn. (past pres.), 3 R's Schoolmen's Club (past pres.), In and About Twin City music Club (past pres.). Club: K.C. Home: 478 W Arlington Ave St Paul MN 55117 Office: 740 W Rose Ave St Paul MN 55117

HEBRON, DELANO LANDAS, radiologist; b. Olongapo City, Philippines, June 9, 1941; s. Desiderio Edquiban and Eugenia Ramos (Landas) H.; A.A., U. Philippines, Quezon City, 1960; M.D., U. of the East, Philippines, 1965; m. Loida V. Niguidula, Aug. 8, 1963; children—Delano Landas, Delon, Melanie. Intern, South Chgo. Community Hosp., 1966; resident in radiology, U. Ill. Hosps., Chgo., 1967-69; chief resident therapeutic radiology service, Hines (Ill.) VA Hosp., 1970; asso. radiologist, St. Mary's Hosp., Waterbury, Conn., 1971; radiologist, Grand Forks (N.D.) Clinic Ltd., 1972—; head dept. radiation therapy, United Hosp., Grand Forks, 1976—; clin. asso. Sch. Medicine, U. N.D. Mem. exec. com. Grand Forks Cub Scout Pack 162, N.D. council, Boy Scouts Am., 1975-76; mem. YMCA, PTA. Diplomate Am. Bd. Radiology, Am. Bd. Nuclear Medicine. Mem. Am. Coll. Radiology, Am. Soc. Therapeutic Radiologists, Am. Soc. Nuclear Medicine, Am. Soc. Abdominal Surgeons, Radiol. Soc. N.Am., 3d Dist. Med. Soc. (N.D. chpt.). Methodist. Club: DeMolay (life mem. Internat. Supreme Council). Contbr. articles to publs., papers to confs. Home: 203 Cleo Court Grand Forks ND 58201 Office: 1000 S Columbia Rd Grand Forks ND 58201

HECK, CHARLES VOISIN, orthopedic surgeon; b. Collinsville, Ill., Aug. 17, 1918; s. Charles John and Ada (Voisin) H.; A.B., U. Ill., 1939, B.S., 1943, M.D., 1943; m. Susan Virginia Jones, July 4, 1948; children—Charles Chandler and Helen Kay (twins). Intern, Ill. Research and Ednl. Hosps., Chgo., 1943-44; resident St. Luke's Hosp., Chgo., 1945-46, preceptor, 1948-50; practice medicine specializing in orthopedic surgery, Chgo., 1948-68; dir. Am. Acad. Orthopaedic Surgeons Chgo., 1968-71, exec. dir., 1972—; research asst. U. Ill. Coll. Medicine, Chgo., 1948-50, asst. prof. orthopedic surgery, 1950-58, asso. prof., 1958-71; asso. prof. Rush Med. Center, 1971-72, prof. 1972—; mem. staff Rush Presbyn.-St. Luke's Med. Center. Bd. dirs. Pub. Service Satellite Consortium, 1975—. Co-trustee Hulbert Fund. Served with M.C., AUS, 1946-48, 1950-51. Diplomate Am. Bd. Orthopaedic Surgery. Mem. A.C.S., Am. Acad. Orthopaedic Surgeons (sec. 1962-67, exec. dir. 1968—), Internat. Soc. Orthopedics and Trauma, Clin. Orthopedic Soc., Inst. Medicine Chgo., Am. Orthopedic Assn., Assn. Ret. Physicians Am. (dir. 1975-77). Presbyterian. Club: Oak Park Country. Contbr. articles on spine and hip to med. jours., also chpts. in books. Home: 906 Fair Oaks Oak Park IL 60302 Office: 430 N Michigan Ave Chicago IL 60611

HECK, ROBERT SKINROOD, physician; b. Mitchell, S.D., Jan. 14, 1929; s. Leo D. and Anna A. (Skinrood) H.; B.A. magna cum laude, U. S.D., 1952; M.D., Northwestern U., 1954; m. Julie Mariann Johnson, Mar. 14, 1968; children—Vicki, Jackie, Robert, Melissa. Intern, Cook County Hosp., Chgo., 1954-55; practice medicine specializing in family practice, Chgo., 1955—; sr. attending Christ Community Hosp., Oak Lawn, Ill., 1970—, program dir. family practice residency, 1973—; prof. family practice, Rush Med. Coll., Chgo., 1972—; pres. Garden Terrace Med. Arts Bldg., 1959—; pres. Bell Acres, Inc. Diplomate Am. Bd. Family Practice. Mem. Am. Acad. Family Physicians, Soc. Tchrs. Family Medicine, Phi Beta Kappa, Phi Beta Pi, Sigma Alpha Epsilon, Phi Eta Sigma. Republican. Mem. United Ch. of Christ. Mason. Home: 4720 W 99th Pl Oak Lawn IL 60453 Office: 8625 S Cicero Ave Chicago IL 60652

HECKADON, ROBERT GORDON, plastic surgeon; b. Brantford, Ont., Can., Jan. 30, 1933; s. Frederick Gordon and Laura (Penrose) H.; B.A., U. Western Ont., 1954, M.D., 1960; postgrad. U. Toronto, 1960-66, U. Vienna, 1966; m. Camilla Joyce Russell, July 11, 1959; children—David, Louise, Peter, William, Barbara. Intern, Toronto Gen. Hosp., 1960-61; asst. resident Toronto Western Hosp., 1961, Toronto Wellesley Hosp., 1962, Toronto Gen. Hosp, 1962-63; resident in plastic surgery St. Michael's Hosp., Toronto, 1963, Toronto Western Hosp., 1964, Toronto Gen. Hosp., 1964, Toronto Hosp. for Sick Children, 1965; asst. resident orthopedics Toronto East Gen. Hosp., 1965-66; practice medicine specializing in plastic surgery, Windsor, Ont., Can., 1966—; mem. staffs Hotel Dieu, Grace, Met. hosps. (all Windsor); cons. staff Windsor Western Hosp.; mem. Essex County Dist. Health Council. Served with RCAF, 1951-56. Fellow A.C.S.; mem. Canadian, Ont., Essex County med. assns., Windsor Acad. Surgery, Royal Coll. Physicians and Surgeons, Can. Soc. Plastic Surgeons. Rotarian. Home: 882 Eastlawn St Windsor ON N8S 3H7 Canada Office: 1368 Ouellette Ave Suite 303 Windsor ON Canada

HECKENBACH, ROY ARTHUR, advt. agy. exec.; b. Fond du Lac, Wis., Feb. 4, 1921; s. Arthur John and Charlotte Josephine (Albee) H.; Ph.B. in Journalism, Marquette U., 1942; m. Virginia Lorraine Burke, Oct. 25, 1947; children—Stephen Arthur, Barbara Anne. Asst. mgr. advt. and pub. relations Milw. div. Standard Oil Co. (Ind.), 1946-47; asst. mgr. advt. X-ray dept. Gen. Electric Co., Milw., 1947-55; account supr. Klau-Van Pietersom Dunlap Inc., advt., Milw., 1955-64; exec. v.p. The Brady Co., advt., Milw., 1964-73; pres. Action Communicators, Inc., Wauwatosa, Wis., 1973—, also dir. Guest lectr. Coll. Journalism, Marquette U., 1970—. Served with AUS, 1942-46. Mem. Bus. Profl. Advt. Assn. (chmn. nat. conv. promotion 1969). Roman Catholic (trustee 1962-69, mem. finance com. 1971-74). Republican. Home: 11726 W Center St Wauwatosa WI 53222 Office: 2525 N Mayfair Rd Wauwatosa WI 53226

HECKER, GEORGE SPRAKE, lawyer; b. St. Louis, Jan. 20, 1922; s. Harold Frederick and Leona (Sprake) H.; B.A. magna cum laude, Amherst Coll., 1943; LL.B., Yale, 1949; m. Susan Strickler Niekamp, Mar. 18, 1960; children—Susan Darcy, Gilbert Cox, Edward Niekamp. Admitted to Mo. bar, 1949; asso. firm Shepley, Kroeger & Hecker and predecessors, St. Louis, 1949-56, partner, 1956-71; partner firm Bryan, Cave, McPheeters & McRoberts, 1971—. Mem. 22d jud. circuit com. Supreme Ct. Mo., chmn., 1971-74. Dir. Beck & Corbitt Co., St. Louis, Rep. United Presbyn. Ch. U.S.A. Gen. Assembly Nat. Council Chs., 1966-76, mem. gen. bd., 1969-76; mem. bd. edn. Sch. Dist. Clayton, Mo., 1965-72, v.p., 1967-70, pres., 1970-72; nat. committeeman Mo. Young Republicans, 1952-53; chmn. St. Louis Met. Vols. for Nixon, 1960. Bd. dirs. Barnard Free Skin and Cancer Hosp., 1951—, sec., 1955-60, pres., 1961-68; bd. dirs. Girls' Home, St. Louis; mem. St. Louis County-Mo. U. extension council, 1973—. Served to capt. AUS, 1943-46. Mem. Am., St. Louis (v.p. 1958-59) bar assns., Mo. Bar, Am. Judicature Soc., Phi Beta Kappa, Phi Delta Phi, Chi Psi. Presbyn. Clubs: University, Noonday, St. Louis Country (St. Louis). Home: 500 E Polo Dr Clayton MO 63105 Office: 500 N Broadway St Louis MO 63102

HECKERMAN, DONALD ARTHUR, mgmt. cons.; b. Cin., Jan. 16, 1947; s. Arthur R. and Marjorie J. (McGraw) H.; B.B.A., U. Cin., 1970, M.B.A., 1971, Ph.D., 1976. Systems and programming cons. 1974-76; lectr. mgmt., seminar leader U. Cin., 1976; lectr. mgmt., mgmt. sci. and data processing Xavier U., Cin., 1976-77; mgmt. cons. Ernst & Ernst, C.P.A.'s, Cleve., 1977—. Mem. Acad. Mgmt., Am. Inst. Decision Scis., Am. Mktg. Assn., Am. Production and Inventory Control Soc., Assn. Time-Sharing Users, Ops. Research Soc. Am., Planning Execs. Inst., Soc. Advancement Mgmt., Inst. Mgmt. Sci., Beta Alpha Psi, Beta Gamma Sigma, Alpha Iota Delta, Sigma Iota Epslion. Clubs: Lakewood Racquet, Shangri-La Water Ski, Terminal Tower Tennis. Author articles. Home: 5264 Victoria Ln North Olmsted OH 44070 Office: 1300 Union Commerce Bldg 925 Euclid Ave Cleveland OH 44115

HECKMAN, FRED PENROSE, real estate exec.; b. Painesville, Ohio, May 25, 1929; s. Harold Wilbert and Pauline Georgia (Effland) H.; grad. high sch.; m. Doris Joan Beebe, June 16, 1951; children—Scott F., Christine Ruth. Clk., Diamond Alkali Co., Cleve., 1947-53; with Wyman Assos., Inc., real estate brokers, Painesville, 1953—, v.p., part owner, 1968—, gen. mgr., 1972-76, pres., co-owner, 1976—, also chief exec. officer. Mem. adv. com. bus. mgmt. program Lakeland Community Coll., 1972-73, also instr.; mem. com. control air pollution adv. Lake County Bd. Health, 1970-73; mem. Lake County Indsl. Devel. Council, 1971; mem. Lake County Devel. Council, 1975—, v.p. adminstrn., 1978—; divisional chmn. United Fund, Eastern Lake C County, 1971. Served with AUS, 1951-52. Mem. Painesville C. of C., Lake County Bd. Realtors (pres. 1971), Ohio Assn. Real Estate Bds. (state chmn. asso. div. 1959-60, dist. v.p. 1972-73). Clubs: Painesville Exchange (pres. 1975), Elks. Home: 7925 Viewmount Dr Painesville OH 44077 Office: 1100 Mentor Ave Painesville OH 44077

HECKMAN, HENRY TREVENNEN SHICK, steel co. exec.; b. Reading, Pa., Mar. 27, 1918; s. H. Raymond and Charlotte E. (Shick) H.; A.B., Lehigh U., 1939; m. Helen Clausen Wright, Nov. 28, 1946; children—Sharon Anita, Charlotte Marie. Prodn. mgr. Republic Steel Corp., Cleve., 1940-42; editor Enduro Era, 1946-51, account exec., 1953-54, asst. dir. advt., 1957-65, dir. advt., 1965—; partner Applegate & Heckman, Washington, 1955-56; advt. mgr. Harris Corp., Cleve., 1956-57. Chmn. bd. Marketing Communications Research Center, 1965. Permanent chmn. Joint Com. for Audit Comparability, 1968—; chmn. publs. com. Lehigh U., 1971-76; pres.'s adv. council Ashland Coll., 1966-76; mem. exec. com. A.R.C., 1968-74; mem. advt. adv. council Kent State U.; exec. com. Republican Finance Com. Served to comdr. USNR, 1942-46, 51-53, Korea. Named to Am. Bus. Press Advt. Effectiveness Hall of Fame, 1967; Advt. Man of Yr., Indsl. Marketing mag., 1970. Mem. Indsl. Marketers Cleve. (past pres.; Golden Mousetrap award 1968), Cleve. Advt. Club (past pres.), Assn. Indsl. Advertisers (pres. 1968-69; chmn. media comparability council 1969—; Best Seller award 1966, G.D. Crain Jr. award 1973), Assn. Nat. Advertisers (dir., com. chmn.), Am. Iron and Steel Inst. (com. chmn. 1961-69), SAR (v.p.), Greater Cleve. Growth Assn. (chmn. indsl. advertisers com. 1973-76). Republican. Clubs: Cleve. Skating; Mid-Day; Cheshire Cheese, Cleve. Grays. Home: 13700 Shaker Blvd Cleveland OH 44120 Office: Republic Bldg Cleveland OH 44101

HECKMAN, STAN P., state and city ofcl.; b. Jefferson City, Mo., Mar. 31, 1943; s. Edwin J. and Marie (Luebbert) H.; student pub. and parochial schs.; m. Rita Bauer, Oct. 8, 1966; 1 dau., DeAnn. Customer engr. Addressograph, Jefferson City, 1965-68; computer operator Mo. Hwy. Patrol, Jefferson City, 1968-69, programmer, 1969-70, systems analyst, 1970-72, systems programming mgr., 1972-76, ops. mgr., 1976—; mayor City of Westphalia (Mo.), 1977—. Chmn., Westphalia Spl. Rd. Dist., 1977—. Served with AUS, 1963-65. Recipient state farmer award Future Farmers Am., 1961. Democrat. Roman Catholic. Clubs: Lions (sec.. 1976; dir. 1977—), Elks. Home: Box 125 Westphalia MO 65085 Office: 1510 Elm St E Jefferson City MO 65101

HEDBERG, GREGORY SCOTT, mus. curator; b. Mpls., May 2, 1946; s. Fred Gustav and Clare Astrid (Nelson) H.; B.A., cum laude, Princeton U., 1968; M.A., N.Y. U., 1970; m. Margaret Joyce Stewart, Sept. 24, 1969. Lectr. curatorial asst. Frick Coll., N.Y.C., 1971-74; curator paintings Mpls. Inst. Arts, 1974—. Club: Racquet and Tennis (N.Y.C.). Home: 1559 Summit Ave St Paul MN 55105 Office: 2400 3d Ave S Minneapolis MN 55404

HEDBERG, PAUL CLIFFORD, radio sta. exec.; b. Cokato, Minn., May 28, 1939; s. Clifford L. and Florence (Erenberg) H.; student Hamline U., 1959-60, U. Minn., 1960-62; m. Juliet Ann Schubert, Dec. 30, 1962; children—Mark, Ann. Program dir. radio sta. KRIB, Mason City, Ia., 1957-58, radio sta. WMIN, Mpls., 1959; staff announcer Time-Life broadcast WTCN AM-TV, Mpls., 1959-61, Crowell Collier broadcast radio sta. KDWB, St. Paul, 1961-62; founder, pres. KBEW Radio Blue Earth (Minn.), 1963—, KQAD Radio AM & FM, LuVerne, Minn., 1971—; pres. Sta. KMRS AM-FM, Morris, Minn., 1971—; founder, pres. Blue Earth Cablevision Inc., 1973—, Courtney Clifford Inc., advt. rep., Mpls., 1977—; founder, owner Market Quoters, Inc., Blue Earth, 1974—; pres., owner KEEZ-FM, Mankato, Minn., 1977—; dir. First Nat. Bank, Blue Earth. Bd. dirs. Minn. Good Roads, v.p., 1976—; bd. dirs. Blue Earth Indsl. Service Corp., pres., 1970-76. Served with USCGR, 1962-70. Recipient Distinguished Service award Blue Earth Jaycees, 1971. Mem. Minn. A.P. Broadcasters (pres. 1966, dir. 1976—), Blue Earth C. of C. (Leadership Recognition award 1967, pres. 1967), Nat., Minn. (dir. 1975—) assns. broadcasters. Lutheran. Clubs: Masons, Kiwanis. Home: Hwy 169 N Blue Earth MN 56013 Office: KBEW Radio Bldg Blue Earth MN 56013

HEDDEN, RUSSELL ALFRED, mfg. co. exec.; b. Kearny, N.J., May 1, 1918; s. George Arthur and Anna (Meyer) H.; B.S. in Mech. Engring., Newark Coll. Engring., 1941; postgrad. Gen. Motors Inst., 1939-40, N.Y.U., 1944-45; m. Dorothy Williams, June 15, 1939; children—Russell Alfred, Susanne (Mrs. John Mouradian), Linda Jean (Mrs. Charles B. Centivany), Nancy Ellen, Richard Earl. Research asso. Nat. Indsl. Conf. Bd., N.Y.C., 1946-48; asst. to pres., budget dir. Carrier Corp., Syracuse, N.Y., 1948-51; controller, dir. mfg. S. Morgan Smith Corp., York, Pa., 1951-59; works mgr. Allis Chalmers Mfg. Co., West Allis, Wis., 1959-62; pres. Sheffield Corp., group mgr. Bendix Corp., Dayton, Ohio, 1962-66; v.p., group exec. Bendix Corp., Southfield, Mich., 1966-69, exec. v.p., 1969, pres. indsl. group, 1970-72; pres., chief exec. officer Kearney & Trecker Corp., Milw., 1972—, also dir.; dir. Nat. Marine Exchange Bank, Milw., Kearney & Trecher Marwin Machine Tools (Holding) Ltd., London, Scully-Jones Co., Chgo., 1967-69, Macklin Abrasives Co., Jackson, Mich., 1967-68, Mich. Spl. Machine Co., Warren, Mich., 1971—. Mem. Industry Adv. Com. on Automation, 1968-71; mem. Greater Milw. Com., 1973—; mem. adv. bd. Milwaukee County council Boy Scouts Am., 1973—. Mem. Fin. Execs. Inst. (vice chmn.), Nat. Machine Tool Builders Assn. (dir. 1969-72), Machinery and Allied Products Inst. (trustee council for technol. advancement 1973—), Am. Def. Preparedness Assn., Nat. Indsl. Conf. Bd., Dayton C. of C. (dir. 1967-69). Republican. Episcopalian (vestryman, sr. warden). Office: Kearney & Trecker Corp 11000 Theodore Trecker Way Milwaukee WI 53214

HEDGCOCK, GRACE HALL, physician; b. Plymouth, Ill., Nov. 16, 1897; d. Robert Sloan and Laura Ann (Bolton) Hedgcock; R.N., Chgo., Wesley Meml. Hosp., 1921; B.S., Northwestern U., 1941; M.D., Woman's Med. Coll., Pa., 1945. Intern, med. residency Queen's Hosp., Honolulu, 1945-47; asst. physician Kalaupapa, Molokai, 1948-50; med. dir. Hale Mohalu, Pearl City, Oahu, 1950-60. Mem. Nat. Republican Club. Mem. Am., Hawaiian med. assns., Honolulu County Med. Soc., Pan-Pacific Surg. Assn. (asso.), Am. Assn. U. Women, Beta Sigma Phi. Congilist. Mem. Order Eastern Star. Home: 2209 St Joe Center Rd Fort Wayne IN 46825

HEDGCOCK, RALPH EVERETTE, constrn. co. exec.; b. Augusta, Ill., Mar. 17, 1896; s. Joseph Madison and Carrie Elizabeth (Griffeth) H.; student Knox Coll., 1915-17; B.S. in Civil Engring., U. Ill., 1922; m. Dorothy M. Loy, June 24, 1929 (dec. June 1956); 1 son, Clark Loy (dec.); m. 2d, Frances Koeberlein, Nov. 26, 1959. With Div. Hwys., State of Ill., Effingham, 1922-28; v.p. Watt Constrn. Co., Winchester, Ill., 1929-36; pres. Mautz & Oren, Inc., Effingham, 1936—. Dir., Asso. Gen. Contractors of Ill., 1969-71. Served with AEF, 1918-19. Mem. Effingham C. of C. (dir. 1959-61), Asso. Gen. Contractors of Ill., Am., Nat., Ill. (pres. Ambraw chpt. 1960-61) socs. profl. engrs., Ill. Christmas Tree Growers Assn., U. Ill. Civil Engring. Alumni Assn. (dir. 1964-72), Am. Legion, V.F.W., Sigma Pi. Republican. Methodist. Mason, Elk. Home: 204 Clark Ave Effingham IL 62401 Office: 406 Jefferson Ave Effingham IL 62401

HEDGER, ROBERT WILLIS, nephrologist; b. Halliday, N.D., Mar. 4, 1939; s. Richard Allen and Agnes Hilda (Hendrickson) H.; B.S., U. N.D., 1962; M.D., Wake Forest U., 1964; m. Kay Alice Letnes, Feb. 3, 1962; children—Kristen, David. Intern Rush-Presbyn.-St. Luke's Med. Center, Chgo., 1964-65, resident, 1967-69; fellow in nephrology, 1969-71; practice medicine specializing in nephrology, 1971—; instr. medicine Abraham Lincoln Sch. Medicine, 1967-70, asst. prof. medicine, 1972—; instr. medicine Rush Med. Coll., 1971; mem. staffs Rush-Presbyn. St. Luke's Med. Center, St. Joseph Hosp., U. Ill. Hosps., Chgo., VA West Side Hosp., Chgo.; clin. ass. prof. medicine U. Ill. Med. Center, 1976—; head sect. nephrology Columbus-Cuneo-Cabrini Hosps., Chgo., 1975; cons. Roosevelt Meml., Ill. Masonic, Augustana, Northwest, St. Mary of Nazareth, Northwest Community Hosps., Chgo. Served with U.S. Army, 1967-67. Named Best attending tchr. dept. medicine Columbus-Cuneo-Cabrini Med. Center, Chgo., 1976. Fellow A.C.P.; mem. Chgo. Soc. Internal Medicine, Am., Internat. socs. nephrology, Ill. Soc. Clin. Nephrologists, Ill. Soc. Internal Medicine, AMA, Ill. State, Chgo. med. socs. Contbr. articles to med. jours. Home: 1013 N East Ave Oak Park IL 60302 Office: 740 N Rush St Chicago IL 60611

HEDLEY, WILLIAM HENBY, chem. co. exec.; b. St. Louis, June 11, 1930; s. William Joseph and Katherine (Henby) H.; B.S., Washington U., St. Louis, 1953, D.Sc., 1957; m. Denise Martineau Coyle, Sept. 14, 1957; children—Charles William, Kathleen Coyle, David William, Claire Cummings. Devel. engr. Mallinckrodt Chem. Works, St. Louis, 1956-58, Weldon Spring, Mo., 1958-61; research chem. engr. Monsanto Research Corp., Dayton, Ohio, 1961-63, sr. research chem. engr., 1963-65, research group leader, 1965-67, research mgr., 1967-69, mgr. 1972—; dir. research Monsanto Enviro-Chem Systems, Inc., 1969-72. Mem. Am. Inst. Chem. Engrs., Sigma Xi, Tau Beta Pi, Kappa Sigma. Republican. Mennonite. Research in systems analysis and engring., pollution assessment and control, process devel. and phys. properties measurement and estimation. Home: 3424 Lenox Dr Dayton OH 45429 Office: Monsanto Research Corp Box 8 Sta B Dayton OH 45407

HEDLEY, WILLIAM JOSEPH, engring. cons.; b. St. Louis County, Mo., Nov. 6, 1902; s. Charles Henry and Elizabeth Frances (Smith) H.; B.S., Washington U., 1925; m. Katherine Henby, May 14, 1927; children—William Henby, Mary Anne Hedley Speer. Draftsman, Miss. Valley Structural Steel Co., Maplewood, Mo., 1925; with Wabash R.R., St. Louis, 1925-57, chief engr., 1957-63, asst. exec. v.p., 1963-64; asst. v.p. Norfolk & Western Ry., St. Louis, 1964-67; cons. U.S. Dept. Transp., Washington, 1968—, Sverdrup & Parcel & Assoc., St. Louis, 1968—. Chmn., Clayton (Mo.) City Plan Commn., 1957-62; mem. St. Louis County Planning Commn., 1958-62; mayor City of Clayton, 1963-67; pres. St. Louis County Municipal League, 1966-67; trustee Washington U., St. Louis, 1959-62. Named Engr. of Year, Mo. Soc. Profl. Engrs., 1964; recipient Alumni citation Washington U., 1966; Achievement award Medal Engrs. Club St. Louis, 1967; Civil Govt. award ASCE, 1969; Hoover medal Joint Bd. Engrs. Found. Soc., 1973; Alumni Achievement award Washington U., 1976. Mem. Joint Council Asso. Engring. Soc. St. Louis (pres. 1951-52), Am. Ry. Engring. Assn. (pres. 1956-57), ASCE (pres. 1965-66), Interprofl. Council on Environ. Design (chmn. 1967), Mo. Soc. Profl. Engrs., Transp. Research Bd., Am. Ry. Bridge and Bldg. Assn., Roadmasters and Maintenance of Way Assn., Am. Rd. Builders Assn., Am. Soc. Planning Ofcls., AAAS, Nat. Def. Transp. Assn., Smithsonian Assos., St. Louis Acad. Sci., Mo. Hist. Soc., Nat. Council State Garden Clubs, St. Louis Council on World Affairs, Internat. Platform Assn., Theta Xi, Tau Beta Pi, Sigma Xi, Chi Epsilon. Republican. Presbyn. Clubs: Saint Louis, Engrs. (pres. 1950-51), Circle (St. Louis); University (Washington). Author: The Achievement of Grade Crossing Protection, 1949; The Effectiveness of Highway-Railway Grade Crossing Protection, 1954; State of the Art Report on Railroad-Highway Grade Crossing Surfaces, 1973. Home: 824 N Biltmore Dr Clayton MO 63105 Office: 800 N 12th Blvd Saint Louis MO 63101

HEDLUND, RONALD DAVID, educator; b. Joliet, Ill., June 16, 1941; s. Henry Gustaf and Betty Marie (Nelson) H.; student Stetson U., summer 1958, Am. U., spring 1962; B.A., Augustana Coll., 1963; M.A., U. Iowa, 1964, Ph.D., 1967; m. Ellen Louise Parrish, Aug. 22, 1964; children—Karen Marie, David Peter. Asst. prof. dept. polit. sci. U. Wis., Milw., 1967-73, asso. prof., 1973-77, prof., 1977—, dir. CETA rev. project; scientist Urban Research Center; mng. partner Wis. Pub. Opinion and Mktg. Research. Ednl. cons. use of videotape medium in polit. sci. instrn., pub. opinion polling techniques, policy research and evaluation techniques. Wis. Legis. Service fellow, 1967-72; NSF grantee, 1966-67, 77-78; Nat. Conf. State Legis. Leaders scholar, 1966-67; Social Sci. Research grantee, 1967-68; U. Wis. Faculty Research grantee, 1974, 76. Mem. Internat., Am., Midwest, So., Southwestern polit. sci. assns., Am. Assn. Pub. Opinion Research. Author: The Conduct of Political Inquiry, 1970; The Job of the Wisconsin Legislator, 1971; Representatives and Represented, 1975. Contbr. articles to profl. jours. Mem. editorial bd. Legis. Studies Quar., Am. Politics Quar. Home: 2114 E Wood Pl Shorewood WI 53211 Office: Dept Polit Sci U Wis Milwaukee WI 53201

HEEB, MAX ALLEN, surgeon; b. Chaffee, Mo., June 25, 1927; s. Arthur and Margaret Katherine Hutton H.; B.S. magna cum laude, SE Mo. State U., 1949; B.S. in Medicine Mo. U., 1951; M.D. cum laude, Washington U., St. Louis, 1953; m. Marianna March Crego, Sept. 1, 1956; children—Christie Sue, Mark Crego, Scott Allen. Intern, Washington U. Sch. Medicine-Jewish Hosp., St. Louis, 1953-54, resident surgery, 1954-58; gen. surgeon Ferguson Med. Group, Sikeston, Mo., 1958—; chief of staff Mo. Delta Community Hosp., Sikeston, 1965, 70-72; surg. cons. Dexter Meml. Hosp., Sikeston, 1967—. Mem. bd. Sikeston Community Schs., 1970—, pres., 1975—. Served with USNR, 1945-46; PTO. Diplomate Am. Bd. Surgery. Fellow A.C.S. (pres. Mo. chpt. 1976-77); mem. Mo. U. Med. Alumni (pres. 1975—), Mo. State Surg. Soc. (council 1974—), SE Mo. Found. for Med. Care (pres. 1976), Alpha Omega Alpha. Home: 928 Hawthorne St Sikeston MO 63801 Office: 1012 N Main St Sikeston MO 63801

HEEREN, JACK MONTGOMERY, electronics mfg. co. exec.; b. Chgo., Dec. 15, 1946; s. Jack W. and Vivian Ione (Stevens) H.: B.A., U. So. Calif., 1970, M.B.A. cum laude, 1971; m. Valery Joyce Croswell, Dec. 27, 1969; children—Daryle, Karie. With Electronic Support Systems Inc., Wood Dale, Ill., 1976—, v.p., 1971-76, gen. mgr. and v.p., 1976—. Mem. U. So. Calif. Alumni Assn., Sigma Chi. Republican. Presbyterian. Club: Univ. (Chgo.). Home: 331 Thornwood Ln Lake Bluff IL 60044 Office: 880 Sivert Dr Wood Dale IL 60191

HEERENS, ROBERT EDWARD, physician; b. Evanston, Ill., July 2, 1915; s. Joseph and Karen (Larsen) H.; A.B., Kalamazoo Coll., 1938; postgrad. U. Ala. Med. Sch., 1939, 41; M.D., Northwestern U., 1944; m. Martha Virginia Lysne, Aug. 21, 1943; children—Kisti Lyn, Martha Jill, Nancy Ann, Robin Jan, Sara Bryce. Intern, U.S. Naval Hosp., Great Lakes, Ill., 1943-44, resident, 1946-47; gen. practice medicine, Rockford, Ill., 1947—; trustee, pres. med. staff Swedish-Am. Hosp.; mem. staffs St. Anthony, Rockford hosps. Pres. Winnebago County Bd. Health, 1961-69, Winnebago Tb Assn., 1960-61; mem. exec. com. Rockford Sch. Medicine, also dir. ind. studies; mem. admissions com. U. Ill. Coll. Medicine, 1970—, promotions com., 1973—, mem. Senate Med. Center, 1975—, also mem. adv. com. on family practice. Bd. dirs. Rockford Community Chest, 1954-60, Vis. Nurse Assn.; mem. Rockford Community Devel. Com.; mem. Community Action Com., 1969-71. Served with M.C., USNR, 1942-47. Diplomate Am. Bd. Family Practice. Mem. Am. Acad. Family Physicians (Ill. del. to congress of dels. 1959-71, mem. pub. relations com. 1967—, chmn. pub. relations com. 1971—, dir., 1970—, exec. com., 1972—, v.p., 1973), Ill. Acad. Gen. Practice (pres. 1958), A.M.A., Ill. (chmn. pub. relations com. 1961-62), Winnebago County (v.p. 1965, pres. 1966) med. socs., Rockford C. of C. (pres. 1962, chmn. edn. com.), Phi Beta Pi. Home: 1910 Bradley Rd Rockford IL 61107 Office: 1309 Second Ave Rockford IL 61108

HEETER, RICHARD DEAN, judge; b. Lewisburg, Ohio, Mar. 14, 1923; s. Otto and Anna (Fouts) H.; student U. Cin., 1945-47; B.A., Wittenberg U., 1950; M. Div., Hamma Theol. Sem., 1955; J.D., Ohio No. Law Sch., 1958; m. Rose Lea McKee, June 13, 1952. Asst. prodn. mgr. Standard Aircraft Products, Dayton, Ohio, 1943-45; salesman classified advt. Springfield (Ohio) Newspapers, Inc., 1950-51; asst. membership sec. Columbus (Ohio) YMCA, 1953-54; asst. program sec. Lima (Ohio) YMCA, 1956-57; asst. minister St. Marks Luth. Ch., Van Wert, Ohio, 1955—; admitted to Ohio bar, 1958, since practiced in Lima; municipal judge, Lima, 1966—, presiding judge, 1968—. Mem. Lima City Council, 1966—. Co-chmn. Lima Area Recreation Study, 1968-69. Treas. Allen County Law Library; bd. dirs. Allen County Comprehensive Mental Health Center, Community Welfare Council; mem. exec. bd. Shawnee council Boy Scouts Am.; bd. dirs. Hamma Theol. Sem., Springfield, O. Served with USNR, 1942-43. Mem. Am., Ohio, Allen County bar assns., Ohio Municipal Judges Assn., N.Am. Judges Assn., Am. Judicature Soc., Blue Key, Tau Kappa Alpha. Delta Theta Phi, Alpha Phi Omega. Republican. Lutheran. Club: Lima Sertoma. Home: 701 W Elm St Lima OH 45804 Office: 217 E High St Lima OH 45802

HEETHUIS, BERNARD GERALD, city ofcl.; b. Muskegon, Mich., Nov. 3, 1921; s. Henry E. and Pearl (Timmer) H.; grad. Howell Sch. Bus. Adminstrn., 1940; m. Anna Kubik, Oct. 24, 1947; children—Bernard P., Thomas H., James M., Patricia A. Clk., Mich. Express, Muskegon, 1940, Shaw-Box Crane Co., Muskegon, 1941-42; owner Heethuis Hardware Store, Muskegon, 1946—; mem. Muskegon City Commn., 1965—; vice mayor City Muskegon, 1971—. Scoutmaster, chmn. troop com. Timber Trails council Boy Scouts Am., 1956-68. Served with USAAF, 1942-46. Recipient Oscar award Boy Scouts Am., 1958. Mem. Mich. (adv. bd. 1952-54), Nat. (adv. com. 1968—) retail hardware assns., U.S. C. of C., Order of Arrow Boy Scouts Am. Republican. Home: 1067 Roberts St Muskegon MI 49442 Office: 460-64 Apple Ave Muskegon MI 49442

HEFFELFINGER, JOHN BROCK, cons. engr.; b. Arkansas City, Kans., July 27, 1917; s. John Byers and Lucile W. (Parmenter) H.; student Bethel Coll., 1934-36; B.S. in Elec. Engring., U. Kans., 1938; M.S., Ohio State U., 1940; m. Georgia Anna Shaw, Sept. 7, 1940; 1 dau., Carol Ann. Design engr. Collins Radio Co., 1940-43, chief field engr., 1943-46; sr. engr. Air Communications, Inc., Kansas City, Mo., 1945, Aireon, Inc., Kansas City, Kans., 1946; asst. prof. Park Coll., 1946-47; cons. radio and TV engr., Kansas City, Mo., 1947—. Registered profl. engr., Mo., Nebr. Mem. I.E.E.E. (sr.), Nat. Soc. Profl. Engrs., Sigma Xi, Tau Beta Pi, Sigma Tau, Eta Kappa Nu, Sigma Pi Sigma, Kappa Eta Kappa. Methodist. Home: 8401 Cherry St Kansas City MO 64131 Office: 9208 Wyoming Pl Kansas City MO 64114

HEFFELFINGER, RICHARD EARL, research chemist; b. Big Prairie, Ohio, Jan. 21, 1922; s. Gust Thomas and Amy Lillian (Norris) H.; student Fenn Coll., 1939-41; A.B. in Chemistry, Wooster Coll, 1949; m. Nella Alberta Brewster, June 11, 1947; children—Susan, Rebecca, Scott. Chemist, Ohio Agrl. Research and Devel. Center, Wooster, Ohio, 1949-51; successively chemist, research chemist, sr. research chemist, asso. sect. mgr. Battelle-Columbus Div., Columbus, Ohio, 1951—. Served with USNR, 1942-43, with USMC, 1943-46. Mem. Soc. Applied Spectroscopy, Ohio Acad. Sci., AAAS, Aircraft Owners and Piolots Assn., ASTM, N.W. Area Council Human Relations. Methodist. Contbr. articles to profl. jours. Home: 2122 Nayland Rd Columbus OH 43220 Office: Battelle Columbus Laboratories 505 King Ave Columbus OH 43201 .

HEFFERNAN, NATHAN STEWART, justice; b. Frederic, Wis., Aug. 6, 1920; s. Jesse Eugene and Pearl Eva (Kaump) H.; B.A., U. Wis., 1942, LL.B., 1948; postgrad. Harvard Bus. Sch., 1943-44; m. Dorothy Hillemann, Apr. 27, 1946; children—Katie (Mrs. Howard Thomas), Michael, Thomas. Admitted to Wis. bar, 1948; asso. firm Schubring, Ryan, Peterson & Sutherland, Madison, 1948-49; counsel Wis. League Municipalities, 1949; research asst. to Gov. Wis., 1949; pvt. practice law, Sheboygan, Wis., 1949-59; partner firm Buchen & Heffernan, 1951-59; asst. dist. atty. Sheboygan County, Wis., 1951-53; city atty. Sheboygan, 1953-59; dep. atty. gen. Wis., 1959-61; U.S. atty. Western Dist. Wis., Madison, 1962-64; justice Wis. Supreme Ct., 1964—. Lectr. municipal corps. U. Wis., Law Sch., 1961-64, lectr. appellate procedure and practice, 1971—, faculty, appellate judges seminar, N.Y. U., 1972—; chmn. Wis. Appellate Practice and Procedures Com., 1975-76. Gen. chmn. Wis. Democratic Conv., 1960, 61. Former mem. bd. Meth. Hosp., Madison; trustee U. Wis. Meml. Union, Wis. State Library; bd. visitors U. Wis. Law Sch. (chmn. 1973-76). Served to lt. USNR, 1942-46. Mem. City Attys. Assn. (past pres.), Am. (spl. com. state-fed. jurisdiction), Wis., Dane County, Sheboygan County bar assns., V.F.W., Wis. Hist. Soc. (curator), Am. Legion, Am. Judicature Soc. (dir.), Am. Law Inst., Inst. of Jud. Adminstrn., Council State Ct. Reps. of Nat. Center for State Cts. (chmn. council 1977), Order Coif, Iron Cross, Phi Delta Phi, Phi Kappa Phi. Congregationalist (past deacon). Home: 17 Thorstein Veblen Pl Madison WI 53705 Office: Supreme Ct Capitol Bldg Madison WI 53702

HEFLIN, TOM PAT, artist; b. Monticello, Ark., July 18, 1934; s. Edward and Mary Modell (Mays) H.; student N.E. La. State U., 1954, Chgo. Art Inst., 1956; m. Luella Mary Keller, Dec. 19, 1955; children—Rebecca Mary, Mark Patrick, Elizabeth, Eron, Sarah. Vice pres. Shostrom Advt., Rockford, Ill., 1956-70; instr. art Rock Valley Coll., Rockford, 1969-71; instr. Burpee Art Mus., Rockford, 1969-71; exhibited in one-man shows at Nat. Design Center, N.Y.C., 1969, Burpee Art Mus., 1970, Carlson Lowe Gallery, Taos, N.Mex., 1975, Sneed-Hillman Gallery, Rockford, 1975; exhibited in group shows in N.Y.C., Chgo., Youngstown, Ohio, Washington, Marietta, Ohio, Rockford; represented in permanent collections including Marietta Coll., U. Ill., Urbana, Burpee Art Mus., First Fed. Savs., Rockford. Winner Franklin Mint Bicentennial Medal Design Competition, 1972; named Rockford Citizen of Year, 1975, 76. Mem. Nat. Soc. Painters in Casein, and Acrylic (1st prize medal 1974), Rockford Art Assn. Author: Quiet Places, Paintings and Writings by Tom Heflin, 1977. Address: 2116 Springbrook Rd Rockford IL 61107

HEGDE, MAHABALAGIRI NARAYAN, speech pathologist; b. Mysore, India, July 2, 1941; s. Narayan G. and Laxmi H.; came to U.S., 1970; M.A., U. Mysore, 1963; Ph.D., So. Ill. U., 1974; m. Prema, May 14, 1966; 1 son, Manu. Asst. prof. psychology All India Inst. Speech and Hearing, Mysore, 1966-70, fellow in clin. psychology, 1963-66; hearing and speech specialist Anna (Ill.) State Hosp., 1972-74; research fellow So. Ill. U., 1971-72; asst. prof. speech pathology Coll. St. Teresa, 1974-75, asso. prof., 1975—, dir. program in communicative disorders, 1974—; cons. in speech pathology. Mem. Indian Psychol. Assn., Am. Speech, Hearing Assn. Author books in Kannada lang.; including: Behavior Therapy, 1971. Contbr. articles to profl. jours. Home: 1535 W 5th St Apt 308 Winona MN 55987 Office: Coll of Saint Teresa Winona MN 55987

HEGG, DAVID LEE, pediatrician; b. Evanston, Ill., Mar. 27, 1931; s. Manne Oscar and Eva Elizabeth (O'Donnell) H.; B.S., St. Mary's Coll., Winona, Minn., 1953; M.D., Loyola U., Chgo., 1957; m. Joan Elizabeth McKendry, July 9, 1955; children—David, Steven, Kevin, Susan, Daniel, Paul, Sharon, Chris. Commd. lt. USAF, 1957, advanced through grades to capt., 1958, discharged, 1965; intern Lackland AFB Hosp., Tex., 1957-58, resident, 1959-61; practice medicine specializing in pediatrics, Kankakee, Ill., 1965—; mem. staff St. Mary's Hosp., Kankakee, Riverside Hosp., Kankakee, Foster G. McGaw Hosp., Maywood, Ill.; cons. pediatrics Div. Crippled Children; clin. asst. prof. dept. pediatrics Stritch Sch. Medicine, Loyola U.; cons. pediatrics Ill. Bd. Vocat. Edn. Mem. Will-Grundy County Comprehensive Health Care Council; mem. exec. com., adviser Kankakee chpt. Nat. Found. March of Dimes; adv. bd. Kankakee area Salvation Army; bd. dirs. Alfred Fortin Villa Learning and Day Care Center. Diplomate Am. Bd. Pediatrics. Fellow Am. Acad. Pediatrics, Royal Soc. Health, Royal Soc. Medicine; mem. Pan. Am. Med. Assn. (diplomate mem.), A.C.P., Ill., Kankakee County med. socs., AMA (Physicians Recognition award 1971, 74, 77), Am. Coll. Sports Medicine, Central Ill. Pediatric Soc. Roman Catholic. Home: Route 2 Box 2 Woodlea Rd Kankakee IL 60901 Office: 401 N Wall St Kankakee IL 60901

HEHMEYER, ALEXANDER, lawyer; b. N.Y.C., Oct. 20, 1910; s. Frederick William and Catherine Enole (Schrader) H.; grad. Montclair (N.J.) Acad., 1928; B.S., Yale U., 1932; LL.B., Columbia U., 1935; m. Florence Isobel Millar, Oct. 10, 1936 (dec. 1967); children—Alexander Millar, Christine McKesson; m. 2d, Sheila Mary Vought, 1968. Admitted to N.Y. bar, 1936, Ill. bar, 1968; asso. firm Cravath, Swaine and Moore, N.Y.C., 1935-40, 44-46; asst. to chmn. Time, Inc., 1940-43; partner firm Paul, Weiss, Rifkind, Wharton & Garrison, N.Y.C., 1946-67; mem. exec. com., dir. Field Enterprises, Inc., Chgo., 1960-75, exec. v.p., gen. counsel, 1967-75; counsel firm Isham, Lincoln & Beale, Chgo., 1976—; past dir. Field Communications Corp., Field Enterprises Ednl. Corp., Field Enterprises Realty Corp., Field Ednl. Publs., Inc., Field Creations, Inc., FSC Paper Corp., Mantistique Pulp & Paper Co., World Book Ednl. Ins. Co., Met. Printing Co.; past mem. mgmt. bd. Kaiser Broadcasting Co., Field Newspaper Syndicate; Field Enterprises Charitable Corp.; dir. Pocket Books, Inc., 1950-57, Am. Research Bur., 1965-69, Telemedia, Inc.; dir, sec., exec. com. Am. Heritage Pub. Co., Inc., 1954-69; dir., v.p. Gahagan Dredging Corp., 1953-70. Legal-econ. cons. Fgn. Econ. Admistrn., 1943-44; vice chmn., counsel

U.S. Econ. Missions, West Berlin, 1952, Gold Coast, 1954. Dir., vice chmn., exec. com. Chgo. Council Fgn. Relations; pres. N.Y. Young Rep. Club, 1944-46; trustee Kent (Conn.) Sch.; trustee, chmn. Midwest adv. bd. Inst. Internat. Edn. Fellow Am. Bar Assn.; mem. Fed., Ill., N.Y. State, Chgo. bar assns., Bar Assn. City N.Y., Phi Gamma Delta. Clubs: University (N.Y.C.); Chicago, Commercial, Racquet, Mid-Day, Saddle & Cycle (Chgo.); Fairfield (Conn.) Hunt. Author: Time for Change, 1943. Home: 20 W Burton Pl Chicago IL 60610 also 57 Owenoke Park Westport CT 06880 Office: One 1st Nat Plaza 42d Floor Chicago IL 60603

HEHN, ANTON HERMAN, mech. engr.; b. Denta, Romania, Feb. 5, 1937; s. Joseph and Mary (Hochbein) H.; came to U.S., 1950; naturalized, 1955; B.S.M.E., Ill. Inst. Tech., 1958; M.S.M.E., Northwestern U., 1961; m. Violet S. Hofmann, Aug. 2, 1958; children—Margaret, Kathleen, Anton J. With Ill. Inst. Tech. Research Inst., Chgo., 1961-68, research engr., 1963-65, mgr., 1965-67, sr. scientist, 1967-68; sr. engr. Gard, Inc., div. GATX, Niles, Ill., 1968-72, program mgr., 1972-77; dir. engring. Graymils Corp., Chgo., 1977—; partner firm Dynamic Technology, Inc., Skokie, Ill., 1967—. Pres. Parent Tchr. League, Skokie, 1976—. Mem. Fluid Power Soc. (pres.-elect, bd. dirs.), Soc. Automotive Engrs., Instrument Soc. Am. Lutheran. Holder numerous patents; contbr. articles to profl. jours. Home: 5100 N Conrad Skokie IL 60076 Office: 3705 N Lincoln Chicago IL 60613

HEIBEL, JOHN THOMAS, electronics co. exec., educator; b. Bklyn., Mar. 22, 1943; s. Gregory John and Margaret Edna (Westervelt) H.; B.S., U. Calif. at Berkeley, 1964; M.S., U. Ariz., 1967, Ph.D., 1969; m. Dorothy Anne Fitchett, Dec. 16, 1967; children—Gregory, Anne. Research chem. engr. Naval Biol. Lab., Oakland, Calif., 1964; instr., fellow U. Ariz., Tucson, 1965-69; systems engr. Indsl. Nucleonics Corp., Columbus, Ohio, 1968, cons., 1969—; vis. prof. Ohio State U., Columbus, 1969, asst. prof. chem. engring., 1970-73, asso. prof. chem. engring., 1974—; pres., chief engr. Indsl. Data Terminal Corp., Columbus, 1975, chief exec. officer, tech. dir., 1976—; vis. prof., scientist Max Planck Inst. fur Stroemungsforschung, Goettingen, Germany, 1973. Recipient Bausch and Lomb award, 1960. Scaife scholar, 1960; Cal. Alumni scholar, 1960; NSF fellow, 1965-69. Mem. Am. Inst. Chem. Engrs. (chmn. Central Ohio sect. 1975), IEEE, Instrument Soc. Am. (Achievement award 1964), Am. Chem. Soc., Am. Soc. Engring. Educators, Sigma Xi. Contbr. articles to profl. jours. Home: 4114 Winfield Rd Columbus OH 43220 Office: 1550 W Henderson Rd Columbus OH 43220

HEIDEMAN, BERT (RONALD) MORTIMER, lawyer, educator; b. Calumet, Mich., Feb. 5, 1909 s. Arthur Leopold and Lempi (Kranck) H.; B.A., U. Mich., 1932; J.D., Detroit Coll. Law, 1937; postgrad. U. Cal., 1939; M.A., U. Mich., 1942, Ph.D., 1952; postgrad. Stanford U., Hoover Library and Inst., 1950-51; m. Katherine Grayson Graham, July 6, 1934; children—Eric Ronald (dec.), Bert Lawrence Karl, Eric Melville Bert. Tchr. Hudson Sch. for Boys, 1933-34; instr. to prof. Detroit Inst. Tech., 1934-42; instr. U. Mich., 1945-49; prof. polit. sci., history Mich. Coll. Mining and Tech., 1949-57; prof. polit. sci. Suomi Coll., 1958—; judge 99th Dist. Ct., 1968-72; lectr. U. Mich. extension, 1948-49, 50-53; Fulbright lectr. U. Abo and U. Turku, Finland, 1953-54. Dept. of State cons. on Finland, 1955—. Chmn. Houghton County Library Bd.; chmn. Community Action Agy., 1968—; bd. dirs. Upper Peninsula Legal Services, Inc. Counsel Houghton County Draft Bd. Mem. edn. pub. information coms. del. Mich. Constl. Conv., 1961-62. Apptd. to Am. Arbitration Assn. Panel of Arbitrators, 1972. Served with OSS, AUS, 1943-45. Recipient commemorative medal U. Turku (Finland), 1955; Admiral's citation Navy League Am., 1971; award of honor Wisdom Soc. Calif., 1972; named Community Leader of Am., 1969, 70, 71. Fellow Intercontinental Biog. Assn.; mem. State Bar Mich. (citation honor), Am. Soc. Engring. Edn. (past pres.), Am. Hist. Assn., Am. Polit. Sci. Assn., Copper Country Bar Assn. (pres.), U. Mich. Alumni Clubs (past pres. 11th dist.), Finlandia Soc. (pres.), Coast Guard Aux. (pub. edn. officer 28th div., comdr. flotilla), Navy League U.S. (judge adv. 1969—), U. Mich. Alumni Assn. (dir. 1963-66), Internat. Platform Assn., Am. Legion, Phi Kappa Phi. Eagle (past local pres.), Lion. Club: University of Mich. Alumni (pres. Houghton-Hancock). Home: 204 Montezuma St Hancock MI 49930

HEIDEMAN, KATHERINE GRAYSON GRAHAM (MRS. BERT M. HEIDEMAN), educator; b. Audubon, Iowa, Apr. 11, 1910; d. James Melville and Katherine (Brown) Graham; student Northwestern U., 1927-28, U. Calif. at Berkeley, summer 1939; B.A., U. Calif. at Los Angeles, 1931; M.A., U. So. Calif., 1934; m. Bert M. Heideman, July 6, 1934; children—Eric Ronald (dec.), Bert Lawrence Karl, Eric Melville Bert. Writer, Collier's New Ency., N.Y.C., 1931-32; tchr. Enterprise Jr. High Sch., Compton, Calif., 1932-34; tchr., head English dept., coordinator dramatics and assembly programs John D. Pierce Jr. High Sch., Grosse Pointe, Mich., 1934-42, 44-46; tchr. English, Kramer Jr. High Sch., Washington, 1943-44; county supt. schs., Houghton County, Hancock, Mich., 1958-63; supt. Houghton County Intermediate Sch. Dist., Hancock, 1963-64, Houghton-Baraga Intermediate Sch. Dist., Hancock, 1964-65, Copper Country Intermediate Sch. Dist., Hancock, 1965—. Sec., Upper Peninsula com. on Mental Retardation, 1967; mem. Suomi Coll. Devel. Council. Mem. adv. com. of 23 for Mich. State Bd. of Edn., 1972—. Named Community Leader Am., 1969, 71; recipient Suomi Coll. award, 1976, Mich. State Bd. Edn. citation, 1976, also tribute resolution Mich. Senate. Mem. Mich. Assn. Intermediate Sch. Adminstrs. (rep. on arts and art edn.), Mich. Assn. Sch. Adminstrs., Mich. Assn. Sch. Bds., Intermediate Supts. Upper Peninsula (sec.), NEA, Mich. Edn. Assn., Mich. Assn. for Emotionally Disturbed Children, Nat. Rehab. Assn., Copper Country Assn. for Retarded Children, AAUW, Mich. Tech. Faculty Women, U. Calif. at Los Angeles Alumni Assn., D.A.R., Calumet Theatre Assn., Internat. Platform Assn., Alpha Delta Kappa, Chi Omega, Phi Beta, Chi Delta Phi. Clubs: Hancock Civic, Hancock Home Study. Home: 204 Montezuma St Hancock MI 49930 Office: 302 Front St Hancock MI 49930

HEIDORN, DONALD GUSTAV, real estate exec.; b. Evanston, Ill., May 6, 1928; s. Gustav Frederick and Laura (Hinz) H.; B.A. in Bus. Adminstrn., Knox Coll., 1950; grad. Realtors Inst. Ill., 1967; m. Bettie Jane Rohlfsen, July 14, 1951; children—Steven, Scott, Bruce, Lisa Beth. Sales rep. Sunbeam Corp., Chgo., 1950-52; zone mgr. mut. fund sales Investors Diversified Services, Inc., Chgo., 1952-54; sales asso. Annen & Busse, Inc. Realtors, Arlington Heights, Ill., 1954-64, sales mgr., 1964-72, v.p., gen. sales mgr., 1972-76; pres. Century 21 Country Squire II, 1976—; mem. real estate adv. bd. Harper Coll., 1972-75. Mem. exec. bd. N.W. Surburban council Boy Scouts Am., 1965—, v.p., 1970-75. Bd. dirs. Mt. Prospect Crusade of Mercy, 1974-75. Served with AUS, 1951-53. Mem. Nat., Ill. assns. realtors, Realtors Nat. Marketing Inst., Soc. Real Estate Appraisers, Chgo. Council Homes for Living Network (pres. 1974-75), NW Surburban Bd. Realtors (dir. 1974—). Lutheran. Home: 517 S Main St Mount Prospect IL 60056 Office: 906 S Roselle Rd Schaumburg IL 60172

HEIDRICH, RUTH ESTELLE, mil. mgmt. exec.; b. San Jose, Calif., Feb. 21, 1935; d. Leslie Angelo Nunes and Florette Thomassen Butcher; B.A., U. Calif., Los Angeles, 1962; M.A., U. Hawaii, 1969; postgrad. Air Force Inst. Tech., 1976-77; m. Robert A. Heidrich, Sept. 17, 1971; children—Laurelle, Karl; 1 stepson, Christopher. Human factors specialist System Devel. Corp., Santa Monica, Calif., 1958-64; guidance counselor U.S. Air Force, Hickam AFB, Hawaii, 1968-73, Wright-Patterson AFB, Ohio, 1973-74, briefing officer Air Force Logistics Command, 1974-75, logistics mgmt. specialist, 1975—; air force cons. to industry; guest lectr. U. Hawaii, 1971, Air Force Inst. Tech., 1975; guest radio, TV. Active Multiple Sclerosis Soc., Boy Scouts Am., Soc. Preservation of Falls of Clyde. K.C. scholar, 1952-53. Mem. Air Force Assn., Am. Def. Preparedness Assn., Soc. Logistics Engrs., Am. Mgmt. Assn., Calif. Scholarship Fedn. (life), Phi Beta Kappa, Sigma Iota Epsilon. Contbr. articles in field to newspapers, mags. Home: 2537 Brown Bark Dr Fairborn OH 45324 Office: AFALD/AQID Wright-Paterson AFB OH 45433

HEIDRICK, GARDNER WILSON, mgmt. cons.; b. Clarion, Pa., Oct. 7, 1911; s. R. Emmet and Helen (Wilson) H.; B.S. in Banking and Finance, U. Ill., 1935; m. Marian Eileen Lindsay, Feb. 19, 1937; children—Gardner Wilson, Robert L. Indsl. dist. sales mgr. Scott Paper Co., Phila., 1935-42; dir. personnel Farmland Industries, Kansas City, Mo., 1942-51; asso. Booz, Allen & Hamilton, Chgo., 1951-53; partner Heidrick & Struggles, Inc., Chgo., 1953—, now chmn. bd. Bd. dirs. Internat. Exec. Service Corps, Keller Grad. Sch. Mgmt., U. Ill. Found. Served with USNR, 1945-46. Mem. Chgo. Assn. Commerce, Ill. C. of C., U. Ill. Alumni Assn. (past pres.), U.S., Ill. srs. golf assns., Phi Kappa Sigma. Clubs: Chicago, Tower, Meadow (Chgo.); Hinsdale (Ill.). Golf (past pres.); University (N.Y.); Country of Fla., Ocean (Delray Beach). Home: 101 S County Line Rd Hinsdale IL 60521 Office: 125 S Wacker Dr Chicago IL 60606

HEIDT, ROBERT SAMUEL, surgeon; b. Covington, Ky., Dec. 12, 1925; s. Harry Herman and Mary Cleo (Meyrose) H.; A.B., U. Cin., 1944; M.D., U. Louisville, 1948; m. Anne Nurre, Nov. 19, 1949; children—Robert, Carol, Tracy, Hollis, Gretchen, Lauren. Intern, resident Christ Hosp., Cin., 1948-51, dir. dept. orthopaedic surgery, 1971—, v.p. med. staff, 1976—; resident orthopaedic surgery Lahey Clinic, Boston City Hosp., 1953-56; practice medicine, specializing in orthopaedic surgery, Cin., 1956—. Asst. clin. prof. U. Cin. Coll. Medicine, 1967—. Pres., Tri Regional Emergency Med. Services, 1976-77; chmn. Ohio State Disaster Com., 1972-77. Bd. dirs. Nat. Found. March Dimes, 1969—, chmn. med. adv. bd., 1973—. Served to capt. USAF, 1951-53. Diplomate Am. Bd. Orthopaedic Surgery. Mem. Cin. Acad. Medicine (pres. 1969-70), Ohio Med. Assn. (del. 1966—), Cin. Acad. Medicine, AMA, Ohio (sec.-treas. 1977—), Tri State, Cin. (past pres.) orthopaedic socs., Phi Delta Theta, Psi Omega, Phi Chi. Clubs: University; Maketewah Country. Home: 630 Evening Star Ln Cincinnati OH 45220 Office: 2340 Auburn Ave Cincinnati OH 45219

HEIFETZ, GARY STEPHEN, lawyer; b. St. Louis, Feb. 20, 1938; s. Israel and Lillian (Glass) H.; A.B. cum laude, Harvard, 1960, LL.B., 1963; m. Julie Ann Nussbaum, Dec. 22, 1968; children—Stephen Robert, Douglas Allen. Admitted to Mo. bar, 1963, Calif. bar, 1964, U.S. Supreme Ct. bar, 1968; atty. Capitol Records, Inc., Los Angeles, 1963-64; practice law, Los Angeles, 1964-66, St. Louis, 1966—; partner Susman, Stern, Heifetz, Lurie, Popkin & Chervitz, 1970—. Mem. Am. Civil Liberties Union. Bd. dirs., v.p., counsel Planned Parenthood Assn. Mem. State Bar Mo., State Bar Cal., Assn. Trial Lawyers Am., Am., Met. St. Louis bar assns. Home: 41 W Brentmoor Park St Louis MO 63105 Office: 7733 Forsyth Blvd 22d Floor St Louis MO 63105

HEIKENEN, PATRICIA SMITH, museum adminstr.; b. Mpls., June 3, 1920; d. Earl Leslie and Alma Helen (Wigand) Smith; B.A. in Journalism, U. Minn., 1942, certificate interior decorating. Extension, 1962; m. Harry Wilbur Heikenen, Sept. 23, 1949 (div. June 1958). Chief copywriter Softlines advt. dept. Gamble-Skogmo, Inc., Mpls., 1943-45; program analyst NBC, N.Y.C., 1945; staff asst. club program. ARC, Manila, P.I., Zama, Japan, Osaka, Japan 1945-47; with decorating studio Dayton's, Mpls., 1957-63; sec. to pres. Bemis Co., Mpls., 1964-65; dir. program and publicity, editor catalogs, publs. Minn. Museum Art, 1965—. Bd. dirs. Minn. UN Assn., 1965-67, v.p., 1966-67, editor Newsletter, 1964-67. Mem. Theta Sigma Phi, Alpha Chi Omega. Episcopalian. Author, editor: (exhbn. catalog) The Introspective Italian, 1973, Kathe Kollwitz, 1973. Home: 3007 Atwood Dr Minnetonka MN 55343 Office: 305 St Peter St St Paul MN 55102

HEIL, RICHARD WENDELL, civil engr.; b. Chgo., Mar. 16, 1926; s. Ralph Waldo and Margaret (Stantesly) H.; B.S. in Civil Engring., U. Ill., 1948; postgrad. U. Chgo., 1965, 66; m. Sarah Jane Olinger, Sept. 28, 1947; children—Nancy Jo, R. Douglas, Margaret Lenore. Mining engr. Oliver Iron Mining div. U.S. Steel Corp., Hibbing, Minn., 1948-55; designer hwys. and bridges Hazelet & Erdal, cons. engrs., Chgo., 1955-58; prin. civil engr. Met. San. Dist. Greater Chgo., 1958—. Scoutmaster Troop 2, Boy Scouts Am., Hibbing, 1950-55. Served with U.S. Army, 1944-46. Registered profl. engr., Ill.; registered structural engr., Ill.; registered sanitarian, Ill., 1967. Fellow ASCE (sec. Ill. sect. 1969-71); mem. Am. Inst. Chem. Engrs., Water Pollution Control Fedn., Central States Water Pollution Control Assn., Lombard Geneal. Soc., Chi Epsilon. Presbyterian. Patentee in field. Home: 30 Arthur Ave Clarendon Hills IL 60514 Office: 5901 W Pershing St Cicero IL 60650

HEILMAN, CECIL CARL, mfg. co. exec.; b. Pomeroy Meigs County, Ohio, Oct. 13, 1912; s. Carl J. and Clara A. (Lightfoot) H.; student Ohio State U., 1929-33; m. Virginia Blanche Smith, June 30, 1935; 1 son, Allen Cecil. With Stansbury Drug Co., Middleport, Ohio, 1935-36, T.H. Davis Co., Pomeroy, Ohio, 1936-41; with Diebold, Inc., Canton, Ohio, 1941—, v.p. mfg. and engring., 1959—. Pres. bd. trustees Canton Christian Home, 1974—; trustee Christian Benevolent Assn., Canton. Mem. Soc. Mfg. Engrs., Am. Inst. Indsl. Engrs., Soc. Mfg. Engrs. Mason. Home: 4459 2d St NW Canton OH 44708 Office: 818 Mulberry Rd SE Canton OH 44711

HEILMAN, JAMES HOWARD, air force officer; b. Seneca County, Ohio, Mar. 13, 1936; s. Howard Briney and Lois Mandana (Doolittle) H.; B.M.E., Ohio State U., 1959; M.S. in Nuclear Engring., Air Force Inst. Tech., 1969; m. Lynda Jane Dicken, June 28, 1959; children—Cheryl Lynn, Jeffrey James. Commd. U.S. Air Force, 1959, advanced through grades to lt. col., 1976; instr. nav., 1960-64; navigator B-52 combat crew, 1964-66; navigator EB-66, 1969-70; nuclear research officer, 1970-74; program mgr., 1975-76; dir. strategic planning, dept. devel. planning Aero. Systems Div., Wright-Patterson AFB, Ohio, 1976—. Decorated Bronze Star, D.F.C., Air medal with 3 oak leaf clusters. Mem. Am. Def. Preparedness Assn., Air Force Assn. Methodist. Home: 3044 Village Green Dr Dayton OH 45432 Office: Deputy for Strategic Systems Wright-Patterson AFB OH 45433

HEILMAN, JOEL CREIGHTON, state ofcl.; b. Frederick, Md., Mar. 11, 1941; s. Albert Henry and Grace Margaret (Snyder) H.; B.A., Mich. State U., 1963; m. Linda Bess Broadbent, Nov. 16, 1962; children—Katherine Linn, John Creighton. Programmer/analyst Oldsmobile div. Gen. Motors Corp., Lansing, Mich., 1963-66; mgr. EDP, J.W. Knapp Co., Lansing, 1966-70; dir. systems devel. Mich. Health and Welfare Data Center, Lansing, 1970—. Mem. Ruffed Grouse Soc. (dir. Lansing 1976—). Home: 1632 Stoney Point Lansing MI 48917 Office: 300 S Capitol St Lansing MI 48926

HEILMAN, RICHARD OWEN, psychiatrist; b. Tomah, Wis., Sept. 22, 1925; s. Adolph and Celia Marie (Gould) H.; B.S. in Zoology, U. Wis., 1950, M.D., 1955; postgrad. U. Minn., 1966; m. Patricia Jeannette Nakashian, Sept. 26, 1964; children—Richard Joseph, Elizabeth Lael. Intern, St. Lawrence Hosp., Lansing, Mich., 1955-56; resident U. Minn. Hosp., Mpls., 1963-66; practice medicine, Stanwood, Mich., 1956-57, Rochester, Minn., 1957-58; acting psychiatrist Willmar (Minn.) State Hosp., 1958-63; dir. drug dependency treatment VA Hosp., Mpls., 1963—; asst. prof. psychiatry and pub. health U. Minn., Mpls., 1968—; sr. psychiat. cons. Hazelden Found., 1964—; lectr. in field. Bd. dirs. Wayside House, 1965—, Eden House, 1971—. Served with USAF 1943-45. Recipient Bronze award V.F.W., 1973. Mem. Am. Psychiat. Assn., Minn. Psychiat. Soc. Home: 2157 Fairmount Ave St Paul MN 55105 Office: VA Hosp 54th St and 48th Ave S Minneapolis MN 55417

HEIMAN, ERNEST JEAN, educator; b. Dubuque, Iowa, Nov. 18, 1930; s. Ernest John and Edna Anna (Wetter) H.; B.S., U. Wis., 1958, M.S., 1961; m. Marian Joan McCray, Apr. 26, 1952; children—Beth, Julie, Kathleen, Joel Willis. Chmn. dept. English, Wisconsin Dells (Wis.) High Sch., 1958-64; coordinator dept. English, Monona Grove High Sch., Madison, Wis., 1964—; cons. U.S. Office Edn. Project English, 1966-67. Served with USAF 1951-55. Mem. NEA (life), Wis. Edn. Assn. (English chmn. 1969-70), Nat. (awards evaluator 1966), Wis. (pres. 1971-72) councils tchrs. English. Co-author: The Dynamics of Language, 1971, American Book Writing Series, 1978; contbr. articles to profl. jours. Home: 5133 Spaanem Ave Madison WI 53716 Office: 4400 Monona Dr Monona WI 53716

HEIMANN, SANDRA ANN WOESTE (MRS. ROBERT A. HEIMANN), financial corp. exec.; b. Cin., Feb. 16, 1943; d. William F. and Margot (Warner) Woeste; student U. Cin., 1961-67; m. Robert A. Heimann, Dec. 7, 1968. Sec. to pres. United Dairy Farmers, Cin., 1959-61; with Am. Financial Corp., Cin., 1961—, corporate sec., 1964—; dir. United Liberty Life Ins., Cin.; sec. Am. Computor Leasing, Cin., 1967—, also dir.; sec., dir. Am. Continental Homes; Sec. Gt. Am. Life Ins. Mem. Cin. Contemporary Arts. Republican. Methodist. Home: 6001 Stirrup St Cincinnati OH 45244 Office: 1 E 4th St Cincinnati OH 45208

HEIMANN, WILLIAM EDWIN, pharm. cons. co. exec.; b. St. Louis, Nov. 20, 1940; s. William Harold and Stella Fern (Spradling) H.; student Mo. Sch. Mines and Metallurgy, 1961; B.S., St. Louis Coll. Pharmacy, 1965; m. Kathleen Locklar, Sept. 30, 1972; 1 dau., Sarah Elizabeth. Vice-pres. Meramec Drugs Inc., 1963-69; pres. Heimann Pharmacy Inc., St. Louis, 1966-69; pres. Pharm. Consultants Inc., Fenton, Mo., 1969—, exec. v.p., 1972-76; adj. clin. instr. St. Louis Coll. Pharmacy, 1976—. Registered pharmacist, Mo., Ill., Fla. Clubs: Masons. Home: 2336 Maybrook St Kirkwood MO 63122 Office: 786 Merus Ct Fenton MO 63026

HEIMBUCH, FLOYD EUGENE, dentist; b. Gering, Nebr., Dec. 22, 1933; s. Immanuel and Lydia (Schmidt) H.; diploma Nebr. Western Coll., 1958; D.D.S., U. Nebr., 1963; m. Sharon J. Meininger, Aug. 11, 1956; children—Paul Anthony, Thomas Allen. Practice dentistry, Alliance, Nebr., 1963—. Box Butte County (Nebr.) pres. Am. Cancer Soc., 1968-70. Ward committeeman Republican party, Alliance, 1968; Rep. del. Box Butte County Conv., 1974. Bd. dirs. Nebr. div. Am. Cancer Soc.; mem. adv. bd. U. Nebr. Dental Coll., 1976-77. Served with USNR, 1952-56; Korea. Mem. Alliance C. of C. (chmn. edn. com. 1969), Am., Nebr. (trustee 1974-76), W. Dist. Nebr. (pres. 1975) dental assns., Xi Psi Phi. Methodist (chmn. council on ministries 1972-73). Lion (pres. 1964, dir.), Elk. Club: Methodist Men's (pres. 1976-77). Home: 707 Black Hills Ave Alliance NE 69301 Office: Sucgang Med Bldg Alliance NE 69301

HEIMBURGER, IRVIN LEROY, thoracic surgeon; b. Tsinan, China, Sept. 28, 1931; s. LeRoy Francis and Margaret Coleman (Smith) H.; A.B., Drury Coll., 1953; M.D. Vanderbilt U., 1957; m. Marcia Enlow, June 30, 1963; children—Angela, Jeffrey, Christian, Jenny. Intern, Vanderbilt U. Hosp., Nashville, 1957-58; resident in thoracic surgery Ind. U. Med. Center, Indpls., 1958-63, faculty, 1964-66, asso. prof. surgery, 1966—; registrar thoracic surgery Leeds, Eng., 1963-64; individual practice medicine, specializing in thoracic surgery Evansville, Ind., 1967—; mem. staffs Deaconess Hosp., St. Mary's Hosp. Mem. A.C.S. (pres. Ind. chpt. 1977-78), Vanderburgh County Med. Soc. (pres. 1977-78), Central Surg. Assn., Soc. Thoracic Surgeons, Internat. Cardiovascular Soc. Contbr. articles to profl. publs., 1960—. Home: 7700 Newburgh Rd Evansville IN 47715 Office: 611 Harriet St Evansville IN 47710

HEIMLICH, HENRY JAY, physician, surgeon; b. Wilmington, Del., Feb. 3, 1920; s. Philip and Mary (Epstein) H.; B.A., Cornell U., 1941, M.D., 1943; m. Jane Murray, June 3, 1951; children—Philip, Peter, Janet and Elizabeth (twins). Intern Boston City Hosp., 1944; resident VA Hosp., Bronx, 1946-47, Mt. Sinai Hosp., N.Y.C., 1947-48, Bellevue Hosp., N.Y.C., 1948-49, Triboro Hosp., Jamaica, N.Y., 1949-50; attending surgeon, div. surgery Montefiore Hosp., N.Y.C., 1950-69; dir. surgery Jewish Hosp., Cin., 1969-77; asso. clin. prof. surgery U. Cin., Coll. Medicine, 1969—; prof. clin. scis. Xavier U., Cin., 1977—. Mem. Pres.' Commn. on Heart Disease, Cancer and Stroke, 1965. Pres. Nat. Cancer Found., 1963-68, bd. dirs., 1960-70; founder, pres. Dysphagia Found.; bd. dirs. Community Devel. Found., 1967-70, Save the Children Fedn., 1967-68, United Cancer Council, 1967-70. Served to lt. (s.g.) USNR, 1944-46. Diplomate Am. Bd. Surgery, Am. Bd. Thoracic Surgery. Fellow A.C.S. (chpt. pres. 1964), Am. Coll. Chest Physicians, Am. Coll. Gastroenterology; mem. Soc. Thoracic Surgeons (founder mem.), AMA (cons. to jour.), Cin. N.Y. Soc. Thoracic Surgery, Soc. Surgery Alimentary Tract, Am. Gastroenterological Assn., Pan Am. Med. Assn., Collegium Internat. Chirurgiae Digestive, Central Surg. Assn. Club: Losantiville Country (Cin.). Author: Postoperative Care in Thoracic Surgery, 1962; (with M.O. Cantor, C.H. Lupton) Surgery of the Stomach, Duodenum and Diaphragm, Questions and Answers, 1965; also contbr. chpts. to books; numerous articles to med. jours. Producer (films) Esophageal Replacement with a Reversed Gastric Tube (awarded Medaglione Di Bronzo Minerva 1961); Reversed Gastric Tube Esophagoplasty Using Stapling Technique; How to Save a Choking Victim: The Heimlich Maneuver. Mem. editorial bd. Emergency Medicine, Reporte's Medicos. Devised Heimlich Maneuver to save victims of food choking, 1974. Home: 17 Elmhurst Pl Cincinnati OH 45208

HEIN, DAVID LEON, diversified industry exec.; b. Cleve., Feb. 4, 1939; s. Oscar Gustav and Helen Rose (Gruss) H.; B.S., Bowling Green State U., 1961; m. Judith Ann Diemert, July 27, 1963; children—Susan, Cathleen, David, Matthew. Audit supr., Ernst & Ernst, Cleve., 1961-65, tax accountant, 1963-64, mgmt. cons., 1965-70; v.p. finance Brewer-Chilcote Paper Co., Cleve., 1970-75, treas., 1972-75, v.p. fin. Chilcote Co., Cleve., 1970—, treas., 1975—; faculty Cleve. State U., 1965-67; dir., cons. Cleve. area small businesses. Adviser, Gt. Lakes Shakespeare Festival, 1965-67. Bowling Green State U. grantee, 1958-61. C.P.A. Mem. Ohio Soc. C.P.A.'s, Alpha Tau Omega. Republican. Roman Catholic. Clubs: Cleve. Athletic, Rocky River Figure Skating (pres. 1977). Home:

21298 Endsley Ave Rocky River OH 44116 Office: 2140 2160 Superior Ave Cleveland OH 44114

HEINDRICHS, ROBERT WINSLOW, real estate exec.; b. East Grand Rapids, Mich., July 12, 1942; s. William and Margaret Dorothy (Gainley) H.; student Grand Rapids Jr. Coll., 1963-65; grad. realtors inst. U. Mich., 1970; m. Jan Chamberlain, Feb. 21, 1970; children—Mary Louise, Teri Lynn. Real estate sales asso. Westdale Co., Grand Rapids, 1964-68, asst. sales mgr., 1968-70, asso. broker, v.p., sales mgr., 1970—. Served with USMCR, 1960-63. Certified mktg.-mgmt. broker. Mem. Grand Rapids Real Estate Bd. (Million Dollar Sales award 1968, sr. sales award 1968, ednl. com.), Nat. Inst. Real Estate Brokers, Nat. Inst. Farm and Land Brokers, Sales and Mktg. Execs. Grand Rapids (v.p.). Home: 2842 Northville Dr NE Grand Rapids MI 49505 Office: 4350 Plainfield St NE Grand Rapids MI 49505

HEINEMAN, MRS. BEN W. (NATALIE), assn. exec. past pres., now bd. dirs., mem. exec. com. Child Welfare League Am.; past pres. Chgo. Child Care Soc.; past chmn. exec. com. United Settlement Appeal; past bd. dirs. Chgo. Fedn. of Settlements, past chmn. Citizens Com. of Adoption Info. Service State of Ill.; bd. dirs. Council for Community Services in Met. Chgo., Erickson Inst. Early Edn., United Way Am., Chgo. Community Fund; mem. woman's bd. U. Chgo.; vis. com. U. Chgo. Sch. Social Service Adminstrn. Address: 180 E Pearson St Chicago IL 60611

HEINEMAN, BEN WALTER, business exec.; b. Wausau, Wis., Feb. 10, 1914; s. Walter Ben and Elsie Brunswick (Deutsch) H.; m. Natalie Goldstein, Apr. 17, 1935; children—Martha Heineman Field, Ben Walter; student U. Mich., 1930-33; LL.B., Northwestern U., 1936; LL.D., Lawrence Coll., 1959, Lake Forest Coll., 1966, Northwestern U., 1967. Admitted to Ill. bar, 1936; individual practice law and govt. service, Chgo., Washington, Algiers, 1936-56; chmn. bd. dirs. Four Wheel Drive Auto Co., 1954-57; now pres. N.W. Industries, Inc., Chgo.; chmn. C.&N.W. Ry. Co., 1956-72; dir., mem. exec. com. 1st Nat. Bank, Chgo.; dir. Field Enterprises, Inc. Chmn., White House Conf. to Fulfill These Rights, 1966, Pres.'s Task Force on Govt. Orgn., 1966-67, Pres.'s Commn. Income Maintenance Programs, 1967-69, Ill. Bd. Higher Edn., 1962-69; trustee U. Chgo.; trustee, mem. investment com. Savs. and Profit Sharing Fund of Sears Roebuck Employees, 1966-71; vis. com. dept. econs. Harvard, 1965-71; trustee, mem. exec. com., chmn. audit com. Rockefeller Found.Fellow Am. Acad. Arts and Scis., Am. Bar Found. (life), Am. Bar Assn.; mem. Am. Law Inst. (life), Ill., Chgo. bar assns., Order of Phi Delta Phi. Home: 180 E Pearson St Chicago IL 60611 Office: 6300 Sears Tower Chicago IL 60606

HEINEMAN, PAUL LOWE, cons. engr.; b. Omaha, Oct. 24, 1924; s. Paul George and Annie L. (Lowe) H.; student U. Omaha, 1942-43; B.C.E., Iowa State U., 1945, M.S., 1948; children—Karen E., John F., Ellen F. Instr. Iowa State U., 1946-48; designer Howard, Needles, Tammen & Bergendoff, Cons. Engrs., Kansas City, Mo., 1948-64, partner, 1965—; v.p. Howard, Needles, Tammen & Bergendoff Internat., Inc., Kansas City, Mo., 1967—. Served with C.E. USNR, 1945-46. Registered profl. engr., Mo., Calif., N.Y., Kans., 22 other states. Fellow ASCE, Am. Cons. Engrs. Council; mem. Am. Ry. Engring. Assn., Am. Concrete Inst., Nat. Soc. Profl. Engrs. Presbyterian (elder 1958—, trustee 1960—). Clubs: Engineers, Rotary (Kansas City). Office: 1805 Grand Ave Kansas City MO 64108

HEINEMANN, LUDWIG GUNTHER, psychiatrist; b. Bickenriede, Germany, May 24, 1934; s. Josef and Mathilde (Maier) H.; came to U.S., 1967; M.D., Bonn (Germany) U., 1962; m. Ilse Quiram, Dec. 22, 1961; children—Iris, Henning. Intern, St. Joseph's Hosp., Herne, Germany, 1961-62; research fellow Max Planck Inst. for Brain Research, Goettingen, Germany, 1964-67; resident, research fellow Mo. Inst. Psychiatry, St. Louis, 1967-72; clin. dir. Psychiat. Service St. Louis County Hosp., 1972—; clin. asst. prof. U. Mo. Med. Sch., 1972—. Mem. Am. Psychiat. Assn., Soc. Psychophysiol. Research. Home: 4652 Spring Dr St Louis MO 63123 Office: 601 S Brentwood St St Louis MO 63105

HEINO, GENE JOHN, bldg. products co. exec.; b. Manitowoc, Wis., Aug. 25, 1950; s. Ed John and Pauline (Masar) H.; B.S. in Mktg. (Athletic scholarship), No. Ill. U., 1972, M.B.A., 1974. Mktg. mgmt. trainee bldg. products div. Abitibi Corp., Chgo., 1974, Kansas City, Mo., 1974-75, area mgr., Des Moines, Iowa, 1975-76, sr. area mgr., Milw., 1976—; grad. teaching asst. No. Ill. U., 1972-74. Recipient Golden Panel award, Abitibi Corp., 1976. Mem. Am. Mktg. Assn., No. Ill. U. Alumni Assn., No. Ill. U. Alumni Varsity Club, Sigma Nu. Club: Tuckaway Country (Milw.). Home and office: 7911 S 68th St Apt 205 Franklin WI 53132

HEINRICH, DONALD CLINTON, swine breeder; b. Versailles, Ind., May 30, 1930; s. Samuel Clinton and Mary Etta (Benham) H.; B.S., Purdue U., 1953; m. Marilyn JoAnn Wagner, Jan. 26, 1952; children—Donna, James, Jill. Tchr. vocational agr. Cowan High Sch. (Ind.), 1953; asst. mgr. Conner Prairie Farms, Noblesville, Ind., 1954-70; v.p. Conner Prairie Swine, Inc., Noblesville, 1970-77, pres., 1977—; treas. Three-Way, Inc., Noblesville, 1968-71; pres. Nat. SPF Accrediting Agy., 1976-77. Named Nobleville Outstanding Young Farmer, Jr. C. of C., 1965. Mem. Ind. Soc. Farm Mgrs. and Rural Appraisers, Ind. Swine Repopulation Assn. (pres. 1969—), SPF (dir. nat. accrediting agy. 1972—, v.p. 1973), Inbred Livestock Registry (pres. 1966—). Methodist (trustee 1969-71, 73—, pres. bd. 1971-73). Mason. Home and Office: Route 1 Box 337-B Sheridan IN 46069

HEINSEN, RICHARD DALE, psychologist; b. Riverside, Ill., May 4, 1941; s. Ralph A. and Elizabeth A. (Van Pelt) H.; student DePauw U., 1959-62; B.A., U. Ill., Chgo. Circle, 1967; M.Ed., U. Ill., Champaign-Urbana, 1970, Ph.D., 1974. Mgmt. cons. Continental Bank, Chgo., 1967-68; counselor, tchr. psychology University High Sch., Urbana, Ill., 1970-73; vis. prof., asso. project dir. U. Ill., Chgo. Circle, 1973; dir. counseling services Lake Park High Sch., Roselle, Ill., 1976—; cons. Chgo. Pub. Schs., 1973-74. Active Common Cause. Served with U.S. Army, 1963-66. Named Outstanding Tchr., University High Sch. Mem. Am. Personnel and Guidance Assn., Am. Sch. Counselors Assn., Am. Psychol. Assn., Phi Delta Kappa. Club: Glen Ayre Racquet. Home: 275 Springhill Dr Roselle IL 60172 Office: Lake Park High Sch 500 W Bryn Mawr Roselle IL 60172

HEINTZ, DANIEL JOSEPH, vocat. counselor; b. Oak Park, Ill., Oct. 4, 1932; s. Daniel J. and Rose (Smith) H.; student St. Thomas Coll., 1950-52; B.S., No. Ill. U., 1958, M.S., 1962; postgrad. Western Mich. U., 1963-70; m. Virginia Grace Niemi, Aug. 22, 1959; children—Janet, Dan, Richard, Mark. Bus. tchr. Chgo. Pub. Schs., 1959-62; class counselor Proviso Twp. High Sch., Maywood, Ill., 1962-68, vocat. coordinator, 1968—, dir. Title I, 1968—; guest lectr. No. Ill. U. Career Seminar, 1971, 1972, Western Mich. U., 1969-71. Selective Service registrar, 1972-75. Served with U.S. Army, 1954-56. Recipient USAF Counselor's Recruitment Citation, 1971. Mem. Nat., Ill. (pres. 1977-78), Suburban (pres. 1973, dir. 1975-76) vocat. guidance assns., Ill., Am. personnel and guidance assns. Roman Catholic. Clubs: Rotary (dir. 1977-78, v.p. elect 1978—). Editor: Vocat. Sch. Book, 1976-77; contbr. chpt. to No. Ill. U. Career Edn. Manual, 1973. Home: 568 Kearsage St Elmhurst IL 60126 Office: 807 S First Ave Maywood IL 60153

HEINTZ, JAMES EDWARD, real estate service exec.; b. Norwalk, Wis., Oct. 10, 1920; s. Edward John and Marcella Beatrice (Gnewikow) H.; B.A. in Polit. Sci., George Washington U., 1965, M.A. in Bus., 1967; grad. Air War Coll., 1964; m. Marian Fischer, Aug. 21, 1943; children—Timothy, Christopher, Linda, Jamie, Julie. Commd. 2d lt., U.S. Air Force, 1943, advanced through grades to col., 1966; command pilot B-17, World War II; comdr., Italy, 1943-44, Berlin Airlift C-54, 1949; mem. NATO staff, Italy, 1951-53, Air Staff, Washington, 1954-58; wing personnel dir. McGuire AFB, N.J., 1958-63; dir. personnel systems HQ Air Def. Command, 1967-69; ret., 1969; adminstr. Michael, Best & Friedrich, 1969-72; exec. dir. Multiple Listing Service, Inc., Milw., 1972—. Decorated Legion of Merit, D.F.C., Air medal, Air Force Commendation medal. Mem. Personnel Mgmt. Assn., Ret. Officers Assn. Clubs: Kiwanis, Exchequer (Milw.). Author: Vote: the UN General Assembly, 1964. Home: 810 Kurtis Dr Elm Grove WI 53122 Office: 807 W Oklahoma Ave Milwaukee WI 53215

HEINTZELMAN, ROSS GARFIELD, state ofcl.; b. Greensburg, Pa., Jan. 2, 1917; s. Ross Garfield and Bertha Lee (Acklin) H.; B.S., Ohio State U., 1948, M.A., 1950; m. Margery Isabel Major, Mar. 17, 1945; children—Christian Lee, Diane Kay. Supr. evaluation programs Timken Co., Canton, Ohio, 1960-73, engr., 1936-60; chief labor relations State Inter-govtl. Personnel Adminstrn., Columbus, 1973-74; adminstrv. staff asst. Indsl. Commn. Ohio, Columbus, 1974—. Councilman, Canton, O., 1957-69; mem. Ohio Ho. of Reps., 1969-72. Served with USAAF, 1943-46. Recipient awards Am. Econ. Found., Polit. Sci. Acad., Police Boys Club, YMCA, Ohio Ednl. Assn.; Canton Tchrs. Man of Year award 1972; Appreciation award Ednl. Community Northeastern Ohio; Canton City Schs. award; Ohio Dental Assn. award; Mayor's citation. Home: 206 Grandview Ave NW Canton OH 44708 Office: Ohio Indsl Commn 65 S Front St Columbus OH 43215

HEINZ, EDWARD N., JR., mfg. co. exec.; b. Chgo., Nov. 27, 1914; s. Edward N. and Adeline (Kelly) H.; B.S. in Chem. Engring., Ill. Inst. Tech., 1937; m. Laurette F. Higgins, Oct. 22, 1943; children—Edward, Raymond, James, Pamela, Laurette, Joan, Mary Jayne. Vice pres., dir. Food Materials Corp., Chgo., 1937-67; pres., dir. Wm. M. Bell Co., Melrose Park, Ill., 1967—. Served with U.S. Army, 1943-46. Mem. Flavor and Extract Mfrs. Assn. U.S. (past pres.), Am. Assn. Candy Technologists (past pres.), Serra Club Chgo. (past pres.), Am. Chem. Soc., Inst. Food Technologists, Am. Assn. Cereal Chemists. Clubs: N. Shore Country (Glenview, Ill.), Lake Shore Athletic Club (Chgo.). Home: 22 Meadowview Dr Winnetka IL 60093 Office: 3312 Bloomingdale Melrose Park IL 60160

HEINZ, LEO GEORGE, real estate broker; b. Hazen, N.D., June 15, 1941; s. George Steven and Pauline (Welk) H.; student Bismarck Jr. Coll., 1972; grad. N.D. Grad. Realtors Inst., 1973; m. Mavis R. Job, Nov. 12, 1966; 1 son, Llewelyn Lee. Owner, pres. Bismarck Realty & Investments Inc., 1970-74; asso. broker Midwestern Realty, Bismarck, 1974—. Served with AUS, 1961-63. Recipient Centurian and Tribune awards Sertoma Internat., 1971, 72. Mem. Bismarck-Mandan Bd. Realtors (pres. 1973), Nat., N.D. (dir. 1973—) assns. realtors, Bismarck-Mandan Bowling Assn. (dir. 1967-71). Baptist. Elk. Club: Sertoma (dir. 1976—). Home: 531 Gary Ave Bismarck ND 58501 Office: 1929 N Kauaney Dr Bismarck ND 58501

HEINZE, ROBERT VALENTINE, cons.; b. St. Paul, Feb. 10, 1892; s. Robert and Elizabeth (Karl) H.; B.A., U. Minn., 1916; m. Mary Wilhelmina Bollinger, Dec. 23, 1917. With Barber Asphalt Paving Co., St. Paul, 1908-12, supr., 1912-16; engring. inspector City of St. Paul, Street Paving Dept., 1912-16; process foreman Acid and Asphalt Works, Standard Oil Co. Ind., various cities, 1916-32; div. supt. petroleum refining Standard Oil Co. N.J., 1932-52; v.p. research and devel. Submerged Combustion Co., Hammond, Ind., 1952-66; cons. heat and fluids processing Selas Corp., Hammond, Ind., 1966—. Mem. tourist com. Aruba, Netherlands, Antilles, 1940-52. Served with AUS, 1917-19. Decorated knight Order of Orange Nassawe Queen Julianna, 1952. Mem. Am. Chem. Soc., Am. Inst. Chem. Engrs., Am. Inst. Chemists. Mason (Shriner). Patentee in field. Address: 6741 Indi Illi Park Hammond IN 46324

HEIPLE, JAMES DEE, judge; b. Peoria, Ill., Sept. 13, 1933; s. Rae Crane and Harriet (Birkett) H.; B.S., Bradley U., 1955; J.D., U. Louisville, 1957; Certificate in Internat. Law, City of London Coll., 1967; grad. Nat. Coll. State Judiciary, 1971; m. Virginia Kerswill, July 28, 1956; children—Jeremy Hans, Jonathan James, Rachel Duffield. Admitted to Ill. bar, 1957, Ky. bar, 1958, U.S. Supreme Ct. bar, 1962; partner firm Heiple and Heiple, Pekin, Ill., 1957-70; circuit judge Ill., 10th Circuit 1970—. Vice pres., dir. Washington State Bank (Ill.), 1959-66; dir. Gridley State Bank (Ill.), 1958-59; village atty., Tremont, Ill., 1961-66, Mackinaw, Ill., 1961-66; asst. pub. defender Tazewell County, 1967-70., legal clerk Ill. Appellate Ct., 1968-70. Chmn. Tazewell County Heart Fund, 1960. Pub. Adminstr. Tazewell County, Ill., 1959-61; sec. Tazewell County Republican Central Com. 1966-70; mem. Pekin Sch. Bd., 1970. Recipient certificate Freedoms Found., 1975, honor medal, 1976. Mem. Am., Ky., Ill. (chmn. legal edn. com. 1972-74, chmn. jud. sect. 1976-77), Tazewell County (pres. 1967-68) bar assns., Ill. Judges Assn. (v.p. 1977-78), Ky., Ill., Pa. hist. socs., Nat. Rifle Assn., S.A.R., Delta Theta Phi, Sigma Nu, Pi Kappa Delta. Methodist. Mason. Clubs: Filson; Union League (Chgo.); Pekin Country; Mo. Athletic (St. Louis); Pendennis (Louisville). Home: 707 S 5th St Pekin IL 61554 Office: Tazewell County Ct House Pekin IL 61554

HEISER, FRANK FRED, trade assn. exec.; b. Cleve., Mar. 13, 1906; s. Fred William and Marian (Williams) H.; student Dyke Coll., 1927; m. Ann Elderkin, Jan. 11, 1975; children by previous marriage—Beryl Marie (Mrs. Clark W. Peck), Marilyn Janice (Mrs. Keith E. Johnson). Mgr., North Olmsted Motor Coach Line (Ohio), 1929-32; owner, operator supermarket, North Olmsted, 1933-40, 46-53; asst. supt. prodn. dept. Fisher Body div. Gen. Motors Corp., Cleve., 1940-46; exec. dir. Cleve. Food Dealers Assn., 1953-71, Ohio Retail Food Dealers Assn., Cleve., 1955-75. Pres. nat. Food Trade Press, 1966-67; mem. Cleve. food industry com., 1953—. Mgmt. trustee health and welfare funds local meat cutters, retail clks. 1953—, chmn., 1965—. Recipient honor award Cleve. Asso. Grocery Mfrs. Reps., 1959, Retail Grocers Assn. Fla., 1967; Grocers Beacon award Shamie Pub. Co., 1968; Nargus Service award, 1972. Mem. Nat. Assn. Retail Grocers (adv. bd. 1956-59), Asparagus Club (pres. 1963-63, scholarship com. 1966-68). Mem. Universalist Church (chmn. trustees). Mason (Shriner). Club: Vermilion (Ohio) Yacht (trustee 1965—, commodore 1965). Home: 13045 W River Rd Columbia Station OH 44028 Office: 4204 Detroit Ave Cleveland OH 44113

HEISER, WALTER CHARLES, librarian, priest; b. Milw., Mar. 16, 1922; s. Walter Matthew and Lauretta Katherine (Kopmeier) H.; A.B., St. Louis U., 1945, A.M., 1947, Ph.L., 1947, S.T.L. 1955; M.S. in L.S., Cath. U. Am., 1959. Joined Soc. Jesus; ordained priest Roman Cath. Ch.; Latin tchr. St. Louis U. High Sch., 1947-50; librarian Divinity Library, St. Louis U., 1955—. Cons. to Cath. supplement Wilson Sr. High Sch. Catalog, 1968—. Mem. Cath. Library Assn., Cath. Theol. Soc. Am. Book review editor Theology Digest, 1963—. Home: 3601 Lindell Blvd St Louis MO 63108 Office: 3655 W Pine Blvd St Louis MO 63108

HEISERMAN, DAVID LEE, educator, author; b. Fostoria, Ohio, July 11, 1940; s. Leland Henry and Maudine E. (Needles) H.; student Ohio State U., 1960-66; m. Judith Ann Hopewell; 1 son, Paul. Research asso., Ohio State U., Columbus, 1965-67; asst. prof. electronics mathematics Franklin U., Columbus, 1968-72; asso. prof. Ohio Inst. Tech., Columbus, 1972—; free lance writer, 1968—; author: Handbook of Small Appliance Troubleshooting and Repair, 1974; Radio Astronomy for the Amateur, 1975; Build Your Own Working Robot, 1976; Handbook of Major Appliance Troubleshooting and Repair, 1977; contbr. articles in field. Served with USN, 1958-60. Republican. Home: 1814 Walden Dr Columbus OH 43229

HEISLER, HAROLD REINHARDT, JR., mgmt. cons.; b. Chgo.; s. Harold Reinhart and Beulah Mary (Schade) H.; B.M.E., U. Ill., 1954. Mgmt. cons. Ill. Power Co., Decatur, 1954—, mem. Nuclear Power Group, Inc., Argonne (Ill.) Nat. Lab., 1955-57; chmn. fossil fuel com., West Central region FPC, Chgo., 1966-68; chmn. evaluation com. Coal Gasification Group, Inc., 1971-75; chmn. Decatur Marine Inc., 1964-66; dir. Indsl. Water Supply Co., Robinson, Ill., 1975-77; pub. speaker in field; mem. Ill. Gov.'s Fuel and Energy Bd., 1970, Ill. Commerce Commn. Fuel and Energy Bd., 1971-75, Ill. Energy Resources Commn. Coal Study Panel, 1976—. Mem. ASME, Nat., Ill. socs. profl. engrs., U. Ill. Alumni Assn., Sigma Phi Delta. Conceptual designer power plant sites and recreational lakes, Baldwin and Clinton, Ill. Home: 1375 W Main St Decatur IL 62522 Office: 500 S 27th St Decatur IL 62525

HEIZER, EDGAR FRANCIS, JR., bus. devel. co. exec.; b. Detroit, Sept. 23, 1929; s. Edgar Francis and Grace Adelia (Smith) H.; m. Molly Bradley Hunt, June 17, 1952; children—Linda Bradley, Molly Hunt, Edgar Francis III; B.S. in Bus. Adminstrn., Northwestern U., 1951; LL.B., Yale U., 1954. Admitted to Ill. bar, 1954; C.P.A., Ill. Auditor, Arthur Andersen & Co., Chgo., 1954-56; staff corporate finance Kidder, Peabody & Co., 1956-58; mgmt. cons. Booz, Allen & Hamilton, 1958-62; staff investments Allstate Ins. Co., 1962-69; chmn., pres., new bus. financier, dir. Heizer Corp., Chgo., 1969—; dir. Amdahl Corp., Sunnyvale, Calif., Computer Consoles, Inc., Rochester, N.Y., Fotomat Corp., Stamford, Conn., Hinde Engring. Co., Highland Park, Ill., IDC Services, Inc., Chgo., ICE, Chgo., Material Services Corp., Elk Grove Village, Ill., Nortec Corp., Santa Clara, Calif., Precision Instruments Co., Santa Clara, Vilcor, Inc., Aspen, Colo., Mem. Nat. advisory com. SBA. Mem. Nat. Venture Capital Assn. (past pres., chmn. bd.), Nat. Assn. Small Bus. Investment Cos. (dir.), Chgo. Soc. Investment Analysts, Delta Upsilon (trustee), Shoreacres Golf Club, Chgo. Curling Club, Econs. Club Chgo., Execs. Club Chgo., Tower Club, Monore Club, Yale Club of N.Y.C. Office: 20 N Wacker Dr Chicago IL 60606

HEJL, JAMES GEORGE, band dir.; b. Caldwell, Tex., Nov. 21, 1939; s. Henry Walter and Annie (Krenek) H.; Mus.B., U. Tex., 1962; Mus.M. (Music Supervision fellow), U. Mich., 1969; m. Patsy Anne Drury, June 8, 1962; children—Sandra, Janice, David. Dir. bands Travis High Sch., Austin, 1962-68; supr. music Eanes Ind. Sch. Dist., Austin, 1969-70; asst. dir. bands U. Tex., Austin, 1970-75; dir. bands Buena Vista Coll., Storm Lake, Iowa, 1975—; cons. to various concert and marching bands. Mem. Tex., Iowa bandmasters assns., Nat. Assn. Coll. Band Dirs., Phi Eta Sigma, Phi Mu Alpha Sinfonia, Kappa Kappa Psi, Pi Kappa Lambda, Phi Beta Mu. Democrat. Presbyterian. Club: Hy-Noon Kiwanis (dir. 1977—) (Storm Lake). Home: 204 W 2d St Storm Lake IA 50588 Office: Buena Vista Coll Storm Lake IA 50588

HELBERG, DAVID STEWART, ophthalmologist; b. Chgo., Sept. 12, 1932; s. Charles and Belle (Mendelsohn) H.; B.A., U. Chgo., 1954, J.D., 1956; M.D., Western Res. U., 1960; m. Barbara Horwitz, June 13, 1954; children—Scott, Pamela, Daniel. Intern, U. Chgo. Hosps., 1960-61, jr. resident, 1961-62, sr. asst. resident, 1962-63; resident Ill. Eye and Ear Infirmary, 1963-64; practice medicine specializing in ophthalmology, Waukegan, Ill., 1964—; mem. staffs Victory Meml., St. Therese hosps., Waukegan, Ill. Diplomate Am. Bd. Ophthalmology. Fellow Am. Acad. Ophthalmology and Otolaryngology; mem. A.M.A., Ill., Lake County (pres. 1975) med. socs., Am., Ill. assns. ophthalmology, Chgo. Ophthal. Soc. Author: Trauma and Disease, 1959. Office: 1702 Washington St Waukegan IL 60085

HELBERG, TERRIE, guidance counselor; b. Chgo., Aug. 3, 1952; d. Joe and Belle (Poremba) H.; B.A., Ohio State U., 1974; postgrad. Loyola U. (Chgo.). Grad. asst. dept. guidance and counseling Sch. Edn., Loyola U., Chgo., 1976-77; fin. cons., publ. relations sec. Old Orchard Bank & Trust Co., Skokie, Ill., 1974-76; facilitator in assertiveness tng. groups and peer counseling groups Greenerfields Continuing End. Center, Northfield, Ill., 1976-77. Vol., Sertoma Vocat. Sch. for Hearing Impaired, Columbus, Ohio, Mem. Am., Ill. personnel and guidance assns. Democrat. Home: 3221 Central Ave Wilmette IL 60091

HELD, ARTHUR HUGO, cons. graphic arts; b. Chgo., Apr. 18, 1913; s. Dr. William and Frances (Cossman) H.; B.S., DePaul U., 1935; m. Harriette Touff, May 29, 1941. Market analyst, 1935; organized own bus. advt. and lithographing Arthur Held, Advt., 1936; sold lithographing bus., retained advt. agency, 1941; active in supervision and mgmt. war prodn. industries since 1941. Dir., Employee Tng. Program, Lithographic Tech. Found. Cons. prodn. sales and mgmt. problems. Trustee Glenbrook San. Dist. Mem. Nat. Rifle Assn. Am., Wilmette Ill., Printer Supplymen's Guild (Chgo.). Club: Honorary mem. Lithographers (Chgo.). Formerly condr. column, pub. by Progressive Syndicate Mags. Author article, Public Relations. Home: 215 Hickory Ct Northbrook IL 60062

HELD, CHARLES HOLBORN, librarian; b. Detroit, Jan. 26, 1929; s. Harold Ernest and A. Irene (Holborn) H.; A.B., Albion Coll., 1950, M.A., 1962; A.M. in L.S., U. Mich., 1952; postgrad. U. Edinburgh (Scotland), 1957; Ph.D., Wayne State U., 1969; m. Nancy J. Graffam, Mar. 25, 1967; children—Heidi, Kirstin. Librarian, tchr. Fordson High Sch., Dearborn, Mich., 1954-63; instr. dept. library sci. Wayne State U., 1963-65; head librarian Albion (Mich.) Coll., 1965—. Asso. prof. library sci. Western Ont. U., 1971. Served with USMCR, 1952-54; maj. AUS Res., 1955—. Mem. Am., Canadian, Mich., Ont. hist. assns., A.L.A., Phi Delta Kappa, Phi Alpha Theta. Rotarian (pres. Albion 1975—). Home: 1155 Rivers Bend Albion MI 49224 Office: Stockwell Meml Library Albion MI 49224

HELFANT, SEYMOUR MEYER, educator; b. N.Y.C., May 8, 1916; s. Henry and Esther (Alterescu) H.; B.S., City Coll. N.Y., 1937; J.D., St. John's U., 1941; M.S., N.Y. U., 1947; m. Thelma Kurinsky Dec. 21, 1947; children—Ronald, Michael, Richard. Co-owner Del Fant Shoes, Far Rockaway, N.Y., 1940-57; mgr. smaller stores div. and specialty stores div. Nat. Retail Mchts. Assn., 1957-68, v.p., mgr. ind. stores div., 1968-69; dir. edn., mgmt. and promotion services, meetings and convs. Internat. Council Shopping Centers, N.Y.C., 1969-77; mem. faculty Columbia (Mo.) Coll., 1977—; lectr. City Coll. N.Y., 1947-73, Bklyn. Coll., 1951-64; mem. N.Y. adv. council for

SBA. Dir. Seminars in Shoe Fitting and Shoe Therapy, Promotion and Mgmt. Seminars; co-dir. Top Mgmt. Seminar. Mem. Am. Mktg. Assn., Am. Soc. for Tng. and Devel., Eta Mu Pi. Club: Masons. Author: Problems of Smaller of Smaller Stores, 1959; Retail Shoe Sales Training Manual, 1960; Operations Manual for Smaller Stores, 2 vols., 1960; The Successful Future of the Independent Retailer, 1960; Profitable Ideas for Smaller Stores, 1961; Increasing Profitability in Today's Retailing, 1963; Training and Motivating Retail Sales People, 1969; Person to Person Selling, 1969; co-author Retail Merchandising and Management with Electronic Data Processing, 1966; Small Store Planning for Growth, pub. 1966; Plan Your Store for Maximum Sales and Profits, 1969. Home: 810A Fairview Rd Columbia MO 65201 Office: Columbia Coll Columbia MO 65201

HELFER, HERMAN HYMAN, glass co. exec.; b. Chgo., Dec. 6, 1919; s. Harry and Sarah (Kurlansky) H.; student Herzl Jr. Coll., 1941; certificate U. Ill. Coll. Pharmacy, 1946; B.S. in Mktg., Roosevelt U., 1973, M.B.A., 1977; m. Frieda Hershkopf, Nov. 16, 1947; children—Joel, Harvey, Gail. With Novelty Glass & Mirror Co., Chgo., 1946—, gen. mgr., sec.-treas., 1960—; pres. Columbia Glass Co., Chgo., 1969—; pres. Energipane Insulating Glass Corp. Instr. Boys State, Springfield, Ill., 1966; chmn. Glazier's Pension and Welfare Funds, Chgo., 1969-73. Served with USAAF, 1943-46. Mem. Am. Legion (post comdr. 1967-68), Assn. Glazing Contractors (pres. 1957-73), Nat. Glass Dealers Assn. (exec. com., pres. elect 1977—, rep. to Consumer Safety Products Commn.), Flat Glass Marketing Assn. (dir.), Nat. Assn. Store Fixture Mfrs. (asso.). Jewish religion (sec., treas. synagogue). Mem. B'nai B'rith. Mason (Shriner). Home: 8937 Forest View Rd Evanston IL 60203 Office: 321 N Pulaski Rd Chicago IL 60624

HELFRICH, ROBERT JAMES, banker; b. St. Louis, July 24, 1948; s. Robert John and Dorothy Agnes (Mc Namara) H.; B.A., St. Benedicts, Coll., 1970; M.B.A., St. Louis U., 1976; postgrad. Grad. Sch. Banking U. Wis., Madison; m. Janet Ruth Niermann, June 1, 1973. With Bank of St. Louis, 1971-73; cashier, asst. v.p., loan dept. supr., investments coordinator Bank of Ladue, St. Louis, 1973—. Mem. Am. Econ. Assn., Bank Adminstrn. Inst., St. Louis Lenders Assn., Am. Inst. Banking, Mo. Bankers Assn., Oceanic Soc. Roman Catholic. Club: Clayton Rugby. Home: 121 Topton Way Clayton MO 63105 Office: 10263 Clayton Rd St Louis MO 63124

HELGELAND, LESTER L., newspaperman; b. Woonsocket, S.D., Nov. 5, 1919; s. S.S. and Anna Florence (Slack) H.; ed. high sch.; m. Irma Rita Olinger, Nov. 27, 1947; children—Patricia, David, Deanna, Mary. Editor, pub. Emery (S.D.) Enterprise, 1945-47; sports editor Mitchell (S.D.) Daily Republic, 1947-53, news service dir., to 1967; exec. editor Yankton (S.D.) Daily Press and Dakotan, 1967—. Chmn. exec. com. vocat. tech. adv. com. U. S.D., Springfield, 1967—; mem. S.D.-Neb. regional com. exec. com., 1967-69, S.D. Regional Med. Program exec. com., 1967-71. Bd. dirs. Yankton Am. Cancer Soc., Black Hills Playhouse, 1975—, Meml. Art Center, S.D. State U., 1977—, S.D. Children's Aid, 1975—. Served with Inf., A.C., AUS, 1942-45. Recipient S.D. 4-H leaders award, 1959, merit award U. S.D. Sch. Bus., 1973, S.D. Future Farmers award, 1963, S.D. State U. Alumni Assn. award, outstanding journalist award S.D. State U., 1964, eminent service award E. River Electric, 1973, Service to Mankind award S.D. Sertoma Club and Yankton Sertoma Club, 1976; named AP Newsman of Yr., 1975. Mem. Am. Legion, V.F.W., Sigma Delta Chi. Elk. Chmn. S.D. Bicentennial Commn., 1970-77. Home: 1003 Mulberry St Yankton SD 57078 Office: Yankton Daily Press and Dakotan 319 Walnut St Yankton SD 57078

HELGESON, DONALD PENFIELD, agr. co. exec.; b. St. Cloud, Dec. 27, 1927; s. Elmer Martin and Mabel Alice (Nelson) H.; B.A., Macalester Coll., 1950; postgrad. U. Minn.; m. Arlene Joan Mittelstadt, Aug. 25, 1950; children—Michael J., Steven D., Scott A., Glen G. Partner, Jack Frost Inc., St. Cloud; dir. Fed. Res. Bank of Mpls., 1975—. Chmn. design and finance St. Cloud Pedestrian Mall, 1971-72. Served with AUS, 1946-47. Mem. Inst. Poultry Industries, Am. Mgmt. Assn., Downtown Assn. (dir. 1973), Minn. Hatchery Assn. (pres. 1955), C. of C. (dir. 1973). Mason. Club: Exchange. Home: North River Rd St Cloud MN 56301 Office: 309 Lincoln St SE St Cloud MN 56301

HELGESON, GERALD DAVID, agr. co. exec.; b. St. Cloud, Minn., Oct. 3, 1933; s. Elmer Martin and Mabel Alice (Nelson) H.; B.A., U. Minn., 1955; m. Ann Peters, Aug. 21, 1954; children—Grant, Kent, Brace, Ginger. Pres., Jack Frost Inc. hatchery, St. Cloud, 1955—; dir., co-owner Met. State Bank of Mpls., Liberty Loan and Thrift, St. Cloud; dir. 1st Am. Nat. Bank, St. Cloud, El Dorado Internat., Inc. Bd. dirs. Govs. Council for Econ. Devel. Mem. Young Pres.'s Orgn. Presbyn. (elder). Elk. Club: St. Cloud Country. Office: 309 Lincoln Ave SE St Cloud MN 56301

HELIE, GILLES AIME, physician; b. Maniwaki, Que., Can., Aug. 9, 1925; s. Oscar and Antoinette (Grignon) H.; B.A., St. Alexander Coll., 1947; M.D., Laval U., 1952; m. Lise Boivin, Sept. 10, 1951; children—Jasmin, Marc, Josee, Michel, Carol, Louise. Intern, Laval U. Hosps., Quebec City, 1951-52; resident Grace Hosp., Detroit, 1952-56; practice medicine specializing in gen. surgery, Sudbury, Ont., Can., 1956—; chief surgery St. Joseph's Hosp., 1958-70, chief staff, 1971—, chief surgery, 1972-73; chief dept. surgery Laurentian Hosp., Sudbury, 1975-77. Bd. regents U. Sudbury, 1969-72. Fellow Royal Coll. Surgeons, A.C.S., Am. Soc. Abdominal Surgeons, Assn. Medecins de Langue Francaise; affiliate Royal Soc. Medicine. Home: 1480 Gennings Dr Sudbury ON Canada Office: 45 Elm St Sudbury ON Canada

HELLAM, LLOYD GEORGE, archtl. cons.; b. Northfield, Minn., Nov. 19, 1923; s. George Robert and Elsie (Johnson) H.; student Dunwoody Inst., 1941-43; m. Sheila Lillian Pauling, Feb. 6, 1946; children—Luann, Pamela, Sandy. Job capt. Irwin E. Engler, Architect, Mpls., 1946-51; archtl. cons. Nat. Gypsum Co., Mpls., 1952, Chgo., 1953-72, Des Plaines, Ill., 1972—. Served with C.E., AUS, 1943-46; ETO. Mem. Constrn. Specification Inst. (dir. Chgo. 1968-70). Moose. Home: 139 Robin Hill Dr Naperville IL 60540 Office: 1400 E Touhy Ave Des Plaines IL 60018

HELLER, GRANT L., neurologist; b. Racine, Wis., Dec. 24, 1930; s. A. Grant and Edythe (Cohen) H.; B.S., Western Reserve U., 1952, M.D., 1956; m. Audrey P. Lecht, Aug. 14, 1954; children—Ronald, Lawrence, Michael, Steven, Brian. Intern, Mt. Sinai Hosp., Cleve., 1956-57; resident in neurology U. Mich. Med. Center, Ann Arbor, 1958-61; practice medicine specializing in neurology, Cleve., 1961—; clin. instr. neurology, Western Reserve U. Served with U.S. Army, 1961-62. Diplomate Am. Bd. Psychiatry and Neurology, Pan-Am. Med. Assn. Fellow A.C.P., Am. Acad. Neurology, Am. Coll. Angiology; mem. U. Mich. Med. Center Alumni Soc. (bd. govs.), Am. Electroencephalographic Soc., Am. Med. EEG Soc., Phi Delta Epsilon nat. treas. Zeta Beta Tau. Contbr. articles in field. Home: 2687 Rochester Rd Shaker Hts OH 44122 Office: 11811 Shaker Blvd Cleveland OH 44120

HELLER, JOHN HENRY, educator; b. Louisville, May 6, 1930; s. Frank Albert and Adeline (Traband) H.; B.S., U. Ky., 1953; M.S., U. Md. (Nat. 4-H fellow), 1960; Dir. Recreation degree, Ind. U., 1969; m. Betty Jane Hamilton, Aug. 25, 1957; children—John Gregory, Bryant Scott, Allison Ann. County extension agt. 4-H, Mich. State U., Port Huron, 1961-63, dist. 4-H field agt. U. Ky., Lexington, 1963-65, state 4-H camping specialist, 1965-70; youth devel. specialist, asso. prof. U. Wis., Madison, 1970—. Mem. nat. task force coms. on camping survey and low-income camps for extension service U.S. Dept. Agr., 1969-70; chmn. nat. 4-H camp com. to rev. trends, programs and facilities, 1976—. Sears & Roebuck human devel. fellow, 1955. Mem. Nat., Wis. assns. extension 4-H agts., Am. (dir. 1976—, chmn. leadership com. 1976), Wis. (dir.) camping assns., Juneau County 4-H Council, Epsilon Sigma Phi. Kiwanian. Presbyn. (deacon 1972—). Home: Route 4 Box 180 Wisconsin Dells WI 53965 Office: 336 Lowell Hall 610 Langdon St Madison WI 53706

HELLER, PHILIP HENRI, physician; b. Des Plaines, Ill., Feb. 6, 1919; s. William Frederick and Magdalene (Henschel) H.; A.B., U. Neb., 1941; M.D. Northwestern U., 1945; m. Ruth Wark, Apr. 28, 1945; children—Jeanne, Philip Henri, Nancy, Patricia, Mary. Intern, St. Lukes Hosp., Chgo., 1944-45; asso. staff St. Francis Hosp., Evanston, Ill., 1946-53; attending staff, staff officer Resurrection Hosp., Chgo., 1952-62, co-dir. family practice residency program, 1978—; attending staff Luth. Gen. Hosp., Park Ridge, Ill., 1959—, v.p., 1970-71, chmn. div. family practice and dir. Family Practice Center and residency program, 1972-77; attending staff Holy Family Hosp., Des Plaines, Ill., 1960-74; asst. prof. Sch. Medicine, U. Ill. Pres., Des Plaines Bd. Health, 1949-63. Served to lt. comdr. USNR, 1945-46, 54-56. Diplomate Am. Bd. Family Practice. Fellow Am. Acad. Family Physicians; mem. Chgo. Med. Soc. (council mem. 1963-71, pres. Irving Park br. 1969-70), Ill. Acad. Family Practice (pres. N. Suburban br. 1959-60), Ill. Med. Soc., AMA, Soc. Tchrs. Family Medicine, Phi Rho Sigma. Congregationalist. Mason. Home: 555 Webford Ave Des Plaines IL 60016 Office: Resurrection Hosp 7435 W Talcott Ave Chicago IL 60631

HELLEWELL, LOUIS PATTERSON, chemist; b. Evanston, Wyo., Nov. 3, 1927; s. Joseph Henry Jr. and Etta Lucille (Patterson) H.; student Brigham Young U., 1947; B.S. in Zoology and Chemistry, U. Wyo., 1950; m. Lorraine Frances Bergren, Aug. 15, 1947; children—Joseph Henry III, Louis Thomas, John R, Judith Lynn, Nancy Anne, Darlene Frances. Tech. trainee Westvaco Chem. Co., Green River, Wyo., 1952-53, process engr., 1953; chem. process shift supr. Intermountain Chem. Co., Green River, 1953-56; asst. to prodn. supt. FMC Corp., 1956-58, sr. chem. process engr., 1958-65, chief chemist, 1965-69; sr. engr. Olin Corp., Baraboo, Wis., 1969-70, sr. project engr., 1970-74, prin. project engr., 1974-75, chief project engr., 1975—; instr. radiol. monitoring/radiation physics Madison Area Tech. Coll., 1970—. Dir., CD, Green River; radiol def. officer, Baraboo, v.p. Jim Bridger council Boy Scouts Am., 1959-63. Named Community Father of Year, 1961. Mem. Am. Assn. Measurements and Control; Sigma Nu, Alpha Epsilon Delta. Mormon. Clubs: Lions Internat. (zone chmn. 1964-65, 72-73), Baraboo Country, Elks. Contbr. articles in field. Baraboo WI

HELLMAN, RICHARD, physician; b. N.Y.C., Jan. 19, 1943; s. Gabriel Michael and Rose (Eventoff) H.; A.B., N.Y. U., 1962; M.D., Chgo. Med. Sch., 1966; m. Sharon Lee Katz, Jan. 28, 1967; 1 dau., Leslie Gayle. Intern, U. Kans. Med. Center, 1966-67, resident in internal medicine and endocrinology, 1967-68, 71-72; asst. prof. medicine U. Mo., Kansas City, 1973-75, asso. prof., 1975—, docent, 1973—; bd. dirs. Prime Health, Kansas City, 1976—; volunteer physician, dir. med. adv. bd. Westport Free Health Clinic, Kansas City, 1972—. Served with USAF, 1968-70. NIH fellow in endocrinology U. Kans., 1972; diplomate Am. Bd. Internal Medicine. Fellow A.C.P.; mem. Am. Diabetes Assn., AAAS. Office: 2411 Holmes St Kansas City MO 64108

HELLYER, ARTHUR LAWRENCE, lawyer, real estate cons.; b. N.Y.C., Oct. 12, 1898; s. Max Edward and Esther (Burroughs) H.; B.A., Tusculum Coll., 1922; LL.B. magnum cum laude, Chgo. Law Sch., 1924; LL.D., St. Joseph's Coll., 1961; m. Irene Mary Connery, Aug. 15, 1921; children—Arthur Lawrence, Irene Hellyer Rodgers, Richard Eugene, Loretta Hellyer Jones. Admitted to Ill. bar, 1925; since practiced in Chgo.; owner Arthur L. Hellyer & Co., Chgo., 1946—; lectr. on real estate, Am. govt. and taxation. Treas., DuPage County, 1934-38, pub. adminstr., 1961-66. Mem. adv. bd. Rosary Coll., River Forest, Ill., 1948-64; trustee St. Joseph's Coll., Rensselaer, Ind., 1950—, chmn., 1966-70; bd. dirs. Ill. Am. Legion Premier Boys State, 1962-69, treas. 1966-69. Served with U.S. Army, World War I; AEF. Recipient Alumni Distinguished Service award Tusculum Coll., 1962. Mem. Chgo. Bar Assn., Chgo. Assn. Commerce and Industry, Chgo. Real Estate Bd., Nat. Assn. Real Estate Bds., Old Timers Baseball Assn., Serra Club Chgo. (trustee 1958-61), Serra Internat. (dist. gov. 1947), Am. Legion (post comdr. 1951, judge adv. dept. Ill. 1948). Address: 111 E Chestnut St Chicago IL 60611

HELM, SHARON MARKS, psychologist; b. Kansas City, Mo., July 26, 1936; d. James Russell and Reva (Luster) Marks; B.A., U. Mo., 1970, M.A., 1974; Ph.D., U. Mo., Kansas City, 1977; children—Shelli, Robin, Terri. Instr. continuing edn. U. Mo., Kansas City, 1973—; dir. Assertive Tng. Inst., Kansas City, 1975—; pvt. practice group, family, individual counseling; cons. in field; mem. faculty Planned Parenthood Jewish Community Center, Johnson County Mental Health Assn. Mem. Profl. Counselors Assn., Internat. Transactional Analysis Assn., Am. Personnel and Guidance Assn., Phi Kappa Phi, Psi Chi, Pi Lambda Theta. Home: 4401 W 94th St Prairie Village KS 66207 Office: 4706 Broadway Kansas City MO 64112

HELMERS, RAYMOND AUGUST HENRY, mag. editor, pub.; b. nr. Percy, Ill., Oct. 5, 1916; s. Herman L. and Mary Pearl (Roberts) H.; student pub. schs.; m. Virginia Thompson, Aug. 16, 1946; children—Raymond August, Ronald Louis. Account exec. Gerald T. LeFever & Assos., Little Rock, 1945-51; sales promotion mgr. Miller Pub. Co., Memphis, 1951-52; mng. editor Furniture Prodn. mag., Nashville, 1952-58; editor Furniture Design Mfg. mag., Chgo., 1958-68, pub., 1968-70, editor, pub., 1970—. Furniture industry mktg. cons., 1966-68; profl. photographer, freelance photo-journalist, 1964—; cons. pub. firm, market research, and chemical co., 1973—. Served with USAAF, 1939-45. Named Polymer Man of the Year, Soc. of Plastics Industry, 1972; entered into Furniture writer's Hall of Fame, Southern Furniture Exposition, NC, 1972. Mem. Forest Products Research Soc. Republican. Contbr. to furniture ency. Home: 124 W Union St Wheaton IL 60187 Office: Suite 2150 222 S Riverside Plaza Chicago IL 60606

HELMICK, KENNETH DALE, counselor; b. Salina, Kans., Sept. 29, 1924; s. Neal and Demaris (Myles) H.; B.A., Kans. Wesleyan U., 1950; M.S., Kans. State U., 1955; Ed.D., Okla. State U., 1968; m. Aileen Barnett, Jan. 26, 1952; children—Ronald, Neal, Bernard, Linda. With Bur. Indian Affairs, Ft. Wingate, N.Mex., 1951-58; guidance dir., Russell, Kans., 1958-60; cons. guidance and testing, Oklahoma City, 1960-65; instr./counselor Okla. State U., 1965-67; counselor, dir. counseling center Central Mo. State U., Warrensburg, 1968—; adj. prof. Eastern Wash. State U., 1970-73, U. N.Y. at Plattesburg, 1973—. Served with arty. AUS, 1943-45; ETO. Decorated Bronze Star. Mem. Mo. Guidance Assn., Am., Mo. psychol. assns., Am. Personnel and Guidance Assn., Phi Delta Kappa. Home: 318 Johnson St Warrensburg MO 64093

HELMKER, JUDITH ANNE, educator; b. Highland Park, Mich., Jan. 22, 1940; d. Theodore Carl and Dorothy Myra (Blitz) Huebner; B.S. in Edn., Central Mich. U., 1961; M.A., Mich. State U., 1968, Ed.S., 1972; m. Lewis James Helmker, Aug. 20, 1960; children—Jon Lewis, Hollie Anne, Shellie Dee. Tchr. phys. edn. Owosso (Mich.) Pub. Schs., 1961—, chmn. paraprofl. com., 1974—, chmn. priority study elementary curriculum council; founder High Sch. Leadership Day Mich., 1965; chmn. Shiawassee (Mich.) Joseph P. Kennedy Spl. Olympics; monitor, instr. ARC; counselor phys. fitness Boy Scouts Am.; sports counselor Girl Guide; bd. dirs. Owosso Area Day Care Center; leader Fair Winds Council Girl Scouts U.S.A.; mem. Adminstrv. bd., children's coordinator, mem. council missions, lay speaker First United Meth. Ch., Owosso; bd. dirs. YMCA, Owosso.; bd. dirs., dir. vols. Owosso Meml. Hosp. Aux. Recipient 10 Yr. service award ARC, 1971; Service award Owosso Meml. Hosp. Aux., 1968. Mem. Am., Mich. (dir., chmn. membership, v.p. phys. edn., pres.) assns. health, phys. edn., recreation, Nat. Mich. edn. assns., Am. Assn. Advancement Control Internat. Biographical Assn., Mich. Girls Athletic Assn. (adviser of Yr. 1965, v.p. 1965;), Saginaw Valley Golf Assn. (rep. assembly), Parent-Tchr. Orgn., Internat. Platform Assn., Mich. Dept. Edn. Referent Group, Delta Psi Kappa. Republican. Clubs: Owosso Country (chmn. golf), Greater Lansing (Mich.) Racquet, Lansing Racquet. Author: Girls' Athletic Associations: Their Organization and Adminstration, 1968; A Manuel of Snowmobiling, 1970; All Terrain Vehicles, 1972; The Autobiography of Pain, 1976; contbr. articles to profl. jours. Home: 2300 Wellington Dr Owosso MI 48867 Office: Owosso Pub Schs W North St Owosso MI 48867

HELMS, JOHN WALKER, consumer products mfg. co. exec.; b. Hattiesburg, Miss., June 21, 1944; s. Jack E. and Nancy Rebecca (Walker) H.; B.A., La. State U., 1966; M.B.A., U. Utah, 1972; m. Linda Helen Lewis, Dec. 9, 1977; children—John Wesley, Rebecca Ann. Product planning mgr. Motorola Inc., Chgo., 1973-75; product mgr. Magnavox Consumer Electronics Co., Ft. Wayne, Ind., 1972-77; new product devel. mgr. Talley Industries, Westclox div., LaSalle, Ill., 1977—. Served with USAF, 1966-73. Decorated Bronze Star. Mem. Am. Mktg. Assn. Home: 208 Bailey Rd Naperville IL 60540 Office: Westclox LaSalle IL 61301

HELMSING, CHARLES HERMAN, ret. bishop; b. Shrewsbury, Mo., Mar. 23, 1908; s. George and Louise (Boschert) H.; ed. St. Louis Prep. Sem., 1922-27, Kenrick Sem., 1927-33; Litt.D. (hon.), Avila Coll., 1962; H.H.D. (hon.), Rockhurst Coll., 1964; LL.D. (hon.), St. Benedict's Coll., Atchison, Kans., 1966. Ordained priest Roman Cath. Ch., 1933; parochial work in parishes St. Liborius, Immaculate Conception, St. Louis Cathedral, 1933-46; prof. religion, history, English, Cathedral Latin Sch., 1934-46; mem. Diocesan Tribunal, 1939; mem. high sch. bd. 1947, asst. supt. high schs. St. Louis Archdiocese, 1936, archdiocesan dir. Soc. for Propagation of Faith, 1947-56, personal sec. and master of ceremonies to Archbishop of St. Louis, 1946; apptd. titular bishop, 1949; consecrated aux. to Archbishop of St. Louis, 1949-56; bishop diocese of Springfield-Cape Girardeau, Mo., 1956-62, Kansas City-St. Joseph, Mo., 1962-77. Mem. secretariat for promotion Christian unity 2d Vatican Ecumenical Council, 1963-76; mem. U.S. Bishops' Commn. for Ecumenical Affairs, 1964-76, chmn., 1969-72; chmn. Spl. Com. for Dialogue with Episcopal Ch. in U.S., 1964-77; chmn. of Catholics, Joint Prep. Commn. for Diologue between Anglican Communion and Roman Cath. Ch., 1966-68; mem. adv. council U.S. Cath. Conf., 1969-72. Decorated Order of Condor (Bolivia). Office: 416 W 16th St Kansas City MO 64105

HELSDINGEN, DANIEL JOHN, advt. agy. exec.; b. Chgo., Aug. 31, 1935; s. Henry Francis and Agnes Catherine (McHugh) H.; B.S. in Commerce, DePaul U., 1957; m. Mary Frances Nicholas, Jan. 25, 1958; children—Patricia, Daniel, Joan, Mary, Thomas. Copywriter, Montgomery Ward, Chgo., 1957-60; asst. mgr. advt. Inland Steel Co., Chgo., 1960-66; nat. ad mgr. Blue Cross Assn., Chgo., 1967; v.p. Edward H. Weiss & Co., Chgo., 1971; became exec. dir. Metropolitan Chgo. Blood Council 1971; now sr. v.p. Lee King & Partners, Inc., Chgo. Chmn. businessmen's task force Ill. Dept. Children and Family Services, 1968-71; trustee Greater Ill. Chpt. Nat. Hemophilia Found., 1976-77. Mem. Blood Banking Task Force (Ill. Dept. Pub. Health), Ill. Assn. Blood Banks, Blue Key, Alpha Chi. Democrat. Roman Catholic. Home: 9021 S Francisco Av Evergreen Park IL 60642 Office: 360 N Michigan Ave Chicago IL 60601

HELSEL, JESS F., metall. co. exec.; b. Deerfield, Ohio, Dec. 22, 1924; s. Jesse A. and Alice Agnes (Bruey) H.; student Kent State U., Akron U., Earlham Coll.; m. Barbara Jene Ebert, Mar. 1, 1947; children—Peter Fredrich, Jessica Jane, Leslie Alison. Supts., Wel-Met Co., Kent, Ohio, 1946-51, plant mgr., Salem, Ind., 1951-55; sales mgr. Ferraloy Co., Salem, 1955-57, pres., 1957-70; gen. mgr. powder metal products div. Gould, Inc., Salem, 1970-73, dir. bus. devel., 1973; pres. Helsel Metall. Co., Campbellsburg, Ind., 1974—, also dir.; pres., dir. Hel-Met, Inc. Mem. Washington County (Ind.) Devel. Council. Served with USMRC, 1942-45. Decorated Purple Heart. Mem. Soc. Automotive Engrs., Soc. Mfg. Engrs., Am. Soc. Metals, Am. Powder Metal Inst., Am. Ordnance Assn., Powder Metallurgy Parts Assn. (pres. 1965-67), Metal Powder Industries Fedn. (pres. 1967-69). Republican. Home: RFD 3 Salem IN 47167 Office: Box 68 State Rd 60W Campbellsburg IN 47108

HELVEY, JERRY L., credit agy. exec.; b. Warsaw, Ind., July 31, 1933; s. B. Leo and Francis W. (Trumbull) H.; B.A., DePauw U., 1955; m. Della R. Phillips, Aug. 7, 1955; children—Lynn A., Jane B. Vice-pres. Joe Mater & Assos., Inc., Warsaw, 1962-66, pres., 1971—; pres. Helvey & Assos., Inc., Warsaw, 1966—; dir. Lake City Bank, Warsaw, Warsaw Ins. Agy., Inc. Pres., Lakeland Community Sch. Corp., 1964-72, Hosp. Authority Kosciusko County, Ind., 1971-74, United Fund Kosciusko County, 1965; mem. Ind. Emergency Med. Services Commn., 1975—; mem. steering com. Kosciusko County Republican Com., 1966—; dir. Oakwood bd. United Meth. Ch., 1976-77. Named Outstanding Young Man of Year for Kosciusko County, Jr. C. of C., 1966; recipient Exec. Achievement award Asso. Credit Bur., 1972, State Leadership award, 1972; Boss of Year award South Bend chpt. Am. Bus. Women's Assn., 1976. Mem. Am. (chmn. nat. legislative council 1972-73), Ind. (Distinguished Service award 1969, dir. 1968-73, 75—, pres. 1977) collectors assns., Asso. Credit Bur. Ind. (pres. 1969-71). Methodist (chmn. task force on camps and confs. 1969-72). Clubs: Masons, Shriners, Kiwanis. Home: Secrist Lake Rural Route 1 Box 533 Leesburg IN 46538 Office: 1015 E Center St Warsaw IN 46580

HEMBROUGH, BETTY LOU, univ. ofcl., counselor; b. Jacksonville, Ill., Oct. 11, 1929; d. Wallace Trabue and Dorothy Lawrnece (Black) Hembrough; A.B., U. Ill., 1951, postgrad., 1953, 61-67; Ed.M., Colo. State U., 1952; postgrad. Washington U., 1960-61, U. Calif. at Los Angeles, 1955. Grad. counselor Colo. State U., 1951-52; head resident counselor, asst. to dean U. Kans., 1953-57; counselor Vocat. Counseling Service of Greater St. Louis, 1957-61;

asst. to dean of women U. Ill. at Urbana, 1961-65, asst. dean student services, 1965—, dir. Office of Women's Resources and Services, 1975—. Mem. edn. com. Ill. Commn. on Status of Women, 1976—; adv. com. on women's studies program Parkland Coll., 1972-75. Mem. Adult Edn. Assn. U.S., Am. Assn. Higher Edn., AAAS, Am. Ednl. Research Assn., AAUW, Am. Personnel and Guidance Assn., Am. Coll. Personnel Assn., Nat. Vocat. Guidance Assn., Nat. Assn. Women Deans, Adminstrs. and Counselors (dir. inst. speakers and cons. 1976—), Nat. Council on Family Relations, Univ. and Coll. Women Ill., Ill. Hist. Soc., Sierra Club, Nat. Wildlife Fedn., Nat. Audubon Soc. Author: (with Miriam A. Shelden) The Student Wife and the Married Woman Student: Their Educational Needs, Desires and Backgrounds, 1964. Editor: Focus on Women: Yesterday, Today and Tomorrow, 1974. Contbr. articles to profl. jours. Home: PO Box 2407 Sta A Champaign IL 61820 Office: 346 Student Services 610 E John St Champaign IL 61820

HEMINOVER, JAMES ARTHUR, veterinarian; b. Waynesville, Mo., May 13, 1944; s. Arthur and Mildred Alma (Davids) H.; D.V.M., Iowa State U., 1973; m. Adela Maria Cijka, May 21, 1966; children—Paul Adam, Pamela Inez, Mark James. Electron microscope technician Nat. Animal Disease Lab., Ames, Iowa, 1964-72, dept. veterinary pathology Iowa State U., 1969-73; student intern Dr. Dale Briley Animal Hosp., Des Moines, 1972-73, veterinarian, 1973-74; pvt. practice veterinary medicine, Des Moines, 1974—; owner, chief veterinarian Kindness Animal Hosp., Des Moines, 1974—; bd. dirs. Animal Rescue League of Iowa, Inc. Served with U.S. Army, 1962-63. Mem. Am. Animal Hosp. Assn., Am., Iowa, Greater Des Moines (pres. 1974) veterinary med. assns. Baptist. Home: 5141 NE 38th St Des Moines IA 50317 Office: 3415 Hubbell Ave Des Moines IA 50317

HEMPE, A(RNOLD) HENRY, lawyer; b. Milw., Mar. 16, 1938; s. Arnold Herman and Marcia (Fleer) H.; B.S., U. Wis., 1962, LL.B., 1965; m. Cornelia Macy Gordon, June 26, 1965; children—Andrew Henry, Amy Heather. Admitted to Wis. bar, 1965; asst. dist. atty. Rock County, Wis., 1965-67, corp. counsel, 1967-72; pres. A. Henry Hempe, S.C., Lawyers, Janesville, 1976—. Mem. Gov.'s Com. on Eminent Domain, 1968; parliamentarian, Rock County Republican Party, 1968-70; mem. rules com. state conv. Republican Party, 1968-69, del., 1967-69, dist. exec., 1967-69, mem. credit com. state conv. 1971; chmn. resolution com. Wis. Fedn. Young Reps., 1969; chmn. Rock County resolutions com., 1969; dir. region VIII Young Rep. Nat. Fedn.; moderator 1st Congregational Ch., Beloit, 1976-77. Served with USMCR, 1961-66. Named Outstanding Young Man of Beloit, 1971-72. Mem. Wis. Assn. County Corp. Counsel (exec. bd. 1968-72, sec.-treas. 1969-70, v.p. 1970-71, pres. 1971-72), State Bar Wis., Am., Rock County, Beloit (v.p. 1972-73) bar assns., Beloit (Wis.) Jr. C. of C. Beloit Booster, 1972. Editor: Wis. Young Republicans, 1968-70; Insight 8 Outlook, 1961-74. Home: 1730 Indian Rd Beloit WI 53511 Office: 13 N Main St Janesville WI 53545

HEMPHILL, MARLIN ROBERT, mortgage banker; b. Tarentum, Pa., Apr. 17, 1916; s. Robert L. and Grace A. (Gillespie) H.; Westminster Coll., 1933-34, U. Pitts., 1940-42; m. Jane E. Best, Sept. 4, 1940; children—Karen E. (Mrs. William A. Pace), Robert M., Denton F. With Allegheny Ludlum Steel Corp., Brackenridge, Pa., 1934-42, asst. sec.-treas. Forging & Casting Corp. 1942-44, works accountant, 1944-50, asst. plant mgr., 1950-54, gen. mgr., 1956-63, gen. mgr. Carmet div., 1954-63, bar products div., Dunkirk, N.Y., 1963-68, asst. to pres., 1968-70; exec. v.p., dir. B.F. Chamberlain Co., 1970—; chmn., treas. Lincoln-Rowe Mortgage Corp.; dir. Novo Indsl. Corp., N.Y.C., Dunkirk Radiator Corp. Pres., S. Oakland County Bd. Realtors, 1975—. Chmn., S. Oakland County YMCA. Mem. Royal Oak (Mich.) Sch. Bd., 1954-63, pres., 1958-63. Trustee Detroit Inst. Tech.; chmn., trustee Oakland County Community Trust. Mem. Engring. Soc. Detroit, Am. Soc. Metals. Am. Soc. Tool Engrs., Nat. Assn. Accountants, Mich. Assn. Realtors (dir.), Dunkirk (dir., pres.), Ferndale (pres.) chambers commerce. Home: 2594 Hounds Chase Rd Troy MI 48098

HENDERLONG, ARTHUR DEAN, agrl. co. exec.; b. Lodi, Ohio, May 19, 1946; s. John Samuel and Selma Marie (Gasser) H.; B.S., Ohio State U., 1969; m. Cynthia Gatti, June 21, 1969; children—Jennifer, Derek Arthur. Salesman, Allied Mills, Inc., Columbus, Ohio, 1969-72, advt. mgr., Chgo., 1972-76, mktg. mgr., 1975—. Served with U.S. Army, 1969-75. Mem. Nat. Agri.-Mktg. Assn. (Achievement award 1974, 75, 76), Alpha Gamma Rho. Republican. Presbyterian. Home: 5851 Chatsworth St Hanover Park IL 60103

HENDERLONG, DONALD EUGENE, rubber products co. exec.; b. Akron, Ohio, Apr. 23, 1930; s. John Samuel and Selma Marie (Gasser) H.; student Miami U., 1948-49; m. Carole Joanne Smith, Sept. 9, 1951; children—Pamela, Deborah, John, Bruce, Dennis. Process engr., gen. foreman Rubbermaid, Wooster, Ohio, 1949-64; foreman Goodrich Rubber Co., Akron, 1964-65; process engr., gen. foreman rubber dept. Sheller Globe Mfg. Co., Chgo., 1965-67; process engr. rubber dept. Brake Parts Co., McHenry, Ill., 1967-73; pres. Don Jon Rubber Co., Inc. (name now Drake Rubber Co., Inc.), McHenry, 1973—; pres. Brake Parts Fed. Credit Union, 1969-73. Trustee Village of McHenry Shores, 1969-76. Served with USAF, 1950-54. Mem. Am. Chem. Soc. (Akron Rubber Group div., Chgo. Rubber Group div.). Home: 502 Amanda Dr McHenry IL 60050 Office: 303 Herbert Rd McHenry IL 60050

HENDERLONG, PAUL ROBERT, agronomist, educator; b. Marshallville, Ohio, Sept. 9, 1937; s. John Samuel and Selma Marie (Gasser) H.; B.S. in Agr., Ohio State U., 1959, M.S., 1961; Ph.D., Va. Poly. Inst. and State U., 1964; m. Mary Ruth Horn, June 8, 1962; children—Jay Paul, Amy Kay, Lisa Ruth. Asst. prof. agronomy W.Va. U., Morgantown, 1964-68; asso. prof. agronomy Ohio State U. and Ohio Agrl. Research and Devel. Center, Columbus, 1968-71, prof., 1971—, chmn. grad. program dept. agronomy, 1977—; vis. prof. pasture agronomy Makerere U., Kampala, Uganda, 1972-73. Mem. Am. Soc. Agronomy, Crop Sci. Soc. Am., Am. Soc. Plant Physiology, Ohio Acad. Sci., Sigma Xi, Gamma Sigma Delta, Delta Theta Sigma, Phi Sigma. Presbyterian (deacon, elder). Asso. editor Agronomy Jour., 1976—. Contbr. articles to profl. publs. Home: 921 Amberly Pl Columbus OH 43220 Office: 1827 Neil Ave Columbus OH 43210

HENDERSHOT, WALTER LEE, ins. co. exec.; b. Belpre, Ohio, Jan. 21, 1930; s. Willie Woodbridge and Bertha Louise (Heintz) H.; B.A., Park Coll., 1973; M.A., Central Mich. U., 1975; m. Patsy Ruth Bridgers, Apr. 6, 1966; children—Ronnald Lee, Janis Lynne, David Michael. Served as enlisted man U.S. Air Force, 1948-68, ret. as master sgt.; supr. City Nat. Bank, Columbus, Ohio, 1968-69; accounting mgr. Educator & Exec. Insurers, Inc., Columbus, 1969-75; dir. accounting JC Penney Casualty Ins. Co., Westerville, Ohio, 1975—; instr. certified profl. sec. courses Nat. Secs. Assn.; mem. vocat. advisory bd. Columbus Pub. Schs., 1974-78. Certified vocat. edn. tchr., Ohio; C.A.M. Mem. Ins. Accounting and Statis. Assn. (pres. Central Ohio chpt. 1975), Adminstrv. Mgmt. Soc. (certification instr., v.p. Columbus chpt. 1978), Office Edn. Assn. (vice chmn. Nat. Bus. Advisory Bd. 1977), Internat. Accountants Soc. Methodist. Club: Kiwanis. Home: 1445 Knollwood Dr E Columbus OH 43227 Office: 800 Brooksedge Blvd Westerville OH 43081

HENDERSON, ALLISON B., physician; b. Orlando, Fla., Oct. 23, 1911; s. Gustavius and Martha (Livingston) H.; B.S., Morehouse Coll., 1933; M.D., Meharry Med. Coll., 1937; m. Bertha George, Nov. 10, 1936. Intern, Cleve. City Hosp., 1937-38, resident, 1938; resident Trinity Hosp., Detroit, 1939-40; practice medicine specializing in insternal medicine, Detroit, 1945—; clin. instr. medicine Wayne U. Med. Sch.; cons. medicine Wayne County Gen. Hosp.; asso. physician Detroit Gen. Hosp. Owner, dir. Dexter Labs. Active YMCA, Boy Scouts Am. Served with AUS, 1941-45. Recipient Laurel Wreath, 1970. Diplomate Am. Bd. Internal Medicine. Fellow A.C.P.; mem. Am. Fedn. Clin. Research, Royal Soc. Medicine (London), Am. Geriatrics Soc., Internat., Am. colls. angiology, Am. Diabetes Assn., Am. Heart Assn., Am. Soc. Hematology, AMA, Detroit Gastroent. Soc., Detroit Physiol. Soc., Wayne County. Detroit med. socs., Internat. Congress Hematology, Internat. Congress of Internal Medicine, AAAS, N.Y. Acad. Sci., Nat. Med. Assn. (editorial bd.), Council for Polit. Edn., Am. Legion, Am. Vets. Com., Booker T. Washington Trade Assn., Alpha Omega Alpha, Kappa Alpha Psi. Contbr. numerous articles to med. jours. Home: 652 Arden Park Detroit MI 48202 Office: 9041 Dexter Blvd Detroit MI 48206

HENDERSON, ARCHIE BOB, coal co. exec.; b. Vienna, Ill., Aug. 22, 1942; s. Everett and Violet (Jackson) H.; J.D., U. Ill., 1966; m. Lynn Anne Keller, Jan. 24, 1964; children—Patricia Anne, Stephen Scott. Admitted to Ill. bar, 1966, U.S. Dist. Ct. Eastern Dist. Ill., 1971; asst. states atty. Saline County, Ill., 1966-69; partner firm Boswell & Henderson Harrisburg, Ill., 1966-69; states atty. Saline County, 1969-72; house counsel Midwest Mortgage Cons., Herrin, Ill., 1972-73; fin. cons., Marion, Ill., 1974; pres., So. Ill. Mining Co., Marion, 1976—; v.p., legal counsel Midwest Mortgage 1972-73. Mem. Ill. Commn. children, 1972-73. Mem. Ill., Am. bar assns., Nat. Dist. Atty. Assn., Phi Alpha Delta. Baptist. Clubs: Young Democrats, Elks. Co-develop econ. method reclamation of coal from coal refuse, 1976. Home: Lomyean Estates Marion IL 62959 Office: PO Box 295 803 E DeYoung Marion IL 62959

HENDERSON, DWIGHT FRANKLIN, educator, univ. dean; b. Austin, Tex., Aug. 14, 1937; s. Ottie Franklin and Leona (Bady) H.; B.A., U. Tex., 1959, M.A., 1961, Ph.D., 1966; m. Connie Chorlton, Dec. 24, 1966; 1 dau., Patricia Ross. Asso. prof. Ind. U., Ft. Wayne, 1966-68, chmn. dept. history, 1968-71, asso. prof. history, 1971—, chmn. arts and scis., 1971-76, dean arts and letters, 1976—. Bd. dirs. Philharmonic Orch., 1973-74, Pub. Transp. Corp., 1975-77. Served with AUS, 1962-64. Tex. Soc. Colonial Dames fellow, 1964-65, 65-66, Ind. U. fellow, 1968, 70, 72. Mem. Orgn. Am. Historians, So. Hist. Assn., Delta Sigma Rho, Phi Alpha Theta. Author: Private Journals of Georgiana Gholson Walker 1963; Courts for a New Nation, 1971. Home: 1730 Kensington Blvd Fort Wayne IN 46805 Office: 2101 Coliseum Blvd E Fort Wayne IN 46805

HENDERSON, EARL WALLACE, JR., architect; b. Mishawaka, Ind., Apr. 5, 1931; s. Earl Wallace and Lida Mae (Gibson) H.; B.Arch., U. Ill., 1954, M.S. in Archtl. Engring., 1959; m. Sally Vicary, June 22, 1957; children—Rebecca, Katherine, Kirstin, Earl Wallace III, Timothy John. Pres Ferry & Henderson Architects, Inc., Springfield, Ill., 1961—; v.p. Springfield Design Center Bldg. Corp., 1965—. Chmn., Hist. Sites Commn., 1967-72; pres. Springfield Central Area Devel. Assn., 1973-74; mem. Auditorium Authority, 1965-69, Springfield Com. for Higher Edn., 1968-69; co-chmn. Capital Bicentennial Commn., 1973-77; chmn. Capital City Plan Commn., 1972-74. Bd. dirs. Ill. Bi-Centennial Commn. Served with C.E., AUS, 1954-56. Mem. AIA (pres. Central Ill. 1966, mem. nat. com. aesthetics 1964-68, nat. com. urban design 1968-71, 73-78), Phi Kappa Sigma. Home: 28 Pinehurst Dr Springfield IL 62704 Office: 1320 S State St Springfield IL 62704

HENDERSON, GEORGE LESLIE, educator, author; b. Brainerd, Minn., Apr. 7, 1925; s. David and Bernice (Froebel) H.; student U. Minn., 1943-44; B.S., U. Ill., 1948, M.Ed., 1954; M.A. for Tchrs., Ind. U., 1966; postgrad U. Chgo., Reed Coll.; m. Miriam Louise Potter. Sept. 1, 1946; children—Larry Wayne, Lee Alan, James Leslie. Tchr. Mansfield, Ill., 1948-51, Toluca, Ill., 1952-55, Dixon, Ill., 1955-59, Moline, Ill., 1960-64; math. dept. head Moline, Ill. Sr. High Sch., 1960-64; math. cons. State Ill. Dept. Pub. Instrn., 1964-66; supr. math. State Wis. Dept. Pub. Instrn., 1966-75; mem. faculty U. Wis., Eau Claire, 1976—. Served with USNR, 1943-46. Mem. Nat. Council Tchrs. Math., Wis. Math. Council. Assn. State Supr. Math. (v.p.). Author: Math. Supervisors Handbook, 1971; The Four Roles of Mathematics, 1971; Let's Play Games in Mathematics, vols. K, 1-7, 1971; Let's Play Games in General Mathematics, 1972; Math Games for Greater Achievement, 1972; Let's Play Games in Metrics, 1973; Math Strikesville, Vols. 3-6, 1975; Introduction to Algebra, 1976; Algebra: A Personalized Approach, 1976; Introduction to Technical Mathematics, 1977; Measure Metric Teachers Guide, 1976; Motor Skills for Kindergarten, 1976; Multidisciplinary Games and Activities for Grades K-3, 1976, for Grades 3-6, 1976; Math Vocabulary Puzzles, Vols. 1-6, 1977. Contbr. articles to profl. jours. Home: 5017 Marathon Dr Madison WI 53705

HENDERSON, GEORGE TRUMBULL, airline exec.; b. Toledo, Ohio, Feb. 4, 1919; s. Clyde C. and Elsie (Norwood) H.; B.S.M.E., Purdue U., 1940; m. Norine Moody, Sept. 20, 1941; children—Larry, Tod, Linda. With United Airlines Inc., Chgo., 1940—, flight mgr., 1955-63, flight operating mgr., 1963-66, dir. flight ops. devel., 1966-77, mgr. B747 ops., 1977—. Dir., Thomas Ford Meml. Library, 1960-66, pres., 1964-66; bd. mem. Community Gen. Meml. Hosp., 1970—; mem. president's council Purdue U. Asso. fellow Am. Inst. of Aero. and Astronautics (chmn. aircraft operations com.); mem. Soc. of Automotive Engrs. (vice-chmn. flight deck com.). Republican. Baptist. Clubs: Masons, Shriners. Home: 208 Briarwood Pass Oak Brook IL 60521 Office: United Airlines Box 66140 Chicago IL 60666

HENDERSON, HAROLD HARRY, mktg. and pub. affairs exec.; b. Atlanta, June 23, 1926; s. Harold and Rose Marie (Sistek) H.; B.S., Valparaiso U., 1950; M.J., Northwestern U., 1952; M.B.A., U. Chgo., 1966; m. Sharon Pavey, July 31, 1954; children—Scott, Todd, Gregg, Brett, Jill, Jeff. Dir. pub. relations YMCA, Chgo., 1952-55; Midwest pub. relations rep. Ford Motor Co., Chgo., 1955-57; mgr. communications Owens-Corning Fiberglas Co., Toledo, 1957-59; v.p., gen. mgr. Burson-Marsteller Asso., Chgo., 1959-62; dir. pub. relations Interlake, Inc., Chgo., 1962-66, dir. pub. relations, advt., civic affairs, 1967-70, v.p. pub. relations and pub. affairs, 1970-74, v.p. mktg. and pub. affairs, 1974—; pub. relations cons. Internat. Harvester Co., Chgo., 1966-67; lectr. on motivation, pvt. enterprise to univs., colls., 1958—; pres. Pub. Relations Clinic of Chgo., 1968-69. Dir., Chgo. Community Ventures, 1972-75, The Tappan Co., 1975—; pres. Persuasion, Inc., Olympia Fields, Ill., 1973—. Served with USNR, 1943-46; PTO. Recipient Service to Youth award YMCA, 1960, award Toledo Community Chest, 1959, various financial relations-communications awards. Mem. Am. Iron and Steel Inst., Pub. Relations Soc. Am., Sigma Delta Chi, Phi Kappa Psi. Clubs: Chicago Headline, Chicago Press, University; Olympia Fields (Ill.) Country. Home: 2841 Chariot Ln Olympia Fields IL 60461 Office: Commerce Plaza 2015 Spring Rd Oakbrook IL 60521

HENDERSON, HOMAN THURMAN, scientist, educator; b. Berea, Ky., Dec. 28, 1932; s. James & Verna (Coontz) H.; Asso. Sci. cum laude, U. Cin., 1954; B.S. in Elec. Engring. and B.S. in Electronic Engring. cum laude, Ind. Inst. Tech., 1958; M.S. in Elec. Engring., So. Meth. U., 1961; postgrad. (NSF grant) Iowa State U., summer 1961, (Ford Found. grant), Mass. Inst. Tech., summer 1963, (NSF faculty fellow 1964); S.M., Harvard, 1967; Ph.D. (So. Meth. U. fellow 1966, NASA traineeship 1966-68), 1968; m. Betty Louise Ross, July 23, 1954; children—Shari Louise, Michael Thurman, Veronica Lynn. Coop. student Gen. Motors Corp. and Westinghouse Corp., Cin. and Dayton, Ohio, 1952-54; machine designer Baldwin-Lima-Hamilton Corp., Hamilton, Ohio, 1954; electronic engr., sr. tech. writer Chance Vought Corp., Dallas, 1958-60; instr. elec. engring. U. Tex. at Arlington, 1960-62, asst. prof., 1962-68; asso. prof. elec. engring. U. Cin., 1968-73, prof., 1973—, mgr. phys. electronics Solid State Electronics Research Labs., 1976, ops. coordinator, 1976-77, dir. grad. studies dept. elec. and computer engring., 1977; indsl. cons. various cos., 1962-78; cons. Nat. Acad. Sci., 1974; dir. research projects solid state electronics, U. Cin., sponsored by NSF, NSAS, Nat. Cash Register, others, 1969-78; bd. sci. advisers KDI Corp.; founding partner Solid State Electronics Research Assos., 1977—; weapons systems engr. LTV Corp., Dallas, summers 1962, 63. Served with AUS, 1954-56. Mem. I.E.E.E. (nat. activities com. 1974-77), Am. Soc. Engring. Edn., Am. Phys. Soc., Am. Cryogenic Soc., N.Y. Acad. Scis., Harvard Grad. Soc., Sigma Xi, Eta Kappa Nu, Tau Beta Pi. Republican. Presbyterian. Club: Harvard (Cin.). Author: (with F.L. Cash) Electrophysical Basis of Materials Science, Electrical Engineering Experiments. Contbr. articles to profl. jours. Home: 3925 Clifton Ave Cincinnati OH 45220

HENDERSON, JEROME D., educator; b. Malone, N.Y., Nov. 19, 1938; s. Robert A. and Charlotte L. (Disque) H.; B.A., Hartwick Coll., 1962; M.A., Temple U., 1964; Ed.D., U. Pitts., 1975; m. Joanne C. Williams, June 20, 1962; children—Kathryn Marie, John Robert, Christopher Daniel, Kevin Lee. Instr. broadcasting Lamar State Coll. Tech., Beaumont, Tex., 1964-65, U. Maine, Orono, 1965-69; asst. prof. Westminster Coll., New Wilmington, Pa., 1969-75, Central Mich. U., Mt. Pleasant, 1975—; involved with various profl. broadcasting activities at several radio stations. Pres., chmn. bd. dirs., U. Maine Employees Credit Union, 1967-69. Mem. Nat. Assn. Ednl. Broadcasters, Broadcast Edn. Assn. (chmn. ednl. materials commn. 1974-76), Mich. Speech Assn. Club: Lions. Developer computer assisted instrn. programs. Home: PO Box 294 Sheperd MI 48883 Office: 342 Moore Hall Central Mich Univ Mt Pleasant MI 48859

HENDERSON, LEONARD LOUIS, research engr.; b. Ordway, Colo., July 9, 1905; s. Leonard Adam and Ellen Wilhelmina (Fritz) H.; student Kans. State U., 1923-25; m. Twila Mae Honfroy, Oct. 8, 1938. Owner Multi-Flow Sales Co., Manhattan, Kans., 1926-33; Vogue Cleaning Co., Springfield, Ohio, 1939-47; pres. 1945-52; pres. Gen. Air Transp. Co., Inc., Springfield, 1946—; pres. Electro-Chem. Research & Engring. Lab., Warren, Ohio, 1952—; cons. in field. Republican. Patentee high speed ignition system, elec. solution control, non-conducting solution moisture meter. Home: 1014 Central Pkwy SE Warren OH 44484 Office: 8137 Market St Warren OH 44484

HENDERSON, MORRIS, health service adminstr.; b. Portageville, Mo., Oct. 31, 1926; s. Dave and Effie (Black) H.; student Stowe Tchrs. Coll., 1944; degree in commerce St. Louis U., 1952, postgrad., 1961-62; postgrad. Am. Coll. Hosp. Adminstrn., 1963; degree in mgmt. Webster Coll., 1977; also seminars; m. Lowell Verniece Battle, Feb. 27, 1947; children—Kenneth Morris, Carlton Eugene. Sales mgr. United Clothing Co., 1950-59; bus. mgr. St. Louis Chronicle Newspaper, 1959-60; with Bank of St. Louis, 1960; adminstr. Peoples Hosp., St. Louis, 1961-66; dir. community involvements Human Devel. Corp., St. Louis, 1966-70; project dir. St. Louis Comprehensive Neighborhood Health Center, Inc., 1970—. Pres. St. Louis County chpt. NAACP, 1955-59, 62-65, past v.p. Mo. conf., mem. nat. nominating com.; mem. County Human Relations Council, 1963; dist. mem. St. Louis area council Boy Scouts Am., after 1960, recipient Certificate of award, 1963; active YMCA, 1955—; mem. St. Louis Mayor's Commn. on Crime; bd. dirs. Ferrier Harris Home for Aged, Inner City Black Athletic Assn., Met. Sickle Cell Anemia Assn., adv. com. Jr. Coll. Dist. Served with AUS, 1945-46. Recipient Distinguished Pub. Service award Mound City Press Club, 1957, Citizen of Year award Radio Sta. KATZ, 1963, certificate award, Jr. C. of C., 1964, numerous citations and Distinguished Service awards. Mem. Nat. Assn. Health Services Execs., Nat. Assn. Neighborhood Health Centers, Hosp. Assn. Met. St. Louis, Peoples Hosp. Assn. (pres. 1959-60), Frontiers, Health Delivery Systems (dir.) Mo. Assn. Social Welfare (dir.), St. Louis Conf. Religion and Race, Am. Pub. Health Assn., Am. Hosp. Assn., United Ch. Men (dir.), Alpha Phi Alpha (life). Baptist (trustee, deacon). Elk, Mason. Contbg. editor St. Louis Am., St. Louis Crusader, St. Louis Argus, People's Guide newspapers, others. Home: 6528 Whitney St St Louis MO 63133 Office: 5471 Dr Martin Luther King Dr St Louis MO 63112

HENDERSON, NORMAN LEE, civil engr.; b. Erie, Pa., Oct. 18, 1925; s. Clyde Samuel and Bessie Ruth (Prindle) H.; B.S., Syracuse U., 1951; m. Dorothy Evelyn Taylor, Nov. 18, 1963; children—Sharon (Mrs. John Bauer), Lorraine (Mrs. Richard Skinner), Susan. Photogrammetrist, U.S. Hydrographic Office, Washington, 1950; stereo operator U.S. Geol. Survey, Arlington, Va., 1951; engr. Ohio Hwy. Dept., Columbus, 1952-56; dir. photogrammetry Photronix, Inc., 1957-60; owner, pres. Henderson Aerial Surveys, Inc., photogrammetric mapping activities, 1960—. Instr. for profl. land surveyors Ohio, 1970—. Bd. dirs. Lake Choctaw Property Owners Assn., 1970-72. Served with USAAF, 1944-46. Registered profl. engr., Ohio, Pa., N.Y., W.Va. Mem. Am. Soc. Photogrammetry (dir.), Ohio Soc. Profl. Engrs. (chpt. v.p.), Legislative Council for Photogrammetry (pres. 1973-74). Republican. Presbyn. Club: Brookside Country. Home: 2800 S Dorchester Rd Columbus OH 43221 Office: 5125 W Broad St Columbus OH 43228

HENDERSON, PAUL TEMPLIN, mech. engr.; b. Chgo., Sept. 20, 1948; s. Harold Charles and Florence Jane (Wilson) H.; B.S. in Mech. Engring., Chgo. Tech. Coll., 1974; m. Bonnie Kip Hiatt, May 4, 1968; 1 dau., Jennifer Diane. Research asst. Materials Research Lab., Inc., Glenwood, Ill., 1968-73; project engr. Allis-Chalmers Corp., Harvey, Ill., 1973—. Vice-chmn. Park Forest (Ill.) All-Am. City Award Task Force, 1977—; bd. dirs. S. Suburban Council on Alcoholism, 1976—. Named Park Forest Jaycee of Year, 1976-77, N.E. Ill. Jaycee of Year, 1976-77, Outstanding Young Man Am., 1977. Mem. ASME, Soc. Automotive Engrs. Club: Park Forest Jaycees (pres. 1977—, dir. 1975-76). Home: 279 Mohawk St Park Forest IL 60466 Office: PO Box 563 Harvey IL 60426

HENDERSON, RONALD SIDNEY, social service adminstr.; b. Indpls., June 13, 1935; s. Charles and Anna Louise (Threet) H.; student Western Mich. U., 1954-55, Wilson Jr. Coll., Chgo., 1958; B.A., Dillard U., 1963; B.A. in Polit. Sci., Tulane U., 1967; postgrad. La. State U., summer, 1968; m. Raljean Haines, June 17, 1960; children—Darryl Keith, Donna, Darri, Dwan. Juvenile counselor Youth Study Center, Dept. of Welfare, New Orleans, 1963-64; research technician dept. of pathology La. State Med. Sch., New Orleans, 1964-65, research asst. dept. of pharmacology, 1965-66; tchr.

L.B. Landry Jr.-Sr. High Schs., New Orleans, 1966-69, also coach basketball and track; exec. dir. Dryades St. Met. Inner-City YMCA, New Orleans, 1969—, cons., 1973—; asst. gen. exec. YMCA of Greater Indpls., 1973—. Dir. Neighborhood Youth Corp. Out-of-Sch. Program, New Orleans, 1969-73; track and field coach So. U., New Orleans, 1970-72. Vice pres. Central City Econ. Opportunity Corp., New Orleans, 1969-70. Mem. leisure recreation com. City of New Orleans Goals to Grow Com., 1969-70, McDonogh Pub. Sch., P.T.A., New Orleans, 1967-73. Mem. mayor's Youth Opportunity Council, New Orleans, 1970-73; mem. spl. com. to evaluate vol. tchrs., Orleans Parish Sch. Bd., City of New Orleans, 1969. Served with USAF, 1954-58. Mem. Assn. Profl. Dirs. YMCA, Nat. YMCA Council (dir. 1972-74), N.A.A.C.P., Alpha Phi Alpha. Mem. Conglist. (Sunday sch. tchr. 1960-62). Home: 8088 Hoover Ln Indianapolis IN 46256 Office: YMCA 222 E Ohio St Indianapolis IN 46204

HENDERSON, WILLIAM STANLEY, JR., banker; b. Waukegan, Ill., May 17, 1933; s. William Stanley and Julia Myrtle (Elmerman) H.; student U. Ill., 1956-59; grad. Sch. for Bank Adminstrn., U. Wis., 1975; m. Knarig Der Hagopian, Sept. 12, 1953; children—Julie Helene, William David. Computer programmer U.S. Govt. Civil Service, Great Lakes, Ill., 1956-59; data processor, sales rep. Nat. Cash Register Co., Chgo., 1959-64; asst. v.p., mgr. data processing Lake Shore Nat. Bank, Chgo., 1964-71; asst. v.p. First Nat. Bank of Lake Forest (Ill.), 1971—; pres. N.Am. NCR Fin. Users Group, 1977-78; lectr. numerous banking groups. Treas., Music Center of Lake County, 1963-65. Served with USAF, 1951-55. Mem. Am. Field Service (v.p. 1968-69), Waukegan Community Players, Tadem Ednl. Soc. Mem. Armenian Apostolic Ch. (chmn. trustees 1966-68). Home: 507 Flossmoor St Waukegan IL 60085 Office: First Nat Bank of Lake Forest Lake Forest IL 60045

HENDRICKS, DONALD RICHARD, arboretum dir.; b. Trenton, N.J., Dec. 31, 1945; s. John Robert and Mildred (Cahall) H.; A.B., Earlham Coll., 1971, diploma in exec. growth, 1975; postgrad. Ball State U.; m. Elaine Gandolph, Mar. 21, 1975. Resident naturalist Hayes Arboretum, Richmond, Ind., 1971-75, asso. dir., 1975-76, dir., 1976—; cons. outdoor labs., environ. edn., starting arboreta. Chmn. Wayne County Multiple Sclerosis Com. Served to capt. U.S. Army, 1966-69; capt. Res. Decorated Bronze Star, Air Medal (2). Mem. Assn. Interpretive Naturalists, Am. Assn. Bot. Gardens and Arboreta, Internat. Soc. Arboriculture, Soc. for Preservation and Use of Resources (ex officio bd.). Quaker. Designer, engr. Ind.'s first solar greenhouse, 1976. Office: Hayes Regional Arboretum 801 Elks Rd Richmond IN 47374

HENDRICKS, GLENN LEROY, distbg. co. exec.; b. Lohrville, Iowa, Dec. 7, 1918; s. Martin Edgar and Cycy Ben (Powers) H.; student pub. schs., Lohrville; m. Irene Josephine Jezek, May 17, 1947; children—Nancy Jo, Scott Ray. With Chader Monarch Co., Des Moines, 1946-56; pres., mgr., owner Central Distbrs. Inc., floor coverings, Des Moines, 1956—. Served as pilot USAF, 1942-46, 51-53. Mem. Nat. Assn. Floor Covering Distbrs., U.S., Des Moines chambers commerce, Nat. Assn. Home Builders, Better Bus. Bur. Republican. Methodist. Clubs: Embassy, Masons (Shriner). Home: 4009 45th St Des Moines IA 50310 Office: 117 College Ave Des Moines IA 50314

HENDRICKSON, DUANE HENRY, realtor; b. Madison, Wis., Apr. 29, 1931; s. Harry E. and Adeline H. (Underdahl) H.; B.B.A., U. Wis., 1956; m. Bonnie L. Byers, Apr. 14, 1958; children—Tanja, Lisa, Leif. Buyer, home furnishings dept. J.L. Hudson Co., Detroit, 1956-59; gen. mgr. Hendrickson's, Inc., Madison, 1959-65; individual practice real estate, Madison, 1965—; faculty mem. Madison Area Tech. Coll., 1971-74. Mem. Madison Bus. and Devel. Commn. 1974-75; mem. exec. com. Dane County Republican Com., 1969, precinct chmn. 1971-73. Served with AUS 1951-53. Mem. Madison Bd. Realtors, Wis. Realtors Assn., Alpha Kappa Psi. Episcopalian. Clubs: Wisconsin Exchange (pres. 1976), Madison Traders (sec.-treas. 1973-75), Four Lakes Yacht, Maple Bluff Country, Elks. Home: 4234 Wanda Pl Madison WI 53711

HENDRICKSON, FRANK SCOTT, dentist; b. Alton, Ill., Jan. 3, 1941; s. Henry Frank and Maxine Katherine (Holliday) H.; student U. Ill., 1959-61, So. Ill. U., 1961-62; D.D.S., Washington U., 1966. Gen. practice dentistry, Granite City, Ill., 1968—. Explorer adviser Cahokia Mounds council Boy Scouts Am., 1971—, now also dist. chmn.; committeeman YMCA, 1972—, United Fund, 1971, 76; mem. Granite City Action Com., 1972—. Served with USNR, 1966-68. Mem. Am. Dental Assn., Madison County, Tri City (pres. 1970-71), Chgo. dental socs., Acad. Gen. Dentistry (Ill. sec. 1975-77, nat. del.), Mo. Bot. Garden, Delta Sigma Delta. Baptist. Club: Optimist (bd. dirs. 1969-71, now youth chmn.). Home: 2967 Madison Ave Granite City IL 62040 Office: 2965 Madison St Granite City IL 62040

HENDRICKSON, MAX SHANNON, elec. engr.; b. Webster City, Iowa, March 20, 1943; s. Aldis Ray and Florence M. (Berkler) H.; B.S.E.E., U. Ariz., 1969. Design engr. E.F. Johnson, Co., Waseca, Minn., 1969-72; design engr. Raven Industries, Sioux Falls, S.D., 1972-75; chief engr. Gerber Electronic, Lock Hugo, Minn., 1975—; sales engr. HC Electronics, Hugo, Minn., 1976—; gen. mgr. Lutronics, Hugo, 1976—; partner Latient Image Photo, Forest Lake, Minn., 1976—; cons. engr. Mitchel & Mitchel, Mpls., 1977—. Mem. St. Paul Amateur Radio Club. Home: 1167 N Shore Dr Forest Lake MN 55025 Office: 15627 Forest Blvd Hugo MN 55038 also 7839 12th Ave S Bloomington MN 55420

HENDRICKSON, T. RICHARD, ednl. adminstr.; b. Brookside, Ky., Nov. 25, 1929; s. Pearl Gilbert and Ora Ruth (Burrell) H.; B.S., Wayne State U., 1961, Ed.Spec., 1974; M.A., Mich. State U., 1965; m. Phyllis Jean Mathews, Dec. 10, 1952; children—Kurt Robert, Melissa Jean. Prin., Oxford Area (Mich.) Community Schs., 1966-68; asst. supt. Novi (Mich.) Community Schs., 1968-72; supt. Williamston (Mich.) Community Schs., 1972-76; tchr. Pontiac (Mich.) Pub. Schs., 1959-63, Waterford Sch. Dist., 1963-66. Pres., Schoolhouse Lake Civic Assn., 1959-61, Greater Waterford Community Council, 1962; dir. Novi Parks and Recreation Commn., 1969-70; charter mem. Waterford Friends of the Library. Active Boy Scouts. Mem. Am., Mich. assns. sch. adminstrs., Mich. Assn. Sch. Bds., Mich. Negotiators Assn., Am. Assn. Curriculum Devel., Mich. Assn. Professions, Mich. Pub. Relations Assn. Baptist. Home: 5094 Shoreline Blvd Waterford MI 48095

HENDRICKSON, THOMAS ATHERTON, lawyer; b. Indpls., May 12, 1927; s. Robert Augustus and Eleanor Riggs (Atherton) H.; B.A., Yale, 1948; LL.B., Ind. U., 1952; m. Sandra Bly Shepard, Feb. 6, 1960; children—Thomas Shepard, Heidi Bly, Melanie Parke. Admitted to Ind. bar, 1952; asso. firm Buschmann, Krieg, DeVault & Alexander, Indpls., 1952-53, Purvis & Hendrickson, 1953-56; dep. prosecutor Marion County, Ind., 1954-57; partner firm. Royse, Travis, Hendrickson & Pantzer, 1956—. Dir. Hamilton Nat. Acceptance Corp.; chmn. Indpls. Bd. Great Books, 1956-57. Dir. Mud Creek Players, Inc., 1962-65; adv. bd. Christamore Aid Soc. Served with USNR, 1945-46. Mem. Am., Ind. (ho. of dels., chmn. group legal services com.), Indpls. (v.p., bd. mgrs. 1972) bar assns. Clubs: Columbia, Indianapolis Sailing Club, Inc. Co-editor: Indianapolis Lawyer, monthly jour. Indpls. Bar Assn., 1969-71. Home: 7979 Lantern Rd Indianapolis IN 46256 Office: 111 Monument Circle 500 Indianapolis IN 46204

HENDRICKSON, WALTER BROOKFIELD, JR., author; b. Indpls., Aug. 24, 1936; s. Walter Brookfield and Marjorie Dorris (Walsh) H.; A.B., Ill. Coll., 1958; postgrad. MacMurray Coll. and U. Ill., 1958-61. Author: Handbook for Space Travelers, 1959; Pioneering in Space, 1961; Reach For the Moon, 1961; The Study of Rockets, Missiles and Space Made Simple, 1963; What's Going on in Space?, 1968; Wild Wings, 1969; Apollo 11: Men to the Moon, 1970; Who Really Invented the Rocket?, 1974; Manned Spacecraft to Mars and Venus, 1975; Illinois: Its People and Culture, 1975; Class G-Zero, 1976; contbr. articles to popular mags. and tech. publs. Mem. Am. Inst. Aeros. and Astronautics, AAAS, Authors Guild, Aviation/Space Writers Assn., Smithsonian Assos., Morgan County Hist. Soc. Democrat. Episcopalian. Club: Rotary Internat. Home and office: 724 W State St Jacksonville IL 62650

HENDRICKSON, WILLIAM CLAIR, architect, engineer; b. Starkweather, N.D., Dec. 9, 1916; s. John Albert and Sena Marie (Ericksted) H.; m. Carolyn Wemett, Dec. 14, 1944; 1 son, Thomas. B.S. in Architecural Engring., N.D. State U., 1941. Registered Structural engr., Minn.; registered architect, Minn., N.D., S.D., Iowa. Jr. engr. CE, USN, 1941-42; comdr. USNR ret.; architect Bettenburg, Townsend, Stolte, Combs, Brainerd, Minn., 1947-55; architect, partner Stegner and Hendrickson, Brainerd, 1955-58 and successor companies, 1958—, offices in Marshall, Minn., 1964—, Edina, Minn., 1975—. Mem. AIA, Minn. Soc. Architects, Nat., Minn. socs. profl. engrs., Am. Concrete Inst., Am. Arbitrators Assn., Minn. Surveyors and Engrs. Soc., Internat. Solar Energy Soc., Sons of Norway, Elks, Lions, Masons, Shriners, Am. Legion, Brainerd Country Club, Sigma Phi Delta. Home: PO Box 732 Brainerd MN 56401 Office: Box 1 Route 11 Brainerd MN 56401

HENDRIX, JACK HALL, judge; b. Orleans, Nebr., Feb. 24, 1922; s. Charles E. and Mary (Hall) H.; B.S. in Edn., U. Nebr., 1947, J.D., 1948; m. Betty L. Parker, Dec. 10, 1943; children—Susan, Lynn, Sally (dec.). Admitted to Nebr. bar, 1948, pvt. practice, Culbertson, Nebr., 1948-49, Trenton, 1949-69; county atty. Hitchcock County, 1949-69; village atty. Trenton, 1949-69, also Stratton; dist. judge 14th Jud. Dist., 1969—. Served to 1st lt. AUS, 1943-46; PTO. Decorated Bronze Star. Mem. Am., Nebr., 14th Jud. Dist. (past pres.) bar assns., C. of C. (pres. 1959), South Platte United Chambers Commerce (pres. 1965-66), Am. Legion, V.F.W., Phi Delta Phi. Mason (dep. grand master), Rotarian (pres. 1954, 71). Home: Trenton NE 69044 Office: Court House McCook NE 69001

HENDRIX, JON RICHARD, educator; b. Passaic, N.J., May 4, 1938; s. William Louis and Velma Lucile (Coleman) H.; B.S., Ind. State U., 1960, M.S., 1963; Ed.D., Ball State U., 1974; m. Janis Ruth Rouhselange, Nov. 24, 1962; children—Margaret Susan, Joann Ruth, Amy Therese. Sci. supr. Sch. Town of Highland, Ind., 1960-71; instr. Ind. U., Gary, 1968-69; asst. prof. biology Ball State U., Muncie, 1972—; cons. State Ind. Dept. Pub. Instrn., 1967-71, Center for Values and Meaning, 1971—; mem. Ind. Sci. Edn. Adv. Bd., Dept. Pub. Instrn., 1967-71. Recipient Outstanding Faculty award in edn. Ind. U. N.W. Campus, 1970, Outstanding Young Educator award Highland Jr. C. of C., 1968; Ball State U. fellow, 1971-73. Mem. Nat. (dir. 1969-71), Ind. (pres. 1968-69) sci. suprs. assns., AAUP, Assn. Supervisors and Curriculum Devel., Nat. Audubon Soc., Nat. Biology Tchrs. Assn., Nat. Sci. Tchrs. Assn. (life), Nat. Soc. Study Edn., Council Elementary Sci. Internat., Central Assn. Coll. Biology Tchrs., Hoosier Assn. Sci. Tchrs. Inc. (dir. 1968-71), Ind. Acad. Sci., Ind. Assn. Tchr. Educators, Ind. Assn. Supervisors and Curriculum Devel., Ind. Biology Tchrs. Assn., Kappa Delta Pi, Phi Delta Kappa. Club:Moose. Author: The Wonder of Somehow, 1974; The Wonder of Someplace, 1974; The Wonder of Sometime, 1974; Becomings: A Parent Guidebook for In-Home Experiences with Nine to Eleven Year Olds, 1974; Becomings: A Clergy Guidebook for Experiences with Nine to Eleven Year Olds and Their Parents, 1974; contbr. articles to profl. jours. Home: 207 Meeks St Muncie IN 47303 Office: Ball State U Biology Dept Muncie IN 47306

HENES, DAVID EDWIN, pub. co. exec.; b. Milw., Feb. 9, 1917; s. Edwin and Alma (Eiring) H.; student Marquette U., 1935-36; B.A., U. Ariz., 1938; m. Kathleen Sullivan, Apr. 18, 1952; children—Susan, Stephen, Peers, Martha. Reporter, Ariz. Daily Star, 1938-39, Tucson Daily Citizen, 1939-40, Milw. Jour., 1940-41, 46-47; mgr. Valley of the Sun Club, tourist promotion orgn., 1947-50; promotion mgr. Phoenix Republic and Gazette, 1950-55, Charlotte Observer, 1955-59; promotion dir. Detroit Free Press, 1959—. Lectr. Am. Press Inst., Columbia. Bd. dirs. Phoenix Desert Bot. Garden, 1952-55, Maricopa County chpt. ARC, Phoenix, 1953-54. Served to 1st lt. AUS, 1942-46. Recipient Silver Shovel award Internat. Newspaper Promotion Assn., 1967. Mem. Mich. chpt. Pub. Relations Soc. Am., Internat. Newspaper Promotion Assn. (pres. 1961-62), Mich. Press Assn. Detroit C. of C., Detroit Advt. Assn. Clubs: Lochmoor, Economic, Adcraft, Detroit Press. Home: 1162 Grayton Rd Grosse Pointe Park MI 48230 Office: 321 Lafayette Detroit MI 48231

HENGEHOLD, LAWRENCE JEROME, data processing exec., univ. ofcl.; b. Cin., Nov. 19, 1939; s. Lawrence Francis and Loretta (Jansing) H.; B.S., So. Ill. U., 1962, M.S., 1968; m. Donna Dale Carman, Dec. 18, 1965; children—Julie Ann, Christina Marie. With computer services dept. So. Ill. U., Carbondale, 1963—, asst. mgr., data processing, 1963-69, coordinator mgmt. systems, 1969-75, asst. dir. computing services, 1975—, lectr. Sch. Bus., 1969-71, asst. prof. Sch. Tech. Careers, 1975—. Mem. Data Processing Mgmt. Assn. (chpt. pres. 1966-67). Home: 1811 W Freeman St Carbondale IL 62901 Office: So Ill U Computing Services Carbondale IL 62901

HENGES, RONALD EDWARD, mfg. co. exec.; b. St. Louis, Oct. 13, 1932; s. J. Gordon and Vera O. (Melsheimer) H.; B.A., Vanderbilt U., 1954; m. Anne Sterry, Sept. 18, 1954; children—Michael, Carolyn, Lawrence. Pres., Keene Corp. Porta-Fab. div., Henges Assos.; v.p. Creve Coeur Camera Co., St. Louis; dir. Constrn. and Mining Services; chmn. bd. Mark Twain Chesterfield Bank. Vice pres. Good Shepherd Sch. for Children; bd. dirs. Parkway Youth Center; chmn. bd. Maryville Coll.; bd. dirs. Nat. Museum of Transport; alderman, City Creve Coeur, 1971-73; dir. Civil Defense, 1965-75. Served with U.S. Army, 1955-57. Mem. Young Pres. Orgn. Clubs: Univ., Media, Mason, Shriner. Home: 13398 Conway Rd St Louis MO 63141 Office: 2319 Grissom Dr St Louis MO 63141

HENKEN, WILLARD JOHN, univ. dean; b. Waupun, Wis., Aug. 15, 1927; s. John Gerrit and Emma Amelia (Korth) H.; B.S., U. Wis., Oshkosh, 1951; M.S., U. Wis.-Madison, 1958, Ph.D., 1966; m. Dolores Ebert, Aug. 26, 1949; children—Thomas, Susan, Richard. Tchr. Cedarburg (Wis.) High Sch., 1951-56; prin., 1956-62; supt. Am. Internat. Sch., New Delhi, India, 1962-64; adminstrv. asst. Sch. Edn., U. Wis., Madison, 1964-66; dean U. Wis. Center, Fond du Lac, 1966—. Chmn. Fond du Lac County Bicentennial Com. Bd. dirs. Fond du Lac County Health Resource Com. Served with USNR, 1945. Mem. Am. Assn. Sch. Adminstrs., U. Wis.-Madison Alumni Assn., U. Wis.-Oshkosh Alumni Assn., Phi Delta Kappa. Home: 736 Nakoma Ave Fond du Lac WI 54935

HENKES, ROBERT JOHN, educator; b. Racine, Wis., Oct. 28, 1922; s. Peter John and Veronica Anatasia (Itsenheiser) H.; B.F.A., Drake U., 1948; M.F.A., U. Wis., 1951; m. Frances Malarney, Apr. 21, 1957; children—Catherine, Anne, Susan, Jane. Art instr. Decorah (Ia.) Pub. Schs., 1948-49, Portage (Ind.) Pub. Schs., 1950-51, 72—; art cons. Kalamazoo Pub. Schs., 1951-65; prof. art Nazareth Coll., Kalamazoo, 1965-72. Art dir. Barbour Hall Mil. Acad., 1965-72; dir. drawing Kalamazoo Inst. Arts, 1958—; dir. Kalamazoo County Children-Parent Workshops, 1965-72; mem. State Mich. Arts Council, 1965-72. Recipient Art award State of Iowa, 1949; Western Art award State Mich., 1957. Mem. Nat., Mich. art edn. assns., Western Arts Assn., Delta Phi Delta. Author: Orientation to Drawing and Painting, 1965; Notes on Art and Art Education, 1969; Eight American Women Painters, 1977. Contbr. articles to profl. jours. Home: 1124 Bretton Dr Kalamazoo MI 49007

HENKIN, PAUL HENRY, educator; b. Los Angeles, Apr. 29, 1940; s. Ahraham Asher and Isabel Valentine (Strauss) H.; A.B., U. So. Calif., 1963; M.A., Washington U., 1971; Ph.D., St. Louis U., 1976. Rehab. coordinator Los Angeles County Dept. Pub. Social Services, 1968; counselor, sch. psychologist Northwest Sch. Dist., Jefferson County, Mo., 1971-72; coordinator Reading and Learning Disabilities Clinic Cemrel, Inc., St. Louis, 1973; coordiantor spl. edn. program Ill. State Community Coll., E. St. Louis, 1974—; cons. Southwest Ill. Regional Spl. Edn. Assn., spl. edn., dists., E. St. Louis. Recipient Howard Paul Wilson Interfaith award, 1963. Mem. Am. Psychol. Assn., Nat. Assn. Sch. Psychologists, Council Exceptional Children, Ill. Psychol. Assn., Midwestern Assn. Behavioral Analysis, Phi Delta Kappa. Democrat. Home: 2257 Summerhouse Dr St Louis MO 63141 Office: 417 Missouri Ave East St Louis MO 62201

HENLEY, FRED LOUIS, state justice; b. Caruthersville, Mo., Oct. 25, 1911; s. Louis Moreau and Dottye Gray (Call) H.; LL.B., Cumberland U., 1934; m. Bernice Chilton, Aug. 3, 1939; children—Sally Kate (Mrs. Gerald Sisson), Lynda (Mrs. James C. Walters), Karen (Mrs. Michael E. Kettler), Joseph. Admitted to Mo. bar, 1935, also U.S. Supreme Ct.; gen. practice, Caruthersville, 1936-64; judge 38th Jud. Circuit Mo., 1955-60; judge Supreme Ct. Mo., 1964—. Chmn. Mo. Hwy. Commn., 1961-64. Served with USAAF, 1942-46; mem. Res. Mem. Am. Bar Assn., Mo. Bar. Mason (Shriner). Home: 1301 Dixon Dr Jefferson City MO 65101 Office: Supreme Ct Bldg Jefferson City MO 65101

HENLINE, FLORENCE, pianist; b. Ft. Wayne, Ind.; d. Samuel and Caroline Dorothy (Mollet) Henline; B.M., Chgo. Musical Coll., 1928; m. Milson Jezek, Sept. 2, 1936. Made first concert appearance at age of 13; appeared with Ill. Symphony and Grant Park Orchs., Chgo. Women's Symphony (ofcl. pianist); accompanist; staff pianist, NBC network, 1930-32; pianist, soloist Chgo. Symphony String Ensemble, 1946-56, Chgo. Pops Symphonette; solo concert engagements in Chgo. and throughout U.S.; soloist Indpls. Symphony String Ensemble, 1970; artist faculty mem. Chgo. Conservatory Coll., 1959—. Judge piano solo contest auditions 35th Ann. Chicagoland Music Festival, 1964, soloists Ann. Young Judea Symphony Orch., 1965, 67. Fellow Internat. Inst. Arts and Letters (life); mem. Chgo. Artists Assn., Lake View Mus. Soc., Musicians' Club of Women, Alliance Francaise (Chgo.), Ill. Opera Guild, Art Inst. Chgo., Mu Phi Epsilon (soloist internat. conv. 1972). Club: Cordon. Home: 9715 S Vanderpoel Ave Chicago IL 60643

HENN, JACK, med. services co. exec.; b. Phila., Sept. 7, 1933; s. William Frederick and Jane Estelle (Ritter) H.; B.S. in Chem. Engring., Princeton U., 1955; M.B.A., Harvard Bus. Sch., 1966; m. Eleanor Ann Shute, Sept. 10, 1955; children—Joan Elizabeth, John Stuart, Karen Louise. Trainee, Scott Paper Co., Chester, Pa., 1955-56; devel. engr. Rohm & Haas Co., Phila., 1959-60, mfg. mgr., 1960-62, salesman, 1962-64; cons., asso. Booz Allen & Hamilton, N.Y.C., 1966-69; v.p. Triangle Corp., N.Y.C., 1969-70; venture mgr. Olin Corp., Stamford, Conn., 1970-71, gen. mgr. consumer products, 1971-76; pres. Telemed Corp., Hoffman Estates, Ill., 1976—. Mem. evangelism commn. Episcopal Diocese of Chgo., 1977—. Served with USN, 1956-59, 63-64. Mem. Health Industry Mfrs. Assn., Princeton Alumni Council (exec. com.). Author: An Electronic Cash and Credit System, 1966. Home: 1380 Lake Shore Dr S Barrington IL 60010 Office: 2345 Pembroke Ave Hoffman Estates IL 60195

HENN, MARY J., physician, educator; b. Fargo, N.D., Jan. 4, 1919; d. Joseph L. and Myrtle (Davenport) Henn; A.B., U. Nebr., 1940, M.D., 1950; M.S., U. Minn., 1944. Intern Research and Ednl. Hosps., U. Ill., 1950-51; fellow Mayo Clinic, Rochester, Minn., 1951-54; asso. prof. internal medicine U. Nebr., 1954-69, prof., 1969—, also asst. dean student affairs. Mem. health council United Community Services, 1958-59; mem. Gov.'s Commn, Status of Women. Bd. dirs. Nebr. Arthritis and Rheumatism Found.; trustee Nebr. Multiple Sclerosis Soc. Diplomate Am. Bd. Internal Medicine. Fellow A.C.P.; mem. Am. Fedn. for Clin. Research. Pan Am. Med. Assn., Am., Nebr. (dir.) diabetes assns., Assn. Am. Med. Colls., Sigma Xi, Delta Delta Delta, Alpha Omega Alpha. Republican. Roman Catholic. Club: Altrusa. Home: 6230 Glenwood Rd Omaha NE 68132 Office: U Nebr Hosp 42d and Dewey Sts Omaha NE 68105

HENN, ROGER EMERSON, pub. adminstrn. exec.; b. Ouray, Colo., Aug. 5, 1917; s. Frank E. and Stella (LaRoche) H.; B.A., U. Denver, 1940; m. Angie Chapman, June 27, 1942; children—Frank Chapman, Patricia Ann, Roger Alan. Statistician, Bur. Census, Washington, 1940-46; field rep. Taxpayers Fedn. of Ill., 1946; exec. sec., Civic League of DuPage County, 1947-49; dir. research Taxpayers Fedn. Ill., 1950-57; chief of staff, appropriations com., Ill. Ho. Reps., 1951, 1953; dir. Ill. Legislative Audit Commn., 1957-59; dir. pub. affairs Union League Club, Chgo., 1959—; exec. sec. Com. on Cts. and Justice. Served with USAAF, 1942-45. Mem. Forward Illinois, Inc. (pres.), Am. Soc. Pub. Adminstrs., Govt. Research Assn., Nat. Municipal League, Chgo. Corral of Westerners (sheriff), Chgo. Mus. Natural History, Newberry Library, Ill., Colo., Ouray, Colo. hist. socs. Club: Union League. Author books mag. articles. Home: 3117 Sprucewood St Wilmette IL 60091 also Ouray CO 81427 Office: 65 W Jackson Blvd Chicago IL 60604

HENNEBERRY, JOHN THOMAS, retail mktg. exec.; b. Chgo., May 12, 1929; s. John Joseph and Catherine Mary (Duffy) H.; student St. Bede Coll., 1948-49, Loyola U., Chgo., 1949-51; m. Nancy May Brown, Sept. 19, 1953; children—John Thomas, Maartin J., Scott M., Ellen M., Catherine M. With Sears, Roebuck & Co., 1953-65, merchandise mgr., St. Joseph, Mo., 1961-63, operating mgr., Grand Island, Nebr., 1963-65; auto center mgr. Montgomery Ward & Co., Harvey, Ill., 1965-66, operating mgr. Waukegan, Ill., 1966-68, merchandise mgr., Evergreen Park, Ill., 1968-69; gen. mgr., dir. store mktg. Farm Stores FS Services, Inc., Bloomington, Ill., 1970—. Active Boy Scouts Am., 1962, 65; com. chmn. Grand Island United Fund, 1964. Served with U.S. Army, 1951-53. Mem. Am. Mktg. Assn. (pres.-chmn. bd. Central Ill. chpt. 1976-77), Bloomington-Normal Advt. and Mktg. Club (pres.-chmn. bd. 1976-77). Roman Catholic. Clubs: Ill. State U. Varsity, Ill. State U. Golf League, Four Seasons, FS Bridge, TWA Ambassadors, Elks. Home: 1 Ridgewood Terr Bloomington IL 61701 Office: 1701 Towande Ave Bloomington IL 61701

HENNEY, ROBERT LEE, assn. exec.; b. Auburn, Ind., Oct. 16, 1933; s. George Kenneth and May (Worble) H.; A.B., Drury Coll., 1955; postgrad. U. Chgo., 1955-57; B.D., Christian Theol. Sem., 1959; M.A., Butler U., 1959; Ph.D., Ind. U., 1964; m. Caroline A. Richards, June 17, 1956; children—Philip L., Linda K. Ordained to ministry, 1954; minister Banquo Christian Ch., 1956-58, Bloomfield Christian Ch., 1958-62, Mountain Grove Christian Ch., 1962-63; dir. literacy edn. Dept. Corrections, State Ind., 1963-64; dir. adult and literacy edn. Bd. Fundamental Edn., Indpls., 1964-68; exec. v.p. Econ. Manpower Corp., N.Y.C., 1968-76; pres. Ednl. Diagnostic Services, Inc., 1975—; dir. EMC Inst., Inc., 1976—. Scoutmaster, Boy Scouts Am., 1945-65; organizer Little League Baseball League, 1957-59. Named Outstanding Young Educator, Jr. C. of C., 1964. Mem. Adult Edn. Assn. U.S.A., Am. Correctional Assn., Am. Soc. Tng. Dirs. Author: Systems for Success, Book 1 and 2, 1964; Systems 3—English, 1974; Systems 3—Mathematics, 1974; Systems 3—Literature, 1975; Systems 3—Science, 1975; Systems 3—Social Studies, 1975; Diagnostic Skill Level Inventories, 1976; The Basic Education Skills Program, 1977. Editor: Educational Facilitators APL Series, 1977. Home: 3903 Bloomingdale St Valparaiso IN 46383

HENNIG, FRANK EDWARD, transp. co. exec.; b. Highland Park, Ill., Aug. 22, 1931; s. William Joseph and Marie (Carlsen) H.; student Northwestern U., 1952-54; B.A., Ariz. State U., 1962; m. Jane Smithson, Sept. 4, 1976. Fin. analyst Dun & Bradstreet, Chgo., 1954-56; bus. mgr. John C. Allen & Sons, Inc., Hinsdale, Ill., 1957-60; controller Itofca, Inc., Clarendon Hills, Ill., 1962-67, v.p. fin., 1968-73, v.p. adminstrn., 1974, v.p. ops., 1975, pres., chief exec. officer, 1976—; dir. Bank of Clarendon Hills, Salt Creek Corp., Hinsdale. Served with USAF, 1950-52: Korea. Mem. Am. Soc. Traffic and Transp., Newcomen Soc. N.Am., Chi Psi. Episcopalian. Clubs: Oak Brook Polo (Ill.); Butler Nat. Golf (Oak Brook, Ill.); Executives, Northwestern U. (Chgo.). Home: 308 Harris Ave Clarendon Hills IL 60514 Office: 2 Walker Ave Clarendon Hills IL 60514

HENNIGAR, LEWIS ALBRO, psychologist; b. Rumford Falls, Maine, July 12, 1908; s. Albro and Rae (Anderson) H.; B.A., Acadia U., 1930; B.D., Andover Newton Theol. Sem., 1933, S.T.M., 1943; Ph.D., Hartford Sem., 1949; postgrad. Purdue U., 1962-63; m. Nettie Mae Hennigar, May 20, 1930; children—Evelyn Mae Hennigar Fairn, Margaret Louise Hennigar Klein. Vis. lectr. Andover Newton Theol. Sch., 1944-48; prof. psychology, chmn. depts. psychology and philosophy Anderson (Ind.) Coll., 1949-74, dir. psychol. clinic, 1949-63; clin. psychologist VA, 1963-68; cons. Anderson Pub. Schs., 1952-55; pvt. practice clin. psychology, Anderson, 1974—. Mem. Ind. Philos. Assn., Am., Midwest psychol. assns. Republican. Baptist. Club: Rotary. Home: 227 7th St W Anderson IN 46016 Office: 222 W 7th St Anderson IN 46016

HENNIGER, BERNARD ROBERT, geologist, educator; b. Zanesville, Ohio, Sept. 8, 1934; s. Bernard Otto and Mildred Helen (Geddes) H.; B.S., Marietta Coll., 1956; M.S. (Ben Weeks scholar), Miami U. at Oxford, 1964; Ph.D., W.Va. U., 1971; m. Marilyn Joyce Lorey, Aug. 6, 1966; 1 dau., Rachele Rene. Exploration geologist Texaco, Inc., Farmington, N.M., 1963-65; geologist U.S. Bur. Mines, Morgantown, W.Va., 1966—; asst. prof. geology W.Va. U., Morgantown, 1968-70; asso. prof. Ashland (Ohio) Coll., 1970—. Cons., 1973—. Served with AUS, 1957-59. Recipient Outstanding Educator award, 1974. Quaker State research grantee, 1965-66. Mem. Geol. Soc. Am., Nat. Geog. Soc., Am. Assn. Petroleum Geologists, Ohio Acad. Sci., Paleontol. Soc., Farmington Geol. Soc., Sigma Xi, Sigma Gamma Epsilon. Mason, K.P. Clubs: Gusher, Rockhounds. Author: Exercises in the Earth Sciences, 1973. Home: 1903 Patricia Ln Ashland OH 44805 Office: Dept Earth Scis Ashland Coll Ashland OH 44805

HENNING, FAY MARIE, ednl. adminstr.; b. Eau Claire, Wis., June 25, 1942; d. Bernard Thomas and Mildred Ione (Strobel) Henning; B.A., Luther Coll., Decorah, Iowa, 1964; M.A., U. Iowa, 1969. Tchr. Spanish, Davenport (Iowa) pub. schs., 1964-69; counselor Slaton (Tex.) pub. schs., 1969-71; social worker, counselor Met. Sch. Dist. Washington Twp., Indpls., 1971-73; dir. edn. and tng. Community Addiction Services Agy., Inc., Indpls., 1973—; co-owner, incorporator The Woman's Touch, Inc., Indpls., 1976—; chmn. Ind. Task Force Certification Substance Abuse Workers, 1976-77; mem. addictions task force Central Ind. Health Systems Agy., 1974—; cons. trainer substance abuse programs, 1975—. Mem. community adv. com. Fairbanks Hosp.; adv. com. Citizens Helping Our Indpls. Children's Edn., 1976—; mem. Westlane Community Sch. Human Relations Task Force, 1971-73. Mem. Am., Ind. personnel and guidance assns., Assn. Counselor Edn. and Supervision, Nat. Women's Polit. Caucus, Common Cause. Home: 2943 N Centennial St Indianapolis IN 46222 Office: 140 E 36th St Indianapolis IN 46205

HENNING, HAROLD WALTER, dentist; b. Lockport, N.Y., Feb. 25, 1919; s. Harold Walter and Erna (Kandt) H.; B.A., North Central Coll., 1941; D.D.S. cum laude, Chgo. Coll. Dental Surgery, 1949; postgrad. U. Ill., Ohio State U. Tchr. zoology, physics, gen. sci., Roseville, Ill., 1941-42. Gen. practice dentistry, Naperville, Ill., 1949—. Amateur coach North Central Coll., Naperville, 1948-62; tchr. swimming, speaker behalf amateur athletics. Mem. Sch. Bd. Naperville, 1954-59. Bd. govs. Nat. Amateur Athletic Union, 1954—, fgn. relations com., 1954—, pres. Central Assn., 1965-66, chmn. U.S. men's swimming com., 1959-65; bd. dirs. U.S. Olympic Com., 1969—, exec. com., 1972-76, chmn. swimming com., 1959-65; organizing com. Pan Am. Games, Chgo., 1959, dir. aquatic competition, 1959; sec.-treas. Amateur Swimming Union of Americas, 1963-71, pres., 1971-75; del. Fedn. Internationale Natation Amateur, 1964—, hon. sec., 1968-72, pres., 1972-76; chmn. exec. com. Olympic Men's and Women's Swimming Trials, 1972, dir. Olympic Games, charge swimming, diving and water polo events, 1972; mgr. U.S. Olympic Swimming Team, Tokyo, 1964, U.S. Pan Am. Team, Mexico, 1955; coach mgr. U.S. Teams to Quatemala and Japan, 1954-62; ofcl. or referree at various internat. games, 1952-68; pres. World Swimming Championships, 1973, 75. Served with USNR, 1942-45. Decorated 1st Order Sports (Egypt); recipient award Internat. Amateur Athlete, 1964; named to Helms Hall of Fame, 1964; Ill. athletic medallion Gov. Ill., 1968; citation and gold medallion Republic of China, 1976; R. Max Ritter medallion, 1976; FINA prize Eminence award, 1976. Fellow Internat. Coll. Dentists; mem. Am., Ill. dental assns., West Suburban and Far West Study Clubs, Fedn. Dentaire Internationale, Acad. Gen. Dentistry. Mason (32 deg.), Lion, Rotarian. Home: Walnut Woods S Julian St Naperville IL 60540 Office: 555 N Washington St Naperville IL 60540

HENNINGS, ROBERT EDWARD, historian; b. Evanston, Ill., Aug. 4, 1925; s. Abraham James and Mervyna Barbara (Dolsen) H.; A.B., Oberlin (Ohio) Coll., 1950; M.A., U. Calif., Berkeley, 1956, Ph.D., 1961; m. Nancy Harriet Wensley, July 21, 1949; children— Deirdre Ellen, Robert Edward, Joseph Turner. Tchr. social studies and English pub. high schs. in Calif. and Ohio, 1953-56; instr. Am. history U. Ky., Lexington, 1961-62; mem. faculty Eastern Ill. U., Charleston, 1962—, prof. history, 1973—, chmn. dept., 1974—; chmn. council faculties to bd. govs. State Colls. and Univs. Ill., 1970-72. Pres., bd. dirs. Charleston Community Theatre, 1972-75. Served with AUS, 1944-46. Mem. AAUP (past chpt. pres.), Am. Assn. State and Local History, Am. Hist. Assn., Coles County, Ill., So. hist. socs., Nat. Trust Historic Preservation, Orgn. Am. Historians. Democrat. Contbr. profl. jours. Home: Bird Hill Route 4 Charleston IL 61920 Office: Dept History Eastern Ill Univ Charleston IL 61920

HENNINGS, THOMAS ARTHUR, restaurant chain exec.; b. Cleve., Jan. 26, 1946; s. Eugene George and Florence Ruth (Helwig) H.; B.S. magna cum laude in Mktg., Bowling Green State U., 1968; m. Melody L. Flood, Sept. 2, 1967; children—Thomas Michael, Traci Lyn. Mem. data processing sales staff IBM, Cleve., 1968; key account salesman Charles Pfizer Inc., Cleve., 1969-70; pres. Piccadilly Parlay Inc., 1970—, Piccadilly Properties Inc., 1973—, and Friar Tucks Party Docks Inc., North Olmsted, Ohio, 1972—, also dir.; dir. S & D Advt. Inc. Ohio Masonic scholar, 1965; Sidney Frohman scholar, 1966; Nat. Food Mktg. scholar, 1967; Sales and Mktg. Execs. scholar, 1968; hon. gov. State of Ohio. Mem. Nat. Restaurant Assn., Phi Eta Sigma, Omicron Delta Kappa, Beta Gamma Sigma, Theta Chi. Lutheran. Clubs: Avon Oaks Country (Ohio); Riverbend Country (Tequesta, Fla.). Home: 31104 Roxbury Park Dr Bay Village OH 44140 Office: 26697 Brookpark Rd North Olmsted OH 44070

HENNIS, HENRY EMIL, research chemist; b. Madelia, Minn., Oct. 23, 1925; s. John Henry and Frieda (Boelter) H.; B.Chemistry, U. Minn., 1950; Ph.D., U. Mo., 1956; indsl. sabbatical U. Munich (Germany), 1968; m. Marian Elizabeth Lovett, Sept. 5, 1951; 1 son, John David (dec.). Grad. asst. U. Mo., Columbia, 1951, 53; asst. instr., 1954-56; research chemist The Dow Chem. Co., Midland, Mich., 1956-57, project leader, 1957-64, group leader, 1964-71, asso. scientist, 1971—. Instr. chemistry Central Mich. U., Mt. Pleasant, 1966-70. Served with USNR, 1943-45, USAF, 1951-53. Mem. Am. Chem. Soc., Research Soc. Am., Luth. Acad. for Scholarship, N.Y. Acad. Scis. Lutheran. Contbr. articles to profl. jours. Patentee in field. Home: 4959 W Baker Rd RFD 3 Coleman MI 48618 Office: 2040 Dow Center Dow Chem Co Midland MI 48640

HENRICHS, HAROLD GARTH, editor; b. Bunker Hill, Ill., Mar. 27, 1903; s. Henry Frederick and Ethel Winifred (Masters) H.; B.A., Eureka Coll., 1925; m. Madge Aurelia Coleman, June 7, 1928; children—Larry L., Carolann (Mrs. Ronald E. Prast). Gen. mgr., dir., pres. Henry F. Henrichs Publs., Inc., Litchfield, Ill., 1940—. Chmn. Litchfield United Fund, 1968; co-chmn. Litchfield Centennial, 1953; mem. adv. bd. St. Francis Hosp., Litchfield, 1967—; chmn. Nat. Christian Men's Fellowship Commn., 1961-63. Trustee Eureka Coll., 1936-63. Named Citizen of Year, Litchfield Jaycees, 1967, Outstanding Christian Laymen Ill. United Ch. Men of Ill., 1969. Mem. Am. Hosp. Assn., White House Retreat League, Litchfield Civic Singers, Montgomery County Hist. Soc., Yokefellows, Psi Alpha Lambda. Rotarian. Author: A Church Board at Work, 1945. Editor: Wild Honey (T.V. Stratton), 1960; He Who Seeks Gold (Everett W. Hill), 1968. Home: East Parkview St Litchfield IL 62056 Office: House of Sunshine Sunshine Park Litchfield IL 62056

HENRIKSEN, CHARLES KENDALL, mech. engr.; b. Rockford, Ill., June 17, 1925; s. John H. and Edith O. (Olander) H.; B.S.M.E., Purdue U., 1948; m. Dorothy H. Hibbits, Feb. 7, 1948; children—David K., Richard L., Mark C. With Johnson Controls, Inc., Chgo., 1948-51, sales engr., Aurora, Ill., 1952-53, br. mgr., Peoria, Ill., 1954-62; cons. engr. Brown, Davis, Mullins, cons. engrs., Champaign. Ill., 1962-73, Phillips Swager Assos., Architects-Engrs., Peoria, 1973—. Sect. chmn. United Fund, Peoria. Served with USN, 1943-46. Recipient Service award Ill. Assn. Sch. Bds., 1973; registered profl. engr., Ill. Mem. Am. Soc. Plumbing Engrs. (pres. Ill. chpt. 1973-76, Merit award 1976), Ill. Assn. Sch. Bds. (chmn. exec. com. 1972-73), Ill. Soc. Profl. Engrs. (vice chmn. local sect. exec. com. 1976-77), Am. Soc. Heating, Refrigeration and Air Conditioning Engrs. (v.p. Central Ill. chpt.), Nat. Soc. Profl. Engrs., Constrn. Specifications Inst. Methodist. Club: Cosmopolitan Internat. Author: (with Jack T. Harroun) Good School Maintenance, 1976. Home: 9300 Timberlane Peoria IL 61614 Office: 3622 N Knoxville Ave Peoria IL 61603

HENRIKSEN, HARRY CHARLES, mus. curator; b. Chgo., Jan. 6, 1932; s. James and Esther Elisa (Schmidt) H.; student Chgo. City Coll., 1949-51; B.A., U. Ill., 1953, M.A., 1957; m. Jeannine Anne Moretti, Nov. 15, 1953; children—Alicia, Erik, Niel. Preparator, Mus. Natural History, U. Ill., Urbana, 1957-66, curator, 1966—, acting dir., 1968. Grant reviewer Nat. Endowment for Humanities, 1974—; cons. Avery Brundage Olympic collection World Heritage Mus., U. Ill., 1977—; cons. Nat. Arts and the Handicapped, 1976—. Test judge U.S. Figure Skating Assn., 1971—; mem. Nat. Indoor Speed Skating Com., 1975; mem. World Short Track Speed Skating Competition Com., 1976. Served with USMCR, 1954-55. Recipient World Short Track Speed Skating Distinguished Service medal, 1976. NSF grantee Mus. Inst., Tucson, 1963. Mem. Am. Anthrop. Assn., Soc. Am. Archaeology, Midwest Museums Conf., Amateur Skating Union U.S. (short track com. 1976-77, Distinguished Service award 1976), U.S. Figure Skating Assn., Fraternal Order Police Speed Skating Club, Amateur Skating Assn. Ill., Old Capitol, Illini (pres. 1969-70) figure skating clubs, Sigma Xi, Phi Sigma. Lutheran. Contbr. articles to profl. jours. Home: 103 E Chalmers St Champaign IL 61820 Office: Mus Natural History U Ill Urbana IL 61801

HENRY, GENE M., heavy equipment mfg. co. exec.; b. Hastings, Nebr., Dec. 2, 1942; s. Ralph R. and May M. (Smith) H.; grad. high sch.; m. Elizabeth Ann Bryant, Oct. 3, 1964; children—Brent Taylor, Tori Lynnette. Spl. products engr. Dairy Equipment Co., Madison, Wis., 1963-69; pres., Monona Tube & Welding, Inc., Mc Farland, Wis., 1971-76, chmn. bd., pres., 1976—. Served with AUS, 1962-63. Mem. Soc. Automotive Engrs. Wis. Ducks Unlimited. Home: 3472 Orvold Park Rd McFarland WI 53558 Office: 5315 Paulson Rd McFarland WI 53558

HENRY, H(AROLD) DALE, realtor; b. DeLeon, Tex., Jan. 21, 1927; s. Wilma H. and Gladys Jane (Bailey) H.; student Lee Coll., 1947-48, U. Tenn., 1948-50, U. Calif. at San Diego, 1959-60; m. Billie Pearl Beck, Sept. 5, 1951; children—James Ray, Brenda Kay, Karen E., Harold Dale II, Robert Gale, Bonita (Mrs. Lewis M. Citro), Glenn Alan. With Rohr Corp., San Diego, 1955-65, gen. supr., mfg. engr., 1960-62, project mfg. engr., 1962-65; sr. tool design engr. Boeing Co., Seattle, 1965-67, prodn. supervisory mgr., 1967-68; salesman Don Ross Realty, Alton, Mo., 1969-70, Shephard Agy., 1970-71; sec., treas. Hightower Henry, Inc., 1971-74; pres. Spring Lakes Estates, 1973-74, Mule Ranch Inc., 1972—; owner, mgr. Henry Real Estate, West Plains, Mo., 1974—; mgr. Park Way Shopping Center, 1975—; dir. Banner Advt. Mem. steering com. West Plains State Sch. for Handicapped, 1975. Served with USNR, 1945-47. Recipient Pride in Excellence award Boeing Co., 1968. Mem. Ozark Trails (pres. 1974), West Plains (dir.) bds. realtors, Mo. Assn. Realtors (dir.). Mem. Assembly of God Ch. Home: Rover Route West Plains MO 65775 Office: PO Box 902 West Plains MO 65775

HENRY, HERMANN RUSSELL, govt. ofcl.; b. Johnson County, Ind., Feb. 12, 1917; s. William F. and Christena (Wilde) H.; student Franklin Coll., 1936-39, Purdue U., 1939-40; m. Rachel Saunders, Sept. 28, 1940; children—Norman, Diane Henry Burford, David S. Operator family farms, 1941—; bd. dirs. Ind. Statewide Assn. Rural Electric Coops., 1973—, sec.-treas., 1976, pres., 1977—. County councilman, 1954-58; mem. Ind. Ho. of Reps., 1959-60; clk. Johnson County, 1965—. Dir. enforcement div. Ind. Pub. Service Commn., 1968-69. Chmn. Johnson County Democratic Com., 1964-72. Mem. United Ch. of Christ. Clubs: Masons, Elks. Home: Rural Route 2 Box 57 Franklin IN 46131

HENRY, JANELL WAGNER, educator; b. Vienna, Mo., May 27, 1953; d. Alfred Louis and Pauline Geraldine (Leach) Wagner; B.S., U. Mo., Columbia, 1974, M.Ed., 1976; m. Dennis Lee Henry, Dec. 21, 1974. Clerical aide U.S. Geol. Survey, Rolla, Mo., summer 1970, cartographic aide full prodn., Rolla, summers 1971, 72, 74; grad. instr. U. Mo., Columbia, 1974-75; math instr. St. Joseph (Mo.) Sch. Dist., 1975—. Mem. Math. Assn. Am., Nat., Mo. councils tchrs. math., Mo., Community tchrs. assns. Methodist. Club: Order Eastern Star. Home: 3816 Seneca St St Joseph MO 64507 Office: 23d and Olive Sts St Joseph MO 64507

HENRY, JOHN ANDREW, state ofcl.; b. Chgo., Sept. 24, 1937; s. George Andrew and Leona Catherine (Kruse) H.; B.S., U. Ill., 1961; M.A. in Adminstrn., Sangamon State U., 1974; m. Rebecca Anne Smith, June 23, 1962; children—Lisa Marie, Andrea Anne. System engr. IBM, Moline, Ill., 1965-68; mgr. data processing Midwest Mfg. Co., Galesburg, 1968-71; mgr. central payroll State of Ill., Springfield, 1971-74, mgr. Service Bur., 1974—; data processing cons., instr. Served to capt. AUS, 1961-65. Mem. Data Processing Mgmt. Assn. Home: 1825 Seven Pines Springfield IL 62704 Office: 801 State Office Bldg Springfield IL 62706

HENRY, JOSEPH PATRICK, chem. co. exec.; b. Mansfield, Ohio, Mar. 3, 1925; s. Harold H. and Louise A. (Droxler) H.; student Bowling Green State U., 1943-44; B.S., Ohio State U., 1949; m. Jeanette E. Russell, Oct. 26, 1957; 1 dau., Jeanette Louise. Ohio sales mgr. NaChurs Plant Food Co., Marion, O., 1949-55; organizer, pres. Growers Chem. Corp., Milan, 1955—, Sandusky Imported Motors, Inc. (Ohio), 1958—; co-owner Homestead Inn Restaurant, Homestead Farms; v.p. Homestead Inn, Inc. Motels, South Avery Corp. Motels; dir. Erie County Bank, Vermilion, Ohio. Served with USMCR, 1943-46; PTO. Mem. Nat. Fedn. Ind. Bus. (nat. adv. council), Ohio Farm Bur. Fedn., NAM, Milan C. of C., Aircraft Owners and Pilots Assn., Internat. Flying Farmers, Ohio Restaurant Assn., Ohio Motel-Hotel Assn., Ohio Licensed Beverage Assn., Am. Horse Show Assn., Nat. Trust for Historic Preservation, Huron County Hist. Soc., Ohio Farm Bur., (pres.), Ohio Internat. (regional dir.) Arabian horse assns., Internat. Platform Assn., Arabian Horse Registry Am. Clubs: Antique Automobile Am., Sports Car Am., N. Am. Yacht Racing Union, Sandusky Yacht, Sandusky Sailing; Ohio State Varsity O Assn. Home: 128 Center St Milan OH 44846 also Homestead Farms Route 1 Milan OH 44846 Office: Growers Chem Corp Box 1750 Milan OH 44846

HENRY, LEE, pollution engr.; b. Skellytown, Tex., Aug. 25, 1930; s. Cecil Truelove and Essie Lavera Henry; B.S., Oreg. State U., Corvallis, 1966; m. Martha Jane Franklin, Sept. 15, 1953; children—Patrick Lee, Jon Thomas, Mark Joseph. Chemist, Oreg. Water Pollution Lab., Portland, 1965-66; dir. labs. Mogul Corp., Chagrin Falls, Ohio, 1967—; mem. sediment control staff NE Ohio Area Pollution Adminstrn.; com. mem. Lake Erie Erosion Project. Mem. Cuyahoga County Planning Commn. Served with USN, 1948-52. Certified source testing specialist EPA. Mem. Cleve. Engring. Soc. (chmn. environ. div.), Nat. Crushed Stone Assn. (chmn. environ. com.), Air Pollution Control Assn., Water Pollution Control Assn., Soc. Indsl. Microbiologists, ASTM. Republican. Mem. Chs. of Christ. Author various chpts. and articles on indsl. waste-water mgmt. and pollution control. Home: 17185 Catsden Rd Chagrin Falls OH 44022 Office: Mogul Corp Laboratory Park Chagrin Falls OH 44022

HENRY, LEROY CHURCH, ammunition mfg. co. exec.; b. Hawthorne, N.Y., June 25, 1923; s. George C. and Ethel (Church) H.; student Mo. Sch. Mines, 1946-48; B.S., S.W. Mo. State Coll., 1950; m. K. Juanita Gilbert, Nov. 28, 1946; children—Richard, Roy, Ross, Rita. Supr. quality control Fairchild Camera & Instrument Corp., Joplin, Mo., 1956-62; engr. Rocketdyne div. N. Am. Aviation, Neosho, Mo., 1962-68; engr. Day & Zimmerman, Inc., Parsons, Kans., 1968-74, dir. stores and transp., 1974-75, plant mgr. Kans. Army Ammunition plant, 1975—. Mem. Carl Junction Sch. Bd., also pres.; scoutmaster, cubmaster Boy Scouts Am.; mgr. Little League, Babe Ruth League. Served with AUS, 1943-45. Recipient Nat. Mgmt. Assn. medallion award, 1977. Mem. Am. Def. Preparedness Assn., Nat. Mgmt. Assn. Methodist. Home: 405 Verbryck Carl Junction MO 64834 Office: Day and Zimmerman US 160 E Parsons KS 67357

HENRY, RACHEL IMOGENE SAUNDERS (MRS. HERMANN R. HENRY), civic worker; b. nr. Franklin, Ind., Mar. 24, 1920; d Arland R. and Imogene (Stewart) Saunders; student Franklin Coll., 1939, Purdue U., 1940; m. Hermann R. Henry, Sept. 28, 1940; children—Pamela (Mrs. Norman E. Stucker) Diane (Mrs. R. W. Burford), David S. Author children stories Johnson County News, Greenwood, Ind., 1952. Mem. Johnson County Sch. Reorgn. Com., 1961-62; bd. mem. United Fund, Johnson County, 1961-65; bd. mem. Gateway Sch. for Retarded Children 1967-71; curator Johnson County Historical Museum, 1972—. Recipient Matrix Table award Franklin Coll., 1969, Rural Life award Kiwanis Club, 1969; named Ky. Col. Mem. Ind. Soc. Mayflower Descendants (sec. 1971-76, dir. 1977), Johnson County Hist. Soc. (pres. 1969-70, award 1971), Delta Delta Delta (pres.), Psi Iota Xi (pres.). Congregationalist (evangelism and devotional chmn. for state bd. 1957-59). Clubs: Women's Study (pres. 1963-64) (Franklin); State Assembly Women's (sec. 1969-71, pres. 1971-73) (Indpls.). Author: Childrens Stories, 1952; Saunders Genealogy, 1966. Home: Route 2 Box 57 Franklin IN 46131

HENRY, RICHARD JAMES, educator; b. Monmouth, Ill., Mar. 6, 1935; s. James William and Elizabeth (Anderson) H.; B.S., Monmouth Coll., 1958; B.S., (univ. scholar), Case-Western Res. U., 1958; M.S. (Hughes fellow), U. Calif., Los Angeles, 1961; Ph.D. (NASA scholar), U. Conn., 1971; m. Sally Ann Platt, June 15, 1958; children—Mark Richard, Scott David, Keith William, Derek George. Engr., Hughes Aircraft Co., Los Angeles, 1958-62; sr. analytical engr., project mgr. Pratt & Whitney Aircraft Co., East Hartford, Conn., 1962-66; instr. math. U. Hartford, 1965-68; guest research scientist Deutsche Forschungs- und Versuchstalt für Luft- und Raumfahrt and U. Stuttgart (Germany), 1969-71; instr. to asso. prof. Black Hawk Coll., Moline, Ill., 1971—. Pres., Warren County Swim Team Parent Assn., 1972-73, United Twp. High Sch. Band Parents, 1977—. Mem. Am. Inst. Aeros. and Astronautics, Instrument Soc. Am., Am. Soc. Heating, Refrigeration and Air Conditioning Engrs., Sigma Chi, Sigma Omicron Mu, Blue Key. Presbyterian. Club: East Moline Newcomers. Home: 2829 8th St East Moline IL 61244 Office: Black Hawk Coll 6600 34th Ave Moline IL 61265

HENRY, ROBERT EDWARD, mech. engr.; b. Lima, Ohio, Nov. 5, 1940; s. Harry William and Anna Rose (Wellman) H.; B.S., U. Notre Dame, 1962, M.S., 1964, Ph.D., 1967; m. Paula Elizabeth Walsh, June 8, 1963; children—Geoffrey, Christopher, Lisa Beth, Robert Edward. Mem. sci. staff Argonne (Ill.) Nat. Lab., 1967-68, 1970—, sect. mgr. out-of-pile reactor expts., 1974—; chmn. mech. engring. dept. Midwest Coll. Engring., Lombard, Ill., 1971—. Served with F.A. U.S. Army, 1968-70. Asso. Midwest U. fellow, 1964-67. Mem. Am. Nuclear Soc. Roman Catholic. Club: Cress Creek Country. Patentee in field. Contbr. articles to profl. jours. Home: 1517 Inverness Ct Naperville IL 60540 Office: 9700 S Cass Ave Argonne IL 60439

HENSCHEN, JAMES LEE, veterinarian; b. St. Mary's, Ohio, May 31, 1939; s. Verlin George and Pauline Elshoff (Poppe) H.; D.V.M., Ohio State U., 1963; m. Jean Ann Gritzmaker, June 25, 1960; children—Jodi Lynn, Jill Ann. Asso. veterinarian Countryside Vet. Center, Westerville, Ohio, 1963-67, owner, 1967—. Mem. Am., Ohio vet. med. assns., Columbus Acad. Vet. Medicine, Am. Assn. Equine Practitioners, 5th Dist. Equine Practitioners Assn., Westerville C. of C. Presbyn. Lion. Home: 205 N Vine St Westerville OH 43081 Office: 10007 N State Rd Westerville OH 43081

HENSELER, DONNA MILLARD, educator; b. Worthington, Minn.; d. Paul A. and Leah S. (Walker) Millard; B.A., Augustana Coll.; M.A., U. S.D.; Ph.D., Mich. State U.; m. Kenneth J. Henseler, Aug. 14, 1951; children—Kevin, Todd, Jay. Instr. U. S.D.; asst. prof. Yankton (S.D.) Coll.; instr. Mich. State U.; now prof. English, head dept. Mt. Marty Coll., Yankton; vis. humanist S.D. Com. Humanities. Recipient James award in writing. Mem. AAUW, AAUP, Modern Lang. Assn., Nat. S.D. Nat., councils tchrs. English, World Future Soc. (S.D. coordinator), Am. Soc. Psychical Research. Contbr. articles poems, short stories to profl. jours.

HENSHEL, RICHARD LEE, sociologist; b. Dallas, Jan. 27, 1939; s. Walter Marcus and Beatrice (Bach) H.; B.A., U. Tex., Austin, 1962; Ph.D., Cornell U., 1969. Asst. prof. sociology U. Tex., Austin, 1968-71; asso. prof. U. Western Ont., London, Can., 1971—; vis. research asso. U. Toronto Centre for Culture and Technology, 1977. Hogg Found. grantee, 1969; Canada Council research grantee, 1972; Canada Council leave fellow 1977. Mem. Am., Internat. sociol. assns., Canadian assns., Sociology Anthropology Assn., Am. Soc. Criminology, World Future Soc. Author: On the Future of Social Prediction, 1976; Reacting to Social Problems, 1976; (with Anne-Marie Henshel) Perspectives on Social Problems, 1973; co-editor: Perception in Criminology, 1975; editor: Futures Canada, 1976-77. Home: 115 Cherryhill Blvd Apt 803 London ON Canada Office: Dept Sociology Univ Western Ontario London Canada

HENSON, JOHN PORTER, equipment co. exec.; b. Girard, Kans., Sept. 25, 1922; s. John Porter and Gladys (deVenny) H.; B.S. in Mech. Engring., Purdue U., 1946; m. Sarah Winslow Hodgdon, Sept. 27, 1947; children—Christena Margaret, John Winslow, David deVenny. Regional mgr. Bendix Westinghouse Air Brake, 1946-59; account exec. Dana Corp., Toledo, 1959-60, sales mgr., 1960-61, asst. gen. sales mgr., 1961-64; sales mgr. Kaydon Engring. Co., Muskegon, Mich., 1964-65; product planning mgr. Clark Equipment Co., Buchanan, Mich., 1965—; exec. engr., 1965-66, v.p. engring. axle div., 1966-72, v.p. mktg., 1972—; cons. on sales and engring. Tremec, 1977—. Served to 2d lt. USMC, 1942-45. Mem. Am. Ordnance Assn., Sec. Automotive Engring., Tau Beta Pi, Pi Tau Sigma, Sigma Chi. Home and Office: 1105 Plym Rd Niles MI 49120

HENZLIK, RAYMOND EUGENE, zoophysiologist, educator; b. Casper, Wyo., Dec. 26, 1926; s. William H. and Adeline (Brown) H.; A.A., Northeastern Neb. Coll., 1946; B.S., U. Nebr., 1948, M.S., 1952, Ph.D., 1960; postgrad. Cornell U., 1961-62, Baylor Med. Coll., 1970-71; m. Wilma Louise Bartels, Oct. 1, 1950; children—Randall Eugene, Nancy Jo. Tchr., York (Nebr.) High Sch., 1948-50; supr. sci. teaching U. Nebr., 1951-53, asst. prof. zoology, 1959-61; tchr. Omaha North High Sch., 1953-56; instr. biology Nebr. Wesleyan U., 1957-59; asst. prof. zoology Ball State U., Muncie, Ind., 1962-67, asso. prof. physiology, 1967-69, prof. physiology, 1969—, also radiol. health officer; postdoctoral research on radioisotopes in marine food chains Radiobiology Lab., U.S. Bur. Comml. Fisheries, Beaufort, N.C., tropical forest radioecology P.R. Nuclear Center, San Juan, 1967, radiotracer methodology Argonne Nat. Lab., 1969. Anatomy consultant Nat. Prescription Footwear Applicators Assn.; lectr. pedorthosis; cons. ednl. affairs Argonne Nat. Lab., also cons. radioecology. Mem. Am. Ecol. Soc., AAAS, Am. Inst. Biol. Scis, Ind. Acad Sci., Sigma Xi, Phi Delta Kappa. Reviewer, referee Jour. Am. Biology Tchr. Research and publs. on radiation biology, ecology of animal communities, ednl. methodology. Home: 3311 Somerset Dr Muncie IN 47304

HERB, EDMUND MICHAEL, optometrist; b. Zanesville, Ohio, Oct. 9, 1942; s. Edmund George and Barbara Rose (Michael) H.; B.S., Ohio State U., 1964, D. Optometry, 1967; m. Mary Ann Wible, June 13, 1964; children—Sara, Andrew. Pvt. optometric practice, Marysville, Ohio, 1967—; pres. Loggerhead Corp., Inc., Marysville, 1971-76, also dir.; owner, breeder Arabian Horses; pres. Saddle Rack & Apparel Inc. Vice-pres. Union County div. Mid Ohio Health Planning Fedn., 1971-75; dir. environmental health, Union County, Ohio, 1971-75. Clin. instr. Coll. Optometry, Ohio State U. Mem. Union County Mounted Deps., Union County Sheriff's Dept. Mem. Am., Ohio optometric assns., Arabian Horse Registry Am., Internat. Arabian Horse Assn., Epsilon Psi Epsilon. Republican. Lion (sec. 1969-70). Home: 18658 Smokey Rd Marysville OH 43040 Office: 303 W 5th St Marysville OH 43040

HERBERT, WILLIAM, engr.; b. Cin., May 27, 1916; s. Joseph Charles and Maude (Johnson) H.; student Xavier U., 1933-34; Chem. Engr., U. Cin., 1938; m. Lois Marie Shields, Nov. 23, 1938; 1 dau., Lois Marie (Mrs. Curtis Lynn Salyers). Plant engr. U.S. Gypsum Co., St. Paul, 1938-40, South Bend, Ind., 1940-42, Philip Carey Mfg. Co., Perth Amboy, N.J., 1945-47; plant mgr. Barrett div. Allied Chem. Corp., Peoria, Ill., 1947-55, dir. operations, N.Y.C., 1955-60; dir. engring. Black Clawson Co., Middletown, Ohio, 1960-74; engr. waste recycling Parsons & Whittemore, N.Y.C., 1974—. Served to lt. (s.g.), USNR, 1942-45. Mem. T.A.P.P.I., (chmn. mech. engring. com. 1972-73), Am. Inst. Chem. Engrs., Middletown Sportsman's Club (dir. 1970-73), Pioneer solid waste resource recovery system; patentee in field. Home: 116 Euclid St Middletown OH 45042 Office: Parsons & Whittemore 200 Park Ave New York City NY 10017

HERBERTT, STANLEY, performing arts adminstr., choreographer; b. Chgo., Apr. 11, 1919; s. Samuel W. and Anna (Sturt) H.; grad. Herzl Jr. Coll., Chgo., 1938; B.Ed., Chgo. Tchrs. Coll., 1942; M.A., Nat. Acad. of Ballet, N.Y.C., 1960. With Chgo. Civic Opera Ballet, 1940-43, San Carlo Opera Ballet, Chgo., 1940-43, Littlefield Ballet Co., Chgo., 1941-42; soloist Ballet Theatre of N.Y., N.Y.C., 1943-47; soloist Broadway musical Carousel, 1947-49, Broadway musical Inside U.S.A., 1947-49; soloist, choreographer Cain Park Summer Theatre, Cleve., 1950-51; propr., dir. Ballet Arts Acad., St. Louis, 1951—; founder, dir. St. Louis Civic Ballet, 1959—. Lectr. St. Louis U., 1965—, Nat. Soc. of Arts and Letters, St. Louis, 1961—, Copper Coin Civic Ballet, Springfield, Ill., 1975—; mem. dance faculty Webster Coll., Webster Groves, Mo., 1976-77; participant Internat. Festival Youth Orchs. and Performing Arts, Aberdeen, Scotland, 1976; choreographer Columbus (Ohio) Ballet Theatre, TV commls.; dir. musical fashion shows for Stix Baer and Fuller Dept. Stores; dir., choreographer ednl. program The History of Dance From Jig to Jet, 1967-76. Mem. dance com. Mo. State Council on the Arts, 1968—. Recipient Edn. for Arts award Stix Baer and Fuller, 1963; Plaque award St. Louis Civic Ballet, 1965; Merit award Fontbonne Coll., 1972; Maharishi award for Celebrations and Fulfillment, 1977; commendations from Mayor St. Louis, 1976, Gov. Mo., 1977. Mem. Assn. Am. Dance Cos., Dance Educators of Am., Am. Dance Guild, Dance Masters of Am. Contbr. articles on dance and choreography to profl. publs. Home: 7548 Parkdale St Louis MO 63105 Office: 7620 Wydown Blvd St Louis MO 63105

HERBST, FREDERICK DANIEL, elec. designer; b. Detroit, Dec. 9, 1921; s. August Jacob and Laura (Stewart) H.; student U. Detroit, 1942-43, Lawrence Tech. Coll., 1943-44; A.S. in Elec. Engring., Detroit Coll. Applied Sci., 1946; m. Virginia Frances Trosell, Aug. 18, 1951; children—James Robert, Timothy Patrick, Frederick Daniel, Laurie Beth. Elec. apprentice Ford Motor Co. and Apprentice Sch., Detroit, 1940; with Ex-Cell-O Corp., Highland Park, Mich., 1940-66, elec. supr., 1945-49, elec. engring. designer, 1950-66; elec. design project engr. Pioneer Engring. & Mfg. Co., Warren, Mich., 1966-67; elec. controls designer Cross Co., Fraser, Mich., 1967—; instr. elec. controls design Detroit Coll. Applied Sci., 1956-57. Chmn. dance com., mgr. youth baseball Berkley (Mich.) Dad's Club. Lutheran. Club: Masons (32 deg., Shriner). Home: 1980 Greenfield Rd Berkley MI 48072 Office: 17801 E 14 Mile Rd Fraser MI 48026

HERBST, WILLIAM HENRY ALBERT, charitable assn. exec.; b. Grand Haven, Mich., Apr. 10, 1915; s. William Emil and Frances Amelia Sophie (Neitring) H.; United Way Am. nat tng. U. Wichita, 1969, U. Wis., 1970; m. Beulah Hope Scott, Aug. 25, 1941; children—Sally-Anne (Mrs. David Noren), William Scott, Kurt Jerome. Enlisted USCG, 1934; advanced through grades to cwo-4, 1946; ret., 1965; sales mgr., pub. relations Welded Products, metal fabricators, Grand Haven, 1965-68; field rep. Mich. United Way, 1968—; exec. dir. Tri-Cities Area United Fund, Grand Haven, 1965—, Greater Holland (Mich.) United Way, 1969—. Cons. to numerous vol. funds. Mem. Grand Haven Harbor Commn., 1965—, Coast Guard Festival Com., Grand Haven, 1965—; pres. Grand Haven Festival Com.; dir. campaign and field services U. Western Mich. Mem. Ret. Officers Assn., V.F.W., Am. Legion. Mason; mem. Order Eastern Star, Elk. Clubs: Spring Lake (Mich.) Country; Holland Country. Home: 1300 Sheldon Rd Grand Haven MI 49417 Office: 33-35 W 8th St Holland MI 49423

HERD, RICHARD MURLEN, oral surgeon; b. Peru, Ind., Sept. 16, 1918; s. Murlen B. and Mary A. (Woolford) H.; A.B. in Chemistry, Ind. U., 1941; D.D.S., St. Louis U., 1945; m. Harriet Jean Erickson, June 27, 1948; children—Richard Murlen, Eric Alan, Dorothy Jean. Intern, U. Oregon Med. Sch., 1947-48, instr. Dental Sch., 1947-48; resident Ind. U. Med. Center, 1948-49; practice dentistry specializing in oral surgery, Indpls., 1960—; chief oral surgeon Louisville Gen. Hosp., 1948-57; asst. prof. oral surgery Louisville Sch. Dentistry, 1948-58; mem. staff St. Francis Hosp., St. Vincent Hosp., Winona Hosp., Community Hosp.; chief oral surgeon Methodist Hosp., 1972-73; mem. faculty Ind. U. Sch. Dentistry, 1976—. Served to lt. USN, 1945-47. Mem. Am., Ind. State dental socs., Am., Great Lakes, Ind. socs. oral surgeons, Ky. Soc. Anesthesia (pres. 1958-59), St. Louis U. Alumni Assn., Omicron Kappa Epsilon, Phi Delta Theta, Xi Psi Phi (pres. 1966-67). Republican. Lutheran. Club: Masons. Contbr. numerous articles on oral surgery to profl. jours.; condr. research in anesthesia; writer, dir. 4 movies in field. Home: 6825 Creekside Ln Indianapolis IN 46220 Office: 3989 Meadows Dr Indianapolis IN 46205

HERDINA, LEO JAMES, dairy co. exec.; b. Sioux Falls, S.D., Jan. 17, 1933; s. Fred Martin and Lillian (Johnson) H.; Accounting degree, Nettelton Coll., 1957; m. Avis K. Schartz, Sept. 9, 1953; children—Stephen, Joseph, Michael, Deborah, Mary. Accountant, Black Hills Milk Producers, Rapid City, S.D., 1957-64, gen. mgr., 1964—. Pres., Black Hills Assn. Retarded Citizens, 1973—. Served with AUS, 1955-57. Mem. Western Dairymen (treas.), S.D. Dairy Assn. (past pres.). Elk. Home: 623 Westwind Dr Rapid City SD 57701 Office: 1130 E St James Rapid City SD 57701

HERDRICH, RALPH COOLEY, steel co. exec.; b. Chgo., May 22, 1913; s. Fredrick H. and Stella Mae (Cooley) H.; student pub. schs.; m. Rita Poblocki, Oct. 4, 1950; children—Ann Elizabeth, Roger Charles. With Inland Steel Co., 1934-46, Briskin Mfg. Co., 1946-52, Rolled Steel Corp., 1952-62; with Tollway Steel and Storage Co., 1962—, pres., 1962—. Mem. Ill. Mfg. Assn., Soc. Automotive Engrs., Melrose Park C. of C. (dir.). Home: 5009 Flanders Rd McHenry IL 60050 Office: 25th Ave and Main St Melrose Park IL 60160

HERFINDAHL, LLOYD MANFORD, artist; b. Emmons, Minn., June 15, 1922; s. Albert and Betsy (Singlestad) H.; student Mpls. Coll. of Art and Design, 1972; pupil Adolph Dehn, 1954-55; also pupil Maurice Ruelle, 1977; studied in Paris, 1969-70. Group shows include: Salon Des Independents, Grand Palais, Paris, 1972, Soc. Academique Des Arts Libraux de Paris, 1972, Bertrand Russell Peace Found. Centenary, Rotunda Gallery, London, 1974-75, Internat. St. Germain Helder Palais, Brussels, Belgium, 1973, Mus. of Modern Art, Paris, 1974, Holy Land Mus., Los Angeles, 1974, Salon de l'Ecole de Thouet, Thovars, France, 1973; one man shows include: Galerie Mouffe, 1974, Bethany Luth. Coll., 1977, U. Minn.; represented in permanent collections: Montvard Mus. of Fine Arts, France, Bethany Coll., Minn., Holy Land Mus., Los Angeles, Eye-O-Graphic Center, Mpls.; paintings include: Portrait of H.M. King Olave V of Norway, Nurse Heritage Series; co-pres. of Internat. Grand Prix of Painting D'Or Beaux Arts, Monte Carlo, Monaco, 1968; art dir. Luth. Sentinel, Luth. Coll., Minn.; art cons. to Boy Scouts of Albert Lea County, 1964-68. Named Hon. Citizen of Mpls., 1977; recipient Queen Fabiola Gold medal award, Belgio-Hispanica, 1973, Silver medal award Soc. D'Encouragement Au Progress, 1974. Mem. Minn. Artists Assn. (fgn. corr. 1974-77), Assn. Belgio-Hispanique, Internat. Platform Assn., Sons of Norway, Internat. Arts Guild. Lutheran. Clubs: Kiwanis, Breakes. Address: 809 John Farry Pl Albert Lea MN 56007

HERGENROTHER, EDWARD LEO, silicone products co. exec.; b. Madison, Wis., Mar. 19, 1927; s. Leo Andrew and Frieda (Aeschliman) H.; B.S., Chem. Engr., U. Wis., 1951; M.B.A., U. Mich., 1962; m. Kathleen Mae Darr, June 18, 1949; children—Susan Lee, Joanne Kay. With Dow Corning Corp., Midland, Mich., 1951—, project mgr., 1963-71, mgr. project engring., 1971-73, mgr. project adminstrn. corporate facilities engring., 1973—. Served with USAAF, 1945-47. Registered profl. engr., Mich., Ky. Mem. Am. Inst. Chem. Engrs., Nat. Soc. Profl. Engrs., Am. Assn. Cost Engrs. Republican. Methodist. Elk. Home: 5703 Summerset Dr Midland MI 48640 Office: S Saginaw Rd Midland MI 48640

HERGUTH, ROBERT J., journalist; b. Chgo.; B.S. in Journalism, U. Mo., 1948; m. Margaret Silsbee; children—Amy Rene, Robert Charles, Mary Jennifer. With Chgo. Daily News, 1954-78, successively reporter, rewrite man, feature writer, columnist; columnist Chgo. Sun Times, 1978—. Served with AUS, Korean Conflict. Home: Wilmette IL 60091 Office: Chgo Sun Times 401 N Wabash Ave Chicago IL 60611

HERING, JAMES STEPHEN, physician; b. Youngstown, Ohio, June 15, 1939; s. Stephen Anthony and Virginia Elizabeth (Simon) H.; B.A., Ohio Wesleyan U., 1961; M.D., Ohio State U., 1965; m. Barbra Anne Bechtle, Dec. 27, 1964; children—James Stephen, Robert C., Thomas D., Stephen D. Intern, Ind. U. Med. Center, Indpls., 1965-66; resident in surgery and thoracic surgery Milw. County Gen. Hosp., 1968-69, Ohio State U. Hosp., Columbus, 1969-73; practice medicine specializing in thoracic surgery, Marion, Ohio, 1973—; mem. staff Marion Gen. Hosp., Hardin Meml. Hosp., Kenton, Ohio, Bucyrus (Ohio) Community Hosp., Grady Meml. Hosp., Delaware, Ohio. Served with USAF, 1966-68. Diplomate Am. Bd. Surgery, Am. Bd. Thoracic Surgery. Mem. A.C.S., AMA, Ohio Med. Assn., Columbus Surg. Soc. Republican. Methodist. Clubs: Kiwanis, Symposiarchs. Home: 1050 Kingwood Dr Marion OH 43302 Office: 367 S Main St Marion OH 43302

HERKNER, MILDRED LUELLA, child psychiatrist, pediatrician; b. Traverse City, Mich., June 21, 1915; s. Oswald and Elsie Agnes (Rickerd) H.; A.B., U. Mich., 1937, M.D., 1940; m. L. Charles Ballance, June 19, 1940; children—Lee Charles, Stephen James, Ann Elizabeth (Mrs. Mark E. Crouch), Robert Alan. Intern, Cleve. City Hosp., 1940-41; resident Children's Hosp. of Mich., 1941-42; sr. resident physician Herman Kiefer Hosp., 1942-43; clin. asst. in pediatrics U. Chgo., 1943; practice medicine specializing in pediatrics, 1944-49, Traverse City, 1951-66; former staff physician Children's Meml. Hosp., Chgo., James Decker Munson Hosp.; resident in adult psychiatry Traverse City State Hosp., 1966-68, clin. dir. children's unit, 1970-73; resident in child psychiatry Hawthorn Center, Northville, Mich., 1968-70, sr. staff, adminstrv. asst., 1973—; cons. Redford Schs., Detroit, 1974, Sarah Fisher Home, Detroit, 1973—. Pres. bd. dirs. YMCA, Traverse City, 1967-68. Mem. A.M.A., Am. Acad. Child Psychiatry, Mich. State Employees Assn. (dir.). Club: Zonta. Home: 1206 Peninsula Ct Traverse City MI 49684 Office: 18471 Haggerty Rd Northville MI 48167

HERMAN, BERNARD, architect; b. Mpls., June 9, 1935; s. John Abbot and Betty (Gilbert) H.; B.Arch., U. Minn., 1958; m. Renee T. London, June 15, 1958; children—Melissa F., Lee R. Draftsman, Thorshov and Cerny, Inc., Mpls., 1959-61; job capt. Cerny Assos., Inc., 1961-64; project architect, asso. firm Miller-Whitehead-Dunwiddie, Inc., 1964-67; architect, corporate v.p. Cottle-Herman Architects, Inc., St. Paul, 1967—; pres. C and H Devel. Co., Inc., St. Paul, 1969—. Campaign com. Gov. Wendell Anderson, 1970; mem. City of New Hope Planning Commn., chmn. design rev. bd., councilman, 1976—; bd. dirs., pres. Community Housing & Service Corp. Mpls.; bd. dirs. Mpls. Fedn. for Jewish Service. Mem. A.I.A., Minn., Mpls. socs. architects, Sigma Alpha Sigma. Democrat. Jewish. Mason; mem. B'nai B'rith. Prin. archtl. works include Betty Crocker Tree House Restaurants for Gen. Mills, Inc., throughout U.S., 1969. Home: 2740 Zealand Ave No Minneapolis MN 55427 Office: 3100 W Lake St Minneapolis MN 55416

HERMAN, EDWARD JOSEPH, dentist; b. Benld, Ill., Aug. 26, 1924; s. Edward Anthony and Josephine Frances (Danis) H.; D.D.S., Wash. U., 1950; m. June Lee Hodgins, May 10, 1952 (dec. June 1962); children—Robert, Thomas; m. 2d, Theresa Ann Riley, Oct. 15, 1964. Intern periodontics St. Louis County Hosp. and Health Dept., 1950-52; pvt. practice dentistry, Brentwood, Mo., 1952—. Vis. instr., lectr. Wash. U., St. Louis U. schs. dentistry. Served with USNR, 1942-45. Mem. Am., Mo. dental assns., St. Louis Dental Soc., Soc. Dental Sci., Acad. Gen. Practice, Gen. Practice, St. Louis Dental research groups, Wash. U. Sch. Dentistry Alumni, Pierre Fauchard Acad., Xi Psi Phi. Club: Forest Hills Country (St. Louis). Home: 12920 Woodlark Ln Town and Country MO 63131 Office: 1617 S Brentwood Blvd Brentwood MO 62144

HERMAN, JOHN ALLEN, editor; b. Willmar, Minn., Apr. 9, 1936; s. Herbert Allen and Mable A. (Boyer) H., student U. Minn., 1955-59; m. Joan Elaine Eddy, Jan. 28, 1967; children—Sarah Elizabeth, Andrew Allen. Field dir. Nat. Small Bus. Assn., Mpls., 1959-60; v.p. Minn. Small Bus. Assn., St. Paul, 1960-61; pub. relations cons., Washington, 1961-66; editor; pub. Washington County Bull., Cottage Grove, Minn., 1966—; pres. Bull. Pub. Corp., Cottage Grove, Minn., 1970—. Mem. state central com. Minn. Republican party, 1970-75; Kandiyohi County chmn. Young Reps., 1964; dep. registrar City of Cottage Grove, 1973—. Recipient State Americanism award Minn. V.F.W., 1970. Mem. Nat., Minn. newspaper assns., Cottage Grove Businessmen's Assn., Washington County, Nat., Minn. hist. socs., Minn. Dep. Registrars Assn. (v.p. 1977—). Nat. Trust Historic Preservation, Minn. Press. Club. Home: 8446 Henna Ave S Cottage Grove MN 55016 Office: 7162 80th St S Cottage Grove MN 55016

HERMAN, ROBERT EDWARD, dentist; b. Manawa, Wis., Feb. 26, 1923; s. Edward Albert and Maryann (Huber) H.; student Wis. State U., Oshkosh, 1940-42, U. Wis., 1942-43; D.D.S., Marquette U., 1946; m. Helen C. Scholtz, May 1, 1946; children—James, Gary, Richard, Steven. Pvt. practice gen. dentistry, Oshkosh, 1946, 48—. Clinician, Minn. Dental Conv., 1954, Iowa Dental Conv., 1955. Regional dir. Wis. Am. Legion Baseball Assn., 1950—, pres., 1965-77. Served as lt. (j.g.) Dental Corps, USNR, 1946-48. Mem. Acad. Gen. Dentistry, Winnebago County (pres. 1960), Fox River Valley (sec. 1967, pres. 1973) dental socs., Am. Legion (past comdr. 1963). Home: 1045 Grove St Oshkosh WI 54901 Office: 424 Washington St Oshkosh WI 54901

HERMANN, DONALD HAROLD JAMES, lawyer, educator; b. Southgate, Ky., Apr. 6, 1943; s. Albert Joseph and Helen Marie (Snow) H.; A.B. (George E. Gamble Honors scholar), Stanford U., 1965; J.D. (John Noble fellow), Columbia U., 1968; LL.M. (Law and Humanities fellow), Harvard U., 1974. Mem. staff, directorate of devel. plans Dept. Def., 1964-65, Legis. Drafting Research Fund, Columbia U., 1966-68; admitted to Ariz. bar, 1968, Wash. bar, 1969, Ky. bar, 1971, Ill. bar, 1972, U.S. Supreme Ct. bar, 1974; mem. faculty U. Wash., Seattle, 1968-71, U. Ky., Lexington, 1971-72; mem. faculty DePaul U., Chgo., 1972—, prof. law, 1973—, dir. acad. programs and interdisciplinary study, 1975-76, asso. dean, 1976—; fellow law and humanities Harvard U., 1973-74; vis. prof. Washington U., St. Louis, 1974, U. Brazilia, 1976; lectr. Latin Am. Soc. Found., 1975—, Sch. Edn., Northwestern U., 1974-76, Christ Coll., Cambridge U., 1977; fellow law and econs. U. Chgo., 1975-76. Bd. dirs. Council for Legal Edn. Opportunity, Ohio Valley Consortium, 1972, Ill. Bar Automated Research Corp., 1975—, Criminal Law Consortium Cook County, 1977—; reporter cons. Ill. Jud. Conf., 1972—. Mem. Am., Ill., Chgo. bar assns., Am. Acad. Polit. and Social Sci., Am. Econ. Assn., Am. Soc. for Polit. and Legal Philosophy, Am. Judicature Soc., Orgn. Am. Historians, Soc. Writers on Legal Subjects, Soc. Am. Law Tchrs., Am. Assn. Law Schs. (del., sect. chmn.), Chgo. Hist. Preservation Soc., Evanston Hist. Soc., Signet Soc. (Harvard). Episcopalian. Clubs: Hasty Pudding (Harvard); Univ., Quadrangle (Chgo.); Univ. (Evanston). Home: 1243 Forest Ave Evanston IL 60202 Office: DePaul U Coll of Law 25 E Jackson St Chicago IL 60604

HERMANN, HARLAND THOMAS, psychiatrist; b. Lincoln, Nebr., June 8, 1919; s. Harold Thomas and Catherine (Morgan) H.; M.D., U. Nebr., 1943; m. Jean Ellison, Feb. 28, 1948; children—Tom, Lucy, Richard. Intern, Meth. Hosp., Omaha, 1944, resident in internal medicine, 1946-47; pvt. group practice psychiatry, Omaha, 1947-56; resident in neuropsychiatry VA Hosp., Omaha, 1956-59; psychiatrist VA, Fort Meade, S.D., 1959—, chief psychiatry and neurology, 1967—; instr. U. Nebr. Med. Coll., 1952-59; cons. West River Mental Health Center, Rapid City, S.D., 1966-75, Luth. Social Service,

1969—; clin. asst. prof. psychiatry U. S.D., 1975—. Served to capt. AUS, 1944-46. Diplomate Am. Bd. Psychiatry and Neurology. Fellow Am. Psychiat. Assn.; mem. Am. Group Psychotherapy Assn., Internat. Transactional Analysis Assn. Mason, Toastmaster, Rotarian. Office: Psychiatry Service VA Hospital Fort Meade SD 57741

HERMANN, JAMES LEE, constrn. co. exec.; b. Sheboygan, Wis., June 21, 1951; s. John and LaVerne Mabel (Maschke) H.; B.S., U. Wis., River Falls, 1973; M.B.A., U. Wis., Oshkosh, 1977; m. Katherine Anne Fengler, July 29, 1972. Controller, Gabe's Constrn. Co., Inc., Sheboygan, 1974-75, controller of corp. and all corporate affiliates, 1975—; dir. Sheboygan Warehouse & Forwarding Co., Inc. Vice chmn. comml. west div. United Fund campaign drive, 1976; mem. budget com. United Fund, 1977. Mem. Sheboygan County Ind. Ins. Agts. Assn. Lutheran. Clubs: Kiwanis, Pine Hills Country. Home: 1720 Sunnyside Ct Sheboygan WI 53081 Office: 2203 S Memorial Place Sheboygan WI 53081

HERMANN, PAUL DAVID, assn. exec.; b. Chgo., Feb. 1, 1925; s. Edgar Paul and Marjory (Alexander) H.; student Lawrence U., 1942-45; B.S. in Bus. Adminstrn., Northwestern U., 1948; m. Joan Louise Mullin, Nov. 10, 1948; children—Bruce Phillip, Susan Marie. Asst. dir. news bur. Ill. Inst. Tech., Chgo., 1945-48; editor Constrn. Equipment Distbn., Chgo., 1948-49; exec. v.p. Asso. Equipment Distbrs., Oak Brook, Ill., 1950—, also pres. Asso. Equipment Distbrs. Research and Services Corp., 1974—. Certified assn. exec. Mem. Am. Soc. Assn. Execs. (pres. 1974, dir. found., mem. past pres.'s council), U.S. C. Of C. (exec. com. Small Bus. Council), Chgo. Soc. Assn. Execs. (pres. 1968-69), Inst. Orgn. Mgmt. (regent 1969-72), Nat. Assn. Wholesaler-Distbrs. (trustee), Pi Delta Epsilon (hon.). Delta Tau Delta. Contbr. articles to profl. jours. and textbooks. Home: 2 S 751 Ave Cherbourg Oak Brook IL 60521 Office: 615 W 22d St Oak Brook IL 60521

HERMANN, ROBERT EWALD, surgeon; b. Highland, Ill., Jan. 28, 1929; s. Ewald Emil and Erna H. (Pabst) H.; A.B. cum laude, Harvard U., 1950; M.D., Washington U., 1954; m. Barbara Bower, Aug. 23, 1952; children—Robert E., Barry C. Intern Univ. Hosp., Cleve, 1954-55, resident in surgery, 1955-61; Crile, Bunts, and Lower fellow in surgery Case-Western Res. U., Cleve., 1961-62, asso. clin. prof. surgery, 1970—; practice medicine specializing in surgery, Cleve., 1962—; mem. staff dept. surgery Cleve. Clin., 1962-69, head dept. surgery, 1969—; bd. dirs. Cancer Center N.E. Ohio, 1974—; bd. trustees Cleve Inst. Music, 1970—, Cleve. Clinic Found., 1976—, Diabetes Assn. Cleve., 1969-71; bd. dirs. Ohio Regional Med. Program, 1970-72. Served to capt. M.C., U.S. Army, 1956-58. Recipient awards Ohio State Med. Assn., 1964; Chgo. Med. Soc., 1966, Am. Acad. Pediatrics, 1967. Diplomate Am. Bd. Surgery (bd. dirs. 1976-81). Fellow A.C.S. (treas. Ohio chpt. 1975—); mem. Am., Eastern., Minn. (hon.), Cleve. (award 1959, pres. 1974-75) surg. socs., Acad. Medicine Cleve. (bd. dirs. 1967-71), Am. Fedn. Clin. Research, Socs. for Surgery Alimentary Tract, Pancreas Club, Surg. Biology Club III., Central Surg. Assn., Whipple Soc., Internat. Soc. Surgery. Contbr. numerous articles to med. jours. Home: 16625 Shaker Blvd Shaker Heights OH 44120 Office: 9500 Euclid Ave Cleveland OH 44106

HERMANSEN, DAVID ROGER, architect; b. Chgo., Jan. 28, 1928; s. Sigurd Oscar and Lillian Dorothy (Larkin) H., m. Evelyn Clara Johnson, Aug. 27, 1949; children—Vicki K., David Scott, Debra Sue; student Wilson Jr. Coll., Chgo., 1948-50; B.S., U. Ill., 1953, M.S. (fellow), 1954. Licensed architect, Kans. With Childs & Smith, Architects. Chgo., 1947-49, Lundeen & Hilfinger, Architects, Bloomington, Ill., 1951-54; instr. U. Kans., Lawrence, 1954-56, asst. prof., 1956-63, asso. prof., 1963-66; asso. prof. architecture Ball State U., Muncie, Ind., 1966-70, prof., 1970—, coordinator programs in archtl. history and preservation, 1973—; cons. Robertson & Ericson, Architects, Lawrence, 1959-65, James Assos., Architects & Engrs., Indpls., 1973—; vis. lectr. Herron Sch. Art, Indpls., 1970-73. Juvenile Officer, Douglas County, Kans., 1954-58; mem. Muncie Historic Preservation Commn., 1977—; bd. dirs. Ball Art Found., 1967-69. Mem. Soc. Archtl. Historians, Assn. Preservation Technologists, Ind., Delaware County hist. socs., Ind. Covered Bridge Soc. (service award 1974), AIA, Ind. Soc. Architects, Hist. Landmarks Found. Ind., Scarab. AIA scholar Cranbrook Seminar, 1964; research grantee Ball State U., 1968; Author: Indiana County Courthouses, 1968; contrbr. articles to profl. jours. Home: 64 Redbud Ln Muncie IN 47302

HERMESMEYER, MICHAEL THOMAS, environ. engr.; b. Quincy, Ill., Nov. 6, 1949; s. Robert Wesley and Norma Mae (Duker) H.; B.S. in Civil Engring., U. Mo., Rolla, 1971; m. Donna Marie Tarne, Aug. 28, 1976. Environ. engr. Ill. Environ. Protection Agency, Chgo., 1972-74; project engr., ops. mgr. by-products div., corporate safety officer Am. Admixtures Corp., Chgo., 1974—; lectr. in field. Mem. Ill. Soc. Profl. Engrs., Water Pollution Control Fedn. Republican. Roman Catholic. Clubs: Mushroom Softball, Oldfield. Home: 108 Winston Ct Bolingbrook IL 60439 Office: 5909 N Rogers St Chicago IL 60646

HERMISTON, RAY TALBOT, educator; b. Ottawa, Ont., Can., Nov. 27, 1935; s. Ross Alan and Elizabeth Gladys (Talbot) H.; B.A., Queen's U., Can., 1959; M.S. (fellow), U. Mich., 1964, Ph.D. (fellow), 1967; m. Mary Kathleen Sullivan, Aug. 23, 1958; children—Sandra Ruth, Andrew John. Tchr., Sudbury (Ont.) High Sch., 1959-60; head phys. edn. dept. Selkirk High Sch., Ft. William, Ont., 1961-63; research dir. faculty phys. and health edn. U. Windsor (Ont.), 1967-69, asst. prof., 1967-69, asso. prof., 1969-74, prof., 1974—; cons. Sports Adminstrn. Centre, Ottawa, Ont., 1972-74, Integration, Inc., Windsor, 1971-76; pres. Minor Hockey League, Windsor, 1970-71. Mem. Canadian Assn. Health, Phys. Edn. and Recreation, Phi Kappa Phi. Contbr. articles to profl. jours. Office: Faculty Phys and Health Edn U Windsor Windsor ON Canada

HERR, RICHARD JOSEPH, art gallery exec.; b. Sheboygan, Wis., Jan. 17, 1937; s. George E. and Molly (Rammer) H.; pvt. study painting and design with Oscar Binder, Stuttgart, Germany, 1955-58; student Marquette U., 1958-60, Layton Sch. Art, 1958-60, U. Wis., 1960-61; children—Gretchen, Kurt, Eric. Owner, dir. Art Independent Gallery, Lake Geneva, Wis., 1968—; sculptor-in-residence The Prairie Sch., Racine, Wis., 1970-71, mem. faculty art dept., 1971-76; mem. faculty U. Wis., Parkside, 1973-74; lectr. in field; one man shows include Reeves Meml. Gallery, U. Wis., Oshkosh, 1967, Univ. Center Galleries, No. Ill. U., DeKalb, 1972, Wustum Mus., Racine, 1973, U. Wis., Parkside, 1976, U. Wis., Whitewater, 1977; two man shows include Gard Gallery, Gary, Ind., 1967, J. Barauch Gallery, Chgo., 1968, Marion Coll., Fond du Lac, Wis., 1968, Atelier Gallery, Milw., 1968, Mt. St. Paul Coll., Waukesha, Wis., 1969, Mt. Mary Coll., Milw., 1970, Carroll Coll., Waukesha, 1975; group shows include Milw. Art Center, 1965, 68, Mid-North Gallery, Chgo., 1966, Deerpath Gallery, Lake Forest, Ill., 1968, Layton Sch. Art, Milw., 1969, Sherbyn Gallery, Chgo., 1970, Crossman Gallery, U. Wis., Whitewater, 1971, Hyde Park Art Center, Chgo., 1972, Wustum Mus., Racine, 1974, North Broadway Gallery, N.Y.C., 1976, others. Served with AUS, 1955-58. Recipient 1st place award for sculpture Stevens Point (Wis.) Fine Arts Festival, 1967, Monument Sq. Art Fair, Racine, 1967, Paine Art Center, Oshkosh, 1967; award for sculpture Deerpath Art Festival, Lake Forest, 1967, Alverno Coll., Milw., 1967, Racine Invitational, Wustum Mus., 1970, 71, 72, 74, Virginia Beach (Va.) Invitational, 1971; Purchase award for permanent collection U. Wis., LaCrosse, 1968, Prarie Sch. Invitational, 1969; Duo Critic's award Chgo. Tribune and Chgo. Art Inst., 1972; numerous others. Mem. So. Assn. Sculptors, Am. Internat. Sculptors, Wis. Art Edn. Assn. (dir.). Sculpture reproduced in Sculpture Casting, 1972, Collage and Assembledge, 1973, Soft Sculpture and Related Soft Art, 1975. Home: 5965 Steele Rd Burlington WI 53105 Office: 706 Main St Lake Geneva WI 53147

HERRE, ERNEST ANDREW, social worker; b. Milw., Jan. 28, 1936; s. Frank Xavier and Marie (Schmid) H.; A.B., Marquette U., 1961; M.S.W., U. Wis., Milw., 1963. Probation and parole agt. Wis. Dept. Pub. Welfare, Milw., 1961-62, social worker, Wales, Milw., 1962-64, Milw. County Protective Services, Milw., 1964-66; supr. staff devel. Milw. County Welfare Dept., 1966—; vis. lectr., prof. social work Marquette U., 1969—. Cons. protective services youth devel. project Wis. Dept. Health and Social Services, 1967-68; participant Council of Internat. Programs in Europe, 1963. Named Social Worker of Year, Nat. Assn. Social Workers, 1968. Mem. Nat. Assn. Social Workers (chmn. Milw. social policy and action commn. 1967-68, exec. bd. Wis. 1967-68, v.p. 1968-69), Cath. Interracial Council (exec. bd. 1965-66), Southeastern Wis. Pub. Welfare Assn. (pres.), Social Welfare Alumni Assn. (pres. 1967-70), Phi Beta Kappa, Alpha Kappa Delta, Pi Gamma Mu. Contbg. author People of Inner Core (North), 1963; Social Workers at Work, 1972. Contbr. articles to profl. jours. Home: 3222 N 46th St Milwaukee WI 53216 Office: 1220 W Vliet St Milwaukee WI 53205

HERRICK, CLAY, JR., civic worker, ret. advt. agy. exec.; b. Cleveland Heights, Ohio, Dec. 15, 1911; s. C. Clay and Alice Mabel (Meriam) H.; B.A. Adelbert Coll. of Western Res. U., 1934; diploma John Huntington Poly. Inst.; m. Ruth Eleanor Penty, Apr. 27, 1935; children—Clay Herrick III, Jill. Pub. relations dir. General Tire & Rubber Co., Akron, 1940-45; creative dir. JP Smith creative printers for Eastman Kodak, Rochester, 1945-48; account exec. Fuller, Smith & Ross, Inc., 1948-58; v.p. Carpenter, Lamb & Herrick, Inc., 1958-64, pres., 1964-73; pres. Western Reserve Press, Inc., 1973—; sr. v.p. Watts, Lamb, Kenyon & Herrick Inc., 1973-74, ret., 1974. Instr. graphics Cleve. State U.; originator, 1st pres. Cleve. Printing Week celebrations. Pres., Early Settlers Assn.; chmn. Cleve. Landmark Commn.; v.p. Shaker Landmarks Commn.; chmn. Cleve. Hall Fame Commn.; v.p. Cleve. Bicentennial Commn.; mem. univ. alumni council Western Res. U.; fund chmn. Cleve. Ch. Fedn.; scoutmaster, cubmaster Boy Scouts Am.; active PTA, ARC; trustee YMCA, Shauffler div. Defiance Coll.; pub. relations bd. United Appeal. Named Cleve. Graphic Arts Man of Year, 1965. Mem. Nat. Cartoonists Soc., Am. Assn. Advt. Agys. (chmn.), New Eng. Soc. (pres., named Man of Year 1977), Cleve. Cultural Gardens Fedn. (v.p.), Shaker Hist. Soc. (pres.). Cleve. Ad Club (v.p.), Founders and Patriots Am. (lt. gov. nat. soc.), Fine Arts Assn. (trustee), Am. Advt. Fedn. (dist gov., named Advt. Man of Year 1974), Intercomm Communications Group (1st pres.), Cleve. Graphic Arts Council (organizer, pres.), Adelbert Alumni Assn. Western Res. U. (pres.), S.A.R. (past pres., sec.-treas. 1974—), Toastmasters Internat. (hon. life), Delta Upsilon, Sigma Delta Chi, Delta Sigma Rho, Pi Epsilon Delta. Presbyn. Club: Cheshire Cheese (past pres. 3 times). Author: But It's So, 1934; Cleveland's Rich Heritage, 1975. Editor, pub. Graphic Artisan; editor Pioneer, others. Home: 16315 Fernway Rd Shaker Heights OH 44120

HERRICK, DONALD WILLARD, ocular surgeon, banker; b. St. Paul, July 6, 1930; s. Willard Robert and Gertrude Evelyn (O'Connor) H.; student Coll. St. Thomas, 1948-51; B.S., U. Minn., 1953, M.D., 1955, postgrad., 1956-61; m. Helen Brooks, Aug. 29, 1953; children—Jane, John W. II, Donald Willard, Robert, Brian, Polly, Richard, Julie. Intern, St. Joseph's Hosp., 1955-56; resident U. Minn. Hosp., Mpls., 1956-61; practice medicine specializing in ocular surgery, St. Paul, 1961—; clin. instr. ophthalmology U. Minn. Med. Sch., 1963—; vice chmn., dir. Heritage State Bank North St. Paul, from 1967, now chmn. bd.; founder, pres. Willard Bank Shares Inc. Served with USAF, 1957-59. Diplomate Am. Bd. Ophthalmology. Fellow Am. Acad. Ophthalmology and Otolaryngology; mem. Minn. Assn. Ophthalmology, St. Paul Ophthalmol. Soc., Pan-Am. Assn. Ophthalmology, Midwest Soc. Physicians and Surgeons (founder, pres.), Am. Assn. Physicians and Surgeons (Ho. of Dels.), Assembly Bank Dirs., Am., Independent bankers assns. Kiwanian. Home: 22 Manitou Island White Bear Lake MN 55110 Office: 215 Kellogg Square St Paul MN 55101

HERRICK, HOWARD DUANE, hosp. adminstr., psychiatrist; b. Brayton, Iowa, Dec. 6, 1925; s. Julius Earl and Myrtle May (Hansen) H.; B.A., U. Omaha, 1951; M.D., U. Nebr., 1956. Intern, So. Pacific Gen. Hosp., San Francisco, 1956-57; resident Univ. Hosp., Omaha, 1957-60; instr., chief alcoholic service Med. Coll., U. Nebr., Omaha, 1962-64, asst. prof. psychiatry, 1974—; asst. supt., chief psychiat. service DeWitt State Hosp., Auburn, Calif., 1964-67; clin. dir. Norfolk (Nebr.) Regional Center and N.E. Mental Health Clinic, 1967-73, supt., regional dir., 1973—; mem. courtesy staff Our Lady of Lourdes, Luth. Community hosps. Served to lt. comdr. USNR, 1960-62. Diplomate Am. Bd. Psychiatry. Fellow Royal Soc. Health, Am. Psychiat. Assn.; mem. A.M.A., Nebr. Med. Assn., Madison Six County Med. Soc., Sioux Psychiat. Soc., A.A.A.S., Am. Med. Soc. on Alcoholism, N.Y. Acad. Scis., N.Am. Assn. Alcoholism Programs, Nat. Council on Alcoholism, Am. Coll. Clin. Pharmacology, Assn. Med. Supts. Mental Hosps., Nat. Assn. Supts. Pub. Residential Facilities for Mentally Retarded. Rotarian. Address: Box 1209 Norfolk NE 68701

HERRICK, JULIA FRANCES, biophysicist; b. nr. St. Paul, Sept. 14, 1893; d. John Willard and Kate E. (Conlin) Herrick; B.A., U. Minn., 1915, M.A., 1919, Ph.D., 1931. Tchr. high sch., Pine City, Minn., 1915-18, Ely, Minn., 1919-20; tchr. Northrup Collegiate Sch., Mpls., 1920-22; asst. prof. physics Rockford Coll., 1922-27; asso. Mayo Grad. Sch. Medicine, 1931-34, instr., 1934-42, asst., then asso. prof., 1946-58, prof. biophysics, 1958; research asso. Cardiovascular Research Lab. U. Wis. Med. Sch., Madison, 1959-60; sr. scientist Vista Lab. Calif. Inst. Tech., 1960-64, cons., 1964-65; sr. research scientist Intersci. Research Inst., Champaign, Ill., 1967-73, vis. prof. Ind. U.-Purdue U., Indpls., 1973-75; Center fellow Indpls. Center for Advanced Research, 1975—. Fellow Am. Phys. Soc., N.Y. Acad. Scis.; mem. Am. Physiol. Soc., AAAS, Am. Assn. Physicists in Medicine, Biophys. Soc., IEEE, Am. Heart Assn., Internat. Soc. Biorheology, Am. Inst. Biol. Scis., Phi Beta Kappa, Sigma Xi, Alpha Gamma Delta. Editor: Biomedical Sciences Instrumentation, vol. 3. Editor-in-chief IRE Transactions in Bio-Med. Electronics, 1953-59. Contbr. articles in field to profl. jours. Home: 1300 W Michigan St Indianapolis IN 46202 Office: 410 Beauty Ave Indianapolis IN 46202

HERRIN, SNYDER E., lawyer; b. Herrin, Ill., Dec. 25, 1903; s. Jeff Snyder and Louisa Clementine (Stearns) H.; student U. Mich., 1921-22; A.B., U. Ill., 1925, J.D., 1927; m. Norma Dot Keen, Aug. 16, 1930; children—Sandra Lou (Mrs. Sandra Plapp), Snyder E. II. Admitted to Ill. bar, 1927; since practiced in Herrin, Ill. Chmn. bd. Herrin Security Bank, 1957—. Govt. appeal agt. Draft Bd., Herrin, 1940-71. Sec. Herrin Bd. Edn., 1928-31; city atty., Herrin, 1935-37, 49-53, 57-69, 76—, Ziegler, Ill., 1934-42; village atty., Cambria, Ill., 1950-62, Bush, Ill., 1966-70; atty. Herrin Park Dist., 1955—, Herrin Mosquito Abatement Dist., 1962—. Served to capt. JAG, AUS, 1942-46. Mem. Ill., Williamson County (pres. 1940-42, 63-64) bar assns., Ill. Trial Lawyers Assn. (hon.), Ill. Assn. Park Dists. (hon.), Am. Legion (comdr. 1952-54), Herrin C. of C. (dir. 1975—), Williamson County Hist. Soc. (pres. 1957-61), Pi Kappa Phi, Gamma Eta Gamma, Democrat. Baptist. Elk, Rotarian (pres. 1932-34). Home: 408 S 12th St Herrin IL 62948 Office: 105 N Park Ave Herrin IL 62948

HERRING, JAMES P., chain food store co. exec.; b. Greenville, N.C., June 29, 1914; s. Leslie Preston and Ruth Harrel (Woodward) H.; ed. pub. schs.; m.; 1 dau., Constance Lee (Mrs. Pieter Mayer); m. 2d, Jean Millicent, May 1, 1965; children—Edward James Leslie, Brenda Harrel. With Walgreen Co. as dir. self-service operations; founder Sav-On Drugs, Inc.; v.p. Kroger Co., 1960-70, pres., chief exec. officer, 1970—, also dir.; pres. supeRx Drugs, Inc., 1961-70; dir. Central Trust Bank. Chmn., Cin. Metro. Nat. Alliance Businessmen, 1971. Bd. dirs. Nat. Center for Resource Recovery, Family Cancer Care, Good Samaritan Hosp. Mason. Clubs: Cincinnati, Hyde Park Country, Commercial of Cincinnati, Queen City, Bankers, Camargo Country; Hound Ears Country (Blowing Rock, N.C.). Home: 8445 Eustisfarm Lane Cincinnati OH 45243 Office: Kroger Bldg 1014 Vine St Cincinnati OH 45202

HERRMANN, ROBERT BERNARD, geophysicist, educator; b. Cin., Dec. 22, 1944; s. William and Bertha H.; B.S., summa cum laude, Xavier U., Cin., 1967; Ph.D., St. Louis U., 1974; m. Marion Klaric, June 19, 1976. Postdoctoral research asso. geophysics Coop. Inst. Research in Environ. Sci., U. Colo., Boulder, 1974-75; asst. prof. geophysics St. Louis, U., 1975—; cons. earthquake engring. Served with C.E., U.S. Army, 1969-71; Vietnam. Decorated Bronze Star. NSF fellow, 1967-69, 71-72. Mem. Seismol. Soc. Am., Am. Geophys. Union, Soc. Exploration Geophysicists, Phi Beta Kappa, Sigma Xi, Sigma Pi Sigma. Roman Catholic. Office: St Louis U PO Box 8099 St Louis MO 63156

HERRON, ORLEY RUFUS, coll. pres.; b. Olive Hill, Ky., Nov. 16, 1933; s. Orley Rufus and Hyllie Ann (Weaver) H.; B.A., Wheaton (Ill.) Coll., 1955; M.A., Mich. State U., 1959, Ph.D., 1965; Litt.D., Houghton (N.Y.) Coll., 1972; m. Donna Jean Morgan, Aug. 24, 1956; children—Jill, Morgan, Mark. Grad. asst., football coach Wheaton Coll., 1955-56; dir. youth River Forest (Ill.) Presbyn. Ch., 1956-58; head resident adviser Mich. State U., 1958-61; dean students Westmont Coll., Santa Barbara, Cal., 1961-67; dir. doctoral program, asso. prof. U. Miss., 1967-68; asst. to pres. Ind. State U., Terre Haute, 1968-70; pres. Greenville (Ill.) Coll., 1970-77, Nat. Coll. Edn., Evanston, Ill., 1977—. Mem. U.S. delegation to represent Pres. at 25th Anniversary Commemorative Ceremonies, UNESCO, 1971; mem. exec. com. Christian Coll. Consortium; mem. Nonpub. Advisory Com. Ill. Bd. Higher Edn. Named Herron Outstanding Citizen of Ill., Greenville Jaycees, 1971; recipient Crusader Century Club Christian Contbn. award Wheaton Coll., 1974. Mem. Nat. Assn. Evangelicals (dir.), Assn. Free Meth. Ednl. Instns. (pres.), Fedn. Ind. Ill. Colls. and Univs. (exec. com.), Am. Council on Edn., Am. Assn. Higher Edn., AAUP, Phi Delta Kappa. Author: Role of the Trustee, 1969; Input/Output, 1970; New Dimensions in Student Personnel Administration, 1970; (casette tape) Governing Higher Education in the 70s, 1970. Home: 32 Linden Ave Wilmette IL 60091

HERSE, BOGUSLAW ADAM, physician; b. Warsaw, Poland, July 20, 1924; s. Adam and Zofia (Kaminska) H.; M.D., Bologna (Italy) U., 1951; m. Lia Poggiolini, Apr. 16, 1950; children—Danielle, Conrad, Natalie. Intern, Columbus Hosp., Chgo., 1952-53; resident in internal medicine, Cook County Hosp., Chgo., 1953-54; gen. practice medicine, Oak Forest, Ill., 1954—; pres. Doctors Ltd., Oak Forest, 1954—; pres. med. staff S. Suburban Hosp., Hazel Crest, Ill., 1962-63, 74-75; med. commr. City of Oak Forest, 1965-67. Served with Polish Armed Forces, 1942-46. Decorated Monte Cassino Cross. Diplomate Am. Acad. Family Practice. Roman Catholic. Home: 16601 Fulton Terr Tinley Park IL 60477

HERSETH, LORNA BUNTROCK, state ofcl.; b. Columbia, S.D., Apr. 5, 1909; d. Albert P. and Ida Louise (Yeske) Buntrock; student No. State Coll., 1927-30, also U. Minn.; m. Ralph E. Herseth, Dec. 23, 1937; children—Karen A. (Mrs. David L. Wee), Connie M. (Mrs. Arnie Stenseth), R. Lars. Tchr. rural sch., then city pub. schs.; dep. county supt. schs.; county supt. Brown County Schs., S.D.; now sec. of state of S.D., Pierre. Active Easter Seal Soc. for Crippled Children and Adults. Treas. Shelby (S.D.) Sch. Bd. Mem. P.E.O. Democrat. Lutheran (Sunday sch. supt.). Home: 707 W Bridgeview Pierre SD 57501 Office: Sec of State State Capitol Pierre SD 57501

HERSHBARGER, ROBERT ALLEN, educator; b. Champaign, Ill., Aug. 30, 1932; s. Lawrence Arlington and Elizabeth Mae (Van Mefer) H.; m. Nancy J. Weeden, Dec. 18, 1954; children—Larry, Delynne, Russell, Mark; B.S., U. Ill., 1955; M.B.A., No. Ill. U., 1970; Ph.D., U. Ga., 1972. Asst. supr. ins. U. Ill., 1959-66; coordinator ins. No. Ill. U., 1966-69; instr. U. Ga., Athens, 1969-71, adviser to chmn. staff benefit com., 1969-71; asst. prof. finance and ins. U. R.I., 1971-74, mem. ins. adv. com. Extension Div., 1973-74; asso. prof. fin. U. Mo.-Columbia, 1974—, mem. industry risk and ins. ednl. adv. com., 1974—; cons. to pub. and pvt. orgns., 1974—. Vice pres., treas. Ins. & Fin. Cons., Inc., 1971-74; mem. adv. com. State Univs. Retirement System, State of Ill., 1965-69; mem. Police and Firemen Retirement Commn., City of Columbia, 1975—. Mem. Am., So., Western risk and ins. assns., Risk and Ins. Mgmt. Soc. Assn., Midwest Bus. Adminstrn. Assn., Central Mo. Estate Planning Council, Ins. Cons. Soc., Phi Gamma Delta, Sigma Iota Epsilon, Beta Sigma Delta, Beta Gamma Sigma, Alpha Kappa Psi. Contbr. articles to profl. jours. Home: 507 Stalcup St Columbia MO 65201

HERSHBERGER, GERALD ROBERT, lawyer; b. Hamden, N.D., Jan. 6, 1917; s. George Robert and Mabel Marie (Clouse) H.; grad. indsl. engring. Gen. Motors Inst., 1939; LL.B., J.D., Wayne State U., 1958; m. Lillian Agnes Mason, Dec. 31, 1942; children—Carole (Mrs. Gary Isom), Trudy (Mrs. Terry Filer), Faye (Mrs. Jack Preston), Gregory, Helen, Gerald, Mark. Tool and die engring. defense work, 1939-43; product engring. work research devel., 1946-61; admitted to Mich. bar, 1958, U.S. patent office, 1960, U.S. Supreme Ct., 1971; practice gen. and patent law, Troy, Mich., 1958—; pres. Ponderosa Realty Co.; pres., owner Snap-Sighter Inc., mfrs. iron dual sight for rifle scopes. Served in Ordnance Corps, AUS, 1943-46. Decorated Victory medal. Recipient 10 yr. grad. key, Gen. Motors Inst., 1956. Mem. Mich. Patent Law Assn., Am., S. Oakland, Oakland County bar assns., Mich. State Bar., Am. Trial Lawyers Assn., Delta Theta Phi, Patent Office Soc. Elk. Patentee vehicle, lighting, timing and warning system, also driving light control. Home and Office: 285 E Long Lake Rd Troy MI 48084

HERSHEWAY, CHARLES EUGENE, mktg. exec.; b. Chgo., Apr. 23, 1933; s. Louis and Jean (Manfre) H.; student U. Ill., 1951-53; B.S., Northwestern U., 1959; m. Shirley Leyendecker, Jan. 19, 1957; children—Deborah Lynn, Louise Jeffrey; m. 2d, Priscilla Karas, Dec. 1, 1974. Editorial dir. Nat. Research Bur., Chgo., 1958-62; promotion mgr. Advt. Publs., Inc., Chgo., 1962-64; advt. mgr. Pfaelzer Bros. div. Armour Co., Chgo., 1964-67, marketing mgr., 1967-70, sales mgr., 1970, v.p. marketing, 1970-74; pres. United Am. Food Processors

Gourmet Fare, 1974-76, Mail Market Makers, Inc., Clarendon Hills, Ill., 1976—. Mem. Percy for Gov. Finance Com., 1965. Served with USMCR, 1952-54, USNR, 1954-58. Mem. Mail Advt. Club Chgo., Chgo. Federated Advt., Premium Industry Club, Sales Promotion Execs., Mail Advt. Author: NRB Retail Advertising and Sales Promotion Manual, vol. I, 1960, vol. II, 1961, vol. III, 1962; M.P. Brown Collection Letter Manual, 1961; Nat. Research Bur. Discount Store Manual, 1961. Contbr. articles to profl. jours. Home and Office: 125 Eastern St Clarendon Hills IL 60514

HERSRUD, LESLIE R., circuit judge; b. Petrel, N.D., Apr. 6, 1914; s. Martin and Luella (Hardy) H.; B.A., St. Olaf Coll., 1935; J.D., U. Minn., 1938; m. Mary L. Smith, Oct. 5, 1942. Admitted to S.D. bar, 1938; practice law Lemmon, S.D., 1938-55; city atty. Lemmon, 1946; presiding circuit judge 8th Jud. Circuit, S.D., 1955—. Bd. dirs. Lutheran Hosps. and Homes Soc., Fargo, N.D. Served with AUS, 1942-45; ETO. Mem. Am., S.D. bar assns., Nat. Conf. State Trial Judges. Lutheran. Home: 304 3d Ave W Lemmon SD 57638 Office: 11 4th St W Lemmon SD 57638

HERTEL, LEONA, religious assn. adminstr.; b. Grand Rapids, Mich.; d. Nicholas and Dena (Timmer) Hertel; grad. high sch. Personal sec. Dr. M.R. DeHaan, founder, tchr. Radio Bible Class, weekly religious broadcast, Grand Rapids, 1941-65, editor newsletter, also contbr., 1953—, corporate sec.-treas., 1963-65, asst. sec.-treas., 1965—, also sec. finance com. Pianist, Calvary Undenominational Ch., 1950—, mem. 50th anniversary com., also sec., 1976—; organist Mel Trotter Mission, 1959—. Contbr. monthly article Discovery Digest. Home: 320 Baynton NE Grand Rapids MI 49503 Office: 3000 Kraft Ave SE Grand Rapids MI 49508

HERTZER, WILLIAM RUDOLPH, staff mem.; b. Emden, Germany, July 19, 1918; came to U.S., 1950, naturalized, 1956; s. Wilhelm Friedrich and Martha Feikea (Meyer) H.; grad. Community Coll., Emden, Germany, 1936; B.A., U. Berlin, 1945; m. Erika Riekena, June 29, 1946; children—Manfred, Sylvia, Sonja, Erika-William. Mgr. liaison office mil. govt., Germany, 1946-48; dir. adult edn. City of Emden, 1948-50, cultural advisor to mayor, 1946-50, licensee Emder Stadt Theater, 1948-50; coordinator linguistic services John Deere Waterloo (Iowa) Tractor Works, 1964—, coordinator metric edn., 1973—; metric cons. Hawkeye Inst. Tech. Mem. Am. Translators Assn., Guild Profl. Translators, Soc. Automotive Engrs., U.S. Metric Assn. (v.p. 1976-77, dir. central area 1978-79). Republican. Methodist. Clubs: Shriner, Mason. Home: 138 Lichty Blvd Waterloo IA 50701 Office: PO Box 270 Waterloo IA 50701

HERWIG, THELMA LANGE (MRS. THEODOR FREDRICK HERWIG), physician; b. Toledo, June 22, 1932; d. Edward Henry and Oleva Henrietta (Edler) Lange; B.S., U. Toledo, 1953; M.D., Ohio State U., 1958; m. Theodor Fredrick Herwig, June 10, 1956; children—Theodor Thomas, Nathaniel Christopher, David Edward. Intern, Mt. Carmel Hosp., Columbus Ohio, 1958-59; family practice medicine, Dublin, Ohio, 1963-67, Columbus, 1967—; employee health physician Riverside Meth. Hosp., Columbus. Mem. A.M.A., Am. Med. Womens Assn. Acad. Medicine Franklin County (med. services com.). Home: 2090 Cheltenham St Columbus OH 43220 Office: 3720 Olentangy River Rd Columbus OH 43214

HERZIG, ADAM HENRY, bearing mfg. co. exec.; b. Jaslo, Poland, Aug. 27, 1924; s. Jacob Joshua and Lea (Goldman) H.; came to U.S., 1973 (Canadian citizen); grad. in Mechanics and Chemistry, Conservatoire National des Arts et Metiers, Paris, 1951; B.Sc., Purdue U.; m. Anne H. Herzig, Mar. 24, 1956; children—Jack J.C., Elise Gina R.R. Export rep. Nadella Needle Bearings Co., France, 1950-52; pres. Internat. Merchandising Corp., N.Am. office of Nadella, Montreal, Can., 1952-70; pres. Nadella Corp., Montreal and Cherry Hill, N.J., 1970-73; pres., dir. Bremen Bearing Co., Inc. (Ind.), 1973—. Pres. B'nai B'rith Lodge L'Alliance, 1962-63. Recipient Silver Cross of Merit, Polish Govt., 1945; Man of Year award State of Israel Bonds, 1973. Mem. Soc. Mfg. Engrs., Computer and Automated Systems Assn., Grad. Soc. Conservatoire National des Arts et Metiers. Jewish. Club: South Bend Country. Home: 3111 Robinhood Ln South Bend IN 46614 Office: Bremen IN 46506

HERZOG, ARTHUR LOUIS, accountant; b. Chgo., May 9, 1904; s. Fred and Caroline (Strey) H.; student Am. Inst. Banking, 1930, DePaul U., 1949, Northwestern U., 1950; m. Lolita H. Stockman, Aug. 20, 1927; children—Phyllis (Mrs. James R. Hartley), Marilyn (Mrs. Max Moore), Sandra N. Auditor, asst. auditor Chgo. City Bank, 1933-47; self-employed as accountant, Chgo., 1948-73; bus. cons., tax analyst, Palos Park, Ill., 1973—; controller, dir. Kemlite Corp., Joliet, Ill.; dir. J.P. Ruklic Screw, Blue Island, Ill.; sec., dir. Mortenson Roofing Co., Chgo., Herman Wilz & Sons, Inc., Chgo. Mem. adv. bd. Community Center Found., Palos Park, 1966-67; mem. Ridge Civic Council, Chgo., 1945-47; treas. Village of Palos Park, 1967-75, mayor, 1975—. Trustee pension and profit sharing plans Kemlite Corp., Fred A. Snow Co., Chgo., J.P. Ruklic Screw Co., Mortenson Roofing Co., Chgo., Herman Wilz & Sons, Chgo., 720 N Mich. Corp., Chgo. Mem. Nat. Soc. Pub. Accountants, Soc. Viticulture and Enology, Beverly Wine and Food Soc. (pres. 1965), Les Amis du Vin, Tower Wine Soc., Ind. Accountants Assn. Ill. (pres. 1964-65, sec. 1963-64, chpt. pres. 1962-63). Republican. Lutheran. Clubs: Country (Midlothian, Ill.); Sons of Bachus; Palos Lions. Address: 12521 91st Ave Palos Park IL 60464

HERZOG, GODOFREDO MAX, physician; b. Chemnitz, Germany, Jan. 12, 1931; s. Heinrich and Louise (Gittler) H.; came to U.S., 1950, naturalized, 1960; B.S., La. State U., 1953; M.D., Washington U., St. Louis, 1957; m. Eva R. Muller, Sept. 2, 1956; children—Jacques A., Patricia M., Elsa M. Intern, Jewish Hosp., St. Louis, 1957-58, Sch. Aerospace Medicine, San Antonio, Tex., 1960; resident in surgery Jewish Hosp., Cin., 1958-59; resident in gynecology and obstetrics Jewish Hosp., St. Louis, 1964-67; instr. obstetrics-gynecology Washington U., St. Louis, 1967—; individual practice medicine, specializing in obstetrics, gynecology St. Louis, 1967—; cons. in field. Med. adviser, bd. dirs. Life Seekers, Planned Parenthood, Abortion Rights Alliance. Served to capt. M.C., USAF, 1959-64. Diplomate Nat. Bd. Med. Examiners, Am. Bd. Obstetrics and Gynecology. Fellow Am. Coll. Obstetrics and Gynecology; mem. AMA, St. Louis County Med. Soc., Pan Am., Israel, Mo. med. assns., Mo., St. Louis gynecol. socs., Am. Soc. Gynecol. Laparoscopists, Am. Fertility Soc. Jewish. Contbr. articles to profl. publs. Home: 9 Wendover St St Louis MO 63124 Office: 1125 Graham Rd St Louis MO 63031

HERZOG, SYLVIA LOUISE, speech pathologist; b. Irvington, Ill., Aug. 2, 1927; d. Julius Alfred and Laura Regina (Hake) Wacker; B.S., U. Ill., 1948, M.S., 1971; m. Roy Martin Herzog, June 27, 1948; children—Linda Herzog Mollman, Garry Steven. Speech therapist Tuscola (Ill.) Pub. Schs., 1948-52; tchr. learning disabilities pub. schs., Champaign, Ill., 1954-57; speech therapist Easter Seal Soc., Danville, Ill., 1955-58; clin. supr. dept. speech and hearing sci. U. Ill., 1973; speech and lang. pathologist Champaign Pub. Schs., 1957—. Pres. bd. dirs. Champaign Sch. Dist. Credit Union, 1957-69. Mem. Ill. Speech and Hearing Assn., NEA, Ill. Edn. Assn., Altrusa Internat., Zeta Phi Eta, Delta Kappa Gamma. Republican. Methodist. Office: 405 E Clark Champaign IL 61820

HESBURGH, THEODORE MARTIN, clergyman, univ. pres.; b. Syracuse, N.Y., May 25, 1917; s. Theodore Bernard and Anne Marie (Murphy) H.; student U. Notre Dame, 1934-37; Ph.B., Gregorian U., 1939; postgrad. Holy Cross Coll., Washington, 1940-43; S.T.D., Cath. U. Am., 1945; hon. degrees Bradley U., LeMoyne Coll., U. R.I., Cath. U. of Santiago (Chile), Dartmouth, Villanova U., St. Benedict's Coll., Columbia, Princeton, Ind. U., Brandeis U., Gonzaga U., U. Cal. at Los Angeles, Temple U., Northwestern U., U. Ill., Fordham U., Manchester Coll., Atlanta U., Wabash Coll., Valparaiso U., Providence Coll., U. So. Calif., Mich. State U., St. Louis U., Cath. U. Am., Loyola U. at Chgo., Anderson Coll., State U., N.Y. at Albany, Utah State U., Lehigh U., Yale, Lafayette Coll., King's Coll., Stonehill Coll., Alma Coll., Syracuse U., Marymount Coll., Hobart and William Smith Coll., Hebrew Union Coll., Cin., Harvard. Entered Order of Congregation of Holy Cross, 1934; ordained priest Roman Catholic Ch., U. Notre Dame, 1943; chaplain Nat. Tng. Sch. for Boys, Washington, 1943-44; vets. chaplain U. Notre Dame, 1945-47, asst. prof. religion, head dept., 1948-49, exec. v.p., 1949-52, pres., 1952—. Former dir. Woodrow Wilson Nat. Fellowship Corp.; mem. Civil Rights Commn., 1957-72; mem. of Carnegie Commn. on Future of Higher Edn.; chmn. U.S. Commn. on Civil Rights, 1969-72; mem. Commn. on an All-Volunteer Armed Force, 1970. Bd. dirs. Am. Council Edn., Freedoms Found. Valley Forge, Adlai-Stevenson Inst. Internat. Affairs; trustee Rockefeller Found., Carnegie Found. for Advancement Teaching, Woodrow Wilson Nat. Fellowship Found., Inst. Internat. Edn., Nutrition Found., United Negro Coll. Fund, others. Recipient U.S. Navy's Distinguished Pub. Service award, 1959; Presdl. Medal of Freedom, 1964; Gold medal Nat. Inst. Social Scis., 1969; Cardinal Gibbons medal Cath. U. Am., 1969; Bellarmine medal Bellarmine-Ursuline Coll., 1970; Meiklejohn award A.A.U.P., 1970; Charles Evans Hughes award Nat. Conf. Christians and Jews, 1970; Merit award Nat. Cath. Ednl. Assn., 1971; Pres.' Cabinet award U. Detroit, 1971; Am. Liberties medallion Am. Jewish Com., 1971; Liberty Bell award Ind. State Bar Assn., 1971; others. Fellow Am. Acad. Arts and Scis.; mem. Internat. Fedn. Cath. Univs., Freedoms Found. (dir., mem. exec. com.), Nutrition Found., Commn. on Humanities, Inst. Internat. Edn. (pres., dir.), Cath. Theol. Soc. Author: Theology of Catholic Action, 1945; God and the World of Man, 1950; Patterns for Educational Growth, 1958; Thoughts for Our Times, 1962; More Thoughts for Our Times, 1965; Still More Thoughts for Our Times, 1966; Thoughts IV, 1968; Thoughts V, 1969; The Humane Imperative: A Challenge for the Year 2000, 1974. Home: U Notre Dame Notre Dame IN 46556

HESKETH, HERBERT THOMAS, physician; b. Grand Forks, N.D., Aug. 13, 1928; s. John and Nellie Merle (Rutherford) H.; B.A. cum laude, Harvard, 1950; M.D., Johns Hopkins, 1954; m. Arline Caroline Heen, June 19, 1951; children—Thomas R., Cheryl A. Intern Henry Ford Hosp., Detroit, 1954-55, resident in anesthesiology, 1955-57; practice medicine specializing in anesthesiology, Park Ridge, Ill., 1959—; head anesthesiology sect. Luth. Gen. Hosp., Park Ridge, 1965—; clin. asso. prof. surgery, Abraham Lincoln Sch. Medicine, 1972—. Served to capt. M.C., USAF, 1957-59. Mem. Am., Ill. med. assns., Chgo. Med. Soc., Am., Ill., Chgo. socs. anesthesiologists. Lutheran (deacon). Home: 869 East Ave Park Ridge IL 60068 Office: 132 S Prospect Rd Park Ridge IL 60068

HESLER, HAROLD PATTON, ret. mech. engr.; b. Alva, Okla., July 24, 1911; s. William Walter and Ethel Carrie (Patton) H.; grad. Kansas City Jr. Coll., 1930; B.S., U. Mich., 1933, M.S. in Mech. Engring., 1934; m. Marxie Squarcia, Nov. 28, 1935; children—Marcia Annette, Toni Gale, Vicki Dale. Design engr., Gen. Electric Co., Schenectady, 1934-39; mech. engr. Standard Oil Co., Chgo., 1939-42; founder Hesler Co. Inc., Prairie Village, Kans., 1945, pres., chmn. bd., 1958-76. Chpt. chmn. Shawnee Mission ARC, Kans., 1970-73, chmn. advisory bd. Heart of Am. div., 1973-75. Served from 1st lt. to lt. col., Ordnance Corps, U.S. Army, 1942-46. Decorated Bronze Star; registered profl. engr., Mo. Mem. ASME, Nat. Soc. Profl. Engrs., Am. Defense Assn., Engrs. Club of Kansas City, Sigma Xi, Iota Alpha, Tau Beta Pi, Phi Kappa Phi. Republican. Methodist. Address: 5327 Canterbury Rd Shawnee Mission KS 66205

HESLING, DONALD MILLS, mech. engr.; b. Dubuque, Iowa, Nov. 3, 1914; s. Francis J. and Mae L. (Mills) H.; student Muskegon Community Coll., 1934-36, U. Mich., 1936-37; m. Rheata E. Peterson, Apr. 2, 1945; children—Donald, Christine, Mary, Carol, Joanne, Terry, Judy, David, Debra, Patrice, Daniel, Dennis, Thomas. Master mechanic Sealed Power Corp., Muskegon, Mich., 1946-50, dir. engring., 1950-52, mgr. mfg. engring., 1952-54, v.p. mfg. engring., 1954-57, v.p. research, engring., 1957—. Mem. IEEE, A.I.M., Am. Mgmt. Assn., Serra Internat., Am. Ordnance Assn., Nat. Bus. AirCraft Assn., Internat. Platform Assn., Soc. Automotive Engrs. Roman Catholic. Home: 1419 Chapel Rd Muskegon MI 49441 Office: 2001 Sanford St Muskegon MI 49443

HESS, BARTLETT LEONARD, clergyman; b. Spokane, Wash., Dec. 27, 1910; s. John Leonard and Jessie (Bartlett) H.; B.A., Park Coll., 1931, M.A. (fellow in history 1931-34), U. Kan., 1932, Ph.D., 1934; B.D., McCormick Theol. Sem., 1936; m. Margaret Young Johnston, July 31, 1937; children—Daniel Bartlett, Deborah Margaret, John Howard and Janet Elizabeth (twins). Ordained to ministry Presbyn. Ch., 1936; pastor Effingham, Kan., 1932-34, Chgo., 1935-42, Cicero, Ill., 1942-56, Ward Meml. Presbyn. Ch., Detroit, 1956-68, Ward U.P. Ch., Livonia, Mich., 1968—. Tchr. ch. history, bible Detroit Bible Coll., 1956—, bd. dirs., 1956—; minister radio sta. WHFC, Chgo., 1942-50, WMUZ-FM, Detroit, 1958-68, WOMC-FM, 1971-72, WBFG-FM, 1972—; missioner to Philippines, United Presbyn. Ch. U.S.A., 1961. Adviser Mich. Synod council United Presbyn. Ch.; mem. com. Billy Graham Crusade for S.E. Mich., 1976. Mem. Organizer Friendship and Service Com. for Refugees, Chgo., 1940. Bd. dirs. Beacon Neighborhood House, Chgo., 1945-52, Presbyns. United for Bibl. Concerns, 1975—; pres. bd. dirs. Peniel Community Center, Chicago, 1945-52. Named Pastor of Year, Mid-Am. Sunday Sch. Assn., 1974. Mem. Cicero Ministers Council (pres. 1951), Phi Beta Kappa, Phi Delta Kappa. Author: (with Margaret Johnston Hess) How to Have a Giving Church, 1974; (with M.J. Hess) The Power of a Loving Church, 1977. Contbr. articles in field to profl. jours. Traveled in Europe, 1939, 52, 55, 68; also in Greece, Turkey, Lebanon, Syria, Egypt, Israel, Iraq; condr. tour of Middle East and Mediterranean countries, 1965, 67, 73, 74, 76, 78. Home: 16845 Riverside Dr Livonia MI 48154 Office: 17000 Farmington Rd Livonia MI 48150

HESS, EDWARD ANTHONY, electromech. and solid state components co. exec.; b. Cin., Sept. 30, 1930; s. Edward August and Clara (Segers) H.; B.S., Xavier U., 1952; postgrad. LaSalle U., 1955-58, Ind. State Tchrs. Coll., 1956, U. Dayton, 1959; M.B.A., U. Calif. at Los Angeles, 1966; m. Virginia Lee Bowen, Oct. 3, 1953 (div. 1968); children—Jennifer, Andrew, Joseph, Matthew, Lynn, Amelia; m. 2d, Shirley Ann Danzeisen, Nov. 13, 1976. Exec. tng. program Pa. R.R. Freight Sales & Service, 1953-57; with Ledex, Inc., Dayton, Ohio, 1960—, product mgr., 1970-71, sales mgr. indsl. markets, 1971-72, comml. markets mgr., 1972-73, gen. sales mgr., 1973-76, mgr. product mgmt., 1976—. Traffic Club Chgo. scholar LaSalle Extension U., Chgo., 1955. Mem. Am. Mktg. Assn., Electronic Industries Assn. (exec. council parts div. 1971-74), Am. Def. Preparedness Assn. Home: 4309 Glen Heath Dr Kettering OH 45440 Office: 123 Webster St Dayton OH 45401

HESS, EDWARD FREDERICK, JR., lawyer, educator; b. Chgo., Jan. 15, 1919; s. Edward Frederick and Rhea Juanita (Hinman) H.; B.S., Northwestern U., 1941; J.D., U. Ill., 1947, M.S., 1963; m. Betty Jane Stone, Nov. 21, 1942; children—Susan Marot (Mrs. Walter R. Popowski), Edward Frederick III. Admitted to Ill. bar, 1948; mem. firm Stone, Stone & Hess, Bloomington, Ill., 1948-52; sr. property adjuster State Farm Mut., Bloomington, 1948-52; asst. reporter of decisions Supreme Ct. Ill., Bloomington, 1953-62; librarian U.S. Ct. Appeals, 9th Circuit, San Francisco, 1963-64; asst. reference librarian, asst. prof. U. Ill., Urbana, 1964-65, asso. prof., asso. librarian, 1965-70, law librarian, prof. library adminstrn., prof. law, 1970—, mem. faculty senate, 1971—. Mem. Adult Edn. McLean County, Bloomington, 1954-54, Bloomington Community and Regional Planning Council, 1948-50; mem. adv. council Bloomington Bd. Edn., 1948-50, chmn., 1950. Served with USNR, 1942-45. Named Man of Year, Jr. Assn. Commerce, Bloomington, 1950. Mem. Internat., Am. (rep. to U.S. Am. Standards Inst. 1969), Chgo. (pres. 1972—) assns. law libraries, Ill. Bar Assn., Nat. Microfilm Assn., Am. Soc. for Information Sci., Spl. Libraries Assn. Club: Exchange (Urbana). Home: 610 W Michigan Urbana IL 61801 Office: U Ill Coll Law Library Champaign IL 61820

HESS, ROBERT BOND, mfg. co. exec.; b. Crystal City, Mo., Aug. 5, 1920; s. Francis J. and Anna M. (Bond) H.; B.S. in Mech. Engring., U. Mo., 1943; M.Engring. Adminstrn., Washington U., 1957; m. Mary Lou Gwinn, June 20, 1943; 1 dau., Sharon Gwinn Hess Summers. Chief components engr. Emerson Electric Co., St. Louis, 1946-59, proposal adminstr., 1959-61, mgr. market planning and research, 1961-62; sales rep. Conductron div. McDonnell Aircraft Co., St. Louis, 1962-65, mgr. product mktg., 1965-67, sales mgr., 1967-69; mgr. product devel. and acquisition Monsanto Co., St. Louis, 1969-71; pres. Low Com Systems Co., St. Louis, 1971-72; sr. v.p. ROI Controls Corp., Princeton, N.J., 1972-73; pres. Blake Assos., Inc., St. Louis, 1972-74; exec. v.p. CE Industries Corp., Belleville, Ill., 1974-75, pres., 1975—, also dir. Served with USAF, 1943-45. Mem. Belleville C. of C. (chmn. mfrs. div. 1975-77), Engrs. Club St. Louis, Ill. Mfrs. Assn., Am. Foundryman Assn. Clubs: Elks, Optimist (Belleville); Media, Ambassadors (St. Louis); Lake St. Louis (Mo.). Home: 531 N Ballas Rd Des Peres MO 63122 Office: PO Box 217 1200 E A St Belleville IL 62222

HESS, ROBERT LEE, educator, univ. ofcl.; b. Asbury Park, N.J., Dec. 18, 1932; s. Henry and Ada (Davis) H.; B.A., Yale, 1954, M.A., 1955, Ph.D., 1960; m. Frances H. Aaron, Apr. 9, 1960; children—Carl, Laura, Jonathan, Roger. Instr., Carnegie Inst. Tech., Pitts., 1958-59, asst. prof. history, 1959-61; asst. prof. history Mount Holyoke Coll., South Hadley, Mass., 1961-64, Northwestern U., Chgo., 1964-65; asso. prof. history U. Ill., Chgo. Circle Campus, 1966-71, prof., 1971—, asso. dean, 1970-72, asso. vice chancellor acad. affairs, 1972—; cons. Center for Study Democratic Instns., Ency. Brit., Ency. Africana, Dictionary Ethiopian Biography, Peace Corps Tng. Program, U. Mass., 1962, Syracuse U., 1965, various univ. presses. Pres., Glencoe (Ill.) Human Relations Com., 1966-68. Ford Found. research travel scholar, 1963; Fulbright scholar, 1956-58; Guggenheim fellow, 1968-69. Fellow African Studies Assn., Middle East Studies Assn. N.Am.; mem. Am. Hist. Assn., Soc. Italian Hist. Studies. Jewish (pres. congregation 1975—). Clubs: Plaza (Chgo.); Mory's and Elizabethan (New Haven). Author: Italian Colonialism in Somalia, 1966; Ethiopia: The Modernization of Autocracy, 1970; A Bibliography of Primary Sources for 19th Century Tropical Africa, 1972; Dictionary of Ethiopian Biography, 1977. Contbr. articles to profl. jours. Home: 648 Country Ln Glencoe IL 60022 Office: Office of Chancellor U Ill Chicago Circle Chicago IL 60680

HESS, STANFORD KENNETH, realtor; b. Hammond, Ind., Oct. 7, 1936; s. Arthur Louis and Gertrude Charlotte (Krim) H.; B.S., Ind. U., 1958; m. Joan Rhoda Korss, June 7, 1974. With Samuel C. Ennis & Co., realtors, Hammond, 1960-63; owner Stanford K. Hess realtor, Hammond, 1965—; dir. Calument Nat. Bank, Hammond. Mem. Hammond Downtown Council, 1967—, Hammond Zoning Bd. Appeals, 1960-62. Mem. at large Calumet council Boy Scouts Am., 1975—; active Ind. U. Found., 1970. Served with AUS, 1959. Mem. Nat. Assn. Real Estate Bds., C. of C. Jewish. Home: 225 Broadmoor St Munster IN 46322 Office: 5246 Hohman Ave Hammond IN 46320

HESS, STANLEY WILLIAM, librarian; b. Bremerton, Wash., July 9, 1939; s. Ray Myron and Kathryn Elaine (Joehnke) H.; student Olympic Community Coll., 1958-60; B.A., U. Wash., 1964, postgrad., 1967-71; M.S. in L.S., Case Western Res. U., 1976. Supr. photograph and slide library Seattle Art Mus., 1964-73; asso. librarian for photographs and slides Cleve. Mus. Art, 1973—. Mem. evaluating panel, adv. com. Slide Buyer's Guide, 1974—; lectr., instr. visual resources in fine arts. Mem. Art Libraries Soc. N.Am. (mem. standards com. 1977—, chmn. sub-com. visual resources 1977—), Coll. Art Assn., Am. Mus. Assn., Spl. Libraries Assn., U. Wash. Alumni Assn. (life), Beta Phi Mu. Episcopalian. Contbr. articles to profl. publs. Home: 2539 N Moreland Blvd Shaker Heights OH 44120 Office: 11150 East Blvd Cleveland OH 44106

HESSER, ERNEST GRANT, bldg. contractor; b. Bowling Green, Ohio, Jan. 11, 1919; s. Ernest George and Ethel (Martin) H.; A.B., Dartmouth Coll., 1941; m. Betty Maescher, Sept. 22, 1944; children—Grant Victor, Peter Langton, John Martin. With Chas. V. Maescher & Co. Inc., Cin., 1946—, sec., 1955-57, exec. v.p., 1957-64, pres., 1964—; former chmn., trustee Constrn. Advancement Program Greater Cin.; mem. nat. panel arbitrators Am. Arbitration Assn.; chmn. Cin. Regional Constrn. Industry Arbitration Com. Active ARC, United Appeal, Boy Scouts Am. Bd. dirs. Gen. Protestant Orphans Home, Thomas More Coll., Cin. Assn. for Blind; founder, v.p., bd dirs. Am. Council for Constrn. Edn. Served to lt. comdr. USNR, 1941-46; ATO, PTO. Fellow Am. Inst. Constructors (v.p., dir.); mem. Asso. Contractors Ohio (pres. 1971, dir.), Asso. Gen. Contractors Am. (nat. dir., pres. Cin. 1970), Allied Constrn. Industries Cin. (pres. 1977 dir.), Ohio, Cin. chambers commerce, Engring. Soc. Cin., S.A.R, Beta Theta Pi (local dir.), Sigma Lamda Chi. Methodist (dir.). Clubs: Dartmouth Cincinnati (pres. 1953, 63), Gyro (pres. 1958-59, dist. gov. 1961-62), University (pres., dir. 1966-73), Cin. Country (dir.); Les Cheneaux Yacht (Mich.). Home: 1130 Rookwood Dr Cincinnati OH 45208 Office: 2106 Florence Ave Cincinnati OH 45206

HESSLER, WILLIAM GERHARD, data processor; b. Chgo., May 20, 1926; s. William Gerhard and Rosemary (Kalb) H.; B.S., Purdue U., 1946; M.B.A., Northwestern U., 1956; m. Kazuko Yonetsu, June 2, 1956; children—Martha, George, Kay, Emmy. Tech. intelligence investigator U.S. Army, Tokyo, Japan, 1947-50, electronics engr., Yokohama, Japan, 1952-54; devel. engr. Western Electric, Cicero, Ill., 1955-61; engring. data processing specialist Goodyear Aerospace Corp., Akron, Ohio, 1961-65, sr. data processing systems analyst Goodyear Tire & Rubber Co., 1965—; tax preparer H & R Block Inc., 1968—. Scoutmaster, Boy Scouts Am., Silver Lake Village, Ohio, 1972-76. Served with AUS, 1950-52. Recipient profl. certificate Data Processing Mgmt. Assn., 1962. Mem. Am. Radio Relay League, Eta Kappa Nu, Alpha Kappa Psi, Alpha Phi Omega, Delta Sigma Phi.

Roman Catholic. Home: 3046 Lake Rd Cuyahoga Falls OH 44224 Office: 1200 E Market St Akron OH 44316

HESTAD, BJORN MARK, metal distbg. co. exec.; b. Evanston, Ill., May 31, 1926; s. Hilmar and Anna (Aagaard) H.; student Ill. Inst. Tech., 1947; m. Florence Anne Ragusi, May 1, 1948; children—Marsha Ann, Patricia (Mrs. James Arthur Hynes), Peter Mark. Sales corr., Shakeproof, Inc., Chgo., 1947-50; indsl. buyer Crescent Industries, Inc., Chgo., 1950-51; purchasing agt. Switchcraft, Inc., Chgo., 1951-73, materials mgr., 1973-74, dir. purchasing, 1974-77; owner Tool King, Northfield, Ill., 1977—. Mgr. youth orgns. Northfield Jr. Hockey Club, 1968-71, Winnfield Hockey Club, 1972-73; bus. mgr. West Hockey Club, 1973-74. Served as cpl. USAAF, 1944-46. Mem. Tool and Die Inst. Republican. Mem. United Ch. Christ. Lion. Home: 850 Happ Rd Northfield IL 60093 Office: 480 Central Ave Northfield IL 60093

HETHERINGTON, JAMES RICHARD, ins. co. exec.; b. Indpls., Feb. 3, 1931; s. Frederick Benjamin and Pauline (Suiter) H.; A.B., Ind. U., 1953; m. Susan Esther Bassett, Jan. 31, 1953; children—Robert Bassett, William Frederick. Reporter, Ind. news editor, Daily Mag. editor Louisville Times, 1955-61; asst. city editor Indpls. Times, 1961-63; editorial editor Sta. WFBM, 1963-74; pub. relations dir. Am. United Life Ins. Co., Indpls., 1974—, v.p., 1977—; lectr. broadcast newswriting Butler U., 1970-75. Bd. dirs. Indpls. Family Service Assn., 1969—, pres., 1974-76. Served with U.S. Army, 1953-55. Recipient Alfred P. Sloan award, 1966; Peabody award for pub. service, 1969; 5 editorial awards Radio-TV News Dirs. Assn. Mem. Pub. Relations Soc. Am., Indpls. Pub. Relations Soc., Life Ins. Advertisers Assn., Sigma Delta Chi (award 1967). Lutheran. Club: Indpls. Press (dir. 1965-68, 75-76, pres. 1967). Home: 7205 Steinmeier Dr Indianapolis IN 46250 Office: 1 W 26th St Indianapolis IN 46206

HETLAND, LARUE ELMER, retail food chain exec.; b. Artesian, S.D., Oct. 21, 1933; s. Elmer Clarence and Edna (Lucid) H.; B.S., U. S.D., 1960; m. Lorma Jane Wittstruck, May 30, 1959; children—James, Nancy, Susan. Dir. advt. Nash Finch Co., Mpls., 1960-75; regional dir. advt. A&P, Indpls., 1975-77; v.p. McGrath Advt. Agy., Indpls., 1977—. Pres. Hopkins (Minn.) Little League, 1973. Served to sgt. USMC, 1954-57. Mem. Internat. Platform Assn. Lutheran. Club: Advt. of Indpls. Home: 8915 Spicewood Ct Indianapolis IN 46260

HETTERICK, DAVID RAYMOND, marketing research cons.; b. Bronx, N.Y., Aug. 11, 1939; s. Raymond Delos and Josephine May (Flick) H.; B.A., St. Olaf Coll., 1961; M.A., Columbia U., 1963; m. Geraldine Ellen Kane, Oct. 15, 1969; children—John, Kathleen, Eileen, Brian, Michael. Statistician, Nat. Council on Aging, 1962-63; mktg. research analyst Nat. Biscuit Co., N.Y.C., 1963-64, mgr. consumer and mktg. research, 1964-68; v.p., dir. research, partner Quatra Mktg. Research, Inc., Edina, Minn., 1968—. Mem. Am. Mgmt. Assn., Am. Mktg. Assn. Home: 5704 Duncan Ln Edina MN 55436 Office: 7200 France Ave S Edina MN 55435

HEUER, MICHAEL ALEXANDER, dentist, educator; b. Grand Rapids, Mich., Apr. 27, 1932; s. Harold Maynard and Gwendolyn Ruth (Kremer) H.; D.D.S., Northwestern U., 1956; M.S., U. Mich., 1959; m. Barbara Margaret Naines, Nov. 23, 1955; children—Kristan M., Karin E., Katrina A. Practice dentistry specializing in endodontics, Chgo., 1959—; teaching asso., asst. prof. Northwestern U. Dental Sch., 1960-66, prof., chmn. dept. endodontics, 1974—; asso. prof. Loyola U. Dental Sch., 1968-73. Sec., chmn. sub-com. MD-156 Am. Nat. Standards Inst.; mem. com. on advanced edn. Commn. Accreditation Dental Edn., 1974-77. Served as lt. Dental Corps, USNR, 1956-58. Diplomate Am. Bd. Endodontics (dir., sec.-treas., pres. 1973-77). Fellow Am. Assn. Endodontists (exec. com. 1967-71), Am. Coll. Dentistry; mem. ADA (cons. council on dental edn., council on dental therapeutics, chmn. sect. on endodontics council on sci. sessions, chmn. council on dental materials and devices 1977—), AAAS, Internat. Assn. for Dental Research, G.V. Black Soc. Northwestern U., Edgar D. Coolidge Endodontic Soc. (trustee), Am. Assn. Dental Schs., Chgo. Odontographic Soc., Pierre Fauchard Acad., Omicron Kappa Upsilon, Delta Sigma Delta, Chi Psi. Contbr. articles to profl. jours. Home: 1461 Lake Shore Dr S Barrington IL 60010 Office: Dental Sch Northwestern U 311 E Chicago Ave Chicago IL 60611

HEUMANN, HERBERT H., fin. and indsl. holding cos. exec.; b. Seward, Nebr., Nov. 18, 1916; s. Fred H. and Caroline (Geseking) H.; B.Sc., U. Nebr., 1939; m. Dorothy Jane Card, Jan. 7, 1940; children—Patricia Lynne, Herbert David. Vice pres. State Securities Co., Lincoln, Nebr., 1940—; v.p., dir. Indal, Inc., Toronto; pres. A & H Realty Co., Lincoln, 1952—, SealRite Industries, Inc., Lincoln, 1953—, N.E. Investment Co., Lincoln, 1956—; pres., dir. 1st City Fin. Corp., Lincoln; dir. 1st Nat. Life Ins. Co., Modern Community Developers Lincoln, Citibank & Trust Co., 1st City Savs. and Loan Assn. Chmn. N.E. Communities Council; mem. charter rev. com. City of Lincoln; dir. Lincoln Action Program. Served with U.S. Army, 1941-47. Decorated Bronze Star, Order Brit. Empire, and others. Mem. Home Builders Assn. Lincoln (past pres.), Lincoln Bd. Realtors (past treas.), Nebr. Manufactured Housing Assn. (dir.), C. of C. Republican. Presbyterian. Club: Rotary (past pres.). Home: 2025 Greenbriar Ln Lincoln NE 68520 Office: PO Box 4593 Lincoln NE 68504

HEUSEL, WILLIAM GEORGE, physician; b. Sutton, Nebr., Feb. 22, 1923; s. Henry Carl and Maude Barbara (Lange) H.; B.S., M.D., U. Nebr., 1961; m. Mona Marlene Larson, Nov. 26, 1959; children—Miriam M., Laurie C., Jonathan W., Karin K. Intern City Hosp., Springfield, Ohio; practice medicine specializing in family practice, Hooper, Nebr., 1962—; vol. faculty U. Nebr. in family practice, Creighton U. Sch. Medicine in pediatrics; med. dir. clinics for migrant workers, Harlingen and Raymondville, Tex., 1971-72, vol. in community devel. El Salvador, India, Am. Friends Service Com., 1953-56; cons. Sch. Allied Health Professions, U. Nebr., 1975. Trustee Immanuel Med. Center. Recipient Volunteer of Year award for work with handicapped children, City of Omaha, 1970. Diplomate, charter fellow Am. Bd. Family Physicians. Mem. AMA, Am. Acad. Family Physicians, Nebr. State Med. Assn., Dodge County Med. Soc., Alpha Zeta. Mem. Soc. of Friends. Lion. Home and Office: Hooper NE 68031

HEUSINKVELD, EDWIN DAVID, ednl. adminstr.; b. Clinton, Iowa, Aug. 21, 1927; s. Edwin David and Rose Viola (Anderson) H.; B.A., Wheaton Coll., 1949; M.A., U. Iowa, 1957, Ph.D., 1964; postgrad. Inst. Ednl. Mgmt. Harvard U., 1973; m. Helen Joan Rod, June 8, 1957; children—David Scott, John Eric, Mark Stephen. Head counselor U. Iowa, Iowa City, 1955-56, asst. counselor of men, 1956-59; dean men Ferris State Coll., Big Rapids, Mich., 1959-64; asst. dean students, 1964-66; asso. dean students Wittenberg U., Springfield, Ohio, 1966-68, dean students, 1968-70, v.p. student services, 1970—, asso. prof. edn., 1968—. Pres. Clark County Alcohol and Drug Council; trustee Clark County Bd. Mental Retardation. Served with USN, 1951-54. Mem. Am. Assn. Higher Edn., Am. Coll. Personnel Assn., Nat., Ohio (pres.) assns. student personnel adminstrs., Phi Delta Kappa, Alpha Phi Omega, Omicron Delta Kappa, Phi Eta Sigma, Sigma Alpha Epsilon. Lutheran. Home: 99 S Broadmoor Blvd Springfield OH 45504 Office: Wittenberg Univ Springfield OH 45501

HEWETT, WILLIAM SHERMAN, II, investment co. exec.; b. St. Paul, July 28, 1924; s. Maurice William and Jesse Lee (Berry) H.; student U. Minn., 1942-43, Universidad de Mexico, 1948; B.A., Wooster Coll., 1949; m. Evelyn Ruth Fischer, Aug. 14, 1948; children—Joanne, Charles, Susan, John, Thomas. With N.Y. Life Ins. Co., Wooster, Ohio, 1949-51; Merrill Lynch, Pierce, Fenner & Smith, Canton, O., 1951-58, Paine Webber Jackson & Curtis, Canton, 1958-62; securities salesman Hayden Miller & Co. div. Stone Webster, Canton, 1962-73, v.p., 1965-73, br. mgr., 1964-73; with Butcher & Singer, 1973-76, Prescott, Ball & Turben, 1976—; real estate developer; tchr. evening sch. investment courses. Served with USN, 1942-46. Clubs: Canton Road Runners, Soaring Thunderbird Gliding, Canton Ski (pres. 1968-69), Keelhaulers Canoe, Toastmasters (pres. club 637, 1951—). Author: Common Stock for the Uncommon Man, 1966. Home: 2380 Saga Circle NE East Canton OH 44730 Office: 412 Mellett Bldg Canton OH 44701

HEWITT, JAMES WATT, lawyer; b. Hastings, Nebr., Dec. 25, 1932; s. Roscoe Stanley and Willa Manners (Watt) H.; student Hastings Coll., 1950-52; B.S., U. Nebr., 1954, J.D., 1956; m. Marjorie Ruth Barrett, Aug. 8, 1954; children—Mary Janet, William Edward, John Charles, Martha Ann. Admitted to Nebr. bar, 1956; practiced in Hastings, 1956-57, Lincoln, Nebr., 1960-61; v.p., gen. counsel Nebco, Inc., Lincoln, 1961—. Vis. lectr. U. Nebr. Coll. Law, 1970-71; dir. Gateway Bank, Lincoln. Mem. state exec. com. Republican party, 1967-70, mem. state central com., 1967-70, legis. chmn., 1968-70. Bd. dirs. Lincoln Child Guidance Center, 1969-72, pres., 1972; bd. dirs. Lincoln Community Playhouse, 1967-73, pres., 1972-73; trustee Bryan Meml. Hosp., Lincoln, 1968-74, 76—, chmn., 1972-74. Served to lt. USAF, 1957-60. Mem. Am. (Nebr. state del. 1972—), Nebr. State (chmn. ins. com. 1972-76), Fed., Lincoln bar assns., Newcomen Soc., Am., Nebr., Lincoln rose socs., Round Table, Beta Theta Pi, Phi Delta Phi. Presbyn. (elder 1962—). Mason (Shriner), Rotarian. Club: University (Lincoln). Home: 2990 Sheridan Blvd Lincoln NE 68502 Office: 1815 Y St Lincoln NE 68501

HEWITT, PATRICIA WIMAN (MRS. WILLIAM ALEXANDER HEWITT), agriculturalist; b. Chgo., Jan. 17, 1925; d. Charles Deere and Pattie (Southall) Wiman; student Conn. Coll. for Women, 1942-44, U. Calif. at Santa Barbara, 1944-45, George Washington U., 1946-47; m. William Alexander Hewitt, Jan. 3, 1948; children—Anna Deere, Adrienne Deere, Alexander Southall. Agriculturist, asst. to mgr. Midvale Farms Corp., Tucson, 1945-47, dir., sec., 1945—, co-owner, 1963; owner, mgr. Friendship Farms, E. Moline, Ill., 1955—; owner, joint mgr. Camelot Vineyards, Rutherford, Calif., 1960—; dir. Diagnostic Data Inc., Mountain View, Calif., 1965-74. Mem. Ill. Racing Bd., 1973—; mem. Jr. League, San Francisco, 1951—; asst. to field dir. A.R.C., 1944-45, service cons., 1950-54; bd. dirs. YWCA, San Francisco, 1951-52, Moline Welfare Agy., 1959-69; mem. Ill.-Iowa Assn. Children with Specific Learning Difficulties, 1970-73; mem. Ill. Zone IV Adv. Council Mental Retardation, 1966-70; mem. Ill. adv. council Edn. Handicapped Children, 1972-75; nat. bd. advisers Nat. Assn. Retarded Children, 1967-71; mem. Nat. Com. on U.S.-China Relations, 1974—; mem. U. Ill. citizens com., 1974—, animal sci. adv. com. Coll. Agr., 1974—; mem. mental health adv. com. Rock Island County Bd. Pub. Health, 1974—; adv. bd. Assn. Retarded Children and Adults of Rock Island County, 1974—; governing life mem Art Inst. Chgo. Bd. dirs. Comprehensive Community Mental Health Center, Rock Island and Mercer counties, Ill; mem. Pres.'s Council Marycrest Coll., Davenport, Iowa, 1969-73; trustee Lincoln Acad. Ill., Rock Island Franciscan Hosp.; chmn. bd. trustees Butterworth Meml. Trust; trustee Arabian Horse Owners Found., Morris Animal Found. Charles Deere Wiman Meml. Trust; mem. corp. vis. com. dept. psychology Mass. Inst. Tech. Mem. Internat. Arabian Horse Assn. (dir. 1964-67). U.S. Modern Pentathlon Assn., Western States Trail Ride, Ind. State Saddle Horses Judges Assn., Am. Horse Shows Assn. (drugs and medications com. 1974—), Arabian Horse Club Registry Am. (governing mem. 1963-64) Art Inst. Chgo. (governing life mem.). Club: Santa Barbara Yacht. Home: 38th St and Blackhawk Rd Rock Island IL 61201 Office: Friendship Farms Box 612 Rural Route 2 East Moline IL 61244

HEWITT, WILLIAM ALEXANDER, mfg. exec.; b. San Francisco, Aug. 9, 1914; s. Edward Thomas and Jeannette (Brun) H.; A.B., U. Calif., 1937; m. Patricia Deere Wiman, Jan. 3, 1948; children—Anna, Adrienne, Alexander. With John Deere Plow Co., San Francisco, 1948-54, v.p., 1950-54; dir. Deere & Co., Moline, Ill., 1951—, exec. v.p., 1954-55, pres., 1955-64, chmn., chief exec. officer, 1964—; dir. Continental Ill. Corp., Continental Ill. Nat. Bank & Trust Co. of Chgo., Am. Tel. & Tel. Co., Continental Oil Co.; mem. internat. adv. com. Chase Manhattan Bank. Founding mem. Bus. Com. for Arts, Emergency Com. for Am. Trade; trustee Calif. Inst. Tech., Nat. Safety Council, Carnegie Endowment for Internat. Peace, 1971-75, Council of Americas, St. Katharine's/St. Mark's Sch., 1965-76; bd. govs. Am. Nat. Red Cross, 1967-70; vis. com. Harvard U. Grad. Sch. Bus. Adminstrn., 1962-67, Grad. Sch. Design, 1967-73, now mem. vis. com. on East Asian studies; incorporator Nat. Corp. for Housing Partnerships, 1968-70; mem. council Stanford Research Inst.; mem. nat. bd. Smithsonian Assos.; mem. Nat. Endowment for Humanities, Trilateral Commn.; mem. Wilson council Woodrow Wilson Internat. Center for Scholars. Served as lt. comdr. USNR, 1942-46. Mem. Farm Indsl. Equipment Inst., the Conf. Bd., Soc. Automotive Engrs., Internat. C. of C. (trustee U.S. council), UN Assn. (dir. 1970-73), Com. Econ. Devel. (hon. trustee); Advt. Council, Inc., Am. Soc. Agrl. Engrs., AIA (hon.), Bus. Council, Council Fgn. Relations, Ill. Council Econ. Edn. (governing mem.), Bus. Roundtable, Nat. Council U.S.-China Trade (dir., vice chmn. 1973-75, chmn. 1975—), U.S.-U.S.S.R. Trade and Econ. Council (dir.), Alpha Delta Phi. Clubs: Pacific-Union (San Francisco); Burlingame (Calif.) Country; Chicago (Chgo.); Bohemian; Pilgrims of U.S. Home: 3800 Blackhawk Rd Rock Island IL 61201 Office: Deere & Co John Deere Rd Moline IL 61265

HEYDE, EDWARD LEE, ophthalmologist; b. Etna Green, Ind., Jan. 10, 1935; s. Claude Edward and Helen Elizabeth (Forney) H.; B.S. in Pharmacy, Purdue U., 1957; M.D., Ind. U., 1967; m. Stephanie Kay Seybert, July 21, 1956; children—Craig Edward, Melissa Kay, Erin Lynn. With Phillips Pharmacy, Goshen, Ind., 1957-58; intern Meml. Hosp., South Bend, Ind., 1966-67; resident in ophthalmology Ind. U. Med. Center, 1967-70; practice medicine specializing in ophthalmology, South Bend, 1970—; mem. staff Meml. Hosp., South Bend, St. Joseph's Hosp., South Bend. Served to 1st lt. M.C., USAF, 1958-61. Mem. AMA, Am. Acad. Ophthalmology and Otolaryngology, Am. Assn. Ophthalmology, Ind. Acad. Ophthalmology. Republican. Presbyterian. Club: Shriners. Home: 17646 Woodridge Ct South Bend IN 46635 Office: 513 N Michigan St South Bend IN 44601

HEYDEGGER, H(ELMUT) ROLAND, chemist; b. Phila., Dec. 3, 1935; s. Helmut and Allyse Theresa (Paulich) H.; B.S., Queens Coll., N.Y.C., 1957; M.S., U. Ark., 1958; Ph.D. (Gen. Electric fellow), U. Chgo., 1968; m. Karen Iversen, Aug. 15, 1970. Research asso. U. Chgo., 1968—; mem. faculty Purdue U., Hammond, Ind., 1970—, asso. prof. chemistry, 1975—; vis. fellow Australian Nat. U., 1976-77; cons. Argonne (Ill.) Nat. Lab., 1973-74; instr. Prairie State Coll., Chicago Heights, Ill., 1961-62; phys. chemist U.S. Bur. Mines, 1958; mem. radiation emergency response com. Ind. Bd. Health, 1973—; vis. research asso. Brookhaven Nat. Lab., Upton, N.Y., 1970; guest scientist Los Alamos Sci. Lab., 1973—. Mem. Am. Chem. Soc., Am. Phys. Soc., Am. Geophys. Union, Geochem. Soc. (charter), Internat. Assn. Geochemistry and Cosmochemistry (charter), Meteoritical Soc. Co-investigator lunar sample analysis project, 1968-71. Contbr. articles to profl. jours. Office: Dept Chemistry Purdue U Hammond IN 46323

HEYMANN, SEYMOUR EDWARD, mfg. co. exec.; B.S., Mass. Inst. Tech., 1939; m. Marion Louise Adams, June 25, 1949; children—Charles Edward, Richard Russell, Robert Owens, Susan Jan, Laurie Ann, James Adams. With Stewart-Warner Corp., 1939-49, gen. sales mgr., 1945-49; asst. to dir. sales Signode Corp., Chgo., 1949-55, mgr. advt. and sales promotion, 1955-66, v.p. marketing service, 1966—. Mem. Am. Marketing Assn., Am. Statis. Assn., Am. Mgmt. Assn. Home: 784 Boal Pkwy Winnetka IL 60093 Office: 3600 W Lake Ave Glenview IL 60025

HEYMANS, EUGENE JOSEPH, JR., banker; b. Mpls., Mar. 23, 1934; s. Gene Joseph and Marjorie Ida (Engstrom) H.; student U. Minn., 1951-53, U. Wis., 1965-67; m. Barbara Louise Dickmeyer, Aug. 18, 1956; children—Richard, Laura, Christopher. Self-employed in agrl. services, Fairfax, Minn., 1956-63; v.p. Bank of Menomonie (Wis.), 1963—, dir., 1963—; dir. Citizens State Bank, Gibbon, Minn., 1958-63. Bd. dirs. Dunn County United Fund. Police commr., Fairfax, 1961-63. Served with AUS, 1954-56. Mem. Am. Inst. Banking, Menomonie Area C. of C., Am. Legion, V.F.W. Roman Catholic. Home: Route 5 Menomonie WI 54751 Office: 605 2d St Menomonie WI 54751

HEYRMAN, DONALD JOSEPH, physician; b. Milw., June 7, 1926; s. Fabian John and Leona Mae (Nackers) H.; student St. Norbert Coll., 1943-44, 1946-48; B.A., U. Wis., 1950; M.D., Marquette U., 1956; m. Catherine Mary Liebmann, June 23, 1951; children—Cathie, Kurt, Mary Lynn, Cynthia, Nancy, Daniel, Thomas, Donald. Intern St. Josephs Hosp., Milw., 1956-57; gen. practice medicine Falls Med. Group, Menomonee Falls, Wis., 1957—, pres., 1970—; pres. Falls Med. Bldg. Co.; mem. staff St. Josephs Hosp., Community Meml. Hosp.; teaching preceptor Marquette U. Sch. Medicine, 1965-69; chief staff, sec.-treas. Community Meml. Hosp., 1965-66, acting chief of staff for devel., 1960-64; mem. exec. com. Pres. Suburban Broadcasting Co., 1963—; asso. clin. prof. medicine Med. Coll. Wis., 1973—, mem. research and adv. com. dept. family practice, 1974-76; mem. cancer com. Wis. Regional Med. Program. Pres. St. Anthonys Sch. Bd., 1966—. Served to 2nd lt. inf. AUS, 1944-46; to 1st lt. M.S.C., 1951-53. Diplomate Am. Bd. Family Practice. Fellow Am. Acad. Family Practice (charter); mem. AMA, Wis., Waukesha County med. socs., Wis. Acad. Family Physicians (speaker 1973-74, dir. 1965-72, pres. 1975—, chmn. bd. dirs. 1976-77), Wis. Heart Assn., Catholic Physicians Guild (sec.-treas. Wis. chpt. 1973-75, pres. Milw. chpt. 1976), Marquette-MCW Med. Alumni Assn. (dir. 1977—), Nu Sigma Nu, Alpha Omega Alpha, Alpha Phi Omega. Roman Catholic. K.C., Rotarian. Home: W137 N7657 North Hills Dr Menomonee Falls WI 53051 Office: N84 W16889 Menomonee Ave Menomonee Falls WI 53051

HIATT, KENNETH B., mfg. co. exec.; b. New Castle, Ind., June 25, 1911; s. Cleodus and Jessie (Leakey) H.; m. Dorothy Mae Cable, Apr. 8, 1972; 1 dau., Judith Ann. Machinist, Chrysler Corp., New Castle, Ind., 1930-40; with W.S. DeMoss & Son Inc., Indpls., 1940—, pres., 1977—, also chmn. bd. Mem. Nat. Tool, Die & Precision Machining Assn. (pres. 1970-71, recipient L.A. Sommer Meml. award 1977), Ind. Mfrs. Assn., Soc. Mfg. Engrs., Nat., Ind., Indpls. C. of C. Clubs: Columbia, Econ. Indpls., Mason, Shriner. Home: 4703 Radnor Rd Indianapolis IN 46226 Office: 660 Virginia Ave Indianapolis IN 46203

HIBBS, JACK EUGENE, librarian; b. Lucas County, Ohio, Jan. 14, 1933; s. Harold Hathaway and Marie Maud (Sponseller) H.; student Kent State U., 1951-53; B.Ed., U. Toledo, 1960, M.L.S., 1969; m. Janet Kay Manley, Dec. 19, 1964; children—Craig Alan, Michele Marie, Stephanie Alane. Clerk, Nat. Lead Co., Toledo, 1954-58; tchr. Toledo Pub. Schs., 1959-60; librarian, Woodville (Ohio) High Sch., 1960-64; tchr. Whitmer High Sch., 1964-65; librarian Northwood High Sch., 1965-69; dir. library Bowling Green State U., Firelands br. campus, 1969-74; research librarian U. Akron (Ohio), 1974—. Trustee Ohio Friends of Library, 1974—, v.p., 1977; trustee Three Seas Inst. Study of World Religions. Mem. ALA, AAUP, Ohio Library Assn. Baptist. Home: 205 Filmore Ave Cuyahoga Falls OH 44221 Office: Bierce Library U Akron Akron OH 44325

HIBBS, WILLIAM GEORGE, ret. physician and hosp. adminstr.; b. Chgo., Dec. 9, 1892; s. William Robert and Anna (Garvin) H.; student Franklin Coll., U. Chgo.; M.D., Rush Med. Coll., 1920; m. Ruth Kerlin, Aug. 10, 1920; children—William, Robert, George. Practice medicine specializing in internal medicine, Chgo. and Franklin, Ind., 1920-54; prof. medicine U. Ill. Sch. Medicine, Chgo., 1940; pathologist Childrens Meml. Hosp., Chgo., 1920-43; med. dir. Presbyn. Hosp., Chgo., 1943-54; Ind. Masonic Home lHosp., Franklin, 1954-59; former mem. coroners adv. com., Chgo. Served with Student Army Tng. Corps, World War I. Home: RFD 1 Box 138 Franklin IN 46131

HIBEN, JOHN, JR., psychologist, clergyman; b. Mpls., Oct. 14, 1924; s. John and Anna (Zustiak) H.; A.B., Bethel Coll. and Sem., St. Paul, 1954, B.D., 1956; M.A., U. Minn., 1960; postgrad. (NSF fellow) State U. Iowa, 1962, U. Kans., 1962-67; m. Marian June George, Sept. 6, 1952; children—Annette Marie (Mrs. James Leon Smith), Virginia Mae, Daniel John. Ordained to ministry Baptist Ch., 1956; minister First Bapt. Ch., Bradley, S.D., 1956-58, First Bapt. Ch., Florence, S.D., 1956-58; asst. prof. psychology Ottawa (Kans.) U., 1961-63; instr. U. Kans., 1963-65, fellow in somatopsychology Kans. Neurol. Inst., 1965-67; sch. psychologist Chilocco (Okla.) Indian Sch., 1967-68; clin. psychologist Parsons (Kans.) State Hosp. and Tng. Center, 1968—. Mem. Kans. Psychol. Assn., Am. Sci. Affiliation, Am. Assn. Mental Deficiency. Contbg. author: Camelot Behavioral Checklist Manual, 1974. Home: 2321 Clark Ave Parsons KS 67357 Office: 2601 Gabriel Ave Parsons KS 67357

HICKEY, JEROME EDWARD, investment banking exec.; b. Chgo., June 25, 1937; s. Matthew J. and Naomi (Pope) H.; B.S. in Econs., Coll. Holy Cross, 1959; M.A. in Philosophy, Boston Coll., 1964; m. Denise Coakley, May 20, 1967; children—Jerome G., Matthew J., Elizabeth T., George S., Peter C. Instr. Cranwell Sch., Lenox, Mass., 1964-66; asso. Paine Webber, Jackson & Curtis, N.Y.C., 1966; with Hickey & Co., Chgo., 1967-72, v.p., 1968-72; v.p. Ralph W. Davis & Co., Chgo., 1972-76, dir., 1973-76; v.p. Dexter Securities Corp., 1976—; mem. Midwest Stock Exchange, 1969—. Bd. dirs. Chgo. Maternity Center. Named An Outstanding Young Man Am., 1970. Mem. Security Traders Assn. Chgo. Clubs: Bond, Economic, Mid-Day (Chgo.); Knollwood (Lake Forest, Ill.). Home: 161 Apple Tree Rd Winnetka IL 60093 Office: 9600 Sears Tower Chicago IL 60606

HICKMAN, SIMEON MARTIN, health ins. co. exec.; b. Sioux City, Iowa, Oct. 10, 1929; s. Simeon M. and Esther (Nixon) H.; B.A. cum laude, Brown U., 1950; m. Marjorie Ann Gibbons, Aug. 11, 1951; children—Paula, Douglas. Actuarial asst. Home Life Ins. Co., N.Y.C., 1950-55; actuary Health Care Service Corp., Chgo., 1955-63, asst. v.p., 1963-67, v.p. fin., 1967-68, treas., 1967—, sr. v.p. fin. and planning, 1968-73, exec. v.p., 1973-76, pres., chief exec. officer, 1976—; chmn. Ft. Dearborn Life Ins. Co., Chgo.; dir. Midwest Data Communication Corp., Blue Cross Assn., Blue Shield Assn., Health Service, Inc., Ft. Dearborn Fire & Casualty Co. Trustee Citizens Info. Service. Served with AUS, 1951-53. Fellow Soc. Actuaries, Acad. of Actuaries; mem. Chgo. Inst. Medicine, Phi Beta Kappa, Sigma Xi. Home: 1932 Central Ave Wilmette IL 60091 Office: 233 N Michigan Ave Chicago IL 60601

HICKMAN, THOMAS ROLAND, architect; b. Dallas, Nov. 6, 1932; s. Willett J. and Mattie O. (Dunlap) H., student U. Okla., 1950-53; B.Arch. (High scholar), U. Wash., 1962; m. Patricia Ann Highfill, Dec. 18, 1955; children—Stacy Ann, Kimberly Ann, Eric Jon; m. Sandra Ann Holland, Sept. 11, 1976. Employee, Bruce Goff, architect, Norman, Okla., 1950-53; architect Kirk, Wallace & McKinley, architects, 1962-64; partner Naramore Bain Brady & Johanson, Seattle, Columbus, Ohio, Anchorage, 1964—, partner-in-charge architecture Columbus office, 1976—. Mem. King County Criminal Justice Coordinating Council, 1973. Dir. Seattle Housing Devel., 1972-74. Served with USNR, 1953-58. Naramore Found. grantee, 1973. Mem. A.I.A., Seattle Urban League (dir. 1972-74). Lion. Club: Corinthian Yacht (dir. 1970-72). Prin. archtl. works include: sci. bldgs. Evergreen State Coll., 1972, Swedish Hosp. Med. Center, 1973, Battelle Commons Conv. Center, Columbus, 1974. Home: 1969 Chatfield Rd Columbus OH 43221 Office: 505 S High St Columbus OH 43215

HICKOX, JOHN EKSTROM, geologist; b. Topeka, Oct. 29, 1925; s. Russel B. and Edna (Ekstrom) H.; B.S., U. Kans., 1949, M.S., 1951; m. Mary L. Parman, Nov. 6, 1949; 1 son, John Eric. Geologist, Texaco, Inc., Mid-Continent area, 1951-63; cons. geologist, 1963—; project supr. Center for Research in Engring. Sci., U. Kans., Lawrence, 1965; asst. research psychologist, Menninger Found., Topeka, 1967-73; geologist Mar-Win Devel. Co., Topeka, 1975—; asst. instr. U. Kans., 1949-51; lectr. Washburn U., Topeka, 1968. Served with AUS, 1943-46. Recipient Haworth honors U. Kans., 1950. Mem. Am. Assn. Petroleum Geologists, A.A.A.S., Geol. Soc. Am., Kans. Geol. Soc., Am. Legion, Sigma Xi, Sigma Gamma Epsilon. Presbyn. (elder 1957-58). Author: (with others) The Permian Reef Complex of West Texas and New Mexico, 1953. Contbr. articles to profl. jours. Home: 3147 Westover Rd Topeka KS 66604 Office: 1271 Woodhull Suite 100 Topeka KS 66604

HICKS, ELDER BARNEY, clergyman; b. Wichita, Kans., July 11, 1907; s. Daniel H. and Carrie (Smith) H.; A.B., Washburn U., 1951; Th.B., Central Baptist Sem., 1934, D.D. (hon.), 1940; D.D., Monrovia Coll. and Indsl. Inst., Monrovia, Liberia, Africa, 1961; m. Effie Mae Hayes, Mar. 9, 1927; (dec. 1960); children—Rose Marie (Mrs. Dewey Sanderson), Milton T., James Edward, E. Barney; m. 2d, Roena S. Starks, Oct. 10, 1961. Ordained to ministry Bapt. Ch., 1934, pastor in Paxico, Kan., 1934-36, Holton and Horton, Kans., 1936-37, Duluth, Minn., 1937-42; exec. sec., missionary Bapt. Conv. of Kans., 1945-56; dir. Bapt. Ednl. Centers of Am. Bapt. Home Mission Socs., 1956-63, asso. dir. community witness program, div. ch. missions, 1963-67, program asso. for inner city work, 1967-69, asst. sec. div. parish devel., 1969-71; regional exec. minister Am. Bapt. Chs. of South, Atlanta, 1971-76; minister coop. relationships Ohio Bapt. Conv., 1976—. Mem. exec. com. Am. Bapt. Eastern Commn. on Ministry, 1975-76; mem. Am. Bapt. Exec. Ministers Council, 1971-76; mem. nat. staff council Am. Bapt. Chs., U.S.A., 1972-76. Bd. dirs. Christian Council Met. Atlanta, 1973-76; trustee Morehouse Sch. Religion, 1974-76. Served from 1st lt. to capt., as chaplain, AUS, 1942-45. Mem. NAACP. Home: 34 S Mulberry St Granville OH 43023 Office: 141 E Broadway Granville OH 43023

HICKS, JAMES THOMAS, physician, lawyer; b. Brownsville, Pa., June 5, 1924; s. Thomas and Florence Julia (O'Donnel) H.; B.S., U. Pitts., 1945, A.B., 1946, M.S., 1946; Ph.D., George Washington U., 1950; M.D., U. Ark., 1956; J.D., DePaul U., 1975; m. Ellen Elliott, Aug. 25, 1950; children—Ellen, Mary Jo. Intern USPHS, Balt., 1958-60; resident VA Hosp., Pitts., 1958-60; admitted to Ill. bar, 1977, Pa. bar; practice medicine specializing in forensic and legal medicine, River Forest, Ill., 1964—; dir. labs. Oak Park (Ill.) Hosp., 1964—; pres. Oakton Service Corp., 1968—. Served with USPHS, 1956-57. Fellow Nat. Cancer Inst., 1949-50. Fellow A.C.P., Internat. Coll. Surgeons; mem. AMA, Sigma Xi. Clubs: Univ., Lake Shore, Oak Park Country. Contbg. editor Hosp. Formulary Mgmt., 1966-70. Home: 7980 W Chicago Ave River Forest IL 60305 Office: 520 Maple Ave Oak Park IL 60304

HICKS, JOHN LESLIE, JR., coll. adminstr.; b. Chambersburg, Pa., Nov. 5, 1927; s. John Leslie and Hulda (Wingert) H.; B.A. in Econs., Gettysburg Coll., 1949; M.S. in Commerce and Finance, Bucknell U., 1950; m. Iris Louise Sheely, July 19, 1950; children—Linda Louise, Jay Leslie. Mgmt. planner Borg-Warner Corp., York, Pa., 1954-58; systems specialist, internal auditor U. Del., Newark, 1958-64; mgr. bus. operations Carnegie-Mellon U., Pitts., 1964-68; dir. bus., finance Denison U., Granville, Ohio, 1968-73, v.p. finance and mgmt., 1973—; cons. Council Advancement Small Colls., Washington, 1971-72. Served with AUS, 1952-54. Mem. Eastern (exec. com., pres.), Ohio (exec. com., pres.), Nat. (chmn. small coll. com., profl. devel. com.) assns. coll. and univ. bus. officers, Indsl. Mgmt. Assn., C. of C., (mem. edn. com., energy com.), Pi Lambda Sigma, Phi Sigma Kappa. Presbyterian (elder). Rotarian. Home: 51 Edgewood Dr Granville OH 43023 Office: Doane Adminstrn Bldg Granville OH 43023

HICKS, SAMUEL IRVING, educator; b. Stormville, N.Y., Apr. 4, 1902; s. Irving J. and Elizabeth (Tripp) H.; A.B., U. Mich., 1924; M.A., Columbia, 1927; Ed.D., Columbia U., 1947; postgrad. N.Y. U., 1931-33; m. Margaret Anderson, Jan. 7, 1924; children—Eleanor (Mrs. Peter Werenfels), Virginia (Mrs. John Karl). Tchr., Boyne City (Mich.) High Sch., 1924-26; prin. jr. and sr. high sch., Dobbs Ferry, N.Y., 1926-29; supt. schs., Central Park, N.Y., 1929-32, Pearl River, N.Y., 1932-58; coordinator services to adminstrs. citizenship edn. project Columbia U., 1954-56; prof. edn. Ohio U., Athens, 1958—, dir. Center for Ednl. Research and Service, 1960-66, coordinator ednl. placement, 1972—; dir. Inst. Edn., Ahmadu Bello U., Nigeria, 1966-70. Mem. Am. Ednl. Research Assn., N.Y. State Ednl. Research Assn. (past pres.), Am. Assn. Sch. Adminstrs., Nat. Conf. Profs. Ednl. Adminstrn., Comparative and Internat. Edn. Soc., Assn. Sch. Bus. Ofcls., Am. Ednl. Fin. Assn., AAUP, Kappa Delta Pi, Phi Delta Kappa. Clubs: Athens Rotary, Rotary (Zaria, Nigeria), Pearl River (past pres.). Home: 48 Briarwood Dr Athens OH 45701 Office: College of Education Ohio University Athens OH 45701

HICKSON, ROBERT COMINS, banker; b. Mt. Gilead, Ohio, Aug. 24, 1928; s. Charles C. and Marian (Sampson) H.; A.B., Ohio Wesleyan U., 1950; M.B.A., Ohio State U., 1952; m. Mary Jean Sturrock, Feb. 13, 1954; children—Robert Comins, Thomas M. With City Nat. Bank & Trust Co., Columbus, Ohio, 1950-51, Ohio Bell Telephone Co., Cleve., 1952-54; partner Hickson Ins.-Realty, Mt. Gilead, 1954—; with Peoples Bank, Mt. Gilead, 1963—, pres., 1967—, chmn. bd., 1963—; vice pres. Peoples Bldg. Finance and Devel. Co., Mt. Gilead, 1967—; dir. HPM Corp.; mem. Ohio Bank Bd., 1976—. Mem. exec. com. Hardinging area council Boy Scouts Am., 1968-74, v.p. 1970-74; chmn. adv. com. Tri-River Vocat. Sch., 1974-75; sec.-treas. Morrow County Found., 1974—; chmn. Republican central com. Morrow County, 1964-68; asso. Ohio Wesleyan U., 1966—; trustee Elyria Meth. Home, 1974—; trustee Marion Concert Assn., 1976—; mem. citizens adv. council Marion Campus, Ohio State U., 1976—. Named Outstanding Young Man Morrow County Jr. C. of C., 1961. Mem. Ohio Bankers Assn. (dir. 1977—), Mt. Gilead C. of C. (past pres.), Morrow County Bd. Realtors (pres. 1977—). Methodist (local lay leader 1971-72, vice chmn. bd. ch. and society, East Ohio Conf., 1973-74). Kiwanian (past pres.). Home: 371 N Main St Mount Gilead OH 43338 Office: Public Sq Mount Gilead OH 43338

HIDA, EDWARD T., hosp. exec.; b. Sacramento, Feb. 8, 1931; B.S., U. Wis., Madison, 1953; M.S.W., Fla. State U., Tallahassee, 1958; C.P.H., U. Calif., Berkeley, 1962; M.S., U. Wis., Milw., 1972; m. Heidi Bentley, Oct. 15, 1960; children—Edward T., Karen, Catherine. Casework supr. Milw. County Dept. Pub. Welfare, 1953-60; med. social worker Muirdale Sanatorium, Milw., 1960-61; chief social worker So. Wis. Colony, Racine, 1962-65; adminstr. community services Milw. County Instn., 1965-74; sr. v.p. DePaul Hosp., Milw., 1974—; advisor Bd. Pub. Welfare, Milw. County Human Rights Commn.; bd. dirs., treas. Milw. Assn. Retarded Citizens; bd. dirs. Milw. Mental Health Assn. Bd. dirs. Dunbar Found., Pilot Club Fund; del. Democratic State Convs., 1968, 72, 76. Recipient citations Milw. County, award Milw. Mental Health Planning Council, Milw. Goodwill Industries. Served with U.S. Army N.G., 1955-63. Certified rehab. counselor. Fellow Am. Pub. Health Assn.; mem. Nat. Assn. Social Workers (past chpt. chmn.), Acad. Certified Social Workers, Am. Coll. Hosp. Adminstrs. Methodist. Home: 2109 N 73d St Wauwatosa WI 53213 Office: 4143 S 13th St Milwaukee WI 53221

HIDORE, JOHN JUNIOR, geographer, educator; b. Cedar Falls, Iowa, July 6, 1932; s. John Henry and Vearle Lluela (Thomas) H.; B.A. in Math. and Earth Sci., State Coll. Iowa, Cedar Falls, 1954; student civil engring. Iowa State U., Ames, 1951-52; M.A. in Phys. Geography, State U. Iowa, Iowa City, 1958, Ph.D., 1960; m. Ruth Olive Norton, June 6, 1954; children—Jill Helen, John Warren. Teaching asst. geography U. Iowa, Iowa City, 1958-59; instr. geography U. Wis., Madison, 1960-62; vis. prof. geography Central Wash. State Coll., Ellensburg, 1962, 64; vis. prof. geography NDEA Inst., Wis. State U., Eau Claire, 1965; asst. prof. geography Okla. State U., Stillwater, 1962-64, asso. prof., 1964-66, dir. NDEA Inst. Geography, 1966; asso. prof. dept. geography U. Ind., Bloomington, 1966-68, acting chmn., 1968-71, prof., 1972-74, 75—. Author: Introduction to Physical Geography, 1967; A Geography of the Atmosphere, 1972; Physical Geography: Earth Systems, 1974; A Workbook of Weather Maps, 1976; contbr. articles, abstracts and book revs. to profl. jours. Home: 4401 Hillview Dr Bloomington IN 47401 Office: Indiana Univ Dept Geography Bloomington IN 47401

HIDVEGI, ERNEST B., orthopedic surgeon; b. Budapest, Hungary, Sept. 24, 1925; s. Istvan and Maria (Kovacs) H.; came to U.S., 1958, naturalized, 1963; M.D., Royal Hungarian U., 1949; m. Tamara Jancewycz, 1966; children—Erica, Andrea. Research asso. Presbyn. Med. Center, U. Ill., Chgo., 1959-61; intern Cook County Hosp., Chgo., 1961-62; resident in orthopedic surgery U. Cin. Med. Center, Childrens Hosp., VA Hosp., Cin., 1963-66; resident in pathology Hosp. Joint Diseases and Med. Center, N.Y.C., 1967-70; mem. attending staff orthopedic surgery Astoria Gen. Hosp., Hillcrest Gen. Hosp., Parkway Hosp., N.Y.C., 1968-70; attending orthopedic surgeon Youngstown (Ohio) Hosp. Assn., 1971—; chief sect. orthopedic surgery Ohio Permanente Med. Group Kaiser Med. Center, Cleve., Parma, Ohio, 1972—. Diplomate Am. Bd. Orthopedic Surgery. Fellow Am. Acad. Orthopedic Surgeons. Contbr. papers to med. jours. Home: 16714 Fernway Rd Shaker Heights OH 44120

HIEBERT, ELIZABETH BLAKE (MRS. HOMER L. HIEBERT), civic worker; b. Mpls., July 18, 1910; d. Henry Seavey and Grace (Riebeth) Blake; student Washburn U., 1926-30; B.S., U. Tex. 1933; m. Homer L. Hiebert, Aug. 29, 1935; children—Grace Elizabeth (Mrs. John E. Beam), Mary Sue (Mrs. Donald Wester), John Blake, Henry Leonard, David Mark. Free lance writer. Sec. Topeka Regional Sci. Fair, 1958-60, mem. bd., 1964—; mem. bd. Topeka Welfare Planning Council, 1958-62, YWCA, 1962—, Kans. Council Children and Youth; water safety instr., swimming instr. for handicapped; active Campfire Girls, Nat. Trust for Historic Preservation, Internat. Oceanographic Found., People-to-People; Fellow Harry S. Truman Library Inst.; mem. bd. Can Help; mem. Topeka Friends of Zoo, Friends of Topeka Library, YMCA, Friends of John F. Kennedy Center Performing Arts, Los Angeles Internat. Fern Soc., Nat. League Am. Pen Women (pres. Topeka), A.A.A.S., D.A.R., Daus. Am. Colonists (mem. bd.), Colo. Hist. Soc., AAUW (bd. mem. 1944-62, 65—, v.p.), New Eng. Women, Washburn U. Alumni Assn., Nat. Wildlife Fedn., Kans. Hist. Soc., N.E. Hist. and Geneol. Soc., Tex. U. Alumni, Am. Home Econs. Assn., Shawnee County Med. Aux., (past pres.) Nat. Audubon, Internat. Platform Assn., Topeka Civic Symphony, Met. Mus. Art, P.E.O. (past local pres. coop. bd.), Topeka Art Guild, Nat. Soc. Ancient and Hon. Arty., Cousteau Soc., Shawnee County Hist. Soc. (dir.), Oceanie Soc., Exec. Female, Delta Kappa Gamma, Delta Gamma. Republican. Methodist (mem. bd. 1963—). Clubs: Capitol Hill, Knife and Fork. Editor children's page Household mag., 1934-39. Home: 1517 Randolph Topeka KS 66604

HIGDEM, ARNOLD PALMER, hist. soc. exec.; b. Bagley, Minn., Feb. 25, 1911; s. Arne J. and Pauline (Haugen) H.; student Hamline U., 1933-34, U. Minn., 1935-36; m. Myrtle A. Grover, Aug. 28, 1937; children—Allyn, Brenton. With U.S. Postal Dept., Bagley, 1929-70; chmn. Clearwater County Hist. Soc., 1965—; dir. No.-Sun Products Corp., Gonvick, Minn. Mem. adv. com. Itasca State Park, 1969—; chmn. Clearwater County Bicentennial Commn., 1974-76; county chmn. Am. Cancer Soc., 1969-74; chmn. Inter County Community Council, 1970-75; mem. Regional Conservation and Devel. Corp., Bagley Indsl. Comm. Bd. dirs. Am. Cancer Soc., Viking Land U.S.A., Mid West Community Devel. Corp. Served with USMCR, 1943-45, 48-52; PTO. Recipient Man of Year award Viking Land, 1975. Mem. Am. Legion (past comdr.), Bagley Civic and Commerce Assn., Sons of Norway (pres. Granlund lodge 1977—). Address: Bagley MN 56621

HIGGINS, JEROME JOHN FOREST, priest, counselor, educator; b. Madison, Wisc., Feb. 7, 1928; s. William Jerome and Dora Agusta (Sell) H.; student St. Lawrence Sem. Coll., 1946-47; B.A. in Philosophy, Mary Immaculate Sem., 1951; M.A. in Theo. Ordination, St. Anthony Sem., 1954; M.Edn. in Ednl. Psychology, Marquette U., 1969; postgrad. St. Thomas Coll., 1969-75, U. Detroit, 1970-71, Azuza Pacific Coll., 1973-74, United Theol. Sem. of Twin Cities, 1972-75. Ordained priest Roman Catholic Ch., 1954; dir. admissions St. Lawrence Sem. High Sch. and Coll., Mt. Calvary, Wisc., 1955-67; dir. guidance St. Mary Springs High Sch., Fond du Lac, Wisc., 1963-67; chaplain, counselor, tchr. Cretin High Sch., St. Paul, Minn., 1967-70; chaplain, tchr., coach Hill Murray High Sch., Maplewood, Minn., 1970—; dir. new programs Nat. Marriage Encounter, St. Paul, 1976—, facilitator marriage enrichment weekends, 1972—; bd. edn. St. Paul Archdiocesan, St. Paul, 1974—. Recipient award for service Knights of Columbus, Supreme Council, 1977. Mem. Am. Personnel and Guildance Assn., Am. Sch. Counselors Assn., Nat. Vocat. Guidance Assn., Minn. Personnel and Guidance Assn., Assn. Christian Therapist, Nat. Council on Family Relations, Minn. Council on Family Relations, Nat. Catholic Edn. Assn., Phi Delta Kappa. Democrat. Roman Catholic. Clubs: Knights of Columbus, (Father Finely Council, Revoux Gen. Assembly). Researcher in ednl. programs; contbr. articles in field. Home 2159 Marshall Ave St Paul MN 55104 Office: 955 Lake Dr St Paul MN 55120

HIGGINS, JOHN RICHARD, lawyer; b. Omaha, Apr. 4, 1922; s. Ray Morten and Eugenie Lucile (Dennis) H.; B.S., U. Nebr., 1947, J.D. (Regents scholar), 1949; postgrad. Northwestern U., 1952, U. Va., Charlottesville, 1970; m. Jessica Martha Stocking, June 7, 1952; children—John Richard, Molly Susan, Ann Elizabeth, Lucy Jean. Admitted to Nebr. bar, 1949; practiced in Grand Island, 1949—; mem. firms Higgins & Higgins, 1949-66, Higgins, Higgins & Huber, 1966—. Adminstrv. asst. to Congressman A.L. Miller, 1951-57; U.S. commr., 1957-71, U.S. magistrate, 1971—. Mem. Grand Island Sch. Bd., 1966—, pres., 1970-71, atty., 1970—. Chmn. Republican party Hall County, 1952-58. Trustee Hazelden Found., 1970-74. Served from pvt. to col. AUS, 1942-47; mil. judge Res. Decorated 6 battle stars, 1 arrowhead (Okinawa), Presdl. Meritorious Achievement medal (2), 1977. Mem. Nebr., Hall County bar assns., Nat. (v.p. western region 1975—, dir. 1977—), Nebr. (pres. 1974-75) sch. bds. assns., VFW (comdr. Hall County 1951), Am. Legion (comdr. 1958), Res. Officers Assn. (state pres. 1957-58, 73-74), Nat. Council Sch. Attys. (exec. bd. 1973—), Delta Theta Phi, Alpha Tau Omega. Mason (Shriner), Elk. Presbyn. (deacon 1966-72). Club: Riverside Golf. Home: 1823 W John St Grand Island NE 68801 Office: Box 1068 1503 W 2d St Grand Island NE 68801

HIGGINS, KENNETH RAYMOND, ednl. adminstr.; b. Akron, Ohio, Sept. 6, 1935; s. Warda Raymond and Lillian Merle (Brotherton) H.; B.S., Wilmington Coll., 1959; M.A., Miami (Ohio) U., 1962; Ph.D., Ohio State U., 1974; m. Wanda Jean Ogle, Feb. 17, 1955; children—Suellen, Scott, Andrew, Kerry. Tchr., counselor Blanchester (Ohio) City Schs., 1958-63; counselor Franklin (Ohio) City Schs., 1963-65; evaluation cons. div. guidance and testing Ohio Dept. Edn., Columbus, 1965-70, dir. testing services, 1970-74, asst. dir. div. guidance and testing, 1974—; vis. prof. Kent State U., 1976. Served with U.S. Army, 1954-56. Mem. Jaycees, Four Seasons Recreation Assn. (pres.), Am., Ohio personnel and guidance assns., Ohio Sch. Counselors Assn., Nat. Vocat. Guidance Assn., Assn. Measuring and Evaluation in Guidance, Nat. Council Measuring in Edn., Phi Delta Kappa. Methodist. Club: Optimists. Author: (with others) What I Have Learned About Reading, 1976; contbr. tests to Ohio Dept. Edn. Home: 136 W Columbus Mount Sterling OH 43143

HIGGINS, RONALD ALLAN, dermatologist; b. Los Angeles, Dec. 6, 1937; s. Chester R. and Beatrice H. (Bennett) H.; B.A. in Chemistry, Central Coll., Fayette, Mo., 1959; M.S. in Microbioligy, U. Mo., 1965, M.D., 1965; m. Ardith Sue Alexander, Mar. 15, 1974; 1 dau., Amy Elizabeth, children by previous marriage—David, Matthew, Danny. Intern Good Samaritan Hosp., Phoenix, 1965-66; resident U. Mo. Med. Center, Columbia, 1966-69; chief dermatology Womack Army Hosp., Fort Bragg, N.C., 1969-71; practice medicine specializing in dermatology, Kansas City, Mo., 1971—; mem. staff St. Joseph Hosp., Kansas City, Mo., Research Hosp., Kansas City, Mo. Served with M.C., U.S. Army, 1969-71. Diplomate Am. Bd. Dermatology. Mem. Johnson County Med. Soc., Kansas City Dermatological Soc., Am. Acad. Dermatology. Home: 3210 W 88th St Leawood KS 66206 Office: 1010 Carondelet Dr Suite 340 Kansas City MO 64114

HIGGINS, RUTH LOVING, ret. educator; b. Columbus, Ohio, June 21, 1895; d. Charles and Jessie Hoover (Schatzman) Higgins; B.A., B.S. in Edn., Ohio State U., 1917, M.A. (scholarship), 1921, Ph.D. (2 fellowships), 1926; postgrad. U. Wis., summer 1922, Cambridge (Eng.) U., summer 1929; LL.D. (hon.), Beaver Coll., 1953. Tchr. history and civics, Ohio high schs., 1917-20, 22-23; instr. history, polit. sci. Elmira (N.Y.) Coll., 1924-25; asst. prof. Earlham Coll., Richmond, Ind., 1925-26; prof., head dept. history and polit. sci. Huntingdon Coll. (formerly Woman's Coll. of Ala.), Montgomery, 1926-34; mem. history faculty U. Ala., summers 1930-31; dean coll., prof. history and govt. Beaver Coll., Glenside, Pa., 1934-60, chmn. dept. history and govt., 1949-60, now emeritus. Mem. Congressman Schweiker's Service Acad. Bd., 1961-64; mem. women's com. Japan Internat. Christian U. Found., 1960—. Trustee Cheltenham Adult Sch., 1940-48, pres. 1943-45. Beaver Coll. clocktower chimes dedicated in honor Ruth Loving Higgins, 1966. Mem. Am. Conf. Acad. Deans (hon. life mem., sec.-treas. 1945-47, editor 1946-48), Am. Acad. Polit. and Social Scis., Am. Hist. Assn., Orgn. Am. Historians (mem. exec. com. 1936-39), Nat. (editorial com. 1935-37), Pa. (chmn. publs. 1938-41) assns. women deans, adminstrs. and counselors, Am. Assn. Higher Edn., Ohio State U. Alumni Assn., AAUW, Ohio Hist. Soc., D.A.R., Delta Kappa Gamma (state founder Ala., Pa.), Phi Alpha Theta. Presbyn. Author: Expansion in New York with Especial Reference to Eighteenth Century, 1931; American Conference of Academic Deans-Developments and Abstracts, 1945-69, 1969; (dramatization) Reflections on Conditions and Events Leading to the Declaration of Independence, 1975; also articles, hist. revs. Home: 5155 N High St Apt 808W Columbus OH 43214

HIGGS, STUART ELDON, elec. engr.; b. Havana, Ill., Oct. 18, 1928; s. John Orville and Elizabeth Irene (Graham) H.; B.S., U. Ill., 1955; m. Helen Mary Tarkany, Oct. 7, 1955; children—David A., Michael C., Cecilia M., Ann C., M. Jane, Mary M., Elizabeth I. Engr.-in-tng. Gen. Motors Corp., Dayton, Ohio, 1955-56; test engr. A.O. Smith, Tipp City, Ohio, 1956-57; gyro test technician Honeywell Aero., Mpls., 1957; civil engr. I, Minn. Hwy. Dept., St. Paul, 1957-58; prodn. engr. Honeywell Ordnance, Hopkins, Minn., 1957-61; GSE designer Lear Siegler Inc., Grand Rapids, Mich., 1961-64; elec. designer Kingscott & Assos., Kalamazoo, 1964-66; chief elec. engr. Durrant, Deininger, Dommer, Kramer, Gordon, Dubuque, 1966-70; elec. engr. Kimmel, Jensen, Wegerer, Wray, Rock Island, Ill., 1970-73; elec./mech. engr. Hynes & Howes, Engring., Inc., Milan, Ill., 1973-74; sr. elec. engr. Beling Engring. Cons., Inc., Moline, Ill., 1974-75; elec. engr. Office State Engr., Pierre, S.D., 1975—. Served with USAF, 1946-49. Registered profl. engr., Ill., Iowa, S.D. Mem. Quint-Cities Joint Engring. Council (chmn. 1974-75), Order of the Engr., Iowa Engring. Soc. (dir. 1974-75, Membership award 1974), Nat. Soc. Profl. Engrs., Am. Soc. Heating, Refrigerating and Air Conditioning Engrs., Nat. Council Engring. Examiners. Republican. Roman Catholic. Editor Engrs. Week Newspaper Supplement, Dubuque Telegraph Herald, 1970. Home: 2834 E Irwin Pierre SD 57501 Office: Office of State Engr Pierre SD 57501

HIGH, CLAUDE, II, employment agy. exec.; b. Marshall, Tex., Nov. 5, 1944; s. Claude and Lola Lee (Jenkins) H.; educated Huston-Tillotson Coll., 1963-64; B.A. in Psychology, U. Mich., 1974; M.A. in Counseling, Oakland U., 1977; m. Nelda Nadine Spencer, Jan. 28, 1964 (div. 1975); children—Kino, Claude 111, Kimberli. Installation, Union rep. Western Electric, Inc. Flint, Mich., 1964-73;

store owner, operator Soul Picnic Store, Flint, 1973-74; caseworker Youth Service Bur., Flint, 1974-75; counselor, coordinator, dir. Pub. Service Employment Agy., 1975—. Mem. coms. advisory Walk In Resource Center, employment task force Flint Community Schs. (certification appreciation), 1975—. Recipient certificate merit Dept. Social Services. Mem. Am. Personnel, Guidance Assn., Nat. Vocat. Guidance Assn. Nat. Employment Counselors Assn. Author: Three M's of Black History. Home: 402 W Russell St Flint MI 48505 Office: 1101 Beach St Flint MI 48502

HIGHAM, ROBIN, educator, editor; b. London, Eng., June 20, 1925; s. Frank David and Margaret Anne (Stewart) H.; came to U.S., 1940, naturalized, 1954; A.B. cum laude, Harvard U., 1950, Ph.D., 1957; M.A., Claremont Grad. Sch., 1953; m. Barbara Davies, Aug. 5, 1950; children—Susan Elizabeth, Martha Anne, Carolee. Instr. Webb Sch. Calif., 1950-52; grad. asst. in oceanic history Harvard U., 1952-54; instr. U. Mass., 1954-57; asst. prof. U. N.C., Chapel Hill, 1957-63; asso. prof. Kans. State U., 1963-66, prof., 1966—; historian Brit. Overseas Airways Corp., 1960-66, 76-78; editor Mil. Affairs, 1968—, Aerospace Historian, 1970—; editor, co-pub. Jour. of the West, 1977—; adv. editor Tech. and Culture, 1967—; mil. adv. editor Univ. Press Ky., 1970-75; lectr. in field. Mem. publs. com. Conf. Brit. Studies, 1965—, chmn. travel com., 1965-66; sec. Tri-Univ. com. to convert U. Kans. Press to Univ. Press Kans., Lawrence, Manhattan and Wichita, 1966-67, search com., 1970-71; adviser Core Collection for Coll. Libraries, 1971-72; chmn., presdl. rep. Pres.'s Com. on Freedom Park and Kans. State U., 1973—. Organizer Gov.'s Conf. Future Rural Kans., 1975. Served with RAF, 1943-46. Named hon. col. Tar Heel Air Force, 1962, Distinguished Personality, Kans. State U., 1967. Social Sci. Research Council nat. security policy research fellow, 1960-61. Mem. Am. Hist. Assn. (permanent liaison officer with Soc. History Tech.), Am. Aviation Hist. Soc., Soc. History Tech. (liaison officer with Am. Hist. Assn.), Air Force Hist. Found., U.S. Naval Inst., Am. Mil. Inst., Orgn. Am. Historians, Am. Inst. Aeros. and Astronautics (mem. standing com. history 1973—), Am. Com. History Second World War (dir. 1973-75, archivist 1977—), U.S., Internat. (editorial bd.) commns. for mil. history. Author: Britain's Imperial Air Routes, 1918-39, 1960; The British Rigid Airship, 1908-31, 1961; Armed Forces in Peacetime: Britain 1918-39, 1963; The Military Intellectuals in Britain: 1918-1939, 1966; A Short History of Warfare, 1966; The Compleat Academic (Macmillan Book Club choice), 1975; Air Power: A Concise History (selection Mil. Book Soc., History Book Club, Flying Book Club). Editor numerous books including Bayonets in the Street, 1969, 75, Civil Wars in the Twentieth Century, 1972, A Guide to the Sources of British Military History, 1972, A Guide to the Sources of U.S. Military History, 1975, The U.S. Army in Peacetime: Essays in Honor of the Bicentennial, 1975; Intervention or Abstention, 1975, Flying Combat Aircraft, Vol. 1, 1975, Vol. 2, 1978. Contbr. numerous articles to profl. jours. Home: 2961 Nevada St Manhattan KS 66502

HIGHLEY, TERRY LEONARD, plant pathologist; b. Anamosa, Iowa, July 3, 1940; s. Charles Leonard and Muriel Frieda (Hanssen) H.; B.S., Iowa State U., 1962; M.S., Oreg. State U., 1964, Ph.D., 1967; m. Barbara Lee McKnight, June 17, 1967; children—Christopher, Stephanie. Research plant pathologist Oreg. State U., Corvallis, 1962-67, U.S. Forest Products Products Lab., Madison, Wis., 1967—. Cons. wood deterioration. Bark and Wood Chemistry fellow, 1962-64, Luther Vinton Rice scholar, 1960-61. Mem. Am. Phytopathol. Soc., Madison Jr. C. of C., Sigma Xi, Phi Sigma, Phi Kappa Phi, Gamma Sigma Delta. Methodist. Contbr. articles to profl. jours. Home: 6302 Romford Rd Madison WI 53711 Office: Walnut St Madison WI 53705

HIGHT, RALPH DALE, physicist, educator; b. San Antonio, Mar. 6, 1945; s. Rolla Angus and Virginia (Goodrich) H.; A.S., San Antonio Jr. Coll., 1964; B.S. with honors in Chemistry and Physics, N. Tex. State U., Denton, 1967, M.S. in Physics, 1969; Ph.D. in Physics, Mont. State U., Bozeman, 1975; m. Sheila Ann Loudat, June 4, 1967; 1 son, Marc Alan. Instr. chemistry N. Tex. State U., Denton, 1965-69, instr. physics, 1969-71; NDEA fellow Mont. State U., Bozeman, 1969, instr. physics, 1971-73, research asst., 1973-75; NSF postdoctoral research fellow U. Toledo (Ohio), 1975-77; instr. physics Bowling Green (Ohio) State U., 1977—; vis. asst. prof. U. Nebr., 1977—; NSF summer fellow La. State U., New Orleans, 1965. Recipient regional award Chem. Rubber Co., 1964. Mem. Am. Inst. Physics, Blue Key, Sigma Pi Sigma. Contbr. articles in field to profl. jours. Home: 5401 Orchard Ln Lincoln NE 68504 Office: Dept Physics Univ Nebr Lincoln NE 68588

HIGLEY, ALBERT MALTBY, JR., constrn. co. exec.; b. Cleve., May 11, 1928; s. Albert Maltby and Mildred (Schuch) H.; B.A., Denison U., 1951; M.B.A., Cornell U., 1954; m. Beverly Gray, June 25, 1955; children—Sharon A., Bruce G., Brian M. Engr., Albert M. Higley Co., Cleve., 1955-60, exec. v.p., 1960-70, chmn. bd., 1970—; dir. Central Nat. Bank of Cleve., Enamel Products Co., Cleve. Sec. Cleve. chpt. A.R.C., 1968-73, 1st vice chmn., 1973-75, chmn., 1976—; trustee Booth Meml. Hosp., 1965-69, YMCA, 1965-68, United Appeal, United Torch, 1976—. Served with AUS, 1951-53; Korea. Clubs: Automobile (dir. 1966), Union, Country (Cleve.). Home: 20776 Sydenham Rd Shaker Heights OH 44122 Office: 2926 Chester Ave Cleveland OH 44115

HILBERT, ANGELIA HULDA, guidance counselor; b. Columbia, Mo., Nov. 26, 1949; d. Ernest Wayland and Opal Elizabeth (Gruebbel) Smith; A.A., Columbia Coll., 1969; B.S., Central Methodist Coll., Fayette, Mo., 1971; M.Ed., U. Mo., 1975; m. Thomas Daniel Hilbert, Aug. 3, 1974. Tchr. 4th grade Daniel Boone Elementary Sch., Warrenton, Mo., 1971-74, elementary guidance counselor, 1974—. Mem. Am. Sch. Counselor Assn., Mid-Mo., Mo. guidance assns., Am. personnel and guidance assns., Mo. Edn. Assn., Women's Internat. Bowling Congress, Delta Kappa Gamma, Beta Sigma Phi. Methodist. Home: 307 Roanoke St Warrenton MO 63383 Office: 302 Kuhl St Warrenton MO 63303

HILBISH, THOMAS, musician, educator; b. Bristol, Ind., Aug. 28, 1918; s. Myron Clay and Lillian Sabina (Stoffel) H.; Mus.B., U. Miami, Coral Gables, Fla., 1941; Mus.M., Princeton, 1948; pvt. study conducting Julius Herford, N.Y.C., 1950-65; postgrad. Columbia, 1950-52, Rutgers U., 1955; m. Barbara E. Smith, July 2, 1950; children—Catherine, Jennifer. Supr. music Princeton (N.J.) Schs., 1948-65; prof., dir. univ. choirs, chmn. conducting dept. U. Mich., Ann Arbor, 1965—. Faculty, Princeton, 1962-63, prof. music, 1967; vis. lectr. Westminster Choir Coll., 1959-64; vis. lectr. music N.Y. U., 1955-56, U. So. Calif., summer 1969, Harvard, summer 1971, Ind. U., summer 1974. Mem. music com. Harvard, 1965-69. Served to lt. AC, USNR, 1941-46. Mem. Am. Choral Dirs. Assn., Phi Mu Alpha, Kappa Sigma. Rotarian. Home: 2189 7th St Ann Arbor MI 48105

HILBOLDT, JAMES SONNEMANN, lawyer, investment adviser; b. Dallas, July 21, 1929; s. Grover C. and Grace E. (Sonnemann) H.; A.B. in Econs., Harvard, 1952; postgrad. U. Chgo., 1952-53; J.D., U. Mich., 1956; m. Martha M. Christian, Sept. 5, 1953; children—James, Katherine Ann, Susanna Jean, Thomas Christian. With comml. banking and trust depts. No. Trust Co., Chgo., 1952-53; admitted to Mich. bar, 1957; practice law, Kalamazoo, 1957—; registered investment adviser, 1971—; sec., dir. Bond Supply Co., Kalamazoo, 1961—; dir. Lafourche Realty Co., Kalamazoo, 1961—, pres., 1971—; dir. Hayes-Albion Corp., Jackson, Mich., Am. Nat. Holding Co., Am. Nat. Bank and Trust Co. Mich., Kalamazoo. Pres., Community Caucus, 1964-66; treas. Kalamazoo Civic Players, 1961-64; alumni rep. sch. and scholarships com. Harvard Coll., 1968—, area chmn. Class of 1952, Fun, 1966, permanent class com. Class of 1952, 1972—, regional dir. Asso. Harvard Alumni, 1973-76. Sec., trustee Power Found., W.P. Laughlin Charitable Found.; former pres. bd. dirs. Southwestern Mich. Tennis Patrons, Inc.; bd. dirs. Kalamazoo Tennis Patrons, Inc., 1974—; former bd. dirs., treas. Chamber Music Soc. Kalamazoo. Served with USMCR, 1946-48. Recipient Barristers award U. Mich. Law Sch., 1956. Mem. Am., Mich., Kalamazoo County bar assns., Owl Club and Hasty Pudding Inst. 1770, Barristers Soc., Phi Delta Phi. Methodist (steward 1961-64). Clubs: Kalamazoo Country, Kalamazoo Figure Skating; Harvard of Western Mich. (pres. 1972-74) (Kalamazoo and Grand Rapids). Home: 4126 Lakeside Dr Kalamazoo MI 49008 Office: American Nat Bank Bldg Kalamazoo MI 49007

HILBORN, JOHN R., ins. co. exec.; b. Oak Park, Ill., Dec. 15, 1928; s. John T. and Evelyn N. (Newcomer) H.; B.A., DePauw U., 1951; M.B.A., Northwestern U., 1956; m. Shirley S. Butcher, Dec. 22, 1950; children—James, Janet, John, Jeffrey. Vice pres., treas. Easterling Co., Wheaton, Ill., 1959-63; tax mgr. Cory Corp., Chgo., 1963-68; v.p., treas. Page Engring. Co., Chgo., 1968-74; v.p. fin. and personnel Map Internat., Wheaton, Ill., 1974-77; spl. agt. Fellinger Corp., Northwestern Life Ins. Co., Chgo., 1977—. Pres., LaGrange Highlands Civic Assn., 1957. Served as 1st lt. USMCR, 1951-53. Home: 4446 Gilbert Ave Western Springs IL 60558 Office: 150 S Wacker Dr Suite 800 Chicago IL 60606

HILDEBRAND, GORDON FRANCIS, drug co. exec.; b. Sheboygan, Wis., Jan. 30, 1917; s. Frank C. and Christina (Uhrig) H.; B.A. cum laude, U. Wis., 1939; m. Marie Brock, July 13, 1940; children—G. Jack, Jan Marie (Mrs. Thomas Cornwall). Mgr., Arthur Andersen & Co., C.P.A.'s, Kansas City, Mo., 1939-52; controller Vitacraft Corp., direct sales, Kansas City, 1955-59; treas. Cencor, Inc., Kansas City, 1952-55; with Campana Corp., Batavia, Ill., 1959—, pres., 1971—; group v.p. Purex Corp., 1972—. Treas. City of Prairie Village (Kans.), 1948-54. C.P.A., Mo., Kans. Mem. Am. Inst. C.P.A.'s, Batavia C. of C., Beta Alpha Psi, Beta Gamma Sigma. Republican. Presbyn. (trustee 1954-59). Elk. Home: 1719 Riverside Ave St Charles IL 60174 Office: Campana Corp Batavia IL 60510

HILDEBRAND, JAMES FREDERICK, dermatologist; b. Howards Grove, Wis., Jan. 25, 1920; s. Gustave J. and Josephine Annette H.; M.D., U. Wis., 1943; m. Marian Esther Towzey, Nov. 5, 1944; children—James R., Carol, Sandra, Michael J., Scott Q., Amy. Intern, Christ Hosp., Cin., 1943-44, resident in internal medicine, 1944-45; practice medicine specializing in internal medicine, 1945—; resident in dermatology Henry Ford Hosp., Detroit, 1953-56; practice medicine specializing in dermatology, 1956—; mem. staff Sheboygan Clinic, 1947—; county coroner Sheboygan County, 1948-53. Served as capt. MC, U.S. Army, 1945-47, MC, USAF, 1953. Diplomate Am. Bd. Internal Medicine, Am. Bd. Dermatology. Fellow Am. Acad. Dermatology; mem. AMA, Wis. Dermatological Soc., Med. Soc. Wis., Sheboygan County Med. Soc. (v.p. 1964). Home: 1739 N 6th St Sheboygan WI 53081 Office: 1011 N 8th St Sheboygan WI 53081

HILDEBRANDT, BRUNO F., educator; b. Goerlitz, Germany, Sept. 26, 1926; s. Otto and Selma (Lange) H.; student Goethe U. (Frankfurt, Germany), 1958; Ph.D., U. Hamburg (Germany), 1963; m. Lieselotte M. Prochnow, Apr. 7, 1949. Came to U.S., 1963, naturalized, 1972. Various teaching positions, Germany, 1960-63; asst. prof. German, U. Colo., Boulder, 1963-65; asso. prof. German, U. Ill., Chgo., 1965-69; prof. German, U. N.D., Grand Forks, 1969—, Hill Family Found. research prof., summer 1971, also dir. grad. studies in German; vis. asso. prof. Ind. U., Bloomington, summer 1967; vis. prof. Middlebury (Vt.) Coll., summers 1968, 69, U. Chgo., 1968, U. Minn., summer 1977; dir. German Linguistic Research Lab., U. Ill., Chgo., 1967, Exam. Center, Deutsches Sprachdiplom fuer Auslaender, Goethe-Inst., U. Ill., Chgo., 1968-69, U. N.D., 1969—. Mem. Found. for Univ. Studies of German People, Modern Lang. Assn., Assn. Am. Tchrs. German, Verein fuer Niederdeutsche Sprachforschung, Linguistic Circle Manitoba and N.D. Author: Experimentalphonetische Untersuchungen zur Bestimmung und Wertung der "durativen Funktion" akzentuierter Vokale, 1963; Drills in German Pronunciation, 1964; Strukturelemente der deutschen Gegenwart shochsprache: Phone und Phonaden, 1976. Contbr. numerous articles to profl. jours. Home: 916 29th Ave S Grand Forks ND 58201

HILDEBRANDT, HERBERT WILLIAM, educator; b. Sheboygan, Wis., Jan. 25, 1931; s. Herbert Herman and Ann (Flemming) H.; B.A., Wartburg Coll., 1952; M.S., U. Wis., 1955, Ph.D., 1958; m. Delores Dorothy Bartels, Aug. 28, 1954; children—Susan, Mark. Instr., U. Wis., Madison, 1957-58; mem. faculty U. Mich., Ann Arbor, 1958—, asst. prof., 1958-62, asso. prof., 1962-71, asst. to pres. sec. of univ., 1965-70, prof. bus. adminstrn., prof. speech, 197; cons. in field.; dir. John Knox Retirement Center. Area Chmn. United Fund, 1966. Served with U.S. Army, 1952-54. Named Outstanding Tchr., Central States Speech Assn., 1961; recipient AMOCO Teaching award, 1977; United Fund Community Award, 1974; Inst. Internat. Commerce grantee, 1972. Mem. Internat. Communication Assn., Am. Bus. Communication Assn., Speech Communication Assn., Am. Inst. Parliamentarians, Econ. Club. Detroit. Lutheran. Author books and contbr. articles in field to profl. jours. Home: 2039 Welch Ct Ann Arbor MI 48103 Office: Grad Sch Bus Univ Mich Ann Arbor MI 48109

HILDRETH, R(OLAND) JAMES, found. adminstr., economist; b. Des Moines, Nov. 26, 1926; s. Roland James and Emma (Lehman) H.; B.S., Iowa State U., 1949, M.S. in Indsl. Econs., 1950, Ph.D. in Econs., 1954; postgrad. in econs., U. Minn., 1950-52; m. May Helen Carlson, June 8, 1947; children—Christine, Jeffrey, Paul. Instr. Augsburg Coll., Mpls., 1950-52; asst. prof. dept. agrl. econs. and sociology Tex. A. and M. Coll., also Tex. Agr. Expt. Sta., 1954-58; research coordinator for West Tex., Tex. Agr. Expt. Sta., 1958-59, asst. dir., 1959-62; asso. mgr., dir. Farm Found., Chgo., 1962-70, mgr., dir., 1970—. Mem. nat. council Boy Scouts Am., 1973-76; adv. com. Council on Rural Health, AMA, 1970—; adv. council on consumer affairs Am. Bankers Assn., 1971-73; citizens adv. com. Coll. Phys. Edn., U. Ill., 1966-69. Bd. dirs. Lutheran Gen. Hosp., Park Ridge, Ill., Nat. Center for Vol. Action. Served with AUS, 1945-47; ETO. Mem. Am. Agrl. Econs. Assn. (pres. 1977-78), Internat. Assn. Agrl. Economists (sec.-treas. 1973—), Am. Country Life Assn. (pres. 1967-69). Contbg. author Changing Patterns in Fertilizer Use, 1968. Editor: Readings in Agricultural Policy, 1967; co-editor, contbg. author Methods for Land Economics Research, 1966. Home: 381 Poplar Ave Elmhurst IL 60126 Office: 600 S Michigan Ave Chicago IL 60605

HILEMAN, KENNETH EUGENE, ins. agy. exec.; b. Dayton, Ohio, June 18, 1934; s. Clyde D. and Alyce L. (Stockslager) H.; B.S., Bowling Green State U., 1956; M.B.A., U. Toledo, 1972; m. Ann Jane Glann, June 29, 1957; children—Lorri Beth, Douglas Glann. Accountant, Ernst & Ernst, Toledo, 1956-63; mgr. pension trust dept. S.G. Carson & Asso., Inc. (co. name changed to Bayer & Assos. 1970), Toledo, 1963—, v.p., 1963—, asso. gen. agt., 1974—; partner Pavos, S.A., San Salvadore, El Salvadore, 1970—, Portage Point Inn, Onekama, Mich., 1973—; v.p., dir. B-C Corp., Toledo, 1968—; dir. Toledo Metal Spinning Co. Bd. dirs. Neighborhood Improvement Found. Toledo, 1965-67, Jr. Achievement, 1973—, Toledo Symphony Orch., 1977—; bd. dirs. Children's Theatre Workshop Toledo, pres. 1970—; trustee Planned Parenthood League Toledo, asst. treas., 1969, 71; bd. mgr. South Toledo YMCA, 1977—. Served with AUS, 1957-58, 61-62. C.P.A., Ohio. Mem. Am. Inst. C.P.A.'s, Ohio Soc. C.P.A.'s, Toledo Area C. of C., Toledo Area Small Bus. Assn. (1st v.p. 1977). Presbyterian (trustee 1969-71, pres. bd. trustees 1971, elder 1977). Home: 3085 Dorian Dr Toledo OH 43614 Office: 200 Libbey-Owens-Ford Bldg Toledo OH 43603

HILL, AVERY, optometrist; b. Evanston, Ill., May 24, 1924; s. William David and Julia Wesley (Avery) H.; D.Optometry, Ill. Coll. Optometry, 1948; m. Eleanor Crawford, Sept. 13, 1947; 1 dau., Colette. Practice optometry, Evanston, Chgo., 1948—; mem. staff Daniel Hale Williams Neighborhood Health Center, 1972—, Childrens Meml. Hosp.; dir. Ill. Vision Services, Inc., Chgo. Mem. Bd. Edn. Evanston Twp. High Sch., 1969—, pres. pro-temp, 1972; mem. steering com. Evanston North Suburban Urban League; mem. lay adv. com. Evanston Twp. High Sch., 1964-67; commr. Evanston Human Relations Commn., 1968-75; active N.A.A.C.P., Norshore Twelve, Inc. Trustee Garrett Theol. Sem., Family Counselling Service of Evanston, Primm Towers Sr. Citizens Home. Served with USAAF, 1943-45; ETO. Decorated Bronze Star with oak leaf cluster. Mem. Am., Ill., Midsouth optometric assns. Home: 3654 Grove St Skokie IL 60076 Office: 4801 W Lake St Chicago IL 60644

HILL, BRUCE MARVIN, scientist, educator; b. Chgo., Mar. 13, 1935; s. Samuel and Leah (Berman) H.; B.S., U. Chgo., 1956; M.S., Stanford, 1958, Ph.D., 1961; m. Anne Edith Gardiner Bruce, Aug. 5, 1972; children—Alec Michael, Russell Andrew, Gregory Bruce. Faculty, U. Mich., Ann Arbor, 1960—, asso. prof. statistics and probability theory, 1964-70, prof., 1970—. Vis. prof. bus. Harvard, 1964-65; vis. prof. systems engring. U. Lancaster (U.K.), 1968-69; cons. IBM, Ford Corp. Grantee, NSF, USAF. Fellow Am. Statis. Assn.; mem. Inst. Math. Statistics, A.A.U.P., Research Club U. Mich., Psi Upsilon, Sigma Chi. Contbr. articles to profl. jours. Home: 1657 Glenwood Ann Arbor MI 48104 Office: Dept Statistics U Mich Ann Arbor MI 48104

HILL, CARL HENRY, data processor, systems cons.; b. Splunge, Miss., Oct. 21, 1918; s. Charles W. and Pearl (Palmer) H.; B.S. in Bus., Northwestern U., 1947; certificate Data Processing Mgmt. Assn., 1956. Systems analyst Internat. Minerals and Chems., Chgo., 1949-56; mgr. machine accounting Benjamine Electric Mfg. Co., Des Plaines, Ill., 1956-57; project planner Pure Oil Co., Chgo., 1957-60; v.p. Nat. Bus. Lists, Chgo., 1960; systems and procedures U. Chgo. Hosps., 1962-74; partner Car-Wal Enterprises, Chgo., 1968—; v.p. Highland Park News Agy.; pres. Viscose, Inc. Served with AUS, 1942-46. Home: 3712 W Montrose Chicago IL 60618 Office: 10400 W Higgins Suite 316 Rosemont IL 60018

HILL, DRAPER, editorial cartoonist; b. Boston, July 1, 1935; s. L. Draper and Jean (Thompson) H.; B.A. magna cum laude, Harvard, 1957; postgrad. Slade Sch. Fine Arts, Univ. Coll., London, Eng., 1960-63; m. Sarah Randolph Adams, Apr. 22, 1967; children—Jennifer Randolph, Jonathan Draper. Reporter, cartoonist Quincy (Mass.) Patriot Ledger, 1957-60; editorial cartoonist Worcester (Mass.) Telegram, 1964-71, Comml. Appeal, 1971-76, Detroit News, 1976—. Bd. dirs. Play of the Month Guild, N.Y.C., 1958—; instr. drawing Worcester Art Sch., 1967-71; one man shows, Germantown Tenn., 1973, Brooks Meml. Art Gallery, Memphis, 1975. Mem. Assn. Am. Editorial Cartoonists (pres. 1975-76), Club: Odd Vols. Author: Mr. Gillray, The Caricaturist, 1965; Fashionable Contrasts, 1966; The Satirical Etchings of James Gillray, 1976; (with James Roper) The Decline and Fall of the Gibbon, 1974. Home: 368 Washington Rd Grosse Pointe MI 48230 Office: 615 W Lafayette Blvd Detroit MI 48231

HILL, HARRY WILLIAMS, newspaperman; b. Sewell, Chile, Nov. 11, 1919 (parents Am. citizens); s. Fred H. and Creta (Williams) H.; student U. Kans., 1936-40; m. Marguerite Donna DeRoos, Sept. 14, 1943; children—Maureen, Jonathan, Brian. News editor Horton (Kans.) Headlight, 1940-42; reporter Clinton (Iowa) Herald, 1945-47; reporter, copyreader Sioux City (Iowa) Jour., 1947-52; with Milw. Jour., 1953—, city editor, 1962-69, asst. mng. editor, 1967—. Lectr. mass communications U. Wis.-Milw., 1971—. Served to 1st lt. USAAF, 1942-45; ETO. Decorated D.F.C., Air medal with 3 oak leaf clusters. Home: 11430 N St James Ln Mequon WI 53092 Office: 333 W State St Milwaukee WI 53201

HILL, JAMES EDWARD, physician; b. Glen Elder, Kans., Apr. 27, 1909; s. Robert William and Lucinda (Copeland) H.; A.B., Friends U., 1930; M.D., Kan. U., 1934; m. Ruth Mary Snyder, June 23, 1935; children—Robert Edward, James Lewis. Intern, St. Francis Hosp., Wichita, Kans., 1934-35; resident Chgo. Eye and Ear Hosp., 1938-40; practice gen. medicine, Conway Springs, Kans., 1935-38; staff Hatcher Clinic, Wellington, Kans., 1940-43, 46-50; practice medicine specializing in ophthalmology, Arkansas City, Kans., 1950—; dir. 1st Fed Savs. & Loan Assn., Arkansas City. Mem. Kans. Bd. Healing Arts, 1964—, now also sec. Served with USNR, 1943-46. Diplomate Am. Bd. Ophthalmology. Fellow A.C.S.; mem. Fedn. State Med. Bds. U.S. (flex test com.). Home: 407 W Vine Arkansas City KS 67005 Office: 2508 Edgemont Dr Arkansas City KS 67005

HILL, JON DE WITT, investment co. exec.; b. Des Moines, July 6, 1935; s. Ward Smith and Jessie Alice (Felix) H.; student Grinnell Coll., 1952-53, U. Vienna, 1953-54; B.A. (Law Sch. Honor fellow), Drake U., 1956; M.B.A., Harvard U., 1961; m. Joan Marie Foreman, Aug. 20, 1955; children—Ted Stephen, Stephanie Paige, Blake Andrew, Chrisjon Michael. Market devel. mgr. Gen. Electric Co., Phoenix, 1961-63; asst. to pres. Howmet Corp., N.Y.C., 1963-65; merchant banking assn. Alex Brown & Sons, N.Y.C., 1966-72; treas., v.p., group exec. Heizer Corp., Chgo., 1972-76; dir. fin. U.S. Ry. Assn., Washington, 1977—; dir. Columbus Dental Co., Bio-Dynamics, Inc., Chalet Susse Internat. V.P., dir. Inverness Assn., 1975-77. Served with USAF, 1956-59. Named Distinguished Military Grad. Drake U., 1956. Mem. Harvard Bus. Sch. Club, Assn. Corporate Growth. Republican. Clubs: Tamarack, Metropolitan, Plum Grove, Harvard. Home: Heather Ln Inverness IL 60067 Office: US Ry Assn L'Enfant Plaza (North) Washington DC 20024

HILL, KEARNEY H.J., educator; b. Pawnee, Okla., Apr. 11, 1933; s. Kearney H. and Bernice (Rengle) H.; A.Sci., Okla. State U., 1963, B.S., 1965; M.S., Kans. State U., 1972; m. Rita M. Karleskint, Aug. 23, 1958. Jr. research engr. Seismograph Service, Tulsa, 1955-56; service mgr., asst. to chief inspector Aerotron Radio Corp., Tulsa, 1956-61; head Instrument div. Quality Control Dept., Midwestern Instruments, Tulsa, 1961; pres. Tultech Electronics Labs., Pawnee, Okla., 1961-65; instr. electronics and math. Classen High Sch., Oklahoma City, 1965-66; electronics instr. Oklahoma City Area Vocat.-Tech. Sch., 1966-67; prof., head dept. computer tech. dept., dir. Computer Center, Kans. Tech. Inst., Salina, 1967—; cons. to CompuServ, Salina, Kans., 1969—. Adviser computer merit badge

Boy Scouts Am., Salina, 1972-74. Mem. Data Processing Mgmt. Assn. (chpt. v.p. 1969-70), Am. Soc. Engring. Edn., Assn. for Computer Machinery, Instrument Soc. Am., IEEE, Assn. Ednl. Data Systems (chpt. pres. elect 1977-78), Phi Delta Kappa, Sigma Tau. Contbr. articles to profl. jours. Home: 857 Navajo St Salina KS 67401

HILL, LEWIS WARREN, city ofcl.; b. Ft. Worth, Feb. 25, 1926; s. Alvin Carnes and Constance (Lewis) H.; B.S. in Design, Inst. Design, Ill. Inst. Tech., 1951; B.A. in Math., U. Minn., 1946; LL.D. (hon.), Loyola U., 1977; m. Dorothy Mae Hey, Sept. 11, 1954; children—Mary Lew, Martha, Katherine, Thomas, David, Sara. Various positions Chgo. Land Clearance Commn., U. Ill. Med. Center, Chgo., Community Conservation Bd., 1951-54; supervising project planner Pub. Housing Adminstrn., Chgo., 1956-57; asst. commr. Dept. Urban Renewal (merged with Community Conservation Bd.), 1957-63, dep. commr., 1963-65, chmn., commr., 1965—; commr. Dept. Devel. and Planning, 1967—; chmn. Comml. Dist. Devel. Commn., 1976—, co-chmn. housing and community devel. programs, 1976—. Sec. Chgo. Plan Commn., Pub. Bldg. Commn.; mem. Econ. Devel. Commn., Chgo. Com. on Criminal Justice, Ill.-Ind. Bi-State Commn., Northeastern Ill. Planning Commn., Commn. on Health Planning and Resources Devel., Chgo. Com. Hist. and Archtl. Landmarks; asst. sec. bd. dirs. Chgo. Boys Club; mem. alumni bd. Ill. Inst. Tech.; asso. trustee U. Chgo. Cancer Research Fund; bd. advisors Catholic Charities Chgo. Served to lt. comdr. USNR, 1944-46. Mem. Am. Inst. Planners (vice chmn. Chgo. sect. 1959-60), Nat. Assn. Housing, Redevel. Ofcls. (chmn. Chgo. chpt. 1959-62), Internat. Fedn. Housing and Planning, Urban Land Inst. (exec. group), Western Soc. Engrs., Chgo. Assn. Commerce and Industry, Lambda Alpha. Roman Catholic. K.C. Mem. Holy Name Soc. Clubs: Tavern, Economic, Svithoid (Chgo.). Home: 5858 N Kenton Ave Chicago IL 60646 Office: City Hall 121 N La Salle St Chicago IL 60602

HILL, MICHAEL EMMANUEL, research adminstr.; b. Balt., Apr. 5, 1943; s. Sidney B. and Margaret W. (Corsey) H.; B.E.E., Am. Inst. Engring. and Tech., Chgo., 1964; B.S. in Gen. Studies, Roosevelt U., Chgo., 1977; postgrad. Northwestern U. Grad. Sch. Bus., 1976-78; children—Michael, Trisha, Tracy. Quality control supr. Pentron Electronics, Chgo., 1964; EDP systems maintenance supr. Spiegel Inc., Chgo., 1964-68; systems analyst and programmer Aetna Bank, Chgo., 1968-69; group leader Ill. Inst. Tech. Research Inst., Chgo., 1969—; pres. Dynamics Devel. Corp., Chgo., 1973-75; v.p. Harthel Computer Services, Chgo., 1976-77. Mem. Chgo. Model Cities Council, 1970-74. Served with U.S. Army, 1960-63. Mem. Nat. Space Inst., Cosmopolitan C. of C. Democrat. Methodist. Home: 7120 S Ingleside Chicago IL 60619 Office: 10 W 35th St Chicago IL 60616

HILL, PAMELA ELLEN, educator; b. Chgo., June 28, 1953; d. David Willis and Joan Marie (Payne) H.; B.S. in Psychology, Western Ill. U., 1974; M.Ed. in Counseling and Guidance, Loyola U., 1975. Family planning counselor Friendship Med. Center, Chgo., 1975; lectr. psychology Chgo. State U., Chgo., 1975; instr. psychology Moraine Valley Community Coll., Palos Hills, Ill., 1975—; research asst. Consumer Analyst, Chgo., 1977—, cons. in field. Bd. dirs. Far South Mental Health Council. Mem. Am. Personnel and Guidance Assn., Assn. of Measurement and Evaluation in Guidance, Assn. Non-White Concerns, Student Personnel Assn. for Tchr. Edn., Alpha Kappa Alpha (treas. Macomb, Ill. 1973). Democrat. Roman Catholic. Home: 1081 W 108th St Chicago IL 60643 Office: 10900 S 88th Ave Palos Hills IL 60465

HILL, RICHARD GLEN, electronic co. exec.; b. Carterville, Ill., Apr. 29, 1917; s. Frank N. and Mable (Mullins) H.; student So. Ill. U., Carbondale, Ill., 1935-37; B.S., U.S. Naval Acad., 1941; m. Nancy Marjory Grant, Sept. 28, 1944; children—Andrea Jhonne, Lisa Margot, Kerren Lee. Commd. ensign U.S. Navy, 1941, advanced through ranks to comdr., 1951, ret., 1961; mil. engr. coordinator Zenith Radio Corp., 1961-70, mgr. govt. engring. support, 1970-71, budget mgr. Engring. and Research div., staff asst. to v.p., video players and audio engring., 1972-77. Decorated Air Medal. Presbyn. Navigated the first successful non-rigid airship flights across the North Atlantic June 1944. Home: 370 S Valley Rd Barrington IL 60010

HILL, RICHARD LEE, mgmt. cons.; b. Coldwater, Mich., July 11, 1931; s. Lloyd Graves and Alice Helen (Lafler) H.; student Tulane U., 1952-53; A.B., Hillsdale Coll., 1956; postgrad. Case Western Res. U., 1962-63; m. Mary Way, Oct. 14, 1956; children—David, Martha, Rebecca, Sarah. Employee relations specialist Gen. Electric Co., Cleve., 1956-57, 60-63, Providence, 1957-60, mgr. union relations, Coshocton, Ohio, 1963-66, div. mgr. employee relations, Pittsfield, Mass., 1966-68; exec. dir. Dow Conf. Center, Hillsdale Coll., Mich., 1968-73; pres. Richard Hill Assos., Inc., Jonesville, Mich., 1973—; mem. faculty Hillsdale Coll., 1968-73; cons. Centro de Produtividade Do Brasil, 1977. Vice pres. Jonesville Bd. Edn., 1972-76. Served with USN, 1949-53. Recipient spl. pub. service award Mich. State Police, 1976. Mem. Am. Soc. Personnel Adminstrn. (accredited, bd. dirs. 1971-74, regional v.p. 1972-73, named regional v.p. of year 1973), Am. Soc. Tng. and Devel., Internat. Orgn. Devel. Registry, Internat. Cons. Found., Orgn. Renewal, Inc., World Future Soc., Omicron Delta Kappa. Author: Role Negotiation for Team Productivity, 1976; Impact—Your Organization and a Changing World, 1977. Home: 316 South St Jonesville MI 49250 Office: Box 195 Suite 2 Olde Italian Villa Jonesville MI 49250

HILL, ROBERT FRANKLIN, nuclear engr.; b. Montrose, Colo., June 28, 1929; s. Frank Cornelius and Charlene Ann (Hubert) H.; Asso. in Sci., Mesa Jr. Coll., 1950; B.S. with distinction, Purdue U., 1953, M.S., 1954; certificate, Oak Ridge Sch. Reactor Tech., 1955; m. Lorraine E. White, Oct. 22, 1972. Nuclear engr. NRB Atomic Energy Commn., Washington, 1955-57; nuclear engr. Gen. Motors Corp., Warren, Mich., 1957-67, supr. Radioisotope Lab., 1967—, radiol. safety officer, 1968—; faculty U. Detroit, 1958-60; treas. Symposium on X-Gamma Radiation, ERDA, 1976; v.p. Strathmore Assn., Troy, Mich., 1976—. Mem. Warren Citizen Adv. Com., 1960-62. Mem. Sigma Xi, Tau Beta Pi. Contbr. articles to profl. jours. Patentee in field. Home: 1207-C Kirts Rd Troy MI 48084 Office: GM Tech Center Research Labs Warren MI 48090

HILL, RUANE BURTON, educator; b. Mondovi, Wis., May 27, 1924; s. Laurence Burton and Velma (Butler) H.; A.B., Beloit Coll., 1948; M.A., Northwestern U., 1949, Ph.D., 1964; m. Marie J. Bergerson, Sept. 3, 1949; children—Gregory, Kristin, Kristofer. Asst. prof. Willamette U., Salem, Oreg., 1949-51; grad. fellow Sch. Speech, Northwestern U., Evanston, Ill., 1951-52; asst. prof. speech Beloit (Wis.) Coll., 1952-55; gen. mgr. WFGM, Fitchburg, Mass. and WMCR, Milford, Mass., 1955-58; asst. prof., gen. mgr. WAER, Syracuse (N.Y.) U., 1958-63; prof. mass communication, gen. mgr. WUWM, U. Wis., Milw., 1963—; faculty U. Mass. extension, 1956-58. Mem. Milw. Radio and TV council, 1963-67; active A.R.C., Milw., 1973—; mem. Greater Milw. Conf. on Religion and Urban Affairs, 1968—. Served as project dir. Corp. for Pub. Broadcasting, Johnson Found., Radio-TV Internat., 1970-76. Served with USAAF, 1943-46. Mem. Nat. Assn. Ednl. Broadcasters (dir. exec. bd. 1973-74), Nat. Ednl. Radio, Assn. Pub. Radio Stas., Broadcast Edn. Assn., Milw. Adult Assn., Milw. Press Club, Milw. Area Broadcast News Assn. (exec. dir. 1969-75), Wis. Broadcasters Assn. (dir., sec. 1965-66). Editor: (with A.E. Koenig) The Farther Vision: ETV Today, 1967, Spanish edit. 1969, Arabic edit., 1975. Home: 3494 N Frederick Ave Milwaukee WI 53211

HILL, RUSSELL EUGENE, artist; b. Duluth, Minn., Aug. 16, 1924; s. Walter Albert and Merle Gertrude (Walker) H.; student pub. schs., Washington; m. Edith Virginia Dunkum, Nov. 3, 1950. Artist, Melpar, Inc., and predecessor firms, Falls Church, Va., 1948-60, illustrator, 1950-55, sr. illustrator, 1955-60; one-man shows include: Tweed Gallery, Duluth, 1965, 73, Duluth Art Inst., 1968, U. Wis., Superior, 1967, 76, Am. Swedish Inst., Mpls., 1966; group shows include: Am. Painters in Paris, 1975, Dept. State's Art in Embassies, 1965-67, 72—, White House Loan, 1969-74; represented in permanent collections: Tweed Gallery, Duluth, Perelman Mus., Phila.; spl. works include: series of paintings on Victorian era objects of the Old West; pvt. art tchr.; lectr. on art and related Victorian era items. Chmn. bd., treas. Douglas County Sheriff's Emergency Patrol; emergency med. technician. Served in U.S. Army, 1943-46. Recipient Pub. Choice award Gettysburg Stam Design Contest, 1963; Best in Show award Internal Revenue Exhibit, 1964; others; elected to Nat. Cowboy Hall of Fame, Oklahoma City, 1974. Mem. Am. Law Enforcement Officers Assn., Wis. Sheriffs and Dep. Sheriffs Assn. Author: Laughter Please, 1963. Home and Studio: Hill Rd Gordon WI 54838

HILL, SANDRA DENISE, ednl. counselor; b. Chgo., June 23, 1949; d. Arthur Derek Coles and Helen Delores (McKinney) Small; B.A. (George M. Pullman scholar, Ill. State scholar, Evanston Women's Assn. scholar), Northwestern U., 1971, M.A. in Counseling, 1974; m. James Allen Hill, Oct. 18, 1969; 1 dau., Janine Nicole. Asst. dean evening div. Northwestern U., 1974-77, asst. dir. fin. aids, 1977—, instr. sociology evening div., 1975. Mem. Am. Personnel and Guidance Assn., Nat., Ill. assns. non-white conerns, Ill. Assn. Fin. Aid Adminstrs., Ill. Assn. Coll. Registrars and Admission Officers, Alpha Kappa Alpha. Methodist. Home: 137 Custer Ave Evanston IL 60202 Office: Northwestern U Rebecca Crown Center 633 Clark St Evanston IL 60201

HILL, THAYER JOHN, JR., EDP tng. adminstr.; b. Aurora, Ill., May 30, 1942; s. Thayer J. and Ruth M. (Friedrich) H.; B.S., N. Central Coll., Ill., 1964; postgrad. Purdue U., U. Chgo., Loyola U., Chgo.; m. Lynn F. Taylor, June 9, 1962; children—David, Kristin. Operator and programmer EDP equipment Peoples Gas Co., Chgo., 1964-66; programmer analyst, systems analyst Pay Line Group Internat. Harvester Co., Broadview, Ill., 1966-69, coordinator office systems, tng. coordinator corporate EDP, Corporate Computer Center, Hinsdale, Ill., 1969-77, mgr. tech. tng., Info. Systems Services, 1977—; established Chgo. Data Processing Edn. Council, 1969; cons. to vendors of tng. packages; instr. Control Data Inst. Author tech. writings in field. Home: 929 Emerald Ln Naperville IL 60540 Office: 903 Commerce Dr Oak Brook IL 60521

HILL, THEODORE ALBERT, psychiatrist; b. Denver, June 12, 1908; s. Albert Lyon and Helen H. (Brown) H.; B.A., U. Calif. at Los Angeles, 1930; M.A., Stanford U., 1931; M.D., Loma Linda U., 1947; m. Eva Grace Harris, June 30, 1934; children—Helen Julia Hill Felicia, Grace Lorraine, Theodora Susan. Adminstrv. analyst Los Angeles County Div. Adminstrv. Research, 1937-40; adminstrv. insp. Dept. Interior, Washington, 1941-42; intern Los Angeles County Gen. Hosp., 1946-47, physician (psychiatry), 1947-50; dir. Adult and Child Guidance Clinic, St. Joseph County, Ind., 1952-56; individual practice medicine specializing in psychiatry, S. Bend, Ind., 1956-68; supt. Dr. Norman M. Beatty Meml. Hosp., Westville, Ind., 1968-72; individual practice medicine specializing in psychiatry, Long Beach and Michigan City, Ind., 1973—; instr. psychiatry Sch. Medicine, Ind. U., 1967-73, asso. prof., 1973—; psychiat. cons. Peace Corps, 1962, LaPorte County Comprehensive Mental Health Center, 1973, Ind. State Prison, Michigan City, 1973-77. Served to maj. M.C., U.S. Army, 1950-52. Diplomate Am. Bd. Psychiatry and Neurology. Fellow Am. Psychiat. Assn. (rep. assembly dist. brs.), Am. Orthopsychiat. Assn.; mem. Am. Group Psychotherapy Assn., No. Ind. Psychiat. Soc. (past pres.). Episcopalian. Home and Office: 1606 Lake Shore Dr Long Beach Michigan City IN 46360

HILL, THOMAS CLARKE, VIII, editor, publisher; b. Broken Bow, Okla., Mar. 16, 1920; s. James Clifford and Lessie Katherine (Graham) H.; M.E., U. Okla., 1939; postgrad. Purdue U., 1956-57, So. Meth. U., 1959-60, La. State U., 1963-64; m. Arlene Mae Wertz, Jan. 7, 1967; 1 son, Thomas Clarke, IX. Owner, operator Hill Oil Co., Long Beach, Calif., 1946-49; sales mgr. Custom Chem. Co., Redondo Beach, Calif., 1948-52; v.p. Am. Ins. Digest, Deerfield, Ill., 1952-55, owner, editor, publisher, 1955—, pres., 1956—; chmn., chief exec. officer Guardian Advisors Corp., Deerfield, 1956—, Hilson Fin. Corp., Rocklin, Calif., 1976—; editor, pub. Ins. Guardian, Deerfield, 1956—; dir. ops. United Nat. Life and 1st United Nat. Corp., Springfield, Ill., 1973-77. Chmn. revenue com. Village of Lincolnshire (Ill.), fin. dir., treas., 1975-76. Served with USNR, 1942-46; ETO, PTO. Named Man of the Year United Nat. Life; Ambassado State of Ariz. Mem. Internat. Platform Assn., Am. Life Underwriters. Mason (32 deg., shriner), mem. Order of Eastern Star. Clubs: Century, 250, Executives, President's, Millionaires, Gaslight. Author: The Case for New Life Insurance Companies, 1969; Life Insurance as an Investment, 1970; Contbr. articles to profl. jours. Home and Office: 64 Berkshire Ln Lincolnshire Sq Deerfield IL 60015

HILL, WALTER WATSON, community center exec.; b. Montgomery, Ala., Feb. 18, 1925; s. John L. Sr. and Irene M. (Jeffers) H.; A.B. in Sociology, Morehouse Coll., 1948; M.Social Work, Atlanta U., 1950; m. Marion Phyllis Jones, Dec. 31, 1950; children—Walter Watson, Patricia F. Boys worker Ada S. McKinley Community House, Chgo., 1951-54; program dir. Neighborhood House Assn., Buffalo, 1954-61; exec. dir. Ann Arbor (Mich.) Community Center, 1961—. Dir. Mich. Savs. and Loan Assn. Instr. field work U. Ill., 1952-54, N.Y.U., 1956-60, U. Mich., 1961—. Mem. spl. com. student problems Mich. Bd. Edn., 1968—; com. racial imbalance Ann Arbor Bd. Edn., 1962-63; dir., 2d v.p. Ch. Mission Help, Buffalo, 1959-61; sec. Ann Arbor City Transit Authority, 1968-74; mem. Mich. adv. commn. Maxey Complex; vice chmn. Washtenaw County Child Care Coordinating Com., 1970-74. Served with USAAF, 1943-46; ETO. Mem. Nat. Assn. Social Workers (chmn. Huron Valley chpt. 1963-64), N.A.A.C.P., Nat. Conf. Social Welfare, Omega Psi Phi. Episcopalian. Home: 701 Sunset Rd Ann Arbor MI 48103 Office: 625 N Main St Ann Arbor MI 48104

HILL, WENDELL TALBOT, JR., pharmacist; b. Phila., Dec. 17, 1924; s. Wendell T. and Mildred (Bailey) H.; B.S., Drake U., 1950; M.S., U. So. Calif., 1954; Pharm. D., 1970; postgrad. U. Calif. at Los Angeles, 1957-64; m. Marcella E. Washington, Aug. 26, 1951; children—Wendell Talbot III, Philip Elliot. Chief pharmacy teaching sect. VA Center, Los Angeles, 1954-57; chief pharmacist Orange County Med. Center, Orange, Calif., 1957-70; asso. prof. hosp. pharmacy Wayne State U., 1970—; dir. pharmacy Detroit Gen. Hosp., 1970—; dir. Drug Information Center, 1970—; dir. Orange County Poison Information Center, 1957-70. Lectr. clin. pharmacy U. So. Calif., 1968-70; pharmacist cons. Calif. Dept. Mental Hygiene, 1966, Cal. Dept. Health Care Services, 1966-71, various hosps. and pharm. mfrs., 1963—. Founder, Orange County Community Action Council 1965; pres. Rehab. Center for Crippled Children and Adults, Orange, 1966-68. Bd. dirs. Easter Seal Soc. Crippled Children and Adults Orange County, 1964-71, pres., 1966-68; bd. dirs. Comprehensive Health Planning Assn. Orange County, pres., 1969-70, YMCA, Orange; pres. bd. dirs. Nat. Council on Pharmacy Continuing Edn., 1974-76. Served with AUS, 1943-46; PTO. Recipient Humanitarian Service award B'nai B'rith, Anaheim, 1968, Alumni Distinguished Service award Drake U., 1975. Mem. Am. Soc. Hosp. Pharmacists (dir. 1968-71, pres. 1972-73), Am., Calif., Mich., Met. Detroit (exec. com. 1975-76) pharm. assns., Southeastern Mich. Soc. Hosp. Pharmacists, AAUP, Calif. Council Hosp. Pharmacists (pres. 1963, 64). Mem. Christian Ch. (elder). Clubs: Rotary, Detroit Cotillion. Author: Recommended Pharmaceutical Practices and Staffing Standards of California State Hospitals, 1966; Pharmaceutical Services for Nursing Homes: A Procedural Manual, 1966. Home: 1969 Orleans St Detroit MI 48207 Office: Wayne State U Coll Pharmacy Detroit MI 48202

HILL, WILBUR THOMAS, osteo. physician, surgeon; b. Colorado Springs, Colo., Aug. 2, 1923; s. Walter L. and Ellen C. (Skinner) H.; student N.E. Mo. State Coll., 1942, 46-47; D.O., Kirksville Coll. Osteopathic Medicine and Surgery, 1951; m. Mary Sibyl Green, Dec. 31, 1942; children—James Wilbur, Roger Earl. Intern Kansas City Osteo. Hosp., 1951-52, gen. practice osteo. medicine and surgery, Liberty, Mo., 1952—; mem. exec. com. Liberty Hosp.; asst. prof. practice, chmn. dept. gen. practice Kansas City Coll. Osteopathic Medicine, chief of staff Center for Health Scis.; chief staff Kansas City Osteo. Hosp. Past pres. Profl. Agy. & Service Corp., also dir.; chmn. bd. Profl. Mut. Ins. Co.; med. examiner FAA, 1971—; med. adviser Liberty chpt. Am. Cancer Soc. Mem. sch. bd. Liberty Pub. Sch. Dist.; v.p., mem. exec. bd. Heart of Am. council Boy Scouts Am., mem. nat. council, bd. dirs. North Central region; bd. dirs. Clay County Youth Center; chmn. bd. Kirksville Coll. Osteo. Medicine and Surgery; pres. adv. bd. Clay County chpt. ARC, bd. dirs. Kansas City Area chpt. Served with AUS, 1943-46; ETO. Recipient Free Enterprise award for outstanding Community Service Sertoma Club, 1970; named Citizen of Year, Mo. Municipal, 1972. Fellow Am. Coll. Osteo. Medicine, Truman Library Assos.; mem. Mo. Assn. Osteo. Physicians and Surgeons (past pres.) (speaker ho. of dels.), Am. Osteo. Assn. (del. ho. of dels.), Liberty C. of C., Met. Kansas City Council Chs. (trustee), Kirksville Osteo. Alumni Assn. (past pres.), Nat., Mo. sch. bd. assns., Clay Platte Bapt. Brotherhood Assn. (past pres.). Baptist (chmn. bd. deacons). Club: Liberty Lions (dep. dist. gov. internat.). Home: 839 Hillside Liberty MO 64068 Office: Westowne Profl Center Westowne VI Liberty MO 64068

HILLARD, ROBERT EARL, accountant; b. Champaign, Ill., Jan. 30, 1945; s. William Earl and Irma Lucille (Cekander) H.; B.S. in Bus., Eastern Ill. U., 1967; M.B.A., U. Mo., St. Louis, 1977; m. Betty Ann Freeberg, Aug. 28, 1966. C.P.A., Peat Marwick Mitchell & Co. St. Louis, 1967-72; mgr. corp. controls Sunmark Co. St. Louis 1972-75; v.p. Northwestern Savs. & Loan Assn. St. Louis, 1976—. Served with USAR, 1967-73. C.P.A., Mo.; certified mgmt. accountant. Mem. Nat. Assn. Accountants, Fin. Mgrs. Soc., Beta Sigma Psi. Lutheran. Home: 12277 Autumn Hill Ct St Louis MO 63043 Office: 3855 Lucas-Hunt St Louis MO 63121

HILLE, FREDERICK E., ins. co. exec.; b. Tabor, S.D., Feb. 13, 1935; s. Edward B. and Theresa H. (Koupal) H.; student U. Notre Dame, 1953; B.A., U. Minn., 1957; m. Ruth L. Carlstrom, June 29, 1957; children—Janice, JoAnn, Frederick. With Prudential Ins. Co., Mpls., 1959-67, Security Life and Accident Ins. Co., Denver, 1967-70, Investers Diversified Services, Mpls., 1971-77; data processing exec. ITT Life Ins. Corp., Thorp, Wis., 1978—. Served with U.S. Army, 1957-59. Mem. Assn. Systems Mgmt., Am. Arbitration Assn. Club: Optimists. Home: 15452 Boulder Creek Dr Minnetonka MN 55343 Office: ITT Life Ins Corp Box E Thorp WI 54771

HILLEBOE, JOHN ALFRED, assn. exec.; b. International Falls, Minn., Mar. 12, 1929; s. Alfred Peter and Margaret Leona (Harrison) H.; B.A., Concordia Coll., 1950; m. Marlys Ann Knudson, Apr. 17, 1951; children—Betsy Joan, Mark Harrison, Margaret Ann, Christian Joseph. Realtor, Amerland Co., Realtors, Fargo, N.D., 1953-70; exec. v.p. Fargo Moorhead Bd. Realtors, Fargo, 1971—; pres. Fargo Moorhead Home Builders Assn., 1962. Instr., N.D. Grad. Realtors Inst., 1969—. Pres., Cath. Family Service, Fargo, N.D., 1977—. Served with AUS, 1951-53. Named Realtor of Yr., Fargo Moorhead Bd. Realtors, 1969. Mem. Nat. Inst. Real Estate Brokers, Fargo Bd. Realtors (pres. 1964), MLS Realtors (pres. 1968), Fargo C. of C. (chmn community improvement com. 1970), Am. Legion, DAV. Elk, Eagle. Home: 2302 S 15th St Fargo ND 58102 Office: 625 Gate City Bldg Box 1756 Fargo ND 58102

HILLER, REMBRANDT CLEMENS, JR., retail co. exec.; b. Indpls., Jan. 11, 1919; s. Rembrandt Clemens and Lillian May (Benedict) H.; B.S., Ind. U., 1940; M.B.A., Northwestern U., 1941; m. Audrey Jeanne Smith, Jan. 22, 1944; 1 son, Mark Clemens (dec.). Trainee Sears, Roebuck and Co., 1941-42, asst. buyer, 1946-48, buyer, 1948-54, asst. mgr. mdse. comparison, 1954-55, asst. to v.p. pub. relations, 1955-57, dir. civic affairs, 1957-62; dir. pub. relations Midwestern territory, 1962—. Lectr. in marketing Northwestern U., 1947-71. Bd. dirs. Met. Chgo. YMCA, Nat. Council YMCAs, Better Govt. Assn., Sears-Roebuck Found. (v.p.), Lake Bluff Chgo. Homes for Children (past pres.), Grad. Sch. Mgmt. Alumni Assn. Northwestern U. Served to lt. USNR, 1942-46. Mem. Ind. Soc. Chgo. (past pres.), Am. Mktg. Assn., Pub. Relations Soc. Am. (pres. Chgo. chpt.), Beta Theta Pi. Methodist. Clubs: University (Chgo.); Glen View (Golf, Ill.). Home: 1100 Long Valley Rd Glenview IL 60025 Office: 7447 Skokie Blvd Skokie IL 60076

HILLERY, JOHN MAURICE, lawyer; b. Chgo., Apr. 10, 1938; s. Martin Matthew and Mary Theresa (Angland) H.; B.S.C. summa cum laude, DePaul U., 1960; J.D., U. Va., 1965; m. Adeline Watson, June 13, 1964; children—Sydney Lawrence, Brendan Sean. Admitted to Ill. bar, 1965; asso. Carroll, Connelly, Hartigan & Hillery and predecessor, 1965—, partner, 1969—. Lectr. bus. law DePaul U., 1965—. Served with AC USNR, 1961-62. Mem. North Suburban Bar Assn. (treas. 1976-77, sec. 1977-78). Lion (treas. Winnetka 1970). Home: 458 Willow Rd Winnetka IL 60093 Office: 1 N LaSalle St Chicago IL 60602

HILLESTAD, ALBERT WILLIAM, clergyman; b. New Richmond, Wis., July 11, 1924; s. Evar and Elenora H.; B.A., U. Wis., 1947; M.Div., Seabury-Western Theol. Sem., 1950; D.D., Nashotah House Sem., 1972; m. Carol Joyce Hutchens, June 19, 1954; children—Mary Harriet, Michael Evar, Elizabeth Ann, William Joseph, James Frederick, Christina Louise, Paul Eric. Ordained priest Episcopal Ch., 1950, consecrated bishop, 1972; curate ch., LaCrosse, Wis., 1950-51; rector ch., Chgo., 1951-57, Carbondale, Ill., 1964-72; vicar ch., Oconto, Wis., 1957-64; Episcopal chaplain Menard and Vienna (Ill.) State Penitentiaries, 1965-72; archdeacon of Cairo, Ill., 1967-72; bishop coadjutor Diocese of Springfield, Ill., 1972, bishop, 1972—. Home: 1109 Williams Blvd Springfield IL 62704 Office: 821 S 2d St Springfield IL 62704

HILLHOUSE, LOUIS EDWIN, data processing exec.; b. West Memphis, Ark., Aug. 7, 1928; s. James Ernst and Faye Lorinne (Lucius) H.; B.S. in Bus. Adminstrn., Washington U., St. Louis, 1962;

m. Mary Elizabeth Waller, Nov. 4, 1950; children—Keith Edwin, David Alan. With McDonnel Co., St. Louis, 1953-66, chief bus. systems programming, 1966; dir. mgmt. info. services Rexall Drug Co., St. Louis, 1966-67; dir. project mgmt.-comml. McDonnell Douglas Automation Co., St. Louis, 1968—. Vice pres. Parkway N. Sr. High Sch. Parent Tchrs. Orgn.; mem. advisory bd. Family and Children's Service of St. Louis. Served with U.S. Army, 1950-52. Mem. Data Processing Mgmt. Assn., Assn. Educators in Data Processing, Am. Mgmt. Assn. Republican. Epsicopalian. Club: Elks. Office: PO Box 516 Saint Louis MO 63166

HILLIS, ELWOOD HAYNES, congressman; b. Kokomo, Ind., Mar. 6, 1926; s. Glen R. and Bernice (Haynes) H.; B.S., Ind. U., 1949, J.D., 1952; m. Carol Hoyne, June 12, 1949; children—Jeffrey H., Gary L., Bradley R. Admitted to Ind. bar, 1952; mem. Ind. Ho. of Reps., 1967-69; mem. 91st to 95th congresses from 5th Ind. Dist. Pres. Elwood Haynes Meml. Charitable Trust; Howard County United Fund, 1969. Served with USAAF, 1944-46; ETO. Mem. Am., Ind., Howard County (past pres.) bar assns., Am. Legion, VFW. Presbyterian. Clubs: Rotary, Elks, Masons, Shriners. Home: 2331 S Wabash Ave Kokomo IN 46901*

HILLMAN, CHARLENE HAMILTON, pub. relations exec.; b. Akron, Ohio; d. Charles E. and Maeton (Anderson) Hamilton; ed. Youngstown Coll., 1940-41, Ind. U. Extension, 1949, 50; m. Robert E. Hillman (separated); 1 son, Robert E. Sales promotion and secretarial work nitrogen div. Allied Chem. Corp., Indpls., 1955-59; mem. Bob Long Assos., Indpls., 1959-62; pub. relations dir. Paul Lennon Advt. Agy., Indpls., 1962-63, Clowes Meml. Hall of Butler U., 1963-64; pub. relations counselor Charlene Hillman Pub. Relations Assos., Indpls., 1964-75; v.p., dir. pub. relations Caldwell-Van Riper, Inc., Indpls., 1975—. Mem. Indpls. Mayor's Communications Task Force, 1968-71. Mem. Pub. Relations Soc. Am. (pres. Hoosier chpt. 1967, 72-73, dist. chmn., nat. dir. 1975-76), Advt. Club Indpls. (Advt. Woman of Year 1969, dir.), Ind. Bus. Communications. (v.p. 1969), Ind. Soc. Assn. Execs., Women in Communications. Club: Indianapolis Press. Editor: Mayflower Warehouseman, 1965-66, Hoosier Ind., 1966—. Home: 9101 Bryant Ln Apt 2A Indianapolis IN 46250 Office: 2600 One Indiana Bank Bldg Indianapolis IN 46204

HILLMAN, DOUGLAS WOODRUFF, lawyer; b. Grand Rapids, Mich., Feb. 15, 1922; s. Lemuel S. and Dorothy (Woodruff) H.; student Phillips Exeter Acad., 1939-40; A.B., U. Mich., 1946; LL.B., 1948; m. Sally Jones, Sept. 13, 1944; children—Drusilla, Clayton. Admitted to Mich. bar, 1948; partner firm Luyendyk, Hainer, Hillman, Karr & Dutcher, Grand Rapids, 1948-65, Hillman, Baxter & Hammond, Grand Rapids, 1965—. Served with USAAF, 1943-45. Decorated Air Medal, D.F.C. Fellow Internat. Acad. Trial Lawyers, Am. Coll. Trial Lawyers, Internat. Soc. Barristers (pres. 1977), Fedn. Ins. Counsel, Internat. Assn. Ins. Counsel; mem. Am., Mich., Grand Rapids (pres. 1963) bar assns., State Bar Mich. Clubs: Athletic; University; Silver Thatch Racquet (Pompano Beach, Fla.). Home: 251 Plymouth Rd SE Grand Rapids MI 49506 Office: Federal Sq Bldg Grand Rapids MI 49502

HILLMAN, STANLEY ERIC GORDON, diversified holding co. exec.; b. London, Eng., Oct. 13, 1911; s. Percy Thomas and Margaret Eleanor Fanny (Lee) H.; ed. Holyrood Sch., also Tonbridge Sch., Eng.; m. May Irene Noon, May 2, 1947; children—Susan Ann, Deborah Ann, Katherine Ann. Came to U.S., 1951, naturalized, 1957. With British-Am. Tobacco Co., Ltd., London and Shanghai, 1933-47; dir. Hillman & Co., Ltd., Cosmos Trading Co., FED Inc., U.S.A., Airmotive Supplies Co. Ltd., Hong Kong, 1947-52; v.p. Gen. Dynamics Corp., 1953-61; v.p., group exec. Am. Machine & Foundry Co., 1962-65; v.p., dir. Gen. Am. Transp. Corp., 1965—; pres., dir. IC Industries, 1968—, vice chmn., 1977—; chmn., chief exec. officer, dir. Ill. Central Gulf R.R., Abex Corp., N.Y.C., Pepsi Cola Gen. Bottlers, Midas Internat., Stone Container Corp., Scott, Foresman & Co., Bandag Corp., Gardner Denver Corp., Avco Corp., Bell & Howell Co., Bliss & Laughlin; trustee Gen. Growth Properties. Adv. bd. Salvation Army, YMCA Met. Chgo.; bd. dirs. Chgo. Lyric Opera; trustee Ill. Inst. Tech. Mem. Am. Def. Preparedness Assn., Assn. U.S. Army, Navy League, Air Force Assn., Newcomen Soc., Soc. Automotive Engrs., Chgo. Assn. Commerce and Industry (dir.), Am. Mgmt. Assn. Clubs: Mid-Am., Econ. of Chgo., Chicago, Exec. (Chgo.); Onwentsia. Home: 1001 Hawthorne Pl Lake Forest IL 60045 Office: 111 E Wacker Dr Chicago IL 60601

HILLMAN, SUE ANN NEWTON, speech pathologist; b. Rockford, Ill., June 27, 1945; d. Russell A. and Alice E. (Kneller) Newton; A.B., Augustana Coll., 1967; M.A., U. Mo., Columbia 1969; m. Arthur Douglas Hillman, Aug. 26, 1967. Speech pathologist Columbia (Mo.) Pub. Schs., 1967-68, 69-70; speech pathologist Des Moines Independent Sch. Dist., 1971—, sign lang. instr., 1975-77; communications cons. Elizabeth J. Ruan Activity Center, 1974-75; chmn. com. communication disability classrooms Heartland (Iowa) Edn. Agency. Licensed speech pathologist, Iowa. Mem. Am. (certificate of clin. competence in speech pathology), Iowa, Central Iowa (pres. 1975-76) speech and hearing assns., NEA, Iowa State Edn. Assn., Council Exceptional Children, Assn. Acoustically Handicapped, Found. Exceptional Children, AAUW, Porsche Club Am., Central Iowa Sailing Assn. Home: 2316 Woodland Ave West Des Moines IA 50265 Office: 2820 Center St Des Moines IA 50312

HILLOCK, DAVID ANTHONY, ednl. adminstr.; b. Chgo., July 29, 1944; s. Charles and Florence (Hillock) Hightower; B.S., Canisius Coll., 1966; M.Ed., Loyola U., Chgo., 1973. Asst. prin. Pulaski Sch., Chgo. Bd. Edn., 1975—. Pres. bd. dirs. El Rincon Community (Methadone) Clinic, Chgo., 1977—, also cons. mental health; mem. Edgewater, Rogers Park community councils, Chgo. Recipient West Towns Youth Services award, 1976. Mem. Am., Ill. (exec. bd. 1977—) personnel and guidance assns., Am. Mental Health Counselors Assn. Democrat. Roman Catholic. Home: 6165 N Winthrop St Chicago IL 60660

HILLS, CARROLL LORAN, educator; b. Oacoma, S.D., May 15, 1925; s. Carroll John and Margaret Ruth (Voorhis) H.; B.S., Black Hills State Coll., 1950; M.A., Stanford U., 1958; postgrad. S.D. State U., summers 1957, 59, 60, 61, 62, 63, 64, acad. year 1963-64; m. Mildred Marie Giedd, Aug. 16, 1947; children—Bradley, Curtis, Kelly Hills Johnson. Tchr. Crook County High Sch., Sundance, Wyo., 1950-51; tchr. chemistry and physics Chamberlain (S.D.) High Sch., 1951-55, Mitchell (S.D.) High Sch., 1955-61; instr. Dakota Wesleyan U., Mitchell, S.D., 1961, asst. prof., 1964, asso. prof., 1968, prof. chemistry, 1971—, chmn. Div. Nat. Sci., 1971—, cir. asso. degree program training med. lab. technicians, 1972—. Troop com. chmn. Boy Scouts Am., Mitchell, S.D., 1972—, pack com. chmn., 1958-60, explorer post com. chmn., 1963-64, explorer adviser, 1964-68. Served with USAAF, 1943-45. Recipient Scoutmasters Arrowhead award, Boy Scouts Am., 1953, Scouters Key award, 1954. NSF grantee, 1957-58, 63-64. Mem. S.D. Acad. Sci. (pres. 1969-70), Sigma Xi. Elk. Home: 1313 E 5th Ave Mitchell SD 57301

HILPERT, BRUNETTE KATHLEEN POWERS (MRS. ELMER ERNEST HILPERT), civic worker; b. Baton Rouge, Feb. 12, 1909; d. Edward Oliver and Orvilla (Nettles) Powers; A.B., La. State U., 1930, B.S. in L.S., 1933; postgrad. Columbia, 1937; m. Elmer Ernest Hilpert, Aug. 1, 1938; children—Margaret Ray (Mrs. L. Bryan Woolley), Elmer Ernest II. Cataloguer, La. State U. Library, Baton Rouge, 1930-36, La. State U. Law Sch. Library, 1936-38; librarian Washington U. Law Sch. Library, St. Louis, 1940-42; reference librarian Washington U. Library, 1952-54; mem. women's adv. bd. Continental Bank & Trust Co., 1970—. Drive capt. United Fund, St. Louis, 1956; del. White House Conf. on Edn., St. Louis, 1962, White House Conf. on Domestic and Econ. Affairs, 1975. Trustee John Burroughs Sch., 1959-63; bd. dirs. Grace Hill Settlement House, 1957-63, v.p., 1960-62; bd. dirs. Internat. Inst., 1964-68, Arts and Edn. Council, 1967—, Miss. River Festival, 1969-75, Community Music Sch., 1972-74, Community Assn. Schs. for Arts, 1974-77, Artist Presentation Soc., 1974-77, Little Symphony Concerts Assn., 1975—, Dance Concert Soc., 1977—, St. Louis Conservatory and Schs. for Arts, 1977—; bd. dirs. St. Louis String Quartet, 1971—, pres., 1975—; bd. dirs. Neighborhood Health Center, 1964-67, sec., 1964-66; pres. Womens Assn. St. Louis Symphony Soc., 1969-71, dir., 1957—; exec. com., bd. dirs. St. Louis Symphony Soc., 1969—, St. Louis Inst. Music, 1971-74. Recipient Woman of Achievement award St. Louis Globe Democrat, 1967. Mem. Nat. Soc. Arts and Letters (dir. 1964-65), Delta Zeta. Republican. Presbyn. Club: Wednesday (rec. sec. 1963-64). Home: 707 Langton Dr St Louis MO 63105

HILSTON, CHARLES RALPH, ednl. assn. exec.; b. Girard, Ohio, Dec. 20, 1930; s. Ralph Wayne and Evelyn (Miller) H.; B.S., Mich. State Normal Coll., 1952; postgrad. Wayne State U., 1956; M.A., Eastern Mich. U., 1959; m. Luella May Cox, Oct. 17, 1959; children—Wayne Charles, Steven Fred, Thomas Christopher, Amylu, Evelyn. Tchr., Hazel Park, Mich., 1955-56, Wyandotte, Mich., 1956-63; prin., Van Wert, Ohio, 1963-65; exec. dir. Ohio Assn. Secondary Sch. Prins. and Ohio Dept. Elementary Sch. Prins., 1965-68; dir. profl. assistance Nat. Assn. Secondary Sch. Prins., Washington, 1968-71; exec. sec. Wis. Secondary Sch. Adminstrs. Assn., Stevens Point, 1971—; cons., lectr. in field. Asst. mgr. Nat. Music Camp, Interlochen, Mich., summers 1957-59; cons. Ohio Sch. Dist. Orgn. Master Plan, 1966; chmn. Wis. Ednl. Goals Task Force, 1972-73, Wis. United Action Council Pub. Edn., 1973; sec.-treas. Wis. Council Sch. Adminstrv. Assns., 1972—; mem. Wis. Center Vocat. Edn., 1972—; chmn. Wis. Sch. Adminstrs., 1974—. Vice pres. Civic Music Assn., Van Wert, 1963-64; active Boy Scouts Am., 1961-63; mem. Ohio selection com. Internat. Farm Youth Exchange, 1965-68; adv. com. Wis. Ednl. Communications Bd., 1974—. Served with USNR, 1953-55. Mem. Phi Delta Kappa. Lutheran. Contbr. articles to profl. jours. Home: 533 Shady Wood Way Madison WI 53714 Office: 1400 E Washington Ave Suite 228 Madison WI 53703

HILTON, LEWIS BOOTH, musician; b. Bulyea, Sask., Can., Nov. 21, 1920; s. George William and Myra Antoinette (Bozarth) H. (parents Am. citizens); B.A., U. No. Iowa, 1942; postgrad. U. Nancy (France), 1938-39; M.A., John Hopkins U., 1946; Ed.D., Columbia U., 1952; m. Mary Jean O'Banion, Mar. 23, 1943. Tchr., Belleville (N.J.) Pub. Schs., 1945, Dowling High Sch., Des Moines, 1946; asso. prof. Drake U., 1946-49; head div. music edn. Washington U., St. Louis, 1951—; writer St. Louis Post Dispatch; author books including: Learning to Teach Through Playing the Woodwinds; editorial bd. Jour. Research Music Edn.; editor Mo. Jour. Research Music Edn.; contbr. articles to profl. jours.; numerous woodwind arrangements, 1975—; composer works including: Polarities for brass quintet, 1977; profl. woodwind player appearing in N.Y.C., Chgo., Des Moines, St. Louis, other cities; Spanish and French translator: former pres. St. Louis chpt. Young Audiences, also Midwest dir. Served with USCG, 1942-45. Recipient numerous grants Washington U. Mem. ASCAP, Music Educators Nat. Conf., Mo. Music Educators Assn., Music Masters (hon.), Community Assn. Schs. Music (bd. dirs.), Nat. Assn. Coll. Wind Percussion Instrs., Phi Mu Alpha Sinfonia, Phi Delta Kappa. Office: Dept Music Washington University Saint Louis MO 63130

HILTON, STANLEY WILLIAM, JR., theatrical mgr.-dir.; b. Phila., Mar. 24, 1936; s. Stanley William and Jennie (Parsons) H.; B.A., Fisk U., 1959; postgrad. Temple U.; m. Inge Himmersbach, Dec. 1962. Office mgr., resource cons., social worker Cook County Dept. Pub. Aid, Chgo., 1961-70; coordinator, ednl. and vocat. counselor Community Coll. Dist., San Francisco, 1971-74; co. mgr. prodn. Hair, San Francisco, 1969; mgr. Orpheum Theatre, San Francisco, 1970; co. mgr. prodns. No Place To Be Somebody, 1971, My Fair Lady, 1973, in San Francisco, also co-mgr. Jesus Christ Superstar, 1973; dir. park and theatre ops. Art Park, Lewiston, N.Y., 1974; exec. dir. Blackstone Theatre, Chgo., 1974—; bd. dirs. Centers New Horizons, Chgo., 1976—. Mem. Assn. Theatrical Press Agts. and Mgrs., Internat. Alliance Theatrical State Employees, Moving Picture Machine Operators U.S. and Can. Office: 60 E Balbo St Chicago IL 60605

HILTY, DOROTHY PAULINE, psychologist; b. nr. Findlay, Ohio, June 30, 1914; d. Christian H. and Minerva (Gilbert) Hilty; A.B., Ohio U., 1937; M.A., Ohio State U., 1938. Asst. dept. psychology Ohio State U., 1939-41; cottage supr. Peter Pan Cottages, Ohio Soldiers and Sailors Orphans Home, Xenia, Ohio, 1941-48, asst. psychologist, 1948-53, psychologist, 1953-75; psychol. cons., 1975—. Past rec. sec., bd. dirs. Greene County Mental Health Assn.; mem. Greene County Bd. Mental Retardation, 1967-73, Greene County Mental Health and Retardation Bd., 1970-73. Mem. Bus. and Profl. Women's Club (1st v.p. 1956-57, named career-woman 1967), Am. Assn. U. Woman (br. sec. 1950), Am., Ohio, Miami Valley psychol. assns., Internat. Council Psychologists, Phi Beta Kappa. Presbyn. Home: 595 Saxony Dr Xenia OH 45385

HIME, WILLIAM GENE, chem. co. exec.; b. Dayton, Ohio, Dec. 31, 1925; s. Raymond and Irma Beatrice (Shawen) H.; B.S., Heidelberg Coll., 1948; postgrad. Northwestern U., 1948-51; m. Nancy Rose Price, Dec. 9, 1950; children—Carolyn Sue, Lisa Ann, Sandra Jean. Research chemist Portland Cement Assn., Skokie, Ill., 1951-54; asst. prof. La. Tech., Ruston, 1954-55; supr. analytical labs. Portland Cement Assn., Skokie, Ill., 1955-65, mgr., 1965-71; v.p., dir. Erlin, Hime Assos., Inc., Northbrook, Ill., 1971—. Cons. Nat. Bur. Standards. Mem. ASTM, Am. Chem. Soc., Soc. for Applied Spectroscopy, Am. Concrete Inst. Presbyn. (elder 1975—). Contbr. articles to profl. jours., chpts. to books. Home: 2701 Fontana Dr Glenview IL 60025 Office: 811 Skokie Blvd Northbrook IL 60062

HIMES, HERBERT DEAN, accountant; b. Orrville, Ohio, May 29, 1952; s. Harley Jean and Ethel Pauline (Amstutz) H.; B.S., Bluffton Coll., 1973; student Ashland Coll., summer 1972, fall 1973; postgrad. U. Akron; m. Debra Jo Streb, June 16, 1973. Partner, Himes Accounting Service, Kidron, Ohio, 1973—. C.P.A. Mennonite. Home: Box 73 Kidron OH 44636 Office: Box 42 Kidron OH 44636

HIMMELFARB, JOHN DAVID, artist; b. Chgo., June 3, 1946; s. Samuel and Eleanor (Gorecki) H.; A.B., Harvard U., 1964, M.A., Grad. Sch. Edn., 1970. Practicing artist, 1970—; one-man shows: Bradley Gallery, Milw., 1974; Ill. Arts Council, 1974; Graphics I&II, Boston, 1974; Ill. Center, Chgo., 1975; art gallery U. Nebr., Omana, 1976; Dorothy Rosenthal Gallery, Chgo., 1976; Included in permanent collections: Art Inst. Chgo., Nat. Collection Fine Art, Fogg Mus. Art, Mus. Art U. Iowa, Ill. State Mus., Minn. Mus. Home: 908 W 19th St Chicago IL 60608

HINDERMANN, MARK JOHN, hwy. contracting co. exec.; b. Mpls., Mar. 18, 1935; s. Winfred Louis and Joyce Irene (Peterson) H.; B.S. in Civil Enging., U. Minn., 1958; m. Suzanne Virginia Strander, Nov. 26, 1960; children—Michael, Matthew, Thomas, Laura, Lisa. Engr., E.C. Bather & Assos., Cons. Engrs., St. Paul, 1957-60; engr. Rochester Sand U Gravel, Inc. (Minn.), 1960-66, pres., 1966—; pres. Wilmar Enterprises, Inc., Rochester, Minn., 1969—; sec.-treas. Rietmann Contracting, Inc., Rochester, 1972—. Div. chmn. United Fund, 1970-71. Served with AUS, 1959. Recipient Boss of Year award Rochester Jr. C. of C., 1972. Registered profl. engr., Minn. Mem. Rochester C. of C. (chmn. transp. com. 1971—), Minn. Soc. Profl. Engrs. (Young Engr. of Year 1969, state dir. 1968—). Republican. Home: 5740 Sumac Ln NE Rochester MN 55901 Office: 4105 E River Rd NE Rochester MN 55901

HINDERY, PHYLLIS CATHERINE, bus. exec.; b. Chgo., Oct. 1, 1947; d. John Anthony and Charlotte Mary (Hayes) Dombeck; B.A., Rosary Coll., 1969; student U. Ill., Chgo. Circle, 1969-70; m. Richard Francis Hindery, Dec. 2, 1972. Asst. personnel mgr. Sears Roebuck & Co., Chgo., 1972-76, staff asst. nat. tng. dept., 1977—. Home: 317 Dean Circle Bolingbrook IL 60439 Office: Sears Tower D/707-1 BSC 34-45 Chicago IL 60684

HINER, ROBERT L., transp. exec.; b. Clinton County, Ind., Nov. 7, 1902; s. Ward Beecher and Vienna Susan (Fleming) H.; m. Margaret Stowers, Oct. 24, 1927; 1 son, Dan Stowers; student Ind. U., 1923. With Am. Red Ball Transit Co., Inc., Indpls., now chmn. bd.; lect. before traffic orgns. and lit. groups; bd. dirs. Household Goods Carriers Bur., Am. Movers Conf. of Washington. Mem. Nat. Def. Transp. Assn. (life), Am. Truck Hist. Soc. (bd. govs.), Ind. Hist. Soc., Traffic Club N.Y.C., Masons, Highland Golf and Country Club, Indpls. Athletic Club. Author: Songs of Life, 1971; On Wings of Words, 1976; contbr. articles to profl. jours. Home: 6430 Central Ave Indianapolis IN 46220 Office: POB 1127 Indianapolis IN 46206

HINER, TRAVIS SCOTT, farm equipment sales co. exec.; b. Kingman, Ariz., Apr. 19, 1944; s. George Franklin and Ruth Irene (Zweiebel) H.; B.A., U. Nebr., 1966, M.B.A., 1968; m. Kathleen Ann Kuxhausen, Feb. 8, 1969. With Hiner Co., Scottsbluff, Nebr., 1968—, sales mgr., v.p., 1974—, pres., 1974—, chmn. bd., 1974—, pres., 1977—; chmn. bd. Hiner Co. Profit Sharing Trust. Chmn. bd. Scottsbluff County Housing Authority; pres. Scottsbluff-Gering Payroll Devel. Corp. Mem. Nat. Farm Equipment Dealers, Midwest Retail Farm Equipment Dealers, Payroll Devel. Found., Scottsbluff C. of C. (life). Republican. Methodist. Clubs: Sertoma (life), Scottsbluff Country (dir.), Elks (life), Nebr. Diplomats. Home: 2325 Park Pl Gering NE 64341 Office: 2401 W 20th St Scottsbluff NE 69361

HINES, JACOB ALBERT, veterinarian; b. West Salem, Ohio, May 1, 1927; s. Miles and Ruth Agnes (Kissane) H.; D.V.M., Ohio State U., 1953; m. Genevieve Mantz, July 13, 1947; children—Ruth, Steven, Sally, Norman, Amy. Pvt. practice vet. medicine, Friendship, Wis., 1953-56, Oxford, Wis., 1956—; dir. M. & I. Westfield Bank. Mem. Marquett County Fair Bd., 1968-74, pres. bd., 1969-71; bd. mem. Westfield Sch. Dist. Sch. Bd., 1970—, Marquette Co. Draft Bd. Bd. dirs. Marquette Rural Health Center. Served with inf. AUS, 1945-47; ETO. Mem. AVMA, Wis., Wisconsin Valley (pres. 1960-61) vet. med. assns., Am. Bovine Practitioners, Wis. Hereford Assn. (pres. 1963), Wis. Cattlemens Assn., Wis. Agr.-Bus. Council, Wis. Live Stock Meat Council, Wis. Live Stock Breeder Assn. (dir.), V.F.W. (comdr. 1964). Presbyn. Lion (pres. 1962). Home: PO Box 7 Oxford WI 53952

HINES, ROGER DWAIN, lawyer; b. Taberville, Mo., Feb. 19, 1934; s. Charles Henry and Mabel (Snider) H.; A.B., U. Mo., 1957, LL.B., 1959; m. Beverly Yvonne Ball, Oct. 13, 1957 (div. 1969); children—Rhonda Deone, Roger Dwain II, Robyn DeAnn. Admitted to Mo. bar, 1959; practiced in Columbia, Mo., 1959—; mem. firm George A. Spencer, 1959-63, Spencer, Hines, Petri, 1963-66, Roger D. Hines, 1966-71, Hines & Southern, 1971-75; city atty., Columbia, 1960-64, Rocheport, Mo., 1962—; municipal judge, Columbia, 1965-75; v.p. Ship Investment, Inc., Columbia, 1964—; pres. Mo. Electric Vehicles, Inc., 1975—; v.p., dir. Mo. Concrete Co., City Quarries, Inc., Huntsdale Sand Co., Richardson & Bass Constrn. Co., Village Marina, Inc. (Lake Ozark, Mo.), Show Case Mart, Inc.; exec. dir. Mo. Coll. for Trial Judges, 1972-74. Asst. pros. atty., Boone County, Mo., 1962. Pres. Boone County Young Democrats, 1962, v.p., 1961; chmn. Trimble for Atty. Gen. Com., 1964. Trustee Graphic Engraving Service Profit-Sharing Trust; dir. Columbia Servicemens Center, 1966—, Boone County Assn. for Retarded Children; chmn. adv. com. Boone County Child Welfare, 1966-67. Served with USNR, 1952-55. Recipient Outstanding Traffic Ct. award Am. Bar Assn., 1971 and 1972. Mem. Mo. (mem. press commn.), Boone County (sec. 1960), Kansas City bar assns., Mo. Municipal and Magistrate Judges Assn. (dir. 1967—, pres. 1970-71), Am. Legion, V.F.W., Jr. C. of C., C. of C., Am. Judicature Soc., Am. Judges Assn., Phi Alpha Delta. Episcopalian. Clubs: Mens, Lincoln Continental Owners. Home: 1215 Frances Dr Columbia MO 65201 Office: Guitar Bldg Columbia MO 65201

HINKLE, CARL, ednl. adminstr.; b. Riverton, W.Va., May 19, 1921; s. Lloyd and Gettie (Hedrick) H.; A.B., Davis-Elkins Coll., 1948; M.A., W.Va. U., 1957; m. Ruth White, Nov. 25, 1953; children—Marcella Lee, Christina Rae, Thomas Carl. Tchr., Carroll County, Ohio, 1948-50; tchr., elementary supr., prin. Columbiana County Schs., 1950-58; local supt. Tuscarawas, Ohio, 1958-66; edn. cons. div. sch. finance Ohio Dept. Edn., 1966-72; supt. Ledgemont Pub. Schs., Thompson, Ohio, 1972-75; supr., prin. Heisley Christian Acad., Mentor, Ohio, 1975—. Active Ledgemont P.T.A.; mem. Tuscarawas Town Council, 1963-64. Served with USNR, 1942-45; PTO. Mem. Nat. Edn. Assn., West Point Grange, 15th Seabee Bn. Assn. (reunion chmn. 1978), Ledgemont Boosters Club. Mem. Christian Ch. (deacon, elder). Club: Men's. Home: 15559 Thompson Rd Thompson OH 44086

HINKS, ROBERT NEWMAN, social service adminstr.; b. Toledo, Oct. 23, 1915; s. Stacey B. and Marguerite E. (Moloney) H.; A.B. in English Lit., U. of Detroit, 1939; M.A. in English Lit., Loyola U., Chgo., 1948; Licentiate in Sacred Theology, West Baden U., 1951; M.S.W., Catholic U. Am., 1954; m. Mary Elizabeth Mannebach, Aug. 7, 1967. Asso. prof. dept. of sociology and social work U. Detroit, 1954-67; clin. social work supr. Regional Consultation Center, Mich. Dept. Mental Health, St. Joseph, 1967-69; exec. dir. Eastern Upper Peninsula Mental Health Center, Sault Ste. Marie, Mich., 1969—. Mem. area planning com., United Community Services of Met. Detroit, com. on urban adjustment. Bd. dirs. A.R.C., mem. adv. bd. Detroit chpt.; founder, trustee Emergency Psychiat. Facilities for Children. Mem. Nat. Assn. Social Workers (dir. Detroit chpt.), Acad. of Certified Social Workers, A.A.U.P., Mich. Soc. Mental Health (dir. Wayne County chpt.) Mich. Assn. for Emotionally Disturbed Children (trustee). Elk. Home: 1900 Ryan St Sault Ste Marie MI 49783 Office: 332 E Spruce St Sault Ste Marie MI 49783

HINMAN, FLOSSIE NORTON, educator; b. London Mills, Ill.; d. Hugh Johnathon and Alice Amanda (Brown) Norton; B.A., Ill. Wesleyan U., 1917; student Western Ill. State U., summers 1930, 44-48, Ill. State U., summers 1950-51; grad. Famous Artists Schs.,

Westport, Conn., 1960; m. Charles William Hinman, July 21, 1919 (div. Sept. 1931). Tchr. Farmington (Ill.) High Sch., 1918, Neponset (Ill.) High Sch., 1919; asst. foreman Blue Bell Corp., Abingdon, Ill., 1930-38; tchr. grade schs., Ill., 1938-44; supt. schs., Camden, Ill., 1946; tchr. high schs., Gladstone, Victoria, Hamilton, and Fulton, Ill., 1947-61. Active Community Fund, 1963. Mem. Knox County Ret. Tchrs. Assn., Ill. Wesleyan U., Western Ill. U. Alumni assns., A.L.A., Ill. Librarians Assn., Nat. Assn. Tchrs. English, N.E.A., Ill. Edn. Assn., Fulton Tchrs. Assn., Oliniana Lit. Soc., Ill. Assn. Sch. Librarians, Alpha Iota. Methodist. Rebekah. Home: 933 W Main St Galesburg IL 61401

HINMAN, FREDERICK RICHARD, assn. exec.; b. Galesburg, Ill., Mar. 1, 1927; s. F. Stanley and Dorothy (McMillian) H.; student Inst. for Orgn. Mgmt., Mich. State U., 1965-71, U. Colo., 1972-73, 74-75, Notre Dame U., 1976-77; m. Betty Lee Courter, Aug. 16, 1948; 1 son, Keith Richard. With Galesburg (Ill.) Register Mail Advt., 1946-50, Fremont (Neb.) Guide and Tribune, 1950-51, Iowa City Press Citizen, 1951-53; with Fed. Discount Corp., 1953-65, advt. mgr., 1957-65; mgr. Chariton (Iowa) C. of C., 1965-68; exec. v.p. Shenandoah (Iowa) C. of C., 1968—. Served with USNR, 1945-46. Named Outstanding Nat. Dir. Iowa Jr. C. of C., 1960. Mem. Iowa Profl. Developers (dir. 1975—), Iowa C. of C. Execs. (pres. 1974), Dubuque Jr. C. of C. (hon. life, pres. 1961-62), Am. Legion. Republican. Roman Catholic. Lion (dir.). Home: 1200 S Center St Shenandoah IA 51601 Office: 403 W Sheridan Ave Shenandoah IA 51601

HINSVARK, INEZ GENIEVE, educator, researcher; b. Brandt, S.D., May 3, 1918; d. Jacob and Clara (Moan) Hinsvark; R.N., Luther Hosp. Sch. Nursing, Watertown, S.D., 1939; A.B., San Francisco State Coll., 1951; M.A., Stanford; Ed.D., U. Calif. at Los Angeles, 1965. Supr., Luther Hosp., 1939-41; staff nurse Community Hosp., Montevideo, Minn., 1941-42; staff nurse Physician and Surgeon Hosp., Glendale, Calif., 1942-44; asst. head nurse Herrick Meml. Hosp., Berkeley, Calif., 1947-51; instr., head dept. clin. nursing S.D. State U., Brookings, 1952-57, dean div. nursing, 1957-67, prof. nursing, 1956-67; prof. Sch. Nursing, U. Wis.-Milw., 1967—, dean, 1967-75; mem. tech. adv. com. on health related curriculums Milw. Pub. Sch. Systems, 1976-77. Mem., chmn. disaster com. Milw. chpt. ARC; chmn. membership services com. S.E. Comprehensive Health Planning Council, 1970-72; mem. Wis. Gov.'s Task Force on Health Policy and Planning, 1971-72; mem. Nat. Adv. Rev. Com. on Constrn. Grants to Schs. Nursing, 1966-74; mem. adv. com. Milwaukee County Hosp. Sch. Nursing, 1971-76; mem. nursing com. Wis. Regional Med. Programs, 1970-75. Served with Army Nurse Corps, 1944-46. Fellow Am. Acad. Nursing; mem. Nat., Wis. edn. assns., Am. Nurses Assn. (commn. on nursing edn., project dir. study on credentialing in nursing 1977—), Nat., Wis. (rep. to joint com. on revision Wis. Nurse Practice Act 1970) leagues nursing, Wis. Nurses Assn. (com. on legislation), Am., Wis. assns. pub. health, Am. Assn. Higher Edn., Nat. Assn. Programmed Instrn., Roy Soc. for Promotion Health, Acad. Polit. and Social Sci., Wis. Hist. Soc., A.A.U.W., Urban League, Pi Gamma Mu, Pi Lambda Theta, Alpha Tau Delta, Phi Kappa Phi, Sigma Theta Tau. Lutheran. Contbr. articles to profl. jours. Home: 3352 N Hackett Ave Milwaukee WI 53211

HINTON, CHARLES FRANKLIN, lawyer; b. Des Moines, June 30, 1932; s. Charles Franklin and Wilma Pearl (Nuzum) H.; B.A., U. Iowa, 1957, J.D., 1959; m. Betty Mae Gray; Dec. 24, 1952 (div. Jan. 1967); 1 son, Charles Franklin III. Admitted to Iowa bar, 1959; practiced in Waterloo, Iowa, 1959—; now prin. Charles F. Hinton Law Firm, Waterloo Asst. Black Hawk County atty., 1960-64; asst. Waterloo city solicitor, 1966-68; spl. prosecutor, 1972—; atty. Heart Fund, 1966-70. Republican committeeman, 1962-64. Served with AUS, 1952-54. Mem. Am., Iowa, Black Hawk County (sec. 1966) bar assns., Am. Trial Lawyers Assn. Methodist (mem. gen. bd. 1964-70). Mason (Shriner), Elk. Clubs: Sertoma Service (Distinguished Club pres. 1967-68, internat. del. 1968); Sunnyside Country (Waterloo). Home: 1815 Winterridge Rd Cedar Falls IA 50613 Office: 751 Progress Ave Waterloo IA 50701

HINZMAN, WAYNE, hosp. adminstr.; b. Avon, S.D., Dec. 26, 1927; s. Harry and Edna (Pudwell) H.; grad. U.S. Air Force Band Sch., 1947, Yankton Coll., 1952; m. Jean M. Heibult, Nov. 20, 1949; children—Larry Wayne, Debra Jean, Diane Lynn. Adminstr. Butler Med. Clinic, Hot Springs, S.D., 1952-72; office mgr. Hills Materials Co., Hot Springs, 1972-75; bus. mgr., controller, asst. adminstr. Campbell County Meml. Hosp., Gillette, Wyo., 1975—. Pres. Hot Springs City Council, 1952-60. Served with USAF, 1946-49. Mem. Hosp. Fin. Mgmt. Assn., Am. Hosp. Assn. (registered med. sec.). Republican. Methodist. Clubs: Lions, Rotary, Mason, Elk. Home: 713 E Iowa St Rapid City SD 57701 Office: 720 W 8th St Gillette WY 82716

HIPPLE, JOHN HENRY, newspaperman; b. Pierre, S.D., Mar. 5, 1928; s. Robert B. and Lois (Henry) H.; B.A., Yale, 1952; m. Dawn Young, Sept. 8, 1952; children—Debra Dawn, Brad Robert, Scott Bowman, Brian Jay. With Pierre Daily Capital Jour., 1952—, mng. editor, 1955—. Active 4-H. Served to sgt. USAAF, 1946-48. Mem. S.D. Press Assn., S.D. Gelbvich Cattle Assn. (hon.), various civic orgns. Home: 415 N Evans St Pierre SD 57501 Office: Pierre Daily Capital Journal 415 S Pierre St Box 878 Pierre SD 57501

HIRD, SAMUEL, automotive and farm equipment co. exec.; b. Edgeley, N.D., Oct. 3, 1927; s. William and Nyva Marie (Johnson) H.; student Dunwoody Inst., 1946-47; m. Lorraine M. Klima, Jan. 31, 1955; children—Kim Samuel, Mark William. Partner, Hird & Sons Inc., Edgeley, 1947—, pres., 1961—; v.p. Hird Implement Co., LaMoure, N.D., 1954—; sec. Hirds Inc., Ellendale, N.D., 1965—. Mem. Edgeley Sch. Bd., 1965—; pres. Edgeley City Council, 1958-66. Mem. subscribers com. N.D. Blue Cross. Served with AUS, 1950-52. Mem. N.D. Implement Dealers Assn. (dir. 1977—), Am. Legion. Clubs: Masons, Elks, Lions, Shriners. Home: 215 2d Ave Edgeley ND 58433 Office: Edgeley ND 58433

HIRE, ROBERT LOWREY, dentist; b. Lake Odessa, Mich., May 3, 1918; s. Loraine Fletcher and Hazel June (Lowrey) H.; B.S., Central Mich. U., 1941; D.D.S., Marquette U., 1950; m. Cecille Jean Moreau, Oct. 18, 1941; children—Brian Lowrey, Laura Jean, Brenton Robert. High sch. tchr., 1941-42; intern Couzens Fund of Detroit, 1950-51; practice gen. dentistry, Petoskey, Mich., 1951-55, Grand Rapids, Mich., 1955—; pres. bd., dir. Dean Lake Med. Bldg.; profl. staff Grand Rapids Osteo. Hosp., 1965—. Nat. alumni pres. Central Mich. U., 1967-69; mem. dental mission to Honduras for United Ch. of Christ, 1966, 68. Trustee West Mich. Environ. Council. Mem. Izaak Walton League Am. pres. Mich. div. 1978, nat. sec. 1978, nat. dir.), Resort Dist. Dental Soc. (v.p. 1954). Conglist. Kiwanian (pres. Grand Rapids 1962). Home: 2424 Elmwood St SE Grand Rapids MI 49506 Office: 2300 3 Mile St NE Grand Rapids MI 49505

HIRN, DORIS DREYER, health services adminstr.; b. N.Y.C., Dec. 3, 1933; d. James M. and Dorothy Van Nostrand (Young) Dreyer; student Colby Jr. Coll., 1951-52, Hofstra U., 1953-56, Northwestern U., 1972-74; m. John D. Hirn, Oct. 27, 1956; children—Deborah Lynn, Robert William. Asst. to adminstr., Albany (N.Y.) Med. Coll., 1962-64; propr., dir. Hickory Hill Camp, Galena, Ill., 1965-72; v.p. Home Health Service of Chgo. North Inc., 1972-74; pres., adminstr. Suburban Home Health Service, Inc., Des Plaines, Ill., 1974—; dir. Avalon Services, Ltd., 1974—. Bd. dirs. Nat. Health Delivery Systems, 1973—, Fox Valley council Girl Scouts U.S., 1965-70. Served with USN, 1951-53. Mem. Am. Mgmt. Assn., Adminstrv. Mgmt. Assn., Ill. Council of Home Health Agys., Nat. Assn. of Home Health Agys., Am. Camping Assn. (dir. Chgo. chpt. 1968-70). Republican. Clubs: Chicago Yacht; Columbia Yacht. Home: 1520 N State Parkway Chicago IL 60610 Office: 2250 E Devon Ave Des Plaines IL 60018

HIRSCH, CHRISTIAN RICHARD, educator; b. LeMars, Iowa, Mar. 6, 1944; s. Chris Richard and Margaret Katherine (Wiltgen) H.; B.A., U. Iowa, 1966; M.A., Creighton U., 1969; M.S., U. Ill., 1970; Ph.D., U. Iowa, 1972; m. Patricia Claire Deegan, June 12, 1965; children—Emily, Anne, Jennifer. Tchr. math. South High Sch., Omaha, 1966-67; chmn. dept. math Notre Dame Acad., Omaha, 1967-69; spl. research asst. Iowa Testing Programs, 1971-72; vis. prof. U. Man., Winnipeg, Can., 1972-73; asso. prof. Western Mich. U., Kalamazoo, 1973—. NSF fellow, 1969-70. Mem. Am. Edn. Research Assn., Math. Assn. Am., Mich. Council Tchrs. Math., Nat. Council Tchrs. Math., Sch. Sci. and Math. Assn., AAUP, Phi Delta Kappa. Democrat. Roman Catholic. Author textbooks; editor jours.; contbr. articles to profl. jours. Home: 2602 Pine Ridge Rd Kalamazoo MI 49008 Office: Dept Math Western Mich Univ Kalamazoo MI 49008

HIRSCH, JAY G., psychiatrist; b. Cleve., Aug. 6, 1930; s. Abe and Bertha (Gusman) H.; B.S., U. Cin., 1950, M.D., 1954; m. Renee B. Schwartz, Oct. 10, 1962; children—Deborah, David, Lauren, Susan. Intern Phila. Gen. Hosp., 1954-55; resident U. Ill. Hosps., 1957-60; practice medicine specializing in psychiatry and child psychiatry, Chgo., 1960-70, Highland Park, Ill., 1970—; resident Inst. for Juvenile Research, Chgo., 1960-62, research child psychiatrist, 1962-66, chief div. preventive psychiatry, 1966-70; dir. Melampus, Ltd.; mem. faculty U. Ill. Coll. Medicine, Chgo., 1959—, asso. prof. psychiatry, 1970-74, prof., 1974—, dir. edn. in child psychiatry and related disciplines, 1973-77. Cons. to several agys. and schs. Mem. Ill. Mental Health Planning Bd., 1967-69, Comprehensive Health Planning Agy. Bd., 1971-74. Vice pres. Kenneth F. Montgomery Found., Chgo., 1965-71; mem. bd. Dr. Martin L. King Family Center, Chgo., 1969-74, Urban Dynamics/Inner City Fund, Chgo., 1970-75. Served to capt. USAF, 1955-57. Fellow Am. Psychiat. Assn., Am. Acad. Child Psychiatry; mem. AMA, Soc. for Research in Child Devel., AAAS, Phi Beta Kappa, Alpha Omega Alpha. Bd. editors Jour. Child Psychiatry, 1972—. Contbr. articles to profl. jours. Home: 591 Stonegate Terr Glencoe IL 60022 Office: 1971 2d St Highland Park IL 60035 also U Ill Dept Psychiatry 912 S Wood St Chicago IL 60612

HIRSCH, LEONARD GEORGE, organizational devel. cons.; b. N.Y.C., Feb. 22, 1939; s. Morris and Jeanette (Fassler) H.; B.A., Hunter Coll., 1962; M.S.W., Adelphi U., 1966; Ph.D., Case Western Res. U., 1975; m. Carolyn Jean Lukensmeyer, Aug. 3, 1968. Group worker East Flatbush YMHA, Bklyn., 1962-64; asst. dir. house plan City Coll. N.Y., 1966-68; asst. prof. dept. social scis. Cleve. State U., 1969-74; chmn. profl. staff, dir. organizational devel. program Gestalt Inst., Cleve., 1971—; pres. Action Research Interventions, Inc., Cleve., 1974—; dir. Congl. Mgmt. Found., Washington, 1976—; cons. organizational devel., White House, Washington, 1977—; orgn. cons. Democratic Nat. Com., 1972-76; advance staff Walter Mondale vice presdl. campaign, 1976; campaign cons. U.S. Senate and Ho. of Reps. NIMH grad. fellow, 1964-66. Mem. Nat. Tng. Labs., Nat. Assn. Social Workers. Democrat. Jewish. Composer numerous songs. Home and Office: 7 Mornington Ln Cleveland OH 44106

HIRSCH, LORE, psychiatrist; b. Mannheim, Germany, July 8, 1908; d. Erwin and Marie (Kiefe) Hirsch; came to U.S., 1940, naturalized, 1946; M.D., U. Heidelberg (Germany), 1937; postgrad. N.Y. U., 1942-43; m. Eugene Hesz, Jan. 25, 1958. Intern, Greenpoint Hosp., Bklyn., 1942-43; resident in psychiatry Bellevue Hosp., N.Y.C., 1943-46, sr. psychiatrist, N.Y.C., 1946-49; sect. chief psychiatry div. VA Hosp., Bronx, N.Y., 1949-54; clin. dir. psychiatry Wayne County Gen. Hosp., Eloise, Mich., 1954-55; dir. out-patient dept. Northville (Mich.) State Hosp., 1955-58; pvt. practice psychiatry, Dearborn, Mich., 1958—; staff Oakwood Hosp., Dearborn, 1958—; asst. prof. psychiatry Wayne State U., Detroit, 1954-55. Pres., Dearborn Health Council, 1960-62. Bd. dirs. YWCA, Dearborn, 1962-70. Recipient Award for leadership City of Dearborn, 1962; award in appreciation of qualities as tchr. Resident Staff Northville State Hosp., 1958. Diplomate Am. Bd. Psychiatry and Neurology. Fellow Am. Psychiat. Assn.; mem. AMA, Internat. Assn. Platform Speakers, Am. Acad. for Religion and Mental Health, Mich. Mental Health Soc., Inter-Profl. Assn. for Marriage, Divorce and Family, Mich. Med. Soc., Mich. Psychiat. Soc., Pan Am. Psychiat. Assn., Assn. Forensic Psychiatry. Unitarian Universalist. Contbr. articles to profl. jours. Home: 212 S Melborn St Dearborn MI 48124 Office: 2021 Monroe Blvd Dearborn MI 48124

HIRSCHBERG, ERWIN EUGENE, fabricated metal products co. exec.; b. Chgo., Aug. 25, 1922; s. Erwin E. and Edith Christine (Nielsen) H.; Prof. degree Chem. Engr., U. Cin., 1950; m. Bertie V. Struyck, July 27, 1945; children—Nicolette C., Scott D. With Eclipse, Inc., fabricated metal products, Rockford, Ill., 1953—, engring. mgr., 1962-70, v.p. engring., 1969—. Bd. dirs. Jr. Achievement Rock River Valley, Inc., 1965—, pres., 1970-71; bd. dirs. Rockford Regional Academic Center. Mem. Ill. Profl. Engr. Examining Com. Served with AUS, 1942-46. Named to Hall of Flame Am. Gas Assn. Registered profl. engr., Ill., Ohio, N.J., Ark. Mem. Am. Inst. Chem. Engrs., AAAS, Nat., Ill. socs. profl. engrs., Air Pollution Control Assn., Combustion Inst., VFW, Pi Kappa Alpha. Club: Kiwanis (Rockford). Patentee in field. Home: 881 Parker Woods Dr Rockford IL 61102 Office: 1665 Elmwood Rd Rockford IL 61103

HIRSCHFELD, STANLEY EDWIN, computer co. exec.; b. New Bremen, Ohio, June 14, 1934; s. Edwin E. and Esther A. (Schmidt) H.; student Heidelberg Coll., 1952-54; B.S., Ohio State U., 1957; m. Dorothy A. Beckett, Nov. 28, 1954; children—Nancy Jane, Jon Scott, Thomas Jeffry. Staff accountant Johnson Atwater & Co., Columbus, Ohio, 1957-62; treas. Am. Fabricated Products, Inc., Indpls., 1962-69; financial analyst Ind. Capital Corp., Indpls., 1969-70; treas. Anacomp, Inc., Indpls., 1970-74, v.p. finance, 1974—. C.P.A., Ind. Home: 6874 Cedarstone Dr Indianapolis IN 46226 Office: 6161 Hillside Ave Indianapolis IN 46220

HIRSCHFELDER, MAX, physician; b. Munich, Germany, Sept. 12, 1910; s. Heinrich and Johanna (Levy) H.; student U. Munich, 1934; M.D., U. Berne (Switzerland), 1935; m. Edith Hirsch, Feb. 19, 1938; children—Dennis, Kemt. Came to U.S., 1936, naturalized, 1939. Asst., Eye Clinic of U. Berne, 1935-36; jr. and sr. resident Ill. Eye and Ear Infirmary, Chgo., 1936-38; supervising physician So. Ill. Trachoma Clinics, 1938-40; attending ophthalmologist St. Mary's Hosp., Centralia, Ill., 1940—; practice medicine specializing in ophthalmology, Centralia, 1940—. Pres., Centralia Cultural Soc., 1969-70. Fellow Am. Acad. Ophthalmology and Otolaryngology, A.C.S.; mem. Chgo. (pres. 1970-71), St. Louis (pres. 1967-68) ophthal. socs. Elk, Rotarian. Club: Meadow Woods (Centralia). Home: 3 Lilac Ln Centralia IL 62801 Office: 408 W 2d St Centralia IL 62801

HIRSCHINGER, LAWRENCE, aviation co. exec.; b. Elwood, Ind., Sept. 3, 1914; s. George Henry and Barbara (Rupp) H.; grad. pub. high sch.; C.A.A. Flight Instr. Certificate, 1939; m. Marilyne Marie Bushhorn, May 31, 1939; children—Sharon Hirschinger Williams, Carol Hirschinger Hooper, Charles. Apprentice mechanic, flight instr. Capitol Airport, Indpls., 1936-37; mgr. Tri-City Airport, Hobbs, Ind., 1938-39; with Muncie (Ind.) Aviation Corp., 1940-61, 64—, v.p., 1964—, also mgr., Muncie airport 1964—, also dir.; asst. mgr. Sky Harbor Airport, Indpls., 1961-64; weatherman WLBC-TV, Muncie, 1953-61. Mem. exec. bd. Delaware County Council Boy Scouts Am., 1965-68. Named Aviation Man Year Ind., 1970. Mem. Muncie-Delaware C. of C. (past dir.), Aviation Assn. Ind. (dir.), Nat. Pilots Assn. (Safe Pilot award 1970), Ind. Airport Ofcls. Assn., Am. Assn. Airport Execs., Quiet Birdman, Indpls. Aero. Club, Internat. Flying Fellowship Rotarians (exec. bd., editor 1971—), Silver Wings, Ox-5 Aviation Pioneers. Republican. Roman Catholic. Rotarian (pres. 1977-78), K.C. Club: Muncie (Ind.), Delaware County Aero (Muncie). Contbg. editor various aviation jours., 1969—. Office: PO Box 1169 Center Pike N Muncie IN 47305

HIRSCHTRITT, GERI MIRIAM RUDNICK, counselor; b. Chgo., Mar. 3, 1947; d. Jack Aaron and Esther (Barad) Rudnick; B.S., U. Okla., 1969; M.A. cum laude, Northeastern Ill. U., 1975; m. Steven Hirschtritt, Aug. 3, 1969; children—Shelly Matthew, Todd. Tchr., Prospect Heights (Ill.) Dist. 27, 1969-73; counselor Psychol. Treatment and Assessment Clinic, Chgo., 1975-76, Psychol. Treatment and Diagnostic Service, Chgo., 1976—; cons. in field. Mem. Am., Ill. personnel and guidance assns., NEA. Jewish. Home: 518 W Barry Ave Chicago IL 60657 Office: 2545 W Peterson Ave Chicago IL 60657

HIRSSIG, JAMES EARL, elec. products co. exec.; b. Toledo, Mar. 9, 1926; s. Frank Edward and Violet L. (Schettler) H.; B.A. with Honors, U. Toledo, 1948; M.B.A., U. Mich., 1950; m. Elizabeth Ann Sauer, Nov. 18, 1950; children—Scott S., Daniel J., Laurie A., Mark W., Sherry A., Jerry J., Gary J. With DeVilbiss, Toledo, 1950-55; sales mgr. Revco, Deerfield, Mich., 1955-67; sales mgr. Kelvinator Comml. Products, Inc., Detroit, 1967-73, export mgr., Manitowoc, Wis., 1970—, advt. mgr., 1970—. Mem. Pres.'s Regional Export Council, 1974—. Exec. bd. mem. Waumegesako council Boy Scouts Am., 1973—; chmn. United Fund, 1970—; chmn. fund raising YMCA, 1970—. Bd. dirs. Manitowoc County chpt. A.R.C., 1974—. Served with AUS, 1943-46. Recipient Pres.'s Export E award, 1973. Mem. Microbiology Tissue Culture Soc., Manitowoc-Two Rivers C. of C. (chmn. fgn. trade), Phi Alpha Theta. Lutheran (trustee 1971—). Home: 2216 Lexington Dr Manitowoc WI 54220 Office: 621 Quay St Manitowoc WI 54220

HIRTZEL, RICHARD DALE, polit. scientist, educator; b. Chgo., Feb. 1, 1929; s. Frederich Edward and Sarah Ferne (Swank) H.; B.S. in Polit. Sci., Brigham Young U., 1956, M.S., 1962; Ph.D., U. Utah, 1967; m. Connie Kay Olsen, Oct. 16, 1964; children—Thomas Dale, Lori Anna, Tammy Rene, Brenda Louise. Supr., office spl. courses and confs. Brigham Young U., Provo, Utah, 1957-61; civilian personnel placement and tng. officer U.S. Govt. in Utah, 1961-63, 65; asst. prof. polit. sci. Winona (Minn.) State Coll., 1966-68; asso. prof. polit. sci. Western Ill. U., Macomb, 1968—; mem. cons. faculty U.S. Army Command and Gen. Staff Coll., 1969—; guest lectr. Nat. Strategy Info. Center, 1969-74. Mem. 20th Congl. Dist. Mil. Acad. Selection Bd., 1969-72. Dir. ann. Boy Scout Merit Badge Pow-Wow, Brigham Young U., 1957-61. Served to 2d lt. U.S. Army, 1950-53; col. Res. Decorated Army Commendation medal. Mem. Res. Officers Assn. (pres. Central Utah chpt. 1960-61), Pi Sigma Alpha. Mem. Ch. of Jesus Christ of Latter-day Saints (pres. Ill. W. dist. mission 1973—). Author: Career Opportunities in Political Science, 1975. Home: 1606 Riverview Dr Macomb IL 61455

HITCHCOCK, JOHN GARETH, judge; b. nr. Ft. Jennings, Ohio, June 10, 1914; s. Roy Clifford and Laura Dell (Adam) H.; LL.B., Ohio State U., 1939; grad. Nat. Coll. State Trial Judges, 1969; m. Helen Marcile Eck, June 10, 1941 (dec. Oct. 1972); children—James Edward, David Louis; m. 2d, Ruth Eleanor Fessel, Aug. 18, 1973. Admitted to Ohio bar, 1939, practiced in Paulding, Ohio, 1939-40, Port Clinton, Ohio, 1946-51; spl. agt. FBI, 1940-42; protection chief Joseph Horne Co., Pitts., 1951-57; investment counselor Federated Investors, Pitts., 1957-59; practice law, 1959-60; judge Ct. Common Pleas Paulding County, Ohio, 1961—. Served from 2d lt. to capt. Corps Mil. Police and Judge Adv. Gen.'s Dept., AUS, 1942-46. Recipient award outstanding service Shawnee council Boy Scouts Am., 1966; Excellent Jud. Service award Ohio Supreme Ct., 1973, 75, 77, Outstanding Jud. Service award, 1974, 76. Mem. Ohio Assn. Common Pleas Judges, Ohio State, Paulding County bar assns., Am. Judicature Soc., Grange. Episcopalian. Republican. Kiwanian (pres. Paulding club 1970, div. lt. gov. 1971). Contbr. book rev. to Am. Bar Assn. Jour., 1955. Home: 302 N Cherry St Paulding OH 45879 Office: Court House Paulding OH 45879

HITCHCOCK, RUTH MARIE, auto dealer; b. Brighton, Iowa, Aug. 15, 1925; d. Howard Reno and Anneta Mary (Weible) Reighard; student Parsons Coll., Fairfield, Iowa, 1941-42, Blackhawk Coll., 1977; 1 dau., Marcy Lee Hitchcock. Sec., Hanssen's Hardware Chain, Davenport, Iowa, 1944-46; accountant Iowa Bearing Co., Davenport, 1946-48; office mgr. Fed. Distbg. Co., Davenport, 1948-55; corp. officer, gen. mgr. Louis Dockterman Chrysler Plymouth, Inc., Davenport, 1955-75; asst. gen. mgr. Kimberly Chrysler Plymouth, Inc., Davenport, 1975-77; gen. mgr. Sweet Datsun, Inc., Galesburg, Ill., 1978—. Pres. N. Harrison St. Bus. Women's Orgn.; chmn. U.S. Singletons Civic Group, elected Miss U.S. Singleton; asst. tchr. mentally retarded. Mem. Accountants of Am. (life), Scott County Auto Dealers Assn., Bus. Mgmt. Soc. Home: 1523 Golden Valley Dr Bettendorf IA 52722 Office: 1621 N Henderson St Galesburg IL 61401

HITE, DAVID L., lawyer; b. Thornville, Ohio, Apr. 30, 1916; s. Frank C. and Mary E. (Pannebaker) H.; B.S., Kent State U., 1938; student Ohio State U., 1945-46; LL.B., Franklin U., 1946; J.D., Capital U., 1966; m. Maxine Whiterbee, July 15, 1943; children—David L., Diane. Admitted to Ohio bar, 1946, U.S. Dist. Ct. So. Dist. Ohio, 1947, U.S. Treasury Dept., 1947; instr. polit. sci. Franklin U., 1946-48; partner Hite and Hite, Utica, Ohio, 1946—; fellow Neuro-Psychiat. Inst., Hartford Conn., 1939; city solicitor, Utica, 1949—; operator Hite farms, 1949—. Trustee Hervey Meml. Library. Served to capt., OSS, 1942-45; ETO. Mem. Am., Ohio State, Licking County, Knox County bar assns. Home: 115 N Main St Utica OH 43080 Office: 26-28 S Main St Utica OH 43080

HITT, WILLIAM DEE, psychologist; b. Lexington, Ky., Feb. 18, 1929; s. Sellers William and Clyde (Barnes) H.; B.A., U. Ky., 1951; M.A., Ohio State U., 1954, Ph.D., 1956; m. Diane Frances Umbaugh, Jan. 26, 1957; children—Jennifer, Jodi, Julie, Jill. Research psychologist Battelle Meml. Inst., Columbus, Ohio, 1957-59, chief of behavioral scis. div., 1959-70, dir. of Center for Improved Edn., 1970-76, program mgr. for edn., 1977—; instr. Ohio State U., Columbus, 1958-63. Chmn. Staff Devel. Com. for Columbus (Ohio), 1972—. Served with USAF, 1951-53. Kellogg grantee, 1972-74. Mem. Am. Psychol. Assn., Assn. for Humanisitc Edn., Sigma Xi. Author: Education as a Human Enterprise, 1973. Home: 223 W

Southington St Worthington OH 43085 Office: Battelle Memorial Institute 505 King St Columbus OH 43201

HIXSON, JOEL DENNIS, mfg. co. exec.; b. Billings, Mont., Nov. 2, 1946; s. Aaron LeRoy and Mary Lillian (Jacobson) H.; B.S., U. N.D., 1968, M.S., 1969; m. Doris Carol Wangen, Aug. 28, 1971; 1 son, Carl Christopher. Nuclear engr., new products program mgr. Medtronic Inc., Mpls., 1969-71, internat. mfg. mgr., 1972-75, dir. corporate mfg. planning and analysis, 1976—. Mem. ASME, Am. Nuclear Soc., Am. Mgmt. Assn., Lutheran. Dir. program to develop world's first nuclear powered cardiac pacemaker. Home: 3417 York Ave N Minneapolis MN 55422 Office: 3055 Old Highway S Minneapolis MN 55418

HJALMARSON, GORDON ROSS, publishing co. exec.; b. Dauphin, Man., Can., Apr. 9, 1926; s. John I. and Holmfridur J. (Johnson) H.; came to U.S., 1942, naturalized, 1950; B.A., Pomona Coll., 1949; M.A., San Francisco State Coll., 1951; postgrad. U. So. Calif., 1953-54; m. Carroll L. Clark, Aug. 9, 1952; children—Gordon Ross II, Melissa Anne, John Clark, Eric Alexander. Sch., univ. tchr., 1951-58; with Houghton Mifflin, Boston, 1958-73; asso. dir. sch. depts., 1968-69, dir. dept., 1969-73, v.p., mem. exec. com., 1973, also dir., 1970-73; pres., dir. Scott, Foresman & Co., Glenview, Ill., 1973—, chmn., chief exec. officer, 1977—; chmn. bd. dirs. Silver Burdett Co., Morristown, N.J., 1975—; chmn. bd., dir. William Morrow, N.Y.C.; dir. South Western Pub. Co., Cin., GLC Ltd. of Can., Toronto, Gage Pub. Co., Toronto. Treas., Huntington Beach (Calif.) Red Cross, 1956; sponsor Met. Council for Ednl. Opportunity, 1970. Mem. Republican Town Com., Wellesley, Mass., 1960. Mem. A.A.A.S., Nat. Council Tchrs. Math, Math. Assn. Am., N.E.A., Nat. Sci. Tchrs. Assn., Phi Delta Kappa. Conglist (moderator 1972-73). Mason. Clubs: Wellesley Country; Union (Boston); Chicago, Executive (Chgo.); President's (N.Y.C.); Sunset Ridge Country (Northbrook, Ill.). Home: 119 Abingdon Ave Kenilworth IL 60043 Office: 1900 E Lake Ave Glenview IL 60025

HO, ANDREW KONG-SUN, educator; b. Hong Kong, Apr. 22, 1939; s. Kaak Yan and Han (Li) H.; came to U.S., 1967, naturalized, 1974; B.Sc., U. Melbourne, 1963, M.Sc., 1965; Ph.D., Monash U., 1967; m. Susan Ju-Chang Wei, Nov. 15, 1969; children—Shirley Ann-Fun, Allan An-Li. NIMH fellow N.Y. U. Med. Center, N.Y.C., 1968-69; research scientist Calif. Dept. Mental Hygiene, Mendocino State Hosp., Ukiah, 1969-70, research specialist, 1970-71; guest scientist Lab. Clin. Scis., NIMH, Bethesda, Md., 1972; asst. prof., asso. prof. Wayne State U., Detroit, 1972-74; asso. prof. pharmacology Peoria Sch. Medicine, U. Ill., 1975—. Research asso. dept. pharmacology San Francisco Med. Center, 1970-71; cons. Spectrum, Inc., N.Y.C. Pharm. Mfrs. Assn. Found. fellow, 1969-71; Beverage Industries Inc. grantee, 1974-75; Nat. Inst. Drug Abuse grantee, 1974-77; Midwestern Alcohol Edn. and Tng. Program grantee, 1977; Ill. Dept. Mental Health contractor, 1977. Recipient NIH Career Tchrs. Devel. award, 1975. Mem. Anatomy Soc. Australia, Anatomy Soc. New Zealand, Australian Physiology and Pharmacology Soc., Research Soc. in Alcoholism, Acad. Med. Educators and Research in Substance Abuse, Rho Chi. Contbr. articles to profl. jours. Office: Dept Basic Scis Peoria Sch Medicine U Ill Peoria IL 61605

HO, RAYMOND YU, mech. engr.; b. Canton, China, July 19, 1921; s. Kee Sheung and Pok Chun (Lo) H.; came to U.S., 1959, naturalized, 1964; B.S. in Mech. Engring., Nat. Chiao-Tung U., China, 1945; postgrad. Ill. Inst. Tech.; m. Julia In-Bong Chan, Dec. 4, 1949; children—Jennifer, Helen, Sharon, Melanie. Prodn. engr. Nat. Carbon (Eastern) Ltd., Hong Kong, 1949-59; engr. Verson Allsteel Press Co., Chgo., 1959-65; mech. engr. Chgo. dist. office Austin Co., 1965-67; research engr. Gen. Am. Research div. GATX, Niles, Ill., 1967-72; research engr. Albright-Nell div. Chemetron Corp., Chgo., 1972-73, mgr. product engring. and service, food equipment div., 1973—. Registered profl. engr., Ill. Mem. Ill. Soc. Profl. Engrs. Home: 8121 Farmingdale Dr Darien IL 60559 Office: 5323 S Western Blvd Chicago IL 60609

HOAD, GRACE HAMILTON, cons. psychologist; b. Detroit; d. James and Jane Ann (Colclough) Hamilton; A.B., U. Mich., 1937, M.S.W., 1942; m. John G. Hoad, Nov. 24, 1937. Supr. pub. welfare, Detroit, 1933-42, Children's Center Met. Detroit, 1947-49; caseworker Community Service, N.Y.C., 1943-45; became psychotherapist, bus. mgr. Birmingham (Mich.) Psychiat. Clinic, 1954—; pvt. practice psychotherapy. Dir., v.p. Hoad Corp., Ypsilanti, Mich., 1957—; v.p. Environment Improvement Corp. Mem. Nat. Assn. Social Workers, Am., Mich. (sec.-treas. 1969-70, sec. 1972, pres. 1974) assns. marriage counselors. Author: Self Damage and the Classroom. Home: 40 Shady Hollow Dearborn MI 48124 Office: 861 Monroe Ave Dearborn MI 48124

HOAD, JOHN GREEN, civil engr.; b. Lawrence, Kans., Sept. 20, 1909; s. William C. and Louis (Green) H.; B.S. in C.E., U. Mich., 1932, postgrad 1932-33, 39-40; m. Grace Hamilton, Nov. 24, 1937. Engr., accountant Pub. Adminstrn. Service, Chgo., 1933; asst. civil engr. Mich. Ferries, 1933-34; with Mich. Hwy. Dept., 1934-37; engr., Detroit Edison Co., 1937-42, power sales engr., 1946-50; engr. Cummins & Barnard, Inc., Ann Arbor, Mich., 1950-53; pres., dir. Lincoln Mining Co., Wallace, Idaho, 1949-53, Hoad Engrs., Inc., Ypsilanti, Mich., 1953—, Environment Improvement Corp., Ypsilanti, 1956—. Served to lt. col. USAAF, 1942-45. Registered profl. engr., Mich., and 35 other states. Fellow Am. Cons. Engrs. Council; mem. ASCE, ASME, Engring. Soc. Detroit, Nat., Mich. socs. profl. engrs., Mich. Engring. Soc., TAPPI, Am. Inst. Cons. Engrs. (pres. 1966—), Delta Upsilon. Clubs: Detroit Athletic, Dearborn Country. Home: 40 Shady Hollow Dearborn MI 48124 Office: 1159 Michigan Ave E Ypsilanti MI 48197

HOADLEY, STEPHEN DAMON, radiation safety ofcl.; b. Washington, Oct. 24, 1939; s. Alfred Damon and Caroline Everet (Warner) H.; student Earlham Coll., 1959-62; B.S., Findlay Coll., 1964; m. Rachel Marie McQuillen, June 21, 1964; 1 dau., Caroline Marie. Radiation technician, Plumbrook Reactor Facility, Sandusky, Ohio, 1964-66; radiation safety engr. Bettis Atomic Power Lab., W. Mifflin, Pa., 1966-71; radiation safety officer, engr. products dept., Monsanto Research Corp., Dayton, Ohio 1971—. Mem. Health Physics Soc. Home: 134 Virginia Ave Centerville OH 45459 Office: Box 8 Station B Dayton OH 45407

HOARE, JAMES PATRICK, chemist; b. Denver, Jan. 9, 1921; s. Patrick Joseph and Mary Josephine (Breen) H.; B.Sc., Regis Coll., 1943; M.Sc., Cath. U. Am., 1948, Ph.D., 1949; m. Therese Clare Tressel, Aug. 29, 1953; children—Karen Marie, Patrick James, John Paul. Instr. physics and chemistry Trinity Coll., Washington, 1949-52, asst. prof., 1952-54; phys. chemist U.S. Naval Research Lab., Washington, 1954-57; prin. research engr. Ford Motor Co., Dearborn, Mich., 1957-60; sr. research chemist Gen. Motors Corp., Research Labs., Warren, Mich., 1960—, sr. tech. staff, 1969—, deptl. research scientist, 1977—. Judge regional, nat. sci. fairs, 1967—; lectr. to sci. clubs, coll. and univ. seminars. Served with USN, 1944-46; PTO. Helen Bonfils scholar, 1939-43; Mullen fellow, 1943-44; Research Corp. grantee, 1952-54. Mem. Am. Chem. Soc., Electrochem. Soc., Internat. Soc. Electrochemistry, N.Y. Acad. Scis., Sigma Xi. Author: The Electrochemistry of Oxygen, 1968. Contbr. articles to profl. jours. Home: 26065 Dover St Detroit MI 48239 Office: Dept 37 12 Mile and Mound Rds Warren MI 48090

HOBAN, THOMAS WILLIAM, assn. exec.; b. Oak Park, Ill., Mar. 7, 1937; s. Edward Charles and Mary Elizabeth (Gaffney) H.; B.S., John Carroll U., 1959; M.S. in Pub. Health, U. Mo., 1969; m. Mary Kay Markey, Aug. 15, 1959; children—Thomas II, Joseph, Edward. Crusade dir. Mo. div. Am. Cancer Soc., 1966-69; exec. dir. Am. Cancer Soc., Mpls., 1963-66, Akron, Ohio, 1960-63; exec. sec. Hennepin County Med. Soc., 1970—; exec. v.p. Physicians Health Plan Greater Mpls., 1975—. Vis. instr. med. residency program U. Minn. and Hennepin County Med. Center, 1973—. Chmn. allocations com. statewide agys. United Fund, 1975-76; pres. Mpls. Vis. Nurse Service, 1975. Bd. dirs. St. Mary's Extended Care Center, Am. Cancer Soc., Hennepin County Acad. Family Physicians, Found. for Health Care Evaluation, YMCA. Mem. Am. Assn. Med. Soc. Execs. Roman Catholic (pres. council ch. 1974-76). Club: Mpls. Athletic. Home: 133 Hawthorne Rd Hopkins MN 55343 Office: 20 Washington Ave S Minneapolis MN 55401

HOBBINS, WILLIAM BELL, surgeon; b. Madison, Wis., Aug. 16, 1924; s. William Suhr and Audrey (Bell) H.; B.S. in Medicine, U. Wis., 1945; M.D., Northwestern U., 1946; m. Paula Ibaugh, Aug. 8, 1975. Intern, Cook County Hosp., Chgo., 1947, surg. resident, 1948-51; surg. resident, Jackson (Wis.) Clinic, 1948; practice medicine specializing in surgery, Madison, Wis., 1951—; mem. surg. staffs, Madison Gen. Hosp., 1951-69, Meth. Hosp., 1965—; cons. surgeon, Watertown Gen., Beaver Dam, Ft. Atkinson Meml., Darlington Meml. hosps.; asst. clin. prof., U. Wis., 1957-68; med. cons. Columbian (S.Am.) Nat. Cancer Inst., establishment of Mass Breast Cancer Screening Program; founder Madison Gen. Hosp. Med.-Surg. Found., 1959, sec., 1959-69; founder, pres. Wis. Breast Cancer Detection Found., 1973—. Councilman, Maple Bluff, Wis., 1955-59; founder, pres., Christ the King Home for Boys and Girls, 1967-74; sr. warden Grace Episcopal Ch., 1963-65; pres. Wis. Ballet Co., 1968-73; commr. Madison Civic Center, 1975—. Served with USNR, 1943-48; served to capt. U.S. Army, 1952-54. Diplomate Am. Bd. Surgery. Fellow A.C.S., Internat. Coll. Surgeons (founder jr. mem. 1951); mem. Wis. Surg. Soc., Dane County, Christian med. socs., Am. Thermographic Soc., Internat. Health Evaluation Assn., Am. Cancer Soc. (pres. Dane County chpt. 1962-65, chmn. 1965-68), Karl A. Meyer Surg. Soc. (sec., treas. 1976—), Club Francais De Telethermographie Clinique, Internat. Soc. Senology, Cook County Hosp. Alumni Assn. Democrat. Contbr. articles to tech., Christian med. publs., presentations, exhibits to med. confs.; organizer, program chmn. Med Am. Breast Cancer Symposia, Madison, 1975, 76. Home: 6005 Hempsted St Madison WI 53717 Office: 121 S Pinckney St Madison WI 53701

HOBBS, HILTON H., banker; b. Tipton County, Ind., Oct. 19, 1915; s. Benjamin and Hazel (Foust) H.; grad. pub. schs.; m. Mildred Eileen Bryant, July 17, 1934; children—Doyle L., Ben B., Nancy May. With Farmers Loan and Trust Co., Tipton, Ind., 1955—, pres., 1958—, chmn. bd. dirs., 1967—. Trustee Tipton County Meml. Hosp. Home: Route 4 Tipton IN 46072 Office: 110 E Jefferson St Tipton IN 46072

HOBBS, LARRY JAY, quality control mgr.; b. Dayton, Ohio, Apr. 10, 1944; s. Carl Edward and Hazel Marie (Gorham) Hobbs; m. Peggy Karnehm, Apr. 17, 1970; 1 dau., Jennifer. B.S., Ohio State U., 1967. Research asso. Charles F. Kettering Research Lab., Yellow Springs, Ohio, 1967-73; quality control supr. Cargill, Inc., Dayton, 1973-74, asst. quality control mgr., 1974-76; quality control mgr. Car-Mi, Inc., Dayton, 1976—. Instr., ARC, 1975—. Mem. Am. Chem. Soc. Am. Assn. Cereal Chemists. Home: 4690 E Ross Rd Tipp City OH 45371 Office: 5640 Brentlinger Dr Dayton OH 45414

HOBBS, LEWIS MANKIN, astronomer; b. Upper Darby, Pa., May 16, 1937; s. Lewis Samuel and Evangeline Elizabeth (Goss) H.; B.E.P., Cornell U., 1960; M.S., U. Wis., 1962, Ph.D. in Physics, 1966; m. Jo Ann Hagele, June 16, 1962; children—John, Michael, Dara. Jr. astronomer Lick Obs., U. Calif., Santa Cruz, 1965-66; asst. prof. astronomy and astrophysics U. Chgo., 1966-72, asso. prof., 1972-76, prof., 1976—; dir. Yerkes Obs., 1974—. Bd. dirs. Assn. Univs. for Research in Astronomy, Tucson, 1974—, Milw. Symphony Assn. of Walworth County (Wis.). Alfred P. Sloan scholar, 1955-60. Mem. Am. Astron. Soc., Am. Phys. Soc., Internat. Astron. Union, Wis. Acad. Scis., Arts and Letters. Contbr. articles to profl. jours. Home: 18 Highland St Williams Bay WI 53191 Office: Yerkes Obs U Chgo Williams Bay WI 53191

HOBBS, MARVIN, engring. exec.; b. Jasper, Ind., Nov. 30, 1912; s. Charles and Madge (Ott) H.; B.S. in Elec. Engring., Tri-State Coll., Angola, Ind., 1930; postgrad. U. Chgo., 1932-33; m. Bernadine E. Weeks, July 4, 1936. Chief engr. Scott Radio Labs., Chgo., 1939-46; cons. engr. RCA, Camden, N.J., 1946-49; v.p. Harvey-Wells Electronics, Southbridge, Mass., 1952-54; asst. to exec. v.p. Gen. Instrument Corp., Newark, N.J., 1958-62; mgr., cons. engr. Design Service Co., N.Y.C., 1963-68, v.p. corp. devel. Gladding Corp., 1968-72, cons., 1972—; dir. A.R.F. Products, Inc., Raton, N.Mex. Mem. Electronics Prodn. Bd., ODM, Washington, 1951-52; operations analyst Far East Air Force, 1945. Recipient Certificate of Appreciation War Dept., 1945, Certificate of Commendation, Navy Dept., 1947. Registered profl. engr., Ill. Life mem. IEEE. Author: Basics of Missile Guidance and Space Techniques, 1959, Fundamentals of Rockets, Missiles and Spacecraft, 1962; Modern Communications Switching Systems, 1974. Inventor low radiation radio receiver. Home: 655 W Irving Park Rd Chicago IL 60613

HOBSON, KENNETH RAY, hosp. adminstr.; b. Hampton, Iowa, June 2, 1925; s. Ray V. and Maude L. (Sherer) H.; B.A., State U. Iowa, 1950; m. Lois A. Sorensen, Aug. 21, 1949; children—Daniel, Kathleen, Joelle. Salesman mut. funds Investors Diversified Service, Hampton, 1950-53; cons. profl. mgmt., Ft. Dodge, Iowa, 1953-57; adminstr. Sioux Valley Meml. Hosp., Cherokee, Iowa, 1957—. Chmn. Cherokee County chpt. A.R.C., 1966; chmn. adv. com. Blue Cross Iowa-S.D. Hosp., 1972; mem. Hill-Burton Adv. Com., 1971—; mem. Iowa Health Planning Council, 1972—; chmn. bd. dirs. Community Chest, Cherokee, 1963-64. Bd. dirs. Sioux City Blue Cross, 1964—. Served with AUS, 1943-46. Mem. Iowa Hosp. Assn. (trustee 1963—, pres. 1973—), Am. Coll. Hosp. Adminstrs., Am. Hosp. Assn. Lutheran (deacon 1965-67). Club: Country (Cherokee). Home: 1 Arrow St Cherokee IA 51012 Office: 300 Sioux Valley Dr Cherokee IA 51012

HOCHGESANG, ROMAN JOSEPH, ret. lumber co. exec., farmer; b. St. Anthony, Ind., June 8, 1915; s. William J. and Philomena (Fleck) H.; student pub. schs.; m. Armellia Buechler, June 14, 1941; children—Phyllis Hochgesang Farley, Glenda Hochgesang Kiefer, Nancy. Pres., Jasper Lumber Co. (Ind.), 1941-77; former owner Hylander Coin Laundry; farmer, 1955—. Served with C.E., U.S. Army, 1942-46. Mem. VFW, Am. Legion, Amateur Trapshooting Assn. Home: 961 3d St Jasper IN 47546 Office: PO Box 59 Jasper IN 47546

HOCHWALD, WERNER, economist, educator; b. Berlin, Germany, Jan. 21, 1910; s. Moritz and Elsa (Stahl) H.; grad. U. Berlin, 1932; Ph.D., Washington U., 1944; m. Hilde Landenberger, Jan. 28, 1938 (dec. June 1958); children—Miriam Ruth, Eve Fay. Came to U.S., 1938, naturalized, 1944. Counsel, Com. on Aid and Reconstrn., Berlin, 1933-38; accountant, St. Louis, 1938-42; instr. Army Specialized Tng. Program, 1942-44; instr. econs., Wash. U., 1944-47, successively asst. and asso. prof., chmn. dept. prof., 1950-63, Tileston prof. polit. economy, 1963—. Cons., U.S. Office Edn., 1967—; dir. Internat. Econ. Research, 1950-55; lectr. Army Fin. Sch., 1950-52; cons. Fed. Res. Bank St. Louis, 1947-58. Mem. Citizens' Budget Com., St. Louis, 1957. Mem. Nat. Planning Assn. (dir. study local impacts fgn. trade), Am. Econ. Assn., Indsl. Relations Research Assn., Econometric Soc., Am. Statis. Assn. (nat. council 1950-52), Econ. History Assn., Am. Farm Econ. Assn., So. (pres. 1966-67), Midwest econ. assns., Conf. Research Income and Wealth, Internat. Assn. Research in Income and Wealth, Nat. Acad. Scis. (project com. 3d hwy. research bd. 1961-64). Author: Local Impact of Foreign Trade, 1960; Design of Regional Accounts, 1962; Essays in Southern Economic Development, 1964; An Economist's Image of History, 1968; The Idea of Progress, 1973. Contbg. author various books, profl. jours. Editor: Design of Regional Accounts, 1961. Home: 6910 Cornell Ave St Louis MO 63130 Office: Washington U St Louis MO 63130

HOCKETT, JAY ANTHONY, dentist; b. Council Bluffs, Iowa, Apr. 2, 1940; s. Penn Thornton and Elizabeth Ann (Pruckler) H.; diploma Grand View Jr. Coll., 1960; B.A., U. Iowa, 1962; D.D.S., 1966; m. Patricia Ann Brown, Dec. 28, 1962; children—Tracy Ann, Kimberly Jane. Practice clin. dentistry Kansas City, Kans., 1969-70, Overland Park, Kans., 1969—. Served with USPHS, 1966-69. Mem. ADA, Johnson County-5th Dist. (sec.-treas. 1972-73, v.p. 1973-74, pres.-elect 1974-75, pres. 1975-76), Kans., Greater Kansas City dental socs. Presbyn. Optimist (v.p. club 1974-75). Home: 4031 W 98th St Overland Park KS 66207 Office: 9036 W 95th St Overland Park KS 66212

HOCKMAN, CHARLES HENRY, neurophysiologist; b. Montreal, Queb., Can., Mar. 15, 1923; s. Charles and Blanche (Lajeunesse) H.; B.A., Queen's U., Kingston, Ont., 1958; Sc.M., Brown U., 1960, Ph.D., 1963; m. Mildred Adele Jardin, Aug. 16, 1952; children—Kenneth Charles, Gail Andrea, Laurie Anne. Asst. prof. neurol. sci. and psychiatry Med. Coll. Va., Richmond, 1962-66; asso. prof. phamacology U. Toronto, 1966-72; asso. prof. basic med. sci. and physiology U. Ill., Urbana, 1972—, chmn. med. physiology program, 1975-77, acting chmn. program in anatomical sci., 1977—. Served with Canadian Mcht. Navy, 1943-45. Canada Council fellow, 1959-61; recipient grants NIH, USPHS, Med. Research Council Can., Can. Dept. Health and Welfare, Ill. Dept. Mental Health. Mem. Am. Physiol. Soc., Canadian Physiol. Soc., Soc. Neuroscience, Sigma Xi. Roman Catholic. Club: K.C. Editor: Chemical Transmission in the Mammalian Central Nervous System, 1976; Editor: Limbic System Mechanisms and Autonomic Function, 1972. Home: 706 Evergreen Circle Urbana IL 61801 Office: Sch Basic Med Sci Med Sci Bldg Univ Ill Urbana IL 61801

HODAN, GERALD JOHN, psychologist; b. Chgo., Feb. 4, 1938; s. John and Evelyn (Hodan) H.; B.A., No. Ill. U., 1964; M.A., Pepperdine U., 1965; Ph.D. (NIMH fellow), U. Okla., 1969; m. Diane A. Jaros, Aug. 31, 1963; children—Michelle, Natalie. Pvt. practice psychology, Milw., 1969—, Winter Haven, Fla., 1971-72; clin. psychologist Milwaukee County (Wis.) Mental Health Center, Milw., 1969-71; dir. satellite clinic Winter Haven (Fla.) Community Mental Health Center, 1971-72; v.p. Behavior & Mgmt. Cons., Inc., Milw., 1972—; child behavior cons. Okla. Head Start, 1967; asso. field assessment officer VISTA, 1968, Peace Corps, 1969; instr. Polk Community Coll., Winter Haven, 1971. Served with USAF, 1957-61. Mem. Am., Fla., Wis., Milw. County psychol. assns. Club: Moose. Home: 900 E Bay Point Rd Bayside WI 53217 Office: 735 W Wisconsin Ave Milwaukee WI 53233

HODAPP, LEROY CHARLES, bishop; b. Seymour, Ind., Nov. 11, 1923; s. Linden Charles H.; student U. Detroit, 1941-42; A.B., U. Evansville (Ind.), 1944; B.D., Drew Theol. Sem., 1947; D.D. (hon.), U. Evansville, 1961; L.H.D. (hon.), Ill. Wesleyan U., 1977; m. Polly Anne Martin, June 12, 1947; children—Anne (Mrs. Thomas Gates), Nancy (Mrs. Kenneth Stofleth). Ordained to ministry United Methodist Ch., 1945; student pastor Asbury Ch., Evansville, 1943-44, Sheepshead Bay, Bklyn., 1945-46; pastor Orleans Ch. Ind., 1947-50, Heath Meml. Ch., Indpls., 1950-54; asso. pastor Meridian St. Ch., Indpls., 1954-61; pastor First Meth. Ch., Bloomington, Ind., 1961-65; supt. Bloomington Dist., 1965-67, Indpls. West Dist., 1967-68, Indpls. N.E. Dist., 1968-70; dir. Council of Ministries, S.Ind. Conf., 1970-76; bishop, Springfield, Ill., 1976—; chmn. Conf. Bd. Social Concerns, Conf. Bd. Ministry, Ind. Council Chs. Legis. Com., Ind. Area TV, Radio and Film Commn.; del. Gen. Conf., 1968, 70, 72, 76, Jurisdictional Conf., 1964, 68, 72, 76; participant Jurisdictional Boundary Com., 1968-72, Gen. Chs. Com. to Study Episcopacy and Dist. Superintendency, 1972-76; mem. tng. team for new D.S.'s and CCOM Dirs., 1970-76; mem. Jurisdictional Urban Network; mem. United Meth. Bd. Ch. and Soc.; mem. governing bd. Nat. Council Chs. Chmn. Bloomington Fair Housing Com., 1963-65; mem. Marion County Crime Commn., 1952-54; mem. exec. com. Monroe County CAAP. Co-editor: Change and the Small Community, 1967. Home: 90 Pebble Beach Dr Springfield IL 62704 Office: 501 E Capitol Ave Springfield IL 62701

HODES, BARNET, lawyer; b. LaSalle, Ill., May 13, 1900; s. Simon and Ruth (Mansfield) H.; J.D., Northwestern U., 1921; m. Eleanor Cramer, 1936; children—Scott, Kay Lynn. Admitted to Ill. bar, U.S. Supreme Ct. bar, 1930, D.C. bar, 1954; practice in Chgo., 1921—; alderman from 7th ward City of Chgo., 1931-33; corp. counsel City of Chgo., 1935-47; lectr. municipal corps. Northwestern U. Law Sch., 1936-40; asst. U.S. coordinator civilian def. Chgo. met. area, 1941-45; impartial arbitrator Ladies Dress Industry, 1946-50. Mem. Ill. State Tax Commn., 1933-35, Chgo. Planning Commn., 1935-42, Chgo. Zoning Bd. Appeals, 1935-47; v.p. Ill. Municipal League, 1936-42; chmn. Patriotic Found. Chgo., 1936—; pres. Nat. Inst. Municipal Law Officers, Washington, 1938-40; bd. govs. Louis A. Weiss Meml. Hosp.; trustee Mus. Contemporary Art, 1967—; vice chmn. Commn. Hist. and Archl. Landmarks Chgo., 1967—. Served to lt. comdr. USCGR, 1944-47. Decorated cross chevalier Legion of Honor (France); recipient Civic Merit award Jr. Assn. Commerce, Chgo., 1934; Chgo. Civil Liberties Com. award for distinguished services, 1939; Decalogue Soc. Lawyers award of merit for distinguished services, 1941; Alumni Service award Northwestern U., 1967, Merit award, 1974; Heritage award Anti-Defamation League, B'nai B'rith, 1973. Mem. Am., Fed., Ill. Chgo. bar assns. Club: Masons. Author: It's Your Money, 1935; Essay on Illinois Taxation, 1936; Law and the Modern City, 1937. Instrumental in having erected in Chgo. the George Washington, Robert Morris, Haym Salomon Monument (declared the 1st sculptural landmark of Chgo. 1971); instrumental in securing commemorative postage stamp honoring Haym Salomon as financial hero of American Revolution. Home: 232 E Walton Pl Chicago IL 60611 Office: 180 N LaSalle St Chicago IL 60601

HODES, SCOTT, lawyer; b. Chgo., Aug. 14, 1937; s. Barnet and Eleanor (Cramer) H.; A.B., U. Chgo., 1956; J.D., U. Mich., 1959; LL.M., Northwestern U., 1962; children—Brian Kenneth, Valery Jane. Admitted to Ill. bar, 1959, D.C. bar, 1962; asso. firm Arvey, Hodes, Costello & Burman, Chgo., 1959-61, partner, 1964—; dir. First Investors Life Ins. Co., Paul Harris Stores, Inc., Indpls. Lectr., Adult Edn. Center, U. Chgo.; chmn. Philippine Exchange Nurses award com., 1966-68; nat. chmn. Lawbooks U.S.A., 1962-71; co-chmn. Chgo. World Friendship Day, 1967. Mem. Ill. Arts Council, 1973-76; mem. vis. com. art dept. U. Chgo. Sec. Citizens for Reelection of Sen. Paul H. Douglas, 1966; mem. 9th dist. Ill. Democratic State Central Com., 1970—. Bd. dirs. Tourism Council Greater Chgo., 1966-74, Michael Reese Hosp. Research Inst., 1965-73. Served to capt., office judge adv. gen. AUS, 1962-64. Named one of Chgo.'s 10 outstanding men Jr. Assn. Commerce and Industry, 1968. Mem. Am., Fed. (chmn. council on financing 1966-67, chmn. younger lawyers div. 1963-64, nat. council, 1965—, dir. Found.; Distinguished Service award 1971, 75), Ill., Chgo. bar assns., Chgo. Art Inst. (life), Chgo. Hist. Soc. (life), Am. Arbitration Assn. (arbitrator), Judge Adv. Gen.'s Assn., Zeta Beta Tau, Tau Epsilon Rho. Jewish (dir. temple). Mason (32 deg.). Clubs: Economic of Chicago, Standard, Union League (Chgo.). Author: The Law of Art and Antiques, 1966; What Every Artist and Collector Should Know About the Law, 1974. Co-editor: Conf. on Mut. Funds, 1966. Contbr. articles to profl. jours. Home: 1240 Lake Shore Dr Chicago IL 60610 Office: 180 N LaSalle St Chicago IL 60601

HODGE, JAMES ROBERT, psychiatrist; b. Martins Ferry, Ohio, Jan. 28, 1927; s. Robert Gabriel and Ethel Melissa (Ashton) H.; B.S., Franklin and Marshall Coll., 1946; M.D., Jefferson Med. Coll., 1950; m. Marilyn Jane Dinklocker, June 10, 1950; children—Sharon Hodge Gertz, Scott. Intern, U.S. Naval Hosp., St. Albans, N.Y., 1950-51; resident Menninger Sch. Psychiatry, Topeka, 1951-52, USN Hosp., Oceanside, Calif., 1952-53, Univ. Hosps., Cleve., 1954-55; USPHS fellow adult psychiatry Sch. Medicine, Case-Western Res. U., Cleve., 1955-56; practice medicine specializing in psychiatry, Akron, Ohio, 1956—; head psychiatry Akron City Hosp., 1962-75, cons. staff, 1975—; adj. prof. psychology U. Akron, 1963—; council chiefs psychiatry Coll. Medicine, Northeastern Ohio U., Akron, 1974-76; chmn. div. mental health scis. Internat. Grad. U., 1976—. Served to lt. USNR, 1944-45, 50-51, 52-54. Recipient spl. recognition award Ohio Psy. Assn., 1976. Fellow Am. Psychiat. Assn., Am. Soc. Clin. Hypnosis, Internat. Soc. Clin. and Exptl. Hypnosis, Acad. Psychosomatic Medicine, Central Neuropsychiat. Assn., mem. Am. Coll. Psychiatrists. Author: Practical Psychiatry for the Primary Physician, 1975. Feature writer Med. Times mag. Producer movie: The Use of Hypnosis in Psychotherapy, 1975. Home: 295 Pembroke Rd Akron OH 44313 Office: 2975 W Market St Akron OH 44313

HODGES, JOHN BLACK, electronics co. exec.; b. Grosse Pointe Farms, Mich., Aug. 27, 1936; s. John Black and Caroline Elizabeth (Hauptman) H.; B.S. in Elec. Engring., U. Mich., 1963; M.S. in Indsl. Mgmt., U. Akron, 1968; m. Janet Rose Merlihan, Aug. 27, 1960; children—Glenn Black, Laura Marie. Mgr. test equipment and test ops. Goodyear Aerospace Co., Akron, Ohio, 1963-74; mgr. mfg. engring. Kelsey-Hayes Co., Brighton, Mich., 1974-75; gen. mgr., chief exec. officer Kent-Moore Instrument Co., Pioneer, Ohio, 1975-77; pres., chief exec. officer, 1977—, also dir.; sr. lectr. dept. indsl. mgmt. U. Akron, 1968-74. Served with USN, 1955-59. Mem. Am. Mgmt. Assn., IEEE, Beta Gamma Sigma. Home: 924 Mayer St Bryan OH 45306 Office: PO Box 507 Industrial Ave Pioneer OH 43554

HODGKINS, EARL WARNER, r.r. engring. assn. exec.; b. Woodsville, N.H., June 30, 1919; s. Earl Warner and Elizabeth (Mitchell) H.; B.S. in Civil Engring., U. N.H., 1950; m. Ruth Abbie Davison, Sept. 23, 1939; children—Earl Warner, Linda Ruth Hodgkins Jacobs, Lorraine Dawn Hodgkins Cunningham. From transferman to messenger to clk. Ry. Express Agy., Woodsville, N.H., 1936-50; structural designer B.& M. R.R., 1950-52, student supr., Greenfield, Mass., 1952; asst. supr. bridges and blgs. Maine Central R.R., Portland, 1953-54, asst. engr. structures, 1954-58; asso. editor Ry. Track and Structures mag., Chgo., 1958-64; asso. engring. editor Ry. Age Weekly, 1958-64; exec. sec. Am. Ry. Engring. Assn., Chgo., 1964-68, exec. mgr., 1968-73, exec. dir., 1974—; exec. vice chmn., engring. div. Assn. Am. R.R.'s, Chgo., 1964-71, exec. dir. engring. div., 1971—. Active local Boy Scouts Am., 1954-60. Served to 1st lt., C.A.C. and Transp. Corps, AUS, 1942-45; ETO. Mem. Am. Ry. Engring. Assn., Am. Ry. Bridge and Bldg. Assn., Roadmasters and Maintenance of Way Assn. Am., Maintenance of Way Club Chgo., Am. Soc. Assn. Execs., Am. Soc. Engring. Edn., ASCE, Council Engring. and Sci. Soc. Execs., Nat. Geog. Soc. Mem. Ch. Jesus Christ of Latter-day Saints. Office: 59 E Van Buren St Chicago IL 60605

HODLMAIR, SCOTLAND ELGIE, real estate broker; b. Chgo., Sept. 1, 1945; s. Charles August and Ruth Elgia (Seldon) H.; student Carthage Coll., 1964-66, U. Minn., 1971; grad. Realtors Inst. Ill., 1969; m. Noreen Ruth Bruns, Nov. 9, 1968; children—Cammi Angela, Allie Teresa. With Eidamiller & Co., Realtors, Des Plaines, Ill., 1967—, partner, 1970—; gen. mgr., partner N.W. Suburban Appraisal Co., Des Plaines, 1971—; owner Wis-Ill Real Estate Co., Des Plaines, 1974—; timber farmer, Mellen, Wis., 1970—. Real estate adviser Girl Scouts U.S.A., Des Plaines, 1974—. Mem. Nat. Assn. Real Estate Bds., Nat. Assn. Ind. Fee Appraisers (sec. 1971-72, pres. 1972-74), N.W. Suburban Bd. Realtors, Ill. Assn. Realtors, Nat. Assn. Real Estate Appraisers, Izaac Walton League. Lion (sec. 1972). Club: Chgo. Yacht. Home: 654 Arlington Ave Des Plaines IL 60016 Office: 680 Lee St Des Plaines IL 60016

HODSON, ARTHUR LOREN, banker; b. Upland, Ind., Dec. 23, 1912; s. Pearl E. and Laura (Gillespie) H.; B.S. in Chem. Engring., Purdue U., 1936; grad. U. Wis. Sch. Banking, 1964; m. Mary Kathryn Speicher, Aug. 12, 1934. Chem. engr. Union Carbide & Carbon Chems. Corp., Fostoria, O. and Charlotte, N.C., 1936-46; mgr. Hodson Farms, Upland, 1946-56, now owner and operator; cashier United Bank, Upland, 1956-64, exec. v.p., 1964-65, pres, 1965—; pres. Central Bank & Trust, Gaston, Ind., 1952-70, chmn. bd. dirs., 1971—; dir., v.p. Citizens Nat. Bank Whitley County, Columbia City, Ind., Citizens Nat. Bank Grant County, Marion, Ind., 1st Valley Bank of Gas City, Ind., Security Bank Elmwood (Ind.), First Nat. Bank Anderson (Ind.), Bank Henry County, Shirley, Ind., Central Bank & Trust Gaston (Ind.), United Bank Upland (Ind.), Grant Life Ins. Co., Marion; dir. Finance & Ins. Co., Inc., Marion, Ind.; owner Art & Mary's Antique Shop, Upland; partner Hodson-Tatman Farm Partnership, 1973—. Mem. Grant County Devel. Com. Financial adviser, mem. investment bd., trustee White's Inst.; bd. dirs. Marion Gen. Hosp. Mem. Upland C. of C. (pres. 1967-68, dir. 1970-73, 74-75), Am. Numis. Assn., Purdue Alumni Assn., Marion Coin Club, Liberty Seated Collectors Club. Republican. Quaker (trustee 1956-64, mem. com. of ministry and council 1960-63, chmn. bldg. com. 1969-70). Home: 10875 E 300 S Hodson Rd Upland IN 46989 Office: 225 N Main St Upland IN 46989

HODSON, DARREL LEROY, lawyer; b. Amboy, Ind., July 20, 1912; s. Charles John and Dora Ellen (Sharp) H.; student Purdue U., 1929-30, U. Wis., 1931; B.S. in Bus. Adminstrn., U. Ind., 1935, J.D., 1937; m. Elaine Emeline Estrich, June 8, 1941; children—John Darrel, James Leroy. Admitted to Ind. bar, 1937; since practiced in Kokomo, partner firm Hodson, Lucas and Hillis, 1938-40, Winslow and Hodson, 1940-42; dir. U.S. Fgn. Claims Commns. in Europe, 1946-47; gen. practice law, 1948-62; partner firm Hodson and Osborn, 1962—; dir., pres. Imperial Properties, Inc.; city judge, Kokomo, 1938; pros. atty. 62nd Jud. Circuit, 194-42, 55-58; county atty., 1950-52. Bd. dirs. Family Service Assn., Inc., 1971-77, United Fund, 1951-52. Served to maj. AUS, 1942-46; col. Res., ret. Decorated Bronze Star. Mem. Am. Legion, C. of C., Am., Ind., Howard County (pres. 1950) bar assns., Judge Advs. Assn. (state pres. 1954-56), Internat. Platform Assn., Res. Officers Assn. Democrat. Methodist. (dir. No. Ind. Conf. Found. 1963-68, dir. dist. missionary soc. 1959-68). Clubs: Kiwanis (v.p. 1955, sec. 1961, dir. Kiwanis Club Found. 1972—), Elks. Home: 1217 W Sycamore St Kokomo IN 46901 Office: 216 E Walnut St Kokomo IN 46901

HOECH, GEORGE PAUL, JR., anesthesiologist; b. Clayton, Mo., Aug. 9, 1932; s. George Paul and Emma Rose (Gassman) H.; A.B., William Jewell Coll., 1954; M.D., Washington U., St. Louis, 1960; m. Joyce Elaine Edson, June 27, 1958; children—Bryan George, Lisa Edson. Intern, Jewish Hosp., St. Louis, 1960-61; resident anesthesiology Presbyn. Hosp., N.Y.C., 1961-63, mem. attending staff, 1965-67; mem. staff Research Med. Center, Kansas City, Mo., 1967—, chmn. dept. anesthesiology, 1975—; asso. clin. prof. anesthesiology U. Mo. Med. Sch., Kansas City, 1974—. Vis. clin. prof. Northwestern U. Med. Sch., 1972; cons. anesthesiology Munson Army Hosp., Ft. Leavenworth, Kan. Served with AUS, 1954-56; fellow dept. biochemistry Columbia Coll. Physicians and Surgeons, 1963-64, fellow dept. anesthesiology, 1964-65. Diplomate Am. Bd. Anesthesiology. Mem. Am., Mo., Jackson County med. assns., N.Y. Acad. Scis. Mo. Baptist (deacon). Home: 11724 Central St Kansas City MO 64114

HOEFT, RICHARD JAMES, educator, coll. adminstr.; b. Wausau, Wis., Mar. 13, 1946; s. Clarence C. and Doris (Bowers) H.; B.S., U. Wis.-LaCrosse, 1969, M.S., 1970, postgrad., 1971; postgrad. U. Wis.-Stout, 1970-71, U. Colo., summers 1973, 74, U. Wis., Madison, 1976. Dir. outdoor recreation U. Wis. at LaCrosse, 1968-69; dir. student activities and housing, 1969—, head resident counselor men's resident hall Western Wis. Tech. Inst., LaCrosse, 1969-76. Mem. City Citizens Com. on Transp., 1973-74; asst. scoutmaster Gateway council Boy Scouts Am., 1966-70, scout camp dir., summers 1971, 72, mem. dist. camping com., 1971-72; chmn. Oktoberfest Parades LaCrosse, 1973-77; bd. dirs. LaCrosse Conv. and Tourist Bur., 1976—; mem. com. Recreation Center, 1971-72; mem. LaCrosse Number One in Am. Commn., LaCrosse Bicentennial Commn., chmn., 1976. Mem. U. Wis. at LaCrosse Alumni Assn. (life), Am., Wis. vocat. assns., Wis. Student Personnel Assn., Am., Wis. personnel and guidance assns., Am., Wis. (exec. bd. 1975-77) coll. personnel assns., Nat. Entertainment Conf. (Wis. unit steering com. 1973—), Am. Coll. Union Internat., Midwest Student Activities Dirs. Assn., LaCrosse Jaycees (dir. 1971-76, dir. Found. 1975—), LaCrosse C. of C., Sigma Tau Gamma Alumni Assn. (sec.-treas. 1971-73), Phi Delta Kappa. Home: 3228 Lauderdale Ct LaCrosse WI 54601 Office: 6th and Vine St LaCrosse WI 54601

HOEHN, JOHN ALBERT, real estate broker; b. Alton, Ill., Mar. 21, 1942; s. John Albert and Alice Ernestine (Norton) H.; B.S., St. Louis U., 1964; m. Sandra Kay Pyle, Apr. 2, 1966; children—Susan, Michael. Sales asso. Sinclair Refining Co., Peoria, Ill., 1964-67; sales cons. Comml. Nat. Realty, Peoria, Ill., 1967-72; v.p., sales mgr. Realty Centre Ltd., 1972-73, pres., 1973—. Mem. Peoria Assn. Commerce, Nat., Ill. assns. realtors, Peoria (dir. 1970-77, pres. 1976-77), Pekin bds. realtors. Home: 300 W Wolf Rd Peoria IL 61614 Office: 4713 W War Memorial Dr Peoria IL 61614

HOEHNEN, DAVID LEE, lawyer; b. Cleve., Dec. 6, 1939; s. Donald Joseph and Anne Elizabeth (Stine) H.; A.B. (scholar), Purdue U., 1962; J.D. (scholar), Washington U., St. Louis, 1965; m. Nora Alice Ogle, Dec. 27, 1961; children—Daniel, Matthew, Julie, Carrie. Admitted to Ohio bar, 1965; partner firm Stotter, Familo, Cavitch, Elden & Durkin, Cleve., 1965-75; founder, gen. counsel pub. interest law firm, 1975—. Lectr. various tax insts. Mem. housing task force Commn. on Cath. Community Action, Cleve., 1972-76; asso. dir., gen. counsel Commn. on Cath. Community Action, 1976—. Mem. Cleve. Bar Assn. (mem. law in urban affairs com. 1972-75), NAACP, Legal Aid Soc. Cleve., Democrat. Roman Catholic. Clubs: City (chmn. club membership com. 1973, dir. 1974-78, pres. 1977), First Friday (table chmn. 1973-75) (Cleve.); Editor: Washington U. Law Quar., 1964-65. Home: 750 Robley Ln Gates Mills OH 44040

HOEKSTRA, BENJAMIN CLARENCE, dentist; b. Chgo., Nov. 8, 1935; s. Benjamin and Clara (Jonkman) H.; B.S., Calvin Coll., 1957; D.D.S., U. Ill., 1960; m. Judith Schelhaas, Sept. 19, 1964; children—Sue Allison, Darrin Benjamin, Amy Kathleen. Practice gen. dentistry, Lansing, Ill., 1963—. Mem. Lansing Sch. Bd., 1970—, Ill. Christian High Sch., 1970-73. Served with USAF, 1960-62; ETO. Mem. Am., Ill., Chgo. dental socs., Acad. Gen. Dentistry. Mem. Christian Ref. Ch. (deacon 1966, 76—). Home: 18844 Wildwood St Lansing IL 60438 Office: 18511 Torrance St Lansing IL 60438

HOEPKER, PAUL GEORGE, computer systems adminstr.; b. Madison, Wis., Feb. 8, 1937; s. George Walter and Loretta Rose (Drunasky) H.; A.A. in Accounting, Madison Bus. Coll., 1957; m. Norma Margaret Walker, Mar. 19, 1960; children—Deborah, David, Andrew. With Am. Family Ins. Group, Madison, Wis., 1961—, sr. programmer, 1966-68, operations mgr., 1968-72, project mgr., 1972-76, dir. systems devel., 1976—. Served with USAF, 1957-61. Mem. Data Processing Mgmt. Assn. (dir.). Roman Catholic. Home: 611 Columbus St Sun Prairie WI 53590 Office: 3099 E Washington Ave Madison WI 53701

HOERNER, MARVIN LAVERN, performing arts agy. exec., gospel singer; b. Arlington Heights, Ill., Mar. 22, 1929; s. Edwin Dewey and Rita (Hoerner) Clink; B.A., Columbia Coll., 1957. Disc jockey Syndicated Overseas, 1959-61; pres. Marve Hoerner Enterprises, Amboy, Ill., Springfield, Ill., Nashville, Tenn., 1959—; pres. Triple T Talent, Amboy, Ill., Springfield, Ill., Nashville, Tenn., 1967—, DeGrande Music/ASCAP, LaCinta Pub. Co.; also gospel singer. Served with AUS, 1950-53. Named to Colo. Country Music Hall of Fame. Mem. Cruz de Oro Assn. (pres.). Author: Reflections of Life through Recitations. Address: Box 99 236 W Bacon St Amboy IL 61310

HOERNER, THOMAS ALLEN, agrl. engr., educator; b. Dubuque, Iowa, Dec. 25, 1934; s. Allen Leroy and Emily Marie (Barmeier) H.; B.S., Iowa State U., 1957, M.S., 1963, Ph.D., 1965; m. Carolyn Ellen Mae Phyfe, June 24, 1955; children—Kim, Michael, Jeffrey, Thomas. Vocat. agrl. tchr. Alburnett (Iowa) Community Sch., 1957-61; instr. Iowa State U., Ames, 1961-66, prof. agrl. engring. dept., 1968—; asst. prof. Pa. State U., University Park, 1966-68; pres. HoBar Enterprises, Inc., 1971-74. Chmn. Nat. Future Farmers Am. Agrl. Mechanics Contest, Kansas City, Mo., 1972-75. Recipient Am. Farmer degree Nat. Future Farmers Assn., 1973. Mem. Am. Assn. Agrl. Engrs., Am. Vocat. Assn., Nat., Iowa vocat. agrl. tchrs. assns., Am. Assn. Tchr. Edn. in Agr., Phi Kappa Phi, Gamma Sigma Delta, Alpha Tau Alpha. Editor: John Deere Pubs., 1972-75; contbr. articles in field to profl. jours. Home: 2824 Ross Rd Ames IA 50010 Office: Room 208 Agrl Engring Dept Iowa State U Ames IA 50011

HOERTEL, WILLIAM WADSWORTH, lawyer; b. St. Louis, Mar. 7, 1930; s. Frederick William and Julia Wadsworth (Hewlett) H.; J.D., U. Mo., 1959; m. Helen Marie Schake, June 18, 1955; children—Edward David, Julia. Admitted to Mo. bar, 1959; individual practice law, Rolla, Mo., 1959—; pros. atty. Phelps County (Mo.), 1961-67, juvenile officer, 1961-75. Trustee John Knox Village, Mo. State Fed. Soldiers' Home, St. James, 1972-74; adv. bd. Meramec Home Health Agy. Served with USN, 1950-54. Mem. Conservation Fedn. Mo., Phi Alpha Delta. Democrat. Lutheran. Home: 612 Salem Ave Rolla MO 65401 Office: 207 Scott Bldg Rolla MO 65401

HOF, JAMES EAGAN, univ. ofcl.; b. Boscobel, Wis., June 28, 1925; s. Samuel M. and Agnes (Eagan) H.; B.A., Bowling Green State U., 1950, M.A., 1951; m. Joyce Stockdale, June 12, 1950; children—Christopher, Catherine, Thomas, Robert, Ann. With Sunbeam Corp., Chgo., 1952-57, dist. sales mgr., Boston, 1956-57; mem. faculty Bowling Green (Ohio) State U., 1951-52, 57—, asst. prof. speech, dir. admissions, 1957-61, dir. alumni affairs, 1960-71, dir. univ. relations, 1963-71, dir. devel., 1971; exec. dir. Bowling Green State U. Found., Inc., 1963-71, v.p. for pub. services, 1971—. Real estate salesman. Active Am. Cancer Soc.; mem. Bowling Green Bd. Edn., 1966-74, pres., 1968; mem. City Planning Commn., 1971-72. Bd. dirs. Blue Cross Northwest Ohio, 1972—. Served with USNR, 1943-46. Mem. Council for Advancement and Support Edn., Bowling Green C. of C. (dir. 1975—), Phi Delta Theta, Omicron Delta Kappa, Pi Kappa Delta. Clubs: Toledo Press; Bowling Green Country. Home: 316 Garden Ct Bowling Green OH 43402

HOFER, ALBERT CORNELIUS, rubber co. exec.; b. Akron, Ohio, Sept. 25, 1920; s. Ernest Edward and Emma (Straub) H.; bus. degree Actual Bus. Coll., 1938-39; student U. Akron, 1940-50; m. Helen Grace Klespies, July 31, 1942; children—Barry A., Diana L., Denise L. Accounting supr. Firestone Tire & Rubber Co., Akron, 1941-53; with Cooper Tire & Rubber Co., Findlay, Ohio, 1953—, mgr. employee services, 1975—; asst. treas. Findlay Warehouse Corp., 1972-76. Republican precinct committeeman, Findlay, 1976—; councilman-at-large City of Findlay, 1970-71, city treas., 1978—; mem. bd., pres. Winnebrenner Meml. Fund, 1975—; chmn. Task Force on Crime and Vandalism, 1976—. Served with USAAF, 1942-45. Mem. Adminstrv. Mgmt. Soc. (Merit Award key 1969, Diamond Merit award 1977), Soc. Pre-Retirement Program Planners, Findlay Area C. of C., Smithsonian Assos., Am. Assn. Ret. Persons, Findlay Area C. of C. Methodist. Clubs: Masons, Shriners, K.T. (Findlay). Home: 608 Yorkshire Dr Findlay OH 45840 Office: PO Box 550 Findlay OH 45840

HOFF, VIVIAN BEAUMONT, composer; b. nr. Fountaintown, Ind., Dec. 17, 1911; d. Robert and Mary Eunice (Logan) Beaumont; student Butler U., Jordan Coll. Music; student piano with Bomar Cramer, Thelma Todd, voice with Elma Igleman, harmony and advanced composition with William Pelz; m. Arville H. Hoff, Apr. 6, 1935. Piano tchr., 1940-50. Chmn., City-Wide July 4th Celebration, Indpls., 1965. Recipient certificate meritorious personal service Indpls. canteen A.R.C., 1946, certificate for entertaining troops, Los Angeles, 1947. Mem. ASCAP, Nat. Assn. Am. Composers and Condrs., Nat. League Am. Pen Women (nat. music editor 1964-68, 72—, pres. Indpls. 1970-72), Nat. Soc. Arts and Letters, Nat. Fedn. Music Clubs (spl. mem.), Indpls. Matinee Musicale. Baptist. Mem. Order Eastern Star. Composer: Father in Heaven and Suite for Piano (7 pieces), 1953-56; Be of Good Courage, 1957; I Look To My Lord, 1960; Keep The Star-Spangled Banner Waving, 1962; also various piano pieces; works performed Christian TV network. Home: 7025 Warwick Rd Indianapolis IN 46220

HOFFLAND, DAVID LAUREN, banker; b. Wheatland, Wyo., June 4, 1933; s. Fred Lauren and Ruth Hazel (Pickerell) H.; A.B. in Bus., San Diego State U., 1955, M.A. in Econs., 1962; m. Marie-Claire Cecile Blouet, May 20, 1960; children—Dorinda Ruth, Timothy David. Vice pres., mgr. bank investment portfolio So. Calif. First Nat. Bank, San Diego, 1961-73; head securities and investments, v.p., bank portfolio mgr. Fifth Third Bank, Cin., 1973—. Treas., Community Concert Assn., San Diego, 1967-73; treas., trustee Community Chest and Council, Cin., 1974—. Mem. Fin. Analysts Soc. Cin., Inst. Chartered Fin. Analysts, Miami Valley Bus. Economists (pres. 1977—), Queen City Municipal Bond Club. Club: Montgomery Swim and Tennis. Contbr. articles to profl. jours. Home: 7705 Shadowhill Way Montgomery OH 45242 Office: 38 Fountain Sq Plaza Cincinnati OH 45202

HOFFMAN, ALBERT ROMAINE, automotive mfg. exec.; b. Auburn, Ind., Dec. 27, 1918; s. Darrel Clyde and Cleora Selma (Wolfe) H.; grad. U.S. Army Command and Gen. Staff Coll., 1957; B.S., U. Md., 1964; M.S. in Bus. Adminstrn., George Washington U., 1965; grad. Indsl. Coll. of Armed Forces, 1965; m. Carol Rose Cullis, Nov. 27, 1943; children—Andrew, Alan, DeeAnn. Enlisted U.S. Army, 1942, commd. 2d lt., advanced through grades to col., 1972; batallion comdr. 806th Engrs., Korea, 1950-52; dir. Systems Def. Supply Agency, 1965-69; dep. comdr. U.S. Army Computer Systems Command, 1969-72, ret. 1972; mgr. planning and devel. parts mktg. and distbn. Chrysler Corp., Center Line, Mich., 1972—. Decorated Legion of Merit with oak leaf cluster, Silver Star, Bronze Star with 3 oak leaf clusters, Army Commendation medal with 2 oak leaf clusters. Mem. Am. Mgmt. Assn., U.S.A. Engr. Hall of Fame. Home: 2035 Wickford Ct Bloomfield Hills MI 48013 Office: 26311 Lawrence Ave Center Line MI 48015

HOFFMAN, CHARLES JACOB, motor carrier exec.; b. Kansas City, Mo., Mar. 1, 1929; s. C.J. and Florence (Brown) H.; B.S., U. Mo., 1950; m. Ellene Thurman, Sept. 1, 1950; children—Steven J., Susan L., Mark C. With Chgo. Kansas City Freight Line, Kansas City, Mo., 1950—, pres., 1962—. Served with USNR, 1946-49. Mem. Regular Common Carrier Conf. (dir.), Am. Trucking Assn. (bd. govs.), Middle West Motor Freight Bur. (dir.), Young Pres.'s Orgn., Kappa Alpha. Home: 8201 Cherokee Circle Leawood KS 66206 Office: 106 W 14th St Kansas City MO 64105

HOFFMAN, DAVID LLOYD, child psychotherapist; b. Merrill, Wis., Dec. 11, 1934; s. Sam S. and Ethelyn Ruth (Andersen) H.; B.A., Lawrence U., 1957; M.A., U. Chgo., 1961; certificate child psychotherapy Chgo. Inst. Psychoanalysis, 1968; div.; 1 son, David Mark; m. 2d, Deborah Hoffman; children—Elyse, Paul. Social worker Winnebago (Wis.) State Hosp., 1958-59, 61-62; family counselor Family Service, Milw., 1962—, supr., cons. child psychotherapy, 1966—, asst. dir. treatment services, 1968-70, dir. treatment services, 1970-72, exec. dir., 1972—; mem. exec. com. Wis. Council Voluntary Family and Children Agys.; chmn. Wis. Assn. Family Service Agys. Bd. dirs. Wis. Council Human Concerns, Milw. Jewish Council. Fellow Am. Orthopsychiat. Assn., Wis. Soc. Clin. Social Workers; mem. Assn. Child Psychotherapists (past pres.), Am., Wis. (past pres.) assns. marriage and family counselors, Am. Acad. Psychotherapists, Execs. United Way Agencies (chmn.). Office: 2819 W Highland Blvd Milwaukee WI 53208

HOFFMAN, ELLEN BARKER, baking co. exec.; b. La Harpe, Kans., Oct. 12, 1920; d. Otis Earl and Gertrude Ellen (Jones) Barker; student Clark's Bus. Coll., Topeka, 1938, U. Kansas City Night Sch., 1947-48; m. Donald D. Hoffman, June 8, 1968. Continuity dir. KMBC-TV, Kansas City, Mo., 1952-58; set dir. Calvin Prodns., film producers, Kansas City, 1958-67; with Interstate Brands Corp., wholesale bakers, Kansas City, 1967—, dir. pub. and consumer communications, 1975—. Mem. rifle shot com. Rockhurst Coll., Kansas City, 1977. Mem. Am. Bakers Assn. (pub. relations com. 1977), Pub. Relations Soc. Am. (dir. Kansas City chpt. 1977—), Kansas City C. of C. Democrat. Episcopalian. Club: Rockhill (Kansas City). Home: 3744 Warwick Blvd Kansas City MO 64111

HOFFMAN, GEORGE WILLIAM, accountant; b. Waukegan, Ill., Nov. 19, 1939; s. Edward Richard and Anna Marie (Titus) H.; B.A. in Bus. Adminstrn., Lake Forest (Ill.) Coll., 1962; m. Janet L. Rowe, Aug. 22, 1974; 1 son, Peter William. Sr. accountant Price Waterhouse & Co., Inc., 1962-66; mem. treas.'s staff United Greenfield Corp., 1966-68; chief fin. officer, sec., dir. J.W. Johnson & Co., 1968-70; treas. Morse/Diesel, Inc., Chgo., 1970-76; mng. partner George William Hoffman, Ltd., P.C., Chgo., 1976—; chmn. bd. dirs. GWH, Inc., 1976—, Interhold, Inc., 1976—. Treas., bd. dirs. So. Sch.; bd. dirs. Pop Warner Little Scholars; del. Republican. State Conv., 1976; mem. businessmen's adv. com. Gov. of Ill. Served with USAR, 1957-65. C.P.A., Ill. Mem. Am. Inst. C.P.A.'s, Ill. Soc. C.P.A.'s, Nat. Assn. Accountants. Clubs: Union League, Met., Young Execs. (Chgo.). Home: 2339 N Commonwealth St Chicago IL 60614

HOFFMAN, GERALD ERNEST, constrn. co. exec.; b. Appleton, Wis., Mar. 28, 1914; s. Paul Edward and Clara Johanna (Kubitz) H.; student Lawrence U., 1932-33; student U. Wis., 1934-37; m. Elaine C. Almlie, May 24, 1949; children—James, Paul, Christine, Thomas. Gen. supt. Hoffman Constrn. Co., Appleton, 1937-43, 47-48; field engr. Austin County (Mich.), Detroit, 1943-44, asst. supt., 1944; v.p., gen. mgr. Hoffman Co. Inc., Appleton, 1948-65, pres., 1965—; pres. First Inc., 1962-74; pres., treas. Hoffman Shopping Center Inc., Appleton; real estate broker, Appleton; dir. Valley Nat. Bank. Active Boy Scouts Am., 1961-64. Bd. dirs. Mut. Service Devel. Corp.; bd. dirs. United Fund, Appleton, 1958-66, chmn. campaign, 1st v.p., 1965. Served to 1st lt. AUS, 1944-47. Mem. Fox River Valley Contractor's Assn. (dir.). Lutheran. Elk. Clubs: Riverview Country, Fox Cities Racquet, Century, Town. Home: 2321 N Oneida St Appleton WI 54911 Office: 2161 S Memorial Dr Appleton WI 54911

HOFFMAN, HARLEY HOWARD, real estate broker; b. Long Lake, S.D., June 8, 1935; s. John F. and Johanna (Zenker) H.; B.S., No. State Coll., 1953; C.L.U., Am. Coll. Life Underwriters, 1967; m. Sharlene J. Koerner, June 8, 1958; children—Blake, Jon, Gregory, Monica, Timothy. Farmer, nr. Long Lake, 1953-58; tchr. Harrison Twp. Sch., Long Lake, 1953-58; salesman Western States Life Ins., 1955-63, Pioneer Mut. Life, Long Lake, 1963—; owner, broker Hoffman Realty, Aberdeen, S.D., 1967—. Asst. drive chmn. United Way, Aberdeen, 1972-73, drive chmn., 1973-74, pres., 1974—, also bd. dirs.; bd. dirs. Aberdeen YMCA. Named Aberdeen Realtor of Year, 1973, S.D. Realtor of Year, 1977; C.L.U., S.D. Mem. Nat. (dir. 1975—), S.D. (pres. 1975, dir.), Aberdeen (pres. 1971) bds. realtors, S.D. Assn. Realtors (nat. dir. 1976—), No. State Coll. Alumni Assn. (v.p. 1969, pres. 1970), C. of C. (indsl. devel. com. 1972—). Lutheran. Clubs: Elks, Sertoma (Aberdeen). Home: Mina SD 57462 Office: 913 6th Ave SE Aberdeen SD 57401

HOFFMAN, JOHN HARRY, lawyer, accountant; b. Chgo., June 18, 1913; s. Dave and Rose (Gewirtzman) H.; J.D., John Marshall Law Sch., 1938; m. Gwen Zollo, Dec. 30, 1949; children—Alana Sue Glickson, Edward Jay, Gayle Beth. Admitted to Ill. bar, 1938, U.S. Supreme Ct. bar, 1956; practiced in Chgo., 1938—; propr. John H. Hoffman & Co., 1952—; partner John H. Hoffman & Co., 1966—; pres. John H. Hoffman, P.C., 1972. Mem. Am., Ill., Chgo. bar assns., Decalogue Soc., Am. Inst. C.P.A.'s, Ill. Soc. C.P.A.'s. Mason (Shriner); mem. B'nai B'rith. Clubs: Covenant (Chgo.); Twin Orchard Country. Home: 239 Valley View Dr Wilmette IL 60091 Office: 221 N LaSalle St Chicago IL 60601

HOFFMAN, KATHRYN ELIZABETH, physician; b. Sandusky, Ohio, Dec. 12, 1910; d. Charles John and Katherine Elizabeth (Rittman) H.; A.B., Denison U., 1932; M.D., U. Mich., 1936. Intern, St. Joseph's Mercy Hosp., Pontiac, Mich., 1936-37; sr. intern obstetrics and gynecology Woman's Hosp., Detroit, 1938-39, resident pathology, 1942; intern Chgo. Lying-in Hosp., 1943-44, resident, 1944-45, asst., 1945-46; practice medicine specializing in gynecology, Cleve., 1946—; mem. staffs Luth. Med. Center; clin. instr. obstetrics Woman's Med. Coll., Phila., 1939-41; asst. visitant obstetrics and gynecology Cleve. Met. Gen. Hosp. and sr. clin. instr. obstetrics and gynecology Case-Western Res. Sch. Medicine, Cleve., 1955-66. Trustee Woman's Gen. Hosp., Cleve. Diplomate Am. Bd. Obstetrics and Gynecology. Mem. Am., Ohio med. assns., Am. Coll. Obstetricians and Gynecologists, Central Assn. Obstetricians and Gynecologists, Am., Internat. fertility assns., Pan-Pacific Surg. Assn., Am. Med. Women's Assn., Cleve. Soc. Obstetricians and Gynecologists, Woman's Med. Soc. Cleve., Acad. Medicine Cleve., Alpha Epsilon Iota. Home: 116 Center St Milan OH 44846

HOFFMAN, LARRY GENE, mus. dir.; b. Paola, Kans., Mar. 12, 1933; s. Jacob E. and Effie (Moore) H.; B.F.A., Drake U., 1954, M.S.E., 1962; m. Mary E. Dixon, June 5, 1954; children—Lawrence Keith, John William. Tchr. art pub. schs., Des Moines, 1954-59, art cons., 1959-62; dir. edn. Des Moines Art Center, 1962-67; dir. Huntington (W.Va.) Galleries, 1967-71, Davenport (Iowa) Municipal Art Gallery, 1971—. Mem. adv. bd. Quad Cities Cultural Survey, 1974-75, electoral bd. United Service Agy., 1962-63; mem. Adult Leadership Council, 1962-63, committeeman Tall Corn council Boy Scouts Am., 1965-66. Mem. Am. Assn. Mus. Cirs., Intermuseum Conservation Assn. (trustee 1974-77), Am. Fedn. Arts, Am. Assn. Museums, Iowa State Art Educators, NEA (artists nomination com. 1969-71), Delta Phi Delta. Rotarian. Episcopalian. Home: 2704 E Garfield St Davenport IA 52803

HOFFMAN, LEONARD, judge; b. Dwight, Ill., Apr. 18, 1918; s. Edward M. and Edna I. (Skidmore) H.; A.B., U. Chgo., 1938, J.D., 1940; m. Marjorie F. Erb, Mar. 9, 1946; children—Valerie, Marjorie, Leonard, Deborah. Admitted to Supreme Ct. Ill. bar, 1940, U.S. Supreme Ct. bar, 1949; gen. practice of law, since 1945; city atty., Morris, Ill., 1949-50; county judge Grundy County, 1950-57; circuit judge 13th Jud. Circuit, 1957—; justice 4th Dist. Appellate Ct., 1959—; dir. Ill. Valley Ice Cream Co., 1st Nat. Bank Dwight (Ill.). Pres. Rainbow council Boy Scouts Am.; chmn. ARC fund campaign, Grundy County, 1948-51. Served in AUS, 1941-45. Named Outstanding Citizen, Morris, 1967. Mem. Grundy County Bar Assn., PTA (pres. Morris, Ill., 1949-50), Ill. Circuit and Superior Judges Assn. (v.p. 1958), Kappa Sigma. Presbyn. Club: Morris Country. Bd. editors U. Chgo. Law rev., 1939, 40. Home: 424 Vine St Morris IL 60450 Office: Court House Morris IL 60450

HOFFMAN, MARION EUREL, fin. co. exec.; b. Matteson, Ill., Jan. 2, 1932; s. Marion Eurel and Christina Irene (Purtee) H.; student Milliken U., 1950; m. Anna Lou Wyatt, Nov. 15, 1953; children—David, Cheryl, Steven, Fianna. Auditor, asst. cashier, asst. v.p. mortgage banking, asst. v.p. installment lending, Ill. Nat. Bank, Springfield, 1950-67; pres. M.E. Hoffman Co., Springfield, 1967—; instr. Ill. Bankers Assn. Sch. Banking, 1961-68, various mortgage banking schs. Mem. Ill. State C. of C., treas., bd. mem. Springfield C. of C., 1960-67; chmn. Springfield Municipal Band Commn., 1960—; active Springfield Central Area Devel. Assn. Mem. Ill. Home Builders Assn., Mortgage Bankers Assn. Am., Ill. State Savs. and Loan League. Republican. Club: Optimist (charter mem, pres. Luncheon Club, 1960). Home: 2234 Warson Rd Springfield IL 62704 Office: 901 S Second St PO Box 1026 Springfield IL 62705

HOFFMAN, PAUL RICHARD, psychologist; b. Hyannis, Mass., Jan. 27, 1929; s. Otto K. and Louisa (Choate) H.; B.A., U. Maine, 1959; postgrad. U. Iowa, 1959-60; Ed.D., U. Ariz., 1961-65; m. Mary Ann Wallbridge, June 17, 1961; children—Alisa Ann, Diana Marie, Carol Ann, Stephen Paul. Chemist, Rubberoid Co., 1948-51; head psychometric unit U. Ariz. Rehab. Center, 1962-63; counseling psychologist VA, 1963-68; dir. Univ. Counseling Center, Inst. Vocat. Rehab., Stout State U., Menomonie, Wis., 1964-68, chmn. Dept. Rehab. and Manpower Services and dir. spl. centers, 1968—; cons. psychologist No. Wis. Colony and Tng. Sch., Narcotic Addict Rehab. Bur. NIMH, Rehab. Services Adminstrn. Mem. Wis. Area III Manpower Council; bd. dirs. Sister Mary Inst. Served with USAF, 1951-55. Recipient Distinguished Citizen's award U. Ariz., 1970. Mem. Am., Wis. psychol. assns., Nat. (Pres.'s award 1974), Wis. rehab. assns., Am. Vocat. Evaluation and Work Adjustment Assn. (past pres., mem. exec. bd.), Internat. Assn. Rehab. Facilities. Contbr. articles to profl. jours. Home: 1113 W 2d St Menomonie WI 54751

HOFFMAN, WILLIAM KENNETH, obstetrician, gynecologist; b. Milw., Jan. 18, 1924; s. William Richard and Marian (Riegler) H.; student U. Wis., 1942-43; student U. Pa., 1943-44, postgrad, 1954-55; M.D., Marquette U., 1947; m. Peggy Folsom, July 28, 1952; children—Janet Susan, Ann Elizabeth. Intern, Columbia Hosp., 1947-48, resident in obstetrics and gynecology, 1948-49, mem. staff, 1949—; preceptor R.E. McDonald, M.D., Milw., 1949-50; resident in obstetrics and gynecology U. Chgo., 1950-51; practice medicine specializing in obstetrics and gynecology, Milw., 1955-74; mem. staff, St Marys Hosp., Luth. Hosp., County Gen. Hosp.; dir. health service U. Wis., Milw., 1974—, cons. Sch. Nursing, 1976-77, mem. instl. rev. bd., 1976—. Mem. Am. Coll. Obstetrics and Gynecology, Wis. Soc. Obstetrics and Gynecology, Am. Cancer Soc. (pub. edn. com. Milw. div.). Home: 4629 N Murray Ave Milwaukee WI 53211

HOFFMANN, CHARLES LEHR, mech. engr.; b. Toledo, Ohio, July 24, 1930; s. Charles W. and Daisy M. (Lehr) H.; B.M.E., U. Detroit, 1954; m. Sally Netz, May 29, 1954; children—Teresa, Christina, Tamara, Tracey. With Ohio Edison, 1954—, ops. supr., Stratton, Ohio, 1967-70, asst. plant supt., 1971-74, plant supt., Toronto, Ohio, 1974—. Roman Catholic. Home: 307 W Lincoln Way Lisbon OH 44432

HOFFMEISTER, ROBERT EDWARD, engine co. exec.; b. Rochester, N.Y., July 13, 1931; s. John Edward and Ruth (Tuthill) H.; B.S., Purdue U., 1953; grad. exec. devel. program Ind. U., 1970; m. Rebecca Jane Burns, June 27, 1964; children—Sharon, James Robert, John Edward, David Joseph. Design, applications engr. Cummins Engine Co., Columbus, Ind., 1953-60, dir. constrn., indsl. service, 1961-65, internat. service and warranty dir., 1965-66, dir. applications engring., 1966-71, exec. dir. product planning, 1971-73, exec. dir. product devel., 1973-74, v.p. product devel., 1974—. Active United Fund drive, Columbus, 1970; crusade chmn. Am. Cancer Soc., 1975. Mem. Soc. Automotive Engrs. (vice chmn. power plant 1964-65, co-chmn. nat. truck meeting 1976), Am. Ordnance Assn., Columbus Area C. of C., Kappa Sigma. Presbyn. (deacon 1965-67, elder 1969-71). Kiwanian. Club: Harrison Lakes Country (Columbus). Home: 4335 N Riverside Columbus IN 47201 Office: 1000 5th St Columbus IN 47201

HOFLING, CHARLES KREIMER, psychiatrist, educator; b. Cin., Apr. 22, 1920; s. Charles A. and Edith (Kreimer) H.; student Ohio U., 1937-39; B.A., U. Cin., 1942, M.D., 1946; m. Madelyn Gibson Laymon, Dec. 24, 1945; children—Deborah Gayle Hofling Witonski, Charles Andrew, Karen Clark, Mark Laymon. Psychiat. resident Cin. Gen. Hosp., 1947-48, 49-50, Menninger Clinic, 1948-49; fellowship May Inst. Med. Research, 1947-48; instr. psychiatry Coll. Medicine, U. Cin., 1950-55, asst. prof., 1955-64, asso. prof., 1964-68, vis. prof., 1968—, lectr. Grad Sch. Arts and Scis., 1957-68; prof. psychiatry, mem. grad. sch. faculty St. Louis U., 1968—; cons. med. dept. Procter & Gamble Corp., 1967-69. Mem. bd. rev. Episcopal Chaplaincy, U. Cin., 1963-68; bd. dirs. Menninger Found., 1974—. Served as capt. USAF, 1952-54. Fellow Am. Coll. Psychiatrists, Am. Coll. Psychoanalysts; mem. AMA, Am. Psychosomatic Soc., AAAS, Pan-Am. Med. Assn., Am. Psychiat. Assn., Assn. Applied Psychoanalysis, Internat. Shakespeare Assn., Soc. Sci. Study of Religion, St. Louis Psychoanalytic Soc. (hon.), Phi Beta Kappa, Sigma Xi, Alpha Omega Alpha. Episcopalian. Clubs: Univ. (Cin. and St. Louis), Cin. Tennis; Cosmos (Washington); Playing Card Soc. (London). Author (with Madeleine Leininger) Basic Psychiatric Concepts, 1961, 3d edit., 1973, Japanese edit., 1968, French edit., 1977; Textbook of Psychiatry for Medical Practice, 1963, 3d edit., 1975, Spanish edit., 1965, 70; (with Paul Ornstein) Memos to Maury, 1968; contbr. articles to profl. jours. Home: 501 N Mosley Rd Creve Coeur MO 63141 Office: 1221 S Grand Blvd Saint Louis MO 63104

HOFMANN, GEORGE FREDERICK, author, historian; b. Cin., Jan. 18, 1935; s. George and Helen K. (Stoppelkamp) H.; B.S. in Bus. Adminstrn., Xavier U., Cin., 1957, M.Ed. in Asian Studies, 1972; M.A. in History, U. Cin., 1970; m. Jane Ann Dobelhoff, Oct. 6, 1956; children—G. Michael, Gregory P., Susanne R. Med. sales rep. Sandoz Pharm. Co., 1960-77; historian, 1970—; author in field of mil. and diplomatic affairs, 1973—; books include: The Super Sixth, 1975; contbr. articles to Dictionary Am. Biography, Mil. Affairs, Armor, Marine Corps Gazette; lectr. diplomatic and modern European history Edgecliff Coll., 1976—. Served with AUS, 1957-59, USAR, 1959-63. U. Cin. grantee, 1977. Mem. Orgn. Am. Historians, Am. Hist. Assn., U.S. Armor Assn., Assn. U.S. Army, Am. Mil. Inst., Phi Alpha Theta. Republican. Roman Catholic. Club: Fairfield Sportsmen Assn. Home and Office: 5575 Little Flower Ave Cincinnati OH 45239

HOFSTATTER, JUNE MARIE EICHENBERG (MRS. FRANK FOX HOFSTATTER), advt. agy. exec.; b. Cleve., Jan. 27, 1925; d. Arthur Conrad and Mattie (Kadlejack) Eichenberg; student Fenn Coll., 1942-43, Baldwin-Wallace Coll., 1943-44; m. Frank Fox Hofstatter, Aug. 22, 1945; children—Caren Lee, Linda Jean, Robert Alan. Exec. sec. Cleve. Graphite Bronze Co., Cleve., 1944-45; v.p. Stahl Assos., 1962—; partner Hofstal Co., Bellevue and Bryan. Ohio, 1959—; co-owner Countyline, shoppers newspaper, Bryan, 1965-67. Mem. Nat. Fedn. Advt. Agencies, Am. Advt. Fedn., Internat. Platform Assn., Women's Advt. Club Toledo, Federated Women's Clubs Bryan (pres. 1966-67). Republican. Presbyterian. Clubs: Sorosis (publicity and program chmn. Bellevue 1960-61); Claire Newcomer (pres. 1966-67), Orchard Hills Country (Bryan). Home: 615 Circle Dr Bryan OH 43506 Office: 1002 Buffalo Rd Bryan OH 43506

HOFSTEDE, ALBERT JOHN, city ofcl.; b. Mpls., Sept. 25, 1940; s. Albert and Florence (Zebro) H.; student U. Minn., 1958-60; B.S., Coll. of St. Thomas, 1964. Land agt. Minn. Park Systems, 1965-66; aide to Gov. Minn., Mpls., 1966; polar panel adminstr., 1966-67; mem. Mpls. City Council from 3d ward, 1967-71; chmn. Twin Cities Met. Council, 1971-73; mayor Mpls., 1974—. Mem. adv. bd. to mgmt. center Coll. St. Thomas. Named Jaycee Man of Year, 1972; Time mag. Leader of Future, 1974; Nat. Jaycees Top Ten Young Men, 1975. Mem. Minn. Soc. Fine Arts, Minn. Orch. Assn. Roman Catholic. Home: 2430 California St NE Minneapolis MN 55418 Office: 127 City Hall Minneapolis MN 55415

HOGAN, CHARLES MARSHALL, lawyer; b. Columbus, Ohio, June 3, 1911; s. Timothy Sylvester and Mary Adele (Deasy) H.; A.B., Xavier U., 1930, M.A., 1972; B.E.E., Purdue U., 1932; LL.B., Capital U., 1939; J.D., DePaul U., 1953, Cin. U., 1954; m. Joan Ziegler, June 22, 1940; children—Timothy, John, Diana, Dennis. Admitted to Ohio bar, 1939, Ill. bar, 1946; examiner U.S. Patent Office, 1942-43; patent atty. Hazeltine Corp., N.Y.C., 1943-44; asso. with Clarence J. Loftus, Chgo., 1946-47; patent atty. AVCO Corp., Cin., 1947-66, gen. patent counsel, 1966-76; cons. on patent law, Cin., 1976—. Vice pres., trustee Ohio Hist. Soc., 1976—. Served with USNR, 1944-46. Mem. Assn. Corp. Gen. Patent Counsel, Am., Cin. (pres. 1961) patent law assns., Am. Hist. Assn. Republican. Roman Catholic. Author: Timothy S. Hogan, Ohio's Crusading Attorney General (1911-14), 1976; contbr. articles to legal jours. 45243

HOGAN, DONALD JOHN, JR., mfrs. rep. co. exec.; b. Evergreen Park, Ill., Feb. 23, 1944; s. Donald John and Jane Francis (Rumpf) H.; B.A., U. Notre Dame, 1965, M.A., 1967; m. Carolyn Vivian Smith, June 12, 1965; children—Judy, Molly, Donald III. Asst. football coach U. Notre Dame, 1964-66; mktg. analyst Shell Oil Co., Chgo., 1967; salesman Donald J. Hogan & Co., Chgo., 1967-69, pres., 1969—; pres. Maintenance of Way Supply Group of Chgo. Chmn., St. Barnabas Athletic Bd., 1969—. Mem. Am. R.R. Engring. Assn. (asso.), Chgo., Northwest maintenance of way clubs, St. Ignatius Alumni Assn. (dir.). Democrat. Roman Catholic. Clubs: Monogram (U. Notre Dame). Home: 1943 W 102d St Chicago IL 60643 Office: 327 S LaSalle St Chicago IL 60604

HOGAN, KEMPF, lawyer; b. East Grand Rapids, Mich., May 11, 1939; s. Romain Grammel and Helen Maude (Kempf) H.; B.B.A., U. Mich., 1961, M.B.A. with distinction, 1965, J.D., 1966; postgrad. Harvard U., 1962; m. Chrystine Wellman Jones, May 21, 1977. Security analyst Detroit Bank & Trust Co., Detroit, 1961-62; tax analyst Standard Oil Co. of N.J., N.Y.C., 1964; admitted to Mich. bar, 1967; asso. firm Poole Littell & Sutherland, Detroit, 1967-71, partner, 1971-76; partner firm Butzel, Long, Gust, Klein & Van Zile, 1976—. Dir. Mich. Nat. Bank-West Metro, Mich. Nat. Bank-Dearborn; asst. sec. Poole Broadcasting Co. Bd. dirs. jr. council Detroit Inst. Arts. Mem. State Bar Mich., Am., Detroit bar assns., Founders Soc. (patron), Friends U. Mich. Mus. Art, Am. Judicature Soc., Phi Kappa Phi, Beta Gamma Sigma, Beta Alpha Psi, Beta Theta Pi, Phi Delta Phi. Presbyn. Clubs: Detroit, Harvard (Detroit); Bloomfield Hills Country. Home: 500 Hawthorne Rd Birmingham MI 48009 Office: 100 W Long Lake Rd Suite 100 Bloomfield Hills MI 48013

HOGAN, TIMOTHY SYLVESTER, judge; b. Wellston, Ohio, Sept. 23, 1909; s. Timothy Sylvester and Mary (Deasy) H.; m. Evalon Roberts, Dec. 27, 1934; children—Nancy Hogan Dutton, Margaret Hogan Wyant, Timothy Sylvester; A.B., Xavier U., 1930, LL.D. (hon.), 1976; J.D., U. Cin., 1931. Admitted to Ohio bar, 1931. Asso. firm Cohen, Baron, Druffel & Hogan, Cin., 1931-66; spl. counsel Ohio atty. gen., 1936-41, 48-50; lectr. trial practice U. Cin. Law Sch., 1950-59; judge U.S. Dist. Ct., So. Dist. Ohio, Cin., 1966—. Democratic nominee Ohio atty. gen., 1946; del. at large Dem. Nat. Conv., 1952; mem. Clermont County Planning Com., 1958-60. Mem. Fed., Ohio, Clermont County, Cin. bar assns., U. Cin., Xavier U., Order of Coif, Phi Delta Phi, Musketeer Club of Xavier U. Home: 3810 Eileen Dr Cincinnati OH 45209 Office: 801 US Post Office and Court House Cincinnati OH 45202

HOGAN, WILLIAM JAMES, physician, clin. scientist; b. Berwyn, Ill., Oct. 26, 1947; s. James Joseph and Ella M. (Bucman) H.; D.Chiropractic, Morton Coll., Nat. Coll. Chiropractic, 1971. Resident diagnosis Nat. Coll. Chiropractic, Lombard, Ill., 1971-72; pvt. practice chiropractic, Detroit, 1972-73, Lombard, 1973—; asst. prof. diagnosis Nat. Coll. Chiropractic, 1973—, dir. diagnosis dept., 1977—, asst. dir. clinic, 1973—, pres. faculty council, 1976—. Mem. Am. Chiropractic Assn., Chi Rho Sigma. Roman Catholic. Home: 2411 57th Ave Cicero IL 60650 Office: 200 E Roosevelt Rd Lombard IL 60148

HOGANSON, SIDNEY J., pub. co. exec.; b. Livermore, Iowa, Mar. 18, 1918; s. Ulysses Sidney and Laura Bernadine (Hazlewood) H.; B.A., U. Iowa, 1939; m. Shirley Marie Heckman, Jan. 14, 1942; children—Russell Sidney, Victoria Lee. Asst. advt. mgr. McGraw Electric Co., 1940-47; advt. dir. Cushman Motors, 1947-49; dir. sales promotion Belnap & Thompson, 1949-51; dir. advt. and sales promotion Cahners Pub. Co., Chgo., 1957—. Bd. dirs. Bur. Bldg. Mktg. Research; mem. bus. adv. com. Bur. Labor Statistics, 1956-57. Served with USAAF, 1943-46. Decorated Bronze Star, Purple Heart, Air medal with 5 oak leaf clusters. Mem. Chgo. Federated Advt. Club, Park Forest Bowling League. Clubs: Eagles, Moose, Ill. Athletic (Chgo.); Sauk Trail Cruising; Tuckaway Golf. Contbr. articles to various jours.; editor bldg. supply newsletter, bulls. Home: 138 Chestnut St Park Forest IL 60466 Office: 5 S Wabash Ave Chicago IL 60603

HOGENDORN, DAVID HARWOOD, radio sta. exec.; b. North English, Iowa, Nov. 14, 1939; s. Carl Leslie and Bertilla Ann (Driscoll) H.; student Parson Coll., 1957-58, U. Iowa, 1958-59; m. Sharon Sue Sweeney, Jan. 2, 1965; children—David Domonic, Shawn Marie, Dustin Driscoll. Editor, Oskaloosa (Iowa) Tribune-Press, 1959-64; prodn. foreman Pioneer-Republican, Marengo, Iowa, 1965-67; owner, mgr., program dir. KNEI Radio, Waukon, 1967—; dir. Northgate Manor Nursing, Inc., Waukon; pres. Waukon Corp., H&H Devel. Co., Waukon. Mem. council Area I Health Planning Council. Mem. Nat., Iowa broadcasting assns., Nat., Iowa press assns., Waukon C. of C. (dir. 1971-75). Club: K.C. Address: Box 151 Waukon IA 52172

HOGUE, ROBERT BRYAN, optometrist; b. Hatfield, Ark., May 5, 1921; s. Joseph Henry and Ruie Beatrice (Kinnerson) Clay; O.D., Ill. Coll. Optometry, 1958; m. Maxine Ralph, Aug. 27, 1945; children—Carol Lynne, Alan Arthur, Leslie Kaye, Mark Patrick, Kellie Ann, Georgette Mary; m. 2d, Pauline Glovack, July 31, 1971. Individual practice optometry, Titusville, Fla., 1959-69, Oscoda, Mich., 1970—, Lewiston, Mich., 1971—. Served with USAF, 1943-55. Mem. C. of C. Home: 3933 W Cedar Lake Rd PO Box 421 Oscoda MI 48750 Office: 309 1/2 State St Oscoda MI 48750 also 219 Kneeland St Lewiston MI 49756

HOGUE, ROBERT DAVID, cons. actuary; b. Rock Island, Ill., Mar. 19, 1939; s. Lawrence David and Madge Marie (Carr) H.; B.S., St. Mary's Coll. of Calif.; m. Catherine Helen Ferry, June 6, 1963; children—Mary, Colleen, Kevin, John, Danelle. Actuarial trainee Occidental Life of Calif., Los Angeles, 1964-67; asst. actuary Hartford

Life Ins. Co. (Conn.), 1967-71; v.p. fin., actuary Lutheran Mutual Life, Waverly, Iowa, 1971-77; cons. actuary Milliman and Robertson, Inc., Chgo., 1977—. Fellow Soc. Actuaries; mem. Am. Acad. Actuaries. Republican. Roman Catholic. Home: Rural Route 1 Waverly IA 50677 Office: 120 S LaSalle St Chicago IL 60603

HOHAUSER, HARVEY RONALD, coll. adminstr.; b. Newark, July 25, 1943; s. Samuel and Dorothy Carol (Dunsky) H.; B.A., Fairleigh Dickinson U., 1965; M.A., Mich. State U., 1966; Ph.D., Case Western Res. U., 1971; m. Andrea Susan Krich, Apr. 4, 1966; children—Jay, Todd. Dir. Lakewood Acad. Center, instr. sociology Cleve. State U., 1968-70; chmn. community services dept., asst. prof. Union Coll. at Cranford, N.J., 1971-73; coordinator, program mgr. univ. year for action Oakland U., Rochester, Mich., 1973-75, asso. dir. Center for Community and Human Devel., 1975—; adj. prof. Cuyahoga Community Coll., Cleve., summer 1970; cons. internat. div. Harcourt, Brace, Jovanovich, N.Y.C., 1972-73; sr. vis. lectr. Mich. State U., East Lansing, 1974; cons. Nat. Adv. Council for Vocat. and Tech. Edn., 1971-73; edn. cons. State Mich. Area Agy. on Aging. Vice pres. Turning Point, 1974-75; mem. Nat. Center for Pub. Service Internship Programs; mem. fund allocation com. United Way of Pontiac, 1973—; mem. state budget com. United Way of Mich., 1976—, bd. dirs., 1977—. Mem. Am. Sociol. Assn., Am. Assn. Higher Edn., Soc. for Experiential Edn. Asso. editor Vol. Adminstrn. Home: 123 Gunder Dr Rochester MI 48063

HOHL, HARVEY EDWARD, govt. ofcl.; b. Rib Lake, Wis., July 21, 1922; s. Anthony Sylvester and Agatha (Seidel) H.; B.S., Marquette U., 1949; M.B.A., DePaul U., 1950; postgrad. U. Wis., 1953-56; m. Kathleen Murphy, June 27, 1953; children—James, Robert, Daniel, Catherine, Edward, Richard, John, Thomas. Asst. bus. mgr. Fournier Inst. Tech., Lemont, Ill., 1950-51; adminstrn. asst. to dean, asst. prof., dir. bus. research, acting dir. Center for Bus. Services, Marquette U., 1951-63; pres. Milw. Research Center, 1963—; chief economist City Milw., 1964-71; dir. Milw. Model Cities Small Bus. Tech. Assistance, 1971-72; comml. devel. officer City Milw., 1973-77; dir. bus. devel. Milwaukee County Exec. Office, 1977—. Served with USMCR, 1942-45. Mem. Am. Econ. Assn., Milw. Research Clearinghouse, Assn. Social Econs., Am. Statis. Assn. Editor: Marquette Bus. Rev., 1959-63. Home: 3259 N 97th St Milwaukee WI 53222 Office: 1744 N Farwell Ave Milwaukee WI 53202

HOHNSTEIN, DALE WILLIAM, supt. schs.; b. Hastings, Nebr., July 24, 1928; s. William and Ella (Yost) H.; A.B., Nebr. Wesleyan U., 1950; M.A., U. No. Colo., 1962; postgrad. Ind. U., 1968; m. Margaret Elizabeth Ohlsen, Oct. 7, 1958; children—Marlan, Brant. Supt. schs., Bushnell, Nebr., 1962-66, Paxton, Nebr., 1966-67, Brady, Nebr., 1969—. Mem. Nebr. Ednl. TV Adv. Council, 1966-67. Served with AUS, 1951-53. Mem. Nebr. Sch. Adminstrs. Assn. Mason (Shriner, 32 deg.). Author: No Season of Calm-The History of the Volga Germans and the Ludwig Hohnstein Family, 1974. Office: Box 68 Brady NE 69123

HOHREITER, JACK EVERT, psychology and mktg. cons.; b. St. Louis, May 30, 1918; s. Erwin Frank and Lola Mehitabelle (Neely) H.; student St. Louis U., 1935-38; B.S. cum laude, Washington U., St. Louis, 1940; postgrad. Ark. U., 1940; M.S., Butler U., 1965; postgrad. Purdue U., 1961; m. June Elise Hays, June 18, 1940; children—Joanne E. Hohreiter Roth, Janis E. Hohreiter Johnson, James E., Jeffery E. Tchr. consol. schs., Normandy, Mo., 1938-42; dep. dir. personnel, also chmn. salary and wage Fin. Center U.S. Army, Indpls., 1946-58, chief test devel. br. and devel. br. Enlisted Evaluation Center U.S. Army, Indpls., 1958-73; co-owner Annie Laurie Interiors, cons. in personnel mgmt., psychology and mktg. Vice chmn. Nat. 500 Race Rally Com., 1973-74. Served to 1st lt. AUS, 1942-46. Mem. Am. Mktg. Assn. (dir. Ind. chpt.), Nat. Vocat. Guidance Assn., Am. Personnel and Guidance Assn., Mil. Testing Assn., Sojourners, Am. Legion, Wally Byam Caravan Club, Pi Mu Epsilon, Phi Delta Kappa. Methodist (adult coordinator 1969-70). Researcher in field. Home: 4809 N Lesley St Indianapolis IN 46226 Office: 6516 N Ferguson St Indianapolis IN 46220

HOKE, GEORGE PEABODY, lawyer; b. St. Paul, Minn., Mar. 18, 1913; s. George E. and Carolyn (Peabody) H.; grad. Shattuck Sch., 1931; A.B. cum laude, Dartmouth, 1935; J.D., Yale, 1938; m. C. Elizabeth Glass, May 25, 1940 (div. Apr. 1963); children—Carolyn Gillet (Mrs. Lane W. Johnson), George, Jared Peabody. Admitted to Minn. bar, 1938, since practiced in Mpls; mem. firm Snyder, Gale, Hoke, Richards and Janes, 1943-57, Wheeler, Fredrikson, Hoke and Larson, 1957-59, Hoke and Larson, 59-75, Hoke, Roehrdanz, Bigelow and Chamberlain, Ltd., 1975—. Mem. Yale Law Sch. Grad. Bd., 1966—; mem. Republican State Central Com., 1940-50; sec., gen. counsel Animal Humane Soc. of Hennepin County; trustee Shattuck Sch., 1940-70. Mem. Am. Arbitration Assn., Minn., Hennepin County, Am. bar assns., Am. Judicature Soc. (state dir. 1950), Am. Law Inst., Beta Theta Pi, Phi Delta Phi (pres. province 1940-65). Episcopalian (vestryman 1950-65). Clubs: Minneapolis, Minneapolis Tennis, Minneapolis Saddle and Bridle, Caballeros del Norte, St. Croix Yacht, Great Lakes Crusing Assn., Yale (N.Y.), Mory's Assn. (New Haven), Swordfish and Mako Shark (New Zealand). Home: 1945 Kenwood Pkwy Minneapolis MN 55405 Office: 212 Ridgewood Minneapolis MN 55403

HOKENSTAD, MERL CLIFFORD, JR., univ. dean; b. Norfolk, Nebr., July 21, 1936; s. Merl Clifford and Flora Diane (Christian) H.; B.A. summa cum laude, Augustana Coll., 1958; postgrad. Durham (Eng.) U., 1958-59; M.S.W., Columbia U., 1962; Ph.D., Brandeis U., 1969; m. Dorothy Jean Tarrell, June 24, 1962; children—Alene Ann, Laura Rae, Marta Lynn. Staff asso. Lower East Side Neighborhoods Assn., N.Y.C., 1962-64; community planning asso. United Community Services, Sioux Falls, S.D., 1964-66; instr. Augustana Coll., Sioux Falls, 1964-66; research asso. Ford Found. Project on Community Planning for Elderly, Brandeis U., Waltham, Mass., 1966-67; dir., prof. sch. social work Western Mich. U., Kalamazoo, 1968-74; dean, prof. sch. applied social scis. Case Western Res. U., Cleve., 1974—; vis. prof. Inst. Sociology, Stockholm, Sweden, 1978; chmn. U.S. com. XVIII Internat. Congress of Schs. of Social Work, 1976; mem. Cleve. Internat. Programs for Youth Workers and Social Workers, Inc., trustee, 1974—; mem. rev. com. Nat. Inst. Alcoholism and Alcohol Abuse, 1974—; mem. edn. and tng. task force Mich. Office Drug Abuse and Alcoholism, 1972-73; mem. com. on community mental health services standards Mich. Dept. Mental Health, 1972-73. Del. assembly United Torch Services, Cleve., 1974—; trustee Alcohol Services Cleve., Inc., 1977—. Named Social Worker of Year, Nat. Assn. Social Workers, 1974; Gerontology tng. grantee, 1967; Rotary Found. fellow, 1958-59. Mem. Acad. Certified Social Workers, Am. Assn. Higher Edn., Am. Sociol. Assn., Council on Social Work Edn., Am. Pub. Welfare Assn., Internat. Assn. Schs. Social Work, Council on Social Work Edn. (del. 1972-75, 77, chmn. ann. program meeting 1973, chmn. com. on nat. legislation and adminstrv. policy 1975), Internat. Council Social Welfare, Nat. Assn. Social Workers, Nat. Conf. Social Welfare, Am. Pub. Welfare Assn., World Future Soc. Club: Men's City (Cleve.). Contbr. articles to profl. jours. Home: 2917 Weymouth Rd Shaker Heights OH 44120 Office: 2035 Abington Rd Cleveland OH 44106

HOLBERT, JOHN EDWARD, farmer; b. Ewing, Mo., Aug. 27, 1930; s. Aura Huse and Margaret Catherine (Daggs) H.; grad. high sch.; m. Lois Jeanette Blake, Oct. 18, 1969; 1 son, John Eric. Owner, Holbert Stock Farm, Ewing, 1948—; dir. Lewis County REA. Served with AUS, 1954-56. Mason, Kiwanian. Address: RD 1 Ewing MO 63440

HOLBROOK, JAMES LANSING, airline pilot; b. Evanston, Ill., Oct. 29, 1942; s. Francis Wayland and Katherine (Colp) H.; B.S., U. Ill., 1964, C.P.A., 1965; M.B.A., Northwestern U., 1965. Auditor, Price Waterhouse & Co., Chgo., 1965-66; budget analyst United Air Lines, Chgo., 1966-69, flight engr., 1969—, mem. pilot's speakers bur., 1969—. Served with AUS, 1966-67. Mem. Air Line Pilots Assn., Phi Gamma Delta. Club: Stick and Rudder (pres. 1973-74, dir. 1969—) (Waukegan). Home: 412 N Green Bay Rd Waukegan IL 60085 Office: United Air Lines PO Box 66100 Chicago IL 60666

HOLCOMB, ALBERT EUGENE, orthodontist; b. Ottumwa, Iowa, May 26, 1914; s. Albert Eugene and Clara D. (Rogers) H.; student Parsons Coll., 1932-35; B.A., U. Iowa, 1935, M.A., 1941, D.D.S., 1950, M.S., 1955; m. Della Mae Stender, June 16, 1937; 1 son, Albert Eugene, III. Tchr. Marengo (Iowa) High Sch., 1936-39, Oak St. Jr. High Sch., Burlington, Iowa, 1939-43; instr. U. Iowa, Iowa City, 1950-54, asst. prof., 1954-55; practice orthodontics, Cedar Rapids, Iowa, 1955—. Mem. bd. Linn County chpt. A.R.C., 1969—. Served with USNR, 1943-45. Mem. Omicron Kappa Upsilon. Elk. Home: 353 Trailridge Rd Cedar Rapids IA 52403 Office: 110 14th St Cedar Rapids IA 52402

HOLDEMAN, RICHARD WENDELL, II, consumer goods mfg. co. exec., psychologist; b. South Bend, Ind., Feb. 19, 1938; s. Richard Wendell and Lillian Estella (Scheib) H.; B.A., DePauw U., 1960; M.S., Purdue U., 1962, Ph.D., 1965; m. Diane Marilynn Grant, Aug. 26, 1961; children—Richard Brewster, Robert Grant, Thomas Edward, John William. Research fellow, teaching asst., admissions counselor Purdue U., 1961-64; research scientist Am. Inst. Research, U. Pitts., 1964-65; v.p. personnel Cosco, Inc., Columbus, Ind., 1965—; instr. Purdue U. at Columbus, 1966-67. Bd. dirs. Opportunity, Inc., 1969-75, pres., 1973-74; bd. dirs. United Devel. Services, 1973-76, Bartholomew County Jr. Achievement, 1969-72, Bartholomew County Hosp. Found., 1971-75; bd. dirs. Children, Inc., 1973—, v.p., 1977; exec. bd. Smith Parent Tchr. Orgn., 1976—, pres., 1977; trustee Columbus Coll., 1970-71. Mem. Am. Psychol. Assn., Am. Soc. Personnel Adminstrn. (accredited exec. in personnel), Am. Soc. Tng. and Devel., Midwest Coll. Placement Assn., Sigma Xi, Psi Chi. Purdue Research Found. grantee, 1964; certified pvt. practice psychologist, Ind. Author: The Evolution of Veterinary Medicine in Indiana, 1965; also Project TALENT Studies. Home: 1825 Park Valley Dr Columbus IN 47201 Office: 2525 State St Columbus IN 47201

HOLDEN, RAYMOND FRANCIS, JR., physician; b. St. Louis, Feb. 2, 1910; s. Raymond Francis and Fern (Reynolds) H.; student Central Coll., Fayette, Mo., 1926-29; B.S., Washington U., St. Louis, 1933, M.D., 1933; m. Gertrude Elsbeth Kies, Aug. 1, 1936; children—John Philip, Rebecca Rae, Raymond Francis. Intern, Barnes Hosp., St. Louis, 1933-35; resident Rockefeller Inst. Hosp., 1935-36; practice medicine specializing in internal medicine, St. Louis, 1937-56; instr. clin. medicine Washington U., 1940-56; med. dir. Mallinckrodt Chem. Works, St. Louis, 1948-53, Wichita div. Boeing Airplane Co., 1956-58; practice medicine specializing in internal medicine, Wichita, Kans., 1958-78; mem. staff Wesley Med. Center, Wichita, 1958—; cons. VA Regional Center. Served to lt. col. AUS, flight surgeon AAF, 1943-46. Diplomate Am. Bd. Internal Medicine. Fellow A.C.P., Am. Geriatrics Soc.; mem. Central Soc. Clin. Research, Harvey Soc. N.Y., Am. Heart Assn., Sigma Xi. Congregationalist. Contbr. articles to med. jours. Home: 262 S Brookside St Wichita KS 67218

HOLECEK, ALLEN ROLAND, designer; b. Berwyn, Ill., Sept. 30, 1944; s. Roland and Sophia (Antzak) H.; m. Doris Elaine Peterson, Feb. 3, 1967; children—Thomas, Ruth; Asso. Sci. in Elec. Engring., Wis. Sch. Engring., Madison, 1964. Staff engr. KDAL-TV, Duluth, Minn., 1967-69, Digital Equipment Corp., Maynard, Mass., 1969-71; devel. engr. Ingersoll Milling Machine Co., Rockford, Ill., 1971-72, chief electronics engr. W.F. and John Barnes, Rockford, 1972-74; owner, operator Creative Controls, Rockton, Ill., 1974—; dir. Midgetronics, Inc., Oregon, Wis. Trustee, Harrison Ch. Mem. Amateur Radio Club. Patentee boolean computer. Office: 15929 Hauley Rd Rockton IL 61072

HOLEWINSKI, FELIX WARNER, educator, historian; b. Milw., Aug. 7, 1943; s. Felix and Celia (Grosman) H.; B.A., Marquette U., 1966; M.A., 1971; D.A., U. N.D., 1978. Tchr. social studies Dominican High Sch., Milw., 1966-67; tchr. history, polit. sci., Webster Sr. High Sch., Webster, Wis., 1967; instr. history U. Wis., Superior, 1975-76, chmn. social studies dept. 1967-77; peer evaluator Webster Sr. High Sch., 1976-77. Chmn. Burnett County Republican Com., Wis., 1968-70; del. to Wis. Rep. Conv., LaCrosse, 1968-69. Recipient teaching assistantship, U. of N.D., 1972-73, teaching intern fellowship, 1975-76. Chmn. St. John the Baptist Parish Council, 1977; mem. Superior Diocesan Pastoral Council, 1976. Mem. Nat., Wis. edn. assns., NW Wis. Educators, Am., Polish Am. hist. assns., The Heraldry Soc. of Can., The Heraldry Soc. of Gt. Britain, Augustan Soc., Noble Co. of the Rose, 13th Internat. Congress on Geneological and Heraldic Sci., Hereditary Order Armigerious Augustians, Wis. Horse Racing Assn., Polish Nobility Assn., Phi Alpha Theta, Pi Gamma Mu. Roman Catholic. Clubs: Royal Order of Piast (Knight), Sovereign Hospitaller Order of St. John (Knight), Military and Hospitaller Order of St. Lazarus of Jerusalem (mem. companion). Contbr. research in field. Home: Rural Route 2 Webster WI 54893

HOLIGA, LUDOMIL ANDREW, metall. engr.; b. Dayton, Ohio, Dec. 7, 1920; s. Andrew and Antonia Margaret (Sefcek) H.; Engr. asso., Sinclair Coll., 1948; B.Sc., Calgary Coll. Tech., 1975, M.M.E., 1976; m. Aryetta Lillian Mernedakis, Feb. 6, 1960; children—David, Carol, Millard, Timothy, Michael. Engr. designer Wright Patterson AFB, Ohio, 1941-54; contract designer Product Design Services, Inc., Dayton, Ohio, 1955-60; with Dayton Progress Corp., 1961—, dir. corp. devel., 1972-73, dir. research and tech. edn., 1974—. Served with USAAF, 1942-45, AUS, 1951-52. Certified mfg. engr. Mem. Soc. Mfg. Engrs. (chmn. standards com. 1963-72), Ohio Research and Devel. Found., Foremans Club, Am. Metal Stamping Assn. Lutheran. Research on cutting clearances for perforating metals in stamping dies. Home: 2025 Oak Tree Dr E Kettering OH 45440 Office: 500 Progress Rd Dayton OH 45449

HOLIHAN, FRANCIS LEONARD, health care adminstr.; b. Syracuse, N.Y., Nov. 15, 1918; s. Thomas Daniel and Agnes (Maroney) H.; student Am. Inst. Banking, 1936-37, Syracuse U., 1937-40, Am. U., 1946-48; B.A., U. Md., 1960; m. Justyne Williamson, Dec. 15, 1943; children—Francis Leonard, Daniel Patrick, Patricia Kay, Michael Stephen, Kathleen Marie. Mgr. div. time sales dept. 1st Trust and Deposit Co., Syracuse, 1936-41; mgr. mortgage loan dept. Fausett & Co., realtors, Little Rock, 1946; served with med. dept. U.S. Army, 1941, advanced through grades to maj., 1945; discharged; returned as maj., Med. Adminstrv. Corps Air Transport Command U.S. Air Force, 1946, advanced through grades to col., 1959; various med. staffing and edn. positions, 1946-56; chief med. liason selection div. Hdqrs., Washington, 1956-60, chief plans and ops. support Hdqrs 15th Air Force, SAC, 1960-64; med. service, hosp. adminstr. Hdqrs 16th Air Force, SAC, Spain, 1964-67, dir. health services mgmt. Air Force Logistics Command, Ohio, 1967-72, ret., 1972; asso. exec. dir. Miami Valley Health Systems Agency, Dayton, Ohio, 1973—; mem. biomed. engring. edn. advisory com. Wright State U., 1974-75; mem. advisory com. Central Service Community, Sisters of the Precious Blood, Dayton, 1975-77. Past pres. Wright Brothers chpt. Armed Forces Mgmt. Assn., 1971. Decorated Legion of Merit. Mem. Assn. Mil. Surgeons U.S., Am. Assn. Hosp. Planning. Fed. Health Care Execs. Inst. Alumni Assn., Ret. Officers Assn., Am. Defense Preparedness Assn., Nat. Histo. Soc. Roman Catholic. Clubs: USAF Officers. Home: 3456 S Dakar Dr Dayton OH 45431 Office: Suite 1349 32 N Main St Dayton OH 45402

HOLINGER, PAUL HENRY, physician, surgeon; b. Chgo., Mar. 13, 1906; s. Jacques Ernst and Cora (Lange) H.; B.S., U. Chgo., 1928; M.S., Northwestern U., 1931, M.D., 1932; m. Julia Campbell Drake, June 26, 1940; children—Lauren Drake, William Jacques, Paul Campbell, Richard Lange. Intern, Albany (N.Y.) Gen. Hosp., 1932-33; resident in otolaryngology U. Ill., 1933-34; asst. in otolaryngology Temple U., Phila., 1934-35; attending bronchologist Children's Meml. Hosp., Chgo., 1936—; instr. to prof. otolaryngology U. Ill., Chgo., 1935—, emeritus since 1974; attending laryngologist St. Luke Hosp., Chgo., 1936-57; prof. Rush Presbyn. St. Luke Med. Center, Chgo., 1957-74, emeritus, 1974—; practice medicine specializing in laryngology, Chgo., 1936—; cons. in field. Chmn. bd. govs. Inst. Medicine Chgo., 1961-66; pres. Ill. div. Am. Cancer Soc., 1965-66; bd. dirs. Swiss Benevolent Soc. Chgo.; trustee Chgo. Med. Sch.; bd. govs. Orchestral Assn. Chgo.; bd. dirs. Am. Bd. Otolaryngology. Fellow A.C.S. (regent 1964-73), Royal Coll. Surgeons Ireland (hon.); mem. AMA, Am. Coll. Chest Physicians, Am. Acad. Ophthalmology and Otolaryngology, Biol. Photog. Assn., Am. Council Otolaryngology, Collegium Otolaryngologicum (hon.), Sigma Xi. Clubs: Univ. Chgo., Casino. Author: (with others) Atlas of Otolaryngology, 1969; editorial bd. nat., internat. med. jours.; contbr. articles to profl. publs. Home: 1500 N Lake Shore Dr Chicago IL 60610 Office: 700 N Michigan Ave Suite 401 Chicago IL 60611

HOLIWELL, GENE ANDREW, realtor; b. Wewoka, Okla., July 24, 1928; s. Wakes and Lena Mae (Matthews) H.; B.S., Kans. State U., 1954, M.S., 1955, postgrad. guidance and counseling, 1976—; m. Bennie Ruth Ware, Oct. 12, 1963; children—Jean, Bradford, Joy. Instr. recreation, Norristown (Pa.) State Hosp., 1956-61; dir. recreation Pennhurst State Sch., Spring City, Pa., 1961-73; civil def. edn. adviser Dept. Edn. Pa., 1973; asst. dir. admissions Millersville (Pa.) State Coll., 1973; res. liaison officer Command and Gen. Staff Coll., Fort Leavenworth, Kans., 1973-77; asso. real estate sales Thorne Realty, Lansing, Kans. Mem. Sch. Bd. Unified Sch. Dist. 207 Fort Leavenworth, Kans., 1974-78. Served with AUS, 1946-49, to col. USAR, 1976—. Fellow Nat. Therapeutic Recreation Soc. (exec. com. 1963-67); mem. Kans. State U. Alumni Assn. (life), Am. Personnel and Guidance Assn., Res. Officers Assn., Assn. U.S. Army. Episcopalian. Clubs: Masons, Lions. Home: 321 Fairlane St Lansing KS 66043

HOLL, JUERGEN FRANZ, radiologist; b. Wilhelmshaven, Germany, Aug. 15, 1934; s. Ernst F. and Kaethe L. (Kock) H.; came to U.S., 1963, naturalized, 1971; D.D.S., U. Hamburg (Germany), 1960; M.D., U. Frankfurt (Germany), 1963; m. Metta Schlotel, Jan. 3, 1962; children—Joern, Tim. Practice medicine specializing in radiology and nuclear medicine, Clinton, Iowa, 1967—; chief of staff Mercy Hosp., Clinton, 1972-75. Diplomate Am. Bd. Radiology, Am. Bd. Nuclear Medicine. Mem. Clinton County Iowa Med. Soc. (pres. 1971). Republican. Lutheran. Office: Mercy Hospital Clinton IA 52732

HOLL, WALTER JOHN, bldg. and interior designer; b. Richardton, N.D., May 14, 1922; s. John and Rose Mary (Raskop) H.; student architecture Internat. Corr. Sch., 1946-47, structural engring., 1959; m. Eleanor Mary Triervieler, Jan. 23, 1943; children—Mark Walter, Michael John, Randall Gregory, Linda Michelle, Timothy James, John Walter. Steel detailer, estimator E.J. Voggenthaler Co., Dubuque, Iowa, 1941-42; engr., methods developer Marinship Corp., Sausalito, Calif., 1942-44; partner Holl & Everly, Dubuque, 1946-47; prin. Holl Designing Co. or W. Holl & Assos., Dubuque, San Francisco, 1947—; cons. Clarke Coll. Art Students, Dubuque, 1953-61. Mem. Dubuque Housing Rehab. Commn., 1975-77, chmn., 1976-77; comdr. USCG Aux., 1976-78, Flotilla, Dubuque. Served with AUS, 1944-46. Mem. Am. Inst. Bldg. Design (recipient awards 1968, 69, 73), Mchts. Mfrs. Club (Chgo.), Am. Soc. Interior Designers (asso.). Roman Catholic. Clubs: Dubuque Golf and Country, Julien Yacht (commodore 1974-75). Patentee castered pallet. Home: 655 Sunset Ridge Dubuque IA 52001 also 41 Gran Via Alamo CA 94507 Office: 655 Sunset Ridge Dubuque IA 52001 also 5735 Diamond Heights Blvd San Francisco CA 94122

HOLLAND, GORDON WILLIAM, telephone co. exec.; b. Harvey, N.B., Can., July 28, 1929; s. William J. and Virginia A. (Wilson) H.; children—Janis, Nancy, Richard; B. Commerce, U. Man., 1951. With Gt. West Life Assurance Co., Winnipeg, Man., 1951-54; underwriting supr. Man. Hosp. Services Assn., 1954-58; chmn. Man. Hosp. Commn., 1965-68; sec. mgmt. com. Cabinet, Govt. of Man., 1968-74; chmn., gen. mgr. Man. Telephone System, Winnipeg, 1974—; dir. Trans-Can. Telephone System, Telesat Can. Bd. dirs. St. Boniface Gen. Hosp., 1974—; bd. govs. Canadian Coll. Health Service Execs. Recipient Can. Centennial medal. Mem. Telephone Pioneers Am. (Man. chpt. 50). Club: Kiwanis of S. Winnipeg. Office: 489 Empress St Winnipeg MB R3C OA2 Canada

HOLLAND, JOHN MADISON, physician, med. adminstr.; b. Holden, W.Va., Oct. 7, 1927; s. Ophia I. and Lou V. (Elliott) H.; B.S. with High Distinction, Eastern Ky. U., Richmond, 1949; M.D., U. Louisville, 1952; m. Mary Louise Bourne, Sept. 2, 1950; children—Dave, Steve, Nancy. Intern St. Joseph Infirmary, Louisville, 1952-53; practice gen. medicine Springfield, Ill., 1955—; med. dir. St. John's Hosp., Springfield, 1971—; clin. asst. prof. family practice So. Ill. U. Sch. Medicine, Springfield, 1975—; project med. dir. Springfield Paramedic Program, 1976—. Mem. Gov.'s prayer breakfast com., 1974—. Bd. dirs. Central Ill. Found. Med. Care. Served to capt., M.C., USAF, 1953-55. Diplomate Am. Bd. Family Practice (charter). Fellow Am. Acad. Family Physicians; mem. Ill. Acad. Family Physicians (pres. 1975—), Christian Med. Soc., Sangamon County Med. Soc. (sec. 1970-71), Alpha Omega Alpha, Phi Chi. Baptist (moderator ch.). Home: 2131 Lindsay St Springfield IL 62704 Office: 700 N 7th St Springfield IL 62702

HOLLAND, NANCY LYNN, counselor; b. Chgo., Sept. 10, 1938; d. Cyrus Elwood and Mary Catherine (Richardson) Holland; B.A., Lake Forest (Ill.) Coll., 1961; M.Ed., DePaul U., Chgo., 1968. Sec., Pullman Standard, Chgo., 1961-62; tchr. Willa Cather Sch., Chgo., 1964-67; counselor John Mills Sch., Elmwood Park, Ill., 1967-68, Elm and Elmwood Schs., 1967-70; counselor Shahonee Jr. High Sch., Northbrook, Ill., 1970-72, Wood Oaks Jr. High Sch., 1972—;

developer sch. counseling programs. Mem. Am., Ill. personnel guidance assns., Am., Ill. sch. counselors assns., NEA, Ill. Edn. Assn., Ill. Elementary Sch. Counselors Assn., Nat. Sch. Counselors Assn., Psi Chi, Kappa Delta Pi, Alpha Phi. Home: 21345 W York Ct Kildeer IL 60047

HOLLAND, RAY LAURIMORE, accountant; b. Rich Hill, Mo., Sept. 10, 1916; s. Ralph Lee and Florence Grace (Horton) H.; A.B., U. Mo., 1937; certificate advanced mgmt. U. Chgo., 1960; m. Thasia G. Field; children—Dennis L., Laurel M., Ray C. Accountant, Arthur Andersen & Co., Chgo. and Seattle, 1940-57, sr. mgr., 1947-57; controller Transunion Corp., Chgo., 1957-65; pvt. practice accounting, Arlington Heights, Ill., 1966—; pres. Holland & Asso., Inc., Arlington Heights, 1972—; dir. Dytec./Central, Inc. Bd. dirs. Christopher Found. C.P.A., Kans., Ill., Wash., Wis., Ohio. Mem. Am. Inst. C.P.A.'s. Home: 1501 Dartmouth Ln Deerfield IL 60015 Office: 121 S Wilke St Arlington Heights IL 60005

HOLLANDER, WILLIAM RALPH, periodontist; b. Evanston, Ill., Sept. 12, 1934; s. Ralph Charles and Agnes (Redfern) H.; D.D.S., U. Iowa, 1958; M.S., U. Nebr., 1967; m. Carol Blessing, June 19, 1955; children—William, Scott, Tod, Vicki. Gen. practice dentistry Sioux City, Iowa, 1958-65, specializing in periodontics, Sioux City, 1967—; chmn. dental assisting program Western Iowa Tech. Coll., 1972; faculty U. Nebr., 1968-69, U. S.D., 1969—. Republican precinct committeeman, 1962-65. Bd. dirs. Delta Dental Plan Iowa, 1975—. Fellow Internat. Coll. Dentistry; mem. Am., Iowa (trustee 1971-76, mem. council on legislation 1973-76, mem. ad interim com. 1973-76, mem. adv. bd. for dental hygienists 1975-76, del. to Am. Dental Assn. 1975—, v.p. 1976, pres. elect 1977), N.W. Dist. (sec. 1963-71, trustee 1971-76) dental assns., Sioux City Dental Soc. (pres. 1974-75), Am. Soc. Periodontists, Am. Acad. Periodontology, Dist. Dental Soc. (sec.), Iowa, Western socs. periodontists, Pierre Fauchard Acad., Psi Omega. Methodist. Mason (Shriner), Kiwanian (pres., dir.). Contbr. to Orban's Periodontics, 1968. Home: 9 W 37th St Pl Sioux City IA 51104 Office: 422 Frances Bldg Sioux City IA 51101

HOLLANDSWORTH, WILLIAM JOSEPH, engring. co. exec.; b. Konnarock, Va., May 26, 1921; s. Guy Melvin and Lillian Fay (Chambers) H.; student Berea Coll., 1938-40, Walton Sch. Commerce, 1940-42, State U. Iowa, 1943-44; B.E.E., Ill. Inst. Tech., 1948; m. Janice Marjorie Kott, Apr. 25, 1942; children—Kathleen Hollandsworth Tanner, Patricia Hollandsworth Winkler, Carol. Mfg. engr. Western Elec. Corp., Chgo., 1945-49; electronic engr. Argonne Nat. Lab., Chgo., 1949-54; staff engr. IBM Corp., Owego, N.Y., 1958-60; project engr. Mo. Research Labs., St. Louis, 1954-58, 60-63, v.p., 1963-76; dir. engring. Hunter Engring. Co., St. Louis, 1976—. Served with AUS, 1942-45. Mem. IEEE. Presbyterian. Club: Masons. Researcher devel. specialized airborne computers, air traffic environment simulation systems, auto service systems. Home: 2425 Oak Springs Ln Saint Louis MO 63131 Office: 11250 Hunter Dr Bridgeton MO 63044

HOLLEB, DORIS BERNSTEIN, economist, urban affairs cons.; b. N.Y.C., Oct. 26, 1922; B.A. magna cum laude, Hunter Coll., 1942; M.A. in Econs., Harvard, 1947; postgrad. U. Chgo., 1959-60, 65-66; m. Marshall M. Holleb, Oct. 15, 1944; children—Alan, Gordon, Paul. Research asst. Harvard Bus. Sch., 1942-43; economist, research div., internat. sect. Fed. Res. Bd., Washington, 1943-44; asst. editor Lake Placid News, 1945; research cons. U.S. Mut. Ins. Assn., 1953; teaching asst. Ill. Inst. Tech., 1954-55; free lance journalist, 1955-63; econ. cons. Chgo. Dept. Devel. and Planning, 1963-64; research asso. Center for Urban Studies, U. Chgo., 1966—, dir. Met. Inst., 1973—, mem. adv. council Adlai E. Stevenson Center for Internat. Studies, 1975—; cons. NSF, OMB, HUD, HEW, Fed. Res. Bd., Ill. Bd. Higher Edn. Mem. citizens adv. com. Ill. Bd. Higher Edn., 1965-71, Ill. Dept. Edn., 1971-74; chmn. Frances W. Parker Sch. Ednl. Council, 1965-71, chmn. parents com., 1959-61; mem. acad. com. Center for Study Democratic Instns., 1975—; mem. Northeastern Ill. Planning Commn., 1973—, sec., mem. exec. com., 1974—, chmn. housing sub-com., 1973-74, by laws sub-com., 1975—, forcasting sub-com., 1976—; bd. dirs. Bright New City Com., Know Your Chgo. Com.; trustee Adlai E. Stevenson Inst., 1972-75; mem. vis. com. Oriental Inst., U. Chgo.; Ill. rep. Conf. on Human Settlements, 1976. Recipient Founders Day award Loyola U., 1974. Mem. Am. Econ. Assn., Am. Soc. Planning Ofcls., Am. Inst. Planners, AAAS, Phi Beta Kappa. Club: Harvard-Radcliffe (bd. dirs.) (Chgo.). Author: Social And Economic Information for Urban Planning, 1968; Colleges and the Urban Poor: The Role of Public Higher Education in Community Service, 1972. Mem. editorial bd. Ill. Issues. Contbr. articles to profl. jours.

HOLLEB, MARSHALL MAYNARD, lawyer; b. Chgo., Dec. 25, 1916; s. A. Paul and Sara (Zaretsky) H.; B.A., U. Wis., 1937; M.B.A., Harvard U., 1939, Indsl. Adminstr., 1941, J.D., 1942; m. Doris Barbara Bernstein, Oct. 15, 1944; children—Alan Reed, Gordon Philip, Paul Daniel. Admitted to Ill. bar, 1947; since practiced in Chgo., partner firm Holleb, Gerstein & Glass, 1951—; chmn. bd. Urban Assos., Inc.; dir. Acorn Fund; vis. lectr. Northwestern U., U. Chgo., 1971. Mem. Ill. appeal bd. SSS, 1961-63; mem. Ill. State Council on Aging, 1961—, chmn., 1973—, chmn. tech. rev. com., 1969—; del. White House Conf. on Aging, 1971; bd. dirs. Hull House, Mus. Contemporary Art; trustee Francis W. Parker Sch., Oriental Inst., U. Chgo, Landmarks Preservation Council; bd. govs. Inst. Psychoanalysis. Served to 1st lt. AUS; PTO. Mem. Am., Internat., Fed., Ill., Chgo. bar assns., Am. Soc. Internat. Law, Am. Inst. Planners, Nat. Assn. Housing and Redevel. Ofcls., Urban Land Inst., Lambda Alpha. Contbr. articles on aging and taxation to profl. jours. Home: 2650 Lakeview Ave Chicago IL 60614 Office: One IBM Plaza Chicago IL 60611

HOLLERAN, BRENT JOSEPH, cardiovascular thoracic surgeon, clin. adminstr.; b. Clinton, Iowa, June 11, 1935; s. Paul B. and Lucille (Lynch) H.; B.A., U. Iowa, 1957, M.D., 1960; m. Johannah Dusseault, Sept. 7, 1963; children—David, Daniel, Johannah. Intern, Cornell Med. Center N.Y. Hosp., N.Y.C., 1960-61, resident in cardiovascular and thoracic surgery, 1961-69, instr. surgery, 1968-69; practice medicine specializing in cardiovascular and thoracic surgery, Dubuque, Iowa, 1969—; chief surg. staff Mercy Med. Center, Dubuque, 1970-76, chief, med. staff, 1977-78. Served to capt. USAF, 1962-63. Diplomate Am. Bd. Surgery, Am. Bd. Thoracic Surgery. Fellow A.C.S. Contbr. articles in thoracic surgery to med. jours. Office: 1000 Langworthy St Dubuque IA 52001

HOLLINGSWORTH, DAVID KIETH, human relations cons.; b. Evansville, Ind., Mar. 1, 1946; s. Carl Joseph and Jean Doris (Hertwick) H.; B.Sc., Marion Coll., 1970; M.Sc., Ind. Univ., 1973; M.Sc., Purdue U., 1977; doctoral candidate Syracuse U., 1 dau., Christina Lee. Clin. dir. Cognition House Res. Center, Indpls., 1975; psychologist Marion County (Ind.) Prosecutor's Office, Indpls., 1975-76; dir. Profl. Human Relations, Inc., Indpls., 1976—; lectr. Ind. U., Purdue U., Indpls. Mem. Am., Ind. personnel and guidance assns., Am. Rehab. Counseling Assn., Am. Psychol. Assn., Assn. Humanistic Psychologists. Club: Hort. Contbr. articles in field to profl. jours. Home: 666 E 66th St Indianapolis IN 46220

HOLLIS, HAROLD BINKLEY, ins. agy. exec.; b. Princeton, Ind., July 18, 1906; s. John S. and Jessie B. (Binkley) H.; B.S., Purdue U., 1928; m. Martha Jane Gehlman, Oct. 15, 1937; children—Richard, John, Barbara (Mrs. John McWalter), Kenneth L. and Nancy J. (twins). Engr., Ill. Hwy. Dept., Paris, 1928, bridge engr., Springfield, 1931-42; civil engr. Mo. Pacific R.R., Nevada, Mo., 1929; purchasing agt. Remington Rand Co., Springfield, Ill., 1942-45; owner ins. agy., Springfield, 1945-73; pres. Hollis-Neff Ins., Inc., Springfield, 1973—. Mgr. baseball team Little League, 1952-54, Pony League, Colt League, 1954-56. Mason (Shriner). Club: Springfield Purdue Alumni (pres. 1937-38, 41-42, 49-50). Home: 1206 W Monroe St Springfield IL 62704 Office: 1001 W Lawrence St Springfield IL 62704

HOLLOWAY, DONALD PHILLIP, librarian; b. Akron, Ohio, Feb. 18, 1928; s. Harold Shane and Dorothy Gayle (Ryder) H.; B.S. in Commerce, Ohio U., Athens, 1950; LL.B., U. Akron, 1955; M.A., Kent State U., 1962. Title examiner Bankers Guarantee Title & Trust Co., Akron, 1950-54; accountant Robinson Clay Product Co., Akron, 1955-60; librarian Akron Pub. Library, 1962-69, head fine arts and music div., 1969-71, sr. librarian, 1972—. Payroll treas. Akron Symphony Orch., 1957-61; treas. Friends Library Akron and Summit County, 1970-72. Mem. Music Library Assn., Am., Ohio, Akron bar assns., Ohio Library Assn., ALA, Nat. Trust for Historic Preservation, Soc. Archtl. Historians, Coll. Art Assn. Club: Nat. Lawyers (Washington). Home: 601 Nome Ave Akron OH 44320

HOLLOWAY, GALE ALLWIN, agrl. engr.; b. Joliet, Ill., Mar. 3, 1944; s. Allwin L. and Eleanor R. (Olson) H.; B.S., Colo. State U., 1968, M.S., 1969; m. Madonna E. Hook, Nov. 30, 1974. Design engr. Internat. Harvester Co., Hinsdale, Ill., 1969-74, project engr., 1974-77, product devel. engr., 1977—. Registered profl. engr., Ill. Mem. Nat., Ill. socs. profl. engrs., Am. Soc. Agrl. Engrs. (chmn. Chgo. sect. 1975, chmn. Ill.-Wis. region 1977), Fluid Power Soc. Home: 9 Berkley St Joliet IL 60432 Office: Internat Harvester Co Hinsdale IL 60521

HOLLOWAY, JAMES ARTHUR, real estate broker; b. Poplar Bluff, Mo., Dec. 7, 1917; s. Edward Otto and Dora (Meadows) H.; B.S. in Edn., S.W. Mo. Coll., 1942; m. Etta Ruth Holloway, children—Bruce Edward, Gary Ira, Keith Arthur, Donna E. Tchr., coach Bradleyville (Mo.) High Sch., 1942; pres. Poplar Land Corp., 1960—; pres. Oakshore, Inc., Poplar Bluff, Reliable Ozark Land, Poplar Bluff; v.p. Lingo Land Inc., Poplar Bluff, 1973—. Mem. Com. to Arrange Parking in Poplar Bluff (Mo.), 1960. Trustee Three Rivers Community Coll., 1966-74. Served with USAAF, 1942-45. Mem. C. of C., Am. Legion, VFW, Amvets (state comdr. 1973-74), Bd. Realtors Butler County (pres. 1973-74), Mo. Assn. Realtors (dir.). Club: WestWood Country. Address: Holloway Bldg Poplar Bluff MO 63901

HOLLOWAY, LAWRENCE MILTON, osteo. physician; b. Kirksville, Mo., Sept. 8, 1913; s. Edward Lee and Vetta (Elmore) H.; student Kirksville Bus. Coll., 1933, NE Mo. U., 1933-36; D.O., Kirksville Coll. Osteopathy and Surgery, 1940; M.D., U. Santo Tomas, 1951; m. Roena Jane Williams, Dec. 24, 1935; children—Lawrence Milton, Lynette Jane. Intern, A.S.O. Hosp., Kirksville, 1939-40, Detroit Osteo. Hosp., 1940-42; gen. practice osteo. medicine, Byron, Mich., 1940-56, specializing in endocrinology, Flint, Mich., 1956—; examining physician Am. Pres. Life Ins. Co.; fellow in surgery Am. Coll. Osteo. Physicians and Surgeons, Byron, 1940-56; instr. Physiol. Chemistry Lab., Kirksville Coll. Osteopathy and Surgery, 1938-40; founder, chief surgeon, chief staff Lawrence Osteo. Hosp., Byron, 1942-56; dir., bus. mgr. L. M. Holloway Clinic; plastic and cosmetic surgeon Flint Gen. Hosp. Pres., L.M. Holloway Mfg. Co., Byron, 1944-47; v.p. Owosso Finance Co. (Mich.), 1952-56, pres., 1956—; adv. bd. Hamilton Internat. Life Ins. Co. Physician, Byron High Sch., 1940-54. Adviser Swartz Creek chpt. Boy Scouts Am.; sec. Orgn. for World Wide Postgrad. Study. Fellow Am. Soc. Clin. Hypnosis (life); mem. Am., Genesee County osteo. assns., Mich. Assn. Osteo. Physicians and Surgeons, Am. Coll. Osteo. Surgeons, Am. Soc. Endocrinology and Nutrition, Am. Soc. Clin. Arthritis, Kirksville Osteo. Alumni Assn., Future Farmers Am. (life), Psi Sigma Alpha. Clubs: Masons (32 deg.), Shriners, Elks, 750 (pres. Mich. chpt. 1958-59, 61, 64-66). Home: 10283 Corunna Rd Swartz Creek MI 48473 Office: G 5200 Corunna Rd Flint MI 48504

HOLLOWAY, WILLIAM JIMMERSON, coll. adminstr.; b. Smithfield, Va., May 6, 1917; s. Arnett Jimmerson and Lucy Pernell (White) H.; B.S., Hampton Inst., 1940; M.A., U. Mich., 1946; Ed.D., U. Ill., 1961; postgrad. Harvard U., 1950; m. Julia Naomi Edmundson June 17, 1944; children—Wendell, Arnett, Lynn. Prin., Union Sch., Hampton, Va., 1946-47; dean students Savannah State Coll. (Ga.), 1947-55; prin Ligon High Sch., Raleigh, N.C., 1956-57; counselor N.C. Central U., Durham, 1959-61; supt. Va. State Sch., Hampton, 1961-65; edn. program officer U.S. Office Edn., Washington, 1965-70; vice provost Ohio State U., Columbus, 1970—, prof. edn., 1970—. Trustee Freedoms Found., 1974, St. Augustines Coll., 1968-77. Recipient Freedoms Found. medal, 1954, Superior Accomplishment award HEW, 1968, Distinguished Alumni award Hampton Inst., 1970, award Nat. Press Inst., 1972; Harvard Far Eastern Studies fellow, 1956. Mem. Am. Assn. Higher Edn., Am. Personnel and Guidance Assn., Am. Assn. Sch. Adminstrs., Alpha Kappa Delta, Phi Delta Kappa, Kappa Delta Pi. Democrat. Presbyterian (elder). Clubs: Lions (pres. 1975); Cosmos (Washington). Editorial bd. Negro Ednl. Rev., 1972. Home: 5140 High St N Apt 313 Columbus OH 43214 Office: 190 Oval Mall N Columbus OH 43210

HOLM, DONALD SUTHERLAND, JR., educator, univ. ofcl.; b. Highland Park, Mich., Oct. 1, 1920; s. D. S. and Louise (Hemeyer) H.; A.B., Oberlin Coll., 1941; M.B.A., Harvard U., 1947; M.A., Ind. U., 1950, Ph.D. (fellow), 1952; m. Marilynn Ruth Lamb, June 8, 1951; children—Donald Sutherland, Elizabeth L. Asst. prof. bus. mgmt. U. Mo., Columbia, 1950-53, asso. prof., 1953-58, prof., 1958—, chmn. dept. bus. mgmt., 1962-65, coordinator M.B.A. program, 1964-65, chmn. dept. mgmt., 1965-69, dir. grad. programs in bus., 1965-70, acting asst. v.p. fin., 1972-73, asst. v.p., asst. treas., 1973-77, treas. and asst. v.p., 1977—; cons. U.S. Dept. Labor, 1960, Comptroller and Budget Dir., State of Mo., 1962, Hawthorn Co., New Haven, Mo., 1963-64, Mo. State Library, 1962-63, M.F.A. Oil Co., Columbia, 1964-65, City of Columbia, 1966, OEO, 1966-67, Mo. Dept. Revenue, 1967, Boone County Hosp., 1968, 73, Am. Coll. Hosp. Adminstrs., 1968-71, Mo. State Hwy. Commn., 1956—, Mo. Savs. and Loan League, 1972. Mem. Mo. Com. on Econ. Devel., 1960-61; chmn. City of Columbia Personnel Adv. Bd., 1963-72; mem. Task Force on Personnel Adminstrn., Mo. State Reorgn. Commn., 1970-71; chmn. Mo. Gov.'s Adv. Council on Employment Security, 1962-65. Served from ensign to lt. comdr. USNR, 1942-46. Recipient Outstanding Achievement award in Aerospace Edn., USAF, 1970. Mem. Acad. Mgmt., U.S. Navy League (dir. 1967-70), Nat., Central assns. coll. and univ. bus. officers. Clubs: Detroit Yacht, Columbia Country (treas., gov. 1966-71); Harvard (N.Y.C.); Mo. Athletic. Author books on labor and unemployment. Contbr. articles on mgmt. to profl. publs. Home: 106 W Ridgeley Rd Columbia MO 65201 Office: 215K University Hall Columbia MO

HOLMAN, CHARLES RAYMOND, osteo. physician; b. Green City, Mo., July 18, 1924; s. Squire Paul and Meeda (Daniel) H.; student N.E. Mo. State Coll., 1942-43, 45-46, Mont. State U., 1943; D.O., Kansas City Coll. Osteopathy and Surgery, 1949. Intern, McDowell Hosp., Phoenix, 1949-50; McLaughlin Hosp., Lansing, Mich., 1957; practice osteo. medicine, Kirksville, Mo., 1949-52, Monterrey, Mex., 1952-53; mem. house staff, practice anesthesiology Cardwell Hosp., Stella, Mo., 1957-61; resident Kirksville (Mo.) Osteo. Hosp., 1961-63; anesthesiologist Lansing (Mich.) Gen. Hosp., 1963—. Served to lt. USAAF, 1943-45; with AUS, 1953-56. Mem. Am. Osteo. Assn., Am. Coll. Osteo. Anesthesiologists. Home: 601 W Illinois St Kirksville MO 63501

HOLMAN, ELWOOD JOSIAH, landscape architect; b. Wauseon, Ohio, July 23, 1930; s. Elwood Josiah and Mildred Alice (Ackerman) H.; B.B.A., Case Western Res. U., 1952; M.Landscape Architecture, U. Mich., 1966; m. Marian Williams McGaw, May 10, 1952; children—James, Thomas, Jeffrey. Asst. mgr. automotive chem. sales Dow Chem. Co., Midland, Mich., 1955-63; v.p., gen. mgr. Johnson & Johnson & Roy, Inc., Ann Arbor, 1966-74; v.p., dir. Colvin, Robinson Assos., Inc., Ann Arbor, 1974—. Mem. Ann Arbor Planning Commn., 1971—, vice chmn., 1974-75, chmn., 1975—. Mem. Am. Soc. Landscape Architects (pres. Mich. chpt. 1972-74), Am. Soc. Planning Ofcls., Tau Sigma Delta. Home: 2011 Geddes Ave Ann Arbor MI 48104 Office: 210 E Huron St Ann Arbor MI 48108

HOLMBERG, JAMES JOHN, electronic component co. exec.; b. Sioux City, Iowa, Sept. 17, 1928; s. James Joseph and Maym Grace (Jacob) H.; B.S. in Commerce, Creighton U., 1951, J.D., 1954; m. Mary Louise Schwery, Oct. 2, 1954; children—James, Mark, Mary Jane, Holly Ann. Admitted to Nebr. bar, 1954; asso. Cropper & Cropper, Omaha, 1954-56; contract coordinator Dale Products, Inc., Columbus, Nebr., 1956-57, engring. adminstr., 1957-58, gen. counsel, 1958-60; sec., gen. counsel Dale Electronics, Inc., Columbus, 1960-63, v.p., gen. counsel, sec., 1963—; sec., treas., dir. Pawnee Scout, Inc. Chmn., Platte County Joint Planning Commn., 1972-76; mem. Nebr. Dept. Labor Adv. Council, 1968-74, Employment Security Council, 1963—. Past pres., bd. dirs. Omaha Archdiocese Bd. Edn.; bd. dirs. Big Brother and Sister Assn. of Columbus, Central Nebr. Tech. Sch. Served with CIC, U.S. Army, 1955-56. Mem. Am., Nebr., Platte County bar assns., Nebr. Assn. Tech. Community Colls. (adv. council), Columbus C. of C. (past pres.), Nebr. Assn. Commerce and Industry. Roman Catholic. Elk. Club: Optimist Internat. (past club pres., dist. lt. gov.). Home: 4809 Country Club Dr Columbus NE 68601 Office: PO Box 609 Columbus NE 68601

HOLMES, BETTY JEAN, librarian; b. Abilene, Kans., Mar. 6, 1929; d. Emery Ray and Ada Leona (Brown) Holmes; student library workshops various colls. and univs., 1947-59. With Abilene Pub. Library, 1947—, asst. librarian, 1948-58, asst., 1958-64, staff asst., 1964-71, asst., 1971-73, library asst., 1973—. Active various civic orgns. and activities; music chmn. Abilene YWCA, 1971-72, v.p., 1972-73, 73-74. Mem. ALA, Mountain Plains, Kans. library assns., Kans. Friends of Libraries, Dickinson County Hist. Soc. Methodist (supt. beginners dept. 1963—, mem. commn. on edn. 1967—, mem. commn. mission 1965—, mem. choir). Club: Ethel Calkins Guild (treas. 1975-77). Home: 911 N Mulberry St Abilene KS 67410 Office: 4th St and Broadway Abilene KS 67410

HOLMES, DOUGLAS MACARTHUR, veterinarian; b. LuVerne, Iowa, Apr. 14, 1942; s. Clifford and Mable H.; student Ft. Dodge Community Coll., 1960-62; B.S., Iowa State U., 1968, D.V.M., 1972; m. Linda D. Clark, Feb. 17, 1961; children—Jeffery D., Todd M., Jennifer L. Gen. practice veterinary medicine, Hampton, Iowa, 1972-73, Waverly, Iowa, 1973-74, Algona, Iowa, 1974—; cons. Felco Lando Lakes. Mem. AVMA, Iowa Veterinary Medicine Assn. Methodist. Clubs: Masons, Shriners. Home and Office: 309 E North St Algona IA 50511

HOLMES, ELWIN LEROY, graphic arts co. exec.; b. Allegan, Mich., Nov. 4, 1921; s. Elwin Delose and Irma Eola (Rowe) H.; grad. high sch.; m. Helen Marie Blanchard, Jan. 30, 1942; children—Elwin Charles, Donald Lee. Printing pressman Kalamazoo Products Co., 1940-42; prodn. foreman aircraft, Ford Motor Co., Willow Run, Mich., 1942-45; printing pressman Kalamazoo Label Co., 1945-62, supt., 1962-73, v.p., 1973—. Mem. Tag and Label Mfrs. Inst. (joint tech. com. 1970-73), Graphic Arts Tech. Found., Printing House Craftsmen. Home: 806 Dayton St Kalamazoo MI 49001 Office: 321 W Ransom St Kalamazoo MI 49006

HOLMES, GLORIA MAUDE HENDREN (MRS. RICHARD L. HOLMES), educator; b. Newark, Ohio, Nov. 5, 1930; d. Walter Ebert and Corinne (Tope) Hendren; B.Ed., Ohio State U., 1952, M.Ed., 1957, postgrad., 1958—; m. Richard Lewis Holmes, July 19, 1959; children—Kimberly Sue, Sally Lou, Kathy Lynn, Jeffery Richard, Nancy Ann, David Michael, Susan Elizabeth. Tchr., Cherry Valley Elementary Sch., Newark, Ohio, 1952-56; grad. asst. lab. sch. Ohio State U., 1956; asso. prof. elementary edn. Ashland Coll., also supr. elementary student teaching, academic counselor, 1956—, founder, dir., supr. Ashland Coll. Kindergarten, 1960-63; mem. curriculum redesign com. tchr. edn. Ohio and Ashland Coll., 1976-77; cons., lectr. Bd. dirs. Ashland Community Day Care Center. Mem. Ashland City Schs. PTA, Ashland Christian Sch. PTA. Active United Appeal; hosp. Vol. ARC, 1956-59; v.p. Women's Missionary Soc. group III Park St. Brethren Ch., 1970-71; staff ch. sch., Bible sch. and youth activities Berean Sunday Sch. Jennings Research scholar, 1974-75. Mem. Ohio, Nat. edn. assns., Ohio, Nat. assns. for higher edn., Ohio Assn. for Tchr. Educators, Nursery-Kindergarten-Primary Assn., Assn. for Supervision and Curriculum Devel., Assn. for Childhood Edn., Am. Assn. Univ. Women, Bus. and Profl. Women's Club, Symphony League, Assn. of Adminstrs., Guidance Assn., Assn. for Exceptional Children, Ohio State U. Alumni Assn., Ohio State U., Ashland Coll. devel. fund assns., N. Central Ohio Tchrs. Assn., Ashland Christian Bus. and Profl. Women's Club, Internat. Reading Assn., Internat. Platform Assn., Phi Delta Kappa, Alpha Delta Kappa, Beta Sigma Phi (pres. Delta Gamma chpt. 1969-70), Kappa Delta Pi (hon.), Xi Iota Alpha. Mem. Order of Eastern Star, White Shrine of Jerusalem, Altrusa Internat. Club: Ashland Coll. Faculty Club, Ashland Coll. Faculty Women's Club (pres. 1959-60), Garden. Author: Handbook for Administrators, Cooperating Teachers, Student Teachers, and College Supervisors-Ashland College, 1957; Handbook for Kindergarten Teachers, 1963; (with Richard L. Holmes) Innovations in Church School Teacher-Education Program, 1972; A Competency Based Program for Teacher Education-Children's Literature, 1974; A Competency Based Program for Teacher Education-Kindergarten Methods, 1974. Home: 452 Hillcrest Dr Ashland OH 44805 Office: Edn Dept Ashland Coll Coll Av Ashland OH 44805

HOLMES, RICHARD LEWIS, sch. adminstr.; b. Ashland, Ohio, Nov. 28, 1927; s. Lewis Mason and Evelyn Lucille (Ledyard) H.; B.S., Ashland Coll., 1965; M.Ed., Kent State U., 1968; postgrad. U. Akron, 1970, Ohio U., 1971; Ed.D (hon.), Lawford State U., 1974; m. Gloria Maude Hendren, July 19, 1959; children—Kimberly Sue, Sally Lou, Kathy Lynn, Jeffery Richard, Nancy Ann, David Michael, Susan Elizabeth. Elementary tchr. Ashland County (Ohio) Schs., 1961-62, Medina County (Ohio) Schs., 1962-67; asst. dir. audio-visual center Kent State U., 1967-68; dir. fed. program, elementary prin. Grant Sch., Wooster, Ohio, 1968-69; dir. ednl. media, coordinator-supr. vocat. edn. Ashland City Schs., 1969—; chmn. policy adv. com. Head

Start Program, Ashland, 1971; pres. Ashland Christian Sch. Parent-Tchr. Fellowship, 1975-76; mem. bd. Christian edn. First Brethren Ch., 1972-76. Served with USAF Res., 1947-55. Mem. Ednl. Media Council Ohio, Assn. Communications and Tech. in Edn., NEA, Ohio Edn. Assn., Nat. Guild Hypnotists, Am. Metalists Assn., Internat. Brotherhood Magicians, Soc. Am. Magicians, Intercontinental Biog. Assn., Phi Delta Kappa, Kappa Delta Pi. Club: Lions (pres., 1966-67). Home: 452 Hillcrest Dr Ashland OH 44805 Office: 1440 King Rd Ashland OH 44805

HOLMES, WILLIAM DEE, utility co. exec.; b. Chgo., Apr. 13, 1929; s. Garrett Arden and Kathleen (Neale) H.; B.S. in Civil Engring. with honors, U. Ill., 1951; m. Patricia Lou Kuebler, Aug. 25, 1951; children—Victoria, Kim, Kam. Staff engr. DeLeuw Cather & Co., Cons. Engrs., Chgo., 1951-56; asst. mgr., treas. Kankakee Water Co. (Ill.), 1957-59, exec. v.p., mgr., 1960-65, pres., mgr., 1965—; dir. Kankakee Fed. Savs. & Loan Assn. Pres. Kankakee Indsl. Devel. Assn., 1965—. County chmn. Cancer Crusade, 1967; county chmn. Am. Heart Assn., 1961, state dir., 1962. Served with AUS, 1952-53. Mem. Am. Water Works Assn. (sect. trustee 1967-72, pres. 1972-73), Nat. Assn. Water Cos. (dir. 1971—), Kankakee C. of C. (pres. 1963-64), U. Ill. Alumni Assn. (dir. 1965-71, pres. 1975-77), Delta Chi (pres. 1951), Phi Eta Sigma, Chi Epsilon, Sigma Tau. Clubs: Masons, Rotary. Home: 1001 Cobb Blvd Kankakee IL 60901 Office: 1000 S Schuyler Ave Kankakee IL 60901

HOLMGREN, LOWELL CARLTON, assn. exec.; b. Rapid City, S.D., June 2, 1931; s. Carl Warner and Clara Annette (Olston) H.; grad. high sch.; m. Deloris Virginia Ellerman, Oct. 10, 1973; children by previous marriage—Michelle C. (Mrs. Paul J. Haedt III), Dayna S. (Mrs. Jimmy McGuire), Cindy J., Charles W., Tim A. With Holmgren's, Inc., comml. printing, Rapid City, 1948-69; salesman Dick Kahler, Inc., Realtors, Rapid City, 1969-75; owner, mgr. Exec. Services Co., exec. sec. Rapid City Multiple Listing Service, exec. officer Black Hills Home Builders Assn., Rapid City, 1975—; exec. sec. Black Hills Bd. Realtors, 1976—. First v.p. Rapid City Parent-Tchr. Council, 1970-72. Mem. S.D. (dir. 1973-74), Black Hills (pres. 1973) bds. realtors, Rapid City C. of C. (mem. sts. and hwys. com. 1970-76). Clubs: Masons (32 deg.), Shrine (pres. Rapid City 1974), Cosmopolitan (sec. 1971-72, pres. 1977-78). Editor, pub. News Nuggets, quar. news mag. Naja Shrine Temple, 1963-64. Home: 2709 Willow Ave Rapid City SD 57701 Office: 919 Main St Suite 213 Rapid City SD 57701

HOLOHAN, O. J., indsl. and interior designer; b. Detroit, Sept. 18, 1936; s. James Frances and Ernestine Flora (Neumann) H.; degree in Indsl. Designs and Interiors, Cleve. Inst. Art, 1961; m. Laurinda Anne Loewe, Oct. 25, 1969; children—Eric James, Shauna Lynn. Illustrator to Pres. D. Eisenhower, 1957-58; art dir. TV sta., Washington, 1958-59; dir. design O.J.K. Designers div. F.W. Roberts, Cleve., 1962-67; pres. O.J. Holohan Assos., Inc., Burton, Ohio, 1967—; judge design juries. Served with U.S. Army, 1957-59. Recipient Merit award Nat. Stationary and Office Equipment Assn., 1962; Design award 2d place Nat. Office Furniture Assn., 1963; Design award, 1965; 1st and 2nd place awards Office Interior Design Mag., 1965; hon. mention award S.M. Hexter Co., 1975. Mem. Inst. Bus. Designers (founding), Zool. Assn. Am., Nat. Office Furniture Assn. Home: 2 Serenity Pk 12175 Snow Rd Burton OH 44021 Office: 1 Serenity Pk 12175 Snow Rd Burton OH 44021

HOLQUIST, RICHARD OSCAR, educator; b. Omaha, Nov. 27, 1934; s. Oscar H. and Emma Caroline (Swanson) H.; A.B., Grinnell (Iowa) Coll., 1957; M.B.A., U. Nebr., Omaha, 1970; Ph.D., U. Nebr., Lincoln, 1974; m. Elinor Gertrude Stenner, Oct. 21, 1961; children—Diana, Cynthia. Mgmt. trainee First Nat. Bank, Omaha, 1958-64; asst. drive-in mgr. Douglas County Bank, Omaha, 1964-66; asst. office mgr. Ralston Purina Co., Omaha, 1966-67; underwriter Mut. of Omaha, 1967-70; instr. U. Nebr., Omaha, 1971-74; asst. prof. bus. adminstrn. Dana Coll., Blair, Nebr., 1944-77; asst. prof. bus. adminstrn., coordinator bus. adminstrn. programs Coll. St. Mary, Omaha, 1977—; cons. mktg. and mgmt. Treas. St. Timothy's Lutheran Ch., Omaha, 1962-66, mem. council, 1971-77. Served with AUS, 1957-58. Mem. Soc. Advancement Mgmt. (faculty adviser), AAUP, Nat. Assn. Accountants, Am. Mktg. Assn., Beta Gamma Sigma. Republican. Author articles in field. Home: 11338 Camden St Omaha NE 68164 Office: 1901 S 72d St Omaha NE 68124

HOLSINGER, ROBERT GEORGE, civil engr.; b. Des Moines, Aug. 2, 1936; s. Stanley Obert and Winifred (Gill) H.; B.S. in Civil Engring., Iowa State Coll., 1959; certificate hwy. traffic, Yale, 1962; M.S. in Civil Engring., U. Nebr., 1977; m. Judith Ann Reynolds, Feb. 27, 1960; children—David, Daniel. Traffic Engr. I, City of Des Moines, 1958-60; asst. city traffic engr., Downey, Calif., 1960-61; city traffic engr., Lincoln, Nebr., 1962-76; engr. Commonwealth Electric Co., Lincoln, 1976-77; engr. Asso. Engrs. Inc., Fort Dodge, Iowa, 1977—; instr., lectr. traffic engring. for transp. safety, Research Center, U. Iowa, 1972, Safety Center, Central Mo. State Coll., 1971-72. Mem. curriculum guide adv. council safety edn. Nebr. Dept. Edn., 1973; dir. Lincoln-Lancaster County (Nebr.) Safety Council, 1967—; hon. life mem. Nebr. PTA. Recipient award of merit for leadership in street constrn. Am. City Mag., 1967, Movite Pres.'s award, 1967. Registered profl. engr., Calif. Fellow Inst. Transp. Engrs. (dir. Mo. valley sect. 1965-68, pres. 1968—; presdl. del. to constl. conv. 1971, nat. policy com. 1976—), Lincoln Engrs. Club (dir. 1971-72, pres. 1973). Presbyn. (deacon 1970—, vice moderator, 1972). Presbyterian (trustee, sec. bd. 1976, chmn. bd. 1977). Mason (Shriner). Contbr. articles to profl. jours. Home: 7721 E Avon Ln Lincoln NE 68505 Office: 1728 Central Ave Fort Dodge IA 50501

HOLT, DONALD HENRY, utility co. exec.; b. Cleve., Jan. 22, 1941; s. Randall N. and Lolia E. (Kinciad) H.; B.S.B.A., John Carroll U., 1964; M.B.A., Case Western Res. U., 1971; J.D., U. Akron, 1976; m. Dianne Williford, May 20, 1970. Mgmt. trainee East Ohio Gas Co., Cleve., 1964, cost analyst, 1967-68, spl. asst. to pres., 1968-69, asst. to pres., 1969—; admitted to Ohio bar, 1977. Trustee Met. Gen. Hosp. Found., United Torch Services, Urban League. Served with AUS, 1965-67. Mem. Greater Cleve., Ohio, Nat. bar assns., Alpha Kappa Psi. Republican. Congregationalist. Club: Rotary. Home: 4400 Clarkwood Pky #412 Cleveland OH 44128 Office: East Ohio Gas Co 1717 E 9th St Cleveland OH 44114

HOLT, JOE D., lawyer, state legislator; b. Mexico, Mo., Aug. 25, 1940; s. Joe P. and Florence S. (Smith) H.; B.A., Westminster Coll., 1962; J.D., U. Mo., 1967; m. Molly F. Deiter, Jan. 25, 1966; children—Ned, Dan, Phil. Admitted to Mo. bar, 1968; mem. firm Holt, Krumm, Hamilton & Shyrock, Fulton, Mo., 1968—; mem. Mo. Ho. of Reps., 1967—, vice chmn. com. agr. and state instns. and properties, 1973-74, chmn. state reorgn. com., 1975-76, chmn. spl. com. on modernization of Gen. Assembly, mem. judiciary com., chmn. rules and joint rules com., majority floor leader, 1977-78, ex-officio mem. all House coms., mem. Atomic Energy Commn. Pres. Young Democrats Callaway County, Mo., 1958-60. Bd. dir. Mid Mo. Council on Criminal Justice, 1969—, Reality House, Columbia, Mo., 1971—. Served with AUS, 1962-64. Recipient Outstanding Legislator award St. Louis Globe-Dem., 1974. Mem. Mo. Bar (mem. cts. and jud. com. 1971—), Callaway County Bar Assn. Presbyn. Mason (Shriner). Club: Optimist (pres. 1971-72). Home: 808 Court St Fulton MO 65251 Office: Room 309 State Capitol Bldg Jefferson City MO 65101 also 413 Court St Fulton MO 65251

HOLT, RICHARD LEE, speech and lang. pathologist; b. Council Grove, Kans., May 7, 1935; s. Clinton Hartwell and Josephine Katherine (Kirkpatrick) H.; B.A., Wichita State U., 1966, M.A. in Logopedics, 1969; M.S. in Spl. Edn. Learning Disabilities, Pitts. State U., 1977; m. Gladys Altagracia Hansen, Dec. 29, 1957; children—Catherine Marie, Susan Anne, Sylvia Louise. Dir. Inst. Logopedics Pittsburg (Kans.) Speech and Hearing Center, 1969-70, 71-75; instr. speech and lang. pathology and audiology U. P.R., San Juan, 1970-71; speech pathologist Crawford County Mental Health Center, Pitts., 1975-77; pvt. practice speech and lang. pathology, Pittsburg, 1977—; bd. dirs. Developmental Learning Center, Pittsburg, 1971-75; adj. prof. Pittsburg State U., 1969-70, 71—; cons. to med. adv. bd. SE Kans. Community Action Program, 1972—. Served with USMC, 1953-57. Mem. Am., Kans. speech and hearing assns., Internat. Assn. Oral Myology, Council Exceptional Children, Orgn. Area Speech Pathologists and Audiologists, Assn. Children with Learning Disabilities, Phi Delta Kappa. Methodist. Home: 2304 S Broadway Pittsburg KS 66762 Office: 114 W 6th St Pittsburg KS 66762

HOLT, WALDO SLY, physician; b. Omaha, July 4, 1924; s. Ralph Waldo and Fara (Sly) H.; A.B., U. Kan., 1945, M.D., 1950; m. Jane Koslowsky, Nov. 24, 1950; children—Barry Alan, Peter Scott. Intern U.S. Naval Hosp., Phila., 1950-51; resident Cleve. Clinic Hosp., 1951-52, Ochsner Found. Hosp., New Orleans, 1954-56; practice medicine specializing in internal medicine, kansas City, Mo., 1956—; mem. staffs St.Mary's, St. Luke's, Bapt. Meml., Research hosps., Kansas City. Mem. med. edn. com. Kansas City, Mo., 1964—. Fellow A.C.P., Phi Sigma; mem. Kan. Acad. Medicine, Jackson County Med. Soc., Am. Soc. Internal Medicine, Jackson County Med. Soc., Am. Soc. Internal Medicine, Mo. Diabetes Assn. (dir.). Home: 5525 Wornall Rd Kansas City MO 64113 Office: 4620 Nichols Pkwy Kansas City MO 64112

HOLT, WILLIAM CARL, JR., mfg. co. exec.; b. Liberty, Mo., July 12, 1947; s. William Carl and Elizabeth Grace (Dearing) H.; B.S. in Chemistry, U. Ill., 1969; m. Barbara Ruth Bosworth, July 31, 1947. Research chemist UOP, Inc., Des Plaines, Ill., 1969-73, research contract adminstr., 1973-75, dist. mgr. div. automotive products, Southfield, Mich., 1976—; exec. dir. Tech. Adv. Bd., Dept. Commerce, Washington, 1975-76. Active Young Republicans, 1969-75; mem. sci. controversy subcom. Pres's. Adv. Com. on Sci. and Tech. Mem. AAAS, Soc. Automotive Engrs. Baptist. Club: Fairland (Dearborn, Mich.). Author: Crisis! Environment and Energy, 1972; editor East-West Technol. Trade, 1976; inventor new class of materials, condrs. organic-ceramics. Home: 6767 E Nashway St West Bloomfield MI 48033 Office: 122 Harvard Plaza 29350 Southfield Rd Southfield MI 48076

HOLT, W(ILLIAM) KERMIT, travel editor; b. Clarksburg, W.Va., Oct. 26, 1916; s. William Tilford and Emelyne (Gregory) H.; A.B., Salem Coll., 1938; M.S. in Journalism, Northwestern U., 1939; m. Gisela Leers, May 7, 1941; children—William Henry, Heidi Marie. Reporter, Clarksburg Exponent, 1937-38, City News Bur., Chgo., 1939; night editor Mil Bur. AP, 1940; reporter Chgo. Tribune, 1940-46, fgn. corr., 1946-48, copy editor, 1948-55, asst. makeup editor, 1955-60, travel editor, 1960—. Served to lt. USMCR, 1942-45. Decorated Purple Heart; recipient Pacific Area Travel Assn. award for best newspaper articles on Pacific, 1962, 65, 70, 71, 73, Trans World Airlines Travel Writing award, 1965, 68, Mark Twain Travel Writing awards, 1960-61, 62-63, George Hedmon award, 1967, Edward Scott Beck award, 1970, Strebig-Dobben Meml. award, 1970; named Salem Coll. Alumnus of Year, 1963, Distinguished W. Virginian, 1971. Mem. Soc. Am. Travel Writers (nat. pres. 1965-67, chmn. bd. 1968-69), Chgo. Press Club (bd. govs. 1965-76, pres. 1975), Sigma Delta Chi. Home: 227 Parkview Rd Glenview IL 60025 Office: Tribune Sq Chicago IL 60611

HOLTERMAN, JAMES LEE, veterinarian; b. Norton, Kans., Sept. 21, 1947; s. Orville William and Pauline Meta (Dietz) H.; student Ft. Hays State Coll., 1965-66; B.S., Kans. State U., 1971, D.V.M., 1973; m. Sandra Kay Haddock, Apr. 2, 1977. Intern, Dykstra Veterinary Hosp., Manhattan, Kans., summer 1971, Norton (Kans.) Veterinary Hosp., summer 1972; veterinarian Liberal (Kans.) Animal Hosp., 1973—. Bd. dirs. S.W. Kans. Humane Soc., 1976—. Mem. AVMA, Kans. Veterinary Med. Assn. Clubs: Pancake Capitol Hi-Flyers (v.p.). Home: 812 N Calhoun St Liberal KS 67901 Office: 730 S Kansas St Liberal KS 67901

HOLTKAMP, DORSEY EMIL, med. research scientist; b. New Knoxville, Ohio, May 28, 1919; s. Emil H. and Caroline E. (Meckstroth) H.; student Ohio State U., 1937-39; A.B., U. Colo., 1945, M.S., 1949, Ph.D., 1951, med. student, 2 1/2 yrs.; m. Marianne Church Johnson, Mar. 20, 1942 (dec. May 1956); 1 son, Kurt Lee; m. 2d, Marie P. Bahm Roberts, Dec. 20, 1957; stepchildren—Charles Timothy Roberts, Michael John Roberts. Teaching asst. in biochemistry, research asst. in biology U. Colo., 1945-46; grad. scholar (univ. fellow) U. Colo. Sch. Medicine, 1946, asst. in biochemistry, 1947-48, research fellow in biochemistry, 1948-51; sr. research scientist Biochemistry sect. Smith, Kline & French Labs., Phila., 1951-57, endocrine-metabolic group leader, 1957-58; head endocrinology dept. Merrell-Nat. Labs. div. Richardson-Merrell, Inc., Cin., 1958-70, group dir. endocrine clin. research med. research dept., 1970—. Fellow AAAS, Am. Inst. Chemists; mem. Am. Soc. Clin. Pharm. and Chemotherapy, Endocrine Soc., Am. Fertility Soc., Am. Chem. Soc., Am. Soc. Pharmacology and Exptl. Therapeutics, Colo.-Wyo., N.Y., Ohio acads. scis., Soc. Exptl. Biology and Medicine, Reticuloendothelial Soc., Am. Inst. Biol. Scis., Nat. Soc. Med. Research, AMA (affiliate), Sigma Xi, Nu Sigma Nu. Republican. Presbyterian. Contbr. articles to sci. publs.; patentee in various phases endocrinology, pharmacology, tumor metabolism, fertility-sterility control, biochemistry, teratology, inflamation and nutrition. Research and devel. new drugs. Home: 9464 Bluewing Terr Cincinnati OH 45241 Office: 110 E Amity Rd Cincinnati OH 45215

HOLTKAMP, STANLEY ALVIN, elec. equipment mfg. co. exec.; b. Centralia, Ill., Jan. 20, 1930; s. Bernard John and Della Ann (Robben) H.; student Northwestern U., 1948-49; m. Norma Jean Garren, Nov. 11, 1950; children—Guy Robert, Mary Ann, Vincent Gerard. With Holtkamp Co., Centralia, 1949—, pres., 1964-69; dir. Highlan Place - B. J. H. Co. Mem. Soc. Automotive Engrs., C. of C. Elk. Home: Rural Route 1 Box 176 Centralia IL 62801 Office: PO Box 567 Centralia IL 62801

HOLTOM, CAROLYN MARJORIE, coll. adminstr.; b. Three Rivers, Mich., Aug. 26, 1925; d. Charles Richard and Ethel Hinckley (Kelsey) Holtom; B.S., Western Mich. Univ., 1946; M.A., U. Mich., 1958, Ph.D., 1964. Occupational therapist U.S. Naval Hosp., Great Lakes, Ill., 1946-51, Rancho Los Amigos Hosp., Hondo, Calif., 1951-52, U. Mich. Hosp., Ann Arbor, 1960-61; instr. Eastern Mich. U., Ypsilanti, 1952-57, asst. prof., 1958-60; asso. dean Chadron State Coll., Nebr., 1965-73, dean of students, 1973—. Dir. Chadron Community Hosp.; mem. council Job Corps, Chadron. Fellow Found. Infantile Parlysis, 1957-58, Office Vocat. Rehab., 1962-64. Mem. Am. Personnel and Guidance Assn., Am. Coll. Personnel Assn., Nat. Assn. Women Deans Adminstrs. and Counselors. Episcopalian. Contbr. articles to profl. jours. Home: PO Box 1206 Chadron NE 69337 Office: Chadron State College Chadron NE 69337

HOLTSBERRY, ALBERT WALTER, retail co. exec.; b. Licking County, Ohio, Sept. 29, 1935; s. Eden Frederick and Vina L. (Hartman) H.; student Ohio U., Athens, 1953-54, Ohio State U., Columbus, 1963-65; children—Rosemary, Theresa, Fred. Sr. systems analyst Scoa Industries, 1964-67; mgr. systems and data processing Am. Standard Co., 1967-70, Big Bear Stores Co., Columbus, 1970—; pres. Big Bear Employees Credit Union, 1974—. Trustee Genoa Conservation Club. Served with USAF, 1954-57. Mem. Assn. Systems Mgmt. (div. dir. Central Ohio chpt. 1972—, pres. 1971-72, internat. qualifications com. 1975-78, Internat. Merit award 1973, Chpt. Service award 1974). Home: 4809 Smoketalk Ln Westerville OH 43081 Office: 770 W Goodale Blvd Columbus OH 43212

HOLVICK, OLAF, II, computer services co. exec.; b. Long Beach, Calif., June 16, 1946; s. Olaf and Elaine Margaret (Klarr) H.; B.S. in Bus. Adminstrn., Babson Coll., 1968; m. Christine Frances Fisher, Dec. 6, 1974; 1 dau., Lindsay Fisher. Mktg. rep. Statis. Analyst Corp., Detroit, 1968-69; mktg. analyst Nat. Bank of Detroit, 1969; group sales mgr. Pathfinder Internat., Detroit, 1969-70; nat. account exec. R.L. Polk and Co., Taylor, Mich., 1970-75; regional mgr. Cutler-Williams, Inc., Dearborn, Mich., 1975—; dir. Interface Systems, Inc., Ann Arbor, Mich., 1972-75. Mem. Econ. Club Detroit, Engring. Soc. Detroit. Republican. Roman Catholic. Clubs: Country of Detroit, Detroit Athletic, Detroit Racquet. Home: 21 Renaud Rd Grosse Pointe Shores MI 48236 Office: 1610 Parklane Towers East Dearborn MI 48126

HOLZER, REGINALD JACK, judge; b. Chgo., Sept. 9, 1927; s. William and Marie (Friedman) H.; B.A., U. Chgo., 1948; J.D., Ill. Inst. Tech.-Chgo.-Kent Coll. Law, 1951; LL.D., Har Etzion U., Israel, 1972; m. Estelle Starkman, Aug. 27, 1950; children—Audrey, Bambi. Admitted to Ill. bar, 1951; practiced in Chgo., 1951-66; legal adviser, hearings referee Ill. Commerce Commn., 1954-60; legal adviser, Sheriff Cook Co., 1962-66; judge Circuit Ct. Cook County, Chgo., 1966—. Mem. faculty Ill. Inst. Tech., Chgo. Kent Coll. Law. Served with USAAF, 1945-47. Recipient award of merit Decalogue Soc. Lawyers, 1957; Golden Key award City of Hope, 1965; State Israel Achievement award, 1965; State Israel Testimonial award, 1967; citation Jewish War Vets. U.S.A., 1967; State Israel Prime Minister's medal, 1970. Mem. Am., Ill., Chgo. bar assns., Ill. Judges Assn. (dir.), Decalogue Soc. Lawyers (past pres.). Jewish (past pres. temple). Mem. B'nai B'rith (past pres. Chgo. Justice lodge). Home: 179 E Lake Shore Dr Chicago IL 60611 Office: Civic Center Chicago IL 60602

HOLZMAN, SHERIDAN VERNE, lawyer; b. Detroit, Jan. 22, 1930; s. Irving V. and Betty (Sipher) H.; B.A., Wayne State U., 1954, J.D., 1955; m. Toby R. Naiman, Mar. 30, 1952; children—Deborah, Brian, Charles, David. Admitted to Mich. bar, 1955—, since practiced in Detroit. Law lectr. U. Mich., 1969-70, Wayne State U., 1970. Chmn., Southfield Democratic Club, 1967-68; mem. Oakland County Dem. Com., 1967—; mem. 17th Dist. Dem. Exec. Com., 1975—. Mem. State Bar Mich., Am. Trial Lawyers Assn., Am. Judicature Soc., ACLU (vice chmn. 1972-75, gen. counsel 1975—). Home: 30485 Old Stream Circle Southfield MI 48076 Office: 1926 First Nat Bldg Detroit MI 48226

HOLZWORTH, WILLIAM ARTHUR, metal health adminstr.; b. Chgo., Oct. 5, 1942; s. Arthur Benjamin and Grace Jeanette (Rylander) H.; m. Susan Jane Fockler, July 6, 1968; 1 dau., Heidi Jane. B.A., Lawrence Coll., 1964; M.A., U. Ill., 1968; intern clin. psychology Galesburg State Research Hosp., 1969-70; counselor, student counseling center U. Ill., Urbana, 1967; teaching asst. child devel. lab. Galesburg (Ill.) State Research Hosp., 1968, teaching asst., psychology dept., 1968-69, psychologist, 1970-74; exec. dir. Spoon River Community Mental Health Center, Galesburg, 1974—. Active United Way of Knox County (Ill.), 1973-74; mem. western counties subregion bd. Ill. Central Health Systems Agency, 1976—. Mem. Am. Psychol. Assn., Tri-County Mental Health Assn., FISH of Galesburg, Phi Beta Kappa, Delta Tau Delta. Contbr. article to profl. jours. Home: 1246 Spruce Ave Galesburg IL 61401 Office: 695 N Kellogg St Galesburg IL 61401

HOMBURGER, RICHARD HANS, educator, accountant; b. Karlsruhe, Germany, Aug. 15, 1914; s. Paul Phillip and Anna (Schuelein) H.; came to U.S., 1940, naturalized, 1945; student Faculte de Droit, Sorbonne, 1934; J.D., U. Zurich, 1937; M.S., Columbia, 1946; m. Ursula Sinell, Dec. 23, 1947; 1 dau., Ann Marie. Dir. bus. adminstrn. W.Va. State Coll., 1946-56, asst. prof., then asso. prof., 1946-56; faculty Wichita (Kans.) State U., 1956—, prof. accounting, 1961—, coordinator grad. studies in accounting, 1962-71. Adviser, Mayor Wichita Com. on Municipal Income Tax, 1956-57. C.P.A., W.Va. Mem. Am. Accounting Assn., Acad. Accounting Historians (1st v.p. 1974-75, trustee; program chmn. 2d world congress 1976), Am. Inst. C.P.A.'s, AAUP, Beta Gamma Sigma. Contbr. to Accountants Ency., articles, revs. to profl. jours. Editor: Wichita State U. Bus. Jour., 1967-69; asso. editor Southwestern Social Sci. Quar., 1960-62. Home: 2519 N Roosevelt Ct Wichita KS 67220

HOMER, GEORGE MOHN, biochemist; b. Cleve., Mar. 28, 1924; s. George Henry and Mary Julia (Mohn) H.; student Ohio U., 1942-43; B.A., Ohio State U., 1948, Ph.D., 1958; M.S., U. Colo., 1951; m. Joanne Ruby Glatte, Sept. 8, 1951; children—Diane Glatte, Cheryl Lee. Research asst. Wyeth Inst. for Med. Research, Phila., 1951-52; research asst. dept. medicine Ohio State U., Columbus, 1952-58; research biochemist Miami Valley Hosp., Dayton, Ohio, 1958-63, asst. dir. research, 1963-65; biochemist Akron (Ohio) City Hosp., 1965—, adj. sci. staff of med. and dental staff, 1974. Lectr. evening coll. U. Akron, 1968-69; instr. chemistry, asso. mem. grad. faculty Youngstown State U., 1973—. Served with USMCR, 1943-45. Diplomate Am. Bd. Clin. Chemists. Fellow Am. Assn. Clin. Chemists (chmn. Ohio Valley sect. 1962-63, chmn. Cleve. sect. 1970-71); mem. Am. Chem. Soc., Nat. Acad. Clin. Biochemists (charter), Ohio State U. Assn., Sigma Xi. Mem. United Ch. of Christ. Contbr. articles to profl. jours. Home: 2953 Overlook Rd Cuyahoga Falls OH 44224 Office: 525 E Market St Akron OH 44309

HOMRIGHAUSEN, RONALD DEAN, clergyman; b. Dover, Ohio, Dec. 28, 1911; s. William Jacob and Laura Gertrude (Stein) H.; A.B., Wittenberg U., 1945; B.D., Hamma Sch. Theology, 1945; m. Carol Louise Allebach, Dec. 22, 1945; children—Sue Keryl Homrighausen Mastick, Paul David, Martha Dianne Homrighausen Brown, Jon Fredric. Ordained to ministry Lutheran Ch., 1945; pastor, evangelist, Bible translator Luth. Ch. Am., Liberia, Africa, 1946-52; pastor Luth. Parish, Middlepoint and Elida, Ohio, 1953-55, First Luth. Ch., Barberton, Ohio, 1956-65, St. James Luth. Ch., East Cleveland, Ohio, 1965-68, Zion Luth. Ch., New Middletown, Ohio, 1968—. Chmn. Citizens for Human Dignity, Youngstown, Ohio, 1972-74; bd. dirs. Wittenberg U., 1961-73, Luth. Campus Ministry Cleve., 1965-68. Mem. Assn. Luth. Pastors Greater Cleve. (sec.-treas. 1966-68), Youngstown Area Luth. Pastors Assn. (sec. 1969-70, pres. 1975-76). Home: 43 Sycamore Dr New Middletown OH 44442 Office: 10857 Main St New Middletown OH 44442

HOMUTH, FLOYD ELLIS, mktg. exec.; b. Woodworth, N.D., June 1, 1917; s. Frederick William and Nina Reynold (Brady) H.; student Jamestown Coll., 1936-37, U. N.D., 1939-40, Northwestern U., 1957-58; m. Joanne Tena Sterkenburg, Nov. 12, 1949; children—Thomas (dec. 1967), Barbara, Kay. Salesman, Nash Finch Co., Minot, N.D., 1941-48; salesman Western Mineral Products Co., Sioux Falls, S.D., 1948-51, regional sales mgr., Mpls., 1952-65; mdse. mgr. B.F. Nelson/Certain-Teed Corp., Mpls., 1965-74; exec. v.p., dir. sales and mktg. Diversified Insulation, Inc., Hamel, Minn., 1974—. Served with U.S. N.G., 1933-36. Mem. Vermiculite Assn. Internat. (pres. 1975-76), Nat. Cellulose Insulation Mrs. Assn. Republican. Episcopalian. Club: Elks. Home: 5124 Valley View Rd Edina MN 55436 Office: PO Box 188 Hamel MN 55340

HONAKER, LINTON RICHARD, ednl. adminstr.; b. Alliance, Ohio, Sept. 29, 1924; s. George R. and Ina (Hobson) H.; B.S., Mount Union Coll., 1948; M.A., Western Res. U., 1949, Ed.D.; m. Betty Lou Baker, Aug. 24, 1947; children—Emily Jean, Diana Lee, Richard, Robert. Tchr. math. Hartville (Ohio) High Sch., 1949-58; high sch. supr. Tuscarawas County (Ohio) Schs., New Philadelphia, 1958-64, supt., 1964—. Exec. com. Agr. Extension Service; mem. State Adv. Com. for Vocat. Agr.; pres. Tuscarawas Valley Mental Health Assn., 1961-63; bd. dirs. Tuscarawas County Guidance Center; treas. Tuscarawas County Guidance Center, Tuscarawas County Crippled Childrens Soc., 1964—; active Boy Scouts Am.; deacon United Ch. Christ; pres. Tuscarawas Valley Comprehensive Mental Health Center. Served with AUS, 1944-46. Named Hon. Ohio Chpt. Farmer, Future Farmers Am. Mem. Northeastern Ohio (pres. 1966-67), Ohio County supts. assns., E. Central Ohio Tchrs. Assn. (pres. 1968), Northeastern Ohio (past pres.), Ohio (past exec. com. mem.) assns. county suprs., NEA, Ohio Edn. Assn., Am., Ohio, Buckeye assns. sch. adminstrs., DAV, Am. Legion. Club: Lions. Home: 724 Oak St NW New Philadelphia OH 44663 Office: 261 W High Ave New Philadelphia OH 44663

HONECK, STEWART GEORGE, lawyer; b. Chgo., Dec. 25, 1906; s. Stewart George and Bertha Ella (Hettinger) H.; J.D. cum laude, Marquette U., 1929; m. Lillian Carter Sewall, Jan. 28, 1939; children—Stewart George, III, June Lynn (Mrs. William Zastrow), Meribeth (Mrs. James Long), Dorothy (Mrs. Kenneth Bergmann). Admitted to Wis. bar, 1929; practice law, Milw., 1930-46, 59—; dep. atty. gen. State of Wis., 1946-57, atty. gen., 1957-59; spl. counsel City of Plymouth (Wis.), 1959-60, Outagamie County, Wis., 1966-68, City of Oak Creek (Wis.), 1972-77, Milw. County Met. Sewage Commn., 1973—; commr. as surrogate for gov. State of Wis., 1977—. Pres. Firemen's Annuity and Bennefit Bd., Milw., 1939-41, Wis. Bd. Bar Commrs., 1974-77. Trustee Family Hosp., Milw., 1960—. Mem. Milw. Bar Assn. (spl. counsel 1955), Milw. Jr. Bar Assn. (pres. 1937), Delta Theta Phi. Presbyn. Mason (33 deg., Shriner). Club: Athletic (Milw.). Home: 323 Grand Ave Thiensville WI 53092 Office: 757 N Broadway Milwaukee WI 53202

HONG, YOU WAH SUU, state ofcl.; b. Chgo., Nov. 14, 1947; s. Suu and Liu (Shee) H.; student Ill. Inst. Tech., 1963-64; B.S., U. Ill., 1969; A.A., Amundsen Coll., 1971; M. Mgmt. in Accounting and Info. Systems, Northwestern U., 1977; m. Deanna Rae Rickert, Aug. 4, 1972; children—Robert, Kimberly Sue. Research analyst U. Ill. Com. on Sch. Math., Urbana, 1965-67; fin. and engring. systems analyst Sargent & Lundy Engrs., Chgo., 1967-72; mgmt. sci. project leader Health and Hosps. Governing Commn., Chgo., 1972-74; mgr. div. info. services Ill. Dept. Mental Health, Chgo., 1974; adminstr. info. services div. Ill. Dangerous Drugs Commn., Chgo., 1974—; dir. I-Tech Capital Group, Y. Hong Assos.; cons. WHO; EDP cons.; lectr. planning and mgmt. info. systems Chgo. State U. Staff aide Pres.'s Council Econ. Advisers, 1970-71; bus. mgr. Harper Theater, 1970-71; mem. Ill. Arts Council, 1971, Hoffman Estate Hosp. Adv. Council, 1977. Recipient Robert Lindblom Pub. Service award Am. Legion, 1965; NSF scholar, 1963-65. Mem. Am. Soc. Pub. Adminstrn., Assn. Computing Machinery, Data Processing Mgmt. Assn., Am. Math. Soc., Ops. Research Soc. Am., Phi Eta Sigma. Contbr. health care articles to various publs. Home: 4413 N Mumford Dr Hoffman Estates IL 60195 Office: 300 N State St Suite 1500 Chicago IL 60610

HOOD, KAY EVE, psychologist; b. Quincy, Ill., Oct. 7, 1944; d. Dorothy M. (Bricker) Ernst; B.A., St. Xavier Coll., Chgo., 1966; M.A., U. Nebr., Lincoln, 1968, Ph.D., 1975; m. Kenneth E. Hood, July 5, 1969. Counselor, U. Nebr., Lincoln, 1970; psychol. intern Inst. Rehab. Medicine, N.Y. U. Med. Center, 1972; community alcoholism educator Appalachian Reg. Hosp., Beckley, W.Va., 1973-74; dir. women's support program U. Nebr., Omaha, 1975—; also adj. asst. profl.; cons. in field. Dir. Omaha Area Council of Alcoholism, 1976—, Nebr. Task Force Woman Alcoholic, 1976—. Grantee U.S. Office Edn., 1976-77. Mem. Am. Psych. Assn., Am. Personnel and Guidance Assn., Soc. Psych. Study Social Issues, Interest Group on the Study of Leisure. Contbr. articles in field to profl. jours. Home: 3139 Mason St Omaha NE 68105 Office: University Nebraska Box 688 Omaha NE 68101

HOOD, SARAH JANE, historian; b. Oakland, Calif., Nov. 6, 1943; d. Matt M. and Norma Emily (Freeouf) Renner; B.A. cum laude, Doane Coll., 1966; M.A. (NDEA fellow), U. Nebr., 1970, Ph.D., 1977; m. John K. Hood, June 10, 1967; 1 son, Justin Kane. Tchr. pub. schs., Ralston, Nebr., 1966-67; instr. history, U. Nebr., Lincoln, 1973-75; asst. archivist Union Pacific Archival Project, Omaha, 1974; lectr. history Creighton U., Omaha, 1975-77. Mem. Am. Hist. Assn., Coordinating Com. on Women in Hist. Profession, Sixteenth Century Studies Conf., Renaissance Soc. Am., Modern Language Assn., NOW. Democrat. Contbr. articles on women in Nebr. history to Nebr. History, 1978. Home: 1725 Grove St Glenview IL 60025

HOODECHECK, ROBERT ALFRED, banker, lawyer; b. Britton, S.D., Apr. 27, 1931; s. Alfred William and Alvina Ursala (Tembrock) H.; Ph.B., U. Notre Dame, 1953; J.D., Georgetown U., 1958; m. Jane Aline Schneider, Sept. 3, 1960; children—Sara Jane, Nancy Ann, Amy Aline. Admitted to Minn. bar, 1958; atty., law clerk U.S. Dist. Court, St. Paul, 1958-59; practice law with firm Brehmer & McMahon, Winona, Minn, 1959-61; trainee, asst. cashier, asst. v.p., Am. Nat. Bank & Trust Co., St. Paul, 1961-68, v.p., 1968-72; sr. v.p., Winona Nat. and Savs. Bank, 1972—. Mem. West St. Paul Charter Commn., 1966-72. Mem. St. Mary's Sch. Bd., 1973. Treas. Minn. Garden Meml. Charitable Trust; bd. dirs. Family Nursing Service, 1970-72; bd. dirs. United Way of Greater Winona, 1975—, campaign chmn., 1974. Mem. Minn., Winona Co. bar assns., D.C. Bar, Nat. Assn. Accountants (bd. dirs. 1968-69), Robert Morris Assos., Serra Club, Phi Alpha Delta, Winona C. of C. K.C., Kiwanian. Club: Winona Country. Office: 204 Main St Winona MN 55987

HOOK, DARYL GAYLE, bus co. exec.; b. Martinsville, Mo., Mar. 13, 1928; s. Thomas Ransom and Minnie Elsie (Glenn) H.; grad. high sch.; m. Dolores Louise Smith, Apr. 12, 1953; children—Deborah Gaylene, Thomas Manford, Warren Lee. Driver, Jefferson Lines Inc., Mpls., 1953-60, supt. div., 1960-69, asst. gen. mgr., 1969-70, v.p., 1970-73, gen. mgr., 1973—, pres., 1974—, also dir.; dir. Jefferson Co., Jeffco. Inc. Pres., gen. mgr. Jefferson Services, Mpls., 1974—. Served with AUS, 1951-53. Mem. South Central (dir.), North Central (dir.), Nat. (dir.) bus traffic assns., Mo. Bus and Truck Assn. (dir.). Methodist. Mason. Home: 235 N Riley St Kansas City MO 64119 Office: 503 6th Ave N Minneapolis MN 55403 also 1212 E 10th St Kansas City MO 64106

HOOKER, ALEXANDER CAMPBELL, JR., educator; b. Detroit, Mar. 24, 1921; s. Alexander Campbell and Harriet Colladay (Gay) H.; A.B., Dartmouth, 1942; A.M., Harvard, 1947; postgrad. Mexico City Coll., 1947-48, Middlebury Coll. Spanish Sch., 1946, 48, 50, 51, D.Modern Langs., 1954; m. Frances Millard Root, June 2, 1945; children—Elizabeth Gay, Jean Campbell. Instr. French, Cambridge Jr. Coll., 1946-47; teaching fellow Romance langs. Harvard, 1948-50; faculty Romance langs. Ripon (Wis.) Coll., 1950—, prof., 1962—, chmn. dept., 1969-74. Served from ensign to lt. USNR, 1942-45. Mem. Modern Lang. Assn. Am., AAUP, Am. Assn. Tchrs. Spanish and Portuguese, Latin Am. Studies Assn., N.Central Council Latin Americanists (pres. 1972-73), Phi Sigma Iota (chmn. policy and expansion com. 1967-71), Rotarian. Author: La novela de Federico Gamboa, 1971. Home: 727 Thorne St Ripon WI 54971

HOOKER, JOHN HENRY, radiologist, clin. dir.; b. Dixon, Mo., Sept. 30, 1924; s. Henry G. and Grace F. (Wells) H.; student U. Mo., 1942-45; M.D., U. Tenn., 1949; m. Betty L. Wells, Apr. 26, 1952; 1 dau., Jennifer L. Intern, Kansas City (Mo.) Gen. Hosp., 1949-50; gen. practice medicine Clarksville, Mo., 1950-55; resident in radiology City Hosp. St. Louis, 1958-61; practice medicine specializing in radiology, Alton, Ill., 1961-77; radiologist Alton Meml. Hosp., 1961-69, dir. dept. radiology, 1969—. Founder, Pride Inc., Alton. Served with U.S. Army, 1956-57. Diplomate Am. Bd. Radiology. Mem. Alton (past pres.), Madison County (past pres.) med. socs., Radiol. Soc. N.Am., Am. Coll. Radiology. Republican. Presbyterian. Office: Alton Memorial Hospital Alton IL 62002

HOOPER, MARY-LOUISE, educator; b. N.Y.C., July 19, 1940; d. Louis Paul and Lillian C. (Palmieri) Biasotti; B.A. in Edn., Kean Coll., N.J., 1962; M.A. in Edn., No. Mich. Univ., 1973; m. Lee P. Hooper, June 29, 1963; children—Steven, Michael. Instr. Wayne Community Coll., Goldsboro, N.C., 1973-74, Fairleigh Dickenson Univ., Teaneck, N.J., 1975; instr., faculty advisor Webster Coll., Wichita, Kans., 1976—, Butler County (Kans.) Community Coll. Inst., 1977—; coordinator Personal Growth Workshop, 1978. Mem. Am. Personnel and Guidance Assn., Assn. for Humanistic Psychology, Phi Kappa Phi. Club: USAF Officers' Wives (2d v.p. 1977-78). Home: 8609 Ent Dr Wichita KS 67210 Office: Webster College 381st CSG/DPT McConnell AFB KS 67221

HOOPS, M. DEAN, educator; b. Killbuck, Ohio, July 17, 1925; s. Elden Mannat and Beulah Marie (Uhl) H.; B.E. cum laude, Kent State U., 1959; M.S., U. Mich., 1961, Ph.D., 1969; m. Deborah F. Fridline, Mar. 21, 1959; children—Heather, Megan. Clinic tchr. Kent (Ohio) State U., 1958-59; tchr. mentally handicapped Battle Creek (Mich.) Pub. Schs., 1959-60; coordinator, inst. spl. edn. Miami U., Oxford, Ohio, 1963-68; asso. prof. spl. edn. U. Md., College Park, 1969-71; asso. prof., chmn. spl. edn. Youngstown (Ohio) State U., 1971-77. Served with AUS, 1943-46. Decorated Purple Heart; recipient Wood badge Boy Scouts Am., 1951; Spl. Edn. Program Devel. grantee HEW, 1972-74. Mem. Am. Assn. Mental Deficiency, Council Exceptional Children, Assn. Childhood Edn., Internat., Am. assns. higher edn., Kappa Delta Pi, Phi Delta Kappa. Clubs: Masons (32 deg.), K.T. Home: 142 Rockland Dr Youngstown OH 44512

HOOTEN, ANN BRATRUD, document analyst; b. Mpls., Apr. 9, 1923; d. Arthur F. and Harriet (Gongol) Bratrud; student Wheaton Coll., 1939-40, Hardin-Simmons U., 1940-43, U. Minn., 1971-75; m. Floyd Hooten, July 12, 1943; children—Susan (Mrs. Robert Vater), Theodor, Rebecca, William. Pvt. practice as document analyst, Mpls., 1958—; v.p., sec. Edie Adams Cut & Curl Beauty Salons, Minn., 1968—. Bd. dirs. Maranatha Home for Aged. Mem. Internat. Assn. for Identification, Ind. Assn. Document Examiners, Bus. and Profl. Women's Clubs Am. Clubs: Christian Women's, Edina Country, Women's (Mpls.). Home: 3806 W Calhoun Blvd Minneapolis MN 55410 Office: 3813 Sheridan Ave S Minneapolis MN 55410

HOOTS, HAROLD RICHARD, newspaper exec.; b. Mattoon, Ill., Oct. 16, 1913; s. Carl E. and Dora D. (Hedges) H.; B.S., James Millikin U., Decatur, Ill., 1941; m. Edith M. Honn, Aug. 19, 1951; 1 son, John E. Engraver, Decatur Herald & Review, 1933-45, supt. engraving dept., 1945-48, prodn. mgr., 1948-50; prodn. mgr. Lindsay-Schaub Newspapers, Decatur, 1950-56, dir. prodn., 1956-68, dir. corporate communications, 1968-77; pres., dir. Lindsay-Schaub Ill., Inc., Lindsay-Schaub Mich., Inc., Lindsay-Schaub Fla., Inc., 710, Inc., Decatur, 1977—; v.p. Maco Engraving, 1953-65; owner, mgr. Buddy Ricks, Hobart Studios, 1953-58; tchr. newspaper electronics courses; mem. coms. Am. Nat. Standards Inst., 1964-70. Mem. Profl. Photographers Am., Photog. Soc. Am., Am. Newspaper Pubs. Assn., Decatur Assn. Commerce. Club: Decatur Camera. Author: Typesetting Practice, 1966. Inventor photo-elec. compensating recording sunshine duration gauge. Home: 4666 Powers Blvd Decatur IL 62521 Office: 123 W North St Decatur IL 62525

HOOVER, EDWIN LEROY, electronics co. exec.; b. Tipton, Ind., Dec. 14, 1927; s. Clifford A. and Juanita A. (Reed) H.; student Marion (Ind.) Coll., 1946, 47; B.E.E., Purdue U., 1949; m. Zylpha L. Baldwin, Aug. 10, 1947; children—Stanley K., Rowena K. Hoover Bickel, Vida L. Hoover Gearhart, Reva. Mem. research staff Purdue U., 1950-56; gen. mgr. Lafayette Radio Supply (Ind.), 1957-64, P/H Electronics, Lafayette, 1965-71; pres. Dayton Electronic Products Co., DEPCO, (Ohio), 1971—. Counselor, Jr. Achievement, 1966-67; active United Fund, 1972; camp v.p. Gideons Internat., 1968-69. Mem. Engrs. Club Dayton. Mem. Wesleyan Ch. (trustee 1971—). Patentee in teaching systems. Home: 4447 Bonnie Brae Valdina OH 45377 Office: 117 E Helena Dayton OH 45404

HOOVER, GEORGE MARION, data processor; b. Williamsburg, Pa., Oct. 2, 1934; s. Charles Wilbur and Nannie (Showalter) H.; student Pa. State U., 1952-53, Wilbur Wright Jr. Coll., 1957-59; Ph.B., DePaul U., 1966; m. Virginia Rose Lazzara, July 20, 1957; children—Gary Alan, Sharon Ann. Lab. technician Underwriters Labs., Inc., Chgo., 1952-56, Cook Electric Co., Morton Grove, Ill., 1956-57; with Kemper Ins. Co., Long Grove, Ill., 1957—, mgr. data processing edn., 1971—. Lectr. on data processing William Rainey Harper Coll., Palatine, Ill., 1972, mem. data processing adv. com., 1972-77; parliamentary procedure cons. and lectr. to various orgns. in met. Chgo. area. Served with AUS, 1953-55. Mem. Am. Inst. Parliamentarians, Chgo. Data Processing Edn. Council. Club: Toastmasters (Long Grove). Home: 4814 Tile Line Rd Crystal Lake IL 60014 Office: Kemper Ins Co Long Grove IL 60049

HOOVER, JAMES EDWARD, pharm. co. exec.; b. Indpls., Dec. 1, 1927; s. Truman Don and Mildred (Mickel) H.; B.S., Purdue U., 1949, M.S., 1950; m. Katherine Cox, May 22, 1954; children—Anne E., David C., Cynthia K. With Eli Lilly & Co., Indpls., 1959—, dir. mfg. ops., Basingstoke, Eng., 1967-72, dir. info. systems devel., Indpls., 1972—; instr. Purdue, 1949-50. Pres., Historic Landmarks Found., 1966; bd. dirs. Central Ind. council Camp Fire Girls, 1977. Served with AUS, 1950-52. Mem. Soc. Advancement Mgmt. (pres. Indpls.), Am. Inst. Chem. Engrs. Republican. Presbyterian. Clubs: Indpls. Athletic, Meridian Hills Country, Masons, Shriners. Home: 6464 Meridian St N Indianapolis IN 46260 Office: 307 McCarty St E Indianapolis IN 46206

HOOVER, ROBERT JAMES, appliance mfg. co. exec.; b. Waterloo, Iowa, Sept. 30, 1925; s. Edgar Lang and Madeline Louise (Beach) H.; B.A., U. Iowa, 1949; m. Ruth Amelia Schultz, June 14, 1946; children—Ann, Mary Beth, Robert John, Kurt, Ellen. Editor bull. Maytag Co., Newton, Iowa, 1949-56, mgr. pub. info., 1956-67, dir. pub. relations, 1967—. Pres. Wartburg Coll. Parents Com., 1971-72; mem. Jasper County Republican Central Com., 1966-73; trustee Iowa-Luth. Hosp., Des Moines, 1967—. Served with U.S. Army, 1943-46, 1950-51; with USCG Aux., 1973—, div. capt., 1977—. Mem. Newton C. of C. (dir. 1964-67), Pub. Relations Soc. Am. (accredited; pres. Iowa chpt. 1971), Iowa Indsl. Editors Assn. (pres. 1955), Maytag Mgmt. Club. Republican. Lutheran (council 1965-68, treas. 1968); Iowa Sailing Assn. (commodore 1976). Clubs: Newton Country; Jaycees (state v.p. 1959), Red Rock Yacht (vice commodore 1977). Home: 1403 W 13th St S Newton IA 50208 Office: The Maytag Co Newton IA 50208

HOOVER, THOMAS HENRY, univ. ofcl.; b. Wilburton, Okla., Sept. 28, 1919; s. Harry and Jessie (Jackson) H.; m. Viola (Kalcik) H.; July 30, 1948; children—Kathleen, Thomas, Ruth, Chris, James; B.A., Pacific Lutheran U., 1959; M.A., U. Wis., 1968, Ph.D., 1970. Commd. 2d lt. U.S. Army, 1942, advanced through grades to lt. col., 1962; mgmt. analyst, Ft. Benning, Ga. and Madigan Army Hosp., Washington, 1952-59, plans and ops. officer Hdqrs. U.S. Army, Europe, Heidelburg, Germany, 1959-62; ret., 1964; asso. prof. mil. sci. U. Wis., Madison, 1962-64, asst. registrar, 1964-66, registrar, 1967—. Chmn. com. on service to mil. families and vets. ARC, 1975—, bd. dirs. Dane County chpt., 1977—; bd. dirs. Wesley Found., 1966-68, M.C.S.H.U.I., Inc., sch. guidance agy., 1968-74. Mem. Am. Assn. Collegiate Registrars and Admissions Officers, Wis. Coll. Personnel Assn., Phi Kappa Phi, Phi Delta Kappa. Author: VOLAR-The Volunteer Army and Social Expectations, 1975. Office: U Wis Madison WI 53706

HOOVER, THOMAS ORLANDO, educator, clin. psychologist; b. Akron, Ohio, Sept. 21, 1946; s. Orlando Oliver and Marie Lacartha (Speicher) H.; B.A., U. Akron, 1968, M.A., 1970, Ph.D., 1975. Grad. asst. psychology U. Akron, 1968-73, dr.'s teaching asst. counseling and spl. edn., 1974—; psychology intern Path Community Mental Health Orgn., Akron, 1973-74; pvt. practice clin. psychology, 1975—; chief outpatient services Cuyahoga Valley Community Mental Health Center, 1976—; cons. Akron Women Against Rape and Suicide Prevention, 1973—. NSF grantee, 1972-73. Mem. Am. Group Psychotherapy Assn., Am. Psychol. Assn., Am. Personnel and Guidance Assn., Soc. Personality Assessment, Psychometric Soc., Sigma Xi, Psi Chi. Contbr. articles to profl. jours. Home: PO Box 5300 Akron OH 44313

HOPE, CATHARINE MARGARET, clubwoman; b. Jefferson City, Mo., Oct. 26, 1898; d. George and Lily (Williams) Hope; B.S. in Edn., U. Mo., 1923. Tchr. Central Sch., Jefferson City, 1923-32; cashier Home Savs. & Loan Assn., Jefferson City, 1935-48; tchr. East Sch., Jefferson City, 1948-63. Mem. aux. Meml. Community Hosp., Jefferson City, 1969—. Mem. Cole County Hist. Soc. (historian 1963-69). Am. Bus. Women's Assn. (Woman of Year 1971), Cole County Area Ret. Tchrs. Assn., Alpha Gamma Delta Alumnae Club (treas. 1966—). Mem. Order Eastern Star. Clubs: Art (pres. 1968-70), Capital City Woman's (corr. sec. 1973—). Address: 318 E McCarty St Jefferson City MO 65101

HOPKINS, B. SMITH, JR., physician; b. Waukesha, Wis., Jan. 12, 1912; s. B. Smith and Sarah Maude (Childs) H.; A.B., Albion Coll., 1932; M.D., Johns Hopkins, U., 1936; m. Louise Varty, June 11, 1936; children—Stephen A., Jonathan W., B. Smith. Intern, Balt. City Hosp., 1936-37, resident in medicine, 1937-38, 39-40; resident in medicine Vanderbilt U. Hosp., Nashville, 1938-39; cons. in internal medicine and rheumatology Carle Clinic Assn., Urbana, Ill., 1940—, mem. staff Carle Found. Hosp., trustee, 1967-71, 74-76; mem. staff McKinley Hosp., Urbana, Charleston (Ill.) Meml. Hosp.; bd. dirs. E. Central Ill. Health Systems Agy., 1974—, pres., 1975—; mem. Statewide Health Coordinating Council, Ill., 1976—. Mem. Champaign County Med. Soc. (past pres.), Ill. Med. Soc. (chmn. health planning com.), AMA, A.C.P., Am. Rheumatism Assn. Clubs: Urbana Exchange, Urbana Golf Country. Home: 606 Delaware St W Urbana IL 61801 Office: 602 University St Urbana IL 61801

HOPKINS, GEORGE THEODORE, dentist; b. St. Joseph, Mo., Jan. 31, 1928; s. George Theodore and Mary Alta (Giseburt) H.; Asso. Sci., St. Joseph Jr. Coll., 1944-46; student U. Mo. at Columbia, 1949; D.D.S., U. Mo. at Kansas City, 1953; m. Wanda Florine Neely, June 10, 1956; children—George Theodore, Kay, Brian. Practice gen. dentistry, St. Joseph, Mo., 1953—. Instr. dental preceptor program U. Mo. at Kansas City, 1971-73. Chmn. Lions. Sight Conservation, 1964-72, 3d v.p., 1973-74. Mem. Community Council, 1962—, chmn. div. task force on edn., 1972-73. Served with AUS, 1946-47; PTO. Mem. N.W. Dental Soc. of Mo. (pres. 1962-63), Mo. Dental Assn. pres. 1974-75). Methodist (chmn. ofcl. bd. of ch. 1965-72). Lion (pres. 1975-76). Home: 1803 Lovers Ln St Joseph MO 64505 Office: 3609 Beck Rd St Joseph MO 64506

HOPKINS, PRUDENCE FERRIER, sch. counselor; b. Newton, Kans., Dec. 18, 1938; d. Leahman Andrew and Eva Marie (Paul) Faulkenbury; B.S., U. Kans., 1961; M.S., Emporia State U., 1976; children—Jennifer Marie, James Andrew, Sarah Elizabeth. Tchr., Topeka Pub. Schs., 1961-68; environ. specialist fed. project, Topeka, 1973-75; tour guide Goodyear Tire and Rubber Co., Topeka, 1973-75; counselor Conway Springs (Kans.) Elementary and Jr. High Schs., 1976—; counselor Wichita Elementary, 1977; mng. dir. domestic goods Establishment for Trade, Commerce and Mfg., 1977—; cons. Topeka Bd. Edn., 1973-74. Vice chmn., curriculum task force chmn. Community Adv. Com. on Edn., 1973-75; pres. Randolph PTA; Republican committeewoman, 1971-75; Shawnee County del. Kans. Rep. Caucus, 1975; election bd. supr., 1971-75. Recipient award of excellence Environ. Edn. Project, 1974. Mem. Am., Kans. personnel and guidance assns., Am. Sch. Counselors Assn., S. Central Counselors Assn., Kans. Mental Health Assn., Kans. Com. on Child Abuse, Episcopalian. Clubs: Beta Sigma Phi.

HOPKINS, RICHARD BRUCE, agrl. engr.; b. Clark's Summit, Pa., Jan. 8, 1920; s. Harry Winter and Avis Holmes (Dorsheimer) H.; B.S., Pa. State U., 1941; M.S., U. Maine, 1952; Ph.D., Mich. State U., 1955; m. Betty Ruedebusch Bleyer, June 21, 1947; children—Richard H., Susan E. Engr., Allis-Chalmers Mfg. Co., Milw., 1941-50; asst. prof. U. Maine, Orono, 1950-53; grad. asst. Mich. State U., East Lansing, 1953-55; design analyst John Deere Product Engring. Center, Waterloo, Iowa, 1955—. Mem. Am. Soc. Agrl. Engrs., Nat. Soc. Profl. Engrs., Soc. Automotive Engrs., Iowa Engring. Soc. (v.p. 1967-68), ASME, Iowa Bd. Engring. Examiners, Sigma Xi, Sigma Pi Sigma. Republican. Methodist. Author: Design Analysis of Shafts and Beams, 1970. Home: 2524 Timber Dr Cedar Falls IA 50613 Office: John Deere Product Engring Center Waterloo IA 50702

HOPKINS, WILLIAM BARTON, JR., charitable instn. adminstr.; b. Idabel, Okla., Nov. 28, 1924; s. William B. and Mary P. (Hinton) H.; B.A. in Econs., Southeastern La. U., 1962; postgrad. La. State U., 1963; m. Rhea Joan Rautio, Aug. 26, 1965; children—Mary Elizabeth, Jonathan Barton. Ins. salesman Life & Casualty So. Nat., Baton Rouge, 1948-59; pub. affairs dir. Minn. Soc. Crippled Children and Adults, Mpls., 1963—; co-chmn. Met. Transit Com. for the Disabled, Mpls., 1974—; cons. on disabled to Minn. Commn. for Handicapped, State Bldg. Code Office, Dept. Natural Resources, Minn. Soc. Architects; designer wheelchair obstacle course exhibit, 1968. Bd. dirs. Islands of Peace Found., Mpls., 1973—. Served with Transp. Corps, AUS, 1943-47. Named Outstanding Social Service Worker, State of Minn., 1974. Mem. Nat., Minn. rehab. assns., Nat. Council Transp. of Disadvantaged. Clubs: Moose, Kiwanis, S.W. Mpls. (pres. 1971-72, lt. gov. 1974-75). Home: 4420 Victory Ave Minneapolis MN 55412 Office: 3915 Golden Valley Rd Minneapolis MN 55422

HOPPER, DARREL GENE, theoretical chemist; b. Stillwater, Okla., June 10, 1944; s. Doyle Houston and Dorthea Elene (Randolph) H.; B.S., Okla. State U., 1966, Ph.D., 1971; m. Chahira Hamed Metwally, Aug. 31, 1969; children—Dalia Lee Elizabeth, Paul Darrel Alexander. Engr., Gen. Electric Co., Mt. Vernon, Ind., 1966; teaching asst. chemistry Okla. State U., Stillwater, 1966-71, research asst., 1967-71, research asst. entomology, 1971, research asso. biochemistry, 1971-72; NRC research asso. Aerospace Research Labs., Wright-Patterson AFB, Ohio, 1972-74; theoretical chemist Argonne (Ill.) Nat. Lab., 1974-77; research asso. prof. Wright State U., Dayton, Ohio, 1977—; staff scientist Sci. Applications, Inc., Dayton, 1977—. NDEA fellow, 1966-69; Petroleum Research Fund fellow, 1969-70; Nat. Research Council asso., 1972-74. Mem. Am. Chem. Soc., Am. Phsy. Soc., Am. Statis. Assn., Quantum Chemistry Program Exchange, Am. Soc. Mass. Spectrometry and Allied Topics, Phi Eta Sigma, Phi Lambda Epsilon. Presbyterian. Contbr. articles to profl. jours. Home: 230 Halifax Dr Vandalia OH 45377 Office: Chemistry Dept and Brehm Lab Wright State U Dayton OH 45435

HOPTON, EUGENE FRANCIS, mfg. co. exec.; b. Kansas City, Kans., Oct. 10, 1907; s. Edward Frederick and May (Dooley) H.; B.A., U. Mich., 1930; m. Marie Emma Carroll, Aug. 13, 1933; children—Gene Hotpon, David, Edward F., Carroll Ann. With Iowa Renderers, Cedar Rapids, 1933-34, mgr., Manchester, Iowa, 1934-36; mgr. N.D. Rendering Co., Bismarck, 1936-37; dir. McIntosh County (N.D.) Welfare, 1937-40; mgr. Montizuma Renderers, Iowa, 1940-48, West Point Renderers (Miss.), 1948-56; dir. engring. Indland Products, Inc., Columbus, Ohio, 1956—. Mem. Nat. Renderers Assn. (nat. pres. 1968-69; Distinguished Service award 1976). Republican. Methodist. Pioneer in cetrifugal separation of rendering; tech. adviser, U.S. del. fats and oils FAO, Rome, 1968-73. Home: 118 Granville Rd W Worthington OH 43085 Office: PO Box 926 Columbus OH 43216

HORAK, PENELOPE CATHERINE, engr.; b. Chgo.; d. Edward Peter and Helene Catherine (Kohes) Horek; B.S., Roosevelt U., 1967, M.P.A. with highest honors, 1972, M.Ph. with highest honors, 1975; postgrad. U. So. Calif. Draftsman, Engring. Services Co., Chgo., 1959-64; draftsman, engr. De Leuw Cather & Co., Cons. Engrs., Chgo., 1964-68; project engr. Nat. Gas Pipeline Co., Chgo., 1968-69; engr. Greeley & Hansen Cons. Engrs., Chgo., 1969-73; staff engr. chmn. div. Quaker Oats Co., Chgo., 1973-74; asst. div. dir. tech. services Fermi Nat. Accelerator Lab., Batavia, Ill., 1974—. Mem. AAUW, Internat., No. Ill. Solar energy socs., Ill. Fedn. Bus. and Profl. Women's Clubs (pres. Hinsdale 1976-77), NOW. Democrat. Home: 5610 Katrine Ave Downers Grove IL 60515 Office: Fermilab PO 500 Batavia IL 60510

HORGAN, EDWARD DANIEL, market research exec.; b. Cin., July 12, 1942; s. Edward Daniel and Gertrude (Hoffman) H.; A.B., U. Cin., 1964; m. Jeanette Yvonne Wray, May 21, 1966; children—Edward IV, Laurie. Dir. control studies Burgoyne, Inc., 1964-68; v.p. mktg. Am. Capital Corp., Cin., 1968-71; dir. research Tempo Research Services, Cin., 1971-73; pres. mktg. Research Services, Inc., Cin., 1973—; instr. mktg. U. Cin., 1970-75. Past pres. Big Bros.; neighborhood leader Charter Parts, 1975; mem. financial com. Bortz for Council campaign, 1977. Recipient Outstanding Service award Big Bros., 1968. Mem. Am. Mktg. Assn. (pres. Cin. chpt. 1977), Mktg. Research Assn., C. Of C. Clubs: Cincinnati, Racquet, Western Hills Country. Home: 346 Neeb Rd Cincinnati OH 45238 Office: 1007 Enquirer Bldg Cincinnati OH 45202

HORITA, KENJI, dentist; b. Fir, Wash., Mar. 15, 1919; s. Seiichiro and Fusayo (Sadakani) H.; A.A., Los Angeles City Coll., 1942; B.A., U. Minn., 1948, B.S., 1952, D.D.S., 1954; m. Betty Lucille Larson, Sept. 6, 1947; children—Daniel John, Leslie Ann, Timothy Lee, Patti Jean, John David, Thomas Fredrick. Practice gen. dentistry, Coon Rapids, Minn., 1954—. Dir. Riverroad Enterprizes, Inc., sec., 1960-69, v.p., 1969—. Clin. instr. dentistry U. Minn., 1954-60, clin. asst. prof., 1960-66, clin. asso. prof., 1967—. Mem. City Planning Commn., Coon Rapids, 1963-66. Served with AUS, 1945-46. Mem. Am. Soc. Dentistry for Children, Minn. Prosthodontic Soc., Minn., Am. dental assns., Mpls. Dist. Dental Soc., Omicron Kappa Upsilon, Delta Sigma Delta. Methodist. (chmn. adminstrv. bd. 1974—). Home: 741 84th Ln NW Coon Rapids MN 55433 Office: 9920 Zilla St NW Coon Rapids MN 55433

HORKHEIMER, RONALD WILLIAM, physician; b. Milw., Aug. 18, 1939; s. Donald Leonard and Wilma Ceclia (Brehl) H.; B.M.E., Marquette U., 1962, M.D., 1967. Rotating intern Mercy Hosp., San Diego, 1967-68; obstetrics-gynecology resident St. Joseph's Hosp., Milw., 1970-71; practice medicine, specializing in emergency medicine, Milw., 1971—; emergency dept. physician Trinity Meml. Hosp., West Allis Meml. Hosp., 1972—; organizing dir., chmn. dept. emergency medicine St. Mary's Hosp., 1973-74. Missionary hosp. physician, Smith Kline & French Fgn. fellow-Sumve Hosp., Tanzania, East Africa, 1967. Served with USNR, 1968-70. Mem. Am. Coll. Emergency Physicians, A.C.S. (regional com. on trauma 1975—), AMA, Wis., Milwaukee County (com. on trauma, emergency med. services com. 1972—) med. socs., Alpha Omega Alpha, Alpha Sigma Nu, Tau Beta Pi, Alpha Kappa Kappa, Pi Tau Sigma. Club: Vagabond Ski. Home: 2914 N 78th St Milwaukee WI 53222 Office: 9997 W North Ave 179 Milwaukee WI 53226

HORN, CARL LEWIS, judge; b. Highland Park, Mich., Aug. 18, 1928; s. Casper Smith and Marie Elizabeth (Beckman) H.; A.B., U. Mich., 1950, J.D., 1952; m. Ann Barton, Feb. 19, 1955; children—Craig W., Marjorie A., Karen J. Admitted to Mich. bar, 1952; asso. firm Harty, Austin and Dingell, Detroit, 1956-59; practiced law, Standish, Mich., 1959-72; pros. atty. Arenac County (Mich.), 1960-72; city atty. Standish, 1960-62; circuit judge 34th Jud. Circuit Mich., Standish, 1972—. Chmn. Republican Committee, 1968-72. Bd. dirs. Standish Devel. Corp. Served with USAF, 1952-56. Mem. Pros. Attys. Mich. (dir. 1968-72), State Bar of Mich., Am. Bar Assn., Am. Judicature Soc., Delta Theta Phi. Methodist (chmn. ch. bd. 1963—). Home: 617 Orchard St Box 749 Standish MI 48658 Office: Courthouse Standish MI 48658

HORN, JAMES EDWARD, rubber products mfg. co. exec.; b. Akron, Ohio, Sept. 6, 1920; s. Paul Edward and Arlene (Robertson) H.; student Baldwin Wallace Coll., 1951-52, Akron U., 1946-49; m. Audrey Marie Grassell, Feb. 28, 1941; children—Ronald, Jean Ann (Mrs. John C. Gillen), James H., Cheryl Lynn (Mrs. Billie D. Tinker). With Crane Packing Co., Vandalia, Ill., 1969—, plant mgr., 1969—. Mem. Vandalia Zoning Commn., 1972—, Fayette County Indsl. Commn., 1971—, Region 14 Manpower Commn., State of Ill. Bd. dirs. Fayette County United Fund Corp., Fayette County Hosp., Vandalia, CEFS Community Action. Served with USAAF, 1944-45. Mem. Vandalia C. of C. (dir.), Chgo. Rubber Group, B.F. Goodrich Foremans Club. Home: 1008 W Jackson St Vandalia IL 62471 Office: PO Box 192 Vandalia IL 62471

HORN, WILFRED, electronic communications corp. exec.; b. Hanover, Germany, Aug. 31, 1947; s. Karl Heinz and Waltraud (Reinike) H.; came to U.S., 1955, naturalized, 1963; B.A., U. Ill., 1969; M.B.A., Loyola U., Chgo., 1973; m. Kim Ann Leader, July 19, 1973. Research, devel. engr. Teletype Corp., 1969-71; sr. market research analyst Brunswick Corp., Skokie, Ill., 1973-76; product planning mgr. Motorola Corp., Schaumburg, Ill., 1976—. Served to capt. USAR, 1969—. Mem. Am. Mktg. Assn., Res. Officers Assn. Republican. Lutheran. Home: 307 Kingsbury Dr Arlington Heights IL 60004 Office: 1301 E Algonquin Rd Schaumburg IL 60196

HORNBY, FREDERICK THOMAS, computer systems analyst; b. Chgo., Nov. 29, 1944; s. Fred J. and Ethel M. (Thomas) H.; student Bradley U., 1962-64; B.B.A., Milton Coll., 1966; m. Cynthia M. Dremel, June 18, 1966; children—Fred, Tamara, Brian. With Walker Mfg. Co. div. of Tenneco, Racine, Wis., 1968—, sr. analyst fin. systems, 1976—. Mem. Gift of Life Com., Kidney Found. Mem. Assn. Systems Mgrs. Lutheran. Home: 4701 N Green Bay Rd Racine WI 53404 Office: 1201 Michigan Blvd Racine WI 53402

HORNE, LEWIS WILLIAM, clin. lab. adminstr., chiropractor; b. Altoona, Pa., Jan. 8, 1926; s. Howard Franklin and Mary Catherine (Lewis) H.; D.C., N.D. cum laude, Nat. Coll. Chiropractic, Chgo., 1949; postgrad. Roosevelt U., 1960-63. Instr. dept. bacteriology and pub. health Nat. Coll. Chiropractic, 1948-52, dir. dept. microbiology and pub. health, 1955-64; supr. Chgo. Med. Arts Lab., 1964-68; supr. Plaza Clin. Lab., Park Ridge, Ill., 1968—. Mem. alumni adv. bd. Franklin Sch. Sci. and Arts. Diplomate Am. Bd. Bio-Analysts. Fellow Am. Coll. Med. Technologists; mem. Am. Soc. Microbiology (25 Year award 1974), Am. Med. Technologists (30 Year award 1975), Am. Inst. Biol. Scis., State Micros. Soc. Ill., Chiropractic Christian Fellowship (faculty advisor), Ill. Soc. Am. Med. Technologists, Ill. Soc. for Microbiology, Delta Tau Alpha (pres. 1948), Chi Rho Sigma. Home: 4829 N Damen Ave Chicago IL 60625

HORNER, DONALD ELVIN, ednl. adminstr.; b. Bad Axe, Mich., Aug. 5, 1938; s. L.W. and Audrey Ann (Elvin) H.; B.A. in Math., Mich. State U., 1963; m. Barbara G. Gilbert, Dec. 19, 1959; children—Bruce, Scott, Christopher. Systems programmer Computer Lab., Mich. State U., East Lansing, 1963-65, mgr. users service, 1965-71, coordinator spl. projects, 1972—. Cons., Nat. Bur. Standards, 1969-70. Served with AUS, 1957-60. Mem. Assn. for Computing Machinery (chpt. chmn. 1965, 69). Kiwanian (dir. Lansing 1969-71, treas. 1972—). Home: 1433 Roxburgh St East Lansing MI 48823

HORNER, THOMAS HARVEY, banker; b. Cleve., Mar. 29, 1928; s. William Wattles and Caroline Clagett (Wattles) H.; B.A., Denison U., 1950; B.B.A., Western Res. U., 1954; m. Virginia Hopkins Jackson, Sept. 15, 1956. Loan officer Central Nat. Bank, Cleve., 1955-63; asst. v.p. Marine Midland Trust Co., Mohawk Valley, Utica, N.Y., 1963-67; v.p. Union Commerce Bank, Cleve., 1967-70; v.p., chief loan officer, dir. Peoples-Mchts. Trust Co., Canton, Ohio, 1970-75; pres., chief exec. officer, dir. Dime Bank, Canton, 1975—; dir. Great Lake Bancshares, Inc. Trustee Canton Art Inst., 1975—, treas., 1977; trustee E. Central Ohio chpt. Am. Heart Assn., 1974; trustee Ohio affiliate, 1976. Served with U.S. Army, 1950-52. Mem. Robert Morris Assos. (pres. No. Ohio chpt. 1973-74), Am. Inst. Banking (grad. certificate 1959), Am. Bankers Assn. (certified comml. lender), Canton Clearing House. Episcopalian. Clubs: Chagrin Valley Hunt, Congress Lake, Canton, Massillon. Office: 301 E Tuscarawas St Canton OH 44702

HORNING, LEORA NORLENE, educator; b. Brooklyn, Mich., Oct. 19, 1916; d. Eben Foster and Belvia (Waters) Horning; B.S., Mich. State U., 1939, M.A., 1946; postgrad. U. Colo., U. Calif. at Los Angeles, U. Nebr. Homemaking tchr. Onsted (Mich.) High Sch., 1939-41; cafeteria mgr., tchr. Eastern High Sch., Lansing, Mich., 1941-44; head dietitian Dow Chmn. Co., Midland, Mich., 1944-45; instr. Mich. State U., 1945-49; head homemaking dept. Saginaw (Mich.) High Sch., 1949-53; homemaking supr., tchr., student tchr. supr. Lakeview Schs., Battle Creek, Mich., 1953-58; asst. prof. vocat. edn. U. Nebr., Lincoln, 1958-61, asso. prof., 1961-62, acting chmn. home econs. edn. dept., 1962-63, asso. prof. home econs. edn., 1963—. Past rec. sec., dir. Hart & Howell Co., Brooklyn; cons. Nebr. Ann. Homemaking Tchrs. Conf., 1958—; speaker Midwest Health Congress, 1974; conf. leader Health Occupations Workshop, Lincoln, 1967, Regional Dietitians Workshop, 1973. Recipient Pub. Relations award Mich. Home Econs. Assn., 1952; Distinguished Service award Adult and Continuing Edn. Assn. Nebr., 1976. Mem. NEA, Nebr. Edn. Assn., Am., Nebr. vocat. assns., Am., Nebr. (pres. 1972) home econs. assns., Adult Edn. Assn. U.S.A., Mo. Valley Adult Edn. Assn. (named Nebr. Adult Educator for 1971), Nat. Assn. Pub. Sch. Adult Educators, Nat., Nebr. assns. student teaching, Nat. Soc. Study Edn., Nat., Nebr. assns. for supervision and curriculum devel., Home Econs. Edn. Assn. (pres. 1975-77), Nat. Assn. Tchr. Educators Home Econs., Am. Bus. Womens Assn. (Bus. Woman of Year 1958, 70), Sigma Kappa. Presbyterian. Club: Toastmistress (past council sec., pres.). Asso. editor: Adult Leadership, 1964-66, 73-76. Home: 10 Gramercy Pl 7111 Old Post Rd Lincoln NE 68520

HORNING, ROSS CHARLES, JR., educator; b. Watertown, S.D., Oct. 10, 1920; s. Ross Charles and Harriett (Meaghan) H.; B.A., Augustana Coll., 1948; M.A., George Washington U., 1952, Ph.D. (Sanders fellow in History), 1958; postgrad. Russian, Inst. of Langs. and Linquistics, Georgetown U., 1952-53. Instr. Wis. State U., Eau Claire, 1958-59; asst. prof. St. John's U., Collegeville, Minn., 1959-64; asso. prof. Russian history and internat. affairs, Creighton U., 1964-68, prof. Russian, Indian and Canadian history, 1968—. Mem. council Nebr. com. for humanities Nat. Endowment for Humanities. Served with USAAF, 1943-46. Fulbright scholarship to India, summer 1967. Mem. AAAS, Am. Assn. For Advancement of Slavic Studies, Am. Hist. Assn., Am. Soc. Internat. Law, AAUP, Orgn. Am. Historians, Conf. on Slavic and European Studies, Assn. Profl. Ball Players, Omaha Urban League, Joslyn Liberal Arts Soc., S.W. Am. Assn. for Advancement Slavic Studies, Western Social Sci. Assn., Am. Fgn. Service Assn., Canadian History Assn., Assn. Canadian Studies in U.S., Western History Assn., UN Assn., Assn. Asian Studies, Omaha Symphony Assn., Assn. Canadienne de Sci. Politique, Internat. Law Assn., Am. Br. Foreign Service Club, Washington, Nebr. Arts Council, Asian Soc., Opera/Omaha, Omaha Press Club, Alpha Sigma Nu. Home: 4955 Cuming St Omaha NE 68132

HORNS, HOWARD LOWELL, internist; b. Buffalo, N.D., July 11, 1912; s. Otto and Crystal (Sherwin) H.; B.A., B.S., U. Minn., 1940, M.B., M.D., 1943; m. Edith Marie Frostenson, Sept. 22, 1940; children—James S., Susan M., William H. Intern U. Minn., Mpls., 1944, resident in internal medicine, 1944-47, asst. prof. 1947-49, asso. prof., 1949-53, prof., 1953—, asst. dean, 1949-53, clin. prof. medicine, 1955—; mem. staff Nicollet Clinic, Mpls., 1955—. Mem. Minn. Bd. Med. Examiners, 1956-75, former pres.; mem. Fedn. State Bds. Med. Examiners, 1956—, pres., 1973-74, mem. liaison com. continuing med. edn., 1975—; mem. Nat. Bd. Med. Examiners, 1975—. Served with M.C., AUS, 1953-55. Diplomate Am. Bd. Internal Medicine. Fellow A.C.P.; mem. Minn. Med. Assn., AMA, Minn. Soc. Internal Medicine (gov. 1971-75). Contbr. articles to profl. jours. Home: 100 Melbourne Ave SE Minneapolis MN 55414 Office: 2001 Blaisdell Ave Minneapolis MN 55404

HORNTHAL, WILLIAM JULIUS, food service industry exec.; b. Chgo., Aug. 6, 1922; s. Philipp J. and Dora (Wolner) H.; B.S., Northwestern U., 1946; grad. Sch. Sales Mgmt. Mktg., Rutgers U., 1954-55; m. Sally Schultz, Sept. 21, 1947; children—Philipp, James. With CFS Continental Inc., 1950—, group v.p., 1966-73, area pres., 1973-75, group pres., 1975—. Chmn. Combined Jewish Appeal Restaurant Assn., 1964-66. Served with AUS, 1943-45. Decorated Bronze Star, Silver Star, Purple Heart. Mem. Sales Mktg. Execs. Chgo., Sales and Mktg. Execs. Internat. Club: Execs. (Chgo). Home: 3940 Loyola Lincolnwood IL 60645 Office: 2550 N Clybourn Ave Chicago IL 60614

HORNYAK, ROY ROBERT, musician, condr.; b. St. Joseph, Mo., Nov. 4, 1925; s. Roy and Mildred (Estes) H.; A.B., Central Meth. Coll., 1948; Mus.M., Ind. U., 1950, Mus.D. in Edn., 1964; m. Mary Margaret Lewis, Aug. 9, 1953; children—Deborah Margaret, Roy Robert. Music supr., dir. bands pub. schs., Rector, Ark., 1948-49; prof. music, dir. univ. bands U. Cin., 1954-70, head music edn. div., 1970-71, asso. dean Coll. Conservatory Music, 1971-74, dir. undergrad. studies, 1971-74, adviser to dean, 1974-75, head performance studies, 1975—; condr., music dir. Cin. Wind Ensemble. Trustee Bapt. Student Found., U. Cin. Served with USNR, 1943-46, 50-53. Recipient Distinguished Alumnus award Central Meth. Coll., 1976. Mem. Music Educators Nat. Conf., Ohio Music Edn. Assn., Coll. Band Dirs. Nat. Assn. (chmn. pub. band music com. 1967-69), Council Research Music Edn., Phi Mu Alpha Sinfonia, Kappa Kappa Psi, Phi Beta Mu. Baptist (deacon). Club: Torch (pres. 1971-73). Address: 5553 Lucenna Dr Cincinnati OH 45238

HORRELL, C. WILLIAM, photographer; b. Anna, Ill., Oct. 15, 1918; s. Clarence W. and Zetta Hileman (Lanier) H.; B.Ed., So. Ill. U., 1942; M.S., U. Ill., 1949; Ed.D., Ind. U., 1955; m. Ettelye Hanser, June 5, 1941; children—Bruce W., Jeffrey L. Mem. staff tng. film preparation unit Scott Field, Ill., 1942-45; owner Horrell Studio, Anna, 1945-49; staff So. Ill. U., Carbondale, 1949—, prof. cinema and photography, 1972—, recipient Good Tchr. award 1972. Awardee contbn. to photog. edn. World Press Assn., 1970. Mem. Assn. Edn. for Journalism, George Eastman House. Mem. United Ch. Christ. Clubs: Lions, Masons. Author: (with Steffes) Introduction and Publications Photography; (with Piper and Voigt) Land Between the Rivers, 1972; (with Harris and Irvin) Rocks and Soils of Southern Illinois, 1977; researcher photog. edn. in higher edn., 1964—. Office: Dept Cinema and Photography So Ill Carbondale Carbondale IL 62901

HORSLEY, JACK EVERETT, lawyer; b. Sioux City, Iowa, Dec. 12, 1915; s. Charles E. and Edith V. (Timms) H.; A.B., U. Ill., 1937, LL.B., 1939, J.D., 1965; m. Sallie Kelley, June 12, 1939 (dec.); children—Pamela, Charles Edward; m. 2d, Bertha J. Newland, Feb. 24, 1950 (dec.); m. 3d, Mary Jane Moran, Jan. 20, 1973; 1 dau., Sharon. Admitted to Ill. bar, 1939, since practiced law Mattoon, Ill.; sr. counsel Craig & Craig, attys. for Ill. Central Gulf R.R. Co., C. & E.I. R.R. Co., Penn Central R.R. Co., Internat. Harvester Co. and other cos.; specializes in defensive trial work; vice chmn. bd., dir. Central Nat. Bank, 1976—; mem. lawyers' adv. council U. Ill. Law Forum, 1960-63; lectr. Practicing Law Inst., N.Y.C., 1967-73, Ct. Practice Inst., Chgo., 1974—, U. Mich. Coll. Law Inst. Continuing Legal Edn., 1968; vis. lectr. Duquesne Coll., Pitts., 1970, chmn. rev. com. Ill. Supreme Ct. Disciplinary Commn., 1973-76. Pres. bd. edn. Sch. Dist. 100, 1946-48; bd. dirs. Moore Heart Research Found., 1969—; narrator Poetry Interludes, WLBH-FM. Served with J.A.G.D., A.C., 1942-46; disch. as lt. col. Fellow Am. Coll. Trial Lawyers; mem. Am., Ill. (mem. exec. council ins. law 1961-63, lectr. ins. law course for attys. 1962, 64, 65), Coles-Cumberland (v.p. 1968-69, pres. 1969-70, chmn. jud. inquiry com. 1976—) bar assns., Assn. Bar City N.Y. (non-resident mem. emeritus), Am. Arbitration Assn. (nat. panel arbitrators), U. Ill. Law Alumni Assn. (pres.), Ill. Def. Counsel Assn. (dir. 1966-67, pres. 1967-68), Soc. Trial Lawyers (chmn. profl. activities 1960-61; dir. 1961-62), Adelphic Debating, Assn. Ins. Attys., Internat. Assn. Ins. Counsel (membership com. 1966-67), Am. Judicature Soc., Appellate Lawyers Assn., Scribe, Delta Phi (mem. exec. com. Alumni Assn., 1960-61), Sigma Delta Kappa. Republican. Christian Scientist. Mason (32 deg.). Author: Trial Lawyer's Manual, 1967; Voir Dire Examinations and Opening Statements, 1968; Current Development in Products Liability Law, 1969; Illinois Civil Practice and Procedure (textbook), 1970; The Medical Expert Witness, 1973; The Doctor and the Law, 1975; The Doctor and Family Law, 1975; The Doctor and Business Law, 1976; The Doctor and Medical Law, 1977. Contbr. Ill. Bar Jour., Def. Law Jour.; contbr. jury instructions and special defenses articles Fedn. of Ins. Council Quar. and Ill. Law Forum, 1958; cons., contbr. Med. Econs., 1969—; legal cons. Mast-Head, 1972—; contbr. RN Mag., 1976—. Home: 50 Elm Ridge Mattoon IL 61938 Office: 1807 Broadway Mattoon IL 61938

HORTON, CHARLES CORNELIUS, pub. co. exec.; b. Jefferson, S.C., Sept. 7, 1920; s. Edward Wilfred and Lula Mae (Munn) H.; B.A., U. S.C., 1941; MsJ, Northwestern U., 1948; m. Phyllis Arleen Thomas, Jan. 6, 1946; children—Linda Ruth, Marion Anne, Carol Arleen. Sales promotion copywriter Dartnell Corp., Chgo., 1947-48; salesman, B.D. Thomas Co., Chgo., 1948-59, advt. salesman, 1950-55, sales mgr., domestic engring., 1955-57; founder, pres. Horton Pub. Co., Skokie, Ill., 1958—. Served with USAF, 1941-45. Republican. Protestant. Contbr. articles in field. Home: 2328 Lincolnwood Dr Evanston IL 60201 Office: 7574 N Lincoln Ave Skokie IL 60076

HORTON, DAVID RICHARD, ins. co. exec.; b. Pawtucket, R.I., Feb. 2, 1941; s. Richard C. and Una M. (Wright) H.; B.A., Dakota Wesleyan U., 1964; postgrad. Life Ins. Agy. Mgmt. Assn. Inst., 1969, 70, 71; m. Barbara A. Schlimgen, May 27, 1961; children—Laura A., Heidi M. Spl. agt. N.Y. Life Ins. Co., Mitchell, 1964-68. Mem., pub. services chmn. Mitchell Life Underwriters (S.D.), 1968-69; owner, gen. mgr. S.D. office Lincoln Mut. Life Ins. Co., Mitchell, 1968—; prof. Dakota Wesleyan U., 1974—. Pres., Mitchell Area Adjustment Tng. Center for Retarded Children, 1972—, chmn. bd., 1972—. Mem. City Planning Bd., Mitchell, 1974—. Founder, David R. Horton Scholarship Fund, Dakota Wesleyan U., 1969-77. Recipient Man of Month award (14) Lincoln Mut. Life Ins. Co., 1969, numerous awards for nat. sales achievement in life ins.; named Mass. Mut. Group Ins. leader, 1972, 76; Alumnus of Yr. award Dakota Wesleyan U., 1975. Mem. Nat. Assn. Life Underwriters (Nat. Quality award 1971-72, 73-74, 74-75), Mitchell Life Underwriters Assn. (pres. 1975-76), Jr. C. of C. (various awards), Dakota Wesleyan U. Alumni Assn. (nat. pres. 1977-78). Methodist (ch. lay leader 1971, chmn. bldg. fund dr.,

1969, chmn. pastor parish relations com. 1974-76). Elk. Home: 1216 Summit Dr Mitchell SD 57301 Office: 1321 N Main Box 176 Mitchell SD 57301

HORTON, GUY MANN, journalist, ednl. adminstr.; b. Apr. 11, 1933; s. Richard H. and Nelia A. (Harrison) H.; B.S., East Tex. State U., 1953, M.S., 1957; postgrad. U. Tex., 1958-59; Ph.D., U. Mo., 1972; m. Linda Ruth Green, Aug. 31, 1959; children—Ellen, Amy. Tchr. of journalism Huntsville (Tex.) High Sch., 1953-54; mem. staff Athens (Tex.) Daily Review, summer, 1954; corr. for Pacific Stars and Stripes, Sendai, Japan, 1954-56; editor U.S. Army newspaper The Cavalier, Tokyo, 1955-56; sports publicist East Tex. State U., Commerce, 1956-57; dir. of journalism Angelo State U., San Angelo, Tex., 1957-60; reporter Standard-Times, San Angelo, 1960-61; pub. relations specialist Tex. A. & M. U., Coll. Sta., 1961-64, asst. prof. journalism, 1964-67; dir. of journalism U. So. Miss., Hattiesburg, 1964-67; mem. pub. relations staff (part-time) U. Mo., Columbia, 1967-68, asst. dir. U. Info. Services, 1968-72, acting dir., 1972-73, dir., 1973—. Mem. Mo. Broadcasters Assn., Council for Advancement and Support of Edn., Pub. Relations Soc. Am., Assn. for Edn. in Journalism, Mo. Press Assn., Kappa Tau Alpha, Sigma Delta Chi. Author: A History of the Athens Review, 1953; contbr. articles to jours. and newspapers. Home: 107 Rockingham St Columbia MO 65201 Office: Univ Missouri 400 Lewis Hall Columbia MO 65201

HORTON, LOWELL WAYNE, educator; b. Oak Hill, Ohio, Oct. 22, 1936; s. Wayne L. and Frances L. (Jones) H.; B.S., Rio Grande Coll., 1960; Ed.M., Ohio U., 1962, Ph.D., 1969; m. Phyllis Bauer, Mar. 2, 1957; 1 son, David. Tchr., Franklin Sch., Circleville, Ohio, 1957-59; prin. McKinley Sch., Xenia, Ohio, 1961-66: asst. prof. edn. dept. Central State U., Wilberforce, Ohio, 1966-68; prof. of edn. No. Ill. U., DeKalb, 1969—. Mem. Assn. Tchr. Educators, Assn. of Supervision Curriculum Devel., Phi Delta Kappa. Author: Learning Center: Heart of the School, 1974; Teacher Education: Trends, Issues, Innovations, 1975. Home: 1203 Elizabeth St DeKalb IL 60115 Office: 170 Gabel Hall Northern Illinois Univ DeKalb IL 60115

HORTON, STANLEY MONROE, educator, writer; b. Huntington Park, Calif., May 6, 1916; s. Harry Samuel and Myrle May (Fisher) H.; B.S., U. Calif., Berkeley, 1937; M.Div., Gordon-Conwell Sem., 1944; S.T.M., Harvard U., 1945; Th.D., Central Bapt. Sem., 1959; m. Evelyn Gertrude Parsons, Sept. 11, 1945; children—Stanley Monroe, Edward Samuel, Faith Evelyn. Instr., Met. Bible Inst., North Bergen, N.J., 1945-48; prof. Bible and Hebrew, chmn. div. Bibl. edn. Central Bible Coll., Springfield, Mo., 1948—; asso. prof. Assemblies of God Grad. Sch., Springfield, 1973—; guest prof. Near East Sch. Bible and Theology, Jerusalem, 1962; books include: Into All Truth, 1955; The Promise of His Coming, 1967; Ready Always, 1974; It's Getting Late, 1975; Welcome Back Jesus, 1975; What the Bible Says About the Holy Spirit, 1976; The Adult Teacher, annual vols., 1952—. Recipient citation for outstanding service Bethel Assembly of God Ch., 1975. Mem. Soc. Bibl. Lit., Am. Sci. Affiliation, Evang. Theol. Soc., Nat. Assn. Profs. of Hebrew, Near East Archaeol. Soc., Nat. Assn. Evangelicals, Calif. Scholarship Fedn. (life), Phi Alpha Chi. Mem. Assemblies of God. Home: 615 W Williams St Springfield MO 65803 Office: 3000 N Grant Ave Springfield MO 65802

HORVATH, JAMES JAY, orthopaedic surgeon; b. Detroit, Apr. 16, 1916; s. Julius Frank and Mary Veronica (Ujfalusi) H.; B.S. in Liberal Arts, Wayne State U., 1944, M.D., 1945; m. Leola H. Montag, Sept. 21, 1946; children—James C., Thomas C., William C., Vikki Lee. Intern, Highland Park (Mich.) Gen. Hosp., 1945-46; resident in gen. surgery St. Joseph Mercy Hosp., Detroit, 1949, resident in orthopedic surgery Harper Hosp., 1951, Children's Hosp., Detroit Gen. Hosp. 1952 (all Detroit); pvt. practice medicine specializing in orthopedic surgery, Detroit, 1953—; chief orthopedic surgery Highland Park Gen., 1958-72, pres. staff, 1960; mem. staff Rehab. Inst., Detroit, pres., 1972; staff Harper, 1953—, chief orthopedic surgery outpatient dept., 1958-68; staff Children's, Detroit Gen., Jennings Meml. hosps., 1953— (all Detroit). Clin. asso. prof. orthopedic surgery Wayne State U. Sch. Medicine, Detroit, 1960—, asst. dean clin. faculty, 1972—. Served with AUS, 1943-45, 46-48. Fellow A.C.S., Clin. Orthopedic Soc., Detroit Acad. Orthopedic Surgeons (pres. 1965); mem. Royal Coll. Medicine-Eng., Am. Acad. Orthopedic Surgeons, Middle Eastern and Mediterranean Orthopedic and Traumatology Soc., Wayne State U. Sch. Medicine Alumni Assn. (pres. 1972), Phi Beta Pi (pres. Kappa chpt. 1956). Mason (Shriner). Contbr. articles to profl. jours. Home: 776 Berkshire Rd Grosse Pointe Park MI 48230 Office: 1553 Woodward Ave Detroit MI 48226

HORVE, LESLIE ALFORD, mech. engr.; b. Decatur, Ill., Dec. 5, 1938; s. Marshall Alford and Louise Ruth (Repak) H.; B.S. in Engring. Physics, U. Ill., 1960, M.S. in Nuclear Engring., 1964; postgrad. U. Conn., 1965-67; M.E., Midwest Coll. Engring., 1971, D.Eng., 1973; m. Betty Kastran, Aug. 21, 1960; children—Deborah, Jeffrey, Susan, Jennifer. Analytical engr., Pratt & Whitney Aircraft Corp., E. Hartford, Conn., 1964-67; application engr. CR Industries, 1967-69, mgr. of shaft seal research, 1969-73, mgr. product engring., 1973-75, dir. engring., Elgin, Ill., 1975—; mem. faculty (part-time) Midwest Coll. Engring., Lombard, Ill., 1967—, Judson Coll., Elgin, Ill., 1968-72. Served to lt. (j.g.), USN, 1960-63. Named Mgmt. Man of the Year, CR Industries, 1970; registered profl. engr., Ill. Mem. Soc. of Automotive Engrs., Am. Soc. Lubrication Engrs., Hanover Park Jaycees. Greek Orthodox. Asso. editor Lubrication Engring., 1976—. Contbr. articles on seals and rubber molding to tech. jours. Home: 515 Rue Chamonix Deer Park Barrington IL 60010 Office: CR Industries 900 N State St Elgin IL 60120

HORWEDEL, LOWELL CHARLES, lubricant co. exec.; b. Cleve., Nov. 27, 1932; s. Albert C. and Mildred (Hackel) H.; A.A., Los Angeles Jr. Coll., 1957; m. Dorothy A. Deupree, June 21, 1958; children—Mary Lee, Nancy Anne, Lowell Charles. Chemist, Vitaminerals, Inc., 1952-54; chemist Electrofilm, Inc., North Hollywood, Calif., 1956-58, chief chemist, 1958-60, research and devel. mgr., 1960-63, product mgr., 1964-65, gen. mgr. lubricants div., 1966-71, exec. v.p. Microseal Corp., 1971-73, pres., 1973-74; pres. Therm-O-Lab Corp., 1974—, E/M Lubricants, Inc., 1974—; v.p., dir. K.N. Thanstrom & Assos., 1977—. Served with AUS, 1954-56. Mem. Am. Chem. Soc., Am. Soc. Lubrication Engrs., Soc. Automotive Engrs., Detroit Engring. Soc., Glass Packaging Inst., Ind. Oil Compounders Assn. Patentee solid film lubricants. Contbr. articles to profl. jours. Home: S Main St Otterbein IN 47970 Office: Hwy 52 NW West Lafayette IN 47906

HORWICH, ROBERT H., research zoologist; b. Paterson, N.J., Dec. 31, 1940; s. Edwin Nathaniel and Edna May (Goldstein) H.; B.A., Rutgers U., 1962; M.S. (Chapman fellow, Orgn. for Tropical Studies scholar), U. Md., 1964, Ph.D. (Natural Resources Inst. fellow, NASA fellow), 1967. Field rep. in India, Smithsonian Inst., Washington, 1967-68; research zoologist Brookfield (Ill.) Zoo, 1970-74; research zoologist Inst. Micro-ontogenetic Ethology and Macro-cosmological Ecology, Gays Mills, Wis., 1974—. Sci. adviser Student Program in Behavioral Research, Brookfield (Ill.) Zoo, 1974; research asso. dept. anatomy U. Chgo., 1970-75; vis. lectr. No. Ill. U., DeKalb, 1974, Chgo. State U., 1975, Grand Valley State Colls., Thomas Jefferson Coll., Allendale, Mich., 1975. Mem. Animal Behavior Soc., Am. Soc. Mammalogists, Phi Sigma. Contbr. articles to profl. jours. Office: Inst Micro-ontogenetic Ethology and Macro-cosmological Ecology RD 1 Box 96 Gays Mills WI 54631

HORWITT, MAX KENNETH, biochemist; b. N.Y.C., Mar. 21, 1908; s. Harry and Bessie (Kenitz) H.; B.A., Dartmouth Coll., 1930; Ph.D., Yale U., 1935; m. Frances Levine, 1933 (dec.); children—Ruth Ann Horwitt Singer, Mary Louise Horwitt Goldman; m. 2d, Mildred Gad Weitzman, Jan. 1, 1974. Research fellow in physiol. chemistry Yale U., 1935-37, lab. asst., 1932-34, asst., 1934-35; dir. biochem. research lab. Elgin (Ill.) State Hosp., 1937-59, L.B. Mendel research lab., 1960-68, hosp. dir. research, 1966-68; asso. dept. biol. chemistry U. Ill. Coll. Medicine, 1940-43. asst. prof., 1943-51, asso. prof., 1951-62, prof., 1962—; prof. dept. biochemistry St. Louis U. Sch. Medicine, 1968-76, prof. emeritus, 1976—; acting dir. div. research services Ill. Dept. Mental Health, Chgo., 1967-68; field dir. Anemia and Malnutrition Research Center, Chiang Mai Med. Sch., Thailand, 1968-69; cons. in human nutrition Rush Med. Sch., Chgo., 1967—. Pres., Kneseth Israel Congregation, Elgin, 1965. Recipient Osborne and Mendel award Am. Inst. Nutrition, 1961. Diplomate Am. Bd. Clin. Chemistry, Am. Bd. Nutrition. Fellow Gerontol. Soc., AAAS, N.Y. Acad. Scis., Am. Inst. Chemists; mem. Am. Soc. Biol. Chemists, Am. Soc. Clin. Nutrition, Soc. Exptl. Biology and Medicine, Soc. Biol. Psychiatry, Assn. Vitamin Chemists, Am. Chem. Soc. Editorial bd. Jour. Nutrition, 1967-71; co-editor Am. Jour. Clin. Nutrition, 1974. Contbr. numerous articles in biochemistry, psychopharmacology and clinical nutrition to profl. publs. Home: 18 York Hills Brentwood MO 63144 Office: 1402 S Grand Blvd St Louis MO 63104

HORWITZ, SAMUEL JACOB, physician; b. Ficksburg, South Africa, July 24, 1931; s. Harry and Lena (Abrams) H.; M.D., U. Cape Town, 1953; m. Eva Hanna Marcks, May 20, 1956; children—Michael Simon, Colin Paul, Naomi Shirley. Came to U.S., 1962, naturalized, 1967. Intern Groote Schuur Hosp., Cape Town, South Africa, 1954; gen. practice medicine, Salisbury, Rhodesia, 1955-62; resident in pediatrics Univ. Hosps. Cleve., 1962-64, now mem. staff; fellow in pediatric neurology Columbia Presbyn. Med. Center, N.Y.C., 1964-67; practice medicine specializing in pediatric neurology, Cleve., 1967—; asst. prof. pediatrics, also asst. clin. prof. neurology Case Western Res. U., Cleve., 1967—. Diplomate Am. Bd. Pediatrics, Am. Bd. Psychiatry and Neurology. Fellow Am. Acad. Pediatrics; mem. A.M.A., Am. Acad. Neurology, Acad. Medicine Cleve., No. Ohio Pediatric Soc. Office: Parkway Med Center 3609 Park E Cleveland OH 44122

HOSACK, ROBERT EUGENE, JR., historian; b. Chanute, Kans., Dec. 20, 1948; s. Robert Eugene and Welthalee (Lasater) H.; B.A. in History, U. Calif., Santa Barbara, 1972. An organizer Neosho Valley Hist. Soc., Chanute, 1975, pres., dir., 1975—, chmn. bd., 1977—; lectr. Neosho County Community Jr. Coll., 1976. Coordinator, McGovern for Pres., Neosho County, 1972; mem. plan com. Chanute Central Bus. Dist. Policy Com., 1977—. Recipient Bicentennial award U.S. Postal Service, 1976. Mem. Am. Hist. Assn., Orgn. Am. Historians, Soc. History Edn., Am. Assn. State and Local History, Western History Assn., Kans., Mo. hist. socs. Democrat. Roman Catholic. Author articles. Home: 218 N Grant St Chanute KS 66720 Office: 201 E Main St Chanute KS 66720

HOSFORD, CLARENCE RALPH, dentist; b. Monticello, Iowa, June 13, 1921; s. Sprague Malon and Kathryn Irene (Brown) H.; student Cornell Coll., 1938-41; D.D.S., State U. Iowa, 1944; m. Virginia Clarissa Sheppard, Aug. 4, 1942; children—Robert Craig, Kay Kristine Hosford Hokanson. Practice gen. dentistry, Monticello, 1946—; mem. Iowa Bd. Dental Examiners, 1975—. Pres. bd. edn. Monticello Community Sch. Dist., 1968-69, 74-75. Served to capt. AUS, 1944-46. Mem. ADA, Iowa Dental Soc. (pres. Dubuque dist. 1973—), Psi Omega, Omicron Kappa Upsilon. Clubs: Masons, Rotary. Home: 128 S Chestnut St Monticello IA 52310 Office: 113 W 1st St Monticello IA 52310

HOSFORD, HARRY WILLIAM, JR., mfg. co. exec.; b. Cleve., Feb. 25, 1922; s. Harry William and Helen Hayden (Harvey) H.; B.M.E., Rensselaer Poly. Inst., 1944; m. Helen Elizabeth Moorehouse, Mar. 15, 1942; children—Ann Hosford White, Hayden, Bill, Peter, Molly. Plant engr. Diamond Alkali Co., Painesville, Ohio, 1946-48; pres. Harco Corp., Cleve., 1948-71, Wright Devel. Corp., 1968-77; chmn. bd. Gilmore Industries, Cleve., 1971-77, also dir.; chmn. bd., pres. MBIS Inc., Cleve., 1977—; dir. Community Nat. Bank, Tel-Fax Corp. Mem. NSC, 1949-52. Served as ensign USNR, 1944-46. Mem. Nat. Assn. Corrosion Engrs., ASME. Episcopalian. Patentee in field. Home: 2078 Lander Rd Mayfield Heights OH 44124 Office: 25865 Richmond Rd Cleveland OH 44146

HOSKINS, HAROLD PAUL, cons. engring. co. exec.; b. Paloma, Ill., Oct. 22, 1908; s. James Ellis and Nettie (Brewer) H.; B.C.E., U. Iowa, 1930; m. Dorothy Lucille Dolan, Feb. 24, 1931; 1 son, James. Materials engr. Ill. Div. Hwys., 1930-36; design engr. Consoer, Townsend & Quinlan, Chgo., 1936-39; field engr. Clay Products Assn., Chgo., 1939-43; chmn. bd., pres. Harold Hoskins & Assos., Lincoln, Nebr., 1944-72; v.p., treas. Western Lab., Lincoln, 1955-72; v.p. Miller Warden Western, Cons. Engrs., Lincoln, 1961-70; chmn. bd. Hoskins-Western-Sonderegger, Planning Engrs., Architects and Photogrammetric Cons., Lincoln, 1972—; nat. dir. Legis. Council Photogrammetry, Washington, 1944-73. Registered profl. engr., Nebr., Iowa, Ill., Minn., Ohio, Mo., Kans., S.D., N.D., Mont., Wyo., Ariz., Colo., Minn. Fellow ASCE; mem. Am. Waterworks Assn., ASTM, Nat. Soc. Profl. Engrs., Am. Soc. Photogrammetry, Am. Congress Surveying and Mapping. Presbyterian. Clubs: Masons, Elks, Country (Lincoln). Home: 2901 Calvert St Lincoln NE 68502 Office: 825 J St Lincoln NE 68501

HOSKINS, JOHN EMMETT, psychologist; b. Detroit, May 9, 1924; s. John Lynn and Annie Laurie (Schrimshire) H.; student U. Mich., 1948-49; B.S., Wayne State U., 1951, Ed.D., 1964; M.A., Western Mich. U., 1959; m. Joyce Margaret Robertson, Mar. 5, 1946; children—Dean William, Deborah Lynn, Karianne Margaret. Exec. trainee, Goodwill Industries, Detroit, 1949-51, exec. dir., Fort Wayne, Ind., 1951-56, Kalamazoo, 1956-60, Detroit, 1960-70; exec. dir. Epilepsy Center Mich., Detroit, 1970-73; pvt. practice clin. and forensic psychology, Grosse Pointe, Mich., 1964—; instr. Wayne State U., 1966—; cons. Social Security Adminstrn., 1962—. Served to capt. USAF, 1942-48. Mem. Am., Mich. psychol. assns., Am. Soc. Clin. Hypnosis, Mich. Soc. Cons. Psychologists, Phi Delta Kappa. Episcopalian. Home: 715 Fisher Rd Grosse Pointe MI 48230 Office: 18633 Mack Ave Detroit MI 48236

HOSKINS, PHILLIP MICHAEL, auditor; b. Bloomington, Ind., Apr. 4, 1948; s. Vernon Festus and Delores Imogene (Houts) H.; student Ind. U. Mem. staff Ind. U. Bookstore, 1972-73; accountant Follett's Bookstore, Bloomington, 1973-74, City of Bloomington, 1974—. Served with USAF, 1966-70; PTO. Mem. DAV (post comdr. 1974, mem. exec. fin. com. Ind. 1973-75), Am. Theatre Organ Soc., Embassy Theatre Found., U.S. Olympic Soc. Episcopalian (lay reader). Home: 317 E Wylie St Bloomington IN 47401 Office: PO Box 1216 Bloomington IN 47401

HOSKINSON, ROBERT EMERY, real estate broker; b. New Lexington, Ohio, Jan. 8, 1921; s. William Emery and Olive Kathryn (Kenyon) H.; grad. high sch.; m. Patricia J. Randles, Sept. 16, 1941; children—Robert Michel, Gene Edward. With Ralston Steel Carl and Columbus Bolt Works, Columbus, Ohio, 1937-42, Hokinson & O'Neil Drywall, Columbus, 1948-64; real estate salesman Robert Hoisington, Columbus, 1964-68; owner, operator Robert Hoskinson Realtor, Galena, Ohio, 1968—. Active Boy Scouts Am., 1952-53, 66-67. Served with AUS, 1942-45; ETO. Decorated Purple Heart. Mem. Columbus Bd. Realtors. Club: Sertoma (pres. 1971-72; life mem.). Address: 6926 Plumb Rd Galena OH 43021

HOSMAN, DAVID WILLIAM, bus. exec.; b. Pittsburg, Kans., July 8, 1946; s. William Samuel and Wilma May H.; B.S. in Bus. Adminstrn., Pittsburg State U., 1970. Mktg. cons. Adventurs Inc., Joplin, Mo., 1970-71; display advt. mgr., classified advt. mgr., then nat. advt. mgr. Stauffer Publs., 1971-73; dir. advt. Hix Corp., Pittsburg, 1974-75; media cons. U. Kans. Media Support, Parsons, Kans., 1975-76; pres. Cor-Mar, Inc., Pittsburg, 1976—. Mem. Am. Mktg. Assn. Contbr. articles in field to profl. jours. Home: 1109 E 10th St Pittsburg KS 66762 Office: 816 E Jefferson Pittsburg KS 66762

HOSSAIN, T. I. M. ZAHUR, gastroenterologist; b. Mymensingh, Bangladesh, Jan. 2, 1940; s. Kasem and Hamida (Munshi) Ali; came to U.S., 1964, naturalized, 1976; M.D., Dacca U., 1962; m. Sadeka Begum, Jan. 17, 1973. Intern, Columbus Hosp., Chgo., 1964-65; resident in internal medicine, Sch. Medicine Wayne State U., Detroit, 1965-68, instr. in internal medicine, 1970-73, asst. prof. medicine, 1973-76; fellow in gastroenterology, Sch. Medicine U. Utah, Salt Lake City, 1968-70; chief gastroenterology sect. VA Hosp., Allen Park, Mich., 1970-76; staff physician, Sherman and St. Joseph Hosps., Elgin, Ill., 1977—. Fellow Am. Coll. Gastroenterology; mem. A.C.P., Am. Soc. Gastrointestinal Endoscopy, Am. Gastroenterol. Assn., Am. Fedn. Clin. Research, AMA, Ill. State Med. Soc. Moslem. Contbr. tech. articles to med. jours. Office: 1795 Grandstand Pl Elgin IL 60120

HOSTENG, DONALD TED, constrn. materials co. exec.; b. Sac City, Iowa, Feb. 21, 1927; s. Theodore M. and Iva (Luke) H.; grad. pub. schs.; m. Marjorie Jean Robson, June 1, 1949; children—Mark, Michael, Craig, Kirk, Scott. Pres., Hosteng Sand & Gravel, Galva, Iowa, 1954—, Hosteng Ready Mix, Sac City, 1962—, Hosteng Concrete & Gravel, Inc., Sac City, 1966—, Farmers Lumber, Sac City, 1966—. Served with USNR, 1945-46. Mem. Sac City C. of C. (pres. 1969-70). Lutheran (treas. 1971—). Club: Kiwanis (pres. Sac City 1971-72). Home: 716 Oak St Sac City IA 50583 Office: 312 Sioux St Sac City IA 50583

HOSTETLER, DAVID LEE, sculptor, educator; b. Beach City, Ohio, Dec. 27, 1926; s. Melwood David and Grace Anna (Penrod) H.; B.S., Ind. U., 1948; M.F.A., Ohio U., 1949; children by previous marriage—Ann Hostetler Lampela, Jane, Jay. Exhibited in one-man shows at Butler Art Inst., Youngstown, Ohio, 1958, Sculpture Center Gallery, N.Y.C., 1965-72, Gilman Galleries, Chgo., 1966, Harmon Gallery, Naples, Fla., 1968, Edna Hibel Gallery, Boston, 1968, Maxwell Galleries, San Francisco, 1969, Downey (Calif.) Museum Art, 1969, Speed Mus., Louisville, 1971, Cultural Arts Center, Canton, Ohio, numerous others; exhibited in group shows at Art U.S.A., N.Y.C., 1958, Wichita (Kans.) Gallery, 1949, Butler Art Inst., Youngstown, 1955-67, 71, Sculpture Center, Gallery, N.Y.C., 1956, 65, 66, 70, 71, Parke-Bernet Galleries, N.Y.C., 1962, Pa. Acad. Fine Arts, Phila., 1966, Emily Lowe Gallery, Miami, Fla., 1966, Smithsonian Traveling Sculpture Exhbn., 1968-69, many others; represented in permanent collections at Canton Art Inst., Miami Museum Modern Art, Ft. Lauderdale Mus., Speed Mus., Louisville, Nat. Geog. Soc., Craftsman in Am., others; various commns. Instr. ceramics Canton Art Inst., 1949-50; instr. ceramics Ohio U., Athens, 1950-56, asst. prof., 1956-61, asso. prof. sculpture, 1961-66, prof., 1967—. Recipient 1st prize Mainstreams, 1969, Marietta Coll., 1969; purchase prize Butler Art Inst., 1970; award Ohio Arts Council, 1971. Served with AUS, 1945-46. Home: Box 989 Athens OH 45701 Office: Sch Art Ohio U Athens OH 45701

HOSTETTER, PHILIP HARVEY, physician; b. Albert, Kans., Apr. 4, 1917; s. Harvey Edgar and Mae Edna (Charlesworth) H.; M.D., U. Kans., 1942; m. Helen Marie Whitwam, Sept. 7, 1941; children—James, Dorothy (Mrs. Warren Brecheisen), Robert, Carol (Mrs. David Pacey). Intern Wichita (Kans.) Hosp., 1942-43; practice family medicine, Baldwin, Kans., 1946-48, Halstead, Kans., 1948-50, Manhattan, Kans., 1950—; mem. staff St. Mary Hosp., Meml. Hosp., Manhattan; dist. coroner, Manhattan, 1957-76; med. dir. Manhattan Mut. Life Ins. Co., 1964—, also dir. Served to capt. M.C., AUS, 1943-46; PTO. Decorated Purple Heart, Bronze Star medal. Diplomate Am. Bd. Family Practice. Fellow Am. Acad. Family Physicians; mem. Kans. Acad. Family Physicians (pres. 1975), AMA, Kans., Riley County (pres. 1957) med. socs. Kiwanian (pres. Manhattan 1968). Home: 2045 Jay Ct Manhattan KS 66502 Office: 821 Poyntz St Manhattan KS 66502

HOTALING, JACK ROBERT, frat. exec.; b. Syracuse, N.Y., June 23, 1931; s. Raymond Main and Thelma May (Legg) H.; B.A., Syracuse U., 1958; m. Virginia Anne Hilmers, July 10, 1971; children—Christopher Paul, Robert Hilmers. Asst. exec. sec. Sigma Alpha Epsilon, Evanston, Ill., 1960-69, exec. sec., 1969—. Dir. Sigma Alpha Epsilon Leadership Found., 1969—. Trustee, sec. Levere Meml. Found.; bd. dirs. Family Counseling Service, Glenview United Fund. Served with USNR, 1952-54. Mem. Evanston Hist. Soc., Am. Soc. Assn. Execs., Fraternity Execs. Assn., Assn. Coll. Frats. (pres. 1973-74). Methodist (ch. fin. commn.). Club: Rotary (dir.). Home: 639 Forest Rd Glenview IL 60025 Office: PO Box 1856 Evanston IL 60204

HOTALING, ROBERT BACHMAN, educator; b. Syracuse, N.Y., July 19, 1918; s. Elliot Danforth and Florence (Bachman) H.; B.S., Syracuse U., 1942; M.Urban Planning, Mich. State U., 1952; m. Janet Kelley, Nov. 20, 1943 (dec.); children—Marilyn Hotaling Knaggs, Brock Elliot, William Austin, Richard Chapman; m. 2d, Jeanne Bryant, July 31, 1971. Staff dir. McFadzean, Everly, Rose & Assos., Chgo., 1946-49; prin. Robert B. Hotaling & Assos., planning cons., Lansing, Mich., 1949-52; dep. dir. state and local planning R.I. Exec. Dept., Providence, 1952-55; city planning dir., urban renewal planner, Portland, Maine, 1955-57; acting dir. Greater Portland Regional Planning Commn., 1956-57; prof. urban planning Coll. Social Sci., prof. continuing edn. Inst. Community Devel., Mich. State U., East Lansing, 1957—; pres. Urban Cons., Inc., Lansing, 1962-66; profl. community planner to Mich. law firms on ct. cases, land developers, state and fed. agys., philanthropic orgns.; mem. State Bd. Registration for Profl. Community Planners, 1967—, chmn., 1970-72, 76-77; mem. Twp. Planning Commn. Meridian Twp., Ingham County, Mich., 1958-70, chmn., 1968-69. Chmn. Meridian Twp. Charter Commn., 1970-72; corr. sec., trustee Mich. Parks Assn., 1960-68. Served to capt. C.E., AUS, 1942-46. Recipient certificate of appreciation for outstanding leadership Meridian Twp., 1970. Mem. Am. Inst. Planners, Nat. Com. on Licensing and Regulation Profl. Planners, Mich. Twps. Assn. (ednl. program cons. 1972—). Christian Scientist. Contbr. articles to profl. jours. Home: 2401 Indian Hills Dr Okemos

MI 48864 Office: Kellogg Center Mich State U East Lansing MI 48823

HOTTLE, DARRELL RIZER, judge; b. Hillsboro, Ohio, Sept. 13, 1918; s. George Emmitt and Alice (Bishop) H.; B.A., Ohio State U., 1940; LL.B., Western Res. U., 1947; m. Catherine Carpenter, Nov. 15, 1947; children—Kay Darlene, Larry Alan. Admitted to Ohio bar 1947, since practiced Hillsboro; city solicitor Hillsboro, 1950; pros. atty. Highland County, 1949-53; judge Common Pleas Court, Highland Co., 1954—. Chmn. co. fund drives, A.R.C., Co. Soc. Crippled Children; v.p. Central Ohio Boy Scouts Am. Sec. Highland Co. Democratic Exec. Com., 1948-50, chmn., 1951-53. Recipient Silver Beaver award Boy Scouts Am. Mem. Am., Ohio State (past exec. com.), Highland County bar assns. United Methodist (del. gen. and world confs.). Clubs: Masons (33 deg.), Elks (past exalted ruler), Rotary (past pres. Hillsboro). Home: 335 W Walnut St Hillsboro OH 45133 Office: Highland County Ct House Hillsboro OH 45133

HOUCHIN, OLLIE BOYD, biochemist; b. Fulton, Mo., Dec. 1, 1913; s. John Lewis and Linnie (Sims) H.; A.B., Westminster Coll., 1935; M.A., U. Mo., 1939; postgrad. Yale, 1940; Ph.D., U. Iowa, 1942; m. Mary Ruth Schroke, Aug. 26, 1939; children—Nancy Ellen (Mrs. David Ladd Swigert), John Frederick. Instr. pharmacology Okla. U. Sch. Medicine, Oklahoma City, 1942-44; asst. prof. biol. chemistry Loyola U. Sch. Medicine, Chgo., 1944-46, U. Louisville, 1946-50; asst. prof. medicine and neurology U. Ark. Med. Center, Little Rock, 1950-58; head, supr. Central Research Labs., Oklahoma Med. Research Found., Oklahoma City, 1958-64; dir. biochemistry Mercy Hosp., Springfield, Ohio, 1964—; mem. staff Mercy Meml. Hosp., Urbana, Ohio, Mercy Med. Center, Springfield, Ohio, Cons. in clin. chemistry Mercy Meml. Hosp., Urbana, Ohio, 1965—. Fellow Am. Inst. Chemists (mem. accrediting com. profl. chemists Ohio chpt. 1971); mem. AAAS, N.Y. Acad. Sci., Am. Assn. Clin. Chemists, Can. Soc. Clin. Chemists, Sigma Xi. Home: 2000 Oak Knoll Dr Springfield OH 45504 Office: 1343 N Fountain Springfield OH 45501

HOUCK, JAMES MCPHERSON, lawyer; b. Greencastle, Ind., Sept. 22, 1921; s. David Worth and Norris (McPherson) H.; A.B., DePauw U., 1943; J.D., Ind. U., 1962; m. Helen Marie Jome, July 1, 1944; children—David Jome and Robert Edgar. Farmer, Greencastle, 1946-59; claims rep. Social Security Adminstrn., Indpls., 1960-62; admitted to Ind. bar, 1962, since practiced in Greencastle; pros. atty. 64th Ind. Jud. Circuit, 1963—. Pres. Putnam County Learning Center, 1975-76. Served with AUS, 1943-46. Mem. Ind. Pros. Attys. Assn. (dir. 1971—, pres. 1976), Ind., Putnam County, Indpls. bar assns., Order of Coif, Sigma Chi. Democrat. Methodist. Home: 724 Terrace Ln Greencastle IN 46135 Office: 11 1/2 S Indiana St Greencastle IN 46135

HOUCK, RICHARD JAMES, ophthalmologist; b. Michigan City, Ind., Apr. 27, 1932; s. Howard Thomas and Marion Elizabeth (Richards) H.; student DePauw U., 1950-53; M.D., Ind. U., 1957; m. Imogene Blair, Dec. 28, 1956; children—Deborah, Richard James, Gregory Thomas. Intern Orange County Hosp., Calif., 1957-58; commd. capt. USAF, 1958, advanced through grades to lt. col., 1970; chief ophthalmology Air Force in France, 1960-63; resident ophthalmology Ohio State U. Hosp., Brooke Gen. Hosp., Armed Forces Inst. Pathology, 1964-65; chief clin. ophthalmology Sch. Aerospace Medicine, 1968-70; ret., 1970; practice medicine specializing in ophthalmology, Michigan City, 1970—. Med. adviser Head Start, 1971-73. Pres. No. Ind. Assn. for Children with Learning Disabilities; mem. adv. com. Mental Health Assn. Ind. Named LaPorte County Physician of Year, Mental Health Assn., 1972. Fellow Am. Bd. Ophthalmology. Mem. Am. Assn. Ophthalmology and Otolaryngology, Aerospace Med. Assn. Home: 2940 Mt Claire Way Michigan City IN 46360 Office: PO Box 556 Beverly Shores IN 46301

HOUGH, JAMES EMERSON, cons. geotech. engr., geologist; b. Paducah, Ky., July 25, 1930; s. Winfred Cyril and Goldie Bernice (Stewart) H.; Asso. Sci., Paducah Jr. Coll., 1951; B.S., U. Ky., 1953, M.S., 1958; m. Valeska Marie Runge, Aug. 11, 1956; children—Jerome Kevin, Christopher Kendal. Asst. geologist Ky. Geol. Survey, Lexington, 1957-58; geologist TVA, Lexington, 1958-59; soil engr. Ky. Hwy. Dept., Frankfort and Lexington, 1959; soil and found. engr. Ill. Div. Hwys., Paris, 1960-63; geol. engr. Geo-Engring. Labs, Mt. Vernon, Ill., 1963; chief engr. Earth Sci. Labs., Cin., 1963; chief engr. James E. Hough & Assos., Cin., 1963—. Elder Presbyterian Ch. Served in C.E., U.S. Army, 1953-55. Registerd profl. engr., Ohio, Ky., Ind., Ill., Va., Pa. Mem. Am. Cons. Engrs. Council, Assn. Soil and Found. Engrs., ASCE, Internat. Soc. Soil Mechanics and Found. Engrs., Geol. Soc. Am., Am. Soc. Photogrammetry, Am. Assn. Petroleum Geologists, Assn. Engring. Geologists, Am. Arbitration Assn., Ohio Assn. Cons. Engrs. (state dir.), Sigma Gamma Epsilon. Club: Masons. Home: 10936 Gosling Rd Cincinnati OH 45247 Office: 3398 W Galbraith Rd Cincinnati OH 45239

HOUGH, JOHN E., mfg. co. exec.; b. Janesville, Wis., July 5, 1916; s. Azel Clarence and Dorothy (Whitehead) H.; A.B., Cornell U., 1937; m. Vivian Swensson, Dec. 28, 1940; children—Gordon Richard, Lawrence A. Pres., Hough Mfg. Corp., Janesville, 1937—. Chmn. Rep. party, Janesville, 1948-52, Rock County (Wis.) Rep. Orgn., 1953-55, 1st Dist. Rep. Orgn., 1958-61; treas. Rep. Party of Wis., 1961-68, state chmn., 1972-74; alt. del. Rep. Nat. Conv., 1968-72; Rep. nat. committeeman, 1968-72; trustee Milton (Wis.) Coll. Mem. Chief Execs. Forum. Clubs: Rotary; Cornell (N.Y.C.); Univ. (Milw.). Home: 1901 Ruger Ave Janesville WI 53545 Office: PO Box 591 Janesville WI 53545

HOUGH, NEAL PATRICK, market research co. exec.; b. St. Louis, Oct. 22, 1940; s. Neal A. and Cathryn (Watson) H.; B.S. in Commerce, St. Louis U., 1963, M.S., 1969; m. Dianne Marie Remley, Dec. 5, 1964; children—Elizabeth, Laura. With Dun & Bradstreet, St. Louis, 1963-65; data processor Honeywell Corp., 1965-66; market researcher Gen. Steel Industries, 1966-68; market research analyst UMC Industries, 1968-69; research account exec. D'Arcy, MacManus & Masius Advt., St. Louis, asso. research dir., 1969-77; v.p. Market Facts, Inc., Chgo., 1977—. Mem. viewers adv. com. Channel 9, 1970. Mem. Am. Mktg. Assn. (treas. St. Louis chpt.). Home: 1308 Central Ave Wilmette IL 60091 Office: 100 S Wacker Dr Chicago IL 60606

HOUGH, RALPH LAMAR, chem. research lab. exec.; b. Springfield, Ohio, Jan. 13, 1930; s. Ralph C. and Ola (Pennsinger) H.; B.A., Wittenberg U., 1954; postgrad. Ohio State U., 1959; m. Lois G. Hallam, July 20, 1963; children—Harold J., Patricia (Mrs. Steven Hickman), Pamela. Engr., Equipment Lab., Wright-Patterson AFB, Ohio, 1955-59; engr. Air Force Materials Lab., Wright-Patterson AFB, 1959-63, research team leader, 1963-66; pres. Hough Labs., Springfield, 1966—; chmn. bd. dirs., pres. Touch of Americana, Inc., Springfield, 1975—. Fellow Am. Inst. Chemists; mem. Am. Soc. for Metals, Am. Chem. Soc., Soc. Aerospace Material and Process Engrs., Internat. Microwave Power Inst., Sigma Xi. Contbr. articles to profl. jours. Home: Box 182 Lewistown OH 43333 Office: PO Box 1505 Springfield OH 45501

HOUGHTON, CHOLM G., trade assn. exec.; b. Goodell, Iowa, May 18, 1913; s. Joseph D. G. and Rose E. (Goodridge) H.; certificate Marshalltown Jr. Coll., 1932; B.A., U. Iowa, 1934; postgrad. Creighton U., 1953; m. Lois Sheaffer, Mar. 3, 1946; children—Gregory S., Marissa Jane. City editor Cherokee (Iowa) Daily Times, 1935-36; editor Garner (Iowa) Leader and Signal, 1936-41; feature writer Dubuque (Iowa) Telegraph-Herald, 1941-42; field dir., asst. dir. dept. pub. info. for midwestern area hdqrs. ARC, 1942-46; mng. editor Lorain (Ohio) Daily Jour., 1946-47; pub. relations dir. Hinky Dinky Stores Co., Omaha, 1947-55; eastern field editor Chain Store Age mag., N.Y.C., 1955-59; asst. dir. dept. pub. info. Am. Meat Inst., Chgo., 1959-63, dir. dept. membership and personnel relations, 1963-74; v.p., dir. dept. info. Livestock Conservation Inst., 1974—. Pres., Garner chpt. ARC, 1940-41, publicity chmn. Douglas County chpt., 1950-53, pres. DuPage County region, 1965-69, chmn. pub. relations com. Mid-Am. chpt., Chgo., 1973; dir. Am. Meat Inst. Center for Continuing Edn., 1963-74. Recipient Nat. award Future Farmers Am., 1969. Mem. Headline Club, Sigma Delta Chi. Clubs: K.C., Rotary (charter pres.); Suburban Press (Chgo.). Contbr. numerous articles to profl. jours. Home: 408 Dawn Ave Glen Ellyn IL 60137

HOUK, RICHARD JOSEPH, geographer; b. Logansport, Ind., Aug. 19, 1921; s. Edward Peter and Florence (Minneman) H.; B.A. in Geography, Ind. U., 1941, M.A. in Geography, 1942; Ph.D. in Geography, Northwestern U., 1950. U.S. State Dept. fellow for Costa Rican research, 1942-43; faculty DePaul U., Chgo., 1950—, asso. prof., 1954-57, prof., 1957—, chmn. dept. geography, 1957-76; preparer programs for CBS, NBC, Sta. WTTW-TV, 1956—; dir. study tours, Europe, Asia, Africa, S. Pacific, 1959—; Enrichment lectr. Royal Viking Line, 1975. Served with USAAF, 1943-46. Decorated caballero Orden de Merito Civil (Spain); Ford Found. fellow for research in Portuguese Africa, 1956-57; Fulbright fellow, Portugal, 1967-68. Mem. Ill. Geog. Soc., Assn. Am. Geographers, Nat. Council Geog. Edn. (treas. 1966-68). Hispanic Soc. Chgo. (pres. 1970), Geog. Soc. Chgo. (pres. 1965-67), Phi Beta Kappa, Sigma Xi, Theta Alpha Phi. Roman Catholic. Contbr. articles to encys. and mags. Office: Dept Geography DePaul U 25 E Jackson Blvd Chicago IL 60604

HOUK, ROBERT WILLIAM, bus. forms mfg. co. exec.; b. Detroit, May 13, 1927; s. Raymond John and Agnes Elizabeth (Morley) H.; B.A., Mich. State U., 1951, M.A., 1956; m. Katherine Rose Seelig, May 15, 1954 (dec.); children—Raymond John, Lisa Caroline. Systems and procedures analyst Ford Motor Co., Dearborn, Mich., 1954-57; asst. sales mgr. Rotary Manifold Forms Corp., Detroit, 1957-66; v.p. sales UFORMA, Inc., Roseville, Mich., 1966-68, chmn. bd., pres., 1968—; chmn. bd. Associated Forms Mfg. Inc., Knoxville, 1975—. Mem. planning com. North trails dist. Boy Scouts Am., 1976—. Served with AUS, 1945-47, 52-54. Recipient Outstanding Service award Printing Industries Am., 1974. Mem. Internat. Bus. Forms Industries (past pres.; recipient presl. citation 1974), Internat. Bus. Forms Industries. Roman Catholic. Home: 3965 Kirkland Ct Bloomfield Hills MI 48013 Office: 27733 Groesbeck Hwy Roseville MI 48066

HOUKES, JOHN MARTIN, librarian; b. Rotterdam, Netherlands, July 7, 1922; s. Frederik J.M. and Johanna E. (Knoops) H.; Philos. license Grand Seminaire, France, 1943-47; M.A., Ind. U., 1961; m. Maxence Daniel, May 3, 1949. Export mgr. Compagnie Meissonnier, Paris, 1948-54; head, freight dept. Ruys & Co., Paris, 1954-59; order accountant Purdue U., 1959-60, asst. order librarian, 1961-63, librarian Krannert Library, 1963—, prof. library sci.; cons. library bldgs. and collections. Mem. Spl. Library Assn., Indsl. Relations Librarians, Com. Univ. Bus. Librarians, Soc. Ind. Archivists, Beta Phi Mu. Roman Catholic. Contbr. articles in field to profl. jours. Home: 1700 Summit Dr W Lafayette IN 47906

HOUPIS, CONSTANTINE HARRY, elec. engr.; b. Lowell, Mass., June 16, 1922; s. Harry John and Metaxia (Gourokous) H.; student Wayne U., 1941-43; B.S., U. Ill., 1947, M.S., 1948; postgrad. Ohio State U., 1952-56; Ph.D., U. Wyo., 1971; m. Mary Stephens, Aug. 28, 1960; children—Harry C., Angella S. Spl. research asst. U. Ill., 1947-48; devel. elec. engr. Babcock & Wilcox Co., Alliance, Ohio, 1948-49; instr. elec. engring. Wayne U., 1949-51; prin. elec. engr. Battelle Meml. Inst., Columbus, Ohio, 1951-52; prof. elec. engring. Air Force Inst. Tech., Wright-Patterson AFB, Ohio, 1952—; guest lectr. Nat. Tech. U. Athens, 1958. Served with AUS, 1943-46. Recipient Outstanding Engr. award Dayton area Nat. Engrs. Week, 1962. Mem. IEEE, Am. Soc. Engring. Edn., Am. Hellenic Edn. Progressive Assn., Tau Beta Pi, Eta Kappa Nu, Sigma Chi. Mem. Greek Orthodox Ch. Author: (with J.J. D'Azzo) Feedback Control System Analysis and Synthesis, 1960, 2d edit., 1966; Principles of Electrical Engineering: Electric Circuits, Electronics, Energy Conversion, Control Systems Computers, 1968; Linear Control Systems Analysis and Design: Conventional and Modern, 1975; (with J. Lubelfeld) Outline of Pulse Circuits; also articles on automatic controls in profl. jours. U.S., Eng., Greece. Home: 1125 Brittany Hills Dr Centerville OH 45459 Office: Air Force Inst Tech Wright-Patterson AFB OH 45433

HOUSE, CHARLES EDWARD, accountant; b. Two Harbors, Minn., Dec. 25, 1939; s. Joe Henry and Helen Catherine (Harkwell) H.; B.A., U. Minn., 1962. Partner firm Stillman, House, Swanson & Co., C.P.A.'s, Duluth, Minn., 1969—. Mem. Minn. Health Coordinating Council, 1976—; treas. United Way of Greater Duluth, 1973-75; adviser ind. study program for hosp. trustees, U. Minn., 1973-76; treas. Health Systems Agy., Western Lake Superior, 1976; bd. dirs. Welch Center, 1975—. C.P.A., Minn. Mem. Minn. Soc. C.P.A.'s (sec. 1976-77), Am. Assn. Comprehensive Health Planning (pres. 1974-75, dir.), Toastmasters Internat. (Outstanding Toastmaster of Year of region 1973). Contbr. articles to profl. jours. Home: 9755 North Shore Dr Duluth MN 55804 Office: 900 Alworth Bldg Duluth MN 55802

HOUSE, DANIEL MURRAY, broadcasting exec.; b. Elizabeth, La., Dec. 29, 1910; s. Archibald Rippon and Mellie (Harris) H.; B.E.E., N.C. State U., 1933; m. Patricia Ruth Logsdon, Dec. 28, 1947; children—Donna L., Rita A. Distbn. engr. Water & Light Commn., Greenville, N.C., 1933-35; transmission, distbn. engr. Ala. Power Co., Birmingham, 1936-40; pres. Planned Music of Ky., Inc., Louisville, 1946—. Scoutmaster, Boy Scouts Am., 1960-61; bd. dirs. Louisville Deaf Oral Sch., Patton Mus. Devel. Fund, Main St. Assn., Louisville. Served from 1st lt. to maj. AUS, 1940-46, col., 1961-62, now col. Res. ret. Mem. Louisville C. of C. (chmn. welcome breakfast com. 1966, chmn. conv. com. 1968-69), Utica Pike Area Assn. (pres. 1967-69), Sales and Mktg. Execs., Louisville Sports Boosters (past pres.), Res. Officers Assn., Internat. Planned Music Assn. (pres. 1965-66), Honorable Order Ky. Cols., Phi Kappa Phi, Theta Tau. Methodist. Clubs: Jefferson; Execs. (past pres.) (Louisville); Pastime Boat (past pres.), Kiwanis (past pres.), Quarterback (pres. 1964). Author: Treatise on Conventions and Tourism. Home: 2107 Utica Pike Jeffersonville IN 47130 Office: 114 W Main St Louisville KY 40202

HOUSE, FRED HAWLEY, dentist; b. Akron, Ohio, July 2, 1918; s. Frank Hawley and Gertrude Louise (Rice) H.; B.S., U. Ala., 1940; postgrad. Case Inst. Tech., 1940-41, Hiram Coll., 1945-46; D.D.S., Western Res. U., 1951; m. Rachel May Weiss, Jan. 21, 1944; children—Betty Jane, Nancy May. Asst. chief chemist Aluminum Co. Am., Cleve., 1940-42; gen. practice dentistry, Garrettsville, Ohio, 1951-66, practice limited to full upper, lower, partial dentures, Cuyahoga Falls, Ohio, 1966—. Cons. dentist Cleve. Browns profl. football team, 1952-62, Middlebury Manor Nursing Home, Inc., 1969—. Republican nominee Sch. Bd., 1954. Served with USAAF, 1942-45; ETO. Decorated Air medal with 3 oak leaf clusters. Mem. Am., Ohio dental assns., Cleve. Dental Soc., Am. Soc. Clin. Hypnosis, 51 Dental Study Club, VFW, Am. Legion, Ohio C. of C., Delta Sigma Delta, Chi Beta Phi. Lutheran. Mason, Eagle, Kiwanian. Pioneer Doc Wholoper fishing lure. Home: 850 Graham Rd Cuyahoga Falls OH 44221 Office: 405 Portage Trail Cuyahoga Falls OH 44221

HOUSE, HUGH BRADFORD, zool. garden adminstr.; b. Buffalo, Wyo., Aug. 21, 1932; s. Martin Samuel and Irene Ruth (Kuiper) H.; B.A. with honors, U. Wyo., 1954, M.S., 1959; postgrad. U. Kans., 1959-60. Asst. dir. Jackson Hole Biol. Research Sta., Moran, Wyo., 1957-61; research asst. Operation Deep Freeze, Antarctica, 1960-61; zoology tchr. Jamaica (West Indies) Sch. Agr., Peace Corps., 1962-64; asst. curator mammals N.Y.C. Zool. Park, 1965-67, curator mammals, 1967-74; asso. dir. animal and plant scis. Minn. Zool. Garden, Apple Valley, 1974—. Served with AUS, 1954-56. Mem. Am. Soc. Mammalogists, Wildlife Soc., AAAS, Am. Assn. Zool. Parks and Aquariums. Home: 22240 Albatross Circle Farmington MN 55024 Office: 12101 Johnny Cake Ridge Rd Apple Valley MN 55124

HOUSER, ARNOLD RICHARD, chiropractor; b. Bklyn., Sept. 13, 1931; s. Floyd M. and Dolly (Eisenbise) H.; D.C., Lincoln Chiropractic Coll., 1961; m. Clorinda E. Tramutolo, June 5, 1969; 1 dau., Cassandra. Practice chiropractic, Glenwood, Ill., 1961—; cons. Nat. Chiropractic Coll. Bd. dirs. Lincoln Chiropractic Coll. Research Fund, Nat. Chiropractic Coll. Served with AUS, 1950-51. Mem. Am. (charter), Chgo. (treas. 1975-76, 76-77), Ill. (treas. 1973-74, 74-75, 2d v.p. 1977) chiropractic socs., Ill. Interprofl. Council Health Professions, Council Roentgenology, Chinese Acupuncture Soc., Am. Legion, Izzak Walton League Am. Clubs: Moose, Elks, Kiwanis (charter mem. Frankfort). Address: 18403 S Halsted Glenwood IL 60425

HOUSER, JON PETER, chiropractor; b. Bklyn., Aug. 27, 1929; s. Floyd Malachi and Dolly (Samish) H.; student Purdue U., 1953-55; D. Chiropractics, Lincoln Chiropractic Coll., 1956; m. Donna R. Youngberg, Dec. 28, 1968; children—Jon Peter, Jennifer Rae, Joi Lynn, Jessica Ruth, Tania Marina. Extern, Spears Chiropractic Hosp., Denver, 1956-57; dir. Palmer Chiropractic Clinic, Harvey, Ill., 1957—. Served with USAF, 1948-52. Diplomate Nat. Chiropractic Bd. Mem. Am., Ill., Chgo. (pres.) chiropractic socs., Am. Acupuncture Soc., Lincoln Chiropractic Coll. Alumni Assn. (pres., dir.). Clubs: Masons, Shriners. Home: Box 184 Rural Route 1 Monee IL 60449 Office: 15412 Turlington St Harvey IL 60426

HOUSER, ROBERT NORMAN, ins. co. exec.; b. Bloomfield, Iowa, Sept. 21, 1919; s. Charles B. and Venna C. (Bartholomew) H.; B.A. summa cum laude, U. Ia., 1947; m. Doris V. Miller, Dec. 18, 1943; children—Theodore Alan, Judith Eileen, James Robert. With Bankers Life Co., 1936-38, 40-43, 47—, asst. actuary, 1953-60, asso. actuary, 1960-63, 2d v.p., actuary, 1963-68, v.p., actuary, 1968-71, v.p., chief actuary, 1972-73, pres., 1973-75, pres., chief exec. officer, 1975—; pres., chmn. BLC Growth & Income Funds, BLC Investment Co.; chmn. BLC Equity Services Corp., BLC Equity Mgmt. Co.; dir. BLC Ins. Co. Mem. adv. bd. Mercy Hosp.; trustee Drake U.; bd. govs. Iowa Coll. Found.; mem. Greater Des Moines Com. Served to 1st lt. USAAF, 1943-45, with USAF, 1961-62. Decorated D.F.C., Air medal. Fellow Soc. Actuaries; mem. Phi Beta Kappa. Home: 2412 48th St Des Moines IA 50310 Office: 711 High St Des Moines IA 50307

HOUSEWORTH, DONALD EUGENE, state prison supr.; b. Three Rivers, Mich., Aug. 21, 1935; s. Samuel Marion and Melba Enid (Muffley) H.; B.A., Western Mich. U., 1959; M.A., Brigham Young U., 1961, Ph.D. (Univ. fellow), 1968; M.A., U. Denver, 1965; children—Corwin Lee, Alicia Ann, Derek Eugene. Staff psychologist State Prison So. Mich., Jackson, 1961-64, adminstr. psychol. services unit, 1972—; dept. chmn. dept. sociology Steven F. Austin State U., Nacogdoches, Tex., 1968-70; asso. prof. sociology Eastern Wash. State Coll., Cheney, 1970-72; tchr. Jackson Community Coll., 1973—; cons. Eastern Wash. Epilepsy Soc., 1970-72. Served with USAF, 1956-58. U. Denver fellow, 1964. Mem. Alpha Kappa Delta, Pi Gamma Mu, Phi Chi. Home: 294 Oakwood Dr Jerome MI 49249 Office: 4000 Cooper St Jackson MI 49201

HOUSFELD, GORDON RICHARD, exec. recruiter; b. Milw., Jan. 19, 1933; s. Emil and Lois R. (Reichenberg) H.; B.B.A., U. Wis., 1955, M.B.A., 1956; m. Carole B. Ferkel, Nov. 22, 1956; children—Susan, Jerrold, Lynn. Cons. firm Ernst & Ernst, Chgo., 1963-65; asso. Arthur Young & Co., Chgo., 1965-67; v.p. Conley Assos., Chgo., 1967-69, pres., dir. 1969—. Served with AUS, 1956-58. Mem. Am. Compensation Assn., Alpha Kappa Psi. Clubs: Chenequa Country, Metropolitan. Home: Beaver Lake Rd Hartland WI 53029 Office: 135 S LaSalle St Chicago IL 60603

HOUSKEEPER, BARBARA ANN ROSSBERG, painter, sculptor, educator; b. Ft. Wayne, Ind., Aug. 25, 1922; d. Clarence Paul and Mary Louise (McCormick) Rossberg; student Knox Coll., 1940-42, R.I. Sch. Design, 1942-43, Art Inst. Chgo., 1943-44; m. Harold Lee Houskeeper, Jan. 5, 1945; children—Lee Paul, Ann Kathryn, Kathryn Louise. Tchr., Arlington Heights (Ill.) Countyside Art Center, 1957—, N. Shore Art League, Winnetka, Ill., 1974—; tchr. Oxbow Summer Sch. of Art, Saugatuck, Mich., 1973—, dir., 1974, 75; tchr. Suburban Fine Arts Center, Highland Park, Ill., 1974—, Morraine Valley Jr. Coll., Palos Heights, Ill., 1976, Columbus Coll., Chgo., 1977—; sculpture commns. include: Am. Bar Assn., Chgo., Kemper Inst. Co. Corp. Collection, Long Grove, Ill., Gould Corp., Palatine, Ill., Ill. Bell Telephone Co., Chgo.; mem. Artemesia Coop. Gallery, Chgo., Zaks Gallery, Chgo. Mem. Arts Club Chgo., Womens Caucus Arts. Episcopalian. Home: 842 Holmes Ave Deerfield IL 60015

HOUSLEY, CHARLES EDWARD, hosp. adminstr.; b. LaFollette, Tenn., Mar. 29, 1939; s. John R. and Hazel Ellen (Byrd) H.; B.S., U. Tenn., 1964; M.B.A. in Hosp. Adminstrn., Xavier U., Cin., 1967; postgrad. health adminstrs. devel. program Cornell U., 1967. Asst. adminstr. East Tenn. Children's Hosp., Knoxville, 1964-65; adminstrv. resident St. Anthony Hosp., Columbus, Ohio, 1966-67, asst. adminstr., 1967-69, asso. adminstr., 1969—. Lectr. on hosp. materiel mgmt. throughout U.S., 1970—; clin. instr. hosp. and health services adminstrn. Ohio State U., Columbus, 1973—, lectr. health care adminstrn., 1972—; preceptor program in hosp. and health services adminstrn. Xavier U., 1968—; vice chmn. shared services com. Franklin County Adminstrv. Council, 1973-74; mem. task force on environ. health concerns on health care facilities Ohio Health Dept., 1975—. Chmn. hosp. div. United Way Campaign, 1973; chmn. hosp. div. Community Health Fair, 1974; active Big Bro. Assn. Trustee, Isabel Ridgway Home for Aged, 1970-75. Recipient appreciation award Columbus Police Dept., 1971, certificate of appreciation United Way Campaign, 1972. Mem. Am., Ohio (materiel mgmt. com. 1975—, Monsignor Griffin award for lit. 1975), Catholic hosp. assns., Am. Coll. Hosp. Adminstrs., Ohio Pub. Health Assn.,

Nat. Mgmt. Assn., Columbus Acad. Med. (courtesy, disaster planning com. 1969—), Young Adminstrv. Colloquium of Central Ohio (past pres.), Columbus C. of C. (fire prevention com. 1975—). Contbr. articles to profl. jours. Home: 2572 Olentangy River Rd Columbus OH 43202 Office: St Anthony Hosp 1450 Hawthorne Ave Columbus OH 43203

HOUSTON, WILLIAM ROBERT MONTGOMERY, ophthalmic surgeon; b. Mansfield, Ohio, Nov. 13, 1922; s. William T. and Frances (Hursh) H.; B.A., Oberlin Coll., 1944; M.D., Western Res. U., 1948; m. Marguerite LaBau Browne, Apr. 25, 1968; children—William Erling Tenney, Marguerite Elisabeth LaBau, Selby Cabot Truitt Vanderbilt. Intern, Meth. Hosp. Bklyn., 1948-49, Ill. Eye and Ear Infirmary, Chgo., 1949-50; resident N.Y. Eye and Ear Infirmary, 1950-52; practice medicine specializing in ophthalmic surgery, Mansfield, 1952—; mem. staffs Mansfield Gen. Hosp., Peoples Hosp., Mansfield, N.Y. U. Bellevue Med. Center, N.Y.C.; asso. prof. clin. ophthalmology N.Y. U. Sch. Medicine. Pres. Mansfield Symphony Soc., 1965-68, Mansfield Civic Music Assn., 1965; mem. Mansfield City Sch. Bd., 1962-65, v.p., 1965. Served to capt. M.C. USAF, 1952-55. Diplomate Am. Bd. Ophthalmology. Fellow Internat. Coll. Surgeons; mem., S.A.R. (color guard 1961-71), Ohio Hist. Soc. (life), N.Y. Geneal. and Biog. Soc. (life), Ohio Geneal. Soc. (trustee 1955—). Address: 456 Park Ave W Mansfield OH 44906

HOUTMAN, THOMAS, JR., research chemist; b. Decatur, Mich., Apr. 5, 1918; s. Thomas and Hattie (Dorlag) H.; A.B., Hope Coll., 1940; M.S., La. State U., 1942; m. Alyda Schuiteman, Dec. 11, 1942; children—Claire, Bruce. With Dow Chem. Co., Midland, Mich., 1942—, research dir. chems., contract projects, hydrocarbons, 1962-76, mgr. employee relations and spl. projects, Mich. div. research and devel., 1977—. Mem. Midland Planning Commn., 1959-62. Mem. Am. Chem. Soc., Sigma Xi. Mem. Ref. Ch. Am. (ch. v.p.). Patentee in field (10). Home: 613 Crescent Dr Midland MI 48640 Office: Dow Chem Co Midland MI 48640

HOVELSRUD, JOHN OLIVER, postal service exec.; b. Mpls., June 18, 1926; s. Julius Oliver and Hazel B. (Johnson) H.; B.A., U. Calif., Los Angeles, 1963; m. Marjory Jean Sandquist, Sept. 11, 1948; children—Jean Ann, John Paul. Br. sales mgr. Minn. Mining & Mfg. Co., St. Paul, 1964-68, nat. sales mgr., 1969-71; v.p. mktg. Ingersoll Rand Co., Los Angeles, 1971-74; circulation mgr. Postal Delivery, Ltd., Beldenville, Wis., 1975—; dir. C.M.E., Ind., Mpls.; lectr. mktg. U. So. Calif., 1973-74. Active. Republican Party, 1965-71. Club: Masons. Home: Route 2 Box 171 Maiden Rock WI 54750 Office: Box 51 Beldenville WI 54003

HOVEN, ARD, clergyman; b. Athena, Oreg., Oct. 21, 1906; s. Victor and Leona (Bodine) H.; B.A., Eugene Bible Coll., 1930, B.D., 1931; B.A., U. Oreg., 1933; M.A., Cin. Bible Sem., 1937; D.S.T., Milligan Coll., 1954; D.D., Ky. Christian Coll., 1954; m. Dorothy Lillian Harris, Sept. 30, 1938; children—Ardis Dee, Vicki Lee. Ordained to ministry Christian Ch., 1933; minister, Ceres, Calif., 1933-34, Cin., 1934-51, Broadway Christian Ch., Lexington, Ky., 1951-66, First Christian Ch., Columbus, Ind., 1966—. Speaker radio program Christians' Hour, 1943—; pres. N.Am. Christian Conv., 1950, mem. continuation com., 1950—; writer weekly Bible Sch. lesson The Lookout, Standard Pub. Co., Cin., 1958—, mem. pub. com., 1957—. Trustee Milligan Coll., Pinkerton High Sch. and Jr. Coll., Ky. Christian Coll. Mem. Bartholomew County Ministerial Assn., Christian Benevolent Assn. Cin. (trustee). Republican. Mason, Rotarian. Author: Christ Is All, 1953; Meditations and Prayers for the Lord's Table, 1962. Home: 3210 Sherwood Pl Columbus IN 47201 Office: First Christian Ch 5th and Lafayette Columbus IN 47201

HOWALD, JOHN WILLIAM, lawyer; b. St. Louis, Dec. 21, 1935; s. Herbert John and Irene Dorothy (Weber) H.; B.S., U. Mo.-Columbia, 1957; LL.B., J.D., St. Louis U., 1962; m. Betty L. Curtis, Feb. 14, 1971; children—Deborah A., Tracy L. (step-dau.), Catherine A., Laura A., John William. Vice-pres. sales Eureka Service & Equipment Co., Eureka, Mo., 1959-62; partner Sheehan, Furtaw & Howald, Hillsboro, Mo., 1963, Thurman, Nixon, Smith & Howald, Hillsboro, 1964-70, Thurman, Nixon, Smith, Howald, Weber & Bowles, Hillsboro, 1970—; dir. LaBarque Enterprises Jefferson County, Rustic Hills Resort Ltd., Bank House Springs. Served to lt. (j.g.), USNR, 1958. Spl. awardee Meramec Basin Assn., 1957-69. Mem. Am., Jefferson County (pres. 1963), Mo. (gov. 1975—) bar assns., Eureka C. of C. (pres. 1962). Home: 3360 Franks Dr House Springs MO 63051 Office: 1 Thurman Ct Hillsboro MO 63050

HOWARD, CHARLES ALLEN, JR., real estate co. exec.; b. Aberdeen, S.D., Aug. 11, 1904; s. Charles Allen and Grace (Brown) H.; student No. State Coll., 1922-23; A.B., Princeton U., 1927; LL.B., Harvard U., 1930. Admitted to N.Y. bar, 1931; practiced in N.Y.C., 1931-42; pres. Howard & Hedger Co., 1946—. Chmn., S.D. Republican Central Com., 1965-71; mem. Rep. Nat. Com., 1965-71; past pres. Aberdeen Community Chest, Aberdeen YMCA; past trustee, vice chmn. bd. Huron (S.D.) Coll. Served to maj. AUS, 1942-46. Decorated Bronze Star. Mem. Aberdeen C. of C. (v.p.). Clubs: Order DeMolay (exec. officer S.D., mem. supreme council), Masons (33 deg.), Shriners, K.T., Rotary (past dist. gov.), Aberdeen Country (past pres.); Prairiewood Golf; Princeton (N.Y.); Nassau (Princeton). Home: 1201 N Main St Aberdeen SD 57401 Office: Box 248 Aberdeen SD 57401

HOWARD, DAN FRANKLIN, artist, educator; b. Iowa City, Aug. 4, 1931; s. Harold M. and Laura (Noregard) H.; B.A., U. Iowa, 1953, M.F.A., 1958; m. Barbara Jean Glaman, Nov. 1, 1958. One-man shows including Masur Mus. Art, Monroe, La., 1965, La. Arts Gallery, Shreveport, 1965, Ft. Smith (Ark.) Art Center, 1967, Southwestern at Memphis, 1968, Ambassador Gallery, Memphis, 1968, Albrecht Gallery, St. Joseph, Mo., 1972, Kans. State U., 1974, U. Ark. at Little Rock, 1976, Sheldon Meml. Art Gallery, Lincoln, Nebr., 1977; exhibited in numerous group shows including Artists of Midwest, Nelson Gallery, Kansas City, Mo., 1967, 69, 73, Contemporary Ams., Ark. Arts Center, Little Rock, 1967, Memphis Acad. Arts, 1968, Ark. Pavilion HemisFair, San Antonio, 1968; Joslyn Art Mus., Omaha, 1975; represented in permanent collections throughout U.S. Faculty, Ark. State U., Jonesboro, 1958-71, asso. prof. art, 1963-71, chmn. div. art, 1965-71; prof. art, head dept. Kans. State U., Manhattan, 1971-74; prof., chmn. dept. art U. Nebr., Lincoln, 1974—. Mem. Nat. Council Art Adminstrs. Pres., Jonesboro Community Concert Assn., 1964-66; mem. Ark. Arts and Humanities Commn., Little Rock, 1966-71. Bd. dirs. State Festival of Arts, Little Rock, 1966-71, Friends of Art Kans. State U., 1971-74. Served with USAF, 1953-55. Recipient numerous nat., regional, state prizes, awards for paintings. Mem. Coll. Art Assn., Am. Fedn. Arts. Mid-Am. Coll. Art Assn. (pres. 1976, dir. 1975—), AAUP, Nebr. Art Assn. Home: 3800 Stockwell Lincoln NE 68506

HOWARD, DEAN CLINTON, musician, educator, painter; b. Cleve., Nov. 17, 1918; s. Thomas Morse and Florence Eleanore (Dean) H.; student Kent State U., 1936-38; grad. Baldwin Wallace Coll., 1941; Mus.B., U. Mich., 1941, Mus.M., 1942; m. Patricia Joan Smith, May 26, 1945; children—Timothy Dean, Thomas Smith, Theodore Scott. Prof. music Buena Vista Coll., Storm Lake, Iowa, 1947-48; prof. music Bradley U., Peoria, Ill., 1948—; clarinetist; one man show Caterpillar World Bldg. and Tech. Center, 1977. Served with USNR, 1943-45. Recipient Putnam award Excellence in Teaching, 1962, Motorola Nat. Watercolor Painting Competition award, 1964; Alumni Music Achievement award Baldwin Wallace Coll., 1976, Americana award Heart of Ill. Fair, 1976, 1st award Bicentennial Art Exhbn. 1976, 1st award and best of show Ill. Art League, 1977. Mem. Danforth Found. Sr. Asso., Am. Soc. U. Composers, Outstanding Educators Am., Phi Mu Alpha, Phi Kappa Phi (hon.). Composer: An Illinois Symphony, Divertimento for Orch., Perspectives for Orch.; numerous works band, chorus, chamber groups; Boats on Peoria Lake, publ. of watercolor painting for Jubilee Coll. restoration. Home: 1814 Bradley Ave Peoria IL 61606

HOWARD, EDWARD NEAL, librarian; b. Carlisle, Ind., Jan. 22, 1920; s. Mervin Christopher and Levada Ellen (Neal) H.; B.A. in English with highest distinction, Ind. U., 1965, M.A. in Library Sci., 1968; m. Elizabeth Joan Wood, Sept. 18, 1977; children—Chris Allen, Helen (Mrs. R. Phillip Thompson). Enlisted U.S. Navy, 1937, advanced through grades to warrant officer, 1955, ret., 1957; prisoner of war Japan, 1941-45; asst. dir. Monroe County Pub. Library, Bloomington, Ind., 1964-66; asst. dir. Bur. Pub. Discussion Ind. U., Bloomington, 1966-67; dir. Vigo County Pub. Library, Terre Haute, Ind., 1968—; adj. asso. prof. Ind. State U., 1972—; vis. instr. Presession, U. Ky., 1971. Mem. Ind. Com. for Humanities affiliate Nat. Endowment for Humanities, 1971-76. Chmn. Mayor's Citizens Adv. Com., Terre Haute, 1969-71; mem. Mid-Am. regional vol. task group United Way Am., 1976—; bd. dirs. Wabash Valley United Way, Terre Haute, 1974—, pres., 1975-76, chmn. bd., 1977—. Recipient John Cotton Dana Publicity award H.W. Wilson Co., N.Y.C., 1969; award of merit, 1974, Labor Day award, 1976 (both Wabash Valley Central Labor Council); Distinguished Service award Terre Haute Jaycees, 1975; named Ind. Librarian of Year Ind. Library Trustees Assn., 1969. Mem. Terre Haute C. of C. (chmn. com. 1970), Ret. Officers Assn., Am. Legion, ALA (mem. council, com. on publishing), Spl. Libraries Assn., Ind. Library Assn. (mem. exec. bd.). Phi Beta Kappa. Republican. Club: Rotary. Editor: Focus on Indiana Libraries, 1966-70. Inventor Orbital Orgn., 1970. Home: 621 S Center St Terre Haute IN 47807 Office: 222 N 7th St Terre Haute IN 47807

HOWARD, HUGH CHARLES, steel co. exec.; b. Milw., Aug. 31, 1929; s. Harry H. and Arlene L. (Schumann) H.; student Elmhurst Coll., 1953; B.S., Walton Sch. Commerce, 1957; m. Jacqueline Rae Jones, Sept. 28, 1957; children—Dawn Marie, Lisa Lynn. Sec.-treas. H. H. Howard Corp., Chgo., 1956—, acting pres., 1964-72, pres., 1972—. Vice pres. Riverside (Ill.) Community Fund, 1973. Served with AUS, 1954-56. Mem. Chicagoland chpt. St. John's Alumni Assn. Presbyterian (elder). Clubs: Union League (Chgo.); Ruth Lake Country (Hinsdale, Ill.); Woods Bathe and Tennis (dir., Burr Ridge, Ill.). Home: 1116 Laurie Ln Burr Ridge IL 60521 Office: 4837 S Kedzie Ave Chicago IL 60632

HOWARD, JACK ROHE, newspaper exec.; b. N.Y.C., Aug. 31, 1910; s. Roy Wilson and Margaret (Rohe) H.; grad. Phillips Exeter Acad., 1928; A.B., Yale, 1932; m. Barbara Baife, Apr. 5, 1934 (dec. 1962); children—Pamela, Michael; m. 2d, Eleanor Sallee Harris, 1964. Reporter Japan Advertiser, Tokyo, Shanghai (China) Evening Post and Mercury, 1932-33; reporter Indpls. Times, 1933-34; asst. telegraph editor, then telegraph editor and news editor Washington Daily News, 1935; staff program dept. radio sta. WNOX, Knoxville, Tenn., also Washington and N.Y.C. offices Continental Radio Co. (now Scripps-Howard Broadcasting Co.), 1936-39; asst. exec. editor Scripps-Howard Newspapers, 1939-42, 45-48, gen. editorial mgr., from 1948; pres., dir. exec. com. Scripps-Howard Newspapers (E.W. Scripps Co.), 1953—; pres., dir. chmn. Scripps Howard Broadcasting Co., 1937-42, 45—; pres. Cleve. Press; dir. Trans World Airlines, Inc.; mem. East Side adv. bd. Chem. Bank N.Y. Bd. dirs. Boys' Clubs Am. Served with USNR, 1942-45; PTO. Mem. Am. Soc. Newspaper Editors, Am. Newspaper Pubs. Assn. (dir.), Inter-Am. Press Assn. (pres. 1965-66), Phillips Exeter Alumni Assn. (pres. 1958-60), Beta Theta Pi, Sigma Delta Chi. Clubs: Dutch Treat, Yale, River, Pilgrims (N.Y.C.); Bohemian (San Francisco); Seawanhaka Corinthian Yacht (Oyster Bay, N.Y.). Address: 200 Park Ave New York City NY 10017

HOWARD, LEROY, JR., educator, evangelist; b. Gary, Ind., July 13, 1949; s. Leroy and Eddie Mae (Griffin) H.; B.S. in Edn., Lincoln U., Mo., 1973, M.Ed., 1974; postgrad. U. Mo., 1974-77. Corrections case worker, counselor Mo. Dept. Corrections, 1974-75; substitute tchr. Columbia (Mo.) Pub. Schs., 1975-76; instr., counselor Upward Bound project Lincoln U., Jefferson City, Mo., 1976—, asst. dir. to dir. cultural enrichment and Upward Bound, 1976—; affiliated Moreno Inst. Psychodrama (Beacon, N.Y.); founder Caravan Fellowship of Mid-Mo.; chaplain Rising Sun Lodge (Columbia); active Operation PUSH (Chgo.), NAACP. Certified tchr., counselor, Mo. Mem. Am. Soc. Group Psychotherapy and Psychodrama, AAUP, Internat. Soc. Gen. Semantics, Am. Personnel and Guidance Assn., Nat. Assn. Speech and Dramatic Arts, Mo. Black Leadership Assn., Rosecrucian Order, Alpha Phi Alpha, Alpha Psi Omega. Baptist. Author: Camp Ground Sugar Grove, 1977. Home: PO Box 1692 Columbia MO 65201

HOWARD, LESTER JAMES, extension adminstr.; b. Charlevoix County, Mich., Sept. 15, 1935; s. Henry Barnabus and Mabel (Osborn) H.; B.S. with honors, Mich. State U., 1957; M.S., Wis. State U., 1968; m. Mary Elizabeth Reich, Aug. 12, 1955; children—Henry A., Harlan J., Jeffrey D. Tchr., audiovisual dir. Cheboygan (Mich.) Area Schs., 1957-67; exec. sec. No. Mich. Fair, Cheboygan, 1960-67; Mich. State U. extension service 4-H youth agt., Ironwood, 1967-69, county extension dir., Gaylord, 1969—; exec. sec., resident agt. No. Mich. Beef Breeders Inc., Gaylord, 1969—. Mem. Cheboygan Agrl. Council, 1959-67. Bd. dirs. Otsego County Fair, Huron Pines Resource Conservation Devel. Project. Kellog Found. grantee, 1972-74, NSF grantee, 1962-67. Mem. Mich. Edn. Assn. (pres. Cheboygan chpt. 1967), Mich. Assn. County Agrl. Agts. (presl. award 1974, dir. 1973-76), Future Farmers Am. (hon.), Alpha Zeta. Rotarian. Home: Route 1 Box 210 Vanderbilt MI 49795 Office: Room 203 County City Bldg Gaylord MI 49735

HOWARD, LOWELL BENNETT, judge, educator; b. New Boston, Ohio, Feb. 12, 1925; s. James Arland and Imogene (Sullivan) H.; B.A., Bowling Green State U., 1947; J.D., Ohio State U., 1949, M.A., 1954, Ph.D., 1975; m. Jeanetta Turner, June 16, 1947; children—Lowell Bennett, Brent Turner, Rebecca Ann. Admitted to Ohio bar, 1950; practiced in Wellston, 1950-51, 54-56, Athens, 1955-71; city solicitor City of Wellston, 1954-56; mem. firm Howard & Gilliland; asst. prof. law Ohio U., Athens, 1955-59, asso. prof., 1959-65, prof., 1965-71, adj. prof. govt. and criminal justice, 1976—; judge Common Pleas Ct. Athens County, Athens, 1971—. Mem., sec. Athens Bd. Zoning Appeals, 1963-66; chmn. Athens Charter Commn., 1969-70. Served with USNR, 1943-46, 51-53. Named Athens County Man of Year, Southeastern Ohio Regional Council, 1972. Mem. Am., Ohio, Athens County (pres. 1968-69) bar assns., Am. Econ. Assn., Am. Polit. Sci. Assn., AAUP, VFW, Am. Legion. Methodist. Club: Rotary. Author: Business Law: An Introduction, 1965. Home: 68 Briarwood Dr Athens OH 45701 Office: Courthouse Athens OH 45701

HOWARD, RICHARD T., veterinarian; b. Des Moines, June 1, 1925; s. Charles and Alice Ann (Coppock) H.; D.V.M., Iowa State U., 1947; m. Elizabeth Louise Pence, July 14, 1947; children—Charles Elbert, Carol Elizabeth, Richard Andrew, Robert Anthony. Pvt. practice veterinary medicine, Kanawha, Iowa, 1947-66; pvt. practice veterinary medicine, specializing in small animals, Ankeny, Iowa, 1966—; dir. Ankeny State Bank. Mem. Iowa (pres. N. Central chpt. 1951), Greater Des Moines veterinary med. assns. Republican. Methodist. Home: 505 SE Sherman Dr Ankeny IA 50021 Office: 103 SE 1st St Ankeny IA 50021

HOWARD, ROBERT PICKRELL, journalist, author; b. New Providence, Iowa, Mar. 18, 1905; s. James R. and Anna (Pickrell) H.; A.B., Cornell Coll., Iowa, 1927; m. Eleanor Nee, Jan. 14, 1934 (dec. Apr. 1971); children—Jane T., Ann H. Condon; m. 2d, Elizabeth T. Appel, Aug. 5, 1972. Mem. staff AP, 1927-42; polit. editor Chgo. Sun, 1942-44; mem. staff Chgo. Tribune, 1944-70, Springfield corr., 1957-70; legis. asst. to atty. gen. Ill., 1970-73. Mem. Ill. Archives Adv. Bd. Mem. Sangamon County (pres. 1970), Ill. State (dir. 1974-77) hist. socs., Ill. State Mus. Soc. (chmn. bd. dirs. 1972-74), Abraham Lincoln Assn. (dir.). Presbyterian. Clubs: Chgo. Press, Sangamo (Springfield). Author: Illinois: A History of the Prairie State, 1972. Address: 2624 E Lake Shore Dr Springfield IL 62707

HOWARD, SHERWIN WARD, coll. adminstr.; b. Safford, Ariz., Feb. 19, 1936; s. Fred Pack and Beatrice S. (Ward) H.; B.S., Utah State U., 1960, M.A., 1964; M.F.A., Yale U., 1966; m. Annette Mina Shoup, June 30, 1961; children—Andrea Lynne, John Stanley, Stephen Ward, David Stowell. Asst. prof. theatre Ohio U., Athens, 1966-69, asst. to provost, 1968-69; asst. prof. theatre Lawrence U., Appleton, Wis., 1969—, asst. to pres., 1969—; mem. faculty for nat. workshops Nat. Assn. Coll. and Univ. Bus. Officers, 1971, 75; cons. planning and budgeting; cons. Council for Advancement of Small Colls., faculty for workshop, 1972; mem. spl. sch. bd. com. to investigate need for new sch. facilities in central city, Appleton, 1970. Served to 1st lt. Chem. Corps, AUS, 1960-62. Winner Sequoia Masque Playwriting Contest, 1968. Mem. Ch. Jesus Christ of Latter-day Saints (full time missionary 1956-58). Author: (with John Dozier) Planning and Budgeting, 1975; author plays staged at Dallas Theatre Centre, Humboldt State Coll., Yale U., Mpls. Theatre in the Round, Ohio U., U. Calif. at Santa Barbara, others; poet. Home: 1525 E Marquette St Appleton WI 54911

HOWARD, WALTER BURKE, chem. engr.; b. Corpus Christi, Jan. 22, 1916; s. Clement and Nell (Smith) H.; B.A., U. Tex., 1937, B.S. in Chem. Engring., 1938, M.S., 1940, Ph.D., 1943; m. Virginia Kentucky Freeman, Feb. 14, 1942; children—Thomas Clement, Virginia Ann. From asst. to sr. chem. engr. Bur. Indsl. Chemistry, U. Tex., Austin, 1939-52; from sr. engr. to scientist Monsanto Chem. Co., Texas City, Tex., 1952-64; mgr. process safety/sci. fellow to sr. engring. fellow Monsanto Co., St. Louis, 1965—. Vice-pres., Texas City Sch. Bd., 1963-64; chmn. bd. dirs. Mainland Opportunity Sch., 1958-61; mem. area council Boy Scouts, 1958-60; active P.T.A. Trustee Austin Presbyn. Theol. Sem., 1961-64. Fellow Am. Inst. Chem. Engrs. (dir.), Austin Engrs. Club (past dir.), Phi Beta Kappa, Sigma Xi, Phi Lambda Upsilon. Presbyn. (elder). Contbr chpts. to books, articles to profl. jours. Patentee in field. Home: 1415 Bopp Rd St Louis MO 63131 Office: 800 N Lindbergh Blvd Creve Coeur MO 63166

HOWARTH, JOSEPH WILLARD, banker; b. St. Anne, Ill., Nov. 11, 1913; s. Joseph Hilmer and Rosemond (Murphy) H.; student Purdue U., 1931-33, Ind. Bus. Coll., 1933-34, Wis. U., 1952-54; m. Belva G. Smith, Jan. 28, 1942; children—Linda Kay, Joseph C. Mgr. Howarth Loan Agy., Pine Village, Ind., 1934; asst. cashier State Bank of Oxford (Ind.), 1946-55, cashier, trust officer, 1955-73, pres., 1973—, also dir. Mem. Warren Sch. Bd., 1950-70, pres., 1966-67. Served as 1st sgt. AUS, 1942-46; PTO. Mem. VFW, Am. Legion. Republican. Mem. Christian Ch. (elder). Clubs: Masons, Lions. Home: 216 S Jefferson St Pine Village IN 47975 Office: State Bank of Oxford Smith and Justus Sts Oxford IN 47971

HOWE, H. PHILIP, banker; b. Manhattan, Kans., July 3, 1932; s. Harold and Ruth Madeline (Riordan) H.; B.S., Kans. State U., 1954; m. Margaret Virginia Griffith, June 1, 1957; children—David, Janet, Evan, Kathleen. Vice-pres., head installment loans Union Nat. Bank, Manhattan, Kans., 1960-68; pres. Kansas State Bank, Manhattan, 1969-73, chmn. bd., 1973—; pres. Griffith Oil Co., Manhattan, 1962-72, chmn. bd., 1972—; v.p. Manhattan Real Properties, Inc., 1963—; v.p. Kans. State Travel Agency, 1968—; pres. Master Med. Corp., 1974—. Bd. trustees Kans. State Endowment Assn., 1976—; bd. trustees St. Mary Hosp., pres., 1975-76; pres. United Way, Manhattan, 1975-76. Served with U.S. Army, 1957-59. Mem. Kans. Bankers Assn., Am. Bankers Assn., Kans. Oilmens Assn., Beta Theta Pi. Roman Catholic. Clubs: Manhattan Country, K.C. Home: 1707 Thomas Circle Manhattan KS 66502 Office: 1010 Westloop Manhattan KS 66502

HOWE, JONATHAN THOMAS, lawyer; b. Evanston, Ill., Dec. 16, 1940; s. Fredrick K. and Rosalie C. (Volz) H.; B.A. with honors, Northwestern U., 1963; J.D. with distinction, Duke U., 1966; m. Lois H. Braun, July 12, 1963; children—Heather C., Jonathan Thomas, Sara E. Admitted to Ill. bar, 1966, Supreme Ct. bar, 1970; partner firm Jenner and Block, Chgo., 1966—; lectr. Ill. Inst. for Continuing Legal Edn., 1967, 68, 70, 72, 73, Am. Law Inst., 1968, Nat. Sch. Bds. Assn., 1973—, Practicing Law Inst., 1974—. Mem. Bd. Edn., Dist. 27, Northbrook, Ill., 1969—, sec., 1969-73, pres., 1973—; mem. exec. com. Northfield Twp. Republican Orgn., 1967-71; Congressional campaign mgr. 13th Congressional Dist., Ill., 1969; mem. bd. deacons Village Presbyn. Ch. of Northbrook (Ill.), 1975—. Mem. Am. (chmn. young lawyers sect. environ. law com. 1967-70, mem. antitrust sect. 1967—), Ill. (co-editor antitrust newsletter 1968-70), Chgo. (chmn. judiciary and bench bar relations com. 1971-72, mem. exec. com. young lawyers sect. 1971-72), D.C. bar assns., Am. Judicature Soc., Am. Soc. Assn. Execs., Ill. Assn. Sch. Bds. (pres. 1977—, dir. 1971—), Chgo. Athletic Assn., Northwestern U., Duke U. alumni assns. Republican. Presbyterian. Clubs: Plaza, Legal (Chicago); Barristers. Author: (with Thomas P. Sullivan) Briefs, Illinois Coal Practice, 1967, rev., 1976; (with Philip W. Tone) Illinois Appellate Practice, 1970, rev. edit., 1973; Real Estate Sales People in the United States, 1977; contbr. articles in field to law jours. Home: 3845 Normandy Ln Northbrook IL 60062 Office: One IBM Plaza Chicago IL 60611

HOWE, RICHARD RAY, lawyer; b. Decatur, Ill., Aug. 23, 1932; s. Elbert Davis and Marie (Harris) H.; A.B., U. Mo., 1954, J.D., 1959; m. Elaine Bondurant, Apr. 17, 1954; children—Richard R., Scott W., Dale A., Tracy. Admitted to Mo. bar, 1959, since practiced in Canton. Mem. Canton Bd. Edn., 1962-68, sec., 1962-67, v.p., 1967-68. Pros. atty. Lewis County (Mo.), 1969-72; commr., also chmn. Commn. to Reapportion Mo. Legislature, 1971. Mem., vice chmn. Mo. Commn. on Human Rights, 1974-76. Chmn., Republican Central Com. Lewis County, 1971-76; chmn. 9th Congl. Dist. Rep. Com., 1974-76. Trustee Canton Pub. Library, 1961-70. Served with USAF, 1955-57. Mem. Am. Bar Assn., Assn. Trial Lawyers Am., Am. Judicature Soc., Alpha Tau Omega, Phi Alpha Delta. Mason, Kiwanian. Home: Rural Route 2 Canton MO 63435 Office: 436 Lewis St Canton MO 63435

HOWE, ROBERT HSI LIN, environ. engr.; b. Swatow, China, Jan. 2, 1922; s. Zulin and Afia (Lin) H.; came to U.S., 1948, naturalized, 1962; B.S., Meth. U., 1943, St. John's U., 1945; M.S., Cornell U., 1949; M. Engring., Cornell, 1950; Ph.D., Purdue U., 1955; D.Sc., World U., 1977; m. Jean Ma, Dec. 23, 1953; children—David Julin, Roberta Carolin, Albert Gillin. Research and teaching asst. Meth. U., Soochow, China, 1943-45, instr., 1945-47; research fellow Purdue U., Lafayette, Ind., 1950-52; engr. Eli Lilly & Co., Lafayette, 1952-55, project engr., 1955-63, sr. engr., 1963-65, research scientist, cons., 1966—; Fulbright-Hays prof. Istanbul Tech. U., 1965-66. Spl. lectr. Milan Poly. U., 1966; sci. program lectr. U.S. Dept. Agr., 1968; lectr. Academia de Sinica, 1968; adj. prof. U. Notre Dame, 1973-74; hon. adviser sci. research Nat. Sci. Council Republic of China, 1974—; adviser-prof. environ. and chem. sci. grad. programs World U., 1976—. Served to lt. Republic of China Army, 1934-37. Recipient Talbert Abrams award Am. Soc. Photogrammetry, 1958, gold award Nat. Accountants Assn., 1959, Indsl. Wastes award Ind. Water Pollution Control Assn., 1965, William-Hatfield award Water Pollution Control Fedn., 1971, Buswell-Porges award Inst. Advanced Sanitation Research Internat., 1972. Diplomate Am. Acad. Environ. Engrs. Fellow Royal Soc. Health, Am. Pub. Health Assn., Inst. Advanced Sanitation Research Internat. (dir. council of fellows U.S. area 1970-75); mem. Nat. Soc. Profl. Engrs. (chpt. v.p. 1959-60), Am. Chem. Soc. (mem. chpt. exec. com. 1976—), Sigma Xi. Kiwanian. Author: Applied Chemistry for Water Purification and Wastes Treatment, Vol. I and II, 1970, 77; Disposal and Handling of Hazardous Chemicals, Vol. I, II and III, 1970-73, Vol. IX, 1976. Contbr. articles to profl. jours. Patentee in field. Home: 106 Drury Ln West Lafayette IN 47906 Office: T8/2 Lilly Rd Lafayette IN 47902

HOWE, WILLIAM FRANCIS, vocat. counselor; b. Ashtabula, Ohio, July 22, 1950; s. Francis X. and Thelma M. (Huhta) H.; B.A., Defiance (Ohio) Coll., 1972; m. Mary Lou Morrissey, Sept. 18, 1976. Youth adviser Ashtabula County Manpower Dept., 1974-75, pub. service advisor, 1975-76, vocat. counselor, 1976; vocat. counselor Lake Erie Consortium, Ashtabula, 1976—; crisis intervention counselor Contact-Ashtabula County. Mem. Am. Personnel and Guidance Assn., Nat. Vocat. Guidance Assn. Roman Cath. Clubs: K.C., Surface Breakers Scuba Diving (pres. 1977). Home: 1636 W 11th St Ashtabula OH 44044 Office: Lake Erie Consortium 4200 Park Ave Ashtabula OH 44004

HOWE, WILLIAM HUGH, artist; b. Stockton, Calif., June 18, 1928; s. Edwin Walter and Eugenia (Mercanti) H.; A.B., Ottawa (Kans.) U., 1951. Exhibited paintings of butterflies at Philbrook Art Center, Tulsa, Ft. Worth Children's Mus., Witte Meml. Art Mus., San Antonio, Anthropology Mus., Chapultepec Park, Mexico City; represented in permanent collections: Cranbrook Inst., Bloomfield Hills, Mich., U. Mich. Exhibits Mus., Ann Arbor, Oak Knoll Mus., Clayton, Mo., Hax Art Center, St. Joseph, Mo., Am. Mus. Natural History, N.Y.C., Central Mo. State Coll., Warrensburg, Mich. State U., East Lansing, U. Wyo. Art Mus., Laramie, San Diego Mus. Nat. History, Balboa Park, U. Ariz., Tucson, Ill. State Mus. Art, Springfield, Mont. Hist. Soc., Helena, Wyo. State Art Mus., Cheyenne, Ariz. State U., Tempe, Milw. Pub. Mus., State Capitol Bldg., Denver, Denver Pub. Library, Kansas City (Mo.) Mus. History Sci., Presdl. Palace, Tamazunchale, Mexico, Ottawa (Kans.) Jr. High Sch., others. Mem. Jour. Lepidopterists Soc., Plaza Art Assn., Burroughs Nature Club, Audubon Soc. Mo., Central States Entomo. Soc., Los Angeles County Mus. Democrat. Episcopalian. Author-artist: Our Butterflies and Moths, 1964; The Butterflies of North America, 1974. Address: 822 E 11th St Ottawa KS 66067

HOWELL, JOHN CHRISTIAN, educator, theol. sem. dean; b. Miami, Fla., Feb. 24, 1924; s. Heman McKenzie and Laura (Anderson) H.; B.A., Stetson U., 1949; B.D., Southwestern Baptist Theol. Sem. 1952, Th.D., 1960, Ph.D., 1975; postdoctorate London Sch. Econ. and Polit. Sci. (Eng.), 1967-68; M.A., U. Mo.-Kansas City, 1973; m. Doris Betty Dooley, Mar. 8, 1947; children—Michael Christian, John Mark. Ordained to ministry Baptist Ch., 1948; pastor First Bapt. Ch., Crowley, Tex., 1950-56, West Bradenton Bapt. Ch., Bradenton, Fla., 1956-60; prof. Christian ethics Midwestern Bapt. Theol. Sem., Kansas City, Mo., 1960—, acad. dean, 1976—; asso. counselor Midwest Christian Counseling Center, Kansas City, 1965—; mem. adv. com. Sex Knowledge Inventory, Form X, Revised, Family Life Publs., Saluda, N.C., 1967—; profl. affiliate, Am. Assn. Pastoral counselors. Served with AUS, 1943-46. Am. Assn. Theol. Schs. fellow, 1967-68. Mem. Nat., Mo. councils family relations, Am. Soc. Christian Ethics, Kansas City Soc. for Theol. Study. Democrat. Author: Teaching about Sex—a Christian Approach, 1966; Growing in Oneness, 1972; Teaching Your Children About Sex, 1973. Home: 5621 N Doniphan Ln Kansas City MO 64118 Office: 5001 N Oak Trafficway Kansas City MO 64118

HOWELL, MARGARET HOFFMANN, counselor; b. Cleve., Dec. 17, 1928; d. Paul Ernst and Mary Margaret (McBride) H.; B.S. in Edn. cum laude, Kent State U., 1953, M.S. in Edn., 1966, Ednl. Specialist, 1971; m. William A. Howell, June 19, 1948; children—William Paul, David Andrew. Tchr., Brimfield Twp. Sch., 1952-54, Cuyahoga Falls (Ohio) Pub. Schs., 1954-69; guidance counselor Roberts Jr. High, Cuyahoga Falls, 1969—. Kent State U. scholar, 1952-53. Mem. Am., Ohio (exec. bd. 1971-73) sch. counselor assns., Am., Ohio personnel and guidance assns., NEA, Ohio Edn. Assn., Cuyahoga Falls Edn. Assn., North Eastern Ohio Tchrs. Assn., Alpha Zi Delta. Mem. Order Eastern Star. Office: 3333 Charles St Cuyahoga Falls OH 44221

HOWELL, RICHARD HIRST, physician; b. Cin., Dec. 29, 1925; s. Thomas William and Ruth Mary (Hirst) H.; B.S., U. Cin., 1948, M.D. cum laude, 1951; m. Mary Phyllis Shofner, Jan. 30, 1947; children—Cynthia A., Thomas W., Barbara R., Janet L., Mary E., Martha J. Intern, resident University Hosp., Ann Arbor, Mich., 1951-53; practice medicine specializing in family practice, Midland, Mich., 1953—; mem. staff Midland Hosp., chief staff, 1962. Served with USAAF, 1944-45. Decorated Air Medal with 3 oak leaf clusters. Diplomate Am. Bd. Family Practice. Mem. Am. Acad. Family Practice (chpt. pres. 1969—), Midland County Med. Soc. (pres. 1958—). Home: 4610 Bristol Ct Midland MI 48640 Office: 4805 Jefferson St Midland MI 48640

HOWELL, ROBERT LEE, clergyman; b. Linton, Ind., July 4, 1928; s. Willard Lynk and Chloe Margaret (Rector) H.; B.A., Mich. State U., 1950; B.D., Va. Theol. Sem., 1958, M.Div., 1958; children—Patrick Houston, Kevin Mark. Ordained to ministry Episcopal Ch., 1958; rector Ch. of Good Shepherd, West Springfield, Mass., 1963-67, St. Chrysostom's Ch., Chgo., 1967—. U.S. founder FISH lay ministry, 1964—; mem. Bishop's Commn. for Edn. and Tng., 1971—, Bishop's Commn. for Human Relations, 1969—; alternate del. Gen. Conv. Episcopal Ch., 1970, 73; mem. clergy selection bd. Chgo. Sunday Evening Club, 1969—; mem. standing com. of diocese Episcopal Diocese Western Mass., 1965-67, chmn. Dept. Missions, 1966-67; lectr. U.S.A., Can., Eng., France. Judge ann. awards to outstanding immigrants Immigrants Service League, 1969—. Bd. dirs. UNICEF, Anglican Fellowship of Prayer, Starfish-Met. Chgo., Living Ch. mag.; mem. Cook County Community Welfare Services Com., 1977—. Served to 1st lt. AUS, 1952-54. Mem. English-Speaking Union (gov. 1974—). Clubs: Racquet, Arts (Chgo.). Author: Fish for My People, 1968; Lost Mountain Days, 1973; The Fish-A Ministry of Love, 1973. Home: 1235 Astor St Chicago IL 60610 Office: 1424 N Dearborn St Chicago IL 60610

HOWELL, THOMAS EDWIN, tractor mfg. co. exec.; b. Peoria, Ill., June 2, 1918; s. Paul Ivan and Mary (DeYoung) H.; student Eureka Coll., 1938; B.S., U. Ill., 1940; m. Elizabeth Jane Higdon, Dec. 24, 1940; 1 dau., Janie (Mrs. James F. Lobig). Br. mgr. Dickinson & Allen Lumber Co., Eureka, Ill., 1940-41; mgr. Alexander Lumber Co., Aurora, Ill., 1942; chief engr. Christopher Aircraft Co., St. Louis, 1943; aircraft tool engr. A.J. Brandt Co., Detroit, 1944; tool designer Caterpillar Tractor Co., Peoria, 1944-45; archtl. designer Lankton, Ziegele & Assos., architects, Peoria, 1946-51; supervising engr. Caterpillar Tractor Co., Peoria, 1951-64, mgr. facilities design, 1965—; prin. Thomas E. Howell, Architect, Peoria, Ill., 1951—. Mem. City of Peoria Bldg. Bd. Appeals, 1958—; chmn. prodn. task force State Emergency Resources Planning Commn., 1964-66. Bd. dirs., v.p. Nat. Inst. for Disaster Mobilization, 1963—; bd. dirs. Ill. Region IV Heart Assn.; trustee Peoria Pub. Library, 1963—, pres., 1972—. Fellow AIA (mem. bldg. industry coordination com. 1969-71, chmn. com. on architecture for commerce and industry 1973—, chmn. com. for architects in industry 1974—); mem. Peoria Assn. Commerce (mem. environmental quality com. 1970—), Am. Phys. Soc., Am. Concrete Inst. (mem. com. on curing 1959-73, com. on pavements and bases 1974—), Acoustical Soc. Am. (mem. com. on noise 1959-65), Nat. Bur. Standards (mem. builders hardware standards com. 1971), Lambda Chi Alpha. Presbyn. Mason. Club: Mt. Hawley Country. Office: 100 NE Adams St Peoria IL 61629

HOWELL, WILLIAM BUSSER, mfg. exec.; b. Hamilton, Ohio, Aug. 29, 1916; s. Robb F. and Celia (Busser) H.; B.S., Ohio State U., 1940; m. Marcia Hobart, Aug. 2, 1941; children—Lucia (Mrs. Stanley Stein), William B., Deborah Hobart, Robb F., II, David Hobart. Sales and service trainee Hobart Mfg., Co., Troy, Ohio, 1940-41; head inspection dept. Motor Generator Corp., Troy, 1941-42; with Hobart Bros. Co., Troy., 1946—; v.p. sales, 1963-71, exec. v.p., 1971—. Bd. dirs. YMCA, Piqua, Ohio, C.C. Hobart Found. Hobart Trade Sch. Served with USNR, 1942-45. Mem. Am. Welding Soc., Beta Theta Pi. Episcopalian. Club: Troy Country (past dir.); Walloon Lake (Mich.) Country; Athletic of Columbus, Varsity O (Ohio State U.). Home: 140 Ridge Ave Troy OH 45373 Office: W Main St Troy OH 45373

HOWERTER, LEE MORGAN, banker; b. Smithfield, Ill., Feb. 26, 1918; s. Carl Clifford and Dolle Grace (Judd) H.; grad. high sch.; m. Vera A. Nayden, Feb. 25, 1941; children—Lee Michael, Leanne Lindauer. With Bath Bros. Men's Wear, Cuba, Ill., 1936-42; asst. cashier Bank Farmington, Ill., 1946, cashier, 1947; cashier Merc. Trust & Savs. Bank, Quincy, Ill., 1953-55, exec. v.p., 1955-57, pres., 1957—, also dir.; dir. Quincy Paper Box Co., Artcraft Co., Quincy. Bd. dirs. Blessing Hosp., Quincy. Served to capt. AUS, 1942-46. Mem. Ill. C. of C. (dir. 1972-74), Am. Legion, V.F.W. Mason. Club: Country (Quincy). Home: 1340 S 22d St Quincy IL 62301 Office: 440 Maine St Quincy IL 62301*

HOWES, MAURICE ALBERT HENRY, metallurgist; b. Birmingham, Eng., Apr. 4, 1930; s. Albert George and Florence Lillian (Williams) H.; B.Sc., London U., 1954, M.Sc., 1956, Ph.D., 1959; m. Mary Haddleton, Aug. 15, 1953; children—Jane Angela, Sally Ruth. Metallurgist, Joseph Lucas Ltd., Birmingham, Eng., 1947-63; devel. engr. Ipsen Industries, Rockford, Ill., 1963-64; chief materials engr. Joseph Lucas Industries Ltd., Birmingham, 1964-66; research dir. IIT Research Inst., Chgo., 1966—, mem. faculty Ill. Inst. Tech., 1968—. Served with Brit. Army, 1955-57. Mem. Am. Soc. Metals, ASTM, Laser Soc. Am., Instn. Metallurgists, Coll. Tech. Birmingham (asso.). Contbr. articles to profl. jours. Patentee in field. Home: 153 Briarwood N Oakbrook IL 60521 Office: 10 35th St W Chicago IL 60616

HOWLAND, ANN, clin. psychologist; b. Cleve., Jan. 7, 1944; d. Richard Moulton Howland and Natalie (Fuller) Howland Merrill; adopted d. William Fessenden Merrill; B.A., Goucher Coll., 1965; M.A., U. Fla., 1971, Ph.D., 1973; m. Gary Steven Sarver, Sept. 5, 1972; children—Andrea Merrill, Joshua Howland. Clin. psychologist, treatment dir. clin. services Mt. St. Mary's Hosp., Nelsonville, Ohio, 1973-75; clin. psychologist, pvt. practice Athens (Ohio) Psychology Clinic, 1975—; chmn. psychology service O'Bleness Hosp.; cons. Parkersburg (W.Va.) Head Start; instr. Case Mgmt. Mental Health Technicians, 1975. Peace Corps vol., Colombia, 1966-68. Mem. Am., Ohio, Southeastern Ohio psychol. assns., Nat. Register Health Service Providers in Psychology, Athens County Humane Soc., Animal Protection Inst., Phi Kappa Phi. Democrat. Clubs: Athens Country, Ponte Vedra (Fla.) Country. Home and office: 6 Berkeley Dr Athens OH 45701

HOWLAND, JOHN PEIRCE, orthodontist; b. Evanston, Ill., June 1, 1933; s. Edgar Gordon and Marian (Peirce) H.; student Tufts Coll., 1951-53; B.S., U. Ill., Chgo., 1955, D.D.S., 1957, certificate in orthodontics, 1963; m. Eleanor Francis Hughes, May 2, 1959; children—John Hughes, Allan Gordon, Edward Everett. Intern, Letterman Army Hosp., 1957-58; commd. 1st lt. U.S. Army, 1957, advanced through grades to lt. col., 1965; ret., 1968; pvt. practice dentistry, Crystal Lake, Ill., 1968—; founder Study Group (German and French) on orthodontics, 1963-67. Cubmaster Black Hawk council Cub Scouts, 1968-76; bd. dirs. YMCA. Named Outstanding Youth Leader Jr. C. of C., 1972; recipient Scouters Key, 1972. Mem. ADA, Ill., McHenry County, Chgo. dental socs., Chgo. (bd. censure 1972), European orthodontic socs., Am., Ill. assns. orthodontists, Midwestern Assn. Orthodontic Soc. (pub. relations com. 1972-76), German Soc. Orthodontists. Congregationalist (diaconate 1968-69). Club: Kiwanis. Home: 6710 W Hillside Rd Crystal Lake IL 60014 Office: 521 Devonshire Rd Crystal Lake IL 60014

HOWLETT, GEORGE FREDERICK, dentist; b. Waupaca, Wis., Apr. 11, 1904; s. John Leo and Leola (Gehr) H.; student No. Mich. U., 1927-29; D.D.S., U. Mich., 1932; m. Noella M. Stenger, June 29, 1935; children—George Frederick Jr., John Leo, Thomas Michael, Dorothea Marianne (Mrs. Peter C. Gottgetreu), Mary Louise (Mrs. Rick Hovde). Accountant J.W. Wells Lumber Co., Iron River, Mich., 1923-27; intern U. Cin. Gen. Hosp., 1932-33; practice dentistry, Green Bay, Wis., 1933—; mem. dental staff St. Vincent Hosp. (pres. 1956-57), Green Bay, Bellin Meml. Hosp. (pres. 1966-68), Green Bay, St. Mary's Hosp. (pres., 1972-73), Green Bay. Treas. Brown County A.R.C., 1935-37. Mem. Am. Dental Assn., Wis. State, Brown Door Kewaunee (pres. 1946-47) dental socs., Am. Rifle Assn. Mason. Club: Sierra. Office: 307 Northern Bldg Green Bay WI 54301

HOWLETT, JAMES LOUIS, lawyer; b. Pontiac, Mich., Dec. 13, 1929; s. Harold Edgar and Lucile (Larson) H.; B.A., U. Mich., 1951, LL.B., 1954; LL.M., N.Y. U., 1958; m. Antoinette Bennardo, Dec. 30, 1961; children—Thomas Harold, Edward Louis. Admitted to Mich. bar, 1954, since practiced in Pontiac and Bloomfield Hills; partner firm Beier, Howlett, McConnell, Googasian & McCann, 1958—. Mem. Pontiac Bd. Edn., 1965-68. Bd. dirs. Pontiac Area United Way, Oakland (Mich.) County Hist. Found., Pontiac Symphony Orch., Pontiac Creative Arts Center, Bloomfield (Mich.) Arts Assn., Mich. Children's Aid Soc., Oakland County chpt. ARC, Friends of Kresge Library, Oakland U., Pres.'s Club Oakland U., Pres.'s Club U. Mich. Served with AUS, 1954-56; PTO. Recipient Distinguished Service award Pontiac Area Jr. C. of C., 1965. Mem. Am., Oakland County bar assns., Cranbrook Sch. Alumni Council, Chi Phi, Delta Theta Phi. Clubs: Orchard Lake (Mich.) Country; City (Bloomfield Hills); Rotary. Home: 2175 N Lake Angelus Rd Pontiac MI 48055 Office: 74 W Long Lake Rd Bloomfield Hills MI 48013

HOWLETT, MICHAEL J., bus. exec.; b. Chgo., Aug. 30, 1914; grad. DePaul U., 1934; m. Helen Geary; children—Michael, Robert, Edward, Catherine, Mary Christine, Helen Marie. Dir. Chgo. area Nat. Youth Adminstrn., 1940-42; exec. dir. Office Orgn. and Administrn. Chgo. Park Dist.; regional dir. OPS, 1951; v.p. Sun Steel Co., Chgo., 1952-60; auditor State Ill., 1960-73, sec. state, 1973-77; pres. Marett Assos., Chgo., 1977—. Del. Democratic Nat. Conv., 1968, 72, 76. Served with USNR, 1942-45. Home: 9630 Winchester St Chicago IL 60643 Office: 55 E Jackson Blvd Chicago IL 60604

HOWLETT, ROBERT GLASGOW, lawyer; b. Bay City, Mich., Nov. 10, 1906; s. Lewis Glasgow and Anne Lucille (Hurst) H.; B.S., Northwestern U., 1929, J.D., 1932; m. Barbara Withey, Sept. 19, 1936; children—Eleanor Howlett Burton, Craig G., Douglas W. Admitted to Ill. bar, 1932, N.Y. bar, 1940, Mich. bar, 1947; mem. firm Schmidt, Howlett, Van't Hof, Snell & Vana, Grand Rapids, 1949—; mem. Mich. Employment Relations Commn., 1963-76, chmn., 1964-76; chmn. Fed. Service Impasses Panel, 1976—; vice-chmn. Fgn. Service Disputes Panel, 1976—; industry mem. shipbldg. commn. Nat. War Labor Bd., 1963-65; spl. asst. atty. gen., dept. aeronautics State of Mich., 1957-61; vis. prof. Mich. State U., East Lansing, 1972, 75. Chmn. Kent County Rep. Com., 1956-61; del. Rep. Nat. Conv., 1960. Mem. Am., Grand Rapids (pres. 1962-63) bar assns., State Bar Mich., Nat. Acad. Arbitrators, Indsl. Relations Research Assn., Soc. Profls. in Dispute Resolution (pres. 1974-75), Assn. Labor Mediation Agys. (pres. 1977-78). Clubs: Kent Country, Peninsular (Grand Rapids). Contbr. articles to profl. jours. Home: 2910 Oak Hollow Dr SE Grand Rapids MI 49506 Office: 700 Frey Bldg Grand Rapids MI 49503

HOWLETT, THOMAS MICHAEL, data processor; b. Green Bay, Wis., Feb. 24, 1941; s. George F. and Noella M. (Stenger) H.; B.A. in Math., Coll. St. Thomas, St. Paul, 1963, M.A. in Teaching, 1964; m. Janet Rae Jacques, June 12, 1971; children—William Casey, Michael James. Dir. data processing St. Norbert Coll., De Pere, Wis., 1969—. Vice chmn. mil. facilities support program N.E. Wis. Tech. Inst.; mem. Mayor's Adv. Com., City of De Pere, 1976—. Served to capt. USMC, 1964-69, maj. Res. Decorated Navy Commendation medal with combat V. Mem. Data Processing Mgmt. Assn., Assn. Small Computer Users in Edn., Marine Corps Res. Officers Assn. (pres. chpt., Wis. councilor), Phi Alpha Theta. Office: St Norbert Coll De Pere WI 54115

HOWSAM, ROBERT LEE, profl. baseball exec.; b. Denver, Feb. 28, 1918; s. Lee W. and Mary (Creley) H.; student U. Colo., 1936-38; m. Janet Johnson, Sept. 15, 1939; children—Edwin, Robert Lee. Gen. mgr., pres. Denver Bears Baseball Club, 1947-60; pres. Denver Broncos Football Club, 1960-61, Howsam-Brown, Inc., Denver, 1961-63; v.p. Westamerica Securities Co., Denver, 1963-64; gen. mgr. St Louis Nat. League Baseball Club, 1964-67; gen. mgr., pres., dir. Cin. Reds, 1967—; past dir. Central Bank & Trust Co., Denver; past pres. Flying Bears, past mem. Mayor Denver Exec. Sports Com.; past bd. dirs., v.p. Am. Assn., Denver Old Timers Baseball Assn., Denver. Mem. Gov. Colo. Conf. Colo. Met. and Urban Problems, 1956; past chmn. Colo. Planning Commn.; chmn. Denver and Colo. Crusade for Freedom, 1952-53; past asso. U. Denver, past dir., v.p. Denver area council Boy Scouts Am. Past mem. bd. mgmt. Denver YMCA. Served with USNR, 1941-46. Named Minor League Exec. of Yr., Sporting News, 1951, 56, Major League Exec. of Yr., 1973; named one of Colo.'s five outstanding young men Colo. Jr. C. of C., 1951, Denver's Young Man of Yr., Jr. C. of C., 1952; named to Colo. Sports Hall Fame, 1971, Cin. Ambassador, 1973; recipient Gold Nugget award Nugget Boosters Club, 1954; Legion of Merit, Order DeMolay, 1955; Exec. of Yr. award Braves 400 Club, Atlanta, 1972; Honor award Nat. Jewish Hosp. and Research Center, 1973; Distinguished Merit award Alpha Sigma Phi, 1974; George Norlin award U. Colo., 1976. Mem. Am. Legion (past post comdr.). Clubs: Press (life), Denver Country, Exec. (past pres.), Pinehurst Country, Rolling Hills Country (1st ann. Personality and Sports award 1956) (Denver); Cincinnati, Hyde Park Country, Queen City (Cin.), Masons (33 deg.), Elks, Rotary. Home: 2444 Madison Rd Cincinnati OH 45208 Office: Riverfront Stadium Cincinnati OH 45202

HOWSER, JOHN WILLIAM, surgeon; b. Chgo., Dec. 27, 1911; s. Reid Owen and Jessie (Johnston) H.; B.A., Cornell Coll, 1933; B.S. in Medicine, Northwestern U., 1934, B. Medicine, 1936, M.D., 1937; m. Lya Fulgenzi, June 10, 1944 (dec.). Intern, Wesley Hosp., Chgo., 1936; intern Cook County Hosp., 1937-38; resident in surgery, 1938-42; practice medicine specializing in surgery, Oak Park, Ill., 1943—; attending surgeon Cook County Hosp., Chgo., 1944-47; chmn. dept. surgery W. Suburban Hosp., Oak Park, 1975—; asso. prof. gen. surgery Rush Med. Coll., Chgo., 1972—; prof. surgery Cook County Grad. Sch., Chgo., 1944—; mem. bd. trustees W. Suburban Hosp., Cook County Grad. Sch. Trustee Cornell Coll., Iowa. Served to capt. M.C., U.S. Army, 1943-44. Fellow A.C.S., Internat. Coll. Surgeons, Chgo. Surg. Soc., AMA. Republican. Methodist. Clubs: Oak Park Country, Masons, Shriners. Contbr. articles in field to surg. and med. jours. Home: 5 Oakbrook Club Dr Oakbrook IL 60521 Office: 715 Lake St Oak Park IL 60301

HOWSON, THOMAS WILLIAM, dentist; b. Kalamazoo, July 1, 1909; s. Ottowell Carmon and Florence Belle (Britton) H.; B.S., Western Mich. U., 1934; D.D.S., U. Mich., 1934; m. Adelaide Elizabeth Everett, Oct. 13, 1934; children—Thomas William, Richard John. Practice gen. dentistry, Kalamazoo, 1934—. Served with AUS, 1942-45. Mem. Am., Mich. dental assns., Kalamazoo Valley Dental Soc. (sec.-treas. 1951-76). Clubs: Masons, Kiwanis. Home: 2317 Tipperary Rd Kalamazoo MI 49008 Office: 905 W South St Kalamazoo MI 49007

HOY, JAMES FRANKLIN, English scholar, educator; b. Wichita, Kans., Dec. 15, 1939; s. Kenneth L. and Marteil (Rice) H.; B.S., Kans. State U., 1961; M.A., Emporia State U., 1965; Ph.D., U. Mo., 1970; m. Catherine June Thompson, Mar. 13, 1965; children—Farrell Alysoun, Joshua Thompson. Instr. English, jr. high sch. Eldorado, Kans., 1963-65; grad. instr. English, U. Mo., Columbia, 1966-70; vis. prof. English, Idaho State U., 1975; asst. prof. English, Emporia (Kans.) State U., 1970-75, asso. prof., 1975—. Mem. Kans. Folklore Soc. (pres. 1974-75). Author: The Language Experience, 1974; asso. editor Heritage of Kans.; Jour. of Great Plains; contbr. articles to scholarly jours. Home: Route 4 Box 68 Emporia KS 66801 Office: Emporia State Univ English Dept Emporia KS 66801

HOYLAND, JANET LOUISE, govt. ofcl.; b. Kansas City, Mo., July 21, 1940; d. Robert J. and Dora Louise (Worley) Hoyland; B.A., Carleton Coll., 1962; postgrad. in music (Mu Phi Epsilon scholar 1966), U. Mo. at Kansas City, 1964-67. Policy writer Lynn Ins. Co., Kansas City, 1963-64; music librarian U. Mo. at Kansas City, 1966-68; benefit authorizer Social Security Adminstrn., Kansas City, Mo., 1969-76, health ins. specialist, 1976—. Piano tchr. Leta Wallace Piano Studio, Kansas City, 1963, 68; piano accompanist Barn Players,

Overland Park, Kan., 1972-75, Off Broadway Dinner Playhouse, Inc., Kansas City, 1973. Co-chmn. Project Equality work area, 1971; work area chmn. on ecumenism Council on Ministries, 1969-70; sec. fair housing action com. Council on Religion and Race, Kansas City, 1968. Active ward and precinct work Democratic Com. for County Progress, 1968. Mem. Women's Div. Kansas City Philharmonic, Friends, of Art Kansas City, Fellowship House Assn. Kansas City, Internat. Platform Assn., Kansas City Mus. Club (chmn. composition dept. 1967-68), Mu Phi Epislon (v.p. Kansas City 1968, sec. 1971, pres. 1975-76), Pi Kappa Lambda. Methodist. Home: 610 W 46th St Kansas City MO 64112 Office: Social Security Administration 2440 Pershing Rd Kansas City MO 64108

HOYT, HAMILTON TAYLOR, lawyer; b. Milw., Feb. 18, 1918; s. Ralph Melvin and Dorothy (Taylor) H.; B.S., Haverford Coll., 1940; LL.B., U. Mich., 1946; m. Grace Koval, July 3, 1965; children—Donald H., Robert D., Mary Lee. Admitted to Wis. bar, 1946; since practiced in Milw., asso. firm Hoyt, Greene, Meissner, and predecessors, 1946-66, partner, 1966—. Served as lt. USNR, 1943-45. Mem. Wis. Bar. Assn. Home: Box 187 Mukwonago WI 53149 Office: 735 N Water St Milwaukee WI 53202

HOYT, JOHN STANLEY, JR., educator; b. Yonkers, N.Y., July 28, 1923; s. John Stanley and Clara (Dean) H.; B. Mech. Engring., Syracuse U., 1948; M.A. in Govt., George Washington U., 1954; Ph.D. in Econs., American U., 1959; advanced mgmt. program, Harvard U., 1963; m. June Cathey Ryfun, June 14, 1948; children—Susan (Mrs. Peter Jasan), Sally Dean. Motive power engr. N.Y.C. R.R., N.Y.C., 1941-50; plant engr. Ednalite Optical Co., Peekskill, N.Y., 1950-51; sr. exec. officer research CIA, Washington, 1951-64; dir. econs. and mgmt. scis. N. Star Research, Mpls., 1964-66; prof. econs., also dir. computer info. systems, head agency info. and journalism dept. U. Minn., St. Paul, 1966-77; dep. dir. Central Solar Energy Research Inst., Eagan, Minn., 1977—. Cons. State Economist Minn., 1967-69; fed. ct. master for legislative reapportionment, Minn., 1972. Chmn. Edina Sch. Bd., 1970—; mem. Edina Planning Commn., 1971. Bd. dirs. Mid-Continent Research and Devel. Council; chmn. bd., also pres. Minn. Assn. Community Service and Continuing Edn. Served with USNR, 1943-45. Mem. Minn. Acad. Sci., AAAS, Tau Beta Pi, Pi Mu Epsilon, Omicron Delta Pi, Pi Tau Sigma, Theta Tau, Phi Kappa Phi. Author: Regional Development Systems in Minnesota, 1968; Personnel Time Management and Effective Administration, 1974. Home: 4812 Dunberry Ln Edina MN 55435 Office: 1256 Trapp Rd Eagan MN 55121

HOZENY, TONY, writer, educator; b. Madison, Wis., Aug. 24, 1946; s. Walter Joseph and Helene Mary (Abel) H.; B.A., U. Wis., 1969; M.A. (Teaching Fellow), Johns Hopkins U., 1972; 1 child, Jesse. Principal, St. Vincent Group Home Sch., Milw., 1969-71; lectr. creative writing U. Wis., Milw., 1971; teaching fellow Johns Hopkins U., Balt., 1971-72; visiting lectr. Rider Coll., Trenton, N.J., 1972-73; publications editor Wis. Public Service Commn., 1974-77; tchr. writing classes, workships at various Wis. colleges; subject of radio profile Sta., WHA, Madison, 1976; interviews with newspapers, Madison, 1974-77; works featured in numerous readings, radio programs throughout Wis. Recipient Leslie Cross award for best full-length fiction by Wis. novelist, 1975; Wis. Arts Bd. Fellow, 1976, grantee, 1977. Author: Driving Wheel, 1974; My House is Dark, 1974. Home: Route 1 Sun Prairie WI 53590 Office: 432 Hill Farms Stste Office Bldg Madison WI 53701

HRACHOVINA, FREDERICK VINCENT, osteo. physician and surgeon; b. St. Paul, Sept. 2, 1926; s. Vincent Frank and Beatrice (Funda) H.; B.A. in Chemistry, Macalester Coll., 1948; D.O., Kirksville (Mo.) Coll. Osteopathy and Surgery, 1956; m. Joan Halverson, July 2, 1955. Chemist, Twin City area, 1948-51; intern Clare (Mich.) Gen. Osteo. Hosp., 1956-57; pvt. practice, Mpls., 1957—. Smith, Kline & French Labs. grantee, 1973. Mem. Am. (council fed. health programs, drug enforcement adminstrn. prescribers working com. 1974-75), Minn. (pres. 1965-66, exec. dir. 1966-74, pub. relations dir. 1974-75) osteo. assns., Assn. Osteo. State Exec. Dirs. (pres. 1970-71, dir. 1971-74), Am. Coll. Gen. Practitioners Osteo. Medicine and Surgery (lectr. Mo. soc.), Minn. Soc. Assn. Execs., Am. Acad. Osteopathy, Minn. Gymnastic Assn. (founder 1962-72), Twin City Model A Ford Club. Mason (Shriner). Clubs: Breakfast, Optimist (dir. Mpls. 1959-62, 69-72, pres. 1970-71, gen. chmn. floor exercise gymnastic program 1959-65), Classic Car Am. (membership chmn. Upper Midwest Region 1977, sec. 1978), Cadillac La Salle. Author: Microscopic Anatomy, 1952; Methods of Development for New Osteopathic Medical Colleges in the Next Millennium, 1977. Contbr. articles to profl. jours. Home: 3655 47th Ave S Minneapolis MN 55406 Office: 202 Inland Bldg 1000 2d Ave S Minneapolis MN 55403

HRECZ, JOSEPH, ednl. adminstr.; b. Warren, Ohio, July 6, 1931; s. Andy and Lydia (Zsegraics) H.; Mus.B., Youngstown State U., 1953; Mus.M. in Edn., U. Colo., 1963; postgrad. U. No. Iowa, 1967-70; m. Rita Arlene Nielsen, Aug. 10, 1963; children—Holly Sue Hrecz Potthoff, Mark Randel. Profl. piano player, 1947—; tchr. pvt. piano lessons, 1951—; bandmaster Garnaville (Iowa) Community Sch., 1957-62, bandmaster and vocal dir., 1964-70; edn. rep. Kepharts Music Center, Decorah, Iowa, 1962-63; vocal music dir. Decorah Community Sch., 1963; vocal music dir. Monticello (Iowa) Community Sch., 1963-64; bandmaster Vinton (Iowa) Community Sch., 1970-71; supt. sch. Martensdale-St. Marys (Iowa) Community Sch., 1971-73, Clay Central Community Sch., Royal, Iowa, 1973—; condr. orch. and chorus, instr. music history European campuses Fgn. Study League, Salt Lake City, summers 1968, 69; condr. community cantata choruses, Monticello, Garnavillo, and Royal, 1963—; adjudicator Iowa State Music Contests, 1967—; piano soloist with various high sch. bands, 1960—; justice of the peace, Clayton County, Iowa, 1965-66. Served to 1st lt. AUS, 1953-56. Mem. NEA (del. conv. 1967-68), Am. Assn. Sch. Adminstrs., Iowa Bandmasters Assn., Phi Mu Alpha Sinfonia, Kappa Delta Pi, Phi Delta Kappa. Lutheran (ch. organist 1967-70, choir dir. 1967—). Club: Lions. Home: PO Box 74 Royal IA 51357 Office: Clay Central Community Sch PO Box 155 Royal IA 51357

HRUBY, FERDINAND JOSEPH, physician; b. Cleve., Dec. 2, 1916; s. Fred Henry and Mary Rita (Kofron) H.; B.S., Georgetown U., 1939, M.D., 1943; m. Mary Jane Parfitt, Mar. 22, 1943. Intern, St. Lukes Hosp., 1943; 1944-45; resident and fellow in medicine Cleve. Clinic, 1945-48; sr. asso. staff physician St. Luke's Hosp., Cleve., 1948—, also sr. asso. in medicine and chief of endocrinology clinic; staff physician Marymount Hosp., Cleve., head div. endocrinology and metabolism, 1956—, chief of medicine, 1957-66. Served with M.C., U.S. Army; C.B.I. Diplomate Am. Bd. Internal Medicine. Fellow A.C.P., Am. Coll. Gastroenterology, Am. Geriatric Soc.; mem. AMA. Clubs: Cleve. Skating, Gonya Shooting. Home: 36805 Miles Rd Chagrin Falls OH 44122 Office: 3461 Warrensville Center Rd Shaker Heights OH 44122

HRUSKA, DOROTHY IRENE GARTAMAKER (MRS. JAMES EMIL HRUSKA), museologist; b. Worthington, Minn., Jan. 20, 1924; d. Ward K. and Mildred Ann (Coon) Gartamaker; student pub. schs., Reading, Minn.; m. James Emil Hruska, Sept. 20, 1941; 1 son, David Kent. Co-dir., curator, guide LeSueur County Hist. Soc. Mus., Elysian, Minn., 1965—. Mem. Waseca Arts Council, 1976-77, Minn. Mus. Edn., 1977; bd. dirs. Gish Families of the World, 1969-76; chmn. baby layette program Pope's Store House, Holy Trinity Parish, Waterville, 1964-69. Mem. Assn. Hist. Adminstrs. (dir. Minn. 1969-71), Minn. Territorial Pioneers (life), Minn. State, LeSueur County (life, pres. 1969, dir. 1970-73) hist. socs., Internat. Platform Assn. Roman Catholic. Editorial adviser Stepping Stones, 1976; contbg. author: LeSueur County Atlas, 1975; Pioneer Chronicles, 1976. Home: 306 West Lake St Waterville MN 56096 Office: PO Box 557 Elysian MN 56028

HRUSKA, JAMES EMIL, museum founder, dir.; b. Waterville, Minn., June 16, 1912; s. Emil and Minnie Mabel (Belden) H.; student W.H. Dunwoody Inst., Minn., 1930; m. Dorothy Irene Gartamaker, Sept. 20, 1941; 1 son, David Kent. Postoffice worker, Waterville, 1931-73; dir. Le Sueur County Hist. Soc. Museum, Elysian, Minn.; adult edn. tchr. Waterville-Elysian Schs., 1976—; lectr. Lake Sakata State Park, Waterville. Mem. Civil Defense dir., 1960-64; mem. Cannon Valley Developmental Assn., bd. dirs., 1970; mem. adv. com. Minn. Agrl. Interpretive Center, 1977-78. Mem. Minn. Territorial Pioneers (life; 3d v.p. 1977-78), Minn. State Hist. Soc., Le Sueur County Hist. Soc. (life mem., pres. 1968-70, 72-77, bd. mem. 1963-71), Minn. State Archeol. Soc., Pioneerland Hist. Assembly (v.p. 1972-73, pres. 1974-75), So. Minn. Hist. Assembly (dir. 1977-78). Roman Catholic. Club: K.C. Established Le Sueur County Hist. Soc. Mus.; asso. editor Stepping Stones 76; contbr. to Minn. Territorial Pioneers' Pioneer Chronicles. Home: 306 W Lake Waterville MN 56096 Office: Box 557 Elysian MN 56028

HRUSKA, KEITH ANTHONY, physician; b. Sidney, Nebr., Aug. 9, 1944; s. Herbert Louis and Ellen (Rauner) H.; M.D., Creighton U., 1969; m. Pamela Jean Higgins, Dec. 27, 1967; children—Kerstin, Keith Jr., Kemper Luke. Intern N.Y. Hosp. Cornell U., 1969-70, resident, 1970-71; med. resident Washington U. St. Louis, 1971-72, renal fellow, 1972-74, asst. prof. medicine, 1974—, med. dir. renal hemodialysis service, 1975-76; med. dir. renal transplant service Barnes Hosp., 1976—. Diplomate Am. Bd. Internal Medicine. Mem. Am. Fedn. Clin. Research, Am., Internat. socs. nephrology, Sigma Xi, Alpha Omega Alpha. Democrat. Roman Catholic. Club: Crystal Lake Country. Contbr. articles to profl. jours. Home: 12355 Creekhaven St St Louis MO 63131 Office: 4550 Scott Ave St Louis MO 63110

HSI, EUGENE YU-TSENG, educator; b. Kiangsu, China, May 25, 1917; s. Teh-Feng and Chu-Siu (Hsu) H.; came to U.S., 1952, naturalized, 1969; B.S., Nat. Central U., China, 1940; M.S., U. Minn., 1954, Ph.D., 1960; m. Siu-Tsun Chang, Jan. 14, 1941; children—Nancy Shi-Heng, Edward Shi-Ping. Instr. Nat. Central U., Chung King China, 1943-44; prof. botany Northland Coll., Ashland, Wis., 1960-64; asso. prof. biology Wayne (Nebr.) State Coll., 1964-68; asso. prof. Southwest State U., Marshall, Minn., 1968-70, prof., 1971—; agrl. cons., Shanghai and Formosa, 1946-52. Co-dir. Minn. Resources Commn. Project, 1974-75. Mem. AAUP, Internat. Assn. Plant Taxonomy, Am. Soc. Plant Taxonomists, Minn. Acad. Scis., Assn. Midwestern Coll. Biology Tchrs. Contbr. articles to profl. jours. Home: 902 Cheryl Ave Marshall MN 56258

HSU, CHARLES FU-JEN, biochemist; b. Kiangsu, China, May 9, 1920; s. Shiu Byao and Yin Tao Hsu; came to U.S., 1958, naturalized, 1969; B.S., Nat. Chung Cheng U., China, 1946; M.S., DePaul U., Chgo., 1961; postgrad. U. Ill. Med. Center, 1961-64; m. Irene Yiu-Yuan Wei, Jan. 15, 1947; children—Phyllis (Mrs. Yon-Shong Shaw), Andrew, Kenneth, Rosa. Asst. chem. engr. Northeast Cement Corp., China, 1946-48; dir. cellulose purification Lin-Tow Co., Taiwan, 1948-50; head tchr. Ga-Yi Indsl. Sch., Taiwan, 1950-52; instr. Taiwan Agr. Coll., 1952-55; asso. prof. Nat. Chung Hsin U., Taiwan, 1955-59; research asso. Ivy Cancer Research Found., Chgo., 1961-64; research chemist G.D. Searle & Co., Chgo., 1964-71, microbiol. biochemist, 1971—. Mem. exec. com. Ill. Inst. Tech. Parent Assn., 1968-75. Recipient Taiwan Govt. award, 1958; Outstanding New Citizen award Citizenship Council Met. Chgo., 1969. Mem. Am. Chem. Soc., N.Y. Acad. Sci., Soc. Indsl. Microbiology. Club: Asian Am. Recreation. Contbr. articles to profl. jours. Patentee in field. Home: 4953 Elm St Skokie IL 60076 Office: Searle Labs PO Box 5110 Chicago IL 60680

HSU, CLEMENT CHING-SHAW, internist, immunologist; b. Taiwan, Oct. 9, 1937; s. Ma-Wong and Yui-Chu (Chen) H.; came to U.S., 1965; naturalized, 1976; M.D., Nat. Taiwan U., 1963; m. Yui-Li Wu, Nov. 20, 1965; children—Felix, Benedict. Intern Jersey City Med. Center, 1965-66; jr. med. resident Montefiore Hosp., Bronx, N.Y., 1966-67; sr. med. resident Boston City Hosp., 1967-68; clin. research fellow in liver disease and nutrition N.J. Coll. Medicine, 1968-69; research asso. dept. pathology Columbia U. Med. Center, N.Y.C., 1969-70; asst. in pediatrics Mt. Sinai Sch. Medicine, N.Y.C., 1970-71, instr. pediatrics, 1970-72; asso. in medicine Northwestern U. Med. Sch., Chgo., 1972-74, asst. prof. medicine, 1974—. Diplomate Am. Bd. Internal Medicine. Mem. Am. Assn. Immunologists, Am. Fedn. Clin. Research, AAAS, Chgo. Assn. Internal Medicine. Contbr. articles to med. jours. Office: 303 E Chicago St Chicago IL 60611

HSU, GRACE HEI-MIN CHEN, clin. biochemist; b. Tainan, Taiwan, Oct. 27, 1940; d. Shou-Tou and Fong-Tuey (Chern) Chen; came to U.S., 1965, naturalized, 1973; B.Sc., Nat. Taiwan Normal U., 1963; M.S., Kans. State Teachers Coll., 1967; Ph.D., U. Ill., 1971; m. Robert Chung-Ching Hsu, Sept. 3, 1966; children—Bradford, Lawrence, Joshua. Teaching and research asst. Cheng-Kung U., Tainan, Taiwan, 1964-65, Kans. State Teachers Coll., 1965-66, U. Ill. at Chgo., 1967-71; vis. fellow dept. chemistry Northwestern U., 1971-72; resident dept. pathology U. Ill. Hosp., Chgo., 1972-74; cons. Clin. Lab., Holy Cross Hosp., Chgo., 1973-74; tech. dir. Clin. Lab., St. James Hosp., Chicago Heights, Ill., 1974—; adj. prof. Coll. Environ. and Applied Sci., Governors State U., Park Forest South, Ill., 1974—. NIH fellow, 1971-72. Mem. Nat. Acad. Clin. Biochemistry, Am. Assn. Clin. Chemists, Sigma Xi. Presbyterian. Home: 1923 W 186th Pl Homewood IL 60430 Office: 1423 Chicago Rd Chicago Heights IL 60411

HSU, JOHN J., psychiatrist; b. China, Oct. 14, 1919; s. Ku Chin and Juen-Mei (Shih) H.; M.D., Coll. Medicine Nat. Central U., Nanking, China, 1944; m. Elizabeth Chang, Oct. 14, 1946; children—James, Nancy, Timothy, Esther, John R. Asst. dept. physiology Coll. Medicine Nat. Central U., 1945-49; pvt. practice, Taipei, Formosa, 1950-54; resident physician Camden (N.J.) County Hosp., 1954-56; resident Pontiac (Mich.) State Hosp., 1957-60, dir. male in-patient dept., 1960-62, dir. research, 1962-65, dir. alcoholism program, 1961-65; pvt. practice psychiatry, Pontiac, 1965-74, Bloomfield Hills, Mich., 1974—; mem. staff dept. psychiatry Pontiac Gen. Hosp., 1963—, chmn. dept. psychiatry, 1973-75; mem. staff St. Joseph Mercy Hosp., 1965—. Pres., Com. on Alcoholism, Pontiac, 1965-66, Oakland County (Mich.) Com. on Alcoholism, 1966-67; bd. dirs. Alcoholics Anonymous, Pontiac, 1965—; mem. med. bd. City Drug Abuse Treatment Program, 1970-74. Fellow Am. Assn. Social Psychiatry; mem. AAAS, Am. Psychiat. Assn., Mich. Psychiat. Soc., AMA, Am. Soc. Clin. Hypnosis. Contbr. articles in field to med. jours. Home: 7224 Old Mill Rd Birmingham MI 48010 Office: 10 W Square Lake Rd Suite 104 Bloomfield Hills MI 48013

HU, CHUNG HONG, physician; b. Taipei, Taiwan, Jan. 1, 1942; s. Sway Wang and Yoh Nee (Lin) H.; came to U.S., 1968, naturalized, 1977; M.D., Taipei Med. Coll., 1966; m. Mimi Wang, Apr. 29, 1968; children—Michael, Mario. Intern, L.I. Jewish Med. Center, Queens Hosp. Center, N.Y.C., 1968; resident U. Ala. Med. Center, Birmingham, 1969; fellow in dermatology Mayo Clinic, Rochester, Minn., 1970-74, instr. Mayo Med. Sch., 1974; practice medicine specializing in dermatology, Cleve., 1975—; asst. dermatologist Univ. Hosps. Cleve., 1975—; asst. prof. Case Western Res. U. Med. Sch., Cleve., 1975—. Served with Navy Republic China, 1966-67. Diplomate Am. Bd. Dermatology, Am. Bd. Dermatopathology. Mem. Soc. Investigative Dermatology, Am. Acad. Dermatology, A.C.P., Cleve. Acad. Medicine, Ohio Med. Assn., Cleve. Dermatol. Soc. Contbr. articles to profl. jours. Home: 3642 Concord Dr Beachwood OH 44122 Office: 2065 Adelbert Rd Cleveland OH 44106

HU, JAMES CHI-NIEN, speech pathologist; b. Taiwan, Feb. 5, 1941; s. Yea Chou and Pea Hua (Lee) H.; came to U.S., 1966, naturalized, 1976; M.A., Wichita State U., 1969; m. Jean F. Horng, Aug. 30, 1969; children—Edwin, Lori. Tchr. high sch. Poo-Yean High Sch., Taiwan, 1965-66; audiologist Ear Nose Throat Specialists' Office, Wichita, Kans., 1968-69; dir. speech and hearing clinic Winfield (Kans.) State Hosp. and Tng. Center, 1969—; cons. in field. Served as 2d lt., Army of Republic of China, 1964-65. Mem. Am. Speech and Hearing Assn., Nat. Assn. Hearing and Speech Action. Baptist. Kiwanis (pres. Winfield 1975-76). Home: 1916 E 14th St Winfield KS 67156 Office: Winfield State Hosp and Tng Center N College St Winfield KS 67156

HUANG, CHAO-YANG, infrared devices co. exec.; b. Taiwan, June 12, 1940; s. Lin-Kun and Geo-Pei (Chow) H.; came to U.S., 1966, naturalized, 1977; Ph.D., U. Mich., 1975, postdoctoral in Mech. Engring., 1975-76; m. Lily Chiu, Sept. 17, 1966; 1 dau., Leta. Teaching and research asst. physicis dept. Nat. Taiwan U., Taipei, 1964-66; sr. scientist Sensors, Inc., Ann Arbor, Mich., 1976-77; scientist Dexter (Mich.) Research Center, 1977—. Mem. Am. Nuclear Soc., Nat. Fire Protection Assn., Optical Soc. Am., Soc. Photo-Optical Instrumentation Engrs., Sigma Xi. Home: 1125 Lincoln St Ann Arbor MI 48104 Office: 7300 Huron River Dr Dexter MI 48130

HUANG, EUGENE YUCHING, civil engr., educator; b. Changsha, China, Nov. 28, 1917; s. Sam and Yi Yun (Chao) H.; came to U.S., 1948, naturalized, 1962; M.S., U. Utah, 1950; D.Sc., U. Mich., 1954; m. Helen W. Woo, Aug. 20, 1955; children—Martha, Pearl, William, Mary, Priscilla, Stephen. Asst. engr., Chinese Nat. Hwy. Adminstrn., 1941-45, asso. engr., 1945-48; research asst. Engring. Research Inst., U. Mich., Ann Arbor, 1953-54; research asst. prof. of civil engring. U. Ill., Urbana, 1954-58, asso. prof., 1958-63; prof. of transp. engring. Mich. Technol. U., Houghton, 1963—; cons. in transp. systems design and soil mechanics, 1954—. Recipient Faculty Research award Mich. Technol. U., 1967; registered profl. engr., Ill., Mich. Fellow ASCE; mem. Am. Soc. Engring. Edn., AAAS, Assn. of Asphalt Paving Technologists, Inst. of Mgmt. Sci., Am. Soc. for Engring. Edn., ASTM, Am. Ry. Engring. Assn., NRC (mem. transp. research bd. 1954), Sigma Xi, Chi Epsilon, Tau Beta Pi, Phi Tau Phi. Episcopalian. Author: Overview of the American Transportation System, 1976; contbr. numerous articles on transp. design systems and research on materials for pavement to profl. jours. Home: 400 Garnet St Houghton MI 49931 Office: Michigan Technological Univ Houghton MI 49931

HUANG, KEE CHANG, med. educator; b. Canton, China, July 22, 1917; s. Chun Yue and M. Lee Huang; B.S., Dr. Sun Yat-Sen U. (China), 1940, M.D., 1940; Ph.D., Columbia, 1953; m. Shou-Shan Chang, Feb. 16, 1947; children—Kou Chu, Anna, Karen. Came to U.S., 1949, naturalized, 1962. Research fellow pharmacology NIH, China, 1940-46; instr. pharmacology Nat. Shanghai Med. Sch., China, 1946-49; fellow Columbia, N.Y.C., 1949-53; research asso. U. Louisville, 1953-56, asst. prof., 1956-59, asso. prof., 1959-63, prof. pharmacology, 1963—; guest scientist Max Planck Inst. für Biophysik, Frankfurt, W.Ger., 1967-68. Recipient Outstanding Basic Sci. Instr. award, 1958, 59, 61, 63, 64, 65, 73, 74. Commonwealth Fund Am. scholar, 1967; NIH spl. fellow, 1967-68. Mem. Am. Physiol. Soc., Am. Soc. Pharmacology and Exptl. Therapeutics, Soc. Exptl. Biology and Medicine, Royal Soc. Medicine (London), Am. Soc. Nephrology, Sigma Xi. Contbr. articles to profl. jours. Author: Outline of Pharmacology, 1971, 2d edit. 1974. Home: 154 Forest Dr Jeffersonville IN 47130 Office: Dept Pharmacology U Louisville Louisville KY 40201

HUANG, LIN YAO, archtl. engring. co. exec.; b. Canton, China, Sept. 19, 1916; s. Doo Dat and Shing (Szeto) H.; came to U.S., 1941, naturalized, 1950; B.C.E., Hang Chow Christian Coll., 1941; M.C.E., U. Mich., 1943, U. Ill., 1944; m. Lena Lum, Sept. 27, 1944; children—Ruth, Janet Huang Preston, Timothy. With firm Smith, Hinchman & Grylls Assos., Inc., Detroit, 1950—, structural engr., 1950-61, chief structural engr., asso., 1961-73, v.p., corporate dir. structural engring., 1973—. Registered profl. engr., Mich., Ariz., Calif., Colo., Fla., N.Y., Washington. Mem. ASCE, Nat. Soc. Profl. Engrs., Am. Concrete Inst., Prestressed Concrete Inst. Home: 4304 Knightsbridge Ln Apt C-4 West Bloomfield MI 48033 Office: 455 W Fort St Detroit MI 48226

HUANG, TEH CHENG, hosp. adminstr.; b. Shanghai, China, Dec. 13, 1918; s. Huay and Falko (Wong) H.; D.V.M., Nat. U. Kwangsi, China, 1943; M.S., State Coll., Wash., 1948, Ph.D., 1951; m. Yu Ying Tsing, July 6, 1948 (dec. Nov. 1967); children—Mary C., Linda C.; m. 2d, Julia Young, June 27, 1974; 1 son, Stephen Wong. Came to U.S., 1947, naturalized, 1958. Govt. veterinarian Nat. Research of Animal Industry, Nanking, China, 1944-47; research asst. Wash. State Coll., 1947-51; research asso. Cornell U., 1951-57; dir. research, asst. dir. lab. Timken Mercy Hosp., Canton, Ohio, 1957-75; pvt. practice vet. medicine, Canton, 1971—. Pres. Stark County Heart Assn., 1968-71, E. Central Ohio Heart Assn., 1973—. Mem. Am. Vet. Med. Assn., Am. Chem. Soc., Am. Clin. Chem. Soc., AAAS, N.Y. Acad. Sci., Am. Assn. Clin. Scientists. Club: Stark County Internat. (pres. 1958-60). Home: 2130 Broad Ave NW Canton OH 44708 Office: 615 Camden SW Canton OH 44706

HUANG, WEN-TZY, pharm. scientist; b. Kaohsiung, Taiwan, China, Mar. 1, 1941; s. Yuan-Cheng and Yu (Hu) Huang; B.S., Kaohsiung Med. Coll., 1965; M.S., U. Iowa, 1969, Ph.D., 1972; m. Daria C. Huang. State hygienic lab. supr. biochem. services U. Iowa, 1972—. Mem. Am., Iowa pharm. assns., Rho Chi. Contbr. articles to profl. jours. Home: 1114 23d St West Des Moines IA 50265 Office: 405 State Office and Lab Bldg E 7th and Court Sts Des Moines IA 50309

HUBBARD, FREDERICK CONGDON, storage co. exec.; b. St. Louis, Mich., May 25, 1916; s. Benjamin Congdon and Mary Paul (Garrett) H.; A.B., U. Chgo., 1938; m. Mildred McElwee, July 12, 1947; children—Thomas Frederick, Amy Louise. Cost accountant Am. Seating Co., Grand Rapids, Mich., 1939-41; with Elston-Richards Storage Co., Grand Rapids, 1946—, v.p., 1949-55, pres., 1955—; pres. Asso. Warehouses Inc., Chgo., 1964-65. Vice pres. Friends of Aquinas Coll. Library, 1971-73, pres., 1974-75. Bd. dirs. Mich. State Accident Fund, 1955—, vice-chmn., 1968—; bd. dirs. Grand Rapids Civic Theatre, v.p., 1964-70. Served to capt. C.E., AUS,

1941-46; ETO. Recipient (with wife) Clay award Grand Rapids Civic Theatre, 1969. Mem. Mich. (dir. 1947-53), Ohio (dir. 1972-74), Ind. (pres. 1976-78) wholesale assns., U. Chgo. Alumni Club (pres. 1940-41). Republican. Episcopalian (vestryman). Mason. Clubs: Exchange (dir. 1957-58), University (Grand Rapids). Home: 3211 Lake Dr SE Grand Rapids MI 49506 Office: 3739 Patterson Ave Grand Rapids MI 49508

HUBBARD, HALSEY FREDERICK, communications exec.; b. Burlington, Wis., Mar. 31, 1907; s. Ira Aldrich and Edith May (Hempstead) H.; student Lawrence Coll., 1925-27; m. Lois Elizabeth Terp, Feb. 3, 1927; children—Emmy Lou, Richard Halsey, Ann Lael, Robert Aldrich, Sandra Jane. Transmission engr. Wis. Telephone Co., Appleton, 1928-42; civilian chief procurement maintenance engring. div. U.S. Army Signal Corps Engring. Lab., 1946-56, chief equipment support agy., 1956-59; U.S. mem. communications staff NATO Internat. Staff, Paris, France, 1959-65; pres. Communications Assos., Inc., Mt. Carmel, Ill., 1965—; pres., chmn. bd. dirs. Mt. Carmel Register Co., 1969-75; pres. Computer Avionics Corp., Mt. Carmel, 1974—, also dir. Served to 1st lt. AUS, 1942-46. Mem. Beta Theta Pi. Elk, Mason (Shriner, 32 deg.). Home: 320 E 3d St Mount Carmel IL 62863 Office: 740 Market St Mt Carmel IL 62863

HUBBARD, ORVILLE L., city ofcl.; b. Apr. 2, 1903; s. Ralph Star and Sylvia Elizabeth (Hart) H.; LL.B., Detroit Coll. Law, 1932; m. Fay Cameron, July 20, 1927. Republican precinct del., Dearborn, Mich., 1932—; asst. atty. gen. State Mich., 1939-40; alt. del. Rep. Nat. Conv., 1940, del., 1952; mem. Wayne County (Mich.) Bd. Suprs., 1942-68; mayor Dearborn, 1942—. Served with USMC, 1922-25; U.S. Army, 1930-37. Recipient Distinguished Citizen award Dearborn C. of C., 1962. Home: 7055 Mead St Dearborn MI 48126 Office: Office of the Mayor Dearborn MI 48126

HUBBARD, STANLEY STUB, broadcast exec.; b. St. Paul, May 28, 1933; s. Stanley Eugene and Didrikke A. (Stub) H.; m. Karen Elizabeth Holmen, June 13, 1959; children—Kathryn, Stanley Eugene, II, Virginia, Robert, Julia; B.A., U. Minn., 1955. With Hubbard Broadcasting, Inc., St. Paul, 1951—, gen. mgr., 1964-65, v.p., gen. mgr., 1965-67, pres., gen. mgr., 1967—; mem. NBC-TV Affiliates Bd., 1967-70. Mem. Gov.'s Crime Commn., 1967-68, Ramsey County Arena Commn., 1970; pres. St. Marys Point Hockey and Figure Skating Assn.; mem. Midway Hosp. Found.; trustee Hubbard Found. Mem. Broadcast Pioneers, Internat. Radio and TV Soc., Minn. Broadcasters Assn. (pres., past dir.), Mpls. C. of C. (dir. 1969), Minn. Flying Farmers, Young Pres.'s Orgn., Minn. Execs. Orgn., Aircraft Owners and Pilots Assn., Air Force Assn., Nat. Rifle Assn., Minneapolis Club, Minnesota Club, St. Paul Athletic Club, Town and Country Club, Tower Club, St. Croix Yacht Club, St. Petersburg Yacht Club, St. Croix Sailing Club. Home: Route 1 Lakeland MN 55043 Office: 3415 University Ave Saint Paul MN 55043

HUBBARD, WILLIS MCCRACKEN, librarian; b. Monmouth, Ill., Sept. 18, 1940; s. Harold Faye and Mary Jane (McCracken) H.; B.A., Monmouth Coll., 1962; M.S., U. Ill., 1963; M.A., So. Ill. U., 1968; m. Marilyn Sue Kessinger, Dec. 29, 1963; children—Laura, Evan. Asst. sci. librarian So. Ill. U., Carbondale, 1963-67, asst. social sci. librarian, 1967-68; head librarian, asst. prof. polit. sci. Eureka (Ill.) Coll., 1968-72, head librarian, dir. instl. research, 1972-77; dir. library Stephens Coll., Columbia, Mo., 1977—. Democratic precinct committeeman Cruger Twp., Woodford County, Ill., 1969-77; 2d v.p. Woodford County Central Dem. Com., 1972-77; mem. bd. auditors Cruger Twp., 1973-77; bd. dirs. Eureka Little League Assn., 1970-71, chmn., 1971. Mem. Jr. C. of C. (chaplain 1969-70, dir. 1969, v.p. 1970-71, state dir. 1972, sec. 1973, treas. 1974, named Jaycee of Year 1973, life mem. 1977), Pi Sigma Alpha. Home: 609 Maplewood Dr Columbia MO 65201 Office: Stephens College Columbia MO 65201

HUBBELL, JOHN GERARD, mag. roving editor; b. N.Y.C., July 14, 1927; s. Lester Sprague and Margaret Ambrose (Malia) H.; B.A., U. Minn., 1950; m. Katherine Hamel Hartigan, June 2, 1956; children—Charles W., John P., Mary Louise, Joseph G., Mary Margaret, William E., Andrew J., Mary Katherine, Mary Jeanne. Asso. editor external house organ Flight Lines Honeywell, Inc., Mpls., 1949-55; staff writer The Reader's Digest Mag., 1955-60, roving editor, Mpls., 1960—. Cons. Boy Scouts Am., 1971-74; Editorial cons. Pres.'s Blue Ribbon Defense Commn. 1970-72. Bd. dirs. Operation Help Other People Everywhere, Northfield, Minn., 1970—. Served with USNR, 1945-46. Recipient Distinguished Service award for book-length spl. feature The Case of the Missing H-Bomb, Sigma Delta Chi. 1966. Mem. Nat. Press Club, Sigma Delta Chi, Delta Kappa Epsilon. Roman Catholic. Club: Mpls. Golf (St. Louis Pk., Minn.). Author: (with James Daniel) Strike in the West, 1963; P.O.W.: A Definitive History of the American Prisoner of War Experience in Viet Nam, 1964-73. Contbr. articles and stories to major mags. Home: 4004 Queen Ave S Minneapolis MN 55410 Office: The Reader's Digest Pleasantville NY 10570

HUBBS, RONALD M., ins. co. exec.; b. Silverton, Oreg., Apr. 27, 1908; s. George W. and Ethel (Burch) H.; B.A., U. Oreg.; m. Margaret S. Jamie, Sept. 9, 1935; 1 son, George J. With St. Paul Fire & Marine Ins. Co., 1936—, asst. to pres., 1948-52, v.p., 1952-59, exec. v.p., 1959-63; pres., chief exec., 1963-68, chmn., 1968-73; pres., chief exec. officer St. Paul Cos., Inc., 1968-73, chmn., 1973—; dir. Western Life Ins. Co., Toro Co., Northwestern Bell Telephone Co.; past chmn. AFIA Worldwide Ins. Bd. dirs. Minn. Council on Econ. Edn.; bd. dirs., founding trustee Twin City Area Ednl. TV Corp.; bd. dirs. emeritus Miller Hosp., St. Paul; trustee James H. Hill Reference Library, Mpls. Soc. Fine Arts, William Mitchell Coll. Law, Coll. St. Thomas, Carleton Coll.; chmn. bd. trustees F.R. Bigelow Found.; trustee, past chmn. Ins. Inst. Am.; mem. consultative council U. Minn. Coll. Bus. Adminstrn.; chmn. pres.'s council St. Catherine's Coll.; gov. Internat. Inst. Seminars, Inc.; elector Ins. Hall Fame. Served from 1st lt. to col. AUS, World War II. Decorated Legion of Merit. Mem. Am. Inst. Property and Liability Underwriters (past chmn., trustee), Minn. Hist. Soc. (pres.) Alpha Tau Omega, Phi Delta Phi. Scabbard and Blade, Friars, Beta Gamma Sigma. Episcopalian (past trustee diocese Minn.). Clubs: Somerset Country; Minn. Home: 1410 Edgecumbe Rd Saint Paul MN 55116 Office: 385 Washington St Saint Paul MN 55102

HUBER, WALTER GLENN, judge; b. Irvington, Nebr., Dec. 24, 1908; s. George F. and Amanda A. (Borup) H.; student U. Omaha, 1926-28; B.A., U. Nebr., 1930, LL.B. cum laude, 1932, J.D., with distinction, 1968; m. Anna M. Hansen, Aug. 24, 1935. Admitted to Neb. bar, 1932; pvt. practice law, Blair, Nebr., 1939-72; dist. judge 6th Jud. Dist. Nebr., Blair, 1972—. County atty., Washington County, Nebr., 1940-46; city atty., Blair, 1941-42. Pres. Nebr. State Rose Soc., Inc., Lincoln, 1973-75. Chmn. Washington County Democrat Party, 1958-60. Bd. trustees U. Nebr. Found., Lincoln, 1972—. Recipient Silver Beaver award Mid-Am. council Boy Scouts Am., 1958. Mem. Washington County Bar Assn. (pres. 1968-72), Phi Beta Kappa. Lutheran. Club: Golf (Blair, Neb.). Author: Deprivation of Parents' Right to Custody of Children in Civil Actions, 1948. Home: Route 2 Blair NE 68008 Office: Courthouse Blair NE 68008

HUBIN, ALLEN JEROME, mfg. co. exec.; b. Crosby, Minn., Mar. 5, 1936; s. Edwin Gustav and Elizabeth (Wall) H.; B.S., Wheaton Coll., 1958; M.S., U. Minn., 1961; m. Marilyn Mae Hagstrom, May 3, 1958; children—Loren Paul, Jennifer Elizabeth, Wendy Evelyn, Daniel Robert, Joy Lynn. With 3M Co., St. Paul, 1961—, patent liaison and info. scientist, 1969-71, tech. patent specialist, internat. div., 1971-75, mgr. tech. edn. and tng., 1975—. Columnist, weekly crime fiction rev. N.Y. Times Book Rev., 1968-71. Mem. Mystery Writers of Am., Am. Soc. Engring. Edn. Presbyterian (elder). Patentee in field polymers, resins and their preparation. Pub., editor Armchair Detective, 1967—; editor Best Detective Stories of Year, 1970-75, Best of the Best Detective Stories, 1971; contbg. editor Ency. Mystery and Detection, 1976. Contbr. to Ency. Brit., 1973, Ency. Americana, 1976; intros. to various other books. Home: 3656 Midland Ave White Bear Lake MN 55110 Office: 3M Co St Paul MN 55101

HUBLY, GENEVIEVE ERLENE, educator, writer; b. Houston, Jan. 20, 1936; d. Anton Thorwald and Alice Geneview (Black) Hubly, Jr.; B.A., Rice U., 1957; M.A., U. Iowa, 1966, M.F.A., 1967; Ph.D., U. Oreg., 1977. Instr. U. No. Iowa, Cedar Falls, 1967-70, asst. prof., 1970—. Mem. Modern Lang. Assn., MW Modern Lang. Assn. Contbr. short stories to pop. mags. Home: 1920 Campus St Cedar Falls IA 50613 Office: Dept English Univ No Iowa Cedar Falls IA 50613

HUBNER, THOMAS ALLAN, airline exec.; b. LaPorte, Ind., Dec. 26, 1940; s. Norman Jacob and Audrey Hattie (Sramek) H.; B.S., Purdue U., 1964; m. Karen Ann Furlong, Mar. 21, 1965; children—Michelle Ann, Thomas Allan, Matthew Aaron. System analyst United Airlines, Chgo., 1965-69; sr. systems analyst Continental Ill. Nat. Bank, Chgo., 1969-71; data processing mgr. Scott Aviation, Lancaster, N.Y., 1971-72; programming mgr. United Airlines, Chgo., 1972—. Pres. Emerson PTA, 1975-76, Wheaton Jaycees, 1976-77. Recipient award of merit United Airlines, 1977; certified data processor; recipient John Armbruster Keyman award Wheaton Jaycees, 1976; named Outstanding Young Man, U.S. Jaycees, 1977. Mem. Sigma Alpha Epsilon. Methodist. Home: 1519 Mayo St Wheaton IL 60187 Office: PO Box 66100 Chicago IL 60666

HUBRICH, RONALD LEROY, apparel wholesale and retail co. exec.; b. Chgo., Oct. 7, 1944; s. Leon Raymond and Jane Pauline (Guzik) H.; B.B.A., Loyola U., Chgo., 1966; M.B.A., Northwestern U., 1967; m. Lois Barbara Franz, May 31, 1969 (dec.); children—Ronald Michael, James Joseph. Sr. auditor Peat, Marwick, Mitchell & Co., Chgo., 1967-70; treas., controller Aparacor, Inc., Evanston, Ill., 1970—. Mem. Am. Inst. C.P.A.'s, Ill. C.P.A. Assn., Immaculate Conception Parochial Sch. Parents Club, Holy Name Soc., Beta Alpha Psi, Beta Gamma Sigma. Roman Catholic. Club: Foresters. Home: 5873 N Overhill Ave Chicago IL 60631 Office: 2500 Crawford Ave Evanston IL 60201

HUCKMAN, MICHAEL SAUL, neuroradiologist; b. Newark, Aug. 20, 1936; s. Louis Fillmore and Mollie (Lehman) H.; A.B., Princeton U., 1958; M.D., St. Louis U., 1962; m. Beverly Joy Blachman, Aug. 2, 1964; children—Andrew Garfield, Robert Steven. Rotating intern Phila. Gen. Hosp., 1962-63, resident in radiology, 1965-68; fellow in neuroradiology Edward Mallinckrodt Inst. Radiology, Washington U., St. Louis, also instr. radiology Washington U., 1968-70; asst. prof. radiology and neurol. scis. Rush Med. Coll., Chgo., 1970-72, asso. prof., 1972—; dir. sect. neuroradiology Rush-Presbyn. St. Luke's Med. Center, 1970—; mem. faculty Cook County Grad. Sch. Medicine, 1972—; cons. in radiology Mt. Sinai Hosp. Served with USNR, 1963-65. Spl. fellow Nat. Inst. Neurol. Diseases and Blindness, 1968-70. Fellow Am. Coll. Radiology; mem. AMA, Ill., Chgo. med. socs., Chgo., Roentgen Soc., Ill., Blockley radiol. socs., Am. Soc. Neuroradiology, Radiol. Soc. N.Am., Assn. Univ. Radiologists, Sigma Xi, Phi Delta Epsilon. Jewish. Mem. editorial bd. of Jour. Computer Assisted Tomography, 1976—. Contbr. articles to profl. jours. Home: 2410 Lincoln St Evanston IL 60201 Office: 1753 W Congress Pkwy Chicago IL 60612

HUDELSON, WILLIAM FRANKLIN, dentist; b. Hibbing, Minn., Sept. 11, 1927; s. Carl William and Helen (Polar) H.; student Hibbing Jr. Coll., 1946-48; B.A., B.S., U. Minn., 1952, D.D.S., 1954; m. Elizabeth Marie Morency, Aug. 7, 1948; childrne—Warren, Vicki, Scott, Karen, Carl, Lee. Practice dentistry, Hibbing, 1954—, asso. Hibbing Dental Service, 1968—; clin. asst. prof. dentistry U. Minn., 1970—; mem. adv. bd. Hibbing Gen. Hosp., 1959—. Chmn., Hibbing Pub. Utilities Commn., 1969—; adv. com. Hibbing Area Tech. Sch., 1959—; bd. dirs. Jr. Achievement of Hibbing; mem. Hibbing Area Redevel. Commn., 1977-78. Served with AUS, 1945-46. Named Library Trustee of Year, State of Minn., 1966. Mem. ADA, Minn. Dental Assn. (pub. policy com. 1967—, legis. com.), Duluth Dist. Dental Soc. (chmn. legis. com. 1970—, v.p. 1975, pres. 1976-77), Omicron Kappa Upsilon. Club: Elks. Home: 2019 11th Ave E Hibbing MN 55746 Office: 2005 E 8th Ave Hibbing MN 55746

HUDGENS, JAMES RUDOLPH, electronics technician; b. Atlanta, June 23, 1923; s. Bennie and Zadie Iola (Hardy) H.; B.S., Benedict Coll., 1950; M.B.A., Central Mich. U., 1978; children—Janice, Joyce, James II; m. Connie R. Poore, Aug. 28, 1972. Asst. in physics, instr. Benedict Coll., Columbia, S.C., 1949-50; clk., Office of Adminstr., Housing and Home Fin. Agency, Washington, 1950-51; radar instr. Keesler AFB, Miss., 1951; electronics communications instr. U.S. Army Signal Corps Sch., Ft. Monmouth, N.J., 1951-62; electronics technician passive devices br., Def. Electronics Supply Center, Def. Logistics Agency, Dayton, Ohio, 1962—, rep. to NATO-U.S. Subcom. on Environ. Test Methods for Elec. and Electronic Component Parts. Pres. Woodside-Cicillion Community Council, Dayton, 1964-71; vestryman St. Augustine Episcopal Ch., Asbury Park, N.J., 1961-62, supt. Sunday sch., dir. religious edn., 1957-62; mem. Dayton Area Episcopal Council, 1970-72; licensed lay reader St. Margaret's Episcopal Ch., Dayton, 1969—; mem. futures planning com. Episcopal Diocese So. Ohio, 1973—. Recipient citation Dayton C. of C., 1970. Served with U.S. Army, 1943-45. Mem. Inst. Environ. Scis., Dayton Audio Club (past pres.), Omega Psi Phi. Author electronics texts for U.S. Army schs. Home: 4912 Shadwell Dr Dayton OH 45416

HUDKINS, DONALD LEROY, prison ofcl.; b. Fulton, Ind., Feb. 26, 1928; s. William Judson and Mildred Iris (Brooker) H.; B.S. in Bus. Adminstrn., Tri-State Coll., Angola, Ind., 1956; m. Julia Anne Carey, Dec. 24, 1948; children—Michael Lee, Renee Marie Hudkins Bell. Correctional officer, counselor, instl. parole officer Ind. State Prison, Michigan City, 1956-63; asst. supt. Ind. State Farm, Greencastle, 1963-69, supt., 1969—. Served with USN, 1946-48, USNR, 1948-53. Mem. Am., Ind. correctional assns., Am., W. Central wardens and supts. assns., Am. Legion. Address: Box 76 Greencastle IN 46135

HUDKINS, STEPHEN JAY, extension adminstr.; b. Rochester, Ind., Dec. 28, 1941; s. Loyal Jud and Deloris Louise (Arven) H.; B.S., Purdue U., 1964; M.A., Ball State U., 1971; m. Mary Loucille Keller, Aug. 23, 1964; children—Katherine Ann, Brian Scott. Soil conservationist U.S. Dept. Agr., Soil Conservation Service, Paoli and Salem, Ind., 1964-66, dist. conservationist, Jasper, Ind., 1966-67, extension agt. youth Purdue U. Coop. Extension Service, Jasper, 1967-68, extension agt. crops, Connersville, Ind., 1968-70, extension soil conservationist, fieldman, state soil and water conservation com. Purdue U., West Lafayette, Ind., 1970-71, extension agt.-coordinator, Tipton, Ind., 1971—; judge Ind. State Fair soil and water conservation, 1970-75. Mem. Tipton County Plan Commn., 1971—; entertainment chmn. Tipton County Pork Festival, 1972; organized Tipton County Soil and Water Conservation Dist., 1974; chmn. bd. trustees Kemp Methodist Ch., Tipton, 1976-77. Mem. Am. Soc. Agronomy, Tipton C. of C., County Extension Agts. Assn. Clubs: Elks, Masons, Rotary (pres. 1975 Tipton), Lions (sec.-treas. Tipton 1966). Author: Soil and Water Conservation around My Home; A Closer Look at Soil and Water Conservation. Home: Rural Route 4 Tipton IN 46072 Office: PO Box 70 Tipton IN 46072

HUDNUT, WILLIAM HERBERT, III, mayor, former congressman, univ. adminstr.; b. Cin., Oct. 17, 1932; s. William H. and Elizabeth (Kilborne) H.; grad. Darrow Sch., 1950; A.B. magna cum laude, Princeton, 1954; B.D. summa cum laude, Union Theol. Sem., 1957; D.D., Hanover Coll., 1967, Wabash Coll., 1969; m. Susan Greer Rice, Dec. 14, 1974; children by previous marriage—Michael, Laura, Timothy, William H. IV, Theodore. Ordained to ministry Presbyn. Ch., 1957; asst. minister Westminster Ch., Buffalo, 1957-60; pastor 1st Ch., Annapolis, Md., 1960-63, 2d Ch., Indpls., 1963-72; mem. 93rd Congress from 11th Ind. Dist.; dir. dept. community affairs Ind. Central U., Indpls., 1975-77; mayor, Indpls., 1977—. Pres. Anne Arundel County Mental Health Assn., 1961-63, Marion County Mental Health Assn. (1965-67), Westminster Found. Purdue U. (1967-72); mem. Central Area council Boy Scouts Am. (1964-72); mem. Bd. Safety, Indpls. Bd. dirs. Flanner House, Indpls., Estelle Peabody Home Manchester, Ind., Family Service Assn., Indpls. Park Sch. Found.; pres. bd. trustees Darrow Sch. Recipient travelling fellowship Union Theol. Sem., 1957. Mem. Phi Beta Kappa. Presbyn. Clubs: Indianapolis Columbia, Woodstock, Princeton. Editor: Union Sem. Quar. Rev., 1956-57. Home: 722 Pine Dr Indianapolis IN 46260 Office: City County Bldg 200 E Washington St Indianapolis IN 46204

HUDSON, HAROLD DON, veterinarian; b. Audrain County, Mo., Nov. 22, 1943; s. Harold F. and Greta Arlene (Boyd) H.; A.A., Hannibal (Mo.) La Grange Coll., 1963; B.S., U. Mo., 1967, D.V.M., 1970; m. Carole Jacqueline Spence, Aug. 30, 1964; children—Dale Brent, Kim Marie. Asso. Clarinda (Iowa) Vet. Clinic, 1970-71; asso. Bethany (Mo.) Vet. Clinic, 1971-72; asso. Vet. Clinic, Mexico, Mo., 1972—. Mem. Am., Mo. vet. med. assns., Am. Assn. Bovine Practitioners, Am. Assn. Swine Practitioners. Baptist. Home: 933 Emmons St Mexico MO 65265 Office: 1624 Hwy 54 E Mexico MO 65265

HUDSPETH, E. RAE, gynecologist: b. Cleburne, Tex., Sept. 9, 1925; d. Ernest William and Minnie Elizabeth (Bankston) Hudspeth; B.S. with high honors, N. Tex. State U., 1947; M.D., U. Tex., 1951. Intern, USPHS Hosp., Seattle, surgeon Fed. Reformatory for Women, USPHS, Alderson, W.Va., 1951-53; resident in obstetrics and gynecology Hutzel Hosp., Detroit, 1953-56, mem. sr. attending staff; practice medicine specializing in gynecology, Grosse Pointe Woods, Mich., 1956-74, in gynecology, 1974—; staff Cottage Hosp., Grosse Pointe, Mich.; clin. instr. Wayne State U. Fellow A.C.S.; mem. Mich., Wayne County med. socs., Am. Coll. Obstetrics and Gynecology, Am. Assn. Gynecol. Laparoscopists. Club: Essex Golf and Country (Windsor, Ont.). Home: 1492 Hollywood St Grosse Pointe Woods MI 48236 Office: 19557 Mack St Grosse Pointe Woods MI 48236

HUEBNER, FRED DUNCAN, lawyer; b. Albia, Iowa, Sept. 28, 1919; s. Fred Cline and Ina Melinda (Duncan) H.; B.A., Iowa Wesleyan Coll., 1943; LL.B., Drake U., 1949, J.D., 1968; m. Lucy Ann Deesz, Sept. 12, 1943; children—Jo Ann Garwood Duncan, Kemp Davis. Admitted to Iowa bar, 1949, since practiced in Des Moines; asso. firm Miller, Huebner & Miller, 1949-50, firm Miller, Davis, Hise & Howland, 1950-53; partner Davis, Huebner, Johnson, Burt, and predecessor firm, 1953-70; partner Hopkins & Huebner, 1970—. Mem. Ia. Indsl. Commrs. Adv. Com., 1960—. Active YMCA; bd. dirs. Little League Baseball, 1960-67. Republican precinct committeeman, 1952. Mem. Am., Polk County, Iowa (past chmn. spl. com. workmen's compensation) bar assns., Iowa Acad. Trial Lawyers, Ia. Def. Counsel, Phi Alpha Delta, Phi Delta Theta. Methodist. Home: 3235 John Lynde St Des Moines IA 50312 Office: Central Nat Bldg Des Moines IA 50309

HUELSBECK, CHARLES JOSEPH, librarian-editor; b. Dedham, Iowa, Jan. 29, 1920; s. Herman Joseph and Mary Anne (Werner) H.; B.A., U. No. Iowa, 1946; M.S., U. No. Colo., 1948; Library certificate, Emporia (Kans.) State U., 1952; M.S. in L.S., U. Wis., 1953; postgrad. U. Iowa, summers 1951, 56, Northwestern U., summer 1960. Instr. English, Creighton U., Omaha, 1947-49, St. Ambrose Coll., Davenport, Iowa, 1949-51; dir. library, publs. adviser U. Maine, Presque Isle, 1953-56; asst. prof., asso. prof. English, guidance cons. Merrimack Coll., North Andover, Mass., 1956-71; dir. Ames Free Library, North Easton, Mass., 1973-74; librarian-editor Iowa Geol. Survey, Iowa City, 1975—. Served with AUS, 1942-43. Mem. Geoscience Info. Soc., Kappa Delta Pi, Pi Gamma Mu. Anglican-Catholic. Author: (with Jayne Harbaugh and Suzan M. Stewart) Iowa Water Resources Data Systems Catalog, 1977. Editor: Iowa Geol. Survey Newsletter, 1975—, Iowa Geol. Survey Staff Notes, 1977—. Contbr. book revs. to America, Catholic World, Sign, 1967-72. Home: Apt 709A 1110 N Dubuque St Iowa City IA 52240 Office: 123 N Capitol St Iowa City IA 52242

HUENEKE, TERRY ALLEN, mktg. adminstr.; b. Milw., Apr. 14, 1942; s. Russell Frank and Naomi Margaret (Esser) H.; Asso., U. Wis., 1966. Asst. advt. mgr. A&P Supermarkets, 1960-69; asst. v.p., mktg. mgr. Career Acad., Milw., 1969-74; dir. U.S. mktg. Manpower Inc., Milw., 1974—; cons. in field. Co-chmn. 1977 Festival of Arts, Milw. Mem. Milw. Advt. Club, Friends of Art Milw. Art Center, AAU. Republican. Episcopalian. Home: 7314 W Marine St Milwaukee WI 53223 Office: 5301 N Ironwood St Milwaukee WI 53201

HUESMANN, L. ROWELL, psychologist; b. Detroit, Jan. 20, 1943; s. Louis E. and Ruth (Rowell) H.; B.S., U. Mich., 1964; M.S., Carnegie Inst. Tech, 1967; Ph.D., Carnegie Mellon U., 1969; m. Penny Graham, May 23, 1964; children—Kim, Graham. Vis. staff scientist, Mitre Corp., Bedford, Mass., 1966; vis. sr. computer analyst Jet Propulsion Lab., Pasadena, Calif., 1970; lectr. dept. psychology Yale U., New Haven, 1968, asst. prof., 1969-73, asso. prof., 1973; asso. prof. psychology and computer sci. U. Ill., Chgo., 1973—; research scientist Naval Personnel Research Center, Point Loma, Calif., 1976; vis. scholar U. Utah, 1976. NIMH grantee, 1970-72, 76—. Mem. Am. Psychol. Assn., Psychometric Soc., Psychonomic Soc., Assn. for Computing Machinery, Sigma Xi. Club: Sierra. Author: Growing Up to be Violent, 1977. Asso. editor Jour. Abnormal Psychology, 1977—. Office: Dept of Psychology Univ of Illinois PO Box 4348 Chicago IL 60680

HUETTNER, DAVID JOSEPH, chemist; b. New London, Wis., Feb. 20, 1938; s. Aloysius Joseph and Margaret Elizabeth (Olson) H.; B.S., St. Norbert Coll., 1960; Ph.D., Wash. State U., 1966; m. Charlotte May Stroobants, Aug. 26, 1961; children—Joseph David, Andrew Joseph, Thomas Joseph, Jennifer Ann. NSF/Petroleum Research Fund postdoctoral fellow U. Mass., Amherst, 1966-68; staff chemist IBM Corp., Endicott, N.Y., 1968-75; asst. prof., research asso. Inst. Paper Chemistry, Appleton, Wis., 1975—. NDEA grad. fellow, 1960-64. Mem. Am. Chem. Soc., Am. Phys. Soc., Alpha Chi Sigma, Delta Epsilon Sigma. Roman Catholic. Patentee in field. Home: 3221 N McDonald St Appleton WI 54911 Office: PO Box 1039 Appleton WI 54911

HUEY, ARTHUR SANDMEYER, petroleum landman, real estate and investment co. exec.; b. Van Buren, Ark., May 18, 1913; s. Richard King and Adele (Sandmeyer) H.; A.B., Amherst Coll., 1935; postgrad. U. Wis., 1939; m. Helen Dorothy Mautz, June 17, 1935; children—Richard King, Arthur Ticknor, Adele Susan, Sara Louise. Asst. dir. Leelanau Schs., Glen Arbor, Mich., 1935-43, headmaster, owner, 1943-54, pres., owner, 1954-64, pres. emeritus bd. trustees; asst. dir. Camp Leelanau, Glen Arbor, 1935-43, camp dir., 1943-54, pres., owner, 1954-72; mgr. Leelanan Homestead Guest Inn, Glen Arbor, 1935-54, owner, 1943-72, pres., 1954-72; pres. ASH, Inc., 1972—. County chmn. Republican Party, 1956-58, fin. chmn., 1951-56; nat. adv. bd. Interlochen Arts Acad.; trustee Asher Student Found.; mem. East Central Regional Bd.-area 2, Boy Scouts Am. Mem. Mich. State, Traverse City Area (Distinguished Service award 1969) chambers commerce, U.S. Ski Assn., Mich. Hotel and Motor Hotel Assn. (past pres., past chmn. exec. bd.), Mich. Skeet Assn. (dir., pres.), Delta Kappa Epsilon. Christian Scientist. Clubs: Masons (32 deg.), Shriners, Rotary; Chgo.; Traverse City Golf and Country; Detroit Gun. Home: Overbrook N Glen Arbor MI 49636 Office: ASH Inc Glen Arbor MI 49636

HUEY, ROBERT NEFF, govt. ofcl.; b. Westhope, N.D., Apr. 29, 1915; s. James Way and Nora L. (Henderson) H.; student N.D. Sch. Forestry, 1933; B.A., Jamestown Coll., 1936; postgrad. U. N.D., 1946; m. Muriel Ekness, Dec. 2, 1945; children—David, Pamela, Paula, Timothy. Dist. mgr. Field Service, U.S. Dept. Commerce, Fargo, N.D., 1946-52; mgr. indsl. dept. Fargo C. of C., 1952-59; asst. dir. N.D. Econ. Devel. Commn., Bismarck, 1959-62, dir., 1962-65; dir. Chgo. Field Office, Bur. Indian Affairs, Indsl. Devel. br., 1965—. Bd. dirs. Cass County chpt. A.R.C. Served with Ordnance Dept., AUS, 1942-45; ETO. Recipient Spl. Achievement certificate Commr. Indian Affairs, 1976. Mem. N.D. Assn. Execs. (v.p.). Presbyterian (elder). Kiwanian (dir.). Home: 2219 Harrison St Glenview IL 60025 Office: 433 W Van Buren Room 929 Chicago IL 60607

HUFENDICK, LAWRENCE HENRY, educator; b. Keokuk, Iowa, Aug. 18, 1935; s. Arthur William and Alma (Miller) H.; B.S., (study grantee) Western Ill. U., 1956, M.S., 1956; M.S., U. Wis.-Milw., 1974; m. Annette Geneen Buss, Aug. 24, 1958; children—Deborah Janel, Jerome Gregory, Jason Anthony. Teaching asst. Western Ill., U., 1955-56; asst. prof. math. Carthage Coll., 1956-63, acting dept. chmn., dept. of math. and physics, 1962-63; asst. prof. math. Carthage Coll., Kenosha, Wis., 1963-64, asst. prof. physics, 1964-68, asst. prof. math., 1968-72; dir. Books, Kenosha, 1972-75, Bushnell, Ill., 1975—; sci. tchr. Bushnell-Prairie City High Sch., 1975-77; tchr. physics Naperville (Ill.) North High Sch., 1977—. Danforth asso., 1961-72. Mem. Ill. 20th Congl. Dist. Adv. Council, 1962; mem. Govs. Conf. for Gifted in Ill., 1963; lectr. space symposium Met. Luth. Council Milw., 1969. Summer study grantee U. Kans. 1957, U. Mich., 1963, U. Calif. at Berkeley, 1964, 67, Oak Ridge Inst. Nuclear Studies, 1965, Stanford, 1968. Mem. Math. Assn. Am., Internat. Platform Assn., Kappa Delta Pi, Sigma Zeta, Kappa Sigma Kappa. Author: Mathematics for The Liberal Arts Student, 1971; Ideas, The Sparks of Life (pseudonym David Spring) 1966; Chart of Education, 1973. Home: 606 N Ellsworth Naperville IL 60540

HUFF, BERNARD LOUIS, JR., biologist, pollution control co. exec.; b. Sainte Marie, Ill., July 25, 1945; s. Bernard L. and Ursula P. (Gangloff) H.; B.S., U. Ill., 1967; M.S., Ohio State U., 1969; Ph.D., Purdue U., 1975; m. Margaret A. Cannon, Aug. 11, 1973; 1 son, Bryan Martin. Biologist, mgr. Cin. office Wapora Inc., research and cons. pollution control, 1974—. Served with AUS, 1969-71. Mem. Entomol. Soc. Am., N. Am. Benthological Soc., Ind. Acad. Sci., Gamma Sigma Delta. Roman Catholic. K.C. Home: 4971 Hawaiian Terr Cincinnati OH 45223 Office: Wapora Inc 5700 Hillside Ave Cincinnati OH 45233

HUFF, FLOYD ALONZO, atmospheric scientist; b. Hilton, N.Y., Aug. 1, 1913; s. Jacob and Anna (Collins) H.; B.S. in Engring., Mich. State U., 1938; student meteorology, U. Chgo., 1942-43; m. Amelia Russi, Aug. 6, 1942. Chem. engr. Eastman Kodak Co., Rochester, N.Y., 1938-42; meteorologist Pan Am. World Airways, 1946-47; with Ill. Water Survey, 1948—, prin. scientist, Urbana, 1972—. Served with USAAF, 1942-46. NSF grantee, 1969-75. Mem. Am. Meteorol. Soc., Am. Geophys. Union, Ill. Acad. Sci., Sigma Xi. Contbr. articles to profl. jours. Home: 2508 Combes St Urbana IL 61801 Office: Ill Water Survey Box 232 Urbana IL 61801

HUFF, JOSEPH WILLIAM, dentist; b. Poplar Bluff, Mo., June 28, 1939; s. John Douglas and Effie (Bocek) H.; student Union Coll., 1958-60, 61-63; D.D.S., St. Louis U., 1967; m. Alyce Fay Chapman, Apr. 11, 1960; children—Dawna Fay (dec.), Donald William. Practice gen. dentistry, Bourbon, Mo., 1969—. Adv. com. Crawford County Child Welfare, 1972—; active Bourbon Booster Club, 1969—. Served with Dental Corps, AUS, 1967-69. Mem. Am., Mo., Greater St. Louis, Ozark dental assns. Seventh-day Adventist (pathfinder dir. 1972, asst. youth leader 1972). Home: Rural Route 1 Box 89 Bourbon MO 65441 Office: 120 S College St Bourbon MO 65441

HUFF, MERRIFIELD WELLS, pub. utility exec.; b. Poplar Bluff, Mo., Aug. 4, 1930; s. William Davis and Mary (Wells) H.; A.B. with honors, Princeton U., 1952; B.J., Mo. U., 1956; m. Bette Lee Brewster, Aug. 25, 1956; children—Susan Victoria, Mark Christopher. Mem. pub. relations dept. Laclede Gas Co., St. Louis, 1956-62; acct. exec. Gardner Advt. Co., St. Louis, 1962-64; dir. advt. and pub. relations The Boatmen's Nat. Bank of St. Louis, 1964-72; dir. info., central region Continental Telephone Service Corp., 1972—. Pub. relations chmn. Children's Home Soc. Mo.; publicity chmn. St. Louis Fall Festival, 1970; v.p. Girl Scout council Greater St. Louis, 1972—. Served with AUS, 1952-54. Mem. Indsl. Press Assn. Greater St. Louis (pres. 1960-61), Internat. Council Indsl. Editors (pres. 1963-64), Met. St. Louis C. of C. (pub. relations chmn. 1970-71), St. Louis Advt. Club, Pub. Relations Soc. Am., Internat. Assn. Bus. Communicators, St. Louis Press Club. Republican. Episcopalian. Club: Univ. Home: 4942 Robert Ave Saint Louis MO 63109 Office: 222 S Central Saint Louis MO 63105

HUFFMAN, JAMES FLOYD, educator; b. Kalamazoo, May 1, 1922; s. Floyd Sampson and Carrie Myrtle (Booker) H.; B.S., Northwestern U., 1948, M.A., 1949; Ph.D., Mich. State U., 1966; m. Martha Alice Neal, June 9, 1946; children—David, Ann. Instr. speech Northwestern U. instr. Iowa State U., Evanston, Ill., 1949; prof. humanities and communication Gen. Motors Inst., Flint, Mich., 1974—, recipient Distinguished Service award; cons. Banking Inst. Am., 1964. Served to 1st. lt. USAF, 1942-45. Decorated 5 battle stars and Air medal. Mem. U.S. Naval Inst., Am. Acad. Polit. Social Sci., Am. Assn. State Local Historians, Nat. Trust for Hist. Preservation, Nat. Office Mgmt. Assn., Beta Theta. Pi. Clubs: Kiwanis Internat. Contbr. film documentaries in field. Home: 1059 W Hemphill St Flint MI 48507 Office: Gen Motors Inst Flint MI 48502

HUFFMAN, JAMES HUDSON, orch. condr.; b. Kansas City, Mo., Aug. 28, 1929; s. LeRoy Bray and Mildred Lee (Hudson) H.; B.S., U. Mo., 1956, M.A., 1957; m. Georgann Lewis, Sept. 3, 1949; children—James Michael, Laura Ann, Elizabeth. Prin. bassist St. Louis Philharmonic Orch., 1957-60, Gary (Ind.) Symphony, 1960-64; with Gary Symphony, several orchs. Chgo. area, including North Shore Symphony, 1964-70; condr. Ft. Dodge (Iowa) Symphony, 1970—; tchr. orchs., Mo., Ind., Ill., Iowa. Served with USAF, 1951-54. Recipient Eldon Jones award U. Mo., 1957. Mem. Music Educators Nat. Conf., Ill., Mo., Ind., Iowa music educators, Am. String Tchrs. Assn., Nat. Sch. Orch. Assn., Ft. Dodge Area Concert Assn. (v.p.), Fine Arts Assn., Phi Mu Alpha. Club: Lions. Home: 3207 10th Ave N Fort Dodge IA 50501 Office: 819 N 25th St Fort Dodge IA 50501

HUFFMAN, PATRICK JOHN, chemist; b. Peoria, Ill., May 8, 1948; s. Patrick Howard and Jane Francis (Hoey) H.; m. Carol Anne Dresch, June 20, 1970; children—John, Jeffrey. B.S., Ill. State U., 1970, M.S., 1973. Certified Class A Waste Treatment Operator, Ill., Certified Pesticide Control Operator, Ill. Tech. Cons. Hawthorne House, Inc., Bloomington, Ill., 1971-72; quality control mgr. Paul F. Beich Co., Bloomington, 1971-73, gen. supr., 1973-74, ops. mgr., 1974—. Mem. Am. Chem. Soc., Environ. Mgmt. Assn., Am. Assn. Candy Techs., Nat. Confectioners Assn., Ill. State Acad. Sci. Recipient Boss of the Year award, Con Brio Chpt. Nat. Secretaries Assn; author: Silver Complexes Containing Pyrazine N-oxides as Ligands, 1974. Office: Beich Rd Bloomington IL 61701

HUFFSTUTLER, DONALD GORDON, mfg. co. exec.; b. Granite City, Ill., Oct. 11, 1938; s. John Gordon and LaVerne Irene (Kahle) H.; student Hofstra U., 1955-59, U. Mo., 1970-71; m. Alice Catherine Sitler, Sept. 6, 1959; children—Donald Gordon, John Robert. Dept. supr. Washington U. Sch. Medicine, St. Louis, 1963-67; instr. Manpower Bus. Tng. Inst., St. Louis, 1967-68; tchr. South County Tech. High Sch., Sunset Hills, Mo., 1968-72; mgr. data processing Prince Gardner Co., St. Louis, 1972—. Served with U.S. Army, 1957, 61-62. Recipient Am. Math. Assn. award, 1954. Republican. Lutheran. Clubs: Castlewood Swim and Tennis. Home: 643 Turfwood Dr Ballwin MO 63011 Office: 1234 S Kings Hwy St Louis MO 63110

HUFFT, JOHN CARLTON, recreational vehicles mfg. co. exec.; b. Sardis, Miss., Oct. 28, 1925; s. Raymond James and Helen Terry (Carlton) H.; B.S., U.S. Naval Acad., 1947; M.S., Rensselaer Polytechnic Inst., 1951; m. Jane Hyndman Fitzcharles, Aug. 15, 1947; children—John C., Kimberly Ann. Commd. ensign, U.S. Navy, 1947, advanced through grades to lt. comdr., 1958; ret., 1959; project engr. Westinghouse Nuclear Energy Systems, Pitts., 1959-69; asst. v.p. Coachmen Ind., Inc., Middlebury, Ind., 1969—. Chmn. Elkhart County Bd. Zoning Appeals; mem. adv. council on continuing edn. Ball State U.; pres. Michiana Watershed of Elkhart County (Ind.). Mem. ASCE, Am. Arbitration Assn. Republican. Methodist. Clubs: Maplecrest Country, Middlebury Civic (past pres.), Elks. Home: 502 S Scott Middlebury IN 46540 Office: Coachmen Ind Box 30 Middlebury IN 46540

HUGENBERG, LAWRENCE WILLIAM, psychologist; b. Cin., July 28, 1953; s. Paul Bernard and Marguerite Marion (Chartier) H.; B.S. in Social Work, Ohio State U., 1974, M.A., 1976; m. Laura Beth Reutter, Aug. 30, 1975. Grad. research asso. Coll. Edn., Ohio State U., 1975-76, coordinator freshman early experiencing program, 1976-77, grad. teaching asso. dept. communication, 1977—; psychology asst. Ohio Youth Commn., Columbus, 1976—. Mem. Am. Personnel and Guidance Assn., Am. Assn. Higher Edn., Am. Coll. Personnel Assn., Assn. Specialists in Group Work, Assn. Measurement and Evaluation in Guidance, Speech Communications Assn., Central States Speech Assn. Democrat. Home: 3003 Ruhl Ave Columbus OH 43209 Office: 2280 W Broad St Columbus OH 43228

HUGGINS, CHARLES BRENTON, physician; b. Halifax, N.S., Can., Sept. 22, 1901; s. Charles Edward and Bessie (Spencer) H.; B.A., Acadia U., 1920, D.Sc., 1946; M.D., Harvard, 1924; M.Sc., Yale, 1947; D.Sc., Washington U., St. Louis, 1950, Leeds U., 1953; Turin U., 1957; Sigillum Magnum, Bologna U., 1964; D.Sc., Trinity Coll., 1965, Wales, 1967, U. Mich., 1968, Med. Coll. Ohio, 1973; LL.D., U. Aberdeen, 1966; D.P.S., George Washington U., 1967; LL.D. (hon.), York U. (Can.); hon. doctorate, U. Calif. at Berkeley, 1968; m. Margaret Wellman, July 29, 1927; children—Charles Edward, Emily Wellman (Mrs. Fine). Intern in surgery U. Mich., 1924-26; instr. surgery, 1926-27; instr. surgery U. Chgo., 1927-29, asst. prof., 1929-33, asso. prof., 1933-36, prof. surgery, 1936—, dir. Ben May Lab. for Cancer Research, 1951-69, William B. Ogden Distinguished Service prof., 1962; Macewan lectureship U. Glasgow, 1958; Chancellor Acadia U., Wolfville, N.S., 1972—. Trustee Worcester Found. Exptl. Biology; hon. trustee Jackson Lab., Bar Harbor, Me.; bd. govs. Weizmann Inst. Sci., Rehovot, Israel. Recipient Charles L. Meyer award for cancer research Nat. Acad. Sci., 1943; Am. Urol. Assn. award for research on male genital tract, 1948; Francis Amory award for cancer research, 1948; AMA gold medals for research, 1936, 1940; Societe Internationale d'Urologie, 1948; Am. Cancer Soc. award, 1953; Bertner award M.D. Anderson Hosp., 1953; award Am. Pharm. Mfrs. Assn., 1953; Gold medal Am. Assn. Genito-Urinary Surgeons, 1955; Borden award Assn. Am. Med. Colls., 1955; decorated Order Pour le Merite, Germany, 1958, Order of The Sun, Peru, 1961; recipient Comfort Crookshank award Middlesex Hosp., London, 1957; Charles Mickel fellow Toronto U., 1958; Cameron prize Edinburg U., 1958; Valentine prize N.Y. Acad. Medicine, 1962; Hunter award Am. Therapeutic Soc., 1962; Lasker award for med. research, 1963; Gold medal for research Rudolf Virchow Soc., 1964, Passano award, 1965; Ramon Guiteras medal and award Am. Urol. Assn., 1966; Centennial medal Acadia U., 1967; Bigelow medal Boston Surgical Soc., 1967; Nobel prize for physiology and medicine, 1966; James Ewing Soc. award, 1975, others. Fellow A.C.S. (hon.), Royal Coll. Physicians (London), Royal Coll. Physicians (Edinburgh) Royal Coll. Surgeons (Can.-hon.); mem. Am. Philos. Soc., Nat. Acad. Scis., Canadian Med. Assn. (hon.), Am. Assn. Cancer Research (hon.), Alpha Omega Alpha. Home: 5807 S Dorchester Chicago IL 60637 Office: 950 E 59th St Chicago IL 60637

HUGHES, CALVIN HOOVER, psychiatrist; b. Clearfield, Pa., Dec. 12, 1928; s. James P. and Bertha Mae (Hoover) H.; B.S., Grove City Coll., 1951; M.D., U. Mich., 1960; m. Wanda Arlena Davis, June 20, 1953; 1 dau., Tammy J. Research asso. Wayne State U., 1951-52; head of mech. heart project research staff Gen. Motors Corp., 1952-56; gen. rotating intern Detroit Meml. Hosp., 1960-61; resident in psychiatry Lafayette Clinic, 1961-64; pvt. practice medicine specializing in psychiatry Harper Woods, Mich., 1964—; attending staff Cottage Hosp., 1974—, acting chief of psychiatry, 1973-74; sr. attending staff Detroit Meml. Hosp., 1970—, acting chief of psychiatry, 1973-74, chmn. continuing med. edn. com.; sr. attending staff South Macomb Hosp.; attending staff St. John's Hosp.; cons. in psychiatry Holy Cross Hosp., Saratoga Hosp., Warren Meml. Hosp.; clin. asst. prof. psychiatry Wayne State U., 1973—; mem. Mich. Bd. Licensing and Regulation Marriage Counselors. Mem. Macomb County Mental Health Bd., 1965-67; bd. dirs. hosps. and homes div. Methodist Ch., 1965-70. Served with U.S. Army, 1946-47. Recipient Outstanding Alumni Achievement award Grove City Coll., 1970. Diplomate Am. Bd. Psychiatry and Neurology. Fellow Am. Psychiat. Assn.; mem. AMA, Mich. Psychiat. Soc. (chmn. pub. info. com.), Mich., Wayne County med. socs., Port Huron Power Squadron. Republican. Presbyn. Clubs: Bayview Yacht, Masons. Address: 19959 Vernier Rd Harper Woods MI 48225

HUGHES, JOHN JAY, clergyman, theologian; b. N.Y.C., May 14, 1928; s. William Dudley Foulke and Marguerite Montgomery (Jay) H.; A.B., Harvard U., 1948; S.T.B., Gen. Theol. Sem., N.Y.C., 1953; Dr. theol., U. Munster (Germany), 1969; Ordained priest Episcopal Ch., 1954; curate Grace Episcopal Ch., Newark, 1953-55; rector St. Johns Epicopal Ch., Bisbee, Ariz., 1956-59; housemaster Collegium Augustinianum, Gaesdonck, West Germany, 1962-65; curate, choirmaster St. Thomas More parish, Munster, 1968-69; vis. prof. U. Louvain, Belgium, 1969; asso. prof. historical theology St. Louis U., 1970-74; adj. prof. history, 1974—; co-dir. finding-list project Center for Reformation Research, St. Louis, 1976, dir. project, 1977-78. Del., Mo. Democratic Conv., 1976. Am. Philos. Soc. grantee, 1974, 75. Mem. AAUP (v.p. 1973-74), Harvard Club St. Louis, Am. Hist. Assn., Am. Cath. Hist. Assn. (exec. council 1975-77), Soc. Ch. History, Conf. British Studies, N. Am. Acad. Ecumenists. Roman Catholic. Author: Absolutely Null and Utterly void, 1968; Stewards of the Lord, 1970; Man For Others, 1971; Zur Frage der anglikanischen Weihen, 1971. Contbr. articles to profl. jours. Home and office: 6825 Natural Bridge St Louis MO 63121

HUGHES, JOHN WILLIAM, veterinarian; b. Tippecanoe County, Ind., Apr. 20, 1947; s. John E. and Fern F. H.; D.V.M., Purdue U., 1971; m. Donna Jean Hughes, Oct. 18, 1972; 1 dau., Luci; stepchildren—Lisa, Lori. Asst. veterinarian Hilltop Animal Hosp., Madison, Ind., 1971-76; owner Hughes Vet. Clinic, Sharpsville, Ind., 1976—. Recipient Pub. Service award Future Farmers of Am., 1976; Service award Tipton County 4-H Clubs, 1976. Mem. Am., Ind. vet. med. assns., Wabash Valley Vet. Dist. (sec.-treas.), Fraternal Order of Police. Republican. Roman Catholic. Clubs: Masons, Elks. Office: Route 2 Sharpsville IN 46068

HUGHES, L.R., III, univ. adminstr.; b. Kansas City, Mo., Aug. 23, 1935; s. Louis Rector Jr. and Mary (Atwood) H.; B.Landscape Architecture in City Planning, U. Fla., 1958; M.S. in Community Devel. and Pub. Health Adminstrn., U. Mo., 1970; m. Saundra Lee Chesney, Oct. 5, 1962; children—Louis Rector IV, Bailey Atwood. Mng. partner Norman Stevens Vending Co., Sedalia, Mo., 1962-66; mgr. Mclaughlin Bros. Furniture Co., Columbia, Mo., 1966-70; v.p. Columbia (Mo.) Coll., 1970-73; judge Boone County, Mo., 1973-75; dir. devel. Cancer Research Center, Columbia, 1973-75; dean univ. relations Lincoln U., Jefferson City, Mo., 1975—. Pres. Downtown Columbia Inc., 1969; chmn. Columbia Planning and Zoning Commn., 1970-71; chmn. Boone County Services Adv. Council, 1972; gen. campaign chmn. Columbia United Way, 1973; founder, bd. dirs. Central Mo. Planned Parenthood Assn., 1970; founding pres. Grand Order Pachyderms Republican Club Mo., 1967-68; mgr. campaign Mo. Rep. Reisch, 1968. Served with C.I.C., AUS, 1958-62; comdr. USAFR, 1977—. Named Outstanding Young Man of Year, (DSA) Jaycees Columbia, 1970. Mem. C. of C. (dir. 1971-73), Am. Inst. Planning, Am. Soc. Landscape Architects, Res. Officers Assn., Phi Kappa Tau. Club: Masons. Co-editor MOHAWK USAFR Newspaper, 1968-77. Author-implementor first 2 year internat. travel adminstrn. coll. asso. degree program in U.S. Home: 1308 Moreau Dr Jefferson City MO 65101 Office: 308 Young Hall Lincoln U Jefferson City MO 65101

HUGHES, LAWRENCE FRANCIS, bus. services co. exec.; b. Queens, N.Y., Mar. 31, 1940; s. Lawrence and Henrietta (Biehl) H.; B.S., Roosevelt U., 1975, postgrad., 1975—; m. Joan Anne Sandvoss, May 7, 1960; children—Lawrence Francis III, Karen. Br. mgr. Potter Instrument Corp., 1962-72; nat. service mgr. Medequip Corp., Park Ridge, Ill., 1972-74; support mgr. Iomec Corp., Elmhurst, Ill., 1974-75; service mgr. Searle Ct. Systems Co., Oakbrook, Ill., 1975—. Mem. Am. Mgmt. Assn., Assn. Field Service Mgrs. (dir. 1977—), Nat. Assn. Field Service Mgrs. Home: 141 Waxwing Ave Naperville IL 60540 Office: 2025 Windsor Dr Oakbrook IL 60521

HUGHES, MARGARET CYRENA, ret. assn. exec.; b. Springfield, Ill.; d. Thomas Patrick and Elizabeth (Donelan) Hughes; student Springfield Jr. Coll., U. Ill. Campaign chmn. Community Fund Assn., 1947-51; exec. dir. Sangamon County Tb Assn., Springfield, 1951-70; exec. dir. Lincoln Land Tb and Respiratory Disease Assn., 1970-76. Pres. Friends of Library, 1956; exec. com. Sangamon County Council Social Agys., 1940-41; pres. Ill. State Assn. Women's Divs. Chambers of Commerce; treas. Springfield Safety Council 1976-77; bd. dirs. Sangamon County Mental Health, 1948-53; Cath. adv. com. Girl Scouts, 1946-51, nat. resettlement adv. com. 1948-53; bd. dirs. St. John's Sanitorium Aux.; mem. mental health div. Ill. Cath. Conf. Bd. dirs. Springfield Safety Council. Recipient Pro Ecclesia et Pontifice medal. Mem. Assn. Commerce and Industry (pres. women's div. 1961-62), Ill. C. of C. (v.p. women's div.), Ill. Conf. Tb Workers (pres. 1961-62), Diocesan Council Cath. Women (past pres.; dir.), Nat. Council Cath. Women (past provincial dir.; chmn. youth com. 1944-51), Louise de Marillac Guild, Sacred Heart Acad. Alumni Assn. (past pres.), Cathedral Altar Soc. (pres. 1956-57), Women's Symphony Guild. Clubs: Zonta (pres. Springfield 1962, area dist. dir. 1963-64); Coterie (dir. 1943-44); Springfield Women's (dir., chmn. safety com., pres.). Home: 417 E Canedy St Springfield IL 62703

HUGO, NORMAN ELIOT, plastic surgeon, educator; b. Beverly, Mass., Sept. 23, 1933; s. Victor Joseph and Helen Bernadette H.; A.B., Williams Coll., 1955; M.D., Cornell U., 1959; m. Geraldine P. Tonry, Oct. 10, 1959; children—Helen, William, Geraldine, Norman, Catherine. Intern, resident Cornell Surg. Service, Bellevue Hosp., N.Y.C., 1959-63; resident N.Y. Hosp.-Cornell Med. Center, 1963-65; chief plastic and reconstructive surgery Michael Reese Hosp., Chgo., 1969-71, Passavant Hosp., Chgo., 1971—; instr. surgery Cornell U., 1965-66; asst. prof. Ind. U., 1966-67, asst. chief plastic surgery, 1966-67; asso. prof. U. Chgo., 1967-69, Northwestern U., 1971—; dir. plastic surgery Lakeside VA Hosp. Served to maj. M.C., AUS, 1967-69. Diplomate Am. Bd. Plastic and Reconstructive Surgery. Mem. Am. Soc. Plastic and Reconstructive Surgeons (bd. dirs. Ednl. Found.), A.C.S., Am. Assn. Plastic and Reconstructive Surgery, Plastic Surgery Research Council, Am. Cleft Palate Soc., Assn. Acad. Surgery, Soc. Head and Neck Surgeons, N.Y. Acad. Sci., AMA, Am. Burn Soc. Clubs: Williams (N.Y.C.); Lake Shore (Chgo.). Home: 1023 Woodland Ave Barrington IL 60010 Office: 707 Fairbanks Ct Chicago IL 60611

HUH, DONG-CHIN, internist, gastroenterologist; b. Korea, Dec. 13, 1938; s. Soo-Young and Sue (Lee) H.; came to U.S., 1967, naturalized, 1977; M.D., Pusan (Korea) Nat. U., 1963; m. Young-Ok Park, Jan. 11, 1966; children—John, Eugene. Intern St. Elizabeth Hosp., Youngstown, Ohio, 1967-68, resident in internal medicine, 1968-71; resident in gastroenterology Cleve. Met. Gen. Hosp., 1971-73; practice medicine specializing in gastroenterology, Woodstock, Ill., 1973—; mem. attending staff Meml. Hosp. McHenry County, Woodstock; cons. staff Sherman Hosp., Elgin, Ill., McHenry (Ill.) Hosp. Diplomate Am. Bd. Internal Medicine, Am. Bd. Gastroenterology. Mem. A.C.P., Am. Soc. Gastrointestinal Endoscopy, McHenry County Med. Soc. Office: 13707 W Jackson St Woodstock IL 60098

HUIZINGA, RALEIGH JAMES, ednl. adminstr.; b. Grand Rapids, Mich., June 7, 1938; s. John and Dorothy (Botting) H.; B.A., Mich. State U., 1961; M.A. (USPHS fellow), Syracuse U., 1964; Ph.D. (U.S. Office Edn. fellow), U. Ariz., 1971; m. Barbara Jean Schuiling, Aug. 17, 1963; 1 son, Christopher Lee. Adminstr. Dallas Ind. Sch. Dist., 1971-75; asst. prof. psychology Health Sci. Center, Grad. Sch. Biomed. Scis., U. Tex., 1971-75, asst. prof. pediatrics Health Sci. Center, Southwestern Med. Sch., 1971-75; exec. dir. Research and Evaluation Center for Learning, Dallas, 1971-75; exec. dir. Groves Learning Center, Minnetonka, Minn., 1975—; adj. prof. spl. edn. Coll. St. Thomas, 1976—; bd. dirs. Nat. Assn. Pvt. Schs. for Exceptional Children, 1977—. Licensed and certified psychologist, Tex.; certified sch. psychologist, Minn.; licensed cons. psychologist, Minn. Mem. Am., Minn. psychol. assns., Council for Exceptional Children, Assn. for Children with Learning Disabilities, Internat. Fedn. of Learning Disabilities, Am. Edn. Research Assn., Am. Assn. Sch. Adminstrs., Kappa Delta Pi. Mem. editorial adv. bd. Jour. Learning Disabilities, 1974—. Home: 1635 Weston Ln Wayzata MN 55391 Office: 2000 Hopkins Crossroad Minnetonka MN 55343

HULL, BETTY JANE, guidance counselor, adminstr.; b. Fremont, Nebr., Oct. 11, 1923; d. Joseph C. and Adda Mary (Guttery) Newsom; A.B., Midland Coll. 1942; student K. Gibbs Sch. 1943; M.A., Case Western Res. U. 1960; m. John R. Hull, May 26, 1944; children—Grover A., John R., Mary Jo, Holly A. Exec. sec. King Features Syndicate, N.Y.C., 1943, FBI, N.Y.C. and Honolulu, 1943-45; tchr. social studies Bay Village (Ohio) Jr. High Sch., 1957-58; tchr., chmn. bus. dept. Bay Village High Sch. 1958-60, guidance counselor, 1960-68, dir. guidance, 1968—; mem. adv. bd. for admissions and registration services Ohio State U., Columbus, 1974—. Recipient Jack M. Scott award for coll. counseling services Ohio Assn. Coll. Admissions Counselors, 1977. Mem. Ohio Assn. Coll. Admissions Counselors (summer workshop com. 1967, 68, 70, 73, 76, chmn. workshops 1971-72, articulation workshops 1966-70, del. nat. assembly 1969-72, pres. 1974-75), Ohio Sch. Counselors Assn. (exec. bd. 1974-76), Nat. Assn. Coll. Admissions Counselors (govt. inter-assn. com. 1975-78), Am., Ohio, NE Ohio personnel and guidance assns., Nat. Vocat. Guidance Assn., Am., W.Shore sch. counselors assns., Nat., Ohio edn. assns., Bay Tchrs. Assn., Delta Kappa Gamma. Contbr. presentations to profl. orgns.; contbr. numerous articles in field to profl. jours. Home: 28924 Lake Rd Bay Village OH 44140 Office: 29230 Wolf Rd Bay Village OH 44140

HULL, JULIUS HENRY, cake decorating equipment mfg. co. exec.; b. Onekama Twp., Mich., Mar. 16, 1919; s. Julius Henry and Emma K. (Peterson) H.; B.A., Mich. State U., 1941; J.D., Georgetown U., 1946; m. Edith June Comrie, Dec. 10, 1940 (dec. Mar. 1952); children—Kathleen Hull Conlin, Charlene (Mrs. Robert Abeyta). Admitted to D.C. bar, Ill. bar; sr. accountant Doty & Doty, C.P.A.'s, Chgo., 1946-60; controller, treas. Wilton Enterprises, Inc., Chgo., 1960—. C.P.A., Ill. Home: 1420 E 156th St Dolton IL 60419 Office: 833 W 115th St Chicago IL 60643

HULL, RONALD EUGENE, communications system adminstr.; b. Rapid City, S.D., May 30, 1930; s. Darrell Clifford and Nettie Faye (Westfall) H.; B.A., Dakota Wesleyan U., 1952; M.S., Syracuse U., 1955; Ed.D., U. Nebr., 1970; m. Naomi Ruth Kaye, June 21, 1953; children—Kevin, Brian, Brandon, Kathryn. Dir., producer Sta. KUON-TV, U. Nebr., Lincoln, 1955-56, production mgr., 1956-61, program mgr., 1961-63, asst. to dir. univ. TV, asst. gen. mgr., since 1970—, prof. of journalism U. Nebr., 1970—; program mgr. of Nebr. Ednl. TV Network, since 1970—; cons. to Vietnamese TV, 1970, 71; TV adviser to S. Vietnam, USIA, 1966-67. Pres. of Lincoln (Nebr.) Symphony, 1976-78; bd. dirs. Willa Cather Mem. Found., Mari, Sandoz Heritage Soc., John G. Neihardt Found.; trustee St. Paul United Meth. Ch., Lincoln. Served with U.S. Army, 1952-54. Named Outstanding Alumnus, Dakota Wesleyan U., 1967. Mem. Nat. Assn. of Edn. Broadcasters. Democrat. Methodist. Clubs: Discussion, Polemica. Co-producer TV programs: Anyone for Tennyson, 1976-78, Menuhin Tribute to Willa Cather, 1974, Vietnam Beyond the Fury, 1972. Home: 3001 Jackson Dr Lincoln NE 68502 Office: PO Box 83111 Lincoln NE 68501

HULL, S. LORAINE BOOS (MRS. JOHN CALKINS HULL), theater actress and dir., civic worker, educator; b. West Bend, Iowa, Aug. 5, 1928; d. Myron Maurice and Vera (Cleal) Boos; B.F.A., Drake U., 1956; M.A., U. Wis., 1971; postgrad. N.Y. U., summer 1966, U. Wis., 1971—; student acting, directing Lee Strasberg and Herbert Berghof, both N.Y.C.; m. John Calkins Hull, Jan. 4, 1949; children—Dianne Lee, Donald John. Theatre actress Drake U., 1946-49, 56, radio sta. and WOI, KRNT, Des Moines, 1946-49, 56; tchr. music elementary sch., West Bend, 1954-55, Truesdale, Iowa, 1956-57; tchr. pub. schs., Fond du Lac, Wis., 1957-65, adminstr., theatre specialist, drama-speech coordinator, 1965-72; actress, play dir. Fond du Lac Community Theatre, 1958—; instr. Lee Strasberg Theater Inst., Los Angeles, 1972—; instr. U. Wis., Fond du Lac, 1971-72; asst. prof. drama Ripon Coll., 1973-75; tchr. acting and creative drama workshops, Sweden, 1971, Ind. Arts Council, 1972, Monaco Internat. Play Festival, 1973, Ark. Arts Council, 1975, So. Calif. Drama Assn., 1975; theatre specialist Fond du Lac Pub. Schs., 1965-73; appeared plays including Roar Like a Dove, 1965, The Irregular Verb to Love, 1965, The Diary of Anne Frank, 1965, The Crucible, 1963, High Ground, 1962, Oh Men, Oh Women, 1961, All My Sons, 1960; dir. plays, programs sta. KFIZ, Fond du Lac, 1965—, sta. WBAY, Green Bay, Wis., 1964, WISN, Milw., 1960-61; movies and comml. actress Kiekhaefer Corp., Fond du Lac, 1957—; actress summer stock, Green Ram Theatre, Baraboo, Wis., 1965; lectr. in field; founder, pres. Fond du Lac County Arts Council, 1968-71, Wis. Community Theatre Assn., 1969-70; U.S. del. Internat. Theatre Congress, Sweden, 1971, Monaco, 1973, Okla., 1975; mem. Wis. Arts Found. and Council Arts Com. 1969-72; founder, U.S. del., 1st pres. N.Am. Regional Theater Alliance, Montreal, 1972—; mem. conf. bd. Wis. Idea Theatre, 1964—, dir., 1964-69, pres., 1968-70; dir. Wis. Community Theatre Assn., 1969—, pres., 1969-70; dir. Fond du Lac Community Theatre, 1958—, pres., 1962-63. Den mother Cub Scouts, Fond du Lac, 1959-62. Ford Found. grantee, 1963-64; recipient Wis. Lunt-Fontaine award for directing 1st pl. play, 1964, 65, 67, 69, 71, 73; ACTA Nat. Merit award for play direction, 1969; Wis. Theatre Woman of Year award, 1969. Mem. Am. Ednl. Theatre Assn., Am. Community Theatre Assn. (dir. of regional play winner 1971, 73; one of six nat. play winners Chgo. 1971, Lincoln, Nebr. 1973, dir. 1970-73, newsletter editor 1970, membership sec. 1970-72, Internat. del. 1971-73), N.Am. Theatre Alliance (pres.), AAUP, AAUW, Fond du Lac Ednl. Assn., Internat. Amateur Theatre Assn., Am. Theatre Assn. (internat. commn.), Wis. Edn. Assn., NEA, ANTA, Wis. Speech Assn., Internat. Platform Assn., Cryonics Soc. Mich., Chi Omega, Theta Alpha Phi, Alpha Psi Omega, Zeta Phi Eta, Pi Beta Epsilon. Presbyterian. Club: Saturday Lecture (pres. 1964). Author: A Theatre Specialist for School and Community Drama, 1972; Inspiring Creativity Through Strasberg Techniques and Creative Dramatics; The Method of Lee Strasberg; contbr. articles to profl. jours. Home: 2308 Takodah Dr Fond du Lac WI 54935

HULL, THOMAS VAN CAMP, librarian, museum curator; b. Noblesville, Ind., Jan. 2, 1925; s. Harry Taffe and Helen (Van Camp) H.; B.A., Hanover Coll., 1949; M.A., U. Ky., 1957. Library asst. circulation dept. Indpls. Pub. Library, 1949-51, sr. librarian sci.-tech. dept., 1952-57; librarian Am. Legion Nat. Hdqrs. Library, Indpls., 1957—; museum curator Am. Legion Nat. Hdqrs. Emil A. Blackmore Museum, Indpls., 1967—; mem. adv. com. Ind. State Library on Area Library Services Authorities, 1972—. Pres., trustee Westfield (Ind.) Pub. Library. Served with AUS, 1943-45. Mem. Spl. Libraries Assn. (pres. Ind. chpt. 1955-56), Am. Legion, Beta Theta Pi. Republican. Episcopalian. Mason (Shriner). Club: Columbia (Indpls.). Author: The First Century: Centennial History of Iota Chapter, Beta Theta Pi Fraternity, Hanover College, 1853-1953, 1953. Home: 420 N Union St Westfield IN 46074 Office: 700 N Pennsylvania St Indianapolis IN 46206

HULLETT, JOHN WAYNE, educator; b. Hiawatha, Kans., May 30, 1942; s. Wayne R. and Opal Marie (Bieri) H.; B.A., U. Denver, 1964, M.A., 1965; m. Leanne Jean Hensley, Apr. 19, 1969; children—Christy, Craig. Instr. dept psychology Augustana Coll., Rock Island, Ill., 1965-70, asst. prof., 1970-76, chmn. dept., 1976—, dir. Fgn. Study Program in Japan, 1977-78; mem. psychiatry curriculum com., guest lectr. Peoria Sch. Medicine, 1974—; cons. Luth. Hosp. Sch. Nursing, 1973—. Vice-pres. Parents Orgn. for Villa de Chantal Sch., 1976-77; cons. Rock Island Bd. Edn., 1974—. Recipient Distinguished prof. award Augustana Coll., 1971; Centennial scholar, 1960-64, Ford Found. fellow, 1962-65, NASA fellow, 1965-66, Lilly Found grantee, 1976. Mem. AAUP, Am., Midwestern psychol. assns., Phi Beta Kappa, Psi Chi, Omicron Delta Kappa. Democrat. Lutheran. Editor: To Know A Child: A Book of Selected Readings, 1974; contbr. articles to profl. jours. Home: 1412 20th St Rock Island IL 61201 Office: Sorensen Hall Augustana Coll Rock Island IL 61201

HULLVERSON, JAMES EVERETT, lawyer; b. St. Louis, Aug. 28, 1928; s. Everett John and Elizabeth (Dwyer) H.; B.A., Yale U., 1950; J.D., St. Louis U., 1953; m. Shirley Marie Shaughnessy, Nov. 18, 1950; children—Susan, Jim. Admitted to Mo., Ill. bar; 1953; partner firm Hullverson & Richardson, St. Louis, 1953-71, Hullverson, Hullverson & Frank, St. Louis, 1971—; lectr., Washington U. Med. Sch., 1972-77; faculty U. Mich. Ann. Advocacy Inst., 1972, Harvard Nat. Coll. Advocacy, 1973. Bd. dirs. Legal Aid Soc., St. Louis, 1968. Named Hon. mem. Mont. Bar, 1972. Mem. Mo. Assn. Trial Lawyers (pres. 1962), Lawyers Assn. St. Louis (pres. 1964), Am. Trial Lawyers Assn. (bd. govs. 1972-75), Mo. Bar (bd. govs. 1976—), Ill. Bar Assn., Inner Circle Advocates, Am. Bd. Profl. Liability Attys. (founding trustee), Internat. Acad. Trial Lawyers. Office: 722 Chestnut St St Louis MO 63101

HULS, JAMES JOSEPH, agrl. mfg. co. exec.; b. Madison, S.D., Aug. 27, 1941; s. Joseph Hubert and Gladys Louise (O'Neil) H.; B.S. in Mech. Engring., S.D. State U., 1964; m. Patricia Delores Shinnick, Oct. 9, 1965; children—James Michael, Nancy Jo, Christopher John. Engr., Feterl Mfg. Co., agrl. equipment, Salem, S.D., 1968—. Cons. in field, 1968—. Served to capt. USAF, 1964-68. Registered profl. engr., S.D. Mem. Am. Soc. Agrl. Engrs., ASME, Air Force Assn., Aircraft Owners and Pilots Assn., Am. Legion (athletic officer 1968-73, post comdr.), Progressive Salem Assn. Elk. Club: McCook Country (pres.). Home: 240 N Pierce St Salem SD 57058 Office: 411 W Center St Salem SD 57058

HULSE, RAYMOND BURRELL, environ. chemist; b. River Rouge, Mich., May 17, 1940; s. Donald Charles and Leota Bessie (Dunsmore) H.; B.S., Baker U., 1965; postgrad. Washington U., 1967-68, Lindenwood Coll., 1976; m. Donna Jean Hoover, Feb. 13, 1965; children—Raymond Brian, Donald Aaron. Tchr. chemistry, head sci. dept. Orchard Farm High Sch., St. Charles County, Mo., 1964-68; chief chemist, head of lab. REBA/RETA/ETS (co. name changed to Envirodyne Engrs., Inc.), 1968—, lab. mgr., 1972—. Active Boy Scouts Am.; bd. dirs. Christian Ch.; pres. Christian Mens Fellowship. Mem. Am. Chem. Soc., Am. Mgmt. Assn., NEA, Mo. Tchrs. Assn. Home: 3010 Sherwood Ln St Charles MO 63301 Office: 12161 Lackland Rd St Louis MO 63141

HULSLANDER, DONALD JOHN, credit union exec.; b. Chelmsford, Mass., Feb. 8, 1916; s. Louis Benjamin and Mary Jane Morrison; student pub. schs., Chelmsford; m. Julia Rebeca Carr, June 7, 1941; 1 son, Donald John. Commd. 2d lt. U.S. Army, 1942, advanced through grades to maj., 1957; retired, 1964; treas., mgr. Franklin County Tchrs. Fed. Credit Union, Columbus, Ohio, 1965—; mem. audit com. Ohio Central Credit Union, Columbus, 1965—. Mem. Credit Union Exec. Soc., Ret. Officers Assn. Republican. Baptist. Clubs: Credit Union Founders. Mason. Home: 3405 Briggs Rd Columbus OH 43204 Office: 3454 N High St Columbus OH 43214

HULTGREN, DENNIS EUGENE, farmer; b. Union County, S.D., Mar. 19, 1929; s. John Alfred and Esther Marie (Johnson) H.; grad. high sch.; m. Nelda Ethelyn Olson, Aug. 3, 1957; children—Nancy (Mrs. Bruce Klemme), Jean (Mrs. Dene Doty), Jahn Dennis, Ruth Dorothy. Farmer, Union County, 1953—; commr., chmn. Union County Planning and Zoning Bd., 1972—. Pres. bd. Union Creek Cemetery, 1958—; pres. bd. mgrs. Union-Sayles Watershed Dist., 1965-70. Treas., mem. bd. W. Union Sch., 1957-67; chmn. Union County Sch. Bd., 1961-68; pres. Alcester (S.D.) Sch. Bd., 1970-77; chmn. Alcester PTA, 1967-68; mem. tech. bd. rev. Southeastern Council Govts., Sioux Falls, S.D., 1976-77; bd. dirs. Siouxland Interstate Met. Planning Council, Sioux City, Iowa, 1977—; sustaining mem. Old Opera House Community Theater, Akron, Iowa; Republican precinct committeeman, 1970—; mem. Union County Rep. Central Com., 1970—. Served with AUS, 1951-53; Korea. Decorated Combat Inf. badge; recipient Best Actor award Old Opera House Community Theatre, 1976. Mem. Farm Bur., Farmer's Union, S.D. Livestock Feeders Assn., Asso. Sch. Bds. S.D. (Merit award 1976), Am. Legion, VFW. Lutheran (mem. bd. 1967-70, lay chmn. 1970, chmn. centennial com. 1974. Address: Hulteboda Farm Box 147 Route 2 Akron IA 51001

HUME, HORACE DELBERT, mfg. co. exec.; b. Endeavor, Wis., Aug. 15, 1898; s. James Samuel and Lydia Alberta (Sawyer) H.; student pub. schs.; m. Minnie L. Harlan, June 2, 1926 (dec. 1972); 1 son James; m. 2d, Sarah D. Rood, Apr. 6, 1973. Stockman and farmer, 1917-19; with automobile retail business, Garfield, Wash., 1920-21, partner and asst. mgr., 1921-27; automobile and farm machine retailer, Garfield, partner, mgr., 1928-35, gne. mgr. Hume-Love Co., Garfield, 1931-35; pres., 1935-57; partner, gen. mgr. H.D. Hume Co., Mendota, Ill., 1944-52; pres. H.D. Hume Co., Inc., 1952—; pres. Hume Products Corp., 1953—; pres., dir. Hume-Fry Co., Garden City, Kans., 1955-73. Mayor, Garfield, Wash., 1938-40. Bd. dirs. Mendota Hosp. Found., 1949—, pres., 1949-54; bd. dirs. Mendota Swimming Pool Assn.; mem. City Planning Commn., 1953-72, chmn. 1953-69; mem. Regional Planning Commn. LaSalle County, Ill., 1965-73; chmn., 1965-71; mem. Schs. Central Com., 1953—, LaSalle County Zoning Commn., 1966—, LaSalle County Care and Treatment Bd., 1970-72; chmn. Mendota Watershed Com., 1967-73. Mem. Am. Soc. Agrl. Engrs., Mendota C. of C. (pres. 1947-49, dir., 1946-49). Republican. Presbyn. (elder) Mason (Shriner), Kiwanian (pres. 1954, dir. 1954, Elk; mem. Order Easter Star. Clubs: Mendota Golf; Lakes (Sun City, Ariz.). Home: 709 Carolyn St Mendota IL 61342 Office: 1701 First Ave Mendota IL 61342

HUMITA, TIBERIUS TED, educator; b. Clui, Romania, Dec. 20, 1913; s. Teodor and Teodosia (Abrudan) H.; student U. Bucharest (Romania), 1937-39, U. Rome (Italy), 1946-50; B.A., Wayne State U., 1958, M.A. in Polit. Sci., Tchrs. Coll., 1960, secondary teaching certificate, 1961; m. Sophie Kisch, Sept. 20, 1954. Came to U.S., 1951, naturalized, 1956. Sec., v.p. Romanian Polit. Refugee Welfare Com., Rome, Italy, 1948-50; worker, timekeeper, payroll clk. Chrysler Corp., Highland Park, Mich., 1951-60; tchr. fgn. langs. Detroit Pub. Schs., 1961—. Corr., Romanian News America, Cleve., 1964—. Romanian cons. Greater Detroit Ethnic Group Project, 1968—. Candidate, Mich. Constl. Conv., 1961; chmn. Romanian sect. nationalites div. Mich. Democratic Com., 1960—, v.p., 1965-66, treas., 1968—. Contbg. mem. Iulia Maniu Found., N.Y., 1965—. Served to 1st lt. Romanian Army, 1939-40. Recipient Service award Nationalites div. Mich. Dem. Com., 1967. Fonds European Secour Etud. Etranger, Switzerland scholar, 1949-50; Nat. Def. Edn. Act grantee N.Y. State U., 1962; Fed. grantee, P.R., 1966. Mem. Internat., Am. polit. sci. assns., Am. Fedn. Tchrs., Am. Acad. Polit. and Social Sci., Mich. Fgn. Lang. Assn., Am. Council Fgn. Lang. Tchrs. Editor Bull. Romanian Am. Nat. Com., Detroit, 1958-63; dir. sci. book exhibit Internat. Congress Dialectology. Louvain, Belgium, 1960. Home: 16424 Lincoln St East Detroit MI 48021 Office: 1000 Scotten St Detroit MI 48209

HUMMER, GLEN SHARP, educator; b. Huntington County, Ind., Feb. 18, 1909; s. Rafe and Fanny Isabelle (Harris) H.; B.S., U. Ill., 1931; postgrad. U. Wash., 1932; M.S., Columbia U., 1939. Tchr., coach Huntington (Ind.) High Sch., 1933-71; asso. prof. phys. edn. Huntington Coll., 1974—, nat. chmn. long distance swimming, 1974—; condr. swimming clinics, Japan. Served with USNR, 1942-45. Mem. Ind. AAU, Skull and Crescent, Phi Epsilon Kappa, Chi Phi. Club: Rotary. Home: Rural Route 8 Huntington IN 46750

HUMPHREY, ESTHER LOUISA GREEN (MRS. HARRY F. HUMPHREY), theatrical printing co. exec.; b. nr. Shelby, Iowa; d. Charles Boyer and Christina Louisa (Kreimeier) Green; m. Harry F. Humphrey, Dec. 24, 1957. Meter record clk. Met. Utilities; owner Film Exhibitors Printing Co., Omaha, 1950—. Recipient Presdl. citation for Nat. Youth Opportunity campaign, 1966, recognition for portrait painting Joslyn Meml. Mem. Nat. Theatre Owners Am., U.S. Figure Skating Assn., Omaha Organ Soc., Phi Sigma Alpha. Episcopalian. Clubs: Happy Hollow, 66 Formal Dancing, Qui Vive Formal Dancing (Omaha). Home: 412 N 96th St Omaha NE 68114 Office: 416 S 14th St Omaha NE 68102

HUMPHREY, MURIEL FAY BUCK, Senator; b. Huron S.D., Feb. 20, 1912; d. Andrew E. and Jessie May (Pierce) Buck; student Huron Coll., 1931-32; m. Hubert Horatio Humphrey (former U.S. Vice Pres.), Sept. 3, 1936 (dec. 1978); children—Nancy (Mrs. C. Bruce Solomonson), Hubert Horatio III, Robert, Douglas. U.S. senator from Minn., 1978—. Office: 2113 Dirksen Senate Office Bldg Washington DC 20510

HUMPHREY, OWEN EVERETT, ednl. adminstr.; b. Wautoma, Wis., Oct. 25, 1920; s. Marion Arthur and Flora Agnes (Helms) H.; B.S., Wis. State Coll., 1947; M.S., U. Ark., 1949; Ed. Specialist, U. Ill., 1954; m. Billye Allene Cox, Apr. 6, 1946; children—Reba (Mrs. James Rick), Ivye. Tchr., Plainfield, Wis., 1941-42, Sheboygan, Wis., 1947-48; prin. Lincoln Elementary Sch., Mattoon, Ill., 1950-55; supervising prin., Peotone, Ill., 1955-57; tchr. Nameoki Elementary Sch., Granite City, Ill., 1957-59; prin. Maryville Sch., Granite City, 1959-67; curriculum coordinator, Granite City, 1967—. Cons. Citizens Adv. Com. for Local Dist. Ednl. Planning, 1972—. Dir., P.T.A. Area Council Mothersingers, Mattoon, Ill., 1951-54, Granite City Area Council Mothersingers, 1958-63. Served with 95th Inf., AUS, 1941-45; ETO. Decorated Bronze Star medal. Mem. Internat. Platform Assn., Nat. Edn. Assn. (life mem.), Assn. Supervision Curriculum Devel., Ill. Assn. Supervision Curriculum Devel., Am. Assn. Sch. Adminstrs., Am. Ednl. Research Assn., Madison County Curriculum Council. Musical compositions: I Should Have Told You, 1965, It Doesn't Matter Now, 1965, Think Kindly of Me, 1965, The Resurrection, 1959; New Jerusalem, 1960; I Will Hold My Master's Hand, 1974; I Remember It All, 1977. Contbr. articles in field to ednl. jours. Home: 18 W Wilson Park Dr Granite City IL 62040 Office: 20th and Adams Sts Granite City IL 62040

HUNG, PAUL P., virologist; b. Taipei, Taiwan, Sept. 30, 1933; s. Yao-Hsun and Shiu-Chin Wu H.; came to U.S., 1955, naturalized, 1963; student medicine Nat. Taiwan U., 1951-53; B.S., Millikin U., 1956; M.S., Purdue U., 1958, Ph.D., 1960; m. Nancy Clark, May 4, 1956; children—Pauline E., Eileen K., Clark D. Research asst. Purdue U., Lafayette, Ind., 1956-60; sr. biochemist Abbott Labs., North Chicago, Ill., 1960-69, asso. research fellow, 1969-73, research fellow, 1973—, head molecular virology lab., 1973—; vis. scholar Stanford Med. Sch., 1969-70; adj. asso. prof. Loyola Med. Sch., Chgo., 1972-76, lectr., 1976—; adj. prof. Northwestern U. Med. Sch., Chgo., 1976—. Mem. Am. Chem. Soc., AAAS, Am. Inst. Chemists, Am. Soc. Biol. Chemists, Am. Soc. Microbiology, Am. Assn. Cancer Research, U. Club Waukegan, Sigma Xi, Phi Lambda Upsilon. Contbr. articles to profl. publs. Home: 2715 Brnot Ave Waukegan IL 60085 Office: Abbott Labs North Chicago IL 60064

HUNGATE, CARROLL PAUL, physician, naval officer; b. Emporia, Kans., July 31, 1904; s. John T. and Meta Bena (Paulson) H.; student Nebr. Wesleyan U., 1921-22, Baker U., 1922-23; A.B., U. Kans., 1925, B.S., 1928, M.D., 1928; postgrad. Harvard, 1929, U. Munich, Vienna, Komenskeho, 1930-31; m. Mary Agnes Patterson, June 23, 1928; children—Mary Agnes (Mrs. R. Kenneth Grubb), Annabel (Mrs. Joseph A. Christy). Intern, Chelsea Naval Hosp., (Mass.), 1928-29, resident, 1929-30; commd. lt. (j.g.), M.C., 1928, promoted capt. 1945; med. officer, 1938-47, sr. med. officer Naval Air Station, Olathe, Kans., 1948-59; ret. 1959; practice medicine, Kansas City, Mo., 1931-40, 1947—; ret. physician Ford Motor Co., Kansas City, Mo.; surg. staff Research Bapt., St. Joseph's, St. Luke's hosps., Kansas City; former instr. preventice medicine Sch. Pharmacy, U. Mo. at Kansas City. Past chmn. health services adv. com. U.S. Civil Def. Council; past cons. AEC, USPHS; mem. bd. Kansas City Council on Alcoholism, 1965—, v.p., 1966; former mem. Mo. Gov.'s Com. Occupation Health and Safety; chmn. Edward Holman Skinner Meml. Trust Fund. Trustee Mo. Valley Coll. Recipient awards Jackson County Med. Soc., U.S. Civil Def. Council, U.S. Civil Def. Adminstrn.; Pfizer award Surgeon Gen. USPHS; Pioneer of Ky. award Harrodsburg (Ky.) Hist. Soc.; keys to cities of Harrodsburg and New Orleans; named Hon. Flight Surgeon, Brazilian Air Force, Wisdom Hall of Fame. Diplomate Am. Bd. Preventive Medicine. Fellow Am. Coll. Preventive Medicine; mem. AMA, Am. Social Health Assn. (past dir.), Mo. (former disaster med. care com.), Jackson County (former mem. emergency med. care com.) med. socs., Mil. Surgeons Assn., Kansas City Social Health Soc. (past pres.), Great Plains (past pres.), Kansas City (past pres.) indsl. med. assns., Am. Med. Writers Assn., AAAS, Am. Assn. Med. History. Am. Soc. Geneology, Mil. Order World Wars, Am. Legion, S.R., Kansas City S.W. Clin. Soc. (pres. 1957), Hungate Hist. Soc. (pres.). Presbyn. Clubs: Univ. (Kansas City, Mo.), Rotary, Masons. Author: History of Hungate Family, Vols. I-V, 1972-75; How to Trace Your Ancestors, 1977. Contbr. articles to profl. jours. Developed traveling exhibit on civil def. and nuclear energy, 1949-50 (now in mus. of physics dept. U.

Kans.). Home: 6845 Oak St Kansas City MO 64113 Office: Profl Bldg Kansas City MO 64106

HUNGERFORD, LUGENE GREEN, nuclear co. exec.; b. Birmingham, Ala., Sept. 1, 1924; d. Wesley Cornith and Anna Mae (Majors) Green; student U. Ala. Law Sch., 1946-48, 1953, 55, U. Tenn., Wayne State U., 1956, 60, Purdue U., 1966, 68; B.S., Birmingham So. U., 1946; M.S., U. Ala., 1950; m. Herbert Eugene Hungerford, Jr., Nov. 4, 1949. Pvt. cons., tutor, 1956-59, 61-64; instr., then asst. prof. physics Wayne State U., 1955-56, 59-60, from adminstrv. asst. to v.p., treas. Calif. Nuclear Co., 1963-68; v.p., treas. Nuclear Mgmt., Inc., Lafayette, Ind., 1968—; dir. Nuclear Engrng. Co., 1969-72; sec., treas., dir. Bio-Service, Inc., 1969—; sec., treas. Mediatech, Inc., 1972-76, dir., 1977—; treas., dir. Chemtree Corp., 1973—. Nat. 2d v.p. Ch. Periodical Club of Episcopal Ch., 1964-67, diocesan dir., 1957-60, provincial dir., 1961-64. Mem. Am. Nuclear Soc., Health Physics Soc., Atomic Indsl. Forum, Am. Phys. Soc., Sigma Xi, Sigma Pi Sigma. Republican. Clubs: Lafayette Country, Purdue Womens. Contbr. articles profl. jours. Home: 7 Knoll Crest Ct West Lafayette IN 47906 Office: 402 Northwestern Ave Suite 112 West Lafayette IN 47806

HUNKINS, DONALD E., banker; b. Flint, Mich., Nov. 6, 1945; s. Bob E. and Virgie M.H.; B.A., Mich. State U., 1971; m. Deborah J. Penrod, June 18, 1966; children—Brett C., Tricia J. Sr. accountant Price Waterhouse & Co., Detroit, 1971-74; internal auditor Ford Motor Co., Dearborn, Mich., 1974-76; v.p. fin. First Midland Bank & Trust Co., Midland Mich., 1976—; treas. First Bank Corp. Bd. dirs. Voluntary Action Center; treas. Ch. of Nazarene, 1972-75, mem. fin. com., 1972-75, chmn. fin. com., 1975—; advisor Jr. Achievement. Served with USAF, 1966-69. C.P.A., Mich. Mem. Am. Inst. C.P.A.'s, Mich. Assn. C.P.A.'s, Mich. State U. Alumni Assn., Beta Alpha Psi. Home: 1210 Evamar St Midland MI 48640 Office: 201 McDonald St Midland MI 48640

HUNSE, TOM SHERIDAN, br. mgr.; b. Chgo., Nov. 3, 1949; s. William Henry and Joan Bernadet (Sheridan) H.; B.S. in Bus., Mktg. and Data Processing, Eastern Ill. U., 1971; m. Karyn Jan Oklepek, Nov. 29, 1969; 1 dau., Kimberly. Programmer, analyst Ohio Med. Products, Madison, Wis., 1971-73; dir. computer services The Wis. Cheeseman, Madison, 1973-75; dir. data processing Benson Optical Co., Mpls., 1975-76; major account rep. Cummins-Allison Corp., Chgo., 1976—; instr. data processing Madison Area Tech. Coll.; cons. Subscription Fulfillment Activities. Bd. mem. Neighborhood Homeowners Assn.; task force mem. Privacy Legislation in Minn. Recipient Citizenship award, S.A.R., 1967. Mem. Wis. Entrex Users Group (charter pres.), Minn. Honeywell Users Group (past pres.), N.W. chpt. Data Processing Mgmt. Assn. (v.p.). Lutheran. Clubs: Southdale Y's Mens. Home: 5622 Hyland Ct Dr Bloomington MN 55437 Office: 7300 France Ave S Edina MN 55435

HUNSTEIN, IRVING JACK, real estate broker, appraiser; b. St. Louis, Nov. 14, 1919; s. Irving Jacob and Edna Louise (Wiese) H.; B.S., Washington U., St. Louis, 1941, M.S., 1946; postgrad. U. Pa.; m. Elsa Muench, Sept. 4, 1946; children—Julia H., Mary M. Hunstein Dobbs, Alice E., James R. Sales mgr. real estate dept. Mercantile Bank, 1952-58; mem. loan office Bank of St. Louis, 1964-66; v.p. Nooney Co., 1966-71; pres. Hunstein Co., St. Louis, 1971—; instr. Washington U., 1944, 50-51, Wharton Sch. U. Pa., 1945-46. Mem. Glendale (Mo.) Planning Commn., 1970—; bd. dirs. St. Louis Altenheim, 1971—. Mem. Soc. Indsl. Realtors (pres. St. Louis chpt. 1974), real estate bds. St. Louis and Mo., Am. Inst. Real Estate Appraisers (pres. St. Louis chpt. 1972). Clubs: Mo. Athletic, Town and Country Tennis, Cool Dell Bath and Tennis (pres. 1975). Home: 1177 Glenway Dr Glendale MO 63122 Office: 11 S Meramec St Saint Louis MO 63105

HUNT, DONALD LEE, banker; b. Searcy, Ark., Sept. 1, 1937; s. Otis Harry and Lola (Davis) H.; B.S. in Bus. Adminstrn., U. Ark., 1960; postgrad. Grad. Sch. Banking, U. Wis., 1967-69; m. Ann Elise Chriten, Dec. 22, 1962 (div. Dec. 1973); children—Donald L., Lisa Ann; m. 2d, Claudia Ann Schulte, June 20, 1975. Nat. bank examiner U.S. Dept. Treasury, Chgo., 1961-66; v.p. First Nat. Bank, Marissa, Ill., 1966-77, pres., chief exec. officer, 1977—; partner Ramsey-Hunt Rentals; owner Angling Antiques, Hunt's Income Tax Service; dir. Marissa Mgmt. Corp. Bd. dirs. Kaskaskia Indsl. Devel. Corp. Served with USAAF, 1961-62. Mem. Bank Adminstrn. Inst. (pres. Southwestern Ill. chpt. 1969), C. of C. (pres. 1968), Jr. C. of C. Baptist. Club: Lions. Home: 911 N Marissa St Marissa IL 62257 Office: 111 N Main St Marissa IL 62257

HUNT, JAMES CALVIN, nephrologist; b. Lexington, N.C., Sept. 11, 1925; s. James Lee and Sarah Della (Frank) H.; A.B., Catawba Coll., 1949; M.D., Bowman Gray Sch. Medicine, 1953; M.Sc., U. Minn., 1958; m. Irene Kivett, Sept. 17, 1949; children—James Calvin, Michael S., Cynthia I. Intern in internal medicine N.C. Bapt. Hosp., Winston-Salem, 1953-54; resident in internal medicine Mayo Grad. Sch. Med., Rochester, Minn., 1954-57, fellow in cardiology and nephrology, 1957-58; practice medicine specializing in cardiology and nephrology, 1958—; instr. medicine Mayo Clinic and Med. Sch., 1958-63, asst. prof., 1963-68, asso. prof., 1968-72, prof., 1972—, chmn. dept. medicine, 1974—, chmn. div. nephrology, 1963-72, asso. dean, 1972-74, cons. 1958—. Pres. Nat. Kidney Found., 1973-76; mem. Nat. Heart, Lung and Blood Adv. Council, 1976—; bd. dirs. Kidney Found. for Upper Midwest, 1976—. Served with USAAF, 1943-46. Recipient Distinguished Alumnus award Catawba Coll., 1974, Bowman Gray Sch. Medicine, 1975. Fellow A.C.P., Am. Coll. Cardiology, Am. Heart Assn. (council on circulation); mem. Internat. Soc. Nephrology, Internat. Soc. Hypertension, Internat. Soc. Cardiology, Am. Soc. Clin. Pharmacology (chmn. renal sect. 1977—), Soc. Nuclear Medicine, Sigma Xi. Author: The Mayo Clinic Renal Diet Cookbook, 1974; contbr. articles to med. jours. Home: 1930 Westfield Ct SW Rochester MN 55901 Office: 200 1st St SW Rochester MN 55901

HUNT, LAMAR, profl. football team exec.; b. 1933; grad. So. Meth. U.; m. Norma Hunt; children—Lamar, Sharon, Clark. Founder, pres. Kansas City Cheifs of Nat. Football League, 1959—; founder, pres. Am. Football League, 1959 (became Am. Football Conf. Nat. Football League 1970), pres. Am. Football Conf., 1970; pres. Kansas City Chiefs to 1977, chmn., 1977—; dir. Great Midwest Corp., Interstate Securities, Traders' Nat. Bank. Bd. dirs. Profl. Football Hall of Fame, Canton Ohio. Named Salesman of Year, Kansas City Advt. and Sales Execs Club, 1963, Southwesterner of Year, Tex. Sportswriters Assn., 1969. Address: c/o Kansas City Chiefs One Arrowhead Dr Kansas City MO 64129

HUNT, ROBERT PAUL, mfg. co. exec.; b. Wooster, Ohio, June 22, 1944; s. Paul Robert and Ruth Irene (Hooser) H.; student Bowling Green U., 1962-63, Ohio State U., 1963-64, Alaska U., 1968; m. Bette Rae Chitwood, Sept. 9, 1972; children—Alexis Leann, Carla Rae. With Ohio Brass Co., Mansfield, Ohio, 1963-66, 69—, transp. mgr., 1970—. Served with USAF, 1966-69. Mem. Central Ohio Traffic Club (dir. 1973-75), Transp. and Distbn. Assn. Methodist. Home: 56 Rambleside Dr Mansfield OH 44907 Office: Ohio Brass Co 380 N Main St Mansfield OH 44902

HUNT, WARREN WILLIAM, dentist; b. St. Paul, Mar. 27, 1932; s. William John and Anna Marie (Greeman) H.; B.S., U. Minn., 1961, D.D.S., 1961; m. Margaret Robertson, July 25, 1959; children—Anne, Melany, David, Margaret. Pvt. practice dentistry, West St. Paul, Minn., 1961—. Clin. instr. U. Minn. Dental Sch., 1961-64. Served with USNR, 1951-55. Mem. U. Minn. Dental Alumni Assn. (pres.), Minn. Soc. Dentistry for Children (pres. 1972), Minn. Acad. Practice Adminstrn. (pres. 1972), Am. Dental Soc. Anesthesiology (pres. Minn. chpt.), St. Paul Dist. Dental Soc. (pres. 1976). Home: 1207 Summit Ct S St Paul MN 55075 Office: 1099 S Robert St West St Paul MN 55118

HUNT, WILLIAM ORLAND, psychotherapist; b. Pontiac, Mich., Jan. 30, 1931; s. Frederick William and Marion Esther (Jones) H.; B.A., Wheaton Coll., 1953; B.D., Conservative Bapt. Theol. Sem., 1956; M.A., City U. N.Y., 1965; Ph.D., Ill. Inst. Tech., 1969; m. Ercel Virginia Webber, Aug. 22, 1953; children—Nancy Jane, Carol Jean. Ordained to ministry Bapt. Ch., 1956; minister Perry (N.Y.) Bapt. Ch., 1958-62, Manhasset (N.Y.) Bapt. Ch., 1962-65; clin. psychologist North Park Clinic, Park Ridge, Ill., 1965-71; pvt. practice clin. psychology, Northbrook, Ill., 1971—; prof. Trinity Evang. Div. Sch., 1972-74; chmn. profl. staff Forest Hosp., Des Plaines, Ill., 1974-75. Fellow Am. Assn. Pastoral Counselors; mem. Am., Ill. psychol. assns., Am. Assn. Marriage and Family Counselors. Home: 1426 Grant Rd Northbrook IL 60062 Office: 655 Landwehr Rd Northbrook IL 60062

HUNT, WILLIAM WOODBURY, sch. adminstr.; b. Chgo., May 21, 1934; s. William Woodbury and Verna (Robinson) H.; B.A., U. Chgo., 1965; m. Elizabeth Yeomans; 1 dau., Katherine; 1 son from previous marriage, Philip. Editor, community organizer Indsl. Area Found., Chgo., 1964-66; editor Commn. on Youth Welfare, Chgo., 1967; evaluation coordinator Model Cities Program, Chgo., 1969-70; dir. program services Chgo. Dept. Human Resources, 1970-73; dir. community affairs Bur. Employment Security Ill. Dept. Labor, Chgo., 1974; dir. pub. services Model Cities Chgo. Com. on Urban Opportunity, 1975; adminstr. Esperanza Sch., Chgo., 1976—. Recipient grant Nat. Endowment Arts, 1968-69, Langston Hughes Meml. prize for poetry, 1974, Ferguson award Friends of Lt., 1976, Ill. Arts Council awards, 1974-76. Mem. Poetry Center at Museum Contemporary Art, Poetry Soc. Am., Modern Poetry Assn. Author: Of The Map That Changes, 1974; poetry editor Chgo. Rev., 1964-66. Home: 1024 11th St Wilmette IL 60091 Office: 520 Marshfield St Chicago IL 60622

HUNTER, CAROL GENE CHEWNING, counselor; b. Covina, Calif., Feb. 15, 1943; d. Eugene Bradley and Esther (Nastri) Chewning; student Westminster Coll., 1960-62; student Calif. State Poly. U., 1962; B.A., Ariz. State U., 1965; M.S., U. Nebr. at Omaha, 1977; m. Terry Alan Hunter, Dec. 29, 1962; children—Christina, Timothy. Tchr., U.S. Armed Forces Inst., Incirlik Air Base, Adana, Turkey, 1965-66, tchr. Dept. Def. Dep. Schs., 1966-67; lectr. Weightwatchers of Rocky Mountain Region, S.D. and Nebr., 1973-76; ednl. asst., counselor Women's Support Programs, U. Nebr. at Omaha, 1976-77, program devel. specialist, advisor Coll. Continuing Studies, 1977—. Troop leader Black Hills council Girl Scouts Am., 1974-75. Mem. Am. Soc. Tng. Dirs., Nebr., Am. personnel and guidance assns., NOW, Nebr. Commn. Status of Women, Assn. Continuing and Higher Edn., N. Central Assn. Counselor Edn. and Supervision, Omaha Area Council on Alcoholism. Club: Officer's Wives Club (Offutt AFB, Nebr.). Home: 808 Bluff St Bellevue NE 68005 Office: Room 35 Coll Continuing Studies Box 688 U Nebr at Omaha Omaha NE 68101

HUNTER, CORNELL CHOATE, banker; b. Newburgh, N.Y., Feb. 3, 1919; s. Dard and Helen Edith (Cornell) H.; B.S., Ohio State U., 1949; m. Irene Rider, Feb. 27, 1943; children—Martha Anna, Edith Cornell. With First Nat. Bank of Chillicothe (Ohio), 1951—, pres., chief exec. officer, chmn. bd., 1972—. Pres. Ross County Hist. Soc., 1975—. Served with U.S. Army, 1944-46. Mem. Am. Numismatic Assn., Soc. Paper Money Collectors (charter). Episcopalian. Clubs: Rotary, Sunset, Symposiarchs, Elks, Am. Legion. Home: 355 W Main St Chillicothe OH 45601 Office: 27 W Second St Chillicothe OH 45601

HUNTER, JACK LAIRD, banker; b. Erie, Pa., Nov. 4, 1927; s. J. Wayne and Marie (Laird) H.; B.A., Syracuse U., 1950; m. Patricia R. Perryman, Dec. 5, 1953; children—David W., Amy J. Trainee, General Electric Co., Syracuse, N.Y., 1954, sales mgr. radio reciever dept., Utica, N.Y., 1962-65, mktg. mgr. audio products dept., Decatur, Ill., 1965-68, gen. mgr., 1968-70; pres. Citizens Nat. Bank, Decatur, 1970—; dir. Lincoln Labs., Progress Industries. Campaign chmn. Macon County (Ill.) United Way, 1973; chmn. coms. for Jr. Coll. Referendum, 1970; Sch. Dist. Bldg. Referendum, 1972; mem. advisory com. Millikin U. Grad. Studies Program, 1974-77; dir. Decatur Meml. Hosp., 1969, chmn. bd. dirs. 1976. Served with USAF, 1950-53. Mem. Decatur C. of C., Assn. for Modern Banking in Ill., Am. Bankers Assn. Clubs: Decatur Country, Decatur, John's Island (Vero Beach, Fla.). Home: 285 Southmoreland Pl Decatur IL 62521 Office: Landmark Mall Decatur IL 62525

HUNTER, LEE, automotive equipment mfg. co. exec., inventor; b. St. Louis, Apr. 27, 1913; s. Lee and Ollie (Stark) H.; ed. Westminster Coll., Fulton, Mo., Washington U., St. Louis; m. Jane Franklin Brauer, 1959; stepchildren—Arthur J. Brauer, Stephen F. Brauer. Draftsman, designer Herman Body Co., 1935-36; founder Lee Hunter Jr. Mfg. Co., 1936; pres. Hunter-Hartman Corp., 1937-42; pres. Hunter Engrng. Co., Bridgeton, Mo., 1947-55, chmn. bd., chief exec. officer 1955—; pres. Hunter Aviation Co., 1955-60; consul of Belgium, 1977—; adv. dir. St. Louis County Nat. Bank, County Nat. Bancorp. Bd. dirs. Webster Coll., Junior Achievement, YMCA; trustee Westminster Coll., Fulton, Mo. Served to 1st lt. C.E., AUS, 1942-46. Recipient Alumni Achievement award Westminster Coll., 1972. Mem. Mo. C. of C., Phi Delta Theta. Presbyterian (trustee). Clubs: St. Louis, Bellerive Country, Strathalbyn, Engineers (St. Louis). Inventor: 1st rapid battery chargers; dynamic lever theory balancing; 1st on car mech. wheel balancer; 1st discharged battery analyzer, wheel alignment, automotive equipment. Home: Hunter Farms 13501 Ladue Rd St Louis County MO 63141 Office: Hunter Engrng Co 11250 Hunter Dr Bridgeton MO 63044

HUNTER, ROBERT LOUIS, personnel mgmt. cons.; b. Scottsville, Ky., June 7, 1919; s. John Andrew and Elsie Hazel H.; A.S., Ohio Mechanics Inst. U. Cin., 1940; m. Sara Louise Day, July 11, 1938; children—Stephan Gareth, Robert Bruce, Mary Beth. Position classifier civilian personnel div. salary wage br. Wright-Patterson AFB, Ohio, 1946-51, dir. classification and wage program Wright Air Devel. Center, 1951-60, staff advisor aero. systems div., 1960-74; pres. Robert L. Hunter & Assos., Springfield, Ohio, 1977—. Former chmn. Springfield (Ohio) Airport Advisory Bd. Served as sgt. U.S. Army, 1943-45. Recipient Medal of Merit Air Force Assn., 1968, 1970, Ohio Man of Year award, 1967, Exceptional Service award, 1975. Mem. Air Force Assn. (charter, past pres. Ohio chpt., Wright Meml. chpt.), Am. Compensation Assn. (past v.p., charter mem.). Clubs: Toastmasters (past v.p.). Home and Office: 2811 Locust Dr Springfield OH 45504

HUNTER, ROBERT SHANNON, lawyer; b. Chgo., Aug. 13, 1919; s. Clyde H. and Florence E. (Geib) H.; J.D., Northwestern U., 1940, LL.B., 1941; grad. Am. Savs. and Loan Inst., 1961; m. Dorothy L. Behrensmeyer, Aug. 1, 1942; 1 dau., Linda L. Admitted to Ill. bar, 1942; asso. firm Taylor, Miller, Busch & Boyden, Chgo., 1942-43; practiced in Quincy, Ill., 1943-57, 1964—; now partner firm Hunter, Hatmacher & Rapp; judge Adams County, 1946-54, 8th Jud. Circuit Ill., 1957-64; pres. Ill. Lawyers Handbooks, Quincy, 1964—; chmn. bd. Quincy-Peoples Savs. & Loan Assn.; dir. Oscar H. Brinks, Inc., O. M. Properties, Inc. Co-founder, 1st pres. Tri-State Civil War Round Table, 1960-61, Adams County Heart Assn., 1950-52, Adams County Cancer Soc., 1948-50. Fellow Ill. Med. Soc. (hon.); mem. Am., Ill., Adams County bar assns., Aircraft Owners and Pilots Assn., Ill. Hist. Soc., Phi Delta Phi, Phi Gamma Delta. Republican. Clubs: Masons (32 deg.), Shriners. Author: Federal Trial Handbook; Trial Handbook for Illinois Lawyers, 1972; Estate Planning and Administration in Illinois, 1970; Private Pilot's Encyclopedia; co-author numerous trial handbooks. Home: 1811 S 24th St Quincy IL 62301 Office: 428 N 6th St Quincy IL 62301

HUNTER, RONALD WESLEY, lawyer; b. Kingsley, Iowa, Jan. 3, 1930; s. Albert W. and Dorothy M. (Barkley) H.; student Waldorf Coll., 1948-49; B.A. magna cum laude, Nebr. State Tchrs. Coll., 1951; B.S., U. Nebr., 1953, J.D. cum laude, 1955; m. Stephanie M.; children—Mark, Steven, Ronald, Ann, Thomas. Admitted to Nebr. bar, 1955, Iowa bar, 1958; asso. firm Swift & Brown, Des Moines, 1957-61; atty. Swanson Enterprises, Omaha, 1961-64; mem. firm Hunter, Houlihan & Katz, Omaha, 1964—; pres., Western Heritage Mus., Omaha, 1976—. Served with CIC, AUS, 1955-57. Club: Rotary. Editor U. Nebr. Law Rev., 1954-55. Home: 509 Ridgewood Dr Bellevue NE 68005 Office: 7100 W Center Rd Omaha NE 68106

HUNTER, RUTH ELIZABETH, research asso.; b. Cleve., May 24, 1920; d. Clarence David and Enid Emily (Boaz) Lloyd; B.S. in Comprehensive Sci., Kent State U., 1965, M.A. in Biology and Journalism, 1969; student Fenn Coll., 1940-41; m. William Bruce Hunter, Apr. 29, 1945; children—Bruce, Donald, Thomas, Jean. Radio engr. Sta. WGAR, Cleve., 1941-45; tchr. math. and sci. Warrensville Heights (Ohio) Pub. Schs., 1965-68, Maple Heights (Ohio) Bd. Edn., 1961-69; research asso. Ohio Dept. Mental Health and Mental Retardation, Research Center, Cleve., 1969-77. Certified tchr. math. and sci., Ohio. Mem. Cleve. Engrng. Soc., Am. Chem. Soc., Assn. Children Learning Disabilities, Arthritis Found., Spectroscopy Soc., Czechoslovak Soc. Am., PTA, Council World Affairs, Iota Sigma Pi. Methodist. Author: (with M.A. Kelsall) Biological Indicator of Summational Exposures to Lead; contbr. articles to tech. jours. Home: 5463 Hollywood Ave Maple Heights OH 44137

HUNTER, VICTOR LEE, furniture co. exec.; b. Garrett, Ind., Mar. 1, 1947; s. John J. and Martha M. (Brown) H.; B.S. in Physics, Purdue U., 1969; M.B.A., Harvard U., 1971; m. Linda Loudermilk, Dec. 20, 1969; children—Jed, Andrew. Dir. mktg. Krueger Co., Green Bay, Wis., 1971-75; pres. Bus. and Instl. Furniture, Milw., 1975—. Methodist. Home: 5509 N Berkeley St Whitefish Bay WI 53217 Office: Bus & Instl Furniture 611 Broadway Milwaukee WI 53202

HUNTINGTON, ROBERT FREEMAN, roofing co. exec.; b. Jeffersonville, Ind., Nov. 17, 1935; s. James Robert and Mildred Virginia (Freeman) H.; student Butler U., 1952-56; m. Mary Ann Busemeyer, Dec. 27, 1957; children—Lynn Ann, James Robert, David Michael. Salesman, AAA Roofing Co., Inc., Indpls., 1958-67, mgr., 1967—, pres., 1975—; pres. A-Tech. Ind., Inc., Indpls., 1976—. Communications dir. 500 Mile Festival Parade, 1975, 76, 77. Mem. Indpls. Heating and Air Conditioning Assn. (dir. 1968), Indpls. C. of C., Indpls. Better Bus. Bur., Assn. U.S.A., Nat. Guard Assn., Aircraft Owners and Pilots Assn. Republican. Roman Catholic. Clubs: Fourwinds Yacht, RLS Flying. Home: 4301 Swanson Dr Indianapolis IN 46208 Office: 910 N Highland Ave Indianapolis IN 46202

HUNTLEY, RICHARD ALLEN, physician; b. Chgo., May 7, 1932; s. Joseph Edward and Emily Rose (Beran) H.; B.S., U. Ill., 1954, M.S., 1956; M.D., U. Bern, Switzerland, 1961; m. Heidi Kraehenbuehl, June 29, 1960. Intern, Hackley Hosp., Muskegon, Mich., 1962; practice medicine specializing in gen. practice, Muskegon, 1963—; mem. staffs Mercy Hosp., Hackley Hosp., Muskegon. Contbr. Muskegon Area Assn. Retarded Children, Indian Funds; patron Hackley-House Heritage Assn., West Shore Symphony Orch.; bd. dirs. Mich. Heart Assn. Archaeol. Indian excavations with Mus. No. Ariz. Fellow Royal Soc. Health (Eng.); mem. AMA, Mich., Muskegon County med. socs., Am. Assn. Foreign Med. Grads., Stratford Festival Assn. Can., Swiss Benevolent Soc. Chgo., Internat. Platform Assn., Mus. No. Ariz. (life), Smithsonian Instn., Chgo. Council on Fgn. Relations, Forum for Contemporary History, Nat. Trust for Historic Preservation, Nat. Hist. Soc. Club: Muskegon Rifle and Pistol. Home: 3685 Farmwood Dr Muskegon MI 49441 Office: 1704 W Sherman Blvd Muskegon MI 49441

HUNTLEY, THOMAS ELLIOTT, clergyman; b. Wadesboro, N.C., June 28, 1903; s. John P. and Lula J. (Brewer) H.; grad. Va. Theol. Sem. and Coll., Lynchburg, Va., 1928; A.B., Morehouse Coll., 1934; postgrad. Atlanta U., 1937; student Union Theol. Sem., N.Y.; D.D., Friendship Coll., Rock Hill, S.C., 1943, Selma (Ala.) U., 1954; m. Kiffie Elizabeth Esther Maddox, Dec. 21, 1933. Ordained to ministry of Bapt. Ch., 1928; pastor of Central Baptist Church, St. Louis, 1942—; founder of Church on Wheels, 1947; leader Nat. Ministers' Prayer March on Washington, 1948; mem. Social Service Commn. Nat. Bapt. Conv., Inc., 1948-52, mem. hist. commn., 1956-58. Formerly mem. pastor's adv. commn. Nat. Council Religious Edn. Founder Nat. Bapt. Pub. House of South India, 1956; chmn. editorial staff fgn. publs. of Bharath Social and Cultural Trust, Publishers of South India, 1957. Recipient Ecumenical Citation. Met. Ch. Fedn., 1958, award, 1973. Mem. N.A.A.C.P., Protestants and Other Americans United For the Separation of Church and State (v.p.), Internat. Platform Assn., Soc. Scientific Study Religion, Phi Beta Sigma. Mason. Author: As I Saw It, 1954; When People Behave Like Sputniks, 1959; The Devil on The Moon, 1960; A Baptist Manifesto in Three Epistles, 1962; Sense and Common Sense in A World of Nonsense. Huntley's Manual for Every Baptist, 1963. Home: 4959 Cote Brilliante St Louis MO 63113 Office: 2842 Washington Ave St Louis MO 63103

HUNTSMAN, JOSEPH WALLACE, trucking co. exec.; b. Uhrichsville, Ohio, Apr. 18, 1914; s. Grover Cleveland and Bertha Mae (Riley) H.; grad. high sch.; m. Dorothy L. Mitchell, Sept. 24, 1945; children—Craig, Doyle, Lori. Driver, Cleve., Columbus, Cin. hwy., 1931-37; driver, foreman, dispatcher Hayes Freight Lines, Akron, 1937-45; foreman, v.p. A.C.E. Transp., Inc., Akron, 1945-61, Akron Chgo., Inc., 1961-68; v.p. ops. and adminstrn. B & L Motor Freight, Inc., Newark, Ohio, 1968—. Mem. Akron Trucking Assn., Ohio Motor Carriers Labor Relations Assn. Club: Masons. Home: 402 Catalina Dr Newark OH 43055 Office: 140 Everett Ave Newark OH 43055

HUPPLER, EDWARD GEORGE, surgeon; b. Watertown, S.D., June 9, 1926; s. Wallace J. and Anna E. (Roche) H.; B.A., U. Minn., 1949, B.S., 1950, B. Medicine, 1952, M.D., 1953, M.Sc. in Surgery,

1956; m. Sylvia Marie Torstad, Dec. 22, 1947; children—Susan M., Edward G., Katherine J., Thomas R., Robert J. Intern, St. Joseph's Hosp., St. Paul, 1952-53; fellow in surgery Mayo Found., Rochester, Minn., 1953-57; surgeon Bartron Clinic, Watertown, S.D., 1964—; asso. prof. South Dakota State U., Brooking. Committeeman, Codington County (S.D.) Republican Com., 1975-78. Served with U.S. Army, 1943-46. Diplomate Am. Bd. Surgery. Fellow A.C.S.; mem. Am. Coll. Chest Physicians, Am. Trudeau Soc., Mayo Alumni Assn., Sigma Xi. Republican. Roman Catholic. Club: Elks. Home: 908 S Lake Dr Watertown SD 57201

HURDLE, ROBERT BRUCE, dentist; b. Maywood, Ill., July 16, 1937; s. John Yale and Elsie Caroline (Nebel) H.; student U. Ill., Urbana, 1955; B.S. in Dentistry, U. Ill., Chgo., 1959, D.D.S., 1961; m. Patricia Ruth Doweidt, June 10, 1961; children—Lynne, Steven. Asso. with Dr. John Ronning, Hinsdale, Ill., 1963-64; pvt. practice dentistry, Downers Grove, Ill., 1964-68; co-founder Drs. Hurdle, Jourgensen, Mitchell and Assos., predecessor to Grove Dental Assos., P.C., 1969—, pres., 1969—, also dir.; mem. staff Hinsdale Sanitarium and Hosp., Hinsdale, Ill.; co-developer Greenbriar Center Office Devel., 1971—, Bolingbrook Med.-Dental Center, 1972—. Chmn. adv. com. Loyola U. Sch. Dentistry Dental Asst. Tng. Program, 1973-74. Mem. membership com. Indian Boundary YMCA, 1966; mem. Downers Grove Jaycees, 1966-67; chmn. for profl. div. Combined Community Appeal, 1968. Served to capt. Dental Corps USAF, 1961-63. Fellow Acad. Gen. Dentistry (dir. Ill. chpt. 1973-75, sec. 1977-78); mem. Am. Dental Assn., Ill., Chgo. dental socs., Far West Dental Study Club (pres. 1974-75), Progressive Club, Am. Acad. Dental Group Practice (sec. 1976—), Ill. Acad. Dental Practice Adminstrn., Midway Acad. Dentistry, Pierre Fauchard Acad., Psi Omega. Lutheran (ch. council 1965-72; chmn. stewardship com. 1969, 70; chmn. meml. com. 1969-71; mem. exec. stewardship com. Ill. synod 1970-75). Home: 1481 Arrow Wood Ln Downers Grove IL 60515 Office: 6800 Main St Downers Grove IL 60515

HURL, RODNEY BECK, physician; b. Shelby, Ohio, Feb. 25, 1930; s. Robert David and Esther Helen (Beck) H.; B.S., Bethany Coll., 1951; M.D., Temple U., 1955; m. Judith Rothrock, July 17, 1954; children—Megan, Marcy, Jeffrey. Intern Mount Carmel Hosp., Columbus, 1955-56, resident, 1959, now mem. staff; practice medicine specializing in family medicine, Marysville, Ohio, 1959—; mem. staff Meml. Hosp., Marysville; dir. Marysville Newspapers Inc.; dir., v.p. Marysville Rest Homes, Inc., Mildon Park Assos., Inc.; dir. Mid Ohio Devel. Corp. Founding chmn. Union County Comprehensive Health Planning Com., 1968-74; mem. Marysville City Recreation and Park Commn., 1973. Mem. finance com. Union County Republican Central Com., 1960—. Trustee Bethany Coll. Served to capt. USAF, 1956-58. Diplomate Am. Bd. Family Practice. Fellow Am. Acad. Family Practice; mem. Am., Ohio med. assns., Union County Med. Soc., Am. Acad. Family Practice, Marysville C. of C. (dir. 1970-74), Culver Summer Schs. Alumni Assn. (v.p.), Phi Beta Pi, Beta Beta Beta, Beta Theta Pi, Gamma Sigma Kappa. Republican. Lutheran (pres. council 1965). Home: 381 Hickory Dr Marysville OH 43040 Office: 211 Stocksdale Dr Marysville OH 43040

HURLEY, JAMES DONALD, JR., lawyer; b. LaSalle, Ill., June 11, 1935; s. James Donald and Emily Elizabeth (Reinhard) H.; B.A., U. Ill., 1957, LL.B., 1959; m. Pamela J. Hurley; children—Katherine, Mary, James Donald III, Ellen. Admitted to Ill. bar, 1959, also U.S. Cts. Appeals, Fed. Dist. Ct., U.S. Tax Ct.; mem. firm Hollerich & Hurley, LaSalle, 1959—; dir. 1st Nat. Bank, Peru, Ill. City atty., LaSalle, 1968-72. Trustee Hollerich Trust. Recipient Distinguished Service award U.S. Jr. C. of C., 1970, Community Service award Ill. Valley Area C. of C., 1970. Mem. Am., Ill., LaSalle bar assns., Internat. Platform Assn., Ill. Valley C. of C. (pres. 1967-68). Elk, Lion. Home: 718 1/2 First St LaSalle IL 61301 Office: 654 First St LaSalle IL 61301

HURLEY, JAMES WILLIAM, diversified holding co. exec.; b. St. Cloud, Minn., July 4, 1939; s. James Warren and Margaret Caroline (Kapphahn) H.; B.S., So. Ill. U., 1967; M.B.A., Northwestern U., 1974. Sr. auditor Arthur Andersen & Co., Chgo., 1968-72; mgr. taxes Oak Industries, Inc., Crystal Lake, Ill., 1972-74; asst. treas. Trans-Union Corp., Lincolnshire, Ill., 1974—. C.P.A., Ill. Mem. Am. Inst. C.P.A.'s, Ill. C.P.A. Soc. Home: 3925 Triumvera Dr Glenview IL 60025 Office: 90 Half Day Rd Lincolnshire IL 60015

HURLOCKER, MARY MARKS, textile researcher; b. Canton, Mo., July 6, 1939; d. Alden Neal and Virginia Kathryn (Tenity) Marks; B.S., U. Mo., 1961; M.S., U. Minn., 1964; postgrad. Fla. State U., 1966-71; postgrad. N.C. State U., 1971-77; m. Lacy Max Hurlocker, Dec. 15, 1973. Student asst. U. Mo., Columbia, 1959-61; grad. asst. U. Minn., St. Paul, 1961-63; lectr. U. Man., Winnipeg, Can., 1963-64; grad. asst., part-time instr. U. Minn., 1964-65; instr. Fla. State U., Tallahassee, 1965-71; grad. asst. N.C. State U., Raleigh, 1972-76; asso. prof. S.D. State U., Brookings, 1976—; cons. in field. Mem. Am., S.D. home econs. assns., Assn. Coll. Profs. in Clothing and Textiles, Am. Assn. Textile Chemists and Colorists, Am. Chem. Soc., ASTM, Phi Upsilon Omicron, Phi Delta Gamma, Gamma Sigma Delta, Sigma Delta Epsilon. Mem. Christian Ch. Contbr. articles to Textile Chemist and Colorist. Home: 720 13th Ave Brookings SD 57006 Office: SD State U HN 445 Brookings SD 57007

HURON, BRUCE CHANEY, hosp. adminstr.; b. Iron Mountain, Mich., Feb. 11, 1931; s. Willis and Eliza Victoria (Chaney) H.; student Colo. Coll., 1949-50, Northwestern U., 1951; B.A., Mich. State U., 1956; m. Mary Katherine Furno, July 12, 1952; children—Jeanna, Bill, Steven, Lisa, Jerry, Sarah. Purchasing agt. Gratiot Community Hosp., Alma, Mich., 1956-60; asst. adminstr. Francis A. Bell Meml. Hosp., Ishpeming, Mich., 1960-64; adminstr. Paul Oliver Meml. Hosp., Frankfort, Mich., 1964—. Bd. dirs. No. Mich. Health Systems Agy., N.W. Mich. Health Services. Served with AUS, 1952-54. Mem. Am. Coll. Hosp. Adminstrs., Frankfort C. of C. (past pres.). Rotarian (pres. Frankfort club 1967). Home: 725 James St Frankfort MI 49635 Office: 224 Park St Frankfort MI 49635

HURSH, DAVID MERCER, pub. co. exec.; b. Lake City, Minn., Mar. 3, 1939; s. Marion Douglas and Laura Ellen (Fershee) H.; B.S., Wheaton Coll., 1964; M.B.A., U. Chgo., 1968; m. Karen Elisabeth Lindved, Dec. 11, 1965. Quality control supr. Gen. Foods Corp., Chgo., 1960-62; mgmt. trainee R.R. Donnelley, Chgo., 1964-68; project mgr., salesman Am. Can Co., Chgo., 1969-71, gen. composition sales mgr., 1972-73, dir. computer services, 1973; dir. mfg. Callaghan & Co., Wilmette, Ill., 1974-76, v.p. mfg., data processing, v.p., 1977—. Served with U.S. Army, 1962-64. Clubs: University, Whitehall (Chgo.). Home: 721 W Diversey Ave Chicago IL 60614 Office: 3201 Old Glenview Rd Wilmette IL 60091

HURST, JAMES WILLIAM, historian; b. Streator, Ill., May 22, 1932; s. George William and Isabelle Bain (Gordon) H.; B.S. in Edn., So. Ill. U., 1956, M.S. in Edn., 1960; certificate advanced study, No. Ill. U., 1972; m. Annabelle Irene Schroedel, Dec. 3, 1954; children—Paula Jean, Jonathan Douglas. Tchr., Hurst-Bush Community High Sch., Hurst, Ill., 1956-60, Joliet (Ill.) Twp. High Sch., 1960-63; prof. history Joliet Jr. Coll., 1963—; active confs. in field. Mem. Bd. Edn. Ill. Dist. 81, 1964-66. Served with USN, 1951-53. Mem. Ill. Social Sci. Assn. (pres. 1977—), Am. Hist. Assn., Orgn. Am. Historians, Mid-West Conf. Brit. Studies, Historians Met. Chgo., Past and Present Soc., Irish Hist. Soc., Ulster Soc. Irish Hist. Studies, Irish Am. Cultural Inst., Phi Delta Kappa, Theta Xi. Episcopalian. Club: Elks. Contbr. articles to profl. jours. Home: 141 W Wood St New Lenox IL 60451 Office: 1216 Houbolt Ave Joliet IL 60436

HURT, JOHN E., lawyer; b. Morgan County, Ind., Nov. 3, 1912; s. William V. and Sarah (Bange) H.; LL.B., Ind. U., 1938; m. Mary Doswell, Feb. 14, 1937; children—Marcia (Mrs. William Gieseke), Nancy (Mrs. Darrell Ewing), John E. Admitted to Ind. bar, 1938; now sr. mem. firm McNutt, Hurt & Blue, Martinsville, Ind. and Indpls.; pres., dir. Morgan County Bank & Trust, Eminence and Mooresville, Ind.; dir. 1st Nat. Bank, Martinsville; pres. Nebo Properties, Nebo Meml. Park, Martinsville. Trustee Kennedy Meml. Christian Home, Christian Theol. Sem.; judge Morgan Circuit Ct., 1952; sec. Ind. Democratic Central Com., 1948-52, chmn. fin. com., legal counsel, 1960-64; sec. Ind. del. Dem. Nat. Conv., 1948, del., 1956, 60, 64, 72. Served with AUS, 1945-46. Mem. Am., Ind., Morgan County, Indpls. bar assns., Bar Assn. 7th Fed. Circuit, Nat. Assn. R.R. Trial Counsel, Am. Judicature Soc., Disciples of Christ Hist. Soc. (trustee), Gamma Eta Gamma, Delta Chi. Mem. Christian Ch. Clubs: Nat. Lawyers (Washington); Indpls. Athletic, Columbia (Indpls.); Masons, Elks, Lions. Address: 910 E Harrison St Martinsville IN 46151

HURWITZ, ARCHIE R., dentist; b. St. Paul, Feb. 8, 1910; s. Joseph B. and Rae (Roe) H.; D.D.S., U. Minn. Dental Sch., 1935; m. Nathalie Helen Bernstein, Aug. 18, 1940; children—Thomas, Barbara (Mrs. Martin P. Lipschultz). Practice dentistry, St. Paul, 1935—; mem. staff St. Paul Ramsey Hosp., 1935—. Dental chmn. Med. Edn. and Research Found., 1968-70. Served to maj. AUS, 1942-46. Fellow Royal Soc. Health, Am. Dental Assn., Am. Soc. Dentistry for Children. Club: U. Minn. Dental Sch. Century. Author: Dentomedical Problems of the Geriatric Patient, 1966. Home: 1245 Stanford Ave St Paul MN 55105 Office: Lowry Med Arts Bldg St Paul MN 55102

HUSAK, JEROME DONALD, assn. exec.; b. Milw., May 25, 1932; s. Lawrence A. and Gertrude (Haeberle) H.; B.S., Marquette U., 1954, M.B.A., 1958; m. Sally A. Vogel, Aug. 18, 1956. Founder exec. sec. Am. Topical Assn., Milw., 1949—, editor Topical Time, 1949—. Recipient Distinguished Topical Philatelist award Am. Topical Assn., 1952; elected to Wis. Philatelic Hall of Fame, 1976. Mem. Am., Nat. philateleic socs., Royal Philatelic Soc. of Can., Assn. Internat. Journalistes Philateliques, Philatelic Press Club. Address: 3306 N 50th St Milwaukee WI 53216

HUSBAND, RICHARD LORIN, SR., bus. exec.; b. Spencer, Iowa, July 28, 1931; s. Ross Twetten and Frances Estelle (Hall) H.; A.A., Rochester State Community Coll., 1953; arts degree U. Minn., 1954; m. Darlene Joyce Granberg, 1954; children—Richard Lorin and Thomas Ross (twins), Mark Thurston, Julia Lynn, Susan Elizabeth. Pres., Orlen Ross Inc., Rochester, Minn., 1962—; partner The Gallery, European antiques, china, gifts, Rochester, 1968—, Millenium III, home furnishings, Rochester, 1975—. Active Episcopal Diocese of Minn., 1951-52, 58—, nat. dept., 1969-73, alt. dept., 1973-75; trustee Seabury Western Theol. Sem., 1975—, exec. com., 1976—; founder Rochester Arts Council, Rochester PTA Community Coll. Scholarship Program, H.D. Mayo Meml. Lecture in Theology, others; pres. Olmsted County (Minn.) Hist. Soc.; b. dirs. Rochester Symphony Orch., Choral, Opera, 1970—; del. Olmsted County Republican Party, 1974—. Recipient Distinguished Service award Rochester Jaycees, 1965, Fifty Mem. award YMCA, 1968, award for Minn. Bicentennial, Gov. Minn., 1976; named 1 of Minn's, 10 Outstanding Young Men, Minn. Jaycees, 1966. Mem. Minn. Home Furnishings Assn. (pres. 1976—, trustee 1968—), First Dist. Hist. Assemlby Minn., Minn. Retail Fedn. (trustee 1972—), Olmsted County Archeology Soc. (founder), Rochester Civil War Roundtable (founder), Rochester Revolutionary War Roundtable (founder), Rochester Arts Council (founder), Am., Nat. (charter), Minn., Norwegian/Am. hist. socs., Minn. Archeology Soc., Am. Assn. State and Local History, U. Minn. Alumni Assn., U. Minn. Alumni Club (chater) Rochester C. of C. Alpha Delta Phi Alumni Assn., Soc. Mayflower Descs., SAR (Minn. trustee), Desc. Colonial Clergy, Sons Union Vets of Civil War, Minn. Territorial Pioneers; Clubs: Rotary (Rochester); Sertoma (Austin) (founder). Speaker, TV and radio appearances in field. Home: 1820 26th St NW Rochester MN 55901 Office: Orlen Ross Inc 400 S Broadway Rochester MN 55901

HUSEBOE, DORIS EGGERS, coll. adminstr., educator; b. Sioux Falls, S.D., Mar. 10, 1933; d. Delbert William and Erna Louise (Schneider) Eggers; student Augustana Coll., Sioux Falls, 1951-53, U. S.D., 1955-56; B.S., Ind. U., 1959, M.S., 1961; m. Arthur Robert Huseboe, May 27, 1953. Pvt. sec. to comdr. Arty. Sch., Ft. Sill, Okla., 1954-55; tchr. Vermillion (S.D.) Jr. High Sch., 1960-61, Patrick Henry Jr. High Sch., Sioux Falls, 1961-66; adminstr., prof. Augustana Coll., Sioux Falls, 1966—. Chmn. youth bd. 1st Luth. Ch., Sioux Falls, 1967-73; bd. dirs. Guthrie Theater Found., 1976—; v.p. Sioux Falls Community Concerts, 1966-73; pres. Sioux Empire Arts Council, 1973-75; bd. dirs. Sioux Empire Youth Orch., 1975—, S.D. Symphony Aux., 1966—; chmn. Sioux Falls March Arts Festival, 1971, 78. Named an Outstanding Young Woman Am., 1968, Faculty-Adminstr. of Year, Augustana Coll., 1976. Mem. AAUW (v.p. Sioux Falls 1965-69), Nat. Council Tchrs. of English, Am., S.D. personnel and guidance assns., Assn. Coll. Unions Internat., Delta Kappa Gamma. Editor Sioux Empire Arts Ann. Calendar, 1968—. Home: 813 E 38th St Sioux Falls SD 57105 Office: Augustana Coll Sioux Falls SD 57102

HUSEMOLLER, ROBERT DEAN, chem. co. exec.; b. Austin, Minn., Sept. 27, 1936; s. Oscar Carl and Florence Louise (Buck) H.; B.A. in Economics and Polit. Sci., St. Olaf Coll., 1958; m. Carolyn Ann Schweigert, June 20, 1959; children—Catherine A., Rebecca L., David R. O., Paul R. Asst. to pres. Schweigart Meat Co., Mpls., 1965-70; new venture mgr. Green Giant Co., Mpls., 1970; pres. Gus Glaser Meat Co., Ft. Dodge, Iowa, 1971-72, Purdy Products Co., Wauconda, Ill., 1976—; nat. sales mgr. Swift Processed Meat Co., Chgo., 1972-74; v.p. Northstar Industries Co., Chgo., 1975— v.p. Lawrence G. Haggerty and Assos., Inc., Chgo., 1976—. Served to capt. USAF, 1958-64. Mem. Chgo. Pres.'s. Assn., Assn. Corp. Growth. Lutheran. Club: Stonehenge Golf. Home: 261 Leon Dr Barrington IL 60010 Office: 1301 N 01 Rand Rd Wauconda IL 60084

HUSSEINY, ABDO AHMED, engr.; b. Estanha, Egypt, July 7, 1936; s. Ahmed and Fahima (Sabbah) H.; B.S., Alexandria (Egypt) U., 1963; M.S., U. Wis., 1967, Ph.D., 1970; postgrad. Queen Mary Coll., London, 1964; engring. tng. sch. Argonne (Ill.) Nat. Lab., 1966; Mass. Inst. Tech., 1973. m. Zeinab Abdel-Salam Sabri, Sept. 23, 1964. Registered profl. engr. Egypt. Asst. engr. Brown Boveri, Vienna, Austria, 1962; instr. Sacred Heart Girl's Coll., Alexandria, 1963-64; instr. elec. engring. U. Alexandria, 1963-64; research asso. U. Wis., Madison, 1970-71; cons. Saudi Arabia and Kuwait, 1971-72; asst. prof. nuclear engring. U. Mo., Rolla, 1972-73; asst. prof. Carnegie-Mellon U., Pitts., 1973-75; cons. Los Alamos (N.Mex.) Sci. Lab., 1974; with Devel. Cons. Assn., Heliopolis, Egypt., 1973; asso. prof. nuclear engring. Iowa State U., Ames, 1975—; cons. Engring. and Tech. Cons. Assos., Alexandria, 1976—; pres. Tech. Internat. Inc., Arlington, Va., 1977—; tech. chmn. 1st Internat. Conf. and Workshops on Iceberg Utilization, 1977—; bd. editors Desalination, The Internat. Jour. of the Sci. and Tech. of Water Desalting and Purification, 1977—. Mem. IEEE, Am. Nuclear Soc. (first chmn. Iowa/Nebr. sect. 1977-78), Am. Phys. Soc., Am. Soc. Engring. Edn., Brit. Nuclear Energy Soc., Inst. Physics (London), Sigma Xi. Author: Modern Vector Analysis, 1963; contbr. articles to profl. jours. Home: 2144 Ashmore Ct Ames IA 50010 Office: 144 Sweeney Hall Ames IA 50011

HUSTON, DONALD BRUCE, research and devel. exec.; b. Colorado Springs, Colo., July 29, 1938; s. Arthur and Anna Elvira (Henderson) H.; A.B., Colo. State Coll., 1961; M.S., Stout State U., 1966; m. Diane Mary Le Roux. Quality control trainee George Banta Co., 1966, plant quality control mgr., 1966-69, project mgr. charge lab. facilities, 1969-74, corp. research mgr., Menasha, Wis., 1974—; vocat. tchr. Menasha Tech. and Vocat. Sch. Served to lt. (j.g.) USNR, 1961-64. Recipient certificate of appreciation Stout State U., 1971. Mem. Graphic Arts Tech. Found., TAPPI, Res. Officers Assn., Naval Res. Assn., YMCA. Clubs: Twin City Rod and Gun, Elks, Masons. Inventor invisible ink process for instant response programmed learning, low cost durable coating method for books used in sch. Home: 1741 Oakridge Ct Menasha WI 54952 Office: George Banta Co Inc Curtis Reed Plaza Menasha WI 54952

HUTCHESON, JOHN MARVIN, JR., med. illustrator; b. Birmingham, Ala., Oct. 13, 1930; s. John Marvin and Bertha Lee (Bryan) H.; B.A., Birmingham So. Coll., 1955; M.S., Med. Coll. Ga., 1958; m. Sharie Lee Clark, Dec. 29, 1967; children—Yancey Bryan, Shelby Lee. Med. illustrator audiovisual sect., Communicable Disease Center, USPHS, Atlanta, Ga., 1958-59, dept. med. illustration U. Fla. Coll. Medicine, Gainesville, 1959-61, sect. med. graphics Mayo Clinic, Mayo Found., Rochester, Minn., 1961—. Mem. Mayo Centennial Commemorative Stamp Com., 1964; sub-chmn. steering com. Rochester Festival of the Arts, 1965; project advisor Rochester's adoption of the 173d Airborne Brigade, 1966; dir. Am. Revolution Bicentennial Commn. Olmsted County, 1975-77. Served with USNR, 1951-53. Recipient Tom Jones award AMA, 1969, Billings Gold medal AMA, 1961, Certificate of Merit, AMA, 1968, Hektoen Bronze medal AMA, 1969. Mem. Assn. Med. Illustrators (editorial bd. 1963-65), Am. Med. Writers Assn., Olmsted County Hist. Soc., History of Medicine Soc., Lambda Chi Alpha. Republican. Methodist. Elk. Clubs: Rochester Coin, Rochester Stamp (pres. 1973-76). Cinematographic co-director movie, Tetanus and its Prevention, 1963. Designed the offcl. cachet cover for the Doctors Mayo commemorative postage stamp, 1964. Numerous contributions to med. texts and jours. Home: 625 6th St SW Rochester MN 55901 Office: 200 First St SW Rochester MN 55901

HUTCHESON, SUSANNA KAYE, editor, writer, advt. exec.; b. ElDorado, Kans., Jan. 8, 1944; d. Harold G. and E. Irene (Wedding) H.; student Butler County Community Coll., 1970-71, Kans. U., 1966-67. Soc. writer Joplin (Mo.) Globe, 1973; writer Antioch (Calif.) Daily Ledger, 1974; advt. mgr. Mulvane (Kans.) News, 1976—, columnist Points to Ponder, 1976—; freelance writer, Specialty Salesman Mag., Am. Salesman, Salesman's Opportunity, others, 1967—; pres. SKAY Features, 1977—, Skay Enterprises, Inc., 1977—; editor Altoona (Kans.) Tribune, 1977—; owner Park City (Kans.) Press, 1977—. Mem. Bus. and Profl. Women, Authors Guild, Authos League Am., Asso. Bus. Writers Am. Republican. Home: PO Box 1583 Wichita KS 67201

HUTCHINSON, JAMES JOSEPH, JR., bank exec.; b. Chgo., Sept. 22, 1947; s. James Joseph and Dorothy (Howell) H.; A.B., Dartmouth Coll., 1969, M.B.A., 1971. Loan officer 1st Nat. Bank of Chgo., 1971-74; exec. v.p. South Side Bank, Chgo., 1974—, also dir.; v.p. Inter-Urban Broadcasting Co., Gary, Ind., 1977—; dir. Interbank Corp. Bd. Dirs. Central YMCA Community Coll., 1977—; mem. edni. policy council Daniel Hale Williams U., Chgo., 1977—; bd. dirs., treas. Ill. Jaycees Children's Camp, 1974-76; S. Central Community Health Orgn.; deacon Chgo. United Ch. Recipient Outstanding Young Man award Chgo. South-End Jaycees, 1973, Ill. Jaycees, 1974; Outstanding Black Businessman award League Black Women, 1977. Mem. Nat. Black M.B.A.'s Assn. Clubs: South-end Jaycees (exec. v.p. 1974-75), Dartmouth (dir. 1974-76) (Chgo.). Home: 6040 S Harper Ave Chicago IL 60637 Office: 4659 Cottage Grove Ave Chicago IL 60653

HUTCHINSON, ROGER LEE, educator, psychologist; b. White River, S.D., Mar. 24, 1933; s. Eugene and Linnet G. Hutchinson; student Dakota Wesleyan U., 1956-58; B.A., State U. Iowa, 1960, M.A., 1961; Ed.D. in Counseling/Psychology, U. S.D., 1969; m. Betsy M. Hutchinson, July 20, 1952; children—Sherry Lynn, Michael Lee, Eric Paul. Housefather, S.D. Children's Aide, Mitchell, 1956-58; tchr. English, Elgin (Ill.) Jr. High Sch., 1960-62; group counselor Kane County Detention Center, 1960-62; guidance dir. Oelwein Community Schs., Iowa, 1962-67; asso. prof. psychology/counselor Ball State U., 1964-69. Cons. Ind. Soldiers' and Sailors' Children's Home, Knightstown, 1969—. Mem. NEA (life), Am. Psychol. Assn., Am. Personnel and Guidance Assn. Contbr. articles to profl. jours. Home: 2505 W Lincolnshire Dr Muncie IN 47304 Office: TC 619 Ball State U Muncie IN 47306

HUTCHISON, CYRIL PAUL, city ofcl.; b. Warnock, Ohio, June 15, 1924; s. Wilson Lee and Martha Elizabeth (Gay) H.; B.S. in Chemistry, Ohio U., 1950; postgrad. Akron U., 1951-55; m. Marian Marjorie Malham, Aug. 19, 1950. Chemist, Brush Berryllium Co., Cleve., 1949-50; with Firestone Tire & Rubber Co., Akron, Ohio, 1950—, tech. service engr., 1964—; chmn. Stow (Ohio) Parks and Recreation Bd., 1965-75; mayor, Stow, Ohio. Bd. dirs. Stow YMCA, 1962—, chmn., 1965-67 mem. central com. Summit County Republican Party. Mem. Stow C. of C., Summit County Mayors Assn., Ohio Municipal League, Mayors Assn. Ohio, Nat. Assn. Rep. Mayors, Phi Kappa Tau. Club: Lions. Home: 3632 Edgewood Dr Stow OH 44224 Office: Stow City Hall 3760 Darrow Rd Stow OH 44224

HUTH, LESTER CHARLES, lawyer; b. Fostoria, Ohio, Nov. 21, 1924; s. Lester George and Helen Margaret (Turner) H.; student John Carroll U., 1948; J.D., U. Notre Dame, 1951; m. Mary Ann Zablocki, Oct. 23, 1954; children—Timothy, Ann, John. Admitted to Ohio bar, 1951; dir. pub. service and safety, Fostoria, 1952-53; practiced in Fostoria, 1954—; asso. atty. Ohio Savs. & Loan Assn., Fostoria, 1970—; legal counsel St. Wendelin Parish, 1968—; U.S. Govt. appeals agt. Draft Bd., 1958-75; city solicitor Fostoria, 1954-56, 58-60, police prosecutor, 1962-68, acting municipal ct. judge, 1970—. Active Boy Scouts Am.; sec.-treas. Karrick Sch. for Handicapped Children, 1959—. Served with Signal Corps, AUS, 1943-45; ETO. Recipient Certificate of Appreciation, Pres. Johnson for service as appeals agt., 1966. Mem. Am., Ohio (criminal justice com. 1973—), Seneca County (pres. 1972-74) bar assns., C. of C. (chmn. legislative com. 1970-71). Democrat. Roman Catholic. K.C. (4 deg.), Elk. Home: 225 E High St Fostoria OH 44830 Office: 112 E North St Fostoria OH 44830

HUTSON, DON, lawyer; b. Kansas City, Mo., Nov. 4, 1931; s. Alpha Henry and Lola (Walmer) H.; A.B. with honors, Central Coll., Fayette, Mo., 1953; postgrad. U. Mo., 1954; J.D. with honors, George Washington U., 1958; m. Betty Jane Switzer, Sept. 7, 1952;

children—Eric, Sheila, Robin, Heather. Ordained to ministry Internat. Conv. Christian Chs., 1949; minister Oak Grove (Mo.) Christian Ch., 1949-53; tchr., coach various Mo. schs., 1952-54; staff asst. to Sen. Stuart Symington, 1955-59; admitted to Mo. bar, 1958; since practiced in Kansas City; mem. firm Hutson, Schmidt, & Hammett 1958—. Asst. pros. atty. Jackson County, 1959-63. Mem. Am., Fed., Kansas City bar assns., Am. Judicature Soc., Am., Mo. trial lawyers assns., Kansas City C. of C., Sigma Epsilon Pi, Phi Alpha Delta (internat. justice 1974—), Pi Kappa Delta. Democrat. Home: 6409 E 64th St Kansas City MO 64133 Office: Traders Bank 1125 Grand Ave Kansas City MO 64106

HUTT, MAX LEWIS, psychotherapist; b. N.Y.C., Sept. 13, 1908; s. Israel and Pauline Hutt; A.B., Coll. City N.Y., 1928, M.S., 1930; postgrad. Columbia; m. Anne Gromet, Feb. 4, 1933. Instr., Ednl. Clinic, Coll. City N.Y., 1928-41, head, 1939-41; dir. Child Consultation Service, Bklyn., 1941-43; lectr. Columbia, 1946; prof., dir. Ph.D. program in clin. psychology U. Mich., 1947-60; pvt. practice clin. psychology, Ann Arbor, Mich., 1960-67; prof. U. Detroit, 1968-73, dir. Psychotherapy Inst., 1969-73, dir. Psychol. Clinic, 1973; pvt. practice, Ann Arbor, 1973—. Cons. in field. Mem. bd. I.M.P.P.A.C. Served with AUS, 1943-46. Decorated Commendation medal. Diplomate Am. Bd. Profl. Psychology (examiner). Fellow Am. Psychol. Assn. (council reps.), Soc. Projective Techniques; mem. Psychologists League (pres. 1939), Mich. Soc. Projective Techniques (pres. 1949), Soc. for Study Social Issues, AAUP, Mich. Soc. Cons. Psychologists, Mich. Psychol. Assn. Author: The Hutt Adaptation of the Bender-Gesalt Test, 1959, 2d edit., 1969, 3d edit., 1977; The Child: Development and Adjustment, 1959; El Nino: Desarrollo y Adaptcion, 1962; Psychology: The Science of Behavior, 2d edit., 1971; co-author: Patterns of Abnormal Behavior, 1957; The Mentally Retarded Child, 1958, 3d edit., 1976; The Child-Development and Adjustment, 1959; Psychology: The Science of Interpersonal Behavior, 1966; An Atlas for the Hutt Adaptation of the Bender-Gesalt Test, 1970; Psychosynthesis: Vital Therapy, 1977. Contbr. articles to profl. jours., chpts. to books, also encys. Home: 21 Regents Dr Ann Arbor MI 48104 Office: 201 S Main St Ann Arbor MI 48108

HUTTIG, JACK WILFRED, ednl. adminstr.; b. Kansas City, Mo., Mar. 13, 1919; s. Alfred and Inez Pearl (Fessler) H.; B.A., Wichita State U., 1970, M.S., 1973; m. Amelia Lovisa Goodman, July 3, 1941; children—Diana Frances, Philip Edward, Pamela Jane, Jack Wilfred. Mgr. mktg. manpower devel. Beech Aircraft Corp., Wichita, 1952-73; dir. Center For Confs. and Instrs., U. Iowa, Iowa City, 1973—. Served with AUS, 1939-45. Recipient Freedoms Found. award, 1950, Internat. award Sales Execs. Club: 1951; award Writers Digest, 1966. Mem. Nat. Univ. Extension Assn., Delta Sigma Pi. Club: Rotary. Books include: Psycho-Sales-Analysis, 1970; 15 Ways to Increase Your Sales, 1972; 1927 Summer of the Eagles, 1977; contbg. editor Profl. Salesman, 1968-69. Contbr. articles to profl. jours. Home: 1204 Village Rd Iowa City IA 52240 Office: 210 Iowa Memorial Union Iowa City IA 52242

HUTZELMAN, PAUL DAVID, pharm. co. rep.; b. Mansfield, Ohio, Aug. 3, 1936; s. William Andrew and Margret E. (Myers) H.; B.Sc., Ohio State U., 1957; m. Kay S. Alexander, June 10, 1955; children—Paul Edward, Phillip Todd. Med. technologists Ohio State U. Hosp. Blood Bank, 1955-57; med. service rep. Parke Davis & Co., Columbus, Ohio, 1958-61, med. surg. sales rep., Dayton, Ohio, 1961-63, area mgr. So. Ind., Floyds Knobs, 1963—. Owner, pres. Falls City (Ind.) Recreation Inc., 1968-70; owner, pres. Colonial Country Club, New Albany, Ind., 1968-70. Chmn. age groups swimming Ky. Assn. Amateur Athletic Union, 1973-75; mem. exec. bd. Rogers Clark Council Boy Scouts Am., 1967-75; founder, chmn. bd. Hoosier Hills Athletic Club Inc., New Albany, 1970—. Recipient Silver Beaver award Boy Scouts Am., 1969. Mem. United Comml. Travelers Assn. (dir.). Methodist (youth coordinator 1970-74). Mason, Rotarian. Address: Route 3 Box 263 Spickert Knob Rd Floyds Knobs IN 47119

HUVOS, KORNEL, linguist; b. Budapest, Hungary, Apr. 25, 1913; s. Laszlo and Ilona (Vajda de Kunagota) Huvos de Botfa; came to U.S., 1956, naturalized, 1961; Bachelier Lettres, U. Paris, 1931; J.S.D., Royal U. Budapest, 1938; Ph.D., U. Cin., 1965; m. Anna Maria Ledniczky, Mar. 25, 1945; 1 son, Christopher. French-German-Hungarian lexicographer Hungarian Acad. Scis., Budapest, 1947-56; news analyst Cin. Times Star, 1956-58; mem. faculty U. Cin., 1958—, Charles Phelps Taft prof. Romance langs. and lits., 1975—, head dept. Romance langs. and lits., 1977—. Woodrow Wilson fellow, 1959; Taft Meml. research grantee. Mem. Modern Lang. Assn., Midwest, South Atlantic modern lang. assns., Am. Assn. Tchrs. French, AAUP, Lit. Club Cin., Pi Delta Phi. Roman Catholic. Author: (with L. Clark Keating) Impressions d'Amérique: Les Etats-Unis dans la litterature francaise contemporaine, 1970; Cinq Mirages Americains: Les Etats-Unis dans l'oeuvre de Georges Duhamel, Jules Romains, Andre Maurois, Jacques Maritain et Simone de Beauvoir, 1972. Contbr. articles to profl. jours. Home: 1600 Thomson Heights Dr Cincinnati OH 45223 Office: Dept Romance Languages Univ Cincinnati Cincinnati OH 45221

HWAY, PHILIP JOSEPH, electronic equipment mfg. co. exec.; b. Berwyn, Ill., Sept. 3, 1946; s. Joseph and Lydia Marie (Gajda) H.; A.B., Harvard U., 1968, M.B.A., 1970; m. Prudence Mary Pick, May 14, 1977; children by previous marriage—Derek Scott, Benjamin Bradford. Indsl. engring. supr. NCR Corp., San Diego, 1972-73; mgmt. devel. asso. Wickes Corp., Saginaw, Mich., 1973-74; sr. asso. Robert H. Hayes & Assos., Inc., Chgo., 1974-76; mktg. mgr. Motorola, Inc., Schaumburg, Ill., 1976—. Precinct capt. Republican party, 1976—. Served in USAF, 1970-72. Home: 2500 Windsor Mall Park Ridge IL 60068 Office: 1301 E Algonquin Rd Schaumburg IL 60196

HYATT, HUDSON, lawyer; b. Cleve., Jan. 1, 1914; s. Harry Cleve and Rose Evelyn (Miller) H.; A.B. cum laude, Adelbert Coll., Western Res. U., 1937, LL.B., 1939; m. Helen Fulmor, Feb. 3, 1940; children—David Hudson, Margaret (Mrs. Ross J. Dixon), Nancy (Mrs. Michael A. Schwartz), Shirley. Admitted to Ohio bar, 1939; asso. Davis & Young, 1939-40; adjudicator Social Security Bd., 1940-42; law clk, U.S. Dist. Ct., 1942-44; atty. Erie R.R. Co., 1946-52; practiced in Cleve., 1952-54; regional atty. Small Bus. Adminstrn., Cleve., 1954-63, asst. regional counsel, 1963-66, dist. atty., 1966-71, dist. counsel 1971-77; lectr. law Coll. Law, Cleve. State U., 1976. Pres., Cleve. Masonic Employment Bur., 1960-63, 1969-70, v.p., 1963-69; pres. Greater Cleve. Vets. Council, 1952-53; bd. control Cleve. Freedom Council, 1961—. Trustee C.L. Jack Meml. Fund. Served from ensign to lt (j.g.), USNR, 1944-46. Mem. Fed. (1st v.p. Cleve. chpt. 1965-66, pres. Cleve. chpt. 1966-67), Am. (chmn. small bus. com. 1965-69), Cleve. Cuyahoga County (editorial bd. bull. 1962-73; chmn. editoral com. 1965-66) bar assns., S.A.R., Am. Legion, V.F.W. (nat. judge adv. gen. 1947-48), Urban League Cleve. Mason (32 deg.). Club: Ripon. Contbg. editor Baldwin's Ohio Legal Forms, 1963, 70, 73, Baldwin's Kentucky Legal Forms, 1963; Carroll and Whiteside's, Forms for Commercial Transactions, 1963. Home: 2648 Euclid Heights Blvd Cleveland Heights OH 44106

HYDE, ALAN LITCHFIELD, lawyer; b. Akron, Ohio, Nov. 4, 1928; s. Howard Linton and Katharine Pennington (Litchfield) H.; A.B., Amherst Coll., 1950; J.D., Harvard U., 1953; m. Charlotte Griffin Ross, July 10, 1954; children—Elizabeth, Pamela. Admitted to Ohio bar, 1953; asso. firm Thompson, Hine and Flory. Cleve., 1953-64, partner, 1964—; hon. mexican consul, Cleve., 1969-74. Sec., gen. counsel Greater Cleve. Growth Assn., 1972-74, dir., 1974—; pres. Planned Parenthood Cleve., 1977—; dir. Cleve. World Trade Assn., 1978—. Mem. Am., Ohio, Greater Cleve., Internat., Inter-Am. bar assns., Greater Cleve. Internat. Lawyers Group (pres. 1976—). Clubs: Union, Tavern, Kirtland Country. Home: Berkshire Rd Gates Mills OH 44040 Office: 1100 Nat City Bank Bldg Cleveland OH 44114

HYDE, HENRY J., lawyer, Congressman; b. Chgo., Apr. 18, 1924; s. Henry Clay and Monica Therese (Kelly) H.; student Duke U., 1943-44; B.S., Georgetown U., 1947; J.D., Loyola U., Chgo., 1949; m. Jeanne M. Simpson, Nov. 8, 1947; children—Henry J., Robert, Laura, Anthony. Admitted to Ill. bar; mem. Ill. Ho. of Reps., 1967-74, majority leader, 1971-72; mem. 94th Congress from 6th Ill. Dist. Served with USNR, World War II; comdr. Res., ret. Mem. Am., Ill., Chgo. bar assns. Home: 1019 W Peterson Ave Park Ridge IL 60068 Office: 1206 Longworth Bldg Washington DC 20515

HYDE, ROBERT C(UNNINGHAM), lawyer; b. Sharon, Pa., Sept. 15, 1903; s. Irvin J. and Elizabeth (Cunningham) H.; grad. Mercersburg Acad., 1921; student Kenyon Coll., 1925; LL.B., City Coll. Law and Finance, 1937; m. Elizabeth Blake Harris, July 5, 1934; children—Robert Blake, Elizabeth Cunningham Nutter. Admitted to Mo. bar, 1937, pvt. practice, Poplar Bluff, 1937—; past pres. Poplar Bluff Industries. Pres. S.E. Mo. council Boy Scouts Am., 1955-58; pres. Poplar Bluff and Butler County United Fund; bd. dirs. Poplar Bluff Sch. Bd., 1957-68, pres., 1966-67. Mem. Am., Mo. (tax com.) bar assns., C. of C. (dir.). Episcopalian (standing com. Diocese Mo. 1960-70, pres. standing com. 1966-67, lay dep. gen. conv., 1973). Contbr. tax articles to legal. jours. Home: 544 N 11th St Poplar Bluff MO 63901 Office: Commerce Bank Bldg Poplar Bluff MO 63901

HYLAND, AIMEE MADELINE, physician; b. Newark, Feb. 22, 1923; d. John Trevithick and Madeline Esther (Ellerman) Wriggins; B.S., Maryville Coll., 1940-44; M.D., Med. Coll. Pa., 1948; postgrad. Fordham U., summer 1944; Physicians Inst., Summer Sch. Alcohol Studies, Rutgers U., summer 1965; m. Jack Hubert Richmond, June 15, 1946 (div. Oct. 1961); children—Lester Daniel, Julia Marie, Eileen Claire; m. 2d, Howard H. Hyland, Aug. 31, 1973. Intern, Easton (Pa.) Hosp., 1948-49; resident Grant Hosp., Columbus, Ohio, 1950-51; resident surgery Univ. Hosp., Columbus, 1951; med. dir. House of Hope for Alcoholics, Columbus, 1961; physician student health service Ohio State U., Columbus, 1961-62; group practice, Oak Hill, Ohio, 1962-63; practice medicine, Middletown, Ohio, 1963—; mem. staff Grant Hosp., Columbus; tchr. med. students as part of residencies at Grant and Univ. hosps.; mem. Nat. Council on Alcoholism, Butler County, Ohio, 1968—, del. nat. meetings, 1969, 70, 71; mem. Easter Seal Soc. for Crippled Children and Adults, Butler County, 1968—, del. nat. meeting, 1970; physician on duty ARC Blood Bank, Columbus, 1952-61; exam. physician Juvenile Center, Columbus, 1952-61, Planned Parenthood Clinics, Columbus and Middletown, 1952—, Endocrinology and Diabetic Clinics, Univ. Hosp., Columbus, 1959-60. Adviser Middletown chpt. Parents Without Partners, 1970—; mem.-at-large adminstrv. bd., council on ministries Methodist Ch., 1976, mem. commn. on evangelism. Diplomate Am. Bd. Family Practice. Charter fellow Am. Acad. Family Physicians; mem. AMA, Butler County, Ohio med. assns., Ohio Acad. Family Physicians, Soc. Prospective Medicine, Am. Med. Soc. on Alcoholism, Christian Med. Soc., Central Ohio Diabetes Assn., Hamilton Civil War Round Table, Middletown C. of C. (legis. action com. 1966—). Republican. Presbyterian (candidate fgn. mission field 1944-53, chmn. mission of ch. com. 1956-57). Home: 136 Eaton Dr Middleton OH 45042 Office: 2226 Central Ave Middletown OH 45042

HYNES, GEORGE PATRICK, librarian; b. Michigan, N.D., Mar. 17, 1910; s. Leo J. and Emma M. (Bunney) H.; B.S. in Edn., U. N.D., 1933, postgrad., 1960; m. Dorothy E. Hennessey, June 11, 1938; children—Wally, Constance, Ronald, Kathleen, Renee. Supt. schs., Carson, N.D., 1938-41, Rocklake, N.D., 1942-46; prin. schs., Neche, N.D., 1941-42; librarian State Jr. Coll., Bottineau, N.D., 1946-64, Marshall-Lyon County Pub. Library, Marshall, Minn., 1964-67, Fort Dodge (Iowa) Pub. Library, 1967—. Pres. PTA, 1961, 67; pres. bd. Corpus Christi Sch., Fort Dodge, 1971. Named N.D. Man of Year in boxing N.D. Golden Gloves, 1959; recipient award for outstanding contbn. to boxing in Iowa, 1975. Mem. ALA, Iowa Library Assn. Democrat. Roman Catholic. Clubs: Eagles (v.p. 1971-72, 75—, pres. 1973-74), K.C. (4 deg.), Elks, Rotary, Lions, Garden. Home: 924 15th Ave Fort Dodge IA 50501 Office: 605 1st St Fort Dodge IA 50501

IACCINO, PAUL A., labor union ofcl.; b. Chgo., Oct. 14, 1917; s. Anthony C. and Rose (Manzella) I.; student Ill. Bus. Coll., 1936-37; m. Marietta H. Smith, Apr. 26, 1941 (dec. Apr. 1973); children—Richard, Gerald, James, William, Diane; m. 2d, Kathrine B. Durham, May 26, 1974. Former musician, dance band leader; employed Hart, Schaffner & Marx Co., 1936-42, Revere Copper & Brass Co., Inc., 1942-52; rep. CIO (now AFL-CIO) to Welfare Council Met. Chgo., 1952-57; sec., treas. Cook County (Ill.) Indsl. Union Council, CIO, 1957-62, asst. to pres. Chgo. Fedn. Labor and Indsl. Union Council AFL-CIO, 1962-68; asst. dir. labor affairs dept. Blue Cross-Blue Shield, 1968-70, adminstr. labor affairs dept., 1970-72, asst. v.p., 1972-74; dir. AFL-CIO Community Services Dept. Crusade of Mercy, 1974—; pres. and founder Italian-Am. Labor Council, 1966-68, sec., 1968-74, treas., 1974-76, mem. bd. dirs., 1976—; chmn. community services com. Chgo. AFL-CIO, 1962-68, dir. community services dept., 1962-68. Bd. dirs., vice-chmn. Met. Chgo. Crusade Mercy, 1965, 66, 67; chmn. Chgo. Mayor's Sr. Citizens Employment Com.; mem. blood bank com. Chgo. ARC, planning com. Ill. Inst. Labor, Health, and Rehab., Ill. Com. Fair Credit Practices, Com. to Form a Pre-Paid Dental Plan, Gov. Ill. Commn. Credit Legis., Gov. Ill. coms. Status of Women and Retardation; mem. ad-hoc com. planning welfare services Proviso Twp.; mem. Ill. Child Labor Com., Ill. Com. on Minimum Wage, Ill. Com. Migratory Labor, Jewish Labor Com.; mem. labor com. Nat. Safety Council; co-chmn. Boys' Town Italy, 1st vice-chmn. Ill. Coll. Podiatric Medicine; bd. dirs. Welfare Council Met. Chgo., Blue Cross, Community Fund. Recipient awards Boys' Town Italy, Italian-Am. Labor Council, Sr. Citizen's Met. Chgo.; Civil Rights award Jewish Labor Com. Home: 3109 Adams St Bellwood IL 60104 Office: 72 W Adams St Chicago IL 60603

IACOCCA, LIDO ANTHONY, automobile mfg. co. exec.; b. Allentown, Pa., Oct. 15, 1924; s. Nicola and Antoinette (Perrotto) I; B.S., Lehigh U., 1945; M.E. (Wallace Meml. fellow), Princeton, 1946; m. Mary McCleary, Sept. 29, 1956; children—Kathryn Lisa, Lia Antoinette. With Ford Motor Co. Dearborn, Mich., 1946—, successively mem. field sales staff, various merchandising and tng. activities, asst. dirs. sales mgr., Phila., dist. sales mgr., Washington, 1946-56, truck mktg. mgr. div. office, 1956-57, car mktg. mgr., 1957-60, vehicle market mgr., 1960, v.p. Ford Motor Co., gen. mgr. Ford div., 1960-65, v.p. car and truck group, 1965-67, exec. v.p. of co., 1967-68, then pres. Ford N.Am. automobile ops., pres. co., 1970—. Mem. Tau Beta Pi. Club: Detroit Athletic. Home: 571 Edgemere Ct Bloomfield Hills MI 48013 Office: American Rd Dearborn MI 48121

IANNONE, LIBERATO ALESSANDRO, cardiologist; b. Winnepeg, Canada, Mar. 13, 1941; s. Giuseppe Luigi and Julia (Valentino) I.; came to U.S., 1945, naturalized, 1956; B.S. cum laude in natural sciences, Niagara U., 1963; M.D., State U. N.Y., Buffalo, 1967; m. Delores Patricia Torres, 1971; children—Timothy, Christopher, Sonya, Sophia. Intern Buffalo Gen. Hosp., 1967-68, resident, 1968-69; cardiology fellow Walter Reed Army Med. Center, 1969-71; staff cardiologist, dir. coronary care unit William Beaumont Army Med. Center, El Paso, Tex., 1971-73, dir. cardiac cathererization lab., 1971-73; staff cardiologist Geisinger Med. Center, Danville, Pa., 1974, practice medicine specializing in cardiology, 1974—; dir. coronary care unit Mercy Hosp., Des Moines, mem. staffs. Meth., Lutheran hosps., Des Moines. Served with U.S. Army, 1969-73. Certified Am. Bd. Internal Medicine. Fellow Am. Coll. Cardiology, Am. Coll. Angiology, Council Clin. Cardiology, Am. Coll. Physicians; mem. AMA, Iowa, Polk County med. socs., Am. Heart Assn. Contbr. articles to med. jours. Home: 2833 SW Calder Des Moines IA 50315 Office: 943 19th St Des Moines IA 50314

IBARRA, JOSE LUIS, psychiatrist; b. Guadalajara, Jalisco, Mex., Sept. 19, 1920; s. Miguel and Maria Luisa (Araiza) I.; came to U.S., 1949, naturalized, 1953; B.S., Universidad Autonoma de Guadalajara, 1939; M.D., Universidad Nacional de Mex., 1946; m. Elizabeth Ann Taylor, July 14, 1944; children—Elizabeth, Luis, Theodore, Patrick, Paul, Michael. Intern, St. Joseph Hosp., Joliet, Ill., 1952-53; resident Manteno (Ill.) State Hosp., 1949-50, Topeka State Hosp., 1950-60; pvt. practice psychiatry, Mex., 1946-49; staff E. Moline (Ill.) State Hosp., 1950-51, 53-58, Topeka State Hosp., 1958; clin. dir. Osawatamie (Kans.) State Hosp., 1960-62; med. dir., adminstrv. dir. Butler County Counseling and Mental Health Center, El Dorado, Kans., 1963-69, cons., 1969; pvt. practice psychiatry, Wichita, Kans., 1969—; teaching staff Wichita State U., 1974—; mem. ednl. com. St. Francis Hosp., Wichita, 1973—, chmn. psychiat. sect., 1972—; cons. Sedgwick County Mental Health Center, VA Hosp., Wichita, Prairie View Hosp., Newton, Kans.; mem. Bd. Health Sedgwick County (Kans.), 1974. Bd. dirs. ARC, Butler County, 1968-69. Fellow Menninger Found.; mem. AMA, Kans., Sedgwick County med. socs., Am., Mid-Continent, Kans. psychiat. assns. Office: Suite 230 1035 N Emporia St Wichita KS 67214

IBSEN, DWAYNE BRADLEY, educator; b. Holdrege, Nebr., Feb. 8, 1944; s. Marvin O. and Louise P. (Burkey) I.; B.A., Kearney State Coll., 1966; postgrad. Wayne State Coll., 1969, U. Oslo (Norway), 1969. Drama instr. Omaha Pub. Sch. System, 1967—; scenic artist Tiffany's Attic Dinner Theatre, Kansas City, Mo., 1975—; artistic dir. Nebr. State Repertory Co. Theatre, Omaha, 1973—. Founder, Spotlight 12 summer theatre, 1967-70; exhibited Haymarket Art Gallery (1st place ink drawing), 1976; dir., producer Shakespeare in Streets of Old Market, 1976. Bd. dirs. Chanticleer Community Theatre, Council Bluffs, Iowa, 1968-71; pres., bd. dirs. Nebr. State Repertory Co. Named Tchr. of Year, Omaha Student Council, 1972; recipient Freedom Found. Tchr. medal, 1973; Design award Met. Actors Guild, 1976. Mem. NEA, Nat. Found. Lit. and Drama in Arts, Am. Theatre Assn., Am. Freedom Found., Nebr., Omaha edn. assns., Asso. Artists Omaha. Home: 4724 Davenport Omaha NE 68132 Office: 4323 N 37th St Omaha NE 68111

ICE, HARRY TREESE, lawyer; b. Paulding, Ohio, Oct. 17, 1904; s. Henry J. and Senna (Treese) I.; A.B., Butler U., 1926; LL.B., Harvard U., 1929; LL.D., Ind. Central Coll., Indpls., 1966; m. Elizabeth McIntyre, July 9, 1932; 1 dau., Marabeth. Admitted Ind. bar, 1929; asso. Ice Miller Donandio & Ryan, Indpls., 1929—, partner, 1934—. Dir., vice chmn. bd. Am. United Life Ins. Co.; dir. Fairbanks Broadcasting Co., Inc.; dir., vice chmn. bd. Union City Body Co. Mem. Constl. Revision Commn., Higher Edn. Coordinating Com.; chmn. Ind. Ethics and Conflicts of Interest Commn.; bd. dirs. United Way of Greater Indpls., Greater Indpls. Progress Commn., Crossroads of Am. council Boy Scouts Am.; trustee Butler U., Christian Ch. Found., Community Hosp. Found.; former trustee Ind. Boys Sch., Ind. Reformatory. Served to lt. comdr. USNR, 1943-45. Mem. Ind. (dir.), Indpls. (dir.) chambers commerce. Mem. Christian Ch. (trustee found.). Home: 6370 Spring Mill Rd Indianapolis IN 46260 Office: 111 Monument Circle Indianapolis IN 46204

ICEMAN, ROBERT LEE, mfg. co. exec.; b. Wooster, Ohio, May 29, 1926; s. Charles Lester and Viola Gale (Bowman) I.; student Ohio Inst. Bus. Sch., 1950-52; m. Perie Helene Williams, Feb. 1, 1947; children—Thomas L., Janet Elaine, Rebecca Lee, Judy Ann. With Wooster Brass Co., 1943, Akron Brass Co., Wooster, 1944; with Gerstenslager Co., Wooster, 1946—, asst. sales mgr. custom body dept., 1960-63, sales mgr. stamping div., 1963-73, mgr. stamping div., 1967-77, pres., 1977—. Mem. village council Shreve, Ohio, 1951-53, pres., 1953-57; mem. bd. edn. Triway Local Schs., Wooster, 1970-78, pres., 1972-73. Served with AUS, 1944-46. Mem. Ohio Sch. Bd. Assn., Am. Legion. Republican. Methodist (trustee 1970-72). Club: Masons (32 deg.). Home: 3474 Shreve Rd Wooster OH 44691 Office: 1425 E Bowman St Wooster OH 44691

ICHORD, RICHARD HOWARD, congressman; b. Licking, Mo., June 27, 1926; s. Richard Howard and Minda (Curtis) I.; B.S., Mo. U., 1949, J.D., 1952; m. Millicent Murphy Koch; children—Richard Howard III, Pamela Lee, Kyle M. Instr. bus. law U. Mo., 1949, 52; admitted to Mo. bar, 1952; mem. firm Lay and Ichord, Houston, Mo., 1952-60; city atty., Houston, 1952; rep. Texas County, Mo. Ho. of Reps., 1953, speaker pro tem, 1957-58, speaker, 1959-60; mem. 87th to 95th Congresses, 8th Dist. Mo. Served AC, USNR, 1944-46. Mem. VFW, Am. Legion, Houston C. of C. Democrat. Mason. Odd Fellow. Home: 116 W Main St Houston MO 65483 Office: Rayburn Office Bldg Washington DC 20515

IDELL, JAMES HAROLD, product design engr.; b. Greeneville, Tenn., Feb. 18, 1946; s. Earl James and Madge Ellen (Rhea) I.; B.S. (scholar), U. Tenn., 1968; M.S. (fellow), N.C. State U., 1971; m. Irma Elaine Carr, July 19, 1969; 1 son, Andrew David. Lab. tech. U. Tenn., Knoxville, 1965-69; grad. research asst. N.C. State U., Raleigh, 1969-71; sr. product design engr. Ford Tractor Ops., Troy, Mich., 1973—. Com. mem. Oakland County (Mich.) Citizens League, 1974—. Served to capt. Ordnance Corps, AUS, 1971-73. Mem. Am. Soc. Agrl. Engring., Alpha Epsilon, Alpha Zeta, Scabbard and Blade. Democrat. Baptist. Home: 2800 Walmsley Circle Lake Orion MI 48035 Office: 2500 E Maple Rd Troy MI 48084

IGLAR, JON LOUIS, librarian; b. Pitts., Jan. 27, 1928; s. Michael Charles and Sophie Elizabeth (Galovic) I.; student U. Pitts., 1949-50, St. Vincent's Coll., 1950-51; A.B., St. Francis Coll., 1953, postgrad., 1953-56; M.L.S., Rosary Coll., 1964; certificate of advanced study U. Ill., 1969; m. Anne Marshall Yoder Brozovic, June 1, 1974; stepchildren—Matthew, Mary Kristen, Mary Susan, John, Michael, Kathryn. Cataloging asst. Law Library, Northwestern U., Evanston, Ill., 1962-63; circulation librarian Law Library, U. Chgo., 1963-64, Harper Library, 1964-65; instr. library sci. U. Ill., Champaign/Urbana, 1967-68; with St. Joseph's Coll. Calumet Campus (name changed to Calumet Coll.), Whiting, Ind., 1965-67, 1968—, now head librarian.

Served with USAF, 1946-49. Mem. ALA, Ind., Cath. library assns., AAUP, Slovak Cath. Sokols, Beta Phi Mu. Editor Mariale, 1954, 55. Home: 1412 Elliott Dr Munster IN 46321 Office: Mary Gorman Specker Meml Library 2400 New York Ave Whiting IN 46394

IGLAUER, ARNOLD, physician, educator; b. Cin., Oct. 31, 1911; s. Charles and Clara I.; student Anitoch Coll., 1928-32; B.M., U. Cin., 1936, M.D., 1937; m. Gene Ach, June 20, 1976; children—Delia Iglauer OHara, Gail. Rotating intern Wis. Gen. Hosp., 1936-37; resident in medicine Cin. Gen. Hosp., 1937-38; research fellow in medicine, cardiorespiratory physiology and cardiorespiratory disease, Harvard U., 1938-40; fellow in cardiology U. Cin., 1944-46, instr. medicine, 1942-48, asst. prof. medicine, 1948—, asst. clin. prof. indsl. medicine, 1955-72, asso. clin. prof. medicine, 1965-71, clin. prof. medicine, 1971—; tng. in peripheral vascular disease Mayo Clinic, Rochester, Minn., 1947, N.Y. U. Postgrad. Med. Sch., 1951; asst. attending physician Cin. Gen. Hosp., 1947-51, attending physician, 1951—; attending physician Jewish Hosp., Cin., 1946—, physician-in-chief electrocardiographic sect., 1961—; attending physician VA Hosp., Cin., 1954-74. Diplomate Am. Bd. Internal Medicine. Fellow A.C.P., Am. Heart Assn. (council clin. cardiology, chpt. pres. 1969-71); mem. Sigma Xi, Cin. Soc. Internal Medicine (pres. 1977). Contbr. articles on cardiovascular and pulmonary problems and drug trials to med. jours. Office: 2825 Burnet Ave Cincinnati OH 45219

IGLEBURGER, ROBERT MARTIN, ret. city ofcl.; b. Dayton, Ohio, Dec. 19, 1909; s. Charles Martin and Cora Belle (Bickel) I.; student Ohio State U., 1929-31; student police adminstrn. Northwestern U., 1954-55; M.Pub.Adminstrn., U. Dayton, 1976; m. Eve Hartman, Nov. 23, 1946; children—Lois Elaine, Debra Gayle; 1 stepson, Gary Tanner. With Dayton Police Dept., 1939-73, capt. in charge traffic sect., 1961-63, capt. in charge uniformed patrol sect., 1963-65, maj. in charge line operations, 1965-67, dir. of police, 1967-73, ret.; resident police adminstr. U. Wis. Law Sch., 1973-74; dir. Dayton Pilot City LEAA Program, 1974—. Served to sgt. AUS, 1942-46; PTO. Mem. Am. Soc. Pub. Adminstrn., Internat. Assn. Chiefs Police. Club: Foreman's (Dayton). Home: 932 Westminster Pl Dayton OH 45419

IGNOFFO, CARLO MICHAEL, insect pathologist-virologist; b. Chicago Heights, Ill., Aug. 24, 1928; s. Joseph and Lucy (Sardo) I.; B.S., No. Ill. U., 1950; M.S., U. Minn., 1954, Ph.D., 1957; m. Florence F. Mielcarek, Sept. 3, 1949. Asst. prof. Iowa Wesleyan Coll., Mt. Pleasant, 1957-59; insect pathologist U.S. Dept. Agr., Brownsville, Tex., 1959-65; dir. entomology Internat. Minerals & Chems. Corp., Wasco, Calif. and Libertyville, Ill., 1965-71; lab. dir. U.S. Dept. Agr., Columbia, Mo., 1971—. Prof. dept. entomology U. Mo., 1974—. Served with Chem. Corps, AUS, 1954-56. Mem. Internat. Orgn. Biol. Control (pres. 1974), AAAS, Am. Inst. Biol. Scis., Soc. Invertebrate Pathology (editorial bd. 1965-68, treas. 1968-70), Entomol. Soc. Am., Mo. Acad. Sci., C. of C. Isolated, commercialized 1st viral pesticide. Patentee in field. Office: PO Box A Research Park Columbia MO 65201

IHDE, GLADYS WILLMA, ret. educator, psychologist; b. Winnebago County, Wis., Nov. 17, 1906; d. William and Ida May (Baumann) Ihde; Ed.B., Oshkosh Tchrs. Coll., 1930; M.S., U. Wis., 1958. Tchr. exceptional children Oshkosh (Wis.) Area Pub. Schs., 1929-60, sch. psychologist, 1960-72; instr. methods of teaching retarded children Wis. State U., Oshkosh, summers 1963-71; vol. tchr. of reading to adults Winnebago County (Wis.), 1972—; prin. G.W. Ihde, psychologist, 1972—; treas. Winnebago County Guidance Center, 1964-66. Bd. dirs. Oshkosh Seniors Center, v.p., 1975-77; bd. dirs. Oshkosh Community Council, treas., 1963-65; bd. dirs. Literacy Services Wis., 1974-77. Boys Club Oshkosh, 1972-77. Named Mental Health Citizen of the Year, Wis. Assn. for Mental Health, 1974; recipient Community Service award Wis. Assn. for Retarded Citizens, 1976, Am. Bicentennial Research Inst. award, 1973; Woman and Boy award, 1976. Fellow Am. Assn. on Mental Deficiency; mem. NEA, Northeastern Wis., Oshkosh edn. assns., Wis. Edn. Council, Nat. Assn. Ret. Tchrs., Am., Midwestern psychol. assns., AAUW, Nat. Assn. Ret. Persons, Nat. Assn. Sch. Psychologists, Nat. Assn. Literacy Advancement, Wis. Sch. Psychologists Assn., Central Wis. Sch. Psychologists, Kappa Delta Pi, Delta Phi, Pi Lambda Theta, Delta Kappa Gamma. Clubs: Altrusa (Oshkosh). Editor: Oshkosh Boys Club Rev., 1976-77, Mental Health Memo, 1969-77. Address: 928 Wright St Oshkosh WI 54901

ILIFF, JOHN EDMUND, clergyman; b. Newark, Mar. 7, 1921; s. George Valentine and Amanda (Zapp) I.; A.B., Franklin and Marshall Coll., 1943; B.D., Lancaster Theol. Sem., 1946, S.T.M., 1975; D.D., Olivet Coll., 1976; m. Jessie Ann Wireback, Dec. 27, 1945; children—Robert, Virginia, Esther, John, Jessie. Ordained to ministry Evang. and Ref. Ch., 1945; pastor, Yukon, Pa., 1945-50; pastor 1st Conglist. Ch., Plentywood, Mont., 1950-55, Watertown, S.D., 1955-57, Boise Idaho, 1957-60, St. Peter's United Ch., Buffalo, 1960-63, 1st Conglist. Ch., Saginaw, Mich., 1963—; bd. dirs. Idaho Conglist. Conf.; bd. dirs., chmn. personnel com. Mich. Congl. Conf.; penal chaplain's adv. com. Mich. Youth com. Buffalo YMCA. Pres. Greater Buffalo Literacy Council, Ada County Mental Health Assn.; pres. bd. dirs. Ada County Mental Health Center; bd. dirs. Idaho Mental Health Assn.; pres. bd. dirs. Saginaw County Info. Center on Alcoholism; dir. Pilgrim Cove Youth Camp; mem. Saginaw Housing Commn. Mem. Saginaw, Buffalo chambers commerce, Saginaw Council Chs. (v.p.), Saginaw Ministerial Assn. (pres.), Council Chs. Buffalo and Erie County (dir., chmn. bd. dirs. social service dept.), Ada County Ministerium (sec.), Wilderness Soc., Nat. Wildlife Fedn., The Remnant, Saginaw Minsterial Assn. (sec.-treas.). Clubs: Masons, Shriners. Contbr. articles to newspapers and religious periodicals. Home: 4125 Studor Dr Saginaw MI 48601 Office: 412 Hayden St Saginaw MI 48607

ILLMER, RUTH (MRS. NORMAN ROUSSEAU), educator; b. Festus, Mo., May 31, 1918; d. Joseph B. and Bertha (Martin) Landau; A.A., Flat River Jr. Coll., 1937; B.A., U. Mo., Kansas City, 1959, M.A., 1966, Ph.D., 1974; m. Herman Illmer, Aug. 25, 1937; children—Charles Richard, Paula Jane (Mrs. Clyde J. West). Elementary tchr. Seemel Sch., Jefferson County, Mo., 1937-38; kindergarten tchr. Porter Sch., Prairie Village, Kans., 1959-64, mem. curriculum com., 1960-62, grade level chmn., 1963-64; teaching fellow U. Mo., Kansas City, 1964-66, instr. elementary edn., 1966-68; lectr. elementary edn., 1966-68; elementary counselor, Grandview, Mo., 1966-68, ednl. cons., 1968-70; ednl. cons. hearing and speech dept. Menorah Med. Center, 1970-72; ednl. cons., dir. Ruth Illmer Assos., 1972—; chmn. dept. edn. Park Coll., Kansas City, Mo., 1974—. Project dir. Title VI Project, Implementation of Comprehensive Ednl. Program for Children with Learning Disabilities; program chmn. Greater Kansas City Nursery Edn. Council, 1968—. Mem. alumni bd. dirs. U. Mo. Life mem. Prairie Village P.T.A. Mem. AAUW (past chmn.), Sch. Edn. Alumni Assn. (pres.), Mo. Assn. for Edn. Young Children (past sec.), Assn. for Children With Learning Disabilities (mem. profl. adv. bd. Kansas City council), Am. Sch. Counselor Assn., NEA, Mo. Tchrs. Assn., Am. Personnel and Guidance Assn., Profl. Counselors Assn., Assn. for Childhood Edn. Internat., Am. Psychol. Assn., Council Exceptional Children, Orton Soc. (mem. bd.). Unitarian. Author: (with Jack Katz) Auditory Problems in Children with Learning Disabilities; No Longer Ignored, Evaluation Diagnosis and Educational Planning for Children with Learning Disabilities. Home: 9671 Reeder Overland Park KS 66214

IMARISIO, JOHN JOSEPH, physician; b. N.Y.C., Sept. 8, 1922; s. Daniel and Ida (Ferrando) I.; A.B., N.Y. U., 1944, M.D., 1950; m. Aili T. Leppanen, Feb. 19, 1955. Intern, Rochester (N.Y.) Gen. Hosp., 1950-51; med. resident Buffalo Gen. Hosp., 1951-52; sr. resident internal medicine State U. N.Y. Service of Kings County Hosp., 1954-56; research fellow biophysics Sloan Kettering Inst., N.Y.C., 1956, also Med. fellow Meml. Hosp., N.Y.C., 1956; individual practice internal medicine, Manhattan, N.Y., 1957-59, also attending physician St. Clare's, Misericordia hosps., N.Y.C.; asst. chief, radioisotope service Hines Hosp., Chgo., 1959-63, also instr. medicine Stritch Coll. Medicine, Chgo.; chief, radioisotope service Cin. VA Hosp., 1963-71; also asst. prof. Cin. Coll. Medicine, until 1971; chief nuclear medicine service Lakeside VA Hosp., Chgo., 1971—; asst. prof. medicine and radiology Northwestern Med. Sch., Chgo., 1971—; dir. nuclear medicine Gottlieb Meml. Hosp., Melrose Park, Ill., 1976—. Served with AUS, 1943-44, 1952-53. Decorated Bronze Star medal. Diplomate Am. Bd. Nuclear Medicine. Mem. AMA, AAUP, N.Y. Acad. Scis., Soc. Nuclear Medicine, Central Soc. Clin. Research, Am. Coll. Nuclear Physicians. Roman Catholic. Contbr. articles to profl. jours. Researcher in med. field; co-inventor radioisotopic constantly monitored perfusion dialysis device; originator in vitro steadystate system for study red cell metabolism. Home: 210 E Pearson Chicago IL 60611 Office: VA Lakeside Hosp 333 E Huron Chicago IL 60611

IMHOF, ANTON B., logging contractor; b. International Falls, Minn., Nov. 12, 1927; s. Otto B. and Mary (Weiss) I.; grad. high sch.; m. Zelah C. Popejoy, June 23, 1951; children—Lynn Anthony, JoAnn Marie, Michael Lee, William Otto. Partner, Otto Imhof & Son, Logging Contractors, Littlefork, Minn., 1951-68, owner Anton Imhof Logging Contractor, 1968—. Mem. Sch. Bd. Littlefork, 1965—. Served with USNR, 1945-47. Mem. Am. Legion. Roman Catholic. Club: K.C. Address: Box 50 Rural Route 1 Littlefork MN 56653

IMHOFF, HAROLD DAVID, cons. engr., land surveyor; b. Eureka, Ill., Apr. 26, 1909; s. Chris D. and Rosa (Barrett) I.; B.S., U. Ill., 1931; m. Lucile Birky, Oct. 25, 1945; children—Rosemary Lucile (Mrs. Rick Law), Richard Birky, Robert Barrett. Civil engr., Woodford County, Ill., 1931-39; county supt. hwys., Eureka, 1939-75; cons. engr., land surveyor, 1975—. Mem. Tau Beta Pi, Sigma Tau, Chi Epsilon, Sigma Epsilon. Home: Box 197 Rural Route 1 Eureka IL 61530

IMHOFF, ROBERT JAY, coll. adminstr.; b. Lakeview, Mich., June 20, 1949; s. Carl A. and Freda B. (Bard) I.; B.A., Spring Arbor Coll., 1972; M.A., Mich. State U., 1975, postgrad., 1977—; m. Jacqueline Faye Mercer, Sept. 2, 1972; 1 dau., Kristin Andrea. Youth guidance dir. Victorious Christian Youth Assn., Flint, Mich., 1972-73; resident dir., instr. Spring Arbor (Mich.) Coll., 1974-75; asst. soccer coach Mich. State U., East Lansing, 1974-75; dir. student devel., head soccer coach John Wesley Coll., Owosso, Mich., 1975—, dean of students, 1976—. Active Gilbert and Sullivan Operetta Co., 1968-71, Youth for Christ Internat., 1972-73. Mem. Nat. Assn. Student Personnel Adminstrs., Am. Personnel and Guidance Assn., Am. Coll. Personnel Assn., Nat. Soccer Coaches Assn., Nat. Assn. Intercollegiate Athletics Coaches Assn., Mich. United Conservation Assn. Home and office: 1020 S Washington St Owosso MI 48867

IMLAY, WILLIAM ELMER, design engr.; b. Lincoln, Nebr., Jan. 7, 1928; s. William H. and Clara (Ullstrom) I.; B.B.A., U. Nebr. at Lincoln, 1951; m. Ethel Irene Hayden, Sept. 24, 1953; children—Elizabeth Ann (Mrs. John W. Wood), Donald M. Salesman, Standard Oil Co. of Ind., Omaha and Grand Island, Nebr., 1953-58; design engr., sec. Benjamin & Assos., Inc., Grand Island, 1958—, also dir. Served with AUS, 1951-53. Licensed city st. and county hwy. supt., certified waste water plant and water works plant operator, Nebr. Mem. Engrs. Club Grand Island (pres. 1968-69), Water Pollution Control Assn., Nat. Water Well Assn. Republican. Methodist. Clubs: Wood River Country, Eagles. Home: 3015 Gladstone Circle Grand Island NE 68801 Office: PO Box 339 Grand Island NE 68801

IMMEL, WILLIAM RAYMOND, accountant; b. Columbus, Ohio, Jan. 30, 1926; s. Raymond Frederick and Helen Barbara (Dietlin) I.; B.S., Franklin U., 1963; m. Mary Katherine Bower, Nov. 23, 1949; children—Gregory, Karen. Payroll clk. Comml. Motor Freight, Columbus, 1948; asst. controller Atlas Linen Supply, Columbus, 1948-61; pvt. practice pub. accounting, Columbus, 1961—; pres. Established Shoe Data, Inc., Columbus, 1972; chmn. bd., sec.-treas. Typog. Press, Inc. Bd. dirs. Fairview Meml. Park. Served with AUS, 1945-47. C.P.A., Ohio. Mem. Pub. Accountants Soc. Roman Catholic. Clubs: Columbus Maennerchor, Shamrock, Sertoma. Home: 68 Amazon Pl Columbus OH 43214 Office: 3526 N High St Columbus OH 43214

IMRIE, WALTER CURTIS, mfg. co. exec.; b. West Newton, Mass., Sept. 18, 1921; s. Gordon MacDonald and Elsie (Smith) I.; B.S., U. R.I., 1944; M.A., Am. U., 1949; m. Mary McIntosh Brookings, July 11, 1945; children—Walter Curtis, John Brookings (dec.), Gordon MacDonald II. With Pan Am. World Airways, Washington, 1946-50; economist CAB, 1951-53; market research Lockheed Aircraft Corp., Marietta, Ga., 1954-63; pres. J.E. Porter Co., Ottawa, Ill., 1964—. Served with USAAF, 1942-45. Clubs: Wings (N.Y.C.); University (Chgo.). Home: 209 Oak Brook Rd Oak Brook IL 60521 Office: 110 N Wacker Dr Chicago IL 60606

INALCIK, HALIL, historian; b. Istanbul, Turkey, May 26, 1916; s. Seyit Osman and Bahriye I.; came to U.S., 1972; Ph.D., U. Ankara, 1942; m. Sevkiye, Jan. 18, 1945; 1 dau., Günhan. Prof. history U. Ankara, 1943-72; prof. Ottoman history U. Chgo., 1972—; vis. prof. Turkish history Columbia U., 1953-54, Princeton U., 1967-68; co-chmn. 1st Internat. Congress on Social and Econ. History of Turkey, 1977. Pres. Internat. Assn. S.E. European Assn., 1972-75. Served with Turkish Army, 1943-46. Rockefeller Found. fellow, 1956; Social Sci. Research fellow, 1975. Fellow Royal Asiatic Soc. (Eng.) (hon.); mem. Am., Turkish, Royal (corr. mem.) hist. socs., Am. Oriental Soc., Am. Acad. Polit. and Social Sci. Author: Tanzimat Reforms and the Bulgarian Question, 1943; Studies on the Reign of Mehmed the Conqueror, 1954; The Ottoman Empire in the Classical Age 1300-1600, 1973. Co-editor: Archivum Ottomanicum, 1969—. Home: 5000 East End Ave Chicago IL 60615 Office: 1130 E 59th St Chicago IL 60637

INCANDELA, JOSEPH ROBERT, elec. co. exec.; b. Chgo., May 28, 1926; s. Joseph C. and Angeline (Micile) I.; student Chgo. Tech. Coll., U. Ill.; m. Rose B. Grippo, Sept. 8, 1948; children—Cathleen, Rebecca, Deborah, Joseph. Estimator, supr. Bern Electric Co., Chgo., 1949-63; pres. New United, Inc., Streamwood, Ill., 1963—. Served with USN, 1944-48, 1952. Mem. Nat. Elec. Contractors Assn. Roman Catholic. Club: Columbian. Home: Box 357 Wayne IL 60184 Office: 1544 Burgundy Pkwy Streamwood IL 60103

INDENBAUM, SAMUEL, physician; b. Detroit, Oct. 5, 1931; s. Meyer and Minnie (Bernstein) I.; B.S. in Chemistry, Wayne State U., 1951, M.D., 1956; m. Valerie Latt, June 24, 1956; children—Michael, Sarah, Amy, Rebecca. Intern, Detroit Recieveing Hosp., 1956-57; resident Mayo Clinic, Rochester, Minn., 1959-63; practice medicine specializing in rheumatology, 1963—; chief of rhematology Woodland, Med. Group, Detroit, 1973—; asst. prof. medicine Wayne State U., 1960—; co-chief div. rheumatology Sinai Hosp., Detroit, 1976—; attending physician Rehab. Inst. Detroit, 1965—. Served with USN, 1957-59. Diplomate Am. Bd. Internal Medicine. Mem. Am. Rheumatism Assn., AMA, Mich., Wayne County med. socs., Am. Congress Rehab. Medicine, Mich. Rheumatism Soc., Pan-Am. Med. Assn., Phi Beta Kappa, Alpha Omega Alpha. Home: 30133 Ponds View Franklin MI 48025 Office: 14800 W Mc Nichols Detroit MI 48235

INGALLINERA, ALBERT JOSEPH, advt. promotions co. exec.; b. Bklyn., May 21, 1947; s. Salvatore J. and Carole M. (Alberti) I.; B.A. in Psychology and Econs., St. John's U., 1970; postgrad N.Y. U.; m. Patricia Brown, May 3, 1968; children—Albert, David. Sales engr. Computer Ribbon Corp., N.Y.C., 1970-71; mktg. rep. Penn Mut., Phila., 1971-74; asst. dir. advt. Dart Industries, Los Angeles, 1974-76; account exec. Mead Digital Systems, Schaumburg, Ill., 1976—; cons. in field. Chmn. fed. title one program Ill. Dept. Edn., 1977. Mem. Direct Mail Mktg. Assn., Midwest Direct Mail Assn., Mpls. Mktg. Assn, Kans. Mail Mktg. Assn. Home: 2016 Farnham Ct Schaumburg IL 60194 Office: 870 E Higgins Rd Schaumburg IL 60195

INGERSLEW, NEILL DENNIS, printing co. exec.; b. Kirksville, Mo., Oct. 6, 1934; s. John P. and Lissa (Madsen) I.; B.S. in Edn., U. Mo., 1958; m. Shirley Ann Bareis, Oct. 8, 1954; children—John, Susan, Cheryl, Nancy. With Western Pub. Co., Hannibal, Mo., 1956—, sales engr., 1964-65, preparatory supt., 1965-67, prodn. mgr., 1967-69, mgr. Data Page div., St. Charles, Mo., 1969-77; v.p., mgr. Lincoln (Nebr.) ops. Metromail, 1977—. Bd. dirs. Hannibal YMCA, 1960—. Republican. Lutheran. Mason (32 deg.), Shriners, Moose. Home: 404 Lincoln St Seward NE 68434 Office: 901 W Bond St Lincoln NE 68521

INGLEFIELD, HOWARD GIBBS, educator, musician; b. Pitts., June 13, 1937; s. Paul Donaldson and Bonita Noss (Gibb) I.; Mus.B., Eastman Sch. Music, U. Rochester, 1959, M.A., 1960; Ph.D., Ohio State U., 1968; m. Suzanne Ogden, Dec. 28, 1959; children—Cynthia Ann, Sylvia Lynn. Instr., Kent (Ohio) State U., 1960-63; teaching asso. music Ohio State U., Columbus, 1963-66; prof. music U. Wis.-Whitewater, 1966—. Mem. Akron (Ohio) Symphony Orch., 1960-63, Columbus Symphony Orch., 1963-66, Milw. Symph. Orch., 1966-69, Waukesha (Wis.) Symphony Orch., 1970-75. Mem. Music Educators Nat. Conf., Wis. Music Educators Conf., Am. Fedn. Musicians, Phi Mu Alpha. Office: Center of Arts U Wis-Whitewater WI 53190

INGMIRE, DAVID BAKER, engr.; b. Saratoga Springs, N.Y., Mar. 3, 1948; s. Haskell Walworth and Mary Elaine (Blackwood) I.; B.S.C.E., Clarkson, Coll., Tech., 1973; m. Mollie Ann Hammond, June 16, 1967; children—David Baker, Christina Hammond. Engring. technician N.Y. State Dept. Transportation, Albany, 1967-69; quality control engr. Asthon Ready Mix, Saratoga Springs, N.Y., 1969-72; project mgr. Law Engring. Testing Co., Detroit, 1973-77; quality control engr., project civil engr., Enrico Fermi II Project Daniel Internat., Monroe, Mich., 1977—. Mem. Am. Concrete Inst., ASCE, Engring. Soc. Detroit. Roman Catholic. Home: 24466 Old Orchard Novi MI 48050 Office: PO Box 1096 Monroe MI 48161

INGRAM, GEORGE ERNEST, data processing cons.; b. Harrisburg, Oreg., Oct. 14, 1925; s. Carl Ernest and Luella Bell (Hall) I.; B.S., Roosevelt U., 1970-73; m. Adelaide Henrietta Erlandson, Oct. 7, 1961; step-children—Larry Dean Messner, Patricia Ann Gutierrez. Sr. staff analyst Chgo. & Northwestern Ry., 1968-72; supr. systems and planning The Austin Co., Des Plaines, Ill., 1972-73; v.p. Algoristic Inc., Barrington, Ill., 1973-75; pres. chmn. bd. Dichotomy, Inc., Wheaton, Ill., 1975—; dir. Algoristics, Inc.; lectr. in field. Mem. Am. Soc. Tool Engrs., Am. Inst. Indsl. Engrs., Data Processing Mgmt. Assn., Pi Sigma Epsilon. Address: 26W482 National Ave Wheaton IL 60187

INGRAM, KENNETH LLOYD, consumer electronics mfg. co. exec.; b. Niles, Mich., Apr. 20, 1928; s. Raymond Gordon and Glennah M. (Lawrence) I.; student DePauw U., 1946-50, U. Colo., 1950; m. Betty Kathryn Neff, June 17, 1950; children—Pamela Sue, Bruce Neff, Scott Lloyd. With Selmer div. Magnovox, Elkhart, Ind., 1952-74, sales promotion mgr., 1961-63, gen. sales mgr., 1963-64, v.p., dir. mktg. and sales, 1964-74; v.p., corp. officer, dir. sales and mktg. Magnavox Consumer Electronics Co., Fort Wayne, Ind., 1975—. Pres. Jr. Achievement Elkhart County, 1972—, bd. dirs., 1970—. Mem. Nat. Assn. Band Instrument Mfrs. (v.p. 1969-70, dir. 1969-72), Music Industry Council (pres. 1974—), Am. Music Conf. (dir. 1970—), C. of C. (dir. 1971—, v.p. 1972). Presbyterian (elder 1962—). Clubs: Masons, Shriners, Rotary (pres. 1974). Home: 4801 Orchard Green Pl Fort Wayne IN 46804

INLOW, DAVID RONALD, food services adminstr.; b. Cheyenne, Wyo., Mar. 18, 1943; s. Gail Maurice and Joanne Francis (Currie) I.; B.A., No. Ill. U., 1965, M.S., 1972; m. Beverly Jean Walden, June 20, 1964; children—Deborah Sue, Robert John, Jennifer Lynn. Food service unit mgr. No. Ill. U., DeKalb, 1965-69, staff asst. to dir., 1969-72; dir. univ. food services Valparaiso (Ind.) U., 1972—; instr. applied food service sanitation Porter County Bd. Health. Bd. dirs. Porter County Vis. Nurses Assn., 1975-77, Porter County Meals on Wheels, Valparaiso U. Credit Union; pres. DeKalb Jaycees, 1970-71. Recipient Distinguished Service award Vis. Nurses Assn.; certified in applied food service sanitation. Mem. Nat., Ind. restaurant assns., Am. Personnel and Guidance Assn., Nat. Assn. Coll. and Univ. Food Services (regional pres.), Vocat. Guidance Assn. Congregationalist. Club: Rotary (dir. 1975-77). Home: 1004 Illinois St Valparaiso IN 46383

INMAN, ROGER JAMES, TV exec.; b. Fort Campbell, Ky., Nov. 14, 1946; s. Lloyd J. and Katherine (Ropiequet) I.; B.A., U. Ill., 1968, M.S., 1975; m. Jonnae Marie Gaston, Jan. 27, 1968; 1 son, Jeffrey Lloyd. Producer, dir. ITV, U. Ill., Urbana, 1975—. Served with USN, 1969-73. Mem. Nat. Assn. Ednl. Broadcasters (state membership coordinator), Kappa Tau Alpha. Home: 907 Country Squire St Urbana IL 61801 Office: 302 Goodwin St N Urbana IL 61801

INNIS, ROBERT WILLIAM, educator; b. Alden, Mich., Oct. 23, 1919; s. William James and Neila (Black) I.; B.S., Central Mich. Coll., 1942; M.S., Stout State U., 1948; Ed.D., Mich. State U., 1956; m. Evangeline Scheffler, June 1, 1946; children—Patricia Ann, Nela Rose. Tchr. rural schs., Kalkasa County, Mich., 1937-40; supt. schs. Williamsburg, Mich., 1946-51; asso. prof. indsl. edn. Bowling Green (Ohio) State U., 1960—. Served to lt. col. USAF, 1942-46, 51-58. Mem. Am. Indsl. Arts Assn., Epsilon Pi Tau, Pi Delta Kappa. Mason (32 deg.). Contbr. articles to profl. jours. Home: 307 Haskins St Bowling Green OH 43402

INSELBERG, EDGAR, plant physiologist; b. Athens, Greece, June 15, 1930; s. Valentin and Louise (Sarfati) I.; B.S., Cornell U., 1953; M.S., U. Ill., 1954, Ph.D., 1956; m. Rachel Medrano Marzan, Aug. 12, 1956. Came to U.S. 1948, naturalized 1963; dir. research Na-Churs Plant Food Co., 1956-61; research asso. U. Pitts., 1961-63, NASA postdoctoral fellow, 1963-65; sr. scientist Volcani Inst., Rehovot, Israel, 1965-66; asso. prof. dept. biology Western Mich. U., Kalamazoo, 1966—. Cons., 1961—. Mem. Am. Soc. Plant Physiologists, Am. Inst. Biol. Scis., Am. Soc. Photobiology, Am. Soc. Agronomy. Research: physiology of ear shoot devel. in corn, radioactive tracer methodology, statistics of radioassay, photosynthesis. Jewish. Address: Biology Dept Western Mich U Kalamazoo MI 49008

INY, GEORGE SALIM, retail co. exec.; b. Teheran, Iran, Sept. 18, 1933; s. Salim J. and Daisy Farah (Djedda) I.; came to U.S., 1948, naturalized, 1959; B.S. in Indsl. Engring., Johns Hopkins U., 1955; B.S. in Bus. Mgmt., U. Balt., 1957; m. Karen Louise Teeven, Dec. 3, 1976. Credit unit mgr. Standard Oil Co., Chgo., 1959-66; asst. v.p. First Nat. Bank of Chgo., 1966-72; sr. v.p. ops. Olympic Savs. & Loan Assn., Chgo., 1974-76; corp. credit mgr. Madigan Bros., Inc., River Forest, Ill., 1972-74, v.p., chief fin. officer, 1976—; guest lectr. Am. Mgmt. Assn., 1971, Morton Coll., 1974-76, Chgo. Midwest Credit Mgmt. Assn. Mem. Internat. Consumer Credit Assn., Nat. Assn. of Credit and Fin. Mgmt., Nat. Retail Mchts. Assn., Chgo. Retail Fin. Execs. Assn. Clubs: Order Eastern Star, Masons. Office: 7440 W Central River Forest IL 60305

IORGULESCU, JORGE, chem. co. exec.; b. Buenos Aires, Argentina, July 12, 1935; s. Nicolas and Ida (Mayer) I.; student La Plata Indsl. Sch. (Argentina), 1948-53; Chem. Engr., La Plata U., 1959; program mgmt. devel. Harvard Bus. Sch., 1970; m. Beatriz E. Cobenas, July 24, 1964; children—Bernardo, Lionel, Andrew. Nylon plant engr. du Pont de Nemours, Ducilo, Berazategui, Argentina, 1959-60, process control chief, 1960; with Liquid Carbonic Argentina Sociedad Anonima Indsl. Coml., Buenos Aires, 1960-67, tech. mgr., 1964-67; prodn. and engring. mgr. Liquid Carbonic Corp. Internat. div., Chgo., 1967-70, v.p. ops., 1970—; dir. Liquid Carbonic Mexico, Sociedad Anonima, Gases Industriales, Sociedad Anonima, Argentina, Liquid Carbonic Venezolana, Liquid Carbonic Argentina, Mitsui Toatsu Liquid Carbonic, Inc., Japan, C.A.F.S.A., Argentina, Alpha Acrux, S.A., Argentina, Liquid Carbonic W. Indies Ltd., Trinidad, others. Cubmaster asst. Boy Scouts Am.; certified swimming ofcl. AAU. Mem. Am. Mgmt. Assn., Am. Inst. Chem. Engrs., Harvard Bus. Sch. Alumni, Council of Ams., Assoc. Harvard Alumni. Home: 504 S Garfield St Hinsdale IL 60521 Office: 135 S LaSalle St Chicago IL 60603

IPES, THOMAS PETER, JR., minister, marriage and family counselor; b. Paterson, N.J., Feb. 25, 1948; s. Thomas Peter and Ruth Lydia (Kroncke) I.; B.A., Columbia Union Coll., Takoma Park, Md., 1970; M.Div., Andrews U., Berrien Springs, Mich., 1973; D.Min., Lancaster (Pa.) Theol. Sem., 1977; m. Mary Anne Simmons, Aug. 16, 1970; children—Christine Marie, Melinda Joy. Ordained to ministry Seventh-Day Adventists Ch., 1972; pastor chs., Pa., 1972-74, Colo., 1974-76; exec. dir. Christian Counseling and Ednl. Center, Newburgh, Ind., 1976—; mem. faculty U. Western Ky.; pres. Ind. Assn. for Couples of Marriage Enrichment; dir., Trustee Nat. Alliance for Family Life, Inc.; speaker on psychology and Bible daily radio program. Mem. Am. Assn. Marriage and Family Counselors, Christian Assn. Marriage Counselors, Am. Assn. Clin. Counselors, Christian Assn. Psychol. Studies, Nat. Assn. Christian Marriage and Family Counselors, Western Assn. Christians for Psychol. Studies, Am. Assn. Sex Educators, Counselors, and Therapists, Assn. for Humanistic Psychology, Nat. Council on Family Relations, Am. Personnel and Guidance Assn., Christian Med. Soc. Author: The Minister and His Library, 1972; Marriage and Family Counseling in the Christian Church, 1977; contbr. articles to profl. jours. Home: Rural Route 6 Box 224 Concord Dr Newburgh IN 47630 Office: 3918 1st Ave Evansville IN 47710

IPINA, JORGE MARIO, state ofcl.; b. Sucre, Bolivia, Jan. 27, 1940; s. Domingo and Rosa Teolinda (Melgar) I.; B.A., Dominican Coll., 1966; M.A., U. Notre Dame, 1968; M.B.A., Western Mich. U., 1974, M.P.A., 1977. With Wolverine World Wide, Inc., Rockford, Mich., 1968-77, market research analyst, 1969-72, mgr. internal mktg. systems, 1972-74, mktg. research mgr., 1974-77; bus. and econ. affairs specialist Office Intergovtl. Relations, Mich. Dept. Mgmt. and Budget, Lansing, 1976—, mgr. research and data standardization unit, 1977—. AID Leadership grantee, 1965. Mem. Am. Mktg. Assn. (dir. chpt. 1971, treas. 1972, sec. chpt. 1973), Am. Econ. Assn., Nat. Assn. Accountants, Municipal Fin. Officers Assn., Inst. Mgmt. Accounting, Am. Footwear Industries Assn. (statis. com. 1974-75, mgmt. scis. com. 1975-76). Home: 228 N Chestnut St Lansing MI 48933 Office: Lewis Cass Bldg Lansing MI 48909

IQBAL, ZAFAR, biochemist, neurochemist; b. Lucknow, India, July 12, 1946; s. Shujaat Ali and Saleha (Begum) Siddiqui; came to U.S., 1972; B.S., Lucknow U., 1961, M.S., 1963, certificate proficiency in French, 1965; Ph.D., All India Inst. Med. Scis., New Delhi, 1971; m. Bernida Lucile Jasiewicz, Nov. 27, 1974. Jr. research fellow Council Sci. and Indsl. Research, India, 1963-66, research fellow, 1967-68; research scholar Directorate Gen. Health Services, India, 1966-67; asst. research officer Indian Council Med. Research, 1968-71; research asso. in physiology, investigator Ind. U. Sch. Medicine, Indpls., 1972—; asst. prof. med. biophysics, 1977—. NIH research grantee, 1973-77, Muscular Dystrophy Assn. Am. research grantee, 1975-77. Mem. Internat. Brain Research Orgn., Internat. Soc. Neurochemistry, Soc. Neurosci., Am. Soc. Neurochemistry, AAAS, Ind., N.Y. acads. scis., Sigma Xi. Contbg. author: Macromolecules in Storage and Transfer of Biological Information, 1969; Macromolecules and Behavior, 1972; Growth and Development of the Brain, 1975; contbr. articles to profl. jours. Home: 8511 N College Ave Indianapolis IN 46240 Office: Physiology Dept Ind U Med Center Indianapolis IN 46202

IRONS, LESTER, lawyer; b. nr. Sullivan, Ind., May 14, 1908; s. Francis F. and Susie (McBride) I.; A.B., Ind. State U., 1929; J.D., U. Mich., 1935; m. Lucy M. Carmony, June 16, 1935; children—David Lester, Martha Jane (Mrs. Kenneth MacKenzie) Admitted to Mo. bar, 1936; mem. legal dept. Gen. Am. Life Ins. Co., 1935-38; gen. practice law, Evansville, Ind., 1938-40; mem. legal dept. Shell Oil Co., St. Louis and N.Y.C. 1940-46; partner Barnes, Hickam, Pantzer & Boyd, Indpls., 1946—. Dir. Lacy Diversified Industries, Inc., Indpls. Mem. nat. council Camp Fire Girls, 1959; mem. bd. dirs. United Fund Greater Indpls. Pres. Ind. Inter-church Center Corp.; chmn., trustee Methodist Hosp., Ind. Central Coll. Recipient Luther Gulick Nat. Camp Fire award, 1961; named Meth. Man of Yr., Indpls. Dist., 1954. Mem. Am., Ind., Indpls. bar assns., Ch. Fedn. Greater Indpls. (pres. 1961-63). Republican. Methodist (lay del. Ind. Conf.). Kiwanian. Home: 8403 Overlook Pkwy Indianapolis IN 46240 Office: Merchants Bank Bldg Indianapolis IN 46204

IRVIN, GERALDINE HALL, psychologist; b. Cambridge, Ohio, Jan. 14, 1925; d. Paul Clark and Elizabeth (Ewers) Hall; B.S., in Edn., Ohio State U., 1945; M.S. in Edn., U. Akron, 1968, Ph.D., 1974; m. William Fay Irvin, Dec. 25, 1948; children—William Paul, James Alan. Tchr., Westerville (Ohio) High Sch., 1945-46; sch. psychologist Kent (Ohio) City Schs., 1969—; instr. part-time U. Akron (Ohio), 1974—; pvt. practice psychology, Akron, 1971—. Certified sch. psychologist, Ohio, licensed psychologist, Ohio. Mem. Nat. Assn. for Women Deans, Adminstrs. and Counselors, Nat. Assn. Sch. Psychologists, Ohio Sch. Psychologists Assn., Am. Personnel and Guidance Assn., Witan (pres. 1966), Phi Delta Kappa, Delta Kappa Gamma. Republican. Lutheran. Home: 2873 Cedar Hill Rd Cuyahoga Falls OH 44223 Office: 321 N DePeyster St Kent OH 44240

IRVIN, KENNETH PAUL mfg. co. exec.; b. Brookville, Pa., Dec. 18, 1933; s. Kenneth Albert and Nellie Beatrice (Davis) I.; B.S. in Bus. Adminstrn., Pa. State U., 1960; m. Katherine Elizabeth Parker, Oct. 22, 1965; children—Elizabeth Anne, Jeanette Kara, Thomas Paul. Salesman gasket div. Armstrong Cork Co., Detroit, 1960-65, mktg. rep., Chgo., 1966-72, indsl. exec. mktg. rep. Milw., 1972—. Chmn. fin., stewardship Brookfield (Wis.) United Methodist Ch.; active Boy Scouts Am. Served with USN, 1952-56. Mem. Soc. Automotive Engrs. Republican. Clubs: Brookfield Tennis, Moorland Tennis, United Meth. Mens. Home and Office 17865 Continental Dr Brookfield WI 53005

IRVINE, JACK DEAN, mfr's. agt.; b. Emporia, Kans., Dec. 28, 1925; s. Alex and Emma Bethia (Piper) I.; B.S.E.E., Iowa State U., 1950; m. Lila Lee Brewer, Feb. 14, 1948; children—Linda Lee, Jack Alex. Installer, Western Electric Co., Iowa area, 1948-50; engr., chief engr. Foxbilt, Inc., Des Moines, 1950-54; dist. mgr. Hydro-Air, Inc., Iowa-Nebr. area, 1955-56; sales mgr., dir. sales, mktg. mgr. Bruning Co., Lincoln, Nebr., 1957-62; pres. dir. Irvine Assos., Inc., W. Des Moines, 1962—; charter mem. Nat. Bur. Standards Advisory Com.; cons. sales and mgmt. Republican. Home: 1900 Prospect Ave West Des Moines IA 50265 Office: 936 8th St West Des Moines IA 50265

IRWIN, GEORGE EARLE, JR., radiologist; b. Kankakee, Ill., Mar. 24, 1919; s. George Earle and Ruth (McBroom) I.; B.S., Northwestern U., 1940, M.S., 1943, M.D., 1944; m. Marguerite Imle, Sept. 19, 1942; children—Patricia McConnell, George Stephen, Janet Johnson. Intern, Evanston (Ill.) Hosp., 1943; resident Wesley Meml. Hosp., Chgo., 1945-48; chief dept. radiology Brokaw Hosp., Normal, Ill., 1948—; attending radiologist Mennonite Hosp., Bloomington, 1948—, St. Joseph Hosp., 1948—; clin. asso. U. Ill. Coll. Medicine, 1973—; dir. Nat. Bank of Bloomington, 1971—; active McLean County Health Dept. Served with AUS, 1944-46. Fellow Am. Coll. Radiology; mem. Radiol. Soc. N. Am., Ill. Radiol. Soc., AMA, Phi Beta Kappa, Alpha Omega Alpha. Presbyterian. Club: Bloomington Country. Home: 44 Sunset Rd Bloomington IL 61701 Office: 703 N East St Bloomington IL 61701

IRWIN, JOHN THOMAS, vocat. guidance counselor; b. Kewanee, Ill., July 31, 1939; s. Edward William and Rosemary (Zeglis) I.; B.A., U. Notre Dame, 1961; M.S. in Edn., No. Ill. U., 1964. Tchr. lang. arts Salt Creek Sch. Dist., Villa Park, Ill., 1961-63; counselor, spl. edn. coordinator Central Community Unit Schs., Burlington, Ill., 1963-77; vocat. guidance coordinator Mid-Valley Area Vocat. Center, Maple Park, Ill., 1977—; mem. Kane County (Ill.) Spl. Edn. Adv. Com. Mem. Am., Ill., Central edn. assns., Am., Ill. personnel and guidance assns., Nat., Ill. vocat. guidance assns., Phi Delta Kappa. Roman Catholic. Home: Box 54 Burlington IL 60109 Office: Mid-Valley Area Vocat Center Maple Park IL 60151

IRWIN, WILLIAM KENNETH, ins. co. exec.; b. Springfield, Ill., Mar. 22, 1925; s. William S. and Ruth (Clark) I.; student Springfield Jr. Coll., 1943, 46, James Millikin U., 1952-53; m. Rosemary McCarthy, Dec. 28, 1950; children—Kathleen, Nancy, Guy, Jane, Julie, John, Rene. Gen. agt. United Home Life Ins. Co., Decatur, Ill., 1951-55; regional sales dir. Franklin Life Ins. Co., Springfield, 1955-58; br. mgr. Gt.-W. Life Assurance Co., Davenport, Ia., 1958-60; pres. Life Securities Ia., Inc., Davenport, 1960—, Financial Security Life Ins. Co., Moline, Ill., 1968—; gen. mgr. Regency Life Ins. Co., Springfield, 1967-70; v.p., sec. Regency Nat. Ltd., 1970—; v.p. Security State Bank, Bettendorf, Ia., 1965-67. Bd. dirs., v.p. Friends of Art. Served with AAC, 1943-46; PTO. Decorated Bronze Star. C.L.U. Mem. Nat. Assn. Life Underwriters, Am. Soc. C.L.U.'s, Internat. Assn. Fin. Counsellors, Internat. Platform Assn., Am. Soc. Pension Actuaries (asso.), Roman Catholic. Clubs: Union League (Chgo.); Univ., Athletic (Iowa City). Home: 935 26th Ave Moline IL 61265 Office: 716 17th St Moline IL 61265

IRWIN, WILLIAM WINSOR, furniture co. exec.; b. Grand Rapids, Mich., Sept. 19, 1910; s. Earle Stephen and Charlotte E. (Neahr) I.; A.B., Princeton U., 1932; m. Mary Louise Huggett, Oct. 18, 1941; children—John Winsor, Earle Stephen II, Mary Elizabeth. Pres. Irwin Seating Co., Grand Rapids, Mich., 1945—, Furniture Mfrs. Warehouse Co., Grand Rapids, 1960—. Bd. dirs. Union Bank & Trust. Bd. trustees Butterworth Hosp., 1963—, pres., 1969—; bd. dirs. Grand Rapids Met. YMCA, 1958-68, pres., 1964-68. Mem. Employers Assn. Grand Rapids (pres. 1969-75), Phi Beta Kappa. Clubs: Kent Country, University (Grand Rapids). Home: 3890 Lake Dr SE Grand Rapids MI 49506 Office: PO Box 2429 Grand Rapids MI 49501

ISAAC, MARGRETHE GLORIA, educator; b. Chgo., May 6, 1927; d. Merle J. and Margrethe D. (Lehmann) Isaac; B.Ed., Chgo. Tchrs. Coll., 1947; M.A., Northwestern U., 1950, Ph.D., 1962. Tchr. Chgo. Pub. Schs., 1947-58; instr. TV Tchrs. Coll., WGN-TV, Chgo., 1958-59; asst. prof. Chgo. Tchrs. Coll., 1959-61; asso. prof. Northeastern Ill. U., Chgo., 1961—, asso. chmn. dept. early childhood edn., 1968-71, 73—. Vis. faculty Northwestern U., summer 1964. Mem. exec. com. Elementary Sch. sect. Nat. Safety Council, 1972—, vice-chmn., 1975-76, chmn., 1976-77, bd. dirs., 1977—, Outstanding Service award, 1977; book reviewer Ill. Reading Service, 1971—. Mem. Chgo. Pub. Schs. Kindergarten-Primary Assn. (pres. 1954-56), Ill. Edn. Assn. (pres. Chgo. div. 1964-65), Ill. Assn. Higher Edn. (pres. 1968-69), Assn. Childhood Edn. Internat., (chmn. various coms. 1954—, v.p. Chgo. area br. 1973-77), NEA, AAUP, AAUW, Alpha Delta Kappa (pres. Ill. Alpha Epsilon chpt. 1957-59, Ill. rec. sec. 1964-66), Pi Lambda Theta (rec. sec. Alpha Zeta chpt. 1965-67, pres. Chgo. area chpt. 1977—), Delta Kappa Gamma, Phi Delta Kappa. Research on profl. problems of beginning tchrs. Home: 700 Victoria Rd Des Plaines IL 60016 Office: Dept Early Childhood Edn Northeastern Ill U Bryn Mawr at St Louis Ave Chicago IL 60625

ISAACS, GERALD LOUIS, EDP adminstr.; b. St. Paul, June 25, 1947; s. Gerald Dewitt and Otellia Ida (Horbach) I.; B.S. in Math., U. Minn., 1969; M.S. in Computer Sci., U. Iowa, 1973; m. Linda Kay Berg, Aug. 24, 1974; children—Joey Allen, Roberta Ann, Robert Paul, Gerald Louis, Nicole Lee. Programmer, 3M Co., St. Paul, 1968-69; programmer software devel. Collins Radio Co., Cedar Rapids, Iowa, 1969-72; programmer analyst Am. Coll. Testing, Iowa City, 1972-73; leader systems devel. project U. Iowa, Iowa City, 1973—; computer and statis cons. Conduit, Westinghouse Learning Corp. Author publs. in computer sci. Home: 707 Iowa St Hills IA 52235 Office: 352 LCM St Iowa City IA 52242

ISAACS, KENNETH S(IDNEY), psychoanalyst, educator; b. Mpls., Apr. 7, 1920; s. Mark William and Sophia (Rau) I.; B.A., U. Minn. 1944; Ph.D., U. Chgo., 1956; postgrad. Inst. Psychoanalysis, 1957-63; m. Ruth Elizabeth Johnson, Feb. 21, 1950 (dec. 1967); m. 2d, Adele Rella Bodroghy, May 17, 1969; children—Jonathan, James; step-children—John, Curtis, Peter and Edward Meissner. Intern, Worcester (Mass.) State Hosp., 1947-48; trainee VA Hosp., Chgo., 1948-50; chief psychologist-outpatient clinic system Ill. Dept. Pub. Welfare, 1949-56; research asso. (asso. prof.) U. Ill. Med. Sch., Chgo., 1956-63; practice psychoanalysis, Evanston, Ill., 1960—; supr. psychiat. residency program Evanston Hosp., Northwestern U., 1972—. Cons. schs., hosps., clinics, pvt. practitioners. Served with AUS, 1943-45; ETO. Mem. Am. Psychol. Assn., AAAS, Chgo. Psychoanalytic Soc., N.Y. Acad. Sci., Sigma Xi. Contbr. articles to profl. publs. Home: 144 Woodstock St Kenilworth IL 60043 Office: 636 Church St Evanston IL 60201

ISAACS, S. TED, chem. engr.; b. Louisville, July 13, 1914; s. Max and Rose (Kaplan) I.; Chem.E., U. Cin., 1936, A.A., 1945; m. Ann Fabe, June 7, 1939; children—Marjorie Jane Susan Lynn. Chem. engr. Standard Oil Co. (Ohio), Latona, Ky., 1936-41; chief instrument engr. Wright Aero. Corp., Cin., 1941-45; sr. process engr. Drackett Co., Cin., 1945-48; pres. The Isaacs Co., Cin., 1948—; v.p. sales Indsl. Engring. Corp., Louisville, 1951-54, pres., 1959-61. Mem. Zero Population Growth; chmn. energy subcom., mem. solid waste subcom. Cin. Environ. Task Force, 1972-73; chmn. energy com. Cin. Environ. Adv. Council, 1976-77; mem. Scientists' Inst. for Pub. Info. Energy Com. Registered profl. engr., Ohio; sr. fluid power technician Inst. for Certification Engring. Technicians. Mem. Engring. Soc. Cin. (life; mem. transp. and energy coms.), Instrument Soc. Am. (sr.), Fluid Power Soc., Fluid Power Distbrs. Assn. (mem. admissions com.), Am. Soc. Technion-Israel (dir. Cin. chpt.), Metric Assn. (v.p. 1967-68), Ohio Environmental Council, Friends of Earth, Environ. Action, Fedn. Am. Scientists, Nat. Intervenors, Sierra Club, Nat., Ohio assns. ry. passengers, Zionist Orgn. Am. (life). Mem. B'nai B'rith. Author articles in profl. jours., also monthly column for Agent and Representative mag., 1964-68. Home: 8080 Springvalley Dr Cincinnati OH 45236 Office: 1840 Amberlawn Dr Cincinnati OH 45237

ISAACSON, BARRY JOEL, corp. exec.; b. Chgo., Apr. 16, 1948; s. William M. and Dorothy (Schlinsky) I.; A.B. in History, U. Ill., 1970, M.A. in Social Studies, 1977. Founder, pres. Atty. Aid Assos., Chgo., 1972—; cons. Mass. Mut. Life In Ins. Co.; developer, instr. course for legal assts., Chgo. city colls. Arbitrator, Better Bus. Bur. Jewish. Home: 2216 N Sedgwick St Chicago IL 60614 Office: 1 E Wacker Dr Chicago IL 60601

ISAACSON, MAX DELMAR, oil co. exec.; b. Madrid, Iowa, May 26, 1932; s. David Richard and Delia Gertrude (Groves) I.; B.A., Drake U., 1954, postgrad., 1977—; m. Elizabeth Ann Fenton, June 19, 1954; children—Scott Lee, Susan Beth, Steven Glen, Stuart David. Reporter, Des Moines Register, 1953-54; editor Drake Times-Delphic, Des Moines, 1953-54; publicist Nat. Speedways, Inc., Des Moines, 1954; subscription fulfillment mgr. Look Mag., Des Moines, 1957-71; adminstrv. v.p. and pub. relations dir. Macmillan Oil Co., Inc., Des Moines, 1971—, also dir. Trustee, Community Blood Bank Central Iowa, 1976—. Served with USAF, 1954-57. Mem. Toastmasters Internat. (Hall of Fame award 1976). Methodist. Clubs: Spiritual Frontiers. Home: 5515 SW 48th Ave Des Moines IA 50321 Office: 4306 2d Ave Box 4968 Des Moines IA 50306

ISELY, CHRISTIAN ROBERT, III, film producer; b. Kilbourn, Wis., Apr. 10, 1917; s. Christian Robert and Myrtle Crossfield I.; B.A., Lawrence Coll., 1938; m. Ruth V. Perry, Feb. 2, 1941; children—Barbara (Mrs. Richard Dedo), Christian Robert IV, Elizabeth (Mrs. Neil Ferrari), Susan, Jeffrey. Photographer, Central Film Service, Chgo., 1939-40; photographer Pilot Prodns., Chgo., 1941-51, producer, 1952-57, pres., Evanston, Ill., 1958—, chmn. bd., 1958—. Served to 1st lt. Transp. Corps, AUS, 1943-44; PTO. Mem. Chgo. Audio-Visual Assn. (dir. 1974—), Tennaqua Tennis Club (pres. 1958-59), Bannockburn Tennis Club. Home: 1230 Elmwood Pl Deerfield IL 60015 Office: Pilot Prodns 1819 Ridge Ave Evanston IL 60201

ISHLER, RICHARD EVES, educator; b. Bellefonte, Pa., Mar. 14, 1934; s. John William and Bessie F. (Eves) I.; B.S., Lock Haven State Coll., 1957; M.Ed., Pa. State U., 1960, Ed.D., 1965; m. Margaret A. Fisher, Dec. 27, 1956; children—Frederick, Theodore. Tchr., Marion Central Sch. (N.Y.), 1957-59; speech therapist York County (Pa.) Schs., 1959-61; elementary prin., Red Lion, Pa., 1961-64; prof. edn., asso. dean U. Toledo, 1965—. Vice-pres. Camp Storer Bd. Mgrs., 1970—. Served with AUS, 1953-55. Mem. Assn. Tchr. Educators (chmn. communications com. 1973—, mem. exec. bd. 1976—), Ohio Assn. Colls. Tchr. Edn. (pres. 1974-75). Author: Creating the Open Classroom: A Handbook for Teachers, 1974; First Steps to the Open Classroom in the Church, 1974. Contbr. articles to profl. jours. Home: 6920 Fredericksburg Dr Sylvania OH 43560 Office: 2801 W Bancroft St Toledo OH 43606

ISQUITH, ALAN JAY, microbiologist; b. Bklyn., Feb. 27, 1936; s. John Henry and Dorothea Margarette (Irish) I.; B.S., Tufts U., 1959; M.S., U. N.H., 1961; Ph.D., Hahnemann Med. Coll., 1966; m. Vivian Judith LaFrance, May 14, 1955; children—Laurel M., Peter K., Matthew A. Microbiologist, U.S. FDA, Washington, 1961-62; group leader microbiology Dow Corning Corp., Midland, Mich., 1968-73, sr. group leader microbiology, 1973-74, sr. group leader health and environ. services, 1974—. World Health Research fellow Johns Hopkins, 1962-63; NIH postdoctoral fellow Temple U. Sch. Medicine, Phila., 1966-68. Mem. Am. Soc. Microbiology, Soc. Indsl. Microbiologists, Am. Assn. Lab. Animal Care, ASTM, Am. Assn. Textile Colorists and Chemists, Sigma Xi. Contbr. articles to profl. publs. Researcher membrane transport, microbial physiology treponemes, NAD biosynthesis, microbiology organosilicones. Patentee in field. Home: 1591 Beth Ann Ct Route 12 Midland MI 48640 Office: CO 3101 Dow Corning Corp 2200 W Salzburg Rd Midland MI 48640

ISRAEL, GEORGE PETZINGER, ins., real estate exec.; b. Eldon, Iowa, Mar. 27, 1927; s. Charles Samuel and Iva Antonette (Petzinger) I.; ed. high sch.; m. Madelyn Lucille Henderson, Nov. 21, 1950; children—Charles Richard, David Lawrence. Farmer, Eldon, 1944—; ins. claims adjuster Underwriters Adjusting Co., Ottumwa, Iowa, 1956-57; owner Finney Ins. Agy., Eldon, 1958—, Israel Real Estate, Eldon, 1968—; sec., treas. Eldon Elevator, Inc., 1967—. Mem. Wapello County Bd. Adjustment, 1969—, chmn., 1972; sec. Wapello County Bd. Rev., 1971—; chmn. Wapello County Soil Conservation Dist., 1970—. Bd. dirs. Wapello County Agrl. Fair Assn. Served with AUS, 1951-52. Mem. S.E. Iowa Bd. Realtors (pres. 1973), Wapello County Farm Bur., Farmers Union, Assn. Ind. Ins. Agts., Iowa Mut. Ins. Agts. Assn. Baptist. Democrat. Mason. Home: RFD 1 Eldon IA 52554 Office: Box 548 Eldon IA 52554

ISSARI, MOHAMMAD ALI, film producer and dir.; b. Esfahan, Iran, Aug. 13, 1924; s. Abbas Bek and Qamar (Soltan) I.; B.A., U. Tehran (Iran), 1963; M.A., U. Calif., Los Angeles, 1968; postgrad. U. So. Calif., Los Angeles, 1969; m. Joan Gura Aamodt, 1953; children—Scheherazade, Katayoun, Roxana. Films officer Brit. Embassy, Brit. Council Joint Film Div., Tehran, 1944-50; asst. motion picture officer USIS, 1950-65; cons. to various Iranian Govt. ministries on film and TV developments, 1950—; ofcl. chief cameraman to Shah of Iran, 1956-65; prof. cinema and coll. communication arts Mich. State U., East Lansing, 1969—, also dir. instructional film and multimedia prodn. Instructional Media Center, 1969—; producer over 1500 ednl., instructional and documentary films, 1956—; free lance film reporter Telenews, UPI, Iran, 1959-61; film adviser to Iranian Oil Operating Cos. in Iran, 1963-65; spl. cons. on edn. and instructional TV, Saudi Arabian Ministry of Info., 1972; project dir., exec. producer Iran Film Series, 1974—; dir. film prodn. workshops Cranbrook Inst., Detroit, 1973-74; tchr. Persian lang. Iran—Am. Soc., Tehran, 1949-59. Founder, exec. sec. Youth Orgn. of Iran, 1951-52; v.p. Rugby Football Fedn., Iran, 1952-53, pres., 1954-55. Recipient Cine Golden Eagle award, 1975, Meritorious Honor award USIA, 1965, Order of Cavalieres, Italy, 1958, Order of Oranje Nassau, Queen Juliana of Holland, 1959, Orders of Kooshesh and Pas, HIM Shah of Iran, 1959, Order of Esteghlal, King Hussein of Jordan, 1960, Order of Sancti Silvestri Papae, Pope John 23rd, 1959. Mem. Anglo-Iranian Dramatic Soc. (dir. 1943-50), Mich. Film Assn. (co-founder 1972, dir. 1972-73), Nat. Assn. Ednl. Broadcasters, Soc. Motion Picture and TV Engrs., Assn. Ednl. Communication and Tech., Acad. Polit. Sci., Assn. Multi-Image, Delta Kappa Alpha. Author: (with Doris Paul) A Picture of Persia, 1977; contbr. articles on ednl. communication and audi-visual instruction to periodicals and profl. jours.; introduced audio-visual edn. in Iran, 1951; established first film festivals in Iran. Home: 4454 Seneca Dr Okemos MI 48864 Office: Instructional Media Center Mich State U East Lansing MI 48824

ITO, JUN, chemist; b. Tokyo, Sept. 25, 1926; s. Tei-ichi and Fumi (Ohki) I.; came to U.S., 1955; M.S., U. Tokyo, 1953, D.Sc., 1962; m. Jean Alice Rogers, May 26, 1971; children—Kenneth, Elliot, John Paul. Instr., U. Tokyo, 1953-55; analytical chemist Harvard U., Cambridge, Mass., 1955-60, research asso., 1965-67, 68-74; lectr. U. Tokyo, 1961-63; chemist Nat. Bur. Standards, Gaithersburg, Md., 1967-68; chemist U. Chgo., 1974-76, sr. research asso., 1977—; cons. Nat. Bur. Standards, Washington, 1968-69, Japan Geol. Survey, 1961-62. Recipient Superior Performance award Nat. Bur. Standards, 1968. Fellow Am. Mineral. Soc., Mineral. Soc. Japan; mem. Am. Chem. Soc., Geophys. Union, Am. Ceramic Soc., Geochem. Soc., Chem. Soc. Japan. Home: 6011 S Ingleside Ave Chicago IL 60637 Office: James Franck Inst U Chgo 5640 Ellis Ave Chicago IL 60637

ITTNER, SCOTT BURRILL, artist; b. St. Louis, Oct. 15, 1901; s. Benjamin F. and Louise (Gundelach) I.; student U. Ill., 1920, Washington U., St. Louis, 1924, 60. One man shows St. Louis Central Pub. Library, 1965, 66, 68, Harmon Galleries, 1972, 78, Mo. Bot. (Shaw's) Garden, 1976, Tower Grove Bank, 1976, all St. Louis; exhibited in group shows Bertrand Russell Meml., London, Eng., Internat. Art Show, N.Y.C., 1970, Robert Paul Gallery, Chgo., 1971, El Paso Tex. Art Mus., 1977, various others; represented in permanent collection Richardson Meml. Library, St. Louis Art Mus.; mem. staff various advt. firms, 1925-55, asso. Glee R. Stocker & Assos., 1945-55. Mem. Friends St. Louis Art Museum, Friends Mo. Bot. (Shaw's) Garden, Sigma Chi. Home: 4067 Magnolia Pl St Louis MO 63110

ITURRALDE, GEORGE, psychiatrist; b. Azul, Argentina, Aug. 7, 1921; s. Cándido Rómulo and Maria Luisa Blanco de Iturralde; came to U.S., 1953, naturalized, 1959; Physician, U. Buenos Aires, 1949, postgrad., 1949-53; m. Maria Angelica Ruiz Mingo, Feb. 18, 1954; 1 son, John Edward. Intern, Zubizarreta City Hosp., Argentina, 1948-50; instr. phys. diagnosis U. Hosp., Buenos Aires, 1949-53; asst. physician Northampton (Mass.) State Hosp., 1954-55; intern Engelwood Hosp., Chgo., 1955-56; resident in psychiatry Washington U., St. Louis, 1956-58; resident in hosp. adminstrn. Neurol. Hosp. Assn., Kansas City, Mo., 1958-59; resident in psychiatry VA Hosp., Kansas City, 1960, staff psychiatrist, 1960-61; pvt. practice medicine specializing in psychiatry and neurology, Prairie Village, Kans., 1960—; fellow in psychiatry U. Kans., 1960-61. Home: 6914 Blue Jacket St Shawnee KS 66203 Office: 7501 Mission Rd Prairie Village KS 66208

IVERSON, DAVID LYNN, ins. co. exec.; b. Vermillion, S.D., Apr. 4, 1948; s. Glenn Lund and Lila Mae (Swanson) I.; B.S., U. S.D., 1970; postgrad. George Washington U., 1971; m. Linda Kay Fisher, Dec. 29, 1967; children—Rachelle Tamara, Meggan Maree, Elyssa Aubrey. Asst. dir. systems services Nat. Blue Shield Assn. Chgo., 1972-77; mgr. ops. support, gov. programs CNA Ins. Co., Chgo., 1977—. Pres. Parent Tchr. Orgn., 1977-78. Served with U.S. Army, 1970-72. Decorated Army Commendation medal. Mem. Health Ins. Assn. Am. Republican. Home: 5569 Arlington Dr Hanover Park IL 60103 Office: CNA Plaza 14-S Chicago IL 60685

IVY, CONWAY GAYLE, elec. products co. exec.; b. Houston, July 8, 1941; s. John Smith and Caro (Gayle) I.; student U. Chgo., 1959-62; B.S. in Natural Scis., Shimer Coll., 1964; postgrad. U. Tex., 1964-65; M.B.A., U. Chgo., 1968, M.A. in Econs., 1972, postgrad. 1972-74; m. Diane Ellen Cole, May 25, 1973; 1 son, Brice McPherson. Geol. asst. John S. Ivy, Houston, 1965-72; securities analyst Halsey Stuart & Co. and successor Bache & Co., Chgo., 1973-74, Winmill Securities Inc., Chgo., 1974; econ. and fin. cons., Chgo., 1974-75; dir. of corporate planning Gould Inc., Rolling Meadows, Ill., 1975—. Mem. Am. Econs. Assn., Phi Gamma Delta. Republican. Author of numerous analytical reports for brokerage industry. Home: 204 Elm Rd Barrington IL 60010 Office: 10 Gould Center Rolling Meadows IL 60008

IZZO, BERNARD PETER, educator; b. Rochester, N.Y., Mar. 21, 1924; s. Joseph Anthony and Assunta (Presutti) I.; Mus.B., Heidelberg Coll., 1948; Mus.M., Am. Conservatory Music, 1949; postgrad. Ariz. State U., 1971; m. Jean Marie Platt, Aug. 20, 1949; children—Thomas Joseph, James Peter, Catherine Sue, John Michael, Patrick Bernard. Instr., Am. Conservatory Music, Chgo., 1949-56, Loras Coll., Dubuque, Ia., 1956-57; asso. prof. N. Central Coll., Naperville, Ill., 1961—; artist mem. Chgo. Lyric Opera, 1956—. Artist mem. Cin. Summer Opera, 1967, 68; solo artist Community Concerts N.Y., 1952-71. Served with AUS, 1943-46. Mem. Am. Fedn. Mus. Artists, A.F.T.R.A., Nat. Assn. Tchrs. Singing, AAUP, Am. Guild Mus. Artists. Roman Catholic. Home: OS 660 Kirk Ave Elmhurst IL 60126 Office: N Central Coll Naperville IL 60540

JABLONSKI, LUCIAN STANLEY, physician; b. Toledo, July 20, 1920; s. Anthoni and Helena Josephine (Nowak) J.; B.S., U. Toledo, 1939; Dr. Osteopathy, Kirksville Coll. Osteo. Medicine, 1942; children—Wanda Marie (Mrs. Terry Hatmaker), Helena Angeline. Intern, Research Hosp., Kansas City, Mo., 1942-43; resident Parkview Hosp., Toledo, 1952-57; practiced medicine, specializing in internal medicine, Toledo, 1955—; chmn. dept. internal medicine Parkview Hosp., 1962—. Sch. physician Dupont High Sch., Bradner High Sch., Lake High Sch., Clay High Sch., Start High Sch., Toledo, 1947—; chmn. dept. sports medicine Ohio AAU, 1965—; pres. physician World Wrestling Championships, 1962, 66, 73, 75. Bd. dirs. NW Ohio Heart Assn., 1976—. Recipient Educator of Year award Parkview Hosp., 1973-74, Meritorious Service award Fedn. Internat. Lutte Amateur, 1962, Gold Key award Amateur Hall of Fame, 1968, Meritorious certificate U.S. Olympic Com., 1960, World Cup, 1973, Soul City Dedicated Service award, Toledo, 1970, Letter of Appreciation, Japanese Army, 1965, Distinguished Service award Japan Gen. Seiichi Yoshie, 1966, Comdrs. Cross, Legion of Merit Fedn. Internationale Des Luttes Amateur, 1976; also 3 certificates of distinction AAU of U.S. Mason (Shriner). Home and office: 1925 Parkwood Av Toledo OH 43624

JACK, DAROLD J., lawyer; b. Cedar Rapids, Iowa, July 28, 1917; s. Edward Darold and Viola Lucille (Mann) J.; B.A., U. Iowa, 1939, J.D., 1941; m. Emily Joanne Robertson, June 14, 1947; children—James Edward, Stephanie Joanne (Mrs. David Scott Hill), Jennifer Mary. Admitted to Iowa bar, 1941, U.S. Supreme Ct., 1976; mem. firms Lundy, Butler & Lundy, Eldora, Iowa, 1941-48, Darold J. Jack, Oelwein, Iowa, 1948—; city atty. Oelwein, 1973—. Mem. Supreme Ct. Grievance Commn., 1974—. Republican committeeman Oelwein 1st Ward, 1960—. Served with USAAF, 1943-46. Mem. Iowa State (mem. bd. govs. 1963-67), 13th Jud. Dist. (pres. 1966-69) bar assns. Clubs: Masons, Elks, Rotary, Glenhaven Country (bd. chmn. 1971). Home: 511 N Frederick Oelwein IA 50662 Office: 8 E Charles St Oelwein IA 50662

JACKLIN, WILLIAM THOMAS, county ofcl., educator; b. Chgo., Dec. 26, 1940; s. Robert Theodore and Florence Carrie (Dombrow) J.; B.S., Roosevelt U., 1967; M.S. in Bus., Ind. U., 1968; m. Bonnie Joy Windquist. Vice pres. Du Page Corp., Lombard, Ill., 1970-73; instr. bus., Coll. Du Page, Glen Ellyn, Ill., 1969—, Elgin (Ill.) Community Coll., 1975—. Chief dep. auditor DuPage County, 1973, county auditor, 1973—. Mem. Ill. Prairie Path; mem. DuPage County Republican Central Com.; treas. Highland Hills Assn., 1975—. Named Most Outstanding DuPage County Pub. Ofcl., Young Republicans, 1976. Mem. Inst. Internal Auditors, Nat. Assn. Accountants (asso. dir.), Am. Accounting Assn., Ill. Assn. County Auditors (sec.-treas. 1976—), Phi Delta Kappa. Christian Scientist. Mason, Rotarian. Home: 411 E 17th St Lombard IL 60148 Office: DuPage Center 421 N County Farm Rd Wheaton IL 60187

JACKMAN, HAROLD DELBERT, civil engineer; b. Columbus, Ohio, July 29, 1946; s. Lawrence Ervin and Xie Mae (Skaggs) J.; B.S. in Civil Engring., U. Cin., 1969, M.S. in Environ. Engring. (Water Pollution Control. Fedn. fellow), 1973. Civil engr. Jennings-Lawrence Co., Washington Court House, Ohio, 1969-72, dir., 1970-72, chief draftsman, head computer sect., 1972-73; pres., system designer Jackman Co., Columbus, 1973-77; computer system designer Hollander Publishing Co., Columbus, 1977—. Mem. builders exchange Columbus Edn. Com.; advisor DeMolay, Columbus, 1967-73; councilor diabetic children Unitarian Ch., 1970-76, mem. com. on single adult programs, 1975, treasurer, 1975—. Mem. ASCE. Home: 857 Bricker Blvd Columbus OH 43221 Office: 12320 Wayzata Blvd Minnetonka MN 55343

JACKMAN, HERBERT LEE, lawyer; b. Lincoln, Nebr., Dec. 29, 1928; s. Ernest Eugene and Ruth Alice (Waggoner) J.; B.S., U. Nebr., 1951, J.D., 1953; postgrad. U. Mich., Northwestern U.; m. Margaret Ann Mulvaney, Aug. 3, 1957; children—Jim, Tom, Bill, Dan, Doug. Admitted to Nebr. bar, 1953; practiced in Franklin, Neb., 1953-55, 1957-61, Grant, Nebr., 1961—; mem. firm Spence & Jackman, 1953-54; dir. Farmers Nat. Bank of Grant. City atty., Franklin, 1953-55; mayor City of Grant, 1964-66; pres. Grant Library Bd., 1971-72. Served with AUS, 1955-57. Mem. Western Nebr. (14th Jud. dist. pres. 1973—), Am., Nebr. (mem. title standards com. 1967—, chmn. title standards 1972—) bar assns. Mason. Rotarian. Republican. Methodist. Home: 305 Sherman Ave Grant NE 69140 Office: 300 Central Ave Grant NE 69140

JACKNOW, DAVID, physician; b. Highland Park, Mich., Nov. 1, 1921; s. Abraham and Fannie (Rovin) J.; student Syracuse U., 1942-43; B.S., Wayne U., 1947, M.D., 1952; m. Muriel Helmstein, June 13, 1948; children—Lisa, Amy, Alan. Research asso. Winthrop-Stearns Co., Detroit, 1947; intern Detroit Meml. Hosp., 1952-53; practice medicine specializing in indsl. medicine and occupational health, Detroit, Warren and Southfield, Mich., 1953—; asso. Detroit Indsl. Clinic, 1953—, pres. clinic group, 1970—; vice chief med. staff Detroit Meml. Hosp., 1970-75; vice chief med. staff South Macomb Hosp., 1970-75, chief med. staff, 1975—; mem. Gov.'s Safety Adv. Council, 1968-70; v.p. Med. Student's Aid Soc., 1966-72. Trustee Detroit-Macomb Hosps. Assn., 1970—. Served with USAAF, 1943-46. Fellow Am. Occupational Med. Assn., Royal Soc. Health (Eng.); mem. Am. Coll. Emergency Physicians (charter), Am. Trauma Soc. (charter), Wayne U. Med. Sch. Alumni Assn. (gov. 1971-74), AMA, Mich., Wayne County med. socs., Phi Lambda Kappa (pres. Detroit alumni club 1964-71). Club: Tam O'Shanter Country. Home: Bloomfield Hills MI 48013 Office: Northland Plaza 20755 Greenfield Rd Southfield MI 48075

JACKOWAY, MARLIN KAY, educator, counselor; b. St. Louis, May 15, 1924; s. Samuel and Sadie (Holiner) J.; B.S. in Bus. Adminstrn., Washington U., St. Louis, 1948, M.A., 1964; Ph.D., St. Louis U., 1971; m. Goldie Duhov, Sept. 1, 1947; children—Judith Lee, Marcia Gay. Tchr., Pattonville Sch. Dist., St. Louis County, Mo., 1959-60, head dept. history, 1960-63, counselor, 1963-66, guidance dir., 1966-74, dir. pupil personnel services, 1974—; asst. prof. U. Mo., St. Louis, 1972—. Served with U.S. Army, 1943-46. Decorated Bronze Star. Mem. Am. Personnel and Guidance Assn., Mo. Guidance Assn., Nat. Rehab. Assn., Am. Edn. Research Assn., Am. Vocat. Edn. Research Assn., Nat. Assn. Pupil Personnel Adminstrs. Jewish. Contbg. author: Current Concepts in Dyslexia, 1971. Home: 11105 Schuetz St St Louis MO 63141 Office: 115 Harding St Maryland Heights MO 63043

JACKSON, CARL ROBERT, obstetrician, gynecologist; b. Mpls., Jan. 8, 1928; s. Carl J. and Mildred J. (Johnson) J.; B.A., Gustavus Adolphus Coll., 1951; M.D., Jefferson Med. Coll., 1956; m. Ann Flesch, Dec. 26, 1967; children—Amy, Carrie, Tom. Intern, St. Mary's Hosp., Duluth, Minn., 1956-57; resident and postdoctoral fellow in obstetrics gynecology U. Wis., Madison, 1957-61; practice medicine specializing in obstetrics gynecology, Madison, 1961—; mem. active staff Madison Gen. Hosp., 1961—, vice chief staff, 1972-74; mem. attending staff Univ. Hosps., Madison; asst. clin. prof. obstetrics gynecology U. Wis., 1971—, mem. high risk obstet. team, 1974-75; chmn. Physicians Alliance, Dane County, Wis. Am. Cancer Soc. fellow, 1960-61; diplomate Am. Bd. Obstetrics Gynecology. Mem. Am. Coll. Obstetrics Gynecology, Central Assn. Obstetricians Gynecologists. Republican. Lutheran. Office: 20 S Park St Madison WI 53715

JACKSON, CHARLES THOMAS, librarian; b. Orient, Iowa, Feb. 26, 1915; s. Charles Thomas and Vida Elizabeth (Buchanan) J.; B.A., State U. Iowa, 1939, M.A., 1946; m. Catherine Alice Benson, Oct. 3, 1937; children—Robert Earl, Verlyn Dean. Sch. supt. Western Iowa, 1939-48; grocer, Early, Ia., 1948-62; dep. grand sec. Iowa Masons, Cedar Rapids, 1962-70, grand sec., grand librarian, 1970—. Councilman, Town of Early, 1950-52, mayor, 1952-58. Home: 298 40th St NE Cedar Rapids IA 52402 Office: 815 1st Ave E Cedar Rapids IA 52406

JACKSON, DAVID ARCHER, educator; b. N.Y.C., Apr. 29, 1942; s. Edwin George and Archer Woodward (Sims) J.; A.B., Harvard U., 1964; Ph.D., Stanford U., 1969; m. Ethel May Noland, June 17, 1966. Fellow Nat. Cystic Fibrosis Research Found., 1969-72; asst. prof. dept. microbiology U. Mich., 1972-77, asso. prof., 1977—. Mem. Am. Soc. Microbiology, Fedn. Am. Scientists. Editor: (with S.P. Stich) The Recombinant DNA Debate, 1978. Home: 301 N Revena Ann Arbor MI 48103 Office: Department of Microbiology University of Michigan Ann Arbor MI 48109

JACKSON, DAVID ARTHUR, metals co. exec.; b. Dublin, Ireland, Feb. 22, 1909 (parents Am. citizens); s. Asher and Edith (Goldwater) J.; B.S., Ill. Inst. Tech., 1937; m. Lauraine Grace Schachter, Nov. 23, 1932; children—Carol Ann Jackson Rice, Sandra Abbie Jackson Cohen, Joan Aileen. Chemist, Interstate Steel Co., 1928-30; chemist, assayer R.W. Hunt Co., Chgo., 1930-37; supt. Div. Lead Co., Chgo., 1937-39; pres. Inland Metals Refining Co., Chgo., 1939—, Lake Calumet Smelting Co., Chgo., 1939—; v.p. Ames Metal Products Co., Chgo., 1960—, Am. Chem. Services Co., Griffith, Ind., 1967—; farmer nr. South Haven, Mich., 1962—. Chem. foundry div. Chgo. Community Fund, 1941; co-chmn. metals div. United Jewish Appeal, 1948—; past treas. South Shore Temple. Registered profl. engr., Ill. Mem. Am. Inst. Mining, Metall. and Petroleum Engrs., Am. Soc. Metals, United Inventors and Scientists Am., Mich. Blueberry Growers Assn. Club: B'nai Brith. Patentee. Home: 2608 N Lakeview St Chicago IL 60614 Office: 651 E 119th St Chicago IL 60628

JACKSON, DON MERRILL, lawyer; b. Kansas City, Mo., Oct. 24, 1913; s. Merrill Marion and Vera (Long) J.; student Harvard U., 1930-31; J.D., U. Mo. at Kansas City, 1936; m. Henrietta J. Boese, Sept. 2, 1933 (dec.); children—Don Merrill, Martha Jackson Layton, Janet Jackson Houghton; m. 2d, Caryle Jean Martin, Nov. 22, 1956. Admitted to Mo. bar, 1936, Mass. bar, 1941; practice law, Kansas City, Mo., 1936—; partner firm Jackson & Sherman, Kansas City, 1961—; mem. Jud. Commn. Clay County (Mo.), 1973-76. City councilman Kansas City, 1951-59; chmn. Kansas City Personnel Bd., 1964-65, Kansas City Plan Commn., 1965-70, Citizens Assn. Kansas City, 1949-50. Served as lt. USNR, 1943-46, 50-51. Fellow Am. Coll. Trial Lawyers, Internat. Acad. Trial Lawyers (dir. 1967-73, 76—), Internat. Soc. Barristers; mem. Am. (chmn. sect. ins., negligence and compensation law 1971-72, sect. del. 1973—), Kansas City, Clay County, Mo., Internat. bar assns., Am. Soc. Hosp. Attys. Clubs: Kansas City, Liberty Hills Country. Contbg. author to textbook: Trials, 1967—. Home: 4620 NE 48th Terr Kansas City MO 64119 Office: 800 Home Savs Bldg Kansas City MO 64106

JACKSON, DOUGLAS NORTHROP, psychologist, educator; b. Merrick, N.Y., Aug. 14, 1929; s. Douglas Northrop and Caya (Cramer) J.; B.Sc., Cornell U., 1951; M.Sc., Purdue U., 1952, Ph.D., 1955; m. Lorraine Jean Morlock, July 28, 1962; children—Douglas Northrop III, Diana, Charles Theodore VI. Research psychologist Menninger Found., Topeka, 1952-53, postdoctoral fellow, 1955-56; clin. psychologist intern U.S. VA, 1951-52, 53-55; asst. prof. psychology Pa. State U., University Park, 1956-61, asso. prof., 1961-64; vis. asso. prof. psychology Stanford U., 1962-64; sr. prof. psychology U. Western Ont., London, 1964—; cons. Ednl. Testing Service, Princeton, N.J., 1958-64, vis. scholar, 1971-72; cons. Research Psychologists Press, Inc., Port Huron, Mich., 1967—. USPHS research fellow, 1955-56; NIMH spl. research fellow, 1962-63, 71. Fellow Am. Psychol. Assn., Can. Psychol. Assn.; mem. Psychometric Soc., Soc. Multivariate Exptl. Psychology (pres. 1975-76), Am. Personnel and Guidance Assn., Sigma Xi. Editor: (with Samuel Messick) Problems in Human Assessment, 1967; contbr. articles to profl. jours. Home: 29 Maldon Rd London ON N6G 1W2 Canada Office: Dept Psychology U Western Ont London ON N6A 5C2 Canada

JACKSON, EDGAR BARTHOLOMEW, JR., physician, educator; b. Rison, Ark., May 30, 1935; s. Edgar Bartholomew and Willie Victoria (Scott) J.; B.A. in Chemistry, Cleve. Coll., 1962; M.D., Case Western Res. U., 1966; m. Thelma Ruth Bennett, June 15, 1957; children—Gary, David, Michael, Laura. Gen. practice internal medicine, Cleve., 19—; dir. M.I.G.H.T. Med. Group, Inc., Cleve., 1974-77; asst. prof. medicine, community health Case Western Res U. Sch. Medicine, Clevel., 1971—, asst. dean, 1971-74. Recipient Robert Devlin award, 1966; diplomate Am. Bd. Internal Medicine. Mem. Cleve. Med. Assn., Cleve. Acad. Medicine. Author: Tracking Down the Sickle Cell, 1977. Office: 2475 E 22d St Cleveland OH 44115

JACKSON, EDWARD FRANKLIN, JR., physician; b. Washington, Feb. 27, 1944; s. Edward Franklin and Hazel Janette (Pickett) J.; B.S., Ohio State U., 1964, M.D., 1968; m. Alice Carolyn Hansen, Jan. 1, 1966; children—Ruth Elaine, Rebecca Carol. Intern, then resident in internal medicine Mt. Carmel Med. Center, Columbus, Ohio, 1968-72; practice medicine specializing in internal medicine, Columbus, 1974—; dir. intensive care unit St. Anthony Hosp., Mt. Carmel East Hosp. Bd. dirs. Hunger Task Force, Columbus. Served as officer M.C., U.S. Army, 1972-74. Decorated Army Commendation medal. Mem. Am., Nat. med. assns., A.C.P., Am. Soc. Internal Medicine, Ohio and Franklin County Acad. Medicine, Alpha Phi Alpha. Baptist. Address: Hazel Pickett Bldg 1043 E Weber Rd Columbus OH 43211

JACKSON, ELMER JOSEPH, natural gas co. exec., lawyer; b. Fairmont, Nebr., Sept. 16, 1920; s. Elmer Ellsworth and Kathleen Johanna (Sullivan) J.; J.D., U. Nebr., 1947; m. Mary Elinor Booth, Sept. 1, 1943; children—Mary Kay (Mrs. Ronald Reeb), Teresa G. (Mrs. William J. Barnthouse), Cecilia A. (Mrs. Shahriar Shadlu), Jean A., Joseph E., James O., Elizabeth J. Admitted to Nebr. bar, 1947; practice of law, Lincoln, 1947-48; with Kans.-Nebr. Natural Gas Co., Inc., Hastings, Nebr., 1952—, v.p., gen. counsel, sec., 1968—, also dir. Mem. Hastings Indsl. Commn., 1966-74, chmn., 1970-74; trustee Nebr. Tax Research Council. Served to lt. col. AUS, 1942-46. Decorated Bronze Star medal, Air medal, Knight of St. Gregory. Mem. Nebr. Assn. Commerce and Industry (chmn. taxation and expenditure council 1967-76), Fed. Energy, Nebr. bar assns., Am. Judicature Soc., Phi Delta Phi. Republican. Roman Catholic (mem. parish council 1970-73). K.C. Club: Lochland Country. Home: 1303 N Briggs Hastings NE 68901 Office: Kans-Nebr Natural Gas Co Inc 300 N St Joseph St Hastings NE 68901

JACKSON, ETHEL CURRY (MRS. RAYMOND T. JACKSON), civic worker; b. Mineral Point, Wis.; d. William Jenkin and Adeline (Argall) Curry; student Northwestern U.; m. Raymond T. Jackson, Sept. 30, 1918 (dec.). Hon. fellow Harry S Truman Library Inst.; mem. U.S. Olympic Com. Mem. Cleve. Council on World Affairs, Cleve. Museum Art, Cleve. Health Mus., Cleve. Mus. Natural History, Musical Arts Assn., Garden Center of Greater Cleve., Women's Com. Cleve. Orch., Northwestern U. Alumni Assn., Cleve. Women's City Club Found., Western Res. Women's Rep. Club, Western Res. Hist. Soc. Cleve., Cleve Inst. Music, Met. Mus. Art N.Y., Friends of Cleve. Library, Friends of Cleve Zool. Soc., Holden Arboretum, Cleve. Play House (women's com.), UN Assn. U.S., Smithsonian Assos. (charter), Nat. Hist. Soc. Methodist. Republican. Clubs: Women's City, Union, Country. Home: 13901 Shaker Blvd Cleveland OH 44120

JACKSON, FREDERICK HERBERT, ednl. orgn. exec.; b. New Haven, May 16, 1919; s. Fred and Mary Elizabeth (Butler) J.; A.B., Brown U., 1941, LL.D., 1968; M.A., U. Pa., 1948, Ph.D., 1950; m. Eleanor Stearns Whittemore, May 2, 1942; children—Isabel Jackson Freeman, David Low. Instr., Marietta (Ohio) Coll., 1948-49, asst.

prof. history, 1949-50; faculty U. Ill., Urbana, 1950-55; program officer Carnegie Corp. of N.Y., N.Y.C., 1955-64; asst. exec. v.p. N.Y. U., N.Y.C., 1964-66, v.p. for humanities and social scis., 1966-67; pres. Clark U., Worcester, Mass., 1967-70; dir. Com. on Instl. Cooperation, Evanston, Ill., 1970—; dir. Stewart Systems Corp., Cambridge, Mass., Paul Revere Variable Annuity Ins. Co. Mem. Rep. Town Meeting, Westport, Conn., 1957-59, 61-67. Served to 1st lt. USAAF, 1942-46. John Hay scholar, 1937-41; Harrison fellow, 1947-48. Mem. Am. Hist. Assn., Am. Assn. Higher Edn., Common Cause (vice chmn. Ill. 1975-77), Phi Beta Kappa. Democrat. Conglist. Clubs: Century, Univ. (N.Y.C.); Cosmos (Washington); St. Botolph (Boston); Cliff Dwellers (Chgo.). Author: Simeon Eben Baldwin: Lawyer, Scholar, Statesman, 1955. Home: 1260 21st St Wilmette IL 60091 Office: 820 Davis St Evanston IL 60201

JACKSON, HARRY CALVIN, mfg. engr.; b. Centerville, Pa., Nov. 19, 1921; s. Leo Harry and Beatrice Marjorie (Bidwell) J.; student Wofford Coll., 1944, Pa. State U., 1947-49; m. Ann Frances Murphy, July 27, 1943. Machine operator Struthers Wells Iron Works, Titusville, Pa., 1941-42; tool and die apprentice Hays Mfg. Co., Erie, Pa., 1946-48; design engr. Autoclave Engrs., Inc., Erie, 1948-52; tool and die maker Kerner Tool & Die Co., Inc., Erie, 1952-54; chief engr., sales mgr. High Pressure Equipment Co., Erie, 1954-61; mktg. mgr. Nat. Forge Co., Irvine, Pa., 1962-67; chief engr. Robinson Clay Products Co., Akron, Ohio, 1968-71; plant mgr. Clow Corp., Summerville, N.J., 1971-74, mgr. mfg. engring., Westmont, Ill., 1974—; dir. High Pressure Equipment, Inc., Erie. Served with USAAF, World War II. Mem. Soc. Mfg. Engrs., Am. Welding Soc. Roman Catholic. Clubs: Elks, Moose. Home: 500 Redondo Dr Apt 307 Downers Grove IL 60515 Office: 40 Chestnut Ln Westmont IL 60559

JACKSON, HARVEY LEWIS, JR., automobile co. exec.; b. Adrian, Mich., Oct. 10, 1946; s. Harvey Lewis and Marion Elizabeth (Engelbach) J.; B.A., Adrian Coll., 1968; postgrad. Mich. State U., 1970-71, Central Mich. U., 1970-72, Eastern Mich. U., 1971-72, U. Mich., 1971-73, Siena Heights Coll., 1973-75; m. Elizabeth Ann Carey, Oct. 10, 1966; children—Amy Marie, Harvey Lewis. Phys. edn. tchr., wrestling coach Onsted (Mich.) High Sch., 1968-71, Madison High Sch., Adrian, 1971-73; athletic dir. Siena Heights Coll., Adrian, 1973-75; exec. sales-mktg. mgmt. John Underwood Chevrolet, Pontiac Olds, Inc., Clinton, Mich., 1975—. Active Boy Scouts Am.; recreation dir. Vols. in Probation, Lenawee County, 1971—; mem. Civitan Internat. Service Club, 1971—. Named Wrestling Coach of Year, Jackson Newspaper, 1970-72; Outstanding Educator of Lenawee County, Adrian Jr. C. of C., 1971-72; Outstanding Young Citizen Am., U.S. Jr. C. of C., 1973. Mem. Nat. Wrestling and Coaches Assn., AAHPER, Southeastern Women's Athletic Conf. (pres. 1974-75), NEA, Mich. Edn. Assn., Nat. Wrestling Coaches and Ofcls. Assn., Mich. High Sch. Coaches Assn., Lenawee County Athletic Assn. (sec. 1970-71), River Raisin Athletic Conf. (pres. 1972-73). Methodist. Club: Elks. Home: 331 S Scott St Adrian MI 49221 Office: Corner State Hwy US 12 and 52 Clinton MI 49236

JACKSON, J. WELDON, judge; b. Belton, Mo., Sept. 9, 1908; s. John and Stella Gertrude (O'Dell) J.; student Mo. U., 1927-28, Warrensburg State U., 1929; m. Olive Mae Herrick, Oct. 10, 1941; children—John, Judith, Linda Jo, Jerald, Janet, Jeffrey, James, Jacquelyn. Presiding judge Cass County (Mo.) County Ct., 1975—. Pres., Citizens Bank of Belton, 1962-74, chmn. bd. dirs., 1975—. Pres., Belton Bd. Edn., 1947-65; city clk., Belton, 1947-60. Trustee Belton-Mt. Pleasant United Fund; bd. dirs. Mid Am. Regional Council; trustee Little Blue Valley Sewer Dist. Served with USNR, 1942-45. Mem. Am. Legion, Cass County Hist. Soc. (v.p.). Democrat. Methodist. Home: 200 Mill St Belton MO 64012 Office: PO Box 276 Belton MO 64012

JACKSON, JOSEPH, banker, accountant, ins. co. exec.; b. Maryville, Mo., July 24, 1934; s. Joseph Ford and Helen Steele (Baker) J.; B.S., U. Mo., 1956, M.A., 1961; postgrad. U. Calif., 1960; m. Sarah Ellan McClure, Dec. 27, 1959; 1 son, Joseph Ford. Accounting instr. U. Mo., 1960-61; auditor Arthur Anderson & Co., Kansas City, Mo., 1961-63; v.p. Citizens State Bank, Maryville, Mo., 1963-66; pres. Jackson Ins. Agy., Maryville, 1966—, First Nat. Bank, Columbus, Kans., 1966—, Columbus Community Devel. Co., 1973—; Mem. advisory council S.E. Kans. Vocat. Tech. Sch., 1969—. Served to lt. USN, 1956-60, C.P.A., Kans. Mem. Beta Theta Pi, Alpha Kappa Psi. Mason (Shriner), Lion (pres. 1974-75). Home: 104 S Vermont St Columbus KS 66725 Office: PO Box 268 Columbus KS 66725

JACKSON, JOSEPH HARRISON, clergyman; b. Rudyard, Miss.; s. Henry and Emily (Johnson) J.; A.B., Jackson Coll., 1927, D.D.; B.D., Colgate Rochester Div. Sch., 1932; M.A., Creighton U., 1933; D.D., Central State Coll., Wilberforce, Ohio, 1954; LL.D., Bishon Coll., Marshall, Tex., 1956; m. Maude T. Alexander; 1 dau., Kenny. Ordained to ministry Baptist Ch.; pastor Olivet Bapt. Ch., Chgo., 1941—. Pres. Nat. Bapt. Conv., Inc., 1953—. Mem. Bapt. World Alliance (exec. com.), Nat. Council Chs. (gen. bd.). Home: 4937 Kimbark Ave Chicago IL 60615 Office: 405 E 31st St Chicago IL 60616

JACKSON, LEON CORNELL, JR., guidance counselor; b. Detroit, July 18, 1941; s. Leon Cornell and Christine Mae (Fletcher) J.; A.A., Los Angeles City Coll., 1972; B.S., Marian Coll., 1974; M.S., Ind. State U., 1976; postgrad. in ednl. mgmt. Ball State U.; children—Leatres D., Andre C., Crystal Lynn. Legal rep. Century Metalcraft Corp., Detroit, 1964-66; sales rep. Summit Labs., Inc., Indpls., 1966-68; credit mgr. Profl. Health Systems, Ann Arbor, Mich., 1968-69; sales rep. Warner-Lambert Pharm., Inc., Morris Plains, N.J., 1969-70; dir. Teen Post, Inc., Los Angeles, 1971-72; joined U.S. Army, 1968, career counselor, Indpls., 1972—; instr. Lockyear Bus. Coll., Indpls., 1976—. Certified probation officer, Ind., Mem. NAACP, Am. Personnel and Guidance Assn., Am. Rehab. Counseling Assn., Assn Non-White Concerns Personnel and Guidance, Parent-Tchrs.-Counselors Orgn. Ind. State Sch. for Deaf. Home: 4360 Winthrop Ave Indianapolis IN 46205 Office: 4881 W 38th St Indianapolis IN 46254

JACKSON, LYDIA OCTAVIA, poet; b. Grafton, N.D., Mar. 5, 1902; d. Karl Olaf and Inga (Schellstad) Svarte; student pub. schs., N.D.; m. Arthur F. Jackson, Dec. 20, 1920; 1 dau., Elizabeth Marjean (Mrs. Leonard Fagerholt). Author: Rhymes for Every Season, 1943; also numerous poems in all types of publs. Publicity chmn. Poetry Day, 1950. Treas. Grafton sch. dist. 22, 1931-61. Recipient Nat. Writers award Farmers Union Ednl. Dept., 1950; named co-asso. poet laureate of N.D., 1975. Mem. Walsh County Sch. Officers Assn. (treas. 1945-62), Midwest Fedn. Chaparral Poets (state regent 1950-51), Nat. League Am. Pen Women, Am. Poetry League, Poetry Soc. of London, Idaho Poets, Writers Guild, Am. Poets Fellowship Soc. (poet laureate 1972-73), World Poetry Day Assn. (membership chmn. N.D. and S.D. 1963—), N.D. Pen Women (compiler Peace Garden of Verses 1967), World Poetry Soc. Intercontinental, Centro Studie Scambi Internazionali (Rome) (recipient Bronze medal 1965, Silver medal 1967). Presbyn. Mem. Order of Eastern Star. Clubs: Riverside Woman's (sec. 1955-57, 59-61, v.p. 1957-59), Sigma Rho Study (v.p. 1950-52, pres., 1952-54, sec., treas., 1958—). Author: Selected Poems, 1962; Pardon My Gaff, 1965. Home: Route 2 Grafton ND 58237

JACKSON, PAUL DOUGLAS, metal co. exec.; b. Kalamazoo, June 28, 1913; s. Arthur A. and Elizabeth (Van Beck) J.; student Western Mich. U., 1931-32; m. Mary Grace Porter, Aug. 12, 1933; children—Patricia Arlene Jackson Vandenberg, Donald Paul. Foreman, gen. supt., factory mgr., v.p., exec. v.p., pres. Durametallic Corp., Kalamazoo, 1933-78, pres., chmn. bd., 1978—; pres. Durametallic Can. Ltd.; v.p., dir. Machine Products N.J.; dir. Durametallic (GmbH), Germany, Durametallic (India) Ltd. Pres. Kalamazoo County Safety Council, 1966-67; treas., trustee, vice. chmn. Kalamazoo Valley Community Coll.; bd. dirs. Jr. Achievement Kalamazoo, 1974-76. Mem. Am. Mgmt. Assn., NAM, Nat. Packaging Mfg. Assn., Kalamazoo C. of C. (past dir.). Clubs: Masons, Shriners, Elks, Kalamazoo Exchange (past pres.), Kalamazoo Execs. (dir. 1969-70). Patentee in field. Home: 5103 Savannah Ave Kalamazoo MI 49004 Office: 2104 Factory St Kalamazoo MI 49004

JACKSON, PRISCILLA THOMSON (MRS. WALTER N. JACKSON), educator, adminstr.; b. Canton, China; d. Joseph Oscar and Ethel (Ramsey) Thomson; student Oberlin Coll., 1939-42; postgrad. U. Chgo., 1942; M.A., Mich. State U., 1971; m. Walter N. Jackson, June 17, 1942; children—Jennifer Agnes Jackson Runquist, Lillian Avis, Nathan Oscar. With continuing edn. div. Oakland U., Rochester, Mich., 1960-72, inst. co-ordinator, 1961-62, instr. creative writing, also asst. dir. confs., 1962, dir. confs., 1963-68, asst. dir. Mott Center Community Affairs, 1965-68, founder and dir. Continuum Center for Women, 1965-69, asst. dean for developmental programs, 1969-72; program dir. div. mgmt. edn. Grad. Sch. Bus. Adminstrn., U. Mich., 1972-73; cons. for spl. programs Univ. Center for Adult Edn., Wayne U.-U. Mich., Detroit, 1972-74; cons. Women-in-Mgmt., 1974—; contbg. editor Washington Newsletter on Women (name changed to Women Today), 1969; originator Place-Finders Confs., 1975—; dir. Conversations Among Women, 1977—. Commr., Oakland County Bd. Social Welfare, 1960-64; mem. bd. confs., inst. sect. Nat. U. Extension Assn., 1964-68, mem. resolutions com., 1973. Recipient Creativity awards (8) Adult Edn. Assn. Mich., Nat. U. Extension Assn., Detroit br. Am. Assn. Tng. Dirs. Mem. Assn. Asian Studies, U.S. Adult Edn. Assn. (chmn. sect. on continuing edn. of women 1969-71, sec. Mich. br. 1972-73), Birmingham (Mich.) LWV (v.p. 1959-60), AAUW, Detroit Women Writers (past prose workshop chmn., founder Oakland U. Writers Conf.), Mich. Partners of Alliance with Brit. Honduras and Dominican Republic (past chmn. women's com.), Women's Econ. Club, Mich. Inter-Profl. Assn. on Marriage, Divorce and the Family. Congregationalist. Club: Village Woman's (Bloomfield Hills). Author: The Continuum Center for Women: Education, Volunteerism, Employment, 1973. Home: 201 E Kirby St Apt 1201 Detroit MI 48202 also RFD Pittsford VT 05763

JACKSON, RANDALL EPHRAIM, educator, inventor; b. Chgo., Dec. 20, 1931; s. Marion Randall and Gladys T. (Butts) J.; student Ill. Inst. Tech., 1950-53; B.S., Roosevelt U., 1962; postgrad. Northeastern Ill. U.; M.A., Governors State U., 1977; children—David, Mark. Machinist and engraver Superior Products, Chgo., 1947-52; cabinet maker J.C.W. Inc., Chgo., 1955-57; coordinator audio-visual Roosevelt U., Chgo., 1958-62, dir. depts. audio-visual and TV, 1968—; pres. Jackson Cabinet Works, Inc., Chgo., 1962-67; cons. communications. Chmn. media subcom. Chgo. Academic Library Council, 1977—. Served in U.S. Army, 1953-55. Mem. Soc. Motion Picture and TV Engrs., Nat. Acad. TV Arts and Scis., Soc. Broadcast Engrs., Assn. Ednl. and Communication Tech., Nat. Assn. Ednl. Broadcasting. Patentee fixture supporting bracket. Office: 430 S Michigan Ave Chicago IL 60605

JACKSON, RAYMOND LAVERNE, cons. engring. co. exec.; b. Kellerton, Iowa, May 2, 1935; s. Oran Stanley and Willette Belle (Smith) J.; student State U. Iowa Coll. Engring., 1953-54, Drake U., 1965-66; A.A., Centerville Community Coll., 1965; B.G.S., U. Nebr., 1972; postgrad. Salisbury State Coll., 1973—; m. Betty Ellen Johnson, June 1, 1974; children—Kaylinda Jeane, Raymond Eugene, Pamela Irene. Engring. asst. Hall Engring. Co., Centerville, Iowa, 1954-56; gas systems supr. Iowa So. Utilities Co., Centerville, 1956-66; dist. mgr. Peoples Gas div. No. Natural Gas Co., Omaha, 1966-69; mgr. program devel. Commonwealth Assos., Inc., Jackson, Mich., 1969-72; gen. mgr. Eastern Shore Gas Co., Snow Hill, Md., 1972-74; mgr. proposals CE-Crest Engring. Co., Tulsa, 1974-75; gen. mgr. Environ. Design Engring. Co., Findlay, Ohio, 1975—; engring. mgmt. cons. utility, petroleum, energy related industry. Pres., bd. dirs. Oskaloosa Musicians Assn., 1963-66; radiol. monitor State Iowa CD Adminstrn., 1966. Mem. Nat. Assn. Corrosion Engrs. (corrosion specialist 1972), ASME, Am. Gas Assn., Findlay Area C. of C. (indsl. devel. and econ. com. 1977), Engring. Soc. Detroit. Republican. Methodist. Clubs: Lions, Elks, Masons, Shriners, Knights Templar of Iowa, Shrine Clown Assn. Home: PO Box 33 1207 Glen Meadow Dr Findlay OH 45840 Office: PO Box 1026 1720 County Rd 300 Findlay OH 45840

JACKSON, REGINALD SHERMAN, pub. relations counselor; b. Newport, R.I., Dec. 25, 1910; s. Sherman Clinton and Gertrude (Miller) J.; student U. Toledo, 1929-34; m. Frances Holland, Jan. 20, 1941; 1 son, Reginald Sherman, Jr. Reporter, Toledo (Ohio) News-Bee, 1937; pub. relations dir. Ohio N.G., 1939-40; account exec. Flournoy & Gibbs, Inc., Toledo, 1945-51, 53-63, v.p., 1963-75, treas., 1967-75; pub. relations dir. Atlas Tours and Travel Service, 1975—. Vice pres., trustee Boys' Club Toledo; trustee Toledo Pub. Library, Toledo-Lucas County Pub. Library. Served from 1st lt. to lt. col. AUS, 1940-46; lt. col. USAR, 1951-60. Decorated Bronze Star with two oak leaf clusters. Mem. Res. Officers Assn. (pres. Toledo 1949), Am. Legion (Toledo post comdr. 1949), Pub. Relations Soc. Am. (pres. N.W. Ohio chpt. 1963, dir., nat. treas. 1972), Toledo Area C. of C. (trustee), Newcomen Soc. N.Am. Congregationalist. Clubs: Masons, Rotary, Toledo Country (past trustee), Toledo Press. Home: 3707 Richlawn Dr Toledo OH 43614 Office: 333 Superior St Toledo OH 43604

JACKSON, RICHARD FIELDING, chiropractor; b. Youngstown, Ohio, Apr. 5, 1914; s. Thomas Henry and Nelle (Shafer) J.; student Youngstown Coll., 1932-33; D.C., Lincoln Chiropractic Coll., 1939, M.C., 1940; D.M., Met. Coll., Cleve., 1941; m. Elizabeth Jeanne Baxter, Dec. 28, 1946; children—Richard Fielding, David Baxter, Gregory Allan, Jeffrey Duane, Kimberly Sue. Clk., Republic Steel Corp., Youngstown, 1932-34; draftsman Gen. Fireproofing Co., Youngstown, 1934-35; practice chiropractics and mechanotherapy, Youngstown, 1941-42, Painesville, Ohio, 1950-70, Edgerton, Ohio, 1971—; orchestral and radio pianist, 1932-35. Served with M.C., USNR, 1942-46. Mem. Am., Ohio State chiropractic assns., Hi Y Club, Sigma Club, Lambda Chi Beta. Republican. Club: Rotary. Home: 308 E River St Edgerton OH 43517 Office: US Route 6 W Edgerton OH 43517

JACKSON, RICHARD LEE, biochemist; b. Indpls., Oct. 8, 1932; s. Ennis Noel and Dola Lavonna (Harris) J.; B.S., Butler U., 1958, M.S., 1962; Ph.D., Ind. U., 1965; m. Ruth Alice Whitehouse, June 21, 1958; children—Joyce Elaine, Valerie Lee. Grad. asst. Butler U., Indpls., 1958-60, lectr. immunology and chemotherapy, 1967; asso. scientist Eli Lilly & Co., Indpls., 1960-62, sr. scientist, 1965-71, research scientist, 1971—. Leader, Girl Scouts Am., 1968-70. Served with USNR, 1952-56. Mem. Am., Ind. pharm. assns., Am. Diabetes Assn., Am. Soc. Neurochemistry, N.Y. Acad. Scis., Sigma Xi. Mem. Christian Ch. Clubs: Masons, K.T., Order Eastern Star. Patentee in insulin field. Home: 951 N Arlington Ave Indianapolis IN 46219 Office: Dept MC413 Eli Lilly & Co 740 S Alabama St Indianapolis IN 46206

JACKSON, ROBERT HOWARD, lawyer; b. Cleve., Dec. 12, 1936; s. Herman Herbert and Frances (Goldman) J.; A.B., U. Ill., 1958; J.D., Case Western Res. U., 1961; m. Donna Lyons, Mar. 22, 1959; children—Karen, Douglas. Admitted to Ohio bar, 1961, since practiced in Cleve.; fin. trial atty. SEC, Cleve., 1961-66; partner firm Kohrman and Jackson, 1969—; dir. Mor-Flo Industries, Inc., Budget Inns of Am., Inc., Stereodyne (Can.), Ltd.; lectr. law Case Western Res. Sch. Law, Cleve., 1967-69. Mem. Am. (chmn. subcom. proxy solicitations, shareholders proposals, fed. securities com. 1970-73), Fed. (chmn. Cleve. chpt. fed. securities com. 1972-73), Internat., Cleve. bar assns. Club: Rowfant. Contbr. articles to legal jours. Home: 3661 Traver Rd Shaker Heights OH 54122 Office: 1600 Central Nat Bank Bldg Cleveland OH 44114

JACKSON, ROBERT WILLARD, architect; b. Salina, Kans., Feb. 5, 1923; s. Solomon Willard and Florence (Woody) J.; B.S., Kans. State U., 1948; M.S., Iowa State U., 1950; m. Thelma K. Dahl, Oct. 21, 1945; children—Jane, Michael, Nancy. Instr., Iowa State U., 1948-49; project architect U.S. Corps Engrs., Kansas City, Mo., 1950-52, 55-57; architect R. W. Jackson, 1952-55; chief regional architect, hosp. facilities div., USPHS, 1957-60; pres. Robert W. Jackson Assos., Inc., 1960—. Served with AUS, 1945-47. Registered architect, 18 states. Mem. AIA, Mo. Assn. Registered Architects, Catholic, Internat., Am. hosp. assns., Beta Theta Pi. Lutheran. Rotarian. Contbr. articles in field to profl. jours.; hosp. architect. Home: 724 W Gregory Blvd Kansas City MO 64114 Office: 4218 Roanoke Rd Kansas City MO 64111

JACKSON, RODNEY NEWLAND, cyto-technologist; b. Chgo., Oct. 30, 1936; s. Raymond and Virginia (Newland) J.; student Lincoln Coll., 1955-56, Ill. Wesleyan U., 1956-57, Ill. State U., 1957, Millikin U., 1958-59; m. Charlotte Elaine Kochendorfer, May 30, 1958; children—Carol Ellen, Beth Ann. Histology technologist Springfield (Ill.) Meml. Hosp., 1959-61, chief cyto-technologist, 1961-65; chief cyto-technologist Passavant Meml. Hosp., Jacksonville, Ill., 1965—; vis. lectr. cyto-tech. and cyto-genetics Passavant Meml. Hosp. Sch. Nursing, MacMurry Coll., Ill. Coll. Bd. Govs. Passavant Meml. Hosp., 1970-73; mem. council local advisers 20th Congl. Dist.; bd. deacons 1st Presbyn. Ch., Jacksonville. Recipient U.S. Army C.E. Pub. Service award, amateur radio, 1969. Mem. Royal Soc. Health, Am. Soc. Clin. Pathologists, Am., Ill. socs. cytology, Jacksonville Area Amateur Radio Club Inc. (pres. 1968), Am. Amateur Radio Relay League (pub. service award 1969, 73). Clubs: Mason. Contbr. articles to Jour. Am. Soc. Med. Tech., 1964; numerous paper presentations Ill. Soc. Cytology, 1974-77. Home: 429 Pendik Rd Jacksonville IL 62650 Office: 1600 W Walnut St Jacksonville IL 62650

JACKSON, WADE MOSBY, assn. exec.; b. Brinkley, Ark., Jan. 30, 1916; s. Alfred Mosby and Claude Keturah (Hallum) J.; student William Jewell Coll., 1933-37, A.B., 1937; student Marquette U., 1958-61, M.B.A., 1961; m. Evelyn Westover Byrd, Jan. 18, 1942; children—Sterling Byrd, Wade Mosby, Kent Turnbull. Commd. 2d. lt. U.S. Marine Corps, 1937, advanced through grades to col., 1957; co. and bn. comdr. 3d. Marine Div., 1942-44; comdr. Inf. Troop Leaders Sch., 1944-45; asst. chief staff Fleet Marine Force, Western Pacific, 1945-47; comdr. 4th Marines, 1953-54; dir. indsl. relations Marine Corps Air Bases, 1954-57; ret., 1957; dir. corporate tng. Allis-Chalmers Mfg. Co., Milw., 1957-61; v.p. mktg. Bank of Milw. & Trust Co., Milw., 1961-64; dir. adminstrn. and planning Bendix Corp., Dayton, Ohio, 1964-71; bus. mgr. Dayton Art Inst., 1972-74; state treas., trustee Ohio Right to Life Soc. Inc., Clin., 1970—; cons. mem. Service Corps Ret. Execs.; lectr. in field. Chmn. U.S. Civil Service Security Screening Bd., 1954-57; mem. N.C. Gov.'s Safety Council, 1955-57; regional adviser SBA, 1958-61; regional del. Boy Scouts Am., 1954-63. Decorated Silver Star. Mem. Nat. Machine Tool Builders Assn., Dayton C. of C., Soc. Advancement Mgmt., Republican. Baptist. Clubs: Dayton Y Athletic, Twin Base Rod and Gun, William Jewell Coll. Century, Wright-Patterson Officers. Editor Principles and Practices of Bus. Mgmt., 1960-61. Contbr. articles to profl. publs. Home: 917 Garrison Ave Dayton OH 45429 Office: 5200 Hamilton St Cincinnati OH 45224

JACKSON, WESLEY EDMUND, veterinarian; b. Wayland, Mich., Aug. 9, 1915; s. Harrison Edmund and Grace Estelle (Gaylord) J.; D.V.M., Mich. State U., 1941; m. Martha Nagelkirk, Nov. 15, 1941; children—Donald, John, Mary Jane, Paul. Field insp. Mich. Dept. Agr., Lansing, 1941-45; pvt. practice veterinary medicine, Moline, Mich., 1945—; v.p., dir. Moline State Bank, 1966—. Mem. Am. Assn. Bovine Practitioners, Moline Bus. Men's Assn. (pres., 1967), AVMA, Mich. Veterinary Med. Assn. Mem. Christian Reformed Ch. Address: 1220 144th St Moline MI 49335

JACKSON, WILBERT, psychologist, educator; b. Birmingham, Ala., Nov. 8, 1922; s. Earl Dallas and Annie Jackson; B.E., Chgo. Tchrs. Coll., 1958, postgrad., 1962-63; M.S., Roosevelt U., 1962; postgrad. Ind. U., 1964, Colo. U., summer 1965; Ed.D., Colo. State Coll., 1968; m. Mentha Anita Bethel, Apr. 24, 1959. Tchr., counselor Chgo. Bd. Edn., 1958-68; dir. counseling center Chgo. State U., 1968-70, asso. dean students, 1970-72, asso. v.p. student affairs, 1972-75, asso. prof. psychology, 1975—. Cons. Volt Tech. Corp., 1968-69, OEO, 1968-69. Served with AUS, 1943-46; PTO. Recipient Student Services award Chgo. State U., 1972, Black Students award, 1973. Mem. Am. Psychol. Assn., Nat. Assn. Student Personnel Adminstrs., Am. Personnel and Guidance Assn., Assn. for Supervision and Curriculum Devel., Phi Delta Kappa. Club: Prairie Tennis. Home: 7141 S St Lawrence Ave Chicago IL 60619

JACOBI, H. PAUL, dentist; b. Dyersville, Iowa, Nov. 2, 1927; s. Fredrick William and Olga (Kiener) J.; D.D.S., Marquette U., 1950; m. Patricia M. Steele, Aug. 9, 1952; children—Fritz, Roger, Curt, Kathy. Gen. practice dentistry, Neenah, Wis., 1950—; internat. lectr. dental mgmt., 1960—; pres. Project P Inc., 1967—, CI-MA-Dent Internat. Ltd., 1972—; advisor Wis. State Bd. Dental Examiners, 1976—. Served to capt. U.S. Army, 1951-53. Fellow Acad. Gen. Dentistry, Royal Soc. Health (Eng.), Acad. Dentistry for Children, Soc. Clin. Hypnosis, Am. Acad. Occlusodontia (asso.); mem. ADA, Assn. Am. Dentists (dir.), Canadian-Am. Med. Dental Assn. (dir.), Acad. Dental Practice Adminstrn., Delta Sigma Delta. Republican. Roman Catholic. Clubs: Rotary, Elks, Lions (pres.). Author: A Dentist's Flight Manual to Success, 1967. Home: 448 Edgewood St Neenah WI 54956 Office: 1215 Doctors Dr Neenah WI 54956

JACOBS, ALFRED GEMIAL, dentist; b. Crystal Falls, Mich., Sept. 2, 1916; s. Abe and Nazira (Mocdece) J.; D.D.S., U. Mich., 1944; m. Phyllis Dickson, Dec. 24, 1943; children—Pamela, R. Scott, Allison. Practice dentistry, Madison, Wis., 1944—; pres. Safe-T-Gard, Madison, 1963—. Served to capt. AUS, 1944-47. Mem. Royal Soc. Health, Fedn. Dentaire Internat., Nat. Sporting Goods Assn. (asso.), ADA, Wis. State, Dane County dental socs. Clubs: Madison, Maple Bluff Country (Madison). Developer form-fitting hot water type athletic teeth protector used in contact sports; lectr. fluoride program. Home: 3428 Viburnum Dr Madison WI 53705 Office: 6911 Raywood Rd Madison WI 53713 also 2701 Marshall Ct Madison WI 53705

JACOBS, ANDREW, JR., congressman; b. Indpls., Feb. 24, 1932; s. Andrew and Joyce (Wellborn) J.; B.S., Ind. U., 1955, LL.B., 1958. Practiced law in Indpls., 1958—; mem. 89th to 92d, 94th to 95th congresses from 11th Ind. dist. Mem. Ind. Ho. of Reps., 1959. Served with inf. USMCR, 1950-52; Korea. Mem. Am. Legion, Indpls. Bar Assn. Democrat. Home: Indianapolis IN Office: Longworth Office Bldg Washington DC 20515

JACOBS, ELMER, grain exporter; b. Springfield, Ill., June 14, 1934; s. Elmer V. and Katherine (Fones) J.; B.S., U. Ill., 1959; m. Arlene L. Jordan, May 8, 1954; children—Lori, Gwen, Paul, Nan, Sam. With Continental Grain Co., 1959—, asst. mgr., Toledo, 1966-67, merchandising mgr., asst. v.p. to regional mgr., v.p., Chgo., 1967-72, v.p., gen. mgr. midwest region, 1972-76; pres. Conti Carriers subs. Continental Grain Co., 1976—; mem. Chgo. Bd. Trade. Mem. agrl. bd. dirs. Oakton Community Coll., Skokie, Ill. Served with U.S. Army, 1952-54. Mem. Nat. Grain and Feed Dealers. Clubs: Union League (Chgo.); Park Ridge Country. Home: 531 N Ashland St Park Ridge IL 60068 Office: 2700 N River Rd Des Plaines IL 60016

JACOBS, FRANCIS ALBIN, educator; b. Mpls., Feb. 23, 1918; s. Anthony and Agnes Ann (Stejskal) J.; B.S., Regis Coll., Denver, 1939; postgrad U. Denver, 1939-41; Ph.D., St. Louis U., 1949; m. Dorothy Caldwell, June 5, 1953; children—Christopher, Gregory, Paula, Margaret, John. Postdoctoral fellow Nat. Cancer Inst., Bethesda, Md., 1949-50; instr. physiol. chemistry U. Pitts. Sch. Medicine, 1951-52, asst. prof., 1952-54; asst. prof. biochemistry U. N.D. Sch. Medicine, Grand Forks, 1954-56, asso. prof., 1956-64, prof., 1964—; dir., research supr. Nat. Sci. Research Participation Program in Biochemistry, 1959-63; advisor directorate for sci. edn. NSF. Mem. Am. Soc. Biol. Chemists, Am. Inst. Nutrition, Soc. Exptl. Biology and Medicine, Am. Chem. Soc. (chmn. Red River valley sect. 1971), AAAS, N.D. Acad. Sci. (editor 1967, 68), AMA, Sigma Xi (pres. chpt. 1965-66), Alpha Sigma Nu, Phi Lambda Upsilon. Contbr. articles to profl. jours. Home: 1525 Robertson Ct Grand Forks ND 58201

JACOBS, HARRY D., JR., broadcasting co. exec.; b. Chgo., Dec. 25, 1928; s. Harry D. and Mary (Mangan) J.; B.A., DePauw U., 1951; M.B.A., U. Chgo., 1962; m. Nancy L. Witte, Sept. 10, 1955; children—Jeffrey, Mary Beth, Cheryl, Christopher. Account exec. Westinghouse Broadcasting Co., Chgo., 1960-65; sales mgr. WMAQ-radio div. NBC, Chgo., 1965-67, gen. mgr., 1967-68, gen. mgr. WMAQ-AM/FM, 1968-72; v.p. Dempsey & Co., 1972—; prin. WROE radio, Neenah, Wis., 1975—; instr. mktg. dept. Loyola U., Chgo., 1966-70. Served with CIC, AUS, 1951-53. Mem. Delta Upsilon. Club: Skokie (Ill.) Country. Home: 175 Spring Ln Winnetka IL 60093 Office: 120 S LaSalle St Chicago IL 60603

JACOBS, HERBERT FRED, tool and die shop exec.; b. Detroit, Nov. 6, 1915; s. William Anthony and Margaret Agnes J.; student pub. schs.; m. Marie Sestock, July 6, 1946. Die maker Murray Body Shop, 1933; die-leader Briggs & Chrysler Co., 1933-62; owner A&O Tool & Die Shop Detroit, 1962-68; committeeman skilled trades UAW, 1946-52, polit. action rep., 1946-52. Served with USNR, 1945-46. Mem. Amvets. Lutheran. Club: Dom Polski. Home: 4363 Barham St Detroit MI 48224

JACOBS, JAN WAYNE, ednl. adminstr.; b. Toledo, Apr. 25, 1935; s. Wayne Edward and June Ellen (Dellinger) J.; B.A. cum laude, U. Toledo, 1957; M.A., U. Mich., 1959, Ph.D., 1965; m. Norma Carolyn Beadle, Dec. 21, 1957; children—Marc Michael, Tammy Lynn. Research asst. U. Mich., Ann Arbor, 1964-65; curriculum coordinator South Reford Sch. Dist., Detroit, 1966-68, asst. supt., 1968-76, supt. schs., 1976—; lectr. Marygrove Coll., Detroit, 1971. Vis. prof. U. Vt., Burlington, 1969, U. Detroit, 1968, No. Mich. U., Marquette, 1967; instr. Schoolcraft Coll., Livonia, Mich., 1966—. Mem. Redford Twp. Occupational Adv. Council, 1968-71. Inst. Devel. Ednl. Activities fellow, 1968, NSF fellow, 1970. Mem. Mich. Assn. Supervision and Curriculum Devel. (bd. dirs. 1969-71), Wayne County Curriculum Dirs. (pres. 1969), Am. Assn. Sch. Adminstrs., Nat. Assn. Secondary Sch. Prins., Nat. Assn. Elementary Sch. Prins., Am. Ednl. Research Assn., Am. Assn. U. Profs., Phi Delta Kappa, Phi Kappa Phi. Presbyn. Home: 21151 Centerfarm Northville MI 48167 Office: 26141 Schoolcraft St Detroit MI 48239

JACOBS, JOHN WILLIAMS, systems and forms co. exec.; b. Jackson, Mich., Oct. 28, 1931; s. William Edson and Luella Fredricka (Walz) J.; A.A., Jackson Community Coll., 1951; B.S., Cleary Coll., 1953; m. Dolores Ann Paquette, Sept. 26, 1953; children—Diane, William, Andres, Julie. Cost accountant Aeroquip Corp., Jackson, 1953-54, asst. personnel dir., 1954-56; sales rep. Uarco, Inc., Jackson, 1956-64; pres. Systems & Forms Co., Inc., Jackson, 1964—. Mem. Nat. Bus. Forms Assn. (dir. 1975—; certified forms cons.). Republican. Methodist. Clubs: Lions, Jackson Country, Clarklake Yacht. Home: 1712 Ottawa Dr Jackson MI 49203 Office: 328 W Franklin St Jackson MI 49201

JACOBS, LOUIS SULLIVAN, architect; b. Chgo., June 11, 1917; s. Morris and Mary J.; B.S. in Architecture and City Planning, Armour Inst. Tech., 1940; M.S. in Indsl. Engring., Ill. Inst. Tech., 1952; Sc.D., in Safety, Ind. No. U., 1972, Ph.D. in Human Engring., 1974. Pres., Louis S. Jacobs & Assos., Chgo., 1945—; prof. archtl. engring. Loop Coll., Chgo., 1967—. Served with USN, 1942-46. Recipient Award of Merit, State of Ill. Office of Civil Def., 1957; Citation Gov. State of Ill. Office Emergency Services, 1964; Citation for Outstanding Pub. Services, Office of Pres. U.S. Emergency Resources Bd., 1967. Mem. AIA, Ill. Soc. Architects (dir. 1976-78), Ill. Soc. Profl. Engrs. (v.p. 1976-78), System Safety Soc. (pres. elect north central chpt. 1978), Nat. Soc. Profl. Engrs., Soc. Am. Registered Architects, ASCE, Western Soc. Engrs., Am. Soc. Safety Engrs., Am. Inst. Indsl. Engrs., Soc. Mfg. Engrs., Vets. Safety, Constrn. Safety Assn. Am., Mil. Order World Wars, Naval Order U.S. Office: 2605 W Pratt Blvd Chicago IL 60645

JACOBS, RAE RODNEY, surgeon, educator; b. Irondequoit, N.Y., Apr. 29, 1936; s. Darwin W. and Maybelle Irene (Smith) J.; B.A., Wheaton Coll., 1958; M.D., U. Buffalo, 1962; m. Pamela Gwin Townsend, July 5, 1975; children by previous marriage—Christopher, Gregory. Intern in surgery E.J. Meyer Meml. Hosp., Buffalo, 1962-63, resident in surgery, 1963-66, chief resident in surgery, 1966-67, Buswell fellow in surg. research, Surg. Research Lab. of E.J. Meyer Meml. Hosp. and the State U. of N.Y., Buffalo, 1967-69; resident in orthopedic surgery Eugene Talmadge Meml. Hosp. and Med. Coll. of Ga., Augusta, 1969-71, chief resident in orthopedic surgery, 1971-72; practice medicine specializing in surgery, Buffalo, 1967-69, Kansas City, Kans., 1972—; asst. clin. instr. surgery State U. N.Y. at Buffalo, 1964-66, clin. instr. surgery, 1967-69; asso. surgeon E.J. Meyer Meml. Hosp., Buffalo, 1967-69; research and edn. asso. VA Hosp., Augusta, 1971-72; attending surgeon Kans. U. Med. Center, Kansas City, 1972—, dir. emergency surg. service, 1972-74, chief amputee clinic, 1973—, chief problem spine clinic, 1977—; asst. prof. surgery Kans. U. Med. Center, 1972-75, asso. prof. surgery, 1975—; attending surgeon VA Hosp., Kansas City, Kans., 1974, co-chief orthopedic sect., 1975-77, chief, 1977—. United Health Found. grantee, 1967, Upjohn Co. grantee, 1973, 75, Kans. U. Med. Center grantee, 1972-73, Alcon Labs. grantee, 1974-76; Zimmer-U.S.A. grantee, 1975, 76; VA grantee, 1975, 76, 77. Diplomate Am. Bd. Surgery, Am. Bd. Orthopedic Surgery. Fellow A.C.S., Am. Acad. Orthopedic Surgery; mem. Greater Kansas City, Midcentral States orthopedic socs., Orthopedic Research Soc., Med. Soc. Kans., Wyandotte County Med. Soc. (mem. emergency med. care council 1973-74), U. Assn. for Emergency Med. Services, Assn. for Advancement of Med. Instrumentation, Am. Trauma Soc. (founding mem. 1974), AMA, Am. Soc. Law and Medicine, Am. Assn. for Surgery of Trauma, Am. Spinal Injury Assn., Internat. Med. Soc. Paraplegia. Contbr. articles on trauma and orthopedic surgery to profl. publs. Home: 7262 Mayfair Dr Merriam KS 66203 Office: Univ of Kansas Medical Center Kansas City KS 66103

JACOBS, STEPHEN LEON, printing co. exec.; b. Indpls., Mar. 20, 1936; s. Morris Louis and Marjorie (Leon) J.; B.S., Ind. U., 1958; spl. courses Carnegie Tech. Inst., 1957; children—Mark Brian, Lisa Ann. Part-owner Success Inc., Indpls., Success Devel. Co., Indpls. Racer, Graphic Arts Co. Inc. Vice pres. fin. com. Crossroads of Am. council Boy Scouts Am.; bd. govs. Jewish Welfare Fedn. Mem. Nat. Catalog Mgrs. Assn. (founder, dir.), Sigma Alpha Mu. Club: Columbia. Home: 8939 Shagbark Rd Indianapolis IN 46204 Office: 1345 W 16th St Indianapolis IN 46202

JACOBS, TIMOTHY WILLIAM, educator; b. Chgo., Aug. 29, 1942; s. William Edward and Margaret Lucille (Hogan) J.; student Loyola U., Chgo., 1963; B.A., DePaul U., 1966, M.A., 1970; m. Madelynn Corbett, June 18, 1966; children—Maureen Elizabeth, Anastasia Eileen. Cashier, City of Chgo., 1961-64; accountant Roto Processing Co., Chgo., 1964-67; tchr. Chgo. Bd. Edn., 1967—, Westinghouse Vocat. High Sch., 1968—. Bd. dirs. Ravenswood Manor Improvement Assn., 1975-76. Mem. Am. Hist. Assn., Chgo. Sch. Architecture Found., Chgo. Tchr.'s Union. Roman Catholic. Home: 4529 N Francisco Ave Chicago IL 60625 Office: 3301 W Franklin Blvd Chicago IL 60618

JACOBSEN, BERNARD MARTIN, broadcasting exec.; b. Clinton, Iowa, Sept. 14, 1917; s. William Sebastian and Mae (Madsen) J.; student Am. U., 1937-40; m. Ruth Irons, Oct. 28, 1952; children—Susan L., Samuel L., Rebecca L., Martha Ann. Asst. producer Double or Nothing radio show WOL, Washington, 1940-41; asst. publicity and pub. relations dir. WLW, Cin., 1946-47; organizer builder WSKI, Montpelier, Vt., 1947; pres., 1947-51; gen. mgr. KROS, Clinton, 1951-73, pres., 1955-73; pres. Jacobsen Co., real estate, 1959—, Clinton TV Cable Co., Iowa Radio Network, 1965-66; dir. Clinton Fed. Savs. & Loan Assn. Mem. Clinton Plan Commn., 1960—, chmn., 1971-73; mng. dir. Clinton Area Devel. Corp., 1975—; mem. Gov.'s Ednl. Adv. Com., 1970-71; mem. Iowa Small Bus. Adv. Council, 1967-68. Served to lt. USNR, 1942-46. Mem. AIM (asso.), C. of C. (past dir.). Episcopalian (vestryman). Home: 1114 10th Ave N Clinton IA 52732 Office: Jacobsen Co Clinton IA 52732

JACOBSEN, EDWARD LEROY, trucking co. exec.; b. Chgo., May 13, 1936; s. Edward LeRoy and Julia (Bodemer) J.; student pub. schs. Chgo.; m. Arlyne N. Grandt, Feb. 14, 1976; 1 dau., Cynthia Lee. Owner, mgr. Jacobsen Trucking Co., Gary, Ind., 1967-74; traffic mgr. Nortown Steel Co., East Chicago, Ind., 1975-77; pres. Cherokee Trucking Inc., Munster, Ind., 1976—; agt. Ace Doran Hauling & Rigging, Daniel Hamm Drayage, 1977—. Mem. Chgo. Suburban Motor Carriers Assn. Episcopalian. Home: 8012 Beech St Munster IN 46321 Office: 7300 15th St W Gary IN 46404

JACOBSEN, ERIC KASNER, cons. engr.; b. N.Y.C., July 21, 1932; s. Henry and Caroline (Kasner) J.; B.C.E., U. Iowa, 1956; m. Dorothy H. Caldwell, Mar. 30, 1957; 1 son, Steven. Structural engr. Stanley Engring. Co., Muscatine, Iowa, 1956-59; asso. dept. mgr. R. W. Booker & Assos., St. Louis, 1959-63; plant mgr. Tri-Cities Terminal div. Nat. Marine Service, Inc., Granite City, Ill., 1963-65; sr. engr. Monsanto Co., 1965-69; chief structural engr. Weitz-Hettalsater Engrs., Kansas City, 1969-72; supr. structural and archtl. engring. Austin Co., Cleve., 1972—; cons. engr. structural and archtl. engring., 1960—. Recipient Eagle Scout award Boy Scouts Am., 1951; registered profl. engr., Ill., N.Y., Iowa, Mo., Wis. Mem. ASCE, ASME, Chi Epsilon. Presbyterian. Home: 16 Louise Dr Chagrin Falls OH 44022 Office: 1245 E 222d St Cleveland OH 44117

JACOBSEN, ERLING ROBERT, electronics engr., govt. orgn. ofcl.; b. Moorhead, Minn., Mar. 7, 1923; s. Robert Thorlief and Sigfrid Lois (Ylvisaker) J.; student math. Augustana Coll., 1940-42, Mass. Inst. Tech., 1942-43, U. M.D., 1949-50; B.S. in Elec. Engring., George Washington U., 1963; postgrad., 1963-65; m. Madeleine Claude Desjardins, Dec. 19, 1966; 1 dau., Dorothy Virginia. Commd. 2d lt. C.E., U.S. Army, 1943, advanced through grades to capt., 1950; instr. Engr. Sch., 1943; research and devel. officer Engr. Bd., 1944-45; asst. to dir. tng. CIC Sch., 1946; intelligence officer, ops. officer, Germany, 1947-51; intelligence officer Fifth Army, 1952; ret., 1952; intelligence officer, acting base chief, project officer, and phys. scientist CIA, Washington, 1952-66; cons. elec. engring., Ill., 1966-68; dir. engring. and research Harrington Signal Co., Moline, Ill., 1968-73; exec. dir. Met. Regional Emergency Communications System, Rock Island, Ill., 1973-77; dir. telecommunications Bi-State Met. Computer Commn., Rock Island, 1977—; mem. Ill. State 911 Advisory Panel, Ill. State 911 Curriculum Devel. and Rev. Com.; instr. George Washington U., 1964, Resident Electronics Tng. Sch., Rock Island, 1966-67, cons. in field. Mem. Rock Island County Criminal Justice Planning Com.; mem. Ill. State Comprehensive Health Planning Advisory Council; chmn. Emergency Med. Services Council Illowa Health Systems Agency; bd. dirs. Illowa Health Planning Council; ex-officio mem. Met. Enforcement Group, Quad-City Law Enforcement and Criminal Justice Tng. Center. Mem. Am. Radio Relay League (life), Nat. Fire Protection Assn., Internat. Municipal Signal Assn., Nat., Ill. soc. profl. engrs., Asso. Pub. Safety Communications Officers (2d v.p. Ill. 1977-78), IEEE, Tau Beta Pi (life). Contbr. articles to profl. jours. Home: 1438 34th Ave Rock Island IL 61201 Office: Scott County Court House 416 W 4th St Davenport IA 52801

JACOBSEN, HOWARD, metal products mfg. co. exec.; b. N.Y.C., Aug. 12, 1921; s. Richard Bernhart and Aagot (Hansen) J.; student N.Y. U., 1940-43, 46-47; m. Betty Pernilla Anderson, June 19, 1943; children—Christine Jacobsen Muenchinger, Howard Emil, Carl Lawrence. Field rep., supr. engring. test dept. Sperry Gyroscope Co., Great Neck, N.Y., 1939-44; salesman Nat. Gypsum Co., Mpls., 1947-49, asst. sales mgr., Chgo., 1951-54, dist. mgr., Detroit, 1954-61; gen. mgr. wholesale div. Nichols Aluminum Co., Davenport, Iowa, 1962-63, v.p. sales, Hinsdale, Ill., 1963-69; v.p., gen. mgr. Amax Aluminum Bldg. Products, Inc., Evansville, Ind., 1969-74; product mgr. Allied Tube & Conduit Corp., Harvey, Ill., 1974—. Served with USN, 1944-46. Home: 1512 N Columbia Naperville IL 60540 Office: Allied Tube & Conduit Corp 16100 S Lathrop Harvey IL 60426

JACOBSEN, ROBERT FRED, archtl., engring. co. exec.; b. Manitowoc, Wis., Mar. 27, 1931; s. Fred Jordan and Esther Mildred (Welk) J.; B.S. in Civil Engring., U. Wis., 1954; m. Marilyn Mae Bruss, June 26, 1954; children—Anne Christine, Kurt Robert. Structural design engr. Ellerbe Architects, Engrs., St. Paul, 1956-60; field engr., constrn. supt. Fegles Constrn. Co., Mpls., 1960-62; field engr. Minn. Mining & Mfg. Co., St. Paul, 1962-63; field engr., dept. mgr. Ellerbe Architects, Engrs., Bloomington, Minn., 1963-74, sr. v.p., 1974—; pres. Bordner Assos., Landmark Devel. Co., FDC Inc., all Bloomington, 1974—. Served to 1st lt. AUS, 1954-56. Mem. ASCE. Home: 6629 Dakota Trail Edina MN 55435 Office: 1 Apple Tree Sq Bloomington MN 55420

JACOBSEN, WINFRED OLSEN, library administr.; b. Marquette, Nebr., Oct. 26, 1914; s. John Andrew and Johanne Elizabeth (Olsen) J.; B.S., U. Nebr., 1939; M.L.S., U. Denver, 1963; m. Frances Irene Turner, July 14, 1946; 1 son, John Craig. Dir. Columbus (Nebr.) Pub. Library, 1961—, Pawnee Regional Library, Columbus, 1965—, No. Library Network, Columbus, 1970—. Chmn., No. Library Adv. Council, 1971-75; 4-H club leader, 1964-69. Served with USNR, 1942-46. Mem. Nebr. Library Assn. (chmn. pub. library sect. 1972-73). Methodist. Lion. Home: Route 1 Box 24 Columbus NE 68601 Office: 2504 14th St Columbus NE 68601

JACOBSON, DANIEL, geographer, educator; b. Newark, Nov. 6, 1923; s. Samuel and Mary (Siegel) J.; B.A., Montclair (N.J.) State Coll., 1947; M.A., Columbia U., 1950; Ph.D., La. State U., 1954; m. Iris M. Blachman, Aug. 18, 1957; children—Lisa, Darryl, Jerrold. Instr. geography U. Ky., 1952-55; instr. geology Bklyn. Coll., 1955-57; asso. prof. geography Montclair State Coll., 1957-65; vis. prof. geography and edn. Mich. State U., East Lansing, 1965-67, prof., 1967—; pres. Nat. Council Geog. Edn., 1968. Author: The Story of Man, 1963; The First Americans, 1969; Great Indian Tribes, 1970; The Hunters, 1974; The Fishermen, 1975; The Gatherers, 1977; editor Peninsular, 1966—. Home: 1827 Mirabeau Dr Okemos MI 48864 Office: Michigan State Univ 518 Erickson Hall East Lansing MI 48824

JACOBSON, HARLAN JEROME, chiropractor; b. Ashby, Minn., Aug. 7, 1937; s. Arthur Oliver and Harriet Junice (Hoff) J.; student Augsburg Coll., 1955-58, Lutheran Bible Inst., 1958; D.Chiropractic, Northwestern Chiropractic Coll., 1964; m. Judy Lucille Skogen, May 25, 1968; children—Shawn Jay, Nicole Teresa. Practice chiropractic medicine, Mpls., 1964-66, Ashby, 1974—; securities account exec. John Kinnard & Co., Inc., Mpls., 1966-69, Bishop & Co., Inc., Mpls., 1969-70; asst. v.p. Gold Chip Securities, Mpls., 1970; owner, operater Jacobson Constrn. Co., Ashby, 1970-74. Dir., promoter various smaller non-pub. cos., Mpls., 1966-70; mem. Trinity Luth. Ch., Ashby, Ashby Health Dept. Mem. Am., Minn. chiropractic assns., Parker Chiropractic Research Found., Sacro-Occipital Research Soc. Internat., Worldwide Christian Chiropractors Assn. Lion (pres. 1978-79). Office: PO Box 235 Ashby MN 56309

JACOBSON, LEONARD LEROY BOLAND, dentist; b. Gordon, Nebr., May 14, 1911; s. Henry Clarence and Sophia Katheryn (Bower) J.; A.B., B.Sc., U. Nebr., 1937; D.D.S., Northwestern U., 1941; certificate Kellog Found., Battle Creek, Mich. and U. Mich. Sch. Pub. Health, 1941; postgrad. U.Ill., 1942, Eastern Ill. U., 1962; m. Fay Darling Shaw, Aug. 29, 1942; children—John Shaw, Katheryn Darling. Chef, Morrison Hotel, Chgo., 1938-41; practice dentistry, Chgo., 1941-44, Lawrenceville, Ill., 1949—; mem. staff Lawrence County Meml. Hosp., 1951—; dir. research and devel. Plywood-Plastics Corp. (now Micarta div. Westinghouse), Hampton, S.C., 1944-46, 1st v.p., asst. to pres., 1946-49; dental adviser Ill. Pub. Welfare, 1960—; instr. Northwestern U., 1942-44; dental cons., 1942-44. Pres., Lawrence County Bd. Health, 1954-71; charter mem. Lawrence County Hist. Soc., 1961, bd. dirs., 1961-67, v.p., 1960—. Fellow Royal Soc. Promotion Health (Eng.); mem. ADA, Ill., Chgo. (asso.), Wabash Valley (ofcl. speaker rep.) dental socs., Am. Acad. Orthodontics (asso.), Am. Inst. Orthodontics (asso.), Wabash Valley Flood Control Assn., Lawrenceville C. of C. (dir. 1948—), Ill. Assn. Bds. Health (pres. 1961-62), Delta Sigma Delta. Republican. Methodist (numerous offices). Clubs: Elks, Lions (pres. 1945-48), Rotary (pres. 1972-73). Home: 1412 Overlook Dr Vincennes IN 47591 Office: 722 S 11th St Lawrenceville IL 62439

JACOBSON, LEONARD OSCAR, food co. exec.; b. Aitkin, Minn., Nov. 2, 1926; s. Oscar Gustaf and Caroline Signe (Eskilson) J.; student Creighton U., 1944-45, U. Minn., Duluth, 1952-53, Mpls., 1956-57; m. Helen Irene Jackman, Jan. 20, 1951; 1 dau., Sara Marie. Dist. mgr., Minn., Curtiss Candy Co., Chgo., 1954-56; div. sales mgr., Minn., Waddell & Reed Inc., Kansas City, Mo., 1956-64; regional sales mgr. Tapserve Corp., Mpls., 1964-66; br. mgr. brokerage office, N.D., Dain Kalman & Quail, Mpls., 1966-69; securities wholesaler Anchor Corp., Elizabeth, N.J., 1969-71; wholesaler mut. funds Security Distbrs. Inc., Topeka, Kans., 1971-76; fin. planner, wholesale, Unimark Ltd., San Rafael, Calif., 1976—; pres. Sara Bay Wild Rice Co.; vice chmn. dir. Minn. Paddy Wild Rice Research Promotion Council; guest lectr. U. N.D. Grad. Sch., Minot (N.D.) AFB. Mem. Minn. Wild Rice Growers Assn. (v.p., dir.). Home: 2720 N Dale St #109 St Paul MN 55113 Office: 3585 N Lexington St St Paul MN 55112

JACOBSON, LOREN JOEL, obstetrician, gynecologist; b. Parshall, N.D., Oct. 28, 1923; s. Phillip Melvin and Nora (Blessum) J.; student U. Willamette, 1944-45; B.S., U. Minn., 1946, M.B., 1948, M.D., 1949; m. Jacqueline Shirley Hanson, June 6, 1947; children—Laurie Jo., Janel Noreen, Steven John, Julie Ann. Rotating intern U. Minn., Mpls., 1948-50; ltd. practice medicine, specializing in obstetrics and gynecology, Mpls., 1952-59; resident in obstetrics and gynecology Mayo Clinic, Rochester, Minn., 1959-61; mem. staff Mpls. Obstetrics and Gynecology Assos., Ltd., 1961—; active staff North Meml. Med. Center, Mpls., Fairview Southdale Hosp. Served as flight surgeon USAF, 1950-52. Mem. Minn. Obstet. and Gynecol. Soc. (pres. 1976), Am. Coll. Obstetricians and Gynecologists (chmn. Minn. sect. 1975-77). Republican. Lutheran. Office: 3366 Oakdale Ave N Minneapolis MN 55422

JACOBSON, MICHAEL HAROLD, educator; b. Lajunta, Colo., Feb. 16, 1945; s. Irving Ralph and Bernice Marie (Rubin) J.; B.S., Loyola U., Chgo., 1967; LL.B., LaSalle U., 1971; M.A., Northeastern Ill. U., 1970; Ph.D., Sussex Coll. (Eng.), 1973. Tchr., Chgo. Bd. Edn., 1967-71, counselor, 1971-76; pres. Chgo. Counseling Assos., 1971-74; regional coordinator Chgo. Region, Effectiveness Tng. Assos., 1972-73; Ill. state rep. Universal Life Ch., 1975—; prof. psychology Foster G. McGaw Grad. Sch., Nat. Coll. Edn., Chgo., 1975—; dir. guidance services Orr High Sch., Chgo., 1976—. Dist. commr., Boy Scouts Am., Chgo., 1975—, asst. dist. commr., 1973-75. Recipient Dist. award of Merit Boy Scouts Am., 1976, named explorer advisor of the year, 1974; decorated Knight Sovereign Order of Lichstenstine; Knight commdr. Order Sursum Corda; Knight Order of Constantine. Mem. Am., Ill. personnel and guidance assns., Am., Ill. sch. counselor assns., Am. Assn. Sex Educators Counselors and Therapists, Assn. for Supervision and Curriculum Devel., Nat. Orgn. on Legal Problems in Edn., Chgo. Prins. Assn., Chgo. Pub. Sch. Counselors Assn., Chgo. Personnel and Guidance Assn., Mensa, Psi Chi, Phi Delta Kappa, Alpha Phi Omega (nat. exec. com. 1974—). Club: Moose. Contbr. articles in field to profl. jours. Home: 4124 N Clarendon Ave Chicago IL 60613 Office: 730 N Pulaski Rd Chicago IL 60624

JACOBSON, NORMAN HARRY, assn. exec.; b. Milw., Sept. 4, 1915; s. John F. and Alma (Kitz) J.; B.A., U. Wis., Madison, 1938; m. Lucille Jay Cunningham, Aug. 14, 1943; children—Judy, Jon, Jill. Supr. indsl. press relations Allis-Chalmers Mfg. Co., Milw., 1938-50; chief indsl. info. br. AEC, 1950-54; editor Electric Light and Power mag., N.Y.C. and Chgo., 1955-62, Atomics and Power Engring. mags., Barrington, Ill., 1962-66; asst. dir. LMFBR Program Office, Argonne (Ill.) Nat. Lab., 1966-70; mgr. publs. Am. Nuclear Soc., Hinsdale, Ill., 1970—; chmn. nuclear div. Am. Power Conf., Chgo., 1972—. Pres. Golf (Ill.) Civic Assn., 1970-71; trustee Village of Golf, 1958-62. Mem. Am. Nuclear Soc., Soc. Tech. Communication, Nat. Assn. Sci. Writers, Council Engring. and Sci. Soc. Execs., Am. Soc. Assn. Execs. Democrat. Lutheran. Club: Chgo. Press. Home: 25 Logan Terr Golf IL 60029 Office: 555 N Kensington Ave LaGrange Park IL 60525

JACOBSON, PAUL, agrl. engr.; b. Harcourt, Iowa, Oct. 23, 1909; s. Frank A. and Pauline (Jacobson) J.; B.S. in Agrl. Engring., Iowa State U., 1932; m. Marion E. Jensen, June 3, 1934; children—Ann K., Mary E., Jean E., Paul A. Area engr. Soil Conservation Service, Shenandoah, Iowa, 1934-44, dist. conservationist, Ft. Dodge, Iowa, 1944-45, zone conservationist, Milw., 1945-54, state cons. engr. for Iowa, Des Moines, 1954-64; drainage and soil conservation specialist Harza Engring. Co., Chgo., 1964—; irrigation specialist spl. mission to Iraq FAO, 1975. Recipient Soil and Water award Am. Soc. Agrl. Engrs., 1973. Fellow Am. Soc. Agrl. Engrs.; mem. Gamma Sigma Delta. Editor sect. on soil and water Agrl. Cultural Engineering Handbook, 1965. Developed system of push-up terraces with tile outlets. Home: Rural Route 1 Dow City IA 51528 Office: Harza Engring Co 150 S Wacker Dr Chicago IL 60600

JACOBSON, PHILLIP GORDON, optometrist; b. Milw., Jan. 27, 1918; s. Morris D. and Edith Mildred (Stein) L.; B.A., U. Wis., 1936; O.D., No. Ill. Coll. Optometry, 1942; m. Charlotte Shapiro, July 22, 1945; children—Eric M., Steven L., Gary J. Practice optometry, Milw., 1946—; pres. Wis. State Bd. Examiners in Optometry, 1960-67. Pres. Vliet St. Assn., 1950-58; mem. Milw. Mayor's Adv. Council, 1950. Served with USAAF, 1943-46. Fellow Am. Sch. Health Assn., Royal Soc. Health; mem. Am. Optometric Found., Nat. Eye Research Found., Am. Optometric Assn., Milw. County Optometric Soc. (pres. 1952, 53, 62, 72-73), Internat. Optometric Fellowship (v.p. 1976-77), Am. Legion (past comdr.). Club: Masons (32 deg.). Home: 2330 W Dickinson Ct 102 North Mequon WI 53092 Office: 8500 W Capitol Dr Milwaukee WI 53222

JACOBY, JOHN STEWART, physician; b. Detroit, Sept. 29, 1930; s. John Cyrenius and Vivian (Brown) J.; student Albion Coll., 1948-51; M.D., Wayne U., 1955; M.P.H., U. Mich., 1959; m. Barbara Ann Dixon, Dec. 18, 1954; children—John D. (dec.), Janet A., James P., Robert P., William J., Thomas R. Intern, Detroit Meml. Hosp., 1955-56, resident, 1958; resident in occupational medicine U. Mich., also Gen. Motors Corp., 1958-59; plant physician Frigidaire div. Gen. Motors Corp., Dayton, Ohio, 1959-61, med. dir. Fisher Body div. Flint #1, Flint, Mich., 1961-67, plant physician Oldsmobile div., Lansing, Mich., 1969-70; med. dir. Ormet Corp., Hannibal, Ohio, 1967-69; med. dir. Mpls. area Honeywell, Inc., 1970-71, med. dir. Honeywell Control Systems, 1972-73, corporate dir. occupational and environ. health, 1973—. Pres. Genesee County Mental Health Assn., 1966; mem. budget com. United Fun, Flint, 1965-67. Served as lt. M.C., USNR, 1956-58. Diplomate Am. Bd. Preventive Medicine. Mem. AMA, Am., North Central occupational med. assns., Am. Acad. Occupational Medicine, Am. Indsl. Hygiene Assn., Minn. Med. Assn., Hennepin County Med. Soc., Minn. Acad. Occupational Medicine and Surgery (pres. 1976). Office: Honeywell Inc Honeywell Plaza Minneapolis MN 55408

JACOBY, ROBIN MILLER, historian; b. Los Angeles, Jan. 22, 1945; d. Robert and Gertrude (Lapidus) Miller; B.A., U. Calif., 1966; M.A., Harvard U., 1968, Ph.D., 1977; m. Jonathan T. Jacoby, June 30, 1968. Asst. prof. history U. Mich., Ann Arbor, 1972—; cons. in field. Ford Found. fellow 1967-70. Mem. Am. Hist. Assn., Mich. Women's Studies Assn., Phi Beta Kappa. Contbr. articles to profl. publs. Home: 1113 Olivia St Ann Arbor MI 48104

JACOKES, LEE EDWARD, ednl. adminstr.; b. Grand Rapids, Mich., Dec. 7, 1938; s. Charles Harold and Mary Lucille (Quinn) J.; B.S., Aquinas Coll., 1961; M.A., U. Detroit, 1964; Ph.D., Mich. State U., 1975; m. Francene Sue Russell, June 23, 1962; children—Renee, Jeannine, Kim. High sch. tchr., counselor Benedictine High Sch., Detroit, 1962-63; clin. psychologist Plymouth State Home and Tng. Sch., Northville, Mich., 1963-64; asso. prof. psychology Aquinas Coll., Grand Rapids, 1964-77, dir. instl. research, 1970-73, acting registrar, 1971-73, dean academic adminstrn., 1973-75, dir. Grad. Mgmt. program, 1977—; lectr. psychology Mercy Central Sch. Nursing, Grand Rapids, 1968-70; clin. psychologist Family Clinic, Grand Rapids, 1965-69. Mem. council cons. Center Environment Studies, Grand Rapids, 1973-74; cons. PreCana Conf., Diocese Grand Rapids, 1968—; statis. analyst campaign staff State Senator John R. Otterbacher, 1972—; trustee Kent County Adult Mental Health Clinic, Grand Rapids, 1966-68, Jellama House, Grand Rapids, 1973-76, Coll. St. Francis, Joliet, Ill., Mental Health Planning sect. W. Mich. Health Systems Agency, Grand Rapids. Kellogg fellow Assn. Ind. Colls. and Univs. Mich., 1972-73; Grand Rapids Found. ednl. grantee, 1972-73. Mem. Am., Mich., Grand Rapids Area (exec. com., membership chmn. 1966-69) psychol. assns., Assn. Instl. Research, Am., Mich. assns. collegiate registrars and admissions officers. Home: 3623 Lake Dr SE Grand Rapids MI 49506

JACOX, JOHN WILLIAM, engring. and consulting co. exec.; b. Pitts., Dec. 12, 1938; s. John Sherman and Grace Edna (Herbster) J.; B.S. in M.E., Carnegie Mellon U., 1962, B.S. in Indsl. Mgmt., 1962; 1 son, Brian Erik. Mfg. engr., Nuclear Fuel div. Westinghouse Elec. Co., Pitts., 1962-65; data processing salesman IBM, Pitts., 1965-66; mktg. mgr. nuclear products MSA Internat., Pitts., 1966-72; v.p. Nuclear Consulting Services, Inc., Columbus, Ohio, 1973—. Coop. edn. adv. com. Otterbein Coll. Mem. ASME (code com. nuclear air and gas treatment, exec. com., legis. services commn., chmn. subcom. testing), Am. Nuclear Soc. (pub. info. com.), Nat. Rifle Rifle Assn. (life). Home: 5874 Northern Pine Pl Columbus OH 43229 Office: PO Box 29151 Columbus OH 43229

JADACH, ALBERT ANDREW, mfg. co. exec.; b. Cleve., Aug. 21, 1928; s. Walter and Gizella (Tolaczynski) J.; B.S. in Engring., U. Mich., 1953, M.B.A., 1955; m. Emily Kaminski, Feb. 8, 1958; children—Christina, Arthur, Nella. Project engr. Dura Corp., Oak Park, Mich., 1956-57, chief engr., 1957-59; plant mgr. Formax Mfg. Co., Detroit, 1959-61, sec.-treas., 1961-62, ops. mgr., 1962-67; gen. mgr. Copco Trailer div. Copco Steel & Engring. Co., South Bend, Ind., 1967-68, v.p. sales, parent co., Detroit, 1968-71; gen. mgr. Indsl. & Automotive Fasteners div. Key Internat., Royal Oak, Mich., 1974-76, plant mgr., 1971-74, dir. corp. devel., Southfield, Mich., 1976—; instr. Wayne State U., 1973—. Mem. Am. Mgmt. Assn., Soc. Automotive Engrs., Am. Soc. Purchasing Agts., Quarterdeck Soc., Royal Oak C. of C. Republican. Roman Catholic. Club: Royal Oak Golf. Patentee Garden Tractor, abrasive wheel, urethane contact wheel, marine container, wheel lug nut. Home: 1820 Vinton Rd Royal Oak MI 48067 Office: 24175 Northwestern Hwy Southfield MI 48037

JAECKLE, CHARLES EISELE, ophthalmologist; b. Jersey City, Mar. 30, 1906; s. August John and Anna (Eisele) J.; student Rutgers Coll., 1922-24; B.S., Columbia U., 1927, postgrad., 1936; postgrad. Upsala Coll., 1935; M.D., N.Y. U., 1940; postgrad. Northwestern U. Med. Sch., 1941-42; m. Elizabeth Robbins, June 7, 1943; children—Robin Ann, Franklin August. House physician and surgeon Orange (N.J.) Meml. Hosp., 1940-41, asst., then attending ophthalmologist, chmn. sec. ophthalmology, 1946-60; resident ophthalmology Wesley Meml. Hosp., Chgo., 1941-42, Passavant Meml. Hosp., Chgo., 1942; Gifford fellow ophthalmology Northwestern U. Med. Sch., Chgo., 1942-43; asst. in ophthalmology Newark Eye and Ear Infirmary, 1946-60; staff to adj. ophthalmologist East Orange (N.J.) Gen. Hosp., 1951-60, attending ophthalmologist, 1960-73; dir. dept. ophthalmology Defiance (Ohio) Hosp., 1960-73, chief of staff, 1964-66, ophthalmologist emeritus, 1973—. Mem. N.J. Commn. for Blind, 1960, White House Conf. on Children and Youth, 1960; cons. USPHS; pres. Med. Eye Services Am., Inc. Trustee Ralph O. Rychener Meml. Fund. Served to capt. M.C., AUS, 1943-46. Recipient Lucien Howe medal AMA sect. opthalmology, 1977. Diplomate Am. Bd. Ophthalmology. Mem. AMA (alt. del. ophthalmology 1969-75, del. 1976—), Am. Assn. Ophthalmology (trustee, sec. 1956-66, editor Ophthalmologist 1960-66, v.p. for sociomed. affairs 1966-70, pres.-elect 1970, pres. 1972-74), N.J. Acad. Ophthalmology (sec. 1954-58, pres. 1958-60), Am. Acad. Ophthalmology and Otolaryngology, Am. Assn. Research in Ophthalmology, Contact Lens Assn. Ophthalmologists (founding trustee), Pan Am. Assn. Ophthalmology, Med. Soc. N.J. (del. 1954-60), Ohio Med. Assn. (del. 1963-69). Presbyterian. Club: Rotary. Home: 229 Riverdale Dr Defiance OH 43512

JAEGER, ARNOLD WILLIAM, state ofcl.; b. Hebron, N.D., Apr. 5, 1923; s. Ernest and Mary (Senne) J.; student Fargo Bus. Coll., 1942, LaSalle Extension U., 1946-47; m. LaVerne V. Gray, July 1, 1945; children—Lauren Lynn (Mrs. Lawrence Magstadt), Lance LaMar. Desk clk. Gardner Hotel, Fargo, N.D., 1942-43; sr. clk. N.D. Unemployment Compensation Div., Bismarck, 1946-47, chief clk., 1947-49, field auditor, 1949-54, claims dep., 1954-59, supr. old age and survivor's ins., 1959-62, chief contbrs., 1962-63, chief retirement and survivor's ins., 1963-65, chief fiscal officer N.D. Employment Security Agys., 1965-73, dir. adminstrv. services, 1973—. Mem. exec. com. United Comml. Travelers Council 325, 1963—, chmn., 1967-68, grand jr. counselor Minn.-N.D. jurisdiction, 1977-78. Bd. dirs. Internat. Assn. Personnel in Employment Security Credit Union, 1966—, pres., 1967-68, v.p., 1968—; bd. dirs. Sch. of Hope (for mentally retarded children), 1967—, v.p., 1968-69. Served with AUS, 1943-46; ETO. Decorated Bronze Star medal; named hon. Ky. Col. Mem. Nat. Conf. State Social Adminstrs. (pres. 1970), Am. Legion. Lutheran. Elk. Home: 1709 Porter Ave Bismarck ND 58501 Office: 1000 E Divide Bismarck ND 58501

JAEGER, DON THEODORE, musician, performing arts adminstr.; b. Port Arthur, Tex., May 10, 1936; s. Lee D. and Mary L. (Garder) J.; student Wichita State U., 1954-56; Mus.B., Oklahoma City U., 1958; postgrad. (Fulbright scholar), Amsterdam Conservatory, The Netherlands, 1958-59, Mozarteum, Salzburg, Austria, 1959; m. Ann Cynthia del Regato, Mar. 30, 1964; children—Jon Eric, Julie Ann. Profl. oboist Wichita (Kans.) Symphony Orch. 1954-56, Oklahoma City Symphony, 1956-58, 60-61, Dallas Symphony Orch., 1959-60, Amarillo (Tex.) Symphony Orch., 1961-62; oboe soloist Alaska Festival Orch., 1961, 63, 64, 67; Chgo. Little Symphony, 1964-67, Lincoln Center; soloist Interlochen (Mich.) Arts Acad. Orch., 1964, instr., 1962-68, dir., 1972-73; instr. music Oklahoma City pub. schs., 1960-61, Amarillo Coll., 1961-62; western states music dir. Young Audiences, Inc., San Francisco, 1968-69, Midwest mus. dir., Midland, Mich., 1969-73; music dir., condr. Midland Symphony Orch., 1969—, exec. dir. Midland Center for the Arts, 1973—. Guest condr. Colorado Springs Orch., 1968-69, Utah All-State Orch., 1972, Kans. All-State Orch., 1973, Detroit Symphony, 1973-74, Flint (Mich.) Symphony Orch., 1974-75, Philharmonic Orch. of Lisbon, 1974, U. Ark. Music Festival, summer, 1971, 73, Wis. State U., 1970, Chattanooga Symphony Orch., 1977, Iowa City Bach Festival, 1977; oboist Today Show NBC, 1964, Interlochen Arts Quintet, 1962-68; mem. faculty Nat. Music Camp, Interlochen, Mich., summers 1960-74; mem. conducting and instructional staff Internat. Jugendorchester, Berlin, Germany, 1965. Bd. dirs. Midland Community Affairs Council; v.p., bd. dirs. Mich. Artrain, Inc. Recipient 3d prize Prague Spring Internat. Competition for Woodwinds, 1959. Mem. Internat. Double Reed Soc., Phi Beta Mu (hon., life), Phi Mu Alpha Sinfonia (award). Editor Double Reed Column, Sch. Musician Mag., 1968—. Rotarian. Mem. United Ch. of Christ. Home: 5801 Highland Dr Midland MI 48640 Office: Midland Center for the Arts 1801 W St Andrews Midland MI 48640

JAFFE, EUGENE J., oral surgeon; b. Chgo., Mar. 6, 1924; s. Harry J. and Dora (Katz) J.; student Wilson City Coll., 1942-43; D.D.S., Loyola U., 1946; m. Adelyne Marshak, Oct. 20, 1946; children—Sally, Patti, Francine. Oral surgery resident Cook County Hosp., 1950-51; pvt. practice oral surgery, Chgo., 1952-69, Oak Lawn, Ill., 1969—. Asst. prof. oral surgery Loyola U. Sch. Dentistry, 1959-67; asst. prof. oral surgery U. Ill., 1967—; clin. asst. prof. surgery Lincoln Sch. Medicine, 1967—; mem. attending staff Cook County Hosp., Michael Reese Hosp. and Med. Center. Served with USAF, 1946-48. Fellow Internat. Assn. Oral Surgeons, Am. Dental Soc. of Anesthesiology; mem. Am., Ill., Chgo. (pres. 1964-65) socs. oral surgeons, Englewood Dental Soc. (pres. 1968-69). Office: 4435 W 95th St Oak Lawn IL 60453

JAFFE, PHILIP MONLANE, chemist, educator; b. Bronx, Aug. 14, 1927; s. Herman and Rose (Friedman) J.; B.S., Coll. City N.Y., 1947; M.S., Bklyn. Poly. Inst., 1952, Ph.D., 1962; m. Mary Abend, June 25, 1950; children—Carl H., Robert T., Steven A. Sr. research chemist Westinghouse Electric, Bloomfield, N.J., 1953-63; head inorganic and analytical sects. Gen. Precision, Little Falls, N.J., 1963-66; head phosphor materials research sect. Zenith Radio Corp., Chgo., 1966-72; prof. chemistry Oakton Community Coll., Morton Grove, Ill., 1970—. Instr. chemistry Bronx Community Coll., 1965, Fairleigh-Dickinson U., Teaneck, N.J., 1964-66, Chgo. City Coll., 1966-68; instr. math. Triton Coll., River Grove, Ill., 1966-68. Active Boy Scouts Am.; mem. Downers Grove Oratorio Soc., 1966-71, N.W. Symphony, 1966—, Newark Wind Quintet, 1961-66. Fellow Am. Inst. Chemists, A.A.A.S.; mem. Am. Chem. Soc., Ill. Acad. Sci., Sigma Xi. Mem. B'nai B'rith. Contbr. articles to profl. jours. Patentee in field. Home: 9818 Maynard Terr Niles IL 60648 Office: 7900 Nagle Morton Grove IL 60053

JAFFEE, LEE S., printing co. exec.; b. N.Y.C., Feb. 1, 1926; s. David and Ethel (Erenberg) J.; m. Fern Block, Feb. 16, 1952; children—Drew, Vickie, Barbara. Prodn. mgr. Parents' Mag., 1946-50, Street & Smith, 1950-51; with Regensteiner Press, Chgo., 1951-71, v.p., gen. mgr., dir., 1968—; pres. Am. Printers & Lithographers div. John Blair & Co., 1972—. Served with AUS, 1943-46. Recipient Human Relations award Am. Jewish Com., 1969. Mem. Printing Industry Ill. (dir.), Chgo. Lithographers Assn. (dir.), Graphic Arts Council Found. (dir.). Home: 1040 Sheridan Rd Glencoe IL 60022 Office: 6701 Oakton St Chicago IL 60648

JAFFERY, SHELDON RONALD, lawyer; b. Cleve., Apr. 22, 1934; s. Dan and Cecelia Shirley (Bailus) J.; B.A. in English, Ohio State U., 1957; B.S. in Edn., Kent State U., 1959; postgrad. U. Calif. at Los Angeles, 1960; J.D., Western Res. U. Law Sch., 1964; m. Judith Ann Friedman, June 23, 1963; children—Kimberly, Jonathan, Jason. Admitted to Ohio bar, 1964, U.S. Supreme Ct. bar, 1970; practiced in Cleve., 1964—; asso. M.D. Barrisch, Cleve., 1964-67, Jerome Silver, Cleve., 1967-68; asso. firm Zellmer and Gruber, Cleve., 1968-71, partner, 1971—; spl. counsel State Ohio, Office Atty. Gen., 1971-74. Pres., dir. Jay-H Investment Co., Cleve., 1968-75; tchr. English, speech, journalism Cardinal High Sch., Middlefield, Ohio, 1959-61. Trustee Hebrew Free Loan Assn., 1976—. Mem. Cleve. (chmn. fine arts com. 1973-75), Ohio bar assns., Assn. Trial Lawyers Am., Vol. Lawyers for Arts, Ohio Acad. Trial Lawyers, Zeta Beta Tau, Tau Epsilon Rho. Home: 23834 Wendover Dr Beachwood OH 44122 Office: 1400 Leader Bldg Cleveland OH 44114

JAFRI, SAIYED QAMAR, construction equipment mfg. co. exec.; b. Akbarpur, India, July 16, 1940; s. Alay Hasan and Safdari Begum (Rizvi) J.; M.S. in Math., Aligarh U., India, 1961; M.S. in Mech. Engring., Tuskegee Inst., 1968; M.B.A. in Mgmt., No. Ill. U., 1978; m. Firdaus Saiyed, Dec. 8, 1972; children—Zaineb Saiyeda, Alay Safdar. Mech. engr. River Valley Project, Ramgania, India, 1963-67; design and project engr. Internat. Harvester, Melrose Park and Antioch, Ill., 1968-76, supr. mktg. dept., Schaumburg, Ill., 1976—. Active, Citizens' Advisory Com. Coll. of DuPage, Glen Ellyn. Recipient Univ. medal Aligarh U., 1961; named Outstanding New Citizen of Year Citizenship Council Chgo., 1976. Mem. Nat., Ill. (named Young Engr. of Year 1974-75) socs. profl. engrs., Am. Mgmt. Assn., Soc. Automotive Engrs., ASME, Assn. M.B.A. Execs., Sigma Iota Epsilon. Republican. Moslem. Patentee in field. Home: 648 Catalpa Ln Bartlett IL 60103 Office: 600 Woodfield Exec Plaza Schaumburg IL 60196

JAGODZINSKI, BENJAMIN ANDREW, physician, surgeon; b. Warsaw, Poland, Feb. 12, 1937; s. Matthew and Marie (Goscinski) J.; B.S., St. Peter's Coll., 1958; M.D., Loyola U., 1962; m. Judith M. Norka, May 26, 1962; children—Susan, Sharon, Caryn, Christine. Intern, Monmouth Med. Center, Long Branch, N.J., 1962-63; obstetrics-gynecology resident Little Co. of Mary Hosp., Evergreen Park, Ill., 1963-64, 66-68, sr. attending physician, cons. 1968—; active attending physician, cons. Christ Hosp., Oak Lawn, Ill., 1968—, Palos Community Hosp., Palos Heights, Ill., 1968—; asso. prof. obstetrics-gynecology Rush Med. Coll.-Presbyn.-St. Luke's Hosp., Chgo., 1970—. Served with U.S. Army, 1964-66. Diplomate Am. Bd. Obstetrics and Gynecology. Mem. AMA (physicians recognition award 1974-77), Am. Coll. Obstetricians and Gynecologists (award 1977), Am. Fertility Soc., Internat. Coll. Surgeons, Am. Assn. Gynecol. Laparascopists, Ill. State, Chgo. med. socs., Chgo. Gynecol. Soc. Roman Catholic. Club: Elks. Office: 3900 W 95th St Evergreen Park IL 60642

JAHN, HARVEY RAYMOND, educator; b. Detroit, May 3, 1936; s. Harvey R. and Eleanor Marie (Hulbert) J.; B.S., U.S. Mil. Acad., 1958; M.A., U. Mich., 1964, Ph.D., 1968; m. Margaret C.; children—Mark, Todd, Cole, Briony. Research, investigator Soviet edn. HEW, Washington and Ann Arbor, 1966-68; asst. prof. legal, internat. founds. edn. U. Nev., Reno, 1968-69; asso. prof. social founds. of edn. Sch. Law, Adrian (Mich.) Coll., 1969-77; asst. prin. Traverse City (Mich.) Jr. High Sch., 1977—; owner, mgr. Jahn's Mile Point Cottages, Central Lake, Mich., 1972—; summer dir. NEA study tours to USSR, 1976—. Served with AUS, 1958-61. NDEA fellow, 1962-65. Mem. Comparative Edn. Soc., Am. Ednl. Studies Assn., West Point Alumni Assn., U. Mich. Alumni Assos., Phi Delta Kappa. Club: Terminal Lake (Mich.) Aux. Author: Reforms in Mathematics Education for Secondary Schools: Historical Trends in Russian and American Education, 1969; contbr. articles to profl. jours. Home: Box 271 Mile Point Central Lake MI 49622

JAIDINGER, JUDITH CLARANN, artist; b. Chgo., Apr. 10, 1941; d. John Henry and Charlotte Violet (Anton) Jaidinger; B.F.A., Sch. Art Inst. Chgo., 1970; m. Gerald Szesko, June 27, 1970; 1 dau. by previous marriage, Loralee C. Kolton. Exhibited in group shows at Honolulu Acad. Art, Joslyn Art Mus., Omaha, N.A.D., N.Y.C., Norfolk (Va.) Mus. Art, Western N.Mex. U., Silver City, Okla. Mus. Art, Oklahoma City, others; represented in permanent collections Minot (N.D.) State Coll., Washington and Jefferson Coll., Washington, Pa., N.Mex. Art League, Albuquerque, Brand Library Art Center, Glendale, Calif., Hunterdon Art Center, Clinton, N.J., Ill. State Museum. Mem. Miniature Art Soc. N.J., Painters and Sculptors Soc. N.J. Home: 6248 N Bell Ave Chicago IL 60659

JAIN, SHARAT KUMAR, psychologist; b. Meerut City, India, Oct. 22, 1940; s. Chandra Prakash and Chhama (Sri) J.; came to U.S., 1969, naturalized, 1974; Ph.D., Agra (India) U., 1967; postdoctoral student U. Man., 1967; postdoctoral fellow U. Minn., 1969; postdoctoral tng. Rutgers U., 1974-76; m. Sudha Jain, Nov. 25, 1962; children—Manoj, Meena, Sanjiv. Personnel mgr. ADL Labs., India, 1960-62; asst. prof. Agra U., 1962-64; civilian scientist Indian Army Hdqrs., New Delhi, 1964-67; staff psychologist Man. Penitentiary, Stony Mountain, 1968; asst. prof. U. Winnipeg (Man.), 1968-69; asso. prof. Central Conn. State Coll., New Britain, Conn., 1969-71; chief psychologyist, dir. research State of Idaho, Boise, 1971-72; prin. clin. psychologist State of N.J., Camden, 1972-75; clin. psychologist VA Hosp., Chillicothe, Ohio, 1975—; instr. Community Coll., Boise U., Rutgers U., Ohio U. Licensed psychologist, Ohio, N.J.; HEW grantee, 1971. Mem. Am. Psychol. Assn., Nat. Bd. Health Providers in Psychology, Internat. Assn. Cross Cultural Psychology, Internat. Assn. Applied Psychology. Author: Abnormal Psychology, 1962; Experimental Psychology, 1962; Developmental Psychology, 1973; Clinical Psychology, 1974; Interpretation of Rorschach Ink Blot Test for Differential Diagnosis, 1975; others; contbr. articles to profl. jours. Home: 83 Fruithill Dr Chillicothe OH 45601 Office: Dept Psychology VA Hosp Chillicothe OH 45601

JAIN, SUSHIL KUMAR, librarian; b. Faridkot, Punjab, India, Sept. 9, 1942; s. Hans Raj Bothra and Kumari Sushila (Rampiyari) J.; B.Ed. in Edn., Govt. Central Tng. Coll., Faridkot, Punjab, 1960; Diploma in Lib. Sci., Punjab. U., 1961; M.A. in Polit Sci., Aligarh Muslim U., 1962; diploma London Sch. Librarianship, U.London, 1965; M.A., Leeds U., 1973; m. Christine Horswell, Apr. 30, 1966. Asst. librarian Ravensbourne Coll. Art & Design, Bromley, Kent Eng., 1962-63; cataloger U. Sask., Regina, 1964-65, ref. librarian, bibliographer to div. social scis., 1966-67; work-study scholar South Asian unit U. Mich., 1965-66; reference librarian Asian Studies bibliographer U. Windsor Ont., 1967-72, resource librarian Inst. Asian Cultures, 1976—, research asso. dept. Asian Studies, 1968-72; assessment dept. Ont. Ministry of Revenue, 1975-76; chmn. Profl. Librarians Assn., U. Windsor, 1969-70; bd. dirs. Inst. Profl. Librarians Ont., 1970-72. Sec., treas. Windsor chpt. Com. for Ind. Can., 1971-72; sec. Council S.E. Asian Studies in Ont., 1971-72. Fellow Royal Commonwealth Soc.; mem. Assn. Asian Studies, Assn. Commonwealth Langs. and Lits., Bibliog. Soc. Can., Canadian Soc. Asian Studies, Linguistic Soc. India. Author: Compiler of Indian Literature in English: A Bibliography in 4 parts, 1965-70; Folklore of India and Pakistan 1965; The Negro in Canada, 1967; The East Indians in Canada, 1971. Home: PO Box

1088 Windsor ON Canada Office: Inst Asian Cultures U Windsor Windsor ON Canada

JAKEWAY, EDWIN WILLIAM, JR., lawyer; b. Flint, Mich., Dec. 7, 1936; s. Edwin William and Lucille (Hodge) J.; A.A., Genesee Community Coll., 1955-57; B.A., Eastern Mich. U., 1958; J.D. (Kiwanis scholar), Detroit Coll., 1961; m. Suzanne Henry, June 23, 1963; children—Craig Edwin, Morgan Henry, Sally Pamela. Admitted to Mich. bar, 1961; asso. firm Ransom and Fazenbaker, Flint, 1962-63, McTaggart and Lattie, Flint, 1964-65; partner firm Neal, Keil, Jakeway and Fazenbaker, Flint, 1965-70, Jakeway, Fazenbaker and Henry, Grand Blanc, Mich., 1970—; asst. prosecutor Genesee County, 1962-63; lectr. various schs. and chs., 1968—. Bd. dirs. Tall Pine council Boy Scouts Am., also atty. Served with Mich. N.G., 1955-62. Mem. Trout Unltd. (pres. Flint chpt. 1971-74), Gideons Internat., Am., Mich., Genesee County (dir. 1971-75) bar assns., Am., Mich. trial lawyers assns. Home: 7338 McCandlish Rd Grand Blanc MI 48439 Office: Bella Vista Mall-Lower Level Grand Blanc MI 48439

JAKSHA, EDWARD ANTON, former telephone co. exec.; b. Calumet, Mich., June 7, 1915; s. Anton and Frances (Spehar) J.; grad. high sch.; m. Marie Josephine Byre, Aug. 26, 1941; children—Michael, Jerome, James. With Western Electric Co., 1936; with Northwestern Bell Telephone Co., Omaha, 1938-77. Pres., Fremont Community Chest, 1955; county chmn. Dodge County Red Cross, 1954; mem. Parks and Recreation Bd., 1958-59. City councilman, 1961-63; finance chmn. Republican party Dodge County, 1960-68. Bd. dirs. YMCA, 1958-62. Served with Signal Corps, USAF, 1942-45; ETO. Recipient George Washington Medal, Freedoms Found., 1959, Distinguished Service award U.S. Jr. C. of C., 1968, Silver Beaver award Boy Scouts Am., 1970, Freedoms Found. award, 1977. Mem. Nebr. Tax Research Council (mem. adv. bd. 1972—), Nebr. C. of C. (mem. exec. bd. 1965-66), Nebr. Polit. Action Council (organizing chmn. 1973-74), Nebr. Tax Forum (pres. 1976-77). Club: Kiwanis (pres. 1968). Home: 13220 Montclair Dr Omaha NE 68144 Office: 100 S 19th St Omaha NE 68102

JAKSTAS, ALFRED JOHN, art museum ofcl.; b. Boston, Oct. 30, 1916; s. Walter John and Julia (Barkevich) J.; A.B., Harvard Coll., 1938; m. Valerie Jeannette Jevaraus, Oct. 11, 1942; children—Janet, Julianne. Teaching fellow Harvard U., 1941-42, conservator Harvard Portrait Collection, 1942-44; conservator Isabella Stewart Gardner Mus., Boston, 1941-61; cons. in conservation of art works to various museums in New Eng., 1945-61; conservator Art Inst. Chgo., 1961—; cons. in conservation of art works to various museums in Midwest, 1961—. Fellow Am., Internat. insts. of conservation of hist. and artistic works. Club: Harvard of Chgo. Home: 400 E Randolph Dr Chicago IL 60601 Office: 125 E Monroe St Chicago IL 60603

JALIL, MAZHAR, entomologist; b. India, June 22, 1933; s. Mohammad Ahmad and Safia (Khatoon) J.; came to U.S., 1967, naturalized, 1973; B.Sc. in Agr., U. Agra (India), 1952, M.Sc. in Agr. in Zoology and Entomology, 1954; M.Sc. in Agrl. Zoology (Lord Belper postgrad. scholar), U. Nottingham (Eng.), 1963; Ph.D. in Biology, U. Waterloo, Can., 1967; postdoctoral U. Ky., 1967-69; m. Betty Ann Lunsford, Feb. 28, 1970; children—Tariq, Khalid. Farm supt. R.A.K. Agrl. Inst., Sehore, India, 1955-56; tchr., lectr. Govt. Coll., Sehore, India, 1956-60; instr. U. Nottingham, 1962-64, U. Waterloo, 1964-67; research asso. U. Ky., 1967-69; entomologist Ohio Dept. Health, Columbus, 1969—. Mem. Acarological Soc. Am., Entomol. Soc. Am., Am. Registry Profl. Entomologists, Islamic Found. Central Ohio. W.V.S. travelling scholar U. Nottingham, 1964; teaching fellow U. Waterloo, 1964-67, Ont. grad. fellow, 1965-67. Contbr. articles to profl. jours. Home: 980 King Ave Columbus OH 43212 Office: Ohio Dept Health PO Box 2568 Columbus OH 43216

JAMES, GORDON DAVID, educator; b. Warren, Ohio, Nov. 27, 1920; s. David R. and Carolyn (Schisler) J.; B.S., Youngstown U., 1942; student Ohio State U., 1947-48, Kent State U. 1958, Columbia U., 1964; m. Mary E. Evans, Mar. 31, 1946; children—Candace Lee (Mrs. Michael Richmond), Timothy Alan, D. Kevin. Tchr. Lordstown High Sch., Warren, 1941-42, 46-52, prin., 1952-58; supt. Gordon D. James Career Center and Lordstown Schs., 1958—. Served with M.C., AUS, 1942-46. Mem. Am., Buckeye assns. sch. adminstrs., Ohio Assn. Local Sch. Supts. (exec. com. 1967-69, pres. 1970, rec. sec. 1972), Ohio Assn. Sec. Sch. Adminstrs., Nat. Assn. Secondary Sch. Adminstrs., Am., Buckeye assns. sch. adminstrs., Ohio Sch. Bds. Assn., Trumbull County Supts. Assn. (pres. 1966-67). Presbyterian (ordained elder). Home: 517 State Rd Warren OH 44483 Office: 1824 Salt Springs Rd W Warren OH 44483

JAMES, GRACE WHITAKER, real estate co. exec.; b. Durham, N.C., Sept. 11, 1921; d. John Wesley and Sudie (Mc Cauley) Whitaker; student Walsh Coll., 1972; m. William Henry Jmaes, June 9, 1939; 1 son, William Henry. Owner, pres. Grace W. James Agy., Canton, Ohio, 1965—. Mem. Nat., Ohio, Canton bds. realtors, Women's Council Realtors. Baptits. Club: Quota. Home: 5615 Fairwood Dr NW Canton OH 44720 Office: 5686 Dressler Rd Canton OH 44720

JAMES, JANE EMERSON, psychologist; b. Creston, Iowa, Oct. 5, 1920; d. Stephen Ray and Meta Florence (Raney) Emerson; B.A., U. Mo., Kansas City, 1968, M.A., 1970; Ph.D., Union Grad. Sch., Yellow Springs, Ohio, 1977; m. Fred Allen James, Sept. 15, 1945; children—John William, Meta Elizabeth. Surveyor, free-lance writer Kansas City (Mo.) Star, 1971-72; counselor Nevada (Mo.) State Hosp., 1972, Nat. Council on Alcoholism, Kansas City, Mo., 1972-77; grant cons. Midwest Research Inst., Kansas City, Mo., 1976-77; founder, pres. Task Force for Women Alcoholics, Inc., 1975-76, exec. bd. advisor, 1976—. Mem. exec. bd. Tracy House; trustee NCA. Mem. Am. Psychol. Assn., Am. Mensa Ltd., Mo. Assn. Alcoholism Counselors, Kans. Alcoholism Counselors Assn. Republican. Clubs: P.E.O. Editor, pub. Emerson Newsletter, 1969-72; editorial referee Jour. Studies on Alcohol, 1972, 74, 76, 77. Research in field of alcoholism and psychology. Contbr. articles to sci. jours. Home: 432 Winnebago Dr Greenwood MO 64034

JAMES, MARION RAY, editor; b. Bellmont, Ill., Dec. 6, 1940; s. Francis Miller and Alma Lorraine (Wylie) J.; B.S., Oakland City Coll., 1964; postgrad. U. Evansville, 1966, St. Francis Coll., 1974-77; m. Janet Sue Tennis, June 16, 1960; children—Jeffrey Glenn, David Ray, Daniel Scott, Cheryl Lynne. Sports and city editor Daily Clarion, Princeton, Ind., 1963-65; English tchr. Jac-Cen-Del High Sch., Osgood, Ind., 1965-66; indsl. editor Whirlpool Corp., Evansville and LaPorte, Ind., 1966-68; indsl. editor Magnavox Govt. and Indsl. Electronics Co., Fort Wayne, Ind., 1968—; pres., editor, pub. Bowhunter mag. Blue-J Pub. Co., Fort Wayne, 1970—. Active basketball program Fort Wayne Police Athletic League; publicity adviser Allen County Soc. Crippled Children and Adults, 1976-77. bd. dirs., mgr. Time Corners Little League. Recipient Best Editorial award United Community Services Publs., 1970-72. Mem. Internat. Assn. Bus. Communicators, Outdoor Writers Assn. Am., Fort Wayne Assn. Bus. Editors (Fort Wayne Bus. Editor of Year 1969, pres. 1975-76), MAGIEC Mgmt. Club, Alpha Phi Gamma, Alpha Psi Omega, Mu Tau Kappa. Club: Toastmasters (Able Toastmaster award). Author: Bowhunting for Whitetail and Mule Deer, 1975; editor: Pope and Young Book World Records, 1975. Home: 9713 Saratoga Rd Fort Wayne IN 46804 Office: 1313 Production Rd Fort Wayne IN 46808

JAMES, O'DESSIE OLIVER, educator, counselor; b. Terry County, Tex., Jan. 13, 1937; d. Doddie Baccus and Willie Mae (Smith) Oliver; B.A., Tex. Tech. U., 1959, M.Ed., 1967; Ed.D. in Guidance and Counseling (Univ. scholar), North Tex. State U., 1975; m. Vernon L. James, July 17, 1976; children—Deborah, Cindy, Huntly. Tchr. pub. schs., Euless, Seminole, Irving, Lubbock, Tex., 1958-67; counselor elementary schs., Lubbock, 1967-68; sch. psychologist, Plainview and Denton, Tex., 1968-69; chmn. guidance program Denton Pub. Schs., 1969-71; pvt. practice marriage and family counseling, Denton, 1971-74; asst. prof. guidance and counseling Wichita (Kans.) State U., 1974—; weekly newspaper columnist on parenting Wichita Eagle and Beacon, 1977—; cons. Head Start, Rural Med. Outreach Program, Infant Stimulation Project, Sedgwick County Juvenile Ct., Wichita Rape Crisis Center, others. Mem. Am., Kans. personnel and guidance assns., Am. Assn. Marriage and Family Counselors (sec. Central Midwest chpt.), Kans. Assn. Counselor Educators and Supervisors (pres.), Nat. Assn. Sch. Psychologists. Author: A Compilation of the Rationale and Research in Play Therapy, 1975; A Historical Overview of Play Therapy, 1977. Contbr. articles to profl. jours. Research on mother-infant bonding. Home: 1925 N Edgemoor St Wichita KS 67208 Office: Wichita State U Coll Edn Wichita KS 67208

JAMES, RICHARD HALE, dentist; b. Emporia, Kans., Apr. 10, 1929; s. William Richard and Vivion Simmons (Hale) J.; B.S., U. Kans., 1952; D.D.S., U. Mo., 1965; m. Ann Louise Jones, Aug. 11, 1949; children—Louise Ann (Mrs. Ronald L. Reno), William David. Geologist, land and geol. div. Phillips Petroleum Co., 1952-58, James & Hutchinson, cons. geologists, 1958-61; pvt. practice dentistry, Emporia, 1965—. Chmn. panel on continuing edn. Kans. Dental Bd., 1975—. Mem. Acad. Gen. Dentistry, Soc. Preservation Oral Health, Am., Kans. State (adv. com. on continuing edn. to State Bd. Dental Examiners 1969-75) dental assns., Fifth Dist. (pres. 1973-74), Flint Hills Dist. (v.p. 1976-77) dental socs., Omicron Kappa Upsilon. Home: 1259 Thompson St Emporia KS 66801 Office: 201 W 12th St Emporia KS 66801

JAMES, WALTER, state ofcl.; b. Mpls., June 8, 1915; s. James Edward and Mollie (Gress) Smoleroff; B.Ch.E., U. Minn., 1938, postgrad, 1945-60; m. Jesse Ann Pickens, Dec. 27, 1948; 1 son, Joel Pickens. Process designer Monsanto Chem. Co., St. Louis, 1940-45; instr. math U. Minn., Mpls., 1945-60, extension div., 1950—; researcher computer based applied math. 3M Co., St. Paul, 1960-68; info. systems planner State of Minn., St. Paul, 1968—. Mem. Am. Math. Assn., AAAS, Sigma Xi. Democrat. Home: 6228 Brooklyn Dr Brooklyn Center MN 55430

JAMES, WARREN EDWARD, educator, musician; b. Xenia, Ohio, Oct. 29, 1922; a. Joshua Byford and Millie (McCoy) J.; student Muskingum Coll., 1940-41; B.S., Ohio State U., 1947, M.A., 1949, Ph.D., 1957; m. Betty M. Smith, 1946 (div.), 1 child, Terri Jan Holderman; m. 2d, Claire Y. Jackson, 1957 (div. 1962), children—Weston Eric, Carson Willard; m. 3d, Martha Boulton, 1968. Instr., Cornell U., 1951-52; instr. Ohio State U., 1952-57; asst. prof. Rutgers U., 1957-59; dir. alcoholism unit Ohio Dept. Health, Columbus, 1960-61; prof. sociology Central State U., Wilberforce, Ohio, 1962—, conductor workshops in improvised music, ethnomusicology, 1976-77; flutist, composer; owner Nada Records, Yellow Springs, Ohio, 1972-77. Served with U.S. Army, 1943-46. Mem. Soc. Ethnomusicology, N.Central Sociol. Assn., Assn. Humanistic Psychology. Author: Alcoholism in Ohio, 1950; editor: Sick Man in Society, 1967; composer: Summer Rain, 1962; composer-producer record album Intersections, 1973. Address: 251 Whitehall Dr Yellow Springs OH 45387

JAMES, WILLIAM ELLERY SEDGWICK, physician; b. N.Y.C., June 1, 1920; s. Ellery Sedgwick and Louise Russell (Hoadley) J.; B.A., Yale, 1942; M.D., Columbia, 1945; m. Mary Ladds, Nov. 18, 1950; children—Sarah L.S., Laura Ladds., Emily Preston. Intern, Mary Imogene Bassett Hosp., 1945-46; asst. resident in medicine Univ. Hosps., Cleve., 1948-49; resident in internal medicine Cleve. VA Hosp., 1949-51; demonstrator dept. preventive medicine Case Western Res. U. Med. Sch., Cleve., 1951-52, now sr. instr. medicine; practice medicine specializing in internal medicine, Cleve. and Shaker Heights, 1952—; active staff St. Luke's Hosp., Cleve.; sch. physician Shaker Heights Schs., 1952-77. Pres. Margaret Wagner House, 1967. Served as lt. (j.g.) USN, 1946-48. Eddie Painton fellow in rheumatic fever, 1952-55. Diplomate Am. Bd. Internal Medicine. Mem. A.C.P., AMA, Ohio Med. Assn., Cleve. Acad. Medicine, Cleve. Diabetes Assn. (trustee 1962-69), Nu Sigma Nu. Republican. Episcopalian. Clubs: Kirtland Country, Montserrat Golf. Home: 2266 Chatfield Dr Cleveland Heights OH 44106 Office: 3461 Warrensville Center Shaker Heights OH 44122

JAMES, WILLIAM JOSEPH, chemist; b. Providence, Sept. 17, 1922; s. Christopher and Rose (Petit) J.; B.S., Tufts U., 1949; M.S., Iowa State U., 1952, Ph.D., 1953; m. Arlene Carll, Aug. 23, 1942; children—Varie Linda James Lynch, Candice Lynn. Predoctoral research fellow in corn products Iowa State U., 1949-53; NIH fellow Pa. State U., 1952; asst. prof. chemistry U. Mo., Rolla, 1953-57, asso. prof., 1957-64, prof., 1964—, dir. grad. center materials research, 1964-75, asso. dir. grad. center materials research, 1975-76, mem. staff Inst. for Chem. and Extractive Metallurgy, sr. investigator materials research, 1976—; indsl. cons., 1957—; abstractor Am. Chem. Soc., 1963—; dir., treas. Mead Chem. Corp., Rolla, 1975—; Fulbright research prof. U. Grenoble (France), 1961-62. Mem. tech. adv. com. St. Louis Regional Council for Growth and Commerce, 1975—. Served with USAAC, 1941-46; PTO. Decorated Air medal; recipient Outstanding Tchr. award Circle K. U. of Mo-Rolla, 1965, Outstanding Research award, 1968, Alumni Merit award for research, 1970; 10 Years Service award Chem. Abstracts, 1972—. Fellow Am. Inst. Chemists; mem. Am. Crystallographic Assn., Electrochem. Soc., Mo. (pres. 1968—), N.Y. acads. scis., Newcomen Soc., Keramos, Alpha Chi Sigma, Sigma Pi Sigma, Phi Lambda Upsilon, Sigma Xi, Alpha Sigma Mu, Phi Kappa Phi, Kappa Sigma. Contbr. articles to profl. publs. Home: Route 1 Rolla MO 65401 Office: Materials Research Center U of Mo Rolla MO 65401

JAMESON, LEE MERLE, dentist; b. Peoria, Ill., May 28, 1946; s. Donovan Edward and Josephine May (Wolf) J.; B.S. in Biology, Bradley U., 1968; D.D.S., Loyola U., Chgo., 1974, M.S. in Oral Biology, 1976; m. Loretta Joan Cuder, July 12, 1975. Sci. tchr. Central High Sch., East Peoria, Ill., 1968-70; gen. practice dentistry, Darien, Ill., 1974-76, Palos Heights, Ill., 1977—; clin. instr. dept. fixed prosthodontics Loyola Dental Sch., Chgo., 1975—. Mem. Am. Dental Assn., Ill., Chgo. dental socs., Am. Coll. Prosthodontists Casso., (1st place Research Competition 1977), Xi Psi Phi, Blue Key. Home: 728 E Berkshire Lombard IL 60148 Office: 7600 College Dr Palos Heights IL 60463

JAMIESON, RICHARD CHANNING, machine tool co. exec.; b. Cin., July 16, 1923; s. Donald Griffith and Elizabeth (Hunt) J.; B.A., Hanover Coll., 1948; m. Margaret Ann Judd, June 19, 1948; children—Beth, Andrew, Melissa. With Carroll-Jamieson Machine Tool Co., Batavia, Ohio, 1951—, gen. mgr., 1960—, sec.-treas., 1956—. Gen. chmn. Batavia Sesquicentennial Celebration, 1964; mem. Batavia Village Council, 1956-58, mayor, 1959-75; mem. Batavia Sch. Dist. Sch. Bd., 1962-70. Served with inf. AUS, 1943-46, 51-53. Decorated Bronze Star. Mem. Phi Delta Theta. Presbyterian (elder). Home: 460 Diana St Batavia OH 45103 Office: 77 Foundry St Batavia OH 45103

JAMISON, WALLACE NEWLIN, clergyman, coll. dean; b. Alexandria, Egypt, Aug. 1, 1918; s. William Brainerd and Gertrude May (Newlin) J. (parents Am. citizens); B.A., Westminster Coll., Pa., 1940, L.H.D. (hon.), 1976; Th.B., Princeton Theol. Sem., 1943; Ph.D., U. Edinburgh, 1948; m. Ruth Dean Galloway, Nov. 16, 1943; children—Kathryn M., Robert N., Mary E., James W. Ordained to ministry United Presbyn. Ch. U.S.A., 1943; pastor United Presbyn. Ch., Indianola, Iowa, 1948-51; chmn. dept. history, dean chapel Westminster (Pa.) Coll., 1951-56; prof. ch. history New Brunswick (N.J.) Theol. Sem., 1956-63, pres., 1963-69; dean coll. Ill. Coll., Jacksonville, Ill., 1970—. Served with Chaplain Corps, USNR, 1943-46. Mem. Am. Hist. Assn., Am. Assn. Acad. Deans, Phi Alpha Theta. Republican. Rotarian. Author: The United Presbyterian Story, 1958; Religion in New Jersey, 1964. Home: 112 Park St Jacksonville IL 62650

JAMRICH, JOHN XAVIER, univ. pres.; b. Muskegon Heights, Mich., June 12, 1920; s. John and Mary (Mudry) J.; B.S., U. Chgo., 1943; M.S., Marquette U., 1948; Ph.D., Northwestern U., 1951; L.H.D., No. Mich. U., 1968; m. June Ann Hrupka, June 26, 1944; children—June Ann, Marna Mary, Barbara Sue. Instr. math. Marquette U., 1946-48; asst. instr. math. U. Wis., 1948-49; asst. dean of men Northwestern U., 1949-51; dean of students Coe Coll., 1951-55; prof. math., dean of faculty Doane Coll., 1955-57; asst. dir. Legis. Survey of Higher Edn. in Mich., 1957-58; prof. higher edn. Mich. State U., 1957-58, dir. Center for Study Higher Edn., 1957-63, asso. dean Coll. of Edn., 1963-68; pres. No. Mich. U., Marquette, 1968—. Dir. Lake Superior & Ishpeming R.R. Cos. examiner No. Central Assn. of Colls. and Secondary Schs.; cons. Ford Found., Ohio Bd. Regents, S.C., Va. Commns. on Higher Edn., U. Chgo., Mich. Bd. of Edn., Thailand Ministry of Edn. Bd. dirs. St. Luke's Hosp., Bay Cliff Health Camp, Marquette; trustee Carthage Coll., Kenosha, Wis. Served to capt. USAAF, 1942-46. Decorated Order of Lion of Finland; recipient Israel City of Peace award, 1974. Mem. Newcomen Soc. N.Am. Home: 537 W Kaye Ave Marquette MI 49855

JAN, GEORGE POKUNG, educator, polit. scientist; b. Peking, China, Jan. 6, 1925; s. Yunan and Tehchieh (Lee) J.; came to U.S., 1955, naturalized, 1969; A.B., Nat. Chengchi U., Nanking, China, 1949; M.A., So. Ill. U., 1956; Ph.D., N.Y. U., 1960; m. Norma Y. Wen, Sept. 28, 1946; children—Gregory, David, Daniel. Mng. editor daily newspaper, pub., editor weekly mag., radio program lectr., newspaper editorial writer, fgn. service intern Ministry Fgn. Affairs Republic of China, tchr., dean schs., dir. lang. sch., 1949-55; instr. Chinese, N.Y. U., 1959-60; asst. prof. polit. sci. No. Ill. U., 1961; from asst. to prof. govt. U. S.D., 1961-68, dir. Summer Inst. Asian Studies, 1964-66; research asso. Social Sci. Found., U. Denver Grad. Sch. Internat. Studies, 1967-68; prof. polit. sci. U. Toledo, 1968—, chmn. Asian Studies program; mem. bd. Toledo Council World Affairs, 1968—; chmn. bd. Jan Jet Corp., Jan Enterprises, Inc. Grantee Asia Soc., Asia Found., Japan Soc., U. Denver, U. Chgo., U. S.D., U. Toledo. Mem. Am., Internat., Midwest polit. sci. assns., Internat. Congress Orientalists, Assn. Asian Studies, Internat. Studies Assn., Phi Beta Kappa, Pi Sigma Alpha, Phi Kappa Phi. Contbr. articles, papers to profl. jours.; author: A Practical Grammar for Jr. and Middle Schools, 1953; A Study of English Words, 1955; The Chinese Commune Experiment, 1964; Government of Communist China, 1966; The International Politics of Asia, 1969. Home: 2253 Goddard Rd Toledo OH 43606

JANARDAN, KONANUR G., educator; b. Konanur, India, Oct. 15, 1934; s. Gundappa Setty V. and Kusumamba G. (Chinnari) J.; came to U.S., 1966; B.Sc. with honours, U. Mysore, India, 1956, M.Sc., 1957; M.A., Pa. State U., 1968, Ph.D., 1970; m. Arundathi Bysani, Feb. 22, 1957; children—Satish, Nanda, Vas. Econ. investigator Planning Commn. Govt. India, 1957-60; lectr. statistics Sri Venkateswara U., India, 1963-66; sr. lectr. U. Mysroe, India, 1964-66; teaching, research asst. Pa. State U., 1966-69, instr. statistics, 1970-71; asst. prof. math. Montclair State U., Upper Montclair, N.J., 1970-71; asso. prof. math. Sangamon State U., Springfield, Ill., 1971—; cons. Ill. EPA. Mem. Am. Statis. Soc., Biometrics, Am. Assn. Math., Phi Mu Epsilon. Contbr. articles to profl. jours. Home: 3017 Clifton Dr Springfield IL 62704

JANATA, RUDOLPH, lawyer; b. Pitts., May 19, 1920; s. Rudolph and Jean (Baker) J.; A.B., U. Pitts., 1941; J.D., Harvard, 1948; m. Mary Jean McCally, Mar. 17, 1951; children—Jeffrey Ward, Julie Ellen, David Wells. Admitted to Ohio bar, 1949; with firm Porter, Wright, Morris & Arthur, Columbus, 1949—. Mem. exec. com., bd. dirs. Ohio Citizens Council, 1963-68; chmn. Ohio Com. on Crime and Delinquency, 1963-65; pres. Columbus Area Council Chs., 1958-60. Bd. dirs. Columbus Met. YMCA, 1965—, pres., 1973-77; trustee Heidelberg Coll., 1965-75, vice chmn., 1967-74; trustee Ohio Legal Center Inst., 1971-75, chmn. bd. trustees, 1974-75; trustee Nat. Council on Crime and Delinquency, 1962-65; bd. dirs. Def. Research Inst., 1970—, pres., 1974-75, chmn. bd. dirs. 1975-76. Served to maj. AUS, 1941-46. Recipient Distinguished Service award U.S. Jaycees, 1953. Fellow Am. Bar Found.; mem. Harvard Law Sch. Assn. Ohio (pres. 1961-62), Harvard Law Sch. Assn. (nat. v.p. 1964-71), Ohio State Bar Assn. (pres. 1972-73), Ohio Def. Assn. (pres. 1967-68), Internat. Assn. Ins. Counsel. Clubs: University (trustee 1961-64, v.p. 1964); Crichton; Harvard; Zanesfield Rod and Gun (trustee 1969—). Contbg. author: Personal Injury Litigation in Ohio, 1965. Home: 6976 Clark State Rd Blacklick OH 43004 Office: 37 W Broad St Columbus OH 43215

JANDACEK, JAMES WARREN, lawyer; b. Evergreen Park, Ill., Oct. 1, 1949; s. George Warren and Joanne Patricia (Leahy) J.; A.B., Cornell U., 1970, M.Engring. in Engring. Physics, 1971; J.D., Harvard U., 1974. Admitted to Ill. bar, 1976; law clk. to Judge Charles M. Merrill, U.S. Ct. Appeals, 9th Circuit, San Francisco, 1974-75; asso. firm Sidley & Austin, Chgo., 1975—. Sec., bd. dirs. Ill. Sci. Lecture Assn., 1975—; mem. jr. governing bd. Chgo. Symphony, 1976—. Mem. Am., Ill., Chgo. bar assns., Assn. ICC Practitioners. Presbyterian. Editorial bd. Harvard Law Rev., 1972-74, note editor, 1973-74. Home: 3027 Scott Crescent Flossmoor IL 60422 Office: Sidley & Austin One First Nat Plaza Chicago IL 60603

JANECKE, ARTHUR THOMAS, physician; b. Chgo., Sept. 18, 1923; s. John Joseph and Pauline Anne (Bennett) J.; M.D., Loyola U., 1947; m. Marion Sylvia Albert, Feb. 15, 1947; children—John Gerard, Thomas Gerard, Martin Gerard, Mary Anne, Beth Anne, Jennifer Marie, Peter Gerard, Julie Anne. Intern Little Co. of Mary Hosp., Evergreen Park, Ill., 1947-48, surg. resident, 1948-49; practice of medicine, Chgo., 1949—; mem. staff Little Co. of Mary Hosp., Evergreen Park, pres. staff, 1971, head dept. family practice, 1964-70; sr. attending staff St. Georges Hosp., Chgo.; head dept. family practice Palos Community Hosp., 1975—. Served to capt. AUS, 1943-46, 55-56. Decorated Commendation Ribbon with metal pendant.

Recipient Physicians Recognition award for continuing edn. AMA, 1969, 71, 73, 76. Diplomate Am. Bd. Family Practice (charter mem.), Pan. Am. Med. Assn. Fellow Am. Acad. Family Practice, Internat. Acad. Proctology; mem. AMA, Ill. State Med. Soc., Chgo. Med. Soc. (br. pres. 1969-70), Am. Acad. Gen. Practice, Cath. Physicians Guild, Right to Life Com. K.C. Home: 12011 S Winslow Rd Palos Park IL 60464 Office: 11110 S Sawyer Ave Chicago IL 60655

JANEVICIUS, VINCAS, neuropsychiatrist; b. Vilnius, Lithuania, July 18, 1922; s. P. and Marija (Rodzevicius) J.; came to U.S., 1951, naturalized, 1957; pre-med. degree U. Vilnius, 1944; M.D., U. Hamburg (Germany), 1949; postgrad. Loyola U., Chgo., 1973, U. Chgo., 1974; m. Anna Balciunas, Jan. 7, 1953; children—Raymond, Richard. Resident, U. Clinics, Hamburg, Germany, 1949-51; intern South Shore Hosp., Chgo., 1952-53; postgrad. tng. in neuropsychiatry Ill. State Psychiat. Inst., Chgo./Research Hosp., Galesburg, Ill., 1955-58; fellow in neuropsychiatry VA West Side Hosp., Chgo., 1960-61; attending physician East Moline State Hosp./Galesburg Research Hosp., 1953-55; chief of service Galesburg Research Hosp., 1958-60; sr. psychiatrist VA Hosp., Danville, Ill., 1961-62; med. dir. Kankakee (Ill.) State Hosp., 1962—; pvt. practice neuropsychiatry, Kankakee, 1964—. Cons. St. Mary's Hosp., Riverside Hosp., local cts., Dwight (Ill.) Women's Reformatory; coroner's physician Kankakee County, 1963—; aviation med. examiner FAA, 1974—. Mem. AMA, Am. Psychiat. Assn., Ill., Chgo., Kankakee County med. socs., Med. Assn. Ill. Dept. Mental Health, World, Ill. Lithuanian med. assns. Ill. State Psychiat. Inst. Alumni Assn., Aircraft Owners and Pilots Assn., Kankakee Valley Pilots Assn., Chgo. Motor Club. Home: 36 Marquette Ln Kankakee IL 60901 Office: 258 E Court St Kankakee IL 60901

JANIS, MICHAEL JAMES, zoo dir.; b. Chgo., Apr. 2, 1947; s. Fabian S. and Phyllis J. (Underwood) J.; m. Victoria Elizabeth Christie, Dec. 23, 1967; 1 dau., Jennifer Lynn. Naturalist, Kingwood Center, Mansfield, Ohio, 1967-68, Forest Preserve Dist. DuPage County (Ill.), Lombard, 1968-69, Fla. State Parks, Ft. White, 1969-70; curator of birds Balt. Zoo, 1970-71; dir. Bolingbrook (Ill.) Park Dist., 1971-73; dir. outdoor edn. Hutchinson (Kans.) Recreation Commn., 1973-75; dir. Harvey County (Kans.) Parks Dept., Newton, 1975-77; dir. Akron (Ohio) Children's Zoo, 1977—. Recipient Distinguished Service award Ill. Assn. Kiwanis Clubs, 1966; named Youth Conservationist of Year, Ill. Wildlife Fedn., 1966; others. Mem. Nat. (certified), Kans. (certified; dir. 1976-77, chmn. pub. info. com. 1976-77), Ohio (certified) recreation and parks assns., Am. Assn. Zool. Parks and Aquariums, Assn. Interpretive Naturalists, Ohio Mus. Assn., Natural Sci. for Youth Found., Kans. Assn. Biology Tchrs., Nat. Audubon Soc., Sand Hills Audubon Soc. (co-founder, dir. 1973-76). Contbr. articles to profl. jours. Office: Akron Children's Zoo 500 Edgewood Ave Akron OH 44307

JANKE, HERBERT GUST, chiropractor, educator; b. Munson, Pa., Mar. 14, 1918; s. Gust and Emma (Ziehmer) J.; B.C., Pa. State U., 1940; D.C., Palmer Coll. Chiropractic, Davenport, Iowa, 1969; m. Lorna Alice Campbell, Oct. 20, 1940; children—Sylvia Janke Kelly, Theodore A. Vets.' agrl. instr. Westmoreland County Schs., Greensburg, Pa., 1946-52; partner Janke's Meats Packing House, Winburne, Pa., 1952-67; instr. Palmer Chiropractic Coll., 1970; practice chiropractics, Davenport, 1970—. Served with AUS. Mem. Am. Legion. Baptist. Clubs: Elks, Lions (pres.). Author: How To Raise Ducks, 1940; Stones Shall Shout, 1970; Yesterday, I Had to Speak a Piece, others. Home: 6204 W Kimberly Rd Davenport IA 52806 Office: 526 W 3d St Davenport IA 52803

JANKLOW, WILLIAM JOHN, atty. gen. S.D.; b. Chgo., Sept. 13, 1939; B.S., J.D., U. S.D.; m. Mary Dean; children—Russell, Pamela, Shawna. Dir., S.D., Legal Aid, 1967-72; chief prosecutor Office Atty. Gen. of S.D., 1973-74, atty. gen., 1975—; practice law, Pierre, S.D., 1972-73. Served with USMC, 1956-59; Vietnam. Mem. Am., S.D. trial lawyers assns., Am. Judicature Soc., Am., S.D. bar assns. Recipient Nat. award for Legal Excellence and Skill, Office of Equal Opportunity Legal Services. Home: 214 S Washington St Pierre SD 57501 Office: Office Atty Gen State House Pierre SD 57501*

JANKURA, DONALD EUGENE, hotel exec.; b. Bridgeport, Conn., Dec. 20, 1929; s. Stephen and Susan (Dirga) J.; B.A., Mich. State U., 1951; m. Elizabeth Deborah Joynt, June 20, 1952; children—Donald E., Stephen J., Daria E., Diane E., Lynn M. Unit mgr. Harding-William Co., 1951; asst. sales mgr. Pick Fort Shelby Hotel, Detroit, 1952; steward, sales mgr., resident mgr. Dearborn Inn (Mich.), 1953-62; mgr. Stouffer's Northland Inn, Southfield, Mich., 1962-66; staff adviser Stouffer Motor Inns, Cleve., 1966-67, v.p., 1968; v.p. Asso. Inns and Restaurants Co. Am., 1968-74, exec. v.p., 1974—; v.p. ARI, Inc., 1974—; sec., v.p. O.P. Baur Confectionery Co., Denver, also dir.; asso. mem. Cleve. Real Estate Bd. Mem. Detroit Hotel Sales Mgmt. Assn. (past pres.), Mich. State U. Hotel Alumni, Mich. Hotel Assn. (sec.-treas., v.p.), Am. (dir.), Ohio (dir.) hotel and motel assns., Nat. Hotel Sales Mgrs. Assn., Phi Kappa Tau. Episcopalian. Clubs: Masons (32 deg.), Shriners. Home: 3249 E Monmouth Rd Cleveland Heights OH 44118 Office: 29425 Chagrin Blvd Cleveland OH 44122

JANNICK, DAVID ARNOLD, clin. psychologist; b. Jefferson City, Mo., Aug. 18, 1947; s. Harry Edward and Genevieve Faith (Curley) J.; B.S., Lincoln U., 1971; M.S., Central Mo. State U., 1973; m. Sandra Lee Gray, Aug. 21, 1970. Fisheries biologist Mo. Conservation Commn., Jefferson City, Mo., 1966-67; psychol. technician Fulton (Mo.) State Hosp., 1971-72, clin. psychologist, 1973-74, supr. Psychol. Services, Maximum Security Unit, 1975—. Workshop leader White House Conf. on Handicapped Individuals, 1976. Served with AUS, 1968-69. Mem. Am., Mo. psychol. assns., Am. Soc. Criminology, Inst. for Reality Therapy, Am. Parapsychol. Research Found., DAV, ACLU, Mo., Great Central States archaeol. socs., Jefferson City Archaeol. Club, Nat. Soc. Pub. Poets. Home: 346 Fredericks Ln Jefferson City MO 65101 Office: Maximum Security Unit Fulton State Hosp Fulton MO 65251

JANNING, MARY BERNADETTE, hosp. adminstr.; b. Custer City, Okla., May 20, 1917; d. Frank R. and Mary Elizabeth (Kreizenbeck) Janning; R.N., St. Francis Hosp. Sch. Nursing, Wichita, Kans., 1942; B.S. in Nursing Edn., Marquette U., 1951, M.S., 1952; certificate in health care adminstrn., George Washington U., 1972. Joined Sisters of Sorrowful Mother, 1936; asst. dir. St. Johns Sch. Nursing, Tulsa, 1952-56; dir. St. Francis Sch. Nursing, Wichita, 1956-65, asso. adminstr., 1972-73, pres., chief exec. officer, 1973—; provincial superior Tulsa Province, Sisters of Sorrowful Mother, 1965-70. Pres., bd. dirs. St. Francis Hosp. and Sch. Nursing, Inc.; chmn. bd. Kans. affiliate Am. Diabetes Assn., 1973-76; sec. bd. dirs. Midway Kans. chpt. ARC. Mem. Kans. Conf. Catholic Health Affairs (pres. 1977), Am. Coll. Hosp. Adminstrs., Am., Kans. (dir.), Cath. hosp. assns., Nat., Kans. leagues for nursing, Hosp. Council Met. Wichita, Wichita Hosp. Adminstrs. Recipient Twenty Year Pin award ARC, 1962; named Alumni Nurse of Year, St. Francis Sch. Nursing, 1972; Author: Life of a Student Nurse, 1961; contbr. chpts. to Nursing Outlook, 1955; The Kansas Nurse, 1958. Home and office: 929 N St Francis Ave Wichita KS 67214

JANNOTTA, NICHOLAS CARMEN, real estate cons. firm exec.; b. Chgo., Apr. 29, 1932; s. Carmen C. and Victoria A. (Dymek) J.; A.A., Wright Jr. Coll., 1951; m. Margaret Miller, Oct. 21, 1961; children—Robert Anthony, Joan Louise, Carol Day. Cost estimator Carmen Constrn. Co., Chgo., 1954-56; with Real Estate Research Corp., Chgo., 1956—, sr. v.p., 1972-74, exec. v.p., 1974—, also dir.; dir. IMC Devel. Corp. Mem. NRC commn. on socitech. systems Transp. Research Bd., Washington, 1974—. Served with AUS, 1952-54. Mem. Am. Inst. Real Estate Appraisers, Am. Soc. Real Estate Counselors, Nat. Assn. Housing and Redevel. Ofcls., Realtors' 40 Club, Lambda Alpha. Club: Union League. Home: 715 S Lincoln Ln Arlington Heights IL 60005 Office: 72 W Adams St Chicago IL 60603

JANOVER, ROBERT H., lawyer; b. N.Y.C., Aug. 17, 1930; s. Cyrus J. and Lillian D. (Horwitz) J.; B.A., Princeton U., 1952; J.D., Harvard U., 1957; m. Mary Elizabeth McMahon, Oct. 23, 1966; 1 dau., Laura Lockwood. Admitted to N.Y. State bar, 1957, U.S. Supreme Ct. bar, 1961, D.C. bar, 1966, Mich. bar, 1973; practice law, N.Y.C., 1957-65; cons. Office of Edn. HEW, 1965, legis. atty. Office of Gen. Counsel, HEW, 1965-66; asst. gen. atty. Mgmt. Assistance, Inc., N.Y.C., 1966-71; atty. Ford Motor Credit Co., Dearborn, Mich., 1971-74; mem. firm. Freud, Markus, Slavin, Toohey & Galgan, Troy, Mich., 1974—. Vice-pres., dir. Oakland Citizens League, 1976—. Served to 2d lt. U.S. Army, 1952-54. Mem. Mich. State Bar, Am., N.Y. State, Detroit bar assns., Bar Assn. D.C., Assn. Bar of City of N.Y. Clubs: Harvard (N.Y.C.). Home: 685 Ardmoor Dr Birmingham MI 48010 Office: 2401 W Big Beaver Rd Troy MI 48084

JANOWICH, WILLIAM ANTHONY, data processing cons.; b. Cleve., Oct. 16, 1945; s. William Andrew and Frances Marie (Szychowski) J.; student parochial schs., Cleve.; m. Johann Burry, Sept. 2, 1967; children—Laura, Mark. Systems programmer Cook United, Cleve., 1967-68; sr. systems cons. White Motors, Cleve., 1969-70; mgr. profl. services, sr. cons. Neoterics, Cleve., 1970-76, br. mgr., 1977. Served with USMC, 1965. Certified data processor. Mem. Data Processing Mgmt. Assn. (dir. 1975-77), Am. Prodn. and Inventory Control Soc. (tchr.). Roman Catholic. Home: 16140 W 130th St Strongsville OH 44136 Office: 1801 E 9th St Cleveland OH 44114

JANOWSKI, BARBARA EDGECOMBE RAY (BARBARA RAY), photographer, writer, lectr.; b. East Liverpool, Ohio, Jan. 14, 1912; d. Arthur Elmore and Elizabeth Birney (Ripley) Edgecombe; high sch. grad.; m. Joseph Earnest Janowski, Aug. 1, 1946; children—Jan Joel, Joel Justin. Proofreader, editor, cost estimator Hawkins & Loomis, 1929-32, McCormick & Henderson, 1932-37, Ill. Typesetters, 1938-40, LaSalle St. Press, all Chgo., 1940-43; owner, operator Barbara Ray Portrait Studio, Gary, Ind., 1943-52; camera page editor Gary Post-Tribune, 1956-71; free-lance writer. Mem. Gary C. of C. Speakers' Bur., 1960-68. Recipient Good Citizenship medal, Ind. Soc. Sons Am. Revolution, 1963. Mem. Gen. Soc. Mayflower Descs. (corr. sec. 1963-64), Ind., Nat. socs. daus. founders and patriots Am., Colonial Dames 17th Century (state 1st v.p. 1963-65, organizing pres. Elder William Brewster chpt. 1961), Nat. Soc. D.A.R. (Ind. state chmn. pub. relations 1961-64, nat. vice chmn. pub. relations East-Central div. 1962-65, regent local chpt. 1964-66, 74-76), Nat. League Am. Pen Women, Profl. Photographers Am., Gary Women's Press Club (sec. 1963-64), Nat. Soc. Magna Charta Dames, Nat. Soc. Women Descs. Ancient and Hon. Arty. Co. (dep. nat. 1971-74), Nat. Soc. Descs. Knights Most Noble Order Garter, Sovereign Colonial Soc., Ams. Royal Descent, Plantagenet Soc., Order of Washington (life), Order of Three Crusades 1096-1192, New Eng. Women, Nat. Soc. Daus. 1812. Home: 149 Morningside Ave Gary IN 46408

JANSEN, BERNARD JOSEPH, engr.; b. Rockville, Minn., Aug. 10, 1927; s. Barney C and Blanche (Brinkman) J.; B.A. cum laude, St. Johns U., Minn., 1950; M.A., St. Louis U., 1952; m. Sarah Kathryn Knight, Dec. 17, 1955; children—Kathryn L., Bernard Joseph, Stephen T., David E. Teaching asst. St. Louis U., 1950-52; mathematician Ballistics Research Lab., Aberdeen (Md.) Proving Ground, 1953-54, summer 1955; instr. math. St. Johns U., Collegeville, Minn., 1954-56; with Univac Def. Systems Co., div. Sperry Rand Corp., St. Paul, 1956—, program mgr., 1967-76, staff cons. engr., 1976—; lectr. math. St. Thomas Coll., St. Paul, 1960-61; mem. com. spaceborne digital computers NASA, 1968-71. Active local Boy Scouts Am., 1946—; pres. home/sch. assn. Highland Roman Cath. Sch., 1974-75. Served with USNR, 1945-46, AUS, 1952-54. Mem. Math. Assn. Am., Sigma Xi, Pi Mu Epsilon. Co-author papers, monograph. Home: 1859 Hillcrest Ave Saint Paul MN 55116 Office: care Sperry Univac Univac Park Saint Paul MN 55165

JANSEN, LAWRENCE FREDERICK, classicist; b. St. Louis, Mar. 2, 1919; s. Lawrence G. and Elizabeth P. (Klostermann) J.; A.B., St. Louis U., 1942, M.A., 1944; S.T.L., St. Marys (Kans.) Coll., 1952. Joined S.J., Roman Cath. Ch., 1937, ordained priest, 1950; asst. prof. Regis Coll., Denver, 1944-47; asst. dean Creighton U., Omaha, 1952-58; asso. dean St. Louis U., 1958-74, prof. classical langs., 1974—. Mem. Nat. Assn. Acad. Affairs Adminstrs. (pres. 1973-75), Jesuit Ednl. Assn., Am. Personnel and Guidance Assn., Classical League, Assn. Am. Med. Colls. Author: Greek and Latin for Scientific Terminology, 1976. Home: Jesuit Hall 3601 Lindell Blvd St Louis MO 63108 Office: St Louis Univ 221 N Grand Blvd St Louis MO 63103

JANSEN, MARY AUDREY, psychologist; b. Pitts., June 23, 1947; d. William T. and Audrey (Standen) Delaney; B.S., U. Dayton, 1968; M.S., Wright State U., 1973; Ph.D., Kent State U., 1977; m. Wayne Allen Jansen, Aug. 24, 1968. Instr. dept. counselor edn. Wright State U., Dayton, 1975; counselor Bur. Vocat. Rehab., Dayton, 1973-75; therapist Good Samaritan Hosp. Community Mental Health Center, Dayton, 1976-77; asst. prof. dept. human resources U. Scranton (Pa.), 1977—; instr. Kent State U., 1975-76, Park Coll. Wright Patterson AFB, 1974-75. Mem. Am., Miami Valley psychol. assns., Am. Personnel and Guidance Assn., Assn. Advancement Behavior Therapy. Office: Dept Human Resources U Scranton Scranton PA 18510

JANSEN, ROBERT JOHN, coll. theatre dir., educator; b. St. Croix Falls, Wis., June 16, 1949; s. Walter and Myrtle Catherine (Hach) J.; B.S., U. Wis., Superior, 1970, M.A., 1972. Dir., Child Drama Center, Calif. State U., Fresno, 1972-76; dir. speech and drama, dir. Daisy Hill Theatre, Coll. St. Scholastica, Duluth, Minn., 1976—; dir., set designer, Palo Alto (Calif.) Childrens Theatre, 1976-77; dir. child and adult theatrical prodns.; cons. creative drama and children's theatre, elementary schs. Named Drama Theatre leader State of Calif., 1975. Home: 1023 W 6th St Duluth MN 55806 Office: Director Speech Drama Coll St Scholastica Duluth MN 55811

JANSMA, THEODORE JOHN, JR., psychologist; b. Phila., Apr. 17, 1943; s. Theodore John and Ruth Virginia (Gezon) J.; B.S., Calvin Coll., 1965; M.A., Mich. State U., 1967; Ph.D., Ill. Inst. Tech., 1971; m. Jo B. Battiston, June 28, 1969. Mental health rehab. counselor Chgo. State Hosp., 1967-69; staff psychologist Charles F. Read Zone Center, Chgo., 1969-71, adminstrv. psychologist, clin. chief service, 1971-72; staff psychologist Pine Rest Christian Hosp., Grand Rapids, Mich., 1972—; dir. dept. psychology, 1977—. adj. asst. prof. psychiatry Mich. State U., 1974—. Exec. dir. Project Talk, 1970-72, Chgo. Registered psychologist, Ill.; certified cons. psychologist, Mich. Nat. Rehab. Study grantee, 1965-67. Mem. Am. Psychol. Assn., Christian Assn. Psychol. Studies, Grand Rapids Area Psychol. Assn. Mem. Christian Reformed Ch. Home: 7434 Thornapple River Dr Caledonia MI 49316 Office: Pine Rest Christian Hosp 6850 S Division St Grand Rapids MI 49508

JANSON, THOMAS RALPH, research chemist; b. Amarillo, Tex., Dec. 31, 1944; s. Raphael Phillip and Marie Irene (Musielak) J.; B.S., St. Louis U., 1966; Ph.D., Case-Western Res. U., 1971; m. Donna Lee Kestler, June 11, 1966; children—David, Timothy, Brian. Asst. chemist Argonne (Ill.) Nat. Lab., 1970—. NDEA fellow, 1966-69. Mem. Am. Chem. Soc. Roman Catholic. Contbr. articles to profl. jours. Patentee in field. Home: 3812 Theodore St Joliet IL 60435 Office: Argonne Nat Lab 9700 S Cass Argonne IL 60439

JANSSEN, DALE HILTON, sales, mktg. and transp. co. exec.; b. Nelson, Neb., Oct. 13, 1921; s. William Fred and Nora Anna (Kramer) J.; student N.W. Mo. State Coll., 1940, Millsaps Coll., 1944-45, Harvard Sch. Bus., 1945; B.S. in Bus. Adminstrn., U. Mo., 1948; m. Lena Louise Gragg, Sept. 12, 1945; children—Deborah Janssen Dyer, Diane Carol Janssen Jensen, Gregory Dale. Research and mktg. asst. Mo. Farmers Assn., Columbia, 1948-49, asst. Fertilizer Chem. Plant, St. Louis, 1950-51, asst. traffic mgr., Columbia, 1952-62, traffic mgr. Soybean Processing Plant Complex, Mexico, Mo., 1963-65; transp. mgr. Soy-Cot Sales Inc., Des Plaines, Ill., 1966—. Merit badge counselor Boy Scouts Am., scoutmaster, 1973; block capt. Mt. Prospect Republican Com., 1972—. Served to lt. (j.g.) USNR, 1942-46. Mem. ICC Practitioners Assn. (chmn. Chgo. chpt.), Nat. Def. Transp. Assn., Res. Officers Assn., Traffic Club Chgo., Omicron Delta Kappa, Phi Kappa Alpha. Presbyterian (elder). Club: Kiwanis. Home: 709 S Can Dota Ave Mount Prospect IL 60056 Office: 2590 E Devon Ave Des Plaines IL 60018

JANSSEN, DONALD PHILLIP, telephone co. exec.; b. Stuart, Iowa, Mar. 20, 1924; s. Philip Bernard and Catherine Margaret (Happe) J.; student Iowa State U., 1942-43, 46-48; m. Katherine Ellen Hulsizer, Apr. 29, 1951; children—Lynn Marie, Kevin Charles. Lineman, Northwestern Bell Telephone Co., Marshalltown, Iowa, 1950-51, engr., 1951-60, dist. engr., 1960—. Vice pres. N.E. Council Alcoholism, 1967-71, pres., 1972—; councilman, Cedar Falls, Iowa, 1966-72. Served with USAAF, 1943-45. Mem. Waterloo, Cedar Falls (dir. 1973—) chambers commerce. Clubs: Sertoma, Elks (Cedar Falls). Home: 625 S Union Rd Cedar Falls IA 50613 Office: 403 Sycamore St Waterloo IA 50703

JANSZ, THOMAS WAYNE, food co. exec.; b. Aurora, Ill., July 13, 1947; s. Nicholas A. and Eileen M. J.; B.S., Aurora Coll., 1970; M.S. in Bus. Mgmt., No. Ill. U., 1971; m. Barbara Mae Raymond, Apr. 11, 1970. New ventures analyst New Product Devel. and Sales 3-M Co., Bedford Park, Ill., 1972-74; mgr. new product devel. and sales All-Steel div. C.I.T. Corp., Montgomery, Ill., 1974-76; group product mgr. Swift & Co., Chgo., 1976—; pres. Purity Products Inc., Naperville, Ill., 1977—; cons. in field. Mem. Aurora Zoning Bd. Appeals, 1972-74. Mem. Am. Mktg. Assn. Roman Catholic. Clubs: Naperville Racquet, Naperville Saddle. Home: 56 Oakwood Dr Naperville IL 60540 Office: 115 W Jackson St Chicago IL 60604

JANUZ, LAUREN ROBERT, direct response mktg. cons.; b. Highland Park, Ill., Jan. 1, 1939; s. Cipron Peter and Elsie (Nelson) J.; student Lake Forest Coll., 1956-58, Northwestern U., U. Detroit; m. Dorothy A. Heuer, Apr. 4, 1964. Pres. Lauren R. Januz & Assos., Inc., Chgo. and Lake Forest, Il., 1958-64; v.p. Pay/Gard Corp., Chgo., 1962-64; salesman Transo Envelope Co. div. Arvey Corp., Chgo., 1964, account exec., Grand Rapids, Mich., 1965, zone sales mgr. Western and Central Mich., 1965-67, Mich. and Ohio 1967-69, gen. mgr., dir. marketing direct mail div., 1969-70; sales mgr. U.O. Colson Co., Paris, Ill., 1970-71; pres. Januz Direct Mktg. Corp., Chgo., Advt. Agy., 1970-76; pres., pub. Januz Mktg. Communications, 1976—; pub. Januz Direct Mktg. Letter, 1974—; pres. Robert Peterson Co., Inc., 1976—; direct mail cons. to Ill. Republican campaigns, 1970-74; instr. Printing Industries Inst. Ill., 1974-76. Pres. Lake Pointe Homeowners Assn., Plymouth, Mich., 1968-70; co-founder Plymouth Twp. Council Homeowners Assns., 1968. Vice chmn. 49th ward Rep. Orgn., Chgo., 1963-64; Rep. precinct committeeman, 1971-75. Mem. Am. Topical Assn. (regional v.p. 1958-71, 2d v.p. 1971-74), Direct Mail Mktg. Assn., Assn. Direct Mktg. Agys., Direct Mktg. Writers Guild, Nat. Mail Order Assn., Philatelic Press Club, Chgo. Assn. Direct Mktg., Newsletter Assn. Am., U.S. Coast Guard Aux. (officer 1974—), Nat. Direct Mail Writers Club, Medinah Press Corp. Clubs: Masons (32 deg.), K.T., Shriners, Order Eastern Star, Toastmasters, Waukegan Yacht; Chgo. Press. Editor Am. Philatelic News, 1969-72; syndicated column The Stamp Collector; direct mktg. columnist Inland Printer, Am. Lithographer Mag. Contbr. articles to mags. Home: 1370 Longwood Rd Forest Haven Lake Forest IL 60045 Office: PO Box 109M Lake Forest IL 60045

JANZEN, ABRAHAM EWELL, hist. soc. adminstr., author; b. Williamsburg, Ukraine, Nov. 22, 1892; s. Abraham H. and Eva (Neufeld) J.; came to U.S., 1904, naturalized, 1913; M.Accts., Salt City Bus. Coll., Kan., 1916; student Tabor Coll., 1919-22; A.B., Kans. U., 1924, M.A., 1927; postgrad. U. Calif. at Berkeley, 1928-30, U. Colo., 1937; m. Zola Bae Lants, Dec. 24, 1917; 1 son, Philip. Tchr. elementary schs. Marion County, Kans., 1911-13; head dept. commerce Tabor Coll., Hillsboro, Kans., 1916-23, head dept. econs., 1924-31, pres., 1934-42, prof., 1942-45; prof. Friends U., Wichita, Kans., 1931-35; exec. sec. Mennonite Brethren Overseas Missions, 1945-60; pres. Mennonite Brethren Hist. Soc. of Midwest, Kans., 1966—; pres. Marion County Hist. Soc., Marion, Kans., 1969—. Mem. Marion County Council on Aging, 1973-75. Named Distinguished Alumnus of Tabor Coll., 1970. Mem. Pi Gamma Mu, Omicron Delta Gamma, Hillsboro C. of C. Mem. Mennonite Brethren Ch. (exec. sec. overseas missions 1945-60, pulpit com. 1936-72). Club: Golden Years of Marion County. Author: Wichita Grain Market, 1928; The Two Kingdoms, 1927; His Second Coming, 1934; Handbook on Peace, 1939; Glimpses of South America, 1944; Africa Mennonite Brethren Mission, 1947; India Mennonite Brethren Mission, 1948; History of Tabor College, Part I, 1958; The Moro's Spear, 1962, and others. Home: 602 S Lincoln St Hillsboro KS 67063 Office: 315 S Lincoln St Hillsboro KS 67063

JANZEN, ERNST KRIJGERS, orthodontist; b. The Netherlands, Sept. 22, 1932; s. Willem Krijgers and Geria (Noteboom) J.; D.D.S., Utrecht State U., The Netherlands, 1957; Ph.D., U. Zurich, Switzerland, 1962; D.D.S., Northwestern U., 1965, M.S., 1965; m. Agnes Pot, Jan. 24, 1959; children—Marita, Annette, Nicolette. Came to U.S., 1962, naturalized, 1967. Pvt. practice dentistry, specializing in orthodontics, Northbrook, Ill., 1966—. Served to capt., M.C., Royal Dutch Army, 1957-59. Recipient 1st prize Ann Research Contest, Am. Assn. Orthodontists, 1966, Milo Hellman Research award, 1966. Mem. Am., European, Ill. (exec. bd.) assns. orthodontists, Am. Dental Assn., Dutch Dental Soc. Republican. Presbyn. (trustee). Rotarian. Contbr. articles profl. jours. Home: 2240 Chestnut St Northbrook IL 60062 Office: 1240 Meadow Rd Northbrook IL 60062

JANZEN, NORINE MADELYN QUINLAN (MRS. DOUGLAS MAC ARTHUR JANZEN), med. technologist; b. Fond du Lac, Wis., Feb. 9, 1943; d. Joseph Wesley and Norma Edith (Gustin) Quinlan; B.S., Marian Coll., 1965; med. technologist St. Agnes Sch. Med. Tech., Fond du Lac, 1966; m. Douglas Mac Arthur Janzen, July 18, 1970. Med. technologist Mayfair Med. Lab., Wauwatosa, Wis., 1966-69; supr. med. technologist Dr.'s Mason, Chamberlain, Franke, Klink & Kamper, Milw., 1969-76, Parkview Med. Assos., Ltd., 1976—. Substitute poll worker Fond du Lac Democratic Com., 1964-65; mem. Dem. Nat. Com., 1973—. Mem. Nat., Wis. (chmn. awards com. 1976-77, co-chmn. Southeastern suprs. group 1976-77, treas. 1977—), Milw. (pres. 1971-72; dir. 1972-73) socs. med. technologists, Alpha Delta Theta (nat. dist. chmn. 1967-69; nat. alumnae dir. 1969-71), Methodist. Home: N 98 W 17298 Dotty Way Germantown WI 53022 Office: 1004 E Sumner St Hartford WI 53027

JARDON, OSCAR MAX, orthopedic surgeon; b. Long Island, Kans., Dec. 23, 1931; s. Robert Fredrick and Dorothy Dee (Yantiss) J.; B.S., Nebr. State U., Kearney, 1953; M.D., U. Nebr., 1957; children—Karla K., Eric M. Practice medicine specializing in orthopedic surgery, Omaha, 1969-77; chief of med. staff Sacred Heart Hosp., Loup City, Nebr., 1961-68; chief resident in orthopedic surgery service U. Nebr., Omaha, 1968-71; asso. prof. dept. orthopedic surgery, 1971—; cons. orthopedic surgery Omaha VA Hosp., 1971—; bd. dirs. Nebr. Arthritis Found., 1971—. Mem. Nebr. Republican Central Com., 1962-67. Served as capt. M.C., U.S. Army, 1958-61; lt. col. USAF Res. Recipient Outstanding Community Service award Loup City C. of C., 1968; R. Shrock award as outstanding orthopedic surgery resident U. Nebr., 1970; diplomate Am. Bd. Orthopedic Surgery. Mem. A.C.S., Am. Acad. Orthopedic Surgery. Contbr. articles to med. jours. Home: 5603 Oak Hills Dr Omaha NE 68137

JARECKI, CLARE FRANK, metalworking machinery co. exec.; b. Grand Rapids, Mich., June 8, 1909; s. Frank J. and Bertha M. (Casper) J.; student Ferris State Coll., 1927-28, J.D. (hon.), 1972; student Mich. Coll. Mining and Tech., 1928-29, Mich. State U., 1929-32; m. Grace Disk, Mar. 5, 1938; children—Judith Claire, Cheryl Nadine. Vice pres., dir. Jarecki Machine & Tool Co., 1931-37, exec. v.p., gen. mgr., 1937-52; pres., gen. mgr., chmn. bd. Jarecki Corp., Grand Rapids, 1952—; pres., dir. Jarecki Products, Inc., Nichols & Cox Lumber Co., North Shore Marina, Inc., Grand Haven, Mich. Treas. bd. Kent County War Bond Drive, 1940; chmn. r.r. expressway relocation Met. Grand Rapids Devel. Assn., 1948-51; chmn. YMCA Indsl. Conf., 1950; chmn. adv. com. Vocat. Centers, 1968; bd. dirs. YMCA, Community Chest, Rehab. League, Mich. State U. Alumni Devel. Bd.; chmn. Mich. State U. Found.; trustee Blodgett Meml. Hosp. Recipient Distinguished Alumnus award Ferris State Coll., 1963, Mich. State U., 1976. Mem. Ferris State Coll. (pres.), Mich. Coll. Mining and Tech. Mich. State U. (vice chmn. devel. fund) alumni assns., Am. Ordnance Assn., U.S., Grand Rapids (past dir., com. chmn.) chambers commerce, U.S. Power Squadron. Clubs: Peninsular, Univ., Grand Rapids Athletic, Kent Country (Grand Rapids); Blythefield Country; Detroit Athletic; Watershed (Grayling, Mich.); Pere Marquette Rod and Gun (Baldwin, Mich.). Home: 2020 Robinson Rd SE Grand Rapids MI 49506 Office: 320 Hall St SW Grand Rapids MI 49502

JARECKI, EUGENE ALOIS, govt. ofcl.; b. Columbus, Nebr., Nov. 5, 1922; s. Dominic Paul and Emelia Veronica (Liss) J.; student Nat. Bus. Inst., Lincoln, Neb., 1941, Creighton U., 1946; B.S., U. Neb., 1950; postgrad. Colo. State U., 1952-54, U. Okla., 1967; m. Jane Marie Arnold, Aug. 22, 1959; children—Marie, Jo Anne, Patricia, Carol. Hydrologist, U.S. Dept. Interior, Grand Island, Neb., 1950-57, supervisory hydrologist, Denver, 1957-64, asst. regional project devel. engr., 1964-68; comprehensive basin planner Great Lakes Basin Commn., Ann Arbor, Mich., 1968-70, asst. planning dir., 1970—. Fed. coordinator Office Emergency Planning, Denver, 1965. Served with USAAF, 1942-45. Mem. Nat., Mich., Colo. socs. profl. engrs., ASCE, Am. Soc. Agrl. Engrs., Am. Water Resources Assn., Mich. Soc. Planning Ofcls. K.C. Club: Toastmasters. Contbr. to profl. publs. in field. Home: 3317 Yellowstone Dr Ann Arbor MI 48105 Office: 3475 Plymouth Rd Ann Arbor MI 48106

JARMAN, DAVID JAMES, automated material handling equipment co. exec.; b. Llwnypia, South Wales, Dec. 1, 1916; s. David James and Beatrice May (Symes) J.; student Inst. Brit. Engrs., 1950; came to U.S., 1960, naturalized, 1966; m. Nellie Clancy, Sept 29, 1943; children—David James, Merlyn Anthony, Staff Brit. I.C. Engine Research Assn., Gt. Brit., 1950-60; pres. Harvey & Jarman Inc., Gt. Brit., 1950-60; chmn. Jarman & Sons, Gt. Brit., 1950-60, 77, pres. Meruvid Ltd., Aurora, Ind., with Continental M.D.M., Aurora, Ind., 1970—, pres., 1971—, chmn, 1972—; cons. in field; asst. pres Campbell Hassfeld Co., Harrison, Ohio, 1967-70; fgn. specialist spl. assignments Ford Motor Co., 1963-66. Councillor Lyming, Hants, Gt. Brit., 1946-60; hon. dep. sheriff Dearborn County, Mich., 1970—. Dir. Aurora Indsl. Park, 1971—. Mem. Nat. Advisory Bd. of Am. Security Council, 1976. Served with RAF, 1934-46. Mem. Reserve Commn. Tng. Corps, 1952-55, Fraternal Order of Police. Mem. Ch. Eng. Clubs: Masons (32 deg.), Bankers, Ambassadors, Congressman's, Dearborn Country. Patentee in field. Home: PO Box 181 Rural Route 3 Aurora IN 47001 Office: PO Box 298 Aurora IN 47001

JARRELL, LLOYD AUBREY, food processing co. exec.; b. Muncie, Ind., Aug. 11, 1919; s. Elsworth Granville and Harriett (Aubrey) J.; student Lake Forest Coll., 1929-31, Ball State U., 1931-32; m. Helen Marjorie Deck, May 24, 1963; 1 dau., Candace Louise. Constrn. supt. Morrow Constrn. Co., Kokomo, Ind., 1940-42; staff asst. R.C.A. Corp., Indpls., 1942-46; owner Jarrell Constrn. Co., Plymouth, Ind., 1946-58; salesman Covina Citrus Corp., Covina, Cal., 1958-61; gen. mgr. juice div. Pacific Hawaiin Products, Plymouth, Ind., 1961-68; v.p., gen. mgr. juice div. Ben Hill Griffin, Inc., Plymouth, Ind., 1968—; dir. Ben Hill Griffin Inc., Frostproof, Fla. Mem. Plymouth C. of C., Mich. Dairymens Booster Assn., Midwest Dairy Products Assn., Ohio Dairymens Booster Assn. Republican. Presbyn. Home: Rural Route #3 Tica Plymouth IN 46563 Office: Rural Route #1 Oak Rd Plymouth IN 46563

JARRELL, ROBERT HOMER, ednl. adminstr.; b. Harrisburg, Ill., July 16, 1923; s. John L. and Catherine (Grace) J.; B.S., U. Ill., 1946; M.S., Ill. Inst. Tech., 1961; m. Elizabeth Jane Beidelman, Feb. 26, 1949; children—Katherine, Michael, Steven, Peter. Accountant, Ill. Farm Supply Co., 1947-50; asst. comptroller Ill. Inst. Tech., 1950-54, comptroller, 1954-62, bus. mgr., 1962—, lectr. in accounting, 1961—. Chmn. edn. div. Ill. Cancer Crusade, Am. Cancer Soc., 1960-63, 65, 66; chmn. adv. bd. Salvation Army Settlement, Chgo.; mem. pub. edn. com. Chgo. unit Am. Cancer Soc., vice chmn., 1974—; mem. adv. com. Sch. Dist. 203, 1967, 71-72; town clk. Lisle Twp., 1973—; jury commr. 18th Jud. Dist. Ill., 1975—; chmn. Lisle Twp. Republican Orgn., 1976—; mem. exec. com. Du Page County Central Rep. Com., 1976—. Mem. Fin. Execs. Inst. (sec. 1964-65), Nat. Assn. Ednl. Buyers (sec.-treas. Ill.-Wis. sect. 1969, chmn. 1971), Nat., Central assns. coll. and univ. bus. officers, Alpha Kappa Psi, Delta Sigma Rho. Republican. Congregationalist. Home: 1204 Cardinal Ln Naperville IL 60540 Office: 3300 S Federal St Chicago IL 60616

JARVIS, CRAIG HOLLOWAY, cons. engring. co. exec.; b. Cleve., June 28, 1947; s. Edwin Richard and Bette (Holloway) J.; B.S., U. Cin., 1970, M.S., 1974; m. Lynette Hammond, Feb. 12, 1977. Head water and sewage dept., san. engr. Warren County (Ohio), Lebanon, 1973-75; project engr. Ohio EPA, Dayton, 1970-73; project mgr.-engr. Pedco, cons. co., Cin., 1975—. Fed. Water Pollution Control Fedn. grantee, 1970-73; registered profl. engr., Ohio, Fla. Mem. ASCE, Am. Water Works Assn., Fed. Water Pollution Control Fedn. Home: 554 Maple Ln Mason OH 45040 Office: 11499 Chester Rd Cincinnati OH 45246

JARVIS, PHILLIP ROBERT, insulated products mfg. co. exec.; b. Winfield, Kans., Feb. 27, 1942; s. Robert Henry and Alta Mae (Dunbar) J.; student U. Kans., 1960-63; B.A., Southwestern Coll. at Winfield, 1964; m. Sandra Marie Haywood, Aug. 25, 1963; children—Jeffrey Phillip, David Alan. Mgr. data processing Jarvis Auto Supply Inc., Winfield, 1963-73; mgr. info. systems Gott Corp., Winfield, 1973—; mem. data processing adv. com. Cowley County Community Jr. Coll. Instl. rep. Boy Scouts Am. Mem. Nat. Assn. Accountants, Winfield Jr. C. of C. (v.p. 1965-66), Nat. Assn. System 3 Users, Wichita Area Assn. System 3 Users. Presbyterian. Club: Winfield Country. Home: Rural Route 5 Winfield KS 67156 Office: 1616 Wheat Rd Winfield KS 67156

JASINSKI, STANLEY KRISTOF, mech. engr.; b. Poland, Feb. 5, 1924; s. Stanley D. and Maria Z. (Krol) J.; m. Ruth Pawletko, Dec. 26, 1955; children—Eve, Kristof. Chief engr. ZML, WZBUP, Warsaw, Poland, 1954-65; project engr. DemagCo., Dusselforf, W.Ger., 1965-67; with Eaton Co., Woodstock, Ont., Can., 1967—, chief design engr., 1970—; dir. HVD-MECH Engring. Ltd. Mem. Assn. Profl. Engrs. Ont., Soc. Automotive Engrs., Fluid Power Soc., Internat. Off Rd. Vehicle Assn. Author: Review of Construction Equipment, 1965. Home: Rural Route 6 Woodstock ON N4S 7W1 Canada Office: 925 Devonshire Woodstock ON Canada

JASPER, ELBERT BAKER, veterinarian; b. Berea, Ohio, May 11, 1923; s. Jay Elbert and Marion Bethia (Baker) J.; student Baldwin Wallace Coll., 1941-42; D.V.M., Ohio State U., 1949; m. Carolyn Agatha Beach, Oct. 27, 1951. Area veterinarian U.S. Dept. Agr., Ohio, 1949-54, Kans., 1955-56, asst. veterinarian in charge State of N.J., 1956-59, asst. veterinarian in charge State of Tenn., 1959-61, mem. program appraisal staff, Washington, 1961-63, veterinarian in charge State of Md., 1963-65, mem. import export staff, Hyattsville, Md., 1965-71; gen. practice veterinary medicine specializing in small animals, Berea, 1973—. Served with Veterinary Corps, U.S. Army, 1944-46; CBI. Mem. Am., Ohio veterinary med. assns., Cleve. Acad. Veterinary Medicine, U.S. Power Squadron. Methodist. Club: Masons. Home and Office: 84 West St Berea OH 44017

JASZCZAK, RONALD JACK, physicist; b. Chicago Heights, Ill., Aug. 23, 1942; s. Jacob and Julia (Gudowicz) J.; B.S. with highest honors, U. Fla., 1964, Ph.D. (NASA fellow), 1968; m. Nancy Jane Bober, Apr. 15, 1967; children—John, Monica. AEC postdoctoral fellow Oak Ridge Nat. Lab., 1968, physicist, 1969; physicist Searle Diagnostics, Des Plaines, Ill., 1971-74, group leader research dept., 1974-77, chief scientist, 1977—. Mem. Soc. Nuclear Medicine, Am. Phys. Soc., IEEE, AAAS, Phi Beta Kappa, Sigma Xi, Sigma Pi Sigma, Sigma Tau Sigma, Phi Kappa Phi. Roman Catholic. Contbr. articles in field to sci. jours.; patentee in field of nuclear med. instrumentation. Home: 2703 N Kennicott St Arlington Heights IL 60004 Office: 333 E Howard St Des Plaines IL 60017

JAUCH, CHRISTIAN MARTIN JOHN, mfg. co. exec.; b. Winsted, Conn., Aug. 19, 1931; s. Christian and Christine (Stegmann) J.; student Rensellaer Poly. Inst., 1949-50; m. Jeannette Marie Thibault, Feb. 9, 1952; children—Christian Martin John, Kathleen Susan. Clock repairman William L. Gilbert, Winsted, Conn., 1947-49, chief draftsman, 1950-52, jr. engr., 1954-55, designer, research and devel., 1956-57; project engr. Seth Thomas Co., Thomaston, Conn., 1955-56; design engr. Haydon div. Gen. Time Co., Torrington, Conn., 1957-65; chief engr. Spartus Corp., Louisville, Miss., 1965-70, dir. new product devel., 1970—. Lt. Burrville (Conn.) Vol Fire Dept., 1960-65; chief Aux Police, Louisville, Miss., 1975-76; ops. officer Louisville CD, 1975-76. Served with U.S. Army, 1952-54. Mem. VFW (life). Patentee several inventions. Home: 128 W Cleveland St Spring Valley IL 61362

JAUTOKAS, VICTOR, electronics engr.; b. Rietavas, Lithuania, Nov. 29, 1929; s. Zigmas and Emilia (Jokubaitis) J.; came to U.S., 1950, naturalized, 1954; B.S. in Elec. Engring., Ill. Inst. Tech., 1963; m. Ruth Kerelis, Aug. 30, 1958; children—Paul, Raminta. Design engr. Chgo. Ry. Equipment Co., 1957-63; project engr. Nat. Video Corp., Chgo., 1963-69; circuit designer Verson Allsteel Press Co., Chgo., 1969-72; communications engr. Chgo. Police Dept., 1972—; cons. to Facilities Design, Ltd. Served with U.S. Army, 1951-53. Registered profl. engr., Ill. Mem. Nat. Soc. Profl. Engrs., Associated Pub. Safety Communications Officers, Am.-Lithuanian Engrs. and Architects Soc., Am. Legion. Democrat. Roman Catholic. Editor Engineering Word, 1974—; author tech. articles in field. Home: 5859 S Whipple St Chicago IL 60629 Office: 1121 S State St Chicago IL 60605

JAVINSKY, PHILLIP ERWIN, engring. co. exec.; b. Mpls., Feb. 13, 1941; s. Simon and Molly (Weinshenker) J.; student Northwestern Electronics, 1964-66; m. Marie Lahusky, Apr. 23, 1962; children—Phillip, Donna, Diane, Stephen. Tech. rep., Honeywell, Inc., Fla., Minn., 1965-72; pres., chmn. bd. J & W Instruments, Inc., Blaine, Minn., 1972—. Served with USAF, 1962. Mem. Soc. Die Casting Engrs. Home: 59 E Golden Lake Rd Circle Pines MN 55014 Office: 9641 Naples St NE Blaine MN 55434

JAY, JAMES M(ONROE), educator; b. Fitzgerald, Ga., Sept. 12, 1927; s. John B. and Lizzie (Wells) J.; A.B., Paine Coll., 1950; M.S., Ohio State U., 1953, Ph.D., 1956; m. Patsie Phelps, June 5, 1959; children—Mark E., Alicia D., Byron R. Postdoctoral fellow Ohio State U., Columbus, 1956-57; from asst. prof. to prof. biology So. U., Baton Rouge, 1957-61; asst. prof. Wayne State U., Detroit, 1961-64, asso. prof., 1964-69, prof., 1969—; pres. Balamp Pub. Co., Detroit, 1971—. Treas. Detroit Council Polit. Edn., 1971-74, 1st v.p., 1975-77, pres., 1977—. Bd. dirs. Met. Hosp. Detroit, 1965-69, sec., 1968-69. Served with AUS, 1946-47. Recipient Probus award, Wayne State U., 1969, Distinguished Alumni award, Paine Coll., 1969. NIH grantee, 1957-72. Fellow Am. Pub. Health Assn.; mem. Am. Chem. Soc., Am. Soc. Microbiology, N.Y. Acad. Sci., Inst. Food Technologists, Soc. Applied Bacteriology (Gt. Britain), Sigma Xi. Author: Modern Food Microbiology, 1970, 2d edit., 1978; Negroes in Science: Natural Science Doctorates, 1876-1969, 1971. Contbr. articles to profl. jours. Home: 4205 Fullerton Detroit MI 48238

JAYABALAN, VEMBLASERRY, nuclear medicine physician, radiologist; b. India, Apr. 3, 1937; s. Parameswara and Janakay (Amma) Menon; came to U.S., 1970; B.Sc., Madras (India) Christian Coll., 1955; M.B., B.S. Jipmer U., India, 1961; Diploma in Med. Radiodiagnosis, U. Liverpool (Eng.), 1967; m. May 2, 1963; children—Kishore, Suresh. Intern, Jipmer Hosp., Pondicherry, India, 1961-62; resident in cardiology K.E.M. Hosp., Bombay, India, 1962-63; resident in radiology Mt. Sinai Hosp., Chgo., 1970-72; fellow in nuclear medicine Michael Reese Hosp., Chgo., 1972-73; dir. nuclear medicine Hurley Med. Center, Flint, Mich., 1973—; asst. clin. prof. radiology Mich. State U. Diplomate Am. Bd. Radiology, Am. Bd. Nuclear Medicine. Fellow Internat. Coll. Physicians; mem. Mich. Coll. Nuclear Medicine (mem. legis. com.), Genesee County Med. Soc. (mem. credential and membership com.), Mich. Med. Soc., Radiol. Soc. N.Am., Am. Coll. Nuclear Medicine, Am. Coll. Nuclear Physicians, Brit. Inst. Radiology, Royal Coll. Radiology, Soc. Nuclear Medicine (mem. program com. Central chpt.). Home: 5495 Floria Dr Swartz Creek MI 48473 Office: Hurley Med Center Flint MI 48502

JAYARAM, BANGALORE-NARAYANA MURTHI, surgeon; b. Shimoga, India, Apr. 13, 1937; s. Bangalore Narayana Murthi and Padmavathi (Sitaramiah) J.; came to U.S., 1963; B.Sc., Central Coll., Bangalore, India, 1955; M.B.B.S., Bangalore Med. Coll., 1962; m. Nalini Lakshmana Rao, Dec. 25, 1972. Intern, Victoria Hosp., Bangalore, 1962-63, Detroit Meml. Hosp., 1963-64; resident in gen. surgery Grace Hosp., Detroit, 1964-67; resident in plastic surgery Northwestern U., Chgo., 1967-70; resident in hand surgery Cook County Hosp., Chgo., 1970-71; practice medicine specializing in plastic surgery, Chgo., 1971—; mem. staff Cook County Hosp., attending surgeon div. plastic surgery, 1971, dep. chmn. div. plastic and reconstructive surgery, 1973; mem. staffs Grant Hosp., Mary Thompson Hosp.; clin. asst. prof. plastic surgery Loyola U. Stritch Sch. Medicine, Maywood, Ill., 1974—. Fellow Royal Coll. Surgeons Can., A.C.S.; mem. India League Am. (dir.). Home: 2756 N Pine Grove St Chicago IL 60612 Office: 1835 W Harrison St Chicago IL 60612

JAYNES, SYDNEY EVANS, orthodontist; b. Twisp, Wash., Sept. 21, 1914; s. Clinton B. and Luella Emily (Johnson) J.; student U. Mo., 1933-34, 35-36; D.M.D., U. Louisville, 1940; M.S., Washington U., St. Louis, 1949; m. Irene Marie Lockwood, Jan. 1, 1937; children—Christian Evans, Philip Conrad, Donald O'Neil, Julie Lu. Dentist, Ky. Dept. Health, 1940-41; hosp. dentist Central State Hosp., Lakeland, Ky., 1941-42; pvt. practice dentistry, Louisville, 1941-42; dental pediatrics instr. Washington U., St. Louis, 1946-49; practice dentistry specializing in orthodontics, Columbia, Mo., 1949—. Orthodontic cons. Stephens Coll., Columbia, Mo., 1951-68, Mo. Crippled Children's Service, 1954—; pres. Columbia Profl. Devel. Corp., 1957—; chmn. Gov's. Commn. Dental Treatment Handicapped Children, 1962-67. Chmn. profl. div. United Fund, 1961, mem. bd., 1962-64; mem. Columbia Parks and Recreation Bd., 1969-72; active Boy Scouts Am. Served as lt. sr. grade USNR, 1943-46. Recipient Silver Beaver award Boy Scouts Am., 1963. Fellow Am. Coll. Dentists, Royal Soc. Health (London); mem. Am. Assn. Orthodontists, Midwestern (pres. 1970-71), Mo. (pres. 1971-72) socs. orthodontists, Central Mo. Dist. (pres. 1954-55), Columbia (pres. 1951-52) dental socs., Am., Mo. (bd. govs. 1959-62) dental assns. Methodist (mem. finance and stewardship commn. 1959-62). Kiwanian. Sci. editor, contbg. editor Mo. State Dental Assn. Jour., 1958-63. Home: 702 Russell Blvd Columbia MO 65201 Office: 1502 E Broadway St Columbia MO 65201

JEAN, RAPHAEL JOSEPH, mech. engr.; b. Cap Haitien, Haiti, Sept. 20, 1953; s. Filip and Mariette (Galland) Jean. B.S. in Mech. Engring., Manhattan Coll., 1975. Lt., U.S. Air Force, Minot AFB, N.D., 1975—. Mem. Soc. of Am. Mil. Engrs., Am. Soc. Mech. Engrs., Am. Nuclear Soc., Air Force Assn., Reserve Officer Assn. Named to Outstanding Coll. Athletes of Am., 1975. Home: 260 Audubon Ave New York City NY 10033 Office: 912 3d Ave NW Minot ND 58701

JECK, HOWARD SHEFFIELD, surgeon; b. N.Y.C., July 14, 1921; s. Howard Sheffield and Norine Harriet (Lever) J.; A.B., Yale U., 1942; M.D., Cornell U., 1945; m. Eileen Isabel McLellan, May 13, 1950; children—H. Sheffield, III, Allister M., Lynne T. Intern in surgery N.Y. Hosp., 1945-46; asst. resident in neurosurgery, 1948-49; asst. resident surgery Cornell div. Bellevue Hosp., N.Y.C., 1949-50; asst. resident surgery VA Med. Teaching Group Kennedy Hosp., Memphis, 1950-52, sr. resident surgery, 1952-53; practice medicine specializing in surgery, Torrington, Conn., 1953-54, St. Joseph, Mo., 1954-56, Oxford, Ohio, 1956—; bd. trustees and dirs. McCullough Hyde Meml. Hosp., Oxford, 1962-69, chmn., 1964-66; asst. prof. clin. surgery Wright State U. Sch. Medicine, 1975—; pres.-elect. med. adv. council Blue Cross of Southwestern Ohio. Served to lt. (j.g.) USN, 1946-48. Diplomate Am. Bd. Surgery. Fellow A.C.S.; mem. AMA, Ohio State Med. Assn., Butler County Med. Soc. (pres. 1976-77), R. F. Bowers Surg. Soc., Assn. Yale Alumni (rep.). Republican. Presbyterian. Clubs: Rotary (Oxford), Oxford Country, Net-Set Tennis; Cin. Yale. Home: 4141 Reily Rd Oxford OH 45056 Office: 5995 Fairfield Rd Oxford OH 45056

JECMEN, JOHN JOSEPH, mfg. co. exec.; b. Chgo., Jan. 16, 1916; s. James and Marie (Steker) J.; student DePaul U., 1933-37, Ill. Inst. Tech., 1942; m. Betty R. Malek, June 18, 1938. Pres., chmn. bd. Harris Preble Co. mfg. elevator doors, Cicero, Ill., 1933—. Mem. NAM, DePaul U. Assos., Nat. Assn. Elevator Contractors, Ill. Mfrs. Assn., Cicero Mfrs. Assn., Internat. Trade Club, Execs. Club Chgo., Chgo. Assn. Commerce and Industry, Finnish-Am., Mid-Am. Arab chambers commerce, C. of C. U.S., U.S., Western golf assns. Moose. Club: Butterfield Country (Oak Brook, Ill.). Patentee in field. Home: 210 Briarwood Pass Oak Brook IL 60521 Office: 4608 W 20th St Chicago IL 60650

JEFFERIES, WILLIAM MCKENDREE, physician; b. Richmond, Va., Oct. 1, 1915; s. Richard Henry and Adeline (Harris) J.; B.A., Hampden-Sydney Coll., 1935; M.D., U. Va., 1940; m. Jeanne Telfair Mercer, Dec. 28, 1946; children—Richard Mercer, Scott McKendree, Colin Tucker, Leslie McLaurin. Intern Mass. Gen. Hosp., Boston, 1940-42; resident 1941-42; practice medicine specializing in endocrinology, Cleve., 1949—; physician-in-charge endocrine clinic and research lab. Univ. Hosp., Cleve., 1949-66; physician-in-charge endocrine research lab. Highland View Hosp., Cleve., 1966-72; cons. endocrinology Euclid (Ohio) Clinic Found., 1972—. Research fellow, com. on growth NRC, 1947-49; instr. McGuire's Univ. Sch., Richmond, Va., 1935-36; asst. clin. prof. med. Case Western Res. U. Served from 1st lt. to lt. col. M.C., AUS, 1942-45. Recipient Van Meter award Am. Thyroid Assn., 1949. Diplomate Am. Bd. Internal Medicine. Fellow A.C.P.; mem. Endocrine Soc., Am. Thyroid Assn., Am. Diabetes Assn., Am. Fertility Soc., AAAS, Am. Fedn. Clin. Research, Central Soc. Clin. Research, AMA, Ohio Med. Assn., Cleve. Acad. Medicine, Raven Soc., Alpha Omega Alpha, Omicron Delta Kappa, Kappa Alpha, Phi Beta Pi. Mem. United Ch. of Christ (chmn. council deacons 1965, trustee). Contbr. articles to publs. Home: 2423 Newbury Dr Cleveland Heights OH 44118 Office: 18599 Lake Shore Blvd Euclid OH 44119

JEFFERSON, ARTHUR, b. b. Ala., Dec. 1, 1938; B.S., Wayne State U., 1960. M.A. in Polit. Sci., 1963, Ed.D. in Curriculum Leadership, 1973; married; 2 children. Asst. region supt. Detroit pub. schs., 1970-71, region supt., 1971-75, interim gen. supt., 1975, gen. supt., 1975—. Mem. Nat., Mich. councils social studies, Assn. Supervision and Curriculum Devel., Am. Assn. Sch. Adminstrs., Mich. Assn. Supervision and Curriculum Devel., Council Basic Edn., Met. Detroit Soc. Black Ednl. Adminstrs., Nat. Alliance Black Sch. Educators, ACLU, NAACP, Wayne State U. Edn. Alumni Assn. (gov. 1968-71), Wayne State U. Alumni Assn. (trustee 1968-71), Phi Sigma Alpha.

Home: 18211 Santa Barbara St Detroit MI 48221 Office: 5057 Woodward Ave Detroit MI 48202

JEFFERSON, HELEN CHANDLER, sch. counselor; b. Chgo., Sept. 13, 1919; d. Edward and Estelle Marie (Thornton) C.; B.S., Northwestern U., 1941; M.A., U. Chgo., 1954; postgrad. Sorbonne, 1965-66; M.A., Roosevelt U., 1976; children—Paul Channing, Kristin Marie. Social worker ARC, Chgo., 1943-44; translator Berlitz Sch. Langs., Chgo., 1951; tchr. elementary sch. Chgo. Bd. Edn., 1956-58, tchr. French, 1958-73, counselor, 1973—; mem. accreditation com. N. Central Secondary Schs., 1969. Mem. Am. Assn. Tchrs. French, Am. Council Teaching Fgn. Langs., Am. Personnel and Guidance Assn., Am. Sch. Counselor Assn., Phi Beta Kappa, Phi Sigma Iota. Home: 400 E 33d St Chicago IL 60616 Office: 936 N Ashland Ave Chicago IL 60622

JEFFERY, ALEXANDER HALEY, lawyer, ins. co. exec.; b. London, Ont., Can., Jan. 29, 1909; s. James Edgar and Gertrude (Dumaresq) J.; student London South Collegiate Inst., 1922-27; grad. U. Western Ont., 1931, Osgoode Hall, Toronto, 1934; m. Eulalie E. Murray, June 29, 1934; children—Alexander M., Judith E. Admitted to Ont. bar, 1934; pvt. practice London, 1934—; pres., gen. counsel The London Life Ins. Co.; pres., dir. Forest City Investments Ltd.; dir. Two Hundred Queens Av. Ltd., London Realty Mgmt. & Rentals Ltd., London Winery, Ltd., Ltd., Canada Trust-Huron & Erie, Thames Valley Investments Ltd. Mem. Parliament for Constituency City of London, 1949-53. Mem. Canada Bar Assn., Am. Assn. Life Ins. Counsel. Anglican. Mason (32 deg.). Clubs: London Hunt and Country, London; Royal Canadian Yacht, University (Toronto); Windsor Yacht; Sarnia Yacht; Trans-Erie Sail; Great Lakes Cruising. Home: 104 Commissioners Rd E London ON N6C 2T1 Canada Office: PO Box 2095 London ON Canada

JEFFREYS, JAMES VICTOR, aero-mech. engr., air force officer; b. Nashville, June 28, 1938; s. James Terry and Jean Young (Stewart) J.; B.M.E., Vanderbilt U., 1961; M.S. in Aero-Mech. Enging., Air Force Inst. Tech., 1967; m. Carolyn Virginia Beam, Sept. 7, 1960; children—Mark, Kathryn, Clara. Commd. 2d lt. U.S. Air Force, 1961, advanced through grades to maj., 1972; mech. engr. USAF Security Service, Washington, 1961-65; aero. engr. Warner Robins Air Logistic Center, Robins AFB, Ga., 1967-69; dep. comdr. Detachment 4 Air Force Procurement Region Far East, Saigon, Vietnam, 1969-70; chief Air Force Logistics Command Corrosion Mgmt. Office, Robins AFB, 1970-74; asst. chief div. tech. services Def. Constrn. Supply Center, Columbus, Ohio, 1974—. Active Central Ohio council Boy Scouts Am. Decorated Bronze Star, Meritorious Service medal (U.S.); Cross of Gallantry with palm (Vietnam); registered profl. engr., Calif. Mem. ASME, Nat. Assn. Corrosion Engrs. (accredited), Soc. Am. Mil. Engrs. (pres. Columbus post 1975), Nat. Rifle Assn. (life), Nat. Eagle Scout Assn., Air Force Assn., Sigma Nu. Methodist. Club: Masons. Home: 306 Jennie Dr Gahanna OH 43230 Office: Def Constrn Supply Center DCSC-SE Columbus OH 43215

JEFFRIES, CHARLES DEAN, univ. adminstr.; b. Rome, Ga., Apr. 9, 1929; s. Andrew Jones and Rachel Lucinda (Ringer) J.; B.S., N. Ga. Coll., 1950; M.S., U. Tenn., 1955, Ph.D., 1958; postgrad. Purdue U., 1955-56; m. Virginia Mae Alford, Sept. 6, 1953. Technician, Ga. Pub. Health Dept., Rome, 1950-51; instr. microbiology Wayne State U., Detroit, 1958-60, asst. prof., 1960-65, asso. prof., 1965-70, prof., 1970, acting chmn. dept., 1972-73, asso. dermatology, 1968—, asst. dean for curriculum affairs, dir. grad. programs Sch. Medicine, 1975—. Fulbright-Hays lectr., Cairo, Egypt, 1965-66; examiner bacteriology Bd. Basic Scis. State Mich., 1967-72, v.p., 1970-72; councilor Am. Assn. Basic Sci. Bds., 1970-72; mem. sci. adv. bd. Mich. Cancer Found., 1970—. Served with AUS, 1951-53. NIH grantee, 1958-70; NSF grantee, 1959-69. Fellow Am. Acad. Microbiology; mem. Am. Soc. for Microbiology (councilor 1976—, chmn. med. mycology div. 1977—), Nat. Registry Microbiologists, Soc. Gen. Microbiology, Soc. Exptl. Biology and Medicine, Internat. Soc. Human and Animal Mycology, Sigma Xi. Contbr. articles to profl. jours. Home: 22513 Raymond Ave St Clair Shores MI 48082 Office: Office Curriculum Affairs Sch Medicine Wayne State U 540 E Canfield Detroit MI 48201

JEFFRIES, DAVID ALAN, electronics co. exec.; b. Lakewood, Ohio, May 17, 1936; s. Charles Mustin and Miriam Lucretia (Crawford) J.; B.S.C., Ohio U., 1958; children—Paul Alan, James David, Juliann. Partner, Brubaker, Helfrich & Taylor C.P.A.'s, Cleve., 1958-71; mgr. Arthur Andersen & Co. C.P.A.'s, Cleve., 1971-74; pres., dir. Winteradio Electronics Corp., Cleve., 1974—. Served with U.S. Army, 1958-64. Mem. Ohio Soc. C.P.A.'s (v.p. 1977—), Am. Inst. C.P.A.'s, Nat. Electronics Distbrs. Assn., Nat. Wholesalers Assn., Electronic Distbrs. Research Inst. (dir., sec.-treas. 1977). Republican. Presbyterian. Club: Cleve. Yachting (dir.). Home: 21215 Detroit Rd Rocky River OH 44116 Office: 1468 25th St W Cleveland OH 44113

JEFFRIES, NEAL POWELL, instn. ofcl., mech. engr.; b. Indpls., Aug. 25, 1935; s. Samson Fredrick and Lucille Davis (Powell) J.; B.S. with high distinction, Purdue U., 1957; M.S. (Whitney Found. fellow), Mass. Inst. Tech., 1958; Engr., Stanford, 1963; Ph.D., U. Cin., 1969; m. Karen Meiks, June 26, 1958; children—Christina Meiks, Kathryn Powell. Specialist heat transfer Gen. Electric, Cin., 1963-65, program mgr., 1965-67, cons., 1967—; research asso. U. Cin., 1967-69, asst. prof. mech. enging., 1969-75; dir. edn. Nat. Center Mfg. Tech., Cin., 1975—; sec., dir. Inst. Tech. Careers, 1976—; dir. Vortec Corp. Faculty, Ohio Coll. Applied Sci., Evening Coll., U. Cin., 1974—. Bd. dirs. Big Bros. Am. Served with USAF, 1958-61. Registered profl. engr., Ohio. Mem. ASME (dir., mem. nat. policy bd., mem. edn. and gen. engring. com. 1974, 75, chmn. continuing edn. 1972—, spl. award 1973), Soc. Mfg. Engrs. (chmn. nat. edn. com. 1975, chmn. adminstrv. council 1976-77), Am. Soc. for Engring. Edn. (mem. continuing edn. com. 1973—), Sigma Xi, Tau Beta Pi, Pi Tau Sigma, Phi Eta Sigma, Phi Delta Theta. Mem. Community Ch. (pres. bd. 1966-69, 71-73). Club: O'Bannon Creek Golf (Cin.). Author: Engineering Fundamentals, 1975. Patentee in field. Home: 3112 Cooper Rd Cincinnati OH 45241 Office: Nat Center for Mfg Tech 5729 Dragon Way Cincinnati OH 45227

JELINEK, LEONARD CHARLES, chem. engr.; b. Chgo., Nov. 21, 1924; s. Charles Edward and Johanna (Vichr) J.; B.S. in Chem. Enging., Tri-State U., Angola, Ind., 1946, hon. profl. degree chem. engring., 1963; m. Marian M. Kenar, May 3, 1953; children—Tom, Christopher, Susan. Chem. lab. instr. Tri-State Coll., 1945; chemist-engr. Allied Chem. & Dye Corp., Chgo., 1946-47; research chemist-engr. Electro-Motive div. Gen. Motors Corp., 1947-53; chem. engr. Liquid Carbonic Corp., Chgo., 1953-54; supervising engr. S&C Electric Co., Chgo., 1954—. Dir. pollution control Village of North Riverside (Ill.), 1973—; instl. rep. Boy Scouts Am., 1969; v.p. Mater Christi Sch. Bd., North Riverside, 1970-71. Recipient citation of merit Chgo. Area Father's Day Council, 1967. Fellow Am. Inst. Chemists (accredited engr.); mem. Am. Chem. Soc., Am. Electroplaters Soc. (certified), Tau Kappa Epsilon. Patentee circuit interrupters. Home: 2449 10th Ave North Riverside IL 60546 Office: 6601 N Ridge Blvd Chicago IL 60626

JELLISON, JAMES LOGAN, II, economist; b. Chgo., June 3, 1922; s. James Logan and Ethel (Reynolds) J.; Ph.B., DePaul U., Chgo., 1943; B.M.E., Northwestern U., 1948; M.B.A., U. Louisville, 1959; m. Charlotte Jean Scott, Oct. 20, 1951; children—James Logan, Jeanene Lynn, Jennifer Lee. Statistician, Petroleum Industry Com. for War, Chgo., 1942-43; purchasing analyst Gen. Electric Co., Lynn, Mass., 1948-49, sales engr., Fort Wayne, Ind., 1950-51, York, Pa., 1952-55, field sales rep., Louisville, 1956-60, mgr. mktg. research, Holland, Mich., 1961—. State and County Conv. del. Republican party, 1964—; bd. dirs. Ottawa County chpt. Nat. Found. Served to 1st lt. AUS, 1943-46, ETO. Decorated Bronze Star, Purple Heart; registered profl. engr. Mem. Am. Mktg. Assn. (pres. W. Mich. chpt. 1970-71), Am. Legion, Elfun Soc., Kappa Sigma. Republican. Unitarian. Club: Holland Country. Home: 729 Lugers Rd Holland MI 49423 Office: 570 E 16th St Holland MI 49423

JELLISON, RICHARD MARION, educator; b. Muncie, Ind., Dec. 26, 1924; s. Carl R. and Leora Melvina (Folkner) J.; B.S., Ball State U., 1948; A.M., Ind. U., 1949, Ph.D., 1953; m. Kathleen Elizabeth Frick, May 5, 1945; children—Richard G., Stephanie L., Leslie N. Instr. history Ind. U., 1952-56; instr. Mich. State U., 1956-58; asso. prof. Eastern Ill. U., 1958-62; prof. Miami U., Oxford, Ohio, 1962—, chmn. dept. history, 1971—; lectr. U. Berlin, 1966, U. Siena, Italy, 1968, Budapest, Hungary, 1974. Served with U.S. Navy, 1942-44. Colonial Williamsburg summer research fellow, 1958-62. Mem. Am. Hist. Assn., Inst. Early Am. Culture, Am. Assn. History Medicine, Orgn. Am. Historians, Internat. Soc. History Medicine, Ohio, Ind., S.C. hist. socs., AAUP (pres. Miami U. chpt. 1967). Author: Society, Freedom & Conscience: The American Revolution in Virginia, Massachusetts and New York, 1976. Contbr. articles to profl. jours. Home: 6345 Fairfield Rd Oxford OH 45056 Office: History Department Miami University Oxford OH 45056

JENDRYSIK, BENJAMIN STANLEY, toy co. exec.; b. Albion Twp., Wis., Mar. 24, 1933; s. Stanley and Mary (Waszak) J.; A.A., Morton Jr. Coll., 1953; student Wright Jr. Coll., 1958-59; m. Eileen Dorothy Augustyn, Sept. 22, 1956; children—Mark, Jill, John. Traffic clk. Victor Mfg. & Gasket Co., Chgo., 1956-57; traffic mgr. Admiral Corp., Chgo., 1957-64; asst. gen. traffic mgr. Walgreen Co., Chgo., 1964-69; traffic mgr. Playskool Inc., Des Plaines, Ill., 1969—. Chmn., Glendale Heights (Ill.) Planning Commn., 1962-65. Served with AUS, 1953-55. Mem. Glendale Heights Jaycees (past pres.), Delta Nu Alpha (past pres.). Home: 101 E Schubert St Glendale Heights IL 60137 Office: 30 E Oakton St Des Plaines IL 60018

JENEFSKY, JACK, wholesale exec.; b. Dayton, Ohio, Oct. 27, 1919; s. David and Anna (Saeks) J.; B.S. in Bus. Adminstrn., Ohio State U., 1941; postgrad. Harvard Bus. Sch., 1943; M.A. in Econs., U. Dayton, 1948; m. Beverly J. Mueller, Feb. 23, 1962; 1 dau., Anna Elizabeth; 1 stepdau., Cathryn Jean Mueller. Surplus broker, Dayton, 1946-48; sales rep. Remington Rand-Univac, Dayton, 1949-56, mgr. AF account, 1957-59, br. mgr. Dayton, 1960-61, regional marketing cons. Midwest region, Dayton, 1962-63; pres. Bowman Supply Co., Dayton, 1963—. Selection adv. bd. Air Force Acad., 3d congl. dist., chmn., 1974—; coordinator Great Lakes region, res. assistance program Civil Air Patrol. Served from pvt. to capt. USAAF, 1942-46; CBI; maj. USAF, 1951-53; col Res. Mem. Air Force Assn. (comdr. Ohio wing 1957-58, 58-59), Res. Officers Assn. (pres. Ohio dept. 1956-57, nat. council 1957-58, chmn. research and devel. com. 1961-62), Dayton Area C. of C., Ohio State U. Alumni Assn. (pres. Montgomery County, Ohio, 1959-60), Nat. Sojourners (pres. Dayton 1961-62). Jewish. Clubs: Harvard Bus. Sch. Dayton (pres. 1961-62), Northmoor (Dayton), Lions. Home: 4534 Skylark Dr Englewood OH 45322 Office: 225 N Irwin St Dayton OH 45403

JENKINS, CARTER, civil engr.; b. Hot Springs, Ark., Nov. 19, 1893; s. Ambroise Driscoll and Rosa Lee (Carter) J.; A.B., Hendrix Coll., 1915; B.C.E. with honors, U. Ill., 1921, M.C.E., 1926; m. Tula B. Blankenship, Mar. 12, 1922; 1 son, Thomas Carter. Hwy. engr. Ill. Div. of Hwys., Elgin, 1921-26; partner with Major W.H. Allen Co., cons. engrs., Des Plaines, Ill., 1926-33; asst. regional officer Nat. Park Service, Dept. Interior, various states, 1933-37; chief engr. Ill. Div. Waterways, 1937-42; coordinator Ill. State Council Def., 1941-43; dir. Ill. Office of Price Adminstrn., Springfield, 1942-46; partner Jenkins, Merchant and Nankivil, cons. engrs., Springfield, 1946-75; prin. C. Jenkins, cons. engr., Springfield, Ill., 1975—. Served to capt., arty., U.S. Army, 1917-1919. Registered profl. engr., Ill., Ind., Ky., Wis., Mich., Ark., Mo. Mem. Nat., Ill. socs. profl. engrs., Ill. Soc. Cons. Engrs., ASCE, Ill. Registered Land Surveyors Assn., Hendrix Coll., U. Ill. alumni assns. Democrat. Methodist. Clubs: Masons (32 deg.), Shriners, Elks. Home: 1702 S 4th St Springfield IL 62703 Office: 801-805 E Miller St Springfield IL 62702

JENKINS, DALE STEVENS, dentist; b. Orient, Ill., Dec. 11, 1915; s. Llewellyn E. and Effie (Stevens) J.; B.S., Blackburn Coll., 1935; D.D.S., Chgo. Coll. Dental Surgery, 1939; m. Maude Elizabeth Wheeler, Aug. 30, 1942; 1 son, Richard. Pvt. practice dentistry, DeKalb, Ill., 1939—; dir. Kishwaukee Community Health Services. Bd. dirs., div. mental health The Kids Place. Served with USAAF, 1943-46. Mem. Acad. of Dentistry, ADA, Ill. (del. 1967, mem. pub. relations com. 1970—), Fox River Valley (pres. 1968-69, dir. 1965-70) dental socs., Ill. Dental Service (committeeman 1972—). Clubs: Elks, Rotary. Home: 1630 N 1st St DeKalb IL 60115 Office: 1606 Sycamore Rd DeKalb IL 60115

JENKINS, EDNA MARGARET, speech and lang. pathologist, audiologist; b. Macon, Ga., Oct. 20, 1924; d. Luther Alvin and Frances Carolyn (Pool) Jenkins; A.B. (scholarship 1939), U. Ga., 1943; M.A., Columbia U., 1952; postgrad. Stanford U., 1951, Northwestern U., 1950-56, So. Ill. U., 1964-67. With Queens Coll. Speech and Hearing Center, N.Y.C., 1946-47, Nat. Hosp. for Speech Disorders, N.Y.C., 1947-48, Conn. Dept. of Health, 1948-50; dir. Speech Correction Program, Rome, Ga., 1950-53; speech and lang. pathologist Elmhurst (Ill.) Pub. Schs., 1954—, cons. lang.-learning disabilities, 1966-71; faculty mem. U. Ga., Rome Center, 1950-53, U. of S.D., 1955, Elmhurst Coll., 1955-60, Chgo. Tchrs. Coll., 1957, Nat. Coll. of Edn., 1973; founder aphasia therapy rehab. center Bellevue Hosp., N.Y.C., 1947; founder forum of the air U. Ga., Rome Center, 1952; cons. Virgin Islands Speech and Hearing Program, 1964, Peace Corps Sch. of Speech, Guatemala, 1974; owner Margo Studios, 1969—. Certificate of clin. competence in speech pathology-audiology. Mem. Am., Ill., Chgo. (officer 1961-64), Ga. (officer 1951-53) speech and hearing assns., Am. Audiology Soc., Council for Exceptional Children (Ill. program advisory com. 1969-70), AAUW, Chgo. Soc. for Gen. Semantics (pres. 1970), Zeta Phi Eta. Contbr. articles in field to profl. jours. Home: 432 N Austin Blvd Oak Park IL 60302

JENKINS, GEORGE HENRY, hosp. adminstrn. exec.; b. Shanghai, China, Oct. 24, 1929 (parents Am. citizens); s. Clarence O. and Efransinia (Pomorenkoff) J.; grad. N.Y. Inst. Photography, 1952; student Purdue U., 1952-55, Ind. U., 1955-58; B.A., Ind. No. U., 1972; M.Ed., Wayne State U., 1976, doctoral student, 1977—; postgrad. U. Mich., 1976-77; m. Madge Marie Vickroy, Aug. 19, 1967. Data processing mgr. Columbia Record Club, Terre Haute, Ind., 1961-63; adminstrv. coordinator Capitol Record Club, Scranton, Pa. and Toronto, Ont., 1963-64; systems coordinator Commn. on Profl. and Hosp. Activities, Ann Arbor, Mich., 1965-66; dir. systems and data processing Nicholson File Co., Anderson, Ind., 1966-69; hosp. adminstr. Wayne County Gen. Hosp.; freelance writer, photographer, 1969—; tchr. photography McComb County Community Coll. Systems Inst., Hazel Park, Mich., 1964-65. Chmn. Speaking Bur., Fort Wayne, Ind., 1958-59; counselor YMCA Rocket and Missile Assn., Milw., 1959-60; chmn. supervisory bd. Eloise Credit Union. Served with USAF, 1948-52. Certified data processor, certified data educator. Mem. Photog. Soc. Gt. Britain, Assn. for Computing Machinery, Human Factors Soc., 8-16 Cine Club Detroit, Assn. for Ednl. Communications and Tech., U.S. Power Squadrons, Photog. Soc. Am. Author: Principles of Stockkeeping, 1965. Home: 23045 Murray Dearborn MI 48128 Office: Wayne County General Hosp Eloise MI 48132

JENKINS, HAROLD RICHARD, library adminstr.; b. Pottstown, Pa., Aug. 23, 1918; s. Stanley Frederick and Flora (High) J.; B.A., Ursinus Coll., 1953; M.A. in L.S., U. Mich., 1956; m. Margaret Houston Leech, Nov. 1, 1957; children—M. Elizabeth, Richard H. Catalog librarian Washington and Lee U., Lexington, Va., 1956-58; dir. Kingsport (Tenn.) Pub. Library, 1958-59, Wise County (Va.) Regional Library, 1959-61, Pottstown Pub. Library 1961-63, Lancaster County (Pa.) Library, 1963-74, Kansas City (Mo.) Pub. Library, 1974—. Bd. dirs. Lancaster Goodwill Industries, 1973-74. Lancaster County Hist. Soc., 1972-73. Served with C.E., AUS, 1941-52. Mem. Mo. Library Assn. (pres. 1977-78), Beta Phi Mu, Pi Gamma Mu. Rotarian. Contbr. articles to profl. jours. Home: 5700 Wyandotte St Kansas City MO 64113 Office: 311 E 12th St Kansas City MO 64106

JENKINS, HARRY GHLEE, ret. retail sales exec.; b. Smithfield, Ill., Sept. 22, 1900; s. Fred Ashton and Lela Sarah (Totten) J.; B.S., Knox Coll., 1928; m. Ruth Jeanette Ramp, Dec. 25, 1928; children—Mary Jane (Mrs. Lloyd Ogilvie), Harry Ghlee. Rural sch. tchr., Fulton County, Ill., 1920-22, Knox County, 1922-23; salesman Wake Electric Co., Galesburg, 1927-28; salesman Montgomery Ward & Co., Galesburg, 1928-29, asst. mgr., 1929-31, store mgr., Burlington, Iowa, 1931-33; plater Casket Hardware Co., Galesburg, Ill., 1933-34; with Sears, Roebuck and Co., 1934-64, successively salesman Davenport, Iowa, asst. mgr., Moline and Decatur, Ill., mgr. Lafayette, Ind. and Waukegan, Ill., 1934-54, gen. mgr. 6 stores, Milw. area, 1954-64; dir. M.T. Linens, Inc., Carlyle, Ill. Chmn. war savs. staff Tippecanoe County, Ind., 1941-43, state chmn. retail div., 1943, co-chmn. Lake County, 1943-45; pres. Community Chest, Waukegan-N. Chgo., 1950-52, bd. dirs., 1944-54, chmn. drive, 1954; chmn. Mayor's Com. for Off-Street Parking, Waukegan, 1953; chmn. drive Victory Meml. Hosp. Bldg. Program, 1953; bd. dirs. Waukegan-N. Chgo. Council Chs., 1951-54; chmn. retail div. Lafayette C. of C., 1940-41, bd. dirs., 1943; pres. Waukegan-N. Chgo. C. of C., 1947-48, chmn. comml. div., 1943-45, bd. dirs., 1945-49; chmn. urban renewal com. Greater Milw. Com., 1961-65, bd. dirs., 1961-65, asso. mem., 1965—; bd. dirs., v.p. Milw. Hosp. Area Planning Com., Inc., 1963, 67; planning adv. council Wauwatosa, 1967-70; mem. Comprehensive Health Planning Agy. Southeastern Wis., Milw. state chmn. Wis. payroll savs. retail div. U.S. Savs. Bonds, 1963; bd. dirs. Better Bus. Bur., 1955-64, v.p., 1957; bd. dirs. mem. exec. com. Milw. chpt. ARC, 1964-66. Mem. Lake County Civic League (dir. 1954), YWCA of Waukegan (chmn. adv. com. 1954), Wis. C. of C. (dir. 1955-57, pres. 1959-60). Methodist (chmn. Capital fund drive spl. gifts div. Eastern Wis. Conf. 1964, trustee, chmn. bldg. com.). Clubs: Masons (32 deg.), Shriners, Wisconsin. Home: 7500 W Dean Rd Apt 312 Milwaukee WI 53223

JENKINS, JAY OLIVER, optometrist; b. Shanandoah, Iowa, Sept. 17, 1900; s. William Henry and Mary Ellen (Wilson) J.; student Lincoln Bus. Coll., 1919-20; grad. Needles Optometric Coll., 1924; postgrad. Coll. Syntonic Optometry; m. Ada Emelia Nyberg, Apr. 22, 1925. Practice optometry, Holdrege, Nebr., 1927-39, North Platte, Nebr., 1940—. Pres. Coll. Syntonic Optometry, North Platte. Charter mem. Optometric Extension Program Nebr. Comdr., Civil Air Patrol Squadron, World War II. Fellow Distinguished Service Optometry, Coll. Syntonic Optometry, Acad. Corrective Optometry. Baptist. Kiwanian. Home: 209 W Circle Dr North Platte NE 69101 Office: 222 W 5th St North Platte NE 69101

JENKINS, LOUIS BURKE, poet, publisher; b. Oklahoma City, Oct. 28, 1942; s. Walter Lee Burke and Genevieve Adelia (Webring) J.; student Wichita State U., 1965-69; m. Ann Louise Jacobson, Dec. 6, 1970; 1 son Lars Peter. Owner, editor, pub. Knife River Press, Duluth, Minn., 1971—; poetry books include The Well Digger's Wife, 1973; editor of Steelhead lit. mag., 1971—; asst. editor Lake Superior Jour., 1976. Home: 2501 Branch St Duluth MN 55812

JENKINS, WALLACE ALFRED, JR., lawyer; b. Cleve., Aug. 23, 1928; s. Wallace Alfred and Florence Ann (McKrell) J.; A.B., Ohio No. U., 1950; J.D., Cleve. State U., 1956, LL.M., 1960; children—Wallace Alfred III, Reed, Mark. Admitted to Ohio bar, 1957, U.S. Supreme Ct. bar, 1971; claims atty. Nationwide Mut. Ins. Co., Cleve. and Canton, Ohio, 1956-64; mem. firm Payne & Payne, 1964—. Served with Signal Corps, AUS, 1951-53. Mem. Parma, Cleve., Cuyahoga County, Ohio bar assns., Ohio Def. Assn. Home: 8455 N Akins Rd North Royalton OH 44133 Office: 2130 Illuminating Bldg Cleveland OH 44113

JENKINS, WALTER KIMBALL, oil co. exec.; b. Council Bluffs, Iowa, July 25, 1929; s. Walter Lot and Ruth Elizabeth (Kimball) J.; B.S. in Chem. Enging., Iowa State U., 1951; M.B.A., State U. N.Y. at Buffalo, 1960; m. Mary Elizabeth Erler, July 25, 1953; children—Donald, Cindy, Nancy, Pat. Ops. supt. U.S. Indsl. Chem. Co., Tuscola, Ill., 1958-64; acting plant mgr. Apple River Chem. Co., East Dubuque, Ill., 1964-67; ops. mgr. Atlantic Richfield Co., Fort Madison, Iowa, 1967-69; project mgr. Procon Inc., gen. contractor petroleum refineries, Des Plaines, Ill., 1970-72; sr. engr. Union Oil Co., Lemont, Ill., 1972—. Co-chmn. steering com. Douglas County Hosp., 1964; active Boy Scouts Am.; chmn.-elect Naperville Council Chs., 1977. Bd. dirs. S.E. Iowa Community Coll.; pres. Naperville Council of Chs., 1978. Served as 1st lt. Signal Corps, AUS, 1951-53. Registered profl. engr., Ill. Mem. Tuscola C. of C. (pres. 1963), Am. Inst. Chem. Engrs. (chmn. Joliet sect. 1976). Presbyn. (dir. ch.). Rotarian. Home: 1156 Elizabeth Ave Naperville IL 60540 Office: Union Oil Refinery Lemont IL 60439

JENKINS, WENDELL LLEWELLYN, mfg. co. exec.; b. Canton, Ohio, July 1, 1907; s. Artemus Llewellyn and Edith (Boucsein) J.; ed. Kenyon Coll., 1930; m. Magdalen Elizabeth Shaeffer, Mar. 29, 1930; children—Thomas Shaeffer, Susan (Mrs. T.R. McClanahan), Patricia Ann. Pres., Midland Implement Co., Canton, 1932-34, Shaeffer Black Co., Canton, 1940-60, W.L. Jenkins Co., Canton, 1948—. Mem. Sarasota Univ. Club, Alpha Delta Phi. Episcopalian. Clubs: Canton City, Oakwood Country, Sarasota Field Yacht; Venice (Fla.) Mission Valley, Patentee in field. Home: 2343 Brentwood Rd NW Canton OH 44708 Office: 1445 Whipple Rd SW Canton OH 44710

JENKS, HALSEY DENTON, retail gas and automotive co. exec.; b. Ypsilanti, Mich., Sept. 2, 1937; s. Halsey Barnes and Rosa Lena (Griggs) J.; A.B., Spring Arbor Coll., 1970; postgrad. Western Mich. U., 1972—. Joined U.S. Army, 1956, advanced through grades to sgt. 1st class, 1965, ret. 1966; partner Arbor Oil Co., Concord, Mich.,

1973—; substitute tchr. Concord Middle Sch., 1972-74. Trustee Village of Concord; chmn. Concord-Pulaski Police Assn., 1971-72. Mem. Orgn. Am. Historians, Concord Heritage Assn. (pres. 1971-73), Concord High Sch. Alumni Assn. (pres. 1977-78). Club: Masons. Home: 216 Hanover St Concord MI 49237 Office: 230 E Jackson St Concord MI 49237

JENKS, WILLIAM THOMAS, real estate appraiser; b. Savanna, Ill., July 14, 1911; s. Fred C. and Ethal L. (Cottral) J.; student Cornell Coll., 1929-30, Loyola U., Chgo., 1931-32, U. Ill., 1950-52, 58; m. Margaret J. Scott, Sept. 3, 1933; 1 son, William Scott. Owner, mgr. real estate cons. office, 1944—; condr. urban econ. studies, market valuations in eminent domain for pvt. clients, pub. agys. Mem. Soc. Real Estate Appraisers (past pres.), Am. Soc. Rural Appraisers. Clubs: Abbey Yacht (Fontana, Wis.), Rockford Skeet Gun, Thunder Rock Gun. Contbr. articles to profl. jours. Home: 1710 Council Crest Rockford IL 61107 Office: 818 Rockford Trust Bldg Rockford IL 61101

JENNER, ALBERT ERNEST, JR., lawyer; b. Chgo., June 20, 1907; s. Albert Ernest and Elizabeth (Owens) J.; m. Nadine Newbill, Mar. 19, 1932; 1 dau., Cynthia Lee; J.D., U. Ill., 1930; LL.D., John Marshall Law Sch., 1952, Northwestern U., 1975, Columbia Coll., 1974, U. Notre Dame, 1975, William B. Mitchel Sch. Law, 1976, U. Mich., 1976; Admitted to Ill. bar, 1930. Mem. firm Jenner & Block, Chgo., 1930—; prof. law Northwestern U., 1952-53. Spl. asst. to atty. gen. Ill., 1956-68; chmn. U.S. Supreme Ct. Adv. Com. on Fed. Rules of Evidence, 1965-75; chmn. Ill. Commn. on Uniform State Laws, 1951—; mem. Nat. Conf. Commn. on Uniform State Laws in U.S., pres., 1969-71; mem. U.S. Supreme Ct. Adv. Com. Fed. Civil Rules, 1960-70; mem. Nat. Conf. Bar Assn. Pres. U.S., pres., 1952-53; mem. U.S. Loyalty Rev. Bd., 1952-53; mem. council U. Ill. Law Forum, 1948-51; sr. counsel Presdl. Commn. to Investigate the Assassination Pres. Kennedy (Warren Commn.), 1964; law mem. Ill. Bd. Examiners Accountancy, 1948-51; mem. Pres.'s Nat. Commn. on Causes and Prevention of Violence in U.S. (Eisenhower Commn.), 1968-69; chief spl. counsel to minority U.S. Ho. of Reps. Judiciary Com. Conducting Impeachment Inquiry on Pres. Nixon, 1974. Bd. dirs. Center for Study Democratic Instns., 1975—; trustee Fund for Republic, recipient Robert Maynard Hutchins Distinguished Service award, 1976; trustee, sec. U.S. Navy Found., 1977—. Recipient Distinguished Service award for outstanding pub. service Chgo. and Ill. Jr. chambers commerce, 1939, U. Ill. Distinguished Alumnus award, 1962, Distinguished Civic Achievement award Am. Jewish Com., 1973, Distinguished Citizens award N.Y. U., 1975; named Chicagoan of Year, Chgo. Press Club, 1975. Fellow Am. Coll. Trial Lawyers (bd. regents, pres. 1958), Internat. Acad. Trial Lawyers; mem. Ill. Soc. Trial Lawyers, Nat. Assn. Def. Lawyers in Criminal Cases, Am. (Ill. state del. ho. of dels. 1948-75, state del. 1975—, chmn. standing com. on fed. judiciary 1965-68, chmn. sect. on individual rights and responsibilities 1973-74, mem. council, sect. on legal edn. gov. 1967-75), Ill. (pres. 1949-50), Chgo. (sec. 1947-49) bar assns., Am. Judicature Soc. (pres. 1958), Am. Inst. Jud. Adminstrn., Bar Assn. U.S. Ct. Appeals (gov.), Am. Law Inst., ACLU (dir. 1976), Order of Coif, Alpha Chi Rho, Phi Delta Phi. Clubs: Skokie Country, Law, Legal, Chgo. Press, Tavern, Chicago. Author, co-author: Ill. Civil Practice, Annotated; Smith-Hurd Ill., Annotated Statutes, 1934-70, 6 vols. on Pleading and Practice Procedure. Mem. permanent editorial bd. Uniform Commercial Code. Contbr. articles to law revs., legal publs. Home: 119 Tudor Pl Kenilworth IL 60043 Office: One IBM Plaza Chicago IL 60611

JENNER, WILLIAM ALEXANDER, govt. ofcl., meteorologist; b. Indianola, Iowa, Nov. 10, 1915; s. Edwin Alexander and Elizabeth May (Brown) J.; A.B., Central Meth. Coll., Mo., 1938; certificate meteorology U. Chgo., 1943; M.Ed., U. Mo., 1947; postgrad. Am. U., 1951-58; m. Jean Norden, Sept. 1, 1946; children—Carol Beth, Paul William, Susan Lynn. Instr. U. Mo., 1946-47; research meteorologist U.S. Weather Bur., Chgo., 1947-49; staff Hdqrs. Air Weather Service, Andrews AFB, Md., 1949-58, Scott AFB, Ill., 1958—, dir. tng., 1960—. Mem. O'Fallon (Ill.) Twp. High Sch. Bd. Edn., 1963—, sec., 1964-71, pres., 1971—; mem. O'Fallon Planning Commn., 1973—. Served with AUS, 1942-46. Recipient Distinguished Service award O'Fallon PTA, 1968. Mem. Am. Psychol. Assn., Wilson Ornithological Soc., Am. Philatelic Soc., Am. Meteorol. Soc., Phi Delta Kappa, Psi Chi. Clubs: Masons, O'Fallon Sportsmen's, Toastmasters Internat. Home: 307 Alma St O'Fallon IL 62269 Office: Scott AFB IL 62225

JENNINGS, FRANCIS PAUL, historian, library adminstr.; b. Pottsville, Pa., Sept. 19, 1918; s. James P. and Della Eleanor (Bierman) J.; B.S. in Edn., Temple U., 1939, Ed.M., 1951; Ph.D. in Am. Civilization, U. Pa., 1965; m. Joan Woollcott, Dec. 6, 1941; children—Michael, Nan, Timothy. Tchr., Phila. pub. high schs., 1941-54; asst. prof. Delaware Valley Coll., Doylestown, Pa., 1961-63; asso. prof. Glassboro (N.J.) State Coll., 1963-66; prof. history Moore Coll. Art, Phila., 1966-68; chmn. dept. history Cedar Crest Coll., Allentown, Pa., 1968-76; dir. Newberry Library Center for History of Am. Indian, Chgo., 1976—; project reviewer Nat. Endowment for the Humanities, 1977. Trustee Universalist Ch. of the Restoration, Phila., 1960-63. Served with U.S. Army, 1942-45. Hon. Research fellow U. London, 1975-76; Am. Philos. Soc. grantee, 1970, 75. Mem. Am. Soc. Ethnohistory (nat. pres. 1973), Orgn. of Am. Historians, Am., Pa. (mem. council 1974-77) hist. assns., Hakluyt Soc. (editorial asst. 1975-76), ACLU (mem. Pa. exec. bd. 1971-76), Hist. Soc. Pa., Am. Studies Assn., Champlain Soc. Democrat. Unitarian. Author: The Invasion of America: Indians, Colonialism and the Cant of Conquest, 1975; contbr. articles on ethnohistory to scholarly jours.; editorial bd. Pennsylvania History, 1972—, Am. Indian Quar., 1977—; editor Indian Bibliog. Series, 1976—. Home: 900 N Lake Shore Dr Chicago IL 60611 Office: Newberry Library 60 W Walton St Chicago IL 60610

JENNINGS, GENE KENNETH, clin. psychologist; b. Georgetown, Ohio, Oct. 28, 1934; s. William Andrew and Alverda Catherine (Warner) J.; B.A., U. Cin., 1957; M.A., Ohio U., 1960; Ph.D. (NSF grantee), Pa. State U., 1971; m. Joyce Marlene Mason, Sept. 3, 1954; children—Julie Lynn, Andrew Mason, Matthew Scot. Psychol. trainee Athens (Ohio) State Hosp., 1957-59; staff psychologist Dayton (Ohio) State Hosp., 1959-61, Adult Psychiat. Clinic, Dayton, 1961-65; clin. psychologist Bair County Mental Health Center, Altoona, Pa., 1965-67; mental health cons. Region H Mental Health, Ebensburg, Pa., 1969-70; sch. clin. psychologist Dept. Exceptional Children, Hollidaysburg, Pa., 1970-72; chief clin. psychologist Child Guidance Clinic, Battle Creek, Mich., 1972—; pvt. practice clin. psychology, Battle Creek, 1976—; part-time instr., lectr. in field, 1961—. Bd. dirs. Blair County Child Devel. Project, 1970-72, Big Bros./Sisters S. Central Mich., 1977—. Mem. Am., Mich., Southwestern Mich. psychol. assns., AAAS, Nat. Council Family Relations. Home: 111 Beachfield Dr Battle Creek MI 49015 Office: 155 Garfield Ave Battle Creek MI 49017

JENNINGS, JAMES BLANDFORD, historian; b. Ironwood, Mich., Jan. 23, 1922; s. Blandford and Anne (Heise) J.; B.E., Ill. State U., 1947, M.Ed., 1948; postgrad. U. Wis., 1950-51, Washington U., 1956, Ripon Coll., 1961, Northwestern U., 1965, Southern Ill. U., Edwardsville, 1970, 71. Instr. polit. sci. and econs. Mc Kendree Coll., Lebanon, Ill., 1948-49; tchr. social studies high sch., Pleasant Hope, Mo., 1950; tchr. history Howe (Ind.) Mil. Sch., 1951-52; tchr. social studies Center Twp. Sch., LaPorte, Ind., 1952-54; tchr. history East High Sch., Aurora, Ill., 1954-67, Maine Twp. High Sch. West, Des Plaines, Ill., 1967-69; instr. history State Community Coll. East St. Louis, 1969—, chmn. humanities, 1972-75. Co-chmn. Search for the Am. Dream in East St. Louis, 1976. Served with AUS, 1943-45. Decorated Bronze Star, Purple Heart with 2 oak leaf cluster Mem. Nat. Forensic League (dist. chmn. 1962-65), Aurora Edn. E. (pres. 1961-62), NEA, Am. Hist. Assn., AAUP, Pi Kappa Delta, Pi Gamma Mu. Home: 2100 Vandalia St Collinsville IL 62234 Office: 417 Misouri Ave East St Louis IL 62201

JENNINGS, NORMAN RODNEY, data processing exec.; b. Pittsburg, Kans., Aug. 14, 1939; s. Frank C. and Edith L. (Gardner) J.; B.S. in Mktg., Calif. State U., Chico, 1966; A.A. in Bus. Adminstrn., Ventura Coll., 1962; m. Barbara Deming, Apr. 15, 1965; children—Rodney Dean, Mark Andrew. Accountant, Texaco Co., Ventura, Calif., 1963-64; field claim rep. State Farm Auto Ins. Co., Ventura, 1966-67; programmer State Farm Fire Ins. Co., Bloomington, Ill., 1967-69, analyst, 1969-73, gen. supt., 1973—. Served with U.S. Army, 1962-63, U.S. N.G., 1963-68. Certified in gen. ins. and mgmt. Ins. Inst. Am.; certified data processor Inst. Certification of Computer Profls. Mem. Data Processing Mgmt. Assn. Home: 1621 Erin St Normal IL 61761 Office: 112 E Washington St Bloomington IL 61701

JENNINGS, WILLIAM GRANGER, real estate and financial exec., investor; b. Evanston, Ill., Aug. 10, 1928; s. Archibald Granger and Florence (Johnson) J.; B.S., Cornell U., 1951; M.B.A., Harvard, 1955; m. Betty Ann Swanson, Apr. 9, 1960; children—Robert William, Elizabeth Ann. With Stewart-Warner Corp., Chgo., 1955-63; v.p., treas. Quinlan & Tyson, Inc., Evanston, 1964-71, exec. v.p., treas., 1971—; exec. v.p., treas. Quinlan & Tyson Mortgage Corp., 1970-72, chmn., treas., 1973—; chmn., treas. Quinlan & Tyson Real Estate Investment Advisors, Inc., 1973-77, pres., 1977—; dir. Community Bank & Trust Co. of Edgewater. Trustee Goodwill Industries. Served to 1st lt. USAF, 1951-53. Mem. ASME, Cornell Soc. Engrs., Inst. Real Estate Mgmt., Real Estate Securities and Syndication Inst., Harvard Bus. Sch. Assn. Clubs: Cornell, Union League (Chgo.); Westmoreland Country, University (Evanston); Kenilworth; Rotary. Patentee in field. Home: 508 Brier St Kenilworth IL 60043 Office: 1569 Sherman Ave Evanston IL 60204

JENS, ELIZABETH LEE SHAFER (MRS. ARTHUR M. JENS, JR.), civic worker; b. Monroe, Mich., Jan. 25, 1915; d. Frank Lee and Mary (Bogard) Shafer; student Kalamazoo Coll., 1932-34, U. Wis., summer 1935; B.S., Northwestern U., 1936; postgrad. Wheaton Coll., summer 1965; L.P.N., Triton Coll., 1969; m. Arthur M. Jens, Jr., Aug. 14, 1937; children—Timothy V., Christopher E., Jeffrey A. Gray Lady, Hines, (Ill.) Hosp., 1948-49, 51-53; vol. Elgin (Ill.) State Hosp., 1958-72; writer Newsletter Vol. Planning Council, 1960-62; mem. Family Service Assn. Du Page County; vol. coordinator for social center for recovering mental patients Du Page County, 1966—; weekly vol. FISH orgn., 1973—. Bd. dirs. Du Page County Mental Health Soc., 1962-68, sec., 1963-64, 65-68, chmn. forgotten patient com., 1963-68, chmn. new projects, 1965-68; co-chmn. Glen Ellyn unit Central Du Page Hosp. Assn. Women's Aux., 1959-60; bd. dirs. chmn. com. on pesticides, Ill. Audubon Soc., 1963-73; mem. Ill. Pesticide Control Com., 1963-73, Citizens Com. Dutch Elm Disease, Glen Ellyn, 1960; bd. dirs. Natural Resources Council Ill., 1961-67, sec., 1961-64; bd. dirs. De Page Art League, 1958-68, chmn. bd., 1961-63, bldg. and grounds, paint-out and spl. memberships chmn., 1963-68, chmn. new bldg. com., 1968-75; bd. dirs. mem. planning com., publicity chmn. Du Page Fine Arts Assn., 1965-67; bd. dirs. Friends Library Glen Ellyn, 1967-68, Rachel Carson Trust for Living Environment 1971-74; bd. dirs., sec. Du Page Mental Health Assn., 1973—; bd. dirs. Du Page County Comprehensive Health Planning Agy., 1976; citizens adv. bd. to mental health div. Du Page Bd. Health, 1977—; mem. Du Page Subarea adv. council Suburban Cook County-Du Page County Health Systems Agy., 1977—; mem. com. on elderly women and widows Ill. Commn. on Status of Women, 1978—; bd. dirs., publicity chmn. DuPage County Council Vol. Coordinators, 1977—. Hon. mention in Nat. Sonnet contest, 1967; Vol. of Year, Ill. Mental Health Assn., 1975. Mem. Wilderness Soc., Du Page County Humane Soc., Du Page County Hist. Soc., Nat., Du Page Audubon socs., Nat Writers Club (monthly meeting chmn. Midwest chpt. 1973-74), Defenders of Wildlife, Theosophical Soc. Am., Nature Conservancy Ill., NAACP, Chgo. Art Inst. (life), Ill. Assn. Mental Health (dir. 1966-68), Pi Beta Phi. Writer column Mental Health and Yor for Press Publs., 1969—. Home: 22 W 210 Stanton Rd Glen Ellyn IL 60137

JENS, STIFEL WILLIAM, cons. civil engr.; b. St. Louis, Aug. 2, 1902; s. William and Laura Julia (Stifel) J.; B.S. in Civil Engring., Washington U., 1932, M.S. in Civil Engring., 1933; m. Henrietta Quinette Cowan, May 28, 1966. Draftsman, St. Louis Frog & Switch Co., 1929-30, Detroit Aircraft Corp., 1929-30; civil engr. Horner & Shifrin Co., St. Louis, 1933-39, partner, 1939-51; prin. Stifel W. Jens, civil engr., St. Louis, 1951-65; partner Reitz & Jens, Inc., St. Louis, 1964-69, sr. v.p., 1969—. Bd. dirs. People's Art Center, St. Louis, 1953-60, v.p., 1959-60; bd. dirs. Spirit of St. Louis Fund, 1960-63, treas., 1962-63. Recipient Alumni Citation award Washington U., 1973, Presidential Commendation for environ. excellence in urban hydrology, 1970; registered profl. engr., Mo., Ill., Minn., Tex. Mem. ASTM (award of appreciation 1974, vice chmn. C-4 1966-74), ASCE, Engrs. Club of St. Louis (award of merit 1964, v.p. 1966-69, pres. 1969-70), Am. Acad. Sanitary Engrs., Am. Geophys. Union, Am. Water Works Assn., Mo. Soc. Profl. Engrs., ASCE Urban Water Resources Research Council (founder 1963, chmn. 1963-69), Sigma Xi, Tau Beta Phi, Pi Mu Epsilon. Clubs: Cosmos (Washington); University (St. Louis). Contbr. articles on urban hydrology and engring. to profl. jours. Home: 536 Purdue Ave University City MO 63130 Office: 111 S Meramec Ave St Louis MO 63105

JENSEN, DONALD ALBERT, automotive mfg. co. exec.; b. San Francisco, Aug. 5, 1915; s. Albert Lund and Ivy (Johnston) J.; A.B., U. Calif. Berkeley, 1937, M.A., 1939; postgrad. Harvard U., 1942; m. Beverly Buchman, Sept. 20, 1969; children—Marilee, Michael, Karen, Christopher, Erick, Jeffrey. County exec., Marin County, Calif., 1954-59; exec. dir. Calif. Air Resources Bd., 1959-65; exec. engr. Ford Motor Co., Dearborn, 1966-70, dir. auto emissions office, 1971-76, dir. auto emissions and fuel economy office, 1977—; asst. prof. Calif. State U., Fresno. Served to comdr. USN, 1942-46; PTO. Mem. U.S. Olympic Team, 1936. Mem. Soc. Automotive Engrs. (recipient Nat. Air Conservation award 1965), Air Pollution Control Assn. (pres. 1970), Motor Vehicle Mfrs. Assn. (chmn. air quality com. 1969-75). Clubs: Dearborn Country, Fairlane, Windemere Island, Eleuthera, Bahamas, Masons, Shriners, Elks. Contbr. articles to profl. jours. Home: 23350 Bonair St Dearborn Heights MI 48127 Office: Ford Motors Co Dearborn MI 48121

JENSEN, EILEEN MARIE, assn. sec.; b. Ravenna, Ohio, Jan. 4, 1919; d. Alfred Frederick and Pearl M. (Cox) Jensen; student Western Res. U., 1936-37, Wilcox Sch. Bus., Cleve., 1942. Hostess, Cafe Rouge Statler Hotel, Cleve., 1939-41; sec. to chief engr. Hollenden Hotel, Cleve., 1941-46; sec. to purchasing agt. Milner Electric Co., Cleve., 1946-49; personnel mgr. Superior Carbon Products Co., Cleve., 1950-53; sec. solicitations dept. Greater Cleve. Growth Assn. (formerly Cleve. C. of C.), 1953-54, sec. to v.p. and sec., 1954-58, sec. to pres., 1959-68, adminstrv. asst., 1968-72, mgr. co. data center, 1972-74, mgr. fin. support rev., 1975—; office sec. Cleve. Tool, Die & Machine Shops Assn. (now Cleve. chpt. Nat. Tool, Die and Precision Machining Assn.), 1953-59, exec. sec., 1969-74; office sec. Soc. No. Ohio Profl. Photographers, Cleve. Soc. Profl. Photographers, 1953-60, exec. sec., 1970-74; office sec. Lake Erie Internat. Vacationland Assn., Cleve., 1954-60. Mem. Am. Bus. Women's Assn. (pres. Moses Cleveland Chpt. 1960, 64, Woman of Year award 1959, Merit award for outstanding service 1964), Exec. Secs. Inc. (v.p. Cleve. chpt. 1969, pres. 1969-70). Clubs: Order Eastern Star, Women's City (Cleve.). Home: 4133 W 143d St Cleveland OH 44135 Office: Union Commerce Bldg Greater Cleve Growth Assn Cleveland OH 44115

JENSEN, EMMANUEL TRANBERG, cons. civil engr.; b. Council Bluffs, Iowa, Nov. 26, 1910; s. Lars Peter and Christina Sophia (Lindhardt) J.; B.S., Iowa State U., 1933, M.S., 1948; postgrad. U. Minn., 1960-62; m. Wilma Mary Westburg, Aug. 15, 1947. Chief engr. Western Contracting Corp., Sioux City, Iowa, 1938-44; project engr. Al Johnson Constrn. Co., Mpls., 1948-50; civil engr. Guy F. Atkinson Co., South San Francisco, Calif., 1950-51; project engr. Donovon-Lovering-Boyle, Pickstown, S.D., 1951-56; civil engr., Winston Bros. Co., Mpls., 1956-58; pvt. cons. civil engr., Minnetonka, Minn., 1958—. Instr. civil engring. U. Minn., 1936-37, structural engring. Iowa State U., 1947-48. Vice pres. Nat. Luth. Alumni Fellowship, 1936-38. Serve to lt. USNR, 1944-45. Fellow ASCE (pres. N.W. sect. 1970-71, dir. 1971-73, vice chmn. nat. constrn. div. 1973-75, chmn., 1975-76, chmn. nat. publs. com. 1971-73), Nat. Model R.R. Assn. (nat. model contest judge 1968), Am. Arbitration Assn. (nat. panel), World Brotherhood Exchange, Phi Kappa Phi. Lutheran. Address: 3620 Fairlawn Dr Minnetonka MN 55343

JENSEN, ERLING N., ret. coll. pres.; b. Des Moines, Sept. 3, 1908; s. Jens Lars and Efra (Nielsen) J.; A.B., Drake U., 1932, LL.D. (hon.), 1969; A.M. (Lydia Roberts fellow), Columbia U., 1933; Ph.D., Iowa State U., 1947; Litt.D. (hon.), Lafayette Coll., 1962; LL.D. (hon.), Muhlenberg Coll., 1969, Lehigh U., 1969; m. Ruth McElhinney, Aug. 9, 1936; children—Richard Erling, Carl Harold, Edward Erik, David Paul. Sci. instr., high sch., prin., 1934-35; prof. sci. Grand View Coll., Des Moines, 1935-43; prof. physics, sr. physicist Inst. for Atomic Research, Iowa State U., 1943-61, prof. physics, 1969-73, prof. emeritus, 1973—; pres. Muhlenberg Coll., Allentown, Pa., 1961-69, pres. emeritus, 1969—. Chmn., Joint Commn. on Lutheran Unity Com. on Colls., 1960-61; chmn. nat. conv. Am. Evang. Ch., 1943-62; del. Luth. World Fedn., Helsinki, Finland, 1963; mem. exec. com. Nat. Luth. Council, 1963-66; del. Luth. Ch. in Am. convs., 1964, 66, 68; del., mem. exec. com. Luth. Council in U.S.A., 1966-69; pres. council Luther Meml. Ch., Des Moines, 1941-42; mem. council St. Pauls Luth. Ch., Allentown, 1962-68; bd. dirs. Luth. Student Found. at Iowa State U.; treas., bd. dirs. Iowa Luth. Campus Mission; mem. Charter Study Commn., Allentown, 1966; mem. exec. com. Commn. on Ind. Colls. and Univs. in Pa., 1965-68, Citizens Com. for Progress Lehigh County (Pa.), 1966-69; active liaison com. from pvt. colls. and univs. Pa. Council Higher Edn., 1967-69; adviser Council Higher Edn., Pa. Bd. Edn., 1969; chmn. bd. dirs. Grand View Coll. and Grand View Sem., 1951-62; bd. dirs. Indsl. Devel. Corp. of Lehigh County, 1964-69, Muhlenberg Med. Center, 1962-69, United Fund of Lehigh County, 1964-69, Allentown-Lehigh County C. of C., 1965-68, Distinguished Service award, 1969, pub. adv. com. Lehigh Valley Hosp. Planning Council, 1969; trustee Grand View Coll. Endowment Fund, 1951-62. Recipient Distinguished Service award, 1965, Double D award, 1968 both from Drake U.; Iowa Tennis Hall of Fame, 1974. Fellow Am. Phys. Soc., Iowa Acad. Sci. (chmn. physics sect. 1946-47); mem. Am. Assn. Phy scis. Tchrs., Am. Fedn. Scientists, Phi Beta Kappa, Sigma Xi, Phi Kappa Phi, Kappa Phi Kappa, Pi Mu Epsilon. Author: College Physics Laboratory Manual, 1944. Contbr. articles on nuclear physics to profl. jours. Home: 2522 Pierce Ave Ames IA 50010

JENSEN, FRED CHARLES, research and devel. engr.; b. Mpls., Jan. 11, 1947; s. Hays Hamilton and Hedwig Elizabeth (Ball) J.; B.S. in Engring. Sci., Fla. State U., 1970; m. Barbara Elizabeth Adamczyk, Sept. 13, 1969. Lab. instr. Fla. State U., Tallahassee, 1968-70; project engr. Tocco div. Park Ohio, Cleve., 1970-72; engring. design dept. head Life Systems, Inc., Cleve., 1972-77; NASA cons. W.L. Tanksley and Assos., Inc., Cleve., 1977—. Registered profl. engr., Ohio. Mem. Am. Soc. Metals, Am. Nuclear Soc., Am. Mgmt. Assn., Nat. Soc. Profl. Engrs., Cleve. East Soc. Profl. Engrs. (chmn. community action com. 1975—). Republican. Roman Catholic. Patentee in field. Home: 1607 Bell St Chagrin Falls OH 44022 Office: 16101 Snow Rd Cleveland OH 44142

JENSEN, HARLAN ELLSWORTH, educator; b. St. Ansgar, Iowa, Oct. 6, 1915; s. Bert and Mattie (Hansen) J.; D.V.M., Iowa State U., 1941; Ph.D., U. Mo., 1971; m. Naomi Louise Geiger, June 7, 1941; children—Kendra Lee (Mrs. Victor Belfi), Doris Eileen, Richard Harlan. Vet. practice, Galesburg, Ill., 1941-46; small animal internship New Brunswick, N.J., 1946-47; small animal practice, Cleve., 1947-58, San Diego, 1958-62, Houston, 1962-67; faculty U. Mo., Columbia, 1967—, chief opthalmology, prof. Vet. Sch., 1967—, asso. prof. ophthalmology Med. Sch., 1972—; cons. to pharm. firms; guest lectr., prof. ophthalmology U. Utrecht (Netherlands) Vet. Sch., 1973; tchr., lectr. various vet. meetings; conducted seminar World Congress Small Animal Medicine and Surgery, 1977. Recipient Am. Vet. Med. Assn.-Gaines award, 1973. Charter diplomate Am. Coll. Vet. Ophthalmologists (v.p. 1970-72, pres. 1972-73). Mem. Am. Vet. Radiology Soc. (pres. 1956-57), Am. Vet. Ophthalmology Soc. (pres. 1960-62), Farm House Frat., Sigma Xi, Phi Kappa Phi, Phi Zeta, Gamma Sigma Delta. Lutheran. Rotarian (pres. Pacific Beach, Calif. 1960-62, pres. Columbia 1977—). Author: Stereoscopic Atlas of Clinical Ophthalmology of Domestic Animals, 1971; Stereoscopic Atlas of Ophthalmic Surgery of Domestic Animals, 1974; co-author Stereoscopic Atlas of Soft Tissue Surgery of Small Animals, 1973; Clinical Dermatology of Small Animals, 1974. Contbr. articles to profl. jours. Inventor instrument for ear trimming in dogs, 1949, breathing apparatus, 1953; designed sound proof animal hosps.; developed 3-D study program for vet. ophthalmology, 1969. Home: 113 W Burnam Rd Columbia MO 65201

JENSEN, JOHN CALLARD, mfg. co. exec.; b. Chgo., Mar. 26, 1910; s. Elmer C. and Mary Dodsworth (Nagel) J.; Ph.B., U. Chgo., 1931; m. Doris Jennette Sanford, May 25, 1940; children—Susan Jensen Butler, Sharon S., Sanford C. Asst. dir. market research, dir. readio research Blackett, Sample, Hummert, Chgo., 1933-38; v.p. advt. Harold Elterich, N.Y.C., 1938-40; v.p. Grant Advt., Mexico City, 1940-42; regional dir. advt. and bus. services Reader's Digest, Chile, 1942-44; pres., founder John C. Jensen Internat., Chgo., 1944-52, South Haven, Mich., 1952-70; pres. Kalamazoo Internat., Inc., 1960—; founder, pres. Agro-Util, Inc. low cost equipment to raise food prodn. in developing nations, South Haven, 1970—; adviser on devel. of Mich. internat. policy and action program, to Gov. Romney, 1965-68; mem. Nat. Export Expansion Council, 1961—. Pres., Camp Fire Girls Council, 1959-61, South Haven Community Arts Council, 1967-69, Human Relations Commn., 1967-69; mem. Port Authority, 1960-64. Mem. Mich. Export Expansion Council, Mich. Partners of the Americas (dir.), Mich. Internat. Council (dir.),

Am. Soc. Agrl. Engrs., World Affairs Council, W. Mich. World Trade Club, C. of C., Phi Kappa Sigma. Episcopalian. Clubs: Kiwanis, South Haven Yacht. Home: 559 Monroe Blvd South Haven MI 49090 Office: 70 Van Buren St South Haven MI 49090

JENSEN, KENNETH RUSSELL, real estate broker; b. Chgo., Oct. 14, 1914; s. John and Elizabeth (Eitel) J.; student Northwestern U., 1932-52; children—James R., Carol Jensen Cory; m. Laura E. Culton, Nov. 2, 1968. Bldg. mgr. Baird & Warner, Chgo., 1935-40, L.J. Sheridan & Co., Chgo., 1940-56; v.p. Crosby Co., Mpls., 1956-69; sr. v.p. IDS Properties, Inc., Mpls., 1969-71; pres. Baker Properties Mgmt. Co., Mpls., 1970-71, Green Tree Bldg. Mgmt. Co., Mpls., 1972—; mem. Mpls. City Assessor's Adv. Com., 1973—, fiscal study com., 1973—. Hon. dir. Central YMCA, Chgo. Mem. Bldg. Owners and Mgrs. Inst. (chmn.), Bldg. Owners and Mgrs. Assn. Internat. (pres. 1971-73), Bldg. Planning Service Council (vice chmn.), Mpls. Downtown Council (dir.), Inst. Real Estate Mgmt. (dir.), Lambda Alpha Land Econs. Frat. Republican. Clubs: Masons, Kiwanis, Interlachen Country, Mpls. Athletic, Marsh Lake Hunting. Home: 219 Ardmore Dr Golden Valley MN 55422 Office: 801 Nicollet Mall Minneapolis MN 55402

JENSEN, LESLIE WARD, telephone co. exec.; b. Aberdeen, S.D., Feb. 12, 1931; s. Leslie and Elizabeth (Ward) J.; A.B., U. Chgo., 1950; LL.B., U. Nebr., 1954; m. Mary Margaret Cook, Aug. 3, 1957; children—Chris, David, Erica, Sharon. Editorial staff Shepards Citations, Colorado Springs, Colo., 1957-62; v.p., Peoples Telephone Co., Hot Springs, S.D., 1962-64, pres., gen. mgr., 1964—; dir. Orgn. for Preservation and Advancement Small Telephone Cos., 1971-72. Mem. Independent Sch. Dist. Bd., Hot Springs, 1967-72; Mem. S.D. Bd. of Regents, 1972—, pres., 1976. Mem. S.D., Bar Assn., Telephone Assn. (S.D.). Democrat Episcopalian. Club: Lions. Home: 346 N 17th St Hot Springs SD 57747 Office: 1510 National Ave Hot Springs SD 57747

JENSEN, LEWIS GERTON, realtor; b. Chetek, Wis., Jan. 7, 1916; s. Lewis and Vivian Loureen (Erickson) J.; grad. high sch.; m. Jane M. Waggoner, Nov. 23, 1950 (dec. 1971); children—Louis Victor, Donald (dec.), Willis (dec.), James Arnold, Lawrence Sampson, Kathleen Jane, Theodore Walter; m. 2d, Jean E. Cooke, July 15, 1975 (div. 1977). Realtor, Lewis Jensen & Son, Chippewa Falls, Wis., 1944-53; realtor, ins. agt. Lewis Jensen Agy., Chippewa Falls, 1953—; pres. Paragon Builders Co. Active Boy Scouts Am., commr. Chippewa Valley council, 1964-70. Mem. Jr. C. of C. (sec.-treas. 1946-50), Nat. Home Builders Assn., Eau Clair Bd. Realtors (sec. 1968). Democrat. Lutheran. Clubs: Masons (32 deg.), Shriners, Moose, Lions (dir.), Chippewa Valley Radio, Order Eastern Star, Ameranth. Home: 510 1/4 N Bridge St Chippewa Falls WI 54729 Office: 510 N Bridge St Chippewa Falls WI 54729

JENSEN, RAYMOND ANDREW, lawyer; b. St. Paul, June 30, 1923; s. Einer Nordall and Laura Camille (Hansen) J.; student U. Wis., 1941-43, U. Calif. at Los Angeles, 1943-44; J.D., U. Chgo., 1950. Admitted to Ill. bar, 1950; atty. Office of Solicitor, U.S. Dept. Labor, Chgo., 1951-53; asst. cashier City Nat. Bank & Trust Co. Chgo., 1953-58; with Dovenmuehle, Inc., Chgo., 1958-73, v.p., 1960-72, counsel, 1958-73, sr. v.p., 1972-73; partner firm Burditt & Calkins, Chgo., 1974—. Mem. Mechanic's Lien Law and Constrn. Financing Study Comm., Ill., 1969-71, Mayor's Adv. Com. Community Renewal Program, Chgo., 1963-68; mem. adv. com. Uniform Land Transactions Act, Nat. Conf. Commrs. Uniform State Laws, 1969-76. Mem. Am. (chmn. real estate financing com. 1968-71, council real property, probate and trust law 1976—), Chgo. (chmn. real property law com. 1968-69) bar assns., Chgo. Mortgage Attys. Assn. (pres. 1963-64), Lambda Alpha. Clubs: Univ. (Chgo.), Cliff Dwellers, Monroe. Contbr. articles to publs. Home: 1555 N Dearborn Pkwy Chicago IL 60610 Office: 135 S La Salle St Chicago IL 60603

JENSEN, WILMA MARY WESTBURG (MRS. EMMANUEL T. JENSEN), assn. exec.; b. Hopkins, Minn., June 11, 1916; d. Andrew Herman and Ida (Anderson) Westburg; B.A., Gustavus Adolphus Coll., 1938; B.L.S., U. Minn., 1940; m. Emmanuel T. Jensen, Aug. 15, 1947. Asst. librarian reference library, U. Minn., Mpls., 1940-43; counsellor for students Nat. Lutheran Council, U. Calif., Berkeley, 1943-47, Iowa State U., Ames, 1947-48; librarian, sec. Donovan-Lovering-Boyle, Contractors, Pickstown, S.D., 1951-56; sec. Luth. World Fedn., Mpls., 1957; sec. bd. Am. missions, Augustana Luth. Ch., Mpls., 1957-62; exec. sec. Luth. Ch. Library Assn., Mpls., 1963—. Nat. del. Luth. Ch. Am., 1966; nat. adv. Lutheran Student Assn. Am., 1946-47. Mem. Minn. Adv. Council on Library Services, 1973-76. Bd. dirs. Com. Am. Missions, Minn., Luth. Ch. in Am., Minnetonka (Minn.) Music Assn. Named World Brother, World Brotherhood Exchange, 1962; recipient Distinguished Alumni citation Gustavus Adolphus Coll., 1974. Mem. Luth. Ch. Library Assn. (nat. v.p., 1962, nat. pres., 1963), Ch. and Synagogue Library Assn. (nat. bd. dirs., nat. v.p. 1970-71, nat. pres. 1971-72), Am., Minn. library assns., Gustavus Library Assos. (nat. v.p. membership 1977-78), United Luth. Ch. Women (life), Alpha Phi Gamma, Iota Beta. Republican. Lutheran. Contbr. articles to profl. jours. Home: 3620 Fairlawn Dr Minnetonka MN 55343 Office: Lutheran Ch Library Assn 122 W Franklin Ave Minneapolis MN 55404

JENSON, JON EBERDT, trade assn. exec.; b. Madison, Wis., Aug. 1, 1934; s. Theodore Joel and Gertrude Beatrice (Eberdt) J.; B.S., U. Wis., 1956; postgrad., Goethe U., Frankfort, 1956; diploma U. Cologne, 1957; m. Jeannette Marie Hasman, May 1, 1976; 2 sons, James, Peter. Staff rep., Forging Industry Assn., Cleve., 1959-63, tech. dir., 1963-65, dir. mktg. and tech. services, 1965-75; exec. v.p., sec. Am. Metal Stamping Assn., Cleve., 1975—; exec. dir., sec. Forging Industry Ednl. and Research Found., Cleve., 1967-75; lectr. N.Y. U., 1973-75. Bd. regents Insts. Orgn. Mgmt. U.S. C. of C., 1977-78. Served with USN, 1958-59. Rotary Internat. fellow, 1956. Mem. Am., Cleve. Socs. Assn. Execs. Clubs: Capitol Hill, Cleve. Athletic. Author Forging Industry Handbook, 1966. Home: 5700 Brookside Rd Independence OH 44131 Office: 27027 Chardon Rd Richmond Heights OH 44143

JEPPESEN, GORDON LUTZ, aerospace co. exec.; b. Chgo., Dec. 5, 1913; s. Gunni and Olga (Lutz) J.; student Crane Jr. Coll., 1932-33; B.S., U. Ill., 1936, M.S., 1938. Research grad. asst. civil engring. U. Ill., Urbana, 1936-38, instr. civil engring., 1938-39; engr. Holabird & Root, architects, Chgo., 1939-40; engr. Goodyear Aerospace Corp., Akron, Ohio, 1940—, mgr. structural analysis, 1948—. Mem. Greater Akron Musical Assn., Akron Art Inst. Recipient Ira Baker award U. Ill., 1936, Roth Meml. trophy Internat. Brotherhood Magicians, 1967, 68, 71, 72. Fellow ASCE, Am. Inst. Aeros. and Astronautics (asso.); mem. Soc. Exptl. Stress Analysis, Soc. Applied Weight Engrs., Internat. Brotherhood Magicians (ring pres. 1968, 73), Sigma Xi, Phi Kappa Phi, Tau Beta Pi, Theta Tau. Home: 2315 Wyandotte Ave Cuyahoga Falls OH 44223 Office: 1210 Massillon Rd Akron OH 44315

JERGER, DOUGLAS CLARK, computer co. exec.; b. Melrose Park, Ill., Nov. 11, 1938; s. Everett Frederick and Dorothy Anna (Wolter) Oehlerking; B.S. in Bus. Adminstrn., Northwestern U., 1959, M.B.A., 1960; m. Margaret Ann Bevans, Apr. 28, 1962; children—Tracy, Mark, Kristin, Daniel. Mem. audit staff Arthur Andersen & Co., Chgo., 1960-65, mgr., 1965-70; v.p. Fortex Data Corp., Chgo., 1970-72, exec. v.p., 1972-76, pres., 1976—. Bd. dirs. Elmhurst (Ill.) Community Chest, 1965—, campaign chmn., 1969-70, pres., 1974-75; active United Way Suburban Chgo., 1971—; mem. Citizens Task Force Elmhurst Unit Sch Dist., 1976. Served with USAR, 1961. Mem. Am. Inst. C.P.A.'s, Ill. C.P.A. Soc., Assn. Govt. Accountants, Assn. Data Processing Service Organizations, Am. Mgmt. Assn., Phi Eta Sigma, Beta Alpha Psi. Home: 216 E St Charles Rd Elmhurst IL 60126 Office: 10 S Riverside Plaza Suite 1560 Chicago IL 60606

JERNIGAN, JAMES LESLIE, broadcasting exec.; b. Pinehurst, N.C., Feb. 26, 1946; s. Melvin H. and Dorothy M. (Kearshner) J.; A.S., Vincennes U., 1972; B.S., Ind. State U., 1975, M.S., 1977; m. Tina Marie Slapar, Mar. 3, 1973. Announcer, Sta. WAOV-AM-FM, Vincennes, Ind., 1970-74; producer dir. Sta. WVUT-TV, Vincennes, 1972-74, gen. mgr., 1976—; asst. prof. broadcasting Vincennes U., 1974—. Author articles and pamphlet in field. Home: 1512 College Ave Vincennes IN 47591

JEROME, JOHN A., psychologist; b. Allen Park, Mich., Aug. 4, 1947; s. John and Helen M. J.; B.S. in Psychology, Mich. State U., E. Lansing, 1965, M.S. in Rehab. Counseling, 1972, Ph.D. in Counseling Psychology, 1978. Chief psychologist Ingham Med. Center Pain Clinic, Lansing, Mich., 1974—; psychophysiologist, sec. Stress Mgmt., Inc., 1976—; instr. Grad. Sch., Mich. State U.; cons. Clinton, Eaton and Ingham Counties Community Mental Health Bd.; Cons. Dept. Def.; prof. edn. Tokyo and Yokohama, Japan, 1977; speaker. NIMH fellow. Mem. Am., Mich. psychol. assns., Am. Personnel and Guidance Assn., Biofeedback Soc. Am., Am. Pain Soc., Univ. Aikido Assn. Home: 2017 Sunnyside St Lansing MI 48910 Office: East Lansing Orthopedic Assn 4528 S Hagadorn Rd East Lansing MI 48823

JEROME, NORGE WINIFRED, nutritionist, anthropologist; b. Grenada, W.I., Nov. 3, 1930; d. Mc Manus Israel and Evelyn Mary (Grant) J.; came to U.S., 1956, naturalized, 1973; B.S. magna cum laude, Howard U., 1960; M.S., U. Wis., 1962, Ph.D., 1967. Asst. prof. U. Kans. Med. Sch., 1967-72, asso. prof., 1972—; dir. ednl. resource centers U. Kans. Med. Center, 1974—; cons. Children's TV Workshop, 1974—; chairperson adv. bd. Teenage Parents Center, 1971-75; mem. planning and budget council, children and family services United Community Services, 1971—; mem. panel on nutrition edn. White House Conf. on Food, Nutrition and Health, 1969; mem. bd. dirs., health care com. Prime Health, 1976—; bd. dirs. Council on Children, Media and Merchandising, 1977—; mem. consumer edn. task force Mid-Am. Health Systems Agy., 1977—. Bd. dirs. Kansas City Urban League. Decorated Dau. British Empire. Fellow Am. Anthrop. Assn. (chairperson com. on nutritional anthropology 1974-77), Soc. Applied Anthropology; mem. Am. Pub. Health Assn. (food and nutrition council 1975-78), Am. Inst. Nutrition, Am. Soc. Clin. Nutrition, Soc. Med. Anthropology, Am. Men and Women of Sci., Nat. Acad. Scis. (world food and nutrition study panel), Soc. Nutrition Edn., Am. Dietetic Assn. Contbr. articles to profl. jours.; asso. editor Jour. Nutrition Edn., 1971-77, nat. adv. council, 1977—; editor Nutritional Anthropology Communicator, 1974—; editorial adv. bd. Med. Anthropology: Cross Cultural Studies in Health and Illness, 1976—. Home: 8135 Halsey St Lenexa KS 66215 Office: 39th and Rainbow Sts Kansas City KS 66103

JERRY, MARJORIE COLLINGS, educator; b. nr. Rockville, Ind., Nov. 7, 1924; d. Ralph W. and Goldie (Thompson) Collings; B.S., Ind. State U., 1947, M.S., 1951, postgrad., 1950-51; postgrad. Purdue U., 1946-47; Ed.D., Ind. U., 1969; m. Robert Howard Jerry, July 23, 1950; children—Robert Howard II, Eleanor Claire. Tchr., Bunker Hill, Ind., 1947, Center Twp. Sch., Fowler, Ind., 1947-50; grad. fellow Ind. State U., Terre Haute, 1950-51, instr., 1966, asst. prof. home econs. 1966-72, asso. prof. home econs., 1972-75, prof., 1976—; coordinator vocat. home econs. curriculum Ind., 1968-72; instr. home econs. edn. Purdue U., Lafayette, Ind., 1951-52; coordinator student tchrs. Ind. U., Bloomington, 1961-66. Vis. instr. Purdue U. at Calumet, Ind., summers 1964, 65. Mem. Am., Ind. (v.p. for ops. 1975-77) home econs. assns., Nat. Assn. Tchr. Educators in Home Economics, Ind. Assn. for Supr. and Curriculum Devel., Am., Ind. vocat. assns., Delta Kappa Gamma, Kappa Delta Pi, Pi Omega Pi, Phi Upsilon Omicron, Psi Iota Xi. Home: 2908 Crawford St Terre Haute IN 47803

JERRY, ROBERT HOWARD, educator; b. Brazil, Ind., July 25, 1923; s. Floyd W. and Zetta (Hoffman) J.; B.S., Ind. State U., 1949, M.S., 1951; Ed.D., Ind. U., 1963; postgrad. Colo. U., 1951; m. Marjorie O. Collings, July 23, 1950; children—Robert Howard II, E. Claire. Elementary tchr., Fowler, Ind., 1949-50; tchr. high sch., Delphi, Ind., 1951-57; prin. Covington (Ind.) High Sch., 1957-60; supt. Worthington (Ind.) Schs., 1961-63; faculty Ind. State U., Terre Haute, 1963—, prof. edn., 1974—. Dep. state supt. pub. instrn. Ind., 1967-69. Served with USNR, 1943-46. Am. Assn. Sch. Adminstrs., Vigo County Exchange Club (pres. 1973-74), Fathers Club (pres. 1972-73), Blue Key, Theta Alpha Phi, Pi Gamma Mu, Phi Delta Kappa, Phi Delta Theta. Mem. Christian Ch. (elder). Home: 2908 Crawford St Terre Haute IN 47803

JERSILD, GERHARDT SAMUEL, lawyer; b. Elk Horn, Iowa, Feb. 9, 1907; s. Thomas Nielsen and Anne (Bille) J.; A.B., U. Nebr., 1928; J.D., U. Chgo., 1931; m. Martha Beck, Feb. 9, 1932; children—Thomas Nielsen, Susan Jersild Kolb. Admitted to Ill. bar, 1931; since practiced in Chgo., mem. firm Tatge & Jersild, 1945-70. Mem. univ. council Valparaiso U.; bd. dirs. United Charities of Chgo., 1956-73, pres., 1963-64. Recipient Useful Citizen citation U. Chgo. Alumni Assn., 1962. Mem. Am., Chgo. bar assns., Order of Coif, Phi Beta Kappa. Lutheran. Clubs: Legal, Univ. (sec. 1958-59, dir. 1956-59) (Chgo.). Home: 1416 Hinman Ave Evanston IL 60201 Office: 209 S LaSalle St Chicago IL 60604

JESSE, WALTER ADOLPH, bldg. contractor; b. Sparta, Wis., Apr. 5, 1903; s. Gustave A. and Tenia (Rich) J.; student pub. schs., Sparta, Wis.; m. Mary Edith Sigler, Mar. 23, 1940. Mason contractor, 1924-34; gen. bldg. contractor, own firm, Akron, Ohio and vicinity, 1934—; pres. Mortar Gun Corp. Am., 1966—. Mem. Asso. Gen. Contractors Am. (Akron chpt. pres. 1952), Akron Gen. Contractors Assn. (pres. 1946-47), Akron Mason Contractors Assn. (pres. 1957-58), Builder's Exchange of Akron and Vicinity (pres. 1953). Mason (32 deg., Shriner, Jester). Inventor and patentee mortar gun. Home: 3094 N Jackson Blvd Uniontown OH 44685 Office: 70 N Howard St Akron OH 44308

JESSEN, ROBERT BRUCE, educator, sociologist; b. Poughkeepsie, N.Y., Nov. 9, 1935; s. Harry John and Mary Elizabeth (Deimling) J.; A.B., Union Coll., Schenectady, 1958; Ph.D., Brown U., 1971; m. Mary Hale Mattice, Aug. 27, 1961; children—Jeannette Marie, Robert Bruce, Scott William, John Joseph, Thomas Page, James Matthew. Case worker Poughkeepsie Dept. Pub. Welfare, 1959-60; tech. officer Bur. Census, 1960; teaching, research asso. Union Coll., 1960-61; research asst. Center for Aging Research, Brown U., 1961-63; asst. prof., then asso. prof. sociology Mary Washington Coll., Fredericksburg, Va., 1964-72; asst. prof. sociology Ind. U., South Bend, 1972—; cons. in field, 1966—; co-propr. Bufhill Collies, Niles, Mich., 1961—. Charter mem. Lake Arrowhead Civic Assn., 1968, pres., 1968-69, v.p., 1970-71, bd. dirs., 1971-72, editor Lake Arrowhead News, 1968-72; pres. Niles Twp. Taxpayers Assn., 1975-77; mayor Brandywine, 1976—; mem. St. Mary's Bd. Edn., 1972. Demographic fellow Population Council, 1963-64; named Tchr. of Year, Mary Washington Coll., 1969. Mem. Population Assn. Am., Internat. Assn. Housing Sci., Am. Sociol. Assn., So. Regional Demographic Group (charter), Michiana Social Scis. Assn. (co-founder), Michiana Kennel Club, Collie Club Am., Assn. Am. Geographers, Alpha Kappa Delta, Delta Chi. Contbr. articles, monographs to profl. jours. Home: 2720 Adams Rd Niles MI 49120 Office: Dept Sociology Ind U South Bend IN 46615

JESSEPH, JOHN ERVIN, educator, surgeon; b. Pasco, Wash., Nov. 6, 1925; s. Harry Ervin and Eula Victoria (Ledgerwood) J.; A.B., Whitman Coll., 1949, D.Sc. (hon.), 1975; M.D., U. Wash., 1953, M.S., 1956; m. Marley M.G. Austin, June 20, 1948; children—Steven A., Jerry M. Intern, King County Hosp., Seattle, 1953-54; resident in surgery U. Wash. Affiliated Hosps., Seattle, 1954-59; asst. prof. surgery U. Wash., Seattle, 1959-62; scientist Brookhaven Nat. Lab., 1962-65; faculty Ohio State U., Columbus, 1965-71, prof., 1967-71; prof. surgery, chmn. dept. Sch. Medicine, Ind. U., Indpls., 1971—. Served with USMCR, 1944-46. USPHS research grantee, 1955-58. Diplomate Am. Bd. Surgery (dir.), Am. Bd. Family Practice. Mem. Am. Surg. Assn., A.C.S., other orgns. Mason. Editor, contbg. author med. books; contbr. articles to profl. publs. Home: 5230 N Meridian St Indianapolis IN 46208 Office: 1100 W Michigan St Indianapolis IN 46202

JESTRAB, FRANK F., lawyer; b. Havre, Mont., Jan. 28, 1914; s. Frank F. and Anna U. (Larson) J.; LL.B. cum laude, Mont. State U., 1938, B.A., 1946; spl. student Harvard Law Sch., 1946-47; m. Elvira Waidt Evensen, Jan. 18, 1952; children—Laural Ann, James David. Admitted to Mont. bar, 1938; mem. legal dept. Anaconda Copper Mining Co., Butte, Mont., 1938-42; practice law, N.Y.C., 1946-48, Houston, 1948-49; lectr. labor law U. Houston, 1948; div. atty. Amerada Petroleum Corp., Casper, Wyo., 1949-51; mem. firm Bjella & Jestrab, Williston, N.D. Mem. Nat. Conf. of Commnrs. on Uniform State Laws, 1956—, mem. exec. com., 1963-68. Served as capt., inf., AUS, 1942-46. Fellow Am. Bar Found.; mem. Internat. Acad. Trial Lawyers, Am., Mont., Wyo., Tex. bar assns., State Bar Assn. N.D. (pres. 1966-67), Bar Assn. City N.Y., Am. Law Inst., Order of Coif. Clubs: Rotary (Williston, district gov. 1950-60), Petroleum (Billings). Home: 217 E 11th St Williston ND 58801 Office: Box 1343 Williston ND 58801

JESUNAS, KENNETH PAUL, physician; b. Chgo., May 31, 1941; s. Paul and Sophie (Ambrose) J.; B.S., U. Ill., 1963, M.D., 1967; intern Cook County Hosp., Chgo., 1967-68; resident Northwestern U., 1968-72; m. Carolyn Carr, Jan. 4, 1969; 1 son, Jason. Asst. chief otolaryngology Brooke Army Med. Center, 1972-74; practice medicine, specializing in otolaryngology, Joliet, Ill., 1974—; mem. staff St. Joseph Hosp., Silver Cross Hosp. Diplomate Am. Bd. Otolaryngology, Nat. Bd. Med. Examiners. Fellow A.C.S.; mem. AMA, Soc. Mil. Otolaryngologists, Am. Acad. Ophthalmology and Otolaryngology, Am. Pharm. Assn., U. Ill. Alumni Assn., Will-Grundy County Med. Soc., Chgo. Laryngol. and Otol. Soc., Alpha Kappa Kappa, Rho Chi, Phi Delta Chi. Home: 110 Rebecca St Joliet IL 60435 Office: 3077 W Jefferson St Joliet IL 60435

JEWELL, DONALD EDWARD, engr.; b. nr. Dodgeville, Wis., Jan. 2, 1915; s. Edward H. and Stella (Lee) J.; B.S., U. Wis., 1947; m. Geraldine R. Wedean, July 22, 1975; children—Lynn K., Jane E., Paul D. Instr., U. Wyo., Laramie, 1947-48, asst. prof., 1949, Oreg. State U., Corvallis, 1949-54; design engr. J.I. Case Co., Rockford, Ill., 1954-57, supr. test ops., 1957-69, product mgr., 1969-70, dept. engr., Bettendorf, Iowa, 1970-75, Racine, Wis., 1975—. Served with USAAF, 1941-45; PTO. Mem. Am. Soc. Agrl. Engrs. (Wis. chmn. 1964-65), Soc. Automotive Engrs., VFW. Methodist. Home: 2001 N Green Bay Rd Racine WI 53405 Office: Tractor Plant 700 State St Racine WI 53403

JEWELL, MARTHA PEARL, mfg. co. exec.; b. Brimfield, Ohio, Oct. 10, 1940; d. Roy Delbert and Johnnie Belle McPherson; m. Richard Lee Jewell, Oct. 13, 1956; children—Melany Elaine, Brian Lee, Kenneth Richard. Sec., treas. Internat. Mag. Service, Kansas City, Mo., 1961-66; bus. adminstr. Blue Ridge Methodist Ch., Kansas City, 1967-70; treas. Arrow Fork Lifts Parts and Mfg. Co., Kansas City, 1971-73, v.p., sales mgr., 1973—. Chmn. Christian Bus. Women Council, Kansas City, 1975; treas. Wesleyan Service Guild, Kansas City. Mem. Sales Mktg. Execs., Material Handling Equipment Distbrs. Assn. Presbyterian. Home: 10400 Walrond St Kansas City MO 64137 Office: 1620 Oakland St Kansas City MO 64126

JEWETT, DENNIS LEE, bus. exec.; b. Jackson, Mich., Sept. 26, 1940; s. Delmar H. and Vera F. J.; C.B.A., 1974; B.S. in Accounting, Loyola U. Chgo., 1976; m. Catherine C. Coller, Dec. 28, 1968; children—Robert, Kristin. Asst. auditor Nat. Bank of Jackson, Mich., 1966-69; auditor 1st Trust Bank of Kankakee, Ill., 1969-71, asst. v.p., 1971-72, v.p., 1972-74, v.p. & cashier, 1975—; instr. in field. Mem. Career Center Advisory Bd., Sch. Dist. Advisory Bd.; chmn. United Fund Div., 1973; mem. United Fund audit Com.; pres. Kankakee Valley Theater, 1975—. Served with USAF, 1961-65. Mem. Kankakee Mgmt. Club, Personnel Mgrs. Club, Am. Inst. of Bankers (pres. local chpt. 1972), Beta Alpha Psi. Club: Lion's. Home: Baker St PO Box 37 Route 3 Kankakee IL 60901 Office: 1 Dearborn Sq Kankakee IL 60901

JEZAK, BERNARD ANDREW, cement co. exec.; b. St. Joseph, Mo., Apr. 6, 1936; s. Andrew and Agnes Margaret (Hruby) J.; student U. Kans., 1954-56; m. Sally Ann Rembolt, June 20, 1959; children—Susan, John. Systems coordinator Service Bur. Corp., Kansas City, Mo., 1960-72; systems analyst Ash Grove Cement Co., Kansas City, Mo., 1972—. Mem. Mid-Am. Planning Commn., 1974—, Mid-Am. Regional Council Open Space, 1971—; mem. Clay County Park Bd., 1972—; planning commr. Gladstone, Mo., 1970; mem. Gladstone Council, 1970—; mayor of Gladstone, 1975-76; mem. Clay County Central Democratic Com., 1972—. Mem. Phi Kappa Sigma. Home: 1611 NE 68th Pl Gladstone MO 64118 Office: 1000 Tenmain Center Kansas City MO 64108

JILANI, ATIQ AHMED, engr.; b. Amroha, India, Feb. 1, 1948; s. Siddiq Ahmed and Nasima (Khatoon) J.; B.E., N.E.D. Engring. Coll., Karachi U., 1969; M.S., Tuskegee Inst., Ala., 1971; m. Khalida Bano Naqvi, Dec. 25, 1975. Script writer Karachi (Pakistan) TV, 1967-70; mem. research staff AEC, Tuskegee, Ala., 1971-71; design engr. Lummus Industries, Columbus, Ga., 1971-73; project engr. Container Corp. of Am., Cedar Falls, Iowa, 1973-74; product engr. Borg-Warner Corp., Chgo., 1974—, mem. cost and productivity com., 1976. Registered profl. engr., Ill. Mem. Nat., Ill. socs. profl. engrs., Am. Soc. Agrl. Engrs., ASME, Soc. Automotive Engrs. Muslim. Contbr. articles to profl. jours. Patentee in field agrl. implements. Home: PO Box 71 Oak Forest IL 60452

JIMERSON, JAMES COMPERE, SR., toxicologist; b. Little Rock, Oct. 10, 1936; s. George Alexander and Lois (Compere) J.; B.A., B.S., Ouachita Bapt. Coll., 1958; postgrad. U. Ark., 1959; m. Ina Sue Jones, Aug. 18, 1957; children—Martha LeAnn, James Compere. Lab. instr.

Ouachita Bapt. Coll., Arkadelphia, Ark., 1957-58; teaching asst. U. Ark., Fayetteville, 1958-59; sr. chemist Allied Chem. Corp., Metropolis, Ill., 1959-62; analytical chemist Tech. Service Labs., P.R. Mallory & Co., Indpls., 1962-65; engring./research group leader Mallory Capacitor Co., Indpls., 1965-72; toxicologist, dept. pathology Wishard Meml. Hosp., Indpls., 1972—; affiliate instr. Ind. Vocat. Tech. Coll. Sr. staff/communication coordinator Office of Civil Def., Indpls. and Marion County, 1965—; bd. dirs. Crossroads of Am. council Boy Scouts Am., 1973—, commr., 1969-72, tng. chmn., 1972-73, dist. chmn., 1973-76; bd. dirs. Marion County unit Am. Cancer Soc. Recipient Silver Beaver award Boy Scouts Am., 1976; Pub. Service award Am. Radio Relay League, 1966, 74; named Man of Yr., Civil Def., 1976. Mem. Am. Chem. Soc., Soc. for Applied Spectroscopy, Coblentz Soc., Am. Acad. Forensic Scis., Central Ind. Clin. Biochem. Forum, Am. Soc. Analytical Toxicologists, Nat. Eagle Scout Assn., Central Ind. VHF/UHF Club. Republican. Baptist. Club: Masons. Patentee. Home: 1820 Fairhaven Dr Indianapolis IN 46229 Office: 1001 W 10th St Indianapolis IN 46202

JINDAL, GOPI RAM, employment co. exec.; b. Julana, India, Aug. 3, 1938; s. Bannari Lal and Bhanga Devi (Gupta) J.; came to U.S., 1959; B.S.E.E., Utah State U., 1961; M.S.E.E., U. So. Calif., 1964; Ph.D., Pa. State U., 1970; m. Usha R. Gupta, Mar. 12, 1967; children—Gorav, Unmaish. Scientist, Ford Motor Co., Dearborn, Mich., 1971; project scientist Enmet Corp., Ann Arbor, Mich., 1972-73; exec. recruiter Mgmt. Recruiters, Ann Arbor, 1973-76; mgr. corp. employment and staffing Sycor, Inc., 1976-77; search and cons. Comp-Tech Search, 1977—; cons. on devel. of instrumentation Kent-Moore Corp., Warren, Mich. Mem. IEEE, Am. Phys. Soc. Hindu. Club: Econ. of Detroit. Contbr. articles to sci. and personnel jours. Home: 2115 Churchill Dr Ann Arbor MI 48103

JOACHIM, PETRONILLA MARY ANN, lawyer, lectr., nun; b. Adrian, Mich.; d. August and Johanna (Führkötter) Joachim; LL.B., Detroit Coll. Law, 1923; LL.M., U. Detroit, 1924; B.A., Siena Hts. Coll., 1926; M.A. in History, Loyola U., Chgo., 1927; Ph.D. magna cum laude, Internat. Cath. U., Switzerland, 1936. Admitted to Mich. bar, 1923, U.S. Supreme Ct. bar, 1936; mem. firm Mayer, Ruby and Joachim, Detroit, 1915-26; joined Sisters of St. Dominic, Adrian, Mich., 1928; prof., chmn. dept. social sci. Siena Hts. Coll., Adrian, 1935—; lectr. various univs. and lit. groups in U.S., 1935—; legal counsel for Dominican Sisters of Adrian Motherhouse, 1928—; organizer, dir. Dominican Camp for Girls, Kelly Island, Lake Erie, 1962-65; atty. for Human Relations Com., City of Adrian, 1967-70; ednl. tour with Am. Express Co. to USSR, 1971. Mem. Gov.'s Fulbright Com. state of Mich., 1966-71; mem. City of Adrian Commn., 1971-74. Named Woman of Year, Alumnae Assn. U. Detroit, 1950; recipient Beta Sigma Phi award Adrian City Area Council, 1976. Mem. Cath. Lawyers Soc., Am. (Plaque award 1976), Mich., Lenawee County bar assns., Am. Econ. Assn., Am. Cath. Sociol. Assn., Assn. Cath. Colls. of Mich. (treas. 1928-33), Nat. Assn. Parliamentarians, Nat. Assn. R.R. Passengers (hon.), Kappa Beta Pi. Democrat. Author: Why I Entered the Convent, 1953; contbr. numerous articles to hist., sociol. and legal jours. Address: Adrian Dominican Sisters 1257 Siena Heights Dr Adrian MI 49221

JOB, RICHARD WILLIAM, mech. engr.; b. Freeport, Minn., Dec. 12, 1939; s. Ralph Leo and Wilhelmina (Wensman) J.; B.M.E., Mich. Technol. U., 1963; m. Jane E. Friberg, May 26, 1962; children—Reba Nell, Sara Jean. Quality control engr. Clinton Engines Corp., Maquoketa, Iowa, 1963-64; design engr. J. I. Case Co., Racine, Wis., 1964-67; project engr. Avco New Idea, Coldwater, Ohio, 1967-70; sr. project engr. Hesston Corp. (Kans.), 1970; sr. project engr. Twin Disc Inc., Racine, Wis., 1970-71; chief engr. test and devel. White Farm Equipment Co., Libertyville, Ill., 1971—. Mem. Soc. Automotive Engrs. Roman Catholic. Home: 549 Longview Dr Antioch IL 60002 Office: Route 45 and Peterson Rd Libertyville IL 60048

JOBE, DONALD LARRY, rec. co. exec., educator; b. Hot Springs, Ark., July 10, 1946; s. William Henry and Belvie Betty (Cheshier) J.; B.S., Western Mich. U., 1969, M.A., 1970, M.A. in Counseling and Personnel, 1975; m. Susan Ann Szewczyk, Sept. 30, 1967; 1 son, Dennis William. Profl. musician, lead vocalist, drummer The Ghosters, 1964—; producer records Ghost Prodns., 1966—; radio announcer Sta. WDOW, Dowagiac, Mich., 1966-67; pres. Ghost-Jobie Records, Kalamazoo, 1965—; tchr. Hopkins (Mich.) High Sch., 1970—, chmn. dept. English, 1972—. Mem. NEA, Hopkins Edn. Assn. (pres. 1974-75), Am. Fedn. Musicians, Journalism Edn. Assn., Speech Assn. Am., Nat. Council Tchrs. of English. Home: 1905 Pesos Pl Kalamazoo MI 49008

JOBES, ALVIN ROY, cons. engr.; b. Roscoe, Pa., Aug. 3, 1925; s. Edgar Robert and Ethel (Langford) J.; student Bethany Coll. (W.Va.), 1943-46; B.S., E.M., W.Va. U., 1950; m. Carol Sarah Bier, May 7, 1948; children—Deborah Ann, Edward Alan, Robert Landon. Engr., sect. foreman Valley Camp Coal Co., 1950-54; design engr., project engr., div. 5 ops. engr. Ohio Dept. Hwys., 1954-63; cons. engr., owner A. R. Jobes and Assos., Inc., 1963-69; pres. Jobes, Henderson & Assos., Inc., 1969—. Served with AUS, 1943-45, ETO. Registered profl. engr. and surveyor, Ohio; profl. engr., W.Va. Mem. Nat., Ohio socs. profl. engrs., Nat., Ohio socs. homebuilders, C. of C., Alpha Sigma Phi. Democrat. Presbyterian. Clubs: Masons (32 deg.), Shriners, Moundbuilders Country. Home: 1574 Russet Ln Newark OH 43055 Office: 80 Westgate Dr Newark OH 43055

JOEHLIN, STANLEY WALBOLT, mfg. co. exec.; b. Toledo, June 19, 1936; s. Homer Wilson and Janis (Walbolt) J.; B.Agrl. Engring. summa cum laude, Ohio State U., 1960, M.S., 1960; m. Dolores Ann St. John, Jan. 14, 1956; children—Linda Ellen, Kenneth Alan, Rebbecca Ann, Scott Arthur. Partner, Homer Joehlin & Son, Curtice, Ohio, 1960-64; with Guardian Industries, Millbury, Ohio, 1964-71, mgr. devel. lab., 1969-70, mgr. research and devel., 1970-71; chief engr., gen. mgr. Glasstech, Inc., Toledo, 1971-77, v.p. ops., 1977—. Com. chmn., Webeloes leader Toledo Area council Boy Scouts Am., 1966-74; v.p. Band Parents Office, 1970-72, pres., 1972-73. Registered profl. engr., Ohio. Patentee gas hearth tempering system. Home: 24678 W Curtice Rd Curtice OH 43412 Office: 801 Front St Toledo OH 43605

JOFFE, BERNARD, accountant; b. Chgo., June 10, 1918; s. Albert Jacob and Sarah (Levin) J.; B.B.A., Northwestern U., 1940; postgrad. Loyola U., Chgo., 1943-44; m. Phyllis R. Levy, Apr. 20, 1966; children—Roberta Lynn Nachman, Nadine Ruth Schwartz; stepchildren—Barry, Jerald, Wendy Joffe Izanuk. Accountant, M. Joffe & Co., C.P.A.'s, Chgo., 1935-44, partner, 1944-69 prin. B. Joffe & Co., C.P.A.'s, Chgo., 1969—; sec., dir. State House Inn, Springfield, Ill., Eldorado Water Co. (Ill.). Treas. Deer Park Civic Assn., 1954-57, v.p., 1958-59. C.P.A., Ill. Mem. Am. Inst. C.P.A.'s, Ill. Soc. C.P.A.'s, Nat. Fedn. Jewish Men's Clubs (Midwest v.p. 1966-73), Alpha Gamma Pi. Jewish (dir. congregation 1958—, v.p. 1965-67). Club: Ner Tamid Men's (pres. 1962-64) (Chgo.). Home: 1310 Ritchie Ct Chicago IL 60610 Office: 105 W Madison St Chicago IL 60602

JOHANNES, KARL ANDREW, mathematician, educator; b. Buffalo, Aug. 30, 1903; s. William Louis and Agnes Laura (Hathaway) J.; A.B., U. Rochester, 1932, A.M., 1933; postgrad. U. Chgo., 1946-50; Ph.D., U. Pitts., 1956; Instr. math. Rochester (N.Y.) Collegiate Center, N.Y. Coll. Forestry, 1933-37; instr. math. Cornell U., Ithaca, N.Y., 1937-38; head of sci. dept. Albany (N.Y.) Acad., 1938-40; instr. Ind. Inst. Tech., Ft. Wayne, 1940-42; instr. Case Inst. Tech., Cleve., 1942-46; instr. math. U. Ill., Chgo., 1946-54, U. Pitts., 1954-55; asst. prof. math. Wis. State U., Whitewater, 1955-57, U. Akron (Ohio), 1957-59; prof. math. U. Wis., Whitewater, 1960-74, prof. emeritus, 1974—. Mem. Math. Assn. Am., Nat. Council Tchrs. Math. Home: 12550 Lake Ave #310 Lakewood OH 44107

JOHANNSEN, KENNETH M., physician; b. Denison, Iowa, Oct. 17, 1930; s. Wilbert and Irene (Krohnke) J.; B.A., State U. Iowa, 1953; M.D., U. Nebr., 1965; m. Audrey J. Leidholdt, Apr. 17, 1953; children—Mark, Jess, Seth. Intern, Bryon Meml. Hosp., 1965-66; gen. practice medicine, Spencer, Iowa, 1966-73; resident in gen. surgery VA Hosp., Des Moines, 1973-77; gen. surgeon Buena Vista Clinic and mem. staff Buena Vista County Hosp., Storm Lake, Iowa, 1977—. Served with USMC, 1953-55. Mem. A.M.A., Ia. Med. Soc. Home: Storm Lake IA 50588

JOHANSEN, ROBERT, artist; b. Kenosha, Wis., Mar. 30, 1923; s. Johan and Dorthea (Nelson) J.; grad. Layton Sch. Art, 1945-47; m. Kathleen Flynn, Jan. 29, 1949; children—Christine, John, Ann, Roberta, Lawrence, Paul. One man shows at Kenosha Mus., Marine Bank, Milw., group shows include Wis. Watercolor Soc., Watercolor Wis., Wustum Mus., Racine Invitational; represented in permanent collections at Borg-Warner, Standard Oil, Marine Bank, Wustum Mus., U. Wis.-La Crosse; comml. artist Eisenberg Studios, Milw. Served with U.S. Army, 1943-45. Mem. Wis., Midwest watercolor socs. Home: 3017 Taylor Ave Racine WI 53405

JOHANSEN, WALTER HENRY, design engr.; b. Lake Preston, S.D., Feb. 9, 1924; s. Henry William and Ellen Marie (Augustsen) J.; student Calif. State Poly. U., 1949-50; B.C.E., State U. Iowa, 1955; m. Mary Louise Kringel, Dec. 31, 1955; children—Patricia Ann, David Alan, Christina Marie. City engr. Wood River (Ill.), 1955-58; sr. design engr. Clark Daily & Dietz, Engrs., Urbana, Ill., 1958-63; v.p., chief san. engr. design sect. Daily & Assos., Engrs., Inc., Champaign, Ill., 1963—, also dir. Served with U.S. Army, 1943-46, 50-52. Decorated Bronze Star; registered profl. engr., Ill. Mem. Nat., Ill. socs. profl. engrs., Theta Tau. Club: Masons (32 deg.). Home: 1104 Hollycrest Dr Champaign IL 61820 Office: 816 Dennison St Champaign IL 61820

JOHANSON, DONALD CARL, anthropologist, educator; b. Chgo., June 28, 1943; s. Carl Torsten and Sally Eugenia (Johnson) J.; B.A., U. Ill., Urbana, 1966; M.A., U. Chgo., 1970, Ph.D., 1974. Asst. prof. dept. anthropology Case Western Res. U., Cleve., 1972—; asso. curator anthropology Cleve. Mus. Natural History, 1972-74, curator phys. anthropology, 1974—; bd. dirs. Found. for Research into Origins of Man. Recipient research grants for anthrop. research Wenner-Gren Found., NSF grants for field research in Ethiopia; NSF trainee, 1966-67; Nat. Inst. Dental Research trainee, 1967-71. Mem. AAAS, Am. Assn. Phys. Anthropologists, Internat. Assn. Human Biologists, Soc. Vertebrate Paleontology, Soc. Study Human Biology, Internat. Assn. Dental Research. Coordinator, co-dir. Internat. Afar Research Expdn. to Ethiopia. Home: 2901 Hampton Rd #18 Cleveland OH 44120 Office: Lab Phys Anthropology Cleve Mus Natural History Cleveland OH 44106

JOHN, ELMER ROY, mgmt. cons.; b. St. Paul, July 28, 1916; s. Gustav H. and Anna (Siering) J.; A.A., Bethel Coll., 1937; B.S. cum laude U. Minn., 1945, M.A., 1952; m. Evelyn C. Rutz, July 22, 1944; children—Gloria Gail, Patricia Ann, Douglas Rychner. Instr., lectr. U. Minn., 1945-49; dir. personnel Midland Coops. Mpls., 1948-59; corporate dir. personnel Gen. Mills, Inc., Mpls., 1959-69; pres. Elmer R. John Assos., Inc., 1969—; pres. Midland Metro Services, Mpls.; chmn. bd., dir. Modern Service Ins. Co., Mut. Service Ins. Cos.; pres., exec. dir. Mantread, Inc., 1976—; dir. Personnel Decisions, Inc., Mpls. Faculty mem. Minn. Met. State Coll., 1972—; asso. clin. prof. U. Minn., 1972—. Past mem. exec. council Viking council Boy Scouts Am.; adv. council Indsl. Relations Center, U. Minn.; mem. Gov.'s Adv. Com. on Mgmt. Devel.; past pres. Twin City chpt. Council Ind. Mgrs., Mpls. Certified Consulting Psychologist, Minn. Fellow Internat. Soc. Advancement Mgmt. Clubs: Athletic, Golf (Mpls.). Home: 2110 Fairmount Ave St Paul MN 55105 Office: Suite 1100 Minnesota Bldg St Paul MN 55101

JOHN, STANLEY ROBERT, computer technologist; b. Huntington Park, Calif., Feb. 11, 1933; s. Rolland Richardson and Helen (White) J.; A.A., San Francisco City Coll., 1956; B.A., U. Calif. at Berkeley, 1958; m. Katherine Mary Kellerup, Mar. 7, 1954; children—Laura, Sharon, Robin. Test engr. Gen. Dynamics, Pomona, Calif., 1958-59, engring. writer, 1959-60, research engr., 1960-66, mgmt. specialist, 1966-67, design specialist, 1967-73, chief computing, Pomona, 1973-75, tech. services specialist, St. Louis, 1975—. Served with USNR, 1951-56. Mem. Assn. Computing Machinery (pres. Arrowhead chpt. 1974), Soc. Mfg. Engrs., San Francisco City Coll. Engring. Soc. Republican. Club: West Alhambra Camera (v.p. 1949). Home: 557 Hickory View Ballwin MO 63011 Office: Pierre Laclede Center Saint Louis MO 63105

JOHNS, MALCOLM MACLEAN, educator, musician; b. Otsego, Mich., Jan. 23, 1915; s. Paul James and Winifred Mae (MacLean) J.; Mus.B., Oberlin Coll., 1938; B.S., Wayne State U., 1940, Mus.M., 1942; Mus.D. (hon.), U. Detroit, 1976; m. Marian Evelyn Johnson, Oct. 2, 1942; children—Cort MacLean, Kristen Reuss Stevens. Tchr., Detroit Pub. Schs., 1938-42, 45-47; faculty Wayne State U., 1947—, now prof. music, choral condr.; organist/choirmaster Grosse Pointe (Mich.) Meml. Ch., 1938-74, Old Christ Ch., Detroit, 1974—. Served with USNR, 1942-45. Mem. Assn. Am. Musicians, Presbyn. Assn. Musicians (past mem. exec. bd.), AAUP, Nat. Music Librarians Assn., Phi Mu Alpha Sinfonia (hon.). Rec. artist of early Am. music. Address: 414 Rivard Blvd Grosse Pointe MI 48230

JOHNSON, ALLAN BERNARD, ins. co. exec.; b. Worcester, Mass., Oct. 2, 1924; s. Bernard William and Eva Eleanor (Lavaley) J.; B.E.E., Worcester Poly. Inst., 1945; m. Doris Marie Klaucke, Sept. 7, 1946; children—Judy, Karen. Exec. asst. Factory Ins. Assos., Hartford, Conn., 1946-64; HPR officer, mgr. HPR dept. Kemper Ins. Cos., Long Grove, Ill., 1964—; sr. v.p. Kemper Internat. Ins. Co.; v.p., dir. Am. Protection Ins. Co. Served with USNR, 1943-46. Registered profl. engr., Calif. Mem. Soc. Fire Protection Engrs., Nat. Fire Protection Assn., Lambda Chi Alpha. Republican. Lutheran (deacon 1967-70). Home: 2241 Shannondale Dr Libertyville IL 60048 Office: Kemper Cos Long Grove IL 60049

JOHNSON, ALLEN DENNIS, owner feed mill; b. Blooming Prairie, Minn., Jan. 2, 1925; s. Elmer R. J. and Edna M. (Dennis) J.; student pub. schs.; m. Dorothy Marie Davis, June 1, 1947; children—David, Gregory, Douglas. Farmer nr. Bixby, Minn., 1945-60; owner Bixby Feed Mill, 1961—; pres. Prairie Farm Service, Inc., 1966—, Sow One, Inc., (both Blooming Prairie, Minn.), 1970—. Bd. dirs. Steele County Fair Bd. Named Outstanding Farmer of Steele County, Owatonna Jr. C. of C., 1959. Methodist (trustee). Clubs: Masons, Shriners, Blooming Prairie Gun and Country. Address: Bixby MN 55916

JOHNSON, ALVIN WAYNE, health care adminstr.; b. Seminole, Okla., Oct. 9, 1915; s. Melvin and Madgie (Lawson) J.; A.B., Anderson Coll., 1949, M.Div., 1963; m. Sylvia Milree Colwell, Aug. 18, 1942; children—Norman Douglas, Gregory Warren. Commd. 2d lt., U.S. Army, 1942, advanced through grades to maj.; ret., 1959; pastor Ch. of God, Cullman, Ala., 1950; nat. coordinator Men of Ch. of God, Anderson, Ind., 1959-68; adminstr. Rolling Hills Skilled Nursing Center, Anderson, 1968-70; adminstr. Americana Health Care Center, Anderson, Ind., 1970—; v.p. Ind. Americana, 1971—. Decorated Bronze Star medal, Purple Heart medal. Mem. Ind., Am. health care assn., Anderson C. of C. (mem. legislative com. 1973-77). Republican. Ch. of God. Kiwanian (lt. gov. Ind. dist. 1973-74). Home: 119 Coventry Dr Anderson IN 46012 Office: 1345 N Madison Ave Anderson IN 46011

JOHNSON, ARCHIE automobile mfg. co. exec.; b. Hattiesburg, Miss., Apr. 3, 1934; s. Joe and Rosie Lee (Carter) J.; student Rust Coll., 1952-53; N.C. A & I U., 1960-62; m. Mary Bradley, Apr., 1963; 1 dau., Gayle. Quality assurance mgr. Gen. Motors Corp., Flint, 1963—. Served with U.S. Army, 1954-56. Mem. Soc. Automotive Engrs., Am. Soc. Quality Control, Omega Psi Phi. Democrat. Methodist. Home: 3656 Evergreen Pkwy Flint MI 48503 Office: Buick Motor Div General Motors Corp 902 Hamilton Ave Flint MI 48550

JOHNSON, ARTHUR SUNE, veterinarian; b. Mpls., Aug. 13, 1927; s. Richard E. and Marie (Johanson) J.; B.S., U. Minn., 1953, D.V.M., 1955; m. Carol Lou Stedman, July 21, 1951; children—Ann Marie, Arthur Mark. Veterinarian, small animal practice All Pets Hosp., Mpls., 1958—; pres. Arthur S. Johnson Corp., investments, 1965—, chmn. bd., 1965—; ordained to ministry Pentecostal Ch., 1969; radio evangelist Selby Gospel Broadcasting, Inc., St. Paul, 1970—; evangelist Harvest Field Mission, Mpls., 1967—, Northside Outreach Worker Program, Mpls., 1971. Precinct chmn. Rep. party, 1966-69; bd. dirs. Kings Acad., Young Am. Encounter. Served with USMCR, 1945-46. Mem. AVMA, Minn. Veterinary Med. Assn., Am., Met. animal hosp. assns., Am. Pub. Health Assn., Nat. Assn. Professions, Full Gospel Businessmen Fellowship Internat., Am. Legion, Gideons Internat. (Bible sec. 1968-71). Clubs: Kiwanis; Forest Hills Golf (Forest Lake, Minn.). Home: 907 51st Ave NE Minneapolis MN 55421 Office: 5100 Central Ave NE Minneapolis MN 54421

JOHNSON, BARRY LEE, clergyman; b. Bloomington, Ill., July 28, 1943; s. James Robert and Elizabeth Carol (Schultz) J.; B.A. in History, Wheaton Coll., 1965; M.Div., Evang. Theol. Sem., 1968; m. Celeste Jane Hoppe, June 10, 1965; children—Tracey Michelle, Dane Christian. Ordained to ministry United Meth. Ch., 1968; asso. minister Bethany United Meth. Ch., Aurora, Ill., 1967-68; sr. minister Bensenville (Ill.) United Meth. Ch., 1968-71, Shiloh Ch., Dayton, Ohio, 1975—; exec. dir. EURISKON, Inc., Chgo., 1971-75; sec. bd. evangelism No. Ill. Conf. United Meth. Ch., 1969-72; cons. United Meth. Ch. Bd. Evangelism, Alaska, Mich., N.Y. confs. Mem. Bensenville Youth Commn., 1969-71. Recipient civic club recognition Rotary, 1969, 75, 77, Lions, 1970, 77, Optimists, 1975, 76, 77, Sertoma, 1976. Mem. Nat. Assn. United Meth. Evangelists, Family Counselors Assn., Bensenville Home Soc., Alcoholic Counselors Assn. Club: Optimists (Dayton). Author: EURISKON'S Personal Planning Manual, 1972; Sometimes There's a Hole in the Ceiling, 1975; contbr. articles to profl. jours. Home: 4165 Colemere Circle Dayton OH 45415 Office: 5300 Philadelphia Dr Dayton OH 45145

JOHNSON, BONNIE JEAN MCKECHNIE (MRS. EMSLEY W. JOHNSON, JR.), bank ofcl., civic worker; b. Stanford, Ky., May 26, 1917; d. Robert L. and Flonnie C. (Hammond) McKechnie; A.B., Butler U., 1938; m. Emsley Wright Johnson, Jr., Oct. 8, 1938; children—Martha Susan (Mrs. William George Batt), Gracia Elizabeth (Mrs. Charles Rutherford Meyer). Piano tchr., 1935-45; substitute high sch. English tchr., 1938-42. Dir. First Bank & Trust Co., Indpls., 1965—, vice chmn. bd., 1972—. Bd. dirs. Indpls. Day Nursery Assn., 1953-59, 71-77, sec., 1955; pres. Aux. Indpls. Day Nursery, 1965-66; mem. Northside bd. Indpls. Symphony, 1957-63; mem. alumni bd. dirs. Butler U., 1970-73, trustee univ., 1972-76; v.p. Day Nursery Found., 1974—; mem. adv. bd. Conner Prairie Pioneer Settlement, 1972—, vice chmn., 1975—; bd. dirs. Methodist Hosp. Ind., 1976—. Mem. D.A.R. (regent 1959-61), Marion County Hist. Soc. (dir. 1971—), Alliance of Indpls. Mus. Art, Kappa Alpha Theta (chpt. adv. bd. 1959-67, chpt. financial adviser 1959-66). Clubs: Fortnightly Literary (pres. 1964-65), Contemporary. Home: 9508 Holliday Circle Indianapolis IN 46260

JOHNSON, CARL ALFRED, JR., tool and mold co. exec.; b. Muskegon, Mich., Mar. 27, 1927; s. Carl Alfred and Verna (McCormick) J.; B.S., U.S. Mil. Acad., 1950; m. Darlene Dewald; children—Terry, Curtis, Carl Alfred III, Gordon; stepchildren—Kevin, Randall. Commd. 2d lt. U.S. Army, 1950; pilot USAF, 1950-56; with Port City Machine & Tool Co., Muskegon, 1956—, pres., 1968—. Mem. Planning Commn. Norton Twp. (Mich.), 1960-65; bd. dirs. YMCA. Decorated D.F.C., Air medal with four oak leaf clusters. Mem. Soc. Mfg. Engrs. (vice-chmn. Muskegon chpt. 1975-76, chmn. 1976-77). Home: 1818 Doris St Grand Haven MI 49417 Office: 560 E Broadway Muskegon Heights MI 49444

JOHNSON, CAROL MARIE, editor; b. Joliet, Ill., Dec. 5, 1927; d. Robey Joseph and Ellen (Ahlstrand) J.; student Joliet Jr. Coll., 1946-48; B.S., U. Ill., 1950. Editorial asst., sec. to editor Bankers Monthly mag., Rand McNally Co., Chgo., 1950-51; editorial asst. Paper Industry mag., Fritz Publs., Chgo., 1951-55; editor Transp. Week newsletter, Transp. Facts, Inc., Chgo., 1955, Salesmaker mag., Gerlach-Barlow Co., Joliet, 1955-57; asso. editor, also prodn. mgr. IGA Grocergram mag., Ind. Grocers' Alliance, Chgo., 1958-73; prodn. editor Electronic Packaging and Prodn. mag. Milton S. Kiver Publs., Chgo., 1974-76; asst. editor Commerce Mag., Chgo. Assn. Commerce and Industry, 1977—. Home: 16 Manor Ct Joliet IL 60436 Office: 130 S Michigan Ave Chicago IL 60603

JOHNSON, CHARLES FARNHAM, mfg. co. exec.; b. Springfield, Ohio, Jan. 2, 1939; s. Charles Farnham and Dorothy (Thomas) J.; A.A., Urbana Coll., 1960; student U. Colo., 1961; B.S., Ohio State U., 1962; m. Sally Louise Robinson, Oct. 15, 1961; children—Amy Louise, William Farnham. Investment counselor Bernard & Co. investment counselors, Columbus, Ohio, 1963-67, Ohio Co. investment banking, Columbus, 1967-69; pres., chmn. bd. Johnson Mfg. Co., Urbana, Ohio, 1969—, Green Halter Co., Urbana, 1969-74; vice pres., dir. Productos Nacionales De Arcilla S.A., Inc., Columbus, 1966—; chmn. bd. Triangle Enterprises, Inc., Columbus, 1970—. Asst. scoutmaster Tecumseh council Boy Scouts Am., 1959-60; trustee Urbana Coll., 1968—, chmn. exec. com., 1969-73, vice chmn., 1973-75, chmn., 1975—; trustee Planned Parenthood, 1969-72. Mem. Nat. Ry. Hist. Soc., Ohio C. of C., Am. Welding Soc., Am. Soc. for Metals. Episcopalian. Home: 1270 S Ludlow Rd Urbana OH 43078 Office: 605 Miami St Urbana OH 43078

JOHNSON, CHARLES PHILIP, agrl. cons. co. exec.; b. Darien, Wis., May 9, 1922; B.A., U. Wis., 1947, L.L.B., 1949. Admitted to Wis. bar, 1949; partner-operator Johnson Farms, Darien, 1950-69, Jon-Dyke, Inc., Agri-Bus., Darien, 1969-75, Johnson & Danielson,

Inc., Ins. and Real Estate, Darien, 1954-74, Darien Hardware Co., 1961-73; prin. C. Phil Johnson, Agcons., Darien, 1976—. Pres. Village of Darien, 1951-52; treas. Darien Consol. Schs., 1960-64, pres., 1965-69; treas. Walworth County March of Dimes, 1950-58; mem. exec. com Walworth County Farm Bur., 1959-59; dir. Wis. div. Nat. Farmers Orgn., 1965-69; area rep. Tri County State Line council Boy Scouts Am., 1954-66; bd. dirs. Wis. Vocat., Tech. Adult Edn., 1972—, Wis. Higher Edn. Aids, 1973—, Wis. Regents, 1976—, Coop. Edn. Service Agy., 1967-71; pres. Wis. Found. Vocat., Tech. and Adult Edn., 1977—. Home and Office: 239 E Jackson St Darien WI 53114

JOHNSON, CHARLES SILAS, banker; b. Muscatine, Iowa, Mar. 1, 1909; s. Raymond E. and Edna I. (Ryan) J.; student Drake U., 1926-29; m. Orpha B. Christian, July 28, 1928; children—Sally Ann (Mrs. Gerald Schomers), Raymond C., Nancy K. (Mrs. Harry Mooney). With Des Moines Nat. Bank, 1924-29; bank examiner State of Iowa, 1929-40; pres. First Nat. Bank of Perry (Iowa), 1940-58; exec. v.p. Brenton Banks, Inc., Des Moines, 1958-74, cons., dir., 1974—; chmn. exec. com., dir. South Des Moines Nat. Bank, 1962—, First Nat. Bank of Perry, 1962—; vice chmn. various Brenton banks in Iowa; chmn., pres. Iowa Bus. Devel. Credit Corp., Des Moines. Chmn. Herman L. Rowley Meml. Masonic Home; pres. Perry Ind. Sch. Dist., 1948-51; chmn. Republican Central Com., Dallas County, 1952-58. Chmn. Dallas County Hosp. Bd., 1952-58. Recipient Outstanding citizen award Kiwanis, 1953, Legion of Honor award Iowa DeMolay, 1969. Mem. Perry C. of C. (pres. 1946, 47). Lutheran. Clubs: Masons, Moose, Rotary (pres. 1950), Elks, Des Moines, Embassy, Bohemian. Home: 7004 Bellaire Ave Des Moines IA 50311 Office: 2928 Ingersoll Des Moines IA 50312

JOHNSON, CHAUNCEY PAUL, financial exec.; b. Detroit, Oct. 25, 1931; s. Chauncey Frederick and Lois Jean (Hon) J.; student Denison U., 1949-51; B.S., Mich. State U., 1953; m. Anne Gayman, June, 1951; children—Julianne, Deborah, Rebecca. Account exec. Robert W. Baird, Milw., 1956-59; pres. Wis. Capital Corp., 1959-64, Reef Club Hotel, Ocho Rios, Jamaica, 1964-66; sr. v.p. Milw. Western Bank, 1967-70; pres. Growth Capital, Inc., Chgo., 1970-72; chmn. bd., pres. Colonial Bank & Trust Co., Chgo., 1972—; Bd. dirs. Am. Field Service; lay dir. St. Patrick's High Sch. Served as capt., USAF, 1953-56. Mem. Belmont C. of C. (1st v.p.), Ill. Bankers Assn. (sec. and gov. Chgo. chpt.), Northside Bankers Assn. (pres.), Lambda Chi Alpha. Clubs: Milw. Athletic. Home: 505 N Lake Shore Dr Chicago IL 60611 Office: 5850 W Belmont Ave Chicago IL 60634

JOHNSON, CLARENCE, JR., civil engr.; b. East Saint Louis, Ill., Dec. 26, 1923; s. Clarence and Kathleen (Clark) J.; B.S. in Bus. Adminstrn., Roosevelt U., 1950; B.S. in Civil Engring., Ill. Inst. Tech., 1963. Draftsman, Babcock & Wilcox Co., Chgo., 1952-58; civil engr. Chgo. Dept. Urban Renewal (formerly Chgo. Land Clearance Commn.), 1959-65, U.S. Steel Corp., Chgo., 1965-72, Roberts & Schaefer Co. div. Elgin Nat. Industries, Inc., Chgo., 1972—. Served with U.S. Army, 1943-46. Mem. ASCE. Office: 120 S Riverside Plaza Chicago IL 60606

JOHNSON, CLIFFORD TERRY, lawyer; b. Bridgeport, Conn., Sept. 24, 1937; s. Clifford Gustave and Evelyn Florence (Terry) J.; grad. Kent Sch., 1956; A.B., Trinity Coll., 1960; LL.D., Columbia, 1963; m. Beverly Lynne Millat, Aug. 22, 1964; children—Laura Elizabeth, Melissa Lynne, Clifford Terry. Admitted to Ohio bar, 1964, since practiced in Dayton; legal dep. Probate Ct. Montgomery County, Ohio, 1964-67; mem. firm Coolidge, Wall, Matusoff, Womsley & Lombard, Dayton, 1967—, partner, 1972—. Lectr., Ohio State Bar Assn. Legal Center Inst., 1969—. Mem. Kettering Med. Center Assos., Kettering Med. Center, Dayton, 1973—, chmn., 1974—. Bd. dirs., pres. Miami Valley Child Devel. Centers, Dayton. Mem. Am., Ohio, Dayton bar assns. Home: 145 W Peach Orchard Rd Dayton OH 45419 Office: 111 1st St Dayton OH 45402

JOHNSON, CRAIG LEOL, lawyer; b. Council Bluffs, Iowa, Apr. 28, 1931; s. Leol Henry and Hazel Grace (Whitney) J.; B.A., Drake U., 1955; J.D., State U. Iowa, 1955; m. Patricia C. Carothers, July 13, 1957; children—Kristen Lea, Kirk Whitney. Admitted to Iowa bar, 1955, since practiced in Marshalltown; partner firm Haupert, Robertson & Johnson, 1959—. Mem. Alumni Council State U. Iowa, 1969—. Bd. dirs. Marshalltown Little League, 1968-70, Marshalltown Area United Way, 1972—. Mem. Marshall County, Iowa, Am. bar assns., C. of C. (dir. 1973—). Home: 1608 Lincoln Way Marshalltown IA 50158 Office: 27 S Center St Marshalltown IA 50158

JOHNSON, CURTIS WILLIAM, ophthalmologist; b. Rockford, Ill., Aug. 10, 1942; s. Arthur William and Mildred Elizabeth (Magnuson) J.; A.B., Drake U., 1964; M.D., U. Ill., 1968; m. Charlotte A. Sullivan, Sept. 25, 1963; children—Jolene Renee, Brett William. Intern, Coll. Med. Sch., U. Tenn., Memphis, 1968-69, resident in internal medicine, 1969-70, resident in ophthalmology, 1970-73; practice medicine specializing in ophthalmology, Clinton, Iowa, 1974—; mem. staffs Jane Lamp, Mercy hosps.; dir., sec., treas. Sta. WHAM, Inc., Memphis, 1972—; pres. Ascension Towers, Inc., Memphis, 1972-73; pres. Bluff Med. Center, Clinton, 1976. NSF Found. grantee, 1963. Diplomate Am. Bd. Ophthalmology. Mem. Am., Iowa (chmn. legis. com.) acads. ophthalmology, Am. Acad. Ophthalmology and Otolaryngology, Am. Assn. Ophthalmologists, Clinton County Med. Soc. (pres.), Phi Eta Sigma, Beta Beta Beta, Phi Delta Theta. Lutheran. Home: 1119 2nd Ave S Clinton IA 52732 Office: 240 N Bluff St Clinton IA 52732

JOHNSON, DALE HARRY, printing co. exec.; b. Rockford, Ill., Mar. 5, 1935; s. Harry Carl and Alice Evelyn (Greenberg) J.; student Rockford pub. schs.; m. Antonietta Lanzetta, Mar. 12, 1967; children—Cindi, Scott, Mike, Todd. With John Green Press, 1953-57; with Johnson Press, Inc., Rockford, 1957—, pres., 1976—; v.p. Am. Color of Phoenix, Am. Color of Houston, Selectability, Versatile Ventures, Inc.; pres. Bishop Printing Co. Republican precinct committeeman, 1976—. Lutheran. Home: 6581 Squire Ln Rockford IL 61111 Office: 2801 Eastrock Dr Rockford IL 61125

JOHNSON, DALE WILLIS, ins. and financial cons.; b. Chgo., July 12, 1936; s. Charles Linn and Marion (Green) J.; student Ripon Coll., 1954-58, Ill. Inst. Tech., evenings 1960-62; m. Mary Anne Ryan, Sept. 19, 1959. Pvt. practice electronics cons., Mount Prospect, Ill., 1958-60; tech. asst. Nat. Electronics, Geneva, Ill., 1960-61, Jefferson Electric, Bellwood, Ill., 1961-62; mem. sales staff Crane Packing Co., Morton Grove, Ill., 1962-67, Dole Valve Co., Morton Grove, 1967-69; dir. tng. Advance Schs., Chgo., 1969-72; marketing and mgmt. cons., 1972-75; ins. and financial cons., Glenview, Ill., 1975—. Spl. adviser Halfway House Program Bd. Ill., 1972—. Precinct capt. Maine Twp. Republican party, 1962-63; spl. adviser, young people's adv. council to Pres. Nixon, 1971-73. Mem. Morton Grove (pres. 1967-68), Glenview (pres. 1972-73), U.S. (dir. 1970-71) jr. chambers commerce, Meeting Planners Internat., Ripon Alumni Club Chgo. (treas. 1968-70). Home: 715 Elmgate Dr Glenview IL 60025 Office: 615 Milwaukee Ave Glenview IL 60025

JOHNSON, DAVID WILLIAM, chiropractor; b. Indpls., Nov. 23, 1944; s. Lowell E. and Theodora C. (Pfeiffer) J.; B.S., Ind. U., 1968, M.S., 1970; B.S., Nat. Coll. Chiropractic, 1971, D. Chiropractic, 1973; m. Barbara Jean Maddox, Aug. 16, 1969; children—Natalie S., Jacquelyn K. Chiropractor Winchester Chiropractic Center, Indpls., 1973—. Mem. Am. Chiropractic Assn. (council clin. nutrition), Sigma Phi Kappa. Methodist. Home: 748 Woodcreek Ct Greenwood IN 46142 Office: 8220 S Madison Ave Indianapolis IN 46227

JOHNSON, DAVID WOLCOTT, psychologist, educator; b. Muncie, Ind., Feb. 7, 1940; s. Roger Wildfield and Francis Elizabeth (Pierce) J.; B.S., Ball State U., 1962; M.A., Columbia, 1964, Ed.D., 1966; m. Linda Mulholland, July 7, 1973; children—James, David, Catherine. Asst. prof. ednl. psychology U. Minn., Mpls., 1966-69, asso. prof., 1969-73, prof., 1973—; organizational cons., psychotherapist. Bd. dirs. Walk-In Counseling Center, 1971-74. Fellow Am. Psychol. Assn.; mem. Am. Sociol. Assn., Am. Ednl. Research Assn. Democrat. Author: Social Psychology of Education, 1970; (with Goodwin Watson), Social Psychology: Issues and Insights, 1972; Reaching Out, 1972; Contemporary Social Psychology, 1973; (with Frank Johnson) Joining Together, 1975; (with Roger Johnson) Learning Together and Alone, 1975, others. Contbr. articles to profl. publs. Home: 162 Windsor Lane New Brighton MN 55112 Office: 330 Burton Hall U Minn Minneapolis MN 55455

JOHNSON, DENNIS CHARLES, mfg. co. exec.; b. St. Louis, Feb. 1, 1943; s. Charles Fred and Virginia Louise (Brown) J.; B.S., U. Mo., 1966; M. Engring. Adminstrn., Midwest Coll. Engring., 1974; m. Joann Pope, June 10, 1966; children—Karen Joann, Michael Dennis. Co-op trainee McDonnell Douglas, St. Louis, 1961-66; instrument engr. Pratt & Whitney Aircraft, West Palm Beach, Fla., 1966-67, East Hartford, Conn., 1967-69; project engr. Ari Industries, Franklin Park, Ill., 1969-73, mgr. engring., 1973—. Mem. Am. Nuclear Soc., ASTM, Instrument Soc. Am. Home: 121 Harrison Ln Hoffman Estates IL 60195 Office: 9000 King St Franklin Park IL 60131

JOHNSON, DENNIS LESTER, ednl. cons. orgn. exec.; b. Hampton, Iowa, Oct. 23, 1938; s. Royden Lester and Lorraine Anita (Rhoades) J.; B.A., Parsons Coll., 1960; m. Carolyn Louise Campbell, Aug. 18, 1963; children—Dené Lynn, Laurie Anne. Admissions officer Parsons Coll., Fairfield, Iowa, 1960-63, regional dir., 1963-65, dir. of admissions counselors, 1965-67; founder Johnson Assos., Inc., Oak Brook, Ill., 1967, pres., 1967—, chmn. bd., 1967—. Bd. dirs. United Cerebral Palsy of Chgo., 1977—, Du Page County (Ill.) Easter Seal Treatment Center, 1975-76. Mem. Am. Assn. for Higher Edn., Soc. for Coll. and U. Planning, Council for Advancement and Support of Edn., Am. Mgmt. Assn., Am. Personnel and Guidance Assn. Presbyterian. Clubs: Oak Brook Bath and Tennis; Executives (Chgo.). Contbr. articles on edn. and mktg. to profl. publs.; columnist Nation's Schools and Colleges, 1974—. Home: 1103 Fairview Ave Lombard IL 60148 Office: 1301 W 22d St Oak Brook IL 60521

JOHNSON, DENNIS WILLIAM, printing co. exec.; b. Rockford, Ill., Mar. 10, 1938; s. Harry C. and Alice E. (Greenberg) J.; student Bethel Coll., 1956-58, Rockford Coll., 1958-59; m. Evelyn Jo Stahl, Aug. 12, 1961; children—Tonya, Cary, Rynn. Sec., treas. H.C. Johnson Press, Inc., Rockford, 1958—; pres. Versatile Ventures, Inc., Rockford, 1966—; sec.-treas. Am. Color Corp., Phoenix, Houston and San Diego, Bishop Printing Co., Rockford, Selectability Inc., Rockford, Johnson Graphics, Inc., Dubuque, Ill. dir. Camelot World Travel, Inc., Rockford, Guaranty Nat. Bank, Rockford. Mem. Bd. Suprs. Winnebago County, Rockford, 1965-68; alderman City of Rockford, 1968—; mem. No. Ill. Law Enforcement Commn., Rockford, 1969-76; bd. dirs. No. Ill. Multiple Sclerosis Bd., 1971-73; co-chmn. Winnebago County Bicentennial Commn., 1976-77; trustee Judson Coll., Elgin, Ill. Named Outstanding Young Legislator, Rockford Jr. C. of C., 1969. Mem. Printing Industry of Ill., Christian Businessmen's Com., C. of C. Republican. Baptist. Home: 3134 Talbot Trail Rockford IL 61111 Office: 2801 Eastrock Dr Rockford IL 61125

JOHNSON, DONALD, constrn. co. exec.; b. Bloomington, Ind., Feb. 14, 1938; s. Aaron Donald and Mary Katherine (Campbell) J.; B.S., Ind. U., 1960, M.B.A., 1961; m. Lois Elese Reid, July 23, 1971; children—Julie Ann, Nancy Ellen. With household soap advt. div. Proctor & Gamble, Cin., 1964; with advt. dept. E.I. duPont de Nemours & Co., Inc., Wilmington, Del., 1965-69; dir. advt. Bell Helicopter, Ft. Worth, 1969-72; partner Realamerica Homes, Ft. Wayne, Ind., 1972-75; owner, pres. Don Johnson Signature Homes, Ft. Wayne, 1975—. Bd. dirs. Better Bus. Bur. Recipient Design for Better Living award Am. Wood Council. Mem. Nat. Home Builders Assn., Ind. Bd. Realtors. Home: 11808 Honey Suckle Ct Fort Wayne IN 46804 Office: 927 S Harrison St Fort Wayne IN 46802

JOHNSON, DONALD RAY, artist, educator; b. Poteau, Okla., Jan. 14, 1942; s. Orville R. and Alma B. (McCullough) J.; B.A., Northeastern State U., Tahlequah, Okla., 1963; M.F.A., U. Okla., 1970, M.A., 1971; m. Eady Joann Remer, Jan. 20, 1963; children—Douglas Edward, Cheri Lynn. Dir. univ. art gallery Emporia (Kans.) State U., 1970-74, asst. prof. art, 1970—; printer for Emilio Amero, Norman, Okla., 1968-70; included in numerous nat. print and drawing exhbns. Served to capt. USAF, 1963-67. Emporia State U. grantee, 1972-74, 75, 76—; Nat. Endowment for Humanities grantee, 1977—. Mem. Coll. Art Assn. Home: 1009 Rural St Emporia KS 66801 Office: Emporia State U Emporia KS 66801

JOHNSON, DOROTHY PHYLLIS, counselor, art therapist; b. Kansas City, Mo., Sept. 13, 1925; d. Chris C. and Mabel T. (Gillum) Green; B.A. in Art, Ft. Hays. State U., 1975, M.S. in Guidance and Counseling, 1976; m. Herbert E. Johnson, May 11, 1945; children—Michael E., Gregory K. Art therapist High Plains Comprehensive Mental Health Assn., Hays, Kans., 1975-76; art therapist, mental health counselor Sunflower Mental Health Assn., Concordia, Kans., 1976—, co-dir. Project Togetherness, 1976-77, coordinator partial hospitalization, 1978—; dir. Swedish Am. State Bank, Courtland, Kans., 1960—, sec., 1973-77. Mem. Kans., Am. art therapy assns., Am. Mental Health Counselors Assn., Am. Personnel and Guidance Assn., Assn. Specialists in Group Work, Phi Delta Kappa. Contbr. articles to profl. jours. Home: Box 164 Courtland KS 66939 Office: 520 B Washington St Concordia KS 66901

JOHNSON, EARLE BERTRAND, ins. co. exec.; b. Otter Lake, Mich., May 3, 1914; s. Bertrand M. and Blanche (Sherman) J.; B.S., U. Fla., 1937, J.D., 1940; m. Peggy Minch, Apr. 30, 1972; children—Earle Bertrand, Victoria, Julia, Sheryl. With State Farm Ins. Cos., Bloomington, Ill., 1940—, regional agy. dir., 1958-60, regional v.p., 1960-65, v.p., sec., mem. exec. com. State Farm Mut. Automobile Ins. Co., 1965—, dir., 1967—, exec. com., 1970; chmn. bd., mem. exec. com., State Farm Life Ins. Co., 1970—, also dir.; mem. exec. com., v.p., dir. State Farm Fire & Casualty Co.; sr. v.p., treas. State Farm County Mut. Ins. Co. Tex.; v.p., dir. State Farm Gen. Ins. Co.; dir., v.p., sec. State Farm Internat. Services, Inc., 1967—. Mem. Gen. Agy. Mgmt. Assn., Agy. Officers Round Table (exec. com. 1970—), Pedlars, Am., Fla. bar assns., Phi Alpha Delta, Phi Kappa Tau. Home: 215 Imperial Dr Bloomington IL 61701 Office: 1 State Farm Plaza Bloomington IL 61701

JOHNSON, EDWARD STONE, puppeteer; b. Almont, Mich., June 27, 1918; s. James Carl and Olive Grace (Junkin) J.; student Highland Park Jr. Coll., 1936-38, Wayne U., 1938-39; m. Frances Elizabeth Radford, July 7, 1951; children—Kathleen Lynn (Mrs. Ivan Kobosh), Gregory Stone, Carl Radford. Propr., Ed Johnson's Marionettes, 1939—; originated one-man marionette show; numerous TV appearances. Served with U.S. Army, 1942-46. Mem. Puppeteers Am. (past pres.), Detroit Puppeteers Guild (founder, past pres.), Motor City Theatre Organ Soc. Author original ednl. stories for schs. Address: 4300 W Highland Rd Milford MI 48042

JOHNSON, ERVIN VICTOR, music co. exec., entertainer; b. Racine, Wis., Sept. 3, 1938; s. Victor and Alice (Hansen) J.; grad. Elsmo Sch. Music, Racine, 1961; m. Karen Sue Peterson, Oct. 16, 1965. Sales mgr. Elsmo Music, Inc., Racine, Wis., 1962-65, Johnson's Music, Inc., Racine, 1965-76; pvt. organ and piano tchr., Racine, 1963—. Lutheran. Composer. Address: 4200 Taylor Ave Racine WI 53405

JOHNSON, EUGENE GUNNARD, exec. mgmt. recruiting cons.; b. Chgo., Feb. 27, 1926; s. Eric Albin and Sophie Rose J.; A.B. in Labor Econs., U. Ill., 1948; postgrad. Northwestern U., 1952, U. Chgo., 1949; m. Shirley Mencel, June 16, 1951; children—Jeffrey Alan, Sheryl Ruth. Factory supt. Turner Mfg. Co., Chgo., 1950-60; v.p. mfg. Mell Mfg. Co., Chgo., 1960-65; founder, owner Met. Bus. Reports Co. Inc., Chgo., 1974—; founder, owner, pres. Johnson & Militante, Inc., Chgo., 1969—. Served with USAAF, 1946-47. Mem. V.F.W., Tau Kappa Epsilon. Methodist. Home: 844 N Florence Dr Park Ridge IL 60068 Office: 5151 N Harlem Ave Suite 305 Chicago IL 60656

JOHNSON, FARNHAM JAMES, rubber co. exec.; b. St. Paul, June 23, 1924; s. William Kendall and Mabel (Wirth) J.; B.S., U. Wis., 1948; student U. Mich., 1943-44; B. Fgn. Trade, Am. Grad. Sch. Internat. Mgmt., 1950, M. Internat. Mgmt., 1978; postgrad. U. Akron, 1977; m. Evelyn Porter Thompson, June 1, 1973. Player, Chgo. Bears Football Team, 1947; internat. rep. Internat. B.F. Goodrich Co., Washington, 1950-51, mgr. Hawaii, 1951-53, internat. rep. Hague, 1954, gen. sales mgr. Goodrich Svenska Gummi A/B, Stockholm, 1955-57, asst. gen. mgr. Phillipines, 1958-61, mgr. internat. accounts N.Y.C. and Ohio, 1962-69, dir. export sales, Akron, 1970-74, dir. mkt. intelligence, 1974—; dir. B.F. Goodrich of Japan Ltd., 1970—. Bd. dirs. Better Boy's Assn. Philippines, 1958-61. Served with USMC, 1943-46. Mem. Rubber Export Assn. (bd. dirs. 1970—), Soc. Automotive Engrs., Marine Corps Res. Officers Assn., Am. Legion, Delta Phi Epsilon, Sigma Phi Epsilon. Republican. Episcopalian. Clubs: Univ. (Akron), W. Club (Wis.), M Club (Mich.), Outrigger Canoe Club (Honolulu), Manila Polo (Philippines), Elks. Office: International B F Goodrich Co 500 S Main St Akron OH 44318

JOHNSON, FREDERIC HENRY, anatomist; b. Geneva, Ill., May 23, 1926; s. Leonard Walter and Helena Elizabeth (Henry) J.; A.B., Cornell U., 1948, A.M., 1950, Ph.D., 1951; children by former marriage—Gary Richard, Frederic Henry. Research asst. Naval Arctic Research Lab., Point Barrow, 1948; research asso. Inst. Research, Walter Reed Army Med. Center, Washington, 1951-52; asst. prof. anatomy U. Oreg., Portland, 1952-53; research asso. Neuropsychiat. Inst., U. Ill., Chgo., 1953-59; dir. neurophysiology lab. Research Inst., U. Buffalo, 1959-61; research neurophysiologist Med. Scis. Research Lab., Miles Lab., Elkhart, Ind., 1961-63; asst. prof. anatomy Temple U., Phila., 1963-67; research asso. neurology Children's Meml. Hosp., Chgo., 1967-69; asso. prof. anatomy Loyola U., Chgo., 1969-70; scholar in residence, also staff Newberry Library, Chgo., 1970-71; scholar Crerar Library, Chgo., 1971—. Pres. Chgo. Ballet Guild, 1961-63. Served with AC, USNR, 1944-46. Mem. Am. Assn. Anatomists, Physiol. Soc. Phila., Am. Soc. Zoologists, Am. Inst. Biol. Sci., AAAS, Am. Soc. Coll. Profs., Fedn. Am. Scientists, Pa. Med. History Soc., Sigma Xi, Phi Kappa Psi, Alpha Kappa Kappa (hon.). Moose. Home: 158 N Humphrey Ave Oak Park IL 60302

JOHNSON, F(REDERICK) GERALD, mfg. co. exec.; b. Alcona, Mich., Aug. 15, 1914; s. Milo N. and Cora (Teeple) J.; student Bay City Jr. Coll., 1931-32; student, U. Mich., 1933-36; m. Edith Viola Panknin, Nov. 23, 1939; children—Richard Allen, Susan Kay Johnson Quinn, Judith Ann. Field salesman Huron Industries, Inc., Alpena, Mich., 1938-42; various positions, 1942-45; field salesman Alert Pipe & Supply Co., Bay City, Mich., 1945-48, mgr. heating dept., 1948-52; asst. sales mgr., mgr. boiler sales Bastian-Morley Co., LaPorte, Ind., 1952-57; gen. sales mgr., heating and air conditioning div. Century Engring. Corp., Cedar Rapids, Iowa, 1957-70, v.p. sales, 1970-75; sales mgr. Century div. Heat Controller, Inc., Jackson, Mich., 1975—; cons. Paul Brysselbout, Architect, 1948-52. Chmn. Alcona County (Mich.) Young Republicans, 1934-38. Mem. Air-Conditioning and Refrigeration Inst. (dir.), Am. Soc. Heating and Air Conditioning Engrs., Old Timers Club of Heating and Cooling Industry, C. of C., Gild Ancient Supplers. Presbyterian. Clubs: Elks, Masons (32 deg.), Shriners, Arbor Hills Country. Home: 3824 Westchester Blvd Jackson MI 49203 Office: 1900 Wellworth St Jackson MI 49203

JOHNSON, HAROLD KENNETH, assn. exec.; b. Hanover, Mass., Oct. 20, 1941; s. Harold Forrest and Marjorie Ruth (French) J.; A.A., Stockbridge Sch. Agr. U. Mass., 1962; B.S. (Ralphs S. Lovett scholar), Ohio State U., 1965; M.S. (Conn. State scholar), U. Conn., 1970; m. Dawn Robie Foote, Sept. 7, 1963; children—Mark Kenneth, Elizabeth Jane. Supr. quality control lab. Dinner Bell Foods, Defiance, Ohio, 1966-67; mgr. quality control Stop & Shop, Inc., Marlboro, Mass., 1969-72; dir. meat merchandising Nat. Live Stock & Meat Bd., Chgo., 1972-74, exec. dir. food sci. div., 1974—; cons. processing and mktg. meats, 1974—. Mem. Am. Meat Sci. Assn. (sec.-treas. 1975—, archivist 1974—, chmn. mktg. com. 1973), Am. Soc. Animal Sci., Inst. Food Technologists, ASTM, Council Agrl. Sci. and Tech., Gamma Sigma Delta. Editor: Meat Management and Operations, 1975; meat co-editor Supermktg. Mag., 1976—. Club: Masons. Contbr. articles to profl. jours. Home: 1907 E Illinois St Wheaton IL 60187 Office: 444 N Michigan Ave Chicago IL 60611

JOHNSON, HARRY CLARENCE, utility exec.; b. Ashby, Minn., Oct. 15, 1913; s. H. Severin and Caroline (Jansen) J.; B.B.A., U. Minn., 1946; m. Elizabeth Ellen Phelps, Sept. 16, 1939 (dec. Dec. 1973); children—Karen (Mrs. Laurence J. Mauer), Stephen Phelps. Accountant, Glacier Park Co. Resort Hotel, East Glacier, Mont., 1937; cost accountant Synder Drug Co., Mpls., 1938; auditor Mpls. Star Tribune, 1938-43; controller St. Paul Foundry & Mfg. Co., 1943-49; comptroller Otter Tail Power Co., Fergus Falls, Minn., 1949—, v.p., chief financial officer, 1970—, treas., 1959—; dir. Northwestern Nat. Bank, Fergus Falls. Pres., dir. Otter Tail Mgmt. Corp., 1969—. Bd. dirs. Lake Region Hosp., Fergus Falls, 1959-77; trustee, pres. First Luth. Ch. Found. Mem. Financial Execs. Inst., N. Central Electric Assn. (treas. 1968-77), Financial Mgmt. Assn., Edison Electric, Thomas Alva Edison Found. Clubs: Rotary, Elks. Home: Route 5 Box 210 Fergus Falls MN 56537 Office: 215 S Cascade St Fergus Falls MN 56537

JOHNSON, HARVEY WILLIAM, ednl. adminstr.; b. Brule, Wis., Oct. 17, 1920; s. William V. and Elizabeth (Mallen) J.; B.S., Wis. State U., 1951, M.E., 1954, Specialist in Edn., 1968; m. Minerva A. Johnson, June 30, 1944; children—Penelope Johnson Hawkins, Christine Sue Johnson Lane, Terry William. Tchr. pub. schs., Hayward, Wis., 1951-52; prin. Cable (Wis.) Union Free High Sch., 1952-54; supt. Joint Sch. Dist. 1, Glen Flora, Wis., 1954-59; supt. South Shore Schs., Port Wing, Wis., 1959-62; supt. Sch. Dist. No. 1,

Shell Lake, Wis., 1962-69, Ashland (Wis.) Unified Sch. Dist., 1969—. Served with USAF, 1942-48. Decorated Air medals (2), D.F.C. Mem. Wis. Assn. Sch. Dist. Adminstrs. (pres. 1971-72), Am., No. Wis. assns. sch. adminstrs., C. of C., Am. Legion, VFW. Clubs: Lions, Rotary, Elks. Home: 1222 10th Ave W Ashland WI 54806 Office: Ellis Ave Ashland WI 54806

JOHNSON, HENDERSON ANDREW, III, dentist; b. Nashville, Dec. 19, 1929; s. Henderson Andrew and Minerva (Hatcher) J., Jr.; B.S., Fisk U., 1950; M.S. in Phys. Edn., Springfield Coll., 1951; postgrad. phys. therapy Med. Coll. Va., 1952; D.D.S., Western Res. U., 1959; m. Gwendolyn Cassie Gregory, June 14, 1952; children—Gregory Paul, Andrea Lynn, H. Andrew IV. Practice dentistry, Cleve., 1959-67, Shaker Heights, O., 1966—; dentist Cuyahoga Hills Boys Sch., Warrensville Heights, O., 1969-70; clin. instr. Sch. Dentistry, Western Res. U., Cleve., 1965-69. Mem. adv. com. child welfare div. City of Cleve., 1966-68; chmn. program com. Cedar YMCA, Cleve., 1968-72; v.p. PACE Assn., 1969-70; mem. Cleve. Welfare Fedn. Budget and Allocation Com., 1967-69; mem. Shaker Heights Library Bd., 1970—, v.p., 1976—; mem. Citizens League Cleve., 1967—. Bd. dirs. Met. YMCA; chmn. bd. trustees Cuyahoga Community Coll., Cleve., 1972-75, chmn. bd. dirs. Cuyahoga Community Coll. Found., 1976—; trustee Cleve. chpt. N.A.A.C.P., 1964-65, Fisk U., Nashville, 1967-76, Urban League, Cleve., 1968-72. Served to 1st lt. USAF, 1952-54. Recipient Community Service awards East Tech. High Sch., 1964, YMCA, 1968, Distinguished Alumnus award Fisk U., 1976. Mem. Cleve., Ohio, Am. dental assns., Am. Soc. Dentistry Children, Fisk U. Gen. Alumni Assn. (pres. 1967-70), Alpha Phi Omega, Sigma Delta Psi, Omega Psi Phi (Citizen of Year award 1974), Sigma Phi. Home: 16506 Fernway Rd Shaker Heights OH 44120 Office: 16611 Chagrin Blvd Shaker Heights OH 44120

JOHNSON, HENRY CLYDE, mfg. co. exec.; b. Niagara Falls, N.Y., June 18, 1914; s. Willis Oscar and Della R. (Hagerty) J.; S.B., S.M., Mass. Inst. Tech., 1936; J.D., Harvard U., 1940; m. Dorothy Diedre Montagu, Feb. 11, 1955; 1 stepdau., Martha Browning Mast. Admitted to Mass. bar, 1940, N.Y. bar, 1940, U.S. Supreme Ct. bar, 1944; asso. firm Phipps, Durgin & Cook, Boston, 1940-41; div. purchasing agt., mgr. planning dept. on staff pres. Philco Corp., Phila., 1946-50; mem. central fin. staff, engring. bd., controller engring. div. Ford Motor Co., Dearborn, Mich., 1950-58; chmn. bd., pres., owner Phil Wood Industries Ltd. (formerly Gar Wood Industries of Can., Ltd.), Windsor, Ont., 1958-69, hon. chmn., 1969—. Mem. Windsor Econ. Com.; benefactor Detroit Inst. Arts; patron mem. Detroit Symphony Orch.; maj. donor Meadowbrook Festival; mem. pres.'s club Oakland U.; trustee, chmn. ednl. policy com. Detroit Inst. Tech. Served from lt. to col. Signal Corps, AUS, 1941-46. Registered profl. engr., Pa. Mem. IEEE (sr.), Am. Bar Assn., Am. Mgmt. Assn. (Personal plaque 1960), AAAS (life), Aircraft Owners and Pilots Assn., Am. Radio Relay League (life), Cranbrook Inst. Sci. (life), Archives Am. Art, Mich. Acad. Sci., Arts and Letters, Assn. Governing Bds. Univs. and Colls., Quarter Century Wireless Assn., Sigma Alpha Epsilon (founder mem.). Episcopalian. Clubs: Econ., M.I.T., Detroit Athletic (Detroit); Otsego (Mich.) Ski; Circumnavigators (N.Y.C.); Harvard (Mich.); Cranbrook Tennis (Bloomfield Hills, Mich.). Patentee automatic tripping snow plow. Home: 3000 Quarton Rd Bloomfield Hills MI 48013

JOHNSON, HUGH ALBERT, physician; b. Mpls., Dec. 14, 1918; s. George A. and Clarice (Bryant) J.; B.S., Northwestern U., 1940, M.D., 1943; M.S. in Plastic Surgery, U. Minn., 1952; m. Madeleine Long, Dec. 19, 1942; children—Cynthia, Daniel Bryant, Madeleine. Intern, Cook County Hosp., Chgo., 1943; resident Mayo Found., Rochester, Minn., 1947-51, asst. to staff, 1951-52; preceptor to Sir Archibald McIndoe, Sussex, Eng., 1952-53; practice medicine, specializing in plastic and reconstructive surgery, Rockford, Ill., 1953—, Phelps, Wis., 1956—; mem. staff Rockford Meml. Hosp., Northwoods Hosp., Phelps; clin. asso. Rockford Sch. Medicine, U. Ill. Fulbright prof. Christian Medi-Coll. and Hosp., Vellore, India, 1958-59, 64; cons. St. Anthony's Hosp. Burn Unit, Rockford; founder Rockford Found. Plastic and Reconstrn. Surgery. Served with USNR, 1943-46. Fellow A.C.S.; mem. A.M.A. (vol. physician to Viet Nam 1969, 73), Ill. State, Winnebago County med. socs., Internat. Coll. Surgeons, Royal Soc. Medicine, Brit. Assn. Plastic Surgeons, Am. Soc. Plastic and Reconstructive Surgery, Am. Found. Plastic and Reconstructive Surgery, Midwestern Assn. Plastic Surgeons (founder), Am. Assn. Plastic and Reconstructive Surgeons, Am. Soc. Aesthetic Plastic Surgery, Am. Soc. Surgery of Hand (asso.), Sigma Nu, Nu Sigma Nu. Clubs: Union League (Chgo.); University, Rotary (Service above Self award 1976) (Rockford, Ill.). Contbr. articles in field to profl. jours. Home: 113 Lawn Pl Rockford IL 61103 Office: 2500 N Rockton Ave Rockford IL 61103 also Northwoods Hosp Phelps WI 54554

JOHNSON, JACK ROSS, computer systems exec.; b. Gibson County, Tenn., Sept. 28, 1934; s. Joseph Odell and Nell Frances (Ross) J.; student Middle Tenn. State U., 1952-53; student Bowling Green Coll. Commerce, 1957-60; m. Linda Lou Woods, Mar. 4, 1963; children—Leigh Ann, Dawn Marie, Stephen Ross. Corporate dir. data processing systems Am. Discount Stores, Mobile, Ala., 1961-63; project mgr. ITT/FEC, Huntsville, Ala., 1963-73; controller, systems mgr. Cardinal Chem. Co., Columbia, S.C., 1973-75; dir. planning and devel. Gilliam Candy Co., Paducah, Ky., 1975-76; mgr. internal control systems dept. U. Cin., Southwestern Ohio Regional Computer Center, 1976-78; corp. planning and control mgr. Robbins & Myers, Inc., Dayton, Ohio, 1978—. Served with USAF, 1953-57. Mem. Assn. Computing Machinery, Data Processing Mgmt. Assn. Presbyterian. Home: 7997 Lebanon Pike Route 48 Waynesburg OH 45068 Office: Winters Tower 2d St Dayton OH 45401

JOHNSON, JACOB RUSSELL, sanitation co. exec.; b. Pittsfield, Ill., Mar. 26, 1948; s. Russell Glen and Myrtle Frances (Ruble) J.; student pub. schs., Pittsfield; m. Wilma Aileen Hall, May 3, 1968. Truckdriver Arthur Crowder Trucking Co., Pittsfield, 1966-69; driver W.W. Sanitation Co., Pittsfield, 1970-74, v.p., mgr. W.W. Sanitation, Inc., after 1974. Bd. dirs. Ch. Nazarene, bus driver, asst. Sunday Sch. supr., 1977, asst. Sunday Sch. tchr., 1975-78. Served with U.S. Army, 1968-69. Decorated Purple Heart, Army Commendation medal with oak leaf cluster (2), Bronze Star with V. Mem. Ill. Solid Waste Assn. (dir. 1976-78). C. of C. (dir. 1977—). Republican. Clubs: Lions. Home: 730 N Jackson St Pittsfield IL 62363 Office: 408 E Washington St Pittsfield IL 62363

JOHNSON, JAMES ALDEN, mgmt. cons.; b. Evanston, Ill., Aug. 4, 1949; s. N. Howard and Elizabeth Jane (Haan) J.; Vice-pres. N. Howard Johnson Inc., mgmt. cons.'s, Park Ridge, Ill., 1974—; lectr. in field. Active Boy Scouts Am., Youth Group Park Ridge Community Ch. Republican. Home: 8904 Jody Ln Des Plaines IL 60016 Office: One N Northwest Hwy Park Ridge IL 60068

JOHNSON, JAMES EDWARD, civil engr.; b. Davenport, Iowa, June 18, 1946; s. Wayne Joseph and Donna Jean (Lee) J.; B.S., Iowa State U., 1969; m. Susanne Eleanor Schaefer, Dec. 28, 1968; 1 son, Christopher Edward. Structural engr. Boeing Co., Seattle, 1969-70; design engr. Harstad Assos., Inc., cons. engrs., Seattle, 1970; asst. city engr. Bettendorf (Iowa), 1970-73; project engr. Cullen, Kilby, Carolan & Assos., cons. engrs., Bettendorf, 1973—. Registered profl. engr., Iowa, Ill. Mem. Nat. Soc. Profl. Engrs., Iowa Engring. Soc. Home: 1845 Providence Dr Bettendorf IA 52722 Office: 1977 Spruce Hills Dr Bettendorf IA 52722

JOHNSON, JAMES EDWARD, educator, psychologist; b. Chgo., May 4, 1939; s. John Robert and Ruth Margaret (Doyle) J.; B.S., Xavier U., Cin., 1962, M.A., 1965; Ph.D. in Clin. Psychology, St. Louis U., 1968; m. Betty Ann Brown, Aug. 10, 1963; children—James Michael, Amy Marie. Sr. staff psychologist Longview State Hosp., Cin., 1968-69; asst. prof. Xavier U., 1968-69; asso. prof. psychology Loyola U., Chgo., 1969—, dir. undergrad. div., 1974—. Cons. VA, 1973—. Bd. dirs. North Town-Rogers Park Mental Health Council, 1970-73. Named Faculty Moderator of Year, Loyola U., 1972, Faculty Member of Year, 1976. Mem. Am., Midwestern psychol. assns., A.A.A.S., A.A.U.P., Psi Chi. Home: 931 Oakwood Ave Wilmette IL 60091 Office: 6525 N Sheridan Rd Chicago IL 60626

JOHNSON, JAMES OWEN, architect; b. Columbus, Ohio, Apr. 20, 1926; s. Sheldon Cornelius and Jewell Frona (Olinger) J.; B.S. in Architecture, U. Cin., 1954; m. Patsy Maureen Risner, Aug. 27, 1952; children—James Owen II, Perian, Gayle. Draftsman, designer Thomas B. Wiggers, Cin., 1954-56; sr. partner Johnson, Ritchhart & Assos., Inc., Anderson, Ind., 1956—. Mem. Anderson Redevel. Commn., 1957-60, Madison County Planning Commn., 1960, Ind. Bd. Registration Architects, 1963-72. Served with USAAF, 1943-46. Mem. A.I.A., Ind. Soc. Architects (1st honor award in design 1962, citation for engring. excellence 1965, pres. Central So. chpt. 1970). Club: Anderson Country. Home: Rural Route 2 Box 157B Pendleton IN 46064 Office: 227 W 11th St Anderson IN 46016

JOHNSON, JANET LESAN, bank exec.; b. Denver, June 1, 1929; d. Walter Glen and Jenne Mae (Richardson) Lesan; student Roosevelt U.; 1 dau., Karen Lee MacDuffie; m. Floyd A. Johnson, June 13, 1958; 1 stepson, Floyd McKenzie. Office mgr. No. Petrochem. Co., Des Plaines, Ill., 1968-72; mgr. mktg. adminstrn., domestic and internat. Advanced Systems, Inc., Elk Grove Village, Ill., 1972-76; mgr. data control dept. Chgo. Title & Trust Co., 1976—. Active PTA, 1960-62; pres. Newcomers Club Des Plaines, 1962. Mem. Adminstrv. Mgmt. Soc. Office: 111 W Washington St Suite 0425 Chicago IL 60602

JOHNSON, JEFFREY ROYCE, utility co. adminstr.; b. Hampton, Iowa, Sept. 26, 1950; s. Eugene Winfield and Kathleen Rose (Hackbarth) J.; B.S. in Engring. Ops., Iowa State U., 1972; M.B.A., Drake U., 1974; m. Kathryn Marie Pecenka, Feb. 14, 1972. Student trainee NASA, Edwards, Calif., 1969, 70; engr. Northwestern Bell Telephone Co., Des Moines, 1972-74, engring. mgr., Cedar Rapids, Iowa, 1974-77, constrn. mgr., Iowa City, 1977—. Mem. Iowa Engring. Soc., Jaycees. Home: 3071 6th St NW Cedar Rapids IA 52402 Office: 830 1st Ave NE Cedar Rapids IA 52401

JOHNSON, JERRY EDWARD, orthodontist; b. Mpls., July 28, 1932; s. Nels Edward and Margaret (Hanson) J.; B.S., U. Minn., 1954, D.D.S., 1956, M.S.D., 1960; m. Jo Eaton, Sept. 4, 1954; children—Peggy, Lynn, Mitchell, Jean. Practice limited to orthodontics, Mpls., 1960—. Clin. instr. U. Minn., 1960-62. Served to lt., Dental Corps, USNR, 1956-58. Mem. Am., Minn. dental assns., Am. Assn. Orthodontists, Midwestern Soc. Orthodontists, Omicron Kappa Upsilon, Delta Sigma Delta. Presbyn. (elder). Rotarian (pres. 1966-67). Home: 5 Circle West Edina MN 55436 Office: Southdale Med Bldg Minneapolis MN 55435

JOHNSON, JOHN ARNOLD, biochemist, educator; b. Cusson, Minn., Dec. 6, 1924; s. John Ivar and Esther Elvera (Hannus) J.; B.A. in Chemistry, U. Minn., 1951, M.S. in Organic Chemistry, 1964, Ph.D. in Biochemistry, 1971; m. Bernetta Elsie Putz, June 16, 1951; children—Linda, Virginia, Mary, Michael, Robert, Caroline. Research chemist Bemis Bag Co., Mpls., 1954-59; scientist dept. dermatology U. Minn., 1960-71; asst. prof. depts. dermatology and biochemistry U. Nebr. Med. Center, 1971-73, asso. prof., 1973—; asso. prof. dept. dermatology Creighton U. Sch. Medicine, 1975—. Served with USAAF, 1943-45. Mem. Soc. Investigative Dermatology, AAAS, Sigma Xi. Home: 3205 N 80th St Omaha NE 68134 Office: 42 and Dewey Sts Omaha NE 68105

JOHNSON, JOHN FOWLER, dentist; b. Wolcott, N.Y., Sept. 23, 1917; s. John F. and Mary (Hay) J.; B.S., U. Mich., 1939, D.D.S., 1950; m. Anne Rynearson, Nov. 15, 1957; children—John Fowler, Jeremy Ann, James Bruce. Tchr. physiology U. Mich. Med. Sch., Ann Arbor, 1939-42; gen. practice dentistry, Flint, Mich., 1950—. Pres. Flint Planned Parenthood, 1967. Served with USAAF, 1941-45, with U.S. Army, 1950-52 to col., 1962, ret. Res., 1970. Fellow in physiology U. Mich., 1939-42. Mem. Am., Mich., Genesee County dental assns., MENSA (sec. Flint 1966). Pioneer in dentistry techniques including use of high speeds with equipment of his own design, full-flow, low vacuum suction. Producer filmed travelogs. Home and Office: 608 Welch Blvd Flint MI 48503

JOHNSON, JOHN HAROLD, mag. publisher; b. Arkansas City, Ark., Jan. 19, 1918; s. LeRoy and Gertrude (Jenkins) J.; student U. Chgo., Northwestern U.; LL.D., Shaw U., Benedict Coll., Carnegie-Mellon Inst., Central State Coll., Eastern Mich. U., Hamilton Coll., Lincoln U., Malcolm X Coll., Morehouse Coll., N.C. Coll., N.C. A. and T. State U., Upper Iowa Coll., Wayne State U., Pratt Inst.; m. Eunice Rivers Walker, June 21, 1941; children—John Harold, Linda Eunice. Pres., pub. Johnson Pub. Co., pubs. Ebony, Jet, Tan, Negro Digest, Ebony Jr.!, mags., Chgo., 1942—; pres. Sta. WJPC, Chgo.; dir. Bell & Howell Co., Marina Bank, Greyhound Corp., Arthur D. Little Inc., Twentieth-Century-Fox Film Corp., Zenith Radio Corp. Mem. Chgo. Mayor's Commn. on Human Relations; v.p. Nat. Urban League; mem. adv. council Harvard Grad. Sch. Bus.; nat. vice chmn. United Negro Coll. Fund; active Chgo. br. ARC; bd. dirs. NCCJ, Chgo., United Charities, Chgo., 4-H Chgo., United Negro Coll. Fund; trustee Tuskegee Inst., Fisk U., Art Inst. Chgo., Boston U. Named one of 10 outstanding young men of year U.S. Jr. C. of C., 1951; recipient Henry Johnson Fisher award Mag. Pubs. Assn., 1972; Communicator of Year award U. Chgo. Alumni Assn., 1974; Columbia Journalism award, 1974; Horatio Alger award, 1966. Fellow Sigma Delta Chi; mem. Mag. Pubs. Assn., Opportunities Industrialization Centers. Home: 1040 Lake Shore Dr Chicago IL 60611 Office: 820 S Michigan Ave Chicago IL 60616 also 1750 Pennsylvania Ave NW Washington DC 20006 also 3600 Wilshire Blvd Los Angeles CA 90005

JOHNSON, JOSEPH BERNARD, lawyer; b. Cambridge, Minn., July 6, 1919; s. Joseph B. and Ruth (Barker) J.; student Carleton Coll., 1938-41; LL.B., J.D., U. Mich., 1948; m. Kathryn M. Dabelstein, Feb. 20, 1943; children—Joseph Bernard III, Christine Ruth. Admitted to Minn. bar, 1948; asso. Holmes, Mayall, Reavill & Neimeyer, Duluth, Minn., 1948-51; partner Reavill, Neimeyer, Johnson, Fredin & Killen & Thibodeau, and predecessor firms, Duluth, 1951-74; pres., sr. mem. firm Johnson, Fredin, Killen, Thibodeau & Seiler, profl. assn., 1974—. Corporate officer, dir. Atwood Larson Co., Halvorson of Duluth Inc., Arrowhead Electric Inc., W.P. & R.S. Mars. Co., Lincoln Stores, Inc., Daugherty Howe Inc., Polar Gas, Inc., Conveyor Belt Service, Inc., Duluth Photographics Inc., Anderson Well-Drilling Inc., Easy Housing Inc.; dir. First Nat. Bank Duluth. Vice chmn. Minn. Bd. Law Examiners, 1956-59. Chmn. budget com. Duluth Community Chest, 1952-63; chmn. Duluth Welfare Council, 1967-70. Bd. dirs. Duluth YMCA, pres. 1977; bd. dirs. St. Luke's Hosp., Duluth, 1970-76; trustee Hunt Scholarship Fund, 1957-69, chmn., 1967-69; bd. dirs., v.p. United Way of Duluth. Served to capt. AUS, 1941-45; now lt. col. Res. Decorated Bronze Star medal with two oak leaf clusters, Purple Heart with two oak leaf clusters (U.S.); Croix de Guerre (France); Fiurre de Gurre (Belgium); Order of Holland (Netherlands). Mem. Am. (taxation sect.), Minn. (bd. govs. 1967-70, chmn. jud. selection com. 1969-73), 11th Dist. (pres. 1966-67) bar assns., Am. Judicature Soc., Duluth C. of C. (chmn. tax and tax laws com.), Duluth Jr. C. of C. (v.p. 1950-51). Republican. Lutheran (chmn. finance, bldg. coms., trustee). Clubs: Northland Country (pres. 1962-63), Kitchi Gammi, Rotary. Home: 3715 Greysolon Pl Duluth MN 55804 Office: First Nat Bank Bldg Duluth MN 55802

JOHNSON, JOSEPHINE LOUISE, counselor, educator; b. Galesburg, Ill., Sept. 22, 1933; d. Harold Leo and Mary Cecile (Myers) Stevens; B.S. in Edn., Western Ill. U., 1955, M.S. in Edn., 1958; Ed.D., U. Wyo., 1972; m. Clarence W. Johnson, Dec. 26, 1954 (dec.); 1 son, Christopher Anthony. Tchr. pub. schs., Del Rio, Tex., 1955, Bushnell, Ill., 1955-58; dir. guidance Bushnell (Ill.)-Prairie City Schs., 1958-70; counselor, dir. student activities Carl Sandburg Coll., Galesburg, Ill., 1971-72; counselor, asso. prof. counselor edn. Western Ill. U., Macomb, 1972—. Mem. Bushnell Bus. and Profl. Women's Club (past pres.), Am., Wyo., Ill. (past pres. chpt. 17) personnel and guidance assns., AAUW, Nat., Ill. edn. assns., Assn. Counselor Educators and Suprs., Am. Coll. Personnel Assn., Delta Kappa Gamma, Phi Kappa Phi, Phi Alpha Epsilon, Kappa Delta Pi, Phi Kappa Delta. Republican. Presbyterian. Clubs: P.E.O. Contbr. articles to profl. jours. Home: 643 Meadow Dr Macomb IL 61455 Office: Sherman Hall Room 127 Western Ill U Macomb IL 61455

JOHNSON, KARL EINAR, engring. and constrn. cons.; b. Kansas City, Mo., Dec. 14, 1915; s. Louis and Ingrid (Nelson) J.; B.M.E., Kans. U., 1938; postgrad. Northwestern U., 1948, 49; m. Lois Marie Friedebach, Aug. 10, 1943; children—Robert Allen Louis, Diane Marie. Central sta. engr. Westinghouse Electric Corp., 1939-42; dist. mgr. J.F. Pritchard & Co., Chgo., 1946-52; exec. v.p. Pritchard Products Co., Kansas City, Mo., 1952-60; v.p. gas div., Kansas City, Mo., 1960-65, sr. v.p., dir., 1965-74; v.p., dir. Pritchard Canadian Ltd., Calgary, 1968-74, Pritchard Internat. Corp., 1970-74; v.p. ISC World Trade Corp., Houston, 1968-74; cons., 1974—. Served to lt. (s.g.) USNR, 1942-46. Mem. ASME (sect. pres. 1961-62), Natural Gasoline Supplymen's Assn. (dir.), Triangle (pres. 1937-38), Tau Beta Pi, Sigma Tau, Pi Tau Sigma. Clubs: Rotary (treas. 1970-71), Indian Hills Country, Mission Hills (Kans.). Patentee in field. Home: 6624 Overhill Rd Shawnee Mission KS 66208

JOHNSON, KENNETH ODELL, systems engr., exec.; b. Harville, Mo., Aug. 31, 1922; s. Kenneth D. and Polly Louise (Wilson) J.; B.S. in Aero. Engring., Purdue U., 1950; m. Betty Lou Jones, Aug. 5, 1950; children—Cynthia Jo, Gregory Alan. Engr., design, quality and production mgmt. Gen. Lamp Co., Elwood, Ind., 1950-51; mem. staff aircraft gas turbine engine design Allison div. Gen. Motors Corp., Speedway, Ind., 1951-66; mem. marine, indstl. gas turbine engine design mgmt. staff Gen. Electric Co., 1966—. Served as pilot USAF, 1942-45. Fellow Am. Inst. Aeros. and Astronautics. Republican. Methodist. Patentee in field. Home: 8360 Arapaho Ln Cincinnati OH 45243 Office: Gen Electric Co M/D K107 Cincinnati OH 45215

JOHNSON, KENNETH ROGER, psychologist; b. Harlan County, Ky., June 24, 1943; s. James Golden and Lillian A. (Stewart) J.; B.A., Cumberland Coll., Williamsburg, Ky., 1966; M.A., U. Toledo, 1968; m. Lois Gaynelle Cooper, Nov. 28, 1963; children—Carles Stewart, Scott Allan. Psychologist in pvt. practice, Toledo, 1969—. NDEA grantee, 1967-68. Mem. Am., Ohio, Northwestern Ohio psychol. assns., Phi Kappa Phi. Club: Maumee Rotary. Home: 2539 Shetland Rd Toledo OH 43617 Office: 5757 Monclova Rd Maumee OH 43537

JOHNSON, KENNETH STUART, publisher and printer; b. Chgo., Aug. 22, 1928; s. William Moss and Lucille (Carsellio) J.; student Wright Jr. Coll., 1949-50, U. Ill., 1951-52; m. Mary Joan Kerber, Aug. 8, 1953; children—Cynthia Diane, Randall, Andrew, Peter. Dir., chmn. Free Press, Inc., Dundee, Ill., 1965—. Served with U.S. Army, 1946-47. Recipient Man and Boy award of Year, 1963. Mem. Cook County Pubs. Assn. (pres. 1963, dir.), Profl. Journalistic Soc., Nat. Editorial Assn., Sigma Delta Chi. Address: Free Press Inc Dundee IL 60110

JOHNSON, LANNY LEO, orthopedic surgeon; b. Highland Park, Mich., Aug. 21, 1933; s. Willard Laverne and Janet Gertrude (Luce) J.; B.S., Mich. State U., 1955; M.D., Wayne State U., 1959; m. Mary Ann Bourne, May 26, 1962; children—Charlotte, Autumn Lynn. Intern, Barnes Hosp., St. Louis, 1959-60, resident, 1960-64; practice medicine specializing in orthopedic surgery, 1964—; mem. staff Ingham Med. Center. Served with USAF, 1964-66. Author: The Comprehensive Arthoscopy of the Knee, 1977. Home: 4584 Comanche Okemos MI 48869 Office: 4528 S Hagadorn East Lansing MI 48823

JOHNSON, LEONARD GUSTAVE, indsl. engring. cons.; b. Negaunee, Mich., Mar. 12, 1918; s. Werner Leonard and Sophia (Larson) J.; A.B., U. No. Mich., 1940; A.M., U. Mich., 1941; m. Taimi Marie Lappi, July 5, 1944; 1 dau., Virginia K. Tchr. high sch. math., Channing, Mich., 1941-42; mathematician Chevrolet div. Gen. Motors Corp., Detroit, 1945-49, reliability scientist research labs. Gen. Motors Tech. Center, Warren, Mich., 1949-74; statis., math. cons. reliability, indsl. engring., Oak Park, Mich., 1974—. Lectr. in field. Mem. Indsl. Math. Soc. (treas. 1952), Soc. Automotive Engrs., Engring. Soc. Detroit, Am. Soc. for Quality Control, Soc. Reliability Engrs., Phi Beta Kappa, Kappa Delta Pi. Author: The Statistical Treatment of Fatigue Experiments, 1964; Theory and Technique of Variation Research, 1964. Home: 31811 Bretz Dr Warren MI 48093 Office: 21900 Greenfield Rd Oak Park MI 48237

JOHNSON, LESTER LARUE, JR., artist; b. Detroit, Sept. 28, 1937; s. Lester L. and Haroldine M. (Stanley) J.; student Wayne State U., 1956-58; B.F.A., U. Mich., 1973, M.F.A., 1974. One-man shows: Gallery 7, Detroit, 1970, 75, Detroit Artists Market, 1972, Flint Inst. Arts, 1973; group shows include: Richmond (Calif.) Art Center, 1965, Butler Inst., Youngstown, Ohio, 1966, Springfield (Mo.) Art Mus., 1966, Internat. Design Center, Los Angeles, 1967, Detroit Inst. Arts, 1968, 74-75, Laguna Beach (Calif.) Art Mus., 1970, Whitney Museum Am. Art, N.Y.C., 1971, 72, 73, Carnegie Inst., Pitts., 1971-72, Smith-Mason Gallery Art, Washington, 1971, others; commn. Detroit Workshop Fine Prints, 1974, also outdoor urban wall mural New Detroit, Inc., 1974; represented in permanent collections: Detroit Inst. Arts, Flint (Mich.) Inst. Arts, Grand Rapids (Mich.) Art Mus., Johnson Pub. Co., Chgo., others, also at various corps. and ednl. instns.; mem. visual arts adv. panel Mich. Council for Arts, 1975. Recipient John S. Newberry purchase prize, also Mrs. Albert Kahn prize 54th Exhbn. for Mich. Artists, Detroit Inst. Arts, 1964, 1st prize painting Mich. State Fair Art Exhbn., 1969, 73, Purchase award Harlem Gallery Square, 1969, 71, 72. Mem. Nat. Soc. Lit. and the Arts, Coll. Art Assn. Am. Home: 8350 E Morrow Circle Detroit MI

48204 Office: Center for Creative Studies Coll Art and Design 245 E Kirby St Detroit MI 48202

JOHNSON, LEWIS NEIL, supt. schs.; b. Anjean, W.Va., Sept. 4, 1940; s. Charles M. and Lillian Bea (Wright) J.; B.S. in Edn., Miami U., Ohio, 1966, M.A., 1968; Ed.D., Ball State U., 1973; m. Joyce Ann Waybright, June 23, 1962; children—Michael Neil, Bryan Lewis. Ins. investigator Retail Credit Co., Dayton, Ohio, 1962-64; 5th grade tchr. Butler Schs., Arcanum, Ohio, 1964-65; social studies tchr. Milton-Union Schs., West Milton, Ohio, 1966-67; asst. prin. Wayne Schs., Dayton, 1967-71; instr. Ball State U., 1971-72; asst. supt. Mad River Schs., Dayton, 1972-74; Mem. Ad Hoc Com. Vocat. Edn. Standards, Columbus, Ohio, 1974—. Mayor, West Milton, 1970-74. NDEA fellow Tex. A. and M. U., 1967; named Outstanding Young Educator in West Milton, Milton-Union Jr. C. of C., 1967. Mem. Am. Assn. Sch. Adminstrs., Ohio Assn. Supervision and Curriculum Devel., Ohio Edn. Assn., Wayne Classroom Tchrs. Assn. (pres. 1967-68), Phi Delta Kappa. Republican. Methodist. Mason; mem. Order Eastern Star. Contbr. reports, articles to profl. jours. Home: 5347 Greengate Groveport OH 43125 Office: 5055 S Hamilton Rd Groveport OH 43125

JOHNSON, LOWELL WARREN, engring. constrn. co. exec.; b. Kansas City, Mo., July 8, 1932; s. Lowell R. and Barbara (Warren) J.; B.S. in Chem. Engring., U. Kans., 1956; postgrad. Ill. Inst. Tech., 1972—; m. Sandra Gail Tabuas, Aug. 21, 1956 (div. Oct. 1971); children—Lisa, Brenda, Deirdra, Craig, Scott, Stephanie; m. 2d, Patricia J. Kontos, Jan. 13, 1974. Chem. prodn. supr. P.P.G. Industries, Barberton, Ohio, 1958-64; prodn. supt. Cabot Titania Inc., Asthtabula, Ohio, 1964-68, Dart Industries-Joliet, Ill., 1968-69; chem. project mgr., chief chem. engr. Hoyer-Schlesinger-Turner Inc., Chgo., 1969—. Served to lt. USNR, 1956-57. Registered profl. engr., Ohio, Ill., Okla. Mem. Am. Inst. Chem. Engrs. Patentee in field. Home: 512 S 8th Ave La Grange IL 60525 Office: 300 W Adams St Chicago IL 60606

JOHNSON, LYLE ROBERT, aircraft and holding co. exec.; b. Seattle, Jan. 12, 1939; s. Lyle Delmar and Virginia Lee (Davis) J.; B.A., U. Wash., 1962, M.B.A. with distinction, 1964; m. Betty Ann Ostendarp, July 2, 1965; children—Nicole Elizabeth, Lyle Robert Morton. Mktg. analyst Nalley's, Inc., Tacoma, 1962-63; fin. analyst Boeing Aircraft Co., Seattle, 1963-64; brand supr. Procter & Gamble Co., Cin., 1964-65; mktg. analyst Dole Co., San Jose, Calif., 1965; mktg. mgr. Louis Sherry, Inc., Long Island City, N.Y., 1966-67; pres., owner U.R.C., Inc., Farmingdale, N.Y., 1967-68; sales mgr., dir. mktg., v.p. mktg. J. Chein & Co., Burlington, N.J., 1968-74; v.p. mktg., dir. Learning Aids Group, Inc., N.Y.C., 1971-73; dir. mktg. Needlecraft div. Quaker Oats Co., Chgo., 1974-76; v.p. mktg. and adminstrn. J.L. Johnson Enterprises Ltd., Northbrook, Ill., 1976—; dir. Autonomic Awareness, Inc., Princeton, N.J., Nassau Design Co., Inc., Garden City, N.Y., Cassette Lending Library, Inc., N.Y.C. Mem. Gov.'s Task Force on Air Transp. Mem. Lower Makefield Civic Assn., Yardley, Pa., 1970-74. Served to lt. comdr. USCGR, 1957-58. Wash. State Legislature grantee, 1964. Mem. Am. Mgmt. Assn. (mktg. council), Sales Execs. Club N.Y., Am. Mktg. Assn., Toy Mfrs. Am., Assn. for Arts, Alpha Kappa Psi. Club: Biltmore Country (Yardley). Author: Alpha Awareness, 1971. Home: 450 Rugby Rd Barrington IL 60010 Office: 450 Anthony Trail Northbrook IL 60062

JOHNSON, SISTER MARIE INEZ, librarian; b. Mitchell, S.D., June 2, 1909; d. Charles and Inez L. (Williams) Johnson; B.A. in English, Coll. St. Catherine, 1929, B.S. in L.S., 1939; M.S., in L.S., Columbia, 1940; postgrad. U. Denver, 1951-52, U. So. Calif., 1953-54. Joined Sisters St. Joseph Carondolet, 1926; tchr. elementary schs. St. Paul, 1930-38; librarian Coll. St. Catherine, St. Paul, 1940-42, head librarian, 1942—. Mem. steering com. U. Minn. Workshop for Librarians, 1956; library cons. survey Mt. Mercy Coll., Cedar Rapids, Iowa, 1963-64; bldg. cons. Fontbonne Coll., St. Louis, 1964—. Mem. Conf. Am. Folklore for Youth, St. Paul Speakers Bur., com. standard catalog for high sch. Cath. Support, Children's Lit. TV Series. Butler Fgn. Study fellow Coll. St. Catherine, 1958. Named Minn. Librarian of Year, 1967. Mem. Am. (various coms.), Cath. (various coms.) library assns. Editor column Cath. Library World, 1954—. Contbr. articles to profl. jours. Address: Coll St Catherine St Paul MN 55116

JOHNSON, MARLENE MARIE, advt. agy. owner; b. Rush City, Minn., Jan. 11, 1946; d. Beauford William and Helen Marie (Nelson) Johnson; B.A., Macalester Coll., 1968. Community organizer Ramsey Action Programs, 1968-69; program dir. St. Paul YMCA, 1969-71; owner, mgr. Split Infinitive, advt. agy., St. Paul, 1970—. Bd. dirs., pres. Face to Face Health & Counselling, Inc., 1976—; bd. dirs., pres. Working Opportunities for Women, 1976—. Chmn. Minn. Women's Polit. Caucus, 1974-76; membership dir. Nat. Women's Polit. Caucus, 1975-77. Mem. Nat. Assn. of Women Bus. Owners, Women in Communication, Macalester Coll. Alumni Assn., Democrat. Home: 30 S St Albans St Saint Paul MN 55105 Office: 400 Sibley St Saint Paul MN 55101

JOHNSON, MARTIN HAROLD, research co. exec.; b. Stoughton, Wis., Mar. 10, 1923; s. Martin Helberg and Sophia Amunda (Christiansen) J.; Chem. Engr., U. Wis., 1944; m. Ruth White, Aug. 24, 1946; children—Martin Harold, Robert, Susan, Katherine. With Ray-O-Vac Co., Madison, Wis., 1944—, asso. dir. research and devel. ESB Inc. Ray-O-Vac Group, 1964-74, v.p. tech. devel., 1974—. Mem. Maple Grove Sch. Bd., 1962-64. Mem. Faraday Soc., Am. Chem. Soc., Electrochem. Soc., N.Y. Acad. Scis. Mem. Moravian Ch. N.Am. (exec. bd.). Patentee in field. Home: 6355 Pheasant Ln RFD 8 Verona WI 53593 Office: 101 E Washington Ave Madison WI 53703

JOHNSON, MARVIN ADOLPH, social worker; b. Platte, S.D., Oct. 6, 1931; s. Adolph Joseph and Emily Eleanor (Fotheringham) J.; B.S. in Sociology, Pasadena (Calif.) Coll., 1956; M.S.W. (Wheat Ridge Found. scholar), U. So. Calif., 1958; postgrad. social psychology, U. Chgo., 1959-61; m. R. Eloise Nelson, Jan. 9, 1954; children—Sonja, Melinda. Family counselor Luth. Family Service, Chgo., 1958-60, Luth. Child Welfare Assn., River Forest, Ill., 1960-61; chmn. div. social work Luth. Gen. Hosp., Park Ridge, Ill., 1962—, tchr. student nurses, 1962-65; part-time practice psychotherapy, 1964—. Cons. in field. Chmn. adv. bd. Community Counseling Center, Des Plaines, Ill., 1966-72; pres. N.W. Suburban Welfare Council, 1964-70; adv. council N.W. Suburban Service Council, 1968-70. Served with U.S. Army, 1953-55. Mem. Nat. Assn. Social Workers, Acad. Certified Social Workers, Am. Assn. Marriage and Family Counselors. Lutheran (past deacon). Home: 412 S Nawata Mt Prospect IL 60056 Office: 1775 Dempster St Park Ridge IL 60068

JOHNSON, MARVIN MELROSE, indsl. engr.; b. Neligh, Nebr., Apr. 21, 1925; s. Harold Nighram and Melissa (Bare) J.; B.S., Purdue U., 1949; postgrad. Ill. Inst. Tech., 1953; M.S. in Indsl. Engring., U. Iowa, 1966, Ph.D., 1968; m. Anne Stuart Campbell, Nov. 10, 1951; children—Douglas Blake, Harold James, Phyllis Anne, Nighram, Melissa. Quality control supr., indsl. engr. Houdaille Hershey, Chgo., 1949-52; indsl. engr. Bell & Howell, Chgo., 1952-54; with Bendix Aviation Corp., Davenport, Iowa, 1954-65, successively chief indsl. engr., staff asst., supr. procedures and systems, 1954-63, reliability engr. Pioneer Central Div., 1963-64, cons., 1964—; lectr. indsl. engr. State U. Iowa, 1963-64; instr. indsl. engring. U. Iowa, 1965-66; asso. prof. U. Nebr., 1968-73, prof., 1973—; U.S. AID adviser mgmt. engring. and food processing Kabul (Afghanistan) U., 1975-76. NSF trainee U. Iowa, 1964-67. Served with AUS, 1943-46, ETO. Registered profl. engr., Iowa, Mo., Nebr. Mem. Am. Soc. Engring. Educators, Am. Statis. Assn., Nebr. Acad. Sci., Am. Inst. Indsl. Engrs., ASME, Ops. Research Soc. Am., Inst. Mgmt. Sci., Sigma Xi, Tau Beta Pi, Pi Tau Sigma. Presbyterian. Home: 2507 Ammon Ave Lincoln NE 68507 Office: 175 Nebraska Hall U Nebr Lincoln NE 68588

JOHNSON, (MARY) ANITA, physician;, med. service adminstr.; b. Clarksburg, W.Va., Oct. 18, 1926; d. Paul F. and Mary Elizabeth (Harris) Johnson; B.S., North Tex. U., 1946; M.D., Woman's Med. Coll. of Pa., 1950; m. Lawrence J. Ciessau, Aug. 22, 1959 (div. 1974); children—Matthew A., Susan E., Sharon L., Mark A. Intern, Baylor U. Hosp., Dallas, 1950-51, resident, 1951-54; practice medicine specializing in internal medicine, Dallas, 1954-58, Chgo., 1958—; instr. internal medicine Southwestern Med. Coll., U. Tex., Dallas, 1954-58; med. dir. YWCA, Dallas, 1955-58; physician infant welfare Chgo. Bd. Health, 1960-63; house physician, emergency physician St. Mary of Nazareth Hosp. Center, Chgo., 1963—, instr. for nurses intensive care unit, 1963—, asst. cardiologist, 1963—. med. dir. Family Care Center, 1973-74; nat. med. dir. Nat. Cath. Soc. Foresters Ins. Co., Chgo., 1975-77; chief med. clinics St. Mary of Nazareth Hosp. Center, 1977—; cons. internal medicine Lisbon VA Hosp., Dallas, 1955-56. Lectr. to community elementary sch. students on opportunities in health field, 1967—. Named Med. Woman of Year, St. Mary of Nazareth Hosp. Center, 1973. Mem. AMA, Ill., Am. socs. internal medicine, Am. Coll. Angiology, Am. Med. Woman's Assn. (regional dir. 1955-58). Ill., Chgo. med. socs., Zeta Phi. Club: Pilot. Home: 1146 N Ashland Ave River Forest IL 60305

JOHNSON, M(ICHAEL) DAVID, registered profl. engr.; b. Terre Haute, Ind., Sept. 29, 1945; s. Herbert Norman and Doris Mae (Nolan) J.; B.S., Ill. Inst. Tech., 1975, M.B.A., 1977; degrees in Lighting Design, Wiring Design and Motor Control Design, Chgo. Elec. Assn., 1972, in Mgmt. and Supervision, Pub. Services Inst. of City Colls. of Chgo., 1976; m. K(athryn) Heather Gillett, July 4, 1969; children—Stephen Matthew, Stephanie Anne. Engring. aide City of San Jose (Calif.), 1965-67; engring. designer Cons.'s & Designers Inc., Palo Alto, Calif. and Chgo., 1967-68; engring. designer Intermatic, Inc., Spring Grove, Ill., 1968-71; engring. constrn. mgr. Met. San. Dist. Greater Chgo., 1971-77; owner Layout Design Specialists, Glenview, Ill., 1974—; village engr. Village of Villa Park (Ill.), 1977—. Adv. mem. U.S. Consumer Product Safety Commn., 1975—. Served with USNR, 1964. Registered profl. engr., Calif., Ill. Mem. Nat. Soc. Profl. Engrs., Am. Assn. M.B.A. Execs., Cons. Engrs. Assn. Chgo., L-5 Soc., Am. Pub. Works Assn., Am. Soc. Certified Engring. Technicians, Costeau Soc., Chess Fedn., Nat. Model R.R. Assn., United Fedn. Planets and Starfleet Command, Inc. Mensa. Mem. Evangel. Covenant. Mng. editor Fleet mag., 1975-76. Home: 442 Michael Manor Glenview IL 60025 Office: 20 S Ardmore Ave Villa Park IL 60181 also PO Box 485 Glenview IL 60025

JOHNSON, MICHAEL LILLARD, educator; b. Springfield, Mo., June 29, 1943; s. Ivan Harold and Margaret Joan (Vernon) J.; B.A., Rice U., Houston, 1965, Ph.D., 1968; M.A., Stanford U., 1966; Lectr. English, Rice U., 1968-69; mem. faculty Kans. U., Lawrence, 1969—, asso. prof. English, 1972—. Ford Found. scholar, 1965; Woodrow Wilson fellow, 1965-66. Mem. Popular Culture Assn., Nat. Council Tchrs. English, Delta Phi Alpha. Author: The New Journalism, 1971; Prometheus Reborn, 1977; Holistic Technology, 1977; (poetry) Dry Season, 1977; also articles, revs. Home: 3029 Rimrock St Lawrence KS 66044 Office: English Dept Univ Kans Lawrence KS 66045

JOHNSON, MILTON KENNETH, realtor; b. Darlington, Wis., June 11, 1907; s. Joseph John and Hilda (Hanson) J.; student Vocational Coll. Madison, 1924-26; m. Hettie Belle Whitford, Dec. 8, 1928 (dec. Nov. 1958); children—Connie Claire (Mrs. Robert L. O'Bryan); m. Helen Mae Kubly, Jan. 8, 1961. Dist rep. Mid-Continent Petroleum Co., 1928-41; owner Johnson Motor Sales, 1941-58; realtor Green County Realty Co., Monroe, Wis., 1958—. Mem. Automobile Dealers Assn. (pres. 1953), Green County Real Estate Assn., C. of C. Moose, Eagle. Club: Country (Monroe). Home: 2241 17th St Monroe WI 53566 Office: 910 17th Ave Monroe WI 53566

JOHNSON, MORRIS ALFRED, biochemist; b. International Falls, Minn., Aug. 3, 1937; s. Alfred and Margaret Veronica (Mannausau) J.; B.S., N.D. State U., 1960, M.S., 1962; Ph.D., Ore. State U., 1966; m. Catherine Anne Kiefer, Aug. 19, 1961; children—Raymond, Sigmond, Armond, Normond. Research asst., asst. prof. biochemistry Inst. Paper Chemistry, Appleton, Wis., 1966-73, chmn. dept. biology, 1970—, asso. prof., 1973—, research asso., 1974—. Mem. Am. Chem. Soc., Am. Inst. Chemists, Sigma Xi, Phi Lambda Upsilon. Roman Catholic. Home: 527 School Rd Route 9 Appleton WI 54911 Office: 1043 E S River St Appleton WI 54911

JOHNSON, ORVILLE URI, metals mfg. co. exec.; b. Scottville, Mich., Jan. 4, 1913; s. Thomas Bone and Vernie (Harrell) J.; grad. pub. schs.; m. Henrietta Jane Hughes, Apr. 15, 1933; children—Betty (Mrs. Carl M. Johnson), Orville E. Machine operator Sealed Power Corp., Muskegon, Mich., 1934-41, dept. foreman, 1941-48; with Aero Mfg. & Machining Co., Muskegon Heights, Mich., 1948—, part-owner, 1947—, sec., 1956—, dir., 1947—; dir. Harbor Steel & Supply Corp., Muskegon, 1956—. Mem. Central Assembly of God Ch. (deacon 1934—). Home: 1301 Chestnut St Muskegon MI 49442 Office: 2724 9th St Muskegon Heights MI 49444

JOHNSON, OSCAR, JR., farms operator; b. St. Louis, Aug. 18, 1905; s. Oscar and Irene (Walter) J.; ed. pvt. schs.; m. Eloise Long Wells, July 12, 1946; 1 dau., Irene Walter Johnson Barnes; stepchildren—Samuel Wistar Polk, Jr., Eloise Wells Polk Spivy. Pres., St. Albans Farms, Inc. (Mo.), 1946—. Pres. St. Louis Symphony Soc., 1933-55, v.p., 1955—; trustee Jacob L. Babler Perpetual Endowment Trust Fund, 1954-70. Recipient award for civic service St. Louis Jr. C. of C., 1936; key to City of St. Louis for service to St. Louis Symphony Soc., 1941. Served with AUS, 1941-42; to lt. comdr., USNR, 1942-45. Mem. Am. Meteorol. Soc., St. Louis Astron. Soc. Republican. Presbyterian. Clubs: St. Louis Country, Racquet, Noonday, Media, Univ., St. Louis (St. Louis); Cypress Point (Pebble Beach, Cal.); Old Capitol (Monterey, Calif.); Trans-Pacific Yacht (Los Angeles). Home: Saint Albans MO 63073 Office: 720 Olive St Saint Louis MO 63101

JOHNSON, PETER OSCAR, wholesale co. exec.; b. Monroe, Wis., Mar. 9, 1938; s. Oscar N. and Mary (Hahn) J.; B.B.A., U. Wis., 1961; m. Martha B. Reuter, Dec. 27, 1966; children—Erik, Lance, Trevor. Vice-pres., Hy Cite Corp., Madison, Wis., 1960-63; nat. sales coordinator Ekco Home Products, Milw., 1964-66; v.p. Hy Cite Corp., Madison, 1966-67, pres., 1968—; dir. Royal Prestige Credit, also treas. Bd. dirs. West Side Hockey Assn., 1976, 77, United Fund, 1974, 75, Little League, 1977; treas.-sec. Applewood Hills Water Utility, also bd. dirs; past pres. Applewood Hills Home Assn. Served with M.C., U.S. Army, 1956-57. Named to Hall of Fame, Ekco Home Products, 1971. Mem. C. of C., U. Wis. Alumni, Big Red Club. Roman Catholic. Home: 7111 Applewood Dr Madison WI 53711 Office: 340 Coyier Ln Madison WI 53713

JOHNSON, RALPH DONALD, agrl. economist; b. Plattsmouth, Nebr., June 22, 1922; s. Arnold Richard and Della (Seydlitz) J.; B.S., U. Nebr., 1948, M.S., 1961, Ph.D., 1971; m. Ruth Marie Smith, June 19, 1948; children—Penny (Mrs. David McCord), Kathy (Mrs. David Kennedy), Ralph Donald, Chris, Heidi, Kim, Jennie. Instr. vocat. agr., Nebr., Iowa, 1948-57; research asst. U. Nebr., 1957-58; agrl. economist commodities econs. div. Econ. Research Service, U.S. Dept. Agr., Lincoln, Nebr., 1958—. Adviser, Better Beef, Inc. Served with USNR, 1942-46. Grad. faculty fellow U. Nebr. Mem. Am., Western, Canadian agrl. econs. assns., Canadian Agrl. Econs. Soc., Gamma Sigma Delta, Omicron Delta Epsilon. Contbr. articles to profl. jours., monographs. Home: 819 N 33d Lincoln NE 68503 Office: 205 Filley Hall Inst Agrl and Natural Resources U Nebr Lincoln NE 68503

JOHNSON, RALPH STANLEY, psychiat. social worker; b. Mpls., July 1, 1935; s. Stanley Gilbert and Vinette (Stromberg) J.; B.A., Augsburg Coll., 1957; M.S.W., Washington U., St. Louis, 1962; m. Alvera Geraldine Olson, Sept. 6, 1958; children—Ann, Alan, Andrew. Caseworker, Isanti County Welfare Dept., Cambridge, Minn., 1958-60; hosp. social worker Moose Lake State Hosp., 1962-64; dir. social work Willmar (Minn.) State Hosp., 1964-67; psychiat. social worker West Central Community Services Center, Willmar, 1967—, asst. dir., 1973—, also dir. The Bridge, 1970—; pvt. practice psychiat. social work, Willmar, 1967—; chmn. Southwest Regional Mental Health Coordinating Com., 1968. Mem. Minn. Welfare Assn. (v.p. 1969), Nat. Conf. Social Welfare, Nat. Assn. Social Workers, Acad. Certified Social Workers. Club: Elks. Home: 1409 Grace Ave Willmar MN 56201 Office: 1125 6th St SE Willmar MN 56201

JOHNSON, RAY ARVIN, constrn. co. exec.; b. Long Prairie, Minn., May 2, 1920; s. Walter David and Rosalind (Hesser) J.; student Iowa State U., 1942, U. Minn., 1948-51, Coll. William and Mary, 1969; m. Kay Meredith Durbahn, May 14, 1960; children—Sherry Kay, Diane Rosalind, Laura Faye. Partner, Johnson Constrn. Co., Litchfield, Minn., 1941; project mgr., Minn. hwy. contracts, 1951-58, constrn. cost estimator, claims negotiator, 1955—; co-founder Johnson Bros. Hwy. & Heavy Constructors, Inc. (now Johnson Bros. Corp.), Litchfield, 1959, v.p., 1959-67, mgr. bridge div., 1960-63, sr. v.p., 1968-72, mgr. underground utilities div., 1961-67, 69-72, mgr. Western div., mgr. Chatfield Dam Stage I and II, 1967-69, mgr. labor relations, 1970-76, chmn. bd., 1973—; dir. Regional Congress Constrn. Employers Minn., 1973-75; instr. Mankato (Minn.) State U., 1975-76. Commr. Minnetonka (Minn.) Park Bd., 1973-75; adv. com. for heavy equipment Vocat. Tech. Inst., Staples, Minn., 1974. Served with USNR, 1942-45. Mem. Asso. Gen. Contractors Am. (nat. heavy and municipal utilities dir. 1973—, mem. nat. joint task force with U.S. Bur. Reclamation 1969-77, mem. equipment expense com. 1974—), Asso. Gen. Contractors Minn. (chmn. hwy. force account com. 1970—, chmn. constrn. equipment cost manual com. 1971—, mem. joint task force com. with Minn. Hwy. Dept. 1971—, hwy. dir. 1973-74, trustee Joint Trusteed constrn. Teamster Funds 1970—), Minn. Moles (co-founder), Soc. Preservation and Encouragement Barbershop Quartet Singing in Am., East Africa Wild Life Soc., Caballeros del Norte. Lutheran. Clubs: Masons (32 deg.), Shriners. Home: 2227 Platwood Rd Minnetonka MN 55343 Office: PO Box 1002 Litchfield Minneapolis MN 55355

JOHNSON, RAY THEODORE, JR., steel co. exec.; b. Chgo., May 13, 1920; s. Ray Theodore and Gladys (Marx) J.; A.B., Denison U., 1942; m. Fayette Hench, Feb. 20, 1943; children—Ray Theodore 3d, William H., Laura E.; m. 2d, Gertrude Cronin, Nov. 23, 1968. Sales clk. Henry C. Lytton & Co., 1942; sales trainee Callaway Mills, Inc., LaGrange, Ga., 1939-40; with Mid-West Forging & Mfg. Co., Chgo., 1946-61, successively dist. sales mgr., sec., asst. treas., 1946-57, sec., exec. v.p., 1957-61; asst. gen. mgr. Forgings div. Portec, Inc., 1961-62, gen. mgr., 1962-75, v.p., group exec. metals products, 1975-77. Active Boy Scouts Am., Community Fund, Jr. Achievement. Served from apprentice seaman to lt., USNR, 1942-46. Mem. Forging Industry Assn., Sigma Alpha Epsilon. Baptist. Home: 36 Kyle Ct Clarendon Hills IL 60514

JOHNSON, RAYMOND JOEL, state ofcl.; b. Duluth, Minn., Sept. 23, 1925; s. Joel and Dorthy May (Sutherland) J.; B.B.A., U. Minn., 1950, S.C.I.E., 1953; M.Ed., Nat. Coll. Edn., 1963; m. Lynnaea Jean Olson, June 25, 1949; children—Scott, Bruce, Mark, Kathryn. Project engr. Champion Motors Co., Mpls., 1951-54; chief indsl. engr. Streater Industries, Spring Park, Minn., 1954-58; exec. dir. CAP and Aviation Edn. bur. Ill. State Div. Aeros., Chgo., 1958—. Vice pres. Balloons & Things, Inc. Exec. sec. Ill. Aerospace Edn. Com., Chgo., 1966—. Former chmn. edn. com. Libertyville (Ill.) Dist. 70 Bd. Edn., 1964—; exec. dir. Ill. Wing Civil Air Patrol, 1958—. Served with USAAC, 1944-45. Mem. Chgo. Soc. Assn. Execs. (dir.), Am. Soc. Assn. Execs., Aviation/Space Writers Assn., Brit. Balloon and Airship Club, Am. Soc. Aerospace Edn. (sec.), Univ. Aviation Assn. Mason. Editor: Illustrated Ency. of Aviation and Space. Home: 817 S 4th St Libertyville IL 60048 Office: 33 W Jackson Blvd Chicago IL 60604

JOHNSON, RICHARD DEAN, pharmacist; b. DeKalb, Ill., July 8, 1936; B.S. in Pharmacy, U. Calif. at Berkeley, 1960; Pharm.D., U. Calif. Med. Center, San Francisco, 1961, M.S. in Pharm. Chemistry, 1962, Ph.D. in Pharm. Chemistry, 1965; m. Paula Jennings, July 26, 1969; children—Janet, Julie, Richard Dean. Practicing pharmacist, San Francisco, 1960-65; teaching asst. phys. chemistry U. Calif., San Francisco, 1962-64, research asst., 1964-65; sect. head pharm. research and devel. Allergan Pharms., Santa Ana, Calif., 1965-67; asso. dir. regulatory affairs Syntex Labs., Palo Alto, Calif., 1967-73; dir. licensing Marion Labs., Kansas City, 1973—; presdl. interchange exec. Dept. Commerce, Washington, 1970-71; lectr. Sch. Bus. Adminstrn., U. S.C., Columbia, 1975—. Registered pharmacist Calif. Fellow Am. Found. Pharm. Edn., Am. Inst. Chemists, Sir Henry S. Wellcome Meml.; mem. AAAS, Acad. Pharm. Scis. (chmn. membership econ. adminstrn.), Nat. Formulary (com. specifications). Contbr. articles to profl. jours. Home: 5330 Ward Pkwy Kansas City MO 64112 Office: 10236 Bunker Ridge Rd Kansas City MO 64137

JOHNSON, RICHARD KENNETH, clergyman, religious orgn. adminstr.; b. Erie, Pa., Sept. 25, 1922; s. William H. and Rosalia L. (Hoig) J.; A.B., Houghton Coll., 1953; M.Div., Union Theol. Sem., 1956; D.D., Mo. Valley Coll., 1971; m. Madelyn Fleming, Apr. 6, 1943; children—Daniel R., Paul H., Carolyn L., Martha L., Stephen W. Ordained to ministry Presbyn. Ch. U.S., United Presbyn. Ch. U.S.A., 1956; pastor Woodburn Presbyn. Ch., Leland, N.C., 1956-59, Westminster Presbyn. Ch., Wilmington, N.C., 1959-74; exec. presbyter NW Mo. Presbytery, Kansas City, Mo., 1965-71, NW Mo. Union Presbytery, 1972, Kansas City, (Mo.) Union presbytery, 1972—; bd. nat. ministries Presbyn. Ch. U.S., 1964-75, pres. nat. mission assn., 1969—, mem. gen. exec. bd., 1975-77; mem. nat. staff United Presbyn. Ch. U.S.A., Presbyn. Ch. U.S., 1971-78; mem. exec. staff Synods of Mid.-Am., 1972—; v.p. Met. Interch. Agy., Kansas City, Mo., 1972-75. Mem. Civil Service Bd., Wilmington, N.C., 1960-64; chmn. Kansas City Community Interagy. Flood Relief Task Force, 1977—; bd. dirs. Southeastern N.C. Mental Health Center, 1960-64, chmn., 1962-64. Served with USAAF, 1941-46; PTO. Decorated D.F.C., Air medal. Fellow (hon.) Truman Library; mem. New Hanover County Ministerial Assn. (pres. 1959-63),

Independence (Mo.) C. of C. Club: Rotary. Home: 3507 Shady Bend Dr Independence MO 64052 Office: 7850 Holmes St Kansas City MO 64101

JOHNSON, RICHARD WILBUR, psychologist; b. St. Cloud, Minn., July 25, 1934; s. Albert Haven and Florence (White) J.; A.B. cum laude, Princeton U., 1956; M.A., U. Minn., 1959, Ph.D., 1961; m. Adelle Clare Dowidat, Nov. 27, 1959; children—Cynthia, Whitney, Kara, Amy. Asst. prof. psychology U. N.D., 1961-65, U. Mass., 1965-68; asso. dir. counseling services, dir. research U. Wis., Madison, 1968—; cons. psychologist VA Hosp., 1966-68, 74—. Mem. Am. Psychol. Assn., Am. Personnel and Guidance Assn. Mem. editorial bd. Jour. Coll. Student Personnel, 1973-76. Contbr. articles to profl. jours. Home: Kathleen St Route 2 Madison WI 53711

JOHNSON, ROBERT DALE, med. soc. exec.; b. Sioux Falls, S.D., Apr. 18, 1943; s. Bernard Dale and Irma May (Gowling) J.; B.S., U. S.D., 1965; m. Teri Lee Sanders, June 12, 1965; children—Julie Jo, Christopher Robert, Nathan Bernard. Dir. pub. and profl. relations S.D. Blue Shield and S.D. State Med. Assn., Sioux Falls, 1966-72; exec. sec. S.D. State Med. Assn., S.D. State Bd. Med. and Osteo. Examiners and S.D. Found. for Med. Care, Sioux Falls, 1972—; bus. mgr. S.D. Jour. Medicine. Mem. adv. bd. S.D. chpt. Am. Assn. Med. Assts. Mem. Sioux Falls C. of C., Am. Assn. Med. Soc. Execs., Delta Tau Delta (dir.). Republican. Episcopalian. Clubs: Masons, Shriners, Elks, Westward Ho Country (Sioux Falls). Home: 2500 S 6th Ave Sioux Falls SD 57105 Office: 608 West Ave N Sioux Falls SD 57104

JOHNSON, ROBERT LEE, rheumatologist; b. Benson, Minn., Apr. 4, 1935; s. Lester Arnold and Maurine Ida (Tavis) J.; student (scholar) Ind. U., 1953-54; A.B. magna cum laude (Minn. Med. Found. scholar), U. Minn., 1957, M.D., 1960; m. Catherine Jane Harris, May 27, 1972; children—Perry Ramsing, Paul Leif. Intern, Denver Gen. Hosp., 1960-61; resident in medicine Mpls. VA Hosp., 1961-62; resident in medicine U. Wis., Madison, 1964-65, USPHS research fellow, 1966-69; arthritis fellow U. Tex. Southwestern Med. Sch., Dallas, 1969-70, asst. prof. dept. internal medicine, 1970-74; asso. prof. internal medicine U. Cin., 1974—. Served with USNR, 1962-64. Arthritis Found. fellow, 1970-72; Merck Faculty Devel. awardee, 1972. Diplomate Am. Bd. Rheumatology, Am. Bd. Internal Medicine. Mem. Am., Ohio rheumatism assns., AAAS, Phi Beta Kappa. Lutheran. Mem. editorial bd. Rheumatism Revs., 1972—. Home: 5455 Lanius Ln Cincinnati OH 45224 Office: 231 Bethesda St 7462 MSB Cincinnati OH 45267

JOHNSON, ROBERT OSCAR, educator; b. Detroit, May 7, 1926; s. Jalmar Oscar and Lydia (Evans) J.; B.S. in Elec. Engring., U. Mich., 1946, in Math., 1946, M.S. in Physics, 1949; M.S. in Math., U. Ill., 1952; Ph.D. in Math., Ohio State U., 1975; m. Hannelore Haselbarth, May 5, 1960; children—Norbert, Dean, Karen. Sr. engr. Internat. Tel.&Tel. Labs., Nutley, N.J., 1950-52; procurement engr. Republic Aviation, Farmingdale, N.Y., 1954; adminstrv. engr. Bendix Corp., Teterboro, N.J., 1954-58; proposal mgr. aerospace div. Walter Kidde & Co., Bellville, N.J., 1958-62; mgr. advanced design Arde Inc., Paramus, N.J., 1963; research specialist N.Am. Rockwell, Columbus, O., 1964-68; engr. Ohio Dept. Transp., Columbus, 1969-75; prof. Franklin U., Columbus, 1968—, Park Coll., Rickenbacher AFB, O., 1975—; ednl. cons. to various colls. and cos., 1975—. Mem. dist. council Boy Scouts Am. 1974. Served with AUS, 1946-47. Mem. Nat. Soc. Profl. Engrs., Am. Soc. Engring. Edn., Math. Assn. Am., Am. Assn. Physics Tchrs., Inst. Math. Statistics, Tau Beta Pi. Contbr. articles to tech. publs. Home: PO Box 30722 Gahanna OH 43230 Office: 201 S Grant Ave Columbus OH 43215

JOHNSON, ROLAND EDWARD, appliance co. exec.; b. Kenosha, Wis., May 14, 1931; s. Edward R. and Clara A. (Blank) J.; B.S., U. Wis., 1953, M.B.A., 1957; m. Mable L. Muller, Aug. 27, 1955; children—Keith E., Carol L. Personnel research specialist Esso Research & Engring. Co., Linden, N.J., 1957-59; mgr. personnel research Whirlpool Corp., Benton Harbor, Mich., 1959-62, dir. of personnel research, 1962-64, dir. orgn. planning, 1964-68, dir. of adminstrv. ops., 1968—; instr. Fairleigh Dickinson U., 1957-59, Mich. State U., 1959-64. Served with U.S. Army, 1953-55. Recipient Research award Indsl. Relations Center, U. Minn., 1960. Mem. Am. Mgmt. Assn., Am. Soc. of Personnel Adminstrs. Club: Elks. Co-editor: Ency of Mgmt., 1978. Home: 4645 Terra Ln St Joseph MI 49085 Office: Administrative Center Whirlpool Corp Benton Harbor MI 49022

JOHNSON, STANLEY HAROLD, printing co. exec.; b. DeKalb, Ill., Dec. 31, 1912; s. Andrew and Anna (Anderson) J.; B.E., No. Ill. U., 1937; m. Virgie May Lee, Jan. 31, 1942; 1 son, David Harold. Supr. accordion dept. Wurlitzer Co., DeKalb, 1932-36; indsl. arts tchr. Ill. Tng. Sch., St. Charles, 1937-39; bindery foreman Hammerich Printing, DeKalb, 1939-42; draftsman engring. dept. Interstate Aircraft Corp., DeKalb, 1942-45; linotype operator, compositor Hammerich Printing, DeKalb, 1945-50; co-owner R & S Johnson Printing Corp., DeKalb, 1950—, sec.-treas., dir., 1950—. Mem. career edn. adv. council DeKalb Community Schs., 1972-73. Mem. Printing Industry Ill., Ill. State, DeKalb chambers commerce, DeKalb County Farm Bur., No. Ill. U. Alumni Assn. Mem. Covenant Ch. (trustee 1955-66, ch. chmn. 1967-69, deacon 1971-72). Club: Kiwanis. Home: Route 2 Rich Rd Sycamore IL 60178 Office: 2205 Sycamore Rd DeKalb IL 60115

JOHNSON, STANLEY RICHARD, JR., mfg. co. exec.; b. Syracuse, N.Y., May 20, 1942; s. Stanley Richard and Margaret Hulda (Stomberg) J., Sr.; A.A., Pasadena City Coll. 1962; B.S., U. Calif. at Los Angeles, 1965; student Calif. State U., 1965-67; m. Kristen Elizabeth Hansen, July 8, 1967; children—Allison Elizabeth, Erik Peter. Research asst. Hyland Labs, Los Angeles, 1966-67, mfg. supr., Costa Mesa, Calif., 1967-72, quality control mgr., Round Lake, Ill., 1973-75, mfg. mgr., 1975—; instr. immunology throughout U.S., S.Am. and P.R. Pres. McHenry Area Rescue Squad, Inc., 1977, 78. Certified paramedic, Ill. Founding mem. Nat. Assn. Emergency Med. Technicians; mem. Am. Mgmt. Assn., Am. Soc. Microbiology, Am. Assn. Trauma Specialists. Patentee (3) in immuno-diagnostics; contbr. numerous tech. exhibits to profl. orgns. Home: 308 N Timothy Ln McHenry IL 60050 Office: Rt 120 at Wilson Rd Round Lake IL 60073

JOHNSON, STEVEN ARNIE, mech. engr.; b. Thief River Falls, Minn., Dec. 23, 1952; s. Arnie W. and Violet (Peterson) J.; A.A., Northland Community Coll., 1972; B. Mech. Engring., U. Minn., 1975, postgrad., 1975; m. Janet M. Carter, June 1, 1973; 1 son, Chriostpher. Engring. asst. U.S. Dept. Agr., Thief River Falls, 1972, Bather, Ringrose & Wolsfeld, Inc., Edina, Minn., 1973, U. Minn., Mpls., 1973-74; research engr. Onan Corp., Mpls., 1975—. Mem. Soc. Automotive Engrs. (Ralph J. Tetor Mini award Twin City sec. 1975), ASME, Engine Mfrs. Assn. (emissions standards com.), Soc. Exptl. Stress Analysis, Combustion Inst. Democrat. Lutheran. Home: 235 Aurora Ln Circle Pines MN 55014

JOHNSON, THEODORE OLIVER, JR., musician, educator; b. Elkhart, Ind., Oct. 9, 1929; s. Theodore Oliver and Harriet Koehler (Herrold) J.; Mus.B., U. Mich., 1951, Mus. M., 1952, D.Mus. Arts (Rackham fellow), 1957; m. Carol Ann Holliff, June 22, 1968; children—Karen, Nancy, Steven. Mem. music-theroy faculty, violinist in faculty string quartet Sch. Fine Arts, U. Kans., 1958-64; mem. music-theory faculty, dept. music Coll. Arts and Letters, Mich. State U., East Lansing, 1964—, prof. music, 1977—, violinist Beaumont String Quartet, 1964—; concertmaster Lansing Symphony Orch., 1967-69, Grand Rapids Symphony Orch., 1972-73; dir. music Bethel Baptist Ch., 1969—; solo recitalist. Served in U.S. Army, 1952-55. Fulbright scholar, 1956-57. Mem. Phi Mu Alpha Sinfonia, Phi Kappa Phi, Pi Kappa Lambda, Phi Eta Sigma. Composer motets. Home: 651 Hillcrest Ave East Lansing MI 48823 Office: 417 Music Practice Bldg Mich State U East Lansing MI 48823

JOHNSON, VINCENT ERWIN, lawyer; b. Montezuma, Iowa, Apr. 13, 1917; s. Axel Emil and Clara Ethel (Burrows) J.; B.S.C., U. Iowa, 1938; J.D., U. Mich., 1947; m. Susan B. Snyder, Sept. 1, 1940; children—Kristin Sue (Mrs. Donald Joseph Armstrong), Vincent Erwin II. Admitted to Iowa bar, 1947, since practiced in Montezuma; dir. Montezuma State Bank. Atty. Poweshiek County, 1956-60; Del., Iowa Rep. Conv., 1964. Mem. Iowa (bd. govs., 1957-59), Poweshiek County (pres. 1952-60), 6th Judicial Dist. (pres., 1965-66) bar assns., Iowa Conf. Bar Assn. Pres.'s (pres., 1957-59), Phi Kappa Sigma. Rep. Methodist. Club: Masons. Home: 1000 E Main St Montezuma IA 50171 Office: 107 S 4th St Montezuma IA 50171

JOHNSON, WILLIAM PAGE, ednl. adminstr.; b. Council Bluffs, Ia., Sept. 25, 1942; s. Efford Wilbert and Jessie Emma (Page) J.; student N.W. Mo. State Coll., 1960-61; B.A., U. Denver, 1964; postgrad. (NSF fellow), U. Nebr., 1965-66; postgrad. Oreg. State U., 1967-68; M.A., U. Iowa, 1972, Ph.D. (Bur. Edn. Handicapped fellow), 1974; m. Vivian Susan Casteel, July 18, 1970. Tchr., coach Council Bluffs Community Schs., 1964-68, Portland (Oreg.) Pub. Schs., 1968-69; tchr., coach Iowa Sch. for Deaf, Council Bluffs, 1969-71; adminstr. Mpls. Pub. Schs., 1973-74, Area Ednl. Agy., Mt. Pleasant, Iowa, 1974-77; supt. Ill. Sch. for the Deaf, Jacksonville, 1976—; cons. Dist. 287 Mpls. Regional Programs for Hearing Impaired, 1973-74; asst. prof. St. Cloud (Minn.) State Coll., 1973-74; with spl. edn. Systems Unlimited, Inc., Iowa City, 1971-73. Named Outstanding Young Educator, Council Bluffs Jr. C. of C., 1968. Mem. Iowa Dirs. Spl. Edn., Council for Exceptional Children, Council Adminstrs. in Spl. Edn., Registry Interpretors for Deaf, Assn. for Retarded Citizens, Council Bluffs Deaf Club. Club: Rotary. Presbyterian (elder 1970—). Home: 125 Caldwell St Jacksonville IL 62650 Office: 125 Webster St Jacksonville IL 62650

JOHNSON, WILLIAM RAYMOND, artist, cartoonist, writer; b. Mpls., Jan. 29, 1922; s. Carl August and Anna Malvina (Anderson) J.; student Dartmouth Coll., 1944-46, Jean Morgan Sch. Art, 1946-48; m. Pauline Vernice Doten, Feb. 2, 1946; children—William Raymond, Jill Anne. Staff artist Am. Seal-Kap Corp., L.I., N.Y., 1948-51; staff artist to art dir. Chartmakers, Inc., 1951-55; free lance artist, cartoonist, writer, N.Y.C. and Mpls., 1955—; art dir., artist Trend Enterprises, St. Paul, 1971—. Mem. Coon Rapids Inds. Devel. Commn., 1969—; active Boy Scouts Am., 1959-69, scoutmaster troop 475, 1962-65; officer, bd. dirs. Levittown Boys Club, L.I., 1959-61. Served with USNR, 1942-46. Recipient Honor certificate Freedoms Found. at Valley Forge for pub. cartoon, 1964. Lutheran. Author-illustrator: Holiday Funtime (juvenile), 1964; weekly sports cartoon Letter from the Twins, 1965-70. Home: 10656 Riverview Pl Coon Rapids MN 55433

JOHNSON, WILLIAM RAYMOND, clergyman; b. Chgo., Feb. 6, 1951; s. Raymond Gottfried and Ruth Elinor (Mathae) J.; B.A., Augustana Coll., Rock Island, Ill., 1973; M.A., State U. Iowa, Iowa City, 1975, Ph.D., 1977; M.Div. candidate, U. Dubuque, 1977; m. Helen Ann Eckhoff, June 9, 1973; 1 dau., Sarah. Terminal operator Augustana Coll. Computer Center, 1971-73; computer-based edn. asst. State U. Iowa, 1973-75; dir. computer resources Loras Coll., Dubuque, 1975-77, acting dir. computer resources, 1977—; ordained to ministry Methodist Ch., 1977; pastor Greeley (Iowa) United Meth. Ch., 1977—; computer cons. U. Dubuque Theol. Sem.; mem. bd. edn. Iowa conf. United Meth. Ch. Certified tchr. secondary sch. math., Iowa, Ill. Mem. Assn. Ednl. Data Systems, Assn. Devel. Computer-Based Instructional Systems, Assn. Computing Machinery, Pi Lambda Theta, Phi Delta Kappa. Home and Office: PO Box 28 Greeley IA 52050

JOHNSTON, BENJAMIN BURWELL, JR., composer, educator; b. Macon, Ga., Mar. 15, 1926; s. Benjamin Burwell and Janet (Ross) J.; B.A., Coll. William and Mary, 1949; student Cath. U. Am., 1944-45; Mus.M., Cin. Conservatory Music, 1950; M.A., Mills Coll., 1952; student U. Calif. at Berkeley, 1950, U. Ill. at Urbana, 1953-55; m. Dorothy Haines, June 1947 (div.); m. 2d, Betty Ruth Hall, Apr. 14, 1950; children—Sibyl Bulluck, Ross Burwell, Christopher Alan. Student composition with Darius Milhaud, Burrill Phillips, Robert Palmer, Harry Partch, John Cage. Prof. music Sch. Music, U. Ill. at Urbana, 1951—, chmn. music planning com. for univ. Festival Contemporary Arts, 1962-65, asso. mem. Center for Advanced Studies, 1966. Chmn. council Newman Center, U. Ill. Served USNR, 1944-46. Guggenheim fellow, 1959-60; Summer Research fellow U. Ill., 1958; Research Bd. grantee, 1965, 69, 70, 71; grantee Nat. Found. on Arts and Humanities, 1966. Mem. ASCAP, Société des Auteurs et Compositeurs Dramatiques, Phi Beta Kappa, Omicron Delta Kappa, Pi Kappa Lambda. Composer: Concerto for Brass, 1951; (for orch.) Passacaglia and Epilogue, 1955, 60, Quintet for Groups, 1965; (ballets) Gambit, 1959, St. Joan, 1955; (operas) Gertrude, or Would She Be Pleased to Receive It?, 1956, Carmilla, 1970; (cantata) Night, 1955; (chorus) Ci-Gît Satie, 1967; Rose, 1971; Mass, 1972; (chamber music) Nine Variations for String Quartet, 1959, String Quartet No. 2, 1964, String Quartet No. 3, 1966; String Quartet No. 4, 1973; Sonata for Two (violin and cello), 1960, Knocking Piece (2 percussionists and grand piano), 1962, Duo (flute and string bass), 1963; One Man (solo for trombone and percussion), 1967; (piano music) Satires, 1953, Celebration, 1953, Sonata for Microtonal Piano, 1965; (for jazz band) Ivesberg Revisited, 1960, Newcastle Troppo, 1960; (songs) Three Chinese Lyrics, 1955, Five Fragments, 1960, A Sea Dirge, 1962; Knocking Piece II, Recipe for a Dancer, Casta Norma, 1968; (song cycle) Seven, 1970, In Memory, 1975, Songs of Innocence, 1975; (with Jaap Spek) Auto Mobile, 1969, Kindergartenlieder, 1969, Knocking Piece Collage, 1969, score for orientation film Mus. History and Tech., Smithsonian Instn., 1968; Vigil, for speaking group, 1976; numerous other compositions. Author articles in field. Home: 1003 W Church St Champaign IL 61820 Office: Sch Music U Ill Urbana IL 61801

JOHNSTON, JOHN LAWRENCE, wire, cable and cord mfg. co. exec.; b. Oak Park, Ill., Aug. 20, 1934; s. John A. and Margaret Mary (Flanagan) J.; B.Sc., Loyola U., Chgo., 1970; M.B.A., U. Chgo., 1972; m. Alice Suzanne Hopkins, Oct. 26, 1957; children—Deborah, Mary Beth, Jean, Michael. Tab operator Belden Corp., Geneva, Ill., 1955-57, cost accountant, 1957-61, inventory control supr., 1961-65, asst. controller, 1965-74, asst. treas., asst. sec., 1974—; dir. Complete Reading Electric & Elec. Splty. Co. Served with AUS, 1957. Mem. Nat. Assn. Accountants. Home: 912 Kehoe Dr Saint Charles IL 60174 Office: 2000 Batavia Ave Geneva IL 60134

JOHNSTON, LEO LORRAINE, constrn. co. pres.; b. Sidney, O., June 1, 1920; s. Leo Cargill and Anna Dolores (Elliott) J.; B.S., Ohio U., 1942; m. Fern Maxine Camplin, Jan. 30, 1942; children—Kay, Cheryl. Founder, pres. Midwest Constructors, Inc., Mansfield, O., 1946—. Chmn., Midwest Utility Service Corp., Mansfield, O., 1967-70, Profl. Bldg. Corp., Mansfield, 1960-63; dir. Richland Trust Co., Mansfield. Chmn. Lake Erie Council Carpenters Benefit Fund, 1966—, Ohio State chmn., 1976-77, Joint Apprenticeship and Tng., 1966—. Bd. dirs. Mansfield Mental Health Center, 1972—, Am. Cancer Soc., 1977—. Served with USNR, 1942-46; ETO. Registered profl. engr., Iowa. Mem. Am. Soc. C.E. (dir. 1972-73), N. Central O. Builders Assn. (pres. 1966-67), Ohio Contractors (chmn. labor relations div. 1969), Nat., Ohio socs. profl. engrs., Cleve. Soc. Engrs. Mason (32 deg., Shriner), Kiwanian (past pres.). Clubs: University, Westbrook Country (pres. 1977). Home: 550 Palomar Dr Mansfield OH 44906 Office: 210 N Illinois Ave Mansfield OH 44905

JOHNSTON, ROBERT PORTER, educator; b. Phila., Oct. 25, 1924; s. Robert Faunce and Irene Titus (Porter) J.; student Girard Coll., 1934-43; B.A., Pa. State U., 1948, M.A., 1951; postgrad. Pa. Acad. Fine Arts, 1951-52, Mich. State U., 1962-65; M.A., U. Wyo., 1958; m. Joyce Elaine Wenthe, June 10, 1962; children—Michael William, Andrew Richard, Paula Rose. Tchr. art Northwood Sch., Lake Placid, N.Y., 1948-49; asst. prof. Hastings (Nebr.) Coll., 1958-62, Mankato (Minn) State U., 1966-67; instr. art Lansing (Mich.) Community Coll., 1964-66; asso. prof. art Western Mich. U., Kalamazoo, 1967—, faculty research fellow, 1970-71; dir. Robert Johnston Gallery, Kalamazoo, 1975—; cons. at colls. and art schs. for Nat. Assn. Schs. Art, 1972—, mem. commn. on accreditation, 1972-75. Ford Found. grantee, 1976. Mem. Coll. Art Assn., Artists Equity Assn. Mem. editorial bd. Minority Voices, 1977—. Contbr. articles to profl. publs. Home: Route 2 Frosty Acres Lawton MI 49065 Office: Art Dept Western Mich U Kalamazoo MI 49008

JOHNSTON, ROBERT WILLIAM, union exec.; b. Ward, Iowa, Apr. 8, 1914; s. Robert and Christina J.; student Albia Jr. Coll., 1936; m. Carol Jeanne Nidy, Mar. 29, 1951; children—Bartly P., Christina, Maribeth, Michael, Kelly. With John Deere & Co., East Moline, Ill., 1937-48; internat. rep. UAW, Des Moines, 1948-56, dir. region 4, Chgo., 1956—; dir. Ill. Dept. Labor, 1961. Mem. Chgo. Human Relations Commn., 1962-67. Home: 50 W Lance Dr Des Plaines IL 60016 Office: 5132 W Harrison St Chicago IL 60644

JOHNSTON, RONALD LEE, dentist; b. Hartford City, Ind., June 25, 1943; s. Donald Willard and Esta Ilene (Cale) J.; student Ind. U., 1964, D.D.S., 1968; m. Linda Helen Hopper, June 13, 1965; children—Melissa Elaine, Ryan Marshall. Pvt. practice dentistry, Indpls., 1970—; instr. Sch. Dentistry, Ind. U., Purdue U., Indpls., 1972—; dental cons. Equitable Ins. Co. Mem. Health Task Force; mgr., coach Indpls. Amateur Baseball Assn., Little League Baseball. Served with USAF, 1968-70. Mem. Am., Ind. dental assns., Indpls. Dist. Dental Soc., Am. Legion, Psi Omega, Alpha Phi Omega. Presbyterian. Club: Masons. Home: 8226 Groton Ln Indianapolis IN 46260 Office: 6545 Carrollton Ave Indianapolis IN 46220

JOHNSTON, WALKER FRANCIS, oil co. exec.; b. Houston, Dec. 4, 1924; s. Walker Francis and Joe Bettie (Miller) J.; B.S. in Chem. Engring., Rice U., 1945, M.S., 1947; m. Karen Lee Tippy, Nov. 26, 1966; children—Kevin, Jo Ann, Craig, Scott, Bradford, Jill. Chem. engr. Pan Am. Refining Corp., Texas City, Tex., 1947-53; group leader chem. engring. Am. Oil Co. subs. Standard Oil Co. (Ind.), Texas City, 1953-57, group leader, sr. chem. engr., 1957, sect. head, sr. chem. engr., 1957-62, asst. dir., Whiting, Ind., 1968-74; dir. Standard Oil Co., Naperville, Ill., 1974—. Served with USNR, 1943-46. Mem. Am. Inst. Chem. Engrs., Am. Chem. Soc. Patentee in field. Home: 6S 671 Millcreek Ln Naperville IL 60540 Office: Standard Oil Co PO Box 400 Warrenville Rd Naperville IL 60540

JOKELA, JOHN MILTON, mfg. co. exec.; b. Detroit, Dec. 8, 1924; s. Henry S. and Mary Elizabeth (Johnson) J.; student Antioch Coll., 1943, U. Ky., 1943; A.B., U. Mich., 1943, postgrad., 1946-49; postgrad. U. Ill., 1967-68; m. Mary Elizabeth Park, Sept. 2, 1949; children—Mary Elizabeth, Jon Brett. With Pitts. Plate Glass Co., 1949-54; with Tempo Products Co., 1954—, v.p., 1967-72, pres., 1972—. Served with AUS, 1943-46. Mem. Automotive Service Industry Assn., Motor Equipment Mfg. Assn., Aircraft Mfrs. and Distbrs. Assn. (dir. 1976—), Aerosol Coating Mfr. Assn. (dir. 1968-70), Sigma Chi. Presbyterian (elder 1963-69, 73—). Clubs: Chagrin Valley Racquet, Hillbrook (Chagrin Falls, Ohio). Home: 184 Willow Ln Chagrin Falls OH 44022 Office: 6200 Cochran Rd Solon OH 44139

JOLLEY, JOY BATES, social worker; b. Grinnell, Iowa, June 30, 1924; d. Roy E. and Katherina Belle (Buchanan) B.; student Iowa; State U., 1942-44; B.A., State U. Iowa, 1947; m. Lewis Ray Jolley, Dec. 10, 1949 (div. 1976); 1 dau., Barbara Jolley Barnhouse. With dept. social services U. Hosp., Iowa City, Iowa, 1947-49; social welfare worker County Dept. Social Services, Grinnell, 1949-50; child welfare worker County Dept. Social Services, Oskaloosa, 1955-69; mental retardation specialist Iowa Dept. Social Services, Des Moines, 1970—. Cons. for establishment Iowa S. Central Mental Health Center, 1959-62, sec. bd. dirs., 1963-66; cons. Dist. XV Iowa Developmental Disabilities Council; sec., bd. dirs. Dist. XV Specialized Child Health Center, 1976—. County organizer Big Buddy System, 1967. Organizer Oskaloosa Child Guidance Council, 1960-61, pres., 1961-64; co-chmn. youth council YW-YMCA, 1966-68; mem. Gov.'s Task Force on Mental Retardation, 1966-67. Bd. dirs. Mahaska County Assn. Retarded Children, 1971—. Mem. Am. Assn. Mental Deficiency, Iowa Welfare Assn., P.E.O., Alpha Xi Delta. Roman Catholic. Clubs: Oskaloosa Women's, Altrusa (Oskaloosa). Home: 1001 N 2d St Apt 5 Oskaloosa IA 52577 Office: PO Box 899 Ottumwa IA 52501

JOLLIFF, CARL R., clin. biochemist, lab. adminstr.; b. Lakewood, Ohio, July 2, 1926; s. Gaither Franklin and Selma Edna (Wolfe) J.; B.S., State U. Iowa, 1949, postgrad., 1949-51; m. Shirley Ann Abbott, June 5, 1948; children—Kathy Lynne Jolliff Harvey, Anne Elizabeth Jolliff Saber. Co-dir. Hastings-Lincoln (Nebr.) Med. Labs., 1951-58; dir. clin. labs. Hastings State Hosp., 1953-56, Lincoln Clinic, 1958—; vis. prof. biology Nebr. Wesleyan U., Lincoln, 1972—; lectr., cons. in field. Sec.-treas. Lincoln Med. Research Found., 1964—. Served with AUS, 1944-46. Am. Cancer Soc. research fellow, 1950. Fellow Royal Soc. Health (London); mem. Am. Acad. Microbiology (specialist microbiologist), Am. Assn. Clin. Chemists (chmn. midwest sect. 1959, 73), N.Y. Acad. Scis., Am. Chem. Soc., Am. Assn. Clin. Chemists, Am. Soc. Microbiology, Sigma Xi. Club: Exec. (pres. Lincoln 1968). Author: (with others) Chemistry for Medical Technologists, 1976; contbr. articles to profl. publs. Home: 1400 Crestline Dr Lincoln NE 68506 Office: Clin Labs Sect Lincoln Clinic PO Box 81009 Lincoln NE 68501

JOLLY, JAMES ALLEN, engring. co. exec.; b. Burlingame, Kans., Feb. 23, 1939; s. James Able and Edna Mae (True) J.; m. Martha Louise Albright, Dec. 27, 1958; children—David, Richard, Anita, Lisa, Jimmy, Bruce. Mech. and elec. designer Burgess, Latimer & Miller, Topeka, Kans., 1959-74; mech. estimator Young Plumbing and Heating, Topeka, 1974-75; exec. v.p. Burgess Engring. Inc., Topeka, 1976—; bd. dirs. Brugess & Assos. Mem. Am. Soc. Heating, Refrigeration and Air Conditioning Engrs., AIA. Home: Rural Route 2 Overbrook KS 66524 Office: 106 E 7th St Topeka KS 66603

JOLLY, JAMES MUMFORD, SR., dentist; b. St. Charles, Mo., May 11, 1918; s. Benjamin Harrison and Margaret Belle (Blackwell) J.; student U. Mo., 1937-40; D.D.S., Washington U., St. Louis, 1943, M.S., 1955; m. Helen Rose Bruns, May 23, 1943; children—James M., Janet Margot, David Bruns. Practice dentistry, Webster Groves, Mo., 1944-46, St. Louis, 1946-51; practice dentistry, specializing in orthodontics, Clayton, Mo., 1955—. Asst. prof. clin. orthodontics Washington U. Dental Sch., 1955-73, asso. prof., 1973—; sec.-treas. Charlevoix Profl. Nursing Home, St. Charles, Mo., 1963—, J.M.S. Realty, St. Charles, 1963—, L. B. Land Co., St. Charles, 1962—, St. Louis Med.-Dental Exchange, 1960—, Washington U. Orthodontic Study Group, 1963-75. Mem. adv. com. St. Charles Sch. Bd. Tech. Sch., 1967-70. Mem. Mo. Dist. Found. Luth. Ch. Served from pvt. 1st class to capt., AUS, 1943, 51-52. Fellow Am. Coll. Dentists; mem. Am., Mo. (bd. govs. 1968-71) dental assns., St. Louis Dental Soc., Am. Assn. Orthodontists, Midwest (historian 1969-73, pres. 1976), Mo., St. Louis (pres. 1963) socs. orthodontists, Am. Soc. Dentistry for Children (pres. Mo. unit 1946), Washington U. Alumni Assn. (pres. 1963), Psi Chi, Xi Psi Phi. Clubs: Clayton; Faculty Conference (St. Louis). Home: 15 Rio Vista St Charles MO 63301 Office: 225 S Meramec Clayton MO 63105

JONA, MARJORIE HELEN PUGH, social worker; b. Mansfield, Ohio, July 18, 1917; d. Walter C. and Hasel (Kennedy) Pugh; student Richland County Jr. Coll., 1934-35, Mansfield Bus. Coll., 1935-36; div. 1956; 1 son, Robert P. K. Clk., Reese Optical Co., Mansfield, 1936-43; sec. P & E. Tile Co., Los Angeles, 1953-54, Hamilton Realty, Mansfield, 1951-52, 55; sales rep. Mid-Ohio Realty, Mansfield, 1955-56; X-ray technologist Mansfield Gen. Hosp., 1956-57, registered X-ray technologist Madison Hosp., Mansfield, 1957-60; with Richland County Welfare Dept., 1960-69, social worker in intake dept. and food stamp dept., 1967-69, adminstrv. specialist, 1975-76, mem. adv. bd., 1969-74; probation officer domestic relations div. Richland County Ct. Common Pleas, 1969-74, Municipal Ct., Mansfield, 1976—. Treas., Malabar Music Parents Club, 1967-68; adv. bd. Richland County Welfare Dept. Mem. Am. Registry Radiol. Techologists. United Methodist. Mem. Order Eastern Star, Rebekah Lodge. Home: 207 S Mulbery St Mansfield OH 44903 Office: City Bldg 30 N Diamond St Mansfield OH 44902

JONAS, GLENN FRANKLIN, exec. search cons.; b. Door County, Wis., May 29, 1934; s. Fred Karl and Esther Cora (Honold) J.; B.M.E., U. Wis., 1961, B.B.A., 1963; m. Rita Marie Koss, June 8, 1963; children—Jory Lynn, Jamey Lea, Glenda Sue, Fredric. Prodn. mgr. indsl. controls div. Square D Co., Milw., 1963-69; materials mgr. and mfg. mgr., switchgear and control div. Allis Chalmers Corp., W. Allis, Wis., 1969-71; planning and control mgr. Johnson Controls Co., Milw., 1970-73; owner, chief exec. officer Jonas & Assos., Inc., Milw., 1973—; guest lectr. U. Wis.-Whitewater, 1973—. Mem. Brown Deer Sch. Bd., 1975—. Served with U.S. Army, 1953-55. Mem. Sales and Mktg. Execs. Milw. (v.p.-edn. 1977—), Met. Assn. Commerce, Pi Sigma Epsilon. Lutheran (past pres. ch. council). Club: Milw. Kiwanis. Home: 9173 N Alpine Ln Brown Deer WI 53223 Office: 3333 N Mayfair Rd Milwaukee WI 53222

JONAS, JIRI, chemistry, educator; b. Prague, Czechoslovakia, Apr. 1, 1932; s. Frantisek and Jirina Jonas; came to U.S., 1965, naturalized, 1972; B.Sc., Czechoslovak Acad. Sci., Prague, 1956, Ph.D., 1960; m. Ana Masiulis, June 1, 1968. Research asso. Czechoslovak Acad. Sci., 1960-65; vis. scientist U. Ill., Urbana, 1965-66, prof. chemistry, 1966—, asso. mem. Inst. Advanced Study, 1976-77. Alfred P. Sloan fellow, 1967-69; Guggenheim fellow, 1972-73; grantee NSF, Air Force Office Sci. Research, ERDA. Mem. Am. Chem. Soc., Am. Phys. Soc., AAAS, Sigma Xi, Phi Lambda Upsilon, Alpha Chi Sigma. Editorial bd. Jour. Magnetic Resonance. Contbr. articles to profl. jours. Home: 2202 Grange Circle Urbana IL 61801 Office: 166 Roger Adams Lab Univ Ill Urbana IL 61801

JONASSEN, GEORGE EINAR, dentist; b. Mpls., Jan. 18, 1914; s. Einar and Genie (Johnson) J.; D.D.S., U. Minn., 1937; m. Velma Erma Bietz, Oct. 5, 1940; children—Robert George, Diane Lynn (Mrs. Rolland Hubert Roers). Dental intern, Mpls. Gen. Hosp., 1937-38; individual practice gen. dentistry, Mpls., 1938-42, Mpls., 1946-58, Edina, Minn., 1958—. Active various capacities Boy Scouts Am., 1926—; a founder, bd. dirs. P.T.A.'s, Richfield. Del. to local and county convs. Republican party. Served with AUS, 1942-46. Recipient Scouters award, Silver Beaver Boy Scouts Am., 1960. Mem. Am., Minn., Southdale dental assns., Mpls. Dental Soc., Acad. Gen. Dentistry (state pres. 1973-74). Conglist. (various offices). Mason (32 deg., Shriner). Home: 6615 Morgan Ave S Minneapolis MN 55423 Office: 6545 France Ave S Edina MN 55435

JONCKHEERE, ALAN MATHEW, physicist; b. Howell, Mich., Feb. 12, 1947; s. August Peter and Elizabeth Gertrude (Nash) J.; B.S. (NSF fellow), Mich. State U., 1969; M.S., U. Wash., 1970, Ph.D., 1976; m. Barbara Jean Minter, Aug. 16, children—Jessica Susan, Laura Jean and Amanda Jean (twins). Instr. physics dept. U. Wash., Seattle, 1969-70, research asst., 1970-76; research asso., physics dept. Fermi Nat. Accelerator Lab., Batavia, Ill., 1976—; researcher elementary particle physics Stanford Linear Accelerator Center, Lawrence Berkeley Lab. (Calif.). Contbr. papers to physics publs. Home: 637 Church St Batavia IL 60510

JONES, A. CLIFFORD, state senator; b. St. Louis, Feb. 13, 1921; s. Wilbur B. and Irene (Clifford) J.; A.B., Princeton U., 1942; J.D., Washington U., St. Louis, 1948; children—A. Clifford, Irene, Wesley, Janet; m. 2d, Nan Thornton, Nov. 1974. City clk. Ladue (Mo.), 1948-50; mem. Mo. Ho. of Reps., Jefferson City, 1950-58, minority floor leader, 1956-58; mem. Mo. Senate, Jefferson City, 1964—, minority floor leader, 1968—; pres. Mo. Polaris Corp., Aluminum Truck Bodies, Inc.; sec.-treas. Hewitt-Lucas Body Co., Inc. Pres. Mo. Assn. for Social Welfare, 1953-54; mem. agy. relations council United Fund, St. Louis, 1950—; bd. dirs. Mo. Mental Health Assn., St. Louis Health and Welfare Council, 1956-59; trustee St. Louis Country Day Sch., 1948-50. Served with USNR, 1942-46; ETO, PTO. Recipient award Jaycees of St. Louis, 1952, Globe Democrat award for pub. service, 1958, 65, 69. Mem. Mo., St. Louis (Bicentennial award) bar assns., Am. Legion, John Marshall Club. Republican. Congregationalist. Clubs: Masons (32 deg.), Shriners, Rotary. Home: 7 Willow Hill Ladue MO 63124 Office: State Capitol Bldg Jefferson City MO 65101

JONES, ALAN PORTER, JR., meat packing co. exec.; b. Milw., Feb. 27, 1925; s. Alan Porter and Eleanor Pratt (Bright) J.; B.A., Harvard U., 1948, M.B.A., 1950; m. Jean E. Drummond, Sept. 12, 1953; children—Richard, Susan, Cynthia, Alexandra. With Jones Dairy Farm, Ft. Atkinson, Wis., 1950—, asst. treas., 1953-61, treas., 1961-74, v.p. and treas., 1974—, also dir.; dir. Bank Ft. Atkinson, PDQ Corp. Bd. dirs. Dwight Foster Pub. Library; mem. Fort Atkinson Sch. Bd., 1968-69; trustee Ripon (Wis.) Coll. Served with inf. U.S. Army, 1943-45. Decorated Bronze Star, Combat Inf. badge. Mem. Newcomen Soc. Republican. Congregationalist. Home: 433 Adams St Fort Atkinson WI 53538 Office: Jones Dairy Farm Fort Atkinson WI 53538

JONES, ANABEL RATCLIFF, anesthesiologist; b. Lafayette, Ind., Sept. 6, 1933; d. Frank William and Mary Rovene (Holt) Ratcliff; A.B., Ind. U., 1955, M.D., 1959; m. Wiley A. Jones, Oct. 4, 1975; 1 son by previous marriage, Warren Lee. Intern, Meth. Hosp., Indpls., 1959-60; resident anesthesiology Ind. U. Med. Center, Indpls., 1960-62; staff anesthesiologist VA Hosp., Indpls., 1962-63; practice medicine, specializing in anesthesiology, Lafayette, 1963—; mem. staff St. Elizabeth Hosp., Home Hosp., Purdue U. Hosp.; instr. Ind. U. Med. Center, Indpls., 1962—. Piano accompanist civic chorus, also combined civic vocal groups; mem. governing bd. Lafayette Symphony Orch., 1971—. Diplomate Am. Bd. Anesthesiology. Mem. Am. Soc. Anesthesiologists, Internat. Anesthesia Research Soc., Pan Am. Surg. Assn., Ind. Med. Assn., Ind. Soc. Anesthesiologists, AMA, Kappa Kappa Kappa, Delta Delta Delta. Methodist. Home: 3301 Cedar Ln Lafayette IN 47905 Office: Life Bldg Lafayette IN 47901

JONES, ANN, educator; b. Pittsburg, Kans., Sept. 9, 1936; d. Russell Robert and Helen Nadine (Schick) Winterbotham; B.A., Baldwin Wallace Coll., 1961; M.Ed., Kent State U., 1976, postgrad., 1976—; m. Robert Ewing Jones, June 13, 1959; children—Russell, Becky, Gary. Tchr. mentally retarded Div. Child Welfare Cuyahoga County (Ohio), 1959-61; career counselor Baldwin Wallace Coll., Berea, Ohio, 1976-77; instr. Lorain County (Ohio) Community Coll., Elyria, 1976—. Mem. Planning Commn. City of Berea; campaign coordinator Democratic Party, Berea, 1975. Mem. Am. Personnel and Guidance Assn., Cleve. Area League Nursing, League Women Voters, Berea Hist. Soc. (mus. chmn.). Home: 612 Barrett Rd Berea OH 44017

JONES, ANNE ATKINS, pub. relations exec.; b. Dayton, Aug. 23, 1951; d. Harold Ray and Barbara Ann (Hedges) J.; Asso. Fine Arts, Sullins Coll., 1971; B.A., U. R.I., 1973; postgrad. Brown U., 1973. Account exec. Horton Church & Goff, Inc., advt., Providence, 1973-74; account exec., pub. service coordinator Sta. WGNG, Providence, 1974-75; dir. pub. relations Intermedia, Inc., adv., Cin., 1975-76; pres. Alias Smith & Jones, Inc., pub. relations, Cin., 1976—; lectr. U. Cin., Xavier U. Festival coordinator Program for Cin.; pub. relations vol. Juvenile Diabetic Found., 1975-76. Recipient Vol. award Hamilton County Juvenile Ct., 1977; Best Research Story daily Am. Heart Assn., 1977, Best Story Ohio award, 1977. Mem. Pub. Relations Soc. Am. (chmn.), Cin. Ad 11 Club (chmn. edn.), Cin. C. of C., Cin. Ad Club, Women in Communications, Publicity Club N.Y. Home and Office: 2356 Park Ave Cincinnati OH 45206

JONES, BRAXTON POLLARD, JR., car wash franchise co. exec.; b. Kansas City, Mo., May 26, 1939; s. Braxton Pollard and Jessie Alice J.; A.B., Rockhurst Coll., 1964, B.S. in Bus. Adminstrn., 1967; m. Sara E. Cain, Dec. 23, 1974; children by previous marriage—Braxton Pollard, Brian Christopher. Accounting mgr. pump div. Colt Industries, Inc., 1959-67; v.p. Keystone Chem., Inc., North Kansas City, Mo. 1967-73; pres., dir. Robo Wash, Inc., Kansas City, Mo., 1973—. Served with AUS, 1957-58. Mem. Am. Mgmt. Assn., Nat. Assn. Accountants, Adminstrv. Mgmt. Assn., Personnel Mgmt. Assn. Mem. Christian Ch. Club: Kansas City Ski. Home: Rural Route 2 Box 29D Louisburg KS 66053 Office: 2330 Burlington North Kansas City MO 64116

JONES, BYRON MAURICE, mining machine co. exec.; b. Indpls., Sept. 5, 1927; s. Floyd H. and Eva Mae J.; B.E.E., Purdue U., 1953; M.E.E., Marquette U., 1974; m. Florence B. Domanski, Oct. 9, 1948; children—Karen, Mark, Douglas. Research engr. Reliance Electric Co., Cleve., 1953-57; chief control engr. Louis Allis Co., Milw., 1957-68; chief engr. Pillar Corp., Milw., 1968-70, Bucyrus-Erie Co., Milw., 1970—. Served with U.S. Navy, 1945-48. Duncan Meter Co. fellow, 1952-53; registered profl. engr., Wis. Mem. IEEE, Tau Beta Pi, Eta Kappa Nu. Patentee in field. Home: 2100 S 148th St New Berlin WI 53151 Office: 1100 Milwaukee Ave South Milwaukee WI 53172

JONES, C. W., banker; b. Murdock, Kans., Oct. 20, 1921; s. Claude C. and Ina E. (Silvius) J.; student Park Coll.; m. H. Florine Johnson, Sept. 15, 1946; children—Marcia (Mrs. Blake W. Foutes), Mark A., Jeffrey L. Pres., Jones Investment Corp., Independence, Mo., 1953—; with Chrisman-Sawyer Bank, Independence, 1962—. Mem. Home Builders Assn., Am. Bankers Assn., Independence C. of C. Baptist. Club: Indian Hills Country. Office: 201 W Lexington St Independence MO 64051

JONES, CHARLES LEWIS, assn. exec.; b. Springfield, Mo., May 12, 1928; s. Charles Archibald and Marie Ethel (Rook) J.; B.A. in English and Journalism, Drury Coll., Springfield, 1954; postgrad. edn. Adelphi U., 1958-62; m. Jeanette Barnett, July 4, 1954; children—Dana Marie, Craig Alan, Angela Sue. Instr. English, drama, speech and journalism high schs., Ill., Mo., N.Y., 1954-68; exec. dir. Mo. Optometric Assn., Jefferson City, 1968-70; exec. v.p. Mo. Hotel and Motel Assn., Jefferson City, 1970—. Eastern N.Y. dir. Nat. Thespian Soc., 1958-64; editor Best of Broadway column Dramatics mag., 1959-64, pres. Little Theatre Jefferson City, 1974. Served with USAAF, 1946-49. Named Hon. citizen of Cork, Ireland, 1974. Mem. Am., Mo. socs. assn. execs., Internat. Soc. Hotel Assn. Execs. (1st v.p. 1978), Ark.-Mo.-Kans.-Okla. Lodging Assn. (sec.-treas. 1974-75), Am. Hotel and Motel Assn. (dir. 1978), Mo. Travel Council (treas. 1977). Home: Route 2 Renns Lake Rd Jefferson City MO 65101 Office: 1800 Southwest Blvd Jefferson City MO 65101

JONES, CHARLES ROBERT, filtration equipment mfg. co. exec.; b. Indpls., Jan. 27, 1940; s. Elmer Fremont and Elizabeth Cecilia (Turner) J.; B.S.M.E., Purdue U., 1963, co-op certificate (Co-op scholar), 1963; m. Dianne Lee Nahmias, Oct. 1, 1965; children—Lisa Renee, Heather Nicole. Co-op student and scholar Peerless Pump Co. Food Machinery Corp., Indpls., 1958-63, engr., 1963-66; asso. engr. Westinghouse Bettis Atomic Power Lab., West Mifflin, Pa., 1966-68, engr., 1968-69; sr. engr. Chambers Co., Shelbyville, Ind., 1969-70, nuclear program mgr., 1971-72; product design supr. Carborundum Filters div. Carborundum Co., Lebanon, Ind., 1972-75, mgr. application engring., 1975—. Served to 1st lt. U.S. Army, 1963-69. Registered profl. engr., Ind. Mem. Am. Nuclear Soc. Home: 923 W 77th N Dr Indianapolis IN 46260 Office: State RD 32 W Lebanon IN 46052

JONES, CLARA ARAMINTA STANTON (MRS. ALBERT D. JONES), librarian; b. St. Louis, May 14, 1913; d. Ralph Herbert and Etta (James) Stanton; student Milw. State Tchrs. Coll., 1929-30; A.B., Spelman Coll., Atlanta, 1934; A.B. in L.S., U. Mich., 1938; D.H.L. (hon.), Shaw Coll., 1975, N.C. Central U., 1976; LL.D., Ball State U., 1976; m. Albert D. Jones, June 25, 1938; children—Stanton William, Vinetta Claire (Mrs. Wesley F. Johnson, Jr.), Kenneth Albert. Asst. librarian Dillard U. Library, New Orleans, 1938-39; library sci. instr. So. U., Baton Rouge, La. summer, 1940, asst. librarian; 1940-41; with Detroit Pub. Library, 1944—, successively youth librarian, adult librarian, chief div., 1951-63 chief dept., 1963-68, neighborhood cons., 1968-70, dir., 1970—. Dir. City Nat. Bank, 1975—. Lectr. and cons. Detroit Commn. on Human Relations, 1945-50. Trustee New Detroit, Inc., 1971—; bd. advisers Wayne State U. Press, 1971—, Western Mich. U. Library Sch., United Found., 1975—. Mem. N.A.A.C.P., A.L.A. (pres. 1976-77), Mich. Library Assn., Women's Internat. League for Peace and Freedom, Assn. for Study of Afro-Am. Life and History, Am. Civil Liberties Union, Your Heritage House. Home: 16631 Princeton Ave Detroit MI 48221 Office: 5201 Woodward Ave Detroit MI 48202

JONES, DAVID FRANCIS, sch. counselor; b. Clinton, Ind., Dec. 17, 1934; s. Richard F. and Gladys J. (Gossett) J.; B.S., Manchester Coll., 1958; M.S., Ind. U., 1966; postgrad. U. Mich., 1971-72, Purdue U., 1975-76; m. Dorothy Faith Brown, Feb. 3, 1961; children—Mark, Craig Alan, Beth Anne, Vera Jean. Tchr., Hobart Twp. (Ind.) Elementary Schs., 1958-59, music tchr., 1959-66; elementary sch. counselor Michigan City (Ind.) Area Schs., 1966-67, Duneland Sch. Corp., Chesterton, Ind., 1967—; guest lectr. Purdue U., 1976-77; cons. Hebrew Day Schs., Hammond, Ind., 1976-77; coordinator, dir. workshops in field. Choir dir. Liberty Bible Ch., 1st Christian Ch.; tenor soloist various area chs. Gen. Electric fellow Ind. U., summer 9175; Ind. Council Social Studies fellow, 1975. Mem. Am., Ind., N.W. personnel and guidance assns. Mem. Christian Ch. Home: Rural Route 1 Box 429 Dickerson Rd Chesterton IN 46304 Office: Yost Sch 100 Beam St Chesterton IN 46304

JONES, DAVID HAMILTON, electronics engr.; b. Yonkers, N.Y., Aug. 18, 1939; s. David Henry and Mildred Anne (Lesnick) J.; Asso. electronics engr., Westchester Community Coll., 1961; certificates in valve engring., digital and process control, computer programming and systems analyst, tech. writing; student Bridgeport U., 1967-68. Systems evaluator, tech. report writer Gemini Mission Control Center, Cape Canaveral, Fla., 1961-62, Houston (Tex.) Manned Spacecraft Center, 1962-63; communications system designer Collins Radio Co., Cedar Rapids, Iowa, 1963-65; designer electronic support systems for first nuclear aircraft carrier Enterprise, Renwar, Inc., N.Y.C., 1959-61; writer tech. manuals and instructional programs for Polaris missile (for Gen. Electric Co.) Miles-Samuelson, Inc., N.Y.C., 1961; reliability engr. Sundstrand Machine Tool Co., Belvidere, Ill., 1973; cons. inter-disciplinary electronics engr., Chgo., 1970—. Rep. State Central Com. of Libertarian Party of Ill., 1976-77. Recipient various awards U.S. Navy Polaris Missile Program, 1961, U.S. Army Pershing Missile Program, 1961, U.S. Air Force Hustler Bomber, 1962; registered profl. engr., N.Y. Mem. Am. Ordnance Assn., Armed Forces Communications and Electronics Assn., Am. Security Council, Air Force Aux., C.A.P., Air Force Assn., Am. Radio Relay League, N.W. Chgo. Libertarian Club, Aircraft Owners and Pilots Assn., Liverpool Motor Club. Contbr. articles on electronics to various trade mags. Home and Office: 1609 N Kilbourn Ave Chicago IL 60639 also Mohawk Motor Inn 1701 Russell St Baltimore MD 21230

JONES, DEBORAH KAY, counselor; b. Terre Haute, Ind., July 27, 1948; d. John Richard and Dolly Dimples (Wilkinson) Jones; stepmother Lorene June (Potts) Jones; B.S., Ind. State U., Terre Haute, 1970; M.S., Ind. U., 1974, postgrad., 1976—. Tchr. music Seeger High Sch., West Lebanon, Ind., 1970-73; freshman counselor Seymour (Ind.) High Sch., 1974—; pvt. tchr. music, as trumpet lessons, 1974—. Asst. dir. Seymour Community Band, 1976—. Mem. Am. Personnel and Guidance Assn., Am. Sch. Counselors Assn., NEA, Ind. Tchrs. Assn., Ind. Juvenile Justice Task Force, Am. Waterski Assn. Club: Elks. Home: 7605 Fawn Ct Columbus IN 47201

JONES, DON L., artist, art therapist; b. Towanda, Pa., Mar. 15, 1923; s. Earl William and Ethel Leona (Peet) J.; student Marietta Coll., So. Methodist U., St. Paul Sch. Theology, Kansas City; m. Eleanor G. Illston, Dec. 24, 1942; children—David Morgan, Amy Leigh, Evan William, Anne Lynne Jones Bennett, Matthew Donald, Peter Whitney. Ordained to ministry Methodist Ch.; pastor Rossville (Kans.) United Meth. Ch., 1949-65; creative arts supr., dir. adjunctive therapy C.F. Menninger Meml. Hosp., Topeka, 1951-67; dir. adjunctive therapy Harding Hosp., Worthington, Ohio, 1967—; adj. prof. art Capital U., Columbus, Ohio, 1976—, Wright State U., Dayton, Ohio, 1976—; executed murals in pub. bldgs. in Rossville; cons. Ohio Dept. Mental Health and Retardation, Ohio Youth Commn., Ohio Commn. on Aging, Ohio Dept. Health, Hosp. Audiences, Inc., Rockefeller Found. Recipient Outstanding Achievement award Harding Hosp. Mem. Am. (life mem., co-founder, pres. 1976-77), Buckeye (co-founder, pres. 1973-74) art therapy assns., Nat. Assn. Activities Therapy and Rehab. Programs Dirs. Democrat. Clubs: Masons; Order Eastern Star. Mem. editorial bd. Internat. Jour. of Art Psychotherapy. Contbr. articles to profl. jours. Home: 823 Franklin Ct Worthington OH 43085 Office: 445 E Granville Rd Worthington OH 43085

JONES, EDGAR RAUM, tax and bus. cons.; b. St. Elmo, Ill., Apr. 13, 1911; s. Curran Newby and Mae M. (Jones) J.; grad. high sch.; IRS spl. courses; m. Florence Hannah Drake, Oct. 20, 1935; children—Joyce Jones Schiska, Norma Elaine. Profl. musician, 1930-39; agt. IRS, 1940-62; pvt. practice accounting and tax cons., Vandalia, Ill., 1962—. Recipient Albert Gallatin award Treasury Dept., 1963. Mem. Nat. Soc. Pub. Accountants, Ind. Accountants Assn. Ill., So. Ill. Sr. Golfers Assn. (dir.). Methodist. Clubs: Moose, Modern Woodman of World, Vandalia Country and Golf (pres. 1954-56, 62-64); St. Elmo Golf. Home: 1024 W Taylor St Vandalia IL 62471 Office: Farmers & Mchts Bank Bldg Vandalia IL 62471

JONES, EDSEL, clergyman; b. Toledo, June 17, 1921; s. Walk James and Ida Florence (Slater) J.; B.R.E., Central Bible Inst., Springfield, Mo., 1951; m. Elsie May Cline, June 9, 1950; children—Janice Marie Jones Joven, Rebecca Diane Jones Farris, Richard Edsel. Ordained to ministry Assembly of God Ch., 1955; pastor Bethel Assembly of God Ch., Mt. Airy, N.C., 1952-57; pastor to deaf Abundant Life Meml., Indpls., 1958-67, Berea Temple, St. Louis, 1967—; tchr. sign lang. to hearing people, 1967—. Served with AUS, 1942-45; ETO. Mem. Registered Interpreters for Deaf (pres. St. Louis chpt.). Home: 3757 Potomac St Saint Louis MO 63118

JONES, EDWARD HENRY, JR., dermatologist; b. Youngstown, Ohio, Sept. 6, 1914; s. Edward Henry and Lulu Adele (Potts) J.; A.B., Western Res. U., 1937; M.D., Washington U., St. Louis, 1942; m. Ruth Virginia Jensen, Feb. 21, 1948; children—Nancy Lou, Keith Powell, Douglas Edward, Ann Mason. Intern, Union Meml. Hosp., Balt., 1942-43, asst. resident in medicine, 1946-47, asst. resident to resident in dermatology Cleve. City Hosp., 1947-50; demonstrator in dermatology Western Res. U., 1948-50; practice medicine specializing in dermatology, Youngstown, 1950—; cons. dermatology Youngstown Hosp. Assn., 1952-76. Served with USN, 1943-46. Decorated Purple Heart; diplomate Am. Bd. Dermatology. Mem. AMA, Ohio State Med. Assn., Mahoning County Med. Soc., Central States, Cleve. dermatol. socs., Am. Acad. Dermatology, Internat. Soc. Tropical Dermatology. Republican. Presbyterian. Club: Masons. Home: 3625 Sampson Rd Youngstown OH 44505 Office: 77 E Midlothian Blvd Youngstown OH 44507

JONES, ELIZABETH BROWN, author, editor; b. Kansas City, Mo., Sept. 27, 1907; d. James Riley and Agnes Julia (Gammage) Brown; student U. Mo.; m. C. Hartley Jones, June 4, 1929; children—Elizabeth Ann, Sara Denise, David Hartley, Phyllis Elaine. Sec., Riley Brown Paint Co., Knasas City, Mo., from 1927, also office mgr.; free lance writer, 1939—; editor Ch. of the Nazarene, Kansas City, Mo., 1962—; cons. in curriculum, 1977—; author of twenty books including: When You Need a Bible Story, 1966, Teaching Primaries Today, 1974, Because God Made Me, 1975, The Story of

God's Love, 1976, Stories of Jesus, 1977; contbr. over 500 poems and short stories for children. Mem. Ch. of the Nazarene. Office: 6401 Paseo Kansas City MO 64131

JONES, ERNEST LEWIS, data systems dir.; b. Winona, W.Va., June 18, 1927; s. Lewis P. and Neva (Goode) J.; student Ohio State U., 1944-45; B.A., Marshall U., 1952, M.A., 1952; m. Patricia Ann O'Connor, Nov. 18, 1950; children—Barbara Carole, Deborah Ann, Sandra Lee. Vets. coordinator, registrar's office Marshall U., 1953, asst. registrar, 1953-55; supr. data processing W.Va. U., Morgantown, 1955-63, asst. dir. Computer Center, 1963-66, dir., 1966-68; dir. Data Systems and Services Ind. U., 1968—, mgr. univ. project GUIDE Internat.; pres. State U. Data Processing Assn., 1970—; cons. Acad. Ednl. Devel.; v.p. Coll. and U. Systems Exchange, 1965, pres., 1966, program com., 1976; chmn. Coll. and U. Machine Records Conf., 1979, bd. dirs., 1977—; guest speaker IBM Exec. Class, 1965-66; mem. survey team A study of Ednl. Statistics in W.Va., W.Va. Bd. Edn., 1960; mem. Faculty Coll. Bus. Mgrs. Inst., U. Ky., 1975. Bd. dirs. CAUSE, 1970-71, project mgr., 1972-73. Served with USAF, 1945-48. Mem. W.Va. Assn. Collegiate Registrars and Admissions Officers (pres.), Assn. Ednl. Data Systems (asso. editor jour.), Assn. Computing Machinery, Sigma Phi Epsilon. Democrat. Club: Morgantown Civitan (past sec.). Contbr. articles to profl. jours. and procs. Home: 4717 E Heritage Woods Rd Bloomington IN 47401 Office: Data Systems and Services 1000 E 17th St Bloomington IN 47401

JONES, ERNEST OLIN, educator, radiation physicist; b. Atlanta, Feb. 1, 1923; s. Ernest and Annie Jane (Bryan) J.; A.B., Emory U., 1948, M.S. (Research Corp. fellow), 1949; M.S., U.S. Naval Postgrad. Sch., 1959; Ph.D., N.C. State U., 1964; m. Dorothy Irene Berg, May 20, 1946; children—Michael Bruce, Jacquelyn Ann (Mrs. Robert H. Hanks). Commd. 2d. lt. U.S. Army, 1950, advanced through grades to lt. col., 1965, dep. dir. div. nuclear medicine WRAIR, 1964-67, dir. div. biometrics, 1967-68; ret., 1968; asso. prof. radiology U. Nebr., Omaha, 1968-72, prof., 1972—. Cons. in field. Decorated Legion of Merit. Diplomate radiol. physics Am. Bd. Radiology, 1975. Mem. Am. Nuclear Soc., Am. Assn. Phys. Medicine (pres. Mo. River Valley chpt. 1972-73), Midlands Soc. Therapeutic Radiologists, Nebr. State Radiol. Soc., Assn. Mil. Surgeons, Am. Coll. Nuclear Physicians, Am. Coll. Radiology. Research minority carrier lifetimes in silicon radiation detectors 1961-64, dosimetry of neutrons in modified research reactor, 1964-67. Home: 12823 Jones St Omaha NE 68154

JONES, FRANK WARREN, township ofcl.; b. LaHarpe, Kans., Dec. 4, 1922; s. Jason Wilson and Bertha (Filson) J.; student Emporia State Coll., 1939-41; B.S. in Civil Engring., Kans. State U., 1943; M.S., U.S. Naval Postgrad. Sch., 1963; m. Mary Catherine Randell, July 23, 1944 (div. Feb. 1967); children—Terry Lee, Dennis Warren, Shirley Kaye, Steven Allen, Connie Linn, Kenneth Stanley, Karl Curtis; m. 2d, Martha Lee Albritton Taylor, Nov. 28, 1969. Engring. draftsman N.Am. Aviation, Inc., Kansas City, 1943-44; civil engr. div. water resources Kans. Dept. Agr., 1946; resident engr. Kan. Hwy. Comm., Hutchinson, 1946-51; now mgr. Saginaw Twp., Mich.; dir. Consol. Savs. & Loan Assn., United Mortgage Co. Served from ensign to lt. (j.g.) USN, 1944-45, recalled 1951, advanced through grades to comdr., 1963, pub. works officer Naval Air Engring Center, Phila., 1965-70. Registered profl. engr., Kans., Colo. Mem. Navy League U.S., Ret. Officers Assn., Fleet Res. Assn., Assn. Navy Civil Engr. Corps Officers, V.F.W. Baptist. Clubs: Rotary Internat., Masons. Home: 5335 Nottingham Dr N Saginaw MI 48603 Office: 4980 Shattuck Rd Saginaw MI 48603

JONES, FREDERICK GOODWIN, metall. engr.; b. Utica, N.Y., Nov. 6, 1935; s. Frederick Goodwin and Ethel Grace (Buell) J.; B.Metall. Engring., Cornell U., 1959; M.S., U. Mich., 1969, Ph.D., 1969; m. Joan Margaret Ellis, June 20, 1959; children—Peggy Ellis, Gwendolyn Anne, Cynthia Joan. Technologist, Oriskany Malleable Iron Co., Inc. (N.Y.), 1957; asst. research metallurgist Spl. Metals, Inc., New Hartford, N.Y., 1958; staff metallurgist Applied Research Lab., Crucible Steel Co. Am., Syracuse, N.Y., 1959-62, Central Research Lab., Pitts., 1962-65; research asst., teaching fellow dept. metallurgy and materials sci. U. Mich., Ann Arbor, 1965-69; pvt. cons. in metall. and magnetic problems, Ann Arbor, 1966-69; sr. devel. engr., magnetic materials bus. sect. Gen. Electric Co., Edmore, Mich., 1969-73; sr. devel. engr. Hitachi Magnetics Corp., Edmore, 1973—. Mem. Citizens' Adv. Com., Alma (Mich.) Sch. Bd., 1972. Bd. dirs., treas. Hoogerland Meml. Workshop, Inc., 1970-73; bd. dirs. Gratiot County United Fund, 1972. NASA trainee, 1967-68, NSF grantee, 1965-69. Mem. Am. Inst. Mining, Metall. and Petroleum Engrs., Am. Foundrymen's Soc., I.E.E.E., N.Y. Acad. Scis., Sigma Xi, Sigma Phi Epsilon, Phi Kappa Phi. Mason (32 deg., Shriner). Methodist. Home: 820 Wright Ave Alma MI 48801 Office: Neff Rd Edmore MI 48829

JONES, GEORGE OVER, ins. co. exec.; b. Toronto, Ont., Can., Aug. 12, 1908; s. Reginald Melville and Muriel Eleanor (Over) J.; student U. Ottawa, 1944-45; m. Agnes Lillian Laderoute, Oct. 7, 1944; 1 dau., Alison M. Jones Watson. With Royal Ins. Co. Ltd. Liverpool, Toronto, 1936-1949; Ont. agy. supr. Nat. Fire Ins. Co. of Hartford, Toronto, 1949-50, supt. for B.C. and Alta., 1950-53; casualty supt. for Can., exec. asst. Legal & Gen. Assurance Soc. Ltd., London, Eng., 1954-55, asst. mgr., 1956; casualty supt. for Can., Am. Fore Ins. Group, Montreal, Que., 1956-58; ins. agt., Sault Ste. Marie, Ont., 1958-62; owner, propr. George O. Jones, Ins., Sault Ste. Marie, 1962—. Served with RCAF, 1943-45. Mem. Composers, Authors and Pubs. Assn. Can. Home and Office: PO Box 986 Sault Ste Marie ON P6A 5N5 Canada

JONES, HAROLD VICTOR, JR., lawyer; b. Franklin, Ind., Jan. 9, 1939; s. Harold V. and Beulah F. (Turner) J.; B.S. in Indsl. Engring., Purdue U., 1961; J.D., Ind. U., 1965; m. Judith Records, Aug. 20, 1960; children—Trent Records, Jennifer. Sales engr. Inland Container Corp., Indpls., 1961-65; admitted to Ind. bar, 1965, U.S. Ct. Appeals, 1973, U.S. Supreme Ct. bar, 1976; asso. firm Trask, Jenkins & Hanley, Indpls., 1965; partner Thompson, Jones, DeClue & Patterson, Columbus, Ind., 1965—. Mem. Bartholomew County Library Assn., 1966-69, pres., 1969; fund raiser United Fund Bartholomew County, 1967-72; chmn. Lugar fund raising dinner, 1972; active in corporate fund raising March of Dimes, 1971, 72; mem. law post adv. com. Hoosier Hills council Explorers, Boy Scouts Am., 1971, mem. dist. exploring com., 1971-72; pres. Bartholomew County Hosp. Found., 1970-71; mem. fin. com. Republican Com. Bartholomew County, 1968; bd. dirs. Distinguished Visitors Services, 1974-77. Mem. Ind., Bartholomew County bar assns., Ind. Trial Lawyers Assn., Columbus C. of C. (chmn. local govt. com.), Phi Delta Phi, Sigma Alpha Epsilon. Mem. Christian Ch. (deacon 1970). Club: Harrison Lake Country (Columbus). Home: 220 19th St Columbus IN 47201 Office: 207 Washington St Columbus IN 47201

JONES, HOWARD VALLANCE, JR., historian; b. Chgo., Apr. 6, 1922; s. Howard Vallance and Frances Ninetta (Edmondson) J.; A.B., Harvard Coll., 1946, A.M., 1947, Ph.D., 1950; m. Ellen Margaret Aakvik, Apr. 21, 1956; children—Catherine Ellen, Howard Vallance III. Asst. prof. history U. N.H., Durham, 1950-53; asst. prof. history U. No. Iowa, Cedar Falls, 1954-56, asso. prof., 1956-63, prof., 1963—. Exec. sec. Uni-Civic Arts Assn., 1975—; music adv. panel Iowa Arts Council, 1977—. Served with U.S. Army, 1942-45. Mem. Assn. Coll. and Community Arts Adminstrs. (pres. 1970-72, Fannie Taylor award 1976), Am. Hist. Assn., Conf. Brit. Studies, Assn. Ancient Historians, Phi Beta Kappa, Pi Gamma Mu. Republican. Episcopalian. Rotarian. Contbr. articles on history, concert mgmt. to profl. publs. Home: 18 Winter Ridge Rd Cedar Falls IA 50613

JONES, (JAMES) WILLARD, food oils co. exec.; b. Ider, Ala., Apr. 5, 1930; s. Lester Lemuel and Ruby (Patterson) J.; student U. Chattanooga, 1955-65; m. Barbara J. Cooper, Apr. 12, 1952; children—Debra Kay, James Willard. Indsl. engr., asst. personnel mgr. Lookout Oil Refining Co., Chattanooga, 1961-65; indsl. engr. food oils div. Armour Food Oils, Chgo., 1965-66; dist. indsl. engr. J.E. Decker & Sons, Dallas, 1966-67; mgr., indsl. engr. and employee relations, asst. plant supt. Capital City Products, Columbus, Ohio, 1967-71; with PVO Internat. Inc., various locations, 1971—, pres., gen. mgr. Central and Eastern div., Boonton, Mo., 1974-75, v.p., gen. mgr. Central div., St. Louis, 1975—. Vice pres. Northwest Civic Orgn., Columbus, 1969-71. Served with AUS, 1951-53. Baptist. Home: 5267 Brass Lantern Pl St Louis MO 63128 Office: 3400 Wharf St N St Louis MO 63147

JONES, JERALD FRANKLIN, broadcasting co. exec.; b. Jackson, Minn., Feb. 2, 1934; s. Byron Spencer and Anna Laura J.; student Internat. Corr. Schs., 1957; m. Betty Darlene Hoffman, Feb. 5, 1956; children—Craig, Dennis, Julie. Transmitter, studio engr. KGLO TV, Mason City, Iowa, 1955-69; asst. chief engr. KAAL-TV, Austin, Minn., 1969-70, chief engr., 1970-71, v.p. engring., 1972—. Mem. on site evaluation group Minn. Vocat. Sch. High Sch. Occupational Adv. Com., Austin; chmn. mem. adv. bd. for electronics Austin Vocat. Tech. Inst. Certified sr. broadcast engr. Mem. Soc. Broadcast Engrs., Soc. Motion Picture and TV Engrs., Popular Rotorcraft Assn., S.E. Minn. Amateur Computer Soc. Home: 306 3d Ave SW Austin MN 55912 Office: 1701 10th Pl NE Austin MN 55912

JONES, JOHN DAVID, cons. engr.; b. Nanty Glo, Pa., Oct. 4, 1923; s. Joseph Louis and Jennie Gertrude (Beutman) J.; student U. Mich., 1949-50; B.S. in Civil Engring., U. Akron, 1952; m. Rose Capriola, Dec. 24, 1942; children—James Steven, Lynn Marie, Stephanie Ann. Field engr. AT & T, Cin., 1952-53, city of Akron, 1953-55, Firestone Tire and Rubber Co., Akron, 1955-58, individual practice cons. engring., Cuyahoga Falls, Ohio, 1958—; pres. John David Jones and Assos., Inc., 1970—. Bd. dirs. Green Cross Gen. Hosp.; elder United Presbyn. Ch. Trustee Cuyahoga Valley Christian Acad. Served with U.S. Army, 1942-45. Decorated Bronze Star medal, Purple Heart with oak leaf cluster. Registered profl. surveyor, Ohio, Pa. Mem. ASCE, Nat. Soc. Profl. Engrs., Am. Congress on Surveying and Mapping, Profl. Engrs. Ohio, cons. engrs. Ohio (v.p.), Water Pollution Control Fedn., Am. Water Works Assn., Phi Sigma Tau, Tau Beta Pi. Mason (32 deg.), Lion. Club: University (Akron). Home: 3192 Hudson Dr Cuyahoga Falls OH 44221 Office: 2162 Front St Cuyahoga Falls OH 44221

JONES, JOHN SILLS, lawyer; b. Evanston, Ill., Dec. 4, 1909; s. Carroll Henry and Helen (Weeks) J.; A.B., Harvard U., 1931, LL.B., 1935; postgrad. U. Munich, 1931-32; m. Ilka Van Leight, Mar. 25, 1948. Admitted to Ill. bar, 1936; with law dept. Chgo. Rapid Transit Co., 1936-42; asso. firm Bell, Boyd & Marshall, 1942-46, William C. Boyden, 1946-57; mem. firm Davis Boyden, Jones & Baer, 1957-70, Davis, Jones & Baer, 1970—. Mem. Am. (mem. com. divorce laws), Ill. (exec. com. family law sect. 1960), Ill. State, Chgo. (co-vice chmn. joint com. codification Ill. family law) bar assns., Am. Acad. Matrimonial Lawyers (gov. v.p., bd. examiners). Home: Glen View Club Golf IL 60029 Office: 120 S LaSalle St Chicago IL 60603

JONES, KENSINGER, advt. agy. exec.; b. St. Louis, Oct. 18, 1919; s. Walter C. and Anna Lee (Kensinger) J.; student Washington U., St. Louis, 1938-39; m. Alice May Guseman, Oct. 7, 1944; children—Jeffrey Kensinger, Janice Ann (Mrs. Jeffrey O. Geary). Exec. v.p., creative dir. Campbell Ewald, Detroit, 1960-68; sr. v.p., exec. creative dir. Leo Burnett, Inc., Detroit, 1968-70, Chgo., 1970-73, regional creative dir., Sydney, Australia, 1973-75, Singapore, 1975—. Screen writer N.Am. Film Acad., Inc. Mem. nat. pub. relations com. Boy Scouts Am., 1965-78; chmn. Pub. Service Communications council, Chgo., 1972-73. Bd. dirs. World Med. Relief, 1960—; chmn. Barry County Econ. Devel. Com.; vice-chmn. Barry County Planning and Zoning Commn., Parks and Recreation Commn.; grants coordinator Barry County, 1977—. Served to sgt. inf. AUS, 1940-45; PTO. Recipient Silver Beaver award Boy Scouts Am., 1968. Clubs: Recess (Detroit); Tavern (Chgo.); author: Enter Singapore, 1975. Contbr. articles to trade jours. Home: 425 Pritchardville Rd Hastings MI 49058

JONES, LARRY DAVID, coll. adminstr.; b. Medina, N.Y., May 17, 1949; s. George William and Ruth Arlene (Nudd) J.; B. Indsl. Engring., Gen. Motors Inst., 1972; M.Ed., Kent State U., 1974. Coop. engr. Harrison Radiator div. Gen. Motors Corp., Lockport, N.Y., 1967-71, research asst., 1972, service coordinator, 1972-73, shipping supr. Packard Electric div., Warren, Ohio, 1973-74; coordinator admissions and counseling Kent State U., Warren, 1974-77, dir. student life, 1977—. Mem. Am. Assn. for Higher Edn., Am. Coll. Personnel Assn., Am. Personnel and Guidance Assn., Nat. Assn. Student Personnel Adminstrs., Ohio Two-Year Coll. Placement Assn., Theta Xi. Democrat. Methodist. Contbr. article to profl. jour. Home: 609 Ridge Rd Apt 102 Newton Falls OH 44444 Office: 4314 Mahoning Ave NW Warren OH 44483

JONES, LARRY LEE, test engr.; b. Niles, Mich., May 23, 1944; s. Lawrence Ernest and Audrey Olive (McCllen) J.; B.S., Western Mich. U., 1969; m. Annie Ruth Boswell, Nov. 17, 1973. Machinist Henco Enterprises, Niles, Mich., 1966; engring. coop. student Clark Equipment Co., Buchanan, Mich., 1967-69, test engr., 1971—; applications engr. Hyster Co., Danville, Ill., 1970-71. Registered profl. engr., Mich. Mem. Soc. Automotive Engrs., Nat., Mich. socs. profl. engrs. Home: 1819 N 5th St Apt F-93 Niles MI 49120 Office: 324 E Dewey Buchanan MI 49107

JONES, LEANDER CORBIN, media specialist; b. Vincent, Ark., July 16, 1934; s. Lander Corbin and Una Bell (Lewis) J.; A.B., U. Ark., Pine Bluff, 1956; M.S., U. Ill., 1968; Ph.D., Union Grad. Sch., 1973; m. Lethonee Angela Hendricks, June 30, 1962; children—Angela Lynne, Leander Corbin. Tchr. English pub. high schs., Chgo. Bd. Edn., 1956-68; vol. English-as-fgn. lang. tchr. Peace Corps, Mogadiscio, Somalia, 1964-66; TV producer City Colls. of Chgo., 1968-73; communications media specialist Meharry Med. Coll., 1973-75; asso. prof. Black Americana Studies Western Mich., U., 1975—; dir. 7 art workshop Am. Negro Emancipation Centennial Authority, Chgo., 1960-63. Served with U.S. Army, 1956-58. Mem. Nat. Assn. Ednl. Broadcasters, DuSable Mus. African Am. History, Assn. for Study African-Am. History, Progressive Prisoners Assn., Theatre Arts, Broadcasting Skills Center, AAUP, Black Child Devel. Inst., Mich. Orgn. African Studies, Nat. Council Black Studies. Dir. play Who's Got His Own, Chgo., 1968-69, Nashville, 1974-75; writer, producer, dir. TV drama: Roof Over my Head, Sta. WDCN, Nashville 1975; designer program in theatre and TV for hard-to-educate; developer edn. programs in Ill. State Penitentiary, Pontiac, and Cook County Jail, Chgo., 1971-73. Home: 2226 S Westnedge Ave Kalamazoo MI 49008 Office: Black Americana Studies Western Mich U Kalamazoo MI 49001

JONES, MABLE VENEIDA, indsl. relations analyst; b. Detroit, Sept. 20, 1950; d. James and Fannie Mae (Williams) J.; B.S. in Spl. Edn., Eastern Mich. U., 1972; M.S. in Guidance and Counseling, Iowa State U., 1973; doctoral candidate Wayne State U., 1975—. Counselor, Wayne State U., Detroit, 1973, asst. dir. Upward Bound, 1974, dir., 1974-75; indsl. relations analyst Ford Motor Co., Allen Park, Mich., 1976—; cons. Wayne State U.; editor Mich. Council Ednl. Opportunity Programs, 1973, treas., 1974, sec., 1975-76. Recipient Key to City of Detroit, Mayor Young, 1975; Certificate of Commendation, Gov. Milliken, 1975. Mem. Am., Mich. (editorial bd. 1977-78) personnel and guidance assns., Wayne State U. Upward Bound Alumni Assn., Wayne State U. Alumni Assn. (pres. 1973-78), Mich. Assn. Non-White Concern in Guidance and Counseling (pres.-elect 1977). Democrat. Roman Catholic. Clubs: Altar Soc., Women of Madonna. Home: 18645 Fenmore St Detroit MI 48235 Office: Ford Motor Co 17000 Oakwood Blvd Allen Park MI 48121

JONES, MARGARET EILEEN ZEE, physician, educator; b. Swedesboro, N.J., June 24, 1936; d. Wilmer and Elsie (Schober) Zee; B.A., U. Pa., 1957; M.D., Med. Coll. Va., 1961; m. John Walker Jones, Aug. 29, 1959; children—John Stewart, Mary Cassaday, Amanda Worthington. Intern, U. Wash., Seattle, 1962-63, resident in pathology and neuropathology 1963-65; resident in pathology Med. Coll. Va., Richmond, 1966-67, instr. pathology, 1967-68, acting dir. div. neuropathology, 1967, 68-69, asst. prof. 1968-69; asst. prof. pathology Mich. State U., East Lansing, 1969-73, asso. prof., 1973—, dir. neurosci. Coll. Osteo. Medicine, 1973—. Lectr. neurosurgery Med. Sch., Yale, 1969—. A.D. Williams summer fellow, 1959, 60; Nat. Inst. Neurol. Diseases and Blindness-NIH fellow, 1970-71. Fellow Am. Soc. Clin. Pathologists; mem. Am. Assn. Neuropathologists, Am. Fedn. for Clin. Research, Nat. Soc. for Programmed Instruction, Soc. Instrnl. Tech., Soc. Neurosci. (pres. chpt. 1974—), Assn. Clin. Scientists. Contbr. articles to tech. jours. Office: Dept Pathology Mich State University East Lansing MI 48824

JONES, MARK ELMER, JR., judge, artist; b. Indpls., Oct. 15, 1920; s. Mark Elmer and Pearl (Campbell) J.; A.B., Roosevelt U., 1948; J.D., Loyola U., 1950; m. Jeanne L. Boger, Apr. 17, 1944; children—Marquita, Marcus, Marvin, Julie. Admitted to Ill. bar, 1950; practiced in Chgo., 1950-63; partner firm McCoy, Ming & Leighton, Chgo., 1957-62; asst. state's atty., Chgo., 1951-57; judge Circuit Ct. of Cook County (Ill.), 1963—. Mem. exec. com. Chgo. br. NAACP, 1959—; bd. dirs. Better Boys Found., Roosevelt U. Alumni, Inst. Cultural Devel., Urban Gateways, South Side Community Art Center; trustee Roosevelt U. Mem. Am., Ill., Chgo., Cook County, Nat. (founding mem., exec. com. jud. council) bar assns. Democrat. Unitarian. Club: Druids. Home: 1137 E 50th St Chicago IL 60615 Office: Chgo Civic Center Chicago IL 60602

JONES, MILO DONALD, mech. engr.; b. Albia, Iowa, July 15, 1924; s. Glenn Nelson and Cora Elizabeth (Smith) J.; B.S., Iowa State U., 1950; m. Phyllis Irene Velten, Apr. 25, 1947; children—Sharon (Mrs. Walter Coppinger), Steven Craig, Cynthia Kay. With Stanley Consultants, Muscatine, Ia., 1951—, head power design dept., 1966-69, prin. project engr., 1969-74, design mgr. power generation, 1974—. Served with U.S. Army, 1943-46. Mem. Nat. Soc. Profl. Engrs., Iowa Engring. Soc. Mason. Home: 36 Geneva Dr Muscatine IA 52761 Office: Stanley Consultants Muscatine IA 52761

JONES, MYRON DOUGLASS, osteo. physician, educator; b. Endicott, Wash., Oct. 27, 1907; s. Albert Terrill and Ruth (Andrew) J.; D.O., Kansas City Coll. Osteopathy and Surgery, 1929; m. Marjorie Shatto, Aug. 12, 1934; children—Myron Douglass, Eula Margaret Jones Johnson, John Phillip. Intern, Lakeside Hosp., Kansas City, Mo., 1930, cons., 1951-72; gen. practice osteo. medicine, Kansas City, 1930-32, 47-49, Milan, Mo., 1932-33, Brumley, Mo., 1933-47; resident in pediatrics Phila. Coll. Osteopathy and Surgery, 1949-51; prof. pediatrics Kansas City Coll. Osteopathy and Surgery, 1951-72; chmn. dept. pediatrics Osteo. Hosps. of Kansas City, 1951-72; cons. Doctor's Hosp., N.E. Hosp.; registered rep. Waddell & Reed, 1972—. Mayor of Brumley, 1936-47. Fellow Am. Coll. Osteo. Pediatricians (pres. 1964-65); mem. Am., Jackson County (pres. 1959-60) osteo. assns., Mo. Assn. Osteo. Physicians, Am. Numis. Assn., Kansas City Numis. Soc. (pres. 1969-70). Methodist (trustee). Clubs: Masons, South Kansas City Bus. (pres. 1960). Home: 6810 N Askew Ave Kansas City MO 64119

JONES, NELSON, marketing exec.; b. Chgo., May 21, 1947; s. George and Rosa Mae (Grant) J.; B.S. in B.A., Roosevelt U., 1969; M.B.A. (Mgmt fellow), U. Chgo., 1974; m. Valerie Ann Hughes, June 21, 1966 (div. 1973); children—Selene Tess, Nelson, Manuel. Sales trainee/sales trainee mgr. Gen. Foods Corp., Chgo., 1968-70; computer marketing rep. IBM, Chgo., 1971-73; program marketing analyst Xerox Corp., Rochester, N.Y., 1973-75; industry account exec. 3M Co., Chgo., 1975-76; asso. dir. mktg. Nat. Minority Purchasing Council, Chgo., 1976-78; mktg. exec. Ill. Bell Telephone Co., Palatine, 1978—. Mem., supporter WTTW/Channel 11, Chgo. Pub. TV, 1977—, Easter Seal Soc., Chgo., 1977—, Masca-Sickle Cell Anemia, 1977—. Boost fellow, Roosevelt U., 1965-69. Mem. Am. Marketing Assn., Assn. of MBA Execs., Nat. Specialty Merchandisers Assn. Contbr. articles in field to profl. jours. Home: 333 E Ontario St Chicago IL 60611

JONES, NINA FLEMISTER (MRS. WILLIAM M. JONES), sch. adminstr.; b. Madison, Ga., July 30, 1918; d. Sumner Lewis and Hallie (Hall) Flemister; A.B., Central YMCA Coll., 1938; M.Ed., Chgo. Tchrs. Coll., 1942; student U. Chgo., 1940-58; Ed.D., Loyola U., Chgo., 1975; m. William M. Jones, Sept. 21, 1940; children—William M. Jr., Steven L. Tchr. Chgo. Bd. Edn., 1942-65; prin. 1966-69, dist. supt. Dist. 2, Chgo., 1969-75, asst. supt. personnel, 1975—. Mem. A.A.U.W., Adminstrv. Women in Edn., Alpha Kappa Alpha, Alpha Gamma Pi. Home: 9156 S Constance Chicago IL 60617 Office: 228 N LaSalle St Chicago IL 60601

JONES, NORMA LOUISE, educator; b. Poplar, Wis.; d. George Elmer and Hilma June (Wiberg) Jones; B.E., U. Wis.; M.A., U. Minn., 1952; postgrad. U. Ill., 1957; Ph.D., U. Mich., 1965. Librarian, Grand Rapids (Mich.) pub. schs., 1947-62; Grand Rapids (Mich.) Pub. Library, 1948-49; instr. Central Mich. U., Mt. Pleasant, 1954, 55; librarian Benton Harbor (Mich.) pub. schs., 1962-63; lectr. U. Mich., Ann Arbor, 1954, 55, 61, 63-65, asst. prof., 1966-68; asst. prof. dept. library sci. U. Wis.-Oshkosh, 1968-70, asso. prof., 1970-75, prof., 1975—; mem. com. on certification of sch. librarians State of Wis., 1972—. Mem. ALA (chmn. reference conf. 1975—), Wis. Library Assn., Am. Assn. sch. Librarians, Phi Beta Kappa, Phi Kappa Phi, Pi Lambda Theta, Beta Phi Mu, Sigma Pi Epsilon. Home: 1220 Maricopa Dr Oshkosh WI 54901

JONES, PAUL ARCHIBALD, radiologist; b. Paxton, Ind., Sept. 27, 1915; s. Edward John and Margaret (Archibald) J.; B.S., Ind. U., 1937, M.D., 1939; m. Carolyn Elizabeth Singer, Dec. 25, 1940; children—Suzanne Elizabeth, Paul Vincent, Jennifer Jayne. Intern, Vancouver (B.C., Can.) Gen. Hosp., 1939-40; resident Duke U., 1946-48; practice medicine specializing in radiology, Zanesville,

Ohio, 1948—; radiologist Good Samaritan Med. Center, Zanesville, 1948—, Bethesda Hosp., Zanesville, 1948—; pres. Radiology Assos. Inc., Zanesville; dir. Ohio Med. Indemnity, 1970—. Bd. dirs. Good Samaritan Med. Center, 1972—, chmn., 1976. Served with M.C., U.S. Army, 1941-46. Fellow Am. Coll. Radiology (bd. chancellors 1964-69); mem. AMA, Radiol. Soc. N.Am., InterAm. Coll. Radiology, Eastern, Ohio, Central Ohio radiol. socs., Ohio Med. Assn., Muskingum County Acad. Medicine. Republican. Methodist. Home: 423 Conventry Circle Zanesville OH 43701 Office: 838 Market St Zanesville OH 43701

JONES, PAUL LAWRENCE, remote computing service co. exec.; b. Phila., Aug. 29, 1936; s. Earl Francis and Elizabeth (Kramer) J.; A.B., Phoenix Coll., 1969; B.A., Cleary Coll., 1975; M.B.A., Eastern Mich. U., 1976; m. Francine Jane Smith, May 30, 1959; children—Judith, Francine, Michael. With computer div. Gen. Electric Co., Phoenix, 1959-69; with Comshare, Inc., Ann Arbor, Mich., 1969—, now v.p.-fin. products services div. Active Boy Scouts, youth baseball and hockey. Served in USMC, 1955-59. Recipient Pres.'s award Cleary Coll., 1975. Mem. Beta Gamma Sigma, Phi Delta Phi. Republican. Roman Catholic. Home: 2209 Delaware Dr Ann Arbor MI 48103 Office: PO Box 1588 Ann Arbor MI 48103

JONES, RALPH, rancher, banker; b. Midland, S.D., Sept. 10, 1903; s. Thomas and Clara Ann (Asman) J.; B.S. in Econs., Huron Coll., 1926; m. Faye Lucille Berry, Sept. 7, 1930; children—Thomas Berry, Ralph David, Jerry Paul, Morris William. Owner, operator Jones Ranch, Inc., S.D., 1926—, pres., dir., 1962—; owner X-Y Ranch, 1926—; dir. First Nat. Bank of Philip (S.D.), 1945—, chmn. bd., 1954—, pres., 1972—; dir. Prairie State Life Ins. Co., Rapid City. Pres. Midland (S.D.) Community Fire Dept., 1945-70; chmn. Common Sch. Dist. Bd. 67, Midland, 1930-56; bd. regents State S.D. for Colls. and Univs., 1959-65; bd. dirs. Midland Community Hosp., 1941-60; trustee Nat. Cowboy Hall of Fame, 1977—. Mem. Am. Cattlemens Assn. (exec. com. 1953-58), S.D. Stock Growers Assn. (pres. 1952-54), Old Stanley County Hist. Soc. (dir.), Pioneers Western S.D. Lutheran. Democrat. Clubs: Masons, Shriners. Home: PO Box 188 Midland SD 57552 Office: First Nat Bank Box 10 Philip SD 57567

JONES, RICHARD CYRUS, lawyer; b. Oak Park, Ill., Oct. 20, 1928; s. Ethler E. and Margaret S. (Stoner) J.; Ph.B., DePaul U., 1960, J.D., 1963; m. Susan Jones; children—Richard C., Carrie, William. Admitted to Ill. bar, 1963; dept. mgr. Chgo. Title & Trust Co., 1947-64; mem. firm Sachnoff, Schrager, Jones & Weaver, Ltd. and predecessor firms, Chgo., 1964—. Instr., Real Estate Inst., Chgo., 1970—. Served with U.S. Army, 1951-52. Decorated Bronze Star medal, Combat Inf. badge. Mem. Am., Ill., Chgo. (com. chmn. 1970-72, 76-77) bar assns., Chgo. Council Lawyers, Delta Theta Phi. Kiwanian. Home: 1044 Forest Ave River Forest IL 60305 Office: One IBM Plaza 47th Floor Chicago IL 60611

JONES, RICHARD DERRAL, accountant; b. Waterloo, Iowa, July 23, 1936; s. Donald Milton and Lavona Adel (Powers) J.; student Coe Coll., 1956-57, LaSalle Extension U., 1956-61; m. Harriet Lorraine Wills, July 27, 1953 (dec. Jan. 1977); children—Judith, Sheryl, Steven, Randall. Printing press operator Cryovac Co., Cedar Rapids, Iowa, 1953-58; pub. accountant L.P. Christensen, accountant, Cedar Rapids, 1958-62; owner R.D. Jones, Accountant, Cedar Rapids, 1962—; dir. Carfrae Meat Co., Mchts. Delivery, Inc., B-J Contract Carriers, Inc., JEB Investments, Inc., CUC, Inc. Mem. accounting adv. com. Area One Community Coll., Calmar, Iowa, 1970-72; mem. Iowa Gov.'s Accounting Practitioner Advisory Com., 1975-78. Mem. Accountants Assn. Iowa (pres. 1970, chmn. legis. com. 1972—), Nat. Soc. Pub. Accountants, Nat. Assn. Accountants, Assn. Enrolled Agts. (dir., v.p. 1975—), Cedar Rapids C. of C., Aircraft Owners and Pilots Assn., Am. Security Council. Methodist (chmn. bd. 1969-71). Clubs: Masons, Shriners, Cedar View Country (dir.); Elmcrest Country. Home: 1404 Linmar Dr NE Cedar Rapids IA 52402 Office: 1120 3d St SE Cedar Rapids IA 52401

JONES, ROBERT, city ofcl.; b. Clarksburg, W.Va., Apr. 2, 1920; s. Milton Doerr and G. Minnie (Klein) J.; B.S., U. Ill., 1943; postgrad. Washington and Lee U., 1945; m. Barbara J. Whitsitt, Oct. 24, 1953; 1 son, R. Gardiner. Food and beverage mgr. Hilton Hotels Corp., Chgo., 1949-60, gen. mgr. catering, 1960-63; v.p. Pick Dining, Inc., Albert Pick Hotels, Chgo., 1964-65; bus. mgr. Met. Fair and Expn. Authority, Chgo., 1965—; v.p. Bertram, Inc., Lake Bluff, Ill., 1963—; v.p. spl. markets Greyhound Food Mgmt. Vice pres. Lake Bluff Park Bd., 1959-60; mem. South Side Planning Bd., Chgo., 1966—; bd. dirs. West Central Assn. Served to capt. AUS, World War II. Mem. Phi Gamma Delta. Author: The President's Own White House Cookbook. Home: 230 E Sheridan Pl Lake Bluff IL 60044 Office: McCormick Place 23d St and South Shore Dr Chicago IL 60602

JONES, RONALD CHALMERS, railway exec.; b. Evansville, Wis., Feb. 27, 1909; s. Edward Marion and Jessie May (Morrison) J.; student U. Wis., Madison, 1926-29; m. Ella Wilhelmine Griswold, Dec. 25, 1937. Accountant, Wis. Conservation Dept., Madison, 1932-37, Oscar Mayer & Co., Madison, 1941-64; sec.-treas. Time Realty Inc., Madison, 1964-76; bd. dirs., sec.—treas. Chgo., Madison & Northern Railway Co., Inc., 1976—. Bd. dirs. Mid-Continent Rwy. Hist. Soc. Inc., 1962-69, treas. 1963-67, 72-74. Served with USNR, 1942-45; ATO, PTO. Mem. Sigma Pi. Mason (Shriner). Editor: Ry. Gazette, 1968-70. Home: 504 E Dean Ave Madison WI 53716 Office: 101 W Beltline Hwy Madison WI 53713

JONES, RONALD LEE, real estate co. exec.; b. Wausau, Wis., Apr. 18, 1947; s. Lee and Evelyn (Everson) J.; A.S., North Central Tech. Inst., 1972; m. Bonnie Witkowski, July 10, 1971; 1 dau., Tara. Salesman, Action Realty, Inc., Schofield, Wis., 1974-76, v.p., dir., 1976—. Mem. exec. com. Democratic Party Marathon County, Wis., 1977-78. Served with AUS, 1967-68. Decorated Army Commendation medal, Purple Heart, Air medal, Combat Infantryman's badge. Mem. Wausau Bd. Realtors (pres. elect 1977, dir. 1977—), Wis. Realtors Assn., Nat. Assn. Realtors, Am. Legion, VFW. Home: 2612 Park Ridge Dr Schofield WI 54476 Office: 928 Grand Ave Schofield WI 54476

JONES, RONALD WILLIAM, container co. exec.; b. Chgo., Mar. 3, 1946; s. William Albert and Genevieve (Breeze) J.; B.S., U. Notre Dame, 1968, M.S., 1971, Ph.D., 1973; m. Virginia Anne Deiss, June 22, 1968; children—Scott, Todd, Holly, Heidi. Fellow in low temperature solid state physics Argonne Nat. Lab., 1971-73; with Sycamore Containers, Inc., Sycamore, Ill., 1973—, gen. mgr., 1975—, v.p., 1976—, also dir. Home: 2009 Arden Place Joliet IL 60435 Office: 215 N Fair St Sycamore IL 60178

JONES, ROSAMOND JANET, educator; b. Canton, S.D.; d. Edward Alfred and Edith (Burns) Jones; B.A. magna cum laude, Sioux Falls Coll., 1932; M.S., Okla. State U., 1940. Tchr. high sch., Western, Nebr., 1932-36, Wright City, Okla., 1936-38; clk. Selective Service Bd., Canton, 1940-41; civilian jr. grade typist Quartermaster Corps, Ft. Meade, S.D., 1941-42; instr. S.D. State Coll., 1942-44; actuarial clk. Bus. Men's Assurance, Kansas City, Mo., 1944-45; tchr. Principia High Sch., St. Louis, 1945-46; instr. U. Wyo., 1946-48; tchr. mathematics Ely (Minn.) Jr. Coll., 1946-52, St. Marys City Jr. Coll., Md., 1952-56; asst. prof. mathematics Bradley U., Peoria, Ill., 1956-64. Mem. AAUW, AAUP, Phi Kappa Phi. Home: Residential Community Apt 402 Cedar Ridge Rd Oconomowoc WI 53066

JONES, SARA S., banker; b. East Liverpool, O., Dec. 17, 1903; d. Samuel William and Fanny (Beardmore) Swindells; student U. Ill., 1922-25; m. Thornton P. Jones, Jan. 13, 1925 (dec.); children—John Milton, Barbara (Mrs. A. H. Greening, Jr.). Pres. Williamsville State Bank (Ill.), 1955-66, chmn. bd., 1966—. Bd. dirs. Lincolnland Lung Assn. Mem. Ill. Fedn. Rep. Women, P.E.O., Kings Daus., Alpha Xi Delta. Methodist. Clubs: Sangamo, Illini Country. Home: Williamsville IL 62693 Office: Williamsville State Bank Williamsville IL 62693

JONES, THOMAS JOHN, steel co. exec.; b. Cin., Mar. 17, 1916; s. Harry Parry and Mary Grace (Jones) J.; Comml. engr., U. Cin., 1939; postgrad. W.Va., Purdue, Cin. univs., 1941-47; m. Pollye Richards Diehl, June 17, 1950; 1 dau., Mary Jane. Field engr. United Fuel Gas Co., Charleston, W.Va., 1939-42; staff engr. Basic Magnesium, Inc., Las Vegas, Nev., 1942; program dir. War Manpower Commn., Cin., 1942-45; tng. dir. The Lunkenheimer Co., Cin., 1945-49; successively engr., asst. chief engr., chief engr., staff asst. to v.p. Wheeling Corrugating Co. div. Wheeling Pittsburgh Steel Corp. (W.Va.), 1950-69, mgr. marketing tech. services, 1969—, also mem. product bd. Tng. chmn. Boy Scouts Am., 1952-64; active Oglebay Inst., Wheeling, 1968—; life mem. P.T.A., pres., 1964, 65. Found. trustee Belmont Tech. Coll. Registered profl. engr., Ohio, W.Va. Mem. Am. Iron and Steel Inst., Am. Soc. C.E., Am. Concrete Inst., Am. Soc. Testing Materials, Internat. Conf. Bldg. Ofcls., Bldg. Ofcls. and Code Adminstrs. Internat., Nat., W.Va. socs. profl. engrs., Smithsonian Instn., Common Cause, Nat. Wildlife Fedn., YMCA, UN Assn. Presbyn. (elder). Mason (Shriner). Home: PO Box 62 St Clairsville OH 43950 Office: 1134 Market St Wheeling WV 26003

JONES, THOMAS KENNETH, JR., radiologist; b. Youngstown, Ohio, Oct. 31, 1934; s. Thomas Kenneth and Julia Marion (Wormer) J.; B.S., Ohio State U., 1955; M.D., Johns Hopkins U., 1959; m. Mary Lou Eichler, Sept. 25, 1956; children—Thomas Kenneth III, Clarissa Ann, Kimberly Erin. Intern surgery Union Meml. Hosp., Balt., 1959-60, resident in gen. surgery, 1960-61; resident in therapeutic radiology Med. Coll. Va., Richmond, 1967-70, instr., 1970; instr. therapeutic radiology U. Minn., Mpls., 1970-71, asst. prof., 1971-73, asso. prof., 1973—. Served with USAF, 1961-67. Mem. AMA, Am. Coll. Radiology, Am. Soc. Therapeutic Radiologists. Republican. Methodist. Home: 7116 West Shore Dr Minneapolis MN 55435 Office: Box 494 Mayo U Minn Hosps Minneapolis MN 55455

JONES, THOMAS OWEN, JR., ednl. adminstr., bus. scientist; b. Washington, June 24, 1935; s. Thomas Owen and Annie Mae (Bell) J.; B.S. in Mech. Engring. U. Pa., 1957; B.S. in Bus. Adminstrn., U. Southwestern La., 1966; M.B.A., George Washington U., 1968, D.Bus. Adminstrn., 1972. Comml. pilot Petroleum Helicopters, Lafayette, La., 1962-66; gen. mgr. Loving Helicopters, College Park, Md., 1967; dir. helicopter ops. Exec. Aviation, Silver Spring, Md., 1968; mktg. specialist Enstrom Helicopters, Washington, 1969; asso. prof. econs., mgmt. USCG Acad., New London, Conn., 1970-71; asst. dean Coll. Bus. Adminstrn., Loyola U., New Orleans, 1971-74; dean Sch. Bus., Eastern Ill. U., Charleston, 1974—; developer 1st degree granting program in energy mgmt. in U.S., 1975. Econ. advisor to Gov. Ill., 1977—. Dir. Living Inc., New Orleans. Served as aviator USNR, 1957-62. Mem. Acad. Mgmt., Am. Mktg. Assn., Financial Execs. Inst., Pi Gamma Mu, Omicron Delta Epsilon, Beta Gamma Sigma. Home: 1811 Meadowlake Dr Charleston IL 61920 Office: Sch Bus Eastern Ill U Charleston IL 61920

JONES, TREVOR OWEN, elec. engr.; b. Maidstone, Eng., Nov. 3, 1930; s. Richard Owen and Rudy Edith (Martin) J.; HNC in Elec. Engring., Aston Tech. Coll., 1952; ONC in Mech. Engring., Liverpool Tech. Coll., 1957; m. Jennie Lou Singleton, Sept. 12, 1959; children—Pembroke Robinson, Bronwyn Elizabeth. Student engr., elec. mechine design engr. Brit. Gen. Electric Co., 1950-57; project engr., project mgr. Nuclear Ship Savannah, Allis Chalmers Mfg. Co., 1957-59; with Gen. Motors Co., Milford, Mich., 1959—, dir. electronic control systems, engring. staff, 1970-72, dir. advance product engring., 1972-74, dir. Proving Grounds, 1974—; dir. Energy Conversion Devices, Inc. Mem. nat. motor vehicle safety adv. council Dept. Transp., 1971, vice chmn. 1972-73, chmn. nat. hwy. safety adv. com., 1976—. Trustee Lawrence Inst. Tech., 1973-76; exec. bd. Clinton Valley council Boy Scouts Am., 1975; bd. govs. Cranbrook Inst. Sci., 1977. Served with Brit. Army, 1955-57. Fellow Brit. Instn. Elec. Engrs., IEEE; mem. Soc. Automotive Engrs., Newcomen Soc., Engring. Soc. Detroit, Am. Def. Preparedness Assn. Republican. Episcopalian. Clubs: Pine Lake Country, Birmingham Athletic; Capitol Hill (Washington). Contbr. articles to profl. jours. Patentee in automotive safety and electronics. Home: 1449 Suffield St Birmingham MI 48009 Office: General Motors Proving Ground Milford MI 48042

JONES, WALTER HEATH, bishop; b. St. Boniface, Man., Can., Dec. 25, 1928; s. Harry Heath and Anne Grace (Stoddart) J.; B.A., U. Man., 1951; B.Th., St. Johns Coll., 1951, S.T.D., 1970; m. L. Marilyn Lunney, Aug. 25, 1951; children—Irene Lenore Jones Mihara, Leah Anne, Barry Malcolm Heath, Kristin Maureen. Ordained priest Episcopal Ch., 1958; founding rector St. Peter's Ch., Flin Flon, Man., 1951-56; rector St. John The Baptist Ch., Winnipeg, Man., 1956-58, St. Mary Ch., Mitchell, S.D., 1958-62; dean Calvary Cathedral, Sioux Falls, S.D., 1968-70; bishop Diocese of Sioux Falls, 1970—. Mem. exec. bd. Sioux council Boy Scouts Am., 1958—. Named hon. citizen, St. Boniface, 1964. Clubs: Masons, Kiwanis. Editor S.D. Churchman, 1962-67. Home: 805 E 32d St Sioux Falls SD 57105 Office: 200 W 18th St Sioux Falls SD 57102

JONES, WALTER LEON, accountant; b. Paris, Ill., Apr. 6, 1940; s. W. Lance and Ruth (Winkler) J.; B.S., Eastern Ill. U., 1965; m. Carla Sue Dee, Aug. 20, 1961; children—Tamera, Jeffrey, Daniel. Cost accountant, Blaw Knox Co., Mattoon, Ill., 1965-66; agt. IRS, Bloomington, Ill., 1966-70; accountant asst. to tax partner Alsup & Assos., Bloomington, 1970; tax mgr. Turnbull & Schussele, Springfield, Ill., 1970-76; pvt. practice accounting, Springfield, 1976—. Mem. finance com. Village of Sherman, 1972-74; mem. citizens adv. com. Sch. Dist. 15, Williamsville, 1974, mem. sch. bd., 1975—. Served with Army N.G., 1957-63. Mem. Am. Inst. C.P.A.'s, Ill. Soc. C.P.A.'s, Sangamon Valley Estate Planning Council. Roman Catholic. Home: 523 Flaggland Dr Sherman IL 62684 Office: 1325 4th St S PO Box 5078 Springfield IL 62705

JONES, WILLIAM AUGUSTUS, JR., bishop; b. Memphis, Jan. 24, 1927; s. William Augustus and Martha (Wharton) J.; B.A., Southwestern at Memphis, 1948; B.D., Yale U., 1951; m. Margaret Loaring-Clark, Aug. 26, 1949; 4 children. Ordained priest Episcopal Ch., 1952; preist-in-charge Messiah Ch., Pulaski, Tenn., 1952-57; curate Christ Ch., Nashville, 1957-58; rector St. Mark Ch., LaGrange, Ga., 1958-65; asso. rector St. Luke Ch., Mountainbrook, Ala., 1965-66; dir. research So. region Assn. Christian Tng. and Service, Memphis, 1966-67, exec. dir., 1968; bishop of Mo., St. Louis, 1975—. Office: 1210 Locust St Saint Louis MO 63103*

JONES, WILLIAM MC KENDREY, educator; b. Dothan, Ala., Sept. 19, 1927; s. William Mc Kendrey and Margaret (Farmer) J.; B.A., U. Ala., 1949, M.A., 1950; Ph.D., Northwestern U., 1953; m. Ruth Ann Roberts, Aug. 14, 1952; children—Margaret, Elizabeth, Bronwen. Asst. prof. English, Wis. State U., Eau Claire, 1953-55; asst. prof. U. Mich., Ann Arbor, 1955-59; mem. faculty U. Mo., Columbia, 1959—, prof. English, 1964—, asso. dean Grad. Sch., 1966-68. Served with U.S. Army, 1946-47. Folger Library summer fellow, 1955; U. Mo. distinguished prof., 1972—. Author: Stages of Composition, 1964; Fiction: Form and Experience, 1969; Guide to Living Power, 1974; (with Ruth Ann Jones) Living in Love, 1976; Speaking Up in Church, 1977. Home: 209 Russell Blvd Columbia MO 65201 Office: Dept English U Mo Columbia MO 65201

JONES, WILLIAM MOSES, ophthalmologist; b. Earle, Ark., Nov. 12, 1898; s. Thomas Caanan and Nancy Emma (Conyers) J.; A.B. in Math. with honors, Fisk U., 1922; M.D., U. Chgo., 1932; m. Geneva May Lacy, Dec. 27, 1934; 1 dau., Jean Andre. Intern, Kansas City (Mo.) Gen. Hosp., 1931-32; resident in ophthalmology U. Chgo.-Billings Meml. Hosp., 1932-37; practice medicine specializing in ophthalmology, Chgo., 1937—; cons. Jackson Park, Woodlawn, Provident, Tamarack hosps.; asso. prof. U. Chgo. Med. Sch., 1954-55; co-owner Walnut Grove Camp, Sturgis, Mich. Mem. Am. Acad. Ophthalmology and Otolaryngology, A.C.S., AMA, Nat. Med. Assn., N.Y. Acad. Scis., Chgo. Med. Soc., Cook County Physicians Assn., Alpha Phi Alpha. Democrat. Conglist. Home: 5234 S Michigan Ave Chicago IL 60615 Office: 7531 Stony Island Ave Chicago IL 60049

JONES, WORTH ROOSEVELT, educator; b. Mortimer, N.C., Mar. 1, 1923; s. Arthur Glen and Lettie Ethel (Gragg) J.; A.B., Lenoir Rhyne Coll., Hickory, N.C., 1948; M.A., Appalachian State U., Boone, N.C., 1952; N.C., Ed.D., Ind. U., 1955; m. Franca Luisa Berlincioni, Oct. 28, 1946; 1 son, William Paul. Dir. Prisoner of War Info. Bur., War Dept., 1946-47; tchr., counselor Hickory (N.C.) city schs., 1948-53; instr., coordinator student activities Appalachian State U., 1953-54; prof., coordinator grad. studies, head specialized sch. services U. Cin., 1955-73; prof. edn., 1973—; cons. in field. Served with U.S. Army, 1943-46. Mem. Am. Personnel and Guidance Assn., Am. Ednl. Research Assn., AAUP, Am. Coll. Personnel Assn., Assn. Counselor Edn. and Supervision, Cin. Guidance and Personnel Assn., Cin. Psychol Assn., Ohio assn. Counselor Edn. and Supervision, Ohio Sch. Counselors Assn., Ohio Sch. Psychologists Assn., Ohio Vis. Tchrs. Assn., Am. Legion, Phi Delta Kappa. Baptist. Author articles. Home: 6896 Greenfield Dr Cincinnati OH 45224 Office: Coll Edn Univ Cincinnati OH 45221

JONLAND, EINAR WILBERT, profl. figure skater; b. Mpls., Oct. 7, 1926; s. Ole and Ida Ovidia (Andersen) J.; m. Mary Catherine Burke, Dec. 8, 1948; children—Brian Charles, Gary Michael, Todd Paul, Eric Daniel. Pres., Michael Kirby Ice Skating Schs., Park Ridge, Ill., 1953-74; head pro Northbrook (Ill.) Sports Complex, 1974—; cons. in field; rector sports Lincoln Acad. Ill., 1970—. Served with Transp. Corps, U.S. Army, 1943-45. Mem. Ice Skating Inst. Am. (exec. bd. 1975—), Amateur Skating Union U.S. (pres. 1971-72), Amateur Skating Assn. Ill. (pres. 1969-70), U.S. Internat. Skating Assn. (life, dir. 1969—), Am. Legion. Republican. Lutheran. Clubs: Lions, Author: Introduction to Ice Skating, 1973. Home: 907 S Washington St Park Ridge IL 60068

JONSON, WILL, architect, artist; b. Chgo., Sept. 20, 1917; s. Alfred and Jessie (Chase) J.; m. Elizabeth Goble, June 25, 1955; children—Barbara Perington, Linda Lakner, Debbie Julian, William A. Pvt. practice architecture and art, Hinsdale, Ill., 1948—. Bd. dirs. Mid-West Art League. Mem. A.I.A., Ill. Soc. Architects. Home: 5729 S Washington St Hinsdale IL 60521 Office: 119 E Ogden Av Hinsdale IL 60521

JOOS, THAD HERMAN, physician; b. Detroit, Aug. 30, 1926; s. Herman C. and Mary (Kelley) J.; student Miami U., Oxford, Ohio, 1944-46; M.D., U. Mich., 1950; m. Suzanne Kottenstette, June 11, 1955; children—Peter H., Susan E., Sarah A. Intern, Henry Ford Hosp., Detroit, 1950-51, resident, 1951-52, 54-55; instr. pediatrics U. Mich., 1955-56; practice medicine specializing in pediatric allergy, Grosse Pointe Woods, Mich., 1956—; mem. staff St. John Hosp., Detroit, Children's Hosp. of Mich., Detroit; clin. instr. pediatrics Wayne State U., 1957—. Served with USN, 1944-45, 52-54. Mem. Am. Acad. Pediatrics, Am. Acad. Allergy, AMA. Republican. Roman Catholic. Club: County of Detroit. Home: 1080 Oxford St S Grosse Pointe Woods MI 48236 Office: 20136 Mack St Grosse Pointe Woods MI 48236

JORDAHL, GENE WALTER, veterinarian; b. Des Lacs, N.D., Jan. 30, 1925; s. Clarence William and Selma Julia (Engen) J.; student Minot State Coll., 1947-50; D.V.M., Iowa State U., 1954; m. Virgene Ruth Hunt, Jan. 6, 1945; children—Connie Jordahl Dilland, Ronald, Marjorie Jordahl Golik, Karen Jordahl Thorson, Rick. Pvt. practice veterinary medicine, Minot, N.D., 1954—; pres. exam. bd. N.D. Bd. Veterinary Med. Examiners, 1970—. Served to lt. USAAF, 1943-46; PTO. Mem. Am., N.D. veterinary med. assns. Lutheran. Clubs: Minot Country, Elks. Home: 1118 Valley View Dr Minot ND 58701 Office: Hwy 83 N Minot ND 58701

JORDAN, ARTHUR EDWARD, educator; b. St. Louis, Aug. 10, 1921; s. Walter Robert and Flora Louise (Fricke) J.; A.B., Harris Tchrs. Coll., 1943; postgrad. Washington U., St. Louis, 1942, 44, 48-50, Kenyon Coll., 1943; M.Ed., Mo. U.-Columbia, 1945, Ed.D., 1959; m. Anna Louise Wehmer, Oct. 29, 1955; 1 dau., Elizabeth Ann. Tchr., Kemper Mil. Sch., Boonville, Mo., 1945-46; tchr. Normandy Sch. Dist., St. Louis County, Mo., 1946-49, adminstr., 1949-58, 59-65; faculty So. Ill. U., Edwardsville, 1965—, asso. prof. elementary edn., 1969—, chmn. dept. elementary edn., 1969-72. Lectr. in field. Served with USAAF, 1943. Mem. Nat. Edn. Assn. (life), Assn. Supervision and Curriculum Devel., Nat. Council Tchrs. Math., A.A.U.P., Nat. Geog. Soc., Smithsonian Assos., Phi Delta Kappa (life), Sigma Tau Gamma. Episcopalian (vestryman). Mason (Shriner). Author: Glossary of Mathematical Terms, 1975; Teaching Mathematics in Elementary School, 1976. Contbr. articles to profl. publs. Home: 7331 Ravinia Dr St Louis MO 63121 Office: Box 122 So Ill U Edwardsville IL 62025

JORDAN, CLIFFORD HOMER, mfg. co. exec.; b. Des Moines, Oct. 17, 1910; s. Talley E. and Lillian Salina (Tilton) J.; student U. Minn., 1928-29; m. V. June Russell, Nov. 22, 1931; children—Richard Talley, Dennis Edward, Linda Kay. Bookkeeper to asst. treas. W.G. Block Co., Davenport, Iowa, 1931-42; with Mc Gladrex, Hansen, Dunn & Co., 1943; sales mgr., v.p., gen. mgr., pres. Kilborn Photo Paper Co., Cedar Rapids, Iowa, 1944-68; pres., chmn. bd. Hwy. Equipment Co., 1958—; pres. Jordan Bldg. Corp., Continental Six, Inc.; dir. Mchts. Nat. Bank. Trustee Coe Coll., St. Lukes Hosp., YMCA. Named Outstanding Mgmt. Man in Iowa, 1962. Mem. Nat. Accountants Soc. Republican. Presbyn. Home: 428 29th St Dr Cedar Rapids IA 52403 Office: 616 D Ave NW NE Cedar Rapids 52405

JORDAN, EARL CLIFFORD, ins. co. exec.; b. Austin, Minn., Dec. 29, 1916; s. Chester R. and Gladys (Ray) J.; A.B., U. Wis., 1939; m. Marion Brannon, Aug. 31, 1940; children—Robert Earl, Julie Ann.

Group supr. Aetna Life Ins. Co., Chgo., 1939-43, asst. gen. agt., Chgo., Albany, N.Y., 1946-48; gen. agt. Mass. Mut. Life Ins. Co., Chgo., 1948—; pres. Planned Futures, Inc.; dir. Nasco Internat., Inc., Ft. Atkinson, Wis., Weatherby Inc.; pres.-elect Life Agy. Mgmt. Conf. Trustee Ill. Children's Home and Aid Soc., past pres.; bd. dirs. U. Wis. Found., Elvehjam Art Center Council U. Wis. Served from pvt. to 1st lt., AUS, 1943-46. Mem. Gen. Agts. and Mgrs. Assn. (pres. Chgo.), Life Ins. and Trust Council Chgo., Chgo. Assn. Life Underwriters, Manila Alumni Assn. (founder, 1st pres.), U. Wis. Nat. Alumni Assn. (past pres., chmn. bd.), Sigma Alpha Epsilon, Fellowship Christian Athletes (treas., dir.), Mass. Mut. Gen. Agts. Assn. (past pres.), Internat. Gen. Agts. and Mgrs. Conf. (pres.). Mason (32 deg.). Clubs: U. Wis., Bob-O-Link Country, Westmoreland Country, Union League, Execs. (Chgo.); Tucson Nat. Golf; Shikar-Safari Internat.; One Shot Antelope Hunt Adventurers; Elgin Golf (Morayshire, Scotland). Home: 1120 Golf View Ln Glenview IL 60025 Office: 111 W Jackson Blvd Chicago IL 60604

JORDAN, LESLIE SPENCE, electronics engr.; b. Roswell, N.Mex., Dec. 23, 1943; s. Jackson Spence and Leona Lorrayne (Burnworth) J.; student Rose Poly. Inst., 1962-65; B.S., Purdue U., 1968; m. Carolyne Bonham, Nov. 24, 1972; children—Tiffany Carolyne, Tyson Nicholaus. Project engr. Essex Group, Inc., Logansport, Ind., 1973—. Mem. Nat. Rifle Assn., Am. Security Council. Author: Electronic Defrost Control, 1973; Electronic Microwave Oven Control, 1974; Electronic Defrost Cycle Control, 1977. Home: 920 19th St Logansport IN 46947 Office: 131 Godfrey St Logansport IN 46947

JORGENSEN, LAVERNIA MAE, educator; b. Luck, Wis., Mar. 2, 1918; d. George and Alice (Christensen) J.; B.S., River Falls (Wis.) State Tchrs. Coll., 1939; M.Ed., U. Minn., 1950; dir. phys. edn. Ind. U., 1955, P.E.D., 1960. Tchr. English and phys. edn., Plummer, Minn., 1941-43, history and phys. edn., Sleepy Eye, Minn., 1943-46; girls' phys. edn., Detroit Lakes, Minn., 1946-49; teaching asst. U. Minn., Mpls., 1949-50; health and phys. edn. Manchester Coll., 1950-55, Ind. U., Bloomington, 1955-56; tchr. health and phys. edn. Eastern Mich. U., 1956-58, U. S.D., 1958-61, Augustana Coll., 1961-63, U. N.D., Grand Forks, 1963—. Recipient honor awards N.D., Central Dist. assns. health, phys. edn. and recreation, 1972; Outstanding Woman N.D. award, 1973; Distinguished Alumnus award U. Wis.-River Falls, 1977. Fellow Am. Sch. Health Assn., AAHPER; mem. AAUP, Am. Corrective Therapy Assn., AAUW, N.D. Health, Phys. Edn., Recreation and Coaches Assn., Nat., N.D. assns. for phys. edn. coll. women, Nat. Recreation and Parks Assn., Soc. Parks and Recreation Educators, Am. Camping Assn., N.D. Park and Recreation Assn., Nat. Found. for Health, Phys. Edn. and Recreation, Am. Numismatic Assn., Ind. U. Alumni Assn., Royal Soc. Health, Internat. Platform Assn., Internat. Recreation Assn., Am. Acad. Sports Medicine, Phi Sigma Alpha (Woman of Year award N.D. Gamma chpt. 1974), Delta Psi Kappa. Republican. Lutheran (deacon). Club: River Bend Country. Contbr. articles in field to profl. jours. Home: 2007 2d Av N Grand Forks ND 58201

JOSAITIS, MARVIN, educator; b. Detroit, Dec. 27, 1941; s. Frank W. and Margaret Agnes (Girard) J.; B.A., Sacred Heart Sem. Coll., 1963; M.A., Eastern Mich. U., 1970, U. Detroit, 1971; postgrad. St. Louis U., 1965, St. John's Provincial Sem., 1963-67; Ph.D., U. Mich., 1977; m. Donna Marie Rimer, Mar. 25, 1970; children—Kateri, Ta'mara, Tarik. Ordained priest Roman Catholic Ch., 1967; asso. pastor St. Michael's Ch., Monroe, Mich., 1967-69; asso. prof. philosophy, English, Monroe County (Mich.) Community Coll., 1969-75; edn. coordinator Alcohol and Drug Abuse program The Ford Motor Co., 1976—. Mem. Monroe County Planning Commn., 1975-76. Named Best instr. Monroe County Community Coll., 1970. Mem. Am. Assn. Higher Edn., Assn. Labor and Mgmt. Cons. on Alcoholism, Assn. Alcoholism Counselors. Home: 2231 Westfield Rd Trenton MI 48183 Office: The Ford Motor Co World Hdqrs The American Rd Dearborn MI 48121

JOSCELYN, KENT BUCKLEY, educator; b. Binghamton, N.Y., Dec. 18, 1936; s. Raymond Miles and Gwen Buckley (Smith) J.; B.S., Union Coll., 1957; J.D., Albany Law Sch., 1960; m. Mary A. Komoroske, Nov. 20, 1965; children—Kathryn Anne, Jennifer Sheldon. Admitted to N.Y. State bar, 1961, U.S. Ct. Mil. Appeals, 1962, D.C. bar, 1967; atty., adviser Hdqrs. USAF, Washington, 1965-67; asso. prof. forensic studies Coll. Arts and Scis. Ind. U., Bloomington, 1967-76, dir. Inst. Research in Pub. Safety, 1970-75; head pub. factors div. Hwy. Safety Research Inst. U. Mich., 1976—; cons. Law Enforcement Assistance Adminstrn., U.S. Dept. Justice, 1969-72; Gov.'s appointee as regional dir. Ind. Criminal Justice Planning Agy., also vice chmn. Ind. Organized Crime Prevention Council, 1969-72; commr. pub. safety City of Bloomington, 1974-76. Served to capt., USAF, 1961-64. Mem. Transp. Research Bd., Nat. Acad. Sci., NRC, Am. Soc. Criminology, AAAS, Soc. Automotive Engrs., Am. Soc. Pub. Adminstrn., Acad. Criminal Justice Scis., Am., N.Y. State bar assns., Internat. Assn. Chiefs Police (asso.), Nat. Safety Council, Sigma Xi. Editor Internat. Jour. Criminal Justice. Home: 2255 Blueberry Ln Ann Arbor MI 48103 Office: Hwy Safety Research Inst U Mich Ann Arbor MI 48109

JOSEPH, EARL CLARK, computer co. exec.; b. St. Paul, Nov. 1, 1926; s. Clark Herbert and Ida Bertha (Schultz) J.; A.A., U. Minn., 1947, B.A., 1951; m. Alma Caroline Bennett, Nov. 19, 1955; children—Alma (Mrs. Richard Chadner), Earl, Vincent, René. Mathematician/programmer Remington Rand Univac, Arlington, Va., 1951-55, supr., St. Paul, 1955-60, systems mgr. Sperry Univac, St. Paul, 1960-63, staff scientist-futurist, 1963—. Vis. lectr. U. Minn., Mpls., 1971—; mem. Sci. and Mgmt. Adv. Com., U.S. Army, 1972-74. Futurist in residence Sci. Mus. of Minn., 1973—. Chmn., Met. Young Adult Ministry, 1967-69; mem. Gov.'s Planning Commn. for City Center Learning, 1968. Served with USNR, 1944-46. Distinguished lectr. I.E.E.E. Computer Soc., 1971-72, 76-78, Assn. Computer Machinery, 1976-78. Mem. I.E.E.E. (sr.), Minn. Futurists (founder, dir., past pres.), World Future Soc., Assn. Computer Machinery (gen. chmn. 1975, pres. chpt. 1976-77), A.A.A.S., Beta Phi Beta. Patents, publs. in field; co-author 18 books. Home: 365 Summit Ave St Paul MN 55102 Office: Univac Park PO Box 3525 St Paul MN 55165

JOSEPH, GERALDINE (GERI) R. MACK (MRS. BURTON M. JOSEPH), Democratic nat. committeewoman; b. St. Paul, June 19, 1923; d. Samuel S. and Edith (Berkovitz) Mack; B.A., U. Minn., 1945; m. Burton M. Joseph, Apr. 2, 1953; children—Shelley M., I. Scott, Jonathan P. Contbg. editor Mpls. Tribune, 1972—; dir. Northwestern Nat. Bank, Hormel Co., Northwestern Bell Telephone Co. Chmn. women's com. Minn. Vols. for Stevenson, 1956; state chairwoman Dem.-Farmer-Labor Party, Minn., 1958-60; subsequently Nat. Dem. committeewoman, vice chmn. Dem. Nat. Com., 1968-70; pres. Nat. Assn. Mental Health, 1968-70; mem. Anti-Defamation League, Gov. (Minn.) Council Youth Tng.; mem. Pres.'s Commn. on Youth Employment, Pres.'s Commn. on Income Maintenance Programs; bd. dirs. Carleton Coll., Northfield, Minn., 1975—. Recipient Sigma Delta Chi award journalism. Mem. Theta Sigma Phi, Delta Phi Lambda. Jewish. Address: 5 Red Cedar Ln Minneapolis MN 55410 and care Mpls Tribune 425 Portland Ave Minneapolis MN 55415

JOSEPH, JAMES ALFRED, govt. ofcl.; b. Opelousas, La., Mar. 12, 1935; s. Adam and Julia (Lee) J.; B.A., So. U., 1956; M. Divinity (Bess and Woodward fellow), Yale U., 1963; L.H.D. (hon.), Shaw U., 1972; m. Doris Taylor, June 27, 1959; children—Jeffrey, Denise. Ordained minister United Ch. of Christ; instr. ethics, admissions officer Stillman Coll., Tuscaloosa, Ala., 1963-64; asst. chaplain Claremont Colls., 1964-67, chaplain, 1969-70; asso. dir. Irwin-Sweeney-Miller, Cummins Engine and Irwin Union Founds., Columbus, Ind., 1967-69, pres. Assn. of Founds., 1970-72; v.p. corporate action Cummins Engine Co., also pres. Cummins Engine Found., Columbus, 1972-77; under sec. U.S. Dept. Interior, 1977—. Lectr. over 50 colls. and univs.; mem. faculty So. Calif. Sch. Theology, 1969-70; mem. adv. com. U.S. Treasury, 1966. Host pub. affairs TV program NBC, Indpls., 1973-76; chmn. Claremont Intercultural Council, 1965-67; chmn. spl. adv. com. World Council Chs., Geneva, Switzerland, 1973—. Trustee, Pitzer Coll., Claremont, Calif., Atlanta U., Union Theol. Sem.; bd. dirs. Council on Founds., 1971—, sec., mem. exec. com., 1972—; bd. dirs. Black Women's Community Devel. Found. Served to 1st lt. U.S. Army, 1956-58. Recipient Business Person of Yr. award NACBS, 1975; Yale Black Alumni award, 1974; Met. Applied Research Center fellow, N.Y.C., 1968; Wilton Park Conf. fellow, Eng., 1971; Danforth Found. grantee Yale, 1961-62. Mem. Alpha Phi Alpha. Co-editor: Three Perspectives on Ethnicity, 1976. Contbr. articles to nat. publs. Home: 1520 Park Valley Dr Columbus IN 47201 Office: 1000 5th St Columbus IN 47201

JOSEPH, MARGUERITE WILSON, state ofcl.; b. Camden, O., Mar. 26, 1919; d. Roeloff H. and Grace D. (Gilpin) Wilson; student Miami U., Oxford, O., 1936-37, 44-45, Baldwin-Wallace Coll., 1937-38; m. Kenneth L. Joseph, Sept. 9, 1938 (div. June 1948); 1 dau., Claudia F. (Mrs. Raymond Hampton). Social worker Ohio State Aid for Aged, Hamilton, 1945-47, Fla. Dept. Welfare, Jacksonville, 1947-48; mgr., owner West Side Drugs, St. Augustine, Fla., 1948-50; radiol. technician St. Joseph's Hosp., Mishawaka, Ind., 1954-56, McCullough-Hyde Hosp., Oxford, 1957-60, Christ Hosp., Cin., 1960-62; test examiner Ohio State Employment Service, Hamilton, 1962-69; coordinator Butler County W.I.N., 1969—. Mem. adv. bd. Miami Valley Tech. Sch., Hamilton, 1967—. Mem. Internat. Assn. Personnel in Employment Security, Nat. Wildlife Assn., Aircraft Owners and Pilots Assn., Soc. Radiol. Technologists, Ohio Civil Service Employees Assn., Internat. Platform Assn. Mem. Order Eastern Star. Contbr. poems to anthologies, mags. including Etude, Silhouette, Am. Poetry, others. Home: 119 N Campus Ave Oxford OH 45056 Office: 112 N 2d St Hamilton OH 45012

JOSEPH, RAMON RAFAEL, physician, educator; b. N.Y.C., May 17, 1930; s. Felix R. and Helen (Espinet) J.; B.S., Manhattan Coll., 1952; M.D., Cornell U., 1956; m. Mary Ann Kowalchik, June 16, 1956; children—Ricardo George, Maria Ann, Lisa Marie. Intern, Meadowbrook Hosp., Hempstead, N.Y., 1956-57, resident, 1957; resident Wayne County Gen. Hosp., Eloise, Mich., 1959-62; practice medicine, specializing in internal medicine and gastroenterology 1962—; dir. gastroenterology Wayne County Gen. Hosp., 1962—, asst. dir. internal medicine, 1964-73, dir., 1973—, pres. med. staff, 1971-72; cons. Annapolis Hosp.; instr. internal medicine U. Mich., 1962-65, asst. prof., 1965-69, asso. prof., 1969-74, prof., 1975—, asst. dean, 1973—; cons. gastroenterology St. Mary Hosp., Livonia, Mich., 1966—. Commr. Community Commn. on Drug Abuse, Livonia and Westland, Mich., 1970-73; mem. Mich. Dept. Edn. Council on Drug Abuse; cons. on drug abuse pub. schs., Livonia, 1968-74; pres. Livonia Sch. Bd. Adv. Council, 1970-71. Served as capt. U.S. Army, 1957-59. Diplomate Nat. Bd. Med. Examiners, Am. Bd. Internal Medicine. Fellow A.C.P.; mem. Am. Fedn. for Clin. Research, Am. Gastroenterol. Assn., A.A.A.S., Assn. Am. Med. Colls., A.M.A., N.Y. Acad. Scis., Detroit Gastroenterol. Soc. (pres. 1969-70), Mich., Wayne County med. socs., Am. Assn. Lab. Animal Sci., Am. Soc. for Gastrointestinal Endoscopy. Roman Catholic. Contbr. articles in field to profl. jours. Home: 5593 Stratford Dr West Bloomfield MI 48033 Office: Wayne County Gen Hosp Eloise MI 48132 also U Mich Med Sch Ann Arbor MI 48104

JOSEPH, RAYMOND PATTON, clergyman; b. Monticello, Iowa, June 2, 1927; s. Raymond Patterson and Alice Reid (Patton) J.; B.S., Geneva Coll., 1951; student State U. Iowa Med. Sch., 1951-52; grad. Ref. Presbyn. Theol. Sem., 1956; m. Alice Muriel Smith, Sept. 3, 1955; children—Brenda and Brian (twins), Philip, Barbara, Rebecca. Ordained to ministry Ref. Presbyn. Ch., 1956; pastor chs., San Diego, 1956-62, Greeley, Colo., 1962-67, West Lafayette, Ind., 1967—; script writer ednl. TV course Midwest Program for Ednl. TV, Purdue U., 1967-69; asso. staff mem. Intervarsity Christian Fellowship. Served with USAAF, 1945-47. Home: 1013 Hillcrest Rd West Lafayette IN 47906

JOSEPH, STANFORD RAYMOND, architect; b. Connersville, Ind., Sept. 7, 1936; s. Abraham and Nellie (Karabell) J.; student Miami U., Oxford, Ohio, 1954-56; B.Arch., Ohio State U., 1960. Pvt. practice architecture, Cin., 1966—; prin. Stan Joseph, Inc., Cin., 1972—, also dir. Mem. AIA, Ohio State U. Alumni Club. Republican. Jewish. Clubs: B'nai B'rith, Crest Hills Country. Home: 2851 Burkhart Ave Cincinnati OH 45213

JOSEPHSEN, GENE, elec. engr.; b. Sparkman, Fla., Apr. 19, 1927; s. Herman and Alice (Lustig) Josephsen; m. Stella Babich, June 19, 1948; children—Richard, James, Cynthia. B.S., Ill. Inst. Tech., 1951; student Northwestern U., 1959-60. Registered profl. engr., Ill. Mgr., Magnetic Recording Systems, Webcor, Inc., Chgo., 1953-64; supr. Stewart Warner Labs., Chgo., 1964-66; group mgr. Electronics Physics Lab., Sears Roebuck & Co., Chgo., 1966—. Troop com. chmn. Dearborn council Boy Scouts Am., 1970-71. Mem. Am. Engring. Assn. (nat. dir. 1966—), Toastmasters Internat., Rho Epsilon, Eta Kappa Nu. Home: 2840 N Parkside St Chicago IL 60634 Office: 925 S Homan Ave Chicago IL 60607

JOSEPHSON, MORTON, psychiatrist; b. N.Y.C., Feb. 2, 1924; s. Isadore and Dora (Schaefert) J.; B.A., Columbia, 1944; M.D., Chgo. Med. Sch., 1950; m. Dorothy Katchkey, Sept. 3, 1950; children—Martin, Steven, Kenneth, Richard. Intern, Harlem Hosp., N.Y.C., 1949-50; resident psychiatry Northport (N.Y.) VA Hosp., 1950-51; resident psychiatry Rochester (N.Y.) State Hosp., 1953-55, mem. med. staff, 1955-59; mem. staff Milw. Psychiat. Hosp., Wauwatosa, Wis., 1959—; clin. dir. Milw. Psychiat. Hosp., 1969—; asst. prof. human behavior Med. Coll. Wis., Milw., 1959-72, asso. prof., 1972—; pvt. practice psychiatry, Wauwatosa, 1959—. Bd. dirs. Mental Health Planning Com. Milwaukee County, 1972-74. Served to 1st lt. M.C. U.S. Army, 1951-53. Diplomate Am. Bd. Neurology and Psychiatry. Fellow Am. Psychiat. Assn.; mem. Wis. Psychiat. Assn. (pres. Milw. chpt. 1969-70), A.M.A. Home: 4059 N 60th St Milwaukee WI 53216 Office: 1220 Dewey Ave Wauwatosa WI 53213

JOSEPHSON, RICHARD JOHN, broadcasting a exec.; b. Monteviedo, Minn., May 24, 1951; s. John Emil and Mary Ann (Olien) J.; B.A., Southwest State U. at Marshall, Minn., 1973; M.S., Murray State U., 1973. Student supr. in charge radio-TV, Southwest State U., 1971-72; program dir., prodn. dir. Murray (Ky.) State U., 1972-73; engr. WLUC-TV, Marquette, Mich., 1973-76; studio supr., producer, dir., 1976—. Mem. Nat. Acad. TV Arts and Scis., Soc. Broadcast Engrs., Nat. Assn. Ednl. Broadcasters, Profl. Assn. Diving Instrs., Am. Radio Relay League, Hiawatha Amateur Radio Assn., Radio Amateur Satellite Corp., Satellite Communicators Club, Alpha Epsilon Rho. Lutheran. Home: 220 Marquette St Apt 1 Negaunee MI 49866 Office: Box 460 Marquette MI 49855

JOSHI, PRAHLAD RAVISHANKAR, indsl. microbiologist; b. Porbandar, India, Apr. 30, 1933; s. Ravishankar Jetharam and Maniben (Ravishankar) J.; B.S., Gujarat U., 1956, M.S., 1959; M.B.A., Ind. No. U., 1974; m. Hansa Hiralal, Feb. 23, 1965; 1 dau., Shephali. Med. technician Indian Council Med. Research, Bombay, 1956-57; tech. asst. Hindustan Antibiotics Research Centre, Poona, India, 1959-61; microbiologist, antibiotics prodn. supt. Cyanamid India Ltd., Bulsar, 1961-70; process engr. Lederle Labs., Pearl River, N.Y., 1970-72; control microbiologist Am. Cyanamid Co., Hannibal, Mo., 1972—. Sec. Sarvodya Mandal, Bulsar, India, 1968-69. Mem. Am. Soc. Microbiology, Soc. Indsl. Microbiology, Am. Mgmt. Assn. Home: 190 Gemini Hannibal MO 63401

JOSLEN, ROBERT ANDREW, hosp. adminstr.; b. Altadena, Calif., June 28, 1929; s. Fred L. and Elsie A. (Westlake) J.; B.S. in Bus. Adminstrn., Anderson (Ind.) Coll. and Theol. Sem., 1952; M.B.A., George Washington U., 1966; m. Eldine Frazee, Dec. 18, 1949; children—Robert, Lisa, Nancy. Adminstrv. asst., adminstrv. resident Washington Hosp., Washington, 1965-67; asst. dir. U. Mo. Med. Center, Columbia, 1967-69, also mem. faculty dept. community health and med. practice U. Mo. Med. Sch.; adminstr. St. Bernard Hosp., Chgo., 1969-73; pres. Saginaw (Mich.) Osteo. Hosp., 1973—; preceptor adminstrv. residents in hosp. adminstrn. George Washington U., 1975—, Trinity U., San Antonio, 1971—. Bd. dirs. Englewood Sr. Citizens Centers, 1969-73, chmn., 1970-71; bd. dirs. Comprehensive Research and Devel., 1971-73, Englewood Manor Apts., 1969-73, Group Health Service Mich., 1975—, Community Hosp. Services, 1973—. Served with AUS, 1946-48. Fellow Am. Coll. Hosp. Adminstrs.; mem. Mich. Hosp. Assn. (trustee; chmn. unemployment compensation com. 1975-77), Mich Osteo. Hosp. Assn. (v.p. 1977—, dir. 1974—), Am. Hosp. Assn., Am. Pub. Health Assn., Acad. Health Care Cons.'s. Clubs: Elks. Kiwanis. Home: 3840 N River Rd Freeland MI 48623 Office: Saginaw Osteo Hosp 515 N Michigan Ave Saginaw MI 48602

JOSLYN, LINDA MAY, clin. psychologist; b. Los Angeles, Dec. 14, 1941; d. Allyn Morgan and Dorothy (Yockel) Joslyn. B.A., U. Calif. at Los Angeles, 1964; M.A., Calif. State U., 1967; Ph.D., U. Kans., 1976. Intern clin. psychology Western Mo. Mental Health Center, Kansas City, 1970-71; staff psychologist adolescent service Western Mo. Mental Health Center, Kansas City, Mo., 1971-73, adolescent unit coordinator, 1973—; cons. Jackson County Juvenile Ct., Kansas City, Mo., 1974, 76, Florence Crittenton Center, Kansas City, 1977—; pvt. practice clin. psychology, Personal and Family Devel. Services, Kansas City, Mo., 1976—; instr. Avila Coll., Kansas City, 1977—; lectr. U. Mo. at Kansas City Med. Sch., 1975—. Bd. dirs. Alternative Opportunities, Inc., Kansas City, Mo., 1976—. Mem. Am., Mo., Greater Kansas City psychol. assns., Internat. Transactional Analysis Assn., Am. Soc. Group Psychotherapy and Psychodrama, Assn. Humanistic Psychology, Assn. Advancement Psychology, Common Cause, U. Calif. at Los Angeles Alumni Assn. Contbg. author Sensitivity Training and the Laboratory Approach, 3d edit., 1977. Office: 3904 Clark St Kansas City MO 64111

JOUNO, RANDOLPH JAMES, historian, personnel mgmt. cons.; b. Minocqua, Wis., Jan. 5, 1907; s. Edwin J. and Rose E. (Krzmarcik) J.; B.A. magna cum laude, St. Thomas Coll., St. Paul, 1929; M.A., U. S.D., 1937; Ph.D., Miss. State U., 1974; m. Dorothy M. Carlson, 1936; 1 dau., Paulette K. Instr. pvt. acad., St. Paul, 1929-39; instr. U.S. history U. Detroit, 1938; civilian personnel officer U.S. Civil Service Commn. and other fed. depts., various locations, 1939-70; lectr. Am. govt. and pub. personnel adminstrn. Miss. State U., 1970-71; personnel mgmt. cons., writer, Falls Church, Va., also St. Paul, 1971—; dir. instr. courses in fed. govt., unemployment ins., personnel mgmt.; officer Twin Cities Fed. Personnel Council. Mem. Am. Hist. Assn., Orgn. Am. Historians, Am. Soc. Pub. Adminstrn. (officer), Twin Cities Fed. Bus. Assn. (officer), Phi Alpha Theta, Pi Sigma Alpha. Democrat. Contbr. articles to newspapers and profl. jours. Home: 870 S Smith Ave St Paul MN 55107

JOURNEY, MARTHA JANE, clin. psychologist; b. Marshall, Mo., July 13, 1950; d. Cecil Eric and Martha Louise (McQuitty) Gray; B.A., Central Mo. State U., 1972, M.S., 1974; M.Ed., U. Mo., Columbia, 1976. Psychologist, Fulton (Mo.) State Hosp., 1973-74; clin. psychologist Higginsville (Mo.) State Sch. and Hosp., 1976—; tchr. psychology Raytown (Mo.) Adult Edn. Certified tchr. behavioral scis. and Spanish, Mo. Mem. Am. Personnel and Guidance Assn., Sigma Sigma Sigma. Methodist. Home: 3517 Blue Ridge St Independence MO 64052 Office: PO Box 522 Higginsville MO 64037

JOY, CHARLES IRVING, lawyer; b. Des Moines, Feb. 19, 1906; s. Maynard I. and Myrtle Leona (Hall) J.; B.S., U. Iowa, 1938, J.D., 1930; m. Loraine Farr, June 18, 1930; children—Virginia (Mrs. Richard L. Poffenberger), James R., William H. Admitted to Iowa bar, 1930; mem. firm Joy & Wifvat, 1950-59, Joy, Wifvat & Poffenberger, 1959-70, Joy, Poffenberger & Joy, 1970—; city atty. City of Perry (Iowa), 1932-36; county atty. Dallas County, 1936-40; counsel, dir. Home Fed. Savs. & Loan Assn., Perry. Mem. Dallas County Sch. Bd., 1945-65. Mem. Am. (chmn. agrl. com., tax sect. 1970-72), Iowa (chmn. pub. info. com. 1966-70, 73-74, pres. conf. of bar assn. presidents 1971-74), Dallas County bar assns., Am. Judicature Soc., Am. Coll. Probate Counsel, Delta Theta Phi. Mason, Elk, Rotarian. Home: 1306 6th St Perry IA 50220 Office: 1215 Warford St Perry IA 50220

JOY, DENNIS MARTIN, physician; b. Lansing, Mich., Dec. 7, 1941; s. George Martin and Geraldine Lucille (Ashbaugh) M. J.; B.S., Mich. State U., 1963, M.S., 1965; M.D., U. Mich., 1971; m. Karen Marie Laine, Sept. 11, 1965; children—D. Martin, Kirsten Marie, Jeffrey Michael. Intern, Bethesda Luth. Hosp., St. Paul, 1971-72; resident in family practice U. Minn. Bethesda Hosp., St. Paul, 1972-74; practice medicine specializing in family practice, Charlevoix, Mich., 1974—; mem. staff Charlevoix Area Hosp., 1974—, chief of staff, 1976. Diplomate Am. Bd. Family Practice. Mem. AMA, Mich. State, No. Mich. med. socs., Am., Minn. acads. family practice, Perinatal Assn. Mich. Home: 301 Central St Charlevoix MI 49720 Office: 724 Park Ave Charlevoix MI 49720

JOYCE, AL JAMES, ins. agency exec.; b. Rockland, Wis., June 18, 1915; s. Charles A. and Winifred A. (Campbell) J.; m. Maurine Walton, Oct. 26, 1944; children—Michael James, Paul Walton, Timothy Alban, Jennifer Anne, Joseph Jay. Ins. agt. Security Mut. Life Ins. Co., 1950-53; pres. Iowa Time Assos., Clear Lake, 1953-65; v.p. equity div. Scarborough & Co., Chgo., 1971-73, cons., 1973-76; pres. Multi-Fin. Cons., Des Moines, 1977—; dir. Capitol Security Ins. Co., 1965-66. Republican. Roman Catholic. Club: Echo Valley Country. Home: 4608 SW 15th St Des Moines IA 50315 Office: 812 Equitable Bldg 6th and Locust Des Moines IA 50309

JOYCE, FLORENCE V. MIENERT (MRS. GEORGE T. JOYCE), civic worker; b. Fosston, Minn., Feb. 13, 1923; s. William P. A. and Clara (Lindfors) Mienert; R.N., Ancker Hosp. Sch. Nursing, St. Paul,

1944; student U. Minn., 1944-45; m. George T. Joyce, Aug. 8, 1946; children—Roberta Eileen Joyce Dreyer, Elizabeth Anne. Bd. dirs. N. Central Iowa chpt. ARC, 1960-66, 67-73, nursing services chmn., 1967—; pres. Vols. Service League, St. Joseph Mercy Hosp., Mason City, Iowa, 1959-61; leader Girl Scouts U.S.A., 1948-66; sec. family and children's services com. Community Planning Council, 1971; bd. dirs YWCA, 1963-66; precinct chmn. Cerro Gordo County Republican Central Com., 1974—. Mem. Nat. Trust Historic Preservation, Cerro Gordo County Med. Aux., Ancker (Hosp.) Alumni Assn., Charles H. MacNider Art Guild (chmn. 1971-72, mems. council 1975—). Club: Mason City Woman's (dir. 1965-75, 76-77, pres. 1969-70). Roman Catholic. Home: 259 N Crescent Dr Mason City IA 50401

JOYCE, JYME RILEY (MRS. WILLIAM JOSEPH JOYCE), univ. ofcl.; b. Joliet, Ill., Sept. 24, 1919; d. John Hopkins and Catherine (Kelly) Riley; student Briarcliff Manor Jr. Coll., 1940; m. William Joseph Joyce, June 5, 1943; children—William Joseph, Judy M. (Mrs. James A. Lang), Catherine M. (Mrs. Paul McManus), Jill (Mrs. Les Kasselman), Mary (Mrs. Gregory J. Hammond). Mem. ladies bd. Loyola University, Chgo. Decorated Lady of the Grand Cross of the Holy Sepulchre. Mem. Cath. Women's League (Joliet). Club: Illinois Club for Catholic Women (Chgo.). Home: 619 Cornelia St Joliet IL 60435 winter Lost Tree Village North Palm Beach FL 33403

JOYCE, WILLIAM JOSEPH, beverage co. exec.; b. Kansas City, Mo., July 29, 1916; s. John M. and Mary Agnes (McCann) J.; student parochial schs.; m. Jyme Riley June 5, 1943; children—William J., Judith Joyce Lang, Catherine Joyce McManus, Jill Joyce Kasselman, Mary Joyce Hammond. Chmn. bd. Ill. 7-Up Bottling Co., Madison 7-Up Bottling Co.; vice chmn., dir. Chgo. 7-Up Bottling Co., N.Y. 7-Up Bottling Co., Joyce Assos., Inc., Joyce 7-Up Bottlers, Inc., Washington 7-Up Bottling Co.; chmn. bd. dirs. Nat. Bank of Joliet (Ill.); vice chmn. bd. Joyce Advt., Inc. Pres., Cath. Youth Orgn.; mem. lay adv. bd. St. Xavier Coll.; trustee St. Francis Coll., Lt. Joseph P. Kennedy Sch., St. Joseph Hosp., Joliet. Decorated knight Grand Cross of Holy Sepulchre, knight Sovereign Order of Malta. Mem. Joliet Assn. Commerce, The Hundred Club of Will County (chmn. bd.), Hundred Club of Cook County (dir.). Clubs: Joliet Country; Minoqua (Wis.) Country; Chgo. Athletic (Chgo.); Chgo. Golf (Wheaton, Ill.); St. Louis; Madison (Wis.); Lost Tree (N. Palm Beach, Fla.). Home: 619 Cornelia St Joliet IL 60435 winter Lost Tree Village North Palm Beach FL 33403 Office: Ill 7-Up Bottling Co Joliet IL 60436

JOYNER, H. SAJON, physicist, med. cons.; b. Ft. Worth, June 6, 1939; s. Howard Warren and Arista (Arnold) J.; student U. Tex. at Arlington, 1957-60; B.S., U. Tex. at Austin, 1962, M.A., 1964; M.S., U. Mo. at Rolla, 1967, Ph.D., 1970; m. Mary Ellen Yankoff, June 15, 1969; children—Mary Elizabeth, Arista Elia, Patricia Danielle. Nuclear engr. Gen. Dynamics, Fort Worth, 1964; asst. prof. dept. mech. engring. Wichita (Kans.) State U., 1969-75, dir. planning, research and devel. U. Kans. Sch. Medicine, Wichita, 1975-77; pres. Kinetic Corp., 1977—. Mem. Am. Phys. Soc., ASME, N.Y. Acad. Scis., Sigma Xi, Pi Tau Sigma, Sigam Pi Sigma, Tau Beta Pi, Phi Kappa Phi. Episcopalian. Home: 16406 E 37th St N Route 1 Towanda KS 67144

JUBA, STEPHEN, mayor Winnipeg (Man., Can.). Office: City Hall Winnipeg MB R3B 1B9 Canada*

JUDD, ROBERT EUGENE, agrl. editor and pub.; b. Emporia, Kans., Sept. 29, 1945; s. Frank Eugene and Roberta Effie (Boles) J.; B.S. in Tech. Journalism, Kans. State U., 1968; m. Ann Miller Harding, June 15, 1968; children—Stefanie Anne, Alex Benjamin. Editor, Kans. 4-H Jour., 1968-69; asso. editor Drovers Jour., 1969-71; editor Better Beef Bus., North Kansas City, Mo., 1971-76; partner Alexander Equipment Co., Amarillo, Tex., 1976—. Pub. cons. Maine-Anjou Mark mag., Am. Breeds Jour. mag. Home: 2110 Violet Lane Liberal KS 67901 Office: Box 7653 Amarillo TX 79109

JUDGE, JOHN EMMET, mktg. cons.; b. Grafton, N.D., May 5, 1912; s. Charles C. and Lillian (Johnson) J.; B.S., U. N.D., m. Clarita Garcia, Apr. 18, 1940; children—Carolyn (Mrs. Samuel Stanley), J. Emmet, Maureen, Eileen, Susan. Asst. to adminstr. Fed. Works Agy., Washington, 1939-42; staff mem. Wallace Clark & Co., mgmt. cons., 1942-46; v.p. Morgan Furniture Co., Asheville, N.C., 1946-48; mgr. financial analysis Lincoln Mercury div., Ford Motor Co., 1949-53, asst. gen. purchasing agt., 1953-55, merchandising mgr., 1955-58, mgr. Mercury mktg., 1958-60, mgr. product planning office, 1960-62; v.p. mktg. services Westinghouse Electric Corp., Pitts., 1963-67; v.p. marketing Indian Head Inc., 1967-68; mktg. cons., Birmingham, Mich., 1968—. Dir. Intertek Industries Inc., Kratos Inc. Mem. nat. adv. com. mktg. to sec. commerce. Chmn. library study com., Birmingham, Mich., 1957; dir. Boysville of Mich., 1957. Mem. Am. Def. Preparedness Assn., Soc. Advancement Mgmt., Engring. Soc. Detroit, Am. Soc. M.E., Nat. Assn. Accountants, Soc. Automotive Engrs., U.S. C. of C. (consumer com.), N.A.M. (mktg. com.), Newcomen Soc. N.Am., Sigma Tau, Alpha Tau Omega. Roman Catholic. Clubs: Detroit Athletic, Economic (Detroit); Orchard Lake County (dir.). Address: Shore Dr Harbor Springs MI 49740

JUDGE, JOHN ROBERT, pathologist, virologist; b. Sharon, Pa., May 13, 1933; s. Nicholas A. and Carmella (Taliano) J.; B.A., Case Western Res. U., 1955, M.S., 1957; M.D., Ohio State U., 1961; m. Helen Louise Kapl, Jan. 8, 1955; children—Michael Raymond, Judith Anne. Intern, St. Lukes Hosp., Cleve., 1961-62; resident Cleve. U. Hosps., 1964-66; resident St. Lukes Hosp., Cleve., 1966-68, mem. staff, 1968-69; dir. pathology Lakewood (Ohio) Hosp., 1970—; asst. clin. prof. pathology Case Western Res. U.; med. cons. Am. Cancer Soc. (local branch). Served with M.C., USN, 1962-64, S.E. Asia. Diplomate Am. Bd. Pathology. Fellow NIH, Am. Cancer Soc.; mem. Cleve. Soc. Pathologists, Cleve. Acad. Medicine, Ohio State Path. Assn., Ohio State Med. Assn., Coll. Am. Pathologists, Am. Soc. Clin. Pathologists, Internat. Acad. Pathology. Republican. Roman Catholic. Clubs: Cleve. Yachting. Author numerous profl. papers; research viral etiology of cancer, 1964-70. Home: 20710 Saratoga Dr Fairview Park OH 44126 Office: 14519 Detroit Ave Lakewood OH 44107

JUDSON, LYMAN SPICER VINCENT, educator, author; b. Plymouth, Mich., Mar. 27, 1903; s. Ernest W. and Fannie Lousie (Spicer) J.; A.B. in Biol. Scis., Albion Coll., 1925; M.S. in Med. Scis., U. Mich., 1929; Ph.D., U. Wis., 1933; postgrad. Sch. Mich. U., 1926, U. Iowa, 1929-30, U. So. Calif., 1927, Harvard U., 1942, U. San Francisco, Palma, Mallorca, Spain, 1967; m. E. Ellen MacKechnie, 1933 (dec. 1964); m. 2d, S. Adele H. Christensen, 1968. Chmn. dept. sci. Las Vegas (Nev.) High Sch., 1925-27; studio dir. Sta. KUSD, 1927-28; chmn. dept. speech Ala. Poly. Inst., Auburn, 1930-31, Kalamazoo Coll., 1936-42; chief motion picture and visual edn. divs. Pan Am. Union, OAS, 1946-50; served to comdr. USNR, 1942-65; mem. joint bd. control USN tng. films, 1944-46; chmn. dept. speech Babson Inst. Bus. Adminstrn., 1950-55; vis. prof. Latin Am. affairs Assn. Am. Colls., 1952; aide Hon. Christian A. Herter, 1954-57; asst. to pres. Alfred U., 1955-57; dir. pub. relations Ripon Coll., 1957-63; lectr. U. Wis., 1963-64; prof. speech Winona (Minn.) State Coll., 1964-71; chmn. bd., treas. Am. Fine Arts Found., Rochester, Minn., 1971—; staff Supreme Allied Comdr. Atlantic, liaison officer staff Supreme Allied Comdr. Europe and European Hdqrs., dir. gen. NATO, 1953-54; spl. mission Vietnam and 7th Fleet, 1966; TV cons. Johnson Found., 1963-64; devel. and long-range planning cons., 1965—; Mem. Explorers Scout bd., cabinet mem., bd. mem., exec. com. mem., treas. Twin Lakes council Boy Scouts Am., 1972-73. Fellow Am. Geog. Soc.; mem. AAAS, Inter-Am. Soc. Anthropology and Geography, Soc. Am. Archeology, Am. Soc. Agrl. Scis., Am. Acad. Polit. and Social Scis., Pub. Relations Soc. Am., Wis. Arts Council, Boston Athenaeum (propr.), Chgo. Art Inst., Assn. Corcoran Gallery Art, Am. Fedn. Arts, Rochester, Walker art centers, Oshkosh Fine Arts Assn., Friends of Bergstrom Art Center, Archeol. Inst. Am. (pres. Winona-Hiawatha Valley chpt.), Friends of Library Oshkosh, Navy League, Sigma Xi, Alpha Phi Omega, Delta Sigma Rho (nat. sec., nat. editor), Tau Kappa Alpha, Pi Kappa Delta, Sigma Delta Chi, Sigma Chi. Episcopalian. Rotarian, Kiwanian. Clubs: Metropolitan Dinner, First Nighters, Explorers (N.Y.C.); Cosmos (Washington). Author: Electrodynamic Recorder, 1930; Objective Studies on the Influence of the Speaker and the Listener, 1930; Combining the Breathing Undae of Speaker and Listener, 1932; Preliminary Study of the Offerings of Speech-Content Courses in the Technical Colleges of the United States, 1932; The Vegetative Versus the Speech Use of Biological Systems, 1932; Basic Speech and Voice Science, 1933; The Fundamentals of the Speaker-Audience Relationship, 1934; Modern Group Discussion, 1935; Manual of Group Discussion, 1936; Public Speaking for Future Farmers, 1936; After-Dinner Speaking, 1937; Winning Future Farmers Speeches, 1939; The Student Congress Movement, 1940; The Monroe Doctrine and the Growth of Western Hemisphere Solidarity, 1941; Voice Science, 1942, rev. edit., 1965; The Judson Guides to Latin America, including: Let's Go to Colombia, 1949, Let's Go to Guatemala, 1950, Let's Go to Peru, 1951, Your Holiday in Cuba, 1952; Report of Command Information Bureau 47 on Operation Inland Seas, 1959; The Interview, 1966; The Business Conference, 1969; Vincent Judson: The Island Series, 1973; Solution: PNC and PNCLAND, 1973; The AQUA Declaration, 1976; numerous other stories, articles and pamphlets. Address: PO Box 769 Rochester MN 55901 also Am Fine Arts Found 307 First Nat Bank Bldg Rochester MN 55901

JUERGENSMEYER, ELIZABETH BOGART (MRS. JOHN ELI JUERGENSMEYER), biologist; b. Columbia, Mo., May 28, 1940; d. Ralph and Frances (Warbritton) Bogart; B.S., Oreg. State U., 1962; M.S. (NSF fellow), U. Ill., 1964, Ph.D., 1967; m. John Eli Juergensmeyer, Sept. 10, 1963; children—Margaret Ann, Frances Elizabeth. Teaching and research asst. U. Ill., Chgo. Circle, 1965-68; asst. prof. biology William Rainey Harper Coll., Palatine, Ill., 1968-69; asso. prof. biology Judson Coll., Elgin, Ill., 1969—. Lay leader Grace Methodist Ch., Elgin. Mem. AAAS, Am. Soc. Zoologists, Genetics Soc., Am. Soc. Protozoologists, Am. Inst. Biol. Sci., N.Y. Acad. Sci. Home: 401 Hazel Dr Elgin IL 60120

JUERGENSMEYER, JOHN ELI, lawyer; b. Stewardson, Ill., May 14, 1934; s. Irvin Karl and Clara Augusta (Johannaber) J.; B.A., U. Ill., 1955, J.D., 1963; M.A., Princeton U., 1957, Ph.D., 1960; m. Elizabeth Ann Bogart, Sept. 10, 1963; children—Margaret Ann, Frances Elizabeth. Faculty, extension div. U. Ill., 1961-63, U. Hawaii, 1958-60; admitted to Ill. bar, 1963; mem. firm Kirkland, Brady, McQueen, Martin & Schnell, Elgin, Ill., 1963-64; founder, sr. partner Juergensmeyer, Zimmerman & Smith, Elgin, 1964—; mng. owner Lawyers Bldg., Inc., 1967—; asst. pub. defender Kane County, 1964-67. Hearing officer Ill. Pollution Control Bd., 1971-74; lectr. Inst. for Continuing Legal Edn., Ill. Bar Assn., 1971-73; asso. prof. Judson Coll., Elgin, 1963—. Chmn. Hiawatha Dist. Boy Scouts Am. Vice pres. Elgin Family Service Assn., 1967-71; sec. Lloyd Morey Scholarship Fund, 1967-73. Commr. Elgin Econ. Devel. Commn., 1971-75; sec. Elgin Twp. Rep. Central Com., 1972—. Adv. bd. Ill. Youth Commission, 1964-68; bd. dirs. Wesley Found. of U. Ill., 1971-75; pres. adv. bd. Elgin Salvation Army, 1973-75. Served to capt. Intelligence Service, USAF, 1958-60. Recipient Anti-Pollution Echo award Defenders of the Fox River, Inc., 1971, Certificate of Merit, Heart Fund, 1971, Outstanding Young Man award Jr. C. of C., Elgin, 1967. Princeton U. fellow, 1955-56, Merrill Found. fellow, 1956-58. Mem. Am. Trial Lawyers Assn., Am., Ill. (chmn. local govt. com. 1974-75), Chgo. (chmn. local govt. com. 1975-76), Kane County bar assns., Am. Arbitration Assn. (arbitrator), Am. Polit. Sci. Assn., Izaak Walton League, Fed. Bar Assn., Phi Beta Kappa, Phi Alpha Delta, Alpha Kappa Lambda. Methodist. Mason (Shriner), Elk, Rotarian (pres. 1977-78). Club: Union League (Chgo.). Author: The President, The Foundations, and The People-to-People Program, 1965. Editor Ill. Bar Assn. Local Govt. Law Newsletter, 1973-75. Contbr. to publs. in field. Office: 5 Douglas Ave Elgin IL 60120

JULIAN, CHARLES LEROY, chiropractor; b. Moline, Kans., Dec. 5, 1929; s. Roy and Kittie Susan (Sallee) J.; D. Chiropractic, Cleve. Chiropractic Coll., 1966; postgrad. Nat. Coll. Chiropractic, 1968-69, 71-74, Tex. Chiropractic Coll., 1974-75; m. Gloria Dean Ray, June 18, 1950; 1 dau., Mona Lynn Julian Fennema. Grocery clk., meat cutter Ray's Market, Independence, Kans., 1952-55; salesman Fuller Brush Co., Independence, 1955-61, Mut. of Omaha, Independence, 1961-62; practice chiropractic medicine, Independence, 1966—; lectr. in field. Served with USN, 1948-49, 50-52. Diplomate Am. Bd. Chiropractic Orthopedics. Mem. Kans. (dist. sec.-treas. 1967-68), Ky. chiropractic assns., Kans. Roentgenology and Orthopedic Assn., Kans. Sacro Occipital Research Soc. Internat. (pres. 1973-74). Methodist. Clubs: Moose (gov. Independence chpt. 1970-71), Promenade Sq. Dance (v.p. 1967). Home: 1516 W Laurel St Independence KS 67301 Office: 1510 W Laurel St Independence KS 67301

JULIAN, CLOYD JAMES, ednl. adminstr.; b. Austin, Ind., Nov. 30, 1910; s. Otto James and Elsie (Mitchell) J.; A.B., DePauw U., 1933, M.A., U. Iowa, 1948; postgrad. Ind. U., 1949-53; m. Elizabeth Brooks, Dec. 25, 1935; children—William B., Joanne E. Tchr., Austin High Sch., 1934-36; tchr., coach George Washington High Sch., Indpls., 1937-51, dept. head, 1946-51, vice prin., 1956-61, prin., 1961—; cons. Indpls. Pub. Schs., 1951-56. Mem. Mayor's Adv. Bd., 1969—. Served with USNR, 1943-46. John Hay fellow; Rector scholar; fellow Ind. Assn. Health, Phys. Edn. and Recreation; named to Ind. Football Hall of Fame, Exchange Club Book of Golden Deeds. Mem. Nat. Assn. Student Councils (adv. bd. 1973-76), Huguenot Soc. Ind., Alpha Tau Omega, Phi Delta Kappa. Methodist. Clubs: Rotary, Masons (32 deg.), Torch. Author: (with James Otto, Edward Tether) Modern Health, 6th edit., 1975; (with Elizabeth Jackson) Modern Sex Education, 2d edit., 1971. Home: 4001 E Kessler Blvd Indianapolis IN 46220

JUNAID, RAJA MUHAMMAD, psychiatrist, educator; b. Gujranwala, Pakistan, July 2, 1939; s. Raja Asgharali and Fatima (Bibi) Khan; came to U.S., 1964; M.D., King Edward Med. Coll., U. Punjab (Pakistan), 1963; m. Susan Mary Nejdl, Dec. 30, 1974; children—Jeffrey, Jon. House surgeon, physician Mayo Hosp., Lahore, Pakistan, 1963-64; intern Glens Falls (N.Y.) Hosp., 1965; resident psychiatry Fairfield Hills Hosp., Newtown, Conn., 1966-68; fellow psychiatry and neurology Yale Med. Sch., 1967-68; psychiatrist Mental Health Inst., Independence, Iowa, 1968-69, asst. chief adult psychiatry, 1969-73, dir. profl. edn. and research, 1973-77; pvt. practice psychiatry, Waterloo, Iowa, 1976—; mem. staff Allen and St. Francis hosps., Waterloo. Clin. instr. U. Iowa, Iowa City, 1973—. Diplomate Am. Bd. Psychiatry and Neurology. Mem. Am. Psychiat. Assn., Am. Assn. Dirs. Psychiat. Residency Tng., Am., Pakistan (life) med. assns. Club: Rotary. Home: 922 Sheridan Rd Waterloo IA 50701 Office: 610 First Nat Bldg Waterloo IA 50703

JUNCHEN, DAVID LAWRENCE, pipe organ mfg. co. exec.; b. Rock Island, Ill., Feb. 23, 1946; s. Lawrence Ernest and Lucy Mae (Ditto) J.; B.S. in Elec. Engring. with highest honors, U. Ill., 1968. Founder, owner Junchen Pipe Organ Service, Sherrard, Ill., 1968—; co-owner Junchen-Collins Organ Corp., Woodstock, Ill., 1975—. Named Outstanding Freshman in Engring. U. Ill., 1963-64. Mem. Am. Inst. Organ Builders, Am. Theatre Organ Soc., Mus. Box Soc., Automatic Mus. Instrument Collectors Assn., Theatre Organ Soc. Australia, Cinema Organ Soc. London, Tau Beta Pi, Sigma Tau, Eta Kappa Nu. Contbr. to Ency. Automatic Mus. Instruments; composer, arranger over 50 music rolls for self-playing mus. instruments. Home: 401 1st St Sherrard IL 61281 Office: 743 McHenry Ave Woodstock IL 60098

JUNE, DOUGLAS EUGENE, mfg. co. exec.; b. Atlanta, Apr. 2, 1927; s. George Warner and Mildred Minnie (Brown) J.; student Coll. Commerce, Mpls., 1947-49, U. Wis., 1960; m. Shirley Ione Steinhoff, Nov. 27, 1949; 1 dau., Kristine Rae. With The Trane Co., diversified industry, LaCrosse, Wis., 1949—, mgr. gen. accounting, 1965-72, mgr. corporate accounting, 1973—; treas., asst. chmn. bd. The Trane Co. Found., Inc., 1970—; mem. audit com. Trane Employees Credit Union, 1960-71, dir., 1977—. Served with USNR, 1945-46. Mem. Am. Inst. C.P.A.'s, Wis. Inst. C.P.A.'s, United Commercial Travelers, Wis. State Com. C.P.A.'s in Industry, V.F.W., Am. Legion. Methodist. Republican. Mason (Shriner). Club: Eagles. Home: 2963 Longview Court LaCrosse WI 54601 Office: 3600 Pammel Creek Rd LaCrosse WI 54601

JUNGBLUT, LEO BERNARD, chiropractor; b. Grand Rapids, Mich., Oct. 8, 1936; s. Theodore and Catherine (Engeldinger) J.; student Aquinas Coll., 1954-56; D. Chiropractic, Palmer Coll. Chiropractic, 1959; m. Giselle Althoff, Aug. 25, 1962. Gen. practice chiropractic medicine, Grand Rapids, 1961-62, Holland, Mich., 1962—. Bd. dirs. Rockley Research Acad. Inc., 1971-72. Recipient Kiwi award Rockley Acad., 1971. Mem. Am., Mich. State (v.p. Dist. 3 1975-76) chiropractic assns. Club: Lions. Home: 965 N Baywood Dr Holland MI 49423 Office: 529 E 16th St Holland MI 49423

JUNGJOHANN, WAYNE VERNON, banker; b. Clinton, Iowa, Dec. 29, 1937; s. Vernon Lloyd and Erma Lillian Emma (Wilke) J.; grad. high sch.; m. Debbie Lou Sidlinger, Apr. 22, 1961; children—Julie Dea, James Edward. Asst. cashier Iowa State Savs. Bank, Clinton, 1961-64, asst. cashier-auditor, 1964-66, auditor, 1966-68, cashier, 1968—, v.p., 1972—. Councilman 7th ward, 1970-71; chmn. Clinton County Regional Planning Commn.; mem. Clinton Planning Commn., 1975—, chmn. spl. projects com.; bd. dirs. Clinton Baseball Club Inc., 1965—, pres., 1974—; bd. dirs. ARC, 1970-71, Salvation Army, 1970-71; auditor United Fund, 1966; mem. Clinton Jaycees Y's Mens Club, 1964, treas., 1964-65; dir. Mississippi Valley Bank Adminstrn. Inst., 1970-71. Served with AUS, 1955-58. Mem. Clinton County Bankers Assn. (pres. 1973), Odeon Assn., Gateway (membership chmn., dir.), Clinton chambers commerce, Clinton Toastmasters (edn. v.p. 1968, 69). Republican. Congregationalist. Clubs: Lions (pres. Clinton 1972), Rotary Valley Oaks Country. Home: 317 35th Ave N Clinton IA 52732 Office: 122 Main Ave Clinton IA 52732

JUNKIN, WALTER EDWARD, photographer; b. Fargo, N.D., Aug. 31, 1933; s. Floyd and Adeline Mary (Howley) J.; student N.D. State U., 1951-54; m. Karen Jean Amundson, Mar. 20, 1954; children—Tracy, Douglas, Matthew. Owner Junkin Studio, portrait photographer, Sauk Centre, Minn., 1956—. Adviser Willmar Tech./Vocational Sch. Photography Course, 1972-74. Mem. Profl. Photographers Am., Minn. (pres. 1974-75), Central Minn. (pres. 1965-66) profl. photographers assns. Mason, Lion (pres. 1970-71). Home and office: 1107 S Main St Sauk Centre MN 56378

JUNKINS, JOHN MERRELL, educator, psychologist; b. Oklahoma City, Aug. 7, 1935; s. John Merrell and Ruth Pearl (Ratliff) J.; B.S., Kans. State Coll., Pittsburg, 1959, M.S., 1963; Ed.D., Okla. State U., 1972; m. Imogene R. Harrall, Mar. 18, 1954; children—Stephen, Gail (Mrs. Gregory W. Sweet), Tommy, Julie. Elementary sch. tchr., Newton and Jasper Counties (Mo.), Joplin pub. schs., 1960-63; faculty Mo. So. State Coll., Joplin, 1963—, asso. prof. psychology, 1972—, head dept., 1975—; part-time clin. psychologist Joplin Regional Diagnostic Clinic, 1967-70. Pres., Joplin R-VIII Bd. Edn., 1974-75. NDEA Inst. fellow, 1967; NSF fellow, grantee, 1965. Baptist. Home: 2722 Wisconsin St Joplin MO 64801

JUPIN, LAURA ROSE, art and pub. relations exec.; b. Champaign, Ill.; d. Charles William and Alice Marshall (Potter) Rose; B.S., U. Ill., 1931, M.A., 1950; postgrad. So. Ill. U.; m. Earl C. Jupin, June 2, 1935 (dec. Nov. 1963); children—Lawrence Earl, Sondra Rose (Mrs. James T. Gillice). Tchr. Mason City Community High Sch., Mason City, Ill., 1931-35; tchr. Young and Antioch Elementary schs., Salem, Ill., 1942-46, Centralia (Ill.) High Sch., 1946; dir. art Centralia City schs., 1948-73; now freelance art and pub. relations. Mem. Ill. Com. Welfare, Marion County; pub. relations coordinator Marion County Am. Cancer Soc. Bd. dirs. Centralia Cultural Soc. Mem. Ill. Edn. Assn. (dir. 1962-65; pres. Kaskaskia Valley 1962), Nat. Sch. Pub. Relations Assn. (Ill. pres. 1967), Ill. Art Edn. Assn. (pres. 1960), Ill., Nat. assn. sch. adminstrs., DAR, Nat. Soc. Magna Carta Dames (life), Marion County Geneal. Hist. Soc. (registrar), Bus. and Profl. Women's Club, Friends of Mitchell Art Mus., Delta Zeta, Delta Kappa Gamma. Mem. Christian Ch. Home: 1063 E McCord St Centralia IL 62801

JUREK, BERNARD JAMES, JR., mech. engr.; b. St. Cloud, Minn., Aug. 19, 1925; s. Ben Joseph and Naomi Louisa (Latteral) J.; B.S., M.E., U. Minn., 1946; m. Eileen Mary Dahl, Feb. 25, 1946; children—Thomas Jon, William Robert, Cherilyn Sue, Connie Louise. With Chevrolet div. Gen. Motors Co., various locations, 1949—, plant mgr. Bay City, Mich., 1967-72, Detroit, 1972-77, mgr. Chevrolet mfg. research and devel., 1977—. Served with USN, 1943-46. Mem. Hamtramck C. of C. (dir.), Soc. Auto. Engrs. Republican. Baptist. Clubs: Masons, Shriners. Huron River Hunting and Fishing. Home: 35675 Congress Rd Farmington Hills MI 48018 Office: 30007 Van Dyke St Warren MI 48090

JUREK, THOMAS FRANCIS, radio sta. exec.; b. Chgo., Aug. 2, 1949; s. Arthur Francis and Lottie Agnes (Glodek) J.; B.A. in Communications, St. Joseph's Coll., Rensselaer, Ind., 1967-71; m. Rosemarie Stalec, Oct. 22, 1977. Mem. staff Sta. WRIN, Rensselaer, 1969-70, part owner, program dir., 1975—; staff Sta. WCRW, Chgo., 1971-73; owner Sta. WFDT, Columbia City, Ind., 1973-75, also newsman, announcer. Mem. Area 3 Regional Plan Commn., 1973-74. Mem. Ind. Broadcasters Assn. Clubs: Elks, Rotary. Home: Panda Apt 6 Rensselaer IN 47978 Office: WRIN Box 282 Rensselaer IN 47978

JURGEMEYER, LOUIS LEROY, lawyer; b. Iowa City, Iowa, May 11, 1918; s. Louis H. and Ida Lee (Cesner) J.; B.A., U. Iowa, 1940, J.D., 1942; m. Margaret W. Andrew, Sept. 2, 1944. Admitted to Iowa bar, 1942; pvt. practice, Clinton, 1946—; mem. firm Jurgemeyer, Frey & Haufe; dir., treas. Clinton Devel. Co., 1953-72. Rep. County chmn., 1950-54, mem. state central com., 1954-59, state chmn., 1957-59, mem. nat. com., 1957-59. Served from pvt. to capt. U.S. Army, 1942-46. Mem. Clinton C. of C. (past pres.), Am., Iowa, Clinton County bar assns., Phi Beta Kappa. Mason. Clubs: Rotary (past pres.), Des Moines, Clinton Country. Home: 222 N 11th St Clinton IA 52732 Office: 209 Wilson Bldg Clinton IA 52732

JURGENS, ROGER EUGENE, dentist; b. Holdrege, Nebr., May 20, 1939; s. Emery Fritz and Ethel Emelia (Anderson) J.; student Luther Jr. Coll., Nebr., 1956-58; B.A. with honors, Kearney (Nebr.) State Coll., 1960; D.D.S. with honors, U. Nebr., 1964, postgrad. othodontics, 1973-75; m. DeAnna Ardell Bruning, Jan. 1, 1961; children—Cynthia Dee, Gregory Lynn, Jennifer Sue. Gen. practice dentistry, Kearney, 1964-72; instr. restorative dentistry U. Nebr. at Lincoln, 1972-73, part time instr., 1968-72, asso. prof. dept. orthodontics, 1975—; pvt. practice orthodontics, Lincoln, 1975—. Mem. exec. com. Good Samaritan Hosp., 1967-68. Pres. Buffalo County unit Am. Cancer Soc., 1967. Bd. dirs. Kearney United Fund, 1967-69, pres., 1969; bd. dirs. Kearney Pub. Schs., 1971-72. Mem. Am., Nebr., Lincoln Dist. (trustee 1977) dental assns., Nebr. N.W. Dist. Soc. (sec.-treas. 1967-68, v.p. 1968-69, pres. 1969-70), Am., Nebr. (dir. 1968-70, sec.-treas. 1970-72, v.p. 1972-73 pres. 1973-74) socs. dentistry for children, N.W. Dist. Soc. Dentistry (del. state 1969-72), Nebr. Soc. Preventive Dentistry (dir. 1973-74), Sertoma Internat. (dir. 1972, 77, v.p.), Am. Assn. Orthodontists, Kearney Jr. C. of C. (v.p. 1966, dir. 1964-66), Alpha Omega, Omicron Kappa Upsilon, Xi Psi Phi, Lambda Delta Lambda, Kappa Mu Epsilon. Lutheran (dir. 1965, 72). Elk. Club: Kearney Country (dir. 1971, 72). Home: 1730 S 77th St Lincoln NE 68520 Office: U Nebr Lincoln NE 68503 also 902 N 70th St Lincoln NE 68505

JURIS, HERVEY ASHER, educator; b. Lawrenceville, N.J., Sept. 5, 1938; s. Edward and Justa (Novik) J.; A.B., Princeton U., 1960; M.B.A., U. Chgo., 1962, Ph.D., 1967; children—Steven Jerome, Robin Lynn. Asst. dean students Grad. Sch. Bus., U. Chgo., 1962-64; asst. prof. U. Wis., Madison, 1965-70, asso. prof., 1970; asso. prof. Grad. Sch. Mgmt., Northwestern U., Evanston, Ill., 1970-75, prof. indsl. relations and urban affairs, 1975—, asso. dean acad. affairs-designate, 1978—. Nat. Center for Health Services Research grantee, 1975-78; Law Enforcement Asst. Adminstrn. grantee, 1970-72; Spencer Found. grantee, 1976-77; Ford Found. grantee, 1977-78. Mem. Am. Economic Assn., Indsl. Relations Research Assn., Indsl. Relations Assn. Chgo. Author: (with Peter Feuille) Police Unionism, 1973. Asso. editor Urban Affairs Quar., 1974—; contbr. articles to profl. jours. Address: 2001 Sheridan Rd Evanston IL 60201

JURSEK, PHILIP DAVID, communications cons.; b. Detroit, Oct. 12, 1939; s. Stanley James and Lauretta Emily (Duprey) J.; A.B., U. Detroit, 1961; M.A., Wayne State U., 1963, Ph.D., 1970; m. Carole Joyce Stewart, Mar. 18, 1967; children—Ned, Elizabeth. Various broadcasting positions, 1957-62; research analyst Campbell Ewald Advt., Detroit, 1962-66; mgr. media info. D'Arcy-MacManus Advt., Bloomfield Hills, Mich., 1966-71; v.p., media and research dir. Foster Advt. Toronto, Ont., Can., 1971-76; v.p. mktg. Swink Inc., 1976—; cons. George Weston Ltd., Maclean-Hunter, Ltd., Hakuhodo Advt., Tokyo, Bur. of Measurement, Ltd., Trans-Public, Ltd.; mem. Global TV Adv. Panel, adviser Fin. Post. Mem. Market Research Soc. (U.K.), Profl. Mktg. Research Soc., Am. Mktg. Assn., Can. Outdoor Advt. Measurement Bur., Print Measurement Bur. Roman Catholic. Contbr. articles to profl. jours. Office: care Swink Inc 333 E Center St Marion OH 43302

JUTZI, BERNHARD FREDERICK, religious assn. exec.; b. Chester, Ill., May 28, 1904; s. Henry Rudolph and Celetha (Gnaege) J.; B.A., Concordia Tchrs. Coll., 1920-25; m. Lottie Rosemary Ludtke, July 23, 1929; children—Bernhard H., Carolyn Sue (Mrs. Ralph N. Gassman), Mary Lou (Mrs. Edgar B. Crutchfield). Prin. St. Paul's Lutheran Sch., Houston, 1925-35; area sales dir. Kitchen Craft Aluminum Co., Houston, 1936, Baton Rouge, La., 1937; mgr. Woltmann Furniture Co., Houston, 1938-63; salesman Eric Moerbe & Co., Realtors, Houston, 1964-67; bus. adminstr. St. Mark's Lutheran Ch., Houston, 1967-69; dir. devel. Lutheran Laymen's League, St. Louis, 1969-71, exec. dir., 1971—. 5th Ward area Air Raid Warden, Houston, World War II. Named Layman of the Year for Greater Met. Houston, Central Activities Council Lutheran Ch., 1960; Layman of Year Lone Star Dist, 1962. Mem. Lone Star Dist. Walther League (pres. 1939-43), Tex. Dist. Bd. Mission Adminstr. Editor: The Houston Lutheran, 1965-69. Home: 14455 Greencastle Apt 3 Chesterfield MO 63017 Office: 2185 Hampton Ave St Louis MO 63139

JUVE, RICHARD HENRY, chem. co. exec.; b. Akron, O., Dec. 31, 1920; s. Walter Henry and Magda Marie (Petersen) J.; student Pa. State U., 1940-42, B.S. in Mineral Econs., 1948; m. Mary Evelyn Moore, June 14, 1947; children—Walter Henry III, John B., Richard C. Trainee, Goodyear Tire & Rubber Co., Akron, 1948-49; asst. mgr. Am. Texolite Corp., Mansfield, O., 1949-50; with tech. service dept. Ferro Chem. Corp., Bedford, O., 1950-53; salesman Americhem, Inc., Cuyahoga Falls, O., 1953-58, pres., 1958—. Served to capt. USMCR, 1942-46. Mem. Am. Mgmt. Assn. (presidents assn.), Soc. Plastics Engrs., Beta Theta Pi. Republican. Club: Sharon Golf (Sharon Center, O.). Home: 2787 N Walnut Ridge Rd Akron OH 44313 Office: 2038 Main St PO Box 375 Cuyahoga Falls OH 44222

JUVE, ROBERT DANIEL, rubber co. exec.; b. Akron, Ohio, June 16, 1917; s. Walter Henry and Magda Marie (Petersen) J.; B.S., Purdue U., 1939; m. Helen Grace Vosburgh, Dec. 31, 1943; children—Jenifer Ann, Kristina (Mrs. Robert Frank Klinkosh), Robert Daniel. Trainee Goodyear Tire & Rubber Co., Akron, 1939-40; in synthetic rubber research, 1940-48, synthetic rubber coordinator, 1948-50; dir. research and devel. Mohawk Rubber Co., 1950-71, dir. materials, compounding and tire scis., 1971—. Mem. Tech. Indsl. Intelligence Com., 1945; copolymer research group War Prodn. Bd., 1942-46. Mem. Am. Chem. Soc., Am. Soc. Testing Materials, Akron Rubber Group, Plastics and Rubber Inst., Beta Theta Pi. Republican. Methodist. Contbr. articles to profl. jours. Home: 444 Rothrock Rd Copley OH 44321 Office: Mohawk Rubber Co 1235 2d Av Akron OH 44309

KAATZ, HERBERT WILHELM GOTTFRIED, aviation mfg. co. exec.; b. Cleve., Apr. 25, 1920; s. Herbert R. and Pauline (Dregalla) K.; A.B., Oberlin U., 1958; m. Mildred N. Fischer, May 3, 1941; children—William H., Lynn R., Donald W. Owner, Photo Shop, Elyria, Ohio, 1939-41; project engr. Romec Pump Co., Elyria, 1941-45; pres. Kenco Products Inc., Lorain, Ohio, 1946-55; pres. Airborne Mfg. Co., Elyria, 1958—, also dir.; dir. JB Systems. Founder Lake Ridge Acad., North Ridgeville, Ohio, 1963, pres., 1964-65, trustee, 1963—. Served with USN, 1945-46. Mem. Am. Phys. Soc., Cleve. Engring. Soc., Gen. Aviation Mfrs. Assn. (dir.), Black River Astron. Soc., Am. Orchid Soc. Lutheran. Clubs: Elyria Country; Beaver Creek Hunt. Patentee in field. Home: 139 Crestview Dr Elyria OH 44035 Office: 711 Taylor St Elyria OH 44035

KABARA, JON JOSEPH, biochem. pharmacologist; b. Chgo., Nov. 26, 1926; s. John Stanley and Mary Elizabeth (Wielgus) K.; B.S., St. Mary's Coll. (Minn.), 1948; M.S., U. Miami, 1950; Ph.D., (Univ. scholar), U. Chgo., 1959; m. Annette Elser Sproull, Aug. 18, 1971; children—Chris Anne, Mary K., Sheila Jon, Pat Lee, Tim S., Steve S. Prof. chemistry U. Detroit, 1965-68; prof., asso., dean Mich. Coll. Osteo. Medicine, Pontiac, 1967-70; prof. asso. dean chemistry Mich. State U., East Lansing 1970-71, prof. biomechanics, 1971—; dir. lab. Spl.-Chem. Labs., Haslett, Mich., 1975—. cons. in neurochemistry and microbiology. Pres., Mich. N.E. PTA, 1959; active Little League, 1973-75. Damon Runyon Cancer fellow, 1949-50, Mt. Sinai fellow, 1949-51; Bishop Heffrom awardee St. Mary's Coll., 1970. Fellow Am. Inst. Chemists; mem. Am. Chem. Soc., N.Y. Acad. Sci., Detroit Physiology Soc., Assn. Analytical Chemists, AAAS, Am. Soc. Clin. Pathologists, Sigma Xi, other orgns. Contbr. articles to profl. publs. Home: 2088 Riverwood Dr Okemos MI 48864 Office: A407 E Fee Hall Mich State U East Lansing MI 48824

KABELE, WALTER AUGUST, mech. engr. and designer; b. Platteville, Wis., May 6, 1915; s. Fred William and Mary Wilhemina (Woolf) K.; mining engr. diploma Wis. Inst. Tech. (now U. Wis.-Platteville), 1941; postgrad. U. Mich., 1969, 71, U. No. Iowa, 1975; m. Lela Mae Jones, June 6, 1942; children—Richard, Dennis, Mary Kabele Juergens, Ruth, Christine. Engr. trainee Fairbanks Morse Co., mfr. pumps and engines, Beloit, Wis., 1941-45; chief engr. div. pumps A. Y. McDonald Mfg. Co., Dubuque, Iowa, 1945-54, Constrn. Machinery Co., Waterloo, Iowa, 1954-77, Enpo-Cornell Pump Co., Piqua, Ohio, 1977—; mem. adv. com. mech. drafting Hawkeye Inst. Tech., 1973-75. Jr. mem. bd. dirs. Allen Meml. Hosp., Waterloo, 1957-65. Mem. Profl. Iowa Engring. Soc. (chpt. charter). Lutheran. Patentee in field. Home: 1814 Wilshire Dr Piqua OH 45356 Office: 420 3d St Piqua OH 45356

KACHRU, BRAJ BEHARI, educator; b. Srinagar, Kashmir, India, May 15, 1932; s. Shyam Lal and Shobhavati Tulsidevi (Tutu) K.; came to U.S., 1963, naturalized, 1969; B.A. with honors, U. Kashmir, India, 1952; M.A., U. Allahabad, India, 1955; diploma applied linguistics U. Edinburgh, Scotland, 1959, Ph.D. (Brit. Council fellow), 1961; m. Yamuna Keskar, Jan. 22, 1965; children—Amita, Shamit. Research fellow Deccan Coll. Research Inst., Poona, India, 1957-58; asst. prof. Lucknow U., India, 1962-63; research asso. U. Ill., Urbana, 1963-64, mem. faculty, 1964—, prof. linguistics, 1970—, head of dept., 1969—, coordinator div. applied linguistics, 1976—; dir. summer program in S. Asian studies, 1967; chmn. regional varieties of English com. Assn. Commonwealth Lit. and Lang., Brisbane, Australia, 1968; mem. lang. com., cons. Am. Inst. Indian Studies, 1971—; cons. Ford Found., 1974-75; mem. lang. and lit. com. S. Asian Regional Council, 1977—. Research fellow Am. Inst. Indian Studies, 1967-68, 70-71, Center Advanced Study U. Ill., 1971-72. Mem. Linguistic Soc. Am. (dir. Linguistic Inst. 1978), Linguistic Soc. India, Am. Oriental Soc., Linguistic Assn. Can. and U.S., Assn. Tchrs. of English to Speakers of Other Langs. Author: A Reference Grammar of Kashmiri, 1966; An Introduction to Spoken Kashmiri, 1973; editor: Dimensions of Bilingualism: Theory and Case Studies, 1976. Home: 2016 Cureton Dr Urbana IL 61801 Office: Dept Linguistics U Ill Urbana IL 61801

KACMARCIK, THOMAS, mfg. co. exec.; b. Ironwood, Mich., Sept. 28, 1925; s. Mathew T. and Mary (Murra) K.; E.E., U. Ga., 1944; m. Josephine Tody, June 19, 1948; children—Sharon, Karen, Thomas, Shirley, James. Pres. F.W. Busch Co., Grafton. Wis., 1960-68; treas., dir. Cargo Ties Co., Cedarburg, Wis., 1968—; pres., dir. Milsted Products Co., Cedarburg, 1964—, Ataco Steel Products Co., Grafton, 1964—; pres. Continental Mfg. Co., Grafton; v.p. prodn. Stamping Corp., Milw.; dir. Snow Mobile Accessories, Inc. Mem. adv. com. Cedarsburg Sch., 1968—. Served as pilot USNR, 1943-48. Mem. Personal Mgmt. Assn. Lion (pres. 1969), Kiwanian (dir.). Home: 9413 Western Ave Cedarburg WI 53012 Office: 1046 Hickory St Grafton WI 53024

KACZMAREK, DONALD THOMAS, elec. and instrumentation project engr.; b. Chgo., Sept. 13, 1930; s. Sylvester and Marie (Aleksy) K.; student U. Ill., 1975; m. Pearl Pogorzelski, Apr. 30, 1955; children—Steven, David. Sr. elec. designer U.S. Industries, Chgo., 1958-65; design supr. United Engrs. & Constructors, Chgo., 1965-68; sr. engr. Kaiser Engrs., Chgo., 1968-69; elec. engr., Brown & Root, 1970-77; design engr. Sargent & Lundy, Chgo., 1970—; instrument and control project engr. Fluor Pioneer Engrs., Chgo., 1977—. Served with AUS, 1951-53; Korea. Registered profl. engr., Wis. Mem. Instrument Soc. Am. Instrumental design and project engring. power plants, nuclear units, steel mills, oil refinery facilities. Home: 3642 S Paulina St Chicago IL 60609 Office: 200 Monroe St W Chicago IL 60606

KACZMAREK, KENNETH KASIMER, automobile mfg. co. exec.; b. Milw., July 2, 1939; s. Arthur J. and Everlyn (Kilps) K.; B.S., Marquette U., 1963; M.B.A., U. Detroit, 1967; m. Carol L. Pietrzak, June 10, 1961; children—June Marie, Jacqueline Ann. Controller AMC Parts div. AM Gen. Corp., South Bend, Ind., 1973, material control mgr. Am. Motors Parts div., Milw., 1974, controller, 1974-77, dir. finance, Wayne, Mich., 1977. Mem. Fin. Exec. Inst., Nat. Assn. Accountants. Home: 3978 Anglia Ct West Bloomfield MI 48033 Office: 32500 Van Born Rd Wayne MI 48184

KADELA, ARNOLD ALEXANDER, tool mfg. co. exec.; b. Chgo., May 22, 1938; s. Alexander and Helen (Sojka) K.; student U. Ill., 1956-57, 59-60; A.A., Wright Jr. Coll., 1976; m. Mary Brown, Oct. 10, 1964; children—James, Karen, David. Corporate sec. Island Saw & Tool Co., Chgo., 1962-64; pres. U.S. Carbide Saw Co., Chgo., 1964-75, Directional Marketing, Inc., 1975—. Served with U.S. Army, 1960-62. Mem. Chgo. Assn. Commerce & Industry. Home: 4002 S Talman Ave Chicago IL 60632 Office: 2527 W Moffat St Chicago IL 60647

KADLUB, KARL JOZEF, psychologist; b. Chgo., Jan. 5, 1926; s. Karol Jozef and Maria (Galik) K.; B.S., U. Ill., 1951, M.S., 1954, Ph.D., 1956; m. Jean Marie Van Arkel, Oct. 10, 1948; children—K. Gregory, Kandace, Rock, Robin. Dir. psychol. services Battle Creek (Mich.) San. Hosp., 1958—; clin. psychologist VA Hosp., Battle Creek, 1956—. Instr., Mich. State U., 1960-66, Battle Creek Community Coll., 1958-60; cons. Battle Creek Dist. Ct., Police, County Sheriff. Mem. Battle Creek Human Relations Commn., 1966-68. Served as USAAF, 1944-46. Mem. Am. Psychol. Assn. Club: Battle Creek Country. Home: 120 W Hamilton Lane Battle Creek MI 49015 Office: 197 N Washington St Battle Creek MI 49016

KADLUBOWSKI, MICHAEL GEORGE, woodworking mfg. co. exec.; b. Reno, Feb. 17, 1945; s. Stanley Lawrence and Constance Sadie (Colby) K.; B.A. in Accounting, North Eastern Ill. U., Chgo., 1978; m. Joanne Damato, Aug. 21, 1971; 1 dau., Michelle Leigh. Chief accountant Pyle Nat. Corp., Chgo., 1969-72; controller Doncor, Inc., Chgo., 1972-73, Emconite div., Chgo., 1973-77; controller Lenc-Smith Mfg. Co. div. Bally Mfg., 1977—. Served with USN, 1965-69. Mem. Am. Accounting Assn., Am. Mgmt. Assn., Shellback Fraternity, Beta Alpha Psi. Home: 329 Loveland Dr Glendale Heights IL 60137 Office: 4616 W 19th St Cicero IL 60650

KAEBITZSCH, REINHOLD JOHANNES, poet; b. Ergolding, Germany, May 18, 1947; s. Johannes Willi and Ludwina Ernestina (Krojer) K.; B.A., Luther Coll., 1969; postgrad. Purdue U., 1969-70; M.A., U. Wis., 1972; m. Lynda Lanier, July 1976. Came to U.S., 1957, naturalized, 1965. Chief, Bur. Critics, United Amateur Press, 1972; fine arts editor New Dimensions, Madison, Wis., 1973, Badger Herald newspaper, U. Wis., Madison, 1973; writer U. Wis. News Service, Madison, 1973-74; teaching asst. German, Purdue U., 1969-70; coordinator pub. relations Elvehjem Art Center, Madison, 1975—; poetry cons. Wis. Acad. Scis., Arts and Letters, 1975—; store detective Tri-State Security, Madison, 1973-74; head security J. C. Penney Co., Madison, 1974—; instr. poetry U. Wis. Extension, 1976—. Bd. dirs. Wis. Regional Writers, 1976—. Mem. Madison Area Writers Assn. (pres. 1976-77). Author: White Marble, 1973; The Blue Sun, 1973; We, 1974; Near the Yellow Shadow, 1975; Fantasy Red, 1975; Georg Trakl's In the Red Forest, 1973; A Poem, Blackberries and a Bottle of Rum, 1975; Carp, a Love Poem and a Mythical Coast, 1975. Mem. editorial bd. Rufus, 1972—; editor-in-chief Hawk and Whippoorwhill Recalled, 1975—; editor The Nat. Locksmith, 1976—; contbg. editor Ozymandias, 1975—. Home: 453 N Baldwin St Madison WI 53703

KAEGEL, RAY MARTIN, real estate and ins. broker; b. St. Louis, Dec. 7, 1925; s. Ray E. and Loyola (Mooney) K.; B.S. in Secondary Edn., Washington U., St. Louis, 1948, M.B.A., 1955; m. Daniel Marilyn Dugger, July 2, 1943. Mgr., St. Louis Amusement Co., Inc., 1941-43, 46-52; gen. mgr. Md. Real Estate & Ins. Agy., Inc., Granite City, Ill., 1953-60; pres., gen. mgr., dir. Kaegel Real Estate & Ins. Agy., Inc., 1961—; sec. Granite City Bd. Realtors, 1959-63, 66-77, pres., 1964-65; sec.-treas. Granite City Multiple Listing Service. Served to lt. (j.g.) USNR, 1943-46. Mem. Nat. (exec. officer's council 1959-77), Ill. assns. real estate bds., Tri-Cities Ind. Ins. Assn. Agts. (pres. 1970-73), Ind. Ins. Agts. Ill., Tri-Cities C. of C. Club: Noonday Optimist. Home: 11255 Ladue Rd Saint Louis MO 63141 Office: 2721 Madison Ave Granite City IL 62040

KAERICHER, JOHN CONRAD, artist, educator; b. Springfield, Ill., June 6, 1936; s. John Henry and Edna Ann (Beckett) K.; B.F.A., Millikin U., 1959; M.F.A., U. Iowa, 1963; student under Mauricio Lasansky, Stuart Edie, James Lechay, David Driesbach. Asst. prof. art Northwestern Coll., Orange City, Iowa, 1963-65, asso. prof., 1965—, chmn. asst. dept., 1963—, dir. art gallery, 1966—chmn. fine arts collection acquistions, 1964—; lectr., cons. in field; exhibited in several one-man shows including Kirkland Fine Arts Center, Millikin U., 1972, Sioux City Art Center; numerous group shows including Central Ill. Ann. Show, Decatur, 1961, Sioux City Ann. Show, 1965, Iowa Gov.'s Office, Des Moines, 1971, Kottler Galleries, N.Y.C., 1973, Paper works, Waterloo (Iowa) Ann. Shows, 1975, Benjamin Galleries, Chgo., 1976, Va. Poly. Inst. Invitational Show, 1976; represented in pvt. and pub. collections. Northwestern Coll. grantee, 1966, 69, 75, 77. Mem. Mid-Am. Coll. Art Assns., Iowa Print Group. Mem. Christian Ch. Home: 615 Arizona St SW Orange City IA 51041 Office: 720 Delaware Ave SW Orange City IA 51041

KAESS, FREDERICK WILLIAM, judge; b. Detroit, Dec. 1, 1910; s. Fred C. and Dorothy (Koch) K.; student U. Mich., 1927-28; LL.B., Detroit Coll., 1932; m. Phyllis Danckmeyer, Dec. 31, 1931; 1 son, Frederick Charles. Admitted to Mich. bar, 1932; individual practice law, 1932-33; municipal justice St. Clair Shores, 1932-33; claims mgr. Mich. Mut. Liability Co., Detroit, 1933-39, 41-45; dep. commr. Mich. Dept. Labor and Industry, 1939-40; mem. firm Davidson, Kaess, Gotshall & Kelly, 1945-53; U.S. atty. Eastern dist. Mich., 1953-60, U.S. dist. judge, 1960—, chief judge, 1969—. Mem. Young Republican Nat. Com., 1941-43; chmn. Wayne County Rep. Com. 1948-52; chmn. Midwest Conf. Young Reps.; gen. counsel Nat. Fedn. Young Reps. Mem. Am., Mich., Fed. (pres. Detroit chpt. 1955-59) bar assns., Internat. Assn. Ins. Counsel, Sigma Delta Kappa. Mason (33 deg., Shriner). Clubs: Country of Detroit, Economic, Caravan Shrine, Noontide, Detroit Press, Crisis. Home: 971 N Oxford Rd Grosse Pointe Woods MI 48236 Office: Federal Bldg Detroit MI 48226

KAFARSKI, MITCHELL I., chem. processing exec.; b. Detroit, Dec. 15, 1917; s. Ignacy A. and Anastasia (Drzazgowski) K.; student U. Detroit, 1939-41, Shrivenham Am. U., Eng., 1945-46; m. Zofia Drozdowska, July 11, 1967; children—Erik Michael, Konrad Christian. Organizer, dir. Artist and Craftsman Sch., Esslingen, Germany, 1945-46; process engr. Packard Motor Car Co., 1941-44; with credit dept. Nat. Bank Detroit, 1946-50; founder, pres., dir. Chem. Processing, Inc., 1950-65; dir., treas. Detroit Magnetic Insp., 1960-65, Packard Plating, Inc., 1962-67; v.p., dir. KMH, Inc., 1960-64; chmn. bd., pres., treas. Aactron, Inc., 1965—. Bd. dirs. U.S.A. Pennsylvania Ave. Devel. Corp., Washington, 1973—; White House rep. opening U.S. Trade Center, Warsaw, Poland, 1972; commr. Mich. State Fair, 1965-72, exec. officer; mem. devel. and planning com. to build Municipal Stadium, 1965-69; patron, mem. Founders Soc. Detroit Inst. Arts; chmn. Am.-Polish Action Council, Inc.; vice chmn. Mich. Nationalities Council; sponsor and host world celebrity for World Preview Mich.; dist. adv. council U.S. SBA, 1971-73; del. White House Conf. on Aging, 1971; trustee Straith Meml. Hosp., Detroit, 1971—, v.p., treas., 1972—, now chmn. bd.; trustee Detroit Sci. Center, 1972—. Served with AUS, 1944-46; ETO. Recipient Nat. award for war prodn. invention, 1943 decorated knight's cross Order of Poland's Rebirth, 1975. Mem. Nat., Mich. (dir. 1966—, pres. 1976) assns. metal finishers, NAM (natural resources com.), Am. Electroplaters Soc., Bloomfield Arts Assn. (fund raising chmn. 1973, dir. 1973—), Cranbrook Acad. Arts. Clubs: Otsego Ski; Capitol Hill (Washington); Detroit Athletic. Home: 240 Chesterfield Bloomfield Hills MI 48013 Office: 29306 Stephenson Hwy Madison Heights MI 48071

KAGAN, SIOMA, educator; b. Riga, Russia, Sept. 29, 1907; s. Jacques and Berta (Kaplan) K.; Diplom Ingenieur, Technische Hochschule, Berlin, Germany, 1931; M.A., Am. U., 1949; Ph.D. in Econs., Columbia U., 1954; m. Jean Batt, Apr. 5, 1947 (div. 1969). Came to U.S., 1941, naturalized, 1950. Sci. asst. Heinrich Hertz Inst., Berlin, 1931-33; partner Laboratoire Electro-Acoustique, Neuilly-sur-Seine, France, 1933-48; chief French Mission Telecommunications French Supply Council in N.A., Washington, 1943-45; mem. telecommunications bd., UN 1946-47, econ. affairs officer, 1947-48; pvt. practice as econ. cons. to govt. and industry; asso. prof. econs. Washington U., St. Louis, 1956-59; staff economist Joint Council on Econ. Edn., N.Y.C., 1959-60; prof. internat. bus. U. Oreg., Eugene, 1960-67, U. Mo., St. Louis, 1967—; faculty leader Exec. Devel. Programs, Columbia U., Northwestern U., NATO Def. Coll., Rome, others. Served with Free French Army, 1941-43. Decorated Legion Honor (France). Fellow Latin Am. Studies Assn.; mem. Am. Econ. Assn., Acad. Polit. Sci., Assn. for Asian Studies. Clubs: University (St. Louis); Conanicut Yacht (Jamestown R.I.). Co-author several books. Contbr. numerous articles profl. publs. Home: 701 S Skinker St Louis MO 63105

KAGE, ARTHUR VINCENT, constrn. co. exec.; b. Buffalo, Apr. 13, 1923; s. Arthur Vincent and Helena (Rech) K.; student Niagara U., 1946-48; B.S. in Civil Engring., Kans. State U., 1951; m. Kathleen Iris

Smart, Mar. 25, 1943; children—Douglas, Karen Lee. With The Austin Co., Roselle, N.J., 1951—, project mgr., 1956-64, asst. dist. mgr., 1964-74, dist. mgr., 1974—; partner Austin Assos., Conn., 1962—; dir. Indsl. Workman's Savs. & Loan Assn., Rahway, N.J. Pres. Clark (N.J.) Municipal Swimming Pool, 1972-74; scoutmaster Union council Boy Scouts Am., 1968-72; coach squash Seton Hall U., South Orange, N.J., 1973-74. Served with U.S. Army, 1942-46. Decorated Bronze Star. Registered profl. engr., N.Y., N.J., Pa., Conn., Mass., D.C., Md., Del., R.I., W.Va., Ky., Minn., Ill., N.H., Vt., Va., Kans., Colo., N.D., Nebr., Mo., Miss., Iowa, Wyo., Ark., Tenn. Mem. Nat. Bd. Engring. Registration, Am. Soc. C.E. Address: Penn Tower Suite 300 3100 Broadway Kansas City MO 64111

KAH, RALPH EDWARD, gynecologist; b. Middletown, Ohio, Apr. 26, 1933; s. Ralph Edward and Zelma May (Sargeant) K.; B.A., M.A., Miami U., 1955; M.D., Ohio State U., 1959, M. Med. Sci., 1964; postgrad. Calif. Western U., 1976; m. Deeann Haney, July 14, 1962; 1 dau., Kathryn Lee. Intern, Ohio State U. Hosps., Columbus, 1959-60, resident in obstetrics and gynecology, 1960-64; practice medicine specializing in gynecology Gynecologic Cons., Inc., Middletown, Ohio; asst. clin. prof. Wright State U. Served to capt. U.S. Army, 1964-66. Mem. AMA (Physicians Recognition award 1976), Ohio State Med. Assn., Am. Coll. Gynecologists, Am. Fertility Soc., Am. Bd. Obstetrics and Gynecology, Am. Assn. Gynecologic Laparoscopists. Episcopalian. Home: 3209 Milton Rd Middletown OH 45042 Office: 20 S Breiel Blvd Middletown OH 45042

KAHLENBECK, HOWARD, JR., lawyer; b. Fort Wayne, Ind., Dec. 7, 1929; s. Howard and Clara Elizabeth (Wegman) K.; B.S. with distinction, Ind. U., 1952; LL.B., U. Mich., 1957; m. Sally A. Horrell, Aug. 14, 1954; children—Kathryn Sue, Douglas H. Admitted to Ind. bar, 1957; partner Krieg, DeVault, Alexander & Capehart, Indpls., 1957—; sec., dir. Maul Tech. Corp. (formerly Buehler Corp.), indsl. equipment mfg., Indpls., 1971—, Am. Monitor Corp., med. equipment mfg., Indpls., 1971—, Am. Interstate Ins. Corp. Wis., Milw., 1973—, Am. Interstate Ins. Co. Ga., 1973—, Am. Underwriters, Inc., ins. holding corp., Indpls., 1973—. Served with USAF, 1952-54. Mem. Am., Ind., Indpls. bar assns., Alpha Kappa Psi, Delta Theta Phi, Beta Gamma Sigma, Delta Upsilon Internat. (dir. 1971—). Lutheran. Home: 6320 Old Orchard Rd Indianapolis IN 46226 Office: 2860 Indiana National Bank Tower Indianapolis IN 46204

KAHLENBECK, PAUL RICHARD, mech. engr.; b. Huntington, Ind., Sept. 24, 1931; s. Henry and Rose Pearl (Lowman) K.; m. Ruby Rosanna Ross, June 10, 1951; children—John, Kim, Joe; B.S. in Mech. Engring., Tri-State Coll., 1957. Program mgr. Cummins Engine Co., Inc., Columbus, Ind., 1967-68, program dir., 1968-70, chief engr., 1970-73, exec. dir. indsl. engring., 1973—; mem. adv. bd. John Wesley Ins. Co. Chmn. bd. trustees Ind. Meth. Conf., South, 1976-78; past pres. Donner Swim Club. Mem. Nat. Fire Protection Assn., Constrn. Industry Mfg. Assn. Home: 3209 Woodlawn Pkwy Columbus IN 47201 Office: 1900 McKinley Ave Columbus IN 47201

KAHLENBERG, KARL WALTER, mfg. co. exec.; b. Two Rivers, Wis., Oct. 29, 1933; s. William John and Mary Cecilia (Marling) K.; B.A., Denison U., 1955; m. Marcia Bilharz, June 21, 1973. With Kahlenberg Bros. Co., diversified mfg. for marine industry, Two Rivers, Wis., 1955—, v.p. marketing, 1970—, advt. mgr., 1963—, dir., 1970—. Mem. Career Edn. Adv. Com., Two Rivers. Vice chmn. bd. Wis. div. Am. Cancer Soc., 1973—, chmn. crusade com. Wis. div., 1972, 73, 74, county pres., 1969-70. Vice chmn. Manitowoc County Republican Com., 1966. Served with U.S. Army, 1956-58. Recipient Elk of the Year award, 1971, award Jr. C. of C., 1960. Mem. Soc. Naval Architects and Marine Engrs., Kappa Sigma. Conglist. Mason (32 deg.), Elk (exalted ruler 1966-67, mem. state house com. 1973, 74). Home: 3414 Adams St Two Rivers WI 54241 Office: 12th and Monroe Sts Two Rivers WI 54241

KAHN, DONALD ROY, surgeon, educator; b. Birmingham, Ala., May 21, 1929; s. Nathan Aaron and Bertha (Goldner) K.; B.S., Birmingham So. Coll., 1950; M.D., Ala. Med. Sch., 1954; m. Ellen Rhee Levy, Aug. 9, 1953; children—Elizabeth, Gayle, Donald Roy, Tamara. Intern, St. Louis City Hosp., 1954-55; resident in surgery U. Mich. Hosp., 1955-61, in thoracic surgery, 1961-63, instr. thoracic surgery, 1963-64, asst. prof. thoracic surgery, 1964-67, asso. prof., 1967-71; prof. surgery, chmn. dept. thoracic surgery U. Wis., Madison, 1971—. Served to capt. USMCR, 1956-58. Diplomate Am. Bd. Surgery, Bd. Thoracic Surgery. Fellow A.C.S., Am. Coll. Cardiology; mem. Assn. Academic Surgeons, Soc. Vascular Surgeons, Mich. Soc. Thoracic Surgeons, John Alexander Am. Thoracic Soc., Am. Heart Assn., Soc. Univ. Surgeons, Soc. Thoracic Surgeons, Am. Assn. Thoracic Surgeons, Transplant Soc. Author: (with W. Wilson and R. Strang) Clinical Aspects of Operable Heart Disease, 1967; contbr. articles on various aspects cardiac surgery and organ transplantation to med. jours. Home: 6410 Antietam Ln Madison WI 53705 Office: U Hosp Dept Surgery U Wis Madison WI 53706

KAHN, GENE RICHARD, communications co. exec.; b. Chgo., Dec. 28, 1930; s. Louis H. and Florence L. (Lieberman) K.; student U., Colo. 1948, U. Ill., 1948-50, Chgo. Acad. Arts, 1951; m. Renee Bernstein, Dec. 5, 1954; children—Gene Richard, Jordan B., Beth E. Sec.-treas. Louis H. Kahn & Sons Inc., Chgo., 1948-68; v.p. mktg. Reliance Products Co., Woonsocket, R.I., 1968; regional sales supr. Fed. Security Systems Co., Jacksonville, Fla., 1969; v.p. mktg. Columbia Video Systems Co., Highland Park, Ill., 1969—; cons., lectr. in field. Pres. Kimballwood Assn., 1971-73, Highland Park Hist. Soc., 1973—. Mem. Highland Park C. of C. (dir. 1977—), Nat. Assn. Ednl. Broadcasters, Assn. for Ednl. Communications and Tech., Ill. Audiovisual Assn. Jewish. Club: Optimists. Home: 848 Kimballwood Ln Highland Park IL 60035 Office: 1805 St Johns Ave Highland Park IL 60035

KAHN, JULIAN, ins. co. exec., mgmt. cons.; b. N.Y.C., Aug. 18, 1932; s. Abraham and Lillian (Fried) K.; B.A., Roosevelt U., 1954; postgrad. U. Chgo. Law Sch., 1954-57; m. Lenore Steinberg, Dec. 26, 1954; children—Cheryl Myra, Louis Frederick. With Office Cook County Probate Ct. Clk., Chgo., 1954, Cook County Clk., 1955, Cook County State's Atty. Office, 1956; head div., pub. utilities insp. Cook Co. Dept. Weights and Measures, 1957; with Chgo. Park Dist., 1958-59; real estate appraiser Cook County Probate Ct., 1958-59; spl. agt. John Hancock Mut. Life Ins. Co., Bellwood, Ill., 1967-68, unit mgr., 1968, asst. gen. agt., 1969, gen. agt., 1969-75; head Julian Kahn Profl. Mgmt. Cons. Founder, chief exec. Drs. Aid. Democratic precinct committeeman, Highland Park, Ill., 1972—. Recipient award leading gen. agt. John Hancock Life Ins. Mem. Nat. Assn. Life Underwriters, Nat. Assn. Securities Dealers (registered rep.), Chgo. Assn. Commerce and Industry (govtl. affairs com. 1967), Bellwood C. of C. (dir. 1971). Home: 1285 Lynn Terrace Highland Park IL 60035 Office: PO Box 105 539 Bellwood Ave Bellwood IL 60104

KAHN, MARK LEO, economist, educator; b. N.Y.C., Dec. 16, 1921; s. Augustus and Manya (Fertig) K.; B.A., Columbia U., 1942; M.A., Harvard U., 1948, Ph.D., 1950; m. Ruth Elizabeth Wecker, Dec. 21, 1947 (div. Jan. 1972); children—Ann Mariam, Peter David, James Allan, Jean Sarah. Asst. economist U.S. OSS, Washington, 1942-43; teaching fellow Harvard U., 1947-49; dir. case analysis U.S. WSB, Region 6-B Mich., 1952-53; econs. faculty Wayne State U., Detroit, 1949—, prof., 1960—, dept. chmn., 1961-68; arbitrator union-mgmt. disputes, specializing in airline industry. Bd. govs. Jewish Welfare Fedn. Detroit, 1976—. Served to capt. AUS, 1943-46. Decorated Bronze Star. Mem. Indsl. Relations Research Assn. (past chpt. pres.), Am. Econ. Assn., AAUP (past chpt. pres.), Nat. Acad. Arbitrators (bd. govs. 1960-62, v.p. 1976-78). Co-author: Collective Bargaining and Technological Change in American Transportation, 1971; contbr. articles to profl. jours. Home: 19541 Cranbrook Dr Detroit MI 48821

KAHN, SOL J(EROME), lawyer; b. Chgo., Sept. 28, 1908; s. Morris and Ida (Slate) K.; LL.B., U. Wis., 1930; m. Miriam Fredricka Posner, Dec. 22, 1935; children—Sandra Kahn Davis, Judith Kahn Posner, Peggy Kahn Jacobson. Admitted to Wis. bar, 1930; engaged in gen. practice, 1930—. Bd. dirs. Nat. Jewish Welfare Bd., Jewish Community Center Milw., NCCJ; mem. exec. com. Milw. County USO Com. Mem. Am., Wis., Milw. bar assns., Am. Judicature Soc. Club: Brynwood Country. Home: 7801 N Club Circle Milwaukee WI 53217 Office: 212 W Wisconsin Ave Milwaukee WI 53203

KAIM, NASEEM THOMAS, dentist; b. Akron, Ohio, July 2, 1925; s. Thomas and Shahda (Fadel) K.; B.S. in Edn., Kent State U., 1950; D.D.S., Ohio State U., 1956; m. Sylvia Irene Talkington, Dec. 31, 1948; children—Thomas Michael, Ronald Joseph, Lisa Anne, Linda Irene. Pvt. practice dentistry, Akron, 1956—; dental dir. Summit County Health Dept., 1956-65. Bd. dirs. Summit County Cancer Soc., 1965-67. Served with USMCR, 1943-46. Decorated Purple Heart. Mem. Am. Dental Assn., Ohio, Akron dental socs., Delta Sigma Delta, Omicron Upsilon. Home: 55 Fir Hill A6B2 Akron OH 44304 Office: 1795 W Market St Akron OH 44313

KAIN, IDA MARIE GROGLOTH, social worker; b. Hammond, Ind., Oct. 26, 1927; d. Frank E. and Marie (DeWald) Grogloth; A.B. (Merit scholar 1948), Ind. U., 1949, M.A., 1954; advanced certificate U. Chgo., 1961; m. Robert W. Pion, Sept. 11, 1949; children—Lynette Marie Pion Bremer, Lynise Louise; m. 2d, John R. Kain, Aug. 14, 1964. Clk., J.J. Woolworth Co., Hammond, 1944-45; sec. Youngstown Sheet & Tube Co., East Chicago, Ind., 1945-47; sec. dept. zoology Ind. U., 1949-50, dept. zoology U. Mo., 1951; clk.-typist Prodn. and Mktg. Adminstrn., U.S. Dept. Agr., Columbia, Mo., 1951-52; caseworker Dr. N. Beatty Hosp., Westville, Ind., 1954-58, placement supr., 1958-60, field work instr., 1957-60; pvt. social worker, part-time, Lake and Porter Counties, Ind., 1959—; social worker Sch. City of Gary (Ind.), 1961-72, field work instr., 1963-70; part-time instr. dept. social work Valparaiso (Ind.) U., 1967-70, asst. prof., dir. field work, 1970—; pvt. cons. Shults-Lewis Children's Home, Valparaiso, 1971-75; social worker Family Service Assn. Porter County, part-time 1969-71; joint-founder Social Work Corp. Am., Inc., 1973, pres., 1974—; sec. N.W. Regional Conf. Social Welfare, 1957-58, bd. dirs., 1961-62, 69-70; organizer Family Service Agy., 1960-61; del. Ind. Gov.'s Conf. on Status Women, 1963; del. Conf. for Advancement of Pvt. Practice in Social Work to Council on Social Work Edn., 1971-74. Recipient award Ind. Mental Health Assn., 1953-54; USPHS grantee for advanced study in social work, 1960; certificates merit Gary Schs., 1965, 66, Valparaiso U., 1967, 68, Psi Iota Xi award, 1954. Mem. Porter County Assn. Mental Health (dir. 1967-69, program chmn. ann. meeting 1968), Lake-Porter Counties Pvt. Practice Social Work Com., Internat. Assn. Pupil Personnel Workers (program chmn., publicity chmn. 1962; workshop leader 1962-63), Ind. Pupil Personnel Assn., Conf. Advancement Pvt. Practice (dir. office publs. 1970-74), Acad. Certified Social Workers, Family Service Assn. Porter County, Nat. Conf. Social Welfare, Ind. Soc. Clin. Social Work, Council Social Work Edn., Nat. Assn. Social Workers (pres. 1968-70, mem. Ind. council 1968-76, pres. 1971-74, chmn. Ind. com. on licensure 1969-74), Delta Phi Epsilon. Home: 1314 Forest Park Ave Valparaiso IN 46383

KAISER, FREDERICK ALFRED, ret. utility exec., civic worker; b. Detroit, Nov. 1, 1897; s. Alfred Frederick and Louise (Hill) K.; student Blackstone Inst., 1922-26, Alexander Hamilton Inst., 1925-29; m. Hazel Kennedy, Mar. 7, 1973. Salesman, Columbia Body Co., Detroit, 1918-22; br. mgr. Denby Motor Truck Co., Portland, Oreg., 1923-26, Los Angeles, 1926-28; spl. rep. Hudson Motor Car Co., 1928-31; salesman, sales mgr., asst. to pres., v.p. sales, exec. v.p., pres. Detroit Stove Co., 1931-53; v.p. sales Mich. Consol. Gas Co., Detroit, 1955-72. Chmn. Mayor's Com. for Indsl. Devel., 1962—; exec. v.p. Detroit Med. Center Corp.; bd. dirs. Harper-Grace Hosps. Mem. Am. Ordnance Assn. (life mem.), Newcomen Soc. N.Am., Detroit Sales Execs. Club (past pres.). Lutheran Clubs: Detroit Golf (past pres.), Detroit Athletic (past dir.), Recess, K.T. Home: 20743 Christine Ct Grosse Pointe Woods MI 48236

KAISER, PAUL JOSEPH, educator; b. Cleveland, July 19, 1946; s. Adelbert K. and Margaret (Bugary) K.; B.S., U. Notre Dame, 1968; M.S., U. Mich., 1970, Ph.D., 1973; m. Kathleen Anne Prendergast, June 27, 1969; children—Carolyn Therese, Kevin Michael. Instr., Tuskegee Inst., 1970-71; asst. prof. math. Lewis U., Lockport, Ill., 1973-76, asso. prof., 1976—. Mem. Am. Math Soc., Associated Colls. Chgo. Area, Joliet Math. Club. Roman Catholic. Contbr. articles to profl. jours. Home: 2104 Midhurst St Joliet IL 60435 Office: Dept Math Lewis U Lockport IL 60441

KAISERMAN, STUART WARREN, real estate exec.; b. Chgo., Nov. 14, 1937; s. Sol Jack and Frances (Weber) K.; B.S. in Bus. Adminstrn., Roosevelt U., Chgo., 1960; m. Geraldine M. Solar, May 30, 1960; children—Jami, Stephanie, Mindy, Daniel, Laurel. Vice pres., dir. Real Estate Capitol Corp., Chgo., 1970; v.p., regional dir. Arlen Realty & Devel. Corp., Chgo., 1972; now chmn. bd. dirs. Hogan & Farwell Marken Realty Group, Chgo.; real estate mgr., adviser Chancery div. Circuit Ct. Chgo.; real estate adviser Prudential Life Ins. Co., Equitable Life Ins. Co., U. Chgo., others. Recipient Real Estate Man of Year award Ill. State of Israel Bonds, 1977. Licensed certified property mgr. Mem. Inst. Real Estate Mgmt., Chgo. Real Estate Bd., Apt. Bldg. Mgrs. Assn., Bldg. Owners and Mgrs. Assn., Prime Ministers Club State of Israel. Jewish. Club: Carlton. Home: 224 Park Ave Highland Park IL 60035 Office: 55 E Monroe St Chicago IL 60603

KAISTHA, KRISHAN KUMAR, toxicologist; b. Sulah, Himachal Pradesh, India, Apr. 6, 1926; s. Mangat Ram and Tara Devi (Mahajan) K.; came to U.S., 1959, naturalized, 1974; B.S. in Chemistry, Punjab (India) U., 1947, B.S. in Pharmacy with honors, 1951, M.S., 1955; Ph.D., U. Fla., 1962; m. Swarn L. Kaistha, Feb. 22, 1948; children—Anita Kaistha Mahajan, Vivek, Vinek. Analytical chemist Punjab (India) Govt. Med. Directorate, 1952-57, chief pharmacist, 1957-59; research fellow State U. N.Y., Buffalo, 1962-63; head pharm. and phytochem. research lab. Punjab Govt., 1964-66; research scientist food and drug directorate Dept. Nat. Health and Welfare, Ottawa, Ont., Can., 1966-69; dir. toxicology labs. State Ill. Dept. Mental Health Drug Abuse Programs, Chgo., 1969-74; chief toxicologist State Ill. Dangerous Drugs Commn., Chgo., 1974—. Research asso. dept. psychiatry U. Chgo., 1969-75. Recipient 1st prize, Lunsford-Richardson award, 1962; Gov.'s Economy Incentive award State Ill., 1973. Diplomate Am. Bd. Forensic Toxicology; certified clin. chemist Nat. Registry Clin. Chemistry. Fellow N.Y. Acad. Sci., Am. Acad. Forensic Scis.; mem. Am. Acad. Clin. Toxicology, Am. Assn. Clin. Chemists, Am. Soc. Pharmacology and Exptl. Therapeutics, Rho Chi, Phi Kappa Phi, Rho Pi Phi. Contbr. numerous research articles to profl. jours. Home: 542 Ashbury Ave Bolingbrook IL 60439 Office: care IIT Research 10 W 35th St Chicago IL 60616

KAKOLEWSKI, JAN WIKTOR, neurobiologist; b. Poznan, Poland, Apr. 16, 1935; s. Wiktor and Malgorzata (Hudalla) K.; M.D., Silesian Acad. Medicine (Poland), 1961; children—Richard, Kirsten, Rebecca, Daniel, Eric, Emily, Johanna. Intern, Warsaw (Poland) Community Hosp. 6, 1959-60; resident Mental Health San., Warsaw, 1960-61; practice medicine specializing in neuro-psychiatry; asst. prof., dir. dept. psychiatry Acad. Medicine, Warsaw, 1962-63; research asso. Galesburg (Ill.) State Research Hosp., 1963-64, Fels Research Inst., Yellow Springs, Ohio, 1965-71; asso. prof. physiology and pharmacology U. S.D. Sch. Medicine, Vermillion, 1971-77; pvt. practice medicine, specializing in brain and behavior disorders, Sioux City, Iowa; staff Winnebago (Wis.) Mental Health Inst., 1977—; adviser to Gayville Devel. Co., 1973—. Nat. Found. March of Dimes grantee, 1974. Mem. Soc. Biol. Psychiatry, Am. Soc. Clin. Pharmacology and Therapeutics, Internat. Assn. Study of Pain, Am. Med. EEG Assn. Research in neurophysiol. mechanisms of behavior and detection of brain trauma. Office: 809 Badgerow Bldg Sioux City IA 51104

KAKONIS, THOMAS EARL, educator; b. Long Beach, Calif., Nov. 13, 1930; s. Gus Peter and Olive May (Woodward) K.; B.A., U. Minn., 1952; M.S., S.D. State U., 1958; Ph.D., U. Iowa, 1965; m. Judith J. Whitlock, May 29, 1971; children—Tom Dion, Daniel James. Prof., U. Idaho, 1958-59, Mankato State Co., 1959-60, No. Ill. U., 1964-66, U. Wis., Whitewater, 1966-68, 69-72, S.D. State U., 1968-69; prof. English, Ferris State Coll., Big Rapids, Mich., 1972—, head dept., English 1972—; cons. Film Counselors, Inc., Med. Group Mgmt. Assos., 1972—. Served with U.S. Army, 1953-55. Nat. Ednowment for Humanities grantee, 1974-75, 77—. Mem. Modern Lang. Assn., Nat. Council Tchrs. English, Popular Culture Assn. Author: The Short Story: Ideas and Backgrounds, 1967; Language, Rhetoric and Idea, 1967; Plays by Four Tragedians, 1968; The Literary Artist as Social Critic, 1969; Forms of Rhetoric, 1969; Strategies in Rhetoric, 1971; Statement and Craft, 1971; From Language to Idea: An Integrated Rhetoric, 1971; Now and Tomorrow, 1971; America: Involvement or Escape, 1971; Scene Seventy: Non-Fiction Prose, 1972; Crossroads: Quality of Life through Rhetorical Modes, 1972; We Have But Faith, 1975; Writing in an Age of Technology, 1977; A Practical Guide to Police Report Writing, 1977. Home: 510 Bailey Dr Big Rapids MI 49307 Office: Ferris State College Big Rapids MI 49307

KALAMAROS, EDWARD NICHOLAS, lawyer; b. Williamsport, Ind., July 5, 1934; s. Nicholas John and Margaret Louise (Riley) K.; B.S. in Edn., Miami U., Oxford, O., 1952; B.S. in Commerce U. Notre Dame, 1956, L.L.B., 1959, J.D., 1959; m. Marilyn Jane Foster, June 14, 1958; children—Alexander, Philip, Anastasia, Timothy. Admitted to Ind. bar, 1959; chief dep. prosecutor 60th Jud. Circuit of Ind., 1963-67; practiced in South Bend, Ind., 1960—. Pres. Edward N. Kalamaros & Assos., South Bend, 1971—. U.S. govt. appeal agt. SSS, 1967-71, adviser to registrants, 1971—; mem. St. Joseph County Tax Adjustment Bd., 1970-73, pres., 1972-73. Sec., v.p., bd. dirs. Council for Retarded of St. Joseph County; bd. dirs., sec. Alcoholism Council. Served with U.S. Army, 1962-65. Mem. Am. Arbitration Assn. (panel of arbitrators), Lawyers and Pilots Bar Assn., Am., Ind., St. Joseph County bar assns., Am. Judicature Soc., Def. Research Inst., Internat. Assn. Indsl. Accident Bds. and Commns., Ind., Am. trial lawyers assns., Comml. Law League. Presbyn. (past deacon, trustee). Mason (32 deg., Shriner). Clubs: Macatawa Bay Yacht; South Bend Press (hon.). Home: 1829 Portage Av South Bend IN 46616 also 5209 Lakeshore Dr Holland MI 49423 Office: Edward N Kalamaros & Assos Tower Bldg South Bend IN 46601

KALASH, WILLARD LOREN, univ. adminstr.; b. Lakefield, Minn., Nov. 8, 1917; s. Felix Loren and Tillie W. (Trosin) K.; B.S., U. Minn.; M.S., St. Cloud State U., 1958; m. Doris Louis Comstock, Aug. 24, 1942; children—Willard Loren (dec.), Susan Marcella. Instr. music Sch. Dist. Freeborn (Minn.), 1941-42; instr. music Sch. Dist. Grove City (Minn.), 1942-47, tchr. social studies, 1942-47, prin., 1945-47; instr. music Sch. Dist. Annandale (Minn.), 1947-60, counselor, 1960-68; counselor St. Cloud (Minn.) State U., 1968-72, dir. counseling center, 1972—; instr. psychology, part time. Recipient Order of Arrow, Boy Scouts Am., 1945. Mem. Central Minn. Counselors Assn. (past pres.), Minn. Personnel and Guidance Assn., Am. Personnel and Guidance Assns., Phi Delta Kappa. Methodist. Club: Lions. Home: 420 N Oak St Annandale MN 55302 Office: Saint Cloud State U Saint Cloud MN 56301

KALBERLOH, RALPH JUNIOR, trade assn. exec.; b. Excelsior Springs, Mo., July 21, 1925; s. Albert Henry and Goldie (Hatfield) K.; student Lincoln U., 1956-57, Mich. State U., 1962-69; m. Joann Fry, Sept. 11, 1943; 1 dau., Kim J.R. Spl. agt. Farm Bur. Ray County, Richmond, Mo., 1952-55; exec. v.p. Mo. Jr. C. of C., Jefferson City, 1955-57; exec. mgr. Mo. Limestone Producers Assn., Jefferson City, 1957-59; exec. dir. Mo. Safety Council, Jefferson City, 1959-61; exec. v.p. Mo. Automobile Dealers Assn., Jefferson City, 1961—; dir. Mark Twain Life Ins. Co. Exec. v.p. Mo. Acceleration Corp. Campaign chmn. Jefferson City, Cole County United Fund, 1968-69; chmn. mayor's adv. commn. reapportionment, 1967-69; sec. Jefferson City Planning and Zoning Commn., 1963-68; mem. Gov.'s Interim Legislative Com., 1960, 68; mem. Home Rule Study Commn., 1960-68; chmn. Greater Jefferson City Trafficways Com., 1968-74; co-chmn. Payroll Bond Issue com., Jefferson City, 1968—. Chmn. bd. regents Inst. Orgn. Mgmt., 1975; pres. Meml. Community Hosp., 1977—; pres. Yesterdays Children Inc. Served to sgt. USAF, 1943-45; ETO. Mem. Automotive Trade Assn. (dir. 1965-67), Automotive Trade Assn. Mgrs. (sec. 1969-70, v.p. 1970-71, pres. 1971-72), Mo. Hwy. Users Conf. (sec. 1966—), Mo. Safety Council (dir. 1961—, treas. 1974, v.p. 1975), Jefferson City (pres. 1960-61), Richmond (pres. 1954-55) jr. chambers commerce, Jefferson City C. of C. (pres. 1965-66), Orgn. Execs. Jefferson City (pres. 1957-58), Am. (dir.), Mo. (pres. 1975) socs. assn. execs., Cole County Hist. Soc. Episcopalian. Rotarian (pres. 1971—), Mason (Shriner). Club: Jefferson City Country. Home: 300 Old Gibler Rd Jefferson City MO 65101 Office: 205 E Capitol St Jefferson City MO 65101

KALES, ROBERT GRAY, bus. exec.; b. Detroit, Mar. 14, 1904; s. William R. and Alice (Gray) K.; grad. Phillips Exeter Acad., 1923; B.S., Mass. Inst. Tech., 1928; M.B.A., Harvard, 1933; m. Jane Webster, Nov. 27, 1932; children—Jane (Mrs. William Hillard Ryan), Robert Gray, William Robert II, Anne Webster (Mrs. Jeffrey M. Howson); m. 2d, Miriam Wallin, Jan. 6, 1945; 1 son, David Wallin; m. 3d, Herma Lou Boyd, Mar. 6, 1951; m. 4d, Shirley L. McBride, Feb. 14, 1961; children—John, Nancy. With Whitehead & Kales Co., Detroit, 1928-31, Union Guardian Trust Co., 1933—; analyst, sec.-treas. Investment Counsel, Inc., 1933-35; founder, pres., dir. Kales Kramer Investment Co., Detroit, 1935—; pres., dir. Indsl. Resources, Inc., Detroit, 1950—, Kales Bldg. Co., 1944—, Midwest Underwriters, Inc., Detroit, 1938—; v.p., dir. Basin Oil Co., Metamora, Mich., 1947—; vice chmn. bd., dir. Whitehead & Kales Co., River Rouge, Mich., 1934—; chmn. bd. Automotive Bin Service Co., Jefferson Terminal Warehouse; dir. Ind. Liberty Life Ins. Co., Grand Rapids, Mich. Mem. adv. com. Patriotic Edn., Inc. Trustee,

Kales Found. Served to lt. comdr. USNR, 1942-44; capt. Res. Mem. Navy League U.S. (pres. Southeastern Mich. council), Mil. Order World Wars (past nat. comdr.-in-chief), S.A.R., Nat. Sojourners, U.S. Naval Inst., Naval Order U.S., Am. Legion, Detroit Power Squadron, Rosicrucian Order, Scarab, Sigma Chi. Episcopalian. Clubs: Masons (K.T.), Bayview Yacht, Country, Detroit Athletic, Players, Detroit, Detroit Curling, Grosse Pointe Hunt, Grosse Pointe Yacht, St. Clair Yacht, University (Detroit); Capitol Hill, Army and Navy, University (Washington); Black River Ranch (Onaway, Mich.); Bloomfield Open Hunt (Bloomfield Hills, Mich.); Longwood Cricket, Union Boat (Boston); Otsego Ski (Gaylord, Mich.); Stone Horse Yacht (Harwich, Mass.); Triton Fish and Game (Quebec City, Que., Can.). Home: 87 Cloverly Rd Grosse Pointe Farms MI 48236 Office: 1900 E Jefferson Ave Detroit MI 48207

KALES, SHIRLEY MCBRIDE (MRS. ROBERT GRAY KALES), club woman; b. Detroit, Feb. 18, 1927; d. Goerge L. and Elsie J. (Storey) McBride; student Wayne State U., 1946-48; student Detroit Conservatory Music, 1948-50; m. Robert Gray Kales, Feb. 14, 1961; children—John Gray, Nancy D. Advt. staff Detroit Evening News Assn., 1949-55; mem. advt. and publicity staff Bielfield Agy., Detroit, 1955-59; mem. advt. and sales dept. Mich. Bell Telephone Co., Detroit, 1959-60; mem. sales promotion and advt. staff Mich. Consol. Gas Co., Detroit, 1960-61. Mem. Detroit Mus. Art Founders Soc., Fine Arts Soc. Detroit, Mich. Anti-Cruelty Assn., Navy League U.S. (v.p. Detroit women's council). Clubs: Women's City (chmn. program com.), Country, Review (pres.), (Detroit); Grosse Pointe (Mich.) Yacht. Home: 87 Cloverly Rd Grosse Pointe Farms MI 48236 Office: 1900 E Jefferson Ave Detroit MI 48207

KALINOS, KATHERINE DIMITRA, microbiologist; b. Springfield, Ohio, Mar. 18, 1933; d. Vangel Christo and Dimitra (Hagegorgeiu) K.; B.A., Wittenberg U., 1958; postgrad. U. Dayton, 1957, 62, Ohio State U., 1960-61. Intern med. technician Springfield (Ohio) City Hosp., 1952-53; med. technologist Mary Rutan Hosp., Bellefountaine, Ohio, 1953-54; asst. chief hematology Mercy Hosp., Springfield, 1954-56, asst. chief chemistry, 1958-59, serologist, 1959-60, chief microbiologist, asst. chief technologist, 1961-70, also teaching supr. bacteriology Sch. Med. Tech.; staff microbiologist Miami Valley Hosp., Dayton, 1970-74; instr. health careers dept. Clark Tech. Coll., Springfield, 1974—. Mem. Registry Med. Tech., Am. Soc. Clin. Pathologists, Am. Soc. Microbiology, Am. Inst. Biol. Scis., Daus. Penelope (pres.), Nat. Registry Microbiolgists, Am. Acad. Microbiology, N.Y. Acad. Scis., Internat. Platform Assn., Internat. Writers Assn. Republican. Roman Catholic. Home: 100 Roseland St W Springfield OH 45503 Office: Clark Tech Coll 570 E Leffel Ln Springfield OH 45505

KALJOT, VICTOR, physician; b. Tartu, Estonia, June 15, 1925; s. Voldemar and Marie (Gruenbaum) K.; M.D., U. Vt., 1955; m. Linda Roose, Aug. 25, 1949; children—Kaarel T., Lena M., Lisa A., Tiina. Came to U.S., 1950, naturalized, 1955. Intern, Mary Fletcher Hosp., Burlington, Vt., 1955-56; resident in internal medicine U. Vt., 1956-57, Boston VA Hosp., 1958-59; resident in cardiology Letterman Gen. Hosp., 1962-63; practice medicine specializing in cardiology Trinity Med Center, Minot, N.D., 1965—, chief med. staff, 1975—, bd. dirs., 1975—; mem. staff St. Joseph's Hosp., Minot. Served to maj., M.C. U.S. Army, 1957-65. Diplomate Am. Bd. Internal Medicine with subsplty. bd. cardiovascular disease. Fellow A.C.P., Am. Coll. Cardiology, Council Clin. Cardiology, Am. Heart Assn., Am. Coll. Chest Physicians. Lutheran. Home: 2111 11th Ave NW Minot ND 58701 Office: 500 Trinity Profl Bldg Minot ND 58701

KALLERUD, MAURITZ JACOB, chem. engr.; b. Chgo., Oct. 25, 1936; s. Mauritz Elner and Catherine (Becker) K.; B.S., Calif. Inst. Tech., 1958; M.S., Mass. Inst. Tech., 1962; m. Sheron Gayle Whitley, Aug. 29, 1964; children—Larry Kevin, Laury Lyn, Mauritz Royce, Roger Dean. Project mgr. Garrett Research & Devel. Co. div. Occidental Petroleum Corp., LaVerne, Calif., 1962-70; devel. engr. Dow Chem. Corp., Denver, 1962; chem. engr. Morton Salt Co., Chgo., 1961, asst. tech. dir., 1970-71, tech. dir., 1971—; chem. engr. Am. Potash & Chem. Co., Trona, Calif., 1958-60, Monsanto Chem. Co., Santa Clara, Calif., 1956-57. Mem. SMRI, 1971—, chmn. tech. com., 1972-74, sec., 1974-75, pres., 1975-76, treas., 1976-77; cubmaster Boy Scouts Am., Claremont, Calif., 1967-68. Served with AUS, 1960. Mem. Am. Inst. Chem. Engrs., Am. Chem. Soc. Home: 1314 Greenwood Ave Wilmette IL 60091 Office: 110 Wacker Dr Chicago IL 60606

KALLESTAD, CHARLES OSBORNE, med. and health service exec.; b. Mpls., Aug. 19, 1936; s. Hursel Osborne and Helen (Dela) K.; B.A., San Jose State Coll., 1964; postgrad. U. Calif. at Los Angeles, 1964-65; LL.B., LaSalle U., 1968; m. Nancy B. Teaching asst. dept. physics San Jose State U., 1963-64; systems analyst Control Data Corp., Los Angeles, 1966-67; asst. mktg. dir. Computer Planning Corp., Los Angeles, 1967-68; chief exec. officer, pres. Kallestad Labs., Inc., Mpls., 1968—. Mem. Tau Delta Phi. Home: 780 Old Crystal Bay Rd Wayzata MN 55391 Office: 1000 Lake Hazeltine Dr Chaska MN 55318

KALLET, HENRY ABRAHAM, pathologist; b. Chgo., Mar. 26, 1935; s. Sam and Kate (Gordon) K.; A.B., U. Chgo., 1954, B.S., 1955; M.D., Northwestern U., 1959; m. Beverley Jean Frommert, July 22, 1967. Intern, U.S. Naval Hosp., San Diego, 1959-60; resident U. Mich. Med. Center, Ann Arbor, 1964-68; instr. pathology, U. Mich., Ann Arbor, 1969; dir. lab., W.A. Foote Hosp., Jackson, Mich., 1969-76; asso. prof. pathology, Mich. State U., Lansing, 1976—; dir. clin. pathology, Jackson Lab. of Clin. Pathology, 1977—. Served to lt. M.C., USN, 1959-63. Mem. Coll. Am. Pathology, Am. Soc. Clin. Pathologists, Soc. Nuclear Medicine. Home: 3324 Bluett St Ann Arbor MI 48105 Office: 569 Wildwood St Jackson MI 49201

KALLICK, CHARLES ARTHUR, physician, educator; b. Chgo., May 10, 1929; s. Sol Z. and Anna (Hirsch) K.; B.S., U. Ill., 1952, M.D., 1954; m. Sonia B. Aamot, Dec. 23, 1956; children—Steven, Karen, Ingrid. Intern, Cook County Hosp., Chgo., 1954-55; resident Presbyn.-St. Luke's Hosp., Chgo., 1967-69; practice medicine, specializing in pediatrics, Lemont, Ill., 1957-67; med. supt. Municipal Contagious Disease Hosp., Chgo., 1969-71; dir. ambulatory pediatrics Presbyn.-St. Luke's Hosp., 1971-73; chief infectious disease service Cook County Hosp., Chgo., 1974—; asso. prof. pediatrics and preventive medicine Rush Med. Coll., 1972—. Served with USNR, 1955-57. Fellow Am. Acad. Pediatrics. Contbr. articles to profl. jours. Home: 181 W 135th St Lemont IL 60439 Office: 1825 W Harrison St Chicago IL 60612

KALLICK-KAUFMANN, MAUREEN, social research adminstr.; b. Chgo., Jan. 15, 1935; d. Irving M. and Jeannette (Welcher) Kallick; student Brandeis U., Ohio State U.; B.A., U. Akron, 1961, M.A., 1962; Ph.D., Purdue U., 1964; m. Felix Kaufmann; children—Julian, Cornelia. Project dir., Kenyon & Eckhardt Advt. Co., N.Y.C., 1964-66, asso. research dir., 1966-67, dir. research services, 1973-74; v.p. Dimensions for Decisions, N.Y.C., 1967-69; sr. asso. research dir. SSC & B Advt. Co., N.Y.C., 1969-73; program dir. econ. behavior program U. Mich. Survey Research Center, Inst. for Social Research, Ann Arbor, 1974—; vis. prof. Baruch Coll., N.Y.C., 1965-69. Bd. dirs. Person-to-Person, N.Y.C., 1967-71. Mem. Am. (sec. treas. div. of consumer psychology 1973-76, pres. 1977-78), Midwestern psychol. assns., Am. Acad. for Polit. and Social Research, Am. Mktg. Assn., Am. Assn. for Pub. Opinion Research. Author: Gambling in America - A Survey of U.S. Households, 1977; contbr. articles in consumer psychology to profl. jours. Home: 1160 Pauline Ann Arbor MI 48103 Office: Univ of Michigan Survey Research Center Ann Arbor MI 48104

KALLSTROM, DAVID H., real estate exec.; b. Akron, Ohio, Mar. 6, 1928; s. Gust R. and Norma P. (Peterson) K.; student Case Inst. Tech., 1945-47; B.S., Ohio State U., 1949; m. Jacqueline V. Kallstrom; children—James D., Neil G. Vice pres. Gust Kallstrom, Inc., builders and developers, Akron, 1949-60; pres. Kallstrom Realtors, Akron, Kallstrom Ins. Agy., Inc., Kallstrom's Comml. & Investment Real Estate, Inc., 1961—; partner Greenfield Co.; guest lectr. Kent State U., 1963-68; cons. Cleve. Trust Co., 1970—. Chmn., Cuyahoga Falls YMCA Bldg. drive, 1960; mem. exec. com. Tri County Regional Planning Commn., 1963-65; mem. Com. of 100, Goals for Greater Akron Area, 1973; trustee The Graefe Found.; mem. adv. commn. to Summit County Govt., 1973. Mem. Appraisal Inst., Soc. Real Estate Appraisers (pres.), C. of C., Akron Area Bd. Realtors. Home: 316 W Streetsboro Rd Hudson OH 44236 Office: 2950 W Market St Akron OH 44313

KALOGERSON, THOMAS ARTHUR, automotive engring. cons., inventor; b. Mpls., May 26, 1928; s. Thomas C. and Selma E. (Sandberg) K.; student Carleton Coll., 1947; E.E., U. Minn., 1950, postgrad., 1953-56; m. Julianne L. Crouch, Mar. 20, 1970; children—Donald A. Debra J.; stepchildren—Donald Hintz, David Hintz, Dale Hintz. Research, sales and prodn. engr. General Mills Inc., 1952-59; sales mgr. Magnetic Controls Corp., Mpls., 1959-66; dir. sales Dexon Inc., Mpls., 1966-67; v.p., dir. Optimizer Industries, Mpls., 1967-76; pres. Kaltron Co., Mpls., 1976—. Served with U.S. Army, 1952-54. Mem. Soc. Automotive Engrs., Am. Radio Relay League, Quarter Century Wireless Assn., Soc. Wireless Pioneers. Clubs: Masons, Shriners. Patentee automobile emission control device (award Minn. Inventors Congress 1970), also auto anti-theft system. Home and office: 7534 Landau Dr Bloomington MN 55438

KALSCH, HUBERT ARTHUR, educator; b. Chgo., Dec. 23, 1933; s. Hubert Theodore and Helen Margaret (Solan) K.; B.S., Chgo. Tchrs. Coll., 1955; M.A., DePaul U., 1964; M.A. in Geography, Chgo. State U., 1969; m. Iris P. Schaefer, June 23, 1962; children—Donald H., Joyce H. Tchr., Chgo. Bd. Edn., 1956-67; asso. prof. social sci. City Coll. Chgo., 1967—, chmn. dept., 1974; instr. geography Chgo. State U., 1975. Served with U.S. Army, 1955-56. NSF study grantee, 1972. Mem. Nat. Council Geographic Edn., Ill. Geographical Soc. Home: 14015 Cheswick Dr Orland Park IL 60462 Office: 7601 Pulaski St Chicago IL 60652

KALSEM, MILLIE E., former hosp. dietitian, investment co. exec.; b. Huxley, Iowa; d. Ole J. and Anna (Nelson) Kalsem; B.S., Iowa State U., 1921; dietetic internship Michael Reese Hosp., Chgo., 1922-23; post grad. student U. Ill. Med. Sch., 1935-36. Tchr. home econs. and physiology, Monticello High Sch., Monticello, Iowa, 1921-22; dietitian Beaver Valley Gen. Hosp., New Brighton, Pa., 1922-23, Iowa Meth. Hosp., Des Moines, Iowa, 1923-27, Ill. Tng. Sch. for Nurses and Cook Co. Sch. Nursing, 1927-38; chief dietitian Cook County Hosp., 1936-62; dir., v.p. Lorraine L. Blair, Inc., investments. Selected by Carrie Chapman Catt as one of 100 Women, Women's Centennial Congress, 1940; recipient Alumni merit award, Iowa State Coll., 1946, Alumni Medal, 1956. Mem. Am. Dietetic Assn. (v.p. 1946-47), Ill. Dietetic Assn. (organizer and 1st pres.), Finance Forum Am. (research chmn. 1954-57), Art Inst. Chgo., Order Knoll (gov. Ill. state found.), Friends of Lit., Omicron Nu, Phi Kappa Phi, Chi Omega. Club: Altrusa (pres. Chgo. 1959-61). Home: 111 Lynn Ave Ames IA 50010 Office: 11 S LaSalle St Chicago IL 60603

KALTENBORN, ARTHUR LEWIS, JR., speech pathologist; b. Oakdale, Pa., Oct. 12, 1913; s. Arthur L. and Effie Gladys (Bower) K.; B.A., Coll. of Wooster, 1937; M.A., Northwestern U., 1948; m. Helen A. Philips, Apr. 2, 1942 (div.); children—David Arthur, Virginia Ann. Instr., Colegio Americano Para Varones, Bogota, Colombia, 1937-38; instr. speech Coll. of Wooster (Ohio), 1938-42, 45-48; instr. U. Tenn., 1948-50; asst. prof. Kent State U., 1950-57, asso. prof., 1957—; cons. in laryngectomee rehab. N.E. Ohio br., mem. exec. com. Portage unit Am. Cancer Soc. Served with inf. U.S. Army, 1942-45; CBI. Mem. Am., Ohio Summit County speech and hearing assns., Speech Communication Assn., AAUP, Ohio Edn. Assn., ACLU, Kent Area Growth Assn. Presbyterian. Author: Voice and Diction-A Handbook, 1970; (with Kendall K. Ward) American-English Pronunciation, 1971; editor Ohio Speech and Hearing Jour., 1950-61. Home: 1370 Athena Dr Kent OH 44240 Office: Sch of Speech Kent State U Kent OH 44242

KAMAKAS, NICHOLAS CONSTANTINE, pediatrician; b. Larisa, Greece, Apr. 27, 1911; s. Constantine Anthony and Aphrodite (Sgouras) K.; M.D., U. Athens (Greece), 1935; m. Alexandra Tourkakis, June 30, 1949; children—Nicholas Peter, Constance Penelope. Intern, Red Cross Hosp., Athens, 1935-36; resident in pediatrics Athens Children's Hosp., 1938-40, Evengelismos Hosp., Athens, 1941-43; pediatrician charge Internat. Red Cross Clinic, 1941-43; Internat. Inst. Edn. fellow to Washington U., Children's Hosp., 1947; resident physician Robert Koch Hosp., St. Louis, 1947-51; resident in pediatrics Presbyn. Hosp., instr. U. Ill., Chgo., 1951-53; practice medicine specializing in pediatrics, Florissant, Mo., 1953—; instr. pediatrics St. Louis U., 1968—. Served to 1st lt., Greek Army, 1940-41, to capt., 1943-45. Diplomate Am. Bd. Pediatrics. Mem. AMA, Am. Acad. Pediatrics, N.Y. Acad. Scis., Mo., So. med. assns., St. Louis Pediatric Soc. Clubs: Masons, Shriners. Home: 3064 Thornbury St Saint Louis MO 63131 Office: 1245 Graham Rd Florissant MO 63031

KAMAL, MOUNIR MARK, research lab. exec.; b. Beirut, Feb. 13, 1936; came to U.S., 1956, naturalized, 1969; s. Rabah and Makkiyeh (Khabbazeh) K.; B.M.E. with honors, Robert Coll., 1956; M.S. in Mech. Engring. and Mechanics, U. Mich., 1958, Ph.D. (Gen. Motors Corp. fellow), 1965; m. Mary Ellen Merrow, June 16, 1962; children—John Robbie, Leila Renee, Lenora Namette. Project engr. AC Spark Plug div. Gen. Motors Corp., Flint, Mich., 1956-59; asso. sr. research engr. Gen. Motors Research Lab., Warren, Mich., 1965-67, supr. research engr., 1968-70, program mgr., 1970-71, asst. dept. head, 1971-77, dept. head, 1977—; del. Internat. Safety Conf., Brussels, 1970; mem. industry com. U. Mich. Coll. Engring. Mem. ASME, Soc. Automotive Engrs., Country Lane Home Owners Assn. (pres. 1966-68), Sigma Xi. Home: 1615 Dutton Rd Rochester MI 48063 Office: Gen Motors Research Lab Twelve Mile and Mound Rds Warren MI 48090

KAMAL, SAMIR, computer center adminstr.; b. Egypt, Mar. 21, 1943; s. Kamal Abdallah and Zezaf Salama (Besada); came to U.S., 1965, naturalized, 1976; M.E.E., Carnegie-Mellon U., 1966; Ph.D. in Computer Sci., Mich. State U., 1972; m. Lilian William Abadeer, June 12, 1966; children—Heba, Mark. Instr. elec. engring. Assuit (Egypt) U., 1963-65; programmer U. Calif. Press, Richmond, 1968; instr. computer sci. Mich. State U., E. Lansing, 1969-71; asst. prof. Wayne State U., Detroit, 1972-75; dir. computer center U. Mich., Flint, 1975—; cons. in field; vis. prof. U. Windsor (Ont., Can.). Recipient faculty research award. Mem. Assn. Computing Machinery (chmn. profl. devel. seminars, treas. Detroit chpt.), IEEE, Assn. Egyptian, Am. Scholars, Sigma Xi. Home: 1976 Canary Ct Troy MI 58085 Office: Computer Center U Mich Flint MI 48503

KAMINSKI, MARGARET JOAN, librarian, writer, pub.; b. Detroit, Mar. 16, 1944; d. John Joseph and Gertrude Agnes (Malak) Kaminski; B.F.A., Wayne State U., 1966, M.S.L.S., 1969. Adult reference librarian Detroit Pub. Library, 1969-74, asst. to coordinator dept. pub. relations, 1974-76, librarian dept. gen. info., 1976—; author books of poetry: Martinis, 1975, La Vida de la Mujer, 1976; columnist Margins, Dame Philology, column on women's writing, 1974—; contbr. poetry, articles, revs. to lit. jours.; pub. Glass Bell Press, 1974—; radio, TV guest; guest lectr., poetry reader; mem. Miles modern poetry com. Wayne State U.; panelist Mich. Poetry Festival. Mem. Moving Out Collective, Detroit Pub. Library Staff Assn. Editor Moving to Antarctica, 1975; editor Moving Out: A Feminist Lit., Arts Jour., 1970—, Detroit Pub. Library Staff News Bull., 1971-73. Home: 5053 Commonwealth St Detroit MI 48208 Office: 5201 Woodward St Detroit MI 48202

KAMINSKY, MANFRED STEPHAN, physicist; b. Koenigsberg, Germany, June 4, 1929; s. Stephan and Kaethe (Gieger) K.; diploma in physics U. Rostock (Germany), 1951; Ph.D. in Physics, U. Marburg (Germany), 1957; m. Elisabeth Moellering, May 1, 1957; children—Cornelia B., Mark-Peter. Came to U.S., 1958. German Research Soc. fellow and grad. asst. in physics U. Rostock, 1950-52; lectr. Rostock Med. Tech. Sch., 1952; German Research Soc. fellow and research asst. Phys. Inst. of U. Marburg, 1953-57, sr. asst., 1957-58; research asso. Argonne (Ill.) Nat. Lab., 1958-59, asst. physicist, 1959-62, asso. physicist, 1962-70, sr. physicist, 1970—, dir. Surface Sci. Center-CTR Program, 1974—. Bd. dirs. Com. 100, Hinsdale, 1970—, pres., 1973; pres. St. Vincent de Paul Soc., Hinsdale, 1972-73. Named Outstanding New Citizen of Year, Citizenship Council Chgo., 1968. Fellow Am. Phys. Soc.; mem. Am. Chem. Soc., Research Soc. Am., A.A.A.S., Union German Phys. Socs., Am. Vacuum Soc. (sr.; chmn. Midwest sect. 1967-68; co-founder Gt. Lakes chpt.; dir.-at-large 1968-70). Author: Atomic and Ionic Impact Phenomena on Metal Surfaces, 1965; also articles profl. jours. Editor: Radiation Effects on Solid Surfaces, 1976; co-editor Surface Effects in Controlled Fusion, 1974, Surface Effects in Controlled Fusion Devices, 1976. Patentee in field. Home: 906 S Park Ave Hinsdale IL 60521 Office: Physics Div Argonne Nat Lab 9700 Cass Ave Argonne IL 60439

KAMM, JACOB OSWALD, economist; b. Cleve., Nov. 29, 1918; s. Jacob and Minnie K. (Christensen) K.; A.B., Baldwin-Wallace Coll., 1940; LL.D., 1963; LL.D., Erskine Coll., 1971; A.M., Brown U., 1942; Ph.D., Ohio State U., 1948; m. Judith Steinbrenner, Apr. 28, 1966; children—Jacob Oswald Kamm II, Christian Philip. Asst. in econs. Brown U., 1942; instr. Ohio State U., 1945; instr. Baldwin-Wallace Coll., 1945-46, asst. prof., 1947-48, asso. prof., 1948, prof., dir. Sch. Commerce, 1948-53; exec. v.p. Cleve. Quarries Co., 1953-55, pres., dir., 1955-67, chmn., chief exec. officer, 1967—; dir., exec. com. United Screw & Bolt Corp.; exec. v.p., treas., dir., then pres. Am. Shipbldg. Co., 1967-69, 73-74; vice chmn., dir. Cardinal Fed. Savs. & Loan Assn. Cleve., MTD Products Inc., Electric Furnace Co., Fairmont Foods Co., Nordson Corp., Bibb Co., Oatey Co., Gowe Printing Co.; mem. investment policy com. Portfolio Adv. Co. Nat. City Bank Cleve.; columnist. Hon. mem. mental health com. Ohio Mental Health Assn.; trustee, mem. exec. com., chmn. investment com. Baldwin-Wallace Coll.; bd. regents State of Ohio; bd. counselors Erskine Coll.; trustee, life fellow Cleve. Zool. Soc., St. Lukes Hosp. Assn. Mem. Am. Econ. Assn., Am. Fin. Assn., Ohio Mfrs. Assn. (chmn. bd. trustees), Royal Econ. Soc., AAUP, Indsl. Assn. N. Central Ohio (pres. 1960), World Wide Acad. Scholars, Assn. Ohio Comdrs., Nat. Alumni Assn. Baldwin-Wallace Coll. (pres. 1961-63), Newcomen Soc. N.Am., John Baldwin Soc., Phi Beta Kappa, Delta Phi Alpha, Delta Mu Delta. Methodist. Clubs: Masons (33 deg.), Shriners; Brown U. (N.Y.C.); Clifton (Lakewood, Ohio); Union (Cleve.); Duquesne (Pitts.); Lake Placid; Pres.'s Ohio State U. Author: Economics of Investments, 1951; Making Profits in the Stock Market, 1952, rev., 1959, 61, 66; Investor's Handbook, 1954; contbg. editor Webster's New World Dictionary; contbr. articles to profl. publs. Home: PO Box 261 Amherst OH 44001 Office: Clevelands Quarries Co Amherst OH 44001

KAMMAN, PAUL WILTON, bakery exec.; b. Versailles, O., Sept. 30, 1918; s. Elmer August and Ruth (Mendenhall) K.; student Wittenberg U., 1936-38; B.S., Ohio State U., 1940; m. Mary Ann Keisler, Mar. 17, 1945; children—Paula (Mrs. John F. Reall), Jane (Mrs. Gerald G. Jacobs), Karol, Paul Wilton. With Am. Bakeries Co., 1938-73, plant supt., N.Y.C., 1947-48, regional prodn. supr., 1948-50, gen. prodn. mgr., Chgo., 1950-69, v.p. prodn., 1969-73; former dir. safety/sanitation Keebler Co.; now regional mgr. Cain Food Industries, Dallas. Served to col. U.S. Army, 1941-45. Mem. Am. Soc. Bakery Engrs. (exec. com. 1969—, pres. 1974). Lutheran. Elk. Address: 1911 Birch Lane Park Ridge IL 60068

KAMMERLING, ERWIN M., internist, gastroenterologist; b. Chgo., Sept. 25, 1918; s. Charles and Rose (Goldflies) K.; B.S. with distinict, Purdue U., 1939; B.S., U. Ill., 1941, M.D., 1943; m. Helen Greenfield, Jan. 23, 1944; children—Robert Charles, Janet Susan, James Michael. Intern, Cook County Hosp., Chgo., 1944, resident in internal medicine, 1947-49; practice medicine specializing in internal medicine and gastroenterology, Chgo., 1949—; mem. staff Weiss Meml. Hosp., pres. staff, 1971-72; cons. Hines VA Hosp.; lectr. internal medicine Abraham Lincoln Sch. Medicine; clin. asso. prof. Chgo. Med. Sch. Served to capt. U.S. Army, 1944-46. Diplomate Am. Bd. Internal Medicine. Fellow A.C.P.; mem. Chgo. Soc. Gastroenterology (pres. 1974-75), Chgo. Soc. Internal Medicine, AMA, Ill., Chgo. med. socs., Am. Gastroent. Assn. Delta Rho Kappa, Sigma Alpha Mu, Phi Delta Epsilon. Jewish. Club: Idlewild Country. Co-author articles in med. jours. Home: 1015 N Grove Ave Oak Park IL 60302 Office: 4640 N Marine Dr Chicago IL 60640

KAMMERLOHR, MORTON A., JR., veterinarian; b. Columbia, S.C., July 1, 1947; s. Morton A. and Maxine (Fogg) K.; student U. Ark., 1965-67; D.V.M., U. Mo., 1973. Mem. staff Northside Animal Hosp., Springfield, Mo., 1973-74; Alpine Vet. Clinic, Alpine, Tex., 1974; asso. veterinarian Cassville Vet. Clinic (Mo.), 1975—. Chmn., Vo-Ag Adv. Council Cassville High Sch., 1976-78. Mem. Am., N.W. Ark., S.W. Mo., Mo. veterinary med. assns., S. Barry County Jr. C. of C. (exec. v.p. 1975-76, pres. 1977-78, named Outstanding Officer 1976), Am. Assn. Equine Practicioners. Episcopalian. Home: PO Box 493 Cassville MO 65625 Office: Bus 37N PO Box 493 Cassville MO 65625

KAMP, EWALD ALBERT, mech. engr.; b. Essen, Germany, May 21, 1914; s. Leopold and Elizabeth (Pollay) K.; came to U.S., 1937, naturalized, 1941; student bus. adminstrn. U. Lausanne (Switzerland), 1933; M.S., Fed. Poly. Inst. (Switzerland), 1937; m. Adele E. Elson, June 2, 1939; children—James Lee, Peggy Ann Kamp Golden, Richard Allan. Research engr. Infilco, Inc., Chgo., 1937-41; div. mgr. Graves Tank & Mfg. Co., E. Chicago, Ind., 1941-46; asst. chmn. Armour Research Found. of IIT, Chgo., 1946-53; dir. engring. The

Englander Co., div. Union Carbide, 1953-64; sr. scientist Union Carbide Corp., Chgo., 1964—. Mem. research and devel. bd. Dept. of Def., 1948-53, mem. guidance com., 1953-63. Mem. Am. Def. Preparedness Assn., TAPPI, Tau Beta Pi. Clubs: Flamingo, B'nai B'rith. Contbr. articles in field to profl. jours.; patentee in field. Home: 5000 S Cornell Ave Chicago IL 60615 Office: 6733 W 65th St Chicago IL 60638

KAMRA, SURJIT SINGH, sci. co. exec.; b. Mailsi, India (now Pakistan), Apr. 12, 1939; s. Tarlok Singh and Raj Kaur (Sandhu) K.; came to U.S., 1970; B.S., Punjab U., 1962; M.S., U. Alta., 1967, M.B.A., 1971; m. Nirmaljit Chawla, Jan. 7, 1969; 1 son, Ajaypreet Singh. Tech. supt. H.M.M. Ltd., Nabha, India, 1962-65; prodn. foreman Palm Dairies, Edmonton, Alta., Can., 1967-69; mgr. quality control Beecham Inc., Racine, Wis., 1971-75; dir. tech. services Foulds Inc., Libertyville, Ill., 1975—; cons. product devel. E. Indian ethnic foods. Rep. Mayor Citizens Com. Desegregation Racine Schs., 1974. Merit scholar Nat. Dairy Research Inst., Karnal, India, 1959, 61. Mem. Inst. Food Technologists (profl.), Am. Assn. Cereal Chemists (profl.). Club: Rotary (sec. Nabha, 1965). Home: 375 Getchell St Grayslake IL 60030 Office: Foulds Inc 520 E Church St Libertyville IL 60048

KAMY, EUGENE MITCHELL, mgmt. cons.; b. Chgo., May 9, 1927; s. Matthew and Marie (Polanski) K.; B.S., U. Ill., 1951; M.S., Loyola U., Chgo., 1957; postgrad. Roosevelt U., 1951-57, Ill. Inst. Tech., 1954-55, DePaul U., 1956-57; m. Margaret Ocsai, Sept. 3, 1949; 1 dau., Deborah Ann. Vice pres. Chgo. Hardware Foundry, N. Chicago, Ill., 1960-67; pres. Eugene M. Kamy & Assos., Inc., Lincolnwood, Ill., 1962—; pres., founder Tolerance Mfg. Co., Waukegan, Ill., 1966-67; pres., treas., founder Profl. Growth Counselors, 1973—; lectr. Sch. Bus. Northwestern U., Evanston, Ill., 1958—; professorial lectr. Grad. Sch. Roosevelt U. Bd. dirs. Indsl. Engring. Coll., Chgo. Registered profl. engr., Ill. Mem. Am. Inst. Indsl. Engrs., Nat. Soc. Profl. Engrs., Am. Prodn. and Inventory Control Soc., Soc. Mfg. Engrs., Ill. Alumni Assn. (life), Delta Sigma Pi, Phi Chi Theta, Psi Chi. Club: Chgo. Farmers. Office: 6677 Lincoln Ave Lincolnwood IL 60645

KAN, FRANK KWOK-YIN, anesthesiologist; b. Canton, China, Apr. 14, 1921; s. Lim-Pak and Wai-Ching (Wong) K.; came to U.S., 1969, naturalized, 1975; student Hsiang Ya Med. Coll., Kweiyang, 1940-42, Changsha, 1947-49, Ling Nan U., Canton, 1949-51; M.B., B.S., U. Hong Kong, 1957; m. Rebecca Luke, July 24, 1948; children—Matthew, Jane, Daniel. House officer, Kowloon Hosp., Hong Kong, 1957-58; med. officer Kwong Wah Hosp., Hong Kong, 1958-61; gen. practice medicine Hong Kong, 1961-69; intern Swedish Hosp., Mpls., 1969-70; resident U. Minn., 1971-73, instr., 1973—; staff anesthesiologist VA Hosp., Mpls., 1973—. Fellow Am. Coll. Anesthesiologists; mem. Am., Minn. socs. Anesthesiologists, Am., Minn., Hennepin County med. assns., Internat. Anesthesia Research Soc. Home: 5601 Washburn Ave S Minneapolis MN 55410 Office: 5400 48th Ave S Minneapolis MN 55417

KANAGA, CLINTON WILLIAMSON, JR., ins. broker; b. Kansas City, Mo., Feb. 28, 1921; s. Clinton W. and Ruth (Smith) K.; B.A., U. Kans., 1942; m. Nina Louise Green, Apr. 30, 1949; children—Stephen C., Carolyn M., William G. With Gambrel Stubbs (merged with Mann-Kline), 1946-49; exec. v.p. Mann-Kline, 1949-68; v.p. Haas & Wilkerson, Kansas City, 1968—; chmn., presiding agt. Jackson County Ins. Commn.; dir. Grandview (Mo.) Bank. Commr., Kansas City Area Transp. Authorily, 1966—, chmn., 1976, 77; pres. Kansas City Bd. Police Commrs., 1977—. Served to maj. USMCR; PTO. Named Outstanding Young Man, Jaycees, 1954; Northland Man of Year, Eagle Scouts, 1977. Mem. U. Kans. Alumni Assn. (nat. dir. 1971-76), Internat. Assn. Chiefs of Police. Democrat. Congregationalist. Clubs: Mercury, Vanguard, Mission Hills Country. Home: 1208 W 65 St Kansas City MO 64113 Office: 3101 Broadway Kansas City MO 64111

KANAN, FANNUN AHMAD, motel exec.; b. Bethlehem, Palestine, June 30, 1928; s. Mohamed A. and Mashiek (Sulamin) K.; m. Elma M., Dec. 2, 1956; children—Renee, Raaji. Came to U.S., 1956, naturalized, 1961. With Arches Internat. Inn, Joplin, Mo., 1956-69, exec. dir., 1961—; chmn. bd. Roadsite Motels USA, Inc., 1971—; dir. Martin Oil Co., Canaan Land Devel. Co. U.S.A. Bd. dirs. Big Bros. Mo., 1956-59. Served with N.G., 1956-59. Mem. C. of C. Clubs: Masons, Lions, Optimist. Home: 3108 Keller Dr Joplin MO 64801 Office: 3535 Rangeline St Joplin MO 64801

KANAROWSKI, STANLEY MARTIN, chemist, chem. engr., govt. ofcl.; b. Beausejour, Man., Can., Dec. 12, 1912; s. Joseph and Caroline K.; came to U.S., 1923, naturalized, 1928; B.S., U. Toledo, 1934; postgrad. Ohio State U., 1938-42, U. Akron, 1943-47, N.Y. U., 1954, Xavier U., 1969; m. Pearl Lewus, Aug. 8, 1936; children—Stanley Martin, Janice Ellen, Nancy Carol. Chemist, chief chemist Ohio Dept. Liquor Control, Columbus, 1936-42; sr. cons. chemist Nebr. Ordnance Plant Firestone Tire and Rubber Co., Fremont, 1942-43; asst. dir. corp. gen. lab., chief factory product, chem. engr., research and devel. compounding engr. Firestone Tire and Rubber Co., Akron, Ohio, 1943-49; lab. dir. asst. research and devel. mgr. Fremont Rubber Co. (Ohio), 1949-52; research and devel. chem. engr. Glass Fibers, Inc., Waterville, Ohio, 1952-53; chief research and devel. chemist-engr., mgr. quality control Dairypak Butler, Inc., Toledo, 1953-60; chief chemist No. Ohio Region Lab. Liquor Control Enforcement Div., State of Ohio, Cleve., 1960-62; research and devel. chemist-engr. Consol. Paper Co., Monroe, Mich., 1962-63; chemist City of Toledo, 1963-64; project engr., head chemist investigations sect. Ohio River Div. Labs., U.S. Army Engr. Div. C.E., 1964-69; project leader, prin. investigator U.S. Army Constrn. Engring. Research Lab., Champaign, Ill., 1969—. Mem. U. Ill. Illini Symphony Orch., 1970—. Recipient Army-Navy E award, 1943. Mem. Am. Inst. Chem. Engrs., Am. Chem. Soc. (mem. rubber div. 1954—), Am. Def. Preparedness Assn. Home: 1404 Garden Hills Dr Champaign IL 61820 Office: PO Box 4005 Champaign IL 61820

KANDRAC, STEPHEN CYRIL, psychologist; b. Berea, O., Feb. 8, 1908; s. Michael and Barbara (Seman) K.; B.A., John Carroll Coll., 1929; M.S., Cath. U., 1938; postgrad. U. Chgo., 1946, U. Cin., 1946-52, 59-60, Ohio State U., 1953; m. Agnes Greenlow, July 24, 1945; children—Michael, Stephen Cyril, Mary, Jean. Personnel officer U.S. Rubber Co., Cleve., 1929-31; supr., investigator Stark County Relief Adminstrn., Massillon, O., 1935-36; social worker St. Mary's Indsl. Sch., Balt., 1938-42; counseling psychologist VA, Cin., 1946-61, chief counseling and rehab., Cin. and Cleve., 1961-73; pvt. practice as psychologist, Rocky River, O., 1973—. Served with AUS, 1942-45. Mem. Am., Ohio psychol. assns., Am. Personnel and Guidance Assn. Home: 19612 Battersea Blvd Rocky River OH 44116

KANE, JACK ALLISON, physician; b. Meadville, Pa., Feb. 28, 1921; s. Thomas Emery and Mildred May (McMahon) K.; B.S., Allegheny Coll., 1944; M.D., Case Western Res. U., 1949; m. Virginia Joan Gasque, Sept. 28, 1946; children—Jeffrey, Marsha, Sharman, Cheryl. Intern, U.S. Naval Hosp., St. Albans, N.Y., 1949-50; fellow in indsl. medicine U. Mich., 1950-51; plant physician Frigidaire div. Gen. Motors Corp., Dayton, 1950-52, med. dir. Central Foundry div., Defiance, Ohio, 1954—; mem. exec. staff Defiance Hosp.; mem. occupational health com. Am. Foundrymen's Soc., Des Plaines, Ill. Pres. Defiance County Tb and Health Assn., 1959-72, Defiance County Bd. Health, 1960—. Served with USNR, 1942-45, 52-54. Diplomate Am. Bd. Preventive Medicine. Fellow Am. Occupational Med. Assn.; mem. AMA, Am., Ohio thoracic socs., Ohio Med. Assn., Defiance County Med. Soc., N.W. Ohio Health Planning Assn. Republican. Home: 2 Mirival Ln Defiance OH 43512 Office: Central Foundry Division General Motors Corp Defiance OH 43512

KANE, LUCILE MARIE, state archivist; b. Maiden Rock, Wis., Mar. 17, 1920; d. Emery John and Ruth (Coty) Kane; B.S., River Falls State Tchrs. Coll., 1942; M.A., U. Minn., 1946. Tchr. Osceola (Wis.) High Sch., 1942-44; asst. publicity dept. U. Minn. Press, Mpls., 1945-46; research fellow, editor Forest Products History Found., St. Paul, 1946-48; curator manuscripts Minn. Hist. Soc., St. Paul, 1948-75; state archivist, 1975—. Fellow Soc. Am. Archivists; mem. Manuscript Soc., Author: A Guide to the Care and Administration of Manuscripts, 2d edit., 1966; Manuscripts Collections of the Minnesota Historial Society, Guide No. 2, 1955; The Waterfall That Built a City, 1966; Guide to the Public Affairs Collection Minn. Historical Soc. 19 Editor: Military Life in Dakota, the Jour. Philippe Régis de Trobriand, 1951; (with June D. Holmquist) The Northern Expeditions of Major Stephen H. Long, 1978. Contbr. articles to profl. jours. Home: 1298 Fairmount Ave St Paul MN 55105 Office: 1500 Mississippi St Paul MN 55101

KANE, RALPH EDGAR, savings and loan exec.; b. Akron, Ohio, July 16, 1921; s. Albert Anton and Ida Martha (Golz) K.; student U. Akron, 1940-42, 46-47, S.D. State Coll., 1943-44; achievement certificate Am. Savs. & Loan Inst., 1953; m. Alice Mabel Zantow, July 2, 1945; children—Paul Anton, Elisabeth Ann. With B.F. Goodrich Co., Akron, 1940-42, 46; with First Fed. Savs. and Loan Assn., Wooster, 1947—, treas., 1950—, advt. mgr., 1960—, controller, 1971—. Chmn., Citizens Com. for Study Local Taxation, Wooster, 1965, Citizens Com. Reapportionment of Wooster, 1968, 71; chmn. bldg. com. Wooster Municipal Bldg., 1960-61; unit treas. Am. Cancer Soc., 1948-52. Councilman-at-large, Wooster, 1958-61. Trustee, Wooster Cemetery Assn., 1960-73. Served with U.S. Army, 1943-46. Named man of the year 20-30 Club Wooster, 1961; recipient award Clipper Graphic Arts, 1973, 74. Mem. Nat. Soc. Savs. and Loan Controllers and Financial Officers (br. operations com. 1963-65), Savs. Instns. Mktg. Soc. (mktg. research com. 1968-71), Am. Savs. and Loan Inst., Ohio Savs. and Loan League (mktg. com. 1974—), Wayne County Builders Exchange, Wooster C. of C., Wayne County Hist. Soc. (treas. 1965-70), Internat. Platform Assn. Republican. Lutheran (endowment treas. 1948—). Kiwanian (pres. 1969). Clubs: 20-30 (pres. 1950), Century (pres. 1971-72) (Wooster). Author: 25 Years of Christmas Poems, 1965; (play) A Modern Version of the Christmas Story, 1967; (play) T.H.E.A.T.R.E., 1975. Home: 315 Oakley Rd Wooster OH 44691 Office: PO Box 385 135 E Liberty St Wooster OH 44691

KANEKO, THOMAS MOTOMI, chemist; b. Tokyo, Japan, Aug. 14, 1914; s. Bert Yosaburo and Miwako (Tokunaga) K.; B.S. in Chem. Engring., U. Utah, 1936, Ph.D., 1956; m. Yoko Moro, Mar. 16, 1957. Assayer, Kennecott Copper Corp., Ruth, Nev., 1936-39; research engr. Mitsubishi Chem. Industries, Tokyo, 1939-41; liaison engr. Mitsubishi Rayon Co., Tokyo, 1950-52; research metallurgist Union Carbide Corp., Niagara Falls, N.Y., 1956-57, Nat. Distillers & Chem. Corp., Cin., 1957-59; sr. research chemist BASF Wyandotte Corp., Mich., 1959—. AEC fellow, 1953-56. Fellow A.A.A.S., Am. Inst. Chemists; mem. N.Y. Acad. Scis., Am. Chem. Soc. (editor Detroit chemist 1953-56), Am. Inst. Chem. Engrs., Am. Inst. Mining and Metall. Engrs., Sigma Xi, Sigma Pi Sigma. Contbr. articles to profl. jours. Patentee in field. Home: 1579 Boxford Rd Trenton MI 48183 Office: 1419 Biddle Ave Wyandotte MI 48192

KANG, BANN, physician; b. Kyungnam, Korea, Mar. 4, 1939; d. Dae Ryong and Buni (Chung) K.; came to U.S., 1964, naturalized, 1976; M.D., Kyung Buk Nat. U., 1963; m. Ung Yun Ryo, Mar. 30, 1963. Intern, L.I. Jewish Hosp./Queens Hosp. Center, N.Y.C., 1964-65, resident in medicine, 1965-67; resident in medicine Kyung Buk Nat. U., Teagu, Korea, 1967-70; fellow in allergy and immunology Creighton U./St. Josephs Hsp., Omaha, 1970-71, Henry Ford Hosp., Detroit, 1971-72, U. Mich. Med. Center, Ann Arbor, 1972-73; asst. prof. Chgo. Med. Sch., 1973-74, Rush Med. Sch., Chgo., 1975—; chief div. allergy and clin. immunology Mt. Sinai Hosp., Chgo., 1973—; practice medicine specializing in allergy/immunology, Chgo., 1973—; mem. staff Mt. Sinai Hosp.; cons. Edgewater, St. Anthony hosps. Diplomate Am. Bd. Internal Medicine, Am. Bd. Allergy and Clin. Immunology. Fellow ACP, Am. Acad. Allergy; mem. Chgo. Allergy Soc., AMA, Am. Fedn. Clin. Research. Contbr. articles to profl. jours. Home: 1555 Astor St Chicago IL 60610 Office: Mt Sinai Hosp 15th St at California Ave Chicago IL 60608

KANGAS, GENE artist, educator; b. Fairport Harbor, Ohio, May 22, 1944; s. Eugene N. and Martha H. (Hendrickson) K.; B.F.A., Miami U., Oxford, Ohio, 1966; M.F.A., Bowling Green U., 1968; postgrad. U. Ky., 1967; m. Linda L. Muse, Jan. 29, 1967; 1 son, Erik. Prof. art U. N.C., 1968-71; prof. Cleve. State U., 1971—; coordinator NBC-TV Spl. Am. Folk Art. Fulbright Hayes awardee, 1968; U. N.C. Research grantee, 1968-70. Commissioned for sculpture in New Cuyahoga County Justice Center, Cleve., 1977. Contbr. articles on Am. folk art to profl. jours. Home: 6852 Painesville-Ravenna Rd Painesville OH 44077 Office: 24th Euclid St Cleveland State U Cleveland OH 44115

KANIA, WALTER THEODORE, dentist; b. Shamokin, Pa., Sept. 25, 1923; s. Steve and Anna (Habura) K.; B.S., Case-Western Res. U., 1948, D.D.S., 1950; m. Jill S. Tussel, July 26, 1952; 1 son, Scott Stephen. Intern St. Lukes Hosp., Cleve., 1950-51; resident in oral surgery Lackland AFB, San Antonio, 1953-55; gen. practice dentistry, Cleve., 1955—; past pres. dental staff S.W. Gen. Hosp. Mem. liaison com. Berea Bd. Edn., 1961-68. Served with USAF, 1953-55. Mem. Am., Ohio dental assns., Cleve. Dental Soc. Home: 16693 Glenridge Ave Cleveland OH 44130 Office: 7155 Pearl Rd Cleveland OH 44130

KANNAPEL, GEORGE DAVID, fabricated metal products co. exec.; b. Palmerton, Pa., Aug. 21, 1933; s. George Charles and Sallie Angelina (Fritch) K.; student Pa. State U., 1951-52; B.S., U.S. Mil. Acad., 1956; postgrad. Lehigh U., 1958-59; m. Louise Amanda Braucher, Aug. 21, 1954; children—Keith David, Lori Ann, Gwynn Marie. Proposal engr. Air Products & Chems., Allentown, Pa., 1957-61; contracts mgr. F.J. Stokes Corp., Phila., 1961-63; mgr. sales CVI Corp., Columbus, O., 1963-73; pres. G.D. Kannapel Co., Columbus, 1973—. Credit officer Air Products Credit Union, 1958-60. Served to 2d lt., inf., AUS, 1956-57. Congl. page, 1950-51. Mem. Atomic Indsl. Forum, Am. Mgmt. Assn., West Point Soc. Central Ohio, Am. Ordnance Assn., Whetstone Boosters Assn. (pres. 1973-74), Columbus C. of C. Republican. Lutheran. Home: 1262 Pepperell Dr Columbus OH 43220 Office: PO Box 20221 Columbus OH 43220

KANTER, CECIL LEE, art exec.; b. Mason City, Iowa, Aug. 11, 1932; s. Cecil and Leora (Curtis) K.; student Chgo. Acad. Fine Arts, 1953-54, Am. Acad. Fine Arts, 1954-56; m. Florence Rose Kanter, Apr. 16, 1955; children—Stephan, Mary, John, Theresa, James, Eric, Margaret. Staff artist Teletype Corp., 1959; graphic artist Booz Allen & Hamilton, 1960-64; art dir. J & J Publs., 1965; art dir. Fry Cons., Chgo., 1966-71; also artist Vanguard & Vicount Greeting Cards, Inc., 1967-68; with A.T. Kearney, Inc., Chgo., 1973—. Committeeman Boy Scouts Am., Spring Grove, Ill., 1970-71. Served with AUS, 1952-54. Mem. Artists Guild Chgo., Implant Mgrs. Assn., McHenry Camera Club (pres. 1966-73, del. 1967-68). Home: 1808 Oakleaf St McHenry IL 60050 Office: 10 N Clark St Chicago IL 60606

KANTER, GERALD ALAN, ins. agy. exec.; b. Detroit, Jan. 6, 1931; s. Phillip L. and Florence (Blumberg) K.; B.A., Mich. State U., 1952; m. Marilyn D. Kates, Apr. 10, 1956; children—Susan G., David M., Sharyn H. Exec. v.p. P.L. Kanter Agy., Inc., 1955-72; pres. N.Am. Assn. Underwriters Corp., Southfield, Mich., 1970-75; v.p. Penn Gen. Agys. of Mich., Inc., Southfield, 1972-76; pres. N.Am. Agys., Inc., Southfield, 1977—; ins. counsel to assns. and spl. risks. Served as 1st lt. U.S. Army, 1953-55; Korea. Named Man of Yr., Life Ins. Leaders Assn., 1961. Mem. Ind. Ins. Agts. Assn., Zeta Beta Tau (pres. 1950-51). Republican. Jewish. Clubs: Masons, Shriner, B'nai Brith; Met. Detroit Ins.; Town and Country (Southfield); Fairlane (Dearborn, Mich.). Home: 29780 Farmbrook Villa Dr Southfield MI 48034 Office: 3221 W Big Beaver Rd Troy MI 48084

KANTOR, MARVIN, educator; b. N.Y.C., May 9, 1934; s. Irving and Sara (Brodsky) K.; Ph.D. (NDEA fellow 1962-64, Horace H. Rackham fellow 1965), U. Mich., 1966; m. Lis Petersen, Aug. 13, 1961; children—Michele, Robert Joseph. Lectr., U. Mich., 1964-65; asst. prof. Bklyn. Coll., 1966-67; asso. prof. Slavic langs. and lits. Northwestern U., 1967—. Served with USMC, 1952-55. Mem. Am. Assn. Tchrs. Slavic, East European Langs., Medieval Acad. Am., Am. Soc. Eighteenth-Century Studies, Ducks Unltd. Jewish. Author: Aspectual Derivation in Contemporary Serbo-Croatian, 1972; Dramtic Works of D. I. Fonuizin, 1974; Vita of Constantine, Vita of Methodius, 1977. Home: 2010 Hawthorne Ln Evanston IL 60201 Office: Dept Slavic Langs and Lits Northwestern U Evanston IL 60201

KANTOR, PAUL BERL, systems cons.; b. Washington, Nov. 27, 1938; s. Harry S. and Anne (Golden) K.; A.B. summa cum laude, Columbia U., 1959; Ph.D. in Physics, Princeton U., 1963; m. Carole Kaplowitz, Feb. 4, 1962; children—Michael, David. Theoretical physicist Brookhaven Nat. Lab., 1963-65; asst. prof. State U. N.Y., Stonybrook, 1965-67; asst. prof. physics Case Western Res. U., Cleve., 1967-69, asso. prof., 1969-73, asso. prof. library sci. and ops. research, 1974-77; systems cons., Cleveland Heights, Ohio, 1977—. Woodrow Wilson fellow, 1959-60; NSF fellow, 1960-63. Mem. Am. Soc. Info. Sci., Soc. Ethnomusicology, Am. Statis. Assn., Am. Phys. Soc., ALA, N.Y. Acad. Scis., Am. Folklore Soc. Home and Office: 3257 Ormond Rd Cleveland Heights OH 44118

KANTROWITZ, ADRIAN, thoracic surgeon; b. N.Y.C., Oct. 4, 1918; s. Bernard Abraham and Rose (Esserman) K.; A.B., N.Y.U., 1940; M.D., L.I. Coll. Medicine, 1943; postgrad. in physiology Western Res. U., 1950; m. Jean Rosensaft, Nov. 25, 1948; children—Niki, Lisa, Allen. Intern, Jewish Hosp., Bklyn., 1944; resident surgery Mt. Sinai Hosp., N.Y.C., 1947; asst. resident Montefiore Hosp., N.Y.C., 1948, resident pathology, 1949, fellow cardiovascular research group, 1949, chief resident surgery, 1950, adj. surg. service, 19S1-55; USPHS fellow cardiovascular research dept physiology Western Res. U., 1951-52, teaching fellow physiology, 1951-52; instr. surgery N.Y. Med. Coll., 1952-55; cons. surgeon Good Samaritan Hosp., Suffern, N.Y., 1954-55; asst. prof. surgery State U.N.Y. Coll. Medicine, 1955-56, asso. prof., 1957-64, prof., dir. surgery 1964-70; mem. staff Maimonides Med. Center, Bklyn., 1955-64, dir. surgery, 1964-70; chmn. dept. surgery Sinai Hosp., Detroit, 1970—; prof. surgery Wayne State U. Sch. Medicine, 1970—. Served to capt. M.C., U.S. Army, 1944-46. Recipient H.L. Moses prize, 1949; 1st prize sci exhibit Conv. N.Y. State Med. Soc., 1952; Gold Plate award Am. Acad. Achievement, 1966; Max Berg award 1966; diplomate Am. Bd. Surgery, Am. Bd. Thoracic Surgery. Fellow N.Y. Acad. Sci., A.C.S.; mem. Internat. Soc. Angiology, Am. Soc. Artificial Organs (pres. 1968-69), N.Y. County Med. Soc., Harvey Soc., N.Y. Soc. Thoracic Surgery, N.Y. Soc. Cardiovascular Surgery, Am. Heart Assn., Am. Physiol. Soc., Am. Coll. Cardiology (Theodore and Susan B. Cummings humanitarian award 1967), Am. Coll. Chest Physicians, Blyn. Thoracic Surgery Soc. (pres. 1967-68), Pan Am. Med. Assn., Soaring Soc., Am. Ski Assn. Contbr. articles to profl. jours. Pub. pioneer motion pictures taken inside living heart, 1950; contbr. to devel. mech. artificial hearts; contbr. to devel. pump-oxygenators for human heart surgery; performed 1st permanent partial mech. heart surgery in humans, 1966; 1st human heart transplant in U.S., Dec. 1967. Home: 70 Gollogly Rd Pontiac MI 48053 Office: 6767 W Outer Dr Detroit MI 48253

KAO, STEPHEN SHENG-TE, engineer; b. Hupeh, China, June 8, 1921; s. Shong Yin and Chi San (Lee) K.; came to U.S., 1959; naturalized, 1968; M.S., lU. Colo., 1948, Carnegie Mellon U., 1961; m. Jean C.H. Tung, Dec. 5, 1948; children—Hugh, June. Prof., chmn. dept. indsl. mgmt. Nat. Cheng-Kung U., Tainan, Taiwan, 1950-59; devel. engr. Blackstone Co., Jamestown, N.Y.. 1961-68; sr. engr. Modine Co., Racine, Wis., 1968—. Mem. Ops. Research Soc. Am., ASME. Republican. Author: Operations Research, 1959; Quality Control. 1958; Production Control, 1957; Application of Operations Research to Optimize Heat Transfer Surface, 1977. Home: 30 Illinois St Racine WI 53405

KAPACINSKAS, JOSEPH, newspaper editor; b. Mazuciai, Lithuania, Oct. 20, 1907; s. George and Teofile (Baskeviciute) K.; came to U.S., 1949, naturalized, 1956; Engr., Tech. Coll., Ausburg, Germany, 1948; B., Allied Inst. Tech., Chgo., 1960; m. Marie Kulikauskas, Dec. 27, 1952; 1 son, Joseph-Vytautas. Employee, City of Kaunas Municipal Govt., Lithuania, 1929-39, Nat. R.R., Lithuania, 1939-44, Nat. R.R., Treuchtlingen, Germany, 1944-45; instr. UNRRA, Weissenburg, Germany, 1946-47; chief electrician Burlington No. R.R., Inc., Chgo., 1951-72; editor Sandara Lithuanian, Chgo., 1973—. Mem. Am. Lithuanian Engrs. and Architects Assn., Lithuanian Journalists Assn., Am. Tool and Mfg. Engrs., AAAS, Internat. Platform Assn., Intercontinental Biog. Assn., Lithuanian Alliance of Am. Author: Siaubingos Dienos-Horrifying Days, 1965; Iseivio Dalia-Emigrant's Fate, 1974. Contbr. articles on Lithuanian culture and social life to newspapers. Home: 6811 S Maplewood Ave Chicago IL 60629

KAPILA, VED PARKASH, engineer, surveyor, builder; b. Lopon, India, Dec. 27, 1932; s. Baboo Ram and Amravati (Vasishta) K.; came to U.S., 1963; naturalized, 1977; student Punjab U., India, 1949-51; Civil engring. Sch., Lucknow, Ind., 1951-53; B.S. in Civil Engring., U. Mich., 1964, M.S. in Civil Engring., 1965; M.B.A., Wayne State U., 1970, value engring. orientation, 1970; m. Pushpa Pipat, Nov. 18, 1952; children—Shashi, Rajnish, Rita, Renu. Engring. sect. officer Punjab State Public Works Dept., India, 1953-63; design, engr. Ayres, Lewis, Norris & May, Ann Arbor, Mich., 1964-65; Obenchain Corp., Dearborn, Mich., 1965-66; v.p., chief civil and structural engr. O. Germany, Inc., Warren, Mich., 1966-76; dir. project services and chief planning and scheduling, chief quality assurance, chief client purchasing Hoad Engrs., Inc., Ypsilanti, Mich., 1976—; owner, pres. Kapila Constrn. Co., cons. civil engr., 1968—. Registered profl. engr. Mich., Ga., Va., Punjab State (India); registered land surveyor, Mich.; licensed builder, Mich.; certified Nat. Council Engring. Examiners.

Mem. ASCE, Am. Concrete Inst., Am. Inst. Steel Constrn., Mich. Soc. Registered Land Surveyors, Am. Soc. Quality Control, Soc. Am. Value Engrs., Nat. Soc. Profl. Engrs. Home: 25039 Branchaster Farmington Hills MI 48018 Office: 1159 E Michigan Ave Ypsilanti MI 48197

KAPLAN, DAVID JOSEPH, food co. exec.; b. Omaha, July 9, 1909; student pub. schs. Omaha. Founder, chmn. bd. Blue Star Foods, Inc., Council Bluffs, Iowa, 1935—. Pres. Christian Home, Council Bluffs, 1971; past mem. pres.'s council Creighton U., Omaha; chmn. adv. bd. St. Albert's Catholic High Sch., Council Bluffs, 1971; mem. council Boy Scouts Am.; lay bd. mem. ednl. fund drive Omaha Archdiocese; mem. archbishop's com. ednl. devel. Omaha Archdiocese Bd. Edn., 1972—; chmn. bd. fund drive Des Moines Diocese; past mem. bd. dirs. St. Joseph Orphanage, Torrington, Wyo., St. Mary's Coll., Omaha; originator, chmn. bd. trustees Mercy Hosp., gen. chmn. fund raising campaign; nat. trustee City of Hope; past lay bd. mem. St. Joseph Hosp., Omaha; past mem. draft bd., Council Bluffs. Decorated knight Order of Holy Sepulchre, 1951, Knight with grand cross, 1955; Knight comdr. Equestrian Order of Holy Sepulchre, 1952, divisional dir.; recipient Coronet medal St. Edward's U., 1963; Pilgrim shell from Latin Patriarch of Jerusalum, 1965; Americanism award Council Bluffs chpt. B'nai B'rith, 1967; Nat. Humanitarian award City of Hope, 1970; J.G. Lemen Humanitarian award, Christian Home Assn. Council Bluffs, 1972; Ben Gershun Meml. award Jewish Welfare Fedn. Council Bluffs, 1976; named to Wisdom Hall of Fame; Nat. Poultry Hall of Fame; adm. in Nebr. Navy. Mem. AIM (pres.'s council 1974), Council Bluffs C. of C. (past dir.). Roman Catholic. Clubs: Happy Hollow, Chalice (Omaha); Council Bluffs Country (past pres.); K.C. (4 deg.); Elks. Home: 9905 Broadmoor Dr Omaha NE 68114 Office: 1023 4th St PO Box 798 Council Bluffs IA 51501

KAPLAN, ETHAN ZADOK, urban planner-analyst; b. Pontiac, Mich., May 9, 1935; s. Morris J. and Certie (Bock) K.; B.A., U. Chgo., 1955, M.A., 1958; postgrad. Washington U. at St. Louis, 1960-62; m. Jane B. Breese, Dec. 23, 1958; children—Mark, Alan. Sr. planner St. Louis County Planning Com., 1962-66, prin. planner, 1967-69; chief advanced planning City Alexandria, Va., 1966-67; research planner Health and Welfare Council St. Louis, 1969—; pvt. cons., 1977—. Mem. St. Louis Census Com., 1975. Served with AUS, 1958-60. Mem. Am. Soc. Planning Ofcls., Am. Statis. Assn., Nat. Con. Social Welfare, Am. Inst. Planners, Am. Sociol. Assn. Home: 7351 Cornell St St Louis MO 63130

KAPLAN, JOEL ROBERT, psychologist; b. Chgo., Aug. 14, 1940; s. Jerome and Phyllis (Rieber) K.; B.A., Washington U., St. Louis, 1962; M.A., Loyola U., 1966, Ph.D., 1970; m. Doreen June Rees, July 25, 1971. Psychologist, Inst. for Psychol. Services, Ill. Inst. Tech., Chgo., 1970-72; dir. psychology dept. Schwab Rehab. Hosp., Chgo., 1973—. NIMH fellow, 1962; registered psychologist, Ill. Mem. Am., Ill. psychol. assns., Am. Congress Rehab. Medicine, Analytical Psychology Club Chgo., Chgo. Psychology Club. Contbr. articles to profl. jours. Home: 516 W Briar Pl Chicago IL 60657 Office: 1401 S California Blvd Chicago IL 60608

KAPLAN, MAURICE, psychiatrist; b. Gorzd, Lithuania, Oct. 10, 1907; s. Eli and Ida (Meyer) K.; came to U.S., 1911, naturalized, 1920; B.S., U. Ill., 1932, M.D., 1935, M.S., 1939. Intern, Detroit Receiving Hosp., 1934-35; resident staff physician Lincoln (Ill.) State Sch. and Colony, 1935-36, Manteno (Ill.) State Hosp., 1936; fellow neuropsychiatry Neuropsychiatric Inst. U. Ill., Chgo., 1936-39; psychoanalytic tng. San Francisco Psychoanalytic Inst., 1949-55; practice medicine, specializing in psychiatry, San Francisco, 1949-59, Chgo., 1960-67, Highland Park, Ill., 1969—; dir. S. Coast Child Guidance Clinic, Costa Mesa, Calif., 1967-69; dir. Child Guidance Clinic of Children's Hosp., San Francisco, 1948-59; cons. dept. psychiatry U.S. Army Letterman Gen. Hosp., San Francisco, 1958-59; asst. instr. psychiatry U. Ill. Coll. Medicine, Chgo., 1936-39, instr. psychiatry, 1940-42, asso. clin. prof., 1961-67; asst. med. dir. Am. Joint Distbn. Com., Paris, 1946-47; asst. dir. children's div. Langley Porter Clinic, U. Calif. Sch. Medicine, San Francisco, 1948-50, lectr. psychiatry, 1948-50; clin. instr. psychiatry U. Calif. Sch. Medicine, San Francisco, 1950-52, asst. clin. prof. psychiatry, 1952-58, asso. clin. prof., 1958-59; lectr. Northwestern U. Sch. Medicine, 1969—; cons. to child guidance services San Francisco Unified Sch. Dist., 1950-59; Fulbright prof., India, 1959-60; cons. Inst. Juvenile Research, Chgo., 1962-67; faculty child therapy program Inst. Psychoanalysis, Chgo., 1962-67; cons. Jewish Family and Community Service, 1962-67, Jewish Vocat. Service, 1963-67, Mary Bartelme Home, 1969—. Fellow Am. Acad. Child Psychiatry, Am. Psychiat. Assn., Am. Orthopsychiat. Assn.; mem. AMA, Am., Internat., Chgo. psychoanalytic assns., Chgo. Med. Soc., Chgo. Council Child Psychiatry, Alpha Omega Alpha, Sigma Xi. Contbr. articles to profl. jours. Address: 572 Cherokee Rd Highland Park IL 60035

KAPLAN, MORRIS, publisher; b. Bklyn., Apr. 8, 1909; s. Simon and Leah (Okin) K.; student Northwestern U. Sch. Journalism, 1928-33; m. Dorothy Weiss, Mar. 28, 1936; children—Kenneth Lawrence, Janet Ann. Editor, Chgo. Peacock Pub. Co., 1927-31; editor Cicero-Berwyn Life printing and Pub. Co. (Ill.), 1933-37; Cicero Berwyn pub. Community Newspaper Pub. Co., 1937-40; pub. Chgo. West Town Publs., 1940-49; asso. pub. Chgo. Lerner Newspapers, 1949-53; pub. West Town Publs., Chgo., 1953—. Mem. adv. bd. Met. Bank and Trust Co. Mem. Art Inst. Chgo., Mus. Contemporary Art, Little Village C. of C. Jewish. Club Kiwanis. Home: 175 Delaware Pl E Chicago IL 60611 Office: 2711 Cermak Rd W Chicago IL 60608

KAPLAN, ROY IRVING, chemist; b. Lexington, Miss., Sept. 19, 1941; s. Samuel and Yetta (Flower) K.; B.S. (academic scholar), U. Miss., 1963; M.S. (NSF scholar), Ga. Inst. Tech, 1966; Ph.D. (Petroleum Research Fund scholar), W.Va. U., 1969; m. Mary Irons, May 14, 1967; children—Deborah Lynn, Sybil Leah. Lab. technician Columbian Carbon Co., Centerville, La., 1963; recitation instr. W.Va. U., Morgantown, 1966-68; group leader Goodyear Atomic Corp., Piketon, Ohio, 1968-73, process tech. supr., 1973-77; with Nalco Chem. Co., Chgo., 1977—; instr. Ga. Inst. Tech., 1963-65, W.Va. U., 1966-68. Mem. Am. Chem. Soc., Sigma Xi, Phi Epsilon Pi. Contbr. articles to chem. jours. Patentee in field. Home: 560 Carriage Hill Dr Naperville IL 60540 Office: 6216 W 66th Pl Chicago IL 60638

KAPLAN, STANLEY MEISEL, psychoanalyst; b. Cin., May 10, 1922; s. Abe and Elka (Meisel) K.; B.S., U. Cin., 1943, M.D., 1946; postgrad. Inst. Psychoanalysis, 1962-67; m. Myran Jarson, June 18, 1950; children—Steven, Barbara, Richard. Intern, Jewish Hosp., Cin., 1946-47, resident, 1947-48; resident psychiatry Cin. Gen. Hosp., 1949-51; fellow in psychosomatics, 1951-52; faculty dept. psychiatry U. Cin., 1953—, prof. psychiatry, 1969—, acting dir. dept. psychiatry, 1975-77; vice-chmn. bd. G & J Pepsi Cola, Inc., Cin. Bd. dirs. Bonds for Israel, Cin., Jewish Vocat. Service, Cin., 1963-67, Travelers Aid Internat., Cin., 1970-73, Cin. Cancer Control Council, 1961-66; mem. allocations com. Community Chest Cin., 1975—. Served with AUS. NIMH fellow, 1954-56. Fellow Am. Psychiat. Assn.; mem. Am. Psychosomatic Soc., Am. Psychoanalytic Assn., AAUP, AMA, Sigma Xi. Contbr. articles to profl. jours. Home: 7216 Willowbrook Ln Cincinnati OH 45237

KAPLAN, STEVEN MAX, scrap steel co. exec.; b. Chgo., Apr. 20, 1942; s. Stanley Medill and Corinne (McCoy) K.; B.A., U. Calif., Los Angeles, 1965; A.M., Harvard U., 1968; m. Linda Langland, Dec. 20, 1976; children—Stanley, Corinne. Vice pres. M.S. Kaplan Co., Chgo., 1968—; instr. economics Roosevelt U., 1968-71. Woodrow Wilson fellow, 1965-66. Mem. Inst. Scrap Iron and Steel (pres. Chgo. chpt. 1976—), Phi Beta Kappa. Home: 505 Lake Shore Dr Chicago IL 60611 Office: 111 E Wacker Dr Chicago IL 60601

KAPPES, PHILIP SPANGLER, lawyer; b. Detroit, Dec. 24, 1925; s. Philip Alexander and Wilma Fern (Spangler) K.; B.A. cum laude, Butler U., 1945; J.D., U. Mich., 1948; m. Glendora Galena Miles, Nov. 27, 1948; children—Susan Lea, Philip Miles, Mark William. Admitted to Ind. bar, U.S. Supreme Ct. bar, 1948; practiced in Indpls., 1948—, asso. firm Armstrong and Gause, 1948-49; asso. law offices C. B. Dutton, 1950-52; partner firm Dutton, Kappes & Overman, 1952—; chmn. bd., dir. Lab. Equipment Corp.; sec., dir. S W, Inc., Midwest Food Center, Inc.; asst. sec., dir. Wellman Dynamics Corp.; sec., dir. Creston Corp.; instr. bus. law Butler U., 1948-49. Counselor, chmn. trust and legal coms. Crossroads of Am. council Boy Scouts Am., 1959—, bd. dirs., exec. com., v.p. adminstrn., 1976—, v.p. fin., 1975-76, pres., 1976—; trustee Children's Mus. Indpls., Washington Twp. Sch. Found., 1967-76. Mem. Am. Judicature Soc., Am. (ho. dels. 1970-71, chmn. lawyers title guaranty fund com. 1971-73), Ind. (ho. dels. 1959—, sec. 1973-74, bd. mgrs. 1975— nominating com., chmn. pub. relations exec. com.), Indpls. (treas. 1959, 1st v.p. 1965, pres. 1970, bd. mgrs. 1976-77) bar assns., Lawyers Assn., Indpls. Legal Aid Soc., Indpls. Jr. C. of C. (past 1st v.p.), Butler U. (bd. govs., past pres.), Mich. alumni assns., Phi Delta Theta, Tau Kappa Alpha. Republican. Presbyterian (pres. bd. trustees, elder). Clubs: Masons (32 deg., past master), Shriners; Lawyers, Gyro (past pres.); Meridian Hills Country. Home: 7450 North Park Ave Indianapolis IN 46240 Office: Guaranty Bldg Indianapolis IN 46204

KARABA, FRANK ANDREW, lawyer; b. Chgo., Jan. 23, 1927; s. Frank and Katherine (Danihel) K.; B.S. with highest distinction, Northwestern U., 1949, J.D., 1951; m. Alice June Olsen, June 2, 1951; children—Thomas Frank, Stephen Milton, Catherine Alice. Admitted to Ill. bar, 1951; teaching asso. Northwestern U. Law Sch., 1951-52; law sec. Ill. Supreme Ct., 1952-53; asso. firm Crowley, Barrett & Karaba, Chgo., 1953-60, partner, 1960-75, mng. partner, 1975—. Dir., Am. Nat. Bank of South Chicago Hgts., Citizens Nat. Bank of Downers Grove, Bensenville State Bank, A & R Printers, Inc., Caron Internat. Inc., The O'Brien Corp. Asst. counsel Emergency Commn. on Crime, Chgo. City Council, 1952; Pres. 7th Av. P.T.A., 1964-66. Bd. dirs. La Grange Little League, 1964-67, pres., 1968. Served with USNR, 1945-46. Mem. Am., Ill., Chgo. (bd. mgrs. 1962-63, chmn. grievance com. 1972—), Order of Coif. Presbyn. (elder). Clubs: Legal, Law. Home: 812 S Stone Ave La Grange IL 60525 Office: 111 W Monroe St Chicago IL 60603

KARAYANNIS, NICHOLAS MARIOS, chemist; b. Athens, Greece, May 30, 1931; s. Marios L. and Antiopi M. (Horsch) K.; came to U.S., 1965; B.S., Nat. Tech. U., Athens, 1955; Ph.D. (Greek Chem. Products & Fertilizers Co. scholar), U. Coll., London, England, 1960; m. Alexandra E. Manolakis, Oct. 1, 1955; children—Marios, Yannis. Sci. adviser Greek Nat. Defense Gen. Staff, Athens, 1961-62; sci. adviser Greek Ministry Coordination, Athens, 1962-65; fuels and lubricants tech. instr. Nat. Tech. U., Athens, 1963-65; research asso. Johns Hopkins, Balt., 1965-67, Drexel U., Phila., 1967-70; sr. research chemist Amoco Chem. Corp., Naperville, Ill., 1970-76, research asso., 1976—. Served with Greek Army, 1959-61. NIH research asso. grantee, 1965-67; U.S. Army Edgewood Arsenal research asso. grantee, 1967-70. Mem. Am. Chem. Soc., N.Y. Acad. Scis., A.A.A.S., Greek Tech. Chamber, Ramsay Soc. Chem. Engrs., Phi Lamda Upsilon. Club: Pebblewood Swim and Racquet. Patentee in field. Home: 15 Pebblewood Trail Naperville IL 60540 Office: Amoco Chemicals Corporation Naperville IL 60540

KARDINAL, CARL GUSTAV, oncologist; b. Downey, Calif., Mar. 31, 1935; s. Gerhard Gustav and Lucille Evelyn (Krueger) K.; B.A., Calif. State Coll., Long Beach, 1961; M.D., Washington U., St. Louis, 1965; m. Martha Parsons Staley, Oct. 21, 1956; children—Lara Lynn, Jeni Jo. Intern, U.S. Naval Hosp., Phila., 1965-66; resident U.S. Naval Hosp., Portsmouth, Va., 1966-69, Phila., 1969-70, Cardeza Found. of Jefferson Med. Sch., Phila., 1970-71; mem. staff U.S. Naval Hosp., Oakland, Calif., 1971-74, Cancer Research Center, Columbia, Mo., 1974, Ellis Fischel State Cancer Hosp., Columbia, 1974—; asso. prof. medicine U. Mo. Sch. Medicine. Chmn. Unitarian Fellowship, Columbia, 1976-77. Served to HM2 Hosp. Corps, USN, 1954-56, to comdr. M.C., 1964-74. Recipient Lange Med. Publs. award, 1965; diplomate Am. Bd. Internal Medicine. Fellow A.C.P.; mem. Assn. Mil. Surgeons of U.S., AMA, Am. Soc. Hematology, Am. Soc. Clin. Oncology. Contbr. numerous articles to med. jours. Home: 1264 Sunset Dr Columbia MO 65201 Office: 115 Bus Loop 70 W Columbia MO 54201

KARDOFF, ALAN DAVID, state agy. cons.; b. Chgo., Jan. 19, 1939; s. Joseph and Mary (Gottlieb) K.; B.S. in Econs., U. Ill., 1961; M.A. in Urban Studies, Loyola U., Chgo., 1968; postgrad. Northwestern U., 1974. Regional unit dir. Welfare Council of Met. Chgo., 1968-69; chief housing and community relations East-West Gateway Coordinating Council, St. Louis, 1969-72; exec. dir. HOPE, Inc., Toledo, Ohio, 1972-73; community devel. cons., Chgo., 1973-75; community devel. planning cons. Village of Skokie (Ill.), 1975; interim exec. dir. SECO, Inc., Balt., 1975; regional cons. for SE Iowa, Iowa State Services for Crippled Children, Ottumwa, 1975—. Community edn. chmn., sec., bd. dirs. Dist. XV, Iowa Dept. Social Services ICF/MR adv. council, 1976—, Dist. XV Child Abuse Coordinating Com., 1976, publicity com., bd. dirs. Parental Stress Services, 1977—, chmn. info. and referral service Social and Health Concerns Project, 1976—. Chmn. community devel. and by-laws coms. Montrose Urban Progress Center Adv. Council, Chgo., 1964-68. Chmn. Lake View br. Chgo. chpt. Am. Cancer Crusade, 1965-66; mem. Toledo Inner-City Housing Task Force, 1972-73, St. Louis Operation Breakthrough Action Team, 1970-71; sec. Northwest Ohio chpt. Ohio Housing Coalition, 1972-73; pres. Park Synagogue Young Adult League, 1967-69; mem. St. Louis Challenge of Seventies Program, 1970-71; del. Iowa State Democratic Conv., 1976; del. Iowa 4th Congl. Dist. Conv., also mem. rules com., 1976; mem. Mahaska County Dem. Central Com., 1976-77; bd. dirs. Japanese Am. Service Com., 1965-68, Met. Black Survival, Inc., pub. relations adviser, 1969-72; mem. exec. bd. Temple Bhai Men's Club, also chmn. pub. relations com. Served with AUS. Recipient Certificate of Recognition Chgo. Community on Urban Opportunity, 1967. Mem. Nat. (nominating com. 1977—), Midwest (mem. program devel. com. 1977—) assns. community health centers, NAACP (publicity com. Ottumwa 1976—), Ottumwa Area C. of C. (human resources com. 1976-77), League of Women Voters, Am. Soc. Planning Ofcls., U. Ill., Loyola U. alumni assns., Alpha Kappa Psi. Contbr. articles on urban devel. to profl. publs. Address: 317 Vanness Apt 202 PO Box 898 Ottumwa IA 52501

KARINATTU, JOSEPH, clin. biochemist; b. India, Aug. 6, 1938; s. Joseph Matthew and Mary Rose (Njarackal) K.; came to U.S., 1963; B.Sc., U. Kerala (India), 1961; M.Sc., U. Delhi, 1963; Ph.D., St. Thomas Inst. Advanced Studies, Cin., 1967; m. Rajamma Mundattuchundayil, Aug. 9, 1963; children—Jeffrey, Jennifer. Biochemist, Jewish Hosp., Cin., 1967-69; dir. dept. clin. biochemistry St. Therese Hosp., Waukegan, Ill., 1969—; vis. prof. Coll. Lake County, Grays Lake, Ill., 1972—. Mem. Am. Chem. Soc., A.A.A.S., N.Y. Acad. Scis., Assn. Clin. Scientists. Home: 344 Birkdale Rd Lake Bluff IL 60044 Office: St Therese Hospital Waukegan IL

KARIOTIS, JOSEPH ANTHONY, ednl. adminstr.; b. Chgo., July 13, 1931; s. Anthony John and Stella (Kourakis) K.; student No. Ill. U., 1950-51, M.S. in Edn., 1961; B.A., Elmhurst Coll., 1958; Ph.D., Waiden U.; m. Anne Paraschos, Sept. 7, 1952; children—Shelley, Anthony, Alexander. Tchr., Roy Sch., North Lake, Ill., 1958-63; prin. Queen Bee Sch., Wheaton, Ill., 1963-64; supt. schs. Dist. 16, Wheaton, 1964—. Served with USAF, 1951-53. Mem. NEA, No. Ill. Prins. Roundtable, No. Ill. Supts. Roundtable, Sch. Assn. Spl. Edn. DuPage County (dir.), Am.-Hellenic Ednl. Progressive Assn. Home: 886 Bryan St Elmhurst IL 60126 Office: 1560 Bloomingdale Rd Glen Ellyn IL 60137

KARKAR, YAQUB NASIF, economist; b. Jerusalem, Jan. 21, 1926; s. Nasif Odeh and Evelyn Jacob (Kishek) K.; student Am. U. Beirut, 1945-47; A.B., U. Calif. at Berkeley, 1949, M.A., 1950; Ph.D., Ind. U., 1964; m. Waltraud Creter Debus, Aug. 21, 1969; 1 dau., Annaluna. Instr., Am. U., Beirut, 1957-60, Villa Madonna Coll., Ky., 1962-63; asst. prof. U. Minn., 1963-66; asst. prof. econs. U. Wis. Center-Marathon County Campus, 1966—, chmn. center system dept. bus. and econs., 1973—, co-dir. project for improvement of econ. learning in Wis., 1973—. Pres., Central Wis. Ballet Found. Served with AUS, 1950-52. Ford scholar, 1961-62. Mem. Am., Midwest, Wis. (co-chmn. meeting 1974) econ. assns., Econ. History Assn., Econ. Historians of Wis., Wis. Collegiate Soccer Assn. (pres. 1973-75). Author: Railway Development in the Ottoman Empire, 1971; also articles. Home: 601 McIndoe St Wausau WI 54401 Office: 518 S 7th Ave Wausau WI 54401

KARKLYS, JOSEPH, elec. engr.; b. Kaunas, Lithuania, Dec. 28, 1927; s. Klemensas and Jolanta (Svarcaite) K.; came to U.S., 1949, naturalized, 1956; B.S. in Elec. Engring., Ill. Inst. Tech., 1957; m. Elvira Kriauciunaite, June 9, 1956; 1 child, Rimas J. Devel. engr. Motorola, Inc., 1957-58; sr. devel. engr. ITT, 1958-63; sr. design engr. Gen. Dynamics Electronics Co., Rochester, N.Y., 1963-66; with Whirlpool Research & Engring. Center, Benton Harbor, Mich., 1966—, sr. research engr., 1971—. Served with Signal Corps, U.S. Army, 1950-52. Mem. Am. Legion, IEEE, Sigma Xi. Republican. Roman Catholic. Office: Whirlpool Research and Engring Center Monte Rd Benton Harbor MI 49022

KARL, GARY WILLIAM, natural resource biologist; b. Waukesha, Wis., Apr. 29, 1937; s. William F. and Marie E. (Koenig) K.; B.S. in Biology and Geography, Carroll Coll., 1960; M.S. in Zoology and Botany, U. Wis.-Madison, 1970; m. Marion D. Tessman, July 30, 1966; children—Susan, Gordon, Janet. Quality control chemist Dairyland Food Labs., Waukesha, 1960-62; research biologist Charles Pfizer Co., Milw., 1962-63; pub. health biologist Wis. Com. on Water Pollution, Madison, 1963-68; natural resource biologist Wis. Dept. Natural Resources, Madison, 1968—. Mem. adv. com. pest mgmt. U. Wis. Extension Program, 1975-76; tech. rep. to Wis. Pesticide Rev. Bd. and Pesticide Council, 1973—. Mem. village govt. adv. com., McFarland, Wis., 1973-76. Bd. dirs. McFarland Hist. Soc., 1973-74. Served with AUS, 1960. Mem. Am. Fishery Soc., North Am. Benthological Soc., Weed Sci. Soc. Am., N. Central Weed Control Conf., Plant Growth Regulator Working Group, Internat. Assn. Great Lakes Research. Lutheran (council 1973-75, pres. 1975). Research on toxic algae in Wis. lakes, pesticide use in Wis. Home: 6308 Lani Lane McFarland WI 53558 Office: Room 1007 4610 University Ave Pyare Sq Bldg Madison WI 53706

KARLOV, BARRY MICHAEL, dentist; b. Chgo., May 14, 1941; s. Sam and Lillian (Segal) K.; B.A., U. Ill., 1964, D.D.S., 1966; m. Dawn Elizabeth Neglia, Sept. 25, 1976; children—Jason Mark, Sarah Elizabeth. Pvt. practice dentistry, Chgo., 1966—; co-owner Midwest Arabians, Northbrook, Ill. Mem. Am. Soc. Preventive Dentistry, Am. Dental Assn., Ill., Chgo. dental socs., Am. Analgesia Soc., Acad. Gen. Dentistry, Internat. Arabian Horse Assn., Tau Epsilon Phi, Alpha Omega. Home: 1281 Ferndale St Highland Park IL 60035 Office: 6212 N Lincoln St Chicago IL 60659

KARLOWSKI, THOMAS RAYMOND, internist; b. Detroit, Jan. 6, 1943; s. Stanley and Sophie (Sohacki) K.; B.S., Wayne State U., 1965, M.D., 1969; m. Diana Lambert, June 21, 1968; children—Thomas Michael, Maria Ann. Intern, William Beaumont Hosp., Royal Oak, Mich., 1969-70; resident in internal medicine Mayo Clinic, Rochester, Minn., 1972-74; practice medicine specializing in internal medicine, Waterloo, Iowa, 1974—; mem. staff St. Francis Hosp., Allen Hosp., Schoitz Hosp.; med. advisor ARC. Served with USPHS, 1970-72. Diplomate Am. Bd. Internal Medicine. Mem. AMA (Physician Recognition awards 1969-72, 72-75), Am. Coll. Physicians, Iowa State Med. Soc., Waterloo C. of C. Roman Catholic. Clubs: Kiwanis, Elks. Research, publs. on vitamin C and common cold. Home: 216 Lovejoy Ave Waterloo IA 50701 Office: 622 W 4th St Waterloo IA 50701

KARMARKOVIC, ALEXANDER, educator; b. Lorain, O., July 17, 1919; s. Stanley and Helen (Radick) K.; B.S., Moorhead State Coll., 1955, M.S., 1957; postgrad. N.D. State U., 1961-62; Ph.D., U. Minn., 1967; certificate Hague Acad. Internat. Law, 1971; m. Ruth Agusta Helgren; children—Carolyn (Mrs. Micky Wagenman), Gloria (Mrs. Larry Ray). Ordained to ministry Assemblies of God Ch., 1942; minister Assemblies of God, Princeton, Minn., 1941-44, Moorhead, 1946-64; asst. prof. polit. sci. Evangel Coll., Springfield, Mo., 1964-66, asso. prof., 1967-76, prof., 1976—, chmn. dept., 1967-70, social sci. dept., 1976—. Republican primary candidate U.S. Ho. of Reps. from Mo. 7th Dist., 1974. Mem. Am., Mo. polit. scis. assns., Conf. on Faith and History. Republican. Kiwanian. Club: University. Home: 1855 Meadow Dr Springfield MO 65804 Office: 1111 N Glenstone St Springfield MO 65802

KARMAZIN, JOSEPHINE ROSE, realtor; b. N.Y.C., Feb. 9, 1922; d. John and Rose Marie (Mares) Karmazin; grad. Bradford Jr. Coll., 1941. Personnel mgr. Kline's Store, Detorit, 1945-53; asst. buyer and advt. Hutzel Store, Ann Arbor, Mich., 1953-55; v.p. personnel and labor relations Karmazin Products Corp., 1955-69; now sales asso. Lee H. Clark, realtor, Grosse Ile, Mich. Chmn. bd. mgmt. Downriver YWCA, 1970-73; chmn. Camp Cavell com. YWCA Met. Detroit, 1974, chmn. expansion com., 1975-76, 3d v.p., 1976—; mem. bd. mgmt. Family Neighborhood Services, 1958-68. Presbyterian (deacon). Club: Grosse Ile Yacht; Soroptimist (pres. 1961, 63) (Wyndotte, Mich.). Home: 22085 Thorofare Grosse Ile MI 48138 Office: 8600 Macomb St Grosse Ile MI 48138

KARMEL, BARBARA MARBUT, educator; b. Denver, Dec. 13, 1932; d. George Carlton and Charlotte Baldwin (Reed) Marbut; B.A., Cornell U., 1954; M.S., Purdue U., 1969, Ph.D. in Organizational Psychology, 1970; m. Kenneth E. Karmel, Aug. 25, 1955 (div. Dec. 1969); children—Kelly Anne, Clayton Reed. Asst. prof. mgmt. Oreg. State U., 1970-74, asso. prof., 1974-75; asso. prof., dir. grad. programs U. Wis., Madison, 1975—; mem. Oreg. Gov's. Mgmt.

Devel. Steering Com., 1972-75; cons., speaker on mgmt. devel. to pub., pvt. orgns. Chmn. Northampton Twp. (Pa.) Sch. Authority, 1963-66; mem. Siuslaw Nat. Forest Advisory Council. Recipient Outstanding Teaching citation Purdue U., 19—; Davis Endowment scholar, 1950-51; Found. for Econ. Edn. fellow, 1971; Oreg. State U. faculty devel. fellow, 1972. Mem. Am. Psychol. Assn., Am. Inst. Decision Scis., Internat. Assn. Applied Psychology, Acad. Mgmt. (rep. at large, bd. govs.), Psi Chi. Home: 6410 Masthead Dr Madison WI 53705 Office: Grad Sch Bus U of Wis Madison WI 53606

KAROL, NATHANIEL H., lawyer, univ. ofcl., cons.; b. N.Y.C., Feb. 16, 1929; s. Isidore and Lillian (Orlow) K.; B.S. in Social Sci., Coll. City N.Y., 1949; M.A. (fellow), Yale U., 1950; LL.B., N.Y. U., 1957, LL.M., 1959, J.D., 1966; m. Liliane Leser, July 20, 1967; children—David, Jordan. Mgmt. trainee Curtiss Wright Corp., Wood-Ridge, N.J., 1956-57; admitted to N.Y. bar, 1957; practiced in N.Y.C., 1957-58; contracting officer USAF, N.Y.C., 1958-62; chief contract mgmt. survey and cost adminstrn. Office of Procurement NASA, Washington, 1962-64; asst. dir. cost reduction, 1964-66; dep. asst. sec. Grants Adminstrn. HEW, Washington, 1966-69; univ. dean City U. N.Y., exec. dir. Research Found., 1969-73; v.p. Hebrew Union Coll., Cin., 1973-75; partner, nat. chmn. consulting services for edn. Coopers & Lybrand, C.P.A.'s, Chgo., 1975—. Cons. to govt. agys. and ednl. instns., 1969—. Served with U.S. Army, 1953-56. Recipient Outstanding Performance award, HEW, 1968, Superior Performance award, 1969. Mem. N.Y. Bar, Nat. Assn. Coll. and Univ. Bus. Officers, Nat. Assn. Coll. and Univ. Attys. Home: 1228 Cambridge Ct Highland Park IL 60035 Office: Coopers & Lybrand 222 S Riverside Plaza Chicago IL 60606

KARP, EDWARD CHARLES, equipment mfg. co. exec.; b. Chgo., May 22, 1917; s. Edward H. and Wilhelmina F. (Schult) K.; B.S., Wheaton Coll., 1939; m. Marian Elizabeth Johnson, June 29, 1940; children—Carol (Mrs. Neal Peterson), Stephen, Charles, Sarah. Process and Plant engr. United Wallpaper Factories, Inc., York, Pa., 1939-40, staff and asst. chief engr., War Contracts div., Chgo. and Montgomery, Ill., 1941-44; plant mgr. and chief engr., Sanitary Scale Co., Belvidere, Ill., 1944-53, v.p., mfg. and engring., 1954-64, v.p. and gen. mgr., 1965—, dir., 1946—; dir. First Nat. Bank, Belvidere, 1973—; mem. industry adv. com. Nat. Sanitation Found., 1958—. Mem. U.S. Nat. Working Group (Scales & Weighing Systems) Internat. Orgn. Legal Metrology, 1977—. Pres. Community Unit Dist. 100 Schs., Belvidere, 1959-70; vice chmn. steering com. Boone-Winnebago Community Coll., 1964; co-chmn. Com. for Rock Valley Coll. Enabling Referendum, 1965; pres. YMCA, 1954-55; past pres. United Fund. Bd. dirs. Highland Hosp., Belvidere. Recipient Community award Doctor of Civic Betterment, Belvidere, 1970-71. Asso. mem. Nat. Conf. on Weights and Measures; mem. Belvidere C. of C. (pres. 1949-50). Mem. Covenant Ch. (trustee 1966-71, chmn. bd. Christian edn., 1958-60). Home: 7942 Revere Circle Belvidere IL 61008 Office: 910 E Lincoln Ave Belvidere IL 61008

KARR, STEPHEN WILLIAM, judge; b. Samos, Greece, June 20, 1919 (parents Am. citizens); s. William and Angeline (Chardoul) K.; A.B., U. Mich., 1941, J.D., 1947; m. Bette J. LaVine, Sept. 16, 1950; children—Carol Jean, Stephen Douglas, Alan William, Catherine Jean. Admitted to Mich. bar, 1947; since practiced in Grand Rapids; partner firm Luyendyk, Hainer, Karr, & Edens, 1950-73; U.S. magistrate U.S. Dist. Ct., 1971—; U.S. commr., 1950-71. Served with OSS, U.S. Army, 1941-45; col. Judge Adv. Gen. Corps ret. Recipient Peace medal, King of Thailand; decorated Army Commendation medal. Mem. Am. Bar Assn., State Bar Mich. Home: 2600 College Ave NE Grand Rapids MI 49505 Office: 666 Fed Bldg Grand Rapids MI 49502

KARRYS, WILLIAM GEORGE, mech. engr.; b. Milw., Nov. 13, 1923; s. George W. and Callope (Stathas) K.; B.S., U. Wis., 1947: m. Effie T. Tarachas, Nov. 25, 1956; children—Kathryn, George, Michael. Indsl. engr. A.O. Smith Corp., Milw., 1947-54: chief indsl. engr. Mech. Handling Systems, Detroit, 1954-55; plant engr. U.S. Steel Corp., Chgo., 1955-56; with Pollak & Skan, Inc., Rosemont, Ill., 19S6—, adminstrv. engr., v.p., 1956-72, pres., 1972—, dir. Served with l)SNR, 1944-46. Mem. Nat., Ill. socs. profl. engrs., ASME, IEEE. Club: Carlton. Home: 150 Eddy Ln Northfield IL 60093 Office: 9575 Higgins Rd Rosemont IL 60018

KASLOW, HAVEN DE LOSS, research biochemist; b. Mora, Minn., Nov. 30, 1910; s. Martin Luther and Flora (Hollister) K.; B.S., N.D. State Coll., 1934; postgrad. Iowa State Coll., 1935-40; m. Ruth Hassinger, Sept. 2, 1944. Grad. asst. chemistry Iowa State Coll., 1936-41; research chemist Corn Products Refining Co., 1941-44; research biochemist Gen. Mills, 1944-62; research asst. biochemistry U. Minn., 1963-64. Freelance cons., 1964—, cons. to v.p. for research Am. Cancer Soc., N.Y.C., 1966—. Fellow Am. Inst. Chemists; mem. A.A.A.S., Am. Chem. Soc. Soc. Rheology, Am. Inst. Physics, N.Y. Acad. Scis. Address: 1430 E Como Blvd St Paul MN 55117

KASMAN, LOUIS PERRY, transp. exec.; b. Bklyn., Apr. 13, 1943; s. Elias and Florence (Dodes) K.; B.A., Williams Coll., 1964; m. Deborah Jean Kehl, Dec. 2, 1972. Dir. adminstrn. and mktg. Air Express Internat., N.Y.C., 1968-72; corp. dir. mktg. Shulman Transport Enterprises, Inc., Cherry Hill, N.J. also gen. mgr. Skycab div., 1972-75; v.p. air freight div. Allied Van Lines, Chgo., 1976—. Served with U.S. Army, 1966-68. Mem. Internat. Airfreight Agts. Assn. (dir.), Nat. Def. Transp. Assn., Delta Nu Alpha. Jewish. Clubs: Wings, Execs. (Chgo.). Author: The Small Package Air Freight Market, 1972; The Economics of Total Cost of Distribution, 1977. Home: 6176 Knoll Ln Ct Clarendon Hills IL 60514 Office: 999 E Touhy Ave Des Plaines IL 60018

KASPER, ROBERT EUGENE, radiologist; b. Sioux Falls, S.D., Sept. 19, 1926; s. Thomas C. and Clara B. (Lillesve) K.; student U. Minn., 1944-46, postgrad. 1953-55; M.D., Marquette U., 1949; m. Rita May Armstrong, July 2, 1954; children—Ann, David, Thomas. Intern Mpls. Gen. Hosp., 1949-50; resident Boston City Hosp., 1952-53, U. Minn. Hosps., Mpls. VA Hosp., 1953-56; practice medicine specializing in radiology, Mpls., 1956—; mem. staffs Swedish Hosp., Waconia Ridgeview, 1956-66; clin. instr., then asst. prof. radiology U. Minn., 1956-67. Served to lt. M.C., USN, 1950-52. Mem. AMA, Minn., Hennepin County med. socs., Mpls. Acad. Medicine, Am. Coll. Radiology, Am. Roentgen Ray Soc., Radiol. Soc. N. Am., Minn. Radiol. Soc. Episcopalian. Club: Minikahda. Contbr. articles to med. jours. Home: 1705 Morgan Ave S Minneapolis MN 55405

KASPERS, LAMBERT MANN, indsl. fasteners mfg. co. exec.; b. Evanston, Ill., Sept. 19, i919; s. Lambert and Florence (Mann) K.; A.B., U. Rochester, 1940; postgrad. in indsl. adminstrn. Harvard U., 1944; m. June Charlotte Motter, June 4, 1944; children—Karen Kaspers Jackson, William F., Richard L., Robert L., John N. With Russell, Burdsall & Ward Bolt & Nut Co., Port Chester, N.Y., 1940-61, plant mgr., 1952-59, asst. gen. mgr., 1959-61; v.p. ops. Knox Glass Co., Inc. (Pa.), 1961-62; v.p., dir. Nat. Screw & Mfg. Co., Cleve., 1962-67; v.p. fastener group, dir. Key Internat. Inc., Dearborn, Mich., 1968—; chmn. bd. Towne Robinson Fastener Co., Dearborn, 1970—; dir. Indsl. and Automotive Fasteners Inc., Royal Oak, Mich., Bear-Kat Products, Inc., Troy, Mich., Fastener Assembly Corp., Troy, Key Korea Co., Ltd., Masan, Korea. Mem. Orange Sch. Dist. Bd. Edn., Pepper Pike, Ohio, 1966-68. Served to lt., Supply Corps, USNR, 1942-45. Mem. Indsl. Fasteners Inst. (chmn. 1975-76), Delta Upsilon. Presbyterian. Clubs: Fairlane (Dearborn); Orchard Lake (Mich.) Country; Cranbrook Tennis (Bloomfield Hills, Mich.). Home: 651 Orchard Ridge Rd Bloomfield Hills MI 48013 Office: 24175 NW Hwy Southfield MI 48037

KASPERSON, RICHARD WILLET, pharm. co. exec.; b. Grand Haven, Mich., June 1, 1927; s. Ernest Richard and Elizabeth (Willett) K.; B.A., Mich. State U., 1949; J.D., Northwestern U., 1958; m. Lucinda Wanner, Nov. 9, 1957; children—David Arthur, Ernest Richard. Admitted to Ill. bar, 1958, U.S. Supreme Ct. bar, 1962; atty.-adviser FTC, Chgo., 1958-61, Washington, 1961-62; v.p. Abbott Labs., North Chicago, Ill., 1962—; Ill. Gov. appointee Food, Drug, Cosmetic and Pesticide Laws Study Commn., 1965-72; industry trustee Food and Drug Law Inst. Bd. dirs. Calorie Control Council. Served to lt. (j.g.) USNR, 1952-54. Mem. Am., Ill., Fed. bar assns., Phi Delta Phi. Home: 954 Western St Northbrook IL 60062 Office: 14th and Sheridan Rd North Chicago IL 60064

KASPRICK, LYLE CLINTON, beverage co. exec.; b. Angus, Minn., Aug. 23, 1932; s. Max Peter and Mary (Taus) K.; B.S. in Bus. Adminstrn. magna cum laude, U. N.D., 1959; m. Harriet Susan Lydick, July 14, 1953; children—Susan, Michael, John; m. 2d, Kathleen M. Westby, June 4, 1977. Tax mgr. Arthur Andersen & Co., Mpls., 1959-69; v.p. Search Investments Corp., Mpls., 1969-77; financial v.p., treas. Tropicana Hotel and Country Club, Las Vegas, 1970-72; chief operating officer Key Pharms., Inc., Miami, Fla., 1972-76, dir., 1976—; dir. Search Investments Corp., 1973-77, Mo Am Co Corp., 1975-76; v.p. MEI Corp., Mpls., 1977—. Speaker before profl. and civic groups. Del. Republican Party dist. and city convs., 1964, 66, 68, 70. Served with USN, 1951-55. C.P.A., Minn. Mem. Am. Inst. C.P.A.'s, Minn. Soc. C.P.A.'s, Nat. Assn. Accountants, Am. Legion. Republican. Roman Catholic, K.C. Home: 7105 Heatherton Trail Minneapolis MN 55435 Office: 733 Marquette Ave Minneapolis MN 55402

KASS, WARREN ALBERT, clin. psychologist; b. Chgo., Jan. 8, 1945; s. Albert Joseph and Wanda Francis (Jaworski) K.; B.S. in Psychology, Marquette U., 1966, M.S. in Clin. Psychology, 1969; Ph.D., St. Louis U., 1973; m. Sandra Ellen Haase, Aug. 31, 1968; twin daus. Instr. psychology, Wis. State U., Eau Claire, 1968-69; psychology intern David P. Wohl Meml. Mental Health Inst., St. Louis, 1970-71; psychol. cons. Juvenile Ct., St. Louis, 1970-72; dir. treatment Magdala Found., St. Louis, 1972—; cons. to spl. project for severe behavior disordered children Hubert Wheeler State Sch., St. Louis, 1975; pvt. practice adolescent and family psychology, St. Louis, 1975—; counselor Neighborhood Youth Corps., Eau Claire, 1969; coordinator vol. program Juvenile Div. Jud. Ct., Hillsboro, Mo., 1971—; cons. ex-offender program City of St. Louis, Seattle, Talbert House; panelist, speaker profl. confs.; mem. faculty Nat. Tng. Inst., 1976-77; mem. advisory com. program for study of crime and delinquency Ohio State U., 1975-76. Mem. Am. Assn. Correctional Psychologists, Am. Correctional Assn. (cons. tech. assistance program 1976—), Am. Psychol. Assn., Assn. for Advancement of Behavior Therapy, Internat. Halfway House Assn. (v.p. dist. V, 1974-77, chmn. research council 1975—, speaker confs. 1974, 1975), Mo. Assn. Community Residential Treatment Centers, Mo. Psychol. Assn. (certified), Mo. Behavior Therapy Assn. (pres., 1977—), St. Louis Br. Assn. for Advancement of Behavior Therapy (com. chmn. 1974). Democrat. Roman Catholic. Contbr. papers to profl. confs., articles to sci. jours. Home: 413 Auber Dr Manchester MO 63011 Office: 1129 Penrose St Saint Louis MO 63107

KASSABAUM, GEORGE EDWARD, architect; b. Atchison, Kans., Dec. 5, 1920; s. George A. and Dorothy (Gaston) K.; B.Arch., Washington U., St. Louis, 1947; m. Marjory Verser, Jan. 22, 1949; children—Douglas George, Ann Denise, Karen Jane. Mem. faculty Washington U., 1947-50; asso. Hellmuth, Yamasaki & Leinweber, 1950-55; prin. Hellmuth, Obata & Kassabaum, St. Louis, 1955—; pres. HoK Devel. Corp.; dir. Tower Grove Bank, St. Louis. Chmn. bd. mgrs. Downtown br. YMCA, 1965-67; trustee Washington U. Served with USAAF, 1945-46. Fellow AIA (pres. 1968-69, chancellor Coll. Fellows 1977-78); hon. fellow Royal Archtl. Inst. Can., Mexican Soc. Architects. Important works include Planetarium St. Louis, U. W. Indies, Bur. Reclamation Office Bldg. (Denver), Dormitories, Classroom Bldgs. Mo. U., Washington U., Equitable Bldg. St. Louis, Health Scis. Center, Buffalo, Dallas-Ft. Worth Airport, Nat. Air-Space Mus., 1st Nat. Bank Dallas. Clubs: Noonday, Media, Racquet, Old Warson. Home: 761 Kent Rd Saint Louis MO 63124 Office: 100 N Broadway Saint Louis MO 63102

KASSEBAUM, JOHN PHILIP, lawyer; b. Kansas City, Mo., Oct. 24, 1932; s. Leonard Charles and Helen (Horn) K.; A.B., U. Kans., 1953; J.D., U. Mich., 1956; m. Nancy Josephine Landon, June 8, 1955; children—John Philip, Linda Josephine, Richard Landon, William Alfred. Admitted to Kans. bar, 1956; partner Kassebaum & Johnson, Wichita, Kans.; chmn., pres. Kassebaum Communications Corp., Radio Sta. KFH Co., Inc., Carey House Square, Inc., Wichita Corp. Chmn., Gov.'s Adv. Commn. on Kans. Instl. Mgmt., 1960-68; pres. Kans. Assn. Mental Health, 1966-67, Wichita Art Mus. Mems. Found., 1968-70; sec. Kans. Found. Behavioral Scis., 1968—; bd. dirs. Wichita Symphony Soc.; trustee St. Joseph Med. Center. Mem. Wichita, Kans., Am. bar assns., Kans. Assn. Def. Counsel, Fedn. Ins. Counsel, Am. Trial Lawyers Assn., Am., English ceramics circles, Keramik-Freunde der Schweiz, U. Kans. Mus. Art (hon. curator ceramics 1960—), Phi Delta Theta, Phi Delta Phi, Omicron Delta Kappa. Episcopalian. Clubs: Union, Down Town Assn., Met. Opera, Racquet and Tennis, Tuxedo (N.Y.C.); Met. (Washington); Yeamans Hall (Charleston, S.C.); Univ. (Kansas City, Mo.); Wichita, Wichita Country. Home: The Carey House Wichita KS 67202 Office: 15th Floor 125 N Market Wichita KS 67202

KASSING, LESTER ALDEN, banker; b. Indpls., Nov. 7, 1930; s. Lester William and Lucile Elizabeth (Roesner) K.; B.S. with distinction, Ind. U., 1956, LL.B. with distinction, 1958; m. Vanita C. Kleinschmidt, May 1, 1954; children—John, Jeffrey, Judson, Jay, Julanne. Asst. trust officer Ind. Bank & Trust Co., Ft. Wayne, 1958-59, trust officer, 1959-60, v.p., trust officer, 1960-62, v.p. comml. loan dept., 1962-67, sr. v.p., 1967-68, exec. v.p., 1968-71, dir. 1969-71; pres., dir. Jefferson Trust and Savs. Bank of Peoria (Ill.), 1971—; faculty Robert Morris Assos. Seminar; lectr. Fed. Res. Sch. Pres. Concordia Luth. High Sch. Assn., 1964-67, Concordia Edn. Found., 1969-70; trustee Proctor Community Hosp.; bd. dirs. Concordia Luth. High. Sch., 1959-71. Served with AUS, 1951-53. Named Distinguished Young Man of Year City of Fort Wayne, Ft. Wayne Jr. C. of C., 1962, Distinguished Young Man of Year Ind., Order of Coif, 1958. Mem. Robert Morris Assos., Am., Ill., Peoria County bar assns., Assn. Modern Banking in Ill. (chmn.), Peoria C. of C. (treas.), Fine Arts Assn., Phi Delta Phi. Lutheran. Clubs: Peoria Country, Creve Coeur (Peoria). Home: 4949 Grandview Dr Peoria IL 61614 Office: 123 SW Jefferson Ave Peoria IL 61602

KASTEN, GEORGE F., banker; b. Milw., Feb. 2, 1912; s. Walter and Anita (Heinemann) K.; A.B., Williams Coll., 1933; m. Janet Mackie, Apr. 26, 1935; children—Walter, George Frederick, Alexander Mitchell, Janet Elizabeth. Asso. 1st Wis. Nat. Bank Milw., 1934-77, chmn. bd., chief exec. officer, dir. First Wis. Corp.; sec., dir. Toepfer & Sons, Inc.; dir. Wis. Power & Light Co., Krause Milling Co., 1st Wis. Trust Co., Harnischfeger Corp., NN Corp., Hometown, Inc., Gilbert Shoe Co., Twin Disc Inc., Wis. Telephone Co. Clubs: Milw., Town, Milw. Athletic, Milw. Country (Milw.). Home: 9325 N Range Line Rd Milwaukee WI 53217 Office: 777 E Wisconsin Ave Milwaukee WI 53201

KASTEN, ROBERT W., JR., congressman; b. Milw., June 19, 1942; s. Robert W. and Mary O. (Ogden) K.; B.A. in English, U. Ariz., 1964; M.B.A., Columbia, 1966. Mgmt. cons., 1966; v.p. mktg., sales mgr., Gilbert Shoe Co., Thiensville, Wis., 1968-74, dir., 1969—; mem. 94th-95th Congress from 9th dist. Wis. Del. Eagleton Inst. Politics Legis. Leadership Conf., Rutgers U., 1973. Mem. Milw. Council on Alcoholism, Inc.; regional dir. Milw. Coalition for Clean Water. Mem. Wis. Senate, 1973-74; alt. del. to Republican Nat. Conv., Miami Beach, Fla., 1972, del., 1976; mem. Wis. Fedn. Young Reps. Bd. dir. Wis. Soc. for the Prevention of Blindness; bd. advisors Student Leadership Services. Named Wis. Conservation Legislator of Year, 1973; recipient Fiscal Integrity award Nat. Taxpayers Union, 1976, Guardian of Small Bus. award Nat. Fedn. Ind. Bus., 1976. Mem. Mequon-Thiensville Jaycees (Jaycee of Year award 1973, past dir.), Nat. Audubon Soc. Episcopalian. Home: Thiensville WI 53092 Office: 119 Cannon Office Bldg Washington DC 20515

KASTEN, WALTER, mfg. co. exec.; b. Berlin, Germany, Aug. 21, 1908; s. Emil and Martha (Wuestenhain) K.; Machienbau degree Deutsche Werke Betriebsfachule, 1928; m. Catherine L. Heenan, May 1, 1934; children—Jane (Mrs. Edward Fontaine), John P., Martha (Mrs. Earl Swartz), Kristin (Mrs. Randolph P. Cohn), Dennis W., William M. Engr., Haug Lab., 1928-29, Skinner Automotive Device Co., 1929-31, Skinner Motors, Inc., 1931-38, Briggs Mfg., 1938-39, Westinghouse Co., 1939-40, Stout Lab., 1940-41, Skinner Purifiers, 1941-47; chief engr. Bendix-Skinner div. Bendix Aviation Corp., 1947-59; dir. engring. Bendis Filters div. Bendix Corp., Madison Heights, Mich., 1959-60, staff asst. to gen. mgr., 1960-64, asst. gen. mgr., 1964-66, gen. mgr., after 1966, former sr. staff exec., ret., 1965; pres. Kasten Inc.; dir. System Asso. Inc. Mem. Soc. Automotive Engrs., Engring. Soc. Detroit, Am. Inst. Aeros. and Astronautics, Club: Torch (Birmingham, Mich.). Patentee in field. Home: 31880 Mountain View Lane Franklin MI 48025 Office: System Asso Inc 55 Park Troy MI 48084

KASTENMEIER, ROBERT WILLIAM, congressman; b. Beaver Dam, Wis., Jan. 24, 1924; s. Leo H. and Lucille (Powers) K.; LL.B., U. Wis., 1952; m. Dorothy Chambers, June 27, 1952; children—William, Andrew, Edward. Branch office dir. Claims Service, War Dept., Philippines, 1946-48; admitted to Wis. bar, 1952; practiced Watertown, Wis., 1952-58; justice of peace, 1955-58. Mem. 86th-95th Congresses from 2d Dist. Wis.; mem. house jud., interior and insular affairs coms.; chmn. judiciary subcom. on cts., civil liberties and adminstrn. of justice. Served from pvt. to 1st lt. Inf., AUS, 1943-46, Philippines. Home: Sun Prairie WI 53590 Office: Office Bldg Washington DC 20515

KASTLER, ELDON LESTER, ednl. adminstr.; b. Valeda, Kans., Aug. 26, 1921; s. Lester John and Lela Frances (Mason) K.; B.S., Kans. State Coll., 1946, M.S., 1951; m. Julia Marie Bronnenberg, Apr. 14, 1940; children—Larry Jon, Linda Jean, Kathryn Sue. Tchr. jr. high sch., Welborn, Kans., 1941-44; athletic dir. YMCA, Pittsburg, Kans., 1946-48; tchr., coach Hickory Grove Sch., Mission, Kans., 1948-54; prin. Tomahawk Elementary Sch., Overland Park, Kans., 1954-55, Hickory Grove Elementary Sch., Mission, 1955-68, Overland Park Elementary Sch., 1968-77, Prairie Sch., Prairie Village, Kans., 1977—. Bd. dirs. Johnson County YMCA, 1961-62, Johnson County chpt. Nat. Found. Served with USMCR, 1944-45. Decorated Purple Heart. Mem. S. Central (treas. 1974-76), Kans. (sec.-treas. 1964-65) assns. elementary sch. prins., Johnson County Elementary Sch. Prins. Assn. (pres. 1959-60), Shawnee Mission Adminstrs. Assn. (pres. 1972-73). Mem. Christian Ch. (deacon 1951-58, 69-71). Club: Optimist (pres. 1961-62, life mem.) (Mission, Kans.). Home: 6725 W 85th Terr Overland Park KS 66212 Office: 6642 Mission Rd Prairie Village KS 66208

KATHAN, RALPH HERMAN, biochemist; b. Chgo., Feb. 1, 1929; s. Herman Joseph and Lena Louise (Hoffman) K.; S.B., U. Chgo., 1949; M.S., U. Ill., 1959, Ph.D., 1961; m. Manijeh Moayeri, Sept. 4, 1976; children—Arthur Eric, Kathryn Jean. Research asso. U. Ill. Coll. Medicine, Chgo., 1961-62, mem. faculty, 1962—, asso. prof. biol. chemistry Sch. Basic Med. Scis., 1971—; chmn., dir. div. biochemistry Cook County Hosp., Chgo., 1971—; asso. mem. commn. influenza Armed Forces Epidemiol. Bd., 1962-68. Served to lt. USN, 1951-55. Mem. Nat. Acad. Clin. Biochemistry, Soc. Complex Carbohydrates, Soc. Exptl. Biology and Medicine, Am. Soc. Biol. Chemists, Am. Assn. Clin. Chemists. Contbr. articles to profl. jours. Home: 1754 N Oak Park Ave Chicago IL 60635 Office: 627 S Wood St Chicago IL 60612

KATO, SHIGEYASU, trade co. exec.; b. Nagoya, Japan, Jan. 6, 1923; s. Shigeyoshi and Torako (Hirao) K.; B.A., Waseda U., 1946; m. Fukiko Shirasu, Nov. 22, 1956; children—Shigeaki, Noriaki. With Mitsui & Co. Ltd., Tokyo, 1946-53, Bangkok (Thailand) office, 1953-56, gen. mgr. iron and steel dept. London office, 1962-66, asst. gen. mgr. spl. steel div. Tokyo office, 1967-71, dep. gen. mgr. steel pipe and tube div., 1971, gen. mgr. 1st. steel export div., 1971-75, sr. v.p. Chgo. office, 1975—. Served with Japanese Navy Air Force, World War II. Mem. Japanese C. of C. and Industry, Japan Am. Soc. Chgo. (v.p. 1975—), Internat. House U. Chgo. (dir. 1975—), Center for Far Eastern Studies. Clubs: Exec. Chgo., Univ. Chgo., Mid-Am., Arts Chgo., Butler Nat. Country. Home: 1555 Astor St Unit 43E Chicago IL 60610 Office: Mitsui & Co USA 303 E Ohio St Chicago IL 60611

KATONA, FLORENCE CIHLAR, librarian; b. Cleve., May 10, 1919; d. Joseph and Nettie (Bruzek) Cihlar; student Western Res. U., 1937-40; B.S., Kent State U., 1966, M.L.S., 1969; m. Frank Katona, Jr., June 8, 1940; children—Sharon Katona Beech, Kenneth R. Librarian, Raymond Sch., Maple Heights, Ohio, 1958-67; tchr. Maple Heights City Schs., 1967; children's asst. librarian Maple Heights Regional Library, 1958-67; children's librarian Warrensville Heights Community Br. Library, 1967-68, Bedford (Ohio) Pub. Library, 1969-71; br. librarian Bedford br. Cuyahoga County Pub. Library, 1971—. Mem. Bedford Community Council, 1972—, treas., 1974—; pres. Maple Heights chpt. Am. Field Service, 1968-70. Mem. Am., Ohio library assns., Bedford Hist. Soc., Zonta, Kappa Delta Pi, Beta Phi Mu. Home: 5258 Joseph St Maple Heights OH 44137 Office: 155 Center Rd Bedford OH 44146

KATOVSICH, DENNIS FRANKLIN, constrn. co. exec.; b. South Bend, Ind., Sept. 3, 1945; s. Thomas Louis and Anna Mary (Kuharic) K.; B.C.E., Tri-State Coll., 1967; m. Jane Ann Wigent, Sept. 9, 1967; children—Sally Ann, Todd Micheal, John Eric. Mech. maintenance supr. Gt. Lakes Steel div. Nat. Steel Corp., Ecorse, Mich., 1967-69; structural engr. Cunningham-Limp Co., Birmingham, Mich., 1969-70, purchasing agt., 1970-72, estimator, 1972-73, project mgr., 1973-75; project mgr. Bay-Con Corp., Sandusky, Ohio, 1975-77, mgr. heavy indsl. group, indsl. div., 1977—. Mem. Ohio Contractor's Polit.

Action Com., 1976; bd. dirs. Sandusky Area Jr. Achievement. Registered profl. engr., Mich., Ohio, Ind. Mem. Nat. Soc. Profl. Engrs., ASCE, Assn. Iron and Steel Engrs. Roman Catholic. Home: 1007 Cove Circle Huron OH 44839 Office: 1630 Sycamore Line Sandusky OH 44870

KATS, BERNHARD ALBERT, physician, educator; b. Almelo, The Netherlands, Apr. 29, 1933; s. Meier Samuel and Margareta Ruth (Mosler) K.; came to U.S., 1972; B.Sc., Huygens Coll., The Netherlands, 1952; M.D., Leiden State U., 1957; M.S. in Aerospace Medicine, Ohio State U., 1974; m. Ahuva Shoshany, July 7, 1963; children—Daniel Meir, Ilana Ruth, Guyora Roger, Michael Erez. Intern Leiden State U. Hosp., 1957-58; intern New Mt. Sinai Hosp., Toronto, Ont., Can., 1958-59, resident in pediatrics, 1959-60; research fellow NIH Hebrew U. Sch. Medicine, Jerusalem, Israel, 1961-62; resident in medicine Donnolo Govt. Hosp., Tel Aviv, Israel, 1962-63; resident in neurology Elisabeth Gasthuis, Haarlem, Holland, 1963; resident in medicine Deer Lodge VA Hosp., Winnipeg, Can., 1963-64, Toronto Gen. Hosp., 1966-67; chief resident Govt. Hosp., Nahariya, Israel, 1968-69; physician Misericodia Hosp., Winnipeg, 1964; attending physician Doctors Hosp., Toronto, 1964-65, Donwood Found., Toronto, 1964-68, Workmens Compensation Hosp. and Rehab. Center, Downsview, Ont., Can., 1965-66; regional flight surgeon Israel Civil Aviation Authorities, Ben Gurion Airport, 1968-72; med. dir. Comprehensive Prison Health Service Ohio Dept. Rehab. and Correction, Chillicothe, 1974-75; internat. sr. med. examiner and accident investigator FAA, 1970—; med. dir. Thumb Dist. Health Dept., 1975—; instr. in aerospace medicine Ohio State U., 1972-74, instr. in medicine, 1975; asso. prof. medicine Mich. State U., East Lansing, 1975—. Served with Dutch Army, 1953-55. Mem. A.C.P., Am. Acad. Med. Dirs., Ohio State U. Hosps. Med. Assn., Assn. Mil. Surgeons U.S., Aerospace, Israel, Dutch, Civil Aviation med. assns., Acad. of Med., Toronto, Flying Physicians Assn., Undersea Med. Soc., Am. Correctional Acad., Mich. Health Officers Assn., Coll. Family Physicians Can., Royal Soc. Medicine London, Coll. Physicians and Surgeons of Ontario, Can. Soc. Aviation Medicine, Soc. Studiosorum Academiae Lugdunum Batavorum (hon. pres. 1955—). Home: 120 Pine St Essexville MI 48732 Office: B-216-B West Fee Hall Coll of Human Medicine Michigan St U East Lansing MI 48824

KATSCHKE, RICHARD NORMAN, pub. relations exec.; b. Chgo., June 23, 1949; s. Norman George and Lucille Victoria (Watson) K.; B.S., No. Ill. U., 1971. Asst. pub. relations dir. Resurrection Hosp., Chgo., 1971-72; pub. relations dir. St. Anthony Hosp., Rockford, Ill., 1972-76; pub. relations specialist U. Chgo., 1976—; pub. relations chmn. Tri-State Hosp. Assembly Conv., Chgo., 1976. Bd. dirs. Rockford Family Consultation Service; bd. dirs., v.p. Rock River Valley Epilepsy Assn. Mem. Pub. Relations Soc. Am., Internat. Assn. Bus. Communicators, Soc. Profl. Journalists, Ill. Hosp. Pub. Relations Soc. (exec. com. 1975-76), Chgo. Council Fgn. Relations, Phi Kappa Sigma. Home: 3111 Jacqueline Dr Rockford IL 61109 Office: 5666 E State St Rockford IL 61101

KATTER, REUBEN LUTHER, research corp. exec.; b. Garner, Iowa, Oct. 13, 1899; s. Fred and Louisa Matilda (Holtkamp) K.; student U. Iowa, 1918-20; B.M.E., U. Minn., 1922; m. Mildred Ruth Johnson, Jan. 16, 1930; 1 dau., Joan Lesley Katter Ludberg. Div. sales mgr. Zenith Radio Corp., Chgo., 1928-32; corp. cons. Halsey Stuart Investment Co., Pitts., 1932—; dir. fin. N. Central Bible Coll., Mpls., 1936-51; registrar, dean Central Bible Coll. and Sem., Springfield, Mo., 1951-55; pres. Theotes-Logos Research Corp., Mpls., 1955—; cons., lectr. in field. Mem. AAAS. Author: The History of Creation and Origin of the Species, 1967; Jesus Christ the Divine Executive, 1977; Creationism: Its Basis, Its Essence, and Its Interwoven Structure, 1978. Home and Office: 4318 York Ave S Minneapolis MN 55410

KATZ, A(DOLPH) EDWARD, psychologist; b. Phila., June 22, 1926; s. Jacob and Sadie (Kaplan) K.; B.S., Purdue U., 1949; Ph.D., U. Chgo., 1956; m. Jeanette Ann Best, June 30, 1951; children—Judith Barbara, Margaret Ann (Mrs. James Pickering), David Martin, Joathan Eric. Research asst. dept. psychology U. Chgo., 1953-55; psychologist Jewish Vocat. Service, Chgo., 1955-56; psychologist Hawthorn Center, Northville, Mich., 1956-61, asso. dir. dept. psychology, 1961-71, dir., 1971—; psychol. cons. Waterford Twp. (Mich.) Pub. Schs. Reading Center, Davis Clinic, Farmington Hills, Mich. Founder, Livonia (Mich.) Citizens for Better Human Relations, 1963, chmn., 1974—; trustee Livonia Bd. Edn., 1964-72, pres., 1968-69. Served to 1st lt. Q.M.C., AUS, 1945-47. Certified cons. psychologist, Mich. Mem. Mich. Psychol. Assn. (exec. council 1964-68, 76—). Home: 16008 Oak Dr Livonia MI 48154 Office: 18471 Haggerty Rd Northville MI 48167

KATZ, ADRIAN IZHACK, physician; b. Bucharest, Romania, Aug. 3, 1932; s. Ferdinand and Helen (Lustig) K.; came to U.S., 1965; M.D., Hebrew U., 1961; m. Miriam Lesser, Mar. 31, 1965; children—Ron, Iris. Research fellow Yale U., 1965-67, Harvard U., 1967-68; intern Belinson Med. Center, Israel, 1961, resident, 1962-65; practice medicine, specializing in internal medicine and nephrology, New Haven, 1966-67, Boston, 1967-68, Chgo., 1968—; mem. staff Albert Merritt Billings Hosp.; head nephrology sect., attending physician U. Chgo. Hosps., 1968—; asst. prof. medicine U. Chgo., 1968-71, asso. prof., 1971-74, prof., 1975—. Fellow A.C.P.; mem. Am. Physiol. Soc., Am. Soc. Clin. Investigation, Am., Internat. socs. nephrology, Central Soc. Clin. Research, N.Y. Acad. Scis. Home: 5219 S Kimbark Ave Chicago IL 60615 Office: 950 E 59th St Chicago IL 60637

KATZ, BERNARD, realtor; b. Chgo., June 1, 1920; s. Harry and Eva (Blank) K.; grad. high sch.; children—Barbara Ann Katz Morelli, David Hamilton. Real estate broker, Chgo., 1951—; pres. Bernard Katz & Co., Inc., Chgo., 1959—, Katz-Weiss Constrn. Corp., 1964—; instr. prins. real estate YMCA Community Jr. Coll., Chgo., 1963. Mem. nat. panel arbitrators Am. Arbitration Assn., 1966—. Served with AUS, 1940-45. Mem. Nat., Ill. assns. realtors, Chgo. (pres. 1973-74), N. Side (pres. 1971) real estate bds., Internat. Real Estate Fedn. Jewish (bd. temple, pres. Men's Club). Clubs: Masons, Shriners. Office: 3120 W Devon Ave Chicago IL 60659

KATZ, DONALD LAVERNE, chem. engr., educator; b. Jackson County, Mich., Aug. 1, 1907; s. Gottlieb and Lucy (Schnackenberg) K.; m. Maxine Crull, Sept. 17, 1932; children—Marvin L., Linda M. Katz Cantrell; m. 2d, Elizabeth H. Correll, Nov. 26, 1965; stepchildren—Richard, Steven, Jonathon. B.S. in Chem. Engring., U. Mich., 1931, M.S., 1932, Ph.D., 1933. Registered profl. engr., Mich., Ill. With dept. chem. engring. Phillips Petroleum Co., Bartlesville, Okla., 1933-36; cons. engr., prof. chem. engring. U. Mich., 1936-77, emeritus, 1977—. Mem. Ann Arbor (Mich.) Bd. Edn., 1948-57. Mem. Am. Inst. Chem. Engrs., ASME, Soc. Petroleum Engrs., Am. Inst. Mech. Engrs., Am. Chem. Soc., Am. Nuclear Soc., AAAS, Am. Soc. Engring Edn., Nat. Acad. Engring. Recipient several awards for excellence in engring. Author numerous books, articles to profl. jours. Home: 2011 Washtenaw Ave Ann Arbor MI 48104 Office: Dept Chem Engring Univ Mich Ann Arbor MI 48109

KATZBERG, ALLAN ALFRED, educator; b. Orcadia, Sask., Can., July 6, 1913; s. Frederick and Ida (Hoffman) K.; came to U.S., 1949, naturalized, 1952; B.Sc., U. Man. (Can.), 1943; M.S., Institutum Divi Thomae (Cin.), 1949; Ph.D., U. Okla., 1956; m. Betty Jeanne Bainbridge, Aug. 10, 1948; children—Allan Alfred, Susan Katzberg Foster, Mary Joanna, Elizabeth Lynne. Tchr. pub. schs. Sask., 1933-37; instr. anatomy U. Okla. Med. Center, Oklahoma City, 1949-56, asst. prof. anatomy, 1956-59; head cellular biology section U.S. Air Force Aerospace Med. Center, Brooks AFB, Tex., 1959-60, dep. chief astrobiology br., 1960-63; asso. prof. physiology U. Sask., Saskatoon, 1963-64; chmn. anatomy S.W. Found. for Research and Edn., San Antonio, 1964-68; asso. prof. biology Western Ill. U., Macomb, 1968-69; asso. prof. anatomy Ind. U. Med. Center, Indpls., 1969-77, prof., 1977—, acting chmn. anatomy dept., 1970-71. Dir. summer seminar Institutum Divi Thomae, Cin., 1961; mem. expedition to collect primates of E. Africa, 1964; cons. U.S. Air Force Arctic Aero-Med. Lab., Fairbanks, Alaska, 1961, Cambridge U., Eng., 1964-65, S.W. Agrl. Inst., Tex., 1965, S.W. Research Inst., Tex., 1966, U. Utah, Purdue U., U. Calif., 1966, Fed. Aviation Adminstr., 1967, U.S. Air Force 6571st Aeromed. Research Lab., Holloman AFB, 1967, Ford Motor Co., 1967. Recipient Ind. State Med. Assn. award, 1971, 72; Eli Lilly award, 1972. Mem. Am. Assn. Anatomists, Tex. Cell and Tissue Culture Assn. (pres. 1960-61), Pan Am. Assn. Anatomists (founder), Sociedad Mexicana de Anatomia (hon. mem.), Royal Microscopical Soc., Youth for Christ (pres. 1963). Baptist (deacon 1955—). Contbr. articles to profl. jours. Home: 944 E Main St Carmel IN 46032 Office: Dept Anatomy Ind U Med Center Indianapolis IN 46202

KATZEL, JEANINE ALMA, journalist; b. Chgo., Feb. 20, 1948, d. LeRoy Paul and Lia Mary (Arcuri) Katzel; B.A. in Journalism, U. Wis., 1970; M.S. in Journalism, Northwestern U., 1974. Publs. editor U. Wis. Sea Grant Program, Madison, 1969-72; editor research div. agrl. sch. U. Wis., Madison, 1972; research editor Prism mag. AMA, Chgo., 1972-73; free lance writer, 1974-75; lit. editor Plant Engring. mag. Tech. Pub. Co., Barrington, Ill., 1975-76, news editor, 1976—. Recipient Elsie Bullard Morrison prize in Journalism, U. Wis., 1969. Mem. Women in Communications, Am. Soc. Bus. Press Editors, Phi Kappa Phi. Home: 16 Boxwood Ln Cary IL 60013 Office: 1301 S Grove Ave Barrington IL 60010

KATZEN, MAXWELL E., lawyer; b. N.Y.C., Dec. 25, 1910; student U. Mich., 1929-30; LL.B., Wayne State U., 1933; m. Ruth Naomi Friedman, Nov. 1, 1942; children—Ann Florence, James Samuel. Admitted to Mich. bar, 1933; mem. firm Schlussel, Lifton, Simon, Rands, Kaufman & Lesinski, Southfield, 1976—. Pres., dir. Theodore Bargman Co., Coldwater, Mich., 1969—, A.W.C. Mfg. Co., Coldwater, Mich., 1973—; sec., dir. Fed. Asphalt Co., Detroit, 1972—. Bd. dirs. Fresh Air Soc. Detroit, 1959—, pres., 1959-62; vice chmn., gov. Cranbrook Acad. Art, Bloomfield Hills, Mich.; trustee Cranbrook Ednl. Community, Theodore and Mina Bargman Found., Camp Oakland; mem. corp. Retina Found., Boston. Mem. Am., Detroit bar assns., State Bar Mich., Am. Judicature Soc. Democrat. Jewish. Club: Standard (Detroit). Home: 23169 Riverside Dr Southfield MI 48034 Office: Suite 500 NBS Financial Center 29201 Telegraph Rd Southfield MI 48034

KATZEN, RAPHAEL, cons. chem. engr.; b. Balt., July 28, 1915; s. Isidor and Esther (Stein) K.; B.Ch.E., Poly. Inst. Bklyn., 1936, M.Ch.E., 1938, D.Ch.E., 1942; m. Selma M. Siegel, June 19, 1938; children—Nancy (Mrs. Richard D. Riedel). Project mgr. Diamond Alkali Co., Painesville, Ohio, 1942-44; mgr. engring. Vulcan Engring. Div., Cin., 1944-53; mng. partner Raphael Katzen Assos., Cin., 1953—; pres. Raphael Katzen Assos. Internat., Inc., 1956—. Mem. Cin. Air Pollution Bd., 1972-76. Recipient Distinguished Alumnus award Poly. Inst. Bklyn., 1970. Fellow Am. Inst. Chemists, Am. Inst. Chem. Engrs., Am. Cons. Engrs. Council; mem. Am. Chem. Soc., Am. Petroleum Inst., Nat. Soc. Profl. Engrs., T.A.P.P.I., A.A.A.S., Sigma Xi, Tau Beta Pi, Lambda Upsilon. Clubs: University (Cin.); Chemists (N.Y.C.). Contbr. articles to profl. jours. Patentee in field. Home: 2868 Alpine Terr Cincinnati OH 45208 Office: 1050 Delta Ave Cincinnati OH 45208

KAUCHER, ROBERT FREDERICK, lawyer; b. East St. Louis, Ill., Feb. 14, 1925; s. Vincent Fred and Mabel Lucy (Gilliland) K.; student Northwestern U., 1946-47; J.D., St. Louis U., 1951; m. Mary Ellen Shepard, June 29, 1947; children—Pamela Ellen, Robert Frederick II, James William. Claim adjuster Travelers Ins. Co., 1951-52; claim adjuster and mgr. Allstate Ins. Co., 1952-63; admitted to Ill. bar, 1952, Mo. bar, Fed. Dist. Ct. bar, U.S. Supreme Ct. bar; practiced in Belleville, Highland, Ill., 1963—; spl. asst. atty. gen. State of Ill. 1969-72. Served with USNR, 1943-46. Mem. Am., Ill., St. Clair County, St. Louis bar assns., Am., Ill. trial lawyers assns., Am. Judicature Soc., Internat. Acad. Law and Sci., Comml. Law League, Am. Arbitration Assn. (arbitrator), Phi Delta Phi. Mason. Home: 309 Harrisburg Dr Belleville IL 62223 Office: 4715 W Main St Belleville IL 62223 also 1115 Washington St Highland IL 62249

KAUFFMAN, DAVID JACOB, mycologist, mktg. exec., former air force officer; b. Indpls., Feb. 27, 1929; s. Arthur Ray and Ruth Elizabeth (Schneider) K.; B.S., Ind. State U., 1959, M.S., 1971; m. Jean Francis Meadows, June 4, 1950; children—Cathy Sue (Mrs. George Smoot), Harold Ray, Cynthia. Asst. mgr. Danner Bros., Indpls., 1942-47; joined USAF, 1948, advanced through grades to master sgt., 1952; served at Baer Field, Ft. Wayne, Ind., O'Hare Field, Chgo., 1950-52; USAF Hosp., Chambley, France, 1961-62; ret., 1968; profl. sales rep. Schering Corp., Terre Haute, Ind., 1960—, mycology research scientist, 1968—. Paramed. missionary United Meth. Ch., Wimbo Nama, Zaire, 1973. Pres. bd. dirs. Happiness Bag Players; active Community Theatre, Terre Haute. Mem. A.A.A.S., Am. Soc. Microbiology, Gideons Internat. (pres. camp 1955-58), South Central Assn. Microbiology, Med. Mycol. Soc. Ams. Elk, Mason (Shriner). Home and Office: 2147 Poplar St Terre Haute IN 47803

KAUFFMAN, EWING MARION, pharm. co. exec., b. 1916; s. John S. and Effie May (Winders) K.; Asso. Sci., Kansas City Jr. Coll.; D.Sci., Union Coll.; m. Muriel Irene McBrien, Feb. 28, 1962; children—Larry, Sue Finsterwald, Julia LaPointe. Founder, chmn. bd. Marion Labs., Inc., Kansas City, Mo., 1950—; owner, pres. Kansas City Royals Baseball Club, 1969—; founder Royals Baseball Acad., Sarasota, Fla., 1970. Mem. Civic Council Kansas City; bd. dirs. Kansas City Sports Commn., Mayor's Corps of Progress; trustee U. Mo. at Kansas City; pres. Ewing M. Kauffman Found. Served with USN. Recipient Horatio Alger award Am. Schs. and Colls. Assn.; Man of Year award Mensa; Mktg. Man of Year Sales and Mktg. Execs. Internat.; Distinguished Service award Fellowship Christian Athletes. Mem. Am. Mgmt. Assn. Clubs: Indian Hills Country, Kansas City, Eldorado Country. Home: 5955 Mission Dr Shawnee Mission KS 66208 Office: Marion Labs Inc 10236 Bunker Ridge Rd Kansas City MO 64137

KAUFFMAN, JOHN DALE, testing co. exec.; b. Chicago Heights, Ill., May 15, 1940; s. Merle Maurer and Mildren Joan (Langbehn) K.; B.S., Bradley U., 1962, M.A., 1964; Ph.D., U. Iowa, 1970; m. Marilyn Joy Goodson, Dec. 27, 1964; children—Heidi Anne, Kirsten Johanna. Math. tchr. pub. schs., Flint, Mich., 1962-63, Lakewood, Ohio, 1963-65; counselor Sudlow Jr. High Sch., Davenport, Iowa, 1965-67; field cons. Iowa Testing Programs U. Iowa, Iowa City, 1967-69; dir. test services Houghton Mifflin Co., Geneva, Ill., 1969-72, coordinator spl. projects-tests, Boston, 1972-74; dir. field services Scholastic Testing Service, Inc., Bensenville, Ill., 1974-77, v.p. mktg., 1977—. Mem. Am. Personnel and Guidance Assn., Assn. for Measurement and Evaluation in Guidance, Council for Exceptional Children, Nat. Council on Measurement in Edn., Phi Delta Kappa. Lutheran. Home: 326 Clearwater Ct Carol Stream IL 60187 Office: 480 Meyer Rd Bensenville IL 60106

KAUFFMAN, LYNN EDWARD, polyethylene film co. exec.; b. Rockford, Ill., Mar. 29, 1940; s. Robert Daniel and Frances Mildred (Chase) K.; grad. high sch.; m. Patricia Ann Roessler, Apr. 15, 1961; children—Steven, Michael, Susan, Joel. Plant mgr. Nat. Poly. Products, Inc., Mankato, Minn., 1958-61; v.p. Universal Poly Film, Inc., Fairmont, Minn., 1961-63; pres., dir. Fairmont Films, Inc. (Minn.), 1963—; dir. Virginia Plastics Inc. (Minn.), Blako Industries, Dunbridge, Ohio. Mem. Fairmont C. of C. Club: Lions. Home: 2077 Knollwood Dr Fairmont MN 56031 Office: 805 E 10th St Fairmont MN 56031

KAUFMAN, ALBERT NICK, mfg. exec.; b. Warsaw, Ind., May 16, 1924; s. Emanuel Kaufman; student Ind. U., 1948; m. Gwendolyn Ione, May 1, 1944; children—Victoria Joyce, Timothy N. With Arnolt Corp., Indpls., 1942-62, advancing through various positions and serving as v.p. mfg., dir., 1953-62; pres. K-T Corp., 1962—; pres., chmn. bd. Kaufman Enterprises, Inc., 1977—. Served with USNR, World War II. Mason (Shriner). Home: 6220 N Chester Ave Indianapolis IN 46220 Office: 850 Elston St Shelbyville IN 46176

KAUFMAN, BURT ALLAN, math. educator; b. Balt., July 19, 1932; s. David and Rose Florence (Levinson) K.; student Sweet Briar Coll. Jr. Year in France Program Sorbonne, Paris, France, 1951-52; B.A., Franklin and Marshall Coll., 1953; LL.B., U. Balt., 1956; M.S., U. Notre Dame, 1962; postgrad. Johns Hopkins, 1956-60; postgrad. U. Mich., 1962-63; m. Paulette Joyce Friedlander, Apr. 11, 1954; children—Terry Morris, Lynn Dee. Tchr. math. Balt. sch. system, 1953-61; math. coordinator Nova Schs., Ft. Lauderdale, Fla., 1963-66; adj. prof. math. Fla. State U., Tallahassee, 1963-65; adj. prof. math. Fla. Atlantic U., Boca Raton, 1965-66; adj. prof. math. So. Ill. U., Carbondale, 1967-74, 77—; dir. Comprehensive Sch. Math. Project, CEMREL, Inc., Carbondale, 1967-75, St. Louis, 1975—. NSF grantee, 1960-63; Esso Found. grantee, 1959. Mem. Nat. Council Tchrs. Math., Math. Assn. Am., Phi Delta Kappa, Pi Lambda Phi. Democrat. Jewish. Author: Operational Systems Games, 1969; Adventures With Your Hand-Calculator, 1977; CSMP Elementary School Program, 1977; also series texts for gifted secondary sch. students, Elements of Mathematics, 1977. Guest editor Ednl. Tech. Mag., Nov. 1973. Contbr. articles to math., edn. jours. Home: 1175 D Appleseed Ln Olivette MO 63132 Office: CEMREL Inc 3120 59th St St Louis MO 63139

KAUFMAN, HARVEY ISADORE, psychologist; b. Virginia, Minn., May 13, 1937; s. Carl and Marcia (Borkon) K.; B.A., U. Minn., 1959, B.S. cum laude, 1960, M.A., 1961; Ed.D., Marquette U., 1967; m. Glenda Markowski, Oct. 16, 1971; children—Jason, Justin. Asst. clin. dir. psychology service Jewish Vocat. Service, Milw., 1965-67; pvt. practice, Fond du Lac, Wis., 1968—; asst. prof. counseling Marquette U., Milw., 1967-71; supr. psychology Children's Consultation Service, Winnebago Mental Health Inst., 1971-74; chief psychologist, dir. neuropsychology lab. Fond du Lac County Mental Health Center, 1974-75, asst. clin. dir., 1975—; instr. U. Wis. at Fond du Lac, 1972—. Chmn. task force on guidance and counseling Gov.'s Commn. on Edn., 1969-70. Mem. Am., Wis. psychol. assns., Phi Delta Kappa, Kappa Delta Pi, Psi Chi. Author: The Kaufman Developmental Schedule, 1975; contbr. articles to profl. jours. Home: 409 Berkeley Pl Fond du Lac WI 54935 Office: 459 E 1st St Fond du Lac WI 54935

KAUFMAN, IRVING H., mktg. cons.; b. Chgo.; Feb. 22, 1925; s. Harry and Becky Kaufman; student Northwestern U.; m. SheliSheila Z. Horwich, Jan. 1, 1956; children—Betty, Harrian, Joel. With Daziens, Inc., N.Y.C., Chgo., 1947-48, Arvin Industries, Columbus, Ind., 1948-52; owner, operator wholesale-retail discount store, from 1952, pres., gen. mgr. to 1964; later mktg. sales cons.; sales v.p. for nat. publishing firm, exec. v.p. Nu-Enamel Co., Chgo., 1967-69; market dir. Allied Paper, Inc., subsidiary Smith-Corona-Marchant, 1970-74; self-employed as mktg. cons. and bus. broker 1974—. Active Boy Scouts Am. Served with U.S. Army, World War II; ETO. Mem. Am. Mktg. Assn., Am. Mgmt. Assn., Internat. Franchise Assn. Home: 145 Manor Dr Deerfield IL 60015 Office: 4747 W Peterson Ave Chicago IL 60646

KAUFMAN, JOANNE KLEIN, mgmt. cons.; b. Cleveland; d. Joseph E. and Martha (Ulmer) Klein; A.B. with honors, Western Res. U., 1958, M.A., 1963; m. James S. Kaufman, 1946; children—Martha J. Kaufman Stone, Peter, Thomas. Manpower program analyst, anti-poverty program Office Equal Opportunity, Dept. Labor, Washington, 1966; cons. U.S. Dept. Commerce, Washington, 1967-68; cons. Cleve. Dept. Pub. Health and Welfare, 1966—, Cleve. Commn. Higher Edn., 1966-76, Office of Edn. and Manpower Tng., HEW, Washington, 1973; mem. staff Vice Pres. Walter F. Mondale, Washington, 1977—; lectr. western civilization Cuyahoga Community Coll., 1966-68, Cleve. State U., 1966-69; pres. Urban Reports Corp. Mem. advance staff Carter-Mondale presdl. campaign, 1976. Mem. Nat. Women's Polit. Caucus, Cuyahoga Women's Polit. Caucus (founder). Clubs: City (Cleve.) Co-author: Teacher Education Centers, Do They Help Student Teachers Attain Their Goals, 1973; Stimulation of Teacher Innovation, 1974; editor: Work and the Nature of Man (Frederick Herzberg), 1964. Home: 2676 E Overlook Rd Cleveland Heights OH 44106 Office: 602 Bond Court Bldg Cleveland OH 44114

KAUFMAN, KIESL KARL, physician; b. Milw., Feb. 22, 1921; s. Aaron and Ida (Cherney) K.; student U. Wis., Milw., 1939-40; B.S., Marquette U., 1943, M.D., 1946; m. Yetta Bodner, Mar. 10, 1946; children—Jay Stuart, Lynne Gail, Jill Kaye. Intern, Mt. Sinai Hosp., Milw., 1946-47; resident in internal medicine, pulmonary disease, VA Hosp., Wood, Wis., 1949-52; asso. clin. prof. medicine, Med. Coll. Wis., Milw., 1952—; asso. attending staff Chest service, Milw. Gen. Hosp., 1952—; attending staff Muridale Sanitarium, Milw., 1954-58; asso. clin. prof. medicine, Med. Sch., U. Wis., Madison, 1974—; med. dir. sch. inhalation therapy, Mt. Sinai Med. Center, Milw., med. dir. respiratory therapy/pulmonary physiology, chief pulmonary diseases, attending staff; cons. staff Deaconess, Family Hosps., Milw. Served to capt., U.S. Army, 1947-49. Diplomate Am. Bd. Internal Medicine, Am. Bd. Pulmonary Disease. Fellow A.C.P., Am. Coll. Chest Physicians, Israel Med. Assn. (Am. Physicians fellow); mem. AMA, Med. Soc. Milw. County, State Med. Soc. Wis., Am. Soc. Internal Medicine, Am. Thoracic Soc., Royal Soc. Medicine, Wis. Lung Assn., Wis. Heart Assn., Milw. Acad. Medicine. Contbr. articles to sci. publs. Home: 7760 N Regent Rd Milwaukee WI 53217 Office: 1218 W Kilbourn Ave Suite 207 Milwaukee WI 53233

KAUFMAN, NATHAN JAY, judge; b. Lemberg, Austria, Nov. 20, 1908; s. David and Rose (Wagner) K.; came to U.S., 1914, naturalized, 1922; LL.B., Detroit Coll. Law, 1929; m. Beatrice Tauber, Dec. 14, 1930; 1 dau., Rose Kaufman Blake. Admitted to Mich., Fed. bars,

1929, practiced in Detroit, 1929-45; asst. pros. atty. Wayne County, Detroit, 1946-53; judge Ct. Common Pleas Detroit, 1953; judge Probate Ct. charge Juvenile Ct., Detroit, 1954-60; circuit judge 3d Jud. Circuit, Wayne County, 1960-75, judge Mich. Ct. Appeals, 1975—. Chmn. equal ednl. com. Detroit Bd. Edn.; mem. bd. Mich. Cystic Fibrosis, Detroit Assn. Retarded Children, Mich. Assn. Emotionally Disturbed Children, City of Hope; del. White House Conf. Children and Youth. Mem. Nat. Juvenile Judges Assn. (mem. exec. bd.), Internat. Juvenile Ct. Judges Assn. (del.). Clubs: Masons, Moose, Odd Fellows, B'nai B'rith. Home: 17533 Freeland St Detroit MI 48235 Office: 900 First Fed Bldg Detroit MI 48226

KAUFMAN, SYDNEY MORTON, metallurgist; b. Elizabeth, N.J., June 14, 1934; s. Alvin and Clara (Fischler) K.; B.S., Carnegie-Mellon U., 1956, M.S., 1960, Ph.D., 1961; m. Nancy Carole Goldberg, Dec. 15, 1956; children—David, Karen, Sara. Research engr. Ford Motor Co., Dearborn, Mich., 1960-65, sr. research engr., 1965-67, prin. research engr. asso., 1967-72, prin. research engr., 1972—. Part-time instr. U. Mich., 1962, Wayne State U., 1964-65. Served to 1st lt., ordnance, U.S. Army, 1956-61. Mem. Am. Inst. Mining, Metall. and Petroleum Engrs., Am. Soc. Metals, Am. Powder Metallurgy Inst., Soc. Automotive Engrs. Patentee in field. Contbr. articles to profl. jours. Home: 14640 Ronnie Lane Livonia MI 48154 Office: Ford Motor Co Dearborn MI 48121

KAUFMANN, FELIX, technol. and planning cons.; b. Berlin, Germany, July 4, 1918; s. Bruno P. and G. Edith (Seligsohn) K.; came to U.S., 1954, naturalized, 1968; B.S. with honors, U. London (Eng.), 1940, D.I.C., 1943; grad. Brit. Inst. Mgmt., 1952; m. Maureen Kallick; children—Ruth, Michael, Julian, Cornelia. Dr. med. research, EGH Labs. Ltd., Manchester, Eng., 1947-51; cons. WHO, Geneva, Switzerland, 1952-55; head makeup dept. Revlon Inc., N.Y.C., 1956; exec. v.p. Kerr Internat. Inc., Detroit, 1957-62; pres. Kerr Italia, SpA, Scafati, Italy, 1959-62; dir. futures program Hudson Inst., Croton, N.Y., 1962-65; mgr. corp. planning Hoffman-LaRoche, N.J., 1965-71; pres. Sci. for Bus. Inc., N.Y.C., 1971—; dir. internat. strategic planning Bendix Corp., Southfield, Mich., 1974-77; cons. to govts. U.S., N.Y. State, India, Pakistan, Romania, Egypt, to WHO, UNITAR, to Johnson and Johnson, Ciba-Geigy; instr. courses grad. sch. bus. U. Pitts., 1972, New Sch. for Social Research, N.Y.C., 1972-73, 73-74, Am. Mgmt. Assn., 1977. Cited in resolution State of Mich. Ho. of Reps. for contbns. to Internat. Congress of Tech. Assessment, 1976. Mem. AAAS, Am. Acad. Polit. and Social Sci., Am. Chem. Soc., Internat. Soc. Tech. Assessment, N.Am. Soc. Corp. Planning, World Future Soc., Newark Center for Tech. Assessment (asso.). Club: Chaos. Author: Decisions, 1972; Organizational Decisions, 1972; World Government and the U.S. National Interest, 1965; (with others) Hypercryogenics, 1963; contbr. articles in field to publs. Home and office: 1160 Pauline Blvd Ann Arbor MI 48103

KAUFMANN, KARL EUGENE, mfg. co. exec.; b. Saginaw, Mich., Feb. 27, 1927; s. Karl E. and Esther G. (Appleby) K.; B.A., U. Minn., 1949; m. Barbara Jane Griebel, Sept. 1, 1949; children—Geoffrey, Nancy. Account exec. KSTP Inc., Mpls., St. Paul, 1949-56; v.p., owner Thermo-Fax Sales, Inc., 1956-62; dist. mgr. 3M Bus. Product Sales, Inc., 1962-68; mktg. mgr. 3M Co., St. Paul, 1968-71, project mgr., 1971-75, advt. and mdse. mgr., 1975—; dir. La Bar, Inc., St. Paul, KOL, Inc., St. Paul. Bd. dirs. Pillsbury Waite Neighborhood Services Inc., Episcopal Community Services Inc.; sr. warden St. Luke's Episc. Ch., 1977; mem. adminstrv. task force Episc. Diocese Minn., 1977. Served with USN, 1945-46. Mem. Direct Mail Mktg. Assn. (certificate of merit 1975), Bus. Profl. Advt. Assn. (Oliver award 1977), Advt. Fedn. Minn., Northwestern Chi Psi. Home: 6405 McCauley Circle Edina MN 55435 Office: 3 M Center 220-10E Saint Paul MN 55101

KAUFMANN, MARION KENNETH, physician; b. Colebrook, O., June 6, 1926; s. Albert Walter and Aldah Wynona (Aiken) K.; B.A., Greenville Coll., 1949; postgrad. Aurora Coll., summer 1949; B.S., U. Ill., 1951, M.D., 1953, postgrad., 1960—; m. Stella Miriam Butcher, Aug. 24, 1948; children—Kenneth Walter, Bruce Gregory, Donald Alan, Gary Bryan, Stella L., Sheryl L., April Dawn. Intern, Cleve. City Hosp., 1953-54; resident gen. surgery Akron (Ohio) City Hosp., 1955; spl. pediatric tng. Akron Children's Hosp., 1957-58; practice medicine, specializing in family practice, Akron, 1955-59, Greenville, Ill., 1959—; mem. staff Ullaut Meml. Hosp., Greenville, chief med. staff, 1967-69, vice-chief, 1971, chief staff, 1976-77; mem. staff St. Joseph's Hosp., Highland; physician, dir. health dept. Greenville Coll., 1959—, asso. prof. biology, 1959—. Pres. Bond County (Ill.) Heart Assn., 1961-62; active coms. Bond County Tb Assn., 1960-71; pres. Am. Cancer Soc., Bond County, 1965, v.p., 1969; state dir. Light and Life Mens Fellowship Ohio Conf. Free Methodist Ch., 1958-59; alumni bd. Greenville Coll., 1960—, alumni chmn. nat. fund, 1967-70. Served with AUS, 1944-46. Recipient Presdl. award Greenville Coll., 1973. Diplomate Am. Bd. Family Practice. Mem. AMA, Ill. (del. 1972-73, 76-78), Bond County (pres. 1965-70) med. socs., Am., Ill. (ins. com. 1967-68, Helvetia chpt. pres. 1969—, del. 1973) acads. family practice, Free Methodist Med. Fellowship (dir. 1963-66), Greenville Coll. Alumni Assn. (pres. 1960-75). Methodist (ofcl. bd. 1959—). Clubs: Greenville Country; Rod and Gun (Greenville, Ill.). Home: 933 N Elm St Route 1 Box 34 Greenville IL 62246 Office: 105 E College Ave Greenville IL 62246

KAUFMANN, STELLA MIRIAM BUTCHER (MRS. KENNETH KAUFMANN), religious Worker; b. Clinton, Ind., Sept. 22, 1922; d. Aaron Edward and Frances Hannah (Phipps) B.; student Greenville Coll., 1940, Terre Haute Comml. Coll., 1942, Ind. State Tchrs. Coll., 1943-45, Aurora Coll., 1949-50, U. Ill., 1950-54; B.A., Greenville Coll., 1954; m. Marion Kenneth Kaufmann, Aug. 24, 1948; children—Kenneth Walter, Bruce Gregory, Donald Alan, Gary Bryan, Stella Louise, Sheryl Lyn, April Dawn. Various positions, Terre Haute and Seymour, Ind., 1941-42; accountant Kroger's Dist. Office, Terre Haute, 1942-47; bookkeeper Greenville (Ill.) Coll., 1947-49; tchr. East View Sch. Dist. 115, Aurora, Ill., 1949-52; accountant, husbands med. bus., Greenville, 1956—. Co-dir. Christian Youth Crusader, Akron, Ohio, 1956-59, Greenville, 1959-63. Mem. W.C.T.U. (state sec. 1968-69, county pres. 1966-68, chpt. treas. 1969-70), Ill. Acad. Gen. Practice Aux., Ill. Med. Soc. Aux., Utlaut Meml. Hosp. (pres. 1968-70, hos. aux. program chmn. 1970-72, chmn. Bazaar 1972), Carolyn Winslow Womens Missionary Circle (v.p. 1968-69). Methodist Editor: Christian Youth Crusader-Heralds, 1960-68. Home: 933 N Elm St Route 1 Box 34 Greenville IL 62246

KAUL, PHILIP GIBBS, physician; b. Holton, Kans., Oct. 14, 1920; s. Frank and Helen Clark (Spears) K.; B.S., Kans. State U., 1942; M.D., U. Kans., 1945; m. Nancy Poteet, Oct. 28, 1950; children—Lucy Helen, Nancy Poteet, Elizabeth Spears, Kathleen, Frank Allen. Intern, U. Kans. Med. Center, 1945-46, resident in internal medicine, 1948-50; pvt. practice internal medicine Kansas City, Mo., 1951—; attending staff St. Luke's and Baptist Meml. Hosps., Kansas City; asst. clin. prof. medicine U. Kans., Kansas City, 1960—. Pres. Kansas City and W. Mo. Heart Assn., 1964-65. Served from 1st. lt. to capt. M.C., U.S. Army, 1946-47. Diplomate Am. Bd. Internal Medicine. Mem. U. Kans. Med. Alumnus Assn. (pres. 1964-65), A.C.P., AMA, Mo. Med. Soc., Jackson County Med. Soc., Am., Mo., Greater Kansas City socs. internal medicine, Republican. Episcopalian. Club: Homestead Country. Home: 5310 Mission Woods Rd Shawnee Mission KS 66205 Office: 4320 Wornall Rd Kansas City MO 64111

KAUPP, VERNE HENRY, project engr.; b. Denver, Apr. 15, 1940; s. Henry and Yvetta Elsie (Pfeiffer) K.; B.S. in Physics, U. Md., 1971; postgrad. U. Kansas., 1975—; m. Sarah Morton Stanish, Feb. 5, 1966; 1 son, Peter Jason. Engr., Martin Marietta Corp., Denver, 1971-74; cons. Earth Resources Tech. Service, Denver, 1974-75; project engr. Center for Research, Inc., U. Kans., Lawrence, 1975—; pres. Systems Tech. and Applied research Corp., 1977—; cons. NASA. Served with U.S. Army, 1962-65. Mem. IEEE Sigma Pi Sigma. Home: 920 W 28th Terr Lawrence KS 66044 Office: 2291 Irving Hill Dr Lawrence KS 66044

KAVANAGH, THOMAS GILES, govt. ofcl.; b. Bay City, Mich., Aug. 14, 1917; A.B., U. Notre Dame, 1938; LL.B. cum laude, U. Detroit, 1943; m. Mary Mahoney, 1939; children—Joseph Hayes, Kathleen Kavanagh Doherty, Thomas Giles, III, Kervin Pedraic. Elected judge Mich. Ct. of Appeals, 1964; justice Mich. Supreme Ct., from 1968, now chief justice. Bd. dirs. Cardinal Newman Found., Wayne State U. Mem. State Bar Mich., Oakland, Detroit bar assns., Catholic Lawyers Soc., Notre Dame Law Assn. Roman Catholic. Office: Law Bldg 2d Floor 525 W Ottawa St Lansing MI 48909*

KAVANAUGH, CHARLES EDWARD, dentist; b. Hamilton, Mo., Sept. 25, 1937; s. Edward C. and Audentia (Miller) K.; B.S., N.W. Mo. State Coll., 1960; D.D.S., U. Mo. at Kansas City, 1964; m. Gladene Sherard, Aug. 30, 1958; children—Kurt Edward, Kent Stewart, Kirby Lee, Kelly Kirk. Resident in orthodontics U. Mo. at Kansas City, 1964-66; practice dentistry specializing in orthodontics, Kansas City, Mo., 1966—, Sedalia, Mo., 1966—, Marshall, Mo., 1969—, Chillicothe, Mo., 1973—, Excelsior Springs, 1974—, Cameron, Mo., 1977—; mem. staff Children's Mercy Hosp.; orthodontic cons. to Mo. Dental Service Corp.; pres. Kirby Devel. Co., Chouteau Profl. Bldg. Inc. Asso. prof. U. Mo. at Kansas City Sch. Dentistry. Bd. dirs. Ernest Shepherd Meml. Youth Center, NWMSU Ednl. Found.; mem. Mo. Bd. Dental Govs. Mem. Am., Mo., Kansas City (dir.) dental assns., Am. Assn. Orthodontists, Kansas City Orthodontic Soc., Mo. Orthodontic Assn., Clay-Platte Dental Soc. (pres. 1969-70), Am. Soc. Dentistry for Children, Am. Numis. Assn., Greater Kansas City Dental Soc. (pres. 1973-74), Pierre Fauchard Acad. Dentistry, Xi Psi Phi. Club: Optimist (zone 1 past lt. gov.). Home: 2600 NE 76th St and Kirby Ln Kansas City MO 64119 Office: 4420 Chouteau Trafficway Kansas City MO 64117

KAVIEFF, SHELDEN MILFORD, sales engr.; b. Detroit, Dec. 9, 1922; s. Otto Henry and Clara (Cannon) K.; B.S. in Mech. Engring., U. Mich., 1947; m. Rosalind Sylvia Rosoff, Oct. 1, 1950; children—Thomas Reid, Elizabeth Anne. Indsl. engr., Mich. Steel Tube Products Co., Hamtramck, 1947; plant engr. of Warren plant, Chrysler Desoto div. Chrysler Corp., 1948-52; sales engr., dist. mgr. Jervis B. Webb Co., Detroit, 1952—; instr. Materials Mgmt. Center, Wayne U., Detroit, 1953-54. Served with USN, 1942-46; PTO. Registered profl. engr., Mich. Mem. Soc. of Automotive Engrs., Engring. Soc. of Detroit, Am. Numismatic Assn., Am. Foundrymans Assn. Unitarian. Clubs: Masons, Shriners; Plum Hollow Country; Pontiac Yacht; Huron River. Contbr. articles on automation to tech. jours.; patentee in field. Office: Webb Dr Farmington Hills MI 48018

KAWAHARA, FRED KATSUMI, chemist; b. Penngrove, Calif., Feb. 26, 1921; s. Kentaro and Kikue (Seo) K.; Ph.D., U. Wis., 1948; postgrad. U. Chgo., 1951-53; m. Sumi Hayami, May 10, 1952; children—Robert K., Kiku S., Richard H. Chemist, Bur. Agr. and Indsl. Chemistry, U.S. Dept. Agr., Peoria, Ill., 1948-51; sr. research scientist Standard Oil Co., Whiting, Ind., 1953-64; chemist EPA, Cin., 1965-66, cons., 1966-68, group leader, 1969-74, research chemist analytical quality control lab., 1974—. Fellow Am. Inst. Chemists; mem. Am. Chem. Soc., ASTM (chmn. infrared com. 1973—), Sigma Xi, Phi Lambda Upsilon. Author: Identification of Petroleum Pollutants. Contbr. articles to profl. jours. Patentee in field. Home: 2530 Eight Mile Rd Cincinnati OH 45244 Office: 1014 Broadway Ave Cincinnati OH 45202

KAY, DICK (RICHARD D. SNODGRASS), TV reporter; b. Delrose, Tenn., July 24, 1936; s. Keby Joe and Ida Belle (Thompson) Snodgrass; m. Kay Sue Johnson, Apr. 16, 1960; children—Steven Anthony, Eric Charles, Brett Alan; B.S. in Speech Edn., Bradley U., 1962. Announcer, WSIV, Pekin, Ill., 1960; news and program dir. Radio Sta. WAAP, Peoria, Ill., 1960-63; reporter WTVH-TV, Peoria, 1963-65; news dir. WFRV-TV, Green Bay, Wis., 1965-68; writer-producer NBC News, Chgo., 1968-70; reporter WMAQ-TV, NBC News, Chgo., 1970—. Mem. North Side Jaycees (hon. dir.; life mem. internat. senate 1977—). Recipient Emmy award Nat. Acad. TV Arts and Scis., 1976. Office: NBC News Merchandise Mart Chicago IL 60654

KAYE, GERARD WALTER, assn. exec.; b. N.Y.C., Sept. 18, 1944; s. Nathan and Sandra Rose (Kohn) Karpf; B.A., DePaul U., 1969; M.A., Roosevelt U., 1971; certificate in psychotherapy Chgo. Med. Sch., 1974; m. Paula Elaine Langfeld, Jan. 28, 1967; children—Michelle Sari, Leora Rachel. Exec. dir. Am. Zionist Youth Fedn., Chgo., 1966-67, dir. youth activities, Chgo., 1967-70; exec. dir. Olin-Sang-Ruby Union Inst., Chgo., 1970—; cons., counselor, practice psychotherapy, Chgo., 1972—; lectr. psychiatry Chgo. Med. Sch., 1972—; lectr. psychology Oakton Coll., Morton Grove, Ill., 1974-75. Bd. dirs. Chgo. Jewish Experience Inc. Fellow Am. Orthopsychiat. Assn.; mem. Am. Personnel and Guidance Assn., Internat. Transactional Analysis Assn., Mensa, Blue Key, Phi Delta Kappa. Home: 8920 Bennett St Evanston IL 60203 Office: 100 W Monroe St Chicago IL 60603

KAYE, JOEL EDMUND, radiologist; b. Cleve., Jan. 21, 1933; s. Norman and Mary (Arnoff) K.; B.S., Ohio State U., 1955, M.D., 1960; m. Monica Bradley, May 6, 1965; children—Ann Kathleen, Clare Monica, Louis David. Intern Mt. Sinai Hosp. Cleve., 1960-61, resident in radiology, 1961-64; instr. radiology Ohio State U., 1964-65; practice medicine specializing in radiology, Mansfield, Ohio, 1965—; trustee Mansfield Gen. Hosp., 1977, pres. med. staff, 1976—; med. dir. Mansfield Cancer Clinic. Diplomate Am. Bd. Radiology, Am. Bd. Nuclear Medicine. Mem. AMA, Ohio, Richland County med. assns., Am. Coll. Radiology, Am. Coll. Nuclear Medicine (sec. Ohio chpt.), Soc. Nuclear Medicine, Radiol. Soc. N.Am., Cleve., Ohio radiol. socs., Soc. Computed Tomography. Clubs: Westbrook Country; Rotary. Home: 551 Forest Hill Rd Mansfield OH 44907 Office: 335 Glessner Ave Mansfield OH 44903

KAYE, STEPHEN JOHN, pub. relations exec.; b. Hillsdale, Mich., Apr. 23, 1943; s. Lester Antone and Marjorie Helen (McColl) K.; B.S., Northwestern U., 1965, M.S., 1966; m. Nancy Jane Wiler, Dec. 18, 1965; children—Stephen Jeffrey, Jennifer Cristin. Mgr. employee communications, pub. relations Morton Norwich, Inc., Chgo., 1966-69; mgr. employee communications Montgomery Ward & Co., Chgo., 1969-70; dir. pub. affairs Consol. Foods Corp., Chgo., 1970-74; dir. pub. relations G. D. Searle & Co., Skokie, Ill., 1974—. Trustee, Library Internat. Relations, Chgo. Mem. Pub. Relations Soc. Am., Chgo. Press Club, Nat. Investor Relations Inst., Phi Gamma Delta, Sigma Delta Chi. Home: 1220 Park Ave W Highland Park IL 60035 Office: 4711 Golf Rd Skokie IL 60076

KAYTON, LAWRENCE, psychiatrist; b. Chgo., Apr. 12, 1938; s. Basil and Belle (Wertheimer) K.; B.A., U. Ill., 1959, M.D., 1963; m. Carole Colvin, June 19, 1960; children—Todd Steven, Cheryl Beth. Intern U. Mich. Hosps., 1964; resident Inst. Psychomatic and Psychiat. Research and Tng., Michael Reese Hosp., Chgo., 1967, chief resident psychiatry, 1967, dir. tng., 1972-76; dir. psychiat. research VA Hosp., Hines, 1976—; asst. prof. psychiatry Pritzker Sch. Medicine, U. Chgo., 1973-76; clin. asso. prof. Loyola U., 1976—; cons. juvenile delinquent program Ill. State Psychiat. Inst., Chgo., 1969-72, sr. cons. in psychiatry, 1976—. Served as officer M.C., AUS, 1967-69; Korea. Decorated Army Commendation medal; recipient David M. Olkon Meml. award U. Ill., 1963; Merk award, 1963; Psychomatic and Psychiatric Inst. Research award Michael Reese Hosp., 1967. Mem. Am. Psychiat. Assn., Am. Assn. Dirs. Psychiat. Residency Tng., A.A.A.S., Am. Soc. Adolescent Psychiatry, Phi Beta Kappa, Alpha Omega Alpha. Author articles in field. Home: 223 W St Charles Rd Elmhurst IL 60126 Office: 111 N Wabash Chicago IL 60609

KAZWELL, ALBERT LEO, dentist; b. Gary, Ind., Apr. 11, 1924; s. Alexander Kazlauski and Eva (Konicki) K.; D.D.S., Ind. U., 1947; m. Helen Marie Geeting, Aug. 10, 1946; children—Richard Douglas, Cynthia Denise Kazwell Carstens, William Albert, Barbara Jane Kazwell Moore, Mary Catherine, John Bryan. Gen. practice dentistry, Cedar Lake, Ind., 1947—; staff mem. Our Lady of Mercy Hosp., Dyer, Ind.; owner resort apt. complex, Englewood, Fla. Served to capt., Dental Corps, AUS, 1953-55. Mem. ADA, Acad. Gen. Dentistry, Acad. Dental Implantology, Cedar Lake, Englewood (Fla.) chambers commerce, Ind. U. Alumni Assn., Am. Legion, Xi Psi Phi. Roman Catholic (parish council). Clubs: K.C. (4 deg.), Lions (sec. 1949), Century, Varsity, Cedar Lake Yacht. Home: 8505 W 141st Pl Cedar Lake IN 46303 Office: 13955 Morse St Cedar Lake IN 46303

KEAIRNS, RAYMOND EARL, dentist; b. nr. Jackson, Ohio, July 27, 1912; s. Gus Earl and Ethel Jane (McClure) K.; student Rio Grande Coll., 1931-33, Ohio State U., summers, 1934-37, 39; D.D.S., Ohio State U., 1943; m. Alice Genevieve Poston, Aug. 21, 1946. Tchr. elementary schs., Jackson County, Ohio, 1933-39; pvt. practice dentistry, Logan, Ohio, 1946—. Pres., Keairns, Inc., Spic and Span Laundromat, Lancaster, Ohio, U-Do-It Laundromat, Logan, Speed Queen Coin-Op Laundry, McArthur, Ohio, Koolway Laundry, U Pick Strawberry Operation. Bd. dirs. Logan chpt. A.R.C. Served with AUS, 1943-46. Mem. Nat. Automatic Laundry and Cleaning Council, Am., Ohio, Logan dental assns. Presbyn. Kiwanian (dir. 1955-57, 62-64). Clubs: Logan Trade, Square Dance. Home: 36660 Hocking Dr Logan OH 43138 Office: 9 E 2d St Logan OH 43138

KEAN, JOSEPH EDWARD, real estate exec.; b. Falls City, Nebr., Aug. 17, 1949; s. Edward Paul and Claudine Annette (Furey) K.; B.S., U. Nebr., 1972; m. Rita Catherine McKenna, July 27, 1974. Sales asso. Town & Country Realty, Inc., Lincoln, Nebr., 1970-71; asso. broker Lincoln Gateway Realty Co., 1971-76; pres. Equity Investment Systems, Ltd., Lincoln, 1972—, Joseph E. Kean Co., 1976—. Active Lincoln-Lancaster County Goals and Policies Com., 1974—. Mem. Neb. Real Estate Polit. Action Com., 1972—, Lancaster County Young Republicans, 1974—. Mem. Lincoln Bd. Realtors (chmn. govtl. affairs com. 1972-77), Nebr. Real Estate Assn., Nat. Assn. Realtors, Nat. Inst. Real Estate Brokers, Kansas City Real Estate Exchange, Lincoln Jaycees (dir. 1973, Key Man award 1973, Man Month Nov. 1972), Lincoln C. of C. (planning, land use com., govtl. affairs com., surface transp. com.), U. Nebr. Alumni Assn. Roman Catholic. Club: Lincoln University. Home: 322 W Lakeshore Dr Lincoln NE 68528 Office: Suite 1212 First Nat Bank Bldg 233 S 13th St Lincoln NE 68508

KEANE, FRANCIS MARTIN, educator; b. Chgo., Nov. 28, 1935; s. Francis and Christina (Daly) K.; LL.B., Blackstone Sch. Law, 1960; B.Sc., Roosevelt U., 1958, M.Sc., 1962; postgrad. Columbia U., 1962-63, U. Chgo., 1965-68; m. Judith Pauline Vertrees, Aug. 8, 1970. Chemist, DeSoto Chem., Chgo., 1959-60; research asso. Royal Vet. and Agrl. Coll., Copenhagen, Denmark, 1961-62; sr. research chemist Stauffer Chem., Chicago Heights, Ill., 1964-65; chmn. sci. dept., tchr. advanced chemistry J.H. Bowen High Sch., Chgo., 1968—. Dir. Faraday Research Inst., Chgo., 1968—; cons. testing labs. and food industry; notary public Ill., 1968—. Recipient Tchrs. award NASA, 1971, 73, Engring. Council Profl. Devel., 1971, 72, 73, Westinghouse, 1971. Fellow Chem. Soc. London; mem. Menninger Found., Nat. Council on Crime and Delinquency, Am. Judicature Soc., Fedn. Am. Scientists, Am. Inst. Chemists, Am. Chem. Soc., Danish Chem. Soc., Ill. Acad. Scis., Nat. Sci. Suprs. Assn., A.A.A.S. Contbg. author Inorganic Syntheses, 1966. Home: 9631 S Houston Ave Chicago IL 60617 Office: 2710 E 89th St Chicago IL 60617

KEANE, JOHN G., business cons.; A.B. in Russian, Syracuse U.; B.S.C. in Bus. Adminstrn., U. Notre Dame; M.B.A. in Mktg., Ind. U.; Ph.D. in Econs., U. Pitts. With U.S. Steel Corp.; later with Booz, Allen & Hamilton; v.p. research, planning dir. J. Walter Thompson, Inc., Chgo.; pres. Managing Change, Inc., Barrington, Ill., 1972—. Mem. Internat. Platform Assn., World Future Soc., N.Am. Soc. for Corporate Planning, Am. Mktg. Assn. (nat. pres. 1976), Econ. Club of Chgo. Contbr. articles to profl. jours. Address: 106 Fox Hunt Trail Barrington IL 60010

KEARNS, CHARLES ALBERT, heavy machinery sales and service co. exec.; b. Herington, Kans., Sept. 8, 1922; s. Charles Edward and Jane Francis (Taylor) K.; student Creighton U., 1940; B.S., Kans. State U., 1949; m. Rae Ruth Loriaux, Jan. 26, 1942; children—Kevin (Mrs. Robert L. McLean), Michael John, Jeffrey Charles, Thomas Patrick. Sales engr. Caterpillar Tractor Co., Peoria, Ill., 1949-51; exec. v.p. Alban Tractor Co., Balt., 1951-67; pres. Capitol Machinery Co., Springfield, Ill., 1967-72; owner, mgr. Kearns Machinery Co., Sioux Falls, S.D., 1972—; dir. Nat. Bank S.D., Sioux Falls, Marley Co., Mission, Kans. Commr., Game, Fish and Parks Dept., State S.D., 1973-76. Bd. dirs. Sioux Empire United Way, Sioux Falls, McKennan Hosp., Sioux Falls; pres. Upper Mo. Water Users Assn. Served with AUS, 1942-45; ETO. Decorated Bronze Star medal. Mem. Ill. Transp. Alliance (pres. 1970-71), Ill. Asso. Gen. Contractors (dir. 1970-71), Sioux Falls C. of C. (dir. 1975-77). Roman Catholic. Home: Box 11A Brandon SD 57005 Office: Box 1307 1001 E 14th St Sioux Falls SD 57101

KEARNS, FRANCIS EMNER, clergyman; b. Bentleyville, Pa., Dec. 9, 1905; s. George Verlinda and Jennie Mae (McCleary) K.; A.B., Ohio Wesleyan U., 1927, D.D., 1954; S.T.B., Boston U. Sch. Theol., 1930; student U. Berlin, U. Edinburgh (Scotland), 1930-31; Ph.D., U. Pitts., 1939; LL.D., Mt. Union Coll., 1965; L.H.D., Ohio No. U., 1965; Pd.D., Baldwin-Wallace Coll., 1966; m. Alice Margaret Thompson, Sept. 1, 1933; children—Rollin Thompson, Margaret Kearns Baldwin, Francis Emner. Ordained to ministry Meth. Ch., 1931; pastor 1st Meth. Ch., Dravosburg, Pa., 1931-32; asso. pastor Christ Meth. Ch., Pitts., 1932-35, Ben Avon (Pitts.) Meth. Ch., 1935-40, Asbury Meth. Ch., Uniontown, Pa., 1940-45, Wauwatosa (Wis.) Meth. Ch., 1945-64; bishop Meth. Ch., Ohio E. area, 1964—; mem. Gen. Bd. Edn. Meth. Ch., 1956-64, curriculum com., 1956-64;

mem. Meth. Inter-bd. Commn. Town and Country, 1964-68, Meth. Gen. Bd. Evangelism, 1965-68; chmn. Inter bd. Commn. Christian Vocations, Meth. Ch., 1964-68; vice chmn. gen. bd. edn. United Meth. Ch., 1968-72, chmn. div. curriculum resources, 1968-72, mem. Program Council, 1968-72, Meth. Corp., 1968-72, vice chmn. div. health and welfare ministries Bd. Global Ministries, 1972-76, mem. Gen. Bd. Global Ministries, 1972-76, mem. Gen. Bd. Ch. and Soc., 1972-76, mem. N. Central Jurisdictional Council on Ministries, 1972-76; mem. gen. assembly Nat. Council Chs., 1965-68; mem. faith and order dept. Ohio Council Chs., pres., 1969-71, mem. gen. bd., 1972-76; Trustee Baldwin-Wallace Coll., Meth. Theol. Sch. in Ohio, Mt. Union Coll., Ohio No. U., Ohio Wesleyan U., Otterbein Coll., United Theol. Sem. Mem. World Meth. Council, Phi Beta Kappa. Clubs: Masons (33 deg.), Rotary. Author: The Church is Mine, 1962; contbr. articles to religious jours. Home: 290 Cottswold Dr Delaware OH 43015

KEATING, DONALD JOHN, electronics engr.; b. Flandreau, S.D., Dec. 30, 1925; s. John Harvey and Verna Anna (Waxdahl) K.; B.S. in Elec. Engring., S.D. State U., 1956, postgrad., 1956-57. Farmer, nr. Flandreau, S.D., 1943-50; teaching asst. S.D. State U., 1955-56; devel. engr. Wright Patterson AFB, Ohio, 1956; instr. elec. engring. S.D. State U., 1956-57; devel. engr. Def. Systems div. Sperry Univac div. Sperry Rand Corp., St. Paul, 1957—, staff engr., group leader, 1974—. Alternate ch. del. Merriam Park Community Council, St. Paul, 1973—. Served with U.S. Army, 1950-52. Mem. IEEE, Nat. Rifle Assn., Antique Aircraft Assn., Aircraft Owners and Pilots Assn., Smithsonian Assos., Sigma Tau, Eta Kappa Nu, Phi Kappa Phi. Republican. Methodist. Clubs: Masons (32 deg.), K.T., Shriners. Home: 1765 Carroll Ave St Paul MN 55104 Office: Sperry Univac PO Box 3525 MSM 6032 St Paul MN 55165

KECK, JAMES MOULTON, advt. agy. exec., ret. air force officer; b. Scranton, Pa., Sept. 4, 1921; s. R. L. and Helen Louise (Walker) K.; m. Barbara Brown Fleck, June 2, 1943; children—Bonnilyn Brown, Thomas James, Allison Sarah; student Brown U., 1939; B.S., U.S. Mil. Acad., 1943; postgrad. Naval War Coll., 1952, Nat. War Coll., 1960. Commd. 2d lt. USAAF, 1943, advanced through grades to lt. gen. USAF, 72; dep. dir. OPS. Strategic Air Command, 1969-70; dep. dir. ops. USAF, 1970-71, dir. plans, 1971-72; comdr. 2d Air Force, 1972-73; vice comdr. Strategic Air Command, 1973-77; ret., 1977; v.p. corporate affairs Bozell & Jacobs, advt. agy., Omaha, 1977—. Vestryman, Episcopal Ch., 1957-60; active Boy Scouts Am., ARC. Decorated D.S.M., Legion of Merit, D.F.C., Air medal. Mem. Air Force Assn., Rotary. Home: 911 S 113th St Omaha NE 68154 Office: 10250 Regency Circle Omaha NE 68114

KECK, ROBERT CLIFTON, lawyer; b. Sioux City, Iowa, May 20, 1914; s. Herbert A. and Harriet (McCutchen) K.; A.B., Ind. U., 1936; J.D., U. Mich., 1939; L.H.D., Nat. Coll. Edn., 1973; m. Ruth P. Edwards, Nov. 2, 1940; children—Robert Clifton, Laura E. Keck Simpson, Gloria E. Keck Sauser. Admitted to Ill. bar, 1939; practiced in Chgo., 1939—, mem. firm Keck, Cushman, Keck, Mahin & Cate, 1939—, partner, 1946—; dir. 1st Ill. Corp., Evanston, Union Spl. Corp., Am. Hosp. Supply Co., Rust-Oleum Corp., Schwinn Bicycle Co., Signode Corp., Methode Electronics, Inc., U.S. Gypsum Co. Chmn. bd. trustees Nat. Coll. Edn.; bd. dirs. Sears Roebuck Found. Served with USNR, 1943-45. Mem. Fed., Am., Ill., Chgo. bar assns., Bar Assn. 7th Fed. Circuit (past pres.), Am. Coll. Trial Lawyers, Phi Gamma Delta. Republican. Clubs: Masons; Westmoreland Country (Wilmette, Ill.); Chgo., Met., Law, Legal, Econ., Execs. (Chgo.); Biltmore Forest Country (Asheville); Glen View (Golf, Ill.). Home: 1043 Seneca Rd Wilmette IL 60091 Office: 233 Wacker Dr Chicago IL 60606

KECK, WILLIAM FRANCIS, certified pub. accountant; b. Aurora, Ill., Aug. 15, 1939; s. William Roswell and Elizabeth Emma (Kurns) K.; B.B.A., U. Notre Dame, 1961; M.S., No. Ill. U., 1968. Accountant, cons. Peat, Marwick, Mitchell & Co., Chgo., 1968-70; internal. auditor Sears, Roebuck & Co., Chgo., 1970-73; accounting mgr. John M. Smyth Co., Chgo., 1973; internal audit mgr. Nat. Student Marketing Corp., Chgo., 1973-76; individual practice as C.P.A., 1977—. Scoutmaster, Sugar Grove (Ill.) Boy Scouts Am., 1963-65; pres. Sugar Grove Vol. Fire Dept., 1970. Trustee Sugar Grove Village Bd., 1965-69, 71-75, chmn. finance com., 1965-69, 71-75. C.P.A., Ill. Mem. Am. Inst. C.P.A.'s, Ill. C.P.A. Soc., Am. Accounting Assn., Nat. Council Dominic Clubs (pres. 1977). Roman Catholic (mem. bldg. com. 1974). K.C., Lion (treas. 1971). Home: Box 281 Maple Ave Sugar Grove IL 60554 Office: 104 E Downer Aurora IL 60507

KEEFE, KENNETH MICHAEL, elec. products mfg. co. exec.; b. Cin., Feb. 10, 1939; s. John Kenneth and Kathryn (Leonard) K.; B.S., Xavier U., 1961; m. Margaret Klee, Sept. 13, 1960; children—Michael, Kelly. With Cin. Fan & Ventilator Co., 1960—, v.p., 1960-65, exec. v.p., 1965-72, pres., 1973—; pres. Hamilton Fan & Blower, Cin., 1973—, Cushman Foundry, Inc., Cin., 1973—, Marken Realty, 1976—. Vice-pres. Turpin Hills Civic Assn., 1971, pres., 1972. Served with AUS, 1962-64. Mem. Young Pres.'s Orgn. Home: 3025 Saddleback Dr Cincinnati OH 45244 Office: 5345 Creek Rd Cincinnati OH 45242

KEEFER, LUCINDA KAY MILLER, county ofcl.; b. Baldwin, Mich., Mar. 25, 1945; d. Marion Leroy and Jane Eilene (Gibson) Miller; student pub. schs., Mason County, Mich.; m. Arthur Milton Spears, Dec. 10, 1977; children by previous marriage—David Martin, Kandice LeNora. Sec., Gordon D. Barney Ins. Agy., Baldwin, Mich., 1964-69; clk./typist Lake County Agrl. Stblzn. and Conservation Service, 1969-70; clk./typist Office of Lake County Clk. and Register of Deeds, Baldwin, 1969-72; county clk. and register of deeds Lake County, Baldwin, 1973—. Sec. Lake County chpt. ARC, 1973—, Lake County Republican Party, 1973—; chmn. Lake County (Mich.) for Milliken Com., 1974. Mem. Nat. Assn. County Recorders and Clks. (dir.), Mich. Assn. County Clks. (3d v.p.), Mich. Assn. Registers of Deeds, Lake County Twp. Officers Assn. (asso.), Lake County Hist. Soc. Congregationalist. Home: Rural Route Box 60 Branch MI 49402 Office: County Bldg Baldwin MI 49304

KEEGAN, JOSEPH HARRY, ednl. adminstr.; b. Monroe, Wis., July 6, 1938; s. Thomas Rudolph and Anna Kathryn (Flannigan) K.; B.S., Colo. State U., 1962; M.Adminstrn., U. Nev., 1970, Edn. Specialist, 1972; m. Beverly Ellen Ericsson, Dec. 27, 1960; children—Kathleen Yvonne, Ann Marie. Tchr. biology Fountain Dist., Fort Carlson, Colorado Springs, Colo., 1962-65; asst. prin., dir. athletics St. Francis DeSales, Denver, 1965-66; tchr., adminstr. Clark County Sch. Dist., Las Vegas, Nev., 1966-70; supt. schs., Belle Fourche, S.D., 1970—; dir. Ericsson Corp., Belle Fourche; sec., dir. Lonesome Country Ltd., 1969—. Mem. Butte County Citizens Drug Com., 1973—; active Boy Scouts; bd. dirs. S.D. Citizens for Modern Cts. Mem. Am. Assn. Sch. Adminstrs., S.D. Sch. Adminstrs., Phi Delta Kappa. Republican. Home: 1212 11th St Belle Fourche SD 57717 Office: 706 Jackson St Belle Fourche SD 57717

KEELER, JAMES HOWARD, mfg. co. exec.; b. Toledo, Oct. 8, 1920; s. Anson Howard and Llenda Lucille (White) K.; B.S., Pa. State U., 1942, Ph.D., 1951; M.S., Stevens Inst. Tech., 1948; m. Irene Krantz, Feb. 17, 1945; children—Kathleen Howard, Clark Alan. Metallurgist Wright Aeronautical Corp., Woodridge, N.J., 1942-47; research asso. Pa. State U., University Park, 1947-50; research asso. research lab. Gen. Electric Co., Schenectady, N.Y., 1951-55, liaison scientist, 1956-59, mgr. materials application, 1959-60, engring. mgr. refractory metals dept. Cleve., 1961-67, mfg. mgr., 1968—. Fellow Am. Soc. Metals (David Ford McFarland award 1961), Am. Inst. Mining, Metallurgical and Petroleum Engrs. (chpt. chmn. 1966-67); mem. Euclid C. of C. (bd. dirs. 1976—), Am. Inst. Mining, Inst. Metals (chmn. 1964-65), Metall. Soc. (bd. dirs. 1964-69). Contbr. articles to profl. jours. Home: 30 Park Ln Chagrin Falls OH 44022 Office: 21800 Tungsten Rd Euclid OH 44117

KEENAN, WILLIAM HERBERT, pub. relations exec.; b. Ravenswood, W.Va., June 3, 1926; s. William Earl and Georgia Della (Morris) K.; student Morris Harvey Coll., 1951. Feature writer, reporter Charleston (W.Va.) Gazette, 1951-56; feature writer Indpls. Star, 1956-61; editor-pub. St. Louis mag., 1962-71; dir. community relations St. Louis Children's Hosp., 197; cons. pub. relations Mid-West Health Congress; cons. Am. Soc. Hosp. Pub. Relations. Served with USNR, 1945-47. Recipient news writing award AP, 1952, Pub. Relations award Mid-West Health Congress, 1972. Mem. Am. Soc. Hosp. Pub. Relations (dir. 1975-76), Pub. Relations Soc. Am., Nat. Assn. Hosp. Deve., Acad. Hosp. Pub. Relations (MacEachern award 1976), Assn. Am. Med. Colls., Nat. Soc. Fund Raisers (dir.), Press Club Met. St. Louis. Republican. Presbyterian. Contbr. features to various publs., including Esquire, St. Louis Post Dispatch. Home: 531 W Jewel Ave Saint Louis MO 63122 Office: 500 S Kingshighway Saint Louis MO 63110

KEENY, MAURICE GARFIELD, physician; b. Pawhuska, Okla., Sept. 22, 1936; s. Maurice Joseph and Elma (Bowman) K.; A.B., Kans. State U., 1962; M.D., U. Kans., 1966; m. Kelly Bracken, Oct. 14, 1977; children—Jeffrey Paul, Mark Daniel, Pamela Ann. Intern Kansas City (Mo.) Gen. Hosp., 1966-67; practice of medicine Keeny-Taylor Clinic, Sedan, Kans., 1967-70, Broadway Med. Clinic, Wichita, 1970—; mem. staff St. Francis Hosp., Wichita. Chmn. bd. Sugar Oil Co., Inc.; pres. Kans. Vets., Inc. Served with USAF, 1954-58. Recipient NIH research grant, 1963-65. Mem. Am. Acad. Gen. Practice, A.M.A., Indsl. Med. Assn., Gt. Plains Indsl. Med. Assn., Kans. Med. Soc., Blue Key, Phi Delta Theta, Phi Beta Pi. Republican. Episcopalian (clk. of vestry 1969). Home: 5 Hillcrest Ave Wichita KS 67208 Office: 841 N Broadway St Wichita KS 67214

KEHL, LEORA ROWENA NEAL, ret. nurse; b. Albion, Ill., Aug. 1, 1910; d. William T. and Clara (Miller) Neal; R.N., Grace Hosp. Sch. Nursing, Detroit, 1932, B.S., Wayne State U., 1948; M.A., Columbia, 1952; m. Charles Herman Kehl, Dec. 21, 1974. Surg. nurse Children's Hosp. of Mich., 1934-36; staff nurse Vis. Nurse Assn., Detroit, 1936-42; supervising nurse Ill. Dept. Health, 1942-45; psychiat. nurse, 1st lt. Nurse Corps, AUS, 1945-46; supr., instr. maternity nursing Butterworth Hosp., Grand Rapids, Mich., 1948-51; hosp. nursing cons. Mich. Dept. Health, Lansing, 1952-75, ret., 1975. Sec., treas. Nurses Assn. Am. Coll. Obstetricians and Gynecologists, 1968-72. Mem. steering com. Isabel Maitland Stewart Research Professorship in Nursing and Nursing Edn., 1960-65. Fellow Royal Soc. Health, Am. Pub. Health Assn.; mem. Am., Mich. nurses assns., Nat., Mich. (membership chmn. 1961-63) leagues nursing, Div. Nursing Edn. Tchrs. Coll. Columbia (treas. 1954-64), Wayne State U. Coll. Nursing, Grace Hosp. Sch. Nursing alumni assns., AAUW, Bus. and Profl. Women, Pi Lambda Theta, Kappa Delta Pi. Roman Catholic. Home: 2324 W 4th Ave Sault Ste Marie MI 49783 also 721 N 66th Ave Hollywood FL 33024

KEHLER, PAUL, physicist; b. Mariampole, Lithuania, Mar. 5, 1931; s. Otto and Wanda (Haak) Kehler; M.S., U. Freiburg (Germany), 1955; m. Luise M. Hofflin, June 4, 1960; children—Elvira, Victoria. Came to U.S., 1956, naturalized, 1962. With Dresser Industries, Dallas, 1956-59, Phillips Petroleum Co., Bartlesville, Okla., 1960-62; with Bell Aerosystems Co., Buffalo, 1963-71; owner, gen. mgr. Frontier Technologies Co., Niagara Falls, N.Y., 1971; pres. Applied Inventions Corp., North Tonawanda, N.Y. and Mishawaka, Ind., 1972—. Mem. Am. Phys. Soc., Am. Nuclear Soc., I.E.E.E. Soc. Profl. Well Log Analysts, Internat. Platform Assn. Contbr. articles to profl. jours. Patentee in field. Home: 17305 Fergus Dr South Bend IN 46635 Office: Box 826 Mishawaka IN 46544

KEIDAN, FRED HANNAN, lawyer; b. Detroit, Nov. 16, 1931; s. Harry Benjamin and Katherine M. (Levenson) K.; B.A., U. Mich., 1952, LL.B., 1955; children—Laura Ruth, Marian R. Admitted to Mich. bar, 1956; asso. firm Watson, Lott & Wunsch, Detroit, 1955-63; partner firm Watson, Wunsch & Keidan, Detroit, 1963-76; of counsel firm Morris Rowland Regan & Prekel, 1977—. Served with AUS, i956-58. Mem. Am., Mich., Detroit bar assns., Maritime Law Assn. U.S. Clubs: Econ., Propeller (Detroit). Home: 2330 Dorchester Troy MI 48084 Office: Suite 504 3001 W Big Beaver Rd Troy MI 48084

KEIL, MARVIN HENRY, assn. exec.; b. Beaver Dam, Wis., Oct. 28, 1902; s. John and Phoebe (Blochwitz) K.; Ph.B., Lawrence Coll., 1925; m. Frances M. Bayer, Aug. 22, 1928 (dec. Oct. 1934); 1 son, John Marvin; m. 2d, Era M. Henderson, June 17, 1936; 1 son, Ward Henderson. Plant mgr. Central Wis. Canneries Inc., 1925-30, distbn. mgr., 1930-41; regional personnel mgr. Green Giant Co., 1941-67; dir. Rochelle Asparagus Co. (Ill.), 1959-65; charter pres. Beaver Dam chpt. Am. Assn. Ret. Persons, 1972-73, asst. dir. for Wis., 1975-76, state dir., 1976—; mem. Dodge County Commn. on Aging, 1974—; dir. Area Agy. on Aging Dist. #1, 1974—. Pres., Wis. Canners and Freezers Assn., 1951-52, dir., 1949-67, trustee pension fund, 1965—; bd. dirs. Nat. Canners Assn., 1953-56; sec.-treas. Brit. W.I. Employers Assn., 1951-64; mem. Beaver Dam City Council, 1952-61; mem. Beaver Dam Fire and Police Commn., 1936-48, 52-77, Wis. Devel. Authority, 1965-69; vice chmn. Fond du Lac conf., mem. bd. So. dist. council Am. Luth. Ch., 1972—, chmn. personnel com., 1974-76. Recipient Employee of Year award Green Giant Co., 1953; Conservation Leadership award Beaver Dam High Sch. Hunting and Fishing Club, 1969; Distinguished Service award Beaver Dam Jaycees, 1969, certificate for service Mayor and Chiefs of Police and Fire Depts., Beaver Dam, 1977. Clubs: Masons, Kiwanis (pres. Beaver Dam 1942, lt. gov. 1944), Order Eastern Star, Fisherman's, Old Hickory Golf, Roamers, Old Guard Soc. Address: 818 Lake Shore Dr Beaver Dam WI 53916

KEIM, EARL GEORGE, JR., realtor; b. Dearborn, Mich., Feb. 26, 1927; s. Earl G. and Gladys (Bourassa) K.; B.S., U. Mich., 1952; m. Musette Townley, Dec. 20, 1952 (div. June 1968); children—Musette, Melissa, Susan, Allison, Ruth Ann; m. 2d, Sharron Tyler Whittier, Dec. 24, 1971. Profl. baseball, Nashville and St. Cloud, summer 1952; salesman West Dearborn Realty, 1952-55, sales mgr., 1955-58; pres., owner Earl Keim Realty, Inc., Dearborn, 1958—. Past chmn. bd. mgmt. Dearborn YMCA. Served with USMCR, 1944-46, M.C. U.S. Army, 1946-48. Mem. Dearborn Bd. Realtors (Realtor of Year 1966, 67, past pres.), Mich. Real Estate Assn. (pres. 1972), Met. Detroit Council Real Estate Bds. (chmn. 1968), Phi Delta Theta. Republican. Methodist. Kiwanian. Home: 30285 Hickory Lane Franklin MI 48025 Office: 28400 Southfield Rd Lathrup Village MI 48076

KEIRNS, HARRY DAYTON, data processing exec.; b. Akron, Ohio, Jan. 25, 1938; s. Harry Austin and Charlotte June (Betz) K.; student Akron U., 1957-68; m. Nancy Cogar, Feb. 20, 1957; children—Susan Marie, Katherine Ann, Roberta Diana. Mgr. systems devel. B.F. Goodrich Tire Co., Akron, 1967-70; pres. AGT, Champaign, Ill., 1970-71; dir. software and date processing Gould, Inc., Boston, 1972; systems mgr. B.F. Goodrich Tire Co., Akron, 1972—. Systems analyst Little Hoover Commn., Summit County, Ohio, 1969. Served with USNR, 1956. Mem. Assn. Computing Machinery, Digital Equipment Corp. Users Group, Vector Gen. Users Group Siggraph, Life Master Am. Contract Bridge League, Mensa. Home: 49 W Garwood Dr Tallmadge OH 44278 Office: 500 S Main St Akron OH 44318

KEISER, ROGER JAMES, architect; b. Estelline, S.D., June 17, 1938; s. Ralph Albert and Marian Theresa (Opland) K.; diploma Winona Sch. Photography, 1958; B.Arch. with distinction, U. Minn., 1966; m. Judith Mary Adams, June 16, 1957; children—Stephanie, Paige. Owner, Keiser's House of Photography, Hutchinson, Minn., 1958-61; project architect Cavin & Page, Mpls., 1966-69, Gingold-Pink, Mpls., 1969-72; owner Keiser Assos., Fergus Falls, Minn., 1972—; pres. Component Bldg. Systems, Inc., Fergus Falls, 1973—. Mem. Heritage Preservation Commn., Fergus Falls, 1974—; mem. State Hosps. Beautification Com., 1977—. Recipient Sweepstakes award Minn. Profl. Photographers Assn., 1959. Registered architect; accredited Nat. Council Archtl. Registration Bds. Mem. AIA, Constrn. Specifications Inst., Minn. Soc. Architects (bldg. code task force 1972-74, legis. com. 1977—), Ottertail County Hist. Soc. Tau Sigma Delta. Lutheran (bldg com. 1973-76). Clubs: Elks, Kiwanis, Leech Lake Yacht. Home and Office: 752 Springen Ave Fergus Falls MN 56537

KEITH, DAMON JEROME, fed. judge; b. Detroit, July 4, 1922; s. Perry A. and Annie (Williams) K.; S.B., W.Va. State Coll., 1943; LL.B., Howard U., 1949; LL.M., Wayne State U., 1956; m. Rachel Boone, Oct. 18, 1953; children—Cecile, Keith, Debbie, Gilda. Admitted to Mich. bar, 1949; atty. Office Friend of Ct., Detroit, 1951-55; mem. Wayne County Bd. Suprs., Detroit, 1958-63; sr. partner firm Keith, Conyers, Anderson, Brown & Wahls, Detroit, 1964-67; U.S. dist. judge Eastern Dist. Mich., Detroit, 1967—; now chief judge U.S. Dist. Ct. Eastern Dist. Mich. Pres. Detroit Housing Commn., 1958-67; co-chmn. Mich. Civil Rights Commn., 1964-67; mem. legal staff Detroit Bd. Edn.; v.p. United Negro Coll. Fund Detroit; 1st v.p. Detroit chpt. N.A.A.C.P. Trustee, Cranbrook Sch., Interlochen Arts Acad. and Mercy Coll., Detroit Art Commn. Served with AUS, World War II. Recipient Alumni citation Wayne State U., 1968; named One of 100 Most Influential Black Americans, Ebony Mag., 1971, 72. Mem. Am., Mich. (commr. 1960-67), Detroit bar assns., Nat. Lawyers Guild, Am. Judicature Soc., AAUP, Alpha Phi Alpha. Methodist (deacon). Club: Detroit Cotillon. Contbr. legal jours. Office: US Dist Ct Rm 720 Federal Bldg Detroit MI 48226

KEITHLEY, RICHARD ERNEST, lawyer; b. Kansas City, Kans., Mar. 12, 1948; s. Marion C. and Elsie V. (Hatch) K.; A.A., Donnelly Coll., 1968; B.A., Kans. U., 1970, J.D., 1974. Admitted to Kans. bar, 1974, Fed. bar, 1974; clk. to Dist. Judge Kenneth Harmon, Leavenworth, Kans, 1973; individual practice law, Kansas City, 1974-75; asst. city atty. City of Kansas City, 1975—; lectr. in field. Democratic nominee Kans. Ho. of Reps., 1972. Mem. Kansas City Jaycees, Phi Alpha Delta, Delta Sigma Phi. Democrat. Episcopalian. Home: 4218 Lathrop Ave Kansas City KS 66104 Office: One Civic Center Plaza Kansas City KS 66101

KEKST, KEEVA JOSEPH, architect, land planner, lectr.; b. Cleve., Mar. 26, 1932; s. Harry and Becky (Azoff) K.; B.Arch., Western Res. U., 1955; m. Joan L. Robbins, Aug. 10, 1952; children—Larry, Audrey, Amy, Nancy, Bradley. With firm Fulton, Krinsky & Delamott, 1955-60; pvt. practice architecture, Cleve., 1960—; city architect, University Heights, O., 1968—. Vice pres. Cleve. Hebrew Schs., Jewish Nat. Fund. Trustee Hillel Found., Western Res. U., 1970—, Bur. Jewish Edn. Cleve., Agnon Sch. Mem. A.I.A. (legislative com. 1968), Architects Soc. Ohio. Home: 2552 Fenwick Rd Cleveland OH 44118 Office: 2800 Euclid Ave Cleveland OH 44115

KELCH, PAUL, univ. adminstr.; b. Cin., May 4, 1916; s. Charles J. Sanzone and Norma Erdmann Sanzone Kelch; B.S., Sul Ross State Coll., 1939, M.A., 1940; m. Audrey J. Becker, Dec. 21, 1941; children—Jeanette, Elaine. Tchr. pub. schs., Edinburg, Tex., 1939-41; enlisted AUS, 1941, advanced through grades to lt. col. Fin. Corps, 1943; ret., 1963; asst. prof. bus. Sul Ross State Coll., Alpine, Tex., 1963-65; asst. prof. bus., sec. adminstrv. council U. Wis., Stevens Point, 1965—. Mem. Univ. Christian Ministry. Mem. Am. Accounting Assn., Wis. Civil Def. and Disaster Assn., Am. Econs. Assn., Am. Legion, Ret. Officers Assn., AAUP, Res. Officers Assn. Author: Programming the Burroughs 205 Computer System, 1963. Address: 24 Ridgewood Dr Park Ridge Stevens Point WI 54481

KELKAR, MANOHAR SHANKAR, physician; b. Dahanu, Maharashtra, India, Oct. 16, 1932; s. Shankar Trimbak and Yamuna Shankar (Marathe) K.; came to U.S., 1962. Intern, Paterson (N.J.) Gen. Hosp., 1962-63; pres. Manohar S. Kelkar, M.D., Inc., Solon, Ohio, 1975—. Pres., Marathi Cultural Assn., Solon, 1976. Mem. Acad. Medicine Cleve., Ohio Med. Assn., Am. Soc. Contemporary Medicine, India Assn. Cleve. Author: Ten Minutes of Asans for Physical Fitness, 1974. Home: 5800 Ledgebrook Ln Solon OH 44139 Office: 34420 Aurora Rd Solon OH 44139

KELLER, CHARLES FREDERICK, realtor; b. Plymouth, Ind., Oct. 10, 1932; s. Charles Frederick and Katherine Elizabeth (Vink) K.; B.A., DePauw U., Greencastle, Ind., 1959; m. Sue Ann Hughes, Oct. 6, 1960; children—Patricia Ann, Mary Elizabeth. Sr. salesman Scott Paper Co., 1960-63; real estate appraiser Ind. Hwy. Commn., 1964-66; real estate appraiser, cons., South Bend, Ind. and Southwestern Mich., 1966—. Instr., Ind. U., South Bend, South Bend-Mishawaka Bd. Realtors. Mem. fund raising com. Century Center, South Bend, 1974; mem. hosp. expansion program, South Bend, 1972-73. Served with USNR, 1951-55; PTO. Decorated Air medal. Mem. Soc. Real Estate Appraisers South Bend (pres. 1975-76), Am. Inst. Real Estate Appraisers (mem. candidate guidance com. Ind. chpt. 1977), Soc. Real Estate Appraisers, Nat. Assn. Realtors, Ind. Assn. Realtors, Econ. Club. Southwestern Mich. Mason. Club: Pickwick (Niles, Mich.). Home: 50600 Mohawk Dr Granger IN 46530 Office: PO Box 142 South Bend IN 46634 also PO Box 341 Niles MI 49120

KELLER, DAVID COE, dept. store exec.; b. Warren, Ohio, Jan. 30, 1921; s. David Claude and Minnie Corlin (Furgerson) K.; B.B.A., Cleve. State U., 1943; m. Gladys Marie Carstens, Jan. 6, 1945; 1 dau., Anne Marie. Staff accountant Touche Ross & Co., Cleve., 1946-49; asst. controller, M. O'Neil Co., dept. store, Akron, Ohio, 1950-56; controller, treas., dir. F.N. Arbaugh Co., dept. store, Lansing, Mich., 1956-59; v.p., treas., dir. Wurzburg Co., dept. store, Grand Rapids, Mich., 1959-72; chief financial officer, v.p., treas. Wieboldt Stores Inc., Chgo., 1972—. Bd. dirs. Jr. Achievement, Grand Rapids, Mich., 1961-69; bd. dirs. Civic Fedn., Chgo., 1974. Served to 1st lt., USMCR, 1943-45. Named Grand Rapids Boss of Year, Am. Women's Clubs, 1969. Mem. Ill. Retail Mchts. Assn. (chmn. tax com.), State St. Council (tax com. 1974), Tau Kappa Epsilon. Mason (Shriner). Office: Wieboldt Stores Inc 1 N State St Chicago IL 60602

KELLER, DEAN HOWARD, librarian; b. Ashtabula, Ohio, May 20, 1933; s. Howard Dean and Fern (Remington) K.; B.A., Kent (Ohio) State U., 1955, M.A., 1958; m. Patricia Lou Scheid, June 9, 1962; children—Jonathon Howard, Jennifer Nancy. Asst. humanities librarian Kent State U., 1958-63, humanities librarian, 1963-66, asso. librarian, readers services and spl. collections, 1967-69, curator spl. collections, 1969—. Lilly fellow U. Ind., 1966-67. Editor: A Fool's Errand, 1969; The Serif, 1967-75. Home: 5887 Roc Marie Ave Kent OH 44240 Office: Kent State Univ Library OH 44242

KELLER, HAROLD WILLIAM, chem. co. exec.; b. Grand Forks, N.D., Aug. 24, 1922; s. Charles Earl and Margaret Ann (Carlson) K.; student U. N.D., 1940-42, 46-48; m. S. Betty Larsen, Oct. 31, 1947; children—Charles William, Kenneth Earl. Asst. dir. research Ill. Water Treatment Co., Rockford, 1952-68, service mgr., 1968-69, mgr. market devel., 1969-72; v.p. Techni-Chem, Inc., Cherry Valley, Ill., 1972-77, pres., 1977—, also corporate exec., dir. Served with USAAF, 1942-46. Mem. Am. Chem. Soc., Am. Inst. Chem. Engrs., Am. Soc. Sugar Beet Tech. Home: 7633 Lucky Ln Rockford IL 61108 Office: 205 E State St Cherry Valley IL 61016

KELLER, HOWARD JOSEPH, printing co. exec.; b. Chgo., Apr. 10, 1906; s. Daniel F. and Mary Louise (Ringler) K.; B.A., Yale, 1927; postgrad. Chgo. Kent Coll. Law, 1930; m. Josephine Kasper Swanson, Feb. 24, 1967; children—Anne H., Howard J. Reporter, Chgo. Herald Examiner, 1927-28; with D.F. Keller Co., Chgo., 1928-65, pres., 1946-65; chmn. Sleepeck Keller Printing Co., Bellwood, Ill., 1965—. Chmn. liaison com. Union Health and Welfare, 1962-70. Clubs: Evanston (Ill.) Golf; Chgo. Yacht; Yale (N.Y.C.). Home: 1410 Sheridan Rd Wilmette IL 60091 Office: 815 25th Ave Bellwood IL 60104

KELLER, JOHN BIDWELL, constrn. co. exec.; b. Columbia, Mo., June 22, 1931; s. Charles Walter and Rowena Rita (Bidwell) K.; B.S., U. Kans., 1952; m. Anne Jackson, June 20, 1953; children—Gilbert Jackson, John Bidwell. Salesman, Denney Machinery Co., Wichita, Kan., 1953-55; pres. Paragon Mech., Inc., Kansas City, Mo., 1955—; pres., dir. Bank of Waverly; pres. Waverly Investment Co., Contrech, Inc.; dir. Plaza Savings Assn., Kansas City, Mo. Mem. Sigma Chi. Presbyn. Clubs: Kansas City, Saddle and Sirloin, Homestead Country. Home: 6431 Wenonga Rd Mission Hills KS 66208 Office: PO Box 4342 Kansas City MO 64127

KELLER, JOHN JEROME, pub. co. exec.; b. Appleton, Wis., Nov. 9, 1918; s. Louis Hugo and Marie Louise (Hollenback) K.; grad. Appleton Bus. Coll., 1938, Coll. of Advanced Traffic, 1942, Interstate Commerce Commn. Law Sch., 1950; certificate Armed Forces Inst., 1945; m. Ethel Doris Courtois, Feb. 19, 1944; children—Robert Louis, James Joseph, Thomas Edward. Traffic supr. Kimberly Clark Corp., Neenah, Wis., 1940-51; admitted to U.S. Interstate Commerce Commn. bar, 1951; v.p., gen. mgr. Kampo Transit, Inc., Neenah, 1950-52; founder, pres., chief exec. Keller Enterprises, Neenah, 1952—; chmn., pres., treas., chief exec. J.J. Keller & Assos., Inc., Neenah, 1953—; prof. transp. econs. and interstate commerce law Wis. Tech. Inst., 1955-65; ednl. chmn. Fox Valley Traffic Club, 1950-55; adv. com. appointee to Ninth Nat. Bank Region Adv. Com., 1976-77. Served to sgt. maj. U.S. Army, 1942-46. Mem. Nat. Soc. of Lit. and the Arts, Interstate Commerce Commn. Practitioners Assn. (life), Delta Nu Alpha (past regional v.p.). Clubs: Butte des Morts Country, BridgKort Racquet, Ringmaster Theatre (Milw.), Am. Legion, Elks. Author and publ. transp. and tech. publs. Home: 2532 Oakcrest Dr Neenah WI 54956 Office: 145 W Wisconsin Ave Neenah WI 54956

KELLER, LOUIS PAUL, elec. engr., engine mfg. co. exec.; b. Columbus, Ind., July 25, 1934; s. J. Keith and Edith Faye (Powell) K.; B.E.E., Purdue U., 1957; m. Roberta Belle Elmore, Nov. 2, 1958; children—Stephen Alan, Linda Marie, Paula June. Foreman of elec. maintenance Cummins Engine Co., Columbus, Ind., 1957-70, gen. foreman of mech. and elec. maintenance, 1970-74, unit mgr. elec. maintenance, 1974-75, mgr. of maintenance, 1975—. Trustee Hope Moravian Ch., sec., 1975—, sec. bd. of elders, 1962-68. Mem. IEEE, Aircraft Owners and Pilots Assn. Club: Masons. Home: 2673 Maple Columbus IN 47201 Office: 1000 5th St Columbus IN 47201

KELLER, MARVIN DAVE, lawyer; b. Hyannis, Nebr., Aug. 22, 1939; s. A.D. and Elsie Grace (Dille) K.; J.D., U. Nebr., 1964; m. Betty Jeanne Foster, June 1, 1968; 1 dau., Marlene; stepchildren—John Hagin II, Matthew Hagin. Admitted to S.D. bar, 1964; since practiced in Sioux Falls, legal asso. Boyce, Murphy, McDowell and Greenfield, 1964-68; partner firm Keller and Parker, 1968-74; dep. states atty., 1969-74, now magistrate 2d Jud. Ct.; mem. spl. com. revise S.D. criminal code, 1975, criminal procedure, 1976, 77; mem. S.D. Jud. Council, 1975—. Mem. State Bar S.D., Am. Bar Assn., Am. Judicature Soc., Minnehaha County Bar Assn. (treas. 1966-68), Am. Contract Bridge League, Kappa Sigma. Republican. Episcopalian (vestryman, 1970-73, chmn. canons com. S.D. diocese 1972). Home: 615 N Summit Ave Sioux Falls SD 57104 Office: 224 W 9th St Sioux Falls SD 57102

KELLER, MAURICE JOSEPH, dentist; b. Newburg, Ind., Oct. 4, 1932; s. Theodore Joseph and Regina O. (Weber) K.; D.D.S., St. Louis U., 1956; m. R. Norine Healy, June 25, 1960; children—Michael, Maureen, John, Anne, Mary. Intern, Louisville Gen. Hosp., 1958-59; pvt. practice dentistry specializing in pedodontics, Evansville, Ind., 1959—; instr. Ind. U., 1964-69. Pres. Evansville Assn. for Retarded Children, 1971-72; treas. Vanderburgh County Tb Assn., 1970-73; bd. dirs. Comprehensive Health Planning Council Tri-State, 1970—. Served to capt. AUS, 1956-58. Mem. Vanderburgh County (pres. 1965-66), 1st Dist. (pres. 1968-69) dental socs. Office: 3700 Bellemeade Ave Evansville IN 47715

KELLER, ROBERT ANTHONY, real estate investment co. exec.; b. Mpls., Nov. 3, 1922; s. Frank Seraphine and Catherine (Morris) K.; student U. Minn., 1940-42, 46-47, Mich. State U., 1942-43; m. Shirley Louise Soderquist, Oct. 11, 1950; children—Frank S., Robert Anthony, Sandra Louise. Pres., Bob Keller & Co., Mpls., 1949-59; founder, pres. Keller Investment Co., Mpls., 1960—. Dir. fund dr. Benilde High Sch., Mpls. Served with USAAF, 1943-46. Mem. Minn. (pres. 1968-69; author code of ethics), Nat. (v.p. 1972) apt. assns., Phi Delta Theta. Democrat. Roman Catholic. Clubs: Interlachen Country; Mpls. Golf; Lafayette (Minnetonka Beach, Minn.). Home and Office: 400 Westwood Dr S Minneapolis MN 55416

KELLER, ROBERT HOWARD, JR., physician; b. Bklyn., Oct. 3, 1942; s. Robert Howard and Christine Marie (Bode) K.; B.A., Fordham U., 1964, M.S., 1966; M.D. cum laude, Temple U., 1970; m. Joan Theresa Flaherty, June 29, 1968; children—Stacy Lynn, Chiara Lynn, Megan Beth, Robert Howard III. Intern, resident in internal medicine U. Rochester-Strong Meml. Hosp., 1970-74; research fellow in immunology Mayo Grad Sch. Medicine, Rochester, Minn., 1974-76, sr. research fellow, 1976-77, asst. prof. immunology, 1977, asso. cons., 1977; asst. prof. medicine Med. Coll. Wis., Milw., 1977—. Diplomate Am. Bd. Internal Medicine; Nat. Arthritis Found. fellow, 1975—; Am. Cancer Soc. grantee, 1976-77. Mem. AAAS, Alpha Omega Alpha, Lambda Nu Chi. Roman Catholic. Contbr. articles to profl. jours. Home: 850 Morningside Ln Elm Grove WI 53122 Office: VA Hospital Wood WI 53193

KELLER, THOMAS WHITNEY, city ofcl., bldg. supply co. exec.; b. Hinsdale, Ill., July 26, 1921; s. Raymond L. and Mildred (Whitney) K.; B.A., Duke U., 1946; m. Marcia E. Marland, Sept. 6, 1951; children—Peter J., Mark T., Marcia E., Scott R. With E.A. Keller Co., LaGrange, Ill., 1946-70, sec., 1949—; pres. TriCounty Land Corp., Lemont, Ill., 1970—; owner Keller Plantations, Holland, Mich.; dir. LaGrange State Bank, Edgewood Bank, LaGrange; v.p., dir. Suburban Credit Bur., LaGrange, 1951-69. Mem. Village of LaGrange Parking Commn., 1957-77; mem. asso. bd. LaGrange Community Meml. Gen. Hosp.; bd. dirs. West Suburban YMCA. Served with AUS, 1942-45. Mem. Am. Legion, Sigma Chi. Methodist. Clubs: Masons, Kiwanis, LaGrange Country. Home: 15346 Leonard Rd Spring Lake MI 49456 Office: 306 New Ave Lemont IL 60439

KELLER, VERA PROKOP, shopping center exec.; b. Oak Park, Ill., July 28, 1924; d. George Gerald and Libuse (Zdenek) Prokop; student Chgo. Profl. Sch. Art, 1942, Am. Acad. Art, 1943; m. Robert E. Keller, Nov. 25, 1954; children—Gwyneth Ann, Marisa Beth. Advt. layout Goldblatt's Dept. Store, Chgo., 1943-47; art dir., mgr. advt. Alden's Retail Stores, Chgo., 1947-51; layout Gimbels and Boston Store, Milw., 1951-55; free lance comml. artist, owner, operator advt. agency, Milw., 1955-61; art, layout, publicity, pub. relations, promotion John Lehrer & Assos., shopping center cons.'s, Milw., Ill., Ind., 1962-66; promotion dir. Capitol Ct., Milw., 1966-70; promotion dir. Southridge and Northridge shopping centers, Milw. and Greendale, Wis., 1970-74, mgr., 1974—; lectr. in field. Pres. Pals Homemakers, 1960, Germantown PTA, 1965; chmn. bd. ARC, 1957-58; adviser March of Dimes, Easter Seals. Mem. Women in Communications, Western Bohemian Fraternal Assn., Milw. Symphony Women's League. Clubs: Milw. Advt. (v.p. 1976-77, treas. 1975-76) Wis. Riders and Exhibitors. Home: N 124 W 14435 Lovers Ln Germantown WI 53022 Office: 5300 S 76th St Greendale WI 53129

KELLERMAN, BERT JOSEPH, educator; b. Pinckneyville, Ill., Aug. 23, 1940; s. Leo Frank and Stella May (Hubler) K.; B.S., So. Ill. U., 1963; M.S., 1966; Ph.D., U. Mo., 1972; m. Mary Ann Oelsen, Aug. 12, 1967. Instr. bus. adminstrn. Southeast Mo. State U., 1965-70, asst. prof., 1972-74, asso. prof., 1974-78, prof., 1978—, chmn. dept. mktg., 1976—; teaching asst. U. Mo., 1970-72; cons. in field. Mem. Am. Mktg. Assn., So., Southwestern mktg. assns., Midwest Bus. Adminstrn. Assn., Advt. Fedn. of Southeast Mo., Cape Girardeau C. of C. Republican. Presbyterian. Club: Lions. Home: 6 S Fountain St Cape Girardeau MO 63701 Office: 900 Normal St Cape Girardeau MO 63701

KELLERMAN, JOHN LEON, lawyer; b. Batesville, Ind., Feb. 21, 1942; s. Sylvester Marion and Adele Elinor (Struewing) K.; A.B., Ind. U., 1964, J.D., 1967; m. Victoria C. Decker, Jan. 5, 1963; children—John Leon, Peter Decker, Clay Matthew, Amy Paige, Adam Wade. Admitted to Ind. bar, 1967; since practiced in Batesville; mem. firm Wycoff, Greeman & Kellerman and predeccessor firm, 1967—; city atty., Batesville, Ind., 1970-72, 76—; town atty., Milan, Ind., 1972—. Chmn. fund-raising drive New Horizons Rehab., Inc., 1972. Vice chmn. Democratic Precinct Com., 1970. Mem. Am., Ind., Ripley County bar assns., Batesville C. of C. (pres. 1976), Batesville Jaycees. Roman Catholic. Lion, Eagle. Home: 429 S Mulberry St Batesville IN 47006 Office: 105 E George St Batesville IN 47006

KELLEY, CARL PHILETUS, athletic assn. exec.; b. Omaha, Oct. 31, 1907; s. Alvin Stingley and Georgia Kate (Gilbert) K.; student U. Nebr., 1928, U. Wis., summer, 1938, Creighton U., 1940; m. Lola Mae Toxword, Oct. 15, 1927; children—Dean L., Marvin C. With Prudential Ins. Co., 1935-66, staff mgr., agt., ret., 1966; pres. Omaha Softball Assn., 1951-77, commr., 1957-77. Dir. Women's Coll. World Series, Omaha, 1969-77. Named to Omaha Softball Hall of Fame, 1966, Amateur Softball Hall of Honor, 1977; recipient numerous plaques and awards, including first Cornerstone award Fellowship Christian Athletes Luth. Laymen, 1973. Mem. Midwest Assn. Amateur Athletic Union (commr. 1970-71, pres. 1968-69), Amateur Softball Assn. (nat. chmn. com. membership 1960-77), Protestant Chs. Athletic Assn. (pres. 1939-74). Baptist (trustee). Mason (Shriner, 32 deg.). Club: Alumni T (Omaha). Contbr. articles to profl. and popular publs. Home: 3712 N 53rd St Omaha NE 68104 Office: 6404 Maple St Omaha NE 68104

KELLEY, CHARLES EDWARD, educator; b. Miami, Mo., Sept. 28, 1913; s. Hiram Oclay and Cecelia (McGrady) K.; B.S. in Edn., Central Mo. State U., 1939; M.A., U. Mo., 1950, Ed.D., 1960; m. Margaret M. Moore, Aug. 17, 1946; 1 son, John Charles. Tchr., Bluff Elementary Sch., Miami, 1934-37; prin. Ballard Consol. Schs., Butler, Mo., 1939-41; supt. Johnstown Consol. Schs., Montrose, Mo., 1941-42; mem. faculty Fayette (Mo.) High Sch., 1942-43, Kemper Mil. Sch., Boonville, Mo., 1943-48, Texarkana (Tex.) Pub. Sch., 1950-51, Wentworth Mil. Acad., Lexington, Mo., 1953-55; mem. faculty Central Mo. State U., Warrensburg, 1955—, prof. math., 1965—, also coordinator grad. math. Mem. Math. Assn. Am. (sect. chmn. 1959-60), Nat. Council Tchrs. Math. (editor newsletter Mo. council 1962-66), Kappa Mu Epsilon, Pi Mu Epsilon, Kappa Delta Pi, Phi Delta Kappa. Home: 1100 S Holden St Warrensburg MO 64093

KELLEY, EDWARD GLENN, artist; b. Nashville, Dec. 17, 1922; s. Michael Francis and Gertrude Louise (Hess) K.; student Watkins Art Inst., 1938-41, Chouinard Art Inst., 1946-48, Ill. Inst. Tech., 1950-53. One-man shows: Chgo. Pub. Library, Riccardo, Dubuque Art Assn., Feingarten Gallery (Chgo.), Monroe St. Gallery, Old Town Art Center, Lake Forest Acad.; exhibited in group shows: Art Inst. Chgo., Pasadena Art Inst., Rockford Art Mus., Frank Oehlschlaeger Gallery, Main St. Gallery, many others; represented in permanent collections: Art Inst. Chgo. Rental and Sales Gallery, Gillman Galleries, Chgo., Vincent Price-Collection; instr. art, Galena, Ill., 1964-68; owner E.G.K. Collectibles and Antiques, Galena. Served with USAAF, 1943-46. Recipient awards Chgo. Magnificent Mile Festival, 1953, 54, 61, Union League Club Chgo., 1959. Life mem. Art Inst. Chgo., Artists Guild Chgo. (awards 1952, 55, 57, 62, 64), Arts Club Chgo., Galena Hist. Soc. Home: 4th and Madison St Galena IL 61036 Office: 305 S Main St Galena IL 61036

KELLEY, FRANK JOSEPH, atty. gen. Mich.; b. Detroit, Dec. 31, 1924; s. Frank Edward and Grace Margaret (Spears) K.; pre-law certificate U. Detroit, 1948, J.D., 1951; m. Josephine Palmisano, June 30, 1945; children—Karen Ann, Frank Edward, Jane Francis. Admitted to Mich. bar, 1952; practice law, Detroit, 1952-54, Alpena, Mich., 1954-61; pub. adminstr. Alpena County, Mich., 1956; atty., Alpena, 1958-61; atty. gen. Mich., 1962—; instr. econs. Alpena Community Coll., 1955-56; instr. real estate law U. Mich. extension, 1957-61. Mem. Alpena County Bd. Suprs., 1958-61; founding dir., 1st sec. Alpena United Fund, 1955; founding dir., 1st pres. Northeastern Mich. Child Guidance Clinic, 1958; pres., dir. Northeastern Mich. Cath. Family Sers. Council, 1956. Mem. Am., 26th Jud. Circuit (pres. 1956) bar assns., State Bar Mich., Internat. Movement Atlantic Union, Nat. Assn. Attys. Gen., Alpha Kappa Psi. K.C. (4 deg.). Office: Law Bldg 525 W Ottawa Lansing MI 48913

KELLEY, FRANK VERNON, psychologist; b. Newport News, Va., Mar. 11, 1931; s. Charles Moyer and Garland (Parker) K.; student Southeastern Bible Coll., Lakeland, Fla., 1951-54; B.S., Malone Coll., 1966; M.S., Ph.D., U. Akron, 1968; m. Margaret Jean Anderson, Jan. 30, 1954; children—Susan, Sandra. Tchr. pub. schs., Barberton, Ohio, 1964-67; psychologist, acad. adminstr. U. Akron, 1967-73; pvt. practice psychology, Akron, Ohio, 1973—; dir. New Hope Press, Stow, Ohio. Bd. dirs. Summit County Bd. Mental Health, 1973, Opportunities Unlimited, 1974, Shelter Care, 1977. Phi Delta Kappa scholar, 1967-68. Mem. Am., Ohio, Cleve. psychol. assns., Ohio, Cleve. acads. cons. psychologists, Am. Acad. Polit. and Social Sci., Phi Delta Kappa, Alpha Kappa Delta, Alpha Sigma Lambda, Kappa Delta Phi. Club: Cascade. Mem. Assemblies of God Ch. (ordained minister 1956). Home: 520 Meredith Ln Cuyahoga Falls OH 44323 Office: 2858 Arlington Rd Akron OH 44312

KELLEY, GAREN NILE, steel co. exec.; b. Moundsville, W.Va., Mar. 2, 1923; s. Roy and Elisabeth (Ruckman) K.; grad. high sch.; m. Naomi L. Hudkins, Oct. 10, 1948; children—Sue Ann, Michael John. Steel supt. Hunkin-Conkey Constrn. Co., Cleve., 1949-58; pres., gen. mgr. Kelley Steel Erectors, Inc., Bedford, Ohio, 1958—; dir. Twinsburg Banking Co. (Ohio). Bd. dirs. Nat. Erectors Assn., Washington. Served with USMCR, 1943-45. Decorated Purple Heart, Gold Star. Clubs: Shaker Heights (Ohio) Union, Cleveland Athletic, Cleveland Racquet; Lost Tree (Palm Beach Fla.). Home: 2978 Courtland Blvd Shaker Heights OH 44122 also 11675 Lost Tree Way Lost Tree Village Palm Beach FL 33408 Office: 7220 Division St Bedford OH 44146

KELLEY, JOHN EDGAR, lawyer; b. Kansas City, Mo., Nov. 18, 1931; s. William and Evelyn (Taylor) K.; B.A., U. Mo., 1955, LL.M. in Urban Affairs, 1970; J.D., Kansas City U., 1958; m. Joanna May Weissbeck, Aug. 24, 1957; children—Kathryn Ann, John Michael. Admitted to Mo. bar, 1958; adminstrv. asst. to Rep. William Randall of Mo., 1958-60; asst. regional counsel SBA, Kansas City, Mo., 1960-62; county counsel Jackson County (Mo.), 1963-65; house counsel Charles F. Curry & Co., Kansas City, 1965-66, 72—; sec., dir. Curry Investment Co., Kansas City, 1975—; exec. dir. Little Blue Valley Sewer Dist., Jackson County, 1969-70; exec. dir. Charter Transition Commn., Jackson County, 1971-72. Mem. Manpower Planning Bd., Jackson County, 1970; campaign dir. Citizens Assn., Kansas City, Mo., 1971, Com. for County Progress, 1966; mem. Urban Ecumenical Com., 1965-66; chmn. Jackson County Dem. com., 1962-64; del. Mo. State Dem. com., 1968-70; sec. Kansas City Bd. Election Commrs., 1973-77, chmn., 1977—. Mem. Fed., Am., Kansas City (sec., dir.) bar assns., Mo. Bar Integrated, Am. Judicature Soc., Phi Delta Phi, Kappa Sigma. Episcopalian. Home: 11 E 109th Terr Kansas City MO 64114 Office: 20 W 9th St Kansas City MO 64105

KELLEY, VERNE ROBERT, social worker; b. Valley Center, Kans., May 23, 1923; s. Verne Leon and Goldie (Redfern) K.; B.A., U. Colo., 1949; M.S.W., U. Denver, 1953; children by previous marriage—Jan, Valerie, Alan; m. Patricia Lou Neal, Aug. 20, 1960; children—Elizabeth, Carolyn. Caseworker, Denver Dept. Welfare, 1949-51; probation officer Milw. Criminal Ct., 1953-55; psychiat. social worker Milw. Child Guidance Center, 1955-60; cons., adminstr. Iowa Mental Health Authority, Iowa City, 1960-67, exec. dir. N.W. Iowa Mental Health Center, Spencer, 1967-69; exec. dir. Mideastern Iowa Community Mental Health Center, Iowa City, 1969—; co-founder, pres. Community Mental Health Centers Assn. Iowa, Inc., 1967-69; founder N.W. Iowa Community Alcoholism Center, 1969; profl. adv. bd. Iowa Assn. Mental Health, 1961-69; co-founder, treas. Iowa City Crisis Intervention Center 1970—; project dir. Rural Communities Learn To Help Themselves, 1972-74. Bd. dirs. Iowa Alcoholism Found., 1968-69, Hoover Health Planning Council Iowa, 1970-73. Served with AUS, 1943-45. Recipient Appreciation award Mental Health Centers Assn. Iowa, 1971. Mem. Acad. Certified Social Workers, Nat. Assn. Social Workers (Social Worker of Year award 1975). Club: Kiwanis. Home: 376 Koser Iowa City IA 52240 Office: 505 E College St Iowa City IA 52240

KELLEY, VERNON EDWARD, labor union ofcl.; b. Tappen, N.D., Jan. 31, 1914; s. Charles E. and Helen C. (Dagan) K.; grad. high sch.; m. Ruby, 1940; 2 children. Bus. agt. local 13 Hotel and Restaurant Employees and Bartenders Internat. Union, 1940-41; personnel mgr. Stone & Webster Engring., 1941-44; with Aluminum Workers Internat. Union, 1946—, sec.-treas. local 205, 1947-53, research and edn. dir., 1953-67, exec. asst. to pres., 1967-75, pres., 1975—. Served in USMC, 1944-46. Office: 818 Olive St Saint Louis MO 63101*

KELLMAN, JEROLD LEE, editor; b. Chgo., Mar. 3, 1945; s. Bernard and Bertha Lillian (Goldberg) K.; A.B., U. Mich., 1967; M.A. (Ford Found. fellow), U. Calif., 1968, Ph.D. (Ford Found. Fellow), U. Calif., 1972; m. Nancy Lou Holleb, May 28, 1967; 1 son, Gabriel. Editor, Publs. Internat. Ltd., Chgo., 1972-74, mng. editor, 1974-75, sr. mng. editor, 1975-77, exec. editor, 1977—. Author: Presidents of the United States, 1975; contbg. author: Ency. Brit. Micropaedia, 1972, Ency. Brit. Yearbook, 1977, Peoples Almanac, 1974, Peoples Almanac II, 1977; contbr. to other hist. publs. Home: 9329 Crawford Ave Evanston IL 60203 Office: 3841 Oakton St Skokie IL 60076

KELLOGG, DARRELL DEAN, lawyer; b. Plainville, Kans., Oct. 29, 1931; s. Orville M. and Cozetta J. (Gager) K.; A.B., U. Kans., 1953; J.D., U. Chgo., 1959; m. Shirley D. Hillyer, Sept. 12, 1953; children—Roxanne, Kevin, Brett. Admitted to Kans. bar, 1959; practiced in Wichita, Kans., 1959—; mem. firm Kahrs, Nelson, Fanning, Hite & Kellogg. Mem. Wichita Bd. Edn., 1967-73. Bd. dirs. Wichita Legal Aid Soc., Urban Ministry, Quivira council Boy Scouts Am.; trustee Wichita Hist. Mus., 1977—; bd. dirs. Historic Cow Town, Wichita, 1977—. Served with USAF, 1953-56. Recipient Wichita Pub. Schs. Citizen's award, 1975. Mem. Am., Kans. (chmn. pub. relations com. 1965-68, chmn. aviation sect. 1973-75, exec. council 1976—), Wichita (pres. jr. bar 1961-62, bd. govs. 1976—) bar assns., Kans. (pres. 1971, del. nat. assembly, 1970-72), Nat. (legis. com. 1971-72) assns. sch. bds., Lambda Chi Alpha. Home: 9820 W 10th St Ct Wichita KS 67212 Office: 220 W Douglas St Wichita KS 67202

KELLOW, KEITH VANCE, dentist; b. Ithaca, Nebr., Jan. 29, 1924; s. Albert Charles Jame and Lena (Trenouth) K.; Regents scholar, Nebr. U., 1941-42, U. Iowa, 1942-43; B.S., Creighton U., 1947, D.D.S., 1952; m. Mary LaVaughn Spurgeon, May 29, 1967. Pvt. practice dentistry, Battle Creek, Iowa, 1952-58, Woodline, Iowa, 1959-67, Belpre, O., 1967—. Instr. sci. North Bend (Nebr.) Pub. High Sch., 1947-48. Served with U.S. Army, 1943-45. Mem. Ohio, Am. dental assns., Muskingham Valley Dental Soc., Delta Sigma Delta. Presbyn. (deacon 1971-73; elder 1974-77). Mason (32 deg.), Lion. Home: 815 Braun St Belpre OH 45714 Office: 517 C Main St Belpre OH 45714

KELLY, BRUCE BIRK, coll. pres.; b. Richmond Heights, Mo., Nov. 14, 1937; s. John Joseph and Laura Johanna (Hugger) K.; m. Mary Lou Rose, June 19, 1958; children—Kimberly, Christopher. B.S. in Edn., S.E. Mo. State U., 1962, M.Ed., 1965; Ed.D., U. Ill., 1968. Tchr. social scis. Pekin (Ill.) Community High Sch., 1962-65; asst. dean students, dir. student loan programs, dean men U. Ill., Champaign and

Chgo. Med. Center, 1965-69; asst. regional dir. Midwest region Am. Coll. Testing Programs, Chgo., 1969-73; mng. partner Rust and Kelly Devel. Corp., Columbia, Mo., 1973-75; asso. dir. admissions, Columbia Coll., 1975-77, dir. admissions, pres., 1977—. Scoutmaster Gt. Rivers council Boy Scouts Am., Columbia. Mem. Am. Psychol. Assn., NEA, Kappa Pi, Kappa Delta Pi, Phi Kappa Delta, Chi Gamma Iota, Kiwanis. Author: Academic Performance and Financial Assistance, 1970. Home: 2215 S Country Club Dr Columbia MO 65201 Office: Columbia Coll 8th St and Rogers St Columbia MO 65201

KELLY, DALE EMERY, cons. engr.; b. Centuria, Wis., Aug. 6, 1923; s. Arthur Emery and Helga Rosemine (Rasmussen) K.; student River Falls State Tchrs. Coll., 1941-42; B.E.E., U. Wis., 1948. With Carl C. Crane, Inc., cons. engrs., 1949-65; owner, mgr. Dale E. Kelly Co., cons. engrs., Belleville, Wis., 1965—; owner, operator Kelly Field, airport, Belleville. Served with USAAF, 1943-45. Decorated Air medal with three oak leaf clusters. Address: Route 2 Belleville WI 53508

KELLY, ERNEST BYRON, JR., investment banker; b. Chgo., Oct. 27, 1915; s. Ernest Byron and Clara (Johnson) K.; A.B., U. Ill., 1937; LL.D. (hon.), Nat. U., San Diego, 1977; m. Kathryn Sumner Canfield, Mar. 7, 1942; children—Ernest Byron III, Michael W. Sales trainee Halsey Stuart and Co., Inc., Chgo., 1937-39, salesman, Detroit, 1940-41, mgr., Detroit, 1946-65, pres., chief exec. officer, Chgo., 1967-70, chmn. bd., chief exec. officer, 1970-76, also dir.; dir. Chgo. Title and Trust Co., 1968-73; v.p. Blyth & Co., Inc., 1965-67; dir., exec. com. Bache & Co., 1973-76, vice-chmn. bd., 1974-76; vice chmn. bd. Bache Halsey Stuart Shields Inc., 1977—, mem. exec. com., dir. Bache Group Inc., 1974—. Mem. Midwest Stock Exchange, asso. mem. Am. Stock Exchange; allied mem. N.Y. Stock Exchange. Mem. City Council Grosse Pointe, Mich., 1963-67; pres. Grosse Pointe Little League, 1963-64; trustee Municipal Adv. Council Mich., 1958-67, chmn., 1967-68; chpt. chmn. United Found. Torch Dr., 1961-65; mem. Wayne County Bd. Suprs., 1965-67. Bd. dirs. Nat. Conf. Christians and Jews, 1968-70; U. Ill. Found., 1973—, Chgo. Youth Centers; trustee, exec. com. Loyola U., Chgo., 1972-76; mem. adv. com. Coll. Commerce and Bus. Adminstrn., U. Ill., 1968—. Served with USNR, 1941-45, ret. lt. comdr. Mem. Securities Industry Assn. Am. (exec. com. Mich. div. 1966-68), Financial Analysts Soc. Detroit, Mil. Order World Wars, U. Ill. Alumni, Chgo. Assn. Stock Exchange Firms (bd. govs. 1970-74, chmn. 1973-74), Chgo. Assn. Commerce and Industry, Nat. Wildlife Fedn., Art Inst. Chgo., Field Mus. Natural History, Chgo. Symphony Orch., Newcomen Soc., Audubon Soc., Delta Kappa Epsilon. Republican. Presbyn. Clubs: Bond (pres. 1952-53), Detroit; Chicago, Mid-America, Attic, Little LaSalle St. (dir.), Metropolitan, Commercial (Chgo.); Wall Street (N.Y.C.); Onwentsia (Lake Forest, Ill.). Home: 501 Cambridge Ln Lake Bluff IL 60044 Office: 135 S LaSalle St Chicago IL 60690

KELLY, GLENN VINCENT, printing co. exec.; b. Britt, Iowa, Mar. 30, 1913; s. Martin Thomas and Anna K. (Sherman) K.; student U. Mo., 1933-38; m. Laurraine Brackette, Aug. 14, 1961; children—Kim Martin, Kirk Vincent. Pres., Kelly Press Inc., Columbia, Mo., 1934—, Graphic Engraving Service, Columbia, 1946-60; dir. Columbia Indsl. Devel. Corp., Silvey Corp., Columbia; co-dir. tourist promotion Great River Rd. Assn. Co., 1965-68; pres. Kelly-Stoddard, Inc., 1965-68; v.p. Kelly Assos., Inc., 1960-70. Mem. Columbia Bd. Health, 1955-60; chmn. Columbia Planning and Zoning Commn., 1961-62; bd. dirs. United Fund, Columbia, 1959-61, Boone County chpt. ARC, 1946-60, YMCA, Columbia, 1958-62, Great River council Boy Scouts Am., 1960-66. Served with C.E., U.S. Army, 1943-46; ETO. Mem. Mo. Press Assn., Printing Industry Am. (dir. 1960-64), Mo. Good Roads Assn., U.S., Mo., Columbia (pres. 1956-57) chambers commerce, Am. Legion, VFW, Am. Feline Soc. (v.p. 1950-72). Democrat. Club: Lions (pres. 1954-55). Home: Route 6 Columbia MO 65201 Office: 201 S 8th St Columbia MO 65201

KELLY, JOHN TERENCE, architect; b. Elyria, Ohio, Jan. 27, 1922; s. Thomas Alo and Coletta Margaret (Conrad) K.; B.Arch., Carnegie Mellon U., 1949; M.Arch., Harvard U., 1951, M.Landscape Architecture (Charles Eliot Norton fellow), 1952. Prin., John Terence Kelly, architect, Cleve., 1954—; vis. critic, lectr. U. Mich., U. Cin., Case Western Res. U., McGill U. Bd. dirs. Nova. Served with inf. AUS, 1943-46. Fulbright fellow, Munich, Germany, 1953. Recipient Cleve. Arts prize in Architecture, 1968. Mem. AIA (nat. com. on design), Am. Inst. Landscape Architects, Am. Inst. Planners, Am. Soc. Planning Ofcls., Western Res. Hist. Soc. Home: 2646 N Moreland Blvd Cleveland OH 44120 Office: 4614 Prospect Ave Cleveland OH 44103

KELLY, JOSEPH FRANCIS, JR., broadcasting co. exec.; b. Bklyn., July 24, 1941; s. Joseph F. and Mary Genevive (Griffin) K.; B.S., Fordham U., 1965; M.B.A., N.Y. U., 1969; m. Sharon Parke, Dec. 26, 1965; children—Steven, Deborah, Michael, David. Bus. mgr. ABC Radio Network, various divs., N.Y.C., 1962-72, account exec., Detroit office, 1972-74, Chgo. office, 1974-75, sales mgr., Detroit Officer, 1975—, v.p., 1977—, regional sales mgr., 1975—; dir. Detroit Radio Adv. Group, 1975—. Bd. dirs. Troy Half-Pint Football, Inc. Mem. Am. Mktg. Assn. Republican. Roman Catholic. Clubs: K.C., Lions, Recess. Home: 5766 Bingham St Troy MI 48098 Office: 20777 W Ten Mile Rd Southfield MI 48075

KELLY, LEONARD MICHAEL, dentist; b. Streator, Ill., July 13, 1908; s. Michael Joseph and Elizabeth Alice (Marley) K.; B.Dental Sci., Loyola U., Chgo., D.D.S., 1933; m. Mary Esther Bermingham, June 30, 1945; 1 son, Leonard Richard. Gen. practice dentistry, Kankakee, Ill., 1934-42; prof. dental prosthodonitcs Northwestern U., 1959-62; practice dentistry specializing in prosthodontics, Kankakee, 1962—. Served with USNR, 1942-45. Fellow Ill. Dental Soc., Am. Coll. Dentists, Midwest Acad. Prosthodontics; mem. Am. Dental Assn., Kankakee Dist. Dental Soc., Am. Prosthodontic Soc., Fedn. Prosthodontic Orgns., Ill. Dental Service, Tau Epsilon Delta. Roman Catholic. Elk. Club: Gaslight. Home: 1122 S Elm Ave Kankakee IL 60901 Office: 450 Kennedy Dr Kankakee IL 60901

KELLY, MARGARET GRIMES, realty exec., artist; b. Denver, Jan. 21, 1902; d. Charles Ysla and Sarah Rosina (Pennebaker) Grimes; B.A., U. Wash., 1923; postgrad. Columbia U., 1924, U. Minn., 1949, Mpls. Sch. Art, 1950-51; m. Charles Joseph Kelly, Jr., Aug. 18, 1928; 1 son, Charles Joseph. Tchr., St. Mary's Sch., Peekskill, N.Y., 1923-24, Miss Spence's Sch., N.Y.C., 1924-28; sales real estate Thorpe Bros., Mpls., 1960-64; owner, broker real estate firm, Wayzata, Minn., 1964—; exhibited in group shows Mpls. Inst. Arts, 1950-52, Minnetonka Center Arts, 1970-71, Lake Minnetonka Garden Club, 1958, 69; diaramas created for Gen. Mills Co. Mpls., Betty Crocker Kitchens, Peavey Co. Founder Minnetonka Art Center, 1950, pres., 1962-64; mem. state adv. com. Citizens for Eisenhower, 1948-49; lobbyist mosquito abatement, anti-billboards, legalized abortion, daylight-saving, tax reform Minn. Legislature, 1949-65; del. Rep. State Conv., 1970; mem. city council Village of Tonka Bay, 1972—; trustee Abbott-Northwestern Hosp., pres. bd. trustees, 1946-47, v.p. bd. trustees, 1968—; trustee Stevens Sq. Home Aged Women, sec. bd. trustees, 1969-70; trustee Minnetonka Garden Club; bd. dirs. Planned Parenthood Minn. Mem. Minn. Bd. Realtors, Wayzata C. of C. (dir. 1975, Citizen of Year 1975), Kappa Kappa Gamma (Achievement award 1975). Clubs: Woodhill Country, Mpls. Home: 4780 Manitou Rd Tonka Bay MN 55331 Office: 429 E Lake St Wayzata MN 55391

KELLY, MICHAEL DANIEL, regional mktg. exec.; b. Rochester, N.Y., Nov. 3, 1946; s. Daniel and Mary (Metchick) Kelly; B.S. in Advt., Ferris State Coll., 1970. With Young & Rubicam, 1970-71, Campbell Ewald Co., Detroit, 1971-72; account exec. Noble Dury Co., Nashville, 1972-76; regional mktg. mgr. Pizza Hut, Lenexa, Kans., 1976—. Home: 11900 W 66th St Shawnee Mission KS 66216 Office: 14975 W 99th St Lenexa KS 66215

KELLY, RAYMOND RANSOME, JR., ednl. adminstr.; b. Chgo., Sept. 9, 1912; s. Raymond Ransome and Bessie Mae (Case) K.; A.B., Ill. Coll., 1935, LL.D., 1969; M.S., Ind. U., 1946; m. Lois Eileen McNeely, Dec. 10, 1938. Tchr. Jr. Mil. Acad., Chgo., 1935-36; head English dept. boxing coach Mo. Mil. Acad., Mexico, 1936-39; English tchr. Howe Mil. Sch., Howe, Ind., 1939-43, head English dept., 1946-48, headmaster, 1948-65, supt., 1965—. Served to lt. (j.g.), USNR, 1943-45. Recipient Educator's medal, Freedoms Foundn., 1974. Mem. Assn. Mil. Colls. and Schs. (pres. 1974-75). Home: 602 Union St Howe IN 46746 Office: Academy Pl Howe IN 46746

KELLY, ROBERT DONALD, mgmt. cons.; b. Chgo., Sept. 14, 1929; s. Donald Francis and Irene Sarah (Gardner) K.; B.S. Indsl. Engring., Iowa State U., 1951; M.S., Purdue U., 1955, Ph.D., 1957; m. Kay Romayne Black, Apr. 25, 1959; children—Kim Robert, Kris Donald, Candis Elizabeth. Faculty, Purdue U., Lafayette, Ind., 1953-57; with A.T. Kearney, Inc., Chgo., 1957—, v.p., 1968—; dir. Allied Farm Equipment, Duff Truck Line, Smith Transp. Co. Mem. bd. edn. Dist. 86, Hinsdale (Ill.) High Sch., 1976—; chmn. bd. trustees Presbyterian Ch., Clarendon Hills, Ill., 1969-72, chmn. bd. deacons, 1966-69. Served to 1st lt. USAF, 1951-53. Mem. Am. Psychol. Assn., Inst. Mgmt. Cons., Sigma Xi. Clubs: Economic, Univ. (Chgo.). Home: 120 S Elm St Hinsdale IL 60521 Office: 100 S Wacker Dr Chicago IL 60606

KELLY, THOMAS JOSEPH, lawyer; b. Chgo., Mar. 1, 1938; s. James J. and Jean M. (Lunny) K.; B.B.A., U. Notre Dame, 1961, LL.D., 1963; m. Gail M. Dina, Nov. 18, 1961; children—Thomas Patrick, Susan Gail, Nancy Jean. Admitted to Ill. bar, 1962; atty. First Nat. Bank Chgo., 1962-67; mem. firm Kelly & Cohler, 1967-68, Pedersen & Houpt, Chgo., 1968—; dir. Chapel Hill Gardens, Inc. Served with AUS, 1962. Mem. Am., Ill. bar assns. Roman Catholic (mem. parish counsel 1973). Asst. editor Notre Dame Lawyer, 1961-62. Home: 1336 Alvin Ct Glenview IL 60025 Office: 180 N LaSalle St Chicago IL 60601

KELMAN, STEPHEN JAY, chiropractor; b. Louisville, Feb. 11, 1944; s. Ben and Billie Ethel (Hark) K.; A.A., U. Louisville, 1968; D.Chiropractic magna cum laude, Palmer Coll. Chiropractic, 1971; m. Delores Sue Callaway, Feb. 11, 1968; 1 son, Jason David. Dir., Chiropractic Arts Center, Fort Wayne, Ind., 1971-72; owner, Three Rivers Chiropractic Center, Fort Wayne, Ind., 1972—. Bd. dirs. Allen County chpt. Am. Cancer Soc., 1976—. Rep., Fort Wayne Jewish Fedn., 1975—; bd. dirs. N.E. Suburban adv. council No. Ind. Health Systems Agy., B'nai Jacob Synagogue, 1973-76; advisor B'nai B'rith Youth Orgn., 1972—. Served with U.S. Army, 1964-66. Recipient Service awards Ind. State Chiropractic Assn., 1974, 75; Ky. Col. Mem. Am. Chiropractic Assn., Ky. Assn. Chiropractors, Ky. Chiropractic Soc., Ind. State Chiropractic Assn., Inc. (dir. 1973-77, 2d v.p. 1977-78), Allen County Chiropractic Soc. (pres. 1973-75), Delta Delta Pi, Pi Tau Delta. Jewish. Mem. B'nai B'rith. Home: 7408 Kingsway Dr Fort Wayne IN 46809 Office: 3310 E State Blvd Fort Wayne IN 46805

KELSEY, GLADYS H., historian; b. Gaylord, Mich., Nov. 2, 1897; d. David A. and Florence (Kittle) Hatt; B.A., U. Mich., 1938, M.A., 1941; Ph.D., Wayne State U., 1968; m. W.K. Kelsey, Nov. 28, 1917 (dec.); children—Barbara Kelsey Madison, Harrison Mitchell, Jane Kelsey Steeh. Corr., N.Y. Times Watchtower, N.Y.C., 1925-39; columnist Detroit Saturday Night, 1924-38; scholar in residence Bridwell Library So. Meth. U., traveling hist. scholar, Peru, Mexico. Author: The Baroque—A Life Style, 1977. Home: Whittier Towers 415 Burns Dr Detroit MI 48214

KELSEY, RIDELL ARCHIBALD, clergyman; b. Oak Park, Ill., May 10, 1917; s. Ridell Archibald and Adah Muriel (Bassett) K.; B.C.S., Drake U., 1939; S.T.B., and S.T.M., Boston U., 1942; postgrad. Willamette U., 1942-45; m. Margaret Eleanor Rupp, Oct. 12, 1941; children—Wayne, Lois, Bruce, Elizabeth. Ordained to ministry, United Meth. Ch., 1942; pastor So. Middleboro and S. Carver, Mass., 1941-42, W. Salem and Summit, Oreg., 1942-45, Mt. Morris, Ill., 1945-49, Evergreen Park, Ill., 1949-60, Sterling, Ill., 1960-63, Brookfield, Ill., 1963—; radio preacher Stas. WEBH and WEAW, 1963-77; mem. bd. evangelism United Meth. Ch., 1976—, sec. No. Ill. Conf. Bd. of Pensions, 1968-76, bd. health and welfare, 1960-68, bd. missions, 1948-52; chaplain CAP, 1963—. Mem. Gross Sch. PTA, Brookfield, 1966-68; bd. dirs. West Cook County Heart Assn., 1969—, chmn. div. Meml. Gifts, 1972—; bd. dirs. Brookfield Swimming Pool Assn., 1969-76; mem. Library Bd., Village of Brookfield, 1975—; bd. dirs. No. Ill. Conf. Credit Union, 1977—. Recipient Meritorious Service award Masons, 1962, Masonic Service award, 1970; Meritorious Service award Chgo. Heart Assn., 1971; Grand Cross of Color, Internat. Order of Rainbow for Girls, 1973. Mem. Disciplined Order of Christ, Brookfield Ministerial Assn. (pres. 1969—), Order of Barnabas, Royal Order Scotland, Order of True Kindred, Order of the Builders, Internat. Biog. Assn., Philalethes Soc., Ill. Hist. Soc., World Meth. Hist. Soc., Clubs: Order Eastern Star, Masons (33 deg., Shriner) (grand chaplain 1962-64), Order of DeMolay (dist. dept. 1962-63). Address: PO Box 132 Brookfield IL 60513

KELSEY, VICTOR ANDREW, food co. exec.; b. Mattawamkeag, Me., Sept. 21, 1936; s. Charles A. and Helen A. (Trueworthy) K.; student Am. Tech. Soc., 1962; diploma Humboldt Inst., 1962; clk.-telegrapher Me. Central R.R., Mattawamkeag, 1955-59; clk.-dispatcher Milw. Motor Transp. Co., St. Paul, 1962-65; transp. coordinator Land O'Lakes, Inc., Albert Lea, Minn., 1965—. Served with U.S. Army, 1959-62. Recipient certificate achievement Tech. Edn. Center Albert Lea, 1971, 72, 73. Mem. Nat. Council Phys. Distbn. Mgmt., Am. Mgmt. Assn., Sertoma Internat. (life). Elk, Moose. Lutheran. Home: Conger MN 56020 Office: 702 13th St Albert Lea MN 56007

KELSO, HAROLD GLEN, physician; b. Newport, Ky., Apr. 1, 1929; s. Harold Glen and Alvina Marie (Hehl) K.; B.S., U. Dayton (O.), 1951; M.D., St. Louis U., 1955; m. Janet Rae Cooper, Aug. 12, 1950; children—Harold Glen III, Susan Annette. Intern St. Elizabeth Hosp., Dayton, 1955-56; practice medicine specializing in family practice, Centerville, O., 1956—; mem. teaching staff St. Elizabeth Hosp., Dayton, O.; mem. staff Kettering (O.) Meml. Hosp., chief staff, 1975-76; asso. clin. prof. family practice Wright State U.; mem. faculty Kettering Coll. Med. Arts; med. dir. Kettering Convalescent Center. Pres., vice mayor, Centerville, O., 1960-62; pres. Bd. Edn., Centerville city schs., 1969-72; trustee Western O. Found. Med. Care. Served with U.S. Army, 1957-59. Diplomate Am. Bd. Family Practice. Fellow Am. Acad. Family Practice; mem. Am., Ohio, Montgomery County (sec. 1970) med. assns., Phi Chi. Rotarian (pres. local club 1974-75). Home: 2212 E Alex-Bellbrook Rd Centerville OH 45459 Office: 330 N Main St Centerville OH 45459

KELSO, JAMES JUDE, obstetrician, gynecologist; b. Washington, July 2, 1933; s. Arthur David and Helen Margaret (Taylor) K.; B.S., U. Md., 1956, M.D., 1958; m. Greta Joyce Johnson, Sept. 3, 1955; children—Leslie Ann, Elizabeth Ann, Karen Leigh, Arthur David, Marianne, Suzanne, James Francis. Intern, Youngstown (Ohio) Hosp., 1958-59; resident in obstetrics and gynecology Georgetown U. Hosp., Washington, 1961-64; practice medicine specializing in obstetrics, gynecology, Des Moines, 1964—; chief med. staff Mercy Hosp., 1973, chief dept. obstetrics and gynecology, 1977—; chief dept. obstetrics, gynecology Broadlawns Hosp., Des Moines, 1977—; dir. Mercy Hosp. Found., Economy Data Products. Served to lt. comdr. USN, 1959-61. Mem. AMA, Iowa State, Polk County med. socs., Am. Coll. Obstetrics and Gynecology, Am. Bd. Obstetrics and Gynecology, Am. Infertility Soc., Iowa Found. Med. Care (dir.). Clubs: Embassy, Des Moines Golf and Country. Home: 2324 Terrace Rd Des Moines IA 50312 Office: 1410 Woodland Ave Des Moines IA 50309

KELSON, ALLEN HOWARD, editor, dining critic; b. Chgo., May 4, 1940; s. Ben and Esther Mae (Ashkin) K.; student U. Ill., Chgo., 1957, U. Ill., Urbana, 1958; B.A. in English, Roosevelt U., Chgo., 1965; m. Carla S. Lipson, Aug. 18, 1966; children—David Lauren, Melina Elisabeth. Catalog copywriter Sears, Roebuck & Co., Chgo., 1962-64, sales promotion writer, 1964-67, spl. projects dir., catalog advt. div., 1967-68; editor-in-chief WFMT Guide, Chgo. Guide, Chgo. mag. WFMT, Inc., Chgo., 1968—; pub. relations and advt. mgr. WFMT, Inc., 1968-70, v.p., dir., 1974—; asso. pub. Chgo. mag., 1977—. Prin. Kelson Kapuler Advt., 1962-68; editor Chgo. GuideBook, 1972-73; lectr. Nat. Retail Mchts. Assn., 1973, Nat. Restaurant Assn., 1975. Mem. adv. staff Walt Disney Magnet Sch., Chgo. Bd. Edn., 1974-75; judge Ill. Women's Press Assn., 1976. Mem. adv. council Internat. Visitors Center, Chgo.; bd. dirs. Friends Highland Park (Ill.) Library. Recipient Merit award Chgo. Advt. Club, 1965, Designer awards Chgo. 4, 1973, 74; award Am. Inst. Graphic Arts, 1976. hon. mem. Duncan Hines Meml. Fellowship, 1q71. Mem. Am. Soc. Mag. Editors. Home: 456 Woodland Rd Highland Park IL 60035 Office: 500 N Michigan Ave Chicago IL 60611

KELTNER, RAYMOND MARION, JR., surgeon, educator; b. Springfield, Mo., Apr. 15, 1929; s. Raymond Marion and Othello Mary (Forgey) K.; B.S., Drury Coll., 1950; B.S. in Medicine, U. Mo., 1955; M.D., Washington U., St. Louis, 1957; m. Carla Ann Clark, May 10, 1974; children—Aintre B., Raymond M., Merl K., Albert D., Gisela W. Practice medicine specializing in surgery, Houston, 1962-63, Houghton, Mich., 1966-68; mem. faculty Washington U. Sch. Medicine, 1963-66; asst. prof. surgery St. Louis U. Sch. Medicine, 1968-71, asso. prof., 1971-76, prof., 1976—, attending surgeon St. Louis U. Hosp., 1968—; chief surgery St. Louis City Hosp. Fellow Am. Coll. Surgeons; mem. AMA (Service Recognition award). Contbr. articles to surg. jours. Office: 1325 S Grand Ave St Louis MO 63104

KELTON, DALE LYNN, mental health adminstr.; b. Poplar Bluff, Mo., Jan. 11, 1940; s. Fred Len and Mildred Helena (Giltner) K.; B.A., So. Ill. U., 1962; M.A., Bradley U., 1967; Ph.D., U. Okla., 1969; m. Dorothy Ann Bailey, Aug. 18, 1962. Clin. psychologist Jacksonville (Ill.) State Hosp., 1963-65, U. Okla. Psychol. Clinic, 1965-69, Helena (Okla.) State Sch. for Boys, 1968-69; dir. edn. and tng. Andrew McFarland Mental Health Zone Center, Springfield, Ill., 1969-73, dep. regional adminstr. Adolf Meyer Center, Decatur, Ill., 1973-75, acting supt., 1974—; regional adminstr. Ill. Dept. Mental Health, Region 3B, 1975—; psychol. cons. Okla. Gov.'s Head Start Program, 1966, Ft. Supply (Okla.) State Hosp., 1967-69; counseling psychologist U. Okla. Counseling Center, 1967-68. Mem. Am. Psychol. Assn. Home: 1410 S Park Ave Springfield IL 62704 Office: 2310 E Mound Rd Decatur IL 62526

KEMBLE, ERNEST DELL, educator; b. Memphis, Dec. 19, 1935; s. Clarance Dell and Lillian Mae (Swett) K.; B.A. cum laude, Memphis State U., 1962; M.A., Vanderbilt U., 1965, Ph.D., 1968; m. Darolis Cathryn Spencer, Aug. 31, 1963; 1 dau., Katrina Coleen. Instr., U. Minn., Morris, 1966-67, asst. prof. psychology, 1968-70, asso. prof., 1970-76, prof., 1976—, U. summer research fellow, 1969, 75, U. grantee, 1969, 70, 74. Research asso. Wis. Regional Primate Center, 1967. NIMH postdoctoral fellow, 1969-70; recipient Horace T. Morse award for contbns. to undergrad. edn., 1977. Mem. A.A.A.S., Animal Behavior Soc., Am., Midwestern psychol. assns., Psychonomic Soc., Sigma Xi. Contbr. articles to profl. jours. Research on functions of limbic system of brain. Home: 105 E 9th St Morris MN 56267 Office: U Minn Dept Psychology Morris MN 56267

KEMENY, GEORGE ORAVEC, physician, clin. dir., educator; b. Tvrdosin, Czechoslovakia, May 18, 1913; s. Sigmund and Jolana (Haas) K.; came to U.S., 1949, naturalized, 1952; M.D., Komensky U., Bratislava, Czechoslovakia, 1937; m. Esther Berkowitz, Apr. 10, 1940; 1 dau., Mary Judith. Chmn. dept. medicine Gen. Hosp., Presov, Czechoslovakia, 1946-49; practice medicine specializing in internal medicine, Wellsville, Ohio, 1951-73; asst. prof. Chgo. Med. Sch., 1973-74; in-patient dir. Family Practice Center MacNeal Meml. Hosp., Berwyn, Ill., 1974-76; asso. prof. dept. family practice Abraham Lincoln Sch. Medicine, Chgo., 1974—; asso. dir. Family Practice Center U. Ill. Hosp., Chgo., 1976—. Served as 1st lt. M.C., Czechoslovakian Army, 1937-39. Diplomate Am. Bd. Family Practice. Fellow Am. Acad. Family Physicians. Contbr. papers to med. jours. Home: 1400 E 55th Pl Chicago IL 60637

KEMP, ARNOLD RAYMOND, mech. engr.; b. Champaign, Ill., Nov. 22, 1918; s. Arnold Raymond and Helen Ruth (Dillon) K.; student U. Ill., 1937-38, Knox Coll., 1938-40; B.S., Bradley U., 1946; m. Mary Elizabeth Quick, Sept. 20, 1941. Mech. engr. John Deere Co., Moline, Ill., 1947-48; design engr. Beling Engring. Cons., Moline, 1948-60; office mgr., Burlington, Iowa, 1961—. Trustee YWCA, 1972—; mem. Bd. Elec. Examiners, Burlington, 1970—. Served with AUS, 1942-45. Mem. Burlington Engrs. Club, Illuminating Engrs. Soc. Methodist. Clubs: Lions, Eagles. Home: 2900 Sunnyside Ave Burlington IA 52601 Office: 214 1/2 N 4th St N Burlington IA 52601

KEMP, GEORGE PENDLETON, state ofcl.; b. Downey, Calif., Mar. 9, 1929; s. George Pendleton, and Violet Snow (Thompson) K.; grad. high sch.; m. Clara Elizabeth Greening, July 1, 1949; children—Gregory, Donna, David. Fed. bank examiner, 1956-61, supervising state bank examiner, state of Mo.; former v.p. Citizens Bank of Pacific (Mo.); now asst. v.p. Bank of St. Louis. Mem. Mo. Bank Mgmt. Com.; instr. East Central Jr. Coll. Scoutmaster, treas. Council 484 Boy Scouts Am., St. Louis, 1970—. Bd. dirs., treas. Springfield Christian Schs., Inc., 1960—. Served with USNR, 1946-48. Mem. Franklin Gasconade Bankers Assn. (pres.) Pacific C. of C. (dir.). Mem. Ch. of Christ (deacon 1967, chmn. finance com. 1968, elder). Lion (v.p. 1963, tail twister 1963), Kiwanian (dir. Pacific chpt.). Home: Rt 4 Box 120 Pacific MO 63069 Office: PO Box 366 Pacific MO 63069

KEMPA, ROY G., market research co. exec.; b. Chgo., June 27, 1945; s. Anthony and Jean (Bolsinga) K.; B.A. in Bus. Adminstrn., St. Ambrose Coll., 1967; M.S. in Mktg., No. Ill. U., 1969; m. Marilyn Kranz, Feb. 8, 1969; children—Maureen, Carolyn, Sherilee. Instr. in bus. orgn. and mgmt. U. Wis., Platteville, 1969-71; dir. market research Chgo. Suburban Paddock Newspapers, Arlington Heights, Ill., 1971-75; mgr. client services Mid-Am. Research Co., Chgo., 1975—; mktg. cons. Paddock Corp., Arlington Heights, 1977—. Lay minister St. Marcelline Roman Catholic Ch., Schaumburg, Ill. Mem. Am. Mktg. Assn. Home: 1020 Sharon Ln Schaumburg IL 60193 Office: 200 E Randolph Dr Chicago IL 60606

KEMPE, ROBERT ARON, instrument co. exec.; b. Mpls., Mar. 6, 1922; s. Walter A. and Madge (Stoker) K.; B.Chem. Engring., U. Minn., 1943; postgrad. Case Western Res. U., 1946-49; m. Virginia Lou Wiseman, June 21, 1946; children—Mark A., Katherine A. Research engr., divisional sales mgr. TRW, Inc., Cleve., 1943-53; v.p. Metalphoto Corp., Cleve., 1954-63, pres., 1963-71; v.p., treas. Horizons Research, Inc., Cleve., 1970-71; pres. Allied Decals, Inc., Cleve., 1963-68; pres. Reuter-Stokes, Inc., Cleve., 1971—. Served to lt. (j.g.) USNR, 1944-46. Mem. Chemists Club N.Y.C., Inst. of Dirs. (London), Am. Nuclear Soc., Sigma Chi. Club: Country (Hudson, O.). Patentee in field. Home: 242 Streetsboro St Hudson OH 44236 Office: 18530 S Miles Pkwy Cleveland OH 44128

KEMPER, CHARLES SAMUEL, dentist; b. Joplin, Mo., Mar. 12, 1933; s. Charles B. and Catharine (Walker) K.; student Joplin Jr. Coll., 1951-52, Washington U., St. Louis, 1952-53, Drury Coll., Springfield, Mo., 1953-54; D.D.S., U. Mo., 1958; grad. Famous Writers Sch., 1976; m. Mary Maurine George, Sept. 20, 1958; children—Kristina Lynn, Samantha Sue. Gen. practice dentistry, Blue Springs, Mo., 1958—; organizer, sole operator charity dental clinic Don Bosco Youth Center, Kansas City, Mo. Mem. Blue Springs C. of C., Kappa Alpha, Psi Omega. Prebyn. (elder). Rotarian. Home: 48 D Lake Tapawingo Blue Springs MO 64015 Office: 1808 W Main St Blue Springs MO 64015

KEMPER, ROBERT GRAHAM, clergyman; b. Alton, Ill., Mar. 31, 1935; s. Robert Chatfield and Virginia (Owens) K.; B.A., Cornell Coll., Mt. Vernon, Iowa, 1957; B.D., U. Chgo., 1961; m. Margery Klontz, Mar. 30, 1959; children—Edward Michael, Virginia Ruth, Mary Elizabeth. Ordained to ministry Congregational Ch., 1961; pastor Newton Falls (Ohio) Congl. Ch., 1961-65, Watchung Ch., Upper Montclair, N.J., 1965-69; editor The Christian Ministry mag., Chgo., 1969—; asso. editor The Christian Century mag., 1969—; sr. minister First Congl. Ch. of Western Springs. Bd. dirs. Chgo. Theol. Sem.; bd. dirs. Lancaster Theol. Sem., mem. Pres.'s adv. council, 1967—; mem. gen. assembly N.J. Council Chs.; vice chmn. Union Montclair Devel. Corp., 1967—; bd. dirs. Children's Aid and Adoption Soc. N.J. Served with USNR, 1957-61. Mem. No. N.J. Assn. Central Atlantic Conf. United Ch. Christ. Clubs: Glen Ridge (N.J.) Country, Kiwanis. Author: An Elephants Ballet, 1977. Contbr. articles to religious publs.; editorial bd. Ministry Mag., 1966—; drama critic Christian Century, 1966-69; columnist A.D. mag. Home: 4325 Grand Ave Western Springs IL 60558 Office: 1106 Chestnut St Western Springs IL 60558

KEMPFER, LESTER LEROY, mcht.; b. Botkins, Ohio. July 28, 1932; s. Roy Agustas and Ruth Caroline (Knasel) K.; student Internat. Corr. Schs., 1969-70; m. Betty Crist, Feb. 6, 1952 (div. Nov. 1970); children—Connie Jo, Mark Leroy; m. 2d, Darlene Reimer, June 23, 1974. Bookkeeper, salesman Moore's, Inc., 1950-52, asst. mgr. to mgr., 1954-57; dept. mgr. Montgomery Ward, 1q57-66; inventory control Bernard Elec. Co., 1966-68; purchasing Westreco, Inc., 1968-71; dept. mgr. Montgomery Ward, 1971-76; owner, mgr. Book Nook & Prints, Marysville, Ohio, 1975—. Served with U.S. Army, 1951-53; Korea. Decorated Army Commendation medal. Mem. Profl. Picture Framing Assn., VFW, Union County Hist. Soc. Lutheran. Author: The Salem Light Guard, 1973. Office: 120 N Main St Maryville OH 43040

KEMPTHORNE, GERALD C., physician; b. Platteville, Wis., Sept. 18, 1930; s. Guy McKinley and Matie (Hugill) K.; B.S., U. Wis., 1956; M.S., Kans. State U., 1957; M.D., U. Md., 1961; m. Maria F.G. Van Everdingen, July 30, 1966; children—Raymond, Guy. Intern Cook County Hosp., Chgo.; practice family medicine, Spring Green, Wis., 1962—; mem. staff Sauk Prairie Meml. Hosp. Chmn. Sauk County Republican Party, 1971-72. Served with USN, 1951-54. Diplomate Am. Bd. Family Practice, Nat. Bd. Med. Examiners. Mem. Am. Acad. Family Practice, AMA, Wis. Med. Soc., Acad. Psychosomatic Medicine, Am. Geriatrics Soc. Club: Lions. Home: RFD 2 Spring Green WI 53588 Office 153 E Jefferson St Spring Green WI 53588

KENAGA, EUGENE ELLIS, ecologist, entomologist; b. Midland, Mich., July 15, 1917; s. Ivan Arthur and Margaret Lena (Supe) K.; B.S., U. Mich., 1939; M.A., U. Kans., 1940; Ph.D., Tokyo U. Agr., 1977; m. Elisabeth Joan Bailey, Oct. 12, 1940; children—Dennis K., Marcia (Mrs. Morgan Edward Davis), David E. Asst. instr. entomology U. Kans., Lawrence, 1939-40; with Dow Chem. Co., Midland, 1940-44, 46—, asso. scientist, 1960—; cons. pesticide wildlife Mich. Dept. Agr., 1965-68, 77, Mich. Dept. Natural Resources, 1966-70, WHO, 1971, EPA, 1972-77, NATO, 1974, Am. Inst. Biol. Scis., 1974, 76, 77, U.S.A-USSR Sci. Info. Exchange, Tbilisi, USSR, 1976. Bd. dirs. Mich. Natural Resources Council, 1966-74, pres., 1972-73; mem. various coms. Nat. Acad. Scis., 1964, 71, 76; bd. dirs. Chippewa Nature Center, 1966-77, pres. 1966-70. Served to lt. USNR, 1944-46. Mem. Am. Ornithologists Union, Internat. Union Pure and Applied Chemistry (pesticide residue com. 1967-71), Nat. Agrl. Chems. Assn. (pesticide wildlife chmn. 1968-77), Entomol. Soc. Am., Ecol. Soc. Am., Wilson Soc., Mich. Audubon Soc. (pres. 1962-64), Sigma Xi, Phi Sigma. Club: Midland Nature (pres. 1953-55). Contbr. articles to profl. jours. and books. Patentee in field. Home: 3309 Isabella Rd Midland MI 48640 Office: PO Box 1706 Midland MI 48640

KENDALL, DONNA JOYCE, coll. ofcl.; b. Milan, Ill., Jan. 15, 1929; d. Orville Daniel and Marie Grace (Hansen) Kendall; A.A., Stephens Coll., 1948; B.A., State U. Iowa, 1950. Reporter, Milan (Ill.) Independent, 1950-56; pub. relations asst. Modern Woodmen of Am., Rock Island, Ill., 1956-57, publs. editor, 1957-60, asst. to pub. relations mgr., 1960-63; corporated pub. relations asst. Title Ins. & Trust Co., Los Angeles, 1963-69; mktg. officer Comml. & Farmers Nat. Bank, Oxnard, Calif., 1969-71; pub. info. dir. Western Ins. Infor. Service, Los Angeles, 1971-73; corporate relations mgr., asst. v.p. Lloyds Bank, Los Angeles, 1973-74; pub. relations dir. Palmer Coll. Chiropractic, Davenport, Iowa, 1974—. Free-lance pub. relations cons. in areas of real estate and politics. Recipient Achievement award Los Angeles Advt. Women, 1968. Mem. Pub. Relations Soc. Am. (dir. Los Angeles, 1966-67, v.p. Quad City chpt. 1978—), Los Angeles Advt. Women (dir. 1967-69, rec. sec. 1972-73, 1st v.p. 1973-74), Los Angeles C. of C. (dir. women's div. 1967-69, 71-74), Calif. Assn. Real Estate Tchrs. (dir. 1965-69), Davenport C. of C., Am. Advt. Fedn., DAR, Alpha Delta Pi, Gamma Alpha Chi. Republican. Methodist. Home: 1804 16th St Rock Island IL 61201 Office: 1000 Brady St Davenport IA 52803

KENDALL, GEORGE PRESTON, ret. ins. co. exec.; b. Seattle, Aug. 11, 1909; s. George R. and Edna (Woods) K.; B.S., U. Ill., 1931; m. Helen A. Hilliard, Sept. 30, 1933; children—George Preston, Thomas C., Helen R. With Washington Nat. Ins. Co., Evanston, Ill., 1931-76, sec., 1950-76, exec. v.p., 1956-62, pres., 1962-67, chmn. bd., 1968-76, also chief exec. officer, dir.; chmn. bd., chief exec. officer, dir. Washington Nat. Corp., 1969-76; dir. State Nat. Bank, Evanston. Served from 2d lt. to 1st lt., inf. AUS, 1942-45. Decorated Purple Heart. Mem. Am. Life Ins. Assn., Health Ins. Assn. Am. (past chmn.), Ill., Evanston chambers commerce, Newcomen Soc. N. Am., Northwestern U., Assos., Nat. Coll. Edn. Assos., Kendall Fellows of Kendall Coll., Theta Chi. Mason (K.T. Shriner). Clubs: Optimist (pres. 1947), Univ. (Evanston); Westmoreland Country (Wilmette, Ill.); Bankers (Chgo.). Home: 70 Indian Hill Rd Winnetka IL 60093

KENDALL, JERRY D., geographer, educator; b. Indpls., May 3, 1940; s. Adrian L. and Edna A. (Farrow) K.; student U. Evansville, 1958-59; B.S., Ind. State U., 1962, M.A., 1966; Ed.D., Ind. U., 1969; m. Karen Sue Cox, June 21, 1962; 1 son, Jeffrey. Asst. prof. geography U. N.D., Grand Forks, 1969-70, U. Evansville (Ind.), 1970—; vis. lectr. Ind. U., 1966-69. Pres., Evansville chpt. Citizens Organized to Protect the Environment; mem. Population Reference Bur. Served with USMC, 1960. NDEA fellow, 1965. Mem. A.A.U.P. (pres. Evansville chpt.), Ind. Acad. Social Scis. (dir.), Nat. Soc. (pres. Evansville chpt.), Assn. Am. Geographers, Am. Geog. Soc., Nat. Council Geog. Edn., Nat. Geog. Soc., Am. Meteorol. Soc., Am. Assn. Higher Edn., Nat. Wildlife Fedn., Gamma Upsilon Theta, Phi Delta Kappa (named Outstanding Am. Educator 1975). Home: 216 S Parker Dr Evansville IN 47714 Office: Dept Geography U Evansville Evansville IN 47702

KENDALL, RICHARD HALE, food co. exec.; b. Indpls., Mar. 24, 1930; s. Max L. and Elberta (Hodson) K.; A.B., Earlham Coll., 1952; M.B.A., Ind. U., 1953; m. Ann Woolley, Sept. 6, 1953; children—Michael F., Thomas H. Bus mgr. Friends United Meeting, Richmond, Ind., 1953-59; v.p., treas. Honeggers & Co., Inc., Fairbury, Ill., 1959-68; v.p. Heath Tecna Corp., Kent, Wash., 1968-71; chmn. bd., chief exec. officer, treas., dir. Maplehurst Farms, Inc., Indpls., 1971—; pres., treas., dir. Advanced Mktg. Systems Corp., Indpls., 1971—; treas., dir. Sr. Trust Corp., Indpls., 1971—; dir., sec. Master Dairies, Inc., 1971—; treas., dir. Maplehurst Deli-Bake, Inc., 1971—; chmn. bd., dir. Maplehurst Deli-Bake/South, Inc., Carrollton, Ga., 1977—, Freshmark Foods, Inc., Indpls., 1977. Mem. nat. export expansion council U.S. Dept. Commerce, 1969-71; mem. spl. levy tax com. State Wash., 1970-71; bd. dirs. Greater Indpls. Progress Com., 1977—; chmn. adminstrn. and orgn. Highline Coll., 1970-71; bd. trustees Earlham Coll., 1977—, Friends United Meeting, 1974—; advisory council Conner Prairie Pioneer Settlement, 1977—, dir. Friends World Com. for Consultation, 1977. Mem. Milk Found. Indpls. (dir. 1971—), Midwest Dairy Products Assn. (dir. 1973—). Clubs: Rotary, Indpls., Meridian Hills Country. Athletic. Home: 7525 N Central Ave Meridian Hills Indianapolis IN 46240 Office: 3745 Farnsworth St Indianapolis IN 46241

KENDALL, ROBERT ANDREW, apparel mfg. co. exec.; b. Winthrop, Mass., July 30, 1934; s. George Allen and Evelyn Lena (Legere) K.; student U. Miami (Fla.), 1956-60; m. Edna MacDonald, May 6, 1971. Mfrs. rep., Salt Lake City and San Francisco, 1960-68; owner, mgr. Golden Rule Vending Co., Oakland, Calif., 1968-73; gen. mgr. Continental Account Servicing House, Inc., St. Louis, 1973-76; pres. Daisy Legs, Inc., St. Louis, 1976—. also dir. Served with USMC, 1954-56. Republican. Roman Catholic. Home: 4400 Lindell St St Louis MO 63108 Office: 2628 Big Bend Blvd St Louis MO 63143

KENDALL, ROBERT LLEWELLYN, contractor; b. Mishawaka, Ind., May 3, 1923; s. Harold E. and Jessie (Pettengill) K.; student pub. schs., Cadillac, Mich.; m. Betty Louise Powers, July 23, 1943; children—Stephen, Jane, Kay, Holly, David, Roberta. Owner, Kendall Constrn. Co., Cadillac, 1945-63, Cadillac Lumber Co.; pres. Robert Kendall, Inc.; v.p. Hungerford Constrn. Co., Jackson, Mich. Mayor, Cadillac, 1953-55; mem. Wexford County Bd. Suprs., County Social Welfare Bd., County and City Planning Bds.; chmn. Bd. Edn., 1948-50; pres. Mich. Extended Care Bldg. Corp. Served from pvt. to capt. USAAF, 1942-45; ETO. Mem. C. of C. (pres. 1958-60), Am. Legion. Presbyterian (deacon). Club: Elks. Home: 340 Edward St Jackson MI 49201 Office: PO Box 499 Jackson MI 49204

KENDLE, JOHN EDWARD, historian; b. London, Apr. 14, 1937; s. Arthur and Sybil Violet Mary (Jordan) K.; came to Can., 1948, naturalized, 1957; B.A., U. Man. (Can.), 1958; Ph.D. (Can. Council fellow), U. London, 1965; m. Judith Ann Halsey, Aug. 3, 1963; children—John Stephen, Andrew Bruce, Nancy Elizabeth. Asst. prof. history U. Man., 1965-70, asso. prof., 1970-75, prof., 1975—; vis. research fellow Australian Nat. U. and Auckland U., 1967-68. Can. Council fellow, 1967-68, 71-72; recipient Research award Can. Council, 1975-76. Mem. Canadian Hist. Assn.,Am. Com. Irish Studies, Royal Commonwealth Soc. Author: The Colonial and Imperial Conferences 1887-1911, 1967; The British Empire-Commonwealth 1897-1931, 1972; The Round Table Movement and Imperial Union, 1975; John Bracken: A Political Biography. Home: 149 The Glen Winnipeg MB R2M 0B5 Canada Office: Saint John's Coll U of Man Winnipeg MB R3T 2M5 Canada

KENDRICK, VIRGINIA CATHERINE (MRS. W. DUDLEY KENDRICK), pianist, composer; b. Mpls., Apr. 8, 1910; d. Ralph and Lelia B. (Hall) Bachman; student music U. Minn., 1928-33; m. W. Dudley Kendrick, Nov. 28, 1934; children—Warren, Nancy (Mrs. Charles Ivey), James, Susan (Mrs. James Williamson), David. Organist, First Ch. of Christ Scientist, Excelsior, Minn., 1962-72, now asst. organist; organ music cons. Schmitt Music Co., Mpls., 1958—; pianist Andahazy Ballet Co., Mpls., 1958—. Mem. Am. Guild Organists, Nat. Fedn. Music Clubs, Sigma Kappa, Mu Phi Epsilon. Composer: Wealth of Mine, 1941; Little Red Hen, 1955; Goody Two Shoes, 1956; From My Window, 1960; Green is the Willow, 1965; Little Miss Whuffit, 1962; White Sky, 1967; Music is Beauty, 1969; Tribute, 1970; Jade Summer, 1971; A Young Boy, 1971; Before the World Was, 1974; Look Unto Me Saith Our God, 1975; I Will Lift Up Mine Eyes Unto the Hills, 1975; Lo, I Am With You Always Unto the End of the World, 1975; Hear My Cry, O God, 1975; The Lord God Omnipotent Reigneth, 1975; arranged hymns by Mary Baker Eddy: Mother's Evening Prayer, Brood O'er Us With Thy Sheltering Wing, In This Soft Velvet Night, Woman in the Shoe. Home: 5800 Echo Rd Shorewood MN 55331

KENDRO, RICHARD JOSEPH, steel co. exec.; b. Canton, O., Dec. 15, 1931; s. Joseph Francis and Anne Marie (Kvasnick) K.; grad. Embry-Riddle Sch. Aviation, 1952; B.S., Kent State U., 1958; m. Barbara Ann Goedicke, July 7, 1956; children—Margo E., Colby E. Display artist C.N. Vicary Co., Canton, 1949-51; salesman Standard Oil Co., Canton, 1955-56; cost analyst E.W. Bliss Co., Canton, 1956-58; plant mgr. Sparta Ceramic Co., East Sparta, O., 1958-66; plant mgr. Good Roads Machinery Corp., Canton, 1966-67; plant mgr. Cleaver-Brooks Co. div. Aqua-Chem., Inc., 1967-71, v.p. mfg. water tech. div., Milw., 1971-73, exec. v.p. water tech div., 1973-74, pres. Cleaver-Brooks div., 1974, v.p. parent co., 1974-76, sr. v.p., 1976—, also dir.; v.p., dir. Cleaver Brooks De Mexico, 1976—, Aqua-Chem, Pty (Australia), 1976—, VP C-B Sales & Service, 1976—; v.p. Maintek, Inc., 1966-68. Exhibited in group shows at Canton Art Inst., 1948, 49, North Canton Art Gallery, 1949, 50; instr. Indsl. Edn. Inst., Inst. for Better Confs. Exec. dir., asst. scoutmaster Buckeye council Boy Scouts Am., 1956-57; pres. P.T.A., 1966-67. Bd. dirs. Community Chest, 1966-67, Am. Boiler Mfrs. Assn., 1975—. Served with USAF, 1951-55. Named to Pa. Sports Hall of Fame. Mem. Internat. Platform Assn., Indsl. Mgmt. Club. Clubs: St. Michaels Mens, Toastmasters (past pres.), Lebanon Country. Office: PO Box 421 Milwaukee WI 53201

KENLY, GRANGER FARWELL, holding co. exec.; b. Portland, Oreg., Feb. 15, 1919; s. F. Corning and Ruth (Farwell) K.; A.B. cum laude, Harvard U., 1941; m. Suzanne Warner, Feb. 7, 1948; children—Margaret Farwell, Granger Farwell. Adminstrv. asst. to v.p. Poole Bros., Inc., Chgo., 1941-42; asst. advt. mgr. Sunset Mag., San Francisco, 1946-47; pub. relations, sales promotion mgr. Pabco Products, Inc., San Francisco, 1947-51; v.p., mgmt. supr. Needham, Louis & Brorby, Inc., Chgo., 1951-60; mgr. mktg. plans dept. Pure Oil Co., Palatine, Ill., 1961-62, v.p. pub. relations, personnel, 1962-66; v.p. pub. affairs Abbott Labs., North Chicago, Ill., 1966-71; v.p. corporate and investor relations IC Industries, 1971—. Mem. 22d Ann. Global Strategy Conf., U.S. Naval War Coll., 1970. Bd. dirs. Evanston Hosp., Lawson YMCA, Chgo.; trustee Ill. Soc. Prevention Blindness, 1958-74. Served to maj. USAAF, 1942-46; ETO. Mem. Newcomen Soc. N.Am., Pub. Relations Soc. Am., Chgo. Assn. Commerce, New Eng. Soc. N.Y.C., Pub. Relations Seminar. Republican. Unitarian. Clubs: Chicago, Economic, University (Chgo.); Glen View Golf (Ill.); Lagunitas Country (Ross, Calif.); Harvard (N.Y.C.). Home: 2204 Thornwood Ave Wilmette IL 60091 Office: 111 E Wacker Dr Chicago IL 60601

KENNA, FRANCIS REGIS, hosp. adminstr.; b. Pitts., July 28, 1932; s. Walter J. and Wilma (Blattner) K.; B.S., Duquesne U., 1954; M.B.A., U. Chgo., 1966; student John Marshall Law Sch., 1967; m. Mary R. Miller, Apr. 24, 1954; children—Regina Mary, Francis Regis, Richard Aloysius, Kathleen Ann, Matthew Scott. Chief pharmacist Homestead Hosp., Pa., 1957; dir. pharmacy Southside Hosp., Pitts., 1957-60; dir. pharmacy U. Chgo. Hosps. and Clinics, 1960-65, adminstrv. asst. pharmacy-central material service, 1965-67, asst. dir., 1967-69, acting dir., 1969, dir., 1969—; asst. prof. grad. program hosp. adminstrn. U. Chgo., 1969—; chmn. Chgo. Hosp. Council, 1977. Pharmacy cons. Am. Hosp. Assn., Chgo., 1961-65. Bd. dirs. Chgo. Hosp. Council, Home Destitute Crippled Children. Ill. Regional Med. Program; trustee Chgo. Home for Incurables. Served with U.S. Army, 1955-57. Mem. Am. (past pres.), Ill. (past pres.) socs. hosp. pharmacists, Am. Pharm. Assn. (past 1st v.p. Chgo. br.), Drug Information Assn. Pharmacy editor Hosp. Topics nat. monthly publ. Contbr. articles profl. jours. Office: 950 E 59th St Chicago IL 60637

KENNEDY, EDWARD EARL, biochem. mfg. co. exec.; b. Evansville, Ind., Jan. 7, 1925; s. Raymond Earl and Hazel May (Krueger) K.; B.S., Purdue U., 1945; A.M., Ind. U., 1948; m. Julia Ruth Bollenbacher, Nov. 19, 1950; children—Jay Douglas, Matthew Curtis. Analytical chemist Eli Lilly & Co., Indpls., 1946-50, mgr. analytical research, 1950-66, dir. corporate quality assurance, 1966-69, plant dir., 1969-70, dir. biochem. mfg., 1970—. Lectr. Purdue U. Extension, Indpls. Active Central Ind. Council Boy Scouts Am., 1964-70, Orgn. Parents and Tchrs., 1970-75. Mem. Am. Chem. Soc. (pres. Ind. sect.), Am. Pharm. Assn., A.A.A.S., Am. Soc. Quality Control, Brendonridge Assn. (dir.). Republican. Presbyn. Home: 5420 Roxbury Rd Indianapolis IN 46226 Office: 302 E McCarty St Indianapolis IN 46202

KENNEDY, GEORGE FRANCIS, publishing co. exec.; b. Providence, R.I., Sept. 23, 1936; s. Amos Huntington and Theresa Catherine (Glancy) K.; B.A., Brown U., 1958; M.A., U. Mich., 1959; Ph.C., U. Mich., 1965. Teaching fellow U. Mich., 1960-63; editor U. Mich. Inst. Sci. and Tech., 1963-66, mng. editor, 1966-68, head publs. 1968-69; publs. dir., pub. info. dir., dir. curriculum devel. High/Scope Ednl. Research Found., Ypsilanti, Mich., 1970-72; gen. mgr. Prakken Publs., Inc., Ann Arbor, 1972—. Mem. adv. council on vocat. edn. Ann Arbor Schs., 1976—. Mem. Am. Mgmt. Assn., Am. Bus. Communication Assn., Soc. Tech. Writers and Pubs., Phi Beta Kappa, Phi Kappa Phi. Democrat. Roman Catholic. Home: 2775 Carmel Ann Arbor MI 48104 Office: 416 Long Shore Dr Ann Arbor MI 48107

KENNEDY, GORDON JAMES, mech. engr.; b. Bucyrus, Ohio, Mar. 7, 1927; s. Milford Joseph and Mildred Marie (Kimble) K.; B.S. in Bus. Adminstrn., Ohio State U., 1951; B.S. in Elec. Engring., Ohio No. U., 1957; postgrad. U. Toledo, 1963-64, Wayne State U., 1973; m. Doris Mae Holsinger, Sept. 9, 1950; children—Suzanne, Margaret, Dwight. Design engr., cost analyzer, Shunk Mfg. Co., Bucyrus, Ohio, 1951-52; chief engr. Transp. Co., Bucyrus, 1952; electro-mech. design engr, No. Electric Co., Galion, Ohio, 1952-55; process instrument engr. Gen. Electric Co., Cleve., 1957-63; instrumentation engr. NASA, Sandusky, Ohio, 1963-71; mech. engr. EPA, Ann Arbor, Mich., 1971—; instr. elec. engring., Cleve. State U., 1961-63. Pres. N.E. Property Owners Civic Assn., Cleve., 1960; precinct committeeman, Cleve., 1960-61. Served with U.S. Army, 1945-49. Mem. Soc. Automotive Engrs. Presbyterian. Club: Masons. Intervened in AEC hearing on constrn. of Davis-Besse Nuclear Power Sta., Port Clinton, Ohio, 1970, 71. Home: 1534 Barrington Pl Ann Arbor MI 48103 Office: EPA 2565 Plymouth Rd Ann Arbor MI 48105

KENNEDY, HAYES, lawyer; b. Joliet, Ill., Sept. 10, 1898; s. Martin Edward and Catherine Ann (Tuohy) K.; Ph.B., U. Chgo., 1922, J.D., 1924; m. Mary Louise Lennon, May 24, 1926; children—Mary Frances, Helen Kennedy Ryan, Hayes, Daniel, James. Admitted to Ill. bar, 1924; since practiced in Chgo., mem. firm Ryan, Condon, & Livingston, 1948-64; gen. claims counsel, asst. gen. counsel The Greyhound Corp., 1948-64; pres., counsel ICMA, Inc., Chgo., 1964—; tchr. Tchr. Loyola U. Law Sch., Chgo., 1926-37; dir. Brach Candy Co., 1931-65. Trustee Lewis Coll., Lockport, Ill., 1960-73. Served with U.S. Army, World War I. Mem. Am., Ill., Will County bar assns., Am. Legion (founder Boys State program in Ill. 1935). Clubs: K.C., Chgo. Athletic. Home: 309 N William St Joliet IL 60435 Office: 1 W Harris St LaGrange IL 60525

KENNEDY, JAMES MARTIN, educator, counselor; b. Columbus, Ohio, Feb. 6, 1936; s. Charles Martin and Mary Veronica (McEwan) K.; B.S. in Edn., Ohio State U., 1964; Ed.M. in Guidance Counseling, Xavier U., 1970; m. Eleanor Rita Hagerty, Dec. 28, 1963; children—Michael Timothy, Kathleen Marie, Theresa Ann, John Patrick, Mary Elizabeth. Tchr., coach Hartley High Sch., Columbus, Ohio, 1964-67; tchr., coach Brunswick (Ohio) Schs., 1967-69, Milford (Ohio) Exempted Village Schs. Vice pres. Guardian Angel Sch. Bd., 1975; bd. Clermont County (Ohio) Mental Helath. Mem. NEA, Ohio, Southwestern, Milford edn. assns., Am., Ohio personnel and guidance assns., Am., Ohio (exec. bd., dist. rep., pres., 1978-79) sch. counselors assns. Democrat. Roman Catholic. Contbr. articles to state guidance newsletter. Home: 1628 Mears Ave Cincinnati OH 45230 Office: 5684 Cromley Dr Milford OH 45150

KENNEDY, JOHN ALLAN, electronics co. exec.; b. Chgo., Dec. 29, 1929; s. John A. and Jane K.; B.S. in E.E., Northwestern U., 1943; m. Mary Ann Bremner, Apr. 29, 1950; children—John, Susan, Vincent,

David, Jane, Mary, James, Madeleine, Lauretta. Sales engr. Motorola, Inc., Chgo., 1947-49; pres. James Electronics, Inc., Chgo., 1950—; pres. Athana, Inc., Torrance, Calif., 1973—. Mem. Ill. Legislature, 1966-67; dir. dept. gen. services State of Ill., 1967-68; v.p. St. Anne's Hosp., St. Elizabeth's Hosp., Chgo. Served to lt (j.g.) U.S. Navy, 1943-47. Mem. IEEE, Instrument Soc. Am. Democrat. Roman Catholic. Clubs: Chgo. Athletic, Old Willow, Sheridan Shore Yacht. Home: 5 Woodley Rd Winnetka IL 60093 Office: 4050 N Rockwell St Chicago IL 60618

KENNEDY, JOHN CHARLES, realtor; b. Huntington, Ind., Nov. 23, 1942; s. Paul E. and Dorothy M. (Bell) K.; B.A., Ball State U., 1971; m. Nancy Jill Hubner, Dec. 9, 1967; children—Christine, Patrick. Salesman, Fisher Givens Realty. Muncie, Ind., 1971-72; mgr. Larry Wells & Assos., Huntington, Ind., 1972-75; owner, mgr. Kennedy, Realtors, Huntington, Ind., 1975—. Adv. bd. Salvation Army; bd. dirs. Huntington County Health Planning Council, Assn. Homes; councilman City of Huntington (Ind.). 1975—. Mem. Nat., Ind. assns. realtors. Clubs: Elk, Kiwanis. Home: 865 Warren St Huntington IN 46750 Office: 231 W Park Dr Huntington IN 46750

KENNEDY, JOHN JOSEPH, educator; b. Cortland, N.Y., Sept. 13, 1914; s. John Austin and Anna Gertrude (Ryan) K.; B.A., U. N.Mex., 1936; A.M., Columbia U., 1938, Ph.D., 1954; m. Elizabeth Carol Riordan, Aug. 19, 1942; children—John Christian, Kathryn Kennedy Bueno. Liaison officer internat. activities Pub. Adminstrn. Clearing House, Chgo., 1938-41; regional specialist Latin Am., Dept. State, Washington, 1941-42, 46-48; vis. prof. U. P.R., 1949-50; asst. prof. polit. sci. U. Notre Dame, 1951-56, asso. prof., 1956-59; prof. U. Va., Charlottesville, 1959-64; prof., dir. Latin Am. studies program Notre Dame (Ind.) U., 1964—; vis. prof. Coll. City N.Y., 1960; cons. Ford Found., Peru and Chile, 1964; Rockefeller Found. affiliate, vis. prof. U. del Valle, Colombia, 1968-71. Served to lt. comdr. USNR, 1942-46. Nat. Council on Religion in Higher Edn. fellow, 1937; postdoctoral fellow Council on Fgn. Relations N.Y., 1958-59. Mem. Am. Polit. Sci. Assn. Democrat. Roman Catholic. Author: Catholicism, Nationalism and Democracy in Argentina, 1958; Over All Development in Chile, 1969. Home: 1937 Inglewood Pl South Bend IN 46616 Office: Box 201 Notre Dame IN 46556

KENNEDY, JOHN XAVIER, banker; b. Chgo., June 10, 1918; s. R. Emmett and Bernadine (Galvin) K.; student Northwestern U., 1946-47; certificate Wharton Sch. Fin. U. Pa., 1964; m. Mary Ann Luke, Nov. 6, 1948; children—J. Luke, Mark, Matthew, Pete, Paul, Kristine. With United Air Lines, Chgo., 1937-41, 46; with Stifel, Nicolaus & Co., Inc., Chgo., 1946-53, bond salesman, 1946-51, buyer, 1951-53; with White Weld & Co., Chgo., 1953-72, municipal bond buyer, 1953-58, mgr. revenue bonds, 1959-63, v.p., 1964-72; v.p. fixed income securities F.S. Moseley & Co., 1972-74; pres. U.S. Securities Corp., 1974-76; v.p. John Nuveen & Co., 1977—; v.p., dir. Stanley Luke Farm, Inc. Mem. devel. bd. Sisters of St. Joseph, La Grange, Ill.; mem. corporate support DePaul U., 1965-66. Served with USAF, 1942-45. Decorated Air medal. Mem. Securities Industry Assn. (chmn. municipal securities com. Central States 1965, mem. municipal fed. legis. com. 1969-71, municipal securities com. 1972), Municipal Fin. Forum, Washington, Bond Club Chgo., Municipal Bond Club Chgo. (past dir.). Home: Route 1 10101 Fifth Ave La Grange IL 60525 Office: 209 S LaSalle St Chicago IL 60604

KENNEDY, KEVIN CURTIS, guidance counselor; b. Sioux Falls, S.D., July 28, 1953; s. Glen Curtis and Catherine Ellen (O'Connor) K.; B.A., Mount Marty Coll., Yankton, S.D., 1976, M.A., U. S.D., Vermillion, 1977. Admissions counselor Mount Marty Coll., Yankton, 1977—. Active Muscular Dystrophy Fund, 1974-75, Heart Fund, 1975-76. Mem. Am. Personnel and Guidance Assn., Alpha Psi Omega. Democrat. Catholic. Contbr. poetry to popular mags. Home: Rte 2 Box 191 Beresford SD 57004 Office: Admissions Mount Marty Coll Yankton SD 57078

KENNEDY, ROBERT LLOYD, architect; b. Mpls., June 2, 1922; s. Frank Bernard and Helen Victoria (Larson) K.; B.Arch., U. Minn., 1949; m. Dorothy Loraine Olson, June 26, 1946; children—Kathleen (Mrs. Gregory Stattine), Robert, Karen, Kristy. Draftsman, Close & Close Architects, Mpls., 1949-52, Samuel T. DeRemer, Grand Forks, N.D., 1952-55; architect DeRemer, Harrie & Kennedy, Grand Forks, 1955-64, Harrie & Kennedy, Grand Forks, 1964—. Dir. S. Forks Shopping Center, 1961-71. Alderman, City of Grand Forks, 1964-68. Served with U.S. Army, 1941-45. Decorated Silver Star. Mem. Alpha Rho Chi. Kiwanian (pres. 1962), Elk. Prin. works include Bek Hall, Smith Hall, Viking Elementary Sch., Franklin Elementary Sch., N.D. Sch. for The Blind, Grand Forks Pub. Library, various office bldgs., South Forks Shopping Center, various commercial bldgs. Home: 3125 Chestnut Grand Forks ND 58201 Office: 600 DeMers Ave Grand Forks ND 58201

KENNEDY, WILLIAM JOSEPH, tool mfg. co. exec.; b. Ponca City, Okla., Oct. 9, 1932; s. William Joseph and Dovie Lee (Bridges) K.; B.M.E. cum laude, U. Okla., 1955: M.B.A., Harvard Grad. Sch. Bus., 1960; m. Mary Louise Rusin, Dec. 26, 1960; children—Elizabeth B., William Joseph. Controller. treas. Dorsett Electronics, Norman, Okla., 1960-63; sr. asso. Booz, Allen & Hamilton, Chgo., 1963-67; dir. mgmt. services Baxter Labs., Inc., Morton Grove, Ill., 1967-70; v.p. Miller & Co., Chgo., 1970-72; v.p. market devel. Ill. Tool Works, Inc., Chgo., 1972—; dir. Miller & Co., Devcon, Ltd. Allocations com. Community Fund of Chgo., 1974-75, agy. and ops. com. 1976-77; group chmn. capital campaign Field Mus. History, 1973-74; mem. capital fund campaign com. Met. YMCA, Chgo., 1976-77: asst. chmn. United Settlement Appeal Fund, 1975; capital fund campaign com. Chgo. Met. Crusade of Mercy, 1977; vice chmn. Met. membership standards com. United Way of Met. Chgo., 1977—, chmn. new applicants com., 1977—; bd. dirs., vice chmn. Duncan YMCA. Served with USAF, 1955-58. Mem. Harvard Bus. Sch. Assn. (mem. exec. council 1972-73), Assn. Corporate Growth, Am. Mktg. Assn., Am. Mgmt. Assn., Ireland-U.S. Council for Commerce and Industry. Clubs: Harvard Bus. Sch. Club Chgo. (pres. 1972-73, sr. adv. com. 1968-77), Economic Club Chgo. (chmn. membership com., exec. com. 1974-75), University Club Chgo., Harvard Club N.Y.C. Home: 571 Hill Ave Glen Ellyn IL 60137 Office: 8501 Higgins Rd Chicago IL 60631

KENNELLY, KAREN MARGARET, historian; b. Graceville, Min., Aug. 4, 1933; d. Walter John and Clara Stella (Eastman) Kennelly; B.A., Coll. St. Catherine, St. Paul, 1956; M.A., Catholic U. Am., 1958; Ph.D., U. Calif., Berkeley, 1962. Joined Order of Sisters of St. Joseph, Roman Cath. Ch., 1954; mem. faculty Coll. St. Catherine, 1957—, prof. history, 1972—, acad. dean, 1971—; co-chmn. Minn. Women Higher Edn., 1976-77; cons.-evaluator N. Central Accreditation Assn., 1974—. Trustee St. Mary's Hosp., Mpls., 1973—. Woodrow Wilson fellow, 1961-62; Fulbright postdoctoral fellow, 1964-65; Am. Council Learned Socs. fellow, 1964; Am. Council Edn. grantee, 1969-70. Mem. Am., Am. Cath. (exec. bd. 1976—) hist. assns., Medieval Acad. Am., Acad. Am. Research Historian on Medieval Spain, Women Historians Midwest, Women High Edn., Cath. League Relgious and Civil Rights (v.p. Minn. 1977—), Phi Beta Kappa. Democrat. Author articles, revs. Address: 2004 Randolph Ave St Paul MN 55105

KENNEY, CHARLES SAMUEL, lawyer; b. Bay City, Mich., July 26, 1917; s. Samuel Charles and Kathern C. (McClellan) K.; B.C.S., Cleary Coll., 1937; B.S., Eastern Mich. U., 1940; J.D., Wayne State U., 1951; m. Ellen G. Hilbert, Oct. 8, 1944; children—Barbara (Mrs. William M. Silvis), Peter C., William S., Scott S. Admitted to Mich. bar, 1952; tchr. Woodland (Mich.) High Sch., 1940-42; auditor Mich. State Accident Fund, 1945-52; partner firm Archer, Kenney, & Wilson, Dearborn, Mich., 1952—. Pres., Western Wayne Homeowners Assn., 1966, Woodland Tchrs. Assn., 1941. Served with U.S. Army, 1942-45. Mem. Dearborn (pres. 1965), Mich., Am. bar assns., Delta Theta Phi. Presbyn. (deacon 1972—). Home: 8909 Beck Rd Plymouth MI 48170 Office: 20390 W Outer Dr Dearborn MI 48124

KENNEY, ROBERT LYLE, city ofcl.; b. Boonville, Mo., July 17, 1941; s. Cecil T. and Juanita Virginia (Wolfe) K.; B.S.B.A., U. Mo., Columbia, 1965; m. Betty Caroline Gieger, June 25, 1967; children—Pamela, Patrick. Cost accountant Remington Arms Co., Lake City Army Ammunition Plant, Independence, Mo., 1966-67; property accountant Independence Power & Light Co., 1967; accounting supr. City of Independence, 1967-71, budget and systems supr., 1971, dir. finance, 1971—. Served with USAFR, 1965-66. Recipient Curators award U. Mo., Columbia, 1959. Mem. Municipal Finance Officers Assn., Nat. Assn. Accountants, Mo. Municipal League, Independence C. of C., Mo. (dir.), Western Mo. (treas.) city clks., finance officers assns. Home: 14608 E 36th Terr Independence MO 64055 Office: 103 N Main St Independence MO 64050

KENNING, NORMAN STEPHEN, data processing exec.; b. Coventry, Eng., Aug. 17, 1916; s. John Henry and Florence Beatrice (McQueen) K.; came to U.S., 1965, naturalized, 1970; student Norwich Inst. Tech., Eng., 1932-34; grad. Brit. Mil. Coll. Sci., 1940-42; m. Mildred Ruth Johnston, Mar. 4, 1967. Pub. carriage officer Scotland Yard, Eng., 1956-60; mgmt. cons. Brisch Birn & Partners, London, 1960-65, Ft. Lauderdale, Fla., 1966-73; mgmt. cons., Midland, Mich., 1974-76; gen. mgr. CFC Data Corp., Inc., Midland, 1976—, dir., 1977—. Bd. dirs. Midland County Rehab. Services for the Handicapped, 1976—. Served with Brit. Army, 1939-56. Named Hon. Citizen of Ft. Worth, 1970. Mem. Inst. of Rd. Transport Engrs., Am. Inst. of Indsl. Engrs., Data Processing Mgmt. Assn., Methods Time Measurement Assn. for Standards and Research. Home: 2801 Gibson St Midland MI 48640 Office: 127 Townsend St Midland MI 48640

KENNY, PHILIP THOMAS, railroad exec.; b. Omaha, Jan. 18, 1930; s. Lee Roy and Clare Gertrude (Connor) K.; student parochial schs., Omaha; m. Jean Marie Welch, June 2, 1956; children—Kathleen Ann, Thomas James, Jane Elizabeth. With Union Pacific R.R., Omaha, 1949—, asst. exec. dir. Nebr. R.R. Assn., 1972-76, exec. dir. assn., 1976—. Served with U.S. Army, 1951-53. Mem. Omaha C. of C., Nebr. Tax Research Council, Nebr. Tax Forum, Nebr. Water Resources Assn., Nebr. Farm Bur. Democrat. Roman Catholic. Clubs: Lincoln Country, Sunset Valley Country, Nebraska, Omaha Press; Capitol Hill (Washington), K.C. Home: 310 S 56th St Omaha NE 68132 Office: Nebr RR Assn 1416 Dodge St Omaha NE 68179

KENT, A. ROBERT, real estate broker; b. Elizabeth, Pa., Dec. 8, 1911; s. John W. and Mary K. (Oriol) K.; B.A., Ohio U., 1933; postgrad. Biarritz Am. U., France, 1945; m. Mary Jo Wintermute, Oct. 20, 1943. Asso. advt. and mktg. depts. several newspapers and bus., Cleve., Weirton, W.Va. and Ambridge, Pa., 1933-52; owner Kent Real Estate, Columbus, Ohio, 1953—; dir. R.R. Savs. and Loan Co., Columbus; pres. Kent Community Sales, Inc., 1964—, Kent Co-ops., Inc., 1962—, 4000, Inc., 1958— (all Columbus). Active Columbus Gallery Fine Arts, 1965—, Columbus Symphony Orch., 1961—, Central Ohio council Boy Scouts Am., United Way Pacesetters Club, 1966—; bd. dirs. House of Hope, Columbus, 1965—, v.p., 1973—. Served with AUS, World War II; ETO. Recipient Grand awards for Advt. Achievement Columbus Dispatch and Citizen Jour., 1973, 74, 75; certificate of Merit Columbus Bd. Realtors, 1960. Mem. Columbus Bd. Realtors, Nat. Assn. Realtors, Bldg. Industry Assn. Central Ohio, Nat. Assn. Home Builders, Columbus Area C. of C., Rolls-Royce Owners Club, Excalibur Assn., Delta Sigma Pi. Republican. Methodist. Clubs: Scioto Country, Brookside Country, Pres.'s Ohio State U., Athletic (Columbus). Home: 4000 Old Poste Rd Columbus OH 43220 Office: Fishinger at Riverside Dr Columbus OH 43221

KENT, ALBERT SYDNEY, bus. services co. exec.; b. Kansas City, Kans., July 19, 1900; s. Albert Sydney and Frances Vandiver (Baldwin) K.; student Kansas City U., 1922-23, Park Coll., 1924-25; m. Helen Marie Ronowicz, May 28, 1934; children—John Otis, Diane. Asst. credit mgr. Nat. Refining Co., Kansas City, Mo., 1918, collection mgr., 1919-20; asst. sales mgr. So. Oil Co., Kansas City, Mo., 1920-22; owner, operator Grease Spot, Kansas City, Kanss., 1923-25; sales mgr. Moore Advt. Co., Kansas City, Kans., 1926-27; founder, owner A.S. Kent & Co., Kansas City, Kans., 1927-78; condr. sales seminars. Sr. counsellor United Comml. Travelers, 1944—; exec. bd., life mem. Wyandotte County Hist. Soc., 1965—; exec. bd. Presbyn. Manor, Kansas City, Kans., 1965—; pres. Wyanodtte County Christian Endeavor, 1923—, United Presbyn. Men of Topeka-Highland Presbytery, 1959—. Served as master sgt., 114th Calvary, U.S. Army, 1925-27. Mem. Kansas City Fgn. Trade Assn. (v.p. 1944-45), Mo.-Kans. Material Handling Soc. (v.p. 1948), Internat. Material Mgmt. Soc., Theta Alpha Phi. Republican. Writer poetry. Home: 2623 N 51st St Kansas City KS 66104 Office: 336 N 7th St Trafficway Kansas City KS 66101

KENT, CALVIN ALBERT, educator; b. Kansas City, Kans., Sept. 8, 1941; s. Homer C. Wright; B.A., Baylor U., 1963; M.A., U. Mo., 1965, Ph.D., 1967; postgrad. U. Va., 1967, Wichita State U., 1972; m. Nita Sue Davis, Aug. 23, 1963; children—Nita Christine, Anna Elaine. Instr. econs. U. Mo., Columbia, 1963-64; instr. social scis. Stevens Coll., Columbia, 1964-67; faculty U. S.D., Vermillion, 1967—, prof. econs., 1973—, dir. pub. fin. studies, 1971—; exec. dir. S.D. Council on Econ. Edn., 1969—; staff counsel taxation coms. S.D. Legislature; cons. S.D. Dept. Rev. Alderman, Vermillion, 1972—, pres. City Council, 1974—; vice chmn. S.D. Municipal League, Dist. 2, 1972-74. Named Outstanding Tchr., U. S.D., 1970-72; NSF awardee, 1974; named Outstanding Young Religious Leader, 1976. Mem. AAUP. Republican. Mem. United Ch. Christ (trustee). Clubs: Masons, Shriners. Author: Indian Poverty, 1969; Taxation of Cooperative Enterprise, 1970; Property Taxes and the Circuit Breaker, 1972; Death Taxes in the American States, 1974; Municipal Regulation and Franchising, 1975. Home: 508 Poplar St Vermillion SD 57069 Office: Dept Econs U SD Vermillion SD 57069

KENT, DONALD LEROY, bus. exec.; b. Lincoln, Nebr., Aug. 11, 1927; s. Roy Jay and Grace Pearl (Scott) K.; ed. Bus. Coll., Enid, Okla.; m. Mary Alice Dishman, May 6, 1956; 1 son, Jay Leroy. Auditor, Champlain Refining Co., Enid, Okla., 1956-59; dir. purchasing, Bethany Med. Center, 1960—. Served with U.S. Army, 1945-56. Mem. Am., Kans. City Area Hosp. Assn., Asso. Purchasing Service. Democrat. Home: 415 #82 Kansas City KS 66112 Office: 51 #12 Kansas City KS 66102

KENT, GEOFFREY, physician; b. Amsterdam, Netherlands, Jan. 30, 1914; s. Jacob and Nelly (Friedland) K.; came to U.S., 1953, naturalized, 1958; M.D., U. Amsterdam, 1939; Ph.D., Northwestern U., 1957; m. Katharine M. Ruscoe, Sept. 22, 1944; children—Jonathan H., Simon R., Paul A., Helen J. Intern, resident Royal Infirmary, Manchester, Eng., 1939-43; chief med. asst., asst. dir. dept. clin. investigation and research Manchester U., 1940-44; sr. registrar Chase Farm Hosp., also London Hosp., London, 1947-50; dir. labs. Gen. and Providence Hosp., Moose Jaw, Sask., Can., 1950-53; asso. dir. pathology Cook County Hosp., Chgo., 1953-57; dir. labs. West Suburban Hosp., Oak Park, Ill., 1958-69; chmn. dept. pathology Chgo. Wesley Meml. Hosp., 1969-73; pathologist-in-chief, dir. labs. Northwestern Meml. Hosp., Chgo., 1973-76; prof. pathology Northwestern U., 1969—. Served to capt. Royal Army Med. Corps, 1944-47. Home: 219 E Lake Shore Dr Chicago IL 60611 Office: 303 E Chicago Ave Chicago IL 60611

KENT, HOMER AUSTIN, JR., clergyman; b. Washington, Aug. 13, 1926; s. Homer Austin and Alice Ethel (Wogaman) K.; B.A. cum laude, Bob Jones U., 1947; B.D. summa cum laude, Grace Theol. Sem., 1950, Th.M., 1952, Th.D., 1956; m. Beverly Jane Page, Aug. 1, 1953; children—Rebecca, Katherine, Daniel. Ordained to ministry Fellowship of Grace Brethren Chs., 1951; mem. faculty Grace Theol. Sem., Winona Lake, Ind., 1951—, dean Sem., 1962-76, pres. Sem. and Grace Coll., 1976—. Mem. Am. Assn. Higher Edn., Evang. Theol. Soc. (chmn. Midwestern sect. 1970-71). Author: The Pastoral Epistles, 1958; Ephesians, The Glory of the Church, 1971; Jerusalem to Rome, Studies in the Book of Acts, 1972; The Epistle to the Hebrews, 1972; Light in the Darkness, Studies in the Gospel of St. John, 1974; The Freedom of God's Sons: Studies in Galatians, 1976. Home: 305 6th St Winona Lake IN 46590 Office: Grace Schools Winona Lake IN 46590

KENT, LEE ANNE, lawyer; b. Evergreen, Ala., Nov. 10, 1926; d. Prinus and Daisy Mae Bradley; B.A., Wayne State U., 1972, M.S. in L.S., 1973, J.D., 1976; m. Earl Kent, Feb. 4, 1950 (div. Mar. 1956). Admitted to Mich. bar, 1976. Stenographer, Internat. Union, UAW, Detroit, 1953-74; librarian Walter P. Reuther Library, Wayne State U., 1974-76; individual practice law, Detroit, 1976-77; hearing officer City of Detroit, 1974—, asst. corp. counsel, 1977—. Pub. mem. Mich. State Elec. Adminstrv. Bd. Mem. Am., Mich., Detroit bar assns., Spl. librariies Assn., Am. Arbitration Assn., Indsl. Relations Research Assn. Home: 1940 Hyde Park Dr Detroit MI 48207 Office: 1010 City-County Bldg Detroit MI 48226

KENT, MELVIN, cons.; b. Newark, Nov. 13, 1929; s. Henry and Pearl (Gould) K.; B.S. magna cum laude, N.Y. U., 1956; M.A., Columbia U., 1960; m. Betsy Madison, June 3, 1965; children—Elizabeth, Michael, Stephan. Personnel exec. Federated Dept. Stores, Columbus, Ohio, 1967-70; owner, pres. Melvin Kent & Assos., Exec. Search Firm, Columbus, 1971—; dir. Madisons, Inc.; instr. Ohio State U., Columbus, 1965-66, Columbus Tech. Inst., 1967-69. Bd. dirs. Mental Health Assn. Ohio; trustee Sr. Citizens Placement Council. Served with AUS, 1948-52. Mem. Beta Gamma Sigma. Club: Winding Hollow Country (trustee). Home: 159 Preston Rd Columbus OH 43209 Office: 250 E Broad St Columbus OH 43215

KENWORTHY, MERRELL T., systems analyst; b. Kokomo, Ind., Aug. 11, 1946; s. Wayne R. and Naomi Gertrude (Henderson) K.; S.B., Mass. Inst. Tech., 1968; postgrad. Syracuse (N.Y.) U., 1968-70; m. Rosalea Kay Farris, Oct. 28, 1974. Programmer, Gen. Electric Corp., Syracuse, 1968-70; instr. Ind. Vocat. Tech. Coll., Kokomo, 1970-73; systems analyst Kokomo Tribune, 1973—. Mem. Assn. Computing Machinery, Math. Assn. Am., Kokomo Mental Health Assn., Kokomo Civic Theatre, Howard County Hist. Soc. Presbyterian. Club: Kokomo Kiwanis. Home: 3110 Orleans Ct Kokomo IN 46901 Office: 300 N Union St Kokomo IN 46901

KENWORTHY, ORVILLE FRANKLIN, ednl. adminstr.; b. Flushing, N.Y., Oct. 7, 1937; s. Orville Owen and Mary Judith (Ferraro) K.; B.A., Coll. Wooster, 1960; M.A., U. Ill., 1961; Ph.D., Mich. State U., 1968; m. Gay Ann Wood, June 30, 1963; children—Stephen, Allison, Meredith. Scenic designer U. Louisville Theatre, 1962-64; tech. dir. Mich. State U. Arena Theatre, 1966-67; asso. prof. theatre, mgr. Univ. Theatre, Purdue U., Fort Wayne, Ind., 1970-77, acting dean Sch. Scis. and Humanities, 1976-77, asst. vice chancellor academic affairs, 1977—, producer Dames At Sea (winner 1972 Am. Coll. Theatre Festival), Marathon 33, 1975, Hair (winner 1976); chmn. house com. Community Center for Performing Arts, 1972—; head judge No. Ind. Region 9 Am. Coll. Theatre Festival, 1974—. Bd. dirs. Ft. Wayne Fine Arts Found., 1972—, v.p., 1973—. Mem. Actors Equity Assn., Am. Theatre Assn., AAUP. Congregationalist (mem. choir). Home: 2029 Forest Valley Dr Fort Wayne IN 46805 Office: 2101 E Coliseum Blvd Fort Wayne IN 46805

KEOGH, JEANNE MARIE, librarian; b. Toledo, Sept. 20, 1924; d. Thomas Leroy and Agnes Mary (Wenzler) Keogh; B.A., Mary Manse Coll., 1946; B.L.S., Western Res. U., 1947. Asst. librarian tech. dept. Toledo Pub. Library, 1946-54; tech. librarian Libbey Owens Ford Co., Toledo, 1954—. Established library Riverside Hosp. Nursing Sch., Toledo, 1950-51; grey lady ARC, Toledo, 1966-70; mem. Transp. Safety Info. Com., 1972—; mem. fin. com. Mary Manse Coll., Toledo, 1972-75. Chmn. bd. Ecumenical Library Toledo, 1976—. Mem. Ohio, Catholic librarian assns., Spl. Libraries Assn. (scholarship com. 1968-74, chmn. 1960-70, 72-74, chmn. Detroit conf. hospitality com., 1970, chmn. metals/materials div. 1977-78), Mary Manse Coll. Alumni Assn. (dir. 1971-76, pres. 1972-73). Club: Quota (Toledo). Home: 3634 Rugby Dr Toledo OH 43614 Office: 1701 E Broadway Toledo OH 43605

KEOUGH, JOSEPH STANLEY, financial exec.; b. Chgo., May 7, 1902; s. Joseph Robert and Agnes (Burns) K.; student St. Meinred Sem., 1919, Internat. Accountants Soc., 1933; A.B., M.A., Magdalen Coll., Oxford (Eng.) U.; postgrad. Sorbonne, Paris, France; m. Mildred Skirvin, May 29, 1931; children—Rosemarie, Joseph P.H. Pub. accountant, 1933—; sr. partner Keough & Root, Bloomington, Ind., 1967—. A founder Boys Club Bloomington, 1950. Bd. dirs. Bloomington parochial sch. fund raising campaign, 1955. Mem. Nat. Soc. Pub. Accountants, Ind. State Bd. Accounting (accreditation council 1974—), Nat. Assn. Accountants (treas. Ind. chpt.). Home: 1612 S Clifton Ave Bloomington IN 47401 Office: 208 N Washington St Bloomington IN 47401

KEPLINGER, STEPHEN ANTHONY, JR., personnel cons. co. exec.; b. Akron, Ohio, Aug. 26, 1949; s. Stephen Anthony and Irene Helen (Lesko) K.; student U. Akron, 1967-69; m. Mary Beth Kopunovitz, May 26, 1973. Dept. mgr. K-Mart, Akron, Ohio, 1969-71; mgr. Gen. Menswear Corp., Akron, 1971-72; cons. Baron Personnel Inc., Akron, 1972-74, pres. Baron Personnel Elyria Inc. (Ohio), 1974—, dist. mgr. Baron Personnel Inc., 1977—. Exec. recording sec. Catholic Youth Orgn. Akron, 1973—. Mem. Nat. Employment Assn., Ohio Pvt. Employment Services Assn., Cath. Slovak Union. Democrat. Roman Catholic. Club: Kiwanis. Home: 525 S Abbe Rd Apt P-11 Elyria OH 44035 Office: 36 Lake Ave Elyria OH 44035

KEPNER, HENRY SIEBER, JR., mathematician, educator; b. Chgo., May 22, 1940; s. Henry Sieber and Inez (Madsen) K.; B.S. in Math., U. Iowa, 1962, M.S., 1964, Ph.D. in Math. Edn., 1970. Instr. math. Univ. Sch., Iowa City, 1963-72; asst. prof. U. Iowa, 1970-72; mem. faculty U. Wis., Milw., 1972—, asso. prof. math. edn., 1975—; dir. summer insts. tchrs. NSF; treas., exec. bd. Wis. Math. Council. Treas., deacon Lake Park Lutheran Ch., Milw. Mem. Nat. Council Tchrs. Math., Math. Assn. Am., Sch. Sci. and Math. Assn., Am. Ednl. Research Assn., Milw.-Area Math. Council, Eastern Wis. Ofcls. Assn. (v.p. 1977), Wis. Umpires Assn. (exec. bd. 1974—). Author articles, tests. Home: 4211 N Prospect Ave Milwaukee WI 53211 Office: Dept Curriculum and Instrn U Wis Milwaukee WI 53201

KEPPLER, ERNEST CARL, lawyer, state senator; b. Sheboygan, Wis., Apr. 5, 1918; s. Ernst John and Meta (Ruge) K.; B.S., U. Wis., 1949, J.D., 1950; m. Bertha L. Zurheide, Oct. 21, 1939; children—Ernest Michael, Mary Elizabeth. Admitted to Wis. bar, 1950, practice in Sheboygan, 1951—; mem. Wis. Gen. Assembly, 1943-45, Wis. Senate, 1960—, senate majority leader, 1969-73, senate v.p., 1973-75. Alderman, Sheboygan, 1941-45, 50-53; asst. dist. atty., Sheboygan County, 1953-55. Served with AUS, 1945-46, 50-51. Recipient Silver Beaver award Boy Scouts Am., Distinguished Eagle Scout award, 1970. Mem. Am. Legion, Am. Vets, V.F.W. Eagle, Mason, Rotarian. Address: 909 New York Av Sheboygan WI 53081

KER, CHARLES ARTHUR, furniture and indsl. products mfg. co. exec.; b. Warsaw, Ind., May 29, 1934; s. Charles Hoskins and Jessie Marie (Anglin) K.; B.A., DePauw U., 1956; M.B.A., Northwestern U., 1957; m. Alice Ann Steele, Sept. 8, 1957; children—Kelly, Karen, Kristin. Cost accountant, financial analyst Eli Lilly & Co., Indpls., 1957-61, head receipts and disbursements Elanco Products div., 1962-65; asst. treas. Dalton Foundries, Inc., Warsaw, 1965-67; treas., 1968-74; pres. Endicott Industries, Warsaw, 1975—; pres. Endicott Ch. Furniture div. Dalton Foundries, Inc., Winona Lake, 1971-74; dir. Lake City Bank, 1973—. Bd. dirs. United Fund of Kosciusko County (Ind.), 1966-76, pres., 1968, chmn. bd., 1969, chmn. gen. campaign, 1974; bd. dirs. Jr. Achievement, Warsaw, 1968-71, pres., 1969-70, treas., 1968-69; bd. dirs. Baker Boys Club, 1966—, treas., 1966-74; bd. dirs. Kosciusko Community YMCA, 1967-68, 77—, Lakeland council Girl Scouts Am., 1969-71, No. Ind. Lung Assn., 1977—. Recipient Distinguished Service award Warsaw Jr. C. of C., 1968. Mem. Warsaw C. of C. (dir. 1968-72, pres. 1970-71, dir. indsl. bd. 1974-76), Financial Execs. Inst. (dir. Ft. Wayne chpt. 1971-73, pres. 1972-73), Ch. Furniture Mfrs. Assn. (dir. 1974-75, pres. 1975). Republican. Presbyn. (deacon 1966-68, moderator 1968, elder 1969-71, trustee 1973-75, pres. 1973-74, sec. 1975). Rotarian (pres. 1975-76, dir. 1968-70, 72-77). Club: Tippecanoe Lake Country (dir. 1974-76, treas. 1975-76). Home: 1607 N Springhill Rd Warsaw IN 46580 Office: Endicott Industries 765 W Market St Warsaw IN 46580

KERBER, DANIEL WILLIAM, farmer, livestock breeder; b. Chatsworth, Ill., May 31, 1908; s. Henry A. and Anna (Froehlich) K.; student pub. schs.; m. Leota C. Feely, Dec. 31, 1935; children—Patricia (Mrs. Leland V. Dehm), Barbara (Mrs. John V. Kane), Donald W., Jerome E., Deborah J. Underwriter, Gleaner Life Ins. Soc., sec., Chatsworth, 1933-46, state officer, 1930-40; livestock farmer, 1935—; breeder of purebred polled Hereford cattle and purebred Yorkshire hogs, 1936—. Chmn. Livingston County Soil Conservation Dist., 1948-51; 4-H club leader, 1950-66; farm stored grain inspector, 1955-68; vice chmn. Livingston County com. Agrl. Stblzn. and Conservation Service, 1968-73, chmn., 1973—. Supr. Charlotte Twp., 1973—. Vice chmn., Twp. Committeemen, 1954-68, Livingston County com., Am. Conservation Service 1969—. Recipient Goodyear Conservation award for exceptional service, 1950, 51. Mem. Livingston County Livestock Boosters Assn. (dir. 1958), Roman Catholic, K.C. (grand knight 1960, 67-68, 72-73), Lion (pres. 1952-58, 66-67, 70-71). Club: Sportsmans (pres. 1947). Address: Rural Route 1 Chatsworth IL 60921

KERBIS, DON KENNETH, tennis club exec.; b. Detroit, Mar. 9, 1935; s. Sam and Helen (Jaffe) K.; B.A., Chgo. Tchrs. Coll., 1958; M.A., Roosevelt U., 1961; M.A., U. Chgo., 1963; children—Julian, Lisa, Kim. Played on tournament tennis tours, 1953-60; owner Don Kerbis Tennis Club, Highland Park, Ill., 1964—; owner, dir. Don Kerbis Tennis Ranch, Watervliet, Mich., 1969—; tennis and program cons.; ct. builder; tchr. of tennis tchrs. Served with AUS, i958-60. Mem. Chgo. Dist. (dir.), U.S. Pro (pres. 1969), Midwest Pro (pres. 1968), U.S. Lawn, Western tennis assns., Am. (nat. standards com.), Midwest camping assns., Chgo. Pvt. Camps Assn. Contbr. articles to tennis mags. Office: 1660 Skokie Blvd Highland Park IL 60035

KERBIS, GERTRUDE LEMPP, architect; B.S., U. Ill.; M.A., Ill. Inst. Tech.; postgrad. Grad. Sch. Design, Harvard, 1949-50; m. Walter Peterhans (dec.); m. 2d, Donald Kerbis (div. 1972); children—Julian, Lisa, Kim. Archtl. designer Skidmore, Owings & Merrill, Chgo., 1954-59, C.F. Murphy Assos., Chgo., 1959-62, 65-67; pvt. practice architecture, Chgo., 1967—; lectr. U. Ill., 1969; asso. prof. William Rainey Harper Coll., 1970-77; asso. prof. Washington U., St. Louis, 1977—; archtl. cons. Dept. Urban Renewal, City of Chgo.; lectr. in field. Mem. Northeastern Ill. Planning Commn., Open Land Project, Mid-North Community Orgn., Chgo. Met. Housing and Planning Council Chgo.; mem. Chgo. Mayor's Commn. for Preservation Chgo.'s Historic Architecture, 1972—. Trustee Chgo. Sch. Architecture Found., 1972-75, Glessner House Found. Fellow A.I.A. (dir. Chgo. chpt. 1971-75, nat. com. architecture arts and recreation, 1972-75, nat. com. design 1974-77); mem. A.A.U.P., U. Ill. Alumni Assn., Ill. Inst. Tech. Alumni Assn., Art Inst. Chgo., A.C.L.U., Chgo. Council Fgn. Relations, Planned Parenthood Assn., Lincoln Park Zool. Soc., Chgo. Women in Architecture (founder 1972), Chicago Arts Club. Prin. works include dining hall U.S. Air Force Acad. (Colo.), Skokie (Ill.) Pub. Library, 1959, Meadows Club, Lake Meadows, Chgo., 1959, Tennis Club, Highland Park, Ill., 1968, 7 Continents Bldg., O'Hare Internat. Airport, 1963, The Greenhouse, 1976, Fugua House, 1977; lectr. Art Inst. Chgo., U. N.Mex., Ill. Inst. Tech., Washington U., St. Louis, Ball State U. Home: 2131 N Clark Chicago IL 60614 Office: 664 N Michigan Ave Chicago IL 60611

KERCHAL, RAYMOND GEORGE, watch and clock mfg. co. exec.; b. Arcadia, Nebr., Feb. 15, 1921; s. Raymond G. and Marie M. (Psota) K.; B.S. in Mech. Engring., U. Nebr., 1949; m. Lydia E. Hosek, Aug. 11, 1941; children—Dennis R., Kenneth D. (dec.), Carolyn J. With Elgin Nat. Watch Co. (Ill.), 1949-64; mgr. mil products Westclox div. Gen. Time Corp., LaSalle, Ill., 1964-68, v.p. ordnance Space and Systems div., Rolling Meadows, Ill., 1968—. Served with USAAF, 1942-46; PTO. Mem. Am. Ordnance Assn., Sigma Tau, Pi Tau Sigma. Elk. Home: 523 N Weston Ave Elgin IL 60120 Office: 1200 Hicks Rd Rolling Meadows IL 60008

KEREKES, JOHN JOSEPH, devel. co. exec.; b. Toledo, Oct. 28, 1949; s. Joseph John and Zelpha Fay (Hayes) K.; student Davis Jr. Coll., 1970-72; m. Sabrina Ann Leighton, Mar. 26, 1976; children by previous marriage—Christine Marie, Mary Francis, Caroline Elizabeth, Catherine Ann. Accountant, Hayes Systems, Inc., Toledo, 1970-71; fin. mgr. Diversified Industries, Toledo, 1971-72; v.p. ops. USI Inc., Toledo 1972—. Served with USAF, 1968-69. Mem. Am. Mgmt. Assn. Republican. Methodist. Home: 3 Birmingham Terr Toledo OH 43605 Office: No 3 2100 Consul St Toledo OH 43605

KERKAY, JULIUS, educator, chemist; b. Sopron, Hungary, Apr. 27, 1934; s. Gyula and Ilona (Hartmann) K.; came to U.S., 1957, naturalized, 1962; B.S. in Chem. Engring., U. Veszprem (Hungary), 1955, M.S., 1956; PH.D., U. Louisville, 1969; m. Betty Marie Thomay, Aug. 27, 1960; children—Laura Beth, Jeffrey Alan. Research asso. Cleve. Clinic, 1958-59; lab. dir. Euclid Clinic Found., Cleve., 1968-70, Internat. Med. Labs., Cleve., 1970-71; faculty Cleve. State U., 1970—, dir. clin. chemistry, 1970—, asso. prof. chemistry, 1974—. Cons., speaker in field; judge N.W. Ohio High Sch. Sci. Fair, 1969—; sci. v.p. Euclid Clinic Research Found., 1969—. Served with U.S. Army, 1960-64. NIH grad. fellow, 1964-68; Hungarian Govt. undergrad. fellow, 1951-56. Diplomate Am. Bd. Clin. Chemistry. Mem. Am. Soc. Clin. Pathology, A.A.A.S., A.A.U.P., Am. Chem. Soc., Am. Assn. Clin. Chemistry, Assn. Clin. Scientists, Cleve. Med. Library Assn., Med. Electronics and Data Soc., Soc. Applied Spectroscopy, Sci. Research Soc. Am., Nat. Acad. Clin. Biochemists, N.Y., Ohio acads. scis., Am. Inst. Chemists, Sigma Xi, Phi Kappa Phi, Phi Lambda Upsilon. Contbr. articles to profl. jours. Home: 8040 Barbara Dr Strongsville OH 44136 Office: Dept Chemistry Cleve State U Cleveland OH 44115

KERN, EDWARD ALLEN, dentist; b. Bellevue, O., Feb. 9, 1919; s. Charles Alfred and Hazel Bertha (Eisenhaur) K.; D.D.S., Ohio State U., 1944; postgrad. U. Mich., 1962; m. Rita W. Barbour, Mar. 20, 1965. Pvt. practice gen. dentistry, Toledo, 1947-62, specializing in endodontics, 1962—. Served with Dental Corps, U.S. Army, 1944-47. Mem. Am. Dental Assn., Dentaire Internationale, Ohio, Toledo (pres. 1970) dental socs., Ohio State U. Alumni Assn. (pres. 1960). Mason (Shriner), Rotarian. Clubs: Toledo, Inverness (Toledo); Dorset (Vt.) Field. Home: 2407 Edgehill Rd Toledo OH 43615 Office: 4253 Sylvania Ave Toledo OH 43623

KERN, JOHN CHARLES, cons.; b. Chgo., May 22, 1925; s. Herbert Arthur and Edith (Speckman) K.; S.B., Mass. Inst. Tech., 1950; postgrad. Harvard U., 1951-53, Northwestern U., 1969-70; m. Anne Rumsey Moreland, Sept. 13, 1958; children—Elizabeth Anne, John Charles, Louise Moreland. Mem. staff div. indsl. cooperation Mass. Inst. Tech., 1951-53; asst. to v.p. research and devel. Royal McBee Corp., West Hartford, Conn., 1954-58; div. mgr. advanced planning and mktg. research Sperry Rand Corp., N.Y.C., 1959-63; dir. planning and devel. Coleman Instruments div. Perkin-Elmer Corp., Oakbrook, Ill., 1964-69; pres. Familia Kern, Inc., P.R. Bd. dirs., mem. exec. com., chmn. fin. com. United Way of Ill.; sec. bd. dirs., mem. exec. com. United Way of Suburban Chgo.; advising trustee Kern Found.; trustee First Ill. Religious and Charitable Risk Pooling Trust, Theosophical Investment Trust; bd. dirs., mem. exec. com. Northwestern Mil. and Naval Acad.; trustee Mus. Contemporary Art, Chgo., Council for Arts at Mass. Inst. Tech. Served with U.S. Army, 1943-46; ETO. Mem. Sigma Xi, Beta Theta Pi. Clubs: Hinsdale Golf; Cliff Dwellers (Chgo.). Address: 341 S Elm St Hinsdale IL 60521

KERN, SISTER MARGARET, adminstrv. nun; b. Bloomington, Ind., Mar. 28, 1926; d. Wendell W. and Loretta Margaret (Torphy) Kern; B.A., St. Mary of the Woods Coll., 1948; M.B.A., U. Notre Dame, 1965; Joined Sisters of Providence, Roman Catholic Ch., 1951; mem. faculty St. Mary-of-the-Woods Coll. (Ind.), 1954-60, subsequently mem. bd.; treas. gen., Sisters of Providence, 1966-72, dir. fin., treas., councilor, 1972—; mem. bd. St. Mary-of-the-Woods Coll. Co-chairperson Region 8 Nat. Cath. Coalition for Responsible Investment, 1976; mem. gov. bd. Interfaith Center on Corporate Responsiblity, 1977. Mem. Conf. Religious Treas. of Ind. and Mich., Am. Mgmt. Assn. Roman Catholic. Office: Sisters Providence S St Mary of the Woods IN 47876

KERNAN, EDWARD JAMES, legal adminstr.; b. Two Harbors, Minn., Mar. 22, 1926; s. Edward James and Edith A. (Scott) K.; B.S., U. Minn., 1948; M.Ed., U. Wis., Superior, 1962; m. Barbara Louise Iverson, Sept. 28, 1948; children—Edward James III, Barbara Lee, James E. Coach and athletic dir. Robbinsdale (Minn.) High Sch., 1948-53, Northland Coll., Ashland, Wis., 1954-64; placement dir. U. Minn., Duluth, 1965; adminstrv. and personnel mgr. Price Waterhouse, Cleve., 1966-73; adminstrv. dir. Sidley & Austin, Chgo., 1974—. Pres. Ashland Little League, 1959-64; pres. Badger-Gopher Conf., 1964-65; chmn. Citizen's Com. for Sch. Bond Issue, Rocky River, Ohio, 1973. Served with USAAF, 1944-45. Mem. Law Office Mgrs. Assn. (dir. 1976-77), Assn. of Legal Adminstrs. (dir. 1977-78), Adminstrv. Mgmt. Soc., Cocker Spaniel Club Midwest. Roman Catholic. Clubs: Brookwood Country, Ill. Athletic. Coached three Badger-Gopher Coll. Conf. basketball championships. Home: 1205 Candlewood Hill Northbrook IL 60062 Office: One First National Plaza Chicago IL 60603

KERNDT, THOMAS MARTIN, banker; b. Lansing, Iowa, July 22, 1917; s. Moritz and Mary (Martin) K.; student Columbia Coll. (now Loras Coll.), 1935-37; B.S., Marquette U., 1939; m. Patricia Ann Reynolds, Feb. 3, 1945; children—Mary Patricia (Mrs. Patrick Ahern), Kathleen Ann (Mrs. Michael Higgins), Gustave William, Thomas Moritz, Peter Reynolds, Ann Louise (dec.), Margaret Mary, Susan Marie, Gretchen Marie, James Michael. With Kerndt Bros. Savs. Bank., Lansing, 1939-42; spl. agt. FBI, 1942-47; with Kerndt Bros. Savs. Bank, 1947—, pres., 1964—; officer, dir. Med. Offices, Inc., 1965—, Lansing Marina, Inc., 1962—. Active various town coms., zoning com., devel. com., Lansing, 1971—. Bd. advisers Viterbo Coll., LaCrosse, Wis., 1960—. Recipient Distinguished Service award Lansing Jr. C. of C., 1969. Mem. Delta Sigma Pi. Republican. Roman Catholic (trustee high sch. 1958-71). K.C. (4 deg.), Kiwanian (pres. 1965). Home: RFD Lansing IA 52151 Office: Main St Lansing IA 52151

KERNS, GERTRUDE YVONNE, sch. psychologist; b. Flint, Mich., July 25, 1931; d. Lloyd D. and Mildred C. Brewer; B.A., Olivet Coll., 1953; M.A., Wayne State U., 1958; postgrad. U. Mich. Sch. psychologist Roseville (Mich.) Pub. Schs., 1958-68, Grosse Pointe (Mich.) Pub. Schs., 1968—; instr. in psychology Macomb Community Coll., 1959-63. Mem. Mich., Am. psychol. assns., Mich., Nat. socs. sch. psychologists, NEA, Psi Chi. Home: 28820 Grant St St Clair Shores MI 48081 Office: 389 St Clair Ave Grosse Pointe MI 48230

KERR, ALBERT EDWARD, constrn. equipment mfg. co. exec.; b. Chgo., Sept. 21, 1914; s. Albert E. and Frances (Sutton) K.; B.M.E., U. Cin., 1937; m. Millicent Griffith, Aug. 25, 1956; children (by previous marriage)—Michele Kerr McLaughlin, David, Lois Kerr Hiner. Designer, Power Press Industry, 1940-56, project engr. Buck div. Desa Industries, 1956-57, chief engr., 1957-66, v.p. sales, 1966-70, pres. material Handling div., Cin., 1970-73; pres. KABS, Inc., Cin., 1973—. Registered profl. engr., Ill. Clubs: Masons (32 deg.), Shriners. Home: 2463 Wenatchee Ln Cincinnati OH 45230 Office: 4030 Mount Carmel Tobasco Rd Cincinnati OH 45230

KERR, CECIL RAYMOND, lumber co. exec.; b. South Gifford, Mo., Nov. 29, 1910; s. Samuel Hayes and Florence Elizabeth (Davidson) K.; student pub. schs.; m. Evadeane Reynolds, Nov. 9, 1937; 1 dau., Marilyn Kerr Royse. Farmer, South Gifford, 1937-55; with LaPlata (Mo.) Lumber Co., 1955—, salesman, 1955-64; buyer, 1964-73, mgr., 1973—. Republican committeeman, 1968-76. Mem. Christian Ch. (deacon, ch. bd. sec.). Clubs: Lions, Masons. Home: PO Box 95 LaPlata MO 63549 Office: PO Box 208 LaPlata MO 63549

KERR, FREDERICK HOHMANN, hosp. adminstr.; b. Pitts., July 11, 1936; s. Nathan F. and Laura (Hohmann) K.; B.A., Pa. State U., 1958; M.P.A., U. Pitts., 1961; 1 dau., Linda Jean; m., Phyllis Jensen, Aug. 21, 1970. Planning intern Allegheny County Planning Commn., Pitts., 1958-59; exec. sec. Fayette County br. Pa. Economy League, Uniontown, 1959, Armstrong County br., Kittanning, 1959-62; exec. sec. Woodbury County Tax Research Conf., Sioux City, Iowa, 1962-65; pub. service dir. City Sioux City, 1965-66; asst. adminstr. St. Luke's Med. Center, Sioux City, 1966-69, asso. adminstr., 1969-71; adminstr. Meml. Hosp., Michigan City, Ind., 1971-75; pres. St. Luke's Hosp., Maumee, Ohio, 1975—; part-time instr. pub. finance and mgmt. Morningside Coll., Sioux City, 1963-66. Dir. Northwest Ohio Data Center, 1975—, pres., 1976—; dir. Clin. Engring. Center Northwest Ohio. Sec., Armstrong County Redevel. Council, 1961-62; Iowa Gov.'s Commn. on State and Local Govt., 1964-65, Intergovtl. Relations Commn., 1966; mem. Sioux City Community Appeals Rev. Bd., 1969-71, chmn., 1970; v.p. LaPorte County (Ind.) Health Planning Council, 1972-74, pres., 1974-75. Bd. dirs. Sioux City Council Community Services, 1965-70; bd. dirs. Hosp. Council Northwest Ohio, 1975—, v.p., 1977—; bd. dirs. Siouxland United Way, 1970-71, chmn. planning div., 1970; bd. dirs. No. Ind. Sch. Radiol. Tech., 1971-75, pres., 1972; bd. dirs. Ohio Hosp. Mgmt. Services, 1976—. Served to 2d lt. U.S. Army, 1958-59. Mem. Am. Soc. Pub. Adminstrn. (pres. Siouxland chpt. 1963-64, nat. council 1966-69), Am. Inter-profl. Inst. (pres. Sioux City chpt. 1968-69), Sioux City Hosp. Council (sec. 1967), Am. Coll. Hosp. Adminstrs., Am. Hosp. Assn., Photog. Soc. Am., Pi Sigma Alpha. Home: 1526 Cherrylawn Dr Toledo OH 43614 Office: 5901 Monclova Rd Maumee OH 43537

KERR, KATHEL AUSTIN, historian; b. St. Louis, Aug. 29, 1938; s. Kathel Bedortha and Ruth Story (Sidebotham) K.; B.A., Oberlin (Ohio) Coll., 1959; M.A., U. Iowa, 1960; Ph.D., U. Pitts., 1965; m. Rita Alexia Butchko, Sept. 2, 1967; children—Julie Ruth, Mary Kathleen, Jonathan Austin. Mem. faculty Ohio State U., Columbus, 1965—, asso. prof. history, 1972—; vis. Fulbright lectr. Waseda U., Tokyo, 1973, U. Tokyo, 1973; coordinator Ohio Historians Media Group, 1974-75. Served with U.S. Army, 1961. Mem. AAUP, Am. Hist. Assn., Orgn. Am. Historians, Ohio Acad. History, Ohio Hist. Soc., Bus. History Conf. Democrat. Author: American Railorad Politics, 1914-1920, 1968; The Politics of Moral Behavior: Prohibition and Drug Abuse, 1973. Home: 3655 Medbrook Way N Columbus OH 43214 Office: 210 W 17th Ave Columbus OH 43210

KERR, WENDLE LOUIS, univ. adminstr.; b. Harlan, Iowa, Dec. 16, 1917; s. Leonard Louis and Clara Carolyn (Wendle) K.; B.S., U. Iowa, 1941, M.S., 1950; m. Mary Eleanor Smith, Apr. 10, 1943; children—James Louis, John David. Sta. pharmacist U. Iowa, Iowa City, 1946-61, instr., 1947-54, asst. prof., 1954-61, asso. prof., 1961—, dir. pharm. procurement, 1961-65, coordinator pharmacy extension services, 1965—. Chief umpire Iowa City Little League, 1954-56; v.p. Iowa City Babe Ruth Baseball, 1957. Bd. dirs. Johnson County Vis. Nurse Assn., 1968-74, v.p., 1973-74. Served with U.S. Army, 1941-46; Res., 1946-70. Mem. Tchrs. Pharmacy Adminstrn. (chmn. 1961-62), Tchrs. Continuing Edn., Am. Soc. Hosp. Pharmacists, Am., Ia. pharm. assns., Ia. Soc. Hosp. Pharmacists, Am. Assn. Colls. Pharmacy, Ia. Res. Officers Assn. (treas. 1968-69, surgeon 1969-72), Sigma Xi, Rho Chi, Sigma Nu. Conglist. Home: 236 Hutchinson Ave Iowa City IA 52240

KERR, WILLIAM EDWARD, JR., author, publishing co. exec.; b. Dalhart, Tex., Jan. 25, 1929; s. William E. and Norma Lucretia (Wightman) K.; B.A., Highlands U., 1950; m. Margaret Elizabeth Dahlbo, Aug. 15, 1953; children—Richard, Kendra. Tchr., Los Alamos (N.Mex.) High Sch., 1950-52; mem. sales staff South-Western Pub. Co., Cin., 1953-62, advt. mgr., 1962-67, dir. ednl. media, 1967—; lectr. audiovisual teaching techniques U. Denver, U. Colo., No. Colo. State U.; author: Dictionary of Accounting Terminology, 1967; (with wife) Think Metric, 1975; co-author: Metric Guide for Educational Materials, 1977; author, dir., producer filmstrips in bus., consumer and metric edn.; metric cons. ednl. materials sector com. Am. Nat. Metric Council. Recipient Student of Yr, award NAM, 1950; Service award Jour. Bus. Edn., 1952. Home: 7859 Ayerdayl St Cincinnati OH 45230 Office: 5101 Madison Rd Cincinnati OH 45227

KERSHAW, BEULAH FRANCES (MRS. BRYAN KERSHAW), music tchr., poet; b. Cloride, Miss., Jan. 9, 1921; d. William Washington and Esther Matilda (Bone) Warren; student pub. schs.; m. Bryan Kershaw, July 10, 1965; children—Georgia Verdon, Sandra Kershaw Gentry. Tchr. piano, organ, guitar and drums, 1962—; writer poetry, 1942—; rec. artist. Vol. worker in rest homes. Mem. Republican Com., Evansville, Ind., Carmi, Ill., 1967—. Author: Poems by Beulah, Vol. I, 1968, Vol. II, 1973. Composer: It Hurts to be Hurt, 1939; Your Woman, 1964; Santa Kissed Me. Home: Route 1 Crossville IL 62827

KERWOOD, JOHN RICHARD, historian; b. Ripley, W.Va., Nov. 7, 1942; s. John Kenna and Delcia Geneva (Hall) K.; B.A., W.Va. Wesleyan Coll., 1964; M.A., Pa. State U., 1967; m. Lynne Irene Nelson, Aug. 15, 1964; children—John Glenn, Jeffrey Nelson. Editor, historian U.S. Capitol Hist. Soc., Washington, 1967-71; dir. regional workshops Am. Assn. State and Local History, Nashville, 1971-72; exec. dir. Montgomery County (Ohio) Hist. Soc., Dayton, 1973-77, Stan Hywet Hall Found., Inc., Akron, Ohio, 1977—; adj. asst. prof. history Wright State U., Dayton, 1975-77; mem. Ohio Com. on Pub. Programs in the Humanities, 1973; adviser mus. programs div. Nat. Endowment for the Humanities, 1974—; vice-chmn. Heritage '76, Dayton-Montgomery County Bicentennial Commn., 1974-76. Trustee, Prince of Peace Ch. of the Brethren, Kettering, Ohio, 1976-77. Recipient George Washington Honor Medal award Freedoms Found. at Valley Forge, 1970; Nat. Hist. Publs. Commn. fellow, 1970-71. Mem. Am. Assn. State and Local History (state membership chmn. 1974—), Soc. Ohio Achivists (council 1973-76), Ohio Museums Assn. (sec. 1977—), Nat. Trust Hist. Preservation, Am. Assn. Museums. Editor: The United States Capitol: An Annotated Bibliography, 1973; (with others) vol. I The Papers of Joseph Henry, The Albany Years, 1797-1832, 1972; The Capitol Dome newsletter, 1967-71; contbr. articles to hist. jours. Home: 2488 Worthington Akron OH 44313 Office: 714 N Portage Path Akron OH 44303

KESKITALO, WALLACE ALBERT, county agt.; b. Republic, Mich., Sept. 3, 1913; s. John O. and Hilda W. (Anttila) K.; B.S., Mich. State U., 1940, M.S., 1956; m. Olive Gwendolynn Kelsey, Sept. 26, 1941 (dec. Nov. 1973); children—John, Patricia Keskitalo Newton, Stewart, Peggy Keskitalo Binoniemi, Pamela; m. 2d, Joyce M. Kalen, Sept. 7, 1976; stepchildren—Gary, David, Brian and Jim Kalen. Tchr., Kellogg Consol. Sch., Augusta, Mich., 1940-42, Shepherd (Mich.) High Sch., 1942-43; loan supr. Farm Security Adminstrn., Ontonogon, Mich., 1943-47; county extension agt. Mich. State U., Houghton, 1947—; mem. Houghton County Soil Conservation Dist. Bd., 1960—, Houghton County Overall Econ. Devel. Dist. Com., 1972—. Chmn. career edn. planning council Houghton, Keweenaw and Baraga County Schs.; mem. bd. edn. Portage Twp. Schs., Houghton, 1958-62, Osceala Twp., 1976; mem. Houghton County Planning Commn., 1962—. Recipient Distinguished Service award Houghton-Keweenaw Soil and Water Conservation Dist., 1977. Mem.

Nat. Assn. County Agrl. Agts. (Distinguished Service award 1974), Epsilon Sigma Phi, Alpha Gamma Rho. Episcopalian (mem. vestry 1974). Home: Box 173 Dollar Bay MI 49922 Office: Courthouse Houghton MI 49931

KESLER, JOHN CHARLES, historian; b. Toledo, Nov. 30, 1941; s. Charles Jay and Constance Kesler; B.S. in Edn., Bowling Green (Ohio) State U., 1969, M.A., 1971; m. Judith Ann Ashcroft, Dec. 22, 1962; 1 dau., Brenda Sue. Grad. teaching asst. Bowling Green State U., 1969-71; mem. faculty Lakeland Community Coll., Mentor, Ohio, 1971—, asst. prof. history, 1971—. Bd. dirs. Lake County Mental Retardation Program, 1976—. Served with U.S. Army, 1959-66; Vietnam. Decorated Air medal, Combat Inf. badge, Army Commendation medal. Mem. Am. Hist. Assn., Hispanic Am. Assn., Soc. Historians Am. Fgn. Policy, Lakeland Faculty Assn. (pres. 1973-74). Democrat. Lutheran. Club: Greene County Sport Parachute. Address: Lakeland Community Coll Mentor OH 44060

KESSINGER, HOWARD DAVID, editor, publisher; b. Wellington, Kans., Oct. 25, 1932; s. Jesse Harrison and Grace (Johnson) K.; student Wichita State U., 1950-52; B.S., Kans. State U., 1957; m. Sharon L. Totten, Sept. 29, 1962; children—Hannah Ann, Sarah Ruth, Mary Catherine, Michael David. Reporter, advt. man Junction City (Kans.) Republic, 1955-58; advt. mgr. Abilene (Kans.) Reflector-Chronicle, 1958-61; mng. editor Oberlin (Kans.) Herald, 1961-66, editor-pub., 1966-75; editor-pub. Marysville (Kans.) Adv., 1975—. Trustee, William Allen White Found. Served with C.E., U.S. Army, 1953-55. Mem. Oberlin C. of C. (pres., 1967, 68), Kans. Press Service (pres. 1976), Kans. Press Assn. (dir. 1968-70), Kans. State U. Alumni Assn. (dir. 1977—), Sigma Delta Chi. Democrat. Episcopalian. Club: Rotary. Home: 1103 Elm St Marysville KS 66508 Office: 107 S 9th St Marysville KS 66508

KESSINGER, MARGARET ANNE, internist; b. Beckley, W.Va., June 4, 1941; d. Clisby Theodore and Margaret Anne (Ellison) Kessinger; B.A., W.Va. U., 1963, M.D., 1967; m. Loyd Ernst Wegner, Nov. 27, 1971. Intern, U. Nebr., 1967-68; resident in internal medicine U. Nebr. Hosp., 1968-70, fellow med. oncology, 1970-72; asst. prof. internal medicine U. Nebr., 1972-77, asso. prof., 1977—; Am. Cancer Soc. fellow, 1971-72. Recipient clin. cancer tng. grant USPHS, 1970-72. Diplomate Nat. Bd. Med. Examiners, Am. Bd. Internal Medicine. Fellow A.C.P.; mem. Am. Soc. Clin. Oncology, Am. Fedn. Clin. Research, Nebr., Greater Omaha med. socs., Sigma Xi. Republican. Methodist. Home: Route 1 Scribner NE 68057 Office: Nebraska Medical Center Omaha NE 68105

KESSLER, CLEMM CROMWELL, III, educator, psychologist; b. Hartford, Conn., Mar. 12, 1941; s. Clemm Cromwell and Elizabeth (Graf) K.; A.B., Bucknell U., 1963; M.S., Western Res. U., 1965; Ph.D., Case Western Res. U., 1967; m. Patricia Jane Catherman, Aug. 31, 1963; children—Dawn Elizabeth, Danielle Ursula. Asst. prof. psychology U. Nebr., Omaha, 1967-70, asso. prof., 1970—. Cons. in field. Mem. Am., Midwestern, Neb. psychol. assns., Psi Chi. Home: Rural Route 2 Glenwood IA 51534 Office: Box 688 Omaha NE 68101

KESSLER, JOHN EDWARD, mfg. co. exec.; b. Champaign, Ill., Aug. 29, 1941; s. Louis M. and Helen Elizabeth (Smith) K.; B.S., U. Ill., 1963, M. Accounting Sci., 1965; m. Nancy Jane Rolfe, Aug. 31, 1963; children—Sherri Marie, Edward Lawrence. Sr. accountant Haskins & Sells, 1965-69; asst. to sr. v.p. adminstrn. Hart Schaffner & Marx, Chgo., 1969-70; regional controller N.Am., IMS Am., Ltd., Des Plaines, Ill., 1970-73; v.p., controller Cummins-Allison Corp., Glenview, Ill., 1973-77; sec.-treas. Ames Supply Co., Downers Grove, Ill., 1977—. Recipient Outstanding Young Man Am. award, 1974, Elijah Watt Sells certificate of hon. mention, C.P.A. exam., 1964, bronze tablet U. Ill., 1963, Haskins & Sells Found. award, 1962. Mem. Ill. Soc. C.P.A.'s, Am. Inst. C.P.A.'s, Am. Accounting Assn., Am. Inst. Corporate Controllers, Alpha Kappa Psi (scholarship medallian), Beta Alpha Psi, Phi Alpha Mu, Phi Eta Sigma, Phi Kappa Phi, Sigma Iota Epsilon, Beta Gamma Sigma, Alpha Kappa Lambda, Delta Sigma Pi (scholarship key). Presbyterian (elder, trustee). Home: 913 69th St Darien IL 60559 Office: 2537 Curtiss St Downers Grove IL 60515

KESSLER, LAWRENCE W., scientist, sci. instrument co. exec.; b. Chgo., Sept. 26, 1942; s. Michael C. and Sue (Sniader) Kessler; m. Gloria M. Lerman, Aug. 23, 1964; children—Jeffrey, Brett, Corey, Brandy. B.E.E., Purdue U., 1964; M.S., U. Ill., 1966, Ph.D., 1968. Mem. research staff Zenith Radio Corp., Chgo., 1968-74: pres. Sonoscan, Inc., Bensenville, Ill., 1974—. Mem. adv. com. HEW, 1973-75. Mem. IEEE (sec.-treas. sonics and ultrasonics div. 1969-71, pres. 1971-73), Am. Inst. for Ultrasound in Medicine, Acoustical Soc. Am., Am. Soc. for Non-destructive Testing, Sigma Xi, Eta Kappa Nu. Editor: Procs. Ultrasonics Symposium, IEEE, Inc., 1970; editor: Acoustical Holography, Vol. 7, 1977. Contbr. articles to tech. jours. Patentee acoustical microscopy, Bragg diffraction imaging, also liquid crystal device. Home: 418 Warren Rd Glenview IL 60025 Office: Sonoscan Inc 720 Foster Ave Bensenville IL 60106

KESSLER, RONALD NORMAN, mktg. co. exec.; b. Youngstown, Ohio, Mar. 25, 1949; s. Milton and Justine K.; B.S., Youngstown State U., 1973; m. Linda Ann Schloss, Aug. 21, 1976. Machine operator Kessler Products Co. Inc., Youngstown, 1964-66, sales, 1967-68, mgr. research and devel., 1969-72; sales staff Space-Links Inc., Youngstown, 1972, mgr. sales and mktg., 1973-74, v.p. sales, 1975-76, pres., 1977—; owner, operator Youngstown Mat Co. Inc., 1976—. Bd. dirs. Jewish Community Center. Mem. Internat. Sanitary Supply Assn., Soc. Plastic Engrs., Nat. Restaurant Assn. Mem. B'nai B'rith. Patentee in field. Home: 4510 Logan Way Hubbard OH 44425 Office: 3031 Market St Youngstown OH 44507

KESSLER, WILLIAM ERTMAN, arthitecture-engrng. co. exec.; b. Detroit, July 3, 1930; s. Ertman William and Pearl Patricia (Alderman) K.; B.S., Eastern Mich. U., 1956; m. Mary Ann Donley, Apr. 11, 1955; children—Lyta, Carol, Frances, Kathleen, Sarah, Paula, Patricia. Nuclear fuel design engr. Westinghouse Electric Corp., Pitts., 1956-61, physcis test engr., Idaho Falls, Idaho, 1961-62; expts. group leader Phillips Petroleum Co., Idaho Falls, 1962-66; project mgr. Consumers Power Co., Jackson, Mich., 1966-75; project mgr. Commonwealth Assos., Inc., Jackson, 1975—; chmn. Argonne Univs. Assn. review com. Components Tech. div. Argonne (Ill.) Nat. Lab., 1972—. Chmn. Region II Comunity Action Agy., 1970-75; mem. planning div. United Way Jackson, 1968-72. Served with AUS, 1951-53. Mem. Am. Nuclear Soc. (chmn. Mich. sect. 1966—). Roman Catholic. Clubs: Midland Country Club, Jackson Raquet Club. Home: 6104 Browns Lake Rd Jackson MI 49203 Office: 209 E Washington Ave Jackson MI 49201

KESSLER, WINIFRED BEAM-FLAUTT, personal and orgn. devel. cons.; b. Memphis, May 1, 1934; d. George Lee and Winifred Antoinette (Peek) Beam; A.B., U. Calif. Berkley, 1956; M.Ed. (sholar), Xavier U., Cin., 1968; postgrad. edn. U. Cin.; m. Thomas J. Flautt, 1955 (div. 1970); children—Madeline T., David G.; m. 2d, Adriaan Kessler, Nov. 2, 1972; stepchildren—Glenn, Sylvia, Marc. Sec. to pres. Maryville Coll., St. Louis, 1952-54; asst., office dean students U. Calif. Berkeley, 1956-57; tchr. Latin, English, Acad. Sacred Heart, Cin., 1957-60; tchr., counselor Convent of Good Shepherd, Cin., 1967-68; tchr. English, Latin, Pub. Schs., Cin., 1968-71; instr. counseling and ednl. psychology U. Cin., 1971-76; prin., con. WBFK Assos., Cin., 1976—; co-dir. Womonspace, Inc., Cin., 1977—. Bd. dirs., edn. chairwoman Cin. Human Relations Commn., 1963-67; bd. dirs., exec. com. Citizens Sch. Com. Cin., 1969—; bd. dirs. Christ Child Day Care Center, Cin., 1960-64; pres. Catholic Interracial council, Cin., 1965-67; bd. dirs. St. Johns Unitarian Ch., 1974-76; mem. priorities com. Community Chest, Cin., 1975—; Maryville Coll. scholar, 1952-55. Mem. Orgn. Devel. Network, Assn. Humanistic Psychology, Am. Psychol. Assn., Am. Personnel and Guidance Assn. Democrat. Unitarian. Club: Womans City, Clifton Meadows Swim/Tennis. Home: 3674 Clifton Ave Cincinnati OH 45220 Office: PO Box 20145 Cincinnati OH 54220

KESTEL, JOHN L., radiologist; b. Remsen, Iowa, July 11, 1899; s. John and Josephine (Osterhans) K.; B.S., Creighton U., 1922, M.D., 1924: m. Elizabeth Watson, Oct. 25, 1930; children—John L., Mary Elizabeth. Intern, St. Joseph's Hosp., Creighton Meml. Hosp., Omaha; fellow in medicine Mayo Found.-U. Minn. Grad. Dept., Rochester, 1925-28; practice medicine specializing in radiology, Waterloo, Iowa, 1928—; mem. staffs St. Francis Hosp., Schoitz Meml. Hosp. Diplomate Am. Bd. Radiology. Fellow Am. Coll. Radiology; mem. Iowa Radiol. Soc. (pres. 1942), Iowa State Med. Soc., AMA, Alumni Assn. Mayo Found., Radiol. Soc. N.Am. Roman Catholic. Club: Elks. Contbr. articles to med. jours. Home: 235 Midlothian Blvd Waterloo IA 50701 Office: 600 Black Bldg Waterloo IA 50703

KESTNBAUM, KATE TRYNIN, business analyst; b. Bklyn.; d. Theodore Norris and Ada (Wilentz) Trynin; A.B., Wellesley Coll., 1956; postgrad. Columbia U., 1956-57; m. Robert Dana Kestnbaum, June 10, 1957; children—Ellen Jean, Meyer II. Tchr., Calif. pub. elementary and secondary schs., 1957-58. Treas., Herrick House Aux., 1960-61, v.p., 1961-62, pres., 1962; founding v.p. jr. group Chgo. Wellesley Club, 1960-62, adv. mem. bd., 1971—; founding pres. Women's bd. Juvenile Protective Assn., 1962-63, bd. dirs., 1962—, sec., 1964-66, v.p., 1967-69, 77—; dist. fund chmn. Wellesley Coll., 1964-68, dist. leadership gifts chmn., 1969-70, vice chmn. Nat. leadership gifts, 1970-71, mem. nat. devel. fund com., 1971-77; women's bd. Met. Chgo. Am. Cancer Soc., 1963-71, chmn. clerical aid dr., 1964, regional vice chmn., 1965, 68, regional chmn., 1966, 69, corr. sec., 1968-69; bd. dirs. Know Your Chgo. Com., 1964—; mem. Chgo. Focus, 1969—; mem. parents' com. Francis W. Parker Sch., 1969-71, 76—. Trustee Hull House Assn., 1968-71. Mem. Soc. Contemporary Am. Art. Jewish. Address: 442 Wellington Ave Chicago IL 60657

KESTNBAUM, ROBERT DANA, mgmt. cons.; b. Chgo., Aug. 5, 1932; s. Meyer and Gertrude (Dana) K.; A.B., U. Chgo., 1951; A.B., Harvard U., 1953, M.B.A., 1955; m. Kate Trynin, June 10, 1957; children—Ellen Jean, Meyer II. Coordinator spl. sales Bell & Howell Co., Chgo., 1959-61, co-founder Robert Maxwell div., 1961, v.p., asst. gen. mgr., 1962-64, gen. mgr., 1964-66; direct mail mgr. Montgomery Ward & Co., 1966-67; pres. R. Kestnbaum & Co., direct mktg. cons., Chgo.; dir. Solar-X Corp., Boston. Bd. dirs. North Side Boys' Clubs, 1960-67, pres., 1965-67; bd. dirs., mem. exec. com. Chgo. Youth Centers, v.p., 1969-71, adminstrv. v.p., 1971-72; vice chmn. campaign for Chgo., U. Chgo. Alumni Fund, 1969-71; bd. dirs. U. Chgo. Alumni Found.; founding co-chmn. Chgo. Forum; founding treas., incorporator Inner City Fund; mem. adv. com. on correctional services Ill. Youth Commn., 1969-70; mem. Gov.'s Adv. Council State of Ill., 1969-72; mem. citizens rev. com. Ill. Bd. Higher Edn., 1971—; vice chmn. operating effectiveness com. Community Fund Met. Chgo., 1972-75, chmn. 1975-77, mem. agy. services com., 1972-77, vice-chmn., 1975-77; pub. mem. devel. com. Jewish Vocat. Service, 1972—; bd. govs. Republican Citizens League of Ill., 1961-63. Served from ensign to lt. (j.g.), USNR, 1955-58. Mem. Chgo. Assn. Direct Mktg. (dir. 1975—), Soc. Contemporary Art, Harvard Bus. Sch. Assn. Chgo. (Ill.). Jewish (trustee congregation 1968—, v.p. 1969-75, treas. 1975—). Clubs: Lake Shore Country (Glencoe, Ill.); Harvard (dir. 1976—), Mid Am. (Chgo.). Home: 442 Wellington Ave Chicago IL 60657 Office: 221 N LaSalle St Chicago IL 60601

KETCHAM, WARREN ANDREW, clin. psychologist; b. Manistee, Mich., June 28, 1909; s. Perry Warren and Anna Ellen (Ulrich) K.; student Albion (Mich.) Coll., 1928-29; B.M., U. Mich., 1932, M.A., 1947, Ph.D., 1951, postgrad. (Hinsdale scholar), 1951-52; m. Edna May Wearne, Nov. 25, 1962. Tchr. supr. music, pub. schs., Reed City, Mich., 1934-36, Melvindale, Mich., 1936-38, Dearborn, Mich., 1939-43; sch. psychologist pub. schs., Ferndale, Mich., 1950-53; prof. ednl. psychology, psychologist Univ. Sch., U. Mich., Ann Arbor, 1953—; pvt. practice clin. and indsl. psychology, Ypsilanti, Mich., 1965—; Fulbright lectr. child devel. U. Leeds (Eng.), 1959; research cons. Am. Sch., Guatemala City, Guatemala, 1959—. Certified psychologist, Mich. Fellow Am. Psychol. Assn.; mem. Nat. Register Health Service Providers Psychology, Mich. Psychol. Assn. Home: 2126 Lakeview Dr Ypsilanti MI 48197 Office: U Michigan School Education Room 2409 Ann Arbor MI 48109

KETEL, W. BRUCE, neurologist; b. Chgo., Dec. 17, 1941; s. Walter H. and Irene G. (Schofield) K.; student Bradley U., 1959-62; B.S., Northwestern U., 1963, M.D., 1966; m. Felicity T. Keily, May 15, 1971; children—Mark A., Derek S. Resident in neurology Northwestern U., Chgo., 1967-72; practice medicine specializing in neurology, Niles, Ill., 1972—; attending neurologist Luth. Gen. Hosp., Park Ridge, Ill., 1972—, Higland Park (Ill.) Hosp., 1972—; cons. in neurology Forest Hosp., Des Plaines, Ill., 1972—; clin. asst. prof. neurology Abraham Lincoln Sch. Medicine, U. Ill. Diplomate Am. Bd. Psychiatry and Neurology. Office: 9101 Greenwood Ave Niles IL 60648

KEUCHER, WILLIAM FREDERICK, clergyman; b. Atlantic City, June 6, 1918; s. Otto Ernest and Margaret (Wilson) K.; A.B., Eastern Coll., St. Davids, Pa., 1942; Th.B., Eastern Bapt. Theol. Sem., 1942, B.D., 1946, D.D., 1971; D.D., Ottawa (Kans.) U., 1953; D.D., Kalamazoo Coll., 1971; m. Edith Warnick Kimber, Nov. 28, 1940; children—Margaret Valerie Keucher Savage, Louise Sherilyn Keucher Cormier. Ordained to ministry Am. Baptist Ch., 1942; pastor Allegheny Ave. Bapt. Ch., Phila., 1942-48, 1st Bapt. Ch., El Dorado, Kans., 1948-52; exec. minister, judicatory head, Kans. Bapt. Conv., Topeka, 1952-70; sr. minister Covenant Bapt. Ch., Detroit, 1970-77, West Bloomfield, Mich., 1977—; mem. bd. internat. ministries Am. Bapt. Chs. U.S.A., 1971-79, pres., 1971, mem. gen. bd., 1972-79; mem. gen. bd. Nat. Council Chs. Christ in Am., 1976-78; vice chmn. Bapt. Joint Com. Pub. Affairs, Washington, 1974-75; mem. adj. faculty service Union Sem., Richmond, Va., 1974, N.Am. Bapt. Sem., 1976-77, No. Bapt. Theol. Sem., 1976. Trustee, Ottawa (Kans.) U., 1953-75, life trustee, 1975—; bd. dirs. Detroit Urban League, 1972—, pres., 1976-78. Author: An Exodus for the Church, 1973; Main Street and the Mind of God, 1974; Good News People in Action, 1975; editor Kans. Bapt., 1952-70; radio pastor Sound of the New Life, Detroit, 1973—. Home: 18225 Coral Gables Blvd Lathrup Village MI 48076 Office: 5800 W Maple Rd West Bloomfield MI 48033

KEVERN, RONALD BAWDEN, coll. adminstr.; b. Pontiac, Mich., June 14, 1933; s. Herbert Stanley and Florence Winifred K.; A.B., Central Mich. U., 1955; M.A., U. Mich., 1961; m. Marilyn Jean Jones, Aug. 20, 1955; children—Debra Jean, Brent Ronald, Bradley Donald. Tchr., Rochester (Mich.) Community Schs., 1955-60, prin., 1960-66, dir. personnel, 1966-68; asst. dir. placement Oakland U., Rochester, 1968-71, dir. career advising and placement, 1971—; cons. Oakland County Youth Assistance Program; mem. speakers bur. Midwest Coll. Placement Council. Vice pres. Rochester Community Schs. Bd. Edn., 1976—; chmn. com. mgmt. Rochester YMCA, 1965-67; vice chmn. Pontiac Area United Fund, 1974; chmn. adminstrv. bd. St. Paul's United Methodist Ch. Recipient Outstanding Service award Pontiac Area United Fund, 1974; service award N. Oakland County Girl Scouts Assn., 1970. Mem. Am., Mich. sch. bd. assns., Midwest Coll. Placement Council, Assn. Sch. Coll. Univ. Staffing, Nat. Edn. Assn., Am. Personnel and Guidance Assn. Home: 207 Orchardale Dr Rochester MI 48063 Office: 201 Wilson Hall Oakland U Rochester MI 48063

KEVLIN, ROSS PATRICK, grain co. exec.; b. New Orleans, Dec. 4, 1931; s. Moffet Henry and Mildred Mary (Brigtsen) K.; B.A., Tulane U., 1954; m. Paulette Renee Waller, Aug. 15, 1961; children—Ross Patrick, Anne. Export traffic mgr. Volkart Bros., Inc., cotton mchts., New Orleans, 1956-60; with Continental Grain Co., Worthington, Ohio, 1960—, mgr. of adminstr. Eastern region, 1976—. Home: 2588 Sonnington Dr Dublin OH 43017

KEYES, JAMES LYMAN, JR., indsl. marketing exec.; b. Peru, Ind., Apr. 27, 1928; s. James Lyman and Mary Edith (Weigel) K.; A.B., Wabash Coll., 1950; M.B.A., Harvard U., 1952. Mgr. Mesabi Range Distributorship, Cummins Engine Co., Inc., Hibbing, Minn., 1958-59, gen. mgr. Cummins Diesel Sales Corp., Columbus, Ind., 1959-61, dir. marketing services, 1961-66, gen. sales mgr., 1966-69, v.p. engine sales, 1969-70, v.p. nat. accounts, 1971-72, v.p. indsl. mktg., 1973-76, pres. Cummins Central Ohio, Inc., Columbus, 1976—. Bd. dirs., exec. com. Nat. Assn. for Retarded Children, 1964-73, v.p., 1969-73. Pres. Ind. Assn. Retarded Children, 1962-65. Served to 1st lt. USAF, 1952-54. Mem. Nat. Assn. Wabash Coll. Men (dir. 1970—, pres. 1974—). Republican. Presbyn. (deacon). Mason (32 deg., Shriner). Home: 1467 B Lake Shore Dr Columbus OH 43204 Office: 101 Phillipi Rd Columbus OH 43228

KEYES, MURRAY ALLISON, data processor; b. Denver, July 6, 1931; s. Henry and Gladys (Allison) K.; B.A., U. Mo., 1954, M.B.A., 1963; m. Carol Van Dyke, Sept. 5, 1954; children—Michelle, Brian, Kirsten. With Bendix Corp., 1958-65, Minn. Mining & Mfg. Co., 1965-68; data processing mgr. Domain Industries Inc., agro products mfg. co., New Richmond, Wis., 1968-74; sr. cons. McDonnell Douglas Automation Co., Creve Coeur, Mo., 1974—. Served with Signal Corps, AUS, 1954-58. Mem. Data Processing Mgmt. Assn., Assn. Systems Mgmt. Club: Lions. Home: 12617 Tallow Hill Ln Creve Coeur MO 63144 Office: PO Box 516 Saint Louis MO 63188

KEYS, CHRISTOPHER BENNETT, educator; b. N.Y.C., Mar. 18, 1946; s. William Walters and Margaret (Forman) K.; B.A., Oberlin Coll., 1968; M.A., U. Cin., 1971, Ph.D., 1973; m. Elizabeth Jaffer, Sept. 14, 1969. Asst. prof. psychology U. Ill., Chgo., 1972—. NIMH trainee, 1968-69, 70-71; U. Ill. grantee; recipient Pub. Service award Cook County, 1974. Mem. Am., Midwestern psychol. assns., Soc. Psychol. Study Social Issues, Orgn. Devel. Network, Assn. Advancement Psychology. Home: 811 Belleforte St Oak Park IL 60302 Office: Dept Psychology Univ Ill Chicago IL 60680

KEYS, MARTHA ELIZABETH, congresswoman; b. Hutchinson, Kans., Aug. 10, 1930; d. S.T. and Clara (Krey) Ludwig; student Olivet Coll., 1946-48; B.A. in Music, U. Mo. at Kansas City, 1952; m. Andrew Jacobs; children—Carol, Bryan, Dana, Scott. Mem. 94th-95th Congresses from 2d dist. Kans. Kans. coordinator McGovern for Pres. campaign, 1972; alt. del. Dem. Nat. Conv., 1972. Bd. dirs. Manhattan Arts Council. Mem. A.A.U.W., Civic Music Club, Common Cause. Home: 2342 Chris Dr Manhattan KS 66502 Office: 1502 Longworth Bldg Washington DC 20515

KEZYS, ALGIMANTAS GEORGE, clergyman; b. Vistvtis, Lithuania, Oct. 28, 1928; s. George and Eugenija (Kolytaite) K.; came to U.S., 1950, naturalized, 1956; M.A., Loyola U. (Chgo.), 1958. Ordained priest Roman Catholic Ch., 1961; photography editor Laiskai Lietuviams, Chgo., 1962-70; photographer-artist, 1957—; exhibited in one-man shows, Ciurlionis Gallery, Chgo., 1963-67, Art Inst. Chgo., 1965; exhibited in group shows, Exphotage Chgo., 1966, Bienal, Sao Paulo, Brazil, 1967; represented in permanent collections Art Inst. Chgo., Mus. Modern Art, N.Y.C., others. Founder, dir. Lithuanian Photo Library, Chgo., 1967—; bd. dirs. Lithuanian Youth Center, Chgo., 1974-77. Author: Sventoji Auka, 1965; Photographs, 1966; I fled Him, down the days and down the nights, 1970; Form and Content, 1972. Editor Lithuanian-Am. Ethnic Ency., 1974—. Home: 5620 S Claremont Ave Chicago IL 60636

KHALAFALLA, SANAA EL-SAYED, metallurgical chemist; b. Mit Yaish, Egypt, July 1, 1924; s. El-Sayed Khalafalla Ali and Ta'hra Solieman (El-Gobeily); came to U.S., 1948, naturalized, 1970; B.Sc. with distinction, U. Cairo, 1944; M.Sc., U. Minn., 1949, Ph.D., 1953; m. Aida Sinbel, Feb. 11, 1957; children—Ashraf, Sammy. Research fellow U. Minn., Mpls., 1961-64; with U.S. Bur. Mines, Twin Cities, Minn., 1964—, research supr., 1966—. Vis. prof. U. Bristol, U.K., 1960-61. Mem. Am. Inst. Mining, Metall. and Petroleum Engrs., Metall. Soc., Iron and Steel Soc., IEEE, Phi Lambda Upsilon, Sigma Xi. Contbr. articles to profl. jours. Patentee in field. Home: 2551 37th Ave S Minneapolis MN 55406 Office: Twin Cities Metallurgy Research Center PO Box 1660 Twin Cities MN 55111

KHALILI, ALI ASGHAR, physician, educator; b. Ardebil, Iran, Feb. 9, 1932; s. Bahlool and Golsoom Khalili; came to U.S., 1958, naturalized, 1970; M.D., Teheran U. Med. Sch., 1957; m. Sandra D. Howard, Feb. 9, 1962; children—Lisa D., Alan J. Intern, Columbus Hosp., Chgo., 1958-59; resident Albert Einstein Coll. Medicine, N.Y. U., 1959-62; practice medicine specializing in phys. medicine and rehab., Chgo., 1965—; asso. prof. dept. rehab. medicine Northwestern U. Med. Center, Chgo., 1968—; dir. neuromuscular diagnostic and research dept. Rehab. Inst. Chgo., 1968-71, cons. physiatrist in spasticity; dir. rehab. medicine Grant Hosp., Chgo., 1968—, chmn. dept., 1976—. Mem. Am. Congress Rehab. Medicine. Named Outstanding New Citizen of Year, Citizenship Council Met. Chgo., 1970. Diplomate Am. Bd. Phys. Medicine and Rehab. Mem. Am. Acad. Phys. Medicine and Rehab., Ill., Chgo. med. socs., A.M.A., Am. Assn. Electromyography and Electrodiagonosis. Contbr. articles to profl. publs. Home: 770 Euclid St Elmhurst IL 60126 Office: 551 Grant Pl Chicago IL 60614

KHALILI, JOSEPH ELIAS, instn. exec., educator; b. Jerusalem, May 17, 1937; s. Elias K. and Emily Khalili; came to U.S., 1958, naturalized, 1972; B.S., Xavier U., 1960; M.A. (Taft fellow), U. Cin., 1961; Ph.D., Sussex (Eng.) Coll. Tech., 1973; m. Rene Jarjoui, Sept. 3, 1961; children—Eli, Emily. Lectr., Libyan Dept. Edn., 1961-62; asst. Beer Zeit Coll., Jerusalem, 1962-64; lectr. Xavier U., Cin., 1965-66; asst. prof. Purdue U., Indpls., 1966-69, Marian Coll., Indpls., 1969-72; personnel dir. St. Augustine Home for Aged, Indpls., 1972—. Polit. commentator Jerusalem Times, 1962-64. Mem. Planning Com. Washington Twp., 1969—. Bd. dirs. Indpls. Council on World Affairs, 1970-72. Mem. A.A.U.P. (pres. Marian chpt. 1970-72), Am. Soc. Internat. Law, Am. Polit. Sci. Assn., Am. Acad. Polit. and Social Sci. Author: Communist China's Interaction with Arab

Nationalists since Bandung, 1970. Contbg. editor The Source, 1972—. Home: 1551 W 79th St Indianapolis IN 46260 Office: 2345 W 86th St Indianapolis IN 46260

KHAMBATA, ADI JEHANGIR, electronics engr., educator; b. Bombay, India, Apr. 8, 1922; s. Jehangir M. and Najoo J. (Vakil) K.; came to U.S., 1956, naturalized, 1959; B.A., U. Bombay, 1944; B.S.E.E. (R.D. Sethna scholar), Milw. Sch. Engring., 1950; m. Ruth Elizabeth Flopper, Mar. 7, 1954; children—Jimmy Adi, Soonoo Ruth, Danny Adi. Customer engr. IBM World Trade Corp., Bombay, 1953-55; jr. cons. Beacons Ltd., Bombay, 1955-56; with Sperry Univac div. Sperry Rand Corp., St. Paul, 1956-75, engring. mgr., 1965-69, staff engr., 1969-75; tchr. St. Paul Tech.-Vocat. Inst., 1975—; tchr. Ramsey Engring. Co., St. Paul, Univac, St. Paul. Pres. Grove Elementary Sch. PTA, St. Paul Park, Minn., 1962-63. Mem. IEEE, Am. Mgmt. Assn., Aircraft Owners and Pilots Assn., Kappa Eta Kappa. Clubs: Southview Country (West St. Paul, Minn.); Rotary (St. Paul). Author: Introduction to Integrated Semiconductor Circuits, 1963 (German transl. 1968); Introduction to Large-scale Integration, 1969 (German transl. 1971, Japanese transl. 1970). Home: 19 Cutler St Saint Paul MN 55119

KHAN, MOHAMMED NASRULLAH, physiologist, veterinarian; b. Hyderabad, India, Oct. 11, 1933; s. Ghouse Mohammed and Hayath (Khatoon) K.; B.V.Sc., Osmania U., India, 1955; M.S., La. State U., 1963, Ph.D., 1970; m. Soraya Khan, Mar. 3, 1957; children—Mahmood, Faiz. Practice vet. medicine, Hyderabad, 1955-58; asst. lectr. Vet. Sch., Rajendranagar, 1958-61; research asst. La. State U., 1961-63, 67-70; instr. Vet. Colls., Hyderabad and Tirupati, 1963-67; asst. prof. City Colls. of Chgo., 1970-72; asso. prof. Lewis U., Schs. of Nursing South Chgo. Hosp. and Little Company of Mary Hosp., Chgo., 1972—; coordinator biology dept. Central YMCA Coll., Chgo. Mem. Andhra Pradesh Vet. Assn. (mng. com. 1960-61), AAUP, AAAS, World Poultry Sci. Assn. H.E.H. The Nizam's fellow, 1961; Ford Found. scholar U. Delhi, 1966; contbr. sci. articles to profl. jours. Home: 8 Gerstung St Park Forest IL 60466

KHANNA, SATISH C., civil engr.; b. Chaniot, Punjab State, India, June 12, 1937; s. Lal C. and Kaushalya Devi (Kapoor) K.; B.A. in Math., Doaba Coll., Punjab, 1956; B.C.E., Punjab Engring. Coll., 1960; M.C.E., Wayne State U., 1972; m. Vinod Bala Kapoor, May 7, 1967; children—Ritu, Rohit, Manish. Civil engr. Punjab Dept. Pub. Works, 1961-71, Land & Sea Corp., Detroit, 1971-72; sr. civil engr. Metro Engrs. Inc., Ypsilanti, Mich., 1972-76, Charles E. Raines Cons. Co., Southgate, Mich., 1977, K-Mart Corp., Troy, Mich., 1977—. Registered profl. engr., Mich. Mem. ASCE. Hindu. Office: K-Mart Corp Design Div 3100 W Big Beaver Rd Troy MI 48084

KHAPOYA, VINCENT BARASSA, educator; b. Kenya, May 15, 1944; s. Gerald Khapoya and Flora Atikinyi (Nangila) Opari; B.S. in Math. and Polit. Sci., Oreg. State U., 1969; postgrad. U. Nev., 1969-70; M.A., U. Denver, 1971, Ph.D. in Polit. Sci., 1974; m. Izzat Gulamani, Apr. 22, 1972. Asst. prof. Afro-Am. studies Met. State Coll., Denver, 1971-72; asst. prof. polit. sci. Oakland U., Mich., 1974—. Mem. Am. Polit. Sci. Assn., Soc. Internat. Devel., African Assn. Polit. Sci., Internat. Studies Assn., African Studies Assn., Pi Sigma Alpha. Home: 1505 Nob Ln Pontiac MI 48055 Office: Oakland U Rochester MI 48063

KHAZEI, AMIR HASSAN, surgeon; b. Tehran, Iran, Jan. 12, 1932; s. Gasem and Esmat (Khaligazam) K.; came to U.S., 1957, naturalized, 1968; B.S., U. Lausanne (Switzerland), 1953, M.D., 1957, Certificat d'Etude Medicale, 1957; m. Mona, June 20, 1958; children—Kimberly, Deborah, Brent, Eric. Intern in internal medicine Hospital Universitaire Nestle, Lausanne, 1955, intern in gen. surgery Centre Hospitalier de Nice (France), 1955; rotating intern Menorah Med. Center, Kansas City, Mo., 1957-58, jr. resident in gen. surgery, 1959-60; surgeon, mem. med. team Internat. Red Cross to Congo, 1961; asst. resident in gen. surgery U. Man. (Can.), Winnipeg, 1960-62, chief resident, teaching fellow in gen. surgery, 1962-63, asso. resident in thoracic and cardiovascular surgery U. Md., 1963-64, chief resident in thoracic and cardiovascular surgery, 1964-65; instr. U. Md. Hosp., 1965-68, asso. dir. shock trauma units, 1966-68; chief thoracic and cardiovascular surgery South Balt. Gen. Hosp., 1965-68: pvt. practice medicine specializing in thoracic and cardiovascular surgery, Elgin, Ill., 1968—; mem. staffs Sherman Hosp., St. Joseph Hosp., Elgin. Diplomate Am. Bd. Surgery, Am. Bd. Thoracic Surgery. Fellow A.C.S., Am. Coll. Chest Physicians; mem. AMA, Md. Surg. Soc., N.Y. Acad. Scis., Ill. State (Gold medal award 1969, Bronze award 1971), Kane County (Ill.) med. socs., Soc. Thoracic Surgeons, Am. Coll. Angiology, Am. Trauma Soc. Author: (with others) Biochemical Engineering Symposium, 1966; contbr. articles to profl. jours.; co-author profl. films. Home: Rural Route 3 Box 218 A Elgin IL 60120 Office: 860 Summit St Elgin IL 60120

KHEDROO, LAWRENCE GLENN, surgeon, educator; b. Chgo., June 9, 1919; s. Khedroo S. and Emma H. (Sargis) K.; D.D.S., Northwestern U., 1942, B.S., M.D., 1946; m. Larna Marilyn Turner, July 5, 1965; children—Susan L., Roberta D., Stephen C., Mark Lawrence. Intern, St. Anne's Hosp., Chgo., 1945-46; resident in gen. surgery St. Elizabeth's Hosp., Chgo., 1949-52; resident in thoracic surgery Municipal Tb Sanitarium, Chgo., 1952-53; practice medicine specializing in surgery, Chgo., 1953—; asst. prof. surgery Rush U. Med. Sch., Chgo., 1972—; mem. sr. surg. staff St. Elizabeth's Hosp., Chgo., 1955—, chmn. tissue com., 1955-58; mem. courtesy surg. staff Lutheran Deaconess Hosp., Chgo., 1958—; chief dept. surgery Alexian Bros. Hosp., Chgo., 1958-60, attending surgeon, 1957—, chmn. dept. edn., 1961-65; mem. surg. staff Highland Park (Ill.) Hosp., 1975—; mem. surg. staff Norwegian Am. Hosp., Chgo., 1968—, mem. med. edn. com., 1971—; mem. surg. staff St. Therese Hosp., Waukegan, Ill., 1969—; mem. surg. staff Swedish Covenant Hosp., Chgo., 1971—; lectr. in surgery, 1975; asso. attending surgeon Cook County (Ill.) Hosp., Chgo., 1972—; clin. asso. prof. dept. anatomy U. Ill. Med. Sch., Chgo., 1950—. Served to 1st lt., M.C., AUS, 1946-47, capt., M.C., AUS, 1953; PTO, Korea. Decorated Bronze Star medal. Diplomate Am. Bd. Surgery, Nat. Bd. Med. Examiners. Fellow A.C.S., Am. Coll. Chest Physicians, Internat. Coll. Physicians, Am. Coll. Emergency Physicians, Pan Am. Med. Assn.; mem. N.Y. Acad. Scis., Sigma Xi, Omicron Kappa Upsilon. Contbr. articles on surgery to profl. jours. Home: 1405 Bob O'Link Highland Park IL 60035 Office: 1344 Shermer Rd Northbrook IL 60062

KHEZRI-YAZDAN, ALI-ASGHAR, metallurgist; b. Yazd, Iran, Apr. 21, 1945: s. Habibollah and Safa (Khajehzadeh) K.; came to U.S., 1964, naturalized, 1976; B.S., No. Mich. U., 1969; M.S., Western Mich. U., 1972; Ph.D., Mich. State U., 1976; m. Naheed Rejaie, Aug. 25, 1971; 1 child, Shabnam. Grad. asst. Western Mich. U., Kalamazoo, 1969-72; grad. asst., instr. Mich. State U., East Lansing, 1972-76; tech. dir. Utilex div. Hoover Ball & Bearing, Fowlerville, Mich., 1973-75, also lectr. in seminars concerning handling and transp. regulations of hazardous materials, process an devel. engring. cons., 1975—; cons. in field. Licensed in indsl. effluent abatement, Mich., 1976; mem. corporate advisory com. on hazardous materials act and acquifier hearings. Mem. Am. Electroplating Soc., Am. Soc. Metals. Recipient Excellence award, Sears Roebuck Co. Muslim. Home: 1563 Cranwood Ct Okemos MI 48864 Office: 425 Frank St Fowlerville MI 48836

KHO, EUSEBIO, surgeon; b. Philippines, Dec. 16, 1933; s. Joaquin and Francisca (Chua) K.: came to U.S., 1964; A.A., Silliman U., Philippines, 1955; M.D., State U. Philippines, 1960; fellow in surgery, Johns Hopkins, 1965-67; m. Grace C. Lim, May 24, 1964: children—Michelle Mae, April Tiffany, Bradley Jude, Jaclyn Ashley. Intern in surgery Balt. City Hosp., 1964-65, resident in gen. surgery, 1965-67; research asso. pediatric surgery U. Chgo. Hosps., 1967-68; resident in gen. surgery, then chief resident U. Tex. Hosp., San Antonio, 1968-70; hosp. surgeon St. Anthony Hosp., Louisville, 1970-72; practice medicine specializing in surgery, Scottsburg, Ind., 1972—; chmn. dept. surgery Scott County Meml. Hosp., 1973—; cons. surgeon Washington County Meml. Hosp., Salem, Ind., also Clark County Meml. Hosp., Jeffersonville, Ind., 1973—; courtesy surgeon Suburban Hosp., Louisville, 1973—. Diplomate Am. Bd. Surgery. Fellow A.C.S.; mem. Am. Coll. Internat. Physicians (founding mem., trustee 1974—), AMA (Physician's Recognition award 1969, 72) Ind., Ky., Ind. Philippine med. assns., Internat. Coll. Surgeons. Presbyterian. Clubs: Optimists, Masons. Home: 14 Carla Ln Scottsburg IN 47170 Office: 137 E McClain Ave Scottsburg IN 47170

KHOSH, JOHN GHOLAM HOSEIN, physician; b. Meshed, Iran, Apr. 21, 1929; s. Hessam and Fatemeh (Tabas) Khoshnevisan; came to U.S., 1957, naturalized, 1970; M.D. summa cum laude, U. Meshed, 1955; postgrad. U. Pa., 1960: m. Mary Nell Sivert, Sept. 1, 1961; children—Sheila June, Deanna June, Lisa June, Lora June. Intern, Cook County Hosp., Chgo., 1957-58; resident in surgery Deaconess Hosp., Cleve., 1959-60, in obstetrics and gynecology, St. Thomas Hosp., Akron, 1959-62, in pathology St. Josephs Hosp., Hamilton, Ont., 1962-63, in surgery, Hamilton Gen. Hosp., 1963-64; practice medicine specializing in obstetrics and gynecology, Strongsville, Ohio, 1965—; mem. staff Fairview Gen. Hosp., Cleve. Diplomate Am. Bd. Obstetrics and Gynecology. Fellow Am. Coll. Obstetrics and Gynecology; mem. Am. Soc. Laparoscopists, Am. Fertility Soc., Cleve. Acad. Medicine, Cleve. Obstetrics and Gynecol. Soc., Ohio Med. Assn. Democrat. Club: Rotary. Office: 12563 Pearl Rd Strongsville OH 44136

KHOSH, MARY SIVERT, psychologist; b. Akron, Ohio, July 28, 1942; d. Floyd Calvin and Mattie Paul (Milwee) Sivert; B.A., U. Akron, 1966, M.S., 1970; Ph.D., Kent State U., 1976; m. John G. H. Khosh, Sept. 1, 1961; children—Sheila June, Deanna June, Lisa June, Lora June. Career counselor Baldwin-Wallace Coll., Berea, Ohio, 1974-75, asst. dir. counseling and advising center, 1975-76, asso. dir., 1976—, dir. articulation project, 1976—; practice psychology, 1977—; cons. in field. Vice pres. SW Gen. Hosp. Jr. Bd., Berea, 1969; guest organist Akron United Meth. Ch., 1961. Mem. SW Gen. Hosp. Med. Wives, 1966-76, pres. 1968-70, Am., Ohio, Cleve. psychol. assns. Nat., Ohio assns. women deans, adminstrs. and counselors, Am. Personnel and Guidance Assn., Am. Coll. Personnel Assn., Fairview Gen. Hosp. Women's Aux. Democrat. Methodist. Contbr. articles to profl. jours. Office: #118 Adminstrn Bldg Baldwin-Wallace Coll Berea OH 44017

KIANI, REZA, physician; b. Shahmirzad, Iran, Feb. 23, 1939; s. Farjollah and Salemeh K.; came to U.S., 1968, naturalized, 1973; M.D., Pahlavi U., Iran, 1966. Rotating intern New Rochelle (N.Y.) Hosp., 1968-69; resident in internal medicine U. Cin. Gen. Hosp., 1969-70, sr. resident in internal medicine, 1970-71; fellow in endocrinology and metabolism Northwestern U. Med. Center, Chgo., 1971-72; fellow in endocrinology and metabolism, instr. medicine, U. Ill. Med. Center, Chgo., 1972-73, asso. in medicine, 1973-74, asst. prof. medicine, attending physician, 1974—; practice medicine specializing in endocrinology and metabolism, Chgo., 1974—; dir. outpatient clinic emergency room, cons. endocrinology, and metabolism Community Gen. Hosp., Sterling, Ill., 1973-74. Diplomate Am. Bd. Internal Medicine. Mem. AMA, (Physician Recognition award, 1971, 73-76), A.C.P. Contbr. articles to med. jours. Home: 360 Versailles Dr Northbrook IL 60062 Office: Dept Medicine Abraham Lincoln Sch Medicine 840 S Wood St PO Box 6998 Chicago IL 60680

KIBBE, JOHN CARTER, lawyer; b. California, Mo., Nov. 2, 1924; s. Edgar Allen and Bess (Carter) K.; student Central Coll., Fayette, Mo., 1941-43, Oreg. U., 1943; A.B., Mo. U., 1948, LL.B., 1950; m. Barbara Hadley, Dec. 26, 1950; children—Ann Kibbe Matthews, John David, Barbara Jane. Admitted to Mo. bar, 1950; since practiced in California, pros. atty. Moniteau County, 1951-64; spl. counsel City of California, 1963-65, city atty., 1965-70; v.p., gen. counsel Moniteau Mills, Inc., 1964-72, pres., 1972-75; mem. firm Kibbe, Crews & Gaw, California and Tipton, Mo., 1973—; pres. Mo. Abstract Co., California, 1974—; dir. The Farmers & Traders Bank; mem. bar com. 26th Jud. Circuit, 1962-70. Chmn. adv. com. trust Elia B. Paegelow; chmn. Moniteau County March Dimes, 1968; trustee Wood Place Library, 1969—. Served from pvt. to technician AUS, 1943-46. Mem. Am., Moniteau County bar assns., Assn. Trial Lawyers Am., Mo. Integrated Bar, Acad. Polit. Sci., Am. Acad. Polit. and Social Sci., VFW (comdr. Post 4345, 1967-68), Am. Judicature Soc., Am., Mo., Moniteau County (dir. 1966) hist. socs., Alumni Assn. Mo. U. (chmn. Moniteau County 1964—), Internat. Soc. Law and Sci., Internat. Platform Assn., Order High Priesthood Mo., Phi Alpha Delta, Alpha Phi Omega. Mem. Christian Ch. (trustee). Club: Masons (past master). Home: Proctor Circle Dr California MO 65108 Office: Kibbe Crews & Gaw California MO 65108

KICE, JACK WILBUR, mfg. co. exec.; b. Wichita, Kans., Jan. 10, 1915; s. James Wilbur and Minnie M. (Winzer) K.; grad. Chgo. Tech. Coll., 1935; m. Anna Ruth Jones, Jan. 1, 1937; children—Richard Lee, Mary Ann Kice Grant, John Edward. Asst. chief engr. Lennox Furnace Co., Marshalltown, Iowa, 1937-40; engr. Strato Lab., Boeing Airplane Co., Wichita, 1940-45; asst. to pres. Coleman Co., Inc., Wichita, 1945-56; v.p. engring. Kice Metal Products Co., Inc., Wichita, 1956-71, chmn. bd., dir. engring., 1971—; pres. C.F.M. Corp., Blackwell, Okla. Registered profl. engr., Kans. Mem. Am. Soc. Heating, Air Conditioning and Refrigeration Engrs., Nat. Soc. Profl. Engrs., C. of C. Republican. Presbyterian. Author tech. papers. Patentee in field of air pollution control, other indsl. air systems. Home: 3021 E Clark St Wichita KS 67211 Office: 2040 S Mead Ave Wichita KS 67211

KICKELS, MARY KAY, coll. adminstr.; b. Chgo., Aug. 16, 1939; d. Gordon J. and Florence M. (McGraw) Kickels; B.A., Rosary Coll., River Forest, Ill., 1961; M.A., Cath. U. Am., 1966; postgrad. (Ford Found. fellow) George Washington U., 1972-73; m. Donald L. Chase, Nov. 8, 1975. Chmn. dept. speech/theatre Nazareth High Sch., La Grange, Ill., 1960-71; media program coordinator/producer, writer Ill. Office of Edn., Springfield, 1971-72; asso. researcher Council Chief State Sch. Officers, Washington, 1972-73; asst. dir. Ednl. Facilties Center, Chgo., 1973-74; chmn. inter-visions dept. Triton Coll., River Grove, Ill., 1974-78, dir. admissions, 1978—; cons. humanities div. Ency. Brit., 1975—; spl. workshop leader Chgo. Consortium Colls. and Univs., 1974—; cons. McDonald's franchise, Ala., Milw. R.R. Mem. Chgo. Friends of the Parks, 1976—; adv. bd. Nat. Indian Employment Council, 1977—. Danforth Found. grantee, 1971. Mem. NEA, Nat. Assn. Curriculum Devel., Assn. Gen. and Liberal Studies, Nat. Assn. Educators in Broadcasting, Nat. Assn. ednl. Tech., Phi Delta Kappa, Rosary Coll. Alunni Assn. (sec., bd. dirs.). Scriptwriter endl. films. Home: 3 N 658 Woodland Dr West Chicago IL 60185 Office: 2000 5th Ave River Grove IL 60171

KIDDLE, LAWRENCE BAYARD, educator; b. Cleve., Aug. 20, 1907; s. Bayard Taylor and Emma Melvina (Volmar) K.; B.A., Oberlin Coll., 1929; M.A., U. Wis., 1930, Ph.D., 1935; m. Allene Cornelia Houglan, June 29, 1932; children—Sue (Mrs. Edward Frederick Meyer), Mary Ellen. Teaching asst. Spanish and French, U. Wis., Madison, 1929-35; instr. Princeton U., 1938-40; asst. prof. Tulane U., New Orleans, 1940-41, asso. prof., 1941-43; asst. prof. Spanish, Romance linguistics U. Mich., Ann Arbor, 1947-48, asso. prof., 1948-54, prof., 1954—; Fulbright prof. linguistics Instituto Caro y Cuervo Bogota (Colombia), 1963-64. Served to lt. comdr. USNR, 1943-47. Decorated comandante Orden Militar de Ayacucho (Peru). Mem. Hispanic Soc. Am. (corr.), Modern Lang. Assn. Am., Am. Assn. Tchrs. Spanish and Portuguese (pres. 1952), Linguistic Soc. Am. Democrat. Editor: (with J.E. Englekirk) Los de Abajo (Mariano Azuela), 1939; Veinte Cuentos Hispanoamericanos del Siglo Veinte, 1956; El Libro de las Cruzes (Alfonso El Sabio), 1961; Cuentos Americanos y Algunas Poesias, 1970. Home: 2654 Englave Dr Ann Arbor MI 48103 Office: U Mich Ann Arbor MI 48109

KIDSTON, ALAN R., lawyer; b. Detroit, Sept. 7, 1928; s. Arthur R. and Gladys (Larder) K.; A.B., U. Mich., 1951, J.D., 1953.; m. Marlowe Anderson, Sept. 2, 1953; children—Adam Stuart, Candace Cecile. Admitted to Ill. bar, 1953; law practice with Chadwell, Keck, Kayser, and Ruggles (and predecessor partnerships), Chgo., 1953-59, partner, 1960-70; sr. v.p., gen. counsel Cherry-Burrell Corp., Chgo., 1970-73; now v.p., gen. legal counsel Ill. Tool Works, Inc., Chgo. Alderman, Park Ridge, Ill., 1965-69. Served with U.S. Army, 1946-47. Mem. Internat., Am., Ill., Chgo. bar assns., Phi Beta Kappa. Clubs: Lawyers, U. Mich. (bd. govs., 1962—, pres., 1966—); Union League (dir. 1972-75), Chicago Yacht, Mid-Day, Law (Chgo.); Park Ridge Country. Home: 715 Elmore St Park Ridge IL 60068

KIDWELL, E. LEE, advt. agy. exec.; b. Morning View, Ky., July 11, 1928; s. James J. and Mary Hazel (Gibson) K.; grad. U. Cin., 1955; B.A., U. Md., 1952, B.S., 1948; m. Norma M. Zeiler, Dec. 23, 1952; children—Toni Ann, Gregory Lee, Bradley James, Christopher Robin. With Osborne-Kemper-Thomas, Inc., advt. agy., Cin., 1955—, v.p. adminstrn., 1967—; pres. Kidwell Mktg. Co. div. Magrish Internat., 1975-76; v.p., gen. sales mgr. Am. Sign & Advt. Services Inc., Cin., 1977—; v.p. product devel. U.M.C. Industries, 1972-75; v.p. mktg., v.p. adminstrn. Osborne-Kemper Thomas div. Hallmark Cards Inc., 1955-72; dir. Wilmington (Ohio) Pub. Co., 1968—; tchr. Shuster Martin Sch., Cin., 1952—. Served with SAC, USAF, 1948-52. Mem. Beta Alpha Psi, Omicron Delta Kappa, Delta Sigma Rho. Clubs: Rotary; Execs. Internat. (Cin.); Businessmen's (Montgomery, Ohio). Home: 7600 Huckleberry Ln Cincinnati OH 45242 Office: Calender Hill Cincinnati OH 45206

KIEFER, JOHN JOSEPH, retail pres.; b. Independence, Mo., Feb. 27, 1932; s. Robert Joseph and Catherine Hester (Smith) K.; student U. Kans., 1959; m. Doris Jean Pratt, Aug. 27, 1958; children—Michael Joseph, Robert David, Alison Ann. Pres., Kief's Record & Hi-Fi, Lawrence, Kan., 1959-71, Kief's Record & Stereo Supply Inc. wholesale, Lawrence, 1971—; owner, developer Holiday Plaza Shopping Center, Lawrence. Served with U.S. Army, 1952-54. Mem. Nat. Assn. Record Merchandisers, Malls Shopping Center Mchts. Assn., V.F.W., Record Merchandisers Am. (nat. youth dir. 1973-74), U. Kans. Alumni Assn. (pres. 1958). Elk. Home: RD 2 Box 71 Lawrence KS 66044 Office: PO Box 2 Lawrence KS 66044

KIEFER, JOSEPH HENRY, med. educator; b. Chgo., Aug. 20, 1910; s. Michael Nicholas and Mary Anna (Seiler) K.; B.S., Northwestern U., 1931, B.M., 1934, M.D., 1935; m. Marie Manning Kinser, July 7, 1945; children—Joseph Henry, Harry K., Marianna S. Intern, then resident urology Cook County Hosp., Chgo., 1935-37: pvt. practice urol. surgery, Chgo., 1937-73; mem. faculty U. Ill. Coll. Medicine, 1937—, prof. urology, 1944—, chmn. div., 1945-60, acting chmn. div., 1968-71; sr. cons. Univ. Ill. Hosps., 1971—; mem. emeritus staffs St. Joseph Hosp., Augustana Hosp., 1971—; Belfield lectr. Chgo. Urol. Soc., 1971. Recipient Distinguished Service award U. Ill. Dept. Surgery, 1959; Centennial award St Joseph Hosp., Chgo., 1969; Alumni Service award DePaul U., Chgo., 1972. Mem. AMA, A.C.S., Ill. (sci. exhibit award 1957), Chgo. (past pres. N. Shore br.) med. socs., Inst. Medicine Chgo., Am. Urol. Assn. (1st prize med. history exhibit 1970, Wirt B. Dakin award 1971), Chgo. Urol. Soc. (past pres.), Am. Assn. Genito-Urinary Surgeons, Soc. Internat. d'Urologie, Soc. Univ. Urologists, Soc. Pediatri Urology, Urology Corr. Club, Soc. Med. History Chgo., Am. Assn. History Medicine, AAAS, Soc. Internat. d'Histoire de Medicine, Ill. Soc. Med. Research, Catholic Physicians Guild Chgo. (past pres.), Chgo. Historians Medicine and Sci., Sigma Xi. Club: Caxton (Chgo.). Author and editor: Davis Memorial Volumne in Medicine History, 1965. Contbr. numerous articles to profl. jours. Home: 1240 W North Shore Ave Chicago IL 60626

KIEFER, ROBERT ALLEN, mech. engr.; b. Chgo., Dec. 17, 1948; s. Adam and Shirley (Kanker) K.; student U. Ill., 1966-68; B.S. in M.E., Ill. Inst. Tech., 1973; m. Patricia Ann Davis, Dec. 21, 1970; 1 dau., Heather Dawn. Mgr. research and devel. Rotary Seal Corp., Chgo., 1968-73; fluid power specialist Miller Fluid Power Co., Bensenville, Ill., 1973-75; field sales engr. Boston Gear Div., Maywood, Ill., 1975; sales mgr. Walter Norris Engring. Co., Chgo., 1975—. Mem. Am. Soc. Mech. Engrs. (asso.), Fluid Power Soc. Home: 8 Chelsea Ln Cary IL 60013 Office: 7800 Merrimac St N Chicago IL 60648

KIEL, O. FREDERICK, psychologist; b. Rapid City, S.D., May 15, 1940; s. Orville Manford and Mabel Anna (Shoemaker) K.; student Macalester Coll., 1960-62; B.A., U. Minn., 1965, Ph.D., 1971; m. Erin V. McNamara, Sept. 2, 1965; children—Kelly, Amy, Bryn Erin. Dir. alcoholism treatment center St. Mary's Hosp., Mpls., 1971-72; co-founder, exec. dir. Center for Behavior Modification, Mpls., 1972-76, chmn. bd. dirs., 1976—; pres. Kiel & Assos., Inc., 1976—, CBM Systems, Inc., 1976—. Lectr., Coll. St. Thomas, St. Paul, 1975—; asst. clin. prof. U. Minn., 1971—; vice chmn. Minn. Bd. Examiners Psychologists, 1974—. Mem. Am. Psychol. Assn., Assn. Advancement Behavior Therapy, Minn. Assn. Advancement Behavior Therapy (past pres.), Minn. Chem. Dependency Assn. Editor: CBM Newsletter, 1973—. Home: 2534 Beverly Rd St Paul MN 55104 Office: 3001 University Ave SE Minneapolis MN 55414

KIELBASA, CLEMENT ALEXANDER, dentist; b. East Chicago, Ind., Nov. 23, 1906; s. Stephan and Angeline (Machalski) K.; student U. Mich., 1926-29; D.D.S., Loyola U., 1934; m. Helen Verjean Sambor, May 29, 1935 (dec. 1975); children—Joan Kielbasa Jankowski, Jean Kielbasa Bochnowski, Geraldine Kielbasa Wadas, Clementine Kielbasa Rucoba, Frederic; m. 2d, Therese Kwasny, Oct. 21, 1977. Individual practice dentistry, East Chicago, 1934—. Mem. ADA (asso.; life), Chgo., N.W., Ind. dental socs., Sacred Heart Soc., Polish Profl. Men's Assn. (pres. 1940), Paderewski Choral Group (pres. 1935-45), Pi Delta Sigma, Delta Sigma Delta. Home: 7142 Hohman St Hammond IN 46324 Office: 3826 Main St East Chicago IN 46312

KIELKOPF, WILLIAM MICHAEL, journalist, educator; b. Ottumwa, Iowa, Nov. 23, 1949; s. William and Marjorie Louise (Howard) K.; B.A., U. Iowa, 1972, M.A., 1977; m. Mary DeNette Guernsey, June 7, 1975. Tchr., English, journalism, head varsity baseball coach, newspaper advisor West Branch (Iowa) High Sch., 1972-75; English tchr. King Edward VII High Sch., Johannesburg, S. Africa, 1976; free-lance writer, 1977—; author feature series on edn. for Johannesburg Star, 1976; author Close Encounters of the South African Kind; reporter Ottumwa Daily Courier and Iowa City Press-Citizen; player American Eagles Internat. Baseball Club, 1976. Mem. Ottumwa Mayor's Adv. Bd., 1967-68; active Democratic Party. Mem. Nat. Council Tchrs. of English, Journalism Edn. Assn., Am. Assn. Coll. Baseball Coaches, Internat. Free Lancers Orgn., Writers in the Pub. Interest, Nat. Writers Club. Home: 49 Bon Aire Iowa City IA 52240

KIENE, RICHARD HOTCHKISS, physician; b. Topeka, Mar. 13, 1910; s. Otto and Alma Ro (Hotchkiss) K.; A.B., U. Kans., 1931; M.D., U. Pa., 1935, postgrad., 1939; m. Edith Elisabeth Swing, June 8, 1935; children—Richard Hotchkiss, Elisabeth Kiene Pace. Intern, San Diego County Gen. Hosp., 1935-36; resident in orthopedic surgery St. Luke's Hosp., Kansas City, 1939-40, Kansas City Gen. Hosp., 1940-41; practice medicine specializing in orthopedic surgery, Kansas City, 1946—; mem. exec. staff St. Luke's Hosp., Kansas City, 1952—, pres. med. staff, pres. hosp.'s Found. for Med. Edn. and Research, 1968-71; chmn. sect. orthopedic surgery Kansas City Gen. Hosp. and Med. Center, 1962-71, acting chmn. dept. surgery, 1966-71; cons. orthopedic staff Children's Mercy Hosp., 1966—; orthopedic cons. VA Hosp., also VA Regional Office, Kansas City; asso. orthopedist Mo. Crippled Children's Service; clin. prof. U. Mo.-Kansas City Sch. Medicine, 1968—; asst. clin. prof. surgery (orthopedics) U. Kans. Sch. Medicine, 1962—. Trustee at large Nat. Soc. for Crippled Children and Adults, 1960-64; pres. Mo. Soc. Crippled Children and Adults, 1958-60, bd. dirs., 1950—; mem. exec. com. Easter Seal Soc. Greater Kansas City, 1950-75, chmn. med. adv. com., 1960-73; bd. dirs. Rehab. Inst., Kansas City, pres., 1969-71. Served from lt. (j.g.) to comdr., M.C., USNR, 1941-45; rear adm. Res. (ret.). Recipient Merit award Jackson County Med. Soc., 1968. Diplomate Am. Bd. Orthopedic Surgery. Fellow A.C.S., Am. Acad. Orthopedic Surgeons, Am. Assn. Surgery of Trauma; mem. Internat. Soc. Orthopedic Surgery and Traumatology, AMA, Am. Orthopedic Assn., Am. Orthopedic Foot Soc., Mo. (del. to AMA 1960-67), Jackson County med. assns., Russell Hibbs, Mid-Central State, Clin. orthopedic socs., Southwestern Surg. Congress, Kansas City Acad. Medicine (pres. 1956), Kansas City Surg. Soc. (pres. 1958-59), Kansas City S.W. Clin. Soc. (pres. 1960), Soc. Med. Cons. to Armed Forces, Naval Res. Assn., Mil. Order World Wars (comdr. 1977), English-Speaking Union (pres. 1972-74), S.A.R., Navy League, Ret. Officers Assn., C. of C. Club: Kansas City Country (dir. 1969). Contbr. articles to profl. jours. Home: 6429 Overbrook Rd Shawnee Mission KS 66208 Office: 4320 Wornall Rd Kansas City MO 64111

KIERNAN, WILLIAM JOSEPH, JR., lawyer; b. Salem, Mass., Mar. 19, 1932; s. William Joseph and Jane Catherine Kiernan; B.S. cum laude, Coll. Holy Cross, 1953; J.D. magna cum laude, Harvard U., 1959; m. Nancy Claire Stirpurko, Nov. 11, 1953; children—Cecilia Jane, William Joseph, Claudia Ellen, Matthew James. Admitted to Wis. bar, 1959; asso. Foley & Lardner, Milw., 1959-66, partner, 1966—. Mem. adv. bd. Salvation Army, 1963-68; bd. dirs. Athletes for Youth, 1969—, Lakeside Community Council, 1966-68; mem. Bd. of Fact Finders, Milw. Catholic Archdiocese, 1971—. Served with USN, 1953-56; Korea. Mem. Am., Wis., Milw. bar assns., League Wis. Municipalities, Nat. Inst. Municipal Law Officers, Am. Trial Lawyers Assn., Municipal Fin. Officers Assn., St. Thomas More Soc. (pres. 1967), Wis. Tax Shelter Council (sec. 1973-74), Miami Estate Planning Inst., Navy League U.S. (judge adv. Milw. chpt. 1971—), Harvard Club Wis., St. Thomas More Soc. (pres. 1967). Roman Catholic. Contbr. articles to various publs. Office: 777 E Wisconsin Ave Milwaukee WI 53202

KIESLING, NORMAN LOUIS, county judge; b. Logansport, Ind., Jan. 31, 1912; s. John W. and Mayme (Scheumann) K.; J.D., Valparaiso U., 1935; grad. Coll. State Trial Judges, Reno, 1974; m. Ruth Bellack, May 29, 1937; children—Marlene Ann (Mrs. John Konsek III), John G. Admitted to Ind. bar, 1935; practice law, Logansport, 1935-59; pros. atty. Cass County (Ind.), 1937-38; judge Circuit Ct. Cass County, 1959—. Mem. Ind. Ho. of Reps., 1949-50. Pres. three Rivers council, v.p. Sagamore council Boy Scouts Am.; active A.R.C. Served with USNR, World War II; PTO. Mem. Ind., Cass County bar assns., Am. Judicature Soc. Lutheran. Elk. Home: 1118 Kiesling Rd Logansport IN 46947 Office: Court House Logansport IN 46947

KIESS, ROBERT DAVID, ophthalmologist; b. Edon, Ohio, Apr. 19, 1914; s. David Theodore and Bertha Laura (Twitchell) K.; B.S., Ohio State U., 1935; M.D., U. Cin., 1943; M.S. in Ophthalmology, U. Mich., 1949; m. Mary Josephine Hannaher, June 3, 1944. Rotating intern U.S. Naval Hosp., Chelsea, Mass., 1943-44, Tulane U. Sch. Grad. Med., 1946-47; served successively as asst. resident, resident, instr. opthalmology U. Mich. Med. Sch., 1947-50; non-resident lectr. ophthalmology Horace H. Rackham Sch. Grad. Studies, U. Mich., 1950-55; practice medicine, specializing in ophthalmology, Toledo, 1950—; clin. asso. surgery Med. Coll. Ohio, 1970—; dir. ophthalmology Toledo Hosp. Trustee, Toledo Soc. Blind, 1960—. Served with M.C., USNR, 1943-46, 53. Named Physician of Year, Toledo Com. to Employ the Handicapped, 1967. Diplomate Am. Bd. Ophthalmology. Fellow A.C.S., N.Y. Acad. Scis.; mem. Sigma Chi, Phi Chi. Clubs: Masons, Toledo, Inverness; Circumnavigators. Contbr. articles to profl. jours. Home: 3316 Christie Blvd Toledo OH 43606 Office: 3939 Monroe St Toledo OH 43606

KIEWIET, PAUL ALAN, advt. exec.; b. Kalamazoo, Jan. 11, 1953; s. Isaac and Nellie (Goldschmeding) K.; A.A., Kalamazoo Valley Community Coll., 1973; postgrad. Western Mich. U., 1974; m. Claude Lucia Svilpe, Sept. 24, 1976. Mgr. dept. Meijer Inc., Kalamazoo, 1969-74; pres. Blue Forest Prodns., Kalamazoo, 1974-75; sales rep. Mut. of Omaha Cos., Kalamazoo, 1975-77; account exec. Central Advt., 1977—. Chmn., Brookwood Creative Centre, 1975. Recipient Sales awards Mut. of Omaha, 1976, Kalamazoo Ad Club, 1975, United of Omaha, 1976. Mem. Nat. Assn. Life Underwriters. Republican. Club: Optimist. Home: 475 Jason Ct Kalamazoo MI 49062 Office: 812 Gull St Kalamazoo MI 49002

KILBURN, RICHARD FRIEND, veterinarian; b. Lodi, Ohio, July 13, 1944; s. Friend Le Roy and Stella Julia (Larsen) K.; D.V.M., Iowa State U., 1968; m. Mary Helen Osth, May 26, 1968; children—Erin Leigh, David Friend. Asso. veterinarian Belmont (Mass.) Animal Hosp., 1968-70, Bulger Animal Hosp., North Andover, Mass., 1970-71; owner, mgr. County Line Animal Hosp., Naperville, Ill., 1971—, Our Animal Hosp., Chgo., 1972-74; dir. Emergency Veterinary Services, Ltd., 1976—, sec., 1977—. Councilor Juvenile Probation of DuPage County, 1976-77. Mem. Am., Ill., DuPage veterinary med. assns., Am. Animal Hosp. Assn. (asso.), Veterinary Radiol. Soc. Republican. Methodist. Clubs: Bus. Men's Flying, Flying Veterinarian, Kiwanis (pres.-elect. Naperville chpt. 1977—). Home: 2204 S Washington St Naperville IL 60540 Office: 2200 S Washington St Naperville IL 60540

KILDEE, DALE E., congressman; b. Flint, Mich., Sept. 16, 1929; s. Timothy Leo and Norma Alicia (Ullmer) K.; B.A., Sacred Heart Sem., 1952; tchr.'s certificate U. Detroit, 1954; M.A., U. Mich., 1961; postgrad. (Rotary Found. fellow) U. Peshawar (Pakistan), 1958-59; m. Gayle Heyn, Feb. 27, 1965; children—David, Laura, Paul. Tchr., U. Detroit High Sch., 1954-56, Flint Central High Sch., 1956-64; mem. Mich. Ho. of Reps. from 81st Dist., 1964-74; mem. Mich. Senate, 1975-77; mem. 95th Congress from 7th Mich. dist., 1977—. Mem. Am. Fedn. Tchrs., Urban League, Phi Delta Kappa. Clubs: K.C., Optimists. Home: 1434 Jane Ave Flint MI 48506 Office: 503 Cannon House Office Bldg Washington DC 20515 also 444 Church St Flint MI 48502

KILGORE, ANNABELLE THOMPSON, guidance counselor; b. Helena, Ark., May 3, 1924; d. Willie P. and Callie L. (Lacey) Thompson; B.A., Roosevelt U., 1959, M.Ed., 1965, M.A. in Counseling and Guidance, 1973; m. Shirley Franklin Kilgore, Aug. 22, 1948; 1 dau., Joyce Evelyn. With personnel dept. Boeing Aircraft Co., Seattle, 1943-45; elementary sch. tchr. City Schs. Gary (Ind.), 1960-72; guidance counselor Emerson High Sch., Gary, 1972—, also basic skills coordinator, test coordinator, career edn. chmn. Recipient Outstanding Alumni award Tuskegee Inst., 1971, award USAF, 1977; named hon. admission counselor U.S. Naval Acad., 1975. Mem. Am. Fedn. Tchrs. (merit award 1971, 74, 75), Am., Ind. personnel and guidance assns., AAUW, Nat. Assn. Study Negro Life and History, NAACP, Tuskegee Alumni Assn. (regional dir. N. Central region), Phi Delta Kappa (pres. Beta Mu chpt.). Democrat. Lutheran. Contbr. articles to profl. publs. Home: 1889 W 20th Ave Gary IN 46404 Office: 716 E 7th Ave Gary IN 46402

KILGORE, JAMES COLUMBUS, educator; b. Ansley, La., May 2, 1928; s. James Wilson and Ruth B. (Armstrong) K.; B.A., Wiley Coll., 1952; M.A. in English, U. Mo. at Columbia, 1963; m. Alberta Gunnels, June 20, 1960; children—Steven, Sheila. Instr. English, Langston High Sch., Hot Springs, Ark., 1954-58, A.M. and N. Coll., Pine Bluff, Ark., 1958-59, Fairlawn (N.J.) High Sch., 1959-60, Central High Sch., Hayti, Mo., 1960-61; instr. Southwest High Sch., Kansas City, Mo., 1963-66; prof. English, Cuyahoga Community Coll., Cleve., 1966—; adj. prof. Afro-Am. lit. Akron (O.) U., 1972; cons. in field, lectr. Black lit. Participant Bread Loaf Writers' Conf., 1970, Cleve. State U. Poetry Center, 1966—. Served with AUS, 1952-54. Recipient So. Edn. Found. award, 1957, Sigginsbottom Found. award U. Mo., 1962. Mem. Nat. Council Tchrs. English, Modern Lang. Assn. Am., Renaissance Soc. Am., Ohio Poets' Assn., Phi Beta Sigma. Baptist. Author poetry books. Contbr. numerous stories, articles, poems to mags. and jours. Home: 2531 Richmond Rd Beachwood OH 44122

KILGOUR, FREDERICK GRIDLEY, librarian; b. Springfield, Mass., Jan. 6, 1914; s. Edward Francis and Lillian Bess (Piper) K.; A.B., Harvard U., 1935, postgrad., 1939-42; postgrad. in L.S., Columbia, 1939-41; m. Eleanor Margaret Beach, Sept. 3, 1940; children—Christopher, Martha, Alison, Meredith. Mem. staff Harvard Coll. Library, 1935-42, OSS, 1942-45; dep. dir. Office Intelligence Collection and Dissemination, Dept. State, 1946-48; librarian Yale Med. Library, New Haven, 1948-65; asso. librarian for research and devel. Yale U. Library, 1965-67; exec. dir. OCLC, Inc., Columbus, 1967—; lectr. history of sci. Yale U., 1950-59, in history of sci. and medicine, 1961-67. Served as lt. (j.g.) USNR, 1943-46. Decorated Legion of Merit. Mem. ALA (Margaret Mann award 1974), Ohio Library Assn. (named librarian of year 1974), Am. Soc. Info. Sci. (recognition of achievement 1974), Library Assn. Australia, Soc. History of Tech. Club: Cosmos (Washington). Author: (with others) Engineering in History, 1956; Library of Medical Institution of Yale College and Its Catalogue of 1865, 1960; The Library and Information Science Cum Index, 1976. Editor: Book of Bodily Exercise (Cristobal Mendez), 1960. Mng. editor Yale Jour. Biology and Medicine, 1949-65; editor Jour. Library Automation, 1968-72. Contbr. articles to profl. jours. Home: 1415 Kirkley Rd Columbus OH 43221 Office: 1125 Kinnear Rd Columbus OH 43212

KILLHAM, ALBERT BENJAMIN, corporate exec.; b. Chgo., June 21, 1936; s. Benjamin John and Alice Henrietta (Freud) K.; A.B., DePauw U., 1958; m. Sue Anne Sutter, Aug. 3, 1957; children—Kimberley, Karen Marie, Benjamin John. Route salesman Sutter's Dairy Products, Inc., Marion, Ind., 1958-59, data processing mgr., 1959-65, staff accountant, 1965-67, asst. comptroller, 1967-72, v.p., 1971-72, corporate dir., 1970-72; accountant, credit mgr. Foster-Forbes Glass Co. div. Nat. Can. Corp., 1972-75; controller Speas Co., Kansas City, Mo., 1975—. Bd. trustees Marion Pub. Library, 1969-75; sec., 1969, pres. 1970. Bd. dirs. Marion Boy's Club, 1969-75. Mem. Nat. Assn. Accountants, Beta Theta Pi. Democrat. Elk. Clubs: Urban League (dir. 1964-65), YMCA Health (dir. 1964), Y's Mens (pres. 1973) (Marion). Home: 9708 Outlook Dr Overland Park KS 66207 Office: 2400 Nicholson Ave Kansas City MO 64120

KILLION, MARK EVEREST, structural engr.; b. Paris, Ill., Oct. 12, 1949; s. Eugene Earl and Audrey Kathleen (Humphrey) K.; B.S. with honors, Rose-Hulman Inst. Tech., 1971; M.S., U. Ill., 1973. Grad. research asst. U. Ill., 1971-73; structural design engr. Dennis Roby & Assos., Decatur, Ill., 1974-77; structural research engr. Custodis Construction, Terre Haute, Ind., 1977—. Served as lt. U.S. Army, 1973-74. Registered profl. engr., Ill., Ind. Mem. Ill., Ind. socs. profl. engrs., ASCE. Methodist. Home: 502 E Jasper St Paris IL 61944

KILLOREN, TIMOTHY JEROME, county ofcl.; b. Chgo., July 10, 1941; s. Jerome and Veronica (Robedeau) K.; B.S. in Bus., So. Ill. U., 1966; m. Valerie R. Clevenger, Nov. 29, 1969. Analyst, salesman computer div. Gen. Elec., Chgo., 1967-70; mgr. Chgo. area, fin. analyst Mgmt. Sci. Inc., Chgo., 1970-71; sr. fin. analyst Combined Ins. Co., Chgo., 1972-73; Florsheim Shoe Co., Chgo., 1972-73; comptroller DuPage County Health Dept., Wheaton, Ill., 1973—; mgmt. cons. SBA, 1971-72; tchr. Coll. of DuPage, 1974-75; mem. Ill. Com. Fiscal Consideration and Audits for Pub. Health Agencies. Treas., commr. Lisle Park Dist., 1972-77; trustee Village of Lisle, 1977—, chmn. fin., police and personnel coms., 1977—; bd. dirs., v.p. Lisle Homeowners Assn., 1975-77. Mem. Municipal Fin. Officers Assn., Ill. Pub. Health Assn. (chmn. audit com. 1973—), Ill. Assn. Pub. Health Adminstrs., Ill. Mgrs. and Mayors Assn. Republican. Roman Catholic. Home: 5130 Main St Lisle IL 60532 Office: 111 County Farm Wheaton IL 60187

KILMAN, JAMES WILLIAM, cardiovascular surgeon, med. sch. and hosp. adminstr.; b. Terre Haute, Ind., Jan. 22, 1931; s. Arthur and Irene Louise (Piker) K.: B.S., Ind. State U., 1956; M.D., U. Ind., 1960; m. Priscilla Margaret Jackson, June 21, 1968; children—James W., Julia Ann, Jennifer Irene. Intern, U. Ind. Med. Center, Indpls., 1960-61, resident in cardiovascular surgery, 1961-66; asst. prof. surgery Ohio State U., Columbus, 1966-73, prof., 1973—, dir. div. thoracic surgery, 1976—, pres. med. staff Univ. Hosp., 1975—; chmn. dept. thoracic surgery Childrens Hosp., Columbus, pres., 1977—. Fellow A.C.S., Am. Coll. Cardiology, Am. Acad. Pediatrics, Am. Coll. Chest Physicians; mem. Acad. Medicine Columbus (pres.), Am. Surg. Assn. Republican. Lutheran. Contbr. papers to profl. jours.; researcher cardiovascular bypass for infants and children and peripheral vascular flow. Home: 4231 Jackson Pike Grove City OH 43123

KILMER, LLOYD WARREN, real estate exec., county ofcl.; b. Stewartville, Minn., Nov. 17, 1920; s. Frank George and Maude Emma (Hiner) K.; B.S., Creighton U., 1949; m. Marie Beckwith, June 28, 1945; children—Lloyd Carlyle, Franklin Ellis. With Wilkie-Beckwith Real Estate Co., Omaha, 1945—, sales broker, 1950—; partner Beckwith Co., real estate brokerage and resident constrn., 1950—; v.p., treas. Conservative Savings and Loan Assn., 1966—; v.p. 1st Fed. Savs. & Loan Assn. Omaha, 1977—. Clk.-comptroller Douglas County, Nebr., 1969-77. Pres., chmn. bd. Forgotten Americans Com., 1970-71; trustee Crowell Meml. Home, Blair, Nebr., 1960-64, Am. Citizens Forum, 1966-70, Nebr. Meth. Hosp. Served with USAAF, 1942-46. Decorated Air medal with 2 clusters. Mem. Ad-Sell League, Pen and Sword Soc., Am. Legion, Internat. Assn. Clks., Recorders, Election Ofcls. and Treasurers (dir., v.p. 1972-75), Nebr. Assn. County Clks. and Register of Deeds (pres. 1974-75), Omaha United Methodist Soc. (pres. 1965-70). Methodist (trustee 1960-71). Mason (32 deg. Shriner). Clubs: Omaha Press, Square and Compass (Omaha). Home: 682 S 84th St Omaha NE 68114 Office: 317 S 17th St Omaha NE 68102

KILSDONK, MARTIN SEXTON, mfrs.' rep.; b. Detroit, June 3, 1926; s. Martin J. and Catherine Ann (Sexton) K.; B.S. in Mech. Engring., U. Notre Dame, 1947; m. Catherine Lee Considine, Nov. 8, 1958; children—Martin W., James R. Mgmt. trainee Clark Equipment Co., 1947-50; systems analyst Ford Motor Co., 1950-55; sales engr. Rollway Bearing Co., 1955-58; dist. mgr. Kaydon Engring. Corp., 1958-61; mfrs. rep. F.W. Lynch Co., Southfield, Mich., 1961—, dir., 1968—. Pres. Westchester Village Assn., Birmingham, Mich., 1966-67. Served with USN, 1944-46, 51-53. Mem. Soc. Automotive Engrs. Republican. Roman Catholic. Clubs: Edgewood Country, Fairlane, Notre Dame. Home: 1832 Long Lake Shores Bloomfield Hills MI 48013 Office: PO Box 2089 Southfield MI 48037

KILTON, FRANCIS JOSEPH, JR., real estate co. exec.; b. Omaha, Oct. 16, 1936; s. Frank Joseph and Josephine Agnes (Ceglar) K.; grad. high sch.; m. Annette Marie Nosek, Sept. 16, 1961; children—Linda M., Frank M. Clk. Union Pacific R.R. Co., Omaha, 1954-63; property mgr. Byron Reed Co., Inc., Omaha, 1963-71, v.p. property mgmt., 1972—. Mem. Sarpy County Planning Commn., 1965—. Served with AUS, 1955-57. Mem. Bldg. Owners and Mgrs. Assn. Omaha (pres. 1976), Inst. Real Estate Mgmt. (regional v.p. 1973). Home: 7959 S 45th Ave Omaha NE 68157 Office: 209 S 19th St Omaha NE 68102

KIM, BYRON B.W., computer systems adminstr.; b. Seoul, Korea, Jan. 22. 1926; s. Kwon K. and Oksoon (Eun) K.; came to U.S., 1953, naturalized, 1965: student Seoul Nat. U. Law Sch., 1948-50; B.A., Lincoln Meml. U., 1957; M.A., U. Ill., 1958; m. Himan Choi, Apr. 1, 1948; children—Raymond, Myong, Florence. Research statistician, sci. programmer Crop-Hail Ins. Actuarial Assn., 1958-66; staff analyst Computer Usage Co., Chgo., 1966-68; systems engr. IBM Corp., Chgo., 1968-70; computer systems mgr. Loyola U. of Chgo., 1970-76, dir. computers, 1976—. Mem. Soc. Certified Data Processors, Assn. Computing Machinery, Data Processing Mgmt. Assn. Home: 2920 W Wilson Ave Chicago IL 60625 Office: Loyola U 2160 S 1st Ave Maywood IL 60153

KIM, CHURL SUK, mathematician, educator; b. Chinhae, Korea, Aug. 6, 1930; s. Buhm Sool and Mall Im (Joo) K.; came to U.S., 1956, naturalized, 1969; B.A., So. Ill. U., Carbondale, 1959, M.A., 1961; Ph.D., U. Okla., 1970; m. Machiko Kono, Mar. 24, 1961; 1 dau., Stella. Asst. prof. math. Ind. U. Southwest, New Albany, 1970-74, asso. prof., chmn. dept., 1974—. USAF research fellow, 1968-70. Mem. Am. Math. Soc., Math. Assn. Am. Club: New Albany Rotary (pres. 1977-78). Home: 903 Woodside Dr New Albany IN 47150 Office: 4201 Grant Line Rd New Albany IN 47150

KIM, DONG-SOO, pediatrician; b. Korea, Aug. 8, 1940; s. Jong-Kwan and Mae-Saol (Shin) K.; came to U.S., 1966, naturalized, 1977; M.D., Chonnam Nat. U., Korea, 1966; m. Sook-Hee Kim, Dec. 9, 1972; children—Ihan, Seran. Intern, St. Peter's Hosp., Albany, N.Y., 1966-67; resident in pediatrics Springfield (Mass.) Hosp. Med. Center, 1967-69; research scientist Birth Defects Inst. N.Y. State Health Dept., Albany, 1969-73; staff physician Hillcrest Center and McPherson Community Health Center, Howell, Mich., 1973—; instr. Albany Med. Coll., 1969-72; asst. clin. prof. dept. human devel. Mich. State U. Diplomate Am. Bd. Pediatrics. Mem. Mich. State Med. Soc., Am. Soc. Human Genetics, Am. Acad. Pediatrics. Contbr. articles in field to med. jours. Home: 510 Aberdeen Way Howell MI 48843 Office: 2900 E Grand River Howell MI 48843

KIM, KYUNG SOO, cardiologist; b. Osaka, Japan, Feb. 11, 1938; s. J.K. and O.B. (Chae) K.; came to U.S., 1967; M.D., Kyungpook U., 1963; m. Chanok Park, Oct. 31, 1970. Intern, Episcopal Hosp., Phila., 1967-68; resident in medicine Pa. Hosp., Phila., 1968-69: fellow in cardiology Cleve. Clinic Found., 1969-73; dir. cardiac catheterization lab. Detroit Gen. Hosp., 1973-74; mem. staff cardiac catheterization lab. St. John Hosp., Detroit, 1974—; instr. medicine Wayne State U., 1973-74. Served to capt. M.C., Korean Army, 1963-67. Diplomate Am. Bd. Internal Medicine. Fellow Am. Coll. Cardiology. Home: 37125 Kelly Rd Mount Clemens MI 48043 Office: 22101 Moross St Detroit MI 48043

KIM, NHAK HEE, dentist; b. Seoul, Korea, Apr. 15, 1929; s. Chung Mok and Bo (Sung) K.: came to U.S., 1954, naturalized, 1972; D.D.S., Seoul Nat. U., 1951. postgrad. Baylor U., 1966; D.D.S., N.Y. U., 1959; m. Oak Sook Chun, June 29, 1957; children—Bill, Jim, Heidi. Asst. prof. dept. periodontics Baylor U., Dallas, 1966-67; pvt. practice dentistry, Muscatine, Iowa, 1970—; adj. asst. prof. U. Iowa, Iowa City, 1972—. Bd. dirs. Muscatine Shelter Work Shop. Mem. Am. Dental Assn., Am. Acad. Periodontology, Am. Coll. Dentists, Korean Acad. Periodontology (founder, pres. 1961). Club: Kiwanis. Home: 19 Colony Dr Muscatine IA 52761 Office: 502 Laurel Bldg Muscatine IA 52761

KIM, SUNG CHUL, mech. engr.; b. Seoul, Korea, Mar. 23, 1934; s. Yu Moon and Eun Dong (Sung) K.; came to U.S., 1957, naturalized, 1968; student Seoul Nat. U., 1953-56; B.S., Bradley U., 1960; M.S., U. Mo., 1962; m. Marilyn Hiroko Suzuki, June 26, 1964; children—Rodney James, Alice Kay. Sr. product engr. heat transfer ITT Bell & Gossett Co., Morton Grove, Ill., 1962—. Served with Korean Army, 1956-57. Mem. ASME, Korean Engrs., Scientists Assn. in Am., Korean Am. Community Service Chgo. Patentee in field. Home: 310 W Norman Ct Des Plaines IL 60016 Office: 8200 N Austin Ave Morton Grove IL 60053

KIMBELL, KENNETH RICHARD, veterinarian; b. Wichita, Kans., Oct. 5, 1943; s. Kenneth Edward Charles and Dorothy (Carr) K.; B.S. in Zoology, Kans. State U., 1966, B.S. in Agr., 1972, D.V.M., 1974; m. Vicky Jo Cotner, Aug. 28, 1964; children—Devin, Darcy, Ashley. Tech. rep. Union Carbide Co., Detroit, 1969-70; veterinarian Kimball Veterinary Clinic, Wichita, 1974—. Mem. Mayor's Sculpture Com.; v.p. Bd. Edn., 1977—; chmn. Wichita/Sedgwick County Task Force on Drug Abuse and Alcohol, Drug Abuse Advisory Bd., Citizens Participation Orgn.; chmn. Kans. Assn. Physically Handicapped. Served with USNR, 1967-69; Vietnam. Mem. Am., Kans., Wichita (v.p.) vet. med. assns., Nat. Wildlife Found., Lefthanders Internat., Kans. State U. Alumni Assn. Episcopalian. Phi Zeta. Club: Kiwanis (v.p. Wichita). Home: 6919 E 14th St Wichita KS 67206 Office: 2046 N Oliver St Wichita KS 67208

KIMBLE, M(ARCUS) ALLEN, minister, instn. adminstr.; b. Sussex, N.J., Oct. 30, 1920; s. Marcus Lynn and Wilhelmina (McConnell) K.; student U. Va., 1941-42; A.B., Wheaton Coll., 1943; M.Div., Princeton Theol. Sem., 1946; D.D., Lake Forest Coll., 1976; L.H.D., Nat. Coll. Edn., 1976; m. Sara Elizabeth Rogers, Aug. 28, 1945; children—Carolyn, Beverly. Ordained to ministry Presbyn. Ch.; asst. minister First Presbyn. Ch., Westfield, N.J., 1946-47; minister Presbyn. Ch., Lawrenceville, N.J., 1947-59, Calvary Presbyn. Ch., Wyncote, Pa., 1959-72; now dir. devel. Presbyn. Home, Evanston, Ill.; master religion Lawrenceville Boys' Sch., 1947-54; moderator Presbytery of New Brunswick; vice moderator Synod of N.J.; mem. gen. assembly com. on budget rev. United Presbyn. Ch. U.S. Trustee Presbytery Phila., Presbytery Chgo. Clubs: Masons; Univ. (Chgo.); Westmoreland Country (Wilmette, Ill.). Contbr. articles to profl. jours. Home: 865 Hiawatha Ln Riverwoods IL 60015 Office: 3200 Grant St Evanston IL 60201

KIMBROUGH, KELSE MCDOWELL, city ofcl., sales rep.; b. Hardin, Mo., Aug. 3, 1924; s. Harry L. and Mayme E. (Kassen) K.; student U. Ill., 1945-46, Rockhurst Coll., 1946-47; m. Mary L. Farris, Mar. 28, 1951; children—Harry L., James M., Mary Suzanne, Patricia Ann, Joan Marie. Mgr. retail lumber co., Norborne, Mo., 1948-63; sales rep. Anton K. Westhe & Co., wholesale lumber, Kansas City, Mo., 1963-68; central sales rep. Am. Creosote Works, New Orleans, 1968—; co-owner, dir. Carr-Co Constrn. Co., Norborne, 1966—; owner K.M. Kimbrough & Assos., real estate brokers, Norborne, 1960—. Exec. dir. Mo. Valley Planning Commn., 1968. Mayor City of Norborne, 1965-76; Republican candidate for Mo. Ho. of Reps., 1968. Bd. dirs. Carroll County Meml. Hosp., 1966-69, 70-73, 75—. Served with USAAF, 1943-45. Decorated Air medal with 6 oak leaf clusters; recipient Hon. Chpt. Farmer award Norborne chpt. Future Farmers Am., 1962. Mem. Am. Legion, V.F.W. K.C. (4 deg.), Lion (charter mem., sec. 1951-52). Address: 615 S Walnut St Norborne MO 64668

KIMBROUGH, ROOSEVELT, dentist; b. Birmingham, Ala., Oct. 4, 1932; s. Jim and Emaline (Robinson) K.; B.S., Roosevelt U., 1958; B.S., U. Ill., 1961, D.D.S., 1962; m. Alberta Bernice Thornton, June 9, 1956; children—Lisa Ann, Keith. Practice gen. dentistry, Chgo., 1962—. Dental cons. Ill. Dental Service Corp. Active Boy Scouts Am. Trustee Faulkner Sch., Chgo. Served with Armed Forces, 1955-57. Mem. Nat., Am. dental assns., Ill., Chgo., Lincoln dental socs. Home: 9117 S Cregier Ave Chicago IL 60617 Office: 7404 S Halsted St Chicago IL 60621

KIMBROUGH, WILLIAM WALTER, III, psychiatrist; b. Cleve., Sept. 26, 1928; s. William Walter and Minerva Grace (Champion) K.; student Cornell U., 1945-46; B.S., U. Mich., 1948, M.D., 1952; m. Jo Ann Greiner, July 6, 1953; children—Elizabeth, Douglas. Intern, Ohio State U. Health Center, Columbus, 1952-53; resident U. Chgo. Clinics, 1955-56, Ypsilanti (Mich.) State Hosp., 1956-59; asso. psychiatrist U. Mich. Health Service, Ann Arbor, 1959-61; practice medicine specializing in psychoanalytic psychiatry, Ann Arbor, 1961—; cons. Atty. Gen. U.S., 1958—, Center for Forensic Psychiatry, 1974—, Brighton Found. for Alcoholism, 1961—. Served to lt. comdr. USPHS, 1953-55. Recipient Physicians Recognition awards AMA, 1972-73. Fellow Am. Acad. Psychiatry and Law, Am. Soc. Psychoanalytic Physicians; mem. Am. Acad. Psychotherapists, Am., Ann Arbor psychiatric assns., Mich. Psychiat. Assn., N.Y. Acad. Sci., AAAS, Sigma Alpha Epsilon, Phi Rho Sigma. Clubs: Ann Arbor Town, Ann Arbor Racquet, Univ.; Little Harbor (Harbor Springs, Mich.). Home: Fair Oaks Ann Arbor MI 48104 Office: 1231 Ferdon Rd Ann Arbor MI 48104

KIMM, JAMES WILSON, cons. engr.; b. Huron, S.D., Sept. 26, 1925; s. Arthur A. and Mary (Fry) K.; B.S., U. Iowa, 1950; m. Dorothy A. Madsen, Aug. 16, 1952; children—Mary L., Jill A., Tobias J. Pub. health engr. Iowa State Dept. Health, Des Moines, 1950-55; head san. engring. report sect. Stanley Engring. Co., Muscatine, Iowa, 1955-61; partner Veenstra & Kimm, Engrs. and Planners, West Des Moines, Iowa, 1961—, West Des Moines Devel. Corp. Served with AUS, 1943-45. Named Engr. Distinction, Engrs. Joint Council. Mem. Iowa Water Pollution Control Assn. (past pres.), Iowa Engring Soc., Nat. Soc. Profl. Engrs., C. of C., Cons. Engrs. Council Iowa, Water Pollution Control Fedn. (dir.), Tau Beta Pi, Chi Epsilon. Presbyterian (elder). Contbr. articles and papers to profl. jours. Home: 3932 Ashworth Rd West Des Moines IA 50265 Office: 300 West Bank Bldg 1601 22 St West Des Moines IA 50265

KIMM, JONG SOUNG, architect; b. Seoul, Korea, Nov. 28, 1935; s. Choon Ki and Chung Sik (Park) K.; came to U.S., 1956, naturalized, 1969; B.Arch., Ill. Inst. Tech., 1961, M.Arch., 1964; student Seoul Nat. U., 1954-56; m. Young Ah Lee, Dec. 27, 1961; children—Florence, Alice, John. Staff architect Ludwig Mies Van Der Rohe, Chgo., 1961-72; prin. J.S. Kimm, Architect, Evanston, Ill., 1972—; asst. prof. architecture Ill. Inst. Tech., 1966, asso. prof., 1972—, asst. dean Coll. Architecture, Planning and Design, 1975. Fulbright-Hays sr. lectr., 1974-75. Mem. AIA, Korean Inst. Architects. Address: 1022 Seward St Evanston IL 60202

KIMMEL, RICHARD LEE, mfg. co. exec.; b. Kenton, Ohio, Jan. 22, 1930; s. Lee Burdette and Lida Bradford (Freed) K.; B.S. in Meteorology, Fla. State U., 1960; M.S. in Edn., U. So. Calif., 1971; m. Shirley Jean Williams, Mar. 20, 1954; children—Cheryl, Kristi, Lisa, Lori, Scott. Commd. lt. U.S. Air Force, 1953, advanced through grades to lt. col., 1969, ret., 1975; v.p. Environ. Improvement Corp., Bellevue, Nebr., 1973—; with Aetna Life & Casualty Co., Omaha, 1975-78; pres., chmn. AK Squared Inc., Bellevue, 1976—. Mem. Nat. Fedn. Ind. Businessmen, Am. Meteorol. Soc., Air Force Assn., Ret. Officers Assn. Republican. Patentee in field. Home: 1403 Lawrence Ln Bellevue NE 68005 Office: 436 Avery Plaza Bellevue NE 68005

KIMMONS, KEITH DEWAYNE, rehab. counselor; b. Chgo.; s. Norman Benjamin and Edith Elizabeth (Hundley) K.; A.A. in Sociology, Olive-Harvey Coll., 1974; B.A. in Psychology, Chgo. State U., 1976; postgrad. in counseling Govs. State U., 1976—. Counselor, Lake County Assn. Retarded Children, Gary, Ind., 1971-72, Chgo. Assn. Retarded Citizens, 1976—. Mem. Am., Ill. (commn. culturalethnic minorities) personnel guidance assns. Home: 9621 Chappel St Chicago IL 60617

KIN, FREDERICK ROBERT, air pollution control cons.; b. Cheshire, Eng., July 27, 1934; s. Hop Chin and Minnie Eleanor (Birse) K.; came to U.S., 1966; B.S. in Chemistry, Liverpool Tech. Coll., 1958; B.S. in Chem. Engring., Birkenhead Coll. Tech., 1965. Plant mgr. J. Bibby & Sons, Liverpool, Eng., 1954-66; air pollution control tech. staff engr. Western Precipitation div. Joy Mfg. Co., Los Angeles, 1966-71; pres. Kin Assos., Inc., Chicago Heights, Ill., 1971—. Mem. Internat. Assn. Pollution Control, Inst. Chem. Engrs. (Eng.), Am. Inst. Chem. Engrs., Air Pollution Control Assn. Office: 276 W 14th St Chicago Heights IL 60411

KINCAID, MARY ELIZABETH, author, illustrator; b. Cleve., June 4, 1923; d. George Walter and Elizabeth (Phillips) Getz; B.A., U. Mich., 1944; m. William Harold Kincaid, Dec. 26, 1945; children—Judith Elizabeth, Jay Alexander, Rebecca Lee. Author-illustrator fgn. lang. comic strip, Contes Français, various Am. newspapers, 1962-66; author, designer, dir. audiovisual film Lang. Strips, 1973-76; co-author bilingual radio series French Minutes, 1973-76; cons. and speaker audiovisual fgn. lang. instructional techniques; contbr. articles to mags. newspapers. Recipient award Mich. Council Arts, 1975-76. Home: 3550 Woodland Rd Ann Arbor MI 48104

KINCHELOE, JOHN ARTHUR, architect; b. Glen Cove, N.Y., Jan. 20, 1936; s. George W. and Alice V. (Moorhead) K.; student U. Ky., 1955-58; B.F.A. cum laude, Ohio U., 1961, B.Arch. cum laude, 1962; m. Mary C. Roland, Mar. 16, 1957; children—Katherine Anne, Deborah Clair, Anna Elizabeth. Engring. asst. Gen. Electric Co., Evendale, O., 1955-57; machine designer Planet Products, Inc., Cin., 1957-59; project architect Van Buren, Blackburn, Columbus, O., 1962-63, McLoney and Tune, Lexington, Ky., 1963-64, Milosevich and Trautwein, Columbus, 1964-66, Ireland and Assos., Columbus, 1966-67; partner Harder and Kincheloe, Columbus, 1967-69; v.p., partner Adams Harder Kincheloe Swearingen, Columbus, 1969—. Mem. Windmill Class Assn., 1970—. Bd. dirs. Camp Willson YMCA, 1970-74. Mem. A.I.A. (Honor award 1971, 73, 74), Constrn. Specifications Inst., Archtl. Historians Soc., Worthington Jaycees. Presbyn. (elder 1962—). Clubs: Kilbourne Dance, Hoover Yacht. Major works include Galbreath Mortgage Co. Bldg., Columbus, 1973, Historic Restoration of Johnston Farm, Piqua, O., 1973, Elliot Vacation House, Apple Valley, O., 1975, Historic Restoration of Zoar Village, O., 1971. Home: 116 Heischman Ave Worthington OH 43085 Office: 960 Kingsmill Pkwy Columbus OH 43229

KINDER, DONALD DEE, mech. engr.; b. Indpls., July 2, 1944; s. Herman Loren and Marian Roberta (Gurney) K.; B.S. in M.E., Purdue U., 1967. Mech. engr. Inland Container Corp., Indpls., 1969-74, R.R. Donnelly & Sons, Dwight, Ill., 1974-77; systems engr. MGD Graphite Systems Cicero, Ill., 1977, resident engr., Cedar Rapids, Iowa, 1977—. Served with AUS, 1967-69. Mem. ASME, Purdue Alumni Assn., Pi Tau Sigma. Democrat. Methodist. Home: 411 Burdette St SW Cedar Rapids IA 52404 Office: 4700 Bowling St SW Cedar Rapids IA 52404

KINDIG, FRED EUGENE, educator, arbitrator; b. York, Pa., Sept. 5, 1920; s. Fred E. and Hattie (Keller) K.; B.S., Pa. State U., 1942; M.S., U. Pitts., 1947, Ph.D., 1951; m. Marie M. Doyle (dec. 1971); children— Pamela M. Bonita K., Gretchen A., Suzanne J.; m. Grace L. Mathison, Aug. 19, 1972. Indsl. engr., supr. Westinghouse Electric Corp., Pitts., 1942-51; asst. to exec. v.p. Phoenix Glass, Monaca, Pa., 1951-53; asst. and asso. prof. U. Pitts., 1953-62; prof., coordinator quantitative methods Ohio State U., Columbus, 1962—. Labor-mgmt. arbitrator, 1953—. Pres., P.T.A., various times; mem. Franklin County 648 Bd. Planning Com., 1975. Mem. Am. Inst. Decision Scis. (v.p., 1969-71), Am. Arbitration Assn., Nat. Acad. Arbitrators, Am. Soc. for Quality Control, Inst. Math. Statistics, Am. Statis. Assn., Operations Research Soc. Am., Alpha Sigma Phi, Tau Beta Pi, Beta Gamma Sigma. Club: Brookside Country. Author: Fundamentals of Statistical Controls and Fundamentals of Linear Programming, 1956. Contbr. articles to profl. jours. Home: 2072 Tremont Rd Columbus OH 43221 Office: Dept Bus Adminstrn Ohio State U Columbus OH 43210

KINDLE, HELEN JOAN SWOVERLAND (MRS. PAUL EUGENE KINDLE), city ofcl.; b. Warsaw, Ind., Feb. 17, 1929; d. Howard Louis and Miriam Pauline (Yeager) Swoverland; student Manchester Coll., 1946-47; grad. Ft. Wayne Internat. Bus. Coll., 1949; m. Paul Eugene Kindle, Dec. 22, 1950; children—Jeffrey Eugene, Ken Eugene. With C. of C., Warsaw, 1949-56, office mgr., 1951-56; clk. to city clk.-treas., Warsaw, 1965-67, clk.-treas., 1968—. Mem. adv. bd. Salvation Army, 1973—; treas., Warsaw-Wayne Twp. Library, 1968-71; mem. Subarea Adv. Council No. Ind. Health Systems Agency, 1976-77. Mem. Internat. Inst. Municipal Clks. (publs. awards com. 1976—), Ind. League Municipal Clks. and Treas. (pres. 1971-72, chmn. edn.-tng. com. clk.-treas. forum 1971 conv.), DAR (treas. 1973-76, regent 1976—). Mem. First Brethren. Club: Order Eastern Star. Home: 1701 E Clark St Warsaw IN 46580 Office: City Bldg E Market St Warsaw IN 46580

KINDNESS, THOMAS NORMAN, congressman; b. Knoxville, Tenn., Aug. 26, 1929; s. Norman G. and Christine (Gunn) K.; A.B. in Polit. Sci., U. Md., 1951; LL.B., George Washington U., 1953; m. Ann G. Hosman, Sept. 15, 1951; children—Sharon L., David T., Glen J., Adam B. Admitted to D.C. bar, 1954; practiced in Washington, 1954-57; asst. counsel Champion Internat. Corp., Hamilton, O., 1957-73; mem. 94th-95th Congress from 8th dist. Ohio, 1975—, mem. judiciary, govt. operations coms. Mem. Hamilton City Council, 1964-69, mayor, 1964-67; mem. Ohio Ho. of Reps., 1971-74. Republican. Home: 328 South D St Hamilton OH 45013 Office: Room 1440 Longworth House Office Bldg Washington DC 20515

KING, ARTHUR MANSFIELD, city ofcl.; b. LeRoy, Ill., Dec. 16, 1902; s. Alpheus Carleton and Estella Jane (Mansfield) K.; B.S., U. Ill.,1928Ill., 1928; m. Berdena Pauline Lee. With A&P Tea Co., Midwest, 1928-52, supt. operations, 1952; exec. v.p. Charles F. Curry real estate, Kansas City, Mo., 1952-68; real estate counselor, 1964—; mayor Weatherby Lake, 1971—. Dir. North Hills Bank; pres. King Investment Co., 1963-74, Weatherby Lake Improvement Co., 1955-57, 69-71. Bd. dirs. Park Coll. Devel. Bd., Jr. Achievement, 1962-70. Mem. S.A.R. (pres. 1974-75, state historian 1974-75), Acacia, Sales Execs. Club, Kansas City Advt., Real Estate Bd. Kansas City. Mason (Shriner, K.T.). Clubs: Wea by Lake Sailing. Home: 10001 NW 75th St Kansas City MO 64152 Office: 7200 Eastise Dr Kansas City MO 64152

KING, BARBARA ANNE, landscape structures mfg. co. exec.; b. Oak Park, Ill., Aug. 6, 1946; d. Ranald E. and Harriett (Anderson) Olson; B.S., Iowa State U., 1968; m. Steven G. King, June 3, 1967; 1 dau., Erin Lee. Home economist Pillsbury Co., Mpls., 1968-71, Barbara Thornton Assos., Mpls., 1971-74; sec. treas. Landscape Structures Inc., Delano, Minn., 1974—, King Assos., Inc., 1973—. Mem. Sigma Alpha Iota, P.E.O., Alpha Delta Pi. Home: 38 Apple Glen Rd Long Lake MN 55356 Office: 300 Dawn Heather Dr Delano MN 53328

KING, CHARLES ROSS, physician; b. Nevada, Iowa, Aug. 22, 1925; s. Carl Russell and Dorothy Sarah (Mills) K.; student Butler U., 1943; B.S. in Bus., Ind. U., 1948, M.D., 1964; m. Frances Pamela Carter, Jan. 8, 1949; children—Deborah Diane, Carter Ross, Charles Conrad, Corbin Kent. Dep. dir. Ind. Pub. Works and Supply, 1949-52; salesman Knox Coal Corp., 1952-59; rotating intern Marion County Gen. Hosp., Indpls., 1964-65; family practice medicine, Anderson, Ind., 1965—; sec.-treas. staff Community Hosp., 1969-72, pres. elect, dir., chief medicine, 1973—, also bd. dirs., 1973-75; sec.-treas. St. John's Hosp., 1968-69, chief medicine, 1972-73, chief pediatrics, 1977—; dir. Rolling Hills Convalescent Center, 1968-73; pres. Profl. Center Lab., 1965—. Vice-chmn. Madison County Bd. Health, 1966-69; dir. First Nat. Bank Madison County, Anderson. Bd. dirs. Family Service Madison County, 1968-69, Madison County Assn. Mentally Retarded, 1972-76. Served with AUS, 1944-46. Diplomate Am. Bd. Family Practice. Recipient Physician's Recognition award AMA, 1969, 72, 75. Fellow Royal Soc. Health, Am. Acad. Family Practice (charter); mem. AMA, Ind., Pan Am. med. assns., Am. Acad. Gen. Practice, Madison County (pres. 1970), 8th Dist. (sec.-treas. 1968) med. socs., Indpls. Mus. Art (corp. mem.). Phi Delta Theta Alumni Assn. (pres. 1952), Phi Delta Theta, Phi Chi. Methodist. Club: Anderson Country. Home: 6414 Rosalind Ln Anderson IN 46011 Office: 1415 Raible Ave Anderson IN 46011

KING, DAVID EDGAR, librarian; b. Waterloo, Ind., Nov. 25, 1936; s. Roy Elmer and Pauline Harriett (Putt) K.; B.S., Ball State U., 1958; M.L.S., Rosary Coll., 1971; postgrad. Hofstra U., 1959. Librarian, Sachem Central Schs., Lake Ronkonkoma, N.Y., 1958-60, U.S. Army Dependent Schs., Germany, 1960-61; vol. U.S. Peace Corps, Philippines, 1961-63; coll. traveler Am. Book Co., N.Y.C., 1963-65; librarian R.R. Donnelley & Sons Co. Chgo., 1965-69; librarian Standard Ednl. Corp., Chgo., 1969—; mem. adv. council U. Ill. Grad. Sch. Library Sci., 1974-77, vis. lectr., summers 1976, 77. Mem. Spl. Libraries Assn. (chmn. pub. div. 1974-75, chmn. conf. 1975, chmn. conf. adv. com. 1976-77, editor pub. div. Bull. 1971-73), ALA (chmn. conf. info. com. 1978), Ill. Library Assn. (chmn. continuing edn. com. 1974), Chgo. Library Club. Contbr. articles to library jours. Home: 2400 Lakeview Ave Chicago IL 60614 Office: 130 N Wells St Chicago IL 60606

KING, DUANE EDWARD, clergyman; b. Skidmore, Mo., Nov. 9, 1937; s. Elza C. and Myrtle Lois (Brown) K.; B.A., Nebr. Christian Coll., 1961, Th.B., 1961; m. Margaret Jean Carr, Aug. 12, 1961; children—Christine Ann, Jonathan Duane. Singer, Watchmen Quartet evang. team, 1958-59, part time 1959—; ordained to ministry Ch. of Christ, 1963; minister Park Av. Christian Ch., Norfolk, Nebr., 1961-68, Central Ch. Christ, Griswold, Iowa, 1968-71, Christ's Ch. of Deaf, Council Bluffs, Iowa, 1971-76; founder Deaf Missions, Council Bluffs, 1971—, also dir. mission. Tchr., Nebr. Christian Coll., 1971—; dean Bible Camp for Deaf, Louisville, Nebr., 1971, 73, 75. Vice pres. Lewis Central P.T.A., 1972-73, pres., 1973-74; cubmaster Boy Scouts Am., 1975-77. Mem. Nebr. Christian Coll. Alumni Assn. (past pres.). Address: RD 2 Council Bluffs IA 51501

KING, FRANKLIN ALEXANDER, r.r. engr.; b. Duluth, Minn., May 2, 1923; s. George Rogers and Gertrude (Greenwood) K.; B.A., U. Minn., 1950; m. Dorothy Ann Haines, Nov. 26, 1960; children—Ralph, Sheila, Phillip. With Duluth, Missabe and Iron Range Ry. Co., Duluth, 1940—, sr. engr., 1973—. Mem. citizens com. to study welfare St. Louis County, Minn., 1972—; active Lake Superior Mus. Transp. and Industry. Mem. St. Louis County (bd. govs.; Pres.'s award 1973), Minn., Ry. and Locomotive hist. socs., Duluth Engrs. Club. Republican. Methodist. Club: Arrowhead Civic. Author: The Missabe Road: The History of the Duluth, Missabe and Iron Range Railway, Golden West, 1972. Home: 529 Ideal St Duluth MN 55811 Office: 200 Missabe Bldg Duluth MN 55802

KING, IMOGENE MARTINA, educator, nurse; b. West Point, Iowa, Jan. 30, 1923; d. Daniel A. and Mary (Schroeder) K.; diploma St. John's Hosp., 1945; B.S. in Nursing, St. Louis U., 1948, M.S. in Nursing, 1957; Ed.D., Columbia U., 1961. Asst. dir. St. John's Hosp., St. Louis, 1947-58; asst. prof. nursing Loyola U., Chgo., 1961-66, asso. prof. nursing, prof. grad. program in nursing, 1972—; asst. chief research Grants br. div. nursing HEW, Washington, 1966-68; prof., dean sch. nursing Ohio State U., Columbus, 1968-72; cons. VA Hosp. Alderman Ward 2, Wood Dale, Ill., 1975-79, chmn. fin. com.; active Addison Art Guild. Mem. Am., Ill. (recipient highest recognition award 1975) nurses assns., 19th Dist. Assn., Ops. Research Soc. Am., Am. Assn. for Higher Edn., Am. Pub. Health Assn., AAAS, Sigma Theta Tau, Alpha Tau Delta. Democrat. Roman Catholic. Contbr. articles in nursing to profl. jours. Office: 6525 N Sheridan Rd Chicago IL 60626

KING, (JACK) WELDON, photographer; b. Springfield, Mo., Jan. 19, 1911; s. Clyde Nelson and Mary Blanche (Murphy) K.; B.A., Drury Coll., 1934, Mus.B., 1934. Chief still photographer African expdns. including Gatti-Hallicrafters Expdn., 1947-48, 12th Gatti Expdn., 1952, Wyman Carroll Congo Expdn., 1955, 13th Gatti Expdn., 1956, 14th Gatti Expdn., 1957; also free-lance photog. expdns., Africa, 1960, 66, 76-77; trips for GAF Corp. to S.Am., 1962, 63, 77-78, Australia and N.Z., 1972-73, also numerous assignments throughout U.S. Served as photographer with Coast Arty. Corps, U.S. Army, 1941-42; PTO; Japanese prisoner of war, 1942-45. Decorated numerous service ribbons and battle stars. Mem. Space Pioneers, Am. Theatre Organ Soc., Humane Soc. U.S., Friends Animals, Nat. Parks and Conservation Assn., Am. Defenders of Bataan and Corregidor, Am. Ex-Prisoners War, Lambda Chi Alpha. Democrat. Roman Catholic. Contbr. to numerous art books including Africa is Adventure, 1959, also French and German edits.; Primitive Peoples Today, 1956; Africa: A Natural History, 1965; South American and Central America, 1967; Animal Worlds, 1963; Living Plants of the World, 1963; The Earth Beneath Us, 1964; Living Trees of the World; The Life of the Jungle, 1970; Living Mammals of the World. Contbr. photographs to mags., encys., textbooks. Address: 1234 E Grand Ave Springfield MO 65804

KING, JAMES ROBERT, mgmt. cons.; b. St. Louis, Sept. 24, 1932; s. Robert Lee and Blanche Mary (Burton) K.; B.S. in B.A., U. Mo., 1958; m. Carolyn Roberson, Mar. 26, 1955; children—Kathryn Lee, James Christopher. With Butler Mfg. Co., Kansas City, Mo., 1958-65, inventory control supr., 1964-65; mgmt. cons. Profl. Mgmt. Midwest, Kansas City, 1965-68; v.p., dir. Wehrenberg & Assos., Wichita, 1968-71; adminstr., sec. Wichita Dental Center, Wichita, 1971-74; adminstr., sec.-treas., v.p. L.C. Harmon Agencies, Wichita, 1974—, also dir.; dir. Jay hawk Accountants, Inc. Served with U.S. Army, 1952-54. U. Mo. curators scholar, 1956. Methodist. Club: Optimist. Home: 308 Fountain St N Wichita KS 67208 Office: 6225 Kellogg St E Wichita KS 67218

KING, JAMES T., educator; b. Evergreen Park, Ill., July 11, 1938; B.A., U. Navarre (Spain), 1961; M.A., DePaul U., 1965; Ph.D. (fellow), U. Notre Dame, 1967; m. Judith Fredo, Aug. 14, 1965. Teaching asst. DePaul U., 1963, U. Notre Dame, 1965-66; asst. prof. philosophy No. Ill. U., DeKalb, 1967-73, asso. prof., 1973—, asso. dean grad. sch., 1974—. Bd. dirs. DeKalb County Villages, Inc. Council Philos. Studies grantee, 1973; Nat. Endowment Humanities grantee, summer 1974. Mem. Am. Philos. Assn., Am. Catholic Philos. Assn., Midwest Soc. Philosophy Edn., Charles S. Peirce Soc., Ill. Philosophy Conf., Hume Soc., Am. Soc. Value Inquiry, AAUP (pres. chpt. 1972-73, chmn. state governance com. 1971-73). Contbr. numerous articles to profl. jours. Home: 731 Hillcrest St DeKalb IL 60115

KING, JOANN ELIZABETH, psychologist; b. Cleve., Aug. 4, 1931; d. Donald and Barbara (Sasek) Vesco.; m. William R. Adrion, Aug. 13, 1949; children—William Donald, Janeen Sue; m. Gregory C. King, Sept. 23, 1966; children—Cynthia Anne, Jeremy Robert. B.S., Ohio State U., 1962, M.A., 1964, Ph.D., 1968. Licensed psychologist, Ohio, 1972. Dir. psychology Fairfield County Mental Health Clinic, Lancaster, Ohio, 1969-74; practice clin. psychology, Columbus, Ohio, 1970—; faculty Ohio State U., 1970-73; asso. staff Riverside Meth. Hosp., Columbus; cons. Ross Labs., Columbus, 1975—; cons. alcoholic unit Riverside Meth Hosp., 1976—. Mem. Am., Ohio, Central Ohio psychol. assns., Am. Soc. Psychologists in Pvt. Practice. Office: 4900 Reed Rd Columbus OH 43220

KING, JOHN CLANCY, architect, engr.; b. Danville, Ill., Aug. 24, 1927; s. Robert Dennis and Ruth Eileen (Hunsaker) K.; B.S., U. Ill., 1952; m. Dolores Ceriotti, Oct. 21, 1950; children—Stephen, Margaret, Mary, John. Partner, Skadden, Sheehan & King, architects, Danville, 1953-65, John C. King, architect, Danville, 1965-67; partner

King & Hible, architects, Danville, 1967-69; prin., John C. King, & Assos., Danville, 1969—; dir. structures D.W. Tyler Co., Danville; Mem. Danville Archtl. Control Bd., 1971-72. Pres. Piankeshaw council Boy Scouts Am., 1973-75; pres. bd. dirs. Danville YMCA, 1968; chmn. bd. dirs. Salvation Army, Danville, 1968. Served with AUS, 1946-47. Recipient Silver Beaver award Boy Scouts Am., 1973; Sear's Farm/City Boy Scout, Philmont tng. scholar, 1967. Mem. Nat. Soc. Profl. Engrs., AIA, Constrn. Specifications Inst. (dir. central Ill. chpt. 1972-73). Roman Catholic (trustee 1974—). Clubs: K.C., Elks, Kiwanis. Prin. archtl. works include Family YMCA, Danville, First Masterplan Danville Jr. Coll. Home: 21 Westwood Pl Danville IL 61832 Office: 907 W Fairchild St Danville IL 61832

KING, KENNETH EDWARD, librarian; b. N.Y.C., July 9, 1925; s. Joseph and Mary (Fereira) K.; B.A., Brown U., 1950; M.L.S., Simmons Coll., 1951; m. Ruth Boulter, Dec. 27, 1951; children—Karen, Kenneth. Coordinator community and group services Detroit Pub. Library, 1956-63, dir. home reading services, 1963-71, asso. dir. br. services, 1971-73; dir. Mount Clemens (Mich.) Pub. Library, 1973—. Mem. Detroit Model Neighborhood Task Force, 1967-68, United Community Services Budget Com., 1965-71. Served with AUS, 1943-46. Decorated Purple Heart; recipient Outstanding Community Service award Greater Mount Clemens C. of C., 1976. Mem. ALA (v.p. adult services div. 1965-66), Mich. Library Assn. (Librarian of Year 1976; 2d v.p. 1967-68). Club: Torch (Detroit). Office: 150 Cass Ave Mount Clemens MI 48043

KING, LEROY HARRY, JR., physician; b. Paducah, Ky., Sept. 4, 1937; s. LeRoy Harry and Goldia Elmarene (Fletcher) K.; A.B., Duke, 1959; M.D., Ind. U., 1964; m. Carol Jane Henzie, July 4, 1974; children—Stephen Lee, Heather Lee, Brandon Williams, Carson Tyler, Travis Warren. Intern Ind. U. Med. Center Hosps, Indpls., 1964-65, resident in internal medicine, 1965-67, fellow in nephrology, 1967-68; instr. dept. medicine Ind. U. Med. Center Hosps., 1968-69: practice medicine specializing in internal medicine and nephrology, Indpls., 1971—; mem. staff Meth. Hosp. of Ind., Indpls., 1971—, co-dir. renal transplant program, 1971—, attending physician, 1971—; mem. staffs Community Hosp. Indpls., 1973—, Winona Hosp., Indpls., 1972—. Served as maj. MC, U.S. Army, 1969-71. Diplomate Am. Bd. Internal Medicine. Fellow A.C.P.; mem. AMA, Am. Heart Assn., Internat., Am. socs. nephrology, Am. Soc. Artificial Internal Organs, Nat. Kidney Found., Am. Fedn. for Clin. Research, Am. Soc. Internal Medicine, Ind. Med. Assn., Marion County Med. Soc., Kidney Found. of Ind. (trustee), Ind. U. Men's Club of Indpls., Beta Theta Pi, Nu Sigma Nu. Republican. Contbr. articles to profl. jours. Home: 7610 Cape Cod Circle Indianapolis IN 46250 Office: 2020 W 86th St Suite 307 Indianapolis IN 46260

KING, LESLIE ALBERT, psychologist, educator; b. Spring Valley, Minn., Feb. 1, 1921; s. Clarence Edward and Anna Rhoda (Hodgson) K.; B.S., Winona State Tchrs. Coll., 1942; M.A., U. Minn., 1947, Ph.D., 1956; m. Gladys Matie Sanford, Apr. 10, 1943; children—Charles, Margaret. Tchr. of sci., pub. schs. of Chatfield, Minn., 1946-47; prin. Amboy (Minn.) High Sch., 1947-49; prof. counseling psychology U. Minn., Mpls., 1951—; cons. psychologist, 1951—. Recipient Outstanding Contbn. to Soc. award Winona State Coll., 1960, Outstanding Profl. in Human Services award Am. Acad. of Human Services, 1974. Mem. Am., Minn. psychol. assns., Am., Minn. personnel and guidance assns., AAUP. Democrat. Unitarian. Research in psychology of learning and counseling techniques. Home: 1625 E River Rd Minneapolis MN 55414 Office: 106 Nicholson Hall Univ of Minn Minneapolis MN 55455

KING, PATRICK JAMES, mfg. co. exec.; b. Chgo., July 13, 1930; s. Edward James and Gladys Helen (Reising) K.; B.S.S., St. Mary's Coll., Winona, Minn., 1953; m. Elizabeth L. Grimm, Oct. 22, 1960; children—Patrick M., Daniel J., Eileen E. Regional sales mgr., nat. merchandising mgr. Motorola Communications div., Chgo., 1960-69; gen. mgr. ITT Mobile Radio div. ITT, N.Y.C., 1969-73; gen. mgr. Electra Co. div. Masco Corp., Indpls., 1973—; guest lectr. Am. Mgmt. Assn. Served to lt. (j.g.) USN, 1953-55. Mem. Radio Club of Am. Clubs: Hillcrest Country (Indpls.); Lake Shore (Chgo.). Home: 6219 Lands End Ln Indianapolis IN 46220 Office: 300 S on E County Line Rd Clumberland IN 46229

KING, ROBERT JAMES, psychologist; b. Logansport, Ind., May 8, 1932; s. William John and Margaret Patricia (Vallely) King; m. Jane Kemper, Oct. 17, 1959; children—Robert, David, Jane, Michael, John. B.S., Loyola U., Chgo., 1955, M.S., 1961: Ph.D., Ill. Inst. Tech., 1973. Registered psychologist, Ill., 1973, Ariz., 1974. Asst. personnel mgr. Gen. Foods Corp., Chgo., 1958-60; personnel mgr. Kaiser Engrs., Chgo., 1960-61; employment mgr. Motorola, Inc., 1961-63, personnel mgr., 1963-65, corp. mgr. personnel testing, 1965-73, corp. dir. human resources, 1973—. Lectr. U. Mich. Indsl. Relations Bur., Loyola U. Grad. Sch. Bus. and Inst. Indsl. Relations, Ill. Inst. Tech. Grad. Sch. Psychology; lectr., cons. Midwest Indsl. Relations Assn. Mem. Am., Ill., Ariz. psychol. assns., Indsl. Relations Assn. Chgo. Extensive research in psychometric testing and evaluations. Home: 1521 S Prospect Ave Park Ridge IL 60068 Office: Motorola Center 1303 E Algonquin Rd Schaumburg IL 60196

KING, THOMAS JOSEPH, physician; b. Chgo., Aug. 17, 1920; s. Thomas and Norah Catherine (Nash) K.; B.S., Xavier U., 1938-42; M.D., Loyola Med. Sch., 1945; m. Agnes Therese Bush, Oct. 30, 1943; children—Thomas, John, Therese (Mrs. Richard Vincent Malak), Gerald, Dennis, Elizabeth, Catherine. Intern Little Co. of Mary Hosp., Evergreen Park, Ill., 1945-46, staff, 1960—, dir. emergency room, 1966-73; practice medicine, Chgo., and Evergreen Park, 1948-58. Athletic dir. Mendel Cath. High Sch., 1960-69. Served with M.C. U.S. Army, 1946-47. Mem. Am., Ill., Chgo. med. socs., Am. Med. Soc. on Alcoholism, Am. Legion (comdr. 1964, 65). Elk. Home: 6241 Forestview Dr Oak Forest IL 60452 Office: Southwest Indsl Clinic 7600 W 119th St Palos Heights IL 60463

KING, WILLIAM FREDERIC, lab. exec.; b. Pontiac, Mich., July 3, 1918; s. Frederic Andrew and Katherine (Meehan) K.; student Gen. Motors Inst., 1936-40; B.S., U. Mich., 1941; m. Mary Aileen Hickey, May 30, 1942; 1 son, Dennis F. With Gen. Motors Research Lab., Warren, Mich., 1941—, jr. engr., 1941-42, research engr., 1946-49, sr. project engr., 1949-53, supr. electromech. applications, 1953-54, asst. head spl. problems, 1954-61, head electromechanics, 1961-70, head vehicle research, 1970-73, acting head biomed. sci., 1972-73, head engring. mechanics, 1973—. Served from ensign to lt. USNR, 1942-46. Mem. Phi Sigma Phi (treas. 1938-39, v.p., chmn. bd. 1939-40), Alpha Tau Iota. Roman Catholic. Clubs: Birmingham (Mich.) Athletic; Detroit Gun. Home: 31781 Bellvine Trail Birmingham MI 48010 Office: 12 Mile and Mound Rds Warren MI 48090

KING, WILLIAM HOUSTON, banker; b. Terre Haute, Ind., May 13, 1937; s. Albert William and Wilma (Leach) K.; B.S., Ind. State U., 1960; postgrad. Nat. Trust Sch., Northwestern U., 1967-68; m. Delores Ann Coons, July 25, 1957; children—Eric, Kurt. Asst. trust officer Terre Haute 1st Nat. Bank, 1958-65; with 2nd Nat. Bank Richmond (Ind.), 1965—, v.p., sr. trust officer, 1969-72, exec. v.p., 1972-74, pres., 1974—, also dir.; dir. Joseph H. Hill Co. County chmn. United Way, 1974, 1st v.p., 1977; pres. Scott Boys Club, 1977; bd. dirs. Reid Meml. Hosp., YMCA, 1973-77. Served with USAF, 1960-66. Recipient Distinguished Service award Richmond Jr. C. of C., 1970, Boss of Year award Am. Bus. Womens Assn., 1972. Mem. Richmond Area C. of C. (pres. 1975). Independent Bankers Assn., Ind. Bankers Assn., Eastern Ind. Econs. Club, Eastern Ind. Estate Planning Council. Methodist. Clubs: Rotary, Elks, Forest Hills Country, Columbia. Home: 321 19th St S Richmond IN 47374 Office: 800 Promendade Richmond IN 47374

KINGDON, ROBERT MCCUNE, historian, educator; b. Chgo., Dec. 29, 1927; s. Robert W. and Anna Catherine (McCune) K.; A.B., Oberlin Coll., 1949; M.A., Columbia, 1950, Ph.D., 1955; postgrad. U. Geneva (Switzerland), 1951-52. Instr., asst. prof. history U. Mass., 1952-57; asst. prof., asso. prof., prof. history State U. Iowa, Iowa City, 1957-65; prof. history U. Wis., Madison, 1965—, mem. Inst. Research Humanities, 1974—, dir., 1975—; vis. instr. Amherst (Mass.) Coll., 1953-54; vis. prof. Stanford, 1964. Bd. dirs. Center Reformation Research, St. Louis, pres., 1967—. Mem. Am. Soc. Reformation Research (v.p. 1970, pres. 1971), Central Renaissance Conf., Renaissance Soc. Am. (exec. bd. 1972—), Internat. Fedn. Socs. and Insts. for Study of Renaissance (sec.-treas. 1967—). Author: Geneva and the Coming of the Wars of Religion in France, 1555-1563, 1956; Geneva and the Consolidation of the French Protestant Movement, 1564-1572, 1967. Editor: (with J. F. Bergier) Registres de la Compagnie des Pasteurs de Geneve au temps de Calvin, 1962—; The Sixteenth Century Journal, 1973—. Contbr. articles to profl. jours. Home: 4 Rosewood Circle Madison WI 53711

KINGET, G. MARIAN, educator, psychologist; b. Belgium, June 2, 1910; d. René Jules Henri and Elisa (Declercq) Kinget; came to U.S., 1948, naturalized, 1951; Ph.D. summa cum laude, U. Louvain (Belgium), 1948, postdoctoral N.Y.U., 1948-49, Columbia, 1949-50. Mem. staff Counseling Center, U. Chgo., 1950-52; asst. prof. psychology Mich. State U., East Lansing, 1952-55, asso. prof., 1955-66, prof., 1966—. Mem. Am., Midwestern Mich. psychol. assns., AAUP. Author: On Being Human, 1975; Psychotherapie et Relations Humaines (translated into Spanish and Portuguese), Vol. II, 1962; The Drawing-Completion Test, 1952; (with Carl R. Rogers) Psychoterapie et Relations Humanies (translated into Spanish, Italian and Portuguese), Vol. I, 1962, Psychotherapie en Menselijke Verhoudingen, 1959. Contbr. chpts. to books. Home: 4583 Nakoma Dr Okemos MI 48864 Office: Michigan State U East Lansing MI 48823

KINIAS, GEORGE ATHANASIOS, environ. engr., coll. adminstr.; b. Distomon, Viotia, Greece, May 15, 1944; s. Athanasios George and Zoe A. Kinias; came to U.S., 1963, naturalized, 1974; B.S. in Civil Engring., Valparaiso U., 1968; M.S.C.E., U. Cin., 1970; m. Carol J. Samuelson, June 7, 1968; children—Thanasis Anthony, Zoe Margaret. Environ. engr. Cin. San. Dist., 1969-70; design engr. Vogt-Ivers Assos., Cin., 1970; lab. dir. No. Labs., Inc., Valparaiso, Ind., 1971-74; asso. prof. Ind. Vocat. Tech. Coll., 1974-76, dir. environ. tng. center, 1976—; cons. environ. control and tng. Served to 2d lt. Greek Army Corps of Engrs., 1970-71. Engr.-in-tng., Ind.; certified waste water treatment plant operators, Ind. Mem. Water Pollution Control Fedn., Am. Water Works Assn., ASCE (chpt. pres.), Ind. Acad. Sci., Nat. Assn. Environ. Edn., Smithsonian Instn., Nat. Ednl. Council Energy and Power, Nat. Environ. Tng. Assn. (nat. pres.). Author, editor tng. manuals. Home: 1703 Rock Castle Dr Valparaiso IN 46383 Office: 1440 E 35th Ave Gary IN 46409

KINNAIRD, CHARLES ROEMLER, lawyer; b. Indpls., July 21, 1932; s. Wayne Davis and Marjorie Goetz (Roemler) K.; A.B., Princeton U., 1954; LL.B., Harvard U., 1961; m. Susan Wiltshire Stempfel, May 28, 1955; children—James R., Christine S., Robert G., Edward W., Keith D. Admitted to Mich. bar, 1962; since practiced in Detroit, asso. Long, Preston, Kinnaird & Avant, 1961-69, partner, 1969—. Trustee Edward C. and Hazel Stephenson Found., 1975—. Served to lt. USNR, 1954-58. Mem. Mich., Detroit, Am. bar assns., Am., Mich. socs. hosp. attys. Clubs: Country of Detroit, Detroit; Belvedere Golf (Charlevoix, Mich.); Princeton of Mich. Contbr. articles to legal jours. Home: 104 Moran Rd Grosse Pointe Farms MI 48236 Office: 4300 City National Bank Bldg Detroit MI 48226

KINNEAR, THOMAS CLIFFORD, educator; b. Toronto, Ont., Can., June 29, 1943; s. John Clifford and Lois Kathleen (Wickett) K.; came to U.S., 1975; B.Com., Queen's U. (Can.), 1966; M.B.A., Harvard U., 1968; Ph.D., U. Mich., 1972; m. Constance Mary Molloy, May 15, 1971; children—Margaret Lynne, James Thomas. Lectr., Queen's U., Kingston, Ont., 1968-69; asst. prof. bus. U. Western Ont., 1971-74; asso. prof. mktg. Sch. Bus. Adminstrn. U. Mich., 1974—; cons. mktg. research. Can. Cooncil fellow, 1970, 71; Seagram's Found. fellow, 1970; Gen. Electric Found. fellow, 1969. Mem. Am. Mktg. Assn., Assn. Consumer Research (exec. sec.). Contbr. numerous articles to profl. jours. Office: Sch of Bus Adminstrn U of Mich Ann Arbor MI 48109

KINNICK, AUGUST EDWARD, real estate broker; b. Coon Rapids, Iowa, Aug. 18, 1928; s. Paul Harold and Dorothy Christina (Sorensen) K.; grad. high sch.; m. Collen JoAnn Davis, June 23, 1948; children—Marcia, Cynthia, Lon, Bryan. Salesman, Armour Agrl. div. W.R. Grace, Bayard, Ia., 1964-67, Am. Cyanamid, Bayard, 1974; dist. sales mgr. Golden Harvest Co., Bayard; farmer/rancher, Bayard, 1949—; real estate broker, Bayard, 1969—. Mem. Bayard Sch. Bd., 1972. Served with U.S. Army, 1946-48. Mem. Nat. Real Estate Bd., Am. Legion. Mason, Odd Fellow. Methodist. Address: Rural Route 1 Box 131 Bayard IA 50029

KINNISON, WILLIAM ANDREW, univ. pres.; b. Springfield, Ohio, Feb 10, 1932; s. Errett Lowell and Audrey Muriel (Smith) K.; A.B., Wittenberg U., 1954, B.S. in Edn., 1955; M.A., U. Wis., 1963; Ph.D. (first Flesher fellow), Ohio State U., 1967; m. Lenore Belle Morris, June 11, 1960; children—William Errett, Linda Elise, Amy Elisabeth. Asst. dean admissions Wittenberg U., Springfield, 1958-65, asst. to pres., 1967-70, v.p. for univ. affairs, 1970-73, v.p. adminstrn., 1973-74, acting pres., 1974-75, pres., 1975—; asst. to dir. Sch. Edn., Ohio State U., Columbus, 1965-67. Mem. Clark County Council Chs., 1963-65; v.p. Springfield Summer Arts Festival, 1971; trustee United Appeals of Clark County. Served with AUS, 1956-58. Mem. Clark County Hist. Soc. (trustee 1963—), Am. Assn. Higher Edn., Orgn. Am. Historians, Am. Coll. Pub. Relations Assn., Springfield Area C. of C. (trustee, v.p. community betterment 1974—), Phi Beta Kappa, Omicron Delta Kappa, Blue Key, Phi Delta Kappa, Kappa Phi Kappa, Pi Sigma Alpha, Tau Kappa Alpha, Delta Sigma Phi. Clubs: Cosmos (Washington); Rotary. Author: Building Sullivant's Pyramid: An Administrative History of the Ohio State University, 1970; Samuel Shellabarger: Lawyer, Jurist, Legislator, 1969; Wittenberg: A Concise History, 1976; also articles. Home: 1820 Timberline Dr Springfield OH 45504

KINSELLA, JAMES JOSEPH, holding co. exec.; b. Peoria, Ill., Sept. 14, 1921. Prin., James J. Kinsella Enterprise Inc., holding co., Peoria, 1977—; founder, mgr. Key Resort Club Am., Peoria, 1977—; founder, owner B.V. Corp., Peoria, 1977—, also dir.; notary public. Mem. Common Cause, Nat. Resources Def. Council. Republican. Clubs: Eagles, Playboy, Loom, Sea World Dolphin, Enterprise, Inc. Home and Office: 206 3d St W Peoria IL 61605

KINSELLA, RALPH ALOYSIUS, JR., physician; b. St. Louis, June 4, 1919; s. Ralph A. and Mabel Lamb (Downey) K.; A.B., St. Louis U., 1939, M.D., 1943; m. Margaret Neville Boyle, Aug. 8, 1947; children—Ralph Aloysius III, Mary, John. Eileen, Michael, Margaret, Matthew, Charles. Intern, Presbyn. Hosp., N.Y.C., 1943; postgrad St. Louis U., 1946-47, mem. faculty, 1948—, prof. medicine, 1972—; chief unit II, St. Louis U. Med. Service, St. Louis City Hosp., 1958—; pres. Inst. Med. Edn. and Research, St. Louis, 1972—. Served with U.S. Army, 1944-46. Charles H. Nielson fellow, 1947-48; John and Mary Markle scholar, 1948-53; diplomate Am. Bd. Internal Medicine. Fellow A.C.P.; mem. St. Louis Soc. Internal Medicine, St. Louis, Mo. med. socs., Endocrine Soc., Soc. Exptl. Biology and Medicine, Central Soc. Clin. Research, Am. Chem. Soc., N.Y. Acad. Scis., AAAS, Sigma Xi. Roman Catholic. Club: Univ. Research in steroid hormonal biochemistry. Home: 6305 Westminster Pl University City MO 63130 Office: 1515 Lafayette Ave St Louis MO 63104

KINSLEY, DANIEL ALLAN (ALLEN EDWARDS), author, bookseller; b. Drexel Hill, Pa., June 4, 1939; s. Daniel and Eva Amelia (Worts) K.; Ph.D. in Near Eastern Studies (hon.), Am. U., Beirut, 1964. Author: The Jewel in the Lotus, 1959, The Cradle of Erotica, 1962, Death Rides A Camel, 1963, The Rape of India, 1966, Erotica Judaica, 1967, Favor the Bold, 1968; editorial adviser Julian Press Library of Sex Research. N.Y.C., 1963-65; asst. mgr. B. Dalton, Bookseller, Prairie Village, Kans., 1969-70, Walden Books, Overland Park, Kans., 1974-76, Clearwater, Fla.. 1977, Kinney Flowers, Clearwater. 1977—. Recipient Knighthood of Mark Twain award Mark Twain Jour., 1967, certificate of merit Cambridge (Eng.) U., 1974. Mem. Nat. Geog. Soc., Little Bighorn Soc.

KINTZ, MARY ELIZABETH, educator; b. Terre Haute, Ind., July 16, 1915; d. Arthur F. and Catherine (Cunningham) Kintz; A.B., Ind. State Tchrs. Coll., 1937, M.A., 1950. Tchr., Harrison Twp.-Vigo County (Ind.) Pub. Schs., 1937-56; counselor Terre Haute City Schs., 1956-62; dean girls Vigo County Sch. Corp., Terre Haute, 1962-65, now counselor, tchr. English, Latin. Mem. Am. Personnel and Guidance Assn., Sigma Kappa. Home: 61 Marigold Dr Terre Haute IN 47803 Office: Sarah Scott Jr High Sch 2000 S 9th St Terre Haute IN 47807

KINYOUN, DALE EDWARD, veterinarian; b. Formoso, Kans., Dec. 28, 1927; s. Robert Roland and Alma Amelia (Ross) K.; D.V.M., Kans. State U., 1951; m. Margaret Mary Cramer, Sept. 17, 1949; children—Joan (Mrs. John T. Ferguson), Jean (Mrs. Randall Folkers), Joseph Walter, Jeffrey Dale, Judith Ann, Jane Mikel. Pvt. practice vet. medicine, Superior, Nebr., 1951—. Mem. Superior Bd. Edn., 1960-64, pres., 1964. Served with USMCR, 1946-48. Mem. Nebr. Vet. Med. Assn. (pres. 1974), Tau Kappa Epsilon. Elk, Eagle. Home: 1263 Commercial St Superior NE 68978 Office: East Hwy 8 Superior NE 68978

KINZER, DONALD LOUIS, historian; b. Kent, Wash., Nov. 9, 1914; s. Addison Louis and Lois Minerva (Fay) K.; B.A., Western Wash. Coll., 1942; B.A., U. Wash., 1947, M.A., 1948, Ph.D., 1954; m. Kathryn Jane Tipton, Aug. 20, 1955: 1 son, William Tipton. Instr., U. Wash., 1954-55; instr. U. Del., 1955-58; asso. prof. Trenton State Coll., 1958-66; asso. prof. Ind. U.-Purdue U., Indpls., 1966-70, prof., 1970—, chmn. dept., 1970—. Served with USAAF, 1942-46. Mem. Am. Hist. Assn., Orgn. Am. Historians, Ind. Hist. Soc., AAUP. Author: An Episode in Anti-Catholicism: The American Protective Association, 1964. Home: 5610 Central Ave Indianapolis IN 46220 Office: Dept History Cavanaugh Hall Ind U Purdue U Indianapolis IN 46202

KIONKA, EDWARD JAMES, lawyer; b. Oak Park, Ill., Feb. 18, 1939; s. Edward Frederick and Antoinette (Harcus) K.; B.S., U. Ill., 1960, J.D., 1962; LL.M. (Krulewitch fellow), Columbia U., 1974; m. Sandra Sellers, Aug. 17, 1958 (div. Apr. 1974); children—Thomas Edward, Meridith Ann, David James; m. 2d, Rebecca Rhodes, Dec. 24, 1975. Admitted to Ill. bar, 1962, Mo. bar, 1977; asso. firm Leibman, Williams, Bennett & Baird (now Sidley & Austin), Chgo., 1962-64; instr. U. Mich. Law Sch., 1964-65; dir. Ill. Inst. for Continuing Legal Edn., Springfield, 1965-67; asst. dean, asst. prof. law U. Ill. Coll. Law, 1967-71; cons. atty., Ill., 1971-72, 75-76; asso. prof. law So. Ill. U., Carbondale, 1973-75, 76-77, prof., 1977—. Spl. counsel gen. govt. com. 6th Ill. Constl. Conv., 1970; cons. to lawyers on civil trials, appeals; mem. adv. council Ill. Inst. for Continuing Legal Edn., 1967-72, 73—, mem. exec. com., chmn. curriculum com., 1967-71. Mem. Am., Ill., Chgo., St. Clair County bar assns., Assn. Trial Lawyers of Am., Appellate Lawyers Assn. (treas. 1974-75, sec. 1975-76, v.p. 1976-77, pres. 1977-78), Am. Judicature Soc., Am. Arbitration Assn., Order of Coif, Phi Delta Phi. Author: Basic Tort Law in a Nutshell, 1977. Asso. editor-in-chief U. Ill. Law Forum, 1961-62; editor Illinois Civil Practice After Trial, 1970. Home: 601 W Main St Carbondale IL 62901

KIPNIS, BARRY EDWIN, accountant; b. Chgo., Nov. 9. 1940; s. Aaron and Faye (Levine) K.; B.S., Ill. Inst. Tech., 1961. Accountant, Checkers, Simon & Rosner, Chgo., 1961-64; partner Kipnis and Co., Chgo., 1964—. Trustee, Congregation Beth Shalom, Northbrook, Ill., 1976. C.P.A., Ill. Mem. Am. Inst. C.P.A.'s, Ill. Soc. C.P.A.'s. Club: B'nai B'rith (dir. 1967-70). Home: 9098 Green Lakes Dr Des Plaines IL 60016 Office: 6160 N Cicero St Suite 610 Chicago IL 60646

KIPP, ROBERT ALMY, city ofcl.; b. Lincoln, Nebr., May 21, 1932; s. Harold Lyman and Constance (Almy) K.; B.S C.E., U. Kans., 1952, M.Pub.Adminstrn. in City Mgmt., 1956; m. Deborah Yvonne Graves, Apr. 29, 1956; children—Steven, David. Instr. Sch. Engring., U. Kans., 1954-55; planning dir., Newton, Kans., 1955-56; asst. city mgr., city planner, Lawrence, Kans., 1956-60; city mgr., Vandalia, Ohio, 1960-63, Fairborn, Ohio, 1963-70; mem. staff City of Kansas City, 1970-73, dir. adminstrn., 1973-74, city mgr., 1974—. Mem. dist. advisory council Ohio Municipal League. Active local Boy Scouts Am. Served with USAF, 1952-54. Mem. Internat. City Mgmt. Assn. (pres. 1977—). Club: Rotary. Home: 72 E 106th Terr Kansas City MO 64114 Office: 414 E 12th St Kansas City MO 64106

KIRACOFE, JOHN HARMON, city mgr.; b. Gomer, Ohio, Feb. 8, 1921; s. Chester Harmon and Martha Jane (Watkins) K.; B.S. in Civil Engring., Ohio No. U., 1954; grad. program in nat. econs. Indsl. Coll. Armed Forces, 1957; certificate in chem. engring. Ohio State U., 1958, U. Md. Law Enforcement Inst., 1965; postgrad in tech. of mgmt. Am. U., 1966; diploma Internat. City Mgmt. Assn. Tng. Inst., 1974; M.Pub.Adminstrn., Nova U., 1977; m. Adeena Mary Miller, Aug. 18, 1946; children—Gregory Lee, Douglas Eugene. Sr. engr. Standard Oil Co. (Ohio), Lima, 1948-60; city engr., Lima, 1960-63, dir. planning, 1963-64; town mgr., Aberdeen, Md., 1964-65; city mgr. Bowie, Md., 1965-69, Berkley, Mich., 1969—; vis. lectr. pub. fin. U. Md., 1966. Mem. Lima Community Devel. Com., 1953; v.p. PTA, 1957; pres. Ottawa Watershed Assn., 1958; chmn. Lima Mayor's Tax Study Com., 1958, Lima Traffic Com., 1960; chmn. Lima Regional Area Transp. Planning Coordinating Com., 1964; bd. dirs. Greater Bowie Bd. Trade, 1966-68; municipal cons. Md. Constl. Conv., 1967; mem. Md. Assn. Housing & Renewal Agys., 1966; chief adviser, bd. dirs. Jr. Achievement, Lima, 1960; bd. dirs. Beaumont Hosp. Authority, Royal Oak, Mich.; mem. phys. edn. com. YMCA; trustee, vice chmn. Southeastern Oakland County Water and Incinerator Authorities,

1969—. Served with USAAF, 1941-45. Recipient Engring. award Lincoln Arc Welding Found., 1953-54, Distinguished Service award Lima Soc. Profl. Engrs. Registered profl. engr., Ohio, Md., Mich., D.C.; registered profl. community planner, Mich. Mem. Lima (past pres.), Ohio (vice chmn. engrs.-in-industry functional group 1957, chmn. young engrs. com. 1958, trustee 1960) socs. profl. engrs., Lima Refinery Foremen's Club (pres. 1956), Md. City Mgrs. Assn. (pres. 1967), Internat. City Mgmt. Assn., Am. Inst. Planners, Mich. Municipal League (transp. com. 1974—, employee tng. adv. com. 1976, 77, workman's compensation ins. adv. com. 1976), Order Engr. Ohio No. U., Mich. Engring. Soc., Am. Acad. Polit. and Social Sci., Acad. Polit. Sci., Inst. Transp. Engrs., So. Mich. Water and Sewer Utilities Assn., Bldg. Ofcls. and Code Adminstrs. Internat., Am. Legion. Clubs: Masons (32 deg.), Shriners, Elks, Lions, Toastmasters Internat. (past area gov., pres., recipient Distinguished Service award 1957). Contbr. articles to profl. jours. Patentee in field. Home: 4218 Cumberland St Berkley MI 48072 Office: 3338 Coolidge Hwy Berkley MI 48072

KIRBY, JAMES ROBERT, ofcl. Dept. Army; b. Logansport, La., July 9, 1924; s. Albert and Marie (Edwards) K.; B.A., U. Md., 1970; M.A., U. Okla., 1972; postgrad. Indsl. Coll. Armed Forces, 1976—; m. Mikiko Takeuchi, Dec. 6, 1950; 1 son, James Robert. With U.S. govt., Guam, 1947-49, engr., Japan, 1949-52, chief engr., 1952-67, chief facilities engr., 1967-73, personnellist, 1973-74; chief recruitment and placement U.S. Army Tank Automotive Command, Warren, Mich., 1974—; prof. pub. adminstr. U. Md., 1973-74; cons. U.S. Army. Adv. bd. UN, 1974—. Served with U.S. Army, 1943-44. Mem. Sci. Acad. Sophia U. Assn. (Tokyo, Japan), U. Okla. Grad. Studies Alumni Assn. Clubs: Masons, Shriners. Home: 28329 Queens Ct Warren MI 48093 Office: US Army Tank Automotive Command Warren MI 48090

KIRBY, THOMAS JOSEPH, JR., ophthalmologist; b. Doucette, Tex., Feb. 14, 1917; s. Thomas Joseph and Mary Ellen (Stanton) K.; A.B., Baylor U., 1938; M.D., Southwestern Med. Coll., 1944; M.S., U. Minn., 1950; m. Mary Elizabeth Willius, May 29, 1947; children—Mary Kirby Ewers, Elizabeth, Jane Kirby Jinks, Thomas. Intern, Brackenridge Hosp., Austin, Tex., 1944; resident Mayo Clinic, Rochester, Minn., 1947-51, cons. in ophthalmology, 1951—, chmn. div. edn. dept. ophthalmology, 1974—, chmn. admissions com., 1974—; fellow in ophthalmology Mayo Found., Rochester, 1947-51, instr. ophthalmology, 1956-63, asst. prof., 1963-73, asso. prof., 1973—; bd. dirs. Joint Commn. on Allied Health Personnel in Ophthalmology, 1973—, pres., 1977. Served to capt. AUS, 1945-47. Mem. Nat. Soc. Med. Research (nat. council 1972—), Assn. Mayo Eye Fellows (dir. 1963-72, sec.-treas. 1963-72), Am. (honor award 1969), Minn. (council pres. 1961-62) acads. ophthalmology, Am. Ophthalmol. Soc., Sigma Xi, Beta Beta Beta, Phi Rho Sigma. Republican. Roman Catholic. Club: Univ. Home: 317 6th Ave SW Apt 308 Rochester MN 55901 Office: Mayo Clinic 200 1st St SW Rochester MN 55901

KIRCHNER, JAMES WILLIAM, elec. engr.; b. Cleve., Oct. 17, 1920; s. William Sebastian and Marcella Louise (Stuart) K.; B.S. in Elec. Engring., Ohio U., Athens, 1950, M.S., 1951; m. Eda Christene Landfear, June 11, 1950 (dec. May 1977); children—Kathleen Ann, Susan Lynn. Instr. elec. engring. Ohio U., 1950-52; mgr. liaison engring. Lear Siegler Inc., Maple Heights, Ohio, 1952-64; coordinator engring. services Case Western Res. U., Cleve., 1964-72, gen. mgr. Med. Center Co., 1972—. Mem. Portage County Republican exec. com., 1961-62; treas. Aurora (Ohio) PTA, 1963-65, v.p. 1965-66; trustee ch., 1963-65, deacon, 1978—. Served with USAAF, 1942-45; PTO. Registered profl. engr., Ohio. Mem. Cleve. (dir. 1969-71), Nat., Ohio socs. profl. engrs., Cleve. Engring. Soc. (chmn. environ. com. 1976), IEEE (sr.), Am. Pollution Control Assn., ASEE. Home: 140 Aurora Hudson Rd Aurora OH 44202 Office: 2250 Circle Dr Cleveland OH 44106

KIRCHNER, JOHN HOWARD, JR., psychologist; b. Passaic, N.J., Dec. 28, 1933; s. John Howard and Anita Gladys (Smith) K.; A.B., U. Ill., 1955; M.A., Northwestern U., 1956, 60, Ph.D., 1964; postgrad. Bradley U., 1965-68; m. Nora Ilse Kuehne, June 16, 1956; children—John Douglas, Gregory Allen. Tchr., high sch., Evergreen Park, Ill., 1956-57, Park Ridge, Ill., 1959-61; asso. prof. Ill. State U., Normal, 1964-71, psychologist, 1965-71; pvt. practice Cashen & Kirchner, Normal, 1969-71; chief psychologist Wood County Mental Health Clinic, Bowling Green, Ohio, 1971-75; exec. dir., chief psychologist Gt. River Mental Health Center, Muscatine, Iowa, 1975—. Served with U.S. Army, 1957-59, 61-62. Diplomate in clin. psychology Am. Bd. Profl. Psychology. Mem. Am., Midwestern, Iowa psychol. assns., Phi Beta Kappa, Phi Delta Kappa, Delta Phi Alpha. Contbr. articles to profl. jours. Home: 2208 Forest Pkwy Muscatine IA 52761 Office: 1608 Cedar St Muscatine IA 52761

KIRCHNER, RICHARD JAY, educator; b. Schenectady, Feb. 17, 1930; s. Richard Jacob and Leah (Williams) K.; B.S., U. Wis., 1952, M.S., 1955, postgrad., 1956; Ed.D., Mich. State U, 1962; m. Barbara Ann Crane, Feb. 2, 1952; children—Richard Alec, Barbara Jayne, Carolyn Diane, Robert Jay, Kathleen Kay. Instr. wrestling and track coach St. Cloud (Minn.) Tchrs. Coll., 1955-56; asst. prof., coaching staff Central Mich. U., Mt. Pleasant, 1956-62, prof. recreation, chmn. dept., 1962—, chmn. pres.'s adv. com.; camp program dir., camp dir. Elkton-Pigeon-Bayport Sch. Camp, Caseville, Mich., 1962; municipal recreation dir. Petoskey (Mich.), 1963, cons., 1964-74; vice chmn. citizens adv. com. Recreation Services div. Mich. Dept. Conservation, 1966-67. Pres. Mt. Pleasant Intermediate Sch. PTA, 1968-69; chmn. tech. planning com. Mt. Pleasant Recreation Commn. Served to capt. USMCR, 1952-54. Mem. AAHPER (v.p. Mich. 1966-67, v.p. Midwest dist. 1973-74), Nat Recreation and Parks Assn., Am. Assn. Leisure and Recreation (nat. pres. elect 1975-76), Am. Camp Assn., Mich. Soc. Gerontology, Outdoor Edn. and Camping Council (charter), Mich. Recreation and Parks Assn. (v.p. 1968-70), Phi Eta Sigma, Phi Epsilon Kappa, Phi Delta Kappa. Home: 6953 Riverside Dr Mount Pleasant MI 48858

KIRK, RUSSELL AMOS, author, editor; b. Plymouth, Mich., Oct. 19, 1918; s. Russell Andrew and Marjorie (Pierce) K.; B.A., Mich. State U., 1940; M.A., Duke U., 1941; D.Litt., St. Andrews U., Scotland, 1952; D.Litt. (hon.), Boston Coll., St. John's U., Loyola Coll.; LL.D. (hon.), Park Coll., Niagara U.; L.H.D. (hon.), Le Moyne Coll., Gannon Coll.; D.J. (hon.), Olivet Coll.; m. Annette Yvonne Courtemanche, 1964; 4 children. Asst. prof. history of civilization Mich. State Coll., 1946-53; Daly lectr. U. Detroit, 1954; mem. faculty politics New Sch. for Social Research, 1959-61; research prof. politics C.W. Post Coll., 1957-69; univ. prof. L.I.U., 1960-69; vis. prof. various univs., 1963-77. Mem. Mich. Am. Revolution Bicentennial Commn. Guggenheim fellow. Sr. fellow Am. Council Learned Socs. Author: Randolph of Roanoke, 1951, 64; The Conservative Mind, 1953, 73; St. Andrews, 1954; A Program for Conservatives, 1954; Academic Freedom, 1955; Beyond the Dreams of Avarice, 1956; The Intelligent Woman's Guide to Conservatism, 1957; The American Cause, 1957; Old House of Fear, 1961; The Surly Sullen Bell, 1962; Confessions of a Bohemian Tory, 1963; The Intemperate Professor, 1965; A Creature of the Twilight, 1966; Edmund Burke, 1967; The Political Principles of Robert A. Taft, 1967; Enemies of the Permanent Things; Observations of Abnormity in Literature and Politics, 1969; Eliot and His Age, 1972; Roots of American Order, 1974; Decadence and Renewal in the Higher Learning, 1978; The Princess of All Lands, 1978; also critical intros. and prefaces to reprints standard scholarly works. Contbr. to scholarly and popular publs., U.S., Can., Gt. Britain, Australia, Norway, Austria, including Sewanee Rev., World Review, Dublin Rev., Yale Rev., Jour. History of Ideas, Annals of Am. Acad., N.Y. Times mag., Fortune, Wall St. Jour., History Today, Sat. Eve. Post, Kenyon Rev., Nat. Rev., The Month, S.W. Rev., Commonweal, Christianity Today, Queen's Quar., America, Contemporary Rev., History Today, 1935—; founder quar. jour. Modern Age; editor quar. Univ. Bookman. Home: Piety Hill Mecosta MI 49332

KIRK, TREVA BENNINGTON, ednl. adminstr.; b. Elyria, O.; d. Newton L. and Phoebe (Athow) Kirk; A.B., Hillsdale Coll., 1930; M.A., U. Mich., 1950; Ed.D., Mich. State U., 1965. High sch. tchr., debate coach, speech dir., softball coach, dir. girl's activities Millington (Mich.) High Sch., 1930-42, high sch. prin., dir. girl's activities, 1942-54, high sch. guidance dir., 1954-56; prin. Millington Community Elementary Schs., 1956—. Mem. State Curriculum Com. Internat. Understanding, 1960—. Mem. Am. Personnel and Guidance Assn., N.E.A., Mich. Edn. Assn., Nat. Dept. Elementary Sch. Prins., Nat. Assn. Women Deans and Counselors, Nat. Council Adminstrv. Women Edn., Nat. Sch. Pub. Relations Assn., Internat. Reading Assn., Delta Kappa Gamma. Home: 4627 E Main St Millington MI 48746 Office: 8664 Dean's Dr Millington MI 48746

KIRK, WILLIAM EDWARD, child psychiatrist, mental health services facility adminstr.; b. Erie, Pa., May 7, 1933; s. Cecil Rayne and Ruth Elizabeth (Weindorf) K.; B.A., Gannon Coll., 1955; M.D., St. Louis U., 1959; m. Jean Marie Vickey, July 19, 1958; children—Douglas, Kathleen, Cynthia, Karen, Jeanmarie, Mary Patrice, Susan, Kristen, Michelle. Intern, St. Francis Gen. Hosp. and Rehab. Inst., Pitts., 1959-60; resident in gen. psychiatry Warren (Pa.) State Hosp., 1960-62; fellow in child psychiatry Children's Psychiat. Hosp., U. Mich., 1962-64; dir. York Woods Center, Ypsilanti, Mich., 1964-77, tng. dir. child psychiatry fellowship program, 1974-76; pvt. practice medicine specializing in psychiatry and child psychiatry, Ann Arbor, Mich., 1972—; mem. staff York Woods Center, Mt. Carmel Mercy Hosp., Detroit; cons. in field. Recipient award for excellence in natural sci. Gannon Coll., 1955; diplomate Am. Bd. Psychiatry and Neurology. Fellow Am. Psychiat. Assn., Am. Orthopsychiat. Assn., Am. Acad. Child Psychiatry; mem. Mich. Psychiat. Soc. (pres.-elect). Roman Catholic. Club: Racquet of Ann Arbor. Contbr. articles to profl. jours. Home: 2900 Provincial St Ann Arbor MI 48104 Office: Mt Carmel Mercy Hosp Dept Child Psychiatry 6071 W Outer Dr Detroit MI 48235

KIRK, WILLIAM JULIAN, graphics co. exec.; b. Middleton, Ohio, Jan. 9, 1913; s. Willian Henri and Catherine Lucille (Julian) K.; B.J., Ohio Wesleyan U., Delaware, 1934; postgrad. U. Cin., 1937-38; m. Beatrice Jane Smith, Sept. 22, 1937; 1 son, William Julian, Jr. With Gibson-Perin Co., Cin., 1935-40; sect. chief Air Service Command HO, Wright Patterson Field, Dayton, Ohio, 1941-44; mil. sales mgr. Tempo Studio, Chgo., 1944-45; pres. Graphic Engring. Service, Chgo., 1945-51; sale mgr. W. A. Brown Mfg. Co., Chgo., 1952; v.p. sales T M Pubs., Chgo., 1953-58; pres. Kirk Tech. Publs. div. Sangamo Electric Co., Des Plaines, Ill., 1959-62; comml. prodn. sales mgr. Televiso Corp., Wheeling, Ill., 1962-66; mng. editor Bus. Graphics, Chgo., 1967; advt., sales mgr. Graphic Arts Pub. Co., Chgo., 1968-76; pres. Quaser Graphics. Inc., Chgo., 1976—; dir. Unit Systems, Inc., Addison, Ill. Mem. Instrument Soc. Am. (sr.). Soc. Reproduction Engrs., Soc. Tech. Writers. Elk. Author: A-N Specifications Guide to Preparation of Technical Data, 1943. Patentee in indsl fields. Home: 90 E Milburn St Mount Prospect IL 60056 Office: 2840 W Fullerton Ave Chicago IL 60647

KIRK, WYATT DOUGLASS, educator, counselor; b. Elgin, Ill., May 10, 1935; s. Wyatt Douglass and Katherine K.: B.S., Western Mich. U., 1963, M.A., 1969, Ed.D., 1973; m. Sarah Virgo, July 9, 1977. Tchr., Benton Harbor (Mich.) High Sch., 1963-67; counselor placement specialist, area 4 coordinator Fort Custer Job Corps Center, Battle Creek, Mich., 1967-68; with counseling and guidance dept. Kalamazoo (Mich.) Pub. Sch., 1968-70; asst. prof., counseling psychologist counseling center, tchr. counselor edn. dept. Western Mich. U., Kalamazoo, 1970—; cons. Rand Corp.. U.S. Office Edn., Nazareth Coll., Kalamazoo, Kalamazoo chpt. planned Parenthood, 1972, Grand Rapids Pub. Sch. System, 1970. Pres. Douglass Community Assn., Kalamaoo; edn. chmn. Northside Devel. Program: vice chmn. 11 Greater Kalamazoo Council; trustee Found.; chmn. Equal Employment, Disadvantaged and Minority. Mem. Am., Mich. personnel and guidance Assns., Nat. Assn. for Non-White Concern, Mich. Coll. Personnel Assn., Mich. Sch. Counselors Assn., Assn. Black Psychologists, Nat. Mich. alliances black sch. educators, NAACP (v.p.), Kappa Alpha Psi. Democrat. Episcopalian. Home: 3625 Kenbrooke Ct Kalamazoo MI 49007 Office: Counseling Center Wester Mich U Kalamazoo MI 49008

KIRKEGAARD, R(AYMOND) LAWRENCE, JR., architect, acoustician; b. Denver, Dec. 11, 1937; s. Raymond Lawrence and Frances Jean (Stocking) K.; A.B., Harvard U., 1960, M.Arch. cum laude, 1964; m. Joslyn Ann Hills, Mar. 23, 1959; children—Dana Lawrence, Jonathan Eric, Bradford Andrew. Cons. archtl. acoustics Bolt, Beranek & Newman, Cambridge, Mass., 1962-64, supervisory cons., regional mgr., Chgo., 1964-75; pres., prin. cons. R. Lawrence Kirkegaard & Assos., Inc., Lombard, Ill., 1976—. Cubmaster, Boy Scouts Am., 1972-74, scoutmaster, 1974-76; co-founder Gingerbread House Presch. Learning Center, 1970. Recipient Citation award for best tech. paper in archtl. acoustics Acoustical Soc. Am., 1972. Mem. Acoustical Soc. Am., AIA, U.S. Inst. Theatre Tech. (exec. bd. Midwest sect. 1972-74). Congregationalist. Club: Harvard (Chgo.). Prin. archtl. works include Tulsa Performing Arts Center, Milw. Performing Arts Center, Mus. Arts Center, Ind. U., Bloomington, McCormick Place, Chgo., Midland (Mich.) Center for Arts, Her Majesty's Theatre, Tehran, Iran, Chgo. Mercantile Exchange, Fort Wayne (Ind.) Amphitheatre, St. Croix Island Center, V.I., Tenn. State Cultural Center, Nashville, Milw. Exposition and Conv. Center, Will County Courthouse, Joliet, Ill., Jondi Shapour U. Performing Arts Center, Ahwaz, Iran, Denver Performing Arts Center, Young People's Theatre, Toronto, Ont., MGM Grand Hotel, Reno, Youth Performing Arts Center, Louisville, music bldgs. Northwestern U., No. Ill. U., U. Wis. at Madison, Mpls. Children's Theatre Complex. Home and Office: 125 Everest Rd Lombard IL 60148

KIRKHUS, HAROLD PRESTON, ret. educator; b. Leland, Ill., July 31, 1910; s. Burton Maynard and Ida (Kittleson) K.; A.B., Bradley U., 1933; M.A., U. Ill., 1938; student Miami U., 1948; m. Ruth Susan Mathre, June 25, 1936; children—John Mark, Mary Jane Kirkhus Hinshaw, Sue Elizabeth Kirkhus Swanson, Karen Jean Kirkhus Mason. Tchr., prin. Newark (Ill.) Pub. Schs., 1933-38; prin. Oswego (Ill.) Consol. Elementary Schs., 1938-43; with Peoria (Ill.) Pub. Schs., 1944-73, tchr., 1944-57, dir. adult edn., 1954-60. dir. ednl. research, 1957-73, ret., 1973. Chmn. pub.-pvt. edn. unit United Fund, 1957-61; exec. sec. steering com. that established Ill. Central Coll., 1966; mem. long range planning com. YMCA; mem. restoration com. Jubilee Coll.; bd. dirs. Peoria Neighborhood House Assn., 1976-77. Recipient merit award Peoria Pub. Sch. System, 1973, certificate of appreciation Peoria Bd. Edn., 1973; Restoration Service award Jubilee Coll., 1976. Mem. Ill. (past pres. Peoria div.), Peoria (past pres.) edn. assns., NEA, Kendall County Tchrs. Assn. (past pres.), Adelphic Nat. Lit. Soc., Am. Ednl. Research Assn., Sons of Norway, Phi Delta Kappa (Distinguished Service Key Edn. 1946, 67, Emeritus Membership award 1973), Kappa Phi Kappa, Pi Kappa Delta, Beta Sigma Mu. Lutheran. Republican. Club: Kiwanis. Home: Peoria IL

KIRKLAND, CHARLES WALTER, JR., dentist; b. Chgo., Nov. 29, 1939; s. Charles Walter and Mary (Smulka) K.; A.A., North Park Coll., 1959, B.S., 1961; D.D.S., Loyola U., 1965. Intern and resident in pediatric dentistry Children's Hosp., Cin., 1965-67; pvt. practice dentistry, Chgo., 1968—; dept. owner and chief dentistry, Laramie Med.-Dental Center, Chgo., 19—. Founder, pres. Kirklands Hobbyland. Mem. Acad. Model Aeros., Am. Kite Flyers Assn., Fedn. Aeronautique Internationale, Nat. Rifle Assn., Ohio Gun Collectors Assn., Lamp Collectors, Aladdin Knights, Xi Psi Phi. Roman Catholic. Contbr. numerous articles on model aviation. Designer remote control device for model aircraft. Home: 5340 W Parker Ave Chicago IL 60639 Office: 125 N Laramie Ave Chicago IL 60644

KIRKPATRICK, GARY LEE, accountant, tax service exec.; b. Davenport, Iowa, Feb. 14, 1945; s. William E. and Ruby B. (Bernauer) Kirkpatrick; student Palmer Jr. Coll., 1966-67, U. Iowa, 1967-69. Tax. cons. H. & R. Block, Davenport, 1970, Tax Corp. Am., Moline, Ill., 1971; owner, operator Kirkpatrick Tax Service, Davenport, 1972—. Served with USNR, 1964-66. Gordon H. Clarke scholar, 1967-69. Mem. U.S. Chess Fedn. (sustaining). Roman Catholic. Clubs: Quad-City Computer, Toastmasters, Illowa Chess (sec. 1976-77). Home: 230 W 3d St Apt 5 Davenport IA 52801 Office: 515 Putnam Bldg Davenport IA 52801

KIRKPATRICK, JAMES C., state ofcl., newspaper publisher; b. Braymer, Mo., June 15, 1905; s. Ray N. and Lena L. (Rea) K.; student Central Mo. State U., U. Mo. Sch. Journalism; m. Jessamine Elizabeth Young, Aug. 18, 1927; 1 son, Don W. Editor, Warrensburg (Mo.) Daily Star-Jour., Jefferson City (Mo.) Post-Tribune and Daily Capitol News; pub. Windsor (Mo.) Rev., 1954-72, Lamar (Mo.) Daily Democrat, 1972-74; former adminstrv. asst. to gov. of Mo.; sec. state State of Mo., Jefferson City, 1965—. Campaign dir. Missourians for Progress, 1962; mem. Mo. Gov.'s Com. on Commerce and Indsl. Devel., 1961-65; mem. Fed. Elections Commn. Advisory Panel, 1975-77. Mem. Mo. Democratic State Exec. Com., 1973—; hon. chmn. Mo. March of Dimes, 1977. Bd. dirs., past chmn. Mo. 4-H Found.; trustee, pres. Central Mo. State U. Recipient Honor scroll Mo. Good Rds. and Sts. Assn., 1968; Honor medal U. Mo. Sch. Journalism, 1969, U. Mo. Faculty-Alumni award, 1972. Mem. Mo. (past pres.), Central Mo. (past pres.) press assns., Nat. Assn. Secs. State (pres. 1973-74), Dem. Editors Mo. (past pres.), Mo. Acad. Squires, Windsor C. of C. (past pres.). Rotarian (past 1st v.p. Jefferson City), Lion (past pres. Windsor). Home: 602B Norris Dr Jefferson City MO 65101 Office: Sec of State Capitol Bldg Jefferson City MO 65101

KIRKPATRICK, JOSEPH FRANCIS, physician; b. Spangler, Pa., Aug. 21, 1930; s. Clement Joseph and Genevieve Marie (Dumm) K.; B.S., St. Francis Coll., 1954; M.D., Georgetown U., 1958; m. Elizabeth Ann Hutchinson, May 5, 1962; children—Colleen, Theresa, Patricia, David, Mary. Intern, Providence Hosp., Washington, 1958-59; resident Balt. Eye-Ear-Nose-Throat Hosp., 1959-62; practice medicine specializing in ophthalmology, Montgomery, Ala., 1962-64, Lancaster, Ohio, 1964—; mem. staff Lancaster-Fairfield County Hosp. Served to capt. M.C., USAF, 1962-64. Diplomate Am. Acad. Ophthalmology and Otolaryngology. Mem. Ohio, Columbus ophthal. socs., Ohio, Fairfield County med. socs., Am. Assn. Physicians and Surgeons, Lancaster C. of C. (dir. 1970-72). Roman Catholic. Home: 108 Terrace Ct Lancaster OH 43170 Office: 1500 E Main St Lancaster OH 43130

KIRKPATRICK, ROBINSON PERKINS, anesthesiologist; b. Utica, O., Apr. 1, 1929; s. Henry Perkins and Iva Myrtle (Lupher) K.; B.Sc., Capital U., 1951; M.D., Ohio State U., 1955; m. Barbara Anne Foster, Mar. 21, 1954; children—Robinson Allen, Andrew Peter, Elizabeth Anne. Intern, Mt. Carmel Hosp., Columbus, O., 1955-56; resident Hines (Ill.) VA Hosp., 1959-61; asst. prof., dir. pediatric anesthesia U. Cin., 1961-65; pvt. practice, Cin., 1965-67, Danville, Ky., 1967-72; dir. respiratory therapy and anesthesiology St. Therese Hosp., Waukegan, Ill., 1972—. Served with USNR, 1957-59. Fellow Am. Coll. Anesthesiology; mem. A.M.A., Ill., Lake County med. socs., Am., Ill. socs. anesthesiologists, Anesthesia Research Soc. Mason. Home: 5023 South Rd Gurnee IL 60031 Office: St Therese Hosp Washington St Waukegan IL 60085

KIRSTEIN, PETER NEIL, historian; b. St. Louis, Dec. 1, 1945; s. Melvin Byron and Kathryn (Kaufman) K.; A.B., Boston U., 1967; M.A., St. Louis U., 1969, Ph.D., 1973. Lectr. history and polit. sci. St. Louis U., 1970-74, St. Louis Community Coll., Meramec, Mo., 1973-74; instr. Ill. Municipal Clk.'s Inst., U. Ill., 1975—; asst. prof. history St. Xavier Coll., Chgo., 1974—. Served with U.S. Army Res., 1968-69. St. Louis U. fellow, 1968, 71-72; fellow Inter-Univ. Seminar Armed Forces and Society, 1975—; grantee Harry S. Truman Library Inst., 1972. Mem. Am. Hist. Assn., Mo. Polit. Sci. Assn., Pi Sigma Alpha, Phi Alpha Theta. Author: Anglo Over Bracero: A History of the Mexican Worker in The United States from Roosevelt to Nixon, 1977; also articles. Office: Dept History St Xavier Coll 3700 W 103d St Chicago IL 60655

KIRSTEINS, ANDREW, surgeon, educator; b. Riga, Latvia, Mar. 11, 1919; s. Ernest and Meta (Starks) K.; came to U.S., 1949, naturalized, 1954; D.V.M., U. Latvia, 1942; M.D., Phillipps U., 1949; M.S. in Surgery, U. Ill., 1954; m. Kaija Inese Ozolins, Aug. 22, 1958; children—Andrew, Astrid. Intern, Evang. Hosp. Chgo., 1950-57; resident in gen. surgery U. Ill. Research Hosp., Chgo. Wesley Meml. Hosp., 1951-55; practice medicine specializing in surgery, Chgo., 1957—; clin. asst. prof. surgery U. Ill., Chgo., 1957—. Served with U.S. Army, 1955-57. Fellow in cancer research U. Ill., 1953. Fellow A.C.S.; mem. AMA, Ill., Chgo. med. socs. Republican. Lutheran. Contbr. articles to profl. jours. Home: 853 East Ave Park Ridge IL 60068 Office: 722 W Diversey Pkwy Chicago IL 60614

KISH, ELMER ANTHONY, cons. engr.; b. Glens Run, O., May 24, 1913; s. Antal and Theresa (Horvath) K.; diploma elec. engring. Am. Sch., 1937; postgrad. Oberlin Coll., 1940-41, Detroit U., 1944-47, Case Inst. Tech., 1949-51; m. Theresa Popp, July 16, 1938; children—Karen Jean, Roger Anthony. Elec. supt. Albert Kahn, Asso. Architects and Engrs., Inc., Detroit, 1942-43; elec. designer Austin Co., spl. engring. div., Cleve., 1941; chief elec. engr. Brooker Engring. Co., Detroit, 1944-47; constrn. mgr. Harley, Ellington & Day, architects and engrs., Detroit, 1947-48; constrn. engr. C. Iber & Sons, gen. contractors, Peoria, Ill., 1948; constrn. mgr. Fulton, Krinsky & DelaMotte, architects, Cleve., 1949-50; asst. chief elec. engr. J. Gordon Turnbull, Inc., cons. engrs., Cleve., 1950-53; chief elec. engr Arthur G. McKee & Co., indsl. div., Cleve., 1954; owner Kish Engring. Co., Lyndhurst, O., 1955—. Registered profl. engr., Ohio, N.Y., Mich., Mo. Mem. Am. Inst. Plant Engrs., Am. Soc. Heating, Refrigeration and Air Conditioning Engrs., Cleve. Engring. Soc., Energy Conservation Council, Nat. Fire Protection Assn. Mason (Shriner). Address: 4837 Fairlawn Rd Lyndhurst OH 44124

KISHNER, MEL, artist; b. Milw., May 17, 1915; s. Samuel and Anna (Horowitz) K.; B.S., Milw. State Tchrs. Coll. (now U. Wis.-Milw.), 1938; m. Jane Elizabeth Pierce, Sept. 30, 1939; children—Minta Ann (Mrs. Jon Walters), Priscilla (Mrs. Herbert Barber), Megan Jane, Jay Mark. Supervising designer WPA Arts Program, 1938; art tchr. Wis. Coll. Music, 1939; artist Milw. Jour. Co., 1940—, art dir. Milw. Newspaper, Inc., 1970—; tchr., artist in residence Exptl. Art Program, practicing and exhibiting fine artist U.S. HEW. Mem. City of Milw. Art Com., 1940. Recipient numerous awards for paintings in nat. and regional exhbns.; named to U. Wis.-Milw. Athletic Hall of Fame, 1973. Mem. U. Wis.-Milw. Alumni Assn. (pres.), Wis. Painters and Sculptors Assn. (pres., dir.), Illustrators and Designers Milw. (pres.), Wis. Watercolor Soc. (v.p.), Sigma Delta Chi. Club: Milw. Press. Home: W269 N1574 Meadowbrook St Pewaukee WI 53072 Office: Jour Sq Milwaukee WI 53201

KISKIS, JAMES MATTHEW, mfg. engr.; b. Springfield, Ohio, Mar. 25, 1932; s. George Charles and Dorothy Jane (Van Gundy) K.; ed. pub. schs., spl. courses; m. Zoie June Addis, May 9, 1953; children—Brenda, James, Thomas, Kenneth, Karen, Daniel, Elaine. Apprentice electrician Internat. Harvester Co., Springfield, Ohio, 1949-53; electrician Robbins & Myers, Inc., Springfield, Ohio, 1954-61, process engr. pump div. Gallipolis, Ohio, 1961-67, inspection supr., quality control mgr., 1967-75, mfg. engr., 1975—. Licensed amateur radio operator, 2d class comml. radiotelephone operator F.C.C. Republican. Roman Catholic. Clubs: Mid Ohio Valley Amateur Radio, K.C. Research and innovations in elec. motor manufacture and design. Home: Rte 2 Box 522 Gallipolis OH 45631 Office: Box 502 Gallipolis OH 45631

KISPERT, DONALD EUGENE, engring. dept. mgr.; b. Clinton, Ind., Sept. 1, 1928; s. Ortie Curtis and Euphemia (Broatch) K.; B.S. in Civil Engring., Ind. Inst. Tech., 1951; m. Nancy Marie Berghoff, Aug. 27, 1950; children—Robert Calvin, Donna Jean, Linda Sue. Field project engr. E.I. DuPont Co., Ind., Ga., N.J., 1951-54, 55-56; constrn. supr. Socony Mobil Oil Co., New Goshen, Ind., 1954-55; field supt. Fruin-Colnon Constrn. Co., Indpls., 1956-59; design engr. Clyde Williams & Assoc., Indpls., 1956-59, E.R. Hamilton & Assos., 1959-60; bldg. and maintenance foreman, mgr. plant engrin. R.R. Donnelley & Sons Co., Warsaw, Ind., 1960—. Bd. dirs. Warsaw YMCA, 1965-72. Served with U.S. Army, 1946-48. Licensed profl. engr., Ind. Mem. Nat., Ind. socs. profl. engrs. Republican. Presbyterian. Clubs: Optimists, Mason. Home: 1933 E Clark St Warsaw IN 46580 Office: RTE 30 W Warsaw IN 46586

KISPERT, ROBERT CHARLES, nuclear materials mfg. co. exec.; b. Cin., Feb. 1, 1936; s. Frank Edward and Rose Mary (Deutsch) K.; B.S. in Chem. Engring., U. Cin., 1960, M.S. in Chem. Engring., 1963. With Nat. Lead Co. Ohio, Cin., 1958—, prodn. supt., 1972-76, sr. staff engr., 1976—. Tchr., U. Cin., 1962-63, Miami Valley Inst. Tech., 1966-68. Dist. campaign chmn. Boy Scouts Am., 1975. Mem. Am. Inst. Chem. Engrs., Am. Nuclear Soc. Republican. Roman Catholic. Patentee in field. Home: 3968 Ruth Lane Cincinnati OH 45211 Office: PO Box 39158 Cincinnati OH 45239

KISS, JANOS, music educator, composer, condr.; b. Hungary, Mar. 21, 1920; s. Andras and Maria (Laszlo) K.; came to U.S., 1956, naturalized, 1973; teaching diploma Bela Bartok Conservatory of Music, Budapest, 1954; conducting diploma People's Ednl. Inst., Budapest, 1956; Franz Liszt Acad. Music, Budapest, 1954-56; m. Josephine Anna Recse, July 27, 1963. Tchr. brasses Cleve. Music Sch. Settlement, 1964—; chmn. music dept. St. Luke Sch., Lakewood, Ohio, 1966-70; dir. orch., composer in residence, tchr. instruments Western Res. Acad., Hudson, Ohio, 1967-72; tchr., composer in residence St. Edward High Sch., Lakewood, Ohio, 1968-74; composer in residence Luth. High Sch., Rocky River, Ohio, 1973—; chmn. music dept. Holy Family Sch., Parma, Ohio, 1974—, St. Ann's Sch., Cleveland Heights, 1974-75; co-founder, condr., music dir. West Suburban Philharmonic Orch., 1969—; hon. mem. Zoltan Kodaly Acad. and Inst., Chgo. Mem. Am. Soc. Univ. Composers, Nat. Assn. Am. Composers and Condrs., Music Tchrs. Nat. Assn., Ohio Music Tchrs. Assn., Cleve. Fedn. Musicians, Am. Music Center, ASCAP. Composer: Spring-At-Last!, 1970; String Bass Concerto, 1970; Flute Concerto, 1970; Concerto for Trombone, 1971; On the Wing, for flute and guitar, 1972; Josepha, quintet for alto recorder with violin, viola, cello and harp, 1973; Concerto for B-Flat Clarinet, with orch., 1974; Celebration and Challenge, for wind ensemble with electronics, 1974; Western Legend, rhapsody for harp and orch., 1975; Twilight Mist, for string quartet and organ, 1975; Impression, for trumpet and piano, 1975; Adagio for Viola, with two violins, cello and harp, 1975; Silent Presence, tone poem for clarinet, viola and organ, 1975; Winter's Sonnet, flute-harp-organ, 1975; Ballet for Harps, 1975; Concerto for violoncello and orch., 1976; Lexington '76, Bicentennial Rhapsody for Orch., 1976; Divertimento, solo violin, solo viola, solo string bass, harp and chamber ensemble, 1977; Episode for oboe, french horn, bassoon and harp, 1977; In Homage for harp ensemble, 1977; Suite in Stilo Antico for orch. with harpsichord, 1977; Salute-in Retrospect, cimbalo solo with orch., 1977; Chorale Prelude, organ, 1977. Home: 229 Bradley Rd Bay Village OH 44140 Office: Cleve Music Sch Settlement Main Sch 11125 Magnolia Dr at Mistletoe Dr Cleveland OH 44106

KISSELL, KENNETH EUGENE, govt. scientist; b. Columbiana, Ohio, June 28, 1928; s. Thomas Franklin and Grace (Messersmith) K.; B.Sc. cum laude, Ohio State U., 1949, M.Sc., 1958, Ph.D., 1969; postgrad. Osservatorio Astrofisico di Arcetri, Florence, Italy, 1969; children—Kevin Douglas, Bradley Thomas. Instrumentation engr. Ohio State U. Rocket Lab., 1948-51; instrumentation physicist Wright Air Devel. Center, Dayton, Ohio, 1951-57; physicist applied mathematics research br. aerospace research lab. Wright-Patterson AFB, Ohio, 1957-59, chief gen. physics research br., 1959-61, research physicist, 1961-66, dir. gen. physics research lab., 1966-72, acting chief surveillance br. reconnaissance and weapon delivery div. air force avionics lab., 1972-76, sr. scientist in aerospace surveillance, 1972—; vis. research prof. U. Florence (Italy), 1969. Recipient Meritorious Civilian Service award Office Aerospace Research, USAF, 1966. NATO grantee, 1972; NSF grantee, 1973. Fellow Am. Inst. Aeros. and Astronautics (asso.), Royal Astron. Soc.; mem. Am. Phys. Soc., Optical Soc. Am., Am. Geophys. Union, Am. Astron. Soc., Instrument Soc. Am. (sr., editor jour. 1962-68), Societa Astronomica Italiana, Internat. Astron. Union, Com. on Space Research, Phi Beta Kappa, Sigma Xi. Contbr. numerous articles to profl. publs., 1953-76; patentee in field; research on solar eclipses, 1954—. Home: 3184 Birchall Dr Dayton OH 45440 Office: Air Force Avionics Lab/RW Wright-Patterson AFB OH 45433

KISSLING, CHARLES DANIEL, clinical psychologist; b. Cleve., Feb. 7, 1919; s. Charles John and Mary Catherine (Schaefer) K.; B.S.M., Baldwin-Wallace Coll., 1940; M.A., Case-Western Res. U., 1942, Ed.D., 1962; postgrad. Fenn Coll., 1946-48; m. Marjorie Jeanne Dreher, Nov. 20, 1948; children—Mary Catherine, Charles Daniel, Judith Anne, Patricia Louise. Counselor, psychologist Cleve. Catholic Diocese, 1958-62; sch. psychologist Lorain (Ohio) Bd. Edn., 1962-67, chief psychologist, 1967-69, psychological evaluator 1969-70; asst. prof. dept. psychology John Carroll U., 1971-74; instr. dept. psychology Cleve. State U., 1965-70; lectr. Lorain County Community Coll., 1964, 69-74; music supr. St. Ignatius Sch. Church, Cleve., 1942-62; consulting psychologist St. Raphael Sch., Bay Village Ohio, 1968-70; St. Mary's Elementary and High Schs., Lorain, Ohio, 1968-69; St. Angela Merici Sch., Fairview Park, Ohio, 1974—; pvt. practice clinical psychology, Rocky River, Ohio, 1964-73, Westlake Ohio, 1973—; mem. profl. advisory bd. Parents Without Partners, Cleve., 1968—. Served with U.S. Army, 1942-45. Licensed psychologist, Ohio. Mem. Am., MW, Ohio, Cleve. psychol. assns., Nat., Cleve. assn. for sch. psychologists, Assn. for Advancement of Ethical Use of Hypnosis, Internat. Soc. for Profl. Hypnosis, Ohio, Cleve. acads. for cons. psychologists, Phi Delta Kappa, Phi Mu Alpha Sinfonia. Home: 3630 Trains End Dr Medina OH 44256 Office: 24700 Center Ridge Rd Westlake OH 44145

KIST, RICHARD JAMES, oral maxillofacial surgeon; b. Eagle Grove, Iowa, Apr. 16, 1930; s. Joseph John and Verna (Klass) K.; D.D.S., State U. Iowa, 1954, M.S.D., 1959; m. Phyllis Ann Comstock, Sept. 30, 1950; children—Mary Kay, Deborah Ann, Suan E., Caroline J. Intern, resident State U. Iowa, 1956-59; pvt. practice oral maxillofacial surgery, Clinton, Iowa, 1959-67; oral surgery cons. VA Hosp., Clinton; mem. advanced cardiac life support affiliate faculty Iowa Heart Assn. Pres. Clinton March of Dimes, 1962, Clinton Symphony Orch., 1964. Served with USAF, 1954-56. Diplomate Am. Bd. Oral Surgery. Founding fellow Am. Coll. Oral Maxillofacial Surgeons; mem. Am., Brit., Internat., Midwestern, Iowa socs. oral surgeons, Clinton County Dental Soc. (past pres.), Nat. Acupuncture Research Soc. Contbr. articles to profl. jours. Home: 1011 9th Ave N Clinton IA 52732 Office: Bluff Med Center Clinton IA 52732

KISTLER, JOHN JOSEPH, JR., civil engr.; b. Lawrence, Kans., June 25, 1926; s. John Joseph and Grace (Olsen) K.; B.S., U. Mich., 1951; postgrad. Western Mich. U., 1962; m. Clare Frances Oberlin, Sept. 5, 1959; 1 dau., Jamie Josephine. Designer, Shaw-Box Crane Div., Muskegon, Mich., 1956-60; chief engr. Standard Iron Works, San Diego, 1960-61; partner T & H Assos., Grand Haven, Mich., 1961-65; pres. Terrill, Kistler & Anderson, Inc., 1965-71; chmn. bd., pres. John Kistler & Assos., Inc., 1971—; dir. College Park Mobile Homes, Grand Traverse Crane Corp. Mem. Grand Haven Econ. Devel. Com. Served with USNR, 1944-46. Registered profl. engr., Ind., Mich., Kans., Ill., Fla. Fellow ASCE (past chpt. dir. and pres.); mem. AIM (pres.'s council), Mich. Soc. Profl. Engrs. (past chpt. pres.), Am. Congress on Surveying and Mapping, Cons. Engrs. Council, Mich. Assn. Professions, Am. Pub. Works Assn., Water Pollution Control Fedn., Muskegon Area, Tri-Cities chambers commerce, Triangle, Phi Gamma Delta. Presbyterian. Clubs: Kiwanis (past pres. Grand Haven), Grand Haven Golf. Home: 15663 Ryan Dr Holland MI 49423 Office: 302 S Beechtree St Grand Haven MI 49417

KITAZUMI, MARIE NAKAMURA, religious assn. exec.; b. Sacramento, Feb. 5, 1921; d. Iwazo and Kishino (Yamamto) Nakamura; student Merritt Sch. Bus., Oakland, Calif., 1939-41, Ind. U. Extension, 1944-46, U. Chgo. Extension, 1955-56, Northwestern U. Extension, 1964-66; m. Tadasu Kitazumi, Dec. 12, 1942 (div. 1962); children—Anita Lin, Constance Marie, Lisa Kishino. Jr. relocation officer War Relocation Authority, Indpls., 1944-46; asst. to chief research analyst Nuernberg Trials, Germany, 1947; office mgr. Chgo. Pottery Co., Chgo., 1950-55; owner Kitazumi Ins. Agy., Waukegan, Ill., 1959-62; adminstrv. asst. Gen. Council on World Service and Fin., United Methodist Ch., Evanston, Ill., 1962-72, asst. gen. sec. Council on Fin. and Adminstrn., 1973—; sec. adminstrv. bd. 1st United Meth. Ch., Evanston, 1970-71. Home: 1425 Sandpebble #336 Wheeling IL 60090 Office: 1200 Davis St Evanston IL 60201

KITCHEN, CARL ROBERT, optometrist; b. Atlantic, Iowa, Nov. 10, 1916; s. Clyde James and Abbie Grace (Acker) K.; student Iowa State Coll., 1936; D.Optometry, No. Ill. Coll. Optometry, 1940; m. Mildred Marie Ihry, Nov. 9, 1946; children—Michal (Mrs. John Moklestad), Jeffrey Carl, John Robert. Pvt. practice optometry, Creston, Iowa, 1940-43, Estherville, Ia., 1946-60, Cedar Rapids, Iowa, 1960—. Chmn. blood procurment Red Cross Blood Bank, 1957; chmn. Estherville Fly-In Breakfast, 1948. Served with USAAF, 1942-45; lt. col. ret., 1968. Decorated Bronze Star medal with oak leaf cluster, Air medal with three oak leaf clusters. Mem. President's Club Ill. Coll. Optometry, Optometric Found., Better Vision Inst., Res. Officers Assn., Am. Legion, V.F.W., Omega Delta. Republican. Episcopalian. Elk, Mason, Kiwanian. Home: 1151 Staub Ct NE Cedar Rapids IA 52402 Office: 4600 1st Ave NE Cedar Rapids IA 52402

KITCHEN, CHARLES WILLIAM, lawyer; b. Cleve., July 17, 1926; s. Karl Kosciusko and Lucille Wilshire (Keynes) K.; A.B., Western Res. U., 1948, LL.B., 1950, J.D., 1950; m. Mary Helen Applegate, July 22, 1950; s. Kenneth K., Guy R., Anne M. Admitted to Ohio bar, 1950; mng. partner firm Kitchen, Messner & Deery, Cleve., 1950—. Served with USAAF, 1944-45. Mem. Cleve. Def. Attys. Group (pres. 1972), Ohio Def. Assn. (pres. 1976), Internat. Assn. Ins. Counsel, Def. Research Inst., Am. Legion, Am., Ohio, Cleve. bar assns., Greater Cleve. Growth Assn., Am. Legion, Citizens League Cleve. Clubs: Avon Oaks Country, Masons. Home: 28949 Turnbridge Rd Bay Village OH 44140 Office: 1305 Superior Bldg Cleveland OH 44114

KITCHEN, DENIS LEE, publisher, artist; b. Milw., Aug. 27, 1946; s. Benjamin Luthor and Margaretha (Margert) K.; B.J., U. Wis. at Milw., 1968; m. Irene Frances Nonnweiler, Feb. 13, 1971 (div. 1977); children—Sheena, Scarlet. Pres., Kitchen Sink Enterprises comic book div. Krupp Comic Works Inc., Princeton, Wis., 1970—, pres. parent co., 1970—; co-founder Bugle-Am., newspaper, 1970—; art dir. Cartoon Factory, Princeton, 1972—; co-pub., art dir. Fox River Patriot, newspaper, 1976—; one-man shows: Priebe Art Gallery, Oshkosh, Wis., 1976, Jewish Community Center, Milw., 1977, Reeve Meml. Union, Oshkosh, 1978; editor Comix Book, N.Y.C., 1974-75; dir. Krupp Mail Order, Inc., Boulder, Colo.; instr. history of comics U. Wis. at Milw., 1972. Socialist Labor party candidate lt. gov. Wis., 1970. Mem. United Cartoon Workers Am. (pres. local). Editor: Snarf, 1972—; Bizarre Sex, 1973—, Death Rattle, 1973—; Wierd Trips, 1974—. Home: RD 1 Box 329 Princeton WI 54968 Office: 114 Washington St Princeton WI 54968

KITCHIN, PAUL CLIFFORD, JR., ret. educator; b. Missoula, Mont., Oct. 18, 1918; s. Paul Clifford and Agnes (Hatch) K.; A.B., Ohio State U., 1946, postgrad. 1954-55; M.A., Kent State U., 1948; m. Virginia M. Stachowicz, May 9, 1942; children—Paul Clifford, Christopher S. Mem. faculty Kent (Ohio) State U., 1948-77, prof. polit. sci., 1972-77, ombudsman, 1970-77; Municipal and local govt. cons. Mem. Bd. Zoning Appeals, Rootstown Twp., Ohio, 1971—, chmn., 1973—. Served with USAAF, 1941-45. Mem. Am. Assn. Higher Edn., Midwest, Am. polit. sci. assns., Ohio Assn. Economists and Polit. Scientists (sec.-treas. 1963-75), AAUP. Home: 5098 Rootstown Rd Ravenna OH 44266 Office: Dept Polit Sci Kent State U Kent OH 44242

KITSIS, LOUIS, candy mfg. co. exec.; b. Nickohiv, Russia, Oct. 24, 1905; s. Sam and Bessie (Goss) K.; came to U.S., 1909, naturalized, 1941; ed. high sch.; m. Florence Sarah Marcus, Mar. 15, 1931; one son, Arlen Thomas. Mgr. LaBovitch Bros. Fruit Co., Mankato, Minn., 1932-40, Mankato Fruit Co., 1940-44; pres. Shari Candies Inc., Mankato, 1944-76, Mpls., 1947—, chmn. bd., 1976—; chmn. bd. Barg & Foster Co., Milw., 1964—; pres. Candymaster Inc., Mpls.; pres. Burton Motor Hotel Inc., Mankato, 1963—; dir. Nat. Bank Commerce Mankato. Pres. B'nai B'rith Mankato, 1934; pres. Mankato Symphony Orch. Bd.; treas. Eclipse Drug Program, also bd. dirs; pres. Mankato Jewish Community Chest, 1945, treas., 1965—; chmn. United Jewish Appeal So. Minn., 1960—; mem. Mankato State Coll. Fine Arts Commn., 1975—; bd. dirs. Minn. B'nai B'rith, Blue Earth County Am. Cancer Soc.; active United Fund. Recipient Golden Deeds award, Exchange Club, Mankato, 1975. Mem. Mankato C. of C. Clubs: Elks, Kiwanis, Masons, Shriners, Standard Mpls., Mpls. Athletic, Quarterdeck, Mankato Country, Southview Country; Mpls. Athletic. Office: 1804 N 2d St Mankato MN 56001

KITT, WALTER, psychiatrist; b. N.Y.C., Dec. 18, 1925; s. Elias and Mary (Opiela) K.; student Coll. City N.Y., 1942-44; A.B. magna cum laude, Syracuse U., 1948; M.D., Chgo. Med. Sch., 1952; m. Terry Escorcia, May 15, 1955 (dec. 1974); 1 son, Gregory; m. 2d, Sally Anderson Chappell, June 22, 1977. Intern Cook County Hosp., Chgo., 1953; resident Neuropsychiat. Inst., U. Ill., Chgo., 1953-56, clin. asst. prof. psychiatry, 1958-64; practice medicine, specializing in psychiatry, Chgo., 1956-63, Munster, Ind., 1963—; clin. psychiatrist Michael Reese Hosp., Chgo., 1957-60, asso. attending psychiatrist, 1960-64; psychiat. cons. Ill. Div. Vocat. Rehab., 1961-64; attending staff Our Lady of Mercy Hosp., Dyer, Ind., 1965—, chmn. div. psychiatry, 1970-72; attending staff St. Margaret's Hosp., Hammond, Ind., 1965—, Inst. Psychiatry at Northwestern Hosp., 1976—; asst. prof. clin. psychiatry Northwestern U. Med. Sch., 1974—. Served with AUS, 1944-46. Mem. AMA, Am. Psychiat. Assn., Lake County Med. Soc., Ill. Psychiat. Soc. Home: 3750 Lake Shore Dr Chicago IL 60613 Office: 7550 Hohman Ave Munster IN 46321

KITTERMAN, JOHN H., physicist; b. Des Moines, July 2, 1937; B.S. in Physics, Kans. State U., 1959, M.S., 1961; Ph.D., Colo. State U., 1970; m. Dee Toothaker, 1960; 4 children. Sr. physicist Babcock & Wilcox Research Center, Alliance, Ohio, 1963-66; grad. research asst. Colo. State U., 1966-69; research specialist, group leader nondestructive testing, gaging and inspection Timken Co., Canton, Ohio. Mem. Am. Phys. Soc., Am. Soc. Metals, Sigma Xi, Sigma Pi Sigma. Author papers in field. Home: 3050 Sheila St NW Massillon OH 44646 Office: Timken Co Research and Devel Dept Canton OH 44720

KITTNER, EDWIN HENRY, mfg. co. exec.; b. Utica, N.Y., Mar. 7, 1925; s. Emanuel Joseph and Genevieve Victoria (Rybicki) K.; B.S. in M.E., Kans. State U., 1950; m. Mary Elizabeth Totten, Oct. 20. 1950; children—Jane Elizabeth, Katherine Ann, Joseph Andrew, John David. Plant engr. Certain-Teed Products Co., Blue Rapids, Kans., 1950-57; chief project engr. Bestwall Gypsum Co., Blue Rapids, 1957-61, project engr. central engring. dept., Paoli, Pa., 1961-63; supt. engring. and maintenance Georgia-Pacific Corp., Blue Rapids, 1963—. Mem. exec. bd. Jayhawk Council Boy Scouts Am., Topeka, Kans., 1950—; mayor, councilman City of Blue Rapids, 1954-61. Recipient Silver Beaver award, 1969. Registered profl. engr., Kans. Mem. Nat. Soc. Profl. Engrs., Kans., Tri-Valley engring. socs. Republican. Roman Catholic. Clubs: Lions (pres. 1955, 65, zone chmn. 1956). Am. Legion, V.F.W. Contbr. articles in field to profl. jours. Home: 604 E Ave Blue Rapids KS 66411 Office: Box 187 Blue Rapids KS 66411

KITTRELL, HAROLD KEITH, assn. exec.; b. Las Anamos, Colo., Dec. 29, 1911; s. Charles Anan and Dassah Mona K.; student No. Iowa U., 1930-32, Northwestern U., 1932-34; m. Avis Tribley, Dec. 12, 1937; children—Charles Anan, Karen Evan. Pres. H.K. Kittrell Co., Inc., Waterloo, Iowa, 1941-64; v.p. Pvt. Enterprise, Inc., Wichita, Kans., 1960; pres. Kitco Internat., Inc., Kansas City, Mo., 1961—; pres. Keith Kittrell & Assos., Inc., Kansas City, 1972—; internat. dir. United Assn. Mfg. Reps., Kansas City, 1975—. Mem. Mfrs. Agents Nat. Assn. (dir.) Republican. Methodist. Clubs: Rotary Internat., Optimists, Kiwanis, Shriner. Home: 213 Terrace Trail W Lake Quivira KS 66106 Office: 808 Broadway Kansas City MO 64105

KITZMILLER, KARL WILLIAM, dermatologist; b. Cin., Sept. 23, 1931; s. Karl Vivien and Mary Agnes (McDevitt) K.; student Xavier U., Cin., 1949-50; B.S., U. Cin., 1953, M.D., 1960; m. Alice Ann Meehan, Jan. 29, 1955; children—Sue Ann, William John, Daniel Joseph, Sarah Mary, Kevin William (dec.), Brian Andrew. Intern, Cin. Gen. Hosp., 1960-61; fellow in dermatology Mayo Clinic, Rochester, Minn., 1961-64; practice medicine specializing in dermatology, Cin., 1964—; asso. clin. prof. dermatology Coll. Medicine U. Cin.; attending staff, chief dermatology Good Samaritan and Deaconess hosps.; cons. Longview State Hosp., Wright Patterson AFB, Dayton, Ohio; courtesy staff Our Lady of Mercy and Holmes hosps.; mem. staffs Children's, Bethesda hosps.; attending staff Christ Hosp., Cin., 1976—, sec. dept. dermatology, 1977—; attending physician Jewish Hosp., 1966—, sec. dept. dermatology, 1977—; attending physician Cin. Gen. Hosp., 1966—. Dir. Mt. Lookout Civic Club, 1970-73, 1st v.p., 1972-73. Served to lt. USAF, 1954-56. Recipient Physicians Recognition award AMA, 1969-73. Diplomate Am. Acad. Dermatology. Fellow A.C.P.; mem. Am., Ohio State (sec. sect. dermatology 1974—) med. assns., Noah Worcester Dermatol. Soc., Acad. Medicine Cin., Soc. Dermatol. Surgery, Chgo., Central States, Cin. (sec. 1973-75, pres. 1975-76) dermatol. socs., Assn. Ohio Commodores, Kidney Found., Cin. C. of C. Roman Catholic. Clubs: Cin. Tennis. Contbr. articles to med. jours. Office: 8040 Reading Rd Cincinnati OH 45237

KIVELA, EDGAR WELTON, govt. ofcl.; b. Montour Falls, N.Y., Aug. 18, 1919; s. Emil Wilfred and Blanche Lorene (Hetchler) K.; B.S., Mich. State U., 1941, M.S., 1944, Ph.D., 1949; m. Lillian Joyce Anderson, Oct. 24, 1947; children—Mark, Laura (Mrs. Victor Nelhiebel), Susan, Paul. Instr. math. Hobart Coll., Geneva, N.Y., 1943; bacteriologist Winthrop Chem. Co., Rensselaer, N.Y., 1944; instr. bacteriology Mich. State U., East Lansing, 1945-47, asst. prof., 1948; asst. chief State Crime Detection and Toxicology Lab., Mich. Dept. Pub. Health, Lansing, 1949-66, chief, 1967—. Adj. prof. Sch. Criminal Justice, Mich. State U., East Lansing, 1974—; lectr. Practising Law Inst., N.Y.C., 1972—, Am. Acad. Judicial Edn., Washington, 1972—. Recipient Winthrop Chem. Co. Presidents award for distinguished service, 1944; Centennial award for distinguished service Mich. Dept. Pub. Health, 1973. Fellow Am. Acad. Forensic Scis.; mem. A.A.A.S., Internat. Assn. Arson Investigators, Nat. Safety Council (mem. com. on alcohol and drugs 1969—), N.Y. Acad. Scis. Home: 4644 Grandwoods Lansing MI 48917 Office: 3500 N Logan St Lansing MI 48914

KIVETT, MARVIN F., anthropologist; b. Nebr., Mar. 10, 1917; s. Thomas and Murl (Mark) K.; A.B., U. Nebr., 1942, M.A., 1948; m. Caroline Ritchey, Sept. 12, 1941; 1 son, Ronald Lee. Archeologist, Smithsonian Instn., 1946-49; mus. dir. Nebr. Hist. Soc., Lincoln, 1949-63, adminstrv. dir., 1963—. Served with AUS, 1942-46. Editor: Nebraska History, 1963—. Contbr. articles to profl. jours. Home: 5425 Franklin Lincoln NE 68506 Office: 1500 R Lincoln NE 68508

KJAR, ROLLAND WILLIAM, educator; b. Lexington, Nebr., July 21, 1932; s. William Carl and Esther Alice (Mitchell) K.; B.A., Gonzaga U., 1955; M.A., U. Kans., 1957; postgrad. Mont. State Coll., 1957-58. Chmn. dept. social studies Duchesne High Sch., St. Charles, Mo., 1964—; instr. N.E. Mo. State Coll., Warrensburg, 1966-72, St. Louis U. 18-18 Program, 1972—. Commr., Mayor's Com. for

Bicentennial, 1972—; chmn. St. Charles Community Council, 1972—; mem. Gov.'s Commn. for Mo. Sesquicentennial, 1972; chmn. St. Charles County Republican Central Com., 1972—; mem. Mo. Rep. State Com., 1972—; Rep. committeeman, St. Charles, 1972—; del. Rep. Nat. Conv., 1976; Presdl. elector, 1976; pres. Grand Order Pachyderms, 1968-70. Recipient Outstanding Tchr. award Jaycees, 1964; U. Kans. research grantee, 1955. Mem. St. Louis Council World Affairs, St. Charles County Jr. Hist. Soc. (dir.). Roman Catholic. Clubs: Kiwanis, K.C. Contbr. weekly hist. series St. Charles Jour., 1968-69. Home: 1865 W Clark St Saint Charles MO 63301 Office: 2550 W Elm St Saint Charles MO 63301

KLAFTER, MELVIN LESLIE, lawyer; b. Chgo., June 29, 1914; s. Samuel E. Klafter; A.B., DePaul U., 1936, J.D., 1938; m. Lynn Dady, Nov. 24, 1959. With Hearst Papers, 1935-38; admitted to Ill. bar, 1938; practiced law, 1939-40; asst. U.S. atty. for No. Dist. Ill., i948-54; partner firm Nathan and Klafter, Chgo., 1954—. Instr. 5th U.S. Army Judge Adv. Gen. Sch., Northwestern U., 1951-52, comdt., 1953-54. Bd. dirs., v.p. U.S.O., 1969—, chmn. membership com., 1971—; trustee Ill. Masonic Med. Center, St. Xavier Coll., Chgo. Served to col., Judge Adv. Gen. Corps, AUS, 1941-46, ret., 1965. Decorated Bronze Star medal, Purple Heart; recipient Distinguished Service award U.S.O., 1971. Mem. Mil. Order of World Wars (comdr. Chgo. 1971, Ill., 1972), Res. Officers Assn. (pres. Ill. dept. 1949), Mil. Order of Purple Heart (chief of staff 1947), Chgo., Fed., Am. bar assns., Am. Judicature Soc., Judge Adv. Assn., Am. Legion, Soc. Fellows De Paul U., De Paul Alumni Assn. (dir. 1968-69, v.p. 1970), Nat. Sojourners, Delta Theta Phi. Clubs: 100 of Chgo., Union League, Exec., Masons (32 deg.), Lawyers Shrine Chgo. (pres. 1977). Home: 219 E Lake Shore Dr Chicago IL 60611 Office: 39 S La Salle St Chicago IL 60603

KLAHN, THOMAS HAROLD, farmer; b. Madison, Wis., June 28, 1949; s. Robert Harold and Meta (Herwig) K.; B.S., U. Wis., 1971, M.S., 1973; m. Judith Ann Applegate, Aug. 19, 1972. Farm mgr., Arlington, Wis., 1973—. Mem. Entomol. Soc. Am., Wis. Alumni Assn. (life), Alpha Gamma Rho. Club: Lions. Address: Rural Route 1 Box 39A Arlington WI 53911

KLAHR, SAULO, physician, educator; b. Santander, Colombia, June 8, 1935; s. Herman and Raquel (Konigsberg) K.; came to U.S., 1961, naturalized, 1970; B.A., Colegio Santa Librada, Cali, Colombia, 1954; M.D., U. Nat., Bogota, Colombia, 1959; m. Carol Declue, Dec. 29, 1965; children—James Herman, Robert David. Intern, Hosp. San Juan de Dios, Bogota, 1958-59; resident U. Hosp., Cali, 1959-61; mem. faculty Washington U. Sch. Medicine, St. Louis, 1966—, prof. medicine, 1972—, dir. renal div., 1972—; asso. physician Barnes Hosp., 1972—; established investigator Am. Heart Assn., 1968-73; mem. adv. com. artificial kidney chronic uremia program USPHS, 1971—; bd. dirs. Eastern Mo. Kidney Found., 1973-75, chmn. med. adv. bd., 1973-74; research com. Mo. Heart Assn., 1973-76. USPHS postdoctoral fellow, 1961-63. Fellow A.C.P.; mem. Am. Soc. Nephrology, Am. Soc. Clin. Investigation, Am. Physiol. Soc., Biophys. Soc., N.Y. Acad. Scis., Central Soc. Clin. Research, Soc. Exptl. Biology and Medicine, Sigma Xi. Author articles, chpts. in books; editor: Differential Diagnosis of Renal and Electrolyte Disorders; editorial bd. Kidney Internat., Proc. Soc. Exptl. Biology and Medicine; asso. editor Jour. Clin. Investigation. Home: 16 Fairwinds Ct Saint Louis MO 63132

KLAINSEK, FRANK, optometrist; b. Chicopee, Kans., Jan. 27, 1907; s. Frank and Teresa (Vodeb) K.; Asso. Arts and Sci., Blackburn Coll., 1938; O.D., Ill. Coll. Optometry, 1948; m. Mary Louise Hatfield, July 25, 1955; 1 dau., Karen Louise. Tchr. elementary sch., Ill., 1939-41; prin. elementary sch., Farmersville, Ill., 1949; pvt. practice optometry, White Hall, Ill., 1949—. Mem. Jerseyville Municipal Band, Virden Concert Band, Carrollton Community Chorus. Served with USAAF, 1942-44. Mem. Nat. Research Eye Found., Ill., Am. optometric assns. Mem. Christian Ch. (deacon, supt. Sunday sch.). Club: Masons. Address: 344 Bruce Dr White Hall IL 62092

KLAMEN, MARVIN MAX, lawyer; b. St. Louis, Mar. 12, 1931; s. Charles and Leah (Markovitz) K.; A.B., Wash. U., St. Louis, 1953, LL.B., 1955; m. Miriam Klausner, Jan. 2, 1976; children—Karen, Jeffrey. Admitted to Mo. bar, 1955, U.S. Tax Ct., 1967; practiced in St. Louis, 1958—; mem. firms Marvin Klamen, 1958-61, Klamen & Grand, 1962-63, Klamen, Fletcher & Weisman, 1964-65, Klamen, Summers, Wattenberg & Compton, 1966-73, Klamen, Summers & Compton, 1974—. Counsel to Planned Indsl. Expansion Authority, City of St. Louis, 1968-71. Bd. dirs. University City (Mo.) Bd. Edn., 1964-66; mem. bd. dirs. St. Louis County Law Library, 1966-74. Served to capt. USAF, 1955-58. Mem. Am. (subcom. chmn. econs. of law office practice, gen. practice section 1974), Mo., St. Louis, St. Louis County bar assns. Contbr. articles to profl. jours. Home: 7 Ridge Top Richmond Heights MO 63117 Office: 7820 Maryland Ave St Louis MO 63105

KLANDERMAN, JOHN WINSTON, psychologist; b. Grand Rapids, Mich., Aug. 1, 1939; s. Gerrit John and Winifred Margaret (Zielstra) K.; A.B., Calvin Coll., Grand Rapids, 1961; M.A., Mich. State U., 1963, Ph.D., 1971; m. Natalie Zwiers, Aug. 12, 1961; children—Kevin, Brian. Tchr. English, Lynden (Wash.) High Sch., 1961-62; psychologist Eaton County Intermediate Sch. Dist., Charlotte, Mich., 1964-67; coordinator psychol. services Sch. Dist. 68, Skokie, Ill., 1968—; asso. grad. faculty Nat. Coll. Edn., Evanston, Ill., 1972—. Mem. Nat. Assn. Sch. Psychologists, Am., Ill. psychol. assns., Phi Delta Kappa. Lutheran. Home: 1316 Gregory St Wilmette IL 60091 Office: 9700 N Crawford St Skokie IL 60076

KLARREICH, HAROLD LEOPOLD, real estate broker; b. Cleve., Oct. 15, 1924; s. Israel Theodore and Eleanor (Weiss) K.; B.S., U. Pa., 1948; J.D., U. Mich., 1950; m. Susan Friedman, Oct. 28, 1950; children—Karin, Betsy, Kathie, Beth. Admitted to Ohio bar, 1951; mem. firm Arthur Miller, Cleve., 1951-52; pres. Klarreich, Wald & Fisher Realty Co., Cleve., 1952—. Dir. Met. Savs. Assn., 1959—, chmn. bd. 1968—; pres. Hebrew Free Loan Assn., Cleve., 1964-66. Instr. real estate Western Res. U., Cuyahoga Community Coll., Dyke Coll., John Carroll U., all Cleve., 1964-71. Pres. Cleve. Campfire Girls, 1970-71, Jewish Community Center, Cleve., 1973—; pres. United Jewish Religious Schs., 1966-69; mem. real estate adv. com. John Carroll Dyke Coll., Cleve. State U., 1972—. Councilman, City of Cleveland Heights, Ohio, 1970-71, 72-73. Trustee Jewish Community Fedn., 1964-67, 69-72, 74—, Cleve. Landmark Commn., 1973-74, Mt. Sinai Hosp., 1976—; trustee Cleveland Heights Landmark Commn., 1973—, chmn. 1973—. Served with U.S. Army, 1943-46. Recipient Kane award Jewish Community Fedn., 1964; named Realtor of Year, Cleve. Real Estate Bds., 1972. Mem. Cleve. Real Estate Bd. (pres. 1964, chmn. 1965), Ohio Assn. Realtors (trustee 1963—), Better Bus. Bur. (trustee 1967-71). Mem. B'nai B'rith (pres. 1958). Club: Oakwood Country (Cleveland Heights). Author: Ohio Supplement for Modern Real Estate Practice, 1972. Home: 1552 Oakwood Dr Cleveland Heights OH 44121 Office: 2717 Lorain Ave Cleveland OH 44113

KLARREICH, SUSAN FRIEDMAN, career counselor; b. Cleve., Jan. 14, 1929; d. Maurice David and Matilda (Saks) F.; B.A., U. Mich., 1950; M.A., Case Western Res. U., 1964, Ph.D., 1973; m. Harold Leopold Klarreich, Oct. 28, 1950; children—Karin, Betsy, Kathie, Beth. Ednl. testing cons. Cleveland Heights Univ. Heights Bd. Edn. (Ohio), 1965-67, Community Action for Youth, Cleve., 1966-67; dir. program devel. Jewish Vocat. Service, University Heights, Ohio, 1968—; guest lectr. Case Western Res. U., Cleve. State U.; project coordinator HEW career equity promotion project. Mem. Am. Personnel and Guidance Assn., Nat. Vocat. Guidance Assn., Nat. Assn. Jewish Communal Service, Am. Arbitration Assn., B'nai Brith Hillel Found. Contbr. articles in field to profl. jours. Home: 1552 Oakwood Dr Cleveland Heights OH 44121 Office: 13878 Cedar Rd University Heights OH 44118

KLASEK, CHARLES BERNARD, ednl. adminstr., ednl. cons.; b. Wilber, Nebr., Dec. 28, 1931; s. Bernard Jacob and Sylvia Frances (Smrz) K.; B.S. with distinction, U. Nebr., 1954; certificate (Fulbright scholar) Inst. for Internat. Ednl. Research, Germany, 1955; M.A., U. Nebr., 1956, Ph.D. in Ednl. Adminstrn., 1971; m. Lila Lee Wanek, Aug. 9, 1953; children—Terese Ann, Steven Charles, Joseph Mark. Tchr. of English, speech and German, Lincoln (Nebr.) pub. schs., 1958-69; exec. dir. Nebr. Council for Ednl. TV, U. Nebr., Lincoln, 1960-63; dir. instructional TV, Santa Ana Unified and Jr. Coll. Dists., Calif., 1963-67; instr. evening classes Calif. State Coll., Fullerton, 1965-67; dir. edn. Ky. Ednl. TV Network, Lexington, 1967-71; instr. instructional TV utilization U. Ky., Lexington, 1968-69; asst. prof. dept. of instructional materials So. Ill. U., Carbondale, 1971-76, asso. prof., 1976—, acting departmental exec. officer of curriculum, instruction and media, 1977, mem. Univ. Task Force on Internat. Edn., 1976-77; UNESCO cons. in utilization and evaluation of ednl. radio and TV, Ministry of Edn., Malaysia, 1974, 75, 72-73; cons. to various pub. schs., San Diego, 1965, New Orleans, 1970, Ill. State U., 1977, Appalachian Ednl. TV Satellite Project, U. Ky., 1977, Nat. Instructional TV Center, Bloomington, Ind., 1967, 68, 69. Mem. Carbondale Bicentennial Commn., 1975-76; mem. Freedom Fest Com., Carbondale, 1976; v.p. council of Epiphany Luth. Ch., Carbondale, 1973, 75, 76-77. Served with U.S. Army, 1954-58. Recipient Academic Excellence award So. Ill. U., 1976; Distinguished Service award City of Carbondale, 1977; named Tchr. of Yr., Coll. of Edn., So. Ill. U., 1977. Mem. Nat. Assn. of Ednl. Broadcasters (field coordinator 1969-71), Assn. for Ednl. Communications and Tech. (dir. 1969-72, mem. certification com. 1975-77), Ill. Audiovisual Assn., Phi Delta Kappa. Lutheran. Club: Kiwanis. Author: Instructional Media in the Modern School, 1972; contbr. articles on ednl. communications to profl. jours.; editor: Action with Kentucky's Children and Youth, 1971. Home: 208 Pine Ln Carbondale IL 62901 Office: Pulliam 323 Southern Illinois Univ Carbondale IL 62901

KLASS, JOSEPH BENJAMIN, psychologist; b. Clinton, Iowa, July 16, 1918; s. Clarence and Harriette Sybil (Miller) J.; B.S., Richmond Profl. Inst., William and Mary Coll., 1951, M.S., 1955; m. Martha Lou Mericle, Aug. 13, 1960; 1 dau., Lisa Ann. Psychologist, Mental Health Inst., Mt. Pleasant, Iowa, 1952-54, East Moline (Ill.) State Hosp., 1954-56, Mich. Dept. Corrections, Jackson, 1956-59; sch. diagnostician Intermediate Sch. Dist., Jackson, 1959-67; sch. psychologist Bi-County Spl. Edn. Co-op., Morrison Ill., 1969-76; pvt. practice, Jackson, 1957—, Clinton, 1967—. Faculty, Jackson Community Coll., 1960-61; officer, dir. Lark Enterprises, Clinton, 1970—. Served with AUS, 1942-46. Mem. Am. Psychol. Assn., Biofeedback Research Soc., Nat. Register Health Service Providers in Psychology. Elk. Club: Arbor Hills Country. Home: 250 Woodlawn Ct Clinton IA 52732 Office: 724 N 2d St Clinton IA 52732

KLAUCK, KENNETH A., psychologist; b. Milw., June 14, 1936; s. Clara M. (Mueller) K.; B.S. with honors, U. Wis., 1962; M.A., U. Ariz., 1966, Ph.D. in Clin. Psychology, 1969. Chief, workshop supr. Jewish Vocat. Service, Milw., 1961-63; psychology cons. Lad Lake, Dousman, Wis., 1969-71; chief restoration unit VA, Wood, Wis., 1969-75, chief psychology service, 1975—; lectr. Marquette U., 1969; asst. prof. Med. Coll. Wis., Milw., 1969—; mem. com. violent behavior and suicide VA Med. Dist. #16, 1977, Region V rep. to fed. agys., 1975. Bd. dirs. Brookfield (Wis.) Youth Adv. Council, 1971-73, Milw. Young People's Club, Inc., 1972. Served with USN, 1954-58. NIMH scholar, 1964-65. Mem. Milw. County, Wis., Am. psychol. assns., Nat. Rehab. Assn., Wis. Rehab. Counseling Assn., Wis. Assn. Alcoholism and Other Drug Abuse, Waukesha County Assn. Mental Health. Home: 13900 W Bluemound Rd Elm Grove WI 53122 Office: VA Center Wood WI 53193

KLAUS, MARK FRANCIS, elec. design draftsman; b. Chgo., Apr. 9, 1953; s. Fred M. and Estelle (Aniszewska) K.; A.A. in Engring., Daley Coll., 1977. Draftsman, House of Stainless, Chgo., 1971; elec. draftsman Goss Printing Co., Cicero, Ill., 1971-73, Aquatechnics, Oak Brook, Ill., 1973-75, sr. elec. draftsman Sargent & Lundy, Chgo., 1975-76; elec. design draftsman Holabird & Root, Chgo., 1976-77, Perkins & Will, Chgo., 1977—. Mem. Landmark Preservation Council, Chgo., 1977. Mem. Am. Inst. for Design and Drafting, Elec. Assn. (cons.). Roman Catholic. Home: 6135 S Kostner St Chicago IL 60629 Office: 309 W Jackson Blvd Chicago IL 60606

KLAUSMEYER, THOMAS HENRY, architect; b. Detroit, Oct. 19, 1921; s. Otto Henry and Lillian (Couch) K.; B.M.E., Purdue U., 1947; B.Arch., B.S. in Archtl. Engring., U. Ill., 1951; m. Doris Irene Pfaffenbach, May 30, 1947; children—John Brian, William Bruce. Pres., Creative Bldgs., Urbana, Ill., 1952-54; project designer Skidmore, Owings & Merrill, Chgo., 1955-58, project mgr., 1966-68; now cons. architect Smith, Hinchman & Grylls Assos., Detroit; project architect, sr. asso. Perkins & Will, Chgo., Washington, 1958-64; project dir., participating asso. Smith, Hinchman & Grylls, Detroit, 1964-66; cons. for hosps. and health profession teaching facilities. Served to 1st lt. USAAF, 1942-46; CBI. Allerton Traveling scholar, 1952; Ryerson Traveling fellow, 1954. Mem. AIA, Assn. Am. Med. Colls., Am. Hosp. Assn., Tau Beta Pi, Kappa Sigma. Home: 1992 Wiltshire Berkeley MI 48072 Office: 455 W Fort St Detroit MI 48226

KLAY, REYNOLD, banker; b. Inwood, Iowa, Feb. 9, 1921; s. John Teunis and Gertrude (Bunning) K.; grad. high sch.; m. Rubye Mae Philipp, June 14, 1949; children—Nancy Jo, James Reynold, Julie Ann. Teller, Little Horn State Bank, Wyola, Mont., 1941-42, 46; asst. cashier 1st Nat. Bank, Luverne, Minn., 1946-54; cashier 1st Nat. Bank, Sauk Centre, Minn., 1954-62; v.p. Nat. Bank of S.D., Huron, 1962-71; exec. v.p. Nat. Bank of S.D., Rapid City, 1971—; dir. Western S.D. Devel. Co., Rapid City, 1973—, chmn. 1973—. Pres. Greater Huron Devel. Corp., 1970-71; treas. Huron United Fund, 1969-70; mem. adv. bd. St. John's Hosp., 1969-71; bd. dirs. Central States Fair, 1971-74. Served with AUS, 1942-45. Mem. S.D. Bankers Assn., Def. Orientation Assn. Republican. Presbyterian. Clubs: Masons, Shriners, Elks, Arrowhead Country (dir. 1973—). Home: 318 N Berry Pine Rd Rapid City SD 57701 Office: PO Box 90 Rapid City SD 57701

KLAYMAN, MAXWELL IRVING, educator; b. Boston, Apr. 30, 1917; s. Joseph and Lena (Seidenberg) K.; B.S. cum laude, U. Mass., 1938; M.S., Iowa State U., 1941; M.A., Harvard U., 1951, Ph.D., 1968; m. Alice Louise Budd, July 22, 1950; children—Judith Ann, Daniel Budd, Naomi Jean. With FAO, UN, Rome, Italy, 1951-62, Cali, Colombia, 1962-64, U.S., 1965-68; prof. econs. State U. N.Y. Coll., New Paltz, 1968-70; prof. mktg. U. Akron (Ohio), 1970-73; grad. prof. bus. adminstrn. Capital U., Columbus, Ohio, 1973—; staff econs. dept. Pahlavi U., Shiraz, Iran, 1975-77, Am. Coll. Switzerland, Leksin, 1977—; cons. Inter-Am. Devel. Bank, 1968-69, Govt. of Can., 1972, U. Ariz. Press, 1971, Clarion State Coll., 1973. Bd. dirs. Akron Civic Forum, 1970—. Served with Q.M. Corps, AUS, 1941-45. Ford Found. grantee, 1965, 66. Mem. Am. Econ. Assn., Assn. Edn. Internat. Bus., Soc. Internat. Devel., Am. Mktg. Assn., Am. Agrl. Econs. Assn., Akron Area C. of C. (program chmn. internat. trade council 1970—). Author: The Moshav in Israel, 1970. Home: 115 Melbourne Ave Akron OH 44313 Office: Am Coll Leksin Switzerland

KLEIMAN, BERNARD, lawyer; b. Chgo., Jan. 26, 1928; s. Isadore and Pearl (Wikoff) K.; B.S., Purdue U., 1951; J.D., Northwestern U., 1954; m. Lenore Silver, Apr. 27, 1959; children—Leslie, David. Admitted to Ill. bar, 1954; practice law in assn. with Abraham W. Brussell, 1957-60; dist. counsel United Steel Workers Am., 1960-65, gen. counsel, 1965—; partner Kleiman, Cornfield & Feldman, Chgo., 1960-75; lectr. in field; negogiator labor disputes. Mem. appraiser selection com. Nat. Accelerator Lab. Site Acquisition Com. Bd. dirs., counsel CARE. Served with AUS, 1946-48. Mem. Am., Ill., Chgo., Allegheny County bar assns., Ill. Labor History Soc., Phi Alpha Delta. Mem. B'nai B'rith. Club: City (Chgo.). Contbr. articles to legal jours. Office: 1 E Wacker Dr Chicago IL 60601

KLEIMOLA, FRANK WILLIAM, nuclear engring. co. exec.; b. Ironwood, Mich., Apr. 6, 1918; s. John and Mary (Saari) K.; A.A., Gogebic Community Coll., 1940; B.S. with honors in Mech. Engring., Mich. Tech. U., 1949; m. Miriam Rachel Syrja, June 12, 1948; children—Daniel, David, Dale, Christine, Ula Marie, Janel. Asso. nuclear engr. Argonne (Ill.) Nat. Lab., 1949-56; nuclear process engr. ACF Industries, Washington, 1956-58; project mgr. Curtiss-Wright Corp., Quehanna, Pa., 1958-60; nuclear engr. Combustion Engring. Inc., Windsor, Conn., 1960-67; prin. nuclear engr. Gilbert/Commonwealth Inc., Jackson, Mich., 1967—; pres. NucleDyne Engring. Corp., Jackson, Mich., 1975—. Served with U.S. Army, 1942-46. Registered profl. engr., Ill., Mich. Mem. Am. Nuclear Soc., Am. Soc. for Metals, ASME, Health Physics Soc. Lutheran. Patentee in field. Home: 5008 Rimers Dr Jackson MI 49201 Office: 728 W Michigan Ave Jackson MI 49201

KLEIN, ALICE JARVIS, civil engr.; b. Mpls., Nov. 17, 1925; d. Matthew George and Mary Margaret (Child) Jarvis; B.C.E., U. Minn., 1947, M.S. in C.E., 1951; m. Morris Jerome Klein, Aug. 24, 1952; children—Matthew Morris, Robert Joseph. Engr., Hitchcock & Estabrook, Mpls., 1947-49, Greeley & Hansen, Engrs., Chgo., 1951-55: substitute tchr. Brookfield (Ill.) Sch. Dist., 1966-72; constrn. coordinator Greeley & Hansen, Engrs., Chgo., 1972—. Mem. Am. Soc. C.E., Nat., Ill. socs. profl. engrs. Methodist. Home: 9417 Jackson St Brookfield IL 60513 Office: 222 S Riverside Plaza Chicago IL 60606

KLEIN, CHARLES HENLE, lithographing co. exec.; b. Cinn., Oct. 5, 1908; s. Benjamin Franklin and Flora (Henle) K.; student Purdue U., 1926-27, U. Cin., 1927-28; m. Ruth Becker, Sept. 23, 1938; children—Betsy (Mrs. Marvin H. Schwartz), Charles H., Carla (Mrs. George Fee III). Pres., Progress Lithographing Co., Cin., 1934-59, Novelart Mfg. Co., 1960—. Mem. Chief Execs. Forum. Clubs: Losantiville Country, Queen City. Home: 6754 Fairoaks Dr Amberley Village Cincinnati OH 45237 Office: Section Rd and PRR Amberley Village Cincinnati OH 45237

KLEIN, CHARLES MOSHER, radiologist; b. Cleve., June 24, 1932; s. Matthew George and Jean Isabel (Mosher) K.; B.S., Western Res. U., 1954, M.D., 1958; m. Barbara Ann Barr, Aug. 20, 1955; children—Janet Ellen, Catherine Elizabeth, James Mosher. Rotating intern St. Luke's Hosp., Cleve., 1958-59; asst. resident radiology U. Mich. Med. Center, 1959-60, resident, 1960-61, jr. clin. instr., 1961-62, Nat. Cancer Inst. fellow, 1961-62; mem. firm Drs. Peck, Means, Straub, et al, Toledo, Ohio, 1964-68; mem. Toledo Radiol. Assos., Inc., 1968—, asst. treas., 1971-73, 77—, treas., 1973-75, pres., 1975-77. Served to lt. comdr. M.C., USNR, 1962-64. Mem. Am. Coll. Radiology (alternate councilor 1976—), Radiol. Soc. N.Am., AMA, Ohio State Med. Assn., Ohio State, Northwestern Ohio (pres. elect 1977) radiol. socs., Acad. Medicine Toledo. Club: Torch (pres. 1971) (Toledo). Home: 5336 Northbrook Ct Sylvania OH 43560 Office: 3939 Monroe St Toledo OH 43606

KLEIN, EDGAR ALBERT, steel co. exec; b. Bellevue, O., Jan. 19, 1912; s. Carl Phillip and Katherine (Hager) K.; grad. high sch; Ph.D. (hon.) Hamilton State U.; m. Pearl Rosina Kochendoerfer, Sept. 24, 1938; 1 son, Carl Raymond. Gen. mgr. Klein Steel Co., Bellevue, 1931-53, pres., dir., partner, 1961—; ind. ins. agt. Edgar A. Klein, Bellevue, 1953-57; engring. dept. Webster Mfg., Inc. Tiffin, O. 1957-58; gen. mgr. engring. and fabricating div. Alert Steel Products Co., Chgo., 1959-60; pres., dir. Klein Steel Co., Bellevue, O., 1961—; partner Klein Steel Supply Co., 1952—. Mem. central adv. bd. Nat. Labor Reform Com.; mem. nat. adv. bd. Am. Security Council; mem. Seneca County Mental Health Assn., Seneca County Humane Soc. Mem. Asso. Industries Cleve., Nat. Fedn. Ind. Bus., Internat. Platform Assn. Roman Catholic, K.C. Home: 25 Charles St Tiffin OH 44883 Office: Lincoln and Buckeye Sts Bellevue OH 44811

KLEIN, GEORGE ROBERT, periodical distbn. co. exec.; b. Washington, Pa., Sept. 28, 1909; s. George Ruttman and Virginia R. (Hickey) K.; B.A., Ohio Wesleyan U., 1930; B.S., Mass. Inst. Tech., 1932; m. Mary Elizabeth Fisher, Jan. 28, 1939. Pres., George R. Klein News Co., Shaker Heights, Ohio, 1940—. Chmn. bd. trustees Ch. of the Saviour, United Methodist, 1960—; vice-chmn., trustee St. Luke's Hosp., 1965—; v.p. bd. mgrs. Central YMCA, 1946-71; trustee Christian Residences Found., 1965—, Goodwill Industries Cleve., 1967-70, Ch. of the Saviour Found., 1962—, N.E. Ohio Conf. Meth. Ch., 1965—, Cleve. Zool. Soc., 1970—; trustee, v.p. Cleve. Play House Theatre; mem. Welfare Fedn. Manpower Commn., 1971-74; pres. Ohio Wesleyan U. Assos., 1960-62; trustee Mus. Arts Assn., 1973—; trustee Play House Found., 1972—, Ohio Wesleyan U., 1971—, Univ. Circle Found., 1974—. Served with USN, 1943-46. Mem. Nat. Bur. Ind. Pubs. and Periodical Distbrs. Assn. (past pres.), Mid-Am. Periodical Distbrs. Assn. (past pres.), Mag. Distributors Research Projects Group (past pres.), Nat. Council Periodical Distbrs. Assn. (past dir.), Ind. Periodical Distbrs. Great Lakes (past pres.), Cleve. Engring. Soc., Sigma Pi Sigma, Pi Mu Epsilon, Omicron Delta Kappa. Clubs: Canterbury Golf; Skating, City, Kiwanis (Cleve.); Rowfant, University, Marco Polo, Union. Home: 23699 Shaker Blvd Shaker Heights OH 44122

KLEIN, PAUL BRINKMAN, advt. co. exec.; b. LaCrosse, Wis., Mar. 24, 1927; s. Edwin M. and Amelia Susan (Brinkman) K.; student U. Frankfort (Germany), 1945-46; grad. diploma Art. Inst. Chgo., 1950; m. Nancy Jewel Slogenhop, June 23, 1951; children—Paula L., Corrin R. With C. Wendel Muench Advt., Chgo., 1953-57, Stevens-Brinkman Agy., 1957-60, O'Toole Inc., advt., 1960-64, Creative Center, 1964—, pres., 1964—; co-owner Petal Post Gallery, South Holland, Ill.; pres. Brinkman Pub. Co., Chgo. Mem. plans commn. Village of South Holland, 1964—; bd. dirs. Howell Neighborhood House, Chgo., 1964—. Served with AUS, 1945-47. Recipient award excellence Soc. Illustrators, N.Y., 1969, Strathmore Paper Co., 1973, Franklin award, 1974; Golden Eagle award Chgo. Fin. Advertisers, 1977. Mem. Artists Guild Chgo. Lutheran. Clubs:

Execs. Chgo., Elks, Lions. Home: 627 E 158th St South Holland IL 60473 Office: 435 N Michigan Ave Chicago IL 60611

KLEIN, STUART MARC, educator; b. Cleve., May 25, 1932; s. George Rockwell and Helen (Levine) K.; B.A., Kent State U., 1954, M.A., 1958; Ph.D., Cornell U., 1963; m. Anne Wood, Dec. 19, 1953; children—Rebecca, Daniel, Michael, Jessica. Mgr. basic personnel research IBM, Armonk, N.Y., 1960-67; prof. U. Ky. at Lexington, 1967-72; prof., chmn. depts. mgmt. and labor relations Cleve. State U., 1972—; adviser Cleve. Personnel Dept. and Dept. Human Resources and Econ. Devel., 1973-75; mem. Manpower Devel. Commn., 1973—. Served with AUS, 1954-56. Ford Found. fellow, 1960-61. Mem. Am. Psychol. Assn., Am. Sociology Assn., Acad. Mgmt., Acad. Scis., Indsl. Relations Research Assn., Phi Kappa Phi. Author: Workers Under Stress, 1971. Home: 2488 Marlboro St Cleveland Heights OH 44118 Office: 1983 E 24th St Cleveland OH 44115

KLEIN, VERN DALE, supt. schs.; b. Mobridge, S.D., Feb. 10, 1932; s. John B. and Caroline (Beyerle) K.; B.S., No. State Coll., S.D., 1961, M.S., 1968; m. Ramona Chamberlin, Oct. 5, 1957; 1 son, Kent Allan. Tchr. pub. schs., Wakpala, S.D., 1961-62, prin., 1962-63, supt., 1963-72; supt. schs., Glenham, S.D., 1970—. Served with U.S. Army, 1952-54. Hon. mem. Sioux Tribe, 1972—. Mem. Am. Legion. Moose. Address: Glenham SD 57631

KLEINERMAN, DAVID, educator; b. Moline, Ill., Oct. 24, 1925; s. Frank and Clara (Bixgorn) K.; B.S., Northwestern U., 1948; M.A., DePaul U., 1954; M.B.A., U. Chgo., 1959; m. Dolores Marcia Zakin, June 20, 1950; children—Barby Ruth, Francee. Staff accountant George Bagley & Co., Chgo., 1948-50; asst. prof. accounting Roosevelt U., 1951-55, asso. prof., 1955-65, prof. accounting, 1965—, v.p., treas., 1965-71, dean Walter E. Heller Coll. Bus. Adminstrn., 1976—; vis. prof. Tel Aviv U., Israel, 1969-71. Cons. Labor-mgmt. relations. Served with USNR, 1944-46. Recipient Ford Found. scholarship, U. Chgo., 1959. Mem. Ill. Soc. C.P.A.s, Am. Accounting Assn., Nat. Assn. Accountants, AAUP, Beta Gamma Sigma. Home: 331 Forestway Dr Northbrook IL 60062 Office: 430 S Michigan Av Chicago IL 60605

KLEINMAN, BENNET, lawyer; b. Cleve., May 25, 1919; s. Samuel and Dorothy (Fine) K.; B.B.A., Cleve. State U., 1940; LL.B., Cleve. Marshall Law Sch., 1947; postgrad. Western Res. U., 1948-51; m. Frances Flacks, Mar. 18, 1944; children—Lee Scott, Judith Ellen Kleinman Hershey. Admitted to Ohio bar, 1947; internal revenue agt. U.S. Govt., Cleve., 1946-48; lawyer, Cleve., 1948—; mem. firm Kahn, Kleinman, Yanowitz & Arnson; tax lectr. Cleve., Cuyahoga bar assns., Cleve. Marshall Law Sch., 1952. Mem. Am. Joint Distbn. Com., 1965—, Am. Assn. Jewish Edn., 1966—, Menorah Park Home for Aged, Cleve., 1960-70; chmn. Jewish Nat. Fund Found.; mem. Nat. Council Am. Israel Pub. Affairs Com.; trustee Jewish Community Fedn. Cleve., Akiva High Sch., Cleve.; past chmn. bd. govs. Cleve. Coll. Jewish Studies; bd. dirs. Cleve. Bur. Jewish Edn., Cleve. Zionist Council, Agnon Day Sch., Histadrut, Citizens League Greater Cleve. Served with AUS, 1943-46. Recipient Bonds for Israel award, 1966; co-recipient Jewish Nat. Fund award, 1972; C.P.A., Ohio. Mem. Ohio, Cleve., Cuyahoga bar assns. Jewish (pres. temple 1972). Club: Hawthorne Valley (past pres. Solon, Ohio). Home: 24675 Hilltop Dr Beachwood OH 44122 Office: Bond Ct Bldg E 9th and St Clair Cleveland OH 44114

KLEINSCHMIDT, ALBERT WILLOUGHBY, milling co. exec.; b. Clinton, Iowa, Mar. 20, 1913; s. Frank Otto and Mable (Fahr) K.; B.S., Iowa State U., 1935, Ph.D., Purdue U., 1941; m. Margaret van Scoyk, Nov. 28, 1943; children—Diane (Mrs. Thomas Lahner), Kay (Mrs. Charles Mella), John. Research chemist Central Soya Co., Decatur, Ind., 1940-44. Beatrice Foods, Chgo., 1944-47, Am. Maize Products Co., Roby, Inc., 1947-57; with J.R. Short Milling Co., Kankakee, Ill., 1958—, lab. mgr., 1963-67, tech. dir., 1967-69, v.p., 1969—. Fellow Am. Inst. Chemists; mem. Am. Chem. Soc., Am. Assn. Cereal Chemists, Am. Oil Chemists Soc., Inst. Food Technologists, Am. Soc. Brewing Chemists, Sigma Xi, Phi Lambda Upsilon, Phi Kappa Phi. Contbr. articles to profl. jours. Patentee in field. Home: PO Box 64 Crete IL 60417 Office: PO Box 866 Kankakee IL 60901

KLEINSMITH, LEWIS JOEL, educator, cell biologist; b. Detroit, Apr. 13, 1942; s. Ralph Louis and Sylvia (Raphael) K.; B.S., U. Mich., 1964; Ph.D., Rockefeller U., 1968; m. Cynthia Weinstein, June 14, 1964; children—Alyssa Jan, Francesca Lynn. Asst. prof. dept. zoology U. Mich., Ann Arbor, 1968-71, asso. prof., 1971-74, prof. div. biol. scis. 1975—. Vis. prof. biochemistry U. Fla. Med. Sch., Gainesville, 1974-75. Recipient Henry Russel award, 1971; Distinguished Service award U. Mich., 1971. Guggenheim fellow, 1974-75. Mem. N.Y. Acad. Scis., Am. Soc. Biol. Chemists, Am. Soc. for Cell Biology, Am. Inst. Biol. Scientists, Phi Beta Kappa, Sigma Xi. Editor: Chromosomal Proteins and Their Role in the Regulation of Gene Expression, 1975. Contbr. chpts. to books, articles to profl. jours. Home: 2642 Essex Rd Ann Arbor MI 48104

KLEMME, LARRY LEE, data processing mgr., cons.; b. Davenport, Iowa, Aug. 14, 1945; s. Oscar Aaron and Margaret Marvella (Hellberg) K.; grad. programmer-analyst, Iowa Tech., 1967; m. Rilla Kay Edwards, Oct. 16, 1965; children—Lonnie Lee, Victoria Kay. Systems analyst, diagnostic programmer Burroughs Corp., Paoli, Pa., 1967-70; data processing mgr. Geneseo Telephone Co., Ill., 1970—; owner, mgr. Larry L. Klemme Computer Services, 1970—. Past v.p. LeClaire (Iowa) Jaycees. Developer langs. for computers. Home: 216 E Ogden Ave Geneseo IL 61254 Office: 111 E 1st St Geneseo IL 61254

KLEPFER, EUGENE WOODS, paper co. exec.; b. Yorktown, Ind., May 28, 1912; s. Edna Woods and Ida Millie (Hollis) K.; B.A., Grinnell Coll., 1936; m. E. Eileen Tharp, Nov. 6, 1937; children—Marilyn C. Klepfer Byers, Susan D. Klepfer Fleck, Eugene W. Salesman, Texaco, Inc., Vincennes and Fort Wayne, Ind., 1936-43; buyer, office mgr. Fort Wayne Corrugated Paper Co., Vincennes, 1943-52, salesman, sales mgr., Hartford City, 1952-59; gen. mgr. Wabash Fibre Box Co. div. Weston Paper and Mfg. Co., Fort Wayne, 1959-66, v.p., gen. mgr., 1969-77. Bd. dirs. YMCA, Fort Wayne, 1969—, trustee, 1975. Mem. Fibre Box Assn. (dir. 1968-70), TAPPI, Ft. Wayne C. of C. (dir. 1969-74, v.p. 1973, treas. 1974-75). Mem. Christian Ch. (elder 1966-69, 70-73). Clubs: Masons (32 deg.), Shriners, Elks, Country, Junto (Fort Wayne). Home: 6921 Blue Mist Rd Fort Wayne IN 46819 Office: PO Box 9310 Baer Field Fort Wayne IN 46809

KLETSCHKA, HAROLD DALE, cardiovascular surgeon, biomedical co. exec.; b. Mpls., Aug. 26, 1924; s. Herbert Leland and Emma Elizabeth (Kopf) K.; A.S., Brainerd (Minn.) Jr. Coll., 1943; B.S., U. Minn., 1946, M.B., 1947, M.D., 1948; LL.B., Blackstone Sch. Law (Ill.), 1970; grad. Air War Coll., 1972. Intern Kings County Hosp., Bklyn., 1947-49; asst. resident surgery Univ. Hosp., Ann Arbor, Mich., 1950-51; resident gen. surgery State U. N.Y. Downstate Med. Center, 1953-54, chief resident thoracic surgery, 1952-53, 54-55; thoracic and gen. surgeon Bratrud Clinic, Thief River Falls, Minn., 1951-52; asst. chief neurosurgery 3275th and 2349th USAF Hosps., Parks AFB, Calif., 1955-56, asst. chief thoracic surgery, 1956, chief thoracic surgery, 1956-57, chief USAF Cardiovascular Research Center, 1957-58; pvt. practice thoracic and cardiovascular surgery, San Francisco and San Jose, Calif., 1958-59; thoracic surgeon VA Hosp., Syracuse, N.Y., 1959-60, chief thoracic surgery, 1960-67; asst. prof. surgery State U. N.Y. Upstate Med. Center, Syracuse, 1959-67, cons. thoracic surgery, 1959-67, USAF med. service liaison officer for surgeon gen., 1964-67; dep. comdr., chief hosp. services 102d TAC Hosp., Phalsbourg Air Base, France, 1961-62; mil. cons. to surgeon gen. USAF, surgeon Hdqrs. Command USAF, 1965-73; aerospace med. cons. to dir. Aerospace Med. Services, Malcolm Grow USAF Med. Center, 1965-73; thoracic surgeon VA Hosp., Houston, 1967-68; thoracic surgeon VA Hosp., Montgomery, Ala., 1968-72, dir. cardiopulmonary labs., 1970-72; chmn. bd., pres., chief exec. officer Bio-Medicus, Inc., Minnetonka, Minn., 1972—; mem. Nat. Council on U.S.-USSR Health Care, Citizen Exchange Corps, N.Y.C., 1976—; mem. exec. com. Council for U.S.-USSR Health Exchange, Boston, 1976—. Campaign mgr. Ind. Republican candidate Dist. 43B, Minn. Ho. of Reps., 1976; mem. nat. adv. bd. Am. Security Council. Diplomate Am. Bd. Surgery, Am. Bd. Thoracic Surgery. Fellow A.C.S.; mem. Am. Heart Assn. (council on basic scis., council on cardiovascular surgery), AAUP, Air Force Assn., U. Minn. Alumni Assn., Am. Soc. for Artificial Internal Organs, Twin City Thoracic and Cardiovascular Surg. Soc., VFW, U. Minn. Alumni Club. Recipient Bausch & Lomb Hon. Sci. award, 1941, IR-100 award for devel. Rafferty-Kletschka artificial heart, 1972, Worldwide Symbolic grad. Air War Coll., 1973, 1st Place award Med./Analytical div. Plastics World, 1976, First prize in Med. div. 8th Bachner award competition, 1976. Club: K.C. (4 deg.) Contbr. chpt. to Progress in Surface and Membrane Science, 1973; Bd. editors, Minn. Medicine, 1960—; editor charge spl. issue Minn. Medicine 49, 1966; Contbr. articles to profl. jours.; patentee in field; pioneer Levowitz-Kletschka fracture. Home: 1925 Noble Dr Minneapolis MN 55422 Office: 15307 Industrial Rd Minnetonka MN 55343

KLEY, ROLAND GOTTLIEB, ret. clergyman; b. Sheboygan, Wis., July 17, 1912; s. Herman Adolph and Caroline (Sieckmann) K.; B.A., Lakeland Coll., 1935; B.D., Mission House Theol. Sem., 1942; M.A., U. Wis., 1959; m. Adeline Wilma Hilmes, June 23, 1938; children—Carol, Susan, Thomas, Stephen. Ordained to ministry United Ch. Christ, 1942; pastor Grace United Ch. of Christ, Wausau, Wis., 1942-45, Kohler, Wis., 1945-50, St. John United Ch. Christ, New Holstein, Wis., 1952-57; librarian Mission House Sem., Sheboygan, 1957-62, United Theol. Sem., New Brighton, Minn., 1962-74; pastor Community United Ch. of Christ, St. Germain, Wis., 1974-77, ret. Author: (with E.C. Jaberg et al) A History of Mission House-Lakeland, 1962; United Theological Seminary: The First Ten Years, 1971. Address: Sheboygan WI 53081

KLIE, GARY YOUNG, mech. contracting co. exec.; b. Ithaca, N.Y., Aug. 22, 1943; s. Hamilton Fuller and Ruth (Young) K.; B.A., Miami U., Oxford, Ohio, 1965; m. Janet Jean Vranich, Apr. 2, 1966; children—Jeffrey Hamilton, Corey Young, Todd Fuller. Exec. v.p. Smith & Oby Co., Cleve., 1965—, also dir. Trustee Cleve. Plumbing Industry. Supplemental Unemployment Benefit Fund Pipefitters Local 120; mem. legis. liaison com. State of Ohio, 1973—. Certified master plumber Ohio. Mem. Mech. Contractors Assn. Cleve. (dir., officer 1976—), Cleve. Plumbing Contractors Assn., Mech. Contractors Assn. Am. Republican. Club: Chagrin Valley Racquet. Home: 8198 Westhill Dr Chagrin Falls OH 44022 Office: 6107 Carnegie St Cleveland OH 44103

KLIE, HAMILTON FULLER, mech. contracting co. exec.; h. Cleve., Nov. 18, 1916; s. Walter and Mabel (Fuller) K.; A.B., Princeton U., 1938; LL.B., Case Western Res. U., 1941; m. Ruth Marian Young, Dec. 21, 1940; children—Gary Y., Kathleen Anne Klie Vranich, Susan Fuller Klie Schroeder. Admitted to Ohio bar, 1941; with firm Baker, Hostetler & Patterson, Cleve., 1941-46; with Smith & Oby Co., Cleve., 1946—, exec. v.p., 1962-74, pres., 1974—; pres. Carnegie-East 61st Co., Cleve., 1946—. Asso. chmn. sect. 4 United Torch Drive, Cleve.; mem. Cleve. Mayor's Equal Employment Opportunity Com., 1970-71; mem. del. assembly Greater Cleve. United Torch Services; life mem. alumni council Univ. Sch.; mem. alumni council Princeton U.; chmn. Constrn. Equal Employment Plan Cleve.; trustee Mech. Contracting Industry Fund Cleve., Cleve. Met. YMCA's. Served to lt. USNR, 1942-46. Mem. Mech. Contractors Assn. Cleve. (pres. 1969-71, chmn. bd. 1974-76), Mech. Contracting Industries Ohio (chmn., trustee legis. liaison com.), Greater Cleve. Growth Assn., Phi Beta Kappa, Phi Delta Phi, Order of Coif. Clubs: Princeton (N.J.) Charter; Hillbrook, Chagrin Valley Racquet (Chagrin Falls, Ohio); Dawn Beach, Oyster Pond Yacht (St. Maarten, N.W.I.); Hermit, Playhouse, Midday, Rotary (sec., community services com.) (Cleve.). Home: 17060 Chillicothe Rd Chagrin Falls OH 44022 Office: 6107 Carnegie Ave Cleveland OH 44103

KLIMEK, RONALD EDWARD, food distbn. and mfg. co. exec.; b. Chgo., July 8, 1942; s. Stanley L. and Adeline A. (Podraza) K.; B.S., St. Marys Coll., 1964; M.B.A., DePaul U., 1966; m. Cecelia A. Schroeder, Oct. 24, 1964; children—Ken, Debbie, Cathy. Gen. accounting Felt Products, Skokie, Ill., 1964; mktg. adminstrn. Frederick Post, Des Plaines, Ill., 1964-66; mktg. research analyst CFS Continental, Chgo., 1966-70, dir. mktg. research, 1970—. Mem. Am. Mktg. Assn., Internat. Food Mfrs. Assn. Home: 2427 Embers St Arlington Heights IL 60005 Office: 2550 Clybourn St Chicago IL 60614

KLINE, JAMES EDWARD, trade assn. exec.; b. Chgo., Feb. 2, 1933; s. Edward James and Grace Frances (Ferrari) K.; student U. Chgo., 1950-52, 57-58, Pomona Coll., 1952-53, Long Beach Coll., 1953-54; m. Karen Lee Oksendahl, Dec. 27, 1968; children—Julia Elizabeth, James Edward. Head activities Rotary Internat., Evanston, Ill., 1957-70; exec. dir. Casket Mfrs. Assn., Evanston, 1970—. Pres., Evanston Young Democrats, 1964-66; mem. Young Democrat Cook County Central Com., 1965; mem. bd. Evanston Regular Dem. Orgn., 1964. Served with AUS, 1954-57. Mem. Am. Soc. Assn. Execs., Expt. in Internat. Living. Rotarian. Home: 428 Washington Ave Wilmette IL 60091 Office: 708 Church St Evanston IL 60201

KLINE, JOYCE CLAIRE (MRS. FLAVIO PULETTI), physician, educator; b. Madison, Wis., July 26, 1929; d. William James and Leta (Shipley) Kline; B.S., U. Wis., 1951, M.D., 1954; m. Flavio Puletti, June 1, 1957. Intern Michael Reese Hosp., Chgo., 1954-55; resident internal medicine St. Mary's Hosp., Madison, Wis., 1955-56; resident radiology Univ. Hosps., Madison, 1956-59, NIH fellow radiation therapy, 1962-63; practice medicine specializing in radiology, Madison, 1959-62; instr. radiology U. Wis. at Madison, 1963-64, asst. prof. radiology, 1964-70, asso. prof., 1971—. Diplomate Am. Bd. Radiology. Fellow Am. Coll. Radiology; mem. AMA, Dane County Med. soc., Radiol. Soc. N.Am., Wis. Radiologic Soc., Am. Soc. Clin. Oncologists, Am. Soc. Therapeutic Radiology, Soc. Nuclear Medicine, Am. Radium Soc., AAAS, AAUP, Am. Women's Med. Assn., N.Y. Acad. Sci., Alpha Epsilon Iota. Home: 4806 Waukesha St Madison WI 53705 Office: 1300 University Ave Madison WI 53706

KLINE, MARY ELAINE GRAVES, educator; b. Clarion, Iowa, Aug. 7, 1920; d. John Preston and Johanna (Stueland) Graves; student Iowa State Tchrs. Coll., 1941-43; B.S. magna cum laude, Kent State U., 1963, M.Ed., 1965, Ed.S., 1976; m. Ralph Olds Kline, June 7, 1946 (dec. 1968); 1 dau., Karilyn Lee. Tchr. rural schs., Pocahontas County, Ia., 1938-42, Everly (Iowa) Consol. Sch., 1943-44, elementary sch., Cuyahoga Falls, Ohio, 1959-65; remedial reading tchr. Cuyahoga Falls City Schs., 1966-68, South Sarasota County Schs., Venice, Fla., 1968-72; reading specialist, Cuyahoga Falls (Ohio) City Sch., 1972—, dir. Right-to-Read, 1975—. Mem. Cuyahoga Falls Edn. Assn. (news editor 1964-66; rec. sec. 1966-67), Akron Area Council Internat. Reading Assn. (sec. 1965-66), Ohio Edn. Assn., NEA, Sarasota County Internat. Reading Assn. (pres. 1970-71, Akron area council pres. 1975-76), Kappa Delta Pi, Delta Kappa Gamma, Alpha Delta Kappa, Phi Delta Kappa. Democrat. Presbyterian (elder). Mem. Order Eastern Star. Home: 2256 11th St Cuyahoga Falls OH 44221

KLINE, RAYMOND ALVIN, elec. engr.; b. Vicksburg, Mich., Apr. 14, 1948; s. Eugene H. and Barbara June (Forsyth) K.; Asso. Sci., Mich. Tech. U., 1971; m. Nancy Lou English, June 30, 1968; children—Shane Leslie, Heidi Rinea. Relay technician Mich. Power Co., Three Rivers, Mich., 1971-72, sr. relay technician, 1973-74, elec. engr. relaying, 1975—. Home: 304 E Cushman St Three Rivers MI 49093 Office: PO Box 413 Three Rivers MI 49093

KLINE, TEX RAY, broadcaster, design engr.; b. Van Buren, Ind., Sept. 14, 1938; s. Ray Loyal and Bernice Eve (Marsh) K.; student DeVry Tech. Inst., Chgo., 1960-61; m. Janet Kay Owens, Dec. 19, 1976; children by previous marriage—Troy Ray, Tracy Rene, Terri Rae. Announcer, program dir. Sta. KTUS, Istanbul, 1957-59; announcer, engr. Sta. WITE, Brazil, Ind., 1962-63, Sta. WGEE, Indpls., 1962-72, Sta. WNTS, Indpls., 1974-76; engr. WPTA-TV, Ft. Wayne, Ind., 1963-64; prodn. mgr. WTAF-TV, Marion, Ind., 1964, WTTV-TV, Indpls., 1964-75; engr., soundstage chief engr. WRTV-TV, Indpls., 1975—; owner Kline's Music Maker Service, 1965—; co-owner, mgr. MidWestern Rec. Studio, 1968-72; dir. engring. Neon Cornfield, 1977—. Candidate for rep. Ind. Legislature, 1976. Served with USN, 1956-59. FCC 1st class radio telephone operator, gen. contractor; recipient award Citizen's Forum Beautification, 1974. Mem. Soc. Broadcast Engrs., Audio Engrs. Soc. Republican. Clubs: Indpls. Advt., Indpls. Press, Masons. Designer multi-media, audio and video equipment for custom applications. Home: 972 W Roache St Indianapolis IN 46208 Office: 1330 N Meridian St Indianapolis IN 46206

KLING, GEORGE ALBERT, radiologist; b. Mt. Clemens, Mich., May 25, 1934; s. Albert Peter and Dorothy Mae (Elson) K.; M.D., U. Mich., 1958; m. Judith Ann Nickel, Aug. 18, 1956; children—Victoria E., Cynthia E., Jeffrey G. Intern, Harper Hosp., Detroit, 1958-59, resident, 1959-62; pres. L. Reynolds Asso., P.C., Detroit, 1975—; chief dept. radiology Harper-Grace Hosp.; mem. staff Children's Hosp.; asst. prof. radiology Wayne State U. Served with M.C., U.S. Army, 1966-68. Decorated Bronze Star; diplomate Am. Bd. Radiology. Fellow Am. Coll. Radiology; mem. AMA, Mich. State, Wayne County med. socs., Am. Roentgen Ray Soc. (mgr.), Mich. Radiol. Soc. (past sec.-treas.), Detroit Gastroent. Soc., Detroit Acad. Medicine, Bockus Internat., Profl. Conv. Mgmt. Assn. Club: Detroit Athletic. Contbr. articles in field to Am. Jour. Roentgenology. Home: 208 Moran Grosse Pointe Farms MI 48236 Office: 3990 John R St Detroit MI 48201

KLINGBEIL, DONALD EDWARD, dentist; b. Ashtabula, Ohio, July 2, 1906; s. Hermand Archibald and Julia Mae (Gallup) K.; D.D.S., U. Pitts., 1928; postgrad. U. Pitts., U. Mich., Ohio State U.; m. Elinor Virginia Poe, June 25, 1931 (dec. Apr. 1951); children—James David, Joel Donald (dec.); m. 2d, Berthe Louise Denhart, June 18, 1955. Gen. practice dentistry, Madison, Ohio, 1928—. Mayor, Village of Madison, 1954-68; chmn. Madison Planning Commn., 1954-68; bd. dirs. YMCA, 1956-57, Lake County chpt. ARC, 1962. Served with USN, 1943-46. Mem. Carriage Assn. Am. (dir. 1964-67), NE Ohio dental assn. (pres.), ADA, Am. Legion, Lake County Hist. Soc., Nat. Trust for Hist. Preservation, Old Mentor Hist. Found., Early Am. Industries Assn. Republican. Methodist. Clubs: Kiwanis (past pres.), Elks, Gyro Internat. Home: 178 E Main St Madison OH 44057 Office: 29 W Main St Madison OH 44057

KLINGEL, MARTIN ALLEN, ins. co. exec.; b. Urbana, Ill., Aug. 27, 1941; s. Allen B. and Mary Margaret O. K.; B.S. with honors, U. Ill., 1964; m. Susan J. Abbott, Aug. 12, 1972; one dau., Katherine A. Coll. agt. Northwestern Mut. Life Ins. Co., Milw., 1963-64, fulltime asso., 1964-68; asso. gen. agt. Robert E. Castelo Gen. Agency, Champaign, Ill., 1968—; co-founder, prin. Dooley's chain, Champaign, 1970—; pres. Nat. Mini Warehouses Co., Urbana, 1973—; pres. K and M Inc., Champaign, 1976—; co-owner, operator Lincoln Lodge, Urbana, 1976—; dir. Busey First Nat. Bank, Urbana. C.L.U., Mem. Million Dollar Round Table (life, qualifying), Republican. Presbyterian. Club: Champaign County Country. Home: 4 Litchfield Ln Champaign IL 61820 Office: 811 W Springfield Ave Champaign IL 61820

KLINGENSMITH, DON JOSEPH, clergyman; b. Lovilia, Iowa, Apr. 1, 1901; s. George Francis and Dora May (Kincaid) K.; A.B., John Fletcher Coll., 1928; M.A., Okla. State U., 1941; M.Div., Garrett Theol. Sem., 1947; m. Thelma Victoria Hyde, Sept. 11, 1930; children—Merle Joseph, Eunice Victoria Klingensmith Evans. Ordained to ministry United Meth. Ch., 1930; supt. Ponca Indian Meth. Mission, Ponca City, Okla., 1936-43; pastor West Wis. Ann. Conf., The Meth. Ch., N.D., 1928-38, West Wis., 1943-50; radio ministry Sta. KBMR, Bismarck, N.D., 1963-71, Sta. KDIX, Dickinson, N.D., 1964-71, Sta. KBOM, Mandan, 1975; pastor Wesleyan Ch., Almont, N.D., 1972—. Hon. chief and councilman Ponca Indians, 1939—; precinct committeeman Republican Com., Mandan, N.D., 1966—; Republican dist. committeeman, Mandan, 1970-72; chmn. N.D. Prohibition Party, 1976, nat. committeeman, 1976. Mem. Meth. Fedn. Social Action, Council Chs. (chmn. Okla. commn. Indian work 1938-43), Nat. Wild Life Fedn., Nat. Writers Club, United Amateur Press, London Poetry Soc. Clubs: Toastmasters, Lions. Translator: New Testament in Everyday English, 1974. Address: PO Box 613 206 Collins Ave Mandan ND 58554

KLINGENSMITH, MRS. DON (THELMA HYDE KLINGENSMITH), ret. ednl. adminstr.; b. Rauville, S.D., May 23, 1904; d. Eber Watson and Ida (Lebert) Hyde; B.A. magna cum laude, John Fletcher Coll., 1928; M.S. in Edn., U. N.D., 1962; m. Don Joseph Klingensmith, Sept. 11, 1930; children—Merle Joseph, Eunice Victoria Klingensmith Evans. Tchr. rural schs., Almont, N.D., 1922-24; exec. sec. Young People's Gospel League, Chgo., 1928-30; asst. supt. Ponca Methodist Indian Mission, Ponca City, Okla., 1936-43; tchr. English, Almont High Sch., 1951-54; supt. schs. Morton County (N.D.), Mandan, 1959-73; v.p. West Wis. conf. Women's Soc. Christian Service, Meth. Ch., 1945-46; sec.-treas. Heart River Gospel Assn., 1950-68, dir., 1950—. Sr. pres. N.D. Young Citizens League, 1963-65; mem. N.D. Mother's Com.; adv. bd. Morton Co. Library, 1960—, trustee, 1977—; bd. dirs. Am. Cancer Soc., 1958-72, pres. sec., 1960-66; treas., dir. Action Com. Environ. Edn., 1968-75; trustee Dickinson Coll. Found., 1967—. Named N.D. Mother of Year, 1965; recipient citation Nat. and N.D. wildlife fedns. Mem. N.D., Am. (mem. seminar to Russia 1969) assns. sch. adminstrs., N.D. County Supts. Assn. (legis. rep. 1963-66), Mountain Plains, N.D. library assns., N.D. Library Trustees Assn. (v.p. 1974—, dir. 1971—, sec. 1971-73), N.D. Wildlife Fedn. Methodist. Clubs:

Zonta (chmn. polit. affairs Area VII 1968-70, del. internat. convs. 1968, 70, 72), Mandan. Editor: Almont Jubilee History Book, 1956, Morton County Elementary Tchrs. Bull., 1959-73. Home: 206 Collins Ave Mandan ND 58554

KLINGER, WILLIAM RUSSELL, educator; b. Columbia City, Ind., Feb. 9, 1939; s. Russell Jennings and Marcella Mae (King) K.; student Marion Coll., 1957-59; B.S., Taylor U., 1961; M.Sc., Ohio State U., 1967, Ph.D., 1973; m. Joanne Lois Clement, July 8, 1960; 1 dau., Nancy. Tchr. math Marion (Ind.) Community Schs., 1961-68; instr. Ohio State U., 1968-73; asso. prof. math., dept. coordinator Marion (Ind.) Coll., 1973—; part-time lectr. Ind. U. at Kokomo, 1973—. Recipient Marion Coll. Prof. of Year award Marion Coll. Students, 1976-77. Mem. Ind. Council Tchrs. Math, Math. Assn. Am., Nat. Council Tchrs. Math, Am. Sci. Affiliation, Phi Delta Kappa. Republican. Wesleyan Ch. Author: (with R.R. Wright) Basic Algebra, 1972. Home: 6970 Mary Ct Marion IN 46952 Office: Dept Math Marion Coll Marion IN 46952

KLINGNER, HAROLD WILLIAM, lawyer; b. Chgo., May 3, 1920; s. Herman and Josephine Marie (Collignon) K.; student Northwestern U., 1938-39, 47-48, Armour Tech. Sch., 1939-41; LL.B., Chgo. Kent Coll. Law, 1950; m. Virginia Grace Bassindale, June 21, 1947; children—Harold W., Thomas D., Susan G., Caron L. Admitted to Ill. bar, 1950, since practiced in Chgo.; asso. firm Guilford R. Windes, 1950-59; mem. firm Windes, Thomas and Klingner, 1959-66, Wooster, Mugalian, Thomas and Klingner, 1966-72; pvt. practice, 1972—. Dir. Cranda Corp., Graphic Products Corp., Type/Graphics Corp. Pres. bd. local improvements Village Arlington Heights (Ill.), 1959-62, 71; chmn. Sch. Dist. No. 25 Caucus, 1955. Served to capt. USMCR, 1942-47. Decorated D.F.C., Air medal. Mem. Am., Fed., Ill., Chgo. (chmn. membership com. 1959-60) bar assns. Lutheran. Home: 1123 N Belmont Ave Arlington Heights IL 60004 Office: 105 W Adams St 37th Floor Chicago IL 60603

KLITZKE, LYLE KENNETH, ednl. adminstr.; b. Ft. Atkinson, Wis., Oct. 2, 1903; s. Charles William and Ethel (Foreman) K.; student Wis. State U., 1922-26; B.S.. U. Ia., 1929; M.A., U. Chgo., 1934; m. Genevieve Smith, June 1, 1928 (dec.); children—Richard, Carol Jean; m. 2d, Irene Schroeder, Apr. 14, 1973. Instr. sci. Beloit (Wis.) Pub. Schs., 1926-28; prin. West Div. Elementary Sch., Des Plaines, Ill., 1928-29, Lincoln Elementary Sch., Maywood, Ill., 1929-35; supt. Dolton (Ill.) Elementary Schs., 1935-41, Somonauk (Ill.) Pub. Schs., 1941-45, (Ind.) Pub. Schs., 1945-49, Plymouth (Ind.) Pub. Schs., 1949-58, Chesterton (Ind.) Pub. Schs., 1959-69, Mundelein (Ill.) Elementary Sch., 1969-74; interim supt. North Boone County (Ill.), 1977—. Mem. Am. Assn. Sch. Adminstrs. (life), Phi Delta Kappa (chpt. pres. 1955). Club: Optimists (treas. Mundelein). Home: 1729 Buckingham St Mundelein IL 60060

KLOEHN, JOHN SHERMAN, orthodontist; b. Appleton, Wis., Feb. 25, 1930; s. Silas John and Irma (Sherman) K.; student U. Wis., 1948-50; B.S., U. Ill. Coll. Dentistry, 1952, D.D.S. with honors, 1954; postgrad. U. Ill., 1956-58; m. Ann Louise Perschbacher, June 26, 1954; children—William John, Julie Ann. Orthodontist, Appleton, 1958—. Bd. dirs. Outagamie County Cancer Soc. Served with Dental Corps, USNR, 1954-56. Diplomate Am. Bd. Orthodontics. Fellow Internat. Coll. Dentists; mem. Am. Assn. Orthodontists, Edward H. Angle Soc. Orthodontists, Wis. Orthodontic Soc. (dir.), Outagamie County Dental Soc. (pres. 1967-68, dir.), Omicron Kappa Upsilon. Republican. Lutheran. Club: Rotary (dir.). Home: 1834 Palisades Appleton WI 54911 Office: 103 W College Ave Appleton WI 54911

KLOEHN, RALPH ANTHONY, plastic surgeon; b. Milw., Dec. 18, 1932; s. Ralph Charles and Virginia Mary (Kosak) K.; B.S., Marquette U., 1954, M.D., 1958; m. Mary Theresa Landers, Nov. 4, 1961; children—Colleen, Gregory, Kristine, Patricia, Timothy, Phillip, Michelle. Intern, Charity Hosp. La., New Orleans, 1958-59; resident in gen. surgery Marquette U., Milw., 1961-65; resident in plastic and maxillofacial surgery U. Tex. Med. Br., Galveston, 1965-68, fellow Shrine Burns Inst., Galveston, Tex., 1965-68; fellow in plastic and reconstructive surgery African Med. and Research Found., Nairobi, Kenya, 1968-69; practice medicine specializing in plastic surgery, Milw., 1969—; clin. instr. plastic surgery Med. Coll. Wis., Milw., 1969—. Served with M.C., USN, 1959-61. Diplomate Am. Bd. Plastic Surgery. Fellow Internat. Coll. Surgeons, A.C.S.; mem. Wis. Soc. Plastic Surgeons (v.p. 1976-78), Milw. County, Waukesha County med. socs., State Med. Soc. Wis., Am. Assn. for Hand Surgery, Am. Cleft Palate Assn., AMA, Am. Soc. Plastic and Reconstructive Surgeons, Am. Trauma Soc., Midwestern Assn. Plastic Surgeons, Singleton Surg. Soc. Contbr. articles to med. jours. Home: 1305 Helene Dr Brookfield WI 53005 Office: 2323 N Mayfair Rd Suite 503 Milwaukee WI 53226

KLOS, JEROME JOHN, lawyer; b. La Crosse, Wis., Jan. 17, 1927; s. Charles and Edna S. (Wagner) K.; B.S., U. Wis., 1948, J.D., 1950; m. Mary M. Hamilton, July 26, 1958; children—Bryant H., Geoffrey W. Admitted to Wis. bar, 1950, since practiced in La Crosse; pres. firm Steele, Smyth, Klos and Flynn. Dir. Home Savs. & Loan Assn., La Crosse, Union State Bank, West Salem, Wis., La Crosse Indsl. Devel., Inc. Mem. La Crosse County Bd., 1957-74, vice chmn., 1972-74; pub. adminstr. La Crosse County, 1962-73. Bd. dirs. West Salem Area Growth, Inc., La Crosse Area Growth, Inc., LaCrosse Community Theatre; trustee Sander and McKinly Scholarship Funds of West Salem Sch. Dist. Fellow Am. Coll. Probate Counsel; mem. Am., Wis. bar assns. Elk, K.C. Home: 346 N Leonard St West Salem WI 54669 Office: 800 Lynne Tower Bldg La Crosse WI 54601

KLOTZ, JOHN MELVIN, nursing asst., ednl. vol.; b. Granite Falls, Minn., Oct. 26, 1946; s. Melvin Herman Henry and Dorothy Theresa (Benson) K.; B.A. cum laude, Luther Coll., 1968, postgrad., 1975; postgrad. Coll. Edn., U. Minn., 1968-76. With VISTA, Ouachita Job Corps Conservation Center, Royal, Ark., 1967; vol. Peace Corps, Iran, summer 1968; taxicab and airport limousine driver Yellow Taxi Co., Mpls., 1968-70, 74-75; nursing asst. Children's Rehab. Center, U. Minn. Hosps., Mpls., 1970-71, Misericordia Gen. Hosp., Winnipeg, Man., Can., 1971-72; warehouseman Employers Overload, Mpls., 1972-73; nursing asst. Met. Med. Center, Mpls., 1973-74, Prospect Park Care Center, Mpls., 1976, Fair Oaks Convalescent Home, Mpls., 1976, Truman Med. Center, Kansas City, Mo., 1976—; crewman Mpls. Fire-Rescue Res., 1976; VISTA vol. Genesis Alternative Sch., Kansas City, 1976; vol. in edn. Westport High Sch., Kansas City, 1977, Longfellow Elementary Sch., 1978. Refused military draft, 1969; refused civilian alternative service, 1971, convicted, 1972, refused presdl. pardon, 1977. Certified nursing asst. Mpls. Area Vocational-Tech. Inst.; certificate in basic rescue Mpls. office CD. Mem. Am. Hist. Assn., Sons of Norway, Midwest Com. for Mil. Counseling, Central Com. for Conscientious Objectors, Phi Alpha Theta. Lutheran. Home: 901 E Linwood Apt 11 Kansas City MO 64109

KLUG, RICHARD PAUL, banker; b. Milw., Sept. 13, 1934; s. Aaron Emil and Theodora Maria (Wendt) K.; B.A., Elmhurst Coll., 1956; grad. U. Wis. Grad. Sch. Banking, 1966; grad. Comml. Lending Sch., U. Okla., 1971; m. Arleen Joann Wittig, Apr. 23, 1958; children—Jeffrey Richard, Jennifer Jo Ann. Mgr. Household Finance Corp., Milw., 1956-60; sr. v.p., sec. to bd. Farmers & Mchts. Bank, Menomonee Falls, Wis., 1960—, dir., 1974—; dir. Leasenu Inc., Anchor Moving & Storage Co. Inc., Middle West Mfg. Co., Inc., Farrell Enterprises, Inc., Slinger Foundry, Inc. Gen. chmn. Menomonee Falls Diamond Jubilee, 1967; area chmn. United Fund, 1968-71; past chmn. Menomonee Falls Youth Center, 1963-65. Chmn. Menomonee Falls Police and Fire Commn., 1962—. Chmn. bd. mgrs. Tri-County YMCA, 1970-73; mem. corp. bd. Met. Milw. YMCA, 1970—; bd. dirs. Waukesha County Mental Health Assn., 1967-68. Served with AUS, 1951-53. Named Man of Year, Menomonee Falls C. of C., 1970. Mem. Wis. Installment Bankers Assn. (pres. 1972), Wis. Bankers Assn. (mem. coms.). Mem. United Ch. Christ. Mason, Rotarian. Home: N87 W15796 Kenwood Blvd Menomonee Falls WI 53051 Office: N88 W16554 Main St Menomonee Falls WI 53051

KLUTZNICK, PHILIP M., religious assn. exec.; b. Kansas City, Mo., July 9, 1907; s. Morris and Minnie (Spindler) K.; student U. Kan., 1924-25, U. Neb., 1925-26; LL.B., Creighton U., Omaha, Neb., 1929, LL.D., 1957; D.H.L. (hon.), Dropsie Coll., 1954, Hebrew Union Coll.-Jewish Inst. Religion, 1957, Coll. Jewish Studies, 1968; LL.D., Wilberforce (O.) U., 1959, Chgo. Med. Sch., 1968, Yeshiva U., 1974, Brandeis U., 1974; m. Ethel Riekes, June 8, 1930; children—Bettylu, Richard (dec.), Thomas Joseph, James Benjamin, Robert, Samuel. Admitted to bar, 1930; U.S. commr. Fed. Pub. Housing Authority, 1944-46; ltd. partner Saloman Bros.; adv. com. Urban Investment and Devel. Co.: dir. First Mark Corp., Mortgage Guaranty Ins. Corp., Milw. Mem. U.S. delegations to UN, 1957, 61, 62; U.S. rep., rank of ambassador, to ECOSOC, 1961-63; mem. President's Adv. Com. on Indo-Chinese Refugees, Bd. dirs. Nat. Jewish Welfare Bd.; chmn. Inst. Jewish Policy Planning; nat. council Boy Scouts Am.; chmn. exec. com. Chicago 21; trustee Eleanor Roosevelt Inst.; bd. dirs. Ednl. Facilities Labs., Creighton U., Roosevelt U., Lyric Opera Chgo., Nat., Bur. Econ. Research vice chmn. bd. dirs., trustee Com. Econ. Devel.; trustee Adlai Stevenson Inst. Internat. Affairs; chmn. governing bd. World Jewish Congress, pres., 1977; Mem. UN Assn. U.S.A. (sr. dir.), Chgo. Assn. Commerce and Industry (dir.), Lambda Alpha, Phi Epsilon Pi (hon.). Mem. B'nai B'rith (hon. internat. pres.) Clubs: Cosmos (Washington); standard, Commercial. Home: 180 E Pearson Chicago IL 60611 Office: 875 N Michigan Ave Chicago IL 60611

KLUVER, HERMAN CHRISTOF, ophthalmologist; b. Audubon, Iowa, Feb. 25, 1902; s. Christian F. and Pauline A. (Hahn) K.; B.S. with honors, U. Chgo., 1924, M.D., 1927; m. Lois Heward Cobb, Dec. 25, 1935; 1 son, Charles Ross Hansen. Intern, Charity Hosp., New Orleans, 1928-29; asst. otolaryngologist Univ. Hosps., U. Iowa, 1929-31, asst. ophthalmologist, 1931-36; practice medicine specializing in ophthalmology and otolaryngology, Fort Dodge, Iowa, 1936—; asso. Martin, Kluver, Coughlan, 1940-50, Kluver, Coughlan & Allen, 1959-68; pres. Melville Farms, Inc., 1959-68; cons. Trinity Regional Hosp., Fort Dodge; mem. med. adv. bd. Selective Service, 1941-42. Served to comdr. USNR, 1942-46. Diplomate Am. Bd. Otolaryngology. Fellow A.M.A., A.C.S., Am. Acad. Ophthalmology and Otolaryngology; mem. Pan Am. Ophthalmology, Am. Soc. Ophthalmology and Otolaryngology Allergy, Ia. Med. Soc., Am. Rifle Assn., V.F.W., Am. Legion. Mason (Shriner), Elk. Author: Cluverii Chronica, 1958, Cluver'sche Familien Archiv, 1961. Contbr. to profl. publs. in field. Home: 331 Wraywood Manor Fort Dodge IA 50501

KNAAK, WILLIAM CHARLES, vocat. inst. adminstr.; b. Swanville, Minn., Jan. 16, 1928; s. William Herman and Elnora Pauline (Rohde) K.; B.S., St. Cloud State Coll., 1951; M.A., U. Minn., 1956, Ph.D., 1969; m. Delores J. McComber, June 2, 1951; children—Frederic, Marcia. Tchr. pub. schs., Rochester, Minn., 1952-54; dir. adult and vocat. edn., pub. schs., White Bear Lake, Minn., 1954-58, asst. supt. bus. and systems devel., 1962-70, supt. spl. intermediate sch. dist. 916 and dir. area vocat. tech. inst., 1970—; asst. dir. vocat. edn., St. Paul, 1958-62; cons. vocat. tech. edn., Sudan, Iran, Venezuela, Saudi Arabia, also various state sch. dists.; lectr. U. Minn., 1962—. Mem. City White Bear Charter Commn., 1960-62; mayor White Bear Lake, 1963-64. Served with AUS, 1946-48. Recipient Gov.'s award, 1963; research award U.S. Office Edn., 1958; mem. internat. commn. on edn. Sudan, 1966. Mem. Am., Minn. assns. sch. adminstrs., Am., Minn. vocat. assns., Minn. Assn. Area Vocat. Tech. Inst. Dirs. (pres. 1973-74), C. of C. Club: Lions. Home: 3515 Jerry St White Bear Lake MN 55110 Office: 3300 N Century Ave White Bear Lake MN 55110

KNAPE, GERALD FRANCIS, dentist; b. Grand Rapids, Mich., June 6, 1928; s. Hubert Francis and Florence Irene (Winterhalter) K.; B.S., Aquinas Coll., 1950; D.D.S., Marquette U., 1955; m. Marilou Rawlings, Sept. 17, 1960; children—Kevin, Michael, Brian. Pvt. practice dentistry, Grand Rapids, 1957-75. Mem. Catholic Social Service Bd. of West Mich. Cath. Diocese, 1967-73, pres., 1973, mem. diocesan bd., 1972-75, pres., 1975. Served to capt., Dental Corps, USAF, 1955-57. Mem. ADA, West Mich. (sec.-treas. 1971-73, pres. 1976-77), Mich. dental socs., Delta Sigma Delta (life mem.). Club: Lions (dist. gov. 1969-70) (Grand Rapids). Home: 820 Washtenaw Dr NE Grand Rapids MI 49505 Office: 4234 Lake Michigan Dr NW Grand Rapids MI 49504

KNAPP, DONALD LEWIS, civil engr.; b. Battle Creek, Mich., Jan. 14, 1933; s. Leo Edgar and Grace Eloise (Tinkler) K.; B.S. in Civil Engring., U. Mich., 1958; m. Marion Lee Pearson, June 30, 1956; children—Lee Ann, Clark Bradford, Kelly Lea. Vice-pres. Spalding DeDecker & Assos., Birmingham, Mich., 1958-72; pres. Donald L. Knapp & Assos., cons. engrs., Birmingham, 1972—. Served with U.S. Army, 1953-55. Recipient Merit award Cons. Engrs. Council, 1967. Mem. Am. Soc. C.E., Oakland County Soc. Profl. Engrs., Mich. Soc. Registered Land Surveyors, Sigma Assn. (dir. 1969—, sec., 1972—). Home: 5570 Lahser Rd Birmingham MI 48010 Office: 1411 N Woodward Ave Birmingham MI 48011

KNAPP, KENNETH RAYMOND, priest, social service adminstr.; b Haubstadt, Ind., Mar. 18, 1937; s. Henry J. and Kathrine M. Gastenveld) K.; B.A., St. Meinrad (Ind.) Coll., 1959; ed. U. Innsbruck (Austria), 1963; M.S. in Counseling, Ind. U. 1968; M.S.W., Catholic U., 1970. Ordained priest Roman Catholic Ch., 1963; asst. pastor St. Wendel parish, Evansville, Ind., 1963-65, family counselor, 1963—; tchr., counselor Mater Dei High Sch., Evansville, 1963-65; supt. Washington Cath. High Sch., Washington, Ind., 1965-67; asso. pastor St Simon parish, Washington, Ind., 1965-67, also counselor; community orgn. worker YWCA, Bethesda, Md., 1968-69; family counselor Cath. Family and Children Service, Fairfax, Va., 1969-70; dir. Cath. Charities Bur., Evansville, 1970—; mem. Priests Senate of Diocese of Evansville, 1970-76, sec., 1971; mem. faculty Pastoral Tng. Inst. for Team Ministry, Mary Manse Coll., summer, 1971; Diocesan dir. of Campaign for Human deve., 1970—, Catholic Relief Service, 1970—; chaplain St. Vincent de Paul Soc., 1970-77; mem. Diocesan Council, Diocese of Evansville, 1970-76, pres., 1973. Pres. Dept. of Human Resources, Evansville, Ind., 1976—; bd. dirs. Community Council, Evansville, 1970-72, Vanderburgh County Council on Aging, 1972-74, Nat. Conf. of Cath. Charities, chmn. of personnel com., 1977—. Mem. Nat. Assn. of Social Workers, Am. Personnel and Guidance Assn., Assn. of Exec. Dirs. of United Way Agys. (sec. 1973-74, pres. 1974-76). Contbr. articles on social work to profl. pubs. Home: 609 Cherry St Evansville IN 47713 Office: 603 Court Bldg Evansville IN 47708

KNAPP, PETER MICHAEL, mgmt. cons., bus. exec.; b. Paterson, N.J., Aug. 11, 1923; s. Joseph William and Mary Frances (Cannon) K.; E.E., Villanova U., 1949; postgrad. Seton Hall U., 1964-66; m. Elizabeth T. McDermott, Nov. 25, 1950 (dec. Apr. 1966); children—Gregory, Kristine, Peter, Paul, Brian; m. 2d, Marjorie F. Newman, June 26, 1971; children—Jane, James, William, Thomas, Nancy, Carol, Linda, Kenneth, Paul. Customer engr. IBM, Phila., 1949-50, Paterson, N.J., 1950-51; engr. Kearfott Co., Little Falls, N.J., 1951-58; chief engr. electro mech. ITT Fed. Labs., Nutley, N.J., 1958-63, dir., 1963-67, engring. mgr., ITT Telecommunications, Milan, Tenn., 1968-70; v.p. ops. Esterline Angus, Indpls., 1970-73, pres., 1973-75; pres. Peter M. Knapp & Assos., 1975; now v.p. ops. Paper Art Co., Indpls.; also cons. in field. Bd. dirs. Am. World Trade Assn., 1974—. Served with USMCR, 1942-45. Mem. Sci. Apparatus Makers Am., Acad. Polit. Sci., V.F.W. Roman Catholic. K.C., Toastmaster, Kiwanian. Clubs: World Trade, Economic. Patentee in field. Home: 6805 Creekside Ln Indianapolis IN 46220

KNAPP, RICHARD WADSWORTH, dentist; b. Rochester, Minn., Mar. 22, 1918; s. Harold Wadsworth and Iva Grace (Cowles) K.; B.B.A., U. Minn., 1948, B.S., 1952, D.D.S., 1953; m. Jean Rudella Johnson, Jan. 9, 1954; children—Scott, Douglas. Pvt. practice dentistry, Rochester, Minn. 1953—. Mem. Am. Dental Assn., Minn., Southeastern, Zumbro Valley dental socs., Omicron Kappa Upsilon. Home: 1527 Graham Court Rochester MN 55901 Office: 410 First National Bank Bldg Rochester MN 55901

KNAPSTEIN, JOHN WILLIAM, rehab. psychologist; b. New London, Wis., June 20, 1937; s. John Joseph and Irene Frances (Peopke) K.; B.A., St. John's U., Collegeville, Minn., 1959; M.A., Marquette U., Milw., 1961; Ph.D., Tex. Tech U., 1970; m. Betty Ann Wilhelm, Nov. 25, 1966; children—John Karl, Susan Elise, Eric Steven. Tchr., Hortonville (Wis.) Union High Sch., 1959-60; counselor Racine (Wis.) Vocat. and Adult Sch., 1961-62; rehab. counseling psychologist John Cochran VA Hosp., St. Louis, 1970-72, Edward Hines (Ill.) VA Hosp., 1972—; instr. U. Mo., St. Louis, 1969-70; asst. prof. So. Ill. U., Edwardsville, 1970-71. Pres. Winston Village 6 Town Home Assn., 1977—. Served with USAF, 1962-66. Marquette U. scholar, 1960-61; Social Rehab. Adminstern fellow, 1966-69; recipient Spl. Service award Cochran VA Hosp., 1972. Mem. Nat. Rehab. Assn., Am., Nat. rehab. counseling assns., Am. Personnel and Guidance Assn., Nat. Vocat. Guidance Assn., Am. Psychol. Assn., Am. Congress Rehab. Medicine. Roman Catholic. Contbr. articles to profl. jours. Home: 120 Pamela Dr Bolingbrook IL 60439 Office: VA Hosp Hines IL 60141

KNECHT, CHARLES DANIEL, veterinarian; b. Halethorpe, Md., Mar. 22, 1932; s. Frank Anthony and Lillian Mary (Smith) K.; B.S., U. Md., 1960; D.V.M., U. Pa., 1956; M.S., U. Ill., 1966; m. Lucretia Jean Hanna, Aug. 14, 1954; children—Charles Mark, Thomas Richard. Staff veterinarian Broad St. Vet. Hosp., Richmond, Va., 1956; vet. practice Verona Rd. Animal Hosp., Pitts., 1958-59, Towson (Md.) Vet. Hosp., 1959-64; instr. to asst. prof. vet. sci. U. Ill., Urbana, 1964-70; prof., chief surgery Coll. Vet. Medicine, U. Ga., Athens, 1970-72; prof., chief surgery, small animal clinic Purdue U., West Lafayette, Ind., 1972—. Served to capt. USAF, 1956-58. Recipient Distinguished Teaching award Upjohn, 1971, Outstanding Tchr. award U. Ga., Athens, 1972, Outstanding Clinician and Outstanding Tchr. award Purdue U., 1973, Outstanding Clinician award, 1975, Purdue Alumni Distinguished Teaching award, 1976. Mem. AVMA, Am. Coll. Surgeons, Am. Coll. Vet. Internal Medicine, Am. Assn. Vet. Clinicians, Am. Assn. Vet. Med. Colls., West Central Ind. Vet. Med. Assn., Sigma Xi, Phi Zeta, Alpha Psi, Omega Tau Sigma, Gamma Sigma Delta. Author: Fundamental Techniques in Veterinary Surgery, 1975. Inventor Knecht Condyle clamp. Contbr. articles to sci. jours. Home: 1220 Ravinia Rd West Lafayette IN 47906 Office: Dept Small Animals Sch Veterinary Medicine Purdue Univ West Lafayette IN 47907

KNEEDLER, CHARLES FORREST, dentist; b. Rockford, Ill., Apr. 14, 1940; s. Forrest Lee and Norma Mary (Jones) K.; B.A., Westminster Coll., 1962; D.M.D., U. Louisville, 1966; m. Katherine Ann Ecker, July 7, 1962; children—Christopher Charles, Lori Anne. Individual practice dentistry, Hartford, Ky., 1966-67, Belleville, Ill., 1967—. Chmn. dental staff St. Elizabeth's Hosp., 1972. Mem. St. Clair County Bd., 1972-76, High Mount Grade Sch. Bd. Edn., 1973; cubscout master, High Mount, 1973-74; chmn. exec. com. Boy Scout Troop, O'Fallon, Ill., 1977—. Bd. dirs., chmn. Swansea Playground; gen. chmn. Belleville United Way, 1974-75. Recipient Distinguished Service award Belleville Jr. C. of C., 1974. Mem. Acad. Gen. Dentistry, Am. Dental Assn., Am. Profl. Practice Assn., Ill., St. Clair Dist. (sec.-treas. 1975, v.p. 1976, pres. 1977) dental socs., Belleville, Swansea chambers commerce, Delta Sigma Delta. Republican. Presbyterian. Clubs: Elks, Optimist (pres. Belleville 1972-73, presdl. citation). Editor for St. Clair County, Ill. Dental Jour., 1972-73. Home: 910 Indian Springs Dr O'Fallon IL 62269 Office: 3700 N Belt W Belleville IL 62223

KNEELAND, LARRY MARSHALL, biochemist; b. Eau Claire, Wis., Aug. 16, 1947; s. Marshall and Rena Genevieve (Erdman) K.; student Albert Ludwigs U., Freiburg, Germany, 1967-68; B.S., U. Wis., 1971. Specialist in pediatrics U. Wis. Med. Center, Madison, 1970-71; scientist Endocrine Labs., Madison, 1972-75, biochemist II, 1975—; founder, exec. dir. Badger Photog. Soc., Inc., 1971—; dir. Madison Community Coop., 1972-75. Mem. 13th Dist. Housing and Zoning Com., Madison, 1973—; mem. Wis. Arts Council, 1973—, Citizens Cable Council, 1973-74. Mem. AAAS, Profl. Photographers Am., Royal Photog. Soc., North Central Camera Club Council (dir. 1975-77, v.p. 1977—) Nat. Audubon Soc., Wis. Acad. Scis., Arts and Letters, Am. Chem. Soc., Soc. Photog. Edn., 13th Dist. Neighborhood Assn. (sec. 1974-75), Sierra Club, Phi Eta Sigma, Alpha Chi Sigma. Home: 601 Wingra St Madison WI 53715 Office: 3301 Kinsman Blvd Madison WI 53704

KNEIP, RICHARD FRANCIS, gov. S.D.; b. Elkton, S.D., Jan. 7, 1933; s. Frank J. and Bernice D. (Pederson) K.; m. Nancy Lou Pankey; children—Kevin, Keith, Kent, Kurt, Paul, Philip, Patrick, Michael. Mem. S.D. Senate, 1964-70, minority leader, 1967-70, gov. S.D., 1970—. Mem. exec. com. Nat. Gov.'s Conf., 1972-73; chmn. Midwestern Gov.'s Conf., 1975-76; chmn. human resources com. Nat. Gov.'s Conf., 1976-77; mem. Adv. Council on Intergovtl. Relations; mem. Old West Regional Commn. Served with USAF, 1951-55. Mem. Am. Legion. Roman Catholic. Address: Exec Office Pierre SD 57501

KNEISLEY, GARY LYNN, broadcasting exec.; b. Painesville, Ohio, Feb. 11, 1941; s. Paul Lawrence and Grace Lucille (Millard) K.; B.F.A., Ohio U., 1965; student Radio Engring. Inst., Sarasota, Fla., 1963; m. Sandra Lee Hausch, June 30, 1962; children—Scot Dwain, Suzanne Beth. Announcer, engr. WPVL Inc., Painesville, 1961-65, program dir., 1965-68; account exec. Nelson Stern & Assos., Painesville, 1968-71; sta. mgr. Lake Communications Corp., Painesville, 1971-74, group dir. ops. and sta. mgr., 1974-76; group dir. ops. WHOK, Inc., Lancaster, Ohio, Capital Communications Inc., Frankfort, Ky.; gen. mgr. Lake Communications Corp., 1976—. Loaned exec. United Way, 1972, 73, mem. pub. relations com., 1971-75; asso. chmn. loaned execs. United Way of Lake County,

1976, 77; v.p. Painesville Area Citizens Com., 1974-75; bd. dirs. Lake County Council of Arts, 1971-75, pres., 1973-74; bd. dirs. YMCA, 1971—, Free Clinic, 1975; trustee, sec. Lake County Devel. Council, 1977-78. Mem. Ohio Assn. Broadcasters. Club: Rotary. Home: 10247 Cherry Hill Dr Painesville OH 44077 Office: 1 Radio Pl Painesville OH 44077

KNEPPER, EUGENE ARTHUR, realtor; b. Sioux Falls, S.D., Oct. 8, 1926; s. Arlie John and May (Crone) K.; B.S.C., Drake U., Des Moines, 1951; m. LaNel Strong, May 7, 1948; children—Kenton Todd, Kristin Rene. Accountant, G.L. Yager, pub. accountant, Estherville, Ia., 1951-52; auditor R.L. Meriwether, C.P.A., Des Moines, 1952-53; accountant govt. renegotiation dept. Collins Radio Co., Cedar Rapids, Iowa, 1953-54; head accounting dept. Hawkeye Rubber Mfg. Co., Cedar Rapids, 1954-56; asst. controller United Fire & Casualty Ins. Co., Cedar Rapids, 1956-58; sales asso. Equitable Life Assurance Soc. U.S., Cedar Rapids, 1958-59; controller Caddis Enterprises, Inc., Cedar Rapids, 1959-61; owner Estherville Laundry Co., 1959-64; sales asso., comml. investment div. mgr. Tommy Tucker Realty Co., Cedar Rapids, 1961-74; owner Real Estate Investment Planning Assos., Cedar Rapids, 1974—; cons. in field; also speaker; guest lectr. Kirkwood Community Coll., Cedar Rapids, Mt. Mercy Coll., Cedar Rapids, Cornell Coll., Mt. Vernon. Active local Boy Scouts Am., YMCA; bd. dirs. Oak Hill-Jackson Outreach Fund, 1970—, pres., 1973-74; bd. dirs. Consumer Credit Counseling Service Cedar Rapids-Marion Area, 1974—, pres., 1974—. Served with USNR, 1945-46. Recipient Storm Manuscript award, 1976. Mem. Nat., Iowa (pres. comml. investment div.) assns. realtors, Nat. Assn. Accountants, Nat. Inst. Real Estate Brokers (membership chmn. Iowa 1972-73), Real Estate Securities and Syndication Inst., Cedar Rapids Bd. Realtors. Methodist. Club: Cedar Rapids Optimist (chmn. boys work com.). Contbr. articles to profl. jours. Home: 283 Tomahawk Trail SE Cedar Rapids IA 52403 Office: 1602 IE Tower Cedar Rapids IA 52401

KNICELY, DAVID ROGER, agrl. engr.; b. Zanesville, Ohio, June 25, 1938; s. Donald Herbert and Margaret Rose (Gosser) K.; B.Agrl. Engring., Ohio State U., 1961; M.S. (teaching and research scholar), Mich. State U., 1963; m. Kathie Irene Ketchum, June 27, 1964; children—Michael David, Monte Edward. Research and devel. engr. research dept. Massey-Ferguson Co., Detroit, 1963-66; research engr. Eaton Corp. Research Center, Southfield, Mich., 1967; product engr. Allis Chalmers Co., Milw., LaPorte, Ind., 1967-69; sr. design engr. FMC Corp., Hoopeston, Ill., 1969—. Registered profl. engr., Ohio. Mem. Am. Soc. Agrl. Engrs., Sigma Xi, Tau Beta Pi. Methodist (trustee 1972-74, 77—, lay leader 1978). Club: Toastmasters (pres. 1973, 78, Outstanding Toastmaster award 1975) (Hoopeston). Patentee in field. Home: 107 Smith Dr Rossville IL 60963 Office: 103 E Maple St Hoopeston IL 60942

KNIERIM, VIRGIL JACOB, metallurgist; b. Adrian, Mich., Aug. 25, 1924; s. Jacob George and Cora Mae (Wood) K.; student Adrian Coll., 1946-48; B.S. in Metal.Engring., Mich. Tech. U., 1951; m. June Lorraine Hiser, June 15, 1947; children—Curtis J., Allyn. Foundry metallurgist Alcoa, Cleve., 1951-53; research metallurgist Bohn Aluminum & Brass Corp., Detroit, 1953-55; devel. engr. Bridgeport Brass Corp., Adrian, 1955-60; staff metallurgist Aeroquip Corp., Jackson, Mich., 1960—; tech. advisor Jackson Community Coll. Served with USMC, 1943-46; PTO. Registered profl. engr., Mich. Mem. Am. Soc. Metals, Nat. Assn. Corrosion Engrs., ASTM, Nat., Mich. socs. profl. engrs., Wire Assn., Alpha Sigma Mu. Methodist. Clubs: Jackson County Outdoor, Masons. Home: 4775 Moon Lake Rd Jackson MI 49201 Office: 300 S East Ave Jackson MI 49203

KNIGHT, LESTER BENJAMIN, cons. firm exec.; b. Albany, N.Y., June 29, 1907; s. Lester B. and Louise (Vaast) K.; M.E., Cornell, 1929; postgrad. Chgo. Kent Coll., 1933-34; m. Elizabeth Field, Mar. 5, 1935; children—Charles Field, Leslie. Chmn. Lester B. Knight and Assos., Inc., Chgo., 1945—; chmn. Lester B. Knight Internat. Corp., Chgo., Universal Castings Corp.; dir. A.B. Knight, Sweden; dir. Knight Wegenstein, London, Eng., Zurich, Switzerland, Dusseldorf, Germany, Vienna, Austria, Florence, Italy. Pres. sponsoring bd. Travelers Aid Soc., Chgo., 1964-65, bd. dirs., 1958—. Mem. Am. Foundrymen's Soc., Am. Soc. M.E., Am. Mgmt. Soc., Indsl. Mgmt. Soc., Chgo. Chamber of Commerce and Industry (dir., v.p. indsl. devel.), Chgo. Assn. Cons. Engrs., Soc. Mil. Engrs. Republican. Clubs: Glenview Golf (Ill.); Economic. Executives Chicago, University (Chgo.); Country of Florida (Golf, Fla.); Ocean (Boynton Beach, Fla.) Delray (Fla.) Yacht; Engineers (N.Y.); Army and Navy (Washington). Home: Glenview Club Golf IL 60629 Office: 549 W Randolph St Chicago IL 60606

KNIGHT, ROBERT DUANE, dentist; b. Humboldt County, Iowa, Oct. 7, 1925; s. Loren L. and Mattie (Mason) K.; student Upper Iowa U., 1946-48; D.D.S., U. Iowa, 1953; m. Julia Caroline Hauth, Aug. 8, 1954; children—William Robert, James Henry, Elizabeth Marie. Pvt. practice dentistry, Ft. Dodge, Iowa, 1953—; mem. staff Trinity East, Trinity West hosps., Ft. Dodge. Bd. dirs. Jerry Rabiner Meml. Boys' Ranch. Served with USNR, 1943-46; PTO. Mem. ADA, Delta Sigma Delta. Lutheran. Club: Elks. Home: 934 15th Ave N Fort Dodge IA 50501 Office: 138 N 9th St Fort Dodge IA 50501

KNIGHT, WILLIAM D., JR., lawyer; b. Rockford, Ill., May 18, 1925; s. William D. and Lela Mae (Clark) K.; A.B., Dartmouth Coll., 1949; J.D., Northwestern U., 1952. Admitted to Ill. bar, 1953; mem. firm Knight & Knight, Rockford, Ill., 1953—. Bd. dirs., counsel Boys Club Assn. of Rockford, 1959—. Served to 1st lt., inf., AUS, 1943-46. Mem. Ill., Winnebago County bar assns., Assn. Ins. Atts., Fedn. Ins. Counsel, Internat. Assn. Ins. Counsel, Def. Research Inst., Am. Legion, Delta Upsilon, Phi Delta Phi. Republican. Methodist. Clubs: Elks, Rockford Country, Univ. (Rockford); Univ. (Chgo.); Lake Geneva Country. Home: 575 S Lake Shore Lake Geneva WI 53197 also 1205 Lundvall Ave Rockford IL 61107 Office: 708 Talcott Bldg Rockford IL 61101

KNIGHT, YALE, optometrist; b. Milw., Oct. 4, 1922; s. Harry and Lillian (Bachman) K.; student U. Wis., 1941-43; O.D., Ill. Coll. Optometry, 1949; children—Harlyne, Eric. Clin. instr. Ill. Coll. Optometry Clinic, 1949; pvt. practice optometry, Milw., 1950, West Allis, Wis., 1951—. Served with USAAF, 1943-45. Mem. Am. Optometric Found., Am., Milw. (dir.), Wis. (keyman legis. com. 1968-73) optometric assns., Nat. Soc. Prevention Blindness, Menninger Found., Air Force Assn., Ill. Coll. Optometry Alumni Assn., U.S. Lawn Tennis Assn. Founder Yale Knight Research award Ill. Coll. Optometry, 1972. Office: 7240 W Greenfield Ave West Allis WI 53214

KNIGHTON, JOSEPH RAYMOND, assn. exec.; b. Chgo., June 1, 1922; s. Joseph Raymond and Eunice Mae (Anderson) K.; student Olivet Coll., 1938-42; Mus.B., Am. Conservatory Music, 1946; Mus.M., Mich. State U., 1947; LL.D. (hon.), Seattle Pacific Coll., 1962; m. Grace Elizabeth Reed, Oct. 13, 1943; children—Nancye, David, Thomas, Michael. Exec. dir. Christian Med. Soc., Oak Park, Ill., 1951-65; founder, pres. MAP Internat., Carol Stream, Ill., 1954—; chmn. Africa Com. for Rehab. So. Sudan, Nairobi, Kenya; exec. com. mem. Health Edn. Econ. Devel., Bangladesh; bd. dirs. Health Edn. Econ. Devel. Haiti, Internat. Afghan Mission, Afghanistan, Christoffel Blindenmission, W.Ger.; cons. to internat. relief, devel. agys. Served with U.S. Army, 1943-46. Decorated knight Order Christopher Columbus (Dominican Republic); knight gt. band Humane Order of African Redemption (Liberia); named Hon. Consul of Dominican Republic for Wheaton, Ill., 1968; recipient Laymen's citation for distinguished service AMA, 1971. Club: Lions (Wheaton). Home: 1120 Lexington St Wheaton IL 60187 Office: PO Box 50 Wheaton IL 60187 also 327 Gundersen Dr Carol Stream IL 60187

KNIGHTON, ROBERT SYRON, neurosurgeon; b. Vallejo, Calif., Aug. 17, 1914; s. David W. and Mae Virginia (Clauson) K.; B.S., Pacific Union Coll., 1939; M.D., Loma Linda U., 1942; m. Cora Louise Taylor, Sept. 9, 1939; children—Robert W., George L., James E., Joan L., Thomas D. Intern, Los Angeles County Gen. Hosp., 1942-43; resident in neurol. surgery White Meml. Hosp., Los Angeles, 1943-44, 46-47; NRC fellow Montreal (Que., Can.) Neurol. Inst., 1947-48; staff neurosurgeon Henry Ford Hosp., Detroit, 1948-52; practice medicine specializing in neurosurgery Detroit, 1948—; mem. staff Henry Ford Hosp., 1948—, chief neurosurgery, 1952-70, chmn. dept. neurology and neurosurgery, 1971—; clin. prof. neurosurgery U. Mich. Med. Sch., 1972—. Served with U.S. Army, 1944-46. Fellow A.C.S.; mem. AMA, Mich. State, Wayne County med. socs., Soc. Neurol. Surgeons, Am. Assn. Neurol. Surgery, Am. Acad. Neurol. Surgeons, Neurosurg. Soc. Am. Contbr. articles to med. jours. Home: 27486 Lathrup Blvd Lathrup Village MI 48076 Office: 2799 W Grand Blvd Detroit MI 48202

KNIGHTON, SAMUEL CURTIS, retail co. exec.; b. Rockford, Ill., Sept. 12, 1938; s. Lester L. and Mary (Nelson) K.; student U. Chgo., 1956-58, Rockford Coll., 1960-72, Am. U., 1969; m. Cheryl A. Peacock, July 22, 1967; children—Teri L., Brent E. Computer operator Anaconda Wire & Cable Co., Sycamore, Ill., 1958-60; data processing mgr. Eclipse Fuel Engring., Rockford, 1960-65; systems analyst Ill. Nat. Bank & Trust, Rockford, 1965-67; dir. data processing H. Douglas Singer Zone Center, Rockford, 1967-73; v.p. Bill Fisher's Appliance & TV Centers, Inc., Cherry Valley Ill., 1973—. Mem. Data Processing Mgmt. Assn. Patentee circuitry parallel multiplication in a digital apparatus. Home: 602 James St Rockford IL 61103 Office: State at Cherry Sts Cherry Valley IL 61016

KNIGHTS, EDWIN MUNROE, pathologist; b. Providence, Dec. 25, 1924; s. Edwin Munroe and Viola Ruth (Koreb) K.; A.B., Brown, 1948; M.D., Cornell, 1948; m. Ruth Lindsay Currie, Sept. 23, 1961; children—Edwin B., Jessie B., Ross D., David J. Intern Bellevue Hosp., N.Y.C., 1948-49; resident in pathology R.I. Hosp., Providence, 1949-50, Henry Ford Hosp., Detroit, 1952-54; asso. pathologist Harper Hosp., Detroit, 1954; dir. labs. Hurley Hosp., Flint, Mich., 1957-62; dir. lab. Providence Hosp., Southfield, Mich., 1963-75, Northland Oakland Med. Labs., Southfield, 1964—; dir. Bio Sci. Labs., Detroit, 1975—; pres. Coll. Terr. Inc., Flint, 1968—, Life Sci. Inc., 1971-72, Vet. Med. Labs., 1973-75; clin. prof. pathology Mich. State U., 1974-75; rep. Comprehensive Health Planning Council South East Mich. Served to lt., USN, 1944-46, 50-52, ETO, Korea. Recipient grants USPHS, 1957-66. Fellow Am. Coll. Physicians, Coll. Am. Pathologists, Am. Soc. Clin. Pathologists (Mich. councilor 1966-68); mem. Oakland County Med. Soc. (pres. 1974), Mich. Soc. Pathologists (pres. 1971), AMA, Internat. Acad. Pathology. Club: Detroit Econ. Author: Ultramicro Methods for Clinical Laboratories, 1957, 2d edit., 1962. Patentee in a buret. Editor: Minicomputers in the Clinical Laboratory, 1970; Lifelines, 1971-75. Contbr. numerous articles to profl. jours. Home: 5153 Echo Rd Bloomfield Hills MI 48013 Office: 24469 Indoplex Circle Farmington Hills MI 48018

KNIOLA, JOHN RAYMOND, photographer; b. Michigan City, Ind., Jan. 23, 1945; s. Raymond Joseph and Phillis Mary (Grott) K.; student Purdue U., 1962, Ray Vogue Sch. Fine Arts, Chgo., 1963-64, Profl. Photographers Sch. Winona Lake, Ind., 1972-74. Photographer, LaPorte (Ind.) Herald Argus newspaper, 1964-65, Michigan City (Ind.) News Dispatch, 1965-69, Pullman Inc. indsl., Chgo., 1969—. Mem. Mid-West Indsl. Photographers, Highland (Ind.) Region Early Ford Club Am. (sec. historian 1971-74), Michiana (Ind.) Model A Club (historian 1971-74), Early Corvette Club Am., Avanti Internat., Corvette Club Am. Roman Catholic. Home: 3717 Brookside St Michigan City IN 46360 Office: 200 S Michigan Ave Chicago IL 60604

KNOCHE, EVERETT, JR., store fixture marketing exec.; b. Crab Orchard, Nebr., July 12, 1930; s. Everett and Blanche Winona (Hadley) K.; student Omaha Sch. Bus., 1947, U. Wis.-Milw., 1953-54; m. Mary Jane Jones, June 29, 1952; children—Everett Eugene, Jeffrey Alan, David Grant. With Store Kraft Mfg. Co., Beatrice, Nebr., 1948—, sales engr., 1955-69, v.p. sales, 1969-76, pres., 1976—, also dir. Served with USNR, 1947-55. Mem. Ch. of Christ (deacon). Mason (Shriner), Elk. Home: 421 N 16th St Beatrice NE 68310 Office: 600 Irving St Beatrice NE 68310

KNOCK, MALCOLM ARGYLE, oil co. exec.; b. Willows, Calif., Apr. 8, 1923; s. Malcolm Argyle and Carolyn (Moon) K.; B.A., U. Calif. at Berkeley, 1949; m. Nancy Barnard, Apr. 13, 1946; children—Kathleen Ann Stokinger, Susan Lynne, Janet Carol Gorin, Judith Nancy. Jr. to mgr. geophysics Amoco Prodn. Co. and predecessor cos., Houston, 1949-50, Yorktown, Tex., 1950, Angleton, Tex., 1950, Mercedes, Tex., 1950, Stanton, Tex., 1952, Lubbock, Tex., 1952, Midland, Tex., 1952-56, Tulsa, Okla., 1951-52, Gretna, La., 1950, Houma, La., 1950-51, Lake Charles, La., 1956-57, Lafayette, La., 1957-59, Edmonton, Alta., Can., 1959-63, Calgary, Alta., 1963-75, Chgo., 1975—. Served with USAAF, 1943-46. Chmn. DuPage County (Ill.) Heart Fund campaign, 1976. Mem. Can. Figure Skating Assn. (dir. 1970-75), Soc. Exploration Geophysicists, Can. Soc. Exploration Geophysicists. Home: 180 Olive St Elmhurst IL 60126 Office: Amoco Prodn Co PO Box 5340AMC 4604 Chicago IL 60680

KNOEDLER, NORMAN ROBERT, devel. engr.; b. Salem, Ohio, Mar. 14, 1941; s. Leland Frederick and Eula Margeret (Hersman) K.; grad. Salem Sch. Trade, 1966; m. Sandra Lee Bak, Nov. 1, 1959; children—Sherene Renee, Debra Lynn, Heidi Lee, Christina Sue, Eric Norman. With N.R.M. Corp., Columbiana, Ohio, 1959—, elec. foreman, 1967-69, designer, 1969-74, project engr., 1974—; instr. Salem Sch. Trades, 1968. Bd. dirs. ARC chpt., 1976—. Mem. IEEE, Salem Hist. Soc. Methodist. Home: 1811 Franklin Rd Salem OH 44460 Office: 400 W Railroad St Columbiana OH 44408

KNOSPE, WILLIAM HERBERT, physician, educator; b. Oak Park, Ill., May 26, 1929; s. Herbert Henry and Dora Isabel (Spruce) K.; A.B., U. Ill., 1951, B.S., 1952, M.D., 1954; M.S. in Radiation Biology, U. Rochester, 1962; m. Adris M. Nelson, June 19, 1954; children—William A., Elizabeth A., David T. Intern, State U. N.Y. at Syracuse, 1954-55; resident in medicine Ill. Central Hosp., Chgo., 1955-56, VA Research Hosp.-Northwestern U., Chgo., 1956-58; practice medicine, specializing in internal medicine, Washington, 1963-66, Chgo., 1967—; attending physician Walter Reed Gen. Hosp., Washington, 1963-64, asst. chief hematology service, chief hematology clinic, 1964-66; asst. attending staff Presbyn.-St. Luke's Hosp., Chgo., 1967, asst. dir. hematology, 1967-74, dir., 1974—, asso. attending staff, 1968-72, attending physician, 1972—; asst. prof. medicine U. Ill. Coll. Medicine, Chgo., 1967-69, asso. prof., 1969—; asso. prof. medicine Rush Med. Coll., 1970-74, prof., 1974—. Served to lt. col. M.C., U.S. Army, 1958-66. Diplomate Am. Bd. Internal Medicine. Fellow A.C.P.; mem. Am. Soc. Hematology, Am. Fedn. Clin. Research, AMA, Central Soc. Clin. Research, Radiation Research Soc., Chgo. Inst. Medicine, Sigma Xi. Research in clin. aspects of leukemia and lymphoma, pathophysiology of hematopoietic stem cells and bone marrow function. Author numerous articles in field. Home: 405 E 7th St Hinsdale IL 60521 Office: 1753 W Congress Pkwy Chicago IL 60612

KNOTE, CHARLES E., lab. exec.; b. Greens Fork, Ind., Feb. 6, 1921; s. Charles E. and Eva Mae (Leisure) K.; B.S., Purdue U., 1942; m. Ruth Alice Rueseler, Oct. 7, 1950; children—Barbara Knote Vardiman, Nancy Knote Evendens, Elizabeth, Patricia, Richard. Farm mgr. Howard Halderman Co., Wabash, Ind., 1943; salesman H.D. Hudson Mfg. Co., Chgo., 1946-48; pest control mgr. trainee Sentinel Insect Control Labs., 1948-49; owner, pres. Cape-Kem Labs., Cape Girardeau, Mo., 1949—; pest control cons. U. Ill., Purdue U., So. Ill. U., U. Mo., industry. Vice pres., mem. bd. Chateau Girardeau, 1974-75; pres. Cape Girardeau Community Concert Assn., 1973-75. Served to ensign, USNR, World War II. Registered profl. entomologist. Mem. Mo. Pest Control Assn. (pres. 1973, profl. service award 1974), Nat. Pest Control Assn. (dir. 1963-66, 73-76), Cape Girardeau C. of C. (Friend of Agr. award 1972), Pi Chi Omega (Profl. Service award 1973). Presbyterian (elder, deacon). Clubs: Masons, Exchange. Editor: Missouri Pest Control Technician Training Manual, 1971; Missouri Pest Control Certification Manual, 1974, 73. Inventor various rodent baits. Home: 2323 Brookwood St Cape Girardeau MO 63701 Office: 33 N Frederick St Cape Girardeau MO 63701

KNOTT, ALBERT PAUL, JR., physician; b. Pitts., Mar. 23, 1935; s. Albert Paul and Fannie (Scott) K.; A.B., Yale U., 1956; M.D., N.J. Coll. Medicine, 1960. Intern D.C. Gen. Hosp., 1960-61, cardiovascular research fellow Michael Reese Hosp., 1961-63; med. resident Hines VA Hosp., 1963-65; practice medicine specializing in cardiology and internal medicine, Chgo., 1967—; mem. staff Rush Presby., St. Lukes Hosp.; cons. cardiologist Daniel Hale Williams Health Center, 1967—; med. dir. Bethany Brethren-Garfield Park Hosp., 1977—; dir. Inner City Industries, Inner City Devel. Co., Inc., Inner City Foods, Templeton Investment Co. Ltd., St. Johns Enterprises Ltd. Mem. Field Mus. Served with USNR, 1965-67. Mem. AMA, Am. Coll. Physicians, Sigma Pi Phi, Phi Rho Sigma. Home: 1501 N State Pkwy Chicago IL 60611 Office: 1753 Congress Pkwy Chicago IL 60607

KNOTT, JAMES LEROY, internist; b. Council Bluffs, Iowa, June 21, 1926; s. Roy Peter and Lillian Bedelia (Peterson) K.; M.D., Creighton U., 1953; m. Margaret Lucille Sluyter, Dec. 23, 1947; children—James Roy, David Lawrence, Paul Douglas Sluyter. Intern, St. Joseph Hosp., Sioux City, Iowa, 1953-54; resident in internal medicine Omaha VA Hosp., 1954-57, staff physician, chief cardiology, 1957-60; chief of staff Jennie Edmundson Meml. Hosp., Council Bluffs, 1969-70, staff physician, 1960—; head dept. medicine and EKG dept. Mercy Hosp., Council Bluffs, 1970-71, 73-74, staff physician, 1960—; med. dir. Iowa Sch. for the Deaf, Council Bluffs, 1963—; pres. Bluffs Med. Assos., P.C.; asst. prof. medicine U. Nebr. Bd. dirs. Hist. Gen. Dodge House; former dir. Council Bluffs C. of C.; bd. dirs. Council Bluffs United Community Service Fund. Served with USNR, 1944-46. Diplomate Am. Bd. Internal Medicine. Fellow A.C.P. (life); mem. Iowa Med. Soc., AMA, Iowa Clin. Soc. Internal Medicine (pres.), Am. Soc. Internal Medicine. Republican. Methodist. Clubs: Council Bluffs Toastmasters (past pres.), Council Bluffs Rotary (pres.). Home: 15 Westlake Village Council Bluffs IA 51501 Office: 302 The Doctors Bldg Council Bluffs IA 51501

KNOUFF, LORENTZ BENNETT, lawyer; b. Zanesville, O., Jan. 29, 1907; s. Washington Irving and Annie Laurie (Bennett) K.; A.B., Otterbein Coll., 1929; J.D., Ohio State U., 1932; LL.M., Columbia, 1933; m. Mary Elizabeth Riley, Sept. 12, 1940. Admitted to Ohio bar, 1932, Ill. bar, 1934; asso. editor Corpus Juris, N.Y.C., 1933-34; practiced in Chgo., 1934—; partner firm Dixon, Todhunter, Knouff & Holmes, and predecessor firms, 1934-68, Knouff & Ley, 1968-73, Knouff, Ley & Davis, 1974—. Pres. John Griffiths Bldg. Corp., 1955—; dir. A.C. Becken Co., Eschner & Keranen, Inc., Henry C. Grebe & Co., Inc., Haddam Co. Traffic commr., Highland Park, Ill., 1948-50; chmn. Barrington Hills Plan Commn., 1959-62; chmn. Barrington Hills Zoning Bd. Appeals, 1962-74; chmn. legal com. Barrington Area Council Govts., 1974—. Bd. dirs., mem. flower show com. Chgo. World Flower and Garden Show, 1958-74; bd. dirs. Am. Ceramic Circle, 1976—. Mem. Ill., Chgo. bar assns., Men's Garden Clubs Am. (past nat. dir.), Antique Automobile Club Am. (pres., dir. Ill. region 1954-55), Rolls Royce Owners Club (dir. Lake Michigan region 1969—), Order of Coif. Clubs: Chicago. Home: Ha'Penny Farm Dundee IL 60118 Office: 33 N Dearborn St Chicago IL 60602

KNOWLES, JEAN TURNBULL (MRS. JAMES KNOWLES, JR.), artist; b. Cambridge, Mass.; d. Frederick Moncrieff and Alice E. (Hilton) Turnbull; grad. Wheelock Coll., 1919; student Boston Mus. Sch., Chgo. Art Inst., U. Calif. at Los Angeles, Washington U.; m. James Knowles June 24, 1922 (dec.); children—James Turnbull, John Hilton. One-woman shows: Belmont Hill Sch., Mass., St. Louis Artists Guild, University City (Mo.) Library; group shows include: St. Louis Art Mus., Artists Guild, Julius Polk Gallery, Pierre Raoul Baptiste Gallery, others. Active St. Louis Symphony Soc. Mem. Friends of St. Louis Art Mus. Republican. Home: 7025 Kingsbury University City MO 63130

KNOX, CHARLES STUART, data processing co. cons.; b. Cedar Rapids, Iowa, Mar. 30, 1922; s. Charles Stuart and Ruth Thatcher (Temple) K.; student Coe Coll., 1940-41; B.S., Iowa State Coll., 1947; m. Gloria Elinor Lehti, Jan. 3, 1948; children—David Stuart, Gary Sinclair. Plant engr. Iowa Mfg. Co., Cedar Rapids, 1948-55; prodn. control asst. mgr. Caterpillar Tractor Co., Peoria, Ill., 1955-60; mgr. data processing Allis Chalmers Co., Milw., 1960-64; mgr. data processing Control Data Corp., Mpls., 1964-67, mfg. cons., 1970-75; mgr. data processing Minn. Mining & Mfg. Co., St. Paul, 1967-70; mfg. cons. Conseru Corp., 1975—; pres. Knox Cons. Services, 1976—; Constable, North Oaks, St. Paul, 1964-66. Served to 1st lt. USAAF, 1942-46. Registered mech. and agrl. profl. engr., Ia. Mem. Sigma Alpha Epsilon. Republican. Presbyterian (deacon 1970). Home and Office: 3 Poplar Ln North Oaks St Paul MN 55110

KNOY, MAURICE GEORGE, plastic mfg. co. exec.; b. Quincy, Ind., Feb. 1, 1912; s. George Granville and Jesse Maude (Cummings) K.; B.M.E., Purdue U., 1933; m. Katharine Livingston Andrew, Sept. 19, 1940; children—Katharine Knoy Crook; m. 2d, Gwendolyn Lee Juergens, Oct. 4, 1958. With Rostone Corp., Lafayette, Ind., 1933—, dir., 1935—, v.p., sec., 1937-63, exec. v.p., treas., 1963-66, pres., 1966—, chmn. bd., 1971—; dir. Lafayette Savs. Bank, Ind. Gas Co., Mycalex and Rosite Ltd., Lafayette Union R.R. Chmn. Purdue Alumni Found., 1963-67, Tippecanoe County chpt. ARC, 1946-48; trustee Purdue U., 1965—, pres., 1967—; bd. dirs. Purdue Research Found., 1957—, St. Elizabeth Hosp., 1960-70, Presbyn. Ch. Found., 1968-70. Mem. Purdue Alumni Assn. (dir. 1957-61), Oriental Inst. Chgo., Antiquarian Soc. Chgo., Audubon Soc., Tau Beta Pi, Pi Tau Sigma, Phi Delta Theta. Presbyterian. Republican. Clubs: Elks;

Lafayette (Ind.) Country; Onwentsia, Old Elm Country (Lake Forest, Ill.); Racquet, Casino (Chgo.); Univ. (Milw.). Home: 1430 N Salisbury St West Lafayette IN 47906 Office: Rostone Corp Rt 52 S Lafayette IN 47902

KNUDTSON, ALLEN DENNIS, banker; b. Whitehall, Wis., May 10, 1947; s. Ingwald Jalmer and Ann (Allen) K.; B.A., U. Wis.-Eau Claire, 1972, postgrad., 1973-74; m. Patricia Ann Goodwyn, Apr. 20, 1968; children—Susan, Nicholas, Katherine. Sales agt. N.Y. Life Ins. Co., Eau Claire, 1972-73; mgmt. trainee Elm-Brook State Bank, Brookfield, Wis., 1974; cashier, 1975—. Unit commr. Boy Scouts Am., 1976. Served with U.S. Army, 1967-70; Vietnam. Mem. Am. Inst. Banking, Bank Adminstrn. Inst. Democrat. Roman Catholic. Club: Edgewood Country (Big Bend, Wis.). Home: 728 N 113d St Wauwatosa WI 53226 Office: 2255 N Calhoun Rd Brookfield WI 53005

KNUTSON, MARLIN JUSTIN, assn. exec.; b. Decorah, Iowa, Mar. 16, 1934; s. Orville A. and Beathe K. (Hovden) K.; B.C.E., Chgo. Tech. Coll., 1960; m. Karen Lee Johnson, June 19, 1958; children—Kari, Katherine, Kevin. With Iowa Dept. Transp., 1954-64; with Portland Cement Assn., 1964-67; with Iowa Concrete Paving Assn., Des Moines, 1967—, exec. v.p., 1967—. Served with U.S. Army, 1953-54. Recipient Certificate of Appreciation, Iowa Dept. Transp., 1976. Mem. Am. Concrete Paving Assn. (dir. 1975-77), Nat. Soc. Profl. Engrs., Iowa Engring. Soc., Nat. Soc. Assn. Execs., Iowa Soc. Assn. Execs., ASCE, Des Moines C. of C. Lutheran. Clubs: Des Moines Engrs., Embassy, Hyperion Field, Elks, (Masons (Shriner). Contbr. articles in field to profl. jours. Home: 2705 Carole Circle Urbandale IA 50322 Office: 1200 35th St West Des Moines IA 50265

KO, PAOSHU, nuclear engr.; b. Shanghai, China, July 13, 1920; s. Kung-cheng and Yun-yu (Che) K.; came to U.S., 1964, naturalized, 1974; Licencie es Scis. and Ingénieur Mécanicien-Electricien, U. l'Aurore, Shanghai, 1942; Docteur en Physique Nucléaire, U. Paris and Inst. Nat. des Scis. et Techniques Nucléaires, 1963; m. Gertrude Sun, Oct. 8, 1950; 1 son, James. Tchr. physics and chemistry sr. high sch. dept. U. l'Aurore, 1942-45; tech. civilian employee U.S. Army Signal Corps, China and Shanghai, 1946; teaching asst. math. Nat. Taiwan U., Taipei, 1947-48; from asst. engr. to chief tech. sect. Taiwan Power Co., 1948-59; research asso. Argonne (Ill.) Nat. Lab., 1957-58; asst. prof. nuclear engring., acting head dept. Nat. Tsing Hua U., Hsinchu, Taiwan, 1959-61; research fellow Centre d'Etudes Nucléaires de Cadarache, St. Paul-lez-Durance, France, 1963-64; asst. prof. physics Manhattan Coll., N.Y.C., 1964-68; sr. engr., fellow engr. nuclear energy systems Westinghouse Electric Corp., Zion, Ill., 1968—. Mem. AAAS, Am. Nuclear Soc., Assn. des Ingénieurs en Génie Atomique. Tech. editor: Outline of Atomic Physics, 1966. Home: 1132 Terre Dr Libertyville IL 60048 Office: 505 Shiloh Blvd Zion IL 60099

KO, SUNG-TAO, surgeon; b. China, June 13, 1940; M.D., Koohsiung Med. Coll., China, 1966. Intern, Mt. Sinai Hosp., Chgo., 1967-68, resident in gen. surgery, 1968-72, fellow in cardiothoracic surgery, 1973-74; clinical instr. surgery Chgo. Med. Sch. Mt. Sinai Hosp., 1974-75, asst. prof. Rush Med. Sch., Mt. Sinai Hosp., 1975—, also asso., attending staff, Mt. Sinai Hosp; courtesy staff Bethesda Hosp.; chmn. dept. surgery Surburban Hosp.; courtesy staff Grant Hosp.; attending staff Good Samaritan Hosp. Fellow Am. Coll. Surgeons, Royal Coll. Surgeons (Can.); mem. Am., Ill., Chgo., medical societies. Office: 30 N Michigan Ave Chicago IL 60602

KOBAK, MATHEW WILLIAM, surgeon; b. Chgo., May 20, 1917; s. Disraeli William and Anna (Braudy) K.; B.S., U. Chgo.; M.D., Rush Med. Sch., 1941; m. Sharon Ann Torreano, Jan. 2, 1976; 1 dau., Caroline Beatrice. Intern, Cook County Hosp., Chgo., 1941-42; resident in pathology Billings Hosp., U. Chgo. Clinics, 1946; resident in surgery Michael Reese Hosp., Chgo., 1947, surg. preceptorship, 1949; sr. asst. resident, fellow Yale U., 1948; practice medicine specializing in surgery Chgo. and Miami, Fla., 1949-76; chief surgeon U.S. VA Hosp., Downey, Ill., 1959; staff VA Lakeside Hosp., Chgo.; asst. clin. prof. surgery Northwestern U. Med. Sch. Served with MC, U.S. Army, 1942-46. Recipient Honors Achievement award Angiology Research Found. and Purdue Frederick Co., 1965-66; diplomate Am. Bd. Surgery. Fellow A.C.S.; mem. AMA, Ill., Chgo. (v.p., past pres. Jackson Park br., councilor Southeastern br.) med. socs. Club: Quadrangle (Chgo.). Author: Studies on the Abdominal Incision, 1965. Contbr. articles to profl. jours. Home: 1700 E 56th St Chicago IL 60637 Office: 333 E Huron St Chicago IL 60611

KOBER, ARLETTA REFSHAUGE (MRS. KAY L. KOBER), ednl. adminstr.; b. Cedar Falls, Iowa, Oct. 31, 1919; d. Edward and Mary (Jensen) Refshauge; B.A., State Coll. Iowa, 1940; M.A., U. No. Iowa; m. Kay Leonard Kober, Feb. 14, 1944; children—Kay Mary, Karilyn Eve. Tchr. high schs., Soldier, Iowa, 1940-41, Montezuma, Iowa, 1941-43, Waterloo, Iowa, 1943-50, 65-67, co-ordinator Office Edn. Waterloo Community Schs., Waterloo, Iowa, 1967—; head dept. co-op. career edn. West High Sch., Waterloo, 1974—. Mem. Waterloo Sch. Health Council; nominating com. YWCA, Waterloo; Black Hawk County chmn. Tb Christmas Seals; ward chmn. ARC, Waterloo; co-chmn. Citizen's Com. for Sch. Bond Issue; pres. Waterloo PTA Council, Waterloo Vis. Nursing Assn., 1956-57, Kingsley Sch. PTA, 1959-60; v.p. Waterloo Women's Club, 1962-63, pres., 1963-64, trustee bd. clubhouse dirs., 1957—; mem. Gen. Fedn. Women's Clubs, Nat. Congress Parents and Tchrs.; Presbyterial world service chmn. Presbyn. Women's Assn.; bd. dirs. Black Hawk County Republican Women, 1952-53, United Services of Black Hawk County, Broadway Theatre League. Mem. AAUW (v.p. Cedar Falls 1946-47), NEA, LWV (dir. Waterloo 1951-52), Black Hawk County Hist. Soc. (charter), Delta Pi Epsilon (v.p. 1966-67), Delta Kappa Gamma. Clubs: White Shrine of Jerusalem, Town (dir.) (Waterloo). Home: 1046 Prospect Blvd Waterloo IA 50701 Office: West High Sch Waterloo IA 50702

KOBLENZ, HOWARD ROBERT, architect; b. St. Louis, Jan. 22, 1943; s. Leonard and Virginia Emily (Papin) K.; student Washington U., St. Louis, 1961-74; children—Lisa, Daniel. Draftsman S. G. Schmidt & Assos., architects, St. Louis, 1963-66, Ralph Fournier, St. Louis, 1966, Jerome Peters, architect, St. Louis, 1966-72; architect, v.p. Jerome Samuel Peters & Howard Robert Koblenz, Inc., St. Louis, 1972-75, Peters, Koblenz and Kreishman, Inc., St. Louis, 1976—. Recipient St. Louis Beautification Commn. award for Renovation Downtown St. Louis Bookstore, 1975. Registered architect, Mo., Ill., Iowa, La. Mem. Constrn. Specifications Inst. Prin. archtl. works include The Plaza at West Port Office and Entertainment Center, St. Louis County, Mo., 1969—. Home: 872 Warwick St St Louis MO 63122 Office: 2025 S Brentwood Blvd St Louis MO 63144

KOBLENZ, MAXINE L., speech and hearing therapist; b. Albany, N.Y., May 23, 1935; Charles and Lillian (Rosen) Levy; Herschel Koblenz, Aug. 12, 1956; children—Marci, Brian. Speech and lang. therapist Cleve. Hebrew Acad., 1977—; originator, coordinator confirmation family learning program Park Synagogue, Cleve., 1977—. Chairperson women's com. Jewish Community Fedn., 1975-77; mem. com. Fedn. for Community Planning, Cleve., 1974-75; chmn. outreach services for youth Jewish Family Service Assn.; mem. womens assn. bd. Coll. Jewish Studies, 1q77—. Mem. Am., Ohio speech and hearing assns. Home: 3175 Falmouth Rd Shaker Heights OH 44122

KOBYLECKY, JOSEPH JOHN, architect, interior designer; b. Chgo., Mar. 26, 1942; s. Miller and Mary Catherine (Stolarczuk/Moran) K.; B.Design in Architecture, U. Ill., 1967; m. Elizabeth M. Kenney, Dec. 21, 1963; 1 dau., Carey Lynn. Draftsman, U. Ill., Chgo., 1964, Kantola-Mizera, Chgo., 1965; architect Hague Richards, Chgo., 1966-73; architect, asso. Warner, Brejcha, Evans & Assos., Homewood, Ill., 1973-75; prin. Joseph J. Kobylecky A.I.A., architect-interior design, Mokena, Ill., 1975—. Corporate sec. Outside/In, Inc., Chgo. Recipient Nat. award Ford Motor Co., 1959. Mem. A.I.A. (chmn. ins. com.), Chgo. Assn. Commerce and Industry, Nat. Trust for Historic Preservation, Mchts. and Mfrs. Club. Home and Office: 184th and Virginia Ln Rural Route #1 Mokena IL 60448

KOCH, ELMER LEONARD, physician; b. Indpls., Apr. 1, 1917; s. Chris and Emma (Lange) K.; A.B., Ind. U., 1939, M.D., 1949; m. Geraldine T. Rea, June 7, 1942 (dec. Nov. 1971); children—Robert L., Byron D., Barbara Joanne; m. 2d, Betty Ann Pollard, Nov. 25, 1972; adopted children—Mary Ann Koch, Frank Koch. Electro-chemist Allison Div. Gen. Motors, 1940-45; intern St. Vincents Hosp., Indpls., 1949-50; practice medicine, specializing in family practice, Danville, Ind., 1950—; med. dir. Ind. Boy's Sch., 1954—; med. adviser Selective Service Bd. 30, Ind., 1954-73; mem. staff Hendricks County Hosp., Danville, Ind., chief staff, 1973-74; staff Meth. Hosp., St. Vincents Hosp., Indpls. Mem. Hendricks County Bd. Health, 1969—. Fellow Am. Acad. Family Practice; mem. Am., Ind., Hendricks County (pres. 1953-55), 7th Dist. (pres. 1955-56) med. assns., Acacia. Methodist (chmn. bd. deacons and trustees 1969—). Mason (K.T.), Rotarian (pres. 1968-69). Home: 301 Bowen St Danville IN 46122 Office: 201 E Columbia St Danville IN 46122

KOCH, GEORGE PAUL, adminstrv. mech. engr.; b. Springfield, Ill., Oct. 21, 1926; s. Fred and Elizabeth (Neuner) K.; B.S. in Mech. Engring., U. Ill., 1951 m. Mary Jean Kruse, June 22, 1952; children—Kathleen Elizabeth, Nina Marlene. Various positions with Allis-Chalmers, Springfield, Ill., 1944-57, project engr., 1957-61, asst. chief engr., 1963-64, chief engr., 1964-66, mgr. engring., 1966-74; project engr. Massey Ferguson Inc., Detroit, 1961-63; mgr. engring. Crawler tractors Fiat-Allis, Springfield, 1974—. Served in USAAF, 1945. Registered profl. engr., Ill. Mem. Soc. Automotive Engrs., U. Ill. Alumni Assn., Ill. Wildlife Fedn., Nat. Rifle Assn. Clubs: Elks, Masons, Springfield Sportsmans. Abe Lincoln Gun. Home: 93 Andover Dr Springfield IL 62704 Office: 3000 S 6th St Springfield IL 62710

KOCH, GUNTER WERNER, dentist; b. Tokiyo, Japan, Nov. 25, 1924; s. Alfred Curt and Anne Margaret (Saul) K.; came to U.S., 1939, naturalized, 1947; student So. Jr. Coll., Chattanooga, 1945; D.D.S., Emory U., 1949; m. Erna Mae Kyle, Sept. 14, 1948; children—Ruth Anne, Gerald Wesley. Pvt. practice dentistry, Bangor, Mich., 1952—. Served with AUS, 1949-52. Mem. Nat. Assn. Seventh Day Adventist Dentists (chpt. pres. 1955). Seventh-day Adventist (elder 1958-75). Kiwanian (pres. 1970-71). Home: Corner M-43 and Apple Blossom Dr Bangor MI 49013 Office: 102 W Monroe St Bangor MI 49013

KOCH, ROBERT LOUIS, II, coating machinery and drying ovens co. exec., city ofcl.; b. Evansville, Ind., Jan. 6, 1939; s. Robert Louis and Mary Loretta (Bray) K.; B.S., U. Notre Dame, 1960; M.B.A., U. Pitts., 1962; m. Cynthia Marian Ross, Oct. 17, 1964; children—David, Kevin, Kristen, Jennifer. Engr. Metalcraft div. George Koch Sons, Inc., Evansville, Ind., 1958-60, Thermal Products div., 1960-62, mgr. Ashdee Div., 1962-64, pres., 1964—; dir., sec., v.p. George Koch Sons, Inc., Evansville, 1973—; dir. Santa Claus Land, Inc., (Ind.), 1972—, Gibbs Aluminum Die Casting, Inc., Henderson, Ky., 1972—; pres. Fesk, Inc., Evansville, 1964—. Mem. Sch. Bd. Screening Com., Evansville, 1971-73; controller City of Evansville, 1976—. Bd. dirs. Jr. Achievement Southwestern Ind., 1969—, ARC, Evansville, 1970—, YMCA, 1973—, Holy Rosary Sch., 1975—; bd. dirs., treas. Cath. Edn. Found., 1973—. Served to 1st lt. U.S. Army, 1960-61. Registered profl. engr., Ind. Mem. Am. Plywood Assn., Screen Printing Assn., Forest Products Research Assn., TAPPI, Soc. Mfg. Engrs., Nat. Soc. Profl. Engrs., Soc. Paint Tech., Nat. Kitchen Cabinet Assn., Tau Beta Pi. Roman Catholic. Clubs: Evansville (Ind.) Country, Kennel, Central Turners, Evansville Petroleum, Tri-State Racquet, Christmas Lake Golf and Country (Evansville). Patentee in field. Contbr. articles to profl. jours. Home: 525 Martins Ln Evansville IN 47715 Office: PO Box 325 10 S 10th Ave Evansville IN 47701

KOCH, WENDELL REUBEN, physicist; b. Phillipsburg, Ohio, Aug. 12, 1909; s. Reuben and Anna Elizabeth (Musselman) K.; B.A. with distinction in Physics, Ohio State U., 1929, M.A., 1932; m. Dorotha Davis, Sept. 6, 1939; children—David Wendell (dec.), Doris Davis Koch Laurini. Physicist, Materials Lab., USAAF, 1929-39; chief physics br. Wright Field, Dayton, Ohio, 1939-51; gen. engr., dep. chief staff plans, then chief resource mgmt. Wright Air Devel. Center, 1951-61; asst. for innovations, dep. for advanced systems planning Aero. Systems div. Wright-Patterson AFB, 1961-69, cons., 1969—; tchr. mechanics Sinclair Coll., Dayton, 1937-38; tchr. advanced optics U. Dayton, 1939; bd. dirs. Honor Seminars Met. Dayton, 1962—. Elder, Dayton Westminster Presbyn. Ch.; enrollment clk. Miami Presbytery, 1974—. Registered profl. engr., Ohio. Fellow AAAS, Ohio Acad. Scis.; mem. Inst. Mgmt. Scis., Am. Inst. Aeros. and Astronautics, Optical Soc. Am., Spl. Libraries Assn., Am. Soc. Info. Sci., World Future Soc. Club: Dayton Torch (pres. 1977). Editorial adviser Beyond The Horizon—Flight in the Atmosphere, 1975-1985, 1966. Address: 560 Monteray Ave Dayton OH 45419

KOCH, WILLIAM ALBERT, recreation exec.; b. Evansville, Ind., Jan. 10, 1915; s. Louis Joseph and Clarice (Ashburn) K.; B.S. in Mech. Engring., Purdue U., 1937; postgrad. U.S. Naval Acad., 1942; m. Patricia Ann Yellig, Dec. 27, 1960; children—William Albert, Kristi I., Daniel L., Philip J., Natalie C. Sales engr. mgr. George Koch Sons, Inc., Evansville, 1937-41, v.p., 1969—; gen. mgr. Santa Claus Land Inc. (Ind.), 1946—; pres. Spencer County Bank, Santa Claus, 1967—, Christmas Lake Agy., Santa Claus, 1968—, Holiday Inn of Jasper (Ind.), 1971—, Carter Clay Corp., Santa Claus, 1969—, Christmas Lake Village, 1966—; Community Natural Gas, 1968—; dir. Spencer Devel. Co., Santa Claus, Richland Devel., Corp. (Ind.). Mem. Gov.'s Commn. To Acquire New Industry for Ind., 1956-65; v.p. Santa Claus Samaritans, 1968—. Pres., Santa Claus Town Bd., 1967—. Trustee St. Meinrod Coll., 1968—. Served to lt. comdr. USNR, 1941-46; PTO. Recipient Outstanding Service to Community award Pres. Nixon, 1972; named Ind. Sachem, Sagamore of Wabash, Rail Splitter, Ky. Col. Mem. Santa Claus C. of C., Christmas Lake Properties Assn. (pres. 1970-71), Lincoln Heritage Trail (dir. 1964—). Methodist. Mason (Shriner). Club: Christmas Lake Golf and Country. Home: Hwy 245 Santa Claus IN 47579 Office: Box 36 Santa Claus IN 47579

KOCH, WILLIAM HENRY, metals co. exec.; b. Wyandotte, Mich., Aug. 12, 1934; s. Anthony Henry and Myrtle Ann (St. Amant) K.; student Internat. Corr. Schs., 1960; m. Marilyn Faye Swain, Dec. 2, 1955; children—Kerry Marie, Denise Ann, Mark William. Metallurgist McLouth Steel Corp., Trenton, Mich., 1952-62; v.p. Metall. Service & Supply, Inc., McKees Rocks, Pa., 1962—; pres. Marko Trucking Corp., New Boston, Mich., 1967—. Served with USN, 1953-54. Mem. Assn. Iron and Steel Engrs., Am. Inst. Mining, Metall. and Petroleum Engrs. Roman Catholic. Club: Grosse Ile Golf and Country. Patentee in field. Home: 3301 Biddle Ave Apt 5-D Wyandotte MI 48192 Office: PO Box 398 McKees Rocks PA 15136

KOCHAR, MAHENDR SINGH, physician, educator; b. Jabalpur, India, Nov. 30, 1943; s. Harnam Singh and Chanan Kaur (Khaturia) K.; came to U.S., 1967; M.B., B.S., All India Inst. Med. Scis., New Delhi, 1965; M.Sc., Med. Coll. Wis., 1972. Intern, All India Inst. Med. Scis. Hosp., New Delhi, 1966, Passaic (N.J.) Gen. Hosp., 1967-68; sr. resident in medicine Allegheny Gen. Hosp., Pitts., 1968-70; fellow in clin. pharmacology Wood VA Hosp., Milw., 1971, attending physician, 1973; fellow in nephrology and hypertension Milwaukee County Gen. Hosp., 1972-73, attending physician, 1973—; attending physician St. Mary's Hosp., 1973—; attending physician St. Michael Hosp., Milw., 1974—, dir. hemodialysis unit, 1975—; asst. clin. prof. medicine and pharmacology Med. Coll. Wis., Milw., 1973-75, asst. prof., 1975-78, asso. prof., 1978—; attending physician St. Joseph's Hosp., Milw., 1975—; cons. nephrology Elmbrook Meml. Hosp., Brookfield, Wis., 1976—; chmn. medicine Northpoint Med. Group, Milw., 1974-75; chief Hypertension Clinic, St. Mary's Hosp., Milw., 1974-75; dir. Milw. Blood Pressure Program, 1975—; dir. Hypertension Clinic, Milwaukee County Downtown Med. and Health Services, 1975—. Fellow ACP, Royal Coll. Physicians Can., Am. Coll. Clin. Pharmacology; mem. AMA, AAAS, Am. Fedn. Clin. Research, Am. Heart Assn., Am. Soc. Nephrology, Am. Soc. Internal Medicine, Am. Med. Writers Assn., Am. Diabetic Assn., Milw. Acad. Medicine. Author: Hypertension Control, 1978. Home: 18630 LeChateau Dr Brookfield WI 53005 Office: 2430 W Wisconsin Ave Milwaukee WI 53233

KOCHELL, RICHARD LEE, gynecologist; b. Williamsport, Ind., Sept. 27, 1937; s. Glen C. and Wilma Jean (Hare) K.; B.S., Purdue U., 1958; M.D., Ind. U., 1962; m. Carol M. Starkey, Aug. 16, 1959; children—Krista, Melissa, Jay-Richard. Intern, then resident in obstetrics and gynecology St. Vincent's Hosp., Indpls., 1962-66; practice medicine specializing in gynecology, Lafayette, Ind., 1966-67, Janesville, Wis., 1967—; mem. staff Mercy Hosp., Janesville, Meml. Hosp., Edgerton, Wis. Served with AUS, 1964-66. Diplomate Am. Bd. Obstetrics and Gynecology. Mem. AMA (Continuing Edn. award 1977), Wis., Rock County med. socs., Am. Coll. Obstetricians and Gynecologists, Am. Soc. Gynecol. Laparoscopists. Republican. Club: Janesville Country. Home: 1000 Laramie Ln Janesville WI 53545 Office: 2020 E Milwaukee St Janesville WI 53545

KOCIAN, MARVIN LEO, fastener mfg. co. exec.; b. Manitowoc, Wis., June 16, 1936; s. Clarence F. and Agnes M. (Muench) K.; ed. U. Wis., 1958; m. Kathryn Ann Miller, Jan. 30, 1965; children—Stephen, Sarah. Personnel mgr. Craft House Plastics, Chgo., 1959-61, Dormeyer Industries, Chgo., 1961-64; sales dept. Carlton Screw Co., Chgo., 1964-69; owner, pres. Komar Screw Chgo., 1969—. Served with U.S. Army, 1957-59. Mem. Chgo. Assn. Commerce and Industry, Chgo. Bolt, Nut and Screw Assn. Roman Catholic. Club: Kenilworth (dir. 1976—). Home: 711 Cummings St Kenilworth IL 60043 Office: 6044 N Pulaski Rd Chicago IL 60646

KOCIOLKO, JOHN STEPHEN, city ofcl.; b. Chgo., Apr. 20, 1949; s. John Ellis and Helen Mary (Rapacz) K.; B.A. with highest honors, De Paul U., Chgo., 1970, M.A. with distinction, 1971; postgrad. Northwestern U., 1971, (Arthur J. Schmitt fellow) Loyola U., Chgo., 1972-75. With fed. research project U.S. Govt., Chgo., 1973; manpower dir. Town of Cicero (Ill.), 1975-77, trustee, 1977—, chmn. Cicero Plan Commn., 1975—; mem. Bd. Edn. Cicero Grade Sch. Dist., 1976-77; lectr. community groups and coll. classes, Chgo., 1972—, Cicero, 1973—. Crusade chmn. Am. Cancer Soc., 1975-76; Cicero community rep. ARC, 1974-76; chmn. Cicero Bicentennial Commn., 1975-76; judge and registrar of election, Cicero, 1972-73; del. Ill. State Republican Conv., 1974, 76; del. county state and nat. Young Republican Convs., 1973-77; commentator St. Mary of Czestochowa Parish, Cicero, 1974—. Ill. State scholar, 1966-70. Mem. Am. Hist. Assn., Hawthorne Businessmen's Assn. (treas. 1973—), Smithsonian Institution Associates, Polish Nat. Alliance, St. Mary of Czestochowa Holy Name Soc. (v.p. 1976-77), Cicero Pastimes Assn., Pi Gamma Mu, Phi Eta Sigma, Delta Epsilon Sigma. Home: 4929 W 31st Place Cicero IL 60650 Office: 4936 W 25th St Cicero IL 60650

KOCOL, RAYMOND JOHN, civil engr.; b. Chgo., May 8, 1927; s. Stanley and Mary (Bodzioch) K.; B.S. in Civil Engring., U. Ill., 1950; M.S., U. Mo., 1954; m. Tommy Sue Moxley, Aug. 14, 1954; children—Stanley, Elizabeth, Katherine, John, David, Jane. Field engr. Ill. Div. Hwys., Elgin, 1950-52; design engr. Western-Knapp Engring. Co., 1952-53; design engr. Bur. Bridges and Buildings, City of Milw., 1954-59, engr. in charge Water Engring. div., 1959—. Served with USMC, 1945-46. Mem. ASCE, Am. Water Works Assn. (chmn. distbn. div. tech. and profl. council 1978—), Nat., Am., Wis. (v.p. Milw. chpt. 1978—) socs. profl. engrs. Roman Catholic. Home: 2923 Marietta St Milwaukee WI 53211 Office: 841 N Broadway St Milwaukee WI 53202

KOCUR, JOHN ANTHONY, mfg. co. exec.; b. Springdale, Pa., May 16, 1927; s. John Alexander and Margaret Teresa (Zbojek) K.; B.A., Duquesne U., 1950; J.D., Georgetown U., 1952; m. Shirley L. Kanaan, Sept. 27, 1952; children—Shirley J., John Anthony, Robert M., Kathy M., Anne L. Admitted to Pa. bar, 1953, Minn. bar, 1971; practiced in Pitts., 1952-64; dep. gen. counsel Crucible Steel Co., Pitts., 1964-69; exec. v.p., gen. counsel Apache Corp., Mpls., 1969—. Served with U.S. Army, 1945-47. Mem. Am., Minn., Pa. bar assns., Delta Theta Phi. Clubs: Wayzata Country, Minneapolis. Home: 18410 29th Ave N Wayzata MN 55391 Office: 1700 Foshay Tower Minneapolis MN 55402

KOEHLER, THEODORE ARMAND, librarian; b. Strasbourg, France, June 23, 1911; s. Albert and Justine (Illig) K.; Licence es Lettres, U. Strasbourg, 1934; S.T.L., U. Fribourg (Switzerland), 1942; postgrad. Vatican Sch. Paleography, 1951-53. Came to U.S., 1969. Joined Soc. Mary; tchr. high sch. Coll. S. Etienne, Strasbourg, France, 1937; ordained priest Roman Catholic Ch., 1941; prof. philosophy Inst. St. Marie, Paris, 1945-51; dir. Marianist Sem., Fribourg, Switzerland, 1954-69; dir., curator Marian Library, U. Dayton (O.), 1969—; dir. Marian Library Pontifical Inst., 1975—. Served to lt. French Army, 1939-41. Mem. Société française d'études mariales (com. mem. 1974), Mariological Soc. Am. (dir. 1970), Academia Mariana Pontificia Internationalis. Author: Le Dieu de Marie, 1959; Mariologia, 6 vols., 1970-75. Editor Marian Library Studies, New Series, 1969—. Contbr. articles to profl. jours. Home: 300 College Park Ave Dayton OH 45469

KOEHN, ENNO, engr., educator; b. Flushing, N.Y., Apr. 29, 1936; s. Theodore John and Anni Margaret (Sievers) K.; B.C.E., Coll. City N.Y., 1957; M.S., Columbia U., 1960; M.C.E., N.Y. U., 1965; summer fellow Mass. Inst. Tech., 1971; Ph.D., Wayne State U., 1975; m. Carol Ann Butcher, Nov. 25, 1967; children—William Enno, James Frederick. Research engr. N.Am. Aviation, Columbus, Ohio, 1957-59; asst. prof. engring. sci. L.I. U., Brookville, N.Y., 1960-66; ednl. specialist IBM, Burlington, Vt., 1966-67; asso. prof. civil engring. Ohio No. U., Ada, 1967-75, prof., 1976—; cons. NSF Sci. Equipment

Program, 1966-67. Mem. steering com. Children's Internat. Summer Villages, 1970-71; campaign chmn., pres. Ada-Liberty Twp. United Way, 1975-77; mem. stewardship com. Ohio synod Lutheran Ch. Am. NSF research grantee, 1964; Fulbright grantee, 1966; Dept. Def. grantee, 1965; registered profl. engr., N.Y., Ohio. Mem. Nat. Soc. Profl. Engrs., Am. Soc. Engring. Edn., ASCE (com. on social and environ. factors in constrn. 1972—, sec. 1976—), AAUP (dir. Ohio No. U. 1971—, treas. 1974—). Clubs: Masons, Rotary. Author: Syllabus for Computer Aided Design, 1970; Computer Programs for Civil Engineering Students, 1972; Physical Testing for Civil Engineers, 1973; Pre Design Cost Estimation Function for Buildings, 1974; Social and Environmental Costs in Construction, 1976; Estimating with Probablistic Unit Costs and Quantities, 1977. Home: Rural Route 1 Box 309 Ada OH 45810 Office: Ohio No U Ada OH 45810

KOENIG, HAROLD HENRY, dental surgeon; b. Edwardsport, Ind., Dec. 14, 1918; s. Herman J. and Nellie M. (Summit) K.; D.D.S., Ind. U., 1940; postgrad. Ohio State U., 1940, Northwestern U., 1940-41; m. Joyce A. Wright, June 17, 1950; children—Keith Alan, Connie Joyce, Penny Sue. Intern, Bellview Gen. Hosp., 1941; practice dental surgery, Rockville, Ind., 1942, 46—; owner Rockville Bowl, 1960—; mem. staff Vermillion County Hosp.; mem. dental staff Rockville Tng. Center. Dist. gov. Ind. DeMolay; gr. lectr. Internat. Order Rainbow for Girls in Ind.; mayor, pres. Rockville Town Bd., 1977—. Served to maj. USAAF, 1943-46. Fellow Royal Soc. Health; mem. U.S. Power Squadron, Am. Legion, Nat. Rifle Assn., Izaak Walton League, ADA, Western Ind. Dental Soc., Ind. Western Horseman's Assn. (pres. 1952), Internat. Soc. Fluoride Research, Ind. Dental Assn., Ind., Rockville (dir. 1968-69) chambers commerce, Psi Omega. Republican. Mem. Christian Ch. Clubs: Masons (32 deg.), Shriners, Elks, Order Eastern Star (worthy grand patron 1968). Address: 220 S College St Rockville IN 47872

KOENIG, RACHEL HOPE, coll. adminstr.; b. Rochester, N.Y., Dec. 28, 1944; d. Fred and Laurena Myrtle (Stiles) K.; B.A., N. Central Bible Coll., Mpls., 1967; postgrad. U. Minn., 1967-68. Coll. recorder N. Central Bible Coll., Mpls., 1967-71, coll. registrar, 1971—. Mem. Upper-Midwest Assn. Collegiate Registrars and Admissions Counselors, Am. Assn. Higher Edn. Am. Assn. Collegiate Registrars and Admissions Officers, Delta Epsilon Chi. Mem. Assembly of God Ch. (jr. high Sunday sch. supt. 1969—, childrens ch. coordinator 1973—). Home: 3806 Toledo Ave N Robbinsdale MN 55422 Office: 910 Elliot Ave S Minneapolis MN 55404

KOEPKE, ROBERT WALTER, med. adminstr.; b. Milw., July 14, 1927; s. Arthur Theodore and Alma Catherine (Luick) K.; student U. Wis., 1964-65, St. Mary's Sch. Nursing, 1965-67, St. Mary's Sch. Anesthesia, 1967-69; m. Audrey C. Shurr, May 21, 1949; children—Robert C., Nancy A., James J., Kurt M., Thomas A. Mgmt. specialist Ford Motor Dealer Devel., Midwest region, 1959; adminstr. Prairie du Chien Gen. Hosp., 1963; adminstr., pres., treas. Holy Cross Hosp., Merrill, Wis., 1969-73; partner Dutchoff & Koepke Anesthesia, Ltd., Dixon, 1973—. Served with Seabees, USNR, 1944-46; PTO. Mem. Am. Assn. Nurse Anesthetists, Merrill C. of C. (dir. 1969-72). Republican. Roman Catholic. Club: Country (dir. 1971—) (Merrill). Home: 1304 Eustace Dr Dixon IL 61021

KOEPP, ALFRED ERNEST, motor co. exec.; b. Barron, Wis., Jan. 8, 1919; s. Ernest Robert and Anna Caroline (Lentz) K.; student La Salle U., 1941, Rice Lake Vocational Sch., 1947; m. Gunvor Christine Moe, Dec. 29, 1942; children—Kathleen (Mrs. Platt), Alfred Ernest, Margaret E. (Mrs. Frederick). With Koepp Trucking Service, Rice Lake, Wis., 1933-55, exec. v.p., 1954-55; agt. N.Am. Van Lines, Rice Lake, 1952-60; with Briggs Transp. Co., St. Paul, 1955—, v.p. claims, 1969—, also dir. Chmn. truck operations for Nat. Def. Transp. Assn. for Stock our Shelters, Mpls. 1963; blood custodian A.R.C., Rice Lake, 1952-60. Served with USAAF, 1942-45. Decorated Bronze Star. Mem. Nat. Freight Claims Council, Minn. Claims Prevention Assn., North Central Claims Council, Assn. Motor Freight Mgrs. (pres. 1963), Mpls., St. Paul traffic clubs, Presbyn. Elk. Home: 3151 Shorewood Dr St Paul MN 55112 Office: 2360 W County Rd C St Paul MN 55113

KOEPPE, RALPH JACOB, social worker, adminstr.; b. Belleville, Ill., Oct. 5, 1912; s. Fred Edward and Anna (Heigele) K.; B.S. in Social Work, Washington U., St. Louis, 1951, M.S.W., 1953; m. Ethel Meyer, Dec. 31, 1941; children—Judith Ann, JoEllen, Ralph Jacob. Warehouse mgr. Ch. World Service, St. Louis, 1946-47; social worker Caroline Mission, St. Louis, 1947-55; exec. dir. Kingdom House, St. Louis, 1955—. Mem. Nat. Assn. Social Workers, Acad. Certified Social Workers. Mem. United Ch. Christ. Home: 10 S Iola Dr Webster Groves MO 63119 Office: 1321 S 11th St Saint Louis MO 63104

KOEPSELL, PAUL LOEL, civil engr., educator; b. Canova, S.D., June 17, 1930; s. Paul Frederick and Anna (Loe) K.; B.S., S.D. State U., 1952; M.S., U. Wash., 1954; Ph.D. (Nat. Sci. fellow), Okla. State U., 1964; m. Delores Lillian Johnson, June 10, 1952; children—Steven, Royal, Pamela. Structural analyst Boeing Airplane Co., Seattle, 1952-57; faculty S.D. State U., Brookings, 1957—, prof. civil engring., 1965—, dir. research and data processing, 1967-75, dir. computing center, 1975—; cons. structural engring. and numerical methods and digital computing. Commr. City of Brookings (S.D.), 1974—. Registered profl. engr., S.D. Mem. Nat. Soc. Profl. Engrs. (nat. dir. 1971—), Assn. for Computing Machinery, ASCE, Am. Concrete Inst., S.D. Engring. Soc., Sigma Xi, Tau Beta Pi, Chi Epsilon. Club: Elks. Home: 1725 Olwien St Brookings SD 57006

KOERNER, WARREN ALDEN, educator, architect, engr.; b. Chgo., Jan. 4, 1907; s. Henry Edward and Dagmar (Larsen) K.; student Eastern Mich. U., 1925-26; B.S. in Architecture, U. Mich., 1931; postgrad. Chgo. Tchrs. Coll., 1949-56, U. Ill., 1951-57; M.A., U. Chgo., 1961; m. Irene Barbara Sinclair, Sept. 3, 1932; children—Warren Sinclair, Beverly Jean. Chief draftsman M.O. Nathan Architect, Chgo., 1924-30; architect Pure Oil Co., Chgo., 1932-34, 37-39, cons., 1940-49; tchr. Chgo. Pub. Schs., 1931-32, 35-37, 39-49, supr. indsl. edn., 1950-65, dir. bur. practical arts and tech. subjects, 1965-72; chmn. ednl. planning Dunbar Vocat. High Sch., Chgo., 1954-55. Mem. explorer com. SW council Boy Scouts Am., 1949-52. Named Outstanding Tchr., Herald Am., Chgo., 1950; recipient Am. Vocat. Assn. Service plaque, 1966, Spl. award Ill. Inst. Tech., 1972; Epsilon Pi Tau Citation 1972; Outstanding Achievement award Ill. Indsl. Edn. Assn., 1972. Registered profl. engr., architect, Ill. Mem. Ill., Ill. Indsl. (pres. 1965-66) edn. assns., Am. (exec. com. ann. conv. 1972), Ill. (dir. 1966, recipient award of merit 1972) vocat. assns., Ill. Council Vocat. Tech. Adminstrs. (v.p. 1959-64, dir. 1971-72), Am. Soc. Engring. Edn., Am. Indsl. Arts Assn., NEA, Nat. Soc. Study Edn., Phi Eta Sigma, Tau Sigma Delta. Mem. United Ch. of Christ. Home: 4608 W 106th St Oak Lawn IL 60453

KOETTING, ROBERT ANTHONY, optometrist; b. St. Louis, Nov. 1, 1925; s. Felix Anthony and Cecilia Catherine (Wuertz) K.; student St. Louis U., 1943-45; D. Optometry, So. Coll. Optometry, 1947; children—Robert Roy, Thomas Tim, Linda Lea (Mrs. Charles Whitney). Practice optometry, St. Louis, 1947—; pres. Eye Lab., Inc., St. Louis, 1964-75. Sec.-treas. Roberts Instrument Co., Inc., 1958-62, Roberts Ophthalmic Instruments, Inc., 1960-62; v.p., Great Rivers Leasing Corp., 1972-75. Mem. adv. com. Family and Children's Service St. Louis, 1970-72. Bd. dirs. St. Louis Optometric Center, 1966-72, pres. bd., 1970-71. Recipient Service award Boys Town Mo., 1959; named Optometrist of the Year, Heart of Am. Contact Lens Soc., 1967. Diplomate Am. Acad. Optometry (chmn. contact lens sect. 1974-76). Fellow Am. Acad. Optometry, S.W. Contact Lens Soc.; mem. Internat. Soc. Contact Lens Specialists, Sociedad Americana Ofthalmologia and Optometria, Am. Optometric Assn. (contact lens chmn.), Heart Am. Contact Lens Soc. (pres. 1966), Am. Soc. Contact Lens Specialists (sec. 1975—). Lion. Contbr. articles to profl. jours. Patentee in field. Home: 230 S Brentwood St Louis MO 63105 Office: 1034 S Brentwood St Louis MO 63117

KOFMAN, SYDNEY, internist, educator; b. Toronto, Can., Dec. 7, 1926; s. Bernard and Bertha (Nachminowitz) K.; M.D., U. Toronto, 1951; m. Doris Sax, Aug. 22, 1959; children—Bonnie, Paul, Clyde, Kerri. Intern U. Ill. Coll. Medicine, 1951-52, resident in internal medicine, 1952-55; asst. prof. medicine, 1960-74, asso. Center for Ednl. Devel., 1970-72; mgr. med. info. Abbott Labs., 1968-70; asst. prof. medicine Rush Med. Coll., Chgo., 1970—; pres. SKM, Ltd., cons. in med. and health edn., Northfield, Ill., 1972—. Diplomate Am. Bd. Internal Medicine. Fellow A.C.P.; mem. AMA, Ill., Chgo. med. socs. Home: 535 Longwood Ave Glencoe IL 60022 Office: 540 Frontage Rd Northfield IL 60093

KOGA, HISAKO MARY, photographer, social worker; b. Sacramento, Aug. 10, 1920; s. Hisakichi Harry and Tsugime (Yoneda) Ishii; B.A., U. Calif., Berkeley, 1942; M.A. (fellow), U. Chgo., 1947; M.F.A., Art Inst. Chgo., 1973; m. Albert M. Koga, June 28, 1947. With Family Service Bur., United Charities Chgo., 1947-52; chief psychiat. social worker Northwestern U. Med. Sch., Chgo., 1952-58; asst. prof. Sch. Social Service Adminstr., U. Chgo., 1959-69; mem. faculty photography dept. Columbia Coll.. Chgo., 1973—; self-employed photographer, Chgo.; exhibited in numerous nat. and local photog. and art exhbns. Bd. dirs. Japanese Am. Service Com., Chgo., 1955-65. Recipient award Ill. Arts Council. 1974. Mem. Soc. for Photog. Edn., Artists League Midwest, Friends of Photography, Nat. Assn. Social Workers, Japan Am. Soc. Chgo. (bd. dirs. 1967—). Home: 1254 Elmdale Ave Chicago IL 60660

KOGAN, BERNARD ROBERT, educator; b. Chgo., May 16, 1920; s. Isaac and Ida (Perlman) K.; A.B., U. Chgo., 1941, A.M., 1946, Ph.D., 1953; m. Irene Wishnewsky, 1962; children—Henry, Sophia, Naomi, Sara. Instr. English, Ind. U., 1946-48; instr. humanities U. Chgo., 1949-51; mem. faculty U. Ill. at Chgo. Circle Campus, 1953—, now prof. English. Author, editor: The Chicago Haymarket Riot: Anarchy on Trial; Darwin and His Critics; Narrative Techniques in the Later Novels of Charles Dickens. Mem. Modern Lang. Assn. Am. Address: 612 Lake Ave Wilmette IL 60091

KOGAN, HERMAN, author, editor; b. Chgo., Nov. 6, 1914; s. Isaac and Ida (Perlman) K.; student Crane Jr. Coll., 1932-33; A.B., U. Chgo., 1936, postgrad., 1936; studied violin with Isidor Braus, harmony and composition with Walter Dellers, 1919-34; m. Alice Marie Schutt, Dec. 28, 1940 (div. 1946); m. 2d, Marilew C. Lowry, Oct. 1, 1950; children—Rick, Mark. High school corr. Chgo. Daily News and Chgo. Evening Post, 1930-32; reporter, rewrite man Chgo. City News Bur., 1935-37; reporter, feature writer, re-write man Chgo. Tribune, 1937-42; with Chgo. Sun, 1942-47, editorial writer, 1943; book editor, drama critic Chgo. Sun-Times, 1951-58; dir. co. relations Ency. Brit., Inc., 1958-61; asst. to exec. editor Chgo. Daily News, 1962-65; asst. gen. mgr. news and newspapers Field Communications Corp., 1965-68; editor Chgo. Sun Times Book Week, 1968-70, Showcase, 1970-75, Show-Book Week, 1975-77; corporate historian Field Enterprises, Inc., Chgo., 1977—. Served with USMC, 1943-46. Recipient Pub. award Geog. Soc. Chgo.; named Chgo. Press Vet. of 1976; Contbn. to Journalism award Am. Newspaper Guild; Adult Edn. Council award Panorama; Communicator of Year award U. Chgo. Alumni Assn. Mem. Chgo. Press Vets. Assn., Art Inst. Chgo. (life), Chgo. Hist. Soc., Nat. Book Critics Circle, Authors Guild, P.E.N., Chgo. Press Club, Phi Beta Kappa (Distinguished Service medal). Jewish. Clubs: Arts, Tavern. Author: (with Lloyd Wendt) Lords of the Levee, 1943; Uncommon Valor, 1947; (with Lloyd Wendt) Bet A Million, 1948; (with Lloyd Wendt) Give the Lady What She Wants, 1952; (with Lloyd Wendt) Big Bill of Chicago, 1953; The Great EB, 1958; (with Lloyd Wendt) Chicago: A Pictorial History, 1959; The Long White Line, 1963; Lending is Our Business, 1966; (with Robert Cromie) The Great Fire: Chicago 1871, 1971; A Continuing Marvel, 1973; The First Century, 1974; (with Rick Kogan) Yesterday's Chicago, 1976; contbr. articles to Nation, New Republic, Liberty, Am. Mag., UN World, Am. Lawn Tennis, Esquire, Fortune, Chgo. History, Ill. Bar Assn. Jour., Firehouse, Midwest. Office: 401 N Wabash Ave Chicago IL 60611

KOGLIN, NORMAN ALFRED, architect; b. Chgo., May 5, 1928; s. Alfred Ernst and Elizabeth Maria (Faselt) K.; B.S. in Architecture, U. Ill., 1951. Architect Skidmore, Owings & Merrill, architects, Chgo., 1957-61; partner Tigerman & Koglin, architects, Chgo., 1961-64; asso. partner C.F. Murphy & Assos., architects, Chgo., 1965-67; pres. Norman A. Koglin Assos., Ltd., Chgo., 1967—; Served with C.E. U.S. Army, 1951-53. Mem. AIA. Clubs: Economic, Monroe, Sports Car of Am. (Chgo.). Office: 111 W Monroe St Chicago IL 60603

KOGUT, KENNETH JOSEPH, cons. engr.; b. Chgo., Dec. 3, 1947; s. Joseph Henry and Estelle Theresa (Swiercz) K.; student Lewis Coll., 1966-68; B.M.E., U. Detroit, 1971, M.E., 1972, postgrad, 1972—; m. Darlene Agnes Jedlicka, June 15, 1974. Mech. engr. Fluor Pioneer Inc., Chgo., 1972-73, cons. engr., 1973-75; project mgr. Engring. Corp. Am., Chgo., 1976-77; cons. pub. utilities Haskins & Sells, Chgo., 1977—. Sloan fellow, 1971-73. Mem. Am. Nuclear Soc., Nat. (asso.), Ill. (asso.) socs. profl. engrs., Blue Key, Tau Beta Pi, Pi Tau Sigma, Polish Nat. Alliance. Address: 5232 W 170th Pl Oak Forest IL 60452

KOH, BYUNG CHUL, educator; b. Seoul, Korea, Apr. 6, 1936; s. Young Whan and Young Sil (Huh) K.; came to U.S., 1959, naturalized, 1971; LL.B., Seoul Nat. U., 1959; M.A., Miami U. at Oxford, O., 1960; M.P.A., Cornell U., 1962, Ph.D., 1963; m. Hae Chung Chun, Feb. 4, 1967; children—Michelle, Christopher. Reporter, Korean Republic English daily, Seoul, 1959; asst. prof. govt. La. State U., Baton Rouge, 1963-65; asst. prof. polit. sci. U. Ill. at Chgo., 1965-68, asso. prof., 1968-72, prof., 1972—. Served to 2d lt. Korean Air Force, 1957-59. U. Ill. faculty research fellow, 1966, 68; NSF fellow, 1970; grantee Social Sci. Research Council and Am. Council Learned Socs., 1974. Mem. Assn. Asian Studies, Am. Soc. Pub. Adminstrn., Am. Polit. Sci. Assn., Am. Soc. Internat. Law. Author: The United Nations Administrative Tribunal, 1966; The Foreign Policy of North Korea, 1969. Contbr. articles to profl. jours. Home: 4207 Woodland Ave Western Springs IL 60558 Office: Dept Polit Sci U Ill Chicago IL 60680

KOH, SEVERINO LEGARDA, mech. engr., educator; b. Manila, Philippines, Jan. 8, 1927; s. Enrique Legarda and Felisa (Un) K.; came to U.S., 1954, naturalized, 1972; student U. Philippines, Manila, 1945-47; B.S. in Meteorology, N.Y. U., 1950; B.S. in Mech. Engring., Nat. U., Manila, 1952; M.S., Pa. State U., 1957; Ph.D. in Engring. Sci., Purdue U., 1962; m. Paz L. Ongjoco, July 19, 1952; children—Amelita P. Koh-Luncsford, Bernadette, Cynthia, Dorothy (dec.), Evangeline. Meteorologist, Philippine Weather Bur., Manila, 1948-54; research asst. Johns Hopkins U., 1954-55; instr. in engring. mechs. Pa. State U., 1955-57; instr. in engring. sci. Purdue U., 1957-59, vis. research asso., 1962-64, asst. prof., 1964-66, asso. prof., 1966-72, prof., 1972—, asst. head div. interdisciplinary engring. studies, 1977—; research asso. Gen. Tech. Corp., West Lafayette, Ind., 1959-61; mech. engr. Gen. Electric Co., Louisville, 1961-62; vis. prof., research asso. Tech. U. Clausthal, Clausthal-Zellerfeld, Germany, 1968-69; vis. prof. Tech. U. Karlsruhe (Germany), 1969, U. Bonn (Germany), 1974-75; dir. Internat. Intertech.; Balik scientist, Philippines, 1976. Recipient Outstanding Teaching award Standard Oil Found., 1967, Outstanding Prof. award Sigma Gamma Tau, 1968, Humboldt award, Germany, 1974, certificate of appreciation Soc. Engring. Sci., 1974; Purdue U. Shreve Hall faculty fellow, 1976; NSF grantee, 1971-74; U.S. Army Research Office grantee, 1972-75. Mem. Soc. Engring. Sci. (founding sec. 1963, sec. 1963-68, dir. 1970-73), ASME, Am. Soc. Engring. Edn., Am. Acad. Mechs., Soc. Rheology, Philippine Profl. Assn., Purdue Filipino Assn., Sigma Xi, Sigma Pi Sigma, Sigma Gamma Tau. Presbyterian. Contbr. numerous articles on continuum mechs., viscoelasticity, elasticity, rheology, composite materials, micormechs., geotech. engring. to tech. jours.; editor Engring. Sci. Perspective, 1976—. Home: 208 E Navajo St West Lafayette IN 47906 Office: Sch of Mech Engring Purdue U West Lafayette IN 47907

KOHEL, JEROME JOSEPH, accountant; b. Menominee, Mich., July 14, 1944; s. George Frank and Anna Barbara (Seifert) K.; B.B.A., U. Mich., 1966; m. Elizabeth Alma Ouellette, July 20, 1968. Accountant, Peat, Marwick, Mitchell & Co., Detroit, 1966-71; mem. finance staff Uniroyal, Inc., 1971-72; corp. controller Master-Craft Corp., Kalamazoo, 1972—, sec., 1975—, asst. treas., 1975-77, treas., 1977—. Bd. dirs. Gull Lake Area United Way; mem. Ross Twp. Planning Commn. Served with USAF, 1967-69. Mem. Mich. Assn. C.P.A.'s, Am. Inst. C.P.A.'s, Kalamazoo Mgmt. Assn. Clubs: Gull Lake Country, Rotary. Columnist Richland Jour. Home: 8226 Lake Vista Richland MI 49083 Office: 831 Cobb Ave Kalamazoo MI 49007

KOH-GUEVARRA, ARSENIA, physician; b. Manila, Philippines, Mar. 14, 1939; d. Eloy T. and Graciana (Saez) Koh; M.D., U. Santo Tomas, Manila, Philippines, 1963; m. Nicanor M. Guevarra, Feb. 15, 1969; children—Nicanor M., Ronald Michael. Intern, Albert Einstein Med. Center, Phila., 1964; resident in internal medicine, Wayne State U., Detroit, 1965-67, fellow in nephrology, 1967-69, clin. instr. Med. Sch., 1970—; physician in charge renal unit, Hutzel Hosp., Detroit, 1970-72; practice medicine specializing in internal medicine, Mt. Clemens, Mich., 1972—. Diplomate Am. Bd. Internal Medicine. Mem. AMA., Am. Soc. Nephrology, Mich. State, Macomb County med. socs., Nat. Kidney Found. Home: Box 33 Mount Clemens MI 48043 Office: 22070 S Nunnely St Mount Clemens MI 48043

KOHLAN, WILLIAM GEORGE, lawyer; b. Mpls., Feb. 13, 1910; s. George and Anastasia (Leschisin) K.; LL.B., Mpls. Coll. Law (William Mitchell Coll. Law), 1932; m. Helen Marie Peterson, Nov. 25, 1947. Admitted to Minn. bar, 1932; practice in Mpls., 1932—; counsel and dir. misc. groups. Mem. Hennepin County Central com. Democratic Farmer Labor party, 1948-67; ward chmn. and ward vice chmn., 1954-59, del. Dem. Farmer Labor convs., 1948-76. Served in USAF, World War II. Recipient medal of Merit, Air Force Assn., 1957; Distinguished Service award Minn. State Bar Assn., 1959, City of Mpls., 1975. Mem. Minn., Hennepin County bar assns., Air Force Assn. (past nat. v.p.), Minn. Wing (AFA) (past comdr.), Air Force Hist. Found., DAV (past judge adv. Minn. dept., past vice comdr. Mpls. chpt.), Mpls. Joint Vets. Council (past pres.). Home: 1610 5th St NE Minneapolis MN 55413 Office: Gorham Bldg Minneapolis MN 55402

KOHLMAN, KENNETH HAROLD, elec. co. exec.; b. Detroit; s. Harold Gustav and Ellen Eleanor (Nordstrom) K.; B.A., Mich. State U., 1958; m. Betty Buell, Oct. 17, 1959; 1 dau., Holly Michelle. Underwriter, Kemper Ins. Co., Chgo., 1958-59; asst. to sales mgr. Brunner & Lay, Inc., Franklin Park, Ill., 1959-60; advt. adminstr. Zenith Sales Corp., Chgo., 1960-69; nat. conv. mgr. Motorola, Schaumburg, Ill., 1969—. Mem. Nat. Trade Show Exhibitors Assn. (past dir.), Soc. Co. Meeting Planners (past dir.), Delta Sigma Pi. Club: Kiwanis. Office: 1301 E Algonquin Schaumburg IL 60172

KOHN, FRANK SOLIS, pharm. co. exec.; b. Bristol, Pa., June 21, 1942; s. Frank S. and Julia E. (Hutchinson) K.; certificate med. tech. Franklin Sch. Sci. and Art, Phila., 1961; A.S., Trenton Jr. Coll., 1963; B.A., N.J. State Coll., 1969; M.S., Drexel U., 1972; postgrad. U. Wis., 1972-75. Virologist, N.J. Dept. Health, Trenton, 1963-69; microbiologist Schering Corp., Cream Ridge, N.J., 1969-70, prodn. mgr., Madison, Wis., 1970-74, mfg. mgr., 1975-76, ops. mgr., 1976—. Cons. microbiologist Bio Search, Inc., 1971-72. Advisor for mgmt. tng. U. Wis., 1977. Recipient Clin. Chem. award Franklin Sch. Sci. and Art, 1961, Pres. award Trenton Jr. Coll., 1963. Mem. Am. Med. Technologists (writing award 1976), Am. Soc. Microbiologists, Am. Acad. Microbiology. Odd Fellow. Club: University. Contbr. articles to profl. jours. Home: PO Box 3184 Madison WI 53704 Office: PO Box 7130 Madison WI 53707

KOHN, RUSSEL FERDINAND, mining cons.; b. Mohawk, Mich., July 17, 1909; s. George F. and Cora (Saam) K.; B.M.E., Mich. Coll. Mining and Tech., 1933; m. Mae Bant, July 17, 1937; 1 dau., Mary Allison. Tchr., Cleveland Cliff Mining Co., Mich., 1936; engr. Pickands Mather & Co., Duluth, Minn., 1937-43; supt. operation, 1947-52, supt. pelletizing, 1952-59; v.p., mgr. Marcona Mining Co., Peru, 1959-64; resident mgr. Goldworthy Mining Proprietary Ltd., 1964-66; cons. engr., mgmt. cons. on mine and iron ore benification, 1967—. Mem. Am. Inst. Mining Engrs. Republican. Club: Masons. Research in devel. of verticle shaft pellitizing furnace and grinding taconite. Address: 810 3d Ave NW Mandan ND 58554

KOHNEN, DAVID ALPHONSE, lawyer; b. Cin., Jan. 7, 1937; s. Ralph B. and Helen H. (Hillenbrand) K.; A.B., Georgetown U., 1959; J.D., U. Cin., 1962; m. Christina C. Sutphin, June 13, 1964; children—Jennifer L., David H., Christopher W. Admitted to Ohio bar, 1962, D.C. bar, 1962; practiced in Washington and Cin.; partner Kohnen & Kohnen. Mem. exec. bd. Cin. Community Chest, 1971-75; mem. Hamilton County Hosp. Commn., 1969—. Bd. dirs. Our Lady of Mercy Hosp. Club: University (Cin.). Home: 4735 Hill Top Ln Cincinnati OH 45243 Office: 4500 Carew Tower Cincinnati OH 45202

KOHNEN, RALPH BERNARD, JR., lawyer; b. Cin., Oct. 22, 1935; s. Ralph Bernard and Helen Rose (Hillenbrand) K.; student U. Fribourg (Switzerland), 1955-56; A.B., Georgetown U., 1957; LL.B., U. Cinn., 1960; m. Nancy Marie Stone, Aug. 20, 1960; children—Ralph William and Allen Stone (twins), Nancy Marie, Daniel Hillenbrand. Admitted to Ohio bar, 1960; partner Kohnen & Kohnen; mem. Ohio Ho. of Reps., 1963-68; mem. Cin. City Council, 1968-73, vice mayor, 1971-72, chmn. finance com., 1971. Dir. Fed. Home Loan Bank Cin. Mem. Cin.-Hamilton County criminal justice regional planning unit Council of Govts., 1972-73, pres., 1972; bd. govs. United Service Orgn., Inc., 1975—. Trustee Cin. Assn. for Blind, Cin., Arthritis Found. Southwestern O.; former trustee Community Improvement Corp. Served with AUS, 1960-61. Mem. Am., Ohio,

Cin. bar assns. Republican. Roman Catholic. Clubs: Cincinnati Country, Racquet, University (Cin.). Home: 2959 Wold Ave Cincinnati OH 45206 Office: Carew Tower Cincinnati OH 45202

KOHR, ROLAND ELLSWORTH, hosp. adminstr.; b. Middletown, O., Dec. 22, 1931; s. Roland Meredith and Mildred (Brandeberry) K.; B.S., U. Cin., 1954; M.H.A. with distinction, Northwestern U., 1959; m. Hilda Louise Scherz, Sept. 6, 1952; children—Linda (Mrs. Paul C. Harper), Roland M., Jeffrey S. Adminstrv. asst., purchasing dir. Bethesda Hosp., Cin., 1958-60; adminstr. William S. Major Hosp., Shelbyville, Ind., 1960-66; adminstr. Bloomington (Ind.) Hosp., 1966—; dir. Ind. Hosp. Service, Inc., Mutual Hosp. Ins., Inc. Pres. Shelby County Mental Health Assn., 1964. Bd. dirs. United Fund of Monroe County; pres. Monroe County United Way. Served to lt. USAF, 1954-56. Recipient Mary H. McGaw award and grant, 1959; Distinguished Service award Shelby County Jr. C. of C., 1965; Named Boss of Year, Monroe County chpt. Am. Bus. and Profl. Women Assn., 1970. Mem. Am. Coll. Hosp. Adminstrs., Ind. Hosp. Assn. (dir. 1970—, chmn. elect), Shelby County C. of C. (v.p. 1965), Am. Legion, Delta Tau Delta (v.p. 1949), Beta Gamma Sigma. Rotarian. Home: 2989 Bankers Dr Bloomington IN 47401 Office: Bloomington Hosp Bloomington IN 47401

KOHRING, GENE WILLIAM, mfg. co. exec.; b. Wood County, Ohio, Feb. 27, 1930; s. Donald Hiser and Olive Mae (Jacobs) K.; student Bowling Green (Ohio) State U., 1953, Brooks Inst. Photography, Santa Barbara, Calif., 1958; m. Shirley Elizabeth Hanf, Nov. 7, 1953; children—Mark D., Darla J., Eric M., Leanne E. With photog. lab. Brush Brillum Co., Toledo, 1948-51; assemblyman Owen Ill. Co., Toledo, 1953; instr. Brooks Inst. Photography, 1953-58; instrumentation photographer Winton Hill Tech. Center, Procter & Gamble Co., Cin., 1958—; cons. in field. Sunday sch. tchr. Hope Lutheran Ch., Cin.; active local Boy Scouts Am., Jr. Achievement. Served with U.S. Army, 1951-53. Mem. Soc. Photog. Instrumentation Engrs., Profl. Photographers Am. Republican. Home: 1647 Millville Shandon Rd Millville OH 45013 Office: 6300 Center Hill Rd Cincinnati OH 45224

KOIVULA, STEVEN JOHN, accountant; b. Waukegan, Ill., June 19, 1949; s. Einar Arnold and Bertha Marie (Vanka) K.; B.A., Augustana Coll., 1971; M.B.A., No. Ill. U., 1973; m. Julie Ann Carlsen, May 29, 1971. Instr. dept. accountancy No. Ill. U., DeKalb, 1973-74; auditor Ernst & Ernst, Chgo., 1974—. C.P.A., Ill. Mem. Ill. Soc. C.P.A.'s, Am. Inst. C.P.A.'s. Republican. Lutheran. Home: 1208 Edwards Ave Saint Charles IL 60174

KOKONIS, NICHOLAS DEMETRIOS, psychologist; b. St. Basil, Tripolis, Greece, June 30, 1941; s. Demetrios and Heliostalachti (Prassas) K.; came to U.S., 1962, naturalized, 1970; teaching certificate Pedagogic Acad., Greece, 1961; B.A., Roosevelt U., 1965, M.A., 1967; Ph.D., Ill. Inst. Tech., 1971; m. Popi Torolopoulou, July 18, 1965; children—Julie, Marian and Christiana (twins). Asst. prof. psychology George Williams Coll., 1968-74; pvt. practice psychology, Skokie, Ill., 1971—. Sch. psychologist Northfield Twp. High Sch. 225, Glenview, Ill., 1974—; cons. psychologist, dept. psychiatry Ill. Masonic Med. Center, Chgo., 1970—, Ill. State Dept. Corrections, Chgo., 1970, La Salle County Mental Health Center, Ottawa, Ill., 1970-71; psychology intern Elgin (Ill.) State Hosp., 1966-67, staff psychologist, 1967-68; community psychology intern Madden Zone Center, Maywood, 1969-70; part-time instr. Ill. Inst. Tech., 1970-73, Roosevelt U., 1972-75, Barat Coll., 1972-73; part-time lectr. St. Dominic Coll., 1966-67, Chgo. City Coll., 1967-68. Vol. youth cons. Ct. of Minors, Greece, 1961-62, YMCA, 1970-71. Mem. Am., Ill. psychol. assns., Hellenic Med. Soc. Ill., Hellenic Profl. Soc. Ill. Author: Poetic Excursions, 1967; Christos' Journal; also articles. Office: 64 Old Orchard Suite 606 Skokie IL 60076

KOKOROPOULOS, PANOS, educator; b. Thessaloniki, Greece, Aug. 10, 1927; s. Constantine and Mary (Carvonides) K.; came to U.S., 1958, naturalized, 1965; B.S. in Chemistry, U. Thessaloniki, 1955; M.S. in Chemistry, U. Dayton, 1964; Ph.D., U. Akron, 1972; m. Carolyn A. Curran, Mar. 26, 1960; children—Mary, Constantine, George. Research chemist U. Dayton Research Inst., 1963-65; asst. prof. chem. tech. U. Akron, 1965-71, dir. Center for Info. Systems, 1965-69, mgr. academic systems and programming, 1969-71, research asso. dept. civil engring., 1971-72; asso. prof. urban and environ. engring., So. Ill. U., Edwardsville, 1973—; cons. in field. Asst. dist. commr. Greek Boy Scouts, 1945-56; mem. troup com. Cahokia Mounds council Boy Scouts Am., 1976—. Served to 2d lt. Greek Army, 1950-52. Fullbright-Smith-Mundt grantee, 1958-59; Guggenheim grantee, 1959-60; Ford Found. grantee, 1959-60. Mem. Solar Energy Soc., Am. Chem. Soc., ASCE, ASTM, Ill. State Acad. Sci. Democrat. Greek Orthodox. Author: (with A. Fatemi, A. Amirie) Political Economy of the Middle East, 1970. Contbr. articles in field to profl. jours. Home: 456 Buena Vista Edwardsville IL 62025 Office: Southern Illinois University at Edwardsville Box 65 Edwardsville IL 62026

KOLAR, OTTO MICHAEL, ednl. adminstr.; b. Berwyn, Ill., Mar. 17, 1940; s. Otto Henry and Emma Elizabeth (Fratrick) K.; A.A., Morton Jr. Coll., 1960; B.S., No. Ill. U., 1962; M.S. in Edn., 1965, Ed.D., 1975; m. Mary Jane Burnett, Aug. 13, 1966; children—Robin Lynn, Deon Michael. Tchr. math. Ridgewood High Sch., Norridge, Ill., 1964-69; instr. math. Triton Coll., River Grove, Ill., 1969-73, asst. dean, 1973—. Mem. adminstrv. bd. Prince of Peace Methodist Ch., Elk Grove Village, Ill., 1971-74; active suburban div. So. Christian Leadership Conf., 1972—. Mem. Assn. for Gen. and Liberal Studies, Ill. Council Community Coll. Adminstrs., Community Coll. Assn. for Instrn. and Tech., Am. Ednl. Research Assn., Phi Delta Kappa. Home: 2500 Lakeview Apt 1805 Chicago IL 60614 Office: Triton College 2000 5th Ave River Grove IL 60171

KOLATALO, WALTER WLADIMIR, surgeon; b. Lwow, Poland, Dec. 11, 1921; s. Nicholas and Madalene (Charkiw) K.; came to U.S., 1952, naturalized, 1957; student U. Lwow Med. Faculty, 1939-44, U. Giessen (Germany) Med. Faculty, 1944-45; M.D., Phillips U., Marburg, Germany, 1948; m. Mirdza Zeilers, Feb. 11, 1947; 1 son, Ihor Jurij. Asst. chief physician Gen. Hosp. Ansbach (Germany), 1948-50; cons. physician Internat. Refugee Orgn., Bremen-Lesum, Germany, 1950-51; intern St. Anthony Hosp., Rockford, Ill., 1952-53, resident in surgery, 1953-55, mem. med. staff, 1955—; resident in surgery VA West Side Hosp., Chgo., 1958-61; practice medicine specializing in surgery, Rockford, Ill., 1961—; mem. staff Swedish Am. Hosp., Rockford Meml. Hosp.; pres. St. Anthony Hosp., 1974-75. Served as maj., M.C., U.S. Army, 1956-57. Diplomate Am. Bd. Surgery. Fellow A.C.S.; mem. Ill., Winnebago County med. socs., AMA, Pan Am. Med. Assn. Catholic. Clubs: Victory Tennis, Wagon Wheel Key. Home: 321 Rockcliff Dr Rockford IL 61108 Office: Doctors Park 5670 E State St Rockford IL 61108

KOLB, ALAN FOSTER, leasing co. exec.; b. New Orleans, Feb. 2, 1944; s. Oris Foster and Ruth (Burns) K.; B.A. in Polit. Sci., Mich. State U., 1965, M.A., 1968; J.D., Ind. U., 1971; m. Linda Louise Derry, June 11, 1967. Residence halls staff Mich. State U., 1965-67; market research analyst Blue Cross, 1968-69; v.p., gen. counsel Sch. Bldgs., Inc., Indpls., 1969—; admitted to Ind. bar, 1972. Mem. Am., Ind., Indpls. bar assns., Ind. U., Mich. State U. alumni assns., Phi Delta Phi. Republican. Episcopalian. Club: Columbia (Indpls.). Home: 3029 Lehigh Ct Indianapolis IN 46268 Office: Ista Center 150 W Market St Indianapolis IN 46204

KOLB, JOSEPH WILBUR, state ofcl.; b. near Princeton, Ind., Jan. 5, 1902; s. Joseph and Margaret M. (Phillips) K.; A.B., Ind. U., 1926, A.M., 1931; postgrad, Evansville Coll., 1948-52, Ind. State Tchrs. Coll., 1950—, Oakland City Coll., 1952—; m. Mary Elizabeth Wolfe, June 21, 1922; children—Unalea (Mrs. Andrew Robb), Mary Lu (Mrs. Thomas Orr). Tchr., adminstr. pub. schs., Neb., Mo., Ill., Ind., 1923-68. Mem. White House Conf. on Aging; mem. Ind. Joint Commn. on Aged and Aging, Nat., Ind., Gibson County ret. tchrs. assns. Del. Dem. Nat. Conv., 1956, 60, mem. platform com., 1972-74. Mem. N.E.A., Am. Assn. Ret. Persons, Wabash Valley Assn. Methodist. Mason (32deg. Shriner); mem. Order Eastern Star. Home: Box 396 Princeton IN 47670

KOLENDA, FRANK DONALD, profl. photographer; b. Grand Rapids, Mich., Mar. 24, 1945; s. Frank Albert and Estelle Stephanie (Jaworowski) K.; B.A., Aquinas Coll., 1967; M.A., Central Mich. U., 1971; student Winona (Ind.) Sch. Profl. Photography, 1973-74; m. Mary Jo Williamson, Aug. 19, 1967; children—Kristine Marie, Steven Donald, William Francis. Tchr. Carson City (Mich.) Elementary Sch., 1967-69, Crystal (Mich.) Elementary Sch., 1969-76; profl. photographer, 1968—; propr. Kolenda Photography, Edmore, Mich., 1968—, Grand Rapids, Mich., 1976—. Recipient spot news award Mich. Press Photographers Assn., 1967; award Mich. Collegiate Press Assn., 1966; recognition in news photography Detroit Press Club, 1969. Mem. Profl. Photographers Am., Carson-City-Crystal Edn. Assn. (pres., negotiator 1972-73). Lion (pres. 1972-73). Home: Route 2 Pine Grove Rd Elmore MI 48829

KOLESAR, EDWARD STEVEN, JR., air force officer; b. Canton, Ohio, June 24, 1950; s. Edward Steven and Margaret Jean (Skolosh) K.; m. Elinor Kropac, Oct. 2, 1976; B.S. magna cum laude in Electronic Engring., U. Akron (Ohio), 1973; M.B.A., Midwestern U., Nebr., 1976; postgrad. Air Force Inst. Tech., 1977—. Coop. engring. student Hoover Co., North Canton, Ohio, 1970-73; commd. 2d lt. USAF, 1973, advanced through grades to capt., 1976; sci. and tech. intelligence analyst Electronics System Div., Hanscom AFB, Mass., 1973-76, instr. systems acquisition and mgmt. sch., 1974-76. Mem. Soc. Am. Mil. Engrs., IEEE, Air Force Assn., Tau Beta Pi, Sigma Tau, Eta Kappa Nu, Omicron Delta Kappa. Decorated Air Force Commendation medal. Office: Air Force Inst Tech/ENA Area C Bldg 640 Wright Patterson AFB OH 45433

KOLFLAT, TOR DAGFIN, cons. design engr.; b. Chgo., Nov. 21, 1925; s. Alf and Bergljot Dagmar (Saetter) K.; B.M.E., Purdue U., 1950, M.M.E., 1954; m. Luetta Robertson, Dec. 17, 1949; children—Karen, Kim, Gail, Leif. Mech. engr. Commonwealth Edison Co., Waukegan, Ill., 1951-54; partner Sargent & Lundy, Chgo., 1954—. Served with USAF, 1943-45. Registered profl. engr., Fla., Ill., Ind., La., Mich., Ohio, Tex. Mem. ASME, Am. Nuclear Soc., IEEE, Atomic Indsl. Forum, Western Soc. Engrs. Clubs: Elks; Union League, Univ. (Chgo.); Westmoreland Country (Wilmette, Ill.). Contbr. articles to profl. jours. Home: 365 Elder Ln Winnetka IL 60093 Office: 55 E Monroe St Chicago IL 60603

KOLLASCH, IRENE HAINES, hosp. purchasing adminstr.; b. Bancroft, Iowa, Dec. 12, 1920; d. Archie Orval and Minnie (Redemske) Haines; A.B., Am. U., 1939; m. Cletus Elbert, Sept. 12, 1945 (dec. 1958); children—Patrick, Mark, Mary; m. 2d, Robert Kollasch, Oct. 5, 1961; 1 dau., Kay. With Met. Life Ins. Co., Algona, Iowa, 1940-43; with Kossuth County Hosp., Algona, 1971—, now purchasing agt. and material mgr. Served with U.S. Navy, 1943-46. Mem. Beta Sigma Phi. Office: Kossuth County Hosp Algona IA 50511

KOLLES, BERTRAND ALOY, optometrist; b. Pierz, Minn., Sept. 25, 1931; s. Albert K. and Sophia (Weidenbach) K.; student St. John's U., 1949-51; B.S., Chgo. Coll. Optometry, 1953, D. Optometry, 1954; m. Irene M. Kuelbs, Dec. 27, 1956; children—Mary, Julie, Joseph, Brett, Camille. Practice optometry, Benson, Minn., 1954-56, St. Paul, 1958—, Roseville, Minn., 1962-73. Served with AUS, 1956-58. Fellow Nat. Eye Research Found., Internat. Soc. Orthokeratology; mem. Am., Minn. optometric assns., Met. (pres. 1971), St. Paul (pres. 1962) optometric socs. Contbr. articles to profl. jours. Inventor gauge for corneal measurements. Home: 965 Lydia Ave St Paul MN 55113 Office: 1790 N Lexington Ave St Paul MN 55113

KOLLINS, MICHAEL JEROME, automotive engr.; b. St. Clairsville, Ohio, Mar. 20, 1912; s. Michael Arthur and Mary Ann (Peck) K.; student City Coll. Detroit, 1928-32; m. Julia Dolores Advent, Jan. 16, 1934; children—Michael Lewis, Richard, Laura. Chief sect. service engring. and tech. data Studebaker-Packard Corp., Detroit, 1945-55; mgr. tech. services Chrysler Corp., Detroit, 1955-64, mgr. warranty adminstrn., 1964-68, mgr. Highland Park Service center, 1968-75; pres. Kollins Design & Engring., Detroit, 1975—. Pres., Oakland (Mich.) U. Chorus, 1969-71; active Birmingham (Mich.) Chorale, Meadowbrook (Mich.) Festival Chorus; mem. adv. bd. Am. Security Council, 1972—. Served with USN, 1942-45. Mem. U.S. Auto Club (vice-chmn. tech. com. 1971—), Am. Automobile Assn. (contest bd.), Soc. Automotive Engrs., Engring. Soc. Detroit (industry ambassador 1972—). Contbr. articles to profl. publs. Designer racing cars, 1932-39, sports cars, spl. luxury vehicles, 1951—, automotive performance and safety devices, 1946—. Home: 821 Highwood Dr Bloomfield Hills MI 48013 Office: Kollins Design & Engring PO Box 214 Bloomfield Hills MI 48013

KOLLKER, JOHN JENNINGS, mortgage co. exec.; b. Evansville, Ind., Oct. 29, 1933; s. John Henry and Marie Josephine (Jennings) K.; B.S., Ind. U., 1955; m. Marie Claire Goodspeed, July 2, 1957; children—Michael, Cynthia, John, Susan. With Assos. Fin. Services Corp., South Bend, Ind., 1955-72, asst. v.p., 1968-72; with Percy Wilson Mortgage & Fin. Corp., Chgo., 1972—, v.p. 1977—. Mem. Mortgage Bankers Assn. Club: Kiwanis. Home: 645 Salem Ct Palatine IL 60067 Office: 221 N LaSalle St Chicago IL 60601

KOLMIN, KENNETH GUY, lawyer, accountant; b. N.Y.C., Oct. 22, 1951; s. Frank William and Edith (Pisk) K.; B.S. summa cum laude in Accounting, State U. N.Y., Albany, 1973; J.D. cum laude, Syracuse U., 1975, M.S. in Accounting, 1975. Intern, Peat, Marwick, Mitchell & Co., C.P.A.'s, Albany, N.Y., 1971-73; adj. instr. Syracuse (N.Y.) U., 1974, teaching asst., 1974-75; admitted to Ill. bar, 1976; tax cons., tax dept. Arthur Young & Co., Chgo., 1976—. Mem. Am., Ill., Chgo. bar assns., Justinian Law Soc., Beta Alpha Psi, Beta Gamma Sigma, Phi Alpha Delta. Home: 40 E Oak St Apt 1807 Chicago IL 60611 Office: One IBM Plaza Suite 3500 Chicago IL 60611

KOLONKO, JOSEPH JOHN, JR., mech. engr.; b. Ashland, Wis., Apr. 17, 1949; s. Joseph John and Eva Frances (Jendrysko) K.; student Northland Coll., 1967-69; B.M.E., U. Wis., Madison, 1972. Research and devel. engr., gear tech. and noise control Cin. Milacron Inc., 1972—. Mem. ASME (Paper award 1974), Soc. Automotive Engrs., Nat. Corvette Owners Assn. Roman Catholic. Home: 3478 Hazelwood Ave Cincinnati OH 45211 Office: 4701 Marburg Ave Cincinnati OH 45209

KOLOSKI, HELEN SPALDING, church exec.; b. Marshfield, Wis., Sept. 19, 1927; d. Thomas Davitt and Helen (Flannigan) Spalding; B.A. magna cum laude, Lawrence U. Wis., 1949; m. Marion J. Koloski, Feb. 2, 1952; children—Paul Joseph, Mary Frances, Peter Andrew, Margart Anne, Martha Jane. Social worker, Catholic Social Services, Columbus, Ohio, 1950-52, 55-56; dir. Marian House rest home for elder, Columbus, 1969-70, Marian House Inc. home for unwed mothers, Columbus, 1970-71; dir. pub. relations Catholic Charities/Social Concerns, Columbus, 1971-75; dir. pub. relations, info. Diocese of Columbus, 1975-77; asst. dir. devel. Ohio Dominican Coll., Columbus, 1977—. Mem. pub. relations com. Ohio Easter Seal, communications com. Ohio Council Churches, pub. relations com. United Way, Communications dept. Cath Conf. Ohio. Ohio State U. scholar, 1949-50. Mem. Pub. Relations Soc. Am., UNDA, Phi Beta Kappa. Roman Catholic.

KOLSRUD, ROGER, musician; b. Minnewaukan, N.D., Dec. 20, 1927; s. Henry G. and Anna (Moen) K.; B.A., Concordia Coll., 1949; postgrad. Syracuse U., 1962, N.D. U., 1965-67; m. Ruth Bierbaum, Mar. 19, 1951; children—Scott (dec.), Timothy, Kari Lynn. Music and sci. tchr., Lynd, Minn., 1949-51; dir. music Mayville (N.D.) Pub. Sch., 1952-71; chmn. music Mayville-Portland High Sch., 1971—; coordinator music and fine arts N.D. Dept. Pub. Instruction; music festival clinician, adjudicator, N.D., Minn., S.D. Mem. N.D. Profl. Rights and Responsibilities Commn., 1964—; mem. N.D. Republican sub-com. fin., 1966—; precinct committeeman, 1968—. Named Tchr. of Year for N.D., 1975. Mem. N.D. Edn. Assn. (pres. 1962), NEA (nat. dir. 1968-77, mem. program and budget com. 1970-73, tchr. rights com. 1974-76, N.D. dir. 1961-77), Am. Legion (post comdr. 1965), VFW, Mayville Civic and Commerce Assn., Music Educators Nat. Conf., N.D. Music Educators (dir. 1959—), Vol. Fire Dept. Lutheran (chmn. congregation 1974-76, dir. ch. choirs). Clubs: Masons, Elks, Eagles. Editor, pub. N.D. Music Educator, 1961—. Home: 428 1st Ave NE Mayville ND 58257

KOLSTAD, JOHN HAESLOOP, ceramic engring. cons.; b. Elmira, N.Y., Feb. 20, 1916; s. Charles A. and Rose (Haesloop) K.; B.S. in Ceramic Engring., Alfred U., 1939; postgrad. Carnegie Inst. Tech., 1940; m. Hazel I. Dreessen, Sept. 28, 1967. Refractory sales trainee Carborundum Co., Perth Amboy, N.J., 1940-41; tunnel kiln operator Am. Radiator & Standard San. Co., Tiffin, Ohio, 1940; tunnel kiln design engr. Allied Engring. div. Ferro Corp., Cleve., 1941-43, constrn. engr., 1946-50, sales engr., 1953-55; brick plant supt. Ragland Brick Co. (Ala.), 1950-53; grinding machinery sales engr. Mfr.'s Equipment Co., Dayton, Ohio, 1954-57; chief design engr. tunnel kiln Interkiln Engring. Co., Atlanta, 1955-57; refractory sales and service engr. Plibrico Sales & Service Co., Atlanta, 1957-59; mfg. research engr. Lockheed Aircraft Co., Marietta, Ga., 1959-60; mfg. devel. engr. Boeing Co., Wichita, Kans., 1960-71, tool liaison man, 1971; ceramic cons., Wichita, 1971—. Sanitarian City-County Health Dept., Wichita, 1971-74. Served with C.E., AUS, 1943-46; ETO. Decorated Bronze Star; registered profl. engr., Kans., Ga. Mem. Am. Ceramic Soc., Inst. Ceramic Engrs., Kans. Engring. Soc., Soc. Aerospace Materials and Process Engrs. (chmn. 1970), Wichita Amateur Radio Club (pres. 1968-69), Am. Legion. Designer pathol. incinerator for Kans. Humane Soc. Contbr. articles on ceramic engring. to profl. publs. Address: 1139 Governeour Ct Wichita KS 67207

KOMIE, STEPHEN MARK, lawyer; b. Chgo., Jan. 22, 1949; s. Leonard and Miriam Ruth (Wineberg) K.; B.A., U. Ariz., 1970, M.A. in Russian History, 1972; J.D., DePaul Coll., Chgo., 1976. Patrolman, Tucson Police Dept., 1972-73; intern Fed. Defender Program, Chgo., 1975-76; admitted to Ill. bar, 1976; individual practice law, Chgo. and Buffalo Grove, Ill., 1976—. Mem. Am. (recipient Silver Key 1976), Chgo., Ill. bar assns., Catholic Lawyers Guild, Chgo. Bar Lawyers Reference Plan, Nat. Assn. Criminal Def. Lawyers, Chgo. Council Fgn. Relations, Mid-N. Assn., Wedgewood Soc. Home: 515 W Belden St Unit 14 Chicago IL 60614 Office: 53 W Jackson Blvd Chicago IL 60604 also 1 Ranch Mart Plaza Buffalo Grove IL 60090

KOMJATHY, ANTHONY TIHAMER, educator; b. Hungary, May 29, 1921; s. Oscar and Margaret K.; came to U.S., 1957, naturalized, 1963; Ph.D., Loyola U., Chgo., 1972; m. Edith Niedzielsky, Dec. 26, 1948; 1 dau., Edith. Served with Hungarian Army, 1949-51; polit. prisoner, 1951-53; various positions, 1956-67; prof. Barat Coll., Lake Forest, Ill., 1967-73, Loyola U., Chgo., 1973-76, now faculty Miss. U. Women, Columbus. Nat. Endowment Humanities grantee, 1972. Mem. Am. Hist. Assn., AAUP. Roman Catholic. Author: The Crises of France's East Central European Diplomacy, 1933-38, 1976. Contbr. articles in field to profl. jours. Home: 7347 N Hoyne St Chicago IL 60645

KOMMER, NORMAN BUD, banker; b. Spencer, Wis., Mar. 29, 1943; s. Norman August and Erma Mary (Stargardt) K.; student Wausau Tech. Inst., 1962; m. Virginia L. Gray, Dec. 29, 1962; children—James, Debbie, Robin, Tammi, Jonalee. Teller, auditor, Central State Bank, Marshfield, Wis., 1963-68; auditor Marquette Nat. Bank, Mpls., 1968-70; asst. cashier Brooklyn Park State (Minn.), 1970-71, Central State Bank, Marshfield, 1971-74: pres. Abbotsford State Bank (Wis.), 1974—. Elder Christ Lutheran Ch. Mem. Am. Inst. Banking (bd. dirs. Wis. chpt. 1q76), Abbotsford C. of C. (v.p. 1977), Ind., Wis. bankers assns., Upper Midwest Agrl. Conf. Home: 205 Elm St W Abbotsford WI 54405 Office: Hwy 13 and 29 Abbotsford WI 54405

KOMOSA, ADAM ANTHONY, educator; b. Pitts., Aug. 24, 1913; s. Simon and Kathrine K.; diploma Advanced Inf. Officers Sch., 1947; certificate The Army Signal Sch., 1952; diploma Air Groun Ops. Sch., 1952; A.A., U. Fla., 1960; B.A., Fla. State U., 1962, M.A., 1963, Ph.D., Inter-American U., 1967; m. Naomi Evlyn Beard, Feb. 11, 1949; children—Katherine Louise, Adam Anthony. Commd. as pvt. U.S. Army, 1932, advanced through grades to lt. col., 1951; radio operator, China, 1935-38; parachute inf. co. comdr, plans and tng officer, World War II, 1942-46; sr. regimental adviser Korean Mil. Advisory Group, 1950-52; gen. staff officer plans and ops., 1956-58; camp dir. nat. rifle and pistol matches, Camp Perry, Ohio, 1957. ret., 1958; prof. history No. Mich. U., 1968—; advisor Am. Security Council. Decorated Silver Star, Bronze Star with Oak Leaf Cluster, Purple Heart and others. Recipient certificate of appreciation U.S. Army Chief of Staff, 1957; Presidential commendation, Sygman Rhee, Pres. of Republic of Korea, 1951; certificate of Merit, Korean Army, 1951; certificate of Recognition, Polish Guard, 1955. Mem. Am. Hist. Assn., Am. Assn. Advancement of Slavic Studies, Polish Am. Hist. Assn., The Kosciuszko Found., Soc. Wireless Pioneers, Phi Kappa Phi, Phi Alpha Theta, Alpha Kappa Psi. Clubs: Marquette Golf and Country, Rotary Internat., Elks. Author: Third Flank Over Sicily, 1963; La Batalla de la Angostura, 1967. Home: 12 Fairway Dr Marquette MI 49855 Office: Northern Michigan University Marquette MI 49855

KOMPASS, EDWARD J., editor; b. Jersey City, Dec. 22, 1926; s. Edward and Margaret (Doran) K.; M.E., Stevens Inst. Tech., 1951; m. Amelia M. Heubel, Sept. 22, 1951; children—Christine (Mrs. Kevin Scully), Daniel, Andrew, Timothy, Matthew, Julie. Jr. engr. Intelectron, Inc., N.Y.C., 1950-52; engr. De Florez Co., N.Y.C., 1952-54; asst. editor Control Engring., McGraw-Hill Pub. Co., N.Y.C., 1954-60, asso. editor, 1960-65; mng. editor control engring.

div. Dun-Donnelley Pub. Co., N.Y.C., 1965-72, editor, Chgo., 1972—. Served with USNR, 1944-46. Home: 793 Burton Dr Lake Forest IL 60045 Office: 222 S Riverside Plaza Chicago IL 60606

KONCELIK, JOSEPH ARTHUR, indsl. designer, educator; b. Islip, N.Y., Apr. 20, 1940; s. Arthur Adam and Marie (Anderson) K.; B. in Indsl. Design, Pratt Inst., 1962; M.A., Stanford, 1963; postgrad. (Fulbright scholar), Royal Coll. Art, London, 1965-66; m. Anastasia Hyrkiel, July 11, 1964; children—David Alban, Joseph Peter. Designer Gen. Motors Corp., Warren, Mich., 1963-65; indsl. design cons. Fairchild Hiller Corp., Bethpage, N.Y., 1966; indsl. designer William Lansing Plumb & Assos., N.Y.C., 1967; asst. prof. Coll. of Human Ecology, Cornell U., Ithaca, N.Y., 1967-73; asso. prof. Coll. of the Arts, Ohio State U., Columbus, 1973—. Adj. prof. indsl. design R.I. Sch. of Design, Providence, 1971, 72, 73, 74. Mem. Gerontological Soc., Assn. for the Study of Man-Environ. Relations, Indsl. Design Edn. Conf. (chmn. graduate edn. and research com.). Contbr. articles on human ecology and indsl. design to profl. publs. Home: 1638 Dollivor Rd Worthington OH 43085 Office: Ohio State Univ Columbus OH 43210

KONDOROSSY, ELIZABETH DAVIS, spl. educator; b. East Canton, Ohio, Dec. 23, 1910; d. William David and Lottie Pearl (Hall) Davis; B.A., Oberlin Coll., 1934; postgrad. (Wall St. Fund Newspaper Fund fellow) U. Mich., 1962; M.Ed., Kent State U., 1968, certificate in spl. edn., 1970; m. Leslie Kondorossy, Jan. 19, 1962. Tchr., East Canton Elementary Sch., 1934-37, Brewster (Ohio) High Sch., 1939-42, Sunbeam Sch. for Crippled Children, Cleve., 1952—; organist First Hungarian Ref. Ch., Cleve., 1948—; pvt. tchr. music, specializing in handicapped children, Cleve., 1952—; organizer, dir. handbell choirs for crippled children and geriatrics; lectr. nat. workshop Am. Guild English Handbell Ringers. lectr. in field. Sec. Cleve. Council Journalism Advisors. Martha Holden Jennings grantee, 1970-71. Mem. Am. Coll. Musicians (faculty), Am. Guild Organists, Council Exceptional Children, Music Educators Assn., Internat. Soc. Music Educators, Nat. Bus. Edn. Assn., Music Tchrs. Nat. Assn. Contbr. articles to profl. jours.; poet librettist for 10 1-act operas, numerous art and religious songs. Home: 14443 E Carroli Blvd University Heights OH 44118

KONDOROSSY, LESLIE, composer, educator; b. Bratislava, Czechoslovakia, June 25, 1915; s. Vincze and Anna (Veress) Toth; came to U.S., 1951, naturalized, 1957; student Franz Liszt Acad. Music, 1936-42, Western Res. U., 1959-63, Sophia U., Japan, summer 1974; m. K. Elizabeth Davis, Jan. 19, 1962. Cantor, Calvinist Ch., Kispest, Hungary, 1932-37; violinist in various orchs., Kispest, 1934-35, Ujpest, 1936-37, Budapest, 1938-43; music critic Film-Theatre-Music mag., Budapest, Hungary, 1938-41; choir dir., organist, church. Regensburg, Germany, 1948-51; tchr. music Cultural Arts Bur., Cleve., 1954-71; appeared in Opera of the Air program, radio sta. WSRS, Cleve., 1955-56; tchr. music, composer Cleve., 1951-61, University Heights, O., 1962—. Major works include The Kossuth Cantata, 1952; (cantata) Lament of the Lord, 1952; (operas) The Pumpkin, 1954, The Voice, 1954, The Midnight Duel, 1955, Two Imposters, 1955, Unexpected Visitor, 1956; String Quartet No. 1, 1960; (cantata) New Dreams for Old, 1961; Concerto for Trombone, 1961, (oratorio) Son of Jesse, 1967; (children's opera-oratorios) Poorest Suitor, 1967, Shizuka's Dance, 1969; Meditation for Organ, 1972, others. Recipient Decoration Medal award Hungarian World Fedn., 1968, (with wife) Martha Holden Jennings Found. award, 1970. Mem. Cleve. Fedn. of Musicians, Am. Guild of Organists, Nat. Music Tchrs. Assn., Nat. Opera Assn., Am. New Opera Theatre Soc. (founder 1953, pres. 1954-58). Address: 14443 E Carroll Blvd University Heights OH 44118

KONICEK, FRANK JOSEPH, gastroenterologist; b. Chgo., June 15, 1938; s. Frank Joseph and Julia (Wisniewski) K.; B.S., Loyola U., 1959, M.D., 1963; m. Marimarie Limbert, June 24, 1961; children—Mark, Annmarie, Daniel, Colleen, Katie. Intern, St. Francis Hosp., Evanston, Ill., 1964-65; fellow in gastroenterology VA, practice medicine specializing in gastroenterology, Chgo., 1971—; pres. Gastroenterology Assos., Chgo.; mem. staff Hines (Ill.) VA Hosp., 1971—, asst. sect. chief gastroenterology, 1971—; mem. staff Ill. Masonic Med. Center, Chgo., 1972—, dir. med. edn., 1972-75, dir. continuing med. edn., 1975—, chief gastroenterology sect., 1972—; instr. medicine Loyola U., 1967-71; instr. U. Ill., Chgo., 1971-72, clin. asst. prof., 1974—. Diplomate Nat. Bd. Med. Examiners, Am. Bd. Internal Medicine. Mem. A.C.P., AMA, Chgo., Ill. med. socs., Chgo. Soc. Gastroenterology, Am. Gastroenterology Assn. Home: 455 Oak Knoll Rd Barrington Hills IL 60010 Office: Illinois Masonic Medical Center 836 W Wellington St Chicago IL 60657

KONIE, JOSEPH C., orthodontist; b. Chgo., Jan. 6, 1932; s. Joseph and Sophie Konieczny; B.S., U. Ill., 1955, D.D.S., 1957, M.S., 1963; 1 dau., Lisa Joy. Practice dentistry specializing in orthodontics, Oak Lawn, Ill., 1963—; instr. U. Ill. Coll. Dentistry, Chgo., 1960-61. Sec. med. field Polands Millenium of Christianity, 1966. Mem. Chgo. Soc. Orthodontists (dir. 1972), Dental Arts Club Chgo. (treas. 1966), Am. Assn. Orthodontists, Ill., Midwestern socs. orthodontists, Orthodontics Alumni Assn., ADA, Ill., Chgo. dental socs., Delta Sigma Delta. Club: Beverly Country. Served to capt. SAC, 1957-59. Home: 4 Cour St Tropez Palos Hills IL 60465 Office: 9501 S Central Ave Oak Lawn IL 60453

KONIE, ROBERT B., real estate and ins. co. exec.; b. Chgo., May 14, 1936; s. Joseph and Sophie (Malkiewicz) Konieczny; B.S., Loyola U., Chgo., 1958, postgrad., 1961. Owner, R.B. Konie & Co., Evergreen Park and Hickory Hills, Ill., 1966—. Served with AUS, 1959-61. Mem. Nat., Ill. assns. realtors, S.W. Suburban Bd. Realtors, Chgo. Bd. Underwriters. Roman Catholic. Club: Elks. Office: 3100 W 95th St Evergreen Park IL 60642

KONIKOW, ROBERT BERNARD, writer, editor, cons.; b. Boston, Apr. 9, 1914; s. Moses Joseph and Rose (Bernard) K.; A.B. cum laude in Math., Harvard U., 1932; m. Ella Klaiman, Sept. 4, 1938; children—Robert Moses, Tobi Harriet (Mrs. Curtiss Hoffman). With various govt. agys., 1940-43; free-lance writer, Washington, 1946-56; editor Advt. & Sales Promotion, Chgo., 1956-69; creative dir. Abelson-Frankel, Chgo., 1969-71; free-lance writer, Chgo., 1971—. Tchr. writing and editing Northwestern U., 1961-63, U. Chgo., 1959-60, Downers Grove (Ill.) Adult Evening Sch., 1963-68. Pres. Downers Grove Friends of the Library, 1968-71, Chgo. Film Council, 1968-71; treas. Community Concert Assn., 1967-69; treas. Midwest Seminar on Videotape and Film, 1972-76, pres., 1977—. Served with AUS, 1943-45. Club: Harvard of Chgo. Author: Discover Historic America, 1973; Sight 'n' Sound Techniques For Sales Meetings and Sales Presentations, 1973; (with Frank E. McElroy) Communications for the Safety Professional, 1975; How to Participate Profitably in Trade Shows, 1976. Home: 4528 Sterling Rd Downers Grove IL 60515

KONKLE, JANET MARIE EVEREST (MRS. ARTHUR JACKSON KONKLE), author, educator; b. Grand Rapids, Mich., Nov. 5, 1917; d. Charles Arthur and Minnie (Koegler) Everest; student Grand Rapids Jr. Coll., 1935-37, U. Mich., 1937-38; B.S., Western Mich. U., 1939; m. Arthur Jackson Konkle, Feb. 14, 1941; children—Kraig Everest, Jill Marie, Dan Jackson. Primary tchr., Grand Rapids, Mich., 1939-60; tchr. kindergarten Forest Hills, Collins Sch., 1960-61, Hillcrest Sch., Grand Rapids, 1961—. Judge cat pet shows, 1961-67, 71. Tchr. photography YWCA, 1953. Recipient numerous photographic awards nat. contests; named Photographer of Year Grand Rapids Camera Club, 1951, 53. Mem. NEA, Mich., Grand Rapids edn. assns., Amateur Photo Club (pres. 1950-52), Grand Rapids Camera Club (sec. 1950-53), Grand Rapids (pres. 1965-67, treas. 1975-77), Mich. (pres. 1969-71) assns. childhood edn., Council of Performing Arts for Children (v.p. 1966-68, dir. 1969-71), Women's Nat. Book Assn., Western Mich. Cat Soc. (pres. 1963), Story Spinners League Grand Rapids, Delta Delta Delta (pres. chpt. 1964-65), Delta Kappa Gamma (chpt. pres. 1968-70). Author: Once There was a Kitten, 1951, 62; The Kitten and the Parakeet, 1952; Christmas Kitten, 1953, 64; Easter Kitten, 1955; Tabby's Kittens, 1956; J. Hamilton Hamster, 1957; Susie Stock Car, 1959; The Sea Cart, 1961, 64; Schoolroom Bunny, 1965; The Raccoon Twins, 1972. Home: 1360 Oakleigh Rd NW Grand Rapids MI 49504

KONNYU, LESLIE, ret. geographer, cartographer, author; b. Tamasi, Hungary, Feb. 28, 1914; s. Joseph and Mary (Polhamer) K.; came to U.S., 1949, naturalized, 1955; diploma Tchrs. Tng. Coll., Hungary, 1933, 44; B.Mus. Edn., St. Louis Mus. and Arts Coll., 1954, diploma cartography, 1957, M.A. in Geography, 1965; m. Elizabeth Gelencser; children—Ernest, Gabriella Konnyu Heizer, Joseph Z. Tchr. elementary sch., Hungary, 1936-42; secondary sch. tchr., Hungary, 1942-44; dir. Refugee Sch., Austria, 1944-49; ch. organist St. Peter's Ch., Jefferson City, Mo., 1949-51; lab. technician Sch. Medicine, Washington U., St. Louis, 1951-55; cartographer Def. Mapping Agy., St. Louis, 1955-73. Dir. Hungarian Radio Program, 1952-58; founder Am. Friends Hungarian Culture, 1959-64; dir. Am. Hungarian Welfare Com., 1956-64; pres. Am. Hungarian Cultural Club, 1967-68; chmn. T.S. Eliot Monument Com., 1972—. Recipient Distinguished Community Service award, St. Louis, 1956; certificate merit lit., London, 1972, certificate merit poetry, 1974. Mem. St. Louis Writers Guild (treas. 1968, historian 1974), St. Louis Poetry Center (v.p., dir. 1973), World Fedn. Hungarian Artists (archivist 1974), Internat. P.E.N., Mo. Writers Guild, Mo. Hist. Soc., Internat. Poetry Assn., Internat. Acad. Poets. Author 23 books in Hungarian, 1 in French, 1 in German; also author: Bond of Beauty, 1959; Against the River, 1961; A History of American Hungarian Literature, 1962; Eagles of Two Continents, 1963; Modern Magyar Literature, 1964; John Xantus, Hungarian Geographer in America, 1965. Editor: Historical Highlights of Cartography, 1965; Hungarians in the U.S.A., 1967; Collected Poems, 1968; Condensed Geography of Hungary, 1971; Acacias: Hungarians in the Mississippi Valley, 1976; editor St. Louis Hungarian weekly, 1957-58; American Hungarian Rev., 1963-74. Home: 5410 Kerth Rd St Louis MO 63128

KONTOGIANNIS, GEORGE J., architect; b. Martins Ferry, O., Oct. 21, 1940; s. John and Athena (Sagia) K.; B.Arch., Ohio U., 1963. With Kellam & Foley, architects, Columbus, O., 1964; project architect Ohio State Architect's Office, 1965; pres. G.J. Kontogiannis & Assos., Columbus, 1965—; dir. Roy-Kon, Inc., Columbus; pres. Colonial Am. Devel. Corp., Columbus, 1971—, G.J. Kontogiannis, Inc., constrn., Columbus, 1973—. Mem. A.I.A., Ohio Architects' Soc., Columbus Jaycees, Wheeling Jaycees, Columbus Apt. Assn., Ahepa. Republican. Mem. Greek Orthodox Ch. Home: 380 S 5th St Columbus OH 43215

KOOI, EARL ROBERT, food co. exec.; b. Morrison, Ill., June 13, 1917; s. Robert and Ethel (Hook) K.; A.B., Central Coll. Ia., 1939; Ph.D. in Chemistry, Iowa State U., 1946; m. Mary B. Barnhart, May 19, 1945; children—Janet, John, Thomas, Robert. Sect. leader research CPC Internat., Inc., Argo, Ill., 1945-61, asst. dir. research, 1961-65, dir. exploratory research, 1965-67, dir. biochem. research, 1967-77, dir. fundamental biochem. research, 1977—. Mem. Am. Assn. Cereal Chemists, Am. Chem. Soc., Am. Soc. for Microbiology, AAAS, Am. Inst. Chem. Engrs., Sigma Xi, Phi Lambda Upsilon, Alpha Chi Sigma. Contbr. chpts. to books, articles to profl. jours. Patentee in field. Home: 1136 S Stone Ave LaGrange IL 60525 Office: CPC Internat Inc Box 345 Argo IL 60501

KOOISTRA, WILLIAM HENRY, psychologist; b. Grand Rapids, Mich., May 20, 1936; s. Henry P. and Marguerite (Brinks) K.; B.A., Calvin Coll., 1957; Ph.D., Wayne State U., 1963; m. Jean Cornelia Heynen, Aug. 24, 1957; children—Kimberly Lynn, William Peter, Kristen Jean, Allison Carol. Psychology intern Lafayette Clinic, Detroit, 1961-62; instr., Wayne State U., Detroit, 1962-63; staff psychologist Pine Rest Christian Hosp., Grand Rapids, 1964, chief psychologist, 1965-67; pvt. practice as clin. psychologist Kooistra, Monsma & Lin, cons. psychologists, Grand Rapids, 1967—. Founder, Project Rehab., Grand Rapids, 1968, bd. dirs., 1969—, pres. bd., 1972-74. Mem. exec. com. Kent County Democratic party, 1969-73, precinct del., 1969—; chmn. Kent County Muskie-for Pres. Com., 1972. Mem. Am. Soc. Psychologists in Pvt. Practice (dir. 1968-75, sec. 1973-75), Christian Assn. Psychol. Studies (v.p. 1968-70), Am., Mich. (dir. 1967-69, 73—, legislative chmn. 1973—), Grand Rapids Area (pres. 1968) psychol. assns., Mich. Soc. Cons. Psychologists (dir. 1969-71). Mem. Christian Reformed Ch. (deacon 1970-72). Club: Press (Grand Rapids). Home: 812 Rosewood Dr SE Grand Rapids MI 49506 Office: 3300 Burton SE Grand Rapids MI 49506

KOPEL, DAVID, educator, psychologist; b. Czenstachowa, Poland, Feb. 22, 1910; s. Joseph and Shandel Mary (Motel) K.; came to U.S., 1913, derivative citizen, 1924; B.S., Northwestern U., 1930, M.S., 1934, Ph.D., 1935; postgrad. Vienna (Austria) Psychoanalytic Soc., 1948-49, U. Chgo., 1950-52. Psychologist, instr. Northwestern U., 1934-38, Chgo. Tchrs. Coll., 1938-43; dir. U.S. Dependent Schs. System, Austria, 1946-47; tchr. edn. specialist U.S. Allied Commn. Austria, 1947-49; faculty Chgo. State U., 1949—, dir. Grad. Sch., 1954-61, prof. psychology and edn., 1959-76, emeritus, 1976—. Faculty, Columbia U., summer 1938, Alameda (Calif.) Guidance Center, summer 1941, Ohio State U., 1942, U. Ill., 1950; cons. in field; pvt. practice psychotherapy, 1952—. Served to 1st lt. U.S. Army, 1943-46. Diplomate Am. Bd. Profl. Psychology. Fellow Am. Psychol. Assn.; mem. Ill. Psychol. Assn., Am. Orthopsychiat. Assn., A.A.U.P., Internat. Comparative Edn. Soc., Internat. Reading Assn. Co-author: Reading and the Educative Process, 1938; Mental Hygiene and Modern Education, 1939; Progress in Clinical Psychology, 1953. Co-editor Ill. Schs. Jour., 1966-68. Contbr. articles to profl. jours. Home: 2231 E 67th St Chicago IL 60649

KOPLIN, ALLEN NORMAN, pub. health physician; b. Hartford, Conn., May 15, 1919; s. Samuel and Belle (Black) K.; B.A., N.Y. U., 1939; M.D., Middlesex Med. Sch., 1943; M.P.H., U. Minn., 1947; m. Pauline Ipsen, July 1, 1946; children—Michael Dean, Kathie Lynn. Intern, Knickerbocker Hosp., N.Y.C., 1943-44; mem. quarantine div. Farm Labor Program, USPHS, Yakima, Wash., 1944-48; area med. adminstr. United Mine Workers Health and Retirement Funds, Birmingham, Ala., 1948-63, Beckley, W.Va., 1963, Knoxville, Tenn., 1963-70, dep. dir., Washington, 1971-75; asso. dir. health Ill. Dept. Pub. Health, Springfield, 1975—; field prof. community medicine Meharry Med. Sch., 1964-70; instr. pub. health edn. U. Tenn., 1964-70; asso. prof. health care planning So. Ill. U., 1975—. Diplomate Am. Bd. Preventive Medicine. Mem. Am., Ill. pub. health assns., Inst. Medicine Chgo. Clubs: Island Bay Yacht (Springfield), Severn Sailing Assn. (Annapolis, Md.). Home: 2953 Battersea Point Springfield IL 62704 Office: 535 W Jefferson St Springfield IL 62761

KOPP, CARL ROBERT, advt. agy. exec.; b. Detroit, Apr. 8, 1921; s. Andrew Russell and Bertha (Hecke) K.; student Ill. Inst. Tech., Advanced Mgmt. Program, Harvard; div.; children—Deborah Ann, Barbara Jane, Jeffrey. Various sales and advt. positions Marathon Corp., 1947-54; account exec. Needham, Louis & Brorby, 1954-55; successively account exec., account supr., mgmt. dir., exec. v.p., pres. Leo Burnett U.S.A., Chgo., 1955-75; pres. Leo Burnett Co., Inc., Chgo., 1975-78, chief exec. officer, 1975—, chmn. bd., 1978—. Mem. Chgo. Crime Commn. Served with AUS, World War II; Korea. Decorated Purple Heart, Bronze Star with V. Home: 505 N Lake Shore Dr Chicago IL 60601 Office: Leo Burnett Co Inc Prudential Plaza Chicago IL 60601

KOPP, LEONARD LEWIS, city ofcl.; b. Kewanee, Ill., Aug. 3, 1917; s. William Ludwig and Selma Marie (Kersten) K.; B.A., U. Iowa, 1957, M.A. (Old Gold fellow), 1958; m. Edna G. Martin, Apr. 7, 1939; 1 dau., Ruth Ann. With Fed.-Mogul Service, Chgo., 1938-49, salesman, 1948-49; parts mgr. Vertrees Motor Co., Iowa City, Iowa, 1949-54; adminstrv. analyst, City of Phoenix, 1958-59, adminstrv. asst. to city mgr., 1959-60; city mgr., Mound, Minn., 1960—. Tchr. municipal adminstrn. and techniques supervision Phoenix Evening Coll., 1959-60. Chmn., West Hennepin County Planning Group, 1968-69. Bd. dirs. Hennepin County League Municipalities, 1969-70, Met. League Municipalities. Served with USNR, 1941-45. Mem. Internat. City Mgmt. Assn., Minn. City Mgrs. Assn. (pres. 1971-72), Met. Area Mgrs. Assn., Am. Legion. Lutheran (pres. 1968-69, 74-75). Rotarian. Home: 2128 Centerview Lane Mound MN 55364 Office: 5341 Maywood Rd Mound MN 55364

KOPPEL, LOWELL B., chem. engr., educator; b. Chgo., Sept. 13, 1935; s. Maurice G. and Mynn (Schultz) K.; B.S., Northwestern U., 1957, Ph.D., 1960, M.S., U. Mich., 1958; m. Barbara J. Parker, June 12, 1957; children—Steven, Sharon, Michael, Lowell. Instr., Calif. Inst. Tech., Pasadena, 1960-61; asst. prof. Sch. Chem. Engring., Purdue U., 1961-64, asso. prof., 1964-67, prof., 1967—, also head sch. chem. engring., 1973—; cons. to industry and govt. Mem. Am. Inst. Chem. Engrs., Am. Chem. Soc. Author: Introduction to Control Theory, 1968; Process Systems Analysis and Control, 1965; contbr. articles to profl. jours. Home: 2234 Carberry West Lafayette IN 47906

KOPPENHAVER, ALLEN J., educator; B.S. in Music, Lebanon Valley (Pa.) Coll.; M.A. in English, Ohio U.; Ph.D. in English, Duke U. Prof. English, Wittenberg U., Springfield, Ohio, chmn. dept., 1969-71; Fulbright lectr. Am. studies Exeter (Eng.) U., 1971-72; opera librettist; performer Springfield Symphony Orch., Wilmington Coll. Chamber Orch. Nat. Endowment for Arts grantee, 1974. Office: English Dept Wittenberg U Springfield OH 45501

KOPS, SHELDON, govt. ofcl.; b. Chgo., Nov. 18, 1923; s. Ben and Sadie (Ticktin) K.; B.S.C., Roosevelt U., 1949, M.S. in Accounting, 1969; m. Shirley Florence Abrams, 1948; children—Frederic D., Richard H., Joanne S. Sr. accountant Silver Millman & Co. C.P.A.'s, Chgo., 1948-52, Lynn & Rubin C.P.A.'s, Chgo., 1952; materials auditor AEC, Argonne, Ill., 1952-56; chief materials mgmt. and safeguards br. ERDA, Argonne, 1956—. Pres. chpt. Am. Jewish Congress, 1964-66. C.P.A., Ill. Served with AUS, 1943-46. Mem. Inst. Nuclear Materials Mgmt. (exec. com.), Am. Inst. C.P.A.'s, Ill. Soc. C.P.A.'s, Am. Nuclear Soc., Research Soc. N. Am., Am. Accounting Assn., AAAS, Sigma Xi. Jewish. Club: Masons. Home: 2510 W Jarvis Ave Chicago IL 60645 Office: 9800 S Cass Ave Argonne IL 60439

KOPULSKY, MARVIN, accountant, educator; b. Chgo., Mar. 19, 1931; s. Reuben and Rose (Richter) K.; B.S., DePaul U., 1953; M.B.A., U. Chgo., 1954; Ph.D., Northwestern U., 1970; m. Barbara Jean Michaelson, June 21, 1953; 1 son, Burton Jay. Self-employed pub. accountant, Chgo.; 1960—; mem. faculty Loyola at Chgo., 1963—, instr., 1963-70, asst. prof., 1970-77, asso. prof., 1977—, also dir. univ. C.P.A. coaching program. C.P.A. Mem. Am. Inst. C.P.A.'s, Ill. Soc. C.P.A.'s, Am. Accounting Assn., Pi Gamma Mu, Beta Gamma Sigma. Home: 5523 N Christiana St Chicago IL 60625 Office: 820 N Michigan Ave Chicago IL 60611

KORE, VALENTINE KARLIS, dentist; b. Riga, Latvia, May 31, 1924; s. Karlis and Helene (Dacjuk) K.; student U. Riga, Latvia, 1943-44, U. Hamburg (Germany), 1949-50; D.D.S., Marquette U., 1959; m. Ruth Blumbergs, July 31, 1955; children—Michael, Eric, Anda. Practice dentistry, West Allis, Wis., 1959—. Cubmaster and scoutmaster Boy Scouts Am., 1967-73. Mem. ADA, Wis., Greater Milw., West Allis dental assns. Home: 12139 W Waterford Ave Greenfield WI 53228 Office: 6531 W Lincoln Ave West Allis WI 53219

KORGIE, JOHN PAUL, computer service exec.; b. Columbus, Nebr., July 5, 1926; s. Joseph Frank and Helen Elisabeth (Rodak) K.; student St. Joseph's Coll., 1940-42, Omaha U., 1966-67; m. Phyllis A. Theran, Aug. 19, 1952; children—Mike, Bill, Kimberly, Jean, Jane, Pat, Nancy, Sheri, Joseph. With Ideal Grocery, Columbus, 1949-53, Consumers PPD, Columbus, 1954-67, PMM & Co., Omaha, Nebr., 1967-68; founder, pres. Data Center of Nebr., Columbus, 1967—; mem. faculty data processing Platte Tech. Coll., 1968-69. Mem. Columbus City Council, 1950-52; chmn. Columbus Airport Authority, 1959-62. Served with USNR, 1944-46. Recipient Profl. Computer Mgmt. award, 1976. Mem. Honeywell Users Group, Am. Legion. Democrat. Roman Catholic. Clubs: Sertoma, Elks, K.C. Home: 935 Lovers Lane Rd Columbus NE 68601 Office: Box 1043 2907 13th St Columbus NE 68601

KORKAN, KENNETH DUNS, aero. scientist; b. Cleve., Nov. 25, 1933; s. George and Emily Rose (Duns) K.; A.A., Santa Monica Jr. Coll., 1959; B.S. in Aero. and Astronautical Engring., Ohio State U., 1963, Ph.D., 1975; M.S., U. So. Calif., 1965; m. Patricia Ann Messina, Aug. 25, 1956; children—Kim Rose, Katherine Jean, David Duns, Kelly Ann. Mem. tech. staff N.Am. Rockwell Corp., Downey, Calif., 1963-69; sr. scientist Systems Research Labs., Inc., Dayton, Ohio, 1969-75; mem. staff Aero. and Astronautical Research Lab., Ohio State U., Columbus, 1975—, instr. aero. engring. dept., 1976—; instr. West Coast U., Orange, Calif., 1966-67. Served with USNR, 1952-56; Korea. Mem. Am. Soc. Engring. Edn., Am. Inst. Aeros. and Astronautics. Contbr. numerous articles in aero. and astronautical engring. to sci publs. Home: 262 Pinney Dr Worthington OH 43085 Office: Dept Aero and Astronautical Engring Ohio State U 2300 W Case Rd Columbus OH 43220

KORLLOS, THOMAS STEPHEN, ednl. adminstr.; b. Homestead, Pa., Aug. 3, 1925; s. Stephen and Sophia (Lagos) K.; A.B. magna cum laude, Youngstown U., 1960; M.A. in Sociology, Kent State U., 1964; Ph.D. in Sociology, Ohio State U., 1976; m. Marion Simon, June 5, 1949; children—T. Stephen, Christopher. Tchr. social studies Howland Schs., Warren, Ohio, 1960-64; asst. prof. Kent State U., 1964-70, asst. dean coll. arts and scis., 1970-73, dean student acad. services, 1973—, co-dir. edn. seminar to USSR, 1971-75, dir., 1976. Served with USAAC, 1944-45. Mem. Am., N.Central sociol. assns., Comparative and Internat. Edn. Soc., AAUP, NEA, Alpha Kappa

Delta, Pi Gamma Mu. Rotarian. Contbr. articles to profl. jours. Home: 1220 Lake Martin Dr Kent OH 44240

KORNEY, JOHN JOSEPH, banker; b. Grand Rapids, Mich., Apr. 24, 1908; s. Onufrey and Anna (Dodyk) K.; A.B., Mich. State U., 1931; LL.B., U. Detroit, 1943, J.D., 1968; m. Margaret E. Ruggles, Feb. 20, 1943; children—J. Douglas, Margaret Anne, Mary Kathleen. Trust officer Bankers Trust Co., Detroit, 1931, v.p., trust officer, 1948-50; trust officer, Bankers-Equitable Trust Co., Detroit, 1950-51; asst. cashier, Bank of the Commonwealth, Detroit, 1951, v.p. 1955—. Mem. Detroit Com. Econ. Devel.; v.p. Ukranian Am. Cultural Com.; mem. Mich. State U. Devel. Fund; budget com. United Community Services of Met. Detroit; mem. Wayne County Bd. Suprs., Mich. Bd. Escheats; chmn. Detroit Bd. Canvassers; mem. jud. and pub. safety com. Wayne County Bd. Commrs. Bd. dirs. Met. Detroit Internat. Inst. Recipient Outstanding Young Man of Year award, Mich. Jr. C. of C.; Major S. Key award Mich. State U., Distinguished Alumni award, 1966. Mem. Am. Hist. Assn., Am. Ordnance Assn., Soc. Genealogists, Am. Acad. Polit. and Social Sci., Am. Finance Assn., Acad. Polit. Sci., Am. (govt. relations council), Mich. (chmn. trust com. 1950) bankers assns., Am. Inst. Banking (pres. Detroit chpt. 1949, nat. vice chmn. conv. 1967), Detroit Life Ins. (v.p. trust council 1949), Detroit Bd. Commerce, Detroit Sportsmens Congress, Mich. State U. Alumni Assn. (exec. bd.), Am. Econ. Assn., Mich. C. of C., Financial Pub. Relations Assn., U. Detroit Law Alumni Assn., Ukranian Profl. Soc. (v.p.), Mich. State Alumni Assn. (dir.), Nat. Assn. Counties (welfare Com.), Mich. United Conservation Clubs (dir.), Mich. Municipal League (trustee), Mich. Assn. Suprs., Mich. Amateur Hockey Assn. (dir.), Detroit Hist. Soc. (dir.), Delta Theta Phi. Democrat. Clubs: University (Detroit); Redwood Golf (Houghton Lake, Mich.); Economic, Detroit Bankers, Ukranian Graduates. Author: Suggested Aids for Drawing Wills and Trusts, 1947. Contbr. articles to profl. jours. Home: 16771 Patton St Detroit MI 48219 Office: Bank of the Commonwealth Dime Bldg Detroit MI 48233

KORNGUTH, STEVEN EDWARD, physiol. chemist; b. N.Y.C., Dec. 1, 1935; s. Eugene I. and Helen (Pardes) K.; B.A., Columbia Coll., 1957; M.S., U. Wis., 1959, Ph.D., 1961; m. Margaret Livens, Aug. 29, 1958; children—Ingrid, David. Staff, N.Y. State Psychiat. Inst., N.Y.C., 1961-63; asst. prof. neurology, physiol. chemistry U. Wis., Madison, 1963-68, asso. prof., 1968-72, prof., 1972—. NIH research, tng. grantee in neurochemistry 1968-73. Mem. Am. Soc. Biol. Chemists, Am. Neurosci. Soc., Internat. Brain Research Orgn. Home: 5702 Hempstead Rd Madison WI 53711

KORNOKOVICH, RONALD JOHN, marketing research co. exec.; b. Cleve., Jan. 2, 1946; s. Ferdinand S. and Marie (Miketo) K.; B.B.A., Cleve. State U., 1969, M.B.A., 1973; m. Judith M. Linden, July 2, 1971. Accountant, Ward Foods, Inc., 1966; trust accountant Nat. City Bank, 1968; sec.-treas. Osborn Survey Service, Cleve., 1969-73, pres., 1973—. Tchr. math. St. Thomas Aquinas, 1969-72. Mem. planning commn. Fairview Park, 1975—, exec. chmn., 1976—. Mem. Market Research Assn. (nat. treas. 1976—, nat. edn. chmn.), Am. Marketing Assn. (nat. conf. treas.), Advt. Club. Club: City (Cleve.). Home: 3129 Creekside Dr Westlake OH 44145 Office: 4231 Fulton Rd Cleveland OH 44144

KOROW, ELINORE MARIA, artist; b. Akron, July 31, 1934; d. Alexander and Elizabeth Helen (Doszpoly) Vigh; grad. Cleve. Inst. Art, 1957; student Siena Heights Coll., 1952-53; m. John Henry Korow, Sept. 28, 1957; children—Christopher, David, Daniel. Staff artist, designer Am. Greetings Corp., Cleve., 1957-58, 71-73; one-woman shows: Design House II, Cleve., 1968, Twinsburg (Ohio) Pub Library, 1969, Cleve. Playhouse, 1973, Halle's Westgate, Fairview Park, 1971, Octogon Galleries, Patterson Library, Westfield, N.Y., 1974, Carousel Dinner Theatre, Ravenna, Ohio, 1975, Chagrin Valley Little Theatre, Chagrin Falls, Ohio, 1976; exhibited in local and nat. group shows, including nat. traveling exhbn. Am. Watercolor Soc., 1973, Kennedy Center Art Gallery, Hiram (Ohio) Coll., 1976; represented in permanent collection Cleve. Playhouse; pvt. instr. portrait painting, 1972—. Recipient Best in Oils award Cleve. Press Club, 1966. Mem. Am. Artists Profl. League, Women's Art Club Cleve. (pres. 1971-72). Roman Catholic. Home: 10469 Deborah Dr Parma OH 44130 Office: 3441 Lee Rd Suite 206 Shaker Heights OH 44120

KORP, OTTO AUGUST, JR., broadcasting co. exec.; b. Omaha, Jan. 29, 1926; s. Otto August and Esther (Lee) K.; grad. high sch.; m. Clara Sue Williams, June 13, 1948; children—Linda Lee, Scott Thomas. Gen. mgr. Western Auto Co., Omaha, 1949-52; mgr. Napanee Resort, Battle Lake, Minn., 1952-58; salesman Fergus Radio Corp., Fergus Falls, Minn., 1956-59; mgr. Factory Outlet Store, Mpls., 1959-61; gen. mgr. Northland Broadcasting Co., Fergus Falls, 1961-67; pres., gen. mgr. Empire Broadcasting Stas., Fergus Falls, 1967—. Chmn. Central Bus. Study Group, Fergus Falls, 1972—; chmn. econ. devel. City of Fergus Falls, 1972—; councilman, Fergus Falls, 1973—; bd. dirs. Indsl. Devel. Park, Protect Citizens Environ. Orgn. Served with USNR, 1943-47. Mem. Minn. Broadcasters Ins. Trust (dir. 1971—), Fergus Falls C. of C. (pres. 1966). Lutheran (ch. council 1968-72). Clubs: Lions (pres. 1965), Elks. Home: Rural Route 4 Fergus Falls MN 56537 Office: 112 E Lincoln St Fergus Falls MN 56537

KORSCHOT, BENJAMIN CALVIN, mut. fund exec.; b. Lafayette, Ind., Mar. 22, 1921; s. Benjamin Garrett and Myrtle Pearl (Goodman) K.; B.S., Purdue U., 1942; M.B.A., U. Chgo., 1947; m. Marian Marie Schelle, Oct. 31, 1941; children—Barbara (Mrs. L. Craig Carver), Lynne (Mrs. Stephen Goeding), John Calvin. Vice pres. The No. Trust Co., Chgo., 1947-64; sr. v.p. St. Louis Union Trust Co., 1964-73, asso. dir., 1968-73; treas., First Union Inc., St. Louis, 1969-73; exec. v.p., dir. Waddell & Reed, Kansas City, Mo., 1973-74, pres., 1974—; pres. United Funds, Inc.; dir. Roosevelt Federal Savs. & Loan Assn., St. Louis, 1969—, United Investors Life Ins. Co., 1974—. Bd. govs. Investment Co. Inst.; bd. dirs. Coll. for Financial Planning. Served to lt. comdr., USNR, 1943-46, 50-52. Chartered financial analyst. Mem. Financial Analysts Fedn. (dir.), Kansas City Soc. Financial Analysts, St. Louis Soc. Financial Analysts (pres. 1968). Republican. Methodist. Club: Bellerive Country (St. Louis); Kansas City, Indian Hills Country. Contbr. articles in field to profl. jours. Home: 8515 Cherokee Pl Kansas City MO 66206 Office: One Crown Center Kansas City MO 64108

KORSVIK, WILLIAM JAMES, banker, economist; b. Chgo., Sept. 9, 1917; s. Oscar J. and Anna (Shine) K.; B.S. in Bus. Adminstrn., Northwestern U., 1949; M.B.A., U. Chgo., 1955; grad. Grad. Sch. Banking, U. Wis., 1951; m. Janet Ruth Greene, Mar. 5, 1949; children—Sherry, Holly, Scott, Heather. With The First Nat. Bank of Chgo., 1935—, asst. cashier, 1949-56, asst. v.p., 1957-61, v.p. research, 1962-74, v.p. internat. banking, 1974—; asso. sec. fed. adv. council Fed. Res. System, 1956—; asso. dir. Grad. Sch. Banking, U. Wis., 1953—. Trustee, treas. Norwegian Am. Hosp.; bd. dirs. Chgo. Theol. Sem. Served with AUS, 1942-45. Mem. Am. Econ. Assn., Am. Finance Assn. Democrat. Conglist. Clubs: Econ., Univ., Bankers, Nat. Economist. Contbg. columnist Chgo. Tribune, 1974—. Home: 1738 Central Ave Wilmette IL 60091 Office: 1 First National Plaza Chicago IL 60670

KORTE, ROBERT THEODORE, mag. editor; b. Columbus, Nebr., Aug. 12, 1934; s. Arthur Theodore and Marie Augustina (Muth) K.; B.A. summa cum laude, Valparaiso U., 1959; m. Kathleen Ann Pribyl, Apr. 23, 1960; children—Michael Robert, Mark Stephen. Actuary, Continental Casualty Co., Chgo., 1959-60; sci. editor Sci. Research Assos., Inc., Chgo., 1960-62; with Heating/Piping/Air Conditioning mag., Reinhold Publ. Co., Chgo., 1962—, mng. editor, 1966-71, editor, 1971—. Freelance ednl. and engring. writing. Chmn. nominating com. Dist. 25 Sch. Bd., Arlington Heights, Ill., 1968; mgr. Little League Baseball, Arlington Heights, 1972-73. Served with arty. U.S. Army, 1955-57. Mem. Am. Soc. Heating, Refrigerating and Air Conditioning Engrs., Am. Contract Bridge League (life master). Democrat. Home: 8912 Route 120 Woodstock IL 60098 Office: Suite 1300 Two Illinois Center Chicago IL 60601

KORTEBEIN, STUART ROWLAND, orthopedic surgeon; b. Evanston, Ill., Apr. 17, 1930; s. Rowland J. and Grace K.; A.A., North Park Coll., 1950; B.S., Wheaton Coll., 1952; postgrad. North Park Theol. Sem., 1952-53; M.D., Loyola U., 1957; m. Alice C. Johnson, July 10, 1954; children—William, David. Intern, Akron (Ohio) Gen. Hosp., 1957-58; resident, 1961-64; resident Hines VA Hosp., 1960, Northwestern U., 1964; practice medicine specializing in orthopedic surgery, Arlington Heights, Ill., 1965—; attending surgeon N.W. Community Hosp., Arlington Heights, 1969—, chief orthopedics, 1976; asso. surgeon Shriners Hosp., Chgo. unit, 1968; v.p. Magnetrans Research and Devel. Corp., 1972—; tech. adviser Juko-Kai Internat., 1970—; instr. emergency med. technician course Harper Coll., 1973—. Deacon, North Haven Covenant Ch., Cuyahoga Falls, Ohio, 1963; Ill. state pres. Jiu Jitsu Black Belt Fedn. Am., 1971-74, Ill. state rep., 1971-74; Sandan instr. Oikiru-Ryu Ju Jitsu, 1977—; water safety instr. ARC, 1949-54; choir dir. First Bapt. Ch., Twenty Nine Palms, Calif., 1959-60; bd. dirs. Chicagoland Drug Prevention Program, 1971—. Served to lt., M.C., USNR, 1958-60. Diplomate Nat. Bd. Med. Examiners. Fellow A.C.S., Am. Acad. Orthopaedic Surgeons; mem. Physicians Martial Arts Assn., Soc. Black Belts Am., AMA (physicians recognition award 1970-80), Christian Med. Soc., Ill. State, Chgo. med. socs., Ill. Orthopaedic Soc., Hakko-Ryu Ju Jitsu Fedn. Contbr. articles to profl. jours. Office: 2010 S Arlington Heights Rd Arlington Heights IL 60005

KORTENHOF, JOSEPH MICHAEL, lawyer; b. Kimberly, Wis., Aug. 18, 1927; s. Joseph Arthur and Marie Anna (Probst) K.; B.A. cum laude, Lawrence Coll., 1950; J.D., U. Mich., 1953; m. Althea I. Hunting, June 7, 1952; children—Elizabeth Ann, Michael, Amy Jo. Admitted to Mo. bar, 1953, since practiced in St. Louis; mem. firm Coburn, Storckman & Croft, St. Louis, 1953-60, partner, 1957-60; mem. firm Kortenhof & Ely, St. Louis, 1960—. Served with USAF, 1945-47. Recipient Trial Lawyer's award Mo. Bar Found., 1962. Mem. Am. Coll. Trial Lawyers, Assn. Civil Defense Counsel, Am. Maritime Law Assn., Am., St. Louis bar assns., The Mo. Bar, Sigma Phi Epsilon. Home: 526 Sheffield Ave Webster Groves MO 63119 Office: Suite 640 Equitable Bldg 10 Broadway St Louis MO 63102

KORTEPETER, FRED TOLIN, realtor; b. Indpls., Aug. 7, 1942; s. Fred Ernst and Ethel Mae (Tolin) K.; student Hanover Coll., 1960-61, Ind. U., 1961-63. Ind. realtor-developer, Indpls., 1963-67; realtor-developer First Bank & Trust Co., Speedway, Ind., 1967-74, Bruce Savage Co., Realtors, Indpls., 1975—. Bd. dirs. Indpls. Humane Soc., 1969—, treas., 1972-73; bd. dirs. Indpls. Mus. Art. Served with AUS, 1963-69. Named one of Indpls.' Most Eligible Bachelors, Indpls. Star, 1972. Mem. Am. Theatre Organ Soc. (dir.), Am. Guild Organists (dir.). Presbyterian. Clubs: Cheltenham (pres. 1970), Masons, Bachelor's (pres. 1971), Columbia, Riviera. Home: Danewood 3235 Pinecrest Rd Indianapolis IN 46234 Office: 6128 N College Ave Indianapolis IN 46220

KOSCIK, RICHARD ALLEN, mech. engr.; b. Chgo., Dec. 17, 1947; s. Edward F. and Irene R. (Kloska) K.; student Western Ill. U., 1966-69; B.S. with honors in Mech. Engring., U. Ill., Urbana, 1971; postgrad. U. Cin., 1975, U. Wis., 1976; postgrad. in bus. adminstrn. Gov.'s State U., 1976—; m. Nancy Erwin, June 26, 1971; 1 son, Scott Michael. Project engr. Deltar Co. div. Ill. Tool Works Inc., Frankfort, Ill., 1971-77, chief engr., 1977—. Mem. Soc. Automotive Engrs., Soc. Plastics Engrs., U. Ill. Alumni Assn., Ill. Tool Works Patent Soc., Tau Beta Pi, Sigma Tau, Pi Tau Sigma. Patentee in field. Office: 21555 S Harlem Ave Frankfort IL 60423

KOSER, PHILLIP JAMES, chem. co. exec.; b. Chgo., Aug. 12, 1934; s. James and Adeline (Lochman) K.; student Ripon Coll., 1952-55. Photoengraving apprentice Barnes Crosby Co., Chgo., 1955-58; with Philip Lochman & Co., Evanston, Ill., 1958—; exec. v.p., 1968—, also dir. Served with AUS, 1956-57. Mason. Home: 9124 Marmora St Morton Grove IL 60053 Office: 2405 Oakton St Evanston IL 60204

KOSHAK, ARTHUR EMIL, paper co. exec.; b. Park Falls, Wis., Mar. 1, 1933; s. Rudy and Alma (Franke) K.; student U. Wis., 1951-53; B.S., U. Omaha, 1963; m. Peggy L. Ray, Feb. 15, 1975; children by previous marriage—Alan, Christine, Randall, Richard; stepchildren—Mike Ray, Mark Ray, Linda Ray, Randy Ray. Joined U.S. Air Force, 1953, advanced through grades to lt. col., 1972, ret., 1974; traffic mgr. Flambeau Paper Co. div. Kansas City Star, Park Falls, Wis., 1974—. Decorated D.F.C., Air medal, Air Force Commendation medal. Mem. Am. Legion. Club: Elks. Home: 884 S 5th Ave Park Falls WI 54552 Office: 200 1st Ave N Park Falls WI 54552

KOSIER, MARY WILKIN, guidance counselor; b. Independence, Kans.; d. Fred Triffany and Grace Elizabeth (McClelland) Wilkin; B.E., Washburn U.; M.Ed., Wichita State U.; m. Charles D. Kosier, Apr. 13, 1952; children—Kathryn Ann Kosier Karnaze, Mary Ann. Tchr. pub. schs., Topeka and Wichita, Kans., Kirkwood, Mo., guidance counselor Derby (Kans.) Sr. High Sch., 1967-71; dir. career devel. program Central Kans. Area Vocat. Sch. Service, 1971—; cons. U.S. Office of Edn.; mem. Kans. Task Force Career Edn., 1973-74, Kans. Career Edn. Input Council, 1976—. Mem. Am. Vocat. Assn., Am. (senator 1977—), Kans. (dir. 1974-75) personnel and guidance assns., Nat. (Merit award 1974; sec. 1975-77, dir. 1975—, del assembly 1973—), Kans. vocat. guidance assns., AAUW, LWV, Am. Sch. Counselors Assn., Phi Delta Kappa. Republican. Methodist. Home: 1115 Pinecrest Ct Newton KS 67114 Office: 218 E 7th St Newton KS 67114

KOSS, JOHN CHARLES, electronics co. exec.; b. Milw., Feb. 22, 1930; s. Earl L. and Eda L. (Kenkel) K.; m. Nancy Lee Weeks, Apr. 19, 1952; children—Michael, Debra, John Charles, Linda, Pam. Founder, Koss Hosp. TV Rental Service, Milw., 1953; founder Koss Electronics (named changed to Koss Corp., 1972), Milw., 1958; founder, pres., chmn. bd., chief exec. officer John C. Koss, Inc., Milw., 1972—; dir. Advanced Healthcare Inc., Heritage Bank of Milw. Chmn., Wis. chpt. Young Presidents Assn., 1974-75, dir. nat. orgn., 1973-77; chmn. Channel 10 Auction, 1974; chmn. Friends of Art, Bal du Lac, Wis., 1971. Bd. dirs. Nat. Jr. Achievement, Milw. Hearing Soc., Milw. Symphony; bd. regents Milw. Sch. Engring. Mem. Am. Mktg. Assn. (Mktg. Man of Year 1972), Research Dirs. Assn. Chgo. (Entrepreneur of Year 1972), Inst. High Fidelity, (pres. 1969-70). Home: 7787 N River Rd Milwaukee WI 53217 Office: 4129 N Port Washington Ave Milwaukee WI 53212

KOSTAL, OTTO ALBIN, cardiologist; b. Potter County, Pa., Mar. 5, 1899; s. Albin and Marie (Bavor) K.; B.Sc., Municipal U. of Omaha, 1921; M.D., U. Nebr., 1923: m. Flo Strickland, Jan. 19, 1926; children—Betty Joan Kostal McBride, Mary Lou Kostal Hartman, Otta A., Jr. Intern, Nebr. Methodist Hosp., Omaha, 1923-24, Gorgas Meml. Hosp., Panama Canal Zone, 1924; gen. practice medicine, Giltner, Nebr., 1925-36, Hastings, Nebr., 1936-46; practice medicine specializing in internal medicine and cardiology, Hastings, 1946—; past pres. staff Mary Lanning Meml. Hosp., Hastings; past chmn. bd. dirs., First Nat. Bank, Hastings. Vice chmn. bd. trustees, Hastings Coll.; mem. adv. council Good Samaritan Village, Hastings. Served as cmdr., USNR, 1943-46. Diplomate Am. Bd. Internal Medicine. Fellow Am. Coll. Cardiology, A.C.P., Internat. Acad. Medicine, Am. Coll. Angiology, Royal Soc. Health (Eng.); mem. Nebr. Med. Assn. (pres. 1962-63), Nebr. Heart Assn. (past pres.), Ancient and Secret Order Quiet Birdmen. Republican. Presbyterian. Clubs: Lochland Country, Mason (Shriner), Royal Order of Jesters, Navy League of the U.S. (past pres.). Contbr. articles in field. Home: PO Box 1004 923 N Elm Ave Hastings NE 68901 Office: PO Box 1004 618 N Denver Ave Hastings NE 68901

KOSTENKO, BARRY MICHAEL, civil engr.; b. Vladivostok, Siberia, Dec. 16, 1912; s. Michael M. and Barbara P. (Novitsky) K.; B.S. in C. E., Ill. Inst. Tech., 1934; m. Helene M. Ullrich, Aug. 22, 1936; 1 dau., Pamela Helene. Came to U.S. 1920, naturalized, 1927. Civil engr. and metallurgist; with Sueske Brass & Copper Co., Chgo., 1934-53; dep. chief staff, staff engr. Com. Finance, City Chgo., 1954-61, dep. budget dir., 1961-73. Commr., pres. West Maywood Park Rd. Mem. Municipal Finance Officers' Assn., Western Soc. Engrs. (chmn. civic com., chmn. transp. engring. sect.), Nat., Ill. socs. profl. engrs., Am. Soc. C.E., Am. Air Mail Soc., Jack Knight Air Mail Soc. Am. Philatelic Soc. Methodist. Asso. editor Am. Air Mail Soc., Air Letter Sheet Catalog. Home: 6772 N Oxford Ave Chicago IL 60631 Office: City Hall Chicago IL 60602

KOSZEWSKI, BOHDAN JULIUS, physician; b. Warsaw, Poland, Dec. 17, 1918; s. Mikolaj and Helena (Lubienski) K.; came to U.S., 1952, naturalized, 1958; M.D., U. Zurich (Switzerland), 1946; M.S., Creighton U., 1956; children—Mikolaj Joseph, Wanda Maria, Andrzej Rohdan. Intern, St. Mary's Hosp., Hoboken, N.J., 1953; resident in pathology U. Zurich, 1944-46, resident in internal medicine, 1946-50, asso. in medicine, 1950-52; practice medicine, specializing in internal medicine, Omaha; staff mem. St. Joseph's Hosp., Luth. Med. Center, Drs., Mercy, and Meth. hosps.; instr. internal medicine Creighton U., 1956-57, asst. prof., 1957-65, asso. prof. internal medicine, 1965—; cons. in hematology Douglas County Hosp., 1959—, Omaha VA Hosp., 1957—. Served with Polish Army, 1940-45. Recipient Honors Achievement award Angiology Research Found., 1964-65. Fellow A.C.P., Am. Coll. Angiology; mem. AAAS, Am. Fedn. Clin. Research, Am., Internat. socs. hematology, AMA. Author: Prognosis in Diabetic Coma, 1952; contbr. numerous articles to med. jours. Home: 8008 Pacific St Omaha NE 68114 Office: 4502 S 42d St Omaha NE 68107

KOTANSKY, DONALD RICHARD, mech. engr.; b. Hinsdale, Ill., July 28, 1939; s. Cyril Methodius and Catherine Marie (Mesich) K.; B. Mech. Engring., Gen. Motors Inst., 1961; M.S. (Gen. Motors Grad. fellow), Mass. Inst. Tech., 1962, M.E., 1964, D.Sc., 1966; m. Gloria Mary Copp, June 23, 1962; children—Steven, Kenneth, Keith. Asst. prof. mech. engring. Purdue U., Lafayette, Ind., 1965-68; project propulsion engr. Gen. Dynamics Corp., Ft. Worth, 1969-70; sect. chief aerodynamics McDonnell Aircraft Co., McDonnell Douglas Corp., St. Louis, 1970—; cons. Allison div. Gen. Motors Corp., Indpls., 1967. Mem. Am. Inst. Aeros. and Astronautics (chmn. St. Louis tech. specialists 1974-75), ASME, Sigma Xi, Tau Beta Pi. Home: 15400 Clover Ridge Dr Chesterfield MO 63017 Office: McDonnell Douglas Corp PO Box 516 St Louis MO 63166

KOTCHE, JAMES RAY, bus. exec.; b. Rockford, Ill., Sept. 6, 1938; s. Gardie James and Corinne Kathern (Kohlbeck) K.; A.A. in Bus., Rock Valley Coll., 1975; m. Ethel Corirossi. Pres. Uncle Sam's, Inc., 1972—. Chmn. bd., sec. Rockford Metro Minority Bus. Devel., Inc., 1971-73; mem. small bus. adv. bd. Rock Valley Coll. Served with USMC, 1955-60. Recipient Nat. Spark Plug of Year award U.S. Jaycees, 1969, 2d pl. Nat. Tavern Owner of Year award, 1974, 1st place Nat. Tavern Owner of Year award, 1975. Mem. Marine Corps League, Rock Valley Ski Assn., Ill. (nat. dir. pub. relations consul 1970-72), Rockford Jaycees (chmn. bd., v.p., pres., dir. 1965—). Clubs: Ski (pres. 1965-66) (Rockford). Author: (with M. Bradley Wood) Drug Abuse, A Community Action Guide, 1970. Home: 3410 Highcrest Rockford IL 61107

KOTIN, LAWRENCE LEWIS, lawyer; b. Chgo., Jan. 5, 1927; s. George N. and Gertrude (Geller) K.; B.S., Northwestern U., 1949, J.D., 1952; m. Marge A. Corboy, Apr. 25, 1965; 1 son, Daniel Michael. Admitted to Ill. bar, 1952, since practiced in Chgo.; mem. firm Corboy & Kotin & Assos., Chgo., 1971-73; individual practice, 1973—. Instr. trial advocacy Ct. Practise Inst. Bd. dirs. Ill. Good Govt. Inst., 1965—. Served with U.S. Army, 1945-46. Mem. Am. Judicature Soc., Am. Trial Lawyers Assn., Am., Ill., Chgo. (mem. grievance com. 1971-74, chmn. hearing panel atty. registration and disciplinary commn. of Supreme Ct. of Ill.) bar assns., Ill. Trial Lawyers Assn. (treas. 1963-67), Bar Assn. 7th Fed. Circuit, Trial Lawyers Club Chgo., Soc. Trial Lawyers, Tau Epsilon Rho. Bd. editors Northwestern U. Law Review, 1951-52. Home: 9334 N Harding Ave Evanston IL 60203 Office: Suite 820 33 N Dearborn St Chicago IL 60602

KOTNIK, RONALD JOSEPH, lawyer; b. Sheboygan, Wis., Nov. 8, 1936; s. Joseph Frank and Margaret (Mervar) K.; B.S., U. Wis., 1959, LL.B., 1962; m. Karen A. Walthers, Feb. 17, 1962; children—Joseph, Jeffrey. Admitted to Wis. bar, 1962, since practiced in Madison; asso. firm Ela, Esch, Hart & Clark, Madison, 1965-68, partner, 1968—. Tchr. Madison Bus. Coll., 1963-65, Am. Inst. Banking, 1964-65. Sec., Poynette (Wis.) Planning Commn., 1967-77; village atty. Poynette, 1966—. Served with USNR, 1953-62. Recipient Knapp Scholarship, U. Wis. Law Sch., 1962. Mem. Am. Trial Lawyers Assn., Wis. Bar Assn., Wis. Sch. Attys. Assn., Am. Numis. Assn., Am. Arbitration Assn. (panel arbitrators 1977), Phi Alpha Delta. Methodist (trustee 1967-70). Club: Elks. Home: Old Settlers Trail Poynette WI 53955 Office: 122 W Washington Ave Madison WI 53703

KOTSONIS, GEORGE NICK, lawyer; b. Sheboygan, Wis., Feb. 5, 1939; s. Nick George and Viola (Spanomihos) K.; B.S., U. Wis., 1962, LL.B., 1965; m. Dianne Chaconas, Aug. 19, 1962; children—Nick, Tia, Gregory, James, Tom. Admitted to Wis. bar, 1965, Fed. Dist. Cts. bar, 1965, U.S. Supreme Ct. bar, 1972; law clk. Wis. Supreme Ct., 1965-66; mem. firm Wickham, Borgett, Skogstad & Powell, Milw., 1966-70; partner firm Niebler & Niebler, 1970-75; partner firm Chronus and Kotsonis, Milw., 1975—. Mem. Am., Wis., Milw. bar assns. Mason (Shriner). Home: 17710 Penbrook St Brookfield WI 53005 Office: 135 W Wells Milwaukee WI 53203

KOTTHA, JAGANNADHAM, biomed. engr., biomed. instrumentation co. exec.; b. Hyderabad, India, July 14, 1943; s. Pulliah and Durgamma (Koppu) K.; came to U.S., 1971; B.S. in Electronics, Osmania U., India, 1967; M.S. with honors, Case Western Res. U., 1975. Jr. tech. officer Electronics Corp. India Ltd., 1968-70; electronic engr. Def. Research & Devel. Lab., Hyderabad, India, 1967-68; biomed. engr. Case Western Res. U., Cleve., 1973-74, U. Hosps., 1973-74; dir. engring. and exec. v.p. Environ. Control of Life Systems, Inc., Cleve., 1974—. Mem. Instrument Soc. Am. (sr.), IEEE, Soc. Advancement of Mgmt., Assn. Advancement of Med. Instrumentation. Home: 2034 Cornell Cleveland OH 44106 Office: 18030 Brook Park Rd Cleveland OH 44135

KOUCKY, JOHN RICHARD, casting co. exec.; b. Chgo., Sept. 21, 1934; s. Frank Louis and Ella Maud (Harshman) K.; B.S. in Metall. Engring., U. Ill., 1957; M.B.A., Northwestern U., 1959; m. Beverly Irene O'Dell, Aug. 16, 1958; children—Deborah Irene, Diane Jean. Gen. supr. product engring. Central Foundry div. Gen. Motors Corp., Saginaw, Mich., 1964-67; asst. gen. mgr. Marion (Ind.) Malleable Iron, 1967-69; mgr. product engring. Wagner Casting Co., Decatur, Ill., 1968-72, mgr. tech. adminstrn., 1972-77, plant mgr. nodular foundry, 1977—. Pres. tennis adv. com. Decatur Park Bd., 1977—. Served to lt. Signal Corps, U.S. Army, 1957. Mem. Am. Soc. for Metals (vice chmn. Central Ill. chpt.), Soc. Automotive Engrs., Am. Foundryman's Soc. (dir. Central Ill. chpt.), ASTM (chmn. nat. com. on malleable iron). Republican. Mem. Christian Ch. Club: Decatur Tennis (pres.), Decatur Racquet. Home: 2210 Gary Dr Decatur IL 62526 Office: PO Box 1319 Decatur IL 62525

KOUMOULIDES, JOHN THOMAS ANASTASIOS, educator, historian; b. Greece, Aug. 23, 1938; s. Anastasios Lazaros and Sophia (Theodosiadou) K.; came to U.S., 1956, naturalized, 1969; A.B., Montclair (N.J.) State Coll., 1960, A.M., 1961; Ph.D., U. Md., 1968; student Fitzwilliam Coll., Cambridge (Eng.) U., 1965-67, vis. fellow, 1971-72. Grad. asst. U. Md., 1961-63; asst. prof. history Austin Peay State U., Clarksville, Tenn., 1963-65, Vanderbilt U., summer 1968; mem. faculty Ball State U., Muncie, Ind., 1968—, prof. history, 1975—. Research grantee Ball State U., 1969, 70, 74, Am. Philos. Soc., 1973; Am. Council Learned Socs. grantee, 1969, 71, 74; Fulbright-Hays research awardee, Greece, 1977-78. Mem. Am., Brit., Cambridge U. hist. assns., Archaeol. Inst. Am., AAUP, Modern Greek Studies Assn., Soc. Promotion Hellenic Studies, Cambridge U. Philol. Assn., Phi Alpha Theta, Alpha Tau Omega. Author: Cyprus and the Greek War of Independence, 1821-1829, 2d edit., 1974; Byzantine and Post-Byzantine Monuments at Aghia in Thessaly, Greece: The Art and Architecture of the Monastery of Saint Panteleimon, 1975; also monographs, articles; editor: Greece in Transition: Essays in the History of Modern Greece 1821-1974, 1977. Home: 810 Wayne St Muncie IN 47303

KOUTOUJIAN, HAGOP KHACHADOUR, chem. engr.; b. Beirut, Lebanon, July 3, 1948; s. Khachadour Hagop and Vartouhi Hagop (Dolabjian) K.; came to U.S., 1974, B.S. in Chemistry, Am. U., Beirut, 1969; M.S. in Chem. Engring., Cleve. State U., 1971. Chief central lab., supr. sulfuric acid plants Lebanon Chems. Co., Selaata, 1969; systems engr. Metito Water Treatment Co., Beirut, 1974; research scholar material properties Thermophysical Properties Research Centre, Purdue U., West Lafayette, Ind., 1974—. Registered profl. engr., Beirut. Mem. Am. Chem. Soc., Am. Inst. Chem. Engrs., Nat. Soc. Profl. Engrs., (legis. com. Purdue chpt. 1977), AAAS, Sigma Xi. Author: Manual on the Electronic and Magnetic and Optical Properties of Materials, 1977. Home: 414 Harrison St West Lafayette IN 47906

KOVACH, BERNARD CLEMENT, publisher; b. Pottsville, Pa., May 26, 1934; s. Stephen Joseph and Ann Mary (Harvilla) K.; B.A., George Washington U., 1955; m. Romayne Postupack, Oct. 1, 1960; children—Elysa, Christopher. Asst. to exec. v.p. Nat. Tire Dealers and Retreaders Assn., Washington, 1955-58; asst. sales mgr. Bacon-Am. Corp., Muncie, Ind., 1958-60; with Bill Communications, Inc., N.Y.C., 1960-72; pres. Hartman Communications, Inc., Akron, Ohio, 1972—; cons. to industry; dir. Bill Communications, Inc Profit Sharing Trust, Tire Retread Info. Bur. Recipient Leadership award Am. Retreaders Assn., 1977. Mem. Young Pres.'s Orgn., Am. Bus. Press. Roman Catholic. Clubs: Fairlawn Country, Akron City, Cherry Valley (Garden City, L.I.). Home: 2449 Stockbridge Rd Akron OH 44313 Office: 77 N Miller Rd Akron OH 44313

KOVACHY, EDWARD MIKLOS, accountant, lawyer; b. Cleve., Mar. 24, 1901; s. Steven Miklos and Helen (Liptay) K.; B.S., U. Pa., 1924; LL.B., cum laude, Cleve. Law Sch., 1929; J.D. cum laude, Cleve. State U., 1969; m. Evelyn Palenscar, Oct. 28, 1944; 1 son, Edward. Accountant, Cleve. Municipal Court, 1925-30; admitted to Ohio bar, 1929; auditor Cleve. Pub. Auditorium, 1930-32; pvt. practice accounting, Cleve., 1932—; mem. law firm Kovachy & Kovachy, Cleve., 1946—, accounting firm Kovachy & Hasman, 1966—; faculty Fenn Coll., Cleve., 1934-52, asso. prof. accounting, 1946-52. Presiding trustee, R.A. Gall Realty Investments. C.P.A., Ohio. Mem. Am. Inst. C.P.A.'s, Ohio Soc. C.P.A.'s (dir. chpt. 1956-57), Am. Assn. Att.-C.P.A.'s, Cuyahoga Bar Assn., Delta Theta Phi. Presbyterian. Clubs: Mason, Shriner, City, Canterbury Golf. Home: 14500 S Park Blvd Shaker Heights OH 44120 Office: 4900 Euclid Ave Suite 404 Cleveland OH 44103

KOVACIK, VICTOR PAUL, mfg. co. exec.; b. St. Louis, Aug. 2, 1927; s. Paul and Anna (Matusovic) K.; B.S., Washington U., St. Louis, 1948; M.S., Purdue U., 1949; diploma Oak Ridge Sch. Reactor Tech., 1951; M.B.A. cum laude, Harvard U., 1957; m. Winifred Ann Hartzell, July 9, 1955; 1 dau., Ellissa. Project engr. Wright Air Devel. Center, Dayton, Ohio, 1949-55; engring. supr. United Aircraft Corp., Boston, Mass., 1956-57; mgr. elec. products dept. TRW, Inc., Cleve., 1957-69; dir. new tech. ventures Studebaker Worthington Corp., N.Y.C., 1969-70; pres. Frolic Friends, Inc., Mentor, Ohio, 1971—; chmn. bd. Cyberex, Inc., Mentor, 1968—; chmn., pres. Mead Dijit, Inc., Dayton, 1973-75, Micromenex Corp., Mentor, 1975—. Served with USNR, 1945-46, USAF, 1953-55. Cupples scholar, 1944; Gottshall scholar, 1945. Mem. IEEE, Soc. Mfg. Engrs., Instrument Soc. Am., Greater Cleve. Growth Assn. Co-author: The Impact of High Temperature Technology, 1957. Contbr. articles to profl. jours. Patentee in field. Home: 522 Saddleback Ln Gates Mills OH 44040 Office: Micromenex Corp 7010 Lindsay Dr Mentor OH 44060

KOVAL, PAUL WILLIAM, lawyer, mech. engr.; b. Wyandotte, Mich., Aug. 1, 1947; s. Paul and Sophie Virginia (Ludwikowski) K.; B.S. in Mech. Engring., U. Mich., 1969, M.S. in Natural Resources, 1973, J.D., 1973; postgrad nuclear engring. Carnegie Mellon U., 1969-70; m. Barbara Bette Granetz, Sept. 2, 1973. Nuclear design and licensing engr. Westinghouse Electric Corp., Pitts., 1969-71; govt. intern air quality and radiation protection div. EPA, Washington, 1972; admitted to Mich. bar, 1973, Alaska bar, 1977; nuclear licensing and environ. compliance atty. Consumers Power Co., Jackson, Mich., 1973—, on leave as atty. firm Graham & James native land claims, environ., oil and gas concerns, Anchorage, 1977—. Leader challenge group 4H, 1975-76. Westinghouse fellow, 1969-70; EPA intern, 1972. Mem. Am., Mich., Alaska bar assns., ASME. Author: Power Facility Planning Within the Michigan Adminstrative System, 1973; co-author: Michigan Environmental Law Handbook, 1975. Club: Lions. Home: 7631 Larme St Allen Park MI 48101 Office: Graham & James 601 W 5th Ave Suite 930 Anchorage AK 99501

KOVARIK, LELAND KENNETH, lawyer; b. Friend, Nebr., Apr. 2, 1938; s. Leland K. and Helen A. (Kunc) K.; B.S., Nebr. Wesleyan U., 1960; J.D., U. Neb., 1966; m. Alice L. Schmer, Oct. 29, 1966; children—James Leland, Mark Leland. Spl. agt. Md. Casualty Co., Omaha, 1960-63; admitted to Nebr. bar, 1966; since practiced in Gering; partner firm Holtorf, Hansen, Kovarik & Nuttleman, Gering, 1966—. Served with N.G., 1956-62. Mem. Assn. Ins. Attys., Def. Research Inst., Am., Nebr., Scott Bluff County bar assns. Elk. Club: Sertoma (Scottsbluff, Nebr.). Home: Route 2 Gering NE 69341 Office: 1715 11th St Gering NE 69341

KOVATS, LESLIE PAUL, chemist; b. Gheorgheni, Romania, May 27, 1934; s. Paul and Katalin (Mendly) K.; came to U.S., 1962, naturalized, 1968; degree in Agrl. Chem. and Food Tech., Poly. U., Budapest, Hungary, 1956; m. Katalin Kolar, Dec. 30, 1961. Research chemist Banting Inst., U. Toronto (Ont., Can.), 1958-62; research chemist Union Starch & Refining Co., Granite City, Ill., 1962-66, Anheuser-Busch, Inc. Corn Products Research, St. Louis, 1966—. Mem. AAAS, Am. Brew Chemists, Am. Assn. Cereal Chemists. Patentee in field. Home: 192 Esquire Dr Granite City IL 62040 Office: 1101 Wyoming St Saint Louis MO 63118

KOVITZ, SEYMOUR J., retail exec.; b. Chgo., Oct. 14, 1917; s. Benjamin and Minnie (Hyman) K.; student Lewis Inst.; B.S., Northwestern U., 1940; m. Elka Pineus, May 10, 1947; children—Jeffrey, Marc, Lorri, Steven. Corr., Armour & Co., Chgo., 1946-47; salesman Big Four Clothing Co., Chgo., 1947-58; pres. Style Center, Inc., Chgo. and Oak Park, Ill., 1958-75, Clothes HQ, Inc., Schaumburg, Ill., 1972—. Vice pres. Beverly Farm Found., Godfrey, Ill., 1974-76. Served to 1st lt. USAAF, 1941-45. Decorated D.F.C. Mem. Nat. Assn. Men's Sportswear Buyers (dir. 1970—). Club: Masons. Co-editor Beverly Farm Reporter, 1969—. Office: 303 Woodfield Mall Schaumburg IL 60195

KOWALL, JAMES L., packaging co. exec.; b. Grand Rapids, Mich., June 19, 1926; s. John B. and Hazel Helena (Haley) K.; grad. Ferris Inst., 1942; m. Elva L. Shults, July 24, 1954. Continuity editor Wood Broadcasting, 1948; midwestern sales mgr. R.H. Young & Son Co., 1949-54; Western Mich. sales rep. Battle Creek Box Co., 1954-60; asst. sales mgr. Consol. Packaging Corp., 1960-66; founder, v.p. Grand Rapids Packaging Corp., 1966-70, Wolverine Packaging Co., Schoolcraft, Mich., 1968-70; founder, pres. Great No. Packaging Corp., Grand Rapids, 1970—, Grand Traverse Packaging Corp., Traverse City, 1974, Huron Packaging Corp., Troy, Mich., 1975, GNP Industries, 1975. Served with USNR, 1943-46. Mem. Soc. Die Casting Engrs., Exec. Soc. Corrugated Sheet Converters (pres. 1972-73), AIM, Assn. Ind. Corrugated Converters (founder, 1st pres. 1973), Nat. Fedn. Ind. Bus., Am. Bus. Clubs, Travelers Protective Soc., NAM. Roman Catholic. Club: Elks. Home: 6965 Oakbrook Dr SE Grand Rapids MI 49508 Office: 4005 Roger B Chaffee Meml Blvd SE Grand Rapids MI 49508

KOYLE, MYRON RAYMOND, bearing mfg. co. exec.; b. Massillon, Ohio, Aug. 8, 1929; s. Ernest R. and Mary Ann (Kane) K.; A.B., Kent State U., 1951; M.A., 1955; m. Adelaine Dorothea Metcalf, June 12, 1954; children—Debra Elaine, Myron Raymond, Douglas Metcalf, Barbara Anne. Indsl. engr. Timken Co., Canton, Ohio, 1955-56, supr. bearing ops., 1956-59, with internat. ops., 1959—, exec. asst. for internat. operations, 1963—. Pres. congregation Our Savior Luth. Ch., Canton, 1974—; active Boy Scouts Am. Served with U.S. Navy, 1952-53. Certified mfg. engr. Mem. Am. Mgmt. Assn., Machinery and Allied Products Inst., Soc. Mfg. Engrs., Am. Soc. Metals, Naval Res. Assn., Kent State U. Alumni Assn. (dir.), Nat. Def. Preparedness Assn. Republican. Club: Brookside Country. Author: (monograph) Physiological Effects of Long-Distance Travel, 1967. Analyst, 1st formulator policy for corporate use of "Jet Lag". Home: 1101 Mile Ave SW Canton OH 44710 Office: 1835 Dueber Ave SW Canton OH 44706

KOZAK, MARTIN JERRY, govt. health adminstr.; b. Chgo., Jan. 19, 1938; s. Isadore and Hilda (Gold) K.; A.B., U. Chgo., 1959; M.B.A., Roosevelt U., 1961; postgrad. Walden U., Naples, Fla., 1972; m. Susan Betsy Alperin, Aug. 11, 1968. With U.S. GAO, Chgo., 1961-68, supervisory mgmt. auditor, 1964-68; audit mgr. Blue Cross Assn., Chgo., 1968-70; sr. audit rev. specialist OEO, Chgo., 1970-73; fin. mgr. Hill-Burton program USPHS, Chgo., 1973-74, asst. regional adminstr., Chgo., 1974—. Active Jewish United Fund, WTTW Channel 11, Ruth Lodge for Handicapped Children, Wilmette (Ill.) Pre-Sch. P.T.A. Served with AUS, 1962. C.P.A., Ill. Mem. Fed. Govt. Accountant Assn. (treas. bd. 1965-67), Am. Coll. Hosp. Adminstrs., Am. Inst. C.P.A.'s, Ill. Soc. C.P.A.'s. (chmn. subcom. health care 1973-75), Am. Accounting Assn., Midwest Bus. Adminstrn. Assn., Assn. Govt. Accountants, Chgo. Art Inst., Field Museum, MENSA. Jewish. Clubs: Whitehall, Highland Park (Ill.) Racquet. Home: 2003 Chestnut Ave Wilmette IL 60691 Office: 300 S Wacker Dr Chicago IL 60607

KOZELKA, EDWARD WILLIAM, seed and feed co. exec.; b. Monona, Iowa, July 19, 1912; s. William Frank and Elizabeth (Tayek) K.; student Loras Coll., 1929-31; m. Beulah Annette Gunderson, Feb. 24, 1941; 1 dau., Gail Kathleen. Gen. mgr. Hall Roberts' Son, Postville, Iowa, 1932-46, v.p., gen. mgr., 1946-75, treas., 1975—; salesman Dean Real Estate, Postville, 1975—; dir. Postville State Bank, Postville Telephone Co. Mem. Postville City Council, 1960-61; pres. Postville Hist. Soc., 1975—; treas. Upper Explorerland Resource, Conservation and Devel. Com., 1969—; chmn. Upper Explorerland Regional Planning Commn., 1971—; chmn. N.E. Iowa River Basin Com., 1976-77; mem. Iowa Policy Adv. Council on Water Quality, 1976-77; mem. citizens adv. Council to Dept. Transp., 1977; mem. planning and fin. com. Postville Hosp., 1959-60; chmn. bldg. com. Postville Hosp., 1960-61; co-chmn. fund-raising com. Postville Good Samaritan Center, 1968; bd. dirs. Big 4 Fair, 1946-74. Recipient Distinguished Service award Jaycees, 1966; hon. future farmer FFA. Mem. Iowa Seed Dealers Assn. (pres. 1972), Iowa Grain and Feed Assn., Western Seed Dealers Assn. Republican. Roman Catholic. Clubs: Kiwanis, Postville Comml. Home: 205 Williams St W Postville IA 52162 Office: PO Box 396 Postville IA 52162

KOZIMER, PHILIP DALE, veterinarian; b. Cleve., July 5, 1949; s. Edward Stanley and Elizabeth (Scharra) K.; B.S., Ohio State U., 1971, D.V.M., 1975; m. Marsha Kay Shipley, Sept. 11, 1971. Pvt. practice Cherandon Veterinary Clinic, North Olmsted, Ohio, 1975—; faculty advisor Polaris Vocat. Sch. Mem. Am., Ohio veterinary assns., Jaycees (chmn. recreation project), Omega Tau Sigma. Home: 21037 Southbend Circle Rocky River OH 44116 Office: 26701 Brookpark Rd Extension North Olmsted OH 44070

KOZLOWSKI, DAVID KARL, ednl. adminstr.; b. Joliet, Ill., Jan. 25, 1943; s. Charles Leonard and Betty (Matuszewski) K.; B.S., No. Ill. U., 1966, M.S., 1968; Ed.D., Wayne State U., 1972; m. Sharon Hucksold, Aug. 20, 1966; 1 son, Dean David. Asst. prof. ednl. communications Temple U., Phila., 1972-74; asst. dean learning resources Triton Coll., River Grove, Ill., 1976—, dir. ind. learning lab., 1974-76; pres., bd. dirs. No. Ill. Learning Resources Coop., 1976-77; bd. dirs. Pa. Learning Resources Assn., 1973-74. Mem. Assn. for Ednl. Communications and Tech., NEA, Ill. Audiovisual Assn., Community Coll. Assn. Instrn. and Tech. Home: Downers Grove IL Office: 2000 5th Ave River Grove IL 60171

KOZLOWSKI, DONALD ROBERT, elec. engr.; b. St. Louis, Dec. 5, 1937; s. Leo William and Dorothy Rose (Adams) K.; B.S.E.E., St. Louis U., 1959; M.S.E.E., Washington U., St. Louis, 1967; m. Patricia Ann Halveland, Nov. 24, 1960; children—Karen, Kathleen, Christine. Engr., McDonnell Douglas Co., St. Louis, 1959-62, sect. mgr., 1965-75, br. chief, 1977—; mgr. program devel. Electronic Specialty Co., Los Angeles, 1962-64; v.p. Aerospace Systems Corp., St. Louis, 1964-65; dir. mission analysis USAF, 1976. Mem. IEEE, Am. Inst. Aeros. and Astronautics, Eta Kappa Nu, Pi Mu Epsilon, Alpha Sigma Nu. Republican. Roman Catholic. Home: 1810 Millshire St St Louis MO 63136 Office: PO Box 516 St Louis MO 63166

KOZY, KENNETH ROBERT, computer co. exec.; b. Chgo., Nov. 9, 1940; s. Felix George and Lillian Martha (Czarnecki) K.; B.S., U. Ill., 1963; M.B.A., U. Chgo., 1969. Systems engr. IBM Corp., Chgo., 1963-69; v.p. systems devel. Computertelic, Inc., Chgo., 1969-71; owner Mgmt. Devel. Orgn., Chgo., 1971—; founder, pres., dir. Info. Cassettes, Inc., Chgo., 1971—; instr. bus. and data processing Central YMCA Coll., Chgo., 1971—, also curriculum adviser. Mem. alumni council U. Chgo. Grad. Sch. Bus., 1972—. Certified data processor, Ill. Mem. Data Processing Mgmt. Assn. (dir. North Shore chpt. 1971-73, v.p. 1973-75, Individual Performance award), Assn. Computing Machinery, Inst. Mgmt. Scis., Ops. Research Soc. Am., Am. Mgmt. Assn., Phi Kappa Theta. Author: Systems Design and Analysis, 1973. Home: 4104 W Nelson St Chicago IL 60641 Office: 645 N Michigan Ave Chicago IL 60611

KRABBENHOFT, KENNETH LESTER, physician, educator; b. Sabula, Iowa, Jan. 7, 1923; s. Lester Henry and Bessie Grant (Thompson) K.; B.A., State U. Iowa, 1943, M.D., 1946; m. Gloria Darlene Eriksen, June 17, 1944; children—Kenneth Lester, Douglas Harold, Karen Ann Krabbenhoft Naegele. Intern, Harper Hosp., Detroit, 1946-47, resident, 1949-52, asso. radiologist, 1952-57, radiologist, 1957—; prof., chmn. dept. radiology Wayne State U., Detroit, 1969—; cons. radiologist VA Hosp., Allen Park, Mich., Children's Hosp. Mich., Crittenton Gen. Hosp., Herman Kiefer Hosp., Nat. Cancer Inst.; mem. Nat. Cancer Adv. Bd., 1970-73; pres. Univ. Emergency Services, P.C., Detroit, 1973—; pres. Detroit Gen. Hosp. Research Corp., 1974—; mem. Environ. Radiation Exposure Adv. Com., 1975—; trustee Am. Bd. Radiology, 1970—, asst. sec., 1974—; alt. del. Internat. Congress Radiology. Served to lt. (j.g.), M.C., USNR, 1947-49. Nat. Cancer Inst. grantee, 1971-75; Nat. Cancer Inst. Specialized Cancer Center grantee, 1973-75. Diplomate Am. Bd. Radiology. Fellow Am. Coll. Radiology; mem. Detroit Acad. Medicine, Detroit Med. Club, AMA (vice chmn. sect. council 1969-71), Mich. State, Wayne County (Mich.) med. socs., Mich. Radiol. Soc. (pres. 1969-70), Am. Radium Soc., Am. Roentgen Ray Soc. (Silver medal 1962), AAAS, Radiol. Soc. N.Am., Inter-Am. Coll. Radiology, Friends of Detroit Pub. Library, Founders Soc. Detroit Inst. Art, State Hist. Soc. Iowa, Mich. Hist. Soc., Lost Lakes Woods Assn., Sigma Xi, Alpha Omega Alpha. Clubs: Masons, Detroit. Asso. editor Am. Jour. Roentgenology, Radium Therapy and Nuclear Medicine, 1958—. Exhibited portable radioactive isotopes for radiography at Smithsonian Instn., 1964-67. Home: 52 Oxford Rd Pleasant Ridge MI 48069 Office: 540 E Canfield St Detroit MI 48201

KRAEMER, BOYD ANDRE, city ofcl.; b. N.Y.C., Jan. 29, 1947; s. Raymond Jacob and Mildred Eileen (Fetterroll) K.; student S.D. Sch. Mines and Tech., 1965-66; B.S., S.D. State U., 1970; m. Kathleen Ann Thompson, Aug. 9, 1969. Landscape contractor Brookings (S.D.) Ind. Sch. Dist. 122, 1968; park caretaker, city forester City of Brookings, 1968-70; dir. parks and recreation City of Wheat Ridge, Colo., 1970-74; landscape supt. Genesee Assos., Denver, 1974; dir. parks, city forester City of Oshkosh (Wis.), 1975—; mem. tech. adv. com. E. Central Regional Planning Commn. Sec., treas. Clear Creek, Inc., Wheat Ridge, 1971—. Mem. Nat., Mid-Continent park and recreation assns., Wis. Parks and Recreation Assn., Wis. Aboretum Assn. Office: City Hall 215 Church Ave PO Box 1130 Oshkosh WI 54901

KRAEMER, HAROLD WILLIAM, lumber co. exec.; b. Melrose, Minn., Aug. 12, 1951; s. Edwin Jack and Mable Barbara (Ohmann) K.; student St. Cloud State U., 1971; m. Mary Ann Wesbur, Mar. 3, 1973; children—Jennifer Ann, Jeremy Aaron, Melanie Jean. Carpenter, Kraemer Lumber Co., Greenwald, Minn., 1969-72, estimator, draftsman, 1972-76, owner, partner, mgr., Melrose, Minn., 1976—. Bd. dirs. Melrose C. of C., 1977—. Served with USMC, 1969-71. Mem. N.W. Lumberman's Assn. Roman Catholic. Clubs: Lions (Melrose), Jaycees (Greenwald), Central Minn. Hoo-Hoo's, Am. Legion. Home: Melrose MN 56352 Office: Kraemer Lumber Co Melrose MN 56352

KRAFT, REYBURN HERMAN, dairy co. exec.; b. Chester, Ill., Dec. 6, 1925; s. Herman F. and Ella (Ahrens) K.; student U. Ill., 1946-48; m. Hazel L. Denny, Dec. 23, 1948; children—Lynn Ann, David Ray. Partner, Chester City Dairy (Ill.), 1948-60; sec., treas. Chester Dairy Co., 1960-62, pres., 1962—. Trustee Chester Library Bd. Served with AUS, 1944-46. Mem. Am. Mgmt. Assn., Am. Legion. Lutheran (elder 1966—). Club: Rotary. Home: 17 Washington St Chester IL 62233 Office: 1915 State St Chester IL 62233

KRAHEL, WILLIAM ALBERT, fin. analyst; b. Martins Ferry, Ohio, Mar. 7, 1948; s. Walter William and Alberta (Kucera) K.; B.S., Wheeling Coll., 1970; m. Jean Marie England, June 1, 1974; 1 son, William A. Accountant, Med. Diagnostic Services div. Chemed Corp., Cin., 1972, accounting mgr., 1972-74; v.p. fin. and adminstrn. Med. Diagnostic Services - Ohio Valley, Cin., 1974-77; sr. fin. analyst Gould Inc., McConnelsville, Ohio, 1977-78, controller, 1978—. Mem. Greater Cin. C. of C. Home: 340 Poplar Dr McConnelsville OH 43756 Office: Ohio State Route 60 McConnelsville OH 43756

KRAHL, ENZO, surgeon; b. Fiume, Italy, Apr. 22, 1924; s. Massimiliano and Camilla (Aub) K.; came to U.S., 1951, naturalized, 1955; M.D., U. Florence (Italy), 1948; m. Anne Katharine Ferbstein, June 14, 1958; children—Edward Alexander, Katharine Frances. Asst. dept. surgery U. Rome, 1948-51, Brit. Council scholar, 1949; fellow in vascular surgery Columbi Presbyn. Med. Center, N.Y.C., 1951-52, fellow in surgery, 1954-55; resident in surgery St. Vincent's Hosp., N.Y.C., 1952-54, chief resident in surgery Akron (Ohio) City Hosp., 1957-58; dir. grad. edn. Akron Gen. Hosp., 1959-60; practice medicine specializing in surgery, Akron, 1958-60, Superior, Wis., 19—; mem. staff Superior Meml. Hosp.; founder Superior Clinic, 1964. Vice pres. Duluth—Superior Symphony; mem. exec. com., bd. dirs. Health Systems Agy. Western Lake Superior. Served as capt. M.C., U.S. Army, 1955-57. Recipient 1st prize for thesis U. Florence (Italy), 1948; United Fund award, 1965; certificate of merit N.Y.C. Civil Def., 1953; diplomate Am. Bd. Surgery. Mem. Douglas County (Wis.), Wis. State (mem. peer review commn.) med. socs., AMA, U.S. Power Squadron, Am. Bridge League. Jewish. Clubs: Kiwanis, Northland Country, Duluth Indoor Tennis, Masons, Shriners. Contbr. articles to med. jours. Home: 3 White Birch Trail Superior WI 54880 Office: 3600 Tower Ave Superior WI 54880

KRALL, JOSEPH I., cardiologist; b. Cleve., Apr. 9, 1938; s. Ellis H. and Margie S. (Straus) K.; A.B., U. Pa., 1960; M.D., State U. N.Y., Buffalo, 1965; m. Mary Ann Lamont, Aug. 24, 1975; children—Roy, Jennifer, Sarah. Intern, Mt. Sinai Hosp., Cleve., 1965-66; resident in cardiology Met. Gen. Hosp., Cleve., also Mt. Sinai Hosp., 1966-70; dir. cardiac catheterization lab. St. Lukes Hosp., Cleve., 1972-74; practice medicine specializing in cardiology, Cleve., 1974—; chief of medicine Shaker Med. Center Hosp., Cleve.; asst. clin. prof. medicine Case Western Res. U. Served to capt. U.S. Army, 1967-73. Diplomate Am. Bd. Internal Medicine, Am. Bd. Cardiovascular Disease. Fellow Am. Coll. Cardiology, Am. Heart Assn. (fellow Council Clin. Cardiology). Home: 3387 Chalfant Rd Shaker Heights OH 44120 Office: 11710 Shaker Blvd Cleveland OH 44120

KRAMER, ALEX JOHN, dentist; b. Aurora, Ill., Dec. 21, 1939; s. Roy Edward and Frances (Astromskis) K.; student Marquette U., 1957-60; D.D.S., U. Ill., 1964; m. Phyllis Gonsky, July 15, 1967. Gen. practice dentistry, Montgomery, Ill., 1966—, Plano, Ill., 1969—; pres. Montgomery Med. Arts Bldg., Inc., 1966—. Mem. exec. bd. Two Rivers council Boy Scouts Am., 1969—, v.p., 1975—. Served as lt. Dental Corps, USNR, 1964-66. Mem. Internat. Acad. Orthomolecular and Preventive Medicine, Internat. Acad. Orthodontics, Am. Soc. Preventive Dentistry, Pierre Fauchard Acad., Am. Soc. Gen. Dentistry, Am. Acad. Gnathologic Orthopedics, Am. Assn. Maxillofacial Orthopedics (charter), ADA, Ill., Fox Valley, Aurora, Chgo. dental socs., U. Ill. Alumni Assn., Dentofacial Orthopedics Study Club Mo. (charter), Nat. Soc. Pershing Rifles, Psi Omega. Roman Catholic. Clubs: Aurora Luncheon Optimist (sec., treas. 1969), Aurora Country. Home: 70 S Gladstone Aurora IL 60506 Office: 115 N Main St Montgomery IL 60538 also 9 N Hugh St Plano IL 60545

KRAMER, ANNE HELEN, personnel adminstr.; b. Bklyn., Aug. 10, 1952; d. William Hans and Rose Martha (Mack) Kramer; B.S. in Phys. Edn., U. Wis., LaCrosse, 1974, now postgrad. in coll. student personnel. Instr., supr. Waukesha (Wis.) Park and Recreation Dept., 1974-76; recreation supr. United Migrant Opportunity Services, Milw., 1974; parts cunter clk. Kuettner Oldsmobile Co., Waukesha, 1974-75; day clk.-bartender Hartbrook Lanes, Hartland, Wis., 1975-76; hall dir. Winona (Minn.) State U., 1977—; acting pres. Sigma Lambd Corp., Alpha Omicron Pi, 1976-77. Mem. Am. Personnel and Guidance Assn., Am. Coll. Personnel Assn. Office: care Student Affairs Winona State U Winona MN 55987

KRAMER, CARL EDWARD, historian; b. New Albany, Ind., May 22, 1946; s. Douglas Manuel and Jane Anastacia (Markert) K.; A.B., Anderson (Ind.) Coll., 1968; M.S., U. Louisville, 1972; M.A., Roosevelt U., 1970; postgrad. U. Toledo, 1972-75. Tchr., intern Urban Tchr. Corps. Chgo. Bd. Edn., 1968-70; population analyst U.S. Bur. Census, Jeffersonville, Ind., 1970-71; research planner Louisville and Jefferson County Planning Commn., Louisville, 1971-72; adj. instr. Inst. Community Devel., U. Louisville, 1976—; archtl. historian Historic Landmarks and Preservation Dists. Comm., Louisville, 1977—; instr. Center for Life Long Learning, Spalding Coll., Louisville, 1977. Mem. exec. bd., v.p. council, Boy Scouts Am., 1977. dist. vice chmn. 1975-77, chmn. long rang planning com., 1977; mem. by laws and auditing com. Silver Creek Hist. Museum; mem. Citizens Met. Planning Council Louisville, William Leckie Grad. scholar, 1974; recipient Nat. Distinguished Service award Order Arrow, Boy Scouts, 1973, Dist. Merit award, 1976. Mem. Am. Hist. Assn., Orgn. Am. Historian, Am. Inst. Planners (asso.), Am. Soc. Planning Ofcls., Community Devel. Soc. Am., World Future Soc., Nat. Trust Historic Preservation, Preservation Alliance Louisville and Jefferson County, Louisville Hist. League, Phi Eta Sigma, Alpha Chi, Phi Kappa Phi, Alpha Phi Gamma, Pi Gamma Mu, Phi Alpha Theta. Democrat. Mem. United Ch. of Christ. Clubs: Filson, Third Century. Contbr. articles to Colloquim, Filson Club History Quar., Louisville Mag. Home: 506 Popp Ave Sellersburg IN 47172 Office: 727 W Main St Louisville KY 40202

KRAMER, CHARLES EUGENE, gear mfg. co. exec.; b. Hamilton, Ohio, Mar. 19, 1910; s. George and Deborah (Begley) K.; B.S. in Mech. Engring., Purdue U., 1940; m. Nelda M. Wood, Aug. 12, 1941; children—Janet Lynn, Robert Michael. Time study engr. Fairfield Mfg. Co., Inc., subs. Rexnord, Inc., Lafayette, Ind., 1940-51, chief indsl. engr., 1951-58, factory mgr., 1958-63, v.p. mfg., 1963-73, pres., chief exec. officer, 1973—; dir. Lafayette Nat. Bank, Schwab Safe Co., Inc. Bd. dirs Lafayette Purdue Research Found.; trustee Lafayette YMCA; Ind. Vocat. and Tech. Coll. Served with U.S. Army, 1944-46. Registered profl. engr., Ind. Mem. Am. Mgmt. Assn., Presidents Assn., ASME, Am. Inst. Indsl. Engrs., Am. Gear Mfrs. Assn. (dir.). Republican. Methodist. Clubs: Lafayette Country, Elks. Home: 300 Valley Lafayette IN 47905 Office: Fairfield Mfg Co Inc US 52 S Lafayette IN 47902

KRAMER, DAVID BRUCE, publisher; b. Keokuk, Iowa, Aug. 12, 1928; s. Verle V. and Sybil (Mershon) K.; B.S., U. Ill., 1951; m. Norma Lee Izard, Aug. 21, 1949; children—Michael, Mark, Lisa. Partner, Kramer Publ. Co., Gibson City, Ill., 1951—. Pres., Fire Protection Dist. Bd. Trustees, 1972—, Gibson Beautification Found., 1975; past pres. Gibson City Plan Commn. Served with AUS, 1950-51. Mem. Ill. Press Assn. (pres. 1972-73), Gibson City C. of C. Lion. Home: 123 W 19th St Gibson City IL 60936 Office: 110 N Sangamon Ave Gibson City IL 60936

KRAMER, DAVID EUGENE, environ. protection engr.; b. Batesville, Ind., Aug. 7, 1950; s. Leonard Francis and Agnes Josephine (Hermesch) K.; B.S. in Agrl. Engring., Purdue U., 1972; M.S., S.D. State U., 1974; m. Cynthia Susan Morris, July 9, 1976; 1 son, Bryan. Soils engr. Claude H. Hurley Co., Elmhurst, Ill., 1974-76; engr. Ill. Environ. Protection Agency, Springfield, 1977—. Mem. Am. Soc. Agrl. Engrs. (asso.), Sigma Xi, Alpha Epsilon. Roman Catholic. Home: Box 369 Pawnee IL 62558 Office: 4500 S 6th St Rd Springfield IL 62706

KRAMER, FREDERICK CLAUDE, photographer; b. Vienna, Austria, Feb. 16, 1914; s. Joseph and Grete Kramer; grad. U. Vienna, 1938; m. Ginette Martin, June 28, 1957; children—Marion, Valerie. Photographer specializing in exec. portraits, Chgo., 1960—. Mem. Am. Humanist Assn. (past pres. Evanston chpt.). Club: Am.-Austria Soc. Midwest. Home: 446 Sandy Ln Wilmette IL 60091 Office: 180 N Wacker Dr Chicago IL 60606

KRAMER, HELEN ANN TOBABEN, librarian; b. Walnut, Kans.; d. Henry J. and Amelia (Munstermann) Tobaben; A.A., Independence Community Coll., 1956; B.S., Kans. State Coll., 1964, M.S., 1976; M.S., Kans. State Tchrs. Coll., 1965; m. Sidney W. Kramer, Feb. 14, 1942 (div. May 1945); 1 son, Jim L. Cons. Roux Distbg. Co., Inc., N.Y.C., 1948-55; 57-63; librarian, asso. prof. librarianship Kans. State U., Pittsburg, 1965—; exec. dir. Nat. Library Week, 1970-72; adviser Alpha Gamma Delta, 1966—. Mem. AAUP (v.p. 1971-73), AAUW, Am., Kans. (exec. council 1969-72) library assns., Phi Theta Kappa, Kappa Delta Pi, Pi Omega Pi, Phi Alpha Theta, Delta Kappa Gamma, Phi Delta Phi. Lutheran. Club: Altrusa. Home: 2001 Countryside Dr Pittsburg KS 67662

KRAMER, JOHN LOUIS, civil engr.; b. Jefferson City, Mo., July 10, 1948; s. Cletus Joseph and Elizabeth Sara (Gerling) K.; B.C.E., U. Mo.-Rolla, 1970. Hwy. engr. trainee Fed. Hwy. Adminstrn., 1971; project engr. Jefferson City Pub. Works, 1971-76; gen. mgr. Traverse Cons., Inc., Jefferson City, 1976—. Bd. dirs. Helias Home Assn. Mem. ASCE, Nat., Mo. socs. profl. engrs., Jefferson City Engrs. Club (chmn. edn. com. 1972-73, chmn. engrs. week com. 1974), Chi Epsilon (sec. 1970), Tau Beta Pi. Roman Catholic. Club: K.C. (4 deg.). Home: 1731 Overlook Dr Jefferson City MO 65101 Office: 707 E McCarty St Jefferson City MO 65101

KRAMER, OSCAR, farmer, county ofcl.; b. Linton, Ind., Apr. 25, 1905; s. Fred J. and Sophia (Strietelemeier) K.; student pub. schs. Stockton Twp.; m. Ruth Swaby, Dec. 22, 1932; 1 dau., Regina R. Farmer, Linton, Ind., 1925—; substitute rural mail carrier, 1923-48; mem. Greene County Council, 1963-67; Greene County commr., 1967-71. Dist. supr. Soil and Water Conservation Dist., 1955-66; pres. Greene County Soil and Water Conservation Dist., 1956-62; mem. Greene County Extension Com., 1951—, Community Study Com., 1967—. Trustee Freeman Greene County Hosp.; mem. adv. com. Vincennes U.; pres. Greene County Hosp. Assn. Mem. Farm Bur., Wabash Valley Assn. (past pres. Greene County chpt.), Linton C. of C. Republican. Mem. United Ch. of Christ (elder). Home: Rural Route 1 Lone Tree Rd Linton IN 47441

KRANITZ, THEODORE MITCHELL, lawyer; b. St. Joseph, Mo., May 27, 1922; s. Louis and Miriam (Saferstein) K.; student St. Joseph Jr. Coll., 1940-41; B.S. in Fgn. Service, Georgetown U., 1948, J.D., 1950; m. Elaine Shirley Kaufman, June 11, 1944; children—Hugh David, Karen Gail and Kathy Jane (twins). Admitted to Mo. bar, 1950, U.S. Supreme Ct. bar, 1955; partner firm Kranitz & Kranitz, St. Joseph, 1950—. Pres. Micropublis, Inc. Active Boy Scouts; pres. St. Joseph Community Theatre, Inc., 1958-60; bd. dirs. United Jewish Fund of St. Joseph, 1957—, pres., 1958-63; sec. Boys' Baseball St. Joseph, 1964-68; trustee Temple Adath Joseph, 1970-74, 77—; bd. dirs. Sholem Temple, 1976—. Served from pvt. to 1st lt. USAAF, 1942-46, ret. capt. USAF Res. Fellow Am. Acad. Matrimonial Lawyers; mem. Am. Legion, Air Force Assn., Res. Officers Assn., Am., St. Joseph (pres. 1977-78) bar assns., Mo. Bar, Am. Soc. Internat. Law, Internat. Acad. Law and Sci., Nat. Assn. Criminal Def. Lawyers. Mem. B'nai B'rith (dist. bd. govs., 1958-61). Author articles in field. Home: 2609 Gene Field Rd St Joseph MO 64506 Office: Boder Bldg 107 S 4th St St Joseph MO 64501

KRANTZ, BEATRICE V., ednl. adminstr.; b. Chgo.; d. Andrew S. and Beatrice K.; B.A., Lake Forest Coll.; M.A. in Public Law, Columbia U.; postgrad. Northwestern U., 1944-60, U. Ill., 1960-62, No. Ill. U., 1964, Ill. Inst. Tech., 1969. Formerly adminstrv. asst. to lawyer, Chgo.; tchr. social studies Deerfield (Ill.) Shields High Sch.; tchr. govt., econs. and history High Sch. Dist. 218, Blue Island, Ill., 1936-47; asst. county supt. schs., dir. tchr. personnel and placement Cook County Schs., Chgo., 1947-51, asst. supt. secondary edn., scholarships, guidance, 1967-70, asst. supt. in charge West area Ednl. Service Region, Cook County, 1970—; adminstrv. asst. to supt. Dist. 88, Du Page County, 1951-59, dean of girls, Elmhurst, Ill., 1960-66; ednl. cons., 1974—. Mem. exec. com. Heart Assn. W. Cook Regions for County. Recipient Distinguished Alumni award Lake Forest Coll., 1976. Mem. NEA, Am. Assn. Sch. Adminstrs., No. Ill. Supts. Round Table, Pan Hellenic Assn., Delta Kappa Gamma, Alpha Xi Delta. Research in field. Office: 1032 Washington Blvd Oak Park IL 60302

KRANTZ, LAWRENCE HENRY, real estate broker, investor, educator; b. Detroit, Nov. 26, 1930; s. Francis Xavier and Edithe Sarah (Kline) K.; engring. certificate Electronics Inst. Det., 1956; B.B.A., Detroit Inst. Tech., 1968; M.A., U. Mich., 1977; 1 dau., Gwendolyn Loretta. With sales mgmt. dept. Texaco Inc., Dearborn, Mich., 1952-59, Pure Oil Co., Detroit, 1959-62; owner, operator Belleville Exway Pure Oil Service Inc. (Mich.), 1963-72; instr. small bus. mgmt. Oakland Community Coll., 1972—; cons. Flag's Restaurant's Inc. Served with U.S. Navy, 1948-52; Korea. Mem. Am. Assn. Accountants. Republican. Home: 12300 Lake Pointe Pass Belleville MI 48111

KRASE, ROGER CURTIS, dentist; b. Kingman, Kans., Nov. 13, 1940; s. Lloyd Cerico and Elizabeth Mary (Hart) K.; B.A., Friends U., 1963; D.D.S., U. Mo., Kansas City, 1968; m. Sandra Jean Ebbs, May 30, 1965; children—Gretchen Elaine, Heather Jane, Charles Quincy. Pvt. practice dentistry, McPherson, Kans., 1970-71; pres. McPherson Health Planning, 1968—. Mem. ADA, Full Gospel Bus. Men's Fellowship Internat. (1st v.p. McPherson chpt. 1977), Am. Soc. Preventive Dentistry. Am. Soc. Dentistry for Children, Kans. Dental Assn. Club: Gideons. Served to lt. USN, 1 968-70. Home: 410 S Ash St McPherson KS 67460 Office: Peoples Bank Bldg McPherson KS 67460

KRATOVIL, ROBERT, lawyer, educator; b. Oshkosh, Wis., May 21, 1910; s. Jacob and Stephanie (Urban) K.; J.D., DePaul U., 1933; m. Ruth Kratovil, Aug. 15, 1952; 1 son, Anthony Robert. Admitted to Ill. bar, 1934; chief title officer Chgo. Title & Trust Co., 1959-62; gen. counsel Chgo. Title Ins. Co., 1962-66; v.p. legal research Chgo. Title & Trust Co., 1966-74, Chgo. Title Ins. Co., 1966-74; faculty John Marshall Law Sch., Chgo., 1975—; instr. real estate law and mortgages Am. Savs. and Loan Inst., 1939-59, DePaul U., Coll. Law, 1947-59, Mortgage Bankers Assn. Am., 1959—; now prof. law John Marshall Law Sch., Chgo. Mem. Am., Ill., Chgo. bar assns., Pi Gamma Mu. Author: Real Estate Law, 6th edit., 1974; Modern Mortgage Law and Practice, 1972; Modern Real Estate Documentation, 1975. Contbr. articles profl. jours. Home: 2772 Garrison Ave Evanston IL 60201 Office: 315 S Plymouth Ct Chicago IL 60604

KRAUSE, ARTHUR WALTER, mfg. co. exec.; b. Milw., Jan. 2, 1919; s. Arthur R. and Selma (Kruse) K.; student U. Wis., evening div., 1947-56; m. Margaret E. Keller, June 21, 1941; 1 dau., Lynn Margaret. Asst. gen. mgr. Delta Mfg. Co., Milw., 1950-54; works mgr. Rockwell Mfg. Co., Pitts., 1954-55; chief methods engr. Controls Co. Am., 1955-59; gen. mgr. Hydraulic Machinery Co., Waukesha, Wis., 1959-62, v.p. fabricated metal products, 1962-64; pres. Hydraulic Power Equipment Corp., Milw., 1964-72; pres. Pettibone Wis. Corp., Milw., 1972—; dir. br. operations Pettibone Corp., Chgo., 1972—. Served with USMC, 1944-46. Republican. Lutheran. Home: 4532 W Fountain Ave Brown Deer WI 53223 Office: 6122 N 76th St Milwaukee WI 53218 also 9501 W Devon Ave Rosemont IL 60018

KRAUSE, EDWARD WALTER, athletic dir.; b. Chgo., Feb. 2, 1913; s. Walter and Theresa (Krauklis) K.; grad. U. Notre Dame, 1934; m. Elizabeth Linden, Aug. 27, 1938; children—Edward Walter, Mary Elise, Philip Charles. Athletic dir., coach St. Mary's Coll., Winona, Minn., 1934-39; line coach Holy Cross Coll., 1939-42; line coach U. Notre Dame, 1942-44, 44-48, head basketball coach, 1942-4, 46-51, asst. athletic dir., 1948-49, athletic dir., 1949—. Dir. First United Life Ins. Co. Pres. Community Chest; chmn. South Bend Recreation Bd.; dir. United Fund, NCCJ; vice chmn. Pan-Am. games. Served as 1st lt. USMCR, 1944-46; mem. Res. Named to Football Hall of Fame Honors Ct., Basketball Hall of Fame. Mem. C. of C. (dir.), Nat. Assn. Collegiate Dirs. Athletics (mem. exec. com. 1972—), Am. Legion. Roman Catholic. Clubs: K.C. (4 deg.), Knights Malta, Eagles, Country. Home: 309 Peashway St South Bend IN 46617 Office: U Notre Dame Notre Dame IN 46556

KRAUSE, PAUL ANTON, counselor; b. Flint, Mich., May 27, 1949; s. Seymour S. and Melba Violet (Simons) K.; B.S. in Bus. Edn., Ferris State Coll., 1971; M.A. in Counseling and Guidance, Central Mich., U., 1972, Ed.S. in Counseling and Psychology, 1975. Humanistic counselor Brandywine Pub. Schs., Niles, Mich., 1972—; instr. Raja Yoga Southwestern Mich. Coll., Dowagiac, Mich., 1973—; co-therapist Family Rap Group Riverwoo Mental Health Dept., Niles, 1975—; instr. Raja Yoga, counselin Grad. Sch. Counselor Edn. and Personal Devel. Central Mich. U., Mt. Pleasant, 1975-76. Mem. Nat., Mich., Brandywine edn. assns., Am., Mich. personnel and guidance assns., Berrien-Cass-Van Buren County Counselors Assn., Himalayan Internat. Inst. Yoga Sci. and Philosophy. Mem. Self-Realization Fellowship Ch. Home: 808 W Front St #86 Buchanan MI 49107 Office: 1700 Bell Rd Niles MI 49120

KRAUTKREMER, JAMES JOSEPH, coop. exec., mayor; b. Jordan, Minn., Apr. 18, 1934; s. James Edwin and Sophia Mary (Hennes) K.; B.Edn., U. Nebr., 1963; m. Shirley Ann Bond, June 1, 1957; children—Julie, Dan, Paul, David. Programmer, Mut. of Omaha, 1953-64; mgr. data processing Kenny Rehab. Found., Mpls., 1964-66; dir. MIS, Midland Coops., Inc. (wholesale), Fridley, Minn., 1966—. Mem. Planning Commn. Brooklyn Park, 1967-70, City Council, 1970-72, mayor, 1972—. Served with AUS, 1954-56. Mem. Assn. for Computing Machinery, Data Processing Mgmt. Assn., NCR Upper Midwest Users Group (dir.), Fedn. NCR Computer Users Groups (pres. 1972-75). Home: 8109 66th Ave N Brooklyn Park MN 55428 Office: I-694 at Main St NE Fridley MN 55421

KRAVETZ, RUSSELL STUART, psychiatrist; b. Lexington, Ky., July 22, 1930; s. Louis and Florence (Byer) K.; B.S., U. Cin., 1950, M.D., 1954; m. Albertta Lee Mayer, May 7, 1959; children—Dayna Ilene, Todd Michael. Rotating intern Cin. Gen. Hosp., 1954-55, jr. resident dept. internal medicine, 1957-58, asst. resident dept. psychiatry, 1958-60, clin. fellow psychosomatic medicine dept. psychiatry, 1960-61, clinician depts. internal medicine and psychiatry, outpatient dept., 1961—, asst. attending psychiatrist, 1961—; practice medicine specializing in psychiatry, Cin., 1961—; asst. dir. psychiat. clinic City Cin. Municipal Ct., 1961-62; asst. clin. prof. dept. psychiatry U. Cin. Coll. Medicine, 1967-73, asso. clin. prof., 1973—; attending staff dept. psychiatry Jewish Hosp., Cin.; active staff dept. neuropsychiatry Christ Hosp., Cin. Trustee Central Psychiat. Clinic, 1973—, Glen Manor Home for Aged. Served as lt. M.C., USNR, 1955-57. Diplomate in psychiatry Am. Bd. Psychiatry and Neurology. Med. Assn., Cin. Acad. Medicine Cin. Soc. Mem. Am., Ohio psychiat. assns., AMA, Ohio Neurology and Psychiatry, Phi Beta Kappa, Alpha Omega Alpha. Home: 7011 Fair Oaks Dr Cincinnati OH 45227 Office: 2607 Burnet Ave Cincinnati OH 45219

KRC, JOHN, JR., chem. crystallographer; b. Chgo., May 17, 1920; s. John and Elizabeth (Babjar) K.; B.S. in Chemistry (scholar), U. Chgo., 1943; student U. Charles IV, Prague, Czechoslovakia, 1946-47; m. Bessie Anna Neboska, Sept. 18, 1949; children—John Conrad, Deborah Lynn, Glen Daniel, Cynthia Louise, George Samuel. Chemist, E.J. Brach and Sons, Chgo., 1947-48, Tucker Corp., Chgo., 1948, Swift & Co., Chgo., 1948; with Armour Research Found., Ill. Inst. Tech., 1949-61, asst. supr. analytical chemistry and explosives research depts., 1954-61; with Parke, Davis & Co., pharmaceuticals, Detroit, 1961—, sr. research pharmacist, 1971—; adj. prof., lectr. U. Mich. Sch. Pharmacy, Ann Arbor, 1967—; cons. in field. Pres. Chgo. sect. Am. Rocket Soc., 1957-58, dir., 1958-61; v.p. Chgo. sect. Am. Inst. Chemists, 1956-57. Mem. sch. bd. Our Shepherd Sch., Birmingham, Mich., 1966-71. Served with USAAF, 1943-45. Decorated D.F.C., Air medal; fellow Inst. Internat. Edn., 1946-47. Mem. AAAS, Am. Crystallographic Assn., Mich. Indsl. Hygiene Soc., Nat. Slovak Soc., Sigma Xi, Phi Beta Sigma. Contbr. articles, chpts. to profl. publs. Home: 26669 Huntington Rd Huntington Woods MI 48070 Office: Parke Davis and Co PO Box 118 Detroit MI 48232

KREBS, CLYDE L., motion picture and communication program producer; b. Warsaw, Ill., Aug. 4, 1922; s. Clyde L. and Ruth Geneva (Griscel) K.; B.B.A., Northwestern U., 1942, postgrad., 1948; m. Cissie A. Draves, Oct. 22, 1949. Sales rep. Capital Airlines, Chgo., 1946, mgr. regional promotion, 1947; sales rep. and engr. Ill. Bell Telephone Co., Chgo., 1947-48; accounting exec. Bills Sales Cons., Chgo., 1948-50; partner Phillips Assos., Chgo., 1950-51; account exec. Sarra Inc., Chgo., 1951-56; v.p., gen. mgr. Galbreath Pictures Inc., Chgo., 1956-60; v.p. nat. sales Reid H. Ray Film Industries Inc., Chgo., 1960-69; pres., dir. Cine-Mark div. Krebs Prodns. Inc., Chgo., 1969—; asso. lectr. Northwestern U., Evanston, Ill., 1949-51. Served with USAAF, 1942-45. Decorated Bronze Star with four oak leaf clusters. Mem. Chgo. Audio-Visual Producers Assn. (dir.), Chgo. Assn. Commerce and Industry. Republican. Presbyterian (elder). Clubs: Lake Shore, Execs., Key. Producer: Steel and America, 1966, Discover America, 1967, The Arizona Adventure, 1971, Impulse 90, 1971, Threshold of Tomorrow, 1971, The Lasting Medium, 1971, A Trail for All Seasons, 1971, Land of the Conquistatores, 1973, Florida—Yours to Discover, 1974, Grand Canyon-An Encounter with Creation, 1976, Chicago is . . .! 1977. Home: 850 DeWitt Pl Chicago IL 60611 Office: 1 IBM Plaza Chicago IL 60611

KREBS, FESTUS JOHN, JR., advt. co. exec.; b. St. Louis, Jan. 31, 1926; s. Festus J. and Marion Alice (Heffernan) K.; B.S., St. Louis U., 1949; postgrad. U. Lausanne (Switzerland); m. Virginia Klohr, June 13, 1953; children—Festus John, Marion Virginia, Carol Marie, Dorothy C. Heffernan, Martin Dean. Vice pres. Char-Lite Mfg. Co., St. Louis, 1955—, dir., 1955—; account exec. and dir. mktg. Roman Co., St. Louis, 1949-58, v.p., 1958-68; founder F.J. Krebs & Assos., Inc., St. Louis, 1968, pres., chmn. bd., 1968—. Co-chmn. Com. for Preservation of Residential Areas in University City, Mo., 1959-65; chmn. sales promotion com. Pres. Eisenhower's Conf. Small Bus., 1958; bd. govs. Lake Forest Trust, Richmond Heights, Mo., 1971-74, trustee, 1974-77; mem. pres.'s council St. Louis U. High, 1971-76; mem. fin. com. Immaculate Ch., 1974—; bd. dirs. Nat. Shrine of Our Lady of the Rivers, 1977—. Served in C.E., U.S. Army, 1944-46. Mem. Am. Mktg. Assn. (dir. 1954-59, pres. St. Louis chpt. 1960-61), Nat. Fedn. Advt. Agys., Nat. Assn. Indsl. Advertisers, Advt. Club St. Louis. Club: Mo. Athletic. Home: 8 Lake Forest Saint Louis MO 63117 Office: 7750 Clayton Rd Saint Louis MO 63117

KREBS, KENNETH ALLEN, dentist; b. Louisville, Aug. 11, 1942; s. Irvin Morris and Shirley (Epstein) K.; student Ind. U., 1960-63; D.M.D., U. Louisville, 1967; clin. certificate periodontics U. Ky., 1970; m. Sandra Yvonne Schwartz, Aug. 22, 1965; 1 son, Mark David. Rotating intern, dental service Michael Reese Hosp. and Med. Center, Chgo., 1967-68, spl. tng. periodontics, 1968-70; practice dentistry specializing in periodontics, Chgo., 1970—; asso. prof. Northwestern U. Dental Sch., 1970—; asst. attending physician, div. dentistry Michael Reese Hosp. and Med. Center, 1970—; cons. periodontics Ill. Bd. Dental Examiners, 1976-77. Mem. ADA, Am. Acad. Periodontology, Ill., Chgo. dental socs., Ill. Soc. Periodontists (pres. 1976-77), Evanston Assn. Dentists (sec.-treas. 1977), Omicron Kappa Upsilon, Phi Kappa Phi. Home: 2738 Birchwood Wilmette IL 60091 Office: 30 N Michigan Ave Chicago IL 60602 also 636 Church St Evanston IL 60201

KRECH, EDWARD M., JR., consumer products co. exec.; b. Paterson, N.J., June 28, 1932; s. Edward M. and Virginia (Pardee) K.; B.M.E., Cornell U., 1955, M.B.A., 1958; m. Joan Gras, Nov. 1, 1953; children—Susan, Edward, Kathleen. With internat. engring. dept. Procter & Gamble Co., 1958—, sect. head European Tech. Center, Brussels, 1966-70, mgr. design and constrn. Procter & Gamble Ltd., Newcastle, Eng., 1970-75, asso. dir. engring. for Asia and Latin Am., Cin., 1975—; instr. U.S. Naval Acad., Annapolis, Md., 1955-57. Served with USN, 1955-57. Mem. ASME, Royal Yachting Assn. Office: Procter & Gamble 6060 Center Hill Rd Cincinnati OH 45224

KRECKE, CHARLES FRANCIS, radiologist; b. Detroit, Dec. 24, 1926; s. Norman W. and Frances Maria (Currie) K.; student U. Notre Dame, 1944-45; B.S., U. Mich., 1948, M.D., 1953; m. Anne Elizabeth McKamy, May 18, 1957; children—Karl Norman, Paul Raymond, Kathryn Anne. Intern, Blodgett Meml. Hosp., Grand Rapids, Mich., 1953-54; resident, Henry Ford Hosp., Detroit, 1954-57; practice medicine specializing in radiology, Birmingham, Mich., 1961-63; radiologist, St. Mary's Hosp., Grand Rapids, Mich., 1963—, dir. radiology, 1968—, vice chief of staff, 1972—; clin. asst. prof. medicine, Mich. State U., 1971-76, clin. asso. prof. radiology, 1976—; pres. Drs. Krecke, Benson, Ashby and Assos., P.C., 1968—; pres. Kent Radiologic Inst., P.C., 1976—. Served with USNR, 1944-46; served with M.C. USAF, 1954-61. Diplomate Am. Bd. Radiology. Mem. AMA, Am. Coll. Radiology, Radiol. Soc. N.Am. Episcopalian. Club: Peninsular. Home: 936 San Lucia Dr SE East Grand Rapids MI 49506 Office: 220 Medical Arts Bldg Grand Rapids MI 49502

KREER, HENRY BLACKSTONE, mktg. and assn. exec.; b. Pitts., Sept. 2, 1923; s. George William and Fay Palmer K.; student Princeton U., 1941-42, Northwestern U., 1946; m. Irene Overman, Dec. 22, 1946; children—Laurene, Linda (Mrs. Thomas Witt). Copy writer Batten, Barton, Durstine & Osborn, Chgo., 1947-51; account supr. Campbell-Mithun Inc., Chgo., 1951-55; owner, operator Henry B. Kreer & Co., Chgo., 1955-68; partner, pres., dir. Stevens Kirkland, Kreer Inc., Chgo., 1968—; pres. Nat. Accounts Mktg., Inc., 1975—; exec. dir. REACT Internat., Inc., 1962—. Chmn. radio subcom. Nat. Industry Adv. Com. FCC, 1967-73. Served to capt. USMCR, 1942-45. Decorated D.F.C., Air medal with 4 clusters. Home: 1904 Glen Oak Dr Glenview IL 60025 Office: 111 E Wacker Dr Chicago IL 60601

KREGEL, ANNA MAY, piano tchr.; b. Nebraska City, Nebr., Apr. 11, 1916; d. Robert W. and Ann (Kerrick) Kregel; B.A. cum laude, Mo. Valley Coll., 1938, Mus.B., 1939; M. Music Edn., U. Mo., Kansas City, 1976. Tchr. high sch., DeWitt, Mo., 1938-39, Kidder, Mo., 1940-42; with Kansas City Star, 1942-44; secretarial position Trans World Airlines, 1945, Thompson Hayward Chem., 1946, Johnson Sales, 1948; exec. sec. Line Material Co., 1949-51, Kansas City Philharmonic, 1951-52, City Plan Dept., Kansas City, Mo., 1952-60; tchr. Woods Studio, 1963-65, Pauline Wright Studio, 1966-70; ch. organist First Ch. Christ Scientist, Merriam, Kans., 1954-59, 73—; pvt. tchr. piano, organ and harmony, Kansas City, Mo., 1961—; piano and organ judge Mid Am. Festival, 1966-68. Judge Spl. Olympics Festival, 1976, 77, 78. Mem. Music Tchrs. Nat. Assn., Mo., Kansas City music tchrs. assn., Federated Music Tchrs. Greater Kansas City, Nat. Secs. Assn. (editor Rainbow chapt. 1948-50), Certified Profl. Secs. Christian Scientist. Home: 2935 Forest Ave Kansas City MO 64109

KREGER, JAMES LEE, ret. ednl. ofcl.; b. Woodward, Okla., Apr. 16, 1908; s. Fenton Jessie and Verna May (Glasscock) K.; B.S. in Edn., S.W. Mo. State Coll., 1930; M.A. in Sch. Adminstrn., Colo. State Coll. Edn., Greeley, 1938; m. Evelyn Boyd, Aug. 31, 1928; children—June (Mrs. Henry E. Botts), Rowena (Mrs. Otis E. Young). Supt. of schs., Nianqua, Mo., 1928-38, Golden City, 1939-42, Miller, 1948-62; personnel adminstr. Riverview Gardens Sch. Dist., St. Louis, 1962-73, ret.; civilian instr. USAAF, Chanute Field, Ill., 1942-43; jr. high prin., Wheaton, Ill., 1943-45. Mem. Chgo. area bd. OPA, 1944-45. Mem. Am. Assn. Sch. Adminstrs., NEA, Mo. Tchrs. Assn., Nat., Mo. socs. bus. adminstrs. United Ch. of Christ. Lion (local pres.). Home: 2900 S 52d St Lincoln NE 68506

KREILICK, MARJORIE ELLEN, artist; b. Oak Harbor, Ohio, Nov. 8, 1925: d. Rolland Chester and Luella Mabel (Smith) Kreilick; B.A., Ohio State U., 1946, M.A., 1947; M.F.A., Cranbrook Art Acad., 1952; F.A.A.R. (Edwin Austin Abbey fellow), Am. Acad. in Rome, 1963; postgrad. Corsi de Cultura sull-Arte Ravennate e Bizantina U. of Bologna (Italy), 1970; m. Allan McNab, Mar. 18, 1972. Instr., Toledo Museum of Art, 1948-51; inst. U. Wis., 1953-58, asst. prof. art U. Wis., Madison, 1958-63, asso. prof., 1963-67, prof., 1967—; apprentice Mosaic Studio of Gulio Giovanetti, Rome, 1956-57; one-man shows include: Architectural League, N.Y.C., 1964, Columbia (S.C.) Mus., 1976, group shows include: Minn. Mus. Art, St. Paul; represented in several permanent collections, including: Mosaic Panel, Pritzker & Pritzker, Nat. Bank Building, Chgo., 1971, also pvt. collections. Recipient Exhbn. Metal and Mosaic prizes Wis. Designer Craftsman, 1958, Palette award, 1959; U. Wis. grantee, 1955, 61, 65, 68, 70, 76, 77; Internat. Design Conf. grantee, 1967. Mem. Nat. Soc. Mural Painters, Pi Lambda Theta, Delta Phi Delta. Home: 2713 Chamberlain Ave Madison WI 53705 Office: 6101A Humanities Bldg U of Wis Madison WI 53706

KREMSNER, FRANK FRED, dept. store exec.; b. Chgo., Nov. 7, 1917; s. Richard and Anna (Blaskovits) K.; grad. high sch. Warehouse foreman Campbell Soup Co., Chgo., 1945-52, Wright Sales, 1952-54; with Goldblatt Bros. Dept. Store, Chgo., 1954—, v.p., dir. ops., 1968—. Served with AUS, 1942-45. Mem. Nat. Guild Profl. and Bus. Graphologists (pres. 1973-77), Internat. Material Mgmt. Soc., Field Mus. Natural History, First Burgenlaender Soc., Soc. of the Little Flower, Am. Legion. Home: 2857 W 55th St Chicago IL 60629 Office: 333 S State St Chicago IL 60604

KRENITSKY, PETER, physician; b. Butler, Pa., June 16, 1935; s. Paul and Anna (Krynicki) K.; B.S., Grove City Coll., 1957; D.O., Kansas City Coll. Osteo. Medicine, 1961; m. Barbara Anne Barone, July 26, 1958; children—Kristin Elena, Kara Leigh. Intern, Detroit Osteo. Hosp. 1961-62, resident in internal medicine, 1962-65; practice osteo. medicine, Detroit, 1965—; chief staff Detroit Osteo. and Bicounty hosp., 1971-73, trustee. 1971-73; clin. prof. Coll. Osteo. Medicine Mich. State U., 1971—; chmn. dept. internal medicine Art Centre Hosp., 1970. Recipient Mosby book award for scholastic excellence, 1961. Mem. Am. Osteo. Assn., Mich. Assn. Osteo. Physicians and Surgeons, Mich. Heart Assn., Am. Coll. Osteo. Internists, Psi Sigma Alpha, Sigma Sigma Phi. Roman Catholic. Club: Detroit Golf. Research in prism optics. Home: 19560 Parkside St Detroit MI 48221 Office: 13355 E 10 Mile Rd Warren MI 48089

KRESS, ROBERT LEE, educator; b. Jasper, Ind., Sept. 22, 1932; s. Oscar Michael and Stella Philomena (Schutz) K.; B.A., St. Meinrad Coll., 1954; S.T.B., U. Innsbruck, 1956, S.T.L., 1958; M.A., U. Notre Dame, 1964; postgrad. Gregorian U., Rome, Italy, 1965-67; S.T.D., Angelicum U., Rome, 1968. Ordained priest Roman Catholic Ch., 1958; supt. Washington (Ind.) Cath. High Sch., 1959-64; lectr. U. Evansville (Ind.), 1967-70, asso. prof. philosophy and religion, 1973—; asst. prof. St. Louis U., 1971-73; lectr. Sch. Medicine, Ind. U., Evansville, 1973—; vis. fellow Princeton (N.J.) Theol. Sem., 1970-71; theol. cons. Ind. Cath. Conf., Canon Law Soc. Am.; lectr. to profl. orgns., colls. Henry J. Grimmelsman fellow, 1964-68; Nat. Endowment for Humanities fellow, 1977; Danforth asso., 1977. Mem. Coll. Theology Soc., Internat. Soc. for Metaphysics, Cath. Theol. Soc. Am., Religious Educators Assn., Council on Study of Religion. Author: Holy Church, Sinful Member, 1968; Whither Womankind? The Humanity of Women, 1975 (Outstanding Book of Yr. award Coll. Theology Soc., 1976); Come, Pilgrim, 1976; Christian Roots, 1977; Holy Church, Sinful Church, 1978. Contbr. articles to New Cath Ency., also popular and scholarly jours. Home: 1712 E Mulberry St Evansville IN 47714 Office: PO Box 329 Evansville IN 47702

KREY, GENEVA MARGARET, educator; b. Hazel Green, Wis., June 6, 1927; s. Thomas J. and Myra (Lenstra) Aide; diploma in elementary edn. Platteville State Tchrs. Coll., 1947; B.S. in Elementary Edn., Wis. State Coll., Platteville, 1956; M.S., U. Wis. at Superior, 1974, postgrad., 1974—; m. Robert D. Krey, June 5, 1951; 1 son, Thomas Robert. Tchr. pub. schs., Reedsburg, Wis., 1947-51, Black Earth, Wis., 1953-54, Lake Geneva, Wis., 1954-68, Superior, Wis., 1969; tchr. adult basic edn. Indianhead Tech. Inst., Superior, 1970-71; instr. reading, dir. reading clinic U. Wis., Superior, 1974-77. Chmn. decorations Douglas County Assn. Retarded Children, 1970. Mem. Internat., Wis., reading assns., Lake Superior Reading Council, Assn. U. Wis. Faculties, Assn. Supervision and Curriculum Devel., U. Wis. Alumni Assn. (life), U. Wis. Platteville Alumni Assn. (life), Phi Delta Kappa. Home: 1107 18th St N Superior WI 54880

KREYKES, GARY DICK, coach, educator; b. Hospers, Iowa, Feb. 16, 1936; s. Dick and Winifred (Mouw) K.; B.A., Westmar Coll., 1960; M.A., No. Colo. State U., Greeley, 1963; m. Myrna Ruth Schalekamp, July 1, 1960; children—Jennifer, Audra. Tchr., coach high sch., Jefferson, S.D., 1960-61, Little Rock, Iowa, 1961-63, Boyden-Hull, 1963-67, U. Wis. at Richland Center, 1967-71, Mont. State U., Bozeman, 1971-72; coach, dir. athletics Muscatine (Iowa) Community Coll., 1972—. Mem. High Sch. Bd. Edn., Richland Center, 1968-71, Muscatine, 1972-73; bd. dirs. YMCA, Muscatine, 1972-78. Served with AUS, 1956-58. Named Coach of Year, Westmar Coll., 1970. Mem. Nat. Basketball Coaches Assn., AAHPER, Phi Delta Kappa. Club: Lions. Home: 132 Middle Rd Muscatine IA 52761 Office: 152 Colorado St Muscatine IA 52761

KRICKER, EDMUND JOSEPH, savs. and loan exec.; b. Portsmouth, Ohio, Aug. 6, 1897; s. George Engelbert and Isabel Agnes (Dunn) K.; student U. Mich., 1917-18, Ohio State U., 1930-31, Ohio Savs. and Loan Acad., 1953; m. Helen Joy Bancroft, Dec. 27, 1954. With First Fed. Savs. and Loan Assn., 1924—, chmn. bd. and loan and investment coms., 1939—; dir. Security Central Nat. Bank. Life bd. dirs. Salvation Army. Mem. Bus. and Profl. Mens Club, Delta Theta Phi. Elk (past exalted ruler, trustee 1946-57), Kiwanian. Club: Portsmouth Yacht (commodore 1942). Home: 2925 Noddin Way Portsmouth OH 45662 Office: First Fed Savs and Loan Assn 843 Gallia St Portsmouth OH 45662

KRIEG, BEVERLY ANN MARRIOTT, guidance counselor; b. Rochester, Ind., Mar. 13, 1951; d. Loren and Lola M. (Finney) Marriott; B.A. in English, Manchester Coll., 1973; M.Ed., Clemson U., 1975; postgrad. Ind. U., 1976—, Ind. State U., 1977—; m. John Mark Krieg, June 2, 1973. Tchr., Culver (Ind.) Community Sch., 1973-74, Southwood Middle Sch., Anderson, S.C., 1974-75; lab. instr. Tri-County Tech. Coll., Pendleton, S.C., 1975-76; guidance counselor Linton (Ind.) High Sch., 1976—. Mem. Am. Sch. Counselors Assn., Am. Personnel and Guidance Assn., Nat. Council Tchrs. English, Ind. Assn. Admissions Counselors, Nat. Geog. Soc. Methodist. Home: 620 N Main St Linton IN 47441 Office: Linton High Sch H and Main Sts Linton IN 47441

KRIEGER, BENJAMIN WILLIAM, paper co. exec.; b. Cin., July 7, 1937; s. William Anthony and Catherine Regina (McDevitt) K.; A.A., U. Cin., 1965; m. Rosemary George, Apr. 12, 1958; children—Gregory, Kenneth, Catherine. With Union Paper & Twine Co. div. Mead Corp., Cleve., 1967—, v.p., 1969-75, gen. mgr. and pres., 1975—; with Chatfield Paper Corp., Cin., 1956-57, asst. sales mgr., 1965-67; pres. Cleve. Graphic Arts Council, 1975; nat. adv. bd. Mead Papers, 1971-73; chmn. nat. adv. bd. Gilbert Paper Co., 1973-75. Trustee No. Hills Assn., 1973-75, pres., 1974-75; active United Appeal Fund drive, Jr. Achievement, Greater Cleve. Growth Assn. Mem. Newcomen Soc., Buckeye Paper Trade Assn., Craftsman Internat., Sales and Mktg. Execs. Cleve., Cleve. Advt. Club, Cleve. Graphic Arts Assn., Advt. Prodn. Club, Hon. Order Ky. Cols., Assn. Ohio Commodores. Republican. Roman Catholic. Club: Chagrin Valley Country. Office: 26401 Richmond Rd Cleveland OH 44146

KRISHNA, GOPAL, anesthesiologist, educator; b. Bombay, India, Sept. 7, 1939; s. Sat and Sarla Devi (Agarwal) Prakash; came to U.S., 1968; B.S., Bareilly Coll., 1957; postgrad. Philipps U., Marburg, W.Ger., 1958-60; M.D., Free U. Berlin, 1963; m. Lillie-Mae Padilla, June 21, 1974. Intern, Berlin City Hosps., 1963-65; resident Neukolln Hosp., Berlin, 1966-68, Ind. U. Med. Center, Indpls., 1968-71; instr. Marion County Gen. Hosp. and Ind. U., 1971-72; asst. prof. anesthesiology Ind. U. Med. Sch., Indpls., 1972—, staff anesthesiologist Med. Center, 1973—. Diplomate Am. Bd. Anesthesiology. Fellow Am. Coll. Anesthesiologists; mem. Internat. Anesthesia Research Soc., Am., Ind., Indpls. socs. anesthesiologists. Office: Dept Anesthesiology 1100 W Michigan St Indianapolis IN 46202

KRIT, ROBERT LEE, med. sch. adminstr.; b. Chgo., Apr. 6, 1920; s. Jacob and Tania (Etzkowitz) K.; B.S. in Commerce, DePaul U., 1946; B.A., N. Park Coll., 1939; m. Susan Nancie Funk, Apr. 9, 1960; children—Melissa, Margaret, Justin. Dir., Chgo. Herald American Mercy Fleet charity drs., 1940-41; asst. exec. dir. cancer research found. U. Chgo., 1947-48; state campaign dir. Am. Cancer Soc., Inc., Chgo., 1948-63; dir. med. devel. U. Chgo., 1963-67; v.p. devel. Chgo. Med. Sch., 1967—; moderator TV series Tension in Modern Living, Drug Abuse, Aging and Retirement, Health and Devel. Children, Cancer, NBC Ednl. Exchange; host producer TV series Med. Looking Glass, Relevant Issues in Health and Medicine, Coping; mem. adv. bd. Central States Inst. for Addiction Services; v.p. Drug Abuse Council of Ill. Served from pvt. to 1st lt., USAAF, 1942-46. Fellow Inst. Medicine Chgo. (co-chmn. com. on pub. info., mem. editorial bd. Proc.); mem. Chgo. Soc. Fund Raising Execs. (pres. 1964-65). Home: 607 Lake Ave Wilmette IL 60091 Office: 233 S Wacker Dr Room 5330 Chicago IL 60606

KRITZ, JERRY RUSSELL, TV exec.; b. Louisiana, Mo., Oct. 15, 1950; s. Gerald T. and Dorothy N. (Ingram) K.; student Westminster Coll., 1968-70; B.S. Communication, Lindenwood Coll., 1972; m. Mary Todd Wise, Aug. 11, 1973. Producer, dir., writer Sta. KETC-TV, St. Louis, 1972-77, mem. exec. staff, 1977—, sr. producer, 1977—. Recipient award of distinction Nat. Assn. State Edn. Officers, 1975, 1st place award Mo. Broadcasters Assn., 1977, St. Louis Emmy award, 1976. Mem. Nat. Assn. Ednl. Broadcasters. Dir. Common Cents, Agy. Instructional TV, 10 part TV series, 1977; producer, dir. Founding Fathers and Edn., pub. service spots, 1976. Home: 32 Old Windmill Rd St Charles MO 63301 Office: 6996 Millbrook Blvd St Louis MO 63130

KROAH, LARRY ALLEN, librarian; b. Saginaw, Mich., Apr. 30, 1948; s. Clarence Mark and Ellen Ethel (Minnich) K.; B.A., Adrian Coll., 1970; M.A., Ohio U., 1972; M.S., U. Ill., 1973. History and Social sci. bibliographer St. Mary's Coll. of Md., St. Mary's City, 1973-74; dir. libraries Am. Coll. Switzerland, Leysin, 1974-77; head librarian Wilmington (Ohio) Coll., 1977—. Mem. Am. Hist. Assn. Mediaeval Acad. Am. Methodist. Home: 220 S 21st St Saginaw MI 48601 Office: Wilmington Coll Library Wilmington OH 45177

KROEMER, JAMES DARRELL, editor; b. Fort Wayne, Ind., Aug. 25, 1946; s. Dolan Edward and Mary Louise (Abram) K.; A.A., Concordia Luth. Jr. Coll., 1966; student Ind. U., 1967-68; m. Cheryl Anne Lips, May 7, 1966; children—Adam, Aaron, Joy. Reporter, Kendallville (Ind.) News-Sun, 1968-69; city govt. reporter Champaign-Urbana (Ill.) Courier, 1969-71; editor, gen. mgr. Auburn (Ind.) Evening Star, 1971—. Mem. DeKalb Meml. Hosp. Corp., 1974—. Recipient awards Hoosier State Press Assn., 1972, 73, 74, UPI, 1976. Democrat. Lutheran (elder 1974-75). Lion. Club: Greenhurst Country. Designer, editor: The Auburn Story, 1972. Home: 331 Ensley Ave Auburn IN 46706 Office: 118 W 9th St Auburn IN 46706

KROEPEL, ROBERT HOWARD, organist, pianist, counselor; b. Melrose, Mass., Feb. 3, 1943; s. Elmer Howard and Mable (Bishop) K.; B.A., Washington U., St. Louis, 1966. Profl. entertainer on piano, organ, Kirkwood, Mo., 1965—; social worker St. Louis State Hosp., 1967-69; pvt. counseling, 1974—; pvt. instr. piano, organ. Mem. Am. Fedn. Musicians, Sigma Chi. Author: Deluxe Encyclopedia of Piano Chords, Piano Rhythm Patterns, Fun with the Organ, Deluxe Encyclopedia of Organ Chords. Address: 916 Poinsetta Ln Kirkwood MO 63122

KROGH, HAROLD CHRISTIAN, educator; b. Cedar Rapids, Iowa, Feb. 1, 1917; s. Hans P. and Dorathea (Meyer) K.; B.S. in Commerce, State U. Iowa, 1939, M.A., 1941, Ph.D., 1953; postgrad. Harvard Grad. Sch. Bus., 1959, N.Y. U., 1964, U. Wis., 1967, Stanford U., 1973, Northwestern U., 1974; grad. Nat. War Coll., 1967, Command and Gen. Staff Coll., Ft. Leavenworth, 1969; m. Bessie Alberta Cummins, May 31, 1942; children—Linda Marie, Richard Alan, Laurie Ellen. Sales, Midland Mortgage Co., Cedar Rapids, 1939-40; instr. econs. U. Ala., Tuscaloosa, 1941-42; personnel officer VA, Des Moines 1946-47; instr., asst. prof., asso. prof. fin. Drake U., Des Moines, 1947-54; asso. prof. bus. adminstrn. U. Kans., Lawrence, 1954-60, prof., 1960—. Cons. to ins. firms, fin. instns., pension funds, 1954—; faculty exchange program U. Costa Rica, summers 1962-63; mem. ins. com. Nat. Collegiate Athletic Assn., Kansas City, Mo., 1962—, chmn., 1977; mem. research com. Internat. Ins. Seminar, Oslo, Norway, 1977. Bd. govs., bd. electors Internat. Ins. Hall of Fame. Served with AUS, 1942-46; col. Res. ret. Mem. Am. Soc. C.L.U.'s, Am. Risk and Ins. Assn. (past pres.), Am., Midwest (past pres.) fin. assns., Fin. Mgmt. Assn., Soc. C.P.C.U.'s, AAUP, Soc. Fin. Analysts, Midwest Bus. Adminstrn. Assn., Midwest Econs. Assn., Kansas City Actuaries Club, Alpha Kappa Psi, Beta Gamma Sigma. Lutheran. Home: 1117 Highland Dr Lawrence KS 66044

KROL, EDWARD J(OSEPH), surgeon; b. Chgo., Apr. 3, 1913; s. Alexander and Mary (Madalinski) K.; B.S., Central YMCA, 1935; M.D., Loyola U., 1939; m. Anne E. Schirvin, Feb. 1, 1942; children—Edwina, Cynthia, Edward, Gerald. Extern, Holy Cross Hosp., Chgo., 1938-39, sr. attending surg. staff, 1948—, pres., chief staff, 1957-59, chmn. dept. surgery, 1959-60, co-chmn. dept. surgery, 1961-62, chmn. exec. bd., 1958-61, sec. exec. bd., 1961-62, now mem. exec. bd.; intern St. Elizabeth's Hosp., Chgo., 1939-40; pvt. practice, Chgo., 1940-42, specializing in surgery, 1945—; postgrad. surg. tng. Cook County Postgrad. Sch., Tufts U., U. Ill., Bunt's Inst. of Crile Clinic, Cleve., U. Minn., U. Kans.; clin. asst. surgery Rush Med. Sch., Chgo., 1940-42; clin. asst. surgery Stritch Sch. Medicine, 1945-50, clin. instr. surgery, 1950—. Chmn. adv. bd. Immaculata Coll., Chgo.; trustee Intestinal Research Inst.; chmn. bd. advisers Shellbourne Center, Valparaiso, Ind.; mem. pres.'s council St. Xavier's Coll., Chgo.; bd. dirs. Polish Med. History and Sci. Found. Served from lt. to capt. M.C., USAAF, 1942-45. Recipient Man of Year award Holy Cross Hosp. Staff, 1971. Diplomate Internat. Bd. Surgery, Am. Bd. Abdominal Surgeons (chmn.), Internat. Bd. Applied Nutrition. Fellow Acad. Psychosomatic Medicine, Internat. Coll. Surgeons, Internat. Acad. Proctology (past trustee, past pres.), Am. Coll. Gastroenterology (pres., trustee), Am. Soc. Abdominal Surgeons (pres.), Am. Coll. Nutrition, Royal Soc. Medicine, AAAS, Am. Geriatric Soc., Internat. Coll. Applied Nutrition (v.p., bd. govs.), Soc. Acad. Achievement, Internat., Am. colls. angiology, Miss. Valley Med. Soc., N.Y. Acad. Sci.; mem. AMA (chmn. gen. surg. sect. 1962—, vice chmn. council gen. surg. sect. 1971—), Am. Thoracic Soc., World Med. Assn., Am. Coll. Chest Physicians, Ill. (ho. of dels.), Chgo. (br. pres., counselor, chmn. ethical relations com.) med. socs., Chgo. Path. Soc., Ill. Acad. Sci., Ill. Soc. Med. Research, Assn. Mil. Surgeons, Polish Med. Alliance (hon.), Assn. Am. Med. Colls., Fedn. Am. Scientists, Lambda Rho. Club: Union League (Chgo.). Editorial staff Am. Jour. Abdom. Surgery, 1962; asso. editor Internat. Jour. Applied Nutrition, 1961; contbg. editor surg. sect. Am. Jour. Proctology, 1952—, Modern Nutrition Jour., 1961—; asso. editor surgery Polish Med. History and Sci. Jour., 1969—. Office: 4255 W 63d St Chicago IL 60629

KROLL, GEORGE, cardiologist; b. Hartford, Conn., May 16, 1922; s. Abrahan Natu and Celia (Fleishman) K.; B.S., Central YMCA Coll., 1944; D.D.S., U. Ill., 1946, M.D. cum laude, 1952, M.S., 1953; m. Helga Wunchova, Apr. 18, 1948. Intern, U. Chgo. Clinics, 1952-53, resident in internal medicine, 1954-55; resident in internal medicine U. Ill. Research and Edn. Hosp., 1953-54; Nat. Heart Inst. Clin. Cardiology fellow, 1955-56. practice medicine specializing in cardiology, Chgo., 1956—; chmn. dept. medicine, dir. internal medicine residency program Edgewater Hosp., Chgo., 1976—; dir. heart sta. VA Lakeside Hosp., 1956-76, chief cardiovascular sect., 1973-76; asso. prof. clin. medicine Sch. Medicine, Northwestern U., 1973-77; prof. medicine U. Health Sci., Chgo. Med. Sch., 1976—. Served to capt. Dental Corps, U.S. Army, 1946-48. Diplomate Am. Bd. Internal Medicine, Am. Bd. Cardiovascular Disease. Fellow A.C.P.; Am. Coll. Cardiology, Am. Heart Assn. (Council Clin. Cardiology), Inst. Medicine Chgo.; mem. Chgo. Soc. Internal Medicine, Am. Fedn. Clin. Research, Sigma Xi, Alpha Omega Alpha. Home: 5733 N Sheridan Rd Chicago IL 60660 Office: 5700 N Ashland Ave Edgewater Hosp Chicago IL 60660

KRONQUIST, SHIRLEY JOYCE, coll. adminstr.; b. Longmont, Colo., Jan. 7, 1929; d. Martin Jess and Vera Mildred (Stansfield) Poling; student Colo. Coll., 1q47-48; B.F.A., U. Colo., 1951; M. Degree, Syracuse U., 1953; m. Dale Parnell Kronquist, Aug. 11, 1957; children—Kimberly Claire, Kevin Dale. Asst. dean women U. Colo., Boulder, 1953-56; indsl. relations counselor Dow Chemical Co., Boulder, 1956-57; asst. dean women Wartburg Coll., Waverly, Iowa, 1957-60; asso. dean students, asst. prof. U Dubuque (Iowa), 1960-63; asst. dean student service John Wood Community Coll., Quincy, Ill., 1975—. Mem. Judges Com. on Juvenile Delinquency, Harney County, Oreg., 1964-65; mem. personnel com., selections and awards com. Two Rivers council Girl Scouts U.S.A., 1976—. Syracuse U. fellow, 1951-53. Mem. Quincy and Adams County Hist. Soc., Am., assns. collegiate registrars and admissions officers, Am., Ill. personnel and guidance assns., Am. Coll. Personnel Assn. Lutheran. Home: 308 Adams St Coatsburg IL 62325 Office: 1919 N 18th St N Quincy IL 62301

KRONSCHNABEL, EDWARD FRANCIS, physician; b. Appleton, Wis., Sept. 9, 1921; s. George J. and Ellen (Hardy) K.; student Coll. St. Thomas, 1938-47; M.D., Marquette U., 1951; m. Shirley Stieghorst, Dec. 30, 1953 (div. 1975); children—Jerome, Mary Sue, Charles. Intern, Evang. Deaconess Hosp., Milw., 1951-52; individual practice medicine, Gwinn, Mich., 1952-57; resident VA Hosp., Wood, Wis., 1957-60; clin. instr. Marquette U., 1957-60; individual practice medicine, specializing in otolaryngic surgery, Marquette, Mich., 1960—; mem. staff Marquette Gen. Hosp., Bell Meml. Hosp., Ishpeming, Mich.; cons. USAF Hosp. K.I. Sawyer AFB, Mich. Bd. dirs. Bay Cliff Health Camp, Marquette. Served with USNR, 1942-45. Diplomate Am. Bd. Otolaryngology. Fellow A.C.S., Am. Broncho-Esophagol. Assn., Am. Acad. Opthalmology and Otolaryngology, Am. Laryngol., Otological and Rhinol. Soc.; mem. AMA, Mich., Marquette-Alger County med. socs., Chgo. Laryngol. and Otol. Soc., Wis. Otolaryngol. Soc. Clubs: K.C., Marquette Golf and Country. Home: 922 Northland Dr Marquette MI 49855 Office: 1414 W Fair Ave Marquette MI 49855

KROSS, MORRIS H., lawyer; b. Kansas City, Mo., May 26, 1932; s. Lee M. and Zelda (Weneck) K.; student Kansas City Jr. Coll., 1949-51; LL.B., U. Mo., 1959. Admitted to Mo. bar, 1959; asso. firm Rogers, Field, Gentry, Benjamin & Robertson, Kansas City, Mo., 1959—, partner, 1967-74; adminstrv. law judge Bur. Hearings and Appeals U.S. Social Security Adminstrn., 1974—. Bd. dirs. Jewish Community Center, Jewish Edn. Council; chmn., Kansas City adult com. B'nai B'rith Youth Orgn., 1969-71; dist. chmn. B'nai B'rith Youth Council, 1971-74; mem. B'nai B'rith Youth Commn., 1971-74; del. Kansas City Jewish Welfare Fedn. on United Jewish Appeal Study Mission to Israel, 1969. Mem. Am., Mo., Kansas City bar assns., Kansas City Lawyers Assn. Jewish (temple bd. dirs.). Mem. B'nai B'rith (lodge pres. 1970, dist. bd. govs. 1971-72). Home: 410 W 111th Terr Kansas City MO 64114 Office: 911 Walnut St Room 1400 Kansas City MO 64106

KROSSNER, WILLIAM JOHN, JR., psychologist, educator; b. Newark, Oct. 19, 1939; s. William J. and Dora (Bruder) K.; B.Chem. Engring., Cornell U., 1961; Ph.D., Harvard, 1965; m. Rhonda A. Parrella, Mar. 4, 1977. Research fellow Harvard Center for Cognitive Studies, 1965; asst. prof. Vassar Coll., Fordham U., 1966-74; asso. prof. psychology and medicine U. Minn., Duluth, 1974—; pres. PsyMinn Corp., Duluth, 1975—; staff psychologist St. Luke's Hosp., 1975—. Pres. Duluth Preservation Soc., 1975—. NIMH predoctoral fellow, 1962-65, Cente for Urban and Regional Affairs grantee, 1974-75. Mem. Am. Statis. Assn., Inst. Math. Statistics, Am., Minn. psychol. assns., Northland Behavioral Sci. Assn. Club: Harvard. Home: 1045 Brainerd Ave Duluth MN 55811 Office: 334 Bohannon Hall U Minn Duluth MN 55812

KROUSE, PAUL CARL, publisher; b. Chgo., May 7, 1937; s. Eugene and Anna (Rothbard) K.; B.S. in Communications, U. Ill., 1959; m. Ann Sharon Wolk, Aug. 8, 1964; children—Amy, Beth, Joey, Katie. Copywriter Montgomery Wards, Chgo., 1960-62; account exec. Arthur Wilk Advt., Chgo., 1962-64; v.p. Real Estate Clearing House, Chgo., 1964-66; adminstrv. asst. Arthur Rubloff & Co., Chgo., 1966-67; pres. Ednl. Communications, Inc., Chgo., 1967—; mem. adv. bd. Distributive Edn. Clubs Am., 1975—. Served with NG 1959-66. Mem. Ednl. Press Assn., Direct Mailers Marketing Assn., Northbrook C. of C., Chgo. Assn. Commerce and Industry, Citizens Adv. Com., Better Bus. Bur. Club: Bannonckburn Tennis and Swim. Home: 3841 Bordeaux St Northbrook IL 60062 Office: 3202 Doolittle St Northbrook IL 60062

KRUCK, DONNA JEAN HAGEMEYER (MRS. MICHAEL ROY KRUCK JR.), ednl. adminstr.; b. Peoria, Ill., Jan. 26, 1930; d. Walter George and Lois Irene (Newburn) Hagemeyer; B.S., Ill. State U., 1962; M.Ed., U. Ill., 1968; m. Michael Roy Kruck, Jr., June 27, 1948; children—Pamela Ann (Mrs. Paul Robert Kokanson), Michael Roy III, Quentin Robert. Tchr. elementary sch., New Lenox, Ill., 1957-62, Lincolnway Area Joint Agreement, Lincolnway High Sch., 1962-67; chmn. spl. edn. dept. Joliet (Ill.) Twp. High Schs., 1967-69, coordinator high schs., 1969-76, dir. alt. schs., 1976—. Mem. Nat., Ill., Joliet (v.p. 1972-73, pres. 1974-76) edn. assn., Am. Assn. Mental Deficiency, Council for Exceptional Children (membership chmn. 1969-71), Am. Bus. Women's Assn. (profl. affairs chmn. 1974-76), Joliet Twp. Tchrs. Assn. (pres. 1974-77), Kappa Delta Pi, Delta Kappa Gamma (research chmn. 1968-70, scholarship chmn. 1970-72, 74-76, project chmn. 1972-74, parliamentarian 1970-72, ceremonies chmn. 1974-76). Lutheran. Club: East Campus Women's. Home: 156 John St New Lenox IL 60451 Office: 201 E Jefferson St Joliet IL 60432

KRUCKENBERG, CORY HENRY, dentist, educator; b. Hartley, Iowa, May 4, 1926; s. Christopher C. and Helen D. (Mayer) K.; A.A., St. Cloud State U., 1953; B.S., U. Minn., 1957, , D.D.S. with honors, 1957; m. Mary Anne, May 15, 1949; children—Christy Lynn, Cory Eugene, Leslie Anne. Practice dentistry, Excelsior, Minn., 1957—; instr. dentistry U. Minn., 1957-62, asst. prof., 1962-71, asso. prof. oral anatomy, 1971—, dir. dental sci., 1972—; cons. to Sch. Dentistry, Saigon, 1972, 73. Mem. Minnetonka Sch. Bd., 1969—; bd. dirs. YMCA, Excelsior, 1959—, United Methodists Missions, 1960—. Served with AUS, 1945-48, 50-51. Named Outstanding Prof., U. Minn. Sch. Dentistry, 1970, Outstanding Community Leader, YMCA, 1973. Mem. Nat. Am. Dental Assn., Minn. Dental Soc., Royal Soc. Health (Eng.). Methodist. Rotarian (pres. 1973-74). Home: 631 3rd St Excelsior MN 55331 Office: 348 2d St Excelsior MN 55331

KRUECKENBERG, KARL LOUIS, coll. adminstr.; b. Milw., May 13, 1942; s. Louis Andrew and Lydia Bertha (Reinke) K.; B.A., Valparaiso U., 1964; M.A. (Rotary Found. fellow, NDEA fellow), State U. N.Y. at Buffalo, 1969, Ph.D., 1977; postgrad. U. Philippines, 1964-65; m. Barbara Ann Beelke, July 10, 1965. Instr. polit. sci. Valparaiso (Ind.) U., 1969-74, dir. ann. giving, 1974—; profl. photographer, 1973—. Mem. Council for Advancement and Support Edn., Profl. Photographers Am., Pi Sigma Alpha. Lutheran. Club: Rotary. Home: 1607 Whittier Park Dr Valparaiso IN 46383 Office: Valparaiso U Valparaiso IN 46383

KRUEGER, ROBERT GEORGE, research microbiologist, immunologist; b. Duluth, Minn., Apr. 22, 1938; s. Emil Robert and Sophia (Dupuis) K.; B.S., Coll. of St. Thomas, 1960; M.S., U. Detroit, 1962; Ph.D. (USPHS grantee), U. Chgo., 1966. m. Delores Ruth James, Aug. 27, 1960; children—Robert George, Sarah Lynn. Asst. prof. microbiology and immunology N.Y. Med. Coll., N.Y.C., 1966-67; asst. prof. microbiology Sch. Medicine U. Wash., Seattle, 1967-71; cons. Mayo Clinic, Rochester, Minn., 1971-75, asso. prof. microbiology, immunology, Mayo Med. Sch., 1972-75; head div. tumor biology, dir. Lab. Viral Oncology Christ Hosp. Inst. Med. Research, Cin., 1975—; asso. prof. microbiology, prof. exptl. medicine U. Cin. Coll. Medicine, 1975—. Mem. Am. Soc. Microbiology, Am. Soc. Immunologists, AAAS, Sigma Xi. Author: Introduction to Microbiology, 1973. Contbr. numerous reviews for sci. jours. Home: 9620 Timbermill Ct Cincinnati OH 45231 Office: Christ Hosp Inst Med Research 2141 Auburn Ave Cincinnati OH 45219

KRUEGER, THOMAS PAUL, neurosurgeon; b. South Bend, Ind., May 22, 1935; s. Paul A. and Ruth Ethel (Jackson) K.; A.B., Ind. U., 1957, M.D., 1960; m. Diane Doubleday, Feb. 2, 1963; children—Debra Lynn, Sheryl Lee, Thomas Paul. Intern, U. Wis. Hosp., Madison, 1960-61, resident in gen. surgery, 1961-62, resident in neurosurgery U. Cin. Med. Center, 1964-68; practice medicine specializing in neurosurgery Neurosurg. Assos., Inc., Evansville, Ind., 1968—; staff neurosurgeon Deaconess Hosp., St. Mary's Hosp., Welborn Meml. Baptist Hosp., all Evansville. Served with USPHS, 1962-64. Diplomate Am. Bd. Neurol. Surgery. Mem. A.C.S., Am. Assn. Neurol. Surgeons, Congress Neurol. Surgeons, Central Neurosurg. Soc., AMA, Ind. State, Vanderburgh County med. socs. Home: 8203 Petersburg Rd Evansville IN 47711 Office: 611 Harriet St Suite 301 Evansville IN 47710

KRUEGER, WILLIAM FREDERICK, lawyer; b. Gillett, Wis., Oct. 12, 1905; s. William Frederick and Augusta (Hintz) K.; student Marquette U., 1924-26; J.D., U. Wis., 1929; m. Zenith Eaton, Sept. 27, 1928; children—William Frederick IV, Marianne (Mrs. Richard A. Knudson). Admitted to Wis. bar, 1929; practiced in Reedsburg, 1929-30, Wausau, 1930—; mem. firm Krueger & Thums, Lusty & Hittner, and predecessor firms; dir. Bank Athens. Tchr. U. Wis. Law Sch., 1973-74. Alderman, Wausau, 1945-50; supr. Marathon County (Wis.), 1945-50; city atty., Wausau, 1950-55, Schofield, Wis., 1942—; village atty., Rothschild 1957—. Bd. dirs. Lakeland Meml. Hosp., 1971-72. Mem. Am., Wis. (bd. govs. 1958-60), Marathon County (pres. 1963-64) bar assns., Benchers Soc. Wis., Wausau C. of C. (dir. 1945-52), U. Wis. Law Sch. Alumni Assn. (dir. 1960-61). Clubs: Masons (33 deg.), Shriners, Wausau (Wis.). Home: PO Box 176 Minocqua WI 54548 Office: PO Box 261 Schofield WI 54476

KRUG, EDWIN HERBERT, advt. exec.; b. South Bend, Ind., June 18, 1938; s. Solomon J. and Lillian (Joshel) K.; B.S., U. Ind., 1960; M.B.A., U. Chgo., 1973; m. Judith Fingeret, Oct. 23, 1963; children—Steven Morris, Michelle Lynn. Auditor, Altshuler, Melvoin & Glaser Co., Chgo., 1961; buyer Warshawsky & Co., Chgo., 1961-63; buyer, mdse. mgr., asst. retail sales mgr. Montgomery Ward & Co., Chgo., 1963-67; account supr. Arthur Wilk Advt. Co., Chgo., 1967-71; sr. v.p. Maxwell Sroge Co., Inc., Chgo., 1971—. Bd. dirs., v.p. Ill. ACLU, 1977. Served with U.S. Army, 1960-61. Mem. Am. Mktg. Assn., Direct Mail Mktg. Assn., Chgo. Assn. Direct Mktg. Co-author mail order workshop textbook. Home: 2770 Sheridan Rd Evanston IL 60201

KRUG, GERHARDT RONALD, machinery co. exec.; b. Evanston, Ill., Aug. 30, 1934; s. Julius William and Clara Eva (Steffens) K.; student Lewis Inst. Sci. and Tech., Lockport, Ill., 1952-55. m. Judith Ann Cotseres, Sept. 10, 1955; children—Colleen, Gerhardt, Kathryn, John, Corey, Lisa and Laura (twins); Field engr. Factory Mut. Engring. Div., Chgo., 1956-60; fire protection engr., corporate safety dir. U.S. Gypsum Co., Chgo., 1960-71; corporate dir. safety Am. Hoist & Derrick Co., St. Paul, 1971—; instr./coordinator Asso. Safety Degree Occupational Safety and Health Technician Program, Inver Hills Community Coll., Inver Grove Heights, Minn.; instr., writer lesson plans Dept. Labor, Occupational Safety and Health Adminstrn. Tng. Inst., Rosemont, Ill.; mem. adv. com. Safety Masters Program, U. Minn., Duluth. Mem. exec. com., power press and forging sect. Nat. Safety Council; community faculty adviser Univ. Without Walls, U. Minn. Registered profl. engr., Calif. Mem. St. Paul Safety Exchange Group, Am. Soc. Safety Engrs., Soc. Fire Protection Engrs., Am. Indsl. Hygiene Assn., Nat. Fire Protection Assn., Nat. Safety Mgmt. Soc., Vets. of Safety. Contbr. articles to safety periodicals. Home: 8344 Windbreak Trail N Lake Elmo MN 55042 Office: 63 S Robert St Saint Paul MN 55107

KRUGER, ELMER LAWRENCE, physician; b. Crosby, Minn., May 5, 1926; s. Elmer Lawrence and Genevieve Grace (Nygaard) K.; student U. Minn., 1946, U. Heidelberg, 1947; B.S., U. Ga., 1948; M.D., Med. Coll. Ga., 1954; m. Margaret Emily Doell, Feb. 23, 1957; children—Heidi, Gretchen, Kathleen, David, Alice, Holly. Intern, Swedish Hosp., Mpls., 1955, Hibbing (Minn.) Gen. Hosp., 1956; gen. practice medicine, Nashwauk, Minn., 1957-71, Hallock, Minn., 1971—; mem. staff Hallock Clinic, Kittson Meml. Hosp., Hallock. Chmn., Cub Scouts, Hallock; dist. commr. Boy Scouts Am.; bd. dirs. Kittson County Day Activity Center. Mem. Am., Minn. med. assns., Range Med. Soc., Hallock Bus. and Profl. Assn. Lion (dir. Hallock). Home: 302 S 2d St Hallock MN 56728 Office: Hallock Clinic Hallock MN 56728

KRUGER, ROBERT LOUIS, pathologist; b. Saline, Mich., Jan. 22, 1934; s. Clarence Edward and Dorothy Vivian (Long) K.; M.D., U. Mich., 1959; m. Beverly Jane Onsted, July 6, 1957; children—Brian Earl, Bruce Elwyn, Bradley Allen. Intern, Brooke Gen. Hosp., 1959-60; resident pathology Nebr. Meth. Hosp., Omaha, 1963-67; pathologist Neb. Meth. Hosp. and Children's Meml. Hosp., Omaha, 1963—; asst. prof. U. Nebr. Coll. Medicine, Omaha, 1975—. Served to capt. AUS, 1959-63. Diplomate Am. Bd. Pathology. Mem. Am., Nebr. med. assns., Omaha Med. Soc., Nebr. Assn. Pathologists (sec. 1971-72), Coll. Am. Pathologists, Am. Soc. Clin. Pathologists, Am. Assn. Blood Banks, Am. Soc. Microbiology, Pediatric Pathology Club, Alpha Kappa Kappa, Phi Eta Sigma. Methodist. Home: 1603 S 79th Ave Omaha NE 68124 Office: 8303 Dodge St Omaha NE 68114

KRUGER, WILLIAM ARNOLD, civil engr.; b. St. Louis, June 13, 1937; s. Reynold and Olinda (Siefker) K.; B.C.E., U. Mo.-Rolla, 1959; M.S., U. Ill., 1968; m. Carole Ann Hofer, Oct. 17, 1959. Civil engr. City of St. Louis, 1959; with Clark, Dietz & Assos., and predecessors, engrs., Urbana, Ill., 1961—, sr. design engr., 1963-67, dir. transp. div., 1968—; instr. Parkland Coll., Champaign, 1972. Served with C.E., AUS, 1959-61. Registered profl. engr., Ill., Mo., Fla., Miss., N.Y., Del. Mem. Nat., Ill. (chpt. pres. 1974, state chmn. registration laws com. 1973), Mo. socs. profl. engrs., ASCE, Am. Pub. Works Assn. (sect. dir. 1974-77), Inst. Transp. Engrs., Met. Assn. Urban Designers and Environ. Planners, Ill. Registered Land Surveyors Assn., Soc. Am. Mil. Engrs., U. Mo.-Rolla Alumni Assn., Theta Tau, Tau Beta Pi, Chi Epsilon, Pi Kappa Alpha. Clubs: Urbana Sportsmans; Ill. Ski. Home: 1811 Coventry Dr Champaign IL 61820 Office: 211 N Race St Urbana IL 61801

KRUIDENIER, DAVID, newspaper publisher; b. Des Moines, July 18, 1921; s. David S. and Florence (Cowles) K.; grad. Phillips Exeter Acad., 1940; B.A., Yale U., 1946; M.B.A., Harvard U., 1948; LL.D., Buena Vista Coll., 1960, Simpson Coll., 1963; m. Elizabeth Stuart, Dec. 29, 1948; 1 dau., Lisa. With Mpls. Star and Tribune Co., 1948-52, now vice chmn.; with Des Moines Register and Tribune, 1952—, pres., pub., 1971—; dir. Des Moines Register and Tribune Co., Iowa-Des Moines Nat. Bank, Nat. By-Products, Inc., Register and Tribune Syndicate, Inc., Iowa Kemper Ins. Co., Jackson (Tenn.) Sun. Pres. Gardner and Florence Call Cowles Found.; trustee Drake U., Iowa Meth. Hosp., Des Moines Art Center, Menninger Found., Civic Center Greater Des Moines, Am. Fedn. Arts, Midwest Research; dir. Audit Bur. Circulations; mem. Yale Devel. Bd. Served with USAAF, 1942-45. Mem. Sigma Delta Chi, Beta Theta Pi, Beta Gamma Sigma. Club: Des Moines. Home: 3409 Southern Hills Dr Des Moines IA 50321 Office: 715 Locust St Des Moines IA 50304

KRUIDENIER, ELIZABETH STUART, state ofcl.; b. Des Moines, Apr. 1, 1926; d. Reece and Ruth (Bewsher) Stuart; student U. Iowa, 1946-47; B.A., Conn. Coll., 1948; J.D., Drake U., 1973; m. David Kruidenier, Dec. 29, 1948; 1 dau., Lisa. Mem. Iowa Civil Rights Commn., Des Moines, 1965-75. Founder Iowa Assn. for UN, 1955; treas. Gardner and Florence Cowles Found.; constl. study chmn. Des Moines League Women Voters, 1960-63; mem. Des Moines Know Your Neighbor Panel, Panel Am. Women, 1960-69. Trustee Grinnell Coll., 1965—. Recipient Jewish War Vets Americanism award; ofcl. ambassador Des Moines, 1964. Home: 3409 Southern Hills Dr Des Moines IA 50321

KRUMHANSL, BERNICE ROSEMARY, phys. therapist, writer; b. Cleve., Apr. 17, 1922; d. Frank Ralph and Anne (Pren) Krumhansl; B.A., Notre Dame Coll., 1943; grad. Cleve. Clinic Found. Staff therapist Assn. for Crippled and Disabled, Cleve., 1944-46; chief phys. therapist St. Alexis Hosp., Cleve., 1946-52; dept. dir. St. Luke's Hosp., Cleve., 1952—; clin. instr. phys. therapy programs numerous univs; lectr. in field; phys. therapy cons. HEW grant Wanless Hosp., Wanless Wadi Chest Hosp., Richardson Hosp. of Leprosy Mission, Miraj, Maharashtra, India, 1966. Mem. Am. Phys. Therapy Assn., Am. Registry Phys. Therapists, Internat. Fedn. Orthopedic Manual Therapists, Sigma Tau Delta (pres. chpt., pres. St. Clair-Superior coalition). Roman Catholic (pres. ch. council). Author: Opportunities in Physical Therapy, 1968, rev. edits., 1974, 77, also articles, juvenile fiction, radio scripts. Contbr. articles to profl. jours. Home: 1167 Addison Rd Cleveland OH 44103 Office: 11311 Shaker Blvd Cleveland OH 44104

KRUMM, CAROL MAE RHODEBACK (MRS. DELBERT RUSSELL KRUMM), librarian; b. Pataskala, Ohio, June 17, 1923; d. Donald F. and Ethel Iren (Stevenson) Rhodeback; B.A., Capital U., 1945; B. L.S., Western Res. U., 1946; m. Delbert Russell Krumm, July 28, 1946; 1 dau., Carolyn (Mrs. Dennis Dean Heffner). Asst., Capital U. Library, Columbus, Ohio, 1941-42, Bexley (Ohio) Pub. Library, 1941-45; asst. librarian Otterbein Coll. Library, Westerville, Ohio, 1946-51; cataloger Ohio State U. Libraries, Columbus, 1952-53, 59-65, catalog maintenance librarian, 1965-71, asst. prof. library adminstr., 1968—, head catalog maintenance and card prodn. div., 1971-72, head bibliog. records div., 1972-76, serials holdings conversion div., 1976—; cataloger Ohio Legis. Service Commn., 1953; serials cataloger Cleve. Pub. Library, 1957-58; cons. Ohio State U. Christian Center Library, 1966-67; librarian E. Linden Evang. United Brethren Ch. Library, 1965-68, Westgate United Methodist Ch. Library, 1970-76; resource leader Children's Work Council, also cons. reading program Ohio SE Conf., Evang. United Brethren Ch., 1960-64. Mem. Am., Ohio, Franklin County library assns., Ohio Valley Group Tech. Service Librarians, Inter-Univ. Library Council, Ch. and Synagogue Library Assn., AAUP. Methodist Clubs: Faculty Women's; Kiwanikwee (chaplain 1972-73). Home: 669 S Kellner Rd Columbus OH 43209 Office: 1858 Neil Ave Mall Columbus OH 43210

KRUMM, JOHN MCGILL, bishop; b. South Bend, Ind., Mar. 15, 1913; s. William F. and Harriett Vincent (McGill) K.; A.A., Pasadena Jr. Coll., 1933; A.B., U. Calif., 1935; B.D., Va. Theol. Sem., 1938, D.D., 1974; Ph.D., Yale U., 1948; S.T.D., Kenyon Coll., Gambler, Ohio, 1962; D.D., Berkeley Div. Sch., Gen. Theol. Sem. Ordained to ministry Episcopal Ch., 1938; vicar Episcopal chs., Compton Lynwood, Hawthorne, Calif., 1938-41; asst. rector St. Paul's Ch., New Haven, 1941-43; rector Ch. of St. Matthew, San Mateo, Calif., 1943-48; dean St. Paul's Cathedral, Los Angeles, 1948-52; chaplain Columbia 1952-65; rector Ch. of Ascension, N.Y.C., 1965-71; bishop of So. Ohio, Episc. Ch., 1971—; vis. lectr. N.T., Berkeley Div. Sch., New Haven, 1942-43, ch. history Va. Theol., Sem., Alexandria, 1942; instr. Prospect Hill Sch., New Haven 1942-43; instr. religion U. So. Calif., 1950-52. Chmn. clergy div. Univ. Religious Conf., Los Angeles; pres. San Mateo-Burlingame (Calif.) Council Chs., 1947-48, Ch. Fedn. Los Angeles, 1951-52; chmn. nat. council Panel of Ams., 1953-61. Trustee Bexley Hall of Colgate-Rochester, Kenyon Coll., Children's Hosp., Cin. Democrat. Clubs: Century Assn. (N.Y.C.); University, Bankers (Cin.). Author: Roadblocks of Faith (with J.A. Pike); What's In a Name: Why Am I an Episcopalian?; Modern Heresies, 1961; The Art of Being a Sinner, 1967; Why Choose the Episcopal Church, 1974. Home: 2001 Calvin Cliff Cincinnati OH 45206 Office: 412 Sycamore St Cincinnati OH 45202

KRUMSKE, WILLIAM FREDERICK, JR., banker; b. Chgo., Dec. 17, 1952; s. William Frederick and Harriet Marie (Piwowarczyk) K.; B.S., Ill. Inst. Tech., 1974; postgrad No. Ill. U., 1976—. Salesman, warehouse mgr. Lus-Ter-Oil Beauty Products, Palos Heights, Ill., 1972-74; pub. relations dir. Crouching Lion Motor Inn, Alsip, Ill., 1974; mgr. food and beverage Inn Devel. & Mgmt., Chicago Heights, Ill., 1974-75; dir. mktg. DeKalb Savings and Loan Assn., DeKalb, Ill., 1975—; mktg. mgr. Jordan Gallagher for State's Atty. campaign, 1976. Mem. Ill. Inst. Tech. Alumni Admission Corps, Am. Mktg. Assn., Savs. Instn. Mktg. Soc. Am., Ill. Savs. and Loan League (mem. mktg. com. 1977—). Republican. Lutheran. Home: 118 Augusta Ave DeKalb IL 60115 Office: 3d St and Locust St DeKalb IL 60115

KRUSE, EDGAR C., hosp. ofcl.; b. Ind., June 15, 1912; s. Henry C. and Emma (Dreyer) K.; student Ind. U.; m. Mildred Kramer, May 15, 1937; children—Dale Keith, Dennis Neal, Donald Edgar. Messenger, jr. exec. Home Tel. & Tel. Co., 1928-48; gen. auditor City Utilities, Fort Wayne, Ind., 1948-52; asst. adminstr. Lutheran Hosp., Ft. Wayne, 1952-59, adminstr., 1959-71, pres., 1971-77; mem. Ind. Bd. Health Regulating and Licensing Council, 1963-67; mem. adv. bd. Sch. Practical Nursing. Bd. dirs. Ft. Wayne chpt. ARC; bd. dirs., exec. com. No. Ind. Health System Authority, 1976—; bd. dirs. Luth. Hosp. Found., 1977—. Mem. Am. Assn. Hosp. Accountants (past pres. Ind. chpt.), Northeastern Ind. Hosp. Council (past pres.), Luth. Hosp. Assn. Am. (dir., past pres.), Tri-State Hosp. Assembly (dir., past pres.), Ft. Wayne C. of C. Clubs: Junto, Fort Wayne Executive (dir., past pres.), 100 Per Cent (dir.). Home: 6037 Ranger Trail Fort Wayne IN 46815 Office: 3024 Fairfield Ave Fort Wayne IN 46807

KRUSE, GERALD STANLEY, computer co. exec.; b. Tecumseh, Mich., Aug. 18, 1941; s. Stanley Howard and Virginia Alice (Peatter) K.; M.B.A., Eastern Mich. U., 1969; m. Penelope Appel, Aug. 19, 1976; children by previous marriage—Gerald Stanley, Christine. Accountant McGladrey, Harrison, Dunn & Co., South Bend, Ind., 1964-66; fin. dir. med. sch. U. Mich., Ann Arbor, 1966-69; cons. Price Waterhouse & Co., Detroit, 1969-71; bus. mgr. Gibraltar (Mich.) Sch. Dist., 1971-74; sr. cons. Arthur Young & Co., Detroit, 1974-76; dir. fin. O'Connor Products Co., Detroit, 1976-77; gen. group mgr. Computer Services Corp., Southfield, Mich., 1977—; adj. instr. U. Mich., 1973-74. C.P.A., Ind. Mem. Assn. Systems Mgmt. Presbyterian. Club: Detroit Yacht. Home: 1470 Iroquois St Detroit MI 48214 Office: 23225 Northwestern Hwy Southfield MI 48075

KRUSE, PAUL WALTERS, JR., physicist; b. Hibbing, Minn., Nov. 24, 1927; s. Paul Walters and Marie Rae (Gibson) K.; B.S., U. Notre Dame, 1951, M.S., 1952, Ph.D., 1954; m. Margaret Mary Fitzpatrick, Jan. 23, 1954; children—Paul II, Robert, John, Mary, Margaret,

Charles, Thomas, Catherine, William. Physicist, Farnsworth Electronics Co., Ft. Wayne, Ind., 1954-56; sr. research scientist Honeywell Corp. Tech. Center, Bloomington, Minn., 1956-59, prin. research scientist, 1959-60, staff scientist, 1960-69, sr. staff scientist, 1969—; panel mem. Pres.'s Sci. Adv. Com., 1969-73; mem. Army Sci. Adv. Panel, 1965—; com. mem. Nat. Materials Adv. Bd., NRC-Nat. Acad. Scis., 1971-72, Adv. Bd. on Mil. Personnel Supplies, 1969-71; mem. planning com. 3d Internat. Photoconductivity Conf., 1968-69; chmn. Army ERADCOM Tech. Com., 1976. Bd. dirs. Benilde High Sch., 1970-74. Recipient H.W. Sweatt award for outstanding sci. accomplishment, 1966; selected by sec. def. for Joint Civilian Orientation Conf. 37, 1967. Fellow Am. Phys. Soc., Am. Inst. Aeros. and Astronautics (asso.); mem. Optical Soc. Am., Am. Def. Preparedness Assn., Assn. U.S. Army, Notre Dame Club of Minn. (pres. 1974-75). Author: (with McGlauchlin and McQuistan) Elements of Infrared Technology, 1961; Contbr. articles to profl. jours.; mem. editorial adv. bd. Optics Letters, 1977—; patentee in field. Home: 6828 Oaklawn Ave Edina MN 55435 Office: Honeywell Corporate Tech Center 10701 Lyndale Ave S Bloomington MN 55420

KRUSINSKI, CLARENCE, architect; b. Chgo., Oct. 3, 1940; s. Clarence John and Evelyn A. (Anders) K.; B.Arch., Ill. Inst. Tech., 1963; m. Josette Nadine Piscitello, Sept. 1, 1962; children—Scott Michael, Brigitta Terese, Mark David, Courtney Josette. Architect, Pace Assos., Chgo., 1963-64, Schipporeit-Heinrich, Inc., Chgo., 1964-67; pres. Clarence Krusinski & Assos., Ltd., Chgo., 1967-77, Miller Krusinski Assos. Ltd., 1977—. Mem. Oak Park (Ill.) Zoning Bd. Appeals; bd. dirs. Chgo. Archtl. Assistance Center, U. Chgo. Cancer Research Found. Recipient Better Homes for Living award. Registered architect, Ill., N.Y., Tex., Ky., Conn. Mem. Nat. Council Archtl. Registration Bds., AIA (1st v.p. Chgo. chpt.), Landmarks Preservation Council, Chgo. Sch. Architecture Found., Ill. Inst. Tech. Alumni Assn. (v.p., dir.). Club: Arts of Chgo. Home: 526 Augusta Oak Park IL 60302 Office: 20 W Hubbard St Chicago IL 60610

KRYSIAK, JOSEPH EDWARD, mech. engr.; b. Cleve., Jan. 13, 1937; s. Edward Aloysious and Anna Margaret (Molinski) K.; B. in Mech. Engring., U. Dayton, 1964, M. in Mech. Engring., 1973. Mech. engr. Air Force Flight Dynamics Lab., Wright-Patterson AFB, Dayton, Ohio, 1965-73; mech. engring. specialist Reliance Electric Co., Euclid, Ohio, 1973-75; mech. engr. Indsl. Applications Internat., Solon, Ohio, 1976—. Recipient 13 invention awards Air Force Flight Dynamics Lab., 1968-74, Outstanding Lab. award, 1966-68. Mem. Am. Soc. for Metals, Math. Assn. Am. Roman Catholic. Club: K. C. Patentee in field. Contbr. articles to profl. jours. Home: 8990 Billings Rd Willoughby OH 44094 Office: 32400 Aurora Rd Solon OH 44139

KUBISTA, THEODORE PAUL, gen. surgeon; b. N.Y.C., July 20, 1937; s. Theodore Anton and Antonette Helene (Balasch) K.; B.S. in Chemistry, Pa. State U., 1959; M.D., U. Pa., 1963; m. Alice Elizabeth Maris, Dec. 26, 1963; children—Theodore Stephen, Christian Gregory. Intern, Hosp. U. Pa., 1963-64; resident in gen. surgery Mayo Grad. Sch. Medicine, Rochester, Minn., 1964-69; gen. surgeon Duluth (Minn.) Clinic, Ltd., 1971—, chmn. dept. gen. surgery, 1975-76; chief of surgery St. Mary's Hosp., 1977—, chmn. dept. inhalation therapy and resuscitation, 1974-76; adv. com. inhalation therapy Coll. St. Scholastica; asst. prof. clin. surgery U. Minn. (Duluth). Served to lt. comdr. M.C., USNR, 1969-71. Decorated Bronze Star with Combat V; recipient Dr. I.S. Ravdin prize in surgery U. Pa., 1963, Priestley prize for surg. research, 1963. Fellow A.C.S. (exec. council Minn. chpt.); mem. AMA, Minn., St. Louis County med. assns., AAAS, Assn. Mil. Surgeons U.S., Minn., Duluth (pres. 1977) surg. socs., Am. Trauma Soc., Minn. Thoracic Soc., Am. Burn Assn., Soc. Clin. Vascular Surgery. Presbyterian. Club: Kitchi Gammi (Duluth). Contbr. articles to profl. jours. Home: 216 N 33d Ave E Duluth MN 55804 Office: Duluth Clinic Ltd 400 E 3d St Duluth MN 55805

KUBO, SAKAE, clergyman, educator; b. Honolulu, May 8, 1926; s. Kumashichi and Teki (Shimota) K.; B.A., Andrews U., 1947, M.A., 1954, B.D., 1955; Ph.D., U. Chgo., 1964; M5.L., Western Mich. U. 1968; m. Hatsuml Sakai, June 27, 1948; children—Wesley, Charlene, Calvin. Tchr., Hawaiian Mission Acad., Honolulu, 1947-48; ordained to ministry Seventh-day Adventist Ch., 1957; minister Hawaiian Mission Conf. Seventh-day Adventists, Hawaii, 1948-50, So. Calif. Conf., Los Angeles, 1950-52; mem. faculty Andrews U., Berrien Springs, Mich., 1955—, prof. N.T., 1966—, Sem. librarian, 1967-77. Mem. Soc. Bibl. Lit., Chgo. Soc. Bibl. Research, Am. Theol. Library Asssn., Chgo. Assn. Theol. Librarians. Author: Readers Greek English Lexicon of the New Testament, 1971; Calculated Goodness?, 1974; Acquitted, 1975; So Many Versions, 1975; Your Summons to Court, 1976; Theological Bibliography, 1977; Contbr. articles to profl. jours. Home: 748 Bluff View Dr Berrien Springs MI 49103 Office: Andrews U Berrien Springs MI 49104

KUBO, YUKIO BRIAN, trading co. exec.; b. Wakayama, Japan, Feb. 17, 1936; s. Seitaro and Fujie (Suhara) K.; came to U.S., 1961; B.A., Internat. Christian U. (Tokyo), 1959; m. Shigeko Imatake, May 15, 1964; children—Steve Satoshi, Ken Takeshi, Naomi. Export sales dept. staff Nissei Sangyo Co., Ltd., Tokyo, Japan, 1959-61, asst. mgr. N.Y. Office, 1961-69, mgr. electronic components and materials Nissei Sangyo America Ltd., Chgo., 1969-73, pres., 1973—, also dir. Mem. Aircraft Owners and Pilots Assn., Ill. Police Fedn. Clubs: TWA Ambassador, Gas Light, Isehara Country. Licensed amateur radio sta. operator. Home: 580 Radcliffe Av Des Plaines IL 60016 Office: 2700 River Rd Des Plaines IL 60018

KUBY, THOMAS EUGENE, pub. relations exec.; b. Cleve., Dec. 13, 1926; s. Paul and Mary Ann (Gabany) K.; B.S., Ohio U., 1955; postgrad. U. Miami, 1962, Princeton U., 1963, U. Fla., 1964, U. Ga., 1964, State U. N.Y., Oswego, 1965, Buffalo, 1967-69, Ind. U., 1966, Case-Western Res. U., 1967-69, Buffalo State U. Coll., 1970-71, U. Mich., 1970-71, Cleve. State U., 1971, Calif. Western U.; m. Barbara Eleanor Asdell, July 12, 1969. Supr. pub. relations advt. Diamond Shamrock, chem. corp., Cleve., 1955-60; supr. creative services and pubs. Brunswick Corp., Chgo., 1960-62; sr. writer, editor, group leader presentations Martin-Marietta Corp., Orlando, Fla., 1962-66; mgr. tech. communications Dix & Eaton, 1968; supr. personnel devel. TRW Inc., Cleve., 1966-68, supr. programs support, 1968-72, dir. communications, 1972-73; vol. faculty State U. Coll., Buffalo, 1967—; cons., tchr. Tom Kuby & Assos., courses and workshops for organizational effectiveness, Chagrin Falls, Ohio, 1966—, Tom Kuby Pub. Relations, 1971—. Founder, bd. dirs. Friends of Maitland Art Research Center, 1965-66; bd. dirs. Greater Maitland Civic Center, 1966. Served with AUS, 1950-52. Recipient Honor medals Freedoms Found., 1958, 1959, 1960, 1961; Outstanding Community Leader award Maitland Civic Center, 1965; Spl. award Sigma Delta Chi, 1955, award Fla. Pub. Relations, 1965; oscar Financial World, 1959, award Cleve. Advt., 1958; Honor medal TRW, Inc., 1971; Community Relations award, Employee Relations award, Government Relations award Greater Cleve. chpt. Pub. Relations Soc. Am., 1971, Golden Achievement award, 1973. Mem. Pub. Relations Soc. Am. (accredited), Creative Edn. Found. (charter mem., colleague), Am. Soc. for Tng. and Devel. Clubs: City, Cleve. Play House. Contbr. numerous articles to profl. pubs. Address: 7236 Chagrin Rd Chagrin Falls OH 44022

KUCERA, KENNETH CHARLES, computer systems co. exec.; b. Chgo., Oct. 2, 1943; s. Irving C. and Helen Anne (Prusha) K.; B.A., B.S., Loyola U., Chgo., 1966; m. Ellen Marie Carll, Jan. 10, 1970; children—Kenneth Carll, Claire Allison. Sr. salesman Mohawk Data Scis., 1969-71; regional mgr. Digital Info. Devices Co., Chgo., 1971-73; mktg. mgr. Complanco Co., Chgo., 1973-74; sales dir. Corning Sci. Micro Systems Inc., Des Plaines, Ill., 1974—; guest lectr. various univs.; cons. to high tech. micro- computer mfrs. Served with Intelligence Corps, U.S. Army, 1966- 69. Decorated Army Commendation medal. Mem. Data Processing Mgmt. Assn., IEEE. Roman Catholic. Home: 1831 Vermont St Rolling Meadows IL 60008 Office: 1111 E Touhy Ave Des Plaines IL 60018

KUCHAR, KATHLEEN ANN, educator, artist; b. Meadow Grove, Nebr., Feb. 4, 1942; d. Alvin Charles and Lenora Leona (Louise) Kuchar; B.A., Kearney State Coll., 1963; M.S., Ft. Hays State U., 1966; M.F.A., Wichita State U., 1974. Tchr. art Minden (Nebr.) Pub. High Sch., 1963-65, elementary art supr., 1963-65; grad. asst. painting Ft. Hays State U., Hays, Kans., 1965-66, asso. prof. art, 1967—. Recipient Max Beckamnn Meml. Scholarship, Bklyn. Museum Art Sch., 1966-67, various cash and purchase awards in numerous art exhbns., 1969, 1970, 1971, 1972, 1975; research grantee in painting and printmaking, Ft. Hays State U., 1975-76. Mem. Women's Caucus for Art, Coll. Art Assn., Kans. Watercolor Soc. Contbr. works to 3rd Midwestern Printmaking Annual, Tulsa, 1976, 1st Nat. Kans. Small Painting, Print and Drawing Exhibn. Home: 2202 Fort St Hays KS 67601

KUCHAR, RUDOLPH JOSEPH, elec. engr.; b. Edmore, N.D., July 2, 1922; s. Rudolph Martin and Anastasia (Matejcek) K.; B.S. in Elec. Engring., U. N.D., 1949; m. Donna Mae Ethel Yeager, June 23, 1949; children—Karen (Mrs. Edwin Aamodt), Robert, William. Engr., Lium, Burdick & MacKichan, Grand Forks, N.D., 1949-52; asso. and elec. engr., head engring. dept. KBM, Inc. (formerly K.B. MacKichan & Assos., Inc.), Grand Forks, 1952-74, pres., chmn. bd., 1974—; dir. Grand Forks Fed. Savs. & Loan Assn. Pres., K.C. Bldg. Assn., Grand Forks, 1973-75. Served with AUS, 1942-46. Registered profl. engr., N.D., Minn. Mem. Am. Cons. Engrs. Council (dir., rural com. chmn. 1970—), N.D. Soc. Profl. Engrs. (dist. dir. 1956-57), Grand Forks C. of C. Roman Catholic. K.C., Elk. Home: 2630 5th Ave N Grand Forks ND 58201 Office: 1604 S Washington St Grand Forks ND 58201

KUCHEL, GAYLON LYLE, educator; b. Kingsley, Iowa, June 27, 1924; s. Philip and Minnie Marie (Lage) K.; B.A., U. Iowa, 1949, M.A., 1950; m. Wanda Mae Bowden, Sept. 14, 1945; children—Wade, Kimberly. Supr., Mut. Benefit H&A Assn., Omaha, 1954-63; from asst. prof. to prof. criminal justice U. Nebr., 1963—. Mem. Nebr. Commn. Criminal Justice, 1967—, Nebr. State Bd. Parole, 1969-70, Nebr. Gov.'s Com. on Jud. and Social Reform, 1971—, Omaha City Personnel Bd., 1968-74. Served with USMCR, 1942-45, with USAF, 1952-54. Mem. Am. Soc. Criminology, Acad. Criminal Justice Scis., Am. Correctional Assn., Internat. Assn. Chiefs of Police, Nebr. (pres. 1976-77), Midwest (2d v.p. 1977—) assns. criminal justice educators, Am. Assn. Wardens and Supts. Contbr. articles to profl. jours. Home: 9133 Dorcas St Omaha NE 68124 Office: PO Box 688 Omaha NE 68101

KUCHERAK, ANTHONY JOHN, charitable assn. exec.; b. Millvale, Pa., Feb. 10, 1917; s. Anton and Sophia (Nemchek) K.; student Ohio U., 1937-38; B.A., U. Miami, 1952; postgrad. in journalism No. Ill. U.; m. Helen Kerston, Aug. 17, 1939; children—Ronald Anthony (dec.), Stephanie. News assignment editor WTVJ-TV, Miami, Fla., 1951-61; dir. pub. relations United Fund Dade County, Miami, 1961-65; dir. radio and TV, Met. Crusade of Mercy, Chgo., 1965-71, dir. media relations, 1971-73, dir. pub. relations, 1974—. Instr. television newswriting U. Miami, evening div., 1955-56. Co-chmn. publicity seminar Welfare Pub. Relations Seminar, 1970. Vice-pres. pub. relations 48th ward Regular Republican Orgn., Chgo., 1965-69. Task force mem. nat. communications adv. com., fund raising adv. com. and nat. profl. adv. com. United Way Am., 1977-78; sec., mem. exec. com. Pub. Service Communications Council, 1977. Served with AUS, 1945-46. Recipient 1st pl. award Fla. Pub. Relations Assn., 1962-63, vol. service award Afro-Am. Family and Community Service Orgn., 1972. Mem. Am. Acad. TV Arts and Scis., Welfare Pub. Relations Forum, Pub. Relations Clinic, Pub. Relations Soc. Am. (chpt. chmn. pub. service com. 1971-72, pub. service award 1972, treas. Chgo. chpt. 1975). Home: 230 E Ontario St Chicago IL 60611 Office: 72 W Adams St Chicago IL 60603

KUCINSKI, LEO, musician; b. Warsaw, Poland, June 28, 1904; s. Ludwik and Kazimira (Sokolowska) K.; came to U.S., 1914, naturalized, 1921; B. Mus., Morningside Coll., 1935, D. Mus. (hon.), 1957; postgrad. Juilliard Grad. Sch., 1930-31; m. Ethel Thompson, June 20, 1928; 1 dau., Lenore. Head string dept. Morningside Coll., Sioux City, Iowa, 1925-50; condr. Lincoln (Nebr.) Symphony Orch., 1932-42, Sioux City Symphony Orch., 1935—; dir. Municipal Band Sioux City, 1929—; guest condr. Mpls. Symphony, Omaha, El Paso (Tex.), Shreveport (La.), Guadalajara (Mexico) orchs.; v.p. Am. Symphony Orch. League, 1946-48; violin soloist; cons. in field. Served to 1st lt., AUS, 1942-45; PTO. Decorated Bronze Star. Recipient civic award medal Sioux City Kiwanis Club, 1939, Sertoma Distinguished Citizen outstanding achievement in music award Sch. Musician mag., 1973, Ia. Gov.'s Music award, 1973. Mem. Am. Bandmasters Assn., Phi Mu Alpha, Phi Beta Mu. Republican. Lutheran. Mason (Shriner), Elk. Author book on Brahms. Contbr. articles to profl. publs. Home: 219 Cook Dr Sioux City IA 51104 Office: 402 Commerce Bldg Sioux City IA 51101

KUECKER, THEODORE EDWIN, shipping agencies exec.; b. Chgo., Feb. 26, 1938; s. Edwin Albert and Mildred E. (Witthoff) K.; student Beloit (Wis.) Coll., 1958, Northwestern U., Evanston, Ill., 1955-60; m. Carol Marie Grining, June 16, 1957; children—Valerie C., T. Scott, Glen D., T. Maxwell. Owner, pres. Kuecker Steamship Services, Inc., Chgo., 1960—; pres. PAD Agy., Inc., Chgo., 1970—; owner, pres. Internat. Cargo Containers, Inc., Chgo., 1971—. Mem. Ocean Freight Agts. Assn. Chgo. (pres. 1972), Lambda Chi Alpha. Republican. Presbyterian. Home: 75 Maple Hill Rd Glencoe IL 60022

KUEHL, HAL C., banker; b. Davenport, Ia., Mar. 21, 1923; s. Donald J. and Martha A. (Sierk) K.; B.B.A., U. Wis., 1947, M.B.A., 1954, postgrad. Grad. Sch. Banking, 1953; m. Joyce M. Helms, May 20, 1950; children—Cynthia Ann, David Charles. With First Wis. Nat. Bank, Milw., 1947—, v.p., 1960-65, exec. v.p. operations, 1965-66, exec. v.p., 1966-69, pres., from 1969, now dep. chmn., chief exec. officer, exec. v.p., dir. First Wis. Bankshares Corp.; pres., dir. 1st Wis. Internat. Bank; chmn. trustee First Wis. Mortgage Co. Mem. Wis. Gov.'s Council on Econ. Devel. Bd. dirs., mem. finance com. Milw. Blood Center; mem. exec. bd. Milw. County council Boy Scouts Am.; bd. dirs., treas. Milw. Voluntary Equal Employment Opportunity Council, Greater Milw. Com.; bd. dirs., mem. exec. com. Milw. div. Am. Cancer Soc.; trustee Citizens Govtl. Research Bur.; bd. dirs. Wis. Taxpayers Alliance, Friends of Art, United Community Services Greater Milw.; mem. corp. Columbia Hosp.; trustee Greater Wis. Found. Inc., Milw. Art Center; trustee, mem. finance com., exec. com. Marquette U. Served with USNR, 1943-45, C.P.A., Wis. Mem. Am. Bankers Assn., Assn. Res. City Bankers, Am. Inst. Banking, Met. Milw. Assn. Commerce, Navy League U.S., Sigma Chi, Episcopalian. Clubs: Milwaukee, Milwaukee Country, University (Milw.). Home: 8156 N Green Bay Rd Milwaukee WI 53209 Office: 777 E Wisconsin Ave Milwaukee WI 53202

KUEHL, WARREN FREDERICK, historian, educator; b. Bettendorf, Iowa, June 14, 1924; s. Gustav Frederick and Elsie Irene (Dobler) K.; B.A., Rollins Coll., 1949, L.H.D. (hon.), 1970; M.A., Northwestern U., 1951, Ph.D., 1954; m. Olga Llano, Sept. 7, 1951; children—Marshall Reed, Paul Bennett. Asst. prof. Rockford (Ill.) Coll., 1955-58; asso. prof. and prof. Miss. State U., State Coll., 1958-64; prof. and head dept. history U. Akron (Ohio), 1964-71, dir. Center for Peace Studies, 1970—; summer faculty Northwestern U., 1963, Duke U., 1964, U. N.C., 1965, Case-Western Res. U., 1968. Mem. Ohio Program in Humanities, 1973-76; mem. council Conf. on Peace Research in History, 1974—. Recipient award for outstanding hist. achievement Ohio Acad. History, 1969. Mem. Am., So. hist. assns., Orgn. Am. Historians, Soc. Historians Am. Fgn. Relations (sec.-treas. 1974—), Consortium on Peace Research and Devel. Author: Blow the Man Down!, 1959; Dissertations in History, 1873-1960, 1965; Dissertations in History, 1960-70, 1972; Hamilton Holt, Journalist, Internationalist, Educator, 1960; Seeking World Order: The U.S. and International Organization to 1920, 1969; gen. editor: Library of World Peace Studies, 1974. Home: 590 Rotunda Ave Akron OH 44313 Office: Dept History U Akron Akron OH 44325

KUEHN, ROBERT OSCAR, lawyer; b. Chgo., Feb. 24, 1943; s. Oscar Raymond and Marie Elizabeth (Renz) K.; B.A., North Park Coll., 1966; J.D., Loyola U., Chgo., 1969; m. Natalie June Benziger, July 8, 1967; children—William Raymond, Natalie Marie, Elizabeth Marion. Admitted to Ill. bar, 1969; asso. firm Williston & McGibbon, Chgo., 1969-71, partner, 1971—. Mem. Am., Ill., Chgo. (uniform comml. code com. 1972-77, probate practice com. 1977—) bar assns., Beta Theta Pi, Phi Alpha Delta. Editorial asst. Western European Labor and the American Corporation, 1968—. Home: 203 N Ashland Ave Park Ridge IL 60068 Office: 20 N Wacker Dr Chicago IL 60606

KUEHNER, GEORGE FREDERICK, dentist; b. Winthrop, Minn., Mar. 9, 1924; s. Charles William August and Clara Elizabeth (Fiss) K.; student St. Olaf Coll., 1942-43, U. Dubuque, 1943-44; D.D.S., Loyola U., 1948; m. Arlene Antramian, Aug. 17, 1951; children—George William, Kathleen Ann. Practice dentistry, New Ulm, Minn., 1948-50, 53—; dir. New Ulm Meml. Found., Highland Homes Corp., Citizens State Bank; commr. Region IX Phys. Devel. Subcommn. Chmn. New Ulm Housing and Redevel. Authority, 1967—. Served with USNR, 1943-45, 50-53. Fellow Internat. Coll. Dentists; mem. Am., Minn. dental assns., So. Minn. Dist. Dental Soc., Pierre Fauchard Acad., Omicron Kappa Upsilon. Lutheran. Lion. Home: 718 S Broadway St New Ulm MN 56073 Office: 16 1/2 N Minnesota St New Ulm MN 56073

KUEHNLE, WALTER REINHART, real estate appraiser, cons.; b. Chgo., June 3, 1902; s. Gustave Albert and Louise (Pracht) K.; student U. Chgo., 1928; m. Mary Alice Ferris, Dec. 24, 1941; children—Corinne Kuehnle Johnston, Christopher Charles, Kathryn Ferris Kuehnle Evans. Partner, G.A. Kuehnle & Son, Chgo., 1922-29; chief real estate Cook County Assessor's Office, Chgo., 1932-35; valuation engr., officer, dir. Harry S. Cutmore & Assos., Chgo., 1931—; pres. Walter R. Kuehnle & Co., Real Estate Appraisers & Cons., Chgo., 1935—; instr. real estate appraising Northwestern U., 1945-52, Central YMCA Coll., 1932-38; pres. Chgo. Real Estate Bd., 1962-63. Mem. regional adv. council War Assets Administrn. Recipient medal of merit El Instituto Mexicano de Valuacion. Mem. Am. Soc. Real Estate Counselors, Am. Inst. Real Estate Appraisers (chmn. edn. com. 1949-50, pres. Ill. chpt. 1947, nat. pres. 1951), Internat. Real Estate Fedn. (pres. real estate appraisal sect. 1972-75, world medal of honor 1974), Pan Am. Union Appraisal Orgns. (pres. 1976—). Author publs. in field. Home: 1351 Edgewood Ln Winnetka IL 60093 Office: 36 S State St Chicago IL 60603

KUENSTER, JOHN JOSEPH, publishing co. exec.; b. Chgo., June 18, 1924; s. Roy Jacob and Kathryn Elizabeth (Holechek) K.; student Mt. Carmel Coll., Niagara Falls, Ont., Can., DePaul U.; m. Mary Virginia Maher, Feb. 15, 1947; children—Kathleen Kuenster Mulcahy, James, Lois Kuenster Fitzmaurice, Virginia Kuenster Friedman, Margaret Kuenster Murphy, Kevin, Mary Frances, Robert. Sports editor The New World, 1946-48; asso. dir. publicity Catholic Youth Orgn., 1946-48; editor The Columbian, 1948-57; staff writer Chgo. Daily News, 1957-65; dir. devel. and pub. relations Mercy Hosp., Chgo., 1965-66; editor Papal Vol. mag., 1966-68; dir. devel. and pub. relations The Claretian Fathers, 1966—; v.p., advt. mgr. Columbian Pub. Co., Chgo., 1963—; editor Baseball Digest, 1969—. Mem. Baseball Writers Assn. Am. (chpt. pres. 1964). Club: K.C. (4 deg.). Home: 9546 S Ridgeway Ave Evergreen Park IL 60642 Office: 221 W Madison St Chicago IL 60606

KUEPER, JOSEPH FRANCIS, calendar printing co. exec.; b. St. Louis, Aug. 31, 1920; s. Leo H. and Elizabeth (Schrewe) Kueper; educated Beaumont Eve. Sch., 1938-42, Wash. U. Eve. Sch., 1939, Western Res. U., 1963; m. Margaret Louise Schroer, June 27, 1952; children—Diane, John. With Skinner & Kennedy Co., St. Louis, 1938—, cost clk., 1939-40, asst. estimator, 1940-41, sec., 1941-45, asst. div. mgr., 1946-60, calendar div. mgr., 1960-75, asst. v.p., 1975—. Served as yeoman 3d class USNR, 1942-44. Mem. St. Louis Advt. Specialist Assn., Certified Advt. Specialists, Specialty Advt. Assn. Internat. Clubs: Norwood Srs. Assn. (sec.). Home: 4310 Melba Ave Normandy MO 63121 Office: 9451 Natural Bridge Rd St Louis MO 63134

KUESPERT, CARL ADOLPH, elec. contracting co. exec.; b. South Bend, Ind., May 31, 1917; s. Adolph O. and Elsie (Rothe) K.; grad. high sch.; m. Lois M. Huff, Jan. 19, 1946; 1 son, William Carl. Apprentice electrician W.D. Hobbick Electric Co., South Bend, Ind., 1935-39, journeyman electrician, 1940—; journeyman electrician South Bend Lathe, 1943; sec.-treas. Hobbick-Kuespert Electric, Inc., South Bend, 1946-63, pres., 1963—. Mem. South Bend City Elec. Exam. Bd., 1964—, South Bend Mishawaka Civic Planning Assn. Served with USNR, 1943-45. Mem. Nat. Elec. Contractors Assn., Am. Turners, Am. Legion, Builders Exchange of St. Joseph Valley, South Bend-Mishawaka C. of C. Mem. United Ch. of Christ. Mason (32 deg.). Home: 2005 Dorwood Dr South Bend IN 46617 Office: 525 S Eddy St South Bend IN 46617

KUGLER, ANNA MARIE, ednl. adminstr.; b. LaHarpe, Ill., Apr. 9, 1941; d. Robert Marion and Evaline Marie (Johnson) Little; B.E., Western Ill. U., 1963; m. Larry Kent Kugler, Dec. 30, 1962; children—Diane Marie, Timothy Kent. English tchr., librarian N.W. Unit Dist., Sciota, Ill., 1963; unit librarian LaHarpe (Ill.) Unit Dist., 1964, 66; English tchr. Bushnell-Prairie City High Sch., Bushnell, Ill., 1967-69, high sch. media dir., 1970—; mem. adv. com. Western Ill. Library System. Mem. NEA, Ill. Edn. Assn., Bushnell-Prairie City Tchrs. Assn. Republican. Methodist. Home: 14 Hiel Dr Bushnell IL 61422 Office: 845 N Walnut St Bushnell IL 61422

KUGLER, WILLIAM JOHN, mus. curator, musician; b. Roberts County, S.D., Sept. 12, 1899; s. Charles and Anne (Washtok) K.; student Woods Sch. Dramatics, Dancing, Music and Theatre, New Orleans, 1927, U. Minn., 1938-41; m. Ida Carolyn Grunke, Nov. 8, 1940. Saxophonist, Bud Ornsby's Ragtime Kids, Rolla, N.D., 1921; band leader; pres. Kugler Music Co., St. Paul, 1938—, Kugler Music and Dance Studios, 1947-61, Musical Instruments Museum, St. Paul, 1962—. Pres., William and Ida Kugler Found. Served with AUS, 1941-42. Mem. Am. Fedn. Musicians, Internat. Council Museums, Am. Assn. Museums, Ethno-Musicology Soc., Am. Wireless Soc., Am. Musical Instrument Soc. Collector mus. instruments. Home: 1124 Dionne St St Paul MN 55113

KUGLITSCH, JOHN FRANCIS, internist; b. Springfield, Mass., Dec. 27, 1942; s. Frank Gabriel and Elizabeth Mary (Frigon) K.; B.S., Marquette U., 1965, M.D., 1969; m. Maureen Rose Hall, Aug. 26, 1967; children—Paul David, Mark Patrick. Intern, St. Joseph's Hosp., Milw., 1969-70; fellow in internal medicine Mayo Clinic, Mayo Grad. Sch. Medicine, Rochester, Minn., 1970-73; practice medicine specializing in internal medicine, Fond du Lac, Wis., 1973—; mem. staff St. Agnes Hosp., 1973—, dir. med. edn., 1975-77. Diplomate Am. Bd. Internal Medicine. Mem. AMA, Am., Wis. socs. internal medicine, Fox Valley Acad. Medicine, A.C.P., Am. Geriatrics Soc., Assn. Hosp. Med. Edn., Continuing Med. Edn. Club Wis., Wis. State, Fond du Lac County med. socs., Mayo Alumni Assn. Club: Elks. Home: 140 Fanna St Fond du Lac WI 54935 Office: Fond du Lac Clinic 80 Sheboygan St Fond du Lac WI 54935

KUHL, LAWRENCE VAN, livestock market exec.; b. Ida Grove, Iowa, July 22, 1914; s. Lawrence William and Jennie E. (Van Wagoner) K.; student Morningside Coll., 1931-33; m. Erma I. Boothby, May 10, 1941; children—Janene (Mrs. Paul E. Rehder), Kathlyn (Mrs. Steven Matre). With Sioux City Stock Yards div. United Stock Yards Corp. (Iowa), 1933—, div. pres., gen. mgr., 1969—; pres. Stock Yards Service & Supply Co., 1969—, Sioux City Terminal Ry. Co., 1974—; dir. Sioux Falls Stock Yards Co., 1957—. Mem. exec. com. Woodbury County Tax Research Com., 1959—. Trustee St. Lukes Med. Center, 1966—, v.p., 1968-73, pres. 1973-75. Served with USAAF, 1942-46. Mem. Am. Stockyards Assn. (chmn. bd. dirs. 1975-77), Internat. Shrine Horse Patrol (v.p. 1972-74), White Horse Mounted Patrol (capt. 1972-74). Methodist (chmn. bd. trustees 1960). Mason (33 deg.), Kiwanian. Home: 4308 Lincoln Way Sioux City IA 51106 Office: 340 Livestock Exchange Bldg Sioux City IA 51107

KUHL, MARGARET HELEN CLAYTON (MRS. ALEXIUS M. KUHL), banker; b. Louisville; d. Joseph Leonard and Maude (Mitzler) Clayton; student Loyola U. Home Study Div., Chgo., 1955—, Buena Vista Coll., Storm Lake, Iowa, summer 1964-65; m. Alexius M. Kuhl, Apr. 21, 1936; children—Carol Lynn (Mrs. Richard Benton Ford), James Michael (adopted). Sales lady, buyer Silverberg, Akron, Iowa, 1924-34; owner dress shop. Fonda, Iowa, 1934-40; librarian, Fonda, 1940-43; bookkeeper, teller First Nat. Bank, Fonda, 1943-44; tchr. librarian asst. Our Lady Good Counsel Sch., Fonda, 1963-70; dir. Pomeroy State Bank, 1959—, pres., chmn. bd., 1975—. Pres. state bd. Women in Community Service, 1970-72, state coordinator, 1973. Recipient Adult Leadership award Cath. Youth Orgn. Sioux City, Iowa, 1967; Nat. Cath. Youth Orgn. award, 1969. Mem. Cath. Daus. Am. (dist. dep. 1964-70, state del. nat. conv. 1968, 62-68, grand regent 1960-61, chmn. ecumenism 1969-71, state treas. 1969-71), Diocesan (chmn. orgn. and devel. 1964-66, pres.), Nat. (sec. diocesan bd., 1966-68, diocesan del. nat. conv. 1962, 64, 68, diocesan pres. 1968, 70, chmn. pub. relations 1962) councils Cath. women, Legion of Mary (pres. curia 1964-70, chmn. curia extension 1960-64), Internat. Biog. Assn., Internat. Platform Assn., Profl. and Bus. Women's Club, Fonda Womens Club, Fonda Country Club. Home: 5th and Queen Sts Fonda IA 50540

KUHL, ROBERT HENRY, surgeon; b. St. Louis, July 9, 1915; s. Robert Joseph and Carolyn B. (Waldemer) K.; A.B., Pa. State U., 1937; M.D., St. Louis U., 1941; student Washington U. Sch. Medicine, 1947; m. Ellen Eudora Hosler, Dec. 24, 1941; children—Marilyn Lee, Katherine Ann, Robert Malcolm, Jon Gregory. Intern, St. Louis City Hosp., 1941-42; resident in surgery St. Louis County Hosp., 1946-50; since practiced medicine, specializing in surgery, Creston, Iowa; sr. surgeon, also one of founders, Creston Med. Clinic, 1953—; dir. Creston Clinic Bldg. Corp., Creston Industries, Inc. Served from 1st lt. to capt. M.C., AUS, 1942-46, 117th Gen. Hosp., Eng., 1943-44, 26th Div., ETO, 1944-45. Diplomate Am. Bd. Surgery. Fellow Internat. Coll. Surgeons; mem. AMA, Iowa, Union County med. assns., Creston C. of C. (dir.). Home: 104 S Park St Creston IA 50801 Office: 526 New York Ave Creston IA 50801

KUHLMAN, JAMES WELDON, county agt.; b. Amarillo, Tex., Feb. 13, 1937; s. Herman and Alma Marie (Gerdsen) K.; B.S., West Tex. State U., 1959; M.S., U. Nebr., 1961; m. Ann B. Davis, Dec. 23, 1967; children—Lisa Ann, Jennifer Shawn. Grad. asst. U. Nebr., Lincoln, 1959-62; extension agt. U.S. Dept. Agr. Extension Service, Buffalo County, Nebr., 1962-67, extension agt. chmn., 1967-72, extension dir., Worth County, Northwood, Iowa, 1972—. Adviser, Northwood Meals on Wheels program, 1974—, bd. dirs., 1975—, pres., 1977—; adminstrv. bd. Northwood United Methodist Ch., 1973—, trustee, 1977—. Served with AUS, 1962. Recipient 4-H Alumni award, 1977. Mem. Am., Iowa, Nebr. Hereford assns., Holstein-Friesian Assn. Am., Iowa State U. Extension Assn. (dist. sec. 1975-76), Northwood C. of C., Nat. Assn. County Agrl. Agts., Worth County (Iowa) Hist. Soc., Alpha Chi, Epsilon Sigma Phi, Gamma Sigma Delta. Lion (v.p. 1975—). Club: Sertoma (pres. 1965-66; distinguished Pres. award 1966). Home: 308 N 12th St Northwood IA 50459 Office: 720 Central Ave Northwood IA 50459

KUHLMAN, PAUL WAYNE, lawyer; b. Carrollton, Mo., Oct. 1, 1940; s. Vernon and Dorothy D. (Sugg) K.; A.B., William Jewell Coll., 1962; J. D., Washington U., St. Louis, 1965; m. Judith Ann Leslie, July 3, 1965; 1 dau., Leslie Elizabeth. Admitted to Mo. bar, 1965; atty. U.S. Dept. Agr., Kansas City, Mo., 1965-67; mem. firm Hale, Coleberd, Kincaid & Waters, Liberty, Mo., 1967-68; partner Von Erdmannsdorff & Kuhlman, North Kansas City, Mo., 1969-74; now prin. in own practice; asst. prof. bus. law William Jewell Coll., 1967-69; chmn. Clay County Continuing Legal Edn./Mo. U., 1972—; chmn. ethics com. Mo. 17th Jud. Circuit, 1976-77, sec. circuit, 1974-76; dir., sec. Farmers Bank, Bogard, Mo.; asso. pros. atty. Clay County (Mo.), 1969—. Bd. dirs. Clay County Sports, Northland Symphonic Assn. Mem. Mo., Kansas City, Clay County bar assns., William Jewell Coll. Alumni Assn. (bd. govs. 1962—). Clubs: Sertoma (Liberty); Kiwanis (past v.p. Leawood, Kans.), Jaycees (Liberty). Home: 12 NW 38th St Kansas City MO 64116 Office: 104 E Franklin St Liberty MO 64068

KUHLMANN, GUSTAVE ADOLF, educator; b. Leoti, Kans., Oct. 6, 1896; s. William Henry and Wilhelmine Johanne (Lohmann) K.; B.A., Concordia Sem., St. Louis, 1922; A.M., Columbia U., 1923; m. Adelaide Dorothy Meyer, Dec. 27, 1928 (dec. Feb. 1953); children—Marjorie Ann Kuhlmann Theimer, Robert Theodore, Ruth Elaine Kuhlmann Ohm, David Gustave; m. 2d, Alma Marie Kruckenberg, Dec. 1, 1957 (dec. May 1974); 1 foster dau., Mary Jean Moore Farley. Asst. prof. St. John's Acad., Winfield, Kans., 1923-27; prof. English and edn. St. John's Coll., Winfield, 1927-73, asst. to pres., 1928-37. Founder, adviser St. John's Reporter, 1921-56; co-founder WL Talent Festival, 1933. Recipient Service award St. John's Coll. Bd. Control, 1973. Mem. Cowley County Hist. Soc. (pres. 1967-73), Speech Assn. Am., Am. Forensic Assn., Central States Speech Assn., Mem. St. John's Coll. Alumni Assn. (pres. 1955-77, service award 1973), Phi Rho Phi. Lutheran (past Sunday sch. supt.). Club: Lions. Author: The Preparation and Publication of Erasmus's Greek New Testament in 1516; Walther League Talent Quest Manual, 1936; editor Phi Rho Pi Persuader, 1940-49; editor-in-chief The Johnnie Heritage, 1893-1976, 1976. Address: Saint John's Coll Winfield KS 67156

KUHN, JOHN RAYMOND, JR., physician; b. Webb City, Mo., June 27, 1902; s. John Raymond and Tinzy Gertrude (Cowan) K.; B.S., Mo. So. State Coll., 1928; M.D., Jefferson Med. Coll., 1930; postgrad. U. Pa., 1931-32. Intern, Gen. Hosp., Kansas City, Mo., 1930-31; gen. practice medicine, Joplin, Mo., 1933—; mem. staff Freeman Hosp., St. John's Med. Center, both Joplin; med. dir. Mo. So. Coll., 1969—; dir. Security Nat. Bank, 1964-66. Student Health and Nursing Bldg. given name of Kuhn Hall, Mo. So. Coll., Joplin, 1970. Mem. Mo., So., Jasper County med. socs., AMA, So. Med. Assn., Samuel D. Gross Assos. Jefferson Med. Coll., C. of C. (dir. 1962-63, 63-64), Kappa Sigma, Alpha Kappa Kappa, U.S. C. of C. Presbyterian (trustee 1964-66). Club: Twin Hills Country (Joplin). Home: 625 Jaccard Pl Joplin MO 64801 Office: 321 Frisco Bldg Joplin MO 64801

KUHN, KAREN ANN KELLOGG, market research exec.; b. Council Bluffs, Iowa, Aug. 23, 1948; d. William E. and Vera L. (Cody) Kellogg; B.A., U. Nebr., 1970; m. Andrew T. Kuhn, Aug. 15, 1969; children—Thomas Andrew, Katherine Kellogg. Statis. clk. market research dept. Valmont Industries, Inc., Valley, Nebr., 1970-72, mktg. research analyst for irrigation product line research, 1972-73, corp. planning and research Agri-Products div., 1973-75, sr. market analyst, 1976, supr. market research sect., 1977—. Mem. Am. Mktg. Assn. (v.p. programs 1976), Mktg. Research Assn., Nat. Agri-Mktg. Assn., Smithsonian Assos., Sigma Kappa, Alpha Lambda Delta. Lutheran. Home: Rural Route 5 Fremont NE 68025 Office: Valmont Industries Inc Valley NE 68064

KUHN, WILLIAM LEO, engring. and mfg. co. exec.; b. Evanston, Ill., July 8, 1929; s. William L. and Helen (Kentlock) K.; student Thornton Coll.; m. Patricia June Cunradi, July 14, 1950; children—William Leo, Patricia Diane, Edward Orin. Project engr. Consol. Welding & Engring. Co., 1955-60; v.p. Capital Engring. & Mfg. Co., Chgo., 1960-69; now pres., owner Worth Engring. & Mfg. Co. Mem. service unit Salvation Army, Chgo. Served with USAF, 1950-52. Registered profl. engr., Ill. Mem. ASME, ASTM, Soc. Mfg. Engrs. (sr. mem.). Clubs: Masons, Lions (past pres. Worth). Home: 10824 S Nordica St Worth IL 60482 Office: 11723 S Austin Ave Alsip IL 60658

KUHRE, BRUCE EDWARD, educator; b. Warren, Pa., Nov. 17, 1936; s. Norman W. and Mary (Rasmussen) K.; A.B. cum laude, Thiel Coll., 1958; M.A., Pa. State U., 1962, Ph.D., 1966; postgrad. U. Calif. at Santa Barbara, 1972; m. Carol M. Stockey, Dec. 31, 1961; children—Siri, Tanja. Instr., asst. prof. sociology Ohio U., Athens, 1965-70, asso. prof., 1970—. Mem. ACLU, 1968—, PTA, 1968—, Indo-China Peace Campaign, 1973-75, Citizens Concerned About World Hunger, 1975—; chmn. Citizens for Better Schs., 1973-75. Danforth Asso. fellow, 1970—; Ohio U. grantee, 1970. Mem. Am., N. Central sociol. assns., Soc. for Sci. Study Religion. Contbr. articles to profl. jours. Field work, Mexico, 1960. Home: RD 2 Box 276 Athens OH 45701 Office: Dept Sociology and Anthropology Ohio U Athens OH 45701

KUKLA, ROBERT JOHN, lawyer, assn. exec.; b. Chgo., Dec. 1, 1932; s. John and Antoinette Marie (Habowska) K.; B.S., Northwestern U., 1954, J.D., 1957; m. Barbara Joan Kafka, Mar. 25, 1973; 1 son, Robert Anthony. Casualty adjuster Allstate Ins. Co., Chgo., 1957; admitted to Ill. bar, 1957 U.S. Dist. Ct. for No. Dist. Ill. bar, 1959; mem. firm Fitzgerald, Petrucelli & Simon, Chgo., 1957-61; mktg., sales distbn. exec. Sears Roebuck & Co., Chgo., 1962-70; self employed author, writer, lectr. TV personality, 1970-72; atty. hearings supr. State of Ill., Chgo., 1972-76; dept. exec. dir Nat. Rifle Assn. of Am.'s Inst. for Legis. Action, Washington, 1976, exec. dir., 1977—, bd. dirs., exec., legis. com., chmn. bylaws com., 1966-76. Founder, pres. Logan Sq. Neighborhood Assn., Inc., 1961-66. Recipient Chicago Certificate of Merit Award, 1970. Mem. Nat., Ill. State rifle assns., Am., Ill. State bar assns., Nat. Justice Found. Am., Am. Numismatic Assn. Clubs: Capitol Hill, NW Gun, Inc. Author: Gun Control, 1973; Ballistics Evidence-Firearms Identification, 1958. Home: PO Box 398 Park Ridge IL 60068 Office: 1600 Rhode Island Ave NW Washington DC 20036

KUKREJA, SUBHASH CHANDER, physician, med. educator; b. Multan, India, July 7, 1946; s. Kanshi Ram and Daya Wanti (Dua) K.; came to U.S., 1969; premed. degree Panjab U., India, 1963; M.D., All India Inst. Med. Scis., New Delhi, 1969; m. Neera Singh, Dec. 7, 1974, Intern, Cook County Hosp., Chgo., 1969-70, resident in internal medicine, 1971-72; resident in internal medicine, Mt. Sinai Hosp. Service, City Hosp., Elmhurst, N.Y., 1970-71; trainee in endocrinology, U. Ill. and VA West Side Hosp., Chgo., 1972-74, staff physician in endocrinology and nuclear medicine, 1974—; asst. prof. medicine, U. Ill., 1974—. Diplomate Am. Bd. Internal Medicine (subsplty. endocrinology), Am. Bd. Nuclear Medicine. Mem. Am. Fedn. Clin. Research, A.C.P., Endocrine Soc., Soc. Nuclear Medicine. Condr. research in field of calcium metabolism and parathyroid physiology. Home: 772 E Parkview Ct Roselle IL 60172 Office: VA West Side Hosp 820 S Damen St Chicago IL 60612

KULACKI, FRANCIS ALFRED, mech. engr.; b. Balt., May 21, 1942; s. Frank Alfred and Ida (Jarowski) K.; B.S. in Mech. Engring., Ill. Inst. Tech., 1963, M.S. in Gas Engring. (Inst. Gas Tech. fellow), 1966; Ph.D., U. Minn., 1971. Jr. engr. Balt. Gas and Electric Co., summers, 1960-63; teaching and research asso. U. Minn., Mpls., 1966-71; asst. prof. mech. engring. Ohio State U., Columbus, 1971 and after, subsequently asso. prof.; cons. in field. Mem. ASME (chmn. Columbus sect.), Am. Soc. Engring. Edn., AAUP., Texnikoi (hon.), Sigma Xi, Tau Beta Pi, Pi Tau Sigma. Roman Catholic. Contbr. articles on heat transfer research, nuclear reactor safety to profl. jours. Home: 2206 Harwitch Rd Columbus OH 43221 Office: 206 W 18th Ave Columbus OH 43210

KULIS, RICHARD WILLIAM, orthodontist; b. Detroit, July 7, 1942; s. William and Eleanor (Rutkowski) K.; B.S., Eastern Mich. U., 1964; D.D.S. magna cum laude, U. Detroit, 1970; M.S., Northeastern U. Dental Sch., 1972; m. Victoria Supkoski, July 4, 1964; children—Jeffery Todd, Richard William. Practice dentistry specializing in orthodontics, Sterling Heights, Mich., 1972—. Vice-pres. Echo Rd Home Owners Assn., 1977. Mem. Am. Assn. Orthodontists, ADA, Great Lakes Soc. Orthodontists, Macomb County Dental Soc., Mich. Soc. Orthodontists, Omicron Kappa Upsilon. Club: Grosse Pointe Yacht. Home: 4920 Echo Rd Bloomfield Hills MI 48013 Office: 8130 Constitution Sterling Heights MI 48078

KULKARNI, BIDY, endocrinologist, educator; b. Maharashtra, India, Apr. 18, 1930; s. Dhondu Y. and Sita (Deshpande) K.; came to U.S., 1961, naturalized, 1973; B.S., Poona (India) U., 1952, M.S., 1956, Ph.D., 1962; m. Suman Sane, May 8, 1957; children—Neela, Bob. Sr. sci. officer Nat. Chem. Lab., Poona, 1966-67; sect. chief steroid chemistry dept. endocrinology S.W. Research Found., San Antonio, 1967-70; asst. prof. dept. obstetrics and gynecology U. Chgo., 1970-73; dir. gynecic endocrinology labs. Michael Reese Hosp., Chgo., 1970-73; dir., asso. prof. reproductive endocrinology Loyola U. Med. Center, Maywood, Ill., 1973—; sci. dir. Loyola U. Perinatal Center, Maywood, 1975—. Recipient grant Center for Population Research NIH, 1972-74; named outstanding new citizen of year Citizenship Council Met. Chgo., 1973. Mem. Endocrine Soc., Soc. Study of Reprodn., World Population Soc., N.Y. Acad. Scis., Ill. Soc. Med. Research, Am. Chem. Soc., AAAS, AAUP. Contbr. articles to profl. jours. Home: 9S155 Nantucket Dr Westmont IL 60559 Office: 2160 S 1st Ave Maywood IL 60153

KULL, CHARLES FREDERICK, JR., securities co. exec.; b. Detroit, Jan. 5, 1922; s. Charles Frederick and Aileen (Nauman) K.; B.S., U. Mich., 1943; m. Patricia Lee Chubbuck, Apr. 15, 1944; children—Charles Frederick III, Edmund Arthur (dec.), Dorothy Ann. Indsl. sales rep. Ford Motor Co., Dearborn, Mich., 1956-58; registered rep. Paine, Webber, Jackson & Curtis, mem. N.Y. Stock Exchange, Detroit, 1959-62; v.p. Anchor Corp., Elizabeth, N.J., 1962-67; US Life Mut. Funds Mgmt. Corp., N.Y.C., 1968-72; account exec., br. mgr. Manley, Bennett, McDonald Co., mem. N.Y. Stock Exchange, Traverse City, Mich., 1972—. Bd. dirs. Grand Traverse Area United Way; chmn. adv. bd. Salvation Army; mem. corp. Traverse City Osteo. Hosp. Served with USNR, 1942-46. Mem. Ret. Officers Assn. Methodist. Mason (K.T.). Club: Kiwanis (Traverse City). Home: 133 Wakulat Dr Traverse City MI 49684 Office: 320 Nat Bank Bldg Traverse City MI 49684

KULP, SAMUEL LESTER, computer systems analyst; b. Mishawaka, Ind., Nov. 23, 1942; s. Lester Charles and Frances Bernice (Chamness) K.; B.S., Purdue U., 1970; m. Constance Lenora White, June 26, 1965. Systems programmer Purdue U. adminstrv. data processing center, West Lafayette, Ind., 1969-70; info. analyst Eli Lilly and Co., Indpls., 1970-73; sr. programmer analyst Am. United Life Ins. Co., Indpls., 1973-78. Scoutmaster, leadership devel. chmn. Boy Scouts Am. (recipient Scouters Key, dist. Merit award, mem. Order of Arrow). Mem. Assn. Computing Machinery (past treas. Central Ind. chpt.). Baptist. Home: 749 Ramblin Rd Greenwood IN 46142

KULTERMANN, UDO RAINER, archtl. historian; b. Stettin, Germany, Oct. 14, 1927; s. Georg and Charlotte (Schultz) K.; student U. Greifswald (Germany), 1946-50; Ph.D. magna cum laude, U. Muenster (Germany), 1953; came to U.S., 1967; m. Judith Danoff, May 10, 1975; children by previous marriage—Martin, Andreas, Eva. Curatorial asst., Kunsthalle, Bremen, Germany, 1954-55; dir. city art museum Schloss Morsbroich, Leverkusen, Germany, 1959-64; lectr. Harvard U., Yale U., U. Calif. at Berkeley and Los Angeles, U. Pa., U. Minn., 1965—; prof. archtl. history Washington U., St. Louis, 1967—; participant 1st Internat. Congress African Culture, So. Rhodesia, 1962; lectr. U. Tel Aviv, U. Haifa, U. Jerusalem, 1972, U. Melbourne, U. Sydney, U. Calcutta, U. Bombay, 1977, U. Cairo, U. Beirut, 1978; participant 2d Arab Biennale Art, Morocco, 1976-77. Author: Architecture of Today, 1958; New Architecture in the World, 1965; History of Art History, 1966; The New Sculpture-Assemblage and Environments, 1967; The New Painting, 1969, rev. edit., 1978; Art and Life—. The Function of Intermedia, 1970; New Realism, 1972; Die Architektur im 20 Jahrhundert, 1977. Home: 6833 Kingsbury St St Louis MO 63130 Office: Washington U St Louis MO 63130

KUMARAN, JAY SAMPATH, veterinarian; b. Mysore, India, Mar. 8, 1940; s. Sampath Devanbu and Anna (Reddy) K.; came to U.S., 1966, naturalized, 1972; B.V.SC and A.H., U. Vikram (India), 1964; M.Sc.D., U. Punjab (India), 1966; 1 dau., Kiran. Research fellow Nat. Dairy Research Inst., Karnal, India, 1964-66; tech. research specialist Delta Primate Research Center, Covington, La., 1966; staff veterinarian Tulane Med. Sch., New Orleans, 1967-68; veterinarian Valparaiso (Ind.) Animal Hosp., 1971-72, Five Points Animal Hosp., Ft. Wayne, Ind., 1972—; founding mem., treas., mem. bd. dirs. Emergency Animal Clinic, Ft. Wayne, 1977—. Active 4-H, Boy Scouts Am., Alliance for Animals. Mem. AVMA, Ft. Wayne Veterinary Med. Assn. (pres. 1971), Ind., N.E. Ind. veterinary med. assns., Am. Animal Hosp. Assn., Nat. Wild Life Health Fedn., Am. Assn. Animal Welfare Veterinarians (charter). Republican. Unitarian. Club: Kiwanis (fund raising chmn. Down Town club 1975, dir. 1974-75, sgt. at arms 1977-78). Author: Sex Chromatin and Applied Cytogenetics, 1965; Artificial Insemination and Animal Reproduction, 1966. Home: 2525 Webster St Fort Wayne IN 46807 Office: 922 Goshen Ave Fort Wayne IN 46808

KUNDERT, ALICE E., state ofcl.; b. Java, S.D., July 23, 1920; d. Otto J. and Maria (Rieger) Kundert; ed. North State Tchrs. Coll. Tchr. pub. schs., Campbell County, S.D., 1939-43, 49-54; from clk to mgr., buyer, dept. store and dress shop, Cal., 1943-48; dept. supt. schs., Campbell County, 1954; county clk of cts., 1955-60; county register of deeds, 1961-68; sec.-treas. Campbell County Republican party, 1962-64, finance chmn., 1962-68, vice chmn., 1964-68; presdl. elector Rep. Party of S.D., 1964; town treas., Mound City, S.D., 1965-68; state auditor, S.D., 1969—. Leader, project leader, 4-H; acting chmn., vice chmn. Black Hills Leaders Lab., exec. sec. citizen's responsibility com. Internat. Leaders Tng. Lab., Ireland, 1963; mem. S.D. Local Study Commn., 1967—; mem. state and local adv. coms. Office Equal Opportunity. Named Outstanding Teen Age Republican adviser, 1971-72, 76; recipient Alumni award No. State Coll. Congregationalist. Author: History of the County of Campbell, 1960. Office: State Capitol Bldg Pierre SD 57501

KUNKEL, LORENZ VICTOR, chem. engr.; b. Olney, Tex., Oct. 24, 1915; s. Victor William and Rosa Elizabeth (Dorpat) K.; B.S., Tex. A. and M. U., 1937; M.S., Tulsa U., 1956; m. Hilda Elizabeth Frank, Nov. 30, 1939; children—Larry Lee, Patricia Ann. Petroleum engr. Humble Oil & Refining Co., Houston, 1937-40; operating engr. Celanese Corp. Am., Bishop, Tex., 1945-48; sr. staff process engr. Amoco Prodn. Co., Tulsa, 1948-73, exec. engr., Chgo., 1973-76; prin. L.V. Kunkel Engring., gas processing cons., Naperville, Ill., 1976—; instr. Command and Gen. Staff Coll., U.S. Army Res. Served to capt. AUS, 1941-45. Decorated Army Commendation medal. Mem. Engring. Soc. Tulsa (dir. tng. and edn.). Contbr. articles to profl. jours. Patentee in field. Home and Office: 1013 Royal Bombay Ct Naperville IL 60540

KUNKLE, CALVIN SYLVESTER, mech. engr.; b. Wauseon, Ohio, Jan. 2, 1937; s. Henry Phillip and Mary Elsie (Cocanower) K.; B.S. in Mech. Engring., Tri State U., 1960; postgrad. Purdue U.; m. Marjorie JoAnn Huard, Aug. 25, 1957; 1 son, Gregory Scott. Process engr. Acme Lees Corp., Muncie, Ind., 1960; exptl. glass research staff Ball Brothers Co., Muncie, 1960-62; project engr. Oakes Mfg. div. FMC Corp., Tipton, Inc., 1962-73, chief engr. fire apparatus ops., 1973—. Dist. rep. Boy Scouts Am., 1970; bd. dirs. United Fund, 1971; mem. entertainment com. Tipton Pork Festival, 1973; supt., elder 1st

Presbyn. Ch., Tipton. Mem. Soc. Auto. Engrs. Republican. Clubs: Kiwanis, Elks. Patentee in field. Home: Route 1 Tipton IN 46072 Office: 516 Dearborn St Tipton IN 46072

KUNKLE, GEORGE ROBERT, environ. scientist; b. Elyria, Ohio, Mar. 27, 1934; s. Harold Ray and Irene Owers (Wallau) K.; B.S., Iowa State U., 1956; M.S., U. Mich., 1958, Ph.D., 1961; m. Sandra Jean Laver, Jan. 25, 1958; children—Karen, Sarah, Robert, Jonathan. Research officer Alta. Research Council, Edmonton, Can., 1960-62; hydrologist Water Resources div., U.S. Geol. Survey, Iowa City, 1962-66; asso. prof. geology U. Toledo, 1966-71; pres., prin. scientist Earthview Inc., Toledo, 1971-77; sr. scientist Jones and Henry Engrs. Ltd., 1977—; lectr. in field. Adv. com. Lucas County Coastal Zone Mgmt., 1977—; bd. dirs. NW Ohio Nat. Resources Council, 1972; environ. adv. com. Toledo-Lucas County Port Authority, 1973—; mem. Ohio Panel Internat. Joint Commn. Reference Group on Gt. Lakes Pollution from Land Use Activities, 1977—. U. Toledo summer faculty fellow, 1969. Mem. Mich. Basin Geol. Soc., Ohio Acad. Sci., Nat. Water Well Assn., Am. Water Resources Assn., Am. Geol. Inst., Sigma Xi, Sigma Gamma Epsilon. Unitarian. Contbr. articles to profl. publs. Home: 5347 Flanders Rd Toledo OH 43623 Office: 2000 W Central Ave Toledo OH 43606

KUNKLER, ARNOLD WILLIAM, surgeon; b. St. Anthony, Ind., Nov. 18, 1921; s. Edward J. and Selma (Hasenour) K.; A.B., Ind. U., 1943, M.D., 1949; m. Muriel Helen Burns, May 22, 1954; children—Lisa, Arnold William, Carolyn, Christine, Phillip, Kevin. Intern Ind. U. Med. Center, Indpls., 1949-50, asst. resident in surgery, also fellow vascular surg. research, 1950-54, resident in surgery, 1954-55; faculty, 1955—, clin. prof. surgery, 1976—; individual practice medicine, specializing in gen. surgery Terre Haute, Ind., 1955—; dir. med. edn. Terre Haute Regional Hosp., 1970—; staff Terre Haute Center Med. Edn., Terre Haute Regional Hosp. Pres. Terre Haute Med. Edn. Found., 1972-73, bd. dirs. 1967—; pres. community adv. council Terre Haute Center Med. Edn., 1976—; treas. Wabash Valley Community Blood Program, 1974—. Served with U.S. Army, 1943-46; ETO. Diplomate Am. Bd. Surgery. Fellow A.C.S. (dir. Ind. chpt. 1973—); mem. Terre Haute C. of C., Vigo County Cancer Soc., Vigo County Med. Soc., Ind., Am., Pan Am. med. assns., Pan Pacific Surg. Assn., Aesculapian Soc. Wabash Valley, Soc. Abdominal Surgeons, Ind. Soc. Chgo. Democrat. Roman Catholic. Club: Country of Terre Haute. Contbr. articles to profl. publs. Home: 3515 Ohio Blvd Terre Haute IN 47803 Office: 1700 N 7th St Terre Haute IN 47804

KUNTZ, EARL JEREMY, telephone communications co. exec.; b. Chgo., July 21, 1929; s. S. Emil and G. Ruth (Beitscher) K.; student Northwestern U., 1948-50; m. Mary M. Kohls, July 28, 1957; children—Karen A., Bradford G. Salesman sales display advt. Chgo. Fgn. Newspapers, Chgo., 1948-50; partner Gen. Bus. Service, Chgo., 1951-59; pres. Gen. Telephone Answering Service, Chgo., 1960—; owner Chgo. Office Forms Co., 1957—; pres. Partimers, Inc., 1970—; mktg. cons., v.p. Phone Aide Co., Inc. div. Wells Gardner Electronics, 1972-76; pres. Telephone Answering Services of Ill., Inc., 1972-74. Vice-pres. PTA, Wilmette, Ill., 1972-73; trustee Communications Research Found., Sausalito, Calif., 1976—; caucus del. Wilmette Sch. Bd., 1973-76. Mem. Assn. Telephone Answering Exchanges (dir.). Clubs: Execs., Monroe (Chgo.). Inventor telephone related devices to improve and simplify communication in telephone answering industry. Office: 30 W Washington St Chicago IL 60602

KUNTZ, HERMAN WILLIAM, otolaryngologist; b. Indpls., June 13, 1902; s. Henry and Marie (Mueller) K.; A.B., Butler U., 1924; M.D., Ind. U., 1927; postgrad., 1935; m. Ethel Cleora Stangle, Nov. 24, 1946; children—Rosemarie, William Henry. Intern, Ind. U. Hosp., Indpls., 1927-28, now staff mem.; gen. practice of medicine, Indpls., 1928-35, specializing in otolaryngology, Indpls., 1935—; mem. staffs Community, Methodist hosps.; instr. otolaryngology Ind. U. Sch. Nursing, 1952-58, asst. prof. emeritus otolaryngology Sch. Medicine, 1975—. Diplomate Am. Bd. Otolaryngology. Mem. Am., Ind. med. assns., Marion County Med. Soc., Am., Ind., Indpls. (pres. 1965-66) ophthalmology and otolaryngology socs., Phi Beta Pi, Delta Chi. Mason (Shriner). Optimist (v.p. 1960-61, Optimist of Year award 1961). Clubs: Columbia; Athenaeum Turners. Home: 2065 Lick Creek Dr Indianapolis IN 46203 Office: 5317 E 16th St Suite 7 Indianapolis IN 46218

KUNTZLEMAN, CHARLES THOMAS, phys. edn. cons.; b. Bloomsburg, Pa., Nov. 4, 1940; s. Walter Allen and Phyllis Winifred (Lehman) K.; A.B., Muhlenberg Coll., 1962; M.Ed., Temple U., 1965, Ed.D., 1976; m. Carol Lee Emhardt, June 9, 1962 (dec.); m. 2d, Beth Ann Garn, Oct. 26, 1974. Instr. phys. edn. Muhlenberg Coll., Allentown, Pa., 1962-66, asso. prof., 1966-67; prin., tchr. New Life Boys Ranch, Harleysville, Pa., 1967-68; dir. student activities, lectr. anatomy, physiology, health and phys. edn. Lehigh County Community Coll., Schnecksville, Pa., 1968-70; v.p., nat. program dir. Fitness Finders, Emmaus, Pa., 1970-74, owner, nat. program cons., 1974—; instr. Jackson (Mich.) Community Coll., Spring Arbor (Mich.) Coll.; mem. Mich. Gov's Council Phys. Fitness and Health, 1976—. Author: The Physical Fitness Encyclopedia, 1970; Activetics, 1975; Color Me Red, 1977; Heartbeat, 1977; Rating the Exercises, 1978; The Exercises Handbook, 1978; also booklets and mag. articles in field. Address: 178 E Harmony St Spring Arbor MI 49238

KUPCINET, IRV, columnist; b. Chgo., July 31, 1912; s. Max and Anna (Paswell) K.; m. Essee Solomon, Feb. 12, 1939; children—Karyn, Jerry; student Northwestern U., 1931; B.A., U. N.D., 1935. With Chgo. Times (now Chgo. Sun-Times), 1935—, columnist Kup's Column, 1943—, host television talk show Kup's Show, 1958—. Conducted Purple Heart Cruise, 1945—; active United Cerebral Palsy Assn., Chgo. Heart Assn., Shimer Coll., Mt. Carroll, Ill. Home: 1040 Lake Shore Dr Chicago IL 60611 Office: 401 N Wabash Ave Chicago IL 60611

KUPERSMITH, FARRELL PRESTON, mgmt. cons.; b. N.Y.C., Apr. 5, 1949; s. Aaron Harry and Cynthia (Skolnick) K.; B.S. with honors, N.Y. U., 1972, M.B.A., 1974; m. Barbara S. Kocolatos, May 27, 1972. Dir. sales and bus. devel. Health Resorts and Spas Corp., Lakewood, N.J., 1970-71, gen. mgr., chief operating exec., 1971-72; mgr. ops. analysis and fin. planning Revlon Internat. Corp. subsidiary Revlon Inc., N.Y.C., 1972-73, dir. fin. planning and asst. to chmn., 1973-74; mgmt. cons. Touche Ross & Co., Detroit and Cleve., 1974—; partner C & F Realty, N.Y.C., 1974—; fin. cons. various charitable orgns. and pvt. trusts, 1974—; guest lectr. internat. finance and market devel. U.S. Dept. Commerce, 1974—. Trustee, Claremore Lodge, 1972-73. Mem. Fin. Mgmt. Assn., Lakewood Hotel Assn. (past trustee), Phi Alpha Kappa (pres. 1972-73). Club: N.Y. U. Author: Avoiding the Commercial Pitfalls of Detente, 1973. Home: 25805 Fairmount Blvd Beachwood OH 44122 Office: 1300 First National Bldg Detroit MI 48226 also 800 Ohio Savs Plaza Cleveland OH 44114

KUPFERBERG, LLOYD SHERMAN, lawyer; b. Chgo., May 11, 1931; s. Emanuel and Lillian (Chalfen) K.; student Northwestern U., 1949-51; B.S., U. Wis., 1953; J.D., Harvard, 1956; m. Barbara Behr, July 22, 1956; children—Susan, Janis, Peter. Admitted to Ill. bar, 1956, since practiced in Chgo.; asso. firm Kahn, Adsit & Arnstein, 1960-63; asso. firm Schwartz, Cooper, Kolb & Gaynor, Chgo., 1963—, partner, 1968—; dir. World's Finest Chocolate, Inc. Mem. sch. bd. caucus, Highland Park, Ill., 1965-72, pres., 1971-72. Bd. dirs. Parent Tchr. Orgn., 1963-64; program chmn. lawyers div. Jewish United Fund, mem. exec. com. Lyric Opera Guild, 1972-75. Served to 1st lt. USAF, 1957-60. Mem. Ill., Chgo. bar assns., Phi Beta Kappa, Artus, Phi Eta Sigma, Pi Lambda Phi. Jewish religion. Mem. B'nai B'rith. Clubs: Standard (Chgo.); Birchwood (Highland Park). Home: 380 Woodland Rd Highland Park IL 60035 Office: 33 N LaSalle St Chicago IL 60602

KUPST, MARY JO, psychologist; b. Chgo., Oct. 4, 1945; d. George Eugene and Winifred Mary (Hughes) Kupst; B.S., Loyola U., Chgo., 1967, M.A., 1969, Ph.D., 1972; m. Alfred P. Stresen-Reuter, Jr., Aug. 21, 1977. Certified psychologist, Ill. Lectr. Loyola U., 1970-71; postdoctoral fellow community psychology U. Ill. Med. Center, Chgo., 1971-72; project dir. experiments in communication of med. info., div. child psychiatry Children's Meml. Hosp., Chgo., 1972-75, project dir. coping in families with a leukemic child, 1976—; instr. psychiatrics/pediatrics Northwestern U., 1973-74, asso., 1974-76, asst. prof., 1976—; practice psychotherapy, Chgo., 1974—. Mem. Am., Ill. psychol. assns., Assn. for Humanistic Psychology, Assn. for Women in Psychology. Contbr. articles to profl. jours. Home: 2779 N Kenmore Ave Chicago IL 60614 Office: Div Child Psychiatry Children's Meml Hosp 2300 Children's Plaza Chicago IL 60614

KURFESS, ROLAND HERMAN, engring. exec.; b. Chgo., Jan. 25, 1936; s. Gregor Joseph and Bernardine (Schobel) K.; B.S. in M.E., Purdue U., 1958, M.S. in Indsl. Engring., 1959; m. Evelyn Mary Haschin, June 7, 1959; children—Judith Ann, Thomas Roland, Stephen Gregory. Chief engr. Dynamic Machine Co., Chgo., 1963-70, v.p. mfg., 1975—; mgr. engring. Courtesy Mfg. Co., Elk Grove, Ill., 1970-75; pres., sr. broker Rino Realty (Palatine, Ill.); v.p. Bertacchi-Kurfess Builders (Palatine). Dir. ecology Village of South Barrington, 1972—. Registered profl. engr., Ill.; certified mfg. engr.; registered real estate broker, Ill. Mem. Soc. Mfg. Engrs., Nat., Ill. (chpt. pres. 1975-76) socs. profl. engrs., Phi Kappa Tau, Pi Tau Sigma, Alpha Pi Mu. Home: Rural Route 3 44 Watergate Dr Barrington IL 60010 Office: 1918 Rand Rd Palatine IL 60067

KURMAN, GEORGE, humanist; b. Tallinn, Estonia, June 10, 1942; s. Hugo and Juta Kurman; came to U.S., 1947; B.A., Cornell U., 1962; M.A., Columbia U., 1966; Ph.D., Ind. U., 1969; m. Tiina Abel, June 12, 1965; children—Ursula, Melba, Iris, Lulu. Faculty Western Ill. U., Macomb, 1970—, asso. prof. English, 1975—. Mem. Assn. for Advancement of Baltic Studies, Am. Comparative Lit. Assn., Modern Lang. Assn. Translator Kalevipoeg, Estonian nat. epic, 1978; author books, contbr. articles to profl. pubs. Home: 1010 E Calhoun St Macomb IL 61455

KURTIS, WILLIAM (BILL) HORTON, broadcast journalist; b. Pensacola, Fla., Sept. 21, 1940; s. William A. and Wilma Mary (Horton) K.; B.S. in Journalism, U. Kans., 1962; J.D., Washburn U., 1966; m. Helen M., July 7, 1963 (dec.); children—Mary Kristin, Scott Erik. News reporter Sta. WBBM-TV, Chgo., 1966-70, anchorman, reporter, 1973—; corr. CBS News, Los Angeles, 1970-73. Served with USMCR, 1962-63. Recipient Chgo. Area Emmy for reporting Chgo. conspiracy trial, 1970, Saigon fall, 1976, Belfast investigation, 1976; Chgo. Area Emmy for individual excellence for performers who appear on camera, 1976; Overseas Press Club award for Saigon Orphans, 1975. Mem. Sigma Delta Chi. Office: 630 N McClurg CT Chicago IL 60611

KUSHNER, FREDERICK R., optometrist; b. Vienna, Austria, Oct. 26, 1914; s. Nathan and Molly (Maier) K.; B.S., U. Vienna, 1938; O.D., Ill. Coll. Optometry, 1946; m. Doris Louise McEarchern, June 26, 1942; children—Kitty Kushner Edler, Kenneth, Roxane. Came to U.S., 1940, naturalized, 1942. Mem. faculty Ill. Coll. Optometry, Chgo., 1946-50, prof., 1950-52, asst. dean, 1950-51, dean, 1951-55; practice optometry, Sheldon, Iowa, 1955—; lectr. various state optometric meetings throughout U.S.; pres. Sheldon Indsl. Devel. Corp., 1971. Trustee Sheldon Community Hosp.; bd. dirs. Sheldon Handicap Village, Sheldon Community Meml. Hosp., Ill. Coll. Optometry; mem. Sheldon Zoning Commn. Recipient Man of Year award Sheldon C. of C., 1961; Optometrist of Year award Iowa Optometric Assn., 1965. Mem. Am. (chmn. nat. com. 1956-69), Iowa (pres. 1963) optometric assns., Sheldon C. of C. (pres. 1968). Club: Masons. Home: 1241 Kahler Ct Sheldon IA 51201 Office: 928 3d Ave Sheldon IA 51201

KUTLER, BENTON, dentist; b. Council Bluffs, Iowa, May 21, 1920; s. Harry and Sarah (Kutler) K.; B.A., State U. Iowa, 1942; D.D.S., Creighton U., 1945; m. Harriet Dorothy Lorkis, June 25, 1944; children—Laura (Mrs. David H. Chait), Robert M., David B., Howard S., Bruce A. Gen. practice dentistry, Omaha, 1946—; asst. prof. preventive medicine U. Nebr. Med. Coll., 1946—, instr. surgery, 1954—; vis. lectr. Creighton U. Coll. Dentistry, 1955-56, clin. instr., 1972—. Chmn., Nebr. Lions Eye Bank, 1960-67; chmn. Nebr. Lions Sight Conservation Found., 1967-68, also trustee. Trustee, Dr. Abe Greenberg Scholarship Found., Anti-Defamation League, Omaha, Omaha chpt. Am. Cancer Soc. Served with AUS, 1943-45; with USNR, 1945-46, 52-54. Recipient Distinguished Service award Nebr. Lions Sight Conservation Found., 1963, 67. Fellow AAAS, Acad. Gen. Dentistry, Internat. Coll. Dentists; mem. Am., Nebr. dental assns., Am. Soc. Dentistry for Children, Omaha Dist. Dental Soc. (asso. editor Chronicle 1951—, pres. 1969-70), Omaha C. of C., Nat. Fedn. Jewish Mens Clubs (regional pres. 1971-73), Sigma Xi. Jewish (trustee synagogue). Lion (dist. gov. 1969-70); mem. B'nai B'rith (lodge pres. 1962-63). Contbg. editor Oral Research Abstracts. Home: 6404 Glenwood Rd Omaha NE 68132 Office: 321 Doctors Bldg Omaha NE 68131

KUTSCHER, GORDON RALPH, educator; b. Jackson, Mo., Jan. 3, 1934; s. Richard Henry and Emilie (Kasten) K.; B.S., S.E. Mo. State Coll., 1957; M.Ed., U. Mo., 1961; student Mo. Sch. Mines, summer 1958; m. Louanna Mae Dickerson, Aug. 15, 1954; children—Richard Gordon, Randy Keith, Robert Clark. Instr. math. Sch. Dist. R-4, Benton, Mo., 1955-57, Rolla (Mo.) Sr. High Sch., 1957-59, head dept. math., 1959-61; sch. psychol. examiner, counselor, dir. guidance Rolla Jr. High Sch., 1962-67; dir. guidance Rolla Pub. Schs., 1967, supr. guidance services Mo. Dept. Edn., 1967-70, asst. dir. Research Coordinating Unit, 1970-71; exec. sec., dir. Mo. Adv. Council Vocat. Edn., 1971—; co-chmn. Nat. Bicentennial Conf. on Vocat. Edn.; del. Mo. Gov.'s Conf. on Edn.; sr. research asst., Freshman orientation counselor U. Mo. at Rolla, summer 1966. Mem. Rolla Community Betterment Program, 1964; past pres. Trinity Lutheran Ch., chmn. bd. stewardship; committeeman explorer post and scout troop Boy Scouts Am.; bd. dirs. Cole County Conservation Commn. Mem. NEA (life), Mo. State Tchrs. Assn., Rolla Community Tchrs. Assn. (past pres.), Phelps County Mental Health Assn. (past pres.), Mo. (past pres.; editor emeritus quar. jour.), South Central (past pres.) guidance assns., Am. Personnel and Guidance Assn., Am. Sch. Counselor Assn., Nat. Vocat. Guidance Assn., Assn. Measurement and Evaluation in Guidance, Am. (life), Mo. vocat. assns., Nat. Assn. Exec. Dirs. State Vocat. Adv. Councils (past v.p.), Phi Delta Kappa (life). Optimist (past pres. Jefferson City, lt. gov. Mo. dist. 1970-71, dist. boys work chmn. 1971-72, dist. community service chmn. 1972-73, dist. oratorical chmn. 1974-75, dist. sec./treas. 1975-76, dist. gov.-elect 1976-77). Author: 1965 Graduates Responses and Data Survey, 1968; Structure, Function and Use of Local Advisory Committees in Vocational Education, 1974; co-author: Handbook for Local Vocational Advisory Committees, 1977; contbr. articles to profl. jours. Home: 1815 Swift's Hwy Jefferson City MO 65101

KUTZ, RALPH GEORGE, clergyman; b. St. Louis, Dec. 31, 1911; s. Joseph A. and Helen M. (Broeckelmann) K.; student St. Louis Prep. Sem., 1925-33, Kenrick Sem., 1933-37, St. Louis U., 1937-39. Ordained priest Roman Catholic Ch., 1937; chaplain Ursuline Novitiate, Festus, Mo., 1937-49; asst. pastor St. Louis Parishes, 1949-54; pastor Wellsville (Mo.), Martinsburg (Mo.) Parishes, 1954-59, Taos (Mo.) Parish, 1966-70, Argyle (Mo.) and Koeltztown (Mo.) parishes, 1970—; mem. faculty Helias High School, 1959-70, chancellor Diocese Jefferson City (Mo.), 1959-70; dir. Diocesan Cath. Charities; instr. St. Louis U., 1937-49; state chaplain Daus. of Isabella, 1968-72. K.C. Editor: Catholic Missourian, 1960-69. Address: Argyle MO 65001

KUTZA, MICHAEL JOSEPH, JR., film festival exec.; b. Chgo., Nov. 28, 1939; s. Michael Joseph and Theresa (Felicetti) K.; student Loyola U., Chgo., 1957-59; B.S., Roosevelt U., 1961; postgrad. Ill. Inst. Design, U. Chgo., 1964. Freelance motion picture cameraman pub. affairs dept. Sta. WGN-TV, Chgo., 1963-64; art dir., pub. relations exec. Milton Shufro & Assos. Chgo., 1964-66; dir. founder Chgo. Internat. Film Festival, Inc., 1964—; free-lance art dir., designer graphics for various film cos. and agys., 1965—; film and media designer Joe Hayes Prodns., N.Y.C., 1965-67; graphic designer Constl. Congress of Internat. Film and Television Students' and Graduates' Assn., Prague, Czechoslovakia, 1969; producer 1970 Spoleto (Italy) Cinema Festival; film editor for Lerner Newspapers, Chgo., 1966—; Am. film critic Il Tempo, Rome, 1976—; film instr. Lewis Coll., Lockport, Ill., 1971; mem., lectr. Chgo. Speakers Bur., div. Chgo. Adult Edn. Council. U.S. chmn. Venice Film Festival, 1971-72, recipient Silver Lion, 1971; U.S. chmn. Tehran Film Festival, 1972-73; U.S. del. Moscow Film Festival, 1971, Taormina (Italy) Film Festival, 1971; chmn. 1st Internat. Film Festival, Lima, Peru, 1973, Delhi, India, 1975. Recipient silver medal Cannes Film Festival du Amateur, 1961. Mem. Profl. Photographers Am., Chgo. Soc. Communicating Arts, Art Dirs. Club Chgo., Tau Kappa Epsilon. Home: 235 W Eugenie St Chicago IL 60614 Office: Chgo Internat Film Festival Inc 415 N Dearborn St Chicago IL 60610

KUZEL, NORBERT RAYMOND, pharmacist; b. Warren, Minn., May 23, 1923; s. John Anton and Anna Matilda (Gust) K.; B.S., N.D. State U., 1948, M.S., 1949; m. Helen Louise Strasser, July 29, 1949; With Eli Lilly & Co., Indpls., 1949—, dept. head, 1959-67, research scientist, 1967-71, research asso., 1971—. Served with USNR, 1944-46. Fellow Am. Found. Pharm. Edn.; mem. Am. Chem. Soc. (chmn. local section 1968), N.Y. Acad. Sci., Instrument Soc. Am., Rho Chi, Phi Kappa Phi. Patentee in field. Contbr. articles to profl. publs. Home: 4611 Berkshire Ln Indianapolis IN 46226 Office: 307 E McCarty St Indianapolis IN 46206

KWAK, JUNKYU CHRISTOPHER, counselor; b. Kangwon-do, Korea, April 22, 1940; s. Hee Chul and Shun Pil (Yim) K.; B.A., U. DongKuk, 1964; M.A., U. Mo., 1975; m. Nancy Louise Yale, Dec. 8, 1972; one dau.—Grace Miriam. Dir. Chrisitan Edn., Korean Reorganized Ch. of Jesus Christ of Latter Saints, 1970-72; staff counselor Research and Guidance Lab., Univ. Wis., Madison, 1976—; cons. in field. Mem. Am. Personnel and Guidance Assn., Assn. Counselor Edn. Supervision. Home: 308 F Eagle Heights Madison WI 53705 Office: 1978 1025 W Johnson St Madison WI 53706

KWAN, FRANCIS P., pediatrician; b. Brit. N. Borneo, Dec. 19, 1929; s. James W.L. and Marie S.Y. (Lou) K.; came to U.S., 1947, naturalized, 1961; A.B. with high honors, U. Ill., 1950; M.S., Northwestern U., 1953; M.D., Med. Coll. Wis., 1957; m. Bernice Edith Nickolaisen, Aug. 10, 1957; children—James, Alexander, Arden, Russell, Mark. Intern, St. Joseph's Hosp., Milw., 1957-58; pediatric resident Milw. Children's Hosp., 1960-62; med. dir. bur. preventable diseases and med. services, Milw. Health Dept., 1958-60; chmn. dept. pediatrics, St. John's Hosp., Rapid City, S.D., 1968-70, pres. med. staff, 1972-73; pres. Rapid City Med. Center, 1977—; clin. asst. prof. in pediatrics, Sch. of Medicine, U. S.D., 1977—; dir. pediatric clinic Mother Butler Center, Rapid City, 1962-70; cons. pediatrician, USPHS Hosps., S.D. Recipient Black Hills Brotherhood award, 1964. Diplomate Am. Bd. Pediatrics. Fellow Am. Acad. Pediatrics; mem. AMA, S.D. State Med. Assn., Black Hills Dist., Rapid City med. socs., Republican. Roman Catholic. Contbr. paper to med. conf., articles to profl. sci. publs. Home: 228 S Berry Pine Rd Rapid City SD 57701 Office: Rapid City Medical Center 728 Columbus St Rapid City SD 57701

KYES, HELEN G. (MRS. ROGER M. KYES), civic leader; b. Marion, Ohio, Dec. 28, 1904; d. Benjamin and Bess (Gilmore) Jacoby; B.A., Oberlin Coll., 1926; m. Roger M. Kyes, June 5, 1931; children—Carolyn, Frances, Katharine, Anne. Sec. pres. Federated Women's Club, Marion, O., 1927-31; bd. dirs. Cleve. Coll. Club, 1936-41, bd. dirs. Cleve. YWCA, 1938-41: mem. bd. Woman's Nat. Farm and Garden 1943-56, 60—, sec., 1943-45, 54-55; dir. Children's Aid and Home Friendless, 1949—, v.p., 1961—; bd. dirs. Brookside Sch., Cranbrook, 1952-58, sec., 1957-58; bd. dirs. Kingswood Sch. Cranbrook, 1968—; charter mem. trustees Oakland U. Found., 1958, v.p. exec. bd., 1960—, trustee, 1970—; mem. Woman's Assn. Detroit Symphony; com. 100 Detroit Met. Opera; capt. spl. gifts Detroit United Fund, 1959-61; mem. Detroit Mus. Art Founders Soc., mem. com. Detroit Foster Home Edn. and Recruitment Program, 1960—. Mem. D.A.R., AAUW (past treas., v.p. Marion) Presbyn. (vice moderator deacons). Clubs: Bloomfield Hills Country, Detroit, Village Woman's; Ocean (Delray Beach, Fla.); Gulfstream Bath and Tennis; Country of Fla.; Little. Home: 945 Cranbrook Rd Bloomfield Hills MI 48013 also 6861 N Ocean Blvd Ocean Ridge FL 33435

KYLE, EARLE FLEETWOOD, JR., publishing co. exec.; b. Mpls., Nov. 17, 1938; s. Earle Fleetwood and Mary Edith (James) K.; B.S. in Physics, U. Minn., 1961; postgrad U. Calif., 1974, U. Minn., 1975; children—Earle F. (dec.), Kimberly Marie, Earle F., Lance William. Pvt. practice electronic design cons., Los Angeles, 1961-63; sr. electronic design engr. Honeywell Aerospace div. Apollo Flight Systems, Mpls., 1963-67; mgr. advanced program devel. Litton Systems, Inc., Mpls., 1967-71; advanced planning specialist 3M Co., St. Paul, 1971-73, sr. physicist Central Research Labs., 1973-77; dir. Carnegie-Mellon Inst., Pitts., 1977—; v.p. ops. Minn. Sentinel Pub. Co., Mpls., 1975—; guest lectr. Luther Coll., Decorah, Iowa, Macalester Coll., St. Paul, Nat. Scholarship Service and Fund for Negro Students; cons. in field. Co-founder Minds For Progress, Inc., Mpls., 1972, bd. dirs., 1972—, sec., treas., 1972, v.p., 1973, pres., 1974, dir. pub. relations, 1975—; bd. dirs. Women Helping Offenders, Inc., 1976—. Recipient Mpls. Star and Tribune Leadership and Service award, 1956; Minds for Progress Service award, 1972; Mpls. C. of C. Future Focus Leadership Program award, 1976-77. Mem. Minn. Newspaper Assn., Minn. Press Club, U. Minn. Alumni Assn., Am. Inst. Physics, 3M Tech. Forum, IEEE, Am. Ordnance Assn., NAACP, St. Paul Urban League, Greater Mpls. C. of C., Alpha Phi Alpha. Author: To Shape The Future, 1975. Producer, moderator (with T.A. Kyle) White Racism, KTCA-TV, St. Paul, 1968. Contbr.

articles to profl. jours. Offices: Twin Cities Courier 84 S 6th St Suite 501 Minneapolis MN 55402 also Carnegie-Mellon Inst 4400 Fifth Ave Pittsburgh PA 15213

KYLE, MARY J., journalist; b. St. Paul; d. Ernest B. and Edith M. (Burnett) James; student U. Minn., Palmer Inst. of Writing, Croydon Inst. of Writing; m. Earle F. Kyle, Nov. 12; children—Shirley Klye Heaton, Robert C., Earlene Kyle Walker, Earle F. Editor and pub. Twin Cities Courier, Mpls., 1967—; pres. Minn. Sentinel Pub. Co., 1967—; editorial commentator Sta. KMSP-TV, 1969—; talk show host Sta. WLOL-AM-FM, 1969—; book reviewer Mpls. Sunday Tribune, 1970—; newspaper columnist, 1948-52; dir. Sta. KTCA-TV, 1973-75; lectr. on human relations, 1967—; mem. adv. bd. Northwestern Nat. Bank, 1975—. Mem. Communications Task Force, Mpls. Urban Coalition, 1972-74; mem. governing bd. YMCA, Mpls., 1970—; mem. Minn. State Bd. Law Examiners, 1977—; bd. dirs. Am. Rehab. Found. Recipient Frank Murray award St. Thomas Coll., 1971, Herman Roe Meml. award, 1967, Human Rights award Jewish Labor Com., 1967, Human Rights award Fezzan Temple Shriners, 1970, Mpls. Distingusihed Served award, 1970, Community Service award Nat. Alliance Businessmen, 1976. Mem. Nat., Minn. newspaper assns., NAACP Minn. Press Club (pres. 1975-76), Minn. Press Women (Journalism award 1976, 77, 78), AFTRA, Greater Mpls. C. of C., Mpls. Urban League (Distinguished Service award 1969), Nat. Newspaper Pubs. Assn., Minn. Council Econ. Edn. (dir. 1975—). Roman Catholic. Home: 3637 4th Ave S Minneapolis MN 55409 Office: 84 S 6th St Minneapolis MN 55402

KYLES, CALVIN EUGENE, airplane mfg. co. exec.; b. Lake Charles, La., Oct. 26, 1937; s. William and Hattie (Hagger) K.; student McNeese State Coll., 1957; B.B.A., Tex. Southern U., 1977; m. Githa Lee Little John, Jan. 5, 1965; 1 dau., Yolanda Yvette. With Riverside Gen. Hosp., Houston, 1964-77, asst. adminstr., 1974-76, project dir. met. health founds. health maintenance orgn. feasibility study, 1974-76; system engr. Automated Health Services div. McDonnell Douglas Co., St. Louis, 1977—. Pres., young adults NAACP, Lake Charles, 1959-61; scoutmaster Boy Scouts Am., 1959-61; pres. PTA Elementary Sch., Houston, 1974-77. Served with AUS, 1961-63. Recipient Parent Year award Fairchild Elementary sch., 1977. Pres. sr. choir St. John Bapt. Ch., Houston. Home: 2008 New Florissant Rd Florissant MO 63033 Office: 5775 Campus Pkwy Hazelwood MO 63042

KYRIAZIS, ANDREAS P., pathologist; b. Aigion, Greece, Jan. 19, 1932; s. Panayiotis and Christina (Demeli) K.; M.D., U. Athens (Greece), 1957; D.Sc. in Pathology, U. Thessaloniki, 1962; Ph.D. on Pathology, Thomas Jefferson U., 1968; m. Aikaterini Iatridou, Dec. 16, 1964. Research asso. in pathology U. Chgo., 1968-70, Seymur Coman fellow in pathology, 1969-70, research asso., asst. prof. pathology, 1970-72, 74-76; asso. prof. dept. pathology U. Cin. Coll. Medicine, 1976—; vis. scientist Argonne Cancer Research Hosp., 1968-72; chmn. dept. pathology Metaxas Meml. Cancer Hosp., Piraeus, Greece, 1972-74. Served to capt. M.C., Greek Army, 1958-60. Research in tumor immunology; connective tissue disorders. Home: 508 Williamsburg Rd Cincinnati OH 45215

KYRIAZOPOULOS, DIMITRIOS GEORGE, mathematician, educator; b. Roino, Tripolis in Greece, Apr. 23, 1931; s. George G. and Elaine (Gavrillos) K.; came to U.S., 1959, naturalized, 1968; B.A., Oklahoma City U., 1963; M.Ed., DePaul U., Chgo., 1969; M.S., Ill. Inst. Tech., 1970; Ph.D., Walden U., Naples, Fla., 1974; m. Susann V. Regas, Aug. 23, 1964; 1 dau., Stella Elaine. Prof. math. Indsl. Engring. Coll., Chgo., 1963-65; dist. mgr. Gestner Corp., Chgo., 1965-66; faculty DeVry Inst. Tech., Chgo., 1966—, prof. math., 1975—; lectr. in field. Pres., founder United Hellenic Voters Ill., 1975—; mem. Clinton Sch. Council, 1972—; exec. com. United Am. Hellenic Congress; v.p. Congress Am.-Hellenic Orgns. Mem. Hellenic Profl. Soc., AAUP, Am. Math. Soc., DePaul, Ill. Inst. Tech., Walden U. (treas. Midwest 1973—) alumni assns., Am. Hellenic Ednl. Profl. Assn. (chpt. pres. 1970—, dist. treas. 1974). Home: 6144 N Rockwell St Chicago IL 60659 Office: 3300 N Campbell Ave Chicago IL 60618

KYVIG, DAVID EDWARD, historian; b. Ames, Iowa, Mar. 8, 1944; s. Edward H. and Wilma (Jessen) K.; B.A., Kalamazoo Coll., 1966; Ph.D., Northwestern U., 1971; m. Barbara Burness, Aug. 19, 1967; children—Jennifer, Elizabeth. Archivist, Office Presdl. Libraries, Nat. Archives, Washington, 1970-71; asst. prof. history, dir. Am. History Research Center, U. Akron (Ohio), 1971—. Mem. Soc. Am. Archivists (com. on urban archives, com. on ethics), Ohio Acad. History, Soc. Ohio Archivists (joint archives-library com.), Orgn. Am. Historians, Am. Hist. Assn., Soc. Historians Am. Fgn. Relations. Author: FDR's America, 1976; Your Family History, 1978. Home: 701 Upper Merriman Arkon OH 44303 Office: U Akron Akron OH 44325

LAATZ, MARY JANE, med. librarian; b. Indpls., Dec. 27, 1916; d. Jacob Philip and Neil (Carey) Laatz; A.B., Butler U., 1938; B.S. in L.S., Western Res. U. 1939. Librarian, Ind. U. Extension Div., Indpls., 1939-41; cataloger, Ind. U. Sch. Medicine Library, 1941-51, reference librarian, 1951, 53-57, acting librarian, 1951-53, med. librarian, 1957—, asst. prof. med. lit., 1957-72, asso. prof. med. lit., 1973—; mem. at large Ind. U.-Purdue U. at Indpls. faculty council, 1974-76. Chmn. Council Midwest Regional Health Scis. Library and Coop. Information Services, 1968-70; Ind. U. rep. at EDUCOM Summer Study on Ednl. Communications Network, 1966; del. Conf. on Interlibrary Communication Network, A.L.A.-U.S. Office Edn., 1970; mem. Midwest Health Sci. Library Network Assembly Resource Libraries, 1973—, chmn., 1975-76. Mem. Med. Library Assn. (mem. scholarship com. 1972-74, chmn. scholarship com. 1973-74), Spl. Libraries Assn. (chpt. pres. 1960-61), John Shaw Billings History Medicine Soc. (sec.-treas. 1965-67), Indpls. Mus. Art, Delta Gamma. Contbr. articles to profl. jours. Presbyn. Home: 6824 Willow Rd Indianapolis IN 46220 Office: Ind U Sch Medicine Library Med Sci Bldg 122 1100 W Michigan St Indianapolis IN 46202

LABATE, CHARLES RAYMOND, printing and paper co. exec.; b. Koppel, Pa., July 4, 1938; s. Raymond Richard and Elda Marie (Nardone) L.; B.S. in Bus., Bradley U., 1960; m. Adolphine Gryzlo, Nov. 20, 1965; children—Constance, Amanda, Lauren. Asst. plant accountant Blaw-Knox Co., East Chicago, Ind., 1961-66; corp. systems mgr. Vulcan Materials Co., Chgo., 1966-69, Bekins Van Lines Co., Hillside, Ill., 1969-70; co-founder, pres. CAL Systems & Forms, Inc., LaGrange, Ill., 1970—. Bd. dirs. Jr. Achievement, East Chicago, 1963-64; treas. East Chicago council Boy Scouts Am., 1964-65. Mem. Data Processing Mgmt. Assn. (dir. Chgo. 1971-74, nat. v.p. 1975-77), Bus. Forms Mgmt. Assn. (treas. Chgo. 1973-74), Nat. Bus. Forms Assn. (membership com.), Bradley U. Alumni Club, Tau Kappa Epsilon. Roman Catholic. Home: 327 Forest Rd Hinsdale IL 60521 Office: 140 N LaGrange Rd LaGrange IL 60525

LABBIE, STEPHEN, clin. psychologist; b. Pitts., Apr. 18, 1944; s. Irwin and Anne (Chawenson) L.; B.A., U. Fla., 1966; M.S., Ill. Inst. Tech., 1972, Ph.D., 1974; m. Linda Fran Weinberg, Aug. 20, 1966; children—Erin Felicia, Elissa Beth. Dir. day care program for retarded children Catholic Welfare Bur., Miami, Fla., 1968-69; grad. asst., counseling center Ill. Inst. Tech., Chgo., 1971-72; clin. intern HEW grant project Health and Hosps. Governing Commn. of Cook County, Chgo., 1972-74; clin. psychologist Du Page County Health Dept., Div. Mental Health, Wheaton, Ill., 1974-75, dir. mental health div. East Satellite, 1975—; pvt. practice, Chgo., 1974—. Supr. masters level psychology students George Williams Coll., Downers Grove, Ill., 1973—. Served with AUS, 1969-71. Mem. Am. Psychol. Assn. (mem. div. counseling 1972—, mem. div. psychotherapy 1973—), Assn. for Advancement Psychology, Nat. Register Health Service Providers in Psychology, Sigma Xi. Contbr. articles to profl. jours. Home: 1133 62d Pl Downers Grove IL 60515 Office: Greenbriar Med Center 6800 S Main St Downers Grove IL 60515

LA BELLE, CHARLES EARL, mech. engr.; b. Laurium, Mich., Apr. 28, 1927; s. Charles Earl and Sigrid Aleda (Jacobson) LaB.; B.M.E., Mich. Technol. U., 1952; grad. bus. adminstrn. Alexander Hamilton Inst., 1959; m. Hilda Alvina Martin, Aug. 11, 1956; children—Charles Earl, Renee Jeanne. Exptl. engr. LeRoi Co., Milw., 1952-55, Clinton Engines Co., Maquoketa, Iowa, 1955-57; project engr. Thomas Industries, Sheboygan, Wis., 1957-63; design engr. Aro Inc., Tullahoma, Tenn., 1963-66; aircraft devel. engr. Continental Aircraft Engine, Muskegon, Mich., 1966-70; research and devel. engr. Roper Corp., Bradley, Ill., 1970-74; div. mgr. product engring. Power Air div. Thomas Industries, Sheboygan, 1974—; curriculum advisor Lakeshore Tech. Inst., Cleveland, Wis., 1974—. Served with USNR, 1945-46. Mem. ASME, Soc. Automotive Engrs., Mich. Technol. U. Alumni Assn. Lutheran. Club: Sheboygan Yacht. Home: Route 2 Box 290 Oostburg WI 53070 Office: 1419 Illinois Ave Sheboygan WI 53081

LA BELLE, WILMA CAROL MARCY, engring. exec.; b. Hay Springs, Nebr., Jan. 16, 1924; d. Orrin Jay and Nelle Edna (Johansen) Marcy; B.S. (grantee), Rensselaer Poly. Inst., 1943, U. Nebr., 1955; children—Judy Thompson, Jay LaBelle, Rose Marie LaBelle, Clark LaBelle. Research engr. Curtiss Wright Corp., 1943-45; engr. USAF, 1945-46; partner LaBelle, LaBelle & Assos., Engrs., 1955-76; pres. Omega Research Corp., Sioux City, Iowa, 1976-77; instr. physics Briar Cliff Coll., 1964-65; cons., lectr. Vice pres. PTA; den mother Boy Scouts Am.; troop leader Girl Scouts Am. Grantee NSF, 1965, Mem. Soc. Women Engrs., Nat. Soc. Profl. Engrs., AAUW (pres. 1965). Methodist. Clubs: Travelers Study (pres.), Hidden Valley Golf, Eastern Star. Home: 23 W 45th St Sioux City IA 51104 Office: Box 354 South Sioux City NE 68776

LABINE, PAUL, chemist; b. Nashua, N.H., June 12, 1943; s. Joseph Urgel and Jeanne Alice (Soucy) L.; B.S., U. Mass., 1964; Ph.D., Mich. State U., 1971; 1 son, Carl. Asst. prof. Purdue U., Indpls., 1969-72; chemist Nalco Chem. Co., Chgo., 1972-73; chief formulation chemist Olin Water Service, Kansas City, Kans., 1973—. Treas. Nelson Square Homes Assn., 1977—. Mem. Am. Chem. Soc. (symposium chmn. for ann. meeting 1978), Nat. Assn. of Corrosion Engrs. (symposium chmn. ann. meeting 1978, vice chmn. com. corrosion in initiators; award 1976). Home: 117 Nelson Circle Olathe KS 66061 Office: 3155 Fiberglas Rd Kansas City KS 66115

LA CAMERA, JOSEPH, JR., counseling psychologist; b. Akron, Ohio, Sept. 15, 1936; s. Joseph and Louise Angeline LaC.; M.A., U. Colo., 1963, Ed.D., 1970; B.A., Hiram Coll., 1959; m. Deanna Ellen, June 10, 1972; children—Lynn Ann, Donald Brett. Tchr., Bath (Ohio) Richfield Sch. Dist., 1959-61; counselor Loveland (Colo.) Sch. Dist., 1962-63; head resident U. Colo., Boulder, 1963-65, program coordinator, 1965-67; dir. housing, residence halls Kent State U., 1967-70; dir. housing Calif. State U., Sacramento, 1971-72; counselor dept. home econs., family ecology, dept. spl. programs Inst. Lifespan Devel. and Gerontology, U. Akron (Ohio), 1972—; cons., lectr. in field; vol. staff Boulder Hospice; workshop staff Akron Suicide Prevention, Regional Conf. Licensed Nurses, Ft. Logan Mental Health Clinic, Denver, Northeastern Ohio univs. colls. medicine, dept. oncology Akron Gen. Med. Center. Mem. Am. Coll. Personnel Assn. (state membership chmn.), Am., Boulder (past pres.) personnel and guidance assns., Nat. Council Family Relations, Found. Thanatology, Phi Delta Kappa. Contbr. to publs. in field. Home: 803 W Market St Apt 4 Akron OH 44303 Office: Testing and Counseling Bur U Akron Akron OH 44325

LACHER, THOMAS FRANCIS, JR., electronic engr.; b. Kalispell, Mont., Nov. 28, 1941; s. Thomas Francis and Jane Allyn (Cockrell) L.; B.S. in Elec. Engring., B.S. in Math., Mont. State U., 1966; M.S. in Elec. Engring., Bradley U., 1969; m. Mary Elnora Beasley, May 11, 1962; children—Thomas Francis, Keri Janel. Research engr. Caterpillar Tractor Co., Peoria, Ill., 1966-73, devel. engr., 1973—. Bd. dirs. FISH of Peoria, 1972-75. Served with USN, 1959-62. Mem. IEEE, U.S. Chess Fedn. Episcopalian. Patentee engine power measuring device. Home: 1204 N Institute Pl Peoria IL 61606

LACHNER, BERNARD JOSEPH, hosp. adminstr.; b. Rock Island, Ill., Oct. 13, 1927; s. Bernard Joseph and Anne Lenore (Canty) L.; student U. Notre Dame, 1945-46, 47-48; B.S., Creighton U., 1950; M.B.A., U. Chgo., 1952; m. Berneice Groen, Aug. 16, 1952; children—Bernard Joseph, Thomas Frederick, James Timothy. From adminstrv. intern to adminstrv. asst. Iowa Methodist Hosp., Des Moines, 1950-54, asst. adminstr. Ohio State U. Hosps., Columbus, 1954-58, asso. adminstr. 1958-62, adminstr., 1962-71; asst. dean Ohio State U. Coll. Medicine, 1961-71, asst. v.p. med. affairs, 1971, v.p. adminstrv. operations, 1971-72, prof. hosp. and health care adminstrn., 1967-72; pres. Evanston (Ill.) Hosp., 1972—; prof. mgmt. Grad. Sch. Mgmt., Northwestern U., 1972—. Mem. Health Services Research Tng. Com. Nat. Center Health Services Research and Devel. U.S. Dept. Health Edn. and Welfare, 1970-71. Chmn. hosp. adv. com. Blue Cross Plan; mem. nat. adv. com. Sangamon State U., Springfield, 1972—; mem. citizens com. U. Ill., 1973—. Adv. bd. Sch. Practical Nursing, Columbus pub. schs.; trustee Mid-Ohio Health Planning Fedn., vice chmn. adminstrs. council, 1968-71; bd. dirs. Ohio League Nursing, 1969-70, Assn. Univs. for Research and Astronomy, 1971-72; bd. dirs. McGaw Med. Center of Northwestern U., 1972—, chmn. adminstrv. com., 1974. Served with AUS, 1946-47. Fellow Am. Coll. Hosp. Adminstrs. (regent 1970-71, bd. govs. 1976—); mem. Am., Ohio (trustee 1963-72, mem. council on legislation 1971-73, mem. ho. of dels., pres. 1969-70), Ill. (trustee-at-large 1973—, exec. com. 1975, chmn. 1976) hosp. assns., Assn. Am. Med. Colls. (mem. council teaching hosps. exec. com. 1971-73), Council Univ. Teaching Hosps., U. Chgo. Hosp. Adminstrn. Alumni Assn. (pres. 1967-68). Kiwanian (trustee 1969-70). Contbr. profl. jours. Home: 2515 Peachtree Ln Northbrook IL 60062 Office: Evanston Hosp 2650 Ridge Ave Evanston IL 60201

LACKENS, JOHN WENDELL, architect; b. Eveleth, Minn., Dec. 27, 1934; s. John Wendell and Dorothy Gertrud (Williams) L.; student Wis. State U., 1952-54; B.A., U. Minn., 1956, B.Arch. with distinction, 1958; M.Arch., Harvard, 1960; m. Barbara Jean Barkhuff, Dec. 28, 1957; children—Gregory David, Catherine Marie. Architect, Thorsov & Cerny, Mpls., 1957-59, Sert Jackson & Gourley, Cambridge, Mass., 1959, The Architect's Collaborative, Cambridge, 1959-60; architect, v.p. Cerny Asso., Mpls., 1960-70; pres., v.p., sec. The Archtl. Alliance, Mpls., 1970—, also dir. Mem. Citizens League of Mpls. and Hennepin County, 1964-71; mem. Mpls. Com. on Urban Environment Task Force on Neighborhood Environment, 1970-71. Bd. dirs. Mpls. Boys Club, 1968—, chmn. bldg. com. 1969—, camp com. mem. 1969—, exec. com., 1974—. Wis. Archtl. Found. scholar, 1956. Recipient Honor award for Valley Sq. Profl. Bldg., Minn. Soc. Architects, 1974, U. Minn.-Duluth Stadium Apts., 1976, Blue Cross and Blue Shield Offices Minn., 1977. Mem. AIA, Walker Art Center, Mpls. Inst. Arts, Harvard Grad. Sch. Design Alumni Assn., U. Minn. Alumni Assn., Mpls., St. Paul chambers commerce; Alpha Rho Chi. Clubs: Harvard, U. Minn. Alumnus. Home: 4915 Garfield Ave S Minneapolis MN 55409 Office: 400 Clifton Ave S Minneapolis MN 55403

LACKIE, RICHARD DAVID, aide to govt. ofcl.; b. Adrian, Mich., Mar. 10, 1932; s. David S. and Ernestine (Scranton) L.; student Adrian Coll., 1950-53; B.B.A., U. Toledo, 1957; m. Beverly J. Garrison, Apr. 4, 1959; children—Karen, John, Joanne. Sales mgr. WABJ, Adrian, 1961-63; sta. mgr. WLEN, Adrian, 1965-76; dist. rep. Congressman Dave Stockman, 1976—. County commr. Lenawee County, 1973—. Served with USNR, 1954-56. Mem. Adrian Jr. C. of C. (dir.). Episcopalian (sr. warden). Rotarian (dir.). Home: 508 N Broad St Adrian MI 49221 Office: 325 S Main St Adrian MI 49221

LA CLAIRE, DAVID BINNEY, photographer; b. Grand Rapids, Mich., July 11, 1929; s. Maurice Carnes and Adeline (Binney) LaC.; student U. Mich. extension, 1951-56; m. Mary Lou Monger, Apr. 5, 1958; children—John Lafayette, Thomas Lucas, Hester Elizabeth. Apprentice, Maurice C. LaClaire, Grand Rapids, 1950-54, partner, 1954-66; pres. LaClaire Portriatur Inc., 1966—, Photog. Colo Service by LaClaire, 1966—. Instr. Winona Sch., Winona Lake, Ind., 1953-61. Mem. Gerald R. Ford Commemorative com., 1975—. Bd. dirs. United Fund, 1968-72, YMCA, 1970-71; bd. dirs. Grand Rapids Art Mus., 1967-76, pres., 1972-73; bd. dirs. Arts Council Greater Grand Rapids, 1969-75, pres., 1973-74; bd. dirs. Torch, 1972-75. Mem. Profl. Photographers Am. (master of photography, 1960), Profl. Photographers Mich. (dir. 1959-62), Soc. Photog. Scientists and Engrs., Cameracraftsmen of Am. (sec., 1968-72), Soc. Am. Photographers. Club: Peninsula. Rotarian (pres. chpt. 1975-76). Home: 7138 Cascade Rd Grand Rapids MI 49506 Office: 2225 Wealthy St SE Grand Rapids MI 49506

LACSINA, EMMANUEL QUIAMBAO, pathologist; b. Manila, Nov. 24, 1937; s. Nicanor Timbol and Sarah Sanchez (Quiambao) L.; came to U.S., 1963, naturalized, 1969; M.D., Far Eastern U., 1963; m. Eva Astrida Grava, Dec. 14, 1963; children—Anita Renee, Ivetta Ann, Deanna Erin. Rotating intern USAF Hosp., Philippines, 1962-63, Deaconess Hosp., Milw., 1963-64; resident in anatomic and clin. pathology Akron (Ohio) City Hosp., 1964-68; asso. pathologist Mercy Hosp., Des Moines, 1972-73; dir. labs. N.W. Community Hosp., Des Moines, 1973—; dep. Polk County (Iowa) Med. Examiners Office, 1973—. Served with AUS, 1968-71. Decorated Army Commendation medal. Fellow Am. Soc. Clin. Pathologists, Coll. Am. Pathologists; mem. Iowa, Polk County med socs. Presbyterian. Club: Hyperion Field. Home: 4505 NW Lovingston Dr Des Moines IA 50323 Office: 1818 48th St Des Moines IA 50310

LACY, EDNA BALZ, mfg. exec.; b. Indpls., Sept. 21, 1906; d. Peter Fred and Lydia (Jose) Balz; B.A., U. Mich., 1928; LL.D., Franklin Coll., 1968; m. Howard John Lacy II, Nov. 29, 1934 (dec. Mar. 1959); children—Margot Diane (Mrs. Robert Eccles), Howard John III, Andre Balz, Stanley Kermit (dec.). Sec., asst. treas. U.S. Corrugated-Fibre Box Co., Indpls., 1952-58, pres., treas., chmn. bd., 1959—; chmn. bd. U.S. Corrugated-Fibre Box Co., Ala., 1969—; pres. Speedway, Inc., also treas., chmn. bd., 1959-64; 1969—; pres., treas., chmn. bd. Lacy Diversified Industries, Inc., 1972—, also div. U.S. Corrugated Fibre Box Co., subs. U.S. Corrugated Fibre Box Co. Ala., Jessup Door Co., Inc., Subsidiary L.D.I. Leasing Inc.; mem. dist. adv. council SBA, 1971—. Bd. dirs. Starlight Musicals, 1959—, Wright Inst. Otology; bd. dirs., mem. exec. com. YMCA Greater Indpls., 1963-72; mem. Nat. Council Met. Opera Assn., N.Y.C., 1965-70; bd. dirs. Ind. Vocational Tech. Coll. Found., United Fund Greater Indpls., Indpls. Goodwill Industries, Community Hosp., Citizens Forum, Indpls. Center for Advanced Research; chmn. Christmas campaign Salvation Army, 1976; bd. dirs. Ind. Symphony Soc., sec. 1972—; bd. govs. Asso. Colls. Ind.; adv. bd. Ind. U.-Purdue U., Indpls., 1975—; trustee Winona Hosp., Indpls., 1965-76; trustee, mem. exec. com., chmn. finance com. Franklin Coll.; gen. campaign chmn. Franklin Coll. Devel. Fund, 1966. Named Sagamore of Wabash by Gov. Handley, 1960; Woman of Year, Ind. Republican Mayors Assn., 1976, Indpls. profl. chpt. Women in Communications, 1976. Mem. Ind. Advocates for Arts, Confederacy Indiana Sachems, Indpls. Women's Symphony Assn., Ind., Indpls. (dir. 1973—) chambers commerce, Athenaeum-Turners, Kappa Alpha Theta. Clubs: Indianapolis Athletic, Woodstock, Columbia, Lambs, Contemporary, Players, Economic (founding, dir. 1974—) (Indpls.); Maxinkuckee Yacht (Culver, Ind.); Capitol Hill (Washington); Union League (Chgo.). Home: 7030 W 79th St Indianapolis IN 46278 Office: 3200 One Indiana Square Indianapolis IN 46204

LACY, EDWIN VEMONT, JR., musician, educator; b. Hopkinsville, Ky., Aug. 1, 1937; s. Edwin Vemont and Lillian Louise (Joiner) L.; B. Mus. Edn., Murray (Ky.) State U., 1960; M. Music, Ind. U., 1966, also postgrad.; m. Beverly Mignonne Broutin, June 5, 1960; children—Edwin Vemont III, Roger Alan. Tchr. Dale (Ind.) Pub. Schs., 1959-61, Robinson (Ill.) Pub. Schs., 1961-65; asst. prof. music Morris Harvey Coll., Charleston, W.Va., 1966-67; asst. prof. music U. Evansville (Ind.), 1967—, chmn. dept. music, 1974-76; mem. Evansville Philharmonic Orch., 1959-65, 67-72, Owensboro (Ky.) Symphony Orch., 1967—. Mem. Internat. Double-Reed Soc. (sec. 1975—), Nat. Assn. Jazz Educators, Music Educators Nat. Conf., Ind. Music Educators Assn., Phi Mu Alpha. Methodist (dir. music 1975-76). Home: 1011 S Vann Ave Evansville IN 47714

LACY, HERMAN EDGAR, mfg. co. exec.; b. Nashville, Sept. 19, 1904; s. Franklin R. and Florence (Single) L.; student Northwestern U., 1928-32; m. Florence E. Dunteman, Nov. 23, 1927; children—Dorothy M. (Mrs. Elliott A. Johnson), Florence E. (Mrs. David H. Pickering), Herman Edgar. Sales corr. Western Electric Co., 1921-25; factory supt. Lacy Products Corp., 1925-35; pres., chmn. bd. Helmco, Inc., 1935-61; pres., gen. mgr. Shamrock Agrl. Enterprises, 1961—; pres., chmn. bd. L.N.K. Devel. Corp.; pres., treas. Hydroforming Co. Am., Inc.; chmn. exec. com. Plaza Drive in Bank; dir. Mid-City Nat. Bank, Mich. Av. Nat. Bank. Mem. Chgo. Merc. Exchange. Served to col. USAF Res. Mem. Am. Mgmt. Assn., Ill. Mfrs. Assn. Home: 4575 Drake Dr Crystal Lake IL 60014

LACY, JACK, econ. devel. commn. ofcl.; b. Rocky Ford, Colo., Feb. 14, 1914; s. John B. and Mayme (Etzel) L.; student U. Colo. Sch. Journalism, 1934-35; m. Madeline Ann Lane, May 16, 1935; 1 son, Jack. City editor World-Ind., Walsenburg, Colo., 1936-40; mgr. La Junta (Colo.) C. of C., 1940-45, St. Joseph (Mo.) C. of C., 1945-47, Pueblo (Colo.) C. of C., 1947-57, Amarillo (Tex.) C. of C., 1957-61; dep. dir. dept. devel. State of N.Mex., Santa Fe, 1961-65; dir. econ. devel. State of Kans., Topeka, 1965-72; dir. Junction City-Geary County (Kans.) Econ. Devel. Commn., 1972—. Faculty, Southwestern Inst. for C. of C. Mgrs., U. Houston, 1947-61, pres., dean faculty, 1956-60; mem. civic devel. com., govt. expenditures com. U.S. C. of C., 1957-61. Served with Colo. Wing, Civil Air Patrol, 1941-45. Mem. Colo. Jr. C. of C. (life), Am. Indsl. Devel. Council. Roman Catholic. K.C. (4 deg.), Elk, Rotarian. Home: 226 W 3d St

Junction City KS 66441 Office: Municipal Bldg Junction City KS 66441

LACY, ROBERT EUGENE, artist; b. Rolla, Mo., Aug. 29, 1943; s. Robert Andrew and Clara Evelyn (Glenn) L.; studied with Earl Strebeck, 1962-67; m. Teresa Louise Durbn, June 18, 1966. Group shows include: Wadsworth Atheneum, Hartford, Conn., 1970, Butler Inst. Am. Art, Youngstown, Ohio, 1969, William A. Farnsworth Art Mus., Rockland, Maine, 1969, Tulsa Arts Council Ann. Exhbn., 1968, Kansas City and City Art Mus. St. Louis, 1968, Springfield (Mo.) Art Mus., 1965, 68; also represented in permanent collections. Recipient 2d Ann. Tulsa award Tulsa Arts Council, 1968. Episcopalian. Address: 517 N Charles Ave Saint James MO 65559

LAD, PRAKASH SHRIPAD, civil engr.; b. Bombay, India, Sept. 7, 1940; s. Shripad Narayan and Sumitra (Rangnekar) L.; came to U.S., 1968, naturalized, 1977; m. Nilima Madan Pai, Apr. 17, 1972; 1 son, Ashvin. Asst. engr. S.B. Joshi & Co., Ltd., Bombay, 1964-65; sub engr. Municipal Corp. of Greater Bombay, 1965-68; civil engr. III bridge office Ill. Dept. of Transp., Springfield, 1969—. Mem. ASCE. Club: Springfield Cricket. Home: 2008 Claremont St Springfield IL 62703 Office: 2300 S Dirksen Pkwy Springfield IL 62703

LADIN, LAWRENCE, textile mfg. co. exec.; b. Mpls., July 1, 1929; s. Jacob Harvey and Mildred Helen (Kelner) L.; student U. Chgo., 1946-48; B.A. in Math., U. Minn., 1951; m. Louise Helen Stern, Dec. 27, 1963; children—Edward, Stephen. With Ladin Industries, Inc., Des Moines, 1952—, pres., 1966—. Pres. Quilting Inst. Am., 1967-68. Mem. Des Moines Planning and Zoning Commn., 1970—; chmn. Iowa Gov's com. on Conservation, 1967-68. Served with USMC, 1951. Mem. Sierra Club (chmn. Iowa chpt. 1970-73). Democrat. Reform Jewish religion. Clubs: Des Moines. Author: TV spl. Before the Pioneers, 1969. Contbr. articles to Des Moines Register. Home: 4235 Foster Dr Des Moines IA 50312 Office: 115 SW 8 St Des Moines IA 50309

LADLEY, CHARLSIE LOUISE, psychologist, counselor; b. Ardmore, Okla., Nov. 10, 1928; d. Charles G. and Willie Louise (Roberson) Thompson; B.A., Fresno (Calif.) State Coll., 1960; M.A., Ariz. State U., Tempe, 1971; Ph.D., Mich. State U., 1975; divorced; children—Toby Louise, William Charles, Cassandra Jane. Tchr., reading specialist schs. in Calif. and Colo., 1959-68; dir. girls guidance Navajo Reservation, Ft. Wingate Elementary Boarding Sch., N. Mex., 1968-71; vocat. rehab. counselor Mich. Dept. Edn., 1972-73, Williamston (Mich.) High Sch., 1973-76; counselor, psychologoist U. No. Iowa, Cedar Falls, 1976—; chmn. Dist.-Wide Career Edn. Com., 1975-76, Career Edn. Planning Dist. 31, 1976; adv. council Lansing (Mich.) Community Coll., 1973-76; chmn. bilingual/bicultural com. Coll. Edn., U. No. Iowa, 1977. Calif. PTA scholar, 1958, Standard Sch. Dist. Tchrs. Club, 1958, Alpha Delta Kappa, 1958. Mem. NEA, Am. Personnel and Guidance Assn., Nat. Assn. Women Deans, Adminstrs. and Counselors, Am. Coll. Personnel Assn., Nat. Vocat. Guidance Assn., Am. Assn. Higher Edn., AAUW, Iowa Women's Polit. Caucus, Phi Delta Kappa, Epsilon Sigma Alpha. Lutheran. Club: Order Eastern Star. Office: Univ No Iowa Cedar Falls IA 5061

LA DU, BERT NICHOLS, JR., educator; b. Lansing, Mich., Nov. 13, 1920; s. Bert Nichols and Natalie Jessie (Kerr) La D.; B.S., Mich. State Coll., 1943; M.D., U. Mich., 1945; Ph.D., U. Calif. at Berkeley, 1950; m. Catherine Shilson, June 14, 1947; children—Elizabeth, Mary, Anne, Jane. Intern, Rochester (N.Y.) Gen. Hosp., 1945-46; research asso. N.Y. U. Research Service, Goldwater Meml. Hosp., N.Y.C., 1950-53; sr. asst. surgeon USPHS, Nat. Heart Inst., 1954-57; surgeon, sr. surgeon, med. dir. Nat. Inst. Arthritis and Metabolic Diseases, 1957-63; prof., chmn. dept. pharmacology N.Y. U. Med. Sch., N.Y.C., 1963-74; prof., chmn. dept. pharmacology U. Mich. Med. Sch., Ann Arbor, 1974—. Mem. adv. com. Roche Inst. Molecular Biology, 1972-74; mem. toxicology adv. com. FDA, 1975-77; mem. nat. adv. com. NIH study sects., 1964-70, Nat. Inst. Arthritis and Metabolic Diseases Council, 1975-78. Served with AUS, 1943-45. Mem. AAAS, Am. Chem. Soc., Am. Soc. Biol. Chemists, Am. Soc. Pharmacology and Therapeutics, Am. Soc. Human Genetics, Biochem. Soc. (Gt. Britain), N.Y. Acad. Scis. Editor: (with others) Fundamentals of Drug Metabolism and Drug Disposition; contbr. articles to profl. jours. Home: 817 Berkshire Rd Ann Arbor MI 48104 Office: 6322 Med Sci Bldg I U Mich Med Sch Ann Arbor MI 48104

LADWIG, HAROLD ALLEN, neurologist; b. Manilla, Iowa, May 11, 1922; s. Ernest and Iva Marie (Allen) L.; B.A., U. Iowa, 1952, M.D., 1947; m. Marjorie Lois Foster, June 26, 1946; children—Stephen Harold, Rosemary Ann. Intern St. Joseph's Hosp., Sioux City, Iowa, 1947-48; resident U. Minn. and affiliated hosps., 1949-50, 52-53; practice medicine, specializing in neurology, Omaha, 1954—; mem. staff, dir. electroencephalographic lab. Archbishop Bergan Mercy Hosp., Omaha, 1965—; instr. neurology U. Minn., Mpls., 1952-53; mem. faculty Creighton U., Sch. Medicine, Omaha, 1954—, asso. prof. neurology, 1966—; pres. Omaha Neurol. Clinic, 1972—; mem. staff Creighton Meml. St. Joseph's Hosp., Nebr. Meth. Hosp., Bishop Clarkson Hosp., Children's Meml. Hosp., Luth. Med. Center, Drs. Hosp. Bd. dirs. Blue Cross Nebr., 1966-76. Served to comdr. M.C., USNR, 1944-45, 50-52. Diplomate Am. Bd. Psychiatry and Neurology, Am. Electroencephalographic Soc. Fellow A.C.P., Am. Acad. Neurology. Presbyn. (elder 1963-69). Home: 1743 S 85th Ave Omaha NE 68124 Office: 8300 Dodge St Suite 202 Omaha NE 68114

LADWIG, RONALD VICTOR, educator; b. Denver, Sept. 10, 1937; s. Howard Victor and Audrey Virginia (Savage) L.; B.A., U. Denver, 1960; M.A., Calif. State U., 1967; postgrad. (advanced fellow) Bowling Green State U., 1970—; m. Gale Louise Childress, May 5, 1962; children—Lance Victor Morris, Christopher Mark. Dir. dramatics Van Nuys (Calif.) Sr. High Sch., 1962-69; chmn. dept. speech and theatre, Ohio No. U., Ada, 1969—, dir. theatre, 1969—. Instr. drama workshop Calif. State U., 1965-67; instr. Am. Drama Workshop, Los Angeles, 1966; dir. honors drama workshop Los Angeles City Schs., 1967, dir. musical theatre arts workshop, 1968-69. Served with USNR, 1955-63. Mem. Am. Theatre Assn., Central States Speech Assn., Lima Area Arts Council, Nat. Soc. Lit. and Arts, Ohio Theatre Alliance, Hardin County Hist. and Archeol. Soc., Phi Delta Kappa, Theta Alpha Phi, Pi Alpha Kappa, Pi Kappa Delta. Home: 546 N Gilbert St Ada OH 45810

LAFEVERS, LARRY EDMOND, food co. exec.; b. Kansas City, Mo., Nov. 1, 1941; s. Edmond James and Veda Elizabeth (Upton) LaF.; student Baker U., 1959-61; B.A., Kans. State Coll., Pittsburg, 1964; m. Gayle Lyn Ireland, Aug. 27, 1963; children—Brett Allen, Cole Evan. Dist. mgr. Libby, McNeill & Libby, 1964-68; partner Allied Meat Co., 1968-70; nat. sales mgr. L'Eggs Products, Inc., Winston-Salem, N.C., 1970-76; nat. sales mgr. Wilton Enterprises Inc. div. Pillsbury Co., 1976-77; dir. nat. accounts and trade relations Borden Foods Sales Co., Columbus, Ohio, 1977—. Mem. Grocery Mfrs. Am., Food Marketing Inst., Heart of Am. Meat Dealers Assn. (past dir.), Nat. Am. Wholesale Grocers Assn., Nat. Assn. Convenience Stores. Methodist. Club: Worthington Hills Country. Office: 180 E Broad St Columbus OH 43215

LAFFER, MOLLY AMELIA BETZ (MRS. WILLIAM G. LAFFER), civic worker; b. Cleve., Nov. 23, 1909; d. Arthur B. and Gertrude (Kreusch) Betz; student Marot Jr. Coll., 1927-29; m. William G. Laffer, May 24, 1930; children—Walter B. II, William G. Jr., Arthur Betz. Bd. dirs. YWCA, Cleve., 1940-48, Campfire Girls, 1968—, Children's Council, 1940-54, Jr. League, 1930—, Friends U. Hosps., 1964-67, Cleve. Mental Health Assn., 1944-54, Cerebral Palsy Assn.; mem. adv. com. Hudson Boys Farm, 1946-52; mem. Ohio Mental Health Com., 1942-54; foreman Grand Jury, Cuyahoga County, Ohio, 1961. Pres. Western Res. Women's Republican Club, 1957-61; mem. exec. com. Cuyahoga County Rep. Com., 1957—. Presbyn. Home: Brookwood Rd Cleveland OH 44124

LAFFER, WILLIAM GILLESPIE, mfg. exec.; b. Cleve., May 14, 1907; s. Walter Ball and Mertice (Gillespie) L.; Ph.B., Yale U., 1927; m. Marian Amelia Betz, May 24, 1930; children—Walter Ball II, William Gillespie, Arthur B. With Cleve. Graphite Bronze Co., 1927-31, 40-52, works mgr., 1946-48, v.p. mfg., 1948-52, pres., 1952-55, pres. Clevite Corp., Cleve., parent orgn., 1955-69, also dir.; chmn. bd. Gould Inc., 1969-72, now dir., cons.; chmn. bd., dir. Reffal Inc., Cleve.; dir. Lamson & Sessions Co., Nat. City Bank of Cleve., Davey Tree Expert Co., Kent, Ohio. Trustee, v.p. Univ. Sch. Clubs: Yale (N.Y.C.); Mayfield Country, Union, The 50 (Cleve.); Bluecoats. Home: Brookwood Dr Lyndhurst Cleveland OH 44124 Office: Brookwood Rd Lyndhurst Cleveland OH 44124

LAFFERTY, DANIEL CHARLES, occupational therapist; b. Detroit, July 5, 1945; s. Charles William and Elspeth Louvenia (Martin) L.; B.S., Eastern Mich. U., 1969, M.A., 1976; Asso. Degree, Washtenaw Community Coll., 1975; m. Lynda Charlene Klaus, Apr. 7, 1969; children—Erin Michelle, Matthew Brandon. Cons., Saginaw County Substance Abuse Services, Saginaw, Mich., 1977—; dir., cons. Saginaw County Central Assessment and Referral Service and Employee Assistance Programs, 1977—; rep. Saginaw County Citizens Adv. Com. on Substance Abuse, 1977—, also mem. staff, cons. com. on case findings. Active Saginaw chpt. Big. Bro.; mem. Fact Finding Com. for Drug Treatment Program Devel.; co-chmn. Com. on Alcohol Treatment Unit Devel., Saginaw County Substance Abuse and Saginaw Community Hosp. Served with U.S. Army, 1968-74; Vietnam. Decorated Bronze Star. Certified occupational therapist. Mem. Am. Personnel and Guidance Assn., Am. Coll. Personnel Assn., Am. Occupational Therapy Assn. (registered mem.), Mich. Assn. Alcoholism and Alcohol Abuse, Mich. Alcoholism Counselors, Alcohol and Drug Problems Assn. N.Am., Phi Kappa Phi. Home: 1700 Weldon St Ann Arbor MI 48103 Office: 610 Perry St 2d Floor Saginaw MI 48602

LAFFERTY, ROBERT CORDER, III, educator; b. Charleston, W.Va., May 15, 1932; s. Robert C. and Edna Jeanne (Corder) L.; B.A., Ohio Wesleyan U., 1958; M.Ed., U. Toledo, 1962; postgrad. Akron U., 1960; m. Diana Salvo, Dec. 27, 1969; children by previous marriage—Bruce Robert, William Roger. Group rep. Aetna Life Ins. Co., Charlotte, N.C., 1958-59; indsl. products salesman Goodyear Tire & Rubber Co., Akron, Ohio, 1959-60; dorm counselor, asst. football and track coach Ohio Wesleyan U., Delaware, 1960-61; grad. asst. football U. Toledo, 1961-62; head track and asst. football coach Marietta (Ohio) Coll., 1962-64, head football and track coach, 1964-66; head track and asst. football coach Coll. Wooster (Ohio), 1966-73; track and field adminstr. AAU of U.S.A., Indpls., 1973-77; track and field cons. Wilkens Internat. Ltd., Waukesha, Wis., 1977—. Cons. Puma Athletic Shoe Co., 1967-68; liaison to men's chmn. and women's chmn. for selection of women's team for World Student Games, 1970; chief field judge Nat. Coll. Athletic Assn. Coll. div. track and field championships, 1972, 73; mem. Nat. Men and Women's track and field com., 1976—. Bd. govs. Nat. Track and Field Hall of Fame U.S. Served with AUS, 1954-56. Mem. AAHPER, Track and Field Writers Am., U.S. Tennis Ct. and Track Builders Assn., Am. Football Coaches Assn., U.S. Track Coaches Assn., Ohio Assn. Track Coaches, Nat. High Sch. Athletic Coaches Assn., U.S. Track and Field Fedn., U.S. Women's Track Coaches Assn., Nat. Coll. Div. Track Coaches Assn., YMCA, Phi Kappa Psi. Elk.

LA FOLLETTE, BRONSON CUTTING, atty. gen. Wis.; b. Washington, Feb. 2, 1936; s. Robert Marion, Jr. and Rachel Wilson (Young) LaF.; children—Robert M., Deborah C.; B.A., U. Wis., 1958, J.D., 1960. Admitted to Wis. bar, 1960, U.S. Supreme Ct., 1966. Individual practice law, Madison, Wis., 1960-62; asst. U.S. atty. Western Dist. Wis., 1962-64; atty. gen. Wis., Madison, 1964-68, 74—; Democratic nominee for Gov. Wis., 1968; lectr. Am. Specialist Abroad Program U.S. Dept. State, India, Sri Lanka, 1965. Mem. Pres.'s Consumer Adv. Council, 1966-69, chmn., 1968-69; bd. dirs. Consumers Union, Inc., 1968-76. Mem. Wis., Dane County bar assns. Office: 114 E State Capitol St Madison WI 53702

LA FOLLETTE, GERRY CAMPBELL, newspaper reporter; b. Corning, N.Y., Jan. 4, 1933; s. Charles DeVon and Elizabeth (Sanborn) LaF.; grad. Phillips Exeter Acad., 1950; B.A. Amherst Coll., 1955; postgrad. Harvard U., 1956-57, Cornell U., 1958-59; m. Susanne Eaglesfield, Sept. 13, 1958; children—Cynthia, Linda, Katherine. With Indpls. Times, 1958, 59-65; polit. reporter Indpls. News, 1965—. Trustee Indpls. Mus. Art., 1969-75. Served with AUS, 1955-57. Recipient Distinguished Reporting award Am. Polit. Sci. Assn., 1966; Nieman fellow Harvard, 1970-71. Mem. Exeter Alumni Assn. Ind. Clubs: Indianapolis Press (pres. 1970); Indiana Amherst (pres. 1965—). Home: 7016 Warwick Rd Indianapolis IN 46220 Office: 307 N Pennsylvania St Indianapolis IN 46206

LAFONT, GERARDO, psychiatrist; b. Palencia, Spain, Sept. 9, 1930; s. Feliciano and Criselda L.; M.D., U. Madrid, 1958; came to U.S., 1959, naturalized, 1968; children—Marcos, Gerard, Michael. Intern St. Johns Hosp., Cleve., 1959-60; resident Mary Mount Hosp., Cleve., 1960-61, T.M. Hosp., Warren O., 1962-63; resident N.Y. Psychiat. Inst., 1965-68; instr. psychiatry Albert Einstein Coll. Medicine, N.Y.C., 1968, asst. clin. prof., 1969; dir. Hunts Point Mental Health Center, Bronx, 1969-70, Stark County Community Mental Health Center, Canton, Ohio, 1970-71; pvt. practice psychiatry, Canton, 1971—. Served with Spanish Air Force, 1957-58. Mem. A.M.A., Am. Psychiat. Assn., Ohio Med. Assn., Stark County Med. Soc. Home: 4319 Guilford Ave NW Canton OH 44709 Office: 907 S Main St N Canton OH 44720

LAFONTANT, JEWEL, former govt. ofcl., lawyer; b. Chgo., Apr. 28, 1922; d. Cornelius Francis and Aida Arabella (Carter) Stradford; B.A., Oberlin Coll., 1943; LL.D., U. Chgo., 1946; m. H. Ernest Lafontant, Nov. 23, 1961 (dec.); 1 son (by previous marriage), John Rogers. Admitted to Ill. bar, 1947, U.S. Supreme Ct. bar, 1949, U.S. Ct. Appeals bar, 1951; since practiced in Chgo.; asst. U.S. atty., Chgo., 1955-58; partner firm Stradford, Lafontant, Fisher & Malkin, Chgo., 1961-73, 75—; dep. U.S. solicitor gen., Washington, 1973-75. Dir., Jewel Cos., Inc., Trans World Airlines, Foote, Cone & Belding, the Bendix Corp.; vice chmn. U.S. Commn. on Internat. Edn. and Cultural Affairs, 1969-73; U.S. rep. 27th Gen. Assembly UN, 1972—. Sec., N.A.A.C.P., 1951-55; v.p. Provident Hosp., 1965-73. Trustee Lincoln Acad., Lake Forest Coll. Mem. Nat. (sec. 1956-61), Chgo. (dir. 1962-64) bar assns., U. Chgo. Law Sch. Alumni Assn. (trustee). Home: 4959 S Greenwood Chicago IL 60615 Office: 69 W Washington Chicago IL 60602

LAFORE, LAURENCE DAVIS, educator, author; b. Narberth, Pa., Sept. 15, 1917; s. John Armand and Anne (Shearer) L.; B.A., Swarthmore Coll., 1938; M.A., Fletcher Sch. Law and Diplomacy 1939, Ph.D., 1950. Mem. faculty Trinity Coll., Hartford, Conn., 1940-42; with State Dept., 1942-43, OWI, 1943-44; asst. press attache Am. embassy, Paris, France, 1944-46; research asso. ECA, 1948; mem. faculty Swarthmore Coll., 1946-69, prof. history, 1960-69; vis. prof. U. Iowa, 1967-68, prof. history, 1969—, chmn. dept., 1974-77. Mem. Am. Hist. Soc. Conf. British Studies, Phi Beta Kappa, Delta Upsilon. Author: (with Paul Beik) Modern Europe, 1958; (novel) Learner's Permit, 1962; (novel) The Devil's Chapel, 1964; The Long Fuse, 1965; (with Sarah L. Lippincott) Philadelphia, The Unexpected City, 1965; (novel) Stephen's Bridge, 1960, (novel) Nine Seven Juliet, 1969; The End of Glory, 1970; (with James Dugan) Days of Emperor and Clown, 1973; American Classic, 1975. Home: 9 Parsons St Iowa City IA 52240

LA FORGE, PAUL EDWARD, constrn. co. exec.; b. Davenport, Iowa, Nov. 18, 1947; s. Paul Francis and Ellen Berniece (Treiber) LaF.; student Labette Community Coll., 1965-67; B.S. in Civil Engring., U. Kans. at Lawrence, 1970, B.S. in Bus. Adminstrn., 1970, m. Linda Joyce Miller, Aug. 24, 1968; children—Natalie Jeanette, Valerie Lynn. Foreman, LaForge & Budd Constrn. Co., Inc., Parsons, Kans., 1962-67, project supt., 1970-72, corporate exec., 1972—; individual practice, Kansas City and Lawrence, Kans., 1968-70. Mem. Nat. Soc. Profl. Engrs., U. Kans. Alumni Assn. Roman Catholic. Home: 526 Joyce Ln Parsons KS 67357 Office: 3101 Main St Parsons KS 67357

LAGE, LOUISE CATHERINE, librarian; b. Davenport, Iowa; d. Otto A. and Louise (Harting) Lage; B.A., Augustana Coll.; B.S. in Library Sci., U. Mich., 1943. Asst. extn. dept. Davenport Pub. Library, 1940-42, head extension dept., 1942-45; asst. librarian Eli Lilly Research Labs., Indpls., 1945-51, asst. chief librarian, 1951-56, chief librarian, 1956—. Dir. Starlight Musicals, 1955—; mem. governing bd. Midwest Regional Med. Library, 1969-73. Recipient Recognition award Indpls. C. of C., 1970, Outstanding Achievement award Augustana Coll., 1975. Mem. Spl. Libraries Assn. (chmn. pharm. sect., sci.-tech. div. 1959-60, pres. Ind. chpt. 1967-68), Am. Soc. Info. Sci., Ind., Med. (chmn. recruitment com. 1951-52, sec. 1952-53, chmn. curriculum com. 1955-56, chmn. pharmacy group 1957-58, dir. 1952-53; mem. exec. com. midwest regional group 1963-69) library assns., Drug Info. Assn., Indpls. Mus. Art, Indpls. Zool. Soc., Children's Mus., Alumni Assn. Augustana Coll. (dir. 1971-74), P.E.O. Presbyn. (elder). Home: 5307 Primrose Ave Indianapolis IN 46220 Office: 307 E McCarty St Indianapolis IN 46206

LAGERLUND, TERRENCE DANIEL, physicist; b. Oak Park, Ill., Aug. 14, 1953; s. Harold and Virginia Marie (Wanamaker) L.; B.A. summa cum laude, Elmhurst Coll., 1970; M.S., Va. Poly. Inst. and State U., 1972, Ph.D., 1975. System programmer, maintenance supr. Particle Physics PDP-8/I computer Va. Poly. Inst., 1972-75; mem. research staff Lab. for Nuclear Sci., Mass. Inst. Tech., Cambridge, 1975—; physicist, elementary particle research CERN, Geneva, 1976—. NSF scholar, 1970-73; Gulf Oil Corp. fellow, 1973-74. Mem. Am. Phys. Soc., Sigma Pi Sigma, Phi Kappa Phi. Home: 23 W 285 Saint Charles Rd Glen Ellyn IL 60137 Office: EP Div CERN CH 1211 Geneva 23 Switzerland

LAGOMARCINO, PAUL ANDREW, psychiat. social worker; b. Clinton, Ia., June 17, 1941; s. Richard Andrew and Nancy (Atlee) L.; B.S., St. Louis U., 1963, M.S.W., 1966; m. Suzanne Kay Zuanut, May 29, 1964; children—Debra Ann, Brian Andrew, Natalie Denise. Social work supr. Alton (Ill.) State Hosp., 1965-67; dir. alcoholic treatment center, 1967-68; pvt. practice as psychotherapist, family, marriage and divorce counselor Psychol. Assos., Alton, Ill., 1968—; dir. Day Treatment Program, Madison County (Ill.) Mental Health Center, Inc., 1968—; field work instr. Wash. U., St. Louis, 1968—, So. Ill. U., Edwardsville, 1970—. Bd. dirs. Vol. Action Center, Alton, 1977—. Mem. Am. Assn. Marriage and Family Counselors (supr.), Am. Group Psychotherapy Assn., Nat. Alliance for Family Life, Ill. Rehab. Assn., Am. Acad. Certified Social Workers. Home: 456 Valley Dr East Alton IL 62024 Office: 307 Henry St Room 402 Alton IL 62002

LAGZDINS, VOLDEMARS, constrn. co. exec.; b. Latvia, Aug. 19, 1921; s. Kriss and Zinaida (Voronkovska) L.; student U. Latvia, 1940-43; grad. LaSalle Extension U., Chgo., 1953; m. Emmy Milda Zons, Sept. 27, 1947. Came to U.S., 1951, naturalized, 1954. Sr. bookkeeper Municipal Constrn. Office, Latvia, 1940-43; adminstr. Internat. Refugee Orgn., Germany, 1946-51; chief accountant, office mgr. Kroll Bros. Co., mfrs. juvenile furniture, Chgo., 1951-57; controller, sec.-treas. Crane Constrn. Co., Inc.; Chgo., 1957—, dir., 1964—; dir. Crane Gen. Inc.; trustee Crane Constrn. Co., Inc. Profit Sharing Trust. Nat. sec. Latvian Welfare Assn., 1956-62, mem. adv. bd., 1962—. Served with Latvian Legion, 1943-46. Home: 425 Elm St Glenview IL 60025 Office: 343 Wainwright Dr Northbrook IL 60062

LAHEY, MICHAEL FRANCIS, dentist; b. Chgo., Oct. 13, 1941; s. Michael Raphael and Frances Jeannette (Steadman) L.; student U. Ill., 1959-60, Ecole Neuchatel (Switzerland), 1963; B.A., Albion Coll., 1964; D.D.S., U. Detroit, 1969; m. Charlene Rene Grismer, Sept. 4, 1971; children—Charles Scott, Lisa René, Kirstie Ann, Megan Ann, Michael Timothy. Chemist, City of Detroit, 1964; Wayne County (Mich.) dep. sheriff, 1965-66; librarian Wayne County Youth Home, 1967-69; pvt. practice dentistry, Detroit, 1969—, Pontiac, Mich., 1974-75; chief staff, chief diagnostic sect. group practice, Pontiac, 1975-76; clin. instr., lectr. U. Detroit Dental Sch., 1969-70, asst. dir. Dental Aux. Utilization Program, 1969-70; mem. ad hoc com. Mich. Dental Plan. Mem. Am., Mich. dental assns., Detroit Dist. Dental Soc. (clinician, editor Eastern Component), Am. Soc. Preventive Dentistry, Chgo. Dental Soc., Fedn. Dentaire Internationale, Internat. Coll. Oral Implantology, Acad. Gen. Dentistry, Detroit Dental Clinic Crown and Bridge Club, Beta Beta Beta, Delta Sigma Delta. Home: 1245 Three Mile Dr Grosse Point Park MI 48230 Office: 17401 Mack Ave Detroit MI 48226

LAHNIERS, CARROLL EDWARD, clin. psychologist; b. Decatur, Ill., June 17, 1944; s. Edward Elda and Frances Maxine (Minor) L.; B.A., Miami (Ohio) U., 1965; M.A., U. Cin., 1968, Ph.D., 1971. Licensed psycholgoist, Ohio Bd. Psychology, 1973. Psychol. technician Knowle Hosp., Fareham, Hants., Eng., 1966-67; psychol. cons. Jewish Hosp., Cin., 1969—, Council of Epilepsy, Cin., 1975—, Mgmt. Design, Inc., Cin., 1974—; faculty U. Cin., 1971—, Xavier U., Cin., 1976—; dir. psychol. services Rollman Psychiat. Inst., Cin., 1971-76; psychol. cons. alcoholism care unit St. Francis Hosp., Cin., 1976—; pvt. practice clin. psychology, Cin., 1971—. Mem. Am., Cin. psychol. assns., Assn. Advancement of Psychology, Nat. Register Health Service Providers in Psychology, Alpha Delta Phi, Psy Chi, Pi Delta Phi. Contbr. articles to profl. jours. Home and office: 1247 Ida St Cincinnati OH 45202

LA HOOD, JOSEPH JOHN, orthopaedic surgeon; b. Detroit, Oct. 18, 1937; s. Tom and Melinia (Simon) La H.; B.S., Georgetown U., 1959, M.D., 1963; m. Elaine Riff, June 3, 1973; children—Lila Marie, Michael Antonios. Intern, New Eng. Med. Center, Boston, 1963-64;

fellow in surgery Mayo Clinic, Rochester, Minn., 1964-66; resident in orthopaedic surgery Wayne State U. Hosp., Detroit, 1968-71; practice medicine specializing in orthopedic surgery, Macomb County, Mich., 1971—; mem. staffs St. Josep, Mt. Clemens, Bon Secours, Cottage hosps., Grosse Pointe, Mich., Holy Cross Hosp., Detroit, S. Macomb Hosp.; instr. orthopaedic surgery Wayne State U., 1972—; orthopedic surgeon staff Macomb County Easter Seal Soc. Crippled Children, 1971—. Served with M.C., USN, 1966-68. Diplomate Am. Bd. Surgery, Am. Bd. Orthopedic Surgery. Fellow A.C.S., Internat. Coll. Surgeons; mem. Am. Acad. Orthopedic Surgery. Republican. Home: 20 Stillmeadow Ln Grosse Pointe Shores MI 48236 Office: 22050 Greater Mack Saint Clair Shores MI 48080

LAHRMAN, DON EUGENE, orthodontist; b. Ft. Wayne, Ind., Mar. 12, 1932; s. Clarence F. and Orpha (Krauter) L.; B.S., Ind. U., 1954, D.D.S., 1957, M.S.D. in Orthodontics, 1965; m. Carolyn Lou Steinbacher, Aug. 29, 1953; children—Lisa Lynn, Don Eugene II. Pvt. practice dentistry, Ft. Wayne, Ind., 1959-62, practice dentistry specializing in orthodontics, Ft. Wayne, 1962—; tchr. Ind. U. at Ft. Wayne, 1966-68. Served as capt. AUS, 1957-59. Mem. Isaac Knapp Dental Soc. (del. 1967-73; pres. 1971-72), Ind., Am. dental assns., Gt. Lakes Soc. Orthodontists, Am. Assn. Orthodontists, Am. Profl. Practice Assn., Ind. Acad. Dental Practice Adminstrn., Found. Orthodontic Research, Am. Cleft Palate Assn., Fedn. Dentaire Internat., Izaak Walton League, Ft. Wayne C. of C. Republican. Lutheran. Author: Clinical Dento-Facial Biometry In Norma Frontalis, 1965. Home: 2933 Covington Lake Dr Fort Wayne IN 46804 Office: 2426 E State Blvd Fort Wayne IN 46805

LAHTI, PAUL THEODORE, gen. surgeon; b. Calumet, Mich., Jan. 20, 1919; s. Waino and Augusta Wilhelmina (Kahara) L.; B.A., U. Mich., 1940, M.D., 1943; m. Elizabeth Margaret Tabar, Apr. 21, 1945; children—Paul Theodore, Carol E., Christine A., James R., Catherine M., Linda E. Intern, surg. resident Grace Hosp., Detroit, 1944-45, 47-49; practice gen. surgery Royal Oak, Mich., 1949—; staff William Beaumont Hosp., Detroit, 1955—, sr. attending surgeon, 1965—. Bd. dirs. Mich. Drs. Polit. Action Com., 1965—; med. Adv. bd. South Oakland Hosp. Authority, 1972—. Bd. dirs. South Oakland br. Mich. Cancer Found., 1958-60, South Oakland YMCA, 1968; pres. South Oakland br. Am. Cancer Soc., 1957; bd. dirs. Mich. Blue Shield, 1968-72. Served with M.C., 1943-45. Diplomate Am. Bd. Surgery. Fellow A.C.S.; mem. Mich. State (council 1972—, del. 1956-72), Oakland County (treas. 1959) med. socs., AMA (del. Mich. 1970-76), Mich. Soc. Gen. Surgeons (pres. 1975-76), Flying Physicians, Nu Sigma Nu. Rotarian. Clubs: Masons (32 deg.), Shriners, Red Run Golf, Royal Oak, Torch Lake Yacht. Patentee sauna heater. Pioneer early discharge of postoperative patients. Home: 831 Jonathan Ln Bloomfield Hills MI 48013 Office: 3600 W 13 Mile Rd Royal Oak MI 48072

LAIDLER, JAMES HAROLD, supt. schs.; b. Windsor, Ont., Can., May 22, 1925; s. John Alfred and Margaret (Cunningham) L.; came to U.S., 1927; naturalized, 1946; B.S., Wayne State U., 1957, M. Ed., 1963, postgrad. 1974—; postgrad. Detroit Coll. Law, 1957-59, Valparaiso U., 1961, Western Reserve U., 1962-63; m. Carolynn J. Scharrer, June 1, 1946; children—Lorraine (Mrs. Richard Hughes), James B., Janet L., Catherine M. Mgmt. positions Ford Motor Co., Dearborn, Mich., 1948-58; tchr. Heintzen Schs., Southgate, Mich., 1958-65; systems analyst mgmt. services Great Lakes Steel, Ecorse, Mich., 1965-67; asst. supt. Gibraltar Sch. Dist., Rockwood, Mich., 1967-71; supt. Morenci (Mich.) Area Schs., 1971-75; supt. Lamphere Schs., Madison Heights, Mich., 1975—. Columnist, Morenci (Mich.) Observer, 1973-75. Cub Scout com. chmn. Boy Scouts Am., Gibraltar, Mich., 1961-66. Mem. Gibraltar (Mich.) Bd. Edn., 1964-67. Served with RCAF, 1943-45; USAF, 1945. Mem. Am., Mich. (mem. in-service com. 1972—, chmn. workshops 1973, 74, 75) assns. sch. adminstrs., Mich. Sch. Bus. Ofcls., Mich. Negotiators Assn., Can. Legion (pres. 1948-49). Roman Catholic (chmn. parish council 1969-71). Elk, Rotarian (pres. 1969-70, 76-77). Home: 30169 Manor Dr Madison Heights MI 48071 Office: Lamphere Schs 31201 Dorchester St Madison Heights MI 48071

LAING, JAMES THOMAS, charitable assn. adminstr.; b. Charleston, W. Va., Jan. 2, 1934; s. James Tamplin and Claire Lenila (Thomas) L.; A.B., Kent State U., 1955, M.A., 1956; postgrad. U. Chgo., 1966, Ohio State U., 1959; m. Barbara Lynn Coe, Sept. 24, 1977. children—Michael Thomas, Susan Kay. Asst. exec. dir. United Community Services, Lorain, Ohio, 1959-64; asso. exec. sec. United Fund of Central Stark County, Canton, Ohio, 1964-69; exec. dir. St. Joseph, Mo., Area United Fund, 1969-73; exec. dir. United Way of St. Joseph County, South Bend, Ind., 1973-76; asso. exec. dir. United Way of Pontiac and North Oakland County (Mich.), 1976—; pres. United Way of Ind., South Bend, 1975-76; mem. manpower devel. com. United Way of Am., 1972—, adv. task force, Mid-Am. Region, 1974—. Instr. sociology Kent (Ohio) State U., 1959-69; field cons. midwest area United Health Founds., Inc., 1967-71; vis. lectr. Oakland U., Rochester, Mich., 1976—. Served with USAF, 1956-59. Mem. Blue Key, Phi Sigma Kappa, Pi Gamma Mu, Alpha Kappa Delta. Home: 5454 Vivian Pontiac MI 48054 Office: 50 Wayne St Pontiac MI 48058

LAIR, DWAYNE EUGENE, agriculturist, farmer; b. Red Oak, Iowa, Oct. 13, 1926; s. Oscar and Dorothy Irene (Carroll) L.; grad. high sch.; m. Marvella Huff, Nov. 27, 1947; children—Cheryl (Mrs. Gary Ray Carter), Dwanella (Mrs. Randall Franklin Snethern), Layne. Truck driver Huff Trucking Co., West Plains, Mo., 1947-50, farmer nr. Hocomo, Mo., 1950-53, 54—; assembly worker Gen. Motors, Kansas City, Kans., 1953; program officer, field asst. U.S. Dept. Agr., West Plains, 1964—; salesman Na-Churs Plant Food Co., 1971-77. Mem. Egypt Grove Sch. Bd., Hocomo, Mo., 1958-59; mem. South Fork (Mo.) Sch. Bd., 1964-65; spl. dep. sheriff, 1970-72, dep. assessor, 1960-68, 70-77. Served with AUS, 1945-46. Mem. Am. Legion, Pork Producers Assn. (dir. 1972-73). Home: Hocomo MO 65691

LAIRD, EVALYN WALSH, lawyer; b. Chgo., Feb. 6, 1902; d. Edward J. and Mae (Tarr) Walsh; J.D., DePaul Law Sch., 1926; Ph.D. (hon.), Hamilton U., 1974; m. Charles Hamilton Laird, Aug. 8, 1925 (dec. 1970); children—Lois (Mrs. Walter P. Hillmann), Betty Ann (Mrs. Donald H. Hillmann), Charles Jr. (dec.), Edward J., Jane Alice (Mrs. Daniel R. Glynn). Admitted to Ill. bar, 1926; practiced in Chgo., 1926—; mng. dir. Edward J. Walsh, ct. reporting, 1950—, owner, 1960—. Former den mother Cub Scouts; past pub. relations chmn. Rogers Park area Girl Scouts U.S.A., Chgo., del. council, mem. council personnel com., 1972-77; past pres. 7th dist. vicarate II, Chgo. Council Catholic Women; mem. Mayor Daley's Com. Women Lawyers; past co-chmn. Ill. Epilepsy League, Inc.; past pres. Glenola Club of Loyola Center. Former co-chmn., Women's Campaign Com. for Esther Saperstein for Senator. Mem. Women's (past mem. speakers bur.; mem. Law Day com.), Chgo. (past house com.; real property com., contracts and titles divs., ecology div. environ. law com., sci. and tech. com.), Ill. (sr. counsellor 1976) bar assns., Chgo. and Cook County Fedn. Women's Clubs (past mem. bd.), Shell Club Field Museum, Field Museum Natural History, Okla., Texas County irrigation and water resources assns., Nat., Internat. wildlife fedns., Angel Guardian Aux., Shedd Aquarium, Internat. Oceanographic Found., Ill. Right to Life Com., U.S. Figure Skating Assn., Big Sisters. Clubs: Skokie Valley Figure Skating; Grand Beach (Mich.) Golf and Social; Glenola (program chmn.). Home: 19259 Pine Ave Grand Beach New Buffalo MI 49117 Office: 127 N Dearborn Suite 1541 Chicago IL 60602

LAIRD, JEAN ELOUISE RYDESKI (MRS. JACK E. LAIRD), author; b. Wakefield, Mich., Jan. 18, 1930; d. Chester A. and Agnes A. (Petranek) Rydeski; Bus. Edn. degree, Duluth (Minn.) Bus. U., 1948; postgrad. U. Minn., 1949-50; m. Jack E. Laird, June 9, 1951; children—John E., Jane E., JoanAnn P., Jerilyn S., Jacquelyn T. Tchr., Oak Lawn (Ill.) High Sch. Adult Evening Sch., 1964-72, St. Xavier Coll., 1974—. Writer monthly column Lady's Circle mag., Time & Money Savers; past travel editor Oldsmobile Mag.; lectr. Mem. Author's Guild, Author's League. Canterbury Writers Club Chgo. (past pres.), Bus. and Profl. Womens Club, St. Linus Guild. Roman Catholic. Author: Lost in the Department Store, 1964; Around The House Like Magic, 1966, How to Get the Most from Your Appliances, 1967; Around the Kitchen Like Magic; For Girls Only—How to Get Along With Boys; Petey Popcorn's Popcorn Party; Barefoot Betsy; What am I?; Her Own Little House; The Plump Ballerina; The Ice Cream Man; The Alphabet Zoo; Fried Marbles & Other Fun Things to Do; Hundreds of Hints for Harrassed Homemakers; numerous booklets for Nat. Research Bur. Contbr. numerous articles to nat. mags. Home: 10540 S Lockwood Ave Oak Lawn IL 60453 also Grand Beach MI 49118

LAIRD, RICHARD H., transp. co. exec.; b. Gulfport, Miss., Jan. 17, 1951; s. Travis H. and Carole A. (Bladon) L.; B.S. in Aero. Sci., Embry Riddle Aero U., 1973; M.B.A., Xavier U., 1977; m. M. Kathleen Miller, Mar. 24, 1976. Cons., Booz Allen & Hamilton, Cin., 1973-75; pres. Am. Helicopters Inc., Cin., 1975-77, dir., 1975—; pres., dir. Am. Group Cos., Inc., Cin., 1976—; dir. Am. Air Services, Inc., Key Aviation, Inc. Served as pilot U.S. Army, 1969-72. Decorated D.F.C., Bronze Star with oak leaf cluster, Purple Heart with 2 oak leaf clusters, Air medal with 25 oak leaf clusters; Cross of Gallantry (Vietnam). Mem. Helicopter Assn. Am., Nat. Air Transp. Assn., Nat. Bus. Aviation Assn. Office: 5706 Hillside Ave Cincinnati OH 45233

LAIRD, SUSAN ZOE, systems officer; b. Dallas, Tex., Oct. 3, 1939; d. Hubert Charles and Helen Field (Grassie) L.; student Mt. Holyoke Coll., 1957-58, Augusta Coll., 1958-59; B.A., Beloit Coll., 1961; M.B.A., DePaul U., 1974. Jr. research analyst Fed. Res. Bank of Chgo., 1961-62; research analyst Res. Ins. Co., Chgo., 1962-65; statis. analyst Booz, Allen & Hamilton, Chgo., 1965-67; systems analyst Continental Assurance Co., Chgo., 1967-69; sr. systems analyst U. Ill., Chgo., 1969-73; systems officer and project mgr. Continental Ill. Nat. Bank and Trust Co., Chgo., 1973—; speaker Women in Computing, Assn. Computing Machinery, 1976, Assn. Systems Mgmt. grantee. Mem. Nat. Assn. Bank Women, Assn. Systems Mgmt., Delta Mu Delta, Kappa Delta. Office: 231 S La Salle St Chicago IL 60693

LAIRD, THOMAS RICHARD, physician; b. Hastings, Nebr., Feb. 2, 1938; s. Bruce and Mabel Fay (Buzzard) L.; M.D., U. Nebr., 1964. Intern, Bryan Meml. Hosp., Lincoln, Nebr., 1964-65; gen. practice medicine, Blue Hill, Nebr., 1965-70; physician emergency room services St. Elizabeth Community Health Center, Lincoln, 1970—. Owner Blue Hill Greenhouses, 1967—. Active Boy Scouts Am. Mem. A.M.A., Nebr., Lancaster County med. socs., Am. Acad. Family Physicians, Aircraft Owners and Pilots Assn., Am. Coll. Emergency Physicians, Order of Arrow, Phi Chi. Republican. Methodist. Home: Box 126 Blue Hill NE 68930 also 3201 N 27th 16 Lincoln NE 68504 Office: 555 S 70th St Lincoln NE 68510

LAKATOS, GEORGE CHARLES, physician; b. Vienna, Austria, May 17, 1923; s. Vicktor Fredrick and Helene (Halmi) L.; came to U.S., 1939, naturalized, 1943; children—Madeleine, Renee, Nicole, Chantalle; B.A., Boston U., 1950; M.D., Bern (Switzerland) Med. Sch., 1956. Intern, Highland Park Gen. Hosp. (Mich.), 1957-58; resident in internal medicine Wayne County Gen. Hosp., Eloise, Mich., 1958-59; practice medicine specializing in internal medicine, Westland, Mich., 1960—; research asso., oncology Wayne County Gen. Hosp., Eloise Mich., 1971—, research grantee, 1973—; mem. staff Annapolis Hosp.; med. dir. Fischer Body Co., Gen. Motors Corp., Livonia, Mich., 1960-61, Detroit House of Correction, 1960-62, Venoy Continued Cre Center, Mayne, Mich., 1976—. Served with AUS, 1943-46: ETO. Mem. AMA, Mich., Wayne County med. socs., Am. Soc. Internal Medicine, Am. Profl. Practice Assn., Internat. Platform Assn. Patentee waste disposal for hosp. beds. Office: 33020 Palmer Rd Westland MI 48185

LAKE, THOMAS PHILIP, radiologist; b. Mpls., Apr. 3, 1938; s. Philip A. and Theodora M. (Soderberg) L.; B.S. summa cum laude, Beloit Coll., 1960; M.D., U. Minn., 1964; m. Joanne R. Zimmerman, June 6, 1960; children—Paul Thomas, Gregory Thomas. Intern, St. Mary's Hosp., Duluth, Minn., 1964-65; resident in diagnostic radiology Mayo Grad. Sch. Medicine, Rochester, Minn., 1967-70; staff radiologist Meml. Med. Center, Springfield, Ill., 1970—; chmn. dept. radiology Springfield Community Hosp., 1977—; clin. asst. prof. radiology So. Ill. Sch. Medicine, Springfield, 1973—, clin. asst. prof. diagnostic radiology, 1973—; treas. Clin. Radiologists, S.C. Served with USNR, 1965-67. Diplomate Am. Bd. Radiology. Mem. Am. Coll. Radiology, Ill. Radiol. Soc., AMA, Ill., Sangamon County med. socs., Phi Beta Kappa. Club: Illini Country (Springfield). Home: 1601 Cherry Rd Springfield IL 62704 Office: Meml Med Center Springfield IL 62702

LALLY, ANN MARIE, ednl. adminstr.; b. Chgo., Sept. 23, 1914; d. Martin J. and Della (McDonnell) Lally; A.B., Mundelein Coll., 1935; A.M., Northwestern U., 1939, Ph.D., 1950; postgrad. Chgo. Tchrs. Coll., Chgo. Art Inst., 1935-36. Tchr., Amundsen High Sch., 1935, Lindblom and Von Steuben high schs., Chgo., 1936-38; chmn. art dept. Schurz High Sch., 1938-40; supr. art Chgo. Pub. Elementary Schs., 1940-48, dir. art Chgo. Public Schs., 1948-57; prin. John Marshall High Sch., 1957-63; supt. Dist. 16, Chgo. Pub. Schs., 1963-64, Dist. 5, 1964—; lectr. Wright Jr. Coll., 1948; instr. creative drawing Chgo. Acad. Fine Art, 1941; instr. interior design Internat. Harvester Co., 1946-48; lectr. in edn. DePaul U., 1952-74; lectr. in edn. and art U. Chgo., 1956-59; lectr. edn., Chgo. Tchrs. Coll., 1960-62. Trustee Pub. Sch. Tchrs. Pension and Retirement Fund Chgo., 1957-71, sec.-treas., 1960-65, pres., 1965-70. Charter mem. women's bd. Loyola U.; charter mem. women's bd. Art Inst., Chgo. Mem. Am., Ill. assns. sch. adminstrs., N.E.A. (life), Ill. Edn. Assn., Dist. Supts. Assn. (pres. 1973-75), Nat. Council Adminstrv. Women in Edn. (profl. relations chmn. 1958-62), Assn. Supervision and Curriculum Devel., Nat. Art Edn. Assn. (mem. council 1956-60), Western Arts Assn. (pres. 1956-58), Internat. Soc. Edn. in Art, Ill. Art Edn. Assn. (pres. 1955), Chgo. Art Educators Assn. (a founder; past v.p., sec. and treas.), Chgo. Pub. Sch. Art Soc., Chgo. Hist. Soc., Am. Assn. U. Women (Chgo. chmn. elementary and secondary edn., dir.-at-large 1962-66), Chgo. Area Reading Assn. (dir. 1963-69), Nat., Ill. assns. secondary sch. prins., Artists Equity Assn., Chgo. Council on Fgn. Relations, Mundelein Coll. Alumnae Assn. (past pres., chmn. bd., Magnificat medal 1964), Pi Lambda Theta, Delta Kappa Gamma. Contbr. articles to art and ednl. jours. Home: 5701 N Sheridan Rd Chicago IL 60660 Office: 4626 N Knox Ave Chicago IL 60630

LAM, TUNG TING, mech. engr.; b. China, Dec. 1, 1948; s. Atilio and Kam To (Nit) L.; came to U.S., 1967; student So. Bapt. Coll., 1967-68; B.S., U. Mo., Rolla, 1970, M.S. in Mech. Engring., 1973; m. Jennifer Lang Hsu, Aug. 10, 1974; 1 dau., Elaine Yachi. Research and teaching asst. U. Mo., Rolla, 1972-74; mech. engr. Black & Veatch Cons. Engrs., Kansas City, Mo., 1974-76, computer applications engr., 1976—. Mem. ASME, Sigma Xi, Pi Tau Sigma. Contbr. articles to profl. jours. Home: 1500 Sioux Dr Olathe KS 66061 Office: 1500 Meadow Lake Pkwy Kansas City MO 64114

LAMB, CHARLOTTE B., realtor; b. Finley, N.D., May 24, 1934; d. Chester and Belle E. (Tuntland) Paulsen; student N.D. State U. at Fargo, 1974—; m. Richard C. Lamb, Aug. 6, 1958; children—Deborah (Mrs. John Verdi, Jr.), Steven Johnk, Lori Johnk. Saleswoman, Twin Town Realty, Moorhead, Minn., 1965-69, Action Realty, Dilworth, Minn., 1969—. Mem. Bd. Realtors, Nat. Inst. Real Estate Bds., Am. Legion Aux. Lutheran. Elkette. Home: 201 4th St NE Dilworth MN 56520 Office: 105 Center Ave Dilworth MN 56529

LAMB, CLIFFORD WILLIAM BILL, sales exec.; b. Danville, Ill., Mar. 15, 1949; s. Clifford Eugene and Beulah Marie (Dollbee) L.; student Atlanta Christian Coll., 1967-69, Danville Jr. Coll., 1970-72; m. Maxine Kay Root, May 24, 1970; children—Jennifer Rene. Mgr., Steak n Shake, Inc., Decatur, Ill., 1969-70; bacteriologist, Lauhoff Grain Co., Danville, 1970-72, coordinator sales service, 1972—. Author: A Comprehensive Discussion of Rodents and Rodent Control, 1975. Home: 2 South St Bismarck IL 61814 Office: 321 E North St Danville IL 61832

LAMB, RICHARD JOSEPH, funeral dir.; b. Evergreen Park, Ill., Sept. 7, 1940; s. Matthew J. and Margaret M. (Lawler) L.; A.B., Holy Cross Coll., 1962; Licensed Funeral Dir., Worsham Coll., 1963; postgrad. U. Chgo., 1965-68; m. Susan Palmgren, Oct. 24, 1964; children—Maureen, Christine, Jennifer, Stephen, Meghan. Corporate sec. Blake-Lamb Funer Homes, Inc., Oak Lawn, Ill., 1975—; pres. 103d St. Oak Lawn Bldg Corp., 1977—; partner Mat-Rich Investments, Oak Lawn, 1963-77, Lamb Flower Shop, Chgo., 1963-76; sec. Lamb Auto Livery. Chmn. Lombard (Ill.) Lilac Festival, 1974-75, Lombard Blood Program, 1975-76. Mem. Nat., Ill. funeral dirs. assns., Funeral Dirs. Services Assn. (dir.), Preferred Funeral Dirs. Internat. (dir.), Am. Thanatalogical Assn., Lombard C. of C. (pres. 1974). Office: 4727 W 103d St Oak Lawn IL 60453

LAMB, THOMAS, naval architect; b. Edinburgh, Scotland, June 2, 1935; s. Thomas and Catherine Gillespie Brownlie L.; came to U.S., 1966, naturalized, 1974; student Her Majesty's Royal Dockyard Tech. Coll., Rosyth, 1951-55; B.S., Kings Coll., Durham (Eng.) U., 1958; m. Isobel Elizabeth Blackie Hogg, Oct. 17, 1959; 1 son, David. Naval architect various shipyards Britain, Denmark, 1958-66; asst. chief naval architect Md. Shipbldg. & Drydock Co., Balt., 1966-70; chief naval architect Seatrain Shipbldg. Corp., N.Y.C., 1970-72; v.p. engring. Com/Code Corp., Alexandria, Va., 1972-74; mgr. comml. ship design Hydronautics Inc., Laurel, Md., 1974-75; v.p. engring. Marinette Marine Corp. (Wis.), 1975—. Mem. Soc. Naval Architects and Marine Engrs., Royal Instn. Naval Architects, Am. Soc. Naval Engrs., Instn. Engrs. and Shipbuilders in Scotland, N.E. Coast Instn. Engrs. and Shipbuilders. Presbyn. Clubs: Riverside Country, Marinette Golf and Country. Contbr. articles to profl. publs. Inventor LNG tank, 1975, ship's accomodation ladder, 1975. Home: 1216 Florence St Marinette WI 54143 Office: Ely St Marinette WI 54143

LAMBERT, CHARLES OTTERBEIN, cons.; b. Barnesville, Ohio, Feb. 22, 1905; s. William Otterbein and Lauretta (Adams) L.; A.B., Otterbein Coll., 1927; B.P.E., George Williams Coll., 1931; m. Bernice Jackson, Sept. 14, 1929, Phys. dir. Northeast Br. Canton (Ohio) YMCA, 1927-29; boys' phys. dir. Chgo. YMCA Wilson Av. Br., 1929-31; youth and phys. dir. Cin. and Hamilton County, Norwood Br., 1931-37; phys. dir. Piqua (Ohio) YMCA, 1937-41, Lincoln, Nebr., 1941-44; exec. sec. Cin. and Hamilton County YMCA Columbia Pkwy. Br., 1944-49, Williams Br., 1949-54; Met. program dir., 1954-64; exec. dir. Powel Crosley Jr. Family Br. YMCA, 1964-70, now cons. phys. fitness program and testing. Mem. Assn. Secs. Presbyn. Kiwanian. Contbr. articles in field to profl. jours. Home: 5767 Belfast Rd Rural Route 3 Batavia OH 45103

LAMBERT, DANIEL MICHAEL, coll. adminstr.; b. Kansas City, Mo., Jan. 16, 1941; s. Paul McKinley and Della Mae (Rogers) L.; A.B., William Jewell Coll., 1963; M.A., Northwestern U., 1965; Ph.D., U. Mo., 1977; m. Carolyn Bright, Dec. 27, 1969; children—Kristian Paige, Dennis McKinley. Asst. to dean Elmhurst (Ill.) Coll., 1963-65; licensed to ministry, Baptist Ch., 1965; asso. pastor Christ Ch., Wellesley, Mass., 1965-66; dean student affairs William Jewell Coll., Liberty, Mo., 1970-76, dean student affairs, asst. to pres., 1977—. Served with U.S. Army, 1966-70. Decorated Bronze Star. Mem. Nat. Assn. Student Personnel Adminstrs., Am. Assn. Higher Edn. Home: 982 Wyckwood Dr Liberty MO 64068 Office: William Jewell Coll Liberty MO 64068

LAMBERT, DENNIS MICHAEL, virologist; b. Chichamauga, Ga., May 12, 1947; s. Marshall Tarver and Mildred Louise (Dennis) L.; B.A., Ind. Central Coll., 1969; M.A., Ind. State U., 1972, Ph.D., 1977; m. Andrea Lee Spencer, Aug. 24, 1968; children—Angela Lynn, Debra Megan. With Univ. Heights Hosp., Indpls., 1965-68, Union Hosp. Lab., Terre Haute, summer 1969; instr. life sci. Ind. State U., Terre Haute, 1974-75; biochem. virologist U. Tex. and S.W. Research Found., San Antonio, 1975-76; asst. investigator Christ Hosp. Inst. Med. Research, Cin., 1976—. Ind. State U. grad. fellow, 1971-74. Mem. Am. Soc. Microbiology, Life Sci. Grad. Student Union (pres. 1973-74), Sigma Xi. Clubs: Toastmasters (Terre Haute, Ind.); Circle K. Home: 4808 Williamsburg Rd NW Cincinnati OH 45215 Office: 2141 Auburn Ave Cincinnati OH 45219

LAMBERT, GUY WILLIAM, dentist; b. Marion, Ill., May 16, 1907; s. William Monroe and Flossie Floyette (Adams) L.; Ed.B. in Sci., So. Ill. U., 1933; D.D.S., St. Louis U., 1938; m. E. Leora Hartley, Oct. 20, 1934; 1 dau., Mary Lynn. Tchr., Ewing (Ill.) High Sch., 1933-34; practice dentistry, West Frankfort, Ill., 1938—. Pres., Pyramid Radio & TV Corp., West Frankfort, 1952—; dir. Bank of West Frankfort. Sr. cons. St. Louis U. Dental Sch., 1937-38; dental cons. Vocational Tech. Inst., So. Ill. U., 1955-60. Chmn., Franklin County March of Dimes, 1960-62; mem. West Frankfort Community Park Bd., 1950-62, pres., 1954-58. Served to maj. Dental Corps, AUS, 1941-46. Recipient Service Achievement award So. Ill. U. Alumni, 1963. Fellow Am. Dental Assn.; mem. Ill. Dental Soc. (mem. com. dental health 1958-68), So. Ill. U. Alumni Assn. (pres. 1958-59). Republican. Presbyn. Mason, Rotarian. Home: 1006 E St Louis St West Frankfort IL 62896 Office: 106 E Oak St West Frankfort IL 62896

LAMBERT, JAMES ARTHUR, otolaryngologist; b. Youngstown, Ohio, Aug. 7, 1941; s. James Jerome and Mary Jane (Gabriele) L.; B.A., Marietta Coll., 1962; postgrad. Youngstown U., 1960, 61; M.D., Western Res. U., 1966; m. Jeannine Marie Dewey, Dec. 29, 1962; children—Diana Caye, Tatia Lenore, Leda Shael, Regina Marie. Commd. ensign U.S. Navy, 1966, advanced through ranks to comdr. MC, 1972; intern Naval Hosp., Phils., 1966-67; resident Naval Hosp., San Diego, 1967-71; chief otolaryngology service Naval Hosp., Gt. Lakes, Ill., 1972-74, discharged, 1974; practice medicine specializing in otolaryngology, Youngstown, 1975—; mem. Fifth Ave. Otolaryngologists, Inc., Youngstown; mem. staffs St. Elizabeth Hosp., Youngstown Hosp. Assn. Diplomate Am. Bd. Otolaryngology, Nat. Bd. Med. Examiners. Fellow Am. Acad. Ophthalmology and Otolaryngology, A.C.S.; mem. Ohio, Mahoning County (treas. 1977—, editor bull. 1976) med. socs. Home: 2760 Belmar Dr Youngstown OH 44505 Office: 1350 Fifth Ave Youngstown OH 44504

LAMBERT, JAMES HOWARD, physician; b. Welch, W.Va., Sept. 22, 1922; s. James Howard and Eliza Ann (Douglas) L.; B.S., U. Ill., 1947, B.S. in Medicine, 1948, M.D., 1950; m. Mary Ann Eck, Feb. 23, 1946; children—James Alan, Gary Douglas, Ann Christine. Intern, St. Joseph Hosp., Joliet, Ill., 1950-51, attending physician, 1951—, past pres. med. staff; practice medicine specializing in family practice, Joliet, Ill., 1951—; attending physician Silver Cross Hosp., 1951-72; partner Joliet Med. Group, Ltd.; asst. prof. dept. family practice Chgo. Med. Sch. Served with AUS, 1943-46. Decorated Bronze Star medal, Combat Inf. badge. Fellow Am. Acad. Family Practice; mem. AMA, Ill., Will County (past pres.) med. socs., Aesculapian Assn. (past pres.), Will County Acad. Family Practice (past pres.). Bd. dirs. Will County United Fund. Presbyterian. Office: 2100 Glenwood Ave Joliet IL 60435

LAMBERT, MILTON HAROLD, petroleum products distbr.; b. Chgo., Apr. 19, 1911; s. Rubin and Esther (Matt) L.; student Crane Jr. Coll., 1929, U. Chgo., 1933; m. Gertrude Ackerman, Oct. 3, 1937; children—Ellen, Barbara, Penny, Felice. With Gen. Gas & Oil Co., Chgo., 1937—, pres., 1978—. Chmn. Skokie (Ill.) Art Festival, 1970-74; Ill. co-chmn. Jackson for Pres. campaign, 1976; founder, former v.p. Lincolnwood Jewish Congregation; founder, pres. Chgo. chpt. Magen David Adom, Israel's ofcl. Red Cross; pres. Prime Minister's Club Bonds for Israel, 1976-78. Named Man of Year City Wide B'nai B'rith Bonds for Israel, 1976, Shomrim Poice Soc. Ill., 1977, Shaare Zadek Hosp. of Jerusalem, 1977. Mem. Midwest Petroleum Marketers Assn. (dir.), Chgo. Oil Men's Club, Ill. Petroleum Marketers Assn., Skokie, North Shore art guilds, Chgo. Cartage Exchange, Ill. Truckers Assn., Nat. Oil Jobbers Council, Am. Israel C. of C. Club: B'nai B'rith. Artist; one-man shows Little Gallery, Riccardo's Restaurant and Art Gallery, Gold Coast Art Shows, Skokie Art Fairs, Lincolnwood Art Fairs. Home: 6418 N Kolmar Ave Lincolnwood IL 60646 Office: 5450 Northwest Hwy Chicago IL 60630

LAMBERT, SAM AMON, county ofcl.: b. LaFollette, Tenn., Nov. 4, 1936; s. Daniel Jefferson and Uhla King (Miller) L.; B.S. in Psychology, E. Tenn. State U., 1964; M.A. in Counseling, Wayne State U., 1972, postgrad., 1973; m. Sharleen Ann Moore, Dec. 30, 1959; children—Katherine, Felicia, Daniel. Caseworker to supr. Youth Assistance Dept. Oakland County (Mich.) Probate Ct., 1965-74, asst. dir., 1974—; pres. advisory bd. Maple Psychiatry Clinic, Birmingham, Mich., 1976; cons. in field. Active, Lakes Area Little League Assn., PTA.; pres. Walled Lake Central Boosters' Club, 1974-76; pres. Peninsular Park Homeowners' Assn., 1969-72. Certified social worker, Mich. Mem. Am. Personnel and Guidance Assn., Mich. Assn. Youth Service Burs. (past pres.), Nat. Council Family Relations, Mich. Juvenile Ct. Officers' Assn., Certified Social Workers Mich., Lambda Chi Alpha. Presbyn. Home: 8056 Farrant St Union Lake MI 48085 Office: 1200 N Telegraph St Pontiac MI 48053

LAMBORN, DAVID JOSEPH, orgn. exec.; b. Canton, Ohio, Feb. 5, 1938; s. Norman Ellsworth and Louise Alberta (Zaiser) L.; B.S., Ohio U., 1961; m. Isobel Donna Allayaud, Dec. 28, 1966; children—Denise Louise, Diane Elizabeth, David Joseph II. Display advt. rep. Telegraph Republican Co., newspaper, Painesville, Ohio, 1962-63; advt. dir. Tusco Grocers, Inc., Dennison, Ohio, 1963-66; sales rep. Engring. Sales Co., Inc., mfrs. agt., Ft. Wayne, Ind., 1966; exec. dir. United Fund Central Tuscarawas County, Inc., Dover, Ohio, 1967-70, Warren County United Appeal, Lebanon, Ohio, 1970-72, Clermont County Health and Welfare Planning Council, Batavia, Ohio, 1970-74, United Way of St. Joseph County (Ind.), 1974—. Guest instr. introduction to social work Clermont br. U. Cin., Batavia, 1972. Mem. com. to initiate program Tuscarawas County (Ohio) Family Service, 1969, Youth Services Bur., Clermont County, 1972; mem. Clermont County Community Council, 1972-73. Bd. dirs. Soap Box Derby, Tuscarawas County, 1965; bd. dirs. Clermont County Community Health Centers, Inc., 1972-74, treas., 1972-73, chmn. finance com., 1972-73; founder Youth Devel. Council, Clermont County. Served with AUS, 1961. Mem. New Philadelphia (Ohio) Jaycees (pres. 1965-66); Ohio Jaycees (state trustee 1965-66). Home: 1728 E Wayne St South Bend IN 46615 Office: 3517 E Jefferson Blvd South Bend IN 46615

LAMBRECHT, ROBERT PALMER, realtor; b. Detroit, Dec. 2, 1936; s. Edward E. and Allene (Palmer) L.; B.S., U. Pa., 1959; m. Virginia McMillan, Dec. 11, 1939; children—Robert Palmer, James McM., Jeffrey F. With Lambrecht Realty Co., Detroit, 1960—, v.p., 1964-69, pres., 1969—. Mem. Gov.'s Task Force Com. on Regional Govt., 1972. Trustee Cottage Hosp., Grosse Pointe; bd. dirs. Detroit Symphony. Served with USAF, 1959-60. Mem. Mortgage Bankers Assn. Mich. (pres. 1972), Detroit Bd. Realtors (pres. 1975), Mich. Assn. Home Builders (dir. 1972—), Mich. Assn. Realtors (dir., dist. v.p. 1974—), Nat. Assn. Home Builders, Young Pres. Orgn., Mortgage Bankers Assn. Am., Nat. Assn. Realtors. Clubs: Detroit, Yondotega, Grosse Pointe, County of Detroit. Home: 56 Oxford Rd Grosse Pointe Shores MI 48236 Office: 3300 City National Bank Bldg Detroit MI 48226

LAMBRECHTS, EMILE DAUMONT, dentist; b. St. Louis, June 5, 1920; s. Emile Daumont and Julia Cecelia (Walsh) L.; student Christian Brothers Coll., 1934-38; D.D.S., St. Louis U., 1945; m. Mary Jane Catherine McCartney, Apr. 22, 1946; children—James Michael, Emile Daumont, Mary Ann, Carol Jane, Robert John. Practice gen. dentistry, St. Louis, 1947—. Health commr., Bellerive Acres Village, Mo., 1967-68; chmn. bd. Bellerive Acres Village, 1965-67. Bd. dirs. Christian Bros. Coll., Clayton, Mo., 1969-71. Served with AUS, 1943-45; served to lt. (j.g.) USNR, 1945-47. Mem. St. Louis Dental Soc. (chmn. info. 1972-76; mem. ins. bd. 1970-73, chmn., 1974, chmn. profl. affairs 1976-77), ADA, Apallonid Guild (exec. sec. 1971—), Psi Omega. Kiwanian (sec. 1960); K.C. (4 deg.). Club: Media (St. Louis). Home: 13050 Woodley Ln St Louis MO 63128 Office: 1723 S Florissant Rd St Louis MO 63031

LAMMERS, PAUL HERMAN, dentist; b. St. Helena, Nebr., Mar. 3, 1899; s. John W. and Anna (Kramer) L.; D.D.S., Creighton U., 1925; m. Mary L. Gerken, Oct. 30, 1925; children—Edward, Anna, Ann (Mrs. Konrad Lasek), Edward. Pvt. practice dentistry, Norfolk, Nebr., 1925-30, Hartington, 1930—. Served with Dental Corps, AUS, 1942-47. Fellow Am. Dental Soc.; mem. Nebr. Dental Soc., Hartington C. of C. (pres. 1949), Psi Omega. K.C. (dist. gov. 1945), Lion. Club: Hartington Country. Home: 503 Broadway Hartington NE 68739 Office: Main St Hartington NE 68739

LAMMERT, ALBERT CHARLES, obstetrician and gynecologist; b. Pitts., June 25, 1923; s. John Harry and Hannah Mae (Barr) L.; B.S., Allegheny Coll., 1944; M.D., Case Western Res. U., 1948; m. Patricia Ann Karnosh, July 9, 1949; children—Linda Anne, Nancy Louise, Gary Karnosh, David Albert. Intern, Western Pa. Hosp., 1948-59; resident in obstetrics and gynecology Univ. Hosps., Cleve., 1950-53; staff Cleve. Clinic, 1955-66; asst. clin. prof. obstetrics and gynecology Case Western Res. U., 1966—, also chief dept. obstetrics Hillcrest Hosp., Mayfield Heights, Ohio, 1975—. Diplomate Am. Bd. Obstetrics and Gynecology. Mem. Am. Coll. Obstetrics and Gynecology, Central Assn. Obstetrics and Gynecology, Ohio Med. Assn., AMA, Cleve. Soc. Obstetrics and Gynecology. Mem. United Ch. of Christ. Club: Shaker Heights Country. Home: 20725 S Woodland Rd Shaker Heights OH 44122 Office: 6803 Mayfield Rd Mayfield Heights OH 44124

LAMMINEN, ARTHUR JOHN, coll. adminstr.; b. Virginia, Minn., Oct. 25, 1912; s. John and Jeannette Maria (Mertala) L.; B.S., Tri State U., 1956, M.A., Mich. State U., 1957; Ph.D., Ind. No. U., 1969; m. Eileen Ruth MacMillen, June 22, 1935; children—Dian (Mrs. Charles M. LaTour), Sue Ann (Mrs. Sixten J. Larsen). Chemurgic researcher Ford Motor Co., Dearborn, 1931-43, supr. indsl. soybean processing, 1943-46; indsl. engring. and mgmt. cons., Dearborn, Mich., Ft. William, Ont., Can., 1946-48; mng. dir. oil seed processing Edible Oils Ltd., Ft. William, 1948-54; adminstrv. asst. to dean Coll. Bus., Grad. Sch., Mich. State U., East Lansing, 1958-62; asst. prof. mgmt. Eastern Mich. U., Ypsilanti, 1962-64, asso. prof. head dept., 1964-66; dir. occupational, vocat., tech. programs Washtenaw Community Coll., Ann Arbor, Mich., 1966—. Mediator, Govt. Mediation Service, Fort William, 1948-51; chmn. Govt. Arbitration Bd., 1951-52. Mem. ASME, Am. Mgmt. Assn., Admintrv. Mgmt. Soc., Creative Edn. Found., Am. Assn. Higher Edn., AAUP, Chemurgic Council, Alpha Kappa Psi. Mason. Home: 1219 Westmoorland Ypsilanti MI 48197 Office: Washtenaw Community Coll Ann Arbor MI 48106

LAMONT, FRANCES STILES (PEG) (MRS. WILLIAM LAMONT), state senator, civic leader; b. Rapid City, S.D., June 10, 1914; d. Frederick Bailey and Frances (Kenney) Stiles; B.A. in Journalism, U. Wis., 1935, M.A., 1936; m. William Mather Lamont, Oct. 6, 1937 (dec. Aug. 1973); children—William Stiles, Nancy Brereton Frances Margaret, Frederick Mather. Lectr. polit. sci. Presentation Coll., 1967-68, bd. trustees, 1969—; mem. S.D. Senate, 1954—, mem. joint appropriations and health and welfare coms. Active A.R.C., 1942-45; mem. S.D. Com. Edn., Gov.'s Com. White House Conf. Aging; organizer, sec. Brown County Mental Health Assn.; bd. dirs. S.D. Mental Health Assn.; state del.-at-large, bd. dirs. Nat. Assn. Mental Health, 1955-57; organizer Northeastern S.D. Mental Health Center, pres., 1958-60: mem. S.D. Women's TV Council, 1955-58; mem. Nat. Women's Adv. Council Civil Def., 1958, organizer, pres. Dacotah Prairie Mus., Inc., 1964-72, mem. Mayor's Study Com. on Low-Rent Housing, 1965—; pres. Brown County Council on Aging, 1961-68; mem. bd. Aberdeen Sr. Center Bd., 1968—; chmn. Gov.'s Com. on Aging, 1962—; gov.'s rep. Nat. Conf. State Execs. on Aging, Washington, 1963, 64, 65; vice chmn. Gov.'s Commn. on Status of Women; mem. Gov.'s Adv. Commn. on Aging, 1968—; chmn. S.D. del., subsect. chmn. White House Conf. on Aging, 1971; mem. S.D. Sr. Citizens Planning Council, 1971-72; mem. Foster Grandparents Council; mem. bd. Girl Scouts U.S.A., chmn. com. of regional bd., 1967-68 health sci. adv. council U. S.D.; v.p. S.D. adv. council Sch. for Deaf, 1976. Named First Lady of Aberdeen for civic achievement, 1954, S.D. Mother of Yr., 1974; recipient Service to mankind award Sertoma Club, 1972, S.D. Ambassador award, 1969. Mem. Am. Assn. U. Women (state bd. 1947-71, state pres. 1958-60, state historian 1961-69, trustee Nat. Edn. Found. 1971-75), DAR, P.E.O., P.T.A. (pres. 1948-49), Brown County Mus. and Hist. Soc. (pres. 1972), Interstate Assn. State Commns. on Status of Women (nat. dir. 1970-72), Nat. Soc. for Historic Preservation (dir.-at-large 1972), Phi Kappa Phi, Theta Sigma Phi, Kappa Alpha Theta, Mortar Bd. Republican (precinct committeewoman 1960—). Episcopalian (vestryman). Home: Meadowlark RFD Aberdeen SD 57401

LAMONT, WILLIAM ALEXANDER, chem. mfg. co. exec.; b. Chgo., Aug. 28, 1923; s. John and Annie Marie (Canning) L.; B.S. in Chemistry, Roosevelt U., 1950; m. Bertha Jane Carney, June 26, 1925; children—Timothy Reed, Terrence Lee, Laurel Anne. Research chemist Armour & Co., Chgo., 1950-53, Argonne Nat. Lab., Lemont, Ill., 1953-55, Nalco Chem. Co., Chgo., 1955-61; research chemist Arthur C. Trask Corp., Argo, Ill., 1961-62, tech. dir., 1962—. Served with USAAF, 1943-46. Mem. Am. Chem. Soc. Presbyn. Elk. Club: Palos Village Players. Contbr. articles to profl. jours. Patentee in field. Home: 12642 London Ln Palos Heights IL 60463 Office: 7666 W 63d St Summit IL 60501

LAMOREAUX, DELORES EVANGELINE TOM LOULA (MRS. LEE V. LAMOREAUX), coop. exec.; b. Phillips, Wis., Dec. 27, 1937; d. Joseph John and Susie (Dill) Tom; grad. high sch.; m. Franklin H. Loula, Sept. 3, 1960 (div. Mar. 1965); m. 2d, Lee V. Lamoreaux, June 7, 1969; 1 dau., Suzette Marie. With Price Electric Coop., Inc., Phillips, 1956—, sec., 1961-66, bookkeeper, 1966, mgmt. asst., 1966-73; owner, operator The Snack Shop, Phillips, 1966-67; owner Phillips Youth Center, 1967-69. Pres. Price Credit Union, Prentice, Wis., 1972—. Mem. Civil Air Patrol, 1959. Methodist (lay speaker Ch. Women's Soc. 1965-70). Mem. Women of the Moose (sr. regent 1957-58). Home: Luger Route Phillips WI 54555

LAMPING, ROBERT LEE, realtor; b. Louisville, July 20, 1931; s. Lewis H. and Nina (Messer) L.; student U. Louisville, 1957-62; m. Rosalie Lloyd, Feb. 7, 1951; children—Linda R., Lou Anne. Sales rep. IH Co., 1954-57; owner, pres. Lamping Real Estate Inc., 1959—, Serenity Inc., 1974-75. Mem. alcohol adv. bd. So. Ind. Mental Health and Guidance, 1974-75. Served with USMCR, 1951-54. Mem. Nat. Assn. Bd. Realtors, Nat. Assn. Home Builders, Nat. Assn. Real Estate Appraisors, Jr. C. of C. (dir. 1962-63). Optimist (past pres.). Club: Clarksville Swim. Home: 100 W Flamingo Dr Clarksville IN 47130 Office: 1110 Eastern Blvd Clarksville IN 47130

LAMSON, ROBERT WADE, mgmt. cons.; b. Cedar Rapids, Iowa, Aug. 27, 1915; s. Louis Bernard and Ruby Marion (Wade) L.; B.S., U. Iowa, 1937; postgrad. George Washington U., 1938, U. Mich., 1938-39; m. Frances Elizabeth Shaum, June 16, 1942; children—Robert Wade, James Shaum. Dir. personnel Container Corp. Am., Wabash, Ind., 1946-53; v.p. Conley Assos. Inc., Chgo., 1953-67; pres. Lamson, Griffiths Assos., Chgo., 1967—; dir. TAB Engrs., Inc., 1975—. Mem. Wilmette (Ill.) Human Relations Com., 1962—, pres., 1963-64; mem. Wilmette Harmony Conv., 1959; chmn. adv. bd. Tri Faith Employment Project, 1965—. Mem. Wilmette Sch. Bd. Caucus, 1959-60, New Trier Sch. Bd. Caucus, 1960-61. Bd. dirs. Chgo. Conf. Religion and Race, 1965—, Wilmette/Kenilworth FISH, 1968—, United Fund Wilmette, 1973—, Ecumenical Inst. Chgo., 1965—, Tarkio (Mo.) Coll., 1972—. Served with AUS, 1942-46; ETO. Decorated Bronze Star, Purple Heart. Mem. Pres.'s Assn. Econ. Club Chgo. Presbyn. (elder). Mason. Clubs: Union League, Tower. Home: 2236 Thornwood St Wilmette IL 60091 Office: 20 N Wacker Dr Chicago IL 60606

LANCASTER, RICHARD KIRBY, physician; b. New Richmond, Ohio, Nov. 3, 1930; s. Richard Gilmore and Laura Marie (Wood) L.; B.S., U. Cin., 1952, M.D., 1956; m. Joan Marg Mehrhoff, Aug. 8, 1953; children—Richard Kirby II, Kathy, Laura and Louise (twins), Cindy, Sharon. Intern, Fitzsimmons Army Hosp., Denver, 1956-57; flight surgeon, Charleston (S.C.) AFB, 1957-59; gen. practice medicine, Cin., 1959—; mem. staff Bethesda Hosp., Cin., Mercy Hosp., Cin.; chief staff Clermont County Hosp., 1970—; health commr. Clermont County 1969—. Mem. Clermont County Bd. Health, 1965-69. Bd. dirs. Tb Assn., 1960-71, Cancer Soc., 1960-71. Served to capt. USAF, 1956-59. Polio Found. grantee, summer 1955. Mem. Phi Chi. Baptist (chmn. bd. deacons 1965-66). Home: 1033 Batavia Pike Batavia OH 45103 Office: 684 Batavia Pike Cincinnati OH 45245

LANCE, GEORGE MILWARD, engring. adminstr., mech. engr.; b. Youngstown, Ohio, Dec. 4, 1928; s. Ray Clifford and Louisa Brigetta (Emch) L.; B.S. in Mech. Engring., Case Inst. Tech., 1952, M.S. in Instrumentation Engring., 1954; m. Phyllis Joanne Sprague, Aug. 9, 1964; children—Kathryn, Deborah, John, Rebecca, George. Instr., Case Inst. Tech., Cleve., 1952-54; research engr. TRW Inc., Cleve., 1954-56; lectr. Washington U., St. Louis, 1956-60; sr. systems engr. Moog Servocontrols Inc., East Aurora, N.Y., 1960-61; asst. prof., then prof. mech. engring. dept. U. Iowa, Iowa City, 1961—, asso. dean engring., 1974—; cons. to McDonnell Aircraft, Boeing Airplane Co., Collins Radio Co., U.S. Army Weapons Command. Served with USN, 1946-48. Registered profl. engr., Ohio, Iowa. Mem. ASME, IEEE, Am. Soc. Engring. Edn., Sigma Xi, Tau Beta Pi, Pi Tau Sigma. Patentee in valves. Home: 609 S Summit St Iowa City IA 52240 Office: Univ Iowa College Engineering Iowa City IA 52242

LANCIONE, BERNARD GABE, lawyer; b. Bellaire, Ohio, Feb. 3, 1939; s. A. G. and Phyllis June (Morford) L.; B.S. in Commerce, Ohio U., 1960; J.D., Capital U., 1966; m. Rosemary; children—Amy Jeanette, Caitin Mountain, Gillian Justin. Statistician, Ohio Dept. Hwys., Columbus, 1961-62; legal aide Office of Ohio Atty. Gen., Columbus, 1962-64; legal aide Nelson Lancione, Lawyer, Columbus, 1964-65; admitted to Ohio bar, 1965, since practiced in Bellaire; asso. A.G. Lancione, 1965-68; partner firm Lancione, Lancione & Lancione, 1968—. Solicitor, City of Bellaire, 1968-72; asst. pros. atty. Belmont County (Ohio), 1969-72. Mem. Ohio Democratic exec. com. 1969-72; pres. Young Dems. of Ohio, 1970-72; mem. Belmont County Dem. Central Com., 1970-76, exec. com., 1974-76; Southeastern Ohio coordinator John Glenn for U.S. Senate, 1973-74; legal counsel Young Dems. Clubs Am., 1971-73. Mem. Am., Ohio, Belmont County (v.p. 1976-77, pres. 1977—) bar assns., Ohio Acad. Trial Lawyers, Am. Judicature Soc., Am. Arbitration Assn. Home: PO Box 1 1425 National Rd Lansing OH 43934 Office: The Profl Complex 38th and Jefferson Sts Bellaire OH 43906

LAND, ROBERT DONALD, mgmt. cons.; b. Niagara Falls, Ont., Can., Feb. 16, 1926; s. Allan Reginald and Beatrice Beryl (Boyle) L.; B.A., U. Toronto, 1948; m. Beverly Grace Hook, July 23, 1955; children—Brian, Diane, Susan. Securities analyst Toronto (Ont.) Gen. Trusts Corp., 1948-50; actuarial accountant Crown Life Ins. Co., Toronto, 1950-53; mgmt. cons. Profl. Mgmt. Detroit, 1953-66, mng. partner, 1964-66; pres. PM Detroit, Inc., Southfield, Mich., 1966—, also dir.; v.p., dir. Black & Skaggs Assos., Inc., Battle Creek, Mich.; pres., dir. Practice Mgmt. Assos. Ltd., Toronto, Ont. Vestryman St. Joseph's Episcopal Ch., Detroit, 1956-59; coach Royal Oak Hockey Assn., Royal Oak, Mich., 1972, 74. Served with Royal Canadian Navy, 1944-46. Certified profl. bus. cons. Mem. Soc. Profl. Bus. Cons. (past dir.), Inst. Certified Profl. Bus. Cons. (past trustee), Nat. Soc. Pub. Accountants, Ind. Accountants Assn. Mich., Wayne County Med. Sch., Windsor Power Squadron, Soc. for Nautical Research. Club: Sheppard (Toronto). Home: 111 Cambridge Blvd Pleasant Ridge MI 48069 Office: 17800 Northland Park Ct Southfield MI 48075

LANDEN, WAYNE LAVERNE, ins. co. exec.; b. Rock Port, Mo., June 16, 1937; s. Axel Harry and Opal (Lindstrom) L.; B.A. in Econs. and Bus. Adminstrn., Tarkio Coll., 1959; postgrad. U. Nebr., 1969-70; m. Marsha Ann Charley, Apr. 4, 1960; children—Lynne, Nancy, Jill, Brian. Underwriter Mut. Omaha Ins. Co., Omaha, 1960-66, work measurement analyst, 1966-68, systems analyst, 1968-72, systems dir., 1972-75, asst. mgr., 1975—, equipment cons., 1976—. Loaned exec. United Community Services, 1971. Asst. ward chmn. Douglas County Republican Com., 1972-74. Bd. dirs. Nebr. Bapt. Conv., Omaha, 1969-74. Served with AUS, 1956-62. Recipient Gold Key award Omaha Jaycees, 1970; named Outstanding Local Chmn., Nebr. Jr. C. of C., 1972. Mem. Nebr. (dir. 1970-71), Omaha (dir. 1964-70, v.p., 1968-70) jr. chambers commerce, Computer Micrographics Tech., Assn. Systems Mgmt. (pres. Omaha chpt. 1976-77), Nat. Microfilm Assn., Alpha Lambda Sigma. Republican. Baptist (ch. bd. dirs. 1966-72, pres. 1968-70). Home: 320 Shorewood Ln Waterloo NE 68069 Office: 3301 Dodge St Omaha NE 68131

LANDER, JOHN CHARLES, instnl. adminstr.; b. Cleve., July 26, 1922; s. John Charles and Pauline Marie (Kikel) Lanzendorfer; B.A., Cleve. State U., 1949; m. Alyce J. Birtic, Feb. 2, 1950 (div. 1975); children—Gary, Janet, Dennis, Betty, Steven. Recreation dir. Woodhill Homes, City of Cleve., 1949-50, Cleve. Bd. Edn., 1950-52; asst. sales mgr. Electric Power Maintenance Co., Cleve., 1952-53; salesman Sears Roebuck Co., Cleve., 1954-56; sr. supervisory buyer Pesco Products div. Borg Warner Corp., 1956-72; cons. State of Ohio, Cleve., 1972-73; supt. Cleve. Reintegration Center, State of Ohio, 1973—. Served in USAAF, 1942-46. Mem. Am. Correction Assn., Internat. Halfway House Assn., Greater Cleve. Correctional Assn., Ohio Courts and Correctional Service Assn. Home: 1906 E 87th St Cleveland OH 44106 Office: 8615 Euclid Ave Cleveland OH 44106

LANDHUIS, LEO RAY, ophthalmologist; b. Marshalltown, Iowa, Apr. 21, 1935; s. Cornelius and Dorothy Lois (Rolston) L.; A.A., Northwestern Coll., 1954; B.S., McPherson Coll., 1969; M.D., U. Iowa, 1959; m. Mary Alice Smith, June 29, 1957; children—Louis Wayne, Mark David, Laura Ann, Mary Jane. Intern, Broadlawns Polk County Hosp., Des Moines, 1959-60; gen. practice medicine Kersten Clinic, Ft. Dodge, Iowa, 1960-64; resident ophthalmology U. Mo. Med. Center, Columbia, 1964-67; instr. ophthalmology Sch. Medicine, U. Mo. at Columbia, 1967-69, asst. clin. prof., 1969—; ophthalmologist Doctors Park, Columbia, 1969-73; ophthalmologist Eye Cons., Inc., Columbia Med. Center; v.p., sec. Drs. Cheek and Landhuis, Eye Consultants, Inc., Columbia, Mo., 1970—; head Lions Eye Tissue Bank of U. Mo., Columbia, 1967-75; med. dir. Lions Eye Tissue Bank of Eye Research Found., Columbia, 1975—; founder Midwest Columbia (Mo.) Regional Hosp. Bd. govs. Eye Research Found. of Mo., Inc.; trustee Mo. Sch. Religion, Columbia. Diplomate Am. Bd. Ophthalmology. Fellow Am. Acad. Ophthalmology and Otolaryngology, Mo. Ophthalmol. Soc., Inc.; mem. AMA, Mo. Med. Assn., Boone County Med. Soc., Eye Bank Assn. Am. (2d v.p.). Presbyterian. Home: 2911 Scott Blvd Columbia MO 65201 Office: Eye Consultants Inc Columbia Med Center 3205 Lansing Ave Columbia MO 65201

LANDIS, FRANK E., lawyer, ins. co. exec.; b. Seward, Nebr., Dec. 27, 1913; s. Harry D. and Mabel Alice (Cattle) L.; student Hastings Coll., 1931-33; A.B., M.A., U. Neb., 1935, LL.B., 1937; m. Ruth Jennings, June 11, 1939; children—Helen, Frank, William, David. Admitted to Nebr. bar, 1937; grad. history asst. U. Nebr., 1938; with Prince & Prince, Grand Island, Nebr., 1938-41; atty. ins. dept. State Nebr., 1941-42, asst. dir. ins., 1946-48; exec. v.p. Universal Surety Co., 1948-51; exec. v.p., sec. Empire Fire & Marine Ins. Co., 1951-64;

pres. Lincoln Bldg. Corp., 1964—, First Fidelity Life Ins. Company, 1965—, Homestead Ins. Co., 1968—. Mem. Nebr. State Bd. Edn., 1954—, v.p., 1957-58, pres., 1959-60, 64-65, 71-72, 77-78. Alt. del. Republican Nat. Conv., 1952, del., 1956, 60. Served from ensign to lt. USNR, 1942-46. Mem. Nebr. Bar Assn. (chmn. ins. sect. 1952), Ins. Fedn. Nebr. (exec. counsel 1951—), Am. Legion (post comdr. 1954-55, dept. comdr. 1960-61), V.F.W., Sigma Chi, Phi Alpha Delta, Theta Sigma Phi, Phi Kappa Delta. Congregationalist. Elk, Rotarian. Home: 2819 Van Dorn St Lincoln NE 68502 Office: Lincoln Bldg Lincoln NE 68508

LANDISS, MARK EUGENE, chem. engr.; b. Alton, Ill., Jan. 7, 1951; s. Robert Eugene and Norma Louise (Lenhardt) L.; B.S. in Chem. Engring., Washington U., St. Louis, 1974. Chemist, Shell Oil Co., Wood River, Ill., 1970, process engr., 1971-73; locksmith Able Key Co., St. Louis, 1971-74; chem. engr. Warner-Jenkinson Co., St. Louis, 1974—, mgr. phys. ops., 1976—. Recipient tech. knowledge award Locksmith Ledger. Mem. Am. Inst. Chem. Engrs. Presbyterian. Club: DeMolay. Home: 5053 Westminster Pl Saint Louis MO 63108 Office: 2526 Baldwin St Saint Louis MO 63106

LANDMAN, DAVID, univ. adminstr.; b. Phila., Oct. 24, 1917; s. Isaac and Beatrice (Eschner) L.; A.B. magna cum laude, Brown U., 1939; M.A., Columbia U., 1963; m. Joan Klein, Sept. 1, 1946 (div. 1963), children—Alicia, Michael Isaac; m. 2d, Hedy Backlin, Dec. 30, 1964. Reporter, Springfield (Mass.) Union, 1939; asso. editor Universal Jewish Ency., N.Y.C., 1939-40, sec. and chief exec., 1950-60; asst. dir. adult edn. Cooper Union, N.Y., 1959-61, chmn. Nuclear Age Conf., 1960, asst. to pres., 1961-63; asso. dir. devel., Princeton U., 1963-69; mem. faculty, dir. info. Harvard Bus. Sch., Cambridge, Mass., 1969-73; lectr. Sch. of Pub. Communication, Boston U., 1973-77; dir. pub. affairs Pathfinder Fund, 1973-77; univ. dir. pub. info. U. Ill., Chgo. and Urbana, 1977—; cons. Lesley Coll., Rider Coll., Levinson Inst. Bd. dirs. Hamilton-Madison House, 1949-69, v.p., 1960-64; chmn. parents com. Windham Coll., 1972-73. Served to maj. AUS, 1941-45. Decorated Bronze Star; Ford Found. fellow to Indonesia, 1955-56. Mem. Am. Soc. Journalists and Authors, Asia Soc., Am. Coll. Pub. Relations Assn., Phi Beta Kappa. Club: Harvard of Boston. Author: Look at America books, 1945-47; (with Joan Landman) Where to Ski, 1949; (with others) Prose by Professionals, 1961; co-editor, America Faces the Nuclear Age 1961; contbr. articles to mags. including Redbook, Coronet, Nation's Bus., New Republic; contbr. profl. articles to jours. and encys. Home: 40 E Cedar St Chicago IL 60611 Office: Office Pub Info U Ill Roosevelt Rd Bldg PO Box 4348 Chicago IL 60680

LANDON, ARNOLD GIFFORD, dentist; b. Silver City, Iowa, Sept. 27, 1911; s. Douglas and Ruth Evangiline (Whipple) L.; B.S., Iowa State U., 1940, D.D.S., 1944; m. Leona Beeler Wright, Oct. 26, 1915; children—Pamela Landon Fallesen, Lovell Theodore. Pvt. practice dentistry, Garner, Iowa, 1946—. Mem. Iowa Dental Health Council, 1970—. Mem. Garner City Council, 1961-62, mayor, 1962-70. Served with USNR, 1931-37, 42-46; comdr. Res. ret. Mem. North Central Dental Soc. (pres. 1958-59), Royal Soc. Health. Presbyn. (trustee, elder 1960-75). Mason (Shriner), Rotarian (pres. 1956-57). Home: 715 Division St Garner IA 50438 Office: 160 W 4th St Garner IA 50438

LANDSBERG, DEAN ARNOLD, psychologist; b. Independence, Mo., Jan. 17, 1946; s. Lewis Emaley and Irene Ester (Shriver) L.; student Graceland Coll., 1964-66; B.S., U. South Ala., 1968; M.S., Central Mo. State U., 1972; m. Janice Lynn Branch, Mar. 9, 1973; children—Dana, Amy. Clin. casework asst. Western Mo. Mental Health Center, Kansas City, 1969-71; psychol. intern, staff psychologist Greater Kansas City Mental Health Found., 1972-73; staff psychologist Marillac Home and Sch., Kansas City, 1973—; pvt. practice psychology Assos. in Psychol. & Family Services, Independence, 1977—. Dir. youth Christ Ch. Unity, 1974—, dir. psychol. services, 1977—. Mem. Greater Kansas City (program chmn. 1975—), Am. (asso.), Mo. (asso.), psychol. assns., Psi Chi. Home: 15316 E 49th St Kansas City MO 64136 Office: 310 W 106th St Kansas City MO 64114 also Suite 152 12401 E 43 St Independence MO 64055

LANDSTROM, DONALD ALBERT, food broker; b. Chgo., Mar. 14, 1929; s. Harlow Albert and Loretta Sophia (Erickson) L.; B.B.A., U. Minn., 1951; m. Marilyn Jean Hicks, June 11, 1955; children—Scott, Gregg. With Fist Brokerage Co., Minnetonka, Minn., 1953—, treas., 1971—, exec. v.p., 1977—, also dir. Served as officer USN, 1951-53. Mem. Inst. Food Technologists. Episcopalian. Home: 2961 Tonkaha Dr Wayzata MN 55391 Office: 6026 Blue Circle Dr Minnetonka MN 55343

LANDWEHR, ARTHUR JOHN, JR., clergyman; b. Highland Park, Ill., Mar. 8, 1934; s. Arthur John and Alice Eleanor (Borchardt) L.; B.A., Drake U.; B.D., Garrett Theol. Sem., 1959; grad. student U. Chgo., 1960-62; postgrad. (fellow) Contemporary Theol. Inst., Montreal, Que., Can., 1969, Stellenbosch Theol. Sem., South Africa, 1973; m. Avonna Lee Mitchell, Sept. 19, 1953; children—Arthur John III, Andrea Lea. Ordained to ministry, United Methodist Ch., 1957; pastor chs., Lyndon, Ill., 1956-59, Marseilles (Ill. United Methodist Ch., 1959-65, Faith United Methodist Ch., Lisle, Ill., 1965-69, First United Meth. Ch., Elmhurst, Ill., 1969-75, First United Methodist Ch. of Evanston, Ill., 1975—; chmn. Commn. on Ecumenical Affairs, United Meth. Ch., 1972-76; faculty mem. Ecumenical Lay Acad., 1970-75; founder Friends of the Christian Inst. of South Africa. Bd. dirs. Ch. Fedn. Greater Chgo.; bd. dirs. John Wesley Theol. Inst.; trustee Garrett Evang. Theol. Sem., 1976—, chmn. com. academic affairs, 1977—. Mem. Am. Acad. Religion, AAAS, Am. Theol. Assn. Rotarian. Author: In the Third Place, 1972. Home: 310 Church St Evanston IL 60201

LANDY, AGATHA HORRIGAN (MRS. THOMAS M. LANDY), realtor; b. Cleve.; d. Lawrence and Catherine (Day) Horrigan; student Cleve. Coll., 1931, John Carroll U., 1932-33; m. Thomas M. Landy, Jan. 23, 1943 (dec. Mar. 1955); children—Thomas M., John C., Philip F., Robert J., Kevin P. Pres., Agatha Horrigan Landy & Sons Inc., Realtors, Cleve., 1956—. Mem. Nat., Cleve. bds. realtors, Internat. Platform Assn. Club: Cleve. Skating. Office: 2647 Berkshire Rd Cleveland OH 44106 Office: 30650 Pinetree St Pepper Pike OH 44124

LANE, DALE WALTER, counselor, adminstr.; b. Adrian, Mich., Sept. 22, 1938; s. Floyd Lorart and Lela Belle (Vansickle) L.; B.A., Andrews U., Berrian Springs, Mich., 1970, M.A., 1971; postgrad. Leadership Devel. Program for Vocat.-Tech. Sch. Adminstrs., U. Mich., 1975; m. Carol Ann Wolf, Jan. 11, 1965; children—Christopher, Todd. With Simplex Paper Corp., Adrian, 1959-67; dir. counseling Lenawee County Vocat.-Tech. Sch., Adrian, 1971—; mem. Mich. Career Edn. Commn., 1976—; chmn. Mich. Supts. Task Force Counseling. Mem. Am., Mich. personnel and guidance assns., Mich. Sch. Counselors Assn. (pres. 1976), Lenawee County Counselors Assn. Club: Kinawis. Home: 1575 Ives St Tecumseh MI 49286 Office: 2345 N Adrian Hwy Adrian MI 49286

LANE, HAROLD EDWIN, educator; b. Malden, Mass., Aug. 19, 1913; s. Edwin George and Annabel (Fraser) L.; B.S., Boston U., 1936, M.A., 1940; m. Constance Mason, June 1, 1940; children—Stephen Winslow, Harold Edwin, Nancy. Asst. sec. Greater Boston Community Fund, 1940-42; sr. economist Nat. War Labor Bd., Boston, also Portland, Oreg., 1942-46; dir. personnel Sordoni Industries, Wilkes-Barre, Pa., 1946-47; v.p. Sheraton Corp. of Am., Boston, 1947-68; v.p. Fred Harvey, Inc., Chgo., 1968-70; asso. prof. Coll. Bus., Mich. State U., East Lansing, 1970—; manpower cons. U.S. Navy; dir. Sheraton-St. Charles Corp., New Orleans; summer sch. instr. Cornell U., 1949-68; spl. lectr. Harvard. Mem. Pres.'s Advisory Com. on Occupational Safety; mem. Council on Pres.'s Plans for Progress; nat. advisory com. Job Corps, Office Econ. Opportunity; chmn. Mich. Wage Deviation Bd.; participant seminar Harvard Bus. Sch., 1963; cons. Ford Found. N.Y., 1963; seminar instr. Am. Mgmt. Assn., 1964. Trustee New Eng. Hotel-Motel and Restaurant Ednl. Found., Inc. Mem. Mass. Audubon Soc. (dir.), Soc. Advancement Mgmt., Am. Mgmt. Assn., Am. Hotel and Motel Assn., Am. Sociol. Assn., Indsl. Relations Research Assn., Nat. Indsl. Conf. Bd., U.S. C. of C. Congregationalist (bd. deacons). Contbr. articles to profl. jours. Home: 4382 Okemos Rd Apt 216G Okemos MI 48864 Office: Coll Business Mich State U East Lansing MI 48823

LANE, JAMES A., lawyer; b. Denver, Nov. 13, 1915; student Regis Coll.; J.D., Creighton U., 1940. Admitted to Nebr. bar, 1940, practiced law, Ogallala. Pres. bd. trustees Nebr. State Colls., 1969. Served to lt. USNR, 1942-45. Fellow Am. Coll. Trial Lawyers; mem. Nebr. (pres. to 1972), Am. bar assns., Am. Trial Lawyers Assn., Am. Judicature Soc., Servientes Ad Legem. Address: Box 119 Ogallala NE 69153

LANE, JOHN CLYDE, chem. engr.; b. Conneaut, Ohio, Oct. 15, 1919; s. Clyde Henry and Nancy Marie (Painter) L.; B.S. (Rochester Prize scholar), U. Rochester, 1942; m. Margaret Adams Hudgins, Dec. 28, 1951; children—John Christian, Anne-Elizabeth. Research engr. Gulf Research & Devel. Co., Pitts., 1942-43, tech. info. specialist, 1943-45, head tech. info. sect., 1945-48; head tech. info. services Inst. Gas Tech., Chgo., 1948-50; research prof., head tech. info. div. Ga. Tech. Engring. Exptl. Sta., Atlanta, 1950-53; tech. analyst, writer Ethyl Corp. Research Labs., Detroit, 1953-54, staff asst., 1954-56, supt. tech. info., Ferndale, Mich., 1956—; trustee Engring. Index Inc., 1966-72. Mem. steering com. Citizens Com. on Edn., Birmingham, Mich., 1958-60. Mem. Am. Chem. Soc., Soc. for Tech. Communication (adv. bd. S.E. Mich. chpt. 1971-72), Internat. Platform Assn., Tau Beta Pi, Theta Delta Chi. Club: Torch (pres. 1968) (Oakland County, Mich.). Author: The Synthine Process, 1948; Technology of the Fischer-Tropsch Process, 1949. Editor: Petroleum Refining Developments, Ethyl Corp. monthly publ., 1954-71, 76—; Internat. Petroleum Refining News Digest, 1975—. Contbr. to publs. in field. Home: 1678 Maryland Blvd Birmingham MI 48009 Office: 1600 W Eight Mile Rd Ferndale MI 48220

LANE, LOUIS, musician, conductor; b. Eagle Pass, Tex., Dec. 25, 1923; s. William Bartlett and Virginia (Gardner) L.; B.Mus. summa cum laude, U. Tex. 1943; Mus.M., Eastman Sch. Music, 1947. Mem. Cleve. Orch., 1947-73, asso. condr., 1960-70, resident condr., 1970-73; condr. Akron (O.) Symphony Orch., 1959—; prin. guest condr. Dallas Symphony Orch., 1973—; guest condr. in Chgo., Seattle, St. Louis, Detroit, Houston, San Antonio, Vancouver, B.C., Can., Montevideo, Uruguay; mus. dir. Lake Erie Opera Theatre, Cleve., 1964-73; co-dir. Blossom Festival Sch. of Cleve. Orch. and Kent State U., 1969-73; adj. prof. music Akron U., 1969—; rec. artist Columbia Records. Served with F.A., AUS 1943-46. Mem. Phi Mu Alpha, Pi Kappa Lambda. Home: 14315 Terrace Rd Cleveland OH 44112 Office: E J Thomas Hall Akron OH 44303

LANE, ORRIS JOHN, JR., civil engr.; b. Sigourney, Iowa, Apr. 21, 1932; s. Orris John and Hester Hanna (Hazen) L.; B.S., Iowa State U., 1957; m. Joan Joyce Nelson, June 19, 1954; children—Jerry Paul, Beth Ann, Dona Sue, Seth Thomas. Asst. dist. materials engr. Iowa Hwy. Commn., Ames, 1957-62, spl. projects engr., 1962-64, portland cement concrete engr., 1964-73, dist. materials engr., Atlantic, 1973—. Project group adv. mem. NCHPR, Washington, 1972—. Served with AUS, 1953-55. Registered profl. engr., Iowa. Mem. Nat. Soc. Profl. Engrs., Iowa Engring. Soc., Orgn. Transp. and State Employees (bd. dirs. 1968—). Methodist. Home: Route 1 Wiota IA 50274 Office: PO Box 406 Atlantic IA 50022

LANE, RICHARD OSCAR, marketing exec.; b. Ironton, Ohio, June 15, 1905; s. Harry Foster and Mary Elizabeth (Hannon) L.; B.Ceramic Engring., Ohio State U., 1930, Profl. Engr., 1940; S.M. in Ceramics, Mass. Inst. Tech., 1936; m. Laura Mae Schindler, Feb. 18, 1949; children—Charles Paul, Richard Allen, Ollire Florence. Ceramic engr. Norton Co., Worcester, Mass., 1930-33; ceramic engr. Macklin Co., Jackson, Mich., 1936-40, v.p., 1950-65; dir. engring. abrasives div. Bendix Corp., Jackson, 1967-70; dir. mktg. Frank Bancroft Co. Inc., Dearborn, Mich., 1970—, cons. in field; mem. safety com. Grinding Wheel Inst., Cleve., 1960-70. Mem. Occupational Safety Commn., Mich., 1969—: chmn. bd. Ella W. Sharp Park, Jackson, 1941-45. Fellow ASME (exec. chmn. prodn. div. 1969-70); mem. Soc. Mfg. Engrs., Am. Soc. Metals, Keramos. Episcopalian. Club: Jackson Rotary (hon.). Contbr. articles to profl. jours. Patentee in field. Home: 878 White Lake Rd Pleasant Lake MI 49272 Office: 23841 Kean Ave Dearborn MI 48123

LANE, ROBERT JOSEPH, motel exec.; b. Port Jervis, N.Y., July 1, 1922; s. Francis Aloyisius and Katherine Berta Ursula (Scarsi) L.; student Georgetown U., 1948-49, John Carroll U., 1958-60; m. Clarissa Geneva Hein, Aug. 16, 1950 (div. 1977); children—Robert, Stephen, Phillip, Eric. U.S. diplomatic courier, 1946-50; sales rep. with various firms, 1953-58; asst. mgr. Statler Hilton Corp., Cleve., 1958-60, Auditorium Hotel, Cleve., 1960-62; auditor, mgr. Howard Johnson Motor Lodges, Cleve., 1962-66; asst. mgr. Sheraton Hotel, Cleve., 1966-69; mgr. Port-O-Call Motor Inn, Brook Park, Ohio, 1969-75; gen. mgr. Exec. Inn, Fairview Park, Ohio, 1976—; developer Villa Valtellina, exec. conf. center, 1977. Served with USAAF, 1942-46; 1st lt. USAF, 1950-53. Winner Mobil Oil 4-Star award, 1973-74. Mem. U.S. Diplomatic Courier Assn. (life), Hotel Motel Sales Mgr. Assn. (v.p. 1961-62). Patentee in field. Home: 5500 Laurent Dr Parma OH 44129 Office: PO Box 81091 Cleveland OH 44181

LANE, RUSSELL WATSON, chemist; b. Morrison, Ill., June 18, 1911; s. Ralph Thomas and Elizabeth Loretta (Alldritt) L.; B.S., Knox Coll., 1933; M.S., Ill. Inst. Tech., 1945; m. Ione Sundberg, June 16, 1934; children—Joan Karen, Patricia Diane. Chemist, Libby McNeill & Libby, Morrison, Ill., 1933-41; research chemist Nalco Chem. Co., Chgo., 1941-45, chief phys. chemist, 1945-47, water treatment engr., 1947-49; chemist Ill. State Water Survey, Champaign, 1949-65, sr. chemist, 1965-77, head chemistry sect., 1977—. Recipient Boss of Year award Champaign-Urbana Jr. C. of C., 1971, Edn. with Industry awards USAF, 1971-74; registered profl. engr., Ill., Calif. Mem. Am. Chem. Soc., Nat. Assn. Corrosion Engrs., Am. Water Works Assn., ASME, ASTM (Max Hecht award 1978), Sigma Xi, Phi Lambda Upsilon. Presbyterian. Club: Lions. Contbr. articles to profl. jours. Patentee in field. Home: 1207 Devonshire Dr Champaign IL 61820 Office: 605 E Springfield Ave Champaign IL 61820

LANE, THOMAS BENTON, dentist; b. Kenosha, Wis., Oct. 25, 1911; s. Hiram Herbert and Jessie (Cooper) L.; student Colby Coll., 1929; B.S., Marquette U., 1935, D.D.S., 1936; m. Eleanore Robinson Jones, July 16, 1938; children—Janet Katherine, Susan (Mrs. Thomas C. Haller), William Stratton. Practice dentistry, Kenosha, 1936-42, 46-78. Mem. exec. council Kenosha council Boy Scouts Am., 1962-73, v.p., 1970. Bd. dirs. A.R.C., Kenosha, 1967-71, chpt. chmn., 1969-71, bd. dirs. LaKeshore Counties chpt., 1971-78, chmn. bldg. com., 1973-78; chmn. Kenosha Bd. Health, 1971-74; bd. dirs. Wiebrecht Found, Milw., 1963-69, pres., 1968-69; bd. dirs., pres. Wiebrecht-Crozat Inst., Milw., 1968—. Served with USNR, 1942-46. Fellow Internat. Coll. Dentists (life, dep. regent 1968-75); mem. Dental Forum (life, pres. 1951), Am. Acad. Periodontology, Am. Acad. Gnathologic Orthopedics (dir. 1968—, sec. 1973-75), Wis. Soc. Dentistry for Children (co-founder 1950; pres. 1952), Wis. Dental Service (dir. 1962-69), Am. (life), Wis. (life) dental assns., Kenosha County Dental Soc. (life), Zeta Psi. Episcopalian. Mason, Rotarian. Home: 1234 Garrett Bay Rd Ellison Bay WI 54210

LANE, WILFRED ROGER, elec. engr.; b. Detroit, June 14, 1954; s. Eldon R. and Anna Marie (Briolat) L.; B.S.E., U. Mich., 1976. Instr. electronic tech. Delta U., University Center, Mich., 1976—; instrument engr. Dow Chem. Co., Midland, Mich., 1976—. Sheldon engring. scholar, 1975-76. Mem. IEEE, Soc. Profl. Engrs., Intrument Soc. Am. Home: 2406 Brookfield Ln Midland MI 48640 Office: Dow Chem Co 800 Bldg Midland MI 48640

LANG, FRANCIS H., lawyer; b. Manchester, Ohio, June 4, 1907; s. James Walter and Mary (Harover) L.; A.B., Ohio Wesleyan Univ., 1929; J.D., Ohio State, 1932; m. Rachel Boyce, Oct. 20, 1934; children—Mary Sue, Charles Boyce, James Richard. Practice of law, East Liverpool, Ohio, 1932-42, 45—; with U.S. War Dept., 1942-45; pres., dir. First Fed. Savs. & Loan Assn.; dir. 1st Nat. Bank East Liverpool, First Nat. Bank Chester, W.Va.; dir., pres. Walter Lang Co., Lang Blue Flame Gas Co., dir., sec., asst. treas. Sayre Electric Contracting Inc., Electric Wholesaling, Inc.; dir., sec. Frank Crook, Inc. Bd. dirs. YMCA, Mary Patterson Meml., East Liverpool, Columbiana County Motor Club; mem. exec. bd. Columbiana council Boy Scouts Am., mem. at large Nat. Council, recipient Silver Beaver award, Silver Antelope award. Trustee Cope Methodist Home. Mem. Ohio State Jr. (past pres.) U.S. Jr. (nat. dir. 1941-42), East Liverpool chambers commerce, Columbiana (past pres.), Ohio, Am. bar assns. Methodist (mem. adminstrv. bd. 1933—, del. World Meth. Conf. 1971, 76, mem. bd. dirs. global ministries 1968-76). Clubs: East Liverpool Country, Rotary (dist. gov. 1973-74). Home: PO Box 103 Highland Colony East Liverpool OH 43920 Office: Potters Savings and Loan Bldg East Liverpool OH 43920

LANG, WILLIAM EDWARD, lawyer; b. Tiffin, Ohio, Sept. 20, 1935; s. William E. and Martha (Lutz) L.; A.B., Ohio No. U., 1957, J.D., 1959; m. Tanyce M. Spitzer, Mar. 21, 1959; children—Gregg, Mark. Admitted to Ohio bar, 1959; practice in Sidney, 1960—; asso. Rodney Blake, 1960-68; city solicitor, Sidney, 1962—. Mem. Shelby County Bar Assn. (pres. 1969, 70). Club: Optimist (charter pres. 1962—) (Sidney). Home: 2033 Wells Dr Sidney OH 45365 Office: 318 S Ohio Ave Sidney OH 45365

LANGE, FREDERICK EMIL, lawyer; b. Washington, May 24, 1908; s. Emil F. and Jane (Austin) L.; A.B., U. Nebr., 1928; LL.B., M.P.L., Washington Coll. Law, 1932; m. Leila M. Benedict, Sept. 11, 1930; children—Frederick Emil, David W., James A. Admitted to D.C. bar, 1932, Minn. bar, 1943; examiner U.S. Patent Office, 1929-35; patent lawyer Honeywell, Inc., 1935-63, mgr. Mpls. patent dept., 1954-63; partner firm Dorsey, Marquart, Windhorst, West & Halladay, Mpls., 1965-73; individual practice law, Mpls., 1973—; spl. lectr. patent law U. Minn., 1949-51; tchr. Minn. Continuing Legal Edn., 1976. Bd. trustees 1st Unitarian Soc., 1970-71; chmn. Minn. br. World Federalists, 1958-60, nat. exec. com., 1958-64; bd. dirs. Group Health Plan, Inc., 1967—, 1st v.p., 1975—; bd. dirs. St. Paul Civic Symphony Assn., 1976—, Environ. Learning Center, 1977—. Recipient Distinguished Service award U. Nebr., 1968. Mem. Am., Minn., D.C., Hennepin County bar assns., Am., Minn. (pres. 1954-55) patent law assns., Am. Judicature Soc. Holder U.S. patents. Home: 25 Paisley Ln Minneapolis MN 55422 Office: 815 Midwest Plaza Bldg Minneapolis MN 55402

LANGELER, GEORGE HARRIS, coll. adminstr.; b. Elmhurst, Ill., Dec. 2, 1927; s. George Adrian and Mary Elizabeth (Santee) L.; B.S., Elmhurst Coll., 1949; M.S., U. Ill., 1950; Ph.D., U. Mich., 1959. Instr. biology Elmhurst Coll., 1950-54, asst. prof. biology, 1954-55, head resident, 1951-55, trustee, 1974—; resident adviser U. Mich., 1955-56, resident dir., 1956-59; acting asso. dean arts and scis. Oberlin Coll., 1959, registrar, 1959-62, dir. financial aid, 1962-64, asso. dean arts and scis., 1964-66, dean of students, 1966—, lectr. biology, 1961—, lectr. human devel., 1975—, dir. human devel. program, 1973-75; examiner, cons. North Central Assn., 1961—, mem. com. on undergrad. edn., 1973-76; affiliate mem., group leader Workshop for Living Learning, N.Y.C., 1975. Mem. Ohio Acad. Sci., Assn. Higher Edn., Nat. Assn. Student Personnel Adminstrs., AAUP, Am. Coll. Personnel and Guidance Assn., Phi Delta Kappa, Phi Kappa Phi. Home: 173 Hollywood St Oberlin OH 44074 Office: 109 Peters Hall Oberlin OH 44074

LANGER, JOHN BOHUMIL, govt. ofcl.; b. Coopersburg, Pa., Dec. 19, 1926; s. John and Mary (Pechacek) L.; A.B., Princeton, 1950; M.A., George Washington U., 1966; grad. Advanced Mgmt. Program, Harvard U., 1971; m. Phyllis Anne Baker, June 27, 1953; children—John, Jane, Susan, Becky. Asst. to dean and to dir. student aid Princeton, 1950-52; personnel officer U.S. CSC, Washington, 1952-57; dir. personnel and security Airways Modernization Bd., Washington, 1957-59; various positions in personnel mgmt., tng. and mgmt. analysis FAA, Washington, 1959-64; asst. to dist. dir. IRS, Balt., 1965-66, asst. dist. dir., Atlanta, 1966-69, dist. dir., Aberdeen, S.D., 1969—; part-time instr. human relations and personnel mgmt. Presentation Coll., Aberdeen, 1970—; instr. law enforcement U. S.D., 1975—, mem. criminal justice studies adv. bd., 1977—. Mem. edn. com. Fairfax County (Va.) Fedn. Citizens Assns., 1962-63; mem. membership com. Nat. Capitol Area Health and Welfare Council 1961-62; chmn. Sand Lake dist. Boy Scouts Am., 1974—; mem. bus. adv. council No. State Coll., Aberdeen, 1974—; mem. Pub. Schs. Adv. Com., Aberdeen, 1974—. Bd. dirs. Aberdeen Area United Way. Served with AUS, 1945-46. Recipient Meritorious award William A. Jump Award Com., 1962. Mem. Atlanta Assn. Fed. Execs. (v.p. 1970), Aberdeen Fed. Execs. Assn. (pres. 1975). Conglist. Contbr. articles to mags. and newspapers. Home: 1003 S Jay St Aberdeen SD 57401 Office: 115 4th Ave SE Aberdeen SD 57401

LANGHAM, MICHAEL, theatrical dir.; b. Somerset, Eng., Aug. 22, 1919; s. Seymour and Muriel (Andrews Speed) L.; student Radley Coll., Abingdon, Eng., 1933-37, London U., 1937-39; D.Litt. (hon.), McMaster U., 1962, St. Scholastica Coll., 1973; LL.D., U. Toronto, 1966; m. Helen Burns, July 8, 1948 (div. 1972); 1 son, Christopher; m. 2d, Ellen Gorky. Engaged in theatrical profession, 1946—; dir. prodns. Arts Council Midland Theatre Co., 1946-48, Sir Barry Jackson's Birmingham Repertory Theatre, 1948-50, Glasgow Citizen's Theatre, 1953-54; artistic dir. Tyrone Guthrie Theater, Mpls., 1971—, including direction Relapse, 1972, Oedipus the King,

1972, 73, The Government Inspector, 1973, The Merchant of Venice, 1973, King Lear, 1974, Love's Labour's Lost, 1974, School for Scandal, 1974; dir. Julius Caesar at Stratford-upon-Avon, 1950, Stratford, Ont., 1955; dir. The Gay Invalid, London, 1950, Pygmalion, London, 1951, The Other Heart, London, 1951; dir. Old Vic Co. prodn. Othello at Berlin Festival, also London, 1951; Brit. Council lectr., Australia, 1952; dir. Richard III, Belgian Nat. Theatre, 1952, The Merry Wives of Windsor, The Hague, 1953; artistic dir. Stratford (Ont.) Shakespearean Festival, 1955—, including direction Hamlet, 1957, Henry IV, Part I, 1958, Much Ado About Nothing, 1958, Romeo and Juliet, 1960, Coriolanus, 1961, Love's Labour's Lost, 1961, Taming of the Shrew, 1962, Cyrano de Bergerac, 1962, Troilus and Cressida, 1963, Timon of Athens, 1963, King Lear, 1964, The Country Wife, 1964, also prodns. Love's Labour's Lost and Timon of Athens at Festival Theatre, Chichester, Eng., 1964; dir. Hamlet, Stratford-upon-Avon, 1956, Merchant of Venice, 1960, Much Ado About Nothing, 1961; dir. Henry V, Edinburgh Festival, 1956, Two Gentlemen of Verona, London, 1957, A Midsummer Night's Dream, London, 1960, Andorra, N.Y.C., 1963; compiler, dir. univ. tour Can. and U.S. on Shakespearean comedy, 1962; author, dir. The Affliction of Love for TV, 1963; artistic cons. LaJolla (Cal.) Theater Project, 1965. Served with Brit. Army, 1939-45. Address: The Guthrie Theater 725 Vineland Pl Minneapolis MN 55403

LANGSTON, JUDY ANN, photographer; b. Evergreen Park, Ill., Jan. 1, 1950; d. John and Marcella (Radicke) Langston; B.A., U. Ill., Chgo., 1973, M.A., Urbana, 1975; postgrad. Ill. Inst. Tech., Universidad Valencia. Photographer, slide and photography library U. Ill., Chgo., 1972-74; sci. photographer Ill. Eye and Ear Infirmary, 1974-76; free lance photographer, Chgo., 1976—; instr. pvt. classes, 1977—. Lydia Bates scholar, 1972-73; certified sci. photographer NIH. Mem. U. Ill. Alumni Assn. One-woman show: Montgomery Ward Gallery, Chgo., 1973; group shows: Hyde Park Art Center, 1973, DePaul U., Chgo., 1973; work published in Artists U.S.A., 1976, 77, 78, 79. Home: 1122 Kemman St LaGrange Park IL 60525 Office: 1516 Taylor St W Chicago IL 60607

LANKER, KARL EMIL, cons. indsl. engr.; b. Absecon, N.J., Aug. 15, 1925; s. Karl Warner and Martha (Jesuncosky) L.; B.S. in Indsl. Engring., Rutgers U., 1951; postgrad. Ohio U., 1972, 74; m. Virginia L. Brown, Sept. 22, 1956; children—M. Kathleen, Debra A. Corporate indsl. engr., mgr. Anchor Hocking Corp., Lancaster, Ohio, 1951-56, chief plant indsl. engr., 1956-59, chief div. indsl. engr., 1959-62, corporate planning coordinator, 1962-65, acting corporate chief indsl. engr., 1965-67; facilities planning mgr. Lancaster Colony, 1967-69; cons. engr., prin. E. Ralph Sims, Jr. & Assos., Inc., Lancaster, 1969—; mem. Active Corps Execs., SBA. Served with USNR, 1943-46; PTO. Registered profl. engr., Ohio, N.J., Calif. Mem. Am. Inst. Indsl. Engrs. (nat. dir. facilities planning and design div. 1975-76), Profl. Engrs. in Pvt. Practice, Internat. Material Mgmt. Soc. (certified), Assn. Mgmt. Cons., Nat. (dir. 1972), Ohio socs. profl. engrs., Soc. Mfg. Engrs. (certified), Lancaster C. of C., Am. Legion, Chi Phi. Methodist. (dir. 1970-73). Elk, Kiwanian. Club: Toastmasters (regional dir. 1954, pres. Lancaster 1975-76). Home: Route 1 1290 Wheeling Rd Lancaster OH 43130 Office: PO Box 646 Lancaster OH 43130

LANKFORD, RONALD BRADLEY, diversified mfg. co. exec.; b. Marietta, Ohio, Sept. 14, 1935; s. Loren Herbert and Mabel Louise (Britton) L.; B.S., Ohio U., 1959; M.B.A., Western Reserve U., 1964; m. Jean Anne Braun, June 7, 1958; children—Kathryn Lynn, Karen Lee, Ronald Bradley. Staff auditor Price Waterhouse & Co., Cleve., 1959-61; accountant William Feather Co., Cleve, 1961-64; v.p. accounting, control Clairmont Transfer Co., Escanaba, Mich., 1964-73; v.p., dir. Peninsula Air Transport Co., 1967-73; v.p. finance Spector Freight System, Inc., Chgo., 1973-77, also Spector Industries, Chgo.; v.p., treas. Buckeye Internat., 1977—, chmn. Buckeye Internat., Ltd., 1977—; instr. Bay de Noc Community Coll., 1965-69. Dir., chmn. Indsl. div., Delta United Services., 1966-73; chmn. fund raising Boy Scouts Am., 1971—. Chmn. Escanaba City Planning Commn., 1966-69; mem. Escanaba Area Sch. Bd., 1968-71. Served with USMCR, 1954-56. C.P.A., Ohio Mem. Am. Inst. C.P.A.'s, Nat. Assn. of Accountants, Am. Trucking Assn. (mem. nat. accounting and finance council 1964—, regional dir. 1971—), Fin. Execs. Inst. Contbr. articles to profl. jours. Home: 11 Shady Ln Ferndale Woods Barrington IL 60010

LANNING, JAMES WILLIAM, publishing co. exec.; b. Logan, Ohio, May 3, 1941; s. Wilbur Warren and Ruth Emily (Dill) L.; B.S., Ohio State U., 1963; m. Ruth Eilene McGrath, Aug. 30, 1969; children—Jennifer, Christina, James. Auditor, AT&T, Columbus, Ohio, 1965-69, Alexander Grant & Co., Columbus, 1969-70; treas. Lincoln Library Encyclopedia, Columbus, 1970—. L.P.A., Ohio. Mem. Pub. Accountants Soc. Ohio, Ohio State U. Assn. (life). Club: Pinehurst Country. Home: and Office: 848 Colony Way Worthington OH 43085

LANNON, JOHN JOSEPH, utility co. exec.; b. Springfield, Ill., Apr. 8, 1937; s. Richard James and Anne (Malone) L.; B.S., U. Ill., 1961; M.B.A., U. Chgo., 1970; m. Arlene Joan Mularski, Sept. 2, 1976; children—John Joseph, Susan Kay, Laura Colleen; stepchildren—Kurt Henry, Karen Joan, Lynne Eileen Feuerschwenger. Accountant Arthur Andersen & Co., Chgo., 1961-66; gen. staff accountant No. Ill. Gas Co., Aurora, Ill., 1966-67, mgr. tech. accounting, 1967-68, asst. comptroller, 1968-70, asst. treas., 1970-71, comptroller, 1971-73, asst. v.p., asst. treas., 1973, treas., 1973-75, v.p., controller, 1975—; dir. State Bank of Saunemin, 1962—. Bd. dirs. Naperville YMCA, Chgo. Community Ventures, Inc. Served with AUS, 1956-58. C.P.A., Ill. Mem. Am. Inst. C.P.A.'s, Accounting Research Assn., Am., Midwest gas assns., Tax Inst. of Am., Sigma Pi, Beta Alpha Psi. Clubs: Executives, Economic (Chgo.). Home: 1716 Towpath Ct Naperville IL 60540 Office: East-West Tollway at Route 59 PO Box 190 Aurora IL 60507

LANO, CHARLES JACK, mfg. co. exec.; b. Port Clinton, Ohio, Apr. 17, 1922; s. Charles Herbin and Antoinette (Schmitt) L.; B.S. in Bus. Adminstrn. summa cum laude, Ohio State U., 1949; m. Beatrice Irene Spees, June 16, 1946; children—Douglas Cloyd, Charles Lewis. With U.S. Gypsum Co., 1941-46, Ottawa Paper Stock Co., 1946-47; accountant Arthur Young & Co., C.P.A.'s, Tulsa, 1949-51; controller Lima div. Ex-Cell-O Corp., 1951-59, electronics div. AVCO Corp., 1959-61, Servomation Corp., 1961; asst. comptroller Scovill Mfg. Co., Waterbury, Conn., 1961-62, comptroller, 1962-67; controller CF&I Steel Corp., Denver, 1967-69, v.p., controller, 1969-70; controller Pacific Lighting Corp., 1970-76; exec. v.p. Arts-Way Mfg. Co., Armstrong, Iowa, 1976—. Served with USMCR, 1942-45, C.P.A., Okla. Mem. Am. Inst. C.P.A.'s, Iowa Soc. C.P.A.'s, Fin. Exec. Inst., Nat. Assn. Accountants, Am. Mgmt. Assn. (lectr. financial control). Office: Arts-Way Mfg Co Armstrong IA 50514

LANTOLF, JOSEPH JOHN, cosmetic and toiletries co. exec.; b. Scarnton, Pa., Aug. 22, 1932; s. John Paul and Mildred Marie (Chiorrizzi) L.; B.S., U. Scranton, 1957; postgrad. St. John's U., L.I. U., 1958; m. Ann Louise Needham, Aug. 23, 1958; children—Holly, Heidi, Paul, Joseph, Heather. Research fellow St. John's U., 1958; research asso. Sterling-Winthrop Research Inst., Albany, N.Y., 1958-61; dir. research and devel. adminstrn. Alberto-Culver Co., Melrose Park, Ill., 1962-76; corporate dir. compliance and quality assurance Hollister Inc., Chgo., 1977—. Pres. Park Manor Civic Assn., 1968; ward capt., 1973; chmn. Little League, Glenview, Ill., 1975. Mem. Soc. Indsl. Microbiology, Am. Soc. Microbiology, Phi Gamma Kappa. Club: K.C. Home: 1821 Harrison St Glenview IL 60025

LANTZ, CHARLES EMIL, lawyer; b. Walnut Grove, Minn., Oct. 20, 1910; s. Charles Emil and Maude Charlotte (Halvorson) L.; student Gustavus Adolphus Coll., 1927-29; B.A., U. Minn., 1931, J.D., 1934; m. Doris L. Greenwood, Nov. 25, 1938; children—W. Charles, Eric John. Admitted to Minn. bar, 1934; since practiced in Walnut Grove; village atty., 1937—; partner Walnut Grove Tribune, 1937-76, also part-time columnist; sec.-treas. Walnut Grove Bldg. & Loan Assn., 1948-71, also dir. Pres. Walnut Grove PTA, 1962-63; sec. Redwood County ARC, 1939-44. Recipient Community Service award Walnut Grove Lions Club, 1970. Mem. Am., Minn. (pub. relations com. 1941—), Ninth Dist. bar assns., Walnut Grove Community Club (pres. 1954), Minn. Press Club (charter), Soc. Am. Magicians, Internat. Brotherhood of Magicians (internat. pres. 1974-75, legal advisor 1976—), U. Minn. Alumni Assn., Redwood County Hist. Soc. Gamma Eta Gamma. Methodist. Author pamphlets on magic. Home: Walnut Grove MN 56180 Office: Walnut Grove MN 56180

LANTZSCH, HANS EDWIN, sch. supt.; b. Krogis, Germany, Aug. 7, 1923; s. Rheinhold Edwin and Louise (Ettmeier) L.; came to U.S., 1927, naturalized, 1934; B.A., Central Mich. U., 1948; M.A., U. Mich., 1950; postgrad. Wayne State U., 1952-63; m. Dora Jablinskey, June 19, 1948; children—James Edwin, Susan Elizabeth, Thomas Paul. Asst. and acting supt. Ecorse (Mich.) Pub. Schs., 1948-67; supt. Trenton (Mich.) Pub. Schs., 1967-71, Gerrish Higgins Sch., Roscommon, Mich., 1971—. Dir. Community Resources Workshop, Mich. State U., 1955-72; asst. dir. NSF Chemistry Inst., Mont. State Coll., 1958. Chmn. sch. liaison Met. Detroit Sci. Fair, 1957-68; mem. com. Wayne County Intermediate Sch. Dist. Occupational Edn., 1969-71. Trustee, Mich. Council for Econ. Edn., 1965-68. Served with AUS, 1943-46. Decorated Bronze Star. Mem. Mich., No. Mich. (pres. 1976-77), Am. (life) assns. sch. adminstrs., Mich. Edn. Assn., Internat. Platform Assn., Phi Delta Kappa (life). Office: Gerrish Higgins Bd Edn Roscommon MI 48653

LANZ, ROBERT WALTER, educator; b. Milw., Aug. 19, 1937; s. Howard Paul and Gladys (Malig) L.; B.S., U. Wis., 1963, M.S., 1965, Ph.D., 1969; m. Janet Fay Straub, Mar. 1, 1958; children—Betty, Laura, Karen. Instr. dept. engring. mechanics U. Wis., Madison, 1963-66; asst. prof. dept. environ. control U. Wis., Green Bay, 1969-73, asso. prof., 1973—. Served with AUS, 1956. Sea Grante Coll. grantee, 1972-74. Mem. Sigma Xi, Phi Tau Sigma. Republican. Lutheran. Home: Route 1 New Franken WI 54229 Office: 120 S University Circle Green Bay WI 54302

LA POINTE, LEON ALVIN, research engr.; b. Monroe, Mich., Nov. 5, 1950; s. Leonard Louis and Angela Marie (Cousino) LaP.; B.S. in Mech. Engring., U. Notre Dame, 1972; m. Michele Janine Morrin, Jan. 18, 1974. Research design engr. Chrysler Corp., 1972-75; research engr. Surface Combustion div. Midland-Ross Corp., Toledo, 1975—. Mem. ASME, Soc. Automotive Engrs. Roman Catholic. Home: 9665 Bay Creek Rd Erie MI 48133 Office: PO Box 907 Toledo OH 43691

LA POLLA, JAMES JOSEPH, pediatrician; b. Youngstown, Ohio, Feb. 27, 1934; s. Dominic Joseph and Ann Patricia (Page) La P.; A.B., Duke U., 1956, M.D., 1960; m. Genevieve Jacobson, Oct. 20, 1962; children—Jim, Ken, Vincent, Mike. Intern, Univ. Hosp., Cleve., 1961-62; resident in pediatrics Babies and Childrens's Hosp., Cleve., 1962-64; practice medicine specializing in pediatrics, Warren, Ohio, 1966—; med. dir. Children's Rehab. Center, Head Start Program, Apple Creek State Inst. for Retarded. Bd. dirs. Trumbull County Mental Retardation Bd., Trumbull County Bd. Mental Health; pres. Howland Local Sch. Bd., 1977-78; exec. bd. N.E. Ohio Sch. Bds. Assns. Served to comdr., USNR, 1964-66. Named Man of Year Jaycees, 1970. Mem. Trumbull County Med. Soc. (exec. com.), Ohio Pediatric Soc. (state chmn. 1972), Ohio Med. Assn., AMA, Ohio Community Theatre Assn. (dir. award 1974). Clubs: Trumbull Country, Buckeye, Howland Rotary (pres.), Shriners. Contbr. articles to profl. jours., chpt. in book. Organized 1st state Olympics for mentally retarded. Home: 707 North Rd SE Warren OH 44484 Office: 8048 E Market St NE Warren OH 44484

LAPOSKY, BEN FRANCIS, comml. artist; b. Cherokee, Iowa, Sept. 30, 1914; s. Peter Paul and Leona Anastasia (Gabriel) L. Free-lance comml. artist, oscillographic designer, 1938; creator electronic abstractions, Oscillons, 1952; one-man shows include: USIA, France, 1956; group shows include: Cybernetic Serendipity, London, 1968; Computer Art, N.Y.C., 1976; contbr. articles to art jours. Recipient Gold Medal award N.Y. Art Dirs. Club, 1957. Home and office: 301 S 6th St Cherokee IA 51012

LARCHER, ANGELO CLEMENT, chiropractor; b. Chgo., Jan. 30, 1924; s. Archangelo C. and Rose (Davis) L.; student Citadel U., 1942-43; Dr. Chiropractic and Naturopathic Dr. cum laude, Nat. Coll. Chiropractics, 1949, postgrad. in acupuncture, 1975; m. Edith L. Rowley, Jan. 12, 1946; children—Cheryl (Mrs. Wayne Ratay), Judith (Mrs. Dominick Christiano) Kathleen (Mrs. Thomas Wilbanks), Floyd, Ronald, Debra (Mrs. Mark Fogarty). Pvt. practice chiropractic medicine, Chgo., 1949—; physician high sch. football teams, Chgo., 1953-76. Health officer City of Palos Heights, Ill., 1959-68; civil def. dir., 1959-64. Bd. dirs. Chgo. Assn. Retarded Children, 1956-76. Served with USAF, 1943-46; PTO. Decorated Bronze Star medal, Silver Star medal. Mem. Ill. (chmn. athletic council), Am. chiropractic assns. Kiwanian (life fellow), K.C. Patentee safer football shoes and helmets. Home: 12542 S 73 Ct Palos Heights IL 60463 Office: 8036 S Western Ave Chicago IL 60620

LARGE, RICHARD LEROY, cons. mech. engr.; b. Wauneta, Nebr., Apr. 29, 1931; s. Everett Leroy and Jessie Mabel (Rathbun) L.; B.S., U. Nebr., 1958; m. Charlotte Mae Holl, Aug. 15, 1954; children—Jon, James, Janelle, Michael. Performance engr. Consumers Pub. Power Dist., Lincoln, Nebr., 1958-63, ops. supr., 1963-64; cons. engr. Tech. Mgmt. Inc., Lincoln, 1964-70; pres. Tech. Mgmt., 1970-71; prin. R.L. Large & Assos., cons. engrs., Lincoln, 1971—. Served with USMC, 1950-52. Registered profl. engr., Nebr., Colo. Mem. ASME (chmn. Nebr., 1969-70, sec. Region VII 1970-72), Lincoln C. of C., Am. Nuclear Soc., Nebr., Nat. socs. profl. engrs., Am. Legion. Republican. Lutheran. Patentee wheel chair devices. Home: 5111 LaSalle St Lincoln NE 68516 Office: 4740 Linden St Lincoln NE 68516

LARKIN, S. LEE, beverage co. exec.; b. Kalamazoo, Apr. 21, 1923; s. Arthur Lee and Annabelle (Smith) L.; B.S., Georgetown U., 1948; A.M. (Heerman's fellow), Washington U., 1957. Asst. history dept. Washington U., St. Louis, 1955-58; pub. relations dir. Harland Bartholemew & Assos., city planning, St. Louis, 1958-59, Internat. Shoe Co., 1959-64, Seven-Up Co., 1964—. Served with USAAF, 1943-45. Mem. Pub. Relations Soc. Am. (chpt. treas. 1963-64), St. Louis Indsl. Press Assn. Presbyn. Club: St. Louis Press. Home: 11891 Cresta Verde Dr Creve Coeur MO 63141 Office: 121 S Meramec Ave St Louis MO 63105

LARMER, OSCAR VANCE, artist; b. Wichita, Kans., July 11, 1924; s. Bert V. and Carrie (Yard) L.; certificate Mpls. Sch. Art, 1947; B.F.A., U. Kans., 1949, M.F.A., U. Wichita, 1955; m. Mary A. Duehring, Dec. 31, 1945; children—Mary Lynn Larmer King, Michael Vance. Asst. dir. Wichita Art Mus., 1953-55; asst. prof. Kans. State U., Manhattan, 1956-63, asso. prof., 1964-69, prof., 1970—, head dept. art, 1957-71; exhibited one-man shows Wichita, Topeka, Kansas City, Salina, Manhattan, 1950-65; exhibited in group shows Joslyn Art Mus., Omaha, Nelson Atkins Galleries, Kansas City, Mo., Wichita Art Mus., many others; represented in permanent collections: Wichita Art Assn., Kans. State U., Manhattan, Kans., U. Wichita, others. Mem. Wichita Artist Guild (past pres.), Soc. Kans. Painters, Prairie, Kans. watercolor socs., Midwest Coll. Art Assn., Kans. Fedn. Art (past pres.). Home: 2441 Hobbs Dr Manhattan KS 66502

LA ROWE, DANIEL DALE, credit union adminstr.; b. Howard County, Ind., July 29, 1908; s. George Edward and Maude Jane (Fisher) L.; student Ind. U. Extension Center, 1953-54; student U. Wis., 1965, 66, 67; m. Edith Bernice Parsons, June 27, 1935; 1 son, Myron Edward. Various positions prodn. and maintenance Continental Steel Corp., Kokomo, Ind., 1929-69; treas., gen. mgr. Continental Fed. Credit Union, Kokomo, part-time 1959-67, full time 1967—; dir. Burlington State Bank (Ind.), 1975—; owner, mgr. farm, Kokomo, 1945—; county commr. Howard County, 1976—. Active Boy Scouts Am., Kokomo, 1948—, institutional rep., 1954-55, scoutmaster, 1955-56, dist. commr., 1959-60, council commr., 1961-62, mem. exec. bd., 1962-75, Silver Beaver award, 1959; pres. Howard County Taxpayers Assn., 1970-75, Kokomo Econ. Devel. Commn., 1973-75; mem. Econ. Devel. Com. Howard County, 1975-76. Councilman at Large, City of Kokomo, Ind., 1972—. Bd. dirs. United Fund, Kokomo, Ind., 1961-68, Family Service, Kokomo, Ind., 1968-73; exec. trustee Ind. Polit. Action Com., 1973, 74, 75. Mem. Credit Union Assn. (pres. N. Central chpt. 1965-66, legis. chmn. N.Central chpt. 1972-75), Credit Union Exec. Soc. Mem. Christian Ch. (trustee 1960-67, elder 1966-75, Sun. sch. tchr. 1955-73). Mason (32 deg.), Lion. Home: 1715 S Webster St Kokomo IN 46901 Office: Continental Fed Credit Union 901 S Courtland Ave Kokomo IN 46901

LA ROWE, MYRON EDWARD, lawyer; b. Indpls., Nov. 22, 1939; s. Daniel Dale and Edith Bernice (Parsons) L.; B.S., U. Wis., 1962, J.D., 1965; m. Rosemary Waeffler, Aug. 24, 1963; children—Mark, Matthew, Christopher, Melinda. Admitted to Wis. bar, 1965; asso. Ksorstad & Stevens, Reedsburg, Wis., 1965-66; partner LaRowe & Gerlach and predecessor firm, Reedsburg, 1966—. City atty. City Reedsburg, 1967—. Mem. State Bar Wis. (mem. com. 1965—, gov. 1975-77, exec. com. 1976-77), Sauk County Bar Assn. (sec. 1965—), Vacationland Alumni Assn. (pres. 1972-73), Am., Wis. bar assns., Am. Judicature Soc. Lion (pres. 1970). Club: Country (pres. 1972-73) (Reedsburg, Wis.). Home: 134 S Oak St Reedsburg WI 53959 Office: 110 Main St Reedsburg WI 53959

LARRANCE, KENNETH S., financial cons.; b. Indianola, Ill., Sept. 10, 1905; s. Thomas H. and Emma (Neal) L.; student Purdue U., 1929; D.B.A., North Central Coll., Naperville, Ill., 1977; m. Leona Peavler, Dec. 17, 1927. With Burroughs Corp., 1930-70, br. mgr., Ft. Wayne, Ind., 1934-37, br. mgr., Indpls., 1937-43, asst. sales mgr., Detroit, 1943-47, br. mgr., Cleve., 1947-52, br. mgr., Chgo., 1952-61, dist. mgr., Chgo., 1961-70; now financial cons.; chmn. bd. Ill. State Bank, Chgo., First Ogden Corp., Naperville; dir. First Security Bank, Wooddale; vice chmn. bd. First Security Bank of Oakbrook; dir. First Security Bank of Addison, First Nat. Bank Deerfield, First Nat. Bank Lincolnshire (all Ill.). Chmn. bd. trustees N. Central Coll., Naperville. Mem. Mich. Blvd. Assn., Inc. (dir.). Clubs: Rotary (dir., v.p. Chgo.), Chicago; Exmoor Country (Highland Park, Ill.); Lake Wales (Fla.); Lake Region Yacht and Country (Winter Haven, Fla.). Home: 750 Exmoor Oaks Dr Highland Park IL 60035 Office: 300 S Michigan Ave Chicago IL 60604

LARRISON, THOMAS RICHARD, ret. indsl. equipment mfr.; b. Grand Island, Neb., Apr. 22, 1911; s. W. S. and Irma (Geer) L.; student pub. schs. Neb.; m. Audrey Bertness, June 8, 1930; children—Thomas Richard, Carol Jo; m. 2d, Helen Metcalfe, July 5, 1947. Various positions in r.r., machine shops, train service, 1927-29; dental lab. technician, Topeka (Kan.) Dental Lab., 1930-34; salesman Richards-Wilcox Mfg. Co., Aurora, Ill., 1935; devel. sales dental products Derlasco Products Co., Portland, Ore., 1936-37; dental tech., 1938; devel. engr. of precision castings and equipment Larrison Dental Lab. and successor corps., 1939-75, ret., 1975; owner, pres. Larmet Co.; Griffith, Ind. Home: 826 Woodside Dr W Griffith IN 46319 Office: 108 N Wiggs St Griffith IN 46319

LARSEN, CURTIS LEROY, paint mfg. co. exec.; b. Escanaba, Mich., May 13, 1934; s. Willmer Oden and Pearl (Lorenson) L.; B.A., Mich. State U., 1958; m. Mary Louise Goetze, Sept. 8, 1956; children—Karen, Gregory. Gen. accounting supr. Commonwealth Assos., Jackson, Mich., 1958-61; mgr. gen. accounting and credit, aircraft div. Aeroquip Corp., Jackson, 1961-65, controller Barco div., Barrington, Ill., 1965-70, asst. sec. corp., 1965-70; v.p. adminstrn. Byron div. Kysor Indsl. Corp., 1970-74; v.p. fin. and adminstrn. Ill. Bronze Paint Co., Lake Zurich, Ill., 1974—. Counselor, Jr. Achievement, 1959-61; pres. Barrington Area United Dr., 1967-68; mem. Met. Crusade of Mercy, 1965-69; personnel and budget com. Countryside YMCA; mem. devel. com. Good Shepherd Hosp.; econs. com. Barrington Area Council Govts. Mem. Barrington C. of C. (pres. 1968-69), Nat. Assn. Accountants, Ill. Mfrs. Cost Assn., Ill. C. of C. Republican. Lutheran. Mason, Rotarian. Home: 357 Beverly Rd Barrington IL 60010 Office: 300 E Main St Lake Zurich IL 60047

LARSEN, JAMES WARNER, mdse. exec.; b. Mpls., Sept. 7, 1926; s. Alvin and Stella Helen (Villesvik) L.; student Dickinson State Coll., 1944-45, Iowa State U., 1945-46; B.S., U. Minn., 1948; m. Shirley May Rolin, Jan. 3, 1951; children—Terry Jane Larsen Hafferkamp, Sydney Lee, Kristi Anne. Athletic coach and tchr. Los Banos (Calif.) Pub. Schs., 1948-51; salesman, sales mgmt. McKesson and Robbins Drug Co., Mpls., 1951-63, v.p. and div. mgr., Cleve., 1963-70, v.p. mktg. devel., N.Y.C., 1970-73, v.p. sales, San Francisco, 1973-75; pres. Gen. Mdse. Distbrs., Topeka, 1975—; bd. dirs. Gen. Mdse. Distbrs. Council. Served with USN, 1944-46. Republican. Lutheran. Clubs: Shawnee Country, Topeka, Rotary (Topeka); Masons (Los Banos); Shriners (Cleve.). Home: 116 Fairlawn Rd Topeka KS 66606 Office: 7215 S Topeka Blvd Topeka KS 66615

LARSEN, LESTER FREDERICK, agrl. engr.; b. Plainview, Nebr., Sept. 4, 1908; s. Daniel and Marie (Petersen) L.; B.S. in Agrl. Engring., U. Nebr., 1933, M.S. in Agrl. Engring. (Univ. fellow), 1939; m. H. Elaine McComb; children—Elaine Marie, Daniel Harvey, Amy Louise, Linda Clare. Assembly line worker Ford Motor Co., Omaha, 1931-33; traveller Internat. Harvester Co., Atwood, Kans., 1933-37; grad. asst. in agrl. engring. U. Nebr., 1937-39, extension engr., 1943-46, engr.-in-charge tractor testing, 1946-76, instr. agrl. engring., 1946-50, asst. prof., 1950-70, asso. prof., 1970-76, ret., 1976; asst. prof. S.D. State U., 1939-43. Fin. sec. Warren United Meth. Ch., Lincoln, Nebr., 1953—. Registered profl. engr. Fellow Am. Soc. Agrl. Engring. (Cyrus Hall McCormick award 1975); mem. Gamma Sigma Delta, Sigma Tau, Alpha Epsilon. Republican. Clubs: Kiwanis, Nat.

Grange, Lincoln Engrs., Lincoln Farmers. Contbr. articles to profl. jours. Home: 1205 N 42d St Lincoln NE 68503

LARSEN, THEODORE EDWARD, electronics co. exec.; b. Harlowton, Mont., Oct. 23, 1927; s. Hans Albert and Anna Marie (Hansen) L.; B.S. in Mech. Engring., Mont. State Coll., 1955; m. Loraine Margaret Eide, June 28, 1952; children—Richard Harvey, Douglas Edward, Nancy Lynn. Design engr. Honeywell Inc., Mpls., 1955-62, tech. dir., Europe, Honeywell GmbH, Frankfurt, Germany, 1962-69, internat. market mgr., Mpls., 1969-73; pres. Detector Electronics Corp., Mpls., 1973—. Mem. planning commn., Bloomington, Minn., 1957-62. Patentee in field. Home: 5812 Jeff Pl Edina MN 55436 Office: 7351 Washington Ave S Edina MN 55435

LARSON, ALLAN LOUIS, educator; b. Chetek, Wis., Mar. 31, 1932; s. Leonard Andrew and Mabel (Marek) L.; B.A., Wis. State U. at Eau Claire, 1954; Ph.D., Northwestern U., Evanston, Ill., 1964. Instr., Evanston, Twp. High Sch., 1958-61; asst. prof. polit. sci. U. Wis., 1963-64; asst. prof. Loyola U., Chgo., 1964-68, asso. prof., 1968-74, prof., 1974—. Norman Wait Harris fellow in polit. sci. Northwestern U., 1954-56. Mem. Am. Polit. Sci. Assn., AAAS, Am. Acad. Polit. and Social Sci., Acad. Polit. Sci., Midwest Polit. Sci. Assn., AAUP, Kappa Delta Pi, Pi Sigma Alpha, Phi Sigma Epsilon. Roman Catholic. Author: Comparative Political Analysis, 1977; (with others) Progress and the Crisis of Man, 1976. Contbr. articles in field to profl. jours. Home: 2015 Orrington Ave Evanston IL 60201 Office: Damen Hall Room 915 6525 N Sheridan Rd Chicago IL 60626

LARSON, ANDREW ROBERT, lawyer; b. Pine County, Minn., Feb. 25, 1930; s. Gustaf Adolf and Mary (Mach) L.; B.A., U. Minn., 1953, B.S. Law, St. Paul Coll. Law, 1956; LL.B., William Mitchell Coll. Law, 1958; m. Evelyn Joan Johnson, Sept. 12, 1953; children—Linda Suzanne, Mark Andrew. With Armour & Co., 1953-56, Minn. Dept. Taxation, 1956-58; admitted to Minn. bar, 1958; individual practice law, Duluth, Minn., 1958—. Municipal judge Village of Proctor, part-time 1961-74; dir., sec. various bus., real estate corps.; pres. firm Larson, Holmstrom, Huseby and Brodin, Ltd. Fin. chmn. Duluth Downtown Devel. Corp.; chmn. Duluth Fair Employment and Housing Commn., 1965-76; vice chmn. Mayor's Arena Auditorium Com., Duluth, 1964-65; mem. State Bd. Human Rights, 1967-73; Midwest regional rep. nat. standing com. on legislation United Cerebral Palsy, 1967-71, bd. dirs. nat. assn., 1971-72; bd. dirs. United Day Activity Center, 1969-76, Am. Cancer Soc., 1973-75, Light House for Blind, 1975—. Recipient awards including Humanitarian Service award United Cerebral Palsy, 1965, Republican party I Care award for work in civil rights, aid to handicapped, 1964, Jr. C. of C. Distinguished Service award, 1965. Mem. Am., Minn. bar assns., Am. Arbitration Assn., Minn. Municipal Judges Assn., Minn. League Municipalities, Hist. Soc., NAACP, ACLU, C. of C., Beta Phi Kappa. Republican. Unitarian-Universalist. Kiwanian. Home: 1831 Arrowhead Rd Duluth MN 55811 Office: 333 W Superior St Duluth MN 55802

LARSON, CARL JACOB, research co. accounting exec., lawyer; b. Brownville, Me., Jan. 31, 1913; s. Peter and Anna Helena (Jacobson) L.; accounting-finance diploma Bay Path Inst., 1932; student in bus. Northeastern U., Springfield, Mass., 1934-36, LL.B., 1942; postgrad. bus. adminstrn. Washington U., St. Louis, 1951-52, U. Mo., 1959-61, U. Dayton, 1968-72; m. Eva Lorene Anderson, Nov. 17, 1956; children—Peter (dec.), Karen (Mrs. W. Michael Meloy), David, Eric. Gen. bookkeeper Fed. Intermediate Credit Bank, Springfield, 1932-42; cost accountant Monsanto Chem. Co., Springfield, 1942-46, supr. gen. accounting, 1946-47, sr. accountant dept. budget exec. div., St. Louis, 1947-52, supr. dept. budget, 1952-58, internal auditor, 1958-60, asst. supr. dept. tabulating, 1960-62; chief auditor Monsanto Research Corp., Miamisburg, Ohio, 1962-64, chief plant accountant, 1964-66, external audit supr., 1966—. Instr. Bay Path Jr. Coll., 1946-47, St. Louis U., 1954-56. Instr. rifle marksmanship YMCA, Kirkwood, Mo., 1958. Mem. Nat. Assn. Accountants (v.p. chpt. 1960-62), Am. Accounting Assn., Nat. Athletic Scholastic Soc., Far Hills Temple Assn. (pres. trustees, Pi Tau Kappa. Presbyn. (treas. bldg. fund 1967-68). Mason (32 deg.). Club: Crestwood (Kettering, Ohio). Genealogist; translator of Swedish. Home: 248 Napoleon Dr Kettering OH 45429 Office: Monsanto Research Corp Mound Lab Miamisburg OH 45342

LARSON, CARL MARTIN, educator; b. Council Bluffs, Iowa, Feb. 11, 1916; s. Carl Emil and Anna (Fredrickson) L.; B.S., U. Ill. at Urbana, 1939; M.B.A., Northwestern U., 1950; m. Mary Jane Jacobson, Mar. 7, 1942; 1 dau., Deborah Rae (Mrs. Jeffrey Poat). Asst. instr. U. Ill., 1946-49, instr., 1949-62, asst. prof., 1962-66, asso. prof., Chgo. campus, 1966-70, prof. mktg., 1970—; cons. in field; dir. Paddock Publs. Inc., Arlington Heights, Ill. Mem. Nat. Council for Small Bus. Mgmt. Devel., nat. steering com. Small Bus. Inst. Served with AUS, 1941-46. Decorated Bronze Star. Mem. Am., So. mktg. assns., Nat. Assn. Mgmt. Educators (v.p. research 1976), Alpha Kappa Psi, Beta Gamma Sigma. Lutheran. Author: (with James Engel and Wayne Tolarzyk) Cases in Promotional Strategy, 1971; (with Robert Weigand and John Wright) Basic Retailing, 1976; Student Guide to Basic Retailing. Contbr. articles in field to profl. jours. Home: 8 N Donald St Arlington Heights IL 60004 Office: U Ill Chgo Circle Campus Box 4348 Chicago IL 60680

LARSON, DAVID ROGER, photographer; b. St. Paul, Oct. 17, 1954; s. Paul W. and Martha M. (Beck) L.; student Apostolic Bible Inst., 1972-74; grad. with honors Minn. Sch. Bus., 1975. Owner, Dave Larson Photography, St. Paul, 1972—; pres. Solar-Aire of Minn., Inc. Recipient several awards in profl. exhbn. Mem. Profl. Photographers Am., Minn. Profl. Photographers Assn. (dir.). Address: 1711 St Mary's Ave St Paul MN 55113

LARSON, DON WAYNE, editor, pub.; b. Alexandria, Minn., Aug. 6, 1929; s. Jay David and Esther Marie (Chase) L.; m. Geil Maria Bundy, Mar. 27, 1949; children—Mark, Bradley, Jill, Steven. News reporter Mankato (Minn.) Free Press, 1946-49, Fort Dodge (Iowa) Messenger, 1950-58; mng. editor Mankato Free Press, 1958-61; bus. and fin. editor St. Paul Dispatch, 1961-73; editor, pub. Corporate Report Mag., Mpls., 1973—. Home: 1074 Linwood Ave Saint Paul MN 55105 Office: 7101 York Ave S Minneapolis MN 55435

LARSON, GERALD LEWIS, elec. engr.; b. Pipestone, Minn., June 15, 1940; s. Albert Lewis and Marguerite Barbara (Kempenich) L.; B.S., Mont. State U., 1966; B.S. in Elec. Engring., Mont. State U., 1966; M.S. in Elec. Engring., Bradley U., 1969; m. Deana Priscilla Estep, Sept. 15, 1962; children—Anita, Eric, Christopher. Research and staff engr., Caterpillar Tractor Co. Peoria, Ill., 1966-73; program mgr., prin. engr. Eaton Corp., Battle Creek, Mich., 1973—; faculty mem. Bradley U., Peoria, 1970-72. Served with USN, 1958-61. Tracey Found. scholar, 1961-66. Mem. IEEE, Instrument Soc. Am. Patentee in infra red temperature sensor, engine running time indicator, also vehicle controls. Home: 113 Terry Ct Battle Creek MI 49015 Office: 463 N 20th St Battle Creek MI 47015

LARSON, GORDON ALBERT, farmer, state legislator; b. Jamestown, N.D., Nov. 7, 1917; s. Albert and Lorena (Nelson) L.; student N.D. State U., 1936-37; B.S., S.D., Sch. Mines and Tech., 1940. Owner, operator farm, nr. Jamestown, 1941—; mem. N.D. Ho. of Reps., 1967—. Mem. exec. bd. Central Dakota Nursing Home, Jamestown. Lutheran. Mason. Address: Route 2 Jamestown ND 53401

LARSON, JOSEPH HENRY, elec. suppliers; b. Roberts, Wis., July 19, 1908; s. Henry Charles and Bridget (Cushing) L.; student River Falls State Tchrs. Coll., 1926-28, U. Wis.-Madison, 1928-30; m. Lucille Oline Olson, Oct. 19; 1 dau., Joy (Mrs. Charles E. Pahl). Pres. J.H. Larson Elec. Co., Eau Claire, Wis., Hudson, Wis., Watertown, S.D., Mpls., 1930—. Mem. Nat. Assn. Elec. Distributors (bd. govs. 1966-70, exec. com. 1972-76). Mason (Shriner), Elks, Rotary). Office: 530 N 3d St Minneapolis MN 55401

LARSON, LARRY KENT, educator; b. Neenah, Wis., Dec. 11, 1936; s. Emil William and Viola Mary (Krasin) L.; A.B., Ripon Coll., 1959; M.S., U. Wis., Madison, 1961, postgrad. 1965, 70, 76; m. Judith Ann Larsen, Dec. 22, 1962. Tchr., Valders High Sch. (Wis.), 1959-60, Roosevelt Jr. High Sch., Beloit, Wis., 1961-62; history tchr., Park High Sch., Racine, Wis., 1962—, cross country coach, 1971—. Mem. Hoy Nature Club Inc. (pres. 1971-73), Wis. AAU (chmn. race walking com. 1969—), Nat. AAU (mem. race walking com. 1969—), NEA, Wis. Edn. Assn., Racine Edn. Assn. Lutheran (elder 1966-70, conv. del. 1968, 70, 76). Author: Sport History as a High School Course, 1973. Home: 909 Ostergaard Ave Racine WI 53406

LARSON, LAWRENCE MYRLIN, surgeon; b. Mpls., Dec. 14, 1903; s. Ludwig Waerbaag and Mary Inga (Nordland) L.; B.A., U. Minn., 1925, M.A., 1929, M.D., 1927, Ph.D., 1932; m. Phyllis Katherine Ells, Nov. 8, 1930; children—Richard Ells, Philips Parker, Stephen Lawrence, David Edmund. Instr. surgery U. Minn. Med. Sch., 1932—; fellow in surgery Mayo Clinic, Rochester, Minn., 1928-32; med. dir. Gamble-Skogmo Co., Am. Linen Co., Patterson Dental Supply, Johnson Inst. Trustee Blake Sch., Hopkins, Minn. Served from lt. comdr. to capt., USNR, 1941-46. Diplomate Am. Bd. Surgery, Am. Bd. Preventive Medicine. Fellow Internat. (regent), Am. colls. surgeons; mem. Western Surg. Soc., Airline Med. Examiners Assn., Aerospace Med. Assn., Minn. Med. Soc., Sigma Xi. Rotarian. Clubs: Athletic, Minikahda. Contbr. to publs. in field. Home: 4700 Townes Rd Minneapolis MN 55424 Office: Gamble Bldg 5100 Gamble Dr Minneapolis MN 55416

LARSON, LEONARD, dentist; b. Oakland, Minn., Feb. 28, 1915; s. Christopher and Louisa (Seim) L.; D.D.S., State U. Iowa, 1938; m. Margaret Roxana Proctor, May 6, 1939; children—Judith (Mrs. Roger Harald), Steven Wayne, David Christopher. Practice dentistry, Spencer, Iowa, 1939-42, 46—; v.p. Profl. Bldg. Inc., Spencer, 1959—. Served with AUS, 1942-46. Mem. Am. Dental Assn., Am. Acad. Gold Foil Operators, Pierre Fauchard Acad., Woodbury Study Club (asst. dir. 1972—), Psi Omega. Methodist. Mason (Shriner), Rotarian. Home: 817 W 10th St Spencer IA 51301 Office: Professional Bldg Spencer IA 51301

LARSON, LESTER GEORGE, state senator; b. Brocket, N.D., Dec. 14, 1914; s. Ole B. and Gunhild (Skjervem) L.; student pub. schs.; m. Clara Amanda Knutson, Nov. 6, 1936; 1 dau., Janet Yvonne. Farmer, Brocket, N.D., 1933—; mem. N.D. Ho. of Reps., 1957-59, 63-65; mem. N.D. Senate, 1965—, now asst. minority floor leader, mem. appropriations com., legis. research com., 1967—. Bd. dirs. Equity Co-op. Elevator Assn., Brocket. Democrat. Home: Route Box 32 Brocket ND 58321

LARSON, LINDA LOUISE, counselor; b. Joliet, Ill., June 13, 1941; d. George Everett and Mary Louise (Wright) Flory; L.P.N., Oak Forest Sch. Practical Nursing, 1962; B.A., Sangamon State U., 1973, M.A., 1974; m. Louis Eugene Laeson, Apr. 20, 1962; 1 son, Brian. Nurse, Silver Cross Hosp., Joliet, Ill., 1962-64; spl. follow up coordinator, psychol. testing coordinator, counselor Christian County Mental Health Assn. 1974—; asso. staff mem. St. Johns Hosp., Springfield; cons. Ill. Heart Assn., 1975-76. Mem. county council PTA, 1971; bd. dirs. ARC, 1974-76, Community Concert Assn., 1973-76. Mem. AAUW, D.A.R., Ill. Assn. Retarded Citizens, Ill. Psychol. Assn., Am. Guidance and Personnel Assn. Presbyterian.

LARSON, MAURICE ALLEN, educator; b. Missouri Valley, Iowa, July 19, 1927; s. Albert Juluis and Grace Elizabeth (Chambers) L.; B.S., Ia. State U., 1951, Ph.D., 1958; m. Ruth Elizabeth Gugeler, Dec. 5, 1953; children—Richard Alan, Janet Ann, John Albert. Chem. engr. Dow Corning Corp., Midland, Mich., 1951-54; teaching asst. Iowa State U., Ames, 1954-55, instr. dept. chem. engring., 1955-58, asst. prof., 1958-61, asso. prof., 1961-64, prof., 1964—. Anson Marston Distinguished prof., 1977—; cons. fertilizer tech. and crystallization, 1960—; cons. AID, Kharagpur, India, 1968; Shell vis. prof. U. Coll., London, Eng., 1971-72; sci. exchange visitor, Czechoslovakia and Poland, 1974. Served with AUS, 1946-47. Recipient H.A. Webber Teaching award Ia. State U., 1967, Western Electric Fund award for teaching Am. Soc. Engring. Edn., 1970, Faculty citation Iowa State U. Alumni, 1972; NSF fellow, 1965-66. Mem. Am. Inst. Chem. Engrs. (pres. Iowa 1970-71), Am. Chem. Soc. (chmn. div. fertilizer and soil chemistry 1975), Am. Soc. Engring. Edn., Sigma Xi, Tau Beta Pi, Phi Lambda Upsilon. Democrat. Methodist. Lion. Author: (with A.D. Randolph) Theory of Particulate Processes, 1971. Contbr. to profl. jours. Home: 2710 Thompson Dr Ames IA 50010

LARSON, OBERT LEROY, banker; b. Worth County, Iowa, Apr. 9, 1916; s. Lauritz Nicholi and Anna Otillie (Storre) L.; student Waldorf Jr. Coll., Forest City, Iowa, 1936; B.A., Luther Coll., Decorah, Iowa, 1939; certificate banking U. Wis., 1967; m. Mary Lou McGrath, June 4, 1944; children—Mary Lynne, John Lauritz. Bookkeeper, Peterson Oil Co., Ft. Dodge, Iowa, 1939-40; retail dealer petroleum products Eagle Grove, Iowa, 1940-41, 46-48; partner Chevrolet/Pontiac retail dealership, Eagle Grove, Iowa, 1948-54, owner, 1954-56; with Security Savs. Bank, Eagle Grove, 1956-66; exec. v.p. Farmers Trust and Savs. Bank, Williamsburg, Iowa, 1966-67, pres., 1967—, chmn. bd., 1972—; chmn. Iowa Bankers and Ins. Services Inc., 1972-75, dir., 1971—. Treas., corr. Rotary Ann Home sr. citizens, 1962-66; treas. Eagle Grove Community Sch. Bd., 1958-66; v.p. Wright County, Iowa Fair Bd., 1951-66; chmn. Iowa County Cancer Crusade, 1975-76; chmn. Iowa County Am. Heart Assn., 1977; mem. Iowa County Airport Commn., 1974—; mem. Iowa County, Iowa Quality Water Study Com., 1977—. Served with USNR, 1941-45. Decorated D.F.C., Air Medal with cluster. Mem. Iowa Independent (dir. 1974-76), Iowa, Am. Independents, Am. bankers assns., Am. Inst. Banking (charter), Eagle Grove C. of C. (pres. 1950, 58), Williamsburg C. of C. (dir. 1967-69), Republican. Lutheran. Clubs: Sport Hill Golf and Country, Rotary (pres. Eagle Grove 1960), Kiwanis. Home: Leo's Blvd Williamsburg IA 52361 Office: 510 Elm St Williamsburg IA 52361

LARSON, PAUL NORDLAND, gynecologist; b. Mpls., May 8, 1906; s. Ludwig W. and Mary (Nordland) L.; M.D., U. Minn.; m. Thelma Larsen, June 23, 1932; children—P. Robert, Kent Charles, Cindy Hinkle. Intern, Hackensack (N.J.) Gen. Hosp.; fellow Mayo Clinic, 1931-34; practice medicine specializing in obstetrics and gynecology, Edina, Minn.; originator Paul Larson Obstet. and Gynecol. Clinic, Mpls. and Edina, 1962-71, ret., 1971—; instr. emeritus U. Minn.; hon. staff N.W. Abbot, Fairview, Meth., Mt. Sinai hosps.; cons. staff St. Gabriel's Hosp. (Little Falls, Minn.); staff emeritus St. Mary's Hosp. (Mpls.); pres. N.W. Hosp., 1961-62. Fellow A.C.S.; mem. Am. Soc. Obstetrics and Gynecology, Internat. Coll. Surgeons, Acad. Medicine Mpls., Am. Coll. Obstetrics and Gynecology, Central States Soc. Obstetrics and Gynecology, Am. Fertility Soc. Clubs: Minikahda (Mpls.), De Anza Country, (Borrego Springs, Calif.). Contbr. articles profl. jours. Home: 5708 S Blake Rd Edina MN 55436 Office: 6517 Drew Ave S Edina MN 55435

LARSON, ROLAND SIGWARD, ednl. cons.; b. St. Paul, Minn., Apr. 18, 1921; s. Laurentius Petrus and Judith Natalia (Cedarbloom) L.; B.S., U. Minn., 1947, M.A., 1949; Ed.D., Mich. State U., 1964; m. Doris Elaine Linell, June 19, 1946; children—Daniel S., Thomas P., Jane L., Mary Lee. Teacher, Fergus Falls (Minn.) Pub. Schs., 1947-48; dir. guidance and counseling LaCrosse (Wis.) Logan High Sch., 1949-52; counselor St. Louis Park (Minn.) Pub. Schs., 1952-59; coordinator of guidance, pupil personnel and spl. edn., 1959-67; v.p., dir. tng. center Search Inst., Mpls., 1967-73; pres. Roland S. Larson & Assos., Mpls., 1974—. Mem. adv. bd. U. Minn. Center for Youth Research and Devel. Served with USNR, 1942-46. Mem. Am. Psychol. Assn., Am. Personnel and Guidance Assn., Am. Soc. Tng. Devel., Am. Sch. Counselors Assn., Nat. Edn. Assn., Minn. Council Family Relations. Lutheran. Author: Values and Faith, 1976. Home and Office: 2442 Gettysburg Av S Minneapolis MN 55426

LARSON, ROLLAND JAMES, supt. schs.; b. Bremen, N.D., Jan. 17, 1934; s. Lester Harold and Palma Miranda (Bergrud) L.; B.S., State Coll., Valley City, N.D., 1955; M.Ed., U. N.D., 1967; m. Alice Joy Ferguson, June 29, 1958; children—Marla, Brent, Sona. Tchr. pub. schs., Wabun, Minn., 1955-56, Hendrum, Minn., 1956-58, Wilton, N.D., 1958-65, Cleveland, N.D., 1965-67, Streeter, N.D., 1967-70; supt. schs. New Salem, N.D., 1970-75; dir. sch. constrn. and pupil transp. N.D. Dept. Pub. Instrn., Bismarck, 1975—. Mem. NEA, N.D. Edn. Assn., N.D. Music Edn. Assn., N.D. Assn. Sch. Adminstrs., (legis. com. 1966—), Am. Assn. Sch. Adminstrs., Music Educators Nat. Conf., Phi Delta Kappa. Lutheran. Lion (sec.-treas. 1968-70). Home: 211 N 5th St New Salem ND 58563 Office: Dept Pub Instrn State Capitol Bismarck ND 58505

LARSON, SANFORD JOHN, physician; b. Chgo., Apr. 9, 1929; s. Leslie S. and Bertha (Doezma) L.; B.A., Wheaton Coll., 1950; M.D. Northwestern U., 1954, Ph.D., 1962; m. Jacquelyn McKay, Aug. 28, 1957;children—Nancy, Michael, Mary. Intern, Passavant Meml. Hosp., Chgo., 1954-55, resident Northwestern U., 1955-57, 59-61, clin. asst. in surgery, 1961-62; dir. neurosurg. edn. Cook County Hosp., Chgo., 1962-63; practice medicine, specializing in neurosurgery, Milw., 1963—; mem. staff Wood VA, Milw. County Gen., Milw. Children's hosps.; cons. Luth. Hosp., Columbia Hosp., Shriners Hosp. for Crippled Children; prof., chmn. dept. neurosurgery Med. Coll. Wis., 1963—. Served to maj. USAF, 1957-59. Diplomate Am. Bd. Neurol. Surgery. Fellow A.C.S.; mem. Am. Assn. Neurol. Surgeons, AMA, Milwaukee County Med. Soc., Am. Assn. Anatomists, Biophys. Soc., Milw. Acad. Medicine, Milw. Neuropsychiat. Soc., Soc. Univ. Surgeons, Soc. Neurol. Surgeons. Home: 8700 W Wisconsin Ave Milwaukee WI 53226 Office: 8700 W Wisconsin Ave Milwaukee WI 53226

LARSON, SIDNEY, educator; b. Sterling, Colo., June 16, 1923; m. George Ann Madden; children—Sara C., Nancy L. Dir. art dept. Columbia (Mo.) Coll.; mural and easel painter; curator art museum State Hist. Soc. Mo.; art conservator; Huntington Hartford fellow; assisted Thomas Hart Benton with Truman Library murals; major art exhbn. designer; artist in residence Spiva Art Center. Mem. Thomas Hart Benton Homestead Commn. Mem. Nat. Soc. Mural Painters, Museum Assos. Address: Columbia Coll Columbia MO 65201

LARSON, WAYNE LEROY, govt. ofcl.; b. LuVerne, Minn., Oct. 7, 1922; s. Andrew and Margaret (Teigen) L.; student U. Mo., 1944-45; B.A., Augustana Coll., 1949; M.S.W., U. Minn., 1957; m. Yvonne A. Norquist, Nov. 27, 1957; children—Andy, John G., Joseph. Dir. LacQue Parle County Welfare Dept., 1951-55; counselor U. Minn., 1955-57; dir. child devel. Center, Minn. Dept. Health, 1957-63; dir. Crow Wing County Welfare Dept., Brainerd, Minn., 1963—; cons. Minn. Health Dept., 1957-63; mem. Minn. Dept. Edn. Title VI Planning Council. Served with A.C., AUS, 1944-45. Mem. Acad. Certified Social Workers. Kiwanian. Home: 1202 9th Ave NE Brainerd MN 56401 Office: Court House Brainerd MN 56401

LARSON, WILFRED LEROY, elec. mfg. co. exec.; b. Bridgewater, S.D., July 9, 1913; s. Luverne P. and Agnes (Akland) L.; student Augustana Coll., 1935-36, RCA Inst., Chgo., 1937-38; m. Irene Ruth Siegele, May 19, 1939; children—Wilfred Wayne, Allan J., Ronald Rey. With RCA Victor Distbg. Corp., Chgo., 1938; successively engring. dept., sales dept., gen. mgr. Carter div. Utah Radio Products, Chgo., 1938-46; founder, pres., chmn. bd., dir. Switchcraft, Inc., Chgo., 1946—. Past pres., dir. Electronic Industry Show Corp., Chgo. Recipient Tiger of Year award Electronic Young Tigers, Inc., 1970; Hall of Fame award Electronic Distbrs. Research Inst., 1973, Electronics Man of Year award, 1977. Mem. Electronic Industries Assn. (gov., v.p., past chmn. exec. com. parts div., mem. exec. com. distbr. products div.; past pres., dir. Central div. distbr. products group, distinguished service award 1975), IEEE (sr.). Lutheran. Clubs: Hunters Country (Richmond, Ill.); Electronic VIP (pres. 1972-74). Home: 15 Rolling Ridge Northfield IL 60093 Office: 5555 N Elston Ave Chicago IL 60630

LARSON, WILLIAM HERBERT, editor; b. LaCrosse, Wis., June 3, 1938; s. George Herbert and Mabel Ingeborg (Carlsson) L.; B.S. magna cum laude, LaCrosse State U., 1960; m. Karen Barbara Nelsestuen, July 30, 1960; children—Christopher William, Andrew Joseph, Daniel James. English tchr. Unified Sch. Dist. 1, Racine County, Wis., 1960-64; editor Western Pub. Co., Inc., Racine, Wis., 1964—, now sr. editor. Lutheran (councilman 1969—, pres. congregation 1972). Author: Let's Go To Animal Town, 1975. Compiler: Stand By for Adventure, 1967; Seven Great Detective Stories, 1968; (with N. Gretchen Greiner) Adventure Calling, 1969. Home: 2321 James Blvd Racine WI 53403 Office: 1220 Mound Ave Racine WI 53404

LARSSON, DOROTHY K. (MRS. KARL G.B. LARSSON), dietitian; b. Indpls., Dec. 26, 1928; d. Ralph and Anna (Klusman) King; B.S., Purdue U., 1950; m. Karl G.B. Larsson, June 9, 1961; children—Gustav Karl, Anna Karla. Dietitian residence halls State U. Iowa, 1951-52; prodn. mgr. tearoom L.S. Ayres, Indpls., 1952-53; became food service mgr. Cin. Milacron, Inc. (formerly Cin. Milling Machine Co.), 1953, now food service dir. Named Food Service Operator of Yr., recipient Silver Plate award Internat. Food Service Mfrs. Assn., 1970; Distinguished Alumni award Purdue U., 1971. Mem. Internat. Platform Assn., Am. Dietetic Assn. (dietetic internship bd. 1964-67), Am. Home Econs. Assn., Ohio, Greater Cin. (v.p. 1970, pres. 1971) restaurant assns., Nat. Indsl. Cafeteria Mgrs. Assn. (pres. 1963-64), Nat. Security Indsl. Assn. (mem. food adv. com.), YWCA, Purdue Alumni Assn. Lutheran. Club: Zonta (v.p. Cin. 1966-67) Home: 2954 Observatory Ave Cincinnati OH 45208 Office: 4701 Marburg Ave Cincinnati OH 45209

LA RUE, DAVID LEE, mfg. co. exec.; b. Ellsworth, Ohio, Oct. 13, 1954; s. Kenneth N. and Gladys May (Calvin) LaR.; student Ohio State U., 1973-74, Youngstown Coll. Bus. and Profl. Drafting, 1975-76. Service mgr. Rent-a-Sport, North Lima, Ohio, 1976-77; design draftsman Buckeye Aluminum Extrusions, Fostoria, Ohio, 1977; change controller Link div. Singer Corp., Houston, 1977—. Mem. Ellsworth Vol. Fire Dept., Clear Lake City Fire Dept., Houston. Mem. Am. Def. Preparedness Assn., Am. Inst. Drafting, Internat. Assn. Arson Investigators. Methodist. Home: 9739 W Hill Dr Canfield OH 44406 Office: 16903 Buccaneer St Houston TX 77058

LASER, WILLIAM CHARLES, seal mfg. co. exec.; b. Hinsdale, Ill., Sept. 11, 1933; s. William Frank and Violet Ruth (Soltwisch) L.; B.S. in Indsl. Engring., Northwestern U., 1958; m. Carlyn Meiners, May 15, 1959; children—Julie, Carla. Exec. v.p. Cartriseal Corp., Wheeling, Ill., 1958-69; v.p. Cartriseal div. Rex Chainbelt, Inc., Wheeling, 1969-70; pres. Seal div. Rexnord, Inc., Wheeling, 1970—, also pres. Bearing div., Downers Grove, Ill. Mem. Ill. Sch. Bd. Dist. 67, Lake Forest; chmn. Planning Com., 1972—. Served with AUS, 1953-55. Mem. Am. Soc. Lubrication Engrs., Am. Inst. Indsl. Engrs. Republican. Presbyn. Club: Knollwood (Lake Forest). Home: 890 Oak Knoll St Lake Forest IL 60045 Office: 634 Glenn Ave Wheeling IL 60090

LASH, KENNETH, educator; b. New Britain, Conn., July 27, 1918; s. Jack Edward and Lillian (Miller) L.; B.A., Yale U., 1939; M.A., U. N.Mex., 1948; postgrad. U. de Lille (France), 1950-51. Instr. dept. English, U. N.Mex., Albuquerque, 1948-54; editor N.Mex. Quar. Rev., Albuquerque, 1951-55; lectr. dept. humanities San Francisco Art Inst., 1959-70, chmn. dept., 1964-70; head art dept. U. No. Iowa, Cedar Falls, 1970-76, dir. humanities program, 1976—; ednl. cons.; mem. role of arts task force Pres.'s Commn. on Mental Health, 1977. Served with USNR, 1943-46. Fulbright scholar, 1950-51; Rockefeller Found. traveling grantee, 1954-55. Mem. Phi Beta Kappa. Writer poetry, drama, fiction, edn., 1946—. Contbg. editor N.Am. Review, 1972—. Home: 2725 Rainbow Dr Cedar Falls IA 50613

LASHER, ESTHER LU (MRS. DONALD T. LASHER), librarian; b. Denver, June 1, 1923; d. Lindley Aubrey and Irma Jane (Rust) Pim; A.A. in Fine Arts, Temple Buell Coll., 1943; B.A., Denver U., 1945, M.A., 1967; M.R.E., Eastern Bapt. Sem., 1948; m. Donald T. Lasher, Apr. 8, 1950; children—Patricia Sue, Donald Aubrey, Keith Alan, Jennifer Luanne. Tchr. pub. schs., Denver, 1945-46; dir. Christian edn. First Bapt. Ch., Evansville, Ind., 1948-50; asst. circulation librarian Evansville (Ind.) Pub. Library, 1950-51; tchr. music Dubois (Ind.) County Schs., 1951-52; br. librarian Jefferson County (Colo.) Pub. Library, 1962-64; acting head, reference librarian Colorado Springs Pub. Library, 1964-67; high sch. librarian Colorado Springs Dist. 2, 1967-68; head music library Butler U., Indpls., 1968-72; cataloger gen. collection Ind. State Library, 1972-77; adult reference librarian Greenwood (Ind.) Pub. Library, 1977—. Leader Hoosier Indpls. council Girl Scouts U.S.A., 1972-73; leader 4-H, Perry County, Ind., 1951-53, Denver, 1956-60; block chmn. Neighborhood Improvement Orgn., 1971-72; mem. Neighborhood Republican Com., 1970-72. Mem. Music Library Assn., Internat. Music Library Assn., Ind. Library Assn., Ind. State Library Staff Assn. (pres. 1976-77), Christian Library Assn., Internat. Platform Assn., Indpls. Mus. Art, Sigma Alpha Iota (adviser 1969-72). Baptist (tchr. Sunday sch. 1968-72; mem. Christian edn. bd. 1969-72, Christian edn. coordinator, 1977—). Club: Order Eastern Star. Home: 4646 Carvel Ave Indianapolis IN 46205 Office: Greenwood Pub Library 310 S Meridian St Greenwood IN 46142

LASHORNE, PAUL RUSSELL, JR., optometrist; b. Indpls., Aug. 3, 1922; s. Paul Russell and Nellie Marie (Ryker) LaS.; Dr. Optometry, No. Ill. Coll. Optometry, 1949; m. Marie Teresa Ryan, May 29, 1948; children—Lynn (Mrs. Tony Gamron), Paula (Mrs. Dwight Sessoms), John, Ellen. Practice optometry specializing in children's and geriatric vision problems, also in mentally disturbed and deaf, Seymour, Ind., 1949—. Cons. for sub-normal vision patients and low-achieving sch. children. Served with USCGR, 1942-45. Decorated Meritorious Service medal. Mem. Seymour C. of C., Am. Legion, V.F.W. Republican. Roman Catholic. K.C. (4 deg.), Elk, Eagle. Home: 437 Mutton Creek Dr Seymour IN 47274 Office: 316 W Tipton St Seymour IN 47274

LASIEWICZ, THADDEUS WALTER, elec. products mfg. co. exec.; b. Chgo., Feb. 8, 1924; s. Walter and Sophia (Szafraniec) L.; B. Mechanical Engring., Cornell U., 1945, postgrad., 1946-48; m. Elizabeth J. Williams, June 27, 1947; children—Thaddeus Walter, Robert, Catherine. Mech. engr. Pitts. Plate Glass Co., Akron, Ohio, 1948; mech. engr. Askania Regulator Co., Chgo., 1949-63; pres. M.E.A., Inc., elec. products, Elk Grove Village, Ill., 1963—; founder, pres. Automatic Indsl. Controls, Elk Grove Village, 1973—; treas. Water Clean, Inc., Hammond, Ind. Mayor, Mentor Ridge Farms, Mentor, Ohio, 1957-58. Served to 2d lt. USAAF, 1943-46. Mem. Assn. Iron and Steel Engrs., Instrument Soc. Am., Assn. Mining and Metall. Engrs., Eastern States Blast Furnace Soc. Home: 1810 Glenview Ave Park Ridge IL 60068 Office: 2600 American Ln Elk Grove Village IL 60007

LASKIN, SYLVESTER, utility co. exec.; b. Duluth, June 18, 1914; s. David and Esther (Kernes) L.; B.Elec. Engring. U. Minn., 1935; m. Betty Cornfeldt, Jan. 12, 1941; children—Eileen (Mrs. James Mitson), Harold, Michael. With Minn. Power & Light Co., Duluth, 1935—, pres., chief exec. officer, after 1969, now chmn. bd. dir. N.W. Bank Corp., First Am. Nat. Bank. Chmn., Minn. Safety Council. Registered profl. engr., Minn. Mem. I.E.E.E. Mason. Home: 3609 E Superior St Duluth MN 55804 Office: 30 W Superior St Duluth MN 55802

LASKOWSKI, LEONARD FRANCIS, JR., microbiologist, educator; b. Milw., Nov. 16, 1919; s. Leonard Francis and Frances (Cyborowski) L.; B.S., Marquette U., 1941, M.S., 1948; Ph.D., St. Louis U., 1951; m. Frances Bielinski, June 1, 1946; children—Leonard Francis III, James, Thomas. Instr. bacteriology Marquette U., 1946-48; grad. fellow St. Louis U., 1948-51, instr. bacteriology, 1951-53, sr. instr., 1953-54, asst. prof. microbiology, 1954-57, asst. prof. pathology, 1957-61, asso. prof. pathology, 1961-69, prof. pathology, 1969—, asso. prof. internal medicine, 1977—; dir. clin. microbiology sect. St. Louis U. Hosps. Labs., 1965—. Cons. clin. microbiology Firmin Desloge Hosp., St. Louis U. Group Hosps., St. Marys Group Hosps.; cons. bacteriology VA Hosp., Asst. dep. chief Pub. Health Lab., St. Louis Civil Def., 1958—; cons. St. Elizabeth's Hosp., St. Louis County Hosp., St. Francis Hosp. Health and tech. tng. coordinator for Latin Am. Peace Corps projects, 1962-66. Served with M.C., AUS, 1942-46. Diplomate Am. Bd. Microbiology. Fellow Am. Acad. Microbiology; mem. Soc. Am. Bacteriologists, N.Y. Acad. Scis., Am., Mo. pub. health assns., Am. Assn. U. Profs., Med. Mycol. Soc. Am., Alpha Omega Alpha. Contbr. articles in field to profl. jours. Home: Route 1 Box 117 Villa Ridge MO 63089 Office: 1402 S Grand Blvd St Louis MO 63104

LASLEY, JACK MOSS, civil engr.; b. Kansas City, Mo., Dec. 14, 1924; s. Erle Wood and Mathilde Christine (Lubert) L.; B.S., U. Kans., 1948, postgrad., 1951-52; m. Evelyn Harrell, June 1, 1947; children—Jeffrey Moss, Lee Ann. Bridge design engr. Kans. Hwy. Commn., Topeka, 1948-51, 54-55; instr. U. Kans., Lawrence, 1951-52; project engr. Indenco Engrs., Inc., San Leandro, Calif., 1955-56; mgr. civil and structural engring. dept. R.W. Booker & Assos., St. Louis, 1956-61; v.p. Thatcher & Patient, Inc., St. Louis, 1961-70; dir. engring. Behlen Mfg. Co. div. of Wickes Corp., Columbus, Nebr., 1970—. Served to lt. C.E. Corps, USNR, 1944-47, 52-54. Registered profl. engr., Nebr., Kans., Okla., Mo., Ill., Ind., Colo.; certified Nat. Council Engring. Examiners. Mem. Nat. Soc. Profl. Engrs., ASCE, Profl. Engrs. Nebr., Metal Bldg. Mfg. Assn. (mem. tech. com. 1971—), Phi Kappa Psi. Elk. Home: 2103 25th St Columbus NE 68601 Office: E Hwy 30 Columbus NE 68601

LASSERS, ELISABETH STERN, child psychiatrist; b. Offenbach, Germany; d. Robert E. and Dora (Metz) Stern; came to U.S., 1940, naturalized, 1946; M.D., U. Ill., 1949; m. Willard J. Lassers, June 30, 1946; 1 dau., Debbie. Intern, Mt. Sinai Hosp., Chgo., 1949-50; fellow Cook County Hosp., Chgo., 1950-51, pediatrics resident, 1951-52; pediatrics resident U. Ill. Research and Ednl. hosps., 1955-56, psychiatry resident U. Cheo. Hosps. and Clinics, 1963-67; med. dir. Ill. Children's Hosp. Sch., Chgo., 1952-53; clin. instr. pediatrics U. Ill., 1954-55, 56-59; practice medicine specializing in pediatrics, Chgo., 1956-59; mem. staff Michael Reese Hosp., 1957-63, dir. Evaluation Center for Handicapped Children, 1960-63; asso. in pediatrics Northwestern U., 1960-63; chief child psychiatry services Ill. Masonic Med. Center, Chgo., 1971-74, cons., 1974—; pvt. practice child and family psychiatry; asst. prof. psychiatry and pediatrics U. Ill., 1967—; lectr. psychiatry U. Chgo. Psychiat. cons. Step Sch., 1967-71, U.S. Children's Bur. fellow Center for Handicapped children, U. Ill., Research and Ednl. Hosps., 1959-60. Diplomate Am. Bd. Pediatrics, Am. Bd. Psychiatry and Neurology, Am. Bd. Child Psychiatry. Fellow Am. Orthopsychiat. Assn.; mem. Chgo. Council Child Psychiatry, Am. Acad. Pediatrics, Chgo. Pediatric Soc. (asso.), Am. Acad. Child Psychiatry, Am. Med. Women's Assn., Am. Psychiat. Assn., Ill. Psychiat. Soc., Soc. for Adolescent Psychiatry. Home: 1509 E 56th St Chicago IL 60637 Office: 111 N Wabash Ave Chicago IL 60602

LASSERS, WILLARD J., lawyer; b. Kankakee, Ill., Aug. 24, 1919; s. Henry and Sylvia (Oppenheim) L.; A.B., U. Chgo., 1940, J.D., 1942; m. Elisabeth Stern, June 30, 1946; 1 dau., Deborah. Admitted to D.C., bar, 1941, Ill. bar, 1942, U.S. Supreme Ct. bar, 1965; individual practice law, Chgo., 1946; practice with Alex Elson, Chgo., 1946-48, Elson and Cotton, 1948-49; atty. RFC. Chgo., 1950-51; atty. Office Price Stablzn., Chgo., 1951-53; individual practice law, Chgo., 1953-60; partner Elson, Lassers and Wolff, Chgo., 1960—; lectr. taxation U. Chgo., 1954-55. Mem. Gov.'s Com. to Study Consumer Credit Laws, 1962-63; chmn. Com. Ill. Govt., 1962-63. Bd. dirs. Ill. div. Am. Civil Liberties Union. Served with AUS, 1943-46. Mem. Ill., Chgo. bar assns., Am. Arbitration Assn. (mem. panel labor arbitrators 1965—). Author: (with Alex Elson) Civil Practice Forms Annotated, Illinois and Federal, 1952, 65; Scapegoat Justice: Lloyd Miller and the Failure of the Legal System, 1973. Home: 1509 E 56th St Chicago IL 60637 Office: 11 S LaSalle St Chicago IL 60603

LASSWELL, TULL CRESS, inventor, chem. co. exec.; b. Springfield, Ill., May 22, 1925; s. Tull Cress and Mary Anne (Selleck) L.; B.S., Northwestern U., 1951; m. Nancy Lee Wheeler, July 22, 1950; children—Tull Wheeler, Marsh Wheeler, Cam Wheeler, Star. Field sales engr. Fansteel Metall. Corp., 1951-53; dist. mgr. Spiegel, Inc., Chgo., 1953-56; prodn. supr. Pillsbury Mills, Springfield, Ill., 1956-58; corp. mgr. Am. Waterlock Corp., Mich., 1958-60; pres. Tri-X Corp., Oxford, Mich., 1960—. Served with Submarine Service USN, 1941-45. Mem. Internat. Brotherhood Magicians, Phi Delta Theta. Patentee in field. Home: 626 Oxford Oaks Ct Oxford MI 48051 Office: 544 Lakeville Rd Oxford MI 48051

LASTORIA, MICHAEL DONALD, coll. dean; b. Cleve., Sept. 21, 1948; s. Michael Angelo and Theresa Marie (Tirabasso) L.; B.S., Rutgers U., 1970; M.S., U. Nebr., Omaha, 1974; certificate, Grace Coll. of Bible, Omaha, 1975; postgrad. Loyola U., Chgo., 1976—; m. Cynthia Shelley Bertram, Aug. 25, 1972. Grad. asst. U. Nebr., Omaha, 1974; head resident adviser Moody Bible Inst., Chgo., 1975-77, asst. dean students, 1977—. Mem. Am. Personnel and Guidance Assn., Am. Coll. Personnel Assn. Home: 538 Germaine St Elk Grove Village IL 60007 Office: 820 N LaSalle Chicago IL 60610

LATHAM, IRIS ANNE, radio broadcaster; b. Coshocton, Ohio, Aug. 14, 1925; d. Raymond Walker and Effie Mae (Bodenheimer) Latham; grad. high sch. Continuity mgr. WGL radio, Fort Wayne, Ind., 1951-54; traffic dir. WHIZ radio, Zanesville, Ohio, 1954-57; women's dir. WANE radio, Fort Wayne, 1957-64; writer, host interview show, producer WGL radio, Fort Wayne, 1964—. Adviser, Social League Interested Women, 1969, Young Republicans Club, 1967-70, YWCA, 1968—; chmn. Judges City Council Internships, 1972; hostess Ind. U. European Tour, 1971. Bd. dirs. March of Dimes Allen County. Recipient George Washington Honor medal Freedoms Found., 1969; Merit citations Mayor Fort Wayne, 1969-71; Sterling Cup award Sterling Mags., 1974; named Notable Woman Broadcaster Family Circle, 1969. Mem. Zonta Internat. (treas., 1971-72), Fort Wayne Press Club. Republican. Baptist. Author, producer, host radio series: They Came to America, The Woman Alcoholic, Europeans Today, Black Legacies, Marriage Today. Home: 235 E Hoover Dr Fort Wayne IN 46816 Office: 2000 Lower Huntington Rd Fort Wayne IN 46809

LATHAM, ROBERT ALLEN, veterinarian; b. Milton Junction, Wis., Nov. 20, 1922; s. Robert Allen and Lillian Gertrude (Schmidt) L.; B.S., U. Ill., 1950, D.V.M., 1952; m. Diana Ruth Dowell, Aug 18, 1951; children—Robert Allen, Timothy John, Benjamin Walter, Katherine Diana. Gen. practice veterinary medicine, Carmi, Ill., 1952, Mt. Carroll, Ill., 1952-55, Erie, Ill., 1955—. Trustee Erie Library Dist., 1970-76; mem. Erie Elementary Sch. Bd., 1963-66. Served with USNR, 1972-76. Mem. Am., Ill. State (pres. 1976), Mississippi Valley (pres. 1964) veterinary med. assns., Ill. Acad. Veterinary Medicine (pres. 1971). Republican. Mem. Christian Ch. (Disciples of Christ). Club: Lions. Editor Ill. State Veterinary Med. Assn. Directory of 1977. Home: 1002 6th St Erie IL 61250 Office: 810 Main St Erie IL 61250

LATHAM, WILBUR JOSEPH, lawyer; b. Alexander, Iowa, Feb. 18, 1912; s. Jesse Llewellyn and Mamie (Meyer) L.; B.S. in Agr., Iowa State U., 1935; J.D. with honors, Drake U., 1967; m. Mary Edney Weatherwax, Jan. 1, 1939; children—Wilbur Joseph, Suzanne (Mrs. Thomas C. Thomsen), Dorothy Jane (Mrs. Steven B. Prater). Field supr. Prodn. Credit Corp., Omaha, 1935-37; asst. mgr. Beneficial Mgmt. Corp., San Diego, 1937-38; auditor Wansley, Crandal & Reuter, C.P.A.'s, San Diego, 1938-39; farm mgr. Met. Life Ins. Co., Ida Grove, Iowa, 1939-43, farm loan rep. farm mortgage div. Iowa br. office, Eagle Grove, 1946-54, mgr. Iowa br., Fort Dodge, 1954-64; admitted to Iowa bar, 1967; partner Johnson, Burnquist, Erb, Latham & Gibb, Fort Dodge. Served as lt. USNR, 1943-46. Mem. Am. Soc. Farm Mgrs. and Rural Appraisers, Order of Coif, Alpha Zeta, Alpha Gamma Rho. Mason (Shriner). Home: 1660 N 23d St Fort Dodge IA 50501 Office: Snell BLdg Fort Dodge IA 50501

LATHEROW, CLIFFORD BRANDON, state legislator; b. Carthage, Ill., Dec. 4, 1915; s. George Alexander and Gail (Miller) L.; B.Ed., Western Ill. U., 1937; m. Betty Hungate, June 26, 1940; children—Linda (Mrs. David Wilson), Donald Brice, Jerry Allen. Tchr., Fountain Green High Sch., 1937-43; owner, operator farm, Carthage, 1940—; mem. Hancock County Bd. Suprs., 1951-65; mem. Ill. Senate, 1965—. Incorporator, Roosevelt Nat. Ins., Springfield, Ill. Del. Republican nat. conv., 1976. Served with USNR, 1943-46. Mem. Am. Legion, V.F.W. Mason (33 degree, Shriner), Elk. Address: Route 3 Carthage IL 62321

LATOURETTE, BRAINERD WILLIAM, JR., county ofcl.; b. St. Louis, June 3, 1930; s. Brainerd William and Evelyn Ruth (Bull) L.; A.N., Westminster Coll., Fulton, Mo., 1952; J.D., Washington U., St. Louis, 1955; m. Nancy McDonald, June 17, 1954; children—Brainerd William III, Suzanne. Admitted to Mo. bar, 1955; sr. partner firm LaTourette, Weyerich & Clinton; city atty., Richmond Heights, 1958-62; mem. St. Louis County Council from 5th dist., 1963—. Trustee St. Louis unit Shriners Hosp., St. Luke's Hosp., St. Louis. Served with U.S. Army, 1955-57. Republican. Clubs: Masons, Shriners, Mo. Athletic, University (St. Louis). Home: 78 Chafford Woods St Louis MO 63144 Office: 11 S Meramec St Clayton MO 63105

LATTA, DELBERT L., congressman; b. Weston, Ohio, Mar. 5, 1920; A.M., LL.B., Ohio No. U.; m. Rose Mary Kiene; children—Rose Ellen, Robert Edward. Admitted to Ohio bar, 1944; state senator, Ohio, 3 terms; mem. 86th to 95th Congresses, 5th Ohio Dist. Republican. Home: Bowling Green OH 43402 Office: House Office Bldg Washington DC 20515

LATTER, MARTIN, wholesale co. exec.; b. N.Y.C., Aug. 11, 1919; s. Harry and Minnie (Stone) L.; B.S., Coll. City N.Y., 1941; m. Patricia Johnson, Dec. 16, 1966; children—Arthur, Howard, Jeffrey. Mdse. mgr. Stevens, Miami, Fla., 1948-54; mdse. mgr. Hinky Dinky Stores, Omaha, 1954-60; corporate v.p., gen. mgr. Eagle Food Stores & May's Drug Co., Milan, Ill., 1960-66; exec. v.p. Haag Drug Co., Indpls., 1966-69; pres. Ronco Teleproducts, Inc., Chgo., 1960—; pres., dir. Pamar Inc., Martin Latter & Assos. Inc., E-Z Open Inc., 1973—; v.p. sales and mktg. Scentex. Inc., Chgo.; dir. Columnist Housewares Rev. Served with AUS, 1941-46. Decorated Purple Heart with clusters, Silver Star, Bronze Star with cluster. Recipient Nat. Merchandiser award, 1964, Am. Jewish Com. award, 1965, Blood Bank award, 1968, D.A.V. award, 1968. Home: 1000 Lake Shore Dr Chicago IL 60611 Office: 3260 W Grand Ave Chicago IL 60651

LATTIMER, RICHARD LEE, archery co. exec.; b. South Bend, Ind., Dec. 6, 1935; s. Clarence Marion and Mary Rosalie (Horvath) L.; B.S., Ind. U., 1957; m. Alice Faye Peters, June 7, 1958; children—Michael John, Elizabeth Ann, Kevin Scott. Market analyst Studebaker-Packard Corp., South Bend, Ind., 1959-62; account exec. Juhl Advt. Agy., Elkhart, 1962-65; advt. mgr. Ekco Products, Inc., Canton, Ohio, 1965-66; account exec. Bonsib Inc., advt. Fort Wayne, Ind., 1966-71; nat. dir. Fred Bear Sports Club, also advt./sales promotion mgr. Bear Archery div. Victor Comptometer Corp., Grayling, Mich., 1972—, editor The Big Sky, 1972—; advisor communications com. Internat. Assn. Fish and Wildlife Agys., Washington. Adult adviser Jr. Achievement, South Bend, 1961; active fund raising United Fund and Fine Arts Found.; chmn. citizens adv. action council Camp Shawono, Office Child and Youth Services, 1974-76; advt. adviser Democratic Party, Allen County, Ind., 1970; dir. No. Ind. fund raising St. Jude Children's Research Hosp., 1970-72; trustee, pub. relations dir. No. Mich. chpt. Multiple Sclerosis Soc., 1972-74. Mem. Am. Mktg. Assn. (charter mem., treas., 1961-62), Nat. Rifle Assn., Grayling Regional C. of C. (dir.), Outdoor Writers Assn. Am. Club: Fred Bear Sports. Author poetry under pseudonym Joshua Carpenter, articles. Home: Rural Route 1 Box 30 Sherwood Forest Grayling MI 49738 Office: Rural Route 1 Grayling MI 49738

LATTIMER-BETHEL, AGNES DOLORES, pediatrician; b. Memphis, May 13, 1928; d. Arthur O. and Hortense Mattie (Lewis) Lattimer; A.B., Fisk U., 1949; M.D., Chgo. Med. Sch., 1954; m. Frank Bethel, Mar. 21, 1971; one son, Bernard Goss. Intern, Cook County Hosp., Chgo., 1954-55, resident in pediatrics, 1955-56; resident in pediatrics Michael Reese Hosp., Chgo., 1956-58; practice medicine specializing in pediatrics, Chgo., 1958-66; dir. div. ambulatory pediatrics Michael Reese Hosp., Chgo., 1966-71; dir. div. ambulatory pediatrics Cook County Hosp., Chgo., 1971—; regional med. cons. Job Corps, Region V, U.S. Dept. Labor, Chgo., 1973-76; clin. instr. preventive medicine U. Ill., 1959-65; clin. instr. pediatrics Chgo. Med. Sch., 1965-66, asst. prof., 1967-68, asso. prof., 1971—; asst. prof. pediatrics U. Chgo., 1970-71. Elsie and Phillip Sang awardee Chgo. Med. Sch., 1968; named distinguished alumnus Chgo. Med. Sch. Alumni Assn., 1971. Diplomate Nat. Bd. Med. Examiners. Fellow Am. Acad. Pediatrics, Inst. Medicine Chgo.; mem. Chgo. Pediatric Soc., Am. Pub. Health Assn., Ambulatory Pediatric Assn., Alpha Omega Alpha, Alpha Gamma Phi. Home: 2138 E 75th St PO Box 426 Chicago IL 60649 Office: 1835 W Harrison St Chicago IL 60612

LATZ, ROBERT, lawyer; b. Mpls., July 15, 1930; s. Rubin and Rose (Arnove) L.; B.S.L., U. Minn., 1952, LL.B., 1954; m. Carolyn Spater, Aug. 6, 1961; children—Ronald, Martin, Michael, Shari Lynn. Admitted to Minn. bar, 1954; asst. atty. gen. Minn., 1955-58; mem. Minn. Ho. of Reps., 1959-66; rep. firm Sachs, Latz & Kirshbaum, Mpls., 1960—. Chmn. Mpls. Urban Coalition Action Council, 1971-72; officer, dir. Greater Mpls. Met. Housing Corp.; del. Democratic Nat. Conv., 1960, 64; chmn. Dem. Farmer-Labor Conv., 1962, 64; candidate atty. gen. Minn., 1966; regent U. Minn., 1975; bd. dirs. Jewish Community Center Greater Mpls. Served with USNR, 1958-60. Mem. Am. Arbitration Assn. (mem. nat. panel arbitrators), Am. Bar Assn. (sects. labor relations and antitrust law), Am. Soc. Law Medicine, Am. Trial Lawyers Assn., Delta Sigma Rho, Sigma Alpha Mu. Jewish. Mason; mem. B'nai B'rith (nat. commr. Anti-Defamation League). Home: 6850 Harold Ave Minneapolis MN 55427 Office: 548 Roanoke Bldg Minneapolis MN 55402

LAU, CHOSEN CHUI-SHUN, physician; b. Hongkong, June 21, 1936; s. Mee Yan and Yuk Chung (Ho) L.; came to Can., 1953, naturalized, 1968; B.Sc., U. Man. (Winnipeg, Can.), 1958, B.Sc. in Medicine, 1962, M.D., 1962; m. Winnifred Lee, May 26, 1962; 1 son, Andrew. Intern, St. Boniface Gen. Hosp., Winnipeg, 1962-63; resident St. Joseph Mercy Hosp., Ann Arbor, Mich., 1963-65, Wayne County Gen. Hosp., Eloise, Mich., 1965-67, in plastic surgery U. Toronto (Ont., Can.), 1967-69; clin. fellow plastic surgery dept. plastic surgery Toronto Gen. Hosp., 1969; practice medicine specializing in plastic, cosmetic and hand surgery, Windsor, Ont., 1970—; dir. regional burn unit Met. Gen. Hosp., Windsor; mem. staff Grace, I.O.D.E., Hotel Dieu hosps., all Windsor. Fellow Royal Coll. Physicians and Surgeons Can., A.C.S.; mem. Canadian Soc. Plastic Surgeons, Am. Soc. Plastic and Reconstructive Surgeons, Am. Burn Assn., Essex County Med. Soc., Ont., Canadian med. assns. Office: 700 Tecumseh Rd E Windsor ON N8X 4T2 Canada

LAU, JACKSON CHART-SUM, architect; b. Canton, China, Apr. 1, 1937; s. King-yuen and Wai-Kwong (Lau) L.; bldg. diploma Hong Kong Tech. Coll., 1957-60; student Purdue U., 1967-70; m. Catherine Wai-ngo Li, Jan. 30, 1964; children—Emily, Scot. Came to U.S., 1967, naturalized, 1973. Designer, E.Y. Wu and Y.S. Shang, architects, Hong Kong, China, 1959-65; asso., H.Y. Chan, architect, Hong Kong,

1965-67; designer, Everett I. Brown Co., architect and engrs., Indpls., 1967-68; project architect McGuire & Shook, Corp., architects, Indpls., 1968-72; architect, Lau & Assos., Inc., Indpls., 1973—. Mem. AIA. Home: 3798 Coventry Way Carmel IN 46032 Office: 1010 E 86th St Indianapolis IN 46240

LAUBACH, JOHN PAUL, food co. exec.; b. Benton, Pa., Mar. 9, 1928; s. Jonathan Paul and Ethel Irene (Bray) L.; B.S., U.S. Naval Acad., 1951; m. Bobbie Lynn Gale, Nov. 5, 1966; children—Sharon, Jonathan. Constrn. exec. J. Paul Laubach Contracting Co., Benton, Pa., 1956-60; mem. tech. and mktg. staff IBM, Phila., White Plains, N.Y., 1961-67; data processing exec. Kraft Foods Co. and Kraftco., N.Y.C., Chgo., 1968-71; dir. info. services Kitchens of Sara Lee div. Consol. Foods Co., Deerfield, Ill., 1972-76; corp. dir. bus. systems Consol. Foods Corp., Chgo., 1976—. Pres., Homeowners Assn.; mem. Northbrook Caucus. Served with USN, 1951-56. Mem. ASCE, IEEE, Soc. for Mgmt. Info. Systems. Clubs: Army-Navy Country Club (Alexandria, Va.), Masons, Consistory, Shriners. Home: 3800 Charles Dr Northbrook IL 60062 Office: 135 S LaSalle St Chicago IL 60603

LAUBENHEIMER, ROGER, dermatologist, educator; b. Richfield, Wis., May 23, 1926; s. William H. and Ida (Beine) L.; B.S., U. Wis., 1948, M.D., 1950; m. Caroline Mahan, Feb. 10, 1951; children—William, Nancy, Kurt, Ann. Intern, Receiving Hosp., Detroit, 1950-51; resident in dermatology U. Wis., Madison, 1952-53; resident and clin. instr. dermatology U. Mich., Ann Arbor, 1953-55; practice medicine specializing in dermatology and chemosurgery, Milw., 1955-77; clin. prof. Med. Coll. Wis. Served with U.S. Army, 1950-52. Diplomate Am. Bd. Dermatology. Mem. Am. Acad. Dermatology, Wis. Dermatological Soc., Milw. Acad. Medicine, Chemosurgery Soc. (charter), Wis. Med. Soc. (del.), AMA, Milw. County Med. Soc. Republican. Congregationalist. Clubs: Rotary, Dairymen's Country, Masons. Contbr. articles in field to profl. jours. Home: 15160 Kings Ridge Ct Brookfield WI 53005 Office: 425 E Wisconsin Ave Milwaukee WI 53202

LAUCK, JACQUELINE ANN, counselor; b. St. Louis, Nov. 27, 1937; d. Harold Joseph and Marie Dorothy (Brewer) Lauck; B.S., So. Ill. U., Edwardsville, 1974, M.S., 1977; children—Steven, Gregory, Carolyn, Patricia, Elizabeth. Tutor So. Ill. U., 1973-74; tchr. East St. Louis Sch. Dist. 189, fall 1974; counselor A.I.D. Inc., Collinsville, Ill., 1975-76; counselor Madison County Council on Alcoholism and Drug Dependency, Alton, Ill., 1976-77; tchr. assertiveness tng., 1976-77; coordinator Metro-E. Title XX Services Project, Lewis and Clark Community Coll., 1977—; tchr. enrichment program Madison County Schs., spring 1973; cons. Belleville (Ill.) Area Community Coll., 1976. Pres. Metro-East Little Theatre Group, Cahokia, Ill., 1969-70; ex-officio dir. Edwardsville Youth Center, 1974. Recipient recognition award A.I.D., Inc., 1976. Mem. Am. Personnel and Guidance Assn., Turtles, Am. Assn. Group Workers, Including Us Feminist Collective, Assn. Women in Psychology, Women's Polit. Caucus. Inventor Acu-step. Address: 1232 St Michael Dr Cahokia IL 62206

LAUCKNER, CONNIE LOUISE PIETROWSKI, market analyst; b. Redwood Falls, Minn., Sept. 1, 1943; d. Stanley Charles and Florence Marie (Klabunde) Pietrowski; B.A., Coll. St. Catherine, 1965, postgrad. (NDEA scholar), Rennes, France, 1966; M.A., U. Mont., 1970; M.B.A., Mankato State U., 1976; m. David E. Lauckner, Dec. 28, 1966. Tchr., Sentinel High Sch., Missoula, Mont., 1965-70; internat. cons. Dittmann Tours, Inc., Northfield, Minn., 1971-72; asst. dir. news bur. Carleton Coll., Northfield, 1973; mktg. rep. Hotels Internat., Inc., Mpls., 1974-75; market research analyst Honeywell, Inc., Mpls., 1976—. Mem. Am. Mktg. Assn., Ops. Research Soc. Am., Alliance Française. Home: 10817 Girard Circle Bloomington MN 55431 Office: 10800 Lyndale Ave S Bloomington MN 55420

LAUDAN, JAMES ALVA, ins. co. exec.; b. Taylor, Tex., Dec. 18, 1915; s. James Verbon and Della Pearl (Barton) L.; B.B.A., U. Tex., 1939; m. Florence Claire Shannon, Sept. 22, 1940; children—Larry L., Kenneth R., Marilyn L. (Mrs. Arthur J. Frankel); m. 2d, Catherine Robbins Hamilton, May 15, 1977. Exec. v.p. Ins. Facilities Corp., Kansas City, Mo., 1957-59; asst. v.p. Holland-Am. Ins. Co., Kansas City, Mo., 1957-59; pres., chmn., Spl. Risks Underwriters Agy., Inc., Kansas City, Mo., 1959-67; exec. v.p., chmn. KLM Investment Corp., Kansas City, Mo., 1964-68; pres., chmn. Al Laudan & Co., Kansas City, Mo., 1964-67; br. mgr. Ranger Ins. Co., Kansas City, Mo., 1967—; treas., dir. FSL Services, Inc., publishers, Overland Park, Kans., 1973-75; dir. Ranger Nat. Life Ins. Co., Houston, 1974—. Vice pres., dir. Hill and Dale Montessori Sch., Overland Park, Kans., 1965-73. Coordinator, Johnson-Wyandotte Counties (Kans.) candidate Kans. ins. commr. Republican party, 1970, 72. Bd. dirs., sec. Kansas City chpt. City of Hope, 1965-67. Served with USNR, 1944-46. Recipient Distinguished Service award Kans. Assn. Ind. Ins. Agents, 1972. Mem. Kans. Assn. Commerce and Industry (mem. pub. affairs council 1973—), Am. Legion. Elk. Clubs: Red Coater; Kansas City Chiefs Football, Friends of Art. Home: PO Box 4311 Shawnee Mission KS 66204 Office: PO Box 8650 Kansas City MO 64114

LAUDICINA, PAUL FRANK, radiol. technologist; b. Chgo., Nov. 4, 1942; s. Frank P. and Ann M. (Alagna) L.; B.A., Northeastern Ill. U., 1974, M.A., 1977; m. Rita Lenore Lewandowski, May 21, 1966; children—Anthony, Michael. Clin. instr. radiology Resurrection Hosp., Chgo., 1966-72; dir. radiol. tech. program Coll. Du Page, Glen Ellyn, Ill., 1972—. Active Boy Scouts Am. Served with USN, 1963-66. Mem. Du Page County X-Ray Soc. (pres., dir., distinguished service award), Am., Ill. (pres., dir.) socs. radiol. technologists, Am. Registry Radiol. Technologists, Coll. Radiol. Scis. (bd. chancellors), Am. Personnel and Guidance Assn. Roman Catholic. Home: 7750 W Victoria St Chicago IL 60631 Office: Coll Du Page Glen Ellen IL 60137

LAUDICK, RICHARD EDWARD, JR., newspaper publisher; b. Ottawa, Ohio, Jan. 11, 1929; s. Richard E. and Edna C. (Gulker) L.; student Bowling Green State U., 1947-48; m. Jeanette Schmitz, Oct. 7, 1950; children—Deborah Laudick Birkemeier, Jeanne Laudick Verhoff, Kevin, Joseph, Annette. Pres., publisher, editor, mgr. Putnam County (Ohio) Sentinel, Ottawa, 1974—. Pres., Putnam County TB Health Assn., 1970-72; pres. Western Ohio Respiratory Health Assn. (now Western Ohio Lung Assn.), 1974-75; chmn. bd. Putnam County (Ohio) Mental Health Clinic, 1974-75; mem. Ottawa Downtown Devel. Com. Mem. Ottawa C. of C. (pres. 1975). Home: 528 E 3rd St Ottawa OH 45875 Office: Box 149 Ottawa OH 45875

LAUER, HAROLD EUGENE, orthodontist; b. Waldo, Ohio, Aug. 17, 1919; s. Herbert Albert and Cloa Melinda (Lehner) L.; B.S., Ohio State U., 1941, D.D.S., 1950, postgrad., 1950-51; m. Ann Riley Nunley, 1975; children by previous marriage—H. Andrew, John Arthur, T. Herbert, Annette; stepchildren—Patricia Nunley, Julia Nunley. Gen. practice dentistry, Columbus, Ohio, 1950-51, practice dentistry specializing in orthodontics, Lima, Ohio, 1952—. Sec., H.L.P. Corp., 1957; dir. Drs. Lauer, Webb, Fowler & McFarland, Inc. Clinician, lectr. Western European Orthodontic Congress, Paris, France, 1964. Pres., Allen County Tb and Health Assn., Lima, 1956-57, Ohio State U. Orthodontic Found., 1965. Bd. dirs. Meml. Hosp. Staff. Served with F.A., AUS, 1941-46. Decorated Bronze Star. Mem. Am., Ohio, Northwestern Ohio dental assns., Am. Assn. Orthodontics, Ohio State Orthodontic Found., Lima Acad. Dentistry, Gt. Lakes Orthodontic Assn., Allen County, Ohio State Univ. Alumni Assn. (past pres.). Lutheran (chmn. devel. and property com.). Elk, Rotarian. Club: Torch (pres. Lima 1966-67). Home: 2614 Shoreline Dr Lima OH 45805 Office: 939 W Market St Lima OH 45805

LAUER, PETER HANS, bus. cons.; b. Hamburg, Germany, May 25, 1918; s. Paul and Mathilde (Winner) L.; came to U.S., 1938, naturalized, 1941; student Northwestern U., 1940-50; M.B.A., U. Chgo., 1956; m. Theresea Paleczny, Feb. 23, 1975; children—Steven K., Linda A. Controller, IIT Research Inst., Chgo., 1945-55; chief financial officer Flexonics Corp., Chgo., 1955-59; controller Interstate-United Corp., Chgo., 1959-64; v.p. finance, dir. Eugene Dietzgen Co., Chgo., 1964-69; pres. Lauer & Holbrook, Inc., Chgo., 1970—. Instr. Grad. Sch. Bus., U. Chgo., 1959-60, Grad. Sch. Bus., DePaul U., Chgo., 1968-72. Served with M.I. AUS, 1943-45. C.P.A., Ill. Mem. Financial Execs. Inst. (Chgo. dir. 1964—), Am. Inst. C.P.A.'s, Ill. Soc. C.P.A.'s. Home: 505 N Lake Shore Dr Chicago IL 60611 Office: 135 S LaSalle St Chicago IL 60603

LAUER, ROBERT HAROLD, sociologist, educator; b. St. Louis, June 28, 1933; s. Earl Ervin and Frances Pauline (Buschen) L.; B.S. in Elec. Engring., Washington U., 1954; M.A., So. Ill. U., 1969, Ph.D., 1970. Asst. prof. sociology So. Ill. U., Edwardsville, 1970-72, asso. prof., 1971-74, prof., 1974—. Asst. chmn. charter rev. com. Town of Florissant (Mo.), 1974, mem. housing appeals com., 1977—. Mem. Am. Sociol. Assn., Midwest Sociol. Soc., Soc. for Cross-Cultural Research, Assn. Vol. Action Scholars, World Future Soc. Democrat. Presbyterian. Author: Perspectives on Social Chage, 1973; Social Problems, 1976; (with Warren Handel) Social Psychology, 1977; Social Problems and the Quality of Life, 1978; editor: Social Movements and Social Change, 1976; contbr. articles to profl. jours. Home: 2545 Guildford St Florissant MO 63033 Office: Box 45 Dept Sociology Southern Illinois Univ Edwardsville IL 62026

LAUFFER, ALICE A., artist; b. Frankfort Twp., Ill., Oct. 25, 1919; d. George Albert and Florence Aubina (Gammon) Lauffer; diploma Chgo. Acad. Fine Arts, 1939; student Sch. of Art Inst. Chgo., 1942-43, 58-62; m. William Frederick Schmidt, June 2, 1950; children—Lora Schmidt Mason, Christine A., David O., William G. Designer, Bates Art Industries, Chgo., 1940-41, Eastern Art Products, Chgo., 1941-43; free-lance designer, Chgo., 1945-58; one-person shows: Chgo. Main Pub. Library, 1972, Ill. Arts Council, Chgo., 1975, Artemisia Gallery, Chgo., 1977; group shows include: San Francisco Mus. Art, 1970, Smithsonian Traveling Exhibition, 1972-74, Nat. Gallery Fine Arts, Washington, 1973-75, Deson-Zaks Group Show, Chgo., 1972, 76, Hyde Pk. Art Center, Chgo., 1976, 1134 Gallery, Chgo., 1976; represented in permanent collections: Art Inst. of Chgo. (Print and Drawing Collection); works include: Beyond Jupiter (lithograph published Landfall Press). Recipient James Broadus Clarke award Art Inst. Chgo., 1969; Purchase award, Drawings U.S.A., Minn. Mus. Art, 1973. Mem. Arts Club Chgo., Chgo. Soc. Artists, W.E.B. Home: 4 E Ohio St Chicago IL 60611 Office: 1017 N Western Ave Chicago IL 60622

LAUGHLIN, CHARLES WALTER, newspaper exec.; b. Indpls., June 22, 1925; s. Charles Wilbur and Emma (Hankins) L.; grad. high sch.; m. Henriette Alida Ooms, July 24, 1945; children—Patricia Alida, Sonja Anna, Marilyn Jo, Gregory Jan. Reporter Anderson (Ind.) Daily Bulletin, 1947, sports editor, 1947-49; with Anderson Newspapers, Inc., 1949—, dir., sec. corp., 1965—, treas., 1967—, asst. gen. mgr., 1967-76, gen. mgr., 1976—; adminstr., trustee Anderson Newspapers Inc. Retirement Trust, 1976—. Mem. Mayor's Adv. Com., 1966; chmn. bus. div. United Fund, 1966, 67; co-chmn. bus. div. campaign Community Hosp., St. John's Hosp., 1967; chmn. St. Mary's Spl. Capital Funds Campaign, 1976; nat. asso. Boys' Clubs Am., 1972—. Bd. dirs. Boys' Clubs, 1964—, exec. com., 1966—, pres., 1966-67; bd. dirs. County Cancer, 1972—. Served with AUS, 1943-46: ETO. Mem. Am. Mgmt. Assn., Inst. Newspapers Controllers and Finance Officers, C. of C., Inland Daily Press Assn., Hoosier State Press Assn., Travelers Protective Assn. (pres., 1951), Internat. Newspaper Advt. Execs. Assn., Miss. Valley Classified Advt. Mgrs. Assn. (pres., 1961). Elk (All-Ind. exalted ruler, 1961), Rotarian (pres. 1964-65; dist. gov. 1976-77). Club: Edgewood Country. Home: 1408 Winding Way Anderson IN 46011 Office: 1133 Jackson St Anderson IN 46015

LAUGHLIN, ETHELREDA ELIZABETH ROSS, educator; b. Cleve., Nov. 13, 1922; d. Edward W. and Marie C. (Solinski) Ross; A.B., Flora Stone Mather Coll., 1942; M.S., Western Res. U., 1944, Ph.D., 1962; m. J. Guy Laughlin, June 14, 1951 (div. June 1956); 1 son, J. Guy. Faculty Loyola U., Chgo., 1948-49, St. John Coll., Cleve., 1949-51, tchr. various schs., 1953-61; faculty Ferris State Coll., 1962-63; prof. chemistry Cuyahoga Community Coll., Western campus, Parma, Ohio, 1963—, dept. head scis., 1965-76; vis. prof. biochemistry Case-Western Res. U., Cleve., 1970-71. Mem. policy com. Coll. Chemistry Consultants service, 1970-76; biochemist in charge animal research Ben Venue Labs., 1947-48, Armour Research Labs., 1948, Western Res. U. Med. Sch., 1942-47; research fellow in biochemistry Cleve. Clinic Hosp. Labs., 1953. Nat. Sci. Tchrs. Assn. grantee, 1957-58, 58-59, NSF grantee, 1958, 60, 61, 63, 77; named Distinguished Grad., Case-Western Res. U., 1968; recipient Outstanding Regional Chemistry Tchr. award Mfg. Chemists Assn., 1973. Mem. N.E.A., Am. Chem. Soc. (chmn. com. on chemistry two-year coll. tchrs. sect. 1974, treas. 1975, chmn. teaching of chemistry com.), Ohio Chemistry Tchrs. Assn., Ohio Jr. Coll. Tchrs. Assn., Nat. Sci. Tchrs. Assn., Ohio Edn. Assn., Nat. Assn. Research in Sci. Teaching, Audubon Soc. (pres. Western Cuyahoga chpt. 1976), Sigma Xi. Club: Sierra. Contbr. articles to publs. Home: 6486 State Rd 12 Concord Sq Village Parma OH 44134

LAUMAN, VONA KATHRYN (MRS. JAMES WESLEY LAUMAN), printing, pub. co. exec.; b. Strawberry Point, Iowa, Nov. 20, 1927; d. Otto Fred and Emma Katherine (Meinken) Weger; B.S.C., U. Iowa, 1950; m. James Wesley Lauman, June 28, 1950; 1 dau., Lori Ann. Sec., Owens Ill. Glass Co., Chgo., 1950-51; sec. to treas. Pacific Coast Coca-Cola Bottling Co., Los Angeles, 1951-53; office mgr. Reynolds Aluminum Co., Indpls., 1953-56; office mgr. Central Pub. Co., Indpls., 1956-59, corporate sec., 1959-65, sales mgr., 1965-69, v.p., asst. gen. mgr., 1969—, also dir.; corporate sec. Weger Farms, Inc., Strawberry Point, Ia., 1969—, also dir. Mem. Ia. U. Alumni Assn., Ind. Bus. Communicators. Republican. Lutheran. Home: 8029 Burn Ct Indianapolis IN 46217 Office: 401 N College Ave Box 1652 Indianapolis IN 46206

LAUN, ARTHUR HENRY, JR., lawyer; b. Milw., May 24, 1930; s. Arthur Henry and Annette (Pfister) L.; B.B.A., U. Wis., 1954, J.D., 1954; m. Marilyn M. Johnson, Feb. 14, 1964; children—Stephen G., Cynthia T., Sharyl K., Steven C., Lisa A. Admitted to Wis. bar, 1954, since practiced in Milw.; mem. firm Quarles & Brady, 1954—, partner, 1962—. Dir. U-Line Corp., Unicare Services, Inc. Mem. Thiensville-Mequon Union High Sch. Dist. No. 1 Sch. Bd., 1965-70; mem. exec. bd. Y-Men's Club; adv. bd. United Fund. Recipient Meritorious Service award YMCA, 1959. Mem. Am. (chmn. com.), Wis. (sect. dir.), Milw. (past com. chmn.) bar assns., Order of Coif, U. Wis. Found., U. Wis. Pres.'s Club, Phi Beta Kappa, Sigma Phi, Phi Delta Phi, Beta Alpha Psi, Beta Gamma Sigma, Delta Sigma Rho, Phi Eta Sigma, Phi Kappa Phi, Iron Cross, Republican. Episcopalian. Exec. editor Wis. Law Rev., 1953-54. Home: 12028 N Lake Shore Dr Mequon WI 53092 Office: 780 N Water St Milwaukee WI 53202

LAUNDRY, MARION SUZANNE TEEUWS (MRS. MELBURN EDWARD LAUNDRY), educator; b. Chgo., Apr. 21, 1933; d. William L. and Marion (Svoda) Teeuws; B.A. in Bus. Econs., Rosary Coll., 1956, M.A. in L.S., 1961; M.Ed., Loyola U., Chgo., 1966; m. Melburn Edward Laundry, May 31, 1958; 1 son, Melburn Edward II. Jr. investment analyst Continental Casualty & Assurance Co., Chgo., 1956-58; tchr. Maywood (Ill.) Bd. Edn., 1958-61; sch. librarian Oak Park (Ill.) Elementary Sch., 1961-66; library cons. USAF, Wiesbaden, Germany, 1966-67; tech. cons. Ill. activities for 1970 White House Conf. Children and Youth, Springfield, Ill., 1967; instr. library sci. Northeastern Ill. State Coll., 1967-69; dir. library tech. edn. Coll. DuPage, Glen Ellyn, Ill., 1969—; mem. Oak Park Lang. Arts Curriculum Com., 1950. Mem. nat. adv. bd. Am. Security Council, Washington, 1974—; bd. dirs., mem. by-laws com. Kidney Found. Ill., 1973—. Mem. ALA (chmn. profl. relations com. 1965-67), NEA, Ill. Edn. Assn. (dist. legislation com. 1965), Ill. (div. exec. bd. mem. 1965-66, editor bull. 1968—), European Sch. library assns., Oak Park-River Forest Art League, AAUW (legis. chmn. 1975—), English Speaking Union, Internat. Platform Assn., U. Chgo. Law Wives, Childrens Reading Round Table, Chgo. Opera Lyric Guild, Chgo. Council Fgn. Relations, AAUP, Frederic Law Olmsted Soc. Riverside, Ill. Fedn. Womens Clubs (ednl. chmn. 1977—), Delta Kappa Gamma, Beta Sigma Phi (chpt. founder, v.p. 1956-57), Pi Gamma Mu, Alpha Phi. Republican. Author: A Basic Reference List for Junior High School Libraries, 1969. Home: 505 Berkley Rd Riverside IL 60546 Office: Coll DuPage Glen Ellyn IL 60137

LAUNIUS, DELMER DWAIN, savs. and loan exec.; b. Ewing, Ill., May 24, 1921; s. Jeff Hillard and Delsie (Jenkins) L.; B.S. in Edn., So. Ill. U., 1949; M.S., U. Ill., 1954, postgrad., 1966, 70; m. Violet Groennert, Dec. 13, 1952; children—Steven, Sherry, Gregory. Vocat. instr. Triad Community Unit 2, St. Jacob, Ill., 1949-70, vocat. dir., 1970—; dir. Troy Savs. & Homestead Assn., Troy, Ill., 1953-67, pres., 1967—; dir. Troy Security Bank; faculty horticulture and fin. Belleville Community Coll., evenings 1969, 71, 72. Mem. Madison County Fair Bd., 1970—. Served with USAAF, 1942-46; PTO. Mem. Ill. Vocat. Assn., Am. Legion, Phi Delta Kappa. Mason (32 deg., Shriner). Home: 108 Elmer St Troy IL 62294 Office: 100 W Market St Troy IL 62294

LAUREN, OSCAR BUD, environ. odor cons.; b. Marinette, Wis., Feb. 12, 1918; s. Isadore and Rose (Brill) L.; B.S., Coll. City N.Y., 1939; children—Howard Keith, Randal Bruce, Sheryl Nan. Pres., Larad Industries, N.Y.C., 1948-66; cons. Rhodia Inc., N.Y.C., 1966-75; prin. Lauren & Assoc., LaGrange, Ill., 1975-77; cons. in field; lectr. in field. Served with USAAF, 1943-45. Decorated Air Medal with 3 oak leaf clusters; recipient Award of Merit, Pollution Engring. Mag., 1975, others. Mem. ASTM (odor com.), Air Pollution Control Assn., Am. Soc. Heating, Refrigerating and Air Conditioning Engrs. Contbr. articles in field to profl. jours. Home: 5805 Rose Ave LaGrange IL 60525 Died Oct. 27, 1977.

LAURENCE, RICHARD ROBERT, educator; b. Knoxville, Tenn., Apr. 22, 1937; s. Robert A. and Sally (Claxton) L.; B.A., U. Tenn., 1959; postgrad. Middlebury Coll., 1959; (Fulbright scholar) U. Vienna, 1959-60; M.A. (Woodrow Wilson fellow, Stanford U. fellow) Stanford U., 1962, Ph.D. (Austrian Govt. Research fellow), 1968; m. Gertraud Fuehrer, July 6, 1961; children—Daniel Robert, Sonya Christina, Alfred James. Instr. dept. humanities Mich. State U., 1966-68, asst. prof., 1968-76, asso. prof., 1976—. Mem. Am. Hist. Assn., Conf. Peace Research in History, Popular Culture Assn. Home: 1572 Cahill Dr East Lansing MI 48823 Office: Dept Humanities Mich State U East Lansing MI 48824

LAURENSON, ROBERT MARK, mech. engr.; b. Pitts., Oct. 25, 1938; s. Robert Mark and Mildred Othelia (Frandsen) L.; student Drury Coll., 1956-58; B.S. in Mech. Engring., Mo. Sch. Mines, 1961; M.S.E. in Mech. Engring., U. Mich., 1962; Ph.D. in Mech. Engring. (NASA tng. grantee), Ga. Inst. Tech., 1968; m. Alice Ann Scroggins, Aug. 26, 1961; children—Susan Elizabeth, Shari Lynn. Dynamics engr. McDonnell Douglas Corp., St. Louis, 1962-64, sr. dynamics engr., 1968-71, group engr., 1971-74, staff engr., 1974-75, tech. specialist, 1975—; mem. conf. organizing com., session chmn. Structures, Structural Dynamics and Materials Conf., 1977, chmn. tech. program, 1978; participant 14th Midwestern Mechanics Conf., 1975; lectr. engring. mechanics St. Louis U. part-time, 1969-71; participant Symposium on Dynamics and Control of Large Flexible Spacecraft, Blacksburg, Va., 1977. Registered profl. engr., Mo. Mem. Am. Soc. Mech. Engrs. (structures materials com. aerospace div., session organizer, chmn. session ann. meeting 1975), Am. Inst. Aeronautics Astronautics, Sigma Xi, Pi Tau Sigma, Tau Beta Pi, Phi Kappa Phi, Sigma Phi Epsilon. Episcopalian (vestryman, sr. warden). Home: 349 Beaver Lake Dr St Charles MO 63301 Office: McDonnell Douglas Corp Box 516 St Louis MO 63166

LAURENTI, JOSEPH LUCIAN, Spanish and Italian scholar, author, educator; b. Hesperange, Luxembourg, Dec. 10, 1931; s. Ernest and Angelina Teresa (Dal Canton) L.; came to U.S., 1949, naturalized, 1952; B.A., U. Ill., 1958, M.A., 1959; Ph.D., U. Mo., 1962; m. A. Luellen Watson, June 10, 1967. Instr. Spanish, U. Mo., Columbia, 1959-62; prof. Spanish and Italian, Ill. State U., Normal, 1962—; U.S. corr. for Quaderni Ibero-Americani, 1972; author numerous books, since 1965, latest being: A Bibliography of Picaresque Literature, 1972; Literary Relations Between Spain and Italy, 1972; The World of Federico Garcia Lorca, 1974; contbr. numerous articles and revs. on Spanish and Italian lit. to scholarly publs. Served with Mil. Intelligence U.S. Army, 1952-54. Recipient Order of Don Quixote. Mem. Modern Lang. Assn., Internat. Assn. of Hispanists, Am. Assn. Tchrs. of Spanish and Portuguese. Democrat. Roman Catholic. Home: 1407 Hanson Dr Normal IL 61761 Office: Stevenson 206 Illinois State Univ Normal IL 61761

LAURENTS, LOUIS VINSON, JR., computer programmer; b. Lake Arthur, La., Apr. 6, 1926; s. Louis Vinson and Evelyn (Greene) L.; m. Jaunita Elizabeth Dickison, July 14, 1947; children—Eileen E., Renee E., Jennie E., Louisa E., Lounita E., Louis Vinson. Instr. tech. tng. command U.S. Air Force, 1946-55, computer programmer, analyst Data Center, Hdqrs. Air Force Logistics Command, Wright Patterson AFB, Ohio, 1955—. Librarian br. geneology library Dayton (Ohio) stake Ch. of Jesus Christ of Latter-day Saints, instr. adult edn. program, established br. genealogy library in Cin., 1966. Served with USAF, 1946-49. Home: 227 Cash Ct Fairborn OH 45324 Office: Data Base and Interface Control Br Directorate Tech Support Wright Patterson AFB OH 45433

LAURILA, HAROLD LAVERN, civil engr., surveyor; b. Ashtabula, Ohio, Dec. 21, 1932; s. John H. and Anna S. (Antila) L.; B.S. in Civil Engring., Ind. Inst. Tech.; m. Dorothy Ruth Shafer, Dec. 21, 1956; children—Mary Elaine, Cathy Lynn, Harold David. With Burgess & Niple Cons. Engrs., Columbus, Ohio, 1958-65; project engr. Packaging Corp. Am., Rittman, Ohio, 1965-68; asst. to pres. Karl R. Rohrer Assos., Inc., Akron, Ohio, 1968—, also pres., mgr. Harold L. Laurila Properties, Rittman, 1968—; cons. engr., Surveyor Karl R.

Rohrer Assos., Inc. (Akron, Ohio). Served to sgt., AUS, 1953-55. Mem. ASCE, Akron Soc. C.E., Nat. Rifle Assn. Republican. Mem. Ch. of Christ (trustee). Participant temporary storage of combined sewer overflows research project, Sandusky, Ohio, 1968-69, project named one of 7 wonders of Ohio, 1969. Home: 55 Bradley St Rittman OH 44270 Office: 3810 Ridgewood Rd Akron OH 44321

LAURINO, ANTHONY C., city ofcl.; b. Chgo., July 27, 1910; s. Vito and Angelina (Minielia) L.; student DePaul U.; m. Marie Batleman, Mar. 11, 1937; children—Marie Angel Laurino D'Amico, William James, Margaret Marie. Precinct capt. City of Chgo., 1934—, ward committeeman, water insp., food insp., alderman City Council. Office: City Hall Chicago IL 60602

LAURSEN, PAUL HERBERT, educator; b. Ord, Nebr., Mar. 28, 1929; s. Ejvind L. and Jacobine E. (Jorgensen) L.; B.A. cum laude, Dana Coll., 1954; Ph.D., Oreg. State U., 1961; vis. scholar U. Calif. at Los Angeles, 1967-68; m. Marcia Gail Thompson, Aug. 23, 1959; children—Brett Paul, Scott Warren. Asst. prof. chemistry Nebr. Wesleyan U., Lincoln, 1959-62, asso. prof., 1962-64, prof., 1964—, head dept. chemistry, 1961-76, chmn. div. natural scis. and math., 1966-67, 68-71, chmn. faculty, 1973-76, acad. dean, 1976—; dir. student sci. tng. projects NSF, 1971-75; dir. Nebr. State Sci. Talent Search, 1974—. Active Boy Scouts Am., 1970-75; treas. Citizens for Environ. Improvement, 1971-73; trustee, gov. Neb. Wesleyan U., Lincoln, 1973-76. Served with Signal Corps, AUS, 1951-53. Recipient honor faculty award Nebr. Wesleyan U. Trustees, 1969, Distinguished Alumnus award Dana Coll., 1975; DuPont teaching fellow, 1958-59; NSF fellow, 1967-68. Mem. Am. Chem. Soc., AAAS, Nebr. Acad. Scis. (pres. 1970-71), Sigma Xi, Phi Lambda Upsilon, Sigma Pi Sigma. Lutheran (mem. exec. com. central dist. Am. Luth Ch. 1972-74). Club: Sertoma (v.p. 1972-73, dir. 1969-71, 72-74, 75-77). Home: 3145 N 70th St Lincoln NE 68507

LAUTERJUNG, MARVIN ALAN, elec. coop. and farm cons.; b. Red Bud, Ill., Dec. 18, 1939; s. Henry Rudolph and Veronica Cecelia (Gross) L.; B.S. in Agrl. Industries, So. Ill. U., 1962; m. Margaret Ann Eberle, Aug. 25, 1962; children—Donald Kent, Anne Marie, Amy Elizabeth. Sales mgr. Bond County Service Co., Greenville, Ill., 1962-64, elevator mgr., 1964-67; farm sales adv. Ill. Power Co., Decatur, 1967-74; elec. coop. and farm adviser, 1974—. Mem. Ill. Farm Electrification Council (4-H com., mem. farm materials handling ct., environ. control ct.). Roman Catholic. Home: 531 S Crea Decatur IL 62522 Office: 500 S 27th St Decatur IL 62525

LAUTZENHISER, NIANN KAY, psychometrist; b. Bryan, Ohio, Jan. 29, 1945; d. Kermit Arden and Luella Marie (Keppler) L.; student Bowling Green State U., 1963, 64, 65; B.S. in Edn., Miami U., Oxford, Ohio, 1966; M.S. in Edn., St. Francis Coll., 1971, M.S., 1975; postgrad. N.W. Tech. Coll., 1976-77. Tchr. math. John F. Kennedy Jr. High Sch., Kettering, Ohio, 1966-69; tchr. math. Angola (Ind.) High Sch., 1969-70, guidance counselor, 1970-75, counseling psychometrist, 1975-77, counseling psychometrist Angola Middle Sch., 1977—. Bd. dirs. Switchboard, Inc., Angola, Community Service, Inc., Angola, sec., 1976. Mem. Nat. Assn. Sch. Counselors (master sch. counselor certificate 1976), Nat. Assn. Sch. Psychologists, Am., Ind., Ohio personnel and guidance assns., NEA, Ind. State Tchrs. Assn., Nat. Council Tchrs. Math., Angola Classroom Tchrs. Assn., AAUW. Lutheran. Office: Route 4 Box 11 A Angola IN 46703

LAUVER, MILTON RENICK, chemist; b. Springfield, Ohio, Sept. 14, 1920; s. Milton and Helen Madera (Renick) L.; A.B., Wittenberg U., 1942; M.S., Case Western Res. U., 1944, Ph.D., 1948; m. Edith Marie Gedeon, July 17, 1948; children—Patricia Ellen, Janet Martha, James Milton, Susan Elizabeth. Research chemist FMC Corp., Carteret, N.J., 1948-53; research chemist Diamond Shamrock Corp., Painesville, Ohio, 1953-58; research phys. scientist Lewis Research Center, NASA, Cleve., 1958—. Co-chmn. Citizens Com. for North Olmsted Pub. Schs., 1967-68. Served with USNR, 1944-46. Mem. Am. Chem. Soc., A.A.A.S. Kiwanian. Home: 28385 Holly Dr North Olmsted OH 44070 Office: 21000 Brookpark Rd Cleveland OH 44135

LAUX, PATRICIA MARIE, editor; b. Clintonville, Wis., Apr. 22, 1943; d. Joseph J. and Adeline E. (Below) Laux; B.A., Coll. of St. Teresa, Minn., 1965. Editorial asst. Prairie Farmer Mag., Chgo., 1966-67, asst. home editor, 1967-69, home editor, 1969-72; tech. editor Metric Publs., Neenah, Wis., 1972-74, asso. editor, 1974-77, gen. editor, 1977—; mem. Nat. Metric Speakers Bur., 1975—. Mem. allocations panel United Way of Neenah, 1977—, mem. citizen agy. team, 1977; chairperson of Vicariate VIII Council, 1976-78; chairperson communications com. St. Gabriel Parish Council, 1973-78. Mem. U.S. Metric Assn., Green Bay Diocesan Pastoral Council. Democrat. Roman Catholic. Home: 2040 Marathon Neenah WI 54956 Office: 145 W Wisconsin Ave Neenah WI 54956

LAVER, GERALD EBY, constrn. co. exec.; b. Elyria, Ohio, May 19, 1924; s. Edmond Ray and Edith Lucille (Eby) L.; student Baldwin Wallace U., 1942; B.B.A. in Mktg., Cleve. State U., 1947; m. Edna Frances Dumont, Apr. 25, 1948; children—Cheryl Ann Laver Linder, Diana Lynn Laver Bowman, Christian Eby. With Dun & Bradstreet, Inc., Cleve., 1947-53, Columbia Gas Co., Elyria, Lorain and Columbus, Ohio, 1953-70; v.p. builder services Galbreath Mortgage Co., Columbus, 1970-73; pres. Marconi Bldg., Inc., 1975—, United Energies, Inc., 1975—, United Energies of W.Va., Inc., 1976—; partner Dumont Sales Co., Columbus, 1958—, also Dumont Bus. Consultants. Chmn. bd. Washington Ave. Christian Ch., Elyria, 1957, N.W. Christian Ch., 1965-66; treas. 125th Anniversary Celebration of Elyria, 1958; elder N.W. Christian Ch., 1974-77; pres. Friendship Village of Columbus, 1976-77. Served with USNR, 1943-46; PTO. Named Young Man of Yr., Elyria Jr. C. of C., 1957, One of Ohio's 10 Outstanding Young Men, Ohio Jr. C. of C., 1958. Mem. Nat. Assn. Home Builders, Home Builders Assn. Greater Columbus. Republican. Mem. Disciples of Christ Ch. Clubs: Optimist, Masons, Shriners. Home: 2487 Chester Rd Columbus OH 43221 Office: 3070 Riverside Dr Columbus OH 43221

LAVIN, CARL HERSHEL, bus. exec.; b. Canton, Ohio, Apr. 11, 1924; s. Leo Benjamin and Dorothy (Weinsweig) L.; B.S., Miami U., Oxford, Ohio, 1947; grad. Advanced Mgmt. Program, Harvard Bus. Sch., 1960; m. Audrey Ann Perlman, Feb. 22, 1953; children—Maud K., Carl Hershel, Franklin L., Douglas B. With Sugardale Foods, Inc., Canton, 1947-69, pres., 1963-69; pres. Homestead Provision Co., Alliance, Ohio, Wadsworth Investment Co., Canton; chmn. Block Coal & Supply Co., Polywood Corp. (both Canton); dir. Performance Polymers, Inc., Cin. Bd. dirs., v.p. Stark Wilderness Center; bd. dirs. Planned Parenthood of Canton, Community Health Planning Council; past bd. dirs. Seven County Alcoholism Council, Canton Jewish Center; chmn. Jewish Welfare Dr. of Canton, 1967. Served in U.S. Army, 1943-45; ETO. Mem. Am. Meat Inst., Nat. Ind. Meat Packers Assn. (past dir.), Ohio Meat Packers Assn., Canton C. of C. (past v.p.). Republican. Jewish. Home: 5240 Plain Center Rd NE Canton OH 44714 Office: Homestead Provision Co 6428 Union Ave PO Box 984 Alliance OH 44601

LAVIN, DAVID J., writer, fast food exec.; b. Canton, Ohio, Aug. 2, 1923; s. William Lewis and Celia (Yassenoff) L.; student U. Wis., 1941-43; B.S., Ohio State U., 1945; Advanced Mgmt. Program, Harvard Bus. Sch., 1959; m. Elinor Rose Golden, June 24, 1951; children—Nancy, Susan, William II. Port and smoked meats dept. mgr. The Sugardale Provision Co., Canton, 1959—, v.p. merchandising, bd. dirs.; chmn., chief exec. officer Sugardale Foods, Inc., 1969-76, pres., 1975-76; chmn. Morgan Restaurants, Inc., 1976—; pres. Niles Realty Co.; past dir. Harter Bancorp.; originator and co-author. with wife Teenage Corner, originally pub. 500 high sch. newspapers, nat. syndication 41 daily newspapers U.S., Can., 1960—; co-founder Camp Conestoga for Boys. Chairman Canton chpt. ARC, Stark County Heart Chpt.; mem. bd. Canton Symphony, hon. bd., 1977; finance and building comm. Canton Philomatheon Soc. for Blind; exec. com., men's chmn. Canton Sesquicentennial; past 1st v.p., mem. bd. Canton Players Guild; pub. dir. Bd. trustees Blue Cross Hosp. plan. Mem. exec. finance committee Stark County Republican Party. Sec. bd. dirs. Walsh College. Recipient certificate of merit Canton Philomatheon Soc. for Blind, Silver Medal award, Advertising Federation of America and Printer's Ink Magazine, 1963. Mem. Canton C. of C., Stark County Hist. Soc. (past dir.), Am. Meat Inst., Harvard Bus. Sch. AMP 36th Class (regional class sec.), Western Res. Acad. Alumni Assn. (v.p.), Arts Unlimited, Musical Arts Assn. Clubs: Canton, Harvard, Canton Advertising (past pres., bd. mem.); Arrowhead Country (bd. mem., treas.); Tamarisk Country; Racquet (Palm Springs, Calif.). Home: 4800 Ellinda Circle NW Rolling Acres Canton OH 44709 Office: 1300 S Main St North Canton OH 44720

LAVIN, ELINOR R. GOLDEN, civic worker; b. Lawrence, Mass.; d. Hy and Jennie (Nicholson) Golden; student Keystone Jr. Coll., 1945-47, N.Y.C. Fashion Acad., 1947-48; m. David J. Lavin, June 24, 1951; children—Nancy Beth, Susan Debra, William II. Fashion designer, N.Y.C.; with Tina Lesser, 1948-49, Hattie Carnegie, Inc., 1949-51; co-writer Teenage Corner column, 1959—. Chmn. women's com. Canton (Ohio) Player's Guild, 1966-69; chmn. women's com. Blossom Music Center, 1968-70, benefit chmn., 1971; chmn. membership drive Canton Art Inst., 1965; mem. women's bd. Aultman Hosp.; mem. women's com. Canton Symphony, Walsh Coll. active United Fund. Mem. Stark County Hist. Soc. Clubs: Arrowhead Country, Canton, Village Country (Canton); Tamarisk Country, Racquet (Palm Springs, Calif.). Home: 4800 Ellinda Circle NW Rolling Acres Canton OH 44709

LAVINE, JOHN MORGAN, newspaper pub., editor; b. Duluth, Minn., Mar. 20, 1941; s. Max H. and Frances (Hoffman) L.; B.A., Carleton Coll., 1963; postgrad. U. Minn., 1963; LL.D., Emerson Coll., 1975; m. Dana Raihill, June 28, 1964 (div. June 1974); children—Miriam Esther, Marc Hoffman. Pub., editor Lavine Newspaper Group, daily newspapers, Chippewa Falls, Portage, Baraboo and Shawano, Wis., 1964—; dir. Cygnet Films, London, Eng. Regent U. Wis. System, 1971—; trustee Coker Coll., Hartsville, S.C., 1970-74; bd. overseers Emerson Coll., 1976; bd. govs. Antioch Coll., interim bd. govs., 1976; mem. regional adv. council Wis. Region of Anti-Defamation League, vice chmn., 1970-74. Named one of 5 outstanding young men in Wis., Wis. Jaycees, 1968; recipient Distinguished Achievement award Carleton Coll. Alumni Assn., 1977. Mem. Am. Soc. Newspaper Editors, Inland Daily Press Assn. (dir.), ACLU (dir. chpt.), Chippewa Falls Area C. of C. (dir.), Nat. Conf. Editorial Writers, NCCJ, Sigma Delta Chi. Mem. B'nai B'rith. Author: Collective Bargaining in Higher Education, 1975. Home: 20 W Central St Chippewa Falls WI 54729 Office: 20-22 W Central St Chippewa Falls WI 54729

LAVITT, BEN, photog. co. exec.; b. Chgo., July 2, 1930; s. Charles and Sara (Solovitz) L.; student U. Ill.; m. Lillian Zimbler, Aug. 2, 1952; children—Alison, Jory. Photographer Eison-Freeman Co., N.Y.C., 1948-54; founder, pres. Astra Photo Services Inc., Chgo., 1954—; pres. Gamma Photo Labs., Chgo. dir. various firms; cons. to editors, writers; judge numerous contests, speaker at schs., various groups on photo processing. Mem. Color Photo Labs. Am., Am. Soc. Mag. Photographers, Profl. Photographers Am. Editor numerous books photography, photo processing. Home: 2466 Ridge Rd Highland Park IL 60035 Office: Gamma Photo Labs 314 W Superior St Chicago IL 60611

LAW, EDWIN B., constrn. exec.; b. Ft. Worth, Aug. 19, 1924; s. Allan B. and Josephine (Parks) L.; student Tex. A. and M. Coll., 1940-42; B.S. in Archtl. Engring., U. Tex., 1949; m. Margaret Ellen Russell, May 29, 1948; children—Patrick E., Michael M., Gregory P., Katherine A., James R. Engr., J.M. Odom Constrn. Co., Austin, Tex., 1947-49; estimator J.W. Bateson Constrn. Co., Dallas, 1949; chief estimator Von Frellick Inc., San Angelo, Tex., 1949-50, Frank E. Blaser Bldg. Co., Wichita, Kans., 1950-52; chief engr. Dondlinger & Sons Constrn. Co., 1953-59; pres., chief exec. officer Law Co., Inc., 1959—; v.p., dir. Law/Kingdon, Profl. Assn. An organizer, dir. Civic Progress Citizens Assn., 1957-63; organizer Citizens for Commn.-Mgr. Plan, 1959; pres. Greater Downtown Wichita, 1963-64; chmn. Wichita-Sedgwick County Met. Area Planning Commn., 1962-63; chmn. bd. Zoning Appeals, 1962-63; bd. dirs. local USO, 1957, NCCJ, United Fund of Wichita and Sedgwick County, Inc. Registered profl. engr., Kans. Named Kans. Outstanding Jaycee by Jr. C. of C., 1958-59. Served to capt., USMC, 1942-46, 52-53. Mem. Nat., Kans., Wichita assns. profl. engrs., Asso. Gen. Contractors (nat. dir., pres. Kans. builders chpt. 1974-75), U.S. (nat. chmn. com. 1970-77), Wichita (pres. 1957) jr. chambers commerce, Wichita C. of C., Sigma Nu. Republican. Roman Catholic. K.C. (4 degree). Clubs: Wichita Country; Office: 313 S Market St Wichita KS 67202

LAW, LYLE BREWSTER, supt. schs.; b. Bordulac, N.D., Feb. 3, 1916; s. Isaac N. and Eugenia (Brewster) L.; B.A., State Tchrs. Coll., Valley City, N.D., 1941; M.A., Colo. State Coll. Edn., 1949; m. Olive Vruwink, Mar. 16, 1940; children—Mary Jo, Janard L. Rural sch. tchr. Bucephalia Ch. Dist., Bordulac, 1934-36; tchr. Wheatland (N.D.) Pub. Schs., 1937-38, Osceola (Wis.) Pub. Schs., 1938-41; tchr. bus. New Richmond (Wis.) High Sch., 1941-42, asst. prin. Osceola High Sch., 1942-45; prin. tchr. bus. Morgan (Minn.) High Sch., 1945-47; supt. schs. Morgan Pub. Schs., 1947—. Sec.-treas. Tomahawk Conf., 1947-48; exec. sec. Tomahawk Conference, 1969-74; mem. dist. com. Minn. High Sch. League, 1949-51, mem. region com., 1950-51, 62-64; v.p. Morgan PTA, 1948-50; sec. Morgan Community Health Assn. 1965—; finance chmn. Salvation Army, 1947—; bd. dirs. Redwood County Day Activity Center, 1969—. Mem. Am., Minn. assns. sch. adminstrs., NEA, Morgan C. of C. Republican. Methodist. Mason, Lion (charter, pres. 1963-64, sec. 1967-71). Address: Morgan MN 56266

LAWERENZ, MARK DAVID, engr.; b. Milw., June 10, 1949; s. Harvey Otto and Anna Elizabeth (Markowski) L.; Asso. Applied Sci., M.E., Milw. Area Tech. Coll., 1969-73; postgrad. in mech. engring. Marquette U., 1973—; m. Susan Patricia Russell, July 17, 1971; children—Matthew James, Carrissa Ann. Sr. draftsman Envirex Inc. Waukesha, Wis., 1972-73; draftsman Compressor div. Allis-Chalmers Corp., Milw., 1973, project coordinator, 1973-78, sales engr., 1978—. Registered profl. engr., Wis. Mem. Inst. for Certification Engring. Technicians (mem. mech. exam. com., certified), Engring. Council for Profl. Devel., Nat., Wis. socs. profl. engrs., Am. Soc. Certified Engring. Technicians, ASME (asso.), Phi Theta Kappa. Lutheran. Home: 413 S Meadow Ct Oconomowoc WI 53066 Office: 1915 S Moorland Rd New Berlin WI 53151

LAWES, BAYARD FRATCHER, press photographer; b. Utica, N.Y., Feb. 23, 1922; s. Richard G. and Ruth (Fratcher) L.; student Mich. State U., 1941-42; m. Jean Fishwild, Nov. 6, 1943; children—Jennifer, Bayard G., Mary Lou, David. Staff photographer Royal Oak (Mich.) Daily Tribune, 1946—, chief photographer, 1950—; with pub. relations dept. William Beaumont Hosp., Royal Oak, 1972—, chief photog. services, 1973—, also dir. audio-visual services; tchr., cons., 1960—; instr. Oakland Police Acad., 1968—; treas. Hosp. Instrnl. Resources Asso., 1974-75; mem. adv. bd. photo class Oakland Community Coll. Bd. dirs. Royal Oak Boys Club. Served as pilot USAAF, World War II; ETO. Recipient numerous nat. citations and awards from nat. and state press orgns.; named Mich. Photographer of Year, 1957, 59. Mem. Nat. (life mem., nat. sec. 1965-66, fellowship award 1966), Mich. (founder, 1st pres. 1963, v.p. 1968—) press photographers assns., Indsl. Photographers Assn. Mich., Sci. Photographers Assn. Mich. (charter sec.-treas.), Acad. Video Communicators (charter treas. 1975, Acad. award Mich. chpt. 1976), Biol. Photog. Assn. Home: 1031 Prairie View Ct Rochester MI 48063

LAWLER, BERNARD JAMES, rehab. counselor; b. Green Bay, Wis., Jan. 9, 1915; s. Patrick Henry and Mary Catherine (Barta) L.; B.S., St. Norbert Coll., 1948; m. Mary Margaret Coleman, Feb. 17, 1942; children—Mary Ann, Susan Ellen, Michael Barta. Psychometrist, ednl. and vocat. guidance counselor St. Norbert Coll., DePere, Wis., 1946-50; rehab. counselor, dir. vocat. rehab. services Curative Workshop Rehab. Center, Green Bay, 1966—; cons. in field. Bd. dirs. Brown County Tb and Health Assn., 1971-72, Halfway House for Alcoholics, Green Bay, 1971—. Served to lt. col. USAAF, 1941-46, USAF, 1950-65. Decorated Air Force Commendation medal. Mem. Nat. Vocat. Guidance Assn., Am. Personnel and Guidance Assn., Nat. Rehab. Assn., Wis. Assn. Alcoholism and Other Drug Abuse, Ret. Officers Assn., Air Force Assn., St. Norbert U. Alumni Assn. Roman Cath. Clubs: Lions, Ret. Officers, K.C. (4 deg.), U. Wis. Varsity. Home: 1404 Servais St Green Bay WI 54304 Office: 2900 University Ave Green Bay WI 54308

LAWLER, WILLIAM EDWARD, JR., co. exec.; b. Chgo., June 19, 1929; s. William Edward and Elizabeth Margarette (Moisand) L.; B.S. in Mech. Engring., Ill. Inst. Tech., 1958; m. Marian S. Drobney, Dec. 28, 1960; 1 dau., Linda Jean. Asso., Am. Engring. & Mfg. Co., San Francisco, 1956-64; pres. Disposal Tech. Inc. (now Controlled Waste Inc.), Chgo., 1964—. Served with AUS, 1945-48; CBI. Decorated Purple Heart; registered profl. engr., 24 states. Mem. Am. Pub. Works Assn., Am. Soc. M.E., Chgo. Builders Club. Developer automated fuel generation process from solid waste. Address: 2536 W 80th St Chicago IL 60652

LAWRENCE, DAVID LONG, radiologist; b. Jamestown, Ky., July 11, 1934; s. Marshall Marvin and Opal H. (Long) L.; B.A., Centre Coll., 1955; M.S., U. Ky., 1958; M.D., U. Louisville, 1962; m. Jeanette Wesley, Jan. 30, 1954; children—Julia Long, David Wesley. Intern, Baroness Erlanger Hosp., Chattanooga, 1962-63; gen. practice medicine, Jamestown, 1963-66; resident U. Louisville Hosps., 1968-71; practice medicine specializing in radiology, 1971—; mem. staffs Mercy Meml. Hosp., Urbana, Ohio, Mercy Med. Center Community Hosp., Springfield, Ohio; instr. dept. radiology U. Louisville, 1970-71; adj. prof. radiation medicine Wittenberg U. Served to lt. comdr. USN, 1966-68. USPHS summer research scholar, 1959; diplomate Am. Bd. Radiology, Nat. Bd. Med. Examiners. Mem. Am. Coll. Radiology, Am., Ohio State med. assns., Clark County Med. Soc., Central Ohio Radiol. Soc. Methodist. Club: Masons. Home: 402 N Broadmoor Blvd Springfield OH 45504

LAWRENCE, DEAN WEBSTER, data processing co. exec.; b. Kansas City, Mo., Sept. 1, 1936; s. Charles Webster and Goldie Bess (Finney) L.; B.S. in Math., Baker U., 1958; certificate in numerical analysis U. Calif. at Los Angeles, 1962; M.A. in Math., U. Kans., 1964. Mathematician, U.S. Naval Ordnance Test Sta., Pasadena, Calif., 1959-62; analyst Midwest Research Inst., Kansas City, 1962-65, mgr. Computer scis. br., 1965-68; v.p., co-founder TransTech Inc., Kansas City, 1968-70; v.p. L & A Computer Industries, Overland Park, Kans., 1970-76; pres. Unimark, Inc., Overland Park, Kans., 1976—; lectr. in computer sci. U. Mo. at Kansas City, 1964-66. Pres. Apollo Gardens Homes Assn., Mission, Kans., 1971-73, also bd. dirs. Mem. Assn. Computing Machinery (pres. 1970-71), U.S. Ski Assn. (dir. 1976—), Alpha Delta Sigma, Pi Mu Upsilon. Club: Kansas City Ski (pres. 1975-76). Contbr. articles to trade jours. Home: 7 Wycklow Shawnee Mission KS 66207 Office: 10520 Barkley St Overland Park KS 66212

LAWRENCE, JAMES ALBERT, ednl. exec.; b. Rockford, Ill., Dec. 30, 1923; s. James A. and Norma (Anderson) L.; B.S., U. Wis., 1947, M.S., 1957 children—Jim, John. Bus. adminstr. Racine (Wis.) Pub. Schs., 1957, J.T. Union High Sch., Milw., 1957-64, Dist. 211 Twp. High Sch., Palatine, Ill., 1964-69, McHenry (Ill.) pub. schs., 1969-72, Ind. Sch. Dist. 12, Circle Pines, Minn., 1972—. Past pres., bd. dirs. Palatine-Schaumburg Credit Union; area bd. dirs. Palatine Community Chest. Served with AUS, 1943-45, 50-53. Decorated Bronze Star medals. Mem. Sigma Alpha Epsilon, Phi Delta Kappa. Rotarian. Home: 10208 N Lever St Circle Pines MN 55014 Office: Centennial Schools Circle Pines MN 55014

LAWRENCE, MERLE, med. educator; b. Remsen, N.Y., Dec. 26, 1915; s. George William and Alice Rutherford (Bowne) L.; A.B., Princeton U., 1938, M.A., 1940, Ph.D., 1941; m. Roberta Ashby Taylor Harper, Aug. 8, 1942; children—Linda Alice (Mrs. E. Robert Nolt, Jr.), Roberta Harper (Mrs. James Edward Henderson), James Bowne. NRC fellow Johns Hopkins Hosp., 1941; asst. prof. psychology Princeton U., 1946-50, asso. prof., 1950-52; asso. research Lempert Inst. Otology, N.Y.C., 1946-52; asso. prof. dept. otolaryngology U. Mich. Med. Sch., 1952-57, prof. otolaryngology, 1957—, research asso. Inst. Indsl. Health, 1952—; prof. psychology U. Mich. Coll. Lit. Sci. and Arts, 1957—, dir. Kresge Hearing Research Inst., 1961—; chmn. bd. Pan-Cayman House, Grand Cayman, B.W.I., 1972—. Cons. to the Surgeon Gens. office U.S. Army advisory com. on research in psychophysiology, 1953-70, advisory com. on aviation medicine, 1963-70; cons. to communicative disorders research tng. com. of Nat. Inst. of Neurol. Diseases and Blindness, communicative scis. study sect. div. of research grants Nat. Inst. Health, 1965-69, chmn., 1967-69, communicative disorders review com. 1972-76, Nat. Advisory Neurol. and communicative disorders and stroke council, 1976-79. Served as naval aviator USNR, 1941-46, 50-51; PTO; Korean conflict. Decorated Purple Heart, sec. Navy Commendation; recipient award merit Am. Acad. Ophthalmology and Otolaryngology, 1965, Am. Otological Soc., 1967, Distinguished Service award Princeton Class of 1938. Rotarian. Home: 2029 Vinewood Blvd Ann Arbor MI 48104

LAWRENCE, NORMAN RICHARD, lawyer; b. Oak Park, Ill., June 9, 1938; s. George Richard and Edith Adrienne (Norman) L.; B.S., U. Ill., 1960, J.D., 1962; m. Kathleen Alice Schmidt, July 1, 1967; children—Deborah, Heather, Bradley. Admitted to Ill. bar, 1962; asso. firm Hart & Banbury, Aurora, Ill., 1962-64; partner firm Hart,

Banbury, Lawrence & Gullstrand, Aurora, 1964-70; pvt. practice law, Aurora, 1970—. Pres. Lawrence Industries, Aurora, 1968— 1250 Gladstone Corp., Aurora, 1974—; v.p. Westwind, Ltd., Aurora, 1973—, Summer Breeze, Ltd., Aurora, 1974—. Dist. chmn. Boy Scouts Am., Aurora, 1968—, legal counsel Two Rivers council, 1966—, exec. bd. Two Rivers council, 1968—. Mem. Ill., Kane County bar assns., Am. Judicature Soc., Estate Planning Council (dir. 1969—), Jaycees, Skull and Crescent, Zeta Psi, Alpha Kappa Psi, Phi Delta Phi. Republican. Conglist. (deacon 1970-74, moderator 1973, trustee 1974-76). Moose, Elk. Clubs: Aurora Flying (dir. 1968-76), Tiger, Phoenix (Aurora). Home: 1319 W Downer St Aurora IL 60506 Office: 30 S Stolp St Aurora IL 60504

LAWRENCE, RICHARD MARSTON, mgmt. cons.; b. Short Hills, N.J., May 1, 1906; s. Frank Luther and Mary Riggs (Lunt) L.; B.S. in Chemistry, U. Cal. at Berkeley, 1926; M.S. in Chem. Engring., U. Ill., 1931; m. Mary Elizabeth Warrington, Aug. 25, 1934 (dec. 1961); children—Dorothy (Mrs. Wayne G. Weber), Katherine (Mrs. James Charles Anderson); m. 2d, Ruth McMillan Ellis, Nov. 28, 1964. Analytical chemist Colgate-Palmolive Co., 1926-29; chem. expert U.S. Tariff Commn., 1931-37; chem. market analyst Atlas Chem. Industries, Wilmington, Del., 1937-47; sr. market analyst Monsanto Chem. Co., St. Louis, 1947-54; dir. bus. research Wyandotte Chems. Corp., Wyandotte, Mich., 1954-57; adviser to v.p. research A.E. Staley Mfg. Co., Decatur, Ill., 1957-61; project mgr. Internat. Minerals & Chem. Corp., Skokie, Ill., 1962-66; mgmt. cons. James Hynes & Co., Chgo., 1967-68; asst. to pres., mgmt. cons. on mergers and finance W.T. Grimm & Co., Chgo., 1968—. Lectr. colls. Mem. adv. com. U.S. Bur. Census, 1951-52; mem. industry devel. coms. Mo., Mich., Ill., 1952-62. Established Mary Lawrence scholastic award Johns Hill Jr. High Sch., Decatur, 1961—. Mem. Am. Chem. Soc., Am. Inst. Chem. Engrs. (chmn. Delaware Valley sect. 1944), Am. Marketing Assn. (pres. St. Louis chpt. 1954), Chem. Market Research Assn. (founding mem. 1940, sec. 1945, v.p. 1952, councillor at large 1953, Distinguished Service award 1976, established R.M. Lawrence award for best paper of year 1976-2000), Ill. State Acad. Sci., Midwest Chem. Marketers, Midwest Planning Assn., Alpha Chi Sigma, Phi Lambda Upsilon, Lambda Chi Alpha. Republican. Presbyterian. Club: Kiwanis. Author: Sources of Information for Industrial Market Research, 1948. Contbr. chpts. to bus. textbooks, articles to chem. jours., papers to profl. socs. Pioneer chem. market research. Home: 134 Sterling Ln Wilmette IL 60091 Office: WT Grimm & Co 135 S La Salle St Chicago IL 60603

LAWRENCE, WILLIAM ROBERT, surgeon; b. Tunnel Hill, Ill., May 17, 1923; s. William Lloyd and Zada Belle (Choate) L.; B.E., So. Ill. Normal U., 1943; A.B., So. Ill. U., 1950; B.S., U. Ill., 1952, M.D., 1954; m. Marilyn Inez Hanna, June 15, 1957; children—Kathryn Rae, Ronald Scott, Richard Kevin. Intern, Illinois Central Hosp., Chgo., 1954-55, resident surgery, 1955-57; resident surgery pathology St. Francis Hosp., Peoria, Ill., 1957-58; chief resident surgery Ill. Central Hosp., Chgo., 1958-60; gen. surgery practice, mem. staff Ill. Central Hosp., Chgo., 1960—; mem. staff S. Suburban Hosp., Hazelcrest, Ill., Ingalls Meml. Hosp., Harvey; spl. examiner Ill. Central R.R., 1960. Served to capt. USAAF, 1943-48. Diplomate Am. Bd. Surgery. Fellow A.C.S.; mem. Am. Assn. Ry. Surgeons, Pan Am. Med. Assn., AMA, Ill., Chgo. med. socs., Am. Geriatrics Soc., Midwest, Ill. surg. socs., Chgo. Inst. Medicine, Alpha Kappa Kappa, Delta Rho, Kappa Delta Pi, Kappa Phi Kappa. Republican. Presbyn. Mason (Shriner). Home: 655 Maple Ct Prestwick Frankfort IL 60423 Office: 5800 Stony Island Chicago IL 60637 also 3235 W Vollmer Rd Flossmoor IL 60422

LAWRENCE, WILLIAM STANTON, planning cons.; b. Little Rock, Jan. 26, 1918; s. James Grayson and Martha Louise (White) L.; student Armour Inst., 1937-39, Chgo. Art Inst., 1946-47; m. Dorothy Marie Kraman, July 26, 1958. Design supt. Bannon & McFayden Constrn. Co., Skokie, Ill., 1939-41; advance base planner for seabee battalion, Bur. Yards and Docks, Chgo., 1942-45; archtl. designer A. Epstein & Sons, architects, Chgo., 1945-46; asso. planner Evert Kincaid & Assos., Chgo., 1948-58; planning and land devel. adviser Ill. State Housing Bd., Chgo., 1950-56; pres., owner, prin. cons. William S. Lawrence & Assos., Inc., planning cons., Chgo., 1947—; dir. Commonwealth Realty & Devel. Group, Inc., Chgo. Mem. Am. Inst. Planners, Am. Soc. Cons. Planners (bd. mem. 1968-71), Am. Soc. Planning Ofcls., Urban Land Inst., Lambda Alpha. Home: 5829 N Keating St Chicago IL 60646 Office: 6330 N Pulaski Chicago IL 60646

LAWRENZ, PAUL HENRY, engineer; b. Peine, Germany, Dec. 6, 1913; s. Paul W. and Alma A. (Vahldiek) L.; came to U.S., 1927, naturalized, 1933; B.S. in Elec. Engring., Wayne State U., 1936, M.S. in Mech. Engring., 1943; m. Eleanor M. Thompson, Aug. 3, 1940; children—Anne, Kay. Heating engr. Mich. Consol. Gas. Co., Detroit, 1936-37; elec. engr. Kelvinator div. Nash-Kelvinator Co., Detroit, 1938-39, standards engr., 1939-44, asst. to v.p. engring., 1944-60; adminstrv. asst. to v.p. Am. Motors Corp., Detroit, 1960-67, mgr. product reliability, 1967-68, safety engr., 1968-73, mgr. exterior lighting, automotive engring., 1973—. Commr. planning dept. Village of Franklin, Mich., 1972—. Mem. Engring. Soc. Detroit, Am. Soc. Heating Refrigeration and Air Conditioning Engrs., Soc. Automotive Engrs. Methodist. Home: 30405 Rosemond Dr Franklin MI 48025 Office: 14250 Plymouth Rd Detroit MI 48232

LAWSON, DONALD ELMER, editor, writer; b. Chgo., May 20, 1917; s. Elmer Daniel and Christina (Grass) L.; B.A., Cornell Coll., Mt. Vernon, Iowa, 1939, Litt.D. (hon.), 1970; student U. Iowa Writers Workshop, 1939-40; m. Beatrice M. Yates, Mar. 30, 1945. Editor, The Advertiser, weekly newspaper, Nora Springs, Iowa, 1940-41; with Compton's Ency., Chgo., 1946-73, mng. editor, 1960-65, editor-in-chief, 1965-73, v.p., 1971-73; exec. editor United Educators, Inc., 1973-74, editor in chief, 1974—. Bd. dirs. Marcy-Newberry Assn. Settlement Houses. Served with USAAF, 1941-45; ETO. Mem. Authors Guild, Chgo. Book Clinic, Internat. Platform Assn., Chgo. Lit. Club, Soc. Midland Authors, Phi Beta Kappa. Methodist. Clubs: Cliff Dwellers, Chicago Press. Author: A Brand for the Burning, 1961; Young People in the White House, 1961, rev. edit., 1970; The United States in World War I, 1963; The United States in World War II, 1963; The United States in the Korean War, 1964; Famous American Political Families, 1965; The War of 1812, 1966; Frances Perkins: First Lady of the Cabinet, 1967; Great Air Battles: World Wars I and II, 1968; The Lion and The Rock, the Story of the Rock of Gibraltar, 1969; Youth and War: From World War I to Vietnam, 1969; Ten Fighters for Peace, 1971; The Colonial Wars, 1972; The American Revolution, 1974; The United States in the Indian Wars, 1975; The United States in the Spanish American War, 1975; The United States in the Mexican War, 1976; The United States in the Civil War, 1977; Education Careers, 1977. Home: 1122 W Lunt Ave Chicago IL 60626 Office: 801 Green Bay Rd Lake Bluff IL 60044

LAWSON, ESTHER CHANEY (MRS. ALBERT THEODORE LAWSON), sch. adminstr.; b. Chgo., July 29, 1930; d. Thomas Roosevelt and Olie Lillie (Ford) Nelson; B.S., U. Ill., 1952; M.A., U. Chgo., 1962; m. Albert Theodore Lawson, May 2, 1954; 1 dau., Laurie Lynne. Primary tchr. Chgo. Bd. Edn., 1952-65, tchr.-counselor, 1965-69; prin. Garrett A. Morgan Elementary Sch., Chgo., 1969-76, Thomas J. Waters Elementary Sch., Chgo., 1976—; cons. resource Wis. Research and Devel. Center, 1973-74. Registrar, 29th dist. S.E. Community Orgn., 1965. Bd. dirs. Marynook Homeowners, 1963—, Potential Sch. for Exceptional Children, 1969-74. Recipient fellowship for outstanding tchrs. Chgo. Bd. Edn., 1964. Mem. Nat. Council Adminstrv. Women, U. Chgo. Alumni, Chgo. Prins. Assn., Samuel Stratton Soc., Individually Guided Edn. Assn., U. Ill. Alumni, Phi Delta Kappa, Delta Kappa Gamma, Delta Sigma Theta. Mem. Ch. of Christ. Pioneer in transfer of adminstrs. for integration Chgo. Pub. Schs. Home: 155 N Harbor Dr Chicago IL 60601 Office: 4540 N Campbell Ave Chicago IL 60625

LAWSON, JUDITH KAREN, rehab. adminstr.; b. Des Moines, Oct. 25, 1942; d. D. Keith and Wilma P. (Johnson) Lawson; A.B., Drury Coll., 1964; M.S., Ill. State U., 1971. Tchr. Oklahoma City Pub. Schs., 1966-69; grad. asst. phys. edn. Ill. State U., Normal, 1969-70; instr. phys. edn. Mo. So. Coll., Joplin, 1970-72; vocat. trainer, educator severly retarded and multiply handicapped Greater Kansas City Found. Mentally Retarded Citizens, 1972-73; evaluation supr., rehab. mgr. mental retardation gov. bd. Wyandotte County, Kans., 1974—. Mem. AAHPER, Okla., Mo. assns. health, phys. edn. and recreation, Nat., Central Assns. phys. edn. coll. women, Nat., Kans. rehab. assns., NE Kans. Rehab. Assn. (v.p. 1975-77), Vocat. Evaluation and Work Adjustment Assn., Kans. Assn. Rehab. Facilities, Am. Personnel and Guidance Assn., Am. Rehab. Counseling Assn., Alpha Phi. Home: 6135 Brooklyn St Kansas City MO 64130 Office: 627 Kansas Ave Kansas City KS 66105

LAWTON, JOHN MILLER, dentist; b. Hancock, Mich., Dec. 20, 1943; s. Robert Augustus and Jane Inez (Miller) L.; student U. Wis.-Madison, 1962-65; D.D.S., Ind. U., 1969; m. Karla Jean McCray, June 21, 1969; children—Daniel Roy, Kimberly Ann, Teri Lynn. Practice dentistry, Hancock, Mich., 1969—. Bd. dirs. United Way. Mem. Am., Mich., Copper Country Dist. (v.p. 1970-72, sec. 1975-77) dental assns., Am. Soc. Dentistry for Children, Ind. U. Alumni Assn. (life), Copper County C. of C., Coast Guard Aux. (flotilla sec., treas.). Psi Omega. Methodist. Rotarian (sec. Hancock), Elk. Home: 326 Mason Ave Hancock MI 49930 Office: 1550 W Quincy St Hancock MI 49930

LAWYER, VERNE, lawyer; b. Indianola, Iowa, May 9, 1923; s. Merrill Guy and Zella (Mills) L.; LL.B., Drake U., 1949; m. Sally Hay, Oct. 5, 1946; 1 dau., Suzanne; m. 2d, Vivian Jury, Oct. 25, 1959; children—Michael, Steven. Admitted Iowa bar, 1949, also U.S. Supreme Ct. bar; practice law, Des Moines, 1949—; mem. firm Lawyer, Lawyer, Dunn & Jackson. Mem. Iowa Aeros. Commn., 1973-75. Trustee ATL Roscoe Pound Found., 1965-71, fellow, 1973—. Recipient Outstanding Law Alumni award Phi Alpha Delta, 1964. Fellow Internat. Acad. Trial Lawyers, Am. Bar Found.; mem. Am. (state chmn. membership com. of ins., negligence and compensation law 1970—), Iowa (spl. comn. on fed. practice 1971—, spl. automobile reparations com. 1972—), Polk County bar assns., Assn. Trial Lawyers Am. (v.p. Iowa chpt. 1956-57, nat. sec. 1963-64, 67-68, gov. 1962-63, mem. internat. aviation com. 1973—, trial advs. scholarship soc. com. 1973—), Iowa Acad. Trial Lawyers (sec.-treas. 1962—, editor Newsbull. 1962—, editor Weekly Verdict Summary 1970—), Assn. Trial Lawyers Iowa, Law Sci. Acad. Am., Lawyer-Pilots Bar Assn., Am. Judicature Soc., World Assn. Lawyers (founding), World Peace Through Law Center, Trial Lawyers Assn. Des Moines, Internat. Soc. Barristers, Phi Alpha Delta, Sigma Alpha Epsilon. Author: Trial by Notebook, 1964; co-author Art of Persuasion in Litigation, 1966; How to Defend a Criminal Case from Arrest to Verdict, 1967. Contbr. articles law jours. Home: 5831 N Waterbury Rd Des Moines IA 50312 Office: Fleming Bldg Des Moines IA 50309

LAX, LOUIS CARL, med. research exec.; b. Toronto, Ont., Can., Apr. 25, 1930; s. Hymie and Rose (Lax) L.; came to U.S., 1961; B.A. magna cum laude, U. Toronto, 1952, M.A., 1953, M.D., 1957, also Ph.D.; m. Evelyn Ruth Richman, June 15, 1958; children—Sharon Elaine, Brian Reuben David, Stuart Allen. Research asst. Banting and Best dept. med. research U. Toronto, 1952-56, fellow, 1956-61; fellow clin. investigation unit Sunnybrook Vets. Hosp., Toronto, 1956-61; asst. scientist, med. research center Brookhaven Nat. Lab., Upton, N.Y., 1961-64, research collaborator, 1964-69; asst. prof. depts. surgery and physiology Sch. Medicine, U. Calif. at Los Angeles Med. Center, 1964-69; sr. clin. investigator, div. hosp. products Abbott Labs., North Chicago, Ill., 1969-71; clin. asso. prof. dept. surgery, div. anesthesiology U. Ill. at Med. Center, Chgo., 1970—; med. dir. Telemed Corp., Hoffman Estates, Ill., 1971-73, v.p., med. dir., 1973—; vis. lectr. Bowman Gray Sch. Medicine, Wake Forest Coll., Winston-Salem, N.C., 1965, cons. to stroke center, dept. neurology, 1965; cons., vis. lectr., dept. radiology Med. Coll. Va., Richmond, 1965-67; cons. div. computer scis. Rand Corp., Santa Monica, Cal., 1965; vis. lectr. dept. biomed. engring. McGill U., Montreal, 1968; research collaborator Nat. Inst. Sci. Research, Santa Monica, Cal., 1968-69; cons. Epoxylite Corp., El Monte, Calif., 1968-69. Mem. AAAS, Biophys. Soc., Canadian Physiol. Soc., N.Y. Acad. Scis., IEEE, Ont. Coll. Physicians and Surgeons. Contbr. articles to profl. jours. Home: 2705 McAree Rd Waukegan IL 60085 Office: Telemed Corp 2345 Pembroke Ave Hoffman Estates IL 60195

LAY, OBERT MERLE, physician-surgeon; b. Aurora, Ill., Jan. 24, 1923; s. Arthur and Lillian (Palmer) L.; A.B., Washington U., St. Louis, 1950, M.D., 1955; m. Sharren Moss, Dec. 24, 1973; children—Barbara, Kim, Christopher, Patrick, Nikki Barr. Rotating intern St. Louis County Hosp., 1955-56, resident in surgery, 1956-59; practice medicine specializing in surgery, Granite City, Ill., 1959—; chief staff St. Elizabeth Hosp., Granite City, 1972-74, chief surgery, 1969-70, chief emergency room, 1974-76, trauma co-ordinator, 1972—, instr. emergency med. technicians and operating room technicians, 1972—; mem. disaster com. and Civil Def., St. Clair and Madison Counties, 1965—; dir. Colonial Bank, Granite City. Served with USAAF, 1943-45. Decorated DFC with clusters, Air medal with clusters; diplomate Am. Bd. Surgery, Pan Am. Med. Assn. Fellow ACS, Am. Soc. Abdominal Surgeons, Internat. Coll. Surgeons, Am. Proctologic Soc.; mem. AMA (physicians recognition award), Am. Trauma Soc., Am. Soc. Colon and Rectal Surgeons, Ill. Trauma Soc. (dir.), Ill. State, Madison County, Tri-City, So. Ill., St. Clair County med. socs., Western Ill. Med. Found. Home: 2216 Woodlawn St Granite City IL 62040 Office: 3165 Myrtle St Granite City IL 62040

LAYBOURNE, GEORGE THOMAS, scientist; b. Springfield, Ohio, July 21, 1929; s. George Thomas and Grace (Tossey) L.; A.B., Wittenberg U., 1955; M.B.A., Am. Internat. Coll., 1962; m. Gail A. Niethamer, July 3, 1953; children—Neal, Ned, Nan. Metallurgist, Internat. Harvester Co., Springfield, 1947-55; chemist Monsanto Co., Columbus, Ohio, 1955-57, sect. leader, Springfield, Mass., 1957-63; sr. quality control engr. USI Film Products, Macedon, N.Y., Bridgeport, Conn., 1963-65; supr. quality control Alamo Co., Stratford, Conn., 1965-67; research supr. Chemplex Co., Rolling Meadows, Ill., 1967—; tchr. Conn. Vocat. Inst., Bridgeport, 1965-67; instr. Elgin Community Coll., 1976—. Mem. Sch. Survey Bd., Hampden, Mass., 1958-59; chmn. Hampden Bd. Assessors, 1960-63; active Boy Scouts Am., 1957—, cubmaster, 1963-67, advancement chmn., 1967-70, chmn. dist. camping commn., 1970-72, chmn. dist. com., 1972-73, adv. bd., 1973-74, council exec. bd., 1974—, recipient Silver Beaver award, 1975; mem. Republican Town Com., Hampden, 1958-63, Trumbull, Conn., 1963-67. Served with AUS, 1951. Mem. Am. Soc. for Quality Control (sect. sec. 1959-61), Soc. Plastics Engrs. (dir. Chgo. sect. 1976—), ASTM (subcom. chmn. 1968-72, com. gen. sec. 1974—). Methodist. Mason. Home: 145 E County Line Rd Barrington IL 60010 Office: 3100 Golf Rd Rolling Meadows IL 60008

LAZAR, HAROLD PAUL, internist, gastroenterologist; b. Ellenville, N.Y., Nov. 19, 1928; s. Ephraim Baruch and Fanny (Springfeld) L.; A.B., cum laude, Harvard, 1948; M.D., N.Y. Med. Coll., 1952; m. Molly Kailen Beck, June 20, 1953; children—Richard Beck, Flora Elizabeth, Emily Jane. Intern, U. Chgo. Clinics, 1952-53; resident in labs. Mt. Sinai Hosp., N.Y.C., 1953-54; resident in medicine Montefiore (N.Y.) Hosp., 1954, Michael Reese Hosp., Chgo., 1957-58; resident in gastroenterology VA Lakeside Hosp., Chgo., 1958-59; individual practice medicine, specializing in gastroenterology, internal medicine Middletown, N.Y., 1959-71, Chgo., 1971—; research asst. gastroenterology Mt. Sinai Hosp., N.Y.C., 1959-66; asst. prof. medicine Northwestern U., Chgo., 1971—; cons. in field; attending physician Northwestern Meml. Hosp., Chgo., 1971—. Served to capt., USAF, 1954-56. Nat. Inst. Arthritis and Metabolic Diseases fellow in gastroenterology, 1958-59. Diplomate Am. Bd. Internal Medicine, Am. Bd. Gastroenterology. Mem. Chgo. Med. Soc., AMA, Am. Gastroenterol. Assn., AAAS, N.Y. Acad. Scis., A.C.P., Chgo. Soc. Internal Medicine, Chgo. Soc. Gastroenterology, Am. Soc. Gastrointestinal Endoscopy, Am. Fedn. Clin. Research. Jewish. Clubs: Harvard (pres. Mid-Hudson Valley 1961-71, dir. Chgo. 1972—); Orange County (N.Y.) Golf. Author: (with Leo Van der Reis). The Human Gut, 1974. Contbr. articles, contbg. author profl. publs. Home: 340 Sheridan Rd Chicago IL 60093 Office: 700 N Michigan Ave Chicago IL 60611

LAZARE, JOHN NICHOLAS, printing co. exec.; b. Chgo., May 24, 1925; s. Nicholas J. and Elizabeth M. (Stapf) L.; ed. Printing Industry Sch. Estimating, Chgo., 1948-49; m. Martha Helfrich, Jan. 8, 1946; 1 son, John Nicholas. Apprentice pressman McCord Printing Co., Chgo., 1946-48, pressman, 1948-52, foreman,1952-64; partner John Lazare Printing Co., Chgo., 1964-75, owner, 1975—. Mem. MidAm. Commodity Exchange, Chgo. Served with USNR, 1943-46; PTO. Mem. Lincoln Park C. of C., VFW, Printing Industry Ill. Inc., North Side Printers Guild Chgo. (dir. 1975-76), Royal Arcanum. Club: Board of Trade Fellowship (dir. 1963-69, v.p. 1970-71, pres. 1972-74). Home: 3971 Oleander Ave Chicago IL 60634 Office: 709 W Wrightwood Ave Chicago IL 60614

LAZARUS, IRWIN PHILIP, indsl. engr.; b. Joliet, Ill., Oct. 19, 1926; s. Meyer and Mildred (Kanne) L.; B.S. in Aero. Engring., Purdue U., 1946, M.S. in Indsl. Engring., 1950, Ph.D., 1952; m. Diana Jean Brodsky, Feb. 13, 1949; children—Mitchell, Daniel, Cathy, Martin. Partner, M.E. Mundel & Assos., Milw., 1949-52, agy. dir. U.S. Army Mgmt. Engring. Tng. Agy., Rock Island, Ill., 1952-57; asst. to pres. Am. Colortype div. Rapid Am. Corp., Chgo., 1957-58, asso. dir. central mgmt. staff Rapid Am. Corp., N.Y.C., 1958-60; cons. Booz, Allen & Hamilton, Chgo., 1960-61, mng. asso. Booz Allen Methods Service, Inc., Chgo., 1961-64, dir. research and edn. Booz, Allen & Hamilton, Inc., Chgo., 1964-70; v.p., dir. Donald R. Booz & Assos., Inc., 1970-76; v.p. Lester B. Knight & Assos. Inc., Chgo., 1976—. Cons. Honeywell, Inc., RCA, Fairbanks-Morse, Mead Corp., Baxter Travenol Labs., McGraw-Edison Co., Harnischfeger Corp., Englander Co., Vendo Co., Fansteel, Inc., Graco, Inc., Internat. Silver Co., Motorola, Inc., others; lectr. various univs. Served to lt. (j.g.) USNR, 1944-47. Registered profl. engr., Cal. Recipient Superior Accomplishment award U.S. Govt., 1954. Mem. Am. Inst. Indsl. Engrs. (v.p. 1957), Am. Soc. Engring. Edn., A.A.A.S. Clubs: Union League, Executives (Chgo.). Research in devel. of predetermined time standards system; analysis of time standards allowances used in U.S. Home: 4032 Tower Circle Skokie IL 60076 Office: 549 W Randolph St Chicago IL 60606

LAZZARA, PHILIP, electric co. exec.; b. Freeman, Ill., Oct. 24, 1915; s. Joseph and Camella (DiMarco) L.; student Armour Inst. Tech., Lewis Inst. Tech., Northwestern U., Art Inst. Chgo.; m. Antoinette Marsillo, Apr. 15, 1950; children—Philip, Joseph, Angelo, Jack, Mary Anne, Nancy, Alan. With Peerless Am., Chgo., 1933-41; design engr. U. Chgo. Site B, 1942-43; prodn. mgr. Huppert Co., Chgo., 1943-46; pres., chief exec. officer Blue M Electric Co., Blue Island, Ill., 1946—; treas. Lazzara Bldg. Corp.; dir. Chgo. City Bank & Trust Co., Chgo. Bancorp. Mem. Sci. Apparatus Makers Assn., Inst. Environ. Scis., Nat. Geog. Soc., Nat. Oceanography Assn., IEEE, Ill. Mfrs. Assn., Cath. Ill. C. of C. Clubs: Executive, Beverly Country (Chgo.); JDM Country (Palm Beach Gardens, Fla.); Odd Fellows. Home: 11867 S Oakley Ave Chicago IL 60643 Office: Blue M Electric Co 138th and Chatham Sts Blue Island IL 60406

LEA, ALBERT ROBERT, mfg. exec.; b. Melrose, Mass., May 27, 1921; s. Robert Wentworth and Lillian (Ryan) L.; A.B., Amherst Coll., 1943; student Harvard Grad. Sch. Bus. Adminstrn., 1943; m. Joyce Winona Padgett, May 17, 1943 (div.); children—Patricia, Jennifer, Anne, Melissa Lea; m. 2d, Helen Clay Jones, May 12, 1961; children—Albert Robert, Robert Wentworth II. Pres. Ashcraft Inc., Kansas City, 1951—, also dir.; pres., dir. Process Plate Co., Trade Plant Inc.; pres., dir. Continental Service Industries, Inc. Served as lt. Supply Corps, USNR, 1943-46. Clubs: Mission Hills Country: University, Kansas City (Kansas City); Metropolitan (N.Y.C.); Surf (Surfside, Fla.). Home: 5021 Sunset Dr Kansas City MO 64112 Office: 816 Locust St Kansas City MO 64106

LEACH, DAVID MASON, lawyer; b. Owatonna, Minn., Sept. 16, 1917; s. Helon E. and Mabelle (King) L.; student U. Minn., 1936-39; B.S. in Law, St. Paul Coll. Law, 1942, LL.B., 1948; m. Lucille A. Dixon, Dec. 24, 1946 (dec. Nov. 1964); 1 dau., Deborah D.; m. 2d, Mary E. Brandley, Mar. 21, 1969. Admitted to Minn. bar, 1949; individual practice law, Owatonna, 1949—; city atty., Owatonna, 1949-64; municipal judge, Owatonna, 1964-72. Bd. dirs. Owatonna Arts Council, 1974—. Served to capt. AUS, 1942-46; lt. col. Res. ret. Mem. City and Village Attys. Assn., League Minn. Municipalities (pres. 1959-60), Am., Minn., Fifth Dist. (past pres.), Steele County bar assns., Am. Judicature Soc., Am. Legion, Owatonna C. of C. (dir. 1972-75), Theta Delta Chi. Episcopalian. Elk. Club: Owatonna Exchange. Home: 424 Prospect St Owatonna MN 55060 Office: 214 S Oak St Owatonna MN 55060

LEACH, FREDERICK DARWIN, artist, educator; b. Arkansas City, Kans., Sept. 19, 1924; s. Fred G. and Edwina (Gist) L.; B.A., Millikin U., 1948; M.A., State U. Iowa, 1949, M.F.A., 1953, Ph.D., 1955; m. Elizabeth Patricia Frye, June 8, 1946; children—Deborah Jane, Dirk Frederick, Elizabeth Katrin, Matthew Frederick. Asst. prof. State U. Ia., 1955; prof. painting, dir. Sch. Art, Ohio U., 1956-68; prof. art Hamline U., St. Paul, 1968—, chmn. dept. art, 1975—. Art tour leader, Europe, Greece, 1965—; editorial bd. mem. Ohio U. Rev. Served with USNR, 1943-45. Decorated D.F.C., Purple Heart, Air medals. Mem. Midwest Coll. Art Conf., Coll. Art Assn., Mid-Am. Coll. Art Assn. (pres. 1977). Contbr. articles to profl. jours.; editorial bd. Hamline Review. Home: 1650 Hewitt Ave St Paul MN 55104

LEACH, JAMES ALBERT SMITH, Congressman; b. Davenport, Iowa, Oct. 15, 1942; s. James Albert and Lois (Hill) L.; m. Elisabeth Foxley, Dec. 6, 1975; B.A., Princeton U., 1964; M.A., Johns Hopkins

U., 1966. Mem. staff Congressman Donald Rumsfeld, 1965-66; U.S. fgn. service officer, 1968-69; spl. asst. to dir. OEO, 1969-70; mem. U.S. Delegation Geneva Disarmament Conf., 1971-72; mem. U.S. Delegation UN Gen. Assembly, 1972; pres. Flamegas Cos.; 1973-76; dir. Fed. Home Loan Bank, Des Moines, 1976; mem. 95th Congress from 1st Iowa Dist., 1977—. Mem. Nat. Fedn. Ind. Bus., C. of C., Rotary Club, Elks, Moose. Home: 2625 Wood Ln Davenport IA 52803 Office: 1724 Longworth House Office Bldg Washington DC 20515

LEACH, JAMES LINDSAY, educator; b. Lawrenceville, Ill., Apr. 9, 1918; s. James Gard and Nellie Irene (Biesecker) L.; B.S. U. N.Mex., 1942; M.S., U. Ill., 1949; Ph.D., Ill. State U., 1974; m. Mary Jane Zipprodt, Oct. 13, 1945; children—Jame Lindsay, Charles Robert, Janet Sue. Faculty U. Ill., Urbana, 1946—, asso. prof., 1949-53, prof., 1953—; mech. engr. foundry div. Gen. Motors, Danville, Ill., 1949-51; engr. Tex. Co. Lawrenceville, 1946-47; cons. in field; vis. prof. Indian Inst. Tech., Kharagpur, 1960-61; Summer Sch. for Engring. Tchrs. India, New Delhi, summer 1964—, 65, Bengal Engring. Coll., Calcutta, 1964, U. Wis., New Delhi, summer 1965, Thermal Fabrication Inst., Coimbatore, India, summers 1966, 67; Survey Tech. Edn., Kenya Vista, 1971, Evaluation and Tng. Tech. Edn. Tchrs., 1972; cons. Acad. Ednl. Devel. and Ministry of Transport, Iran, 1976. Served to lt. col. USAAF, 1943-45. Recipient citation Am. Soc. Die Casting Engrs., 1975. Mem. Am. Soc. Mech. Engrs., Am. Soc. Mil. Engrs., Am. Soc. Petroleum Engrs., Nat. Soc. for Engring. Edn., Nat. Soc. Profl. Engrs., Sci. Research Soc. Am., Fedn. Am. Scientists, Am. Foundrymen's Soc. (dir. Central Ill. chpt. 1960—, citation 1968). Author: (with others) Manufacturing Processes and Materials for Engineers, 2d edit. Contbr. articles to profl. jours. Home: 910 N Broadway Urbana IL 61801 Office: Foundry Laboratory University of Illinois Urbana IL 61801

LEACH, RONALD LEE, diversified industry exec.; b. Athens, Ohio, Aug. 22, 1934; s. Ralph and Lelia Celesta (Woodruff) L.; B.S., Ohio U., 1958; m. Marilyn Rose Dreger, Sept. 3, 1956; children—Cynthia Diane, Mark Ronald, Douglas Ralph. With Ernst & Ernst, C.P.A.'s, Cleve., 1960-70, mgr., 1967-70; asst. to v.p., controller Eaton Corp., Cleve., 1970-72, asst. controller fin. accounting, 1972-77, controller, 1977—, also dir. Served to 1st lt. USAF, 1958-60. C.P.A., Ohio. Mem. Greater Cleve. Growth Assn., Am. Inst. C.P.A.'s, Ohio Soc. C.P.A.'s, Am. Accounting Assn., Fin. Execs. Inst. (sec. 1976, chmn. nat. com. govt. bus. 1977), Nat. Assn. Accountants, Beta Alpha Psi, Pi Gamma Mu, Beta Gamma Sigma. Mem. Ch. of God (trustee 1969-74, 75—, treas. 1968—). Home: 7419 Gerald Dr Middleburg Heights OH 44130 Office: 100 Erieview Plaza Cleveland OH 44114

LEAHY, JAMES MICHAEL, real estate broker; b. Milw., Mar. 20, 1943; s. Robert Eugene and Virginia Estelle (Drolshagen) L.; student Mich. State U., 1965; m. Janet Arlene Ahern, Feb. 3, 1967; 1 dau., Kelly. Vice pres. Leahy Builders, Inc., Birmingham, Mich., 1965-67; salesman Weir, Manuel, Snyder & Ranke, Inc., Realtors, Birmingham, 1967-72, mgr., Troy, Mich., 1973—. Mem. bd. mgmt. YMCA, 1969-73, mem. bd. pub. relations com., 1970-71, chmn. phys. com. and mems., 1971-72. Served with Air NG, 1965-66. Mem. Birmingham Jr. C. of C. (chmn. youth devel. 1969), Birmingham-Bloomfield Bd. Realtors (chmn. profl. standards com. 1977), Sigma Alpha Epsilon. Roman Catholic. Home: 3790 Estates Dr Troy MI 48084 Office: 4700 Rochester Rd Troy MI 48084

LEAL, VICTOR LUCIANO, sch. adminstr.; b. E. Chicago, May 3, 1939; s. Victor Luciano and Clara (Schenk-Gonzalez) L.; B.S., Ind. U., 1961, M.S., 1964, Ed.D., 1976; m. Nilsa Cabrera, June 19, 1964; 1 dau., Lyzette Marie. Tchr. elementary sch. East Chicago, Ind., 1961-68, jr. high counselor, 1968-70, asst. prin. high sch., 1970-73, dir. pupil personnel services, 1973—. Named outstanding young man East Chicago Jaycees, 1971. Mem. Am. Assn. Sch. Adminstrs., Nat. Orgn. Legal Problems Edn., Internat. Assn. Pupil Personnel Workers, Am., Ind. personnel and guidance assns., Am. Vocat. Assn., NW Ind. Assn. Profl. Attendance Counselors and Social Workers, Phi Delta Kappa. Democrat. Home: 1412 N Dwiggins St Griffith IN 46319 Office: 2700 Cardinal Dr East Chicago IN 46312

LEANEAGH, JERRY DEL, publisher; b. Algona, Iowa, Nov. 11, 1932; s. Del and Arlouine (Palmer) L.; B.S., Iowa State U., 1954; student U. Heidelberg, Germany, 1956, Drake U., 1958-60; m. Sandra Leaneagh; children—David, Alan, Joan, John, Beth Ann, Randy, Tammy. Sales engr. Westinghouse Elec. Corp., Des Moines, 1957-60; pres. Directory Service Co., Algona, 1961—; Area chmn. Iowa Coll. Found. Served with AUS, 1955-57. Recipient Distinguished Services award, Algona, 1963. Mem. Aircraft Owners and Pilots Assn., Internat. Platform Assn., Young Presidents Orgn. Home: Burt IA 50522 Office: Directory Service Co Hwy 18 E Algona IA 50511

LEAR, JOHN, writer, editor; b. nr. Allen, Pa., Aug. 10, 1909; s. Charles D. and Esther M. (Sourbeer) L.; grad. high sch.; Sc.D. (hon.), Dickinson Coll., 1968; m. Dorothy Leeds, Sept. 26, 1931 (dec. May 1965); m. 2d, Marie Nesta, Aug. 28, 1966. Editor, Daily Local News, Mechanicsburg, Pa., 1927-28; reporter The Patriot, Harrisburg, Pa., 1928-34; writer-editor A.P., Phila., Chgo., N.Y.C., Washington, Buenos Aires, roving assignments Eastern U.S., Can., S.A., 1934-42; coordinator information staff gov. P.R., 1942-43; radio news writer Press Assn., N.Y.C., 1943; free lance mag. corr., 1944-48; mng. editor Steelways mag., 1948-49; chief articles editor Collier's mag., 1949-50, asso. editor, 1950-53; cons. publs. IBM Corp., 1953-54; dir. spl. atomics and automation studies Research Inst. Am., 1954-55; sci. editor Sat. Rev., 1956-71, sr. editor, 1971-72; v.p. communications Bauer Engring. Inc., 1972-73, v.p., chief editor Bauer, Sheaffer and Lear, Inc., 1972-75; chief editor Keifer & Assos., Inc., 1975-76; Am. corr. New Scientist, London, 1956-62; cons. Russell Sage Found., 1967-68, cons. com. pub. policy Nat. Acad. Engring., 1972—, Inst. Social Research, U. Mich., 1972-73; columnist King Features Syndicate; sci. cons. Crown Pubs. Inc., 1974; cons. Office Tech. Assessment, U.S. Congress, 1975—, Acad. Forum, Nat. Scis., 1976, Rockefeller Found., 1977. Recipient Distinguished Pub. Service award Sigma Delta Chi, 1950, 61; Westinghouse award AAAS, 1951; Albert Lasker Med. Journalism award, 1952. Mem. Soc. Profl. Journalists Sigma Delta Chi. Clubs: Chgo. Headline, Chgo. Press. Author: Forgotten Front, 1942; Kepler's Dream, 1965. Home: Lake Point Tower 505 N Lake Shore Dr Chicago IL 60611

LEARNED, CHARLES ALDEN, securities exec.; b. Stafford, Kans., Sept. 14, 1933; s. Wilmer Harrison and Vivian Edith (Hendershot) L.; B.S., Sterling Coll., 1955; m. Jean Starbuck, June 13, 1954; 1 son, Rodney David. Cashier municipal bond dept. Small-Milburn Investment, Inc., Wichita, Kans., 1956-58; mgr. municipal bond dept. Stockyards Nat. Bank, Wichita, 1958-64; exec. v.p., mgr. municipal bond dept. Mid-Continent Securities Corp., Wichita, 1964-68; v.p., mgr. municipal bond dept. Columbian Securities Corp., Wichita, 1968—; pres., dir. Learned Investments, Inc., Wichita, 1970—. Recipient Merit award Adminstr. Mgmt. Soc., 1971, Diamond Merit award, 1974. Mem. Adminstrv. Mgmt. Soc. (chpt. pres. 1970-72, dir. edn. div. on internat. bd. dirs. 1972-74), Wichita Ind. Bus. Assn., C. of C. Mem. Evang. Free Ch. Clubs: Wichita Racquet, Wichita Shocker, Knife and Fork, Masons, Shriners, Moose (life), Kiwanis. Home: 6705 Magill St Wichita KS 67206 Office: 321 E William St Wichita KS 67202

LEASE, THOMAS CHARLES, dentist; b. Salem, Ohio, Nov. 9, 1941; s. Donald Earl and Evelyn Louise (Horch) L.; B.A., Ohio State U., 1963, D.D.S., 1967; M.S.D., Ind. U., 1971; m. Carolyn Jean Walker; 1 dau., Dawn Dee. Asso. prof. periodontics Washington U., Sch. Dental Medicine, 1971—, also practice dentistry ltd. to periodontics, Creve Coeur, Mo., 1972—. Served to lt. comdr., Dental Corps, USNR, 1967-69. Mem. Am. Acad. Periodontology, Am., Mo. dental assns., Midwest Soc. Periodontology, Greater St. Louis Dental Soc., Mo. Soc. Periodontists, Mo. Valley Study Club, Pi Kappa Alpha, Psi Omega, Kappa Kappa Psi. Home: 224 Corral Trail Ellisville MO 63011 Office: 443 N New Ballas Rd Creve Coeur MO 63141

LEATHERMAN, LOWEN AUDRED, dentist; b. Wichita, Kans., June 11, 1947; s. Benny Audred and Glenna Marlyn (Albers) L.; B.A., Emporia State Coll., 1970; D.D.S., U. Mo., 1975; m. Virginia Lynn Burris, July 24, 1976. Gen. practice dentistry, Wichita, Kans., 1975—; instr. Penn Valley Jr. Coll., Kansas City, Mo., 1974—; instr. Wichita State U., 1976—. Mem. Am., Kans. dental assns., Wichita Dental Soc. Home: 2200 South Rock Rd Wichita KS 67207 Office: 8015 Peach Tree Ln Wichita KS 67207

LEATHERWOOD, PAUL RANDOLPH SCOTT, JR., pub. relations exec.; b. Hanover, Pa., Sept. 27, 1932; s. Paul Randolph Scott and Elizabeth Wilson (Chesley) L.; student Western Md. Coll., 1954-55, Balt. Coll. Commerce, 1962-70; m. Joan Evelyn Stimax, Sept. 10, 1955; children—Cherie Lynn, Laurie Ann. Supr. facilities services Bendix Field Engring. Corp., Owings Mills, Md., 1961-64, pub. relations coordinator, services supr., 1964-66, dir. pub. relations, Columbia, Md., 1966-70; regional mgr. pub. relations West Coast, Bendix Corp., Sylmar, Calif., 1970-73, regional mgr. pub. relations Midwest, South Bend, Ind., 1973-75, group dir. pub. relations Automotive Control Systems Group, 1975-76, dir. advt. and communications, 1976—. Served with USAF, 1949-53. Mem. Pub. Relations Soc. Am. (accredited), Jr. C. of C. Internat. (life). Club: South Bend Press. Home: 52743 Sporn Dr South Bend IN 46635 Office: 401 N Bendix Dr South Bend IN 46634

LEBENS, JOHN CASPER, elec. cons.; b. St. Louis, July 31, 1911; s. John Casper and Katherine Gertrude (Lally) L.; B.E.E., Washington U., St. Louis, 1932, M.E.E., 1933; m. Jeannette Lewald, June 7, 1934; 1 son, Charles Alfred. Elec. engr. Bussmann Mfg. div. McGraw Edison Co., St. Louis, 1935-48, chief engr., 1948-56, v.p., 1956-64, cons., 1964-77; pres. Lebens Assos., St. Louis, 1964—, Bridge Holding Corp., St. Louis, 1974—; guest lectr. Moore Grad. Sch. Pa. U., 1950-56. Active St. Louis Regional Commerce and Growth Assn., Mo. Hist. Soc., St. Louis Art Mus., Mo. Bot. Garden, McDonnell Planetarium. Registered profl. engr., Mo. Fellow IEEE; mem. Nat. Soc. Profl. Engrs., St. Louis Elec. Bd. Trade, Soc. Automotive Engrs., Nat. Elec. Mfrs. Assn., Am. Soc. Metals, Tau Beta Pi, Sigma Xi, Pi Mu Epsilon. Republican. Roman Catholic. Clubs: St. Louis, Mo. Athletic, Engrs. Contbr. articles on elec. protection to tech. jours. Home: 4 Briarcliff Saint Louis MO 63124

LEBIT, EDWARD ALAN, lawyer; b. Chgo., Oct. 23, 1936; s. Joseph Morton and Lillian (Inbinder) L.; A.B., Western Res. U., 1958; J.D., Cleve. Marshall Law Sch., 1965; m. Barbara Lou Biederman, Apr. 7, 1963; children—Lynn Ellen, Leslie Susan. Accountant, Soloway &Von Rosen, Cleve., 1960-61, Laks & Wynbrandt, Cleve., 1961-62; internal revenue agt. U.S. Treasury Dept., Cleve., 1962-65; admitted to Ohio bar, 1965; partner McCarthy, Lebit, Crystal, Kleinman & Gibbons Co., L.P.A., Cleve., 1970—; guest lectr. Cleve. Marshall Law Sch., 1965-71, lectr. Bread and Butter seminars, 1965-71; lectr. Ohio Bar Assn., 1971—. Served with AUS, 1959-60. C.P.A., Ohio. Mem. Am., Ohio, Cuyahoga, Cleve. bar assns. Asso. editor Ohio Probate Law Practice and Forms (Merrick Rippner), 1964. Home: 1902 Camberly Dr Lyndhurst OH 44124 Office: Illuminating Bldg Cleveland OH 44113

LEBRENZ, EUGENE RICHARD, educator; b. Teaneck, N.J., Aug. 3, 1941; s. George F. and Leanore (Fallot) L.; B.B.A., Upsala Coll., 1963; M.B.A., Seton Hall U., 1967; M.A., No. Ill. U., 1972, Ed.D., 1974. Fin. analyst N.J. Bank & Trust Co., Paterson, 1963-66; div. credit mgr. Am. Hosp. Supply Corp., Edison, N.J., 1966-68; corporate credit supr. Hoffmann-LaRoche, Inc., Nutley, N.J., 1968-69; coordinator financial mgmt. program, prof. fin. and econs. Coll. DuPage, Glen Ellyn, Ill., 1969—; cons. Tech. Adv. Service, Phila., 1971—. Mem. Am., Midwest, Ill. econs. assns., Nat. Bus. Edn. Assn., Midwest Fin. Assn., Beta Gamma Sigma, Alpha Kappa Psi, Delta Pi Epsilon. Author: Economics and Capitalism, 1971; The Business of Finance, 1971. Home: 23 W 267 Windsor Dr Glen Ellyn IL 60137 Office: Coll DuPage Glen Ellyn IL 60137

LE BRUN, JOHN LEO, educator; b. Geneva, N.Y., Aug. 8, 1934; s. Ralph Leo and Mary Elizabeth (Petro) LeB.; student St. Andrew's Seminary, 1952-54; A.B., U. Rochester, 1957; M.A., Boston Coll., 1962; Ph.D., Case Western Reserve U., 1971; m. Priscilla Sue Costich, Aug. 12, 1961; children—Joseph Andre, Lisette Johanna. Lab. technician U. Rochester Atomic Energy Project, 1954-55; tech. writer and editor Gen. Dynamics Corp., Rochester, N.Y., 1958-60; prof. history Baldwin-Wallace Coll., Berea, Ohio, 1963-64, Kent State U., Salem, Ohio, 1964—. Vice-chairperson St. Michael Parish Council, Canfield, Ohio, 1972-76; chairperson Community Life Commn. of Youngstown (Ohio) Diocesean Pastoral Council, 1974—; mem. social concerns dept. Cath. Conf. Ohio, 1975—; central com. Synod of Diocese of Youngstown, 1975—; vice chmn. State of Ohio Faculty Senate, 1970—; adv. com. to chancellor Ohio Bd. Regents, 1975—; tng. chairperson Western Reserve Dist. Mahoning Valley Council Boy Scouts Am., Youngstown, 1976—; mem. planning council Youngstown United Appeal, 1976—. Served with S.C., U.S. Army, 1957-58. Fox fellow, 1961-62. Recipient District award of Merit Mahoning Valley council Boy Scouts Am., 1975. Mem. Am. Hist. Assn., Am. Studies Assn., Orgn. Am. Historians, Council on Peace Research in History, Ohio Hist. Assn., Ohio Acad. History, Canadian Hist. Assn., AAUP, Soc. Tech. Communication, Am. Catholic Hist. Assn. Roman Catholic. Home: 85 Cardinal Dr Canfield OH 44406 Office: Kent State University Box 91 Salem OH 44460

LE BRUN, VIVIAN LUCILLE DAVIS (MRS. DONALD EDWARD LEBRUN), co-owner theatre; b. Ayersville, Ohio, Nov. 29, 1909; d. John Edgar and Nettie Ann (Eis) Davis; student pub. schs.; m. Donald Edward LeBrun, July 5, 1932; children—Suzanne LeBrun Cook, Donald Davis. Staff writer South Whitley (Ind.) Tribune, 1947-58, accounts exec., advt. dept., 1958; photographer, columnist Warsaw-Times-Union, Warsaw, Ind., 1947-72; co-owner, co-mgr. Kent Theatre, South Whitley, Ind., 1957—. Organizing regent Seek's Village, 1976—. Recipient award for oil painting Whitley County Art Guild Show, Columbia City, 1973. Mem. Gen. Fedn. Women's Clubs (county pres. 1941-42, dist. pres. 1956-58), Internat. Platform Assn., Nat. League Am. Pen Women, Nat. Writers Club, Ft. Wayne Hist. Soc., DAR (chpt. regent 1972-74, 76, chmn. motion pictures and TV Ind. chpt. 1976-78), Ladies Aux. V.F.W. (post pres. 1945), Whitley County Artist Guild, Ind. Museum Soc. (dist. dir. 1973-75). Methodist. Clubs: Order Eastern Star (worthy matron 1944-45), White Shrine Jerusalem. Address: 106 N Maple St Box 495 South Whitley IN 46787

LEBRYK, EDWIN FRANK, microscopist; b. East Chgo., Ind., Jan. 28, 1924; s. Walter and Stephanie (Bernacke) L.; student Detroit U., 1942-43, N.D. A. and M. U., 1943-44; student Ill. Inst. Tech., 1965-66, student McCrone Research Inst., 1966; m. Shirlee M. Hands, Aug. 5, 1950; children—Judith Ann Lebryk Millspaugh, Sharon Kay. Lab. technician Inland Steel Co., East Chicago, 1942; sr. devel. operator Sinclair Refining Co., East Chicago, 1946-65; research microscopist Atlantic Richfield Co., Harvey, Ill., 1965—. Instr. Acad. Sci., Chgo., 1972—; cons. State Microscopical Soc. Ill. Student Affiliate, 1973—. Explorer adviser, organizer, Boy Scouts Am., East Chicago, 1946-72, mem. council, 1950-72. Pres. ARCO Credit Union, Harvey, Ill., 1971—. Served as sr. sgt., USAAF, 1943-46. Recipient 25 Year Service award, Credit Union ARCO, 1974; 35 Yr. Service award, Boy Scouts Am., 1970. Fellow Royal Microscopical Soc.; mem. Am. Legion, Electron Microscopical Soc. Am., Midwest Soc. Electron Microscopists, Quekett Microscopical London, State Microscopical Soc. Ill. (pres. 1969-70; editor centennial volume 1972—). Cons. for Microscopy Tech. Series, 1970—. Home: 1713 Ridge Rd Munster IN 46321 Office: 400 E Sibley Blvd Harvey IL 60426

LECHIARA, JOSEPH MICHAEL, accountant; b. Smithers, W.Va., Aug. 17, 1935; s. Joseph Carvelli and Virginia Mary (Paterno) L.; student Morris Harvey Coll., 1953-55; B.B.A., Marshall U., 1958; m. Phyllis Ann Brewer, Aug. 25, 1957; children—Victoria Lynn, Elizabeth Ann, J. Michael. With Ernst & Ernst, C.P.A.'s, Akron, 1960—, partner, 1972—. Asso. editor Akron Bus. and Econ. Rev. 1970-71. Served with AUS, 1958-60. C.P.A., Ohio. Mem. Am. Inst. C.P.A.'s, (dir. 1968-69), Ohio Accounting Council (pres. 1970-71), Ohio Soc. C.P.A.'s, Nat. Accounting and Finance Council, St. Hilary Holy Name Soc. (sec. 1970-71), Robe Honorary Soc., Sigma Phi Epsilon. Clubs: Fairlawn Country, Akron City, University. Home: 2386 Brice Rd Akron OH 44313 Office: 1 Cascade Plaza Akron OH 44308

LECHNER, GEORGE WILLIAM, gen. and vascular surgeon; b. Denver, July 30, 1931; s. Frank Clifford and Hazel Mae (Elkins) L.; student U. N.Mex., 1948-49; B.A., Pacific Union Coll., 1952; M.D. summa cum laude, Loma Linda U., 1956; m. Betty Jane Baumbach, Aug. 3, 1952; children—Kathleen Ann, Elaine Marie, Carol Jean, Patricia Louise, James Richard. Instr. surgery Wayne State U., Detroit, 1963-64; intern Pontiac (Mich.) Gen. Hosp., 1956-57; resident in surgery Harper Hosp., Detroit, 1957-58, Wayne State U. Hosps., 1961-64; pvt. practice medicine specializing in surgery, Dayton, Ohio, 1964—; dir. surgery sect. 3, Kettering Med. Center, Dayton, 1967—, also dir. emergency medicine residency; mem. active staff Kettering Med. Center; adj. faculty Kettering Coll. Med. Arts; pres. Kettering Emergency Room Corp.; asso. clin. prof. surgery Wright State U., 1975—. Trustee, mem. exec. com. bd. Kettering Med. Center, 1971-74; trustee Spring Valley Acad., 1973—, pres., 1973-75. Served with AUS, 1958-61; Japan. Diplomate Am. Bd. Surgery; recipient C.V. Mosby award for acad. excellence, 1956. Fellow A.C.S.; mem. Midwest Surg. Assn., Dayton Surg. Soc., AMA, Ohio and Montgomery County med. socs., Am. Coll. Emergency Room Physicians, AAAS. Seventh-day Adventist. Republican. Club: Rotary. Home: 920 Butte Creek Circle Dayton OH 45459 Office: 2801 Far Hills Ave Dayton OH 45419

LECKIE, JAMES ROBERT, mgmt. cons. co. exec.; b. Chgo., Mar. 11, 1939; s. Robert Fulton and Olive Harriet (Brumnill) L.; B.A., DePauw U., 1962; m. Kathryn Newell Urban, Aug. 11, 1962; children—Scott Andrew, James Robert III. Bus. mgr. Roger's Chevrolet Co., Rantoul, Ill., 1962-64; gen. mgr. Jocke Buick Co., Chgo., 1964-66; comptroller, Z Frank Chevrolet, Chgo., 1966-68; mgr. mgmt. service Killam & DeValk, C.P.A.'s, Chgo., 1968-70; pres., Keys Communication Ltd., Elmhurst, Ill., 1970—; dir. Keys Communications Ltd., Keys Marketing, MS Key Services, Ltd., The Leckie Assos. Contbg. lectr. DePauw U., Northwood Inst., 1973—. Mem. Elmhurst C. of C., Automotive Old Timers (life), Delta Chi. Republican. Methodist (mem. finance com. 1972—). Kiwanian. Contbr. articles to profl. jours. Home: 925 S Yale St Villa Park IL 60181 Office: 188 Industrial Dr 18A Elmhurst IL 60126

LE CLAIRE, HENRI, physician; b. Lewiston, Me., Mar. 23, 1908; s. Dominique and Valada (Roy) LeC.; M.D., Loyola U. Med. Sch., 1940; m. Dorothy Maier; children—Andre, Henri Robert, Laureanne. Intern, Christ Hosp., Cin., 1940-41; resident Chgo. Tumor Inst., 1950-51; practice medicine, specializing in radiology, Cin., 1952—; cons. radiologist Highland County Hosp., Hillsboro, Ohio, 1954—; cons. radium therapist Deaconess Hosp., Cin., 1960—. Am. Cancer Soc. fellow Barnard Skin & Cancer Hosp., St. Louis, 1951-52. Mem. AMA, Am. Radium Soc Radiol. Soc. N. Am., Am. Coll. Radiology. Republican. Clubs: Cuvier Press, Internat. Bacchus, Am. Angus Assn., Ohio Thoroughbred Horsemen's Assn., Chevalier De La Chaine Des Rotisseurs. Contbr. monographs to profl. jours. Home: 1075 Eversole Rd Cincinnati OH 45230 Office: 19 Garfield Pl Suite 735 Cincinnati OH 45202

LE COMPTE, GARÉ, psychologist; b. Chgo., Sept. 15, 1937; s. Edward Winston Groshell and Clair Agnew LeCompte; B.A., U. Wash., 1959, M.A., Am. U., 1967, Ph.D., 1970; Ph.D., Case-Western Res. U., 1978; m. Dorothy Joan Bookhamer, Jan. 28, 1961; children—Michele, Nicole, Andre. Nat. def. analyst U.S. Govt., Washington and Boston, 1960-62; vis. prof. Syrian U., Damascus, Syria, 1962-63; research coordinator spl. projects Gen. Dynamics Corp., Groton, Conn., 1964-67; sr. research scientist, dir. social sci. research Conn. State Research Commn., Hartford, 1967-71; dir. research N.Y.-Pa. Health Mgmt. Corp., Binghamton, N.Y., 1971-73; dean, prof. behavioral sci. Ohio Coll. Podiatric Medicine, Cleve., 1973—; bd. dirs. Inst. Middle Eastern and N. African Affairs, Highgate Social Research Center; mem. faculty U. Hartford (Conn.), 1967-71. Bd. dirs. Family and Children's Services of So. Tier, N.Y., 1971-73. Strong Found. fellow, 1963-64. Mem. Am. Psychol. Assn., Am. Pub. Health Assn., Assn. Advancement Behavior Therapy, Psychiat. Sociology and Med. Sociology, Research Com. Internat. Sociol. Assn. Episcopalian. Contbr. articles on health and mental health service systems to profl. jours. Home: 22361 Rye Rd Shaker Heights OH 44122 Office: 10515 Carnegie Ave U Circle Cleveland OH 44106

LE CRONE, NORMAN JAMES, constrn. co. exec.; b. Columbus, Mar. 18, 1913; s. Francis Garfield and Carrie (Jaycox) LeC.; ed. North High Sch., Columbus, 1932; m. Estelle Louise Dyer, July 20, 1934; children—Carolyn Dianne (Mrs. Elsworth Boyer), Sharon (Mrs. Robert Love), Norman, Rosalie (Mrs. Lamar Reynolds). Owner, operator N.J. LeCrone Constrn. Co., Columbus, 1936—; dir. Columbus Bldg. Exchange, 1952—. Mem. Engrs. Club Columbus, Columbus C. of C., Ohio Contractors and Am. Rd. Builders Assn. Methodist. Lion, Mason. Home: 2315 Haverford Rd Columbus OH 43220 Office: 1575 Harmon Ave Columbus OH 43223

LEDINKO, NADA, educator; b. Girard, O., Dec. 16, 1924; s. John Daniel and Zora Maria (Valencic) L.; B.S., Ohio State U., 1946; M.S., Pa. State U., 1949; Ph.D., Yale U., 1952. Chief virologist, research career devel. awardee Nat. Cancer Inst., Bennington, Vt., 1965-71; prof. biology U. Akron (Ohio), 1971—. Nat. Cancer Inst. spl. postdoctoral fellow, 1962-65, Poliomyelitis Research Fund fellow,

1953-56, Damon Runyon Fund grantee, 1970-73, Nat. Cancer Inst. grantee, 1967-76. Mem. Tissue Culture Soc., Am. Soc. Microbiology, Am. Assn. Cancer Research, Sigma Xi, Phi Beta Kappa, Phi Kappa Phi. Contbr. articles to profl. jours. Home: 566 Haskell Dr Akron OH 44313 Office: Dept Biology U Akron Akron OH 44325

LE DUC, DON RAYMOND, lawyer; b. S. Milwaukee, Wis., Apr. 7, 1933; s. Raymond Joseph and Roberta (Jones) Le D.; B.A., U. Wis., 1959, Ph.D., 1970; J.D., Marquette U., 1962; m. Alice Marie Pranica, Oct. 24, 1959; children—Paul, Marie. Admitted to Wis. bar, 1962; asso. firm Arnold, Murray & O'Neill, Milw., 1962-63; Ford fellow comparative law U. Wis., Madison, 1963-64, prof., 1973—; individual practice law, Green Bay, Wis., 1964-67; chief counsel Wis. Dept. Ins., Madison, 1967-69; asst. prof. communication law U. Md., College Park, 1970-71; asso. prof. communication law Ohio State U., Columbus, 1971-73; dir. Comparative Telecommunications Research Center, Madison, since 1974—. Chief counsel Wis. Gov.'s Task Force on Telecommunications, 1971-72; cable TV adv. com FCC, 1972—. Served as spl. agt., CIC, U.S. Army, 1954-57. Awardee Ohio State U., 1971, Wis. Alumni Research Found., 1974, 75, 77. Mem. FCC, Wis. bar assns., Broadcast Edn. Assn., Internat. Inst. Communication. Republican. Roman Catholic. Author: Cable Television and the FCC, 1973; Issues in Broadcast Regulation, 1974; contbr. articles to profl. publs.; editor Client mag., 1972—. Home: 305 Cheyenne Trail Madison WI 53705 Office: Vilas Communication Hall U Wis Madison WI 53706

LEE, DONG SUNG, physician, anesthesiologist; b. Pyung-Buk, Korea, Jan. 1, 1933; s. Yi Bae and Soon Myong (Jie) L.; came to U.S., 1967; grad. Seoul Nat. U., 1953; M.D., Seoul (Korea) Nat. U., 1957; m. Yung Sim Kang, Feb. 1, 1959; children—Janet, Sharyl, Jill, John, David, Grace, Betty. Intern DePaul Hosp., Norfolk, Va., 1967-68; resident in anesthesiology St. Elizabeth Hosp., Youngstown, Ohio, 1968-71; partner Bel-Park Anesthesia Assos., Inc., Youngstown, 1971—. Served as med. officer to maj. Korean Air Force, 1957-67. Recipient Hon. Citizenship, State of Tex., 1963. Diplomate Am. Bd. Anesthesiology. Fellow Am. Coll. Anesthesiology; mem. Am., Ohio State med. assns., Am., Ohio socs. anesthesiologists. Home: 940 Royal Arms Dr Girard OH 44420 Office: St Elizabeth Hospital Youngstown OH 44505

LEE, DOUGLAS ALLEN, musician, educator; b. Carmel, Ind., Nov. 3, 1932; s. Ralph Henley and Flossie Ellen (Chandler) L.; B. Music, DePauw U., Greencastle, Ind., 1954; M.Mus., U. Mich., 1958, Ph.D., 1968; m. Beverly Ruth Haskell, Sept. 21, 1961. Asst. prof. piano Mt. Union Coll., Alliance, Ohio, 1959-61; prof. music lit. and piano Wichita (Kans.) State U., 1964—; instr. Nat. Music Camp, Interlochen, Mich., 1959-62; editor Am. Music Tchr., 1970-72; adjudicator Nat. Guild Piano Tchrs., 1960, 61. Served with AUS, 1955-57. Mem. Am. Musicol. Soc., Am. Soc. 18th Century Studies, Music Tchrs. Nat. Assn., Wichita Area Piano Tchrs. League (chmn. 1967-69), Pi Kappa Lambda, Phi Kappa Phi. Episcopalian. Author: The Works of Christoph Nichelmann: A thematic index, 1971; Christoph Nichelmann: Two Concertos, 1977; also articles. Home: 6420 Oneida St Wichita KS 67206 Office: Dept Musicology Wichita State Univ Wichita KS 67208

LEE, E(UGENE) STANLEY, engr.; b. Hopeh, China, Sept. 7, 1930; s. Ing Yah and Lindy (Hsieng) L.; came to U.S., 1955, naturalized, 1961; M.S., N.C. State U., 1957; Ph.D., Princeton U., 1962; m. Mayanne Lee, Dec. 21, 1957; children—Linda J., Margaret H. Research engr. Phillips Petroleum Co., Bartlesville, Okla., 1960-66; asst. prof. Kans. State U., Manhattan, 1966-67, asso. prof., 1967-69, prof. Coll. Engring., 1969—; prof. U. So. Calif., Los Angeles, 1972-76. Research grantee NSF, 1971—, Office Water Resources, 1968-75, EPA, 1969-71, Dept. Def., 1967-72. Mem. Am. Inst. Chem. Engrs., Soc. Indsl. and Applied Math., Ops. Research Soc. Am., Sigma Xi, Tau Beta Pi, Phi Kappa Phi. Author: Quasilinearization and Invariant Imbedding, 1968; editor Energy Sci. and Tech., 1975—; asso. editor Jour. Math. Analysis and Applications, 1974—, Computers and Math. with Applications, 1974—. Home: 109 Frick Dr Manhattan KS 66502 Office: Coll Engring Kans State U Manhattan KS 66502

LEE, GILBERT BROOKS, research asso.; b. Cohasset, Mass., Sept. 10, 1913; s. John Alden and Charlotte Louise (Brooks) L.; B.A., Reed Coll., 1946; M.A., New Sch. Social Research, 1949; m. Marion Corrine Rapp, Mar. 7, 1943 (div. Jan. 1969); children—Thomas Stearns, Jane Stanton, Frederick Cabot, Eliot Frazar. Asst. psychologist Civil Service, Psychophysics of Vision, U.S. Naval Submarine Base, New London, Conn., 1950-53; research asso. Project Mich., Vision Research Labs., Willow Run, 1954-57; research asso. dept. ophthalmology U. Mich., Ann Arbor, 1958-72, sr. research asso., 1972—. Precinct del. Democratic County Conv., Washtenaw County, 1970, 74; treas. Dem. party, Ann Arbor, Mich., 1971-72, 74-75; chmn. Precinct Election Inspectors, 1968-75. Served to capt. AUS, 1942-46, 61-62. Mem. Optical Soc. Am., A.A.A.S., Assn. Research in Vision and Ophthalmology, Nation Assos., A.C.L.U. Contbr. articles to profl. jours. Home: 901 Edgewood Ave Ann Arbor MI 48103

LEE, HI BAHL, physician; b. Ahndong, Korea, Jan. 9, 1942; s. Woo Sung and Pil Joo Lee; came to U.S., 1968; M.D., Seoul Nat. U., Korea, 1965; m. Jung Hee Kwon, Jan. 5, 1972; children—Kang Hahn, Kang Nak. Intern, Western Pa. Hosp., Pitts., 1968-69; resident internal medicine Mt. Sinai Hosp., Mpls., 1969-70; resident Wayne State U., Detroit, 1970-72, fellow nephrology, 1972-74; attending physician nephrology Meml. Med. Center. Springfield, Ill., 1974—, also asst. clin. prof. medicine So. Ill. U., 1974—; cons. in nephrology St. John, Springfield Community hosps. (Springfield), Decatur (Ill.) Meml. Hosp., Passavant Meml. Hosp., Jacksonville, Ill., St. Anthony Hosp., Effingham, Ill., Alton (Ill.) Meml. Hosp. Served with M.C., Korean Army, 1965-68. Diplomate Am. Bd. Internal Medicine. Mem. Am., Internat. socs. nephrology. Home: 149 Cypress Point Springfield IL 62704 Office: 1st and Miller Sts Springfield IL 62705

LEE, J. MURRAY, educator; b. Spokane, Wash., Oct. 25, 1904; A.B., Occidental Coll., 1926; A.M. Columbia U., 1928, Ph.D., 1934; m. Myrtle F. Lee; children—Lorna Lombard, Lawrence K. Tchr. city schs., Burbank, Calif., 1926-29, dir. research, 1929-36, dir. curriculum and research, 1936-37; asst. prof. edn. U. Wis., 1937-41; dean Sch. Edn., dir. summer sessions, prof. edn. State Coll. Wash., 1941-54, prof. edn., 1941-56; prof. elementary edn. U. Miami, 1956-58; chmn. dept. elementary edn. So. Ill. U., 1958-68, prof. elementary edn., 1968-73, prof. emeritus, 1973—; summer vis. prof. Tchrs. Coll., Columbia, 1932, Coll. William and Mary, 1935, U. Tex., 1936-37, U. Hawaii, 1951, U. Colo., 1956, Mich. State U., 1958, U. So. Calif., 1961; vis. lectr. Yale U., 1952-53; also cons. pub. sch. survey of Utah. Served to lt. comdr. USNR, 1943-45. Mem. Ill. Adv. Com. for Gifted. Mem. Dept. Elementary Sch. Prins., NEA; mem. AAAS, Edn. Research Assn., Phi Delta Kappa. Co-author: The Child and His Curriculum, The Child and His Development; author: Elementary Education: Today and Tomorrow, 2d edit., 1972. Foundations of Elementary Education, 1969. Home: 907 Taylor Dr Carbondale IL 62901

LEE, JAMES CHEN-MING, chemist; b. Taipei, Taiwan, Feb. 19, 1944; s. Ben-Shin and Fan-Fung (Huang) L.; came to U.S., 1971, naturalized, 1977; B.S., Chung Yuan Christian Coll., 1968; M.S., Eastern N.Mex. U., 1973; m. Ching-Ling Wu, Nov. 16, 1970; 1 son, Yueh Zenas. Research asst. Nat. Tsing Hua U., Taiwan, 1968-69; tchr. chemistry Du Shi High Sch., Taiwan, 1969-71; teaching asst. Eastern N.Mex. U., Portales, 1971-73; chemist Thompson-Hayward Chem. Co., Kansas City, Kans., 1974—. Mem. Am. Chem. Soc. Home: 10805 W 95th Terr Overland Park KS 66214 Office: 5200 Speaker Rd Kansas City MO 66106

LEE, JOON JA KIM, anesthesiologist; b. Seoul, Korea, Apr. 5, 1945; d. Young Bin and Jung Sook (Lee) Kim; M.D., Ewha Womans U., Seoul, Korea, 1970; postgrad. U. Minn., 1972-75; m. Kyoo Won Lee, July 17, 1970. Rotating intern Severance Hosp., Seoul, 1970-71, St. Paul-Ramsey Hosp., St. Paul, 1971-72; resident anesthesiology U. Minn. Hosps., Mpls., 1972-75, physician, instr. dept. anesthesiology, 1975—. Mem. AMA, Am., Minn. socs. anesthesiologists, Internat. Anesthesia Research Soc. Home: 1998 Brewster St St Paul MN 55108 Office: Dept of Anesthesiology Univ of Minnesota Hospitals Minneapolis MN 55455

LEE, JOSEPH JOOINN, educator; b. Seoul, Korea, Dec. 20, 1934; s. Kyungsoo and Myungsook (Lee) L.; came to U.S., 1957, naturalized, 1969; B.A., Chosun Christian U., 1957; M.A., U. N.D., 1958; Ph.D., U. Ill., 1962; m. Claire Youngsook Chu, June 15, 1963; children—Arthur, Andrew, Albert. Instr., U. Minn., Morris, 1961-62, asst. prof., 1962-65, asso. prof., 1965-70, prof. polit. sci., 1970—, vice-chmn. div. social scis., 1973—. Adviser, Minn. Humanities Commn., 1972—. Recipient Teaching award Horace T. Morse-Standard Oil Found., 1973, award NSF, 1965, award Outstanding Educators Am., 1972. Postdoctoral Cross disciplinary fellow, 1969-70, Nat. Endowment Humanities fellow, 1967, Weil Found. fellow, 1967, Ednl. Devel. Program grantee, 1972-73, Grad. Sch. Faculty research grantee, 1966-67, Minn. Humanities Commn. grantee, 1972-74, Nat. Humanities Inst. fellow, 1977-78. Fellow Soc. Values in Higher Edn.; mem. AAUP, Am., Midwest, Minn. (pres. 1973-74) polit. sci. assns., Minn. Acad. Sci. (chmn. polit. sci. sect. 1972-73). Author: The Second Renaissance: The Quest of Utopia, 1957; The Status of Political Theory in the Study of Politics, 1965; Democracy on Trial in Asia, 1967; Authoritarianism: Transitional Democracy in Asia, 1968; Komeito: Sokagakkai-ism in Japanese Politics, 1970; The impact of Religion on Political Development, 1972; Anarchism Reconsidered: Is Anarchism an Anachronistic Ideology?, 1975. Co-editor: Politics and You: Issues in Contemporary Theory and Practice of Politics, 1976. Home: 4400 Tyrol Crest Golden Valley MN 55416

LEE, JUNG KI, clin. psychologist; b. Seoul, Korea, Oct. 18, 1936; s. Pyung Hack and Kap Sil (Kim) L.; came to U.S., 1961, naturalized, 1970; B.A., Sun Kyun Kwan U., Seoul, 1960; M.A. in Psychology, Western Mich. U., 1966; postgrad. U. Akron, 1968-71; Ph.D. in Clin. Psychology, Tenn. Christian U., 1975; m. Joann Bangyul, Dec. 30, 1967; children—James Wook, Rochelle Mia. Licensed psychologist, dir. work adjustment services Vocat. Guidance & Rehab. Services, Cleve., 1968—; pvt. practice Cleve., 1970-76; pres. Psycho-Vocational Cons., Inc., Cleve., 1976—. Speaker, Nat. Rehab. Conf., Las Vegas, 1974, Cin., 1975; tchr. Cuyahoga Community Coll., 1968-71. Mem. Am., Ohio, Cleve. psychol. assns., Assn. Advancement Psychologists, Cleve. Acad. Cons. Psychologists. Olympic wrestler, 1960. Home: 17022 Eagle Nest Circle Strongsville OH 44136 Office: 666 Euclid Ave Suite 725 Cleveland OH 44114

LEE, KYO RAK, radiologist; b. Seoul, Korea, Aug. 3, 1933; s. Ke Chang and Ok Hi (Um) L.; came to U.S., 1964, naturalized, 1976; M.D., Seoul Nat. U., 1959; m. Ke Sook Oh, July 22, 1964; children—Andrew, John. Intern, Franklin Sq. Hosp., Balt., 1964-65; resident U. Mo. Med. Center, Columbia, Mo., 1965-68; instr. dept. radiology U. Mo., Columbia, 1968-69, asst. prof., 1969-71; asst. prof. dept. radiology U. Kans., Kansas City, 1971-76, asso. prof., 1976—. Served with Republic of Korea Army, 1950-52. Diplomate Am. Bd. Radiology. Recipient Richard H. Marshak award Am. Coll. Gastroenterology, 1975. Mem. Am. Coll. Radiology, Assn. Univ. Radiologists, Kans. Radiol. Soc., Greater Kansas City Radiol. Soc., Wyandotte County Med. Soc. Presbyterian. Contbr. articles to med. jours. Home: 9800 Glenwood St Overland Park KS 66212 Office: 39th St and Rainbow Blvd Kansas City KS 66103

LEE, KYU YAWP, educator; b. Pyongyang, Korea, Apr. 8, 1925; s. Young K. and Cha (Song) L.; came to U.S., 1947, naturalized, 1959; B.A., Mich. State U., 1953, B.S., 1954, M.S., 1957, Ph.D., 1960; m. Susie Roe, June 14, 1953; children—Irene, Nelson K., Wilson. Asst. prof. Chgo. Med. Sch., 1966-68; asst. prof. U. Nebr., Omaha, 1968-70, asso. prof. biochemistry Med. Sch., 1970—; asso. prof. Courtauld Inst. Biochemistry, U. London, 1968. Vis. scientist molecular oncology U. Tokyo, Japan, 1972. Pres., Burke High Sch. P.T.A., 1973. Recipient Distinguished Research award Chgo. Med. Sch., 1967; Am. Cancer Soc. research grantee, 1964, NSF Research Council travel grantee, 1966. Mem. Am. Chem. Soc., Am. Oil Chemists Soc., A.A.A.S., Biochem. Soc. (London), N.Y. Acad. Scis., Sigma Xi. Author: Interdisciplinary Experimental Cell Biology and Biochemistry, 1971. Patentee in field. Home: Route 5 Box 74B Council Bluffs IA 51501

LEE, MARGARET, newspaper editor; b. Northfield, Minn., Jan. 5, 1921; d. Edward S. and Ferne Josephine (Thompson) Lee. With accounting dept. John W. Thomas Co., Mpls., 1943-44; reporter-bookkeeper Northfield News, 1944-54, news editor, 1954-56, asso. editor, 1956-62, mng. editor, 1962-67, editor, 1967—. Bd. dirs. Northfield Future, Inc. Recipient numerous writing awards Minn. Press Women, Nat. Fedn. Press Women. Mem. Minn. Press Women (editor Gopher Tidings 1959—, past pres.), Nat. Fedn. Press Women (past regional dir.), Minn. Newspaper Assn. (past com. chmn.), Bus. and Profl. Womens Club (past pres. Northfield, dist. chmn.), Northfield Improvement assn. (past sec.), Northfield Hosp. Aux., Northfield Arts Guild, Minn., Rice County (v.p., dir.), Northfield (a founder, charter mem., sec. 1975—) hist. socs., HATPIN. Club: Minnesota Press (charter mem., dir.). Home: 1012 Union St Northfield MN 55057 Office: Northfield News Northfield MN 55057

LEE, NELDA KAYE, structural engr.; b. Carrollton, Ala., Sept. 14, 1946; d. Milton Horace and Euna Faye (Johnson) Lee; B.S. in Aerospace Engring., Auburn U., 1969. Structural and mech. design engr. McDonnell Douglas Corp., St. Louis, 1969—, named participant in personal devel. program, 1976. Named Accident Prevention counselor St. Louis area Dept. Transp. and FAA, 1977. Mem. Am. Inst. Aeros. and Astronautics, Soc. Women Engrs., Mo. Pilots Assn., Greater St. Louis Flight Instrs., Ninety-Nines, Inc., Whirly-Girls, Inc. No. 247 (scholar, 1977), St. Louis N. County Tennis Assn., McDonnell Douglas Corp. Tennis League, Delta Zeta. Baptist. Clubs: Internat. Toastmistress; Ski (McDonnell Douglas Corp.). Home: 1816 Exuma Dr St Louis MO 63136 Office: PO Box 516 St Louis MO 63166

LEE, PAUL WARREN, govt. recreation dept. leader; b. St. Petersburg, Fla., Jan. 4, 1948; s. Paul William and Lilly Evelyn (Smith) L.; B.A. in Music Edn., Ohio State U., 1970, M.A. in Music Edn., 1975; M.Div., Methodist Theol. Sch., Delaware, Ohio, 1974; postgrad. Capital U. Law Sch., 1974-75. Ordained to ministry Methodist Ch., 1971; asso. minister Thurman Av. Methodist Ch., Columbus, Ohio, 1966-69; ambulance driver, attendant Columbus Ambulance Service, 1970-72; recreation leader sr. citizens Columbus Dept. Recreation, 1971—, also asso. minister First Conglist. Ch., Columbus, 1971-73; owner Lee Aviation, Columbus, 1965—; musical performer, 1965—; mem. Registry Emergency Med. Technicians, 1973—; mem. Columbus Civic Ballet, 1972—. Coach, ofcl. football Ohio High Sch. Athletic Assn., Columbus, 1972—; mem. Columbus Aux. Police Dept., 1973—. Mem. Common Cause, Pub. Citizens, Ohio Parks and Recreation Assn., Nat. Recreation and Parks Assn., Fraternal Order of Police Assn., Central Ohio Soaring Assn., various community theater groups. Home: 551 E Deshler Ave Columbus OH 43206 Office: 2385 Mock Rd Columbus OH 43219

LEE, RALPH LAWRENCE, real estate appraiser; b. Omaha, Nov. 12, 1921; s. Alf Lawrence and Barbara Louise (Howard) L.; student Mpls. Bus. Coll., 1948-49; student U. Minn., 1963, 73, U. Chgo., 1967, U. Detroit, 1965; m. Ethel L. Friberg, Feb. 26, 1957; children—Richard, Donovan, Ted, Diane. Estimator constrn. Anchor Block Co., St. Paul, 1954-59, part owner, dir., 1955-59; owner Chisago St. Croix Real Estate Appraisal Service, Chisago City, Minn., 1967-70, Pequot Lakes (Minn.) Real Estate, 1970—; appraiser right of way div. Minn. Hwy. Dept., St. Paul, 1962-68; real estate appraiser, cons. First Fed. Savs. and Loan Assn., Brainerd, Minn., 1962—, La Salle, Ruppert & Lowe, Mpls., 1967—; pub. The Pequot Progressor (now Country Echo), 1971-73. Chmn. edn. com. Brainerd (Minn.) Bd. Realtors, 1972, pres., 1973; instr. real estate Globe Bus. Coll., St. Paul, 1968-69, Brainerd (Minn.) Area Vocat. Tech. Sch., 1969—; co-program chmn., speaker indsl. seminar Am. Soc. Appraisers Augsburg Coll., Mpls., 1968. Bd. dirs. Minn. Child Evangelism, Inc., 1960-70, pres. St. Paul br., 1967-68. Served with USAAF, 1941-45. Named Minn. Realtor of Year, Minn. Assn. Realtors, 1973. Mem. Am. Soc. Appraisers (sr.; sec. twin city bd. examiners 1966-68), Nat. Inst. Farm and Land Brokers, Gideons Internat. (pres. St. Paul camp 1962), Pequot Lakes C. of C. (sec. 1971). Home: Upper Loon Lake Box 10 Pequot Lakes MN 56472 Office: Pequot Lakes Real Estate Box 10 Highway 371 Pequot Lakes MN 56472

LEE, ROBERT EDWARD, chem. co. exec.; b. Quincy, Mass., Mar. 16, 1931; s. John Percy and Adrienne Rita (Kelcourse) L.; B.S. in Chem. Engring. with honors, Northeastern U., 1953; M.B.A. with honors, U. Mich., 1961; m. Loretta G. Gerulski, Oct. 30, 1954; children—Richard A., Cathryn A., Kevin J. Project leader styrene polymerization Dow Chem. Co., Midland, Mich., 1953-59, dir., 1959-61, dir. Saran devel., 1961-62, applied research dir., 1962-63, films research dir., 1963-68, films tech. service and devel. mgr., 1968, films research and devel. tech. dir., 1968—. Charles Hayden scholar, 1948. Registered profl. engr., Mich. Mem. Am. Inst. Chem. Engrs., Tau Beta Pi. Elk. Patentee in field. Home: 377 Llanberis Dr Granville OH 43023 Office: Granville Research and Devel Center Dow Chem Co Granville OH 43023

LEE, ROBERT MICHAEL, communications co. exec.; b. Mpls., July 17, 1940; s. Stanley Christopher and Rose Ann (Sannes) L.; student U. Minn., 1958-59; certificate Brown Inst. Broadcasting, 1959-60; m. Nancy J. Johnson, May 22, 1965; children—Kevin, Kenneth. Announcer, radio sta. WMNE, Menomone, Wis., 1961-62; announcer, newsman radio sta. KYSM, 1962; news dir. radio station WWAM, WWTV-FM and TV sta. WWTV, Cadillac, Mich., 1964—. Chmn. broadcast wire study com. Mich. Asso. Press, 1970—. Chmn. Cadillac Community Council, 1966-67; chmn. Cadillac Citizens Adv. Com., 1967; sec. Cadillac Charter Commn., 1971-72. Served with AUS, 1962-64. Decorated Army Commendation medal; recipient Spl. Recognition award Mich. Environmental Health Assn., 1972; award Mich. Farm Bur., 1975. Mem. Radio-TV News Dirs. Assn. Home: 1946 W Chestnut St Cadillac MI 49601 Office: Dighton Rd Cadillac MI 49601

LEE, SANG HAN, engr.; b. Korea, Dec. 5, 1935; s. Jang Woo and Sumyun (Kim) L.; came to U.S., 1956, naturalized, 1968; B.S., Ind. Inst. Tech., 1960; M.B.A., U. Chgo., 1968; m. Hansoon Kim, Nov. 3, 1961; children—Edmund, Susanne, Thomas. Project engr. Internat. Harvester Co., Melrose Park, Ill., 1960-67; mgr. engring. Pullman Standard div. Pullman, Inc., Hammond, Ind., 1967—. Registered profl. engr., Ill. Mem. ASME. Patentee in field. Home: 18500 Center Ave Homewood IL 60430 Office: 1414 Field St Hammond IN 46320

LEE, SHERMAN EMERY, art museum dir.; b. Seattle, Apr. 19, 1918; s. Emery H. and Adelia (Baker) L.; B.A., M.A., Am. U.; Ph.D., Western Res. U.; m. Ruth A. Ward, Sept. 3, 1938; children—Katharine C., Margaret A. (Mrs. Arne L. Gray), Elizabeth K. (Mrs. William Chiego, Jr.), Thomas W. Curator, Far Eastern art Detroit Inst. Art, 1941-46; with dept. Arts and Monuments div. civil information and edn. sect., gen. hdqrs. Supreme Comdr. Allied Powers, Tokyo, 1946-48; asst. dir., then asso. dir. Seattle Mus. Art, 1948-52; curator Oriental art Cleve. Mus. Art, 1952—, dir., 1958—; lectr. art history U. Wash., 1948-52; lectr. art history Western Res. U., 1958, prof. art, 1962—; cons. com. Artibus Asiae. Trustee Cleve. Art Assn. Served from ensign to lt. (j.g.), USNR, 1944-46. Decorated Legion of Honor, Order North Star, Order Sacred Treasure 3d class (Japan). Mem. Am. Acad. Arts and Scis., Am. Assn. Museums, Coll. Art Assn., Assn. of Art Mus. Dirs. (past pres.). Clubs: Union (Cleve.); Century Assn. (N.Y.C.). Author: Chinese Landscape Painting, 1954, rev. 1962; (with Wen Fong) Streams and Mountains Without End, 1955, Japanese Decorative Style, 1961; History of Far Eastern Art, 1964, rev. edit., 1973; (with W. K. Ho) Chinese Art Under the Mongols, 1968. Home: 2536 Norfolk Rd Cleveland OH 44106 Office: 11150 East Blvd Cleveland OH 44106

LEE, SHU CHING, educator; b. Feng-cheng, Liao-ning, China, Nov. 29, 1907; s. Fang Chen and Hsiao Mai (Chao) L.; B.A., Nat. Tsing Hua U. (China), 1935; M.A., U. Wis. (Tsing Hua U. fellow 1936-38), 1938; Ph.D., U. Chgo., 1950; m. Ting Lan Chung, Dec. 30, 1964; children—Yun-Sheng, Sandra P.S. Came to U.S., 1945, naturalized, 1958. Asst. prof. sociology dept. sociology U. Oreg., 1952-53; asst. prof. dept. sociology-anthropology Wash. U., 1953-56; research asso. U. Chgo., 1956-58; asso. prof. sociology Southeast Mo. State Coll., 1958-63; asso. prof. sociology U. S.D., 1963-65, prof., 1965-68; prof. sociology U. Dayton, 1968-69; prof. sociology Ohio U., 1969-77; ret., 1977. Am. Philos. Soc. grantee, 1951-52, NIH grant, 1964-65. Mem. Am. Sociol. Assn., Population Assn. Am., Soc. for Study of Social Problems, Internat. Sociol. Assn. Contbr. articles to profl. jours., also books. Home: 14 Canterbury Dr Athens OH 45701 Office: 213 Carnegie Hall Athens OH 45701

LEE, SONG PING, physician; b. Tsao-Tun, Taiwan, Dec. 2, 1934; s. Tsang-Lang and Chu-Ying C. L.; came to U.S., 1965, naturalized, 1977; B. Medicine, Nat. Taiwan U., 1961, M.D., 1961; m. Li-Ying Chen, Apr. 13, 1965; children—Donald, Edward, Andrew. Intern, Pottsville (Pa.) Hosp., 1965-66; sr. resident Univ. Hosp., Nat. Taiwan U., Taipei, 1965; chief resident in otorhinolaryngology Pottsville (Pa.) Hosp., 1966-68, Boston City Hosp and New Eng. Med. Center Hosp., Boston, 1969-72; teaching fellow Tufts Med. Sch., Boston, 1971-72; otolaryngologist, head neck surgeon Topeka Med. Center, 1972—, chmn. exec. com., 1975—; practice medicine specializing in otolaryngology Topeka, 1972—; cons. in field. Diplomate Am. Bd. Otolaryngology. Fellow A.C.S., Am. Acad. Ophthalmology and Otolaryngology; mem. Shawnee County, Kans. med. socs., AMA, Am. Council Otolaryngology, Kansas City Soc. Ophthalmology and Otolaryngology, Centurian Club Deafness Research Found. Author: Otologic Assessments—Physiological Measures of the Audio-Vestibular System, 1975. Home: 210 Yorkshire Rd Topeka KS 66606 Office: 918 W 10th St Topeka KS 66604

LEE, SUNG HO, psychiatrist; b. Seoul, Korea, June 28, 1934; s. Suk K. and Chung W. (Kim) L.; came to U.S., 1964, naturalized, 1976; M.D., Yonsei U., 1959; M.Sc., Ohio State U., 1969; m. Myung Ha, Nov. 17, 1959; children—Benjamin, May. Rotating intern Seoul Red Cross Hosp., 1959-60; resident in psychiatry Yonsei U. Hosp., 1960-62, Ohio State U., 1965-67, Brentwood Hosp., Los Angeles, 1967-68; asst. prof., chmn. dept. psychiatry Ewha U. Hosp., Seoul, 1968-70; clin. dir. unit B, Broughton State Hosp., Morganton, N.C., 1970-71; chief psychiat. service Dayton (Ohio) VA Med. Center, 1970-76, sr. psychiatrist, 1976—; pvt. practice specializing in psychiatry, Dayton, 1975—; asst. clin. prof. Ohio State U. Med. Sch., Wright State U.; cons. in field. Diplomate Am. Bd. Psychiatry and Neurology. Mem. AMA, Korean, Montgomery County med. assns., Am. Psychiat. Assn. Methodist. Contbr. articles to med. jours. Home: 7706 Normandy Ln Dayton OH 45459 Office: 2801 Far Hills Ave Dayton OH 45419

LEE, TED J., ins. cons.; b. Pasco, Wash., Nov. 19, 1927; s. Bertram B. and Marie H. (Palmer) L.; B.A., U. Minn., 1945; C.L.U., 1961; m. Carolyn May Fawcett, Mar. 19, 1949; children—Geoffrey B., Nancy Lee Dahl, Susan J., John K., Barbara A. Founder, pres. of co. specializing in retirement plans, financial and estate planning, Duluth, Minn., 1958—; co-founder Sch. Bus. and Econs., U. Minn., Duluth; speaker, cons., tchr. in field. Served with USMC, 1945-47. Mem. Am. Soc. C.L.U.'s, Minn., Arrowhead (past pres.) assns. C.L.U.'s, Life Leaders Minn., U. Minn. Alumni Assn. Republican. Conglist. Club: Kitchi Gammi (Duluth). Home: 1941 Woodland Ave Duluth MN 55803 Office: 806 First Nat Bank Bldg Duluth MN 55802

LEE, THOMAS GERALD, ins. co. exec.; b. Cin., Sept. 17, 1937; s. Lowell Jay and Dorothy Charolett (Meinberg) L.; B.B.A. in Accounting, U. Cin., 1960; m. Gail Howard, Sept. 16, 1959; children—Cynthia Ann, Gary Michael, Steven Jay. Underwriting services mgr. Sentry Life Ins. Co., Stevens Point, Wis., 1961-65; v.p. underwriting Horace Mann Educators Corp., Springfield, Ill., 1965-71, v.p. data processing, 1971-73, pres. Datamann, Inc., subsidiary, 1972-73; v.p. adminstrn. Am. Bankers Life Corp., Miami, 1973-75; v.p. mktg. ops. Horace Mann Educators Corp., Springfield, Ill., 1975—; dir. Educators Life Ins. Co., Horace Mann Investors, Inc. Am. Treas. Lincolnland Project Misdemenant, 1970-74. Fellow Life Mgmt. Inst.; mem. Chartered Life Underwriters, Am. Bus. Club, Springfield Jr. C. of C. (v.p. 1972). Office: 1 Horace Mann Plaza Springfield IL 62715

LEE, TONG HUN, educator; b. Seoul, Korea, Nov. 20, 1931; s. Chong Su and Yun (Lee) L.; came to U.S., 1955, naturalized, 1968; B.S., Yon-Sae U., 1955; Ph.D., U. Wis., 1961; m. Yul Jah Ahn, June 11, 1960; children—Bruce Keebeck, James Keewon. Asst. prof. econs. U. Tenn., Knoxville, 1962-64, asso. prof., 1964-67; prof. econs. U. Wis., Milw., 1967—. NSF grantee, 1965-67, 73-75. Mem. Am. Econ. Assn., Am. Fin. Assn., Am. Statis. Assn., Econometric Soc. Author: Interregional Intersectoral Flow Analysis, 1973. Contbr. articles to profl. jours. Home: 7250 N Wayside Dr Milwaukee WI 53209

LEE, WILLIAM CHAE-SIK, physician; b. Pyongyang, Korea, May 30, 1926; s. Pyong Ho and Kyong-Sook (Ahn) L.; M.D., Seoul (Korea) Nat. U., 1951; postgrad. Dallas Theol. Sem., 1953-54; M.S., U. Minn., 1959; student acupuncture Kyong Hee U., Seoul, Korea, 1972, U. Vienna (Austria), 1973, Osaka (Japan) Med. U., 1974; m. Grace Koom-Soon, Dec. 30, 1955; children—Victor Lewis, Leonard William, Marie Grace, Michelle Vidle. Came to U.S., 1953, naturalized, 1970. Intern, United Hosp., Port Chester, N.Y., 1954-55, Orange County Gen. Hosp., Orange, Calif., 1955-56; resident Lloyd Noland Hosp., Faifield, Ala., 1956-57, U. Minn. Hosps., Mpls., 1957-59, also fellow; dir. dept. anesthesiology Hibbing (Minn.) Gen. Hosp., 1959—, dir. sch. anesthesia for nurses, 1967—, med. dir. inhalation therapy dept., 1968—. Cons. Chisholm (Minn.) Meml. Hosp., 1965—. Med. co-chmn. Civil Def., Hibbing, 1964—. Served to capt. M.C., Korean Army, 1951-53. Diplomate Am. Bd. Anesthesiology. Fellow Am. Coll. Anesthesiologists, Am. Coll. Chest Physicians; mem. Nat. Acupuncture Research Soc., Internat. Assn. Study Pain, Am. Med. Soc. Vienna, Internat. Anesthesia Research Soc., N.Y. Acad. Scis., Minn., Am. socs. anesthesiologists, Minn. Med. Assn., A.M.A. Home: 207 Highland Dr Hibbing MN 55746 Office: 2015 4th Ave E Hibbing MN 55746

LEE, WILLIAM JOHNSON, lawyer, state ofcl.; b. Oneida, Tenn., Jan. 13, 1924; s. William J. and Ara (Anderson) L.; student Akron U., 1941-43, Denison U., 1943-44, Harvard U., 1944-45; LL.B., Ohio State U., 1948. Admitted to Ohio bar, 1948, Fla. bar, 1962; research asst. Ohio State U. Law Sch., 1948-49; asst. dir. Ohio Dept. Liquor Control, chief purchases, 1956-57, atty. examiner, 1951-53, asst. state permit chief, 1953-55, state permit chief, 1955-56; asst. counsel, staff Hupp Corp., 1957-58; spl. counsel City Attys. Office Ft. Lauderdale (Fla.), 1963-65; asst. atty. gen. Office Atty. Gen., State of Ohio, 1966-70; adminstr. State Med. Bd. Ohio, Columbus, 1970—; pvt. practice law, Ft. Lauderdale, 1965-66; acting municipal judge, Ravenna, Ohio, 1960; instr. Coll. Bus. Adminstrn., Kent State U., 1961-62. Mem. pastoral relations com. Epworth United Meth. Ch., 1976; chmn. legal aid com. Portage County, Ohio, 1960; troop awards chmn. Boy Scouts Am., 1965; mem. ch. bd. Melrose Park (Fla.) Meth. Ch., 1966. Mem. Am. Legion, Fla., Columbus, Akron, Broward County (Fla.) bar assns., Delta Theta Phi, Phi Kappa Tau, Pi Kappa Delta. Served with USAAF, 1942-46. Editorial bd. Ohio State Law Jour., 1947-48. Home: 4893 Brittany Ct W Columbus OH 43229 Office: Suite 1006 Borden Bldg 180 E Broad St Columbus OH 43215

LEE, WOODROW, hosp. adminstr.; b. Chgo., Feb. 4, 1931; s. Arve and Stella Henrietta (Hanson) L.; student U. Hawaii, 1948-49; B.A., Lake Forest Coll., 1952; M.H.A., U. Minn., 1954; m. Marilyn Jean Loafman, Mar. 6, 1957; children—Mark Alan, Martha Lynne, David Arve, Daniel Glen. Adminstrv. resident St. Luke's Hosp., Milw., 1953-54; asst. dir. John D. Archbold Meml. Hosp., Thomasville, Ga., 1956-60; adminstr. McCune-Brooks Hosp., Carthage, Mo., 1960-65; adminstr., dir. St. John's Hosp., Joplin, Mo., 1965; adminstr. Audrain Med. Center, Mexico, Mo., 1966—; clin. asso. prof. grad. program in health services mgmt. U. Mo., Columbia, 1966—. Pres. Mo. Hosp. Councils, 1964, 68, 70; chmn. Permanent Blue Cross Orgn. Central Mo., 1970-72, mem. Blue Cross Hosp. Adv. Com., 1973—; adminstr. Audrain County (Mo.) Health Unit, 1966—; mem. pres.'s council Nat. Health/Welfare Retirement Assn., 1974—, mem. nominating com., 1977; mem. adv. group Area II, Health Systems Agy., 1977—; local registrar vital statistics, 1978—. Served with AUS, 1954-56. Mem. Am. Coll. Hosp. Adminstrs., Mo. Hosp. Assn. (trustee 1973-77, treas. 1974-76), Mexico C. of C. (dir. 1971-75). Presbyn (elder 1974-77). Rotarian (sec. 1976-78, treas. 1978). Club: Mexico Country. Home: 722 E Monroe St Mexico MO 65265 Office: 620 E Monroe St Mexico MO 65265

LEE, YIEN-HWEI, physician, pharmacologist; b. Taiwan, China, Oct. 20, 1937; s. Yann-fang and Chao-ti-mei (Shen) L.; came to U.S., 1964, naturalized, 1975; B.M., Nat. Taiwan U., 1963; Ph.D., U. Calif. at Los Angeles, 1968; m. Shaw-guang Lin, Aug. 4, 1968; children—Yishane Isa, Yiying Jiuana, Yiking Kevin. Research asso. Neuropsychiat. Inst., U. Calif. at Los Angeles, 1966-68; sr. research pharmacologist G. D. Searle & Co., Skokie, Ill., 1968-72; sect. head Abbott Labs., Abbott Park, Ill., 1972-76; staff physician Edgewater Hosp., Chgo., 1976-77, St. Joseph Hosp., Chgo., 1977—. Served to 2d lt. Chinese Air Force, 1963-64. Mem. Am. Soc. Pharmacology and Exptl. Therapeutics, Inc., A.A.A.S., Formosan Med. Assn., N.Y. Acad. Scis. Nat. Taiwan U. Med. Sch. Alumni Assn. (pres. 1969-71), ACP, Am. Chem. Soc., Sigma Xi. Home: 907 Wexford Ct Libertyville IL 60048

LEECE, CURTIS THOMPSON, photographer, educator; b. Detroit, Oct. 15, 1932; s. Perry Curtis and Mildred Christine (Thompson) L.; A.A.S., Rochester (N.Y.) Inst. Tech., 1952; postgrad. Bay City (Mich.) Jr. Coll., 1956-57; m. Gayle Elizabeth Koehler, Sept. 18, 1957 (div. Sept. 1972); children—Catherine Gayle, David Curtis; m. 2d, Judith Lynne Perry, Oct. 15, 1972. Staff photographer Saginaw (Mich.) News, 1957—; free-lance comml. and indsl. photographer, Saginaw, 1964—; instr. photography Saginaw Valley Coll., 1973—; dir. Delta Coll. Summer Festival of Art Photography Workshop, 1969-73. Bd. dirs. Saginaw Symphony Assn., 1970-74; trustee Saginaw Art Mus., 1970—, pres. bd., 1972-74. Served with AUS, 1953. Recipient Photo Competition first prize Mich. Asso. Press, 1957, 3d prize, 1976; Regional Art Show first prize Flint (Mich.) Inst. Arts, 1970, others. Mem. Nat. Press Photographers Assn. Exhibitor in several one-man shows in Saginaw area, 1970-75; regular juryman in photo competitions in Mid-Mich. area, 1970-75. Home: 3534 Linger Ln Saginaw MI 48601 Office: 203 S Washington St Saginaw MI 48607

LEEDY, EMILY L. FOSTER (MRS. WILLIAM N. LEEDY), state ofcl.; b. Jackson, Ohio, Sept. 24, 1921; d. Raymond S. and Grace (Garrett) Foster; B.S., Rio Grande Coll., 1949; M.Ed., Ohio U., 1957; postgrad. Ohio State U., 1956, Mich. State U., 1958-59, Western Res. U., 1963-64; m. William N. Leedy, Jan. 1, 1943; 1 son, Dwight A. Tchr. Frankfort (Ohio) pub. schs., 1941-46, Ross County Schs., Chillicothe, Ohio, 1948-53; elementary and supervising tchr. Chillicothe City Schs., 1953-56; dean of girls, secondary tchr. Berea City Schs., 1956-57; vis. tchr. Parma City Schs., 1957-59; counselor Homewood-Flossmoor High Sch., Flossmoor, Ill., 1959-60; teaching fellow Ohio U., 1960-62, asst. prof. edn., 1962-64; counselor, asso. prof. Cuyahoga Community Coll., Cleve., 1964-66; dean women Cleve. State U., 1966-67, asso. dean of student affairs, 1967-69; dir. guidance Cathedral Latin Sch., Cleve., 1969-71; dir. women's services div. Ohio Bur. Employment Services, Columbus, 1971—. Cons. in edn. Mem. adv. com. S. W. Community Info. Service, 1959-60; mem. bd. mgmt., chmn. youth com. YWCA, 1964-70; mem. group services council Cleve. Welfare Fedn., 1964-67; bd. dirs., program study com. Cleve. Met. YWCA, 1966-72, v.p., 1967; adv. council Ch. in World Neighborhood Youth Corps, 1965-66; v.p., legis. com. Cleve. Council Status Women, 1969-70, pres., 1970-72; pres. Ohio Commn. Status of Women, 1970-71. Mem. AAUW, Am., Northeastern Ohio (sec. 1958-59, exec. com. 1963-64, pub. relations chmn. 1962-64, newsletter chmn., editor, 1963-64, del. nat. assembly, 1959, 63) personnel and guidance assns., Nat. Vocat. Guidance Assn., Am. Coll. Personnel Assn., Am., Ohio sch. counselors assns., Am. Rehab. Counseling Assn., Nat., Ohio assns. women deans and counselors (program chmn. 1966-67, newsletter editor 1967-69, com. status women 1968-69), Cleve. Counselors Assn. (sec. 1964, v.p. 1965, pres. 1966), NEA, Assn. Higher Edn., AAUP, Ohio Edn. Assn., Ohio Assn. Gifted Children, League Women Voters, Cleve. Mental Health Assn., Columbus Bus. and Profl. Women's Club, Phi Delta Gamma, Delta Kappa Gamma. Clubs: Women's City of Cleveland (mental health com. progress women com.); Zonta (dir. 1968-70, treas. 1970-72, dist. chmn. status of Women 1970-72, internat. com. on status of women 1975—) (Berea). Home: 580 Lindberg Blvd Berea OH 44017

LEEKLEY, ROBERT MITCHELL, chemist; b. Montrose, S.D., July 18, 1911; s. Thomas Bales and Beulah Ella (Briggs) L.; B.S., Dakota Wesleyan U., 1933; M.A., U. S.D., 1934; Ph.D., U. Minn., 1938; m. Lorna Dugal McCartney, June 14, 1941; children—Lorna Lou (Mrs. Richard L. Kaluzny), Robert McCartney, Jay Thomas. Research chemist E.I. duPont de Nemours & Co., Wilmington, Del., 1938-45; with Springdale Labs., Stamford, Conn., 1945-62, asso. research dir., 1951-62; with Inst. Paper Chemistry, Appleton, Wis., 1963-76, sr. research asso., 1967-76, graphic arts cons., 1976—. Mem. Am. Chem. Soc. (chmn. western Conn. sect. 1953, councilor 1957-59), TAPPI (editorial bd. 1973-75), Tech. Assn. Graphic Arts. Conglist. Home: 75 Fox Point Dr Appleton WI 54911

LEEMON, JOHN ALLEN, lawyer; b. Hoopeston, Ill., Jan. 12, 1928; s. Allen Wallace and Eva Carol (Merritt) L.; B.S., U. Ill., 1950, LL.B., 1952; m. Sally P. Pierce, July 14, 1951; children—John P., Lisa A. Admitted to Ill. bar, 1952; practiced in Savannah, Ill., 1952-54, Mt. Carroll, Ill, 1954—; mem. firms Eaton & Leemon, 1956-66, Eaton, Leemon & Rapp, 1967, Leemon & Rapp, 1968-70; dir. Mt. Carroll Fire Ins. Co. Mem. Am., Ill. (negligence council 1961-66, grievance com. inquiry div. 1967-70), Carroll County, Whiteside County bar assns. Mason (Shriner). Home: Rural Route Box 108 Mt Carroll IL 61053 Office: National Bank Bldg Mt Carroll IL 61053 also State Bank of Shannon Bldg Shannon IL 61078

LEENHOUTS, KEITH JAMES, former judge, assn. exec.; b. Grand Rapids, Mich., Oct. 17, 1925; s. William James and Dorothy (Champion) L.; B.A., Albion Coll., 1949; J.D., Wayne State U., 1952; m. Audrey Doris Saari, June 27, 1953; children—William James, David John, Daniel S. (dec.), James Edward. Admitted to Mich. bar, 1953; practice law, Royal Oak, Mich., 1953-59; mem. firm Dell, Heber & Leenhouts, Royal Oak, 1953-59; from municipal ct. judge to Mich. Dist. ct. judge, 1959-69; pres. Vol. In Probation, Inc., Royal Oak, 1969-71; dir. Vols. In Probation div. Nat. Council on Crime and Delinquency, 1972—. Lectr. Nat. Coll. State Trial Judges, 1967, Nat. Coll. State Judiciary, 1972, numerous seminars; cons. Law Enforcement Assistance Adminstrn.; prin. investigator Nat. Insts. Mental Health, 1965-69. Active YMCA, Boys Club. Bd. dirs. ACTION, 1972. Served with USAAF, 1944-46. Recipient Halpern award Nat. Council on Crime and Delinquency; Distinguished Service award Jaycees; Distinguished Alumni award Albion Coll., 1967; Distinguished Service award Wayne State U., 1970. Mem. Mich. State Bar (chmn. com. on probation), Am. Judicature Soc. (dir. 1969-70), North Am. Judges Assn. (v.p. 1962-65, awards). Methodist (trustee, Sunday sch. tchr.). Lion. Author: First Offender, 1971; A Father...A Son...And a Three Mile Run, 1975. Contbr. numerous articles to pop. mags., profl. jours. Home: 830 Normandy St Royal Oak MI 48073 Office: 200 Washington Square Plaza Royal Oak MI 48067

LEEP, GUS WEAURTON, JR., paint co. exec.; b. Louisville, Feb. 18, 1925; s. Gus Weaurton and Mariam Virginia (Blackerby) L.; B. Chem. Engring., U. Louisville, 1945, M. Chem. Engring., 1950; postgrad. Columbia, 1949; m. Bernice Alberta Olsen, Nov. 10, 1945; children—Jeffrey Allen, Susan Joyce. Lube oil research Tex. Co., Port Arthur, Tex., 1948-49; titanium metal research Nat. Lead Co., South Amboy, N.J., 1950-51; product devel. engr. Permacel Tape Corp., New Brunswick, N.J., 1951-55; chief chemist William F. Zummach, Inc., Milw., 1955-62; chief chemist Ill. Bronze Paint Co., Lake Zurich, Ill., 1962-68, v.p. research and devel., 1969—. Mem. chem. technician adv. com. Coll. Lake County, 1973—; sec.-treas. Lake Zurich Indsl. Council. Served with USNR, 1943-46; PTO. Fellow Am. Inst. Chemists; mem. Chgo. Soc. Paint Tech. (treas. 1972-73, sec. 1973-74, v.p. 1974-75, pres. 1975-76), Nat. Paint and Coatings Assn. (chmn. spray paint mfrs. com. 1976, 77), Wheeling Instrumental League (treas. 1970-71), Theta Tau. Republican. Presbyn. Contbg. editor: Science of Aerosol Packaging, 1971. Home: 437 Regent Dr Buffalo Grove IL 60090 Office: 300 E Main St Lake Zurich IL 60047

LEET, RICHARD EUGENE, mus. dir., artist; b. Waterloo, Iowa, Sept. 11, 1936; s. Arthur John and Gladys F. (Simmons) L.; B.A., U. No. Iowa, 1958, M.A., 1965; postgrad. U. Iowa, 1961-64; m. Kay Annette Whitney, June 26, 1960; children—Kimberly Renee, Todd Whitney. Art instr. Oelwein (Iowa) Jr. and Sr. High Sch., 1958-65; dir. Charles H. MacNider Mus., Mason City, Iowa, 1965—; exhibited in group shows Iowa Artists, Des Moines Art Center, Iowa State Fair Art Salon, Des Moines, Butler Inst. Am. Art, Youngstown, Ohio, El Paso (Tex.) Mus. Art, Springfield (Mo.) Art Mus., Joslyn Art Mus., Omaha, many others; one-man shows Hamline U., St. Paul, 1968; Luther Coll., Decorah, Iowa, 1968, Sioux City (Iowa) Art Center, 1968, 75, Blanden Meml. Art Gallery, Ft. Dodge, Iowa, 1967, Fisher Community Center, Marshalltown, Iowa, 1967, Charles H. MacNider Mus., 1970, Charleston (W.Va.) Art Gallery at Sunrise, 1972, others; represented by Percival Galleries, Des Moines. Mem. Iowa Arts Council, 1970-76. Mem. Am. Assn. Museums, Midwest Mus. Conf. (pres. 1972-73). Methodist. Rotarian. Illustrated book Dr. Garbee's Wild Game Dinners, 1964. Author, monthly art column Mason City Globe-Gazette, 1968—. Home: 1149 Manor Dr Mason City IA 50401 Office: 303 2d St SE Mason City IA 50401

LEFFLER, MARLIN TEMPLETON, cons.; b. Union County, Ind., Feb. 28, 1911; s. John Cochran and May Pearl (Templeton) L.; A.B., Miami U., 1932; M.A., U. Ill., 1933, Ph.D., 1936; postgrad. Harvard, 1950; m. Martha A. Driscol, Dec. 23, 1933; children—Susan (Mrs. Michael Baker), Mary (Mrs. John Rutgers), Ann (Mrs. John Hartshorne). Research chemist Abbott Labs., North Chicago, Ill., 1936-45, asso. dir. research, 1946-55, dir. research liaison, 1956-71, cons., 1971—. Trustee Village of Lake Bluff, Ill., 1944-53; bd. dirs. Am. Cancer Soc., Lake County, Ill. Mem. AAAS, Am. Chem. Soc. (chmn. med. div. 1954-55), Gordon Research Conf. (chmn. med. chemistry 1950), Phi Beta Kappa, Sigma Xi. Club: Bay and Gulf (Siesta Key, Sarasota, Fla.). Patentee in field. Home: 615 Smith Ave Lake Bluff IL 60044

LEFFMAN, PETER LAWRENCE, physician; b. Aug. 7, 1933; s. Alfred A. and Ann E. (Wertheim) L.; B.S., U. Ill., 1954, M.D., 1958; m. Mary Elizabeth Allen, Sept. 14, 1959; children—Michael, Ruth, David. Intern, Michael Reese Hosp., Chgo., 1958-59; resident U. Ill. Research and Ednl. Hosps., 1959-62; practice medicine specializing in otolaryngology, Quincy, Ill., 1964—; partner Quincy Clinic, 1967—; chief dept. surgery Blessing Hosp., Quincy, Ill.; mem. staff St. Mary Hosp., Quincy. Mem. Quincy Youth Commn., 1971—; mem. Mayor's Citizens Adv. Council, Quincy, 1968—. Served with USAF, 1962-64. Fellow Am. Acad. Ophthalmology and Otolaryngology; mem. AMA, Ill., Adams County med. and Rotarian. Home: 17 Ridgewood Dr Quincy IL 62301 Office: 1400 Main St Quincy IL 62301

LEFTIN, GARY WAYNE, civil engr.; b. Cin., Feb. 20, 1944; s. Charles Zook and June (Wagner) L.; Asso. Civil Engring. Tech., Ohio Coll. Applied Sci., 1964; B.S. in Bldg. and Civil Tech., Mo. Western Coll., 1973; m. Linda Pauline Thompson, Apr. 15, 1967; children—Adeana Ranae, Chad Wayne. Coop. student City of Cin. Engring. Dept., 1964; instrument man Ky. Div. Hwys., Frankfort, 1964-65; survey crew party chief Howard, Needles, Tammen & Bergendoff, Kansas City, Mo., 1966-69; civil engr. City of St. Joseph (Mo.), 1969—. Mem. supervisory bd. St. Joseph Credit Union, 1972—. Served with USCGR, 1965-71. Mem. Am. Soc. Certified Engring. Technicians (charter), Mo. Assn. Registered Land Surveyors, Inst. Certified Engring. Technicians. Methodist (mem. ch. bd.). Eagle. Home: 2806 Doniphan St St Joseph MO 64507 Office: Room 204 City Hall St Joseph MO 64501

LEGGETT, GLENN, mfg. co. exec.; b. Ashtabula, Ohio, Mar. 29, 1918; s. Glenn H. and Celinda (Sheldon) L.; A.B., Middlebury (Vt.) Coll., 1940, LL.D., 1971; M.A., Ohio State U., 1941, Ph.D., 1949; L.H.D., Rockford Coll., 1967, Ripon Coll., 1968, Grinnell Coll., 1975; Litt.D., Lawrence U., 1968; LL.D., Morningside Coll., 1975; m. Doris Ruth James, June 14, 1941 (dec.); children—Leslie Ann (Mrs. David K. Leonard), Susan Cady (Mrs. Michael Baxter Jones), Celinda Sheldon (Mrs. Ray Riecke), Joanna Ruth; m. 2d, Mrs. Russelle Seeberger Jones, Mar. 11, 1973; children—Brian Edward Jones, Sarah Lorene Jones. Instr., English, Mass. Inst. Tech., 1942-44; instr., then asst. prof. English, Ohio State U., 1946-52; asso. prof. English, U. Wash., 1952-58, asst. to pres., 1958-61, vice provost, 1961-63, provost, 1963-65; prof. English, pres. Grinnell Coll., 1965-75; v.p. Deere & Co., Moline, Ill., 1975—. Mem. commn. English, Coll. Entrance Exam. Bd., 1957-65, trustee, 1965-76, chmn., 1972-74; chmn. Conf. Coll. Composition, 1959; chmn. Iowa Assn. Pvt. Colls., 1969-71, Asso. Colls. Midwest, 1971-73, Iowa Coll. Found., 1974-75; trustee Ill.-Iowa Assn. Children with Learning Disabilities, 1976—, pres., 1977—; trustee Marycrest Coll., 1975—; bd. dirs. Quad Cities Grad. Study Center, 1975—, chmn., 1977—; curator Stephens Coll., 1976—. Served with USNR, 1944-46. Mem. Modern Lang. Assn., Nat. Council Tchrs. English (chmn. coll. sect. 1963-65, chmn. survey undergrad. curriculum in English 1964-68, chmn. nominating com. 1967), Chi Psi. Conglist. Author: (with Mead & Charvat) Handbook for Writers, 6th edit., 1974; A Conservative View, The New Professors, 1960. Editor: Twelve Poets, 1959; (with Daniel and Beardsley) Theme and Form: An Introduction to Literature, 4th edit., 1975; (with Daniel) The Written Word, 1960; (with Steiner) Twelve Poets, Alternate Edition, 1967. Address: care Deere & Co John Deere Rd Moline IL 61265

LEGGETT, KERRY EUGENE, publisher; b. Kansas City, Mo., Nov. 19, 1933; s. Eugene Clements and Irma (Ellis) L.; student U. Nebr., 1951-53, Kearney (Nebr.) State Coll., 1953-54; m. Carol Jeanne Kwiatkowski, June 20, 1963; children—Susan, Sheri, Shannon. Editor, Ord (Nebr.) Quiz, weekly, 1963-65, pub., 1966—; pres. Quiz Graphic Arts, Inc., Ord, 1966—. Pub. speaker several states and Can. Served with AUS, 1955-56. Mem. Nebr. Press Assn. (past pres.). Republican. Methodist. Home: 2510 K St Ord NE 68862 Office: 305 S 16th St Ord NE 68862

LEGGITT, DOROTHY, educator; b. Oblong, Ill., Feb. 19, 1903; d. Clarence C. and Louise Frances (Muchmore) Leggitt; diploma Eastern Ill. State U., 1923; Ph.B., U. Chgo., 1930, M.A., 1933, postgrad., intermittently, 1937-62. Tchr. rural schs., Jasper & Crawford Counties, Ill., 1920-22; tchr. high sch., Glen Ellyn, Ill., 1923-35; lectr., prof. No. Ill. State U., DeKalb, 1936-37; tchr. social studies, counselor Clayton (Mo.) pub. schs., 1937-52; tchr. Decatur (Ill.) pub. schs., 1952-54, Park Ridge (Ill.) pub. schs., 1954-61; reading specialist Joliet (Ill.) Jr. Coll., 1961-62, Niles West High Sch., Skokie,

Ill., 1962-63; reading cons. Kenosha High Schs., Kenosha, Wis., 1963-65; head study skills dept. Palm Beach (Fla.) Jr. Coll., 1965-73, prof. emeritus, 1973—; summer lectr. various colls. and univs. Field rep. grad. edn. and social sci. depts. U. Chgo.; mem. found. bd. Eastern Ill. U. Recipient Walgreen Found. award in social, econ. and polit. instns., 1948, scholarship award Pi Lambda Theta, 1948, Distinguished Alumni award Eastern Ill. U., 1974. Mem. Newberry Library Assn. (asso.), NEA, AAUW. Author: Basic Study Skills and Workbook, 1942. Contbr. articles to profl. jours. Home: 401 S LaSalle St Chicago IL 60605 Office: PO Box 1432 Chicago IL 60690

LE GRAND, CLAY, justice state supreme ct.; b. St. Louis, Feb. 26, 1911; s. Nic and Mary (Leifield) LeG.; student St. Ambrose Coll., 1928-30; J.D., Cath. U. Am., 1934; m. Suzanne Wilcox, Dec. 30, 1935;children—Mary Suzanne (Mrs. Thomas J. Murray), Julie, Nicholas W. Pvt. practice law, 1934-57; judge Dist. Ct., Iowa, 1957-67; justice Ia. Supreme Ct., Des Moines, 1967—. Lectr. St. Ambrose Coll., 1957-67. Recipient Alumni Achievement award Cath. U. Am., 1969; award merit St. Ambrose Coll. Alumni Assn., 1976. Mem. Am., Iowa, Scott County bar assns., Am. Judicature Soc., Inst. Jud. Adminstrn. Home: Rural Route 1 LeClaire IA 52753 Office: State House Des Moines IA 50319

LEHMAN, CHARLES DWIGHT, meat processing co. exec.; b. Goshen, Ind., May 3, 1938; s. Dwight K. and Esther I. (Thomas) L.; B.S., Miami U., Oxford, Ohio, 1960; M.B.A., U. Cin., 1962; m. Myrna A. Widmeyer, Nov. 19, 1960; children—David, Michelle. Market research analyst Mercedes-Benz Sales Inc., South Bend, Ind., 1962-63; sales cons. Ind. Bell Telephone Co., South Bend, 1963-64; market research mgr. Richardson Homes Corp., Elkhart, Ind., 1964-67; market research specialist Oscar Mayer Co., Madison, Wis., 1967-74; market research product planning mgr. Chef's Pantry, Sandusky, Ohio, 1974—. Instr. in marketing mgmt. Ind. U., South Bend, 1963-66; part-time instr. supervisory devel. Tech. Coll., Madison, 1972-73. Job devel. capt. Nat. Alliance of Businessmen program, Madison, 1972-74, com. mem. student summer Employment Program, Madison, 1972, chmn., 1973-74; part time instr. mktg. Bowling Green U. at Huron (Ohio), 1975—. Served with AUS, 1960-66. Mem. Am. Mktg. Assn. (treas. Michiana chpt. 1965-66), Internat. Food Service Mfrs. Assn. (market research com. 1971—), Madison East Hockey Assn. (dir. 1972-73), Elvehjem Neighborhood Assn. (pres. 1970), Sigma Phi Epsilon. Home: 1217 Laguna Dr Huron OH 44834 Office: Sandusky OH

LEHMAN, CLYDE FREDERICK, pub. utilities adminstr.; b. Kenyon, Minn., July 16, 1917; s. Clarence F. and Olga L. (Ness) L.; student U. Wis., 1953, U. Ill., 1964; m. G. Jeanne Smith, Dec. 10, 1938; 1 dau., Roberta Jeanne (Mrs. Ronald L. Bourget). Chief engr. North Star Creamery, Kenyon, Minn., 1940-47; city engr. City of Kenyon (Minn.), 1948-52; supt., mgr. Dept. Pub. Utilities, City of Chippewa Falls (Wis.), 1952—. Pres. Wis. Waste Water Operators Conf., 1967-68, chmn. edn. com., 1974-75; instr. Dept. Natural Resources edn. program on water and wastewater, Eau Claire, Wis., 1969-75. Pres. Chippewa Found., 1971-72. Mem. Water Pollution Control Fedn. (William O. Hatfield award 1965), Am. Water Works Assn. (chmn. mgmt. edn. com. Wis. sect. 1974-76, Willing Water award 1963), Central States Water Pollution Control Assn. (chmn. pub. relations com. 1955-56, Operator of the Year award 1965), Sentral States Select Soc. of Sanitary Sludge Shovelers, Nat. Safety Council, Chippewa Falls C. of C. (dir. 1963-75), Columbus Assn. Catholic (pres. bd. 1971-73). K.C. Club: National Exchange of Chippewa Falls (dir. 1974-75). Home: 715 Water St Chippewa Falls WI 54729 Office: 30 W Central St Chippewa Falls WI 54729

LEHMAN, DAVID OWEN, lawyer; b. Decatur, Ill., Nov. 9, 1947; s. Charles Owen and Beulah Løbdill) L.; B.A., Harvard U., 1969; J.D., U. Pa., 1973; English-Speaking Union scholar Univ. Coll., London, 1970-71. Admitted to Ill. bar, 1973; law sec. to Justice Walter V. Schaefer, Supreme Ct. Ill., 1973; to Judge John Minor Wisdom, U.S. Ct. Appeals 5th Circuit, 1974; asso. firm Walsh, Case & Cogle, Chgo. Mem. Am., Ohio, Ill., Chgo. bar assns. Office: Suite 1100 104 S Michigan Ave Chicago IL 60603

LEHMAN, RICHARD LEROY, lawyer; b. Johnstown, Pa., Feb. 4, 1930; s. John S. and Deliah E. (Chase) L.; A.B. in Social Work, U. Ky., 1957; LL.B., U. Detroit, 1960. Admitted to Mich. bar, 1961; since practiced in Detroit; mem. firm Garan, Lucow, Miller, Lehman, Seward & Cooper; dir. Bros. Specifications Inc., Detroit. Vis. lectr. U. Detroit Law Sch., 1970—, also adviser student bar assn. Bd. dirs. Old Newsboys Goodfellow Fund of Detroit. Exec. bd. pres.'s cabinet U. Detroit. Served to 1st. lt. AUS, 1947-53. Mem. Am., Detroit bar assns., State Bar of Mich. (mem. negligence council 1972-75), Am. Judicature Soc., Assn. Def. Trial Counsel, Def. Research Inst., U. Ky. Alumni Assn., U. Detroit Law Sch. Alumni Assn. (dir. 1970—, pres. 1973-75), Am. Arbitration Assn. Home: 4052 Waterwheel Ln Bloomfield Hills MI 48013 Office: 561 E Jefferson Ave Detroit MI 48226

LEHMANN, M. DRUE, speech pathologist; b. Columbus, Ohio, Feb. 29, 1948; d. Selmar Lee and Clara Frances (Ketner) L.; B.S., Bowling Green State U., 1971; M.A., Ohio State U., 1973; Speech pathologist Sacred Heart Hosp., Allentown, Pa., 1973-75; instr. speech pathology U. Cin. Med. Center, 1974—; clin. speech pathologist Holmes Hosp., Cin., 1974—. Mem. Am., Ohio, S.W. Ohio (exec. council) speech and hearing assns., Aphasiology Assn. Ohio. Roman Catholic. Home: 727 Dixmyth Apt 216 Cincinnati OH 45220 Office: Holmes Hosp Eden and Bethesda Sts Cincinnati OH 45219

LEHMBERG, STANFORD EUGENE, historian, educator; b. McPherson, Kans., Sept. 23, 1931; s. Willard Eugene and Helen (Stanford) L.; B.A., U. Kans., 1953, M.A., 1954; Ph.D. (Fulbright fellow), Cambridge (Eng.) U., 1956; m. Phyllis Barton, July 23, 1962; 1 son, Derek Grantham. Mem. faculty history U. Tex., Austin, 1956-69; prof. history U. Minn., Mpls., 1969—; trustee Hist. Soc. Episcopal Ch. Guggenheim fellow, 1964-65. Fellow Royal Hist. Soc. Author: Sir Thomas Elyot, 1962; Sir Walter Mildmay, 1964; The Reformation Parliament, 1970; The Later Parliaments of Henry VIII, 1977. Home: 2300 S Willow Ln Minneapolis MN 55416 Office: Univ Minnesota Dept History Minneapolis MN 55455

LEHNER, PAUL MICHAEL, real estate mgmt. and devel. exec.; b. Mishawaka, Ind., Dec. 5, 1941; s. Paul Mathias and Margaret D. (Van Acker) L.; B.B.A. summa cum laude, U. Notre Dame, 1963; M.B.A., Harvard U., 1969; m. Linda Suzanne Smith, Aug. 5, 1967; children—Suzanne Michelle, Paulyn Marie. Mem. cons. group Irwin Mgmt. Co., Columbus, Ind., 1969, real estate projects coordinator, 1970-76, v.p. real estate, 1977—; pres., dir. Nashville Internat. Trading Co., Inc., 1977—. Pres., Brown County Bd. Zoning Appeals; vice chmn. Brown County Planning Commn.; trustee Town of Nashville, (Ind.); county rep. Sen. R. Lugar. Served with USN, 1964-66. Mem. C. of C., Internat. Council Shopping Centers, Nat. Assn. Homebuilders, Bd. Realtors. Roman Catholic. Home: Artists Dr Route 3 Box 17 Nashville IN 47448 Office: 235 Washington St Columbus IN 47201

LEHR, GLENN CARLTON, dentist; b. Grand Rapids, Mich., Apr. 16, 1934; s. Glenn Cecil and Nella (Van Ian Waarden) L.; student Mich. State U., 1952-55; B. Gen. Edn., U. Neb., 1962; D.D.S., U. Mich., 1968; m. Maria Rhodes, Jan. 25, 1959; children—Glenn Christopher, Michael David, Victoria Alice. Individual practice dentistry, Manchester, Mich., 1968—. Lectr. profl. orgns. Active Boy Scouts Am. Served to capt. USAF, 1955-64. Mem. Am. Soc. Preventive Dentistry (nat. dir. 1974—), Mich., Chgo., Detroit dental socs., Vedder Soc. Crown and Bridge Prosthodontics, Bunting Periodontal Study Club, Detroit Clinic Club, Manchester C. of C. (pres. 1972-73). Home: 19220 Sanborn Rd Manchester MI 48158 Office: 500 Galloway Dr Manchester MI 48158

LEIBOVICH, HERMAN, utility co. exec.; b. St. Louis, Apr. 3, 1930; s. Abe and Helen (Goldstein) L.; B.J., U. Mo., 1951; m. Eve Blinder, May 29, 1955; children—Steven, Gary, Richard, Susan. With Union Electric Co., St. Louis, 1953—, asst. dir. advt. and pub. relations mgr., 1966-72, asst. mgr. pub. info., 1972—. Served with USAF, 1951-53. Named outstanding mem. Jr. Advt. Club, 1957. Mem. Pub. Relations Soc. Am. (sec. 1975-76, dir. 1977), Pub. Utilities Advt. Assn. (region chmn. 1971-72, dir. 1976—). Jewish. Clubs: Jr. Advertising (pres. 1958), Advertising (bd. govs. 1970-76), Press (St. Louis). Home: 14193 Parliament Dr Chesterfield MO 63017 Office: 1 Memorial Dr St Louis MO 63166

LEICHT, GERALDINE RUSSELL, sch. counselor; b. New Era, Mich., Apr. 4, 1918; d. Robert Winfield and Clara Maude (Olson) Russell; B.S., Western Mich. U., 1966; M.S., Purdue U., 1969; m. Willard S. Leicht, June 14, 1942 (dec.); children—W. Jeffrey, Mary E., Cheri C., Gregory B. Tchr., Oceana County (Mich.) pub. schs., 1936-43; clerk typist War Dept., various military bases, 1943-46; legal sec. firm Wm. J. Balgooyen, Muskegon Heights, Mich., 1946-50; elementary tchr. Fairview Sch., Grand Rapids, Mich., 1962-64; tchr. elementary sch., Long Grove, Ill., 1966-69, counselor, 1969—. Named Educator of Year Willow Grove Sch. Buffalo Grove Jaycees, 1966; NDEA grantee oral language So. Ill. U., 1967; Ednl. Profl. Devel. Act grantee guidance and counseling Purdue U., 1968-69. Mem. Am., Ill. NW Suburban personnel and guidance assns., Nat. Vocat. Guidance Assn., AAUW (charter mem., sec. Barrington Area Branch, 1974-76), Nat., Ill. (v.p. dist.) edn. assns. Mem. Community Ch. Home: 24 N Hwy 59 Barrington IL 60010 Office: Route 2 Box 287 Long Grove IL 60047

LEIDIG, MELVIN DWIGHT, minister, counselor; b. Pompeii, Mich., Aug. 3, 1925; s. Reuben G. and Emily May (Teuscher) L.; diploma Ontario Mennonite Bible Inst., 1954; A.A., Delta Coll., 1960; B.S., Western Mich. U., 1970, M.A., 1972; m. Lois Arlene Gisel, June 19, 1954; children—Shari Jean, Debra Anne. Ordained to ministry Mennonite Ch., 1955; pastor Grace Chapel, Saginaw, Mich., 1955-72, Moorepark Mennonite Ch., Three Rivers, Mich., 1972-74, 1st Mennonite Ch., Canton, Ohio, 1974—; social worker Saginaw Pub. Schs., 1968-70; counselor Dept. Labor, Battle Creek, Mich., 1970-72; social worker Starr Commonwealth for Boys, Albion, Mich., 1972-73, Jenkins Rehab. Center, Kalamazoo, 1974. Recipient Community Leaders and Noteworthy Americans Award, 1973-74. Adv. com. Sch. Supts., 1975-76; mem. Mayor's Task Force on Crime, 1975-76; task force Stark Tech. Coll., 1976-77. Mem. Nat. Assn. Social Workers, Christian Assn. Psychol. Studies, Am. Personnel and Guidance Assn., Nat. Assn. Christians In Social Work, Nat. Chaplains Assn., Mental Health Profls., Evang. Ministers Stark County (sec.-treas. 1977), Assn. Christian Marriage Counselors, Alpha Psi Omega. Contbr. articles to religious mags. Home and Office: 1939 3d St SE Canton OH 44707

LEIDNER, BURTON RICHARD, counseling psychologist; b. Cleve., Nov. 28, 1928; s. Edward A. and Agnes (Zweig) L.; B.S. summa cum laude, Ohio State U., 1950; M.A., Columbia U., 1951; postgrad. U. Wis., 1954-55, Case-Western Res. U., 1958-59; Ph.D., U. Sarasota, 1973; m. June Ethel Schwartz, June 12, 1954; 1 dau., Ellen Beth. Supr. instrumental music pub. schs., Willard, Ohio, 1951-53, Xenia, Ohio, 1953-54; grad. teaching fellow U. Wis., 1954-55; asst. prof. Auburn U., 1955-56; asso. prof. Hartwick Coll., 1956-58; counseling psychologist U. Tex. at Austin, Testing and Counseling Center, 1959-60; mgmt. appraisal and devel. specialist United Air Lines, Chgo., 1961-62; mgr. employee counseling, testing and appraisal programs IBM Space-Missile Guidance Center, Owego, N.Y., 1962-65; dir. counseling services Orange County Community Coll., Middletown, N.Y., 1965-66; adult and continuing edn. specialist Zanesville br. campus Ohio U., 1966-68; counseling psychologist, asst. prof. Lorain County Community Coll., 1968-76, asso. prof., 1976—; orgn., mgmt. devel. cons. Nat. Cash Register Co., Bendix-Westinghouse, Ohio Ferro Alloys, Romec div. Lear Siegler, Inc., Elyria Savings & Trust Nat. Bank, Elyria (Ohio) C. of C.; lectr.-demonstrator hypnosis; lectr. on alcoholic problem at mgmt. level in Am. bus. and industry, also on misuse of psychol. measurement in employment and promotion process. lectr. motivation, productivity, and employee attitudes. Mem. Am. Personnel and Guidance Assn., AAUP, Am. Coll. Personnel Assn. (mem. Com. XI on student personnel programs; speaker nat. conv. 1975, 77), Phi Delta Kappa, Phi Mu Alpha, Kappa Phi Kappa, Phi Eta Sigma. Clubs: Masons, Rotary (former dir.), Vermilion Boat. Contbr. articles to profl. jours. Home: 3400 Wooster Rd Suite 311 Rocky River OH 44116 Office: 1005 N Abbe Rd Elyria OH 44035

LEIDNER, HAROLD EDWARD, lawyer; b. Cleve., Aug. 23, 1937; s. Nathan Nelson and Therese Loretta (Burdine) L.; A.B., Cornell U., 1959; LL.B., Western Reserve U., 1963; m. Barbara Ann Weinberger, Dec. 15, 1965; children—Kenneth Jason, Andrew Mitchell. Admitted to Ohio bar, 1963; since practiced in Cleve.; partner Fuerst, Leidner, Dougherty & Kasdan Co., L.P.A., 1971—; dir. Shawnee Plastics Inc., Kuttawa, Ky. Trustee Cleve. Opera Co. Served to lt. comdr. JAG, USNR. Mem. Am., Ohio, Cleve. bar assns., Am. Arbitration Assn. (arbitrator). Republican. Clubs: Cornell, Mill Creek Racquet (Cleve.); Curzon House (London, Eng.). Law editor Webster's New World Dictionary of the American Language, 1970. Home: 2709 Belvoir Blvd Shaker Heights OH 44122 Office: 1500 Terminal Tower Bldg Cleveland OH 44113

LEIF, CLAUDE (BUD) PETER, realtor; b. Cole Harbor, N.D., July 3, 1920; s. John J. and Frances A. (Feyen) L.; student St. Mary's Coll., 1938, Austin Jr. Coll., 1940; B.B.A., U. Minn., 1943; m. Alice Mae Ankeny, Oct. 9, 1943; children—Jerome, Georgia (Mrs. E. LaVallie), Paul, Keith, Gregory, Lawrence, Joseph, Donald, Daniel, Mary, Steven. Gen. mgr. Miller Real Estate Co., Austin, Minn., 1946-58, partner, 1954-58; gen. mgr. Miller Molde Constrn. Co., Austin, Minn., 1946-58; gen. mgr., sec. Miller Home Devel., Inc., Austin, 1946-60, 70—; prin. Bud Leif Real Estate and Ins. Co., Austin, Minn., 1958—; sec. Crestwood Home Devel., Inc., 1970—. Active Twin Valley Council Boy Scouts Am., 1952-75, chmn. Austin Council, 1962—; mem. com. United Fund, Austin, 1958—. Served with AUS, 1943-46; ETO. Recipient Silver Scout award, 1973. Mem. Austin C. of C., Austin Bd. Realtors (pres. 1962, 77, 78), Nat. Bd. Realtors, Minn. Assn. Mutual Agts., Am. Legion, V.F.W., U. Minn. Alumni Assn., St. Mary's Coll. Alumni Assn., Alpha Kappa Psi. K.C. (4 deg.), Eagles, Moose. Home: 500 17th St SW Austin MN 55912 Office: 807 W Oakland Austin MN 55912

LEIGH, FRED DURSHEE, physician; b. Mt. Carroll, Ill., Jan. 22, 1920; s. Fred Clair and Myrtle Ruth (Wachtel) L.; m. Helen Elsie Isaacs, July 25, 1943; children—Susan Leigh Kingston, Frederic, Tom; B.A., Cornell Coll., 1941; B.S., U. Ill., 1942, M.D., 1943; intern Cook County Hosp., Chgo., 1944; resident R & E Hosp.-U. Ill. Coll. Medicine, 1946. Practice medicine, specializing in obstetrics and pediatrics, Freeport, Ill., 1946-48, Huron, S.D., 1948—; v.p. Huron Clinic Found.; faculty U. S.D. Med. Sch.; chief of staff St. Johns Regional Med. Center. 1976. Pres. Huron Arena Assn. Mem. Am., S.D. (pres.) med. assns., Huron Dist. Med. Soc., Am. Coll. Obstetrics and Gynecology, Am. Acad. Pediatrics, S.D. Pediatric Soc., S.D. Obstetrics Soc., Huron C. of C. (pres.), Mason, Shriners, Elks, Rotary (pres.). Recipient award S.D. Jr. C. of C. Contbr. articles to profl. jours. Home: 1751 McClullen Dr Huron SD 57350 Office: Huron Clinic Huron SD 57350

LEIGH, ROBERT LAWTON, bldg. products co. exec.; b. Peru, Ind., June 26, 1912; s. Roy Leighton and Kathryn Lorraine (Lawton) L.; B.S., Mich. State U., 1933; m. Mary Maxine Boozer, Dec. 20, 1941; children—Mary Elizabeth (Mrs. James Kinnebrew), Lorraine Kathryn, Robert Lawrence. Pres., Air Control Products, Inc. (name changed to Leigh Products, Inc. 1962), 1938-70, chmn. bd., 1971—; treas. Leigh's of Western Mich., Inc., Grand Rapids, Mich., 1975—; Rotarian. Home: 648 Manhattan Rd Grand Rapids MI 49506 Office: 2627 East Beltline SE Grand Rapids MI 49586

LEIGHNINGER, DAVID SCOTT, cardiovascular surgeon; b. Youngstown, Ohio, Jan. 16, 1920; s. Jesse Harrison and Marjorie (Lightner) L.; B.A., Oberlin Coll., 1942; M.D., Case-Western Res. U., 1945; m. Margaret Jane Malony, May 24, 1942; children—David Allan, Jenny. Intern, U. Hosps. Cleve., 1945-46; research fellow cardiovascular surgery research lab. Case-Western Res. U. Sch. Medicine, Cleve., 1948-49, 51-55, 57-67; resident U. Hosps. Cleve., 1949-51, Cin. Gen. Hosp., 1955-57; pvt. practice medicine, specializing in cardiovascular surgery, Cleve., 1957-70; pvt. practice, specializing in cardiovascular and gen. surgery Edgewater Hosp., Chgo., 1970—; staff surgeon, also co-dir. surg. intensive care unit Edgewater Hosp. and Mazel Med. Center, Chgo., 1970—; instr. surgery Case-Western U. Sch. Medicine, 1951-55, sr. instr. surgery, 1957-64; asst. prof. surgery, 1964-68, asst. clin. prof. surgery, 1968-70; asst. surgeon U. Hosps. Cleve., 1951-68; asso., courtesy staff mem. or cons. staff mem. of Marymount Hosp., Cleve., Mt. Sinai Hosp., Cleve., Geauga Community Hosp., Chardon, Ohio, Bedford (Ohio) Community Hosp., 1957-70. Tchr. tng. courses in cardiopulmonary resuscitation for police, fire and vol. rescue workers, numerous cities, 1962-70. Served to capt. M.C., AUS, 1946-48. Recipient Chris award Columbus (Ohio) Internat. Film Festival, 1964, numerous other awards for scientific exhibits from various nat. and state med. socs., 1953-70; USPHS grantee, 1949-68. Fellow Am. Coll. Cardiology, Am. Coll. Chest Physicians; mem. AMA, Ill. State, Chgo. med. assns., Mont Ried Surg. Soc. (Cin.). Contbr. numerous articles in field to profl. jours.; contbr. numerous chpts. to med. texts. Spl. pioneer research (with Claude S. Beck) in Physiopathology of coronary artery disease and cardiopulmonary resuscitation; developed surg. treatment of coronary artery disease; achieved first successful defibrillation of human heart, first successful reversal of fatal heart attack; provided first "intensive care" of coronary patients. Home: 1124 Midway Rd Northbrook IL 60062 Office: 5700 N Ashland Ave Chicago IL 60660

LEIGHNINGER, MARGARET JANE MALONY (MRS. DAVID S. LEIGHNINGER), artist; b. Dayton, Ohio, Sept. 14, 1918; d. William A. and Pearl (Leihgeber) Malony; student Kent State U., 1936, Western Res. U., 1948, Case Western Res. U., 1964-68, Cleve. Art Inst., 1968, Chgo. Art Inst., 1970; B.A., Mundelein Coll., 1973; m. David S. Leighninger, May 24, 1942; children—David Allan, Jenny. Social worker, Youngstown, Ohio, 1937-42; nursery sch. tchr., 1947-48, 49-52; record room librarian U. Hosps. Cleve., 1942-46, 52-56; exhibited in one-man shows at Fine Arts Assn., Willoughby, Ohio, Fenn Coll., The Brewery Works Fine Arts Salon, Cedarburg, Wis., Ozaukee Art Center, Cedarburg; exhibited in group shows at Malvina Freedson Galleries, Shaker Art Show, Mundelein Coll., 1971, Larew's Art Galleries, Evanston, Ill., North Shore Art League Ill., Nat. shows in Colo., Ala., Fla., N.J., N.Y., Calif., Tex., Okla., La., Ohio and others; represented in permanent collections Willoughby Fine Arts Assn. Patron Northwestern U. Friends of Art; sustaining mem. Evanston Art League, mem. Ozaukee Art Center, Wis. Painters and Sculptors Assn., Northbrook Art League. Mem. Cleve. Acad. Medicine, Heart Assn. Northeastern Ohio, Women's Art League Cleve., Edgewater Wives Med. Staff, Edgewater Service Club, N. Shore Med. Soc. Aux. Home: 1124 Midway Rd Northbrook IL 60062

LEIGHTON, GEORGE NEVES, judge; b. New Bedford, Mass., Oct. 22, 1912; s. Antonio N. and Anna Sylvia (Garcia) Leitao; A.B., Howard U., 1940; LL.B., Harvard, 1946; LL.D., Elmhurst Coll., 1964, John Marshall Law Sch., Southeastern Mass. U., 1975; m. Virginia Berry Quivers, June 21, 1942; children—Virginia Anne, Barbara Elaine. Admitted to Mass. bar, 1946, Ill. bar, 1947, U.S. Supreme Ct. bar, 1958; partner Moore, Ming & Leighton, Chgo., 1951-59, McCoy, Ming & Leighton, Chgo., 1959-64; judge Circuit Ct. Cook County, Ill., 1964-69, Appellate Ct., 1st Dist., 1969-76, U.S. Dist. Ct., 1976—. Commr., as mem. character and fitness com. for 1st Appellate Dist., Supreme Ct. Ill., 1955-63, chmn. character and fitness com., 1961-62; mem. joint com. for revision jud. article Ill. and Chgo. bar assns., 1959-62, joint com. for revision Ill. Criminal Code, 1959-63; chmn. Ill. adv. com. U.S. Commn. on Civil Rights, 1964; mem. pub. rev. bd. UAW, AFL-CIO, 1961-69. Asst. atty. gen. State of Ill., 1950-51; pres. 3d Ward Regular Democratic Orgn., Cook County. Ill., 1951-53, v.p. 21st Ward, 1964. Bd. dirs. United Ch. Bd. for Homeland Ministries, United Ch. of Christ. Board directors Grant Hosp., Chgo. Served from 2d lt. to capt., inf. AUS, 1942-45. Decorated Bronze Star; recipient Civil Liberties award Ill. div. Am. Civil Liberties Union, 1961; named Chicagoan of Year in Law and Judiciary, Jr. Assn. Commerce and Industry, 1964. Fellow of Am. Bar Found.; mem. Howard U. Chgo. Alumni Club (chmn. bd. dirs.), John Howard Assn. (dir.), Chgo., Ill. bar assns., N.A.A.C.P. (chmn. legal redress com. Chgo. br.), Nat. Harvard Law Sch. Assn. (mem. Council), Phi Beta Kappa (hon.), Gamma of D.C. Contbr. articles to legal jours. Home: 8400 S Prairie Av Chicago IL 60619 Office: Dirksen Fed Bldg Chicago IL 60604

LEIGHTON, PAUL WILLIAM, publishing co. exec., mgmt. cons.; b. Eden, Idaho, Jan. 4, 1920; s. Ralph Edward and Hazel Elma (Shields) L.; B.C.E. with honors, Cornell U., 1942; m. Greta Wilcox, Dec. 9, 1944; children—Christy E., Ann S., Mark W., Rebecca J. Asst. mgr. battery div. Socony, Mobil Oil Co., N.Y.C., 1946-50; partner K.E. Hughes Co., N.Y.C., 1952-56; regional sales mgr., advt. mgr., asst. to v.p., battery sales Globe Union Inc., Milw., 1956-60; marketing mgr., 1960-64, v.p. marketing, battery div., 1964-67, v.p. marketing, pub. relations, corporate, 1967-68, v.p. corp., gen. mgr. centralab semiconductor div., 1968-70, v.p. corp., gen. mgr. battery div., 1970-73; pres. Hammond Pub. Co. Inc., Milw., 1973—; exec. v.p. PMA Corp., mgmt. cons. Bd. dirs. Milw. Rescue Mission, 1970—, Friendship Village. Served as capt. AUS, 1942-46, 50-52. Mem. Gideons. Republican. Presbyn (elder). Rotarian. Home: 513 Bel Aire Dr Thiensville WI 53092 Office: 115 E Wells St Milwaukee WI 53202

LEIMKUHLER, GUS ERNEST, JR., librarian; b. North Kansas City, Mo., June 30, 1926; s. Gus Ernest and Elsie Willmetta (Millsap) L.; B.S. in Edn., U. Mo. at Columbia, 1950; M.S. Edn., U. Mo. at Kansas City, 1955; m. Lois Marjorie Darby, June 25, 1950; children—Ann Darby, James Kenton. Tchr. jr. high sch. North Kansas City Sch. Dist. 74, 1950-52, tchr. high sch., 1952-63; head librarian North Kansas City High Sch., 1963—, yearbook adviser, 1954-68. Mem. bd. Free Pub. Library Bd., North Kansas City, 1954, 55, ARC, Clay County, Mo., 1968-71; bd. mgrs. Kansas City area Am. Field Service, also U.S. adv. bd., 1974-76, del. 2d World Congress, Pawling, N.Y., 1976. Served with inf. AUS, 1944-46. Mem. North Kansas City Community Tchrs. Assn. (pres. 1959-60), Mo. Assn. Sch. Librarians, Mo. State Tchrs. Assn. (pres. 11th dist. librarians 1971-72), NEA. Republican. Methodist. Club: Old Pike Country (pres. 1967, v.p. 1968). Graphics cons. Legacy of Leadership, 1970—. Home: 206 NW 59th St Gladstone MO 64118 Office: 23d and Gentry North Kansas City MO 64116

LEIN, MALCOLM EMIL, museum dir.; b. Havre, Mont., July 19, 1913; s. Emil A. and Ruth (Fredeen) L.; student U. Wis., 1930; B.Arch., U. Minn., 1936; m. Miriam Balliet Bend, Apr. 13, 1939; children—Eric Manning, Kristin Anker, R. Kurt Harrison. Asst. head constrn. dept. F.W. Woolworth Co. Dist. Office, Mpls., 1936-41; pvt. practice architecture and design, St. Paul, 1946—; pres. Minn. Museum of Art, 1947—; pres. Design Consultants, Inc., St. Paul, 1949—. Mid-West Credit Corp., St. Paul, 1959—, Desconi Corp. Served to col., C.E., AUS, 1941-46; CBI. Mem Am. Assn. Museums, Am. Fedn. Art, Archives Am. Art, Res. Officers Assn., Air Force Assn. Home: 361 Summit Ave St Paul MN 55102 Office: 305 St Peter St Paul MN 55102

LEININGER, ELMER, chemist; b. Milw., Apr. 19, 1900; s. Philip Henry and Louise (Hardtke) L.; B.S., Carroll Coll., 1923; postgrad. U. Wis., 1923-24; M.S., Mich. State U., 1931; Ph.D., U. Mich., 1941; m. Hazel Ann MacNamara, Dec. 30, 1924 (dec. June 1961); 1 dau., Mary Louise (Mrs. Allan David Reese); m. 2d, Byrnice L. Dickinson, 1964. Instr. chem. Mich. State U., 1924-30, prof. chemistry, head analytical chemistry sect. 1930-65, prof. emeritus, 1965—; chem. cons., 1965—, Sec., dir. Geneva Lake Civic Assn., 1968-76. Mem. Am. Chem. Soc., Am. Philatelic Soc., A.A.A.S., Sigma Xi, Alpha Chi Sigma, Phi Lambda Upsilon. Republican. Club: Lake Geneva Country. Editorial adv. bd. Analytical Chemistry. Contbr. articles to profl. jours. Address: S Lake Shore Dr Rural Route 1 Box 238 Lake Geneva WI 53147

LEININGER, HAROLD VERNON, microbiologist; b. Baton Rouge, June 18, 1925; s. Wilfred Clarence and Georgia Tennessee (Carpenter) L.; B.S., La. State U., 1948, M.S., 1950; m. Emma Elizabeth McBride, June 3, 1950; 1 son, Harold Vernon. Food and drug insp. FDA, New Orleans, 1950-51, microbiologist, Washington, 1951-57, project officer Atomic Test Site, Mercury, Nev., 1957, research microbiologist, Washington, 1957-63, liaison microbiologist, Washington, 1963-69, dir. Mpls. Center for Microbiol. Investigations, 1969—. Lectr., U. Wis., Madison, 1968, U. Wis., River Falls, 1973, U. Minn., 1970. Served with USNR, 1943-46. Recipient FDA award of merit, 1977. USPHS fellow, 1948-49. Mem. Am. Soc. Microbiology, Inst. Food Tech., Internat. Assn. Milk, Food and Environmental Sanitarians, Inc., Assn. Food and Drug Ofcls. (mem. sci. and tech. com. 1972-77), Assn. Ofcl. Analytical Chemists (gen. referee 1965-70), Henrici Soc., Minn. Sanitarians Assn., Central States Assn. Food and Drug Ofcls. Episcopalian (vestryman 1965). Author: (with McConnell, Mathews, Spiher) Civil Defense Information for Food and Drug Officials of the United States, 1955, 2d edit., 1956. Contbr. articles to profl. jours.; chpt. to Compendium of Methods for Microbiological Examination of Foods, 1976. Home: 3329 Sycamore Trail SW Prior Lake MN 55372 Office: 240 Hennepin Ave Minneapolis MN 55401

LEINONEN, ELLEN ANNA, educator; b. Houghton, Mich., Oct. 15, 1912; d. Matt and Maria (Gustava) Leinonen; certificate in Dental Hygiene, U. Mich., 1949, B.S. with distinction, 1956, M.S. in Anatomy, 1962; Ph.D. (Dr. A.L. Legro research scholar, Teaching fellow, Simpson Meml. Inst. fellow), Ohio State U., 1967. Instr. dentistry U. Mich. at Ann Arbor, 1949-62, asst. prof. dentistry, 1965—, asst. prof. anatomy Med. Sch., 1971—; dental hygienist, Ypsilanti, Mich., 1949-50, Canton Center, Mich., summer 1950, Wayne, Mich., 1950-52, Ann Arbor, 1953-55. Fellow Simpson Meml. Inst. U. Mich. Mem. N.Y. Acad. Scis., Am. Assn. Anatomists, Am. Inst. Chemists, AAAS, Dental Hygienists Assn., AAUP, Smithsonian Instn., Sigma Xi, Sigma Delta Epsilon, Pi Lambda Theta, Sigma Phi Alpha (pres. 1970-71). Republican. Lutheran. Clubs: Zonta International (mem. exec. bd. 1970-73), Business and Professional Womans (Ypsilanti, Mich.). Contbr. chpts. to books in field. Home: 3093 Lexington Dr Ann Arbor MI 48105

LEISEN, RICHARD JOSEPH, clergyman; b. St. Cloud, Minn., Apr. 26, 1930; s. Othmar and Cecelia Anna (Moser) L.; student Crosier Sem. and Coll., 1944-50; B.A., St. John's U., 1956; M.S.W. (NIMH fellow), Fordham U., 1956. Ordained priest Roman Catholic Ch., 1956; asst. pastor Catholic chs., Pierz and St. Cloud, 1956-63; dir. Cath. charities, Diocese St. Cloud, 1965—. Pres. Key-Row Community housing devel. low-income families, 1968—. Vice pres. Big Bros., 1970—, YMCA, 1969-71; mem. community adv. council St. Cloud, Hosp., 1969-71; mem. steering com. Joint Religious Legis. Com. Minn., 1970-71; mem. operating com. St. Benedict's Center; bd. dirs. Region 7W Devel. Commn., Crosier Apostolate, Central Minn. Health Systems Agy. Mem. Minn. Cath. Conf. (social action chmn.), Minn. Assn. Voluntary Social Service Agys. (chmn.), Minn. Conf. Cath. Charities (pres. 1968-70), Minn. Welfare Assn. (regional resolutions chmn. 1967-77), Nat. Conf. Cath. Charities (housing commn., 1970-74), Crosier Alumni Assn. (pres., 1969-72). K.C. Home: 1726 7th Ave St Cloud MN 56301 Office: 1726 7th Ave S St Cloud MN 56301

LEISER, BURTON MYRON, educator; b. Denver, Dec. 12, 1930; s. Nathan and Eva Mae (Newman) L.; B.A., U. Chgo., 1951; M.H.L., Yeshiva U., 1956; Ph.D. (Univ. fellow), Brown U., 1968; m. Barbara Hurowitz-Tabor, June 9, 1967; children by previous marriage—Shoshana, Illana, Phillip; step children—Ellen, David, Susan. Instr. philosophy Fort Lewis Coll., Durango, Colo., 1963-65; asst. prof. philosophy N.Y. State U., Buffalo, 1965-68; asso. prof. philosophy, 1968-70; vis. asso. prof. Judaic studies Sir George Williams U., Montreal, Que., Can., 1969-71, asso. prof. philosophy, 1971-72; prof. philosophy Drake U., Des Moines, 1972—, chmn. dept., 1972—. Bd. dirs. Bur. Jewish Edn. of Des Moines, 1973-76, Polk County Mental Health Assn., 1974-76. Democratic Party Dist. Committeeman, Des Moines, 1974. N.Y. State U. Research Found. grantee, 1967-68, Meml. Found. for Jewish Culture grantee, 1970-71, Exxon Edn. Found. grantee, 1973-74, Mem. AAUP, Authors Guild, Am. Philos. Assn., Am. sect. Internat. Soc. Legal and Social Philosophy, Soc. Bibl. Lit., Am. Acad. Religion, Soc. Philos. and Pub. Affairs, Soc. for Polit. and legal Philosophy, Am. Profs for Peace in Middle East (nat. exec. com.). Jewish. Author: Custom, Law, and Morality, 1969, Liberty, Justice, and Morals, 1973. Home: 900 45th St West Des Moines IA 50265 Office: Dept of Philosophy Drake Univ Des Moines IA 50311

LEISETH, ROBERT VERNON, banker, former state legislator; b. nr. Sisseton, S.D., Apr. 29, 1928; s. Soren Henry and Bertha (Jordahl) L.; B.A., Concordia Coll., 1956; m. Marilyn Kathleen Johnson, Aug. 4, 1957; children—Bruce Robert, Jon Robert, Kristi Kay. Asst. nat. bank examiner U.S. comptroller of currency, Mpls., 1956-59; exec. v.p., dir. 1st Nat. Bank, Detroit Lakes, Minn., 1959-66; pres., dir. Norman County State Bank, Hendrum, Minn., 1967, Norman County Agy., Inc., Hendrum, 1967—, Detroit Lakes Advt., Inc. (Minn.), 1968—; pres. C.K. of Sioux Falls, Inc. (S.D.), 1972—. Republican precinct chmn., Detroit Lakes, 1962—, Becker County chmn., 1963-66; mem. Minn. Senate, 1966-69; treas. 7th dist. Rep. Central Com., 1973-76, chmn. 7th dist. Rep. Exec. Com., 1976—. Mem. steering com. C-400 Club Concordia Coll., Moorhead, Minn., 1966—. Recipient Pres.'s award Concordia Coll., 1976. Mem. Am. Legion, Sons of Norway. Rotarian (pres. Detroit Lakes 1967-68). Home: Route 2 Box 190 B Lake Park MN 56554

LEIST, CARL CLINTON, lawyer; b. Circleville, Ohio, Oct. 23, 1909; s. Clinton Augustus and Elizabeth F. (Crist) L.; B.A., Capital U., 1930; J.D., Ohio State U., 1933; m. Geraldine C. Merrill, Oct. 14, 1932; 1 son, Warren Carl. Admitted to Ohio bar, 1933, since practiced in Circleville; mem. firm Leist & Kitchen, 1933—, sr. mem., 1953—; city atty. Circleville, 1934-40. Dir., Atty., 1st v.p. First Nat. Bank Circleville, 1953—; dir., treas., mem. counsel Scioto Bldg. & Loan Co. Circleville, 1944—. Chmn., Pickaway County chpt. ARC, 1937-45; Pickaway County appeals agt. SSS, 1950-72; mem. Circleville City Sch. Dist. Bd. Edn., 1943-61, pres., 1948-61. Chmn. Pickaway County Democratic Exec. Com., 1942-48, chmn. county Dem. central com., 1948-50. Mem. Pickaway County (past pres.), Ohio, Am. bar assns., Pickaway County Law Library Assn. (chmn. 1970—, trustee), Circleville C. of C., Delta Theta Phi. Lutheran (chmn. ch. council 1954-76, pres. congregation 1954-76). Elk, Rotarian. Home: 205 Northridge Rd Circleville OH 43113 Office: 105 W Mound St Circleville OH 43113

LEIST, JOHN WRIGHT, psychiatrist; b. Columbus, Ohio, Apr. 14, 1919; s. Joseph Wright and Laura Frances (Cotter) L.; B.A., Ohio State U., 1940, M.D., 1943; m. Florence Taylor, Aug. 31, 1940 (div. 1944); children—Patricia, Anne; m. 2d, Louise Fredericka Hauser, Aug. 7, 1952; children—Andrew, Matthew. Intern San Diego County Gen. Hosp., 1944, St. Clare's Hosp., N.Y.C., 1946-47; resident psychiatry Halloran VA Hosp., S.I., Northport VA (N.Y.) Hosp., Croton Manor, Croton-on-Hudson, N.Y., 1947-50; practice medicine specializing in psychiatry, N.Y.C., 1950-53, Columbus, 1953—; vis. psychiatrist Children's Mental Health Center, Columbus, 1954-57; cons. psychiatrist Boy's Indsl. Sch., Lancaster, Ohio, 1957-61; cons. psychiatrist Juvenile Diagnostic Center, Columbus, 1962-71; chief psychiatrist Juvenile Diagnostic Center, Columbus, 1971-72; cons. psychiatrist Central Ohio Mental Health Clinic and Guidance Center, Delaware, 1970—; cons. psychiatrist Tng. Instn. Central Ohio, Columbus, 1972-76; cons. psychiatrist Div. Forensic Psychiatry, State Ohio Dept. Mental Health and Mental Retardation, Dayton, 1973—; cons. psychiatrist Human Resources Mental Health Center, Columbus, O., 1973-76; cons. psychiatrist Franklin County Children's Services, Columbus, 1973-74; cons. staff Grady Meml. Hosp., Delaware, Ohio, 1977—. Pres., Del. Community Chorus, 1974-76. Served with AUS, 1944-46. Fellow Assn. Advancement Psychotherapy; mem. Ohio State Med. Assn., N.Y. County, Franklin County med. socs., Am., Ohio psychiat. assns., Neuropsychiat. Soc. Central Ohio, Franklin County Mental Health Assn. (sec. 1963-65, v.p. 1966, dir. 1958-66), N.Y. County Med. Soc., Central Ohio Correctional Assn. (pres. 1966). Presbyn. Composer various songs. Home: 144 W Fountain Ave Delaware OH 43015 Office: 1864 Summit St Columbus OH 43201

LEITH, JAMES CLARK, economist; b. Brandon, Man., Can., Dec. 9, 1937; s. James Scott and Bertha Miriam (Clark) L.; B.A., U. Toronto, 1959; M.S., U. Wis., 1960, Ph.D., 1967; m. Carole Ann Mason, Aug. 29, 1964; children—James, Deborah, Jonathan. Fgn. service officer, Govt. of Canada, 1961-64; asst. prof. U. Western Ont., 1967-71; vis. lectr. U. Ghana, 1969-71; asso. prof. econs. U. Western Ont., London, 1971-78, prof. econs., 1978—, chmn. dept., 1972-76. Vis. research fellow Inst. Internat. Economic Studies, U. Stockholm, 1976-77. Mem. Canadian, Am. econs. assns., Royal Econ. Soc., Econ. Soc. Ghana. Author: Foreign Trade Regimes and Economic Development: Ghana, 1974; (with P.T. Ellsworth) The International Economy, 1975; editor: (with D. Patinkin) Keynes Cambridge and the General Theory, 1977. Home: 80 Friars Way London ON N6G 2B2 Canada Office: Dept Econs Univ Western Ont London ON N6A 5C2 Canada

LEITHERER, ARTHUR EUGENE, milling co. exec.; b. Winnetka, Ill., July 2, 1914; s. Philip Oswald and Martha Anna (Zschau) L.; Ph.B., DePaul U., 1939; M. Traffic and Transp. Law, Coll. Advanced Traffic, 1949; m. Frances Brown, Dec. 26, 1951; children—Philip John, Thomas Paul. With Chgo. Cold Storage, 1933-38, Montgomery Ward, Chgo., 1938-42, Corn Products Refining (now CPC Internat.), 1942-52; with Allied Mills, Inc., Chgo., 1952—, now v.p. transp. Past gen. chmn. Midwest Adv. Bd. Registered practioner, ICC. Mem. Am. Soc. Traffic and Transp. (founder), Nat. Assn. ICC Practioners, Nat. Freight Traffic Assn., Nat. Indsl. Traffic League (past pres.), Am. Feed Mfrs. Assn. (past chmn. traffic exec. com.), Transp. Club (Internat. Transp. Man of Year 1974). Club: Traffic (past pres.) (Chgo.). Home: 801 Inverness Rd Lisle IL 60532 Office: 110 N Wacker Dr Chicago IL 60606

LELAND, GARY LEROY, ins. co. exec.; b. Winfield, Kans., Nov. 16, 1938; s. Harold B. and Doris L. (Buss) L.; student Ark. City Jr. Coll., 1956-57; B.B.A., Wichita State U., 1965; m. Joan Margaret McGowan, Jan. 17, 1960. Operator data processing credit dept. Goodyear Tire & Rubber Co., Wichita, Kans., 1960-63; payroll accountant accounting dept. Kans. Gas & Electric Co., Wichita, 1963-64; accounting supr. Farm & Ranch Life Ins. Co., Inc., Wichita, 1964-67, treas., 1967-71, sec.-treas., 1971—, v.p., 1972—; sec. Lockeford Vintner Corp. div. (Calif.), 1972—; asst. sec., asst. treas. Farm & Ranch Financial, Inc., Wichita, 1972—. Served with USNR, 1957-60. Mem. Data Processing Mgmt. Assn. (pres. Wichita chpt. 1974-75). Home: 425 N Yale Wichita KS 67208 Office: 1069 Parklane St Wichita KS 67218

LELIAERT, RAYMOND MAURICE, mech. engr.; b. Grinnell, Iowa, Sept. 17, 1921; s. Gustave N. and Martha (Vanden Bossche) L.; B.S., U. Notre Dame, 1949; m. Lois Mary Zubler, Mar. 10, 1945; children—Raymond, Mark, Karen (Mrs. Thomas VanMeter), Mary (Mrs. Dennis Rader), Diane (Mrs. Reid Webster), Martha, Christopher, Judith, Barbara. With Wheelabrator-Frye Inc., Mishawaka, Ind., 1940—, dir. research and devel., 1966—. Served with USNR, 1942-46; PTO. Mem. Air Pollution Control Assn., Am. Soc. M.E., Am. Foundrymen's Soc. (research bd.), Am. Soc. Metals. Roman Catholic. K.C. Club: University. Patentee in field. Home: 3612 Brentwood Dr South Bend IN 46628 Office: 400 S Byrkit St Mishawaka IN 46544

LE MAR, WILLIAM BERNHARDT, civil engr., educator; b. Rapid City, S.D., Sept. 24, 1922; s. Harold Diehl and Luella (Petersen) LeM.; student Va. Mil. Inst., 1939-41; B.A. in Engring., Stanford, 1943; M.Engring. in Civil Engring., Yale, 1947; postgrad. Army War Coll., 1970; m. Mary Alma Soule, June 15, 1953 (div. 1967); 1 son, Wade H.M. Draftsman, Anaconda Copper Mining Co., N.Y.C., 1948; structural draftsman N.Y., N.H. & H. R.R., New Haven, 1948-50; dir. engring. P.F. Petersen Baking Co., Omaha, 1950-57, v.p. prodn., 1957-60; civil engr. U. S. Army Corps Engrs., Omaha, 1961; asst. prof. dept. civil engring. U. Nebr., Omaha, 1961-64, asso. prof., 1964—. Dir. Omaha Tng. Course for Sewage Treatment Plant Operators, 1963-70; mem. augmentation faculty U.S. Army Command and Gen. Staff Coll., Ft. Leavenworth, Kan., 1968-75. Served to 1st lt. AUS, 1943-46; col. Res., ret. 1975. Decorated Bronze Star medal, Meritorious Service medal. Registered profl. engr., Nebr., Iowa. Mem. Am. Soc. C.E., Profl. Engrs. Nebr., Yale Engring. Assn., Assn. U.S. Army, Navy League U.S., Res. Officers Assn., Omaha Com. on Fgn. Relations (exec. com.), Council Abandoned Mil. Posts, Phi Alpha Theta, Gamma Alpha. Presbyn. Clubs: Omaha Press, Omaha Engineers; Army and Navy (Washington). Home: 666 N 58th St Omaha NE 68132

LEMBERGER, LOUIS, pharmacologist, physician; b. Monticello, N.Y., May 8, 1937; s. Max and Ida (Seigel) L.; B.S. magna cum laude, Bklyn. Coll. Pharmacy, L.I. U., 1960; Ph.D. in Pharmacology, Albert Einstein Coll. Medicine, 1964, M.D., 1968; m. Myrna Sue Diamond, 1959; children—Harriet, Margo. Pharmacy intern VA Regional Office, Newark, summer 1960; postdoctoral fellow Albert Einstein Coll. Medicine, 1964-68; intern medicine Met. Hosp. Center, N.Y. Med. Coll., N.Y.C., 1968-69; research asso. NIH, Bethesda, Md., 1969-71; practice medicine specializing in clin. pharmacology, Bethesda, 1969-71, Indpls., 1971—; clin. pharmacologist Lilly Lab. for Clin. Research, Eli Lilly & Co., Indpls., 1971-75, chief clin. pharmacology, 1975—; asst. prof. pharmacology Ind. U., 1972-73, asst. prof. medicine, 1972-73, asso. prof. pharmacology, 1973-77, prof. pharmacology, 1977—, asso. prof. medicine 1973-77, prof. medicine and psychiatry, 1977—, mem. grad. faculty, 1975—; adj. prof. clin. pharmacology Ohio State U., 1975—; physician Wishard Meml. Hosp., 1976—; cons. U.S. Nat. Commn. on Marihuana and Drug Abuse, 1971-73, Canadian Commn. of Inquiry into Non-Med. Use of Drugs, 1971-73; guest lectr. in various univs., 1968—. Post adviser Crossroads of Am. council Boy Scouts Am., 1972—. Served with USPHS, 1969-71. Fellow A.C.P., N.Y. Acad. Scis.; mem. Am. Soc. Pharmacology and Exptl. Therapeutics (com. div. clin. pharmacology 1972—), AAAS, Am. Soc. Clin. Pharmacology and Therapeutics (chmn. neuropsychopharmacology sect. 1973—, chmn. fin. com. 1976—), Am. Soc. Clin. Investigation, Collegium Internat. Neuro-Psychopharmacologicum, Am. Fedn. Clin. Research, Central Soc. Clin. Research, Am. Coll. Neuropsychopharmacology, Soc. Neurosci., Sigma Xi, Alpha Omega Alpha, Rho Chi. Jewish. Author: (with A. Rubin) Physiologic Disposition of Drugs of Abuse, 1976; contbr. numerous articles on biochemistry and pharmacology to sci. jours.; editorial bd. Excerpta Medica, 1972—, Clin. Pharmacology and Therapeutics, 1976—, Psychopharmacology, 1975—. Home: 7521 Colony Circle Indianapolis IN 46260 Office: Lilly Lab Clin Research Wishard Memorial Hosp Indianapolis IN 46202

LEMBERGER, ROBERT ALOIS, cons. engr.; b. St. Louis, July 10, 1934; s. Alois A. and Marie (Stukejergen) L.; B.S. in Physics, U. Mo., Rolla, 1959, B.S. in Civil Engring., 1960; m. Beverly L. Birmingham, Feb. 14, 1959; 1 son, John Robert. Mgmt. trainee Proctor & Gamble Mfg. Co., St. Louis, 1960-63; instr. U. Mo., Rolla, 1963-66; partner Mo. Engring. Co., Rolla, 1966—; chmn. bd. dirs. Am. Planning Corp., Rolla, 1965; dir. Mo. Engring. Corp. of the Ozarks, Camdenton, Mo. Mem. Maries County (Mo.) Sch. Bd., 1975—. Served with AUS, 1953-55. Mem. Mo., Nat. socs. profl. engrs., Mo. Assn. Registered Land Surveyors, Kappa Alpha. Lion. Home: Vienna MO 65582 Office: PO Box 13 Rolla MO 65401

LEMING, JOHN CURTIS, mech. engr.; b. DuQuoin, Ill., Dec. 24, 1919; s. Clarence and Agnes (Schmitt) L.; B.S. in Mech. Engring., U. Ill., 1941; m. Leila Marie Edrington, June 20, 1942; children—Patricia Ann. John Michael, Curtis Edrington. Engring. research design and devel. Wright Aero. Corp., N.J., 1941-54; sales mgr. Gear Grinding Machine Co., Detroit, 1954-59; gear grind machine div. mgr. Mich. Tool Co., 1959-67; v.p., dir. engring. Overton Gear & Tool Corp., 1967-72; chief engr. Arrow Gear Co., Downers Grove, Ill., 1972—; gearing cons., 1954—. Served with USAAF, 1945-46. Recipient Edward P. Connell award Am. Gear Mfrs. Assn., 1973. Mem. Am. Gear Mfrs. Assn., Indsl. Math. Soc., Engring. Soc. Detroit, Air Force Assn., Am. Ordnance Assn. Patentee in field. Home: 2S-180 Stratford Rd Glen Ellyn IL 60137 Office: 2301 Curtiss Downers Grove IL 60515

LEMKE, ARTHUR ATHNIEL, hydraulic and san. engr.; b. Watertown, Wis., Feb. 26, 1913; s. Frederick William and Ruth Wilhelmina (Hauser) L.; B.S. in Civil Engring., U. Wis., 1934, M.S. in Civil Engring., 1935, C.E., 1946; m. Rosalie Priscilla Lyga, July 18, 1936. Jr. chemist and engring. aide Wis. Hwy. Commn., 1935-36; instr. civil engring. Lewis Inst., Chgo., 1936-40; instrumentman, also chief party Chgo. Park Dist., 1940-42; with Chgo. Pump, environmental equipment div. FMC Corp., Chgo., 1942—, san. engr., 1942-46, sr. san. engr., 1946-48, asst. mgr. application engring., sewage equipment engring. dept., 1948-52, mgr., 1952-64, supr. process engring., 1964-72, sr. project engr., 1972—, patent liaison, 1971—. Registered profl. engr., Ill., Wis. Diplomate Am. Acad. Environmental Engrs. Fellow ASCE; mem. Water Pollution Control Fedn., Internat. Assn. for Hydraulic Research, Phi Eta Sigma, Chi Epsilon. Contbr. to profl. publs. Patentee sewage systems. Home: 3329 Noyes St Evanston IL 60201 Office: FMC Corp 1800 FMC Dr W Itasca IL 60143

LEMMON, DALLAS MARION, educator; b. Goshen, Ind., Apr. 29, 1933; s. Dallas Marion and Anne Emily (Sailor) L.; student Western Mich. Coll., 1951-52, Purdue U., 1952-53; B.S. with distinction, U. Mich., 1957; M.A., Ind. U., 1966, Ph.D., 1970; m. Kathlene Sutton, Apr. 10, 1966; children—Lynn C., Marianne E. Geologist, N.W. Prodn. Corp., Rock Springs, Wyo., 1956-57; teaching asst. Ind. U., Bloomington, 1962-64; instr. U. Hawaii, Honolulu, 1964-66; chmn. dept. English, Kankakee (Ill.) Community Coll., 1968-69; instr. english and film Coll. DuPage, Glen Ellyn, Ill., 1969—. Research cons., reviewer Prentice-Hall, Inc., 1974—. Bd. dirs. Assn. Advancement Human Understanding. Served with AUS, 1958. Mem. Modern Lang. Assn., Nat. Council Tchrs. English, Centro Studi E Scambi Internationale (mem. internat. com. 1970-71), Sigma Gamma Epsilon. Author: Fire Mountain, 1967; Sweet-tooth, Blood-tooth, 1968; Third Days, 1968, 5-4-3-2, 1971. Contbr. poems to various publs.

LEMMON, KENNETH WAYNE, psychologist; b. DuQuoin, Ill., June 21, 1938; s. Haley Norbert and Lillie Bell (Downen) L.; B.A., U. Corpus Christi, 1966; M.A., Tex. A and I. U., 1967; postgrad. Wayne State U., 1969-71; m. Mary Aldora Greer, Jan. 24, 1959; children—Sonya Kim, Bradley Wayne. Instr. psychology Mobile Coll., 1968-69, U. Windsor (Ont., Can.), 1969-71; lectr. Wayne County Community Coll., 1970-71; teaching fellow Wayne State U., 1969-70, instr., 1973-74; asst. prof. psychology Center for Creative Studies, Coll. Art and Design, 1971—; med. hypnotist; photographer; psychol. cons. to industry. Mem. exec. com. bd. dirs. YMCA, Royal Oak, Mich., 1975—; chmn. bd. dirs. Coastal Bend Habilitation Bd., Corpus Christi. Served with U.S. Army, 1957-58. Whitehall fellow,

1967-68; Tex. A. and I. U. grantee, 1966-68; Nat. Bd. Ministries grantee, 1968-69. Mem. Am., Mich. psychol. assns., AAUP, Am. Sociol. Assn. Episcopalian. Club: Forestors. Author: A Glossary of Statistical Terms, 1971; contbr. articles to profl. jours. Home: 923 W Eleven Mile Rd Royal Oak MI 48067 Office: 245 E Kirby St Detroit MI 48202

LEMON, HENRY MARTYN, physician, educator; b. Chgo., Dec. 23, 1915; s. Harvey Brace and Louise (Birkhoff) L.; B.S., U. Chgo., 1938; M.D. cum laude, Harvard U., 1940; m. Harriet Tuxbury Qua, May 3, 1941; children—Elizabeth Anne (Mrs. Wendell E. Carr), Harvey Brace, Stanley Moncrief, David Tuxbury, Jennifer Jane (Mrs. Dennis Dewitt); m. 2d, Dorothy Cambell, May 28, 1976. Intern, Billings Hosp., Chgo., 1940-41, asst. resident medicine, 1941-42; asst. in dept. medicine U. Chgo., 1942-43; chief med. resident U. Hosp., Boston, 1946-48; instr. medicine Boston U., 1946-48, asst. prof. medicine, 1948-54, asso. prof. medicine, 1954-61; dir. Eugene C. Eppley Cancer Inst., U. Nebr. Coll. Medicine, Omaha, 1961-68, prof. internal medicine, 1961—; cons. internal medicine VA, Boston, Omaha, 1950—. Bd. dirs. Mass., Nebr. div. Am. Cancer Soc. Served to capt. M.C. AUS, 1943-46; col. Res. Recipient Distinguished Service award U. Chgo. Med. Alumni, 1952; 3 awards merit AMA Sci. Exhibits, Distinguished Teaching award U. Nebr. Med. Center, 1976. Diplomate Am. Bd. Internal Medicine, Am. Bd. Med. Oncology. Fellow A.C.P.; mem. AMA, Am. Assn. Cancer Research, Endocrine Soc., Ewing Soc., Central Soc. Clin. Research, Res. Officers Assn. Republican. Unitarian. Rotarian. Research air-borne infection, cytodiagnosis pancreatic cancer, transplantation human cancer to hamsters, 1952, estrogen imbalance in breast cancer, endocrine and chemotherapy cancer, reduction of toxicity in cancer chemotherapy, estriol prevention breast cancer, carcinogenesis breast, leukemia and lymphoma, 1940—. Home: 10805 Poppleton Ave Omaha NE 68144 Office: Dept Internal Medicine U Nebr Omaha NE 68105

LEMON, WILLIAM JOSEPH, transp. exec. ; b. Bayville, N.J., Sept. 22, 1922; s. William and Mary (McGurty) L.; grad. high sch.; m. Eileen Arnheim, June 1, 1968; children—Ellen, William, Barbara. Traffic supr. Safeway Stores, Inc., N.J., 1938-42; mgr. Spector Freight System, Ind., N.Y., 1945-48, operations mgr. Eastern div., 1948-52, dir. operations, Chgo., 1952-57, dir. labor relations, 1957-62, v.p. labor relations, Chgo., 1962-73, v.p. indsl. relations, 1973—. Served with USAAF, 1942-45. Mem. Am. Legion, Am. Trucking Assn. (regional vice chmn., chmn. indsl. relations com.), Motor Carrier Employer Conf. Central States (chmn. bd.). Home: 1132 Royal St George Dr Naperville IL 60540 Office: 1050 Kingery Hwy Bensenville IL 60106

LE MOYNE, NOEL JOSEPH, market analyst; b. Dayton, Ohio, Oct. 3, 1939; s. Joseph Hastings and Katherine (Cooper) LeM.; B.S., Miami U., Oxford, Ohio, 1962; M.B.A., U. Mich., 1966; m. Doris Lee Stallard. Market research analyst Standard Oil Co. of Ohio, Cleve., 1966-68; sr. market analyst R.G. Barry Co., slipper mfg., Columbus, 1968—. Marketing cons. Loaned exec. United Way, 1972; active Big Bros. Served as 1st lt. USAF, 1962-65. Mem. Am. Marketing Assn. (pres. Central Ohio chpt. 1971-73), Am. Footwear Industries Assn. (mktg. info. com.). Home: 636 Fleetrun Ave Columbus OH 43230 Office: 13405 Yarmouth Dr NW Pickerington OH 43147

LENAGAR, GLENN ROBERT, JR., archtl. engr.; b. Kansas City, Mo., Feb. 4, 1924; s. Glenn Robert and Hazel (Huston) L.; B.S., U. Kans., 1951; m. Jenson M. McGinnis, Nov. 1, 1958. Engr., plant engring. Gen. Motors Corp., Kansas City, Mo., 1951-57, J.F. Pritchard Co., Kansas City, 1957-59; project engr. Gordon Johnson Co., Kansas City, 1959-62; mech. engr. King Radio, Olathe, Kans., 1962-63. Wilcox Electric Co., Kansas City, 1963-64 Bonzer Electronics Co., Shawnee Mission, Kans., 1964-65; plant engr. Kansas City Structural Steel Co. (Kans.), 1965—. Served with USAAF, 1942-48. Mem. Nat. Soc. Profl. Engrs., Kans. Engring. Soc., Amvets (past pres.), Sigma Nu. Patentee in field. Home: 7101 Linden Rd Prairie Village KS 66208 Office: 2100 Metropolitan Ave Kansas City KS 66106

LENARDSON, JAMES DUANE, electric co. exec.; b. Riga, Mich., June 8, 1924; s. James Wesley and Viola Martha (Becker) L.; student U. Detroit, 1941-43; B.S. in Mech. Engring., U. Ill., 1946; m. Raye Evelyn Lauderdale, Dec. 23, 1945; children—Linda Lee, Cynthia Sue, James Raymond, Richard Lee. Jr. through sr. engr. Toledo (Ohio) Edison Co., 1946-55, constrn. engr., 1955-68, plant mech. engr., 1968-70, quality assurance mgr., 1970-77, quality assurance dir., 1977—; also cons. Active Boy Scouts Am. Served to comdr. USN, 1943-46. Registered profl. engr., Ohio, Calif. Mem. ASTM, Am. Concrete Inst., ASME (nat. code coms.), Am. Soc. for Quality Control (nat. standard com.), Am. Soc. for Nondestructive Testing, Nat. Rifle Assn., U. Ill. Alumni Assn., Nat. Wildlife Fedn., Am. Audubon Soc., Ducks Unltd. Republican. Lutheran. Lectr., speaker on tech. engring. Home: 7360 Wild Haven Park Lambertville MI 48144 Office: 300 Madison Ave Toledo OH 43652

LENERTZ, ALOYS FRANK, real estate broker; b. Canby, Minn., Nov. 7, 1913; s. Anthony T. and Anna M. (Dartman) L.; B.S., U. N.D., 1936; m. Edith Mae Bjorge, Nov. 16, 1946; children—Jane Kay (Mrs. Gary J. Marsden), Barbara Ann (Mrs. Don R. Wetter), Nancy Lee (Mrs. Stephen M. Shermoen). Ins. broker W.A. Alexander & Co., Chgo., 1941-42; owner, operator Lenertz Ins. Agy., Grand Forks, N.D., 1946-72; owner Lenertz Realty, Grand Forks, 1963—. Served with USNR, 1942-46. Mem. Nat. Assn. Realtors, VFW. Elk. Home: 506 Harvard St Grand Forks ND 58201 Office: 201 S 4th St Grand Forks ND 58201

LENGEL, LELAND LEVI, educator; b. Concordia, Kans., May 16, 1934; s. Charles Harrison and Minnie Louise (Dangberg) L.; A.B., McPherson Coll., 1956; M.A., Duke, 1962; Ph.D., U. Ore., 1968; m. Nancy Jane Keim, May 31, 1957; children—Douglas Alan, Carolyn Jean. Teaching asst. U. Oreg., Eugene, 1960-63; faculty, dept. history McPherson (Kans.) Coll., 1963-74, 77—, asso. dean acad. affairs, 1974-77. Democratic precinct committeeman, McPherson, 1974—. Rockefeller Bros. Theol. fellow, 1958-59. Mem. ACLU, Sierra Club, Phi Alpha Theta. Mem. Ch. of Brethren. Home: 321 N Olivette St McPherson KS 67460

LENHART, MILTON JOHN, obstetrician and gynecologist; b. Campbell, Ohio, Feb. 6, 1932; s. Milton Stephen and Anna (Van Such) L.; student DePauw U., 1949-50; B.S., Ohio State U., 1953, M.D., 1957; m. Roberta Rubenstahl, Nov. 28, 1959; children—Milton G., Denise, Lisa, Lorraine. Intern, St. Elizabeth Hosp., Youngstown, Ohio, 1957-58; resident in obstetrics and gynecology Akron (Ohio) City Hosp., 1960-64; practice medicine specializing in obstetrics and gynecology, Youngstown, 1964—; sec. obstet. and gynecol. dept. Youngstown Hosp. Assn., 1971-76, vice chief of obstetrics and gynecology, 1976-77, chief, 1977—. Pres. St. Edward's PTA, 1976. Served with USNR, 1958-60. Diplomate Am. Bd. Obstetrics and Gynecology. Mem. Ohio, Mahoning County med. socs., AMA, Am. Coll. Obstetrics and Gynecology, Cleve., Youngstown socs. obstetrics and gynecology, Am. Assn. Gynecol. Laparoscopists, Am. Fertility Soc. Roman Catholic. Club: Jewish Community Center. Home: 2225 5th Ave Youngstown OH 44504 Office: 1005 Belmont Ave Youngstown OH 44504

LENNERTZ, RAYMOND, bus. cons.; b. Ft. Benton, Mont., May 27, 1921; s. Peter and Bertha (Kramer) L.; B.S. in Chemistry, U. Notre Dame, 1943; m. Rosemary Hornett, Apr. 8, 1944; children—Thomas, William, Mary. Founder, pres. Colonial Drug Co., Gary, Ind., 1951-71, Tyler Labs., Gary, 1957-71, Char-Steak House, Chgo., 1966-71, Valparaiso Pharmacy (Ind.), 1961-72, Western States Char-Steak House, Chgo., 1967-71; partner Kings Pharmacy, Homewood, Ill., 1962-70, Reister, Lennertz & Assos., Highland, Ind., 1970—. Served as lt. (j.g.) USNR, 1944-47. Decorated 5 Bronze Stars. Rotarian. Club: Gary Country. Home: 530 W 56th Pl Merrillville IN 46410 Office: 9001 Indianapolis Blvd Highland IN 46322

LENNON, DELORES RAE FRANCISCO, tchr. aide, wig and make-up artist; b. Mpls., July 11, 1940; d. Clarence Frank and Ruth Evelyn (Hayden) Francisco; student Macalester Coll., 1958, Minn. Sch. Bus., Ritter's Beauty Sch., 1960, Rasmussen Sch. Bus. (Bus. and Profl. Women's Found. grant), 1969; B.S. in Elementary Edn. (fed. grants), U. Minn., 1974, postgrad., 1974—; postgrad. U. Newcastle (Eng.), 1977-78; m. John Wermuth Lennon, Oct. 28, 1961 (div.); children—Gretchen Anne, John Edward; m. 2d, Morris L. Paterson, Feb. 8, 1975 (dec. May 1976). Telephone operator Northwestern Bell Co., 1956-57; instr. Sillouette Figure Form Internat., 1958; swimmer Water Ballet Corps Al Sheehan's Aqua Follies, summers 1957-59; sec., receptionist Mpls. Woman's Club, 1958; Hotel Pick-Nicollet, Mpls., 1958, Hotel Leamington, Mpls., 1959; pvt. sec. Home of the Good Shepherd, St. Paul, 1960; hairdresser Ritter's Beauty Shop, St. Paul, 1961; asst. wig maker Tyrone Guthrie Theatre, Mpls., 1968-69; tchr. Pine Point Exptl. Indian Sch., Pondsford, Minn., 1976; sec., receptionist St. Paul Pub. Schs., also tchr. aide; free-lance wig and make-up artist; drama resource tchr. Blake Schs., Hopkins, Minn., 1974-75; founder Delores Unltd., Inc.; artist, arts adminstr. Community Programs in Arts and Scis. Vol. United Fund, 1965; model Goodwill Aux.; leader Camp Fire Girls; co-chmn. Tyrone Guthrie Theatre Teen Bd., 1964-65. Mem. Gallanteers Minn. Mus. Art, Puppeteers Am., Internat. Juggler's Assn., Mpls. Soc. Fine Arts, Walker Art Center, Nat. Soc. Lit. and Arts, Met. Children's Theatre Assn. (v.p.), Nat. Assn. Gifted Children, Am. Orff-Schulwerk Assn., Minn. Assn. Edn. Young Children, NOW, Minn. Edn. Assn., Nat. Soc. Lit. and Arts, Nat. Council Tchrs. English, League Women Voters (del. Met. council 1963-66), Minn. Woman's Polit. Caucus, Minn. Sci. Fiction Soc., Internat. Platform Assn., Minn. Civil Liberties Union, Nat. Consortium Options Pub. Edn., Phi Beta Kappa, Phi Beta (grantee), Phi Delta Kappa. Unitarian. Home and Office: 1867 Princeton Ave Saint Paul MN 55105

LENNOX, MARJORIE ELIZABETH, govt. ofcl.; b. Omaha, Sept. 10, 1938; d. George Banks and Viola Marjorie (Richards) Lennox; B.S. in Edn., U. Nebr., Lincoln, 1962, M.A., 1970. Tchr. Omaha elementary pub. schs., 1962-71; real estate salesman Grice and Co., Omaha, 1968-71; equal opportunity specialist Omaha area office Dept. Housing and Urban Devel., 1972—. Treas. Omaha chpt. Links, Inc., 1969-75, chairperson constn. com. Central Links, Inc., 1973-74, Central area rep. research com. nat. orgn., 1969-70. Dist. rep. Nebr. Democratic Conv., 1967; mem. Omaha Charter Revision Conv., 1973. Bd. dirs. Danner Meml. Children's Center, 1971-72, Girls Club Omaha, 1973—. Fellow Tri-Univ. Project Elementary Edn./English; recipient certificate of award Central Area Links, 1972. Mem. Am. Acad. Polit. and Social Scis., Am. Soc. Pub. Adminstrn., Conf. Minority Pub. Adminstrs., Internat. Platform Assn., Nat. Assn. Human Rights Workers, Nat. Assn. Real Estate Brokers, Nat. Assn. Women Deans, Adminstrs. and Counselors, ACLU, Nat. Urban League, NAACP, Nat. Fedn. Settlements and Neighborhood Centers. Episcopalian (deacon). Author: Education for the '70's, 1970. Home: 722 JE George Blvd Omaha NE 68132 Office: 7100 W Center Rd Omaha NE 68106

LENNOX, RAND TRU, clothing mfg. co. exec.; b. Cleve., Jan. 20, 1944; s. Richard Theodore and Mary Rose (Felber) L.; B.S. in Econs., John Carroll U., 1965; m. Leilani M. Petrovich, Aug. 28, 1965; children—Heather, Rand, Richard, David. Systems programming mgr. Bobbie Brooks, Inc., Cleve., 1971-73, dir. data processing and planning, 1973-76, dir. mgmt. info. services, 1976—. Served with U.S. Army, 1966-67. Mem. Am. Mgmt. Assn., Mensa. Roman Catholic. Club: K.C. Home: 6793 Brandywine Rd Parma Heights OH 44130 Office: 3830 Kelley Ave Cleveland OH 44114

LENOX, RICHARD LOUIS, mfg. co. exec.; b. Piqua, Ohio, May 26, 1924; s. Roy Laverne and Anna Marie (Schulz) L.; B.M.E., U. Cin., 1949; m. Mildred Elaine Puthoff, Sept. 25, 1949; children—Elizabeth E., Barbara E., Marcia A. Asst. supt. power and maintenance Hobart Corp., Troy, Ohio, 1949-56, dir. facilities engring., 1959—; plant engr. John Oster Mfg. Co., Milw., 1956-59. Served with U.S. Navy, 1944-45. Registered profl. engr., Ohio. Mem. Troy C. of C., Ohio Mfrs. Assn., Pi Tau Sigma, Tau Beta Pi. Republican. Club: Dolphin Swim (dir. 1971-73). Home: 1450 Cornish Rd Troy OH 45373 Office: 711 World Headquarters Ave Troy OH 45374

LENTFER, RICHARD HERMAN, realtor; b. Chgo., Apr. 19, 1936; s. Herman Henry and Elsie Elizabeth (Michaelis) L.; m. Sharon Louise Davis, Sept. 13, 1959; children—Sheryl Lynn, Susan Elizabeth; A.A., Thornton Jr. Coll., 1957. Mgr., v.p. Braun & Aldridge, Inc., Orland Park, Ill., 1959-65; owner, pres. Rich Constrn. Co., Orland Park, 1965-72; owner, pres. Rich Real Estate, Inc., Orland Park, 1969—. Pres., chmn. bd. dirs. Orland Park Crusade of Mercy. Licensed real estate broker, Ill. Mem. Nat., Ill. assns. realtors, Realtors Nat. Mktg. Inst., Southwest Suburban Bd. Realtors (pres. 1978, dir., Realtor of Year 1975), Southwest Suburban Multiple Listing Service, Internat. Real Estate Fedn., Ill. Farm and Ranch Multiple Listing Service, Ill. Farm and Ranch Assn. Realtors, All Points Relocation Service, Soc. Real Estate Appraisers (asso.), Profl. Real Estate Brokers Assn., Orland Park (pres., dir.), Palos Heights (pres., dir.) chambers commerce. Clubs: Orland Park Lions Orland Park Rotary Club (pres., dir.), Southwest Suburban Shrine, Medina Temple Shrine. Office: 14340 La Grange Rd Orland Park IL 60462 also 7001 W 127th St Palos Heights IL 60463

LENTZ, DANIEL MARVIN, application engr.; b. Milw., July 24, 1949; s. Frank Hugo and Arlyne Dorothy (Caspary) L.; B.S. in Engring. with honors, U. Wis., Milw., 1971, M.S., 1972. Teaching and project asst. U. Wis., Milw., 1971-73; engr. Hatco Corp., Milw., 1974; exec. dir. Wis. chpt. Am. Inst. Aero. and Astronautics, Milw., 1974-77; application engr. Vilter Mfg. Corp., Milw., 1977—; speaker before community groups on space exploration; chmn. Dividends from Space. Recipient numerous citations Am. Inst. Aero. and Astronautics. Asso. fellow British Interplanetary Soc.; mem. Am. Inst. Aero. and Astronautics, Royal Aero. Soc., Dividends from Space, Am. Soc. for Aerospace Edn., Am. Soc. for Engring. Edn., Soc. for Tech. Communications, Am. Soc. of Heating, Refrigeration and Air Conditioning Engrs., ASME, Am. Inst. Chem. Engrs., German Rocket Soc., The World Future Soc., Phi Kappa Phi, Tau Beta Pi. Roman Catholic. Author mgmt. guidebooks for Wis. tech. socs.; contbr. articles on space exploration to newspapers. Home: 3228 N 26th St Milwaukee WI 53206 Office: 2217 S 1st St Milwaukee WI 53207

LENTZ, JAY ALDEN, psychologist, educator; b. Kansas City, Mo., July 15, 1943; s. George Arthur and Eunice Rachel (Keith) L.; A.B., U. Mo., Columbia, 1965, M.A. in Edn., U. Mo., 1970, M.A. in Clin. Psychology, 1971, M.A. in Counselor Edn., 1974, Ph.D. in Counselor Edn., 1977; m. Julia Jayne Almack, Feb. 9, 1974. Tchr. trainee Peace Corps Liberia Project, 1965-66; mgmt. trainee, supr. Allstate Ins. Co., 1967-68; tchr. Kansas City (Mo.) Sch. Dist., 1968-70; grad. research asst., office of med. edn. Sch. Medicine, U. Mo., Kansas City, 1971-72, research asso., office med. edn., 1972, adminstrv. asso., asso. dir. student affairs, office of dean, 1972-73, coordinator employee tng. and devel., 1973-75, edn. coordinator Center for Mgmt. Devel., Sch. of Adminstrn., 1975—; pvt. practice counseling and cons. psychologist, Kansas City, 1971—. Mem. Am. Personnel and Guidance Assn., Am. Psychol. Assn., Am. Soc. for Tng. and Devel., Internat. Transactional Analysis Assn., Orgn. Devel. Network. Home: Route 1 M68 Lake Lotowana MO 64063 Office: 5347 Rockhill Rd Kansas City MO 64110

LENZ, RALPH CHARLES, JR., adminstrv. aero. engr.; b. Beatrice, Nebr., Oct. 27, 1919; s. Ralph Carl and Lois Elsie (Sutliff) L.; B.S. in Aero. Engring., U. Cin., 1943; M.S. (Sloan fellow), Mass. Inst. Tech., 1959; m. Mary Ellen Stone, Feb. 5, 1945; children—Lois Ellen, Linda Ann. Aero. engr. Glenn L. Martin Co., Omaha, 1943-45; aero. engr. U.S. Air Force, Wright Patterson AFB, Ohio, 1947-53, chief, plans div., aero systems div., 1954-74; sr. research engr. U. Dayton (Ohio) Research Inst., 1974—; lectr., cons. tech. forecasting. Served as aero. engr. USAAF, 1945-46. Mem. Air Force Assn. (Aerospace Power award 1974), Am. Inst. Aeros. and Astronautics, World Future Soc., Sigma Xi. Co-founder, editor Technol. Forecasting and Social Change, 1969. Home: 895 Meadow Ln Xenia OH 45385 Office: Univ Dayton Dayton OH 45469

LENZO, ANTHONY SAMUEL, educator, interior designer; b. East Chicago, Jan. 22, 1925; s. Carmelo and Antonia Lenzo; B.S., Ind. U., 1949, M.S., 1961; Ed.D., Nova U., 1975; m. Valerie Zawada, Oct. 10, 1968; children—Anthony Joseph, Julianne Marie, Holly Marie. Mgr. bus. and advt. Our Sunday Visitor, Gary, Ind., 1955-67; communications media cons. N.Y.C. and Chgo., 1954-56; radio-TV producer Kenyon & Eckhart Advt. Agy., Chgo., 1956-57; coordinator resource learning center Gary (Ind.) Pub. Schs., 1957-62; dir. instructional media East Chicago (Ind.) Pub. Schs., 1972-77; cons. vocat. resources, 1977—; pres. Crown Point Creative Interiors, Inc., Crown Point, 1977—. Pres., East Chicago Community Council, 1973-77; sec. Riley Cultural and Arts Assn., 1972—; pres. East Chicago Hist. Soc., 1976; mem. exec. bd. Nat. Council Encouragement Patriotism. Served with AUS, 1943-46, 49-52, Col. Res. Recipient Nat. Tchrs. medal Freedoms Found., 1965; named Ind. Mr. Patriot, Ind. State Legislature, 1976. Mem. Gary Fedn. Tchrs. (trustee), North-West Ind. Council Tchrs. Unions (pres.), Mil. Order World Wars, Res. Officers Assn., Gary Assn. Childhood Edn. (chmn. publicity), Assn. Ednl. Communications Tech., Nat. Ednl. Broadcasters Assn., Am. Legion (awards chmn.), Phi Delta Kappa (sec.). Roman Catholic. Clubs: Elks, Lions (dir.). Home: 8425 Morse Pl Crown Point IN 46307 Office: 210 E Columbus Dr E East Chicago IN 46312

LEON, ARTHUR SOL, cardiologist; b. Bklyn., Apr. 26, 1931; s. Alex and Anne (Schrek) L.; B.S. with honors in Chemistry, U. Fla., Gainsville, 1952; M.S. in Biochemistry, U. Wis., Madison, 1954, M.D., 1957; m. Gloria Rakita, Dec. 23, 1956; children—Denise, Harmon, Michelle. Intern, Henry Ford Hosp., Detroit, 1957-58; fellow internal medicine Lahey Clinic, Boston, 1958-60; fellow cardiology U. Miami (Fla.) Sch. Medicine, Jackson Meml. Hosp., Miami, 1960-61; chief gen. medicine, cardiology, dir. intern edn. 34th Gen. U.S. Army Hosp., Orleans, France, 1961-64; research cardiologist Walter Reed Army Inst. Research, Washington, 1964-67; dir. Hoffmann-La Roche Clin. Pharmacology Research Unit, Newark (N.J.) Beth Israel Med. Center, 1969-73; instr. dept. medicine Coll. Medicine and Dentistry N.J., Newark, 1967-69, asst. prof., 1969-72, asso. prof., 1972-73; asso. prof. cardiology and clin. pharm., physiol. hygiene, nutrition and physiology Med. Sch. and Sch. Pub. Health, U. Minn., Mpls., 1973—; dir. grad. studies, applied research and labs., lab. physiol. hygiene U. Minn., 1973—; col., chief cardiology 5501 U.S. Army Hosp., Ft. Snelling, Minn., 1973—; mem. Med. Evaluation Team Gemini and Apollo Projects, Washington, 1964-67. Served with M.C., U.S. Army, 1961-67. Recipient Amos Alonzo Stagg Phys. Fitness medal, 1963; Am. Heart Assn. fellow, 1960-61. Fellow Am. Coll. Cardiology, Am. Coll. Chest Physicians, Am. Coll. Clin. Pharm., N.Y. Acad. Sci., Am. Coll. Sports Medicine (trustee 1976-78, v.p. 1977-78); mem. Am. Physiol. Soc. Clin. Pharm. and Therapeutics, Am. Heart Assn., Am. Fedn. Clin. Research, Am. Soc. Biol. and Exptl. Therapeutics, Phi Beta Kappa, Phi Kappa Phi. Jewish. Contbr. articles in field of exercise physiology, exercise in prevention, treatment of coronary heart disease, cardiology, biochemistry, clin. pharmacology to med. jours., books. Participant White House Conf. Health and Physical Activity, 1976. Home: 9701 Oak Ridge Trail Minnetonka MN 55343 Office: Lab Physiol Hygiene U Minn Stadium Gate 27 Minneapolis MN 55455

LEONARD, ALBERT EDWIN, dentist; b. Columbus, Ohio, May 1, 1920; s. Walter Adelbert and Belma Ruth (Brown) L.; B.A., Ohio Wesleyan U., 1942; D.D.S. cum laude, Ohio State U., 1954; m. Helen Margaret Haney, Oct. 12, 1946; children—Beverly (Mrs. Vernon Reding), Barbara (Mrs. Jeffrey Jones). Gen. practice dentistry, Logan, Ohio, 1954—; dir. Citizens Bank of Logan; chief dental staff Hocking Valley Community Hosp., 1973—. Served to capt. USMCR, 1942-46. Mem. Am., Ohio dental assns., Hocking Valley Dental Soc. (pres. 1966-67), Delta Dental Plan Ohio (trustee), Phi Delta Theta, Delta Sigma, Omicron Kappa Upsilon. Republican. Methodist (chmn. council ministries 1969-70). Rotarian. Clubs: Hocking Hills Country (pres. 1967). Home: 143 Wilson Ave Logan OH 43138 Office: 8 E Hunter St Logan OH 43138

LEONARD, ARCHIBALD THANE, cons. psychologist; b. Vermontville, Mich., Oct. 21, 1917; s. Archie George and Mable Groves (Cook) L.; B.S., Wayne State U., 1941, M.A., 1946; postgrad. Mich. State U., 1946-48; m. Anne B. Cronick, Oct. 12, 1957. Chief psychologist Grand Rapids (Mich.) Child Guidance Clinic, 1948-58; cons. psychologist, North Muskegon, Mich., 1958—. Cons. to pvt. agys., local and state govt. agys. Host, moderator ednl. series WGRD radio sta., Grand Rapids, 1950-52; host drug abuse informational series WMKG-TV sta., Muskegon, 1968; host mental health info. series WMUS radio sta., Muskegon, 1962-64. Chmn. bd. Lincoln Found., Grand Rapids, 1950-56. Mem. Am., Mich. psychol. assns., Mich. Soc. Cons. Psychologists, Nat. Rehab. Soc., Mich. State Med. Soc. Home: 302 3rd St North Muskegon MI 49445 Office: 435 Whitehall Rd North Muskegon MI 49445

LEONARD, GEORGE ADAMS, grocery chain exec.; b. Clinton, Iowa, June 16, 1924; s. George Tod and Lola Francis (Follett) L.; m. Ella Viola Converse, Nov. 5, 1948; children—Carolyn C., George Tod, Craig C., Julie A.; A.B., U. Mich., 1946, J.D., 1951. Admitted to Mich. bar, Ohio bar; asso. firm Slyfield, Hartman, Reitz & Tate; atty. Kroger Co., Cin., 1956-59, asst. sec., 1959-60, supervising atty., 1960-63, gen. atty., 1963-69, v.p., 1969-70, sec., gen. counsel, 1970—. Served with USAF, 1942-46. Decorated DFC, Air Medal. Mem. Am., Mich., Ohio, Cin. bar assns., Queen City Club, Kenwood Country

Club. Home: 10307 Crestwind Circle Cincinnati OH 45242 Office: Kroger Co 1014 Vine St Cincinnati OH 45201

LEONARD, HARRY ELVIN, indsl. relations cons.; b. Ottowa, Ill., Mar. 5, 1899; s. Andrew and Hannah (Weberg) L.; student U. Minn., 1920-21; m. Louise Anne Olson, May 13, 1940; children—Terri Lou (Mrs. Gordon Buhrer), Jacqueline Lee (Mrs. Robert Posner). With No. States Power Co., Mpls., 1923-40; asst. bus. mgr. Local 160 Internat. Brotherhood Elec. Workers, Mpls., 1940-41, union organizer, 1942-43, bus. mgr., 1944-64; maintenance supr. East Side Neighborhood Services, Mpls., 1966-67; indsl. relations cons. Minn. Nurses Assn., St. Paul, 1968—; arbitrator for pub. employees of State of Minn., 1973—. Dir., Service Savs. and Loan Assn., St. Paul, 1956-66; instr. labor relations U. Minn. Evening Sch., 1950-51. Mem. exec. com. Citizens League Greater Mpls., 1953-54; mem. staff Coummunity Chest, Mpls. 1944; commr. Mpls. Charter Commn., 1958-70, chmn., 1963-64. Chmn. 3d Ward Democratic Farmer Labor Club, 1941-46; del. Dem. Nat. Conv., 1948. Bd. dirs. Hennepin County Cancer Soc., 1959-71, hon. life mem., 1971—, 2d v.p., 1963-66. Served with U. S. Army, 1918. Named Labor Man of Year Mpls. Jr. C. of C., 1958. Mem. Amicus, Assn. for Non-Smokers Rights. Unitarian. Mason (Shriner), Eagle (life). Home: 2939 Grand St NE Minneapolis MN 55418 Office: 1821 University Ave St Paul MN 55104

LEONARD, LEO DONALD, ednl. sociologist; b. Salt Lake City, Nov. 23, 1938; s. Leo Bradford and Florence (Robbins) L.; B.S., U. Utah, 1961, student U. Wash., 1961-62, 64-65; M.S., Utah State U., 1967, Ed.D., 1969; m. Marilynn Rae Hoyt, Jan. 2, 1962; 1 son, Richard Corey. Acting head King County Dept. Mental Health and Adoptions, Seattle, 1962; dir. programs and youth Snoline YMCA, Seattle, 1962-64; instr. Shorecrest High Sch., 1967-68, Roy (Utah) High Sch., 1966-67; instr. ednl. sociology Utah State U., 1968-69; prof. edn. U. Toledo, 1969—; univ. coordinator Catholic Diocese of Toledo Curriculum Devel. Project, 1970-75; coll. dir. Canadian Dissemination Project, 1971-74; bd. dirs. Internat. Tchrs. Edn. Council, 1970—. Bd. dirs. Toledo Symphony Orch., 1970—. Fellow Internat. Tchr. Edn. Council, 1971—; Fulbright scholar, Africa, 1967; grantee U.S. Office Edn-Tchr. Corps, 1970, many others. Mem. Am. Assn. Individual Guided Edn., Am. Edn. Research Soc., Comparative Edn. Soc. U.S., Comparative Edn. Soc. Can., Phi Kappa Phi, Phi Alpha Theta, Phi Delta Theta. Author: (with Robert T. Utz) The Building Skills for Competency Based Teaching, 1974, The Foundations of Competency Based Education, 1975, A Competency Based Curriculum, 1971; (with others) 7 instructors guides for individually guided edn.; contbr. articles to profl. jours. Home: 4643 Sheringham Ln Sylvania OH 43560 Office: Coll Edn U Toledo Toledo OH 43606

LEONARD, PAUL JAMES, welding accessory mfg. co. exec.; b. Bristol, Va., Sept. 6, 1913; s. Isaac G. and Nancy (Davis) L.; student DeForests Sch. Radio, 1931-32, Bryant and Stratton Sch. Bus., 1939-40; m. Jane A. McKee, Oct. 13, 1938; children—Angeline Jane (Mrs. Thomas Kregel) Paul Andrew, Nancy Sue, Cynthia, Mark. Announcer, Sta. WOPI, Bristol, 1932-36; radio and air operations Am. Airline, Inc., 1936-40; airline dispatcher All Am. Aviation, Inc., Pitts., 1940-41; exec. sec. Egg Driers, Inc., Cedarburg, Wis., 1941-43; mng. partner Absogood Packing Co., Jackson Mo., 1943-47; pres. Wagner Mfg. Co. (now Lenco, Inc.), Jackson, 1948—, also dir.; pres. Redarco, Inc.; dir. Lenco Welding Accessories, Ltd., Windsor, Ont., Can., Lenco de Mexico, S.A., Monterrey. Commr., Boy Scouts Am., Jackson. Mayor of Jackson (Mo.); non-partisan candidate for gov. of Mo. Served with AUS, 1944-45. Mem. Am. Welding Soc. (sustaining), Jackson C. of C., Internat. Platform Assn. (bd. govs.), Am. Assn. Mental Deficiency. Methodist. Mason (320, Shriner), Rotarian (past pres. Jackson). Home: 823 E Washington St Jackson MO 63755 Office: 319 W Main St Jackson MO 63755

LEONARD, ROY JUNIOR, educator; b. Central Square, N.Y., Aug. 17, 1929; s. Roy Jackson and Margaret Elizabeth (Keller) L.; B.S., Clarkson Coll. Tech., 1952; M.S., U. Conn., 1954; postgrad. Mich. State U., 1954-55; Ph.D., Iowa State U., 1958; m. Edith Campbell Gilmore; children—Robert J., Constance J. Asst. prof. civil engring. U. Del., Newark, 1957-59; asso. prof. civil engring. Lehigh U., Bethlehem, Pa., 1959-65; spl. projects engr. Dames and Moore, geotech. cons., N.Y.C., 1965; prof. civil engring. U. Kans., Lawrence, 1965—. Cons. E.H. Richardson & Asso., Newark, Del., 1957-65, Kansas City (Mo.) Testing Lab., 1967—, Burns & McDonnell, Kansas City, 1967—. NSF fellow, 1963-65. Registered profl. engr., N.Y., Pa., Kans., Mo. Fellow ASCE; mem. Assn. Engring. Geologists, Soc. Mining Engrs., Am. Soc. Engring. Edn., Chi Epsilon. Episcopalian. Home: Route 4 Box 241 Lawrence KS 66044

LEONARD, THEODIS RAYMOND, elementary sch. tchr.; b. Schlater, Miss., Feb. 3, 1934; s. Joseph Richard and Lelia Alvenia (Williams) L.; A.A., Crane Jr. Coll., 1961; B.Ed., Chgo. Tchr.'s Coll., 1965, M.S.Edn. in Sch. Guidance, 1975; m. Essie Mae Tate, Dec. 26, 1957; children—Doris Renee, Valerie Faye, Theodis Raymond Jr., Curtis Allan. Maintenance man Wieboldt Stores, Evanston, Ill., 1958-59, Plastic Contact Lens, 1959-65; tchr. pub. elementary schs., Chgo., 1965—, tchr. reading, 1969-71, co-author gifted disadvantaged program, 1971—. Mem. Lawndale Community Council. Served with USAF, 1953-57. Recipient certificate commendation Ill. Office Edn., 1973, tchr. of yr. Gregory Sch., 1974, parent of yr. Corkery Sch., 1977; Northeastern Ill. U. fellow, 1971. Mem. Assn. for Gifted, Am. Personnel Guidance Assn., Chgo. Tchrs. Union, Marcy Newberry Assn. (dir.). Methodist. Home: 4111 W 21st Pl Chicago IL 60623 Office: 3715 W Polk St Chicago IL 60624

LEONIDA, DOMINGO DOMINIC JOSEPH, physician; b. Honolulu, July 3, 1927; s. Fernando Gabriel and Fortunata (Ragas) L.; B.S., Marquette U., 1951; M.S., U. Cin., 1953, M.D., 1959; M.P.H., U. Mich., 1962; m. Madelaine Ching Hua Kao, Aug. 7, 1954; children—Mark Huaming Patrick, Clara HuaCin Catherine. Intern, Mercy Hosp., Toledo, Ohio, 1959-60; resident U. Mich. Hosp., Ann Arbor, 1961-62; research biochemist U.S. Indsl. Chem. - Nat. Distillers Corp., Cin., 1955-56; epidemiologist Ohio Dept. Health, Columbus, 1962-64, chief chronic diseases, 1964-65; mem. staff Physicians Alcohol Inst. Studies, Rutgers U., New Brunswick, N.J., 1964; med. dir. immunol. activities and grants, epidemiologist N.Y. Dept. Health, Albany, 1964-67; med. dir. Skokie (Ill.) Health Dept., 1967-69, Kenosha (Wis.) Health Dept., 1969-71; family practice, indsl. practice medicine, Lincoln, Ill., 1971—; instr. Coll. Medicine, Ohio State U., 1963-64, spl. edn. Ill. State U., 1973-74, coll. medicine, U. Ill., Peoria, 1971-77; mem. staff Meth. Hosp., Peoria, Pekin (Ill.) Hosp., Warner Hosp., Clinton, Ill. Chmn. camping health safety coms. Kenosha council Boy Scouts Am., 1970-71. Served with M.C., U.S. Army, 1946-48, M.C., USN, 1960-61. Mental health profl., Hamilton, Ohio. Fellow Am. Coll. Preventive Medicine, Am. Acad. Family Practice; mem. AAAS, Ecol. Soc. Am., AMA, Ill. State, Logan County Med. Socs., Am. Heart Assn. (Chgo. Br.), N.Y. Pub. Health Assn. Roman Catholic. Club: Rotary (Skokie, Ill., 1967-69, Kenosha, Wis., 1969-71, Peoria/Pekin, Ill., 1971-73). Contbr. articles to med. jours. Home and Office: 42 Northbrook St Lincoln IL 62656

LEPARD, CECIL WARD, physician; b. Otsego, Mich., Sept. 11, 1901; s. Warren Ward and Daisy (O'Fallen) L.; A.B., U. Mich., 1924, M.D., 1928; m. Elisabeth Fikes, June 20, 1940; 1 dau., Robin (Mrs. Jorg Lehnert). Resident U. Mich. Med. Center, Ann Arbor, 1928-32; practice medicine specializing in ophthalmology, Detroit, 1932-73, Grosse Pointe, Mich., 1954—; ophthalmologist-in-chief Children's Hosp. of Mich., Detroit, 1946-69; mem. staffs Jennings Meml. Hosp., Detroit, Bon Secours Hosp., Grosse Pointe; instr. U. Mich., Ann Arbor, 1930-32; clin. prof. ophthalmology Wayne State U., Detroit, 1946-73; instr. Am. Acad. Ophthalmology & Otolaryngology, 1946-71. Mem. Mich. Opthalmological Soc. (founder, pres. 1946-47), Detroit Med. Club (pres. 1968), Am. Acad. Opthalmology & Otolaryngology. Clubs: Country of Detroit, Detroit Boat. Home: 237 Ridge Rd Grosse Pointe Farms MI 48236 Office: 413 Fisher Rd Grosse Pointe MI 48230

LEPLEY, DERWARD, JR., cardiovascular surgeon; b. Viola, Wis., Jan. 10, 1924; s. Derward and Eva (Blakeley) L.; M.D., Marquette U., 1949; m. Ardis Pobanz, June 12, 1949; children—Stephen, Larry, Diane, Heide. Rotating intern Wis. Gen. Hosp., Madison, 1949-50; resident in gen. surgery Wood VA Hosp., 1952-56, resident in thoracic surgery, 1956-58; research fellow Nat. Heart Inst., U. Minn., Mpls., 1958-59; practice medicine, specializing in cardiovascular surgery; faculty Marquette U., Milw., 1956-58, 59-70, asso. prof. surgery, 1963-68, prof. surgery, 1968-70, chmn. dept. thoracic-cardiovascular surgery, 1968-74; mem. staff Milw. County Hosp., 19—, chief of cardiovascular surgery, 1962-74; attending staff Milw. Children's Hosp., VA Hosp., chief thoracic-cardiovascular surgery St. Luke's Hosp., 1962-72; clin. prof. surgery Med. Coll. Wis., Milw., 1970—. Served with USN, 1941-45, USNR, 1950-52. Named Alumnus of the Year Marquette U., 1977, Alumnus of Year Marquette U. Alumni Assn., Wisconsite of Year Am. Broadcasting Assn. Diplomate Am. Bd. Surgery, Am. Bd. Thoracic Surgery. Fellow A.C.S.; mem. Am. Assn. Thoracic Surgery, Am. Coll. Cardiology, Am. Heart Assn., AMA, Am. Thoracic Soc., Central Surg. Assn., Milw. Acad. Medicine, Milw. Acad. Surgery, Milw. County, Wis. med. socs., Soc. Thoracic Surgeons, Soc. Univ Surgeons, Wis. Surg. Soc., Internat. Cardiovascular Soc. Am. Coll. Chest Physicians, Wis. Heart Assn. (past pres.). Contbr. numerous articles in med. jours. Home: 12600 W Stephen Pl Elm Grove WI 53122 Office: 9800 W Bluemound Rd Milwaukee WI 53226

LEPUCKI, RICHARD JOHN, elec. engr.; b. New Brunswick, N.J., Aug. 28, 1949; s. Peter and Edna (Garbosky) L.; B. Engring. with honors, Stevens Inst. Tech., 1971; postgrad., U. Akron, 1974-76. Elec. engr. Babcock and Wilcox Research Center, Alliance, Ohio, 1972—. Mem. IEEE. Designer research test facility, nuclear reactor emergency core coolant system, research facilities in nuclear safety and performance. Home: 721 Mill Circle Alliance OH 44601 Office: 1562 Beeson St Alliance OH 44601

LERNER, ALBERT MARTIN, physician, educator; b. St. Louis, Sept. 3, 1929; s. Bernard and Sarah L.; m. Helen Saperstein, June 1966; children—Joshua, Emily, Joel, Elizabeth; B.A., Washington U., St. Louis, 1950, M.D., 1954; intern Barnes Hosp., St. Louis, 1954-55, sr. asst. resident, 1958-59; asst. resident Boston City Hosp., 1957-58. Diplomate Am. Bd. Internal Medicine, Pan Am. Med. Assn. (life mem. 1968). Served as med. officer USPHS, 1955-57; sr. asst. surgeon, lab. investigator Nat. Inst. Allergy and Infectious Diseases, 1955-57; research fellow medicine Thorndike Meml. Lab., Boston City Hosp. and Harvard Med. Sch., 1959-62; fellow Med. Found. Greater Boston, Inc., 1960-63; research asso., dept. biology Mass. Inst. Tech., 1962-63; chief infectious diseases Detroit Gen. Hosp., 1963-73, asso. in medicine, 1963-65, asso. in pathology, 1964-65, dir. bacteriology lab., 1964-69, clin. cons., 1969—, attending active staff in medicine, 1965-67, cons. pathology, 1965—, sr. attending staff, 1967—; cons. infectious diseases VA Hosp., Allen Park, Mich., 1963—, Sinai Hosp. of Detroit, 1964—; mem. asso. staff Harper Hosp., Detroit, 1964-67, asso. physician, mem. teaching staff, 1967-74, mem. active staff, physician dept. medicine, sect. internal medicine, 1975; chief dept. medicine Hutzel Hosp., Detroit, 1970—; mem. cons. staff, dept. pediatric medicine Childrens Hosp. of Mich., 1971—; mem. ad hoc adv. com. Antiviral Substances Program, Nat. Inst. Allergy and Infectious Diseases, 1971; external reviewer for research grants Med. Research Council, Ottawa, Ont., Can., 1973; cons. Nat. Inst. Dental Research, 1974; asso. prof. medicine, chief div. infectious diseases Wayne State U. Sch. Medicine, 1963-67, asso. in microbiology, 1963—, asso. in pathology, 1964—, prof. medicine, chief div. infectious diseases, 1967—, Staff award by sr. class, 1974; prof. pro-tem, dept. medicine William Beaumont Army Med. Center, El Paso, Tex., 1974; invited lectr. Johann Wolfgang Goethe U., Oberursel, Germany, 1974; vis. prof. infectious diseases Cleve. Clinic, 1974; vis. prof. dept. medicine U. Pa., 1976; test com. for medicine Nat. Bd. Med. Examiners, 1971-74; allergy and infectious diseases tng. grant com. NIH, 1971-73; advisory com. Fedn. Am. Socs. Exptl. Biology. Fellow A.C.P. (govs. adv. com. Mich. 1974—, chmn. continuing edn. com. Mich. chpt. 1976—), Am. Coll. Clin. Pharmacology; mem. Am. Soc. for Microbiology, N.Y. Acad. Scis., Am. Fedn. for Clin. Research (pres. Ann Arbor-Detroit-Toledo-Lansing chpt. 1967-68), Infectious Diseases Soc. Am., Central Soc. for Clin. Research, Am. Soc. for Clin. Investigation, Am. Assn. Immunologists, Soc. for Exptl. Biology and Medicine, Am. Pub. Health Assn., Detroit Med. Club, Wayne County Med. Soc. (chmn. med. sect. 1970-72), Am. Assn. Physicians, Mich. Found. for Infectious Diseases (pres. 1976), Probus Club Detroit (5th Ann. award for acad. achievement 1967), Phi Lambda Kappa (award for outstanding contbn. to research, teaching and acad. medicine 1969). Asso. sci. editor Mich. Medicine, 1968-70; contbr. articles to profl. jours. Home: 3570 Tuckahoe St Birmingham MI 48010 Office: 4707 St Antoine St Detroit MI 48201

LERNER, ALFRED, real estate investor; b. N.Y.C., May 8, 1933; s. Abraham and Clara (Abrahamson) L.; B.A., Columbia, 1965; m. Norma Wokloff, Aug. 7, 1955; children—Nancy Faith, Randolph David. Sales rep. Broyhill Furniture Factories, 1957-58, Baumritter Corp., 1958-63; distbr. Bassett Furniture Co., 1963-65; pres. Randolph Distbg. Co., 1963-65; chmn., chief exec. officer Multi-Amp Corp., Dallas, Realty Refund Trust, Cleve., pres., chief exec. officer Refund Advisers, Inc., Mid-Am. Mgmt. Corp., partner Mid-Am. Cos., Cleve.; dir. Capital Nat. Bank. Served to 1st lt. USMCR, 1955-57. Mem. Young President's Orgn., Nat. Assn. Real Estate Investment Trusts. Jewish. Clubs: Beechmont, Commerce (Cleve.); Harmonie (N.Y.C.). Home: 18020 S Woodland Rd Shaker Heights OH 44120 Office: 1101 Euclid Ave Cleveland OH 44115

LERNER, LOUIS ABRAHAM, diplomat; b. Chgo., June 12, 1935; s. Leo Alfred and Deana (Duskin) L.; student U. Chgo., 1951-54, Scandinavian seminars, Copenhagen, Denmark, 1956-57; B.A., Roosevelt U., 1960; m. Susan Winchester, July 22, 1957; children—Lucy Alix, Jane Chelsea Reporter, North Town News Chgo., 1954-56; corr. Accredited Home Newspapers Am., Chgo., Copenhagen, 1956-58; exec. Lerner Home Newspapers Chgo., 1959—, publisher, 1969-77; U.S. ambassador to Norway, 1977—; dir. Myers Pub. Co., Lincoln-Belmont Pub. Co., pres. Lerner Suburban Communiciations. Mem. Nat. Commn. on Libraries and Information Sci., 1971—, Walker Art Center, Mpls., Chgo. Mus. Contemporary Art, Stedjelik Mus., Amsterdam. Bd. dirs. Chgo. Better Bus. Bur., Lyric Opera Guild, Suburban Newspaper Research Center, Suburban Newspapers Am.; bd. dirs., v.p. Chgo. Pub. Library. Recipient Pub. Service award Accredited Home Newspapers Am., 1960. Mem. North Town C. of C. (dir. 1963-65), Am. Acad. Polit. and Social Sci., A.L.A., Newspaper Soc. London, Web Offset Newspaper Assn. (London), Sigma Delta Chi. Democrat. Clubs: Headline, City (bd. govs. 1966-69) (Chgo.). Home: 442 W Wellington Chicago IL 60657 Office: Am Embassy Oslo Norway

LE ROY, GEORGE WILLARD, state hist. park supt., curator; b. Spokane, Wash., Sept. 26, 1920; s. George Washington and Geneva Alice (Grigware) LeR.; student numerous mil. schs., 1943-63; m. Gladys Pauline Petersen, Feb. 9, 1973; children by previous marriage—Cheryl (Mrs. Douglas Mill), Larry, Patricia (Mrs. Milton Hemingway). Active duty with Air Corps, AUS, 1942-63; head ranger Ocean City State Park, Aberdeen, Wash., 1963-64; dir. Buffalo Bill's Ranch, State Hist. Park, North Platte, Nebr., 1964—. Chmn., Cancer Drive, North Platte, 1970; co-chmn. Centennial Com., North Platte, 1973; mem. Greater Community Forum, North Platte, 1974-75; mem. Visit North Platte, Inc., 1974-75; co-chmn. Bi-Centennial Com., North Platte, 1975—; comdr. 4th Security Batallion, Nebr. State Guard, 1970-75. Recipient Eyes on Nebr. award Nebr. Optometric Assn., 1969; Col. of Cody Scouts Hon. Citation award City of North Platte, 1973; named Admiral, Nebr. Navy, 1950, 65. Mem. Am. Legion. Kiwanian (charter pres. 1964). Narrator weekly program radio sta. KODY, North Platte, 1964—. Address: Buffalo Bill's Ranch Rural Route 1 North Platte NE 69101

LEROY, ROBERT PIERRE, hotel exec.; b. Jersey City, Aug. 22, 1924; s. Elie Pierre and Helen (Wright) L.; student Loyola U., Los Angeles; m. Florence Simmons, June 15, 1957; children—Patria Anne, Robert David. Exec. Hilton Hotels Corp., 1952-61, Pick Hotels Corp., 1961-75; exec. v.p. hotel div. IDS Properties, Inc., 1976-77; v.p., gen. mgr. Drake Hotel, Chgo., 1977—. Served with USNR, 1942-46. Recipient Hall of Fame Hospitality Industry award, 1969; named Mr. Gourmet, 1969. Mem. Internat. Wine and Food Soc. (Chgo. and London), Postgrad. Wine Coll., Connoiseurs Internat., Culinary Inst. Am. (dir.). Home: Drake Hotel Apt 952 140 E Walton St Chicago IL 60611 Office: Drake Hotel 140 E Walton St Chicago IL 60611

LE SAGE, LEO GAY, nuclear engr.; b. Concordia, Kans., Apr. 15, 1935; s. Leo S. and Margaret Caroline (Gay) LeS.; B.S. in Engring. Physics, U. Kans., 1957; M.S. in Engring. Sci., Stanford U., 1962, Ph.D. in Nuclear Engring., 1966; m. Carolyn Lee Bailey, June 22, 1958; children—Annette Gay, Marietta Lee. Nuclear engr. div. applied physics Argonne (Ill.) Nat. Lab., 1966-73, program mgr., 1973—, asso. dir. div. applied physics, 1975—. Served with USN, 1957-61. AEC fellow, 1961-65. Mem. Am. Nuclear Soc. (nat. program com.). Methodist. Contbr. numerous articles on physics of fast breeder reactors to profl. publs. Home: 233 James Ln Naperville IL 60540 Office: Bldg 316 Argonne Nat Lab Argonne IL 60439

LESLIE, LOREN RICHARDSON, state health ofcl.; b. Chester, Iowa, Aug. 26, 1934; s. Carl William and Viola Mildred (Souhrada) L.; B.A., U. Minn., 1955, B.S., 1958, M.D., 1958; m. Arlene Sylvia Kivell, July 24, 1955; 1 son, Magnus Carl Loren. Intern, Mercy Hosp., Toledo, O., 1958-59; resident dept. phys. medicine U. Minn., 1963-65; with Olmsted Med. Group, Rochester, Minn., 1961-63; dir. Sister Kenny Inst., Mpls., 1967-73; pres. Am. Rehab. Found., Mpls., 1973-76; dir. chronic diseases Minn. Dept. Health, 1976—. Asst. clin. prof. U. Minn., 1965—. Mem. adv. council for mental health Minn. Dept. Pub. Welfare, 1969-70; mem. adv. com. for handicapped children Minn. Dept. Edn., 1970-71; mem. Pres.'s Com. on Employment of Handicapped, 1973-77. Bd. trustees Northlands Regional Med. Program, St. Paul, Mpls. Med. Center, Minn. Heart Assn., Minn. Cancer Council. Served with USNR, 1959-61. Diplomate Am. Bd. Phys. Medicine and Rehab. Mem. Am. Acad. Phys. Medicine and Rehab., Am. Coll. Hosp. Adminstrs. Home: 16248 Ringer Rd Wayzata MN 55391 Office: 717 Delaware SE Minneapolis MN 55440

LESLY, PHILIP, pub. relations counsel; b. Chgo., May 29, 1918; B.S. with honors, Northwestern U., 1940; m. Ruth Edwards, Oct. 17, 1940 (div. Dec. 1971); 1 son, Craig. Copywriter advt. dept. Sears Roebuck & Co., 1940-41; asst. dir. pub. relations Northwestern U., 1941-42; account exec. Theodore R. Sills & Co., Chgo., 1942-43, v.p., 1943-45, exec. v.p., 1945; dir. pub. relations Ziff-Davis Pub. Co., 1945-46; v.p. Harry Coleman & Co., 1947-49; pres. Philip Lesly Co., Chgo. and Toronto, 1949—; dir. Tisdall, Clark, Lesly & Partners (Toronto); lectr., speaker on pub. relations, pub. opinion, social dynamics. Bd. dirs. Nat. Safety Council, 1967-70; mem. Chgo. Crime Commn., 1977—. Mem. Pub. Relations Soc. Am. (Silver Anvil award 1946, 63, 66), Internat. Pub. Relations Assn. Club: Mid-Am. (Chgo.). Author: (with others) Public Relations: Principles and Procedures, 1945, Everything AND the Kitchen Sink, 1955; The People Factor, 1974; editor: Public Relations in Action, 1947; Public Relations Handbook, 1950; Lesly's Public Relations Handbook, 1971, 78; author bi-monthly jour. Managing the Human Climate, 1970; contbr. articles to U.S., Brit. and Canadian mags. Home: 155 Harbor Dr Chicago IL 60601 Office: 33 N Dearborn St Chicago IL 60602

LESNER, SAMUEL JOEL, columnist, critic; b. Chgo., Feb. 16, 1909; s. Jacob and Syma (Jenkins) L.; student Am. Conservatory Music, 1929-33; m. Esther M. Malkin, Apr. 6, 1941; children—Roberta L. (Mrs. Charles B. Bernstein), Judy Sue (Mrs. Robert L. Holstein). With Chgo. Daily News, 1928—, nightlife reviewer, 1941—, radio-TV columnist, also music and movie critic, 1945—. Tchr. recorder adult edn. program Chgo. YMCA, 1947—. Served with M.C., AUS, 1944-45. Mem. Chgo. Press Club, Sigma Delta Xi. Jewish (trustee temple). Home: 9230 Bennett Ave Chicago IL 60617 Office: Chgo Daily News 401 N Wabash Ave Chicago IL 60611

L'ESPERANCE, WILFORD LOUIS, economist; b. N.Y.C., Dec. 9, 1930; children—Annette, Suzanne, Claire, Wilford L.; A.B., Columbia Coll., 1951; M.S., Columbia U., 1952; Ph.D., U. Mich., 1963; m. Barbara Manochio, May 4, 1957. Math. analyst Ordnance Corps, U.S. Army Guided Missile Devel. Div., Huntsville, Ala., 1953-55; lectr. prins. of econs., bus. statistics, econ. history Ind. U., Ft. Wayne, 1956-60; mktg. research analyst Gen. Electric Co., N.Y.C., Ft. Wayne, 1952-53, 55-60, cons., 1965; research asst. dept. econs. U. Mich., 1961-63; economist Bur. Comml. Fisheries, Dept. Interior, Ann Arbor, Mich., 1962-63, cons., Sandusky, Ohio, 1963-65; asst. prof. dept. econs. Ohio State U., Columbus, 1963-66, asso. prof., 1966-70, prof., 1970—, instr. exec. devel. program Div. Continuing Edn., 1970-75; pres. Midwest Econometrics, Inc., Columbus, 1973—; cons. Indsl. Nucleonics Corp., Columbus, 1965, Dwight Spencer & Assos., 1966, Battelle Columbus Labs., 1967, 73, Ohio Dept. Econ. and Community Devel., 1967-70, 73, Convair div. Gen. Dynamics Corp., San Diego, 1969, Ohio Power Siting Commn., Columbus, 1974; mem. Gov.'s Task Force on Lake Erie Fishery, Ohio Dept. Natural Resources, 1973-74, Population Study Group of Environ. Health Com., Office Comprehensive Health Planning, Ohio Dept. Health, 1973-76. Tech. adv. group Mayor's Econ. Devel. Council, Columbus, 1975-77, panel econ. advisers for John Glenn, Ohio Democratic candidate for U.S. Senate, 1974. Bur. Comml. Fisheries Dept. Interior research grantee, 1963-64, Coll. Research Com., Coll. Commerce and Adminstrn. research grantee, 1965-66, Ohio Dept. Devel. research grantee, 1967-68, Coll. Research Com., Coll. Social and Behavioral Scis. research grantee, 1969, 76. Mem. Am. Econ. Assn., Am. Statis. Assn. (pres. Columbus chpt. 1968), Econometric Soc., Regional Sci. Assn., Ohio Assn. Economists and Polit. Scientists, Ohio Acad. Sci., AAUP, N.Y. State Soc. Cin., Ohio, Worthington hist. socs. Club: Hoover Yacht (fleet capt. 1972). Author: (with others) Columbus Area Economy-Structure and Growth, 1950-1985, 1966; Modern Statistics for Business and Economics, 1971; The Structure and Control of a State Economy, 1976; contbr. articles on econs. to profl. jours. Home: 296 Acton Rd Columbus OH 43214 Office: Ohio State U 1775 S College Rd Columbus OH 43210

LESSEN, GRACE LEOLA, librarian; b. Pleasant Plains, Ill.; d. William Alexander and Becky Ann (Haynes) Plunkett; A.A., Lincoln Coll., 1932; B.S., U. Ill., 1942, M.S., 1947, M.S. in L.S., 1962; postgrad. U. Ill., U. Chgo.; m. W.G. Lessen, Apr. 15, 1934; children—Larry, Sue Lessen Kanaby. Tchr., Logan County (Ill.) Rural Schs., 1930-39; tchr. English dept. Lincoln (Ill.) High Sch., 1953-54, Beason (Ill.) High Sch., 1955-66; asst. prof. English, Lincoln Coll., 1966-69, asst. librarian, 1969-70; instr. use of library facilities, asst. dir. learning center Spoon River Coll., Canton, Ill., 1970-72. Mem. Nat., Ill. edn. assns., Ill. Library Assn., Modern Lang. Assn., Assn. Coll. and Research Libraries, Ill. Assn. Sch. Librarians, AAUW (mem. state bd. on edn. 1949-55), Kappa Delta Pi. Methodist. Home: 707 N Union St Lincoln IL 62656

LESSEN, LARRY LEE, lawyer; b. Lincoln, Ill., Dec. 25, 1939; s. William G. and Grace L. (Plunkett) L.; B.A., U. Ill., 1960, LL.B., 1962; m. Susan M. Vaughn, Dec. 5, 1964; children—Laura, Lynn, William. Admitted to Ill. bar, 1962; practiced in Danville, 1962—; law clk. Fed. Dist. Ct., 1962-64; asso. firm Sebat, Swanson & Banks, 1967-68, partner, 1968—; asst. States Atty. Vermilion County, Ill., 1965-66; asst. Atty. Gen. Vermilion County, 1968-70; atty. City of Danville, 1970-73; U.S. magistrate, bankruptcy judge Eastern Dist. Ill., 1973—. Pres. Family Service Bur., Danville, 1972—, also dir. Mem. Am., Ill., Fed., Vermilion County bar assns., Nat. Conf. Bankruptcy Judges. Elk. Home: 21 Shady Ln Danville IL 61832 Office: 306 Adams Bldg Danville IL 61832

LESTER, ROBERT RIDENOUR, indsl. exec.; b. Denver, May 14, 1894; s. John Calvin and Kate Louisa (Ridenour) L.; Litt.B., Princeton, 1916; m. Ruth Flower, Sept. 26, 1925; s. Ruth (Mrs. R. Flower L. Hund), Virginia (Mrs. W.C. Buckner). Buyer, Ridenour Baker Wholesale Grocery Co., 1920-25; mgr. Mut. Transfer & Storage Co., 1921-25; asst. v.p. Fidelity Nat. Bank, 1926-33; bank liaison officer Mo. Fed. Housing Adminstrn., 1934-35; pres., chmn. bd., chief exec. officer Mut. Transfer Co., and successor firm KCTW Industries, Inc. and subsidiaries, Kansas City, Mo., 1937—. Trustee Elmwood Cemetery Soc. Mem. Am. Field Service, 1916-17. Served to lt. (j.g.) USN, 1917-18. Mem. Kansas City C. of C., Am. Warehouseman's Assn. Rotarian. Clubs: University, Kansas City Country. Home: 11131 Holly St Kansas City MO 64114 Office: 1701 Liberty St Kansas City MO 64102

LE TARTE, CLYDE EDWARD, univ. adminstr.; b. Muskegon, Mich., Aug. 22, 1938; s. Harold and Ellen Lucille (Bullman) LeT.; A.B., Hope Coll., 1960; M.A., Mich. State U., 1964; Ed.D. (Mott fellow), Mich. State U., 1969; m. Kathleen Coutlette, June 18, 1967; children—Richard Michael, Rhonda Lynn. Tchr., Mt. Morris (Mich.) Jr. and Sr. High Sch., 1960-63; dir. community edn. Muskegon Pub. Schs., 1965-67; cons. Mich. Dept. Edn., Lansing, 1967-69; prof. sch. adminstrn. Eastern Mich. U., Ypsilanti, 1969-77, asso. dean Grad. Sch., 1971-77; v.p. acad. affairs Triton Coll., River Grove, Ill., 1977—. Dir. Custom Mfg. Service, Inc. Mem. Nat. Community Edn. Assn. (pres. 1966-67, exec. sec. 1970-71), Mich. Pub. Sch. Adult Edn. Assn. (v.p. 1971), Mich. Community Sch. Edn. Assn. (dir. 1971), Mich. Council Grad. Deans (chmn. com. on post baccalaureate experiences 1974-77), Phi Delta Kappa. Presbyterian (elder). Author: (with Jack Minzey) Community Education: From Program to Process, 1972. Editorial bd. Community Edn. Jour., 1971—. Contbr. articles to profl. jours. Home: 663 Highland Glen Ellyn IL 60137

LETMAN, SLOAN TIMOTHY, III, lawyer, educator; b. Chgo., Aug. 4, 1947; s. Sloan Timothy and Amy Estelle (Branche) L.; B.A., Loyola U., Chgo., 1968, M.A., 1971; J.D., DePaul U., 1975; m. Clyniece L. Watson, July 7, 1973. Admitted to Ill. bar, 1977; community center asst. dir. Blessed Sacrament Parish, Chgo., 1967-68, coordinator day camp, 1968; instr. Resurection and Santa Maria Addolorata schs., Chgo., 1969; neighborhood worker Chgo. Dept. Human Resources 1969-70; lectr. Malcolm X Coll., Chgo., 1972-74; lectr. Loyola U., Chgo., 1972-74, prof. criminal justice, 1977—; lectr. citizen info. service League Women Voters, Chgo., 1972-74; supr. investigations Office Profl. Standards, Chgo., 1974-77. Bd. dirs. Hyde Park Community Conf., 1975-76; Catholic Interracial Council, 1970-74; mem. Council on Youth Ministry, Archdiocese of Chgo. Mem. Loyola Urban Studies Assn., Acad. Criminal Justice Scis., Soc. Police and Criminal Psychology (Ill. state coordinator, chmn. standing com. minorities), Ill. Athletic Club, Alpha Phi Alpha. Contbr. articles in field to profl. jours. Home: 1461 E 56th St Chicago IL 60637 Office: 820 N Michigan Ave Chicago IL 60611

LETTS, ROBERT MERVYN, orthopedic surgeon; b. Killarny, Man., Can., June 29, 1940; s. Alfred Cyril and Grace Elizabeth (Nicholson) L.; B.Sc., U. Man., 1964, M.D. with honors, 1964; M.Sc., Queens U., 1970; m. Marilyn Jones, May 21, 1964; children—Ian Michael, Eric Matthew. Intern St. Boniface Gen. Hosp., Winnipeg, Man., 1964-65; resident Nat. Def. Med. Center, Ottawa, Ont., Can., 1965-68; practice medicine, specializing in orthopedic surgery, Winnipeg, 1968—; orthopedist-in-chief Children's Hosp., Winnipeg, 1972—; asso. surgeon Shriners Hosp. for Crippled Children, Winnipeg; asst. prof. surgery U. Man., 1972—. Served with RCAF, 1965-68. Fellow Royal Coll. Surgeons (Can.). Home: 2575 Assiniboine Crescent Winnipeg MB Canada Office: Childrens Centre Bannatyne Ave Winnipeg 9 MB Canada

LETWENKO, EDWARD STANLEY JOHN, greeting card co. exec.; b. Chgo., Sept. 19, 1930; s. John and Rose (Czwakiel) L.; student Chgo. Acad. Fine Arts, 1946-49, Famous Artists, 1949-52, Harper Coll., 1969-70; m. Roberta Jean Alheim, July 7, 1956; children—Kathryn Elizabeth, Michael Paul. Advt. prodn. dept. Marshall Field & Co., Chgo., 1953-55; freelance fashion illustrator dept. stores, 1955-59; with United Card Co., Rolling Meadows, Ill., 1959-77, v.p., creative dir., 1960-77; creative dir. Gallant Greetings Corp., 1977—; graphic designer, art dir. Playboy Greeting Cards, 1975—. Cons. Nat. Paper Adv. Bd., 1970-71; illustrator children's books; creator syndicated comic strip. Mem. Artists Guild, Nat. Art Dirs. Club, Soc. Am. Artists, Soc. Typographic Arts. Home: 159 Jamison Ln Hoffman Estates IL 60172 Office: 2725 W Fullerton Ave Chicago IL 60647

LETZE, BERNARD JULIAN, air transp. service exec.; b. Watertown, S.D., July 8, 1927; s. Paul Bernard and Mable Sophia (Wangen) L.; student pub. schs.; m. Darlene E. Schaack, Feb. 9, 1952; children—Alan, Bonnie, Kay, Paula. Asst. pressman Watertown Pub. Opinion, 1944-45; asst. airport mgr. Watertown Municipal Airport, 1947-54, airport supt., 1954—. Mem. League Municipalities Airport Adv. Com., 1966—. Served with AUS, 1946-47. Mem. Am. Assn. Airport Execs. Home: Bldg 113 Airport Watertown SD 57201 Office: Airport Watertown SD 57201

LEUNG, MOW-WO, mech. design engr., restaurant exec.; b. Canton, China, Aug. 5, 1942; s. Yuen-Wing and Yuk-Wan (Chow) L.; came to U.S., 1969, naturalized, 1977; B.S. in Mech. Engring., Nat. Taiwan U., 1967; M.S. in Mech. Engring., U. Miss., 1973; m. Der-Ling Huah, Nov. 9, 1974; 1 son, Eric Hao-Ming. Programmer, U. Miss. Computer Center, 1971-73; owner Dragon House Chinese Restaurant, Oxford, Miss., 1972-75; partner King's Chop Suey, Chgo., 1976—, also mech. design engr. Cardwell Westinghouse Co., Chgo., 1974-78; mech. engr. U.S. Industries Co., Chgo., 1978—. Mem. ASME. Research on alternative method of solving problem of large deflections of nonlinear viscoelastic columns. Home: 10244 S 82d Ave Palos Hills IL 60465

LEUSCHEN, JAMES WALTER, telephone co. exec.; b. Panama, Iowa, Aug. 20, 1940; s. Walter N. and Cornelia M. (Hoffman) L.; A.B. in Polit. Sci., Creighton U., 1962; m. M. Patricia Oppold, June 8, 1963; children—Susan, Paul, Kate. Adminstrv. intern Internal Revenue Service, 1962; exec. sec. U.S. Civil Service Bd. of Examiners, 1963; trainee, mgmt. devel. program Northwestern Bell Telephone Co., Omaha, 1963, editorial asst., 1964, advt. and news supr., 1965-71, pub. info. supr., 1971-74, Nebr. pub. relations supr., 1974—. Vol. pub. relations cons. Met. YMCA, Henry Doorly Zoo, United Way, Joslyn Art Mus., Old West Trail Found., Nebr. Council on Econ. Edn.; bd. dirs. Nebr. Community Improvement Program. Co-recipient nat. award for best print advt. United Way, 1976; named Outstanding Young Omahan, Omaha Jr. C. of C., 1975. Mem. Pub. Relations Soc. Am. (accredited, dir. Nebr. chpt.), Nebr. Telephone Assn., Nebr. Press Assn., Omaha Press Club (dir.), Omaha Fedn. Advt. (dir.). Roman Catholic. Home: 5210 Davenport St Omaha NE 68132 Office: 100 S 19th St Omaha NE 68102

LEVANDOWSKY, ANTON DANILOVITCH, govt. ofcl.; b. Washington, Aug. 26, 1932; s. Daniel Wladimirvitch and Evelyn Isabel (Mooney) L.; student U. Md., 1950-52; A.B., Antioch Coll., 1958; M.A., U. Mich., 1959, M.P.H., 1972; m. Marcia Elizabeth Mathiasen, June 23, 1956; children—Darrel Andrew, Gregory Erik. Human factors specialist System Devel. Corp., Santa Monica, Calif., 1959-61; engring. psychologist Gen. Electric Co., Phila., 1961-62; sr. engr. Philco-Ford Corp., Palo Alto, Calif., 1962-64; ops. analyst Stanford Research Inst., Menlo Park, Calif., 1964-66; sr. systems analyst Litton Industries, Sunnyvale, Calif., 1966-68; sr. project analyst Serendipity, Inc., Los Altos, Calif., 1968-69; sr. research scientist Am. Insts. for Research, Pitts., 1969-72; asst. regional health adminstr. for planning and evaluation Region V, USPHS, HEW, Chgo., 1972—. Mem. Dist. 11 Bd. Edn., Medinah, Ill., 1977—. Served with USAF, 1955-56. Mem. Am. Pub. Health Assn., Am. Psychol. Assn., Human Factors Soc. (pres. San Francisco chpt. 1967-68). Home: 649 E Devon Ave Roselle IL 60172 Office: USPHS Region V US Dept Health Edn and Welfare 34th Floor 300 S Wacker Dr Chicago IL 60606

LEVANTROSSER, FREDERICK CARL, civil engr., automobile co. exec.; b. Detroit, Apr. 20, 1938; s. Frederick R. and Grace E, (Schroeder) L.; B.S., Wayne State U., 1960, M.S. in Civil Engring., 1967; M.B.A., Mich. State U., 1973; m. Barbara Chaplin, July 1, 1961; children—Laura Beth, Sandra Kay, Debra Sue. Civil engr. Gen. Motors Corp., Detroit, 1959-61; service engr. The Boeing Co., Seattle, 1961-63; civil project engr. Giffels & Rossetti, Detroit, 1963-64; sr. civil engr. Ford Motor Co., Dearborn, Mich., 1964-76, mgr. environ. control, utilities and fuel conservation, automotive assembly div., 1976—. Mem. founder's soc. Detroit Inst. Arts; benefactor Allen Park (Mich.) Symphony Orch.; mem. Duvall PTA. Recipient Am. Legion award, 1953; Boch and Lomb Sci. award, 1956. Registered profl. engr., Mich. Mem. Am. Soc. C.E., Wayne State U., Mich. State alumni assns. Phi Beta Kappa, Chi Epsilon. Mason (Shriner, 32 deg.). Author: Impact of Metrication on the Construction Industry, 1973. Home: 22834 Park Ave Dearborn MI 48124

LEVENFELD, MILTON ARTHUR, lawyer; b. Chgo., Mar. 18, 1927; s. Mitchell A. and Florence B. (Berman) L.; B.A., U. Chgo., 1947, J.D., 1950; m. Iona W. Wishner, Dec. 18, 1949; children—Barry, David, Judith. Admitted to Ill. bar, 1950; asso. firm David Altman, 1951-60; partner Altman, Levenfeld & Kanter, Chgo., 1961-64, Levenfeld, Kanter, Baskes & Lippitz, Chgo., 1964—; dir. Lawndale Trust & Savs. Bank. Bd. dirs. Spertus Coll. Judaica, Council Jewish Elderly, Jewish Fedn. Chgo.; co-gen. chmn. Chgo. Jewish United Fund, 1977—. Served with USNR, 1944-45. Mem. Am., Ill., Chgo. bar assns., Am. Technion Soc. Chgo. (dir.). Jewish. Writer, lectr. in fed. taxation. Home: 866 Stonegate Dr Highland Park IL 60035 Office: 10 S LaSalle St Chicago IL 60603

LEVER, ALVIN, architect, med. and sci. facilities devel. firm exec.; b. St. Louis, Jan. 27, 1939; s. Jack I. and Sabina (Vogel) L.; B.S. in Archtl. Scis., Washington U., St. Louis, 1961, B.Arch., 1963; postgrad. in Architecture for Civil Def. U. Mich., 1963; m. Norine Sue Schwedt, Jan. 27, 1963; children—Daniel Jay, Michael Leonard. Project architect firm Sir Basil Spence, Architect, Edinburgh, Scotland, 1963-65; v.p. med. facilities firm Hellmuth, Obata & Kassabuam, Inc., Architects, St. Louis, 1965-72; v.p. facility planning and adminstr. Michael Reese Med. Center, Chgo., 1972-74; v.p., gen. mgr. Apelco Internat. Ltd., Northbrook, Ill., 1974—. Archtl. critic U. Edinburgh, 1964-65, mem. lab. design commn., 1964-65; thesis adviser Washington U., 1968-69, guest lectr., 1968-69, speaker, mem. faculty conf. for med. facility design, 1973; mem. adv. bd. St. Louis Model Cities Program, 1966-67; cons. to industry on systems planning for hosps. Mem. rev. bd. Operation Breakthrough, St. Louis, 1969. Registered architect, Mo., Ill. Mem. A.I.A., Am. Hosp. Assn. (juror, exhibitor nat. annual archtl. exhibit 1969-74), Am. Assn. Hosp. Planners, No. Ill. Venture Assn., World Trade Council, Chgo. Assn. Commerce, Industry, Med. Research Inst. Council. Jewish religion. Club: Waukegan (Ill.) Yacht. Home: 1040 Ridgewood Dr Highland Park IL 60035 Office: 3192 Doolittle Dr Northbrook IL 60062

LEVI, EDWARD HIRSCH, atty. gen. U.S.; b. Chgo., June 26, 1911; s. Gerson B. and Elsa B. (Hirsch) L.; Ph.B., U. Chgo., 1932, J.D., 1935, L.H.D. (hon.); J.S.D. (Sterling fellow 1935-36), Yale U., 1938; LL.D., U. Mich., 1959, U. Calif. at Santa Cruz, Jewish Theol. Sem. Am., U. Iowa, Brandeis U., Lake Forest Coll., U. Rochester, U. Toronto, Yale U., U. Notre Dame, Denison U., U. Nebr., U. Miami, Boston Coll., Yeshiva U., Columbia, Dropsie U., U. Pa.; L.H.D., Hebrew Union Coll., DePaul U., Loyola U., Kenyon Coll., Bard Coll., Beloit Coll.; m. Kate Sulzberger, June 4, 1946; children—John, David, Michael. Admitted to Ill. bar, U.S. Supreme Ct. bar, 1945; asst. prof. U. Chgo. Law Sch., 1936-40, prof. law, 1945-75, 77—, dean, 1950-62, provost univ., 1962-68, univ. pres., 1968-75, pres. emeritus, 1975—, Karl Llewellyn Distinguished Service prof. (on leave), 1975-77, Glen A. Lloyd distinguished service prof., 1977—; atty. gen. U.S., 1975-77; Thomas Guest prof. U. Chgo., summer 1960, guest prof. U. Colo., summer 1960; past Benjamin N. Cardozo lectr., Randolph Tucker lectr.; spl. asst. to atty. gen. U.S., Washington, 1940-45; 1st asst. war div. Dept. Justice, 1943, 1st asst. antitrust div., 1944-45; chmn. interdeptl. com. on monopolies and cartels, 1944; counsel Fedn. Atomic Scientists with respect to Atomic Energy Act, 1946; counsel subcom. on monopoly power Judicary Com., 81st Congress, 1950. Mem. research advisory bd. Com. Econ. Devel., 1951-54; bd. Social Sci. Research Council, 1959-62, Council Legal Edn. and Profl. Responsibility, 1968-74; mem. Citizens Commn. Grad. Med. Edn., 1963-66, Commn. Founds. and Pvt. Philanthropy, 1969-70, Pres.'s Task Force Priorities in Higher Edn., 1969-70, Sloan Commn. Cable Communications, 1970, Nat. Commn. on Productivity, 1970-75, Nat. Council on Humanities. Hon. trustee U. Chgo.; trustee Internat. Legal Center, 1966-75, Woodrow Wilson Nat. Fellowship Found., 1972-75, Inst. Psychoanalysis Chgo., 1961-75, Urban Inst., 1968-75, Mus. Sci. and Industry, 1971-75, Russell Sage Found., 1971-75, Aspen Inst. Humanistic Studies, 1970-75, Inst. Internat. Edn. (hon.), 1969. Decorated Legion of Honor (France); recipient Distinguished Citizen award Ill. St. Andrews Soc., 1975, Fed. Bar Assn. award, 1975; Herbert H. Lehman Ethics medal Jewish Theol. Sem., Miami, Fla., 1976; Learned Hand medal for excellence in fed. jurisprudence Fed. Bar Council, N.Y.C., 1976; Wallace award Am.-Scottish Found., 1976; Morris J. Kaplun Meml. prize, 1976. Fellow Am. Acad. Arts and Scis., Am. Bar Found.; mem. Am., Ill., Chgo. bar assns., Am. Law Inst. (council), Am. Judicature Soc., Phi Beta Kappa, Order of Coif. Clubs: Century (N.Y.C.); Chgo., Comml., Standard, Quadrangle, Econ., Mid-Am. (Chgo.); Columbia Yacht; Cosmos (Washington). Author: Introduction to Legal Reasoning, 1949; Four Talks on Legal Education, 1952; Point of View, 1969; The Crisis in the Nature of Law, 1969; editor: Gilbert's Collier on Bankruptcy (with J. W. Moore), 1936; Elements of the Law (with R. S. Steffen), 1950; editorial bd. Jour. Legal Edn., 1956-58; asso. editor Natural Law Forum, 1956-68; bd. editors Ency. Brit., 1968-75. Office: U Chgo Law Sch 5801 Ellis Ave Chicago IL 60637

LEVI, JAMES HENRY, judge; b. Stevens Point, Wis., July 16, 1913; s. Harry J. and Mary (Murphy) L.; student Wis. State Coll., 1931-33; LL.B., U. Notre Dame, 1937; m. Eugenia Carberry, Feb. 17, 1945; children—Thomas, Michael, Mary, Martha, John, James, Joan. Admitted to Wis. bar, 1937; with claims dept. Hardware Mut.-Sentry Life Ins., Stevens Point, 1937-41; practice law, Stevens Point, 1945-51; dist. atty., 1948-51; judge Portage County (Wis.), 1951-68; circuit judge 7th Wis. Circuit, 1969—. Mem. Stevens Point Bd. Health, 1949-69; mem. adv. com. Wis. Mental Health Assn., 1961-68; lay bd. advisers St. Michael's Hosp., Pacelli High Sch., Stevens Point. Served from pvt. to maj. USAAF, 1942-45. Decorated Papal Honor, Knight Holy Sepulchre. Mem. State Bar Wis., Portage County Bar Assn., Wis. Bd. Juvenile Ct. Judges (pres. 1957), Wis. Bd. Circuit Judges, D.A.V., Am. Legion. K.C. (vice supreme master 1977—), Elk; mem. Cath. Order Foresters. Club: Serra (pres. 1963-64) (Stevens Point). Home: 1516 Wisconsin St Stevens Point WI 54481 Office: County-City Bldg Stevens Point WI 54481

LEVICH, CALMAN, educator; b. Iowa City, Iowa, May 26, 1921; s. Jacob and Edith (Subotnik) L.; B.S. cum laude, Morningside Coll., 1949; Ph.D., Cath. U. Am., 1966; m. Eva Belle Lindas, Sept. 22, 1946; children—Judith, David, Rebecca, Miriam. Enlisted U.S. Navy, 1941, advanced through grades to comdr., 1965, ret., 1967; prin. investigater Naval Med. Research Inst., Bethesda, Md., 1950-61; research projects dir., prin. investigator Armed Forces Radiobiology Research Inst., Bethesda, 1961-67; asso. prof. physics Central Mich. U., Mount Pleasant, 1967-68, prof. and chmn. physics dept., 1970—; chmn. dept. physics Seton Hall U., South Orange, N.J., 1968-70. Mem. Biophys. Soc. (charter), Radiation Research Soc., Am. Assn. Physics Tchrs., AAUP, AAAS, Sigma Xi, Sigma Pi Sigma, Zeta Sigma. Home: 805 Douglas St PO Box 492 Mount Pleasant MI 48858

LEVIN, BARRY LIVINGSTON, educator; b. N.Y.C., May 5, 1918; s. Benjamin Bernard and Genevieve Rose (Livingston) L.; B.A., N.Y. U., 1941; M.S., Boston U., 1946; Ph.D., Columbia U., 1969; m. Ruth Kaplan, Dec. 2, 1957; 1 dau., Susan. Mental health cons. Div. Community Mental Health, Tex. Health Dept., Austin, 1953-55; acting dir., asso. dir. dept. community mental health, Eric County, Buffalo, 1958-67; asst. dir. community mental health State Fla. Dept. Mental Health and Mental Retardation, Tallahassee, 1967-69; prof. social work U. Mo., Columbia, 1969—; vis. prof. U. So. Calif. Andrus Gerontology Center, cons. So. Calif. Health Tng. Center, 1976-77. Rep. City Council PTA, 1972-73; program cons. Mo. Foster Parents Assn., 1974, 75. Served with U.S. Army, 1942-46. NIMH research fellow, 1956-57. Fellow Am. Pub. Health Assn. (chmn. mental health sect.); mem. Nat. Assn. Social Workers, Am. Psychol. Assn., Gerontol. Soc., Mo. Assn. Mental Health (dir., v.p.), Boone County Mental Health Assn. (dir.), Justinian Soc., Kappa Delta Pi. Club: B'nai B'rith (v.p., treas.). Home: 1021 Duke St Columbia MO 65201 Office: 715 Clark Hall Columbia MO 65201

LEVIN, CARL MILTON, lawyer, city ofcl.; b. Detroit, June 28, 1934; s. Saul R. and Bess L. (Levinson) L.; B.A., Swarthmore Coll., 1956; LL.B., Harvard, 1959; m. Barbara Halpern, Aug. 31, 1961; children—Kate, Laura, Erica. Admitted to Mich. bar, 1959, practice in Detroit, 1959-64; asst. atty. gen., gen. counsel Mich. Civil Rights Commn., Detroit, 1964-68; chief dep. defender Detroit Defender's Office, 1968-69; mem. Detroit City Council, 1970-77, pres., 1974-77. Instr. Wayne U. Law Sch., Detroit, 1970, U. Detroit, 1966, 68. Mem. Am., Mich., Detroit bar assns. Democrat. Home: 20044 Renfrew Rd Detroit MI 48221 Office: City-County Bldg Detroit MI 48226

LEVIN, CHARLES LEONARD, justice state supreme ct.; b. Detroit, Apr. 28, 1926; s. Theodore and Rhoda (Katzin) L.; B.A., U. Mich., 1946, LL.B., 1947; m. Patricia Joyce Oppenheim, Feb. 21, 1956; children—Arthur, Amy, Fredrick. Admitted to Mich. bar, 1947, N.Y. bar, 1949, U.S. Supreme Ct. bar, 1953, D.C. bar, 1954; practiced in N.Y.C., 1948-50, Detroit, 1950-66; partner Levin, Levin, Garvett & Dill, Detroit, 1951-66; judge Mich. Ct. Appeals, Detroit, 1966-73; justice Supreme Ct. Mich., 1973—. Mem. Mich. Law Revision Commn., 1966. Trustee Marygrove Coll., Detroit, chmn., 1971-74. Mem. Am. Law Inst. Home: 18280 Fairway Dr Detroit MI 48221 Office: Travelers Towers Box 9 26555 Evergreen Southfield MI 48076

LEVIN, COLMAN, mktg. cons. firm exec.; b. Boston, Dec. 29, 1933; s. Myer Joseph and Ethel Ruth (Agoos) L.; A.B., Brown U., 1955; M.B.A., U. Chgo., 1957. Regional mktg. analyst N. Central region Montgomery Ward & Co., Chgo., 1962-64; asso. Howard L. Green & Assos., Inc., Birmingham, Mich., 1965-71, v.p., 1972—. Bd. dirs. Am. Jewish Com., Detroit, 1969—; founder Detroit Area Council Experiment in Internat. Living, 1965, bd. dirs., 1965—. Served with U.S. Army Chem. Procurement, 1957-59. Mem. Am. Mktg. Assn., Am. Statis. Assn., Brown U. Club Mich. (dir. 1972—, pres. 1972-74). Home: 426 N Fox Hills Dr Bloomfield Hills MI 48013 Office: 1025 E Maple St Suite 200 Birmingham MI 48011

LEVIN, DIANE, pub. relations exec.; b. N.Y.C., July 31, 1930; d. Harry H. and Goldie (Friedman) L.; B.A. cum laude in Journalism and Polit. Sci., Syracuse U., 1951. Mem. editorial staff Fairchild Publs., Chgo., 1951-52; mng. editor Hyde Park Herald, Chgo., 1952-53; reporter Advt. Age, Chgo., 1953-54; asso. editor external publ. Nat. Assn. Bedding Mfrs., Chgo., 1954-56; asst. dir. pub. relations Michael Reese Hosp. and Med. Center, Chgo., 1956-58; account supr. Daniel J. Edelman, Inc., Chgo., 1958-68; v.p. Harshe-Rotman & Druck, Inc., Chgo., 1968-75; dir. underwriting devel. Sta. WTTW-TV, Chgo., 1976—. Mem. Pub. Relations Soc. Am. (accredited, pres. Chgo. chpt. 1977). Office: 5400 N Saint Louis Ave Chicago IL 60625

LEVIN, LUCIENNE YVONNE, psychologist, social worker; b. Brussels; d. Samuel and Mary Anne (Bromet) Polak; came to U.S., 1946, naturalized, 1949; M.S.W. summa cum laude, Inst. Social Work, Brussels, 1940; M.A., Wayne State U., 1955; m. David B. Levin, May 19, 1946; 1 son, William Samuel. Head of social service Associationdes Juifs de Belgique, 1942-45; prin. welfare officer camps UNRRA in Germany, 1945-46; clin. psychologist Northville (Mich.) State Hosp., 1955-59; sch. psychologist, Livonia, Mich., 1959-64; coordinator psychology dept. Lincoln Park (Mich.) Pub. Schs., 1964-71; cons. Southgate (Mich.) Bd. Edn., 1972-76; prin. Lucienne Y. Levin, clin. psychologist, Southfield, 1955—; dir. seminars for writers Wayne U., 1973—. Mem. Am., Mich. psychol. assns., Mich. Soc. for Group Psychology (sec. 1964-66), Mich. Assn. Sch. Psychologists (sec. 1960-62), Wayne State U. Alumni, Hadassah. Contbr. poems to lit. publs.; contbr. short stories to French lit. publs.; contbr. articles in social work to profl. jours.; developer, co-author test for measurement of self concept in kindergarten children, 1967, French edit., 1977. Home: 22343 Le Rhone Southfield MI 48075

LEVIN, MAX, liquor co. exec.; b. New Orleans, Mar. 7, 1919; s. Louis and Esther (Yuspeh) L.; ed. Tulane U.; m. Flory Liebmann, Sept. 5, 1940; children—Jack, Carol Ann, Linda Louise. Sales rep. Schenley Industries Inc., New Orleans, 1945-49; sales mgr., Gulftex Drug Co. Inc., Houston, 1949-56, gen. mgr., 1956-58; pres. Liberty Liquor Distbrs. Inc., Springfield, Mass., 1958-68, W & S Merchandisers, Inc., Chgo., 1967—. Trustee Pension Fund Liquor and Allied Workers Union Local #3. Recipient Man of Year award Ill. Liquor Stores Assn., 1977. Mem. Ill. Restaurant Assn., Ill. Wholesale Liquor Dealers Assn., Wine and Spirits Wholesalers of Am., Ill. Liquor Assn. of City of Hope, Chgo. C. of C., Conv. Bureau. Home: 1144 Mayfair Ln Glencoe IL 60022 Office: 3600 S Racine Ave Chicago IL 60609

LEVIN, MORRIS JACOB, lawyer; b. St. Louis, Aug. 30, 1909; s. Barnett and Jeannette (Rosenblatt) L.; J.D., Washington U., St. Louis, 1930; m. Betty M. O'Brien, Jan. 8, 1972; 1 son from previous marriage—Roger B. Admitted to Mo. bar, 1931, since practiced in St. Louis; partner Levin & Weinhaus, 1959—. Mem. Mo. Bar (chmn. labor law sect. 1974-75). Home: 55 Clermont Ln Ladue MO 63124 Office: Levin & Weinhaus Exec Bldg 515 Olive St St Louis MO 63101

LEVIN, MURIEL IMOGENE (MRS. SHELDON LEVIN), educator; b. Chgo., Apr. 8, 1922; d. Joseph E. Kramer and Anne (Kleinberg) Heller; B.S., Northwestern U., 1963, M.A., 1971; m. Sheldon Levin, Nov. 29, 1944; children—Carol, Diane Levin Woodley, Larry. Tchr. voice tng. Columbia Coll., Chgo., 1964-66; tchr. acting voice Goodman Theatre Sch., Chgo., 1965-68; tchr. drama Evanston (Ill.) Twp. High Sch., 1970-71; tchr. drama and English, Chgo. Pub. Schs., 1972—; now chmn. performing arts dept. New Orr High Sch.; theatre coach Northwestern U., summer 1973. Television script writer; actress Country Club Theatre; dir. Hull House, Goodman Theatre, Drama Club, Evanston. Mem. Ill. Theatre Assn. (v.p.). Home: 3180 Lake Shore Dr Chicago IL 60657 Office: Orr High Sch Pulaski and Chicago Ave Chicago IL 60624

LEVIN, MURRAY LAURENCE, physician, educator; b. Boston, Nov. 14, 1935; s. Martin Marney and Matilda (Drobnis) L.; A.B., Harvard, 1957; M.D. cum laude, Tufts U., 1961; m. Joan Erma Solomon, May 30, 1961; children—Russell Jay, Cynthia Ann. Intern, Beth Israel Hosp., Boston, 1961-62, resident internal medicine, 1962-64; research fellow U. Tex., Dallas, 1964-66; faculty Northwestern U. Med. Sch., Chgo., 1966—, asso. prof. medicine, 1972—; chief renal sect. VA Lakeside Hosp., Chgo., 1972-76, chief med. service, 1976—. Mem. sci. adv. bd. Kidney Found. Ill., 1973—; mem. research award rev. com. Chgo. Heart Assn. NIH fellow, 1965-66; NIH grantee, 1967-70; Chgo. Heart Assn. grantee, 1973—. Mem. Am. Fedn. for Clin. Research (nat. com. on social issues 1974—, Midwest pres. 1974-75), Central Soc. Clin. Research (chmn. publs. com. 1975—), Internat., Am. socs. nephrology, AAAS, N.Y. Acad. Sci., Midwest Salt and Water Club, Central Clin. Research Club. Contbr. to publs. in field. Home: 368 Jackson Av Glencoe IL 60022 Office: Med Service VA Lakeside Hosp 333 E Huron St Chicago IL 60611

LEVIN, RICHARD MICHAEL, bus. exec.; b. Chgo., Apr. 16, 1925; s. Jacob and Marion (Berger) L.; B.S., U. Pa., 1947; m. Carol Ann Hoffman, June 30, 1951; children—Nancy, Michael, Ann. With Jason-Empire, Inc., Kansas City, Mo., 1949—, v.p., 1952-58, pres., chief exec. officer, 1958—; dir. Overland Park State Bank (Kans.). Mem. Civic Council Kansas City. Pres., Jewish Vocational Service of Kansas City, 1969-70, bd. dirs., 1960—; bd. dirs. Menorah Med. Center, United Hias Agy., N.Y.C.; v.p. Jewish Fedn. Council, Kansas City, New Reform Temple; bd. dirs. Kansas City Area council Boy Scouts Am., Jr. Achievement. Served with inf. AUS, 1943-46. Decorated Purple Heart. Club: Oakwood Country. Home: 835 W 64th Terr Kansas City MO 64113 Office: 9200 Cody St Overland Park KS 66214

LEVIN, STUART FRANKLIN, theatre exec.; b. Cleve., June 15, 1933; s. Samuel Allen and Cecelia (Ellerin) L.; student Cleve. Play House Sch. of Theatre, 1947-51; m. Carol Barbara Lessin, Sept. 21, 1975; 1 son by previous marriage Jonathan Erwin; stepchildren—Marc Alan Resnik, Deborah Joy Resnik. Dir. WJW-TV, Cleve., 1952-60; radio, tv producer, dir., writer Comstock Advt., Buffalo, 1960-62; producer Actor's Theatre, Hollywood, Calif., 1962-66; dir. Children's and Youth Theatres, Cleve. Play House, 1966-71; dir. Musicarnival Winter Theatre and Sch., also prodn. mgr. Summer Theatre, 1971-74; producer Showplace Theatre, 1975; exec. dir. Stu Levin Prodns., 1975—; pres. Cleve. Youth theatre, 1976—; drama critic radio and TV, 1976—. Mem. Cleve. Play House Acting Ensemble, 1949-51, 66-71. Mem. AFTRA (mem. bd. 1975—, treas. 1976—), Nat. Assn. Television Arts and Scis. (chmn. entertainment com. 1975—), Am. Ednl. Theatre Assn., Actor's Equity Assn. Home and office: 5129 Chickadee Ln Lyndhurst OH 44124

LEVINE, ALFRED DAVID, film producer; b. Cleve.; s. Manuel and Jessie (Bialosky) LeV.; grad. Western Res. U., 1937; postgrad. Ohio State U. Law Sch., 1938; m. Frances Elaine Leberman, Jan. 16, 1948. Advt. and sales promotion staff Cleve. News, 1939-42; advt. dir. Cunningham Drug Stores, Detroit, 1946; mdse. mgr. Goldblatt Bros., Chgo., 1947; Midwest mgr. Chen Yu Cosmetics, Chgo. 1948; dir. advt. Cunningham's Detroit, 1949; account exec. Snader Telescriptions, Chgo., 1950-51; sales mgr. Consol. Television, Chgo., 1952-54; gen. mgr. Sportlite Films, Chgo., 1955—, also head film producer. Head law enforcement com. Lakeview Citizens Council, Chgo., 1958; vice chmn. cleanup com. N.E. Neighbors, 1961; mem. Com. 100, Jewish Fedn. Chgo., 1962; vice chmn. communications div. Combined Jewish Appeal, 1960-67; mem. com. Woodlawn Assn., 1966. Active Ill. 9th dist. campaign Decker for Congress, 1964. Served to capt. USAAF, 1942-45; ETO. Decorated Bronze Star, Presdl. citation with cluster. Mem. Western Res. U. Alumni Assn. (chmn. Chgo. chpt. 1957-60, mem. fund raising com. Millis Sci. Bldg., 1964), Wyo. Hunters Protective Assn. Clubs: Chgo. Press, Indianapolis Athletic. Producer and distbr. sports ednl. films, for libraries, instns., bus., including films Drivers Choice, Indpls., 1964, 64, Women's World of Golf, 1971. Home: 2970 Lake Shore Dr Chicago IL 60657 Office: 20 N Wacker Dr Chicago IL 60606

LEVINE, BERNARD HAROLD, realtor, food service co. exec.; b. Eau Claire, Wis., June 29, 1925; s. Alvin A. and Eleanor (Kasper) L.p studIL.; student St. Thomas Coll., St. Paul, 1942-43, Doane Coll., 1943-44, Harvard, 1944-45, U. Wis., 1943, 47; m. Joy Shirley Baar, Apr. 22, 1948; children—Stephanie Ann, Lori Jill, Daniel Edward. With Debutante Dress Mfg. Sales, Chgo., 1947-48, Wareham-Burns, Ottowma, Iowa, 1949; owner Radio Advt., Miami, Fla., 1950-51; mgr. Fashion Store, Wausau, 1951-60; B.H. Levine Realty, Wausau, 1961—; chmn. bd. Chips Food Service, Inc., fast-food franchises, Wausau, Wis., 1966—; pres., dir. Chips of Wausau, 1965—, Chips of Merrill, Inc., 1970—; dir., officer No. Realty, Inc., Allied Investors Inc., Nitschke-Levine, Inc.; pres., dir. VIP Inc., 1968—, Log Cabin Kitchen Inc., 1974—; dir. Shops Internat., Inc., cons., Lake Geneva, Wis. Served to ensign Supply Corps, USNR, 1943-47; PTO. Recipient city beautification award, 1976. Mem. Nat. Assn. Realtors, Wausau Area C. of C., Nat. Assn. Corporate Real Estate Execs., Wis. Restaurant Assn., Am. Bonanza Soc., Aircraft Owners and Pilots Assn. Mem. B'nai B'rith. Home: 1031 Weston Ave Wausau WI 54401 Office: 114 Grand Ave Wausau WI 54401

LEVINE, DAVID SANDER, mgmt. engring. cons.; b. Toledo, Ohio, Nov. 10, 1940; s. Norman Nathan and Dorothy Sarah (Davis) L.; B.S. in Engring. Physics, Toledo U., 1962; M.S. in Engring. Sci., Rensselaer Poly. Inst., 1965; postgrad. U. Dayton, 1976—. Sr. engr. advanced power systems, Prett and Whitney Aircraft, E. Hartford, Conn., 1962-65; sr. research engr. systems analysis and ops. research, Rockwell Internat., Columbus, Ohio, 1966-68; project mgr. systems analysis, Battelle Meml. Inst., Columbus, 1969-70; chief econ. planning services Ohio Dept. Econ. and Community Devel., 1971, chief internal systems group, 1972-73, controller and mgr. fin. dept., 1973-75, dir. adminstrv. services div., 1975; pres. David S. Levine and Co., Columbus, 1975—; dir. Energy Horizons, Inc., Columbus; part time instr. mathematics, Columbus Tech. Inst. Registered profl. engr., Ohio. Mem. Ops. Research Soc. Central Ohio, Tau Beta Pi. Contbr. research reports to publs. Home and Office: 2436 Hardesty Dr S Columbus OH 43204

LEVINE, DONALD NATHAN, sociologist, educator; b. New Castle, Pa., June 16, 1931; s. Abe and Rose (Gusky) L.; A.B., U. Chgo., 1950, M.A., 1954, Ph.D., 1957; postgrad. U. Frankfurt (Germany), 1952-53; m. Ruth Weinstein, Aug. 26, 1967; children—Theodore, William, Rachel. Asst. prof. sociology U. Chgo., 1962-65, asso. prof., 1965-73, prof., 1973—; cons. Ethiopian affairs to U.S. Govt. Recipient Quantrell award U. Chgo., 1971. Mem. Internat. Soc. Comparative Study of Civilization, Am. Sociol. Assn. Jewish. Author: Wax and Gold: Tradition and Innovation in Ethiopian Culture, 1965; Georg Simmel on Individuality and Social Forms, 1971; Greater Ethiopia; The Evolution of a Multiethnic Society, 1974. Office: 1126 E 59th St Chicago IL 60637

LEVINE, EDWARD STANTON, accountant; b. Kansas City, Mo., Oct. 8, 1935; s. Joseph and Mildred Jeanette (Sandhaus) L.; B.S. in Bus. Adminstrn., U. Mo., 1957; m. Joe Ann Berkowitz, Jan. 2, 1970; children—H. Terry, Marcia L., Robyn R. Admitted as non-attorney U.S. Tax Court, 1964; partner Haith, Weinstein & Levine, C.P.A.'s, Kansas City, Mo., 1968-74, Alexander Grant & Co., Kansas City, Mo., 1974—. Fund raiser Nat. Jewish Hosp., Denver, 1967, Menorah Med. Center, Kansas City, 1973—; fund raiser Jewish Fedn. and Council, 1967—, mem. budget com., religious, ednl., cultural subcom., 1971—; mem. dist. council, asst. scoutmaster Boy Scouts Am., 1970-75; treas., bd. dirs. Kansas City Cardiac Exercise Rehab. Program, 1976—; treas., bd. dirs. Inst. for the Achievement of Human Potential of Greater Kansas City, Mo., 1965-72; bd. dirs. Jewish Vocat. Service, 1973—; bd. dirs. Am. Heart Assn., 1973—, treas., mem. exec. com., 1977—. Served to capt. AUS, 1957-68. C.P.A., Mo., Kans. Mem. Am. Inst. C.P.A.'s (profl. devel. com. 1967-71), Mo. Soc. C.P.A.'s (taxation com. 1971—), Kans. Soc. C.P.A.'s. Mason (32 deg., Shriner); mem. B'nai B'rith (mem. bd. Kansas City 1964—). Home: 9908 Catalina Overland Park KS 66207 Office: 1600 Mercantile Bank Tower Kansas City MO 64106

LEVINE, FRANKLIN ROBERT, toy co. exec.; b. Chgo., May 30, 1934; s. Oscar and Freda L.; B.S.M.E., U. Ill., 1956; m. Joan R. Aron, Dec. 26, 1956; children—Edward, Paul, Sue. Engr. Underwriters Labs., Inc., Chgo., 1956-57; Motorola Corp., Chgo., 1957-58; dir. quality control Apeco Corp., Evanston, Ill., 1958-76; dir. quality assurance Playskool, Inc., Chgo., 1976—. Served with U.S. Army, 1956-62. Mem. Am. Soc. Quality Control, ASME, ASTM. Office: 4501 Augusta Chicago IL 60676

LEVINE, HELEN SAXON (MRS. NORMAN D. LEVINE), med. technologist; b. San Francisco; d. Ernest M. and Ann (Bello) Saxon Dippel; A.B., U. Ill., 1939; m. Norman D. Levine, Mar. 2, 1935. Supr. Lab. San Francisco Dept. Pub. Health Tb Sanatorium, 1944-46, U. Ill. Health Services, Urbana, 1952-65; research asso. immunobiology, zoology dept. U. Ill., 1965—. Mem. AAAS, Am. Pub. Health Assn., Ill. Acad. Sci., Am. Soc. Med. Technologists, Am. Soc. Clin. Pathologists, Cancer Prevention Study Group, AAUP, Ill. Heart Assn., Sigma Delta Epsilon. Research and pubs. on devel. antigens against round worm parasites. Home: 702 LaSell Dr Champaign IL 61822 Office: Morrill Hall Urbana IL 61801

LEVINE, ISAAC JACOB, internist; b. Glasgow, Scotland, Aug. 18, 1923; s. Calman and Minnie (Bloch) L.; came to U.S., 1934, naturalized, 1941; student Cornell U., 1941-43, St. Louis U., 1944; B.S., U. Nebr., 1947, M.D., 1949; m. Dian Bernstein, Feb. 8, 1969; children—Joseph, David, Charles; step-children—William Kurtz, Michael Kurtz, Craig Kurtz. Intern, Jewish Hosp., Cin., 1949-50; resident in internal medicine Jewish Hosp., Cin., 1950-51, Univ. Hosp., Iowa City, Iowa, 1953-55; practice medicine specializing in internal medicine, Cin., 1955—; mem. McHenry (Ill.) Med. Group, 1958-60; instr. medicine U. Cin.; co-founder pulmonary unit Jewish Hosp.; sr. cons. physician Social Security Adminstrn.; life ins. examiner; FAA examiner; Am. Heart Assn. rep. for McHenry County, 1958-60. Served with M.C., USAF, 1951-53. Diplomate Am. Bd. Internal Medicine. Fellow Am. Coll. Chest Physicians; mem. Acad. Medicine Cin., Ohio Med. Assn., AMA, Am. Lung Assn., Ohio Thoracic Soc., Phi Delta Epsilon. Club: Amberley Swim. Research in pulmonary lavage, subacute bacterial endocarditis. Home: 6770 Fair Acres Dr Cincinnati OH 45213 Office: 8228 Winton Rd Cincinnati OH 45331

LEVINE, JAMES, condr.; b. Cin., 1943; ed. Juilliard Sch. Music. Asst. condr. Cleve. Orch., 1964-71; prin. condr. Met. Opera, N.Y.C., 1973-76, music dir., 1976—; musical dir. Chgo. Symphony Orch. Ravinia Festival, 1973—; musical dir. Cin. Symphony Orch. May Festival, 1974-77; guest condr. appearances; recs. include Verdi operas Giovanna D'Arco, I Vespri Siciliani, Rossini opera Barber of Seville, Bellini opera Norma, Mahler symphonies 1, 2, 4, 6, 8, 10. Address: care Ravinia Festival Assn Ravinia Park Highland Park IL 60035

LEVINE, MAITA FAYE, educator; b. Cin., Oct. 17, 1930; d. Aaron and Jessie (Byer) Levine; B.A., U. Cin., 1952, B.Ed., 1953, M.A. in Teaching, 1966; Ph.D., Ohio State U., 1970. Tchr., Woodward High Sch., Cin., 1953-63; instr. math. U. Cin., 1963-70, asst. prof. math., 1970-76, asso. prof. math. edn., 1976—; writer Nat. Longitudinal Study Math. Abilities, Sch. Math. Study Group, Stanford, Calif., 1963, Am. Coll. Testing Program, Iowa City, 1973—; lectr. NSF Insts., Kenyon Coll., 1960-61, U. Cin., 1962—. Faculty fellow NSF, 1968-69. Mem. AAUW, Math. Assn. Am., Nat. Council Tchrs. Math., AAUP, Assn. Women in Math., Sch. Sci. and Math. Soc., Commn. on History Math., Sigma Xi, Phi Beta Kappa, Delta Kappa Gamma. Democrat. Jewish. Home: 1106 Lois Dr Cincinnati OH 45237

LEVINE, NORMAN DION, educator; b. Boston, Nov. 30, 1912; s. Max and Adele (Daen) L.; B.S., Iowa State U., 1933; Ph.D., U. Calif. at Berkeley, 1937; m. Helen Marie Saxon, Mar. 2, 1935. Asst. dept. zoology, U. Calif., Berkeley, 1933-37; from asst. to prof. Coll. Vet. Medicine and Zoology, U. Ill., Urbana, 1937—, dir. Center for Human Ecology, 1968-74. Chmn. tropical medicine and parasitology study section NIH, 1965-69, ad hoc com. on health sci. achievement award program, 1965, animal resources adv. com., 1971-75. Served to maj. U.S. Army, 1942-46. Decorated Bronze Star. Recipient various research and tng. grants from NIH and NSF. Mem. Am. Micros. Soc. (pres. 1968-69, hon. mem.), Soc. Protozoologists (pres. 1959-60, exec. com. 1960—, hon. mem.), Am. Soc. Profl. Biologists (pres. 1966-68), Ill. Acad. Sci. (pres. 1966-67), AAAS (council, 1963-66, 69), Am. Soc. Parasitologists, Am. Bd. Microbiology (gov. bd. 1959-64), Phi Sigma (hon. life). Author: Protozoan Parasites of Domestic Animals and of Man, 1961, rev. 1973; Nematode Parasites of Domestic Animals and of Man, 1968; Coccidian Parasites of Rodents, 1965; Coccidian Parasites of Ruminants, 1970; Human Ecology, 1975. Editor: Malaria in the Interior Valley of North Am., 1964; Natural Nidality of Transmissible Diseases, 1966; Natural Nidality of Diseases, 1968; Animal Ecology, 1972. Editor Jour. Protozoology, 1965-71. Home: 702 LaSell Dr Champaign IL 61820 Office: Coll of Vet Medicine U Ill Urbana IL 61801

LEVINE, ROBERT SIDNEY, orthopaedic surgeon; b. Detroit, Aug. 1, 1942; s. Joseph and Bertha (Berkowitz) L.; B.A., U. Mich., 1963; M.D., Wayne State U., 1968; m. Faye Paula Chernikov, May 7, 1970; children—Aviva Rebecca, Rachel Anne. Intern and resident in gen. surgery St. Joseph Mercy Hosp., Pontiac, Mich., 1968-70; resident in orthopaedic surgery Wayne State U. Affiliated Hosp., Detroit, 1970-73; practice medicine specializing in orthopaedic surgery, Pontiac, 1973—; clin. asst. prof. orthopaedic surgery Wayne State U., Detroit; adj. asso. prof. bioengring. Wayne State U.; coordinator Amputee Clinic, Detroit Gen. Hosp.; cons. orthopaedic surgeon Oakland County Hosp.; mem. staff St. Joseph Mercy Hosp., Pontiac Gen. Hosp.; mem. Stapp Car Crash Conf. Adv. Com. Served to lt. comdr. M.C. USNR. Diplomate Am. Bd. Orthopaedic Surgery. Fellow A.C.S., Am. Acad. Orthopaedic Surgeons; mem. AMA, Am. Assn. Automotive Medicine, Wayne State U. Med. Alumni Assn. (pres. 1977-78). Jewish. Contbr. articles in field to profl. jours. Home: 3845 Shellmarr Ln Bloomfield Hills MI 48013 Office: 880 Woodward Ave Suite 104 Pontiac MI 48053

LEVINE, STANLEY ROBERT, urologist; b. Bklyn., June 26, 1931; s. Max and Paula (Golub) L.; B.S., Tulane U., 1954, M.D., 1956; m. Susan Settel, July 2, 1974; children—David, Richard, Thomas (dec.), Sara, Michael, Elizabeth, Emily. Intern, Touro Infirmary, New Orleans, 1956-57, resident in gen. surgery, 1957-58; pvt. practice medicine specializing in urology, Lake Forest, Ill., 1963—; mem. staff Highland Park Hosp., Ill., Lake Forest Hosp., Ill.; cons. Hines VA Hosp., Ill., Ill. Inst. Tech. (research projects), Chgo., Mediphone, Chgo., Fertility Inst.; asso. prof. Loyola Med. Sch., Chgo., 1966-68; clin. asso. prof. urology U. Health Services Chgo. Med. Sch., 1975—; dir. clinic services Midwest Population Center, Chgo., 1970—. Served with USAF, 1958-60. Diplomate Bd. Urology. Fellow Am. Coll. Surgeons, Royal Soc. Health, London; mem. Am. Assn. Sex Educators and Counselors (certified sex therapist), Am. Urologic Assn., Chgo. Urologic Soc., Fertility Soc., Pan Am. Surgical Soc., May Clinic Alumni Assn. (fellow urology, 1960-63). Contbr. articles in field to Jour. Urology, Brit. Jour. Urology. Office: 320 E Vine Ave Lake Forest IL 60045

LEVINE, STUART GEORGE, educator; b. N.Y.C., May 25, 1932; s. Max and Jean (Berens) L.; A.B., Harvard, 1954, M.A., Brown U., 1956, Ph.D., 1958; m. Susan F. Matthews, June 6, 1962; children—Rebecca, Aaron, Allen. Teaching fellow Brown U., 1956-57; instr. English, U. Kans., Lawrence, 1958-61, asst. prof., 1961-64, asso. prof. Am. studies, 1964-66, prof., 1966—, dept. founder, chmn., 1963-70; vis. prof. U. Mo., Kansas City, 1966, U. S.D., 1963, Kans. State U., 1965, Calif. State U. at Los Angeles 1968, 70; scholar in residence U. Ariz., 1972-73; Fulbright prof. U. La Plata (Argentina), 1962, U. Costa Rica, 1965, 67, Nat. Autonomous U. Mexico, 1972; profl. concert musician, 1955-58, 73—, music commentator Concert Network, Boston, N.Y.C., Providence, Hartford, New Haven, White Mountains, 1955-58. Regional chmn. Harvard Coll. Fund. Recipient Anisfield Wolf award (with others) Saturday Rev., 1968, citation Nat. Conf. Christians and Jews, 1969. Mem. Am. Studies Assn. (mem. exec. com. nat. meeting 1965-66, pub. com. nat. meeting 1965-66), Midcontinent Am. Studies Assn., (mem. exec. and editorial bds. 1960—). Editor-in-chief: American Studies, 1960—. Editor The Am. Studies Series, 1965—. Author: (with N.O. Lurie) The American Indian Today, 1968, Caffin's The Story of American Painting, 1970; Edgar Poe, Seer, and Craftsman, 1972. Editor: (with Susan F. Levine) The Short Fiction of Edgar Poe: An Annotated Edition, 1976. Home: 1846 Barker St Lawrence KS 66044

LEVINE, WALTER ELI, engring. mgr.; b. New Haven, Oct. 17, 1929; s. Philip Hyman and Celia (Gordon) L.; B.S.M.E., Worcester Poly. Inst., 1953; postgrad. U. Conn., 1956; m. Sharon K., Oct. 16, 1977; children—Scott E., Craig M., Cheryl A. Research engr. Worthington Corp., Holyoke, Mass., 1953-56; project engr. Edwards Co., Norwalk, Conn., 1957-62; mktg. specialist Dresser I.V.I. Div., Stratford, Conn., 1962-69; indsl. sales mgr. Consol. Controls Corp., Bethel, Conn., 1970-71; engring. mgr. Bindicator Co., Port Huron, Mich., 1972—. Mem. Instrument Soc. Am. (sr.). Club: Masons. Patentee in field. Home: 3150 Westhaven Dr Port Huron MI 48060 Office: 1915 Dove St Port Huron MI 48060

LEVINGER, HAROLD LEE, mcht.; b. Yankton, S.D., Jan. 13, 1928; s. Harold W. and Lerena (Fantle) L.; student Yankton Coll., 1945-46; B.S., U. Nebr., 1950; m. Saundra L. Lavin, Oct. 24, 1954; children—Michael, Janet, Deborah. Engr., Silas Mason Co., Pickstown, S.D., 1949, Grand Island, Nebr., 1950-51; engr. Mpls. Honeywell Co., 1953-55; pres., dir. Fantle-Sioux City Co. (Iowa), 1955—; pres., dir. Fantle-Marshalltown Co.; sec., dir. Fantle Bros. Co., Fantle-LaCrosse Co., Fantle-Austin Co., Fantle-Ft. Dodge Co. Gen. chmn. United Jewish Campaign, Sioux City, 1969. Sec. bd. dirs. Harold and Lerena Levinger Found.; bd. dirs. Sioux Land Mdse. Council; bd. dirs., past pres. Jewish Fedn. Sioux City; past pres. Siouxland Better Bus. Bur. Served with C.E., AUS, 1951-53. Decorated Bronze Star medal. Recipient Harold and Bernice Goldstein Young Leadership award, 1968. Mem. Sioux City C. of C. Jewish religion (trustee temple). Kiwanian. Mason; mem. B'nai B'rith. Home: 3656 Maplewood Sioux City IA 51104 Office: 504 4th St Sioux City IA 51102

LEVINSOHN, SIDNEY HARVEY, pharmacy co. exec.; b. St. Paul, Jan. 17, 1930; s. Max L. and Dorothy (Titner) L.; B.S., U. Minn., 1955; m. Joan R. Cramer; Mar. 21, 1959; children—Loren, Craig. Owner, operator Carlson Drug and Rental Co., Mpls., 1970; partner Pharmacy Corp. Am., 1973—; instr., cons. in field. Group leader Give & Take Drug Center. Served to capt. USAF, 1956-67. Mem. Am. Soc. Cons. Pharmacists, Minn., Am. Pharm. Assn., Nat. Assn. Retail Druggists, Direct Mail Advt. Assn., Am. Diabetic Assn. Jewish. Clubs: Temple Israel Mens. Author: How to Be Your Own Boss Though You Work for Someone Else; How to Ask for a Raise and Get It . . . in Ten Minutes Flat; author, editor The Gerigram Newsletter; patentee in field. Home: 3224 Cavell Ln Minneapolis MN 55426 Office: 422 S 7th St Minneapolis MN 55415

LEVINSON, CHARLES BERNARD, architect, educator, real estate developer; b. Youngstown, O., Dec. 15, 1912; s. Al and Goldye (Davis) (L.; B.S. in Architecture, U. Cin., 1934; m. Doris Mombach, Nov. 10, 1940; children—Ronnie Ann (Mrs. John Shore), Barbara Jean (Mrs. Ronald Stern), Suzanne (Mrs. Ralph Stern). Draftsman, Gulf Refining Co., 1934-35; designer Hunt and Allan, 1935-36; pvt. practice architecture, 1936-39; partner Al Levinson Co., 1940; partner Steelcraft Engring. Co., 1941-44; v.p. Steelcraft Mfg. Co., 1945-51, exec. v.p., 1951-66, pres., 1966-69, chmn. bd., 1969-70; v.p. Knapp Bros. Mfg. Co., 1949-51, pres., 1951-65, pres.-treas., 1965-68; v.p., sec. Charbert Industries, Inc., 1950-66, chmn. bd., 1966—; v.p., sec. ALCO Bldg. Products Co., 1950-70, Leesburg Realty Co., 1952-76; v.p., Candle-Lite, Inc., Leesburg and Cin., 1952-66, pres. 1967—; v.p. Steelcraft Realty Co., 1953-58; sec.-treas. ABCO Tool & Die Co., 1953-65, v.p., sec., 1965-70; v.p., treas. Rosscraft Industries, Inc., 1954-62; pres. Colonial Village, Inc., 1962-68; v.p., Steelcraft Mfg. Co. Can. Ltd., Malton, Ont., 1962-65; v.p., sec. Oceanautic Mfg. & Research Co., 1968-70; asst. prof. Coll. Design Architecture Art, U. Cin., 1970— Bd. dirs. Big Brothers Am., 1955-66, spl. projects, com. 1965, v.p. 1957; bd. trustees Big Brothers Assn. Cin., pres., 1953-54; active Citizens Com. on Youth, Cin., pres. 1960-63, fed. projects bd. chmn. 1965-67; mem.-at-large Nat. Com. for Children and Youth, 1966-69, nat. adv. com., 1970, steering com. nat. leadership council, 1966, treas., 1966; bd. dirs. Nat. Com. for Employment of Youth, 1962-68, vice-chmn., 1968; mem. nat. council Am. Jewish Joint Distbn. Com., 1967-69; asso. mem. Cin. Montessori, Soc., Inc., 1966-70; ad hoc adv. steering com. 1970 White House Conf. on Children and Youth, 1966-70; bd. trustees Jewish Fedn. Cin., 1968—; adv. Determined Young Men, Cin., 1969; trustee Cin. Ballet Co., 1968—, pres., 1969-75; chmn. bd. Contemporary Arts Center, 1969-71; mem. president's com. Dept. Labor 50th Anniversary, 1963; mem. spl. project Cin. Youth Commn., 1963-64; seminar chmn. Mid-Decade Conf. on Children and Youth, 1966; mem. adv. com. on young workers U.S. Dept. Labor, 1962-63; campaign chmn. Cin. Jewish Welfare Fund, 1966-67, chmn. men's div., 1967-68; adviser Gen. Subcom. on Labor, for Youth Employment Opportunities Act of 1961; adviser Gen. Subcom. on Edn. for Youth Employment Act of 1963; bd. dirs. Better Housing League of Cin., 1950; bd. govs. Cin. Renewal Corp., 1958. Vice-pres. The Levinson Found., Cin., 1951-76; v.p., treas. Charles B. Levinson Found., 1970; trustee The Jewish Hosp., Cin., 1968-75, Cin. Symphony Orch., 1971-76; exec. com. Fountain Square Sculpture Fund, Cin., 1970-71; bd. dirs. Jewish Community Center, Cin., 1955—; bd. dirs. Home for the Jewish Aged, Cin., 1955—, v.p., 1962. Named Top 10 Dad by Cin. Jr. C. of C., 1959; Boss of the Year, Cin. and Internat. PBX Clubs, Cin., 1960; recipient merit award Social Service Assn. of Greater Cin., 1962; citation Citizens Com. on Youth, Cin., 1963. Mem. Producers Council, Inc. (mktg. devel. com. 1966), AIA, Queen City Assn., Cin. Charter Com. Jewish. Mason; mem. B'nai B'rith. Clubs: Losantiville Country, Cincinnati, Queen City. Home: 1400 Highland Towers Cincinnati OH 45202 Office: 720 DuBois Tower Cincinnati OH 45202

LEVINSON, JOSEPH EMANUEL, physician; b. Cin., Apr. 7, 1920; s. Samuel W. and Rebecca (Lewin) L.; student Columbia U., 1937-40; A.B., Stanford U., 1941; M.D., U. Cin., 1944; m. Marianne Freiberg, Mar. 21, 1945; children—Steven H., Henry S., Richard Peter. Intern, Cin. Gen. Hosp., 1944-45, asst. resident medicine, 1947-48; asst. resident medicine Cin. Jewish Hosp., 1948-49, chief resident medicine, 1949-50; clin. and research fellow in medicine Mass. Gen. Hosp., Harvard Sch. Medicine, 1950-52; instr. medicine U. Cin. Coll. Medicine, 1952-59, asst. clin. prof., 1959-67, asso. clin. prof., 1967-69, asso. prof., 1969-73, prof. medicine, 1973—, asso. prof. pediatrics, 1972-77, prof., 1977—; dir. div. pediatric rheumatology Children's Hosp. Med. Center, 1974—; cons. HEW. Mem. exec. com. Arthritis Found., 1972-73. Served to capt. M.C., AUS, 1945-47, 53. Mem. Am. Rheumatism Assn. Contbr. to profl. jours. Home: 437 Rawson Woods Ln Cincinnati OH 45220 Office: U Cin Coll Medicine Cincinnati OH 45267

LEVINSON, MONTE JAY, physician; b. Oak Park, Ill., July 19, 1933; s. Chester S. and Evelyn (Beller) L.; B.S., U. Ill., 1954, M.D., 1957; m. Sophie Sebebrenick, May 12, 1963; children—Victor Isaiah, Linda Vivienne. Intern, Michael Reese Hosp., Chgo., 1957-58, fellow gastrointestinal research dept. Med. Research Inst., 1958-59, hosp. resident in internal medicine, 1961-63, chief Wednesday Internal Med. Clin., Mandel Clinic, 1963-72, mem. staff dept. internal medicine, 1963-75, attending physician, 1972-75, med. dir. med. group S.C., 1972-75; cons. physician Div. Adult Health and Aging, Chgo. Bd. Health, 1961-63, research physician, 1963-66; clin. instr. medicine Chgo. Med. Sch., 1963-66; practice medicine specializing in internal medicine, Chgo., 1965-72; clin. asst. prof. medicine Pritzker Sch. Medicine, U. Chgo., 1972-75; asso. attending physician Evanston (Ill.) Hosp., 1975—, co-investigator Aspirin Myocardial Infarction Study, 1975; asst. prof. clin. medicine Northwestern U., Chgo., 1975, mem. exec. com. for clin. diagnosis, 1976—; attending physician dept. internal medicine Presbyn. Home, Evanston, 1976—; mem. Skokie (Ill.) Bd. Health, 1970-72. Served to lt. M.C., USNR, 1959-61. Diplomate Am. Bd. Internal Medicine. Fellow A.C.P., Inst. Medicine Chgo.; mem. Am. (fellow Council on Epidemiology), Chgo. (info. and referral com. 1970-72, health care research and devel adv. group 1974-75) heart assns., Internat. Soc. Cardiology, Chgo. Soc. Internal Medicine, Am. Physicians Fellowship, Group Health Assn. Am. (ad hoc com. med. dirs. 1974-75), Heart Assn N. Cook County (curriculum devel. com. 1976—). Jewish. Contbr. articles to profl. jours. Home: 2149 Central Park Ave Evanston IL 60201 Office: 636 Church St Evanston IL 60201

LEVITT, SEYMOUR HERBERT, physician, educator; b. Chgo., July 18, 1928; s. Nathan E. and Margaret (Chizever) L.; B.A., U. Colo., 1950, M.D., 1954; m. Phillis Jeanne Martin, Oct. 31, 1952; children—Mary Jeanne, Jennifer Gaye, Scott Hayden. Resident U. Cal. at San Francisco Med. Center, 1957-61; instr. U. Mich. Med. Sch., 1961-62, U. Rochester (N.Y.) Med Sch., 1962-63; asso. prof. U. Okla. Med. Sch., 1963-66; prof. radiology, chmn. div. radiotherapy Med. Coll. Va., Richmond, 1966-70; prof., head dept. therapeutic radiology U. Minn., 1970—; cons. radiotherapist VA Hosp.; mem. exec. bd. Joint Com. for End Result Reporting and Cancer Staging; trustee Am. Bd. Radiology; mem. com. on radiation oncology studies Nat. Cancer Inst. Served with M.C., AUS, 1955-57. Fellow Am. Coll. Radiology (steering com. council); mem. Radiol. Soc. N. Am., Am. Radium Soc., Am. Roentgen Ray Soc., Soc. Chairmen Acad. Radiation Oncology Programs (pres.), Soc. Nuclear Medicine, Am. Soc. Therapeutic Radiologists (exec. bd.), Phi Beta Kappa, Alpha Omega Alpha. Home: 6413 Cherokee Trail Minneapolis MN 55435 Office: U Minn Hosp PO Box 494 Minneapolis MN

LEVY, BENJAMIN, elec. engr.; b. Kansas City, Mo., Mar. 14, 1915; s. Benno Joseph and Estella Madeline (Brew) L.; student Kansas City Jr. Coll., 1932-34; B.S., U. Kans., 1937, postgrad., 1947-50; m. Margaret Eva Partello, Mar. 4, 1955. Engr. estimator Kansas City (Mo.) Power & Light Co., 1939-41; asst. engr. U.S. Army Engrs., Omaha, 1941-43; instr. elec. engring. U. Kans., Lawrence, 1947-50; staff engr. Sandia Corp., Albuquerque, 1950-51; research engr. U. Mich., Ann Arbor, 1951-56; staff engr. Boeing Airplane Co., Seattle, 1956; research engr. U. Mich., Ann Arbor, 1956-70; elec. engr. U.S. Air Force, Wright-Patterson AFB, Ohio, 1972—. Cons. elec. engring., 1953—. Served to lt. USNR, 1943-46. Decorated Air medal. Mem. Am., Motor City theatre organ socs., Detroit Theater Organ Club, Triangle Fraternity, Sigma Xi. Patentee silent air compressor, 1954. Home: 113 Worden Ave Ann Arbor MI 48103

LEVY, DAVID HYMAN, physician; b. Syracuse, N.Y., Sept. 29, 1907; s. Morris and Nellie (Stolufsky) L.; B.S., Ind. U., 1932, M.D. cum laude, 1934. Intern, Ind. U. Hosps., 1934-35; practice medicine specializing in family practice, Youngstown, Ohio, 1935—; mem. staff St. Elizabeth's Hosp.; police surgeon, 1968—. Diplomate Am. Bd. Family Physicians. Fellow AMA; mem. Ohio Med. Assn., Mahoning County Med. Soc., Am. Inst. Assn., Mahoning County Acad. Family Physicians. Democrat. Clubs: Masons, Kiwanis. Home: 1310 5th Ave Youngstown OH 44504 Office: 414 Home Savs Bldg Youngstown OH 44503

LEVY, DONALD MORRIS, plastic surgeon; b. New Orleans, May 20, 1935; s. Leo and Leontine (Capdepon) L.; M.D., La. State U., 1959; m. Mary Cahlamer, May 30, 1974. Intern, Touro Hosp., New Orleans; gen. surg. resident, Mayo Clinic, Rochester, Minn., also resident in plastic surgery; asso. prof. plastic surgery, Med. Coll. Wis., Milw.; dir. hand surgery Rheumatic Disease Center, Columbia Hosp., also chmn. dept. plastic surgery; nat. lectr. in field; pres. Spanish Village Co., Phoenix. Served to maj., USAR. Named Man of Year, Milw. Cosmopolitan Club. Mem. AMA, Med. Soc. Milw. County, Am. Soc. Aesthetic Plastic Surgery, A.C.S., Am. Burn Assn., Wis. Soc. Plastic Surgeons, Am. Soc. Plastic and Reconstructive Surgeons, Am. Cleft Palate Assn., Wis. Alumni Mayo Clinic. Contbr. articles to med. publs. Home: 3205 W County Line Rd Milwaukee WI 53217 Office: 425 E Wisconsin Ave Milwaukee WI 53202

LEVY, JOEL C., lawyer; b. South Bend, Ind., Oct. 22, 1937; s. Ira and Lillian (Cooper) L.; B.S. in Bus. Adminstrn., Ind. U., 1959, J.D., 1962; m. Judith N. Amdur, June 4, 1961; children—Janice Ruth, Julie Ann. Admitted to Ind. bar, 1962; since practiced in Hammond; asso. Singleton, Levy & Crist, and predecessor, 1962-66, partner, 1967—; lectr. Valparaiso U. Sch. Law, Purdue U., Hammond, Ind. Chmn. local rule revision com. U.S. Dist. Ct. No. Ind., 1971-72; atty. Hammond Sch. Bd., 1968-70. Bd. dirs. Legal Aid Soc., Gary, Ind.; pres. local PTA. Mem. Am., Ind. State, Hammond (treas. 1966-68) bar assns., Am. Judicature Soc., Northwest Ind. Council Lawyers (v.p. 1972), Phi Delta Theta, Zeta Beta Tau. Jewish religion. Mem. B'nai B'rith (sec.). Home: 9124 Walnut Dr Munster IN 46321 Office: 9013 Indianapolis Blvd Highland IN 46322

LEVY, JOEL HOWARD, chem. co. exec.; b. N.Y.C., Jan. 7, 1938; s. David M. and Mildred (Davidoff) L.; B.Ch.E., Coll. City N.Y., 1960; M.S., Poly. Inst. Bklyn., 1968; m. Renee Fenchel, Aug. 18, 1963; children—Seth Evan, Alissa Cheryl. Project leader Princeton Chem. Research, Inc. (N.J.), 1964-68, mgr. polymer devel., 1968-70, plant mgr., 1970-72; plant mgr. Hydron Lab., Inc., New Brunswick, N.J., 1972-74; process devel. supr. Sun Chem. Corp., Carlstadt, N.J., 1974-75; supr. residue products research and devel. chems. div. Quaker Oats Co., Barrington, Ill., 1975-78; mgr. process engring.-sweeteners Searle Chems. Inc., Skokie, Ill., 1978—. Served with AUS, 1961. Mem. Am. Inst. Chem. Engrs. (exec. com. N.J. sect.). Home: 311 Burr Oak Ct Deerfield IL 60015 Office: Searle Chems Inc Skokie IL

LEVY, VIRGIL LOUIS, dentistry research cons.; b. Ligonier, Ind., Dec. 20, 1917; s. Louis L. and Ruth Ellen (Todd) L.; student Ind. U., 1935-36; student Ball State U., 1936-39, Northwestern U., 1939-40; D.D.S., Loyola U., Chgo., 1948; m. Jean Ann Hughes, Sept. 5, 1941; children—Laura Ruth (Mrs. Frank Celarek), Todd Hughes, Lydia Ellen (Mrs. Michael Panyard), Lisa Ann (Mrs. David Augustyniak), Thaddeus Louis. Resident surgery, anesthesiology Cook County Hosp., Chgo., 1948-50, Loyola U., Chgo., 1951; pvt. practice specializing in oral and facial surgery, Fort Wayne, Ind., 1950-73; mem. profl. attending staffs Lutheran Hosp., also St. Joseph Hosp., both Fort Wayne, 1950-78; mem. vis. staff Parkview Meml. Hosp., Fort Wayne, 1950-75; research cons. Preventive Dentistry Research Inst. Inc., Ind. U., Fort Wayne, 1974-75; profl. cons. Aetna Life & Casualty Ins. Co., Fort Wayne, 1974-78. Cons. oral surgery VA Hosp., Fort Wayne, 1955-73. Pres., lay adv. bd. St. Vincent's Home, Ligonier, 1965-66; bd. dirs. St. Anne's Home, Fort Wayne, 1977—. Served to master sgt., AUS, 1942-46. Mem. Isaac Knapp Dist. Dental Soc. (pres. 1965-66), Am., Ind. dental assns., Internat., Am., Ind., Great Lakes socs. oral surgery, Am., Ind. socs. anesthesiology, Cook County Hosp. Assn. oral surgeons, Logan-Brophy Meml. Soc. Oral Surgeons, St. Apollonia Guild (Fort Wayne-South Bend Diocese pres. 1958-66), Fort Wayne Civil War Round Table (pres. 1965-66, 75-76), Crosier Lay Apostolate, Sigma Tau Gamma, Xi Psi Phi. Roman Catholic. K.C. (4 deg.), Elk. Address: 2937 Westbrook Dr Fort Wayne IN 46805

LEWIN, PHILIP MARTIN, banker; b. Chgo., Jan. 15, 1935; s. Lewis Birkwood and Sadie Z. (Edelstein) L.; B.S., Northwestern U., 1956; m. Judith Ann Langert, Mar. 1, 1958; children—Stanton, Stephanie. With Continental Ill. Nat. Bank and Trust Co., Chgo., 1956—, asst. cashier, 1960-66, 2d v.p., 1966-69, v.p., 1969-70, head new bus. task force, 1970-75; pres., chief exec. officer Drovers Nat. Bank Chgo., 1975-76; pres., chief operating officer Exchange Nat. Bank, Chgo., 1976—; vice-chmn. Exchange Internat. Corp., pres., 1977—; vice chmn. Am.-Israel Bank, Tel Aviv, 1977—. Asst. treas. Ill. div. Am. Cancer Soc., 1966-69, treas., 1970-75, vice chmn., 1975-77, chmn., 1977—. Bd. dirs. Hebrew Theol. Coll., 1968-69. Served with AUS, 1957. Mem. Am. Israel C. of C. (bd. dirs. 1960—). Home: 720 Oakton St Evanston IL 60202 Office: 130 S LaSalle St Chicago IL 60690

LEWIS, BETTY CARROLL (MRS. THOMAS A. LEWIS), clubwoman; b. St. Paul, Apr. 27, 1920; d. Charles Parnell and Lydarene (Bryan) Carroll; student Coll. St. Catherine, 1938-40; m. Thomas A. Lewis, Sept. 21, 1940; children—Thomas Andrew, Carol Ann Lewis Anderson, Mary Beth Lewis Pates. Mem. exec. com. Stritch Ann. Award Dinner, 1957—; exec. com. presentation ball Order of Lafayette, 1960—; fellow St. Joseph Coll., 1962—; treas. women's bd. Mercy Hosp., Chgo., 1969-71; mem. women's bd. Loyola U., Chgo., 1963—, DePaul U., Chgo., 1968-71; v.p. DuPage County women's bd. Am. Cancer Soc. Mem. Ill. Club for Cath. Women (v.p. 1968-73). Clubs: Fidelitas Women's (v.p. 1970-72), Butterfield Country, Union League (Chgo.); White Lake Yacht, White Lake Golf (Whitehall, Mich.). Home: 21 Spinning Wheel Rd Hinsdale IL 60520

LEWIS, BUELL LAUGHLIN, dentist; b. Calvin, N.D., July 8, 1920; s. Samuel McLean and Annie Christina (McLean) L.; B.A., Valley City State Coll., 1943; B.S., U. Nebr., 1948, D.D.S., 1950; postgrad. U. Minn., 1957; m. Virginia Lucille George, Sept. 23, 1944; children—Nancy Kay, Peggy Rae. Practice dentistry, Grand Forks, N.D., 1950—. Mem. Gov's. Com. for Vocational Rehab. Services, 1968-69. Served with USNR, 1943-46. Mem. Am. Soc. Dentistry for Children, Nat. (del. 1971-72), N.D. State (pres. 1972-73) dental assns., Grand Forks (pres. 1955, 61), N.E. Dist. (pres. 1957, 63) dental socs., Xi Psi Phi. Presbyn. (elder). Mason (Shriner), Elk, Kiwanian. Club: Grand Forks Country. Home: 2617 Olson Dr Grand Forks ND 58201 Office: 410 First Nat Bank Bldg Grand Forks ND 58201

LEWIS, CARY BLACKBURN, JR., educator, accountant, lawyer; b. Chgo., Sept. 13, 1921; s. Cary Blackburn and Bertha (Mosley) L.; A.B., U. Ill., 1942; M.B.A., U. Chgo., 1947; J.D., DePaul U., 1966; Advanced Mgmt. certificate Harvard, 1971; m. Eleanor Taylor, Feb. 28, 1943; 1 dau., Cheryl (Mrs. Walker Beverly IV); m. 2d, Mary Lewis, Dec., 1970; 1 son, Cary B. III. Asst. prof. accounting Ky. State Coll., Frankfort, 1947-50; asso. prof. So. U., Baton Rouge, 1950-51; sr. auditor M.T. Washington C.P.A.'s, Chgo., 1951-53; auditor Collier-Lewis Realty Co., 1953-70; auditor A.A. Rayner & Sons, 1960-72; tchr. Chgo. Pub. Schs., 1951-57; asso. prof. law, accounting Chgo. Tchrs. Coll., Chgo., 1957-65, budget coordinator, 1966-67; asso. prof. law, accounting Ill. Tchrs. Coll., 1965-67, Chgo. State Coll., Chgo., 1967-70; prof. Chgo. State U., 1970—, spl. asst. to v.p., 1976-77. C.P.A., Chgo., 1950—; lawyer, Chgo., 1966—. Budgetary cons. OEO; ednl. cons. to HEW; auditing cons. to Dept. Labor; mgmt. cons. to Black Econ. Union, 1969—; chmn. edn. adv. com. N.A.A.C.P., 1966—. Served to 2d. lt. AC, AUS, 1942-54; C.P.A., Ill. Mem. Am., Ill., Chgo. bar assns., Am. Assn. Accountants, Am. Assn. U. Profs., Am. Bus. Law Assn., Am. Judicature Soc., Am. Inst. C.P.A.'s. Club: Chgo. City. Author: How To Take an Inventory, 1948; Directory of Negro Business of Baton Rouge, La., 1950. Contbr. Bus. Men's Guide, 1971. Home: 18252 S California Ave Homewood IL 60430

LEWIS, DANIEL EDWIN, lawyer; b. Goshen, Ind., May 2, 1910; s. Daniel Arthur and Emma John (Williams) L.; A.B., Hanover Coll., 1932; M.S., Ind. U., 1939; J.D., Valparaiso U., 1949; m. Annette Jean Fewell, July 28, 1934; children—Daniel Edwin, Nancy Jean (Mrs. Glenn Lee Haswell). Tchr. high sch., Knox, Ind., 1932-35; tchr., athletic coach high sch., LaPorte, Ind., 1935-43; dir. indsl. relations Allis Chalmers Mfg. Co., LaPorte, 1943-55; admitted to Ind. bar, 1949, since practiced in LaPorte; partner firm Newby & Lewis, 1955-59, Newby, Lewis & Kaminski, 1959—; instr. mgmt. Purdue U., LaPorte, 1944, Ind. U., LaPorte, 1945. Pres. United Fund of Greater LaPorte, 1957, 65; chmn. LaPorte chpt. A.R.C., 1948; vice chmn. Pottawattomie council Boy Scouts Am., 1963-69; pres. Family Service Assn. LaPorte County, 1975-77; pres. LaPorte Bd. Edn., 1952-55, LaPorte County Human Relations Commn., 1967-68; chmn. LaPorte Bicentennial Plaza Meml. Com.; ambassador Asso. Colls. Ind. Bd. dirs. LaPorte YMCA, pres., 1960-62; Recipient Alumni Achievement award Hanover Coll., 1965; named Outstanding Citizen of LaPorte, LaPorte Jr. C. of C., 1955. Mem. Am., Ind., Ind. State, LaPorte County bar assns., Am. Arbitration Assn., LaPorte Athletic Club (pres. 1949), Phi Delta Kappa, Phi Alpha Delta, Phi Delta Theta. Presbyn. (Elder). Elk, Mason, Kiwanian (pres. 1954) Home: 207 Edgewood Lane LaPorte IN 46350 Office: 916 Lincoln Way LaPorte IN 46350

LEWIS, EDMUND JEAN, internist; b. N.Y.C., Nov. 10, 1936; s. Herbert P. and Sylvia (Roth) L.; B.S., McGill U., 1958; M.D., U. B.C., 1962; children—Diane, Susanne. Intern, Johns Hopkins U., 1962; mem. house staff Johns Hopkins, 1962-65; research fellow Harvard, 1965-66, 68-70, asst. prof., 1970-71; asso. prof. medicine U. Chgo., 1971-73; prof. medicine, dir. sect. nephrology Rush Med. Coll., Chgo., 1973—. Chmn. med. adv. bd. Kidney Found. Ill., 1972-74, mem. exec. com., bd. dirs., 1972-77. Served with USPHS, 1966-68. Recipient Hamber Gold medal, U. B.C., 1962, Horner Gold medal, 1962. Mem. Johns Hopkins Med. and Surg. Soc., Am. Fedn. Clin. Research, Am. Soc. Nephrology, Transplantation Soc., Chgo. Med. Soc., Am. Soc. Internal Medicine, AMA, Alpha Omega Alpha. Contbr. articles to med. jours. Home: 333 E Ontario St Chicago IL 60611 Office: 1753 W Congress Pkwy Chicago IL 60611

LEWIS, EDWARD EARL, publisher; b. Royal Oak, Mich., Mar. 9, 1926; s. Arthur Earl and Rose Martha (Gerboth) L.; B.S., Ball State, 1959; m. Jean Elizabeth Sanborn, Sept. 23, 1952; children—Steven Edward, Jon Richard, Brian Arthur. Newspaper reporter The Star, Muncie, Ind., 1944-46, The Statesman, Salem, Oreg., 1946-48; editor Jour. Gas City, Ind., 1949-51; editor The Argus, Brighton, Mich., 1953-55; writer Chrysler Corp., Detroit, 1955-58; pub. relations Wyandotte Chems., Wyandotte, Mich., 1958-61; advt. mgr. Gelman Instrument Co., Ann Arbor, Mich., 1962-66; founder pub. co. as Gelman subsidiary, 1966, owner, pres., treas. Ann Arbor Sci. Pubs., Inc., 1971—. Instr. Cleary Coll., Ypsilanti, Mich., 1964. Mem. Bd. Edn., Chelsea, Mich., 1968-70. Served with USNR, 1943-44. Mem. Indsl. Editors Assn. Detroit (past pres.). Mason. Club: Chelsea Rod and Gun. Home: 314 E Middle St Chelsea MI 48118 Office: 230 Collingwood St Ann Arbor MI 48106

LEWIS, ELDWYN ERNEST, educator; b. St. Louis, July 18, 1941; s. Brutus Clay and Jewell Juanita (Wilson) L.; student Harris Tchrs. Coll., 1960-62; B.A., So. Ill. U., 1965; M.A., St. Louis U., 1970, postgrad., 1971—. Recreation leader trainee St. Louis div. Recreation, St. Louis, Mo., 1966-67; group social worker Plymouth House, St. Louis, 1962; playground leader trainee St. Louis Div. Recreation, 1962-63, recreation leader, 1963-64; dir. group services Plymouth House-Group Social Work, St. Louis, 1964-65; supr. I, St. Louis div. Recreation, 1965-70; tchr. St. Louis Bd. Edn., 1966-67; asst. prof. sociology Meramec Community Coll., 1970-73; instr. sociology in AfroAmerican studies St. Louis U., 1973—, also dir. AfroAmerican Studies Inst., 1974—. Bd. dirs. Divorce Counseling Service, Providence Group Home. Served with AUS, 1967-69. Mem. Mo. State Tchrs. Assn., Am. Sociol. Assn., Soc. Psychol. Study of Social Problems, A.A.U.P., A.C.L.U., Mo. Sociol. Soc., Internat. Communications Assn., Am. Acad. Polit. and Social Sci., A.A.A.S., African Studies Assn., Caribbean Studies Assn., Nat. Council Family Relations, Am. Assn. Marriage and Family Counselors, Omega Psi Phi. Lodge: The Rosicrucian Order. Home: 1412 Bluebird Terr St Louis MO 63144 Office: 221 N Grand Blvd St Louis MO 63103

LEWIS, EUGENE WILLIAM, III, lawyer; b. Detroit, July 20, 1940; s. Eugene William, Jr. and Margaret B. (Bornhauser) L.; B.A., Brown U., 1962; J.D., U. Mich., 1965; m. Ann Louise Bearden, May 15, 1965 (div.); children—Eugene William IV, Michael L.; m. 2d, Katherine Ann Krieghoff, Apr. 28, 1972; 1 son, James Timmons. Admitted to Mich. bar, 1966, U.S. Circuit Ct. Appeals, 1966, U.S. Supreme Ct. bar, 1969; asso. firm Dahlberg, Mallender & Gawne, Detroit, 1965-70, McInally, Rockwell & Brucker, Detroit, 1971-74; partner firm Morris, Rowland, Regan & Prekel, Troy, Mich., 1975—. Bd. dirs., asst. treas., asst. sec. Mich. Humane Soc.; trustee Detroit Orthopedic Clinic. Mem. Am., Detroit bar assns., State Bar Mich., Am. Judicature Soc., Detroit Hist. Soc., Detroit Zool. Soc., Southeastern Mich. Tennis Assn. (dir., treas. 1967—), Brown U. Alumni Assn. (pres. 1969-71, dir. 1969—), Phi Delta Phi. Republican. Presbyn. Clubs: University,

Economic (Detroit); Grosse Pointe. Home: 378 Hillcrest Rd Grosse Pointe Farms MI 48236 Office: 3001 W Big Beaver St Suite 504 Troy MI 48084

LEWIS, FRED, chemist; b. Snow Hill, N.C., Oct. 2, 1938; s. Walter Lewis and Patsy (Waters) L.; B.S., Johnson C. Smith U., 1963; M.S. in Chemistry, L.I. U., 1970; certificate in polymer characterization Stevens Inst. Tech., 1970; M.S. in Occupational and Environ. Health, Wayne State U., 1977; m. Nancy Lena Morris, June 14, 1968. Chemist, Fisher Sci. Co., Fair Lawn, N.J., 1963-68; chemist Celanese Plastic Research Center, Clark, N.J., 1968-70; supr. analytica lab. Reichhold Chemicals Inc., Tuxedo Park, N.Y., 1970-72; research engring. asso. Ford Motor Co., Mt. Clemens, Mich., 1972—. First v.p. Macomb County NAACP, pres., 1975-76; adviser Jr. Achievement. Mem. Am. Chem. Soc., Am. Microchem. Soc., ASTM, Mich. Indsl. Hygiene Assn., Alpha Phi Alpha, Jonson C. Smith Alumni Assn. (midwest dir.). Club: Masons. Home: 20228 Great Oaks Circle S Mt Clemens MI 48043 Office: 400 Groesbeck Hwy Mt Clemens MI 48043

LEWIS, GEORGE WILLIAM, physician; b. St. Paul, Ind., Oct. 13, 1933; s. George M. and Isabelle (Turner) L.; A.B., DePauw U., 1955; M.S., Purdue U., 1957; M.D., Ohio State U., 1962; m. Patricia K. Macy, Sept. 16, 1953; children—Cathy, George, Gregory, John. Intern, Grant Hosp., Columbus, Ohio, 1962; resident in obstetrics and gynecology Ohio State U. Hosp., Columbus, 1963-67; practice medicine specializing in obstetrics and gynecology Central Ohio Med. Clinic, Columbus, 1969—; mem. staff Ohio State U., Grant, Mt. Carmel, St. Ann's hosps. (all Columbus); mem. med. adv. bd. Planned Parenthood; team physician Upper Arlington High Sch. Bd. dirs. Upper Arlington Boosters Club, 1976—. Served with USAF, 1968-70. Rector scholar, 1951-55; USPHS fellow, 1963-66; Am. Cancer Soc. fellow, 1967; recipient Bausch and Lomb award, 1951, Roche award, 1960, Hofheimer prize, 1960. Diplomate Am. Bd. Obstetrics and Gynecology. Mem. Columbus Obstetrics and Gynecology Soc., Acad. Medicine Columbus and Franklin County, Ohio Med. Assn., Planned Parenthood Internat., Am. Fertility Soc., Sigma Xi, Alpha Omega Alpha, Delta Kappa Epsilon, Phi Chi. Methodist. Contbr. articles to profl. jours. Home: 4081 Fenwick Rd Upper Arlington OH 43220 Office: 497 E Town St Columbus OH 43215

LEWIS, HERSCHELL GORDON, advt. and motion picture exec.; b. Pitts., June 15, 1926; s. Calvin Emanuel and Geraldine (Waldman) L.; B.S., Northwestern U., 1946, M.S., 1947; Ph.D., Mid-Western U., 1955; m. Barbara Rosebaum, 1948 (div.); children—Michael David, Robert Dale; m. 2d, Helene Comm, 1973. Pres. Lewis & Martin Films, Inc., 1952-59, Comml. Syndicated Films, Inc., 1956-59; pres. Mid-Continent Films, Inc., 1959-62, Creative Communications, Inc., 1960-69, Mayflower Pictures Inc.; treas. B. I. & L. Releasing Corp.; chmn. Lewis-Nelson-Kahn Co., 1969-74; pres. Lewis-Andrews Theatres, 1970-74; chief officer Communicomp, Highland Park, Ill., 1974—. Served from pvt. to aviation cadet USAF, 1943-45. Mem. Soc. Comprehensive Medicine, Screen Dirs. Guild, Soc. Clin. and Exptl. Hypnosis, Acad. TV Arts and Scis., Soc. Motion Picture and TV Engrs., A.A.A.S., Pub. Relations Soc. Am., Sigma Delta Chi. Club: Variety. Author: Facts on Franchises, 1963; The Businessman's Guide to Advertising and Sales Promotion, 1974; How to Handle Your Own Public Relations, 1976. Home: 1988 Green Bay Highland Park IL 60035 Office: 454 Central Ave Highland Park IL 60035

LEWIS, LAURA ANN PENN, health educator; b. Winston-Salem, N.C., Aug. 17, 1931; d. Cicero Garland and Velma Francis (Tatum) Penn; B.S., N.C. Central U., 1953, M.S. in Pub. Health, 1959; m. Julian Leigh Lewis, Dec. 28, 1957; children—Julian Leigh, Gary Scott. Teen-age program and camp dir. YWCA, Winston-Salem, 1954-58; tchr. Winston-Salem Pub. Schs., 1959-60; adult activities dir. YWCA, Winston-Salem, 1961-62; health educator Family Health Assn. Cleve., 1963-64; tchr. Cleve. Job Corps Center for Women, 1966-67; med. social worker Cleve. Met. Gen. Hosp., 1967-69; adoption case worker Cath. Family and Children's Services, Cleve., 1970-75; project dir. Cleve. Pub. Schs., 1975—. USPHS fellow, 1958-59. Mem. Am., Northeastern Ohio personnel and guidance assns., AAUW, N.C. Central U. Alumni Assn., Ohio Assn. Secondary Sch. Adminstrs., Alpha Kappa Alpha. Home: 3397 Daleford Rd Shaker Heights OH 44120

LEWIS, LOWELL CHARLES, supt. schs.; b. Ingraham, Ill., Dec. 6, 1920; s. Morton and Mae (Birch) L.; A.B., DePauw U., 1946, M.A., 1953; student Eastern Ill. U., 1941, U. Ill., 1951; m. Oneida Geneva McAdams, Mar. 15, 1946; children—Danny Morton, Lyndall Dean, Reba Cheryl, Glenda Faye. Tchr. high sch. Dieterich, Ill., 1946; radio announcer and news editor, sta. WCRA, Effingham, Ill., 1947-48; reporter Effingham Daily News, 1949; prin. Edgewood (Ill.) Grade Sch., 1949-55; supt. schs. Effingham County (Ill.), 1955—. Distbn. center chmn. So. Ill. Am. Field Service, 1961, 62; mem. Effingham County Am. Field Service adv. com., 1957—, pres., 1963; mem. Ill. Reading Service Bd. Served from 2d lt. to capt. inf. AUS, 1942-46. PTO. Decorated Bronze Star medal with arrowhead. Mem. N.E.A., Am. Legion, 40 and 8. V.F.W., Effingham County Regional Hist. Soc., Ill. Hist. Soc. Men's Hall Assn., Effingham County Old Settlers Assn. (pres.), Ill. Assn. County Supts. Schs. (pres. 1967-68), Am. Assn. Sch. Adminstrs., Phi Delta Kappa. Republican. Mem. Christian Ch. Mason (worshipful master 1960). Lion (charter: past pres.). Home: 306 Wabash Ave Effingham IL 62401 Office: Courthouse Effingham IL 62401

LEWIS, MYRON FRANCIS, religious orgn. adminstr.; b. Quincy, Ill., Sept. 11, 1913; s. John W. and Ollie Pearl (Jones) L.; B.A., Quincy Coll., 1935; M.A., Mercer U., 1936; postgrad. La. State U., 1936-39, U. N.C., 1939-41; m. Janet Hanel, July 6, 1961. Asst. prof. sociology Loyola U., New Orleans, 1950-51; lectr. sociology Am. U., Washington, economist Fed. Govt. Service, 1951-53; dir. research, tng. Wells Orgns. ch. fund raising, Chgo., 1953-58; with Lutheran Stewardship Counselors, Milw., 1958—, pres., 1959—. Served with USNR, 1945-46. Rockefeller Found. fellow, 1939-41. Fellow Am. Sociol. Assn., Religious Research Assn. Home: 4475 W Dean Rd Milwaukee WI 53223 Office: Lutheran Stewardship Counselors PO Box 16523 Parklawn Sta Milwaukee WI 53216

LEWIS, RICHARD CURTIS, paper co. exec.; b. Chgo., Nov. 19, 1923; s. Roy Alexander and Maud Esther (Curtis) L.; B.A., Northwestern U., 1946; m. Miriam A. Wennekendonk, May 6, 1970; children—John, Marcy. Salesman, Reliable Paper Co., 1951-57; v.p., dir. sales Hobart Mc Intosh Paper Co., Elk Grove, Ill., 1957-75; pres., chmn. bd. Lewis & Gould Paper Co., Inc., Northfield, Ill., 1975—. Served to lt. (j.g.) USNR, 1943-45; ETO, PTO. Mem. Book Mfrs. Inst. Clubs: Chgo. Yacht, Ocean Reef, Milw. Yacht, Westmoreland Country. Office: 550 Frontage Rd 3015 Northfield IL 60092

LEWIS, RICHARD EUGENE, health care exec.; b. Republic, Pa., July 3, 1936; s. Benjamin Eugene and Ellamae (Smithley) L.; B.S. in Econs. and Bus. Adminstrn., Ind. Central Coll., 1968; m. Elizabeth Lola Jennings, Jan. 25, 1958; children—Lorri Ann, Kimberly Beth. With Diamond Chain Co., Indpls., 1959-72, asso. engr., 1959-66, asst. advt. mgr., 1966-67, advt. mgr., 1968-69, mgr. distbr. sales, 1969-73; marketing dir. Jackson Enterprises, Inc., Indpls., 1973-75; adminstr. Turtle Creek Convalescent Center, 1975-77, Greenview Manor Inc., 1977—. Republican precinct committeeman, 1966-70. Mem. Am. Coll. Hosp. Adminstrs., Am. Coll. Nursing Home Adminstrs., Am., Ind. health care assns., Am. Marketing Assn., Sales and Marketing Execs. Baptist. Mason. Home: 8542 Ridge Hill Dr Indianapolis IN 46217 Office: 1700 N Illinois St Indianapolis IN 46202

LEWIS, ROBERT LINUEL, JR., accountant; b. East Liverpool, Ohio, Jan. 12, 1943; s. Robert L. and Barbara (Gabor) L.; A.S., Point Park Coll., 1962; B.S.B.A. in Accounting, Geneva Coll., 1969; m. Kathleen Anne Meehan, Mar. 7, 1964; children—Judith Regan, Maureen Anne, Robert L. III, Megan Michelle, Colleen Regina. Cost accountant Pittsburgh Forgings Co., Coraopolis, Pa., 1962-63; jr. accountant S. R. Snodgrass & Co., C.P.A.'s, Mentor, Ohio, 1964-68, resident partner, 1969-70, gen. partner, 1971—. Instr. accounting Community Coll. of Beaver County (Ohio), 1969-70, Geneva Coll., 1970-74. C.P.A., Pa., Ohio. Mem. Am. Inst. C.P.A.'s, Am. Accounting Assn. Roman Catholic. Rotarian (sec. Mentor club 1976-77). Home: 9190 Idlewood Dr Mentor OH 44060 Office: 8925 Mentor Ave Mentor OH 44060

LEWIS, ROBERT OWEN, surgeon; b. Carmi, Ill., Oct. 13, 1927; s. Henry and Helen (Peterson) L.; B.A., DePauw U., Greencastle, Ind., 1950; B.A., U. Ill. Coll. Medicine, 1952, M.D., 1954; m. Eleanor De Vries Lewis, 1958; children—Gregory J., Robert D., John Henry. Intern, Presbyn. Hosp., Chgo., 1954-55, resident in gen. surgery, 1955-59; mem. staff Community Hosp., Ottawa, Ill., 1959—, also mem. exec. bd.; asst. prof. surgery U. Ill. Coll. Medicine. Elder Presbyterian Ch. Recipient Distinguished Service award U. Ill. Dept. Surgery, 1969. Diplomate Am. Bd. Surgery. Fellow A.C.S.; mem. AMA, Ill. State, LaSalle County med. socs., Ill. Surg. Soc. (dir. exec. bd.). Home: 325 E Pearl St Ottawa IL 61350 Office: 1703 Polaris Circle Ottawa IL 61350

LEWIS, RONALD ANTHONY, electronic engr.; b. Green Bay, Wis., May 29, 1933; s. Lester Samuel and Genevieve Victorean (Smeester) L.; Asso. Sci., DeVry Tech., 1957; A.A., Wright Coll., 1963; B.S., Roosevelt U., 1970; m. Sarah Carpenter, Oct. 23, 1965; children—Matthew, Jonathan, Emily. Research asso. bio-engring. lab. Northwestern U., 1962-64, Inst. Communicative Disorders, 1965-68; research asso. bio-engring. lab. U. Tex., 1964-65; dir. electronics Loyola U. Med. Center, Maywood, Ill., 1968—. Served with U.S. Army, 1953-55. Certified clin. engr., Assn. Advancement Med. Instrumentation. Sr. mem. IEEE, Instrument Soc. Am. Patentee disposable telemetric device, disposable thermometer. Home: 1085 Bernard Dr Buffalo Grove IL 60090 Office: 2160 S 1st Ave Maywood IL 60153

LEWIS, SALLY BUTZEL (MRS. LEONARD THEODORE LEWIS), civic worker; b. Detroit, June 29, 1912; d. Leo Martin and Caroline (Heavenrich) Butzel; B.A., Vassar Coll., 1934; m. Leonard Theodore Lewis, Apr. 4, 1935; 1 son, Leonard Theodore. Mem. Women's City Club of Detroit, 1932-67, dir., 1935-38; dir., chmn. community services com. Village Woman's Club of Birmingham-Bloomfield dir. Franklin-Wright Settlement, Inc., Detroit, 1939—, pres. 1959-80; trustee Oakland County Children's Aid Soc., 1950-64; mem. exec. com. Detroit Fedn. Settlements, 1961; mem. steering com., women's orgn. United Fund, 1960-61; mem. Oakland planning div. United Community Services, Met. Detroit, 1959-70; membership chmn. Bloomfield Art Assn., Birmingham, Mich.; mem. scholarship com. Meadow Brook Sch. Music, Meadow Brook Festival, Rochester, Mich.; treas. Cranbrook Music Guild, Inc., 1959, dir., 1958-63, sec., 1960-61; mem. women's com. Cranbrook Galleries Art, Bloomfield Hills; exec. com. Meadow Brook Festival, Rochester, Mich., 1969-76; bd. dirs. Oakland U. Found., 1975—, Mich. Opera Theatre, 1977—. Mem. Nat. Council Jewish Women, Am. Jewish Com., Women's Assn. Detroit Symphony, Friends Detroit Symphony. Mem. Women's Nat. Farm and Garden. Clubs: Village, Ibex. Home: 1421 Lochridge Rd Bloomfield Hills MI 48013

LEWIS, SHIRLEY ANN, ednl. adminstr.; b. Pekin, Ill., Oct. 21, 1934; d. James Warren and Nora Mae (Sweany) Lewis; B.S., U. Ill., 1956; M.A., U. Mich., 1967. English and journalism tchr. Barrington (Ill.) Consol. High Sch., 1956-58, Carl Sandburg High Sch., Orland Park, Ill., 1958-59, USAF Dependent Schs., Eng., 1959-60, Ger., 1960-61; English and journalism tchr. Riverside-Brookfield Twp. (Ill.), 1960-66, counselor, 1967-68, adminstr., 1968—. Recipient Outstanding Tchr. award USAF Europe, 1961. Mem. Am. Personnel and Guidance Assn., Am. Sch. Counselors Assn., Ill. Women Deans and Counselors, Delta Kappa Gamma, Phi Kappa Phi. Methodist. Home: 65 Longcommon Rd Riverside IL 60546 Office: Ridgewood and Golf Rds Riverside IL 60546

LEWIS, THOMAS ANDREW, investment co. exec.; b. Chgo., May 12, 1918; s. Frank J. and Julia (Deal) L.; student Coll. St. Thomas, St. Paul, 1937-38, DePaul U., 1938-39, Northwestern U., 1946-47; LL.D. (hon.), St. Joseph Coll., Rensselaer, Ind., 1963; m. Elizabeth Carroll, Sept. 21, 1940; children—Thomas Andrew, Carol Ann (Mrs. R.A. Anderson), Mary Beth (Mrs. L.A. Pates). Partner, Stifel, Nicolaus & Co., Inc., Chgo., 1946-58; registered rep. White, Weld & Co., 1958-67, F.S. Moseley & Co. (now Moseley, Hallgarten, Estabrook, Inc.), Chgo., 1967-75, v.p., 1973—; dir. E. Systems, Inc., Dallas, 1973—; dir. Chgo. Molded Products, Inc., 1974—. Financial adviser Serra Internat. Fund, 1971—. Mem. adv. bd. Ill. Masonic Hosp., Chgo., 1973—; mem. adv. council Nat. Inf. Mus., Columbus, Ga., 1970—. Chmn. bd. St. Xavier Coll., Chgo., 1970-75; chmn. bd. St. Catherine Coll., St. Paul, 1971-75; dir. Catholic charities citizens bd. Loyola U., Chgo., 1966-75; bd. dirs. U.S.O., N.Y.C., chmn., Chgo.; trustee, fellow St. Joseph Coll., 1954—. Served from pvt. to capt. AUS, 1942-46. Decorated Silver Star, Bronze Star with cluster, Purple Heart with cluster (U.S.); Croix de Guerre with gold star (France); named Knight Lazarus Jerusalem Knight of Justice, Mil. and Hosp. Order of St. Lazarus, 1972; named to Inf. Hall of Fame, Ft. Benning, Ga., 1969. Mem. Mil. Order World Wars (comdr. Chgo. chpt. 1957-58; Nat. Citation award 1973), Serra Club Chgo. (pres. 1958-59, internat. treas. 1962-63, pres. internat. found. 1968-71), Whitelake Golf and Yacht Club. Republican. Roman Catholic. Clubs: Union League (Chgo.), Butterfield Country. Home: 21 Spinning Wheel Rd Hinsdale IL 60521 Office: 135 S LaSalle St Chicago IL 60603

LEWIS, TOM F., surgeon; b. Middleport, Ohio, July 12, 1908; s. Tom F. and Laura (Wells) L.; M.D., Ohio State U., 1932; m. Beatrice Torbert, 1934; children—Tom T., Susan Lewis Forster, James F., Carol Lewis Giessler; m. 2d, Ellen Maxwell, 1973. Intern, Miami Valley Hosp., Dayton, Ohio, 1932-33; resident in surgery and gynecology Ohio State U., 1933-36, asst. in surgery, 1936-38, instr., 1938-42; practice medicine specializing in surgery, Columbus, 1936—; mem. staff Mt. Carmel Hosp., bd. trustees emeritus; clins. asst. prof. Ohio State U., 1942-74, clin. asso. prof., 1975—. Diplomate Am. Bd. Surgery. Mem. A.C.S. (liaison fellow Commn. on Cancer 1977; past pres. Ohio chpt.), Acad. Medicine Columbus and Franklin County (past pres.), Columbus (founder, past pres.), Ohio State (past pres., founder) surg. socs., Ohio State Med. Assn., AMA, Ohio State U. Med. Alumni Assn. (past pres.). Clubs: Scioto Country, Athletic. Home: 1733 Merrick Rd Columbus OH 43212 Office: 350 E Broad St Columbus OH 43215

LEWIS, WAYNE DOUGLAS, sociologist, educator; b. Washington, D.C., June 12, 1947; s. Joseph Henry and Sarah Elizabeth (Daily) L.; A.B., U. Ga., 1969; M.A., U. Del., 1975. Teaching fellow sociology U. Del., Newark, 1971-75; instr. sociology St. Meinrad (Ind.) Coll. Liberal Arts, 1971-74, asst. prof., 1975—; instr. Vincennes U., Jasper, Ind., 1977—. NSF trainee, 1971. Mem. Am. Sociol. Assn., N. Central Sociol. Soc., AAUP. Home: PO Box 391 English IN 47118 Office: H320 St Meinrad Coll Liberal Arts St Meinrad IN 47577

LEWIS, WENDELL PHILLIPS, dentist; b. Henning, Minn., Mar. 11, 1915; s. Arthur John and Clara Eugenia (Quan) L.; D.D.S., U. Minn., 1939; m. Lois Dorothea Tang, Mar. 15, 1941; children—Laura, Donald, Linda. Dental intern Mpls. Gen. Hosp., 1939-40, mem. dental staff, 1940-43; pvt. practice dentistry, Mpls., 1940-43, Albert Lea, Minn., 1946—. Mem. Minn. People-to-People Dental Mission to Europe, 1974. Served with USNR, 1943-46; capt. Res. ret. Mem. Am., Minn., S.E. Dist. dental assns., Acad. Gen. Dentistry (state bd. dirs. 1972-73), Naval Res. Assn., Ret. Officers Assn., Assn. Mil. Surgeons U.S., V.F.W., Am. Legion, War Dads, Psi Omega. Club: University of Minnesota Alumni. Home: 914 Clausen Ave Albert Lea MN 56007 Office: 435 Bridge Ave Albert Lea MN 56007

LEWIS, WILLIAM ELLSWORTH, judge; b. Garrett, Ind., May 22, 1917; s. Sherman and Grace (Brown) L.; LL.B., Ind. U., 1951; m. Garnet Irby, Apr. 1, 1939; 1 dau., Janice (Mrs. Charles E. White). With U.S. P.O., Kokomo, Ind., 1937-41; admitted to Ind. bar, 1951; practice law, Kokomo, Ind., 1951-62; judge Superior Ct., Kokomo, 1963—. Served with AUS, 1942-45; ETO. Republican. Home: 2915 Dellwood St Kokomo IN 46901 Office: Courthouse Kokomo IN 46901

LEWIS, WILLIAM FRANKLIN, marketing cons., educator; b. Jackson, Mich., Oct. 20, 1941; s. Francis Christopher and Marion Geraldine (Booth) L.; grad. A.G.S. Jackson Community Coll., 1961; B.A. in Econs., Spring Arbor Coll., 1967; M.B.A. in Marketing, Mich. State U., 1969; Ph.D. in Marketing, U. Cin., 1976; m. Dorothy Jean Solberg, Aug. 5, 1967. Instr., Spring Arbor (Mich.) Coll., 1968-69; teaching fellow U. Cin., 1970-73, asst. prof. marketing Xavier U., Cin., 1973-76; asst. prof. of marketing Miami U., Oxford, Ohio, 1976—; guest speaker sta. WVXU-FM, 1974, 75; credit corporate treasury dept. Chrysler Corp., 1969-70; cons. in marketing to govt. agys. and various bus. firms, 1968—; pres. W.F. Lewis Associates, Inc., Cin., 1977—. Served with USNR, 1959-65. Mem. Am. (v.p. 1977-78), So. marketing assns., Acad. Mgmt., Product Devel. and Mgmt. Assn., Sales and Marketing Execs., Mu Kappa Tau (nat. pres. 1977-79), Beta Gamma Sigma, Pi Sigma Epsilon, Sigma Iota Epsilon. Baptist. Contbr. articles in field to profl. publs. Home: 1539 Karahill Dr Cincinnati OH 45240 Office: Marketing Dept Miami Univ Oxford OH 45056

LEWY, ROBERT BARNARD, physician; b. Chgo., Oct. 4, 1909; s. Alfred and Minnie (Barnard) L.; B.S., U. Chgo., 1930, M.D., 1935; children—Margery (Mrs. Melvyn Rieff), Alfred James. Intern Cook County (Ill.) Hosp., 1934-36, resident, 1936-37; practice medicine specializing in otolaryngology, Chgo., 1937—; sr. attending staff Michael Reese Hosp.; cons. Municipal Contagious Disease Hosp., Chgo., 1937—. Clin. prof. otolaryngology Abraham Lincoln Sch. Medicine U. Ill., Chgo., 1937—. Served to lt. col. AUS, 1941-46. Recipient Arquin prize, 1937, Miss. Valley Med. Soc. prize, 1941, Barraquer prize, 1966. Mem. Am. Laryngol. Assn. (1st v.p. 1970-71), Chgo. Laryngol. and Otological Soc. (pres. 1963), Triological Soc. (v.p. 1973-74), Sigma Xi, Alpha Omega Alpha. Club: Quadrangle (Chgo.). Inventor surg. instruments. Home: 5530 South Shore Dr Chicago IL 60637 Office: 25 E Washington St Chicago IL 60602

LEY, ROBERT EARL, JR., dentist; b. New Philadelphia, Ohio, Sept. 30, 1918; s. Robert Earl and Mary Zula (Fisher) L.; student Ohio Wesleyan U., 1936-38; D.D.S., Ohio State U., 1943; m. Suzanne Abbott Weible, Oct. 16, 1943; children—Robert Earl III, Sally, Jeanne (Mrs. Roy Leatherbury), Suzanne, Janet, Mary Lynn, Heather. Pvt. practice dentistry, Dover, Ohio, 1946—; dental staff Union Hosp., Dover. Councilman at large City of Dover, 1954-60. Served with Dental Corps, USNR, 1943-46; PTO. Mem. Pierre Fouchard Acad., Am. Dental Assn., Am. Dental Soc. Anesthesiology, Ohio State, Tuscarawas County (pres. 1954-55) dental socs., Am. Legion, Psi Omega. Republican. Moravian (trustee, pres. bd. 1972-73). Mason (Shriner), Elk, Kiwanian. Home: 1 Parkview Dr Dover OH 44622 Office: 129 W 2d St Dover OH 44622

LEY, ROBERT JOSEPH, lawyer; b. Joliet, Ill., Sept. 29, 1918; s. James Joseph and Anna Clara (Schuster) L.; A.B., U. Ill., 1939; J.D., DePaul U., 1946; m. Janet Elizabeth Musselman, July 20, 1943; children—Ellen (Satenstein), Caroline Elizabeth, George Musselman, Catherine Sharrin. Admitted to Ill. bar, 1942; since practiced in Chgo.; mem. firm Knouff, Ley & Davis, and predecessor firms. Dir. Apollo Colors Inc., W.W. Engring. Co., W.W. Mfg. Co., London Chem. Co., Inc., Henry C. Grebe & Co., Inc. Mem. Winnetka Caucus Com., 1953-54, 59-60; trustee Village of Winnetka, 1968-72. Mem. citizens bd. Loyola U., Chgo., 1961—; bd. mgrs. Florence Crittenton Anchorage, Chgo., 1967-72; bd. dirs. Mental Health Assn. Greater Chgo., 1968-73. Served with USNR, 1942-45; now lt. comdr. Res. ret. Mem. Chgo. Bar Assn. (chmn. state and municipal taxation com. 1966-67, mem. nominating com. 1973), Delta Kappa Epsilon. Republican. Roman Catholic. Clubs: Mid-Day (Chgo.); Vintage Sportscar (dir.). Home: 436 Linden St Winnetka IL 60093 Office: 33 N Dearborn St Suite 2011 Chicago IL 60602

LEYDA, WILLIAM DAVID, oral surgeon; b. New Castle, Pa., Aug. 2, 1936; s. Wallace Benjamin and Alice Virginia (Thompson) L.; D.D.S., Ind. U., 1960; m. Jean Elaine Bushong, June 11, 1960; children—Douglas William, Jill Elaine, David Andrew. Intern Ind. U. Med. Center, Indpls., 1960-61, resident, 1961-63; practice oral surgery, Kokomo, Ind., 1963—; chief dental staff Howard Community Hosp., Kokomo; cons. Pulaski Meml. Hosp., Winimac, Ind. Bd. dirs. United Way, 1976-79. Diplomate Am. Bd. Oral Surgery. Fellow Internat. Coll. Dentists, Am. Coll. Oral and Maxillo-facial Surgeons (founder); mem. Am., Ind. dental assns., Wabash Valley Dental Soc. (pres. 1971-72), Am., Ind. (dir. 1972-74, sec.-treas. 1974-77, v.p. 1977-78), Great Lakes socs. oral surgeons, Kokomo-Howard County C. of C. (scholarship chmn. 1970-72, v.p. econ. devel. group, dir. 1974-77, v.p. community and govtl. affairs 1977-78), Ind. Alumni Assn. (pres. Kokomo chpt. 1968-69). Presbyn. Clubs: Y Men's (pres. 1972-73), Rotary (pres. 1977-78). Home: 2509 Greentree Lane Kokomo IN 46901 Office: 3429 Lafountain St Kokomo IN 46901

LEYMASTER, GLEN R., assn. exec.; b. Aurora, Nebr., Aug. 17, 1915; s. Leslie and Frances (Wertman) L.; m. Margaret Hendricks, June 20, 1942; children—Mark H., Mary Beth, Lynn F.; A.B., U. Nebr., 1938; M.D., Harvard U., 1942; M.P.H., Johns Hopkins, 1950; intern, asst. resident, resident Harvard Med. Service, Boston City Hosp., 1942-44. Instr. medicine Johns Hopkins Med. Sch., 1944-46, instr., asst. prof. bacteriology Sch. Pub. Health and Hygiene, 1946-48; asso. prof. pub. health, instr. medicine U. Utah Sch. Medicine, 1948-50, prof., head dept. preventive medicine, asst. prof. medicine, also dir. univ. health service, 1950-60; adviser med. edn.-preventive medicine ICA, Bangkok, Thailand, 1956-58; asso. sec. council med. edn. and hosps. AMA, Chgo., 1960-63, dir. dept. undergrad. med. edn., 1970-75; pres., dean Women's Med. Coll. Pa., 1964-70; exec. dir.

Am. Bd. Med. Specialties, Evanston, Ill., 1975—. Mem. Am., Ill., Chgo. med. assns., Inst. Medicine Chgo., Phi Beta Kappa, Sigma Xi, Alpha Omega Alpha. Contbr. articles in field to profl. jours. Home: 1155 Michigan Ave Wilmette IL 60091 Office: 1603 Orrington Ave Evanston IL 60201

LEYPOLD, GREGORY GEORGES, real estate broker; b. Aurora, Ill., Apr. 26, 1947; s. Francis Georges and Madeline Jean (Sturm) L.; student No. Ill. U., 1966; m. Karen Cecile Over, July 6, 1968; children—Bradley Georges, Kristine Jenine, Barry Georges. With R.J. Honig & Asso., Lockport, Ill., 1969—, mgr. br. office, 1970-72, gen. mgr., 1973—. Speaker at local schs., also real estate confs. Mem. Nat. Assn. Real Estate Bds., Asso. Joliet Will County Bd. Realtors (pres. 1973), Joliet Will County Bd. Realtors, Ill. Assn. Real Estate Bds. (mem. asso. div.). Home: 412 E 12th St Lockport IL 60441 Office: 113 E 9th St Lockport IL 60441

LI, CHAO-CHIUNG, architect; b. Hai-Nan Island, Nov. 20, 1949; s. Lung-Fu and Sung-Tong (Wang) L.; came to U.S., 1974; M.Arch., Washington U., 1975; m. Tresa C. S. Chen, Nov. 4, 1974. Draftsman Planned Projects, Inc., St. Louis, Mo., 1975; archtl. designer Wedemeyer, Cernik & Corrubia, Inc., St. Louis, Mo., 1975-76; archtl. designer Warren & Goodin, Inc., Springfield, Mo., 1976-78; project architect Harold A. Casey & Assos., Springfield, 1978—. Mem. exec. com. Chinese-Am. Architecture Soc., St. Louis, 1977. Serviced with Chinese Army, 1972-74. Exhibited one-man show, Tunghai U., Taiwan, 1972, Washington U., 1974, Southwest Mo. State U., 1977. Confucianist. Home: 2930 E Madison Springfield MO 65802 Office: 412 Holland Bldg Springfield MO 65806

LI, CHARLES SHUHANG, plastic surgeon; b. Formosa, China, Aug. 1, 1930; s. Tzau and Siang (Hsu) L.; came to U.S., 1950, naturalized, 1965; B.S. magna cum laude, St. Benedict's Coll., 1954; M.D., St. Louis U., 1957. Intern, St. Mary's Hosp., St. Louis, 1957-58; resident in gen. surgery St. Vincent Charity Hosp., Cleve., 1958-61, sr. resident, 1961-62, resident in plastic surgery Columbia Presbyn. Med. Center, N.Y.C., 1962-64; fellow in surgery of hand Roosevelt Hosp., N.Y.C., 1964; practice medicine specializing in plastic and reconstructive surgery and surgery of hand, Parma, Ohio, 1964—; asst. clin. prof. plastic surgery Case Western Res. U., 1972—. Diplomate Am. Bd. Surgery, Am. Bd. Plastic Surgery. Mem. AMA, Ohio State Med. Assn., Cleve. Acad. Medicine, Cleve. Surg. Soc., A.C.S., Ednl. Found. of Am. Plastic and Reconstructive Surgery, Inc., Am. Soc. Plastic and Reconstructive Surgeons, Ohio Valley Plastic Surgery Soc., Webster Soc. Columbia, Am. Soc. Surgery of Hand, Pan-Pacific Surg. Assn., Presbyterian Hosp. Alumni Assn., Roosevelt Hosp. Alumni Assn. Roman Catholic. Contbr. articles in field to profl. jours. Home: 5377 W Ridgewood Dr Parma OH 44134 Office: Med Arts Center 6681 Ridge Rd Suite 303 Parma OH 44129

LIACOPOULOS, VAN PETER, mfg. co. exec.; b. Fond Du Lac, Wis., July 26, 1938; s. Peter A. and Dena (Condel) L.; B.S. in Engring. Sci., U.S. Naval Acad., 1962; m. Nancy Mistrioty, Dec. 29, 1962; children—Peter, Dena, Jimmy. Mem. navy marine mktg. staff Cuttier-Hammer Co., Milw., 1967-69; maintenance engr. Pabst Brewing Co., Milw., 1969-72; plant engr. Albert Trustel Packing Co., Lake Geneva, Wis., 1972-74; dir. mfg. services A. F. Gallun & Sons, Milw., 1974—. Served with USN, 1962-67, to lt. comdr., USNR, 1967—. Greek Orthodox. Home: 1740 Whitemont St Brookfield WI 53005 Office: 1818 N Water St Milwaukee WI 53201

LIAN, TECK SENG, psychiatrist; b. Sitiawan, Malaysia, Jan. 29, 1933; s. Choon Chiau and Bee Gim (Tan) L.; came to U.S., 1953, naturalized, 1965; B.S. summa cum laude, Tenn. Wesleyan Coll., 1957; M.S., Tulane U., 1960, M.D., 1960; m. Margaret Ellen McAllister, Sept. 9, 1961; children—Melinda, Jennifer, Timothy. Intern Saginaw (Mich.) Gen. Hosp., 1960-61, sr. attending psychiatrist, 1970—, chmn. child psychiatry dept., 1970—, chmn. peer rev. in psychiatry, 1973—, chmn. dept. psychiatry, 1977—, mem. exec. bd., 1977—; resident psychiatry Traverse City (Mich.) State Hosp., 1964-67; fellow Saginaw Valley Child Guidance Clinic, 1967-68; pvt. practice psychiatry, Saginaw, 1968—; psychiat. cons. Saginaw Community Hosp.; sr. attending psychiatrist St. Luke's Hosp., Saginaw. Served to capt. M.C., USAF, 1961-64. Diplomate Am. Bd. Psychiatry and Neurology. Fellow Royal Soc. Health; mem. Am. Psychiat. Assn., A.M.A., Aerospace Med. Assn., Pan Am. Med. Assn., Mich., Saginaw County med. assns., Saginaw County Med. Soc. (chmn. medico-legal com. 1975) Rotarian (chmn. crippled children com. Saginaw 1975). Club: Germania (Saginaw). Home: 6 Ghia Ct Saginaw MI 48602 Office: 4595 State St Saginaw MI 48603

LIAO, KUN TWU, physician; b. Yun-Lin, Taiwan, Dec. 12, 1932; s. Wan Neu and Ye How (Lee) L.; M.D., Nat. Taiwan U., 1958; m. Grace Ya-Sin Yen, Dec. 25, 1959; children—Angela, Jimmy, Margie. Resident surgery Nat. Taiwan U. Hosp., Taipei, 1960-63; intern Balt. City Hosp., 1963-64; resident surgery Del. Hosp., Wilmington, 1964-65; resident pathology Wilmington (Del.) Med. Center, 1965-69; fellow pathology Washington U., St. Louis, 1969-70; asst. pathologist Barnes Hosp., St. Louis, 1970-71; pathologist Clin. Labs. St. Louis, 1971—; dir. labs. Wood River Twp. Hosp. (Ill.), 1971; cons. pathologist Washington County Hosp., Nashville, Ill., St. Mary's Hosp., Christian Welfare Hosp., Centerville Twp. Hosp., all East St. Louis, Ill., Incarnate Ward Hosp., St. Louis, St. Joseph Hosp., St. Charles, Mo. Served with Nationalist Chinese Army, 1958-60. Diplomate Am. Bd. Pathology. Mem. AMA, Am. Soc. Clin. Pathologists, Coll. Am. Pathologists, Mo., So. med. assns., St. Louis Med. Soc. Home: 128 Gunston Hall Ct Chesterfield MO 63017 Office: 11636 Adminstration Dr Creve Coeur MO 63141

LIAO, SHU-CHUNG, chemist; b. Taiwan, Oct. 18, 1939; s. Chi-Chun and Cheung-Hsien (Lin) L.; B.S., Nat. Taiwan U., 1963; Ph.D., U. Western Ont., 1970; m. Pi-Wu Liu, Sept. 18, 1971; children—Ann, Susan. Research asso. dept. chemistry and macromolecular research center U. Mich., Ann Arbor, 1970-71, research asso. Sch. Pub. Health, 1972-73; sr. research asso. Climax Molybdenum Co. of Mich., Ann Arbor, 1973—. Exec. Taiwanese Christian Conf., Mich., Ohio, Ky. region, 1975; treas. Asian Presbyn. Caucus-Synod and Ann Arbor Taiwanese Christian Ch., 1977-78. Mem. Am. Chem. Soc. (analytical chemistry div.). Home: 2166 Yorktown Dr Ann Arbor MI 48105 Office: 1600 Huron Pkwy Ann Arbor MI 48105

LIBERTINY, GEORGE ZOLTAN, research engr.; b. Szolnok, Hungary, June 14, 1934; s. Arpad Pal and Ilona (Szendrei) L.; came to U.S., 1963, naturalized, 1974; B.Sc., U. Strathclyde, Glasgow, Scotland, 1959; Ph.D., U. Bristol (Eng.), 1964; m. Anna Vizvardi, 1956; children—Thomas, Karen. Engr., English Elec. Co., Ltd., Whetstone, 1959-60; asst. prof. mech. engring. U. Miami, Coral Gables, Fla., 1963-65, asso. prof., 1965-68; asso. prof. mechs. and aerospace engring. Ill. Inst. Tech., Chgo., 1968-71; sr. research engr. Ford Motor Co., Dearborn, Mich., 1971-73, prin. research engr. asso., 1973—; cons., expert witness design, stress and materials related to product liability cases. Ford Found. scholar, 1957-59, 60-63. Mem. Soc. Automotive Engrs. (R.R. Teetor award 1967), ASME, Am. Soc. Engring. Edn., Inst. Mech. Engrs. (Eng.), Soc. Exptl. Stress Analysis, Sigma Xi. Contbr. articles to profl. jours. Patentee in field. Office: Ford Motor Co American Rd Dearborn MI 48121

LICCARDI, EDWARD PAUL, electric contracting co. exec.; b. Cleve., Sept. 17, 1928; s. Dominic and Grace (Zicarelli) L.; student Cleve. Trade Sch., 1950-54; m. Edith Marie Caterini, May 8, 1954; children—Linda Marie (Mrs. Stephen Barbour), Cheryl Ann. With Max Oster Electric Co., Cleve., 1954—, pres., 1973—. Pres., Italian-Am. Cultural Found., Cleve., 1977—; pres. United Community Blood Center, Parma, Ohio, 1972—. Served with AUS, 1950-52. Mem. Cleve. Engring. Soc., Internat. Brotherhood of Elec. Workers, Am. Assn. Blood Banks, Cleve. Builders Assn. Roman Catholic. Home: 7830 Royal Ridge Dr Parma OH 44129 Office: 3907 Perkins Av Cleveland OH 44114

LICHTWARDT, HARRY EDWARD, physician, surgeon; b. Rio De Janeiro, Brazil, Dec. 16, 1918; s. Henry Herman and Ruth (Moyer) L.; A.B., Oberlin Coll., 1940; M.D., Washington U., 1943; m. Genevieve Isabelle Merry, July 28, 1947; children—Ronald Arthur, Gregory Edward. Intern Woman's Hosp., Detroit, 1943-44, surgery resident, 1946-47; resident surgery Dearborn VA Hosp., 1947-48; urology resident Wayne County Gen. Hosp., Eloise, Mich., 1948-51; practice medicine specializing in urology, Royal Oak, Mich., 1951—; chief urology Wm. Beaumont Hosp., Royal Oak, 1955—; vice chief urology, instr. Wayne County Gen. Hosp., 1958-65. Chmn. bd. mgmt. Birmingham (Mich.) YMCA, 1966-68. Served with M.C., AUS, 1944-46. Decorated Bronze Star. Diplomate Am. Bd. Urology. Fellow A.C.S.; mem. AMA, Mich., Oakland County med. socs., Am. Urol. Assn. (sec. North Central sect. 1971-74, pres. 1975). Club: Orchard Lake Country. Home: 4805 N Harsdale Bloomfield Hills MI 48013 Office: 3535 W 13 Mile Rd Royal Oak MI 48072

LIDDELL, LEON MORRIS, educator, librarian; b. Gainesville, Tex., July 21, 1914; s. Thomas L. and Minnie Mae (Morris) L.; B.A., U. Tex., 1937, J.D., 1937; B.L.S., U. Chgo., 1946; grad. study Internat. Law, Faculty of Polit. Sci., Columbia. Admitted to Tex. bar, 1937; claims dept. Hartford Accident and Indemnity Co., Houston, 1937-38; pvt. practice Gainesville, 1938-39; claim dept. Pacific Mutual Life Ins. Co., Kansas City, Mo., 1939-41; asst. prof. law and law librarian U. Conn., 1946-47; asst. prof. law U. Minn., 1949-50, asso. prof. law and law librarian, 1950-54, prof., 1954-60; prof. of law, law librarian U. Chgo., 1960-74, emeritus, 1974—; librarian, prof. law Northwestern U., Chgo., 1974—. Served from 2d lt. to maj. AUS, 1941-46. Mem. Tex. State Bar, Am. Assn. Law Libraries, Spl. Libraries Assn. Home: 880 Lake Shore Dr Chicago IL 60611 Office: 357 E Chicago Ave Chicago IL 60611

LIDMAN, J(OHN) KIRBY, transp. planner; b. Dickens, Iowa, July 12, 1930; s. John Harold and Marie (Sorenson) L.; B.S., Iowa State U., 1961. Mem. Iowa Hwy. Commn., 1958-60, 61-62; wind-tunnel design engr. airframe and rotorcraft div. B & C Splty., Inc., Ames, Iowa, 1963-69; project engr. Iowa Hwy. Commn., 1969—. Registered profl. engr., Iowa. Fellow Brit. Interplanetary Soc. (asso.); mem. Soc. for Indsl. and Applied Math., Am. Inst. Aeros. and Astronautics, Air Force Assn., Civil Air Patrol, Soaring Soc. Am., ASCE, Exptl. Aircraft Assn., Nat. Aeros. Assn., Nat. Soc. Profl. Engrs. Home: 607 Carroll Av Ames IA 50010 Office: Iowa Dept Transp Ames IA 50010 50010

LIEB, BERNARD, physician; b. N.Y.C., Oct. 14, 1918; s. Louis and Anna (Hausfresser) Liebschutz; B.S., N.Y. U. Coll. Arts and Scis., 1938, postgrad., 1938-40; M.B., Chgo. Med. Sch., 1943, M.D., 1944; m. Minnie Brainin, June 20, 1943; children—David B., Richard L., Linda K. Intern Beth Moses Hosp., Bklyn., 1944; practice medicine specializing in family practice, Chgo., 1946—; chief staff South Chgo. Community Hosp., 1970—. Served with USNR, 1945-46. Diplomate Am. Bd. Family Practice. Charter fellow Am. Acad. Family Physicians; mem. A.M.A., Ill., Chgo. med. socs., Am. Heart Assn., Alumni Assn. Chgo. Med. Sch., Phi Beta Kappa. Jewish. Office: 11141 S Kedzie Ave Chicago IL 60655

LIEBENOW, ROLAND RUDOLPH, ins. co. med. dir.; b. Jefferson County, Wis., Sept. 17, 1922; s. Rudolph F. and Elma L. (Loper) L.; B.S., U. Wis., Madison, 1944, M.D., 1948; m. Martha E. Anderson, May 5, 1950; children—Linda S., Ronald M., Kurt S. Intern, Colo. Gen. Hosp., Denver, 1948-49; gen. practice medicine, Stevens Point, Wis., 1949-50; practice medicine specializing in medicine and surgery, Lake Mills, Wis., 1950-67; asst. med. dir. Northwestern Met. Life Ins. Co., Milw., 1967—; teaching asst. in anatomy Med. Sch., U. Wis., 1944, research asst. in pharmacology, 1946-47; mem. med. staffs Deaconess Hosp., Milw., Watertown Meml., Ft. Atkinson Meml. hosps.; pres. exec. com. Marquardt Manor Nursing Home, Watertown, Wis., 1972-74; pres. med. staff St. Mary's Hosp., Watertown, 1959; vice chief of staff Ft. Atkinson (Wis.) Meml. Hosp., 1967; clin. instr. Med. Coll. Wis., 1976—. Chmn. troop com. Sinnissippi council Boy Scouts Am., 1965-76; vice chmn. bd. elders Lake Mills Moravian Ch., 1972-75. Served to capt. M.C., U.S. Army, 1953-55. Named Alumnus of Year, Lake Mills Alumni Assn., 1972. Diplomate Am. Bd. Family Practice; certified Bd. Life Ins. Medicine. Fellow Am. Acad. Family Practice; mem. Jefferson County (pres. 1959-60), Wis. State med. assns., AMA, Assn. Life Ins. Med. Dirs., Aerospace Med. Assn., Soc. for Prospective Medicine, Am. Legion, Phi Kappa Phi. Republican. Clubs: Northwestern Mut. Stamp (pres. 1972-76), Wis. Fedn. Stamp Clubs, Philatelic Classics Soc., Masons. Co-author monograph on chloroform, 1951. Home: 309 Lakeview Ave Lake Mills WI 53551 Office: 720 E Wisconsin Ave Milwaukee WI 53202

LIEBERMAN, DAVID JOSEPH, county ofcl.; b. Phila., Feb. 2, 1928; s. Wolf Meyer and Anne (Elman) L.; student Temple U., 1946; M.D., Jefferson Med. Coll., Phila., 1950; postgrad. U. Pa., 1952-53, 66; M.P.H., Harvard U., 1966. Rotating intern Phila. Gen. Hosp., 1950-52; camp physician Camp Pinecrest, Dingman's Ferry, Pa., 1951; ship surgeon Grace Line, N.Y.C., 1952-53; resident gen. surgery Albert Einstein Med. Center, Phila., 1953-56; tour physician Harlem Globetrotters Basketball Exhbn. World Tour, 1956; practice medicine specializing in gen. surgery Albert Einstein Med. Center, Phila., 1956-59; instr. surgery Albert Einstein Med. Center, No. Div., 1956-59, Albert Einstein Med. Center Sch. Nursing, 1956-59, Temple U. Sch. Medicine, 1956-59; asso. surgeon Rush Hosp. for Diseases of Chest, 1956-59; surgeon Home for the Jewish Aged, 1956-59; mem. courtesy surg. staff Germantown Hosp., Rolling Hill Hosp., 1956-59; ship surgeon U.S. Lines, N.Y.C., 1960; chief surg. services Warren (Pa.) State Hosp., 1960-64; physician I, Pa. Dept. Health, Bur. Field Services, 1964-65; asst. health dir. Phila. Dept. Pub. Health, Bur. Dist. Health Services, 1966-67; dir. Bur. Med. Policies and Standards, Office Med. Services and Facilities, Pa. Dept. Pub. Welfare, Harrisburg, 1968-69, med. assistance adminstr. Bur. Med. Assistance, Office Family Services, 1967-68; exec. med. dir. med. assistance program N.Y.C. Dept. Health, 1969-71; dir. Dept. Ambulatory Care Services and Community Medicine, French and Polyclinic Med. Sch. and Health Center, N.Y.C., 1971-74; dir. Monroe County Health Dept., Monroe County Med. Examiner, Monroe, Mich., 1975—; lectr. U. Mich.; mem. tech. adv. council Mich. Cancer Found. Community Outreach Detection and Care Project; mem. Coordinating Council Agencies Monroe County; mem. Monroe County Substance Abuse Adv. Council. Chmn. physicians subcom. United Way of Monroe County, Inc., 1975, chmn. profl. div., 1976; bd. dirs., pres. elect Monroe Boys Club, 1976—; bd. dirs. Monroe chpt. Mich. Soc. Mental Health; chmn. Monroe County Health Planning Council, Monroe County Emergency Med. Service Council; health services coordinator Monroe County Office Civil Preparedness; bd. dirs. Monroe County Commn. Aging, Monroe County Opportunities Program. Recipient Dr. Francis W. Shain Prize, Gold medal in surgery Jefferson Med. Coll., 1950, Best Resident prize, Albert Einstein Med. Center Phila., 1956; USPHS traineeship grantee, 1965-66. Fellow Am. Pub. Health Assn., Am. Assn. Pub. Welfare Med. Dirs., Royal Soc. Health; mem. Am. Acad. Health Adminstrn., Am. Pub. Welfare Assn., Am. Coll. Preventive Medicine, Mich. Pub. Health Assn. (membership com. 1976—, sec. adminstrn. div. 1976—), Mich. Health Officers Assn. (dir. 1977—, sec. 1976-77), Mich-Alcohol and Addiction Assn., Mich. Emergency Services Health Council, Mich. Environ. Health Assn., Physicians Forum, Mich. State, Monroe County med. socs. Home: 3861 N Custer Rd Monroe MI 48161 Office: 650 Stewart Rd Monroe MI 48161

LIEBERMAN, STANLEY BERTRAM, real estate broker; b. Trenton, N.J., Mar. 31, 1938; s. Abram Herbert and Freida (Chamowitz) L.; A.B. in Bus. Mgmt., Rutgers U., 1960; children—Louis, Jonathan, Rebecca. Sales mgr. Am. Photograph Corp., N.Y.C., 1960-67, Root Photographers, Chgo., 1968-71; pres. Lieberman Inc., Realtors, Buffalo Grove, Ill., 1971—, Video Homes of Am., Inc., Buffalo Grove, 1972—; instr. real estate prins. Harper Coll., Palatine, Ill. Police and fire commr. City of Buffalo Grove, 1971-75; founder, pres. Congregation Beth Judea, 1968-70; treas. United Synagogue of Am. Midwest, 1970. Served as 1st lt. U.S. Army, 1960. Mem. N.W. Suburban Bd. Realtors (pres.), Realtors Nat. Mktg. Inst. Clubs: Rotary (past treas.), B'nai B'rith. Home: Rural Route 2 Box 459 Mardan Woods Long Grove IL 60047 Office: 400 W Dundee Rd Buffalo Grove IL 60090

LIEBERMANN, THOMAS ROBERT, engine co. exec.; b. Arad, Romania, Nov. 22, 1949; s. Geza Andrew and Bella (Schachter) L.; came to U.S., 1966, naturalized, 1974; B.A. in Sociology, U. Pa., 1972, B.C.E., 1975, M.B.A., 1975. Profl. soccer player Boston Minutemen, 1974; chief subject diver Inst. Environ. Medicine, Phila., 1970-71, research technician, 1970-75; asst. to exec. v.p. and gen. mgr. Cummins Engine Co. Inc., Columbus, Ind., 1975-76, mgr. major constrn. bus., 1976—. Mem. ASCE, Assn. M.B.A. Execs. Club: Amateur Soccer. Home: 3121 Wedgewood Ct Columbus IN 47201 Office: 1000 5th St Columbus IN 47201

LIEBERT, LUCILLE A., psychologist; b. Coffeyville, Kans., Feb. 10, 1934; d. Albert L. and Mamie Josephine (Jordan) Liebert; B.M., Kans. State Coll. of Pitts., 1955; M.A., U. of Notre Dame, 1968; post-grad. U. of Mo., Kans. City, 1976—. Tchr. music Coffeyville, Kans., 1955-67; tchr. music Holy Name Jr. High Sch., Coffeyville, 1964-67; dir. counseling services Marymount Coll., Salina, Kans., 1968-71; pvt. practice psychology Psychological Services, Kans. City, Mo., 1971—; profl. cons. Catholic Diocese of Kans. City and St. Joseph, Mo., 1971, Catholic Diocese of Jefferson City, Mo., 1975—. Mem. Mo., Kans., Am. psychological assns., Am. Personnel and Guidance Assn. Roman Catholic. Home: 9100 Riggs Ln Overland Pk KS 66212 Office: 1207 Grand Ave Kansas City MO 64106

LIEBLER, EDWARD CHARLES, veterinarian, constrn. co. exec.; b. Brown City, Mich., Apr. 6, 1939; s. Harris D. and Golda Elfleda (Hollenbeck) L.; B.S., Mich. State U., 1962, D.V.M., 1964; m. Carol Sue Kerrins, Sept. 10, 1960 (div. 1972); children—Juli Kristina, Edward Jae; m. 2d, Sharon D. Willis, Nov. 2, 1973. Individual practice vet. medicine, Caro, Mich., 1964-72; founder, pres. Liebler Constrn. Co., 1966—, Caro Land Devel. Corp., 1971-73; dir. Caro Devel. Corp., 1977—. Chmn. Citizens Com. to Become City, 1969-70; bd. dirs. Mich. Eye Collection Center, Inc.; mem. Tuscola County Republican exec. com., 1976—. Mem. Mich. (ethics com. 1969-70), Thumb (pres. 1967-68) vet. med. assns., Home Builders Assn. Thumb (pres. 1971), Nat. Home Builders Assn. (dir. 1974-75, 77—). Mason, Lion (pres. 1968-69, zone chmn. 1972-73, dep. dist. gov. 1973-75). Club: Amateur Radio (Caro). Home: 645 Westchester Dr Caro MI 48723 Office: 429 N State St Caro MI 48723

LIEBMAN, MONTE HARRIS, educator, former psychiatrist; b. Milw., July 20, 1930; s. William and Ida (Zaichek) L.; B.S., U. Wis., 1953, M.D., 1957; 1 dau., Lori Kay. Intern, Mount Zion Hosp., San Francisco, 1958; resident psychiatry VA Hosp., Palo Alto, Calif., 1959; psychiatry fellow Marquette U., Milw., 1960-62; practice medicine, specializing in psychiatry, Milw., 1962—; staff Mount Sinai Hosp., Milw., 1962—; asst. clin. prof. Med. Coll. Wis., Milw., 1962-75; psychotherapy supr. Mount Sinai Med. Center Clinic and Clergy, Milw., 1965-74; cons. tchr. Central State Hosp., Waupuh, Wis., 1974-75; cons. Pub. Health Center, Waukesha, Wis. community health aid program, 1972-73; tchr. adult non-credit sch. Marquette U., 1974—; facilitator Free U., Milw., 1975—; counselling instr., pres. bd. dirs. Pregnancy Aftermath Helpline, Milw., 1976—. Fellow Am. Soc. Psychoanalytic Physicians; mem. The Sayers, Internat. Soc. Psychiatric Research, Milw. Mental Health Assn., Wis. Concerned Citizens for Life. Author: Communications from the Private World of a Psychiatrist, Counselor's Handbook on Hysteria and Schizophrenia, What Is Love and How to Find It; Introduction to Psychotherapy, Elements for Contemporary Counseling and Development, all in 1977; exec. editor Med. Psych. Publications; contbg. editor: Pasticcio, 1973 (booklet). Home: W310 N6431 N Beaver Lake Rd Hartland WI 53029 Office: 2040 W Wisconsin Ave Milwaukee WI 53233

LIEBOLD, MARY JANE, real estate and ins. agy. exec.; b. Chgo., June 5, 1925; d. Oscar Paul and Mary Albina (Hancock) Larson; student St. Agnes Acad., 1938-42; m. William E. Liebold, Feb. 11, 1955 (dec.). Sec.-treas. McClain-Matthews Agy., Inc., Indpls., from 1957, now v.p. Past pres. Indpls. chpt. Womens Council Indpls. Real Estate Bd.; past corporate sec. Indpls. Bd. Realtors. Mem. Ind. Real Estate Assn. (dir.), Nat. Assn. Real Estate Bds. (chmn. com. Indpls. chpt. Womens Council), Womens Council Realtors (past state pres., past gov. Ind., regional v.p.). Club: Altrusa (past pres., corr. sec.). Home: 7799 Landings Dr Indianapolis IN 46240

LIECHTI, HARRIS NELSON, educator; b. Des Moines, Aug. 20, 1935; s. Frederick Sinon and Dorothy Mabel (Nelson) L.; B.A., U. Mich., 1957, M.A., 1958, Ph.D., 1968; m. Marya Beth Adams, Oct. 31, 1970; children—Sean Adam Nelson, Taya Maxon. Writer/producer/dir. Armed Forces Radio and TV Service, Hollywood, Calif., 1959-60; floor mgr./film editor U. Mich. TV Center, Ann Arbor, 1960-61; asst. reports officer U.S. Office of Edn., Washington, 1962-63, 66-68; asst. prof. speech U. Wis.-Oshkosh, 1968-73, dir. TV services, 1969-75, asso. prof. speech, 1973—; pres. Oshkosh Cinema Guild, 1975-76. Served in U.S. Army, 1958-60. Recipient Regents-Alumni award U. Mich., 1953. Mem. Speech Communication Assn. (nat. steering com. for Young Turks 1969-70), Nat. Assn. Ednl. Broadcasters, Broadcast Edn. Assn., World Future Soc., Am. Film Inst., Oshkosh Symphony Assn., Friends of Paine Mus. Democrat. Unitarian. Producer TV shows: Joyful Banners: Calder and the Arts, 1974; Fields of Grace: The Art of Léon Lhermitte, 1975; others. Home: 823 Washington Ave Oshkosh WI 54901 Office: Dept Speech U Wis Oshkosh WI 54901

LIECHTY, G(EORGE) FREDERICK, hosp. service exec.; b. Monroe, Ind., Jan. 1, 1914; s. M. Simon and Rosina (Wittwer) L.; B.S., Eastern Mich. U., 1938; M.B.A., U. Mich., 1940; m. Helen Holly Van

Sickle, June 23, 1945; children—Susan, John, Thomas, Jane. Bus. mgr. U. Mich. Hosp., Ann Arbor, 1941-45; branch mgr. Blue Cross-Blue Shield, Chgo., 1945-47, asst. dir., 1947-63, v.p. marketing, 1963-67, sr. v.p. marketing, 1967-73, sr. v.p. corp. affairs, 1973—. Lectr. Sch. Hosp. Adminstrn., Northwestern U., Evanston, Ill., 1946-50; trustee Meth. Student Found., Northwestern U., 1952-58; mem. Evanston High Sch. Bd. Edn., 1965-72. Trustee Northwestern Meml. Hosp., Chgo., 1969—; bd. dirs., exec. com. Chgo. Lung Assn., 1974—. Mem. Am. Mgmt. Assn., Am. Pub. Health Assn., Ill. Hist. Soc., Ill. C. of C., Chgo. Assn. Commerce and Industry, Chgo. Athletic Assn., Field Mus. Natural History. Club: Executives (Chgo.). Rotarian (Chgo. pres. 1963—). United Methodist (del. No. Ill. Conf. 1959-75; chmn. adminstrv. bd. 1964-66, mem. bd. trustees 1971—, chmn. 1973-74). Home: 2436 Central Park Ave Evanston IL 60201 Office: 233 N Michigan Ave Chicago IL 60601

LIEDHOLM, CARL EDWARD, educator; b. Long Beach, Calif., July 22, 1940; s. George Edward and Marian (Folts) L.; B.A., Pomona Coll., 1961; Ph.D., U. Mich., 1965; m. Margaret Edith Osgood, Nov. 29, 1963; children—Kathleen Elizabeth, Erik Allen. Adviser, acting dir. Economic Devel. Inst., U. Nigeria, Enugu, 1965-67; asst. prof. econs. Mich. State U., E. Lansing, 1967-69, chmn. Econs. Dept., 1969-74, prof. econs., 1974—. Cons. to U.S. Agy. for Internat. Devel., 1973—, Rockefeller Found., 1969. NDEA fellow, 1961-65; Yale U. vis. fellow, 1974; Sussex U. (Eng.) vis. fellow, 1975. Fellow African Studies Assn.; mem. Am. Econs. Assn., Nigeria, Royal econ. socs., Phi Beta Kappa. Club: Cal. Cello. Author: Growth and Development of Nigerian Economy (with Carl Eicher), 1970. Author: The Indian Iron and Steel Industry: An Analysis of Comparative Advantage, 1974. Home: 830 Wildwood St East Lansing MI 48823

LIEM, DANIEL TIANG HAM, physician; b. Sepandjang, Indonesia, June 15, 1937; s. Ibrahim Hien Sing and Rachel (Tjaij Nio Tjoa) L.; doctorandus, U. AirLangga, Surabaja, Indonesia, 1960; M.D., Wilhelm's U., Muenster, Germany, 1962, Ph.D., 1964; m. Rebecca I. Tanutama, Sept. 19, 1969; children—Nathania Ruth, Joel Jonathan, Jesse Joshua. Resident Henry Ford Hosp., Detroit, 1965-68, Victoria Hosp., London, Ont., Can., 1969-71; practice medicine specializing in internal medicine and allergy, Windsor, Ont., Can., 1971—; mem. staffs Grace Hosp., Hotel Dieu Hosp., Met. Gen. Hosp., Windsor Western Hosp. Fellow Royal Coll. Physicians Can.; mem. Canadian, Ont. med. assns., Essex County Med. Soc., Christian Med. Soc. Can.; asso. mem. Am. Acad. Allergy, Mich. Allergy Soc. Home: 4021 Kennedy Dr East Windsor ON N9G 1X9 Canada Office: 1100 Ouellette Av Windsor ON Canada

LIEN, ANDREW CLYDE, women's figure salon exec.; b. N.Y.C., Jan. 19, 1943; s. Julius Martin and Sylvia (Schotter) L.; B.A., City Coll. N.Y., 1964; M.B.A., N.Y. U., 1966; m. Claire Abby Levine, June 3, 1965; children—Christopher Adam, Rebecca Anne. Various exec. positions mktg. Procter & Gamble Co., domestic, 1966-72, Internat., 1973-75; dir. new bus. devel. Gillette Co., Boston, 1975-77; pres., chief exec. officer Elaine Powers Figure Salons, Milw., 1977—; lectr. in field. Active Jr. Achievement, Boy Scouts Am. Mem. Am. Mgmt. Assn., Manila Polo Club, N. River Racquet Club. Home: 9736 N Lake Dr Milwaukee WI 53217 Office: Elaine Powers Figure Salons 105 W Michigan St Milwaukee WI 53203

LIERLEY, EARL CLEON, automotive aftermarket mfg. co. exec.; b. Council Bluffs, Iowa, Jan. 2, 1917; s. Otis W. and Claudia M. (Ferris) L.; grad. high sch.; m. Geraldine Walenz, Nov. 7, 1942; children—Kathleen (Mrs. Robert E. Eppler), Karen (Mrs. Harold Bowman), Patrice, Michael. Bus. mgr., sec.-treas. J.V. Thorndike Inc., Omaha, 1935-63; pres., gen. mgr. Universal Mfg. Co., Algona, Iowa, 1963—; pres. Allied Sales Co., Algona, 1963—. Bd. dirs. Midwest Employers Council, Omaha. Mem. Ford Authorized Remanufacturers Assn. (chmn. 1967, dir. 1972—), Algona C. of C. (pres. 1966). Rotarian (pres. 1968). Home: 169 South Hwy Algona IA 50511 Office: 405 Diagonal St Algona IA 50511

LIETH, HELMUT SIEGFRIED, plastics co. exec.; b. Halle, Germany, July 20, 1936; s. Leo and Elisabeth (Schmidt) L.; m. Ute Bickenbach, Mar. 21, 1963; children—Anne, Frank; came to U.S., 1963; student NAO Coll. Engring., Cologne, Germany, 1963. Plant mgr. United Thread Mills, N.Y.C., 1963-65; nat. sales mgr. Deutz Diesel Corp. subs. KHD, Hicksville, N.Y., 1965-73; v.p., gen. mgr., sec. Schuberth Corp., Holland, Ohio, 1973—. Mem. Internat. Trade Assn. (dir. Toledo Area). Home: 5254 Fredelia Dr Toledo OH 43623 Office: 1510 Albon Rd Holland OH 43528

LIEU, JOHN, physician; b. Hankow, China, Aug. 15, 1904; s. Fan Hou and Sing Ten (Chen) L.; M.D., St. John's U., Shanghai, China, 1926; D.T.M., Liverpool (Eng.) U., 1939; m. Dorothy A. Irwin, Aug. 31, 1974; children—John, Gladys. Came to U.S., 1959, naturalized, 1964. Supt. Works & Mine Hosp., Tayeh, Hupeh, China, 1928; asst. med. officer, Shanghai Municipal Council, 1929-36; doctor-in-charge Municipal Hosp., Shanghai, 1936-45; chief surgeon Soochow (China) Hosp., 1945-46; pvt. practice, Soochow, 1946-49, Columbus, Ohio, 1962—; chief surg. dept. Municipal Sixth Hosp., Shanghai, 1949-57; asst. port health officer, Hongkong; dir. Emerick Hosp., Columbus State Inst., 1961-65; mem. staff Grant Hosp., Columbus. Rockerfeller scholar, 1940. Fellow Royal Soc. Health, Eng.; mem. Am., Ohio med. assns., Acad. Medicine, AAAS, Ohio Acad. Sci. Presbyn. (deacon 1968). Home: 645 Neil Ave Columbus OH 43215 Office: 370 E Town St Columbus OH 43215

LIFSCHULTZ, PHILLIP, merchandising corp. exec.; b. Oak Park, Ill., Mar. 5, 1927; s. Abraham Albert and Frances (Siegel) L.; B.S., U. Ill., 1949; J.D., John Marshall Law Sch., 1956; m. Edith Louise Leavitt, June 27, 1948; children—Gregory Ross, Bonnie Gail, Jodie Ann. Tax mgr. Arthur Andersen & Co., Chgo., 1957-63; asst. controller taxes, ins. Montgomery Ward & Co., Inc., Chgo., 1963-67, divisional v.p. taxes, 1967-69, v.p. taxes, 1969—; dir. Montgomery Ward Realty Corp., M-W Properties Corp., Montgomery Ward Devel. Corp.; v.p., dir., Randhurst Corp., Mount Prospect, Ill., 1965-77. Lectr. accounting, taxation DePaul U. Evening Div., Chgo., 1957-61. Mem. adv. bd. Auditor Gen. Ill., 1965-73, chmn. adv. bd., 1972-73; chmn. Transition Task Force to Ill. Dept. Revenue, 1972-73. Mem. adv. council Coll. Commerce and Bus. Adminstrn., U. Ill. at Urbana-Champaign. Served with AUS, 1945-46. C.P.A., Ill. Mem. Ill. Bar Assn., Tax Execs. Inst. (dir. Chgo. chpt.), Nat. Retail Mchts. Assn. (chmn. taxation com. 1975—), Am. Retail Fedn. (chmn. com. taxation and fiscal policy 1971-73), Internat. Fiscal Assn., Am. Inst. C.P.A.'s, Ill. Soc. C.P.A.'s, Nat. Assn. Tax Adminstrs., Internat. Assn. Assessing Officers, Civic Fedn. (dir. 1975—, chmn. tax reform com. 1973), Nat. Tax Assn. Tax Inst. Am., Tau Delta Phi, Beta Alpha Psi. Clubs: Standard, Executives (Chgo.). Home: 976 Oak Dr Glencoe IL 60022 Office: One Montgomery Ward Plaza Chicago IL 60671

LIFTON, HERMAN MANUEL, dentist; b. Detroit, Apr. 3, 1919; s. Isidore and Esther (Zieve) L.; student Wayne State U., 1939-40; D.D.S., U. Detroit, 1943; m. Pola W. Winokur, Sept. 17, 1944; children—Estralee, Cathy, James. Pvt. practice gen. dentistry, Melvindale, Mich., 1946—. Served with Dental Corps, U.S. Army, 1943-46. Mem. Am., Mich. dental assns., Detroit Dist. Dental Soc., Am., Acad. Oral Medicine, Am. Soc. Preventive Dentistry, Mich. Soc. Psychosomatic Dentistry, Am. Acad. Gen. Dentistry, Chgo. Dental Soc., So. Acad. Clin. Nutrition, Royal Soc. Health, Am. Soc. Clin. Hypnosis, Inst. Myofunctional Therapy, Touch for Health, Nutrition Today, Pierre Fauchard Soc., Russell B. Bunting Periodontal Soc., Alpha Omega. Jewish. Clubs: Shriner, Mason. Home: 23417 Riverview Dr Southfield MI 48034 Office: 2920 Oakwood Blvd Melvindale MI 48122

LIGGETT, DELMORE, educator, cons.; b. Rising Sun, Ind., May 19, 1906; s. Harvey C. and Lydia Belle (Hannah) L.; B.S., Ind. U., 1941; D. Psychology in Metaphysics, D. Metaphysics, Indpls. Coll. of Divine Metaphysics, 1966, D.D., 1968. Prin. Cass-Union Sch., 1931-42; postmaster, Rising Sun, 1942-45; prin. Freedom, Ind., 1949-53; tchr. English Aurora (Ind.) High Sch., 1953-68. Cons. Ind. State Tchrs. Assn., Nat. Edn., World Field Research. Trustee BonDurant Agape Ministry, 1966—. Recipient certificate of Appreciation Nat. Police Officers Assn., 1970. Fellow World Acad.; mem. Nat. Hist. Soc. (founder), Ohio-Switzerland Counties Ret. Tchrs. Assn. (pres. 1975—), UN Assn. of U.S., Internat. Platform Assn., OAS. Democrat. Methodist. Clubs: Century, Am. Traveliares, World Traveler. Home: Box 35 RD Suite 1 Rising Sun IN 47040

LIGHT, GERALD SIDNEY, pediatric nephrologist; b. Melfort, Sask., Can., July 11, 1940; s. William Harold and Ella Viola (Elsner) L.; came to U.S., 1965; M.D., U. Sask., 1965; m. Gloria Elaine Joyner, Jan. 26, 1973. Intern, McLaren Hosp., Flint, Mich., 1965-66; resident in pediatrics U. Mich., Ann Arbor, 1966-68; dir. pediatric edn. Hurley Med. Center, Flint, Mich., 1968-69; fellow in pediatric nephrology U. Mich., Ann Arbor, 1969-70; coordinator renal unit Hurley Med. Center, 1970—; practice medicine specializing in pediatric nephrology Flint, 1970—. Recipient Urban Gareau award, 1965; Mott Children's Center scholar, 1966-68, Mich. Kidney Found. scholar, 1969-70. Fellow Am. Acad. Pediatrics; mem. Mich. Kidney Found., Transplant Soc. Mich., Am. Acad. Nephrology, Internat. Acad. Nephrology. Contbr. articles to profl. publs. Home: 5414 N Dyewood St Flint MI 48504 Office: G-1071 Ballenger Hwy Suite 31 Flint MI 48504

LIGHTBOURN, GEORGE ALLEN, urologist; b. Miami, Fla., July 7, 1933; s. Carol Allenmore and Dorothy Burnell (Dames) L.; B.A., Fisk U., 1954, M.A., 1956; M.D., Meharry Med. Coll., 1963; m. Jean Powell, Apr. 11, 1956; children—Andrea, Linda, Tracey, Rose, George. Practice medicine specializing in urology, Detroit; mem. staff Harper-Grace Hosp., Children's Hosp. of Detroit, St. Joseph Mercy Hosp., Kirwood Gen. Hosp., SW Detroit Hosp. Served with U.S. Army, 1956-58. Diplomate Am. Bd. Urology. Fellow A.C.S. Contbr. articles to med. jours. Office: 3800 Woodward St Detroit MI 48201

LIGHTFOOT, LYLE EUGENE, architect; b. Kansas City, Kans., Feb. 7, 1921; s. Alma Lincoln and Mary Agusta (Opperman) L.; B.S., Iowa State U., 1945; m. Anna Mae Pennick, Oct. 25, 1944. Architect, asso. Gentry & Voskamp-Architects, Kansas City, Mo., 1955-63; architect Boyer & Biskup-Architects, Omaha, 1963-66; asso., chief architect Bucher & Willis, Salina, Kans., 1966-74; individual practice, Salina, 1975—; mem. Salina Planning Commn. Recipient Design award, Stran Steel Corp., 1967. Mem. A.I.A. Republican. Mem. Reorganized Ch. of Jesus Christ of Latterday-Saints. Mason. Home: 1007 Scott St Salina KS 67401 Office: 431 North 13th St Salina KS 67401

LIISTE, LENNART LESTER, businessman; b. Mpls., Sept. 8, 1914; s. John Wilhelm and Alma Rebecka (Tuominen) Lillberg; educated in Finland; m. Anna Liisa Lammi, Oct. 9, 1939; children—Helen, Elizabeth, Patricia. With Dayton-Hudson, Mpls., 1948 and after; dir. Anna-Liisa's Nursery Sch., Mpls., 1951-64; pres. Finn Port Co., Mpls., 1969—. Served with Finnish Army, 1939-44. Mem. Nat. Retail Merchants Assn., Finnish-Am. Soc. (pres. 1962, exec. dir. 1971—). Lutheran. Home: 1027 Rhode Island Ave N Minneapolis MN 55427 Office: 4944 Xerxes Ave S Minneapolis MN 55410

LILJEQUIST, JON LEON, educator; b. Chgo., Apr. 24, 1936; s. Leon R. and Muriel (Staples) L.; B.S., U. Ill., 1958; J.D., Loyola U., Chgo., 1964; m. Bonnie Barrow; children—Lisa, Laura, Lars. Design engr. Outboard Marine Corp., Waukegan, Ill., 1958-60; instr. U. Ill., Chgo., 1960-63; law asso. Hofgren Webner Allen, Stellman and McCord, Chgo., 1963-64; asst. prof. law and engring U. Ill., Chgo., 1964—; chief patent counsel Appleton Electric Co., Chgo. part-time, 1966-73; pres., founder Timark. Registered profl. engr., Ill. Mem. Am. Bar Assn., Chgo. Patent Law Assn. Patentee in field. Home: 801 S Elmhurst Ave Mount Prospect IL 60056 Office: U Ill Chicago Circle Chicago IL 60680

LILLARD, JOHN STOLL, investment counselor; b. Cin., May 31, 1930; s. William Parlin and Margaret Scott (Stoll) L.; B.A., U. Va., 1952; M.B.A., Xavier U., 1961; m. Paula Polk, Sept. 12, 1953; children—Lisa, Lynn, Pamela, Angeline, Paula. Investment counselor Haydock, Peabody & Hawley, 1955-59; investment counselor Scudder, Stevens & Clark, Cin., 1959-64, gen. partner, 1964-77; pres. Scudder, Stevens & Clark, Inc. (Ill.), Chgo., 1971-77, chmn. bd., 1973-77, chmn. finance, budget and analyst coms. of bd. dirs., 1975-77, nat. mktg. dir., 1976-77, spl. partner, 1977—; dir. Scudder Realty Advisers, Inc., 1973-77; dir. United Data Processing Services, Clem Corp. Mem. fin. com. Community Chest of Greater Cin., 1970-71; active United Appeal, United Fine Arts Funds; trustee Cin. May Festival, 1963-68, pres. bd., 1965-67; trustee Cin. Union Bethel, Hamilton County Diagnostic Clinic, Childrens Home, Boys Clubs Greater Cin., Hillsdale-Lotspeich Schs., Hull House Assn., Old Peoples Home, Chgo., Ill. Childrens Home and Aid Soc., Chgo. Orchestral Assn.; trustee Cin. Symphony Orch., 1965—, pres., 1968-71; trustee, mem. exec. com. Ravinia Festival Assn. Served to lt. (j.g.) USN, 1952-55. Mem. Cin. Soc. Fin. Analysts (past pres.), Queen City Assn. (past pres.). Clubs: Miami of Ohio (past pres.); Racquet (past pres.), Queen City, Commercial, Commonwealth (Cin.); Camargo (past treas., mem. bd. govs.); Onwentsia (Lake Forest); Tavern (Chgo.). Home: 1300 N Waukegan Rd Lake Forest IL 60045 Office: 111 E Wacker Dr Chicago IL 60601

LILLIE, RICHARD HORACE, surgeon; b. Milw., Feb. 3, 1918; s. Osville Richard and Sylvia Grace (Faber) L.; B.S., Haverford Coll., 1939; M.D., Harvard U., 1943; M.S. in Surgery, U. Mich., 1950; m. Jane Louise Zwicky, Sept. 24, 1949; children—Richard Horace, Diane Louise. Intern, U. Mich. Hosp., Ann Arbor, 1943-44, resident, 1946-50; chief of surgery, Milw. Hosp., 1968—; practice medicine specializing in surgery, Milw., 1951—; clin. prof. Med. Coll. Wis.; pres. Lillie 18-94 Corp.; v.p. Waukesha Motor Inns. Bd. dirs. Goodwill Industries. Served with M.C. AUS, 1944-46. Mem. Am. Bd. Surgery, A.C.S., Central Surg. Assn., AMA, Wis. Surg. Soc. Episcopalian. Clubs: Milw. Athletic, Univ. of Milw., Milw. Yacht, Town. Contbr. articles to surg. jours. Home: 6500 N Lake Dr Milwaukee WI 53217 Office: 811 E Wisconsin Ave Milwaukee WI 53202

LILLY, ALFRED FORREST, JR., ins. co. computer planning exec.; b. Aruba, Netherlands Antilles, Dec. 4, 1938; s. Alfred Forrest and Bertha May (Walsh) L. (parents Am. citizens); A.A., Johnson County (Kan.) Community Coll., 1974; B.A., Rockhurst Coll., 1978; m. Loree Adele Plattner, Jan. 27, 1972; children—Diana Laurene, Jennifer Ann, Robert Kyle. Asst. mgr. computer programming Kansas City (Mo.) Life Ins. Co., 1965-67; supr. computer services, 1967-73, dir. computer ops., 1973-75, dir. computer planning, 1975—. Mem. Citizens Assn., Kansas City, Mo., 1962. Served with Signal Corps, AUS, 1956-59; Korea, 1958-59. Mem. Univac Users Assn., Univac Sci. Exchange (sec. Kansas City chpt. 1976-77, vice chmn. 1977-78), Kansas City Jr. C. of C. Methodist. Home: 7701 Westgate Dr Lenexa KS 66216 Office: PO Box 139 Kansas City MO 64141

LILLY, ROGER MCKINLEY, guidance dir.; b. Huntington, W.Va., Jan. 26, 1946; s. Van M. and Kathleen B. (Smith) L.; B.A., Marshall U., Huntington, 1968, M.A., 1970; divorced; children—Anna Jo and Amy Lynn (twins). Dir. biology dept. Russell (Ky.) Ind. Schs., 1968; dir. guidance Magnolia High Sch., Wetzell County Schs., New Martinsville, W.Va., 1970-71, Green Local Schs., Franklin Furnace, Ohio, 1971—; v.p. So. Ohio Sch. Employees Credit Union. Mem. Am. Personnel and Guidance Assn., Nat., Ohio edn. assns., Scioto Area Counselors Assn. (past pres.), Green Local Tchrs. Assn. (chief negotiator). Democrat. Presbyterian. Home: 2212 Inwood Dr Huntington WV 25701 Office: Route 1 Franklin Furnace OH 45629

LIM, TOH-WOON, dentist; b. Fukien, China, Jan. 18, 1948; s. Si-Sin and Po-Sio (Kwa) L.; came to U.S., 1971, naturalized, 1978; B. Dental Surgery, Inst. Medicine, 1971; D.M.D., Tufts U., 1973, postgrad periodontics, 1975. Staff dentist R.I. Hosp., Providence, 1974; staff periodontist Woodstock Hosp., McHenry Hosp., Crystal Lake, Ill., 1976—. Mem. Chgo., McHenry County dental socs., Am., Ill. dental assns., Am. Acad. Periodontology. Methodist. Office: 111 Virginia St Crystal Lake IL 60014

LIMBACHER, JAMES LOUIS, film librarian; b. St. Marys, Ohio, Nov. 30, 1926; s. Fritz J. and Edith (Smith) L.; B.A., Bowling Green State U., 1949, M.A., 1954; M.S. in Edn., Ind. U., 1955; M.S. in L.S., Wayne State U., 1972. Audio-visual librarian Dearborn (Mich.) Dept. Libraries, 1955—; instr. history and appreciation motion picture Univ. Center for Adult Edn., Detroit, 1965-72, Marygrove Coll., 1966-67, Wayne State U., 1973—. Recipient Mich. Librarian of Yr. award, 1974. Mem. Am. Fedn. Film Socs. (nat. pres. 1962-65), Ednl. Film Library Assn. (nat. pres. 1966-70), Soc. for Cinema Studies, Soc. for Cinephiles, Alpha Tau Omega, Theta Alpha Phi, Omicron Delta Kappa, Beta Phi Mu. Author: Four Aspects of the Film, 1969; A Reference Guide to Audiovisual Information, 1972; Film Music: From Violins to Video, 1973; The Song List, 1973. Editor: Using Films, 1967, Feature films on 8 and 16, annually 1968—; Remakes, Sequels and Series, 1978. Contbr. monthly record column Previews, 1963-77, weekly column to Dearborn Press, 1956-73. Home: 21800 Morley Av Dearborn MI 48124 Office: Henry Ford Centennial Library Dearborn MI 48126

LIMBERG, FRANKLIN HAROLD, pharm. co. exec.; b. Marinette, Wis., July 21, 1943; s. Franklin William and Genieve Sarah (Boivin) L.; B.S., Marquette U., 1966; M.S., Wichita State U., 1968; m. Carol Ann Wenderoth, 1944; children—Franklin C., Jason W., Neal J. Research scientist Wyeth Labs., West Chester, Pa., 1968-70; dir. quality control Badger Labs., Jackson, Wis., 1970-74; dir. quality control Marion Health and Safety div. Marion Labs., Rockford, Ill., 1974—. Mem. Health Industries Assn., Am. Pharm. Assn., AAAS. Home: 3543 Montlake Dr Rockford IL 61111 Office: 1515 Elmwood Rd Rockford IL 61101

LIMJOCO, URIEL ROMEY, surgeon; b. Philippines, May 11, 1935; s. Emilio Tinchuangco and Clara Jugo (Romey) L.; came to U.S., 1961, naturalized, 1972; A.A., M.D., U. Philippines, 1957; M.S., U. Wis., 1966; m. Carolyn Jo Olson, Aug. 22, 1964; children—Lucy, Lisa, Jeffrey, Laura, Jennifer, Victoria. Instr. anatomy U. Philippines Med. Sch., 1957-61; resident in surgery U. Wis. Hosp., 1962-67; staff surgeon VA Hosp., Madison, Wis. also instr. surgery U. Wis. Med. Sch., 1967-69; practice medicine specializing in surgery, Menomonee Falls, Wis., 1969—; mem. staff Community Meml. Hosp., Menomonee Falls, chief surgery, 1972-74, pres. med. staff, 1977-78; mem. staff Elmbrook Hosp., Brookfield, Wis. Bd. dirs., chmn. pub. edn. com. Wis. div. Am. Cancer Soc., 1974—, pres. Waukesha County unit, 1973-75. Diplomate Am. Bd. Surgery. Fellow A.C.S.; mem. Wis. Surg. Soc., Milw. Acad. Surgery, Waukesha County Med. Soc. (chmn. pub. relations com. 1975—). Republican. Roman Catholic. Club: North Hills Country. Contbr. to med. jours. Home: W213 N5349 Adamdale Dr Menomonee Falls WI 53051 Office: N84 W16889 Menomonee Ave Menomonee Falls WI 53051

LIN, JOHN YEN, physician; b. Taiwan, China, Feb. 26, 1937: came to U.S., 1965, naturalized, 1977; M.D., Nat. Taiwan U., 1963; m. Elena Wu, Apr. 4, 1965; children—Stephen, Patricia, David. Intern, Edward Hosp., Naperville, Ill., from 1973, Good Samaritan Hosp., Downers Grove, Ill., 1973-77; gen. practice resident Sharon (Pa.) Gen. Hosp., 1965-67; resident in internal medicine Louis A. Weiss Hosp., Chgo., 1967-71; resident in pulmonary diseases Hines (Ill.) VA Hosp., 1971-73; practice medicine specializing in pulmonary disease, Bolingbrook, Ill.; attending physician Edward Hosp., Good Samaritan Hosp. Mem. AMA, Dupage County Med. Soc. Club: Bolingbrook Rotary. Office: 257 N Schmidt Rd Bolingbrook IL 60439

LIN, KUANG-MING, mech. engr.; b. Taipei, Taiwan, Mar. 10, 1932; s. Ruey-chia and Yu-twan (Hsu) L.; B.S., Nat. Taiwan U., 1956; M.S., Auburn U., 1958; Ph.D., Mich. State U., 1964; m. Pi-yau Fu, Mar. 25, 1962; children—Patricia, Rhoda, Janice, Diane. Asst. instr. Mich. State U., 1958-60; asst. prof. engring. mechanics Tri-State Coll., 1961-63; asst. prof. engring. sci. Tenn. Tech. U., 1964-66, asso. prof., 1966; prin. research engr. Teledyne Brown Engring. Co., 1966-68; staff engr. tech. center Dana Corp., Toledo, Ohio, 1968-73, dep. dir. Asia-Pacific, 1973-75, mgr. internat. planning, 1975—; asso. prof. U. Ala., Huntsville, 1966-68; dir. Najico-Spicer Co., Tokyo, 1974-75. Registered profl. engr., Ohio. Mem. ASME, Soc. Automotive Engrs., ASCE, Pi Mu Epsilon. Home: 3851 Fairwood Dr Sylvania OH 43560 Office: 4500 Dorr St Toledo OH 43697

LIN, ROBERT KWAN-HWAN, educator; b. Canton, China, July 7, 1937; s. Chuan Foo and Wei Chin (Chen) L.; B.A., Nat. Taiwan U., 1960; M.L.S., U. Okla., 1965; M.A., U. Mich., 1972; m. Deborah Shock Kai Shieh, Feb. 22, 1964; children—Hsia Pin, Hsia Lynn, Hsia Min. Instr. English, Chungli High Sch., Taiwan, 1961-63; reference librarian Woodbury Coll., Los Angeles, 1966; asst. librarian, instr. library sci. Culver-Stockton Coll., Canton, Mo., 1966-70, asso. librarian, asst. prof. history, 1970-74, head librarian, asst. prof. Asian history, 1974—. vis prof. history and English, Soochow U., 1977-76. Mem. Canton Pub. Library Bd., 1973—. Club: Canton Roundtable. Author: Common Expressions in Chinese and English, 1975. Contbr. articles to profl. publs. Home: 700 White St Canton MO 63435 Office: Culver-Stockton Coll Canton MO 63435

LINCOLN, JAMES HELME, ret. judge; b. Harbor Beach, Mich., Aug. 26, 1916; s. Burr B. and Esther (Hoare) L.; A.B., U. Mich., 1938; LL.B., Detroit Coll. of Law, 1943; m. Mary F. Kimmerling, June 21, 1941; children—Janet (Mrs. David Stoller), David, Edward, Linda. Admitted to Mich. bar, 1946; practiced law, Detroit, 1946-49; mem. firm Griffith, Williams, Griffiths, Detroit, 1948-54; spl. asst. U.S. atty., Detroit, 1948-51; mem. Common Council City of Detroit, 1954-60; judge of probate Wayne County (Mich.) Juvenile Ct., Detroit, 1960-77. Mem. Nat. Council Juvenile Ct. Judges Assn. (v.p. 1968-71, pres. 1971—). Author: Anatomy of a Riot, 1967. Home: 1829 South Shore Rd Harbor Beach MI 48441

LINCOLN, KENDALL T., engring. co. exec.; b. Adrian, Mo., Aug. 23, 1932; s. Howard Thomas and Frances Eddith (Timmons) L.; B.S. in Bus. Adminstrn., U. Mo., 1954; m. Patricia Lee Gratz, Apr. 6, 1957; 1 dau., Debra Lee. Auditor U.S. Army Audit Agy., Denver, 1954-55; accountant firm Peat, Marwick, Mitchell & Co., Kansas City, Mo., 1957-63; controller firm Howard, Needles, Tammen & Bergendoff, Kansas City, Mo., until 1974, finance dir., 1974-76, asso., dir. finance, 1976—. Cons. Engr., Kansas City, 1963—. Served with AUS, 1955-57. C.P.A., Mo., Kans. Mem. Am. Inst. C.P.A.'s, Mo. Soc. C.P.A.'s, Nat. Assn. Accountants, Financial Execs. Inst., Profl. Services Bus. Mgmt. Assn., Beta Gamma Sigma. Home: 5623 Lamar St Mission KS 66202 Office: 1805 Grand Ave Kansas City MO 64108

LIND, ARTHUR CHARLES, physicist; b. Chgo., May 28, 1932; s. Arthur L. and Mildred E. (Loetz) L.; B.S. in Physics, U. Ill., 1955; Ph.D. in Physics, Rensselaer Poly. Inst., 1966; m. Barbara Ann Collins, Sept. 1, 1957; children—Julie Ann, Catherine Elizabeth, Charles Collins. Engr. Knolls Atomic Power Lab., Schenectady, 1958-60; scientist Watervliet (N.Y.) Arsenal, 1963-66; sr. group engr. McDonnell Douglas Astronautics Co., St. Louis, 1966-70; scientist McDonnell Douglas Research Labs., St. Louis, 1970—. Served with AUS, 1956-58. Recipient Bausch and Lomb Hon Sci. award, 1951. Mem. Am. Phys. Soc., Am. Chem. Soc., Internat. Soc. of Magnetic Resonance, AAAS, IEEE (sec. combined microwave group 1969-70). Presbyn. (deacon 1969—). Author: Electromagnetic Theory and Antennas, 1963. Contbr. articles to profl. publs. Home: 15450 Country Mill Ct Chesterfield MO 63017 Office: Radiation Sciences Dept McDonnell Douglas Research Labs St Louis MO 63166

LIND, EARL R., pub. service exec.; b. Chgo., Feb. 1, 1920; s. Stanley C. and Emma May (Saumer) L.; A.B., Ind. U., 1947, M.A., 1948; postgrad. Am. U., 1948, fellow Nat. Inst. Pub. Affairs; m. Alice May Crundwell, June 16, 1947; children—Karen May, Ingrid Alice. Various positions Inland Steel Co., Chgo., 1939-47, 49-50; cons., com. on appropriations U.S. Senate, 1948, 50-51; mgr. office standards and methods J. T. Ryerson & Sons, Chgo., 1951-60; sr. cons. A.T. Kearney & Co., Chgo., 1960-64; Am. Appraisal Co. mgr., mem. relations Ill. C. of C., Chgo., 1964-65; pres. Better Bus. Bur. Met. Chgo., 1965—. Past trustee LaGrange Village Bd.; bd. dirs. Council Better Bus. Burs. Served with AUS, 1942-46. Lutheran. Mason. Club: Executive of Chicago (dir.). Contbr. articles to profl. jours. Office: 35 E Wacker Dr Chicago IL 60601

LINDAHL, RAYMOND FLORUS, hearing and speech agy. exec.; b. nr. Benton Harbor, Mich., May 13, 1932; s. Earnest William and Hattie (Arent) L.; A.A., Lake Mich. Community Coll., 1957; B.S., Wayne State U., 1959, M.Ed., 1964; m. Joyce Janet Brunke, June 18, 1955; children—Julie Ann, David Ray. Speech and hearing cons. Detroit Bd. Edn., 1959-64; exec. dir. Detroit Hearing and Speech Center, 1964—. Survey cons. Commn. Accreditation of Rehab. Facilities, 1972. Mem. speakers bur. Detroit United Found., 1965-77. Served with AUS, 1952-54. Mem. Nat. Assn. Execs. (chmn. 1969-70), Am., Mich. (v.p.) speech and hearing assns., Nat. Assn. Hearing and Speech Agencies. Baptist. Home: 20430 Roxana St East Detroit MI 48021 Office: 19185 Wyoming St Detroit MI 48221

LINDBERG, HARRY CHESTER, JR., high sch. drama dir.; b. Bklyn., Aug. 29, 1927; s. Harry Chester and Freda Sophia (Nelson) L.; student U. Ill. at Chgo., 1948-50; B.T.A., Pasadena (Cal.) Playhouse Coll. Theatre Arts, 1952, M.T.A., 1953; postgrad. Northwestern U., 1956-57. Dir., Geller Prodns., Hollywood, Cal., 1953-54; dir. drama Rockford (Ill.) West Sr. High Sch., 1954—. Served with AUS, 1945-47. Decorated Certificate of Achievement; recipient Excellence in Directing award U. Ill. at Chgo., 1950. Mem. Internat. Thespian Soc. (sponsor troop), Am. Theatre Assn., Ill. Speech and Theatre Assn. Home: 2226 N Rockton St Rockford IL 61103 Office: 1900 N Rockton St Rockford IL 61103

LINDBLOM, LAWRENCE A(NDREW), ins. co. exec.; b. Manhattan, Kans., Aug. 3, 1922; s. Lawrence Andrew and Verna (McCoin) L.; B.S., Kans. State U., 1948; m. Bonnie Howell, Sept. 14, 1946; children—David Mark, Jon Andrew. Asst. underwriter Farm Bur. Mut. Ins. Co., Inc., Manhattan, Kans., 1946-48, 64—, also mem. mgmt., investment com.; chief accountant Kans. Farm Life Ins. Co., Inc., Manhattan, 1948-51, controller, asst. treas., 1951-57, treas., asst. mgr., 1958-64, v.p., gen. mgr., 1964—, also mem. mgmt., investment com.; mem. mgmt. and investment com. KFB Ins. Co., Inc., Kans. Farm Bur., Inc.; dir., vice chmn. Kans. Life and Health Ins. Guaranty Assn. Vice chmn. Community Chest, Manhattan, 1952, bd. dirs., 1952-53; mem. exec. bd. dirs., v.p. Coronado area council Boy Scouts Am., mem. Nat. Council, 1963-71; mem. Manhattan City Planning Bd., 1963-69; mem. Manhattan City Commn., 1969-71; chmn. Pott County, Riley County, City of Manhattan Regional Planning Commn., 1969-72; chmn. Big Lakes Area Planning Commn., 1972-73. Served with USMC, World War II. C.L.U. Mem. Kans. Life Ins. Execs. Assn. (past pres.), Actuaries Club Kansas City, Farm Bur. Accountants Nat. Association (past v.p.), Ins. Accounting and Statis. Assn. (past regional vice pres.), U.S., Kans., Manhattan (dir.) chambers commerce, Am. Council Life Ins., Inst. Life Ins., Nat. Pilots Assn., Internat. Platform Assn. Republican. Methodist. Clubs: Lions, Manhattan Country (past pres., dir.), Elks. Home: 540 Wickham Rd Manhattan KS 66502 Office: 2321 Anderson St Manhattan KS 66502

LINDBORG, DANIEL ROBERT, dentist; b. LaPorte, Ind., May 21, 1918; s. Daniel Jonathan and Lilly Naomi (Olson) L.; B.S., Ind. U., 1940, D.D.S., 1943; m. Millicent L. Plantz, Mar. 6, 1948; children—Daniel F., Richard R., Douglas A., David W. Intern Forsythe Dental Infirmary, Boston, 1943-44; practice dentistry, South Bend, Ind., 1946—. Pres. United Health Found., 1968-70. Trustee Wittenberg U., 1961-71. Served with Dental Corps, USNR, 1944-46. Fellow Am. Coll. Dentists; mem. North Central (pres. 1965-66), St. Joseph County (pres. 1963-65) dental socs., Ind. U. Sch. Dentistry Alumni Assn. (pres. 1972-73), Xi Psi Phi. Club: South Bend Kiwanis (pres. 1970-71). Home: 52650 Brooktrails South Bend IN 46637 Office: 801 N Michigan St South Bend IN 46601

LINDEBERG, RICHARD THEODORE, savs. and loan exec.; b. Sioux City, Iowa, Dec. 5, 1919; s. Elmer Theodore and Ethel Marian (Carvel) L.; B.S. in Indsl. Engring., Iowa State U., 1946; m. Joan Wilson, July 15, 1942; children—Richard W., Stephen C., Elizabeth Ann, John Barbour, Nancy Joan. Exec. v.p. Conservative Mortgage Co., Sioux City, 1949-54; chmn. bd., chief exec. officer, dir. First Fed. Savs. Ft. Dodge (Iowa), 1954—; past dir. Fed. Home Loan Bank, Des Moines. Past vice chmn. Ft. Dodge Planning and Zoning Commn.; past pres. Ft. Dodge Bd. Realtors. Pres., Trinity Regional Hosp., Ft. Dodge. Served with USAAF, 1942-45. Decorated Bronze Star, Air medal with two oak leaf clusters. Mem. Iowa Savs. and Loan League (past chmn.), Iowa Mortgage Bankers Assn. (past pres.), Sigma Alpha Epsilon. Presbyn. (elder). Club: Fort Dodge Country. Home: 825 Forest Ave Fort Dodge IA 50501 Office: 825 Central Ave Fort Dodge IA 50501

LINDELOW, OLAF VICTOR, physician; b. Minot, N.D., June 10, 1924; s. Olaf Vidner and Ethel Frances (Johnson) L.; B. Chem. Engring., U. Minn., 1945; M.D., U. Pa., 1951; m. Betty Jean Bell, Sept. 11, 1950; children—David, Susan, John, Nancy. Intern, George F. Geisinger Meml. Hosp., Foss Clinic, Danville, Pa., 1951-52, resident in internal medicine, 1952-54; resident in internal medicine Cleve. (Ohio) Clinic Found., 1954-55; mem. dept. internal medicine Mid Dakota Clinic, Bismarck, N.D., 1955—; mem. staff St. Alexius Hosp., Bismarck, Bismarck Hosp.; instr. U. N.D. Med. Sch., 1976—; bd. dirs. N.D. Blue Shield, 1966—. Served with USNR, 1942-46. Diplomate Am. Bd. Internal Medicine. Fellow A.C.P.; mem. Am., N.D. med. assns., 6th Dist. Med. Soc. Clubs: Exchange, Masons. Home: 1117 W Highland Acres Rd Bismarck ND 58501 Office: Mid Dakota Clinic 9th and Rosser Ave Bismarck ND 58501

LINDEMANN, JOHN ARMIN STOY, pharmacist; b. Chgo., Oct. 30, 1928; s. Armin S. and Ellen D. (Hellstrand) L.; B.S. in Zoology, U. Ill., 1950, B.S. in Pharmacy, 1954; m. Joan F. Murphy, June 9, 1951; children—Gayle Ellen, Kathleen Joan, Corinne Elizabeth, John Arthur S. Owner, Lindemann Pharmacy, Deerfield, Ill., 1951—; dir. Deerfield Savs. & Loan Assn. Trustee Village of Deerfield, 1961-65; bd. dirs. Highland Park Hosp., 1965-69. Served to capt. USAF, 1955-57. Mem. Deerfield C. of C. (dir. 1958-65). Club: Thorngate Country. Home: 2200 Wilmot Rd Bannockburn IL 60015 Office: 758 Deerfield Rd Deerfield IL 60015

LINDEN, HENRY ROBERT, research exec.; b. Vienna, Austria, Feb. 21, 1922; s. Dr. Fred and Edith (Lermer) L.; B.S., Georgia Sch. Tech., 1944; M.Chem. Engring., Poly. Inst. of Bklyn., 1947; Ph.D., Ill. Inst, Tech., 1952; m. Natalie Govedarica, 1967; children by previous marriage—Robert, Debra. Came to U.S., 1939, naturalized, 1945. Chem. engr. Socony Vacuum Labs., 1944-47; various mgmt. positions Inst. of Gas Tech., Chgo., 1947-61, dir., 1961-69, exec. v.p., 1969-74, pres., trustee, 1974—; pres. Gas Devels. Corp., 1973-77, chmn., 1973—; pres., dir. Gas Research Inst., 1976—; trustee Argonne Univs. Assn.; dir. So. Natural Resources, Inc., Reynolds Metals Co. Research asso. prof. Ill. Inst. Tech., 1954-61, adj. prof. gas engring., 1961—; mem. steering com. on exec. adv. com., mem. supply tech. adv. com. Gas Policy Adv. Council, FPC, 1975—; mem. commerce tech. adv. bd. Panel on Project Independence Blueprint, 1974-75; mem. gen. adv. com. ERDA, 1975-77. Recipient award of merit, distinguished service award, operating sect. Am. Gas Assn., Walton Clark medal Franklin Inst., 1972. Fellow Am. Inst. Chem. Engrs., Inst. of Fuel; mem. Nat. Acad. Engring., Am. Chem. Soc. (recipient H.H. Storch award 1967, councillor 1967—, chmn. div. fuel chemistry 1967), Am. Soc. Assn. Execs., Am. Gas Assn., Am. Petroleum Inst. Contbr. tech. articles to profl. jours. Holder U.S. and fgn. patents in fuel tech. Home: 1515 N Astor Chicago IL 60610 Office: 3424 S State St Chicago IL 60616

LINDER, GEORGE ELISHA, box co. exec.; b. Centralia, Ill., Nov. 27, 1913; s. Harry H. and Grace (Hammers) L.; student Ind. U., 1932-35; m. Mary Josephine Knight, Sept. 30, 1937; children—Heidi Ann, Christina Jo, George Knight. With sales dept. Container Corp. Am., Chgo., 1935-37; div. sales mgr. Am. Coating Mills, Elkhart, Ind., 1937-51; pres. No. Box Co. Inc., Elkhart, 1951—; dir. First Nat. Bank, Elkhart; sec. Ivy Terrace Inc., Goshen, Ind., 1962—, treas., 1962—, also dir. Lutheran. Home: 1320 W Lexington St Elkhart IN 46514 Office: 1328 Mishawaka St Elkhart IN 46514

LINDER, MICHAEL GARY, pension cons.; b. Santa Ana, Calif., Aug. 14, 1945; s. P.A. and Beatrice E. L.; B.A. in Mgmt. Systems, Calif. State Coll., Fullerton; m. Betty A. Scalzitti, June 3, 1972; children—Anthony M., Joseph M. Sales rep. Mut. of Omaha, Chgo., 1968-75; regional sales mgr. TIPS Ins. for Minn., Wis., Ill., Ind., Ohio and Mich., 1975-76; regional sales mgr. Reliance Ins. Co., Merrilville, Ind., 1976-77; owner, pres. Creative Ins. Concepts, Inc., Merrilville, 1977—. Mem. Internat. Health and Welfare Found. Republican. Methodist. Office: Suite 322 S 1000 E 80th Pl Merrillville IN 46383

LINDERMAN, CHARLES R., pub. relations ofcl.; b. Wolf Point, Mont., June 28, 1922; s. Charles Raymond and Martha Bertha Finstad L.; student Park Coll., Kansas City, Mo., 1977; m. Florence Rowe, Oct. 19, 1952; children—Cheryl Rae Boggio, Darlene Mae Rolczynski. Commd. 2d lt., CAP, USAF, 1968, advanced through grades to maj., 1977; various positions in recruiting advt., publicity, Air Force info., 1954-67, pub. info. officer community relations Wright-Patterson AFB, Ohio, 1968-73, supr. community relations Office Info., 1975—; dir. Heritage Resource Services, Inc., Dayton. Chmn. Am. Revolution Bicentennial Com. '76, Fairborn, Ohio, 1974—; treas. Concerned Citizens of Fairborn, 1973-75. Bd. dirs. Fairborn Civic and Cultural Center Com. Served with AUS, 1940-45. Decorated Bronze Star medal. Harry S. Truman Library Inst. fellow, 1975-76. Mem. Smithsonian Assos., Air/Space Writers Assn., Aviation Hall of Fame (charter), Co. Mil. Historians, Ohio Valley Mil. Soc., Nat. Hist. Soc., Ohio Hist. Soc. Mason (Shriner), Rotarian. Author: Stars in Stripes, 1970; American Freedom Plane, 1976. Home: 1463 Maplegrove Dr Fairborn OH 45324 Office: Office Information 2750ABW/OI Wright-Patterson AFB OH 45433

LINDESMITH, LARRY ALAN, physician; b. Amarillo, Tex., July 27, 1938; s. Lyle J. and Imogene Agnes (Young) L.; B.A., U. Colo., 1959; M.D., Bowman-Gray Sch. Medicine, Wake Forest Coll., 1963; m. Diane Joyce Bakken, Nov. 22, 1973; children—Robert James, Lisa Ann, Abigail Arleen. Intern, U. Chgo., 1963-64; resident internal medicine U. Colo. Med. Center, 1964-66; fellow pulmonary disease U. Colo. Med. Center and Webb-Waring Inst. Med. Research, 1966-67; physician, chief sect. pulmonary physiology dept. internal medicine Gundersen Clinic, Ltd., LaCrosse, Wis., 1969—; med. dir. blood gas lab. LaCrosse Luth. Hosp., 1969—; mem. courtesy staff consultations in pulmonary disease St. Francis Hosp., LaCrosse, 1971—; instr. clin. elective in pulmonary disease Gundersen Clinic, U. Wis. Med. Sch., 1974—. Served to maj., M.C., U.S. Army, 1967-69. Diplomate Am. Bd. Internal Medicine. Fellow Am. Thoracic Soc.; mem. Am. Assn. Respiratory Therapy, Am. Coll. Chest Physicians (adviser to com. on pulmonary rehab. 1974—), Wis. Lung Assn. (dir. 1972—, pres. 1975-77), Wis. Respiratory Care Soc. (med. adviser 1974-75), Wis. Thoracic Soc., AMA, Wis., LaCrosse County med. socs. Republican. Lutheran. Home: Route 1 Woodhaven Dr LaCrosse WI 54601 Office: 1836 South Ave LaCrosse WI 54601

LINDGREN, D(ERBIN) KENNETH, JR., lawyer; b. Mpls., Aug. 25, 1932; s. Derbin Kenneth and Margaret (Anderson) L.; B.S., U. Minn., 1954, J.D., 1958; m. Patricia Ann Ransier, Dec. 17, 1955; children—Christian Kenneth, Carol Ann, Charles Derbin. Admitted to Minn. bar, 1958, U.S. Supreme Ct. bar, 1968; gen. practice law Mpls., 1958—; mem., dir. Larkin, Hoffman, Daly & Lindgren, Ltd., Mpls., 1960—. Dir. Hirshfield's Inc., Irathane Internat., Inc. Mem. Bd. Edn. Ind. Sch. Dist. 274, Hopkins, Minn., 1970-76, chmn., 1972-76. Served as lt. USAF, 1955-57. Fellow Am. Coll. Probate Counsel; mem. Am., Minn. Hennepin County bar assns. Lutheran. Clubs: Minneapolis Athletic, Interlachen Country. Contbr. articles to profl. jours. Home: 225 Hawthorne Rd Hopkins MN 55343 Office: 1500 Northwestern Financial Center 7900 Xerxes Ave S Minneapolis MN 55431

LINDHOLM, WILLIAM CHARLES, clergyman; b. Perry, Iowa, Mar. 20, 1932; s. Lester Leander and Elizabeth (Winegar) L.; B.A., Augustana Coll., 1954; M. Div., Lutheran. Sch. Theology, 1958; m. Patricia Ann Schneider, Feb. 14, 1953; children—Jonell, Jana, William Charles. Ordained to ministry Lutheran Ch., 1958; pastor Grace Luth. Ch., East Tawas, Mich., 1958-70, Hope Luth. Ch., Oscoda, Mich., 1958-70, Holy Cross Luth. Ch., Livonia, Mich., 1971—. Chmn. bd. Michi-Lu-Ca Conf. Center, Fairview, Mich., 1962-69; bd. dirs., mem. exec. bd. Mich. Synod Luth. Ch. in Am., 1968—; organizer, chmn. Nat. Com. for Amish Religious Freedom, 1957—. Mem. Internat. Transactional Analysis Assn. Editor Mich. Synod News. Home: 15343 Susanna Circle Livonia MI 48154 Office: 30650 Six Mile Rd Livonia MI 48152

LINDHOUT, WILLIAM PIERCE, architect; b. Grand Rapids, Mich., Sept. 22, 1924; s. Pierre and Trixie Mae (Pierce) L.; student Mich. State Coll., 1942-43; B.Arch., U. Mich., 1950; m. Betty Burlingham Cole, Feb. 4, 1950; children—David Cole, Piet William. Draftsman, Chris Steketee, Grand Rapids, 1947, J. & G. Daverman, Grand Rapids, 1947-48, Thomas Tanner, Ann Arbor, Mich., 1949, Leo M. Bauer, Detroit, 1950-53; asso. architect Leo. M. Bauer & Assos., Detroit, 1953-57; archtl. practice, Livonia, Mich., 1957—; owner Lindhout Assos., Livonia, 1969—; dir. Livonia Indsl. Devel. Corp. Mem. archtl. adv. com. Schoolcrft Coll., 1968—. Mem. City of Livonia Zoning Bd. Appeals, 1957-64. Served with USNR, 1943-45. Decorated D.F.C., Air medal (5). Mem. A.I.A., Mich. Soc. Architects, Livonia C. of C. (pres. 1975), Sigma Phi. Rotarian (pres. 1971). Clubs: Meadowbrook Country; Kandahar Ski. Prin. archtl. works include: Clay Elementary Sch., Ward Presbyn. Ch., Lindhout Bldg., Unity Ch., St. Matthews Ch., St. Pauls Luth. Ch., (all Livonia), First Meth. Ch., St. Joseph. Home: 37655 Margareta St Livonia MI 48152 Office: 18518 Farmington Rd Livonia MI 48152

LINDNER, CARL H., diversified financial holding co. exec.; b. Dayton, 1919. Chmn. bd., pres. Am. Financial Corp., Cin.; pub. Cin. Enquirer; chmn. bd., pres. Gt. Am. Ins. Co., Cin.; chmn. bd. Provident Bank, Cin., Hunter Savs. Assn., Cin., United Liberty Life Ins. Co.; partner United Dairy Farmers Investment Co., Cin. Home: 8555 Shawnee Run Rd Cincinnati OH 45243 Office: 1 E 4th St Cincinnati OH 45202

LINDNER, KENNETH EDWARD, univ. adminstr.; b. LaCrosse, Wis., Nov. 29, 1922; s. Henry B. and Cora (Ward) L.; B.S., Wis. State U., 1949; M.A., U. Iowa, 1953, Ph.D., 1966; m. Ila M. Jacobson, Feb. 28, 1947; children—Diane, Charles, Barbara, Nancy, John, Sara. High sch. chemistry tchr., Black River Falls, Wis., 1949-55; prof. chemistry Wis. State U., LaCrosse, 1956-67; head acad. affairs Wis. State U. System, Madison, 1967-70; pres. U. Wis., LaCrosse, 1971-72, chancellor, 1972—. Cons. radiation chemistry Dairyland Power Coop., LaCrosse Boiling Water Reacter, 1966-67; cons. radiation safety Gunderson Clinic, Luth. Hosp., LaCrosse, 1966-67; cons.-examiner N. Central Assn. Colls. and Secondary Schs., 1972—. Served with AUS, 1942-45. Mem. Internat. Radiation Protection Soc., Am. Chem. Soc. Health Physics Soc. Home: 147 S 13th St LaCrosse WI 54601 Office: U Wis LaCrosse WI 54601

LINDQUIST, DANIEL ARDEN, soil conservation engr.; b. Funk, Nebr., Oct. 15, 1932; s. John Albert and Ruby Elizabeth (Bengtson) L.; B.S., U. Nebr., 1954, B.S. in Agrl. Engring., 1960; m. Phyllis Marie Johnson, Sept. 5, 1953; children—Greg, Genice, Paul, Nancy. Agrl. engr. Soil Conservation Service, U.S. Dept. Agr., Shenandoah, Iowa, 1960-64, hydraulic engr., Des Moines, Iowa, 1964-68, supervising hydraulic engr., Columbus, Ohio, 1968-73; soil conservation engr. Iowa Dept. Soil Conservation, Des Moines, 1973—. Served with AUS, 1954-56. Registered profl. engr., Iowa. Mem. Am. Soc. Agrl. Engrs., Soc. Preservation and Encouragement of Barbershop Quartet Singing in Am. Lutheran. Home: 4515 Beavercrest Dr Des Moines IA 50310 Office: Grimes State Office Bldg Des Moines IA 50319

LINDQUIST, DONALD RODNEY, educator; b. Alexandria, Minn., Nov. 4, 1927; s. Oscar Daniel and Esther (Sundberg) L.; m. Elda Freeberg, May 28, 1949; children—David, Daniel, Douglas, Debbie, Denise. With Barrs Cities Service, 1948-50, M.R. Thompson, 1950-52, Socony Mobil, 1952-55 (all Alexandria, Minn.); supr. Park Region Pub. Co., 1957-69; instr. Alexandria Area Tech. Inst., Alexandria, Minn., 1969—, chmn. faculty council, 1976-77. Mem. exec. bd. Alexandria (Minn.) Edn. Com., 1974-75; precinct caucus chmn., Alexandria, Minn., 1973-74. Served with USNR, 1945-48. Mem. Profl. Photographers Am., Am. Legion, Graphic Arts Internat. Union. Democrat. Lutheran (chmn. ch. council 1972). Club: Snowmobile (Alexandria, Minn.) (pres. 1969-70). Contbr. photographs to Race and Rally mag., 1970-75. Home: Route 3 Alexandria MN 56308 Office: 1600 Jefferson St Alexandria MN 56308

LINDQUIST, NORMAN CHARLES, communications co. exec.; b. Chgo., July 23, 1916; s. Nels H. and Harriet (Hudella) L.; student Coll. Commerce, DePaul U., 1942-46; m. Margaret M. McGorrin, May 6, 1944. Sr. copywriter Commonwealth Edison Co., 1945-47; v.p. TV Advt. Prodns., Inc., 1947-48; creative dir. Malcolm-Howard Advt. Agy., 1948-50; v.p. Atlas Film Corp., 1950-55; account exec. Wilding, Inc., 1955-57; network sales rep. Liv-United Artists, 1957-60; v.p. sales Fred A. Niles Communications Centers, Inc., Chgo., 1960—; mem. mktg. faculty DePaul U.; condr. seminars in field. Bd. assos. DePaul U. Recipient Outstanding Service award Heart Assn., 1955. Mem. Am. Acad. Television Arts and Scis. (bd. govs. 1962-64), Nat. Visual Presentation Assn. (pres. 1965-66), Broadcast Advt. Club (treas. 1954-56), Chgo. Advt. Club (v.p. 1957-58), Sales and Mktg. Execs. Assn. Chgo. (treas. 1969-70), Broadcast Pioneers, Chgo. Film Council. Club: Lake Shore (Chgo.). Home: 200 Golf Terr Wilmette IL 60091 Office: 1058 W Washington Blvd Chicago IL 60607

LINDSAY, EARL EDWARD, veterinarian; b. Massillon, Ohio, July 26, 1926; s. Earl Thomas and Grace Edna (Stover) L.; D.V.M., Ohio State U., 1954; m. Nancy Lou Schick, June 13, 1954; children—Thomas Earl, Melinda Jane. Gen. practice veterinary medicine Canton (Ohio) Veterinary Hosp., 1954, N. Lawrence, Ohio, 1954—; lectr. in field. Pres. Tuslaw Sch. Bd., 1974-75, v.p., 1972, 73; deacon Christ United Presbyn. Ch., Canton, Ohio, 1972-76, elder, 1977—. Served with USAF, 1945-47. Mem. Am., Ohio veterinary med. assns., Am. Assn. Bovine Practioners, Ohio State U. Pres. Club, Ohio State U. Faculty Club, Ohio State U. Century Club. Clubs: Tuslaw Lions (charter mem.), Masons. Home: 13467 Lincoln St NW North Lawrence OH 44666

LINDSAY, JUNE CAMPBELL MCKEE, communications exec.; b. Detroit, Nov. 14, 1920; d. Maitland Everett and Josephine Belle (Campbell) McKee; B.A. with honors in Speech (McGregor Fund Mich. grantee), U. Mich., 1943; Electronics Engring. certificate Signal Corps Ground Signal Service, 1943; postgrad. (Inst. Gen. Semantics grantee), U. Chgo., 1944-45, N.Y. U. (Armour grantee), 1945-46, Columbia U., 1946-47, Wayne State U., 1960-64, U. Mich., 1964-70; m. Powell Lindsay, Nov. 25, 1967; 1 son, Kristi Costa-McKee. Coordinator, activator McKee Prodns., Detroit, 1943-56; Being Unltd., 1957—; info. dir. Suitcase Theatre, Inc., Lansing and Ann Arbor, Mich. Cons. Cornelian Corner Detroit, Inc., 1957-63, Islamic Center Found. Soc., Detroit, 1959-62, City Ann Arbor Human

Relations Commn., 1966-68, Urban Adult Edn. Inst., Detroit, 1968-69, Mich. Bell Telephone Co., Detroit, 1969, African Art Gallery Founders, Detroit Inst. Arts, 1964, WKAR-TV, Mich. State U., 1971—. Bd. dirs. Mus. Youth Internat., Saline, Mich. Chaplain's asst. Univ. Hosp., Ann Arbor, 1971-72; program dir. People-to-People, Ann Arbor, 1971-72; Suitcase Theatre tour coordinator Brit. Empire's Leprosy Relief Assn., 1972—; assembly cons. Baha'i Faith, 1960—. Recipient Award for Excellence Mich. Ednl. Assn., 1971, Mich. Assn. Classroom Tchrs., 1972. Mem. Soc. for Individual Responsibility, Am. Women in Radio and TV Broadcast Pioneers, Am. Fedn. Advt., Internat. Platform Assn. Home: 2339 S Circle Dr Ann Arbor MI 48103

LINDSAY, POWELL, theatre exec.; b. Phila.; s. Henry and Addie (Trower) L.; B.A., Va. Union U., 1935; postgrad. Yale, 1936-37; m. June Campbell McKee, Nov. 25, 1967. Writer, dir., producer, star numerous plays for stage (Broadway and on tour), screen and broadcast, 1936—; writer spl. studies for N.A.A.C.P. and Mayor's Com. City of Detroit, 1957-64; research analyst, legis. service bur., Mich. Legislature, Lansing, 1965—; exec. dir. Suitcase Theatre, Inc., Lansing, 1970—; partner Lin-Mar Prodns., 1967-69, Lindsay-Costa-McKee Liaison Agy., 1968—, Being Unlimited, 1960—; co-founder Harlem Suitcase Theatre, 1937, Negro Playwrights Co., 1940. Mem. founders com. African Art Gallery, Detroit Inst. Arts, 1962-65; youth chpt. dir. People-to-People Internat., 1971—. Writer pub. relations for U.S. Senator Philip A. Hart, 1958, Mich. Gov. John B. Swainson, 1961. Bd. dirs. Musical Youth Internat., 1971—. Mem. Citation of Appreciation, City of Lansing, 1970, Mich. Legislature, 1971, Award for Excellence, Mich. Edn. Assn. and Mich. Assn. Classroom Tchrs., 1972. Mem. Research Assn. for Mich. Negro History (founder pres. 1965-69). Bahai Faith (chmn. teaching com. Detroit assembly 1961-63). Home: 2339 South Circle Dr Ann Arbor MI 48103 Office: 409 W Kalamazoo St Lansing MI 48933

LINDSAY, ROBERT, educator; b. Durham, N.C., Nov. 27, 1924; s. Albert and Emily Frances (Sheridan) L.; B.A., U. Wis., 1953, M.A., 1954; Ph.D., U. Minn., 1965; m. Mary Anne Phillips, Jan. 3, 1950; children—Phillips S., Nancy B. Reporter, commentator, news dir. WKOW, UPI, WIBA, WHA-TV, Madison, Wis., 1947-50, 54-57; faculty U. Wis., Madison, 1952-57; faculty U. Minn., Mpls., 1957—, prof. mass communication and internat. relations, 1971—. Sr. program specialist for space communication UNESCO, Paris, France, 1968-69; vis. prof. U. Wis., Madison, 1959-65; lectr. univs. and journalism tng. centers Belgium, Bolivia, Brazil, Ecuador, France, Mexico, Hong Kong, Thailand, Malaysia, Singapore, U.K.; U.S. Dept. State specialist Latin Am., S.E. Asia, Africa, 1965-78; chmn. Internat. Communication Devel. Council, Midwest Univs. Consortium for Internat. Activities, 1970-72; news service U. Wis., U.S. Navy Journalist Sch., Great Lakes, Ill., Defense Information Sch., Ft. Slocum, N.Y. Mem. citizens adv. com. Twin City Area Ednl. TV Corp., 1975—. Served with USMC, 1941-45, 50-52. Found. for Pub. Relations Research and Edn. fellow, 1959, 67; Office Internat. Programs grantee, 1971; U. Minn. grantee, 1967. Recipient Ariel award, Mpls. Citizens Com. on Pub. Edn., 1960; named Outstanding Instr., U. Minn., 1963. Mem. Inst. Internat. Communications, Internat. Assn. for Mass Communication Research, Internat. Communication Assn., Internat. Studies Assn., Internat. Press Inst., Institut Internat. de Droit Spatial, Soc. for Internat. Devel., World Future Soc., British Inst. for Internat. and Comparative Law, Centre d'Etude des Consequences Generales de Grandes Techniques Nouvelles, Canadian Inst. Internat. Affairs, Communication Assn. Pacific, Asian Mass Communication Research and Information Centre, Inter-Am. Press Assn., Latin Am. Studies Assn., Am. Soc. Internat. Law, AAAS, Fgn. Policy Assn., Soc. Profl. Journalists, Radio-TV News Dirs. Assn., Am. Soc. for 18th Century Studies. Clubs: Geneva Press (Switzerland); Minnesota Press, University. Author: This High Name, 1956. Conbr. articles to profl. and scholarly jours. Home: 11 Hillside Court St Paul MN 55108 Office: 111 Murphy Hall U Minn Minneapolis MN 55455

LINDSHIELD, JAMES HARVEY, air force officer; b. Lindsborg, Kans., June 12, 1945; s. Theodore Howard and Lois Edith Hendershott (Shores) L.; B.A., U. Kans., 1967; M.B.A., U. Utah, 1972; m. Ann Elizabeth Dunkley, Jan. 26, 1974; children—Christopher James, Matthew John. Commd. 2d lt., USAF, 1967; advanced through grades to capt., 1970; logistics mgr. Udorn Royal Thai AFB, 1968-69, Forbes (Kans.) AFB, 1967-68, RAF, Alconbury, Eng., 1970-72; chief supply and transp. div. USAF Aerospace Guidance and Metrology Center, Newark, Ohio, 1973-74; logistics mgr. Joint U.S. Mil. Adv. Group, Thailand, 1975-77; staff logistics officer Hdqrs. Tactical Air Command, Langley AFB, Va., 1977—. Decorated Meritorious Service Medal. Mem. Acad. Mgmt., Am. Acad. Arts and Scis., Am. Acad. Polit. and Social Scis., Am. Econ. Assn., Am. Finance Assn., Am. Mgmt. Assn., Am. Soc. Pub. Adminstrn., Brit. Inst. Mgmt., Nat. Tax Assn., Inst. Mgmt. Sci., Royal Econ. Soc., Soc. Econ. Analysis, World Future Soc. Episcopalian. Elk. Home: 226 S Washington St Lindsborg KS 67456

LINDSTROM, RUSSELL JOSEPH, banker; b. DeKalb, Ill., June 26, 1915; s. Joseph Benjamin and Mabel Ellen (White) L.; student No. Ill. U., 1933-35; m. Doris G. Eckberg, Aug. 20, 1939; children—Karren (Mrs. Arthur Lee Maercker), Dona (Mrs. William A. Leppanen), Cheryl (Mrs. John W. Countryman). Teller, First Nat. Bank, DeKalb, 1941-45, asst. cashier, 1945-52, asst. v.p., 1952-53, v.p., 1953-57, cashier, sec. to bd., 1955-57, exec. v.p., 1957—, asst. trust officer, dir., 1963-66, exec. v.p., dir., sec. to bd., 1966—. Mem. DeKalb Park Bd., 1945-52, treas. DeKalb Municipal Bank, 1944—; mem. DeKalb Pub. Library, 1949—, pres., 1965—. Trustee, pres. Jacob Haish Meml. Hosp., 1948-52, DeKalb County Tb. Assn., 1947-52. Mem. Am. Fedn. Musicians (local pres. 1945-46), DeKalb County Bankers (pres. 1944). Lutheran. Mason (32 deg. Shriner), Lion, Elk (state treas. 1971-75). Home: 330 S 9th St DeKalb IL 60115 Office: 141 W Lincoln Hwy DeKalb IL 60115

LING, ALEXANDER, neurol. surgeon; b. Tientsin, China, June 24, 1922; s. Ping and Clara (Soo-Hoo) L.; came to U.S., 1941, naturalized, 1943; B.S., St. John's U., Shanghai, 1941; M.D., Washington U., St. Louis, 1944; m. Apr. 1, 1946; children—Alexander, Cynthia. Intern, Union Meml. Hosp., Balt., 1944-45; resident in surgery Columbia-Presbyn. Hosp., N.Y.C., 1947-49; resident in neurol. surgery Cleve. Clinic, 1949-52; chief sect. on neurol. surgery Fairview Gen. Hosp., Fairview Park, Ohio, 1956—. Served to capt. M.C., U.S. Army, 1945-47. Fellow A.C.S.; mem. Am. Assn. Neurol. Surgeons, Congress Neurol. Surgeons. Presbyn. Club: Rotary. Home: 2660 River Oaks Rocky River OH 44116 Office: 507 Westgate Med Arts Bldg Fairview Park OH 44126

LING, JOHN FRANCIS, physician; b. Hebron, Ind., Aug. 17, 1916; s. Francis E. and Lulu Mae (Benkie) L.; B.A. in Chemistry, Ind. U., 1938, M.D., 1941; m. Mildred Grace Thomas, Feb. 1, 1942; children—Ninetta Diane, Elizabeth Jane, John Francis. Intern, Ind. U. Med. Center, Indpls., 1941-42, resident in internal medicine, 1945-47, resident in cardiovascular disease, 1947-49; practice medicine specializing in internal medicine and cardiovascular disease, Richmond, Ind., 1949—; asst. medicine Ind. U.; chief of med. staff Reid Meml. Hosp., Richmond; cons. internal medicine Richmond State Hosp. Served with U.S. Army, 1942-45. Decorated Bronze Star; diplomate Am. Bd. Internal Medicine. Fellow A.C.P., Am. Coll. Cardiology; mem. AMA, Ind., Wayne County med. assns., Am. (dir. 1967-74), Ind. (pres. 1966) heart assns., Ind. U. Sch. Medicine Alumni Assn. (pres. alumni council 1970). Methodist. Club: Rotary. Home: 6 Parkway Ln Richmond IN 47374 Office: 1250 Chester Blvd Richmond IN 47374

LING, JOSEPH TSO-TI, mfg. co. exec.; b. Peking, China, June 10, 1919; s. Ping Sun and Chong Hung (Lee) L.; B.C.E., Hangchow Christian Coll., Shanghai, China, 1944; M.S. in Civil Engring., U. Minn., 1950, Ph.D. in San. Engring., 1952; m. Rose Hsu, Feb. 1, 1944; children—Lois (Mrs. Benjamin Olson), Rosa-Mai (Mrs. Michael Ahlgren), Louis, Lorraine. Came to U.S., 1948, naturalized, 1963. Civil engr. Nanking-Shanghai R.R. System, 1944-47; research asst. san. engring. U. Minn., 1948-52; sr. staff san. engr. Gen. Mills, Inc., Mpls., 1953-55; dir. dept. san. engring. research Ministry Municipal Constrn., Peking, 1956-57; prof. civil engring. Bapt. U., Hong Kong, 1958-59; head dept. water and san. engring. Minn. Mining & Mfg. Co., St. Paul, 1960-66, mgr. environmental and civil engring., 1967-70, dir. environmental engring. and pollution control, 1970-74, v.p., 1975—. Adv. mem. on air pollution Minn. Bd. Health, 1964-66; mem. Minn. Gov.'s Adv. Com. on Air Resources, 1966-67; mem. adv. panel on environmental pollution U.S. C. of C., 1966-71; mem. chem. indsl. com., adv. to Ohio River Valley Water Sanitation Commn., 1962—; mem. environmental quality panel Electronic Industries Assn., 1971—; mem. environmental quality com. Nat. Assn. Mfrs., 1965—; mem. Pres.'s Adv. Bd. on Air Quality, 1974-75; vice chmn. environmental com. U.S. Bus. and Industry Adv. Com. to OECD, 1975—. Trustee Belwin Outdoor Lab., St. Paul; bd. dirs. Fresh Water Biol. Found., Northwest Area Found., St. Paul Area YMCA, Midwest China Study Center, Minn. Environmental Sci. Found. Woodrow Wilsor Sr. fellow, 1975—. Registered profl. engr., Minn., Ala., N.J., Okla., W.Va., N.Y., Ill., Ind., Pa., Mich. Fellow Am. Soc. C.E.; mem. Nat. Acad. Engring., Am. Acad. Environmental Engrs., Minn. Assn. Commerce and Industry (chmn. water mgmt. com. 1967-72), Am. Water Works Assn., Air Pollution Control Assn. (dir.), Mfg. Chemists Assn. (mem. solid waste mgmt. com. 1969—), Water Pollution Control Fedn. Club: Rainbow (Mpls.). Contbr. articles to profl. jours. Home: 2090 Arcade St St Paul MN 55109 Office: 3M Co Box 33331 St Paul MN 55133

LINGREN, RONALD HAL, state legislator; b. Gowrie, Ia., June 26, 1935; s. Herbert George and Zula Melissa (Bolton) L.; B.S., Ia. State U., 1960, M.A., U. Ia., 1961, Ph.D., 1965; children—Scott Allen, Kristin Lee. Psychol. cons. Jefferson County Schs., Fairfield, Ia., 1961-62; asst. dir. Pine Sch. research project, U. Ia. Hosp., Iowa City, 1962-64, cons. child psychiatry clinic, 1963-65; faculty U. Wis., Milw., 1965-74, dir. Center for Behavioral Studies, 1965-74, on leave, 1975—; mem. Wis. Assembly, 1975—. Served with AUS, 1953-55. Recipient Outstanding Service awards Nat. Assn. Sch. Psychologists, 1970, 72; Outstanding Service award Wis. Assn. Sch. Psychologists, 1971. Mem. Nat. (dir. 1969-71), Wis. (pres. 1969-71) assns. sch. psychologists, Wis. Council of Assns. of Pupil Services (pres. 1974). Contbr. articles to profl. jours. Home: W149 N8301 Norman Dr Menomonee Falls WI 53051 Office: State Capitol Madison WI 53702

LINK, ARTHUR A., gov. of N.D.; b. nr. Alexander, N.D., May 24, 1914; ed. N.D. Agrl. Coll.; m. Grace Johnson; 6 children. Farmer-rancher, Alexander; mem. 92d Congress from N.D. 2d dist.; gov. of N.D., 1973—. Chmn. N.D. State Adv. Council Vocational Edn., 1969-71; past mem. McKenzie County Welfare Bd. Former mem. Randolph Twp. bd.; mem. N.D. Ho. of Reps., 1946-70, minority leader, speaker of house, 1965; active N.D. Nonpartisan League. Bd. dirs. Williston U. Center Found. Lutheran (past council pres.). Lion. Address: Governor's Residence 1131 N 4th St Bismarck ND 58501

LINK, NANCY CAROL, hosp. adminstr.; b. Chgo., June 11, 1938; d. Gail Fenton and Ruth Marie (Neuman) Link; student Carthage Coll., 1956-58, Lyons Twp. Jr. Coll., 1958-59; certificate Northwestern U., 1960; postgrad. Alverno Weekend Coll., 1978. Asst. med. record librarian Mac Neal Meml. Hosp., Berwyn, Ill., 1960-61, chief med. record librarian, 1961-62; asst. med. record librarian La Grange (Ill.) Community Meml. Hosp., 1962-63; med. record librarian Milw. County Gen. Hosp., 1963-67; chief registered record adminstr. Doctors Hosp. Complex, Milw., 1967-69, New Berlin (Wis.) Meml. Hosp., 1969-72, St. Anthony Hosp., Milw., 1972-74, Misericordia Community Hosp., Milw., 1974-77, dir. rummage and bake sales, 1975; various positions for Burlington R.R., Chgo., 1955-56; swimming instr. YMCA, La Grange, Ill., 1954-55, office clk., 1954-56. YMCA del. at Young Adult Conf., Bodensee, Germany, summer, 1963; counselor Bible Camp, Tower Hill, Mich. Mem. Am., Wis., Southeastern Wis. assns. of med. record adminstrs., Am. Bus. Women's Assn. Lutheran. Home: 1606 Swartz Dr Waukesha WI 53186

LINKMEYER, LARRY LEE, electronic technician; b. Milan, Ind., Apr. 30, 1938; s. Denton Harry and Henrietta Amelia (Cosby) L.; student DeVry Tech. Inst., 1956-58, RCA Schs., 1958-59; m. Margaret Ann Henschen, Nov. 13, 1965; children—Jon Mark, Laurie Ann, Michael Alan. Auto mechanic Schwanholts, Aurora, Ind., 1958-60; appliance serviceman Gambles', Aurora, 1960-62; chem. technician Monsanto Co., Addyston, Ohio, 1962-66; micro electronic design technician Procter & Gamble Co., Cin., 1966—; cons. Megalogic Corp., Brookville, Ohio. Democrat precinct committeeman, 1962—; mem. bd. edn. St. Mary's Sch., 1977—. Served with U.S. Army, 1958. Mem. Amateur Radio Relay League. Roman Catholic. Home: 45 Country Hills Dr Aurora IN 47001 Office: 5299 Spring Grove Ave Cincinnati OH 45217

LINN, DAVID, judge; b. Augustow, Poland, Mar. 20, 1917; s. Israel Berel and Rose (Hirschfeld) L.; came to U.S., 1922, naturalized, 1935; A.B., U. Chgo., 1938, J.D., 1940; m. Doris Sandra Ellison, Jan. 2, 1948; children—James Barry, Lesley Rae. Admitted to Ill. bar, 1940, since practiced in Chicago; asso. judge Circuit Ct. of Cook County, 1971-76; justice Appellate Ct. of Ill., 1976—; instr. U.S. Judge Adv. Gen. Dept.; lectr. profl. socs. Commr., Ill. Commn. Human Relations, 1966-68. Mem. Constl. Conv., Ill., 1969-70. Treas., bd. dirs. S.E. Community Orgn. Served to capt. U.S. Army, 1941-45. Decorated Bronze Star medal; recipient certificates of merit Chgo. Bar Assn., Decalogue Soc., 1967. Fellow Internat. Acad. Law and Sci., Am. Acad. Matrimonial Lawyers (bd. govs.); mem. Decalogue Soc. (bd. govs.), Ill. Judges Assn. (dir.), Ill. (sect. chmn.), Chgo. (com. chmn.), S. Chgo. (pres., bd. govs.) bar assns., Judicature Soc., Law Inst., Phi Beta Delta. Clubs: Quadrangle, Convenant of Ill. (Chgo.). Mem. editorial planning bd. Ill. Family Law, 1967. Contbr. articles to profl. jours. Office: 30th Floor Daley Center Chicago IL 60602

LINN, EDWARD THEODORE, constrn. co. exec.; b. Peoria, Ill., Jan. 14, 1933; s. Oscar and Lelia (Mellert) L.; student U. Ill., 1950-51; Northwestern U., 1953; B.S., Bradley U., 1956; m. Judith Arline Buffum, Aug. 29, 1954; children—Nancy Ann, Diana Jean, Edith Annette. Hydraulics engr. John Deere, Moline, Ill., 1956-58; pres. Linn Materials, Inc., Canton, Ill., 1958—, Canton Concrete Products, Canton, 1967—, Material Cartage, Inc., Canton, 1970—; pres. Liverpool Materials Co., Canton, 1970—, Linn Farms, Inc., Canton, 1970—, Linn Devel. Corp., Canton. Bd. dirs. Canton Assn. Commerce and Industry, 1966-72, pres. bd., 1971. Served with USNR, 1952-54. Mem. Phi Sigma Phi. Methodist (bd. mem. 1958—). Mason (32 deg.). Club: Creve Coeur (Peoria, Ill.). Home: 150 Middle Park Dr Canton IL 61520 Office: Box 539 Canton IL 61520

LINNARD, LAWRENCE GILBERT, photographer, film lectr.; b. Princeton, Ill., Nov. 30, 1901; s. August J. and Carolina (Johnson) L.; B.S., U. Ill. at Champaign-Urbana, 1925; m. Margaret Murray Horn, Jan. 1, 1926; children—Carolyn Elizabeth (Mrs. Arthur E. Tissol), Lawrence Murray. Apprentice, Vitale & Geiffert, Landscape Architects, N.Y.C., 1927-33; landscape architect U.S. War Dept., Washington, 1933-34; landscape architect Ohio State Hwy. Dept., Toledo, 1934-37; pvt. practice landscape architecture and site planning, Toledo, 1934-62, Detroit, 1934-62; photographer, film lectr. African and Alaskan wildlife, numerous cities, U.S. and Can., 1961—. Fellow Am. Soc. Landscape Architects (pres. 1951-52); mem. Mich. Acad. Arts, Scis., and Letters, Engring. Soc. Detroit, Detroit chpt. Explorers Club of N.Y., Detroit chpt. Circumnavigators Club of N.Y., Internat. Torch Club, East African Wildlife Soc. Home: 618 Pierce St Maumee OH 43537

LINSLEY, SCOTT ELLSWORTH, cons.; b. St. Paul, June 4, 1910; s. Sam Ellsworth and Lydia Bertha (Sperling) L.; B.E.E., U. Minn., 1932, postgrad. 1932-33; m. Virginia Marie Gadbois, May 31, 1938; children—Scott John, William Emery, Craig Anson, Teschon Cather'ne. Jr. engr., bldg. operator, asst. plant operator Mpls-St. Paul Sanitary Dist., St. Paul, 1935-41, asst. plant operator, 1951-52, asst. chief engr., 1968-70, gen. supt. operations, Metropolitan Wastewater Treatment Plant, Metro Sewer Bd., 1970-72, mgr. Capital Improvements Program, 1972-75, cons., 1975—. Mem. Citizens League, St. Paul, 1967—; mem. Clear Air Clear Water, St. Paul, 1963—. Served to maj., AUS, 1941-44; served to maj., USAF, 1944-51. Recipient Arthur Sidney Bedell award, Water Pollution Control Fedn., 1971. Registered profl. engr., Minn. Diplomate Am. Acad. Environmental Engrs. Am. Acad. Sanitary Engrs. Mem. Central States Water Pollution Control Assn. (pres. 1968-69), IEEE, Water Pollution Control Fedn., Tau Beta Pi, Eta Kappa Nu. Episcopalian. Club: Engrs. (Mpls.). Patentee in field. Home: 1076 W Hoyt Ave St Paul MN 55117

LINSMAYER, JOHN JAMES, paper co. exec.; b. Mpls., Sept. 3, 1929; s. Carl P. and Ruth (Fitzpatrick) L.; student U. Minn., 1947-50; m. Karen Anne Cody, Apr. 28, 1967; children—David, Anne, Jane, Stephen, Mary. Self-employed in ins. sales field, 1952—; mem. sales staff Murphy Ins. Agy., Mpls., 1965—; pres. Mpls. Wool Co., 1964—; pres. Battin Paper Products, Inc., Mpls., 1967—. Served with Air Corps USNR, 1951. Roman Catholic. Elk. Clubs: Minneapolis Golf, Minneapolis Athletic. Home: 250 Yosemite Circle Golden Valley MN 55422 Office: 100 1st St N Minneapolis MN 55401

LINTON, ADAM LUNN, physician; b. Selkirk, Scotland, Sept. 23, 1932; s. Walter and Mary (Grant) L.; M.B., Ch.B., U. Edinburgh, 1955; m. Margaret Slimman, Oct. 11, 1957; children—Anne, Judith, Alistair. Intern Dumfries, Scotland, 1956-57; lectr. medicine U. Glasgow (Scotland), 1960-70; cons. physician Western Infirmary, Glasgow, 1966-70; chief of medicine, dir. renal unit Victoria Hosp., London, Ont., also prof. medicine U. Western Ont., 1970—; mem. Victoria Hosp. Trust. Served with Brit. Army, 1956-58. Fellow Royal Coll. Physicians (Edinburgh, Glasgow and Can.), ACP; mem. Am. Soc. Nephrology, Assn. Canadian Univ. Profs. Medicine, Internat. Soc. Nephrology. Contbr. articles to profl. jours. Home: 266 Regent St London ON Canada Office: Victoria Hospital London ON Canada

LINTS, CARLTON EUGENE, educator; b. Ilion, N.Y., Dec. 31, 1930; s. Wesley Albert and Margaret Hazel (Parker) L.; B.A. in Biology, Northwestern U., Evanston, Ill., 1956; Ph.D. in Psychology, U. Chgo., 1965. Asst. prof. psychology No. Ill. U., DeKalb, 1965-66, 68-70, asso. prof. psychology, 1970—, also Center for Biochem. and Biophys. Studies, 1975—, chmn. biopsychology, 1970-73, 75—. Served with USN, 1948-52. Decorated Presdl. Unit Citation medal, Korean ribbon with four oak leaf clusters (UN). Hon. mem. Brit. Brain Research Assn., European Brain and Behavior Soc.; mem. A.A.A.S., Am., Midwest psychol. assns., Soc. Neurosci., Sigma Xi. Contbr. articles in field to profl. jours. Home: 2525 Old Tavern Rd Lisle IL 60532 Office: Dept of Psychology Northern Ill Univ DeKalb IL 60115

LINTZ, ROBERT CARROLL, banker; b. Cin., Oct. 2, 1933; s. Frank George and Carolyn Martha (Dickhaus) L.; B.B.A., U. Cin., 1956; m. Mary Agnes Mott, Feb. 1, 1964; children—Lesa, Robert Carroll II, Laura, Michael. Staff accountant Alexander Grant & Co., Cin., 1958-60; dist. dir. credit and bus. devel. Uniroyal Inc., Memphis, 1960-65; sr. v.p., treas. Am. Fin. Leasing & Services Co., Cin., 1965-76, also dir.; exec. v.p. Provident Bank, Cin., 1975—. Trustee St. Francis-St. George Hosp., Cin. Served to capt. AUS, 1956-58, 61-62. Mem. Beta Alpha Psi. Republican. Roman Catholic. K.C. Home: 5524 Palisades Dr Cincinnati OH 45238 Office: One E 4th St Cincinnati OH 45202

LINVILLE, MALCOLM EUGENE, JR., educator; b. Kansas City, Mo., Mar. 30, 1935; s. Malcolm Eugene and Maebell Leanda (Reimert) L.; m. Duana Mae Rankin, Feb. 1, 1939; children—Deborah, Douglas. B.A., Kansas City U., 1957, M.A., 1963; Ph.D., U. Mo., 1973. Intern psychol. testing Fitzsimmons Hosp., Denver, 1959, Psychol. Inst., Walter Reed Hosp., Los Angeles, 1960; neuro-psychiat. intern Fitzsimmons Hosp., 1961; intern counseling U. Mo. at Kansas City, 1970. Teacher, Baptiste Jr. High Sch., Hickman Mills, Mo., 1962-64; psychologist, dir. spl. edn. Prairie Sch. Dist., Prairie Village, Kans., 1964-69; prof. Sch. Edn., U. Mo. at Kansas City, 1969—. Bd. dirs. New Sch. of Human Edn., 1975—; chairperson adv. com. Human Resources Corp., 1977. Mem. Am. Assn. Higher Edn., Am. Assn. Mental Deficiency, Am. Personnel and Guidance Assn., Am. Psychol. Assn., Phi Delta Kappa, Pi Lambda Theta. Contbr. articles to profl. jours. Home: 7400 Wyoming St Kansas City MO 64114 Office: Univ Mo Kansas City MO 64110

LIONBERGER, ERLE TALBOT LUND, polit. orgn. ofcl.; b. St. Louis, Apr. 29, 1933; d. Joel Y. and Erle (Harsh) Lund; student Mary Inst., 1951; A.B., Vassar Coll., 1955; m. John S. Lionberger, Jr., June 23, 1956; children—Erle Talbot, Louise Shepley. Republican committeewoman Hadley Twp., St. Louis County, 1965—, mem. St. Louis County Rep. Central Com., 1965—; alternate del. Rep. Nat. Conv., 1968, del., 1972, 76; mem. Rep. State Com., 1968—. Regional chmn. United Fund, 1964; area chmn. Arts Council Drive, 1965; chmn. St. Louis Preservation Pilgrimage, 1974. Bd. dirs. Friends of Winston Churchill Meml., 1975-76; mem. exec. bd. Mo. Bot. Garden, 1977—; mem. St. Louis County Hist. Bldg. Commn., 1976—. Mem. Jr. League St. Louis, Nat. Soc. Colonial Dames Am. (Mo. bd. dirs. 1976—, hist. properties chmn. 1975—), Landmarks Assn. St. Louis (dir. 1973-76, landmarks rep. Cultural Educators Roundtable 1976—). Address: 21 Dartford St St Louis MO 63105

LIPINSKI, WALTER CHARLES, elec. engr.; b. Chgo., Jan. 5, 1927; s. Walter Louis and Emily (Kretowicz) L.; B.S., U. Ill., 1950; M.S., Ill. Inst. Tech., 1963, Ph.D., 1969; m. Jo Ann Miller, Jan. 13, 1951; 1 dau., Marjorie. Asst. elec. engr. Argonne (Ill.) Nat. Lab., 1950-56, asso. elec. engr., 1956-74, sr. elec. engr., 1974—, mgr. instrumentation and control section, 1960-75. Dean grad. sch. Midwest Coll. Engring.,

Lombard, Ill., 1973-76; cons. to adv. com. on reactor safeguards U.S. Nuclear Regulatory Commn., 1964—; U.S. del. to Internat. Electrotech. Commn., 1964—. Pres. S.W. Suburban Community Concert Assn., Oak Lawn, Ill., 1965-67. Served with AUS, 1945-46. Registered profl. engr., Ill. Mem. IEEE, Am. Nuclear Soc., U. Ill. Alumni Assn., Ill. Inst. Tech. Alumni Assn., Phi Kappa Phi, Sigma Xi, Tau Beta Pi, Sigma Tau, Eta Kappa Nu, Pi Mu Epsilon, Phi Eta Sigma, Chi Gamma Iota. Methodist. Mason (Shriner). Author chpt. 8 Reactor Handbook, 2nd edit., vol. IV, 1964. Home: 9816 S Kilbourn Ave Oak Lawn IL 60453 Office: 9700 S Cass Ave Argonne IL 60439

LIPOWITZ, JONATHAN, chemist; b. Paterson, N.J., Apr. 25, 1937; s. Alex and Esther (Knoble) L.; B.S., Rutgers U., 1958; Ph.D., U. Pitts., 1964; m. Evelyn Ruth Jacobs, Dec. 25, 1961; children—Robert Allen, Suzanne Joyce. Postdoctoral fellow Pa. State U., University Park, 1964-65; project chemist Dow Corning Corp., Midland, Mich., 1965-74, sr. project chemist, 1974-75, asso. scientist, 1975—. Midland County del. to Mich. Democratic Conv., 1972; Dem. precinct del., 1970-76. NSF predoctoral fellow, 1962-64. Mem. Am. Chem. Soc., ASTM, Am. Assn. Textile Chemists and Colorists, Sigma Xi. Unitarian. Contbr. articles to sci. jours. Home: 1524 Dilloway Dr Midland MI 48640 Office: Dow Corning Corp Research Dept Midland MI 48640

LIPPERT, CLARISSA START, journalist; b. St. Louis, Mar. 28, 1917; d. George Michael and Ada (Huebel) Start; B.J., U. Mo., 1936; m. E. Gary Davidson, May 14, 1938 (dec.); 1 son, Bruce Benton Davidson; m. 2d, Raymond J. Lippert, Dec. 21, 1972. Feature writer St. Louis Post-Dispatch, 1938-72, columnist The Little Woman, 1955-72, The Happy Gardener, 1972—; owner, operator Blue Barn antique shop, 1972—; editor Humane Soc. News, 1958-75; columnist This Day Mag., 1966-71, Youth Speaks Up, KSD-TV, 1960-61. Chmn. adv. com. St. Louis County Child Welfare, 1954; mem. Mo. Gov.'s Commn. Status of Women, 1964, 66-67, 70-74; co-chmn. Jefferson County Christmas Carols Assn., 1969. Bd. dirs. St. Louis Met. Ch. Fedn., Webster Groves (Mo.) Hist. Soc.; mem. met. bd. YMCA, 1968-75. Named Woman of Year, St. Louis Women's C. of C., 1955; Ecumenical Woman of Year, Met. Ch. Fedn. St. Louis, 1968, Outstanding Woman in Communications, 1968, Advt. Woman of Year 9th Dist. AAF, 1970. Mem. Mo. Press Women (pres. 1963-65), Am. Newspaper Guild, D.A.R., Theta Sigma Phi (award 1958; past pres.), Gamma Alpha Chi. Republican. Clubs: Women's Advt. (pres. St. Louis 1949-50); Fenton (Mo.) Garden. Author: God's Man, the Story of Pastor Niemoeller, 1959; When You're a Widow, 1968; Never Underestimate the Little Woman, 1969; Look Here, Lord, 1972; Flowers Forever, 1974; Webster Groves, 1975. Home: Box 196 Route 4 High Ridge MO 63049 Office: St Louis Post-Dispatch 1133 Franklin Ave St Louis MO 63101

LIPPERT, DAVID JAMES, journalism educator; b. Kenosha, Wis., May 23, 1919; m.; 4 children; B.A. in Econs., U. Wis., 1941, M.A. in Journalism, 1947, postgrad., 1962-64; Ph.D., So. Ill. U., 1969. Asso. editor Wis. State Employee mag., 1947-53; gen. assignment reporter Madison (Wis.) Capital Times, 1947-50; State Capital Bur. chief Milw. Sentinel, 1950-62; lectr. journalism U. Wis., 1962-64; head journalism program Wis. State U., Oshkosh, 1966—, chmn. dept. journalism, 1968—. Mem. Wis. Gov.'s Com. on Employment Physically Handicapped, 1950-60. Mem. Milw., Madison press clubs, Assn. Edn. in Journalism, Nat. Council Coll. Publs. Advisers, Am. Soc. Journalism Sch. Adminstrs., Wis. Press Assn., Wingspread Conf., Sigma Delta Chi, Phi Gamma Delta, Kappa Tau Alpha, Pioneer Yacht Club. Home: 1135 Elmwood Ave Oshkosh WI 54901

LIPPERT, DONNA RAU HARNESS, chemist; b. La Porte, Ind., May 5, 1948; d. Harry N. and Mary (Maxey) Harness; B.S., Valparaiso U., 1969; m. Gerald E. Lippert, Dec. 15, 1972. Tech. trainee main chem. lab., metall. dept. Burns Harbor plant Bethlehem Steel Corp., Chesterton, Ind., 1969-71, engr., main chem. lab., 1971-73, chief spectrographer, metall. dept., main chem. lab., 1973-75, tin plate engr., metall. dept., sheet and tin mill, 1975-76, asst. chem. supr., metall. dept., sheet and tin mill, 1976—. Democrat. Lutheran. Home: MR Box 4E Franklin St Chesterton IN 46304 Office: Box 248 Sheet & Tin Mill Bethlehem Steel Corp Chesterton IN 46304

LIPPERT, MARGARET JEAN SEAY, physician; b. Birmingham, Ala., Feb. 15, 1932; d. James Elbert and Ethlyn Louise (Hill) Seay; m. David James Lippert, June 18, 1960; children—Kathryn Louise, James Seay, William Leahy; A.B., Bryn Mawr Coll., 1954; M.D., Ala. Med. Coll., 1958. Intern, then resident psychiatry Univ. Hosps., Madison, Wis., 1958-62. Service chief child-adolescent unit Mendota (Wis.) State Hosp., 1962-67; cons. Coop. Ednl. Services Agy. #13, Waupun, Wis., 1966-70; staff psychiatrist Winnebago State Hosp., Oshkosh, Wis., 1966-67; cons. Oshkosh pub. schs., 1969-72; psychiatrist Winnebago Guidance Clinic, 1973—; pvt. practice medicine, specializing in psychiatry, 1962—; mem. faculty U. Wis. Med. Sch., 1963-67. Trustee, 1st Congl. Ch., Oshkosh, 1974-75; Girl Scout leader, 1973-74; Cub Scout den mother, 1974-75; bd. dirs. Big Bros. Fox Valley, 1973-75. Mem. AMA, Wis. Med. Soc., Winnebago Med. Soc., No. Wis. Psychiatry Assn. (sec. 1973-75), Dane County Psychiat. Assn. (sec. 1966-67), AAUW, U. Wis. Faculty Dames (v.p. 1973-74), Kappa Delta, Brewsters Club. Recipient Dutch Uncle award Big Bros., 1972-76, Vol. of Year award, 1972-73. Address: 1135 Elmwood Ave Oshkosh WI 54901

LIPSCHULTZ, M. RICHARD, accountant; b. Chgo., July 5, 1913; s. Morris David and Minnie (Moskowitz) L.; student Northwestern U., 1930-35; J.D., De Paul U., 1948; m. Evelyn Smolin, May 16, 1945 (dec. 1963); m. 2d Phyllis Siegel, July 11, 1965; children—Howard Elliott, Carl Alvin, Saul Martin. Admitted to Ill. bar, 1948; auditor State of Ill., Chgo., 1938-41; conferee Internal Revenue Service, Chgo., 1941-49; tax accountant A.I. Grade & Co., C.P.A.s, Chgo., 1949-50; sr. partner Lipschultz Bros., Levin and Gray and predecessor firms, C.P.A.s, Chgo., 1950—; financial v.p., dir. Miller Asso. Industries, Inc., Skokie, 1973-74; dir. Miller Builders, Inc.; dir., chmn. exec. com. Portable Electric Tools, Inc., Geneva, Ill., 1963-67; mem. exec. com. Midland Screw Corp., Chgo., 1958-66; faculty John Marshall Law Sch., 1951-64. Bd. dirs., sec., treas. Phil Pekow Family Found.; pres. bd. dirs. Lipschultz Bros. Family Found. Served with USAAF, 1943-46. C.P.A., Ill. Mem. Ill. Soc. C.P.A.'s, Am. Inst. C.P.A.'s, Am., Fed., Chgo., Ill. bar assns., Decalogue Soc. Lawyers, Am. Legion, Nu Beta-Epsilon. Mem. B'nai B'rith. Clubs: Standard (Chgo.); Ravinia Green Country (Deerfield, Ill.). Contbr. articles to profl. jours. Home: 1671 E Mission Hills Rd Northbrook IL 60062 Office: One Concourse Plaza Skokie IL 60076

LIPSCHULTZ, MAURICE ALLEN, machinery co. exec.; b. Chgo., Aug. 5, 1912; s. Isadore M. and Minnie (Tuchow) L.; student Crane Jr. Coll., 1928-29, U. Chgo., 1929-30; m. Sarah Goldsher, Aug. 29, 1934; children—Nathan M., Arthur H., Martin P. Pres. Malco Machinery Co., Chgo., 1939—; sec.-treas. Continental Drill Corp., Chgo., 1951-65; chmn. Viking Drill and Tool Co., St. Paul, 1965—; chmn. Reltool Corp., St. Paul, 1965—; chmn. Namco Corp.; partner Namco Mgmt. Co.; treas. Conwell Bldg. Corp., 1960—; dir. AIM Cos., Detroit, 1969—. Mem. art vis. com. U. Chgo.; mem. art adv. bd. Spertus Mus. Bd. dirs. Gottlieb Meml. Hosp., Museum Contemporary Art, Chgo., Evanston (Ill.) Art Center, D'Arcy Galleries, Loyola U., Chgo., Ukrainian Mus. Modern Art. Jewish religion (dir. temple). Mason. Club: Covenant (Chgo.). Home: 1342 Jackson Ave River Forest IL 60305 Office: 214 S Clinton St Chicago IL 60606

LIPSCOMB, JAMES FREDRICK, pub. co. mktg. officer; b. Milw., Mar. 16, 1922; s. Fred A. and Viola M. (Katz) L.; student Marquette U., 1939-42, B.S. in Bus. Adminstrn., 1946; student Washington-Jefferson Coll., 1942-43, U. W.Va., 1943; m. Alice Ann Tierney, Oct. 24, 1944; children—James, Paul, John, Patricia (Mrs. Patrick Geary), Virginia (Mrs. Thomas Baas), Susan (Mrs. Craig Supanich), Mary (Mrs. Douglas Hudson), Katherine, Jean, William, David, Margaret. Computer salesman Univac Corp., Milw., 1946-65; corp. data processing mgr. Western Pub. Co., Inc., Racine, Wis., 1965-72, asst. to v.p., dir. mktg., 1972—. Republican committeeman, River Hills, Wis., 1958-66; mem. Planning Commn., Village of River Hills, 1962—. Served with AUS, 1942-46. Mem. Am. Legion, Delta Sigma Pi. Republican. Roman Catholic. Home: 1040 W Greentree Rd Milwaukee WI 53217 Office: Western Pub Co Inc 1220 Mound Ave Racine WI 53404

LIPSITT, HARRY ALLAN, metallurgist; b. Detroit, June 7, 1931; s. Murray Jack and Betty Jean (Killen) L.; B.S., Mich. State U., 1952; M.S., Carnegie Mellon U., 1955, Ph.D., 1956; m. Donna Louise Lego, June 16, 1956; children—David Allan, Bruce Martin, Mark Andrew, Eric William. Task scientist Aerospace Research Labs., Wright Patterson AFB, O., 1956-58, project scientist, 1958-60, group leader metallurgy and mechanics research, 1960-75, group leader high temperature materials Air Force Materials Lab., 1975—. Sabbatical visitor metallurgy dept. U. Cambridge (Eng.), 1963-64; liaison scientist Materials, Office Naval Research, London, Eng., 1967-69. Water safety instr. trainer coordinator Western O. div. A.R.C., 1975—, sailing instr. trainer, 1975—. Served with USAF, 1956-58. E.I. duPont de Nemours & Co., Inc. fellow, 1953-56. Recipient Exceptional Civilian Service award, USAF, 1966. Mem. Am. Inst. Mining, Metall. and Petroleum Engrs., Tau Beta Pi, Sigma Pi Sigma, Sigma Xi. Club: The Bath (London, Eng.). Contbr. articles to profl. jours. Home: 1414 Birch St Yellow Springs OH 45387 Office: AFML/LL Wright Patterson AFB OH 45433

LIPSITZ, DAVID ALAN, clin. psychologist; b. St. Louis, Sept. 24, 1943; s. Ellis Sigmund and Edith May (Vorhaus) L.; B.A., Miami U., 1965; M.Ed., U. Mo. at Columbia, 1968; Ph.D., St. Louis U., 1973; m. Judith Miriam Robkin, Aug. 18, 1968; children—Daniel, Emily. Staff psychologist Child Center of Our Lady of Grace, St. Louis, 1972-73; clin. psychologist Midwest Clinic, Inc., St. Charles, Mo., 1973—; cons. Youth in Need, St. Charles; mem. adv. bd. Washington U. Child Guidance Clinic, St. Louis, 1973—. Bd. dirs. Jewish Family and Children's Service, St. Louis. Served with AUS, 1967-73. Certified psychologist, Mo. Mem. Am., Mo. psychol. assns., Nat. Health Registry for Psychology, St. Louis Soc. Psychologists. Jewish. Clubs: Westwood Country, Town and Tennis, Inc. Home: 512 White Rose Ln Olivette MO 63132 Office: 1360 S 5th St Saint Charles MO 63301

LIPSKI, JOHN GABRIEL, psychiatrist; b. Krakow, Poland, July 7, 1914; s. Stanley and Irene (Wyczolkowski) L.; came to U.S., 1947, naturalized, 1951; student Johanni Casimiriensis U. (Poland), 1933-39; Faculty Medicine, U. Edinburgh (Scotland), 1946; B.Sc., Wayne State U., 1950; m. Eleanor Lorraine Respondek, July 29, 1944; children—Jan Alexander, Irene (Mrs. Nicola), Roberta Jean (Mrs. Mays), Laura Ruth, Lillian Marie. Intern, Henry Ford Hosp., Detroit, 1951-53; indsl. physician Packard Motor Car Co., Guimares Clinic, Marygrove Clinic, Detroit, 1953-58; gen. practice medicine, Rogers City and Posen, Mich., 1958-63; resident psychiatry Traverse City (Mich.) State Hosp., 1963-68, staff psychiatrist, 1967-69; med. dir. Petoskey (Mich.) Area Mental Health Clinic, 1969-75; chief dept. psychiatry and neurology Burns Clinic Med. Center, Petoskey, 1970-75; psychiat. cons. Lockwood-MacDonald Hosp., Petoskey, 1971-72. Cons. to intermedial sch. dist., dist. cts.; chief of staff Rogers City Gen. Hosp., 1960-62; chief women's div., chmn. group therapy com., dir. shelter workshop Traverse City (Mich.) State Hosp., 1967-68. Bd. dirs. Area Mental Health Clinic, Petoskey, 1971-72, Big Bros. Am., N.W. Mich., 1972-75. Recipient Am. Med. Assn. award for continuing edn., 1972. Fellow Royal Soc. Health (London); mem. A.M.A., Am., Canadian psychiat. assns., Mich. Assn. Neuro-Psychiat. Physicians, Alpena-Alcona-Presque Isle County (pres. 1961), No. Mich. (treas. 1975-76) med. socs. Home: 450 Country Club Rd Petoskey MI 49770 Office: 560 W Mitchell St Petoskey MI 49770

LISIO, DONALD JOHN, historian, educator; b. Oak Park, Ill., May 27, 1934; s. Anthony and Dorothy (LoCelso) L.; B.A., Knox Coll., 1956; M.A., Ohio U., 1958; Ph.D., U. Wis., 1965; m. Suzanne Marie Swanson, Apr. 22, 1958; children—Denise Anne, Stephen Anthony. Mem. faculty overseas div. U. Md., 1958-60; asst. prof. history Coe Coll., Cedar Rapids, Iowa, 1964-69, asso. prof., 1969-74, prof., 1974—, chmn. dept., 1973—; mem. exec. com. Cedar Rapids Com. Historic Preservation, 1975—; William F. Vilas research fellow U. Wis., 1963-64. Served with U.S. Army, 1958-60. Recipient Outstanding Tchr. award Coe Coll., 1969; Nat. Endowment for Humanities fellow, 1969-70; Am. Council Learned Socs. fellow, 1977-78. Mem. Orgn. Am. Historians, Am. Hist. Assn., AAUP, ACLU, Common Cause. Episcopalian. Author: The President and Protest: Hoover, Conspiracy, and the Bonus Riot, 1974; contbr. author: The War Generation, 1975. Contbr. articles to hist. jours. Home: 4203 Twin Ridge Ct SE Cedar Rapids IA 52403 Office: Coe College Cedar Rapids IA 52401

LISMAN, WILLIAM FRANKLYN, elec. equipment mfg. co. exec.; b. Linton, Ind., Apr. 6, 1903; s. Andrew Mack and Mary Lola (Stockrahm) L.; B.E.E., Rose Poly Inst., 1924, Dr. Eng., 1967; m. Rosanne Lieser, June 10, 1937; 1 dau., Susan Ann Lisman Hultquist. Engring. and mktg. positions Gen. Electric Co., Ft. Wayne, Ind., also Cleve., 1924-34; chmn., pres. Leland Electric Co., Dayton, Ohio, 1934-52; v.p. Brown-Brockmeyer Co., Dayton, 1952-54; chmn., chief exec. officer Furnas Electric Co., Batavia, Ill., 1954—; dir. Sola-Basic Industries Inc., Milw., 1st Nat. Bank Batavia, Batavia Savs. & Bldg. Assn. Bd. dirs., v.p. Valley Indsl. Assn., 1966-72; bd. dirs. Furnas Found.; trustee Furnas Trust, Community Hosp. Men's Found. (pres. 1957-59). Mem. IEEE, NAM, Nat. Elec. Mfrs. Assn., Soc. Advancement Mgmt., Ill. (dir. 1964-72), Batavia (pres. 1956-58) chambers commerce, Lambda Chi Alpha. Republican. Roman Catholic. Home: 335 North Ave Batavia IL 60510 Office: 1000 McKee St Batavia IL 60510

LISON, JAMES J., JR., state ofcl.; B.A., St. Norbert Coll., 1942; m. Marian Kehl; children—Kathy, Peter, Susan, Joan. Wis. adj. gen., 1969-77, dep. adj. gen., 1977—. Mem. Wis. Am. Revolution Bicentennial Commn. Served from 2d lt. to capt., AUS, 1942-45, ETO; brig. gen. Wis. N.G. Decorated Legion of Merit, Bronze Star medal. Mem. N.G. Assn. U.S., Wis. N.G. Assn., Am. Legion, V.F.W., 32d, 42d inf. div. vets. assns. Home: 310 Yosemite Trail Madison WI 53705 Office: 3020 Wright St Madison WI 53701

LISSNER, ARTHUR BART, plastic surgeon; b. N.Y.C., Oct. 2, 1929; s. Arthur and Leona (Brophel) L.; B.S. cum laude, Georgetown U., 1951; M.D., Jefferson Med. Coll., 1955; m. Adrienne Hessel, June 19, 1954; children—Lee, Amy, Chris, Ken, Cindy, Jenny, Kathy, Mike. Resident gen. surgery Cornell Div. Bellevue Hosp., N.Y.C., 1958-61; resident plastic surgery Columbia U., 1961-63; asst. instr. surgery St. Louis U., 1965—; practice medicine specializing in plastic surgery, St. Louis, St. Charles, Florissant, Mo., 1963—; chief surgery Christian Northwest Hosp., Florissant, 1970-73; pres. Plastic Surgery Consultants Ltd., 1972—. Served to lt. M.C. USNR, 1956-58. Diplomate Am. Bd. Plastic and Reconstructive Surgery. Fellow A.C.S.; mem. AMA, St. Louis County Med. Soc., St. Louis Surg. Soc., Am. Soc. Plastic and Reconstructive Surgery. Home: 13 Royale Ct Lake Saint Louis MO 63367 Office: 1245 Graham Rd Florissant MO 63031

LIST, DAVID PATTON, lawyer; b. Belvidere, Ill., Feb. 4, 1920; s. Raymond Ford and Marguerite (Patton) L.; A.B., Dartmouth Coll., 1942; LL.B., Harvard U., 1948; m. Patricia Porter, Jan. 7, 1949; children—John, Victoria, David Patton. Admitted to Ill. bar, 1948; since practiced in Chgo., partner firm Sidley & Austin, and predecessors, 1955—. Served with AUS, 1942-45. Fellow Am. Coll. Trial Lawyers; mem. Am., Ill. State, Chgo. bar assns., Legal Club Chgo., Law Club Chgo. Republican. Episcopalian. Clubs: Westmoreland Country, Univ. of Chgo. Address: 1 First National Plaza Chicago IL 60670

LISTER, COLIN HOLDEN, hockey club ofcl.; b. Perth, W. Australia, July 7, 1927; s. George Holden and Elinor (Daly) L.; student pvt. schs., Perth; came to U.S., 1958, naturalized, 1961. Teller, Commonwealth Bank of Australia, Perth/Sydney, 1942-51; clk. Lex Garages, London, 1952; asst. cashier Bank of Montreal (Que., Can.), 1953-58; partner, dir. Komet Hockey Club, Fort Wayne, Ind., 1958—, treas., 1960—, bus. mgr., 1958—. Bd. dirs. Urban Youth Ventures, Inc., Ft. Wayne, 1976-77. Mem. Ind. Amateur Baseball Congress (sec. 1969—). Mem. Calvary Temple. Club: Rotary. Home: 1025 Ridgewood Dr Fort Wayne IN 46805 Office: 4000 Parnell Ave Fort Wayne IN 46805

LISTON, GEORGE EDWARD, art instr.; b. Medina, Ohio, Aug. 14, 1930; s. Lewis Edward and Sara Mae (James) L.; A.B., Otterbein Coll., 1952; postgrad. Ohio No. U., 1952-53, U.S. Armed Forces Inst., 1954-56; M.Ed., Miami U., 1958; postgrad. Miami U., Ind. U., 1958-61, Wright State U., 1976-77; m. Jane Britannia Devers, June 2, 1953; children—Jefferson Edward, Jonathan Devers. Tchr. English, art Logan County (Ohio) Schs., 1952-53; art instr. Troy (Ohio) City Schs., 1953-54; elementary and jr. high art instr. Kettering (Ohio) City Schs., 1956—; tchr. Kettering Adult Sch., 1962-72. Supr. arts and crafts City of Kettering, 1966-76; artist; works exhibited juried shows in Dayton. Chmn. supervisory com., mem. bd. dirs. Dayton Tchrs. Fed. Credit Union, also v.p., 1975-76, pres. bd. dirs., 1977-78. Served with USNR, 1954-56. Recipient classroom tchrs. medal Freedoms Found., 1965; certificate of merit in fine arts Ohio No. U., 1953; letter commendation City Beautiful Council Dayton, 1972; Martha Holden Jennings scholar, 1974-75. Mem. Otterbein Alumni Assn. (pres. Miami Valley chpt. 1962-63), Oakwood Speech Parents (treas. 1970-72), Ohio Edn. Assn., Kettering Classroom Tchrs. Assn. (pres. 1962-64), NEA (life), Engrs. Club Dayton, Dayton Soc. Painters and Sculptors (chmn. bd., pres. 1970-73). Methodist. Home: 111 Oakwood Ave Dayton OH 45409 Office: 3301 Shroyer Rd Kettering OH 45429

LISZESKI, JOSEPH MICHAL, dentist; b. Cleve., Sept. 29, 1939; s. Joseph Walter and Martha (Pizon) L.; student U. Dayton, 1957-60, John Carroll U., 1959; D.D.S., Case Western Res. U., 1964; m. Beverley Ann Svec, Aug. 31, 1963; children—Joseph, Lisa, David, Lawrence, Theodore, Julie, Theresa. Asst. records' librarian Univ. Hosps., Cleve., 1961-62; med. technician St. Vincent Charity Hosp., Cleve., 1962-64; gen. practice dentistry, 1964—; mem. dental staff Elyria Meml. Hosp., 1976—. Vice pres. Catholic Youth Orgn., 1956-57, pres., 1958-59; scout master Boy Scouts Am., 1976—. Recipient Medallion Circle award Confraternity of Holy Name, 1972. Mem. Am., Ohio, Lorain County dental assns., Internat. Acad. Preventive Medicine, Am. Bowling Congress, Holy Name Soc. (v.p. 1966-68, pres. 1968-70, sec. 1971-72), Sigma Delta Pi, Psi Omega (sec. 1963-64), Democrat. Roman Catholic (lay minister 1971—). Home: 8233 Avon Belden Rd North Ridgeville OH 44039 Office: 8225 Avon Belden Rd North Ridgeville OH 44039

LIT, ALFRED, exptl. psychologist, educator; b. N.Y.C., Nov. 24, 1914; s. Zachary Oscar and Elsie (Jaro) L.; B.S., Columbia U., 1938, A.M., 1943, Ph.D., 1948; m. Imogene Speegle, Jan. 27, 1947. Lectr. optometry Columbia U., 1946-47, instr. optometry, 1947-49, asst. prof. optometry, 1949-52, asso. prof. optometry, 1952-56, also mem. staff research project between dept. psychology and U.S. Office Naval Research, 1949-56; research psychologist Vision Research Labs., U. Mich., Ann Arbor, 1956-59; head human factors engring. staff Bendix Systems Div., Ann Arbor, 1959-61; prof. psychology, elec. scis. and systems engring. Sch. Engring. and Tech., So. Ill. U., Carbondale, 1961—, also mem. exec. com. engring. biophysics program and molecular sci. doctoral program. Served to 1st lt. USAAF, 1943-46. Recipient Sigma Xi-Kaplan Research award So. Ill. U., 1971; Am. Acad. Optometry grantee, 1948, State of Ill. Dept. Mental Health grantee, 1962-64, NSF grantee, 1962-68, Eye Inst. of USPHS grantee, 1962-77. Fellow Am. Psychol. Assn., AAAS, Am. Acad. Optometry, Optical Soc. Am., Psychonomic Soc., N.Y. Acad. Sci.; mem. Soc. Engring. Psychologists; Midwestern Psychol. Assn., Nat. Acad. Scis. (nat. research council com. on vision 1960—), Human Factors Soc., New York County Optometric Soc. (pres. 1954-55), Assn. for Research in Vision and Ophthalmology, Sigma Xi (pres. chpt. 1967-69). Sci. referee Am. Jour. Optometry, 1973—; mem. editorial adv. bd. Vision Research, 1974—. Contbr. articles on psychology and vision research to profl. jours. Home: Route 1 Box 164A Murphysboro IL 62966

LITOT, EDWARD FRANCIS, clergyman; b. Fort Wayne, Ind., June 18, 1922; s. Francis E. and Bernadette C. (Forbing) L.; student St. Joseph Coll., 1940-42; St. Meinrad Major Sem., 1942-47. Ordained priest Roman Catholic Ch., 1947; asst. pastor St. Vincent Ch., Elkhart, Ind., 1947-51; dir. Gary (Ind.) Alerding Settlement House, 1953-67; asst. pastor St. Joseph's Ch. Dyer, Ind., 1951-53; pastor, 1967—. Dir. Diocesan Info. Bur., Gary, 1957—; diocesan dir. Council Cath. Men, 1964—; chmn. Diocesan Ecumenical Commn., 1964—; diocesan dir. Confrat. Christian Doctrine, Gary Diocese, 1957-63; chaplain Gary Police, 1964-67, Ind. Guard Res., 1965—; diocesan consultor, 1969; diocesan dir. cemeteries, 1971—; pro-synodal judge, 1971. Pres., Frontiers Internat., Gary, 1967. Dir. Northwestern Ind. Council Chs., 1965—. Named Domestic prelate Pope John XXIII, 1962, monsignor, 1962. Mem. Ind. Cath. Conf. (pub. relations com. 1966—), Gary Fellowship Ministers, Gary C. of C. Editor: Gary edit. Our Sunday Visitor, 1957—. Home: 440 Joliet St Dyer IN 46311 Office: 3855 Broadway Gary IN 46401

LITOWSKY, JACK MORTON, educator; b. Mpls., May 29, 1936; s. Nathan and Mildred (Yablonsky) L.; B.S., U. Minn. at Mpls., 1959. Tchr. speech and theatre arts Montrose County High Sch., Montrose, Colo., 1959-61; tchr. speech and theater arts Mpls. Pub. Schs., 1961—; co-creator Mpls. Youth theater, 1977. Mem. center arts council Walker Art Center, Mpls., 1969. Served with Minn. Air N.G., 1954-59, USAF, 1961-62. Rockefeller grantee for Tyrone Guthrie

Theater, 1969. Mem. Nat. Collegiate Players, AFTRA, Am. Fedn. Tchrs., Mpls. Area Council Tchrs. English. Co-creator Mpls. Pub. High Sch. Student Residency Program at Tyrone Guthrie Theater, 1969; creator Theater Is TV show WCCO-TV, Mpls., 1969, Sch. and Community Theater Two, 1973, Sch. and Community Theater Three, 1974, Mpls. Sch. and Community Theater Co-op, 1975. Home: 3733 Gettysburg Ave N Minneapolis MN 55427

LITSCHER, DANIEL WORDEN, elec. co. exec.; b. Grand Rapids, Mich., July 22, 1912; s. Christian Joseph and Sarah Ann (MacNeil) L.; A.B., Harvard Coll., 1934, postgrad., 1934-35; m. Elizabeth Williams Nind, Mar. 14, 1942; children—Sarah Jane Litscher Milkins, Ann Litscher Bergesen, Mary Christina Litscher Miles. Tchr., co-partner Kent Country Day Sch., Grand Rapids, 1935-39; warehouseman, counter salesman Litscher Elec. Co., Grand Rapids, 1939-41, office, credit mgr., 1941-42, 46-49, gen. mgr., 1949-68, pres., 1968-77, chmn. bd., 1977—. Bd. dirs. Tb, Health and Emphysema Soc. Western Mich., 1971—; exec. com. Western Mich. Tourist Assn., 1976—. Served to lt. col., F.A. and M.I., U.S. Army, 1942-46. Mem. Nat. Assn. Elec. Distbrs. (dir. 1969-74, trustee edn. found. 1974—), Grand Rapids Area C. of C. Republican. Episcopalian. Club: Kent Country. Home: 2346 Lake Dr SE Grand Rapids MI 49506 Office: 910 Scribner Ave NW Grand Rapids MI 49504

LITTLE, ARTHUR DILLARD, coll. theater dir.; b. Thomasville, Ga., Oct. 31, 1911; s. Arthur Dillard Harmon and Carolyn Scarlett (Atkinson) L.; student U. N.C. at Chapel Hill, 1927-30, Clifford Brooke Acad. Dramatic Arts, 1933-34, The Studio of Acting, 1934-36; L.H.D. (hon.), Earlham Coll., 1976— m. Sara Jones, Nov. 30, 1940; 1 son, Jon Dunwody. Dir. Macon (Ga.) Little Theater, 1939-42; edn. sec. Civilian Pub. Service Camp, Gatlinburg, Tenn., 1943-46; with fgn. service sect. Am. Friends Service Com., Phila., 1946-47; dir. theater Earlham Coll., Richmond, Ind., 1947—, prof. at large, 1977—. Ford Found. Japanese Studies grantee, 1962-63; Fulbright fellow to Japan, 1966-67. Mem. Am. Theater Assn., Japan Soc. Author: St. Francis, a Noh play, U.S., 1970, Japan, 1975. Home: 606 College Ave Richmond IN 47374

LITTLE, BERNARD HAROLD, mfg. co. exec.; b. Pitts., Oct. 19, 1921; s. Robert E. and Irene (Jamison) L.; student Robert Morris Coll., 1947-49; m. Bernadeen; children—Michele, Dorothy, Richard. With Ernst & Ernst, C.P.A.'s, 1949-59, mgr., 1957-59; with Ohio Brass Co., Mansfield, 1959—, v.p. finance, dir., 1967—, sec.-treas., 1961—; chmn. Tax Council, Inc., Washington. Trustee Mansfield Univ. Found. Served with USAAF, 1943-47. Mem. Ohio Mfg. Assn. (trustee, v.p.). Home: PO Box 1481 Mansfield OH 44901 Office: 380 N Main St Mansfield OH 44902

LITTLE, CLARENCE WILBUR, JR., foundry cons.; b. Crowley, La., Apr. 28, 1923; s. Clarence Wilbur and Adelia (Faulk) L.; student La. Poly. Inst., 1940-44; B.E.E., Johns Hopkins U., 1948, D.Eng., 1952; m. Eleanor MacWithey, June 12, 1945; children—Nancy Lee (Mrs. Glenn David Ahrens), Jonathan Avery, Christopher Mark, Peter Coffman, Martha Lee, Sarah Palmer, David Stanley, Paul Drake. Supr. physics and elec. research Allis-Chalmers Mfg. Co., West Allis, Wis., 1952-57; group leader C-Stellarator Assos. James Forrestal Research Center, Princeton, N.J., 1957-59, dir. ops., 1959-61; v.p. research and devel. Waukesha Foundry Co., Inc. (Wis.), 1961-72, exec. v.p., 1972-74, v.p., gen. mgr. manufactured products div., 1974-76, also dir.; cons., program coordinator dept. engring. and applied sci. U. Wis.-Extension, 1976—; pres., dir. Dutch Hollow Lake Property Owners Assn., LaValle, Wis., 1974—. Active Boy Scouts Am. Served with USNR, 1944-46. Mem. Hydraulic Inst., Internat. Conf. on Standards, Sigma Xi, Lambda Chi Alpha, Tau Beta Pi, Alpha Phi Omega. Mem. Ch. Jesus Christ of Latter-day Saints. Contr. articles to tech. jours. Patentee in field. Home: 441 Summit Point Dr LaValle WI 53941 Office: 432 N Lake St Madison WI 53706

LITTLE, ERVIN DEWEY, JR., advt. and pub. relations co. exec.; b. Flint, Mich., Jan. 16, 1925; s. Ervin Dewey and Mary Blanche (Anderson) L.; B.A., U. Mich., 1949; M.A., U. Mo., 1951; m. Dorothy Marie Veal, Aug. 9, 1947; children—Gregory, Melinda, Randolph. Asso. editor Haywood Pub. Co., Chgo., 1951-56; asst. editor World Book Ency., Chgo., 1956-57; mgr. pub. relations Spector Freight System, Chgo., 1957-60; writer Jam Handy Orgn., Detroit, 1960-64; mgr. pub. relations Mich. Blue Shield, Detroit, 1964-67; dir. community relations Wyandotte (Mich.) Gen. Hosp., 1967-73; owner Dewey Little & Assos., Royal Oak, Mich., 1974—; editor, pub. Mich. Health Educator Mag., 1976—. Safety chmn. Starr Sch., Royal Oak, 1968-69; com. mem. Boy Scouts Am., Wyandotte, 1969-70. Served with inf. AUS, 1943-45. Decorated Purple Heart. Recipient Pub. Relations Contest First prize Am. Trucking Assn., 1958; three Internat. MacEachern Pub. Relations Contest awards Am. Acad. Hosp. Pub. Relations, 1970, 71. Mem. Pub. Relations Soc. Am., Am. Soc. Hosp. Pub. Relations Dirs., Mich. Hosp. Pub. Relations Assn. (state pres. 1971, pres. southeast chpt. 1974-75), Detroit Press Club, Sigma Delta Chi. Address: 2902 Glenview Av Royal Oak MI 48073

LITTLE, JAMES REICHARD, dentist; b. St. Paul, Jan. 13, 1920; s. Joseph Monroe and Elizabeth (Reichard) L.; D.D.S., U. Minn., 1943; m. Janet Mae Coates, Sept. 4, 1943; children—John Coates, Laura Elizabeth. Practice gen. dentistry, St. Paul, 1946—. Bd. dirs. St. Paul Area Health Council; mem. Ramsey County Health Interagy. Com. Served to maj. Dental Corps, AUS, 1943-46. Fellow Am. Coll. Dentists (pres. Minn. sect. 1965), Internat. Coll. Dentists; mem. Am. (spl. cons. 1972—, cons. nat. bds., council nat. bd. exams. 1977—), Minn. (com. chmn. 1952—) dental assns., St. Paul Dist. Dental Soc. (exec. council. 1950—), U. Minn. Dental Alumni Assn. (pres. 1963), Minn. State Bd. Dentistry, Am. Assn. Dental Schs. (spl. cons. 1972—), Minn. Acad. Restorative Dentistry, Fedn. Assns. Health Regulatory Bds. (dir.), Am. Assn. Dental Examiners, Exec. Council (pres. 1974-75), St. Paul Jr. C. of C., Sigma Alpha Epsilon. Republican. Unitarian. Mason, Rotarian. Clubs: Town and Country. Home: 2022 Summit Ave St Paul MN 55105 Office: 1371 W 7th St St Paul MN 55102

LITTLE, MARTHA LOUISE, clin. psychologist; b. Evansville, Ind., Mar. 28, 1914; d. Harry Wilson and Dora (Haussermann) L.; B.A., Wellesley Coll., 1935; M.A., Middlebury French Sch., 1942; M.A., Cath. U. Am., 1959, Ph.D., 1967. Clin. psychologist, research asst. NIMH, Bethesda, Md., 1955; clin. psychology trainee VA Clinics and Hosp., Washington and Balt., 1955-57; clin. psychology intern Columbus (Ohio) Psychiat. Clinic, 1957-58; clin. psychologist Dayton (Ohio) State Hosp., 1958-59, Fairfax-Falls Church (Va.) Mental Health Center, 1961-63, Adult Psychiat. Clinic, Dayton, 1963-66; supervising clin. psychologist Oneida County Dept. Mental Health, Utica, N.Y., 1966-68; chief clin. psychologist Sinnissippi Mental Health Center, Dixon, Ill., 1968-70; pvt. practice clin. psychology, Dixon, 1970—. Certificate in applied psychiatry for tchrs. Wash. Sch. Psychiatry, 1955; licensed certified clin. psychologist, N.Y., Ohio, Ill., Fla. Diplomate Am. Bd. Profl. Psychology. Mem. Am., Ill., Ohio, N.Y. psychol. assns., Am., Ill. group psychotherapy assns., Ohio Acad. Cons. Psychologists, Am. Soc. Psychologists in Pvt. Practice, Psychologists Interested in Study of Psychoanalysis. Home: 210 1/2 N Dixon Ave Dixon IL 61021 Office: 357 W Everett St Dixon IL 61021

LITTLE, RICHARD ALLEN, educator; b. Coshocton, Ohio, Jan. 12, 1939; s. Charles Milton and Elsie Leanna (Smith) L.; B.Sc., Wittenberg U., 1960; M.A., Johns Hopkins U., 1961; Ed.M., Harvard, 1965; Ph.D., Kent State U., 1971; m. Gail Louanne Koons, June 12, 1960; children—Eric Andrew, Joan Alice, Stephanie Ann. Tchr. math, counselor, coach Culver (Ind.) Mil. Acad., 1961-65; instr., curriculum specialist Nigerian Project, Harvard U., Cambridge Mass. and Aiyetoro, Nigeria, 1965-67; instr. math. Kent State U., Stark and Canton, Ohio, 1967-69, asst. prof., 1969-74, asso. prof., 1974-75; asso. prof. math. Baldwin Wallace Coll., Berea, Ohio, 1975—. Bd. dirs. Canton Symphony Orch., 1973-75; chmn. bd. deacons Holy Cross Lutheran Ch., Canton, 1971-74. Gen. Motors scholar, 1956-60; Ford Found. fellow, 1960-61; NSF fellow, 1963-64. Mem. Greater Canton (exec. com. 1968-72, pres. 1969-70), Ohio (dir. 1968—, pres. 1974-76), Nat. councils tchrs. math, Math. Assn. Am. (editor newsletter 1977—). Republican. Clubs: Oakwood Tennis. Home: 243 Kraft St Berea OH 44017 Office: Dept Math Baldwin Wallace Coll Berea OH 44017

LITTMANN, MARTIN FREDERICK, metallurgist; b. Brazil, Ind., Feb. 9, 1919; s. Walter Arnold and Magdalene Marie (Mueller) L.; Ch.E., U. Cin., 1941, M.S., 1943; m. Anna Lou Aker, Oct. 28, 1944; children—Carol Littmann Prahl, Daniel. With Armco Steel Corp., Middletown, Ohio, 1941-43, research asst., 1943, jr. research engr., 1944-45, research engr., 1945-52, sr. research engr., 1952-68, prin. research asso., 1968—. Pres. Madison Twp. (Ohio) Improvement Assn., 1953-63; mem. Butler County (Ohio) Planning Commn., 1967—, v.p., 1971-76, pres., 1976—. Armco Steel fellow, 1941-43. Registered profl. engr. Ohio. Mem. Am. Inst. Mining, Metall. and Petroleum Engrs., IEEE, Sigma Xi, Tau Beta Pi, Alpha Chi Sigma, Phi Lambda Upsilon. Republican. Lutheran (bd. stewardship 1969-73, dist. sec. Luth. Laymens League 1974—). Contbr. articles to profl. jours. Patentee in field. Home: 1050 Knoll Ln Middletown OH 45042 Office: Armco Steel Corp Middletown OH 45043

LITTON, STEPHEN FREDERICK, orthodontist, anatomist; b. Bklyn., Jan. 8, 1943; s. Murray A. and Eda (Schwartz) L.; B.A., U. Minn., 1965, B.S. with distinction, 1965, D.D.S., 1967, certificate orthodontics, 1970, PH.D., 1972; m. Bonnie Lee Tarnoff, July 4, 1965; children—Jeremy, Jonathan. Teaching asst. dept. anatomy U. Minn., 1967-72; research fellow Sch. Dentistry U. Minn., 1967-72, asst. prof. dept. anatomy, 1972—; practice dentistry, Mpls., 1967-70, practice orthodontics, Mpls., 1970—. Asst. dir. orthodontics Children's Hosp., Mpls., 1972—. Recipient W. H. Crawford award Minn. sect. Internat. Assn. Dental Research, 1965; USPHS fellow, 1967-72. Mem. Internat. Assn. Dental Research, Am. Assn. Orthodontists, Am. Dental Assn., Omicron Kappa Upsilon, Sigma Alpha Mu, Alpha Omega. Home: 1850 Kelly Dr Minneapolis MN 55427 Office: 717 Winnetka Ave Minneapolis MN 55427

LITTRELL, KENNETH EARL, mail order co. exec.; b. Arizona, Nebr., Jan. 3, 1915; s. Earl Nelson and Henrietta (Langdale) L.; student Morningside Coll., 1934-35, U. Nebr., 1936-37; B.A., Neb. Wesleyan U., 1939; postgrad. George Williams Coll., 1939; M.B.A., U. Chgo., 1950; m. Helen Louise Opp, Dec. 16, 1938; children—Gayle Louise, Richard Earl. With Montgomery Ward, Chgo., 1940-46; with Aldens, Inc., Chgo., 1946—, operating mgr., supt., adminstrv. asst. to v.p., 1958-59, gen. mgr. catalog offices, 1959-65, gen. mgr. Gambles catalog office, 1965—; mgr. indsl. operations Foster & Gallagher, Peoria, Ill.; bd. dirs. W.M. Tyler Corp., Skokie, Ill. Chmn. Skokie Archtl. Commn., 1956—; mem. Skokie Recreation Commn., 1956—; founder Home Owners Council, 1955, pres., 1955-57; pres. Niles Twp. Sch. Bd. Assn., 1956; pres. Sch. Dist. Number 219, 1960-61; chmn. spl. edn. com., 1963; chmn. Downtown Redevel. Commn., East Peoria, Ill.; labor negotiator City of East Peoria. Named Man of Year, Niles Twp. Jr. C. of C., 1957; recipient award for service to edn. Skokie C. of C., 1960. Mem. Am. Soc. Personnel Adminstrs., NAM (mem. indsl. relations com.), Adminstrv. Mgmt. Soc. (v.p., now pres. Peoria chpt.), Am. Inst. Parliamentarians, Chgo. Assn. Commerce and Industry, Am. Mgmt. Assn., Highview Home Owners Assn. (pres.), Alpha Psi Omega, Mason (Shriner), Rotarian (pres. East Peoria). Home: 821 Highview Rd East Peoria IL 61611 Office: 6523 N Galena Rd Peoria IL 61601

LITVAG, IRVING R., univ. adminstr.; b. St. Louis, Sept. 5, 1928; s. Joseph and Ida (Rosenberg) L.; student U. Mo., 1946-47; A.B., Washington U., 1950; m. Ilene Doris Gallop, June 3, 1962; children—Julie, Joseph. Newswriter, reporter KMOX radio, St. Louis, 1950-57; advt. and pub. relations writer Krupnick & Assos., Inc., St. Louis, 1957; dir. pub. relations Jewish Fedn. St. Louis, 1958-61; dir. spl. events Washington U., St. Louis, 1961-73, dir. spl. projects Sch. Dental Medicine, 1973—. Recipient 1st prize Nat. Playwriting competition Webster Groves Theater Guild, 1956. Mem. Authors Guild, Soc. Profl. Journalists. Jewish. Author: Singer in the Shadows, 1972; The Master of Sunnybank: A Biography of Albert Payson Terhune, 1977. Home: 655 Fairways Circle St Louis MO 63141 Office: 4559 Scott Ave St Louis MO 63110

LITVIN, ROBERT LOWELL, mech. contractor exec.; b. Chgo., Oct. 27, 1925; s. Thomas Henry and Theresa (Bellak) L.; B.S.C.E., U. Ill., 1946; m. K. Jean Gault, Sept. 18, 1976; children—Marilyn Beth, Michelle Ann, Robert, William. With Thomas H. Litvin Co., Chgo., 1938-46, 46— pres., 1969—; with Thoro, Inc., Chgo., 1964—, pres., 1969-76, chmn. bd., 1976—; gen. partner C.S.A. Asso. Ltd., Chgo., 1967—, 40 E. Oak St. Apts., Chgo., 1967—, Harbor House Ltd., Chgo., 1967—; partner 180 N. Michigan Ave. Bldg., Chgo., 1967-69; mech. contractor in plumbing and fire protection; chmn. No. Ill. Regional Bargaining Council Plumbing Industry. Author (with others) Chgo. Plan, 1969-70, chmn. plumbing industry operating com., 1970—. Trustee Carl Howard Litvin fellowship for Leukemia Research; bd. dirs. Mt. Sinai Med. Research Found., Mt. Sinai Hosp. Med. Center, Young Men's Jewish Council, Chgo. Youth Centers, Rest Haven Convalescent Hosp., Deborah Boys Club; founder Technion U. Israel, Hebrew U.; bd. govs. State of Israel Bonds, chmn. bldg. trades State of Israel Bonds: active Combined Jewish Appeal. Served with USNR, 1943-45. Mem. Plumbing Contractors Assn. (co-chmn. labor relations com.), Plumbing Council (dir. 1968-70), ASCE, Am. Soc. San. Engrs., Am. Soc. Plumbing Engrs., Am. Legion, Sigma Alpha Mu. Jewish (v.p. temple). Club: Standard (Chgo.). Home: 180 E Pearson St Chicago IL 60611 Office: 1355 W Washington Blvd Chicago IL 60607

LITWILLER, OTTO BRYAN, dentist; b. Hopedale, Ill., Aug. 4, 1901; s. Jacob T. and Mary Ann (Wittrig) L.; student Ill. State U., 1920-23; B.S., U. Ill., 1928, D.D.S., 1928, grad. oral surgery, 1942; student Lewis Inst., 1924-26; m. Imogene Mowat, Mar. 16, 1931; 1 son, Gavin Dee. Athletic coach, tchr. sci. Witt (Ill.) High Sch., 1922-24; practice dentistry, Peoria, Ill., 1928—; asst. oral surgery U. Ill. at Chgo., 1938-42; mem. staff Proctor Hosp. Mem. subcom. oral cancer Ill. div. Am. Cancer Soc.; mem. Gov.'s Commn. to Study Pub. Health, 1966-70; chmn. Peoria County Cancer Soc.; mem. Peoria Council Alcoholism. Fellow Am., Ill. dental socs., Royal Soc. Health (Eng.), Am. Coll. Dentistry; mem. Am. Acad. Oral Pathology, Peoria Dist. Dental Soc. (pres. 1941-43). Mem. 1st Federated Ch. (mem. council, trustee). Mason (Shriner), Rotarian. Clubs: Creve Coeur, Peoria Country, Knife and Fork (pres. 1940-44), Illini (pres. 1934) (Peoria). Home: 501 Main St Peoria IL 61602 Office: 1101 Main St Peoria IL 61606

LIU, CHUN NAN, engine lathe co. exec.; b. Taiwan, Mar. 29, 1942; s. Chin Chen and Chien (Lo) L.; came to U.S., 1970; M.M.E., Ill. Inst. Tech., 1973; m. Anita Sia Kee, Aug. 14, 1971; children—Christine K., Edward Quincy. Stationery engr. Oak Park (Ill.) Hosp., 1970-73; mech. engr. Sverdrup & Parcel Assos., St. Louis, 1973-74, Laramore, Douglas & Popham, Chgo., 1974-76; owner, pres. The Evenhanded Co., Skokie, Ill., 1976—; cons. to power plant industry. Registered profl. engr., Ill., Mo.; lic. marine 3d engr., China, Liberia. Mem. ASME, Am. Inst. Plant Engrs. Club: Formosan of Am. Developer computer-oriented stress analysis of orthotropic plate with 2 holes, 1973. Home and Office: 4539 W Howard St Skokie IL 60076

LIU, EDWARD CHUNG-HONG, design engr.; b. Tainan, Taiwan, Aug. 17, 1940; s. Seifu and Tsi-Fang (Chuang) L.; came to U.S., 1968, naturalized, 1976; B.S. in Chem. Engring., Chung Yuan Coll. Engring., Taiwan, 1963; M.S. in Chem. Engring., U. Mo., Rolla, 1971; m. Ingrid Yin-Guey Tzeng, Apr. 12, 1969; children—Jean Ju, Jasper Edward. Process engr. Kaohsiung Oil Refinery, Chinese Petroleum Corp., 1965-68; sr. instrument engr. Catalytic, Inc., Phila., 1973-74; design engr. Ashland Chem. Co., Dublin, Ohio, 1975—; cons. Mem. Am. Inst. Chem. Engrs., Instrument Soc. Am. Club: Formosan of U.S.A. Office: PO Box 2219 Columbus OH 43216

LIU, HENRY, educator; b. Peking, China, June 3, 1936; s. Yen-Huai and Remei (Bardina) L.; B.S., Nat. Taiwan U., 1959; M.S., Colo. State U., 1963, Ph.D., 1966; m. Dou-Mei Chow, Dec. 16, 1964; children—Jerry B., Jason C. Asst. prof. civil engring. U. Mo., Columbia, 1965-69, asso. prof. civil engring., 1969-77; vis. prof. Nat. Taiwan (China) U., 1971-72; faculty adviser Chinese Student Assn., U. Mo., Columbia, 1972-75. Dept. Interior grantee, 1966-68, 76-78. Registered profl. engr., Mo. Mem. ASCE (chmn. aerodynamics com. 1976—), Am. Soc. Engring. Edn., Internat. Assn. Hydraulic Research, Sigma Xi. Contbr. articles to profl. jours. Home: 2001 Rose Dr Columbia MO 65201

LIU, PAUL CHI, oceanographer; b. Chefoo, China, June 18, 1935; s. Joseph Tzu-chien and Agatha I-ming (Wang) L.; came to U.S., 1959, naturalized, 1972; B.S., Nat. Taiwan U., 1956; M.S., Va. Poly. Inst., 1961; postgrad. Cornell U., Wayne State U.; Ph.D., U. Mich., 1977; m. Teresa Sheau-mei Wang, Jan. 30, 1965; 1 dau., Christina. Research phys. scientist C.E., U.S. Army, Lake Survey Dist., Detroit, 1965-71; research phys. scientist Lake Survey Center, Nat. Oceanic and Atmospheric Adminstrn., Detroit, 1971-74, phys. scientist Great Lakes Environ. Research Lab., Ann Arbor, 1974—. NOAA fellow, 1971-72. Mem. Am. Geophys. Union, Am. Meterol. Soc., ASCE, Internat. Assn. Great Lakes Research, Sigma Xi, Phi Kappa Phi. Contbr. articles to profl. jours. Home: 2939 Renfrew St Ann Arbor MI 48105 Office: 2300 Washtenaw St Ann Arbor MI 48104

LIU, RUEY-WEN, educator; b. Kiang-en, China, Mar. 18, 1930; s. Yen-sun and Wei-en (Chang) L.; came to U.S., 1951, naturalized, 1956; B.S., U. Ill., 1954, M.S., 1955, Ph.D., 1960; m. Nancy Shao-lan Lee, Aug. 18, 1957; children—Alexander, Theodore. Asst. prof. U. Notre Dame (Ind.), 1960-63, asso. prof., 1963-66, prof. elec. engring., 1966—; vis. prof. U. Calif. at Berkeley, 1965-66, Nat. Taiwan U., Taipei, China, spring 1969, Universidad de Chile, Santiago de Chile, summer 1970. Trustee Calif. Buddhism Assn., 1974-76. U. Ill. fellow, 1954; Gen. Electric fellow, 1958; NSF grantee, 1962. Mem. N.Y. Acad. Sci., Am. Math. Soc., IEEE, Soc. Indsl. and Applied Maths., Sigma Xi, Tau Beta Pi, Pi Mu Epsilon. Contbr. articles to profl. jours. Home: 1929 Dorwood Dr South Bend IN 46617 Office: Dept Elec Engring Notre Dame U Notre Dame IN 46556

LIVELY, JOHN KENNETH, pub. relations exec.; b. Marshalltown, Iowa, June 11, 1933; s. Kenneth Verlou and Helen Irene (Ethington) L.; A.B., Cornell Coll., Mt. Vernon, Iowa, 1955; M.S. (Lydia Roberts fellow), Columbia, 1956. With UPI, N.Y.C., 1955-56; news editor KFJB Radio, Marshalltown, 1958-63; night news editor WHO-AM-FM-TV News, Des Moines, 1963-66; mgr. audio-visual, pub. relations Minn. Mining & Mfg. Co., St. Paul, 1966—. Served with AUS, 1956-58. Mem. Pub. Relations Soc. Am. Mason. Home: 4504 Belvidere Ln Edina MN 55435 Office: Bldg 216-3S 3M Center St Paul MN 55101

LIVELY, RODGER MARSHALL, instructional services coordinator; b. Cin., Jan. 1, 1941; s. Marshall Everett and Gladys Irene (Smith) L.; B.A., Georgetown (Ky.) Coll., 1963; M.A., Ind. U., 1966; m. Harriet Neil Sprouse, July 12, 1969. Instr., Va. Commonwealth U., Richmond, 1965-66, instr., FM gen. mgr. Georgetown Coll., 1966-67; dir. TV, instr. U. Mass., Amherst, 1967-68; dir. instructional services Mt. Wachusett Community Coll., Gardner, Mass., 1968-73; dir. outreach and growth Burncoat Baptist Ch., Worcester, Mass., 1973-74; coordinator instructional services Muskegon (Mich.) Community Coll., 1974—; cons. in field. Chmn. bd. Christian edn. Burncoat Bapt. Ch., 1972-73; chmn. communications com. First Bapt. Ch., Muskegon, 1975-76, exec. producer Ecclesia Prodns., 1976—; chmn. bd. Montachusett Youth for Christ, 1969-70; dir. Living Word, weekly TV program, 1977. Mem. Assn. Ednl. Communications and Tech., Nat. Assn. Ednl. Broadcasters, Community Coll. Assn. Instrn. and Tech., NEA, Mich. Edn. Assn., Pi Kappa Delta. Home: 564 Wind Drift Ln Spring Lake MI 49456 Office: 221 S Quarterline Rd Muskegon MI 49442

LIVENGOOD, ROGER LYNN, accountant; b. Maryville, Mo., Aug. 1, 1949; s. Stanley Lynn and Betty Joan (Carpenter) L.; student pub. schs., Burlington Junction, Mo.; m. Donna Francis Wood, July 5, 1969; children—Dana, Robert, Curtis Lyle. Bookkeeper, Mayfield Pipeline Constrn. Co., Tarkio, Mo., 1968, Consumers Oil Co., Maryville, 1968-69; bookkeeper, tax preparer Livengood Accounting, Tarkio, 1969-73; individual practice accounting and taxes, Burlington Junction, 1973—. Youth counselor Meth. Ch. Mem. Am. Soc. Tax Cons.'s. Clubs: Lions (pres.), Elmo Community Betterment. Home: Rural Route 3 Box 157 Burlington Junction MO 64428 Office: PO Box 183 Burlington Junction MO 64428

LIVERS, DAVID LINN, JR., educator; b. Concordia, Kans., Jan. 29, 1926; s. David Linn and Helen Lenore (Willert) L.; B.S., Kans. State U., 1950, M.S., 1954; Ph.D., U. Iowa, 1963; m. Phyllis Eleanor Taplin, May 20, 1951; children—Daniel, Cynthia, Stefanie, Jeffrey. Tchr. sci. and math. Fostoria (Kans.) Rural High Sch., 1950-51; high sch. prin. Olsburg (Kans.) High Sch., 1951-53; supt. schs., Beattie, Kans., 1953-55; high sch. prin. consol. schs., Cimarron, Kans., 1955-59; grad. asst. U. Iowa at Iowa City, 1959-62; asst. prof. edn. Ill. State U., Normal, 1962-64, asso. prof. edn., 1964-69, prof. edn., 1969—. Cons., U.S. Office Edn.; mem. nat. adv. bd. Control Data Inst. of Control Data Corp., Mpls.; test cons. regional office Ill. State Div. Vocat. Rehab., Bloomington; dir. Specialty Oriented Student Research Program, State of Ill., 1969-73; cons. for two vocat. films. Bd. dirs. McLean County (Ill.) Family Service, 1964-69, pres. 1969; mem. steering com. Singing Y'ers boys choir, Bloomington, 1973-75. Served with USMCR, 1944-46; PTO. U.S. Office Edn. grantee, 1967, Ill. State Div. Vocat. and Tech. Edn. grantee, 1968-71. Registered psychologist, Ill. Mem. Ill. Guidance and Personnel Assn. (pres. 1975-76); Ill. Vocat. Guidance Assn. (pres. 1972-73), Am. (chmn.

awards com. 1970—), Ill. vocat. assns., Am. Personnel and Guidance Assn. (chmn. nat. membership com. 1969—), N.E.A. (life mem.), Am. Psychol. Assn., Am. Sch. Counselors Assn., Assn. for Counseling, Edn. and Supervision, Phi Delta Kappa, Kappa Delta Pi, Theta Xi. Author: (with Kenneth Hoyt) Basic Research Facts for Studying Specialty Oriented Studys, 1972; (with Kenneth Hoyt) SOS Guidance Research Booklets, Nos. 235-280, 1971-72; chpt. in Counselor's Handbook (ed. Gamsky and Coughlan), 1974. Contbr. several articles in field to profl. jours. Home: 8 Grandview Dr Normal IL 61761

LIVINGOOD, CLARENCE S., dermatologist; b. Elverson, Pa., Aug. 7, 1911; s. Clarance A. and Eliza (Zerr) L.; B.S., Ursinus Coll., 1932; M.D., U. Pa., 1936; m. Louise Sinclair Woelpper, Oct. 24, 1947; children—Wilson, Louise S., Clarence, Susan, Elizabeth. Asst. prof. dermatology U. Pa. Med. Sch., 1946, Grad. Sch., 1946; prof., chmn. dept. dermatology Jefferson Med. Sch., Phila., 1948-49; prof., chmn. dept. dermatology U. Tex. Sch. Medicine, 1949-53; chmn. dermatology dept. Henry Ford Hosp., Detroit, 1953-76, chmn. emeritus, 1976—; team physician Detroit Tigers baseball club; clin. prof. dermatology Sch. Medicine, U. Mich., 1971—; civilian cons. dermatology Surgeon Gen. U.S. Army; mem. com. on cutaneous diseases AFEB. Sec.-gen. XII Internat. Congress of Dermatology; AMA residency review com. for dermatology; exec. com. Am. Bd. Med. Specialties, 1974-76; adv. com. Nat. Disease and Therapeutic Index. Trustee Dermatology Found., recipient Meritorious Achievement certificate, 1975; bd. dirs. Council Med. Specialty Socs., 1977—, also mem. liaison com. grad. med. edn. Served to lt. col. M.C., AUS, 1942-46. Decorated Bronze Star, Legion of Merit; recipient certificate Dermatology Found. Diplomate Am. Bd. Dermatology (exec. sec.). Fellow Am. Acad. Dermatology (dir., past pres., Gold Medal 1975), A.C.P.; mem. AMA (ho. dels., chmn. sect. dermatology 1959, del. 1968—), Soc. Investigative Dermatology (past pres.), Am. Dermatol. Assn. (past pres., dir.), Coll. Physicians Phila., Mich. (past pres.), Phila dermatol. socs., Med. Cons. Soc. World War II, Assn. Mil. Dermatologists, Detroit Acad. Medicine, Mich. Med. Soc. (mem. jud. council), Assn. Dermatology of Argentina (corr.); hon. mem. Danish Soc. Dermatology, Yugoslavian, Israel, Pacific dermatol. socs., Dermatol. Soc. Indian Assn. Dermatologists, Brit. Assn. Dermatology. Clubs: Grosse Pointe; Witenagemote (Galveston); Detroit Boat. Author: (with D. M. Pillsbury, M. B. Sulzberger) Manual of Dermatology. Editorial bd. AMA Archives of Dermatology, Excerpta Medica, Conn's Current Therapy, Jour. of Geriatrics. Contbr. articles to med. jours. Home: 345 University Pl Grosse Pointe MI 48230 Office: Henry Ford Hospital Detroit MI 48202

LIVINGSTON, A. EDWARD, physician; b. Bloomington, Ill., Sept. 26, 1912; s. Milton R. and Florence M. (Griesheim) L.; A.B., U. Mich., 1933; M.D., Northwestern U., 1938; m. Zelona Worden, Aug. 9, 1941; children—Milton R., Peter A., Laurie Anne, Ellen Sue. Intern, Iowa Meth. Hosp., Des Moines, 1937-38; resident in internal medicine Denver Gen. Hosp., 1938-41; practice internal medicine, Bloomington, Ill., 1945—; internist, pres. McLean County Internal Medicine Assos., Bloomington, Ill.; clin. asso. prof. U. Ill. Served to lt. col. M.C., U.S. Army, 1941-45. Diplomate Am. Bd. Internal Medicine. Fellow A.C.P., Am. Coll. Cardiology, Am. Coll. Chest Physicians; mem. Ill. State Med. Soc. (trustee 1970-76), McLean County Med. Soc. (past pres.), AMA. Republican. Jewish. Club: Bloomington Country. Home: 1110 E Monroe St Bloomington IL 61701 Office: 326 Fairway Dr Bloomington IL 61701

LIVINGSTON, BURT R., mech. equipment mfg. co. exec.; b. Monroe, Iowa, June 24, 1919; s. Ralph B. and Adda C. (Culver) L.; B.S. in Engring., Iowa State U., 1949; m. Junella Morris, Dec. 4, 1943; children—Juliann, James, Jeffrey. With Maytag Co., Newton, Iowa, 1949—, chief engr., 1954-63, mgr. maintenance and constrn., 1963—; dir. Newton Home Savs. & Loan Assn. Mem. engring. adv. council Iowa State U., 1967-70; chmn. Iowa Bd. Engring. Examiners, 1975—. Chmn. Citizens for Schs., Newton, 1968. Bd. dirs. Community Chest. Served with AUS, 1942-45. Registered profl. engr., Iowa. Mem. ASME, Nat. Soc. Profl. Engrs., Iowa Engring. Soc. pres. 1965, Distinguished Service to Profession award 1971), Nat. Mgmt. Assn. Lutheran (council 1952-60). Elk. Home: Rural Route 5 Newton IA 50208 Office: Maytag Co Newton IA 50208

LIVINGSTON, DAVID THOMAS, employee benefits researcher; b. Buffalo, May 25, 1936; s. David Henry and Dorothy Margaret (Thomas) L.; B.A. magna cum laude, Westminster Coll., 1958; M.A. in Pub. Adminstrn. (Lent Upson fellow), Wayne State U., 1960; Ph.D. (Fels Doctoral fellow), Wharton Sch., U. Pa., 1970; m. Judith Ann Reif, Mar. 30, 1964; 1 son, David Aron. Instr., U. Wis.-Milw., 1962-66; sr. researcher Citizens' Govtl. Research Bur., Milw., 1966-69; survey analyst, dir. research Internat. Found. Employee Benefit Plans, Brookfield, Wis., 1969-76, also mem. editorial bd. major publs.; dir. research Tolley Internat. Corp., 1976—. Program coordinator Taft-Hartley Funds Monthly Cassette Service, Brookfield, 1972—; speaker on employee benefit topics at insts. and seminars. Ford Found. Urban Research grantee, 1962-65. Mem. Am. Polit. Sci. Assn., Phi Kappa Tau. Author: Growth and Development of Jointly Trusteed Funds: A Historical Perspective, 1973; Research Report on Collection of Contributions to Taft-Hartley Trusts, 1974; Research Report on Investment Practices Among Taft-Hartley Pension Funds, 1975; Fiduciary Liability for Taft-Hartley Funds: A Comparison of Coverages, 1975. Editor: Trustees Handbook: Primer for Trustees of Taft-Hartley Welfare and Pension Plans, 1970. Contbr. articles to profl. jours. Home: 17360 Country Lane Brookfield WI 53005 Office: PO Box 69 Brookfield WI 53005

LIVINGSTON, ROBERT LEIGH, minister; b. Pittsfield, Mass., May 21, 1941; s. Henry Richmond and Eleanor R. (Buck) L.; A.B., Bates Coll., 1963; M.Div., Andover Newton Theol. Sch., 1967; m. Susan Rollins Drury, Aug. 8, 1964; children—Mark, Kerry. Ordained to ministry United Ch. of Christ, 1966; asso. pastor Central Ch., Worcester, Mass., 1966-68; asso. chaplain Cranbrook Sch., Bloomfield Hills, Mich., 1968-75, chaplain, chmn. dept. religion and human devel., 1975-77; pastor St. John's United Ch. of Christ, Niles, Mich., 1977—; bd. dirs. Christian communication council Met. Detroit Chs., 1974-77. Mem. Am., Mich. personnel and guidance assns., Am. Assn. Sex Educators, Counselors, Therapists, S.W. Mich. Assn. United Ch. Christ. Home: 1408 Chicago Rd Niles MI 49120 Office: 601 Sycamore St Niles MI 49120

LIVINGSTON, VON EDWARD, lawyer; b. New Boston, Ill., Dec. 10, 1903; s. Warren F. and Katherine M. (Bridger) L.; B.A. magna cum laude, Knox Coll., 1925; J.D., U. Chgo., 1928; m. Katharine True, Aug. 2, 1928; children—Katharine (Mrs. William E. Evans), Mary (Mrs. Brant R. Moore), Martha (Mrs. Don McCoy). Admitted to Ill. bar, 1928; atty. firm Cooke, Sullivan & Ricks, Chgo., 1928-39; partner Lawyer, Anderson & Livingston, Chgo., 1939-41; gen. counsel Ind. Service Corp., 1941-45, Ind. & Mich. Electric Co.; sr. partner Livingston, Dildine, Haynie & Yoder, Ft. Wayne, Ind., and predecessor firm, 1945—. Dir., mem. exec. com. Peoples Trust Bank & Financial, Inc.; dir. Petrusco Realty, Inc., Mktg. Enterprises, Inc.; mem. com. character and fitness Ind. Supreme Ct.; past hon. Ind. asst. atty. gen. Dir., past pres. Ft. Wayne Charity Horse Assn.; fellow Ind. Inst. Tech.; mem. nat. bequests com. DePauw U. Pres. Ft. Wayne Bd. Aviation Commrs., 1950-58; mem. Allen County Republican Com. Served to 1st lt., U.S. Army, 1925-30. Mem. Ft. Wayne C. of C. (past dir.), Ind. Soc. Chgo., Newcomen Soc., Internat. Platform Assn., Phi Beta Kappa, Sigma Delta Chi. Conglist. Clubs: Masons (Shriners, 32 deg.), Fort Wayne Rotary (past pres.), Ft. Wayne Country, Summit, Quest (past pres.) (Ft. Wayne); Columbia (Indpls.). Home: 5219 Hickory Ln Ft Wayne IN 46825 Office: Lincoln Tower Ft Wayne IN 46802

LL, TZE-CHUNG, educator; b. China, Feb. 17, 1927; s. Ken-hsiang and Yu-hsien (Chang) L.; LL.B., Soochow U., 1948; grad. Chinese Research Inst. Land Econs., 1952; LL.M., So. Meth. U., 1957; LL.M., Harvard, 1958; M.S., Columbia, 1965; Ph.D., New Sch. for Social Research, 1963; m. Dorothy In-lan Wang, Oct. 21, 1961; children—Lily, Rose, Dist. judge, China, 1949-51; div. head dept. law Ministry Nat. Def., China, 1951-56; asst. prof. library sci., asst. librarian Ill. State U., 1965-66; asst. prof. polit. sci. and library sci. Rosary Coll., River Forest, Ill., 1966-70, asso. prof. library sci., 1970-74, prof., 1974—. Dir. Nat. Central Library, China, 1970-72, cons., 1974—; chmn. Grad. Inst. Library Sci., China, 1971-72; nat. vis. asso. prof. Nat. Taiwan U., 1969. Pres., Chinese-Am. Ednl. Found., Chgo., 1968-70; adviser Friends of Soochow, Los Angeles, 1974—; mem. Nat. Council Cultural Renaissance, 1971—; pres. Chinese Culture Service, 1974—. Recipient Elsie O. and Philip D. Sang Excellence in Teaching award Rosary Coll., 1971, Outstanding Educator award, 1973. Mem. Chinese Am. Librarians Assn. (pres. 1974-76, chmn. 1976—), ALA, Assn. Am. Library Schs., Chinese Library Assn. (gov. 1971-72), Internat. Assn. Orientalist Librarians (area rep. 1971-76). Asso. editor Law Digest, China, 1951-53; editor Jour. Library and Information Sci., 1974—. Contbr. articles to profl. jours. Home: 1104 Greenfield Ave Oak Park IL 60302 Office: Roseary Coll River Forest IL 60305

LLOYD, JOHN HENRY, railroad co. exec.; b. Glasgow, Mont., July 27, 1917; s. John Henry and Edith (Wright) L.; B.S., U. Pa., 1941; m. Dorothy Rigg, Sept. 17, 1944; children—Edith Leone, John Henry III, Robert, Joseph. Brakeman, G.N. Ry. Co., Havre, Mont., 1941-42, asst. to master mechanic and travel car insp., 1941-42, trainmaster, 1945-50; with C., R.I. & P. Ry. Co., 1951-56, 58-61, asst. supt., 1951, supt., 1951-52, asst. gen. mgr., 1953-56, gen. supt. motive power, v.p. ops., 1958-61; gen. mgr. Alaska R.R., Anchorage, 1956-58; v.p. ops. Mo. Pacific R.R. Co., St. Louis, 1961-68, exec. v.p., 1968-72, pres., chief exec. officer, 1972—. Served to lt. USNR, 1942-45. Mem. Phi Delta Theta. Republican. Episcopalian. Clubs: Old Warson Country, University, Missouri Athletic; Media, Union League (Chgo.). Home: 5 Indian Creek Ln St Louis MO 63131 Office: 210 N 13th St St Louis MO 63103

LLOYD, ROBERT DEAN, photographer; b. Springfield, Ill., Mar. 30, 1949; s. Dean Stanley and Norma Mae (Whitler) L.; student E. Tex. State U., 1968-70; B.S. in Agr., U. Ill., 1971; m. Edna Mae Roberts, Aug. 16, 1969; 1 son, Ronald Dean. Owner, Lloyd Studios, portrait-comml. photography, Virden, Ill., 1971—. Mem. Profl. Photographers Am., Asso. Profl. Photographers Ill., Wedding Photographers Am., Aircraft Owners and Pilots Assn., Farm Bur., Delta Tau Delta. Mem. Christian Ch. Rotarian (pres. Virden club 1977-78). Club: Edgewood Country (Auburn, Ill.). Home: Route 2 Girard IL 62640 Office: East Side Square Virden IL 62690

LO, RAYMOND C., elec. engr.; b. China, July 15, 1944; s. David C. and Margaret M. (Lee) L.; came to U.S., 1961, naturalized, 1968; B.S. in E.E., Milw. Sch. Engring., 1968; m. JoAnn Joy Thoenes, Feb. 15, 1964; 1 dau., Jennifer. Electronics engr. Addressograph Multigraph Corp., Cleve., 1968-74; sr. devel. engr. Motorola, Inc., Schaumburg, Ill., 1974—. Mem. IEEE. Home: 1270 Bristol Ln Hanover Park IL 60103 Office: 1301 E Algonquin Rd Schaumburg IL 60196

LOACH, PAUL ALLEN, educator; b. Findlay, Ohio, July 18, 1934; s. Leland O. and Dorothy E. (Davis) L.; B.S., U. Akron, 1957; Ph.D., (USPHS Predoctoral fellow), Yale U., 1961; postgrad. U. Calif. at Berkeley, 1961-63; m. Patricia Ann Johnson, Dec. 28, 1957; children—Mark, Eric, Jennifer. Asst. prof. chemistry Northwestern U., Evanston, Ill., 1963-68, asso. prof. chemistry, 1968-73, prof. chemistry, 1973-74, prof. biochemistry and molecular biology and chemistry, 1974—. Cons., Argonne Nat. Lab., 1971—. Recipient Research Career Devel. award USPHS, 1971-76; NSF grantee, 1963-76, USPHS research grantee, 1965-77. Mem. Am. Assn. Biol. Chemists, AAAS, Am. Chem. Soc., Biophys. Soc., Am. Soc. Photobiology. Asso. editor Photochemistry and Photobiology, also Biophysics of Structure and Mechanism, 1974—. Contbr. articles to profl. jours. Home: 2219 Lincolnwood Dr Evanston IL 60201

LOBENTHAL, RICHARD HENRY, assn. exec.; b. N.Y.C., July 29, 1934; s. Joseph S. and Sallie (Schwartz) L.; A.B., U. Chgo., 1954, postgrad., 1955; postgrad. L.I. U., 1956, N.Y. U., 1957; children—Joshua, Adam, Lisa, Debra. Mem. treatment staff U. Chgo., 1951-53; acting dir. Boys House Community Service Soc., N.Y.C., 1956-58; with Anti-Defamation League of B'nai B'rith, Tex., Okla., N.C., Va., 1959-64, Mich. regional dir., Detroit, 1964—. Cons. N.Y. Dept. Labor, 1958-59; affiliated for spl. assignments U.S. vol. orgns. UNESCO, 1958; part-time faculty dept. sociology Wayne State U., Detroit, 1966-73; faculty adviser, founder Pub. Interest Research Group in Mich., 1971-73; cons. social sci. div. Coll. Lifelong Learning, 1974—; part time faculty dept. sociology U. Detroit, 1975—, cons., guest lectr. Urban Extension div., 1972—, field-work faculty grad. schs. social work, 1968—; guest faculty Divine Word Internat. Centre for Religious Edn., London, Ont., Can., 1971-73; field work faculty grad. schs. social work Mich. State U., James Madison Coll., 1970—; faculty U. Mich., Dearborn; adviser Nat. Center for Urban Ethnic Affairs, Detroit, 1970—; pvt. cons. civil rights; radio commentator Sta. WDET-FM; nat. cons. to police depts. Mem. bd. Narcotics Addiction Rehab. Coordinating Orgn., Detroit; chmn. coordinating council on human relations City Detroit, 1965—; mem. state bd., exec. com. Mich. Congress Parents and Tchrs., 1968-73; human relations cons. Detroit council PTA, 1966—; mem. human relations curriculum com. Mich. Dept. Edn., 1969—; mem. Detroit Mayor's Neighborhood Preservation Com., 1965; mem. community relations adv. com. New Detroit, 1971-73; mem. Interfaith Action Council Detroit, 1968—, Citizens for Advancement Pub. Edn., 1966—; mem. com. on pub. edn. Mich. Council Chs., 1968—; mem. Mich. adv. com. U.S. Commn. on Civil Rights, 1972—; mem. adv. task force Project Compact, 1973—; advisory com. Farm Worker's Edn. Fund, Archdiocese of Detroit. Bd. dirs. Urban Alliance, People Acting for Change Together, Neighborhood Service Orgn., Detroit Indsl. Mission, Health Resource Program; bd. dirs., corporate sec. Nat. Center for Resources on Instl. Oppression, Detroit, 1970—; Mem. Nat., Mich. (past pres.) assns. human rights workers, Am. Sociol. Assn., Soc. for Psychol. Study Social Issues, AAUP. Author: (with Gregory Squires) Affirmative Action: Guide to the Perplexed, 1977. Home: 8151 Lincoln Huntington Woods MI 48070 Office: 163 Madison St Detroit MI 48226

LOBMEYER, RAYMOND JOSEPH, design engr.; b. Garden City, Kans., Dec. 24, 1935; s. Louis and Anna Marie (Ohmes) L.; B.S., Kans. State U., 1961; postgrad. Iowa State U., 1969-70, Iowa U., 1972, LaSalle Extension U., 1962-67; m. Patricia Ann Moritz, Aug. 23, 1958; children—Raymond, DeAnn, Susan, Janet. Sr. engr. John Deere Dubuque Tractor Works (Iowa), 1961-77, project engr. John Deere Product Engring. Center, Waterloo, Iowa, 1977—. Active Boy Scouts Am. Treas. Town of Sageville, Iowa, 1968-69, town clk., 1968-77; mem. Dubuque County Met. Area Planning Commn., 1966-67. Served with USAF, 1953-57. Mem. Am. Soc. Agrl. Engrs., Soc. Automotive Engrs., Nat. Soc. Profl. Engrs., Iowa Municipal Finance Officers Assn., Great River Rd. Assn. Roman Catholic. K.C. Club: Toastmasters (Dubuque). Home: 129 Prospect Hill Circle Waterloo IA 50701 Office: John Deere Product Engring Center PO Box 270 Waterloo IA 50704

LOBSTEIN, OTTO ERVIN, clin. biochemist; b. Nestemice, Czechoslovakia, Apr. 12, 1922; s. Robert and Fritzi (Adler) L.; came to U.S., 1946, naturalized, 1949; B.Sc., U. London (Eng.), 1945; Ph.D. in Biochemistry, Northwestern U., 1952; postgrad. U. So. Calif., 1960-61, U. Calif. at Los Angeles, 1962; m. Miriam Thelma Goldberg, Apr. 11, 1952; children—Dennis David, Harvey Roy, Heidi Melina. Asst. research chemist Messrs. Howard & Sons, Ltd., London, 1942-46; biochemist I, Elgin (Ill.) State Hosp., 1947-48; fellow surgery and biochemistry Northwestern U. Med. Sch., Chgo., 1948-52; research asso. U. So. Cal., Los Angeles, 1952-53; owner, research dir. Pvt. Clin. Labs., Los Angeles, 1952-64; asst. prof. biochemistry Loyola U., Los Angeles, 1964-65; clin. biochemist St. Elizabeth Hosp. and Med. Center, Lafayette, Ind., 1965-76; dir. clin. chemistry Mt. Sinai Hosp., Chgo., 1976—; vis. research prof. U. Redlands (Calif.), 1959-65; adj. prof. biochemistry Purdue U., Lafayette, 1968-76; prof. biochemistry and pathology Rush U. and Med. Coll., Chgo., 1976—. Active Boy Scouts Am.; pres. Civic Theater of Greater Lafayette, 1970-72. Served with Ordnance Corps, AUS, 1946-47. Recipient Tng. awards, Boy Scouts Am., 1964-69, Scouter's Keys award, 1969, Silver Shofar Nat. award, 1972, Arrowhead Honor award, 1965. Diplomate Am. Bd. Clin. Chemistry. Fellow AAAS, Am. Inst. Chemists, Am. Assn. Clin. Chemists; sr. mem. Am. Chem. Soc.; mem. Ill. Soc. Med. Research, N.Y. Acad. Scis. Contbr. articles to profl. jours. Home: 2920 Priscilla Ln Highland Park IL 60035 Office: Mt Sinai Hosp Med Center Dept Pathology 2755 W 15th St Chicago IL 60608

LOCARNI, RICHARD GLENN, marble co. exec.; b. Carthage, Mo., Aug. 24, 1930; s. Alfred Dreyfus and Freda Olga (Nyberg) L.; B.Arch., Mass. Inst. Tech., 1953; m. Norma Kay Neubert, Dec. 9, 1960; 1 son, Richard Glenn. Vice pres. Locarni Marble Co., Carthage, 1956—. Lectr. archtl. history and restorations, 1968—; dir. Bldg. Stone Inst., 1976—. Chmn., Carthage Historic Homes Tour, 1970; v.p. Carthage Council on Arts, 1970-71, pres., 1975; mem. Jasper County Devel. Assn., 1971. Served to 1st lt., AUS, 1954-56. Mem. Marble Inst. Am. (dir. 1971, pres. 1973), Carthage Arts and Crafts Assn. (pres. 1969-70, v.p. 1974-75), Carthage C. of C. (pres. 1971). Rotarian (pres. Carthage 1970-71). Home: Route 4 Carthage MO 64836 Office: Box 716 Carthage MO 64836

LOCKE, GILES RICHARD, radiologist; b. Youngstown, Ohio, Jan. 12, 1937; s. Giles R. and Mildred (Gray) L.; B.A., DePauw U., 1958; M.D., Western Reserve U., 1962; m. Judith Blang, Aug. 2, 1958; children—Rick, Jon, Mark, Mike. Intern, Milw. County Hosp., 1962-63; resident U. Iowa, Iowa City, 1963-66; chmn. radiation oncology Decatur Meml. Hosp., Decatur, Ill., 1968-75; chmn. radiology, 1974—; pres. X-ray Service Corp., 1975—; clin. asso. U. Ill.; cons. Ill. Cancer Council; regional asst. dean U. Ill., mem. exec. com. Sch. Basic Med. Scis. Served with U.S. Army, 1966-68. Recipient Distinguished Service Award, Jaycees, 1972. Mem. AMA, Am. Coll. Radiology, Am. Soc. Therapeutic Radiologists, Radiology Soc. N.Am., Am. Cancer Soc. (pres. Macon County). Presbyterian. Clubs: Decatur Country (bd. dirs.). Office: 2300 N Edward St Decatur IL 62526

LOCKE, PHILIP FRANCIS, judge; b. Rockford, Ill., Aug. 10, 1912; s. Richard Foss and Grace (Hench) L.; student U. Ill., 1931-32; A.B., North Central Coll., Naperville, Ill., 1938; LL.B., John Marshal Law Sch., 1949; m. Marjorie Ryan, May 4, 1943; children—Philip F., Janice L. Admitted to Ill. bar, 1949, practiced in Glen Ellyn, 1949-58; judge Probate Ct., DuPage County, Ill., 1958-64; judge 18th Jud. Ct., Wheaton, Ill., 1964—. Served to capt. USAAF, World War II. Mem. Am. Legion. Conglist. (chmn. bd. trustees). Mason (Shriner). Home: IN131 Indianknoll Rd West Chicago IL 60185 Office: DuPage County Ct House Wheaton IL 60187

LOCKER, THOMAS, artist; b. N.Y.C., June 26, 1937; s. Bernard and Nan (Alpern) L.; B.A., U. Chgo., 1960; M.A., Am. U., 1963; m. Maria Ritter, June 1973; children—Aaron Thomas, Joshuah Bernard. One-man shows Banfer Gallery, N.Y.C., 1964, Washington Gallery of Art, 1964-65, Gilman Gallery, Chgo., 1964, 67, 68, Vincent Price Gallery, 1970, 71, Rex Evans Gallery, Los Angeles, 1971, R.S. Johnson Gallery, 1972, Reflections Gallery, Atlanta, 1973, Oehlechlager Gallery, Chgo., 1975; exhibited in group shows Rex Evans Gallery, Los Angeles, 1968, Gallery of Contemporary Artists, N.Y.C., 1968-69; represented in permanent collections John Herron Mus., Indpls., Chgo. Arts Council, Chgo.; prof. Shimer Coll., Mt. Carroll, Ill. Served with AUS, 1956-64. Home: Rural Route 1 Elizabeth Massbach IL 61028

LOCKHART, MARY MALISSE FOSTER (MRS. THEODUS A. LOCKHART), educator; b. Oxford, Miss., July 2, 1918; d. William Henry and Zella (Kirkwood) Foster; B.S., Lane Coll., 1940; postgrad. Alcorn A. and M. Coll., summers 1941, 42, St. Mary Coll., 1961, 62; M.S., Kans. State Tchrs. Coll., 1965; postgrad. Bradley U., 1968, Wheaton Coll., 1969, No. Ill. U., 1969, Nat. Coll., 1970, U. Ill., 1970, (fellow) Ill. State U., 1971; postgrad. in mental retardation Holland, Norway, Denmark Sweden, 1971; m. Theodus A. Lockhart, June 19, 1943; children—Theresa Vonetta (Mrs. William Harper), Rosalyn Valere (Mrs. Reginald Carr), Theodus A. Tchr., Taylor (Miss.) High Sch., 1940-41, Noxapater (Miss.) High Sch., 1941-42, Oxford (Miss.) Sch., 1942-44; tchr. spl. edn. Nettie Hartnett, Leavenworth, Kan., 1963-68; tchr. ednl. mentally handicapped Edison Jr. High Sch., 1968-69; tchr. Evaluation and Tng. Center Lyons (Ill.) Twp. High Sch., 1969—. Leader, Girl Scouts U.S.A., 1949-61, now bd. dirs. Dupage County council; mem. Leavenworth County Mental Health Assn., 1966-68; mem. directory bd. Headstart, LaGrange, Ill., 1973—; mem. S.E. Quadrant citizen's adv. bd. to DuPage County Health Dept.; active YWCA. Recipient Medgar Evers award NAACP, 1975. U. Kan. fellow orthopedically handicapped, 1966; U. Ill. fellow mental retardation, 1970. Mem. NEA, Nat. Rehab. Assn., League Women Voters, Helping Hand Handicapped Assn., Lyons Twp. High Sch. Faculty Assn., Council for Exceptional Children, AAUW, Farm Club Handicapped Assn., Ill. Edn. Assn. (mimority caucus), Lane Coll. Alumni Assn., Am. Legion Aux. (pres. 1959-60), NAACP (life; v.p. 1967, chairperson life membership LaGrange Br. 1975—), Delta Kappa Gamma, Sigma Gamma Rho, Delta Sigma Gamma. Methodist. Mem. Order Eastern Star (past matron). Home: 821 S Williams Apt C404 Westmont IL 60559

LOCKOS, DEBORAH GAY, educator; b. St. Louis, Nov. 12, 1953; d. George Louis and Ethel (Anagnostaras) L.; B.S. in Edn. (Univ. Scholar), U. Mo., 1975. Office worker Bellerive Country Club, Creve Coeur, Mo., 1969-74; Title I math. tchr. Ritenour Sch. Dist., Overland, Mo., 1975-76, 8th grade math. tchr., 1976—; cottage parent St. Louis County Detention Center, Clayton, Mo., 1976—; cartographer, 1977—. Mem. Nat. Council Tchrs. Math., U. Mo.-St. Louis Alumni Assn., Am Fedn. Tchrs., Math. Assn. Am., Mo. Tchrs.

Assn., Kappa Delta Pi. Home: 8 Lawrence Dr Saint Louis MO 63141 Office: 2d and Arsenal Sts Saint Louis MO 63118

LOCKS, HERZL BEN-ZION, mech. engr.; b. Chgo., Jan. 3, 1940; s. Herman H. and Martha Mildred (Kritchevsky) L.; B.S. in Mech. Engring., Ill. Inst. Tech., 1962; m. Hannah Jane Sonnabend, Aug. 23, 1964; children—Rebecca Michelle, Daniel William. Thermodynamicist Chrysler Space div., New Orleans, 1964-68; engr., programmer Avondale Shipyards, New Orleans, 1968; project engr. Clinton Corn Processing Co., Clinton, Iowa, 1969-71; pres. H.B. Locks & Asso., Bettendorf, Iowa, 1972-76; project engr. Anheuser-Busch, St. Louis, 1976—. Lectr., Davenport (Iowa) Community Schs., 1975-76, mem. adv. com. maintenance tgn., 1975-76. Registered profl. engr., Ill., Iowa. Mem. Am. Soc. Mech. Engrs., Nat. Soc. Profl. Engrs., Bettendorf Jr. C. of C. Jewish religion. Specializing in design of chem. process piping systems, bulk materials handling systems, air pollution control, heating, ventilating and air conditioning. Home: 12080 Sprucehaven Dr Creve Coeur MO 63141 Office: Anheuser-Busch 721 Pestalozzi St St Louis MO 63118

LOCKSHIN, JERROLD LEON, truck leasing exec.; b. Youngstown, Ohio, Jan. 30, 1928; s. Nathan A. and Mary (Richstone) L.; B.S. in Bus. Adminstrn., Ohio State U., 1950; m. Phyllis Oster, Mar. 11, 1951; children—Lawrence J., Thomas A., Cathy J. Salesman, Fame Beverage Co., 1953-59, v.p., 1957-60; pres. A-1 Truck Service, Inc., Canton, Ohio, 1960—; pres. Nat. Truck Leasing System. Precinct committeeman Stark County Democratic Party; chmn. bd. Shaaray Torah Synagogue. Served to capt., AUS, 1950-53. Clubs: Masons, Shriners. Home: 716 24th St NE Canton OH 44714 Office: 1324 3d St SW Canton OH 44706

LOCKWOOD, FRANK JAMES, mfg. co. exec.; b. San Bernardino, Cal., Oct. 30, 1931; s. John Ellis and Sarah Grace (Roberts) L.; student S.E. City Coll., 1955, Ill. Inst. Tech., 1963-64, Bogan Jr. Coll., 1966; m. Roberta Mae Morse, May 7, 1977; children—Fay (Mrs. Mark Huegelmann), Frank, Hedy (Mrs. Michael Machala), Jonnie, George, Katherine, Bill, Dena, Kevin, Michael, Tony Potmas. Gen. foreman Hupp Aviation, Chgo., 1951-60; dept. head UARCO, Inc., Chgo., 1960-68; pres. Xact Machine & Engring. Co., Chgo., 1968—, also chmn. bd., dir.; pres. Ratchford Tool Corp., Ill. Nat. Corp. Cons. engr. Served with USNR, 1948-50. Named Chicago Ridge (Ill.) Father of Year, 1964. Mem. Ill. Divers Assn. (pres. 1961-62). Mason (32 deg., Shriner). Club: Starcraft. Patentee in field. Home: 7011 W Archer Ave Chicago IL 60638 Office: 7011 W Archer Ave Chicago IL 60638

LOCKWOOD, GEORGE J., newspaper editor; b. Albany, N.Y., Aug. 19, 1931; s. James D. and Evelyn (Weinstein) L.; B.A., Syracuse U., 1953; M.A., U. Minn., 1957; m. Eileen Chamberlain, Sept. 3, 1955; children—Audrey, Cary, Noah, Jason. Reporter, Milw. Jour., 1956-58, asst. picture editor, 1958-62, roto editor, 1962-66, picture editor, 1966-69, editor Sunday mag., 1969-72, spl. sects. editor, 1972-77, asst. mng. editor, 1977—; lectr. journalism U. Wis., Milw., 1966-74; discussion leader Am. Press Inst., 1970—. Wood badge course dir. East Central region and Milw. council Boy Scouts Am., 1958—. Served with USNR, 1953-55. Recipient Pulitzer prize for meritorious pub. service, 1967, Meeman Conservation award, 1967, Freedoms Found. medal, 1965, Silver Beaver award Boy Scouts Am., 1969. Mem. Milw. Press Club, Acacia, Sigma Delta Chi. Kappa Tau Alpha, Alpha Phi Omega, Tau Theta Upsilon. Author: Cartoons of R. A. Lewis, 1968. Home: 2607 E Wood Pl Milwaukee WI 53211 Office: 333 W State St Milwaukee WI 53201

LOCKWOOD, JOHN PATTERSON, switch co. exec.; b. Bridgeton, N.J., Dec. 19, 1924; s. Lee John and Frances Mary (Patterson) L.; B.S. in Mech. Engring., Northwestern U., 1950; m. Evelyn May Anderson, June 9, 1951. Project engr. Micro Switch div. Honeywell Co., Freeport, Ill., 1950-56, supr. lab. exptl. unit, 1956-68, sr. engring. cons., 1968-72, lab supr., 1972-74, ops. mgr. D.C. Control Motors div., 1974-75, dir. quality assurance, 1975—. Tchr., lectr. archaeology, technico-legal subjects. Mem. Oriental Inst. of U. Chgo., Archaeol. Inst. Am. (pres. Rockford, Ill. chpt. 1970-72), Am. Schs. Oriental Research, Palestine Exploration Fund, Brit. Sch. Archaeology in Jerusalem (Israel), Freeport C. of C. Presbyn. (elder). Mason. Clubs: Germania Club of Freeport. Author: Applying Precision Switches, 1st and 2d edits., 1972. Contbr. articles on elec. switching to profl. jours. Developer first precision switch for use at 1000 deg. F. Home: 1015 S Benson Blvd Freeport IL 61032 Office: Micro Switch Div Honeywell Co Chicago and Spring Sts Freeport IL 61032

LOCKWOOD, THOMAS MORROW, surgeon; b. Toronto, Ont., Can., Feb. 25, 1917; s. Thomas Clarence and Bessie (Morrow) L.; B.A., McGill U., 1938, M.D.C.M., 1942; m. Dorothy Sydney Staniforth, Feb. 6, 1943; children—Donald, Della Ann (Mrs. Peter Hill), Martha, Kenneth. Intern, Royal Victoria Hosp., Montreal, Que., Can., 1942-43, 46-47, McGill Inst. Pathology, 1947-48; resident Childrens Meml. Hosp., Montreal, 1948-49; surgeon, also pres. Lockwood Clinic, Toronto, 1949-57; surgeon North York (Ont.) Branson Hosp., 1957-58, Mississauga (Ont.) Hosp., 1958—; cons. surgeon Queensway and Oakville hosps. Council mem. Ont. Health Ins. Plan, 1966-72. Bd. dirs. Mississauga Hosp. Found. Served as lt. comdr. Canadian Navy, 1943-46. Fellow Royal Coll. Physicians and Surgeons Can., A.C.S., Am. Coll. Chest Physicians; mem. Ont. Coll. Physicians and Surgeons (council 1971-77), Ont. Med. Assn. (dir. 1960-65), Mississauga Hosp. Med. Staff (pres. 1970-72), Am. Thyroid Assn., Theta Delta. Rotarian. Clubs: Badminton and Racquet (Toronto); Caledon (Ont.) Ski. Contbr. articles to med. jours. Home: 2192 Parker Dr Mississauga ON Canada Office: PO Box 72 Mississauga ON Canada

LODER, DWIGHT ELLSWORTH, bishop; b. Waverly, Nebr., July 8, 1914; s. William and Alice C. (Snyder) L.; A.B., U. Nebr., 1936; S.T.B., Boston U. Sch. Theology, 1939; D.D., Hamline U., 1951; D.D., Garrett Theol. Sem., 1955, Albion Coll., 1968; Dr. Sacred Theology, Dickinson Coll., 1966; L.H.D., Willamette Coll., 1966; LL.D., Baldwin-Wallace Coll., 1976; m. Mildred Ethyl Shay, Sept. 17, 1939; children—Ruth Ann (Mrs. James C. Burnecke), William, David. Asso. pastor 1st Congl. Ch., Stoneham, Mass., 1937-39; ordained to ministry Meth. Ch., 1939; mem. Central N.Y. Conf., 1939-47, Minn. Conf., 1947-57, Rock River Conf., 1957—; pastor, North Towanda, Pa., 1939-41, Blossburg, 1941-47; minister Hennepin Av. Ch., Mpls., 1947-51, minister worship, 1951-55; pres. Garrett Theol. Sem., Evanston, Ill., 1955-64; bishop Mich. area United Meth. Ch., 1964-76. Lectr. 8th ann. Ministers' Convocation of So. Cal., 1956; lectr. Glide Sch. Evangelism, San Francisco, 1960; rep. theol. edn. on ministerial exchange World Meth. Council, 1959—, N.Am. Faith and Order Study Conf., World Council Chs., 1957; del. Gen. Conf. Meth. Ch., 1960, 64; del. North Central Jurisdictional Conf., 1960, 64; mem. univ. senate Meth. Ch., 1963-65; Fondren lectr. So. Meth. U., Dallas, 1965; mem. exec. com. World Meth. Council, 1970—, mem. bd. 1973—, pres. Am. sect., 1977—; pres. Council Bishops, 1974-75. Mem. North Central Jurisdictional Commn. on Higher Edn., Commn. to Chaplaincy, 1964-72, Membership Commn. on Chaplains, 1966-72; mem. Mich. Officer's Compensation Commn., 1968-75; chmn. Com. on Equal Opportunity, 1969-71; pres. Nat. div. Bd. Missions, 1968-72; mem. Gov.'s Crime Commn. Trustee Ohio No. U., Ohio Wesleyan U., Baldwin-Wallace Coll., Otterbein Coll., Mt. Union Coll., Riverside Meth. Hosp.; former trustee Evanston Inst. for Ecumenical Studies. Recipient Founder's award W. Va. Wesleyan Coll., 1966; Distinguished Alumni award Boston U. Mem. Am. Assn. Theol. Schs., Assn. Meth. Theol. Schs. (pres. 1960), Commn. on Ecumenical Consultation, Alpha Kappa Psi (hon.). Mason (Shriner). Club: Executives (Chgo.). Home: 31 Meadow Park Ave Columbus OH 43209 Office: The Motorists Bldg 471 E Broad St Columbus OH 43215

LODGE, JAMES ROBERT, educator; b. Downey, Iowa, July 1, 1925; s. Ferrel Labon and Margaret Clara (Elliott) L.; B.S., Iowa State U., 1952, M.S., 1954; Ph.D., Mich. State U., 1957; m. Jean Agnes Wessel, June 15, 1947; children—Julie Beth, James Robert. Research asst. Mich. State U., East Lansing, 1954-57; research asso. U. Ill. at Urbana, 1957-60, asst. prof. reproductive physiology, 1960-63, asso. prof. reproductive physiology, 1963-69, prof. reproductive physiology, 1969—. Participant, Internat. Cong. Reproduction, Trento, Italy, 1964, Paris, France, 1968, Krakow, Poland, 1976. Asst. coach girls softball Babe Ruth Little League, Urbana, 1972-74. Served with AUS, 1944-46. Recipient Outstanding Instr. award Dairy Club of U. Ill., 1969; NIH Research fellow, 1969. Mem. Am. Physiol. Soc., AAAS, Soc. Study Reprodn., Am. Dairy Sci. Assn., Am. Soc. Animal Sci., Soc. Cryobiology, N.Y. Acad. Sci., Sigma Xi, Phi Kappa Phi (mem. scholarship com. 1970-73, chmn. 1973), Gamma Sigma Delta. Methodist (mem. commn. edn. 1975-78). Mason. Contbr. numerous articles to profl. jours. Home: 1701 S Cottage Grove St Urbana IL 61801

LODGE, RHEA EWALD (MRS. L. HARVEY LODGE), writer, editor, state ofcl.; b. Detroit; d. William Rudolph and Rhea Elizabeth (Allen) Ewald; student Wellesley, Coll., 1937-39, U. Mo. Journalism Sch., 1940-42; m. Robert Brigham Ellery, Oct. 17, 1942 (dec. July 1945); 1 son, Robert Brigham (dec. 1969); m. 2d, Robert Kingsbury Vietor, Sept. 2, 1947; 1 son, Carl Frederick III; m. 3d, L. Harvey Lodge, Oct. 16, 1971 (dec. May 1976). Wire editor Pontiac (Mich.) Press, 1945-47, women's editor, 1957-60; editor Lakeland Tribune, 1960-63, account exec. A. R. Gloster Agy., Detroit, 1963-66; dir. pub. relations, continuing edn. at Oakland U., Rochester Mich., 1965-68; free lance pub. relations cons., Birmingham, Mich., 1967-70; writer, photographer News-Tribune Publs., Inc., 1968-71; pres. Vietor-Lodge Assos., 1970-72; pub. relations specialist, exec. asst. to dir. Mich. Dept. Labor. Chmn. community drives; spl. asst. Meadow Brook Music Festival, Rochester, Mich.; mem. State adv. council for bicentennial; bd. dirs. Center for Barrier Free Environment. Mem. League Women Voters (dir. 1953), Founders Soc. Detroit Inst. Arts, Nat. Fedn. Press Women, Women in Communications (sec. 1968-69, chpt. treas. 1941-42). Alpha Phi. Clubs: Detroit Press, Economic of Detroit, Mich. Womens Press, Nomads, Wellesley; House and Senate (past treas., Lansing); Deer Lake Racquet. Address: 5881 Dixie Hwy Waterford MI 48095

LODWICK, ROSS WILLIAM, engr.; b. Youngstown, Ohio, Oct. 6, 1925; s. Ross Olen and Elizabeth Svea (Johnson) L.; B.S., Case Western Res. U., 1949; m. Dorothy Frances Simcox, Mar. 18, 1954; children—Kevin William, Karen Elizabeth. Engr., Youngstown Sheet & Tube Co. (Ohio), 1952-58; plant engr. Am. Welding & Mfg. Co., Dietz Road, Warren, Ohio, 1958-68; cons. in gen. engring., Poland, Ohio, 1968-77; chief engr. Niles Expanded Metals Co. (Ohio), 1977—. Mem. Am. Soc. for Metals, Am. Welding Soc. Republican. Lutheran. Inventor closed loop electro-hydraulic servo system for resistance welding 1968. Home: 8631 Pittsburgh Rd Poland OH 44514 Office: 310 N Pleasent St Niles OH 44446

LOEB, JOHN WILLIAM, supermarket chain exec.; b. Chgo., Mar. 9, 1937; s. Herbert A. and Minnabel (Coleman) L.; B.A., U. Mich., 1958; m. Susan Jane Mesirow, Sept. 4, 1957; children—Lori, Julie, Caren. With Hillman's Inc., Chgo., 1958—, dept. mgr., 1959-61, store mgr., 1961-63, dir. grocery merchandising, 1964-67, v.p., dir. merchandising, 1967-70, dir., 1968, exec. v.p., gen. mgr., 1971-72, chmn. bd., chief exec. officer, 1973—; dir. Ranger Cartage Co. Mem. Chgo. Crime Commn., 1970; bd. dirs. Better Boys Found., pres., 1976-77. Mem. Chicago Assn. Commerce and Industry (mem. consumer affairs com. 1970—). Jewish. Club: Lake Shore Country. Home: 367 Charal Ln Highland Park IL 60035 Office: 28 W Washington Chicago IL 60602

LOEB, VIRGIL, JR., physician; b. St. Louis, Sept. 21, 1921; s. Virgil and Therese (Meltzer) L.; student Swarthmore Coll., 1938-41; M.D., Washington U., St. Louis, 1944; m. Lenore Harlow, Sept. 8, 1950; children—Katherine Loeb Barksdale, Elizabeth, David, Mark. Intern, Barnes and Jewish hosps., St. Louis, 1944-45; resident, research fellow Washington U. and Barnes Hosp., 1949-52, mem. med. faculty, 1951—, prof. clin. medicine, 1978—, research in med. oncology and hematology, 1951—, dir. Central Diagnostic Labs., Barnes Hosp., 1952-68; cons. Nat. Cancer Inst., 1966—, chmn. cancer clin. investigation rev. com., 1966-69; mem. staff numerous hosps., 1951—; mem. VA Oncology Merit Rev. Bd., 1971-75; mem. Polycythemia Vera Study Group, NIH, 1966—, S.E. Cancer Study Group, 1956—. Bd. dirs. St. Louis and Mo. div. Am. Cancer Soc.; bd. dirs. St. Louis Blue Cross. Served with M.C., AUS, 1945-47. Diplomate Am. Bd. Internal Medicine. Fellow A.C.P.; mem. Central Soc. Clin. Research, Inst. Medicine, Am. Assn. Cancer Research, Am. Soc. Clin. Oncology, Am. Fedn. Clin. Research, Internat., Am. socs. hematology, St. Louis Soc. Internal Medicine, Alpha Omega Alpha, Sigma Xi. Contbr. articles to med. and sci. jours., chpts. to books. Home: 24 Deerfield Rd Saint Louis MO 63124 Office: 4989 Barnes Hosp Plaza Saint Louis MO 63110

LOEFFLER, HEINZ H., paper co. exec.; b. Germany, July 9, 1910; s. Julius and Carola (Bechmann) L.; student Ecole Superieure de Commerce, Neuchatel, Switzerland, U. Chgo.; m. Jean C. Campbell, Aug. 31, 1946; children—Susan L. Bainbridge, Patricia Lynne. Stock clk. Robert Reis & Co., N.Y.C., 1928; clk. McGlynn & Co., N.Y.C., 1928-29; salesman Kupfer Bros. Paper N.Y.C., Chgo., 1929-33; pres., Chgo., 1936-48; pres. Exeter Paper Co., Inc., Chgo., 1948—, also chmn. bd.; dir. Handschy Chem. Co., Mem. Co. Mem. Am. Security Council. Mem. exec. com. Nat. Com. for Employer Support of Guard and Res.; bd. dirs. Navy Supply Corps Found. Served from lt. (j.g.) to lt. comdr. USNR, World War II; rear adm. Res. ret. Mem. Indsl. Packaging Engrs., Am. Acad. Polit. Sci., Council Fgn. Relations, Lake County Civic League, Packaging Inst., Ill. C. of C., Navy League (dir. Chgo. council), Naval Res. Assn., Nat. Paper Box Assn. (dir.), Navy Supply Corps Sch. Alumni Assn. (dir.), Marine Corps Res. Assn., Air Force Assn., Nat. Strategy Info. Center, Naval Order U.S., Holy Name Soc. Rotarian. Clubs: Executives, Mid-America, Internat. Trade (Chgo.). Home: Rural Route 1 Box 178 Long Grove IL 60047 Office: 730 N Franklin St Chicago IL 60610

LOEFFLER, ROBERT JAMES, hist. site ofcl., educator; b. Worcester, Mass., Oct. 20, 1922; s. Guy James and Elvira Christiana (Nordquist) L.; B.A. cum laude, Syracuse (N.Y.) U., 1948; M.S., U. Wis., 1950, Ph.D., 1954; m. M. Jane Lomen, June 16, 1956; children—Leslie, Nathan, Catherine, Clay. Asst. prof. botany Concordia Coll., Moorhead, Minn., 1954-63, asso. prof., 1964-65, prof., 1969-70, ret., 1973; site mgr. S.G. Comstock Hist. House Minn. Hist. Soc., Moorhead, 1974—. Research fellow Royal Ont. (Can.) Mus., Toronto, 1970-71; pres. Comstock Hist. House Soc., 1974. Served with M.C., AUS, 1943-46. Mem. Bot. Soc. Am., Am. Inst. Biol. Sci., Minn. Edn. Conservation Council (chmn. 1962-63), Ecol. Soc. Am., Am. Fern Soc., Am. Soc. Limnology, Oceanography, Sigma Xi, Gamma Alpha. Home: 704 8th St S Moorhead MN 56560 Office: 506 8th St S Moorhead MN 56560

LOEHNERT, JOHN TYLER, savs. and loan exec.; b. Cleve., June 3, 1923; s. Frank and Elizabeth (Brightman) L.; B.A. in Econs., Denison U., 1947; m. Gail Kathleen Pritchard, June 29, 1946; children—Leslie Ann, John Tyler, Gail Brooke, Todd P. Restauranteur, Granville, Ohio, 1947-51; asst. basketball coach Denison U., 1947-51, head basketball coach, 1951-53; mgmt. trainee Dollar Fed. Savs. & Loan Assn. (co. name changed to Dollar Savs. Assn. 1973), Columbus, Ohio, 1953, asst. v.p., 1957-63, v.p., 1963—. Chmn. Franklin County Cancer Soc. Crusade, 1970; mem. Bexley (Ohio) City Council, 1978—; pres. Stelios M. Stelson Found., 1976. Served with USN, 1943-46; PTO; ret. capt. Res. Recipient Meritorious Community Service award, Sec. of Navy, 1971; Distinguished Community Service award City of Bexley, 1972; Gold Wreath Recruiting award U.S. Navy, 1976. Mem. Pub. Relations Soc. Am., U.S. Savs. and Loan League, Inst. Fin. Edn., Res. Officers Assn., Am. Savs. and Loan Inst. (pres. Columbus chpt. 1962), Ohio Savs. and Loan League, Navy League U.S. (pres. Columbus counci 1966), Omicron Delta Kappa. Republican. Episcopalian. Clubs: Athletic (Columbus); Masons (Granville); Kiwanis (pres. 1957) (Columbus). Home: 120 N Cassingham St Bexley OH 43209 Office: 1 E Gay St Columbus OH 43215

LOENDORF, WILLIAM ROGER, electronic engr.; b. Racine, Wis., July 21, 1948; s. Thorwald Christian and Edna Lillian (Henriksen) L.; B.S. in Engring. Sci., U. Wis. at Parkside, 1971; M.E.E., Colo. State U., 1973. With Unico, Inc., Franksville, Wis., 1973—, project engr., 1973-75, software devel. mgr., tchr. tech. courses, 1975—; part-time lectr. in elec. engring. and computer sci. U. Wis. at Parkside, Kenosha; mem. electronic tech.-computer adv. com. Gateway Tech. Inst., Racine, 1975—. Registered profl. engr., Wis. Mem. IEEE, Nat. Soc. Profl. Engrs., Data Processing Mgmt. Assn., U. Wis. at Parkside Alumni Assn. (vice chmn., bd. dirs. 1973—), Eta Kappa Nu. Lutheran. Clubs: Unico, Inc. Employees (v.p.). Home: 1406 Summit Ave Racine WI 53404 Office: 3725 Nicholson Rd Franksville WI 53126

LOENING, KURT LEOPOLD, chem. abstracts service exec.; b. Berlin, Germany, Jan. 18, 1924; s. Kurt Edgar and Vera (Brill) L.; came to U.S., 1942, naturalized, 1945; B.S. in Chemistry, Ohio State U., 1944, Ph.D., 1951; m. Helen Margaret Clark, Nov. 15, 1945; children—Philip Daniel, Thomas Clark. Asst. editor Chem. Abstracts Service, Ohio State U., Columbus, 1951-54, asso. editor, 1955-59, sr. asso. editor, 1960, head nomenclature dept., 1961-62, asso. nomenclature dir., 1963, dir. nomenclature, 1964—; chmn. interdivisional com. nomenclature and symbols Internat. Union Pure and Applied Chemistry, also mem. commns. Served with AUS, 1942-44. Mem. Am. Chem. Soc. (chmn. nomenclature com. 1964), AAAS, Sigma Xi. Author (with Adams and Fernelius) Notes on Nomenclature, a regular column in Jour. of Chem. Edn., 1971—. Contbr. articles to profl. jours. Home: 2064 Inchcliff Rd Columbus OH 43221 Office: Chemical Abstracts Service care Ohio State U Columbus OH 43210

LOENSER, LARRY ELDON, county extension dir.; b. Geneseo, Ill., Mar. 18, 1944; s. Eldon William and Wilma Irene (Mohler) L.; B.S., Ia. State U., 1966, M.S., 1976; m. Eugenie Loralee Rice, June 10, 1966; children—Rebecca, Michael, Christina. Prodn. supr. Internat. Harvester Co., E. Moline, Ill., 1966-70; county extension dir. Butler County, Allison, Iowa, 1970-72, Black Hawk County, Waterloo, Iowa, 1972—; mem. local arrangements com. World Food Conf., Iowa State U., 1976. Mem. Black Hawk County Bicentennial Commn. bd., 1974-75; exec. com. dir. N.Central Iowa Health Planning Council, 1971-72; adv. com. Area VII Dept. Social Services, 1971-72; chmn. Black Hawk County Rural Devel. Com., 1972—. Mem. Iowa State U. Extension Assn., Cedar Falls C. of C., Waterloo C. of C., Phi Kappa Phi, Epsilon Sigma Phi, Phi Delta Kappa. Lutheran. Rotarian. Home: 206 Devlin Circle Cedar Falls IA 50613 Office: 1022 W 5th St Waterloo IA 50702

LOESCH, KATHARINE TAYLOR (MRS. JOHN GEORGE LOESCH), educator; b. Berkeley, Calif., Apr. 13, 1922; d. Paul Schuster and Katharine (Whiteside) Taylor; student Swarthmore Coll., 1939-41, U. Wash., 1942; B.A., Columbia U., 1944, M.A., 1949; postgrad. Ind. U., 1953; Ph.D., Northwestern U., 1961; m. John George Loesch, Aug. 28, 1948; 1 son, William Ross. Instr. speech Wellesley (Mass.) Coll., 1949-52, Loyola U., Chgo., 1956; asst. prof. speech Roosevelt U., Chgo., 1957, 62-65; faculty U. Ill. at Chgo. Circle, 1968—, asso. prof. communications and theatre, 1970—. Recipient Golden Anniversary Prize award Speech Assn. Am., 1969. Am. Philos. Soc. grantee, 1970. Mem. Am. Soc. Aesthetics, Linguistics Soc. Am., Speech Communication Assn., Modern Lang. Assn. Home: 2129 N Sedgwick St Chicago IL 60614 Office: Dept Communications and Theatre U Ill Chicago IL 60680

LOESCHER, GILBERT DAMIAN, polit. scientist, univ. dean; b. San Francisco, Mar. 7, 1945; s. Burt G. and Helene A. Loescher; B.A., St. Marys Coll. Calif., 1967; Ph.D. (Montague Burton research fellow), London Sch. Economics Polit. Sci., 1975; m. Ann Dull, Sept. 25, 1971; 1 dau., Margaret. Prin., Am. Community Sch., London, 1969-71; vis. asst. prof. polit. sci. U. Notre Dame (Ind.), 1975-76, asst. academic dean Coll. Arts Letters, asst. prof. dept. govt., 1976—; bd. dirs. Ind. Consortium Internat. Programs. Roman Catholic. Author: Chinese Way, 1974; Human Rights, 1978; Human Rights and American Foreign Policy, 1978. Office: Univ Notre Dame 101 O'Shaughnessy Hall Notre Dame IN 46556

LOEWEN, ELEANOR MARIE, church ofcl.; b. Calgary, Alta., Can., Dec. 20, 1938; d. Martin Abram and Sarah (Neumann) Loewen; came to U.S., 1967; B.A. in Music, Goshen (Ind.) Coll., 1967; M.S. in Edn., Ind. U., 1971. Head resident Goshen Coll., 1967-68; counselor Am. Sch. of Kinshasa (Zaire), 1971-73; dir. career counseling and placement Bluffton Coll., 1973-76; dir. student services Gen. Conf. of the Mennonite Ch., Newton, Kans., 1976—; dir. career planning and placement Bethel Coll., 1977—. Mem. Am. Personnel and Guidance Assn., Nat. Vocat. Guidance Assn., AAUW, Pi Lambda Theta. Home: PO Box 461 North Newton KS 67117 Office: PO Box 347 Newton KS 67114

LOFGREN, KARL ADOLPH, surgeon; b. Killeberg, Sweden, Apr. 1, 1915; s. Hokan Albin and Teckla Elisabeth (Carlsson) L.; student Northwestern U., 1934-37; M.D., Harvard U., 1941; M.S. in Surgery, U. Minn., 1947; m. Jean Frances Taylor, Sept. 12, 1942; children—Karl Edward, Anne Elizabeth. Intern, U. Minn. Hosps., Mpls., 1941-42, Mayo Found. fellow in surgery, 1942-44, 46-48; asst. surgeon Royal Academic Hosp., Uppsala, Sweden, 1949; asst. to surg. staff Mayo Clinic, Rochester, Minn., 1949-50, cons. sect. peripheral vein surgery, 1950—, instr. in surgery Mayo Grad. Sch. Medicine, 1951-60, asst. prof. surgery, 1960-74, comdg. officer USNR Med. Co. Mayo Clinic, 1963-67, head sect. peripheral vein surgery, dept. surgery, 1966—; asso. prof. surgery Mayo Med. Sch., Rochester, 1974—; cons. surg. staff Rochester Meth. Hosp. and St. Mary's Hosp.

Mem. adv. bd. Salvation Army of Rochester, 1959—, pres., 1962-63. Served to capt., M.C. USNR, 1944-46. Decorated Bronze Star. Diplomate Am. Bd. Surgery. Fellow A.C.S.; mem. Internat. Cardiovascular Soc., Minn., Swedish (hon.) surg. socs., Mil. Surgeons, So. Minn. Med. Assn. (pres. 1972-73), Swiss Soc. Phlebology (co-worker), Sigma Xi. Baptist. Club: Rotary of Rochester. Contbr. articles to profl. jours. and textbooks. Home: 1001 7th Ave NE Rochester MN 55901 Office: Mayo Clinic Rochester MN 55901

LOFTIS, GENE AUSTIN, coll. adminstr.; b. Ada, Okla., Aug. 27, 1928; s. Marrol Franklin and Ruth Gladys (Sterling) L.; B.S., East Central State Coll., 1952; M.Ed., U. Okla., 1953, Ed.D., 1966; m. Delma Joyce Murdock, Dec. 22, 1950; children—Pamela Joyce, Jonalyn Kay, Randall Gene. Bus. tchr. Alanreed (Tex.) Schs., 1952, Classen High Sch., Oklahoma City, 1953-57; instr. Adult Inst., Oklahoma City, 1955-57; asso. prof., asst. chmn. dept. bus. Central State U., Edmond, Okla., 1957-67; prof., head dept. bus. adminstrn. and bus. edn., also chmn. div. practical and fine arts S.E. Mo. State U., Cape Girardeau, 1967-76, dean Coll. Bus., 1976—. Served with USN, 1946-49; PTO. Mem. Mo. Edn. Assn., Nat. Bus. Edn. Assn., Delta Pi Epsilon. Baptist (deacon). Toastmaster, Optimist. Home: 2302 Brookwood Dr Cape Girardeau MO 63701

LOFTON, C(HARLOTTE) A(NITA) MARYJOE, educator; b. Chgo., May 14, 1943; d. Stephen Kenneth Sr. and Lilliard Mardre (Reams) Lofton; B.A. in English, Roosevelt U., 1974. Instr. creative writing Chgo. City Jr. Coll., 1974-75; dir. Hyde Park Multi-Media Tutoring Center, Chgo., 1975—; adj. instr. U. Without Walls program Shaw U., Raleigh, N.C., 1974—; exec. pres. St. Michael's Lit. Services. poetry cons. News in Mass Media, Writer's and Educator's Media Workshop, Gary, Ind., 1973; cons. Internat. Black Writers Conf.; instr. Poetry Workshop, Chgo., 1972; poetess; poet Ill. Art Council Poets-in-the-schs. program, 1975—; part-time faculty Daniel Hale Williams U. Mem. PUSH, Union Black Artists. Mem. Religious Soc. of Friends (chmn. social concerns 1965-67). Mem. Mayan Order. Contbg. author: Night comes Softly, 1970; New Voices in Black Poetry, 1972. Home: care L Lofton 7927 S Perry Ave Chicago IL 60620 Office: Daniel Hale Williams U 5247 W Madison Ave Chicago IL 60644

LOFTUS, GARY JOSEPH, civil engr., businessman; b. New Albany, Ind., June 29, 1951; s. Francis Jerome and Mary Jean (Shirley) L.; B.S. in Civil Engring., Purdue U., 1973; m. Debra Kay Bennett, Sept. 20, 1974; children—Rebecca Jean, Kathy Jo. Engr., Ind. State Hwy. Commn., 1973-74; asso. Ron Vuckson & Assos., Engrs., New Albany, Ind., 1974—; surveyor Floyd County (Ind.) Surveyor's Office, 1974; partner Loftus Constrn. Co., New Albany, 1970—, Korner Kitchen and Floyd Central Hardware, New Albany, 1977—. Mem. Nat. Soc. Profl. Engrs. (pres. chpt. 1976-77), ASCE, Nat. Retail Hardware Assn. Democrat. Roman Catholic. Club: K.C. Home: Rural Route 2 Box 467A New Albany IN 47150 Office: Rural Route 2 Box 397T New Albany IN 47150

LOGAN, JOHN STERLING, engr.; b. Helena, Mont., Feb. 23, 1934; s. William Ernest and Florence (Snow) L.; B.M.E., Pa. State U., 1956; m. Gwendolyn June Bickford, Nov. 7, 1959; 1 son, John Sterling. Supv. heavy vehicle chassis sect. Ford Motor Co., Dearborn, Mich., 1965-72, mgr. product engring. dept. transp. systems ops., 1972-76, mgr. transp. systems, diversified products ops., 1976-77, mgr. spl. projects vehicle research N.Am. auto ops., 1977—. Served with U.S. Army, 1957. Registered profl. engr., Mich. Mem. Soc. Automotive Engrs., Mich. Engring. Soc. Patentee in automated transp. systems. Home: 24444 Emerson St Dearborn MI 48124 Office: Ford Motor Co Amer Rd Dearborn MI 48124

LOGAN, JOHN WESLEY, JR., civil engr.; b. Chgo., Aug. 15, 1954; s. John Wesley and Martha Elizabeth (Peterson) L.; B.C.E., Purdue U., 1975. Engr., Peoples Gas Light & Coke Co., Chgo., 1973; structural engr. Eastman Kodak Co., Rochester, N.Y., 1974; staff engr. Amoco Oil Co., Chgo., 1975, 76-77, project engr., 1977—. Mem. Nat. Soc. Profl. Engrs., ASCE, Nat. Soc. Black Engrs., Nat. Tech. Alliance. Democrat. Methodist. Home: 9352 King Dr Chicago IL 60619 Office: 200 E Randolph Dr Chicago IL 60601

LOGAN, LLOYD, pharmacist; b. Columbia, Mo., Dec. 27, 1932; s. Henry B. and Eva G. (Nelson) L.; student Purdue U., 1951-52, Belleville Jr. Coll., 1953-54; B.S. in Pharmacy, St. Louis Coll. Pharmacy, 1958; m. Lottie A. Pecot, Aug. 16, 1958; children—Terri Lynn, Connie Renee, Gerald Brian, Michael Steven, Kevin Craig. Staff pharmacist St. Louis U. Hosp., 1958-59, chief pharmacist, 1959-67, dir. pharmacy and purchasing, 1966-69; owner Mound City Pharmacy, St. Louis, 1962—; sec. Rhodes Med. Supply, Inc., St. Louis, 1968-72. Asst. dir. purchasing services Daus. of Charity Shared Services Assn.; mem. shared services adv. panel Am. Hosp. Assn.; pres. People, Inc., St. Louis, 1967-68; mem. YMCA; mem. adv. com. HELP, Inc., St. Louis; treas. Page Community Devel. Corp., St. Louis, 1971-73; trustee Lindell Hosp., St. Louis; mem. sch. bd. St. Engelbert Sch., 1969-76, pres., 1973-76; mem. St. Louis Archdiocesan Sch. Bd., 1976—, pres., 1977—. Served with USAF, 1952-56. Mem. Am., Nat., Mound City (pres. 1964) pharm. assns., Am., St. Louis socs. hosp. pharmacists, Nat. Assn. Retail Druggists, Chi Delta Mu (sec. 1967-69, pres. 1973-74). Roman Catholic. Patentee. Home: 6055 Lindell Blvd Saint Louis MO 63112 Office: 2715 N Union Blvd Saint Louis MO 63113

LOGAN, SANDRA SIMMS, lawyer; b. Quincy, Fla., June 8, 1942; d. Waymon Arthur and Pollie Bell (Preston) Simms; B.S., Fla. A. and M. U., 1968; M.S. (So. fellow), U. Okla., 1970; J.D., Cleve. State U., 1974; children—June Yvette, Anthony Trenton, Jeffrey Simms. Admitted to Ohio bar, 1976, since practiced in Cleve. Recipient Moot Ct. Award for Outstanding Advocacy, 1974. Mem. Cuyahoga, Cleve. bar assns., Assn. Trial Lawyers Am., Soc. for Study of Social Issues, Phi Alpha Delta. Republican. Clubs: Group 500. Home and office: Park Centre 1700 E 13th St Cleveland OH 44114

LOGAN, SERGE EDWARD, editor, wax co. exec.; b. Chgo., Feb. 7, 1926; s. Carl and Alexandra (Honcharik) L.; student Superior (Wis.) State U., 1946-48; B.A. magna cum laude, U. Minn., 1950. Reporter, asst. city editor, Sunday editor Racine (Wis.) Jour.-Times, 1950-60; publs. mgr. S. C. Johnson & Son, Inc., Racine, 1960-65, community affairs mgr., editor, 1965-68, communications mgr., 1968-71, communications dir., 1971—, editor Johnson Mag., 1960—. Active as scoutmaster, explorer adviser, commnr., mem. exec. bd. SE Wis. council Boy Scouts Am., 1951—, pres., 1966-68; sec. Johnson Wax Fund, Inc., 1965-68; pub. relations chmn. United Fund, 1967, 70, 72, 73. Served with USNR, 1944-46; PTO. Named Outstanding Young Man of Year, Racine Jr. C. of C., 1961; recipient Silver Beaver award Boy Scouts Am., 1963, Silver Antelope, 1973. Am. Polit. Sci. Assn. Congl. fellow on Senate staff Hubert H. Humphrey, Ho. of reps. staff James Wright, 1956-57. Mem. C. of C. (publs. com. 1967—), Internat. (conf. program chmn. 1977), Wis. (officer, dir.) assns. bus. communicators, Phi Beta Kappa. Methodist (steward). Home: 1737 Wisconsin Ave Racine WI 53403 Office: 1525 Howe St Racine WI 53403

LOGSDON, JOHN DAVID, lawyer, educator; b. Fort Smith, Ark., May 18, 1935; s. Hill Frank and Ruby (King) L.; B.S., U. Tulsa, 1957, M.B.A., 1958; J.D., U. Kans., 1961; m. Marcia Janice Hall, June 21, 1959 (dec. Nov. 15, 1976); children—J. David, Ann E., Karen D., Douglas A. Instr. U. Kans., Lawrence, 1958-61, asst. prof., 1964-67; lectr. Washburn U., Topeka, 1961-64; partner Sinderson, Jenning & Mueller, C.P.A.'s Kansas City, Kans., 1967-69; pvt. practice law, 1969—. Lectr. bus. adminstrn. U. Mo., Kansas City, 1967-68, asso. prof. accounting, 1968-72, prof., 1972—. Asst. sec., treas. Ednl. Found. Kans. Soc. C.P.A.'s. Served to capt., judge adv. gen. corps, USAF, 1961-64. C.P.A., Kans. Mem. Kans. Soc. C.P.A.'s (bd. dirs.), Am. Inst. C.P.A.'s, Am. Accounting Assn., Am., Kans. bar assns., Am. Assn. Atty.-C.P.A.'s, Am., Midwest bus. law assns., Am. Econ. Assn., Lambda Chi Alpha, Delta Sigma Pi, Phi Delta Phi, Beta Gamma Sigma. Republican. Presbyn. Home: 6440 Wenonga Rd Mission Hills KS 66208 Office: 5110 Cherry Kansas City MO 64110

LOGUE, THOMAS JOSEPH, lawyer; b. Pana, Ill., July 6, 1930; s. Wayne Edward and Dorothy Ellen (Kelligar) L.; B.A., U. Ill., 1952, LL.B., 1956; m. Mary Ann Laurent, Aug. 25, 1951; children—Michele, Bridget, Edith, Mary, Thomas, Kathleen, Gretchen, Dan, Terrence, Michael, Chris. Admitted to Ill. bar, 1956, to practice before Ill. and Fed. Cts.; partner firm Glenn & Logue, Mattoon, Ill., 1966—; asst. states atty. Coles County, Ill., 1966-68; city atty. City of Mattoon, 1961-65. Mem. Coles County Democratic Central Com., 1962-68. Served with AUS, 1952-54. Mem. Am., Ill., Coles-Cumberland (v.p.) bar assns., Am., Ill. trial lawyers assns., Am. Legion. Roman Catholic. K.C., Elk, Moose. Home: 3920 Western Ave Mattoon IL 61938 Office: 901 Charleston Ave Mattoon IL 61938

LOHMAN, BERNEICE THOMAS KNAGGS (MRS. BEN E. LOHMAN), bus. and club woman; b. Ovid, Mich., Nov. 22, 1905; d. Frederick Arthur and Evalena (Vosburgh) Thomas; diploma Baker Bus. Coll., 1925; student Central Mich. U., 1923; LL.B., Blackstone Inst. Law, Chgo., 1930-42; m. Daniel A. Knaggs, Mar. 11, 1944 (dec. Aug. 1957); m. 2d, Ben E. Lohman, Dec. 27, 1958. Legal sec. firm Smith, Hunter & Spaulding, St. Johns, Mich., 1925-26; Person, Marshall & Palm, Lansing, Mich., 1927-29, Office Atty. Gen. Mich., 1933-35, Miller, Canfield, Paddock & Stone, Detroit, 1937-39; com. clk. Mich. Ho. of Reps., Lansing, 1927, sec. to speaker of house, 1929-33, statistician ways and means com., 1939, 41-61; sec. to chmn. Mich. Liquor Control Commn., 1935-37, Mich. Dept. Labor and Industry, 1939-41; also licensed real estate saleswoman. Nurses aide A.R.C., Mich., 1942—; sec. Monroe County Hist. Soc., 1948-50, v.p., 1950-52, pres., 1954-56, bd. dirs. Southeastern Mich. Tourists Assn., 1956-58; sec. Sesquicentennial Com. Battle River Raisin; chmn. impact Civil War on farming in Mich., Civil War Centennial Observance Commn., 1960-65; mem. Monroe County Hist. Com., 1976—, sec., 1977—. Vice pres. Mich. Fedn. Republican Women's Clubs, 1943-44, mem. election bd., Monroe, Mich., 1952-56; mem. State Employees Retirement Bd., 1970—, chmn., 1973, vice chmn., 1975; sec. Monroe County Rep. Com., 1952-53, mem., 1969—; pres. Republican Woman's Club, Monroe, 1973-77. Recipient citation of appreciation Vets. Fgn. Wars, 1945, also Citizens' award; award of merit A.R.C.; citation Mich. Ho. of Reps., 1961; citation D.A.V., 1964. Mem. Mich. Hist. Soc. (trustee 1946-48, award of merit), Daus. Am. Colonists (chpt. regent 1971-73, state regent 1973-76, nat. v.p. Middle West sect. 1976—), D.A.R. Episcopalian. Mem. Order Eastern Star. Home: 610 E Elm Ave Monroe MI 48161 also 2618 Lake Shore Dr Fennville MI 49408

LOHMAN, KEITH DOUGLASS, ednl. adminstr.; b. Milw., Nov. 27, 1942; s. Walter Henry and Marjorie Jean (Raatz) L.; B.S., Carroll Coll., 1964; M.S., U. Wis. at Milw., 1966; Ed.D., U. No. Colo., 1971; m. Romayne Carol Beuthling, June 6, 1970. Instr. sociology U. Wis. at Whitewater, 1966-69, asso. dean student life, coordinator counseling programs, 1973—; instr. sociology U. No. Colo., 1969-70; vice prin. Mukwonago (Wis.) High Sch., 1971-72; alcohol awareness and alcohol edn. coordinator, U. Wis. Served with USAR, 1967-73. Mem. Am., Wis. coll. personnel assns., Am. Personnel and Guidance Assn., ACLU (mem. student rights com.), Phi Delta Kappa. Lutheran. Home: PO Box 277 Palmyra WI 53156 Office: 101 Salisbury St U Wis Whitewater WI 53190

LOHMANN, WILLIAM TOMBAUGH, architect; b. Burlington, Iowa, June 12, 1928; s. Carl John and Helen Rachel (Tombaugh) L.; student Burlington Jr. Coll., 1946-47; B.S., Iowa State U., 1950; postgrad. Ill. Inst. Tech., 1956-58; m. Evelyn Day Ward, July 15, 1951; children—Catherine Day Lohmann Ricketts, Melanie Ann. Draftsman Dane D. Morgan & Assos., Burlington, 1954-57; project adminstr. Robert Babbin & Assos., Chgo., 1958-62; specification writer Bertrand Goldberg Assos., Chgo., 1963-67; chief specifier C.F. Murphy Assos., Chgo., 1968—. Lectr. several Midwest campuses; mem. Nat. Delphi Panel of Benz Nat. Surveys, Somerville, N.J., 1975—. Mem. Constrn. Industry Affairs Com. Chgo., 1967-69, 70—; mem. City of Chgo. Com. on Standards and Tests, 1973—. Served with USAF, 1950-54. Recipient Constrn. Specifications Inst. Region 7 Dirs. award, 1974, others. Fellow Constrn. Specifications Inst.; mem. ASTM, Am. Inst. Architects (chmn. specifications subcom. 1974—), Constrn. Specifications Inst. (chpt. pres. 1969-70). Methodist. Contributing editor Progressive Architecture mag., 1975—. Home: 1232 Maple Ave Evanston IL 60202 Office: 224 S Michigan Ave Chicago IL 60604

LOHUTKO, CONRAD ANTHONY, govt. social scientist; b. Detroit, Sept. 5, 1944; s. Floryan Anthony and Virginia Elizabeth (Barber) L.; A.B., Dickinson Coll., 1966; A.M., St. Louis U., 1970, Ph.D. candidate, 1976; m. Sandra Lee Moore, Apr. 17, 1967; children—Eric Conrad, Kurt Charles, Matthew Moore, Karen Virginia, Amy Davis, Janet Lynn, Sara Ellen. Dir. community relations Asso. Industries of Mo., St. Louis, 1968; spl. asst. to pres. St. Louis U., 1970-71; sr. position classification specialist U.S. Army Aviation Systems Command and U.S. Army Automated Logistics Mgmt. Systems Agy., St. Louis, 1971—. Lectr. polit. sci. St. Louis U., 1970—. Polit. strategist Independent Colls. and Univs. Mo., 1970-71. Served to 1st lt. AUS, 1968; Viet Nam. Crown Zellerbach Found. fellow, 1970-71. Mem. Am., Midwest polit. sci. assns., Alpha Chi Rho, Pi Sigma Alpha, Alpha Sigma Nu. Republican. Mem. Christian and Missionary Alliance Ch. (elder 1974-75). Author: Is the United States Part of the Inter-American System?, 1971; Political Interests in Conflict: The Politics Behind the Passage and Funding of the Missouri Tuition Assistance Bill, 1977; The Centrality of Position and Pay Management, 1975. Home: 7504 Knackstedt St St Louis MO 63116 Office: 12th and Spruce Sts St Louis MO 63102

LOJACONO, MARIE SHIYA, speech pathologist; b. Ashtabula, Ohio, Jan. 2, 1933; d. Leo Kallil and Renee (Saad) Shiya; student Fredonia State Tchrs. Coll., 1951-52; B.A., Mich. State U., 1955; m. Emil Frank Lojacono, Aug. 18, 1956; children—Gregory, Lisa, Mark, Beth. Speech pathologist Pontiac (Mich.) Pub. Schs., 1955-56, Lansing (Mich.) Pub. Schs., 1956-58, Portland (Mich.) Pub. Schs., 1958-59; speech and hearing pathologist Buffalo Hearing Center, 1961-62; tchr. cleft palate Buffalo Children's Hosp., 1963-66; speech therapist schs. Denison, Tex., 1966-67, Cranberry, N.J., 1968-71, Western Springs, Ill., 1972-73, La Grange, Ill., 1973-74, Lisle, Ill., 1975-76, St. Joan of Arc Sch., Lisle, Ill., 1976—. Mem. Am. (certified speech pathologist), Ill., Western Suburban, Du Page County speech and hearing assns. Democrat. Roman Catholic. Home: 5217 Harvey Ave Western Springs IL 60558 Office: St Joan of Arc Sch 4913 Kingston St Lisle IL 60532

LOLLAR, ROBERT MILLER, indsl. mgmt. exec.; b. Lebanon, Ohio, May 17, 1915; s. Harry David and Ruby (Miller) L.; Chem.E., U. Cin., 1937, M.S., 1938, Ph.D., 1940; m. Dorothy Marie Williams, Jan. 1, 1941; children—Janet Ruth (Mrs. David Schwarz), Katherine Louise (Mrs. James Punteney, Jr.). Cereal analyst Kroger Food Found., Cin., 1935-37; devel. chemist Rit Product div. Corn Products, Indpls., 1937-39, 40-41; asso. prof. U. Cin., 1941-59; tech. dir. Armour & Co., Chgo., 1959-73; mgmt. and tech. cons., pres. Lollar and Assos., 1973—; tech. dir. Tanners' Council Am., Cin., 1975—. Dir. OSRD, 1942-45. Recipient Alsop award Am. Leather Chemists' Assn., 1954. Mem. Am. Leather Chemists Assn. (pres., editor-in-chief), Inst. Food Technologists, Am. Chem. Soc. (nat. councillor), Am. Soc. Quality Control, World Mariculture Soc., Sigma Xi, Tau Beta Pi, Alpha Chi Sigma. Address: 5960 Donjoy Dr Cincinnati OH 45242

LOMAN, FRANCES RATNER, accountant; b. N.Y.C., Sept. 20, 1913; d. Harry E. and Goldie (Oppenheim) Ratner; B.A., Hunter Coll., 1934; M.B.A., City U. N.Y., 1962; postgrad. Northwestern U., 1962, U. Chgo., 1964-65; m. Charles Loman, Nov. 15, 1941; children—Robert, Richard. Pvt. tchr., tutor, N.Y., 1934-37; bookkeeper Continental Supply, wholesale paper, N.Y., 1937-45; controller J. Eisenberg & Co., textile converters, N.Y., 1945-59; accountant East Chicago Heights Utility Corp., 1959-64; pvt. practice C.P.A., East Chicago Heights, Ill., 1964—. Dir. Community and Econ. Devel. Assn. Cook County (Ill.), Inc., 1969—; bd. dirs. East Chicago Heights Community Service Center, Inc., 1969—; mem. Community Devel. Bd., Village of East Chicago Heights, 1976—. Mem. Plan Commn., Village East Chicago Heights, 1963—. Recipient urban service award Office Econ. Opportunity, 1967. Mem. Am. Inst. C.P.A.'s, Ill. Soc. C.P.A.'s, Am. Women's Soc. C.P.A.'s, Cosmopolitan C. of C., Beta Gamma Sigma. Address: 1433 E 15th St East Chicago Heights IL 60411

LOMBARDY, ROSS DAVID, food co. exec.; b. Cleve., Mar. 20, 1920; s. David Ross and Minnie (Roberto) L.; student pub. schs.; m. Louise Adelaide McMahon, Oct. 28, 1940; children—Louise, Ross David, David J., Kathleen L., Mary A., Thomas J. Pres. David Lombardy Co., Cleve., 1942-57; v.p., sec. Seaway Foods, Inc., Bedford Heights, Ohio, 1957—. Recipient Grocery Man of Year award, 1973. Mem. Internat. Order Alhambra (Grand Comdr.). Roman Cathloic (pres. Holy Name Soc. 1955). K.C. (4 deg.). Club: K-C (trustee South Euclid, Ohio). Home: 4991 Countryside Ln Lyndhurst OH 44124 Office: 22801 Aurora Rd Bedford Heights OH 44146

LONE, FRANK JOHN, physician; b. Winnipeg, Man., Can., Apr. 7, 1922; s. John and Helen (Bytnar) L.; M.D., L.M.C.C., U. Man., 1945; m. Isobell Mary Barron, Sept. 23, 1946; children—Barbara (Mrs. Fergus Penner), Monica, Cynthia (Mrs. Thomas Fisher). Intern Winnipeg Gen. Hosp., 1944-45; gen. practice medicine, Killarney, Man., 1946-56; dir. labs. St. Joseph's and Port Arthur Gen. Hosps., Thunder Bay, Ont., 1960—; lectr. microbiology Lakehead U. Chmn. utilization Task Force on Health of Fed. Govt. of Can.; fellow cancer Meml. Hosp. for Cancer (N.Y.C.). Gov. Lakehead U. Fellow Royal Coll. Physicians and Surgeons of Can.; mem. Hosp. Med. Records Inst. (past chmn.), Ont. Assn. Pathologists (v.p.), Canadian, Ont. med. socs., Am. Soc. Clin. Pathologists, Canadian, Ont. assns. pathologists. Home: 35 S High St Thunder Bay ON Canada Office: St Joseph's General Hospital Thunder Bay ON Canada

LONEY, RICHARD HUGH, telephone co. exec.; b. Elkhart, Ind., Dec. 5, 1931; s. Hugh Willard and June Adeline (Sands) L.; grad. pub. schs.; m. Jean Lorraine Coggan, May 31, 1953; children—Stephen Andrew, Michael Hugh, Betsy Sue. With Gen. Telephone Co. of Ind., 1950—, gen. service mgr., 1975-77, gen. retail sales mgr., 1977—. Mem. youth com. Lafayette YMCA, 1964-66; scoutmaster Anthony Wayne council Boy Scouts Am., 1966-71; mem. Fort Wayne (Ind.) Fire Commn., 1978—. Served with AUS, 1954-56. Republican. Episcopalian. Club: Ft Wayne Diving. Home: 6324 Holgate Dr Fort Wayne IN 46816 Office: 8001 Hwy 24 W PO 1201 Fort Wayne IN 46801

LONG, ALAN, psychologist; b. Logansport, Ind., Apr. 5, 1942; s. Joe D. and Ruby P. (Searer) L.; B.S., Manchester Coll., 1964; M.S., Purdue U., 1965; Ph.D., Fielding Inst., 1974. Sch. counselor, psychol. specialist Hammond (Ind.) Schs., 1965-68; sch. psychologist 3 Coops., Ind. and Ill., 1969-72; vocat. psychologist L.A.P.S.E., La Grange, Ill., 1973-75; pvt. practice psychology, Homewood, Ill., 1975—; bd. dirs. S. Suburban Council on Alcoholism, 1976—. Pres. N. Manchester Civic Symphony, 1962-64. Registered psychologist, Ill.; NDEA fellow Ind. U., 1966. Mem. Acad. Psychologists in Marital and Family Therapy, Am., Ill. psychol. assns., Assn. Advancement Behavior Therapy, Assn. Advancement Tension Control, Soc. Personality Assessment, Biofeedback Soc. Am., Ill. (dir. 1975-76, pres. 1976-77). Club: Rotary. Author numerous papers on biofeedback. Office: 18019 Dixie Hwy Box 284 Suite 1D Homewood IL 60430

LONG, CLAYTON LEWIS, adminstrv. power systems engr.; b. Corvallis, Oreg., July 18, 1924; s. Clayton Lewis and Lucille (Townsend) L.; B.S. in Civil Engring., Union Coll., 1950; m. Norma Eileen Akitt, July 5, 1945; children—Gary Norman, Carolyn Lucille, Nancy Marion, Patricia Maureen. Various engring. positions Gen. Electric Co., Schenectady, 1950-52, start-up engr., 1954-56, project engr., 1956-70; mgr. project ops. Allis Chalmers Power Systems Inc., W. Allis, Wis., 1970—. Mem. Am. Nuclear Soc. Lutheran. Home: 15000 San Marcos Ct Brookfield WI 53005 Office: Allis Chalmers Power Systems 1135 S 70th St West Allis WI 53051

LONG, DAVID DESMOND, dentist; b. Oak Park, Ill., Dec. 7, 1941; s. Fleming Desmond and Mary Louise (Bowker) L.; student Drake U., 1959-61; D.D.S., Washington U., 1965; m. Linda Lee Larson, June 8, 1959; children—Tad David, Robb Dana, Dyke Desmond. Practice dentistry, Galesburg, Ill., 1965-66, 68—. Mem. East Galesburg (Ill.) City Council, 1969-70. Served to capt. Dental Corps, AUS, 1966-68. Mem. Am. Soc. Preventive Dentistry, Prairie Valley Dental Soc. (pres. 1972-73). Rotarian. Home: Rural Route 4 Galesburg IL 61401 Office: 940 N Henderson St Galesburg IL 61401

LONG, DAVID HAROLD, city ofcl.; b. East St. Louis, Ill., July 31, 1939; s. Walter and Violet J. Long; B.S. in Bus. Adminstrn., So. Ill. U., 1970, M.B.A., 1970; m. Willie Mae Hudson, Dec. 21, 1964; children—Christopher Walter, Johnathan Justin. With Union Electric Co. Mo., St. Louis, 1960-71, residential sales rep., 1969-71; exec. dir. Model Cities program, then asst. dir. community devel. City East St. Louis, 1971-76, exec. dir. planning dept., 1976—; mem. trust com. Metro-East Health Services Council; cons. in field. Sec. trustees Mt. Pisgah Baptist Ch., E. St. Louis. Served with USMCR, 1957-60. Recipient various certificates of merit, achievement. Mem. Nat. Community Dirs. Assn., Urban League, Am. Soc. Pub. Adminstrs., Am. Inst. Planners, Conf. Minority Pub. Adminstrs., Alumni Assn. So. Ill. U. Club: Masons. Home: 623 N 80th St East St Louis IL 62201 Office: 320 N 10th St East St Louis IL 62201

LONG, ERNESTINE MARTHA JOULLIAN, educator; b. St. Louis, Mo., Nov. 14, 1906; d. Ernest Cameron and Alice (Joullian) Long; A.B., U. Wis., 1927; M.S., U. Chgo., 1932; Ph.D., St. Louis U., 1975. Tchr. scis. Normandy High Sch., St. Louis, 1927-64; with City St. Louis Health Dept. and Maternal Child Health Div., Children's Bur., Washington, 1964-66; tchr. Red Bud (Ill.) High Sch., 1966-71, St. Louis pub. schs., 1971-75; asso. research cons. U. Mo.-St. Louis, 1976—. Mem. Am. Personnel and Guidance Assn. (treas. St. Louis br. 1954), Am. Chem. Soc., Central Assn. Sch. Sci., Math. Tchrs., A.A.A.S., Am. Physics Tchrs. Assn., Am. Inst. Physics, Mo. Assn. Microbiology, Am. Soc. Curriculum Devel., Am. Guild Organists, N.E.A. Home: 245 N Price Rd St Louis MO 63124 Office: Stadler Hall 219 8001 Natural Bridge Rd St Louis MO 63121

LONG, G(EORGE) DONALD, electronic mfg. co. research adminstr.; b. Elizabeth, N.J., Nov. 12, 1929; s. George Davis and Lillian Mary (Meagher) L.; B.S. in Engring. Physics, Lehigh U., 1951; Ph.D. in Physics, U. Pa., 1956; m. Lucille Audrey Thomas, Sept. 6, 1952; children—Thomas Donald, Jennifer Alison. Research scientist Honeywell Inc., Bloomington, Minn., 1955-60, research sect. head, dept. mgr., 1960-77, mgr. corp. material scis., 1977—. Fellow Am. Phys. Soc.; mem. IEEE, Sigma Xi, Tau Beta Pi. Author: Energy Bands in Semiconductors, 1968. Spl. research on solid state materials and devices, 1953—. Home: 4801 Barbara Dr Hopkins MN 55343 Office: Corporate Tech Center 10701 Lyndale Ave S Bloomington MN 55420

LONG, HOMER J., univ. dean; b. Bolchow, Mo., Aug. 6, 1921; s. Homer L. and Beulah R. Long; B.S. in Edn., N.W. Mo. State U., 1949; M.Ed., U. Mo., Columbia, 1951, Ed.D., 1969; m. Myrtice E. Carr, May 16, 1953; children—Jeffrey T., Kara M. Tchr., coach, guidance counselor schs. in Mo., 1950-56; dean of men S.W. Mo. State U., Springfield, 1956-67, dir. Counseling Center, 1962-64, asso. dean students, 1968—; pres. Mo. Coll. Testing Program, 1966. Pres. Wesley Found., Springfield, 1965; pres. area commn. higher edn. and campus ministries United Methodist Ch., 1976-80. Served with AUS, 1942-46. Mem. Am. (br. pres.), Mo. personnel and guidance assns., Am., Mo. (membership chmn. 1953) sch. counselors assns., Mo. Coll. Personnel Assn. (pres. elect 1977), Nat. Vocat. Guidance Assn. (pres. Ozark br. 1958), Dist. Guidance Assn. (pres. 1958), Am. Coll. Personnel Assn. (chmn. commn. for new and developing state divs. 1978—, mem. task force on alternative futures for student affairs 1978—), Phi Kappa Phi, Phi Delta Kappa. Home: Route 9 Box 470F Springfield MO 65804 Office: SW Missouri State U 901 S National St Springfield MO 65802

LONG, JOHN MARSHALL, med. and health care computer cons., educator; b. Norfolk, Va., July 28, 1928: s. Samuel J. and Maud Leigh (Everett) L.; B.S. in Math., Coll. William and Mary, 1950; M.S. in Math., Mich. State U., 1952; Ed.D. in Statistics, U. Va., 1960; m. Luella Clemons, Nov. 24, 1960; children—Samuel Clifford, Virginia Leigh, Paul Nelson. Asso. engr. Douglas Aircraft Corp., Santa Monica, Calif., 1953-54; asst. prof. math. Norfolk Coll. William and Mary, 1954-58, asso. prof. math., 1958-61, chmn. dept., 1959-61; head div. biometry U. Ark. Med. Center, Little Rock, also dir. research computer lab. of Med. Sch., 1962-67, asso. prof. biometry, 1962-69, prof. 1969-71, asst. dean, 1967-69, dir. computing facility, 1967-71; prin. med. cons. profl. services div. Control Data Corp., Bloomington, Minn., 1971-76; asso. prof. surg. scis. and biometry U. Minn., Mpls., 1975—. Cons., Prin. Pembroke Assn. Tenn., 1966; cons. Ark. Regional Med. Program, 1967-71; cons. Econ. Research Analyst, Inc., Ark., 1971; cons. Indian Health Mgmt. Corp., Rosebud, S.D., 1973-76. Chmn. com. to develop Ark. State Center for Health Statistics, 1969-71. Bd. dirs. Bus. and Profl. Group Am., Nashville, 1968-71; founder, pres. Am. Family Life, Inc., 1976—. Served with USAF, 1950-52. NSF Summer research grantee U. Fla., 1960, U. Okla., 1961; NIH Computer grantee U. Ark. Med. Center, 1962-67. Mem. A.A.U.P. (pres. chpt. 1958-59), Va. Acad. Scis. (chmn. statistics sect. 1961-62), Am. Ednl. Research Assn. (nat. membership com. 1964-67), Soc. for Computer Medicine, Sigma Xi, Phi Delta Kappa. Rotarian. Contbr. articles to profl. jours. Developer Nat. Migrant Student Record Transfer System, 1969-71, Humins Project, 1965-71. Home: 6120 Zenith Ave S Edina MN 55410 Office: Dept Surgery U Minn Minneapolis MN

LONG, LARRY RUSSELL, cons. civil engr.; b. Warsaw, Ind., Sept. 19, 1949; s. Russell Harry and Ester May (Shand) L.; B.C.E., Purdue U., 1972; m. Diana Kay Unruh, Aug. 22, 1969; children—Brian Larry, Benjamin David. Structural engr. Clyde E. Williams & Assos., South Bend, Ind., 1976—. Served with USAF, 1972-76. Registered profl. engr., Miss., Ind. Mem. ASCE, Nat. Soc. Profl. Engrs., Soc. Am. Mil. Engrs. Home: 67636 Sycamore Rd North Liberty IN 46554 Office: PO Box 3629 South Bend IN 46619

LONG, PAUL ALAN, treatment center exec.; b. Ossian, Ind., Dec. 13, 1941; s. Otho Washington and Helen May (Houser) L.; B.A. St. Francis Coll., Fort Wayne, Ind., 1968, M.S., 1971; m. Sharon Edith Renz, Nov. 14, 1964; children—Penelope Anne, Phillip Andrew. Caseworker, Fort Wayne (Ind.) Children's Home, 1967-68; therapist St. Vincent Villa, Fort Wayne, 1968-71; treatment dir., co-founder St. Vincent Treatment Center, residential home for emotionally disturbed boys, Fort Wayne, 1971, exec. dir., 1971—. Mem. Am. Correctional Assn., Ind. Assn. Residential Child Care Agys., Phoenix Volunteer Assn. (founder, dir. 1971—). Office: St Vincent Treatment Center 2000 N Wells St Fort Wayne IN 46808

LONG, ROBERT MICHAEL, county drug abuse program adminstr.; b. Milw., Nov. 27, 1946; s. Robert R. and Veronica (Tracy) L.; B.B.A., U. Wis., Milw., 1969, M.S., Whitewater, 1973; m. Diane Clare Laidlaw, Oct. 3, 1970; Dir. social studies program, teacher Walker Point Middle Sch., Milw., 1970-71; dir. Rock County Summer Program for Youth, Rock County Manpower Program, Janesville, Wis., 1974; dir. youth services Crossroads Counseling Center, Janesville, Wis., 1973-77; project supr. Intensive Drug & Alcohol Abuse Program, Rock County, Janesville, Wis., 1977—. Bd. dirs. Crossroads Counseling Center; Beginnings Group Home; Janesville Youth Program; Rock County Health Assn. for Mental Health. Mem. Am. Personnel Guidance Assns., Am. Mental Health Counselors Assn., Am. Assn. Correctional Psychology. Home: 2005 S Oakhill Ave Janesville WI 53545 Office: PO Box 351 Rock County Health Care Center Janesville WI 53545

LONG, ROLAND JOHN, secondary sch. prin.; b. Chgo., Nov. 15, 1921; s. John and Lillian Catherine (Sigmund) L.; B.S., Ill. State Normal U., 1949; M.A., Northwestern U., 1951; Ed.D., Ill. State U., 1972; m. Valerie Ann Zawila, Nov. 13, 1954; children—Ronald J., Thomas E. Instr. of social sci. Ball State U., Muncie, Ind., 1951; comdt. Morgan Park Mil. Acad., Chgo., 1952-54; tchr. history Hyde Park and Amundsen high schs., Chgo., 1955-62; prin. Hubbard Elementary Sch., Chgo., 1962; founder, prin. Hubbard High Sch., Chgo., 1963—; mem. doctoral advisory com. of Ill. State U., 1973-75. Mem. Chgo. Police Dist. 8 steering com., 1974-77; bd. dirs. West Communities YMCA, Chgo., Greater Lawn Mental Health Center, Chgo. Served to 1st lt., inf., U.S. Army; ETO. Decorated Silver Star, Purple Heart, Bronze Star; Ford Found. fellow, 1973; recipient Sch. Mgmt. citation Ill. Gen. Assembly, 1972. Fellow (hon.) Harry S. Truman Library Inst.; mem. Ill. Assn. for Supervision and Curriculum Devel., Nat. Assn. of Secondary Sch. Prins., Am. Legion, Phi Delta Kappa, Pi Gamma Mu, Kappa Delta Pi. Club: Elks. Author: Dr. Long's Old-Fashioned Basic Report Card and Parent Helper, 1977. Home: 6701 N Ionia Ave Chicago IL 60646 Office: 6200 S Hamlin Ave Chicago IL 60629

LONG, TIMOTHY SCOTT, chemist; b. Racine, Wis., Dec. 20, 1937; s. Leslie Alexander and Esther Agnet (Sand) L.; B.A., Winona State U., 1975; children—Corinne Susan, Christine Ann. Lab. technician Ladish Co., Cudahy, Wis., 1957; spectroscopist A. O. Smith Corp., Milw., 1958-62; staff chemist IBM, Rochester, Minn., 1962—. Mem. citizens adv. com. Rochester Area Vocat.-Tech. Inst., 1970-77. Mem. Soc. Applied Spectroscopy (chmn. Minn. sect.), ASTM. Lutheran. Contbr. articles to profl. jours. Office: Hwy 52 N Dept 314/004-1 Rochester MN 55901

LONG, WILLIAM FREDERICK, physicist; b. Burlington, Iowa, Oct. 15, 1951; s. Leslie James and Avis Ione (Dodge) L.; B.S., Iowa State U., 1973; M.S., U. Wis., 1974. Research asst. dept. physics U. Wis., Madison, 1973—. Mem. Am. Phys. Soc., Phi Kappa Phi, Pi Mu Epsilon. Research in phenomenology of elementary particle interactions; contbr. articles to profl. jours. Home: 502 N Frances St Apt 501E Madison WI 53703 Office: Dept Physics Univ Wis Madison WI 53706

LONG, WILLIS FRANKLIN, elec. engr., educator; b. Lima, Ohio, Jan. 30, 1934; s. Jesse Raymond and Cerelda Elizabeth (Stepleton) L.; B.S. cum laude in Engring. Physics, U. Toledo, 1957, M.S. in Elec. Engring., 1962; Ph.D. (NSF Sci. Faculty fellow), U. Wis., 1970; m. Ginger Carol Miller, Oct. 17, 1959; children—Andrew, Kristin, David. Project engr. Doehler-Jarvis div. Nat. Lead Co., Toledo, 1957-60; instr. elec. engring. U. Toledo, 1962-66; lectr. elec. engring. U. Wis., Madison, 1968-69, asst. prof. elec. and computer engring., 1969—; mem. tech. staff Hughes Research Labs., Malibu, Calif., 1969-73, cons., 1973—; asst. prof. engring. U. Wis.-Extension, 1973-75, asso. prof., 1975—, program dir. elec. power systems, 1973—. Cons. Eprad Corp., Toledo, 1964, Owens Corning Fiberglas Corp., 1965-66, Los Angeles Dept. Water and Power, 1975—; mem. adv. com. energy conservation Wis. Dept. Industry, Labor and Human Relations, 1975—. Mem. Common Cause, 1971—; treas. Manna, Conejo Valley Food Bank, 1972-73. Scoutmaster Boy Scouts Am., 1958-59. Precinct worker for McCarthy, 1968, McGovern, 1972. Served to 1st lt. Signal Corps, AUS, 1957-58. Registered profl. engr., Ohio, Wis. Mem. I.E.E.E. (sr.), CIGRE, Sierra Club (exec. com. Wis. chpt. 1974, vice chmn. 1975, chmn. 1976), Sigma Xi, Phi Kappa Phi, Tau Beta Pi. Mem. United Ch. of Christ (dir. 1975—). Contbr. articles to profl. publs. Patentee power switching. Home: 1444 E Skyline Dr Madison WI 53705

LONGFELLOW, LAYNE ALLEN, psychologist, educator; b. Jackson, Ohio, Oct. 23, 1937; s. Hershel Herman and Opal Edna (Pursley) L.; B.A. magna cum laude with honors in Psychology, Ohio U., 1959; M.A. (Woodrow Wilson fellow NSF fellow), U. Mich., 1961, Ph.D., 1967; postgrad. (NIMH post-doctoral fellow, resident fellow) Center for Studies of the Person, 1968-70. Instr. U. Mich., Ann Arbor, 1967; asst. prof. psychology Reed Coll., Portland, Oreg., 1967-68; asst. prof. psychology Prescott (Ariz.) Coll., 197O-71, asso. prof., 1971-72, chmn. dept., 1971-72, acad. v.p., 1972-74; adj. prof. Union Grad. Sch., 1971—, Humanistic Psychology Inst., 1974—; profl. asso. Center for Applied Behavioral Scis., Menninger Found., Topeka, 1975; dir. seminars Center Applied Behavioral Scis., 1976—; lectr., cons. stress reduction. Founder, dir. Psycreation, Inc., La Jolla, 1969-70; cons. in ednl. planning, group dynamics, organizational behavior. Mem. Am. Psychol. Assn., Assn. for Humanistic Psychology, ACLU, Phi Beta Kappa, Phi Kappa Phi, Psi Chi, Omicron Delta Kappa, Beta Theta Pi. Author: Body Talk, 1970; The Feel Wheel, 1972. Composer: Ten Songs, 1969; An Uncommon Festival of Christmas-Sixteen Carols, 1974. Address: Menninger Found Box 829 Topeka KS 66601

LONGMAN, WILLIAM MCQUILKIN, pub. opinion research co. exec.; b. Page County, Iowa, Nov. 7, 1921; s. William H. and Ruth E. (McQuilkin) L.; B.S., U. Nebr., 1942; m. Eleanor E. Watson, Apr. 17, 1943; children—James W., Robert W., Carol A. Research dir. Central Surveys, Inc., Shenandoah, Iowa, 1947-50, exec. v.p., 1950-60, pres., 1960—; dir. Home Savs. & Loan Assn., Shenandoah, 1974—. Vice chmn. planning and zoning com. Shenandoah, 1953—: state exec. finance com. Rep. Com. of Iowa 1970-75. Trustee Jay Trust, Shenandoah, 1974—; bd. dirs. S.W. Iowa Cosmetology Coll., Shenandoah, 1973—; trustee, treas. Shenandoah Industries, Inc., 1955—. Served to maj., AUS, 1942-46. Named Young man of the Year, Shenandoah Jr. C. of C., 1956. Mem. Shenandoah C. of C. (pres. 1956-57, dir. 1955-57, 64-66), Omaha/Lincoln Mktg. Assn. (pres. 1965-66), Sigma Chi. Presbyn. Elk. Home: 25 Mayridge Dr Shenandoah IA 51601 Office: 111 N Elm St Shenandoah IA 51601

LONGO, MICHAEL ANTHONY, govt. ofcl.; b. Cicero, Ill., Nov. 7, 1914; s. Nicholas and Julia (Garippo) L.; student U. Ill., 1932-36; m. Pauline Lipps, May 14, 1944; children—Michelene (Mrs. Kenneth Smith), Gerard. Chief investigator Air Pollution Control, Cicero, 1966—; field rep. World Book Ency.; dir. Fireside Fed. Savs. and Loan Assn., Fireside Service Corp., Cicero, Michael A. Longo Ins. Spl. asst. to Congressman Henry J. Hyde, 6th Ill. Dist., 1975—. Constable, Cicero, 1960-64; chmn. Cancer Crusade, Cicero, 1971—, chmn. Cicero Unit, 1976-77. Precinct capt. Republican Orgn., Cicero, 1946—; trustee Town of Cicero, 1974—. Bd. dirs. Central Suburban unit Am. Cancer Soc., 1972—, Cicero Pub. Library, 1964—, Community Chest, Cicero. Served with AUS, 1942-46; ETO. Mem. Order Sons Italy Am., Holy Name Soc., St. Vincent de Paul Soc., VFW. Roman Catholic. Club: West Suburban Exec. Breakfast (charter, dir. 1976-77). Home: 1232 S 51st Ave Cicero IL 60650 Office: 6140 W Cermak Rd Cicero IL 60650

LONGWORTH, DAVID WILLIAM, orthodontist; b. Mpls., Sept. 11, 1929; s. Herbert Wade and Pauline (Green) L.; B.S., U. Minn., 1957, D.D.S., 1959, certificate orthodontics, 1962; m. Jacquelyn Lorraine Taylor, July 4, 1953; children—James, Polly, Taylor, Nancy, Barbara, Dana, Lisa. Practice dentistry, Lake Norden, S.D., 1959-62; practice orthodontics, Watertown, S.D., 1963—, Brookings, S.D., 1970—, Sisseton, S.D., 1972—. Served with USN, 1947-53; lt. comdr. Res. ret. Decorated Air medal with two gold stars. Mem. Am. Dental Assn., Flying Dentists Assn., Soc. Preservation and Encouragement of Barbershop Quartet Singing in Am., Internat. Platform Assn., Psi Omega, Gideons. Republican. Episcopalian. Mason (32 deg.). Home: 523 1st Ave SE Watertown SD 57201 Office: 6 1/2 S Broadway St Watertown SD 57201

LONNBERG, CHARLES MITCHELL, librarian; b. Jetmore, Kans., Nov. 1, 1926; s. Earl and Winnie May (Braddock) L.; B.S. in Music, Kans. State Tchrs. Coll., 1949, M.S. in Music, 1953; study in Rome, Italy, 1954; M.A. in L.S., Ind. U., 1964; m. Evelynne Dreger, Aug. 17, 1957; children—William Charles, Thomas Robert. Tchr. music Copeland (Kans.) High Sch., 1949-50; prof. music Anderson (Ind.) Coll., 1955-66, dir. Ednl. Research and Resource Center, dir. library services, 1966-69; librarian, prof. library sci. Ind. State U. at Evansville, 1969—. Active PTA, Friends of Willard Library. Bd. dirs. Anderson Fine Arts Center, 1966-69, Anderson Concert Series, 1962-69. Served with AUS, 1950-52. Mem. ALA, Ind. Library Assn., AAUP, Audubon Soc., Phi Mu Alpha Sinfonia, Sigma Tau Gamma. Methodist. Club: Musicians (Evansville). Home: Route 1 Box 315B Evansville IN 47712

LONNING, PHILIP EUGENE, clin. psychologist; b. Thor, Iowa, July 22, 1932; s. Lennie B. and Leone B. (Hanson) L.; B.A., U. No. Iowa, 1957; M.A., U. No. Colo., 1960; Ph.D., Iowa State U., 1969; m. Carole Ann Yohn, June 4, 1960; children—Elizabeth Ann, James Brian. Tchr. bus. edn., Garner, Iowa, 1957-59; high sch. guidance dir., Garner, 1959-62; guidance cons., Humboldt and Pocahontas Counties, Iowa, 1962-75; coordinator of consultants Area V Edn. Assn., Ft. Dodge, Iowa, 1975-76; clin. psychologist, Ft. Dodge, 1970—; vis. prof. Iowa State U., 1968, Drake U., 1971, Buena Vista Coll., 1977. Pres., Zion Luth. Ch., 1975-77; active Lions Club, 1960-70, Assn. for Crippled Children & Adults, 1970—. Mem. Am. Personnel and Guidance Assn., Iowa Psychol. Assn., Phi Delta Kappa. Republican. Lutheran. Home: 404 11th St SW Humboldt IA 50548 Office: 320 S 12th St Fort Dodge IA 50501

LONQUIST, BERTEL ARTHUR, mech. engr.; b. Chgo., Sept. 4, 1926; s. Arthur and Elizabeth (Huhta) L.; B.S. in M.E., Northwestern U., 1946; m. Leota Jean Gardner, Sept. 25, 1948; children—Gary Gardner, Nancy Jean. Jr. engr. Swift & Co., Chgo., 1946-47; engr. Shaw, Naess & Murphy, Chgo., 1947-49; project engr. Schmidt, Garden & Erikson, Chgo., 1949-71; v.p. Environ. Systems Design, Inc., Chgo., 1971—. Pres., Niles Twp High Sch. Booster Club, 1969. Served with USNR, 1944-46. Registered profl. engr., Ill., Wis., Ind., Pa., W.Va., Colo. Mem. Nat., Ill. socs. profl. engrs., Am. Soc. Heating, Refrigeration and Air Conditioning Engrs., Pi Tau Sigma. Lutheran (trustee 1960-63). Home: 2820 Dryden Ct Arlington Heights IL 60004 Office: 35 E Wacker Dr Chicago IL 60601

LOOFT, WALTER GENE, mech. engr.; b. Ottawa, Ill., Feb. 26, 1938; s. Henry Charles and Margery V. (Moss) L.; B.S. in Engring., Purdue U., 1960; m. Beverly Jean Milburn, June 7, 1959; children—Annette, Steven P., Mark A. Conveyor application engr. Chain Belt Co., Milw., 1961-63; bearing application engr. Rex Chainbelt Inc., Downers Grove, Ill., 1964-65, supr. design, 1966-68, mgr. engring., 1969-76, mgr. sales and engring., 1976—; head U.S. del. to Internat. Standards Orgn. meeting, Cologne, W.Ger., 1975, 76, mem. del., Moscow, 1977. Pres. Baseball Leagues, Lisle, Ill., 1973-75; sec. Lisle Sch. Bd., 1976, pres., 1977—; bd. dirs. YMCA, 1972-74. Registered profl. engr., Ill.; recipient Distinguished Vol. Service award Lisle Park Dist., 1973. Mem. Soc. Automotive Engrs., Am. Nat. Standards Inst. Presbyterian. Home: 5831 Queens Cove Lisle IL 60532 Office: 2400 Curtiss Ave Downers Grove IL 60515

LOOKER, JACK DEVON, retail exec.; b. Richmond, Ind., June 10, 1933; s. Harold Homer and Susie Elizabeth (Carter) L.; student Ind. Tech. Coll., 1956-57; m. Bernice Ann Frey, Apr. 28, 1962; 1 son, Shane Devon. Draftsman, Stamco, Inc., New Bremem, Ohio, 1957-60; sales engr. Scott Equipment Co., Dayton, Ohio, 1960-66; regional sales mgr. Manatrol div. Perry-Fay, Inc., Elyria, Ohio, 1966-70; owner, operator Nu-Hy Co., Indpls., 1970—, also pres. Vectrol, Inc., Indpls., 1973—. Served with USNR, 1951-55; Korea. Mem. Fluid Power Soc., Am. Def. Preparedness Assn. Mem. Ch. of the Brethren. Club: Heather Hills Country. Home and office: 2310 Herod Ct Indianapolis IN 46229

LOOMIS, CHARLES WAYNE, career planning service exec.; b. Madison County, Iowa, Mar. 17, 1940; s. Homer Hill and Wilma Lucille (McNichols) L.; B.A., Anderson Coll., 1962; M.Ed., Kent State U., 1967; m. Nancy Lynn Daft, Dec. 11, 1976. Vocat. rehab. counselor Ohio Bur. Vocat. Rehab., Dayton, 1963-64; dir. rehab. services Goodwill Industries & Rehab. Clinic, Canton, Ohio, 1966-69; pres. Career Devel. Center, Inc., Columbus, Ohio, 1969—, also chmn. bd. Chmn. bd. ARCraft of Franklin County (Ohio), program for mentally retarded, 1973-74. Served with AUS, 1962-63. Mem. Am., Ohio psychol. assns., Am. Personnel and Guidance Assn., Nat., Ohio (dir. 1973-76) rehab. assns., Bus. & Profl. Mens Assn. Office: 3100 Sullivant Ave Columbus OH 43204

LOOMIS, HOWARD KREY, banker; b. Omaha, Apr. 9, 1927; s. Arthur L. and Genevieve (Krey) L.; A.B., Cornell U., 1949, M.B.A., 1950; m. Florence Porter, Apr. 24, 1954; children—Arthur L. II, Frederick S., Howard Krey, John Porter. Mgmt. trainee Hallmark Cards, Inc., Kansas City, Mo., 1953-56; sec., controller Mine Service Co., Inc., Fort Smith, Arkansas, 1956-59; controller Electra Mfg. Co., Independence, Kans., 1959-63; v.p., dir. The Peoples Bank, Pratt, Kans., 1963-65, pres., dir., 1966—; pres., dir. Central States, Inc., Pratt, 1970-76; dir. Garland Coal & Mining Co., Ft. Smith, Ark. Pres. Cannonball Trail chpt. ARC. Bd. dirs. Kans. Devel. Credit Corp., Topeka. Served with AUS, 1950-52. Mem. Pratt Area C. of C. (past pres.), Kans. Assn. Commerce and Industry (dist. v.p.), Kans. Bankers Assn. (governing council), Fin. Execs. Inst., Sigma Delta Chi, Chi Psi. Republican. Presbyn. Elk, Rotarian. Club: Park Hills Country. Home: 502 Welton St Pratt KS 67124 Office: 222 S Main St Pratt KS 67124

LOOMIS, SALORA DALE, psychiatrist; b. Peru, Ind., Oct. 21, 1930; s. Salora Dale and Rhea Pearl (Davis) L.; A.B. in Zoology, Ind. U., 1953, M.S. in Human Anatomy, 1955, M.D., 1958; m. Carol Marie Davis, Jan. 3, 1959; children—Stephen Dale, Patricia Marie. Intern, Cook County Hosp., Chgo., 1958-59; resident psychiatry Logansport (Ind.) State Hosp., 1959-60, Ill. State Psychiat. Inst., Chgo., 1960-62; staff psychiatrist Katharine Wright Psychiat. Clinic, Chgo., 1962-65, dir., 1965—; cons. Ill. Youth Commn., 1962-64; asst. dir. Northwestern U. Psychiat. Clinics, Chgo., 1963-65; attending psychiatrist, also vice-chmn. dept. psychiatry St. Joseph Hosp., Chgo., 1964—; psychiat. cons. Ill. Dept. Pub. Health, 1967—; attending psychiatrist, also chmn. dept. psychiatry Ill. Masonic Med. Center, Chgo., 1970—. Instr. psychiatry Northwestern U. Med. Sch., Chgo., 1962-64, asso., 1964-67; lectr. psychiatry and neurology Loyola U. Med. Sch., Chgo., 1964-65, asso. 1965, asst. prof., 1965-73; asso. prof. psychiatry U. Ill. Coll. Medicine, Chgo., 1973—. Diplomate Am. Bd. Psychiatry and Neurology. Fellow Am. Coll. Psychiatrists, Am. Psychiat. Assn., Acad. Psychosomatic Medicine; mem. A.M.A., Ill. State (chmn. council on mental health and addiction 1974-75, chmn. joint peer rev. com. 1975—), Chgo. med. socs., Ill. Psychiat. Soc. (chmn. ethics com. 1974-75) Assn. Dirs. Ill. Gen. Hosp. Psy. Services (pres. 1977—). Home: 321 Franklin St Geneva IL 60134 Office: 700 N Michigan Av Chicago IL 60611 also 923 W Wellington Av Chicago IL 60657

LOOTS, ROBERT JAMES, lawyer; b. Havelock, Iowa, Mar. 6, 1931; s. John William and Anna Mary (Livingston) L.; B.A., U. Iowa, 1953, J.D., 1958; m. Mary Esther Ladd, June 28, 1954; children—James Mason, Margaret Mary, Catherine Ann. Admitted to Wis. bar, 1958, Iowa bar, 1959; practiced in Milw., 1958—; partner firm Gibbs, Roper, Loots & Williams, Milw., 1963—. Served with USNR, 1953-56. Mem. Am., Wis., Milw. bar assns., Order of Coif, Omicron Delta Kappa, Phi Delta Phi, Delta Tau Delta. Republican. Methodist. Club: University (Milw.). Editor Iowa Law Rev., 1957-58. Home: 9931 N Otto Rd 2W Mequon WI 53092 Office: 757 N Broadway Milwaukee WI 53202

LOPATA, HELENA ZNANIECKI, sociologist; b. Poznan, Poland, Oct. 1, 1925; d. Florian Witold and Eileen (Markley) Znaniecki; came to U.S., naturalized, 1946; B.A., U. Ill., 1946, M.A., 1947; Ph.D., U. Chgo., 1954; m. Richard Stefan Lopata, Feb. 8, 1946; children—Theodora Karen, Stefan Richard. Lectr., U. Va. extension, Langley AFB, 1951-52, DePaul U., Chgo., 1956-60; mem. faculty Roosevelt U., Chgo., 1950-69, asso. prof. sociology, 1967-69; prof. sociology Loyola U., Chgo., 1969-70, chmn. dept., 1970-72, dir. Center Comparative Study Social Roles, 1972—. Bd. dirs. Polish Acad. Arts and Scis. in Am., 1976—; exec. bd. Cana Conf., 1971-74. Mem. Mayor's council for Senior Citizens and the Handicapped, 1975—, on Manpower and Economic Advisors, 1975—; mem. nat. commn. on Families and Pub. Policies, 1977—. Research grantee Chgo. Tribune, 1956, Adminstrn. on Aging, 1967-69, Social Security Adminstrn., 1971—. Fellow Midwest Council Social Research on Aging (pres. 1968-70, postdoctoral tng. dir. 1971—), Am. Sociol. Assn. (chmn. sect. on family 1976, chmn. sect. sex roles 1975, Sorokin awards com. 1970-73, publ. com. 1972-73, nominations com. 1975-77), Soc. Study Social Problems (v.p. 1975 mem. C. Wright Mills awards com. 1976, chmn. 1977), Ill. Sociol. Assn. (pres. 1969-70); Gerontol. Soc.; mem. Internat. Geront. Soc., Nat. Council Family Relations, Midwest Sociol. Soc. (asso. editor quar. 1969-72, pres. 1975-76), Sociologists for Women in Soc. Author: Occupation: Housewife, 1971; Widowhood in an American City, 1972; Marriages and Families, 1973; Polish Americans: Status Competition in an Ethnic Community, 1976; Women As Widows, 1978; contbr. numerous articles to profl. jours. Editor: Research in the Interweave of Social Roles: Woman and Men, 1978. Address: Loyola Univ 6525 N Sheridan Rd Chicago IL 60626

LOPATA, RICHARD STEFAN, mgmt. cons.; b. Chgo., Nov. 30, 1925; s. Stefan Carl and Helen (Janus) L.; B.S. in Mktg., U. Ill., 1947, M.S. in Econs., 1948; Ph.D. Program Certificate in Philosophy, Northwestern U., 1964; m. Helena Znaniecki, Feb. 9, 1946; children—Stefan Richard, Theodora Karen. Instr. mktg. U. Ill., Urbana, 1947-48; instr. econs. and mktg. U. Mass., Amherst, 1948-49; sr. asso. Poetzinger, Dechert & Kielty, sales and mktg. firm, Chgo., 1949-51; asst. prof. econs. U. Va., Newport News, 1951-52; professorial lectr. mktg. DePaul U., Chgo., 1954-61; pres. Mktg. Mgmt., Inc., cons. firm, Chgo., 1957-59; v.p. McCann-Erickson Advt. Co., Chgo., 1959-61; pres. The Lopata Corp., cons. firm, Chgo., 1959-63; prin. A.T. Kearney & Co., Inc., cons. firm, Chgo., 1963-72; cons., investor Sam Assos. Inc., Chgo., 1972—; dir. Recording Dynamics, Inc., Nashville, 1974—; dir. Colo. Shelter Systems, Inc., Hayden, Colo., 1972—. Served with USMCR, 1942-44; as asst. comptroller Tactical Air Command, USAF, 1950-52. Mem. Am. Mktg. Assn., Am. Econ. Assn., Am. Arbitration Assn. (panel mem. 1973—), Alpha Delta Sigma, Chi Phi. Rotarian. Contbr. numerous articles in field to profl. jours. Home: 1017 Grove St Evanston IL 60201 Office: 30 W Washington St Chicago IL 60602

LO PATIN, LAWRENCE HAROLD, real estate exec.; b. Detroit, Sept. 20, 1925; s. Henry and Mary (Harelik) LoP.; LL.B., Wayne State U., 1950; m. Florence R. Grossman, Dec. 3, 1950; children—Mark, Norman. Founder, pres. L.H. LoPatin & Co., Detroit, 1959—; co-founder, chief financial officer Windsor Raceway Holdings, Inc., 1962-66; founder, pres. Capital Adv., Inc., Detroit, 1963—; founder, pres. Am. Raceways Inc. (formerly Mich. Internat. Speedway, Inc.), Detroit, 1967-70; founder, pres. Retail Site Selection Group; mem. staff Applied Mgmt. and Tech. Center, Wayne State U., 1971—; founder Surg. Centers Mich. Inc., 1976—; owner, operator Bagel Nosh of Mich., Inc., 1977—. Mem. Nat. Assn. Real Estate Bds., Internat. Council Shopping Centers, Am., Mich. land devel. assns., Urban Land Inst. Home: 28545 River Crest Dr Southfield MI 48075 Office: Suite 403 28333 Telegraph Rd Southfield MI 48076

LOPEZ, ALFONSO ASTRERO, JR., surgeon; b. Naga City, Philippines, Aug. 5, 1939; s. Alfonso Lopinto and Josefina (Astrero) L.; M.D., U. of East, 1963; m. Pazcelita Valeriano, Oct. 15, 1965; children—John Vincent, Julie Lisa, Alfonso, III. Intern, Edgewater Hosp., Chgo., 1965-66; resident in gen. surgery Ft. Howard VA Hosp., Balt., 1966-69, Saginaw (Mich.) Cooperative Hosps., Inc., 1969-71; surg. house physician Marymount Hosp., Cleve., 1971-72; practice medicine specializing in surgery Mercy Hosp., Benton Harbor, Mich., 1973—, vice chmn. dept. surgery, 1976-78, chmn. dept. surgery, 1978—; mem. staff Meml. Hosp., St. Joseph, Mich., 1973—. Diplomate Am. Bd. Surgery. Fellow ACP; mem. Soc. Abdominal Surgeons, AMA, Soc. Philippine Surgeons of Am. Home: 2833 Marilynn Dr Saint Joseph MI 49085 Office: 1901 Niles Ave Saint Joseph MI 49085

LOPEZ, ROBERT ANTHONY, librarian; b. Fayetteville, N.C., June 27, 1925; s. Anthony C. and Laura (Raynor) L.; student U. Fla., 1946-48; B.A. in Journalism, Emory U., 1950. Editor, New Smyrna (Fla.) Beach News, 1950-53; night supr. library Mpls. Star & Tribune Co., 1953-59; head librarian Mpls. Star & Tribune Co., 1959—. Served with USNR, 1942-46. Mem. Spl. Librarian Assn., Minn. Press Club, Sigma Delta Chi, Delta Tau Delta. Home: 4200 N 45th Ave Robbinsdale MN 55422 Office: 425 Portland Ave Minneapolis MN 55415

LOPEZ-DELGADO, VALENTIN, physician; b. Tuy, Spain, June 18, 1925; s. Pablo and Jacinta (Delgado Martin) Lopez Blanco; M.D., U. Valladolid, Spain, 1953; m. Margaret Leone (Hutchinson), July 29, 1966; children—David-James, Margot-Pilar. Family physician, Badajoz, Spain, 1953-54; intern Brantford (Ont., Can.) Gen. Hosp., 1959-61; hosp. med. officer St. Joseph's Hosp., Hamilton, Ont., 1961-64; anesthesia tng., Hamilton Gen. Hosp., also Wellesley Gen. Hosp. (both Ont.), 1964-68; pvt. practice ltd. to anesthesia, Spain, 1969-71, St. Thomas-Elgin Gen. Hosp., St. Thomas, Ont., 1971—. Served as med. lt., Spanish Army, 1954-59. Roman Catholic. Club: Rotary. Home: 22 Applewood Crescent St Thomas ON N5R 1H2 Canada

L'ORANGE, FINN FAYE, dentist; b. Phila., May 20, 1911; s. Otto Henrik and Anne A'Munda (Gabrielsen) L.; D.D.S., Western Reserve U., 1938; m. Margaret Elizabeth Hickson, Nov. 25, 1937; children—Mundalea (Mrs. Donald F. Lindow), Deborah Karen, Martha Jane, John Otto II. Intern, St. Luke's Hosp., Cleve., 1938-39; pvt. practice dentistry, Cleve., 1939—; mem. asso. dental staff surgeon St. Luke's Hosp., 1939-77; clin. instr. prosthodontia Case Western Reserve U. Dental Sch., 1970—. Served to lt. col. AUS, 1942-46, 61-62. Fellow Acad. Gen. Dentistry; mem. Pierre Fauchard Acad., Acad. Gen. Dentistry, Am., Ohio dental assns., Ohio State (pres. 1956-58), Cleve. (pres. 1955-56) socs. dentistry for children, Cleve. Dental Soc., Cleve. Acad. Dental Studies, Delta Sigma Delta. Republican. Methodist. Home: 2665 Endicott Rd Shaker Heights OH 44120 Office: 11811 Shaker Blvd Cleveland OH 44120

LORANTH, LESLIE Z., librarian; b. Celldomolk, Hungary, Feb. 4, 1929; s. Julius and Margaret (Grof) L.; diploma Eotvos Lorand U. Budapest, 1947-53, student Sch. Polit. Econs., 1947-48; M.S. in L.S., Western Res. U., 1967, postgrad. Case Western Res. U., 1968-69; m. Alice Nagypataky, Apr. 17, 1954; 1 dau., Kinga. Came to U.S., 1957, naturalized, 1963. Lexicographer, Hungarian Nat. Acad. Sci., Budapest, 1953-56; tchr. Corvin Matyas High Sch., Budapest, 1952-56; librarian Millis Sci. Center Western Res. U., Cleve., 1966-67; head librarian Lorain County Community Coll., Elyria, Ohio 1968-75, dir. library and instructional media, 1976—. Mem. A.L.A., Ohio Library Assn. Home: 378 Bradley Rd Bay Village OH 44140 Office: 1005 N Abbe Rd Elyria OH 44035

LORD, JAMES LAWRENCE, ednl. exec.; b. Peoria, Ill., June 20, 1915; s. Joseph and Ellen Cecelia (Driscoll) L.; B.S., St. Louis U., 1950; m. Dorothy Marie Boble, Sept. 27, 1944; children—James L., Terence G., Michael J., Christine Marie, Thomas A. Dir. devel. St. Vincent's Hosp., St. Louis, 1955-67; provincial cons. Western Province Daus. Charity St. Vincent de Paul, St. Louis, 1967-73; dir. devel. De Paul Community Health Center, St. Louis, 1973-76; dir. devel. Cardinal Newman Coll., 1976—. Ambassador, United Fund, 1964-67. Served with AUS, 1942-46. Mem. Hosp. Assn. Met. St. Louis (chmn. pub. relations com. 1960-62), Nat. Assn. Pvt. Psychiatric Hosps., St. Louis U. Arts and Sci. Alumni (pres. 1957), Acad. Hosp. Pub. Relations, Nat. Assn. Hosp. Devel., St. Louis Press Club, St. Andrew's Soc. Roman Catholic (extraordinary minister 1971—). Club: Norwood Hills Country (St. Louis). Home: 4128 Ammann Ln Northwoods MO 63121 Office: 7701 Florissant Rd St Louis MO 63121

LORD, WILLIAM HERMAN, theatre cons.; b. Providence, Feb. 28, 1931; s. Herman Maurice and Gertrude (Thompson) L.; B.A., U. Evansville (Ind.), 1953; M.A., Northwestern U., 1961; m. Catherine Lynn Ball, Sept. 14, 1957; children—Jennifer Lynn, Louise Giovanna. Lighting dir. Bosse (Ind.) High Sch., 1947-49, Evansville (Ind.) Community Players, 1947-53, also tech. dir. Evansville Coll. Theatre, 1950-53; with R.H.M. Stage Equipment Co., Indpls., 1955-57; scenic carpenter WFBM-TV, Indpls., 1957-58; tchr. speech and tech. theater, also prodn. supr. sch. theatre No. Central High Sch., Indpls., 1958—; owner, pres., dir. Theater Assos., Inc., Indpls., 1957—; owner William H. Lord theatre cons., Indpls., 1961—. Bd. dirs. Footlite Musicals Co., Indpls., 1958-60. Served with AUS, 1953-55. Decorated Am. Spirit Honor medal. Mem. Ind. State Tchrs. Assn., U.S. Inst. Theatre Tech., Ind. Speech Assn., Speech Communications Assn., Am. Theatre Assn., Illuminating Engrs. Soc. (mem. com. theatre, television and film lighting), Conservation Specifications Inst., Alpha Psi Omega, Pi Delta Epsilon, Tau Kappa Alpha, Lambda Chi Alpha. Presbyn. (elder 1971-73). Author: Installing a Theatre Lighting System, 1977. Contbr. series of articles on stage lighting to Dramatics Mag., 1970-71. Home: 9210 N College Ave Indianapolis IN 46240

LORE, IRVING ALLAN, lawyer; b. Milw., Feb. 28, 1916; s. Michael and Jean (Dinerstein) L.; B.A., U. Wis., 1935; J.D. (Burr W. Jones law scholar), 1937; m. Clarissa Lerner, Feb. 4, 1940; children—Nancy (Mrs. Stephen E. Einhorn), Eileen (Mrs. Fred G. Gosman). Fellow, Office Atty. Gen. Wis., Madison, 1936-37; admitted to Wis. bar, 1937, U.S. Supreme Ct. bar, 1942; practiced in Milw., 1937—; counsel Wis. Hotel Industry in Labor Mgmt. Relations, Milw., 1947—. Bd. dirs. Wisconsin Hotel-Motel-Resort Assn., Greater Milw. Hotel-Motel Assn.; mem. employee relations com. Am. Hotel-Motel Assn. Mem. Milw. Devel. Group; chmn. Community Chest Drive hotel div.; chmn. profl. div. United Fund Campaigns, 1971, 72. Bd. dirs. United Way of Greater of Milw., Inc., Milw. Found., Milw. Jewish Community Center; mem. Greater Milw. Com.; bd. dirs. Milw. Jewish Fedn., Nat. Jewish Welfare Bd. Nat. Council, Am. Jewish Joint Distbn. Com. Milw. Sch. Engring. trustee Walter Schroeder Scholarship Fund, Marquette U.; mgmt. trustee Milw. Hotel Industry Health and Welfare Trust Fund; bd. dirs. Milw. Jewish Home for the Aged; trustee Mt. Sinai Med. Center. Served to lt. (j.g.) USNR, 1943-45. Mem. Am., Wis. (labor relations com.), Milw. (labor law com.) bar assns., Assn. Trial Lawyers Am., Wis. Acad. Trial Lawyers, U. Wis. Alumni Assn., Wis. Law Sch. Alumni Assn., Milw. Assn. Commerce (bd. dirs.), Am. Judicature Soc., Milw. Downtown Assn. (dir.), Wis. State C. of C. (labor relations com.), Artus, Order of Coif. Jewish (dir. and trustee congregation). Mason (32 deg. Shriner). Club: Milw. Athletic. Editor: Wis. Law Rev., 1935-37; also numerous articles in field to law revs. Home: 1610 N Prospect Ave Milwaukee WI 53202 Office: 161 W Wisconsin Ave Milwaukee WI 53203

LORENZEN, GEORGE ARTHUR, motor transp. co. exec.; b. Davenport, Iowa, May 6, 1927; s. Arthur Henry and Clara Katherine (Dohrn) L.; B.S., Iowa State U., 1950; m. Marilyn Purcell, June 20, 1953; children—James A.; Jeffrey G., Scott D., Nancy A. Payroll clk. Dohrn Transfer Co., Rock Island, Ill., 1950-53, asst. operations supt.; 1953-56, sec., 1956-63, exec. v.p., sec., 1963-70, pres., 1970—; dir. First Nat. Bank, Rock Island, Ill., 1970—. Sec.-treas. Salvation Army, Davenport, 1966-68, bd. dirs., 1963—; bd. dirs. United Community Services, Davenport, 1970-73; trustee Dohrn Found., Davenport Rotary scholarship Trust, 1971-73. Served with USNR, 1945-46, AUS, 1951-52. Mem. Am. Trucking Assn. (bd. govs. 1964—), Ill. C. of C. (dir. 1972—, exec. com. 1972—, regional v.p. 1976), United Indsl. Council (dir. 1973—), Iowa Motor Truck Assn. (dir. 1975—), Beta Theta Pi. Republican. Episcopalian (vestryman 1962-74, sr. warden 1974—). Clubs: Davenport Country (pres. 1968-69); Davenport Outing; Crow Valley Country; Lindsey Boat. Home: 2738 Elm St Davenport IA 52803 Office: 4016 9th St Rock Island IL 61201

LORGE, GERALD DAVID, lawyer, state senator; b. Bear Creek, Wis., July 9, 1922; s. Joseph J. and Anna M. (Peterson) L.; J.D., Marquette U., 1952; m. Christina C. Ziegler, Apr. 15, 1958; children—Robert G., William D., Anna Marie, Julie Agnes. Admitted to Wis. bar, 1952; gen. practice, Bear Creek, 1951—; mem. Wis. Gen. Assembly, 1951-54, Wis. Senate, 1954—, past chmn. com. on committees, past chmn. com. on judiciary and ins., past mem. com. on interstate co-operation, past mem. com. on legislative procedure, now mem. Com. on Audit, Ins. Laws Revisions. Mem. Wis. Legis. Council, Interstate Coop., past chmn. Justice and Law Enforcement Study com. Midwestern Council Govts., also past mem. jud. council; mem. ins. laws rev. com. Served with USMCR, 1942-45. Mem. Am., Wis., Outagamie bar assns., Nat. Conf. Ins. Legislators (dir. 1971-73, pres. 1973), Am. Legion. Republican. K.C. Clubs: Bear Creek, Outagame Conservative. Home: Route 1 Bear Creek WI 54922 Office: PO Box 47 Bear Creek WI 54922 also Room 337 S State Capitol Madison WI 53702

LORMAN, MILTON, state legislator, scrap processing co. exec.; b. Fort Atkinson, Wis., July 27, 1927; s. Louis R. and Clara (Walach) L.; B.B.A., U. Wis., 1950, J.D., 1953; m. Barbara Kailin, Feb. 1, 1953; children—Carol, William, David. Operations mgr. Lorman Iron & Metal Co., Inc., Fort Atkinson, Wis., 1953-63, pres., 1968—; mem. Wis. Assembly from 39th Dist. Municipal judge City of Fort Atkinson, Wis., 1960—; asst. dist. atty. Jefferson County, Wis., 1954-56. Mem. sch. bd., Fort Atkinson, Wis., 1968—; mem. bd. Sinnissippi Council, Boy Scouts Am., Fort Atkinson, Wis., 1974—; mem. S.Central Wis. Criminal Justice Planning Council, 1971—, v.p., 1975—; pres. City of Fort Atkinson (Wis.) Band, 1965, ARC, Fort Atkinson, Wis., 1957. Chmn. bd. dirs. Milw. Symphony Fort Atkinson area Concert Assn., 1971-73; chmn., v.p. Madison Jewish Welfare Council, 1972. Served with USNR, 1945-46. Recipient Jr. C. of C. Man of the Year award, 1958; Distinguished Service award, Fort Atkinson Lions Club, 1973; Employer of the year award, Jefferson County Assn. Retarded Children, 1973. Mem. Wis. Mfrs. Assn., Am., Wis., Jefferson County bar assns., Wis. Municipal Justice Assn., Am. Judicature Soc., Am. Legion, Inst. Scrap Iron and Steel (v.p. 1974-75, pres. 1976-77), Nat. Assn. Recycling Industries, Fort Atkinson High Sch. Alumni Assn. (pres. 1958), U. Wis. Alumni Assn. (chpt. pres. 1968), Train Collectors Assn., Antique Automob'le Club Am., Nat. Model Railroaders Assn., Classic Automobile Club Am., Model A Restorers Club. Mason (Shriner), Lion, K.P. Home: 712 Frederick St Fort Atkinson WI 53538 Office: 115 Lorman St Fort Atkinson WI 53538

LORNITZO, FRANK ADAM, biochemist; b. N.Y.C., Dec. 18, 1926; s. Frank Charles and Ella Marie (Krupicka) L.; student Antioch Coll., 1944-46; B.S., U. R.I., 1955; M.S., U. Wis., 1956, M.S. in Philosophy, 1958; m. Elizabeth Mary Colwell, July 12, 1958; children—Steven Frank, Morris Frederick, Hannah Jan. Research chemist Tb research lab. VA Hosp., Enzyme Inst. U. Wis., Madison, 1958-72; research chemist Lipid Metabolism Lab. VA Hosp., Madison, 1972—. Mem. Am. Chem. Soc., Am. Soc. Cell Biology, N.Y. Acad. Sci., Am. Soc. Microbiology, Sigma Xi. Mem. Soc. Friends. Contbr. articles to profl. jours. Patentee in field. Home: 705 Riverside Dr Madison WI 53704 Office: VA Hosp Overlook Terr Madison WI 53705

LORTON, STEPHEN GREGORY, film producer/writer; b. Whitehall, Ill., Dec. 11, 1937; s. William Jess and Margaret Louise (Mitchell) L.; m. Betsy James Sloan, July 13, 1974; B.S., So. Ill. U., 1959. Reporter, Radio Sta. WICC, Bridgeport, Conn., 1962-63; editor New York Times, 1963-70; editorial writer, spokesman NBC (WKYC-TV), Cleve., 1970-74, documentary film writer, producer, 1974—. Trustee, Not Alone, Inc. Mem. Nat. Acad. Television Arts and Scis. (Emmy award 1976), Cleve. Press Club. Recipient Gold plaque Chgo. Internat. Film Festival, 1975, 76, Outstanding Television Program award Nat. Assn. Television Program Execs., 1976, Gold medal V.I. Film Festival, 1976; named Outstanding Young Man, Cleve. Area Jr. C. of C., 1973. Home: 27900 N Woodland Rd Pepper Pike OH 44124 Office: 1403 E 6th St Cleveland OH 44114

LO SASSO, ALVIN MICHAEL, physician; b. Vandergrift, Pa., May 17, 1936; s. Alvin M. and Rose (Pagano) L.; B.S., Duke U., 1958; M.D., Ohio State U., 1963; M.S. in Pharmacology, Ind. U., 1967; m. Anita Gore, Sept. 9, 1967; children—Michael, Laura. Intern Ind. U. Med. Center, Indpls., 1963-64, resident in anesthesiology 1964-67, asst. prof. anesthesiology, 1967-71, asso. prof., 1971—, cons. intensive care units, 1967—, med. dir. respiratory therapy, 1967—. Mem. Am., Ind. socs. anesthesiologists, Internat. Anesthesia Research Soc., Marion County Med. Assn., Indpls. Soc. Anesthesiologists. Home: Box 89-6 Route 3 Zionsville IN 46077 Office: 1100 W Michigan St Indianapolis IN 46202

LOSSE, CARL HERBERT, librarian; b. Milw., Feb. 7, 1914; s. Herbert Alfred and Lydia Agnes (Ulbricht) L.; B. Ed., Milw. State Tchrs. Coll., 1936; M.S. in L.S., Case Western Res. U., 1953; m. Arlyle Mansfield, Jan. 20, 1962. With Milw. Pub. Library System, 1937-77, spl. services reference librarian, 1953-77. Mem. ALA, Spl. Libraries Assn., Arlis/NA, Internat. Platform Assn., Am. Philatelic Soc., Soc. Philatelic Ams., Royal Arcanum, DeMolay (mem. adv. bd. 1954—), Great Books Discussion Groups (leader 1963-64). Presbyterian (tchr.; treas.; library cons., deacon 1973—). Mason (K.T., 32 deg., Shriner). Clubs: Temple Stamp (Milw.); Masonic Stamp (N.Y.C.). Contbr. articles to Masonic mags. Home: 4124 W Fond du Lac Ave Apt 6 Milwaukee WI 53216

LOTHE, INGEBORG OLINA VLKEN (MRS. IRVIN EUGENE LOTHE), club woman; b. Spring Prairie, Wis., Sept. 16, 1915; d. Jens and Helga (Midthun) Vlken; student pub. schs.; m. Irvin Eugene Lothe, June 16, 1938; 1 dau., Jean Marie. Pvt. sec., cashier Great No. Life Ins. Co., Madison, Wis., 1935-38. Pres. Poynette (Wis.) Woman's Club, 1954-56, rec. sec., 1963-64; sec. Columbia County (Wis.) Fedn. Women's Clubs, 1956-58; 1st v.p. 2d Dist. Fedn. Women's Clubs, 1957-58, pres., 1958-60; state corr. sec. Wis. Fedn. Women's Clubs, 1960-62, rec. sec., 1964-66, 2d v.p., 1966-68, 1st v.p., 1968-70, pres., 1970-72, rep. joint com. edn., 1962—, also chmn. mem. revisions com., 1964-66, mem. resolutions com., 1966-68; chmn. Gen. Fedn. Women's Clubs, 1972-74, 2d v.p. Miss. Valley conf., 1972-74, 1st v.p. Gt. Lakes conf., 1974—, nat. conservation chmn., 1974-78; state treas. Wis. Assn. Am. Council for Better Broadcasts, 1960-63; mem. bd. control Coop. Ednl. Service Agy. No. 12 in Wis., 1965-67; sec. Columbia County Coll. Bd., 1965-71 Dist. bd. mem. Blackhawk Council, Girl Scouts U.S.A., Madison, 1954-57; local solicitor ARC, 1965; bd. dirs. Joint Com. Edn., chmn., 1969-71; mem. State com. Farm and City Council, 1971—; adv. cons. Environment Wis., 1972-73; dir. Joint Com. on Edn. Wis., 1972-73; adv. council Wis. MacKenzie Environ. Center, 1975—. Clk. Bd. Edn., Poynette, Wis., 1953-67; mem. People to People. Trustee Greater Wis. Found., 1971-73, Columbia County Home and Farm Bd., 1975—; bd. dirs. Crusade for Cleaner Environment, Wis. Youth Symphony Orch., 1975—. Mem. Nat., Wis. assns. parliamentarians, Am. Council Better Broadcasts, Nat., Wis. congresses parents and tchrs. Home: 204 E Washington St Poynette WI 53955

LOTHRINGER, ROBERT ALAN, banker; b. Davenport, Iowa, Dec. 25, 1923; s. Alfred Otto and Emma Christine (Schunter) L.; B.S.C., U. Iowa, 1947; m. Dorothy Rose Walter, June 27, 1948 (dec. Dec. 1970); children—Ann Christine, Peter Alan, Sarah Ellen; m. 2d, Matilda Krysa, June 10, 1972. Asst. mgr. wholesale dept. Sheaffer Pen Co., Ft. Madison, Iowa, 1947-48; teller City Nat. Bank, Clinton, Iowa, 1948-51; asst. sec.-treas. Clinton Fed. Savs. and Loan, 1951-60; pres., chief exec. officer Clinton Nat. Bank, 1960-74; exec. v.p. First Nat. Bank Muscatine, 1974—, also dir.; dir. Midwest Data Processing, Inc.; dir. Clinton Devel. Co. Mem. Clinton Community Sch. Bd., 1959-74; mem. budget com. United Way Muscatine; v.p. Illowa council Boy Scouts Am. Bd. dirs. Mercy Hosp., Clinton, Sharar Found. for Clinton Community Coll., Clinton, YMCA. Recipient Silver Beaver award Boy Scouts Am., 1965. Mem. Beta Theta Pi, Delta Sigma Pi. Republican. Lutheran (past pres. ch. council). Kiwanian, Rotarian. Home: 703 Sunrise Circle Muscatine IA 52761 Office: First National Bank Muscatine IA 52761

LOTITO, FRANK G., ins. co. exec.; b. Chgo., Nov. 23, 1909; s. James and Angeline (Lotito) L.; student Loyola U. night sch., 1931-37; m. Hilda A. Coteus, May 26, 1938; children—John F., Janice E. Agt., Lincoln Nat. Life Ins. Co., Chgo., 1939-47, gen. agt., 1952-74, sr. v.p., 1974—; asst. mgr. Prudential Ins. Co., Chgo., 1947-52. Chmn. Am. Cancer Soc., Skokie, Ill., 1966. Mem. Life Agy. Mgrs. Chgo. (sec. treas., pres. 1959-60), Chgo. Assn. Life Underwriters, (dir. 1959-61), Chgo. Estate Planning Council, Life Agy. Mgrs. K.C. (grand knight Skokie council 1957-59). Home: 8033 Kostner St Skokie IL 60076 Office: 10 S Riverside Plaza Chicago IL 60606

LOTTES, JOHN WILLIAM, coll. pres.; b. Mpls., Apr. 8, 1934; s. Otto Herman and Edith (Wittkopf) L.; A.A., Concordia Coll., St. Paul, 1953; B.F.A., Mpls. Sch. Art, 1960; postgrad. U. Iowa, 1967; m. Nancy Judith Sawyer, Apr. 27, 1957; children—John Erich, Andrew Charles, Rachel Lee. Dean coll., registrar Kansas City (Mo.) Art Inst., 1966-68; dir. planning and devel. Corcoran Gallery and Sch. Art, Washington, 1968-69; asst. to pres. acad. affairs Calif. Coll. Arts Crafts, Oakland, 1969-70; pres. Kansas City Art Inst., 1970—. Chmn. bd. dirs. Union Ind. Colls. Art, 1977—, Kansas City Regional Council Higher Edn., 1976—; v.p. bd. dirs. Nat. Assn. Schs. Art, 1976—, City of Fountains Found., 1974—; mem. Internat. Relations Council Kansas City, 1970—. Home: 6108 Morningside Dr Kansas City MO 64113 Office: 4415 Warwick Blvd Kansas City MO 64111

LOTZ, HERBERT KARL, psychologist; b. Guenterod, Germany, Mar. 14, 1920; s. Karl and Maria Elisabeth (Hehl) L.; came to U.S., 1929, naturalized, 1944; student Drake U., 1938-39; B.S., Iowa State U., 1942; M.A., U. Iowa, 1947; postgrad. U. Wash., 1949-50; m. Janet Sladden Howell, May 29, 1948; children—Kathryn Ann, Steven Karl, Richard Paul, William Howell. Jr. psychologist Iowa Dept. Social Welfare, 1946-49, sr. psychologist, 1951-53; area psychologist Ill. Office Pub. Instruction, 1954-56, chief area psychologist, 1956-63; psychologist Henry County Coop. for Psychol. Services, 1963-69; chief psychologist Henry-Stark Counties Spl. Edn. Coop., Kewanee, Ill., 1969—; pvt. practice psychology, Galesburg, Ill., 1955—; contract psychologist Ill. Div. Vocat. Rehab., 1963—; cons. Fed. Disability Program, 1964—, Positive Attitudes, Inc., 1975-76; mem. psychologist exam. com. State Ill. Dept. Registration and Edn., 1976—. Bd. dirs. Positive Attitudes, Inc., 1969-75. Served with U.S. Army, 1943-46. Diplomate in sch. psychology Am. Bd. Profl. Psychology; listed Nat. Register Health Providers in Psychology Mem. ACLU (treas. Western Ill. chpt. 1973—), AAAS, Am. Orthopsychiat. Assn., Am. Assn. Mental Deficiency, Council Exceptional Children, Am., Ill. (treas. 1977—) psychol. assns. Mem. Soc. of Friends. Club: Rotary (Cambridge, Ill.). Home: 220 N Chambers St Galesburg IL 61401 Office: PO Box 597 600 N Lexington St Kewanee IL 61443

LOTZ, JANET HOWELL, psychologist; b. Springfield, Ohio, June 4, 1923; d. Folger Branson and Catherine Sladden (Tordt) Howell; student Earlham Coll., 1941-43; B.A., U. Iowa, 1945, M.A., 1948; m. Herbert Karl Lotz, May 29, 1948; children—Kathryn A., Steven K., Richard P., William H. Jr. psychologist Div. Child Welfare, State of Iowa, 1947-49; psychologist Knox-Warren Spl. Edn. Dist., Galesburg, Ill., 1964—, intern supr., 1968-70; psychologist Warren Achievement Sch., Monmouth, Ill., 1972-73; individual practice, Galesburg, 1962—; cons. psychologist Headstart Program, Galesburg. Mem. Am. (asso.), Ill. psychol. assns. Democrat. Quaker. Home: 1018 S Farnham Galesburg IL 61401 Office: 531 Oak St Galesburg IL 61401

LOUDEN, JONATHAN ERNST, librarian; b. Painesville, Ohio, Feb. 12, 1942; s. Eugene Belat and Carol Elaine (Cook) L.; B.S., Defiance Coll., 1965; M.S.L., Western Mich. U., 1966; m. Beverly June Yarnell, Sept. 3, 1963; children—Amy Orcelia, William Eugene, Jennifer Jean. Bookmobile librarian State Library Ohio, 1962-65, supr. bookmobiles, Napoleon, 1966-67, instl. cons., 1967-68; dir. Gallia County (Ohio) Dist. Library, 1968-77; joint dir. Gallia County Dist. Library, 1971—; chmn. Ohio Valley Regional Film Circuit, 1971—; owner The Alcove, Gallipolis, Ohio, 1973—. Mem. Ohio Library Assn. Rotarian. Home: Route 1 Thurman OH 45685 Office: 3d and State Sts Gallipolis OH 45631

LOUDENBACK, LYNN JOSEPH, mktg. specialist; b. Wenatchee, Wash., Sept. 3, 1936; s. Everett Charles and Ida Pearl (Coons) L.; B.A., Wash. State U., 1958; M.B.A., U. Wash., 1963, Ph.D., 1969; children—Ross Cameron, Aaron Christian. Asst. prof. mktg. U. Nebr., Lincoln, 1967-72, asso. prof., 1972-75; prof. mktg., chmn. dept. indsl. adminstrn. Iowa State U., Ames, 1975—; vis. prof. U. Queensland, Brisbane, Australia, summer 1973; cons. various fgn. and domestic firms. Mem. Am. (dir. 1973-75), So. mktg. assns. Author: Anthology of Practical Marketing, 1976; contbr. articles in field to profl. jours. Office: Dept Indsl Adminstrn Iowa State U Ames IA 50011

LOUDON, ROY VIRGIL, JR., univ. ofcl.; b. Shelby, N.C., Aug. 19, 1924; s. Roy Virgil and Nellie Veronica (Dailey) L.; B.S., U. Nebr., 1950, M.A., 1953, Ed.D., 1967; m. Elizabeth Louise Willie, Feb. 14, 1947; children—Catherine Loudon Williams, Michael Roy, John Louis, Timothy Dale, Joseph Paul, Lee Stephen. Ins. agt. Allstate Ins. Co., Lincoln, Nebr., 1953-55; ins. and retirement officer U. Nebr., Lincoln, 1955-57, dir. personnel, 1957-77, adminstr. personnel and risk mgmt., 1977—. Risk mgmt. cons. Mem. Lincoln Catholic Sch. Bd., 1969-73, pres., 1971-73; mem. Lincoln Charter Revision Com., 1968-72; mem. Gov.'s Com. Implementation State Employees Collective Bargaining Act, 1969. Served with USAAF, 1942-46. Mem. Univ. Ins. Mgrs. Assn. (dir. 1970-73), Am. Soc. Ins. Mgmt. (sec. 1973, v.p. 1974, pres. 1975), Coll. and Univ. Personnel Assn., Am. Legion. Home: 635 S 36th St Lincoln NE 68510 Office: Adminstrn Bldg U Nebr Lincoln NE 68508

LOURENCO, RUY VALENTIM, physician, educator; b. Lisbon, Portugal, Mar. 25, 1929; s. Raul Valentim and Maria Amalia (Gomes-Rosa) L.; came to U.S., 1959, naturalized, 1966; B.S., U. Lisbon, Portugal, 1947, M.D., 1951; m. Susan Jane Loewenthal, Jan. 18, 1960; children—Peter Edward, Margaret Philippa. Intern, Lisbon U. Hosp., 1951-53, resident internal medicine, 1953-55, instr., 1955-59; fellow dept. medicine Columbia-Presbyn. Med. Center, N.Y.C., 1959-63; asst. prof. medicine N.J. Coll. Medicine, Jersey City, 1963-66, asso. prof., 1966-67; attending physician, also dir. respiratory physiology lab. Jersey City Med. Center, 1963-67; asso. prof. medicine and physiology U. Ill. Coll. Medicine Chgo., 1967-69, prof., 1969—; dir. respiratory research lab. Hektoen Inst., Chgo., 1967-70; dir. pulmonary medicine Cook County Hosp., Chgo., 1969-70; dir. pulmonary sect. and labs. U. Ill. Med. Center, Chgo., 1970-77, physician in chief, 1977—; chmn. dept. medicine U. Ill. Abraham Lincoln Sch. Medicine, 1977—. Cons. task force on research in respiratory diseases NIH, 1972, mem. study sect., 1972-76, mem. review bd. for Spl. Centers of Research program, 1974; cons. career devel. program VA, 1972—; mem. Nat. Com. Review Sci. Basis of Inhalation Therapy, 1973-74. Bd. dirs. Chgo. Lung Assn., 1974—. Fellow Am. Coll. Chest Physicians (pres. Ill. chpt. 1974-75); mem. Am. Fedn. Clin. Research, Am. Physiol. Soc., Am. Soc. Clin. Investigation, Am. Thoracic Soc. (chmn. sci. assembly 1974-75), Central Soc. Clin. Research (councillor 1973—), Soc. Exptl. Biology and Medicine, Sigma Xi. Editorial bd. Jour. Lab. and Clin. Medicine, 1973—. Contbr. numerous articles on pulmonary diseases, respiratory physiology and biochemistry to profl. jours. Home: 417 Sunset Ln Glencoe IL 60022 Office: 840 S Wood St Chicago IL 60612

LOUSBERG, PETER HERMAN, lawyer; b. Des Moines, Aug. 19, 1931; s. Peter J. and Ottilia M. (Vogel) L.; A.B., Yale, 1953; J.D. cum laude, U. Notre Dame, 1956; m. JoAnn Beimer, Jan. 20, 1962; children—Macara Lynn, Mark, Stephen. Admitted to Ill. bar, 1956, Fla. bar, 1972; clk. Ill. Appellate Ct., 1956-57; asst. states atty. Rock Island County, Ill., 1959-60; partner firm Klockau, McCarthy, Lousberg, Ellison & Rinden, Rock Island, Ill., 1960—. Opinion commentator radio sta., WHBF, 1973-74; lectr. Ill. Inst. Continuing Edn., Ill. Trial Lawyers seminars. Chmn. crime and juvenile delinquency Rock Island Model Cities Task Force, 1969; chmn. Rock Island Youth Guidance Council, 1964-69; adv. bd. Ill. Dept. Corrections Juvenile Div., 1976—; Ill. commr. Nat. Conf. Commrs. Uniform State Laws, 1976—; treas. Greater Quad City Close-up Program, 1976-77. Bd. dirs. Rock Island Indsl.-Comml. Devel. Corp., 1977—; bd. govs. Rock Island Community Found., 1977—. Served to 1st lt., USMC, 1957-59. Fellow Am. Bar Found.; mem. Am., Ill. (past gov. 1969-74, chmn. spl. survey com. 1974-75), Rock Island bar assns., Rock Island C. of C. (treas. 1975, 2d v.p. 1976, 1st v.p. 1977), Am., Ill. (bd. mgrs. 1974—) trial lawyers assns., Am. Judicature Soc., Nat. Legal Aid and Defenders Assn. (chmn. membership campaigns for Ill. 1969-71, for Midwest dist. 2 1974-75), U.S. Power Squadron. Roman Catholic. Rotarian. Clubs: Notre Dame, Quad Cities (Rock Island). Contbr. articles to profl. jours. Home: 2704 27th St Rock Island IL 61201 Office: 1808 3d Ave Rock Island IL 61201

LOUTHAN, WILLIAM CARL, educator; b. Akron, Ohio, Mar. 6, 1943; s. Harvey Forest and Dorothy Grace (Wegmiller) L.; B.A. with distinction, Ohio State U., 1965, M.A., 1967, Ph.D., 1970; m. Leslie Lee Koons, Sept. 10, 1966; children—Lauren Stephanie, Mark Alan. Grad. research asso. Ohio State U., Columbus, 1968-69, grad. teaching asso., 1969-70; asst. prof. govt. and pub. adminstrn. Am. U., Washington, 1970-72, acad. dir. Washington semester program, 1971-72; asst. prof. politics and govt. Ohio Wesleyan U., Delaware, 1972-74, acting chmn. dept., 1973, 75, asso. prof., 1975—, dean acad. affairs, 1977—; co-dir. Midwest Inst. Social Research, 1976—. NDEA fellow, 1968-70. Mem. Law and Soc. Assn., Policy Studies Orgn., Am., Midwest, So. polit. sci. assns., Ohio Assn. Polit. Scientists and Economists, Phi Beta Kappa, Pi Sigma Alpha, Phi Eta Sigma. Kiwanian. Author: Republicans and Democrats: Similarities and Differences, 1974; The Politics of Justice, 1977. Asso. editor Electionews, 1971-72. Contbr. articles to profl. jours. Home: 653 Presidential Way Delaware OH 43015

LOVAN, OWEN LEE, paper co. exec.; b. Salina, Kans., Oct. 30, 1922; s. Owen L. and Myra (Rhodes) L.; B.S., U. Nebr., 1948; m. Mary Patricia Tomlinson, Dec. 27, 1957; children—Victor, Andrew. Buyer, Hall Bros., Inc., Kansas City, Mo., 1948-50; sales rep. Wertgame Paper Co., Kansas City, Mo., 1951-55, div. sales mgr., Wichita, Kans., 1955-58; partner Liberty Paper Co., Wichita, 1958-59, pres., 1959—. Served with USAAF, 1942-45; lt. col. USAF Res., ret. Mem. Wichita Area C. of C., Res. Officers Assn. (past pres. dep. Kans.), Sigme Alpha Epsilon. Clubs: Wichita, Lancers, Mason, Kiwanis (pres. North Wichita Club). Contbr. articles to trade publs. Home 2 Sequoia St Wichita KS 67206 Office: 550 Commerce St S Wichita KS 67202

LOVE, JOHN, JR., educator; b. Paris, Tex., Jan. 26, 1916; s. John and Stella Maude (Reynolds) L.; A.B., U. Mo., 1939; B.Mech. Engring., 1951, M. Mech. Engring., 1953; Ph.D., Okla. State U., 1966; m. Marjorie O. Zoeller, May 18, 1942. Conductor, Mo. Kan. Tex. R.R., Parsons, Kan., 1939-49; asst. prof. mech. and aerospace engring. U. Mo., Columbia, 1951-54, asso. prof. mech. engring., 1958—; mgr. requisition engring. Gen. Electric Co., Norwood, Ohio, 1954-58. Engring. cons. Black & Veatch, cons. engrs., 1973—. NSF sci. faculty fellow, 1962-63. Registered profl. engr., Mo. Mem. Am. Soc. Testing and Materials (chmn. energy com. 1973—), Columbia Audubon Soc. (dir. 1966-68), Sigma Xi, Tau Beta Pi, Pi Tau Sigma, Alpha Chi Sigma. Mem. editorial bd. Elsevier Sci. Pub. Co., 1974—. Home: 1501 St Christopher St Columbia MO 65201

LOVE, LEON, univ. adminstr.; b. N.Y.C., Sept. 7, 1923; s. Isidore and May (Simon) L.; B.S., City Coll. N.Y., 1943; M.D., Chgo. Med. Sch., 1946; m. Rita Levinthal, June 17, 1956; children—Jonathan, Matthew, Emily. Intern, St. Barnabas Hosp., Newark, 1946, St. Johns Hosp., L.I., 1947; resident, Hosp. Joint Diseases, N.Y.C., 1949, Bellevue Hosp., N.Y.C., 1950-52; practice medicine specializing in radiology, N.Y.C., 1951; radiologist, dir. Cook County Hosp., Chgo., 1961-69; chmn. dept. radiology Loyola U. Med. Sch., Chgo., 1969—. Served to capt., M.C., AUS, 1952-54. NIH grantee, 1951. Fellow Am. Coll. Radiologists; mem. Alpha Omega Alpha. Editor, Viewbox, Ill. Med. Jour., 1961—. Home: 235 Hawthorn St Glencoe IL 60022 Office: 2160 S 1st Ave Maywood IL 60153

LOVE, MAHLON LLOYD, automotive engr.; b. Orion, Ill., Feb. 22, 1924; s. Mahlon Lloyd and Ethel Maria (Andereck) L.; student Blackburn Coll., 1942-43, U. Ill., 1943; m. Ruth Fairbanks, Sept. 20, 1946; children—Lonnie, Nancy. With John Deere East Moline Works, East Moline, Ill., 1944—, sr. engr., 1965—. Mem. Soc. Automotive Engrs., Am. Soc. Agrl. Engrs., Farm Bur. Presbyn. Mason. Patentee in field. Home: Rural Route 1 Osco IL 61274 Office: 1300 13th St East Moline IL 61255

LOVE, NORRIS, sch. adminstr.; b. Chgo., Dec. 13, 1936; s. Harold Norris and Anne (Schuttler) L.; A.B., Princeton U., 1958; M.B.A., Stanford U., 1960; m. Marcena Pickett Waterman, Sept. 12, 1959; children—Kathryn, Anne, Sara. Mktg. research supr. D'Arcy Advt., Chgo., 1960-64, account exec., 1964-66; mgr. Mid Am. Research Assos., Chgo., 1966-68; mgr. mktg. research dept. D'Arcy Advt. Co., Chgo., 1967-68; asso. research dir. Campbell-Mithun Advt. Co., Chgo., 1968-72; v.p., asso. dean Advanced Mgmt. Inst., Lake Forest, Ill., 1972—; dir. radio sta. KBOA, KTHS. Bd. dirs., trustee Chgo. Zool. Soc., mem. exec. com., 1975—; treas. Lake Mich. Fedn., Chgo., 1970-77; bd. Christian edn. Winnetka Congregational Ch. (Ill.), 1975-77; bd. dirs. Crisis Homes, Park Ridge, 1977—; active Shedd Aquarium, Chgo.; coach Winnetka Park Dist. Mem. Am. Mktg. Assn. Republican. Clubs: Chgo., Chgo. Golf, Tawas Beach, Duck, Anglers Chgo., Pheasant Valley Hunting; Trout Unltd. (dir. Chgo. 1976—). Home: 1175 Pelham Rd Winnetka IL 60093 Office: Advanced Mgmt Inst Lake Forest Coll Lake Forest IL 60045

LOVEJOY, LEONARD JAMES, pub. relations exec.; b. Topeka, Kans., Apr. 5, 1931; s. Leonard Mark and Margaret Mary (Zeller) L.; Ph.B., Marquette U., 1953; m. Julianne Rolla, May 29, 1954; children—Valerie, Christopher, Kimberly, Leslie, Julianne, Geoffrey. Writer, ARC, Chgo. chpt., 1956-58; publicity mgr. U.S. Gypsum Co., Chgo., 1958-62; dir. pub. relations Holtzman-Kain Advt. Co., Chgo., 1962-64; account supr. Philip Lesly Co., Chgo., 1964-65; account supr. Burson-Marsteller Co., Chgo., 1965-68, client services mgr., 1968, v.p., 1969, group v.p., 1972-76, asst. gen. mgr., 1976—; dir. Mark Lovejoy & Assos. Chmn. ARC Fund Drive, Westmont, Ill., 1960; agy. chmn. Girl Scout Fund Drive, Chgo., 1972; bd. dirs. Pop Warner Little Scholars, Inc., 1975—. Served with U.S. Army, 1953-56. Mem. Pub. Relations Soc. Am. (Silver Anvil award 1972, 1973), Publicity Club of Chgo. (Golden Trumpet award 1973, 74), Sigma Delta Chi. Roman Catholic. Club: Union League (Chicago). Home: 205 S Catherine La Grange IL 60525 Office: 1 E Wacker Dr Chicago IL 60601

LOVELESS, BILLY G., realtor; b. Boonville, Ind., Oct. 27, 1932; s. John M. and Vera T. (Pate) L.; A.B., B.S., Oakland City Coll., 1954; M.A., Ind. State U., 1959; m. Sara Mae Creek, Aug. 12, 1956; children—Sara Jean, Jane Ellen. Tchr. Wadesville (Ind.) High Sch., 1954-59; tchr. North Posey (Ind.) High Sch., 1959-63, asst. prin., 1964-69; owner, real estate broker Flack Realty & Ins. Co., Princeton, Ind., 1969—. Served with USNR, 1953. Mem. Gibson-Pike Bd. Realtors (pres. 1972), Nat., Ind. assns. realtors, Nat. Inst. Real Estate Bds., Soc. Real Estate Appraisers, Am. Inst. Real Estate Appraisers. Mason (Shriner, Scottish Rite). Club: Princeton Civitan (pres. 1966, 73). Home: 426 Lincoln Ave Princeton IN 47670 Office: 115 S Main St Princeton IN 47670

LOVELL, EDWARD GEORGE, mech. engr.; b. Windsor, Ont., Can., May 25, 1939; s. George Andrew and Julia Anne (Kopacz) L.: m. Ellen Mary Tyler, Oct. 23, 1964; children—Elise Ondine, Ethan Tyler. B.S., Wayne State U., 1960, M.S., 1961; Ph.D., U. Mich., 1967. Registered profl. engr., Wis. Asst. prof. engring. mechanics U. Wis., Madison, 1968-72, asso. prof., 1972—; structural engr. Pratt and Whitney Aircraft, E. Hartford, Conn., Boeing Co., Seattle, Ford Motor Co., Troy, Mich., Bur. Naval Weapons, Washington. Mem. ASME, Am. Acad. Mechanics. NATO sr. fellow in sci., U. Manchester (Eng.), 1973; NASA, Nat. Acad. Sci. fellow, 1967; NSF fellow, 1961. Mem. Sigma Xi, Tau Beta Pi, Phi Kappa Phi. Contbr. tech. articles to jours. ASME, ASCE, Am. Inst. Aeros. and Astronautics, Am. Nuclear Soc. Home: 7781 Cherrywood Ln Rural Route 7 Verona WI 53593 Office: 1425 Johnson Dr U Wis Madison WI 53706

LOVESTEDT, STANLEY ALMER, dentist; b. Iliff, Colo., June 7, 1913; s. Almer Jonas and Helen S. (Swedensky) L.; B.S., U. So. Calif., 1938, D.D.S., 1938; M.S., U. Minn., 1945; m. Seiberta Lee Conklin, Sept. 7, 1940; children—Priscilla (Mrs. Michael J. Strand), Helen (Mrs. William W. Pye), Robert A. Fellow Mayo Found. Med. Edn. and Research, Rochester, Minn., 1938—, cons. 1943—; prof. clin. dentistry Mayo Grad. Sch., 1969-72; prof. dentistry Mayo Med. Sch., 1973—. Mem. study sect. Nat. Inst. Dental Research, 1964-68; dental rep. Minn. Cancer Council, 1975—. Mem. Minn. Orch. in Rochester Com., 1969-73; pres. Rochester Arts Council, 1972. Served as maj. AUS, 1953-55. Diplomate Am. Bd. Oral Surgery. Mem. Am. Coll. Dentists (regent 1961-65, pres. 1968-69, chmn. oral cancer liasion com. 1964-71), Am. Acad. Oral Pathology, Am. Acad. Dental Radiology, Am. Soc. Oral Surgery, Fedn. Dentaire Internationale, Sigma Xi. Club: University. Contbr. to profl. publs. in field. Home: 1520 8th Ave NW Rochester MN 55901 Office: 200 1st St SW Rochester MN 55901

LOVINGER, WARREN CONRAD, univ. pres.; b. Big Sandy, Mont., July 29, 1915; s. Wilbur G. and Ruth (Hokanson) L.; B.A., Mont. State U., 1942, M.A., 1944; Ed.D., Columbia, 1947; m. Dorothy Blackburn, Aug. 14, 1937; children—Patricia Mae, Jeanne, Warren C. Tchr. Mont. pub. schs., 1937-42; instr. Mont. State U., 1943-44; asso. sec. Am. Assn. Colls. Tchr. Edn., 1947-51; pres. No. State Tchrs. Coll., Aberdeen, S.D., 1951-56, Central Mo. State U., Warrensburg, Mo., 1956—. Mem. S.D. com. State and White House Conf. on Edn., 1954-56; coordinator four state project on personal and family living, 1954-56; mem. Nat. Commn. on Accrediting, 1960-61; mem. Commn. Colls. and Univs., North Central Assn., 1953-57, 60-63; pres. Council Pub. Higher Edn. Mo., 1973-74, exec. com., 1972-74. Served as lt. USNR, 1944-46. Mem. Am. Assn. Coll. Tchr. Edn. (mem. exec. com. 1956-60, 62-66, pres. 1963-64, rep. to Internat. Council on Edn. for Teaching, 1964, mem. evaluative criteria com. 1966-70), Am. Assn. State Colls. and Univs. (chmn. com. on studies 1966-69, dir., 1969-77, pres. 1974-75, del. to People's Republic of China 1975, to Republic of China 1976), Nat. Council Accreditation Tchrs. Edn. (chmn. visitation and appraisal com., 1960-62, mem. coordinating bd. 1966-72), Am., Mo. assns. sch. adminstrs., Am. Legion, North Central Assn. Coll. and Secondary Schs. (supr. leadership tng. project 1957-58), Am. Social Health Assn. (mem. ednl. adv. com. 1954—), Mo. State Tchrs. Assn. (exec. com., chmn. tchrs. edn. and profl. standards com. 1959-66), NEA (chmn. nat. States com. 1961-62), Columbia Alumni Assn., C. of C. (dir. 1959-61, 63-65, 69-71, 73-75), UN Assn., Phi Delta Kappa, Kappa Delta Pi. Presbyn. (elder). Mason, Rotarian (pres. 1953-54). Author: General Education in Teachers Colleges, 1948. Contbr. articles to profl. jours. Home: 518 South Holden St Warrensburg MO 64093

LOWE, EARL WARDLE, ret. powder metal co. exec.; b. Omaha, Dec. 11, 1898; s. John Moses and Grace (Wardle) L.; student Iowa State Coll., 1917-18; m. Ruth Marie McKeon, July 4, 1920; 1 dau., Patricia Jane (Mrs. William D. Kinsell, Jr.). Salesman various firms, 1921-32; pres. Security Analytical Service, 1932-40; exec. v.p. McAleer Mfg. Co., 1940-46; pres. Greenback Industries, Inc., 1946-72. Served with U.S. Army, 1917-19. Mem. Am. Soc. Metals, Am. Ordnance Assn., Am. Soc. Testing Materials, Bklyn. Bot. Soc., Am. Nutrition Soc., Am. Powder Metallurgy Inst., Metal Powder Producers Assn. (pres. 1961-62), Metal Powder Industries Fedn. (pres. 1963-66, Distinguished Service award 1968). Clubs: Admiral, Ambassador, Detroit Athletic, Econ. (Detroit); Marco Polo (N.Y.C.); Internat. (Chgo.). Research in microstructures powder metal compacts; developer colored photog. processes for colored transparencies for reflected light for microstructures of powdered metal specimans. Home: 915 Pilgrim Rd Birmingham MI 48009

LOWE, E(DWARD) JOSEPH, physician; b. Jamaica, W. Indies, July 19, 1935; s. Phillip and Irene (Wong) L.; B.A., Chico State Coll., 1962; M.D., Loma Linda U., 1967. Intern, Washington Adventist Hosp., Takoma Park, Md., 1967-68, house physician, 1968-70; resident U. Md. Hosp., Balt., 1970-72; gen. practice medicine, Piqua, Ohio, 1972—; med. dir. Shelby County (Ohio) Bd. Health, Sidney, 1973—. Diplomate Am. Bd. Family Practice. Fellow Am. Acad. Family Physicians; mem. Ohio Acad. Family Physicians, AMA, Ohio Med. Assn., Miami County Med. Soc. Adventist. Club: Sugarmill Woods Country. Home: 107 Parkridge Pl Piqua OH 45356 Office: 113 Cassell St Piqua OH 45356

LOWE, GEORGE WASHINGTON, JR., transp. cons., piano tchr.; b. Columbia, Ky., Mar. 18, 1919; s. George Washington and Fannie Sophronia (Faulkner) L.; student Lindsey Wilson Jr. Coll., 1936-37, Draughan's, Dwyer's Consol. Bus. Colls., 1943-50, Pearson Music Sch., 1941-45; Ind. U., 1944-45, Central Beauty Coll., 1961-62, Famous Writers Sch., 1966-67. Office mgr. United Laundries and Dry Cleaners, 1943-46; asst. traffic mgr. Republic Creosoting, 1947-48; rate analyst I.R.C. & D., Carolina Motor Express, 1948-56; rate analyst United Trucking, Middlestates Motor Freight, Consol. Freightways, Inc., 1956-69; rate analyst accountant Ryder Truck Lines, Inc., 1969-76; transp. cons., owner, operator Lowe Traffic Service, Brownsburg, Ind., 1976—; pvt. tchr. piano and organ, Brownsburg, 1972—; lectr. on music and transp. Ward chmn. Republican party, Marion County, Ind., 1954-55. Mem. Am. Theater Organist Soc., Internat. Platform Assn., Mid Am. Rate Council, Ind. Theatre Organists Soc. Author: Octave Theory, 1972. Home: 203 Gordon Ct Brownsburg IN 46112 Office: 44 W Main St Brownsburg IN 46112

LOWE, JAMES BROWNE, lawyer; b. Winfield, Kans., Jan. 24, 1935; s. John and Vera Elizabeth (Browne) L.; B.S., U. Kans., 1956, M.S., 1959, LL.B., 1962; m. Eleanor Ann Hawkinson, Aug. 20, 1961; children—Sarah Ann, Michael Browne, John Willard. Admitted to Mo. bar, 1962, since practiced in Kansas City; dir. Kuraner, Dingman, Schwegler, Kinton & Lowe, profl. corp. Chmn. men's div. Heart of Am. United Campaign, 1973; treas. Kansas City br. Common Cause, 1972-73. Mem. Johnson County Republican Central Com., 1973. Bd. dirs. Family and Children's Services, Kansas City, Mo., pres., 1977-78; bd. dirs. Heart of Am. United Way, United Community Services; mem. adv. bd. Salvation Army. bd. deacons Village United Presbyn. Ch., 1977-79. Served with USNR, 1956-58; comdg. officer USCG Res. unit, Kansas City, Mo. Mem. Am., Mo., Kansas City (bd. govs.) bar assns., Kansas City Lawyers Assn. (pres. jr. sect. 1969-70), Delta Upsilon. Club: Homestead Country (Prairie Village, Kans.). Home: 3301 W 68th St Mission Hills KS 66208 Office: Commerce Bank Bldg Kansas City MO 64106

LOWE, ROBERT CLINTON, steel products co. exec.; b. St. Louis, Oct. 6, 1918; s. Robert M. and Eunice (Coates) L.; B.S., U. Pitts.; m. Pauline C. Artz, Oct. 5, 1940; children—Robert Clinton, Paula Carol, Diane Louise. Asst. sec.-treas. Coates Steel Products Co., 1940-52, exec. v.p., treas., 1952-60, pres., 1960—; dir. 1st Nat. Bank. Chmn. Greenville Airport Authority. Mem. Am. Inst. Mining Metall. and Petroleum Engrs., Am. Soc. Metals, Kappa Sigma. Presbyn. Clubs: Glen Echo Country, Greenbriar Country, Sunset Hills Country, Mo. Athletic (St. Louis); Union (Cleve.); Lehigh Country (Allentown, Pa.); Highland Country; Burning Tree (Washington). Home: 422 E Main St Greenville IL 62246 Office: Box 185 Greenville IL 62246

LOWE, ROY GOINS, lawyer; b. Lake Worth, Fla., Apr. 8, 1926; s. Roy Sereno and May (Goins) L.; A.B., U. Kans., 1948, LL.B., 1951. Admitted to Kans. bar, 1951; gen. practice, Olathe, 1951—; mem. firm Lowe, Terry & Roberts and predecessor, 1951—. Served with USNR, 1944-46. Mem. Bar Assn. State Kans., Johnson County Bar Assn., Am. Legion, Phi Alpha Delta, Sigma Nu. Republican. Presbyn. Home: 701 W Park Olathe KS 66061 Office: Colonial Bldg Olathe KS 66061

LOWEKE, GEORGE PAUL, educator, author; b. Detroit, Feb. 5, 1902; s. Herman Friedrich Ludwig, Jr. and Martha (Zieske) L.; student U. Chgo., 1926; A.B. with distinction, U. Mich., 1931, M.A., 1932; Ph.D., U. Berlin, 1936; M.M.E., Chrysler Inst. Engring., 1939; m. Lolamae Weians, June 22, 1937; children—Joan Virginia, Lowell Paul Weians. Head math. dept. Kans. Wesleyan U., Salina, 1936; editor Babson Statis. Orgn., Wellesley Hills, Mass., 1936-37; project engr., instr. Chrysler Inst. Engring., Highland Park, Mich., 1937-42; instr. engring. mechanics dept. Wayne State U., Detroit, 1942-45, asst. prof., 1945-51, asso. prof., 1951-68; cons. Novamatic Products Co., 1945-52; author: The Political Plague in America, 1964; A Mathematical Development for Prime Numbers, 1968; The Lore of Prime Numbers, 1978; contbr. articles in engring., math. and astronomy to sci. publs. Pres. Rosemond Estates Assn., 1959-63; candidate for Oakland County Rep. Del., 1966. Simon Mandelbaum scholar, 1931. Mem. Math. Assn. Am., Indsl. Math. Soc., Am. Mus. Natural History. One of first instrs. of space flight in U.S., 1957. Home and Office: 6886 W Harbor Dr Box 623 Elk Rapids MI 49629

LOWER, JOHN JOSEPH, elec. coop. ofcl.; b. Rushville, Ind., Nov. 24, 1921; s. John W. and Favora Francena (Goddard) L.; student Ball State U., 1939-40; m. Edna D. Nixon, Nov. 26, 1942; children—Judith Elaine, Steven Joe, Mark Allen. Lineman, serviceman, power use advisor Rush County Rural Electric Coop., Rushville, Ind., 1949-59; gen. mgr. Southeastern Mich. Rural Electric Coop., Adrian, 1959-66; ins. salesman Preferred Risk Mut. Ins. Co., Huntington Woods, Mich., 1966-67; cost accountant Am. Chain and Cable Co., Adrian, 1967; mem. services dir., dept. head Shelby County Rural Electric Membership Coop., Shelbyville, Ind., 1967—; chmn. Shelby County Extension Bd., program devel. Ind. REMC mem. services assn.; bd. Home Builders Assn. Shelby County, cons. session Am. Inst. Coops., Mich. State U., 1965. Bd. dirs. Shelby County Assn. Retarded Citizens, 1973—; trustee and deacon Ch. of Christ. Served with U.S. Army, 1943-46. Decorated Bronze Star (3), Dutch Lanyard, Belgian Fourragère; recipient 4-H Electric Leader certificate, 1976, Joseph P. Kennedy Jr. Found. award, 1972, Ind. Vocat. Clubs of Am. outstanding service award, 1975, certificate for spl. service, 1977. Mem. Internat. Assn. Elec. Insps. (dir., pres. Ind. Chpt., 1976-77), IEEE (asso.), Coop. Editorial Assn., Ind. Electric Heating Inst. (dir., pres. 1971-72), Ind. REMC Mem. Services Assn., NRECA Mem. Services Assn. (winner ann. reports contest 1974, 75, 76), Food and Energy Council, Ind. Farm Electrification Council, Shelby County C. of C. (chmn. pub. relations com. 1971-72-73, chmn. community devel. com. 1973-74, 74-75, 76-77). Editor Rush County REMC monthly newsletter Electralite, 1950-59, Shelby County monthly newsletter Watts News, 1967—. Home: Route 2 Rolling Ridge Box 44C Shelbyville IN 46176 Office: 1504 S Harrison PO Box 100 Shelbyville IN 46176

LOWERY, JOHN FREEMAN, marketing exec.; b. St. Louis, May 10, 1940; s. Freeman John and Annabelle (Hoerr) L.; B.S., St. Louis U., 1962, postgrad., 1963-65; postgrad. So. Meth. U., 1968; m. Sharon Pappenfus, Jan. 25, 1969; 1 son, Bradley John. Research asso. D'Arcy Advt. Co., St. Louis, 1962-65; research analyst Needham, Harper & Steers, Advt., Inc., Chgo., 1965-68; account exec. Marketing and Research Counselors, Inc., Dallas, 1968-74, v.p., dir. Chgo. Office, 1974—. Served with USCGR, 1962. Mem. Am. Marketing Assn. (chpt. treas. 1970-71). Home: 1509 Hyde Park Lane Naperville IL 60540 Office: 2905 Butterfield Rd Oak Brook IL 60521

LOWNEY, ROGER GORDON, ednl. adminstr.; b. Superior, Wis., June 7, 1935; s. Ray Samuel and Esther Lorraine (Alexson) L.; student U. Wis. at Stout, 1953-55; B.S., U. Wis. at Superior, 1959, M.E., 1962, Ed.S., 1968; postgrad. U. Mont., 1963, Wash. State U., 1974; Ph.D., U. Wis. at Madison, 1977; m. Kathleen Margaret Wells, Nov. 17, 1956; children—Darcy, Michael, Scott, Dana. Tchr., coach, prin. high sch. Cameron (Wis.) Pub. Schs., 1959-63; supt. schs., Hawkins (Wis.) Pub. Schs., 1963-64; supt. schs. Stratford (Wis.) Pub. Schs., 1964-70; supt. schs. Merrill (Wis.) Pub. Schs., 1970-77, Longview (Wash.) Pub. Schs., 1977—. Bd. dirs. Daniel Boone Nat. Found.; bd. dirs. T.B. Scott Library, Merrill, Wis. Recipient Acad. Profl. Devel. award, 1974; Danforth fellow, 1974. Mem. Am. Assn. Sch. Adminstrs., Merrill C. of C., Wis. Assn. Sch. Dist. Adminstrs. (dir. 1974), Phi Delta Kappa. Club: Lions (v.p. 1968). Home: 3170 N Ammons Dr Longview WA 98632 Office: 2715 Lilac St Longview WA 98632

LOWRANCE, EDWARD WALTON, educator; b. Ogden, Utah, June 17, 1908; s. Samuel Franklin and Edith May (Sandusky) L.; student Utah Westminster Coll., 1926-28; A.B., U. Utah, 1930, A.M., 1932; Ph.D., Stanford, 1937; postgrad. U. Kans., 1944-45; m. Rhoda Elizabeth Patton, June 21, 1935; children—Margaret Ann (Mrs. Jack F. Allman), Janet. Rockefeller research asst. in embryology Stanford U., Palo Alto, Calif., 1934-36, 37-38; instr. zoology U. Nev., Reno, 1938-39; asst. prof., 1939-43, asso. prof., 1943-49, chmn. dept. biology, 1947-49; asst. prof. anatomy U. S.D. Sch. Medicine, Vermillion, 1949-50; asso. prof. anatomy U. Mo. Sch. Medicine, Columbia, 1950-55, prof., 1955—. Acting asso. prof. anatomy Sch. Medicine, U. Kans., Lawrence, 1944-46; state sec. Mo. State Anatomical Bd., 1969—. Rosenberg research fellow in biology, Stanford U., 1936-37. Fellow AAAS; mem. Am. Assn. Anatomists, Am. Microscopical Soc., Western Soc. Naturalists, N.Y. Acad. Scis., Mid-Mo. Camera Club, Sigma Xi, Phi Kappa Phi, Phi Beta Pi. Mem. Christian Ch. Contbr. articles to profl. jours. Home: 103 Thistledown Dr Columbia MO 65201

LOWRY, CLAUDE MAGNUS, neurologist; b. Hamilton, Ohio, Feb. 15, 1923; s. Ray Smith and Helen Corinne (Herner) L.; A.B., DePauw U., 1945; M.D., U. Mich., 1948; m. Mary Adele Rhodes, June 14, 1947; children—Bruce Allen, Janet Claire, Scott R., Carol Sue. Intern, U. Mich. Hosp., 1948-49, resident in neurosurgery, 1949-52; practice medicine specializing in neurology, Ann Arbor, Mich., 1957—; mem. staff St. Joseph Mercy Hosp.; instr. neurology U. Mich. Med. Center; acting chief neurology VA Hosp., Ann Arbor; cons. in neurology Saginaw (Mich.) VA Hosp., Mercywood Hosp., Ann Arbor. Served with USNR, 1944; to capt. USAF, 1952-54. Mem. AMA, Am. Acad. Neurology, Mich. Neurol. Assn., Mich. State, Washtenaw County med. socs. Home: 1707 Shadford Rd Ann Arbor MI 48104 Office: 326 N Ingalls St Ann Arbor MI 48104

LOWRY, EARL CRANSTON, physician; b. Robeson County, N.C., July 20, 1907; s. Fuller and Jessie (Hatcher) L.; B.Sc., U. Chattanooga, 1927; M.D., Vanderbilt U., 1933; m. Olivia King, May 23, 1936; children—Anne King Sistrunk, Olivia Rose Odom. Intern, St. Thomas Hosp., Nashville, 1933-34, resident in surgery and urology, 1934-37; commd. 1st lt. M.C., U.S. Army, 1933, advanced through grades to col., 1944; chief dept. surgery Lawson Gen. Hosp., 1940-43, Oliver Gen. Hosp., 1946-50, Gorgas Hosp., Canal Zone, 1950-53; chief dept. urology Letterman Gen. Hosp., San Francisco, 1957; profl. dir. Office Dependents Med. Care, Dept. Def., Washington, 1957-58; prof. clin. surgery U. Ga. Med. Sch., Augusta, 1946-50; ret., 1958; pres., chief exec. officer Iowa Med. Service (Blue Shield), Des Moines, 1958-66. Diplomate Am. Bd. Urology. Decorated Legion Merit. Fellow A.C.S., Internat Coll. Surgeons, Royal Soc. Medicine (London); mem. Am. Urol. Assn., Pan Am. Med. Assn., Des Moines C. of C. (chmn. health com. 1964-65). Democrat. Methodist. Contbr. articles to profl. jours. Home and Office: 5403 Harwood Dr Des Moines IA 50312

LOWRY, ORVAL EARL, mktg. research co. exec.; b. Wahoo, Nebr., Nov. 26, 1892; s. Oliver Perry and Julia Caroline (Odwalker) L.; B.A., Grinell Coll., 1917; m. Constance Lesley Platt, Aug. 18, 1924; children—John Earl, Thomas Boyne. Asst. v.p. Northwestern Bell Telephone Co., Omaha, 1919-57; v.p. Allen & Reynolds Advt. Agency, Omaha, 1957-65; pres. Lowry Research Co., Omaha, 1965—. Served with U.S. Navy, 1917-18. Mem. Am. Mktg. Assn. (v.p. Omaha-Lincoln chpt. 1960-61), Phi Beta Kappa. Republican. Presbyterian. Clubs: Masons (past master), Omaha Ad (pres. 1927-28). Home and Office: 5308 Nicholas St Omaha NE 68132

LOWRY, RAYMOND WILMOT, JR., optometrist; b. Worthington, Minn., Mar. 30, 1926; s. Raymond Wilmot and Ermyl (Long) L.; B.S., Pacific U., 1949; D. Optometry, 1951; M.S., 1958; m. Elfreda Ione Kolsch, Apr. 10, 1954; children—Todd Christian, Raymond Wilmot III, Christopher Allen. Pvt. practice optometry, Worthington, 1951—; fellow Gesell Inst. Child Devel., New Haven, 1955-57; lectr. children's vision-reading in U.S. and Can., 1959-62; dir. Minn. Optometric Extension Program, 1959—; dir. adult reading classes Nobles, Martin, Pipestone county libraries, 1954-62. Pres., United Fund, 1960, Youth Commn., 1959, Concert Assn., 1960-61; pres. Nat. Soc. Developmental Vision Care. Served with USNR, 1944-46; PTO. Recipient Distinguished Service award Worthington Jr. C. of C., 1955, Fellow Am. Acad. Optometry, A.A.A.S.; mem. Am., Minn. (award 1960) optometric assns., Coll. Optometric Vision Devel. (pres.), Internat. Reading Assn., Optometric Extension Program, Better Vision Inst., Am. Optometric Found., Minn. Automobile Assn. (dir.). Presbyn. Mason (Shriner), Kiwanian (pres. Worthington 1963, lt. gov. 1966). Author: (with Richard Apell) Preschool Vision, 1959; Optometric Rapid Reading, 1963; Handbook for Developmental Optometrist, 1970. Contbr. articles profl. jours. Home: 1600 South Shore Dr Worthington MN 56187 Office: 319 11th St Worthington MN 56187 also 202 W 37th St Sioux Falls SD 57105

LOWRY, SHELDON GAYLON, educator; b. Cardston, Alta., Can., Aug. 25, 1924; s. Marcellus Anderson and Rose Belle (Wood) L.; m. Gloria Groneman, Apr. 3, 1946; children—Pamela, Martha, Kristine, Amanda Lee. B.A., Brigham Young U., 1946; M.A., Mich. State U., 1950, Ph.D., 1954. Certified marriage counselor, 1973. Instr. Mich. State U., 1951-52; research asso. Health Info. Found., N.Y.C., 1952; asst. prof. N.C. State Coll., 1952-57; asst. prof. sociology Mich. State U., 1957-59, asso. prof., 1959-65, prof., 1965—, asso. chmn. sociology, 1966-69, dir. multidisciplinary program, 1970—, asst. dean for grad. and undergrad. edn., 1975—. Mem. Am. Sociol. Assn., Rural Sociol. Soc. (pres. 1976-77), Nat. Council Family Relations, Am. Assn. Marriage and Family Counselors, Alpha Kappa Delta, Epsilon Sigma Phi. Editor: Rural Sociology, 1963-65; co-author: 10-Year Cumulative Index To Rural Sociology, 1965; contbr. articles in field to profl. jours. Office: Michigan State Univ Social Science Multidisciplinary Program East Lansing MI 48824

LOWRY, WENDELL WILLIS, automotive engr.; b. Napoleon, Ohio, Feb. 5, 1916; s. Joseph Eliot and Loal Pearl (Miller) L.; B.S. in Aero. Engring., Ind. Tech. Coll., 1939; m. Marjorie Louise Provonzie, Dec. 2, 1967; children—David J., Louise A. Head aero. engring. dept. Ind. Tech. Coll., Fort Wayne, 1942-43; aircraft engr. United Air Lines, Cheyenne, Wyo. and Chgo., 1946-47; program mgr. automotive tools and equipment U.S. Army, Toledo, 1949-62; program mgr. combat vehicles U.S. Army Weapons Command, Rock Island, Ill., 1962-66; v.p. mfg. Bear Mfg. Co., Rock Island, 1966-74; gen. engr. quality engring. div. Gen. Thomas E. Rodman lab. Rock Island Arsenal, 1974-77, chief, pre-issue engring. br. maintenance directorate U.S. Army Armament Readiness Command, 1977—. Served with Combat Aircraft Service, USNR, 1943-46; PTO. Mem. Am. Def. Preparedness Assn. Co-patentee dynamic wheel alignment machine and hydraulic brake tester for automotive use. Home: 16128 US Route 67 Milan IL 61264 Office: Gen Thomas E Rodman Lab Rock Island Arsenal Rock Island IL 61264

LOYD, HERMAN THEODORE, food service exec.; b. Phillipsburg, Kans., Mar. 17, 1931; s. Elmer Francis and Martha Gertrude (Foster) L.; B.B.A., Washburn U., 1958; m. Donna Marie Hoverson, Feb. 1, 1953; children—Brenda Ellen, Bruce Lane. With Fleming Co., Inc., Oklahoma City, also Wichita, Kans., 1958-62, Galloway Sales, Inc., Wichita, Kans., 1962-64, Instnl. Sales, Inc., Kansas City, Kans., 1964-66; v.p. Lady Baltimore Foods, Inc., Kansas City, 1967-77, Isis Foods, Inc., 1977—. Served with USAF, 1951-55. Presbyn. Home: 9001 W 71st St Shawnee Mission KS 66204 Office: 1500 W 12th Kansas City KS 64101

LUBARSKY, ANATOLY, orthodontist; b. Ukraine, Russia, Feb. 22, 1940; s. Ivan and Nina; came to U.S., 1958, naturalized, 1963; student Purdue U., 1959-61; B.S., Ind. U., 1963, M.S., 1967, D.D.S., 1968, Ph.D. certificate, 1969, Orthodontics, 1970; m. Martha Jean Otteson, Mar. 9, 1963; children—Michael Anthony, Tina Marie. Practice dentistry specializing in orthodontics, Bloomington, Ind., 1970—. Nat. Inst. of Dental Research fellow, 1968-70. Mem. Bloomington Dental Soc. (pres. 1976), Am. Dental Assn., Am. Assn. of Orthodontists, Am. Soc. of Dentistry for Children. Contbr. articles on salivary gland research to profl. jours. Home: 319 Lookout Ln Bloomington IN 47401 Office: 515 Woodscrest Dr Bloomington IN 47401

LUBAS, THADDEUS JOHN, data processing mgr.; b. Reading, Pa., Dec. 24, 1931; s. John and Martha L.; B.B.A., U. Miami, 1954; m. Helen Irene Allan, Nov. 24, 1960; 1 dau., Tracy. Regional audit mgr. Montgomery Ward Co., Kansas City, Mo., 1957-59, catalog house controller, Balt., 1960-62, corp. systems devel. mgr., 1962-70, corp. systems planning mgr., 1971-72, data processing security, v.p., sec.-treas., 1972-73; group mgr. data processing Foster and Gallagher, Peoria, Ill., 1975—. Bd. dirs. N.W Mental Health, Arlington Heights, Ill., 1970-75. Served to capt. USAF, 1954-57. Roman Catholic. Clubs: U. Miami Alumni, Peoria YMCA. Home: 309 W Eagle Nest Dunlap IL 61525 Office: 6523 N Galena Rd Peoria IL 61601

LUBBERS, LELAND EUGENE, sculptor, educator; b. Stoughton, Wis., June 6, 1928; s. Lubbert Eike and Marguetite (O'Brien) L.; A.B., St. Louis U., 1952, M.A., 1953, Ph.L., 1954, S.T.L., 1960; Docteur de l'universite de Paris, U. Paris, 1963. Joined Soc. of Jesus, 1946; asst. prof. Creighton U., Omaha, from 1965, asso. prof., chmn. fine arts dept., 1967-72; exhibited sculpture Galerie Marcel-Lenoir, Paris, Sheldon Gallery U. Nebr., Lincoln, Coll. St. Mary, Omaha, Duchesne Coll., Omaha, Mus. Jacksonville, Fla., Centennial Invitational Joslyn Mus., Omaha, Frye Art Mus., Seattle; exhibited paintings St. Joseph Coll., Phila.; exhibited group show Chgo. Response, 1968, Gallery at the Market, Omaha, 1971, Northwest Biennial, Brookings, S.D., 1972, Time Plaza, Milw., 1973, Ward-Nasse Gallery, N.Y., 1974; represented in permanent collections Sheldon Gallery, Duchesne Coll., Ward-Nasse Gallery, Co-op Gallery, Omaha, Kans. State U.; designer, Sculptor Sets for FIDELIO for Seattle Opera, Doan Coll., Concordia Coll., Stuhr Mus.; designer-collaborator electronic operatic piece Canisius Coll. Centennial, Albright-Knox Gallery. Participant Art in Embassies, State Dept. Recipient Best Sculpture award Midwest Biennial, Joslyn Mus., Omaha, 1976. Mem. Nebr. (dir.), Met. (dir., sec. exec. com. 1966—) arts councils, Asso. Artists, Omaha Ballet Soc. (pres. 1968-70, bd. dirs.), Omaha Acad. Ballet (pres. 1968-75). Home: 2500 California St Omaha NE 68131

LUBBOCK, JAMES EDWARD, writer, photographer; b. St. Louis, Sept. 12, 1924; s. Winans Fowler and Hildegard Beauregard (Whittemore) L.; B.A. in English, U. Mo., 1949; m. Charlotte Frances Ferguson, Aug. 24, 1947; children—Daniel Lawrason, Brian Wade, Kathleen Harper. Asst. editor St. Louis County Observer, 1949-51; staff writer St. Louis Globe-Democrat, 1951-53, state editor, 1954-56; mng. editor Food Merchandising mag., 1956-57; free-lance indsl. writer-photographer, St. Louis, 1958—. Served with Signal Corps, U.S. Army, 1943-46. Mem. Soc. Profl. Journalists, Sigma Delta Chi, St. Louis Press Club, ACLU, Common Cause. Liberal Democrat. Home and Office: 10734 Clearwater Dr Saint Louis MO 63123

LUBELFELD, JERZY, electronic engr.; b. Warsaw, Poland, Oct. 29, 1907; s. Benedict Florian and Regina (Lilienthal) L.; m. Joan Hawley Elliott, Aug. 24, 1948; 1 son, Nicholas; came to U.S., 1948, naturalized, 1953; B.Sc. in Math., U. Warsaw, 1927; Dipl. Eng., Mil. Tech. Coll., 1930. Commd. ensign Polish Navy, 1929, advanced through grades to comdr., 1945; instr. elec. communications Polish Army and Navy schs., 1931, asst. prof., 1936; mgr. elec. workshops Naval Yard, Gdynia, 1933-36; prof., head dept. elec. communications Naval Tng. Center, 1936-39, Polish Naval Establishment in Eng., 1945-48; ret., 1948; asst. prof. math. U. Detroit, 1948-54; asso. prof. electronic engring. Air Force Inst. Tech., Wright-Patterson AFB, Ohio, 1954—, chmn. vis. lectr. program Sch. Engring., 1957-74. Recipient Spl. Recognition certificate Air Force Inst. Tech., 1974. Mem. Am. Soc. Engring. Edn., IEEE (Harrel V. Noble award Dayton chpt. 1976), Polish Inst. Arts and Scis. in Am., Tau Beta Pi, Eta Kappa Nu. Author: (with C.H. Houpis) Pulse Circuits, 1966; contbr. tech. articles to profl. jours. Home: 4411 Lambeth Dr Dayton OH 45424 Office: Air Force Inst Tech Sch Engring Wright-Patterson AFB OH 45433

LUBENS, HERMAN MICHAEL, physician, allergist; b. N.Y.C., Nov. 22, 1913; s. Bernard and Pauline (Hirsch) L.; B.S., N.Y. U., 1933; M.D., Berlin (Germany) U., 1938; m. Frances Richman, Sept. 22, 1946; children—Perry Robert, Jonathan Martin, Richard Matthew, Pauline Bonnie. Intern Lincoln Hosp., Bronx, N.Y., 1938-41, pediatric house doctor, 1941-42, pediatrics fellow, 1945-46, mem. pediatrics staff, 1947-54; contagion resident Willard Parker Hosp., N.Y.C., 1947; mem. staff Flower-Fith Av. Hosp., Lincoln Hosp., Lebanon Hosp., Met. Hosp., Fordham Hosp., Mt. Sinai Hosp., Hackensack (N.J.) Hosp., Barnett Meml. Hosp., Paterson (N.J.) Gen. Hosp., to 1956; cons. pediatrician, head sch. health services N.Y.C. Health Dept., 1948-51, diagnostic epidemiologist, 1948-51; practice medicine specializing in allergy, Dayton, Ohio, 1956—; cons. allergist Children's Med. Center of Dayton; mem. staff Dayton Miami Valley Hosp., St. Elizabeth Hosp.; mem. staff, dir. Allergy-Immunology Clinic, Good Samaritan Hosp., Dayton. Instr. pediatrics Lincoln Sch. Nurses, 1948-50; clin. instr. pediatrics N.Y. Med. Coll., 1950-53; now asso. clin. prof. pediatric allergy U. Cin., Wright State U., Dayton; asso. clin. prof. allergy and immunology Ohio U. Nat. trustee Asthmatic Children's Found., Asthma Inc. Served to capt. M.C., AUS, 1942-45. Decorated Bronze Star. Diplomate Am. Bd. Pediatrics, Am. Bd. Allergy and Immunology. Fellow Am. Coll. Allergists; mem. Am. Acad. Allergists, Assn. Am. Physicians and Surgeons, Bronx Pediatric Soc., Montgomery County, Ohio med. socs., A.M.A., Am. Pub. Health Assn., Jewish War Vets. Mem. B'nai B'rith. Contbr. articles to profl. jours. Patentee anesthetic patch. Home: 396 Elm Grove Dr Dayton OH 45415 Office: Harries Bldg Dayton OH 45402

LUBITZ, JOSEPH MORTON, pathologist; b. N.Y.C., July 1, 1910; s. Jacob M. and Lena (Pachehek) L.; B.A., N.Y. U., 1933; M.D., U. Munich (Germany), 1936; m. Ina Maria Van Treeck, June 13, 1940; children—Joan Grosz, Peter. Intern, St. Mary's Hosp., Milw., 1936-37; resident Milw. County Hosp., 1937-40; chief of lab service VA Hosp., Woods, Wis., 1946-57; practice medicine, specializing in pathology, Milw., 1946—, Oconomowoc, 1963—; mem. staff Oconomowoc (Wis.) Meml. Hosp., Sacred Heart Rehab. Hosp., Milw.; cons. Milw. County Gen. Hosp., VA Hosp., Wood; clin. prof. pathology Med. Coll. Wis., 1946—. Dir. Waukesha County Marine Bank. Mem. adv. group Wis. Regional Med. Program, 1971—. Mem. Elmbrook (Wis.) Sch. Bd., 1953-67; mem. Fire and Police Commn., Brookfield, 1956-69. Bd. dirs. Friends of U. Wis., Waukesha, 1970—; trustee De Paul Rehab. Hosp., Milw., 1972—, Sacred Heart Rehab. Hosp., Milw., 1973—. Served with USPHS, 1940-46. Diplomate Am. Bd. Pathology. Mem. AMA, A.C.P., Coll. Am. Pathologists, Am. Soc. Clin. Pathologists, Am. Assn. Blood Banks, Wis. Med. Soc. (chmn. commn. on govtl. affairs). Home: 2828 Interlaken Dr Oconomowoc WI 53066 Office: Med Coll Wis Milwaukee WI 53233

LUBY, ELLIOT DONALD, psychiatrist; b. Detroit, Apr. 3, 1924; s. Albert A. and Ida (Zussman) L.; student Kalamazoo Coll., 1943-44, U. Chgo., 1944-45; B.S., U. Mo., 1945-47; M.D., Washington U., St. Louis, 1949; m. Ideane Maura Levenson, June 28, 1950; children—Arthur, Howard, Joan. Intern, Receiving Hosp., Detroit, 1949-50; resident psychiatry Yale U., New Haven, 1952-54; chief adult services Lafayette Clinic, Detroit, 1957-64, clin. dir., 1964—; cons. psychiatry Sinai Hosp., Detroit; prof. psychiatry Sch. Medicine, Wayne State U., Detroit, 1965—, prof. psychiatry and law Law Sch., 1965—. Pres. Comprehensive Psychiat. Services, Southfield, 1972—. Served to sr. asst. surgeon USPHS, 1950-52. Recipient teaching awards Wayne State U. Med. Sch., 1965, 67, gold medal award Am. Acad. Psychosomatic Medicine, 1962. Diplomate Am. Bd. Psychiatry and Neurology. Fellow Am. Psychiat. Assn., Am. Coll. Psychiatrists; mem. Am. Psychosomatic Soc., Sigma Xi. Contbr. to publs. in field. Home: 4467 Stony River Dr Birmingham MI 48010 Office: 21415 Civic Center Dr Southfield MI 48076

LUCAS, CHRISTOPHER JOHN, educator; b. Indpls., Feb. 21, 1940; s. Marshal P. and Ada Doreen (Holden) L.; student Butler U., 1958-59; B.A., Syracuse U., 1962; postgrad. Garrett Theol. Sem., 1962-63; M.A. in Teaching, Northwestern U., 1964; Ph.D., Ohio State U., 1967; m. Teresa Marie Stout, July 1, 1967; Tchr. secondary schs., Chgo., 1963-64; teaching asso. Ohio State U., 1964-67; prof. edn. U. Mo., Columbia, 1967—. Co-dir. U.S. registration Internat. Summer Courses, U. Salzburg, Austria, 1965-72. Fellow Philosophy of Edn. Soc.; mem. Comparative and Internat. Edn. Soc., Am. Ednl. Studies Assn. (pres. 1976-77), History Edn. Soc., Phi Beta Kappa, Kappa Delta Pi, Phi Delta Kappa. Author: What is Philosophy of Education?, 1969; Our Western Educational Heritage, 1972; Challenge and Choice in Contemporary Education, 1976. Home: RD 4 Columbia MO 65201

LUCAS, GLENNARD RALPH, chemist; b. Marissa, Ill., Feb. 22, 1916; s. Glenn C. and Besse (McQuilken) L.; B.S., Monmouth Coll., 1938; Ph.D. (univ. fellow), Columbia U., 1942; m. Elva F. Bowley, Aug. 20, 1941; children—Jane (Mrs. Greg Furch), Robert Bowley. Chemist, Gen. Electric Co., Pittsfield, Mass., 1942-52, mgr. process engring., Waterford, N.Y., 1952-56, mgr. advance product devel., Pittsfield, 1956-58; research dir. Signode Corp., Glenview, Ill., 1958—. Adviser, Jr. Achievement, Pittsfield, 1957-58. Area dir. Glenview Cacucus Party, 1961, 63. Trustee Glenview Library Bd., 1971-77, pres., 1975-77. Columbia fellow, 1941-42. Fellow AAAS; mem. Am. Mgmt. Assn., Am. Chem. Soc., Soc. Plastics Engrs., Sigma Xi. Republican. Methodist. Rotarian. Patentee in field polymers, plastics and pkg. materials. Home: 1011 Hunter Red Glenview IL 60025 Office: 3650 W Lake St Glenview IL 60025

LUCAS, ROBERT ROTGER, criminal justice cons.; b. San Francisco, Mar. 26, 1925; s. Harold Andreas Lucas and Catherine Elizabeth (Fitts) Lucas Wayland; A.B., U. Calif., 1948, M.A., 1951; m. Ann Bowler, Dec. 18, 1955; children—John Gordon, Jeffrey Bowler, Andrew Robert. Dep. probation officer Santa Clara County Juvenile Probation Dept., San Jose, Calif., 1951; field probation officer Contra Costa County Probation Dept., Richmond, Calif., 1952-56; with Calif. Dept. Corrections, 1956-68, classification and parole rep. Calif. Mens Colony, San Luis Obispo, 1962-68; state dir. Ill. com. Nat. Council on Crime and Delinquency, Chgo., 1968-71, dep. dir. urban services, Homewood, Ill., 1971-73; coordinator Safer Found., Chgo., 1973—, dir. community edn., 1975—. Condr. field research HUD, Balt., Indpls., Des Moines, Richmond, Calif., 1973; bd. dirs. Chgo. Welfare Pub. Relations Forum. Served with AUS, 1943-46. Honored by Gov. Ill. for service to Ill. Law Enforcement Commn., 1971. Mem. Am. Soc. Pub. Adminstrn., Nat. Audubon Soc. Office: Room 400 343 S Dearborn St Chicago IL 60604

LUCAS, WILDER, lawyer; b. St. Louis, Aug. 29, 1901; s. George Herman and Kittiebelle (Wilder) L.; matura gymnasium, U. Zurich (Switzerland), 1920; student U. Lausanne (Switzerland), 1920-21; A.B., LL.B., Washington U., St. Louis, 1924; m. Ruth Houck, Aug. 22, 1932; children—Wilder George, Ruth Virginia (Mrs. Richard Raycraft). Admitted to Mo. bar, 1924; practiced in St. Louis, 1924—; mem. firms Finley, Sullivan & Lucas, 1941-51, Finley, Lucas & Arnold, 1951-57; now partner Lucas & Murphy. Lectr. internat. law Washington U., 1951. Pres., Internat. Inst., St. Louis, 1938-41, St. Louis Soc. Crippled Children, 1954-56. Hon. Austrian consul, 1931-38. Trustee various family trusts. Decorated Golden Cross of Honor (Austria). Fellow Am. Coll. Trial Lawyers; mem. Bar Assn. Met. St. Louis, Internat., Am. (past exec. com. internat. sect.), Mo. bar assns., Internat. Assn. Ins. Counsel, Maritime Law Assn. U.S. (v.p. 1961-62). Club: Noonday (St. Louis). Home: 7050 Westmoreland Dr University City MO 63130 Office: Laclede Gas Bldg 720 Olive St St Louis MO 63101

LUCCA, JOSEPH SALVATORE, structural engr.; b. Sicily, Italy, June 17, 1951; s. Vincent and Teresa (Valvo) L.; came to U.S., 1954, naturalized, 1959; B.C.E., Ill. Inst. Tech., 1973. Structural engr. Fluor Pioneer, Chgo., 1973-75, A. G. McKee, Chgo., 1975-77; structural design group leader, project coordinator Barber Greene, Aurora, Ill., 1977—. Ill. State scholar, 1969-73. Mem. ASCE, Cousteau Soc. Roman Catholic. Club: Alfa Romeo Owners. Home: 818 N 16th Ave Melrose Park IL 60160 Office: 400 N Highland Ave Aurora IL 60507

LUCCHESI, CLAUDE A., chemist; b. Chgo., Apr. 20, 1929; s. Nello and Anna (Bellizia) L.; B.S., U. Ill., 1950; Ph.D., Northwestern U., 1954; m. Ruth Alice Wellstein, Oct. 24, 1954; children—Nello William, Kent Gregory. Leader spectroscopy group Shell Devel. Co., Houston, 1954-56; dir. analytical research Sherwin Williams, Chgo., 1956-61; mgr. analytical and phys. chemistry Mobil Chem. Co., Edison, N.J., 1961-66; mgr. central coatings lab. Mobil Chem. Co., Edison, N.J., 1966-68; lectr., dir. analytical services, chemistry dept. Northwestern U., Evanston, Ill., 1968—. Cons., Sherwin Williams. Fellow Am. Inst. Chemists; mem. Am. Chem. Soc. (councilor 1973—, chmn. Chgo. sect. 1977-78), Soc. Applied Spectroscopy (chmn. Chgo., 1958), Sigma Xi, Phi Lambda Upsilon, Alpha Chi Sigma. Unitarian. Contbg. editor Jour. Analytical Chemistry, 1974—. Contbr. profl. jours. Home: 127 Riverside Dr Northfield IL 60093 Office: Dept Chemistry Northwestern Univ Evanston IL 60201

LUCEY, JOHN WILLIAM, educator; b. Winthrop, Mass., Aug. 21, 1935; s. John F. and Margaret A. (Doyle) L.; B.S., U. Notre Dame, 1957; M.S. (AEC fellow), Mass. Inst. Tech., 1963, Ph.D., 1965; m. Nancy T. Brozovich, Aug. 31, 1957; children—Josephine, John Michael, Thomas, Christopher. Asst. prof. nuclear engring. U. Notre Dame (Ind.), 1965-68, asso. prof., 1968—. Mem. Ind. Radiation Emergency Response Com., 1974—. Served with USNR, 1957-60. Mem. Am. Nuclear Soc., Am. Soc. Engring. Edn., AAUP, AAAS, Soc. History of Technology, Sigma Xi. Democrat. Roman Catholic. Home: 307 E Pokagon St South Bend IN 46617 Office: Univ Notre Dame Mechanical Engineering Dept Notre Dame IN 46556

LUCEY, PATRICK JOSEPH, ambassador; b. La Crosse, Wis., Mar. 21, 1918; s. Gregory C. and Ella (McNamara) L.; student St. Thomas Coll., St. Paul, 1935-37; B.A., U. Wis., 1946; hon. degrees St. Norbert's Coll., DePere, Wis., Northland Coll., Ashland, Wis.; m. Jean Vlasis, Nov. 14, 1951; children—Paul, Laurie, David. Mem. Wis. Ho. of Reps., 1948-50; dir. Wis. Democratic Party, 1951, chmn., 1957-63; mgr. campaign for Thomas E. Fairchild, 1952, James E. Doyle, 1954, Sen. William Proxmire, 1957; Wis. Dem. nat. committeeman, 1964; lt. gov. Wis., 1964-66, gov., 1971-77; U.S. ambassador to Mexico, 1977—. campaign aide Robert F. Kennedy, 1968. Chmn. Nat. Democratic Gov.'s Conf., Gt. Lakes Govs.' Conf.; mem. Nat. Advisory Commn. Productivity and Work Quality; mem. Com. 100 for Nat. Health Ins.; mem. Nat. Com. Pub. Financing Elections. Wis. chmn. Kennedy Meml. Library Fund. Former trustee Wis. Investment Bd.; mem. Dem. Nat. Com. Home: 99 Cambridge Rd Madison WI 53704 Office: Am Embassy (Mexico) Dept State 2201 C St NW Washington DC 20520

LUCIDO, JOSEPH LOUIS, surgeon; b. St. Louis, Mar. 19, 1911; student Washington U., St. Louis, 1928-30; B.S., St. Louis U., 1933, M.D., 1937; intern St. Louis City Hosps., 1937-38, resident surgery, 1938-40, 46-47; resident surgery Chatham Meml. Hosp., Elkin, N.C., 1940-41; resident thoracic surgery VA Hosp., St. Louis, 1947-49. Diplomate Am. Bd. Surgery, Am. Bd. Thoracic Surgery. Practice medicine specializing in thoracic surgery, St. Louis, 1949—; mem. active staff Mt. St. Rose Hosp., Firmin Desloge Hosp., Glennon Meml. Hosp., St. Louis County Hosp., St. Marys Health Center; mem. cons. staff Alexian Brothers Hosp., Luth. Med. Center, Christian Hosp. N.W., St. Anthonys Hosp., Mo. Pacific Employee Hosp. Assn., Incarnate Word Hosp., DePaul Hosp., St. Johns Mercy Hosp., St. Louis State Hosp., Mo. Baptist Hosp., St. Louis City Hosp.; mem. emeritus hon. staff Bethesda Hosp., Deaconess Hosp.; attending and cons. thoracic surgeon VA Hosp., St. Louis, and Jefferson Barracks, Mo.; cons. thoracic surgeon Ft. Leonard Wood Base Hosp., USAF, Scott Air Base; prof. clin. surgery and thoracic surgery St. Louis U. Fellow A.C.S., Southwestern Surg. Conf.; mem. AMA, Mo., St. Louis med. socs., St. Louis Surg. Soc., Am. Trudeau Soc., St. Louis Tb. Soc., Royal Soc. Medicine, Alpha Omega Alpha, Mo. Athletic Club. Contbr. articles to profl. jours. Home: 6 Bellerive Acres Saint Louis MO 63121 Office: 1035 Bellevue Ave Saint Louis MO 63117

LUCKER, GILES WESLEY, real estate broker; b. Wheeling, W. Va., Nov. 22, 1934; s. Walter B. and Maude Ann (Leyland) L.; student Wittenberg U., 1934-35; m. Mary A. Baldy, Jan. 23, 1947; 1 dau., Linda L. (Mrs. Thomas McCord Paris). Owner, mgr. Lucker Realty Co., Mpls., 1947—; pres. Fairview Realty & Investment Co., Mpls., 1955—, Trenton Properties, Mpls., 1969—, Equitable Mortgage Investment Co., Mpls., 1963—, Wesley Investment Co., Rekeul Investment Co. Served with C.E. AUS, 1943-46. Decorated Purple Heart. Mem. Soc. Exchange Counselors, Mpls. Bd. Realtors, Minn. Property Exchangers, Uptown Business Men's Assn., Inst. Certified Bus. Counselors, Fla. Real Estate Exchangors. Republican. Lutheran. Mason (32 deg., Shriner). Home: 4100 Parklawn Ave Edina MN 55435 Office: 1406 W Lake St Minneapolis MN 55408

LUCKHARDT, HENRY JOSEPH, optometrist; b. Chgo., Nov. 8, 1913; s. Louis Joseph and Tillie (Swiercz) L.; student Central YMCA Coll., 1936-37, Northwestern U., 1942-43; O.D., Monroe Coll. Optometry, 1947; m. Annie L. Vitale, June 3, 1939; children—Sharon (Mrs. Thomas Plonka), Carol (Mrs. Anton Rodde). Pvt. practice optometry, Brookfield, Ill., 1947-50, Westmont, Ill., 1950—; guest lectr. Ill. Coll. Optometry. Dir. 1st Ogden Corp., Bank of Westmont; 1st sec. Bank of Wood Dale, Bank of Downers Grove. Mem. optometric adv. com. Ill. Dept. Pub. Aid, 1967—, chmn., 1972; bd. dirs. Conservation Inst., also treas.; pres., dir. Vision Bldg. Found.; mem. optometric adv. com. Triton Coll., 1973—. Mem. Westmont Planning Commn., 1968-69, chmn., 1970. Mem. Ill. Optometric Assn. (pres. 1971, treas. 1972), West Suburban Optometric Soc. (pres. 1952), Omega Epsilon Phi. Republican. Roman Catholic. Moose, Lion. Home and office: 136 N Cass Ave Westmont IL 60559

LUCKINBILL, MERLE ERVIN, rancher, recreation exec.; b. Coon Rapids, Iowa, Aug. 23, 1930; s. Clinton Harold and Helena Winona (West) L.; student Denver U., 1949-51; m. Helen Margaret Schaafsma, Aug. 23, 1958; children—Clinton, Cynthia, Susan. Apprentice cement constrn. Schaafsma Bros. Constrn. Co., Bellflower, Calif., 1957-60, asst. foreman, 1960-67; owner, operator Bar-L Ranch, beef ranch and children's vacation ranch, Guthrie Center, Iowa, 1967—. Scoutmaster Mid. Ia. council Boy Scouts Am., 1969-70, 70-71. Served with USAF, 1951-55; ETO, Korea. Recipient Outstanding Achievement award Mo. Mil. Acad., 1974. Mem. Am. Camping Assn., Am. Beef Producers. Presbyn. (elder 1968-73). Address: Rural Route 2 Box 263 Guthrie Center IA 50115

LUCY, DAVID CARTIER, assn. exec.; b. St. Louis, Mar. 13, 1943; s. Gregory Ramsey and Catherine Mary (Cartier) L.; student U. Mo., 1961-62, Washington U., 1963-66; B.A., U. Mo., 1969. Dir. membership Farm Equipment Mfrs. Assn., St. Louis, 1967-71; dir. membership, asso. editor Nat. Farm and Power Equipment Dealers Assn., St. Louis, 1971-73; exec. v.p. Ind. Implement Dealers Assn., Indpls., 1973—. Served with AUS, 1968-69. Mem. Am. Soc. Assn. Execs., Ind. Soc. Assn. Execs., Ind. Implement Dealers Services, Inc. (dir. 1973—), Ind. Implement Dealers Ins. Trust, Inc. (chief adminstrv. officer, trustee 1973—), Ind. Agribus. Club, Inc. (dir. 1974—), Ind. Retail Council, Ind. Better Bus. Bur., Ind. Farm Safety Council, Ind. Farmer-Retailer Com., Coalition Retail Assns., Assn. Farm and Power Equipment Mgrs. (dir. 1976—). Mason (32 deg., Shriner). Editor, pub. The Pinion, 1974—. Home: 5826 San Clemente Lane Indianapolis IN 46226 Office: 6112 N College Ave Indianapolis IN 46220

LUDWIG, ARNOLD FRANCIS, candy co. exec.; b. Toledo, May 30, 1934; s. Clarence J. and Helen D. (Pry) L.; B.S. (scholar), U. Wis., 1956, B.B.A., 1958; m. Betty Jean Bubolz, Dec. 31, 1958; children—Wendy Lou, Timothy Daniel. Dir. quality control Babcock Dairy Co., Toledo, 1958-60; v.p., co founder Seaway Candy Co., Toledo, 1960-69; pres., founder Ludwig Candy Co., Manteno, Ill., 1969—, also dir. Chmn. music program Manteno Bi-Centennial, 1976. Mem. U. Wis. W Club (dir.), Am. Mgmt. Assn. (pres.), Wis. Agrl. and Life Scis. Alumni Assn. Republican. Roman Catholic. Club: Moose. Home: Rt 1 Manteno IL 60950 Office: 395 Locust St S Manteno IL 60950

LUDWIG, CLIFFORD EARLE, hosp. adminstr; b. Painesville, Ohio, June 22, 1929; s. Milton John and Esther (Bechtel) L.; B.A., Ohio Wesleyan U., 1951; M.B.A., Northwestern U., 1953; m. Patricia Cope, Aug. 1, 1953; children—Karen Sue, Kimberly Ann. Auditor, Price Waterhouse Agy., Cleve., 1953-55, sr. staff supr. auditor, 1959-63; budgets and measurements analyst Gen. Electric Co., Nela Park lamp div., 1956-57, supr. gen. accounting miniature and photo lamps, 1957-58, distbn. cost analyst, 1958-59; comptroller Univ. Hosps., Cleve., 1963-69, asst. adminstr. fiscal affairs, 1969—. Served with AUS, 1953-55. C.P.A., Ohio. Mem. Ohio Soc. C.P.A.'s, Am. Inst. C.P.A.'s, Northeastern Ohio Hosp. Mgmt. Assn., Greater Cleve. Hosp. Assn. (mem. financial mgmt. com. 1963—). Home: 1020 Piermont Rd South Euclid OH 44121 Office: 2065 Adelbert Rd Cleveland OH 44106

LUDWIG, FRED ALBERT, JR., mental health ofcl.; b. Waterloo, Ill., Aug. 2, 1927; s. Fred A. and Pauline (Hern) L.; A.B., U. Ill., 1949, M.A., 1971; M.S.W., Washington U., St. Louis, 1952; m. Virginia Goodwine, Aug. 13, 1949; children—Philip, Susan, Ann, Peter. Social worker Ill. Soldiers and Sailors Children's Sch., Normal, 1952-54; social worker Mental Health Assn. and Center, Springfield, Ill., 1954-57, exec. dir., 1957—; individual practice counseling, part-time 1958—; mem. faculty Lincoln Land Community Coll.; asso. psychiatry So. Ill. Sch. Medicine. Bd. dirs. Springfield and Sangamon County Community Action, 1965—, exec. com., 1968—; bd. dirs. Kemmerer Children's Home, 1966—, pres., 1970-73. Mem. Nat. Mental Health Assn. (membership sec. staff council 1963-65, nominating com. 1965-67), Ill. Assn. Mental Health Center Adminstrs. (pres. 1968), Am. Orthopsychiat. Assn., Nat. Assn. Social Workers (v.p. Ill. council). Presbyn. (elder 1967). Contbr. articles to profl. lit. Home: 11 Linden Lane Springfield IL 62707 Office: 707 N Rutledge Springfield IL 62703

LUDWIG, MARVIN JAY, coll. adminstr.; b. Sioux City, Iowa, Aug. 29, 1926; s. L. Harrison and Naomi K. (Strayer) L.; A.A., North Park Coll., 1948; B.A. in Phys. Edn., Ohio Wesleyan U., 1952; L.H.D. (hon.), George Williams Coll., 1975; m. Ruth Marilyn Bjorkman, June 10, 1952; children—Marshall, Robin, Rhonda. Youth dir. Marion (Ohio) YMCA, 1949-55; sec. program, devel. Ethiopian Addis Ababa, YMCA, 1955-59, nat. gen. sec., Ethiopia, 1959-67, advisor nat. bd., Ethiopia, 1967-68, dir. world service and income prodn. Internat. div. YMCA, 1969-73, dep. exec. dir., 1973-75, now mem. Great Lakes Regional Council; pres. Defiance (Ohio) Coll., 1975—. Mem. Am. Council Edn., now mem. Great Lakes Regional Council; bd. dirs. Defiance Hosp. Served as sgt. 1943-45. Recipient Haile Selassie Prize Trust award for outstanding achievements in humanitarian activities, 1964. Paul Harris fellow. Mem. Assn. Am. Colls., Assn. Ind. Colls. and Univs., Ohio Coll. Assn., Ohio Found. Ind. Colls. Mem. United Ch. of Christ. Clubs: Rotary (found. fellowship 1955; past pres. Addis Ababa chpt.). Contbr. articles to profl. jours. Home: 705 E High St Defiance OH 43512 Office: The Defiance Coll 701 N Clinton St Defiance OH 43512

LUDWIG, R. ARTHUR, lawyer; b. Milw., Apr. 25, 1929; s. Arthur H. and Marie (Hebien) L.; B.B.A., U. Wis., 1954, LL.B., 1955, Dr. Juris Sci., 1966; m. Evelyn L. Amacher, May 21, 1971. Admitted to Wis. bar, 1955; since practiced in Milw.; mem. firm Ludwig and Shlimovitz, S.C., 1972—. Dir., sec. Delta Printing Co., Milw., 1972—. Dir. River Woods Family Campground Inc., 1974—; dir., pres. Packaging Design Inc., 1971—; dir. Apt. Coin Laundry, 1976—. Mem. Am. (co-chmn. com. on legal problems of aged 1974—), Wis. (sec. treas. bankruptcy, insolvency and creditors rights sect. 1968—), Milw. (staff Milw. lawyer), 7th Circuit bar assns. Editor Bankruptcy Newsletter, 1965—. Home: 5524 N 13th St Milwaukee WI 53209 Office: 1845 N Farwell Milwaukee WI 53202

LUEBBERS, RAYMOND JULIUS, rubber co. exec.; b. Dayton, Ky., Nov. 15, 1920; s. Julius and Elizabeth Frances (Dehnert) L.; Chem. Engr., U. Cin., 1943; m. Mary Ann Romocean, Feb. 10, 1945; children—Raymond J., Rosemary E., James M., Marilyn S. Tire devel. engr. Firestone Tire & Rubber Co., Akron, Ohio, 1943-54, tech. mgr. tire plants, 1954-60, dir. for quality control, 1960-64, dir. tire prodn., 1964-70; dir. mfg. services B.F. Goodrich Co., Akron, 1971-72, dir. engring., 1972-73, v.p. engring. and mfg. services, 1973-75, v.p. ops., 1975—. Pres. Green Local Bd. Edn., 1967—. Bd. dirs. Akron Jr. Achievement. Mem. Ohio Hist. Soc. Home: 4715 Christman Rd Akron OH 44319 Office: BF Goodrich Co 500 S Main St Akron OH 44318

LUECKERATH, ELMER WILLIAM, reliability engr.; b. Ferguson, Mo., May 14, 1913; s. John William and Anna Elizabeth (Langenegger) L.; B.S., Washington U., St. Louis, 1936; m. Leta Helen Story, May 8, 1976. Engr., Anheuser Busch, Inc., St. Louis, 1936-41, U.S. Corps of Engrs., St. Louis, 1941-44, Monsanto Chem. Co., St. Louis, 1946-49, Union Elec. Co., St. Louis, 1949-56, McDonnell-Douglas Corp., St. Louis, 1956-60; sr. research engr. Falstaff Brewing Co., St. Louis, 1960-68; engr. Miles Labs., Granite City, Ill., 1968-71; engr. U.S. Army Aviation Systems Command, St. Louis, 1971—. Mem. Ferguson Citizens Com., 1955—; treas. Ferguson Twp. Republican. Club, 1969-71. Served to lt., USNR, 1943-46. Recipient letter of commendation Am. Soc. Brewing Chemists, 1967, Pres. Falstaff Brewing Co., 1968, certificate of outstanding professionalism Hughes Helicopters, 1976, letter of appreciation Gen. Stevens U.S. Army, 1976. Mem. Nat., Mo. socs. profl. engrs., Am. Inst. Aeros. and Astronautics, Am. Def. Preparedness Assn. Baptist. Clubs: Discussion, Engrs. (St. Louis). Home: 231 Olympia Dr Ferguson MO 63135

LUEDTKE, ROLAND ALFRED, lawyer; b. Lincoln, Nebr., Jan. 4, 1924; s. Alfred C. and Caroline (Senne) L.; B.S., U. Nebr., 1949, LL.B., 1951; m. Helen Snyder, Dec. 1, 1951; children—Larry O., David A. Admitted to Nebr. bar, 1951; practiced in Lincoln, 1951—; mem. firm Kier, Cobb & Luedtke, 1961-69, Kier & Luedtke, 1969-73, Luedtke, Radcliffe & Evans and predecessor, 1973—; dep. sec. state State of Nebr., Lincoln, 1953-60; spl. legislative liaison Nebr. Dept. State, Lincoln, 1953-60; corps and elections counsel to sec. state, Lincoln, 1960-65; state senator Nebr. Unicameral Legislature, 1967—, speaker, 1977-78. Exec. sec. Neb. Gov.'s Com. Refugee Relief, 1954-58; conferee Nat. Conf. Judiciary, Williamsburg, Va., 1971, Nat. Conf. Corrections, Williamsburg, Va., 1971; del. Nat. Conf. Criminal Justice, Washington, 1973. Past pres. Lancaster County Cancer Soc.; dist. v.p., finance chmn. Boy Scouts Am. Treas., Nebr. Young Republicans, 1953-54; jr. pres. Founders Day Nebr. Rep. Com., 1958-59; chmn. Lancaster County Rep. Com., 1962-64. Bd. dirs. Concordia Coll. Assn., Seward, Nebr., pres., 1962-66; bd. dirs. Lincoln Luth. Sch. Assn., pres., 1964-65. Served with AUS, 1943-45; ETO. Decorated Bronze Star, Purple Heart; recipient Distinguished Service award Concordia Tchrs. Coll., 1976. Mem. Am., Nebr. (spl. com. juv. law revision), Lincoln bar assns., Am. Legion, Lincoln Jr. C. of C. (dir. 1955-57, v.p., 1956-57), Nat. Conf. State Legislators (chmn. criminal justice task force and consumers affairs com., mem. exec. com.), Am. Judicature Soc., Delta Theta Phi. Lutheran (pres. ch. 1971-74). Club: Sertoma (pres. 1962-63, chmn. bd. 1963-64) (Lincoln). Home: 327 Park Vista Lincoln NE 68510 Office: Exec Bldg Lincoln NE 68508

LUEKER, ERWIN LOUIS, educator; b. Dover, Ark., Dec. 15, 1914; s. Charles Henry and Louise Caroline (Harms) L.; student St. Paul's Coll., 1933-35; B.D., Concordia Sem., 1939; M.A., Washington U., St. Louis, 1940, Ph.D., 1942; m. Anna Marie Schick, May 2, 1943; children—Erwin Louis, Lisette Louise (Mrs. Robert Gibson), George Schick, Jonathan Charles. Ordained to ministry Lutheran Ch., 1942; pastor, Luth. Meml. Ch., Richmond Heights, Mo., 1943-46; prof. lang. and humanities St. Paul's Coll., Concordia, Mo., 1946-55; prof. theology and philosophy Concordia Sem., St. Louis, 1955-74; prof. theology Concordia Sem. in Exile, St. Louis, 1974—, dir. corr. Sch., 1957-69, dir. Grad. Sch., 1965-66, dir. research ch. and ministry, 1962-72. John W. Behnken fellow, 1970. Mem. Internat. Platform Assn., Am. Philos. Assn., Luth. Acad. for Scholarship. Author: The Author of Hebrews—A Fresh Approach, 1946; Concordia Bible Dictionary, 1963; (with R. Caemmerer) Church and Ministry in Transition, 1964; Change and the Church, 1968; Structured Musings of EL, 1968; For Anna Marie, 1973. Editor Luth. Cyclopedia, 1954—. Contbr. articles to profl. jours. Home: 7049 Camden Ct University City MO 63130

LUELOFF, JORIE ANNE PAYNE (MRS. RICHARD FRIEDMAN), journalist; b. Milw.; d. R.T. and Marjorie (Kaltenbach) Lueloff; student U. Geneva and Inst. des Hautes Etudes Internationales (Switzerland), 1961; B.A., Mills Coll., 1962; postgrad. Georgetown U. Sch. Fgn. Service, 1963; m. Richard Friedman, May 1, 1971. With CIA, Washington, 1962-63; newsfeature writer A.P., N.Y.C., 1964-65; news reporter, newscaster NBC News, Sta. WMAQ-TV, Chgo., 1965—. Mem. Jr. Governing Bd. Chgo. Symphony. Mem. Chgo. Acad. TV Arts and Scis. (dir.). Club: Chicago Press. Office: NBC News Merchandise Mart Chicago IL 60654

LUEMPERT, ARTHUR GEORGE, program mgr.; b. Broadview Heights, Ohio, Apr. 22, 1931; s. Arthur John and Myrtle Margaret (Siebert) L.; B.S. in Elec. Engring., Ohio U., 1954; postgrad. Xavier U., 1959-60, Cin. U., 1956-59; m. Graclyn Jean Smith, Oct. 23, 1955; children—Arthur Frederick, Amy Lynne, Molly Ann. Head electronics sect. U.S. Army, Fort Belvoir, 1954-56; engr. AVCO Mfg. Corp., Cin., 1956-60; project engr. Sparton Electronics, Jackson, Mich., 1960-66, program mgr., 1968—; asst. chief engr. Gen. Dynamics Corp., Rochester, N.Y., 1966-68. Trustee Clark Lake Sch. Bd.; chmn. Boy Scouts Am., 1968—. Served with AUS, 1954-56. Mem. IEEE, Nat. Security Indsl. Assn., Am. Ordnance Assn. Clubs: Order Eastern Star, Masons. Patentee in expendable timer, expendable airborne bathermograph. Home: 150 Lakeview Dr Clark Lake MI 49234 Office: 2400 E Ganson St Jackson MI 49202

LUESCHEN, GUENTHER RUDOLF FRIEDO, educator; b. Oldenburg, Germany, Jan. 21, 1930; s. Gustav Anton and Elsa Elisabeth (Magnus) L.; came to U.S., 1966, student U. Cologne, 1953-55, U. Bonn, 1955-57, 60; Ph.D., U. Graz (Austria), 1959; m. Klara M. Mertens, Dec. 22, 1958; children—Birgit, Gerhard. Project dir. U. Cologne, Germany, 1961-65; prof. U. Bremen, Germany, 1965-71; asso. prof. sociology U. Ill., Urbana, 1966-71, prof., 1972—. Philipp Noel Baker award ICSPE/UNESCO, 1974; vis. scholar U. Mich., 1960-61. Mem. Internat., Am., German sociol. assns. Author: Kleingruppenforschung und Gruppe im Sport, 1966; Soziologie der Familie (with E. Lupri), 1970; The Cross-Cultural Analysis of Sport and Games, 1970; Die Soziologie des Sports, 1976. Contbr. articles to profl. jours. Home: 10 Shuman Circle Urbana IL 61801 Office: Dept Sociology Univ Ill Urbana IL 61801

LUFF, EARL THOMAS, steel exec.; b. Palmyra, Nebr., Jan. 8, 1906; s. Thomas Eligah and Maude Mary (Arnold) L.; B.S., U. Nebr., 1928; m. Florence Flodden, Jan. 19, 1929; children—Earlene, Lyall. Engr. Cudahy Packing Co., Omaha, 1928-29, Concrete Engring. Co., Omaha, 1929-30; sales engr. Lincoln Steel Corp. (Nebr.), 1931, sales mgr., 1933-35, gen. mgr., 1935-46, pres., 1946-72, chmn. bd., 1972—; chmn. bd. Northland Steel Co., Billings, Mont., Lincoln/Northland Inc., 1975—; dir. S.W. adv. bd. Comml. Fed. Savs. & Loan of Omaha; partner 2LK Horse & Cattle Co. Pres. Lincoln Builders Bur., 1938-39, Dir. Lincoln Children's Zoo, 1962-71; pres. Lincoln YMCA, 1961-62; dir. Belmont Community Center, 1948-54, Lincoln Council Christians and Jews, 1960-63, Lincoln Council Alcoholism, 1962-68. State dir. Bus.-Industry Polit. Action Com.; past v.p. Salt-Wahoo Watershed Dist.; mem. Lincoln City Planning Commn., 1956-66; dir. Lower Platte South Natural Resources Dist., 1973-75; mem. Nebr. Soil and Water Conservation Commn., 1957-70, chmn., 1966, mem. counciling com. on ch. and soc. U.P. Ch. U.S.A., 1960-68; past v.p. Nebr. Synod council Presbyn. Men. Trustee Hastings Coll., 1948—, Nebr. Ind. Coll. Found., 1959-62; bd. dirs. Nebr. Council on Alcohol Edn.; treas. Nebr. Resources Found., 1968-76; mem. adv. bd. St. Elizabeth Hosp., 1965-70. Mem. Asso. Industries Nebr. (past pres.; Nebr. Bus. and Industry Man of Year 1959), Asso. Industries Lincoln (past pres.), Nebr. Engring. Soc. (past pres.), Nebr. (pres. 1963-65), Lincoln (past pres.) chambers commerce, Transp. Assn. Am. (past state chmn.), Nebr. Appaloosa Horse Club (past pres.), NAM (past dir.), Theta Xi (past nat. pres.), Sigma Tau. Presbyn. (elder). Rotarian (past pres.). Clubs: Lincoln Dinner (past pres.), Lincoln University. Home: 3501 W Pershing Rd Lincoln NE 68501 Office: 545 W O St Lincoln NE 68501

LUGAR, RICHARD GREEN, U.S. senator; b. Indpls., Apr. 4, 1932; s. Marvin and Bertha (Green) L.; B.A., Denison U., 1954; B.A., M.A. (Rhodes scholar), Oxford (Eng.) U., 1954-56; m. Charlene Smeltzer, Sept. 8, 1956; children—Mark, Robert, John, David. With Thomas L. Green & Co., Indpls., 1960—, v.p., treas., 1960-67, sec.-treas. 1967—; treas. Lugar Stock Farm Inc., Indpls., 1960—; mayor city Indpls., 1968-75; U.S. Senator from Ind., 1977—. Mem. Adv. Commn. on Intergovtl. Relations, 1968-75, vice chmn., 1970-75; mem. adv. council U.S. Conf. Mayors, 1969-75; pres. Nat. League Cities, 1970-71; mem. regional export expansion council Dept. Commerce, Indpls., 1967-73. Incorporator, 1st v.p. Community Action Against Poverty Bd., Indpls., 1965-67; mem. Indpls. Bd. Sch. Commrs., 1964-67, v.p., 1965; mem. Nat. Adv. Commn. on Criminal Justice Standards and Goals, 1971-72. Mem. adv. com. Marion County Republican Com., 1966—; keynoter Ind. Rep. Conv., 1968, del., 1970, 72; mem. platform com. Rep. Nat. Conv., 1968, 72, Keynote speaker, 1972. Bd. dirs. Hawthorne Settlement House Indpls.; mem. exec. com. Indpls. Symphony Orch., 1964-66; trustee, vice chmn. Ind. Central Coll.; trustee Denison U., Indpls. Center Advanced Research, 1973-76; trustee, past mem. bldg. fund com. Westview Hosp.; mem. Nat. 4-H Service Com.; bd. visitors Joint Center for Urban Studies, Harvard-Mass. Inst. Tech. Served to lt. USNR, 1957-60. Named Outstanding Young Man, Indpls. Jr. C. of C., 1966. Mem. Washington High Sch. Men's Club (pres. 1966-68), Phi Beta Kappa. Methodist. Rotarian (v.p. Indpls. 1967-68). Home: 7841 Old Dominion Dr McLean VA 22101 Office: 5107 Dirksen Senate Office Bldg Washington DC 20510

LUHMAN, WILLIAM SIMON, govt. ofcl.; b. Belvidere, Ill., May 15, 1934; s. Donald R. and H. Elizabeth (Rudberg) L.; A.B., Park Coll., 1956; M.A., Fla. State U., 1957. City planner, City of Moline, Ill., 1959-64; planning dir. Rock Island County, Rock Island, Ill., 1964-66; exec. dir. Bi-State Met. Planning Commn., Rock Island, 1966-71; dir. regional devel. Northeastern Ill. Planning Commn., Chgo., 1971-74, asso. dir., 1975-76, dep. dir., 1977—. Vis. instr. Augustana Coll., Rock Island, 1967, 69. Mem. adv. council profl. devel. Center for Govt. Studies, No. Ill. U., 1976-80. Served with AUS, 1957-59. Mem. Am. Soc. Pub. Adminstrn., Am. Soc. Planning Ofcls., Internat., Ill. city mgmt. assns. Home: 1538 Fremont St Belvidere IL 61008 Office: 400 W Madison Chicago IL 60606

LUHNOW, RAYMOND BERTRAM, JR., cons. engr.; b. Kansas City, Mo., May 3, 1923; s. Raymond Bertram and Jeanette Elizabeth (McVey) L.; B.S. in Elec. Engring., U. Ill., 1944; M.B.A., U. Mo., 1964; m. Ruth E. Anderson, Sept. 6, 1947; children—Raymond Christian, Mark Frederick, Steven Kirk, Nancy Ruth. Design engr. Burns & McDonnell Engring. Co., Kansas City, 1946—, partner, 1964-74, pres., 1974—. Dir. Helping Hand Inst.; gov. Am. Royal Assn.; trustee Midwest Research Inst. Served with USNR, 1943-46. Registered profl. engr., Mo., Kans., N.Y., N.J., Pa., Conn., Del., Mass., D.C.; registered profl. planner, N.J. Mem. Am. Soc. Heating, Refrigerating and Air Conditioning Engrs., Kansas City C. of C., Nat. Soc. Profl. Engrs., IEEE, Soc. Fire Protection Engrs. Presbyterian (elder). Clubs: Engrs., Carriage (bd. dirs.). Contbr. articles tech. jours. and mags. Home: 6510 Rainbow Ave Shawnee Mission KS 66208 Office: 4600 E 63d St Kansas City MO 64141

LUHR, ADELHEID WILHELMINE, constrn. co. exec.; b. Fountain, Ill., Apr. 8, 1917; d. Lorenz George and Emma Sophia (Rustsberg) Schanz; student pub. schs.; m. Eugene Luhr, Sept. 6, 1936 (dec. 1958). Sec.-treas. Luhr Bros. Inc., Columbia, Ill., 1948—. Bd. dirs. Meml. Hosp., Belleville, Ill., 1965—, Ill. South Conf. United Ch. of Christ, 1970-77, Eden Theol. Sem., St. Louis, 1976—. Mem. Nat. Assn. Women in Constrn. Republican. Club: Waterloo Country. Home: 1034 Main St N Columbia IL 62236 Office: 1020 Main St N Columbia IL 62236

LUICK, HAROLD LEE, recording co. exec.; b. Des Moines, May 14, 1930; s. George Jacob and Charlotte Elizabeth (Willshaw) L.; student Am. Inst. Bus., 1954-56; m. Carolyn J. Moore, Dec. 12, 1960; children—Karla, Michael Sanford. Research and devel. engr., Delvan Mfg. Co., West Des Moines, Iowa, 1959-73; pres., engr., gen. mgr. KAJAC Record Corp., Carlisle, Iowa, 1975—. Musician, 1948—. Mem. Carlisle City Council, 1973-74. Mem. Colo. Music Festival. Served with USAF, 1950-53; Korea. Named to Colo. Hall of Fame award, 1973; named Band of year by Profl. Musician and Entertainers Club of Iowa, 1975. Mem. Am. Fedn. Musicians, Profl. Musicians and Entertainers Club Iowa (founder 1963), Iowa Sound Promotion and Advt. Execs. Pres., founder Midwest Entertainment Rev./newspaper, 1971-75. Home: 110 Garfield St Carlisle IA 50047 Office: 155 1st St Carlisle IA 50047

LUKANCIC, LOUIS PAUL, physician; b. Joliet, Ill., Dec. 15, 1933; s. Louis and Paula (Matko) L.; B.S., U. Ill., 1956, M.D., 1958; m. Barbara J. Liesse, Aug. 27, 1960; children—Louis Roy, Steven Paul, Mary Teresa, Paula Jean, Catherine, Carolyn. Intern, resident St. Francis Hosp., Peoria, Ill., 1958-60; gen. practice medicine, Spring Valley, Ill., 1962—; mem. staff, also governing bd. St. Margaret's Hosp., Spring Valley, 1970-76; pub. health officer, Spring Valley, 1971—. Dir. Spring Valley City Bank, 1970—. Chmn. Red Cross Blood Bank, 1967—. Mem. Ill. Valley YMCA, 1970-73; bd. dirs. United Fund, Ill. Valley, 1970-73. Served with M.C., USAF, 1960-62. Mem. A.M.A., Am. Assn. Gen. Practice, Ill., Bureau County med. socs., Rotarian (pres. 1972-73). Home: Oakdale Ct Deerpath Spring Valley IL 61362 Office: 207 E St Paul St Spring Valley IL 63162

LUKAS, JOSEPH, automotive engr.; b. Sausininkai, Lithuania, Jan. 27, 1942; s. Vincentas and Magdelena Victorija (Pranskevicius) Lukasevicius; came to U.S., 1949, naturalized, 1960; student Aquinas Coll., 1960-62; B.S., Western Mich. U., 1965. Engr., Gen. Motors Proving Ground, Milford, Mich., 1965, 68, project engr. Diesel Equipment div. Gen. Motors Corp., Grand Rapids, Mich., 1969—. Served with AUS, 1965-68. Mem. Soc. Automotive Engrs. (treas. Western Mich. sect. 1976-78), Soc. Automotive Engrs. Roman Catholic. Home: 622 Tremont Ct NW Grand Rapids MI 49504 Office: 2100 Burlingame SW Grand Rapids MI 49501

LUKE, LEON VICTOR, dentist; b. Mt. Clemens, Mich., Sept. 1, 1924; s. Leon and Jeanette (Kosinski) L.; B.S., Holy Cross Coll., 1947; D.D.S., U. Detroit, 1951; m. Elizabeth Susan Palinko, June 1951 (div. Dec. 1968); children—Eliz, Jeanette, Leon Steven, Thomas Edward, Michael David; m. 2d, Sandra K. Harton, Feb. 8, 1969; step-children—Richard Turner Riggs, Russell Steven Riggs. Practice gen. dentistry, East Lansing, Mich., 1951—. Clin. instr. Lansing Community Coll., 1972. Mem. Central Dental Soc. (pres. 1961), Mich. Dental Assn. (chmn. govt. affairs com. 1965-72). Home: 1630 Walnut Heights Dr East Lansing MI 48823 Office: 121 Burcham St East Lansing MI 48823

LUKEN, THOMAS A., Congressman; b. Cin., July 9, 1925; A.B., Xavier U., 1947; postgrad. Bowling Green State U., 1943-44; LL.B., Salmon P. Chase Law Sch., 1950; m. Shirley Ast, 1947; 8 children. Admitted to Ohio bar, 1950; practiced in Cin.; city atty. City of Deer Park (Ohio), 1955-61; Fed. dist. atty., 1961-64; mem. Cin. City Council, 1964-67, 69-71, 73, mayor, 1971-72; mem. 94th-95th congresses from 2d Ohio Dist.; chmn. Cin. Law Observance Com. Served in USMC, 1943-45. Mem. Am. Legion, Jaycees (life). Club: K.C. Office: Room 1131 Longworth House Office Bldg Washington DC 20515*

LUKENS, DONALD E. (BUZ), mgmt. cons., state senator, former congressman; b. Harveysburg, Ohio, Feb. 11, 1931; s. William Arthur and Edith (Greene) L.; student Ohio State U., 1950, Baylor U., 1955. Acting minority counsel house rules com. U.S. Ho. of Reps., 1961-63; nat. chmn. Young Republican Nat. Fedn., also mem. exec. com. Rep. Nat. Com., 1963-65; mgmt. cons., 1965—; mem. 90th-91st Congresses 24th dist. Ohio; mem. house sci. and astronautics com., house post office and civil service com.; now mem. Ohio Senate, minority whip. Mem. Middletown (Ohio) Civic Assn.; chmn. Ohio Am. Bicentennial Commn.; active Heart Assn., Boy Scouts Am., Am. Cancer Soc., Muscular Dystrophy Assn., Multiple Sclerosis Assn. Served with USAF, 1954-60; maj. Res. Mem. Middletown C. of C., Sertoma, Farm Bur., Toastmasters Internat. Delta Chi, Ahepa. Mason (Shriner), Kiwanian. Office: State Senate Columbus OH 43215

LUM, MARY DANG ONG (MRS. GWON H. LUM), govt. ofcl.; b. Oakland, Calif., Nov. 30, 1923; d. Young Tung and Grace (Gee) Ong; A.B., U. Calif. at Berkeley, 1945, M.A. in Statistics, 1946; m. Gwon H. Lum, June 19, 1949; children—James, Donald, Penny, Carol, Robert, Gary. Teaching asst. math. U. Calif. at Berkeley, 1945-46, Mich. State Coll., East Lansing, 1947-48; teaching and research fellow U. Mich., Ann Arbor, 1948-49, research asst. Aero. Research Center, Willow Run, 1949-50; math. statistician Aero. Research Lab., Wright-Patterson AFB, Dayton, Ohio, 1951-68, sr. operations research analyst Hdqrs. Air Force Logistics Command, 1968—. Cons. statistics. Mem. Am. Statis. Assn., Inst. Math. Statistics, Internat., Assn. for Statistics in Phys. Scis., Phi Beta Kappa, Sigma Xi, Pi Mu Epsilon. Club: Circle Eight Square Dance (Dayton). Research on error analysis and reliability components guided missiles, hierarchal models in design of expts., character errors in error-correcting codes for ternary reception, math. evaluation grain counts in enlaged photographs, comparison of some forecast methods. Home: Rural Route 1 Box 19 Fairborn OH 45324

LUMICAO, BENJAMIN GUIAB, physician; b. Philippines, Mar. 15, 1936; s. Tomas B. and Josefina (Guiab) L.; came to U.S., 1962, naturalized, 1976; M.D., U. of East, Quezon City, Philippines, 1961; m. Felicitas Evangelista, May 4, 1965; children—Benjamin, Robert F. Intern, St. Peters Hosp., Albany, N.Y., 1962-63; resident in internal medicine Ill. Masonic Hosp., Chgo., 1963-64; resident in internal medicine Passavant Meml. Hosp., Chgo., 1964-66, chief resident, 1966-67; fellow in cardiology Northwestern U. Med. Sch., 1967-68, U. Ala., 1968-69; practice medicine specializing in internal medicine and cardiology, Chgo., 1969—; attending physician Northwestern Meml. Hosp., 1969—, dir. coronary care unit Passavant Pavillion, 1975—; asst. prof. medicine Northwestern U. Med. Sch. Diplomate Am. Bd. Internal Medicine. Asso. fellow Am. Coll. Cardiology; mem. A.C.P., Chgo. Soc. Internal Medicine. Home: 2629 Kingston Dr Northbrook IL 60062 Office: 707 N Fairbanks Ct Chicago IL 60611

LUMMIS, JOHN MICHAEL, funeral dir.; b. Quincy, Ill., May 1, 1949; s. John Burdeen and Dorothy Pearl (Akers) L.; student Central Mo. State Coll., 1967-68, Quincy Coll., 1971; grad. Ind. Coll. Mortuary Sci., 1972; m. Marcia Rae Leenerts, Mar. 23, 1968; children—Todd, Brett, Scott, Heather. Apprentice, Hufnagel Funeral Chapel, Mt. Sterling, Ill., 1972-73; owner, operator Ward Funeral Home, Pleasant Hill, Ill., 1973—. Mem. founding bd. Pike County Ambulance Service, 1976; bd. dirs. Illini Community Hosp., 1977; treas. United Methodist Ch. Served with U.S. Army, 1969-70. Decorated Army Commendation medal; registered emergency med. technician, Ill. Dept. Pub. Health. Mem. Nat., Ill. funeral dirs. assns., Asso. Funeral Dirs., Federated Funeral Dirs. Am., Pleasant Hill Jr. C. of C. (sec.-treas. 1974, 75, external v.p. 1976). Clubs: Masons, Lions. Home and Office: 502 S Main St Pleasant Hill IL 62366

LUND, HANS ERNEST, county ofcl.; b. Cedar Falls, Iowa, Sept. 9, 1928; s. Hans M. and Ellen J. (Peterson) L.; student U. Iowa, 1966-67, Iowa State U., 1967-70; m. Frances A. Good, Jan. 15, 1949; children—Steven R., Chryse E., Frank A., Barbara L., Jeanne G., Mary K. With U. Iowa Printing Service, Iowa City, 1948-65; assessor, Washington County, Iowa, 1965—. Mem. sch. bd., Riverside, Iowa, 1957-62, mayor, 1962-64. Served with USN, 1946-48. Mem. Internat. Assn. Assessing Officers (mem. adv. com. on r.r. and utility property 1974-75), Iowa Certified Assessors, Iowa State Assessors Assn., Am. Soc. Appraisers (sr. mem.). Lutheran. Mason, Lion. Author: Personal Property, 1973. Office: 210 W Main St Washington IA 52353

LUND, STEWART HELMER MURPHY, lawyer; b. Webster City, Iowa, July 20, 1911; s. Frank Joel and Grace Elizabeth (Bishop) L.; student Webster City Jr. Coll., 1933; LL.B., Drake U., 1942; m. Bernice E. Sealine, Oct. 4, 1947; children—Caryl (Mrs. Roger Scheffer), Janice (Mrs. Gary Johnson). Truck driver Western Gravel Co., 1930; room clk., bookkeeper Boss Hotels, Webster City, 1931-32, Beloit, Wis., 1932-35; dist. sales and engring. positions Gen. Refrigeration Corp., Beloit, 1936-39; admitted to Ia. bar, 1942; practiced in Webster City, 1946—, city atty., 1957-58. Mem. adv. council Drake U. Law Sch., 1970—. County dir. Civil Def., 1947-59; mem. Iowa Gov.'s Com. Jobs for Vets., 1971—. Served as lt. USNR, 1942-45; PTO. Mem. Am., Hamilton County (pres. 1952, 64), 11th Jud. Dist. (sec. 1963-72), Iowa (bd. govs. 1970-73), Jud. Dist. 2-B (bd. govs. 1974—) bar assns., Am. Legion (mem. nat. Americanism commn. 1954-72, nat. exec. committeeman 1972—), Iowa Def. Counsel (pres. 1976-77). Lutheran. Kiwanian, Moose, Elk. Club: Webster City Country. Home: 728 Elm St Webster City IA 50595 Office: 623 2d St Webster City IA 50595

LUNDAHL, BETTY LEE, counselor; b. Moline, Ill., July 21, 1924; d. Leroy Walter and Sophie W. (Larson) L.; B.A., Augustana Coll., Rock Island, Ill., 1946; M.Ed., Loyola U., Chgo., 1964; postgrad. Purdue U., 1967-73. Tchr. sci. and health Columbia Jr. High Sch., Hammond, Ind., 1948-60; tchr. sci. and health Gavit Jr. Sr. High Sch., Hammond, 1960-62, counselor, 1962-64, dean girls, dir. student activities, 1964-75, acting asst. prin., 1967-68; counselor Morton Sr. High Sch., Hammond, 1975—. Mem. Ind. State, N.W. Ind. (sect. sec., div. meetings 1955; chmn. 1956), Hammond tchrs. assns., NEA, Am., Ind. personnel and guidance assns., AAHPER, Delta Kappa Gamma. Lutheran. Author numerous tchr. and student handbooks. Home: 8931 Woodward Ave Highland IN 46322 Office: 6915 Grand Ave Hammond IN 46323

LUNDE, HAROLD IRVING, retail chain exec.; b. Austin, Minn., Apr. 18, 1929; s. Peter Oliver and Emma (Stoa) L.; B.A., St. Olaf Coll., 1952; M.A., U. Minn., 1954, Ph.D., 1966; m. Sarah Jeanette Lysne, June 25, 1955; children—Paul, James, John, Thomas. Asso. prof. econs. Macalester Coll., St. Paul, 1957-64; financial staff economist Gen. Motors Corp., N.Y.C., 1965-67; corporate sec. Dayton-Hudson Corp., Mpls., 1967-70; mgr. planning and gen. research The May Dept. Stores Co., St. Louis, 1970-72, v.p. planning and research, 1972—. Bd. regents Augusburg Coll., Mpls. Mem. Am. Econ. Assn., St. Louis Corp. Growth Assn., Am. Statis. Assn., Nat. Assn. Bus. Economists, Planning Execs. Inst., Phi Beta Kappa. Club: Minneapolis. Home: 11746 Westham Dr St Louis MO 63131 Office: 611 Olive St St Louis MO 63101

LUNDELL, ARTHUR FREDERICK, publisher; b. Milw., Dec. 30, 1930; s. Arthur E. and Margaret Alice (Pletka) L.; B.A. in Journalism, U. Mont., 1953; m. Beverly Jane Wolff, Dec. 29, 1951; children—Laura J., Nancy A. News editor Broadcaster-Censor, Viroqua, Wis., 1955-64, co-pub., 1964—. Served with USAF, 1953-55. Mem. Wis. Newspaper Assn., Viroqua Area C. of C. (exec. sec. 1958-60). Lutheran. Home: 317 Terrace Ave Viroqua WI 54665 Office: 122 W Jefferson St Viroqua WI 54665

LUNDELL, WILLIAM WARNER, pub. relations counsel; b. Mpls., Nov. 28, 1900; s. Carl Warner and Wilhelmina (Carle) L.; A.B. magna cum laude, U. Minn., 1924; S.T.B., Harvard, 1927; postgrad. Sorbonne-U. Paris, 1928; m. Melania Valle, July 15, 1931 (dec.). With Christian Sci. Monitor, 1927-29, N.Y. World, 1928-31, Boston Herald, 1930-31; news and sports commentator sta. WBZ, Boston, 1930-31; dir. spl. events NBC, N.Y.C., 1931-36; owner pub. relations bus., N.Y.C., 1937-42; with Gen. Motors Corp., Trenton, N.J., 1942-47; dir. pub. relations Mpls.-Moline, Inc., Hopkins, Minn., 1948-67, White Materials Handling div. White Motor Corp., 1968—, Greater Mpls. C. of C., 1968-71. Bd. dirs. Minn. Masonic Home, Mpls.; mem. pub. relations Com. Farm and Indsl. Equipment Inst. Mem. Nat. Republican Publicity Com., 1936. Named Hon. State Farmer, Future Farmers Am., 1969; recipient Distinguished Humanitarian Service award Masonic Grand Lodge, 1965, Nat. Distinguished Service award Future Farmers Am., 1972. Mem. Mpls. C. of C. (Distinguished Service award 1965, promotion com. 1964—), Am. Vocational Assn., Pub. Relations Soc. Am., Phi Beta Kappa, Lambda Alpha Psi. Unitarian. Mason (32 deg., Knight Comdr., Shriner; grand orator Minn. 1970). Club: Minn. Press, Harvard of Minn. Home: 745 Fillmore St NE Minneapolis MN 55413 Office: 130 9th Ave S Hopkins MN 55343

LUNDGREN, KATHLYN IOLA KING, librarian; b. Clark, S.D., Oct. 24, 1919; d. Charles Eugene and Jennie (Patterson) King; B.S., Mankato State Coll., 1941; M.A., U. Denver, 1968, also postgrad.; m. George Andrew Lundgren, June 4, 1942 (div. 1977); children—Thomas George, Genevieve Kathleen. Tchr. elementary sch., Danube, Minn., 1941-42; adult and children's librarian McCook (Neb.) Pub. Library, 1960-62; librarian Hannibal (Mo.) High Sch., 1962-64; elementary librarian, Scottsbluff, Neb., 1964-67; dir. Library Services Center, Scottsbluff, 1966-70, elementary library coordinator, 1966-70; coordinator media resources, audiovisual librarian, instr. children's lit. Neb. Western Coll., Scottsbluff, 1970—, librarian, summer 1969. Library cons. to ednl. instns., also H.W. Wilson Children's Catalog. Bd. dirs. SALINET, U. Denver Grad. Library Sch., 1973—. Mem. Mayor's Commn. Status of Women, Scottsbluff, 1975—; mem. Nebr. Commn. on Status of Women, 1976-79, treas., 1976-78. Mem. ALA (mem. jr. coll. bibliography com., sec. 1976-77), Nebr. (mem. sch. library devel. com. 1966—, sec. state sch. library sect. 1967-68, state pres. 1970-71), Mountain Plains library assns. (sec. 1970, pres. 1973-74), NEA, Nebr. (dist. pres. library sect. 1967—, pres. 1970-71), Scottsbluff (sec. 1965—) edn. assns., Am. Coll. Reference Librarians (sec. community/jr. coll. sect.), AAUW (local pres. 1972-74, state v.p. 1975—), P.E.O. (pres. local chpt. 1970), Beta Phi Mu. Episcopalian (guild pres. 1967-69). Mem. Order Eastern Star. Mem. cons. editorial bd. advisers Denison Co., 1967-71, book reviewer, 1966-71; reviewer Sch. Library Jour. Home: 2807 18th Ave Box 1086 Scottsbluff NE 69361

LUNDH, SVERRER HAAKON, clergyman; b. Grove City, Pa., May 12, 1929; s. Sverrer Haakon and Karen (Flock) L.; B.A., B.S., Bowling Green State U., 1953; certificate in theology, Luther Theol. Sem., 1957; M.A., U. N.D., 1970; postgrad. Chapman Coll., 1974-77. Ordained to ministry, Am. Lutheran Ch., 1957; pastor McGregor (N.D.) Luth. Parish, 1957-62, Douglas-Rural Minot Luth. Parish, Douglas, N.D., 1962-68, Mekinock (N.D.) Luth. Parish, 1968-74; asso. pastor parish edn. Christ Luth. Ch., Minot, N.D., 1974—. Mem. dist. com. Boy Scouts Am., Minot, 1974—, mem. council exec. bd., chmn. Protestant relations com., Grand Forks, N.D., 1968-74, Silver Beaver award, 1963. Mem. Am. Sociol. Assn., Nat. Council Family Relations, League of Norsemen, Alpha Phi Omega. Kiwanian. Home: 528 17th St NW Minot ND 58701 Office: 502 17th St NW Minot ND 58701

LUNDHOLM, EUGENE THEODORE, librarian; b. Superior, Wis., Oct. 21, 1922; s. Herman Eugene and Esther Maria (Paulson) L.; B.S., Superior State Coll., 1947; M.A., U. So. Calif., 1956; M.S. in Library Sci., 1959; children from previous marriage—Dagmar Elise, Gregory Paul, Jeffrey Lee. Tchr., pub. schs., Los Angeles County, 1947-56; librarian Los Angeles Pub. Library, 1956-67; librarian Calif. Luth.

Coll., Thousand Oaks, 1960-61; librarian U. Wis., Superior, 1967—, asst. prof., 1967—, also instr. psychology dept. Regional investigator Center for UFO Studies and Mut. UFO Network, Aerial Phenomena Research Orgn., Tucson; lectr. parapsychology. Spl. dep. sheriff Douglas County. Vice pres. Superior Bd. Edn., 1968-73. Served with AUS, 1943-45. Mem. ASCAP, Internat. Poetry Assn. (edit. cons. Orbis mag., 1973), Chaparral Poets Calif., Mantinee Musicale, Internat. Platform Assn., Mensa, Alpha Psi Omega, Epsilon Phi, Sigma Pi Sigma, Sigma Tau Gamma. Composer musical The Power of Suggestion, 1960; contbr. poetry various mags. and anthologies. Home: 2202 Hughitt Ave Superior WI 54880 Office: Hill Library Univ Wis Superior WI 54880

LUNDQUIST, MYRTLE VERNICE, educator, author; b. Chgo.; d. Martin Luther and Anna Emily (Lorenz) Lundquist; B.A., U. Chgo., 1951, M.A., 1963. Editor, The Commentator, Fed. Res. Bank Chgo., 1942-60; tchr., Wheeling, Ill., 1960-65, Schaumburg, Ill., 1965—. Mem. Women in Communications, Internat. Assn. Bus. Communications, AAUW, NEA, Indsl. Editors Assn. Chgo., Thimble Guild, Thimble Collectors. Author: The Book of a Thousand Thimbles, 1970; Thimble Treasury, 1975. Contbr. articles to mags. Home: 630 Prairie Ave Wilmette IL 60091

LUNDQUIST, VIRGIL JOHN PERSHING, surgeon; b. Kanduyohi, Minn., Jan. 1, 1918; s. August and Olga S. (Skoglund) L.; B.A., Gustavus Adolphus Coll., St. Peter, Minn., 1938; M.D., U. Minn., 1943; m. Irma E. Olson, July 3, 1940; children—Karen, Kipton, Karna, Kada. Intern, U.S. Naval Hosp., Bremerton, Wash., 1942-43; resident U. Minn. Hosp., U.S. VA Hosp., Mpls.; practice medicine specializing in surgery, Mpls., 1950—; mem. staff Met. Med. Center, Fairview Hosp. Served with M.C., USN, 1942-47. Diplomate Am. Bd. Surgery. Fellow A.C.S.; mem. AMA, Minn., Hennepin County med. socs., Minn., Mpls. surg. socs., Mpls. Acad. Medicine. Lutheran. Clubs: Shriners, Mpls. Athletic. Home: 4805 Sunnyside Rd Edina MN 55424 Office: 1202 Metropolitan Med Bldg Minneapolis MN 55404

LUNDSTROM, RAY MAX, coll. adminstr.; b. Little River, Kans., Oct. 1, 1930; s. Fred Niles and Agnes Elmira (Case) L.; A.A., Hutchinson Jr. Coll., 1950; B.A., Kans. State Coll., Pittsburg, 1954, M.S., 1955; ed.D., U. Kans., 1966; m. Margaret Eleanor Gowans, Dec. 28, 1951; children—Elaine Lynette, Marjorie Eleanor. Tch., Clearwater (Kans.) High Sch., 1955-56, Parkview High Sch., Springfield, Mo., 1956-58; placement dir. Wayne (Nebr.) State Coll., 1958-66, asst. dean adminstrn., 1966-71, v.p. adminstrn., prof., 1971—. Served with AUS, 1951-53. Mem. Nat. Assn. Coll. and Univ. Bus. Officers, C. of C., Phi Delta Kappa. Presbyn. (elder 1974—). Kiwanian. Home: 204 W 10th St Wayne NE 68787

LUNSETH, JOHN BENTLEY, surgeon; b. Grand Forks, N.D., Oct. 22, 1927; s. Oscar and Sophia Bergetta (Bentley) L.; B.S., U. N.D., 1952; postgrad. Harvard U., 1954; Ph.D., U. Minn., 1966; m. Cleone Beverly Nasset, July 16, 1947; children—John Bentley II, Steven Henry, Mark Peter, Michele Cleone, Susan Ann. Intern surgery U. Minn. Hosps., 1954-55; resident in thoracic and cardiovascular surgery U. Minn., 1955-64, VA Hosp., Mpls., 1968-69; staff surgeon U. Minn. and VA Hosp., Mpls., 1964-70, asst. prof. surgery, 1966-70; staff surgeon Met. Cardiovascular Assn., St. Paul, 1971—; individual practice medicine specializing in thoracic and cardiovascular surgery, St. Paul, 1971—; clin. asst. prof. surgery U. Minn., Mpls., 1974-76, clin. asso. prof., 1977—. Served with Med. Service Corps. to 1st lt., U.S. Army, 1946-49; Japan. Clin. investigator VA Hosp., Mpls., 1968-70. Mem. Am. Heart Assn. (pres. St. Paul div. 1976), Ramsey County, Minn., Am. med. assns., St. Paul, Minn. surg. socs., Twin Cities Thoracic and Cardiovascular Surgery. Republican. Lutheran. Home: 1386 Grantham St St Paul MN 55108 Office: 862 Central Medical Bldg St Paul MN 55104

LUPSE, RAYMOND SIMON, obstetrician, gynecologist; b. Girard, Ohio, Jan. 22, 1911; s. Simon G. and Helen (Haner) L.; B.A., Ohio U., 1932; M.D., Case Western Res. U., 1937; m. Helen Ann Manning, June 14, 1975; children by previous marriage—Linda R., Raymond M. Intern, Youngstown (Ohio) Hosp. Assn., 1937-38, resident in medicine, 1938-39; resident in obstetrics and gynecology Univ. Hosps., Cleve., 1939-42; practice medicine specializing in obstetrics and gynecology, Youngstown, 1942—; dir. dept. obstetrics and gynecology Youngstown Hosp. Assn., 1952-54, 67-69, lectr. Sch. Nursing, 1942-57. Treas. Youngstown Charity Horse Show, 1958-61. Recipient award for contbn. to sports Mahoning Valley High Sch. Coaches Assn., 1972; certificate of merit Green and White Club of Athens, 1963; diplomate Am. Bd. Obstetrics Gynecology. Fellow A.C.S., Am. Coll. Obstetrics Gynecology (founding), Internat. Coll. Surgeons; mem. Am. Cancer Soc. (med. trustee Ohio div., exec. com. Ohio div.), Case Western Res. Sch. Medicine (trustee), Ohio U. (pres. Greater Youngstown alumni chpt., Merit Certificate 1963) alumni assns. Clubs: Rotary, Kiwanis, Elks, Youngstown, Youngstown Country, Duquesne Hunting and Fishing, Masons, Shriners, Mahoning Bridle and Saddle (bd. dirs. 1957-60). Home: 4078 Sampson Rd Youngstown OH 44505 Office: 3100 Market St Youngstown OH 44507

LURIE, LOIS BENDES, ednl. diagnostician, therapist; b. Mpls., Sept. 22, 1926; d. Jacob Harry and Pauline Pearl (Berman) Bendes; B.A., U. Mich., 1948; M.A., Northwestern U., 1969; m. Howard James Lurie, May 20, 1951; children—James Harrison, Frederick Allan, Katherine Sue. Speech therapist Rockford (Ill.) Coll., 1948, Wyandotte (Mich.) Pub. Schs., 1948-50, Michael Reese Hosp., Chgo., 1950-53; diagnostician learning disabilities, tchr., Highland Park (Ill.) Sch. Dist., 1969—; tchr. edn. program Inst. Psychoanalysis, 1975-77; coop. supr., student tchrs. in learning disabilities Northwestern U., Evanston, Ill.; mem. working com. Ill. Guide Lines Learning Disabilities, 1977; participant conf. on learning disabilities Chgo. Fedn. Union Am. Hebrew Congregations, 1973, participant nat. conf., 1977—. Home: 911 Rollingwood Dr Highland Park IL 60035 Office: 2075 Saint Johns Ave Highland Park IL 60035

LURIE, MAX LEONARD, psychiatrist; b. Cin., Aug. 5, 1920; s. Louis A. and Osna (Bernstein) L.; B.S., U. Cin., 1941, M.D., 1943; m. Miriam Rudnick, Apr. 23, 1944; children—Ona R., Ellen S. Intern, Cin. Gen. Hosp., 1944; resident psychiatry Ill. Neuropsychiat. Inst., Chgo., 1945, Psychopathic Hosp., Iowa City, Iowa, 1946; pvt. practice medicine, specializing in psychiatry, Cin., 1948—; sr. active staff Jewish Hosp., Cin.; mem. staff Christ Hosp., Cin. Gen. Hosp., Emerson North Hosp. (all Cin.); asso. clin. prof. psychiatry U. Cin., Coll. Medicine, 1973—. Bd. dirs. Children's Protective Service, 1963—. Served to capt. M.C., AUS, 1946-48. Fellow Am. Psychiat. Assn.; mem. A.M.A., Ohio Med. Assn., Ohio Psychiat. Assn., Cin. Psychiat. Soc., Central Neuropsychiat. Assn., Acad. Medicine Cin. Contbr. articles to profl. jours. Home: 7402 Willowbrook Ln Cincinnati OH 45237 Office: 270 Doctors Bldg 19 Garfield Pl Cincinnati OH 45202

LUSBY, LARRY LEE, sales exec.; b. Dayton, Ky., Jan. 28, 1942; s. Curtis J. and Alvera Alma (Glick) L.; A.A., U. Cin., 1968, B.S., 1971; m. Martha Ann Schultze, Mar. 1, 1974; children—Kimberly Beth, Amanda Gwen. Sales rep. Comml. Solvents Corp., Cin., 1971-72, Staley Chem. Co., Decatur, Ill., 1972-75; account exec. H.S. Crocker Co., Inc., Cin., 1975—; cons. chemist. Served with USAR, 1966—. Mem. Delta Sigma Pi. Democrat. Methodist. Club: Moose. Composer: High School Days, 1959. Home: PO Box 241 West Chester OH 45069 Office: 10150 Alliance Rd Cincinnati OH 45242

LUSCH, ROBERT KARL, telecommunications co. exec.; b. Toledo, Dec. 3, 1940; s. Harry J. and Christina Delia (Ludgate) L.; student U. Toledo, 1963; certificate in indsl. psychology Elgin (Ill.) Community Coll., 1964; m. Sharon Reynolds, Oct. 31, 1959; children—Douglas, Michael, Tamiko, Maria, Melissa, Timothy. Div. sales mgr. Sears Roebuck Co., Monroe, Mich., 1960; staff supr. Western Electric Co., Plymouth, Mich., 1961-70, supr. on loan N.Y. Telephone Co., N.Y.C., 1971, on loan New Eng. Tel. & Tel. Co., Salem, Mass., 1972, supr. installation, Detroit, 1973-75; pres. Inland Seas Telecommunications Co., Monroe, Mich., also organizer, founder, chmn. bd., 1976—. Mem. Solicitations Com. City of Monroe, 1973—, chmn., 1974—. Served with USN, 1958-59. Mem. Monroe County C. of C., Mich. Ind. Telephone Assn., Asso. Telephone Answering Service Exchanges, Am. Numis. Assn., Token and Medal Soc., Telephone Artifacts Assn. Republican. Roman Catholic. Club: K.C. Home: 417 Arbor St Monroe MI 48161 Office: 2 E 1st St Monroe MI 48161

LUSK, JEANNETTE CRAWFORD (MRS. ROBERT DAVIES LUSK), publisher; b. Huron, S.D., Aug. 1, 1905; d. Coe I. and Lavinia (Robinson) Crawford; student Coe Coll., 1923; student Huron Coll., 1924-26, L.H.D. (hon.), 1976; m. Robert Davies Lusk, Jan. 5, 1927 (dec. Dec. 1962); 1 dau., Victoria Coe. Pres., Huron Pub. Co., 1963—; pub. Daily Plainsman, Huron, 1963—; pres. Dakota West Corp., 1963—. Mem. S.D. State Bldg. Authority, 1967-68; charter mem. S.D. Fine Arts Council, 1966-70. Bd. dirs. Huron United Fund, 1966, chmn. fund dr., 1967; charter mem. bd. S.D. Meml. Fine Arts Center, pres., 1969-75; trustee Huron Coll., 1967-73. Recipient Woman of Yr. award Huron Bus. and Profl. Women, 1972, S.D. Gov.'s award for outstanding support of arts, 1973; Distinguished Pub. Service award S.D. State U. Alumni Assn., 1976. Mem. P.E.O., Kappa Tau Alpha (hon.), Delta Kappa Gamma (hon.). Episcopalian. Home: 265 5th St SE Huron SD 57350 Office: 49 E 3d St Huron SD 57350

LUSK, PEGGY JUNE, educator; b. Springfield, Mo., Aug. 31, 1925; d. James G. and Cecile C. (Slagle) Lusk; B.A. magna cum laude, Drury Coll., 1947; M.A., Syracuse U., 1950. Field dir., camp dir. Girl Scouts U.S.A., Springfield, Mo., 1945-48; student dean Syracuse (N.Y.) U., 1948-50; resident counselor Winthrop Coll., Rock Hill, S.C., 1950-52; asst. dean women, instr. Ohio Wesleyan U., 1952-58; dean students U. Chgo., 1958-60; counselor Presbyn. St. Luke's Hosp., Chgo., 1961-68; staff counselor Rush Presbyn. St. Luke's Med. Center, Chgo., 1968—; cons. in field. Drury Coll. scholar, 1943-47; Syracuse U. fellow, 1948-50; Danforth fellow, 1956. Mem. Am. Camping Assn., Nat., Ill. leagues nursing, Ill. Assn. Women Deans Adminstrs. Counselors (pres. 1977-79), AAUP, Am. Assn. Personnel and Guidance, AAUW, League Women Voters, Ill., Am. personnel and guidance assns., Drury Coll. Alumni Assn. (chpt. pres.), Nat. Assn. Women Deans, Adminstrs. and Counselors, Mortar Board, Pi Lambda Theta, Phi Gamma Nu, Pi Beta Phi. Home: 5725 S Holmes Ave Clarendon Hills IL 60514 Office: 1743 W Harrison St Chicago IL 60612

LUSK, ROBERT CLIFFORD, ednl. cons.; b. New Kensington, Pa., Oct. 30, 1915; s. Randall Edgar and Nell (Farneth) L.; A.B., U. Mich., 1938; M.Ed., Wayne U., 1951, Ed.D., 1956; m. Miriam Louise Lattin, Feb. 3, 1940; children—Judith, Jon, David, Jill. Tchr. pub. schs., Trenton, Mich., 1940-43; faculty mem. Edison Inst., Greenfield Village, Mich., 1946-52, Wayne U., 1952-54; dir. ednl. services Automobile Mfrs. Assn., Detroit, 1954-72; cons. edn. and pub. relations Lusk Co., 1972—; adjunct asso. prof. U. Mich., 1972—. Pres. Wayne State Alumni, Wayne State Fund. Served with USN, 1944-46. Decorated 7 battle stars; recipient Mich. Citizen Edn. award. Mem. Nat. Edn. Assn., Am. Vocat. Assn., Pub. Relations Soc. Am. (accredited), Mich. Indsl. Edn. Assn. Author: Michigan Men, 1966; Michigan Women, 1967; Michigan's Historic Sights, 1968; editor automobiles of Am., 1956-72; cons. editor Random House Dictionary, 1968; What It Takes to Make Your Car, 1956-72. Address: 16007 Curtis St Detroit MI 48235

LUSTED, LEE BROWNING, radiologist; b. Mason City, Iowa, May 22, 1922; s. George Charles and Maude (Browning) L.; B.A., Cornell Coll., 1943, D.Sc., 1963; M.D., Harvard, 1950; m. Winifred Chamberlin, Aug. 24, 1943; children—Lee Browning II, Hugh S. Intern, Mass. Meml. Hosp., Boston, 1950-51; resident in radiology U. Calif., 1951-54, asst. prof. radiology, 1954-56; asst. radiologist NIH, Bethesda, Md., 1956-58; asso. prof. radiology U. Rochester, 1958-62, prof. biomed. engring., 1960-62; sr. scientist Oreg. Primate Research Center, Portland, 1962-68; prof. radiology U. Oreg. Med. Sch., 1962-68; prof., chmn. dept. radiology Stritch Sch. Medicine, Loyola U., Maywood, Ill., 1968-69, also asso. dean profl. affairs; chief of staff Loyola U. Hosp., 1968-69; prof., vice chmn. dept. radiology U. Chgo., 1969—. Lectr. XII Internat. Congress Radiology, Tokyo, 1969. Trustee Cornell Coll. Fellow Am. Coll. Radiology (chmn. common efficacy studies 1971—), N.Y. Acad. Sci., AAAS, IEEE. Author: Atlas of Roentgenographic Measurement; Prime; Introduction to Medical Decision Making. Contbr. numerous articles to sci. jours. Home: 990 Lake Shore Dr Apt 9C Chicago IL 60611 Office: Dept Radiology Univ Chgo 950 E 59th St Chicago IL 60637

LUTES, MARYBELLE PEARSON, mfg. co. exec.; b. Chgo., Apr. 12, 1921; d. Carlo Arnold and Annie Laura (Fasten) Pearson; student U. Wis., 1937; m. John R. Lutes, June 20, 1941; children—Jacqueline Karen, John. Sec., Ind. Rating Bur., South Bend, 1949-52; legal sec. to atty., Dowagiac, Mich., 1952-64; co-partner John R. Lutes Co., Niles, Mich., 1952—, sec.-treas. Mem. Election Canvas Bd., Niles, Mich., 1963-70. Republican. Home: 1205 Sassifras Ln Niles MI 49120 Office: 1400 Chicago Rd Niles MI 49120

LUTH, DAVID EUGENE, rehab. adminstr.; b. Yankton, S.D., May 30, 1948; s. Willis and Donna (Couch) L.; B.A., Yankton Coll., 1973; postgrad. U. S.D.; m. Mary Louise MacClure, July 3, 1971; 1 son, Justin. Recreation therapist S.D. Human Services Center, Yankton, 1965-69, activity dir., 1969-73; dir., mgr. N.E. Nebr. Rehab. Services, Bloomfield, 1973-75; exec. dir. Service Industries, Inc., Redwood Falls, Minn., 1975—; mem. Gov.'s Regional Council for Handicapped; bd. mem. S.W. Minn. Developmental Disabilities Council; charter bd. mem. Continuing Edn. Com. in Mental Retardation. Mem. Nat., Minn. rehab. assns. Democratic Farm Labor Party. Methodist. Clubs: Jaycees, Masons, Shriners, Elks, Toastmasters, DeMolay. Home: PO Box 333 600 E Broadway Redwood Falls MN 56283 Office: PO Box 248 1317 E Bridge St Redwood Falls MN 56283

LUTHER, DON PRESTON, assn. exec.; b. Flint, Mich., Dec. 8, 1920; s. Clarence Dar and Hazel Rhea (Crandall) L.; student U. Mich., 1952; B.A., Wayne State U., 1976; m. Frances Almeda Denton, June 3, 1943; children—Darleen R. Luther Hatt, Norma O. Luther Claxton. Asst. ct. reporter St. Clair County, Port Huron, Mich., 1942; sec. San Diego Employers Assn., 1946-49; exec. sec. The Economic Club Detroit, 1949-64, asst. to pres., 1964-68, exec. dir., 1968—. Co-chmn. Mich. Rendezvous at EXPO 70, 1969-70; pres. Los Buenos Vecinos de Detroit, Spanish good neighbors club, 1958-59; bd. dirs. Lula Belle Stewart Center, 1976—. Served with USNR, 1942-45. Mem. Pub. Relations Soc. Am. (chpt. chmn. pub. service com. 1975—), Circumnavigators, Detroit Press. Episcopalian. Rotarian. Home: 15989 Woodland Dr Dearborn MI 48120 Office: 920 Free Press Bldg Detroit MI 48226

LUTTRULL, JAMES DAVID, coll. dean; b. Evansville, Ind., Jan. 5, 1933; s. Amon Leroy and Ruth (Leverich) L.; student Asbury Coll., 1950-51; B.A., U. Evansville, 1954; M.S., Ind. State U., 1957; postgrad. Atlanta U., U. Minn., Ind. U., Ball State U.; m. June Crossman Simpson, Dec. 8, 1951; children—Sandra, James David, Cheryl, Ruth, Linda. Tchr. English, Bremen (Ind.) Pub. Schs., 1954-57; asst. prin. Twp. Schs., Bourbon, Ind., 1957-60; dir. guidance Ind. State U. Lab. Sch., Terre Haute, 1960-62; guidance dir. Tri Twp. Schs. Corp., Boubon, 1962-64; dean students, asso. prof. edn. Marion (Ind.) Coll., 1964—. Precinct capt. for Democratic mayoral candidate; County chmn. Republican senatorial candidate. NDEA fellow, summer 1959. Mem. Am., Ind. personnel and guidance assns., Assn. Counselor Edn. and Supervision, Am., Ind. coll. personnel assns. Lay leader, tchr. and supt. Sunday Sch. dist. men's pres. Wesleyan Ch. Republican. Home: 515 W 5th St Marion IN 46952 Office: 4201 Washington St S Marion IN 46952

LUUS, GEORGE AARNE, physician; b. Estonia, Apr. 23, 1937; s. Edgar and Aili (Poldmaa) L.; M.D., U. Toronto (Ont., Can.), 1962; m. Margit Jaanusson, Sept. 14, 1962; children—Caroline Anna Elizabeth, Clyde Gregory Edgar, Lia Esther Isabelle. Intern Toronto East Gen. and Orthopaedic Hosp.; practice medicine specializing in family medicine, Sault Ste Marie, Ont., 1963—; mem. Algoma Dist. Med. Group, 1966—; sec. med. staff Gen. Hosp., 1972—, v.p., bd. dirs., 1973. Adv. bd. Can. Scholarship Trust Found., 1976-77. Mem. Algoma West Med. Acad., Acad. Medicine Toronto. Club: Rotary. Home: 42 Linstedt St Sault Ste Marie ON Canada Office: 240 McNabb St Sault Ste Marie ON Canada

LUX, LAWRENCE EMMETT, engr.; b. Chgo., June 7, 1942; s. Lawrence Aloysius and Mary Irene (Emmett) L.; student Chgo. Tchrs. Coll., 1961-64, Ill. Inst. Tech., 1964-66, U. Wis., 1966-74; m. Paulette Nields, Nov. 23, 1974. With Edwin Hancock Engring. Co., Forest Park, Ill., 1964-66; asst. village engr., engring., planning and traffic dept. Oak Lawn, Ill., 1966—; part-time instr. land planning Moraine Valley Community Coll., Palos Hills, Ill. Mem. dist. gov.'s adv. cabinet, 1971—; trustee Lions of Ill. Found. Mem. Am. Water Works Assn., Am. Pub. Works Assn., Am. Soc. Planning Officials, Am. Forestry Assn., South Suburban Water Operators Assn. (past pres.). Democrat. Roman Catholic. Lion. Club: Bonehead's Social and Athletic. Home: 10801 S Keating St Oak Lawn IL 60543 Office: 5252 W James St Oak Lawn IL 60453

LUZADRE, JOHN HINKLE, obstetrician, gynecologist; b. Logansport, Ind., Dec. 4, 1921; s. John Franklin and Mary Louise (Hinkle) L.; B.S., U. Pitts., 1942, D.D.S., 1945; M.D., Duke U., 1951; m. Barbara Louise Cary, Sept. 24, 1949; children—John Cary, Jo Ann, Robert Allan, David James, Timothy Hart. Instr., U. Pitts., Sch. Dentistry, 1947; intern Henry Ford Hosp., Detroit, 1951-52, resident in obstetrics and gynecology, 1952-55; practice medicine specializing in obstetrics and gynecology, Grosse Pointe Farms, Mich., 1955—; mem. staffs St. John Hosp., Detroit, Cottage Hosp., Grosse Pointe Farms. Served as capt. Dental Corps U.S. Army, 1945-47; ETO. Diplomate Am. Bd. Obstetrics and Gynecology. Fellow A.C.S., Am. Coll. Obstetrics, Gynecology; mem. Continental Gynecologic Soc., Alpha Omega Alpha. Republican. Presbyterian. Clubs: Country of Detroit; Hillsboro (Fla.); Tennis House (Grosse Pointe Farms). Home: 1311 Devonshire Rd Grosse Pointe Park MI 48230 Office: 18430 Mack Ave Grosse Pointe Farms MI 48236

LYALL, JAMES MORRIS, psychologist; b. Cleve., July 19, 1949; s. Robert Edward and Marjorie (Fishe) L.; B.A., John Carroll U., 1970, M.A., 1973; Ph.D., U. Akron (Ohio), 1977; m. Janet Mary Brunecz, May 18, 1973. Social worker, psychologist Ohio State Reformatory, Mansfield, Ohio, 1972-74; rehab. counselor Bur. Vocat. Rehab., Canton, Ohio, 1974-75; psychologist Behavioral Science Center, Ravenna, Ohio, 1975-76, Counseling Psychology Services, Akron, 1976—; cons. VA Guidance Center, Akron, 1976—. Mem. Am. Psychol. Assn., Am. Personnel and Guidance Assn., Am. Rehab. Counselor's Assn. Home: 1003 Greenfield SW Canton OH 44706 Office: 806 W Market St Akron OH 44309

LYBROOK, ROBERT BURKE, judge; b. Gary, Ind., Jan. 11, 1914; s. Bird Hugh and Hazel Katherine (Todhunter) L.; LL.B., Ind. U., 1937; m. Josephine E. Miller, Apr. 25, 1940; children—Robert E., Jo Katherine Lybrook Durkott, Mary Eliz Lybrook Phariss. Admitted to Ind. bar, 1937; practiced in Franklin, Ind., 1942-54, Nashville, Ind., 1967-71; pros. atty. 8th Jud. Circuit Ind., Franklin, 1946-50, circuit judge, 1954-67; judge Ind. Appellate Ct., Indpls., 1970, Ind. Ct. Appeals, Indpls., 1972—. Served with USNR, World War II. Mem. Am. Judicature Soc. Republican. Clubs: Masons, Elks, Columbia (Indpls.). Home: Route 8 Martinsville IN 46151 Office: State House Indianapolis IN 46204

LYDDON, JAMES HAMILTON, investment co. exec.; b. Kansas City, Mo., May 10, 1924; s. George Dana and Ethel Paige (Branigar) L.; B.S., U. Colo., 1948; m. Margaret Claire Carswell, June 12, 1946; children—Judith Ann, Margaret Sue, Kathryn Grace, Nancy Claire, James Hamilton. Pres., dir. Midwest Precote Co., 1948-70, Universal Pipeline Co., 1954-70, Summitt Investment Co., Kansas City, Mo., 1955—, Underground Storage Co., 1964-70, Underground Devel. Co., 1964-70, Randolph Investment Co., Kansas City, Mo., 1966—; v.p., dir. Gracewell, Inc., 1950-70, Kansas City Dock & Storage Co., 1953-65, Midwest Paving Co., 1955-70; dir. Kansas City Bank & Trust Co., Kansas City Bancshares, Inc., 1977—. Bd. dirs. Southtown YMCA, 1971—, Cardiac Center, Children's Mercy Hosp., 1964-70, Research Med. Center, 1974; trustee Park Coll., Parkville, Mo., 1974—; pres., treas. bd. edn. Kansas City Sch. Dist., 1974—; deacon Country Club Christian Ch., 1974—. Served as aviator USN, 1942-45. Mem. Nat. Crushed Stone Assn., Nat. Agr. Limestone Inst., Nat. Asphalt Paving Assn., Heavy Constructors Assn. (dir. 1964-66), Navy League U.S., Beta Theta Pi (alumni pres.). Democrat. Clubs: Masons, Shriners, Rotary, Liberty Hills Country, Homestead. Home: 1025 W 61st Terr Kansas City MO 64113 Office: 800 W 47th St Kansas City MO 64112

LYDIC, FRANK AYLSWORTH, riverman, poet; b. Farnam, Nebr., Jan. 22, 1909; s. Robert Johnston and Lula Ethel (Aylsworth) L.; B.F.A., Kearnsey (Nebr.) State Coll., 1931; m. Florence Faye Meadows, July 2, 1934; children—Marcelle, Bernice Joy (dec.), Robert Norman. Tchr. schs., Calif., 1931-56; riverman various vessels Mississippi River, 1961—; del. Nat. Maritime Union Conv., 1966, 69, 72, 76. Served in U.S. Mcht. Marine, 1943-48, 56-61. Mem. Am. Acad. Poets, Western Writers Am. (asso.), Nebr. Writers Guild, Nebr. Poets Assn. (asso.), Ill. State Poetry Assn., Chgo. Poets and Patrons. Democrat. Author: Desert Lure, 1971; Rhymes of a Riverman, 1973; When My Stretch on the River is Done, 1974; Nebraska! Oh Nebraska, 1975; San Francisco Revisited, 1976; At the Little Bighorn, 1976. Home: Gen Delivery Joliet IL 60431 Office: care Nat Maritime Union 310 N Ottowa St Joliet IL 60435

LYDON, DANIEL PATRICK, assn. exec.; b. Chgo., Mar. 19, 1924; s. John Joseph and Delia Theresa (Geraghty) L.; student DePaul U., 1946-49; m. Mary Louise Genette, Oct. 20, 1951; children—Daniel John, Patricia Delia, John Joseph, Stephen Michael. Reporter, editor Garfieldian Publs., Chgo., 1952-57; dir. pub. info. City of Chgo., 1957-68; exec. dir. Plumbing Council Chicagoland, 1968—; sec.-treas. San Jose Cable TV Corp., 1968—. Chmn., Chgo.'s St. Patrick's Day Parade, 1955-57, coordinator, 1958—; mem. adv. com. Sec. State Ill. Communications, 1972-76. Served with U.S. Army, 1943-45; ETO. Recipient Journalism award Ill. Press Assn., 1954, 55, 56. Mem. Am. Soc. San. Engring. (sec. Ill. chpt. 1971-75), Press, Publicity clubs, Chgo. Hist. Soc., Chgo. Press Vets. Assn., Am. Soc. Assn. Execs. Club: Irish Fellowship (dir.), Execs. (Chgo.). Editor: Pan-American Games, 1959 Yearbook; Comprehensive Plan of Chicago, 1966. Home: 11 Evergreen St Elk Grove Village IL 60007 Office: 1400 W Washington St Chicago IL 60607

LYLE, WILLIS EDWIN, veterinarian; b. St. Clairsville, Ohio, Apr. 30, 1922; s. Edwin Ray and Lena Agnes (Boyd) L.; D.V.M., Ohio State U., 1944; M.S., U. Wis., 1951; m. Mildred Ellen Todd, Mar. 18, 1944; children—Robert, Thomas, Ted, Janet. Veterinarian, Edgerton, Wis., 1944-50; extension veterinarian U. Wis., Madison, 1950-51; veterinarian, Deerfield, Wis., 1952-62; dir. Wis. Animal Health Labs., Madison, 1962-77; adminstr. animal health div. Wis. Dept. Agr., Madison, 1977—; lectr. in field. Mem. Deerfield Sch. Bd., 1962-68; dir. Coop. Ednl. Service Area, 1966-68. Served with U.S. Army, 1943-44. Mem. Am. Assn. Veterinary Lab. Diagnosticians (pres. 1970), AVMA, Wis. Veterinary Med. Assn. (pres. 1963), U.S. Animal Health Assn. Club: Lions. Home: Route 1 PO Box 303H Edgerton WI 53534 Office: 6101 Mineral Point Rd Madison WI 53705

LYMAN, HOWARD B(URBECK), psychologist; b. Athol, Mass., Feb. 12, 1920; s. Stanley B(urbeck) and Ruth Mary (Gray) L.; A.B., Brown U., 1942; M.A., U. Minn., 1948; Ph.D., U. Ky., 1951; m. Patricia Malone Taylor, May 4, 1966; children—David S., Nancy M., D. Jane; stepchildren—Richard P., Martha C., Robert M. and David P. Taylor. Acting dir. student personnel E. Tex. State Tchrs. Coll., Commerce, 1948-49; counselor, research asst. univ. personnel office U. Ky., Lexington, 1949-51; research psychologist tests and measurements U.S. Naval Exam. Center, Norfolk, Va. and Gt. Lakes, Ill., 1951-52; asst. prof. psychology U. Cin., 1952-62, asso. prof., 1962—; dir. Acad. Edn. and Research in Profl. Psychology Ohio 1975—. Served with AUS, 1942-46. Licensed psychologist, Ohio. Fellow Am. Psychol. Assn.; mem. Ohio (dir. 1960—, Distinguished Service award 1974), Midwestern, Cin. psychol. assns., Assn. Measurement and Evaluation in Guidance, Nat. Council Measurement in Edn., Psi Chi. Author: Single Again, 1971; Test Scores and What They Mean, 3d edit., 1978; editor Ohio Psychologist, 1967—. Home: 3422 Whitfield Ave Cincinnati OH 45220

LYMAN, JANICE KAY, social worker; b. Macon, Mo., Jan. 3, 1945; s. John Thomas and Lorene (Nisbeth) L.; student Culver Stockton Coll., 1963-66; A.B., North East Mo. State U., 1971, M.A., 1977. Social worker Div. Family Services, Macon, Mo., 1966-69, div. mental health Kirksville (Mo.) Regional Center for the Developmentally Disabled, 1970—. Religious edn. scholar CulverStockton Coll. Mem. Am. Personnel and Guidance Assn. Mem. Ch. Disciples of Christ. Home: 210 Jackson St Macon MO 63552 Office: 1702 E Laharpe St Kirksville MO 63501

LYMAN, RICHARD OLNEY, rancher, county ofcl.; b. Mpls., Aug. 17, 1939; s. Richard Brackett and Mary Francis (Olney) L.; student Carleton Coll., 1957-59; B.S., U. Minn., 1961, postgrad. 1964-65; postgrad. Vanderbilt U., 1961-62; m. Martha Norman Anderson, July 23, 1969; children—Andrew Norman Richard, John Lockhart, Charles Benjamin. Tchr. Peace Corps, Ethopia, 1962-64; turkey rancher nr. Chanhassen, Minn., 1965—. Chmn. Carver County United Fund, Chanhassen, Minn., 1969-70; adviser Jr. Achievement, 1972-73; chmn. Chanhassen Planning Commn., 1968; vice chmn. Met. Park Open Space Task Force, 1972; mem. Criminal Justice Adv. Commn., 1969-72; treas. Minnetonka Montessori Schs., 1974—; chmn. Chanhassen Park Bd., 1967; elected to Carver County Bd. Commrs., 1968-72, chmn. Welfare Bd., 1970-72, created Carver County Dept. Pub. Works, Chaska, Minn., 1972; sec. Carver County Sheriffs Civil Service Bd., 1973—. Rep. precinct chmn. 1970. Mem. bd. govs. U. Minn., 1960-61, pres. 1960-61; mem. bd. dirs. Minn. Internat. Center, 1973. Ralston Purina scholar, 1960. Mem. Alpha Zeta, Gamma Sigma Delta, Conglist. Rotarian. Club: Mpls. Home: Route 1 Box 607 Excelsior MN 55331

LYNCH, CHARLES THEODORE, scientist, adminstr.; b. Lima, Ohio, May 17, 1932; s. John Richard and Helen (Dunn) L.; A.A., George Washington U., 1953, B.S. in Chemistry, 1955; M.S., U. Ill., 1957, Ph.D. in analytical chemistry, 1960; m. Betty Ann Korkolis, Feb. 3, 1956; children—Karen Elaine, Charles Theodore, Richard Anthony, Thomas Edward. Grad. teaching asst. U. Ill., 1955-60; research materials engr. and lead scientist, USAF Materials Lab., Wright-Patterson AFB, O. 1962-66; chief advanced metall. studies br., USAF-AFML, Ohio, 1966-72, sr. scientist, 1969-76, sr. scientist environ. effects, 1976—; lectr. in chemistry Wright State Campus, Miami (Ohio) State U., Dayton, 1964-66; Air Force liaison mem. Materials adv. bd. panel on solid processing Ad Hoc Com. on ceramic Process; mem. AIME-IMD Composites Com, 1968-75; mem. DoD Interagy. Panel on Stress Corrosion; mem. AFML Post-doctoral Com.; co-chmn. Dayton Conf. Composite Materials 1970; mem. adv. bd. Sci. and Engring. Inst. Dayton, 1969-71. Mem. Fairborn (Ohio) Pub. Sch. PTA, pres. 1967-69; choir dir. Wright-Patterson AFB Chapel II, 1960-64; mem. George Washington U., Traveling Troubadours, 1950-55; choir dir. Trinity United Ch. Christ, Fairborn, 1968—. Served to 1st lt. USAF, 1960-62, capt. Res. NSF fellow, summer 1959. Recipient numerous USAF patent awards; Award for Scientific Achievement, 1968. Mem. Am. Chem. Soc. (treas. Dayton sect. 1966), Am. Inst. Mining, Metall. and Petroleum Engrs. (mem. corrosion resistant metals com. 1974—, mem. composite materials com. 1968-75), Am. Ceramic Soc., AAAS, Ohio Acad. Sci., Sci. Research Soc. Am., N.Y. Acad. Scis., Alpha Chi Sigma, Omicron Delta Kappa, Phi Lambda Upsilon, Delta Sigma Rho. Baptist (choir dir.). Patentee in field. Contbr. articles to profl. jours.; editor Handbook of Materials Sci. series, 1974, 75; author: Book on Composites, 1970. Home: 387 Cherrywood Dr Fairborn OH 45324 Office: Metals and Ceramics Div Air Force Materials Lab Wright Patterson AFB OH 45433

LYNCH, CHARLES THOMAS, educator; b. Waterbury, Conn., Oct. 10, 1918; s. Charles T. and Sara (Carroll) L.; student U. of Ala., 1935-37, Mich. State U., 1960; B.A., Western Mich. U., 1963, M.A., 1966; Ph.D., Southern Ill. U., 1972; m. Helen Victoria Kaliss, Aug. 4, 1941; children—C. Thomas, Jean Lynch Julian, Christopher. Announcer, producer, writer at commercial radio stations Waterbury, Conn., Tallahassee, Fla., Phila., Lansing, Mich., 1938-49; program mgr., exec. producer Fetzer Broadcasting Co., Kalamazoo, Mich., 1949-67; asst. prof. radio TV, radio station mgr., Southern Ill. U., Carbondale, 1967-74, asso. prof., chmn. radio/TV, 1974—; lectr. Western Mich. U., Kalamazoo, 1966-67; cons. Kalamazoo (Mich.) Valley Community Coll., 1965. Pres. Community Theatre Assn. of Mich., 1963-65; pres. Kalamazoo Civic Theatre, 1962-64; pres. Kalamazoo Area PTA, 1960-61; mem. Southern Ill. Chpt. of U.N. Assn. Bd., 1968-77. Recipient Broadcast Preceptor award Broadcast Industry Conf., 1976. Mem. Nat. Acad. TV Arts & Sci., Nat. Assn. Ednl. Broadcasters, Broadcast Edn. Assn., Speech Communication Assn., Soc. Profl. Journalists, Am. Film Inst., Ill. News Broadcasters Assn., Alpha Epsilon Rho, Phi Kappa Phi. Roman Catholic. Contbr. numerous articles, documentary in field. Home: 125 Roxanne St Rural Route #6 Carbondale IL 62901 Office: Radio TV Dept Southern Ill U Carbondale IL 62901

LYNCH, DARREL LUVENE, educator; b. Dewey, Okla., Feb. 6, 1921; s. Homer Dee and Della Iola (Elam) L.; B.S., U. Ill., 1947, M.S., 1948, Ph.D., 1953; M.S. chemistry, U. Del., 1957; m. Dorothy Eileen Banner, Jan. 22, 1949; children—Alan D., Francis L., Alice R., Margaret L. Asst. prof. U. Del., 1952-58, U. Alta. (Can.), 1958-60; asso. prof. chemistry Ga. So. Coll., Statesboro, 1960-62; prof. microbiology No. Ill. U., DeKalb, 1962—. Cons., Environ. Analysts, Inc., Batavia, Ill., 1973—. Served with AUS, 1943-46. Recipient grant Del. Research Found., 1952. Mem. Ill. Acad. Sci., Am. Soc. Microbiology. Democrat. Mem. Disciples of Christ. Editor Jour. Transactions, Ill. Acad. Sci., 1968-70. Home: 306 Dresser Rd DeKalb IL 60115 Office: Dept Biological Scis No Ill Univ DeKalb IL 60115

LYNCH, GEORGE ARTHUR, physicist; b. Titusville, Pa., May 4, 1938; s. Harvey Thomas and Georgianna Beatrice (Porter) L.; B.S. in Engring. Physics, Wright State U., 1974; m. Lucille Joyce Rocco, May 9, 1959; children—Kim R., Tammy A., Terri J. Research devel. specialist USAF, Dayton, Ohio, 1964-74, physicist acoustics, 1974, physicist electro-optics, 1974—. Commr., Boy Scouts Am., 1973; chmn. Mad River Sch. Bd. Adv. Com.. 1974. Served with USAF, 1956-64. Decorated AF Commendation Medal. Mem. Ohio Soc. Profl. Engrs., IEEE, Am. Legion, DAV, Greene County Fish and Game Assn., Ohio Congress Parents and Tchrs. (hon. life). Club: Wright Patterson AFB Rod and Gun (past pres.). Home: 5649 Hunters Ridge Dayton OH 45431 Office: FTD ETS Wright Patterson Air Force Base OH 45433

LYNCH, JACK CHARLES, broadcasting exec.; b. Lidgerwood, N.D., Mar. 29, 1921; s. Jack Francis and Alice (Mapes) L.; student St. Thomas Coll., 1939-40, Wis. State Coll. at LaCrosse, 1945-46; m. Mayme Quale, Jan. 30, 1942; children—Jack, Michael, Kathleen, Shannon. Announcer radio sta. WMIN, Mpls. St. Paul, 1939-40, radio sta. WKBH, LaCrosse, 1942-46; announcer radio sta. KWLM, Wilmar, Minn., 1940-42, sales mgr., 1946-68, mgr., 1968—. Mem. Minn. Higher Edn. Coordinating Commn., 1965—, pres., 1973; mem. Willmar Sch. Bd., 1960-69, pres., 1966-68; mem. New Ulm (Minn.) Diocesan Sch. Bd., 1969-72; mem. Karishon Dist. exec. bd. Viking council Boy Scouts Am., 1956—, chmn., 1956-61; mem. Kandiyohi County (Minn.) Fair Bd., 1956—; mem. Willmar United Fund Bd., 1955—, pres., 1955-56; state chmn. Brotherhood Week NCCJ, 1960. Mayor of Willmar (Minn.), 1973-76. Served with USAAF, 1942-45. Recipient Silver Beaver award Boy Scouts Am., 1962. Roman Catholic. Lion, K.C. Home: 618 W 10th St Willmar MN 56201 Office: Station KWLM Willmar MN 56201

LYNCH, JOHN JAMES, judge; b. Chgo., June 28, 1915; s. John Joseph and Mary C. (Duffin) L.; B.A., Ohio State U., 1938, J.D., 1940; m. Vernie Rogan, Sept. 13, 1947 (dec. May 1968); children—John, Arlene, Dennis; m. 2d, Emma Gentile Bartholomew, Aug. 9, 1975. Admitted to Ohio bar, 1940; spl. agt. FBI, 1940-43; practice law, Youngstown, 1946-65; asst. atty. gen., 1959-63, judge Ct. of Appeals, 7th appellate dist. Ohio, 1965—, chief justice, 1977—. Mem. Ohio Ho. Reps., 1949-58, chmn. Democrat mems. policy com., 1957; chmn. Mahoning County com. Bus. and Profl. Men and Women for Kennedy-Johnson, 1960. Served with AUS, 1943-46. Mem. Am., Ohio, Mahoning County bar assns., Ohio State Alumni Assn., Amvets, Am. Legion, Nat. Counter Intelligence Corps Assn. Democrat. Roman Catholic. K.C. Home: 2718 Normandy Dr Youngstown OH 44511 Office: Ct House Youngstown OH 44503

LYNCH, SISTER MARGUERITE, nun, counselor; b. Chgo., Aug. 18, 1927; d. Patrick J. and Mary A. (Burke) Lynch; B.A., Rosary Coll., 1950; M.A., Loyola U., 1960. Joined Sisters of St. Joseph, Roman Catholic Ch., 1945; prin. St. Mary Sch., Riverside, Ill., 1958-61, St. Margaret Mary Sch., Chgo., 1969-72; dean studies Sisters of St. Joseph, LaGrange, Ill., 1972-77; dir. guidance Nazareth Acad. High Sch., LaGrange, 1977—; adminstr. ORFF Music Camp, LaGrange, 1974-77; liason with No. Ill. U., Dekalb, 1975; mem. Ednl. Com. of Mental Health, La Grange, Ill., 1975—; sch. bd. caucus La Grange Sch., 1975—; mem. com. La Grange Summer Employment Program, 1976. NSF grantee, Beaver Coll., Phila., 1973; selected for Vocat. Guidance Inst. Ill. Inst. Tech., Chgo., 1968; Ill. State Bd. Edn. grantee, Normal, Ill., 1976. Mem. Am., Ill. personnel and guidance assns., SW Suburban Guidance Dirs., Nat. Catholic Guidance Assn. Home: 1515 W Ogden Ave LaGrange IL 60525 Office: 1209 W Ogden Ave LaGrange IL 60525

LYNCH, RAYMOND PATRICK, pediatrician; b. Evergreen Park, Ill., Apr. 15, 1937; s. Bernard Michael and Leah Ida (Dunham) L.; M.D., Loyola U., Chgo., 1962; m. Roberta Caliendo, Aug. 6, 1960; children—Debra, Joe, Karen, Cheryl, Raymond, Andrea. Intern, Cook County Hosp., Chgo., 1962-63; resident in pediatrics Children's Meml. Hosp., Chgo., Evanston, Ill., 1966-67; practice medicine specializing in pediatrics, St. Paul, Minn., 1968—; clin. instr. U. Minn. Sch. Medicine. Diplomate Am. Bd. Pediatrics. Fellow Am. Acad. Pediatrics. Roman Catholic. Office: 233 Smith Ave St Paul MN 55101

LYNCH, ROBERT EMMETT, educator; b. Chgo., Feb. 5, 1932; s. Joseph Burke and Mildred Cecilia (Bildhauser) L.; student Cornell U., 1949-55, B.Engring. Physics, 1955; M.S., Harvard, 1959, Ph.D., 1963; m. Martha Bolling Hacker, Oct. 8, 1955; children—Barbara, William, Pamela. Sr. research mathematician Gen. Motors Research Labs., Warren, Mich., 1961-64; asst. prof. U. Tex. at Austin, 1964-66, asso. prof., 1966-67; asso. prof. Purdue U., West Lafayette, Ind., 1967—. Served with USAF, 1955-57. Mem. Am. Math. Soc., Am. Assn. Math., Soc. Indsl. and Applied Math, Sigma Xi. Author: (with John R. Rice) Computers: Their Impact and Use; with introduction to Basic, 1975; Computers Their Impact and Use; with structured programming in Fortran, 1977; Computers Their Impact and Use; with structured programming in PL/I, 1977. Home: 105 E Navajo St West Lafayette IN 47906 Office: Div Math Sci Purdue Univ West Lafayette IN 47907

LYNCH, WILLIAM ERNEST, JR., physician; b. Omaha, Jan. 24, 1938; s. William Ernest and Gertrude Catherine (McKenna) L.; M.D., Creighton U., 1963; m. Virginia Rae Wiltse, Aug. 29, 1964; children—Michael, Joseph, Danniel, Charles, Peter, Katherine. Intern, Creighton U., 1963, resident in medicine, 1964-66, fellow in cardiology, 1966-68; practice medicine specializing in cardiology, Springfield, Ill., 1974—; asso. dir. cardiology Meml. Hosp., Springfield, 1970-74; mem. staff St. Johns Hosp.; clin. asst. prof. medicine So. Ill. U., 1975—. Chmn. Sangamon County Heart Assn., 1971-72, 73. Served to maj. USAF, 1968-70. Diplomate Am. Bd. Internal Medicine (subsplty. cardiovascular disease). Fellow Am. Coll. Cardiology, Council Clin. Cardiology, Am. Heart Assn.; mem. A.C.P., AMA, Ill., Sangamon County med. assns., Springfield Med. Club. Republican. Roman Catholic. Home: 1600 Illini Rd Springfield IL 62704 Office: 801 7th St N Springfield IL 62702

LYNN, EDWARD RANDALL, hosp. adminstr.; b. Oak Park, Ill., Oct. 6, 1931; s. Albert Edward and Margaret Lucille (Fell) L.; B.S., U. Ill., 1953; M.H.A., U. Minn., 1957; m. Elma Harriet Fendley, Mar. 12, 1955; children—Ruth Emily, Alice Jane. Adminstrv. resident Abbott Hosp., Mpls., 1956-57, asst. adminstr., 1957-61, asso. adminstr., 1961-66; adminstr. Jennie Edmundson Meml. Hosp., Council Bluffs, Iowa, 1966—; dir. Council Bluffs Savs. Bank, Banks of Iowa, Council Bluffs Investment Co. Mem. Gov.'s Com. Physicians Assists; preceptor health adminstrn. U. Minn., also clin. faculty study program hosp. or health care facility adminstrs. Pres. Council Bluffs Bd. Health, 1968, 72; dir. Council Bluffs Family and Child Services, 1971-72; bd. dirs. Omaha-Council Bluffs Family and Child Services, 1974—, treas., 1976-77; pres. United Fund of Council Bluffs, 1971, dir., 1971-74; pres. Health Planning Council of Midlands, 1973-76; asso. chmn. finance campaign United Community Services of Omaha, 1970; dir. Health Planning Council of Iowa, 1971-72; dir. Western Iowa and S.D. Blue Cross. Pres. bd. dirs. Council Bluffs Library, 1973-74; bd. dirs. Omaha Henry Doorly Zoo, Riverfront Communities Devel. Found., Hist. Gen. Dodge House, 1972-76. Served to 1st lt. M.C., AUS, 1953-55. Mem. Iowa, Omaha (pres. 1973, 74) hosp. assns., Am. Coll. Hosp. Adminstrs., Nat. League Nursing, Alpha Kappa Psi. Presbyn. (elder). Club: Lake Shore Country (Council Bluffs). Home: 303 Oak Park Rd Council Bluffs IA 51501 Office: 933 E Pierce St Council Bluffs IA 51501

LYNN, ELIZABETH MEAGHER, mgmt. training specialist; b. Oshkosh, Wis.; d. Joseph E. and Gertrude J. (DeYoung) Meagher; B.A., Marygrove Coll., Detroit, 1960; M.A., Villanova U., 1962; M.Ed., Columbia U., 1971; Ph.D. Ind. U., 1974; m. Lowell A. Lynn. Chem. sales corr. Westvaco, 1963-65; English tchr. Phila. Bd. Edn., 1965-66; film production coordinator Marathon Internat. Productions, 1966; broadcast editor Nat. Assn. Broadcasters, Code Authority, 1966-67; writer 21st Century, CBS-TV and Nat. Citizens Com. for Pub. Broadcasting, 1967-68; lectr. City Coll. N.Y., 1968-71; asso. instr. Ind. U., 1971-74; instr. Cuyahoga Community Coll., Cleve., 1974-75; sr. research asso. Case Western Res. U., Cleve., 1975-76; communications cons., profl. lectr., Cleve., 1976-77; staff asso.-training Standard Oil Co. (Ohio), Cleve., 1977—; speaker, cons. corps., univ. schs. mgmt., profl. assns.; speech writer, lectr.; editorial reviewer profl. manuscripts for ERIC, Wadsworth and Addison-Wesley pub. orgns. Grantee, Nat. Inst. Edn., Ind. U., Pi Lambda Theta, Hunter Coll. (CUNY), Villanova U.; fellow Columbia U. Mem. Am. Arbitration Assn., Am. Soc. Training Dirs., Speech Communications Assn., Am. Bus. Communication Assn., Internat., Central States communication assns. Author: Improving Classroom Communication, 1976; co-author U.S. Govt. HEW report: The Role of the Professional Nurse in Primary Health Care. Contbr. articles to profl. jours., ERIC system. Office: Standard Oil Co (Ohio) Midland Bldg Cleveland OH 44115

LYON, GEOFFREY DALE, material handling co. exec.; b. Niles, Mich., Apr. 17, 1945; s. Theodore Richard and Donna Nell (Folkman) L.; B.A., Mich. State U., 1967; M.B.A., Western Mich. U., 1969; m. Lynne Brockman, Aug. 3, 1968; children—Chad, Jason. Mgr. mktg. service Graphic Arts Center Clark Equipment Co., Dowagiac, Mich., 1971-73; corporate market analyst, Buchanan, Mich., 1973-76; regional bus. mgr. Clark Equipment Credit Corp., Buchanan, 1976-77, sr. bus. mgr., 1977—. Served with U.S. Army, 1969-71. Mem. Am. Mktg. Assn. (dir. Mich. chpt. 1973-75, treas. 1975). Republican. Presbyterian. Clubs: Elks, Orchard Hills Country, Michiana Courthouse. Home: 1405 Sioux Trail Niles MI 49120 Office: 128 E Front St Buchanan MI 49107

LYONS, BERNARD PATRICK, newspaper editor; b. Chelsea, Mich., July 17, 1922; s. Henry Hugh and Helen (Burg) L.; B.A., U. Mich., 1947, certificate journalism, 1947; m. Anita C. McClear, Nov. 24, 1945; children—Dawn, William, Jill. Reporter Port Huron (Mich.) Times Herald, 1947-50, city editor, 1950-53, editorial writer, 1959-62, mng. editor, 1962-73; editor Lafayette (Ind.) Jour. & Courier, 1973-76, adminstrv. editor, 1976—; editor Marysville (Mich.) Jour., 1953-58, St. Clair (Mich.) County Press, 1958-59. Pub. info. chmn. United Community Chest, St. Clair County, 1968; pres. Internat. Symphony Orch., Sarnia, Ont., Can. and Port Huron, 1967-69, Port Huron Cultural Com., 1961-64. Sec. adv. bd. Mercy Hosp., Port Huron, 1973; bd. dirs. Port Huron Mus. Arts and History, 1968-73, Lafayette Art Assn., 1975—; trustee LaFayette Symphony Orchestra, 1974—. Served with USAF, 1943-45; ETO. Mem. Mich. A.P. Editorial Assn. (pres. 1973-74), Hoosier State Press Assn., A.P. Mng. Editors Assn. Roman Catholic. Clubs: Univ. Press of Mich. (pres. 1968-69); Lafayette Country. Home: 3600 Cypress Ln Lafayette IN 47904 Office: 217 N 6th St Lafayette IN 47901

LYONS, BEULAH M. WALLAR (MRS. LAWRENCE RUPERT LYONS), Christian Sci. practitioner; b. Canton, O., Jan. 27, 1912; d. Lee E. and Viola (Clinger) Wallar; student pub. sch.; m.2d, Lawrence Rupert Lyons, Feb. 19, 1937 (dec. Mar. 1972); children—Wilma (dec.), Jack Victor (dec.). Joined Christian Sci. Ch. Toledo, 1943. Christian Sci. Mother Ch., Boston, 1944: 1st reader Christian Sci. Ch., Waterloo, Iowa, 1951-53, 2d reader, Enterprise, Ala., 1959; now practitioner. Dir., bylaw com. chs. at Waterloo, Cedar Rapids, Iowa, Enterprise, Ala., Ottumwa, Iowa. Adviser, Christian Sci. Coll. Orgn., Coe Coll., 1962-64. Mem. Christian Sci. Assn. Leslie Leland C.S.B. Toledo (dir. 1961-64, chmn. bd. 1963-64), Internat. Platform Assn., Marine Corps League Aux. (life; past pres.), Daus. Am. (hon. life). Home: 2875 Mt Vernon Rd SE Cedar Rapids IA 52403

LYONS, DON CHALMERS, oral surgeon; b. Jackson, Mich., May 5, 1899; s. James White and Estelle May (Stonerod) L.; D.D.S., U. Mich., 1921, M.S. in Oral Surgery, 1932; Ph.D., Mich. State U., 1935; m. Gertrude Campbell Rosecrans, Sept. 28, 1922; children—Don Chalmers, Roger, Shirley. Intern Bellevue Hosp., N.Y.C., 1921; fellow, intern Mayo Clinic, Rochester, Minn., 1921-23; practice oral surgery and oral medicine, Jackson, 1923—; mem. staff Jackson Osteo Hosp.; vis. oral surgeon, mem. staff Albion (Mich.) Community Hosp.; mem. exec. com. oral surgery, cons. oral surgery and medicine W.A. Foote Hosp., Jackson; cons. oral surgery Mercy Hosp., Jackson; Fulbright prof. oral medicine and surgery U. San Marcus, Lima, Peru, 1961, U. Central and U. Cuenca, Ecuador, 1963; Fulbright prof. oral medicine, pathology and oral surgery U. Tehran (Iran), 1966-67. Scoutmaster Land of Lakes council Boy Scouts Am., 1939-55, v.p. council, 1950, mem. exec. com., 1945—, mem.-at-large Nat. council, 1965—. Served with M.C., U.S. Army, 1918. Recipient Distinguished Service certificate U.S. Jr. C. of C., 1935, Silver Beaver award Boy Scouts Am., 1950. Diplomate Am. Bd. Oral Medicine. Fellow Am. Pub. Health Assn., A.A.A.S., Am. Med. Writers Assn. (dir. 1959), Am. Acad. Oral Medicine (pres. 1958-59, Samuel Miller Meml. award 1969, Diamond Service award 1975, editor newsletter), Am., Internat. colls. dentists; mem. Am. Dental Assn. (life), Mich. (life), Jackson Dist. (pres. 1929) dental socs., Jackson Acad. Medicine and Dentistry, Am. Soc. Bacteriologists, Research Soc. Am., Am. Dental Editors Soc., Fedn. Dentaire Internationale, Sigma Xi, Phi Sigma, Omicron Kappa Upsilon, Delta Sigma Delta, Phi Delta Theta. Republican. Episcopalian. Clubs: Jackson (Mich.) Country; Circumnavigator. Author: Esenciales de Cirugia Oral, 1964; contbr.

chpts. to Oral Diagnosis and Treatment, 1946, 57; Diagnostica Tratiemento Buccal, 1957; Oral and Facial Signs and Symptons of Systemic Disease, 1968. Contbr. numerous sci. articles to profl. jours. Co-chmn. publ. com. Jour. Oral Medicine. Home: 512 S Wisner St Jackson MI 49203 Office: 420 W Michigan Ave Jackson MI 49201

LYONS, J. ROLLAND, civil engr.; b. Cedar Rapids, Iowa, Apr. 27, 1909; s. Neen T. and Goldie N. (Hill) L.; B.S., U. Iowa, 1933; m. Mary Jane Doht, June 10, 1924; children—Marlene Lyons Sparks, Sharon Lyons Hutson, Lynn Lyons Dunas. Jr. hwy. engr. Works Projects Adminstrn. field engr. Dept. Transp., State Ill., Peoria, 1930-31, civil engr. I-IV Central Office, Springfield, 1934-53, civil engr. V, 1953-66, municipal sect. chief, civil engr. VI, 1966-72. Civil Def. radio officer Springfield and Sangamon County (Ill.) Civil Def. Agy., 1952—. Recipient Meritorious Service award, Am. Assn. State Hwy. Ofcls., 1968; 25 Yr. Career Service award, State Ill., 1966; Certificate Appreciation, Ill. Municipal League, 1971. Registered profl. engr., Ill.; registered land surveyor, Ill. Mem. Ill. Assn. State Hwy. Engrs., State Ill. Employees Assn., Am. Pub. Works Assn., Am. Assn. State Hwy. Ofcls., Amateur Trapshooters Assn. Clubs: K.C., Sangamon Valley Radio; Lakewood Golf and Country. Address: 3642 Lancaster Rd Springfield IL 62703

LYONS, JAMES DAVID, bus. services exec.; b. Chgo., Jan. 6, 1935; s. Fred L. and Agnes V. (Brown) L.; student U. Ill., 1953-54; B.S., Rutgers U., 1956; m. Mary Lou Fisher, July 21, 1956; children—David, James, Dennis, Deborah. With A.C. Nielsen Co., Northbrook, Ill., 1958—, exec. v.p. and gen. mgr. media research div., 1974—, pres. and chief exec. officer media research services group, 1977—, also dir. Served with U.S. Army, 1955-57. Mem. Am. Mgmt. Assn., Am. Mktg. Assn. Clubs: Univ. Club of N.Y., Mich. Shores (Wilmette, Ill.). Home: 416 Woodstock Ave Kenilworth IL 60043 Office: Nielsen Plaza Northbrook IL 60062

LYONS, JERRY LEE, engr.; b. St. Louis, Apr. 2, 1939; M.E., Okla. Inst. Tech., 1964. Registered profl. engr., Calif.; certified mfg. engr. in product design. Project engr. Harris Mfg. Co., St. Louis, 1964-70; project engr. Essex Cryogenics Industries, Inc., St. Louis, 1970-73; mgr. engring. research Fluid Controls div. Chemtron Corp., St. Louis, 1973—; pres. Yankee Ingenuity Inc., St. Louis, 1974—. Mem. St. Louis Soc. Mfg. Engrs. (vice chmn., 1975, 77) Soc. Mfg. Engrs. for Registration in Mo. (chmn. 1976), Nat. Fluid Power Assn. (mem. com. 1974-76), ASME (sr. com. mem. ops., applications and components div. 1975—), Am. Security Council (mem. nat. advisory bd. 1975—), Nat. Soc. Profl. Engrs., Mo. Soc. Profl. Engrs., Soc. Mfg. Engrs., Instrument Soc. Am., St. Louis Engrs. Club (award of merit 1977). Author: Lyons Encyclopedia of Valves, 1975; ISA Handbook Control Valves (with J.W. Hutchinson), 1976; ISA Control Valve Study Series on Acuators and Accessories, 1977; The Valve Designers Handbook, 1977; contbr. articles, papers to profl. jours. Home: 7535 Harlan Walk St Louis MO 63123 Office:

LYONS, THOMAS HARSHMAN, librarian; b. Detroit, Apr. 15, 1923; s. Ward Irving and Margaret Smith (Peters) L.; student Olivet Coll., 1940-43; B.A., Wayne State U., 1947, M.S. in Edn., 1949, Edn. Specialist in Instructional Tech., 1977; A.M. in L.S., U. Mich., 1964; m. Harriet Ann Hamilton, July 8, 1944; children—Norman Hamilton, David John, Thomas Michael. Tchr., librarian West Bloomfield Schs., Orchard Lake, Mich., 1949-67; librarian, audio-visual dir. Northwood Inst., Midland, Mich., 1967-74; asso. prof., dir. audio visual services Oakland U., Rochester, Mich., 1974—. Active Inst. Sch. Library Personnel Western Mich. U., 1965, Media Inst. Mich. State U., 1968-69. Served with AUS, 1943-46. Mem. Mich. Library Assn., Assn. for Ednl. Communications and Tech., Mich. Assn. for Media in Edn., AAUP, Mich. Soc. Instructional Tech. Home: 2315 Cheltingham Sylvan Lake MI 48053 Office: Audio Visual Services Varner Hall Oakland U Rochester MI 48063

LYSNE, ALLEN BRUCE, health care adminstr.; b. Owen, Wis., Nov. 8, 1938; s. Almond Palmer and Helen Adeline (Childs) L.; student U. N.D., 1959, Minot State Coll., 1958; med. technologist, 1961; m. Sharon Kay Reiger, Aug. 24, 1967; children—Bruce Allen, Brooke Renae. With Indian Health div. USPHS, 1961, Dr. Salsbury's Labs., Charles City, Iowa, 1962, Luth. Hosps. and Homes Soc., Gillette, Wyo., 1962-63, Lake Region Clinic, Devils Lake, N.D., 1963-69; adminstr. Meml. Hosp., Maddock, N.D., 1969-76; dir. ops. N.D. Health Care Rev., Inc., 1976—. Bd. dirs. Central Flyway Health Planning Council, Continuing Edn. for Med. Technologists in N.D.; chmn. adv. bd. Benson County Welfare Area Adminstrs. Commn. Mem. N.D. Hosp. Assn. Roman Catholic. Home: 2038 8th St NW Minot ND 58701 Office: 3415 N Broadway Minot ND 58701

LYTLE, CLIFFORD FRANKLIN, accountant; b. Marquette County, Wis., Mar. 22, 1918; s. Ira Garfield and Lillian Maria (Wing) L.; B.B.A., Madison Coll., 1936; postgrad. Englewood Coll., 1938, U. Rome (Italy), 1943-45, Internat. Accountants Soc., 1947-49; m. Irene Mae Peters, June 14, 1941; children—Thomas F., Terrance L., Sally J. Stenographic reporter com. on judiciary and joint com. on finance Wis. State Senate, Madison, 1937, 39, 41; with Erie R.R. Co., Chgo., 1942-43, 45-46; bus. mgr. Hudson Motor Car Co., Milw., 1947-50, asst. zone mgr., 1950-52; pvt. practice accounting, Waukesha, Wis., 1952—. Justice of the Peace, Big Bend, Wis., Waukesha County, 1950-53; charter mem. Waukesha Meml. Hosp., 1957—. Served with AUS, 1943-45. Recipient Ford Motor Co. Bus. Mgmt. award, 1961-74; Diamond award Chrysler Motor Corp., 1957; named to Nat. Accountants Honor Roll, Pontiac Motor Div., 1964-76. Mem. Wis. Assn. Accountants, Nat. Soc. Pub. Accountants, Buick Motor Div. Honor Accountants Club. Home: 1226 Downing Dr Waukesha WI 53186

MA, ALEX, surgeon; b. Toronto, Ont., Can., June 6, 1930; s. Timothy K. Wou and Anna (Lee) M.; M.A. in Physiology and Biochemistry, U. Toronto, 1954, M.D., 1958; m. Grace Ling, June 20, 1959; children—Brian Andrew, Enid Ann, Alison Celeste, Charles Edward, Peter Timothy. Intern Toronto Gen. Hosp., 1958-59; resident Toronto East Gen. Hosp., 1959-61, U. Hosp., Saskatoon, Sask., 1961-63; fellow surgery U. Sask., 1963-64; mem. staff Mississauga (Ont.) Hosp., 1965-69, 70—, Oasis Hosp., Abu Dhabi, Arabian Gulf, 1969-70, 72, 75. Chmn. bd. Young Men's Christian Inst., Toronto, 1972—. Fellow Royal Coll. Physicians and Surgeons Can. Presbyn. (elder, chmn. Com. Christian edn.). Address: 687 Sir Richards Rd Mississauga ON Canada

MA, CYNTHIA SANMAN, computer systems analyst; b. Hong Kong, May 16, 1940; d. Pin-San and Soo-Hin (Wong) Chan; came to U.S., 1961, naturalized, 1977; B.S., Siena Coll., 1962; M.S., Fla. State U., 1966, Ph.D., 1969; m. Pang-Fai Ma, June 4, 1966; children—Alvina, Arnold. Statistician, Community Studies Inst., Kansas City, Mo., 1962-63; computer programmer Fla. State U., 1966-67, instr., systems analyst, 1967-69; asst. prof., research systems analyst Ball State U., Muncie, Ind., 1969-72, asso. prof. dept. fin. and mgmt., 1972—; cons. Data Dynamics, Tallahassee, 1970. Mem. Am. Statis. Assn., Assn. Systems Mgmt., Computing Machinery Assn., Am. Assn. Sch. Adminstrs., Delta Kappa Pi. Roman Catholic. Author: Introduction of Computers, 1978. Home: 2608 W Purdue Ave Muncie IN 47304 Office: Dept Mgmt Ball State U Muncie IN 47306

MAAHS, WERNER H., foods co. exec.; b. Milw., Jan. 15, 1927; s. William H. and Marie (Mueller) N.; grad. N. Division High Sch., 1944; m. Gladys M. Anderson, June 24, 1950; children—Sandra Marie, Nancy Jean, Christine Lynn, David, Judy. Dir. Alto Shaam, Inc., Milw., 1955-63, past dir., now v.p. marketing; v.p. Chicken Delight, Inc., Rock Island, Ill., 1956-63, past dir.; past pres. Chicken Delight of Calif., Los Angeles; past pres. Franchise Devel. Corp.; pres. Buffalo Bill's Steak Village, Inc.; pres. M & M Enterprizes, Inc.; partner Linkletter, Maahs, Bolte & Asso., bus. and mgmt. counselors; dir. Buffalo Bill's Steak Village of Can., Ltd.; pres. Buffalo Bill's Enterprises Inc., Buffalo Bill's Properties Inc.; v.p. Fitzgerald, Maahs, Miller, Inc.; Capt. Jim's Seafood Galley; v.p., dir. Adventure Prodns. Inc., Hollywood, Cal.; gen. mgr. Franchise Travelodge Internat.; nat. investment cons. Hanna Industries, Portland, Ore.; dir. Robson Systems Inc., Van Nuys, Calif. Mem. ethics com. Internat. Franchise Assn. Bd. dirs. U. Calif. Los Angeles Campus Ministry Council. Lutheran (past pres.). Contbg. author: Franchise Today. Home: N 63 W 33959 Lake View Dr Oconomowoc WI 53209

MAAS, JOHANNES, ch. denomination pres.; b. Paterson, N.J., Sept. 8, 1936; s. Cornelius and Agnes (Nawyn) M.; A.B., Alma White Coll., 1958; B.D., Evang. Bible Sem., 1962, Th.M., 1963, Th.D., 1964; M.Ed., U. Pitts., 1967; m. Julia Dawn Bartlett, Jan. 21, 1961; children—Johanna Ruth, Jonathan Hans, Joel Cornelius-Jyoti. Ordained to ministry Wesleyan Meth. Ch., 1955, Wesleyan Tabernacle Assn., 1977; gen. evangelist Wesleyan Meth. Ch. Am., 1960-64; pres. Praise Rec. Co., Paris, Ohio, 1964—; bus. mgr. Allegheny Wesleyan Coll., Salem, Ohio, 1968-69; pres. Calvary Christian Coll., Paris, 1970-76; founder, internat. pres. Calvary Missionary Assn. of India, 1974—; gen. mgr. radio sta. WMCM, Paris, 1975-76; pres. Calvary Missionary Assn. Chs., 1973—; pres., founder Calvary Christian Children's Homes, India, 1974—; conv. speaker Indian Ch. of God, 1974, 75, 76, 77; founder Agnes Maas Meml. Children's Home, Tadepallegudem, India, 1977. Trustee, Aldersgate Sch. Religion, Salem, 1969—; pres., bd. dirs. Wesleyan Missionary Council, Decatur, Ill., 1972-74; pres. Worldwide Faith Missions, 1977—. Mem. Wesleyan Ednl. Assn. Am. (nat. sec., dir. 1968-74). Home: 12790 Warren Rd NE Paris OH 44669 Office: Calvary Missionary Assn Paris OH 44669

MAASBERG, ALBERT THOMAS, chem. co. exec.; b. Bronx, N.Y., Feb. 10, 1915; s. Albert Paul and Lillian Genevieve (Harlach) M.; student Syracuse U., 1932-36; B.S. magna cum laude, N.Y. State Coll. of Forestry, 1936; m. Margaret Celeste Haley, May 31, 1941; children—Thomas Albert, Michael William. Tech. dir. plastics prodn. dept. Dow Chem. Co., Midland, Mich., 1954-56, dir. research and devel. Midland div., 1956-63, dir. contract research, devel. and engring., govt. and pub. relations, 1963-75; with research and devel. dept. Dow Chem. Co., 1976—. Pres. Paul Bunyan Council Boy Scouts Am., Midland, 1965-68. Bd. dirs. United Community Fund of Midland County, Mich., 1968-74. Served to lt. col., AUS, 1936-75. Decorated Army Commendation medal. Recipient Trailblazer award Boy Scouts Am., 1963, Silver Beaver award, 1966. Fellow Am. Inst. Chem. Engrs.; mem. Am. Chem. Soc., T.A.P.P.I., Winterfield Conservation Club, Sigma Xi. Rotarian. Club: Midland Country. Patentee in field. Contbr. articles to profl. jours. Home: 3220 Noeske St Midland MI 48640 Office: Dow Chem Co Bldg 566 Midland MI 48640

MAASS, VERA SONJA, psychologist; b. Berlin, Germany, July 6, 1931; d. Willy Ernst and Walli Elisabeth (Reinke) Keck; came to U.S., 1958, naturalized, 1970; B.A., Monmouth Coll., 1971; M.A., Lehigh U., 1974; Ph.D., U. Mo., 1977; m. Joachim A. Maass, Dec. 24, 1954. Teaching asst. Lehigh U., Bethlehem, Pa., 1971-72; tutor in adult basic edn. Teaching Assistance Orgn., Kansas City, Mo., 1973-74; grad. research asst. U. Mo., Kansas City, 1974-76; intern U. Ky. Med. Sch., Lexington, 1975-76; psychologist-therapist Dunn Mental Health Center, Richmond, Ind., 1976—; developer, conductor workshops in rational behavior therapy, Lexington, 1975-76, Richmond, 1976-77; v.p. Vitatronics, Inc., Wall, N.J., 1969—. Mem. Am. Personnel and Guidance Assn., Nat. Council Family Relations, Internat. Assn. Applied Psychology, Psi Chi. Contbr. articles to profl. jours. Home: PO Box 923 Richmond IN 47374

MAAZEL, LORIN, conductor, violinist; b. Paris, France, Mar. 6, 1930 (parents U.S. citizens); s. Lincoln and Marie (Varencove) M.; Mus.D. (hon.), U. Pitts., 1965; H.H.D., Beaver Coll., 1973; m. Miriam Sandbank, June 18, 1952; 1 dau., Anjali. Debut as conductor, 1938, condr. major orchs. U.S. 1938—, festivals in Edinburgh (Scotland), Bayreuth (Germany) and Salzburg (Germany), 1952—; world tours include Japan, Latin Am., Australia, USSR; dir. Deutsche Oper Berlin and Radiosymphonic Orch., Berlin, 1964—; condr., dir. Cleve. Orch.; recording for London Records, Vienna Philharmonic. Office: care of S Hurok 730 Fifth Ave New York City NY 10019 also Cleveland Orch 11001 Euclid Ave Cleveland OH 44106

MABEL, THOMAS ARTHUR, physician; b. Hammond, Ind., Dec. 4, 1941; s. Arthur A. and Wilma L. (Shrock) M.; A.B., Ind. U., 1964, M.D., 1970; m. Nancy L. Barnes, June 17, 1967; children—Andrew Joseph, Leann Kristin. Intern, Meth. Hosp., Indpls., 1970-71, resident in family practice, 1973-74; practice family medicine, Noblesville, Ind., 1975—. Served with USAF, 1971-73. Diplomate Am. Bd. Family Practice. Mem. Am. Acad. Family Physicians, Flying Physicians Assn., Sigma Alpha Epsilon. Clubs: Kiwanis, Elks. Home: 1222 Willow Way Noblesville IN 46060 Office: 110 Lakeview Dr Noblesville IN 46060

MABLEY, JACK, newspaperman; b. Binghamton, N.Y., Oct. 26, 1915; s. Clarence Ware and Mabelle (Howe) M.; B.S., U. Ill., 1938; m. Frances Habeck, Aug. 29, 1940; children—Jill, Ann, Pat, Robert. With Chgo. Daily News, 1938-61, beginning as reporter, then writer, columnist; columnist Chgo. American, 1961-66, asst. mng. editor, from 1966, asso. editor Chgo. Today, 1967-74; columnist Chgo. Tribune; lectr. in journalism Northwestern U., 1949-50. Pres., Village of Glenview (Ill.), 1957-61. Served from ensign to lt. USNR, 1941-45. Home: 2275 Winnetka Rd Glenview IL 60025 Office: 435 N Michigan Ave Chicago IL 60611

MAC ADAMS, RICHARD JOSEPH, engring. cons.; b. N.Y.C., Mar. 27, 1925; s. Robert J. and Josephine (Ziegler) MacA.; B.S., Lehigh U., 1946; m. Geraldine M. Mitchell, Oct. 23, 1948; children—Monica M., Michael R., Melanie R. With Pure Oil Co., Toledo, Ohio, 1946-60, Allied Chem. Corp., Buffalo, 1960-62, Toledo, 1962-65; with Samborn, Steketee, Otis & Evans, Inc., Toledo, 1965—, v.p., 1973—. Registered profl. engr, Ohio. Mem. Ohio Soc. Profl. Engrs., C. of C., Am. Inst. Chem. Engrs., Tau Beta Pi. Home: 7066 Edinburgh Dr Lambertville MI 48144 Office: 1001 Madison Ave Toledo OH 43624

MACARTNEY, FRANK P., aviation exec.; b. St. Paul, Dec. 16, 1931; s. Grant Street and Hope (Drezmal) M.; student Yale, 1949-50; m. Barbara Kelly, June 25, 1955 (div. 1964); children—Grant Street II, Kenneth H. m. 2d, Mary Larson, Sept. 15, 1972. Engring. staff Gen. Motors, 1957-58; pres., Aerodynamics, Inc., Pontiac, Mich., 1959—. Served with USAF, 1952-57. Home: 191 Erin Castle Dr Rochester MI 48063 Office: Box 508 Pontiac MI 48056

MACATOL, FORTUNATO RIBAGORDA, pathologist; b. 1943; s. Segundo Rullon and Rosario (Ribagorda) M.; M.D., Cebu Inst. Medicine, 1967; m. Sally Elizabeth Snead; children—Michael Christopher, Matthew Jonathan. Intern, DePaul Hosp., Norfolk, Va., 1968-69, resident anatomic and clin. pathology, 1969-73; asso. pathologist Marietta (Ohio) Meml. Hosp., 1973-75, dir. lab., 1975—; instr. physiology and pharmacology Cebu Inst. Medicine, 1967-68. Diplomate Am. Bd. Pathology. Fellow Am. Coll. Pathology, Am. Soc. Clin. Pathologists; mem. AMA (physician recognition award 1974-77), Washington County Med. Soc. (pres. 1977), Ohio Med. Assn. Club: Marietta Country. Office: Marietta Memorial Hospital Marietta OH 45750

MAC CALLUM, GERALD CUSHING, JR., educator; b. Spokane, Wash., June 16, 1925; s. Gerald Cushing and Grace C.D. (Hallahan) MacC.; student Wash. State Coll., 1946-48; B.A., U. Calif. at Berkeley, 1950, M.A., 1954, Ph.D., 1961; postgrad. (Fulbright scholar) Oxford U. (Eng.), 1958-59; m. Paulette Naomi Griffith, 1951 (dec. 1975); m. Susan Louise Feagin, 1977; 1 dau., Deborah Ellen. Instr., Cornell U., Ithaca, N.Y., 1959-61; asst. prof. U. Wis., Madison, 1961-65, asso. prof., 1966-69, prof. philosophy, 1969—, chmn. dept., 1970-72; vis. asso. prof. U. Wash., Seattle, 1965-66. Served with AUS, 1943-46. Am. Council Learned Socs. fellow, 1969-70. Mem. AAUP, Am. Soc. Polit. and Legal Philosophy, Council Polit. Studies, Am. Philos. Assn. (sec.-treas. western div. 1967-69, chmn. com. on status and future of profession 1973-76). Contbr. articles in field to profl. and legal jours. Home: 726 Copeland St Madison WI 53711

MAC CARTHY, JOHN PETERS, trust co. exec.; b. St. Louis, Apr. 6, 1933; s. John Donald and Ruth (Peters) MacC.; A.B., Princeton U., 1954; LL.B., Harvard U., 1959; m. Talbot Leland, June 21, 1958; children—John Leland, Talbot Peters. Admitted to Mo. bar, 1959; partner Bryan Cave McPheeters & McRoberts, St. Louis, 1959-69; sec. 1st. Union Co., bank holding co., St. Louis, 1969—, also dir.; sec. St. Louis Union Trust Co., 1969-72, exec. v.p., 1972-75, pres., 1975—, also dir.; dir. KSH Inc., Ocean Drilling and Exploration Co., Miss. Lime Co. Trustee Washington U., St. Louis, 1972—, St. Louis Art Mus., 1976—, St. Louis Country Day Sch., 1973—. Served with USNR, 1954-56. Mem. Am., St. Louis bar assns. Clubs: Noonday, Racquet, Bogey, St. Louis Country. Home: 6 Robin Hill Ln Saint Louis MO 63124 Office: 510 Locust St Saint Louis MO 63101

MACDONALD, JAMES M., II, finance co. exec.; b. Chgo., May 19, 1934; s. James M. and Jean (Macdonald) M.; ed. U. Tex., 1955; B.S., U. Ill., 1962; m. Myriam T. Hoppe, Dec. 23, 1967; 1 son, James III. Account exec. James Talcott, Inc., Chgo., 1962-66, Mills Factor Corp., Chgo., 1966-67; asst. mgr. secured lending div. Exchange Nat. Bank, Chgo., 1967-68; sales mgr. ITT-Comml. Discount Corp., Chgo., 1968-71; v.p. Asso.'s Corp. N. Am., Chgo., 1971-75, Exchange Nat. Bank Chgo., 1975; pres. Walter Middleton & Co., Evanston, Ill., 1975—; sec., treas. Rally Round Game Co., Inc., Evanston, 1964—. Vice pres. Young Republicans Cook County, 1965. Served with USAF, 1954-58. Named Outstanding Air Man of Year, SAC, Austin, Tex., 1955, London, 1957. Mem. Ill. C. of C. Home and Office: 1010 Seward St Evanston IL 60202

MACDONALD, JOHN BERNARD, dept. store exec.; b. Jerome, Ariz., Mar. 14, 1923; s. John Bernard and Martha Marie (Wilson) MacD.; B.S.C., U. Santa Clara (Calif.), 1949, grad. student bus. mktg., 1968-70; m. Velma Dolores Keller, Feb. 10, 1952; children—Jack, Michael, Debra, Gregory. Trainee, mdse. mgr. Montgomery Ward & Co., Calif., Utah and Oreg., 1949-54; store mgr. Spiegel's, Calif., 1954-59; with J.M. McDonald Co. div. Gambles, Mpls., 1959—, store mgr., Santa Clara, San Jose, Calif., 1959-70, v.p. sales, mem. exec. com., Hastings, Nebr., 1970-75, v.p. for advt. and sales promotion, 1975-76, vice chmn. and sales promotion officer, office of pres., 1976—. Bd. dirs. Better Bus. Bur. Santa Clara, 1965-68; mem. bd. distributive edn. com. San Jose (Calif.) High Sch., 1968; hon. dir. Santa Clara Philharmonic, 1965; adv. com. San Jose City Coll., 1967-68. Served with USNR, 1942-46. Named Nat. Retailer of Year, Brand Name Found., 1968; recipient Coopers Nat. Jockey award merit, San Jose, 1968. Mem. Alumni Assn. U. Santa Clara. Democrat. Roman Catholic. Home: 3100 Park Lane Dr Apt 6 Hastings NE 68901 Office: 2635 W 2d St Hastings NE 68901

MAC DONALD, LEO HADLEY, SR., lawyer; b. St. Louis, Mar. 15, 1934; s. Bernard Callaghan and Alice Dean (Hadley) MacD.; B.S., Spring Hill Coll., Mobile, Ala., 1956; J.D., St. Louis U., 1960; m. Susan Elizabeth George, July 7, 1962; children—Paul Mullen, Mary Hadley, Leo Hadley, Patricia George, Suzanne Dean, Mark Callaghan, Kathleen King. Admitted to Mo. bar, 1960, U.S. Supreme Ct. bar; practice in St. Louis, 1970—; partner firm Sumner, Hanlon, Sumner, MacDonald & Nouss, P.C., 1970—; spl. asst. atty. gen., Mo., 1962, 71; asst. circuit atty., St. Louis, 1960-69, spl. asst. circuit atty., 1969-71; instr. law St. Louis U. Law Sch., 1965-68, guest lectr. Commerce Sch., 1967-68; guest lectr. U.S. Narcotic Bur., 1969, St. Louis Police Acad., 1961-68. Dir. B.C. MacDonald & Co., Hadley Dean Glass Co., St. Louis. Treas. local Boy Scouts Am., 1971-73; bd. dirs. St. Louis Greater Alliance, 1972-74; trustee, sec.-treas. Maryland Terrace, 1970-75; trustee Spring Hill Coll., 1962-64. Served to 1st lt. AUS, 1957-58. Decorated Distinguished Mil. Service award. Mem. Am., Mo., St. Louis, St. Louis County bar assns., St. Louis Jr. C. of C., St. Louis City Lawyers Assn., Alpha Sigma Nu, Phi Delta Phi. Kiwanian. Co-author: Termination of Parental Rights, 1962. Home: 7254 Maryland St St Louis MO 63130 Office: 7733 Forsyth Blvd St Louis MO 63105

MAC DONALD, MARIE GENEVA (MRS. KING RUFUS MACDONALD), journalist; b. Ozark, Ark., June 1, 1910; d. Matthew J. and Edna Mae (Barclift) Self; occasional student Wichita State U.; m. King Rufus MacDonald, Aug. 2, 1931; (dec. Oct. 7, 1966); 1 son, Ronald (dec.); step-daus. Marion Lam, Dorothy Cardell, Molly Baca. Reporter soc. dept. Wichita Eagle, 1942-47; women's editor Wichita Beacon, 1947-49; dir. women's activities, broadcaster Radio Sta. KFBI, 1949-56, KARD-TV, 1956-58; asst. program dir. Radio Sta. KFH, 1958-61; publicity dir. YWCA, 1961-63; feature writer Wichita Eagle & Beacon, 1965-76; promotion rep. Wichita Hist. Cowtown Village, 1977—; columnist, Person to Person, Party-Line Farm Jour., 1973-75. Mem. pub. information com. A.R.C., 1952-60, regional pub. information coordinator, 1963-66, bd. dirs., 1970-74; mem. pub. information com. Kans. div. Am. Cancer Soc., 1972—. Recipient 1st Pl. award Nat. Fedn. Press Women, 1955, 69, Kans. Optometric Soc. Writing award, 1970. Mem. Internat. Platform Assn., Am. Women Radio and TV (pres. Wichita chpt. 1975), Women in Communications (pres. Wichita profl. chpt. 1971), Wichita (pres. 1950), Kans. (Sweepstakes award 1970, pres. 1952) press women. Home: 836 Coolidge St Wichita KS 67203

MAC DONALD, MARSHALL ALLEN, allergist; b. Alma, Mich., Sept. 14, 1915; s. Edward Blake and Lois Ludington (Fraker) MacD.; B.Sc., Alma Coll., 1936; M.D., U. Mich., 1940; m. Helen Margaret Johnson, July 11, 1942; children—Lois Ruth, Mary Anne, Charles Allen. Intern, Receiving Hosp., Detroit, 1940-41, resident in internal medicine, 1946-48; instr. internal medicine Wayne State U. Med. Sch., Detroit, 1941-42; practice medicine specializing in allergy, Kalamazoo, 1948—; mem. staff Borgess Hosp., Bronson Methodist Hosp.; adj. prof. clin. medicine Western Mich. U.; asst. clin. prof.

medicine U. Mich. State Sch. Human Medicine. Served to capt. AUS, 1942-43. Diplomate Am. Bd. Allergy and Immunology. Fellow Am. Coll. Allergy; mem. AMA, Am. Acad. Allergy, Midwest Allergy Forum, Mich. Allergy Soc., Mich. State Med. Soc., Kalamazoo Acad. Medicine. Methodist. Home: 2824 Hill 'n Brook Dr Kalamazoo MI 49008 Office: 352 Bronson Med Center 252 E Lovell St Kalamazoo MI 49006

MAC DONALD, PAIGE LEE, counselor; b. East St. Louis, Apr. 7, 1955; d. Harold A. and Virginia (Bowers) Dashner; student Millikin U., 1972-73; B.A., St. Louis Washington U., 1975, M.A.Ed., 1976; m. Robert Callen MacDonald, Dec. 21, 1974. Tchr., owner Sch. Baton, Dupo, Ill., 1970—; counselor Jennings (Mo.) High Sch., 1975-76, tchr. music sch. dist., 1976—; music therapist Barnes Children's Hosp., 1974-75. Tchr., Vacation Bible Sch., 1970-75; ambassador St. Louis Council World Affairs, 1972. Mem. Am. Personnel and Guidance Assn., Assn. Humanistic Edn. and Devel., NEA, Mo. Edn. assn., Jennings Community Tchrs. Assn., Women's Panhellenic Assn., Mortarboard, Pi Beta Phi, Mu Phi Epsilon. Republican. Lutheran. Alto soloist with St. Louis Symphony, Carnegie Hall, 1977, Powell Symphony Hall, St. Louis, 1974—. Home: 11022 Whitbyhall Dr Bridgeton MO 63044 Office: Ferguson Florissant Sch Dist Florissant MO 63031

MAC DONALD, RAYMOND WILBUR, union ofcl.; b. Hanford, Calif., Apr. 2, 1938; s. Wilbur John and Rose (Carillo) MacD.; B.A., San Diego State Coll., 1964, postgrad., 1964-65. Sr. electronics devel. technician Gen. Dynamics Corp., 1959-65; research asst. research dept. AFL-CIO, Washington, 1965-66, dir. research and edn. Internat. Molders' and Allied Workers Union, Cin., 1966-68, economist, Washington, 1968-70, dir. research Allied Indsl. Workers, Milw., 1970-72, 75—, dir. contract and research dept. Lithographers and Photoengravers Internat. Union, 1972, economist, country dir. Asian-Am. Free Labor Inst., Manila, Philippines, 1972-74; lectr. econs. U. Cin., 1967-68, U. Hawaii Labor-Mgmt. Center on Pay Bd. procedures, 1972, Labor-Mgmt. Dispute Settlement, U. Philippines Law Center, Quezon City, 1974-75; lectr. Am. labor law U. Saigon (South Vietnam), 1974; mem. labor research adv. council Bur. Labor Statistics, U.S. Dept. Labor, 1968—, chmn. productivity, tech. and growth com., 1968-70. Bd. dirs. Clergy Econ. Edn. Found., 1968-72. Mem. Indsl. Relations Research Assn., Internat. Assn. Machinists, Newspaper Guild, Am. Fedn. Tchrs., Arbitration Assn. Philippines, Manila Overseas Press Club. Contbr. articles to profl. jours. Office: 3520 W Oklahoma Ave Milwaukee WI 53215

MAC DONALD, RICHARD VINCENT, JR., mech. engr.; b. Verona, Pa., Oct. 27, 1932; s. Richard Vincent and Alice Loraine (McDade) MacD.; student Tex. A. and M. Coll., 1950-52, U. Utah, 1952-53; m. Elizabeth Ann Weber, Feb. 20, 1960; children—Patrick, Maureen, Colleen, Timothy, Brendan, Bethiah. Project mgr. Natkin & Co., Denver, 1962-67, A.M. Kinney, Inc., Cin., 1969-72; chief design and drafting Vulcan Cincinnati, Inc., Cin., 1972-74; mechanic design project engr. A-E Design Assos. Inc., 1974—. Tchr. confrat. Christian doctrine St. Bernard's Sch., Cin. Mem. legis. ednl. com. White Oak Improvement Assn., 1971-74; mem. N.W. Sch. Bd., Hamilton County, Ohio, 1974—. Mem. central com. Cin. Democratic party, 1972-74; precinct exec. Green Twp. Dem. party, 1972-74. Home: 5950 Jessup Rd Cincinnati OH 45239 Office: 1329 Arlington St Cincinnati OH 45239

MACDONALD, ROBERT DICKSON, shoe mfg. co. exec.; b. South Bend, Ind., Mar. 14, 1937; s. Charles A. and Dorothy (Dickson) MacD.; B.S. in Mktg., Northwestern U., 1959; m. Anita Olson, Sept. 23, 1960; children—William Robert, Scott Robert. Account exec. Needham, Harper & Steers, Chgo., 1961-66; account exec. Leo Burnett Co., Chgo., 1966-68; gen. mgr. Roblee div. Brown Shoe Co., St. Louis, 1968-77, gen. mgr. Roblee and Pedwin divs., 1977—. Served with USMC, 1959-60. Mem. Nat. Shoe Retailers Assn. (mem. men's style com. 1976—), Nat. Shoe Travelers Assn., Two/Ten Nat. Found. Club: Town and Country Racquet. Office: PO Box 354 Brown Shoe Co Roblee Div St Louis MO 63166

MAC DONALD, WILLIAM BURKE, counselor; b. Chgo., Dec. 19, 1942; s. William Charles and Mary Jane (Burke) MacD.; A.B., Regis Coll., 1964; M.Ed., Loyola U., 1968; m. Mary E. Kotre, Dec. 28, 1968; 1 dau., Colleen. Tchr. Lindop Sch., Broadview, Ill., 1964-67; guidance dir. Miner Jr. High Sch., Arlington Heights, Ill., 1967-70; counselor Addison (Ill.) Trail High Sch., 1970—; instr. Effectiveness Tng. Assn., Solona Beach, Calif., 1973—. Mem. Nat. Edn. Assn., Am. Fedn. Tchrs., Am. Personnel and Guidance Assn. Roman Catholic. Home: 208 Dunlap Pl Schaumburg IL 60194 Office: 213 Lombard Rd Addison IL 60101

MAC DOUGAL, GARY EDWARD, indsl. products mfg. co. exec.; b. Chgo., July 3, 1936; s. Thomas William and Lorna Lee (McDougall) MacD.; B.S. in Engring., U. Cal. at Los Angeles, 1958; M.B.A. with distinction, Harvard, 1963; m. Julianne Laurel Maxwell, June 13, 1958; children—Gary Edward, Michael Scott. Cons., McKinsey & Co., N.Y.C. and Los Angeles, 1963-68, partner, 1968-69; chmn. bd., chief exec. officer Mark Controls Corp. (formerly Clayton Mark & Co.), Evanston, Ill., 1969—, also pres., 1971-75; dir. United Parcel Service Am. Inc., Greenwich, Conn., Union Camp Corp., Wayne, N.J., Maremont Corp., Chgo.; dir., mem. exec. com. Sargent-Welch Sci. Co., Skokie, Ill. Instr. U. Cal. at Los Angeles, 1969. Trustee U. Cal. at Los Angeles Found. Served to lt. USNR, 1958-61. Mem. Kappa Sigma. Episcopalian. Clubs: Harvard of N.Y.; Economic, Harvard Business School (Chgo.). Contbr. articles to profl. jours., chpts. to books. Home: 591 Plum Tree Rd Barrington Hills IL 60010 Office: 1900 Dempster St Evanston IL 60204

MACENSKI, CHARLES WILLIAM, JR., assn. exec.; b. Hammond, Ind., Dec. 13, 1936; s. Charles William and Olga (Lecyk) M.; B.S., Purdue U., 1959, M.S., 1963; m. Nancy Carole Daniel, June 7, 1958; children—Charles Daniel, Christopher Lee, Mark Robert. Pharmacist, Fifield Pharmacy, Hammond, Ind., 1959-60; profl. rep. E.R. Squibb & Sons, Hammond and Madison, Wis., 1960-61, 63-64; with AMA, Chgo., 1964—, exec. asst. div. sci. activities, 1970-74, exec. asst. office of exec. v.p., 1974—. Mem. Sigma Xi, Alpha Chi Rho, Rho Chi. Ukrainian Orthodox. Home: 1538 Janice Ln Munster IN 46321 Office: 535 N Dearborn St Chicago IL 60610

MAC GIBBON, JAMES DUNCAN, radiologist; b. Mpls., Feb. 13, 1935; s. Everett Elsworth and Lucinda (Hedding) Mac G.; B.A., U. Minn., 1956, M.D., B.S., 1960; m. Janice Roberta Booker, Aug. 22, 1959; children—Susan Anne, Bruce Everett, Nancy Lynn. Intern, Mpls. Gen. Hosp., 1960-61; resident in radiology VA Hosp., Mpls., 1964-67, U. Minn., Mpls., 1964-67; practice medicine specializing in radiology, Edina, Minn., 1968—; mem. staffs Suburban Radiologic Cons. Ltd., Fairview Hosp., Mpls., Fairview Southdale Hosp., Edina. Served with M.C. USAF, 1962-63. Mem. AMA, Minn. State Med. Assn., Hennepin County (Minn.) Med. Soc., Minn. State Radiol. Soc., Am. Coll. Radiology, Radiol. Soc. N.Am. Roman Catholic. Clubs: Decathlon Athletic, Olympic Hills Golf. Home: 6601 Iroquois Trail Edina MN 55435 Office: 471 Southdale Med Bldg Edina MN 55435

MACHINIS, PETER ALEXANDER, civil engr.; b. Chgo., Mar. 12, 1912; s. Alexander and Catherine (Lessares) M.; B.S., Ill. Inst. Tech., 1934; m. Fay Mezilson, Aug. 5, 1945; children—Cathy, Alexander. Civil engr. Ill. Hwy. Dept., 1935-36 engr., estimator Harvey Co., Chgo., 1937; project engr. PWA, Chgo., 1938-40; supervisory civil engr. C.E., Dept. Army, Chgo., 1941—: partner MSL Engring. Consultants, Park Ridge, Ill., 1952—. Mem. Civil Def. Adv. Council Ill., 1967—. Served with USAAF. 1943-45; ETO. Registered profl. engr., Ill. Fellow ASCE; mem. Nat. Soc. Profl. Engrs., Am. Congress Surveying and Mapping, Soc. Am. Mil. Engrs., Assn. U.S. Army, Greek Orthodox (ch. trustee). Home: 10247 S Oakley Ave Chicago IL 60643 Office: 536 S Clark St Chicago IL 60605

MACHMUELLER, VILAS EDWARD, paper co. exec.; b. Wausau, Wis., Nov. 12, 1928; s. Paul Ludwig and Adela Anna (Yanke) M.; student Marathon County Tech. Sch., nights 1960-65; m. Sharon Lee Otto, Apr. 4, 1952; children—Linda, Jeffrey. With Weyerhaeuser Co. (and predecessors), Rothschild, Wis., 1947—, maintenance supt., 1973-74, mgr. utilities engring., 1974-76, supt. utilities engring. and maintenance, 1976—. Owner, operator rental properties. Sec., Weston San. Dist., 1960-65, supr., 1965-71, town chmn., 1971—, Water Utility Commn. Mem., 1969—; mem. Marathon County Bd. Suprs., 1972-76; mem. Regional Planning Commn., 1971—. Served with USNR, 1945-47, 50-51: Korea. Mem. Wis. Towns Assn., Am. Water Works Assn., Wis. Valley Suprs. Club, Wis. Suburban League. Mem. United Ch. Christ. Mason, Moose, Elk. Home: 1415 McIntyre Ave Schofield WI 54476 Office: PO Box 200 Weyerhaeuser Co Rothschild WI 54474

MACHTINGER, LAWRENCE ARNOLD, mathematician, educator; b. St. Louis, Mar. 11, 1936; s. Harry and Evelyn Z. (Pultman) M.; B.S., Washington U., St. Louis, 1959, A.M., 1963, Ph.D., 1965; m. Doris Mae Diamant, June 21, 1964; children—Marc Diamant, Rebecca Eve. Asst. prof. math. Webster Coll., Webster Groves, Mo., 1964-65, St. Louis U., 1965-66, Ill. Inst. Tech., 1966-72; asso. prof. math. Purdue U., North Central Campus, Westville, Ind., 1972—; cons. in field. Mem. math. adv. council Ind. Dept. Pub. Instrn., 1974-76; mem. sch. accreditation team North Central Assn., 1971. NDEA fellow, 1959-62; NSF grantee, 1968-71, 74-75. Mem. Am. Math. Soc., Math. Assn. Am., Nat., Ill. councils tchrs. math., Met. Math. Club Chgo., Tau Beta Pi, Pi Mu Epsilon. Research, publs. in field. Home: 2930 Alexander Crescent Flossmoor IL 60422 Office: Dept Math Purdue U N Central Campus Westville IN 46391

MACHULAK, EDWARD LEON, corp. exec.; b. Milw., July 14, 1926; s. Frank and Mary (Sokolowski) M.; B.S. in Accounting, U. Wis., 1949; student spl. courses various univs.; m. Sylvia Mary Jablonski, Sept. 2, 1950; children—Edward A., John E., Lauren A., Christine M., Paul E. Pres., chmn. bd. Commerce Capital Corp. (reorganized and renamed Commerce Group Corp. 1971), Milw., 1962—; dir. Gen. Lumber & Supply Co., Inc., Draco Labs., Inc., Parkway Land Corp., Med. Systems, Inc., Bus. Analysis Corp., Gem. Nat. Distbrs., Inc., Land Resources Co., Nu-Air Humidifier Corp., Continental Recreation Corp., Environment Dynamics Corp., Glen's for Men, Inc., Homestead Convalescent Center, Inc., Bea Kay Real Estate Corp., San Luis Estates, Inc., San Sebastian Gold Mines, Inc., Edios Corp., Homespan Realty Co., Inc., Universal Developers, Inc., Piccadilly Advt. Agy., Inc., Himount Land, Inc., The Oaks of Carmel, Inc., Amglo Industries, Inc. Mem. nat. small bus. investment co. adv. council Small Bus. Adminstrn., 1972-74, co-chmn., 1973-74; mem. Wis. Small Bus. Investment Co. Council, 1970-74, chmn., 1974; mem. Wis., Milw. bds. realtors, 1955—. Financial adv. mem. planning com. Marmion Mil. Acad., Aurora, Ill., 1967-71, lay trustee, 1967—. Mem. adv. bd. Jesuit Retreat House, Oshkosh, Wis., 1966-68. Served with AUS, 1945-46. Mem. Am., Nat. (award for distinguished service to small bus. 1970, mem. exec. com., bd. govs. 1970-74), Regional (pres. 1971-72) assns. small bus. investment cos. K.C. (4 deg.), Elk. Clubs: Senior Citizens of Wauwatosa (organizer, treas. 1958); Milwaukee Athletic, Tripoli Golf (Milw.); Chemist's, Canadian (N.Y.C.). Home: 903 W Green Tree Rd River Hills WI 53217 Office: 6001 N 91st St Milwaukee WI 53225

MAC INTYRE, PATRICIA NELLE, speech-lang. pathologist; b. E. Cleveland, Ohio, July 2, 1923; d. Robert Isadore and Blanche Esther (Schlesinger) Grossman; B.A., Western Reserve U., 1945; M.A., Case Western Reserve U., 1968; m. William James MacIntyre, Sept. 16, 1947; children—Kathleen Suzanne, Steven James. Staff mem. dept. speech pathology Soc. Crippled Children, Cleve., 1968-75, clin. dir., 1975—; clin. instr. dept. speech communication Case Western Res. U., 1973—; adj. asst. prof. dept. communication Cleve. State U., 1973—. Bd. dirs. Flora Stone Mather Coll., 1957-61. Certificate clin. competence speech pathology; Receptive-Expressive Lang. Tng. Program grantee, 1976—. Mem. Am., Ohio, Northeastern Ohio (v.p. 1973) speech and hearing assns. Home: 3108 Huntington Rd Shaker Heights OH 44120 Office: 11001 Buckeye Rd Cleveland OH 44106

MACIUSZKO, JERZY JANUSZ, educator; b. Warsaw, Poland, July 15, 1913; s. Bonifacy and Aleksandra (Lipman) M.; M.A., U. Warsaw, 1936; M.S. in L.S., Western Res. U., 1953; Ph.D., Case Western Res. U., 1962; m. Kathleen Lynn Post, Dec. 11, 1976. Came to U.S., 1951, naturalized, 1957. Insp. Brit. Ministry of Edn. Polish Secondary Schs., Eng., 1946-51; head John G. White dept., Cleve. Pub. Library, 1963-69; chmn. dept. Slavic Studies Alliance Coll., Cambridge Springs, Pa., 1969-73, chmn. div. Slavic and modern langs., 1973-74; prof., library dir. Baldwin-Wallace Coll., Berea, Ohio, 1974—. Lectr. in Polish language, lit. Case Western Res. U., Cleve., 1964-69. Dir. Alliance Coll. Year Abroad program at Jagellonian U., Cracow, Poland, 1969-74. Served with AUS, 1945-46. Recipient Doctoral Dissertation award Kosciuszko Found., 1967, Hilbert T. Ficken award, 1973. Mem. Am. Assn. of Tchrs. of Slavic and East European Langs. (chpt. pres. 1965-66), ALA (chmn. slavic subsect. assn. of coll. and research libraries 1968-69), Am. Assn. Advancement of Slavic Studies, Modern Lang. Assn., Polish Inst. Arts. and Scis., Polish Am. Hist. Assn., Case Western Res. U. Library Sch. Alumni Assn. (pres. 1970-71), Slavic Honor Soc. Clubs: Rowfant (Cleve.). Home: 133 Sunset Dr Berea OH 44017 Office: Ritter Library Baldwin Wallace Coll Berea OH 44017

MACK, DOUGLAS ARCHIBALD, pub. health adminstr.; b. Waterloo, Que., Can., Mar. 28, 1935; s. Edwin William and Frieda Maron (Ball) M.; came to U.S., 1956, naturalized, 1963; student La Sierra Coll., 1956-59; B.A., Andrews U., 1960-62; M.D., Loma Linda U., 1967; M.P.H. (USPHS grantee, Mich. Dept. Pub. Health fellow), U. Mich., 1971; m. Ailene Stella Brock, Mar. 27, 1955; children—Judith, Sherry, Sandra, Rhonda. Intern, Hinsdale (Ill.) Hosp., 1967-68; gen. practice medicine, Wakefield, Mich., 1968-69; dir. pub. health Branch-Hillsdale-St. Joseph Dist. Health Dept., Coldwater, Mich., 1969-76, Kent County (Mich.), 1976—; chief medical examiner Kent County, 1976—; exec. dir. Community Health Services, Grand Rapids, Mich., 1976—; asso. prof., office health service edn. and research Coll. Human Medicine, Mich. State U., East Lansing, 1973-76. Mem. S. Central Mich. Health Planning Council; mem. adv. com. to state dir. pub. health on food sanitation services. Bd. dirs. Southwestern Mich. Tb and Respiratory Disease Assn. Mem. A.M.A., Am., Mich. pub. health assns., Mich. Health Officers Assn. (sec. 1974—, pres. elect), Mich. State Med. Soc., Alumni Assn. Andrews U. (dir. 1970—). Home: 122 Forest Hills Ave SE Grand Rapids MI 49506 Office: 1619 Walker NW Grand Rapids MI 49504

MACK, IRVING, physician; b. Vilna, Poland, Apr. 15, 1919; s. Meilach and Rebecca (Zelcer) M.; came to U.S., 1921, naturalized, 1927; B.S., U. Chgo., 1939, M.D., 1942; m. Jean Charlotte Tarrant, Nov. 8, 1959 (dec. Nov. 1969); children—Melissa, Susan. Intern Cook County Hosp., Chgo., 1942-43; sr. resident medicine Michael Reese Hosp., Chgo., 1944-45, sr. fellow dept. cardiovascular research, 1945-46, research asso. Cardiovascular Inst. of hosp., 1946-59, roentgenologic cons. of inst., 1950-55, chest cons. Psychosomatic and Psychiat. Inst. of hosp., 1950—, chief Thursday chest clinic of hosp., 1952-73, attending physician dept. thoracic medicine of hosp., 1947-73, sr. attending physician, 1973—; practice medicine, specializing in internal medicine, Chgo., 1946—; clin. asso. prof. medicine Chgo. Med. Sch., 1949-73; clin. prof. medicine Pritzker Sch. Medicine, U. Chgo., 1973—; cons. Herrick House for Rheumatic Fever, 1948-54. Mem. exec. com. Michael Reese Hosp., 1962-66; trustee Michael Reese Hosp. and Med. Center. Recipient Freer medal, dept. medicine U. Chgo. Coll. Medicine, 1942. Diplomate Am. Bd. Internal Medicine, Nat. Bd. Med. Examiners. Fellow A.C.P., Am. Coll. Chest Physicians (chmn. sect. on electrocardiography 1953-59, mem. com. on postgrad. courses 1955-66), Am. Coll. Cardiology: mem. Am. Fedn. for Clin. Research, Am. Thoracic Soc., Am. Heart Assn., Am. Psychosomatic Soc., Assn. Am. Med. Colls., Am. Soc. Internal Medicine, Am. Assn. History of Medicine, AAAS, AMA, Am. Acad. Tb Physicians, Chgo. Soc. Internal Medicine, Chgo. Inst. of Medicine, Phi Beta Kappa, Sigma Xi, Alpha Omega Alpha. Author numerous articles in med. jours. on cardiac arrythmias, rheumatic heart disease, electrocardiography, pulmonary physiology, emphysema, Tb and related fields. Mem. editorial bd. Cardiology, 1958-67. Home: 5490 S Shore Dr Chicago IL 60615 Office: 104 S Michigan Ave Chicago IL 60603

MACK, RAYMOND WRIGHT, educator; b. Ashtabula, Ohio, July 15, 1927; s. Wright R. and Hazel E. (Card) M.; A.B. with honors, Baldwin-Wallace Coll., 1949; M.A., U. N.C., 1951, Ph.D., 1953; m. Barbara Leonard, Mar. 1948 (div. 1953); 1 son, Donald Gene; m. 2d, Elizabeth Ann Hunter, Oct. 16, 1953; children—Meredith Lou, Julia Glen, Margaret Kingsley. Asst. prof. sociology and anthropology U. Miss., 1953; faculty Northwestern U., 1953—, asso. prof. sociology, 1957-62, prof. sociology, 1962—, chmn. dept., 1959-67, dir. program Bell System execs., 1958-59; dir., Center for Urban Affairs, 1968-71, v.p., also dean faculties, 1971-74, provost, 1974—. Fellow Am. Sociol. Assn. (v.p. 1972-73); mem. Midwest Sociol. Soc. (pres. 1968), Alpha Kappa Delta (pres. 1966-68); Soc. for Study of Social Problems (pres. 1969). Author: (with Freeman and Yellin) Social Mobility, 1957; (with Kimball Young) Sociology and Social Life, 1959, Transforming Am., 1967. Editor: (with Kimball Young) Principles of Sociology: A Reader in Theory and Research 1960; Race, Class and Power, 1963; Our Children's Burden, 1968; The Changing South, 1970; Prejudice and Race Relations, 1970. Asso. editor: Sociol. Quar., 1958-61. Editor, The American Sociologist, 1968-70. Home: 2233 Orrington Ave Evanston IL 60201 Office: Rebecca Crown Center Northwestern U Evanston IL 60201

MACK, ROBERT EMMET, hosp. adminstr., physician; b. Morris, Ill., 1924; M.D., St. Louis U., 1948. Intern, St. Mary's Hosp. Group, 1948-49, asst. physician; asst. resident, then resident internal medicine St. Louis U., 1949-52; asst. chief radioisotope clinic Walter Reed Army Med. Center, Washington, 1954-56; chief med. service, chief radioisotope service St. Louis VA Hosp., 1956-61; vis. physician St. Louis City Hosp., 1957-61; chmn. dept. medicine Woman's Hosp., Detroit, 1961-66; dir. Hutzel Hosp., Detroit, 1966-71, pres., 1971—; asst. prof medicine St. Louis U., 1957-61; asso. prof. medicine Wayne State U., 1961-66, prof., 1966—. Diplomate Am. Bd. Internal Medicine. Mem. AMA, Am. Fedn. Clin. Research, Central Soc. Clin. Research, Am. Endocrine Soc., Am. Physiol. Soc. Address: 4707 St Antoine Blvd Detroit MI 48201

MACK, WALTER MERRIMAN, automobile co. exec.; b. Chgo., July 22, 1925; s. Walter Adams and Viola Antionette (Merriman) M.; B.A., U. Chgo., 1948; m. Suzanne Charbonneau, Nov. 20, 1948; children—Elaine, Linda, Stephen. Owner, Mack Cadillac Corp., Chgo., 1946-64, Mt. Prospect, Ill., 1964—; owner Mack Leasing Co., Chgo., 1956-64, Mt. Prospect, 1964—; owner M & M Enterprises, Inc., Mt. Prospect, Ill., 1971—. Dir. C.L.C. Corp. Owner, WEXI-FM, Arlington Heights, Ill., 1967-72. Served with AUS, 1943-46. Mem. Chgo. Auto Trade Assn. (dir. 1965-69), Delta Kappa Epsilon. Roman Catholic. Clubs: Glen View (ILL.), Shoreacres, Chicago; Lyford Cay (Bahamas). Office: 303 W Rand Rd Mount Prospect IL 60056

MACK, WILLIAM JESS, dentist; b. Charleston, W.Va., Sept. 10, 1938; s. Steven Joseph and Frieda (Campbell) M.; student Drake U., Des Moines, 1956-59; D.D.S., State U. Iowa, 1963; m. Judith Louise Erickson, June 14, 1963; children—Scott, Jeff, Steve, John. Individual practice dentistry, Phoenix, 1965-66, Davenport, Iowa, 1966—; Served to lt. USNR, 1963-65. Mem. Am., Ariz., Iowa dental assns., Scott County Dental Soc. (v.p. 1972), Am. Soc. Preventive Dentistry, Davenport Dist., Christian dental socs., Am. Soc. Dentistry Children, Davenport C. of C., Sigma Phi Epsilon, Delta Sigma Delta. Rotarian. Home: 4465 Spring Davenport IA 52807 Office: NW Tower 100 E Kimberly Rd Davenport IA 52806

MACKAY, JOHN RICHARDSON, lawyer; b. Chgo., Oct. 7, 1917; s. John Miller and Isabel (Mackay) M.; student Loyola U., Chgo., 1945; J.D., John Marshall Law Sch., Chgo., 1949; children—John Richardson, James D. Admitted to Ill. bar, 1950; underwriter, claims atty. Hartford Accident & Indemnity Co., Chgo., 1940-51; practice law, Wheaton, Ill., 1951—; spl. asst. atty. gen. Ill., 1956-59; chmn. Senator Percy's com. to study fed. jud. dists. in Ill.; mem. Gov.'s Task Force on Law and Edn. Mem. Ill. (pres. 1974-75, bd. govs. 1967—), DuPage County (pres. 1965-66) bar assns., Ill. Bar Officers Conf. (pres. 1966-67), 7th Dist. Fedn. Local Bar Assns. (pres. 1957-58). Club: Masons. Office: 422 W Wesley Wheaton IL 60187

MAC KAY, LEO STEVEN, automotive industry exec.; b. Blawnox, Pa., Aug. 6, 1914; s. Joseph and Ann (Cush) MacK.; student Carnegie Inst. Tech., 1936; m. Cecelia F. Kost, June 15, 1940; 1 son, Jon Charles. Purchasing agt. Blaw-Knox Co., 1932-46; dir. purchases Kaiser-Frazer Co., 1946-53; v.p. procurement Willys Motors, Inc., Kaiser-Jeep Corp., Toledo, 1954-69; v.p. operations AM Gen. Corp., subsidiary Am. Motors Corp., Wayne, Mich., 1970—. Clubs: Detroit Athletic, Dearborn Country, South Bend Country. Home: 6611 Parkway Circle Dearborn Heights MI 48127 Office: 32500 Van Born Rd Wayne MI 48184

MACKEL, AUDLEY MAURICE, dentist; b. Natchez, Miss., Oct. 1, 1904; s. Robert and Emma Irine (Williams) M.; student Natchez Coll., 1919-21, Atlanta U., 1921-22; D.D.S., Meharry Dental Coll., 1927; m. Rosetta Libian Lloyd, June 18, 1927; children—Audrose, Charles Banks, Audley Maurice, Harriett Gatlin, Lyvonne, Wilbert Washington, Gwendolyn, Marilyn. Gen. practice dentistry, Natchez, 1927-30, 38-56, Monroe, La., 1930-48, Chgo., 1956—. Vice pres. Tri-State Med. Dental Pharm. Assn., 1929; pres. Miss. Dental Soc., 1940; commr. Joint Commn. Accrediation Dental Labs. U.S.A., 1962-71. Founder, exec. sec. Natchez br. N.A.C.C.P., 1951, mem.

nat. bd., 1953-57; pres. nat. parents council Bennett Coll., 1955; mem. gen. bd. edn. A.M.E. Ch., 1956-60, pres. laymen 8th Episcopal Dist., 1954; founder, pres. Monroe Civic League, 1933; chmn. edn. com. Natchez Bus. and Civic League, 1954; bd. dirs., exec. com. Southtown br. Met. YMCA Chgo., 1962-72; dist. commr. Adams County (Miss.) dist. Boy Scouts Am., 1942, Englewood dist., Chgo., 1958. Trustee Campbell Coll., Jackson, Miss. Recipient award certificate Pres. Roosevelt, 1940, Inter Deniminational Minister Civic League Ill., 1964. Mem. Am., Nat. (pres. 1953), Ill. dental assns., Chgo., Lincoln dental socs., South Shore Valley Community Assn. (dir.), Kappa Alpha Psi. Mem. A.M.E. Ch. (trustee). Mason (32 deg.). Home: 9113 S Constance St Chicago IL 60617 Office: 1025 W 63d St Chicago IL 60621

MAC KENZIE, JOHN ROBERT, physician; b. Egmondville, Ont., Can., Apr. 26, 1930; s. Robert Edwin and Ella Jane Charters (Chesney) MacK.; M.D., U. Toronto (Ont.), 1954; m. Priscilla Sutherland, Oct. 1, 1955; children—Dawneen, Robert G., Daphne J., Douglas J. Intern Toronto Western Hosp., 1954-55, Hosp. for Sick Children, Toronto, 1955; practice medicine specializing in family practice, Sarnia, Ont., 1955—; mem. staffs Sarnia Gen. Hosp., St. Joseph's Hosp.; dir. Physician's Services, Inc., 1963-72; dir., pres. Lambton Med. Arts, Inc., 1957—, Desimac Investment Ltd., 1966—; hon. med. adv. Royal Life Saving Soc. Can., 1954-65. Bd. dirs. Physician's Services Inc. Found., 1970-77. Mem. Coll. Family Practice, Assn. Canadian Underwater Councils. Conservative. Clubs: Craigleith Ski, (Collingwood, Ont.); Sarnia Riding. Home: 1375 Robin Ln Sarnia ON Canada also Scenic Cave Rd Colingwood ON Canada Office: 168 Essex St Sarnia ON N7V 4R9 Canada

MAC KENZIE, ROBERT DOUGLAS, biochemist; b. Chgo., Aug. 18, 1928; s. Vernon Gordon and Alice (Rasmussen) MacK.; B.S., U. Cin., 1952; M.S., Mich. State U., 1954, Ph.D., 1957; m. Ruth Ann Noelcke, Sept. 6, 1952; children—Robert Bruce, Barbara Alice, Catherine Ann, Deborah Ruth. Research chemist William S. Merrell Co., Reading, O., summer 1952, research biochemist, 1957-63, sect. head, 1963—; grad. asst. Mich. State U., East Lansing, 1953-54, spl. research grad. asst., 1954-57; sect. head cardiovascular and neurological diseases dept. Merrell Nat. Labs., Cin., 1971—, head hematology sect., 1973—. Adj. asso. prof. biochemistry U. Cin., 1967-69. Served with AUS, 1946-48. Mem. Am. Heart Assn. (mem. council thrombosis 1971, speakers bur. 1972, mem. pub. edn. sub-com. 1973), Am. Chem. Soc., A.A.A.S., N.Y. Acad. Sci., Am. Mgmt. Assn., Sigma Xi. Patentee in field. Home: 6229 Savannah Ave Cincinnati OH 45224 Office: 110 E Amity Rd Cincinnati OH 45215

MAC KEOWN, GRAEME JACK, mgmt. cons.; b. East Orange, N.J., Dec. 15, 1930; s. Graeme Jack and Caroline (Ulrich) MacK.; student physics U. N.C., 1950-55; student math. Columbia U. and Rutgers U., 1956-59; m. Marjorie Jane Gabriel, Dec. 31, 1966; children—Graeme Jack III, Christopher Jearvey. Mfg. mgr. ITT, 1955-59; project engr. Honeywell EDP, Boston, 1959-63; space systems mgr. Gemini Spacecapsule and F-4 Phantom projects McDonnell Douglas Corp., St. Louis, 1963-67; research engr. Olin Corp., East Alton, Ill., 1967-69; engring. specialist Parsons Brinckerhoff-Tudor-Bechtel, Atlanta, 1972-75; mgmt. cons. Grahm Assos., Vandalia, Ohio, 1975-77. Served with AUS, 1950-60. Mem. ASME, N.Y. Acad. Scis., Soc. Am. Mil. Engrs. Club: Atlanta Press. Contbr. articles profl. jours. Holder 3 U.S. patents. Home and office: 308 S Brown School Rd Vandalia OH 45377

MACKEY, DIANA PARSONS, employment counsellor; b. Columbus, Ohio, Mar. 26, 1946; d. Reid Ivan and Charleen Lois (Krieg) Parsons; B.A. in Edn., Miami U., Oxford, Ohio, 1968; m. Ralph Trannett Mackey, Nov. 1, 1969; children—Michelle, Jon. Asst. librarian Columbus Pub. Library, 1968-70; sales and adminstrv. placement counsellor Snelling & Snelling, Columbus, 1976—. Co-founder S.E. Civic Assn., Columbus, 1974, pres., 1976—; Democratic candidate for county commr., 1976. Soroptimist scholar, 1964. Mem. Franklin County Women's Polit. Caucus, Miami U. Alumni, Ohioans for Utility Reform, NOW, Kappa Delta Alumnae. Home: 1340 Wilson Ave Columbus OH 43206 Office: 8 E Broad St Columbus OH 43215

MACKEY, ELIZABETH JOCELYN, musicologist; b. Corbin, Ky., Oct. 30, 1927; d. Elbert Thomas and Flora (Bryant) Mackey; B.S., Peabody Coll., 1948; B. Music, Greensboro Coll., 1953; M. Music, U. Mich., 1956, Ph.D., 1968. Tchr. music pub. schs. N.C., Calif., 1948-55; asst. prof. music Indiana (Pa.) State Coll., 1956-58; asso. prof. Minot (N.D.) State Coll., 1964-67; asst. prof. musicology Ball State U., Muncie, Ind., 1969-74, asso. prof., 1974—. Dir. choir Holy Trinity Luth. Ch., Muncie, 1969—. Fulbright scholar Berlin, 1961-62; AAUW fellow, 1963-64. Mem. Pi Kappa Lambda, Sigma Alpha Iota (nat. program counselor 1968—, Sword of Honor, Rose of Honor). Home: 803 Riverside Ave Muncie IN 47303

MACKEY, ORMA EVERETT, corp. exec.; b. nr. Centralia, Mo., Oct. 18, 1900; s. Cebern Bennett and Daisy Della (Young) M.; student Chillicothe Bus. Coll., 1918-19; m. Cleo Carrie Mitchell, Dec. 21, 1919; children—Orma E., William Everett, Shirley Delphene (Mrs. Kenneth Ray Hammond), Glenda Colleen (Mrs. William B. Severin, Jr.). Served as vice president Audrian County Agr. Conservation Assn., 1934-37, pres., 1937-40, 41-46; sec.-dir. Consol. Electric Coop., Mexico, Mo., 1938-70; pres. Zeeway Products, Inc., 1954—, Mexico Egg Ranch, Inc., 1961—, Mackey-Snell Co., Inc., 1962-66, Mackey Investment Co., 1962—; dir. Family Benefit Investment Co., 1st Nat. Bank, 1958—, Family Benefit Life Ins. Co. Pres. Mo. State REA Assn., 1962-65; dir., chmn. agr. hall fame com. Nat. REA, 1966-70; pres. Agrl. Hall Fame and National Center. Bd. dirs. Naylor Sch. Dist., Audrain County 1930-46, chmn. Audrain County Sch. Bd. Assn., 1943-47; mem. Audrain County Com. for War Bonds and USO, 1943-44; chmn. Audrain County Fair Fund Drive, 1955. Named hon. col. staff of gov. of Mo., 1965. Mem. Internat. Platform Assn., C. of C. (past v.p., past dir.), Audrain County Real Estate Bd. (dir.), Audrain County Farm Bur. (past pres.), Audrain Co-op. Assn. (past pres.), Audrain County Bd. Realtors (past pres.), Mo. Limousin Breeders Assn. (dir.). Baptist. Home: RFD 3 Centralia MO 65240 Office: 217 W Jackson Mexico MO 65265

MAC KICHAN, KENNETH ALLEN, hydrologist; b. Sanilac County, Mich., Oct. 27, 1911; s. John Allen and Anna Pearl (Brooks) MacK.; A.A., Port Huron Jr. Coll., 1932; B.S., U. Mich., 1934, M.S., 1935; m. Lois Alma Deyton, May 1, 1943; children—John, Robert, Margaret. Jr. draftsman Mich. Hwy. Dept., Lansing, 1935; civil engr. Appalachian Forest Expt. Sta., Asheville, N.C., 1935-38; hydraulic engr. U.S. Geol. Survey, Asheville, 1938-41, Charleston, W.Va., 1941-51, Washington, 1951-61, chief hydraulic studies sect. Gen. Hydrology Br., 1955-61, dist. engr. quality Water Br., Ocala, Fla., 1961-65, dist. chief Water Resources Div., Lincoln, Nebr., 1965—. Active Boy Scouts Am. Registered profl. engr., W.Va., Md. Fellow ASCE; mem. Am. Geophys. Union, Am. Water Works Assn., Water Pollution Control Fedn., Am. Water Resources Assn. (sect. sec.-treas. 1971-72), Nebr. Acad. Sci., Nebr. Irrigation Assn., Sigma Xi. Contbr. articles to profl. jours. Home: 2570 Woods Blvd Lincoln NE 68502 Office: Room 406 Fed Office Bldg and Courthouse 100 Centennial Mall N Lincoln NE 68508

MACKIW, THEODORE, educator; b. Strutyn, Ukraine, May 30, 1918; s. Ivan and Maria (Jankiw) M.; came to U.S., 1950, naturalized, 1956; Ph.D., Frankfurt (Germany) U., 1950; postgrad. Seton Hall U., 1951-54; m. Ellen Kraus; 1 son, Stephen. Instr., Seton Hall U., 1950-54; tchr. Blue Ridge Country Day Sch., Milwood, Va., 1954-55, Cushing Acad., Ashburnham, Mass., 1955-56; vis. prof. history Schwyz (Switzerland) Coll., 1956-57; prof. Lane Coll., 1957-58; tchr. Hamden Hall Country Day Sch., Hamden, Conn., 1958-60; asst. prof. U. R.I., 1960-62; prof. Slavic studies, dir. Soviet area studies U. Akron, 1962—; head search sect. documents intelligence UNRRA; postdoctoral research fellow Yale U., 1959-60; NDEA grad. fellow Ind. U., 1967. Mem. AAUP, AAAS, Am. Assn. Tchrs. of Slavic and E. European Langs., Am. Hist. Assn., Shevchenko Sci. Soc. Author: Mazepa im Lichte der zeitgenoessischen deutschen Quellen (1639-1709), 1963; Prince Mazepa: Hetman of Ukraine, 1687-1709, 1967. Office: U Akron Akron OH 44325

MAC LAREN, DAVID SARGEANT, pollution control equipment co. exec.; b. Cleve., Jan. 4, 1931; s. Albert Sargeant and Theadora Beidler (Potter) MacL.; A.B., Miami U., Oxford, Ohio, 1955; m. Suzanne Moler, June 19, 1954; children—Alison, Carolyn, Catherine. Mgr. Jet Aeration Co., Cleve., 1958-60, chmn. bd., pres., 1961—; founder, chmn. bd., pres. Air Injector Corp., Cleve., 1958—; founder, pres. Fluid Equipment, Inc., Cleve., 1962-72, chmn. bd., 1962-72; founder, pres. T&M Co., Cleve., 1963-71, chmn. bd., 1964-71; founder, pres. Alison Realty Co., Cleve., 1965—, chmn. bd., 1967—; founder, pres. Mold Leasing, Inc., Cleve., 1968-71; dir. Gilmore Industries, 1975-77. Mem. tech. com. Nat. Sanitation Found., Ann Arbor, Mich., 1967—. Mem. Republican State Central Com., 1968-72, Cuyahoga County Rep. Central Com., 1968-72; registered legis. agt. 110th Ohio Gen. Assembly, 1973-74. Served with arty. AUS, 1955-58. Certified scuba diver; internat. diving certificate. Fellow Royal Soc. Health (London, Eng.); mem. Nat., Ohio environ. health assns., Nat., Ohio water pollution control fedns., Nat. Precast Concrete Assn., Am. Pub. Health Assn., Gullwing Club, Ohio Gun Collectors Assn., Defenders Wildlife, Com. Humane Legislation, Friends of Animals, Am. Mgmt. Assn., Mercedes Benz Club N.Am. (pres. 1968), U.S. Martial Arts Assn. (black belt, instr.), Jiu-Jitsu/Karati Black Belt Fedn., Scottish Tartans Soc., Clan MacLaren Soc., Vintage Sports Car Club, Nat. Audubon Soc., Ferrari Club Am., Fraternal Order Police, Cleve. Animal Protective League, Highland Heights Citizens League, SAR, Internat. Platform Assn., Delta Kappa Epsilon (nat. dir. 1974—; dir. Kappa chpt. assn. 1969—). Clubs: Mentor Harbor Yachting; Cleveland Skating, Cleveland Racquet, Country. Patentee in field. Home: 21176 Brantley Rd Shaker Heights OH 44122 Office: 750 Alpha Dr Cleveland OH 44143

MACLAUGHLIN, HARRY HUNTER, Judge; b. Breckenridge, Minn., Aug. 9, 1927; s. Harry Hunter and Grace (Swank) MacL.; B.B.A. with distinction, U. Minn., 1949, LL.B., J.D., 1956; m. Mary Jean Shaffer, June 25, 1958; children—David, Douglas. With Gen. Motors Corp., Mpls., 1949-52, Minn. Mining Co., St. Paul, 1952-54; law clk. to Justice Frank Gallagher Minn. Supreme Ct., 1955-56; admitted to Minn. bar, 1956; practice law, Mpls., 1956-72; partner firm MacLaughlin & Harstad, 1960-72; asso. justice Minn. Supreme Ct., 1972-77; U.S. dist. judge Dist. of Minn., 1977—; lectr. U. Minn. Law Sch., 1973—; part-time instr. William Mitchell Coll. Law, St. Paul, 1958-63. Mem. Mpls. Charter Commn., 1966-72, Minn. State Coll. Bd., 1971-72, Minn. Jud. Council, 1972; nat. adv. council Small Bus. Adminstrn., 1968-70. Served with USNR, 1945-46. Mem. Am., Minn., Hennepin County bar assns., Am. Trial Lawyers Assn., Beta Gamma Sigma, Phi Delta Phi. Methodist. Bd. editors Minn. Law Rev., 1954-55. Home: 2301 Oliver Ave S Minneapolis MN 55405 Office: US Court House Minneapolis MN 55401

MAC LEAN, LOWE (SANDY), univ. adminstr.; b. Laurium, Mich., June 24, 1934; s. Angus Lowe and Marion (Stannard) MacL.; B.A., No. Mich. U., 1956; M.A., Mich. State U., 1960; postgrad. U. No. Ia., 1960-63; Ed.D., Ind. U., 1967; m. Judith Ellen Rea, July 12, 1969; children—Kent Allen, Brian Lowe. Tchr., coach Crystal (Mich.) Community Schs., 1958-59; grad. adviser Mich. State U., 1959-60; dir. Men's Halls U. No. Ia., 1960-63; head counsellor Ind. U., 1963-66; asst. dean students, prof. edn. U. Mo. at Columbia, 1966-70; dean students Eastern Mich. U., 1970-76, asso. v.p. student affairs, 1976—. Chmn. Ypsilanti Summer Festival Commn., 1975; chmn. adv. council Ypsilanti Sch. Dist., Title VII. Mem. exec. bd. of bd. govs. Washtenaw United Way. Served with AUS, 1956-58. Mem. Am. Coll. Personnel Assn. (coordinator govt. relations 1976—), Am. Assn. Higher Edn., Am., Mich. personnel and guidance assns., Nat. Assn. Student Personnel Admnstrs., Mich. Coll. Personnel Assn., Tau Kappa Epsilon, Phi Delta Kappa. Rotarian (pres. 1975-76). Home: 209 Elm St Ypsilanti MI 48197

MAC MAHAN, HORACE ARTHUR, JR., phys. geographer; b. Freeport, Maine, Aug. 13, 1928; s. Horace Arthur and Anne Louise (Skagen) MacM.; B.A., U. Maine, 1954; M.S., U. Utah, 1963; Ed.D., U. Colo., 1967; m. Marcia Jeanne Wollum, Jan. 28, 1965; 1 dau., Kerri. Staff asst. Earth Sci. Curriculum Project, Boulder, Colo., 1963-64; asso. prof. earth sci. State U. Coll., Oneonta, N.Y., 1967-68; asso. prof. secondary edn. Weber State Coll., Ogden, Utah, 1968-69; prof. geography and geology Eastern Mich. U., Ypsilanti, Mich., 1969—; cons. Hubbard Sci. Co., Northbrook, Ill., 1970—. Served with USN, 1947-49. Mem. Am. Assn. Higher Edn., AAAS, Assn. Edn. Tchrs. of Sci., Council Geog. Edn., Nat. Assn. Geology Tchrs., Nat. Sci. Tchrs. Assn., N.Y. Acad. Sci., Kappa Delta Pi, Phi Delta Kappa. Author: Investigating the Dynamic Earth, 1974; Stereogram Book of Contours, 1972. Home: 1303 Collegewood Ave Ypsilanti MI 48197

MAC MAHON, HAROLD BERNARD, mfg. co. exec.; b. Newton, Mass., Nov. 15, 1917; s. Harold A. and Alma A. (McCabe) MacM.; B.S. in Edn., Boston U., 1940; m. Mary M. Savage, Jan. 1, 1942; 1 dau., Karen D. MacMahon Levisay. Plant mgr. Bassick div. Stewart-Warner Corp., Spring Valley, Ill., 1958-66, controller Alemite and Instrument div., Chgo., 1966-73, asst. gen. mgr., 1973-74, gen. mgr. Hobbs div., Springfield, Ill., 1974—, v.p., 1976—; dir. Springfield Marine Bank. Dir., Greater Springfield Indsl. Devel. Council, 1976-77. Served with U.S. Army, 1943-45. Mem. Soc. Automotive Engrs., Newcomen Soc. N.Am., Ill. C. of C., Kappa Delta Phi. Club: Sangamo (Springfield). Home: 23 The Country Pl Springfield IL 62703 also 260 E Chestnut St Chicago IL 60611 Office: Yale Blvd and Ash St Springfield IL 62705

MAC MASTER, DANIEL MILLER, museum pres.; b. Chgo., Feb. 11, 1913; s. Daniel Howard and Charlotte Louise (Miller) MacM.; student Lakeside Press Tng. Sch., 1930-31, U. Chgo., 1931-34, L.H.D., Lincoln Coll., 1970; m. Sylvia Jane Hill, Feb. 22, 1935; children—Daniel Miller, Jane Irene (Mrs. Robert W. Lightell). Mem. staff Mus. Sci. and Industry, Chgo., 1933—, acting dir., 1950, dir., 1951-72, pres., trustee, 1968—; gen. mgr. Chgo. R.R. Fair, 1948-49. Dir. Hyde Park Bank & Trust Co. Dir. Floating Seminar to Greece, 1960; guest mus. cons. Fed. Republic of Germany, 1961; U.S. State Dept. specialist on mus. in Dublin, Essen, Berlin, Stockholm, 1963. Mem. Homewood (Ill.) Bd. Edn., 1945-49, pres., 1948-49; sec. State Ill. Higher Edn. Commn., 1955-59; mem. U. Ill. Citizens Adv. Com. 1945—. Bd. dirs. Internat. Coll. Surgeons Hall of Fame; hon. bd. dirs. Chgo. Chamber Orch., pres., 1970-71; dir. emeritus Monmouth Coll.; trustee Adler Planetarium, Sears-Roebuck Found., 1970-73, U. Chgo. Cancer Research Found.; vice chmn. bd. govs. Chgo. Heart Assn.; mem. Nat. 4-H Service Com.; citizens bd. U. Chgo., Lincoln Acad. Ill. Decorated Golden Cross Royal Order Phoenix (Greece); Officer's Cross Polonia Restituta (Poland); Grand Badge of Honor (Austria); Golden Badge of Honor (Vienna), Grand Badge Honor of Burgenland (Austria); Officer's Cross 1st Class Order Merit (Germany); Oskar von Miller Gold medal Deutsches Mus.; Munich, Germany; Order Cultural Merit (Poland); officer Order of Merit (Luxembourg); recipient Patriotic Civilian Service award U.S. Army. Fellow Assn. Sci.-Tech. Centers; mem. Kappa Sigma. Clubs: Tavern, Quadrangle, Comml. (Chgo.). Author: Exploring the Mysteries of Physics and Chemistry (with others), 1938. Book reviewer. Contbr. to newspapers, mags., encys. Home: 910 Bruce Ave Flossmoor IL 60422 Office: Museum of Science and Industry 57th St and South Lake Shore Dr Chicago IL 60637

MACNAUGHTON, DAVID RAYMOND, elec. co. exec.; b. Jersey City, Aug. 26, 1920; s. David Raymond and Agnes Alexandra (Miller) M.; student St. Peters Coll., 1937-42; B.S. in Econs., U. Pa., 1946; m. Esther Rose Dietz, Oct. 25, 1947; children—Esther, David, Michael. Account analyst Nat. City Bank N.Y., N.Y.C., 1937-42; with Gen. Electric Co., 1946—, supr. personnel accounting Chem. div., 1948, mem. Corporate audit staff, 1948-52, mgr. budgets and measurements Switchgear div., Phila., 1952-53, mgr. finance, 1953-55, mgr. finance Lamp div., Cleve., 1955-57, mgr. financial planning and analysis, Cleve., 1960—, mgr. finance Atomic Products div., Hanford, Wash., 1958-60. Tchr. Gen. Electric Tng. courses, 1961—. Pres., West Geauga Booster Club, 1963-67, treas., 1964-66, finance officer, 1962—. Bd. dirs. Geauga br. Cleve. YMCA, Served with USAAF, 1942-43. Named Man of the Year, Geauga YMCA, 1972. Mem. Sigma Chi. Episcopalian. Club: Mayfield Village Racquet. Home: 9401 Wilson Mills Rd Chesterland OH 44026 Office: Nela Park East Cleveland OH 44112

MAC NEVEN, ROBERT WILLIAM, educator; b. nr. Gaylord, Mich., Feb. 21, 1915; s. William and Ruth (Quistgaard) MacN.; B.S., Kansas City Tchrs. Coll., 1938; M.A., Columbia, 1946; m. Pauline Marie Adamek, Sept. 5, 1937; 1 son, William Joseph. Tchr., head tchr., prin. Kansas City (Mo.) Pub. Schs., 1938-51, dir. dept. pupil services, 1951-62, dir. youth devel. project, 1962-64; spl. cons. Kansas City Commn. Human Relations, City Kansas City, 1964-67; asst. supt. schs. charge human relations Kansas City Pub. Schs., 1967-70, asst. supt. sch. support and devel., 1970-74, asst. supt. accountability personnel and research, 1974—. Mem. Coll. Entrance Exams. Bd. Pres. Regional Health and Welfare Council, 1963-66; v.p. nat. council YMCA's, 1968-71. Bd. dirs. Gillis Home, 1962-66, Council for Handicapped, 1963-70; bd. dirs. Kansas City Assn. Mental Health, 1966-70, past pres.; bd. dirs. Greater Kansas City chpt. A.R.C., 1970-73, Nat. Conf. Christians and Jews, 1973—; mem. adv. bd. Kansas City Urban League, 1966—; bd. dirs. Mattie Rhodes Center, 1976—. Recipient Schoolman of Year award Freedoms Found., 1973; Distinguished Educator award Acad. Fellows, C.F. Kettering Found., 1976. Fellow Inst. Devel. Ednl. Activities, Charles F. Kettering Found., 1969, 73, 75, 76. Fellow Am. Orthopsychiat. Assn.; hon. fellow Harry S. Truman Library Inst.; mem. Internat. Assn. Pupil Personnel Workers, Am. Soc. Pub. Adminstrn., Am. Assn. Sch. Personnel Adminstrs., Nat. Assn. Intergroup Relations Ofcls., Kansas City St. Andrews Soc. (past pres.), Kansas City Edn. Assn., Nat. Assn. Sch. Execs., Mo. Tchrs. Assn., Am., Mo. assns. sch. adminstrs., Assn. for Supervision and Curriculum Devel., Mo. Assn. Social Welfare, N.E.A., Phi Delta Kappa. Democrat. Presbyn. Home: 224 E 60th St Kansas City MO 64113 Office: 1211 McGee St Kansas City MO 64106

MAC NIDER, JACK, cement co. exec.; b. Washington, Feb. 21, 1927; s. Hanford and Margaret Elizabeth (McAuley) MacN.; B.A., Harvard U., 1950, M.B.A. with distinction, 1952; m. Margaret Hansen, Sept. 9, 1950; 1 son, Charles Hanford. With U.S. Steel Corp., 1952-54; with Northwestern States Portland Cement Co., Mason City, Iowa, 1954—, v.p., asst. gen. mgr., 1959-60, pres., gen. mgr., 1960—, also dir.; dir. First Nat. Bank Mason City; pres., sec.-treas., dir. Mason City Hotel Corp.; trustee Equitable Life Ins. Co. of Iowa. Pres. N. Iowa Med. Center; trustee Midwest Research Inst., Kansas City, Mo., Beloit (Wis.) Coll.; pres. Iowa Coll. Found., 1962. Served with USMCR, 1944-45. Mem. Young Pres.'s Orgn., Portland Cement Assn. (chmn. 1974-76, dir.), Iowa Mfrs. Assn. (chmn., dir. 1971-72), Mason City C. of C. (pres. 1962), Am. Legion (past post comdr.). Republican. Congregationalist. Clubs: Masons; Euchre and Cycle, Mason City Country (Mason City); Mpls.; Univ. (Chgo.); Des Moines; Tavern. Home: Box 623 Mason City IA 50401 Office: Box 1008 Mason City IA

MACSAI, JOHN, architect; b. Budapest, Hungary, May 20, 1926; s. Francis and Margaret (Rosenfeld) Lusztig; came to U.S., 1947, naturalized, 1954; Baccalaureate summa cum laude, Kolcsey Gimnasium, Budapest, 1944; student Atelier Art Sch., Budapest, 1941-43, Poly. U., Budapest, 1945-47; B.Arch. magna cum laude, Miami U., Oxford, Ohio, 1949; m. Geraldine Marcus, May 7, 1950; children—Pamela, Aaron, Marian, Gwen. Archtl. designer Skidmore, Owings & Merrill, Chgo., Pace Assos., Chgo., Raymond Loewy Assos., Chgo., 1949-55; partner Hausner & Macsai, Chgo., 1955-71, Campbell & Macsai, Chgo., 1971-74; prin. John Macsai & Assos. Architects Inc., Chgo., 1975—; prof. architecture U. Ill., Chgo. Circle Campus. Chmn., S.E. Council Integrated Communities, 1968-70; past mem. housing adv. com. Chgo. Commn. on Human Relations; past bd. dirs. South Shore Commn., Jewish Council on Urban Affairs, Jewish Family and Community Service, Adult Edn. Council. Recipient 13 award citations Chgo. chpt. AIA. Mem. AIA. Jewish (past v.p. synogogue). Author: High Rise Apartment Buildings—A Design Primer, 1972; Housing, 1976. Important works include N.O.R.C. Bldg. U. Chgo., High Energy Physics Bldg. U. Chgo., Social Service Center U. Chgo., Harbor House Apt. Bldg., Chgo., Malibu East Apt. Bldg., Chgo., Volkswagen Midwest Hdqrs., Northbrook, Water Tower Inn, Chgo., Hyatt House Hotel, Lincolnwood, M.L. King Community Services Center, Chgo., Jackson Park Hosp., Chgo. Home: 1207 Judson Ave Evanston IL 60202 Office: 168 N Michigan Ave Chicago IL 60601

MADDEN, THOMAS JOSEPH, JR., electronic engr.; b. Chgo., Feb. 26, 1931; s. Thomas Joseph and Doris Amanda (Oksnee) M.; B.S. in Elec. Engring., U. Ill., 1953; m. Marjorie June Forbes, Jan. 31, 1953; children—John, James, Jeffery. Electronic engr. Ralph M. Parsons, Pasadena, Calif., 1953-54, Farnsworth Electronics, Ft. Wayne, Ind., 1956-57; project engr. Cook Electric Co., Morton Grove, Ill., 1957-65; mgr. Word processing engring. A. B. Dick Co., Chgo., 1967—. Served with U.S. Army, 1954-56. Mem. League Am. Wheelmen. Lutheran. Patentee in field. Home: 428 Lilac St Elk Grove IL 60007 Office: 2200 Arthur Ave Elk Grove IL 60007

MADDIN, MICHAEL WARREN, lawyer; b. Detroit, May 18, 1940; s. Milton Maurice and Esther (Loewenberg) M.; B.A., U. Mich., 1962; J.D., Wayne State U., 1965; m. Donna Sue Hartman, Dec. 28, 1966; children—Melissa Joy, Marc Robert, Martin Brian. Admitted to Mich. bar, 1966; practiced in Detroit, 1966-72, Southfield, Mich., 1972—; mem. firms Milton M. Maddin, 1966, Maddin & Maddin, 1967—. Bd. dirs. Jr. div. Jewish Welfare Fedn. Detroit, 1967-71, mem. exec. com., 1969-71, pres., 1970-71, campaign coordinator,

1971-72, bd. govs., 1976—; liaison to Jewish Vocat. Service bd. dirs. 1968-69; mem. liaison bd. dirs. Jewish Community Center, 1969-70; liaison dir. Fresh Air Soc., 1970-71, bd. dirs. 1971-77, chmn. community relations com., 1976-77, mem. program com., 1971—, research and devel. coms., 1971-77, budget and fees com., 1977—; mem. nat. young leadership cabinet United Jewish Appeal, 1972—, regional chmn., 1975—, mem. exec. com., 1976—. Mem. Am., Southfield, Detroit bar assns., State Bar of Mich., Am. Judicature Soc. Mason. (Shriner). Clubs: University of Michigan Club of Detroit, Standard (dir.), Franklin Hills Country, Economic (Detroit) Home: 3257 Parkland Dr West Bloomfield MI 48033 Office: 1618 Travelers Tower Southfield MI 48076

MADDIN, MILTON MAURICE, lawyer; b. San Francisco, Jan. 10, 1902; s. Morris and Esther (Shambrum) M.; student Detroit City Coll., 1919; A.B., U. Mich., 1922; LL.B., 1925; m. Esther Loewenberg, Feb. 26, 1937; children—Michael Warren, Richard Joel, Rosalyn Faye. Admitted to Mich. bar, 1925; practice of law, specializing in corporate and real property law. Gov., mem. exec. com. Jewish Welfare Fedn. Detroit, 1958—; bd. dirs. United Jewish Charities, 1958—; bd. dirs. Fresh Air Soc., 1944—, pres., 1949-51; bd. dirs. Jewish House of Shelter, 1942—, pres., 1934-36; bd. dirs. Jewish Vocational Service, 1956—; bd. dirs. Sinai Hosp., Detroit, 1959—, pres., 1968—, bd. dirs. Tamarack Authority, 1954—; trustee Cloverhill Park Cemetery, 1948—, pres., 1955-61. Served as lt., AUS, World War II. Mem. Mich. Assn. of Professions, Am., Detroit bar assns., State Bar Mich., Am. Judicature Soc., Lawyers Club U. Mich., Scabbard and Blade, Pi Lambda Phi. Mason (Shriner, 33 deg.) Clubs: Intercollegiate (pres. 1927-28), Covenant (dir.), Standard (dir. 1952-56), Standard City (dir., pres. 1959). Franklin Hills Country (pres. 1969-70) (Detroit). Home: 25230 Southfield Rd Southfield MI 48075 Office: 16th Floor Travelers Tower Southfield MI 48076

MADDIN, RICHARD JOEL, lawyer; b. Detroit, Oct. 30, 1942; s. Milton Maurice and Esther (Loewenberg) M.; B.A., Mich. State U., 1964; J.D., U. Detroit, 1967; m. Nancy Jo Spilker, Dec. 22, 1971; 1 son, Russell Bruce. Admitted to Mich. bar, 1968; partner firm Maddin & Maddin, Southfield, Mich., 1969—. Mem. Am. Judicature Soc., Am. Trial Lawyers Assn., Am. Bar Assn., U. Detroit, Mich. State alumni clubs. Clubs: Masons, Shriners, Economic (Detroit). Home: 28515 Balmoral Way Farmington Hills MI 48018 Office: 1618 Travelers Tower Southfield MI 48076

MADDOX, ARNOLD WAYNE, engr.; b. Kansas City, Mo., Mar. 28, 1933; s. Hugh Maxwell and Anna Allene (Cobb) M.; B.S. in Mech. Engring., U. Mo., Rolla, 1955, Profl. Aerospace Engr., 1977; M.S. in Mgmt. Sci., U. So. Calif., 1972; m. Carolyn Marie Daniels, Sept. 4, 1955; 1 dau., Lisa Marie. Dep. chief engr. aerothermodynamics McDonnell Douglas Astronautics Co.-West Santa Monica, Calif., 1965-68, program mgr., 1968-70; corp. mgr. tech. planning McDonnell Douglas Corp., St. Louis, 1972—; v.p., treas. Instacomp Inc., 1968-72; adj. faculty Webster Coll., Webster Groves, Mo. Served with U.S. Army, 1957. Registered profl. engr., Mo. Mem. AAAS, ASME, Inst. Mgmt. Sci. Home: 13346 Amiot Ct Saint Louis MO 63141

MADDOX, LUCY JANE, librarian, educator; b. Port, Okla., Apr. 6, 1922; d. Robert T. and Tollie (Pierce) Maddox; A.A., Central Coll., 1942; A.B., Seattle Pacific Coll., 1944; M.A., Colo. State Coll., 1948; M.L.S., U. Mich., 1956, Ph.D., 1958. Instr. speech and English, Eaton (Colo.) Pub. High Sch., 1945-48; dean women, asst. prof. speech and English, Spring Arbor (Mich.) Coll., 1948-51, 52-53; asso. prof. speech and English, Seattle Pacific Coll., 1951-52; librarian, prof. English, Owosso (Mich.) Coll., 1953-55, chmn. div. lit., langs. and fine arts, 1958-59; asst. dept. library sci. U. Mich., Ann Arbor, 1957-58; dir., instr. library technician program Ferris State Coll., Big Rapids, Mich., 1959-62; library curriculum coordinator Spring Arbor (Mich.) Coll., 1962-63; dir. library, prof. English, 1963—. Lectr. library sci. U. Mich., Ann Arbor, part-time, 1957-65; vis. instr. library sci. Colo. State Coll., Greeley, summers 1958-61, 65, 66. Christian Librarians fellow. Mem. Mich. Library Assn. (vice chmn. dist IV 1961-62, chmn. dist. II 1967-68), Conf. Christianity and Lit., Assn. for Gen. and Liberal Studies, Mich. Acad., Beta Phi Mu. Free Methodist. Home: 174 E Harmony Rd Spring Arbor MI 49283

MADDOX, WALTER DONALD, oral surgeon; b. Chgo., Apr. 5, 1932; s. Walter Blake and Dominica (Cresto) M.; B.S., Northwestern U., 1955, D.D.S., 1957; M.S., U. Minn., 1963; m. Mary Myster, Aug. 20, 1955; children—Susan Anne, Linda Ellen, Charles David, Stephen Douglas. Resident oral surgery Mayo Clinic, Rochester, Minn., 1960-63; pvt. practice oral surgery, Kankakee, Ill., 1964—; pres. dental staffs Riverside, St. Mary's hosps. Cons. Kankakee State Hosp. Chmn. bd. trustees Kankakee Community Coll.; bd. dirs. Kankakee chpt. Am. Cancer Soc. Served as lt. comdr. USNR, 1957-59. Diplomate Am. Bd. Oral Surgery. Fellow Am. Dental Soc. Anesthesiology; mem. Am. Dental Assn., Ill., Kankakee Dist. (pres. 1971), Chgo. dental socs., Am., Ill. (sec.), Gt. Lakes socs. oral surgeons, Internat. Assn. Oral Surgeons, Sigma Xi, Psi Omega. Presbyn. (elder). Elk, Rotarian. Contbr. articles to dental jours. Home: 1471 Budd Blvd Kankakee IL 60901 Office: 401 N Wall St Kankakee IL 60901

MADDOX, WILLIAM CLARENCE, pedodontist, photographer; b. Dayton, Ohio, June 30, 1927; s. Clarence William and Olive Myrtle (Althouse) M.; B.S. in Edn., Ohio State U., 1950, D.D.S., 1954, pedodontic certificate, 1956, M.Sc., 1967; m. Roberta Lee Clark, Aug. 16, 1952; children—Rickey William, Marjorie Lee, Winifred Ann. Practice pedodontics, 1954—; instr. pedodontics Ohio State U., 1956-66, asst. prof., 1966-67; asso. staff Children's Hosp., Columbus, 1956—; pres. bd. Riverglen Profl. Bldg., Inc., Worthington, Ohio, 1964-66, 73-76. Asst. dist. commr. Central Ohio council Boy Scouts Am., 1960-66, dist. chmn., 1966-67. Mem. bd. edn. Worthington Christian Schs., 1972. Served with USNR, 1945-46. Fellow Am. Acad. Pedodontics, Pierre Fauchard Acad.; mem. Ohio Soc. Pedodontists (pres. 1968-69), Ohio Soc. Dentistry Children, (pres. 1957-58), Columbus Soc. Dentistry Children (pres. 1956-57), Photog. Soc. Am., Profl. Photographers Am., Profl. Photographers Ohio, Phi Delta Theta, Psi Omega, Alpha Phi Omega. Club: Ohio State University Faculty. Home: 267 Highgate Ave Worthington OH 43085 Office: 3722 J Olentangy River Rd Columbus OH 43214

MADDUX, KENNETH CARL, mech. engr.; b. Cin., June 24, 1946; s. Paul E. and Ruth L. (Schmithorst) M.; B.S. with honors in Mech. Engring., U. Cin., 1969; M.S. with honors in Mech. Engring., Purdue U., 1971; m. Elizabeth Jean Ror, June 20, 1969; 1 son, Jonathan A. Engr., Cin. Milacron Co., Cin., 1969; instr. mech. engring., Purdue U., 1969-71; mgr. dei design group Structural Dynamics Research Corp., Cin., 1971—, also cons. engr. Registered profl. engr., Ohio. Mem. ASME, Soc. Automotive Engrs., Soc. Mfg. Engrs., Ohio Soc. Profl. Engrs. Presbyterian. Club: Terrace Park Swim and Tennis. Inventor device in field. Office: 5729 Dragon Way Cincinnati OH 45227

MADELINE, STEPHEN EUGENE, automobile mfg. co. exec.; b. Phila., Aug. 21, 1932; s. Stephen and Jean (Fallotico) M.; A.B., La Salle Coll., 1954; M.B.A., U. Detroit, 1965; m. Elizabeth A. Gallen, Sept. 12, 1959; children—Stephanie, John. Gen. reporter Phila. Daily News, 1954-56; editor employee newspaper Food Fairs Stores, Inc., 1957-59; with Ford Motor Co., Dearborn, Mich., 1961—, stockholder relations mgr., 1975-77, Midwest regional pub. relations mgr., 1977—. Mem. Pub. Relations Soc. Am. (Silver Anvil award 1972), Am. Mgmt. Assn., Nat. Investor Relations Inst., Chgo., Detroit press clubs. Club: Chgo. Mid-Am. Contbr. short stories and articles to Redbook Mag., Detroit News Sunday Mag., Phila. Bull. Sunday mag. Office: 1 E Wacker Dr United of America Bldg Chicago IL 60601

MADEY, RICHARD, educator; b. Bklyn., Feb. 23, 1922; s. Elia Doher and Dorothy Ann (Diab) M.; B.E.E. (Conn. Alumni scholar), Rensselaer Poly. Inst., 1942; Ph.D. in Physics, U. Calif. at Berkeley, 1952; m. Mary Lou Kirch, Sept. 8, 1951; children—Doren Louise, Diane Claire, Daryl Jane, Richard Kirk, Ronald Eliot, Randall Clarke. Elec. engr. Allen B. Dumont Labs., Passaic, N.J., 1934-44; physicist Lawrence Radiation Lab., Berkeley, 1947-53, guest scientist, 1971, 73; asso. physicist Brookhaven Nat. Lab., Upton, L.I., N.Y., 1953-56, guest scientist, 1961, 74; scientist Republic Aviation Corp., Farmingdale, N.Y., 1956-58, sr. scientist, 1958-61, chief staff scientist modern physics, 1961-62, chief applied physics subdiv. of research div., 1964; prof. physics Clarkson Coll. Tech., Potsdam, N.Y., 1965-71, chmn. dept., 1965; prof. physics, chmn. dept. Kent (Ohio) State U., 1971—. Cons. Ross Radio Corp., Berkeley, 1952-53, West Coast Electronics Lab., Willys Motors Co., Oakland, Calif., 1954-55, Kaiser Aircraft & Electronics Corp., Palo Alto, Calif., 1955-56, Health and Safety Lab., U.S. AEC, N.Y.C., 1965-75, ERDA, 1975-77, Dept. of Energy, 1977—; guest scientist Nevis Cyclotron Lab., Columbia U., Irvington-on-the-Hudson, N.Y., 1955, 75, 77, Foster Radiation Lab., McGill U., Montreal, Que., Can., 1967, 68, NRC, Ottawa, Ont., Can., 1968, 69, 70, Nuclear Structure Lab., U. Rochester (N.Y.), 1970, Lawrence Berkeley Lab., 1971, 72, 77, Ind. U. Cyclotron Facility, Bloomington, 1975—, Cyclotron Lab., U. Md. at College Park, 1973, 74, 75; prin. investigator U.S. Air Force, 1963-75, AEC, 1967-75, ERDA, 1975-77, Dept. Energy, 1977—, NSF, 1971—, Nat. Cancer Inst., NIH, 1973—, NASA, 1974—. Served from ensign to lt. (j.g.), USNR, 1944-46. Decorated Naval Ordnance Devel. award (U.S.); Letter Commendation (Brit. Admiralty); recipient Army-Navy "E" award, 1943. Registered profl. elec. engr., Calif. Fellow N.Y. Acad. Scis., AAAS; mem. Inst. Colloid and Surface Sci., IEEE, Ohio Acad. Scis., AAUP, Am. Geophys. Union, Am. Phys. Soc., Am. Nuclear Soc. (membership com. 1962-63; membership com. shielding, dosimetry div. 1964-65, nominating com. 1965-66, exec. com. 1966-68; chmn. membership com. aerospace div. 1962-63, exec. com. 1963-65, treas. 1964-65; dir. N.Y. met. sect. 1960-61, spl. program chmn. 1960-62, sec. 1962-63, vice chmn. 1963, chmn. 1964, award 1965), Sigma Xi, Sigma Pi Sigma, Eta Kappa Nu, Pi Delta Epsilon. Author: (with Robert M. Winter) Modern Physics, 1971. Contbr. numerous articles tech. lit. Patentee in field. Home: 215 Overlook Dr Kent OH 44240

MADIGAN, EDWARD R., congressman; b. Lincoln, Ill., Jan. 13, 1936; s. Earl T. and Theresa (Loobey) M.; grad. bus. Lincoln Coll., 1957; L.H.D. (hon.), Lincoln Coll., 1975; m. Evelyn George, Sept. 1, 1954; children—Kim, Kellie, Mary. Mem. 93-95th Congresses from Ill. 21st dist., mem. agr. com., also interstate and fgn. commerce com. Mem. Ill. Ho. of Reps., 1966-72. Recipient Outstanding Legislator award Ill. Assn. Sch. Supts., Outstanding Achievement award Lincoln Coll. Alumni Assn. Named Outstanding Freshman Congressman Nat. R.R. Unions. Home: 308 Pulaski St Lincoln IL 62656 Office: 1514 Longworth Bldg Washington DC 20515

MADISON, FREDERICK WILLIAM, physician; b. Mazomanie, Wis., Dec. 22, 1899; s. Joseph Frederick and Ethel (Blair) M.; B.A., U. Wis., 1921, M.A., 1922; M.D., Columbia U., 1924; m. Geraldine Conover, June 9, 1928; children—Nancy, Sarah, Frederick. Practice medicine specializing in internal medicine, Milw., 1927—; chief of staff Columbia Hosp., Milw., 1941-52; asst. clin. prof. medicine Med. Coll. Wis., Milw., 1933-38, asso. clin. prof., 1938-53, clin. prof., 1953—; bd. dirs. Associated Hosp. Service, Milw., 1960-72, Milw. Blood Center, 1946—. Served with M.C., U.S. Army, 1918-19. Recipient Alumni citation U. Wis., 1966. Diplomate Am. Bd. Internal Medicine. Mem. A.C.P. (gov., v.p.), Milw. Acad. Medicine, AMA. Republican. Episcopalian. Author: Etiology of Agranulocytic Angina, 1934. Home: 1919 N Summit Ave Milwaukee WI 53202

MADISON, ROBERT P., architect; b. Cleve., July 28, 1923; s. Robert J. and Nettie (Brown) M.; student Howard U., 1940-43; B. Arch., Western Res. U., 1946-48; M.Arch., Harvard, 1952; m. Leatrice L. Branch, Apr. 16, 1949; children—Jeanne Marie, Juliette Branch. Mem. various archtl. firms, 1948-52; instr. Howard U., 1952-54; pres. Madison-Madison, internat. architects, engrs. and planners, Cleve., 1954—; dir. Indsl. Bank of Washington. Vis. prof. Howard U., 1961-62; lectr. Western Res. U., 1964-65. Mem. U.S. Architects Tour Team People's Republic China, 1974. Mem. tech. adv. com. Cleve. Bd. Edn., 1960—; adv. com. Cleve. Urban Renewal, 1963—; mem. fine arts adv. com. to mayor Cleve.; mem. Council for Coll. of Architecture, Cornell U. Trustee Case Western Res. U., Glen Oak Sch.; bd. dirs. Jr. Achievement Greater Cleve. Served to 1st lt. inf. AUS, 1943-46. Decorated Purple Heart (U.S.); Fullbright fellow 1952-53. Fellow A.I.A. (chpt. pres., nat. task force for creative econs. 1973), mem. Architects Soc. Ohio, Epsilon Delta Rho, Alpha Phi Alpha, Sigma Pi Phi. Club: City (Cleve.). Prin. works include U.S. Embassy Office Bldg., Dakar Senegal, 1966. Home: 2339 N Park Blvd Cleveland Heights OH 44106 Office: 1900 Euclid Ave Cleveland OH 44115

MADRIGRANO, JOSEPH FRANK, wholesale co. exec.; b. Kenosha, Wis., Sept. 6, 1919; s. Eugene F. and Mimi M. (Lamacchia) M.; grad. Coll. Commerce, 1939; m. Shirley Engdahl, Nov. 28, 1945; children—Joseph Frank, Glenn, Mary Joy, Karen, Gene, Daniel. Gen. mgr. E.F. Madrigrano Distbg. Co., 1952; pres. Triangle Wholesale Co., Kenosha, 1952—; chmn. bd. Seven Up Bottling Co. of Kenosha, Racine and Walworth, 1962; v.p., organizer Am. State Bank; dir. G. LeBlanc Corp.; partner Lakeland Distbg. Co. Former pres., dir. Italian Am. Soc. Mem. Nat. Beer Wholesale Assn., Wis. Beer Distbrs., Italians of Am. Descent. Roman Catholic. Clubs: Moose, Eagles, Kenosha Country, Italian Bus. Men's. Home: 4919 Harrison Rd Kenosha WI 53142 Office: 2119 81st St Kenosha WI 53140

MADSEN, GEORGE FRANK, lawyer; b. Sioux City, Iowa, Mar. 24, 1933; s. Frank Olaf and Agnes (Cuhel) M.; B.A., St. Olaf Coll., Northfield, Minn., 1954; LL.B., Harvard, 1959; m. Magnhild N. Norstog, June 28, 1959; 1 dau., Michelle Marie. Admitted to Ia. bar, 1961, Ohio bar, 1960; with firm Martin, Browne, Hull & Harper, Springfield, Ohio, 1959-61; with firm Shull, Marshall & Marks, Sioux City, 1961—, now partner. Chmn. Siouxland area endowment fund drive St. Olaf Coll., 1964. Mem. Sioux City Zoning Bd. Adjustment, 1964. Bd. dirs., sec. Boys' Club Sioux City, 1969-73. Served as officer USAF, 1954-56. Mem. Am., Iowa, Woodbury County bar assns., St. Olaf Coll. Alumni Assn. (pres. Siouxland chpt. 1963-64), Phi Beta Kappa (pres. Sioux City chpt. 1966-67, 73-74), Pi Gamma Mu. Lutheran (pres. congregation 1962-63). Club: Sioux City Country. Editor: Marshall, Iowa, Title Opinions and Standards, 1977, 2d edit., 1978. Home: 3916 Sylvian Way Sioux City IA 51104 Office: Box 3166 Sioux City IA 51102

MADSON, CARLISLE, land surveyor; b. Wichita Falls, Tex., Apr. 3, 1920; s. Carlisle and Merlon Mae (Dennison) M.; student U. Minn., 1938-40, 50-56; m. S. Arleen Severson, May 22, 1948; children—Peggy Annette, John Carlisle, James Arby. Draftsman, Minn. Hwy. Dept., 1941; engring. aid, spl. engring. div. Third Locks Project, C.Z., 1942-43; draftsman, party chief A.C. Smith Co., 1946-50; sr. engring. aide, party chief City of St. Louis Park (Minn.), 1950-56; prin. land surveyor, exec. v.p. Schoell & Madson, Inc. cons. engrs. and land surveyors, Hopkins, Minn., 1956—; surveyor Carver County, 1970—; partner Carben Surveying Reprints. Served with AUS, 1943-46; CBI. Fellow Am. Congress Surveying and Mapping; mem. Minn. Land Surveyors Assn. (Ann. Achievement awar 1971; historian, past pres.), Hennepin County Surveyors Assn., Minn. Surveyors and Engrs. Soc., Wis., Iowa socs. land surveyors, Mont. Assn. Registered Land Surveyors, Tex. Surveyors Assn., VFW, Am. Legion, Confederate Air Force, Minn. Hist. Soc., Danish Am. Inst. Republican. Congregationalist. Club: Interlachen. Home: 209 Shady Oak Rd Hopkins MN 55343 Office: 50 9th Ave Hopkins MN 55343

MADURA, FREDERICK JOSEPH, corp. exec.; b. Chgo., Apr. 4, 1938; s. Walter Joseph and Helen Ann (Stanek) M.; B.A., Northwestern U., 1960; postgrad., 1960-61; M.B.A., U. Chgo., 1969; m. Patricia Diane O'Rielly, Dec. 28, 1959; children—Michele A., Laurie A., Mark F. Statis. analyst Aldens, Inc., Chgo., 1961-62, new credit mgr., 1963-65, credit research mgr., 1966-69, group mgr. research and circulation, 1969—. Vice pres., Am. Direct, Inc., Chgo., 1971—; lectr. in field. Mem. Am. Mktg. Assn., Am. Statis. Assn., Inst. Mgmt. Sci., Ops. Research Soc., Direct Mktg. Assn., Northwestern U. Alumni Assn., Theta Xi. Home: 22 Williamsburg Terr Evanston IL 60203 Office: 5000 W Roosevelt Rd Chicago IL 60607

MADURA, JAMES ANTHONY, physician; b. Campbell, Ohio, June 10, 1938; s. Anthony Peter and Margaret Ethel (Sebest) M.; A.B., Colgate U., 1959; M.D., Western Res. U., 1963; m. Loretta Jayne Souak, Aug. 8, 1959; children—Debra Jean, James Anthony II, VikkiSue. Intern, Ohio State U., Columbus, 1963-64; resident in surgery, 1966-71; practice surgery, Indpls., 1971—; mem. staff Ind. U. Hosp., 1971—, Indpls. VA Hosp., 1971—, Wishard Meml. Hosp., Indpls., 1971—; asst. prof. surgery Ind. U. Med. Sch. Indpls., 1971-75, asso. prof., 1976—. Dir. safety and health Indpls. Youth Hockey League, 1975-77. Served with AUS, 1964-66: Vietnam. NIH surg. trainee, 1967-71. Diplomate Am. Bd. Surgery. Fellow A.C.S.; mem. Assn. Acad. Surgeons, Ind. Med. Assn., Marion County Med. Soc., Sigma Xi. Roman Catholic. Clubs: Columbia, Elks. Contbr. articles to profl. jours. Home: 9525 Copley Dr Indianapolis IN 46260 Office: 1100 W Michigan St Indianapolis IN 46260

MAEDA, IKUO, orthopaedic surgeon; b. Sendai Japan, Sept. 8, 1934; s. Yukio and Katsuko (Asano) M.; M.D., Nippon Med. Sch., 1959; m. Carole Lynne Webster, June 29, 1963; children—Christopher Michael, Jill Kristen. Intern, Buffalo Gen. Hosp., 1960-61; resident Youngstown (Ohio) Hosp., 1961-63, Childrens Hosp., Buffalo, 1964-65; pvt. practice orthopedic surgery, Canfield, Ohio, 1967—; mem. staff, chief orthopedic surgery Youngstown Hosp. Assn. mem. council of chief orthopedics Northeastern Ohio U. Diplomate Am. Acad. Orthopedic Surgeons. Home: 4229 Oak Knoll Dr Youngstown OH 44512 Office: 6470 Tippecanoe Rd Canfield OH 44406

MAG, ARTHUR, lawyer; b. New Britain, Conn., Oct. 11, 1896; s. Nathan Elihu and Rebecca (Goldberg) M.; A.B., Yale, 1918, J.D., 1920; LL.D., U. Mo., 1974; m. Selma Rothenberg, Nov. 7, 1925 (dec. Oct. 1930); children—Josephine Selma (Mrs. Randall), Helen Louise (Mrs. Wolcott); m. 2d, Charline Weil, Nov. 24, 1932. Admitted to Conn. bar, 1920, Mo. bar, 1920; since practiced in Kansas City, Mo.; with Stinson, Mag, Thomson, McEvers & Fizzell, 1924—; chmn. exec. com. Host Internat., Inc., Los Angeles, chmn. bd. Schutte Lumber Co.; dir. First Nat. Bank Kansas City, Mo., Standard Milling Co., L.B. Price Merc. Co., St. Louis, Hereford Redevel. Corp., First Nat. Charter Co., Price Candy Co., Marley Co., Rival Mfg. Co., Gold, Inc., Denver, Helzberg's Diamond Shops, Kansas City, Rothschild & Sons, Kansas City, Z Bar Cattle Co. Mem. Mo.'s Commn. for White House Conf. on the Aging; co-chmn. Gov.'s Task Force on Role Pvt. Higher Edn., 1970; mem. Gov.'s Citizens Com. on Crime and Delinquency, 1966-68; mem. citizens study com. Kansas City-Jackson County Health Services, 1968; chmn. Greater Kansas City liaison com. Regional Med. Program Kans. and Mo., 1952-66; mem. Mayor's Commn. Civil Disorder, Kansas City, 1968. Hon. chmn. bd., trustee Menorah Med. Center; trustee Midwest Research Inst.; mem. NIMH, HEW, 1955-59; Nat. Adv. Council Mental Health; pres. Greater Kansas City Mental Health Found., 1952-56; trustee U. Mo.-Kansas City, Menninger Found., Topeka, Kans., Frederic Ervine McIlvain Trust, Carl W. Allendoerfer Meml. Library Trust, Carrie J. Loose Fund, Harry Wilson Loose Trust, Edward F. Swinney Trust, Sadie Danciger Trust, Kansas City Assn. Trusts & Founds., Menorah Found. Med. Research, Mo. Bar Found.; hon. chmn. bd. dirs. Menorah Med. Center; curator Stephen's Coll., 1967-72; mem. adv. bd. Kansas City Area council Boy Scouts Am. Served in U.S. Navy, 1918. Recipient Pro Meritis award Rockhurst Coll.; Mr. Kansas City 1964 award; chancellors medallion U. Mo. at Kansas City, 1965, Law Day award, 1966, Civic Service award Hebrew Acad. Greater Kansas City, 1975. Fellow Am. Coll. Hosp. Adminstrs., Am. Bar Assn.; mem. Mo., Kansas City bar assns., Lawyers Assn. Kansas City, Assn. of Bar City N.Y., Mo. Acad. Squires, Newcomen Soc. N.Am., Yale Law Sch. Assn. (hon. mem. exec. com.), Order Coif (hon.), Delta Sigma Rho. Republican. Clubs: Yale (N.Y.C.); Kansas City, Oakwood Country (Kansas City); Reform (London, Eng.); Standard (Chgo.). Author: Trusteeship, 1948. Home: 5049 Wornall Rd Kansas City MO 64112 Office: 2100 Ten Main Center PO Box 19251 Kansas City MO 64141

MAGEE, LAURA JEAN, arts edn. cons.; b. Lake Cormorant, Miss., May 10, 1938; d. Julius E. and Ottomece (Price) Magee; B.F.A., Newcomb Coll. Tulane U., 1959; M.A., La. State U., 1970; Ed.D., Ariz. State U., 1973. Instr. art Delgado Coll., New Orleans, 1964-68; grad. teaching asst., art, La. State U., Baton Rouge, 1968-70, Ariz. State U., Tempe, 1971-73; asst. prof. art Drake U., Des Moines, 1973-76; cons. arts edn. Iowa Dept. Pub. Instrn., Des Moines, 1976—; TV cons. IPBN, Des Moines, 1974—; media cons. Phoenix Coll., 1972; TV cons. Sta KAET, Tempe, 1971-72. Mem. Nat. Art Edn. Assn. (co-chmn. documentation evaluation 1977). Author publs. in field. Home: 1430 20th St Apt 7 West Des Moines IA 50265 Office: Iowa Dept Public Instruction Grimes State Office Bldg Des Moines IA 50319

MAGNER, JOHN MARSHALL, entomologist; b. Webster Groves, Mo., May 4, 1913; s. John Henry and Maybelle Charlotte (MacKenzie) M.; student Iowa State U., 1935-36; B.A., U. Ill., 1939; m. Ernestine Marie Thro, Feb. 3, 1946; children—John Marshall, Charles Roland, Robyn MacKenzie, David Thro, Thomas Eyssell. Entomologist, U.S. Dept. Agr., Mo., Ill. and Mont., 1933-42; sr. entomologist Monsanto Co., St. Louis, 1946—; instr. Endicott (Mass.) Jr. Coll., 1939-40, St. Louis YMCA, 1949, Washington U., St. Louis, 1947-48. Mem. Planning Commn. City of Webster Groves (Mo.), 1959-60, liaison with park and health commns., 1961-70, city councilman, 1960-70; dir. Hist. Soc., 1970-72, v.p., 1973, pres., 1974-76; mem. Mo. Gov's. Environ. Pollution Com., 1970-72; mem. adv. com. curriculum pest control St. Fair Community Coll., 1972-75;

active Boy Scouts Am. Served with U.S. Army, 1942-45. Mem. AAAS, Am. Inst. Biol. Scis., Am. Mosquito Control Assn., Am. Ornithol. Union, Nat. Pest Control Assn., Entomol. Soc. Am. (pres. N.C. br. 1966), Entomol. Soc. Wash., Nat. (del. 1947, 50-55, 69), Mo., St. Louis (pres. 1973, 74) Audubon socs., St. Louis Acad. Sci., Sigma Xi, Webster Groves Nature Study Soc. (pres. 1946-47). Club: Masons. Contbr. articles to profl. jours.; patentee in field. Home: 516 Bacon Ave Webster Groves MO 63119 Office: 800 N Lindbergh Blvd Saint Louis MO 63166

MAGNES, G(ERALD) DONALD, dentist; b. Chgo., Sept. 27, 1933; s. Herman S. and Fae (Ray) M.; B.S., U. Ill., 1956, D.D.S., 1958; m. Loretta Bass, Aug. 5, 1956; children—Scott A., Craig N. Individual practice dentistry, Chgo., 1958—. Cons., Warner-Chilcott Labs., Morris Plains, N.J., 1964—; instr. U. Ill. Coll. Dentistry. Recipient certificate recognition Am. Dental Assn., 1967; award winning exhibit Nat. Am. Dental Assn., 1967; donor sci. exhibit U. Ill. Med. Sch., 1968. Fellow Royal Soc. Health; mem. Am. Dental Assn., Chgo. Dental Soc., Am. Cancer Soc. (speaker 1969-70), U. Ill. Alumni Assn., Alpha Omega. Contbr. articles to profl. jours. Home: 4625 West Grove Skokie IL 60076 Office: 2601 W Peterson Ave Chicago IL 60659

MAGNUSON, PAUL ARTHUR, lawyer; b. Carthage, S.D., Feb. 9, 1937; s. Arthur and Emma Elleda (Paulson) M.; B.A., Gustavus Adolphus Coll., 1959; J.D., William Mitchell Coll. Law, 1963; m. Sharon Schultz, Dec. 21, 1959; children—Marlene, Margaret, Kevin, Kara. Registrar, William Mitchell Coll. Law, St. Paul, 1959-60; claim adjuster Agrl. Ins. Co., 1960-62; clk. Bertie & Bettenberg, 1962-63; admitted to Minn. bar, 1963; mem. firm LeVander, Gillen, Miller & Magnuson, South St. Paul, Minn., 1963—; dir. Ithaca Corp., St. Paul, Trossen Wright Assos., Architects, Inc., St. Paul. Mem. Met. Health Bd., 1970—, Northlands Regional Med. Program, 1972—; mem. Citizens League, 1971, bd. dirs., 1973—. Mem. Dakota County Republican Com., 1965—, chmn., 1967-70; dist. chmn. Young Reps. League Minn., 1965, nat. committeeman, 1965-66, state chmn., 1966-67, Quie vol. com., 1971; asso. mgr. LeVander for Gov. campaign, 1966. Bd. dirs. St. Paul area Young Life. Mem. Am., Minn., 1st Jud. Dist. (pres. 1976—), Dakota County bar assns., Am. Trial Lawyers Assn., Am. Judicature Soc., St. Paul C. of C., S.E. Met. C. of C., Gustavus Adolphus Alumni Assn. (pres. 1968-70) Alpha Kappa Psi, Delta Theta Phi, Phi Alpha. Presbyterian (mem. council 1964-70, pres. 1968-70, ruling elder 1976—). Kiwanian (dir. 1966-69). Clubs: St. Paul Athletic, Southview Country. Home: 3047 Klondike Ave N Lake Elmo MN 55042 Office: Drovers Bank Bldg South St Paul MN 55075

MAGRATH, C(LAUDE) PETER, univ. pres.; b. N.Y.C., Apr. 23, 1933; s. Laurence Wilfrid and Guilia Maria (Dentice) M.; m. Sandra Hughes, June 18, 1955 (div. 1977); 1 dau., Valerie Ruth; m. 2d, Diane Skomars, Mar. 25, 1978; 1 stepdau., Monette Fay; B.A., U. N.H., 1955; Ph.D., Cornell U., 1962. Faculty, Brown U., 1961-68, prof. polit. sci., 1967-68, asso. dean Grad. Sch., 1965-66; dean Coll. Arts and Sci., U. Nebr., 1968-69, dean of faculties, 1969, interim chancellor, 1969, interim v.p. U. Nebr. System, 1971-72, prof. polit. sci., 1968, vice chancellor for acad. affairs, 1972; prof. polit. sci. State U. N.Y. at Binghamton, 1972-74; pres. U. Minn., Mpls., 1974—. Mem. Am., Midwest polit. sci. assns., Orgn. Am. Historians, Phi Beta Kappa, Phi Kappa Phi, Pi Gamma Mu, Pi Sigma Alpha. Author: The Triumph of Character, 1963; Yazoo: Law and Politics in the New Republic, The Case of Fletcher v. Peck, 1966; Constitutionalism and Politics: Conflict and Consensus, 1968; The American Democracy, 1973. Home: 176 N Mississippi River Blvd Saint Paul MN 55104 Office: Morrill Hall U Minn Minneapolis MN 55455

MAGY, ROBERT ALVIN, promotion agy. exec.; b. Detroit, May 6, 1942; s. Morris and Mildred Margaret Plepler M.; B.A., U. Minn., 1966; m. Bonnie Gayle Rosenbloom, July 1, 1965; children—Chana, Dov Ber. Tech. writer N. Ordnance div. FMC Corp., Mpls., 1966-69; promotion specialist Control Data Corp., Mpls., 1969-72, MTS Systems Corp., Mpls., 1972-74; communications specialist mgr. Cardiac Pacemakers Inc., St. Paul, 1974-76; pres. Market Impact Internat., Mpls., 1976—. Bd. dirs. Torah Acad., Mpls. Mem. Pub. Relations Soc. Am., Am. Heart Assn., Torah Umesorah, Merkos L'Inyonie Chinuch-Lubavitch. Producer-narrator B'nai Shalom Show, KUXL radio sta., Mpls., 1968-72. Home: 2836 France Ave S Minneapolis MN 55416 Office: Market Impact Internat 2836 France Ave S Minneapolis MN 55416

MAH, CHONGGI LAURENCE, radiologist; b. Tokyo, Jan. 19, 1939; s. Haesong F. and Wesun C. (Park) M.; came to U.S., 1966, naturalized, 1976; M.D., Yonsei U., Seoul, Korea, 1963; m. Joungyon Hwang, Sept. 17, 1966; children—Francis, Andrew, John. Intern, Miami Valley Hosp., Dayton, Ohio, 1966-67; resident VA Hosp., Dayton, 1967-68, Ohio State U. Hosp., Columbus, 1968-70; instr. Ohio State U., 1970-71; asst. prof. radiology and pediatrics Med. Coll. of Ohio at Toledo, 1971-75, clin. asst. prof., 1975—; practice medicine specializing in radiology, Toledo, 1975—; mem. Toledo Radiol. Assos., Inc. Served with Korean Air Force, 1963-66. Recipient Golden Apple award Med. Coll. of Ohio at Toledo, 1975, Korean Lit. award Korean Lit. Pub. Co., Seoul, 1976. Mem. AMA, Am. Coll. Radiology, Radiol. Soc. N.A., Soc. Pediatric Radiology, Ohio State Radiol. Soc. Author: (poetry) Quiet Triumph, 1963; Second Winter, 1965; Well-Tempered Music, vol. 1, 1968, vol. 2, 1972; A Flower in the Border, 1976. Home: 4357 Bromley Dr Toledo OH 43623 Office: 3939 Monroe St Toledo OH 43606

MAHAFFEY, MARYANN, social worker, city ofcl., educator; b. Burlington, Iowa, Jan. 18, 1925; d. Kent and Nelle (Widener) Mahaffey; B.A., Cornell Coll., Mt. Vernon, Iowa, 1946; M.S.W., U. So. Calif., 1951; m. Herman Dooha, June 8, 1950; 1 dau., Susan Margaret. Recreation dir. Japanese Relocation Center, Poston, Ariz., 1945; with Seattle YWCA, 1946-49, Girl Scouts Met. Detroit and Indpls., 1951-54, Merrill-Palmer Inst., 1954-56, 59, United Cerebral Palsy Assn. Chgo., 1956-57, Brightomoor Community Center, 1959-63; program coordinator, social service dir. Detroit Foster Homes project Merrill-Palmer Inst., 1963-65; prof. Sch. Social Work, Wayne State U., Detroit, 1965—. Pres. pro tem Detroit City Council, 1974—. Commr., Mich. Nutrition Commn., 1974—; chairperson Mich. Coalition Better Health Care; vice chmn. com. on battered women and domestic violence Detroit Police Commn., 1977—; legislative rep., chmn. Mich. Social Work Council, 1965-68; conf. chmn. Nat. Confs. on Foster Care for Emotionally Disturbed Children, 1964-66; v.p. Detroit Fedn. Settlements, 1961-63; chmn. recreation and social services com. Youth Opportunity Council, Detroit, 1967; cons. Fedn. for Aid to Dependent Children, 1961-67; chmn. Detroit Mayor's Common Council Task Force on Hunger and Malnutrition, 1970-74; trustee U.S. Dist. Ct. Pre-Trial Agency, 1975—. Mem. exec. bd., policy com. 17th Dist. Democratic party, 1969-74; spokeswoman Mich. Dem. party women's caucus, 1972-74. Bd. dirs. Met. Detroit YWCA, 1971-74. Fellow Am. Orthopsychiat. Assn.; mem. Nat. Assn. Social Workers (mem. nat. bd., Detroit Social Worker of Yr, 1974, pres. 1975-77), N.O.W., Council on Social Work Edn., Nat. Conf. on Social Welfare, Acad. Certified Social Workers (charter), Mich. Women's Polit. Caucus, Am. Acad. Sci., Am. Fedn. Tchrs., N.A.A.C.P., Am. Civil Liberties Union. Home: 19468 Avon St Detroit MI 48219 Office: City-County Bldg Detroit MI 48226

MAHAN, GENEVIEVE ELLIS, sociologist; b. Canton, Ohio, Aug. 1, 1909; d. William and Lillian (Ellis) Mahan; A.B., Western Res. U., 1931, A.M., 1941; postgrad. (Ford Found. fellow) Yale, 1952, Akademie fur Politische Bildung, Tutzing, Germany, 1963. Tchr. high schs., Canton, 1937-52; research asst. dept. sociology Yale, 1953-55; lectr. sociology Walsh Coll., Canton, 1970—. Participant Instns. Atlantic and European Cooperation Seminar, Portugal, 1970. Trustee, Stark County Psychiat. Found., 1961-68. Fellow Am. Sociol. Assn.; mem. Internat. Sociol. Assn., Eastern Sociol. Soc., Am. Acad. Polit. and Social Sci., Nat., Ohio (exec. bd. 1962-69, pres. 1965) councils for social studies, A.A.A.S., Am. Assn. U. Women (mem. exec. bd. Canton 1966-67), Ohio Acad. Sci., Ohio Soc. N.Y. Clubs: Canton Womans, Canton College. Research in polit. caricature, 1955—. Home: 804 5th St NW Canton OH 44703

MAHAN, HAROLD DEAN, museum exec.; b. Ferndale, Mich., June 11, 1931; s. Elbert Verl and Jo Ann Magdeline (Upton) M.; m. Mary Jane Gardiner, June 9, 1954; children—Michael, Eric, David, Christopher, Thomas; B.A., Wayne U., 1954; M.S., U. Mich., 1957; Ph.D., Mich. State U., 1964. Prof. biology Central Mich. U., 1957-73, dir. Center for Cultural and Natural History, 1970-72; pres. Environ. Enterprises, Inc., Mt. Pleasant, Mich., 1970-73; dir. Cleve. Mus. Natural History, 1973—; adj. prof. Case-Western Res. U., 1973—; resident scientist Museo de Historia Natural, Cali, Colombia, 1968; v.p. Midwest Museums Conf., 1974—. Mem. Airport Commn. Mt. Pleasant, 1965-68; pres. Mich. Audubon Soc., 1972-73; mem. Ohio Natural Areas Council, 1974—; trustee Shaker Lakes Regional Nature Center, Holden Arboretum (corporate bd.), Greater Cleve. Garden Center, Univ. Circle, Inc. Mem. Ohio Museums Assn. (pres. 1976—), Sigma Xi, Phi Kappa Phi, Phi Sigma, Beta Beta Beta, NSF faculty fellow Mich. State U., 1965. Clubs: Cleve. Playhouse, Rowfant; Explorers (N.Y.C.). Author: (with George J. Wallace) An Introduction to Ornithology, 1975; editor: The Jack Pine Warbler, 1965-72; Nature columnist Cleve. Press, 1973-74; book rev. editor Explorer mag., 1974—; contbr. articles to profl. jours. Home: 28050 Gates Mills Blvd Pepper Pike OH 44124 Office: Mus Natural History Wade Oval University Circle Cleveland OH 44106

MAHANNA, SIMON ALBERT, construction mgmt. co. exec.; b. St. Louis, Sept. 14, 1948; s. Simon Albert and Patricia Ruth (Swift) M.; B.S., U. Mo., 1970, M.S., 1975; m. Debra Ann Brady, July 24, 1971. Civil engr., City of St. Louis, 1970-72; sr. planning engr. Bechtel Power Corp., 1973-76; project engr. McCarthy Bros. Co., St. Louis, 1976-77; sr. v.p. Escrow Mgmt., Inc., Crestwood, Mo., 1977—; pres. Profl. Devel. and Mgmt. Services, 1977—, dir. Served with U.S. Army, 1969-77. Registered profl. engr., Mo., Calif. Mem. ASCE, Mo. Soc. Profl. Engrs., Am. Fedn. Scientists. Maronite Catholic. Office: 9920 Watson Rd Suite 110 Crestwood MO 63126

MAHER, CORNELIUS CREEDON, III, chemist; b. Bklyn., Jan. 30, 1949; s. Cornelius Creedon and Hester (Sullivan) M.; B.S., Boston Coll., 1969; M.S., U. Mich., 1973, Ph.D., 1976; m. Lynn Marie Elliott, July 15, 1972; children—Christa, Cornelius Creedon IV, Kimberley. Summer research fellow Brookhaven Nat. Lab., 1969; teaching fellow U. Mich., 1969-70, 71-72, Inst. for Environmental Quality fellow, 1972-74, research fellow, 1974-76, lectr., 1976; research asso. Children's Hosp. Med. Center, Boston, 1976—; indsl. toxicologist West Allis (Wis.) Meml. Hosp., 1977—. Mem. Am. Chem. Soc., AAAS, DAV, Am. Inst. Chemistry, Soc. Applied Specialities, Am. Indsl. Hygiene Assn., Alpha Chi Sigma, Phi Lambda Upsilon. Home: 1863 N 71 St Wawatosa WI 53213 Office: West Allis Meml Hosp 8901 W Lincoln Ave West Allis WI 53227

MAHER, DAVID WILLARD, lawyer; b. Chgo., Aug. 14, 1934; s. Chauncey Carter and Martha (Peppers) M.; A.B., Harvard, 1955, LL.B., 1959; m. Jill Waid Armagnac, Dec. 20, 1954; children—Philip Armagnac, Julia Armagnac. Admitted to N.Y. bar, 1960, Ill. bar, 1961; practiced in Chgo., 1961—; asso. Kirkland & Ellis, and predecessor firm, 1960-65, partner, 1966—. Lectr. DePaul U. Coll. Law. Bd. dirs. Chgo. Better Bus. Bur. Served to 2d lt. USAF, 1955-56. Mem. Am., Ill., Chgo. bar assns. Republican. Roman Catholic. Clubs: Bull Valley Hunt, Chicago Literary, Tavern. Home: 311 Belden Ave Chicago IL 60614 Office: 200 E Randolph Dr Chicago IL 60601

MAHER, JAMES BERNARD, mech. engr.; b. Salt Lake City, Feb. 13, 1925; s. James Bernard and Julia Margret (Hearley) M.; student Creighton U., 1942-43; B.M.E., U. Utah, 1948; postgrad. U. Colo., 1967-68. With Chgo. Bridge and Iron Co., Oak Brook, Ill., 1949—, asst. chief engr., 1971—, chief mech. engr., 1958-77, dir. research, 1977—. Served with USAF, 1943-46. Decorated Air medals, D.F.C. Mem. ASME, Western Soc. Engrs. Roman Catholic. Club: K.C. Contbr. articles to profl. jours. Patentee in field. Home: 20 N Tower Rd Oak Brook IL 60521 Office: Chgo Bridge & Iron Co Route 59 Plainfield IL 60544

MAHLSTEDE, JOHN PETER, ednl. adminstr.; b. Cleve., June 5, 1923; s. John Adrian and Gretchen M. (Boddy) M.; B.S., Miami U., Oxford, Ohio, 1947; M.S., Mich. State U., 1948, Ph.D., 1951; m. Alberta J. Lindquist, Aug. 20, 1948; children—Deborah, Barbara, Cynthia, John. Asst. prof. horticulture Iowa State U., Ames, 1951-55, asso. prof., 1955-57, prof., 1957—, head. dept. horticulture, 1961-65, asst. dir. Ia. agr. and home econs. experiment sta., 1965-66, asso. dir., 1966—, adminstrv. bd., 1968—, asso. dean, 1975—. B.Y. Morrison lectr. U.S. Dept. Agr., 1973. Faculty rep. Iowa State U.-Big Eight Conf., 1971—. Bd. dirs. Ames YMCA, Campfire Girls. Pres., YMCA Swim Assn., 1968-69, Ames A.A.U. Swim Team, 1969-70. Served with USAF, 1943-45. Decorated D.F.C., Air medal with 8 oak leaf clusters. Mem. Am. Soc. for Hort. Sci. (pres. 1971-72), Iowa State Hort. Soc. (award 1970), Internat. Plant Propagators Soc. (pres. 1962-63, pres. Eastern region 1961-62, award 1967), Soc. Iowa Florists (merit award 1968). Kiwanian (pres. Ames club 1963-64). Author (with E.S. Haber): Plant Propagation, 1957. Home: 1530 Roosevelt St Ames IA 50010

MAHMOOD, KHALID, physician; b. Gujranwala, Pakistan, Feb. 15, 1938; s. Mohammad Saied and Mumtaz Begum (Ata Mohammad) Mazharie; came to U.S., 1971, naturalized, 1977; F.Sc., Govt. Coll., Abbottabad, Pakistan, 1956; B.Sc., U. Punjab, Lahore, Pakistan, 1960; M.B., B.S., King Edward Med. Coll., Lahore, 1962; m. Patricia Hope Ashleman, June 15, 1975; 1 dau., Farrah Renee. Intern, Danbury (Conn.) Hosp., 1963-64, Lewis Gale Hosp., Roanoke, Va., 1964-65; resident otolaryngology Albert Einstein Coll. Medicine, N.Y.C., 1965-69; research fellow otolaryngology U. Toronto (Ont., Can.), 1969-70; practice medicine, specializing in otolaryngology, Toronto, 1971, Sandusky, Ohio, 1972—; mem. staff. cons. Providence Hosp., Chief div. otolaryngology, 1974—; mem. cons. staff, chief otolaryngology Good Samaritan Hosp., 1972—. Bd. dirs. Erie County (Ohio) Unit Am. Cancer Soc. Fellow A.C.S., Am. Acad. Ophthalmology and Otolaryngology; mem. AMA, Erie County Med. Soc., Ohio State Med. Assn. Research on tritiated thymidine study of irradiated cancer larynx, 1968-69. Home: Sandusky OH Office: 1221 Hayes Ave Sandusky OH 44870

MAHMOUD, ALY AHMED, educator; b. Cairo, Egypt, Jan. 25, 1935; s. Ahmed Aly and Amina Mohammed (Rashwan) M.; came to U.S., 1960, naturalized, 1970; B.Sc. with distinction and honors (Nat. Honor student), Ain Shams U., Cairo, 1958; M.S., Purdue U., 1961, Ph.D., 1964; m. Lucinda Lou Keller, Dec. 20, 1962; children—Ramy, Samy. Instr. elec. engring. Ain Shams U., 1958-60; asst. prof. elec. engring. U. N.B., Fredericton, 1964; research engr. No. Electric Research and Devel. Lab., Ottawa, Ont., Can., summer 1964; asst. prof. elec. engring. U. Asyut (Egypt) 1964-66; sr. research elec. engr. Naval Civil Engring. Lab., Port Hueneme, Calif., 1968-69, summer 1970; asst. prof. U. Mo., Columbia, 1966-71, asso. prof., 1971-73, prof. elec. engring., 1973-76; prof. elec. engring., program mgr. Power Affiliates Research Program, supr. Power System Computer Service, Iowa State U., 1976—. Vis. prof., cons. Nat. Research Center, Cairo, and Ain Shams U., 1964-66; cons. various indsl. firms, 1964—. Vice chmn. Water and Light Adv. Bd. City of Columbia, 1973—. Am. Friends of Middle East fellow, 1960-68. Mem. Am. Men and Women of Sci., I.E.E.E., Power Engring. Soc., Am. Phys. Soc., Egyptian Profl. Engring. Soc., Am. Soc. Engring. Edn., Mo. Acad. Sci., Sigma Xi, Tau Beta Pi, Eta Kappa Nu. Patentee in field. Contbr. articles to profl. jours. Home: 230 Trailridge Rd Ames IA 50010

MAHONEY, EDWARD STEPHEN, lawyer; b. N.Y.C., July 17, 1928; s. Edward Stephen and Mary Ann (Brief) M.; student Butler U., 1949-52; LL.B., Ind. U., 1956; m. Carol Jean Klitzke, Mar. 31, 1956; children—Melinda, William, Laura. Admitted to Ind. bar, 1956; claims adjuster Continental Casualty Co., Indpls., 1953-56; pvt. practice, Kokomo, 1956—; partner firm Lacey, O'Mahoney, Mahoney, Angel & Jessup, 1966—; city atty., Kokomo, 1971. Republican candidate for Ind. Ho. Reps., 1960. Bd. dirs. Youth Services Bur., Kokomo, 1970-71. Served with USAAF, 1946-49. Mem. Am. Trial Lawyers Assn. Presbyn. (elder, clk. session 1966-69). Moose, Elk. Home: 1500 Kirk Row Kokomo IN 46901 Office: 518 N Main Kokomo IN 46901

MAHR, ALLAN DAVID, poet; b. Belleville, Ill., Jan. 7, 1910; s. Allan D. and Sadie Lee (Duffy) M.; student St. Louis U. Extension, 1953, also Mo. U. Extension; m. Cora Belle Sanders, Dec. 14, 1941; children—Cosandra Lee, Allan David, Michael Anthony, Noel Kriston, Jan Corlus, Dale Brian, Coraminita Elizabeth, Coralicia Dawnisse. Author over 2000 poems, 1936—: Eye of the Heart, 1973; tapes of 88 poems donated to Tape Talk for the Blind, Webster Groves, Mo.; contbr. poetry to various lit. publs. and anthologies; poems displayed in collections of Winston Churchill Meml. Library, Kennedy Meml. Library, L.B. Johnson Meml. Library, The Truman and Tom Dooley Room at Notre Dame, Forest Park Community Coll., Florissant Valley Community Coll. Sec., treas. Holy Ghost council Boy Scouts Am., 1960-65. Recipient various awards including Hon. Mention, St. Louis Poetry Center, 1965, Dag Hammarskjold award Poems of Decade Anthologies, Eng. Mem. Acad. Am. Poets of N.Y., Ariz. Poetry Soc., Avalonian Writers of San Angelo (Tex.), McKendree Writers, Centro Studi Escambi of Rome. Roman Catholic. Address: 4838 Cote Brilliante Saint Louis MO 63113

MAHRT, DELMAR HERMANN, radiologist; b. Colon, Nebr., Jan. 9, 1936; s. Herman Jurgens Frederick and Kathleen Mercedes (Hoffsteter) M.; M.D., U. Nebr., 1960; m. Dorothea Ann Wetzel, Dec. 19, 1975. Intern, Immanuel Hosp., Omaha, 1960-61; resident in radiology Washington U., St. Louis, 1961-64; attending radiologist Reid Meml. Hosp., Richmond, Ind., 1964-65; attending therapeutic radiologist Wm. Beaumont Hosp., Royal Oak, Mich., 1965—; pres. Oakland County (Mich.) unit Am. Cancer Soc., 1974-76. Mem. Mich. Soc. Therapeutic Radiologists (pres., chmn. bd.), Oakland County Med. Soc. (sec.). Lutheran. Home: 855 N Pemberton Rd Bloomfield Hills MI 48013 Office: 3601 W 13-Mile Rd Royal Oak MI 48072

MAIER, HENRY W., mayor; b. Dayton, Ohio, Feb. 7, 1918; s. Charles Jr. and Marie L. (Kniseley) M.; B.A., U. Wis., 1940; M.A., U. Wis.-Milw., 1964; m. Mary Ann Monaghan, June 25, 1941; children—Melinda Ann (Mrs. Carlisle), Melanie Marie. Mem. Wis. Legislature, 1950-60, minority floor leader for Senate, 1953, 55, 57, 59; mayor of Milw., 1960—. Adv. bd. U.S. Conf. Mayors'; mem. Nat. Adv. Com. on Hwy. Safety. Served to lt. USNR, World War II; PTO. Mem. Nat. League of Cities (past pres.). Democrat. Author: Challenge to the Cities, 1966. Home: 1919 N Summit Ave Milwaukee WI 53202 Office: City Hall Milwaukee WI 53202

MAIER, IRWIN, newspaper exec.; b. Mellen, Wis., July 25, 1899; s. Louis A. and Mary E. (Ryan) M.; A.B., U. Wis., 1921, LL.D., 1964; L.H.D., Marquette U., 1965; D. Pub. Service, Northland Coll., 1973; m. Loraine Greve, Apr. 9, 1926; children—Sally Ann (Mrs. Thomas L. Tolan, Jr.), Mary Clare (Mrs. Conrad P. Bittner), Victor Irwin, John Peter. Chmn. bd. Jour. Co., pubs. Milw. Jour., Milw. Sentinel and operators radio sta. WTMJ, WTMJ-TV, Milw. Recipient award for distinguished service U. Minn. Sch. Journalism, 1962; Vocational Service award Rotary Club Milw., 1964; Frye Community Service award Milw. Found. Com. 1965; Silver medal Advt. Fedn. Am.-Printers Ink mag., 1965, Distinguished Service award Wis. Alumni Assn., 1966, award for outstanding service to secondary edn., nat. com. on secondary edn. Nat. Assn. Secondary Sch. Prins., 1973; Distinguished Service award Wis. Newspaper Assn., 1976; Pub. Service award Pub. Expenditure Survey Wis., 1977. Mem. Milw. Assn. Commerce, Greater Milw. Com. (founder 1939), Newspaper Advt. Execs. Assn., Am. Newspaper Pubs. Assn. (dir., dir. bur. advt. 1943-57, chmn. 1951-52, pres. 1962-63), Sigma Delta Chi, Chi Phi, Phi Kappa Phi. Clubs: University, Athletic, Milwaukee Country, Rotary (Milw.), Milwaukee. Home: 2620 E Newberry Blvd Milwaukee WI 53211 Office: 333 W State St Milwaukee WI 53201

MAIER, PAUL LUTHER, author, clergyman, educator; b. St. Louis, May 31, 1930; s. Walter A. and Hulda (Eickhoff) M.; A.B., Concordia Sem., 1952, B.D., 1955; student Harvard U., 1948-50, M.A., 1954; postgrad. Heidelberg U. (Germany), 1955; Ph.D. summa cum laude, U. Basel (Switzerland), 1957; m. Joan M. Ludtke, June 17, 1967; children—Laura Ann, Julie Joan. Ordained to ministry Lutheran Ch., 1958; Luth. campus chaplain Western Mich. U., Kalamazoo, 1958—, prof. history, 1959—. Recipient Harvard Detur award, 1950, Alumni award for teaching excellence Western Mich. U., 1974. Mem. Am. Hist. Assn., Bach Soc. Kalamazoo. Author: Caspar Schwenckfeld, 1959; A Man Spoke, A World Listened, 1963; Pontius Pilate, 1968; First Christmas, The True and Unfamiliar Story, 1971; First Easter, The True and Unfamiliar Story, 1973; First Christians, Pentecost and the Spread of Christianity, 1976; editor: The Improvement of College and University Courses in the History of Civilization, 1965; contbr. articles in field to gen. and profl. jours. Home: 8383 W Main St Kalamazoo MI 49009

MAIER, WILLIAM CONRAD, lawyer; b. St. Louis, Apr. 4, 1934; s. Joseph Thomas and Clara Katherine (Schmidt) M.; B.S., St. Louis U., 1956, J.D., 1963; m. Jo Ann Malwitz, Oct. 10, 1964; children—William Conrad, Robert Lewis. Admitted to Mo. bar, 1963; partner firm Dubail, Judge, Kilker & Maier, St. Louis, 1963—. Instr. Sch. Law, St. Louis U., 1964-65. Served to lt. USNR, 1956-60. Mem. Am., Mo., St. Louis bar assns., Alpha Sigma Nu, Phi Delta Phi. Home: 874 Amersham Dr St Louis MO 63141 Office: 1 Mercantile Center Suite 3210 St Louis MO 63101

MAINEN, EUGENE LOUIS, sales exec.; b. Balt., May 9, 1940; s. Allan and Gertrude (Rose) M.; B.S., U. Md., 1963; M.S., U. Iowa, 1965, Ph.D. (U.S. Army Research fellow), 1966; m. Barbara Louise Karl, Aug. 14, 1966; children—David, Sarah. Research chemist 3M

Co. Central Research Lab., St. Paul, 1967-69; photog. research chemist 3M Italia and 3M U.K., 1969-70, polyester devel. chemist, St. Paul, 1970-71, x-ray tech. service specialist, 1971-73; x-ray customer service supr. Photog. Products div. 3M Co., St. Paul, 1973-76, tech. market mgr. X-ray products, 1976—. Mem. Am. Chem. Soc., Sigma Xi, Alpha Chi Sigma. Mem. B'nai B'rith. Home: 11544 Fetterly Rd Minnetonka MN 55343 Office: 3M Center Bldg 223-2SW St Paul MN 55101

MAINONE, ROBERT FRANKLIN, naturalist; b. Flint, Mich., Feb. 11, 1929; s. Robert Henry and Nell Claudine (Phillips) M.; B.S., Mich. State U., 1951, B.S.Forestry, 1952, M.S., 1959; postgrad. U. Utah, 1955; m. Carolyn Beryl Bothwell, Aug. 12, 1972. Ranger, naturalist Rocky Mountain Nat. Park, Estes Park, Colo., 1957, Everglades Nat. Park, Homestead, Fla., 1958; zookeeper Antelope Zoo, Lincoln, Neb., 1959; jr. curator Detroit Zool. Park, 1959-60; interpretive naturalist Kalamazoo Nature Center, 1961-66; interpretive ecologist Kellogg Bird Sanctuary Mich. State U., Augusta, 1967—. Served with USAF, 1953-56. Recipient Harold G. Henderson award Haiku Soc. Am., 1977. Mem. Ecol. Soc. Am., Assn. Interpretive Naturalists, Wilderness Soc., Archaeol. Soc. Mich., Arctic Inst. N.Am., Nat. Fedn. State Poetry Socs., Poetry Soc. Mich. Author: (poetry) An American Naturalists Haiku, 1964, Parnassus Flowers, 1965, Where Waves Were, 1966, This Boundless Mist, 1968, Shadows, 1971, Young Leaves, 1974; High on the Wind, 1976. Home: Route 3 Box 485 Delton MI 49046 Office: Kellogg Bird Sanctuary Route 1 Augusta MI 49012

MAINWARING, ROSSER L., physician; b. Detroit, Jan. 15, 1923; grad. Wayne State U., also M.D.; m.; 4 sons, 1 dau. Intern, resident surgery, resident pathology Detroit Receiving Hosp.; pathologist dir. labs. Blood Bank, Oakwood Hosp.; clin. prof. pathology Wayne State U.; commr. med. lab. personnel Am. Soc. Clin. Pathologists, 1970—; bd. dirs., mem. exec. com. Am. Blood Commn., 1975—. Recipient John Elliott Meml. award Am. Assn. Blood Banks, 1969. Mem. Am. Soc. Clin. Pathologists (past pres.; Burdick award 1977), Mich. Assn. Blood Banks, Mich. Cancer Found., Mich. Soc. Pathologists. Home: 24601 Fairmont St Dearborn MI 48124

MAJETI, SATYANARAYANA, adminstrv. chemist; b. Kakumanu, India, June 15, 1941; s. Sreeramulu and Basavapunnamma (Addepalli) M.; came to U.S., 1965; B.Sc., Andhra U., India, 1962; M.Sc., Banaras Hindu U., 1964; Ph.D., U. Calif., Los Angeles, 1969; m. Vimala Alapati, June 10, 1967; children—Srinivas, Ravindra. Research asso. chemistry Banaras Hindu U., Varanasi, 1964-65; teaching asso. chemistry U. Calif., Los Angeles, 1965-67, acting asst. prof., postdoctoral fellow, 1969-70; research chemist, group leader Procter & Gamble, Cin., 1970—; lectr. chemistry U. Cin. Mem. Am. Chem. Soc., Am. Soc. Photobiology, Am. Acad. Dermatology, Sigma Xi. Contbr. articles in field to profl. jours.; patentee in field. Home: 7477 Greenfarms Dr Cincinnati OH 45224 Office: Procter Gamble Winton Hill Tech Center Cincinnati OH 45224

MAJHER, EDWARD ALLEN, ednl. adminstr.; b. Cleve., Apr. 5, 1940; s. Edward and Verna (Lang) M.; B.S. in Bus. Adminstrn., Dyke Coll., 1962; student Baldwin-Wallace Coll., 1958-59; m. Judith Turner, Aug. 28, 1962; children—Cynthia, Matthew. Asst. supr. Fed. Res. Bank, Cleve., 1963-68; sr. auditor Ernst & Ernst, Cleve., 1968-71; asst. controller Central Security Nat. Bank, Lorain, Ohio, 1971; controller Lakeland Community Coll., Mentor, Ohio, 1971—. Councilman, City of Mentor on the Lake, Ohio, 1976-77. Registered pub. accountant, Ohio. Mem. Nat. Assn. Accountants (dir. Cleve. E. chpt. 1976—), Am. Mgmt. Assn. Club: Masons. Home: 5606 Marine Pkwy Mentor on the Lake OH 44060 Office: I-90 and State Route 306 Mentor OH 44060

MAJURY, ARTHUR STUART, physician; b. Belfast, No. Ireland, Jan. 4, 1919; s. Matthew and Florence (Stuart) M.; M.B., B.Ch., B.A.O., Queen's U., Belfast, 1941; m. Edna Margaret Huss, July 20, 1948; children—Susan Fiona, Diana Margaret. Intern Royal Victoria Hosp., Belfast, 1941-42; resident Royal Victoria, also City Hosp., Belfast, 1947-53; practice medicine specializing in gynecology and obstetrics, Winnipeg (Man., Can.) Clinic, 1953—; mem. staffs Health Scis. Center, Grace Hosp., Winnipeg; asst. prof. dept. obstetrics and gynecology U. Man., 1960—. Bd. dirs. Soc. Crippled Children and Adults, Winnipeg Clinic Research Inst. Served with RAF, 1942-46. Fellow Royal Coll. Obstetricians and Gynecologists (London, Eng.), Am. Coll. Obstetricians and Gynecologists; mem. Canadian Gynecol. Soc., Soc. Obstetricians and Gynecologists of Can. Clubs: Manitoba; Winnipeg Winter. Home: 148 Elm St Winnipeg MB R3M 3P1 Canada Office: 425 St Mary's Ave Winnipeg MB R3C 0N2 Canada

MAKELY, WILLIAM ORSON, editor; b. N.Y.C., Dec. 31, 1932; s. Ralph G. and Helen (Craig) M.; B.S., U. Wis., 1955; M.A., U. Chgo., 1961; m. Ethel Neil Dee, Dec. 20, 1958; children—Jennifer, Katherine, Gordon. Asst. librarian Oriental Inst. Library U. Chgo., 1958-59; asst. prof. humanities Rose-Hulman Inst. Tech., Terre Haute, Ind., 1961-64; asst. prof. English, Roosevelt U., Chgo., 1964-69; sr. index editor World Book Ency., Chgo., 1969—; free-lance writer and indexer; author books, stories and poems, 1965—. Home: 4730 Main St Downers Grove IL 60515 Office: World Book Encyclopedia Merchandise Mart Plaza Station 32 Chicago IL 60654

MAKI, PAULA SPROULL DENNIS, speech pathologist; b. Hollywood, Calif., Dec. 20, 1948; d. Paul Louis and Suzanne (Sproull) Dennis; student Coll. of the Desert, Palm Desert, Calif., 1966-67, Colo. Alpine Coll., Steamboat Springs, 1967-68; B.S., Ball State U., Muncie, Ind., 1970; M.A., Mich. State U., 1974; m. Michael Frank Maki; 1 son, Michael Paul. Speech pathologist Eastern Upper Peninsula Intermediate Sch. Dist., Sault Ste. Marie, Mich., 1970-72, also cons.; speech pathologist Lansing (Mich.) Head Start Program, 1972-73; speech pathologist Head Start Program, Chippewa-Luce-Mackinac Community Action, Human Resource Authority, Inc., Sault Ste. Marie, 1974—; cons. Tri-county Health Depts. Active, Pregnancy Guidance Services. Mem. Luce County Hist. Soc., Am. (certificate of clin. competence), Mich. speech and hearing assns. Club: Newberry Country. Home: Rural Route 1 Box 154 Newberry MI 49868 Office: PO Box 373 Sault Ste Marie MI 49783

MAKKAI, ADAM, linguist, lexicographer, poet; b. Budapest, Hungary, Dec. 16, 1935; s. John D. and Rózsa (Ignácz) M.; came to U.S., 1957, naturalized, 1963; student U. Budapest, 1954-56; B.A. cum laude in Slavic Langs., Harvard U., 1958; M.A. (Ford Found. fellow, Wilson fellow) in Gen. Linguistics, Yale U., 1962, Ph.D. (Jr. Sterling fellow) in Gen. Linguistics, 1965; m. Valerie June Becker, June 5, 1966; 1 dau., Sylvia. Tchr. of Latin, German, Russian and French, Iolani Coll. Prep. Acad., Honolulu, 1958-60; lectr. in Russian, U. Hawaii, Honolulu, 1958-60; instr. in Russian, Yale U., New Haven, 1962-63; vis. asst. prof. linguistics U. Malaya, 1963-64; asst. prof. linguistics and Russian, Occidental Coll., Los Angeles and asst. prof. English, Calif. State U., Long Beach, 1966-67; asst. prof. linguistics U. Ill. at Chgo. Circle campus, 1967-69, asso. prof., 1969-74, prof., 1974—: researcher in computational linguistics Rand Corp., Santa Monica, Calif., 1965-66; founder Zoltán Kodály Hungarian Cultural Soc. Chgo., 1968, pres., 1968—; Found. exec. dir. of Lacus, Inc., 1974—, dir. publs., 1974—, chmn. bd., 1974—; author: Idiom Structure in English, 1973; Readings in Stratificational Linguistics, 1973; A Dictionary of Space English, 1973; maj. contbr. The Living Webster's Encyclopedic Dictionary of the English Language, 1971; Szomj és ecet (collected poems in Hungarian), 1966; co-editor The Poetry of Hungary; contbr. poetry to English and Hungarian anthologies; contbr. numerous articles on linguistics and semantics to linguistic jours.; editor Forum Linguisticum, 1976—; editorial bd. Indian Jour. Linguistics, 1975—, Studi Italiani della Linguistica Teorica ed Applicata, 1975, Ótágú Síp, 1973-76. NSF grantee, 1965-66, Paderewski Found. and Internat. Devel. Found. Travel grantee, 1963-64. Mem. Linguistic Soc. Am., Modern Lang. Assn. (chmn. spl. interest group on gen. linguistics 1977-78), Internat. Linguistic Assn. (mng. editor jour. 1973-74). Home: 360 MacLaren Ln Lake Bluff IL 60044 Office: Dept Linguistics U Ill Chicago Circle PO Box 4348 Chicago IL 60680

MAKY, WALTER, lawyer; b. Cleve., June 4, 1916; s. Viktor and Saimi (Pahkala) M.; B.S., Cleve. State U., 1940, J.D., 1947; m. Helen Marian Rancken, Dec. 3, 1938; children—Pamela (Mrs. Ronald Boyarsky), Bonita (Mrs. Stephen Swift). Spot welder Gray Wire Specialty Co., 1934-37; trouble shooter Ohio Bell Telephone Co., 1937-38; patent agt. Parker-Hannifin Corp., 1938-45; admitted to Ohio bar, 1947; since practiced in Cleve.; mem. firm Donnelly, Maky, Renner & Otto, Cleve., 1945—. Consul of Finland, State Ohio, 1951—. Mem. Am., D.C., Cleve. bar assns., Nat. Council Patent Law Assns. (councilman 1972-73), Am., Cleve. (pres. 1971-72) patent law assns., Bar Assn. Greater Cleve. Club: Ashtabula Country (Ohio). Home: 33320 Cromwell Dr Solon OH 44139 Office: 601 Rockwell Ave Cleveland OH 44114

MALANY, LE GRAND LYNN, state ofcl.; b. Chgo., May 14, 1941; s. LeGrand Franklin and Marion (Jaynes) M.; B.S. in Engring. Physics, U. Ill., 1964, J.D., 1970; m. Barbara Bumgarner, June 26, 1965; children—LeGrand Karl, Siobhan, Carleen. Asst. astronomer Adler Planetarium, Chgo., 1960-63; research asst. Portland Cement Research Assn., Skokie, Ill., 1964; instr. dept. gen. engring. U. Ill., 1965-70; project dir. driver control program U.S. Dept. Transp., 1971-73; asso. drivers license adminstr. State of Ill., Springfield, 1973-74, asst. auditor gen., 1977—; expert U.S. Fed. Energy Adminstrn., 1974; counsel juvenile div. Circuit Ct., Sangamon County, Ill., 1973-75; chief counsel Ill. Dept. Motor Vehicles, Springfield, 1974. Trustee Meret Center, Inc., 1973-75. Registered profl. engr., Ill. Mem. Am. Phys. Soc., Nat., Ill. socs. profl. engrs., Am., Ill. bar assns. Developer statewide motorcycle driver licensing program. Home: 600 S Rosehill St Springfield IL 62704 Office: 524 S 2d St Springfield IL 62706

MALAS, CORNELIA, bus. exec.; b. Cin.; d. John C. and Katherine (Farres) Malas; student U. Cin., 1940-42; bus. certificate Littleford Nelson Bus. Coll., 1943; student Schuster Martin Sch. Drama, 1943; certificate Patricia Stevens Modeling Sch., 1944; student Campbell Bus. Coll., 1956. Head central filing dept. Gruen Watch Co., Cin., 1945-50; expediter purchasing dept. MacGregor Sport Products, Cin., 1950-57; personnel adminstr. Eagle-Picher Industries, Inc., Cin., 1957—. Chmn. Rosie Reds Night at Crosley Field, Rooters Organized to Stimulate Interest and Enthusiasm in Cin. Reds Baseball Team, 1967, v.p., 1972, pres., 1975-76, trustee, 1971-79; mem. women's com. Nat. Gov.'s. Conf., 1968; mem. ticket com. Cin. Symphony Orch., 1968; publicity chmn. May Festival, 1969, mem. women's com., 1971-73; solicitor Fine Arts Fund, 1974-75; judge Jr., Achievement, 1965, 67. Mem. Nat. Secs. Assn. (pres. Ohio div. 1969-70), Internat. Women's Personnel Assn., Women's Personnel Assn. Cin. (dir.), Am. Mgmt. Assn., Internat. Platform Assn., Cin. Opera Guild, Alpha Delta Pi. Clubs: Hyde Park Golf and Country, Cincinnati, Internat. Toastmistress, Williams (pres. 1966-67). Home: 715 McMakin St Cincinnati OH 45232 Office: 580 Bldg Cincinnati OH 45202

MALASKY, PAUL MICHAEL, profl. mil. officer, auto exec., design exec., law enforcement technologist; b. Detroit, Sept. 14, 1927; s. Peter and Pauline (Kuntz) M.; student Case Inst. Tech., 1941, U.S. Mil. Acad., 1942; B.S., Army War Coll., 1945, M.S., 1947; degree in Police Sci. and Criminal Justice, Nat. Commn. on Law Enforcement Standards, 1977; m. Barbara Marinovic, Oct. 15, 1949. Enlisted U.S. Army, 1942, advanced through grades to maj., 1956; confdl. M.I. assignments; ret., 1957; with Ford Motor Co., Dearborn, Mich., 1957-65, design mgr., 1965; with Chrysler Corp., Detroit, 1965—, chief research vehicle design, 1965-70, internat. design exec., 1977—; bomb disposal and hazardous devices specialist, 1944—; design cons. handicapped equipment U. Mich. Recipient Exemplary Police Service awards Am. Police Acad.; decorated Legion of Merit, Silver Star, Bronze Star, Combat Infantryman Badge, Purple Heart; awarded 40 formal disclosures and patents. Mem. Soc. Automotive Engrs., Detroit Engring. Soc., Indsl. Designers Soc., Internat. Assn. Chiefs Police, Mich. Assn. Chiefs Police, Nat. Sheriffs Assn., Am. Law Enforcement Assn., Nat. Law Enforcement Acad., Internat. Acad. Criminology, Am. Police Acad., Res. Officers Assn., Am. Def. Preparedness Assn., Assn. Former Intelligence Agts., Am. Legion, DAV. Home: 4000 Overlea Ct Bloomfield Hills MI 48013

MALASTO, ARTHUR STEVEN, hosp. adminstr.; b. Berwind, Colo., Sept. 11, 1924; s. James and Catherine Lena (Mauro) M.; B.S., Millikin U., 1952; M.S., Northwestern U., 1957; m. Irene Rose Karlowsky, Jan. 19, 1945; children—Judy Leetz, Charles, Steven, James, Linda, Thomas. Bus. mgr. Gibson Community Hosp., Gibson City, Ill., 1953-54; asst. adminstr. Porter Meml. Hosp., Valparaiso, Ind., 1954-55, adminstr., 1955—. Asst. prof., vis. lectr. Valparaiso U., 1972-73. Pres., Ind. Adv. Comprehensive Health Planning Council, 1972-73; chmn. Porter County United Fund drive, 1968; mem. univ. council Valparaiso U., 1972. Bd. dirs., mem. exec. com. Blue Cross-Blue Shield, Ind., Tri-State Hosp. Assembly (pres. 1976). Served with AUS, 1943-45. Fellow Am. Coll. Hosp. Adminstrs.; mem. Ind. Hosp. Assn. (pres. 1964-65), Greater Valparaiso C. of C. (pres. 1970-71). K.C. (Ind. Cath. Layman of Year 1964, 4 deg.), Rotarian (pres. 1966). Home: 458 Glendale Blvd Valparaiso IN 46383 Office: 814 LaPorte Ave Valparaiso IN 46383

MALCHAREK, GERHARD, dentist; b. Ottice, Czechoslovakia, June 22, 1931; s. Arnost Engelbert and Hedwig Marie (Peterek) M.; came to U.S., 1951, naturalized, 1954; A.A., North Park Jr. Coll., Chgo., 1956; B.S. in Edn., Western Ill. U., Macomb, 1959; B.S. in Dentistry, U. Ill., 1964, D.D.S., 1966; m. Aileen Joanne Sandberg, Dec. 19, 1964; children—Marianne, Paul. Tchr. sci. high schs., Chgo., 1959-61; dentist div. dental health Ill. Pub. Health Dept., 1966-67, Warren G. Murray Children's Center div. mental retardation Ill. Dept. Mental Health, Centralia, 1967—; pvt. practice, Irvington, Ill., 1968—. Served with AUS, 1952-54. Mem. Am. Dental Assn., Ill., So. Ill. dental socs., Acad. Gen. Dentistry, Res. Officers Assn. U.S. Author article. Home: PO Box 239 Irvington IL 62848 Office: Irvington Med Center Irvington IL 62848

MALCOLM, RUSSELL LAING, JR., pathologist; b. Ann Arbor, Mich., Dec. 21, 1929; s. Russell Laing and Bernice Francis (Staebler) M.; A.B., Earlham Coll., 1951; M.A., Ind. U., 1960, M.D., 1960; m. Ann Elizabeth Wissler, Aug. 15, 1956; children—Christine Laing, Albert Staebler, Melissa Ann. Intern Marion County Gen. Hosp., Indpls., 1960-61; resident in pathology Ind. U. Med. Center, 1961-65, chief resident-instr. pathology, 1964-65; asso. pathologist Middletown (Ohio) Hosp. Assn., 1965—; instr. U. Cin. Med. Sch., 1965-72. Served with USN, 1951-55. Clin. fellow Am. Cancer Soc., 1964-65. Diplomate Am. Bd. Pathology. Fellow Coll. Am. Pathologists; mem. AMA, Am. Soc. Clin. Pathologists, Internat. Acad. Pathology, AAAS, S.W. Ohio Heart Assn. (pres. 1973-75). Republican. Quaker. Home: 8000 W Alexandria Rd Middletown OH 45042 Office: 105 McKnight Dr Middletown OH 45092

MALEY, CHARLES DAVID, lawyer; b. Highland Park, Ill., Aug. 18, 1924; s. Lyle West and Irene (Davis) M.; A.B., State U. Iowa, 1948; J.D., De Paul U., 1952; m. Mildred J. Tobin, Apr. 27, 1957; 1 dau., Annabel Irene. Admitted to Ill. bar, 1952, U.S. Supreme Ct. bar, 1956; asso. firm Friedlund, Levin & Friedlund, Chgo., 1952-58; pvt. practice law, Chgo., 1958-68, Lake Bluff, Ill., 1966-72, Lake Forest, Ill., 1972—; pub. adminstr. Lake County, 1971-74. Asst. district commr. Boy Scouts Am., 1963-65. Mem. Lake County Republican Central Com., 1967-72, 76—, Rep. State Com., 1971-74. Served with AUS, 1943-46, Decorated Purple Heart with oak leaf cluster, Bronze Star Medal. Mem. Am., Seventh Circuit, Ill., Chgo., Lake County bar assns., Am. Judicature Soc., Chgo. Law Inst., S.A.R., Am. Legion (post comdr. 1967-68, 74-77, service officer 1968-69), Am. Arbitration Assn. (mem. panel 1965-67), Lake Forest C. of C., Phi Gamma Delta, Phi Alpha Delta. Republican. Presbyn. Kiwanian (bd. govs. 1976—). Clubs: Capitol Hill (Washington); Tower (Chgo.). Home: 241 W Washington St Lake Bluff IL 60044 Office: 711 McKinley Rd Lake Forest IL 60045

MALINOWSKI, ARTHUR ANTHONY, labor arbitrator, educator; b. Chgo., Apr. 4, 1929; s. Ignatius and Sophie (Data) M.; B.S., DePaul U., 1956, J.D. (Chgo. Title and Trust scholar), 1960; M.S., Loyola U., 1958; Ph.D., Ill. Inst. Tech., 1971; m. Theresa Helen Ecimovich, Feb. 18, 1967; children—Arthur, Mary, Sarah. Faculty Inst. Indsl. Relations Loyola U., Chgo., 1963—, asst. prof. dept. econ., 1971—; labor arbitrator, 1960—. Mem. Office of Collective Bargaining, State of Ill., 1974—. Served with AUS, 1951-53. Recipient Loyal Inst. Social and Indsl. Relations award, Loyola U., 1958. Mem. Nat. Acad. Arbitrators (regional chmn. 1971—, bd. govs. 1976—), Ill., Chgo. bar assns., Advocates Soc., Phi Alpha Delta, Alpha Sigma Nu, Sigma Iota Epsilon, Pi Gamma Mu. K.C. Home: 9240 Major Ave Morton Grove IL 60053 Office: 820 N Michigan Ave Chicago IL 60611

MALIS, LOUISE (MRS. LOUIS A. MALIS), pub. relations cons.; b. Atlanta, Apr. 6, 1921; d. Benjamin and Helen (Aarons) Clein; grad. Wright Jr. Coll., Chgo., 1939; student Northwestern U., 1939-40; m. Louis Albert Malis, Fab. 20, 1943; children—Susan Linda, Amy Beth. Mem. PTA, 1949—, various local and council positions, 1949-54, sch. edn. chmn. Chgo. region Ill. Congress Parents and Tchrs., 1954-58, v.p. Chgo. region, 1958-60, pres., Chgo. region, 1960-62; pub. relations exec. Inst. Internat. Edn., Chgo., 1962-71; cons. Frank H. Cassell & Assos., 1973-74; dir. pub. relations Rehab. Inst. Chgo., 1973-77. Mem. curriculum council Chgo. Bd. Edn., 1954-58, 60-62; sec. Mayor's Commn. on Sch. Bd. Nominations, 1960, 61; adv. bd. Nat. Humanities Inst.; mem. Chgo. Bd. Edn., 1964—; mem. steering com. Midwest Program on Airborne TV Instruction, Chgo., 1960-62; Chgo. del. to Conf. on Out-of-Sch., Unemployed Youth, Washington, 1961; v.p. Council Great City Schs., 1977—, adv. mem. Jewish Children's Bur.; bd. govs. Aspira, Inc.; mem. exec. com. Chgo. Metro History Fair, 1977. Named Woman of Year, Gregorian Soc., 1976. Mem. Ill. (hon. life), Nat. (hon. life) congresses parents and tchrs. Democrat. Jewish. Contbr. articles to ednl. publs. Home: 5757 Sheridan Rd Chicago IL 60660

MALLAS, KENNETH MURIAL, supt. schs.; b. Boone, Ia., Oct. 19, 1932; s. Jack Peter and Goldie Marie (Coleman) M.; B.S., Ia. State U., 1955; Ph.D., 1971; M.S., Drake U., 1962, S.Ed., 1965; m. Shirley Ann Schultz, May 25, 1955; children—Jeffrey Lee, Angela Lynn. Tchr., Maquoketa, Ia., 1960-63; supt. Central Dallas Community Sch., Minburn, Ia., 1963-72, Corning (Ia.) Community Sch., 1972—. Mem. Gov.'s Rural Policy Council, 1972. Bd. dirs. Adams County Fair, 1972—, Adams County Agrl. Extension Council; mem. State Adv. Council and Coordinating Com. for Improvement Edn. in Iowa. Served with arty., AUS; lt. col. Iowa N.G. Mem. Adams Community Indsl. Devel. Corp., Phi Delta Kappa. Mem. Reorganized Ch. Latterday Saints (elder). Home: RD 4 Corning IA 50841 Office: 904 8th St Corning IA 50841

MALLAY, JAMES FRANCIS, boiler mfg. co. exec.; b. Morristown, N.J., Dec. 8, 1936; s. Paul C. and Rachel R. (Jones) M.; B.S., Lafayette Coll., 1959; M.S., Mass. Inst. Tech., 1961; m. Mary Louise Egert, June 12, 1960; children—Cynthia J., Russell J. Engr., Babcock & Wilcox, Lynchburg, Va., 1961-62, lead engr., 1965-69, mgr. safety analysis, 1969-71, mgr. licensing, 1971-75, mgr. liquid metal fast breeder reactor components, Akron, Ohio, 1975—. Served to capt. AUS, 1962-65. Registered profl. engr., Ohio, Va. Mem. Am. Assn. Physics Tchrs., Am. Nuclear Soc., ASME. Methodist. Home: 378 Summit St Wadsworth OH 44281 Office: 1570 S Hawkins Ave Akron OH 44320

MALLERS, GEORGE PETER, lawyer; b. Lima, Ohio, Apr. 28, 1928; s. Peter G. and Helen (Daskalakis) M.; B.S., Ind. U., 1951; J.D., Valparaiso U., 1955; m. Rubie Loomis, Feb. 2, 1950; children—Peter G. II, William G., Elaine. Admitted to Ind. bar, 1955; practiced in Ft. Wayne, 1955—; mem. firm Adair, Perry, Beers, Mallers & Larmore, 1955—; county atty., Allen County, Ind., 1964-73; pres. Mallers Theatres, Ft. Wayne, 1949—, Holiday Theatres, Inc., Mallers Mgmt., 1964—, Muncie Theatres, Inc., 1966—, Lansing Theatres, Inc., 1968—, Mallers & Spirou Enterprises, Inc., 1971—, Georgetown Square Theatres I & II, 1971—, Stage Door, Inc., 1972—, M-S Amusement Corp., 1972—, Georgetown Lounge & Restaurant, Inc., 1972—, Mallers-Spirou Mgmt. Corp., 1973—, Georgetown Bowl, Inc., 1976—. Pres., Village Little League, Ft. Wayne, 1962-64, Hoevelwood Civic Assn., 1959-61; mem. Allen County Police Merit Bd., 1967-77. Pres., Allen County Young Republican Club, 1956-58; asst. to Rep. county chmn. Allen County, 1958—. Mem. Am., Ind., Allen County (sec., dir. 1961-63) bar assns., Am. Judicature Soc., Phi Alpha Delta. Office: Ft Wayne Nat Bank Bldg Fort Wayne IN 46802

MALLETT, CONRAD LE ROY, city ofcl.; b. Ames, Tex., Feb. 22, 1928; s. LeRoy Raymond and Mary Lonnie (Thierry) M.; student U. Detroit, 1950-52; B.S., Wayne State U., 1957, Ed.D., 1972; M.A., U. Mich., 1962; m. Claudia Gwendolyn Jones, Nov. 29, 1952; children—Conrad, Lydia Gwendolyn, Veronica Thierry. Clk., U.S. P.O., 1947-52; patrolman Detroit Police Dept., 1952-57; tchr. Detroit Bd. Edn., 1957-64; supr. Mayor's Youth Employment Project, 1964-65; Mott fellow, Mott instr. U. Cin. Preparation Program, Flint, Mich., 1965-66; exec. sec. I mayor Detroit, 1966-68; dir. community extension programs, div. urban extension Wayne State U., Detroit, 1968-70, dir. Office Neighborhood Relations, 1970-73; v.p. acad. affairs Wayne County Community Coll., Detroit, 1973-77; dir. transp. City of Detroit, 1977—. Mem. tech. adv. team Met. Detroit Citizen's Devel. Authority, 1967—; cons. Project Save our Schs., 1964—; treas. Esther R. LaMarr Meml. Found., 1967—. Precinct del. 1st Congl. Dist., 1966—, vice chmn., 1966-68; dir. Detroit Housing Commn., 1969-70; mem. Wayne County Bd. Commrs., 1971—. Bd. dirs. YMCA, Col. Placement Corps. Served with USAAF, 1946-47. Mem. N.A.A.C.P., Trade Union Leadership Council, Phi Delta Kappa,

Kappa Alpha Psi. Home: 2030 W Boston St Detroit MI 48206 Office: 1301 E Warren Ave Detroit MI 48207

MALLORY, ARTHUR LEE, state ofcl.; b. Springfield, Mo., Dec. 26, 1932; s. Dillard A. and Ferrell (Claxton) M.; B.S. in Edn., S.W. Mo. State Coll., 1954; M.Ed., U. Mo. at Columbia, 1957, Ed.D., 1959; L.H.D., S.W. Bapt. Coll., 1972; m. Joann Peters, June 6, 1954; children—Dennis Arthur, Christopher Lee, Stephanie Ann, Jennifer Lyn. History supr. U. Mo. Lab. Sch., Columbia, 1956-57; asst. to supt. schs. Columbia Pub. Schs., 1957-59; asst. supt. schs. Pkwy. Sch. Dist., St. Louis County, Mo., 1959-64; dean evening div. U. Mo. at St. Louis, 1964; pres. S.W. Mo. State Coll., Springfield, 1964-70; commr. Dept. Elementary and Secondary Edn., Jefferson City, Mo., 1971—. Pres. Great Rivers council Boy Scouts Am., 1971-73. Mem. bd. A.R.C. Cole County; mem. adv. com. Mo. 4-H Found., 1974; mem. Gov.'s Council on the Arts, 1965-66; mem. St. Louis Ednl. TV Comm. Bd.'s Adv. Council KETC-TV, Mo. Law Enforcement Assistance Council, Juvenile Delinquency Task Force, Task Force Commn. States; mem. Uterine task force Am. Cancer Soc.; chmn. com. bds. So. Bapt. Conv., 1973, mem. exec. bd. Mo. Bapt. Conv., 1972-75, 77—. Bd. dirs. Mid-Continent Regional Ednl. Lab., Midwestern Baptist Theol. Sem., 1968—, Internat. House, U. Mo., 1956-59, trustee Meml. Hosp., Jefferson City, William Jewell Coll. Mem. Am., Mo., S.W. Mo. assns. sch. adminstrs., NEA, Mo. State Tchrs. Assn., Mo. Congress Parents and Tchrs. (hon. life). Baptist (deacon). Mason (33 deg.), Rotarian. Home: 3261 S Ten Mile Dr Jefferson City MO 65101 Office: 100 E Capitol Ave Jefferson City MO 65101

MALLORY, TROY L., accountant; b. Sesser, Ill., July 30, 1923; s. Theodore E. and Alice (Mitchell) M.; student So. Ill. U., 1941-43, Washington and Jefferson Coll., 1943-44; B.S., U. Ill., 1947, M.S., 1948; m. Magdalene Richter, Jan. 26, 1963. Staff sr., supr. Scovell, Wellington & Co., C.P.A.'s, Chgo., 1948-58; mgr. Gray, Hunter, Stenn & Co., C.P.A.'s, Quincy, 1959-62, partner, 1962—. Mem. finance com. United Fund, Adams County, 1961-64. Bd. dirs. Woodland Home for Orphans and Friendless, 1970—. Served with 84th Inf. Div. AUS, 1942-45. Decorated Purple Heart, Bronze Star. Mem. Quincy C. of C. (dir. (1970-76), Am. Inst. C.P.A.'s, Ill. Soc. C.P.A.'s. Rotarian (dir. Quincy 1967-70, pres. elect 1977-78). Home: 51 Wilmar Dr Quincy IL 62301 Office: 200 Quincy Peoples Bldg PO Box 32 Quincy IL 62301

MALLOZZI, PHILIP JAMES, physicist; b. Norwalk, Conn., Feb. 12, 1937; s. Philip and Jennie (Saltarelli) M.; B.A., Harvard, 1960; M.S., Yale, 1962, Ph.D., 1964; m. Judy Ju-Yuan Wang, July 29, 1961; children—Stephen Alexander, Lisa Valerie, Richard Philip, Julie Marie. Instr. physics Yale, New Haven, 1964-66; sr. scientist Battelle Meml. Inst., Columbus, Ohio, 1966-70, head laser applications center, 1970—. Mem. Am. Phys. Soc., Sigma Xi. Inventor in field. Contbr. articles to profl. jours. Home: 2088 Tremont Rd Columbus OH 43221 Office: 505 King Ave Columbus OH 43201

MALMIN, OSCAR, dentist; b. Boise, Idaho, Aug. 7, 1924; s. Carl and Emma Lena (Benkenstein) M.; D.D.S., Western Res. U., 1952; certificate U.S. Naval Dental Sch., 1954; M.Sc., Ohio State U., 1963. Practice dentistry, Scobey, Mont., 1960-61, Akron, Ohio, 1954-60, 63—. Served with A.C., USNR, 1943-46, Dental Corps, 1952-54. Mem. Am. Dental Assn., Ohio, Akron dental socs., Am. Soc. Dentistry for Children, Am. Soc. Preventive Dentistry, Delta Sigma Delta. Author: The Shot That Kills. Patentee dental, med., indsl. devices. Home and office: 127 E Wayne Ave Akron OH 44301

MALMSTROM, GREGORY BRUCE, city ofcl.; b. Sioux City, Iowa, Mar. 12, 1937; s. Arthur Raymond and Marion Bernice (Moe) M.; student Iowa State U., 1955-57; m. Janice Rae Carpenter, Nov. 15, 1959; children—Bruce Allan, Janine Renee, Jill Renee. Survey instrumentman City of Sioux City, Iowa, 1958-67, survey party chief, 1968-69; asst. city engr., City of Webster City, Iowa, 1969-73, dir. pub. works, 1973—. Mem. Am. Pub. Works Assn., Inst. for Certification of Engrng. Technicians, Soc. Land Surveyors of Iowa. Meth. Mason. Mem. Order Eastern Star. Kiwanian. Home: 815 Prospect St Webster City IA 50595 Office: 4002d St Webster City IA 50595

MALNAK, ALLEN BERT, internist; b. Du Quoin, Ill., Oct. 12, 1928; s. Nathan Hyman and Rae (Cornick) M.; B.S., Roosevelt U., Chgo., 1950; B.S., U. Ill. Coll. Medicine, 1952, M.D., 1954; m. Tillie Shaewitz, Aug. 14, 1955; children—Nancy, Scott, Wendy, Peter. Intern, Cook County Hosp., Chgo., 1954-55; resident in internal medicine U. Ill. Hosps. and West Side VA Hosp., Chgo., 1955-58; chief resident in internal medicine Mt. Sinai Hosp., Chgo., 1960-61; sr. attending physician Gottlieb Meml. Hosp., Melrose Park, Ill., 1962—, chmn. dept. internal medicine, 1969-70, 72-74, pres. med. staff, 1974-75; clin. asst. prof. Stritch Sch. Medicine, Loyola U., Maywood, Ill., 1969—. Served as capt. USAR, 1958-60. William J. Cook scholar, 1946-50. Diplomate Am. Bd. Internal Medicine. Mem. AMA, Ill., Chgo. med. assns., Am. Heart Assn., Chgo. Backgammon Club. Clubs: Whitehall (Chgo.); Friends of Acapulco. Contbr. articles to med. jours. Home: 2215 Whiteoak Dr Northbrook IL 60062 Office: Gottlieb Hosp 8720 W North Ave Melrose Park IL 60160

MALONE, FRANCIS EDWARD, accountant; b. Kempton, Ill., Jan. 18, 1907; s. Frank Mark and Julia Kathern (Walgenback) M.; A.A. in Commerce, Springfield Coll. Ill., 1954; B.S.C., U. Notre Dame, 1956. Mgr., Walgenback-Walker Farm, near Kempton, 1930-42; chief statis. clk. U.S. War Dept., McCook Army Air Field, McCook, Nebr., 1945-46; bookkeeper and office mgr. Tombaugh-Turner Hybrid Corn Co., Pontiac, Ill., 1946-47; safety responsibility evaluator Ill. Div. Hwys., Springfield, 1947-49; agrl. statistician U.S. Dept. Agr. Bur. Agrl. Econs., Springfield, 1949-53; sr. accountant Raymond E. Rickbiel, C.P.A., 1955-61, Ernst & Ernst, Springfield, 1961-62; pvt. practice pub. accounting, Springfield, 1963—. Served to sgt. USAAF, 1942-45. Mem. Am. Accounting Assn., Air Force Assn., Am. Legion (adj. post 1973—), Alumni Assn. U. Notre Dame, Te Deum Internat. (sec.-treas. Ill. chpt. 1962-65), Thomist Assn. (chmn. Burse Ill. chpt. 1957-62), K.C. Home and office: One Maple Ln Kempton IL 60946

MALONE, JOHN MICHAEL, obstetrician, gynecologist; b. Toledo, Jan. 15, 1927; s. Louis Pierre and Laurette Elizabeth (Bartley) M.; student U. Detroit, 1944-47; M.D., St. Louis U., 1951; m. Thereza de Quieros Mattoso, May 22, 1950; children—John, Mary Thereza, Louis, Thomas, Mark, James, Susan. Intern, Mt. Carmel Hosp., Detroit, 1951-52, resident in obstetrics and gynecology, 1952-55, pres. med. staff, 1978; practice medicine specializing in obstetrics and gynecology, Farmington Hills, Mich., 1955—; tchr. med. students Wayne State U. Served with USNR, 1945-46. Fellow A.C.S.; mem. Mich. (chmn. jud. com. 1977—), Wayne County med. socs., AMA, Am. Coll. Obstetricians and Gynecologists, Central Assn. Obstetricians and Gynecologists, Mich. Soc. Obstetricians and Gynecologists (pres. 1974-75), Nat. Fedn. Cath. Physicians (pres. 1968-69). Republican. Roman Catholic. Club: K.C. Home: 17225 Melrose St Southfield MI 48075 Office: 27970 Orchard Lake Rd Farmington Hills MI 48018

MALONE, ROBERT NEAL, chem. co. exec.; b. Elyria, Ohio, Oct. 5, 1923; s. William Walter and Carolyn (McHugh) M.; B.S., Bowling Green State U., 1950; m. Roberta Mae Borradaille, July 22, 1950; children—Robert William, Rhonda Jan. Territorial salesman Phillip Morris Ltd., Inc., Sandusky, Ohio, 1950-51; mgr. Gray Drug Co., Sandusky, Ohio, 1951-52; v.p. Damon Chem. Co., Alliance, Ohio, 1952—, also dir.; v.p. Monad Co.; dir. Lien Chem., Monad Co., Carnation Investment Co.; cons. AIMS Staff, Arby's Internat., Inc. Served with USAAF, 1943-46. Decorated Presdl. citation. Mem. Internat. San. Supply Assn., VFW. Clubs: Alliance Country, Marlington Booster, Elks. Home: 120 E Carol St Alliance OH 44601 Office: PO Box 480 Alliance OH 44601

MALONEY, JOHN CLEMENT, advt. co. exec.; b. Laurel, Nebr., Aug. 19, 1929; s. Clement Mathew and Annette (McCabe) M.; B.A., U. Nebr., 1951; M.S., Purdue U., 1953, Ph.D., 1954; m. Maybelle Margaret Reinsch, Aug., 1950; children—Connie (Mrs. Leland Robinson), Sheila, Barbara, Jane, Lynn. Mgr. personnel testing Mpls. Honeywell Co., 1954-55; dir. market research Omar, Inc., Omaha, 1955-58; mgr. research and devel. Leo Burnett Co., Chgo., 1958-66; research dir. Urban Journalism Center, asso. prof. advtg. and journalism Northwestern U., 1966-72; v.p. research Arthur Meyerhoff Assos., Inc., Chgo., 1972—. Cons. various ednl. and research founds., corps., govt. agys. Ford Found. grantee, 1968-69. Mem. Am. Psychol. Assn. (dir. consumer psychology div. 1964-65), AAUP (pres. Northwestern U. chpt. 1970), Am. Mktg. Assn., AAAS. Contbr. articles to profl. jours. Home: 147 Plumtree Rd Deerfield IL 60015 Office: Arthur Meyerhoff Assos Inc 410 N Michigan Ave Chicago IL 60611

MALOON, JAMES HAROLD, airline exec.; b. Union City, Ohio, June 22, 1926; s. Charles E. and Bertha (Creviston) M.; A.B., Miami U., Oxford, Ohio, 1949; M.A., Ind. U., 1951, Ph.D., 1960; children—Sharon Maloon Wilt, Craig J., Elizabeth M. Maloon TerHaar, Douglas C.T. Dir. fin. State of Ohio, 1959-62; exec. v.p. Reston Va., Inc., 1963-64; sr. v.p., chief fin. officer, dir. Columbia Gas System Service Corp., 1965-72; exec. v.p., dir. Pan Am World Airways, 1972—; dir. Intercontinental Hotels Corp., Falcon Jet Corp., Liberian Devel. Corp., Grand Central Bldg. Corp., Fred F. French Investing Corp. Served with USNR, 1944-45. Mem. Am. Econ. Assn., Nat. Tax Assn. Clubs: Sky, University; Fairfield (Conn.) Hunt. Home: 6000 Olentangy River Rd Delaware OH 43015 also 200 E 66th St New York City NY 10021

MALOON, JERRY LEE, physician, lawyer, medicolegal cons.; b. Union City, Ind., June 23, 1938; s. Charles Elias and Bertha Lucille (Creviston) M.; B.S., Ohio State U., 1960, M.D., 1964; J.D., Capital U. Law Sch., 1974; m. Gabriella Thomas, Mar. 21, 1970; children—Jeffrey Lee, Jerry Lee II; 1 stepson, Michael Thomas Gibson. Intern, Santa Monica (Calif.) Hosp., 1964-65; tng. psychiatry Columbus (Ohio) State Hosp., 1969, Menninger Clinic, Topeka, Kans., 1970; clin. dir. Orient (Ohio) State Inst. for Mentally Retarded, 1967-69, chief of staff, 1971—; asso. med. dir. Western Electric, Inc., Columbus, 1969-71. Guest lectr. law and medicine Orient State Inst., also Columbus State Inst., 1969-71. Served to capt. M.C., AUS, 1965-67. Fellow Am. Coll. Legal Medicine; mem. A.M.A., Indsl. Med. Assn., Columbus and Franklin County Acad. Medicine, Ohio Med. Assn., Am., Ohio, Columbus bar assns., Ohio State U. Alumni Assn., U.S. Trotting Assn., Am. Profl. Practice Assn. Home: 3535 Henderson Rd Columbus OH 43220 Office: Orient State Inst Orient OH 43146

MALSON, JOHN RAYMOND, accountant; b. Berlin, Wis., Aug. 28, 1911; s. John Michael and Stella Ann (Wolnick) M.; student Green Lake Normal, 1930-31, Fountain City Bus. Coll., 1931-33, Fond du Lac Bus. Coll., 1933-34, Chgo. Commerce Sch., 1936-43; m. Harriet Ann Hoffmann, Nov. 24, 1934; children—Joan (Mrs. William Brunet), Milton, James, Ginny (Mrs. Tom Mattison), John Raphael, Patricia (Mrs. John Hanrahan). Music tchr. various rural schs., 1936-38; court house clk., Fond du Lac, Wis., 1938-40; time, cost clk., Giddings & Lewis Machine Co., Fond du Lac, 1940-43; sr. accountant R. Mabie & Assos. C.P.A.'s, Stevens Point, Wis., 1943-45; office procedure coordinator Northern Furniture Co., Sheboygan, Wis., 1945-47; pvt. practice accounting, Fond du Lac, Wis., 1947—; exec. dir., pres. Mel-So'nance Nat. Music Inc. Justice of Peace, Fond du Lac City, 1956-57. Craft instr. Badger Council Boy Scouts Am., 1948. Served with AUS, 1943. Mem. Nat. Soc. Pub. Accountants, Wis. Assn. Accountants, Am. Soc. Composers, Authors, Publishers, Wis. Regional Writers Assn., Travelers Protective Assn., Fond du Lac County Hist. Soc., Fond du Lac Writers Work Shop. Eagle, Moose. Co-author (with others): Portfolio of Accounting Systems for Small and Medium-Sized Businesses, 2 vols., 1968. Author, composer Christmas, patriotic songs, ballads; producer L.P. album Christmas Is In The Air. Home: 150 W Scott St Fond du Lac WI 54935 Office: 150 W Scott St Fond du Lac WI 54935

MALTZ, ROBERT, surgeon; b. Cin., July 21, 1935; s. William and Sarah (Goldberg) M.; B.S., U. Cin., 1958, M.D., 1962; m. Sylvia Moskowitz, Aug. 24, 1958; children—Mark Edward, Deborah Lynn, Steven Alan, David Stuart. Intern, Cin. Gen. Hosp., 1962-63; resident Barnes Hosp., St. Louis, 1965-69; asst. prof. surgery Stanford U. Med. Center, Palo Alto, Calif., 1969-71; asso. prof. otolaryngology U. Cin. Med. Center, 1971—. Mem. brotherhood bd. Rockdale Temple, Cin., 1975—. Served in USAF, 1963-65. USPHS fellow, 1968-69; Eli Lilly Co. research grantee, 1971, 76; Burroughs Wellcome Co. research grantee, 1972; diplomate Am. Bd. Otolaryngology. Fellow Am. Coll. Surgeons; mem. Am. Acad. Ophthalmology Otolaryngology, Am. Acad. Facial Plastic and Reconstructive Surgery, Am. Assn. Cosmetic Surgeons (sec.-treas.), Royal Soc. Health (Eng.), Am. Council Otolaryngology, Pan Am. Assn. Otorhinolaryngology and Bronchoesophagology, Internat. Acad. Cosmetic Surgery. Clubs: Amerley Village Swim and Tennis, Queen City Racquet, Losantiville Country, B'nai B'ith. Home: 2601 Willowbrook Dr Cincinnati OH 45237 Office: 2825 Burnet Ave Cincinnati OH 45219

MAN, JEROME VICTOR, mfg. co. exec.; b. Chgo., Mar. 22, 1924; s. Harry and Celia (Silverman) Friedman; B.S., Ill. Inst. Tech., 1950; m. Marilyn Ravin, June 11, 1948; children—Jacqueline Man Fredricks, Diane Man Henderson, Norman, Carol, Tina. Chief engr. Allied Radio, Chgo., 1945-48; service mgr. Hallicrafters, Chgo., 1948-50; with Electronic Engrs., Chgo., 1950—, chmn. bd., 1975—; with Internat. Rec. Co., Chgo., 1964—, chmn. bd., 1975—. Tchr. adult edn. classes Deerfield (Ill.) High Sch., 1972-74, Maine High Sch., Park Ridge, Ill., 1970-75. Commr. East Skokie (Ill.) Drainage Dist., 1973—; chmn. USO Gifts in Kind Com., Chgo., 1964—; committeeman West Deerfield Twp. Ill., 1970—. Served with USAAF, 1942-45. Registered profl. engr., Ill. Mem. Nat. Soc. Profl. Engrs., Chgo. Audio and Acoustic Group, Sigma Alpha Mu. Mason. Patentee in field. Home: 3377 Old Mill Rd Highland Park IL 60035 Office: 1639 Evergreen St Chicago IL 60622

MAN, PANG LING, physician; b. Hong Kong, July 11, 1934; s. Kwong Cheung and Loy Ho (Wong) M.; came to U.S., 1964; M.D., Sun Yat-Sen U. (China), 1958; m. Wo Hop Lam, Apr. 18, 1958; children—Ching, Dick, Linda. Clin. dir. Eastern State Hosp., Lexington, Ky., 1967-71; clin. instr. psychiatry U. Louisville, 1967-71; dir. research, asso. dir. edn. Northville (Mich.) State Hosp., 1971—; clin. asst. prof. psychiatry Wayne State U., Detroit, 1971—; cons. dept. psychiatry VA Hosp., Allen Park, Mich., 1976—. Recipient John W. Barr Jr. prize U. Louisville, 1970, others; grantee in psychopharmacology. Mem. Am. Psychiat. Assn., Mich. Psychiat. Soc., Wayne County Med. Soc., AAAS, Sigma Xi. Author: Handbook of Acupuncture Analgesia, 1973; Principles and Practice of Acupuncture Analgesia, 1975. Contbr. articles to med. jours. Home: 21237 Summerside Ln Northville MI 48167 Office: Northville State Hosp Northville MI 48167 also 16800 W 12 Mile Rd Southfield MI 48076

MANALICH, RAMIRO, educator; b. Havana, Cuba, Oct. 20, 1917; s. Ramiro and Amparo (Rodriguez-Morejon) M.; came to U.S., 1960, naturalized, 1970; B.Letters and Sci., LL.D., Havana U., 1950, Litt.D., 1951; m. Mercedes Torron, Mar. 23, 1956; 1 son, Ramiro. Prof. Spanish and English, J. Lopez Gt. Comml. Acad., Havana, 1951-57; prof. Spanish, Concordia Coll., Moorhead, Minn., 1963-66, N.D. State U., nights, 1964-66, U. Wis.-La Crosse, 1966—, Luther Coll., Deborah, Iowa, 1965-66; asso. dir. Center Latin Am., U. Wis.-Milw., 1974—; admitted to Havana bar, 1950; atty. Cuban Ministry Def., 1949-52; mem. firm Gutierrez-Manalich, Havana, 1955-58; sec.-gen. Havana Docks Corp., also Havana Steamship Conf., 1949-58; atty. Cuban Match Industry, 1957-58. Provincial del. Cuban Revolutionary Party, 1957-58, sec.-gen. lawyers div., 1957-58. Mem. Assn. U. Wis. Faculties, Am. Assn. Tchrs. Spanish and Portuguese, Wis. Humanities Com., N. Central Council Latin Americanists, Caribbean Studies Assn., Sigma Delta Pi. Author: Hispanoamerica: Enfoque Historico, Cultural, Politico, Economico, Social y Literario, 1970; also brochures, articles. Roman Catholic. Home: 4091 Terrace Dr La Crosse WI 54601

MANATT, RICHARD, educator; b. Odebolt, Iowa, Dec. 13, 1931; s. William Price and Lucille (Taylor) M.; B.Sc., Iowa State U., 1953, M.S., 1956; Ph.D., U. Iowa, 1964; m. Sally Jo Johnson, Aug. 20, 1952; children—Tamra Jo, Ann Lea, Joel Price; m. 2d, Jacquelyn M. Nesset, Feb. 25, 1970; 1 dau., Megan Sue. Prin. Oskaloosa (Iowa) Schs. 1959-62; research asso. U. Iowa Iowa City, 1962-64; asst. prof. Iowa State U., Ames, 1964-67, asso. prof. ednl. adminstrn., 1967-72, prof., sect. leader ednl. adminstrn., 1972—, chmn. dept. ednl. adminstrn., 1970—. Cons. program planning for com. colls. and pub. schs. Served with AUS, 1953-55. Mem. N.E.A., Nat. Assn. Secondary Sch. Prins., Am. Assn. Sch. Adminstrs., Phi Kappa Phi, Phi Delta Kappa, Delta Chi. Democrat. Methodist. Author: Educator's Guide to the New Design. Home: 2926 Monroe Dr Ames IA 50010

MANCO, HUGO RUPERTO, paint co. exec.; b. Lima, Peru, Apr. 22, 1930; s. Pedro Hugo and Dona Rosaura (Moscoso) M.; came to U.S., 1950, naturalized, 1975; B.A. (Scholastic fellow), Baker U., 1954; postgrad. Columbia U., 1954; m. Janet Elizabeth Richmond, Apr. 22, 1968; children—David Hugo, Donna Maria, Daniel Kerr, Monica Marie, Jessica Elizabeth. Tech. dir. Longwear Paint Co., North Kansas City, Mo., 1954-60, Great Western Paint Co., Kansas City, Mo., 1960-65; plant mgr. Morris Paint Co., Kansas City, 1965-68; research scientist Farmland Industries, North Kansas City, 1968—. Mem. Kansas City Soc. Coatings Tech. (pres. 1977-78), Hispanic C. of C. of Greater Kansas City (dir. 1977—). Republican. Roman Catholic. Home: 410 NW Sagamore Ln Kansas City MO 64116 Office: 103 W 26th Ave North Kansas City MO 64116

MANCUSO, JAMES VINCENT, automobile dealer; b. Batavia, N.Y., June 18, 1916; s. Benjamin J. and Laura (LaRussa) M.; student Gen. Motors Inst., Flint, Mich., 1949; m. Clarissa R. Pope, Sept. 8, 1945; children—Richard J., Robert P., Linda M., Laura L. Salesman, C. Mancuso Son, Inc., 1934-39, gen. mgr., 1939-42; gen. mgr. Batavia Motors, 1945-49; sales rep. Cadillac Motor Car div. Gen. Motors Corp., 1950-53; pres., gen. mgr. Mancuso Chevrolet, Skokie, Ill., 1953-74, chmn. bd., 1974—; pres. Village Cadillac, Barrington, Ill., 1974-76, chmn. bd., 1976—; pres. Genesee Corp.; dir. First Nat. Bank of Skokie, Lake States Ins. Co.; adv. council Consol. Am. Life Ins. Co. Bd. dirs. Greater Chgo. Better Bus. Bur., chmn. pub. relations com., 1969-71. Gen. mgr. Niles Twp. Community Fund, 1955; trustee Skokie Valley Community Hosp.; pres. Skokie's All American City Com., 1961, chmn., 1967; dir. Auto Industry Hwy. Safety Commn., 1965-69; chmn. Niles Twp. Jud. Reform Com., 1963, pres. Niles Twp. Service Sta. Mgmt. Tng. Program, 1971. Served from pvt. to maj. USAAF, 1942-46. Recipient Skokie's Man of Year Abraham Lincoln medal, 1960; 1 Skokie's top 10 civic leaders, 1959; Outstanding Community Service award Skokie League Womens Voters, 1963. Mem. Am. Legion, Nat. Auto Dealers Assn. (dir., regional v.p., chmn. pub. relations com.), Assn. Employers Ill. (dir.), C. of C. (pres. 1956), Chgo. Auto Dealers Assn. (dir. 1959-68), Chgo. Met. Chevrolet Dealers Assn. (pres. 1957-59), Chgo. Automobile Trade Assn. (v.p. 1960-61), Chgo. Met. Chevrolet Dealers Advt. Assn. (pres. 1969-70). Roman Catholic. Clubs: Rotary (past pres.), Evanston Golf (pres. 1969, dir.). Home: 17 Longmeadow Rd Winnetka IL 60093 Office: 4700 Golf Rd Skokie IL 60076

MANDARINO, RALPH JOSEPH, JR., accountant; b. Chgo., Dec. 1, 1937; s. Ralph Joseph and Mae (Suchy) M.; B.S. in Accounting with honors, U. Ill., 1962; m. Eileen Emily Kuczek, Feb. 3, 1962; children—Robert, Susan, Patti. Partner in charge adminstrv. group and profl. devel. dept. Peat, Marwick, Mitchell & Co., Chgo., 1962, partner in charge audit dept., Detroit, 1977—. Gen. chmn. Chgo. Jaycees and Mayor Daley's Summer Jobs for Youth, 1969, 72, 73; dir. Chgo. Jr. Assn. Commerce and Industry, 1969-70; regional chmn. Winnetka (Ill.) Community House fund raising program, 1972; trustee fin. devel. com., v.p. men's council Mus. Contemporary Art, pres. council, 1977—; v.p., bd. dirs. Music of the Baroqué; mem. Renaissance Center. Served with USMCR, 1956-59. Mem. Am. Inst. C.P.A.'s Ill. Soc. C.P.A.'s (tchr. 1969, chmn. pub. service and info. com. 1974), Mich. C.P.A. Assn., Am. Mgmt. Assn. (tchr. 1970—), U. Ill. Commerce Alumni Assn. (dir.), Sigma Iota Epsilon, Beta Alpha Psi. Clubs: Univ. Chgo. (fin. com.); Toastmasters (pres. chpt. 1973). Home: 30 Lee Gate Ln Grosse Pointe Farms MI 48236 Office: 200 Renaissance Center Detroit MI 48243

MANDEL, SHELDON LLOYD, dermatologist; b. Mpls., Dec. 6, 1922; s. Maurice and Stelle N. M.; B.A., U. Minn., 1943, B.S., 1944, M.B., 1946, M.D., 1946; 1 dau. by previous marriage, Melissa Ann. Intern U. Okla. Hosp., 1946-47; trainee Valley Forge Hosp., 1947-49; fellow Grad. Sch. U. Minn., 1949-53; resident (preceptee Dr. H.E. Michelson) VA Hosp., 1949-53; practice medicine specializing in dermatology, Mpls., 1953—; asso. prof. dermatology U. Minn., 1970—, course dir. resident-staff seminars in dermatology, 1972—; mem. staffs Northwestern Hosp., Abbott Hosp., Mpls. Served to capt. M.C. AUS, 1947-49. Diplomate Am. Bd. Dermatology. Fellow Am. Acad. Dermatology; mem. AMA, Minn., Hennepin County med. socs., Mpls. Acad. Medicine, AAUP, Noah Worchester, Minn. (past pres.) dermatol. socs., Pan Am. Med. Assn. Clubs: Mpls. Athletic, Mpls. Golf. Contbr. articles to med. jours. Home: 2828 Burnham Blvd Minneapolis MN 55416 Office: 715 Med Arts Bldg Minneapolis MN 55402

MANDELBAUM, HARRY DAVID, fin. planner; b. Cin., July 7, 1932; s. Max and Bessie (Goodman) M.; B.S., Xavier U. (Cin.), 1955, M.S., 1958. Prin. fin. planner, Cin., 1960—. Active Republican Workshops of Ohio, Inc., 1960—, county pres., 1961-62, state bd. dirs., 1966-67, county bd. dirs., 1968-69. Served with U.S. Army, 1952-54. Mem. Inst. Certified Fin. Planners, Internat. Assn. Fin. Planners, Coll. Fin. Planning, VFW. Jewish. Club: Kiwanis. Home:

7504 Tiki Ave Cincinnati OH 45243 Office: 108 W Third St Cincinnati OH 45202

MANDELL, MAURICE IRA, mktg. scientist, educator; b. N.Y.C., Oct. 23, 1925; s. Benjamin David and Myn (Lester) M.; B.S., N.Y. U., 1947; M.B.A., Syracuse U., 1949; D. Bus. Adminstrn., Ind. U., 1953; m. Natalie Eldredge Gould, July 29, 1956; children—David Gould, Lisa Rose. Instr. mktg. Syracuse (N.Y.) U., 1948-50; asst. prof. mktg. Western Res. U., Cleve., 1951-53; prof. Bowling Green (Ohio) State U., 1953—, chmn. dept. mktg., 1965—; Fulbright prof. Turun Kauppakorkeakoulu, Turku, Finland, 1956-57; Ford Found. cons. Inst. Bus. Adminstrn., Dacca, Bangladesh, 1967. Found. Econ. Edn. fellow, 1953, 62; Am. Assn. Advt. Agys. fellow 1963. Mem. Am. Mktg. Assn., A.A.U.P., Am. Acad. Advt., Omicron Delta Kappa, Alpha Delta Sigma, Beta Gamma Sigma, Theta Chi. Author: Advertising, 1968, 2d edit., 1974. Contbr. articles, revs. to profl. publs. Home: 10 Parkwood Dr Bowling Green OH 43402

MANDELL, STEVEN LESLIE, educator; b. Newark, Aug. 10, 1944; s. Herbert and Gail Pearl (Lavich) M.; B.A., Lehigh U., 1966, B.S. in Chem. Engring., 1967; M.B.A., U. Pa., 1969; D. Bus. Adminstrn., George Washington U., 1975; m. Colleen Jane Bailik, July 12, 1969; children—Hollis Elizabeth, Zachary Jonathan. Systems engr. IBM, Fairfax, Va., 1969-70; asso. dir., computer specialist U.S. Civil Service Commn., Washington, 1972-75; asst. prof. information systems Bowling Green (O.) State U., 1975—, dir. Mgmt. Information Inst., 1977—; cons. Bur. Land Mgmt., AID. Served to capt. U.S. Army, 1970-72. Decorated Army Commendation medal. IBM fellow, 1968-69; Am. Metal Climax scholar, 1966-67; Bowling Green U. grantee, 1976-77. Mem. Acad. Internat. Bus. Club: Bowling Green Tennis. Author: The Management Information System is Going to Pieces, 1975; Multinational Corporate Computer Systems, 1975; Organizational Intelligence Networks, 1977; Principles of Data Processing, 1977; PLI/PLC: A Short Course, 1977. Home: 1059 Bourgogne St Bowling Green OH 43402 Office: Quantitative Analysis Bowling Green State U Bowling Green OH 43402

MANDELSTAMM, JEROME R., lawyer; b. St. Louis, Apr. 3, 1932; s. Henry and Estelle (London) M.; A.B., U. Pa., 1954; LL.B., Harvard U., 1957; m. Ann Callahan Gagliardi, Nov. 9, 1973. Admitted to Mo. bar, 1957; since practiced in St. Louis, partner firm Greenfield, Davidson, Mandelstamm & Voorhees, 1969—. Mem. St. Louis County Bd. Election Commrs., 1973-77; bd. dirs. Legal Aid Soc. City and County St. Louis, 1967-75, pres., 1969-70; bd. dirs. Lawyers Reference Service Met. St. Louis, 1976—, Mo. Legal Aid Soc., 1977—. Served with AUS, 1957. Mem. Am., Mo. bar assns., Bar Assn. Met. St. Louis (chmn. urban affairs com. 1971-75, v.p. 1974-75, treas. 1975-76). Home: 915 S Bemiston Clayton MO 63105 Office: 1516 Chemical Bldg 721 Olive St Saint Louis MO 63101

MANDERS, KARL LEE, neurol. surgeon; b. Rochester, N.Y., Jan. 21, 1927; s. David Bert and Frances Edna (Cohan) M.; student Cornell U., 1946; M.D., U. Buffalo, 1950; m. Ann Laprell, July 28, 1969; children—Karlanna, Maidena, Karl, Kerry, Kristine. Intern, U. Va. Hosp., Charlottesville, 1950-51, resident in neurol. surgery, 1951-52; resident in neurol. surgery Henry Ford Hosp., Detroit, 1954-56; practice medicine specializing in neurol. surgery, Indpls., 1956—; med. dir. Community Hosp. Rehab. Center for Pain, 1973—; chief med. and surg. neurology Community Hosp., 1977; coroner Marion County (Ind.), 1977; pres. Manders-Marks, Inc.; pres. Bioscan Inc. Served with USN, 1952-54. Fellow A.C.S.; mem. AMA, Am. Assn. Neurol. Surgery, Congress Neurol. Surgery, Internat. Assn. Study of Pain, Am. Assn. Study of Headache, N.Y. Acad. Sci., Am. Coll. Angiology, Am. Soc. Contemporary Medicine and Surgery. Home: 5845 Highfall St Indianapolis IN 46226 Office: 5506 E 16th St Indianapolis IN 46218

MANDOLINI, ANTHONY MARLO, accountant; b. Chgo., Mar. 9, 1933; s. Primo Mario and Rose (Pieroni) M.; B.S. in Accounting cum laude, U. Notre Dame, 1954; m. Lorraine Vivian Kargol, June 26, 1954; children—Gregory Anthony, Mark Allan, David James, Anthony Michael, Lori Ann. Staff accountant Peat, Marwick, Mitchell & Co., Chgo., 1954-57, mem. mgmt. cons. dept., 1957-58, mgr., 1961, mem. state and local govt. dept., 1962, partner, 1964—, partner in charge dept., 1966—. Pres. council St. Ignatius High Sch., Chgo.; mem. State of Ill. Intergovtl. Coop. Commn., 1973. Bd. dirs., pres. Civic Fedn. Chgo. Named One of Ten Outstanding Young Men, Chgo. Jr. Assn. Commerce and Industry, 1968; recipient Distinguished Service award Ill. Auditor Pub. Accounts, 1967. C.P.A., Ill., Ia., Ga. Mem. Am. Inst. C.P.A.'s (com. govtl. accounting 1968—, chmn. ad hoc com. on intergovtl. audit standards 1971-72, chmn. task force model state laws, chmn. task force spl. municipalities com.), Municipal Finance Officers Assn. U.S. and Can. (accounting com. 1972—, bond disclosure guidelines com. 1976), Ill. Soc. C.P.A.'s (dir.), Notre Dame Club Chgo. (gov.), Am. Water Works Assn. (Mgmt. Div. award 1966), Fed. Govt. Accountants Assn., Nat. Council Govt. Accountants (exec. com.), Nat. Council Tchr. Retirement, Hosp. Finance Mgmt. Assn. (past pres., dir.), Internat. Bridge, Tunnel and Turnpike Assn. K.C. Club: Notre Dame Monogram. Contbr. articles to profl. jours. Home: 1429 Elizabeth Ln Glenview IL 60025 Office: 222 S Riverside Plaza Chicago IL 60606

MANELLI, DONALD DEAN, writer, producer motion pictures; b. Burlington, Iowa, Oct. 20, 1936; s. Daniel Anthony and Mignon Marie M.; B.A., U. Notre Dame, 1959; children by former marriage—Daniel, Lisa. Communications specialist Jewel Cos., 1959; script writer Coronet Films, Chgo., 1960-62; freelance writer, 1962-63; creative dir. Fred A. Niles Communications Centers, Chgo., 1963-67; sr. writer Wild Kingdom, NBC-TV network, also freelance film writer, 1967-70; pres. Donald Manelli & Assos., Inc., Chgo., 1970—. Recipient internat. film festival and TV awards. Mem. Writers Guild Am., Nat. Acad. TV Arts and Scis., Outdoor Writers Assn. Am. Clubs: Whitehall, Mid-Town Tennis (Chgo.). Office: 307 N Michigan Ave Chicago IL 60601

MANFRE, THOMAS STEVEN, air freight transp. co. exec.; b. Chgo., Dec. 21, 1942; s. Thomas and Ceceilia (Kwiatkowski) M.; student Coll. Advanced Traffic, Chgo., 1965-67, Loyola U., Chgo., 1967-72; m. Sharon L. Jozwiak, July 24, 1965; children—Susan, Karen, Thomas. Mgr. customer service and claim dept. Terminal Transport Co., Chgo., 1963-65; mgr. internat. service dept. Consol. Freightways Inc., Chgo., 1967-69, asst. terminal mgr. C.F. Package div., 1967-69, ops. mgr. C.F. Air Freight div., 1969-70; founder, owner Internat. Air Services Ltd., Chgo., 1970-71, now dir.; founder, owner, pres., chmn. bd. Performance by Air, Inc., Chgo., 1971—. Served with U.S. Army, 1965-67; Vietnam. Mem. Air Freight Forwarders Assn., Internat. Air Transport Assn. Roman Catholic. Home: 732 Tomlin Dr Burr Ridge IL 60521 Office: PO Box 66397 Chicago IL 60666

MANFRO, PATRICK JAMES (PATRICK JAMES HOLIDAY), radio artist; b. Kingston, N.Y., Dec. 30, 1947; s. Charles Vincent and Anna Agnes (Albany) Manfro; Asso. Sci. in Accounting, Ulster Coll., 1968; diploma Radio Electronics Inst., 1969; m. Janice Lynn Truscott, July 5, 1975. Program dir., radio artist WKNY, Kingston, 1966-70; radio artist WPTR, Albany, N.Y., 1970, WPOP, Hartford, Conn., 1970, CKLW, Detroit, 1970-71, WOR-FM, N.Y.C., 1971-72, CKLW Radio, Detroit, 1972—. Radio cons.; adviser New Contemporary Sch. Announcing, Albany, 1973—; comml. announcer radio, television, 1970—. Judge, Miss Mich. Universe Pageant, 1970. Mem. N.Y. State N.G., 1968-74. Recipient 5 Year Service ribbon N.Y. State, 1973; named Runner-up Billboard Air Personality awards, 1971. Mem. AFTRA, Smithsonian Assos., BMI Songwriters Guild. Club: Dominion Golf and Country. Home: 1637 Goyeau St Windsor ON Canada Office: 1640 Ouellette Windsor ON N8X 1L1 Canada

MANGIE, RONALD EUGENE, dentist; b. Youngstown, Ohio, Feb. 16, 1937; s. James Carl and Helene Dolores (Del Signore) M.; B.S. in Bacteriology, Ohio State U., 1958, D.D.S., 1964; postgrad. oral surgery St. Elizabeth Hosp., Youngstown, Ohio, 1964-65; m. Davene Louise Ucello, Dec. 27, 1960; children—David, Rhonda, Dara, Douglas, Ronald Eugene, Dana. Practice dentistry, Youngstown, 1965—; mem. teaching staff St. Elizabeth Hosp., 1965—, also chmn. edn. com. dental resident program Dental Clinic. Owner, founder cattle-raising farm REM Rolling Acres; owner Ye Olde Butcher Shoppe, 1976—. Mem. Nat. Rehab. Assn. (cons. 1969—), Am. Endodontic Soc., Acad. Gen. Dentistry, Holy Name Soc., Corydon Palmer Soc., Am. Dental Assn., Internat. Assn. Orthodontics, Eta Sigma, Psi Omega. Club: Fonderlac Country (Poland, Ohio). Home: 6166 Middletown Rd New Middletown OH 44442 Office: 495 Southern Park Mall Youngstown OH 44512

MANGOLD, JOHN EARL, banker; b. Ryan, Iowa, Nov. 19, 1924; s. Raymond E. and Blanche M. (McEnany) M.; B.S. in Commerce, U. Iowa, 1950, J.D., 1953; grad. U. Wis. Sch. Banking, 1961; certificate Am. Inst. Banking, 1962; m. Mary Veronica Duggan, Aug. 20, 1947; with Mchts. Nat. Bank, Cedar Rapids, Iowa, 1953—, asst. cashier, 1959-61, v.p., 1961-70, sr. v.p., 1970—. Vice pres. Banks of Iowa Inc., 1970. Served with 106 Inf. div., AUS, 1944-46. Recipient Fetzer Meml. award Cedar Rapids Jr. C. of C., 1955; certified comml. lender. Mem. Am., Iowa State bar assns., Am. Inst. Banking (chpt. founder, charter pres. 1954, dist. asso. councilman 1958-61), Phi Alpha Delta. Republican. Roman Catholic. Elk, K.C. Club: University Athletic (Iowa City, Iowa). Home: 306 Red Fox Rd SE Cedar Rapids IA 52403 Office: Mchts Nat Bank Cedar Rapids IA 52401

MANHEIM, THEODORE, librarian; b. Detroit, July 21, 1921; s. Louis and Frances (Kellman) M.; B.A., Wayne State U., 1943; B.L.S., U. Mich., 1947, M.L.S., 1948; m. Rose Jaffe, Oct. 7, 1950 (dec. Nov. 1966); children—Rhonda, Sandra, Bruce. Head ednl. div. Wayne State U. Libraries, Detroit, 1949—, cooperating faculty, 1961—; vis. lectr. U. So. Fla., Tampa, 1964, 71; mem. exec. bd. Detroit Children's Book Fair, 1963-68. Trustee John H. Trybom Meml. Collections, Dept. Indsl. Edn., Wayne State U. Served with AUS, 1943-45. Mem. AAUP. Author: Culturally Disadvantaged: A KWOC Index, 1966; Sources in Educational Research, 1969; reviewer Am. Reference Books Ann., 1970—. Home: 20230 Annchester St Detroit MI 48219

MANIS, LAURA GLANCE, counselor; b. Chgo., May 25, 1924; d. Nathan and Minnie (Walters) Glance; B.Edn., Chgo. Tchrs. Coll., 1945; M.A., Western Mich. U., 1965; m. Jerome G. Manis, May 31, 1949; children—Robert Manis, Lisa Manis. Personnel dir. Doctors Hosp., N.Y.C., 1949-51; counselor Climax-Scotts High Sch., Climax, Mich., 1965-66; counseling psychologist Western Mich. U., Kalamazoo, 1966—, dir. Center for Womens Services, 1975—. cons. in field; dir. Kalamazoo Consultation Center, 1976-79; dir. Planned Parenthood Mich., 1975-78. Danforth grantee, 1975-76. Mem. League Women Voters (pres. 1964-67), ACLU Southwestern Mich. (v.p. 1974-75), Am., Mich. personnel and guidance assns., Assn. for Specialists in Group Work, Am. Coll. Personnel Assn., Mich. Assn. for Specialists in Group Work, N.O.W. Democrat. Author: Womanpower: A Manual for Workshops in Personal Effectiveness, 1977; contbr. articles to profl. jours. Home: 3607 Middlebury Rd Kalamazoo MI 49007 Office: Counseling Center Western Mich Univ Kalamazoo MI 49008

MANLEY, MYRL OTIS, coll. pres.; b. Stockton, Ill., July 11, 1913; s. Otis Albert and Katie C. (Nadig) M.; B.A., Emmanuel Missionary Coll., 1935; postgrad. U. Mich., 1935; M.A., Pacific Union Coll., 1948; Ed.S., Stanford, 1956, M.A.T., 1964, Ph.D., 1966; m. Gertrude Elizabeth Sherman, Aug. 19, 1934; children—James Otis, Robert Elliott. Tchr. Cedar Lake (Mich.) Acad., 1935-40, Vincent Hill Sch. and Coll., India, 1941-43; pres. Spicer Meml. Coll., Kirkee, India, 1944-46, Burma Union of Seventh-day Adventists, 1946-51; prin. Vincent Hill Sch., India, 1952-62; chmn. dept. world mission and comparative religions Andrews U., Berrien Springs, Mich., 1966-69, v.p. student affairs, 1969-73; pres. Union Coll., Lincoln, Nebr., 1973—. Mem. Am. Assn. Sch. Adminstrs., Phi Delta Kappa. Home: 4840 Bancroft St Lincoln NE 68506

MANLEY, ROBERT EDWARD, lawyer, economist; b. Cin., Nov. 24, 1935; s. John M. and Helen (McCarthy) M.; B.S., Xavier U., 1956; M.A., U. Cin., 1957; J.D., Harvard U., 1960; student London Sch. Econs. and Polit. Sci., 1960; m. Roberta Anzinger, 1972. Teaching fellow econs. U. Cin., 1956-57; admitted to Ohio bar, 1960; since practiced in Cin. Adj. prof. econs. Xavier U., 1962-73; lectr. law Salmon P. Chase Law Sch., 1965-73; vis. lectr. community planning U. Cin., 1967-73, adj. asso. prof. urban planning, 1973—. Chmn. environ. adv. council City of Cin., 1975-76. Trustee Hope Cincinnati, Albert J. Ryan Found., Cin. Legal Aid Soc.; mem. Pub. Defender Commn. Hamilton County (Ohio), 1976—. Served to capt. AUS. 1961. Fellow Cin. Coll. Philosophers; mem. Am., Ohio, Cin. bar assns., Am. Judicature Soc., Law and Society Assn., Am. Econ. Assn., Am. Acad. Polit. and Social Scis., Xavier, Cin. alumni assns., Harvard U. Law Sch. Assn., Alpha Sigma Nu (nat. dir. 1966-76), Tau Kappa Alpha, Omicron Delta Epsilon, Phi Alpha Delta. Republican. Roman Catholic. Clubs: Queen City, Harvard. Contbr. articles to profl. jours. Home: Dexter and Wold Cincinnati OH 45206 Office: Carew Tower Cincinnati OH 45202

MANLEY, THOMAS ROGER, educator; b. Yonkers, N.Y., June 26, 1935; s. Samuel Roger and Agnes Teresa (Sullivan) M.; B.S., U.S. Naval Acad., 1958; M.S., Rensselaer Poly. Inst., 1965, Ph.D., 1972; m. Eleyse Therese Connell, June 7, 1958; children—Robert C., Catherine A., Joan M., Thomas Roger. Missile devel. engr., mgr. Cape Canaveral, Fla., also Vandenberg AFB, Cal., 1958-62; missile combat crew comdr. SAC, Denver, 1962-64; chief systems integration Titan III Space Launch Vehicle, Cape Canaveral, Fla., 1965-69; prof. mgmt. and organizational behavior Air Force Inst. Tech., 1972—, internal cons. U.S. Air Force, 1972—; cons. Mich. Bell, N.Y. Telephone. Served with USAF, 1958—. Fellow Inter-Univ. Seminar Armed Forces and Soc. Mem. Acad. Mgmt., Am. Psychol. Assn., Am. Inst. Decision Scis., U.S. Naval Inst., U.S. Naval Acad. Alumni Assn., Epsilon Delta Sigma, Alpha Iota Delta. Republican. Roman Catholic. Home: 1188 Rona Pkwy Dr Fairborn OH 45324 Office: Air Force Inst Tech Wright Patterson AFB OH 45433

MANN, DAVID DOUGLAS, English scholar, educator; b. Oklahoma City, Sept. 13, 1934; s. Loftin Harry and Jeannette (Kneer) Mann-Lackey; B.S., Okla. State U., 1956, M.A., 1963; Ph.D., Ind. U., 1969; m. Catherine Elizabeth Hoyser, June 18, 1972. Instr., Leelanau Schs., Glen Arbor, Mich., 1962-63; instr. Wabash Coll., 1965-67; asso. prof. English, Miami U., Oxford, Ohio, 1968—; cons. Am. Assn. Higher Edn. Vice pres. Oxford (Ohio) Chamber Symphony, 1969-70. Served with USNR, 1956-59. Folger Shakespeare Library fellow, 1970; Miami U. Research grantee, 1973, 77; Nat. Endowment for the Humanities grantee, 1976. Mem. Modern Lang. Assn., Midwestern Modern. Lang. Assn., Charles Lamb Soc., Samuel Johnson Soc. of Midwest, Childrens Literature Nat. Assn. Editor: A Concordance To the Plays of William Congreve, 1973; asst. editor: Old Northwest, 1975—; contbr. articles in field to profl. jours. Home: 327 E Vine St Oxford OH 45056 Office: English Department Miami University Oxford OH 45056

MANN, DONALD NATHANIEL, broadcasting exec.; b. Chgo., Dec. 15, 1920; s. Henry J. and Rose (Bonner) M.; B.S., Northwestern U., 1942; M.A., Columbia U., 1946; J.D., John Marshall Law Sch., 1948; m. Rhoda Fiener, Nov. 8, 1952; children—Gary Kevin, Eric Scott, Holly Jada. Program dir., asst. communications mgr. KWWL, Waterloo, Iowa, 1948-49; gen. mgr. comml. mgr. WKNK, Muskegon, Mich., 1949-51; account exec. WBBM Radio & TV CBS, Chgo., 1951-54; gen. mgr. WOKY-TV, Milw., 1954; mgr. spl. projects, account exec. WBBM Radio, 1954—; prof. communications Columbia Coll., Chgo., 1967; dir. Cosmopolitan Bank and Trust Co.; pres. Am. Coll. Radio Arts, Crafts and Scis., Chgo., 1961—. Asst. chmn. communications div. Combined Jewish Appeal, Chgo., 1959-69; dir. Niles Township (Ill.) Community Concerts, 1961—; co-chmn. Red Feather Dr., Chgo., 1960; pres. Timber Ridge Home Owners, Skokie, Ill., 1957-60; mem. Chgo. Council on Fgn. Relations, 1965—, Chgo. Crime Commn.; pres. Bus. and Profl. Men City of Hope Chgo., 1961; chmn. humanitarian awards Easter Seals, 1977—; hon. chmn. Am. Diabetes Bike-A-Thon, 1977; pres. Skokie (Ill.) Caucus Party, 1957-64; master Chancery Village Ct. of Skokie, 1962; police and fire commr. Skokie, 1965; pres. Deere Park, 1970—; trustee, chmn. 50th ann. com., dir. research bd. Mt. Sinai Hosp.; trustee John Marshall Law Sch. Served with AUS, 1942-46. Named Radio Man of Year, Am. Coll. Radio, 1964; recipient Distinguished Alumni award John Marshall Law Sch., 1968; trustee Columbia Coll. Mem. Ill. State, Am., 7th Fed. Dist., Chgo. bar assns., Am. Fedn. Musicians, Am. Judicature Soc., Sales Execs. Club, Alpha Sigma Iota, Grocery Sales Mfg. Execs., John Marshall Alumni Assn. (pres. 1971—), Decalogue Soc., Am. Legion, Jewish War Vets., Merchandising Execs. Club. Jewish (trustee temple). Clubs: Elks, B'nai B'rith, Standard, Variety Chgo. Co-author: Pvt. Droop Has Lost The War, 1944; author: History of Sault St Marie; How to Become Your Company's Top Salesman through Showmanship. Home: 111 S Deere Park Dr Highland Park IL 60035 Office: WBBM Radio CBS 630 N McClurg Ct Chicago IL 60611

MANN, JOHN C., lawyer; b. Latham, Ill., Oct. 12, 1898; s. Frank and Josephine (Canary) M.; student James Millikin U., 1917-19; J.D., U. Ill., 1922; m. Irene Watkins, Mar. 26, 1927; 1 dau., Linda. Admitted to Ill. bar, 1922; practiced law in Decatur, Ill., 1923-34; law dept. Chgo. Title & Trust Co., Chgo., 1934-63, asso. gen. counsel, 1960-63. Served pvt. U.S. Army, World War I. Mem. Ill., Chgo. bar assns., Order of Coif, Sigma Alpha Epsilon, Phi Delta Phi. Club: Glen Oak Country. Author: Title Examinations Involving Chancery Proceedings, 1948; Illinois Chancery Procedure and Forms, 1969; Escrows; Their Use and Value, 1949, 75; Joint Tenancies Today, 1956; Is Joint Tenancy the Answer, 1953; Joint Tenancy and Survivorship Problems in Estate Planning, 1975. Editor: (with John Norton Pomeroy, Jr.) Pomeroy's Specific Performance of Contracts, 3d edit., 1926. Contbr. various articles to legal publs. Home: 515 N Main St Apt 3CS Glen Ellyn IL 60137 Office: 111 W Washington St Chicago IL 60602

MANN, JOHN MC GREGOR, lawyer; b. Chgo., June 25, 1924; s. Lester Bradwell and Helen Barbara (Moore) M.; B.S. in Mech. Engring., B.S. in Bus., U. Colo., 1949; J.D., Georgetown U., 1952; M.P.L., John Marshall Law Sch., 1958; m. Grace E. Reed, June 16, 1956 (dec. May 22, 1976); children—John McGregor, Kathryn Alice; m. 2d, Elsie W. Cox, Dec. 19, 1976. Civil engr. Hughes Constrn. Co., Washington, 1949-50; typist U.S. Patent Office, Washington, 1950, patent examiner, 1951-52; admitted to Ill. bar, 1953; patent lawyer Brown, Jackson, Boettcher & Dienner, Chgo., 1952-54; patent lawyer McWilliams and Mann, Chgo., 1954—, partner, 1957—. Sec. C.A. Young Products Corp. Vice pres. Prospect Sch. PTA, Clarendon Hills, Ill., 1964-65, pres., 1965-66; pack chmn. Cub Scout Pack 251, Clarendon Hills, 1967-68; vice chmn. Clarendon Hills Community Caucus, 1969-70, chmn., 1971-72; chmn. Clarendon Hills Zoning Bd. Appeals, 1973-74, mem. plan commn., 1975—. Served with C.E., AUS, 1943-45. Recipient Eagle Scout award Boy Scouts Am., 1938. Mem. Am., Ill., Chgo. bar assns., Am., Chgo. (treas. 1973-74) patent law assns., Christian Legal Soc. (dir. 1969-72), ASME, Chgo. Engrs. Club, Chgo. Natural History Mus., Am. Legion, Patent Office Soc. Washington, Kappa Sigma, Delta Theta Phi. Republican. Episcopalian. Clubs: Union League (Chgo.); Three Lakes (Wis.) Rod and Gun (sec.-treas. 1976—). Co-author: Patent, Trademark and Copyright Tax Guide, 1965, rev. edit., 1970. Contbr. articles profl. jours. Home: 41 Golf Ave Clarendon Hills IL 60514 Office: 53 W Jackson Blvd Chicago IL 60604

MANN, RICHARD EUGENE, psychiatrist; b. Muncie, Ind., Dec. 25, 1931; s. George and Louise (Wellinger) M.; B.S., Ball State U., 1956; M.D., Ind. U., 1957; m. Barbara Jean Irwin, June 27, 1954; children—Richard Eugene, Kimila Sue, Kurt, Douglas, Kara Lynn. Resident in psychiatry Ind. U. Med. Center Hosps., 1958-61; pvt. practice psychiatry, Fort Wayne, Ind., 1963—; pres. Psychiat. Services, Inc., Fort Wayne, 1973—. Cons. Chatham County (Ga.) Mental Health Clinic, 1961-63. Mem. Internat. Assn. Applied Hypnosis, AMA, Am. Psychiat. Assn., Am., Internat. group psychotherapy assns., Ind. State Med. Assn. Rotarian. Served with USNR, 1961-63. Home: 1316 Old Lantern Trail Fort Wayne IN 46825 Office: 1405 N Anthony Blvd Fort Wayne IN 46805

MANN, ROBERT DAVID, lawyer; b. Chgo., May 27, 1941; s. Robert Lewis and Leona (Merillat) M.; B.A., Depauw U., 1963; J.D., Ind. U., 1966. Admitted to Ind. bar, 1966, practiced in Bloomington; partner firm Baker, Barnhart, Andrews, Baker & Mann, 1966-73, Cotner, Mann & Chapman, 1974—. Pres. bd. Monroe County Mental Health Clinic; bd. dirs. Monroe County Mental Health Assn.; chmn. Bloomington Bd. Pub. Safety, 1973—. Mem. Am., Ind., Monroe County bar assns., Ind. Trial Lawyers Assn., Greater Bloomington C. of C. (sec., dir. 1971-74), Delta Chi, Phi Delta Phi. Mason. Office: PO Box 176 Bloomington IN 47401

MANN, SUSIE HAIRE, ednl. counselor; b. Scooba, Miss., Apr. 28, 1929; d. Thomas and Deseree (Birch) Haire; B.S., Tuskegee Inst., 1951, M.S., 1952; M.A., St. Louis U., 1971, also postgrad.; m. George L. Mann, July 6, 1961; children—Doris Elise, Lucia Carol. Instr., dietitian Jackson (Miss.) Coll., 1952-54; tchr. East St. Louis, Ill., 1954-70, counselor high sch., 1970—; cons. in field. Active University City Library, PTA, Assn. Retarded Children. Carnegie Found fellow, 1950-51; James Fund grantee, 1952. Mem. Mo. Assn. Social Welfare (pres. St. Louis Bridge unit 1976—), Am. Bridge Assn. (sr. life master), Am. Fedn. Tchrs., Am., Mo., Ill. personnel and guidance assns., St. Clair County Tchrs. Planning Inst.-County Mental Health Bd., NAACP, League Women Voters, Tuskegee Alumni Assn. (life), Alpha Kappa Alpha, Beta Kappa Chi. Democrat. Methodist. Home: 8303 Amherst St St Louis MO 63132 Office: 910 Summit St East St Louis IL 62201

MANNARINO, ANTONIO DOMENICO, physician; b. Crotone, Italy, Nov. 20, 1927; s. Antonio G. and Eugenia (Borrelli) M.; came to U.S., 1952, naturalized, 1957; M.D., U. Bari (Italy), 1951; m. Catherine Colosimo, Dec. 31, 1952; children—Maria, Eugenia, Antonio Domenico, Francesco. Intern, St. Elizabeth Hosp., 1953-55; resident VA Hosp., Dayton, Ohio, 1958-61, Ohio State U., Columbus, 1961-63; dir. clin. labs. Greene Meml. Hosp., Xenia, Ohio, 1963—, Clinton Meml. Hosp., Wilmington, Ohio, 1967—; asso. clin. prof. pathology Wright State U., Dayton, 1976—; clin. instr. pathology Ohio State U. Med. Sch., Columbus, 1963—. Bd. dirs. Dayton chpt. ARC, 1972. Fellow Coll. Am. Pathologists, Am. Soc. Clin. Pathologists; mem. Ordine Dei Medici of Italy, Ohio Med. Assn., Ohio Soc. Pathologists, Greene County Med. Soc. (past pres., del.). Roman Catholic. Club: Xenia Rotary. Home: 2970 Cathy Ln Dayton OH 45429 Office: Greene Meml Hosp Xenia OH 45385

MANNE, MARSHALL STANLEY, periodontist; b. St. Louis, Nov. 16, 1933; s. Emil and Lillian (Iuster) M.; A.B., Washington U., St. Louis, 1956, D.D.S., 1960; M.S. in Periodontia, Ind. U., 1964; children—Matthew Jared, Malissa Beth. Individual practice periodontia, St. Louis, 1964—; instr. Ind. U., 1963-64; asst. prof. Washington U., 1964-69, asso. prof., 1969—; mem. staff Belleville Meml., St. Elizabeth, Faith, Deaconess hosps., St. Louis; cons. dental detachment Scott AFB. Mem. Mo. State Bd.; bd. dirs. Greater St. Louis Dental Soc. Served to capt. AUS, 1960-62. Diplomate Am. Bd. Periodontology. Mem. Am. Dental Assn., Am. Acad. Periodontology, Am. Acad. Oral Pathology, Internat. Assn. Dental Research, Midwest, Ill., Mo. socs. periodontology, St. Louis Soc. Dental Research. Home: 14475 Greencastle St Louis MO 63017 Office: 777 S New Ballas St Louis MO 63141

MANNEY, RUSSELL FIELD, JR., printing co. exec.; b. Detroit, Oct. 11, 1933; s. Russell Field and Mildred Allison (Lamb) M.; student Trinity Coll., 1950-51; B.B.A., U. Detroit, 1959; postgrad. Mich. Sch. Theology, 1963-68; m. Mary Janet Fairbanks, June 9, 1955; children—Russell III, Timothy, Thomas. Controller, City of Troy, Mich., 1959-61, City of Grosse Pointe Woods, Mich., 1961-64; city mgr., Harper Woods, Mich., 1964-68; pres. Prescot Press, Inc., Roseville, Mich., 1968—. Pub. accountant, 1959—; treas., dir. Metamora Hills, Inc., Metamora, Mich., 1965—; instr. Wayne State U., 1971-72. Leader, Cub Scouts, Boy Scouts Am., Harper Woods, 1973-76; mem. Harper Woods Dads' Club, 1973—. Bd. dirs. Harper Woods Citizens for Good Govt., 1969-70. Mem. Roseville C. of C. (sec., dir.), Detroit Club Printing House Craftsmen. Episcopalian (finance chmn. Mich. diocese chpt., vestryman, dir. religious edn. 1973—, ch. treas. 1971—). Home: 18987 Huntington Harper Woods MI 48225 Office: 17971 Eleven Mile Roseville MI 48066

MANNING, JOHN WARREN, III, surgeon, educator; b. Phila., Nov. 24, 1919; s. John Warren and Edith Margaret (Reagan) M.; M.D., U. Pa., 1943; m. Muriel Elizabeth Johnson, Oct. 11, 1944; children—John Warren, Melissa Ann, Susan Jane. Intern, VA Hosp., Phila., 1944; practice medicine specializing in surgery, Saginaw, Mich., 1946-47; resident in surgery, Saginaw Gen. Hosp., also U. Mich., 1947-50; practice medicine specializing in surgery, Saginaw, 1950—; asso. clin. prof. surgery Mich. State U.; mem. active and sr. staff Saginaw Gen. Hosp., St. Luke Hosp., St. Marys Hosp.; cons. VA Hosp. Served with M.C. USN, 1944-46. Diplomate Am. Bd. Surgery. Fellow A.C.S., Am. Soc. Abdominal Surgeons, Am. Coll. Angiology. Home: 203 Ardussi St Saginaw MI 48602

MANNING, OWEN DUNCAN, utilities co. exec.; b. Turnersville, Ky., Oct. 18, 1920; s. George E. and Grace Lee (Baugh) M.; B.E.E., U. Ky., Lexington, 1939; m. Sue Ella Reynolds, Sept. 2, 1942; children—Bonnie, Jeannie, Michael, Deborah. Chief engr. Fleming-Mason Elec. Coop., Flemingsburg, Ky., 1948-50; instr. Ohio State U., 1950-55; gen. mgr. Frontier Power Co., Coshocton, Ohio, 1955—; v.p. Nat. Rural Utilities Coop. Fin. Corp., 1971—; dir. Ohio Rural Electric Supply Corp., Buckeye Power, Inc., 1st Nat. Bank Coshocton. Pres. Coshocton County Regional Planning Commn., 1967-76; mem. Coshocton County Airport Authority, 1965—; bd. dirs. Coshocton County Meml. Hosp., 1972—; past pres., dir. Muskingum Valley council Boy Scouts Am., 1955. Served in U.S. Army, 1942-45. Decorated Purple Heart; recipient Silver Beaver award Boy Scouts Am., 1957; Good Will Ambassador award Coshocton Area C. of C., 1969; Outstanding Service award Nat. Rural Electric Corp., 1964. Mem. Ohio Rural Electric Mgrs. Assn., C. of C. Coshocton (pres. 1966), Rotary, Farm Bur., Cosocton Grange. Democrat. Mem. Central Christian Ch. Contbr. articles in field to profl. jours. Home: Route #1 Coshocton OH 43812 Office: 770 S 2d St Coshocton OH 43812

MANSAGER, FELIX NORMAN, appliance mfg. co. exec.; b. Dell Rapids, S.D., Jan. 30, 1911; s. Hoff and Alice (Qualseth) M.; LL.D., Capital U., 1967, Strathclyde U. (Scotland), 1970; D.H.L. (hon.), Malone Coll., 1972; Pd.D. (hon.), Walsh Coll., 1974; H.H.D., Wartburg Coll., Waverly, Iowa, 1976; m. Geraldine Larson, July 5, 1931; children—Donna (Mrs. Harlan Hogsven), Eva Kay (Mrs. Walter Sieverts), Douglas Norman. With Hoover Co., 1929—, v.p. sales, North Canton, Ohio, 1959-61, exec. v.p., 1961-63, exec. v.p. Hoover Group, 1963-66, pres., chmn. bd., Hoover Co./Hoover Worldwide Corp., 1966-75, now mem. exec. com., dir., 1976—; dir. Harter Bank & Trust Co. Trustee-at-large, mem. exec. com. Ind. Coll. Funds Am.; trustee Grad. theol. Union Cal., Eisenhower Exchange Fellowships, Gustavus Adolphus Coll., Augustana Coll., Sioux Falls, S.D. Ohio Found. Ind. Colls.; bd. govs. Ditchley Found. Decorated chevalier Legion of Honor (France); Knight Order Brit. Empire; chevalier Order Leopold (Belgium); Knight 1st class Order St. Olav (Norway); Order al Merito (Italy); grand officer Dukes Burgundy; recipient awards Brit. Inst. Marketing, 1971, Canton C. of C., 1971, Vassa U. (Finland) Medal of Honor, 1972. Fellow Univ. Coll., Wales. Mem. Council on Fgn. Relations, Pilgrims U.S., Newcomen Soc. in N.Am., World League Norsemen (hon.), Assn. Ohio Commodores, Beta Sigma Gamma (hon.). Mason (32 deg.), Rotarian. Clubs: Congress Lake Country (Canton, Ohio); Metropolitan (N.Y.C.) (Washington). Home: 3421 Lindel Ct NW Canton OH 44718

MANSDORF, SEYMOUR ZACK, indsl., environ. health scientist; b. Akron, Ohio, Jan. 6, 1947; s. William and Dorothy M.; B.A., U. Akron, 1969; M.S., U. Mich., 1972; postgrad. Drexel U., 1974-75; m. Marsha Bennington, Dec. 23, 1968; children—Brett Edward, Bart Allen. Group leader biomed. research U. Akron, 1968-69, ops. mgr., 1969-71; programmer U. Mich., Ann Arbor, 1972-73; scientist, trustee Creative Biology Lab., Barberton, Ohio, 1976—; lectr., cons. in field. Trustee Forest Hills Co-op., 1972. Served to capt., Med. Service Corps., U.S. Army, 1973-76. USPHS grantee, 1972. Mem. Am. Inst. Biol. Scis., Ohio Acad. Scis., Am. Pub. Health Assn., Nat. Environ. Health Assn., AAAS, Am. Indsl. Hygiene Assn., Phi Sigma, Lambda Chi Alpha. Lutheran. Research in slow-release, especially to control aquatic weeds. Patentee in field. Home: 2455 Deepridge Circle Akron OH 44313 Office: Creative Biology Lab 3070 Cleveland-Massillon Rd Barberton OH 44203

MANSEN, HARRY G., patent counselor; b. Boras, Sweden, July 16, 1900; s. Carl Albin and Gerda Josefina (Bergstrand) M.; grad. mech. engring. Chalmers Inst. Tech. (Sweden), 1922; LL.B., LaSalle Extension U., Chgo., 1965; m. Lennah Dale Johnston, June 9, 1951; children—Anne Sophie (Mrs. Fred Lundquist), David Joel. Came to U.S., 1940, naturalized, 1952. Pvt. engring. practice, Sweden and U.S., 1922-27; tchr., dean engring. Engring. Schs., Katrineholm and Malmo, Sweden, 1927-30; asso. firm A.W. Anderson, Patentbyra, Malmo also Stockholm, Sweden, 1930-34; owner H.G. Mansens Patentbyra, Malmo, 1934-40; internat. patent cons., Chgo. also Evanston, Ill., 1940—; chief patent dept. Elgin Softener Corp. (Ill.), 1942-49; chief patent dept., Edwards Valves Inc., East Chicago, Ind., 1951-56; with Singer, Stern & Carlberg (merged with Hill, Gross, Simpson, Van Santen, Steadman, Chiara & Simpson 1972), attys. and counsellors at Law, Chgo., 1951—. Mem. Internat. Patent and Trademark Assn., Nat. Patent Council, Chalmers Engrs. Soc., Swedish Engrs. Soc. Chgo., U.S. Patent Office Bar, Internat. Platform Assn., Am.-Scandinavian Found., Conglist. Author: Boilers, 1931; Heating, Ventilation and Sanitation, 1932. Patentee water conditioner valves. Home: 1312 Livingston St Evanston IL 60201 Office: Sears Tower 233 S Wacker Dr Chicago IL 60606

MANSER, GEORGE ROBERT, ins. co. exec.; b. Mpls., May 7, 1931; s. George Louis and Helen Blanche (Krusemark) M.; A.A., B.S., U. Minn., 1958; M.B.A., Capitol U., 1974; m. Jeanne De Wolf Seebe, June 21, 1952; children—Richard Louis, Ronald Alan, Pamela Ann, Michael Wayne. Youth dir. Union Congl. Ch., Mpls., 1955-58; exec. dir. Minn. Republican Party, 1958-61; adminstrv. asst. Gov. Minn., 1961-63; ins. salesman, sales mgr. N.Am. Equitable Life Assurance Co., Columbus, Ohio, 1964-68, pres., 1969—; pres. Brookings Internat. Life Ins. Co. (S.D.), 1968—; pres., chief exec. officer, dir. N.Am. Nat. Corp.; dir. N.Am. Equitable Life Assurance Co., Brookings Internat. Life Ins. Co., Asset Data Systems, Inc., Parkview Nursing Home, Cardinal Foods, Inc., Redding Inc. Extradition referee State of Minn., 1961-63; mem. Met. Airports Commn., 1966-67. Former trustee Yankton (S.D.) Coll.; former chmn. bd. trustees Found. N. Congl. Ch. Columbus. Served with USAF, 1951-55. Mem. Nat. Assn. Life Underwriters, Newcomen Soc. Mem. United Ch. of Christ. Mason. Club: Worthington Hills Country. Home: 756 Highland Dr Columbus OH 43214 Office: 1015 E Broad St Columbus OH 43205

MANSFIELD, LOIS EDNA, educator, mathematician; b. Portland, Maine, Jan. 2, 1941; d. Robert Carleton and Mary Josephine (Bowdish) Mansfield; B.S., U. Mich., 1962; M.S., U. Utah, 1966, Ph.D., 1969. Tchr. Rowland Hall-St. Marks Sch., Salt Lake City, 1962-65; vis. asst. prof. Purdue U., 1969-70; asst. prof. computer sci. U. Kans., 1970-74, asso. prof., 1974—; vis. asst. prof. math. U. Utah, 1973-74, NASA trainee, 1967-69 vis. scientist Institute for Computer Applications in sci. and engring. NASA, 1977; mem. advisory panel computer sci. and engring. NSF, 1975—. Mem. Am. Math. Soc., Assn. Computing Machinery, Soc. Indsl. and Applied Math. Contbr. articles to profl. jours. Home: DD 211 Bristol Terrace Lawrence KS 66044 Office: Dept Computer Sci Univ of Kansas Lawrence KS 66045

MAPLE, FRANCIS MARION, gastroenterologist; b. Spiceland, Ind., Mar. 28, 1922; s. Fredrick Marion and Dora Belle (Wagoner) M.; B.S., Ind. U., 1946, M.D., 1950; m. Margaret Ruth Feeny, July 28, 1946; children—John Fredrick, Margaret Anne, Louise Kay, Thomas Edward. Intern, U. Wash. Hosp., Seattle, 1950-51, resident in internal medicine and gastroenterology, 1951-54; cons. in gastroenterology and internal medicine Smith-Glynn-Callaway Clinic, Springfield, Mo., 1954—; cons. in gastroenterology U.S. Med. Center, Springfield, 1970—; chief of staff St. John's Hosp., Springfield, 1969-71; pres. Mo. Health Data Corp., Jefferson City, Mo.; clin. asso. prof. gastroenterology U. Mo., Kansas City. Pres., Springfield Area Council of Chs., 1970-72. Served with USN, 1943-46. Diplomate Am. Bd. Internal Medicine. Fellow Am. Coll. Gastroenterology, A.C.P.; mem. AMA, Mo. State Med. Assn., Greene County Med. Soc., Royal Soc. Medicine, Am., Mo. (pres. 1969-71) socs. internal medicine. Republican. Episcopalian. Clubs: Hickory Hills Country, Kiwanis (pres. 1959) (Springfield). Home: 2115 E Edgewood Springfield MO 65804 Office: 1211 S Glenstone St Springfield MO 65804

MAPLES, JERRY STEVEN, banker; b. Grinnell, Iowa, Sept. 16, 1939; s. Grant Marvin and La Dean Frances (Schultz) M.; B.A. in Bus. Adminstrn., Cornell Coll., 1961; M.A. in Mktg., U. Iowa, 1964; postgrad seminars Northwestern U., U. Wis., U. Iowa, Harvard; m. Judith Rae Bezanson, July 3, 1964; children—Jeffrey, Jason, Joy. Mgmt. trainee Eastman Kodak Co., Rochester, N.Y., 1964-65, Continental Ill. Nat. Bank & Trust Co., Chgo., 1965-66; pres. and chief exec. officer Jackson State Bank, Maquoketa, Iowa, 1966—, asst. v.p., 1966-68, v.p., 1968-72, trust officer, 1966-72, exec. v.p., 1971-74, also dir.; dir. MorAm. Fin. Corp., Cedar Rapids, Iowa, First Trust & Savs. Bank, Wheatland, Iowa. Chmn., dir. Jackson County Cancer Soc., 1967-71; bd. dirs. Jackson County Red Cross, 1974-75, Maquoketa Indsl. Devel. Com., 1968-70, Timber City Devel. Corp., 1971—. Served with AUS, 1961-62. Mem. Am., Iowa (lobbyist to state legis.) bankers assns., Bank Adminstrn. Inst. (v.p. and dir. Eastern Iowa chpt. 1975—). Methodist. Club: Rotary. Contbr. articles to profl. jours. Home: 806 Country Club Dr Maquoketa IA 52060 Office: 120 S Main St Maquoketa IA 52060

MAPLES, ROBERT HENRY, design engr.; b. Little Rock, Jan. 28, 1939; s. Robert Thomas and Mandy Marie (Fowler) M.; student pub. schs., Little Rock; m. Patricia Helen Wampole, June 6, 1975; children—Robert, Maureen; stepchildren—Craig, Brian, Kevin. Controller supr. satellite tracking network Bendix Corp., Greenbelt, Md., 1963-67; mission support programmer RCA, Greenbelt, 1968-71; sr. asso. engr. Litton Industries, College Park, Md., 1972-73; sr. systems software design engr. Systems Tech. Assos., Falls Church, Va., 1973-75; sr. systems design engr. ITT, Des Plaines, Ill., 1975—. Served with AUS, 1957-63. Network controller and mission controller, NASA, Apollo 11 moon launch. Mem. Amateur Satellite Corp. (founding), Rock Creek Amateur Radio Club. Democrat. Methodist. Home: 1125 Price Dr Elgin IL 60120 Office: 2000 S Wolf Rd Des Plaines IL 60018

MARBLE, EDWIN JOHNSTON, urologist; b. Liscomb, Iowa, Feb. 20, 1907; s. Pearl Leonidas and Telena Estella (Johnston) M.; B.A., U. Iowa, 1928, M.D., 1931; m. Patricia Mary Reynolds, June 25, 1943; children—Michael Raymond, Jennifer Mary. Intern, Charity Hsop., New Orleans, 1931-33, resident, 1935-37; practice medicine, Liscomb, 1933-35, specializing in surgery and urology, Marshalltown, Iowa, 1937-60, specializing in urology, 1960-77; mem. staffs Marshalltown Hosp., Newton Hosp., Grinnell Hosp. Served with USMC, 1941-46. Diplomate Am. Bd. Urology. Mem. Am. Urol. Assn., Am. Assn. Clin. Urologists, Pan Am. Med. Soc., Iowa Med. Soc., Iowa Urological Soc. Republican. Episcopalian. Clubs: Lions (pres. 1957), Masons. Contbr. articles to profl. jours. Home: 1710 W Lincolnway Marshalltown IA 50158 Office: 112 S 2d Ave Marshalltown IA 50158

MARCH, KENNETH ALAN, research co. exec.; b. Chgo., Jan. 14, 1948; s. Joseph Frank and Mary Ann (Swistek) Marciniak; B.S. cum laude, Loyola U. (Chgo.), 1969, M.A., 1972, Ph.D. summa cum laude, 1973; m. Mary Marchlewski, 1973. With Chgo. Read Mental Health Center, 1971-72; research asst. dept. psychology, Loyola U., Chgo., 1972-73, lectr. in psychology, 1973; account research mgr. Sieber & McIntyre, Inc., Chgo., 1973-76, dir. market research, 1977—. Arthur J. Schmitt fellow, 1972-73. Mem. Am. Psychol. Assn., Ill. Psychol. Assn., Midwestern Psychol. Assn., Am. Marketing Assn., Evanston Tennis Assn. Club: Touhy Tennis. Contbr. articles in field to profl. jours. Home: 944 Michigan Ave Evanston IL 60202 Office: 625 N Michigan Ave Chicago IL 60611

MARCHI, MICHAEL, physician, surgeon; b. Capannori, Italy, June 5, 1932; s. Narciso and Elisa (Fontana) M.; came to U.S., 1957, naturalized, 1963; student U. Pisa (Italy), 1951-57; M.D., U. Ill., 1963; m. Elizabeth F. Domingsil; children—Michaela Andria, Michael Paul. Practice medicine specializing in family practice, Chgo., 1966—; attending physician Resurrection, Ravenswood, St. Elizabeth hosps., Chgo.; clin. asso. in medicine Abraham Lincoln Sch. Medicine, Chgo., 1972—. Diplomate Am. Bd. Family Practice. Fellow Am. Acad. Family Physicians; mem. AMA, Ill., Chgo. med. socs., Soc. Tchrs. Family Medicine. Office: 7407 W Irving Park Rd Chicago IL 60634

MARCHMAN, MARTHA JEAN DAWSON, civic worker; b. Muncie, Ind., Aug. 15, 1915; d. Emmet H. and Elsie (Fields) Dawson; student Ind. U., 1941-42; m. Watt Pearson Marchman, Nov. 27, 1963; children—Susan Jean (dec.), David Watt. Asst. supr. Ohio Bell Telephone Co., Tiffin, 1934-40; credit mgr. Sears, Roebuck & Co., Tiffin, 1959-61; teller First Nat. Bank, Tiffin, 1961-63. Chmn. landscape com. Met. Park Bd. Adv. Com., 1971-74. Mem. Fremont (pres. 1971-73, trustee), Lakeside (auditor 1975, pres. 1977) fedns. women, Audubon Soc. (charter mem., dir. Pres. R.B. Hayes chpt. 1970-73). Republican. Club: Cosmopolitan (sec. 1967-69, auditor 1975-76) (Fremont, Ohio). Home: 1500 Buckland Ave Fremont OH 43420

MARCHMAN, WATT P(EARSON), librarian, historian; b. Eatonton, Ga., Sept. 1, 1911; s. Watt Pearson and Mary (Hudson) M.; A.B., Rollins Coll., 1933, A.M., 1937; student Duke, 1936; m. Virginia Orebaugh, Oct. 16, 1937 (dec. June 1960); 1 son, David; m. 2d, Martha J. Dawson McGrain, Nov. 27, 1963. Instr., Georgia Mil. Acad., 1934; sec. Rollins Press, Inc., Winter Park, Fla., 1934-40; archivist Rollins Coll., 1935-40, dir. alumni placement service, 1937-40; librarian, corresponding sec., Florida Hist. Soc., 1939-42; sec., dir. research Rutherford B. Hayes & Lucy Webb Hayes Found.; dir. Rutherford B. Hayes Library, Fremont, Ohio, 1946—; mgr. Rutherford B. Hayes State Meml., 1950—. Trustee, sec. St. Augustine (Fla.) Pub. Library, 1942, Birchard Pub. Library of Sandusky County, 1968—. Served in signal corps, AUS, 1943-46; ETO. Recipient merit citation Martha Kinney Cooper Ohioana Library Assn., 1971. Mem. Am. Assn. State and Local History, Soc. Am. Archivists, Soc. Am. Historians, Ohio (Exec. board 1952-53), Martha Kinney Cooper Ohioana (trustee 1970—), Birchard (sec. 1959—, trustee) library assns., Am. Hist. Assn., Ohio, Fla. hist. socs., Ohio Acad. of History (award of Merit 1969), Manuscript Soc. (v.p. 1950-64), Hist. Assn. So. Fla., Phi Delta Theta. Clubs: Rotary (local pres. 1963-64) (Fremont, Ohio); Rowfant (Cleve.). Author monographs on historical subjects; exec. editor: Hayes Hist. Jour., 1976—; contbr. to periodicals; editorial bd. Northwest Ohio Quar. Home: 1500 Buckland Ave Fremont OH 43420 Office: Rutherford B Hayes Library Fremont OH 43420

MARCINIAK, EDWARD ALLEN, urban cons.; b. Chgo., Dec. 21, 1917; s. Walter and Hattie (Kleszcz) M.; A.B., Loyola U., 1939, M.Social Adminstrn., 1942; LL.D., St. Joseph's Coll., 1964; m. Virginia Volini, Apr. 25, 1953; children—Catherine Vianney, Christina Maria, Francesca Louise, Claudia Noel. Instr sociology Loyola U., 1939-49; dir. div. labor studies Sheil Sch. Social Studies, 1943-53; internat. v.p. Am. Newspaper Guild, 1955-60; dir. Chgo. Commn. Human Relations, 1960-67; dep. commr. Chgo. Dept. Devel. and Planning, 1967-72; pres. Inst. of Urban Life, prof. urban studies, Loyola U., Chgo., 1973—. Founder, Nat. Cath. Social Action Conf., 1953, treas,, 1959-71; mem. com. social devel. U.S. Cath. Conf., 1967-71; mem. Ill. Urban Edn. Commn., 1969-73; chmn. Cath. Sch. Study Commn. Chgo., 1970-72. Bd. dirs. Great Books Found., Fund for Faith and Freedom, bd. dirs., vice chmn. Catholic Theol. Union; chmn. bd. Nat. Center for Urban Ethnic Affairs, Washington. Recipient awards including Archbishop Noll award Nat. Fedn. Cath. Coll. Students, 1963, Clarence Darrow Humanitarian award, 1964; Aquinas award Aquinas Coll., 1965. Mem. Indsl. Relations Research Assn. (chpt. pres. 1958-60), Nat. Assn. Intergroup Relations Ofcls. (dir. 1965-69), Am. Soc. Planning Ofcls., Blue Key, Alpha Kappa Delta, Phi Alpha Rho. Author: Tomorrow's Christian, 1969; Reviving An Inner City Community, 1977. Contbr. articles to various publs. Home: 1341 W Catalpa Ave Chicago IL 60640 Office: 14 E Chestnut Chicago IL 60611

MARCINIAK, GARY STEPHEN PAUL, research engr., designer; b. Medina, N.Y., May 6, 1953; s. LaVern William and Beatrice Jane (Burbules) M.; A.A.S., Milw. Sch. Engring., 1973. Designer HVAC, Manci & Haning Co., Brookfield, Wis., 1973-74; instrumentation designer Honeywell Inc., Milw., 1975; HVAC process designer Joseph Schlitz Brewing Co., Milw., 1975-77, research engring. technician, designer, 1977-78; design engr. Grunau Co., Milw., 1978—; cons. solar heat recovery. Mem. . Soc. Heating, Refrigerating, and Air Conditioning Engrs., Inst. Certification Engring. Technicians, Wis. Soc. Certified Engring. Technicians, Internat. Solar Energy Soc., Solar Energy Industries Assn. (profl.), Am. Bowling Congress. Roman Catholic. Home: 1827 E Newton Ave Shorewood WI 53211 Office: Grunau Co 307 W Layton Ave Milwaukee WI 53201

MARCINKOSKI, ANNETTE MARIE, educator; b. Akron, Ohio, Aug. 2, 1933; d. Frank J. and Barbara (Popielarczyk) Marcinkoski; B.S., U. Akron, 1955; M.A., U. Mich., 1959. Tchr. Flint (Mich.) Pub. Schs., 1955-63, tng. tchr. Coop. Tchr. Edn. Program, 1963-69, elementary tchr., 1969—. Active Big Sister program; sponsor Jr. Red Cross, 1959-63; tchr. Confraternity of Christian Doctrine. Mem. United Tchrs. of Flint (del. rep. assembly), Mich. Edn. Assn. (pres. Region X, 1977—), NEA (regional dir. 1973-77), Elementary, Kindergarten and Nursery Educators, Mich. (treas. 1970-72, pres. 1973-75), Flint (sec. 1959-62) assns. childhood edn., Assn. Childhood Edn. Internat., AAUW (v.p. 1967-69, area rep. in edn. 1969-72), Theta Phi Alpha (adviser Gen. Motors Inst. chpt. 1973—, chmn. bd. dirs. 1975—), Delta Kappa Gamma, Cath. Bus. Women (sec. 1970-72), Flint Area Reading Council, Mich. Reading Assn. (del. council state orgns. 1974-76). Home: 1911 Laurel Oak Dr Flint MI 48507 Office: 1402 W Dayton St Flint MI 48504

MARCOS, JOSE MARIANO, physician; b. Palencia, Spain, Mar. 19, 1930; s. Mariano and Encarnacion (Herrero) M.; Bachelor Degree, LaSalle Coll., Palencia Spain, 1947; M.D., U. Valladolid, 1953; m. Teresa McInnis, June 5, 1965; children—Xavier, Vincent. Chest physician Cindad Sanatorial de Tarrasa, Barcelona, Spain, 1953-54; gen. practice medicine, Rivas de Campos, Palencia, Spain, 1954-55, Noviercas, Soria, 1955-56; resident radiology Residencia Sanitaria Fernando Primo de Rivera, Guadalajara, Spain, 1956-59; jr. intern Brantford Gen. Hosp., (Ont., Can.), 1959-60; sr. intern Scarborough Gen. Hosp., 1960-61; asst. resident therapeutic radiology Princess Margaret Hosp., Toronto, Ont., Can., 1962-64; chief resident therapeutic radiology Ont. Cancer Found., Kingston Cancer Clinic, 1964-68; gen. practice medicine, Windsor, Ont., Can., 1968-72; chest physician Ont. Dept. Health, Ottawa, Ont., Can., 1972—, now physician in charge. Office: 1015 Merivale Rd Ottawa ON K1Z 6A6 Canada

MARCUS, CARLTON PARKS, JR., feed co. exec.; b. Birmingham, Ala., Oct. 19, 1925; s. Carlton Parks and Thelma (Alexander) M.; B.S., U. Md., 1949, M.S., 1952; m. Louvera A. Hudson, Feb. 3, 1948; children—Carlton Parks, Lynne M., Bruce H. Research scientist U.S. Dept. Agr., 1950-53; dir. research Buntings' Nurseries, Selbyville, Del., 1953-59; sr. tech. salesman Shell Chem. Co., 1959-67; with Milk Specialties, Inc., Dundee, Ill., 1967—, v.p. mktg., 1970—. Village trustee Sleepy Hollow (Ill.), 1970-71; pres. bd. commrs. Dundee Twp. Park Dist., 1971—. Served with AUS, 1943-45. Decorated Bronze Star with oak leaf cluster. Mem. Phi Kappa Sigma. Congregationalist (chmn. bd. trustees 1970-71). Home: 304 North St Dundee IL 60118 Office: Box 278 Dundee IL 60118

MARCUS, RICHARD ALAN, lawyer, mfg. co. exec.; b. N.Y.C., Aug. 25, 1933; s. Berthold and Dorothy (Kerstien) M.; A.B., Coll. City N.Y., 1954; J.D., U. Va., 1959; m. Davys Kay Weisberg, June 4, 1961; children—Barbara Jo, Kimberly Ellen, Scott Arak. Admitted to N.Y. bar, 1960, Va. bar, 1959, Minn. bar, 1962, Fla. bar, 1960,; pvt. practice law, asso. Bernard C. Fuller, Miami Beach, Fla., 1960-62; asso. Robins, Davis, & Lyons, Mpls., 1962-64; counsel, v.p. Napco Industries, Inc., Hopkins, Minn., 1964—; v.p., dir. Mass Merchandisers, Inc., Napco Industries (Can.) Ltd., Napco Industries G.m.b.H., Denver Aviation Corp., Airline Support Co., Inter-Ad, Inc., Star Leasing Corp. Served with AUS, 1954-56. Mem. Am., N.Y., Va., Fla., Minn. bar assns., Nat. Soc. Corporate Planning, Am. Mgmt. Assn., Phi Delta Epsilon, Sigma Nu Phi. Jewish religion. Mason. Home: 14121 Stonegate Ln Hopkins MN 55343 Office: 1600 Second St S Hopkins MN 55343

MARCUS, RICHARD EARL, physician; b. Milw., Apr. 11, 1916; s. Max and Celia (Grodin) M.; B.S., U. Wis., 1937, M.D., 1940; m. Francelle Wohl, Jan. 3, 1942; children—Carlyn (Mrs. Sören Ekström), Richard Max, Elizabeth. Resident Milw. County Gen. Hosp., 1941-42; resident U. Ill. Eye and Ear Infirmary, 1946-48, asst. to F.L. Lederer, 1948-50; practice medicine specializing in otology, Chgo., 1948-53, Los Angeles, 1954-55, Winnetka, Ill., 1955-60, Skokie, Ill., 1960—; clin. prof. otolaryngology U. Ill. Coll. Medicine, Chgo., 1946—; asso. prof. U. Calif. Coll. Medicine, Los Angeles, 1954-55; founding mem., exec. dir. Inst. for Hearing and Speech, Winnetka, 1962—; vis. prof. U. Colo. Coll. Medicine, Denver, 1966. Guest lectr. XIII Congresso Pan-Americano, 1972; faculty First Symposium Neurol. Surgery of the Ear, 1977. Bd. dirs. Chgo. Hearing Soc., 1952-55. Served from 1st lt. to maj. USAAF, 1942-46. John and Mary R. Markle Found. scholar in med. sci., 1951. Diplomate Am. Bd. Otolaryngology. Mem. AMA, Chgo. Laryngol. and Otol. Soc. (pres. 1976-77), Am. Acad. Opthalmology and Otolaryngology (award of merit 1971), Am. Laryngol., Rhinol. and Otol. Soc., Am. Neurotology Soc. (founding mem.; pres. 1969-70), Winnetka Tennis Assn. (founding mem.; sec.-treas. 1960-63, pres. 1964-65), Sigma Xi. Clubs: Tavern (Chgo.); Lake Shore Country (Glencoe). Author: Electroencephalography in the Diagnosis of Hearing Loss in the Very Young Child, 1949; Ototoxic Medication in Premature Children, 1963; Vestibular Function and Additional Findings in Waardenburg's Syndrome, 1968; Reduced Incidence of Congenital and Prelingual Deafness, 1970; Cochlear and Neural Disease: Classification and Otoaudiologic Correlations, 1974; Cochleoneural Hearing Loss Treated With Acupuncture, 1974; Inner Ear Disorders in a Family with Sickle Cell Thalassemia, 1976; Clinical Audiology: The Auditory Profile, 1977. Office: 64 Old Orchard Skokie IL 60076

MARCZYNSKI, THADDEUS JOHN, educator; b. Poznan, Poland, Nov. 30, 1920; s. John Adam and Wanda Catherine (Sielski) M.; M.D., Med. Sch. of Jagiellonian U. and Acad. of Medicine (Cracow, Poland), 1951; Sc.D., Acad. Medicine (Cracow, Poland), 1959; m. Barbara Konieczny, Oct. 10, 1956; children—Gregory Thaddeus, John Thaddeus. Came to U.S., 1964, naturalized, 1973. Asst. physician dept. medicine Mil. Hosp., Cracow, Poland, 1951-52; emergency physician Ambulance of the City of Cracow, Poland, 1953-54; sr. research asst. dept. pharmacology Acad. Medicine, Cracow, Poland, 1956-62, asst. prof. pharmacology, 1962-64; asst. prof. pharmacology U. Ill. at Chgo., 1964-69, asso. prof. pharmacology, 1969-73, mem. Intercampus Bioengring. faculty, 1973—, prof. dept. med. psychology and dept. bioengring. Grad. Coll., 1973—, prof. pharmacology Sch. Basic Med. Scis., 1973—, prof. pharmacology Abraham Lincoln Sch. Medicine, U. Ill. at Chgo., 1974—. Vis. scientist Brain Research Inst. U. Calif. at Los Angeles, 1961-62. Recipient Rockefeller Found. fellowship, 1961-62. Mem. AAAS, Am. Soc. Pharmacology and Exptl. Therapeutics, Soc. Neurosci., N.Y. Acad. Sci. Contbr. numerous articles to specialized jours. Home: 1217 Hinman St Evanston IL 60202 Office: 835 S Wolcott Chicago IL 60612

MARDELL, CAROL DOLORES, psychologist; b. Chgo., Nov. 30, 1935; d. Albert and Lee (Mandel) Goldstein; children—Benjamin, Dina, Ruth. B.S., U. Ill., 1956; M.A., U. Chgo., 1958; Ph.D., Northwestern U., 1972. Elementary teaching certificate, 1956; supervisory certificate, 1969; learning disabilities certificate, 1970; adminstrv. certificate, 1970; sch. psychologist certificate, 1973; adminstrv. certificate with supt. endorsement, 1974; registered psychologist, Ill. Classroom tchr., Skokie, Ill., 1956-59, sch. psychometrist, 1959-60; pvt. practice psychology, Skokie, 1962-65; tutor, Skokie, 1965-68; learning disabilities tchr., Highland Park, Ill., 1969-70, learning disabilities cons., 1970-71; research project dir. Ill. Office Edn., Chgo., 1971-73; asst. prof. Northwestern U., Evanston, Ill., 1973-74; asso. prof. Northeastern Ill. U., Chgo., 1974—, co-dir. Spl. Edn. for Presch. Children Project, 1976—; mem. Ill. Early Childhood Task Force, 1972-73; bd. mem. Fund for Perceptually Handicapped Children, 1973—; mem. State Task Force for Child Care Tng., 1973-75; editorial bd. Jour. Learning Disabilities, 1976; asso. editor Exceptional Children, 1977. Mem. Am. Psychol. Assn., Council for Exceptional Children, Assn. Children with Learning Disabilities, Nat. Assn. for Edn. Young Children, Alpha Lambda Delta, Kappa Delta Pi, Pi Lambda Theta, Phi Kappa Phi, Phi Delta Kappa. Author: (with Dorothea S. Goldenberg) Developmental Indicators for the Assessment of Learning, 1973; contbr. articles in field to profl. jours. Home: 1233 Lincoln Ave S Highland Park IL 60035 Office: 5500 N St Louis Ave Chicago IL 60625

MARDIGIAN, EDWARD STEPHAN, machine tool co. exec.; b. Stambul, Turkey, Oct. 25, 1909; s. Stephan and Agavine (Hagopian) M.; came to U.S., 1914, naturalized, 1929; student Wayne U., 1932-34; m. Helen Alexander, June 5, 1938; children—Marilyn, Edward, Robert. Asst. tool engr. Briggs Mfg. Co., Detroit, 1935-37, chief tool engr., Eng., 1937-45, chief project engr., 1945; owner, operator Mardigian Corp., Warren, Mich., 1948-69, Marco Corp., Warren, 1954, bought Buckeye Aluminum Co., Wooster, Ohio, 1956, Mardigian Car Corp., Warren, 1966—; pres. Hercules Machine Tool & Die Co., Warren, 1973—; chmn. bd. Central States Mfg. Co., Warren, 1973—. Pres. Armenian Gen. Benevolent Union Am., 1972—; chmn. Chief Exec. Forum, Warren, 1974. Decorated medal St. Gregory by Vasken 1st Supreme Patriarch of All Armenians, 1966; named Man of Year Diocese Armenian Ch. N.Am., 1977. Home: 1525 Tottenham Rd Birmingham MI 48009 Office: Hercules Machine Tool & Die Co 13920 E Ten Mile Rd Warren MI 48089

MARDIS, HAL KENNEDY, urol. surgeon; b. Lincoln, Nebr., Apr. 4, 1934; s. Harold Corson and Marie (Swaim) M.; B.S., U. Nebr., 1955, M.D., 1958; m. Janet Reimer Schenken, June 22, 1956; children—Michael Corson, Anne Lucile, Jeanne Marie. Intern Charity Hosp. La., New Orleans, 1958-59, resident surgery, 1959-63; practice medicine, specializing in adult, pediatric urology Omaha, 1965—; instr. medicine La. State U., New Orleans, 1961-62, instr. urology, 1963-64, asst. prof., 1964-65; asso. prof. U. Nebr., Lincoln, 1965—; cons. urologist birth defects Spl. Treatment Center, Children's Hosp., Omaha, 1965—; staff Methodist, Clarkson, Immanuel, Children's and Univ. hosps., Omaha, 1965—. Bd. dirs. Omaha Symphony Assn., 1969—, sec., 1971—, pres., 1975—. Diplomate Am. Bd. Urology. Fellow A.C.S.; mem. Soc. Pediatric Urology, Am. Coll. Nuclear Medicine, Soc. Pediatric Urology, Soc. Nuclear Medicine, Royal Soc. Medicine, Am. Assn. Clin. Urologists, Am. Urol. Assn., A.M.A., So. Med. Assn., Omaha-Midwest Clin. Soc. Republican. Mason (Shriner). Contbr. articles to profl. jours. Home: 9465 Pauline St Omaha NE 68124 Office: 8300 Dodge St Omaha NE 68114

MARECEK, LYNN MARIE, educator; b. Chgo., May 11, 1951; d. Hugh H. and Martha E. (Kalchbrenner) Brown; B.S. (Pres. scholar), Valparaiso U., 1973; M.S., Purdue U., 1976; m. Gerald Marecek, June 16, 1973. Tchr. high sch. math. Sch. Town of Highland (Ind.), 1973—; guest lectr. math. Purdue U. Calumet Campus, Hammond, Ind., 1977—. Recipient S. C. Johnson Outstanding Chemistry Student award Valparaiso U., 1970. Mem. Nat. Council Tchrs. Math., Am. Math. Soc. Lutheran. Home: 17786 Arlington Dr Country Club Hills IL 60477 Office: 9135 Erie St Highland IN 46322

MARECEK, MILAN, typographer; b. Berwyn, Ill., Sep. 5, 1920; s. John and Anna (Sefcik) M.; student pub. schs.; m. Adeline Anna Wagner, Nov. 16, 1941; children—Marcia Jan. Michael X. Trainee, Lake Shore Press, Keystone Typesetting, Guzik Press, Webb-Linn Printing, 1936-41; retail grocery bus. and linotype foreman 20th Century Press, 1946-51; owner G & R. Typesetting Co., Cicero, Ill., 1951—; sec.-treas. G & R Typesetting Co. Served with USAAF, 1942-45. Decorated D.F.C. with 1 cluster, Air medal with 3 clusters. Mem. V.F.W. (life). Lutheran. Mason (Shriner), Elk, Lion. Club: Czechoslovak Typographic, Dobrovsky. Home: 8006 Winter Circle Dr Downers Grove IL 60515 Office: 5105 W Roosevelt Rd Cicero IL 60650

MARGOLIN, ROBERT J., lawyer; b. Kansas City, Mo., Mar. 21, 1935; s. Abraham E. and Florence (Solow) M.; A.B., Dartmouth Coll., 1957; LL.B., J.D., U. Mich., 1960; m. Dorothy Macy, Sept. 20, 1958; children—Kathryn Ruth, Charles David. Admitted to Mo. bar, 1960; practice law, Kansas City, Mo.; mem. firm Margolin & Kirwan; pres., dir. Twin Oaks, Inc., Kansas City, 1968—; sec.-treas., dir. Kansas City Kings; dir. Indian Springs State Bank, Kansas City. Bd. counsellors Menorah Center; bd. dirs. Jewish Vocat. Service, Jewish Community Center. Mem. Am., Mo., Kansas City, Jackson County bar assns. Office: 1000 United Mo Bank Bldg Kansas City MO 64106

MARGRAFF, HOWARD DAVID, inland port adminstr.; b. St. Louis, Nov. 19, 1930; s. Howard David and Mary Ann (Hoffman) M.; Asso. Arts and Sci., St. Louis U., 1958, B.S., 1962; certificate Dale Carnegie Inst., 1964; m. Rae Jean Alice Schulte, Nov. 25, 1954; 1 dau., Kathleen Marie. Mgr. coll. bookstore St. Louis U., 1949-51; clk. Daniel Hamm Drayage Co., St. Louis, 1953-58, asst. traffic mgr., 1958-63, traffic mgr., safety dir., 1963-65, mgr. freight div., 1965-73; mgr. sales and service St. Louis Terminals Corp., 1973-75, v.p., gen. mgr., 1975—, also dir.; mgr. sales and service Granite City Terminals Corp. (Ill.), 1973-75, v.p., gen. mgr., 1975—; mgr. sales and service Mid-South Terminals Corp., 1973-75, also dir.; dir. Mid-South Terminal Corp., Mid-West Terminal Corp., Kare Realty Co. Chmn. bd. adjustments City of Dellwood (Mo.), 1972-75; pres. Ferguson Twp. Democratic Com., Township, 1972-74, now dir. Served with USMC, 1951-53. Mem. Inland Rivers Ports and Terminals (dir.), Nat. Waterways Council, St. Louis Labor Relations and Mediation Assn., Am. Warehousemen's Assn., Traffic Club St. Louis (dir.), St. Louis Coal Club (dir.), Goaltenders (dir.), St. Louis Ambassadors, Holy Name Soc., Daily World Missions, Legion of 1000 Men, Delta Nu Alpha (dir.). Clubs: Mo. Athletic, Media, Propellor (St. Louis). Home: 1911 Hudson Rd St Louis MO 63136 Office: 1 N Market St St Louis MO 63102

MARGULIES, SEYMOUR, physicist, educator; b. Jaslo, Poland, Oct. 3, 1933; s. Morris and Ruth (Kalb) M.; came to U.S. 1939, naturalized, 1950; B.E.E., Cooper Union, 1955; M.S. in Physics, U. Ill., 1956, Ph.D., 1962; m. Cecile Stoller, Jan. 25, 1959; children—Jonathan, Daniel. Nat. Acad. Scis./NRC postdoctoral fellow Max Planck Institut für Kernphysik, Heidelberg, Germany, 1961-63; research asso. Nevis Labs., Columbia U., 1963-65; asst. prof. physics U. Ill. at Chgo. Circle, 1965-69, asso. prof., 1969—; vis. scientist Argonne Nat. Lab., summer 1967, Fermi Accelerator Lab., Batavia, Ill., winter 1973. Mem. 57th St. Art Fair, Inc., Chgo., 1973—, chmn., 1976. Raytheon predoctoral fellow, 1958-59; NSF grantee, 1973—. Mem. Am. Phys. Soc., Sigma Xi. Co-translator: Pauli Lectures on Physics, 1973; contbr. articles to profl. jours. Home: 1623 E Hyde Park Blvd Chicago IL 60615 Office: Dept Physics U Ill Chicago Circle Chicago IL 60680

MARIN, ALLAN MARSHALL, advt. co. exec.; b. Chgo., Aug. 30, 1912; s. Jacob A. and Gertrude R. (Simon) M.; Ph.B., U. Chgo., 1934; m. Mildred Lady, Dec. 24, 1950; children—Richard Allan, Pamela Margaret. With Gimbel Bros., Milw., 1934; radio advt. John Blair & Co., Chgo., 1935; advt. dir. Dr. Peter Fahrney & Sons Co., Chgo., 1936-42; pres. Allan Marin & Assos., Inc., advt. agy., Chgo., 1946—; pres. Kemar Corp., tech. book pubs., Chgo., Mag. Market Place, Inc., mag. brokers, Chgo.; officer, dir. Greater Tex. Co., Inc., Houston; pres. Phone Devices Corp. Mem. Evanston Plan Commn., 1962-70, chmn., 1967-70. Served with USAF, 1942-45. Home: 1047 Forest Ave Evanston IL 60202 Office: 624 S Michigan Ave Chicago IL 60605

MARINE, JULIA MASON LANG (MRS. ROY MILTON MARINE), educator; b. Rockport, Ind., June 26, 1908; d. Shirley Charles and Maud (Mason) Lang; student Monticello Coll., 1924-26; A.B., Evansville Coll., 1928; M.S. in Edn., Ind. U., 1944; m. Joseph Emerson Welborn, June 6, 1930 (div. 1939); children—Joseph Keith, Kent Lang; m. 2d, Roy Milton Marine, Dec. 26, 1944. With attendance dept. Evansville (Ind.) Pub. Schs., 1940-42; asst. to dir. student personnel Coll. Edn., Ind. U., Bloomington, 1942-44; asst. to dean Ohio State U. Coll. Arts and Scis., Columbus, 1945-57, asst. sec., 1957-62, sec., 1962-68, asst. dean, sec., 1968-74, emeritus, 1974. Recipient Distinguished Service award Ohio State U., 1975. Mem. AAUW, Pi Lambda Theta, Alpha Lambda Delta. Clubs: Faculty (membership com. 1966-68), Faculty Women's (pres. 1956-57), Univ. Women's. Home: 4759 Scenic Dr Columbus OH 43214

MARINELLI, ANNE VERA, librarian; b. Hibbing, Minn.; d. John and Concetta (Varriano) Marinelli; diploma Hibbing Jr. Coll., 1927; B.A., U. Wis., 1929; B.S. in Library Sci., Columbia, 1931, postgrad., 1934-35, 37, 40; postgrad. Inst. U. Chgo., 1947; M.A. in Italian and Library Sci., U. Ill., 1948; postgrad. U.S. Dept. Agr. Grad. Sch., 1951, (Rackham Research grant). U. Mich., 1952-59; diploma U. Perugia (Italy), 1951; postgrad. archival mgmt. course Nat. Archives and Recs. Service, GSA, 1959. Tchr., Hibbing Pub. Schs., 1929-30; jr. asst. librarian N.Y. Pub. Library, N.Y.C., 1930-32, sr. asst. librarian, 1933-35, asst. br. librarian, 1935-37; head librarian, instr. library methods Coll. St. Teresa, Winona, Minn., 1937-38; head catalog dept. Scoville Library Carleton Coll., Northfield, Minn., 1938-44; head libraries Chishom (Minn.) Pub. Schs., 1944-45; bibliographer U. Ill. at Urbana Library, 1945-52; asst. prof. Grad. Sch. Library Sci., Fla. State U., 1953-55; asso. prof. Grad. Sch. Library Sci., Tex. Woman's U., 1956-60; head librarian Hibbing Jr. Coll., 1960-73, ret., 1973; spl. assignment Pan Am. Union Library, Washington, 1949; spl. asst. to librarian Library of Congress, 1950; Fulbright lectr., cons. Italian libraries and librarians, 1951-52; chairperson seminars on libraries and librarianship, Rome, also Florence, Naples, Italy, 1952; adminstrv. asst. to Am. chmn. Internat. Fedn. Library Assns. Congress, Washington, 1950; del. Nat. Commn. UNESCO Conf., 1959. Mem. Hibbing Am. Revolution Bi-Centennial Com., Hibbing. Decorated Knight Order Star of Solidarity (Italy); recipient Amita award merit, 1967, Golden Anniversary award merit Hibbing State Jr. Coll. Alumni Assn., 1967, Hibbing High Sch. F. Bellamy award outstanding alumna, 1968, Internat. Rotary-Hibbing Service award, 1974. Mem. ALA, Assn. Coll. and Research Libraries, Round Table on Library Service Abroad (charter), Hibbing Community Coll. Alumni Assn. (exec. Sec. 1973—, permanent chairperson awards com.), Assn. Am. Library Schs., Amita (hon. chairperson), U. Ill. Library Assn., Hibbing First Settlers' Assn., Am. Assn. Ret. Persons, U. Ill., U. Wis. alumni assns., Nat., Minn. ret. tchrs. assns., Columbia U. Alumni Fedn., Smithsonian Instn. Assos., Met. Mus. Art Nat. Assn., Fulbright Alumni Assn., Iota Kappa Gamma, Alpha Beta Alpha, Pi Lambda Theta, Beta Phi Mu. Contbr. articles to U.S. and fgn. profl. jours. Home: 909 Minnesota St Hibbing MN 55746

MARINO, CHARLES JOSEPH, govt. ofcl.; b. Litchfield, Ill., May 30, 1926; s. Joseph and Lucille (Valerio) M.; B.C.S., St. Louis U., 1952; M.S., Webster Coll., 1977; m. Laura Eugenia Donadon, Apr. 15, 1950; 1 son, Charles Joseph. Personnel asst. Kroger Co., St. Louis, 1946-48; asst. placement dir. St. Louis U., 1948-50, placement dir., 1950-57, dir. personnel and placement, 1957-67; dir. manpower mgmt. Blue Cross Hosp. Service, Inc., St. Louis, 1967-75; exec. asst. to dir. health and hosps. City of St. Louis, 1975—. Mem. adv. bd. Met. Coll. St. Louis U.; bd. dirs. Helpers of the Holy Souls, St. Louis, Urban League St. Louis; chmn. CSC of St. Louis. Served with USMCR, 1944-46. Mem. Midwest Coll. Placement Assn. (v.p. 1955), Am. Arbitration Assn. Am. Inst. Mgmt., Am. Soc. Personnel Adminstrn., Adminstrv. Mgmt. Soc., Am. Personnel and Guidance Assn., NEA, Indsl. Relations Club St. Louis (pres. 1975). Home: 7161 Lindenwood Saint Louis MO 63109

MARK, HARRY BERST, JR., chemist; b. Camden, N.J., Feb. 28, 1934; s. Harry Berst and Placid (Truschess) M.; B.A., U. Va., 1956; Ph.D. in Chemistry, Duke U., 1960; m. Frances Elizabeth Gray, Aug. 20, 1960; children—David Joseph, Sarah Elizabeth, Steven Frederick. Postdoctoral research asso. U. N.C., Chapel Hill, 1960-62; postdoctoral research fellow Calif. Inst. Tech., Pasadena, 1962-63; asst. prof. chemistry U. Mich., Ann Arbor, 1963-67, asso. prof., 1967-70; prof. chemistry, chmn. analytical chemistry div. U. Cin., 1970-76, head dept. chemistry, 1976—; vis. prof. Université Libre, Brussels, 1970; pres. Coast Assos., Inc., 1973—; profl. race car driver USAC, 1963—. Mem. Am. Chem. Soc., Electrochem. Soc., AAAS, Western Electroanalytical-Theoretical Soc. (nat. sec.-treas.), Soc. Applied Spectroscopy, N.Y., Ohio acads. sci., Am. Inst. Chemists, AAUP, Sigma Xi, Phi Lambda Upsilon, Alpha Chi Sigma, Theta Chi, Phi Kappa Phi. Author: (with G.A. Rechnitz, R.A. Greinke) Kinetics in Analytical Chemistry, 1968; (with J.S. Mattson) Activated Carbon, Surface Chemistry and Absorption from Solution, 1971; (with R.D. Sacks) Simplified Circuit Analysis: Digital-Analog Logic, 1972; editor: (with J.S. Mattson and H.C. MacDonald, Jr.) Computers in Chemistry and Instrumentation, vols. 1-7, 1971-77; (with S. Fujiwara) Computer Assisted Chemical Research Design, 1975; contbr. numerous articles on electrochemistry and analytical chemistry to profl. jours. Home: 6122 Dryden Ave Cincinnati OH 45213

MARK, JACK CHARLES, gas co. exec.; b. Mpls., Aug. 10, 1930; s. Abraham and Betty (Herzbach) M.; B.A., U. Minn., 1952, M.A., 1956; m. Marjorie Ellen Robinson, Dec. 19, 1965; children—Jonathan David, Brian Alan. With Minn. Gas Co., 1956—, advt. supr., 1959-62, asst. mgr. mdse. sales, 1962-63, mgr. advt. and sales promotion, 1965-73, mgr. consumer communications, 1973—, dir. consumer communications, 1974; instr. Sch. Journalism and Mass Communications, U. Minn., 1968—. Mem. Am. (mem. mktg. research, communications residential advt. com. 1966—), Midwest (chmn. advt. sect. 1966-72) gas assns., Advt. Club Minn. (dir. 1965, pres. 1969), Am. Mktg. Assn., Pub. Utilities Commn. Assn. (pres. 1974), Sigma Alpha Mu, Sigma Delta Chi. Mason (Shriner). Home: 3735 Glenhurst Ave Minneapolis MN 55416 Office: 733 Marquette Ave Minneapolis MN 55402

MARK, NORMAN BARRY, journalist; b. Chgo., Sept. 6, 1939; s. Arthur I. and Belle (Harman) M.; B.S., Northwestern U., 1961; m. Rhoda Kravets, Feb. 2, 1963; children—Geoffrey Wayne, Joel Richard. With Chgo. Daily News, 1966—, daily radio-TV columnist, 1969-75; critic at large for CBS, Chgo., 1973—; host WFLD-TV, Chgo., 1977—, WAIT-AM. Instr. Columbia Coll., Chgo., 1974-75, Roosevelt U., Chgo., 1975—. Media cons. Regional Transit Authority Election Campaign, Chgo., 1974. Served with Ill. Nat. Guard, 1963-69. Recipient AP News-feature writing award, 1968. Mem. Newspaper Guild, A.F.T.R.A., Writers Guild W. Contbr. articles to profl. jours. Author: Norman Mark's Chicago, 1977; (with others) The San Francisco Weight Loss Method, 1975, also various television scripts and plays produced in regional theaters. Office: 401 N Wabash St Chicago IL 60611

MARKENDORF, ARTHUR CARY, sociologist, anthropologist; b. Louisville, July 16, 1921; s. Karl Schoenfield and Elsie (Kiefer) M.; A.B., U. Mich., 1948, M.A., 1955, Ph.D., 1962; postgrad. U. Minn., Ariz. State U.; m. Joyce Faye Webb, Aug. 25, 1966; 1 dau., Karla. Asst. prof. ednl. sociology Los Angeles State Coll., 1959-60; asst. prof. sociology Western State Coll. Colo., 1962-66; asso. prof. sociology Wittenberg U., 1966-67; prof. sociology-anthropology, chmn. dept. Washburn U., Topeka, 1967—. Bd. dirs. Seven-Step Found., Topeka, Topeka Halfway House, Voluntary Action Center, Topeka. Served with USAAF, 1942-43. Mem. AAAS, Am. Anthrop. Assn., Am. Population Assn., Central States Anthrop. Assn., Phi Delta Theta, Phi Kappa Phi. Home: 65 Pepper Tree Ln Topeka KS 66611

MARKHAM, CLARENCE MATTHEW, JR., publishing co. exec.; b. San Antonio, June 20, 1911; s. Clarence Matthew and Lena (Dillwood) M.; student Wittenberg Coll., 1933-35; m. Olga Hughes, July 23, 1935; children—Clarence Matthew III, Melvin, Olga, Pierre, Leslie. Founder Bellmen Porters Assn., Springfield, O., 1933; operator porter and news butcher service Cin. and Lake Erie R.R. Co., Toledo, 1933-37; supt. dining car service Ann Arbor R.R. Co., Toledo, 1937-38; founder Travelers Research Pub. Co. Inc., Chgo., 1942, editor, pub., 1942—. Democrat. Roman Catholic. Home: 8034 S Prairie Ave Chicago IL 60619 Office: 11717 S Vincennes Ave Chicago IL 60643

MARKHAM, THOMAS NEWTON, physician; b. Middletown, Conn., Nov. 8, 1934; s. Clyde Newton and Hazel Elmire (Brown) M.; B.S., Tufts U., 1956; M.D., St. Louis U., 1960; M.P.H., U. Mich., 1967; children—Eleanor Marie, Julia Ann, Cynthia Rae. Intern, Firmin DesLoge Hosp., St. Louis U., 1960-61; resident U. Mich., Ann Arbor, 1964-67; commd. lt. USN, 1961, advanced through grades to capt., 1975; dir. biomed. scis. Naval Submarine Med. Research Lab., 1967-71; dir. occupational environ. health service Naval Regional Med. Center, Oakland, Calif., 1971-74; head Navy Environ. Health Center, 1974—; sr. med. officer Project Tektite I, 1968-69. Mem. Am. Occupational Med. Assn., Am. Acad. Occupational Medicine, Undersea Med. Soc., Aerospace Med. Assn., Am. Pub. Health Assn., Am. Congress Govtl. Indsl. Hygienists. Home: 3420 Sunbury Ln Cincinnati OH 45239 Office: 3333 Vine St Cincinnati OH 45239

MARKIEWICZ, WIGDOR, psychiatrist; b. Lomza, Poland, Jan. 3, 1920; s. Hirsh and Chana (Sokolower) M.; came to U.S., 1949, naturalized, 1955; student T. Kosciuszko Jr. Coll., 1935-37; student Faculty Medicine U. Wilno (Poland), 1937-39, U. Lwow (Poland), 1939-41; M.D., Kharkov Med. Inst., 1941; m. Sarah Pruszczanski, Mar. 18, 1941; children—Susan (Mrs. Robert McNeil), Dorothy (Mrs. Robert Haccoun), Debra Ann. Intern, St. Anne's Hosp., Chgo., 1953-54; resident in internal medicine St. Alexis Hosp., Cleve., 1954-55; resident psychiatry Fairhill Psychiat. Hosp., Cleve., 1965-68; gen. practice of medicine USSR, Poland, Germany and U.S., 1941-55; practice medicine specializing in internal medicine, Cleve., 1955-65, specializing in psychiatry, 1965—; clin. dir. Fairhill Mental Health Center, Cleve., 1970-76; dir. residency tng., 1976—; mem. staffs Huron Rd. Hosp., Cleve., Windsor Hosp., Chagrin Falls, Ohio, Woodruff Hosp., Cleve. Diplomate Am. Bd. Neurology and Psychiatry. Mem. Am., Ohio med. assns., Am., Ohio psychiat. assns., Cleve. Acad. Medicine, Cleve. Soc. Neurology and Psychiatry. Office: 2231 Taylor Rd Cleveland Heights OH 44112

MARKING, T(HEODORE) JOSEPH, JR., transp. and urban planner; b. Shelbyville, Ind., June 28, 1945; s. Theodore Joseph and Alvena Cecelia (Thieman) M.; B.A., So. Ill. U., 1967, M.S., 1972; m. Kathy K. Hagerman, Nov. 25, 1969. Intelligence research specialist Def. Intelligence Agy., Washington, 1967-68; planner I, St. Louis City Plan Commn., 1970; transp. planner Alan M. Voorhees & Assos., St. Louis, 1970-74, sr. transp. planner, 1974—. Mem. Am. Inst. Planners (asso.), Am. Soc. Planning Ofcls., Mo. Planning Assn., Assn. Am. Geographers, Traffic Engrs. Assn. of Met. St. Louis. Home: 2308 Charlemagne Dr Maryland Heights MO 63043 Office: 12161 Lackland Rd St Louis MO 63141

MARKLEY, ROGER BRUCE, accountant; b. Bluffton, Ind., Feb. 25, 1921; s. Herman Roderick and Beulah May (Harmon) M.; B.A., Internat. Coll., 1940; postgrad. Ball. State U., Oxford (Eng.) U., others; m. Betty June Sheffer, Feb. 14, 1942; children—Jeffrey Bruce, Patrice Faye, Rodney Lee. Commd. pvt. USAAF, 1941, advanced through grades to maj. U.S. Air Force, 1961, ret., 1964; controller Rockledge Products, Inc., Portland, Ind., 1964-69, Jay Petroleum, Inc., Portland, 1970-74; treas. Puterbaugh's Inc., Wehrly Motor Sales Inc. (both Portland) auditor OEO, 1964-74; pvt. practice as accountant, auditor, tax cons., Portland, 1964—; mgr. Wabash Village Apts., Nashville, Ind. Tchr. accounting and bookkeeping Purdue U. Farm Schs., 1968-74. Leader Jay County 4-H Club, 1964-69; area camping dir. Boy Scouts Am., Portland, 1938-42. City councilman City of Portland, 1958-62. Bd. dirs. Jay County Fair Assn., 1968-74. Decorated Purple Heart, Air medal; recipient award Am. Legion, 1962, State of Ind., 1962. Mem. Nat., Ind. (chpt. pres. 1968-69) assns. pub. accountants, Am. Legion (treas. 1964-70), Res. Officers Assn. U.S., V.F.W., Jay County Horse Club (pres. 1967-69). Methodist (treas. 1966-71). Mason; mem. Order Eastern Star. Home: Rural Route 3 Artist Dr Nashville IN 47448 Office: Wabash Village Rural Route 2 Nashville IN 47448

MARKOS, CHRIS, real estate appraiser; b. Cleve., Nov. 25, 1926; s. George and Bessie (Papathopoulos) M.; B.A., Western Res. U., 1960; LL.B., LaSalle Law Sch., 1964; m. Alice Zaharopoulos, Dec. 11, 1949; children—Marilyn, Irene, Betsy. Real estate broker Bklyn. Realty, 1952-63; v.p. Herbert Laronge, Inc., Cleve., 1963-76; pres. Calabese, Davis & Markos, Inc., 1976—; real estate instr. Case Western Res. U., 1963-68, Cuyahoga Community Coll., 1969—, Cleve. State U., 1973—, Nat. Inst. Brokers. Named Cleve. Realtor of Year, 1976. Mem. Cleve. Area Bd. Realtors (pres. 1974, chmn. bd. 1975), Am. Right of Way Assn., Ohio Assn. Real Estate Bds. (mem. edn. steering com., trustee), Am. Soc. Appraisers (chpt. pres. 1973-74, state dir. 1975). Home: 7927 Seth Paine St Brecksville OH 44141 Office: 2728 Euclid Ave Cleveland OH 44115

MARKOVITZ, RICHARD ERNEST, process equipment mfg. exec.; b. North Tonawanda, N.Y. Dec. 15, 1925; s. Gabriel and Ivy (Schofield) M.; B.S. in Mech. Engring., U. Buffalo, 1950; m. Ardith Ina Mahl, June 4, 1949; children—Kirk, Clark, Amy. Design engr. Adsco Industries, Buffalo, 1950-55; asst. mgr. engring. Blaw Knox Co., Buffalo, 1955-63; mgr. engring. Brighton Corp., Cin., 1963-77, v.p. engring., 1977—. Served with USN, 1944-46. Mem. ASME; asso. mem. Am. Welding Soc. Republican. Lutheran. Author papers in field. Address: 1762 Clayburn Circle Cincinnati OH 45240

MARKS, BISSELL EUGENE, educator; b. Linden, W.Va., Jan. 19, 1925; s. Floyd Harrison and Leah (Bissell) M.; B.A., Ashland Coll., 1954, B.S., 1954; M.Ed., KentState U., 1957; m. Marie Faith Saunders, Sept. 20, 1942; children—Eugenia, Larry. Tchr., dir. guidance Alliance (Ohio) City Schs., 1954-57; clin. psychologist Ohio Dept. Mental Hygiene and Correction, 1957-59; psychologist pub. schs., Marietta, Ohio, 1959-61; test coordinator, sch. psychologist, supr. sch. psychology internship program North Royalton (Ohio) City Schs., 1961—; pvt. practice psycho-ednl. rehab., marriage counseling; instr. Baldwin Wallace Coll., 1963, Cuyahoga Community Coll., 1963—. Trustee, staff psychologist Area Drug Action Com. City liaison officer N. Roylton Bicentennial Commn.; speakers bur. Cyahoga Valley Recreation Area. Served with USAAF, 1943-45; now capt. Res. Mem. Nat., Ohio, Royalton edn. assns., Ohio Psychol. Assn., Sch. Phsychologists Ohio, Am. Personnel and Guidance Assn., Cleve. Air Force Res. Officers Assn. (v.p.). Methodist. Mason (32 deg., Shriner), Kiwanian. Home: 9799 Independence Dr North Royalton OH 44133

MARKS, EDWARD GRAUMAN, lawyer; b. Cin., Jan. 11, 1941; s. Grauman and Louise E. (Dreyfoos) M.; B.F.A., U. Cin., 1963, J.D., 1967; m. Anita L. Stith, Aug. 7, 1965; children—Alison Louise, Amy Rochelle. News writer, reporter, producer Taft Broadcasting Co., Cin., 1959-63, radio broadcaster, newsman, 1963-64; admitted to Ohio bar, 1967; partner firm Marks, Goldsmith & Weiner, 1967—. Lectr. on broadcast law U. Cin., Coll. Conservatory Music. Sec. Cin. Music Hall Assn., 1974—. Trustee Rockdale Temple, The Corbett Found. Mem. Am., Ohio (council dels., chmn. pub. relations com. 1977—), Cin. (chmn. pub. relations sect. 1971-74, 76—, exec. com. 1974-76) bar assns. Club: Cincinnati Civic (pres. 1969-70). Home: 203 Wilmuth Ave Wyoming OH 45215 Office: 707 First Nat Bank Bldg Cincinnati OH 45202

MARKS, ERNESTINE LE ETTA BROWN (MRS. SAMUEL MILTON MARKS), frat. exec.; b. Topeka, Feb. 16, 1917; d. Raymond Clyde and Etta Philena (Dewey) Brown; B.S., Purdue U., 1939; m. Samuel Milton Marks, Nov. 15, 1941; 1 son, Samuel Milton. Alumnae v.p. nat. council Alpha Xi Delta, 1965-68, membership v.p., 1968-71, collegiate v.p., 1971-74, nat. pres., 1974—. Den mother Boy Scouts Am., 1951-53. Trustee Alpha Xi Delta Found., 1965—. Mem. Purdue Players, Women's Soc. Christian Service, Tippecanoe County Hist. Assn., St. Elizabeth Hosp. Aux. Methodist. Clubs: Twelve to Twenty (chmn. 1957), Purdue Women's (treas. 1963-64) (West Lafayette, Ind.), Lioness (1st v.p.). Author: (with Mrs. Richard L. Saunders) Alpha Xi Delta Membership Manual, 1970. Designer Penman Award for Alpha Xi Delta Frat., 1967. Home: 124 Seneca Ln West Lafayette IN 47906 Office: 8702 Founders Rd Indianapolis IN 46205

MARKS, ERWIN, mgmt. cons.; b. Chgo., July 4, 1937; s. Samuel and Mary (Pollyea) M.; B.A. with honors, Chgo. State U., 1958; M.A., Northwestern U., 1960; m. Deborah F. Weinstein, Aug. 24, 1958; children—James, Margaret, Jonathan. Cons. mgr. Price Waterhouse & Co., Chgo., 1964-71; v.p. On-Line Decisions, Inc., 1971-74; v.p. Lester B. Knight & Assos., Inc., 1974—. Home: 401 Voltz Rd Northbrook IL 60062 Office: 549 W Randolph St Chicago IL 60606

MARKS, GREGORY ALLAN, univ. adminstr.; b. Milw., May 26, 1939; s. Allan Charles and Jane (Eberhardt) M.; B.A. with distinction and honors in Polit. Sci., U. Mich., 1962, M.A. in Math., 1963, postgrad., 1963—; m. Carolyn Lois Geda, Apr. 20, 1968; children—Cynthia Jane, Eleanor Lynn. Computer programmer data processing sect. Inst. for Social Research, U. Mich., Ann Arbor, 1964; computer programmer tech. services Inter-Univ. Consortium for Polit. Research, Inst. for Social Research, U. Mich., 1964-65, asst. dir. tech. services, 1965-66, supr. programming, 1966-67, asst. dir., 1968—; head computer support Center for Polit. Studies Inst. for Social Research, 1970—; lectr. polit sci. dept. U. Mich., 1971. Mem. Am., Midwest, Western polit. sci. assns., Assn. for Computing Machinery, Am. Statis. Assn., Am. Sociol. Assn., A.A.A.S., IEEE, Pi Sigma Alpha. Democrat. Contbr. to profl. publs. Home: 1737 Sanford Place Ann Arbor MI 48103 Office: 4258 ISR Center for Political Studies Box 1248 Ann Arbor MI 48106

MARKS, JEROME, city ofcl.; b. St. Louis, Aug. 10, 1922; s. Harry Ely and Frieda (Meyer) M.; B.J., U. Mo., 1948; m. Helen Z. Patek, Dec. 9, 1948; children—Gail Ellen, Joy Arlene. Newspaper reporter in Minn., Tex., Kans. and Iowa and editor Chgo. bur. Internat. News Service, 1948-68; asst. to exec. dir. N.E. Minn. Devel. Assn., 1969-71; account exec. J.F.P. and Assos., Duluth, 1971-72; dir. indsl. devel. Seaway Port Authority, Duluth, Minn., 1972—; pres. Metro Duluth Econ. Devel. Assn., 1972—; mem. Mayor Duluth Com. Econ. Devel. Served with Signal Intelligence, AUS, World War II. Recipient Journalism award Sigma Delta Chi. Mem. Minn. Indsl. Devel. Assn., Kappa Tau Alpha. Home: 1201 Brainerd Ave Duluth MN 55811 Office: City Hall 5th Ave W and 1st St Duluth MN 55802

MARKUS, RICHARD, judge; b. Evanston, Ill., Apr. 16, 1930; s. Benjamin and Ruby Irene M.; B.S. magna cum laude, Northwestern U., 1951; J.D. cum laude, Harvard U., 1954; m. Carol Joanne Slater, July 26, 1952; children—Linda, Scott, Kent. Admitted to D.C. bar, 1954, Ohio bar, 1956; appellate atty. civil div. Dept. Justice, 1954-56; partner Sindell, Sindell, Bourne, Markus, Stern & Spero, Cleve., 1956-73, Spangerberg, Shibley, Traci, Lancione & Markus, Cleve., 1973-76; judge Spangenberg, (Ohio) Ct. Common Pleas, Cleve., 1976—; instr. Mass. Inst. Tech., 1952-54; adj. prof. Cleve. State U. Law Sch., 1960—; instr. Case Western Res. U. Law Sch., 1972—; co-founder Nat. Advocacy Coll., 1970; mem. Nat. Commn. on Med. Malpractice, 1971-73. Trustee, Roscoe Pound Found. Mem. Am. Trial Lawyers Assn. (pres. 1970-71), Ohio Acad. Trial Lawyers (pres. 1965-66), Nat. Inst. Trial Advocacy (trustee vice chmn.), Phi Beta Kappa, Pi Mu Epsilon, Delta Sigma Rho. Author: Trial Handbook for Ohio Lawyers, 1973; editor Harvard Law Rev., 1952-54; Ohio Localizer P.I.A.D.D., 1967; contbr. articles to profl. jours. Home: 4769 Edenwood Rd South Euclid OH 44121 Office: Justice Center Cleveland OH 44113

MARKUS, ROBERT MICHAEL, newspaper columnist; b. Chgo., Jan. 30, 1934; s. David White and Anna (Tonkonogy) M.; B.J., U. Mo., 1955; m. Leslie Winnifred Ator, Aug. 25, 1962; children—Catherine Mary, Patricia Ann, Michael Hughes. Asst. state editor Moline (Ill.) Dispatch, 1955-59; copy editor Chgo. Tribune, 1959-66, sports columnist, 1966—. Served with U.S. Army, 1956-58. Named Ill. Sports Writer of Yr., 1972, 73, 74; recipient Nat. Headliner award for sports columns, 1973. Mem. Baseball Writers Assn. Am., Football Writers Assn. Am., Profl. Football Writers Assn., Am. Auto Racing Writers and Broadcasters Assn. Home: 402 Willow Rd Winnetka IL 60093 Office: 435 N Michigan Ave Chicago IL 60611

MARKUSEN, RICHARD JOSEPH, EDP exec.; b. Racine, Wis., Nov. 22, 1944; s. Earl Joseph and Marie Agnes (Nielsen) M.; B.S. in Applied Math. and Engring. Physics, U. Wis., Milw., 1968. Systems specialist Gettys Mfg., Racine, 1975-77, operations coordinator, 1977—. Served with USAF, 1968-72. Decorated Air Force Commendation medal. Mem. EDP Mgrs. Assn. Office: 2700 Golf Ave Racine WI 53404

MARLOW, FRANK WESLEY, statistician; b. Ft. Worth, Dec. 6, 1918; s. Frank W. and Josephine Gay (Bullard) M.; m. Helen Louise Hellerud, June 12, 1942; children—Terence, Joan; B.A., U. Iowa, 1940. Sr. statis. analyst, sr. methods accountant, staff statistician, survey statistician Southwestern Bell Telephone Co., St. Louis, 1941—. Bd. dirs. Salem Meth. Ch., 1970—; treas. St. Louis hdqrs. Telephone Credit Union, 1954-75; dir. Mo. Credit Union League, 1969—; pres. Gateway Chpt. Credit Unions, 1975. Mem. Am. Mktg. Assn. (dir. St. Louis chpt. 1970—, v.p. 1974, treas. 1975-76). Club: Hacienda Bath and Tennis. Home: 12017 Villa Dorado Dr St Louis MO 63141 Office: 1010 Pine St St Louis MO 63101

MARLOW, MARGARET ANN, historian; b. Dover, Ohio, July 11, 1927; d. George N. and Della (Bingham) Marlow; B.S. in Edn., Kent State U., 1950, M.A., 1950, postgrad. 1953, 58; postgrad. Western Res. U., 1951; U. Colo., 1960. Tchr., Eastlake Jr. High Sch., Willoughby, Ohio, 1951-53, East Canton (Ohio) High Sch., 1953-54; asso. prof. Monticello Coll., Godfrey, Ill., 1954-71; prof. Lewis and Clark Community Coll., Godfrey, 1971—; coordinator history and pol. sci. Ill. Great Tchrs. Seminar, 1972, chmn. curriculum com., 1972—. Mem. friends div. St. Louis Art Mus., 1972—. Recipient Monticello Coll. Distinguished Service award, 1964. Mem. Am. Hist. Assn., Modern History Soc., Soc. for History Edn., AAUP, Phil Alpha Theta, Pi Gamma Mu. Home: 724 Lafayette Ave Godfrey IL 62035 Office: Lewis & Clark Community Coll Godfrey IL 62035

MARNELL, RICHARD THOMAS, physician, educator; b. Hoboken, N.J., May 25, 1927; s. Francis X. and Mabel (Fitzpatrick) M.; B.S., St. Peters Coll., Jersey City, N.J., 1950; M.D., State U. N.Y., 1955; m. Maria A. Strong, Aug. 23, 1954: children—Francis X., Mary A., Stephen F., Christopher M., David M., Sean D., Nicole. Intern, St. Raphael Hosp., New Haven, Conn., 1955-56, resident in medicine, 1956-59; NIH research fellow U. Cin., 1959-62, asst. prof. medicine Coll. Medicine, 1962-74, clin. asso. prof. medicine, 1974—; practice medicine specializing in endocrinology, Cin., 1974—. Fellow Am. Coll. Physicians. Contbr. articles to med. jours. Home: 359 Warren Ave Cincinnati OH 45220

MARNER, DAVID LLOYD, lawyer; b. Riverside, Iowa, June 14, 1933; s. Ray I. and Lydia M. (Miller) M.; B.A. magna cum laude, Coe Coll., 1955; J.D. with distinction, U. Iowa, 1958; m. Pauline E. Frank, Aug. 19, 1955; children—David Lloyd, Trenton P., Paula L. Admitted to Iowa bar; asso. Young law firm, Wellman, Iowa, 1958-59; asso., then partner firm Nazette, Hendrickson, Marner and Good, Cedar Rapids, Iowa, 1962—; legislative asst. to Congressman James E. Bromwell, 1962-66. Dir. Exchange State Bank, Springville, Iowa, Cedar Rapids Baseball Club, Inc. Mem. Cedar Rapids Estate Planning Council. Adviser Kirkwood Community Coll.; pres. local PTA, 1972. Bd. dirs. Iowa Children's and Family Services, Des Moines, United Cerebral Palsy Center, Youth Council Cedar Rapids, Jr. C. of C. Charities, Inc. Served with USAF, 1959-62. Iowa Centennial scholar; Frederick S. Murray Internat. Relations scholar. Mem. Cedar Rapids Jr. (v.p. 1965), Cedar Rapids chambers commerce, Linn County (dir.; past sec.-treas), Iowa, Am., Sixth Jud. Dist. (pres. 1977), bar assns., Cedar Rapids Law Club (dir.), Christian Legal Soc., Phi Beta Kappa, Phi Kappa Phi, Pi Kappa Delta. Presbyterian. (trustee). Clubs: Thursday Noon Optimist (pres. 1972), Cedar Rapids Country. Contbr. articles to legal jours. Home: 2114 Greenwood Dr Cedar Rapids IA 52403 Office: 200 1st St SW Cedar Rapids IA 52404

MAROLD, FRANK, corporate exec.; b. St. Marys, Pa., Jan. 19, 1925; s. Vincent and Anna (Mahnick) M.; B.S. in Metallurgy, Pa. State U., 1945; m. Sara Piperato, Dec. 20, 1952; children—Robinne, Francine, Franklin, Lisa, Vincent. Mgmt. trainee, sales rep. Allis-Chalmers Mfg. Co., Milw., 1945-51; sales mgr. Shahmoon Industries, N.Y.C., 1951-57; v.p. sales Atlantic Metal Hose Co., N.Y.C., 1957-59; v.p. marketing Griffin Pipe Products Co. div. Amsted Industries, Inc., 1959-65, exec. v.p., 1965-66, pres., 1966-74; pres., dir. Glamorgan Pipe & Foundry Co., Inc. subsidiary Amsted Industries, 1972-74; v.p. Amsted Industries Inc., 1974—; dir. Kemlite Corp., Joliet, Ill. Mem. Am. Soc. Plastics Engrs., Am. Water Works Assn., Am. Ceramic Soc., Am. Marketing Assn. Clubs: Executive, Economic, University (Chgo.), St. Charles Country. Home: 502 Willow Ln Geneva IL 60134 Office: 3700 Prudential Plaza Chicago IL 60601

MARONEK, JAMES EDWARD, theatre scene designer, educator; b. Milw., Dec. 4, 1931; s. Frank Raymond and Gladys (Parker) M.; student U. Wis., 1952-53; B.F.A., Art Inst. Chgo., 1953, M.F.A., 1958; m. Carole Anita Rudzina, Oct. 31, 1970; children—Michael, Nicholas, Gayle Ann. Asso. prof. Goodman Sch. Drama, Chgo., 1959—. Designer, Peninsula Players, Wis., 1950-53, NBC-TV, Chgo., 1957-58, Edgewater Beach Playhouse, Chgo., 1958-61, Acad. Playhouse, Lake Forest, Ill., 1967, 69, Ravinia Drama Festival, Highland Park, Ill., 1968-69, U. Chgo., 1966, Hull House, Chgo., 1964, U.S. Fla., 1972, Columbia Coll. at Chgo., 1969, Lyric Opera Chgo., 1976; indsl. shows IBM, RCA, Admiral, Zenith, Gen. Electric, Philco-Ford; sr. resident designer Goodman Theatre Chgo., 1959-71; designer 1st Chgo. Center, 1974; contbg. editor, arts critic Chgo. mag., 1973-77; one man shows Hull House Gallery, 1964, Artists Guild Chgo., 1965. Served with AUS, 1953-55. Recipient Joseph Jefferson awards best scenic design Goodman Theatre, 1974, best lighting design Organic Theatre, 1976. Mem. U.S. Inst. Theatre Tech., Am. Theatre Assn., AAUP, United Scenic Artists of Am. (pres. 1968—). Author: Designers Notebook, 1971. Home: 2113 Park Ln Highland Park IL 60035

MAROSKY, JOHN EDWIN, endodontist; b. Indpls., July 3, 1941; s. Clarence H. and Wilma J. Marosky; A.B., Ind. U., 1963, D.D.S., 1967, M.S.D., 1975; m. Janet Sue Adams, Dec. 26, 1965; children—Julie Kay, Jill Suzanne. Practice dentistry, Indpls., 1969—. Instr., Ind. U. Sch. Dentistry, 1969-73, asst. prof., 1975—. Served to capt. AUS, 1967-69. Decorated Bronze Star Medal. Mem. Am., Ind., Indpls. dental assns., Harry J. Healey Endodontic Study Club (sec.-treas.), Hamilton Study Club, Am., Ind. assns. endodontists, Alpha Tau Omega. Mem. Christian Ch. (pres. Ind. Men's Fellowship 1974). Contbr. articles to profl. jours. Home: 5959 Cape Cod Ct Indianapolis IN 46250 Office: 1010 E 86th St Winterton Indianapolis IN 46240

MARQUETTE, RAYMOND EUGENE, auto club exec.; b. Indpls., June 19, 1929; s. Grover Cleveland and Minnie (Heinz) M.; B.S. in Journalism, Ind. U., 1951; m. Jacqueline Lou Maddox, Feb. 3, 1951; children—Donald Ray, Denise, Lisa Marie. Sportswriter, Indpls. News, 1951-64, author weekly auto racing column, 1969—; sportswriter Indpls. Star, 1964-77; dir. pub. affairs U.S. Auto Club, 1977—. Tchr. journalism Ind. Central Coll., 1966-71. Recipient Henry McLemore award as outstanding motor sports writer, 1971; Sportswriting of Year awards Indpls. Press Club, 1959, 67, 68; also basketball and auto racing contest awards. Mem. U.S. Basketball Writers Assn. (pres. 1963, sec., treas., editor 1969—), Am. Automobile Racing Writers and Broadcasters Assn. (v.p. 1972-74) Nat. Motorsports Assn., Sigma Delta Chi, Sigma Pi. Author: Indiana University Basketball, 1975; The Perfect Season, 1976. Home: 1425 E Banta Rd Indianapolis IN 46227 Office: 4910 W 16th St Speedway IN 46224

MARQUIS, GERALDINE MAE HILDRETH (MRS. FORREST W. MARQUIS), educator; b. Ankeny, Iowa, Aug. 8; d. Vernon Otto and Alma Leona (Woods) Hildreth; student U. No. Iowa; M.A., Drake U., 1972; m. Forrest William Marquis; 1 son, Robert William. Elementary tchr., Ankeny and Ft. Dodge, Iowa, 1944-49, 56—; organizer Ft. Dodge Coop. Nursery Sch. Mem. NEA, Iowa, Ft. Dodge edn. assns., Assn. Childhood Edn. Internat. (Ia. pres. 1974-77), Nat. Assn. Edn. Young Children, Civic Music Assn., TTT Nat. Soc., Delta Kappa Gamma (local pres. 1974-77), Phi Sigma Alpha. Republican. Methodist. Home: 814 N 16th St Fort Dodge IA 50501 Office: 615 N 16th St Fort Dodge IA 50501

MARRON, MICHAEL THOMAS, educator; b. Buffalo, Jan. 31, 1943; s. Thomas Urban and Anna Alberta (Bloom) M.; B.S., U. Portland, 1964; M.A., Johns Hopkins U., 1965, Ph.D. (NIH fellow), 1969; m. Mary Elizabeth O'Brien, July 2, 1966. Research asso. Theoretical Chemistry Inst., Madison, Wis., 1969-70; asst. prof. U. Wis., Parkside, Kenosha, 1970-73, asso. prof. chemistry since, 1973—. Mem. Racine (Wis.) Air Pollution Control Appeals Bd., 1971-76. Mem. AAAS, Wis. Acad. Sci., Arts and Letters, Am. Phys. Soc., Sigma Xi, Phi Lambda Upsilon. Contbr. articles in field to profl. jours. Home: 1307 Main St Racine WI 53403 Office: U Wis-Parkside Kenosha WI 53140

MARSCHALL, VERNELL LEE, mineral exploration co. exec.; b. Fargo, N.D., June 24, 1946; s. Albert David and Delores Esther (Marquardt) M.; student Columbia Basin Coll., 1964, Eastern Wash. State Coll., 1965-69; m. Susan Frances Carrington, May 11, 1974; 1 son, Nathan. Field foreman Bear Creek Mining Co., western Mont., 1967-68; head surveyor Kenneth L. Preston Mining Engring. Co., No. Idaho, 1969; asst. geophys. technician, Noranda Exploration Inc., Reno, 1970; chief geophys. technician, Rhinelander, Wis., 1971—. Mem. Soc. Exploration Geophysicists, Prospectors and Developers Assn., Trout Unlimited (pres. N. Woods chpt. 1976-77), Ducks

Unlimited, Central Wis. Retriever Club, Wis. Amateur Field Trial Club, Sierra Club. Mem. United Ch. Christ. Geophys. discoverer Pelican River ore deposit Oneida County, Wis., 1973. Home: 4342 Lake Mildred Rd Rhinelander WI 54501 Office: PO Box 7 Rhinelander WI 54501

MARSEE, CARL WAYNE, mfg. co. exec.; b. Middlesboro, Ky., Sept. 12, 1939; s. Troy McKinley and Flora Bell (Hensley) M.; A.A. in Accounting, Miami Jacobs Coll., 1959; student Giffen Coll., 1962; B.A., Ind. No. U., 1975; m. Diana Fay Taylor, May 16, 1960; 1 son, Jeffrey Wayne. Salesman, Anchor Sales Corp., Celina, Ohio, 1959-60, sales mgr., 1964-71, v.p., 1968-73; quality assurance inspector Nat. Seal Co., Van Wert, Ohio, 1961-62; salesman Western & So. Ins. Co., St. Marys, Ohio, 1963-64; v.p. Speicher Bros., Inc., Celina, 1968-73; pres., gen. mgr. Speicher Corp., Celina, 1974—, C-Mar Corp., Celina, 1974—; chmn. bd. Celular Corp., Celina. Mem. finance com. St. Paul's United Methodist Ch.; trustee Giffen Coll., 1971-72; v.p. Coop. Extension Service. Mem. Am. Soc. Agrl. Engrs., Land Improvement Contractors Assn. (asso. dir.), Distbn. Contractors Assn. (asso. dir.), Young Pres.' Orgn., C. of C. (v.p.), Worldwide Sportsmen's Club. Republican. Clubs: Summit, Grand Lake Racquet, Masons, Shriners, Elks. Home: 317 Magnolia St Celina OH 45822 Office: 600 E Wayne St Celina OH 45822

MARSH, DON E., supermarket exec.; b. Muncie, Ind., Feb. 2, 1938; s. Ermal W. and Garnet (Gibson) M.; B.A., Mich. State U., 1961; m. Marilyn Faust, Mar. 28, 1959; children—Don Ermal, Arthur Andrew, David Alan, Ann Elizabeth, Alexander Elliott. With Marsh Supermarkets, Inc., Yorktown, Ind., 1961—, pres., 1966—, also dir.; dir. Am. Guaranty, Inc., Am. Nat. Bank & Trust Co., Kokomo Land Inc., Marsh Pension Plan, Circle Velley Farms, Gt. Lakes, Inc., Mid States Finance, Mundy Realty, Nationwide, Inc., John Marshall Life Ins. Co., Panorama, Inc., Village Pantry, Inc.; dir. Central Ind. Better Bus. Bur., Central Ind. Retail Council, Food Industry Good Govt., Super Market Inst. Mem. advisory bd. Jr. Achievement; mem. Nat. Commn. Unemployment Compensation. Mem. Ind. (dir.), Indpls., Muncie, Delaware County (dir.) chambers commerce, Newcomen Soc. N. Am., Internat. (dir.), Nat. assns. food chains, Am. Mgmt. Assn., Young Presidents Assn., Food Merchandisers Edn. Council, Nat. Assn. Convenience Stores, Phi Sigma Epsilon, Lambda Chi Alpha. Mason, Elk, Rotarian. Clubs: Columbia (Indpls.); Delaware Country (Muncie); World Trade. Home: 50 Warwick Rd Muncie IN 47304 Office: Marsh Supermarkets Inc PO Box 155 Yorktown IN 47396

MARSH, EDWIN THOMAS, artist-potter; b. Winchester, Ky., Feb. 11, 1934; s. Howard Thomas and Bessie Anise (Gamboe) M.; B.S., U. Louisville, 1960; apprentice to Totaro SaKuma, Mashiko, Japan, 1961-62; student at Engakuji Temple, Japan, 1963; apprenticeship Kei Fujiwara, Japan, 1963-64; M.A., Ind. U., 1970; m. Virginia Jean Stein, Dec. 27, 1968; 1 dau., Rebekah Jean; children by previous marriage—Amy, Beth, Dan. Practicing prodn. studio potter, 1958—; founded Marsh Pottery, Sellersburg, Ind., 1965, designed and built present facilities in Borden, Ind., 1968—; prof. fine arts Allen R. Hite Art Inst., U. Louisville, Ky., 1970—; one-man shows: Art Center Gallery, Louisville, Swearingen-Byck Gallery, Louisville, The Gallery, Bloomington, Ind., N. Mo. State U. Mus., Shirokiya, Tokyo; group shows include: Mid-West Crafts, Evansville, Ind., J.B. Speed Mus., Louisville, Walker Art Center, Mpls., Mus. Modern Art, Kamakura; represented in permanent collections: The Ashland Oil Co., Columbus Mus. Fine Arts, Ohio State U., Ind. U., State U. Iowa, Duke U., Brown U., U. Notre Dame, Mus. Modern Art Japan, The Renwick Gallery, The Smithsonian Inst. Mem. Am. Craftsmen's Council, Nat. Council on Edn. for the Ceramic Arts, AAUP. Home: Route 2 Box 657 Borden IN 47106 Office: Fine Arts - U Louisville Louisville KY 40208

MARSH, FRANK, state ofcl.; b. Norfolk, Nebr., Apr. 27, 1924; s. Frank and Delia (Andrews) M.; B.S. in Edn., U. Nebr., 1950; m. Shirley Mac McVicker, Mar. 5, 1943; children—Sherry Anne Marsh Tupper, Dory Michael, Stephen Alan, Corwin Frank, Mitchell Edward, Melissa Lou. Builder, tchr., businessman, 1946-52; sec. state Nebr., 1953-71, lt. gov., 1971-75, state treas., 1975—. Mem. State Canvassing Bd., State Claims Bd.; govt. liaison adviser Mayor's Com. Internat. Friendship; past pres. Nat. Council Community Services to Internat. Visitors; internat. trustee Am. Field Service/Intercultural Programs, U. Nebr. Fgn. Student Host Program; bd. dirs. Am. Youth Hostels, Inc. Mem. Combined Orgn. Police Services, Am., Nebr. correctional assns., Central States Corrections Assn. (past pres.), Capitol City Footprinters, Nebraskaland Found., Nat. Assn. State Treasurers (sr. v.p.), Midwest Internat. Trade Assn. (dir.), V.F.W., Am. Legion, Scottish Soc. Nebr., Nebr. Hist. Soc., Lincoln Chamber Soc. Orch., D.A.V., Native Sons and Daus. (life), U. Nebr. Alumni Assn. Republican. Methodist (chmn. adminstrv. bd.). Clubs: Sertoma, Lincoln Gem and Mineral, Lincoln Stamp, Polemic. Home: 2701 S 34th St Lincoln NE 68506 Office: State Capitol Bldg Lincoln NE 68509

MARSH, HOMER ELLSWORTH, assn. exec.; b. Plymouth, Ind., Apr. 19, 1912; s. Marion Oscar and Pearl Ione (Ritter) M.; B.S., Ind. U., 1935, postgrad., 1935-36; m. Hazel Gladys Monce, May 24, 1941. Instr. sch. bus. adminstrn. Ind. U., 1935-36; dir. research and statistics Unemployment Compensation Div., State of Ind., 1936-44; cons. bur. labor statistics U.S. Dept. Labor, 1942-44; dir. research Nat. Tax Equality Assn., Chgo., 1944-48, 49-62, exec. sec., 1962-70, cons., 1970-75, pres., 1975-77; dir. research Nat. Asso. Businessmen, Inc., Washington, 1948, now mem. bd. Mem. Govtl. Research Assn., Nat. Tax Assn., Internat. Fiscal Assn., Am. Acad. Polit. and Social Sci., Beta Gamma Sigma. Author: (with Thomas W. Rogers) Bibliography of Public Employment Offices, 1935; Solvency of Indiana Unemployment Compensation Fund, 1943; Cooperative Expansion in the Petroleum Industry, 1944; Super-Cooperatives in the Field Purchasing, 1944; Tax Free Manufacturing Cooperative Corporations, 1945; Subsidized Cooperatives in the Marketing Field, 1945; Cooperative Competition in New England, 1946; The Facts in the Matter, 1947; The Other Tax Exempts, 1947; Tax Escaping Cooperatives Engaged in Grocery Distribution, 1949. Contbr. to trade publs. Home: PO Box 485 Plymouth IN 46563

MARSH, JEREMIAH, lawyer; b. Freeborn County, Minn., June 5, 1933; s. Howard E. and Mildred (Larson) M.; A.B. magna cum laude, Harvard U., 1955, J.D., 1958; m. Marietta Cashen, June 16, 1956; children—Howard, Kimberley, Courtney, Christopher. Practice law, Chgo., 1958-62; legis. asst. to Sen. Edward M. Kennedy, Washington, 1963-64; mem. firm Hackbert, Rooks, Pitts., Fullagar & Poust, Chgo., 1964-68; spl. counsel to Gov. Ogilvie, Chgo., Springfield, Ill., 1969-72; mem. firm. Hopkins, Sutter, Mulroy, Davis & Cromartie, Chgo., 1973—; mem. faculty John Marshall Law Sch., 1959-68, 75—; mem. Nat. Conf. Commrs. Uniform State Laws, 1969-73, 77—; chmn. Ill. Adminstrv. Rules Commn., 1977—. Treas., bd. dirs. gateway House Found.; mem. adv. council Misericordia Home. Mem. Am., Ill., Chgo., 7th Circuit, Fed. bar assns., Selden Soc., Am. Judicature Soc., Supreme Ct. Hist. Soc., Law Club, Chgo. Assn. Commerce and Industry. Home: 456 Elder Ln Winnetka IL 60093 Office: 1 First Nat Plaza Chicago IL 60603

MARSH, ROBERT CHARLES, writer, music critic; b. Columbus, Ohio, Aug. 5, 1924; s. Charles L. and Jane A. (Beckett) M.; B.S., Northwestern U., 1945, A.M., 1946; Sage fellow Cornell U., 1946-47; postgrad. U. Chgo., 1948; Ed.D., Harvard, 1951; postgrad. U. Oxford, 1952-53, U. Cambridge, 1953-56; m. Kathleen C. Moscrop, July 4, 1956. Instr. social sci. U. Ill., 1947-49; lectr. humanities Chgo. City Jr. Coll., 1950-51; asst. prof. edn. U. Kansas City, 1951-52; vis. prof. edn. State U. N.Y., 1953-54; humanities staff U. Chgo., 1956-58, lectr. social thought, 1976; music critic Chgo. Sun-Times, 1956—. Nat. adv. com., project for tng. music critics U. So. Calif., 1964-72. Ford Found. fellow, 1965-66. Episcopalian. Club: Tavern (Chicago). Author: Toscanini and the Art of Orchestral Performance, 1956, revised edit., 1962; The Cleveland Orchestra, 1967. Editor: Logic and Knowledge, 1956; contbg. editor High Fidelity, 1955-66, 71-77. Office: 1825 N Lincoln Plaza Chicago IL 60614 also Chgo Sun-Times 401 N Wabash Ave Chicago IL 60611

MARSHALL, ALBERT P(RINCE), librarian; b. Texarkana, Tex., Sept. 5, 1914; s. Early and Mary (Bland) M.; A.B., Lincoln U., 1938; B.S. in L.S., U. Ill., 1939, M.A., 1953; m. Ruthe Langley, June 12, 1941; 1 dau., Satia Yvette (Mrs. James E. Orange). Asst. librarian Lincoln U., 1939-41; librarian Winston-Salem (N.C.) Tchrs. Coll., 1941-48; univ. librarian Lincoln U., 1950-69; dir. library Eastern Mich. U., Ypsilanti, 1969-72, dean acad. services, 1972-76, prof. library service, 1977—. Mem. Mayor's Commn. on Race Relations, Winston-Salem, 1946-48, Commn. Human Relations, Jefferson City, Mo., 1953-56. Chmn. ALA-ACRL Audio Visual Com., 1967-69. Mem. Harry S. Truman Library Inst., 1968—; mem. adv. council Internat. Book Year, 1971-72; mem. bd. cons. Nat. Endowment for the Humanities, 1977; cons. in field. Active Boy Scouts Am. Bd. dirs. Community Center Assn., 1955-69, Child and Family Service Assn. Washtenaw County, 1972-75, Washtenaw County chpt. Mich. Heart Assn.; sec., bd. dirs. Washtenaw County Opportunities Industrialization Centers. Served with USCGR, 1943-45. Recipient Distinguished Alumni award Lincoln U., 1965. Mem. Am. (chmn. nominating com. 1965-66; mem. council 1964-67, 2d v.p. 1971-72), Mo. (pres. 1961-62; chmn. college and univ. library devel. com. 1964-66; citation 1969), Mich. (2d v.p. 1972-73), N.C. Negro (v.p. 1947-48) library assns., NAACP (pres. state conf. of brs. 1954-55), Alumni Assn. Lincoln U. (alumni sec.; editor bull. 1956-67), Am. Legion, Am. Hist. Assn., Am. Assn. Higher Edn., Assn. for Study of Afro-Am. History, Alpha Phi Alpha (achievement award 1975), Delta Phi Delta. Methodist (sr. steward, vice chmn.). Rotarian. Club: Business and Professional (treas. 1972—). Author: Soldier's Dream: Centennial History of Lincoln University, 1966. Home: 1616 Gregory St Ypsilanti MI 48197 Office: Center Ednl Resources Eastern Mich Univ Ypsilanti MI 48197

MARSHALL, CHARLES ORR, JR., lawyer; b. Omaha, Apr. 9, 1911; s. Charles Orr and Ahlene (Cox) M.; B.S.E., U. Mich., 1931; J.D., Loyola U., Chgo., 1935; m. Juanita Ruth Lang, July 2, 1932; children—Orr, Ahlene Marshall Welsh, Delmar, Suzanne Marshall Nevius. Admitted to Ill. bar, 1935, Ohio bar, 1938; asso. firm Gillson, Mann & Cox, Chgo., 1931-35, Williams, Bradbury, McCaleb & Hinkle, Chgo., 1935-37; partner Marshall & Yeasting, Toledo, 1937—; pres. Patent Annuity Mgmt. Inc., Toledo, 1973—. Mem. Am., Toledo bar assns. Republican. Presbyterian. Clubs: Toledo, Inverness (Toledo). Home: 1716 Secor Rd Toledo OH 43607 Office: Edward Lamb Bldg Toledo OH 43604

MARSHALL, FLOYD WILLIAM, coll. pres.; b. Quincy, Ill., July 24, 1921; s. William A. and Hattie C. (Leu) M.; B.S., Calif. Coll. Commerce, 1955; M.A., Gem City Coll., 1958; Ph.D., Inst. Social Research, Switzerland, 1969; m. Frieda V. Dege, July 21, 1944; children—Bruce T., Janice E. Office mgr. Gem City Coll., Quincy, 1940-42, office mgr., corp. sec., 1946-54, pres., 1955—; adminstr. Good Samaritan Home for Aged, 1955; pres. Kansas City Sch. Watchmaking, Argent, Inc., Greenmount Cemetery Assn. UN Day chmn. City of Quincy; mem. Region 12 Manpower Tech. Adv. Com.; pres. West Central Ill. Lung Assn.; seal sale chmn. Adams County Tb Assn.; crusade chmn. Am. Cancer Soc.; treas. Adams County Mental Health Assn. Named Exec. of Year, Nat. Secs. Assn., 1966, hon. mem. Quinsippi chpt. 1961. Mem. Ill. Bus. Schs. Assn. (past pres.), Assn. Ind. Colls. and Schs. (bd. dirs. 1962-65), Accredited Ill. Bus. Schs. (v.p. 1970), Ill. Bus. Edn. Assn. (dir.). Clubs: Masons, Quincy High Twelve. Editor: Principles of Accounting, 1966. Home: 166 Kentucky St Quincy IL 62301 Office: 700 State St Quincy IL 62301

MARSHALL, GEORGE BADGLEY, judge; b. Columbus, Ohio, Apr. 23, 1906; s. George Sidney and Alice (Badgley) M.; B.A.; Ohio State U., 1928, L.D., 1931; m. Pauline Blanton, June 27, 1942; 1 son, George Blanton. Admitted to Ohio bar, 1931, pvt. practice Columbus, 1931-54; judge Ct. of Common Pleas, Franklin County, 1954—. Mem. Ohio Ho. of Reps., 1939-44, 47-49, Senate, 1950-51. Served from lt. (j.g.) to lt. USNR, 1943-45, PTO. Mem. Am., Ohio, Columbus bar assns., Am. Judicature Soc., S.A.R., Phi Beta Kappa. Mason (32 deg.). Clubs: Executives, Torch. Home: 2175 West Lane Ave Columbus OH 43221 Office: Hall of Justice 369 South High St Columbus OH 43215

MARSHALL, HERBERT A., lawyer; b. Clinton, Ill., Aug. 20, 1917; s. Harry A. and Andrea (Pederson) M.; A.B., Washburn U., 1940, LL.B., J.D., 1943; m. Helen Christman, May 3, 1941; children—James A., Thomas A., Mary Marshall Nichols. Admitted to Kans. bar, 1943; law clk. U.S. Ct. Appeals, 1943-44; asst. county atty. Shawnee County (Kans.), 1944-50; individual practice law, Topeka, 1944—; mem. firm Marshall, Hawks, McKinney & Hendrix, 1946—; instr. practice ct. Washburn U. Law Sch., 1963—; mem. Kans. Supreme Ct. Nominating Commn., 1968—. Fellow Am. Coll. Trial Lawyers; mem. Kans. (exec. council 1968—, v.p. 1977), Topeka (pres. 1968) bar assns., Topeka C. of C. Presbyterian (trustee, elder). Clubs: Masons, Elks, Moose, Topeka Optimist. Home: 4722 Brentwood St Topeka KS 66606 Office: Mchts Bank Bldg Topeka KS 66612

MARSHALL, JOHN HART, biophysicist; b. Chgo., Feb. 14, 1925; s. Thomas Linder and Elizabeth Webster (Carpenter) M.; A.B. magna cum laude, Harvard U., 1945; Ph.D. (AEC fellow), Mass. Inst. Tech., 1952; m. Constance Edmonds Leighton, May 21, 1955; children—Deborah (Mrs. James Little Woodward), Nancy (Mrs. Preston Goddard Athey). Research asso. Radioactivity Center, Mass. Inst. Tech., Cambridge, 1952-55; asst. physicist radiol. research div. Argonne (Ill.) Nat. Lab., 1955-59, biophysicist, 1960-70, sr. biophysicist, 1971—, group leader radioisotope toxicity Center for Human Radiobiology, 1970—. Co-chmn. Symposium on Cancer Mechanisms, Argonne, 1974; chmn. task group Internat. Commn. on Radiol. Protection, London, Eng., 1968—; mem. com. 23 Nat. Com. on Radiation Protection, Washington, 1966-74. Served with USNR, 1942-46. Mem. Radiation Research Soc., Orthopaedic Research Soc. (mem. program com. 1965-68). Republican. Episcopalian. Club: Hinsdale (Ill.) Golf. Author: Theory of Alkaline Earth Metabolism, 1964; (with Liniecki, Mays and others) Alkaline Earth Metabolism in Adult Man, 1973; (with Groer) Theory of the Induction of Bone Cancer by Alpha Radiation, 1977. Home: 108 Briarwood Ln Oak Brook IL 60521 Office: 203-B-121 Argonne National Laboratory Argonne IL 60439

MARSHALL, KENNETH ERIC, scientist; b. Kings Lynn, England, Oct. 25, 1930; s. William and Effie (Coates) M.; came to Canada, 1967, naturalized, 1975; B.Sc. in Zoology, U. London, 1951; m. Dorothy Kindred Edgar, Oct. 18, 1958; children—Lynn Susan, Karina Joyce, Kenneth William Edgar. Librarian Freshwater Biological Assn., Ambleside, England, 1955-64; science librarian U. London, Englefield Green, Surrey, England, 1964-67; head library and publ. services Freshwater Inst., Fisheries and Environment Can., Winnipeg, Man., 1967—. Mem. Inst. for Info. Science, Canadian Assn. for Info. Science (pres. 1975-76), Am. Assn. for Info. Science, Spl. Libraries Assn., Canadian, Man., English library assns. Mem. Anglican Ch. Club: Falcon Yacht (commodore 1977). Author: Index to Journal of Ecology, Vol. 21-50, 1933-62, 1966. Home: 653 Patricia Ave Winnipeg MB R3T 3A8 Canada Office: 501 University Crescent Winnipeg MB R3T 2N6 Canada

MARSHALL, MILLARD RAY, surgeon, corporate med. dir.; b. Clinton, Ind., Oct. 9, 1915; s. Millard Fillmore and Lottie (McAdams) M.; B.S., U. Ind., 1938, M.D., 1939; M.S. in Surgery, U. Mich., 1948. Practice medicine specializing in surgery, cons. surgeon, Gary, Ind., 1952-63; asso. med. dir. Inland Steel Co., East Chicago, Ind., 1963-65; plant surgeon, Gary Works U.S. Steel Co., 1965-69; med. dir. Corn Products, CPC Internat., Argo, Ill., 1969—. Health commr., Indian Head Park, Ill., 1975—. Diplomate Am. Bd. Surgery. Pres. NW Ind. Heart Assn.; fellow Am. Coll. Surgeons, Am. Occupat. Med. Assn., Am. Acad. Occupational Medicine, Med. Dirs. Club Chgo. Home: 118 Cascade Dr Indian Head Park IL 60525

MARSHALL, ROBERT E., dentist; b. Columbia, Mo., Oct. 31, 1921; s. Robert E. and Mary Essie (Tolleson) M.; D.D.S., St. Louis U., 1944; m. Sally Helen Brownfield, Mar. 8, 1952; children—Robert E. Lee, Lesa Ann. Individual practice dentistry, Lee's Summit, Mo., 1946—. Pres. dental corp., Lee's Summit, Mo., 1972—. Served with Dental Corps, USNR, 1942-46. Mem. Am., Mo., Greater Kansas City dental assns., Acad. Gen. Dentistry, Mo. Pilots Assn., Flying Dentists Assn., C. of C. Rotarian. Home: 215 Woodbine Ave Lee's Summit MO 64063 Office: 319 Southeast Main Lee's Summit MO 64063

MARSHALL, ROBERT FRANKLIN, clergyman; b. Geneva, Ill., Aug. 26, 1920; s. George L. and Helen Edith (Faitz) M.; student Cornell Coll., 1938-42, U. Chgo., 1943-45, Chgo. Theol. Sem., 1943-46; m. Doris J. Klass, Aug. 15, 1948; children—Stephen, Barbara, Robert S., John, Joy. Ordained to ministry Unitarian Universalist Ch., 1963; asst. minister First Congl. Ch., Cedar Rapids, Iowa, 1938-40; minister Monmouth-Baldwin Community Meth. Parish (Iowa), 1940-42, Birmingham (Mich.) Unitarian Ch., 1962—; with ednl. dept. UAW-CIO, 1947-48; owner, operator Bob Marshall's Book Shop, Ann Arbor, Mich., 1949-67, Ypsilanti, Mich., 1956-62. Officer Oakland County (Mich.) OEO, 1964-67, Pontiac (Mich.) Opportunities Industrialization Center, 1974—; founder CORE, 1942, Citizens for Suburban Responsibility, 1969; bd. dirs. ACLU, 1966-70. Mem. Concerned Clergy of Greater Pontiac, League Indsl. Democracy, NAACP, Common Cause, Workmen's Circle, Unitarian Universalist Ministers Assn., Workers Def. League, Urban League, Interfaith Com. to Support Farm Workers, Friends of Haifa U. Democrat. Book editor Jour. Religious Humanism; contbr. articles to numerous publs. Recognized by Guinness Book of Records for preaching world's longest sermon (60 hours, 31 minutes), 1976. Home: 952 Wimbleton St Birmingham MI 48008 Office: 651 N Woodward St Bloomfield Hills MI 48010

MARSHALL, RONALD CLEMENS, orgn. exec.; b. Detroit, July 21, 1944; s. Anthony J. and Edith M. (Webb) M.; B.A., Mich. State U., 1967; M.A., Wayne State U., 1970. Labor market analyst State of Mich., 1967; tchr. elementary sch., 1968-69; a founder Project Headline, community health service agy., Detroit, 1970, dir. drug prevention programs, 1970—, alcoholism therapist, 1974-76, sr. therapist, 1977—; mem. faculty Wayne County Community Coll., 1970-72. Mem. Wayne County Drug Edn. and Tng. Task Force, 1974; co-chmn. New Detroit Inc. Black Applied Research Drug Team, 1972. Bd. dirs. Narcotics Addiction Rehab. Coordinating Corgn., 1973—, Heartline Inc., 1975—, South Eastern Mich. Substance Abuse Council, 1975—. Recipient awards for work in drug abuse field. Mem. Internat. Transactional Analysis Assn. (clin. mem.). Author article. Home: 13375 Jane St Detroit MI 48205 Office: 18820 Hayes St Detroit MI 48205

MARSTELLER, WILLIAM A., advt. exec.; b. Champaign, Ill., Feb. 23, 1914; s. P. L. and Minnie (Finder) M.; B.S., U. Ill., 1937; m. Gloria Crawford, Apr. 22, 1938; children—Elizabeth A. (Mrs. Stuart M. Gordon), Julie. Reporter, Champaign News-Gazette, 1932-37; agy. counselor Mass. Mut. Life Ins. Co., Chgo., 1937-41; advt. and sales promotion mgr. Edward Valves, Inc., East Chicago, Ind., 1941-43, sec., 1943-45, v.p., dir., 1945-51; mgr. advt. and market research Rockwell Mfg. Co., Pitts., 1945-49, v.p., 1949-51; pres. Marsteller Research, Inc., Chgo., 1951—; pres. Marsteller Inc., 1951-60, chmn., 1960-76, chmn. exec. com., 1976—; chmn. Burson-Marsteller, Assos., 1953-68, Marsteller Internat., S.A., Geneva, Switzerland, 1961—. Trustee Barnard Coll., Whitney Mus. Am. Art; mem. U. Ill. Pres.'s Club, Barnard Council. Recipient Achievement award U. Ill., 1973; Pres.'s award, 1976. Mem. Am. Mgmt. Assn. (dir.), Am. Assn. Advt. Agys., Chgo. (pres. 1945-46), Nat. (pres. 1947-49) indsl. advertisers assns., Football Writers Assn. Am., AAUP, U. Ill. Found. Art Inst. Chgo. (life), Sigma Chi. Clubs: California (Los Angeles); Tavern, Mid-America, Arts (Chgo.); Pinnacle (N.Y.C.); Duquesne (Pitts.). Author: The Wonderful World of Words, 1972. Contbr. articles to mktg. and advt. publs. Home: 900 Lake Shore Dr Chicago IL 60611 also 1060 Fifth Ave New York City NY Office: 1 E Wacker Dr Chicago IL 60601 also 866 3d Ave New York City NY 10022

MARSTON, ANSON DAY, ret. army officer, educator; b. Ames, Iowa, May 20, 1905; s. Anson and M. Alice (Day) M.; B.S. in Civil Engring., Iowa State Coll., 1925; M.S., U. Wis., 1926; E.E., Iowa State Coll., 1931; grad. Command Gen Staff Coll., 1948, Air War Coll., 1949, Indsl. Coll. Armed Forces, 1954; D.Sc. (hon.), U. Omaha, 1968; m. Virginia J. Hibbard, Sept. 6, 1927 (dec. June 1973); children—Alice Virginia (Mrs. Keith R. Barney, Junior), Lucy Jeannette (Mrs. Peter A. Carruthers); m. 2d, Margaret Pentzien, Dec. 19, 1973. Indsl. engr. Kansas City Power & Light Co., 1926-41; officer U.S. Army, 1941-60, ret. 1960; col. office Chief of Engrs., Washington, 1956-58; dep. div. engr. Missouri River Div., Omaha, 1958-60; prof. engring. U. Nebr. at Omaha, 1960-70, head dept., 1963-68, acting dean engring., 1966-67, dean, 1967-70; dir. pub. works City of Omaha, 1961-62. Vice pres. Mid-Am. council Boy Scouts Am., 1964—, recipient Silver Beaver award. Mem. Nebr. Bd. Examiners Profl. Engrs. and Architects, 1961-73. Chmn. Omaha City Planning Bd., 1962-74. Decorated Legion of Merit with oak leaf cluster, Bronze Star medal with oak leaf cluster; chevalier Legion of Honor, Croix de Guerre avec palme (France); Officer, Order Brit. Empire; Ulchi Distinguished Service Medal with silver star (Korea). Registered profl. engr., Nebr. Fellow Am. Soc. C.E.; mem. Am. Soc. Engring. Edn., Nat. Soc. Profl. Engrs., Soc. Am. Mil. Engrs. Episcopalian. Rotarian. Clubs: Omaha, Omaha Country, Omaha Press. Home: 412 N 61st St Omaha NE 68132

MARSZALEK, THEODORE DAVID, city ofcl., accounting co. exec.; b. Chgo., Dec. 16, 1952; s. Theodore and Marcella (Samp) M.; B.A. with high honors, DePaul U., 1975. Internal auditor City of Chgo., 1975—; owner TDM Co., Chgo., 1976—. Treas., 41st ward Young Democratic Orgn., 1977, precinct capt. Regular Dem. Orgn., 1977—; lector St. Thecla Roman Catholic Ch., 1974—. Mem. Beta Alpha Psi. Home: 6251 N Neenah Ave Chicago IL 60631

MARTA, JOHN B., JR., radiologist; b. Laurium, Mich., July 29, 1932; s. John B. and Mary T. (Silva) M.; student Mich., Tech. U., 1950-52; M.D., Marquette U., 1957; M.S., U. Minn., 1963; m. Louise P. Koopikka, June 8, 1957; children—Michael, Michele, Lisa, David. Intern Receiving Hosp., Detroit, 1957-58; fellow in radiology Mayo Clinic, Rochester, Minn., 1960-63; practice medicine specializing in radiology, Lansing, Mich., 1963-67, St. Paul, 1967—; instr. anatomy Mich. State U., 1965-67; instr. dept. radiology and nuclear medicine U. Minn., 1967—; mem. staffs United Hosps., Childrens Hosp., St. Joseph Hosp., St. John's Hosp. Pres. Mounds View Sch. Dist. PTA, 1971-72. Served with MC USAF, 1958-60. Joseph Collins scholar 1956-57; recipient Russell Carman award Mayo Clinic Dept. Roentgenology, 1963. Mem. AMA, Ramsey County, Minn. State med. socs., Am. Coll. Radiology, Radiol. Soc. N.Am., Am. Roentgen Ray Soc., Soc. Nuclear Medicine. Roman Catholic. Club: Elks. Contbr. articles to med. jours. Home: 11 Ridge Rd St Paul MN 55110 Office: 940 Lowry Med Bldg St Paul MN 55102

MARTELL, RONALD EUGENE, lawyer; b. Mpls., July 31, 1936; s. Michael Joseph and Pearl Elsie (Wester) M.; B.S. in Law, U. Minn., 1959, J.D. cum laude, 1960; m. Elizabeth Ann Porter, Dec. 23, 1961; 1 dau., Judith Marie. Admitted to Minn. bar, 1960; partner Burkard & Martell, 1960-66; asso. Faricy, Moore, Costello & Hart, St. Paul, 1966-71; partner Moore, Costello & Hart, St. Paul, 1971—. Spl. hearing officer U.S. Dept. Justice, 1965-66; lectr. continuing legal edn. U. Minn., 1971-75. Mem. Am. (regional chmn. pub. contract law sect. 1974—, regional chmn. constrn. law com. litigation sect. 1976—), Minn. (sec. ct. rules com. 1974-77, chmn. 1977—) Hennepin County, Ramsey County bar assns., Am. Bd. Trial Advocates (asso., sec. Minn. chpt. 1973-76, pres. 1976-77), St. Paul Athletic Club, Am. Arbitration Assn. (mem. nat. panel arbitrators 1974—), Theta Chi, Phi Delta Phi. Home: 5145 35th Ave S Minneapolis MN 55417 Office: 1400 Northwestern National Bank Bldg St Paul MN 55101

MARTELLARO, JOSEPH ALEXANDER, educator; b. Rockford, Ill., July 20, 1924; s. Vito and Mary (Ciaccio) M.; A.B., U. Notre Dame, 1956, M.A., 1958, Ph.D., 1962; m. Loretta W. Kowalski, Aug. 25, 1945; children—Joseph M., Charles S., David M. Asso. prof. econs. Ind. U., South Bend, 1966-67; prof. econs. No. Ill. U., DeKalb, 1967—, asso. dean grad. sch., 1969-73, acting dean grad. sch., 1973-74. Pres. Martell Radio and Appliances, Inc., South Bend, 1947-57, bd. dirs. 1953-57. Served to maj., U.S. Army Res., 1960-61, 72—. Fulbright research grantee to Italy, 1960-61, Argentina, 1964, 65. Mem. Am. Econ. Assn., Assn. for Comparative Econ. Author: Economic Development in So. Italy, 1950-60, 1965; contbg. author: Perspectives for Teachers of Latin Am. Culture, 1971. Contbr. articles to profl. jours. Home: 1702 Margaret Ln DeKalb IL 60115

MARTENS, LESLIE VERNON, educator, dentist; b. Peoria, Ill., Oct. 15, 1938; s. Vernon Christ and Lydia Rachel (Wiesenburger) M.; B.S., Bradley U., 1959; D.D.S., Loyola U., Chgo., 1963; M.P.H., U. Minn., 1969; m. Judith Ann Siegert, July 15, 1961; children—Michael, Philip, Eric, Pamela. Practice dentistry, Peoria, 1963, Mpls., 1969—; asso. prof. Sch. Dentistry and Sch. Pub. Health, U. Minn., Mpls., 1969—, dir. team dentistry program, 1971—. Preventive dentistry cons. Cambridge State Hosp. for Mentally Retarded, 1968-77, Mpls. Pub. Sch. System, 1969—, Minnetonka Pub. Sch. System, 1969-76, Mpls. Health Dept., 1969-77; cons. dept. dentistry HEW, USPHS, 1973—. Mem. citizens adv. com. Anoka Hennepin Sch. Dist. 11, 1972-73. Served to maj. AUS, 1963-68. Recipient Outstanding Achievement award Internat. Coll. Dentists, 1963. Mem. Am. Dental Assn., Am. Pub. Health Assn., Am. Soc. for Preventive Dentistry, Am. Soc. Dentistry for Children, Internat. Assn. for Dental Research, Behavorial Scientists in Dental Research, Delta Sigma Delta, Omicron Kappa Upsilon. Contbr. research articles to book chpts., dental and pub. health jours. Home: 6956 161st Ln NW Anoka MN 55303 Office: 5831 Brooklyn Blvd Minneapolis MN 55429

MARTENS, RAINER, psychologist; b. Russelsheim, W.Ger., Nov. 8, 1942; s. Vernon F. and Anna (Trause) M.; came to U.S., 1946, naturalized, 1951; B.S., Kans. State Tchrs. Coll., 1964; M.S., U. Mont., Missoula, 1965; Ph.D., U. Ill., 1968; m. Marilyn Kay Pohlman, Jan. 21, 1961. Head wrestling coach U. Mont., 1965; tchr. social sci., coach Hellgate High Sch., Missoula, 1965-66; research asso. prof. Children's Research Center, U. Ill., Champaign, 1968—, dir. motor performance and Play Research Lab., 1973-75; prof. dept. kinesiology U. Waterloo, Ont., 1975-76; prof. dept. phys. edn. U. Ill., Champaign, 1976—; Series editor phys. edn. Harper & Row, 1971—. Mem. N.Am. Soc. Psychology of Sport and Phys. Activity (sec.-treas. 1971—; pres. 1973—), AAHPER (research council). Author: Sport Competition Anxiety Test; Social Psychology and Physical Activity, 1975; editor-in-chief Human Kinetics; contbr. articles to profl. jours. Home: 27 Fields E Champaign IL 61820 Office: 213A Huff Gymnasium U Ill Champaign IL 61820

MARTENS, THEODORE GLENN, ophthalmologist; b. Rochester, N.Y., Apr. 2, 1917; s. Theodore Henry and Florence Anna (Ackerman) M.; B.A., Colgate U., 1939; M.D., U. Rochester, 1943; M.S. in Ophthalmology, U. Minn., 1947; m. Mary Jean Becker, June 26, 1942; children—Nancy Martens Dawson, Linda Martens Smedes, Robert, David. Intern, Strong Meml. Hosp., Rochester, 1943; resident in ophthalmology Mayo Clinic, Rochester, 1943-47; practice medicine specializing in ophthalmology, Fall River, Mass., 1947-49; ophthalmologist Truesdale Clinic, Fall River, Mass., 1947-49; cons. Mayo Clinic, Rochester, 1949—; asso. prof. ophthalmology U. Minn., 1962—; police surgeon Rochester, 1963—. Trustee, treas. Rochester Found., 1961—. Served to capt. USCG, 1962-68. Fellow Am. Acad. Ophthalmology and Otolaryngology; mem. AMA, Minn., Zumbro Valley med. socs., Soc. Research in Ophthalmology. Contbr. articles on ophthalmology to med. jours. Author: (with K.N. Ogle and J.H. Dyer), Ocular Muscle Imbalance, 1967. Home: 815 8th St SW Rochester MN 55901 Office: 200 1st St SW Rochester MN 55901

MARTH, ELMER HERMAN, bacteriologist; b. Jackson, Wis., Sept. 11, 1927; s. William F. and Irma A. (Bublitz) M.; B.S., U. Wis., 1950, M.S., 1952, Ph.D., 1954; m. Phyllis E. Menge, Aug. 10, 1957. Teaching asst. bacteriology U. Wis., Madison, 1949-51, research asst., 1951-54, project asso., 1954-55, instr. bacteriology, 1955-57, asso. prof. food sci. and bacteriology, 1966-71, prof., 1971—; with Kraft, Inc., Glenview, Ill., 1957-66, research bacteriologist, 1957-61, sr. research bacteriologist, 1961-63, group leader microbiology, 1963-66, asso. mgr. microbiology, 1966; mem. Intersoc. Council on Standard Methods for Exam. Dairy Products, 1968—, chmn., 1972—. Sec., Luth. Acad. Scholarship, 1961-71. WHO travel fellow, 1975; recipient Pfizer award for research, 1975; Educator award for research and teaching in food hygiene, 1977. Mem. Am. Soc. Microbiology, Am. Dairy Sci. Assn., Internat. Assn. Milk, Food, and Environ. Sanitarians, Inst. Food Technologists, AAAS, Council Biology Editors, Sigma Xi, Alpha Zeta, Kappa Eta Kappa, Phi Sigma, Delta Theta Sigma, Gamma Alpha. Contbg. author: Fundamentals of Dairy Chemistry, 1965, rev. edit., 1974; Standard Methods for Examination of Dairy Products, 1967, rev. edit., 1972; Residue Reviews, 1965, 66; Ency. Chem. Tech., 1967; Laboratory Manual Food Microbiology, 1968; Laboratory Manual General Bacteriology, 1957; editor Jour. Milk and Food Tech., 1967-76, Jour. Food Protection, 1977—; contbg. author: Byproducts from Milk, 1970; Low Temperature Preservation of Food and Other Biological Material, 1973; Ency. Food Technology, 1974; Staphylococci and their Significance in Foods, 1976; Food Microbiology: Public Health and Spoilage Aspects, 1976; contbr. articles to profl. jours. Patentee in field. Home: 3414 Viburnum Dr Madison WI 53705

MARTIN, CHARLES ALLEN, aero.-mech. engr.; b. Detroit, Apr. 3, 1938; s. Joseph Allen and Anna Lorretta (Piontkowski) M.; B.S. in Aero. Engring., Wayne State U., 1961, M.S. in Engring. Mechs., 1963, M.M.E., 1975; m. Jeanette Bienko, Aug. 31, 1963; children—Jacqueline Marie, Christopher Charles. Product design engr. Ford Motor Co. Engring. & Research Center, Dearborn, Mich., 1962-63; instr. in engring. mechs. U. Detroit, 1964-65; asso. prof. mech. engring. Gen. Motors Inst., Flint, Mich., 1965-75; vis. scientist NASA Johnson Space Center, Houston, 1975; product research mgr. Ex-Cell-O Aerospace Devel. Center, Walled Lake, Mich., 1975—. Mem. Soc. Automotive Engrs., ASME, Am. Inst. Aeros. and Astronautics (chmn. Mich. sect. 1977-78). Roman Catholic. Home: 16884 Renwick St Livonia MI 48154 Office: 850 Ladd Rd Walled Lake MI 48088

MARTIN, CHARLES LEWIS, orgn. exec.; b. Hebron, Ohio, Apr. 30, 1915; s. Harold W. and Elta M. (Emswiler) M.; B.S., Ohio U., 1941; M.A., Ohio State U., 1947; postgrad. U. Colo., 1948, Northwestern U., 1953-55, U. Ill., 1958-59, 69-70; m. Ola Belle Miller, Aug. 22, 1936; children—Carolyn (Mrs. Thomas R. Argust), Mariann (Mrs. James W. Weinstein). Prin. Bloom Twp. Elementary Sch., Lithopolis, Ohio, 1936-38, Bremen (Ohio) Elementary Sch., 1938-42, South Elementary Sch., Lancaster, O., 1942-48; prin., adminstrv. asst., dist. 102, LaGrange, Ill., 1948-56; dir. spl. Edn., LaGrange, 1956-74; exec. dir. West Suburban C. of C., La Grange, 1974—. Cons. spl. edn. adminstrn., throughout Ill., 1958—; instr. adminstrn. and supervision Nat. Coll., Evanston, Ill., No. Ill. U., 1968—. First v.p. Central Baptist Children's Home, Lake Villa, Ill., 1970—. Pres. Ill. Adminstrs. Spl. Edn., 1964-65; pres. Council Adminstrs. Spl. Edn., 1967-68, now hon. life mem.; mem. Cook County Adv. Com. Spl. Edn., Council for Exceptional Children, State Adv. Council Profl. Soc. Served with USNR, 1944-46. Recipient Distinguished Service award Ill. Council for Exceptional Children, 1970, Outstanding Service award Ill. Adminstrs. Spl. Edn., 1974; C. Lewis Martin Center dedicated in his honor, 1975. Mem. Nat., Ill. edn. assns., Comparative Edn. Soc., S.W. Suburban Mental Health Assn. (founder 1954), Ill. Assn. C. of C. Execs. (scholarship to Mgmt. Inst. Notre Dame). Kiwanian (pres. 1965-66). Clubs: First Chicago Torch (pres. 1971-72), Toastmaster (hon. life). Author: Exceptional Children—A Special Ministry, 1968; God's Plan for Me, 1969. Contbr. articles on edn. to profl. and religious jours. Home: 814 Community Dr LaGrange Park IL 60525 Office: 112 N LaGrange Rd La Grange IL 60525

MARTIN, CHARLES WELDON, electronics co. exec.; b. Indpls., Dec. 22, 1915; s. Charles and Glenn (Ridenour) M.; student Purdue U. and Ind. U. extensions; m. Helen Jane Lowry, Mar. 4, 1937; 1 dau., Lynne Rose. Laborer, Ermet Mfg. Co., 1937-39; bookkeeper Pa. Oil Co., 1939-40; clk. N.Y.C. R.R., 1940-41; mgr. statis. quality control U.S. Rubber Co., 1941-46; farm mgr., 1946-49; clk. inventory control Stokeley VanCamp Foods, 1949; mgr. quality control switch div. P. R. Mallory Co., 1950-55; owner service sta., 1955-56; gen. mgr. Aircraft & Electronics Specialties, Avon, Ind., 1956-71, pres., 1971—; v.p. Cal. Automatic Control Service, Fullerton, 1959—. Cons. Mason (Shriner). Club: Highland Country. Home: 7225 Kingsford Dr Indianapolis IN 46260 Office: PO Box 126 Plainfield IN 46168

MARTIN, CLARENCE SAMUEL, physician and surgeon; b. nr. Springfield, Minn., Mar. 13, 1918; s. Johannes Theophilus and Elizabeth Beatrice (Romig) M.; B.S., Moravian Coll., Bethlehem, Pa., 1939; M.D., U. Pa., 1943; postgrad. Harvard U. Med. Sch., 1946-47; m. Dora E. Wolsky, Mar. 13, 1946; children—Jonathan, Timothy, Michael, Peter, Tamara. Rotating intern Presbyn. Hosp., Phila., 1943-44; resident physician Elwyn (Pa.) Tng. Sch., 1947-48; gen. practice medicine and surgery, Kensal, N.D., 1948-61, Medina, N.D., 1961—; physician, surgeon Medina Med. Center, 1961—. Nat. bd. dirs. Security Internat. Ins. Co. Founder, Christian Constl. party of Republic, 1962, chmn. N.D., 1963-68; nat. chmn. Constn. parties U.S. and affiliated Parties, 1968-72; exec. sec. 3d Continental Congress, 1968—; mem. Internat. Com. Monetary Reform, 1970—. Served to capt. M.C., AUS, World War II; maj. Civil Air Patrol. Recipient Liberty award Congress Freedom, 1971. Diplomate Nat. Bd. Medical Examiners. Mem. Hist. Preservation and Exploration Soc. (founder). Author: The Declaration of the Third Continental Congress, 1968; (juveniles) The Mouse and The Moon, 1958; Jo Jo, 1958; Credo Hoc, 1973; author, compiler: To Be Free, The Rebirth of A Nation, 1976. Address: Medina ND 58467

MARTIN, CLAUDE RAYMOND, JR., marketing cons., educator; b. Harrisburg, Pa., May 11, 1932; s. Claude R. and Marie Teresa (Stapf) M.; B.S., U. Scranton, 1954, M.B.A., 1963; Ph.D., Columbia U., 1969; m. Marie Frances Culkin, Nov. 16, 1957; children—Elizabeth Ann, David Jude, Nancy Marie, William Jude, Patrick Jude, Cecelia Marie. Newsman, sta. WILK-TV, Wilkes-Barre, Pa., 1953-55; news dir. sta. WNEP-TV, Scranton, Pa., 1955-60; dir. systems Blue Cross & Blue Shield Ins., Wilkes-Barre, 1960-63; lectr. in mktg. St. Francis Coll., Bklyn., 1964; lectr. in mktg. U. Mich., Ann Arbor, 1965-68, asst. prof., 1968-73, asso. prof., 1973-77, prof., 1977—; dir. Huron Valley Bank, Ann Arbor, 1977—; cons. in mktg. to various fin. instns., 1966—. Served with USN, 1955-57. Mem. Acad. of Mktg. Sci., Am., Southwest mktg. assns., Bank Mktg. Assn., Assn. for Consumer Research, Am. Collegiate Retailing Assn. Roman Catholic. Contbr. articles on mktg. analysis and consumer research to profl. jours. Home: 1116 Aberdeen Dr Ann Arbor MI 48104 Office: Graduate School of Business Administration Univ of Michigan Ann Arbor MI 48109

MARTIN, CLYDE VERNE, psychiatrist; b. Coffeyville, Kans., Apr. 7, 1933; s. Howard Verne and Elfrieda Louise (Moehn) M.; student Coffeyville Coll., 1951-52; A.B., U. Kans., 1955, M.D., 1958; M.A., Webster Coll., St. Louis, 1977; m. Barbara Jean McNeilly, June 24, 1956; children—Kent Clyde, Kristin Claire, Kerry Constance, Kyle Curtis. Intern, Lewis Gale Hosp., Roanoke, Va., 1958-59; resident psychiatry, U. Kans. Med. Center, Kansas City, Mo., 1959-62; staff psychiatrist Neurological Hosp., Kansas City, 1962; pvt. practice psychiatry, Kanasa City, Mo., 1964—; med. dir., mem. bd. dirs. Mid-Continent Psychiatric Hosp., Olathe Kans., 1972—; adj. prof. psychology Baker U., Baldwin City, Kans., 1969—; pres., editor Corrective and Social Psychiatry, Olathe, 1970—. Bd. dirs. Meth. Youthville, Newton, Kans., 1965-75, Spofford Home, Kansas City, 1974—. Served to capt., USAF, 1962-64. Fellow Royal Soc. Health; mem. AMA, Am., Mid-Continent psychiatric assns., Assn. for Advancement Psychotherapy, N.Y. Acad. Sci., Aerospace Med. Assn., Phi Beta Pi, Pi Kappa Alpha. Methodist (del. to Kan. E. Conf. 1972—, bd. global ministries 1974—). Club: Carriage; Kansas City. Mason. Contbr. articles to profl. jours. Home: 5531 E Mission Dr Mission Hills KS 66208 Office: 800 W 47th St Suite 318 Kansas City MO 64110

MARTIN, DAUN HACKETT, psychologist; b. Western Mills, N.Y., Jan. 13, 1939; d. John Maynard and Elnor (White) Hackett; m. Jack R. Martin, June 13, 1971; children—DeKristie, Mindee, John Matthew; B.S., Okla. State U., 1962, M.S., 1964, Ph.D., 1967; student U. Kans., 1973-74. Psychologist, Huntsville-Madison County Mental Health Center, Huntsville, Ala., 1966-72; asso. prof. Oakwood Coll., 1967, Ala. A. and M. U., 1970, U. Ala., 1965-71; cons. Marshall Space Flight Center, 1972, Huntsville Hosp., 1971-72, Spl. Peace Officers Standards and Tng. Commn., Ala., 1972; psychologist Residential Treatment Program for Disturbed Adolescents, Mpls., 1975-77; psychologist Child Guidance Clinic, Greater Winnipeg (Man., Can.) Sch. Dist., 1976-77; asst. clin. prof. div. psychiatry U. N.D. Med. Sch., 1975-77; dir. Children-Adolescent Services, S.E. Mental Health and Retardation Center, Fargo, N.D., 1974-77; exec. dir. Alger-Marquette Mental Health Center, Marquette, Mich., 1977—; mem. council on services Nat. Council Community Mental Health Centers, 1976—; mem. N.D. Gov.'s Juvenile Justice Adv. Council, 1976; cons. spl. edn. N.D. Dept. Pub. Instruction, 1975—. Chmn. Mayor's Coordinating Council for Youth, Fargo, 1976—; bd. dirs. Fargo YMCA. Mem. Assn. Advancement of Behavior Therapy, Am., Ala., N.D. psychol. assns. NDEA scholar, 1962-65; Recognition of Distinguished Service award Huntsville-Madison County Mental Health Center, 1972. Contbr. articles to profl. jours. Office: 425 Fisher St Marquette MI 49855

MARTIN, DAVID FOSTER, opera co. exec.; b. Rochester, N.Y., Dec. 10, 1937; s. Vaughan Foster and Alvera (Barber) M.; Mus.B. with distinction, Eastman Sch. Music, 1960, Mus.M., 1961, performer's certificate in opera, 1961; postgrad. Ind. U., 1967-69; m. Patricia Louise Paslay, Apr. 4, 1957 (div.); children—David Thoreau, Suzanne Elizabeth, Tatjana Lauraine, Cynthia Jane; m. Elizabeth Holleque, Aug. 13, 1976. Profl. opera and concert singer in U.S., Germany and Switzerland, 1961-67; leading baritone Ind. Opera Theater, Bloomington, 1967-69; artistic dir., producer, condr., gen. mgr. Fargo-Moorhead Civic Opera, Fargo, N.D., 1971—. Artist-in-residence, asst. prof. music Concordia Coll., Moorhead, Minn., 1969-73. Mem. Am. Guild Performing Arts, Am. Guild Musical Artists. Home: 1036 E 2d St #144 West Fargo ND 58078 also 1294 Richmond Rd Winter Park FL 32789

MARTIN, EDWARD MOSS, civic exec. sec.; b. Chgo., Sept. 24, 1895; s. Edward Philetus and Leila Adams (Moss) M.; student Wheaton (Ill.) Coll. Acad., 1908-12; A.B., Oberlin (Ohio) Coll., 1916; M.A., Inst. for Pub. Adminstrn., N.Y.C., 1921; Ph.D., U. Chgo., 1938; m. Ethel Austin, Oct. 4, 1924. Newspaper reporter City News Bur., Chgo., 1916-17; sci. asst. USPHS, Detroit and Waterbury, Conn., 1917-20; municipal research N.Y. Bur. for Municipal Research, 1922-24; exec. dir. pub. affairs Union League Club, Chgo., 1924-60, publ. mgr. and editor Union League Men and Events, 1925-60, exec. dir., asst. corp. sec. Union League Civic and Arts Found., 1949-74; exec. sec. Citizens' Assn. Chgo., 1942-50, also dir. Chmn. Ill. Council on Govt. Personnel; sec.-treas. Ill. Council Mgr. Conf. Bd. dirs., sec. Citizenship Council Met. Chgo.; bd. dirs., vice chmn. Municipal Art League Chgo.; bd. dirs., v.p. Citizens Greater Chgo. Recipient Citizens of Greater Chicago honor award, 1958; named to Sr. Citizen Hall of Fame, City of Chgo., 1971. Mem. Nat. Municipal League, Internat. City Mgmt. Assn., Am. Judicature Soc., Tennyson Soc. Clubs: Union League (recipient citation for pub. service 1958), Chaos (Chgo.). Author: The Role of the Bar in Electing the Bench, 1936. Contbr. articles to various publs. Home: Apt 4932 300 N State St Chicago IL 60610 Office: 65 W Jackson Blvd Chicago IL 60604

MARTIN, ETHEL AUSTIN (MRS. EDWARD MARTIN), nutritionist, dietitian b. Storm Lake, Iowa, July 14, 1893; d. George Winchester and Evaline L. (Hurd) Austin; B.S., S.D. State U., 1916, D.Sc. (hon.), 1955; M.S., Columbia, 1923; postgrad. U. Chgo., 1924-26; m. Edward Moss Martin, Oct. 4, 1924. Tchr. State Coll. for Women, Denton, Tex., 1919-22, U. Ill., 1923-24, U. Chgo., 1925-29; dir. nutrition service Nat. Dairy Council, 1929-51. Del. to 12th Internat. Dairy Congress, Stockholm, Sweden, 1949; tchr. Northwestern U., 1957-59; mem. adv. com. nutrition sect. Chgo. Bd. Health, 1957—; mem. Food and Nutrition Research Adv. Com. of U.S. Dept. Agr., 1950-59. Mem. Am. Dietetic Assn., Am., Ill. (chmn. health and welfare sect.) home econs. assns., Chgo. Nutrition Assn. (past pres.). Chgo. Nutrition Council (past pres.), Sigma Xi, Phi Upsilon Omicron, Kappa Mu Sigma, Sigma Delta Epsilon. Author: Roberts Nutrition Work with Children, 1954, 4th edit., 1978; Nutrition in Action, 4th edit., 1978; Nutrition Education in Action, 1963. Home: 300 N State St Chicago IL 60610

MARTIN, FREDERICK STANTON, veterinarian, cons. co. exec.; b. Danville, Ill., Sept. 14, 1946; s. Edward Rhodes and Helen Marie (Stanton) M.; B.S. in Animal Sci., Purdue U., 1971, D.V.M., 1971; m. Dorothy Sue Claypool, Mar. 10, 1976; stepchildren—Bret Ashley, M. Troy. Horse trainer, various locations, 1964-72, blacksmith, 1965-76, practice veterinary medicine and surgery, West Lafayette, Ind., 1971, Covington, Ind., 1971—; propr., owner Martin Veterinary Clinic, Covington, 1971—; dir. Martin Profl. Cons., Covington, 1971—; insp. veterinarian Fountain County Humane Soc.; rifle instr. Bd. dirs. Citizen Scholarship Found. of Covington, 1964-65. Recipient Purdue U. Acad. Pres.'s award, 1970. Mem. Am. Assn. Equine Practioners, Ind. Equestrian Assn., AVMA, 7th Dist. Veterinary Med. Assn., Am. Animal Hosp. Assn. (asso.), Internat. Veterinary Acupuncture Soc., Quarter Horse Assn., Purdue Alumni Assn. Presbyterian. Clubs: Masons (32 deg.), Shriners, Lions. Contbr. articles on veterinary medicine to profl. jours. Home: Rural Route 1 Covington IN 47932 Office: 1320 Pearl St Covington IN 47932

MARTIN, GEORGE JEROME, psychiatrist; b. Kaukauna, Wis., Apr. 6, 1916; s. Mark William and Julia Laura (Sweeney) M.; A.B., U. Wis., 1938, M.D., 1941; m. Mary McCarty, Mar. 11, 1967; children—George Jerome, Sheryl, Mary Kay, Marcia. Intern, John Sealy Hosp., Galveston, Tex., 1941-42; resident Boston Psychopathic Hosp., 1942-43, Pa. Hosp., Phila., 1943-44; dir. Norristown (Pa.) State Hosp., 1947-53; practice medicine specializing in psychiatry Milw., 1953—; mem. staff Milwaukee County Gen. Hosp.; asso. prof. psychiatry Med. Coll. of Wis., Milw., 1960—. Served to maj. AUS, 1944-47. Harvard fellow, 1942-43; Rockefeller fellow, 1943-44. Fellow Am. Psychiat. Assn.; mem. Am. Psychoanalytic Assn., Wis. Psychiat. Assn. Address: 2277 N Lake Dr Milwaukee WI 53202

MARTIN, GEORGE THOMAS, judge; b. Chgo., Sept. 22, 1906; s. Thomas William and Ann (McEnteggart) M.; A.B., U. Mich., 1929, J.D., 1931; m. Helen M. Elliott, Aug. 7, 1936. Admitted to Mich. bar, 1931, since practiced in Dearborn; municipal judge, 1943-67; Wayne County Circuit Ct. judge, 1967—. Mem. Nat. Council Family Relations; active Dearborn council Boy Scouts Am.; pres. Dearborn Community Fund; founder Dearborn Sch. for Parents (George T. Martin Sch. named in his honor). Trustee, pres. Dearborn Sch. Bd., 1933-43. Trustee, pres. Dearborn Y.W.C.A., bd. dirs. Dearborn YMCA, Dearborn Boys' Club, Dearborn Health Council, Detroit

Family Service Soc. Recipient Best Municipal Ct. award Am. Bar Assn. Mem. Am., Mich., Dearborn bar assns., Am. Judicature Soc., Mich. (past pres.), Nat. (past pres.), Wayne County (past pres.) Assns. municipal judges, Wayne County Municipal Judges Assn. (pres. Naval Res. Council Dearborn. Kiwanian (pres. East Dearborn). Home: 16140 Woodland St Dearborn MI 48120 Office: Old County Bldg Detroit MI 48226

MARTIN, HARRY EDWARD, sch. adminstr.; b. Wellston, Ohio, Feb. 13, 1916; s. John Harrison and Goldie (Stephenson) M.; B.S. in Edn., Ohio State U., 1942, M.A., 1947; m. Carolyne Elizabeth Jenkins, Aug. 11, 1939; children—John Stephen, Ann, Michael David. Elementary tchr., Wellston, 1939-43; prin. elementary sch., Delaware, Ohio, 1946-49; prin. high sch., Franklin, Ohio, 1949-50, Bryan, Ohio, 1950-55, Lima, Ohio, 1955-60; supt. Lima Pub. Schs., 1960-65; prin. Chillicothe (Ohio) High Sch., 1966—. Mem. adv. com. Lima State Hosp., 1960-65. Bd. dirs. Lima YMCA, United Fund, Lima, Lima Symphony Orch. Served to lt. USNR, 1944-46; PTO. Mem. NEA, Ohio Edn. Assn., Am., Ohio assns. sch. adminstrs., Nat., Ohio (exec. com. 1969—) assns. secondary sch. prins. Methodist (ofcl. bd). Mason. Lion. Home: 1237 Dolphin St Chillicothe OH 45601

MARTIN, JERRY THOMAS, chemist; b. Plum City, Wis., Nov. 6, 1934; s. Lester Christian and Paula Marie (Gfall) M.; B.S., U. Wis., Milw., 1960; m. Agnes I. Brion, July 14, 1956; children—Roy, Roberta, Brian. Analytical chemist Globe Union Inc., Milw., 1960-62; chemist Milw. Rd., 1962-66; adv. engr. IBM, Rochester, Minn., 1966—; instr. chemistry Rochester Community Coll., 1975—. Mem. Dist. 810 Bd. Edn., 1971—. Served with U.S. Army, 1954-56. Mem. Am. Chem. Soc. Roman Catholic. Club: K.C. Patentee in field. Home: 910 3d Ave NW Plainview MN 55964 Office: 314/004 Hwy 52N Rochester MN 55901

MARTIN, JOHN BRUCE, chem. engr.; b. Auburn, Ala., Feb. 2, 1922; s. Herbert Marshall and Lannie (Steadham) M.; B.S., Ala. Poly. Inst., 1943; M.Sc., Ohio State U., 1947, Ph.D., 1949; m. Mildred Jane Foster, Aug. 7, 1943 (dec. Nov. 1960); children—Shirlie, John Bruce II, Richard Kipp; m. 2d, Phyllis Barbara Rodgers, June 25, 1963. Grad. asst. Ohio State U., 1946-47, Procter & Gamble fellow, 1947-48, asst., 1948-49, lectr. 1949-67, adj. asso. prof., 1967-75; process devel. engr. Procter & Gamble Co., Cin., 1949-55, mgr. personnel and tng., research and devel. 1955-67, coordinator orgn. devel., research and devel., 1967-77, market research, 1977—. Served with AUS, 1943-46. Decorated Air Medal, Bronze Star medal with oak leaf cluster; named Distinguished Alumnus, Ohio State U. Coll. Engring. Fellow Am. Inst. Chem. Engrs. (named Chem. Engr. of Year, Ohio Valley sect. 1971, chmn. Ohio valley sect. 1965-66, dir. 1968-70); mem. Engring. Soc. Cin. (dir. 1967-69, pres. 1972-73), Tech. and Sci. Socs. Council (pres. 1972-73), Am. Soc. Engring. Edn., Am. Chem. Soc., Sigma Xi, Tau Beta Pi, Phi Kappa Phi, Alpha Tau Omega, Alpha Phi Omega, Phi Lambda Upsilon, Pi Tau Chi. Republican. Mem. Disciples of Christ Ch. Home: 644 Doepke Ln Cincinnati OH 45231 Office: Procter & Gamble Co 299 E 6th St Cincinnati OH 45202

MARTIN, JOHN EDWARD, physician; b. Rockford, Ill., Dec. 28, 1937; s. Charles Edward and Marion (Hoffman) M.; B.S., Drake U., 1959; M.D., U. Ill., 1964; m. Jeanette Walters, Feb. 27, 1960; children—Paul, David, Steven, Anne, Karen. Intern, Cook County Hosp., Chgo., 1965-66; resident West Side VA and Univ. Ill. hosps., Chgo., 1968-71; fellow in pulmonary disease Presbyn.-St. Lukes Hosp., Chgo., 1971-72, dir. pulmonary lab., 1972-74; instr. Rush Med. Coll., Chgo., 1972-77, asst. prof. medicine, 1977—; dir. pulmonary medicine, chmn. dept. medicine Grant Hosp., Chgo., 1974—; dir. pulmonary function lab. respiratory therapy Holy Cross Hosp. at Chgo., 1972—; asst. attending Presbyn.-St. Luke's Hosp., Chgo., 1971—. Diplomate Am. Bd. Internal Medicine with supsplty. in pulmonary medicine. Fellow Am. Coll. Chest Physicians; mem. AAAS, ACP, AMA, Am., Ill. thoracic socs., Ill., Chgo. med. socs., Chgo. Soc. Allergy, Chgo. Soc. Internal Medicine. Contbr. articles to profl. jours. Home: 4318 Grand St Western Springs IL 60558 Office: 551 Grant Pl Chicago IL 60614

MARTIN, JOHN THOMAS, physician; b. Cleve., June 8, 1924; s. Clarence Henry and Clara (Feeney) M.; student Miami U., Oxford, Ohio, 1941-43; M.D., U. Cin., 1948; m. Marion Elizabeth George, Feb. 18, 1946; children—Thomas Reed, David Byrd, Richard George, Janet Elaine, Patricia Lucile, Robert Willard. Resident in anesthesiology USAF Hosp., Lackland AFB, San Antonio, also U. Tex. Med. Br., Galveston, 1953-55; asst. dir. USAF Sch. Anesthesiology, Lackland AFB Hosp., 1955-57; practice medicine specializing in anesthesiology, Dallas, 1957-58; cons. in anesthesiology Mayo Clinic, Rochester, Minn., 1958-72, head sect. anesthesiology, 1966-72, sr. cons. anesthesiology, 1972; chmn. dept. anesthesiology Ochsner Med. Center, New Orleans, 1972-74; asso. prof. clin. anesthesiology Mayo Grad. Sch. Medicine, U. Minn., Rochester; asso. prof. surgery Tulane U. Sch. Med., New Orleans, 1972-74; prof. anesthesiology Med. Coll. Ohio, Toledo, 1974—. Mem. Rochester Civic Music Bd., 1963-64, chmn., 1964; mem. Rochester Symphony Orch., 1963-72. Served with M.C., AUS, 1943-44, to maj. M.C., USAF, 1949-57. Diplomate Am. Bd. Anesthesiology. Fellow Am. Coll. Anesthesiologists; mem. Am., Minn. med. assns., Am. (chmn. com. on hosp. planning and constrn.), Minn. (pres. 1966), Ohio socs. anesthesiologists, Internat. Anesthesia Research Soc. (trustee 1966—), Am. Med. Writers Assn. (pres. N. Central chpt. 1970-71), Sigma Xi, Sigma Chi, Phi Chi. Asso. editor Anesthesia and Analgesia-Current Researches, 1968-77. Home: 4605 Woodland Ln Sylvania OH 43560 Office: Dept Anesthesiology Med Coll Ohio Toledo OH 43614

MARTIN, JOSEPH MARION, computer services adminstr.; b. Reesville, Ohio, May 3, 1942; s. Joseph M. and Mary Lou (Hudson) M.; student Cin. Bible Sem., 1960-62, U. Cin., 1965-66; B.A., B.Th., Nebr. Christian Coll., 1977; m. Sharon S. Case, June 22, 1963; children—John Christopher, Meredith Lynn. Accountant, Heekin Can Co., Cin., 1961-66; computer operator and programmer County of San Bernardino, Calif., 1967-69, dir. computer services N.E. Tech. Community Coll., Norfolk, Nebr., 1974—. Served with USAF, 1966-73. Mem. Honeywell Users Group Small and Medium Systems, Honeywell Users Ednl. Systems. Republican. Mem. Christian Ch. Club: Rotary. Home: 311 N 13th St Norfolk NE 68701 Office: 801 E Benjamin Ave Norfolk NE 68701

MARTIN, LUTHER WASHBURN, broadcasting co. exec.; b. Wichita, Kan., July 31, 1919; s. Luther and Mabel St. Clair (Washburn) M.; grad. high sch.; m. Jeanne Frances Reynolds, Dec. 24, 1939; children—Lynn, Judy (Mrs. Robert L. Miers), Tara (Mrs. George W. Calhoun), Kurt, Marta. Ordained to Ministry Ch. of Christ, 1941; staff engr. sta. KWTO, Springfield, Mo., 1938-45; dir. engring. stas. WGAA, WRLD, Cedartown, West Point, Ga., 1945-47; owner, gen. mgr. sta. KTTR, Rolla, Mo., 1947-68; v.p. sta. KALV, Martin Broadcasting Corp., Alva, Okla., 1968—, sta. KVLH, Garvin County Broadcasting, Inc., Pauls Valley, Okla., 1973—. Vice pres. Triad Printing Corp., Rolla, 1960-70, chmn. bd., 1970-77; sec.-treas. Show-Me Electronics, Inc., Rolla; sec. Mo. Cable Co., Inc., Columbia; sec. Radio & Television Supply, Inc., Sedalia. Radio cons. engr. FCC, Washington, 1945-47. Mem. nat. council Fla. Coll. at Temple Terrace. County chmn. Phelps County Republican Party, 1966-70, 76—; mem. Phelps County Rep. Central Com., 1966—. Recipient Boss of Year award Rolla Jr. C. of C., 1967; also numerous pub. service honors, Rolla. Mem. Soc. Broadcast Engrs. (sr.), Phelps County Hist. Soc. (life). Club: Optimists. Staff writer Searching the Scriptures, 1965—; contbr. numerous articles religious jours. Home: 707 Salem Ave Rolla MO 64501 Office: 1200 E Hwy 72 Rolla MO 65401

MARTIN, MICHAEL EDWARD, chiropractor; b. North Platte, Nebr., Mar. 6, 1946; s. Ned and Ellen M. (Eshelman) M.; student Kearney State Coll., 1964-66; D. Chiropractic, Northwestern Coll. Chiropractic, 1969; m. Virginia Kay Dunn, June 28, 1967; children—Jennifer Kay, Michael Edward. Practice chiropractic, Ogallala, Nebr., 1970-74, North Platte, Nebr., 1975—; pres. Chiropractic Life Center, North Platte, 1975—. Mem. Neb. Chiropractic Physicians (dir. 1975—), Am. Chiropractic Assn., Parker Chiropractic Research Found., Life Found. Atlanta. Mason. Home: Rural Route 2 Box 62N7 Ogallala NE 69153 Office: 1849 W A St North Platte NE 69101

MARTIN, ORVILLE WELLS, JR., assn. exec.; b. Oshkosh, Wis., Aug. 13, 1923; s. Orville Wells and Priscilla (Lucas) M.; B.A., U. Md., 1964; m. Alice May Duncanson, Apr. 6, 1946; 1 dau., Pamela. Enlisted in U.S. Army, 1942, commd. 2d lt., 1943, advanced through grades to col., 1970; assigned China, France, Germany and Korea; editor Armor, 1967-71; editor in chief Mil. Rev., 1971-74; ret., 1974; dir. adminstrv. services State Hist. Soc. Wis., Madison, 1974—. Dir. Council Abandoned Mil. Posts-U.S.A., 1968—, pres., 1971-74; mem. bd. advisers U.S. Commn. Mil. History, 1973. Decorated Legion of Merit, Bronze Star, Meritorious Service medal; Croix de Guerre (France). Mem. Am. Assn. State and Local History, Am. Soc. Pub. Adminstrn., Am. Hist. Assn., Western History Assn., Nat. Trust Historic Preservation, Company Mil. Historians, state hist. socs. Ill., Kan., Minn., Wis., Ohio, Soc. Mayflower Descs., S.A.R., Am. Mil. Inst., U.S. Armor Assn. (sec.-treas. 1967-71), USCG Aux. Episcopalian. Editorial adv. bd. Mil. Affairs, 1974—. Home: 209 N Yellowstone Dr Madison WI 53705 Office: 816 State St Madison WI 53706

MARTIN, PAUL JOSEPH, biomed. engr., cardiovascular physiologist; b. Hammond, Ind., May 22, 1936; s. Joseph E. and Verna Catherine (Heidgerken) M.; B.E.E., U. Tex., 1961; M.S. in Biomed. Engring., Drexel Inst. Tech., 1962; Ph.D., Case Western Res. U., 1967; m. Jeanne Theresa Oubre, Sept. 10, 1960; children—Mar Kay, Barry, Craig, Colleen. Steel rigger, electronic technician Page Communications Engrs., Inc., Greenland, 1959; research fellow Latter Day Saints Hosp., Salt Lake City, 1962-63; sr. research biomed. engr. Technology Inc., Dayton, Ohio, 1963-64; research asso. dept. investigative medicine Mt. Sinai Hosp., Cleve., 1967-72, head bioengring. sect., dept. investigative medicine, 1972—; asso. prof. physiology and biomed. engring. Schs. Medicine and Engring., Case Western Res. U.; teaching cons. Ohio Coll. Podiatric Medicine; chmn. research study sect. N.E. Ohio affiliate Am. Heart Assn. Served with USN, 1954-57. Am. Heart Assn. grantee, 1966—; NIH grantee, 1968—; NIH fellow, 1964-67. Mem. Am. Physiol. Soc., Biomed Engring. Soc., IEEE, Sigma Xi, Eta Kappa Nu. Roman Catholic. Club: Coventry Neighbors. Asso. editor Am. Jour. Physiology, 1976—; mem. editorial bd. Circulation Research, 1976—; contbr. to jours. in field. Home: 2099 Lamberton Rd Cleveland Heights OH 44118 Office: Dept Investigative Medicine Mount Sinai Hosp University Circle Cleveland OH 44106

MARTIN, RAY CHARLES, ins. co. exec.; b. Marshall, Wis., Sept. 27, 1921; s. Ernie Maynard and Lena Elizabeth (Haldiman) M.; student pub. schs., Marshall; m. Esther Disch, Aug. 31, 1955. Sales rep. Equitable Life Assurance Soc. U.S., Madison, Wis., 1951—; exec. dir., Wis. Assn. Life Underwriters, Madison. Vice chmn. Citizens for Better Govt., Madison, 1972-77; sec.-treas. Life Underwriters Polit. Action Com., Wis., 1971-77; registered lobbyist Wis. Assn. Life Underwriters. Mason (Shriner). Club: Madison Curling. Home: 3805 Nakoma Rd Madison WI 53711 Office: 4513 Vernon Blvd Madison WI 53705

MARTIN, ROBERT ALLEN, industrialist; b. Alburnett, Iowa, Jan. 13, 1939; s. Robert William and Evelyn Elaine (Helbig) M.; B.A., B.S. in Elec. Engring., U. Iowa, 1962; M.B.A., Northwestern U., 1964; m. Margaret Ann Cunningham, Dec. 26, 1964; 1 son, Robert William. With Motorola Communications and Electronics Chgo., 1962-65, mgr. tech. computer ops., 1964-65; with Syntronic Instruments, Inc., Addison, Ill., 1964-68, v.p. engring., dir. operations, 1967-68; founder, pres., chmn. bd. Nationwide Electronic Systems, Inc., Streamwood, Ill., 1968—, chief exec. com., 1970—; founder, chmn. bd. Martin's Marine, Door County, Wis., 1970—; founder, chmn. bd. Engring. Devel. Corp., Chgo., 1972—; founder, chmn. bd., pres. Internat. Investments, Inc., Chgo., 1973—; founder, pres., chmn. bd. Martin Communication Corp., Dallas, 1974—; founder, pres., chmn. bd. Martin Devel. Corp., Chgo., 1974—; founder, pres., chmn. bd. Martin Farms, Cedar Rapids, Iowa, 1975—. Committeeman Republican Party, DuPage County, Ill., 1970-74; active Boy Scouts Am., 1963—; mem. adv. bd., fin. bd. Ill. Retired Folks Found., 1970-74; dir. Ill. Found. Boys Clubs, 1974—; pres. Sr. Citizens Help Group, 1971-73, dir., 1973—; founder, exec. dir. Equipment for the Blind Found., 1972. Recipient numerous civic, shooting and rifleman, bus. awards latest including Achievement award Advt. Assn. Am., 1974, Gold medal Assn. Commerce and Industry, 1975, Grand Entrepreneur Gold medal Am. Assn. Entrepreneurs, 1975, White Hat award Mchts. Council Cedar Rapids, 1975, Pub. Service award Ill. Indsl. Assn., 1976. Mem. IEEE (past chmn. regional sect.), Am. Vacuum Soc., Internat. Physics Soc., Instrument Soc. Am., Fin. Execs. Assn., Am. Mgmt. Assn. (mem. adv. bd.), Interstate Bus. Assn. (trustee), Great Lakes Assn. (dir.), and others. Clubs: Ephraim (Wis.) Yacht, Beaver Island Yacht, Chgo. Yacht, Lions, Barrington Archery and Gun. Patentee in field. Author: The Best There Is; No Second Fastest Gunfighters; Real Truth in Accounting; There Is No Such Thing as a Good Loser; Who's Watching the Watchers?; Real Research or Repeat?; The Young Are Intelligent, The Old Are Experienced. Contbr. articles to jours., mags. Home: Barrington Hills IL 60010 Office: 1536 Brandy Pkwy Streamwood IL 60103

MARTIN, ROBERT COOLIDGE, city mgr.; b. Chgo., Aug. 19, 1930; s. Robert C. and Grace (Farmer) M.; B.S. in Bus. Adminstrn., N. Central Coll., Naperville, Ill., 1954; M.A. in Pub. Adminstrn., U. Minn., 1967; m. Agnes Kluzneski, Nov. 23, 1963; children—Margaret Louise, Grace Marie. With steel co., 1955-63; asst. city mgr., St. Louis Park, Minn., 1963-69; city mgr., Ft. Atkinson, Wis., 1969—; dep. sheriff, Jefferson County, instr. extension div., U. Wis. Mem. exec. bd. Fort Meml. Hosp., Hoard Hist. Soc.; bd. dirs. Fort Atkinson Found. Served with USAF, 1949-52. Recipient Safety award Nat. Safety Council, 1967. Mem. Am. Soc. Pub. Adminstrn. (pres. 1974), Am. Pub. Works Assn., Internat., Wis. (pres. 1972, exec. bd. 1973—) city mgmt. assns., Am. Legion, U. Minn. Alumni Assn. (past pres., award 1973). Rotarian (past pres.). Author chpt. in book, articles. Home: 1122 Janette St Fort Atkinson WI 53538 Office: 101 N Main St Fort Atkinson WI 53538

MARTIN, ROBERT JAMES, surgeon; b. Omaha, Oct. 16, 1936; s. James Wicher and Frances Olivia (Dickerson) M.; B.S., U. Nebr., 1957, M.D., 1961; m. Nancy Lyn Janssen, July 10, 1960; children—Susan Jane, James Robert. Intern, Nebr. Methodist Hosp., Omaha, 1961-62; resident in surgery U. Kans. Med. Center, Kansas City, 1962-66; practice medicine specializing in surgery, Cherokee, Iowa, 1968—; mem. staff Sioux Valley Hosp.; cons. surgeon State Mental Health Inst., Cherokee, 1968—. Mem. Cherokee Community Sch. Dist. Bd. Edn., 1969—, pres., 1974-75. Served as capt. USAF, 1966-68. Diplomate Am. Bd. Surgery. Fellow A.C.S.; mem. AMA, Theta Nu, Phi Chi, Sigma Nu. Republican. Home: 700 Walnut St Cherokee IA 51012 Office: 213 N 2d St Cherokee IA 51012

MARTIN, ROBIN MICHAEL, photographer; b. Farnham, Surrey, Eng., May 27, 1941; s. Edwin Bennie and Bette L.M. (Marshall) M.; grad. schs., Eng.; m. Maxine Gayle Huston, Sept. 3, 1966; children—Robin Allison, David Craig. Photographer, studio mgr. Victor Azia Photography, London, Ont., 1958-63, James Photo (Chatham), Ltd., Chatham, Ont., 1963-71; owner Michael Martin Photography, Chatham, Ont., 1971—. Mem. provincial consultive com. for photographic programs Ont. Govt. Dept. Cols. and Univs., 1973-74. Adv. bd. photog. programs Fanshaw Coll., London, Ont., 1974-75; bd. dirs. Kent County Crippled Children's Treatment Centre. Mem. Profl. Photographers Can. (v.p. 1972-73), Profl. Photographers Am. (portrait councilman 1973-74), Profl. Photographers Ont. (pres. 1972). Clubs: Kiwanis, Rotary, Kinsmen. Address: 12 Grand Ave W Chatham ON N7M 5K5 Canada

MARTIN, ROGER BOND, landscape architect; b. Virginia, Minn., Nov. 23, 1936; s. Thomas George and Audrey (Bond) M.; B.S., U. Minn., 1958; M. Landscape Arch., Harvard, 1961; m. Janis Ann Kloss, Aug. 11, 1962; children—Thomas, Stephen, Jonathan. Asst. prof. U. Calif. at Berkeley, 1964-66; asso. prof. U. Minn., Mpls., 1966, prof., 1968—, chmn. dept. landscape architecture, 1968-77; owner Roger Martin & Assos. site planners land architects, Mpls., 1966-68; prin. Interdesign, Inc., Mpls., 1968—. Mem. N.G., 1962. Mem. Am. Soc. Landscape Architects (past pres. Minn. chpt. 1970-72), Nat. Council Instrs. Landscape Architecture (pres. 1973-74). Home: 2912 45th Ave Minneapolis MN 55406 Office: Arch Bldg U Minn Minneapolis MN 55455

MARTIN, ROSS LLOYD, real estate and devel. exec.; b. Vancouver, B.C., Can., Apr. 20, 1939; s. Ross Wilson and Violet (Smith) M.; B.Commerce, U. B.C., 1962; M.B.A., U. Calif. at Berkeley, 1963; m. Irene Goss, Sept. 2, 1960; children—Eric Steven, Michael Ryan. Marketing mgr. T. Eaton Co., 1964-66; marketing mgr. Beaver Lumber Co. Ltd., Winnipeg, Man., 1966-71; owner, mgr. R. L. M. Enterprises Ltd., Genesis Marketing Orgn. Ltd., Servall Mgmt. Ltd.; dir. Danaba Ltd., Traditional Homes, Zealous Investments, 800 Devel. Group, Century Investments, Vancouver; lectr. U. Man., Winnipeg, Can., 1966—. Mem. Am. Marketing Assn. (founder Winnipeg chpt. 1967, Canadian dir.), Am. Mgmt. Assn., C. of C., Beta Gamma Sigma. Mason. Home: 1529 Elite Rd Mississauga ON Canada

MARTIN, STANLEY WILBUR, hosp. cons.; b. Cleve., Nov. 20, 1916; s. Stanley and Effie May (Fritz) M.; diploma Dyke Bus. Coll., Cleve., 1936; B.S., Western Res. U., Cleve., 1949; M.H.A., Washington U., 1951; m. Constance Lev-Lyons, June 26, 1948; children—Stanley Lyons, Dawn Marie. Food broker Gen. Brokerage Co., Cleve., 1943-45; indsl. engr. Republic Steel Corp., 1945-46; personnel mgr. Cleve. Steel Barrel Co., 1947; resident St. Mary's Hosp., Rochester, N.Y., 1951, asst. adminstr., 1952; adminstr. Wood River Twp. Hosp., Wood River, Ill., 1952-53; asst. adminstr. Lutheran Hosp. of Milw., Inc., 1953-55, exec. dir., 1955-74, pres., 1975-76, cons., 1977—. Adv. bd. Booth Meml. Hosp., Wauwatosa, Wis., 1966-75, chmn. hosp. adv. council, 1970-73; pres. Milw. Regional Med. TV Network, 1967-69. Fellow Am. Coll. Hosp. Adminstrs. Mem. Am., Wis. hosps. assns., Royal Soc. Health Eng., Hosp. Council Greater Milw. Area (pres. 1961, chmn. purchasing com. 1965-76), Employers Assn. (dir. 1966-67), Am. Protestant Hosp. Assn. (mem. govt. relations council 1967-70). Club: Milwaukee Athletic. Home and office: 6301 Washington Circle Wauwatosa WI 53213

MARTIN, THOMAS BROOKS, wax co. exec.; b. Butler, Pa., Nov. 24, 1920; s. James Campbell and Pauline (Brooks) M.; student Millersville State Tchrs. Coll., 1940-41, Carnegie Inst. Tech., 1941-42; B.S. in Commerce, Grove City Coll., 1947; m. Helen B. Spicer, May 31, 1947; 1 son, Thomas Brooks. Indsl. engr. Armco Steel Co., Butler, 1941-44; household products salesman S. C. Johnson & Son, Inc., Phil., 1947-50, service products supr., 1950-53, service products dist. mgr., 1953-55, sales tng. dir., 1955-58, advt., merchandising dir., 1958-63, pub. relations dir., 1963-64; v.p. pub. and personnel relations, corporate officer, 1967-70, v.p. pub. affairs, 1970—; pres., gen. mgr. Johnson Wax Way Centers, Inc., Racine, Wis., 1965-67; pres. Century Corp., Johnson Real Estate Corp.; dir. Meadow Lake Realty Co., Inc., Heritage Bank, Racine, Racine Environment Com. Bd. dirs. Pub. Affairs Council, Racine Environment Com. Non-Profit Housing Corp.; trustee Prairie Sch., Johnson Wax Fund; mem. Task Force of Nat. Urban Coalition. Republican. Presbyn. Clubs: Racine Country, Somerset. Home: 5131 Starlight Dr Racine WI 53402 Office: 1525 Howe St Racine WI 53403

MARTIN, THOMAS HERMAN, otolaryngologist; b. Chatham, Ont., Can., Oct. 18, 1934; s. Lawrence Victor and Emily Dora (Sperling) M.; diploma Ont. Agrl. Coll., 1955; M.D., U. Western Ont., 1964; m. Karen Elizabeth Stover, June 19, 1965; children—Lawrence Victor, Carolyn, Emily, Dayton. Intern, Grace Hosp., Detroit, 1964-65; resident surgical training otolaryngology, Westminster, Victoria, St. Joseph's hosps., London, Ont., Can., 1965-69; practice medicine specializing in otolaryngology, Chatham, Ont., Can., 1970—; chief surgery dept. St. Joseph's Hosp., Chatham, 1972—; chief otolaryngology service, St. Joseph's Hosp., Pub. Gen. Hosp., Chatham, 1971—. Adviser Kent County Hearing Soc.; pres. Kent County Progressive Conservative Polit. Soc.; bd. dirs. Chatham Jr. Achievement. Pres.'s fellow U. Western Ont. Fellow Royal Coll. Surgeons (Can.); mem. Kent County Med. Soc. (treas. 1973, pres. 1977-78). Clubs: Chatham Curling; Kent Men's, Ont. Agrl. Coll. Century (charter), Rotary (dir., pres. 1977-78), Masons (32 deg.), U. Western Ontario Founders (founder.). Contbr. to profl. publs. in field. Home: Rural Route 4 Chatham ON Canada Office: 11 Grand Ave W Chatham ON Canada

MARTIN, THOMAS JOHN, savs. and loan co. exec.; b. Chgo., July 3, 1925; s. John and Rose (Barranco) Martino; student Wright Jr. Coll., 1946; B.A., Beloit Coll., 1950; postgrad. Northwestern U., 1950; standard diploma Am. Savs. and Loan Inst., Chgo., 1958, grad. diploma, 1959, grad. sch. diploma and Key, 1967; m. Carol Lorraine Klima, June 30, 1951; children—John Charles, Lawrence Thomas, Sylvia-Rose, Donald, Marjorie, Celeste. Agt., Fidelity Mut. Life Ins. Co. Phila., Chgo., 1950-51; with Celkay Enterprises, Inc., North Riverside, Ill., 1951—, sec.-treas., dir., 1956—; with Clyde Savs. & Loan Assn., North Riverside, 1951—, v.p., 1964-71, sr. v.p., 1971-74, exec. v.p., dir., 1974—; pres. Clyde Service Corp., 1971—, also dir.; instr., Am. Savs. and Loan Inst., Chgo., 1964-66, mem. grad. sch. thesis rev. bd., 1967-75. Mem. Cicero Progress Com., 1970-75; bus. chmn. Cicero Cancer Crusade, 1971; mem. gen. occupation adv. com.

Morton Coll., Cicero, 1973—. Served with Signal Corps, AUS, 1943-46. Recipient citation of recognition for highest scholastic achievement Chgo. chpt. Am. Savs. and Loan Inst., 1958. Mem. Soc. Real Estate Appraisers, Savs. Instns. Mktg. Soc. Am. (charter to 1976), Czechosolovak Savs. and Loan League (v.p. 1967-68, pres. 1969-70), West Towns, (asso.), DuPage bds. realtors, Inst. Fin. Edn. (bd. govs. Chgo. 1965-74, pres. 1973), Cermak Rd. Bus. Assn., Cicero (pres. 1967-69, dir. 1961-74), North LaGrange (Ill.) Park Assn. (pres., 1957). Republican. Roman Catholic. Home: 4721 Howard Ave Western Springs IL 60558 Office: 7222 W Cermak Rd North Riverside IL 60546

MARTIN, THOMAS LYLE, JR., univ. pres.; b. Memphis, Sept. 26, 1921; s. Thomas Lyle and Malvina (Rucks) M.; B.E.E., Rensselaer Poly. Inst., 1942, M.E.E., 1948, Dr. Engring., 1967; Ph.D., Stanford, 1951; m. Helene Hartley, June 12, 1943; children—Michele Marie, Thomas Lyle III. Prof. elec. engring. U. N.M., 1948-53; prof. engring. U. Ariz., 1953-63, dean engring., 1958-63; dean engring. U. Fla., Gainesville, 1963-66; dean engring. So. Meth. U., Dallas, 1966-74; pres. Ill. Inst. Tech., Chgo., also IIT Research Inst., 1974—. Dir. Stewart-Warner Co., Inland Steel Co., Mark Controls, Amsted Industries, Gas Devel. Corp. Mem. Dallas-Fort Worth Regional Airport Bd., 1970-74. Bd. dirs. Museum Sci. and Industry, 1975—, Inst. Gas Tech. Served to capt. Signal Corps, AUS, 1943-46. Decorated Bronze Star medal. Fellow IEEE; mem. Nat. Acad. Engring., Sigma Xi, Tau Beta Pi, Eta Kappa Nu, Sigma Tau. Author: UHF Engineering, 1950; Electronic Circuits, 1955; Physical Basis for Electrical Engineering, 1957; Strategy for Survival, 1963; Electrons And Crystals, 1970; Malice in Blunderland, 1973. Home: 990 Lake Shore Dr Apt 19C Chicago IL 60611

MARTIN, WILFRED SAMUEL, ret. business exec.; b. Adamsville, Pa., June 11, 1910; s. Albert W. and Elizabeth (Porter) M.; B.S., Iowa State U., 1930; M.S., U. Cin., 1938; m. Elizabeth Myers, July 9, 1938; children—Peter, Judith (Mrs. Peter Kleinman), Nancy (Mrs. Richard Foss), Paula. Chem. engr. process devel. dept. Procter & Gamble Co., Cin., 1930-50, mgr. drug products mfg., 1950-51, asso. dir. chem. div., 1952-53, dir. product devel., soap products div., 1953-63, mgr. mfg. and products devel. Food Products div., 1963-71, sr. dir. research and devel., 1971-75. Mem. Wyoming (Ohio) Bd. Edn., 1961-69, pres., 1965-68. Bd. dirs. Indsl. Research Inst., 1964-68, v.p., 1968-69, pres., 1969-71; chmn. trustee Ohio Presbyn. Homes, Columbus, Ohio, 1959-69, 73—; vice chmn. bd. trustees Pikeville (Ky.) Coll., 1973-76, chmn. bd. trustees, 1976—. Mem. Am. Chem. Soc., Am. Inst. Chem. Engrs., AAAS, Soc. Chem. Industry, Am. Oil Chemist Soc., Engring. Soc. Cin., N.Y. Acad. Scis., Am. Mgmt. Assn. (research devel. council 1974—). Club: Wyoming Golf (Cin.). Home: 504 Hickory Hill Ln Cincinnati OH 45215

MARTIN, WILLIAM BRADLEY, physician; b. Knife River, Minn., Apr. 12, 1918; s. Edward Thomas and Jane (Ellis) M.; diploma with distinction Duluth Jr. Coll., 1937; B.S. with distinction, U. Minn., 1939, M.B., 1941, M.D., 1942, M.S. in Medicine, 1949; m. Dorothy Ann Eusterman, Nov. 5, 1949; children—William Bradley III, Diane, Charlaine, Todd, Quentin, Maureen. Intern. Milwaukee County Hosp., Wauwatosa, Wis., 1941-42; fellow med. edn. Mayo Found., Rochester, Minn., 1946-49; practice medicine specializing in internal medicine, cardiology, Duluth, Minn., 1953-65; vis. cons. St. Josephs Hosp., Superior, Wis., 1951-65; poison control officer St. Lukes Hosp., Duluth, 1958-65, electrocardiographer, 1955—; cons. Lakeview Meml. Hosp., 1958-65; staff Miller Meml. Hosp., Duluth, 1953-65; co-chmn. Duluth Cardiac Research Lab., 1959-65; vis. cons. St. Marys Hosp., Superior, 1951-65; chief cardiology VA Hosp., Dayton, Ohio, 1965-70; clin. mgr. Upjohn Co., Kalamazoo, 1970—, chief clin. cardiology research, 1973—; staff, Bronson Meml. Hosp., 1970—; dir. Bronson/Upjohn Hypertension Clinic, Kalamazoo, 1973—. Bd. dirs. Kalamazoo Heart Assn., 1970—, pres., 1974; bd. dirs. Mich. Heart Assn., 1976—; mem. Human Use com. Western Mich. U., 1975—. Served from lt. (j.g.) to lt. comdr. USNR, 1942-46; PTO. Recipient E. Starr Judd Prize, 1949. Diplomate Am. Bd. Internal Medicine and subspeciality cardiovascular disease. Fellow A.C.P., Am. Coll. Chest Physicians, Am. Heart Assn. Council Clin. Cardiology, Am. Coll. Cardiology; mem. Interurban Acad. Medicine (pres. 1958), Minn. Heart Assn. (past dir.), Am., Minn. State med. assns., St. Louis County Med. Soc. (chmn. diabetes com. 1957-60, chmn. pub. health and reference com. 1961—), Minn. Soc. Internal Medicine, Minn. Soc. Study Diseases Heart and Circulation (sec. 1963), Am. Diabetes Assn., Alumni Assn. Mayo Found., Holy Name Soc., Miami Valley Heart Assn. (dir., v.p.), Nu Sigma Nu. Contbr. articles on cardiac diagnosis, use of statistics in diagnosis, lipid lowering drugs, vaso-dilators in hypertension, measurement cardiac output. exptl. cardiac defects, prostaglandins in peripheral vascular disease to med. jours. Home: 2526 Pine Ridge Rd Kalamazoo MI 49008 Office: Upjohn Co Bldg 24-2 Kalamazoo MI 49001

MARTIN, WILLIAM WOODROW, tractor co. exec.; b. Ottawa, Kans., June 19, 1924; s. Charles Henry and Mary Elizabeth (Koontz) M.; B.S. in Indsl. Mgmt., U. Kans., 1949; m. Betty Louise Chubb, Dec. 20, 1947; children—Gregory Jennings, Janet Louise, Judith Ellen. Propr., W.W. Martin Constrn. Co., Fort Scott, Kans., 1946-49; pres. Martin Tractor Co., Inc., Topeka, 1957—; chmn. bd. Martin Co. Inc., Topeka, 1967—; dir. First Nat. Bank Topeka, Southwestern Bell Telephone Co., St. Louis, Gas Service Co. Inc., Kansas City, Mo. Vice chmn. Topeka Urban Renewal Agy., 1960-64; mem. State of Kans. Pooled Money Investment Bd.; chmn. Gov.'s Task Force on Effective Mgmt. Precinct committeeman Republican Party, Topeka; mem. exec. com. Kans. Rep. Com.; chmn. 2d Congl. Dist. Republican. Exec. bd. Kans. U. Sch. Bus.; alumni bd. Kans. U. Served with Q.C., AUS,1943-46; PTO. Mem. Kans. Assn. Commerce and Industry (pres., dir.), N.A.M. (dir.), Greater Topeka C. of C. (past pres.), Asso. Industries Kans. (pres. 1968-70), Kans. U. Alumni Assn. (exec. v.p.), Phi Delta Theta. Methodist (trustee 1971—). Mason (32 degree, Shrine, Jester), Rotarian (past pres. Topeka). Home: 3162 Shadow Ln Topeka KS 66604 Office: 1737 SW 42d St Box 1698 Topeka KS 66601

MARTINDALE, JOHN HENRY, JR., metal bldg. contractor; b. Knox County, Ind., Jan. 30, 1925; s. John Henry and Jennie L. (Church) M.; grad. Purdue U., 1950; postgrad. Vanderbilt U., Ind. U.; m. Betty R. Misner, Dec. 23, 1949; children—Michael, Janice, David, Doris. Owner, Pebco, metal bldg. contractor, Brownstown, Ind., 1966—. Served to maj. USAAF, 1943-45, USAF, 1951-53. Mem. ASCE, Metal Bldg. Dealers Assn. (dir. Ind. chpt.). Mason. Author tech. handbook. Contbr. articles to profl. jours. Address: Route 1 Brownstown IN 47220

MARTINDALE, ROBERT MALCOLM, business exec.; b. Springfield, Mass., Oct. 13, 1933; s. Kirby Willard and Laura (Taylor) M.; B.A., Syracuse U., 1956; m. Mary Margaret Cummings, Feb. 12, 1955; children—David Charles, Gregory Scott, James Thomas, Michael Edward, Jeffrey John. Staff announcer Civic Broadcasting Corp., 1954-56; asst. v.p., dir. advt. Marine Midland Trust Co., Syracuse, N.Y., 1956-61, asst. v.p., 1961—, asst. sec. Marine Midland Corp., Buffalo, 1961-64, asst. v.p., 1964-66; v.p., dir. marketing and pub. relations Tex. Bank & Trust Co., Dallas, 1966-67; pres. Midwest Bank Card System, Inc., Chgo., 1967-70; v.p., dir. marketing LaSalle Nat. Bank Chgo., 1970-71; pres. Hughes-Martindale and Assos., Inc., Chicago, 1971—. Mem. Bank Pub. Relations and Marketing Assn., Am. Inst. Banking (mem. faculty), Chgo. Financial Advertisers. Methodist (trustee). Home: 20 W Lonnquist Blvd Mount Prospect IL 60056 Office: 188 Industrial Dr Elmhurst IL 60126

MARTINEAU, JAMES PHILLIP, lawyer; b. Madison, Wis., Oct. 5, 1929; s. James Anthony and Louise Carol (Thompson) M.; A.B., U. Wis.; LL.B., Harvard U.; m. Sara Cordelia Newhart, June 12, 1957; children—Catherine, James, Helen. Partner law firm Lindquist & Vennum, Mpls. Mem. Met. Transit Commn.; bd. dirs. Children's Theatre Co. Served to lt. j.g. USN, 1952-55. Democrat. Club: Mpls. Home: 1929 Kenwood Pkwy Minneapolis MN 55405 Office: 80 S 8th St Minneapolis MN 55402

MARTINEK, OTTO CHARLES, savs. and loan exec.; b. Chgo., Jan. 14, 1922; s. Vincent and Anna (Vachuda) M.; student Northwestern U., 1942, Am. Savs. and Loan Inst., 1949, Savs. and Loan Grad. Sch. U. Ind., 1959; m. Grace Jane Andreasen, Jan. 26, 1952; 1 son, Robert Charles. Exec. v.p. Olympic Savs. & Loan Assn., Berwyn, Ill., 1946-72; pres., chief exec. officer Republic Fed. Savs. & Loan Assn., Chgo., 1972-75; pres., dir. Republic Fed. div. First Fed. Savs. Chgo., also sr. v.p. First Fed. Savs. Chgo., 1975—; past dir. Am. Savs. and Loan Inst.; pres. Chgo. area Council Insured Savs. Assns., 1977—; founding pres. Savs. Assn. Council, 1970-71. Bd. dirs. Boys' Club, Cicero, Ill.; bd. dirs. Greater SW Service Corp., 1976-77; pres., chmn. bd. SW Devel. Corp., 1977. Served with USAAF, 1942-46. Mem. Pub. Relations Soc. Am. (past pres.), Chgo. Lawn C. of C. (v.p.), Amvets (comdr. post 1950), Ill. Savs. and Loan League (dir. 1975-78), Savs. Inst. Mktg. Soc. Am. (charter), Soc. Savs. and Loan Controllers, Am. Legion. Methodist (chmn. fin. commn. 1973-75). Clubs: Masons, Shriners, Elks (past exalted ruler). Home: 4125 Howard Ave Western Springs IL 60558 Office: 6222 S Kedzie Ave Chicago IL 60629

MARTINEK, ROBERT GEORGE, biochemist; b. Chgo., Nov. 25, 1919; s. Anton and Agnes (Simon) M.; B.S. in Pharmacy, U. Ill., 1941, B.S. in Medicine, 1945, M.S. in Biochemistry, 1943; Pharm. D., U. So. Calif., 1953; m. Lydia Mildred Chab, July 12, 1952. Research analytical chemist AMA, Chgo., 1950-55; sr. chemist in nutritional research and devel. Mead Johnson & Co., Evansville, Ind., 1955-56; sr. profl. asso. biochemist Butterworth Hosp., Grand Rapids, Mich., 1956-58; clin. chemist, head biochem. lab. Iowa Meth. Hosp., Des Moines, 1958-62; clin. chemist, head quality control Chgo. Dept. Health Labs., 1962-65; chief lab. improvement sect. Ill. Dept. Pub. Health Labs., Chgo., 1965—; dir., cons. Lab-Line Instruments Co.; lectr. U. Ill., Chgo.; mem. subcom. on temperature measurement Nat. Com. Clin. Lab. Standards. Served as 1st lt. Med. Service Corps U.S. Army, 1951-52. Recipient Scholarship award Rho Chi, 1938-39; Ebert award U. Ill. Coll. Pharmacy, 1941; Pub. Health Service award Ill. Assn. Clin. Labs., 1970. Fellow Am. Inst. Chemists (accredited, life); mem. AAAS (life), Am. Pharm. Assn. (life), AMA (affiliate), Nat. Geog. Soc. (life), Am. Inst. Econ. Research, Nat. Registry Clin. Chemistry (accredited clin. chemist), Am. Bd. Bioanalysis (certified), Sigma Xi, Phi Kappa Phi, Rho Chi. Mem. Libertarian Party. Unitarian. Author: Technical Characteristics of Clinical Laboratory Instruments, 1967; MED Equipment Buyers Guide, 1974; contbr. numerous articles to profl. publs.; asso. editor Jour. Am. Med. Tech., 1966-77; editorial cons. Med. Electronics, 1970-77; patentee in field. Home: 4736 N Tripp Ave Chicago IL 60630 Office: 2121 W Taylor St Chicago IL 60612

MARTINELLI, DAVID FORTUNATO, mfg. co. exec.; b. Chgo., Apr. 4, 1943; s. David Innocente and Inez Joan (Frigo) M.; B.S. in Polit. Sci., Loyola U., Chgo., 1966, also M.B.A. in Fin.; m. Sandra L. Wiencek, Aug. 8, 1968. Mem. contract adminstrn. staff Hallicrafters Corp., Rolling Meadows, Ill., 1968-69, Gen. Time Corp., Rolling Meadows, 1969-70; adminstr. U. Chgo., 1971-74; sr. contract adminstr., nuclear contract adminstrn. Graver Tank & Mfg. Co., E. Chicago, Ind., 1974-75; sr. coordinator Inst. Gas Tech., Chgo., 1975; mgr. contracts and def. contracts Blaw-Knox Foundry & Mill Machinery, E. Chicago, 1976—; cons. grant and contract adminstrn. and negotiations. Certified profl. contracts mgr. Home: 10153 S 87th Ave Palos Hills IL 60465 Office: 4440 Railroad Ave East Chicago IN 46312

MARTINO, JOSEPH PAUL, research scientist; b. Warren, Ohio, July 16, 1931; s. Joseph and Anna Elizabeth (Kubina) M.; A.B., Miami U., Ohio, 1953; M.S., Purdue U., 1955; Ph.D., Ohio State U., 1961; m. Mary Lou Bouquot, May 18, 1957; children—Theresa, Anthony, Michael. Commd. 2d lt. U.S. Air Force, 1953, advanced through grades to col., 1973; project engr. Armament Lab., Wright-Patterson AFB, Ohio, 1955-58; mathematician Office of Sci. Research, Washington, 1961-62; staff scientist Avionics Lab., Wright-Patterson AFB, 1972-73; dir. engring. standardization Def. Electronics Supply Center, Dayton, Ohio, 1973-75; ret., 1975; research scientist U. Dayton Research Inst., 1975—. Fellow IEEE; mem. Ops. Research Soc. Am., Inst. Mgmt. Scis., Am. Inst. Aeros. and Astronautics. Roman Catholic. Author: Technological Forecasting for Decisionmaking, 1972; asso. editor Tech. Forecasting and Social Change Jour., 1968—. Home: 819 N Maple Ave Fairborn OH 45324 Office: Research Inst U Dayton Dayton OH 45469

MARTINSONS, ALEKSANDRS, research chemist; b. Borshom, Russia, Nov. 30, 1912; s. Aleksandrs and Hildegard (Kevai) M.; student U. Riga (Latvia), 1935-39, U. Kiel, 1949-50; M.S., U. Mich., 1955; m. Herta Gutmanis, June 11, 1939; children—Hugo-Maris, Alexander. Came to U.S., 1950, naturalized, 1956. Sr. research chemist Am. Potash & Chem. Corp., Henderson, Nev., 1957-60; sr. research chemist PPG Industries Inc. Tech. Center, Barberton, Ohio, 1960—. Mem. Electrochem. Soc. Holder numerous U.S., fgn. patents. Home: 135 Westview Ave Wadsworth OH 44281 Office: PO Box 31 Barberton OH 44203

MARTIS, LEO, pharmacologist; b. Bombay, India, June 3, 1945; s. Gregory and Apolina (Desa) M.; came to U.S., 1968, naturalized, 1972; B.S. in Chemistry, U. of Mysore, India, 1965; B.S. in Chem. Tech., U. Bombay, 1968; M.S. (John B. Quick fellow) in Pharm. Chemistry, U. Wash., 1970, Ph.D. (Rubenstein fellow), 1973; m. Jacintha B. Castalino, June 10, 1975. Research asso., dept. of neurosurgery Sch. of Medicine, U. Wash., Seattle, 1973-74; sr. research scientist Baxter-Travenol Labs., Morton Grove, Ill., 1974-76; mgr. biochem. pharmacology, 1976—. Sec., treas. Indian Students Assn., U. Wash., Seattle, 1972-74. Mem. Am. Chem. Soc., Am. Pharm. Assn., AAAS, Rho Chi. Roman Catholic. Contbr. numerous articles on pharm. research to sci. jours. Home: 8901 Western Des Plaines IL 60016 Office: 6301 Lincoln Ave Morton Grove IL 60053

MARTS, FREDERICK DUANE, pipeline co. exec.; b. Kansas City, Kans., Nov. 20, 1925; s. Fred Henry and Clara Gladys (Harrel) M.; B.S., Finlay Engring. Coll., 1949; postgrad. U. Pitts., 1966; m. Nina Erlene Miller, Aug. 31, 1947; children—Jennifer E., Jeffrey D. Engr. Panhandle Eastern Pipe Line Co., 1950-51, sr. engr. Platte Pipe Line Co., 1951-58; pres. Jayhawk Pipeline Corp., Wichita, Kans., 1958—. Served with USAAF, 1943-45. Registered profl. engr., Mo. Mem. Am. Petroleum Inst., Am. Mgmt. Assn. Republican. Methodist. Mason (Shriner). Home: 354 Ralstin St Wichita KS 67209 Office: 202 W 1st St Wichita KS 67201

MARTYNIUK, OSYP, architect; b. Ceniv, Berezany, Western Ukraine, July 17, 1931; s. John and Maria (Mandzij) M.; came to U.S., 1949, naturalized, 1955; B.Arch., Okla. State U., 1956; M.Arch., Cranbrook Acad. Art, 1961; m. Anna Chmil, Aug. 28, 1955; children—John W., Andrew O., Maria M., Irene A. Designer, Glen Paulsen & Asso., architects, Bloomfield Hills, Mich., 1960-63, Minoru Yamasaki & Asso., Birmingham, 1963-64; prof. Sch. Architecture, Kent (Ohio) State U., 1965—; partner McWilliams, Martyniuk, Schidlowski, architects, Kent, 1970—. Recipient sch. medal AIA, 1956; Edward J. Delaney scholar, 1955-56, Illumination Engring. Research Inst. grantee, 1972-75. Mem. AIA, Assn. Collegiate Schs. of Architecture, Assn. Archtl. Historians, AAUP, Ukrainian Engrs. Soc. Am., Phi Kappa Theta, Tau Sigma Delta (hon.). Ukrainian Catholic. Club: Kiwanis. Home: 549 Bowman Dr Kent OH 44240

MARTZ, GEORGE E., lawyer; b. Indpls., Apr. 26, 1926; s. Joseph Arthur and Addie May (Hoss) M.; B.S., Ind. U., 1949, J.D., 1957; m. Patricia Lee Terry, Dec. 29, 1973; children by previous marriage—George E., Linda, Steven, Dennis, Christopher, Kimberly. Admitted to Ind. bar, U.S. Supreme Ct. bar, Ct. of Mil. Appeals bar, U.S. Dist. Ct. bar, Circuit Ct. of Appeals bar; practice law, Indpls., 1957—; chief pub. defender Marion County Criminal Ct., 1959-62; spl. trial dep. Marion County prosecutor's office, 1975. Sec., dir. Dunkin Mobile Homes Ind., Inc., Instant Living Fla., Inc. Served with USAAF, 1943-44, USAF, 1949-53. Mem. Am., Ind., Indpls. bar assns., Am., Ind. Trial Lawyers Assns., Am. Judicature Soc., Smithsonian Inst., Frat. Order Police (asso.), Phi Alpha Delta. Democrat. Presbyterian (elder). Mason (Shriner). Home: 9060 Stonegate Rd Indianapolis IN 46227 Office: 915 First Federal Bldg Indianapolis IN 46204

MARTZ, LYLE ERWIN, chem. engr.; b. Grand Rapids, Mich., Feb. 15, 1922; s. Cleon Russell and Katherine (Meulenberg) M.; student Grand Rapids Jr. Coll., 1939-41; B.S. in Chem. Engring., U. Mich., 1943; m. Thea May Burkhardt, June 7, 1952; children—Janice, Lori. With Dow Chem. Co., Midland, Mich., 1946—, research specialist, 1972—. Served with AUS, 1944-46. Mem. Am. Inst. Chem. Engrs., Am. Chem. Soc. Patentee in field. Home: 2008 Airfield Ln Midland MI 48640 Office: Dow Chem Co Midland MI 48640

MARTZIAL, TERRENCE JOSEPH, JR., dentist; b. Youngstown, Ohio, Feb. 27, 1933; s. Terrence Joseph and Elizabeth Carmella (Perruzzi) M.; student Youngstown State U., 1951-52; student Western Res. U., 1952-54, D.D.S., 1958; m. Patricia Jean Agnone, June 22, 1957; children—Josephine Lucia, Terrence Joseph III, Lisa Ann. Practice dentistry, New Middletown, Ohio, 1960—. Active Boy Scouts Am. Served to capt. USAF, 1958-60. Recipient Outstanding Pub. Service award Children's Dental Health, 1969; Dental Sci. Clinic award Corydon Palmer Dental Soc., 1968. Fellow Royal Soc. Health (London); mem. Am., Ohio (mem. council on dental pub. health and information) dental assns., Corydon Palmer Dental Soc. (pres. 1973-74). Roman Catholic. Lion (pres. New Middletown 1963). Home: 8126 Thunderbird Ct Poland OH 44514 Office: 10282 Main St New Middletown OH 44442

MARUYAMA, HENRY HATSUO, tech. specialist engr.; b. Rocky Ford, Colo., Oct. 20, 1923; s. Zengoro and Koto (Awa) M.; student Santa Rosa (Calif.) Jr. Coll., 1942; B.S. in Physics, U. Mich., Ann Arbor, 1947; m. Haruko Okuda, June 23, 1957. Chemist Pontiac Motor Car div. Gen. Motors Corp., 1958; tech. specialist engr. Engring. and Research Office, Chrysler Corp., Highland Park, Mich., 1958—. Served with inf. AUS, 1944-45. Decorated Bronze Star, Purple Heart. Mem. Soc. Automotive Engrs., Nat. Inventors Council, VFW. Democrat. Methodist. Inventor mech. devices, 1944—. Home: 5137 Buckingham Pl Troy MI 48098 Office: 12800 Lynn Townsend Dr Highland Park MI 48231

MARUYAMA, MAGOROH, anthropologist; b. 1929; B.A. in Math., U. Calif., Berkeley, 1951; postgrad. U. Munich, 1954-55, U. Heidelberg, 1955; Am.-Scandinavian Found. fellow, U. Copenhagen, 1955-57; Ph.D. (Swedish State fellow), U. Lund, 1959. Jr. research psychologist Inst. Human Devel., U. Calif., Berkeley, 1960-62; research asso. Inst. for Study Human Problems, Stanford U., 1962-64; community devel. specialist in Aleut villages in Alaska destroyed by tidal wave, 1964; sr. counselor Parks Job Corps Center, OEO, Pleasanton, Calif., 1965; research asso. Inst. for Study Crime and Delinquency, Sacramento, 1965-67, Lemberg Center for Study Violence, Brandeis U., 1967-69; vis. research fellow Culture and Mental Health Program, Social Sci. Research Inst., U. Hawaii, 1970-71; vis. prof. computer sci. and communication studies Antioch Coll., Yellow Springs, Ohio, 1971-72; prof. systems sci. Portland (Oreg.) State U., 1973—; vis. prof. anthropology U. Ill., Urbana, 1976—; cons. Calif. Dept. Pub. Health, 1960-62, Calif. Dept. Mental Hygiene, 1963-64, Dept. Interior, 1964, OEO, 1966-67, Nat. Bur. Standards, 1971, U.S. C.E. Inst. for Water Resources, 1972-75, Canadian Fed. Ministry State for Urban Affairs, 1974-75, NASA, 1975. Fellow Am. Anthrop. Assn.; mem. AAAS, Am. Soc. Planning Ofcls., Am. Psychol. Assn., Am. Sociol. Assn. Recipient Distinguished Article of Year award Am. Scientist, 1963; contbr. sci. articles to profl. jours. Office: Dept Anthropology U Ill Urbana IL 61801

MARVIN, JAMES CONWAY, librarian; b. Warroad, Minn., Aug. 3, 1927; s. William C. and Isabel (Carlquist) M.; B.A., U. Minn., 1950, M.A., Library Sch., 1966; m. Patricia Katharine Moe, Sept. 8, 1947; children—Heidi C., James Conway, Jill C., Jack C. Librarian, City of Kaukauna (Wis.), 1952-54; chief librarian City of Eau Claire (Wis.), 1954-56; dir. Cedar Rapids (Iowa) Pub. Library, 1956-67; dir. Topeka Pub. Library, 1967—; vis. faculty Kans. State Tchrs. Coll., 1970—; ALA-Rockefeller Found. vis. prof. Inst. Library Sci. U. Philippines, 1964-65. Served with USNR, 1945-46. Mem. ALA, Philippine (life), Kans., Iowa (past pres.) library assns., Johnson Soc. Club: Rotary (past pres.). Home: 40 Pepper Tree Ln Topeka KS 66611 Office: 1515 W 10th St Topeka KS 66604

MARVIN, WILLIAM SIBLEY, lumber co. exec.; b. Warroad, Minn., Aug. 25, 1917; s. George Griffin and Almina (Gibson) M.; B.S., U. Minn., 1939; m. Margaret Isabelle Wallin, 1940; children—Frank R., Margaret Ann (Mrs. Paul S. Johnson), John W., George G., Susan, Robert W. With Marvin Lumber & Cedar Co., Warroad, 1939—, now pres., chmn. bd.; pres. Marvin Windows Ltd., Winnipeg, Man., Can. Bd. dirs., past chmn. Warroad Hosp. Bd., gen. chmn. fund raising com., 1960. Mem. Nat. Woodwork Mfrs. Assn. (dir. 1968-70), Northwestern Minn. Mfrs. Assn. (pres. 1970-71), Ponderosa Pine Woodwork Assn. (dir. 1967-69, 71—), Warroad C. of C. (pres. 1942), Tau Kappa Epsilon. Republican. Episcopalian. Home: Warroad MN 56763 Office: Marvin Lumber & Cedar Co Warroad MN 56763

MARVY, JAMES, photo. designer; b. St. Paul, Mar. 8, 1945; s. William and Rose (Goldberg) M.; A.A., U. Minn., 1965. Owner, Marvy Advt. Photography, photog. illustrator-designer, Hopkins, Minn., 1964—, clients include 3M, Pillsbury, Westbend, Gen. Mills, Green Giant, Am. Express, TWA. Tchr. advanced photography Mpls. Coll. Art and Design, 1974. Recipient various regional and nat. photography awards, including awards Art Dirs. Club, 1973, 1974, nat. award Creativity 74, 1974, Creativity 75, 1975, Creativity 76, 1976, also Communications Arts award. Mem. Profl. Photographers

Am., Minn. Profl. Photographers Assn., Photog. Soc. Am., Minn. Comml. Indsl. Photographers Assn., Royal Photog. Soc. Gt. Britain. Art Dirs. Club Mpls. St. Paul, (Best of Show award, Nat. Creativity award 1974, 75, 76, Andy award), Advt. Club Minn. Home: 1721 Mt Curve Ave Minneapolis MN 55403 Office: 41 12th Ave N Hopkins MN 55343

MARX, EDWIN JOSEPH, electronics co. exec.; b. Mineola, L.I., N.Y., Mar. 20, 1929; s. Joseph Allen and Nina (Beedon) M.; A.A., Flint (Mich.) Jr. Coll., 1950; B.A., Mich. State U., 1952; m. Goldie Gladys Main, June 23, 1956; children—Gregory Michael, Catherine Angela, Brian Christopher. Electronic lab. technician, field engr., devel. engr. AC Spark Plug div. Gen. Motors Corp., Flint, 1954-58, sales analyst, resident sales engr., 1958-60, coordinator advt. and sales promotion, 1960-62; advt. and sales promotion mgr. Delco Radio div. Gen. Motors Corp., Kokomo, Ind., 1962-72, merchandising mgr. Delco Electronics div., 1972—; cons. Ind. U., 1974—. Active Boy Scouts Am., 1959-72; bd. dirs., pres. Devon Woods Rolling Acres Homeowners Assn., 1969-74. Served with AUS, 1952-54. Republican. Roman Catholic. Home: 4700 Mayfield Dr Kokomo IN 46901 Office: 700 E Firmin St Kokomo IN 46901

MARZOLF, STANLEY S(MITH), educator; b. Aurora, Ill., Oct. 18, 1904; s. George E. and Cora E. (Smith) M.; A.B., Wittenberg U., 1926; M.A., Ohio State U., 1930, Ph.D., 1937; m. Helen M. Gooding, Mar. 1, 1934; children—George Richard, John Edward. Tchr. chemistry Bucyrus High Sch. (Ohio), 1926-30; psychologist Ohio Dept. Pub. Welfare, Columbus, 1930-35; asst. prof. psychology Ill. State U., Normal, 1937-42, asso. prof., 1942-46, prof., 1946-68, Distinguished prof., 1968-72, prof. emeritus, 1972—. Sec.-treas. Ill. Bd. Examiners in Psychology, 1958-61. Fellow Am. Psychol. Assn.; mem. Ill. Psychol. Assn. (pres. 1954), Am. Assn. Psychol. Bds. (pres. 1962). Author: Studying the Individual, 1941; Psychological Diagnosis and Counseling in the Schools, 1956. Contbr. to profl. jours., psychol. textbooks. Home: 806 Hester Ave Normal IL 61761

MARZOTTO, ESIO JAMES, indsl. engr.; b. Ojibway, Windsor, Ont., Feb. 21, 1932; s. Antonio and Giuseppina (Pasqualatto) M.; B.S., Wayne State U., 1968, M.S., 1972, postgrad. 1973—; m. Kathleen Maria Shaughnessy, Nov. 24, 1956. TV technician CKLW-TV, Windsor, 1954-59; asst. dir. engring. CJAY-TV, Winnipeg, Man., Can., 1959-62; labour relations officer Can. Broadcasting Corp., Ottawa, Ont., Can., 1962-63; tech. supr. Media Centre, U. Windsor, 1966-69, dir., 1966—, instr. communications studies univ., 1973—. Chmn. communications com. United Way, 1977; bd. dirs. Children Achievement Assn. Windsor. Mem. Soc. Motion Picture and TV Engrs., Assn. Ednl. Communications and Tech., Assn. Media and Tech. in Edn. Can., Nat. Assn. Ednl. Broadcasters, Assn. Profl. Engrs. Ont. Roman Catholic. Clubs: K.C., Order of Alhambra, Rotary. Home: 1183 Highland Ave Windsor ON N9A 1R6 Canada Office: U Windsor Windsor ON N9B 3P4 Canada

MARZULLO, VITO, city ofcl.; b. Senerchia, Italy, Sept. 10, 1897; s. Anthony and Anna (Cerasale) M.; came to U.S., 1910, naturalized, 1921; student pub. schs.; m. Letizia Cozzi, June 11, 1922; children—Helen (Mrs. Michael Dimperio), William V., Adeline (Mrs. Ralph Malorano), Robert D., Ann (Mrs. Anthony De Maria), Eleanor (Mrs. Robert Masciola). Clk., Office of Treas. Cook County; dep. bailiff Chgo. Municipal Ct., sect. foreman Chgo. Dept. Sanitation, ward supt.; alderman Chgo. Mem. Ill. Ho. of Reps.; Democratic committeeman 25th Ward. Roman Catholic. Home: 823 S Oakley Blvd Chicago IL 60612 Office: City Hall Chicago IL

MASCIO, JOHN JOSEPH, lawyer; b. Steubenville, Ohio, Sept. 9, 1940; s. John Ubaldo and Elizabeth Julie (Calabria) M.; B.A., Coll. Steubenville, 1962; J.D., Ohio No. U., 1965; m. Virginia Vance, Mar. 27, 1965; children—John Jeffrey, David Paul, Karen Lynn. Admitted to Ohio bar; mem. firm Sferrella & Mascio, Steubenville, 1965-66, Kimble, Evans & Mascio, Steubenville, 1966-70, Evans & Mascio, Steubenville, 1970-76, Mascio & Blake, 1976—. Legal adviser Steubenville Air Pollution Bur., 1969-71. Solicitor, Village of Wintersville, Ohio, 1968-71, City of Steubenville, 1972—; spl. counsel to Ohio Atty. Gen., 1977—. Trustee Jr. Achievement, Steubenville, 1969-72. Mem. Am., Ohio (past mem. unethical practice com.), Jefferson County (past sec.-treas) bar assns., Am. Judicature Soc., Jeffersonian Lodge (past pres., trustee, Ahepa, Delta Theta Phi, Alpha Phi Delta. Elk (past exalted ruler), Eagle, Lion, K.C. Club: Serra. Home: 567 Braebarton Blvd Steubenville OH 43952 Office: 4110 Sunset Blvd Steubenville OH 43952

MASHAW, LANE HICKS, civil engr., educator; b. Lewisville, Ark., Sept. 24, 1925; s. Andrew Louis and Mattie Aurilla (Thatcher) M.; B.S., U. Ill., 1946; M.S., U. Iowa, 1966; m. Hazel LaVerne Brown, Mar. 31, 1945; children—Gayle Leslie McEvoy, Drew Vincent Mashaw. Asst. city engr. City of Champaign (Ill.), 1946-48; staff Warren & Van Prang, cons.'s, Decatur, Ill., 1948-57; city engr. City of Rockford (Ill.), 1957-60; pub. works dir. City of Iowa City (Iowa), 1960-64; asso. prof. civil engring. U. Iowa, Iowa City, 1964-74; prof. civil engring. Iowa State U., Ames, 1974—. Mem. Plan Commn. City of Iowa City, 1967-69; mem. Johnson County Conservation Commn., 1970-74. Served with USNR, 1943-46, 51-53. Grantee EPA, 1970-74, U.S. Dept. Interior, 1972-74; registered profl. engr. Iowa. Mem. Nat. Soc. Profl. Engrs., Iowa Engring. Soc., Am. Soc. Engring. Edn., Am. Pub. Works Assn. Presbyterian. Home: 2749 Cleveland Ave Ames IA 50010 Office: 112 Marston Hall Iowa State U Ames IA 50010

MASLIN, MEYER, ednl. adminstr.; b. Chgo., June 22, 1925; s. Morris and Sarah (Calisoff) M.; B.A., Roosevelt U., 1952, M.A., 1955; postgrad. Northwestern U., 1956-57; m. Charlotte Sternberg, June 20, 1948; children—Lynn Frances, Claudia Rachel. Tchr., Peterson Sch., Chgo., 1952-58, Von Steuben High Sch., Chgo., 1958-59; tchr. early childhood edn. edn. and child psychology Roosevelt U., 1959-64; prin. Oriole Park Sch., Chgo., 1961—; supr. tchrs. Sierra Leone project Peace Corps, 1964; gen. mgr. Maslin Investment Co., Chgo. Served with inf. AUS, 1943-46; ETO. Mem. Chgo. Prins. Assn. (sec. aux. II 1966-67), Chgo. Area Reading Assn. (chmn. dist. 1968-71), Am. Contract Bridge League (life master), Roosevelt U. Alumni Assn. Home: 5906 N Clark St Chicago IL 60660 Office: Oriole Park Sch 5424 N Oketo Ave Chicago IL 60656

MASON, ALICE FRANCES, artist; b. Chgo., Jan. 16, 1895; d. Philip Jacob and Franciska (Zschuppe) Kolb; B.S., Northwestern U., 1917; B.F.A., Art Inst. Chgo., 1935, M.F.A., 1944; m. Dr. Michael L. Mason, Dec. 28, 1921. Exhibited Art Inst. Chgo., 1937-40, 46, 49, 51-52, 54-55, Pa. Acad., 1938-39, 53, 56, Corcoran Gallery, 1941, internat. color lithography exhibit Cin. Art Mus., 1949, 51, 53, 55, Soc. Am. Graphic Artists, N.Y., 1952-55, Library Congress, 1952-55, 57, Union League Art Club, Chgo., 1957, 61, 63, 65, 72, Boerner Bot. Gardens, Milw., 1970, Chgo. Pub. Library, 1971; works represented in permanent collections Met. Mus., Library Congress, U. Chgo., others; one-man show paintings and color lithographs Chgo. Pub. Library, 1961, 71, A.C.S., 1964; juried exhbns. Hunterdon County Art Center, 1958-65, Conn. Acad. Fine Arts, 1955, 56, 58, 59, 64, 65; also represented Art Rental and Sales Gallery, Art Inst. Chgo., 1962—; by invitation Chgo. Pub. Library Print Show, 1965; one man shows Quincy (Ill.) Art Center, 1950, 66. Tchr. lithography Summer Sch. Paintings, Mich., 1953. Recipient 1st prize Art Mus. New Britain (Conn.) Inst., purchase prize, 1953; prize Municipal Art League, 1957, purchase prize Union League Civic and Arts Found., 1972. Mem. Chgo. Soc. Artists (pres. 1954-55, 56-57, 58-59, dir. 1959—, 1st v.p., 1964-67), Hunterdon County, Conn. acads. fine arts, Renaissance Soc. (bd. mem. 1959-67, hon. dir. 1968—), Alpha Omicron Pi. Clubs: Cordon (past pres.), Arts (Chgo.). Address: 9775 W Huron River Dr Dexter MI 48130

MASON, ARVIS JERRY, nursing home adminstr.; b. Princeton, Ind., June 27, 1920; s. James Levi and Lavenia Luella (Mason) M.; student Walbash Valley Coll.; m. Virginia Lee Goldman, Apr. 29, 1950; children—Rena Arwan (Mrs. Kent Smith), Bennet Paul, Arvis Jerry, Gina. Real estate broker, Princeton, 1946-60; adminstr. Pine Lawn Manor of Creeks Inc., Sumner, Ill., 1960—, owner, 1976—. Served with AUS, 1940-45. Mem. V.F.W. Moose. Address: PO Box 186 Sumner IL 62466

MASON, EARL JAMES, JR., physician; b. Marion, Ind., Aug. 26, 1923; s. Earl James and Grace A. (Leer) M.; student Marion Coll., 1940-41; B.S. in Medicine, Ind. U., 1944, A.B. in Chemistry, 1947, M.A. in Bacteriology, 1947; Ph.D. in Microbiology, Ohio State U., 1950; M.D., Western Res. U., 1954; m. Eileen Gursansky, Dec. 2, 1967. Teaching asst. dept. bacteriology Ind. U., 1945-47; research fellow depts. ophthalmology and bacteriology Ohio State U., Columbus, 1947-48, teaching asst. dept. bacteriology, 1948-50; Crile research scholar Western Res. U., Cleve., 1951-53; Damon Runyon cancer research fellow dept. pathology Western Res. U.-Cleve. City Hosp., 1951-56; dept. chief dept. pathology USPHS Hosp., San Francisco, 1956-58; fellow pathology U. Tex. Postgrad. Sch. Medicine, M.D. Anderson Hosp. and Tumor Inst., Houston, 1958-59; asst. prof. dept. pathology Baylor U. Coll. Medicine, 1959-60; asst. pathologist Jefferson Davis Hosp., 1959-60; asst. pathologist Michael Reese Hosp. and Med. Center, Chgo., 1960-61; asso. dir. dept. pathology, dir. dept. biol. scis. Mercy Hosp., 1960-65; dir. labs. St. Mary Med. Center, Gary and Hobart, Ind., 1965—; asso. prof. pathology Chgo. Med. Sch., 1966—; clin. prof. pathology Ind. U. Med. Sch., 1976—. Diplomate Am. Bd. Pathology, Am. Bd. Nuclear Medicine. Mem. Coll. Am. Pathologists, Am. Assn. Pathologists and Bacteriologists, Am. Soc. Clin. Pathologists, Internat. Acad. Pathologists, Am. Soc. Exptl. Pathology, Am. Assn. Cancer Research, Am. Assn. Blood Banks, Soc. Nuclear Medicine, Lake County Med. Soc., Am. Soc. Cytology, Sigma Xi. Research on cellular origin of antibodies and virus-cell interactions. Home: PO Box 485 7 Summit Rd Ogden Dunes Portage IN 46368 Office: 540 Tyler St Gary IN 46402

MASON, EDWARD EATON, surgeon, educator; b. Boise, Idaho, Oct. 16, 1920; s. Edward Files and Dora Bell (Eaton) M.; B.S., U. Iowa, 1943, M.D., 1945; Ph.D. in Surgery, U. Minn., 1953; m. Dordana Fairman, June 24, 1943; children—Daniel Edward, Rosemary, Richard Eaton, Charles Henry. Intern, U. Minn. Hosps., Mpls., 1945-46, resident in surgery, 1948-52; prof. surgery U. Iowa, Iowa City, 1953—. Served to lt. USN, 1946-48. Diplomate Am. Bd. Surgery. Mem. AMA, Iowa Med. Soc., Johnson County Med. Assn., Soc. Exptl. Biology and Medicine, Am. Thyroid Assn., A.C.S., Central Surg. Assn., Iowa Acad. Surgery, Soc. Univ. Surgeons, AAAS, Internat. Soc. Surgery, Iowa Clin. Surg. Soc., Am. Surg. Assn. Presbyn. Contbr. articles in field to profl. publs. Home: 5 Melrose Circle Iowa City IA 52240 Office: Dept Surgery Univ Hosps Iowa City IA 52242

MASON, JOHN EDWIN, clin. psychologist; b. Wadsworth, Ohio, Dec. 9, 1926; s. Lee Dwight and Ruth Elmira (Rickel) M.; A.B., Baldwin-Wallace Coll., 1949; M.A., Kent State U., 1955; Ph.D., Mich. State U., 1962; m. Annabel Nicholl, June 21, 1953; children—Melody Ann, Melissa Lynn. Tchr. sci.-math. Highland Schs., Medina, Ohio, 1952-54; asst. chief, psychology service, VA Hosp., Battle Creek, Mich., 1962—. Served with USNR, 1945-46, 1950-51. Mem. Am., Mich., Southwestern Mich. (pres. 1972) psychol. assns., Sigma Phi Epsilon (pres. 1948), Phi Mu Alpha Sinfonia. Mason. Home: 271 Gregg Dr Battle Creek MI 49017 Office: VA Hosp Battle Creek MI 49016

MASON, MEARLE D., lawyer; b. Nowata, Okla., Mar. 1, 1921; s. Mearle D. and Lois (Kellogg) M.; A.B., Kans. State Coll., 1943; LL.B., J.D., U. Mich., 1949; m. Dorothy Ann Altepeter, Mar. 7, 1946; children—Steven F., L. Lorrain, Dana K. Admitted to Kans. bar, 1949; asso. mem. firm Ratner & Allen, Wichita, 1949-50; pres. Wasco Instruments Co., Wichita; partner firm Hill & Mason, Wichita, 1950—; municipal ct. judge, Wichita, 1973—; city atty. Mulvane (Kans.), 1970—; pres. Prepaid Legal Services of Kan., Inc. Bd. dirs., sec.-treas. Clear Lakes, Inc., Wichita, 1968—. Served to lt. USNR, 1943-46; PTO. Mem. Sedgwick County-Wichita (pres.), Wichita (pres.) bar assns., Kappa Delta Kappa. Republican. Methodist. Club: Lions. Home: 3109 N St Clair St Wichita KS 67204 Office: 810 W Douglas St Suite C Wichita KS 67203

MASON, MILDRED JUNE, sch. counselor; b. Poland, Ohio, Dec. 26, 1924; d. Harry Albert and Elizabeth May (Myers) Kariher; student Case Western Res. U., 1943-45; B.A., M.S. in Edn., Youngstown State U., 1965-73; postgrad. Kent State U., 1973-74; children by former marriage—Robert, Thomas, Samuel, Carol, Ruth, Donald. Farmer, New Middletown, Ohio, 1930-68; tchr. Columbiana (Ohio) Schs., 1966-69; counselor Elyria (Ohio) City Schs., 1969—. Active PTA; dir. youth choir Old Springfield United Ch. Christ, 1960-65; adult ednl. adviser Case Western Res. U. Mem. Am., Ohio personnel and guidance assns., Am., Ohio sch. counselors assns., Ohio Vocat. Assn., Nat., Ohio, Elyria edn. assns. Republican. Mem. United Ch. Christ. Home: 508 Debby Ln Elyria OH 44035 Office: Franklin Jr High Sch 446 W 11th St Elyria OH 44035

MASON, NORMAN RONALD, endocrinologist; b. Rochester, Minn., Nov. 20, 1929; s. Harold Lawrence and Margaret Maude (McKenzie) M.; B.S., U. Chgo., 1953; M.A., U. Utah, 1956, Ph.D., 1959; m. Nancy May Bumgarner, June 24, 1953; children—Charles Norman, Susan Elizabeth. Instr. biochemistry Sch. Medicine U. Miami (Fla.), 1959-60, research asst. prof., 1960-64; investigator Howard Hughes Med. Inst., Miami, 1959-64; sr. physiologist Eli Lilly & Co. Research Labs., Indpls., 1964—. Mem. Endocrine Soc., Am. Chem. Soc., A.A.A.S. Research on hormone action, ovary physiology, metabolism. Home: 7301 Steinmeier Dr Indianapolis IN 46250 Office: Eli Lilly & Co Research Labs Indianapolis IN 46206

MASON, RONALD JAMES, educator; b. Windsor, Ont., Can., Oct. 11, 1929; s. James Henry and Sarrannie (Howarth) M.; brought to U.S., 1939, naturalized, 1946; B.A., U. Pa., 1957; M.A., U. Mich., 1957, Ph.D., 1964; m. Carol Ann Irwin, Dec. 13, 1958; children—Victoria Anne, Peter Alden. Asst. dir., curator anthropology Neville Pub. Mus., Green Bay, Wis., 1958-61; lectr. dept. anthropology Lawrence U., Appleton, Wis., 1961-62, asst. prof., 1962-66, asso. prof., 1966-71, prof., 1971—. Mem. Wis. Historic Preservation Rev. Bd., 1972—. Served with USAF, 1950-54. NSF research grantee, 1967-68; recipient research medal Wis. Archeol. Soc., 1968. Fellow A.A.A.S., Am. Anthrop. Assn.; mem. Soc. for Am. Archaeology, Wis. Archeol. Survey (pres. 1966-68). Author: Late Pleistocene Geochronology and the Paleo-Indian Penetration into the Lower Michigan Peninsula, 1958; Two Stratified Sites on the Door Peninsula of Wisconsin, 1966. Contbr. articles to profl. jours. Home: 620 E South River St Appleton WI 54911

MASON, VIRGINIA LILLY (MRS. JAMES MASON), civic worker; b. Chgo., Feb. 25, 1908; d. Paul Foster and Ione J. (McBroom) Lilly; grad. Chgo. Tchrs. Coll., 1927; student U. Chgo.; m. James Mason, Oct. 17, 1931; children—Eleanor (Mrs. Carl C. Hanke, Jr.), Frances Virginia (Mrs. Joel P. Smith), John Paul. Ednl. cons. Carson Pirie Scott & Co., Chgo., 1963-73. Chmn. edn. com. Chgo. Commn. Human Relations, 1952-70; pres. Citizen's Sch. Com. Chgo., 1953-57; mem. Nat. Citizen's Council Better Schs., 1956-60; vice-chmn. Ill. Citizens Edn. Com., 1959-64; chmn. adv. bd. to urban youth program Chgo. Pub. Schs., 1964-70, chmn. distributive edn. adv. com., 1969—, pres. distributive edn. adv. council, 1970-72; mem. staff DuPage County Nutrition Program, 1974-77. Chmn. sch. and child com. Mayor's Commn. on Youth Welfare, 1956-60. Mem. bd. mgrs. Met. Chgo., YMCA, 1955-71, mem. bd. Ill. area, 1955-60, mem. nat. council, 1958-64; world service chmn. S.W. Surburban YMCA, Chgo., 1964; mem. Nat. Citizens Com. for Support Pub. Schs., mem. bd. Girl Scouts Chgo., 1958-60; trustee Garrett Theol. Sem., 1970-74; mem. staff George Williams Coll. Camp. Recipient award City Chgo. Commn. Human Relations, 1950, award Citizens Schs. Com., 1957, award YMCA Met. Chgo., 1970. Home: 65 Brewster Ln LaGrange Park IL 60525

MASOPUST, JOSEPH FRANCIS, travel assn. exec.; b. N.Y.C., Mar. 4, 1914; s. John and Frances (Schima) M.; B.A., Fordham U., 1933; m. Hollis Hutchinson, Nov. 20, 1945. Exec. sec. N.Y.C. Employees Retirement System, N.Y.C., 1940-70; pres. Nemaha County Devel. Corp., Auburn, Nebr., 1970—; pres. Peru (Nebr.) State Achievement Found., 1975—; v.p. N.Y.C. Civil Service Retired Assn., N.Y.C., 1971—; chmn. Tri-state Mo. River Tourism Corp., Peru, 1975—; dir. Bank of Peru, 1975—, Maverick, Media Inc., 1976—. Mem. adv. bd. Peru State Coll., 1975—. Served with USAF, 1942-46. Mem. Am. Indsl. Devel. Council, Inc. Nebr. Diplomats. Clubs: Elks, Kiwanis. Home: 1916 8th St Peru NE 68421 Office: Peru State Coll Peru NE 68421

MASOTTI, LOUIS HENRY, educator; b. N.Y.C., May 16, 1934; s. Henry and Angela Catherine (Turi) M.; A.B., Princeton U., 1956; M.A., Northwestern U., 1961, Ph.D., 1964; m. Iris Patricia Leonard, Aug. 28, 1958; children—Laura Lynn, Andrea Anne. Fellow, Nat. Center for Edn. in Politics, 1962; asst. prof. Case Western Res. U., Cleve., 1963-67, asso. prof., 1967-69, dir. Civil Violence Research Center, 1968-69; sr. Fulbright lectr. Johns Hopkins U. Center for Advanced Internat. Studies, Bologna, Italy, 1969-70; asso. prof. Northwestern U., Evanston, Ill., 1970-72, prof. polit. sci., 1972—, dir. Center for Urban Affairs, 1971—. Cons. to numerous publs. and govtl. agys.; vis. asso. prof. U. Wash., summer 1969. Research dir. Carl Stokes for Mayor of Cleve., 1967; mem. Cleveland Heights Bd. Edn., 1967-69; adviser to various congl. and gubinatorial campaigns, Ohio, Ill., N.J. Served to lt. USNR, 1956-59. Recipient Distinguished Service award Cleve. C. of C., 1967; numerous fed. and found. research grants, 1963—. Mem. Am., Midwest (v.p. 1976-77) polit. sci. assns., Soc. for Study of Social Problems. Author: Education and Politics in Suburbia, 1967; Shootout in Cleveland, 1969; A Time to Burn?, 1969; Suburbia in Transition, 1973; The New Urban Politics, 1976; The City in Comparative Perspective, 1976; co-editor: Metropolis in Crisis, 1968, 2d edit., 1971; Riots and Rebellion, 1968; The Urbanization of the Suburbs, 1973. Editor Edn. and Urban Soc., 1968-71, Urban Affairs Quar., 1973—. Home: 2700 Grant St Evanston IL 60201

MASSA, RICHARD WAYNE, author, educator; b. Carona, Kans., May 2, 1932; s. Columbo and Ella (Whitehead) M.; B.J., U. Mo., Columbia, 1954, M.A., 1955; postgrad. U. Ark., 1964-65; m. Teresa Ramirez, Mar. 19, 1971; children—Tod, Daphne, Sara. Instr. journalism U. Mo., Columbia, 1954-55, Miss. State Coll. Women, Columbus, 1957-58; instr. journalism and English, U. Sci. and Arts Okla., Chickasha, 1958-69; v.p. Interpersonal Communications Cons., Oklahoma City, 1969-71; instr. journalism N.E. Mo. State U., 1971-72, Mo. So. State Coll., Joplin, 1972—; cons., speech writer for polit. candidates, 1968-72; dir. pub. relations workshops govt. agencies, 1970—. Co-editor and co-author: Contemporary Man in World Society, 1969; Philosophical Man, His Quest for Values, 1969; Aesthetic Man: His Contemporary Values, 1970; Inquisitive Man, 1970; Technological Man, 1971. Home: 2005 E 24th St Joplin MO 64801 Office: Missouri Southern State Coll Joplin MO 64801

MASSEY, JAMES EARL, clergyman; b. Ferndale, Mich., Jan. 4, 1930; s. George Wilson and Elizabeth (Shelton) M.; student U. Detroit, 1949-50, 55-57; B.Th., B.R.E., Detroit Bible Coll., 1961; A.M., Oberlin Grad. Sch. Theology, 1964; postgrad. U. Mich., 1967-69; D.D., Asbury Theol. Sem., 1972; postgrad. Pacific Sch. Religion, 1972; m. Gwendolyn Inez Kilpatrick, Aug. 4, 1951. Ordained to ministry Church of God, 1951; asso. minister Ch. of God of Detroit, 1951-53; sr. pastor Met. Church of God, Detroit, 1954-76, pastor-at-large, 1976; speaker Christian Brotherhood Hour, 1977—. Prin. Jamaica Sch. Theology, Kingston, Jamaica, 1963-66; campus minister Anderson (Ind.) Coll., 1969-77, asst. prof. religious studies, 1969-75, asso. prof., 1975—; chmn. Commn. on Higher Edn. in the Church of God, 1968-71; vice-chmn. Bd. Publs. Church of God, 1968—. Dir. Warner Press, Inc. Mem. Corp. Inter-Varsity Christian Fellowship. Served with AUS, 1951-53. Mem. Nat. Assn. Coll. and Univ. Chaplains, Nat. Com. Black Churchmen, Nat. Negro Evang. Assn. (bd. dirs. 1969—). Author: When Thou Prayest, 1960; The Worshipping Church, 1961; Raymond S. Jackson, A Portrait, 1967; The Soul Under Siege, 1970; The Church of God and the Negro, 1971; The Hidden Disciplines, 1972; The Responsible Pulpit, 1973; Temples of the Spirit, 1974; The Sermon in Perspective, 1976. Editorial bd. The Christian Scholar's Rev. Home: 1138 Kingsmill Rd Anderson IN 46012

MASSIE, CHARLES LLEWELYN, health orgn. exec.; b. Lee's Summit, Mo., June 28, 1910; s. John Edmund and Minnie Lavina (Kennedy) M.; student Dickinson Secretarial Coll., 1931, Finlay Engring. Coll., 1934, U. Mo., 1965, U. Utah, 1966-72; m. Alice Ream Tucker, Aug. 3, 1929; children—Charles, Robert, Dennis, Alicia (Mrs. Carl W. Hunt). With Task Force Organized Group Hosp. Service (Blue Cross), Kansas City, Mo., 1939-41; adminstrv. officer, services analyst U.S. Ry. Mail Service, Kansas City, St. Louis, 1941-70; mng. carrier Govt. Employee Hospital Assn., Inc., Kansas City, Mo., 1960-75; pres. Govt. Employees Hospital Assn., Inc., 1949-75, dir., 1941—. Dir. Am. Bank & Trust Co., Kansas City, Mo. Bd. dirs. Ry. Mail Hospital Assn., Inc., 1941—, pres., 1949-75. Mem. Mo. Gov.'s Adv. Council on Alcoholism and Drug Abuse, 1971-74. Bd. dirs. Center for Spl. Problems, Kansas City, 1970—, pres., 1970, 75; bd. dirs. Nat. Council on Alcoholism, Kansas City, 1966—, pres., 1971; bd. dirs. Armour Meml. Home, Kansas City, 1969-76, Independence Council of Services, 1971—, Zionic Research Inst., Independence, 1973-76, Independence House, Inc., 1974-76. Mem. Am. Pub. Health Assn., Group Health Assn. Am., Royal Soc. Health (London). Mem. Reorganized Ch. of Jesus Christ of Latter-day Saints (ordained minister 1965). Mason. Author: Family Ministry in Alcoholism, 1968, rev. edit., 1970. Home: 1225 W 25th Terr Independence MO 64052 Office: 35 W 40th St PO Box 10304 Kansas City MO 64111

MASSIE, THOMAS ANDREW, indsl. engr.; b. Columbus, Ohio, June 25, 1941; s. Ralph Andrew and Florence Marie Massie; B.S. in Indsl. Engring., San Jose (Calif.) State U., 1965; M.B.A., Golden Gate U., San Francisco, 1973; m. Maria del Carmen Flores, Apr. 20, 1967; children—Michael Andrew, Robert Andrew, Jennifer Ann. Civilian indsl. engr. USAF, AFLC/XOMCE, McClellan AFB, Calif., 1970-74, ATC/XPMMM, Randolph Field AFB, Tex., 1974-76, AFLC/DPQQL, Wright-Patterson AFB, Ohio, 1977—. Served to capt. USAF, 1965-70. Registered profl. engr., Tex. Mem. Nat., Tex. socs. prof. engrs. Republican. Roman Catholic. Clubs: Chess, Cath. Men's. Home: 1523 Salem Ave Apt 9 Fairborn OH 45324 Office: AFLC/DPQQL Wright-Patterson AFB OH 45433

MASSMAN, VIRGIL F., library adminstr.; B.A. in English, St. John's U.; M.A. in English, U. Minn.; M.A. in L.S.; Ph.D. in L.S., U. Mich., married; 3 children. Head reference librarian Bemidji (Minn.) State Coll., 1960-65; asso. prof. English U. of S.D., 1965-66; dir. libraries, 1966-71; exec. dir. James J. Hill Reference Library, St. Paul, 1971—; cons. in field. Mem. AAUP, Am., Minn. (mem. advisory council 1971-75; chairperson academic div. 1974) library assns., Minn., S.D. hist. socs. Contbr. articles in field to profl. jours. Home: 3411 Vivian Ave Saint Paul MN 55112

MASTER, LAWRENCE STANLEY, educator; b. N.Y.C., Dec. 14, 1933; s. Moses and Anne Helen (Rodnick) M.; B.S., U. Louisville, 1956; M.S., Ind. U., 1963, Ed.D., 1969; m. Nancy Louise Briggs, Jan. 31, 1970; 1 dau., Mary Anne. Tchr., Jefferson County (Ky.) Pub. Schs., 1961-64; vice prin., guidance dir. Bloomington (Ind.) Met. Schs., 1964-66; coordinator interstate programs Ind. Dept. Pub. Instrn., Indpls., 1966-67; asso. dir. Ind. U. Upward Bound Program, Bloomington, 1967-68; field and editorial dir. Ind. Assn. Jr. and Sr. High Sch. Prins. Assn., 1968-69; asso. prof. edn., coordinator continuing edn. Coll. Edn., U. Wis.-Oshkosh, 1969-76; social studies and lang. arts cons. Keystone Area Edn. Agency State of Iowa, Dubuque, 1976—. vis. prof. edn. Ind. U., S.E., New Albany, 1974, 77. Cons. various high schs., Wis., 1969-76; chmn. various North Central Assn. evaluations, Wis. and Ind., 1968-76. Exec. bds. dirs. Twin Lakes and Bay Lakes councils Boy Scouts Am., 1971-76, dir. chmn. Winnebago Dist., Bay Lakes council, 1971-75, award of Merit, Winnebago Dist., Twin Lakes council, 1973. Served with inf. AUS, 1956-58. Mem. Wis. Assn. Curriculum and Supervision (mem. exec. bd. 1972-74), Wis. Reading Assn. (exec. bd. 1972-76, editor jour. 1972-76), Oshkosh Area Reading Council (pres. 1973-75), Fox Valley Curriculum Study Council (exec. sec. 1970-74), Ind. U. Alumni Assn. Wis. (pres. 1970-72), Phi Delta Kappa (pres. 1976-77). Mason (Shriner), Kiwanian (dir. 1971-74). Contbr. articles to profl. jours. Home: 3670 Pennsylvania Ave Dubuque IA 52001

MASTICS, ALEC A., lawyer; b. Cleve., Nov. 2, 1903; s. Elmer William and Ida Marie (Walter) M.; A.B., Western Res. U., 1925, J.D., 1927; m. Marianne M. Matousek, July 29, 1944. Admitted to Ohio bar, 1927, since practiced in Cleve. and Bay Village. Chief counsel for Ohio, Ky. and W.Va., W.L.B., 1943-47; regional atty. to acting chmn. bd. Wage Stblzn. Bd., 1951-53; yachting editor Cleve. Plain Dealer, 1943—. Chmn. Ohio cosmopolitan com. for Sen. Robert Taft, Sr., 1950. Recipient Thomas Fleming Day award for editorials on boating, 1966. Mem. Great Lakes Hist. Soc. (v.p., trustee), Inter-Lake Yachting Assn. (commodore 1961; chmn. trustees), U.S. (hon. life), Cleve. (comdr. 1943) power squadrons, U.S. Yacht Racing Union. Club: Cleve. Yachting (commodore 1957). Home and office: 26500 Lake Rd Bay Village OH 44140

MASUDA, GEORGE THEODORE, bishop; b. Mpls., Mar. 3, 1913; s. Roy T. and Minnie (Gilbertson) M.; B.A., Carleton Coll., Northfield, Minn., 1934; B.D., Seabury Western Sem., Evanston, Ill., 1942, D.D., 1965; m. Jeanne Bennett, Oct. 20, 1951; children—David, Michael. Ordained to ministry Episcopal Ch., 1942; vicar in Whitefish, Mont., 1942-48; rector in Billings, Mont., 1948-65; bishop of N.D., 1965—. Home: 707 S 8th St S Fargo ND 58102 Office: 809 S 8th Ave S Fargo ND 58102

MATALAMAKI, WILLIAM, ednl. adminstr.; b. Floodwood, Minn., June 14, 1917; s. Matt and Mary (Kalpio) M.; B.S., U. Minn., 1942, M.S., 1953; Ph.D., U. Wis., 1960; m. Margaret Marie Myers, Sept. 11, 1942; children—Judith Marie (Mrs. Jack Gerlinger), William Michael. Instr. vocat. agr., prin. high sch., Bigfork, Minn., 1942-45; instr. vocat. and vets. agr. Esko High Sch., 1945-49; prin. N. Central Sch. Agr., Grand Rapids, Minn., 1949-56; prof., supt. N. Central Sch. and Expt. Sta., Grand Rapids, 1956—. Cons. Ford Found. and U. Minn. to Chile, S.Am., 1965; dir. First Nat. Bank, Grand Rapids, 1964—. Mem. Arrowhead Regional Devel. Commn., 1972—. Trustee Charles K. Blandin Found.; chmn. Itasca County Welfare and Hosp. Bd.; mem. Minn. Synod. Luth. Social Service Bd.; bd. dirs. Range Center, Inc., Minn. Lions Eye Bank. Recipient Good Govt. award Grand Rapids Jr. C. of C., 1960, 25 Year Service award U. Minn.; State Farmer degree Future Farmers Am., 1960. Mem. Minn. Vocat. Agr. Instrs. Assn. (pres. 1948-49), Minn. Alumni Assn. (chpt. pres. 1957), Minn. Arrowhead Assn., AAAS, Grand Rapids C. of C. (past pres.), Phi Delta Kappa. Lutheran (chmn. bd. 1960-66). Mason, Lion (dist. gov. 1966-67, mem. dist. gov.'s cabinet), Toastmaster. Editor: N. Central Quar., 1956—. Address: N Central Expt Sta Grand Rapids MN 55744

MATALON, JOHN GEORGE, religious store exec.; b. Peoria, Ill., Feb. 6, 1921; s. John Joseph and Agnes Marcella (Bybokas) M.; student Bradley U., 1938-40; B.S., U. Ill., 1942; m. Arvilla Marie Klika, July 17, 1976; stepchildren—Michael, Patrick, John and Thomas DuPree. Service rep. Caterpillar Tractor Co., 1946-53; sr. engr. Westinghouse Electric Corp., 1954-60; chief engr. Hancock Industries, Jackson, Mich., 1960-61; staff engr. Bendix Corp., Kansas City, Mo., 1961-76; gen. mgr. Soc. St. Vincent de Paul Store, Kansas City, Kans., 1976—, also dir. Served with USNR, 1944-46. Mem. Am. Def. Preparedness Assn., Nat. Conf. Cath. Charities. Republican. Roman Catholic. Clubs: Hillcrest Country, K.C. (4 deg.). Home: 5001 Reed Rd Mission KS 66202 Office: 814 Osage St Kansas City KS 66105

MATASOVIC, JOHN LOUIS, welding supply and equipment co. exec.; b. Chgo., Sept. 4, 1916; s. John J. and Marie (Bielek) M.; grad. pub. schs., Chgo.; student U. Ill., 1942-43; m. Stella Butkauskas, Feb. 26, 1938; children—Linda, Marilyn. Chief insp. Nat. Certified Welding Bur., Chgo., 1940-45; instr. piping trade Chgo. Bd. Edn., Washburne Trade Sch., 1940-45; pres. Universal Welding Supply Co., New Lenox, Ill., 1944—; pres. Oxo Welding Equipment Co., New Lenox, 1944—. Mem. Am. Welding Soc., Am. Hereford Assn. Roman Catholic. Author: Pipefitters Layout Guide, 1945. Patentee electric welding and gas welding apparatus. Home: Route 1 Mokena IL 60448 Office: Cedar and Oak Sts New Lenox IL 60451

MATASOVIC, STELLA, mech. products co. exec., ranch exec.; b. Lovington, Ill., July 19, 1916; d. Charles K. and Agnes (Nickus) Butkauskas; B.E., Ill. State Normal U., 1935; m. John L. Matasovic, Feb. 26, 1938; children—Linda Swiercinsky, Marilyn. Tchr. elementary sch., Pana, Ill., 1935-37; partner OXO Welding Equipment Co., New Lenox, Ill., 1944—; partner Universal Welding Supply Co., New Lenox, Ill., 1944—; mgr. Oxo Hereford ranches, Mokena, Ill., 1952—. Mem. Nat. Welding Supply Assn., New Lenox C. of C. (sec. 1969), Am. Nat. Cattlemen's Assn., Ill., Colo. hereford assns., Am. Hereford Aux. (pres. 1969-70), Ill. Beef Aux. Home: Rural Route 1 Mokena IL 60448 Office: Cedar and Oak Sts New Lenox IL 60451

MATCHETT, HUGH MOORE, lawyer; b. Chgo., Apr. 24, 1912; s. David Fleming and Jennie E. (Moore) M.; A.B., Monmouth (Ill.) Coll., 1934; J.D., U. Chgo., 1937; m. Ilo Venona Wolff, May 12, 1956. Admitted to Ill. bar, 1937, since practiced in Chgo. Served with USNR, 1942-46; MTO, PTO; lt. comdr. JAGC, USNR. Mem. Fed. (chmn. mil. law com. Chgo. chpt. 1954-55, mem. com. 1960-61), Am., Ill., Chgo. bar assns., Judge Advs. Assn., Tau Kappa Epsilon, Phi Alpha Delta. Republican. Presbyterian. Counsel in litigation establishing rule that charitable instns. are liable in tort to extent of their non-taxable funds. Home: 5834 S Stony Island Ave Chicago IL 60637 Office: 10 S La Salle St Chicago IL 60603

MATCZYNSKI, AVALON NOLEN, sch. counselor; b. Kansas City, Mo., Nov. 18, 1932; d. Thomas J. and Estella (Banks) Nolen; B.S., Lincoln U., Jefferson City, Mo., 1953; postgrad. Central State U., Wilberforce, Ohio, 1958-59; M.S., Miami U., Oxford, Ohio, 1968; certificate adminstrn., Wright State U., Dayton, Ohio, 1975; m. Thomas J. Matczynski, Aug. 8, 1970; 1 son, Mark Damian. Tchr. comml. edn. Sedalia, Mo., 1953-54; elementary tchr., Dayton, Ohio, 1959-68, elementary counselor, 1968-69, 71-73; counselor Patterson Vocat. Coop. High Sch., Dayton, 1968-71, Stivers-Patterson Vocat. High Sch., Dayton, 1973—; cons. in field. Adviser Del-Teen Club, Dayton, 1966—. Martha Jennings Holden scholar, 1968-69. Mem. Am., Miami Valley personnel and guidance assns., Am., Ohio sch. counselors assns., Dayton, Ohio edn. assns., Delta Sigma Theta. Democrat. Roman Catholic. Home: 1752 Burroughs Dr Dayton OH 45406 Office: Patterson Coop High Sch 1313 E 5th St Dayton OH 45403

MATEESCU, SONJA KATHERINE TOPLAK, dentist; b. Maribor, Yugoslavia, Dec. 2, 1931; d. Joseph Glavina and Antonia (Gombac) Glavina; came to U.S., 1957, naturalized, 1962; student stomatology, U. Ljubijana, 1954-56; student medicine U. Vienna, 1956-57. B.S., Western Reserve U., 1961, D.D.S., 1962; m. 2d, Gheorghe Mateescu, Nov. 24, 1974; children—Vesna Toplak, Bogdan Toplak. Gen. practice dentistry, Ohio, 1962—; clin. instr. Sch. Dentistry Cleve. Western Reserve U., 1973—. Mem. ADA, Acad. Gen. Dentistry, Am. Assn. Women Dentists. Roman Catholic. Office: 6420 St Clair Cleveland OH 44103

MATHEIN, EDWARD ALBERT, dentist; b. Jackson, Mich., Nov. 13, 1941; s. Albert Henley and Margaret Mary (Dalton) M.; student Jackson Community Coll., 1959-61; D.D.S., U. Detroit, 1965; m. Jeanine Ann Matthews, June 19, 1965; children—Ann Marie, Lori Anne. Gen practice dentistry, Jackson, 1967—; pres. Blue Ribbon Investments, 1976—. Treas. Cascades, Essex, Crieglow Civic Assn., 1972—; co-chmn. March of Dimes, 1975-76; chmn. awareness program Jackson County Bi-Centennial Com., 1975-76; pres. Jackson Profl. Plaza Condominium Assn., 1976—. Served with USNR, 1965-67. Mem. Am., Mich., Jackson (v.p. 1977-78) dental assns., Mich. Assn. Professions, Am. Analgesia Soc., Am. Soc. Preventive Dentistry, Am. Endodontic Soc., Acad. Gen. Dentistry, Jackson Dist. Dental Soc. (sec.-editor 1975-76, treas. 1976-77, v.p. 1977-78, dir.), Jackson Jaycees (dir. 1973-74), Nat. Wildlife Assn., Fedn. Ind. Bus., U. Detroit Alumni Club, Jackson C. of C., Blue Ribbon Investment Club (v.p.), Xi Psi Phi. Club: Century (Detroit). Editor: Jackson District Dental Soc. Newsletter, 1969-76. Home: 2058 Wildwood Ln Jackson MI 49203 Office: Jackson Profl Plaza 306 W Washington Ave Jackson MI 49201 Jackson MI 49203

MATHENY, STANLEY HOWARD, lawyer; b. Carthage, Ill., Sept. 10, 1934; s. Jesse Edwin and Zula Myrtle (Hardy) M.; A.B., Wabash Coll., 1956; J.D., Ind. U., 1959; m. Nancy Ellen Cain, June 15, 1957; children—Deborah, Thomas, Susan, Jill. Admitted to Ind. bar, 1959; practiced in Shelbyville, 1959-60, Huntington, 1960—; dep. pros. atty., 1962-63; city judge, 1963-67; city atty. City of Huntington, 1968-75. Dir., Community State Bank, Huntington. Republican precinct committeeman, 1962-64, 66-74. Recipient Gavit award Ind. U. Sch. Law, 1959. Mem. Am., Ind., Huntington County (pres. 1963) bar assns., Am. Acad. Social Sci., Delta Tau Delta. Methodist. Mason (Shriner), Odd Fellow, Elk. Club: Optimist (Huntington). Home: RR 8 Box 193 Huntington IN 46750 Office: 45 W Market St Huntington IN 46750

MATHER, BETTY BANG, musician, educator; b. Emporia, Kans., Aug. 7, 1927; d. Read Robinson and Shirley (Smith) Bang; B.Mus., Oberlin Conservatory, 1949; M.A., Columbia U., 1951; m. Roger Mather, Aug. 3, 1973. Mem. faculty U. Iowa, Iowa City, 1952—, prof. music, 1973—; leader workshop Baroque Interpretation for Woodwinds, Coe Coll., 1975, 76. Author: Interpretation of French Music from 1675-1775, 1973; (with David Lasocki) Free Ornamentation for Woodwind Instruments from 1700-1775, 1976. Editor: 30 Virtuosic Selections in the Gallant Style for Unaccompanied Flute, 1975; Opera Duets Arranged for Two Flutes by Berbiguier, 1976. Contbr. articles to profl. publs. Home: 308 4th Ave Iowa City IA 52240 Office: Sch Music U Iowa Iowa City IA 52242

MATHER, EDWARD LYLE, accountant; b. Colby, Kans., Oct. 5, 1924; s. Edward Elmer and Gertrude I. (Ritchey) M.; B.S., Kans. State U., 1949; m. Marian Sarah Roberts, Feb. 17, 1952; children—Pamela, Karen, Paula, Donald. Office mgr. Wheatbelt Pub. Power, Sidney, Nebr., 1951-58; chief accountant Hill County Electric, Havre, Mont., 1960-66; accountant Farmers Union Elevator, Gurley, Nebr., 1967-74; village clk. accountant Village of Gurley, 1967—; pvt. practice as pub. accountant, Gurley, 1974—. Chmn. or co-chmn. Ft. Sidney Days, 1953-55; cubmaster Cub Scouts, Gurley, 1971-73; scoutmaster Boy Scouts Am., Gurley, 1974-75; treas. Sch. Bd. Edn., Gurley, 1970-75; bd. dirs. Nebr. Centennial Parade, 1967, co-chmn., 1967; bd. dirs. Cheyenne County Centennial Parade, 1970, sec., 1970, co-chmn., 1970; treas. Christian Ch., 1975. Mem. Nat. Soc. Pub. Accountants. Mem. Christian Ch. (treas. 1956-60). Mason. Home: Box 73 Gurley NE 69141

MATHER, ROGER FREDERICK, musician, educator; b. London, May 27, 1917; s. Richard and Marie Louise (Schultze) M.; came to U.S., 1938, naturalized, 1948; B.A. with honors, Cambridge (Eng.) U., 1938, M.A. (hon.), 1941; M.Sc., Mass. Inst. Tech., 1940; m. Betty Louise Bang, Aug. 3, 1973; children by previous marriage—Arielle Diane, Christopher Richard. Research metallurgist Inland Steel Co., East Chicago, Ind., 1940-42; chief metallurgist Willys-Overland Motors Co., Toledo, 1942-46, Kaiser-Frazer Corp., Willow Run, Mich., 1946-50; project mgr. U.S. Steel Corp., Pitts., 1950-61; dir. research and engring. Mine Safety Appliances Co., Pitts., 1961-62; mem. staff research div. E. I. DuPont de Nemours Co., Wilmington, Del., 1962-63; br. chief nuclear power tech. NASA, Cleve., 1963-73; lectr. Sch. Music U. Iowa, 1973—; condr. flute clinics workshops. Registered profl. engr., Ohio, Mich., Pa. Mem. Am. Musical Inst. Soc., Am. Recorder Soc., Nat. Flute Soc., Nat. Assn. Mus. Inst. Technicians, Galpin Soc., Am. Inst. Mining, Metall., Petroleum Engrs., Am. Soc. Metals, Am. Inst. Aeros., Astronautics, ASME, ASTM, Soc. Automotive Engrs., Mensa, Pennsylvania Soc. Contbr. articles on engring., flute to profl. jours. Home: 308 Fourth Ave Iowa City IA 52240 Office: Sch Music U Iowa Iowa City IA 52242

MATHESON, WILLIAM ANGUS, JR., farm machinery co. exec.; b. Oregon City, Oreg., Dec. 6, 1919; s. William Angus and Maude (Moore) M.; B.S. in Bus. Adminstrn., Lehigh U., 1941; m. Jeanne Elyse Manley, Feb. 14, 1942; children—Jeanne Sandra, Susan Manley, Bonnie Ann. Procurement engr. Office Chief of Ordnance, 1942-43; mgr. contract sales Eureka-Williams Corp., Bloomington, Ill., 1946-49; dist. sales mgr. Perfex Corp., Milw., 1949-51; v.p. sales Internat. Heater Co., Utica, N.Y., 1951-53; sales mgr. heating div. Heil Co., Milw., 1953-55; v.p. sales, dir. Portable Elevator Mfg. Co., Bloomington, 1955-70; exec. v.p. portable elevator div. Dynamics Corp. Am., 1971-75, pres., 1975—, dir., 1971—. Bd. dirs. Jr. Achievement Central Ill., 1959-71, pres. Bloomington dist., 1964. Served from pvt. to 1st lt. AUS, 1943-46. Mem. Farm Equipment Mfrs. Assn. (dir. 1961—, pres. 1969, treas. 1970—), McLean County Assn. Commerce and Industry (pres. 1974), Truck Equipment and Body Distbrs. Assn. (co-founder 1963), Am. Legion, Flying Farmers, Nat. Pilots Assn., Chi Phi. Republican. Presbyterian. Clubs: Rotary, Bloomington Country, Masons, Shriners. Home: 1404 E Washington St Bloomington IL 61701 Office: PO Box 2847 920 E Grove St Bloomington IL 61701

MATHEWS, ADELE, newspaper editor; b. Chgo., May 27, 1946; d. Leo and Miriam (Givel) Lebow; B.A., cum laude, U. Ill., 1968; m. James John Mathews, 1968. Reporter, Hollister Newspapers, 1968; editor Bankers Life and Casualty Co., 1969-72; reporter Pioneer Press Inc., 1973, mng. editor Lake Forester, Wilmette, Ill., 1975—. Mem. Suburban Newspapers Am. Office: 444 Central Ave Highland Park IL 60035

MATHEWS, FRED L., optometrist; b. Atlanta, Mich., Mar. 28, 1929; s. James Wilbert and Lena Lois (McCoy) M.; student Central Mich. U., 1948-49; O.D., So. Coll. Optometry, 1949-52; m. Lathelda Joyce Livingston, June 28, 1953; children—Scott, David. Practice optometry, Dowagiac, Mich., 1952—. DIr. Community State Bank Dowagiac. Mem. Cass County Planning Commn., 1972—. Chmn. bd. trustees Southwestern Mich. Coll., 1964—. Served with AUS, 1946-47. Named Citizen of Year Dowagiac Elks, 1967; Fred L. Mathews Library Southwestern Mich. Coll. named for him. Mem. Am., Mich. (Educator of Year award 1966) optometric assns., Southwest Mich. optometric Soc., Mich. Community Coll. Assn. (dir. 1970—, pres. 1972), Assn. Community Coll. Trustees (dir.), Dowagiac C. of C. (dir. 1953-63, pres. 1957). Lion (past pres. Dowagiac chpt.), Elk. Home: Route 2 Dowagiac MI 49047 Office: PO Box 506 Dowagiac MI 49047

MATHEWS, HENRY JAMES, dentist; b. Aurora, Ill., Oct. 9, 1915; s. Christopher John and Emilie Marie (Birkholtz) M.; student Loyola U., 1935-36; D.D.S., Chgo. Coll. Dental Surgery, 1940; m. Floretta Esther Guemmer, May 10, 1947; children—Beth Ann, Jeanne Kay, James Henry. Individual practice dentistry, Chgo., 1940—; sec. dental staff Holy Cross Hosp., 1952. Bd. dirs. No. Ill. dist. Lutheran Ch.-Mo. Synod, 1973—. Served to maj. Dental Corps, AUS, 1942-45. Fellow Royal Soc. Health, Am. Coll. Dentists; mem. Am. Dental Assn., Chgo. (pres. 1973-74), Englewood (pres. 1958-59) dental socs., Odontographic Soc. Chgo., Pierre Fauchard Acad., Acad. Gen. Dentistry, Fedn. Dentaire Internat., Ill. Soc. Med. Research, Internat. Assn. Anesthesiologists. Lutheran (chmn. bd. elders 1964, chmn. bd. Christian edn. 1967). Home: 4618 Clausen Ave Western Springs IL 60558 Office: 6745 W 63d St Chicago IL 60638

MATHEWS, JOHN ANDREW, optometrist; b. Montmorency County, Mich., Oct. 8, 1922; s. James Wilbert and Lena Lois (McCoy) M.; D.Optometry, No. Ill. Coll. Optometry, 1948; m. Shirley Ruth Langton, Oct. 26, 1951; children—James, Mary, Julie, Lois, Kent, Douglas, Lori. Pvt. practice optometry, Three Rivers, Mich., 1949—. Dir. Three Rivers (Mich.) Savs. & Loan Assn., 20th Century Guardian Life Ins. Co., Battle Creek. Mem. St. Joseph County Bd. Election Canvassars, 1966-70. Served with USAAF, 1942-46; lt. col. Res., ret. 1969. Decorated Air medals. Mem. Am., Mich. optometric assns., Southwestern Mich. Optometric Soc. (pres. 1968-71), Am. Legion, V.F.W., Res. Officers Assn. U.S. (life), Nat. Rifle Assn., Three Rivers C. of C., Mich. Assn. Professions. Club: Farm Bur. Home: Rural Route #2 Box 396 Three Rivers MI 49093 Office: 3 1/2 N Main St Three Rivers MI 49093

MATHEWS, PAUL HIPPOLYTE, oral surgeon; b. Cleve., Mar. 1, 1929; s. Hippolit and Cecelia (Majewski) Matuzeski; A.B., Western Res. U., 1951, D.D.S., 1955; postgrad. U. Pa., 1955-56; m. Christine Helene Mosinski, June 2, 1956; children—Paula Ann, Robert Christopher, Mary Louise, Christine Julie. Intern, Central Dispensary and Emergency Hosp., Washington, 1956-57; resident Henry Ford Hosp., Detroit, 1959-61; pvt. practice oral surgery, Cleve., 1961—; mem. staffs Deaconess Hosp., Luth. Med. Center, Cleve.; asst. clin. prof. oral surgery Sch. Dentistry, Case Western Res. U., Cleve., 1961—. Mem. Independence (Ohio) Sch. Bd. Edn., 1970-74, pres. bd., 1972-73; mem. Cuyahoga County Bd. Edn. Served to lt. USNR, 1957-59. Diplomate Am. Bd. Oral Surgery. Fellow Internat. Coll. Dentists; mem. Internat. Assn. Oral Surgeons, Am., Cleve. socs. oral surgeons, ADA, Ohio, Cleve. dental assns., Pierre Fauchard Acad. (co-chmn. Ohio sect.), Omicron Kappa Upsilon, Delta Tau Delta, Delta Sigma Delta. Roman Catholic. Club: Cleveland Soc. Poles. Home: 1595 Arthur Ave Lakewood OH 44107 Office: 14701 Detroit Ave Lakewood OH 44107

MATHEWS, THOMAS EDWARD, optometrist; b. Atlanta, Mich., Sept. 24, 1930; s. James Wilbert and Lena Lois (McCoy) M.; student Western Mich. U., 1952-53; D.Optometry, So. Coll. Optometry, 1957. Pvt. practice optometry, Three Rivers, Mich., 1957—. Cons. Three Rivers Environ. Control Bd., 1971—. Chmn., Three Rivers Water Pollution Subcom., 1971. Charter mem. St. Joseph County chpt. Michianna Watershed, Inc., 1963—, legis. chmn., 1965-71. Bd. dirs. Mich. Assn. Professions, 1973—. Served with USAF, 1951-52. Mem. Am., Mich. (legis. keyman 1967-77; named Optometrist Year 1970-71) optometric assns., Am. Optometric Found., D.A.V., Three Rivers C. of C., Omega Epsilon Phi. Baptist. Lion. Patentee in field. Home: Rural Route # 4 Box 106 Three Rivers MI 49093 Office: 3 1/2 N Main St Three Rivers MI 49093

MATHEWS, THOMAS OSBORN, newspaper editor and pub.; b. Fairfield, Ill., Apr. 17, 1911; s. Thomas Eugene and Lucretia (Harry) M.; student U. Ill.; m. Marjorie Cunningham, Oct. 15, 1939; children—Charles Preston, Thomas Osborn. Reporter, Wayne County Press, Fairfield, 1931—, editor, pub., since 1937; dir. Fairfield Nat. Bank, Thalatta Inc. Trustee Fairfield Meml. Hosp., Wayfair Restorium. Mem. Nat. Newspaper Assn., Ill. Press Assn. (past pres.). Republican. Methodist. Clubs: Rotary, Elks, Shriners. Home: 500 E Center St Fairfield IL 62837 Office: 213 E Main St Fairfield IL 62837

MATHEWS, WILLIAM STEWART, judge; b. Cin., Aug. 9, 1926; s. J. Stewart and Viola (Richardson) M.; B.A., U. Cin., 1952, LL.B., 1953; children—Stewart Mathews, Patricia, James (dec.). Admitted to Ohio bar, 1953; gen. practice, Cin., 1953-59; asst. pros. atty. Hamilton County, O., 1959-65; judge Cin. Municipal Ct. 1965-67, Hamilton County Municipal Ct., 1967-68. Ct. of Common Pleas

Hamilton County, Cin., 1968—. Served with USAAF, 1944-48. Club: Blue Horizon Travel (trustee, sec.-treas.). Home: 980 Springbrook Dr Cincinnati OH 45224 Office: Ct House Cincinnati OH 45202

MATHEWSON, HUGH SPALDING, physician, educator; b. Washington, Sept. 20, 1921; s. Walter Eldridge and Jennie Lind (Jones) M.; student Washburn U., 1938-39; A.B., U. Kans., 1942, M.D., 1944; m. Hazel Marie Jones, July 7, 1952; children—Jane (Mrs. Gary Holcombe), Geoffrey K., Brian E., Catherine E., Jennifer A. Intern, Wesley Hosp., Wichita, Kans., 1944-45; resident U. Kans. Med. Center, Kansas City, 1946-48; practice medicine specializing in anesthesiology, Kansas City, Mo., 1948-69; chief anesthesiologist St. Luke's Hosp., 1948-69; med. dir., sect. respiratory therapy U. Kans. Med. Center, Kansas City, Kans., 1969—, asso. prof., 1969-75, prof., 1975—; examiner schs. respiratory therapy, 1975—; oral examiner Nat. Bd. Respiratory Therapy; mem. Council Nurse Anesthesia Practice, 1974—; dir. Empire State Bank. Trustee Kansas City Mus. Served to lt. comdr. USNR, 1956. Recipient Bird Lit. prize Am. Assn. Respiratory Therapists, 1976. Mem. Mo. (pres. 1963), Kans. (pres. 1974-77) socs. anesthesiologists, Council Kan. Med. Soc., Sigma Xi, Phi Beta Kappa. Club: Carriage (Kansas City, Mo.). Author: Structural Forms of Anesthetic Compounds, 1961; Respiratory Therapy in Critical Care, 1976; Pharmacology for Respiratory Therapists, 1977; contbr. numerous articles to profl. jours.; editorial bd. Anesthesia Staff News, 1975—. Home: 6523 Overbrook Rd Shawnee Mission KS 66208 Office: 39th and Rainbow Sts Kansas City KS 66103

MATHIAS, FRANK FURLONG, historian, educator; b. Maysville, Ky., May 23, 1925; s. Charles Lindsay and Nancy Browning (Furlong) M.; A.B., U. Ky., 1950, M.A., 1961, Ph.D., 1966; m. Florence Risque Duffy, Aug. 23, 1958; children—Nancy, Frank, Susan. Salesman, P. Lorillard Tobacco Co., Eastern Ky., 1953-57; asst. prof. history W.Va. Tech. U., 1962-63; asst. prof. history U. Dayton (Ohio), 1963-70, asso. prof., 1970-75, prof., 1975—, Newberry Library fellow, 1977. Named Prof. of Yr., U. Dayton, 1975. Democrat. Author: Albert D. Kirwan, 1975; Incidents and Experiences in the Life of Thomas W. Parsons, 1975. Home: 2728 Corlington Dr Dayton OH 45440 Office: Univ Dayton Box 155 Dayton OH 45469

MATHIEU, JOSEPH EDWARD, automotive exec.; b. Chgo., Jan. 20, 1929; s. Arthur J. and Julia M. (McHale) M.; student U. Notre Dame, 1946-47; m. LaVerne Deichen, Feb. 4, 1950; children—Edward, Douglas, Joan, Richard, Thomas, Eliazabeth, Claudia, Paula. Owner, Mathieu Bldg. Center, Blue Island, Ill., 1950-64, Bauer Buick Co., Harvey, Ill., 1963—. Treas., Catholic Ch. Extension Soc., 1964—; mem. Harvey (Ill.) Planning Commn., 1952-54; S. Suburban chmn. Heart Fund, 1956-57; bd. dirs. Ingalls Meml. Hosp., Harvey, 1969—. Mem. S. Suburban C. of C. (past pres.), Chgo. Met. Buick Dealers Assn. (past pres.), Buick Dealers Assn. (chmn. advt. com. 1973-74), Chgo. Automobile Trade Assn. (dir. 1974—). Home: 1447 Brassie St Flossmoor IL 60422 Office: 15400 Dixie Hwy Harvey IL 60426

MATHIS, JACK DAVID, advt. agy. exec.; b. La Porte, Ind., Nov. 27, 1931; s. George Anthony and Bernice (Bennethum) M.; student U. Mo., 1950-52; B.S., Fla. State U., 1955; m. Phyllis Dene Hoffman, Dec. 24, 1971; children—Kane Cameron, Jara Dene. With Benton & Bowles, Inc., 1955-56; owner Jack Mathis Advt., 1956—. Mem. U.S. Olympic Basketball Com. Recipent citation Mktg. Research Council N.Y. Mem. Alpha Delta Sigma. Author: Valley of the Cliffhangers; creative cons. motion picture That's Action!, 1977. Home: 1323 Woodland Dr Deerfield IL 60015 Office: Box 714 3501 Woodhead Dr Northbrook IL 60062

MATHIS, JOHN FREDERICK, JR., telephone co. account exec.; b. Cairo, Ill., Nov. 1, 1946; s. John Frederick and Pauline Frances (Vaughn) M.; student Floissant Valley Community Coll., 1969, U. Mo., St. Louis, 1970-73, Washington U., 1974-77; m. Carol Jean Waser, May 20, 1971; 1 dau., Jennifer Michelle. Clk., Hammond Sheet Metal Co., St. Louis, 1964-65; printing press operator Emerson Electric Co., St. Louis, 1965-66; coin collector, 1969-70, Southwestern Bell, St. Louis, communications rep., 1971, sales and service rep., 1971, spl. rep., 1973, coin supr., 1974, account exec., 1975—. Served with USN, 1966-68. Mem. Am. Mktg. Assn. Republican. Roman Catholic. Home: 10903 Carrollwood St St Louis MO 63128 Office: 7216 Lanham St St Louis MO 63143

MATHIS, THELMA ATWOOD, artist; b. Creal Springs, Ill.; d. Hubert L. and Mima (Hutchison) Atwood; B.S., So. Ill. U., 1955, M.F.A., 1957; student Art Students League, 1957-59; m. John A. Mathis, Sept. 1, 1928 (div. 1950); children—John Atwood, Shirley (Mrs. Frank Woosley), James Stevens. One-man shows So. Ill. U., 1957, 59, Sparta (Ill.) Pub. Library, 1960, Art Mart, Inc., St. Louis, 1961, St. Louis Artists Guild, 1962; two-man show Madison Galleries, N.Y.C., 1963; juried N.Y.C. Center, 1958, 59, Madison Sq. Garden, N.Y.C., 1958, Nat. Old Testament, St. Louis, 1961, 62, Mo. Art Show, St. Louis City Art Mus., 1954, 55, Nat. Arts & Crafts, Wichita, Kans., 1953, 55; instr., asst. prof. art dept. Midwestern Coll., Denison, Iowa, 1965-70. Recipient Grand prize oil and drawing DuQuoin State Fair, 1955, 56, 58, 59. Mem. St. Louis Artists Guild, Am. Assn. U. Women, Pi Lambda Theta. Baptist. Home: Box 13 Pinckneyville IL 62274 Office: 508 W Randolph St Pinckneyville IL 62274

MATHISON, ARDEN EARLE, agrl. engr.; b. Grafton, N.D., Nov. 24, 1939; s. James Edwin and Mabel Adeline (Arneson) M.; Asso. Sci., Wahpeton State Sch. Sci., 1959; B.S., N.D. State U., 1962; m. Kathleen Marie Sheehan, July 23, 1966; children—Arlene Mary, Ann Marie, Helen Kay. Drainage engr. Bur. Reclamation, Bismarck, N.D., 1962-63, Riverton, Wyo., 1963-64, Great Falls, Mont., 1964-66, Minot, N.D., 1966—. Served with AUS, 1963. Recipient Scholarship, Rural Electric Adminstrn., 1962. Registered profl. engr., N.D. Mem. Am. Soc. Agrl. Engrs. Club: Toastmasters (sergeant at arms 1972-73) (Minot, N.D.). Eagle. Home: 2116 1st Ave SW Minot ND 58701 Office: 2045 3d St NW Minot ND 58701

MATHUES, THOMAS OLIVER, auto mfg. co. exec.; b. Dayton, Ohio, Jan. 26, 1923; s. John Leslie and Florence (Killen) M.; student Grove City Coll., 1944-45, U. Ill., 1945-46; B.M.E., Gen. Motors Inst., 1947; m. Patricia McFarland, May 20, 1944; children—Thomas P., Rebecca, John, Jennifer. With Inland div. Gen. Motors Corp., Dayton, 1940—, gen. mgr., 1966—. Mem. Area Progress Council, Dayton; chmn. Dayton Mayor's Council Econ. Advisers; trustee Blue Cross Southwestern Ohio; bd. dirs. U. Dayton; trustee, chmn. Engring. and Sci. Found.; bd. regents Gen. Motors Inst., Flint, Mich. Served with USNR, 1944-46. Mem. Ohio C. of C. (v.p., dir.), Soc. Automotive Engrs., Phi Gamma Delta. Mem. Christian Ch. Club: Sycamore Creek Country. Patentee in field. Home: 6040 Mad River Rd Dayton OH 45459 Office: 2727 Inland Ave Dayton OH 45407

MATHUR, BHAGWAN PRAKASH, physicist; b. Rampur, India, June 23, 1938; s. Satya Prakash and Rama M.; came to U.S., 1967; B.Sc., Agra (India) U., 1958, M.Sc., 1961; Ph.D. in Physics, Rajasthan U., Jaipur, India, 1967; m. Kumud Mathur, Nov. 8, 1962; children—Vishal, Ankur, Manjari. Lectr. Khalsa Coll., Patiala, India, 1961-63; sr. research fellow Rajasthan U., 1963-66; asst. prof. physics Kurukshetra (India) U., 1966-67; research asso. in physics Yale, 1967-69, Columbia, 1969-70, Inst. Gas Tech., Chgo., 1973-74, Research Inst. Engring. Scis. Wayne State U. Dept. Chem. Engring., 1974—; research asso., interim asst. prof. chemistry U. Fla., 1970-73. Mem. Am. Phys. Soc., Nat. Acad. Scis. of India. Hindu. Research, publs. on physics and chemistry of atomic and molecular collisions, diffusion, thermal diffusion and intermolecular forces in gases, isotope separation, mass spectrometry of pollutants in combustion processes. Home: 15815 Scott Dr Apt 102 Taylor MI 48180 Office: Research Inst Engring Scis Coll Engring Wayne State U Detroit MI 48202

MATIASKA, ERNEST ALLAN, instruments and controls engring. co. exec.; b. Cleve., Nov. 20, 1930; s. Charles A. and Emma (Hanzlik) M.; B.M.E., Cleve. State U., 1963; m. Barbara Ann Yonchak, Sept. 23, 1967; children—Douglas, Carla. Devel. project engr. Bailey Meter Co., Wickliffe, Ohio, 1959-63, mgr. engring. test lab., 1963-66, mgr. product reliability and testing, 1966-69, mgr. product engring., 1969—; U.S.A. expert to Internat. Electrotech. Commn., 1976—. Served with USAF, 1951-55; Korea. Mem. ASME, ASTM, Instrument Soc. Am., Inst. Environ. Scis., Sci. Apparatus Makers Assn. Home: 21990 Roberts Ave Euclid OH 44123 Office: 29801 Euclid Ave Wickliffe OH 44092

MATOVICH, MICHAEL, educator; b. E. Chicago, Ind., Mar. 13, 1925; s. John and Stana (Savich) M.; A.B., Ind. U., 1950, M.S., 1964, Ed.S., 1967, Ed.D., 1972. Ins. investigator Retail Credit Co., Hammond, Ind., 1950; with Combustion-Engring., Inc., East Chicago, Ind., 1951-60; auto salesman Gibson Motor Sales, East Chicago, 1960; with East Chicago Sch. System, 1960—, tchr. social sci. Roosevelt High Sch., 1973—. Served with USNR, 1943-46. Mem. Nat. Soc. for Study of Edn., Assn. for Supervision and Curriculum Devel., Ind. Council of Social Studies, Internat. Platform Assn., Early Am. Soc., Nat. Hist. Soc., Phi Delta Kappa. Democrat. Inventor, tri-colored tail-light system for automobiles, 1949, also printed indicia for coordinated identification of related articles. Home: 4332 Ivy St East Chicago IN 46312

MATSAKIS, NICHOLAS DEMETRIOS, dentist; b. Canonsburg, Pa., Mar. 8, 1914; s. Demetrios Nicholas and Sophia (Constantinides) M.; diploma Pan Cyprian Sem., Cyprus, 1929-32; D.D.S., Washington U., St. Louis, 1940; m. Theodora L. Papageorge, Dec. 2, 1945; children—Aphrodite (Mrs. Russell Scarato), Demetrios, Elias. Tchr. Greek Parochial Sch., Steubenville, O., 1933-34, Lowell, Mass., 1934-36, St. Louis, 1936-39; practice dentistry, St. Louis, 1940—. Chmn., Justice for Cyprus Com., 1955—; hon. consul of Cyprus, St. Louis, 1970—, Washington, 1970—; active Boy Scouts Am., 1960-64. Served to maj. AUS, 1942-46. Mem. Am., Mo., St. Louis dental assns., Hellenic Am. Dental Soc., St. Louis Dental Sci. Soc., Order of Ahepa, St. Louis Council World Affairs, Am. Hellenic Vets. Assn., Hellenic Am. Progressive League, Pan-Karpahtian Soc., Homer Soc. Mem. Greek Orthodox Ch. Home: 1410 Jamaica Ct St Louis MO 63122 Office: 3192 Watson Rd St Louis MO 63139

MATSON, JAMES EVANS, anesthesiologist; b. St. Clairsville, Ohio, Nov. 6, 1926; s. Lester and Kathering (Evans) M.; student Denison U., 1944-45; B.A., Ohio State U., 1946, M.D., 1950; m. Ruth Roberta Moon, June 17, 1950; children—Sally Jayne, John Evan, Jennifer Ruth, Melissa, James Todd. Intern, resident Ohio State U. Hosp., 1950-52; resident Univ. Hosps. Cleve., 1954; practice medicine specializing in anesthesia, Columbus, Ohio, 1955—; asso. dir. dept. anesthesia Ohio State U. Hosps., 1955-59; founding mem., pres. White Cross Riverside Anesthesiology Service, 1959—; chief sect. anesthesia, chmn. pulmonary services com. Riverside Meth. Hosp., pres. med. and dental staff, 1972-73, trustee, mem. exec. com., com. Sch. Nursing, 1974—; mem. faculty Coll. Medicine Ohio State U., 1955—. Trustee Lake Hill Inc., 1968—. Served with USNR, 1944-45, 52-54; capt. M.C. Res. Diplomate Am. Bd. Anesthesiology. Mem. AMA, Am. Soc. Anesthesiologists, Ohio State Med. Assn., Ohio (dist. dir. 1966-68, pres. 1970-71), Columbus (past pres.) socs. anesthesiologists, Acad. Medicine Columbus and Franklin County (chmn. membership com. 1969-70, editor bull. 1975-77, pres. elect). Presbyterian (trustee ch. 1969—). Club: Masons. Home: 6562 Plesenton Dr Worthington OH 43085 Office: 3535 Olentangy River Rd Columbus OH 43215

MATSON, VIRGINIA MAE FREEBERG (MRS. EDWARD J. MATSON), educator, author; b. Chgo., Aug. 25, 1914; d. Axel George and Mae (Dalrymple) Freeberg; B.A., U. Ky., 1934; M.A., Northwestern U., 1941; m. Edward John Matson, Oct. 18, 1941; children—Karin (Mrs. Rudolf A. Renfer, Jr.), Sara M. (Mrs. Carl B. Drake III), Edward Robert, Laurence D., David O. Tchr. high schs., Chgo., 1934-42, Ridge Farm, 1944-45, Lake County Pub. Schs., 1956-59; founder, pres. Grove Sch., 1958—. Treas. Ill. Council on Exceptional Children; mem. woman's council Brain Research Found., U. Chgo., 1966—. Recipient Humanitarian award Ill. Med. Soc. Women's Aux. Mem. Friends Lit. Democrat. Author: Shadow on the Lost Rock, 1958; Saul, the King, 1968; Abba, Father (Friends Lit. Fiction award 1972), 1970; Buried Alive, 1970; A School for Peter, 1974. Home: 950 N St Mary's Rd Libertyville IL 60048 Office: 40 E Old Mill Rd Lake Forest IL 60045

MATSUMOTO, GEORGE MASARU, dentist; b. San Francisco, Nov. 3, 1916; s. Ben Toyomatsu and Teruko (Taniguchi) M.; A.B., U. Calif. at Berkeley, 1940; D.D.S., Loyola U., Chgo., 1949; m. Masako Ishii, Jan. 8, 1946; 1 son, Gregory Yutaka. Pvt. practice dentistry, Chgo., 1950-68; asst. prof. anatomy and histology Loyola U. Dental Sch., 1950-58; clin. investigator NIH, 1968-72; staff dentist Ill. Dept. Mental Health, 1968-76; chief hosp. dental service Lincoln (Ill.) Developmental Center, 1976—; guest lectr. oral medicine Parkland Coll., Champaign, Ill., 1968—. Served with AUS, World War II. Fellow Royal Soc. Health; mem. Am., Ill., Chgo. dental assns., Am. Soc. Geriatric Dentistry (sec. 1969-72). Home: 2724 N Mildred Ave Chicago IL 60614

MATSUSHIMA, AKIRA PAUL, internat. co. exec.; b. Tokyo, July 7, 1937; s. Hiromasa and Tomiko (Watanabe) M.; came to U.S., 1970; B.S., Waseda U., Tokyo, 1961, M.S. in Mech. Engring., 1964; m. Kathleen Sue Rowland, Aug. 18, 1968; children—John Hikaru, Karen Emi. Asst. mgr. research and devel. Nippon Oil Seal Industry, Tokyo, 1965-67, mgr. research planning, 1968-70; dir. engring. NOK-USA, Inc., Los Angeles, 1970-72, v.p., 1973-74, exec. v.p., Chgo., 1975—, dir., 1971—; Japanese Govt. del. to Internat. Standardization Orgn., 1973—. Adv. bd. Christopher House, Chgo., 1977—; ch. officer, 1972-74, 77—. Mem. Soc. Automotive Engrs. (adv. bd. seals com. 1974—), Am., Japan socs. lubrication engrs., Nat. Soc. Profl. Engrs., Japan Soc. M.E., N.W. Suburban YMCA. Presbyterian. Contbr. articles to tech. jours. Patentee sealing device; holder numerous Japanese patents in field. Home: 633 S Bristol Ln Arlington Heights IL 60005 Office: 1350 Kirk St Elk Grove Village IL 60007

MATTA, RAM KUMAR, aero., acoustic engr.; b. Karachi, India (now Pakistan), May 9, 1946; s. Madhavdas Lalchand and Damyanti (Ahuja) M.; came to U.S., 1967, naturalized, 1976; B. Tech., Indian Inst. Tech., New Delhi, 1967; M.S., U. Minn., Mpls., 1969, Ph.D., 1973; m. Linda Carole Russell, July 1, 1972. Engring. trainee Automobile Products Co. India, Bombay, summer 1965, MAN Industries, Jaipur, India, summer 1966; grad. asst. mechanics U. Minn., Mpls., 1967-68, research asst., 1968, teaching asso., 1968-69, research asso., 1969, research fellow, 1969-73; acoustics engr. advanced engring. and tech. program dept. engring. div. aircraft engine group Gen. Electric Co., Evendale, Ohio, 1973-75, mgr. turbomachinery acoustics, 1975-76, mgr. component acoustic tech., 1976-77. Exec. mem., vol. Minn. Internat. Center, Mpls., 1970-72; chmn. Citizens Com. for Community Devel., Forest Park, Ohio, 1975-76. Merit scholar, also Dir.'s Gold Medal, Indian Inst. Tech., 1967; grad. tuition scholar U. Minn., 1968. Mem. Am. Inst. Aeros. and Astronautics, Sigma Gamma Tau. Contbr. articles to profl. publs. Patentee in field. Home: 823 Carpenter Rd Loveland OH 45140 Office: N144 Gen Electric Co Cincinnati OH 45215

MATTESON, DONALD WAYNE, electronics exec.; b. Jackson, Mich., Sept. 5, 1922; s. William A. and Vera M. (Wright) M.; certificate Ill. Inst. Tech., 1942; Asso. Sci. Jackson Jr. Coll., 1948; postgrad. U. Mich., 1949; B.S., Eastern Mich. U., 1973; m. Sally A. Hamilton, Feb. 14, 1944; children—Robert Wayne, William Hillary. Pres., Matteson Electronics, Inc., Jackson, 1949-51, 52-55; sales engr., contracts adminstr. Lear, Inc., Grand Rapids, Mich., 1955-57; product sales mgr. Sparton Electronics Div., Jackson, 1957-59; pres. Cosmic Voice, Inc., Jackson, 1959-76; curatorial cons. Henry Ford Mus., Edison Inst., Dearborn, Mich., 1976—. Faculty, Jackson (Mich.) Community Coll. Served to lt. col. USAAF, World War II, USAF, 1951-52. Mem. Air Force Assn., Res. Officers Assn., Old Car Clubs. Presbyn. (deacon). Rotarian. Patentee in field. Home: 1399 Badgley Rd Jackson MI 49203 Office: 1399 Badgley Rd Jackson MI 49202 also Henry Ford Mus Edison Inst Dearborn MI 48121

MATTHEWS, FRANK THOMAS, JR., retail co. exec.; b. Astoria, N.Y., Dec. 19, 1930; s. Frank Thomas and Elizabeth Mary (Murray) M.; student Queens Coll., N.Y.C., 1949-51; m. Ann Alfano, June 5, 1954; children—Frank Thomas III, Patrick T., Darren T. Display designer John H. Beyer, N.Y.C., 1953-55; with Montgomery Ward & Co., N.Y.C., 1955-65, Chgo., 1965-73; corporate v.p. advt. and sales promotion, store design constrn., display Gamble-Skogmo Inc., Mpls., 1973—. Served with U.S. Army, 1951-53. Mem. Minn. Advt. Rev. Council, Minn. Boys Club. Republican. Roman Catholic. Home: 6611 Pawnee Rd Edina MN 55435 Office: 5100 Gamble Dr Minneapolis MN 55417

MATTHEWS, JOHN EDWIN, adv. cons.; b. Ashland, Ohio, Mar. 6, 1913; s. Lloyd Monroe and Lucille (Bushnell) M.; B.A., Ohio Wesleyan U., 1935; m. Sylvia E. Canaday, June 18, 1962; children—Michael, Joan, Anne Alexandra. Copywriter, Meermens, Inc., Cleve., 1940-41, Howard Swink Advt., Marion, O., 1941-43; creative dir. Roy S. Durstine, Inc., Cin., 1946-48; copy supr. Young & Rubicam, Inc., Chgo., 1948-51; sr. v.p., exec. creative dir. Leo Burnett Co., Inc., Chgo., 1951-69, dir., exec. com., 1961-69; pres. John E. Matthews Ltd., advt. cons., pub., lectr., Glen Ellyn, Ill., 1964—; chmn. plans bd. Draper Daniels, Inc., Chgo., 1972-76. Pres., Central W. Suburban chpt. Muscular Dystrophy Assn., Wheaton, Ill., 1968-69. Served with AUS, 1943-46. Mem. Phi Kappa Psi. Republican. Methodist. Club: Mid-Am. (Chgo.). Author: The Copywriter, The Chief Executives Journal of Capitalistic Advertising. Address: 268 Cumnor Ave Glen Ellyn IL 60137

MATTHEWS, JOSEPH DUDLEY, dentist; b. Valley Falls, Kans., Apr. 25, 1927; s. John Clarence and Noma Merle (Lewis) M.; A.B., Washburn U., 1954; D.D.S., U. Mo., 1959; m. Maralee Ann Alexander, Jan. 27, 1951; children—Paula Clarine, Pamela Jo, Joseph Dudley, Sara Lee, William Sidney, Vera Ann. Gen. practice dentistry, Leavenworth, Kans., 1959—. Mem. County Pub. Health Bd., 1970—. Served with USNR, 1945-46. Mem. Am. Dental Assn., Northeast Dental Soc. (pres. 1962), Pierre Fauchard Acad., Xi Psi Phi. Methodist (trustee ch. 1970—). Mason. Club: Golden Spade (Kansas City). Home: 2200 Sunset Ct Leavenworth KS 66048 Office: 515 1/2 Delaware St Leavenworth KS 66048

MATTHEWS, PAULINE ANNA, ednl. adminstr.; b. Bloomington, Ill., Nov. 6, 1933; d. Harvey Raymond and Helen Louise (Devore) Storm; B.Mus., Bradley U., 1955; M.S., Western Ill. U., 1976, postgrad., 1977—; children—Sherri, Mark, Berkley. Dir. Matthews Music Co. Studio, 1955-72; musician, hostess Channel 19, Peoria, Ill., 1970-74; dir. student services Graham Hosp. Sch. Nursing, Canton, Ill., 1972-77; developmental edn. coordinator Community Workshop Training Centers, Inc., Canton, 1977—; cons. in field. Adv. bd. Spoon River Coll., 1974-77, LPN Vocational Program, Spoon River Coll., 1976-77; exec. bd. Multiple Sclerosis of Peoria, 1970-77; mem. Fulton County Bd. Citizens for Mental Health, 1974-77, Fulton County Assn. Mental Retarded and Handicapped, 1977—; mem. bd. United Way. Bradley U. scholar, 1952-55. Mem. Am., Ill. personnel and guidance assns., Ill. Assn. Student Fin. Aid Adminstrs., Midwest Assn. Student Fin. Aid Adminstrs., Nat. Assn. Student Fin. Adminstrs., Altrusa Internat., Lambda Chi Omega, Sigma Alpha Iota, Sigma Kappa. Roman Catholic. Contbr. articles in field to profl. jours. Home: 12 N C Ave Canton IL 61520 Office: 500 N Main St Canton IL 61520

MATTHEWS, REX DONALD, city ofcl.; b. Davenport, Iowa, Jan. 3, 1930; s. Nickolas Arthur and Velma Josephine (Schroeder) M.; student St. Ambrose Coll., 1947-49; B.S., Iowa State U., 1954; m. Marilyn Jane Klehn, Sept. 24, 1955; children—Julianne, Gina Louise. With engring. dept. City of Davenport, 1953-54, project engr., 1955-57, city engr., 1957-59, dir. pub. works, 1959—. Served with AUS, 1951-53. Mem. Am. Pub. Works Assn. (hon.), Davenport N.W. Turners Club, Tau Lambda Rho (hon.). Presbyterian. Elk. Home: 1918 W Garfield St Davenport IA 52804 Office: 226 W 4th St Davenport IA 52801

MATTHIAS, RUSSELL HOWARD, lawyer; b. Milw., Aug. 7, 1906; s. Charles G. and Lena (Martin) M.; A.B., Northwestern U., 1930, J.D., 1932; m. Helene Seibold, Dec. 28, 1932; children—Russell Howard, William Warrens, Robert Charles. Admitted to Ill. bar, 1933; spl. asst. to atty. gen. of U.S., Railroad Retirement Act, 1934-35; sec. Ill. Fraternal Congress, 1935-40, 45-60; partner Meyers and Matthias, Chgo., 1951—; sec., dir. Supervised Investors Services Inc.; pres., dir. Mattco, Inc.; sec., treas., dir. Supervised Investors Icome Fund, Inc., Technology Fund, Inc., Supervised Investors Summit Fund, Inc., Supervised Investors Growth Fund, Inc., Kemper Income and Capital Preservation Fund, Inc., Kemper Money Market Fund, Inc.; v.p., gen. counsel, dir. Bankers Mut. Life Ins. Co.; gen. counsel, dir. United Founders Life Ins. Co. Ill., United Founders Life Ins. Co. Okla.; gen. counsel, dir. Wesco, Inc.; dir. Old Orchard Bank & Trust Co., Republic Nat. Life Ins. Co., Dallas. Mem. drafting com. Ill. Ins. Code, 1938, annotating com., 1940; mem. La. Ins. Code Drafting Com., 1948. Trustee Luth. Gen. Hosp., Valparaiso U. Law Sch. Served from capt. to lt. col. AUS, 1942-46. Recipient alumni award Northwestern U., 1973. Mem. Lutheran Brotherhood (v.p., dir., gen. counsel), Internat. Assn. Life Ins. Counsel, Phi Delta Theta. Republican. Lutheran. Clubs: Indian Hill Country; University, Mid-Day (Chgo.); Kenilworth; Army and Navy (Washington); Minneapolis; Country of Orlando, Citrus (Orlando Fla.). Home: 1500 Sheridan Rd Wilmette IL 60091 Office: 230 W Monroe St Chicago IL 60606

MATTHIES, FRED JOHN, archtl.-engring. co. exec.; b. Omaha, Oct. 4, 1925; s. Fred J. and Charlotte Leota (Metz) M.; B.S.C.E., Cornell U., 1947; postgrad. U. Nebr., 1952-53; m. Carol Mae Dean,

Sept. 14, 1947; children—John Frederick, Jane Carolyn. Civil engr. Henningson, Durham & Richardson, cons. engrs., Omaha, 1947-50, 52-54; sr. v.p. for devel. Leo A. Daly Co., architects, engrs., planners, Omaha, 1954—; lectr. on doing bus. with fed. govt. presented paper on alternative energies Internat. Seminar on Engring. in Cold Regions, 1978. Mem. central com. Douglas County (Nebr.) Republican Party, 1968-72; regent Augustana Coll., Sioux Falls, S.D., 1976—; bd. dirs. Orange County Lutheran Hosp. Assn., Anaheim, Calif., 1961-62; bd. dirs. Lutheran Hosp., Omaha, 1978. Served to 1st lt. USMCR, 1943-46, 50-52. Registered profl. engr., Iowa, Nebr., Wash., Calif., Fla. Fellow ASCE, Instn. Civil Engrs. (London); mem. Air Force Assn., Am. Acad. Environ. Engrs. (diplomate), Am. Waterworks Assn., Nat. Soc. Profl. Engrs. Am. Legion. Republican. Lutheran. Clubs: Happy Hollow Country, Rotary. Contbr. articles to Proc. ASCE, Cons. Engr. Mag. Home: 337 S 127th St Omaha NE 68154 Office: 8600 Indian Hills Dr Omaha NE 68114

MATTILA, JOHN PETER, economist; b. Hayfield, Minn., Oct. 27, 1943; s. John Matt and Barbara Lenore (Johnson) M.; B.A., U. Mich., 1965; Ph.D., U. Wis.-Madison, 1969; m. Mary Jo Kalsem, Jan. 27, 1968. Asst. prof. econs. Ohio State U., Columbus, 1969-73; asst. prof. Iowa, State U., Ames, 1973-76; asso. prof., 1976—; cons. HUD, Nat. Planning Assn., Irwin Publishers. Research grantee Manpower Adminstrn. U.S. Dept. Labor; Ford Found. dissertation fellow. Mem. Am. Econ. Assn., Indsl. Relations Research Assn. Home: 1723 Maxwell Ave Ames IA 50010

MATTLER, ALBERT ANTHONY, priest, counselor; b. St. Louis, Feb. 4, 1930; s. Albert and Alberta Virginia (Sucher) M.; B.A., Kenrick Seminary, 1952; M.Ed., St. Louis U., 1958. Ordained priest Roman Catholic Ch., 1956; asso. pastor Holy Cross Ch., St. Louis, 1956-57; asst. pastor Corpus Christi Parish, Jennings, Mo., 1957-58, St. Philip Neri Parish, St. Louis, 1958-63; tchr. Merch High Sch., University City, Mo., 1959-74; asso. pastor St. Joseph's Parish, Clayton, Mo., 1963-68; asso. pastor St. Jude's Parish, St. Louis County, Mo., 1968-74; pastor Holy Martyrs Ch., Japan, Mo., 1974—; team priest for marriage encounter, 1974—. Mem. Am., Mo., St. Louis personnel and guidance assns. Home and Office: Route 1 Box 376 Sullivan MO 63080

MATTOX, AUDREY BLANCHE (MRS. THOMAS C. MATTOX), real estate broker; b. Fayetteville, Ark., Oct. 21, 1893; d. Jesse Benton and Mary Elizabeth (Woolverton) Easter; student Northeastern State Tchrs. Coll., Tahlequah, Okla., 1910-11; m. Thomas C. Mattox, Mar. 31, 1915; 1 dau., Thelma Carden (Mrs. Leonard C. Smith). Tchr., Cherokee and Adair counties, Okla., 1910-14; tchr. accounting El Dorado (Kan.) Bus. Coll., 1919-20; real estate broker, El Dorado, 1940—. Named Realtor of Year, 1972. Mem. El Dorado Devel. Co., 1971—. Mem. El Dorado C. of C., Bus. and Profl. Women's Club (Woman of Year 1974), El Dorado Ins. Women (founder 1949, pres. 1949-50), Butler County Real Estate Bd. (founder 1947), D.A.R. (chaplain 1971—), Am. Legion Aux., V.F.W. Aux. Mem. order Eastern Star, White Shrine. Methodist. Home: 330 W Central El Dorado KS 67042

MATTSON, EDWARD NEIL, pub. co. exec.; b. Warren, Minn., Sept. 26, 1926; s. Edgar N. and Ann (Swanson) M.; B.A., U. Minn., 1948; m. Marilyn J. Erickson, Sept. 10, 1950; children—John, Kathryn, Jean, Eric, Brian, Duane, Kendell, Angela. Asst. to pub. Patchogue (N.Y.) Advance, 1948-49; with Warren (Minn.) Sheaf, 1949—, mng. editor, 1955—; v.p. Thief River Falls (Minn.) Times, 1971—. Chmn. Marshall County Republican Party orgn., 1956-57. Served with AUS, 1944-45. Recipient Silver Beaver award Boy Scouts Am., 1959. Mem. Minn. Hist. Soc. (pres. 1970-74), Minn. Newspaper Assn. (dir. 1976—), Sigma Delta Chi, Phi Gamma Delta. Lutheran (chmn. ch.). Elk. Home: 615 N 5th St Warren MN 56762 Office: Warren Sheaf Warren MN 56762

MATTSON, JOHN GARY, social worker; b. Paton, Iowa, June 3, 1938; s. Lyle Milton and Ruth (Cochran) M.; student Boone Jr. Coll., 1956-57, Brigham Young U., 1957; B.A., U. Iowa, 1961; M.A. in Social Work, Ind. U., 1965; m. Shirley Westrum, Aug. 17, 1958;children—Stephanie, John, Jay. Team social worker Woodward State Hosp. (Iowa), 1962-63, group worker, 1966-67, caseworker, 1965-67, community cons., 1965-68, intake supr., 1967-68; dir. social services Exceptional Persons, Inc., Waterloo, Iowa, 1968—. Adj. instr. U. No. Iowa, 1973-76. Mem. regionalization com. State Progressive Action for Retardation, 1966-67; scuba instr. YMCA, Indpls. and Boone, Iowa, 1961—; mem. Boone Underwater Rescue Unit, 1965—; mem. Cedar Valley Underwater Search and Recovery Unit, 1972—; mem. state adv. com. CORE, 1976—; mem. Dist. 7 Title XX Adv. Com., 1976—. Served with N.G., 1955-63. Named Outstanding Young Educator, Boone Jr. C. of C., 1966; recipient Service to Mankind award Cedar Falls Sertoma Club, 1974. Mem. Nat. Assn. Social Workers (past pres. Northeast Iowa), Acad. Certified Social Workers, Am. Assn on Mental Deficiency. Baptist (trustee). Home: 3807 Hudson Rd Cedar Falls IA 50613 Office: Box 690 Waterloo IA 50704

MATTSON, PETER ROLAND, electric mfg. co. adminstr.; b. Oakland, Calif., Apr. 15, 1931; s. Edward Carl and Anna Christina (Gustavson) Mattson; m. Roberta Mae Francine, Jan. 17, 1954; children—Pamela, Bruce. B.S. in Marine Engring., Calif. Maritime Acad., 1953; postgrad. San Jose State Coll., 1955-56. Licensed engring. officer U.S. Merchant Marine. With Gen. Electric Co., Chgo., 1956—, dist. mgr. generation equipment sales, 1969—. Home: 1333 Glenwood Ave Glenview IL 60025

MATTSON, ROGER ALBERT, psychiatrist, flight surgeon; b. Ishpeming, Mich., May 12, 1938; s. Albert John and Anita Lucille (Laurie) M.; student Suomi Coll., 1956-57; B.A., No. Mich. U., 1959; M.D., U. Mich., 1963; m. Karen Alice Filby, June 6, 1964; children—David, Kari, Amy, Sara. Intern St. Mary's Hosp., Duluth, Minn., 1963-64; resident psychiatry Mayo Clinic, Rochester, Minn. and VA Hosp., Mpls., 1967-70; psychiatrist, flight surgeon USAF Res., Mpls., 1967—; practice medicine specializing in psychiatry, Duluth, 1970—; mem. staff St. Mary's Hosp., Duluth, 1966—, St. Luke's Hosp., Duluth, 1966—, Miller-Dwan Hosps., Duluth, 1970—, Douglas County Hosp., Wentworth, Wis., 1970-75; asso. clin. prof. psychiatry U. Minn., Duluth, 1975—. Active Boy Scouts Am. Mem. Adv. bd. Suomi Coll., 1968—. Served with USAF, 1964-67. Diplomate Am. Psychiatry and Neurology. Mem. St. Louis County, Minn. State, Am. med. assns., Am. Psychiat. Assn., Res. Officers Assn. Home: 1501 Cliff Ave Duluth MN 55811 Office: 1015 Med Arts Bldg Duluth MN 55802

MATUSZEWSKI, STANLEY, clergyman; b. Morris Run, Pa., May 4, 1915; s. Andrew and Mary (Czekalski) M.; grad. St. Andrew's Prep. Sem., Rochester, N.Y.; student La Salette Coll., Hartford, Conn., Scholastic Sem., Altamont, N.Y. Ordained priest Roman Catholic Ch., 1942; disciplinarian, prof. classics, La Salette Sem., Olivet, 1942-46, dir., 1948—; superior Midwest province LaSalette Fathers; founding editor Our Lady's Digest, 1946—; exec. bd. Nat. Catholic Decency in Reading Program; faculty adv. Midwest Conf. of Internat. Relations Clubs sponsored 1944 in Chgo. by Carnegie Endowment for Internat. Peace. Trustee Nat. Shrine of Immaculate Conception, Washington. Honored by Rochester, N.Y. Centennial Com. 1934 as Monroe County (N.Y.) orator. Mem. Mariological Soc. Am. (1954 award), Missionaries of Our Lady of La Salette, Catholic Press Assn., Canon Law Soc., Catholic Broadcasters' Assn., Religious Edn. Assn., Polish-Hungarian World Fedn. (trustee). K.C. Author: Rochester Centennial Oration; Youth Marches On. Home: Box 777 Twin Lakes WI 53181

MATVEIA, KENNETH WAYNE, paper co. exec.; b. Kalamazoo, May 31, 1920; s. Ernest C. and Katherine (Heinrich) M.; B.S., Internat. Corr. Schs., 1956; m. Mary Patricia O'Conner, July 3, 1940; children—Donna, Donald, Kenneth II. With Bryant Paper Co., Kalamazoo, 1939-41, lab. asst., Kalamazoo, 1941-43; asst. supt. mfg. Time, Inc., Kalamazoo, 1946-47; div. supt. mgr. St. Regis Paper Co., Kalamazoo, 1947-49; chemist KVP Co., Kalamazoo, 1949-56, tech. asst., v.p. sales, 1956-62; tech. coordinator KVP Sutherland, Kalamazoo, 1962-64, account exec., 1964-66; marketing mgr. Brown Co., Kalamazoo, 1966-72, mgr. tech. services, 1972-74, mgr. converting mfg., 1974-76, mgr. tech. services and parchment mfg., 1976—. Mem. Kalamazoo Twp. Planning Commn., 1962—. Served with AUS, 1943-46. Mem. T.A.P.P.I., Tag and Label Mfrs. Inst., Nat. Flexible Packaging Assn. Lutheran. Elk. Home: 1530 Vickery Dr Portage MI 49081 Office: 243 E Paterson St Kalamazoo MI 49007

MATZ, MILTON, clin. psychologist, rabbi; b. N.Y.C., June 30, 1927; s. Joshua E. and Sonja (Kiat) Matz; m. Anne L. Jaburg, June 20, 1952; children—Deborah, David. B.A., Yeshiva U., 1947; M.H.L., rabbinic ordination, Hebrew Union Coll., 1952, D.D. (hon.), 1977; Ph.D., U. Chgo., 1966. Certification Ohio Psychol. Assn. Bd. Examiners Psychologists, 1966; Licensed, Ohio Bd. Psychology, 1973. First lt. USAF, 1952-54; asst. rabbi Kehilath Anshei Maariv Temple, Chgo., 1954-57; rabbi Congregation B'nai Jehoshua, Chgo., 1957-59; dir. pastoral psychology, asst. rabbi The Temple, Cleve., 1959-66; sr. staff psychologist Fairhill Psychiat. Hosp., Cleve., 1966-69; adj. prof. Cleve. State U., 1966-70; clin. instr. Case-Western Res. Sch. Medicine, 1966-73, asst. clin. prof., 1973—, dir. Pastoral Psychology Service Inst., 1973—; pvt. practice in clin. psychology, Cleveland Heights, Ohio, 1966—. Sec., v.p. Greater Cleve. Bd. Rabbis, 1964-66; bd. mem. Jewish Children's Bur. and Bellefaire Jewish Community Center, Cleve., 1952-64; advisory bd. Div. Child Welfare, Cuyahoga County, Ohio, 1962-66; founding mem. Cuyahoga County Community Mental Health and Retardation Bd., Cleve., 1967-71, chmn., 1972-73; chmn. Central Conf. Am. Rabbis Com. on Judaism and Health, N.Y.C., 1975—. Fellow Am. Assn. Pastoral Counselors; mem. Am., Ohio psychol. assns., Am. Assn. Pastoral Counselors. Author numerous papers and articles on treatment of marital conflict and grief, primary prevention of mental illness, psychology and religion, and pastoral tng.; recipient commendation for outstanding leadership in mental health Bd. Commrs. of Cuyahoga County, 1973. Home: 3346 Stockholm Rd Cleveland OH 44120 Office: 5 Severance Circle Cleveland OH 44118

MATZ, ROBERT DENNIS, dentist; b. Canton, Ohio, June 7, 1939; s. Carl Leroy and Lena Mary (Jossie) M.; D.D.S., Ohio State U., 1963; m. Shirley Ann Ray, July 8, 1962; children—Jeffrey, Joel, Sharon. Practice dentistry, Ashland, Ohio, 1965—; mem. staff Samaritan Hosp., Ashland. Served with AUS, 1963-65. Mem. Ashland (past pres.), Mansfield, Central Ohio (pres. elect) dental socs., Am. Dental Assn., Delta Sigma Delta. Republican. Mem. Ch. of Christ (deacon). Kiwanian. Home: 1284 US Route 42 RD1 Ashland OH 44805 Office: 144 Claremont Ave Ashland OH 44805

MATZ, ROGER ELWOOD, newspaper editor; b. Waterloo, Iowa, Nov. 16, 1938; s. Edward H. and Myldred (Holm) M.; student U. No. Iowa, 1958-59, Mankato State Coll., 1967-68; grad. U. Minn., 1977; m. Judith Ann Bruch, Apr. 12, 1958; children—Michael, Michelle, Christopher, Jason. Reporter, Waterloo Daily Courier, 1959-61, bur. chief, 1962-64, asst. state editor and farm editor, 1964-66; regional editor Sentinel, Fairmont, Minn., 1966-67, mng. editor, 1967-72, editor, 1973-74; pub. New Ulm (Minn.) Daily Jour., 1974—; chmn. Minn. AP newswriting contest, 1969—; v.p. New Ulm Bus. Dists., Inc., 1977. Pres., Budd Elementary Sch. PTA, Fairmont, 1969—; chmn. exec. com. Twin Valley council Boy Scouts Am., 1968-69. Recipient Minn. Edn. Assn. Sch. Bell award, 1967. Mem. Minn. AP (pres. 1977), New Ulm C. of C. Lutheran (chmn. bd. deacons). Home: 51 Lincoln Ln New Ulm MN 56073 Office: 303 N Minnesota St New Ulm MN 56073

MATZER, JOHN NICHOLAS, JR., city mgr.; b. Yonkers, N.Y., Dec. 7, 1934; s. John Nicholas and Helen Mary (Sommers) M.; B.A. in Polit. Sci., Rutgers U., 1956, M.A. (grantee), 1957, postgrad., 1957-61; certificate U.S. Dept. Agr. Grad. Sch., 1972; m. Lorraine Carhart, June 11, 1954; children—Christine, Cheryl Anne, John Nicholas III. Adminstrv. intern, City of Phila., 1957-58, adminstrv. analyst, 1958-60; research asso. Bur. Govt. Research, Rutgers U., 1960-61, field rep. Urban Studies Center, 1961-62; with city adminstrn., Trenton, N.J., 1962-70, city adminstr., 1964-70; village mgr., Skokie, Ill., 1970—; instr. Rutgers U., 1962-70, Rider Coll., 1963-64, Roosevelt U., 1970—, Inst. Tng. Municipal Adminstrn., Ill. City Mgmt. Assn., 1972—, Ill. Inst. Tech., 1975—. Mem. legis. com. N.J. League Municipalities, 1965-70, mem. pension study com., 1965. Chmn. pub. employees div. Skokie Valley United Crusade, 1972, bd. dirs., 1972—, gen. campaign chmn., 1973, pres., 1975; trustee Social Service Council Greater Trenton, 1969-71; chmn. com. municipal and govtl. mgmt. William Rainey Harper Coll., 1976—. Mem. Am. Soc. Pub. Adminstrn. (nat. council 1969-72, pub. adminstrn. rev. editorial bd. 1970-72, pres. N.J. 1967-68, council Chgo. 1972—), Internat. City Mgmt. Assn. (mem. Acad. Profl. Devel., com. mgmt. labor relations 1974-76), Municipal Finance Officers Assn., Municipal Finance Officers Assn. (nat. com. innovative fin. policy, planning and mgmt. for smaller govtl. units), Chgo. Met. City Mgmt. Assn. (dir.). Author: Techniques of Negotiating with Public Employee Organizations, 1970; Personnel Management: A Guide for Small Local Governments, 1975 also articles. Home: 7412 Keeler St Skokie IL 60076 Office: 5127 Oakton St Skokie IL 60076

MATZKO, MICHAEL NEWTON, safety engr.; b. Butler, Pa., Nov. 17, 1940; s. Michael Frank and Elizabeth Ann (Palace) M.; B.A., Washington and Jefferson Coll., 1962; m. Pamela Dunning Zelt, Mar. 4, 1967; 1 son, David Michael. Loss prevention and loss prevention account rep. Liberty Mut. Ins. Co., Boston, 1969-72; corp. safety dir. Nat. Homes Corp., Lafayette, Ind., 1972-74, mgr. corp. safety and security, 1974-75, mgr. corp. safety, security and group ins., 1975—; lectr. to profl. groups on safety. Mem. Tippecanoe County (Ind.) CD Advisory Council, 1974—. Served to capt. U.S. Army, 1962-68; Vietnam. Decorated Air medal with 12 oak leaf clusters. Mem. Am. Soc. Safety Engrs., Am. Soc. Indsl. Security, Nat. Safety Council (exec. com. constrn. sect.), Nat. Fire Protection Assn., Nat. Soc. Profl. Engrs. (affiliate), Phi Alpha Theta. Republican. Presbyterian. Home: 2790 Linda Ln West Lafayette IN 47906 Office: PO Box 680 401 S Earl Ave Lafayette IN 47902

MAU, GORDON ELLIOTT, san. engr.; b. Britt, Iowa, Jan. 2, 1920; s. Walter Harry and Marea Sophia (Milbrandt) M.; B.C.E., U. Iowa, 1943; Ph.D., 1958; M.S., Harvard U., 1948; m. Marie Charlotte Votava, May 9, 1959; children—Barbara, Roberta, Russell. Constrn. engr. Dravo Corp., Pitts., 1943-44; san. engr. Iowa Dept. Health, 1945, UNRRA, China, 1946-47; chief water pollution control Kans. Bd. Health, 1948-56; san. engr. Edlger Engring. Co., Wichita, 1957-58; san. and project engr. Parsons Corp., Dacca, Pakistan (now Bangladesh); 1959-65; pvt. engring. cons., New Hampton, Iowa, 1965—; chmn. Iowa Chem. Tech. Commn., 1970—. WHO fellow to Eng. and Germany, 1952. Mem. Am. Water Works Assn., Water Pollution Control Fedn., ASCE, Chi Epsilon. Address: Rural Route 3 New Hampton IA 50659

MAUGANS, JOHN CONRAD, lawyer; b. Miami County, Ind., May 10, 1938; s. Willis William and Evelyn Jeannette (Mills) M.; A.B., Manchester Coll., 1960; LL.B. with distinction (Krannert scholar), Ind. U., 1962, J.D., 1970; m. Judith M. Gallagher, Jan. 24, 1960; children—Lisa Denise, Stacy Erin, Kristen Cherie. Admitted to Ind. bar, 1962; with firm Barnes, Hickam, Pantzer & Boyd, Indpls., 1962-63; practice in Kokomo, 1966—; partner firm Bayliff, Harrigan, Cord & Maugans, 1969—; guest lectr. Coll. Bus., Manchester Coll. Chmn. Howard County fund dr. Manchester Coll., 1971; bd. dirs. Tribal Trials council Girl Scouts U.S.A., 1977—. Served to capt. AUS, 1963-66. Mem. Am., Ind., Howard County bar assns., Am., Ind. trial lawyers assns., Manchester Coll. Alumni Assn. (chmn. area chpt. 1970), Manchester Coll. M. Alumni Assn. (pres. 1972), Order of Coif, Phi Delta Phi. Presbyterian (elder). Contbr. articles to legal jours. Home: 2013 S Malfalfa Rd Kokomo IN 46901 Office: Box 2249 402 Southway Blvd Kokomo IN 46901

MAULDIN, WILLIAM H., cartoonist; b. Mountain Park, N.Mex., Oct. 29, 1921; s. Sidney Albert and Edith Katrina (Bemis) M.; ed. pub. schs., N.Mex. and Ariz.; student art Chgo. Acad. Fine Arts; M.A. (hon.), Conn. Wesleyan U., 1946; L.H.D. (hon.), Lincoln Coll., 1970; Litt.D. (hon.), Albion Coll., 1970, N.Mex. State U. at Las Cruces, 1972; m. Norma Jean Humphries, Feb. 28, 1942 (div. 1946); children—Bruce Patrick, Timothy; m. 2d, Natalie Sarah Evans, June 27, 1947 (dec. Aug. 1971); children—Andrew, David, John, Nathaniel; m. 3d, Christine Ruth Lund, July 29, 1972. Cartoonist, St. Louis Post-Dispatch, until 1962, Chgo. Sun-Times, 1962—; tech. adviser, actor in movie Teresa, 1950; actor The Red Badge of Courage, 1950. Served with AUS, 1940-45; with 45th Div. (worked part time on div. newspaper); transferred to Mediterranean edit. Stars and Stripes, 1943; participated in campaigns, Sicily, Italy, France, Germany. Decorated Purple Heart, Legion of Merit; recipient Pulitzer prize for cartoons, 1944, Pulitzer prize for satiric comment on plight of Boris Pasternak, 1958; Sigma Delta Chi journalism award for cartoons, 1964, 70, 72, Distinguished Service award, 1969; Prix Charles Huard de dessin de presse Found. Pour L'Art et la Recherche, 1974. Fellow Sigma Delta Chi. Author, cartoonist: Up Front (Book of the Month Club selection), 1945; Back Home (Book of the Month selection), 1947; cartoonist: Star Spangled Banter, 1941; Sicily Sketch Book, 1943; Star Spangled Banter (separate collection of cartoons), 1944; Mud, Mules and Mountains (Italy), 1944; This Damn Tree Leaks (Italy) 1945; A Sort of a Saga, 1949: Bill Mauldin's Army, 1951; Bill Mauldin in Korea, 1952; What's Got Your Back Up?, 1961; I've Decided I Want My Seat Back, 1965; The Brass Ring, 1972 (Book of Month Club selection). Address: care Chgo Sun-Times Chicago IL 60611

MAURER, C. JACKSON, railroad exec.; b. St. Louis, June 12, 1922; s. C. E. and Lillian (Meier) M.; B.S. in Aero. Engring., Parks Air Coll., St. Louis U., 1942; B.S. in Bus. Adminstrn., Washington U., 1947, M.A. in Econs., 1949; m. Charlotte M. Fisher, Mar. 3, 1951; children—Robert, Ellen, John. Service engr. Curtiss Wright Corp., 1942-44; flutter and vibration engr. CBS, St. Louis, 1945-47; treas. Miss. River Fuel Corp., St. Louis, 1947-61; asst. v.p. finance Mo. Pacific R.R., 1961, controller, 1962-64, asst. to pres., 1964-67, sec., treas., 1972—; v.p. finance C. & E.I. R.R., 1967-72; sec., treas. T. & P. Ry., 1972-76; dir. New Orleans & Lower Coast R.R. Co. Faculty bus. div. So. Ill. U., Edwardsville, part-time 1970-71. Mem. Financial Execs. Inst., C. of C., Am. Mgmt. Assn., Nat. Assn. Accountants. Club: Media. Home: 4 Hawbrook Lane Kirkwood MO 63122 Office: 210 N 13th St St Louis MO 63103

MAURER, IRVING J., ret. ins. exec.; b. Marshfield, Wis., May 11, 1905; s. Joseph F. and Anna M. (Geiger) M.; student Central State Tchrs. Coll., 1924-25; m. Kathryn Fischer, Oct. 30, 1933; children—John I., Mary Ann Maurer O'Hara. Underwriter, salesman Hardware Mut. Casualty Co., 1925-29; with Am. Family Mut. Ins. Co., Madison, Wis., 1929-77, successively pres., chmn. bd., and dir., ret., 1977; pres., dir. Am. Family Life Co., 1957-77; chmn. bd., dir. Am. Standard Co., 1961-77; pres., dir. Nall Co., Conf. Mut. Casualty Cos. Trustee Wis. Council Safety, Medic Alert Trust Found. Mem. Nat. Assn. Ind. Insurers (chmn.), Nat. Alliance Businessmen (chmn. Madison chpt.), Ins. Soc. U. Wis. (hon. life), Nat. Assn. Mut. Ins. Cos., Wis., U.S. chambers commerce Madison Art Assn. Clubs: Rotary, Maple Bluff, Madison. Home: 1029 Spaight St Madison WI 53703 Office: 3099 E Washington Ave Madison WI 53708

MAURICE, S. JOSEPH, physician; b. Chgo., Sept. 3, 1935; s. Samuel J. and Jennie (Colletti) M.; B.S., Loyola U., Chgo., 1956, M.D., 1960; m. Nancy L. Larkin, June 29, 1963; children—Samuel, Joseph, Gregory. Intern Cook County Hosp., Chgo., 1960-61; resident in surgery West Side VA Hosp., Chgo., 1963-67; practice medicine specializing in surgery, Chgo., 1967—; mem. staff Loretto Hosp., Oak Park Hosp., Gottlieb Hosp. Served as flight surgeon USAF, 1961-63. Fellow A.C.S.; mem. Ill. Surg. Soc., Internat. Coll. Surgeons, AMA. Office: 5428 W Addison St Chicago IL 60651

MAURY, ROBERT LEE, geotech. engr.; b. Covington, Ky., July 29, 1932; s. Charles Claudes and Katherine Lucille (Purdy) M.; B.S., Fla. State U., 1961; m. Sheila Rose George, Apr. 6, 1964; children—Kathy, Debbie, Jereme. Geotech. engr. Universal Engring. Co., Merritt Island, Fla., 1962-70, Pittsburg Testing Labs., Miami, 1970-73, Hurst-Rosche Engrs., Hillsboro, Ill., 1975—; systems analyst Grumman Aircraft Engring. Corp., Kennedy Space Center, Fla., 1965-70; remote sensing scientist Fla. Dept. Transp., Tallahassee, 1973-75; cons. in field. Served with USN, 1951-55; Korea. Registered engring., profl. geologist, profl. engr., gemologist Ill. Mem. Nat. Soc. Profl. Engrs., Assn. Engring. Geologists, Soc. Exploration Geophysicists, Am. Inst. Mining, Metall. and Petroleum Engrs., Am. Soc. Photogrammetry, Gt. Brit. Gemological Assn., Accredited Gemologist Assn., Gemological Inst. Am. Republican. Baptist. Home: 1408 Vandalia St Hillsboro IL 62049 Office: 1400 E Tremont St Hillsboro IL 62049

MAUS, DONALD JAMES, computer system exec.; b. May 26, 1948; s. Rodney A. and Dorothy M. (Bohlman) Data Processing, Thornton Community Coll., 1969; m. Mary Eileen Burke, July 5, 1972; children—Laura Ann, Brian Edward. Applications analyst Call-a-Computer, Chgo., 1967-69; EDP mgr. Asso. Material Handling Industries, Alsip, Ill., 1969-77; dir. data services, owner Multiwave Digital Systems, Richton Park, Ill., 1977—; tchr. computer programming Thornton Community Coll., 1969-70. Certified data processor. Mem. Assn. Computer Programmers and Analysts, Assn. for Computing Machinery, Assn. Time Sharing Users. Developer computerized modeling and simulation tool for analysis of warehouses and material handling systems. Home and office: 4221 Greenbrier Ln Richton Park IL 60471

MAUS, JOHN HALL, physician; b. Ayr, Ont., Can., Mar. 28, 1918; s. Jairus Wilton and Elizabeth Ann (Baxter) M.; M.D., U. Toronto, 1942; m. Shirley Sloan Foster, Oct. 30, 1943; children—J. Roger, Elizabeth F. Maus Snider, Linda Ann Maus Murphy, Natalie Jean Maus Fisher, Margaret H., K. Laurie. Rotating intern Met. Gen. Hosp., Windsor, Ont., Can., 1942, 46-47; practice medicine specializing in cancer treatment by surgery and radiotherapy, 1947—; dir. Ont. Cancer Found. Windsor Clinic, 1963—. Served with Royal Canadian Army, 1943-46. Fellow Am. Coll. Radiology, Royal Coll. Physicians; mem. Canadian, Ont. med. assns., Essex County Med. Soc. (pres. 1973—), Canadian Assn. Radiologists, Am. Soc. Therapeutic Radiologists, Radiol. Soc. N.Am., Am. Coll. Radiology, Acad. Surgery Windsor (charter mem.), Am. Radium Soc. Club: Rotary (dir. 1974-76, v.p. 1977-78). Editorial bd. radiotherapy and roentgenology The Year Book of Cancer, 1965-68. Home: 269 Reedmere Rd Windsor ON N8S 2L3 Canada Office: 2220 Kildare Rd Windsor ON N8W 2X3 Canada

MAUSEL, PAUL WARNER, geographer, educator; b. Mpls., Jan. 2, 1936; s. Paul George and Esther Victoria (Sundstrom) M.; B.A. in Chemistry and Geography, U. Minn., 1958, M.A. in Geography, 1961; Ph.D., U. N.C., 1966; m. Jean Frances Kias, July 2, 1966; children—Paul Brandon, Catherine Suzanne. Asst. prof. geography Eastern Ill. U., Charleston, 1965-70, asso. prof., 1970-71; asso. prof. geography Ind. State U., Terre Haute, 1971-75, prof., 1975—, dir. Remote Sensing Lab., 1975—; research geographer Lab. Applications of Remote Sensing, Purdue U., West Lafayette, Ind., 1972-73; soils geographer cons. U. Mo. at Columbia, summer 1974; lectr. in field. Mem. Assn. Am. Geographers, Am. Geog. Soc., Soil Sci. Soc. Am., Am. Soc. Photogrammetry, Sigma Xi. Contbr. articles to profl. publs. Home: Rural Route 32 Box 105 Terre Haute IN 47803

MAUSETH, JAMES OLIVER, librarian; b. Rice Lake, Wis., June 18, 1927; s. Oliver S. and M. Llewellyn (Stout) M.; B.A., Macalester Coll., 1952; M.A., U. Minn., 1953. Asst. librarian Carthage Coll. (Ill.), 1953-59;asst. librarian No. State Coll., Aberdeen, S.D., 1959-61, asso. dir. library 1961-66, acting dir. library, 1966-67, dir. library, 1967—. Mem. ALA, AAUP, Geneal. Soc. N.J., S.D., Mountain Plains library assns., Phi Delta Kappa. Elk. Home: 1223 S Main St Aberdeen SD 57401

MAUTHE, HOWARD, physician; b. Des Moines, July 27, 1915; s. Walter and Jennie (Flanigan) M.; B.S., U. Chgo., 1935, Ph.D., 1941, M.D., 1943; m. Agatha Otto, June 22, 1940; children—Howard George, Martin, Andrew, Daniel. Tchr., Milw. Pub. Schs., 1935-39; instr. physiology Mich. State U., 1940; gen. med. practice, Orangeville, Ill., 1947-49; resident radiology Milw., 1949-51; practice radiology Fond du Lac, Wis., 1951—; clin. prof. radiology Med. Coll. Wis., Milw., 1959—. Mem. Fond du Lac Bd. Edn., 1962-65; mem. Fond du Lac City Common Council, 1967-69. Served to lt., M.C. USNR, 1943-47. Mem. A.M.A., state and county med. socs., Am. Coll. Radiology, Radiol. Soc. N. Am., Wis. Radiol. Soc. Home: 3802 DeNeveu Ln Fond du Lac WI 54935 Office: 104 S Main St Fond du Lac WI 54935

MAUTZ, BERNHARD FREDERICK, paint co. exec.; b. Madison, Wis., May 12, 1936; s. Bernhard and Jane (Fuller) M.; B.A., U. Wis., 1960; m. Louise Urquhart, Feb. 15, 1958; children—Allison, Bernhard Frederick. With Mautz Paint Co., Madison, 1958—, exec. v.p., 1968-74, pres., 1974—; dir. First Wis. Nat. Bank, Madison. Bd. dirs. Madison chpt. A.R.C. Served with AUS, 1957-59. Mem. Nat. Paint Coatings Assn. (chmn.), Rotarian. Clubs: Maple Bluff Country, Madison. Home: 659 Farwell St Madison WI 53704 Office: 939 E Washington St Madison WI 53701

MAUZEY, ARMAND JEAN, physician; b. Findlay, Ill., Apr. 18, 1907; s. George Washington and Catherine E. (Cloos) M.; A.B., Eureka (Ill.) Coll., 1928; B.S., U. Ill., 1931, M.D., 1932; postgrad. U. Pa., 1937-38; M.Sc., U. Pa., 1940, D.Sc., 1948; m. Virginia E. Tompkins, May 25, 1945; children—Katherine E., John M., Suzanne R. Surveyman, U.S. Engrs., East St. Louis, Ill., Coal Creek, Tenn., Washington, summers 1925-29; intern St. Lukes Hosp., Chgo., 1932-33; gen. practice medicine, Shelbyville, Ill., 1934-36; resident in obstetrics and gynecology U. Ill. Coll. Medicine, Chgo., 1938-40, now clin. asso. prof.; practice medicine specializing in obstetrics and gynecology, Elmhurst, Ill., 1952—; cons. gynecologist Cook County Hosp., Chgo., 1946-49, Elgin (Ill.) State Hosp., 1949-52, Booth Meml. Hosp., Chgo., 1952-58; chmn. dept. obstetrics and gynecology Elmhurst Meml. Hosp., 1954-58, 66-67; pres. med. staff Meml. Hosp., DuPage County, Elmhurst, 1968-69. Bd. dirs. Elmhurst YMCA. Recipient 25 Year Teaching award U. Ill. Coll. Medicine; Achievement Citation award Eureka Coll., 1968; named to Athletic Hall of Fame, Eureka Coll., 1970. Served from 1st lt. to maj. M.C., AUS, 1941-46; ETO. Diplomate Am. Bd. Obstetrics and Gynecology. Fellow A.C.S.; mem. A.M.A., Ill. (chmn. sect. obstetrics and gynecology 1951-52), Du Page County med. socs., Am. Coll. Obstetrics and Gynecology, Internat. Coll. Surgeons, Chgo. Gynecol. Soc., N.Y. Acad. Scis., Huguenot Soc. S.C., Nat. Huguenot Soc., Va. Hist. Soc., SAR, Huguenot Soc. London, Lambda Chi Alpha, Alpha Kappa Kappa. Republican. Episcopalian. Mason. Contbr. articles to med. jours. and hist. mags. Home: 21 Spinning Wheel Rd Apt 6A Hinsdale IL 60521

MAVEC, BRUCE VAN, real estate exec.; b. Cleve., May 14, 1950; s. Frank Van and Mary Coletta (Goggin) M.; A.B., Kenyon Coll., 1972; m. Katherine Joan Hanson, Aug. 17, 1974. Pres., chief exec. officer Royal Am. Corp., Cleve., 1972—; pres. Royal Am. Mgmt. Co., Cleve., 1972—; pres. Mavec Investment Co., Cleve., 1972—; dir. Telerama Inc., cable TV., Cleve., 1971-72, Kaiser Broadcasting, Oakland, Calif., 1971-73. Mem. Inst. Real Estate Mgmt., Area Bd. Realtors, Apt. Home Owners Assn. Cleve. (v.p. 1973-75), Kenyon Alumni Assn. Cleve. (v.p. 1974-75), Alumni Council Univ. High Sch., Alpha Delta Phi. Episcopalian. Clubs: Canterbury Country, Cleve. Athletic, Kirtland Country, Mayfield Village. Home: 9120 Martin Rd Mentor OH 44060 Office: Royal Am Corp 27691 Euclid Ave Cleveland OH 44132

MAVES, BARBARA ANN BANER, social service adminstr.; b. Chgo., Apr. 14, 1934; d. Charles Martin and Ella (Detweiler) Baner; student Eureka Coll., 1952-53; B.S., Bradley U., 1957; student Howard County Jr. Coll., 1957-58, N.Y. State Coll. at Buffalo, summer 1961; M.A., Ball State U., 1965; m. Ronald Stanley Maves, Dec. 30, 1955 (div. Aug. 1974); children—Scott Stanley, Steven Snyder. Women's staff writer Peoria (Ill.) Jour. Star, 1954-55; tchr. Big Spring (Tex.) Ind. Sch. Dist., 1956-58; pub. relations Gen. Mills, Buffalo, 1959; home economist Ind. & Mich. Electric Co., Marion, Ind., 1963-66; with Muncie (Ind.) Community Schs., 1966-70; dir. Ind. Consumer Adv. Council, Dept. Commerce, 1970-71; supervising tchr. Ball State U., Muncie, 1968-71; mem. pub. relations staff Roudebush for U.S. Senate, 1970; community program cons. Gov.'s Office Community Affairs, 1971; v.p. consumer sales div. Investment Diamonds, Inc., 1971-72; dir. Indpls. Mayor's Office Consumer Affairs, 1972-73; adminstr. ops. div. Community Service Program, City of Indpls., 1973-74; exec. dir. Planned Parenthood of E. Central Ind., Muncie, 1974—; mem. Dental Research Council NIH, Bethesda, Md., 1975-77. Co-chmn. 5th Congl. Dist. Young Republicans, 1966-67; co-chmn. Delaware County Young Republicans, 1967-69, chmn., 1969-70; state program chmn. Ind. Young Rep. Fedn., 1967-68, state co-chmn., 1968-70; mem. Ind. Rep. Central com., 1968-70; mem. Rep. nat. com. voter registration, 1968; chmn. Ind. mil. absentee voting, 1968; membership chmn. Young Rep. Nat. Fedn., 1969-71; bd. dirs. Ind. Health Council, 1975—, Bethel Home Place for Boys, 1977—. Mem. Am., Ind. home econs. assns., AAUW, Mortar Bd. Methodist. Club: Altrusa. Home: 2508 W Twickingham Dr Muncie IN 47304 Office: 4020 Rosewood Ave Muncie IN 47314

MAVIS, FREDERIC THEODORE, cons. engr.; b. Crocketts Bluff, Ark., Feb. 7, 1901; s. Martin John and Hinda (Cassens) Mewes; B.S. in C.E., U. Ill., 1922, M.S., 1926, C.E., 1932, Ph.D., 1936; postgrad. Technische Hochschule Karlsruhe, 1927-28; m. Edith Frances Foley, June 7, 1930. Office engr. charge of design Kelker, DeLeuw & Co., Cons. Engrs., Chgo., 1922-27; Freeman fellow ASCE, 1927-28; asst. prof. to dept. head U. Iowa, also cons. engr. Iowa Inst. Hydraulic Research, 1928-39; prof., head dept. civil engring. Pa. State Coll., 1939-44, Carnegie Inst. Tech., 1944-57; dean engring., prof. U. Md., 1957-67; ret., 1967; cons. engr., Macomb, Ill., 1967—; rep. Nat. Acad. Scis.-NSF, 1955-63. Recipient Wason medal for research Am. Concrete Inst., 1958; registered profl. engr., registered structural engr., Ill. Fellow ASCE; mem. ASME, Am. Waterworks Assn., Soc. Am. Mil. Engrs., Am. Soc. Engring. Edn., Sigma Xi, Tau Beta Pi, Phi Kappa Phi, Chi Epsilon, Pi Tau Sigma, Pi Kappa Phi. Republican. Club: Rotary. Author: (with Edith F. Mavis) Four Hundred Wildflowers in McDonough County, 1972; Construction of Nomographic Charts, 1939. Cons. editor Civil Engring. Series, 1948-54. Contbr. articles to profl. jours. Home: 215 W Piper St Macomb IL 61455

MAVRELIS, WILLIAM PETER, physician, surgeon; b. Waterloo, Iowa, Jan. 12, 1912; s. Peter L. and Amelia (Commandros) M.; student Iowa State Tchrs. Coll., 1930-32; B.S., U. Minn., 1934, M.D., 1937; m. Cornelia MacDonald, Mar. 1, 1938; children—Penelope, Amy, Peter. Intern, St. Francis Hosp., Peoria, Ill., 1936-37, resident, 1937-38; jr. pathology resident Cook County Hosp., Chgo., 1938-42, sr. pathology resident, 1942, sr. pathologist, 1946-50; pathologist, clin. pathologist Ill. Central Community Hosp., 1950-77; asst. prof. Northwestern Med. Sch., 1946-77; police surgeon, Chgo., 1957-77. Sec. bd. dirs. Ill. Central Community Hosp., 1974—. Served to lt. col. U.S. Army, 1942-46. Diplomate Am. Bd. Path. Anatomy. Mem. AMA, Am. Assn. Rwy. Surgeons, Assn. Practitioners and Infection Control, Am., Ill. assns. blood banks, Ill., Chgo. med. assns., Chgo. Path. Soc., Chgo. Gas Chromotography, Chgo. Mycol. Soc. Greek Orthodox. Clubs: Beverly Hills Tennis; Chgo. Athletic Assn. Home: 614 S Lombard Ave Oak Park IL 60304 Office: 5800 Stony Island Ave Chicago IL 60637

MAWBY, RUSSELL GEORGE, found. exec.; b. Grand Rapids, Mich., Feb. 23, 1928; s. Wesley Gray and Ruby (Finch) M.; B.S. in Agr., Mich. State U., 1949, Ph.D. in Agrl. Econs., 1959, LL.D., 1972; M.S., Purdue U., 1951, D.Agr. (hon.), 1973; D.H.L. (hon.), Luther Coll., 1972, Alma. Coll., 1975, Nazareth Coll., 1976; LL.D. (hon.), N.C. A and T State U., 1974; D.Pub. Adminstrn. (hon.), Albion Coll., 1976; D.C.L. (hon.), U. Newcastle (Eng.), 1977; m. Ruth Evelyn Edison, Dec. 16, 1950; children—Douglas James, David Randall, Karen Sue. Asst. dir. 4-H and youth devel. Co-op. Extension Service, Mich. State U., 1956-64, instr., 1952-59, asso. prof., 1959-61, prof., 1961-64; dir. div. agr. W. K. Kellogg Found., Battle Creek, Mich., 1964-67, v.p. programs, 1966-70, pres., 1970—; dir. Kellogg Co., 1974—. Cons. U. Nigeria, 1963; grad. prof. Cornell U., 1962. Trustee Youth for Understanding, 1973—; bd. dirs. Gateway Tech. Inst. Found., Kenosha, Wis., 1977—. Served with AUS, 1953-55. Recipient Distinguished Service award U.S. Dept. Agr., 1963, Distinguished Alumni award Mich. State U., 1971, Alumni award Nat. 4-H Club, 1972, Distinguished Eagle Scout award Boy Scouts Am., 1973, Achievement award Fla. A and M U., 1973; nat. partner in 4-H award USDA Extension Service, 1976; hon. fellow Spring Arbor (Mich.) Coll., 1972; decorated knight first class Royal Order St. Olaf, 1974 (Norway); knight's cross Order Dannebrog 1st Class (Denmark); Mem. U.S., Mich. adult edn. assns., Am. Agrl. Econ. Assn., Epsilon Sigma Phi (certificate of recognition 1974), Phi Kappa Phi, Alpha Zeta, Alpha Gamma Rho (dir. 1976—, Man of Year award Chgo. Alumni chpt. 1976). Home: 8400 39th St Augusta MI 49012 Office: 400 North Ave Battle Creek MI 49016

MAWICKE, ALBERT THOMAS, ednl. materials exec.; b. Chgo., July 16, 1921; s. Henry J. and Margaret (Mann) M.; student Northwestern U. 1943, U. Chgo., 1956; m. Dorothy Harris, Oct. 16, 1943 (dec.); children—Jeffrey J., Paul D., Ann M.; m. 2d, Grayce Cahoon, May 15, 1977; stepchildren—Susan, Kathryn Washam. With Pontiac Graphics Corp., Chgo., 1946-50, salesman, 1950-52, sales mgr., v.p.; 1952-59 sales mgr., v.p., div. mgr., 1959-63; with Field Enterprise Ednl. Corp. (name changed to World Book Childcraft Internat. 1977), 1963—, regional mgr., 1966-68, asst. sales mgr., 1968-69, sales mgr., zone 5, 1969—, zone 1, 1970-74, br. mgr., 1975—; lectr., cons. Printing Industry Ill., Northwestern U., Craftsmen Clubs, various printers, mfrs., art groups. Served to capt. AUS, 1942-46; ETO. Decorated Bronze Star medal. Mem. Phi Kappa Sigma. Home: 19 Lakeshore Dr Clarendon Hills IL 60514 Office: 503 Lockport St Plainfield IL 60544

MAXFIELD, DONALD VINCENT, ins. exec.; b. Centralia, Ill., Apr. 19, 1914; s. Hurem Allen and Blanche (Copple) M.; B.S. in Accounting, U. Ill., 1936; m. Elizabeth A. Hartz, May 19, 1945; children—James Allen, Susan Mary. Sr. accountant Grey, Hunter, Stenn, C.P.A.'s, Marion, Ill., 1936-39; asst. to controller Ill. Agrl. Assn., Chgo., 1939-41; asst. controller Clinton Foods (Iowa), 1945-50; systems analyst Hotpoint, Inc., Chgo., 1950-51; contoller Peter Fox Brewing Co., Chgo., 1951-53; asst. auditor Northern Trust Co., Chgo., 1953-57; asst. v.p., asst. controller Continental Casualty Co., Chgo., 1957-58, controller, 1958-60, v.p., 1960-62; v.p., treas. Canteen Corp., Chgo., 1962-64, fin. v.p., 1964-68, adminstrv. v.p., 1968, also dir. sub.'s; fin. v.p. Ky. Fried Chicken Corp., Nashville, 1968-70, pres. chief exec. officer, treas. Satellite 3 in 1 Corp., Atlanta, 1970-71; v.p. fin. Equity Nat. Industries, Atlanta, 1971-73; controller Central States S.E. and S.W. areas Health Welfare and Pension Funds, Chgo., 1973—, dir. Mdse. Nat. Bank Chgo. Served to maj. AUS, 1941-45. Decorated Purple Heart. Mem. Fin. Execs. Inst., Am. Mgmt. Assn., Nat. Rifle Assn. Home: 1207 Inverleith Rd Lake Forest IL 60045 Office: 8550 W Bryn Mawr Chicago IL 60631

MAXMEN, HAROLD AARON, endodontist; b. Detroit, Jan. 26, 1909; s. Samuel Joseph and Anna (Galison) M.; Ph.C., Wayne U., 1931, B.S., in Pharmacy, 1932; D.D.S., U. Detroit, 1936; m. Ethel Tucker, July 3, 1941; children—Jerry Samuel, Robert Leslie. Sr. dentist in charge Oakland County, Children's Fund Mich., 1936-37; supervising asso. dentist, Detroit Dept. Health Dental Clinics, 1937-45; individual practice endodontics, Detroit, 1939-63, Southfield, Mich., 1963—; cons. Sinai Hosp., Detroit, 1976—. Bd. dirs. Mich. chpt. Am. Cancer Soc., trustee, 1974-76; pres. Detroit Dist. Dental Soc. Found., 1973-74. Recipient merit award Detroit Dist. Dental Soc., Sinai Hosp. of Detroit, Certificate of Merit R.A. Sommer Endodontic Study Club U. Mich., 1976. Diplomate fellow Am. Bd. Endodontics. Fellow Acad. Internat. Dentistry, Internat. Coll. Dentists (recipient Brother's Keeper award 1971), Am. Coll. Dentists; mem. Am. Assn. Endodontics, Detroit Dental Clinic Club, Am., Mich. (pres. 1950) socs. dentistry for children, Mich. Assn. Endodontists (founding pres. 1962-63), Mich. State (com. edn. and specialties), Detroit Dist. (chmn. health edn., trustee Found.), dental socs., U. Detroit Dental Alumni Assn. (pres.), ORT (founder Detroit chpt.), AAAS, Detroit Clinic Club (hon. life), Alpha Omega (merit award). Contbr. articles to dental jours. Home: 23087 Riverside Dr Southfield MI 48075 Office: Northland Med Center Southfield MI 48075

MAXON, HARRY RUSSELL, internist; b. Muncie, Ind., Aug. 28, 1941; s. Harry Russell and Mary Evelyn (Fox) M.; B.A., Stanford, 1963; M.D. with honors, Tulane U., 1967; m. Mary Isabelle Moss, June 17, 1967; children—Harry Russell, IV, Mary Evelyn Ashley Layden. Intern, Naval Hosp., Portsmouth, Va., 1967-68, resident in internal medicine, 1968-71; spl. research fellow in nuclear medicine Cin. Gen. Hosp., 1973-74; practice medicine specializing in thyroidology, Cin., 1974—; asst. prof. radiology (nuclear medicine) U. Cin. Coll. Medicine, 1974—, asst. prof. medicine (endocrinology), 1974—; mem. staff Holmes Hosp., Cin., 1974—, also chmn. med. records com.; mem. staff Jewish Hosp., Cin., 1974—; spl. cons. thyroid effects of ionizing radiation to Brookhaven Nat. Lab., Nuclear Regulatory Commn., Nat. Council Radiation Protection; cons. MEDCO Peer Review, Inc.; dir. Maxon Corp., Muncie; v.p., dir. Assos. in Nuclear Medicine, Inc., Cin. Served with USN, 1967-73. Diplomate Am. Bd. Internal Medicine, Am. Bd. Nuclear Medicine; decorated Navy Commendation Medal. Mem. AMA, A.C.P., Am. Thyroid Assn., Ohio Med. Assn., Am. Soc. Nuclear Medicine, Soc. Internal Medicine Cin., Cin. Acad. Medicine. Republican. Episcopalian. Contbr. numerous articles to med. jours. Office: Cin Gen Hosp Cincinnati OH 45267

MAXWELL, FLORENCE HINSHAW (MRS. JOHN WILLIAMSON MAXWELL), civic worker; Nora, Ind., July 14, 1914; d. Asa Benton and Gertrude (Randall) Hinshaw; B.A. cum laude, Butler U., 1935; m. John Williamson Maxwell, June 5, 1936; children—Marilyn, William Douglas. Coordinate, Sight Conservation and Aid to Blind, 1962-73, nat. chmn. bd. dir., 1969-73; active various fund drives; chmn. jamboree, hostess coms. North Central High Sch., 1959, 64; Girl Scouts U.S.A., 1937-38, 54-56; mus. chmn. Sr. Girl Scout Regional Council, 1956-57; scorekeeper Little League, 1955-57; bd. dirs. Nora Sch. Parents' Club, 1958-59, Eastwood Jr. High Sch. Triangle Club, 1959-62, Ind. State Symphony Soc. Women's Com., 1965-67, 76—, Symphoguide chmn., 1976—; vision screening Indpls. innercity pub. sch. kindergartens, pre-schs., 1962—; asst. Glaucoma screening clinics Gen. Hosp., Glendale Shopping Center, City County Bldg., Am. Legion Nat. Hdqrs., Ind. Health Assn. Conf., 1962—; chmn. sight conservation and aid to blind Nat. Delta Gamma Found., Indpls., Columbus, O., 1969-73; mem. telethon team Butler U. Fund, 1964; symphoguide hostess Internat. Conf. on Cities, 1971, Nat. League of Cities, 1972. Recipient Cable award Delta Gamma, 1969, Outstanding Alumna award, 1973; Key to City of Indpls., 1972. Mem. Nat., Ind. (dir. 1962—, exec. com. 1971—, Sight Saving Award 1974) socs. for prevention blindness, Delta Gamma (chpt. golden anniversary celebration decade and communication chmn. 1975; nat. chmn. Parent Club Study Com. 1976-77; Service Recognition award 1977). Republican. Address: 1502 E 80th St Indianapolis IN 46240

MAXWELL, JACK ERWIN, automobile co. exec.; b. Cleve., July 17, 1926; s. Fred A. and Gertrude F. (Haug) M.; B.S. in Mech. Engring., Case Inst. Tech., 1949; M.B.A., Harvard, 1952; children by previous marriage—Laura Jane, Fredric, Elizabeth Grant, Carla Moore, Linda Hanson; m. 2d, Martha Jane Miller, Dec. 28, 1966. Indsl. engr. Lincoln Electric Co., Cleve., 1952-53; mgr. purchase analysis Ford Motor Co., Dearborn, Mich., 1953-57; v.p. Booz, Allen & Hamilton, Inc., Detroit, 1957-69; v.p. corp. devel. Am. Motors Corp., Detroit, 1969-71, v.p. adminstrn., 1971-76, v.p. non-automotive subsidiaries, 1976—. Served with USNR, 1944-46. Mem. Harvard Bus. Sch., Case Inst. Tech. alumni assns., Blue Key, Tau Beta Pi, Theta Tau. Presbyn. Clubs: Harvard Business School, Detroit Economic, Detroit Athletic, Detroit Yacht. Home: 3541 Bradway Blvd Birmingham MI 48010 Office: 27777 Franklin Rd Southfield MI 48034

MAXWELL, MADALYN, lawyer; b. Nashville, Ill., Jan. 9, 1926; d. Judge Ralph L. and Beulah (House) Maxwell; student Whitworth Coll., 1943-45; B.S., U. Ill., 1947, M.A., 1949; m. Thomas H. McGary, 1968. Admitted to Ill. bar, 1951; practiced in Nashville, Ill., 1951-53; with inheritance tax div. Ill. Atty. Gen. Office, Springfield, 1953-55, asst. atty. gen. in charge pub. assistance claims enforcement div., 1956—; asst. to treas. Sangamo Electric Co., Springfield, Ill., 1955-56. Vol. worker Springfield Meml. Hosp. Mem. Am., Ill., Sangamon County bar assns., Ill., Washington County, Sangamon County hist. socs., Am. Judicature Soc., Urban League, Altar Guild, Chgo. Council Fgn. Relations. Episcopalian. Club: Pilot (Springfield). Home: 1100 Orendorff Pkwy Springfield IL 62704 Office: Ridgely Bldg Springfield IL 62706

MAXWELL, STEPHEN LLOYD, dist. ct. judge; b. St. Paul, Jan. 12, 1921; s. Stephen L. and Ethel Mae (Howard) M.; B.S.L., St. Paul Coll., 1951, LL.B., 1953; B.A., Morehouse Coll., 1942; m. Betty Virginia Mae Rodney, May 8, 1943; children—Stephen L. III, Rodney D. Zone dept. collector Bur. Internal Revenue, Mpls., 1945-46, auditor, St. Paul, 1948; accountant St. Paul Municipal Auditorium, 1948-51; spl. agt. investigator OPS, St. Paul/Mpls., 1951-53; gen. practice law, St. Paul, 1953-59; asst. Ramsey County atty., St. Paul, 1959-64, 67; corp. counsel City of St. Paul, 1964-66; municipal judge City St. Paul, 1967-68; judge Dist. Ct., 1968—. Republican candidate for Congress 4th Dist., Minn., 1966. Active Boy Scouts Am. Bd. dirs. ARC, Minn. Safety Council, Hamline U. Sch. Law; bd. regents St. John's U.; pub. corporate mem. Blue Cross and Blue Shield of Minn., 1977—, United Hosps. Inc., 1975—. Served with USCGR, 1942-45; now capt. USNR. Mem. Minn., Ill. bar assns., St. Paul-Mpls. Com. on Fgn. Relations. Episcopalian. Home: 882 Carroll Ave St Paul MN 55104 Office: Court House St Paul MN 55102

MAY, ALONZO GAIL, cons. engr.; b. Island Park, Iowa, Feb. 21, 1914; s. Alonzo M. and Elizabeth (Williams) M.; B.S. in Mech. Engring., U. Kans., 1938; m. E. Madelene Wells, Dec. 24, 1939; children—Gary Gail, Carol Sue. Jr. engr., resident engr., asst. prin. engr. Black & Veatch, cons. engrs., Kansas City, Mo., 1938-48; partner Lutz & May Co., cons. engrs., Kansas City, 1948-60; partner May Engring. Co., Kansas City, 1960—. Mem. ASME, Nat., Mo. socs. profl. engr., Tau Beta Pi, Theta Tau. Club: Engineers (Kansas City). Home: 5830 Fontana Dr Shawnee Mission KS 66205 Office: 7140 Wornall Rd Kansas City MO 64114

MAY, ARNOLD NICHOLAS, constrn. co. exec.; b. Spring Grove, Ill., June 9, 1917; s. Frank and Mathilda (Kattner) M.; B.A. in Archtl. Engring., U. Ill., 1942; m. Margaret Mary Fosket, June 26, 1948; children—Joanne, Robert, Melissa, Pamela, Marianne, A. Stephen. Engring. adviser to Ambassador to Republic of China, 1947-48; with J.G. White, engrs., N.Y.C., 1949-50; owner Arnold May Builders, Inc., Richmond, Ill., 1950—. Chmn. county mental health bd., 1973-75; pres. McHenry County (Ill.) Mental Health Center, 1967-68; chmn. bd. dirs. McHenry County Cancer Soc., 1965-71. Served to maj. C.E., AUS, 1942-46. K.C. (4 deg.). Home: 9622

Hideaway Ln Richmond IL 60071 Office: 9716 N Rt 12 Richmond IL 60071

MAY, EUGENE PINKNEY, psychologist; b. Louisville, May 1, 1931; s. Eugene Pinkney and Amanda Miller (Baskette) M.; B.A., George Peabody Coll., Nashville, 1953, M.A., 1966; Ph.D., U. Ill., Urbana, 1971. Tchr., Dade County, Fla., 1962-66; counselor Dade County schs., 1966-71; head resident, supervising counselor Hendrick House, Urbana, 1970-71; grad. counselor, research asst. U. Ill., 1969-71; psychologist VA Hosp., Cleve., 1971—; pvt. practice, Cleve., 1973—; cons. psychologist, mem. adj. med. staff dept. psychiatry Evening Mental Health Clinic, Cleve. Met. Gen. Hosp., 1974—; counselor Peace Corps advanced tng. project for Korea, summer 1966. Mem. Am., Ohio, Cleve. psychol. assns., Assn. Humanistic Psychology, Am. Personnel and Guidance Assn., Assn. Counselor Edn. and Supervision, Cleve. Acad. Cons. Psychologists, U. Ill. Alumni Assn., Phi Delta Kappa, Kappa Delta Pi. Author articles in field. Home: 2641 Euclid Heights Blvd Cleveland Heights OH 44106 Office: 10701 E Boulevard Cleveland OH 44106

MAY, ROBERT PORTER, electronics co. exec.; b. Mohawk, N.Y., Jan. 28, 1934; s. Calvin Andrew and Lila Marie (Porter) M.; B.S., Syracuse U., 1956; postgrad. Marshall-Wythe Sch. Law, Coll. William and Mary, 1970, George Washington U., 1973; m. Mary Ann Sullivan, Sept. 3, 1967; children—Susan Michele, Kelly Ann. Auditor, U.S. Air Force Auditor Gen., Utica, N.Y., 1957-60; price analyst U.S. Air Force, Griffiss AFB, Rome, N.Y., 1960-63; mgr. purchasing Page Communications Engrs., Washington, 1963-65; mgr. contracts Litcom div. Litton Industries, New Rochelle, N.Y., 1965-69; mgr. contracts Cin. Electronics Corp., 1969—. Certified profl. contracts mgr. Mem. Nat. Def. Preparedness Assn., Nat. Contract Mgmt. Assn., Assn. Old Crows, Nat. Security Indsl. Assn., Cin. Electronics Mgmt. Club (past pres.). Republican. Clubs: Masons, Shriners. Home: 8825 Tammy Dr West Chester OH 45069 Office: 2630 Glendale-Milford Rd Cincinnati OH 45241

MAYBA, IHOR, orthopaedic surgeon; b. Vegreville, Alta., Can., May 23, 1931; B.S., U. Man., 1952, M.D., 1957. Fellow Canadian Royal Coll. Surgeons in gen. surgery and orthopaedic surgery; intern St. Boniface Hosp., Winnipeg, Man., Can., 1956; resident Winnipeg Gen. Hosp., Royal Victor, Shriners hosps., Montreal, Que., Can.; practice medicine specializing in orthopaedic surgery, Winnipeg, 1967—; orthopaedic surgeon Man. Clinic, 1962—; mem. staffs Winnipeg, Gen., Winnipeg Children's, Winnipeg Misericordia hosps.; clin. instr. orthopaedics U. Man., 1967—. Diplomate Am. Bd. Surgery. Mem. Ukrainian Nat. Home Assn., Winnipeg Orthopaedic Soc., Ukrainian Profl. and Businessmen's Club. Office: Man Clinic 790 Sherbrooke St Winnipeg MB R3A IM3 Canada

MAYBERG, DONALD MAC MILLAN, psychiatrist; b. Mpls., Oct. 31, 1924; s. Marc Norman and Grace Margaret (Challman) M.; B.A., U. Minn., 1948, M.D., 1952; m. Betty Lou Davis, Oct. 29, 1971; children—Stephen, Susan, Marc, Nancy, Barbara. Intern, Madigan Army Gen. Hosp., Tacoma, 1952-53; resident in psychiatry U. Minn. Hosps., Mpls., 1954-57; instr. psychiatry U. Minn., 1957-58; practice medicine specializing in psychiatry, Mpls., 1958—; clin. asso. prof. psychiatry U. Minn.; dir. psychiat. edn. and tng. Abbott-Northwestern Hosp., Inc.; cons. Dept. Def., FAA, McGraw-Hill Publs. Served to capt., USAF, 1942-46, 52- 54. Fellow Am. Psychiat. Assn.; mem. Am., Minn. (pres.) psychiat. assns., AMA, Family and Children's Assn. (bd. dirs.), Hennepin County Psychiat. Soc., Hennepin County Med. Assn., Alpha Delta Phi, Nu Sigma Nu. Presbyterian. Contbr. to Modern Medicine, 1954-59. Office: 4225 Golden Valley Rd Minneapolis MN 55422

MAYBERRY, THOMAS ARNOLD, real estate broker; b. Sherburn, Minn., Dec. 23, 1937; s. Thomas and Mildred Irene (Hanson) M.; grad. high sch.; 1 dau., Michelle M. Owner, operator Mayberry Lanes, St. James, Minn., 1964—; owner St. James Hotel and Cate, 1966—; broker, owner T.A. Mayberry Realty and Mayberry Realty Inc., St. James, 1970—; developer Mayberry Hills Colonial Manor Apts., Riverine Hills housing devel. Bd. dirs. Hi-Way 60 Commn., 1971-73, pres., 1972. Mem. Nat., Minn., St. James assns. realtors, Minn. Bowling Assn. (dir. 1970—), Nat., Minn. bowling proprs. assns., C. of C. (pres. 1972, 77). Shriner Republican. Presbyterian. Home: Route 2 St James MN 56081 Office: 119 S 7th St St James MN 56081

MAYBERRY, WILLIAM EUGENE, physician; b. Cookeville, Tenn., Aug. 22, 1929; s. Henry Eugene and Beatrice Lucille (Maynard) M.; student Tenn. Technol. U., 1947-49; M.D., U. Tenn., 1953; M.S. in Medicine, U. Minn., 1959; intern U.S. Naval Hosp., Phila., 1953-54; resident Mayo Grad. Sch. Medicine, Rochester, Minn., 1956-59; m. Jane G. Foster, Dec. 29, 1953; children—Ann Graves, Paul Foster. Mem. staff New Eng. Med. Center, Boston, 1959-60, Nat. Inst. Arthritis and Metabolic Diseases, 1962-64; staff Mayo Clinic, Rochester, 1960-62, 64—, cons. internal medicine, endocrine research and lab. medicine, chmn. dept. lab. medicine, 1971-75, bd. govs., 1971—, vice chmn., 1974-75, chmn., 1976—, chief exec. officer, 1977—; asst. in medicine Tufts U. Med. Sch., 1959-60; faculty Mayo Grad. Sch. Medicine and Mayo Med. Sch., 1960—, now prof. lab. medicine. Trustee, Mayo Found., 1971—, vice chmn., 1974—. Diplomate Am. Bd. Internal Medicine. Fellow A.C.P.; mem. Am. Thyroid Assn., Am. Chem. Soc., Am. Fedn. for Clin. Research, Endocrine Soc., Central Research Club, Central Soc. for Clin. Research, Sigma Xi. Clubs: Rochester Golf and Country, Mpls. Recipient Distinguished Alumni award Tenn. Technol. U., 1976; NIH research fellow, 1959-60, Am. Cancer Soc. research fellow, 1962-64; NIH research grantee, 1965-71; mem. editorial bd. Jour. of Clin. Endocrinology and Metabolism, 1971-73; contbr. articles to profl. jours. Home: 705 SW 8th Ave Rocheste MN 55901 Office: 200 SW 1st St Rochester MN 55901

MAYER, JAMES ANDREW, newspaper exec.; b. Clarksville, Iowa, Sept. 24, 1930; s. George Jacob and Clara Dina (Lubben) M.; B.A., U. Iowa, 1952; m. Marjorie Aileen Nettleton, June 6, 1953; children—April Jolene Mayer Acton, Kelly James, Melody Ann, Brant Anthony. News editor Marengo (Iowa) Pioneer-Republican, 1954-63; editor, 1963-68; editor, pub. Anamosa (Iowa) Jour., also Eureka, 1968—; dir., pres. Anamosa Newspapers, Inc. Dist. committeeman Boy Scouts Am., 1971. Trustee, v.p. Anamosa Pub. Library; trustee Anamosa Community Hosp. Served with USAF, 1952-54. Mem. Iowa Press Assn., Nat. Editorial Assn., Internat. Soc. Weekly Newspaper Editors, Izaak Walton League (Founder's award 1964, chpt. sec. 1969-73), Am. Legion, Anamosa C. of C. (bd. dirs. 1970-71; named Businessman of Year 1974), Sigma Delta Chi. Roman Catholic. K.C., Kiwanian (pres. 1966), Rotarian (bd. dirs. 1970-71, pres. 1978-79). Home: RFD 3 405 N Ford St Anamosa IA 52205 Office: 111 N Ford St Anamosa IA 52205

MAYER, JAMES JOSEPH, judge; b. Shelby, Ohio, Oct. 13, 1920; s. Guss J. and Julia (Haley) M.; student DeSales Coll., Toledo, 1938-40; J.D., Ohio No. U., 1946; m. Margaret Jane Basinger, Sept. 28, 1946; children—Julia, James, Philip, Barbara, Mark, Margaret, Matthew, John and Luke (twins), Theresa. Admitted to Ohio bar, 1947, U.S. Supreme Ct. bar; sr. mem. Mayer & Larson, 1949-50, Mayer, Larson & Arbaugh, 1950-52, Mayer & McClellan, 1952-55, Mayer, McClellan, Christiansen, & Johnson, 1955-56, Mayer, McDermott & Assos., 1956-59; asst. pros. atty. Richland County. Ohio, 1949-52; judge Common Pleas Ct., Richland County, Mansfield, Ohio, 1959—; judge Muskingum Watershed Conservancy Dist., 1959—. Mem. Ohio Central and Exec. Coms. Dem. Party, 1958-59; chmn. Richland County Dem. Exec. Com., 1958-59. Served with AUS, 1942-45; PTO. Recipient Carl V. Weygandt award Supreme Ct. Ohio, 1972, 73, also Outstanding Judicial Service awards, 1974, 75, Superior Judicial Service award, 1976; testimonials Mansfield Edn. Assn., Richland County Bar Assn., Richland County Med. Soc., Richland County Council AFL-CIO, SSS. Mem. Ohio, Richland County bar assns., Common pleas Judges Assn. Ohio. Roman Catholic. Republican. Home: RD 11 Fleming Falls Rd Mansfield OH 44903 Office: 50 Park Ave E Mansfield OH 44902

MAYER, JEAN LOIS, community health educator; b. Cleve., May 12, 1931; d. Lewis Everett and Irene Marguerite (Warren) Yost; B.A., Denison U., Granville, Ohio, 1953; M.A., Mich. State U., 1975; m. Endre Agoston Mayer, June 17, 1956; children—Susan Jean, Sandra Jane, Warren Endre. Service rep. Ohio Bell Telephone Co., 1953-57; field dir., camp coordinator Camp Fire Girls, Pontiac, Mich., 1968-72; asst. to producer Sta. WXYZ-TV, Southfield, Mich., 1972-73; Christian edn. resource person First Baptist Ch., Mt. Clemens, Mich., 1975—; community health educator Am. Cancer Soc., Southfield, 1976—. Chmn. Birmingham (Mich.) Dial-a-Ride Study Com., 1976—. Mem. AAUW, Am., Mich. personnel and guidance assns., Mich. Assn. Group Workers, Mich. Assn. Agy. Workers. Am. Baptist. Club: Altrusa. Author articles. Home: 945 Poppleton St Birmingham MI 48008 Office: 15800 W McNichols Detroit MI 48076

MAYER, OSCAR G., meat packing co. exec.; b. Chgo., Mar. 16, 1914; s. Oscar G. and Elsa (Stieglitz) M.; A.B., Cornell U., 1934; m. Rosalie Harrison, Nov. 21, 1942; children—Oscar Harrison, Donald Lawrence, William Edward. With Oscar Mayer & Co., 1936—, v.p. ops., 1950-53, exec. v.p., 1953-55, pres., 1955-66, chmn. bd., 1966-73, chmn. exec. com., 1973-77, also dir., 1939—; trustee Northwestern Mut. Life Ins. Co.; dir. Wis. Telephone Co., Fed. Res. Bank of Chgo. Mem. bus. sch. council U. Chgo.; hon. trustee Com. for Econ. Devel.; bd. dirs. U. Wis. Found.; bd. dirs. U. Wis. Found., Lyric Opera Chgo. Clubs: Chgo.; Maple Bluff Country, Madison (Madison, Wis.). Home: 722 Wilder Dr Madison WI 53704 Office: 713 First Wisconsin Plaza Madison WI 53703

MAYER, RAYMOND RICHARD, educator; b. Chgo., Aug. 31, 1924; s. Adam and Mary (Bogdala) M.; B.S., Ill. Inst. Tech., 1948, M.S., 1954, Ph.D., 1957; m. Helen Lakowski, Jan. 30, 1954; children—Mark, John, Mary, Jane. Indsl. engr. Standard Oil Co., Whiting, Ind., 1948-51; organizational analyst Ford Motor Co., Chgo., 1951-53; instr. Ill. Inst. Tech., Chgo., 1953-56, asso. prof., 1958-60; asst. prof. U. Chgo., 1956-58; Walter F. Mullady prof. bus. adminstrn. Loyola U., Chgo., 1960—. Served with USNR, 1944-46. Ingersoll Found. fellow, 1955-56; Machinery and Allied Products Inst. fellow, 1954-55; Ford Found. fellow, 1962. Mem. Acad. of Mgmt., Am. Econ. Assn., Am. Statis. Assn., Am. Inst. for Decision Scis., Nat. Assn. Purchasing Mgmt., Polish Inst. Arts and Scis. in Am., Alpha Iota Delta, Alpha Kappa Psi, Beta Gamma Sigma. Author: Financial Analysis of Investment Alternatives, 1966; Production Management, 1962, rev. edit., 1968; Production and Operations Management, 1975; Capital Expenditure Analysis, 1978. Home: 2111-B Sherman Ave Evanston IL 60201 Office: 820 N Michigan Ave Chicago IL 60611

MAYER, RICHARD, JR., newspaper editor; b. Sioux City, Iowa, May 26, 1923; s. Richard P. and Laura Wilma (Rouse) M.; B.S., Washburn U., 1949; postgrad. Kans. U., 1951-52; m. Anna Marie Simons, Oct. 29, 1950; children—Deborah, Bryce, Jill, Mike, Amy. Mem. staff Clay County (Nebr.) News, 1952-53; editor North Vernon (Ind.) Plain Dealer and Sun, 1954—. Sec. North Vernon Park Bds., 1959—. Mem. Hoosier State Press Assn. (dir.), North Vernon C. of C. (dir., pres.). Home: 12 Hare Ln North Vernon IN 47265 Office: 528 E O & M Ave North Vernon IN 47265

MAYERSAK, JEROME STEPHEN, urologist; b. Superior, Wis., July 4, 1938; s. Joseph Walter and Libby Jean (Conroy) M.; B.A., Johns Hopkins, 1960; M.D., George Washington U., 1964; m. Priscilla M. Kurtzweil, Mar. 27, 1976; dau., Kathlyne Mary. Intern dept. surgery George Washington U. Hosp., Washington, 1964-65, resident in urology, 1966, chief resident, 1968; resident in surgery D.C. Gen. Hosp., 1965-66, resident in urology, 1966-67, sr. resident, 1967; resident in urology George Washington U. Sch. of Medicine, 1966-69; sr. resident VA Hosp., 1968, chief resident, Washington, 1969; practice medicine specializing in urology, Wisconsin Rapids, Wis., 1969-71, Merrill, Wis., 1971—; urologist Med. Arts Group, Wisconsin Rapids, 1969-71; mem. staff Taylor County Meml. Hosp., Medford, Wis., 1970—, Holy Cross Hosp., Merrill, Wis., 1971—, Tri-County Meml. Hosp., Whitehall, Wis., 1971—, v.p. med. staff, 1975—; mem. cons. staff Riverview Hosp., Wisconsin Rapids, 1970-75, Sacred Heart Hosp., Tomahawk, Wis., 1971—, Wild Rose (Wis.) Community Meml. Hosp., 1970—, Neillsville (Wis.) Meml. Hosp., 1969—; jr. cons. to St. Elizabeth's Hosp., Washington, 1968-69; urologist J.S. Mayersak Service Corp., Merrill, 1971—; cons. urologist Langlade County Meml. Hosp., Antigo, Wis., Eagle River (Wis.) Hosp., Park Falls (Wis.) Hosp. Chmn. adv. airport com. to Airport Commn., Merrill, Wis., 1970-75; bd. dirs. Tri-County Meml. Hosp. Fellow William Beaumont Hon. Research Soc., St. George Cancer Soc.; mem. AMA, State Med. Soc. Wis., Am. Assn. of Physicians and Surgeons, Am., Internat. socs. of nephrology, Minn., Twin Cities urol. socs., Flying Physicians Assn., Wis., Lincoln County (pres. 1974-78), Aerospace med. socs., Internat. Soc. Nephrology, Am. Soc. Microbiology, A.C.S., Va. Acad. Scis., Pan Am. Med. Assn., Renal Physicians Assn. (ho. dels. 1977—), Royal Soc. of London, Asociacion Medica Panamericana, Socieded Equatoriana de Urologia (hon.), Am. Fertility Soc., Internat. Platform Assn., Wis. Physicians Union (pres. 1973—), AAAS, Sigma Xi, Nu Sigma Nu. Club: Elks. Home: 717 Tee Lane Dr Merrill WI 54452 Office: 712 E 2d St Merrill WI 54452

MAYERSDORF, ASSA, physician; b. Israel, Sept. 21, 1937; M.D., Hebrew U.-Hadassah Med. Sch., Jerusalem, 1963; m. Nira Mayersdorf, 1965, 2 children. Intern, Hadassah-Hebrew Univ. Hosp., Jerusalem, 1962-63, resident in medicine, 1963; house officer neurosurgery Tel-Hashomer Govtl. Hosp., Israel, 1964-66; asst. resident dept. neurology Balt. City Hosp., 1966-68; asst. resident in neurology Johns Hopkins Hosp., Balt., 1968-69, chief resident, 1969; fellow Johns Hopkins Univ. Sch. Medicine, 1966-69; instr. div. neurology U. Fla. Coll. Medicine, Gainesville, 1970, asso. mem. Center for Neurobiol. Scis., 1970; chief sect. neurology Soroka Med. Center, Univ. Center for Health Scis., Ben-Gurion Univ., Beer-Sheva, Israel, 1971-74, guest lectr. Faculty Scis., 1971-74; asst. prof. dept. neurology U. Minn. Sch. Medicine, Mpls., 1974—; dir. Epilepsy Treatment Center VA Hosp., Mpls., 1974—. Bd. dirs. Minn. Epilepsy League, 1975—, sec., 1977—. Served with Israel Def. Armed Forces, 1963-66. Diplomate Am. Bd. Neurology and Psychiatry. Mem. Am. Acad. Neurology, Am. Epilepsy Soc., Epilepsy Found. Am., Eastern Assn. Electroencephalographers, Israel Med. Assn., Israel Neurol. Soc. Israel Soc. Electroencephalography. Office: Epilepsy Treatment Center VA Hosp 54th St and 48th Ave S Minneapolis MN 55417

MAYFIELD, ELI BURTON, JR., dentist; b. St. Louis, Nov. 24, 1902; s. Eli Burton and Ida May (Conrad) M.; D.D.S., St. Louis U., 1903; m. Ruby May Radley, May 29, 1924 (dec. Sept. 17, 1967); children—Burton Walter, Ruby Radley (Mrs. Bruce Mitchel Benthin). Practice dentistry, St. Louis, 1932—. Served to capt. AUS, 1941-45; PTO. Mem. Am., Mo. dental assns., Greater St. Louis Dental Soc., Mo. Soc., S.A.R. Mason. Home and office: 6908 Natural Bridge St St Louis MO 63121

MAYL, JACK JOSEPH, lawyer; b. Dayton, Ohio, June 21, 1930; s. Eugene Aloysius and Helen Irene (Cooper) M.; B.S. cum laude, U. Notre Dame, 1952; J.D., Georgetown U., 1958; m. Gay Reddig, Apr. 8, 1972. Admitted to Ohio bar, 1960; partner firm Murphy & Mayl, Dayton, 1960—; dir. Central Pharmacal Co., Seymour, Ind., R.L. Consol. Inc., Cleve. Trustee Cath. Social Services Miami Valley. Served to lt. USNR, 1953-56. Mem. Internat., Inter-Am., Am., Ohio, Dayton bar assns., Nat. Assn. Criminal Def. Lawyers, Antique Automobile Club Am., Rolls Royce Owners Club, Phi Alpha Delta. Clubs: Lawyers, Dayton Country, Dayton Racquet. Home: Plantation Ln Kettering OH 45419 Office: 2660 Winters Bank Tower Dayton OH 45402

MAYLATH, DONALD OLIVER, food co. exec.; b. Granite City, Ill., Dec. 9, 1933; s. Aladar and Mary Margaret (Petesh) M.; B.S., U. Ill., 1955; postgrad. St. Louis U., 1959-62, U. Minn., 1963-68; children—Pamela, Mark, Carol. Reporter, St. Louis (Mo.) Globe-Democrat, 1955-56; asst. advt. mgr. Bemis Co., Inc., St. Louis, 1958-63, market research analyst, Mpls., 1963-67, asst. pricing mgr., 1967-68; mgr. marketing research Miles Labs., Inc., Union Div., Granite City, Ill., 1968-71, mgr. marketing research, Marschall Div., Elkhart, Ind., 1971-75, mgr. marketing services, 1976—. Served with U.S. Army, 1956-58. Mem. Am. Marketing Assn., Inst. of Food Technologists, European Chem. Marketing Research Assn., European Assn. for Indsl. Marketing Research, European Marketing Assn., Internat. Market Research Assn., Sigma Delta Chi. Roman Catholic. Club: Elks. Home: 51068 Shady Ln Elkhart IN 46514 Office: 1127 Myrtle St Elkhart IN 46514

MAYMAN, MARTIN, educator; b. N.Y.C., Apr. 2, 1924; s. Abraham and Anna (Mann) M.; B.S., Coll. City N.Y., 1943; M.S., N.Y. U., 1947; Ph.D., U. Kans., 1953; m. Rosemary Walker, Oct. 12, 1960 (div.); children—Sara, Stephen, Daniel. Clin. psychologist Menninger Found., Topeka, Kans., 1944-46; clin. instr. U. Kans. and Winter VA Hosp., Topeka, 1946-51; dir. psychol. training Menninger Found., Topeka, 1951-65; prof. psychology U. Mich., Ann Arbor, 1966—, also co-dir. Psychol. Clinic; vis. prof. U. Colo., Denver; 1965-66, U. Calif. at Berkeley, 1966; faculty Topeka Psychoanalytic Inst., 1960—, Mich. Psychoanalytic Inst., Detroit, 1967—. Participant Nat. Conf. on Profl. Tng. in Clin. Psychology, 1960. Fellow Am. Psychol. Assn., Am. Bd. Examiners Profl. Psychology; mem. Mich. Psychoanalytic Assn., Topeka Psychoanalytic Assn., Soc. for Personality Assessment (pres. 1967-68). Adv. editor Jour. Consulting Psychology, 1965-70, Psychotherapy, 1975—. Author: Psychoanalytic Research: Three Approaches to the Experimental Study of Subliminal Processes, 1973; (with K. A. Menninger and P. Pruyser) The Vital Balance, 1963; (with K. A. Menninger and P. Pruyser) A Manual for Psychiatric Case Study, 2d edit., 1963. Home: 230 Wildwood Ann Arbor MI 48104

MAYNARD, H. GLENN, educator; b. Sterling, Ill., May 12, 1927; s. H.E. and Bernece H. (Deem) M.; B.S., No. Ill. U., 1949; M.S., U. Ill., 1952; Ed.D., U. No. Colo., 1960; m. M. Lynn Thomas, Dec. 27, 1947. Classroom tchr. Yorkville (Ill.) Pub. Schs., 1949-51; tchr., coach Hinckley (Ill.) Pub. Schs., 1951-53, prin., 1951-53; asst. supt. Milledgeville (Ill.) Pub. Schs., 1953-57; asst. prof. edn. State U. N.Y. at Oneonta, 1957-60; asst. prof. Kent (Ohio) State U., 1960-65, asso. prof., 1965-69, prof. ednl. adminstrn., 1969—, coordinator Grad. Sch. Edn., 1970—; pres. Cricket Press, Inc., Kent, 1972—; cons. Peat, Marwick, Mitchell & Co., 1968-70; cons. in field. Recipient Service to Edn. award Phi Delta Kappa, 1974, Honor Key award Kappa Delta Pi, 1974. Mem. Nat. Middle Sch. Assn. (dir. 1972-75, pres. 1973-74). Club: Lions (dir. 1971-77, pres. 1975-76). Author: (with H.D. Behrens) The Changing Child, 1972; mng. editor Middle Sch. Jour., 1973-76. Home: Box 666 Kent OH 44240

MAYNARD, MARIANNE, educator; b. Detroit, Oct. 3, 1931; d. Henery and Hazel Loise (Shaw) Maynard; B.A., Wayne State U., 1953, M.A., 1955; Ph.D., U. Wis., Madison, 1976. Tchr. art, pub. schs. Detroit, Inkster, Mich., 1954-57; occupational therapist Soc. for Crippled Children, Cleve., 1957-59, St. Joseph Mercy Hosp., Ann Arbor, 1957-59, Ann Arbor VA Hosp., 1959-60; mental health cons., dir. occupational therapy tng. and staff devel. Wis. Dept. Health and Social Services, Madison, 1964-72; mem. faculty continuing edn. dept., U. Wis., 1972-76; asso. prof., dir. continuing edn. Eastern Mich. U., Ypsilanti, 1976—. Mem. Am., Mich. occupational therapy assns., Adult Edn. Assn. U.S.A., Am. Personnel and Guidance Assn., Assn. Humanistic Edn., Comprehensive Health Planning Council Southeastern Mich., Delta Sigma Theta, Pi Lambda Theta. Contbr. articles to profl. jours. Home: 1056 Greenhile Dr Ann Arbor MI 48105 Office: Dept Continuing Edn Eastern Mich U Ypsilanti MI 48197

MAYO, GEORGIA THELMA RILEY (MRS. HARRY RELVIA MAYO), banker; b. Macon, Mo., Sept. 16, 1897; d. Andrew Edwin and Elizabeth Ann (Archer) Riley; student Mo. Wesleyan Coll., 1918-19, 19-20, Kirksville State Coll., 1921; m. Harry Relvia Mayo, Aug. 30, 1922 (dec. Sept. 1961); children—Elizabeth Ann (Mrs. Robert Sibbit), George Edwin, Harry Riley (dec.), John William. Tchr. pub. schs., Brookfield, Mo., 1920-21, Mendon, Mo., 1921-22; with Peoples State Bank, Spickard, Mo., 1961—, v.p., dir., 1962—. Sec., Mo. Ninth Congl. Republican Com., 1962-67. Pres., Mo. dept. Am. Legion Aux. 1941-42, mem. exec. com., 1937—, dir. Mo. Girls' State 1949, 51-53; conf. sec. Christian social relations Methodist Woman's Soc. Christian Service, 1963-67. Mem. D.A.R. (past regent), Order Eastern Star (past matron), Marquis Biog. Library Soc. Home: 1225 E 13th Ct Trenton MO 64683 Office: PO Box 458 Trenton MO 64683

MAYO, SAMUEL TURBERVILLE, educator; b. Century, Fla., Dec. 25, 1921; s. Arthur David and Mildred Louise (Ward) M.; B.E.E., Auburn U., 1943; M.A., Emory U., 1951; Ph.D., U. Minn., 1956; m. Melba Virginia Hendricks, Aug. 28, 1949; 1 dau., Melissa. Elec. engr. Gen. Electric Co., Syracuse, N.Y., Bridgeport, Conn., Schenectady, Lynn, Mass. and Atlanta, 1946-48; instr. elec. tech. Ga. Inst. Tech., Atlanta, 1948-49; research asst. Bur. Edn. Research, U. Minn., Mpls., 1951-54; dir., div. edn. measurements Council on Dental Edn., ADA, Chgo., 1954-55; instr., asst. prof., asso. prof. Loyola U., Chgo., 1955-66; prof. ednl. psychology, 1966—; vis. asso. prof. U. So. Calif., summer 1962; cons. ednl. psychology and research. Bd. dirs. Chgo. Internat. Program for Youth Leaders and Social Workers, 1967—, v.p., 1969-71. Served to lt. USNR, 1943-46. Fellow Am. Psychol. Assn., AAAS; mem. Am. Statis. Assn. (dir. Chgo. chpt. 1977-78), Am. Ednl. Research Assn., Nat. Council on Measurement in Edn. (treas. 1964-69), Psychometric Soc., U.S. Power Squadron (admissions chmn. Skokie Valley 1967-72, mem. nat. instruction techniques com. 1972—), Sigma Xi (chpt. pres. 1973-74), Phi Delta Kappa (chpt. v.p. 1953-54). Contbr. articles to profl. jours.; editor (rev.) Psychometrika, 1967-75. Home: 2525 Park Ln Glenview IL 60025 Office: 820 N Michigan Ave Chicago IL 60611

MAYO, WILLIAM LEONARD, assn. exec., educator; b. Detroit, May 31, 1931; s. William Neale and Laverne Julia (Leonard) M.; B.A. in Geography, U. Mich., 1953, M.A. in Geography, 1954, M.A. in Edn., 1959, Ph.D. in Edn. and Geography, 1964. Asst. dir. Cleve. Center, Ohio U., 1964-65; dean edn. Curry Coll., Milton, Mass., 1965-74; pres., exec. dir. Am. Soc. Environ. Edn., Park Forest S., Ill., 1972—; Univ. prof. environ. edn. Govs. State U., Park Forest S., 1974—. Winston Churchill traveling fellow, 1967. Fellow Royal Geog. Soc.; mem. Internat. Geog. Union (del. 1966, 68), Internat. Tchr. Edn. Council (trustee). Author: The Development and Status of Secondary School Geography, 1965; People, Planet and Progress, 1975; other books. Contbr. numerous articles on ecology, geography, edn. to periodicals, profl. jours. Home: PO Box 36 Crete IL 60417 Office: care Governor's State U Park Forest S IL 60466

MAYRON, LEWIS WALTER, chemist; b. Chgo., Sept. 20, 1932; s. Max and Florence Minette (Brody) M.; B.S., Roosevelt U., 1954; M.S., U. Ill., 1956, Ph.D., 1959; m. Ellen Rae Lester, Nov. 23, 1958; children—Leslie Hope, Eric Brian. Research, teaching asst. dept. biol. chemistry U. Ill., Chgo. Profl. Colls., 1954-59; research asso. dept. biochemistry and nutrition U. So. Calif. Sch. Medicine, Los Angeles, 1959-61; instr. dept. biol. chemistry U. Ill. Coll. Medicine, Chgo., 1961-62; leader biochemistry group Tardanbek Labs., Chgo., 1962-63; sr. devel. chemist Abbott Labs., North Chicago, Ill., 1963-64; asst. spl. staff Michael Reese Hosp. and Med. Center, Chgo., 1965-66, research asso. dept. allergy research, 1964-66; biochem. cons. N.W. Community Hosp., Arlington Heights, Ill., 1966-67; asst. prof. biochemistry, physiology Loyola U. Sch. Dentistry, Chgo., 1968-71; research chemist VA Hosp., Hines, Ill., 1968—. Guest investigator Argonne (Ill.) Nat. Lab., 1973—. Mem. Skokie Flood and Water Pollution Commn., 1971-74; chmn. Skokie Environment Commn., 1973—; mem. fed. exec. bd. Energy Conservation Com., 1974-75; pack cubmaster, Skokie, 1974-75. Recipient sci. award Ill. Assn. Clin. Labs., 1970; named Laureat of Genia Czerniak prize for nuclear medicine and radiopharmacology Ahavot Zion Found. Israel, 1974. Mem. Biochem. Soc. (London), Am. Assn. Clin. Chemists, AAAS, Soc. Exptl. Biology and Medicine, Am. Soc. Photobiology, Soc. Nuclear Medicine, Soc. Clin. Ecology, Sigma Xi. Home: 5437 Suffield Terr Skokie IL 60076 Office: VA Hosp Nuclear Medicine (151/115) Hines IL 60141

MAYS, WALTER JUANO, actuary; b. Medon, Tenn., May 23, 1913; s. Walter Thompson and Elna Leonora (Vantreese) M.; B.S. with high distinction, Murray State Coll., 1934; M.A., Vanderbilt U., 1935; m. Ella Lucille Hearn, July 7, 1935; 2 sons, Walter Allan, John Hearn. Tchr., prin. pub. schs. Chester County, Hamilton County, Tenn., 1935-41; actuarial asst. Vol. State Life Ins. Co., Chattanooga, 1941-47; asst. actuary Liberty Life Ins. Co., Greenville, S.C., 1947-51; actuary Imperial Life Ins. Co., Asheville, N.C., 1951-57; asso. actuary Western and Southern Life Ins. Co., Cin., 1957—. Translator Internat. Visitors Center, Cin., 1966—; lt. col. and aide-de-camp, staff of Gov. of Miss., 1977—. Mem. Am. Acad. Actuaries, Soc. Actuaries (asso.), Southeastern Actuaries Club (charter, v.p., 1951-52, pres., 1952-53), Actuaries Club of Ind., Ky., Ohio, Math. Assn. Am., Am. Oriental Soc. Contbr. research papers to publs. U.S., Eng., Ger. Home: 6565 Stewart Rd Cincinnati OH 45236 Office: 400 Broadway St Cincinnati OH 45202

MAYS, WILLIAM OSCAR, physician; b. Little Rock, Jan. 21, 1934; s. William O. and Belandis (Smith) M.; B.S., Howard U., 1956; M.D., U. Ark., 1960; m. Elaine Fisher, Aug. 24, 1957; 1 son, William O. Gen. practice internal medicine, Detroit, 1966—; mem. Comprehensive Health Planning Council Southeastern Mich., 1970—; dir. Blue Cross Blue Shield Mich., 1972-75; pres., chmn. bd. Mich. HMO Plans, Inc., Detroit, 1974—; pres. Detroit Med. Found., 1971—. Served to capt. M.C. U.S. Army, 1962-63. Recipient Outstanding Health Care certificate Mich. Ho. of Reps., 1976. Office: 2200 Edison Plaza 660 Jones St Detroit MI 48226

MAYUGA, EDGARDO GUEVARRA, anesthesiologist; b. Philippines, Aug. 3, 1936; s. Arsenio M. Mayuga and Trinidad J. Guevarra; M.D., U. Santo Tomas, Manila, Philippines, 1960; m. Emma Villaneuva Matundan, May 30, 1967; children—Edgardo L., Eric J. Intern, Bon Secours Hosp., Balt., 1963-64; resident Barnes Hosp., Washington U. Med. Center, St. Louis, 1971-72; practice medicine specializing in anesthesiology, St. Louis, 1972—; staff anesthesiologist St. Mary's Hosp., St. Louis, St. Anthony's Med. Center, St. Louis. Diplomate Am. Bd. Anesthesiology. Fellow Am. Coll. Anesthesiologists; mem. AMA, Am. Soc. Anesthesiologists, St. Louis Med. Soc. Home: 12474 S Forty Dr Saint Louis MO 63141 Office: Saint Anthony's Med Center 10010 Kennerly Rd Saint Louis MO 63128

MAZEWSKI, ALOYSIUS ALEX, lawyer, pub. co. exec.; b. North Chicago, Ill., Jan. 5, 1916; s. Felix and Harriet (Konieczny) M.; J.D., DePaul U., 1940; m. Florence Heider, June 27, 1948; children—Aloysius A., Marilyn. Admitted to Ill. bar, 1940, pvt. practice law, Chgo., 1940-67; master in chancery Cir. Ct. Cook County (Ill.), 1964-66; mem. Arbitration Bd.; pres. Polish Nat. Alliance, 1967—, Alliance Printers & Pubs. Inc. Pres., Polish Am. Congress, 1970—, U.S. alt. del. UN, 25th Assembly, 1970; bd. dirs. pres. Vol. Action Com., 1968—, Chgo. Council Fgn. Relations, 1969—; vice-chmn. bd. trustees Alliance Coll. Served to maj. AUS, 1941-45. Mem. Chgo., Fed., Am., Ill. bar assns., Am. Judicature Soc., Am. Acad. Matrimonial Lawyers, Amvets (past comdr.), Am. Legion, Polish Legion Am. Vets., Advs. Soc. (pres. 1964). Club: Lions. Home: 3813 Medford Circle Northbrook IL 60062 Office: 6100 N Cicero Ave Chicago IL 60646

MAZUR, BOLESLAW, dental educator; b. Struga, Poland, Oct. 19, 1918; s. Ignacy and Rozalia (Wieczorek) M.; came to U.S., 1949, naturalized, 1956; student U. Hamburg, 1946, 47-49; D.D.S., U. Ill., 1956, M.S., 1961, certificate in fixed partial prosthodontics, 1961; m. Krystyna Pellech, Apr. 30, 1974. Prisoner of war in Germany, 1939-45; instr. U. Ill. Coll. Dentistry, Chgo., 1956-61, asso. prof., 1964-70; asst. prof. W.Va. U. Sch. Dentistry, Morgantown, W.Va., 1961-63; prof. Sch. Dentistry, Loyola U., Chgo., 1970—; lectr. to various profl. groups and orgns. Mem. Am. Dental Assn., Am. Acad. Crown and Bridge Prosthodontics, Am. Equilibration Soc., Fedn. Dentaire Internationale, AAAS, N.Y. Acad. Scis. Collaborator: Current Clinical Dental Terminology, 1974. Home: 67 Cherry St Roselle IL 60172 Office: 55 E Washington St Chicago IL 60602

MAZUR, CONRAD FRANCIS, chem. co. exec.; b. Milw., Nov. 7, 1934; s. Conrad Frank and Blanche (Kubacki) Mazurkiewicz; B.S., U. Wis., 1957; m. Judith Norene Froberg, June 14, 1956; children—Cynthia, Michael, Steven, Douglas, Gregory. Engr. Oilgear Co., Milw., 1957-58; engr. Consol. Thermoplastics, Chippewa Falls, Wis., 1959-63, mgr., 1964-67; sr. product specialist Rexall Chem. Co., Odessa, Tex., 1963-64; mgr. Amoco Chems. Corp., Chippewa Falls, 1967-71, gen. mgr. mfg., Chgo., 1971-75, ops. mgr. custom div., St. Paul, 1975—. Active Boy Scouts Am. Bd. dirs. United Fund, 1967-70. Served to lt. AUS, 1957. Mem. Soc. Plastics Engrs., Chippewa Falls Jr. C. of C. (pres. 1963, recipient Distinguished Service award 1970), C. of C. (v.p. 1969-71). Elk (exalted ruler 1966-67). Home: 28 Peninsula Rd Dellwood MN 55110 Office: 45 E Maryland Ave St Paul MN 55117

MAZZAFERRI, ERNEST LOUIS, endocrinologist; b. Cleve., Sept. 27, 1936; s. Joseph and Nettie Marie M.; B.S. cum laude, John Carrol U., 1958; M.D., Ohio State U., 1962; m. Florence Mildred Marolt, Nov. 23, 1957; children—Patricia, Michael, Sharon, Ernest. Intern, Ohio State U., Columbus, 1962-63, resident, 1967-68, asst. prof. medicine, from 1970, asso. prof., 1972-76, prof., 1976—, dir. div. endocrinology and metabolism, 1974-78; prof., chmn. dept. medicine Coll. Medicine, U. Nev., Reno, 1978—. Served to lt. col. USAF, 1964-72. Diplomate Am. Bd. Internal Medicine, Am. Bd. Endocrinology Metabolism. Fellow A.C.P.; mem. Endocrine Soc., Am. Diabetes Assn., Am. Fedn. Clin. Research, Am. Thyroid Assn., Central Soc. for Clin. Research, Alpha Omega Alpha. Republican. Roman Catholic. Author: Endocrinology Case Studies, 1971; editor: Endocrinology, A Review of Clinical Endocrinology, 1974. Home: 4266 Mumford Dr Columbus OH 43220 Office: 410 W 10th Ave Columbus OH 43210

MAZZUCA, LOIS CAMILLE, coll. cons.; b. Chgo., May 10, 1941; d. Lewis D. and Camille Carol (Parrillo) Mazzuca; B.A., Marycrest Coll., 1963; M.A., Northeastern Ill. State U., 1970. Tchr., counselor Notre Dame High Sch., Chgo., 1963-68; asso. dir. admissions Marycrest Coll., Davenport, Ia., 1968-70; counselor Prospect High Sch., Mt. Prospect, Ill., 1970-71; coll. cons. High Sch. Dist. 214, Rolling Meadows, Ill., 1971—. Vice chmn. Wood Dale Planning Bd., 1972-77; chmn. Wood Dale Bicentennial Commn., 1976; trustee, Addison Twp., 1977—; mem. Wood Dale Youth Commn., 1973. Recipient Youth Achievement award, Chgo. Daily News, 1959; Vol. Service award, Dept. Mental Health, State of Ill., 1965-68; Distinguished Service award Ill. Bicentennial Commn., 1976. Mem. Nat., Ill. assns. coll. admissions counselors, Am., Ill. personnel and guidance assns. Republican. Roman Catholic. Club: Chgo. Council on Fgn. Relations. Contbr. articles in field to profl. jours. Home: 288 Charmille Ln Wood Dale IL 60191 Office: 2901 Central Rd Rolling Meadows IL 60008

MC ADOW, JERRY E., lawyer; b. Lima, Ohio, Aug. 2, 1941; s. Emit Walter and Kathryn D. (Painter) McA.; B.A., U. Wis., 1964; J.D., U. Denver, 1967; m. Carol M. McLean, Aug. 10, 1963; children—Kathryn Jo, Gary D. Admitted to Wis. bar, 1967; asso. firm Isaksen, Werner, Lathrop & Heaney, Madison, 1967-70, partner, 1970—. Mem. budget com. United Way of Dane County, 1970—. Mem. Am., Wis., Dane County bar assns. Rotarian (pres. 1973-74, dir. 1971-75). Home: 5518 Dorsett Dr Madison WI 53711 Office: 122 W Washington Ave Madison WI 53703

MC ALEECE, DONALD JOHN, educator; b. Detroit, May 26, 1918; s. Joseph Patrick and Kathryn (DeLeeuw) McA.; B.S., Purdue U., 1952; M.A., Ball State U., 1968; m. Margaret Ann Mull, Nov. 25, 1954; children—Stephen Donald, Michele Denise. With Gen. Electric Co., Ft. Wayne, Ind., 1936-66; faculty Purdue U., Ft. Wayne Campus, 1966—, prof. dept. mech. engring. tech., 1966—; design engr. advanced safety research Ford Motor Co., Dearborn, Mich., 1972. Job placement cons. Outreach Office, Nat. Alliance of Businessmen, Ft. Wayne, 1968; indsl. engr. cons. Am. Hoist & Derrick Co., Ft. Wayne, 1969; mech. and indsl. engr. cons. Franklin Electric Co., Ft. Wayne, Ind., 1970. Served with AUS, 1946-47. Recipient Ralph R. Teetor award Soc. Automotive Engrs., 1972. Ednl. Profl. Devel. Act Afro-Am. Studies grantee, 1971. Mem. Am. Soc. Engring. Edn., Am. Tech. Edn. Assn., Soc. Automotive Engrs. (Outstanding Faculty Advisor Service award 1974), Soc. Am. Mil. Engrs., ASME (chmn. program com. 1971-75), Am. Soc. Heating, Refrigeration and Air Conditioning Engrs. (mem. nat. engring. council profl. devel. accreditation team), United Comml. Travelers, Pi Tau Sigma. Baptist (deacon 1968-72). Mason (Shriner). Home: 4426 Dicke Rd Fort Wayne IN 46804

MC ALINDON, JAMES DANIEL, surgeon, hosp. adminstr., educator; b. Bay County, Mich., May 19, 1926; s. James Peter and Anna Mary (Potla) McA.; B.S., U. Detroit, 1950; M.D., Loyola U., Chgo., 1954; m. Mary Naomi Solomon, Nov. 25, 1961; children—Robert, Donald, James, Peter, Mary. Resident in surgery Georgetown U. Hosp., Washington, 1955-59; dir. med. edn. St. Joseph Hosp., Flint, Mich., 1963-67; chmn. dept. surgery McLaren Gen. Hosp., Flint, 1969—; clin. asst. prof. surgery Mich. State Med. Sch., East Lansing, 1970 and after, subsequently asso. clin. prof. surgery. Served with USN, 1944-46. Diplomate Am. Bd. Surgery. Fellow A.C.S. Contbr. article to med. jours. Home: 1423 Oxyoke Dr Flint MI 48504

MC ALLISTER, CHARLES JOSEPH, educator, architect; b. Chgo., Nov. 1, 1927; s. Robert Edward and Edith (Imrie) McA.; B.Arch., U. Ill., 1953; M.S., Ill. Inst. Tech., 1966; m. Elsie Viola Wilson, Sept. 1, 1951; children—Janis, Nancy, Robert, Kent. Archtl. draftsman, firm Mielke & Smith, Architects & Engrs., Chgo., 1953-55; job capt., Perkins & Will, Architects & Engrs., Chgo., 1955-57; project architect firm Bachman & Bertram, Architects & Engrs., Hammond, Ind., 1957-62; asso. prof. archtl. tech., dept. constrn. tech., Purdue U. at Hammond, 1962-70, head dept., 1970—; archtl., city planning cons., 1962—. Pres. Munster (Ind.) Community Swim Assn., 1975-77. Served with USNR, 1946-47. Mem. AIA. Baptist. Home: 1410 Tulip Ln Munster IN 46321 Office: 2233 171st St Hammond IN 46323

MC ALLISTER, LESTER GROVER, JR., clergyman, educator; b. Little Rock, Oct. 12, 1919; s. Lester Grover and Clara Edna (Brown) McA.; A.B., Transylvania Coll., 1941; B.D., Lexington Theol. Sem., 1944; postgrad. U. Cal. Berkeley, 1949-50; Th.D., Pacific Sch. Religion, 1953. Ordained to ministry Disciples of Christ Ch., 1944; nat. dir. Youth Work, Disciples of Christ, Indpls., 1945-50; asso. minister Univ. Christian Ch., Berkeley, 1950-53; asso. prof. religion Bethany (W.Va.) Coll., 1953-55, provost, prof., 1955-62; prof. modern ch. history Christian Theol. Sem., Indpls., 1962—; vis. prof. Overdale Coll., Birmingham, Eng., 1960; guest preacher Renfield St. Ch. of Scotland, Glasgow, 1962. Del. Western Hemispheric Youth Conf., Cuba, 1946, World Youth Conf., Oslo, Norway, 1947; mem. World Christian Youth Com., Lund, Sweden, 1947; chmn. youth, div. Christian edn. Nat. Council Chs., 1948-51; exec. com. World Conv. Chs. Christ, 1965-70. Named Distinguished Alumnus, U. Ark., Little Rock, 1964. Mem. AAUP, Am. Soc. Church History, Theta Phi, Pi Kappa Alpha. Clubs: Authors' (London, Eng.); Royal Scottish Automobile (Glasgow); Indianapolis Athletic, Highland Golf and Country (Indpls.). Author: Thomas Campbell: Man of the Book, 1954; Life of Z.T. Sweeney, 1967; Alexander Campbell at Glasgow U., 1970; co-author Journey on Faith: A History of the Christian Church-Disciples of Christ, 1975. Home: 5937 Deerwood Ct Indianapolis IN 46254

MC ALPIN, JOSEPH MARK, dentist; b. Marion Ill., Sept. 10, 1924; s. Mark L. and Eliza (McLaren) McA.; D.D.S., Washington U., St. Louis, 1952; m. Suzanne Cochran, June 25, 1947; children—Carol Cochran, Laura Elizabeth. Pvt. practice dentistry, Marion, 1953—. Co-chmn. Marion United Fund Drive, 1969, also bd. dirs., pres., 1974; chmn. Community Heart Fund Drive, 1956; chmn. finance campaign Pyramid dist. Boy Scouts Am., 1958. Bd. dirs. Marion Civic Center, 1974-75, chmn. patron series, 1976-78. Served with AUS, 1943-46. Mem. Am. Dental Assn., Ill., So. Ill. Dist. dental socs., Little Egypt Dental Research Group (pres. 1966-67). Methodist (chmn. ofcl. bd. 1965-67, com. on finance 1969-70, com. on personnel 1969-70, com. on nominations 1971, stewardship com. 1974, trustee 1970-71, pres. United Meth. men 1971, chmn. pastor-parish relations com. 1973, chmn. com. on fin. 1978). Elk, Rotarian (pres. Marion 1961-62). Home: 411 E Everett St Marion IL 62959 Office: 202 W Main St Marion IL 62959

MC ANDREW, GORDON LESLIE, supt. schs.; b. Oakland, Calif., Aug. 29, 1926; s. James and Margaret (Watts) McA.; A.B., U. Calif. at Berkeley, 1948, M.A., 1952, Ph.D., 1962; m. Doris McGarry, Sept. 12, 1948; children—Kevin Regan. Tchr. and sch. adminstr., Oakland, 1949-64; dir. N.C. Advancement Sch. and Learning Inst., 1964-68; supt. Gary (Ind.) Pub. Schs., 1968—; cons. Office Econ. Opportunity, 1965—, U.S. Office of Edn., 1965—. Served with USAAF, 1944-45. Home: 6225 Forest St Gary IN 46403 Office: 620 E 10th St Gary IN 46402

MC ANDREWS, JAMES PATRICK, lawyer; b. Carbondale, Pa., May 11, 1929; s. James Patrick and Mary Agnes (Walsh) McA.; B.S. in Accounting, U. Scranton, 1949; LL.B., Fordham U., 1952; grad. Real Estate Inst., N.Y. U., 1972; m. Mona Marie Steinke, Sept. 4, 1954; children—James P., George A., Catherine M., Joseph M., Michael P., Anne Marie, Edward R., Daniel P. Admitted to N.Y. State bar, 1953, Ohio bar, 1974; asso. James F. McManus, Levittown, N.Y., 1955; atty. Emigrant Savs. Bank, N.Y.C., 1955-68; counsel Tchrs. Ins. and Annuity Assn., N.Y.C., 1968-73; asso. firm Thompson, Hine & Flory, Cleve., 1973-74, partner, 1974—: mem. law faculty Am. Inst. Banking, 1968-69. Served with JAGC, USAF, 1972-74. Mem. Am., Ohio, Cleve. bar assns., Am. Land Title Assn., Urban Land Inst., Internat. Council Shopping Centers, Am. Legion. Roman Catholic. Contbr. articles to profl. publs. Home: 2971 Litchfield Rd Shaker Heights OH 44120 Office: 1100 Nat City Bank Bldg Cleveland OH 44114

MC ANDREWS, JEROME FRANCIS, chiropractor; b. Davenport, Ia., Apr. 7, 1933; s. Patrick William and Ruth Louise (Pellegrin) McA.; D.Chiropractic, Palmer Coll. Chiropractic, 1956; student U. Ia., 1958-61; m. Joan Dorothy Utroska, Oct. 25, 1958; children—Patrick William, Jennifer Anne, Stephanie Joan, Andria Jeanne, Laura Lynn, Kathleen Sue. Dir. clinic, instr. Palmer Coll. Chriopractic, 1961-63, chmn. chiropractic scis. div., 1964-66, admissions dir., asst. to pres., 1967-70; individual practice chiropractic, Fulton, Ill., 1970—; exec. dir. Found. Advancement Chiropractic Tenets and Sci. Served with USNR, 1953-55. Fellow Internat. Chiropractors Assn. (exec. dir. 1971—); mem. Am. Soc. Assn. Execs., AAAS, C. of C. Republican. Roman Catholic. Home: Rural Route 3 Davenport IA 52804 Office: 741 Brady St Davenport IA 52803

MCAULEY, PATRICK CAMPBELL, psychologist; b. Evanston, Ill., Apr. 9, 1944; s. Robert Francis and Ruth Isabell (Campbell) McA.; B.A., DePaul U., Chgo., 1965; M.A., Loyola U., Chgo., 1970, Ph.D., 1970. Grad. asst. Loyola U., Chgo., 1968-70; substitute tchr. high sch. math., Chgo., 1971-73; dir. research Nat. Council on Drug Abuse, 1972-74; psychometrician RPR, Inc., Chgo., 1973; research cons., psychologist various orgns., pvt. industries, and state offices, including State of Ill., 1974, also U.S. Virgin Islands; cons. Edgewater Uptown Community Mental Health Council. Served with USNR, 1965-66; Vietnam. Mem. Am. Psychol. Assn., Math. Assn. Am., Soc. Indsl. Applied Maths., AAAS, Met. Math Club, Internat. Personnel Mgmt. Assn., Psi Chi. Contbr. articles to profl. jours. Home and Office: 4278 N Hazel Chicago IL 60613

MC BAIN, RUSSELL LYLE, govt. ofcl.; b. Melville, N.D., July 31, 1925; s. George and Hattie (Mellon) McB.; B.S., Jamestown Coll., 1950; M.Ed., U. N.D., 1956; m. Violette Bradburn, June 7, 1947, (dec. 1967); children—Scott Alan, Paula Rae; m. 2d, Delores J. Hell, Feb. 9, 1974; children—Duane Hell, Kathy Hell, Kristy Hell. Tchr., various schs., 1953-59; customs insp., port dir. customs U.S. Customs Service, Walhalla, N.D., 1959—. Mem. Walhalla Sch. Bd., 1967—, pres., 1973—. Served with USNR, 1944-46. Decorated Purple Heart medal. Named Outstanding Handicapped Citizen, Walhalla, N.D., 1972. Mem. Am. Legion (comdr. 1969-70), D.A.V. Presbyterian (elder 1954—, moderator 1964-65, stated clk. 1968-72). Clubs: Masons, Shrine, Elks, Walhalla Country (sec.-treas. 1968-76). Home: Walhalla ND 58282 Office: Box 146 Rural Route 1 Walhalla ND 58282

MC BEAN, ROBERT PARKER, civil engring. cons.; b. Chilliwack, B.C., Can., May 6, 1939; s. Wilfred Parker and Mabel Irene (Gauthier) McB.; B.Applied Sci., U. B.C., 1962, M.A. Sc., 1965; Ph.D., Stanford U., 1968; m. Marilyn Elizabeth Cumming, June 30, 1962; children—Christine, Kenneth, Scott. Structural engr. H.A. Simons Ltd., cons. engrs., Vancouver, B.C., 1962-63; structural engr. Phillips, Barratt & Partners, cons. engrs., Vancouver, 1964; research engr. Hooley Engring. Ltd., cons. engrs., Vancouver, 1965, John A. Blume & Assos., cons. engrs., San Francisco, 1966; instr. civil engring. Stanford U., asst. prof. civil engring. U. Mo., Columbia, 1968-71, asso. prof., 1971-74; head structural analysis group Black & Veatch, cons. engrs., Kansas City, Mo., 1974—. Recipient Faculty/Alumni gold medal award U. Mo., 1972, outstanding tchr. engring. award U. Mo., 1971. Mem. ASCE, Nat., Mo. (chmn. profl. engrs. in edn. 1974) socs. profl. engrs., Sigma Xi. Home: 10330 Russell St Overland Park KS 66212 Office: 1500 Meadowlake Pkwy Kansas City MO 64114

MC BRIDE, LLOYD MERRILL, lawyer; b. Corydon, Iowa, July 20, 1908; s. Ernest Eugene and Jeannie (Randolph) McB.; A.B., Carleton Coll., Northfield, Minn., 1930; student Harvard U., 1931-32; J.D., Northwestern U., 1934; m. Alice Rowland, June 8, 1935; children—Patricia Ann, Barbara Jean. Admitted to Ill. bar, 1934, since practiced in Chgo.; with firm Stearns & Jones, 1934-41, partner in successor firm Stearns & McBride, 1941-43, McBride & Baker, 1943-58, McBride, Baker, Wienke & Schlosser, 1958—; dir. Morton-Norwich Products, Inc.; sec., dir. Stenographic Machines, Inc., Morton Chem. of Can., Ltd., Bayou Corp., Vermilion Corp.; v.p., dir. Bornquist, Inc., Meric, Inc.; dir. Essex Terminal Ry. Co.; dir. Canadian Salt Co. Ltd., Canadian Rock Salt Co. Ltd., Morton Terminal, Ltd., Stenning Industries, Inc., Wallace Bus. Forms, Inc., Federick Ryder Co. Republican. Clubs: Tower, Mid-Am., Racquet (Chgo.). Home: 1550 N State Pkwy Chicago IL 60610 Office: 110 N Wacker Dr Chicago IL 60606

MC BRIDE, NANCY ALLYSON, counselor; b. Lakewood, Ohio, June 15, 1952; d. Harold Jackson and Mary Alice (Inman) McBride; student U. N.C., Greensboro, 1970; Ind. U., 1971; B.A. magna cum laude, Oakland U., 1977. Office mgr. alternative lifestyles YMCA North Oakland County, Pontiac, Mich., 1975, counselor, office mgr.

creative outlooks, 1977—; program dir., corp. sec. Alternative Lifestyles, Inc., Pontiac, 1975-77. Mem. Am., Mich. personnel and guidance assns., Assn. for Humanistic Edn. and Devel., Mich. Assn. for Agy. Counselors, Mich. Alcohol and Addiction Assn., Mich. League for Human Services, Oakland Area Counselors Assn. Contbr. poetry, research, articles in field. Home: 2072 Rhine Rd West Bloomfield MI 48033 Office: 131 University Dr Pontiac MI 48058

MC BRIDE, ROBERT, ELLSWORTH, mgmt. cons.; b. Ridgely, Md., Apr. 13, 1927; s. Henry Ellsworth and Mabel Elizabeth (Barnes) McB.; B.S., Mass. Inst. Tech., 1947; children—Jann Ellyn, Nancy Jayne, Robert Arnold. With sales, mktg. Gen. Electric Co., Mass., N.Y., 1947-63; v.p. mktg. Colt Firearms, Hartford, Conn., 1963-64; group v.p. Applied Power Industries, Milw., 1964-72; pres. Remac Assos., Ltd., Milw., 1972—. Mem. IEEE, Sales and Mktg. Execs., Tau Beta Pi. Republican. Congregationalist. Club: Masons. Home and Office: 1070 Pilgrim Pkwy Elm Grove WI 53122

MCBRIDE, ROBERT LAWRENCE, judge; b. Dayton, Ohio, Mar. 11, 1910; s. Mark S. and Mary C. (Hemler) McB.; B.A., U. Dayton, 1932, LL.B., J.D., 1934; m. Evelyn K. Lewis, Feb. 22, 1938 (dec. Dec. 1960); children—Robert Lewis, Andrew; m. 2d, Noreen O'Leary, Oct. 14, 1961. Admitted to Ohio bar, 1934; pvt. practice as asso. McConnaughey, Shea, Demann & McConnaughey, 1934-43; instr. bus. law U. Dayton, 1942-43; judge Dayton Municipal Ct., 1946-53; judge Common Pleas Court of Montgomery County, Ohio, 1953-75, presiding judge, 1972-75; judge Ct. of Appeals, 2d dist., Dayton, 1975—. Served with USNR, 1943-46. Mem. Am., Ohio, Dayton bar assns., Ohio Common Pleas Judges' Assn. (pres. 1961-62), Ohio Judicial Conf. (chmn. 1964-66), Ohio Municipal Judges' Assn. (v.p., 1952-53). Author: The Art of Instructing the Jury, 1969; also articles. Office: Courts Bldg Dayton OH 45402

MC BRIDE, WILLIAM LEON, philosopher, educator; b. N.Y.C., Jan. 19, 1938: s. William Joseph and Irene May (Choffin) McB.; A.B., Georgetown U., 1959; postgrad. U. Lille, 1959-60; M.A., Yale U., 1962, Ph.D., 1964; m. Mary Angela Barron, June 12, 1965; children—Catherine, Kara. Instr. philosophy Yale U., 1964-66, asst. prof., 1966-70, asso. prof., 1970-73; asso. prof. philosophy Purdue U., West Lafayette, Ind., 1973-76, prof., 1976—. Pres. Highland Sch. PTA, Lafayette, Ind., 1977—. Fulbright scholar, 1959-60; Woodrow Wilson fellow, 1960-61; Social Sci. Research Council fellow, 1963-64; Morse fellow, 1968-69; David Ross research grantee, 1974. Mem. Am. Philos. Assn., AAUP, Am. Soc. Polit. and Legal Philosophy, Soc. Phenomenology and Existential Philosophy (exec. co-sec. 1977—), Assn. Amis Romain Rolland. Author: Fundamental Change in Law and Society: Hart and Sartre on Revolution, 1970; The Philosophy of Marx, 1977. Home: 744 Cherokee Ave Lafayette IN 47905 Office: Dept Philosophy Purdue U West Lafayette IN 47907

MC BURNEY, GEORGE WILLIAM, lawyer; b. Ames, Iowa, Feb. 17, 1926; s. James William and Elfie Hazel (Jones) McB.; B.A., State U. Iowa, 1950; J.D., 1953; m. Georgianna Edwards, Aug. 28, 1949; children—Hollis Lynn, Jana Lee, John Edwards. Admitted to Iowa bar, 1953, Ill. bar, 1954; practiced in Chgo., 1953—; with firm Sidley & Austin and predecessor firm, 1953—, partner, 1964—. Mem. Chgo. Crime Commn., 1966—. Trustee, pres. Old Peoples Home City Chgo.; trustee, counsel The Georgian, Evanston, Ill. Served with inf., AUS, 1944-46. Mem. Am. Judicature Soc., Am., Ill., Chgo. bar assns., Law Club Chgo., Legal Club Chgo., Bar Assn. 7th Fed. Circuit, Am. Arbitration Assn. (panel), Nat. Coll. Edn. (bd. assos.), Phi Kappa Psi. Omicron Delta Kappa, Delta Sigma Rho, Phi Delta Phi. Republican. Presbyterian. Clubs: Union League, Mid-Day, Monroe (Chgo.); Westmoreland Country (Wilmette). Editor: Iowa Law Rev., 1952-53. Home: 1110 13th St Wilmette IL 60091 Office: One First Nat Plaza Chicago IL 60603

MC CABE, JOHN CHARLES, III, educator, writer; b. Detroit, Nov. 14, 1920; s. Charles John and Rosalie (Dropiewski) McC.; Ph.B., U. Detroit, 1947, M.F.A. in Theatre, Fordham U., 1948; Ph.D. in English Lit., U. Birmingham (Eng.), 1954; m. Vija Valda Zarina, Oct. 17, 1958; children—Linard Peter, Sean Cahal and Deirdre Rose (twins). Profl. actor appearing mainly in summer theatres, 1938—; producer-dir. Milford (Pa.) Playhouse, summers 1948-53; producer N.Y. U. Summer Theatre, Sterling Forest, 1963-65; instr. speech and theatre Wayne U., 1948-51, Coll. City N.Y., 1955; mem. faculty N.Y. U., 1956-68, prof. dramatic art, chmn. dept., 1962-66, prof. ednl. theatre, chmn. dept., 1966-68; chmn. dept. drama and theatre arts Mackinac Coll., Mackinac Island, Mich., 1968-70; author in residence Lake Superior State Coll., Sault Ste. Marie, Mich., 1970—; producer-dir. Mackinac Coll. Summer Theatre, 1968-70; founder The Sons of the Desert, group devoted to works Laurel and Hardy, 1963. Served with USAAF, 1943-45; ETO. Mem. Shakespeare Assn. Am., Actors Equity Assn., Cath. Actors Guild Am., Baker St. Irregulars, Players Club (N.Y.C.). Author: Mr. Laurel and Mr. Hardy, 1962, rev. edit. 1966; George M. Cohan: The Man Who Owned Broadway, 1973; The Comedy World of Stan Laurel, 1975; Laurel and Hardy, 1975; (with G.B. Harrison) Proclaiming the Word, 1976. Home: Box 363 Mackinac Island MI 49757 Office: Lake Superior State Coll Saulte Ste Marie MI 49783

MC CABE, JOSEPH E., coll. pres. emeritus; b. Bridgeville, Pa., Apr. 23, 1912; s. John S. and Rebecca (Fife) McC.; B.A., Muskingum Coll., 1937, D.D., 1957; M.A., Ohio State U., 1940; B.Th., Princeton Theol. Sem., 1943, Th.M., 1947; Ph.D., U. Edinburgh (Scotland), 1951; LL.D., Monmouth Coll., 1959; L.H.D., Waynesburg (Pa.) Coll., 1965; Litt.D., Coll. St. Thomas, 1966; m. Margaret V. Welch, Apr 1, 1944; children—Jonathan B., Alice E. Asst. dean of men Muskingum Coll., 1937-38, field rep., admissions counsellor, 1938-39; grad. counsellor to freshmen Ohio State U., 1939-40; ordained to ministry Presbyn. Ch., 1943; minister 1st Presbyn. Ch., Lambertville, N.J., 1946-53; critic student preaching Princeton Theol. Sem., 1950-56; sr. minister Presbyn. Ch. of Chestnut Hill, Phila., 1953-58; pres. Coe Coll., Cedar Rapids, Iowa, 1958-70, chancellor, 1970-77, pres. emeritus, 1977—; moderator Presbytery New Brunswick, Presbyn. Ch. U.S.A., 1953; mem. com. consolidations Presbyn. Ch. U.S.A. and United Presbyn. Ch. N.Am., 1957—; mem. Commn. on Ecumenical Mission and Relations. Mem. alumni council Muskingum Coll.; trustee Presbytery Phila.; chmn. bd. trustees Beirut Coll. Women. Served as chaplain USNR, 1943-46. Mem. Presbyn. Coll. Union (pres.), Asso. Colls. Midwest (chmn. bd.), Navy League (chaplain), Res. Officers Assn. Iowa (chaplain). Club: Rotary. Author: The Power of God in a Parish Program, 1959; Service Book for Ministers; Challenging Careers in the Church, 1966; Your First Year at College: Letters to a College Freshman, 1967; Reason, Faith and Love, 1971; Better Preaching and Better Pastoring, 1973; contbr. to religious publs. Home: 163 Thompson Dr SE Cedar Rapids IA 52403

MC CAFFREE, MARY KATHERINE, physician; b. Schell City, Mo., Feb. 24, 1933; d. William Taylor and Katherine Peterson (Grinstead) McCaffree; student Cottey Coll., 1951-52; A.B., U. Mo., 1956, M.D., 1963. Intern, St. Luke's Hosp., St. Louis, 1963-64; resident internal medicine U. Mo. Med. Sch., Columbia, 1964-67; practice medicine specializing in internal medicine, St. Joseph, Mo., 1967-70, Jefferson City, Mo., 1971—; mem. staff St. Mary's Hosp., pres. staff, 1976; sec. hosp. staff Meml. Community Hosp., Jefferson City, 1975. Mem. advisory com. Jefferson City Sch. Practical Nursing, 1976-77; advisory bd. St. Mary's Hosp., Jefferson City, 1977. Mem. A.C.P., Am. Philat. Soc., Am., Mo. (vice-councilor 5th dist. 1977), So., Cole County, med. assns., Am. Soc. Internal Medicine, Am. Heart Assn., Kansas City S.W. Clin. Soc., U. Mo. Med. Alumni Assn. (bd. govs. 1977). Home: 903A Southwest Blvd Jefferson City MO 65101 Office: 1505 Southwest Blvd Jefferson City MO 65101

MC CAIN, JAMES ALLEN, state ofcl., former univ. pres.; b. York, S.C., Dec. 8, 1907; s. Frank Pickering and Julia (Allen) McC.; A.B., Wofford Coll., Spartanburg, S.C., 1926, LL.D., 1951; M.A., Duke U., 1929, Ed.D., Stanford U., 1948; D.Sc., Andhra Pradesh State U. (India), 1967; LL.D., Mont. State U., 1964, Colo. State U., 1965; m. Janet McLean Henry, Dec. 18, 1930; 1 dau., Sheila Janet. Asst. prof. English and journalism Colo State Univ., 1929-34, asst. to pres., 1934-39, dean student personnel, 1939-41, dean vocational edn. and guidance, dir. summer session, 1941-42; pres. Mont. State U., 1945-50; pres. Kans. State U., 1950-75; sec. human resources State of Kans., 1975—; dir. Dunlap & Assos., Inc., Stamford, Conn., Security Benefit Life Ins. Co., Topeka, Manhattan Mut. Life (Kan.), Helena br. Fed. Res. Bank Mpls., 1948-50; mem. adv. com. Export-Import Bank of Washington, 1961-70. Trustee Eisenhower Exchange Fellowships, 1960—; mem. Eisenhower Presidential Library; adv. bd. Kans. Office Econ. Analysis; bd. dirs. Kans. Research Found.; mem. Pres.'s Commn. Olympic Sports, 1975. Served from lt. (j.g.) to lt. comdr. USNR, 1942-45, officer-in-charge enlisted classification program USN. Eisenhower Internat. Exchange fellow, 1957; with ICA program India, 1960; cons. Iranian univs., 1969. Mem. Am. Psychol. Assn., Am. Council Edn. (commn. internat. edn. 1964-67), Mid-Am. State Univs. Assn. (pres. 1965-66), Kans. Acad. Sci., Phi Kappa Phi, Sigma Upsilon, Pi Delta Epsilon, Iota Lambda Sigma. Rotarian. Clubs: Kansas City; University (N.Y.C.). Co-author: Vocational Education, 1942. Author: Education in the Armed Services, 1945. Home: 1711 Sunny Slope Ln Manhattan KS 66502

MC CAIN, WINFIELD REYNOLDS, accountant; b. New Underwood, S.D., June 5, 1912; s. Merle A. and Mary Eliza (Reynolds) McC.; student S.D. Sch. Mines, 1930-31; m. Dorothy Agnes Read, July 4, 1936 (dec. Dec. 1961); children—John B., Charles E., Janet R. McCain Greer, Anne A. McCain Raga; m. 2d, Gratia Jones Engberg, Apr. 25, 1968. Asst. cashier First Nat. Bank Black Hills, Rapid City, S.D., 1933-47; acting sec. Rapid City (S.D.) C. of C., 1947-48; sales rep., traveling auditor Buckingham Transp. Co., Rapid City, 1948-60; pvt. practice as accountant, Rapid City, also Hill City, S.D., 1960—; owner, operator Circle S Motel, Hill City, 1970-76; credit mgr. Ray Dental Group, Rapid City, 1977—. Organizer, Rapid City Youth Center, 1943-47, Rapid City YMCA, 1948-51, Rapid City Community Chest, 1945-47; pres. S.D. Jr. C. of C., 1946-47. Recipient Distinguished Service award Rapid City Jr. C. of C., 1945. Mem. Hill City Motel Assn. (dir. 1971-75), Rapid City, Hill City (pres. 1972-74, dir. 1972—) chambers commerce, Black Hills Assn. Chambers Commerce (v.p. 1973—). Republican. Episcopalian. Clubs: Masons, Elks, Rotary. Address: Hill City SD 57745

MC CALL, ENNIS, lawyer; b. Wilmington, Del., June 16, 1912; s. Leroy Davidson and Gertrude Viola (Ennis) McC.; B.A., State U. Iowa, 1934, J.D., 1936; m. Jane Bradley, Jan. 9, 1942; children—Deborah, Bradley. Admitted to Iowa bar, 1936, since practiced in Newton; city atty., Newton, 1946-51; dir. Thombert Inc., Pyramid Inc., Gyroplane Air Transp. Inc. Pres., bd. dirs. Maytag Park; sec., bd. dirs. Newton Meml. Scholarship. Served to lt. col. USAAF, 1940-46, USAF, 1951-52. Decorated Bronze Star, Presdl. citation. Mem. Am., Iowa, Jasper County (pres. 1960) bar assns. Presbyterian (mem. session). Mason. Home: 1113 S 12th Ave W Newton IA 50208 Office: Newton Home Savs and Loan Bldg Newton IA 50208

MC CALL, JAMES LODGE, metallurgist; b. Morristown, N.J., June 3, 1935; s. George L. and Florence (Lodge) McC.; B.Metall. Engring., Ohio State U., 1958, M.S., 1961; m. Constance Cornett, Sept. 8, 1956; children—Jeffrey J., Elizabeth L. Mgr. materials characterization Battelle-Columbus (O.) Labs., 1957—. Mem. Internat. Metallographic Soc. (dir. 1970-74), Am. Soc. Metals, Ohio Soc. Profl. Engrs.; Electron Midrobeam Soc. Am., Electron Microscope Soc. Am., Central Ohio Metallographic Soc., Wire Assn. Author: Microstructural Analysis: Tools and Techniques, 1973; Specimen Preparation Techniques for Optical and Electron Microscopy, 1974; Microstructural Analysis, vol. 1, 1973, vol. 2, 1974, vol. 3, 1975. Editor Metallography, 1970-75, Sliplines, 1974-75. Home: 2144 Tremont St Columbus OH 43221 Office: 505 King Ave Columbus OH 43201

MC CALL, JOSEPH FRANCIS, musician, educator; b. Balt., Aug. 14, 1929; s. John Harold and Margaret Amanda Ruskell McC.; A.A., St. Mary's Sem., 1949; A.B., Loyola U., Balt., 1951; Mus. B., Peabody Conservatory Coll., 1954, Mus. M., 1956; postdoctoral studies Eastman Sch. Music, 1959-63, Johns Hopkins, 1955-56; m. Heide Ruth Schaefer, 1971. Faculty vocal music, chmn. dept. So. High Sch., Balt., 1955-59; dir. choir Mt. St. Agnes Coll., Balt., 1955-57; dir. Glee Club, Loyola Coll., Balt., 1957-59; faculty Valparaiso U. (Ind.), 1960—, asso. prof. voice, 1967—, chmn. concert program, 1971—; concert baritone. Mem. Gary Docesan Liturgical Comm., 1968-70; co-chmn. Met. Opera Contest, No. Ind. Dist., 1972—. Mem. Assn. Coll. and Univ. Community Arts Adminstrs., Phi Mu Alpha Sinfonia. Club: Cliff Dwellers (Chgo.). Composer masses, other works. Home: 3 Napoleon St Valparaiso IN 46383

MC CALL, KENNETH DEARDORFF, former govt. ofcl.; b. Culver, Kans., July 31, 1906; s. Ira Wilson and Hattie Elnora (Deardorff) McC.; B.S., Kans. Wesleyan U., 1928; B.S. in Civil Engring., Kans. State U., 1934; m. Vernal Faye Venter, Aug. 21, 1930; children—Kenneth Deardorff, Theresa (Mrs. Thomas Earl Beebe), Frederick. Tchr. high sch., Gaylord, Kans., 1928-29, Portales, N.Mex., 1929-32; irrigation engr. State of Kans., Garden City, 1934-41, Topeka, 1941-44; city engr., Garden City, Kans., 1944-45; chief hydrology, asst. area engr. Bur. Reclamation, Oklahoma City, 1945-54, Little Rock, 1952-53, engr. charge field studies for law suit, El Paso, 1954-56; sec. southwest field com. Office of the Sec., Dept. Interior, Tulsa, 1956, Muskogee, Okla., 1956-64, regional coordinator southwest region 1964-69. Registered profl. engr., Kans. Mem. ASCE, Sigma Tau. Presbyterian (elder 1948-52, 57-63, 70-76), Rotarian, Lion. Home: Box 65 Route 3 Osceola MO 64776

MC CALL, KENNETH DEARDORFF, JR., dentist; b. Manhattan, Kans., Nov. 30, 1932; s. Kenneth Deardorff and Vernal Faye (Venter) McC.; student Monmouth Coll., 1950-51, Tex. Western Coll., 1954-56, Okla. A. and M. U., 1956; D.D.S., St. Louis U., 1960; m. Madge Rose Boswell, June 29, 1958; children—Denise Rose, Brian Kenneth, Sharon Faye. Pvt. practice dentistry, Centralia, Ill., 1960—. Tchr. dept. dental assisting Kaskaskia Coll., 1970-73. Bd. dirs. ARC, 1962-63, United Fund, Centralia, Ill., 1965; pres. Centralia Little Theatre Group, 1973-74, 77. Served with AUS, 1952-54. Mem. Am. Dental Assn., Marion County Dental Soc., Centralia Jr. C. of C. (pres. 1963), Acad. Gen. Dentistry, Am. Soc. Clin. Hypnosis, Centralia Cultural Soc. (dir. 1976—), Tau Kappa Epsilon, Delta Sigma Delta. Presbyterian (elder 1963-73). Elk, Rotarian (dir. 1974-75, pres. 1977-78). Club: Meadow Woods Country (Centralia). Home: 22 Edgewood Lane N Centralia IL 62801 Office: 1501 E 2d St Centralia IL 62801

MC CALL, MAURICE HENDERSON, univ. ofcl.; b. Hampton, Va., Mar. 8, 1943; s. Morris O. and Bennie E. (Staton) McC.; B.F.A., Carnegie Inst. Tech., 1966, M.F.A., 1967; D.Mus. Arts (So. Edn. fellow), U. Cin., 1975; m. Ernestine Foreman, Aug. 28, 1976. Instr. music Hampton (Va.) Inst., 1967-70; lectr. Afro-Am. musical history U. Cin., 1971-75, acting asst. to dean, 1974-75, exec. asst. to dean, 1975-76; registrar Clermont Coll., Batavia, Ohio, 1976—. Dir. minority affairs radio sta. WGUC-FM, Cin., 1973-74; cons. on minority broadcasting Corp. for Pub. Broadcasting, Washington, 1974-75; guest lectr. Afro-Am. music St. Joseph's Coll., Rensselaer, Ind., summers 1974, 75, 76. Mem. adv. council Beamon-Hough Arts Fund, Cin., 1975—. Bd. dirs. Jewish Community Center Concert Series, Newport News, Va., 1969-70. Recipient Ganzel award for Music Composition Cin. Lit. and Mus. Soc., 1973. Mem. Assn. of Black Electronic Communicators (sec. 1974-75). Home: PO Box 20108 Cincinnati OH 45220 Office: 105 Clermont Coll Batavia OH 45103

MC CALL, ROBERT BOOTH, psychologist, educator; b. Milw., June 21, 1940; s. John I. and Blanche (Booth) M.; A.B., DePauw U., 1962; M.A., U. Ill., Ph.D. (USPHS fellow), 1965; m. Rozanne Allison, June 13, 1962; children—Darin Scott, Stacey Allison. NSF postdoctoral fellow Harvard U., Cambridge, Mass., 1965-66; asst. prof. U. N.C., Chapel Hill, 1966-68; chmn. dept. psychology, sr. scientist, chief perceptual-cognitive devel. sec. Fels Research Inst., Yellow Springs, Ohio, 1968-77; asso. prof. Antioch Coll., Yellow Springs, 1968-77; fellow Boys Town (Nebr.) Center for Study Youth Devel., 1977—. Recipient several NIH grants; Grant Found. grantee, 1972. Fellow Am. Psychol. Assn. (conv. program chairperson, exec. council div. 1976-77), AAAS, Soc. for Research in Child Devel., Internat. Soc. for Study of Behavioral Devel., Lambda Chi Alpha, Sigma Xi, Phi Beta Kappa. Author: Fundamental Statistics for Psychology, 1975; Intelligence and Heredity, 1975; 4 monographs; contbr. numerous articles to profl. jours.; editorial bd. Child Devel., 1975, Jour. Exptl. Child Psychology, 1976, Intelligence, 1976; reviewer jours. Office: Boys Town Center Study Youth Development Boys Town NE 68010

MC CALLUM, CHARLES EDWARD, lawyer; b. Memphis, Mar. 13, 1939; s. Edward Payson and India Raimelle (Musick) McC.; B.S., Mass. Inst. Tech., 1960; Fulbright scholar U. Manchester (Eng.), 1960-61; J.D., Vanderbilt U., 1964; m. JoAnn Hepinstall, Sept. 21, 1974; children—Florence Andrea, Printha Kyle, Chandler Ward Payson. Admitted to Mich. bar, 1964; asso. firm Warner, Norcross & Judd, Grand Rapids, Mich., 1964-69, partner, 1969—; rep. assemblyman State Bar of Mich., 1973—; lectr. continuing legal edn. programs. Chmn. Grand Rapids Transit Authority, 1976—, mem., 1972—; mem. council Nat. Municipal League, 1971—; trustee Grand Rapids Art Mus., 1976—, Butterworth Hosp., 1977—; ednl. counselor Mass. Inst. Tech., 1974—; chmn. Vanderbilt Law Sch. Devel. Com., 1976—. Woodrow Wilson fellow, 1960-61. Mem. Am., Tenn., Mich., Grand Rapids bar assns., Grand Rapids C. of C. (pres. 1975, bd. dirs. 1970-76), Order of Coif, Sigma Xi. Clubs: Kent Country, Grand Rapids Athletic, Peninsular. Home: 7519 Woodvale St SE Grand Rapids MI 49508 Office: 900 Old Kent Bldg 1 Vandenberg Center Grand Rapids MI 49503

MC CALLUM, CHARLES RAY, found. cons.; b. Orange, N.J., Apr. 15, 1922; s. Charles Ray and Esther Locke (Worden) McC.; B.A., Amherst Coll., 1947; postgrad. Yale Drama Sch., 1947-49; m. Patricia Ann Flynn, Sept. 25, 1954. Producer, At War with the Army, N.Y.C., 1949; mng. dir. Woolhouse Players, Woodstock, Vt., 1949-51, Rutland (Vt.) Players Club, 1949-51; spl. instr. Milw. Downer Coll., 1956-64; mng. dir. Milw. Repertory Theatre, 1964-74; cons. Found. for Extension and Devel. Am. Profl. Theatre, 1974—; mng. dir. Milw. Ballet Co., 1977—; guest lectr. arts adminstrn. Sch. Bus., U. Wis., Madison; adj. prof. Sch. Fine Arts, U. Wis.-Milw., 1975—; 2d v.p. Wis. Arts Council, 1970-73. Bd. dirs. Valley Studio, Wis. Mime Co., 1975—. Served with USAAF, 1943-46. Mem. Nat. Theatre Conf., State Hist. Soc. Wis. (bd. curators 1966—), Gambrinus Soc. (sec. 1968—). Club: University (Milw.). Home: 5070 Holy Hill Rd 167 Hubertus WI 53033 Office: PO Box 92516 Milwaukee WI 53202

MC CALLUM, DONALD ROY, lawyer; b. Appleton, Wis., July 21, 1930; s. Roy and Ann Cyrilla (Gerrits) McC.; B.S., U. Wis.-Madison, 1957, J.D., 1960; m. Diane M. Esch, Nov. 17, 1956; children—Douglas, Michael. Admitted to Wis. bar, 1960; practice law, Madison, 1960—; spl. asst. dist. atty. Dane County, Wis., 1959-61, dep. dist. atty., 1961-66; asso. law firm Jasper, Winner, Perina and Rouse, Madison, 1966-70; partner firm Winner, McCallum and Sautoff, Madison, 1970—; lectr. U. Wis.-Madison, 1965, 67, trial instr., 1973; chmn. CSC, Madison, 1972, mem. 1969-72. Chmn. Dane County Brotherhood Week, 1965. Bd. dirs. Dane County Legal Services Center, 1968—, sec., 1972—. Served with USMCR, 1950-52. Mem. Am., Dane County (chmn. criminal law com. 1969—) bar assns., State Bar Wis., Dane County Criminal Bar Assn. (pres. 1969), Am. Trial Lawyers Assn. Club: Nakoma Country (Madison). Home: Route 3 Box 232 Stoughton WI 53589 Office: 111 S Fairchild Madison WI 53703

MC CALLUM, WALTER EDWARD, dentist; b. Hendersonville, N.C., Mar. 13, 1936; s. Walter E. and Lucy Lillian (Jones) McC.; B.S., U. Pitts., 1958, D.D.S., 1962; m. Dolores Johnson, July 8, 1961; children—Robin, Todd. Pvt. practice dentistry, Waukegan, Ill., 1965—. Dental officer, candidate guidance officer U.S. Naval Acad., 1962—; clin. instr. dental assisting program Lake County Jr. Coll., also co-chmn. gen. adv. com. Mem. Big Brother program Genesee St. YMCA, Waukegan, Ill., 1969-70; mem. Senator Adlai Stevenson's selection bd. for nominations to U.S. Mil. Acad., 1972—. Bd. dirs. The Lake County Urban League, 1966—, pres., 1971-73; bd. dirs. Lake County Community Action Project, 1965-70, treas., 1967-70; bd. dirs. United Way of Lake County, 1973-75. Served with USNR, 1965—; now comdr. Res. Mem. Nat. Naval Officers Assn., Am. Dental Assn., Lincoln, Lake County, Chgo. dental socs., Waukegan Dental Study Group, NAACP (branch bd. dirs. 1969-70), Waukegan-North Chgo. C. of C. (mem. edn. com. 1970-71), Alpha Phi Alpha. Home: 594 Audubon Pl Highland Park IL 60035 Office: 1800 Grand Ave Waukegan IL 60085

MC CAMLEY, PETER JOHN, chemist; b. Wis. Rapids, Sept. 20, 1932; s. Howard J. and Jennie A. (Minta) M.; B.S., U. Wis., 1960; m. Theresa Sopa, Sept. 16, 1961; children—Maureen, Patrick, Mary. Research chemist Fiberite Corp., Winona, Minn., 1960- 72, mgr. research and devel., 1973-74, product mgr., 1975—. Served with U.S. Army, 1954-56. Mem. Am. Chem. Soc., Soc. Plastic Engrs. Roman Catholic. Clubs: Lions (past pres.), VFW, YMCA. Home: 1212 Birch Fountain City WI 54629 Office: 515 W 3d St Winona MN 55987

MC CANDLESS, BARBARA J., state ofcl.; b. Cottonwood Falls, Kans., Oct. 25, 1931; d. Arch G. and Grace (Kittle) McCandless; B.S., Kans. State U., 1953; M.S., Cornell U., 1959; postgrad. U. Minn., 1962-66, U. Calif. at Berkeley, 1971-72; m. Allyn O. Lockner, 1969. Home demonstration agt. Kans. State U., 1953-57; teaching asst. Cornell U., 1957-58, asst. extension home economist in mktg.,

1958-59; consumer mkgt. specialist, asst. prof. Oreg. State U., 1959-62; instr. home econs. U. Minn., St. Paul, 1962-63, research asst. agrl. econs., 1963-66; asst. prof. Coll. Home Econs., U.R.I., Kingston, 1966-67; asso. prof. family econs., head mgmt., housing equipment dept. Coll. Home Econs., S.D. State U., Brookings, 1967-73; asst. to sec. S.D. Dept. Commerce and Consumer Affairs, Pierre, 1973—. Mem. Nat. Council Occupational Licensing, dir., 1974-75, v.p., 1975—. Mem. Am. Mktg. Assn., Am. Council on Consumer Interests, League of Women Voters, S.D. Consumers League, Nat. Council Family Relations, Am. Agrl. Econs. Assn., Am. Home Econs. Assn., Kans. State U. Alumni Assn., Pi Gamma Mu. Club: Brookings Country. Research on profl. and occupational licensing bds. Address: 1100 E Church St Pierre SD 57501

MC CANDLESS, PERRY G., educator, historian; b. Lincoln, Mo., Dec. 9, 1917; s. William Albert and Edith Amelia (Graves) McC.; B.S., Central Mo. State Coll., 1941; M.A., So. Meth. U., 1948; Ph.D., U. Mo., Columbia, 1953; m. Opal Alpha Braland, July 5, 1947; children—Richard Lee, Anne Christine. Instr. history, Central Mo. State U., Warrensburg, Mo., 1948-49, asst. prof., 1949-50, 53-56, asso. prof., 1956-60, prof. 1960—, head Dept. History, 1965-69. Served with USAAF, 1941-45. Recipient award of Merit, Am. Assn. State and Local History, 1974. Mem. Organization of Am. Historians, State Historical Soc. Mo., Mo. State Tchrs. Assn. Democrat. Methodist. Author: Missouri: Then and Now, 1976; A History of Missouri, Vol. II, 1820-1860; contbr. numerous articles in field. Address: 609 Christopher St Warrensburg MO 64093

MC CANN, DAVID FRANCIS, lawyer; b. Dunlap, Iowa, Nov. 5, 1928; s. Edmund Ralph and Ethel Fern (Howe) McC.; B.S., Creighton U., 1951, LL.B., 1957; m. Ethel Mildred Dinneen, June 4, 1955; children—Mary C., David J., Terrance M., Stephen J., Kathleen E., Margaret R., Michael John. With Employers Mut. Casualty Co., Omaha, 1957-58, First Trust Co., Lincoln, Nebr., 1958-61; admitted to Iowa bar, 1958, Nebr. bar, 1957, U.S. Supreme Ct. bar, 1973; mem. firm. Dippel & McCann, Council Bluffs, Iowa, 1961—. Instr. real estate law Iowa Western Community Coll., 1970—; bd. dirs., sec. Petersen Radio Co., Council Bluffs, 1972—. Mem. Iowa Council Social Services, 1969-74, chmn., 1971-72; mem. Pottawattamie County Bd. Social Welfare, 1967-68, chmn., 1968. Bd. dirs. Mental Health Center, Council Bluffs. Served with AUS, 1951-54; lt. col. Army Res. Mem. Iowa, Nebr. bar assns., Res. Officers Assn., Am. Legion. Democrat. Roman Catholic. Clubs: Elks, Cosmopolitan. Home: 510 Forest Dr Council Bluffs IA 51501 Office: 403 First Nat Bank Bldg Council Bluffs IA 51501

MC CANN, JAMES I., audio-video prodn. services co. exec.; b. Mpls., Aug. 18, 1942; s. James Louis and Artemise Joan (Pohl) McC.; student St. Cloud State Coll., 1963-64; B.A., U. Minn., 1967; m. Felicia Jean Finsterwalder, Sept. 2, 1967; 1 son, Aaron James. Salesman, Scott Paper Co., Mpls., 1968-69, sr. salesman, 1969, midwest area mgr., 1969-70; pres., dir. mktg. Meta-Com, Inc., Mpls., 1970—. Served with USN, 1960-63. Office: Meta-Com Inc 707 W Broadway St Minneapolis MN 55411

MC CANN, MARY KATHLEEN, social worker; b. Milw., Dec. 4, 1944; d. Ray Thomas and Annetta Mary (O'Connor) McCann; B.A. in Psychology cum laude, U. Wis., Madison, 1967, M.S. in Counseling and Guidance, 1970. With United Calif. Bank, 1967-68; social worker Milw. County Dept. Pub. Welfare, 1971—. Active Milw. Jr. League. Mem. Am. Personnel and Guidance Assn., Phi Kappa Phi. Home: 2733 N Cramer St Milwaukee WI 53211 Office: 1220 W Vliet St Milwaukee WI 53205

MC CANN, WILLIAM ALBERT, real estate co. exec.; b. Chgo., Oct. 7, 1937; s. William Ambrose and Louise (Shover) McC.; student Thornton Jr. Coll., 1955-56; Asso. Bus. Adminstrn., Central Jr. Coll., 1958-64; m. Louise M. Stahmer, Sept. 17, 1966; children—Brian, Kathleen, Michael, Charmaine, William. Loan officer, appraiser Central Fed. Savs. & Loan, Cicero, Ill., 1958-60; field supr., appraiser Mid Am. Appraisal Co., Chgo., 1960-62; owner, pres. William A. McCann & Assos., Inc., Chgo., 1962—, treas., 1974—. Chmn. Ill. Savs. & Loan Commn., 1972-75. Mem. Am. Inst. Real Estate Appraisers, Soc. Real Estate Appraisers, Ill. Assn. Certified Real Estate Appraisers, Am. Right of Way Assn., Chgo. Real Estate Bd., Nat. Assn. Real Estate Bds., Mich. Ave. Club, Lambda Alpha (hon.). Office: 180 N LaSalle St Chicago IL 60601

MC CANN, WILLIAM DALE, printing co. exec.; b. Cin., Apr. 21, 1929; s. Bernard H. and Madeline Mary (Schilling) McC.; grad. pub. high sch., 1947; m. Louise Wilcox, May 6, 1950; children—Sheryl (Mrs. Chas. T. Sturgeon), Kelly Ann. Asst. procurement supr. Joseph E. Seagram & Sons, Lawrenceburg, Ind., 1947-51; credit mgr., dealer, store mgr. Firestone Tire & Rubber Co., Cin., 1951-57; co-pub., bus.-prodn. mgr. Register Printing Co., Inc., Lawrenceburg, Ind., 1957—. Mem. Hoosier State Press Assn., Suburban Newspapers of Am., Nat. Newspaper Assn., Ind. Democratic Editorial Assn., Lawrenceburg Merchants Assn. (pres. 1970-71). Lion, Kiwanian. Home: 401 Porter St Cleves OH 45002 Office: Register Printing Co Inc 126 W High St Lawrenceburg IN 47025

MC CANSE, JAMES EDSON, agrl. engr.; b. LaGrande, Oreg., July 2, 1929; s. Edson Rodney and Lydia Bertha (Sailer) McC.; B.S. in Agrl. Engring., Oreg. State U., 1951, M.A. in Agrl. Engring. Soils and Agrl. Econs., 1963; m. Lillian May Griffin, Sept. 11, 1947; children—Sandra McCanse Wood, James Rodney, Donald Edson, Richard Lee, Bruce Dean. Plant mgr. Simplot Soil Builders, Garfield, Wash., 1954-55; mgr. fertilizer dept. Columbia Farm Supply, Walla Walla, Wash., 1955-57; design engr. John Deere Indsl. Works, Moline, Ill., 1957-62; chief engr. Wood Bros. div. Hesston Corp., Oregon, Ill., 1962-67, 68—, Brady Corp., Des Moines, 1967-68; owner, propr. grain farm, Oregon. Mem. Am. Nat. Standards Inst. safety standards com.; past alderman, Moline. Mem. Am. Soc. Agrl. Engrs. (compaction study com.), Soc. Automotive Engrs., Aircraft Owners and Pilots Assn. Republican. Mem. Reorganized Ch. of Jesus Christ of Latter Day Saints (priest, pastor Rockford br. 1969). Clubs: Masons, Rotary (chpt. pres.). Patentee in field. Address: Route 3 PO Box 23 Oregon IL 61061

MC CARTEN, JOHN JAMES, lawyer; b. Marshalltown, Iowa, May 18, 1916; s. Frank T. and Agnes (Coulton) McC.; B.S.C., Creighton U., 1938, J.D., 1940; m. Maureen Riley, June 16, 1947; children—Jean, Paul, Mary, Riley. Admitted to Iowa bar, 1940, Minn. bar, 1940; practiced in Sioux City, Iowa, 1940-41; mem. firm Dell & McCarten (name later changed to McCarten & Tillitt), Alexandria, Minn., 1946—; pres. Alexandria Telephone Co., 1955-70, Alexandria Interurban Telephone Co., 1955-70, Alexandria Telephone Cable Co., 1965-70; pres. United Utilities Inc. (merger Alexandria Telephone Co., Alexandria Interurban Telephone Co., Alexandria Telephone Cable Co.), 1970—; E.F.I. Co., lakeshore devel., 1958—, Tentelino Enterprises, Inc., theatres; sec. Central Minn. TV Co. (KCMT TV-FM, Alexandria, Sta. KNMT-TV, Walker, Minn.), 1955, Minn. All-Channel Cable Vision Inc., 1964—, Alexandria; gen. mgr. Riley Co., S.D., 1950—; asst. sec. Bellanca Aircraft Corp., 1955-64, v.p., 1966—; Douglas County atty., 1951-66; chmn. lay sch. bd. St. Mary's Sch., 1965-68; chmn. lay adv. bd. Mercy Hosp., 1955-69; chmn. Douglas County Hosp. Bd. Served as lt. USAAF, 1941-46. Decorated D.F.C., Air Medal; Knight of St. Gregory. Mem. Am., Fed., Minn. (bd. govs.), Iowa, 7th Jud. Dist (pres. 1964-65) bar assns., Soc. Hosp. Attys., Am. Judicature Soc., Nat. Dist. Attys.' Assn., Am. Mgmt. Assn., Am. Inst. Mgmt., Am. Legion (past comdr.), V.F.W., Gamma Eta Gamma. Roman Catholic. Clubs: K.C. (4 deg.), Elk, Eagle, Kiwanis, Mpls. Athletic, Alexandria Country. Home: Blakes by the Lakes Alexandria MN 56308 Office: Alexandria Bank and Trust Bldg Alexandria MN 56308

MC CARTER, CHARLES CHASE, lawyer; b. Pleasanton, Kans., Mar. 17, 1926; s. Charles Nelson and Donna (Chase) McC.; B.A., Principia, 1950; J.D., Washburn U., 1953; LL.M., Yale, 1954; m. Clarice Blanchard, June 25, 1950; children—(Charles) Kevin, Cheryl Ann. Admitted to Kans. bar, 1953, U.S. Ct. Appeals D.C., 1957, U.S. Ct. Appeals 10th Circuit, 1961, U.S. Supreme Ct., 1962, Mo. bar, 1968; asst. atty. gen. Kans., Topeka, 1954-57; appellate counsel FCC, Washington, 1957-58; asso. firm Weigard, Curfman, Brainerd, Harris and Kaufman, Wichita, Kans., 1958-61; gen. counsel Kans. Corp. Commn., Topeka, 1961-63; partner McCarter, Frizzell & Wettig, Wichita, 1963-68; chmn. HRDAB, City of Wichita, 1967-68; partner McCarter & Badger, Wichita, 1968-73; pvt. practice law, St. Louis, 1968-76; partner firm McCarter & Greenley, St. Louis, 1976—; law lectr. Washburn Law Sch., Topeka, 1956-57; mem. govtl. adv. council Gulf Oil Corp., 1977—. Dir. Peace Haven Assn., Inc. Apptd. by gov. of Tex. to legal com. Interstate Oil Compact Commn., 1961. Served wtth USNR 1944-46. Mem. Am., Kans., Mo. bar assns., Am. Legion, VFW, Native Sons and Daus. Kans. (pres. 1957-58), Principia Dads Club (bd. dirs.), Kappa Sigma, Delta Theta Phi. Republican. Club: Clayton (St. Louis). Contbr. articles in field to profl. jours. Asso. editor Law Review, Washburn U. 1953; nat. Moot Ct. winner, 1953. Home: 23 Chapel Hill Estates St Louis MO 63131 Office: 230 S Bemiston St St Louis MO 63105

MC CARTHY, DANIEL JOSEPH, microscopic scientist, educator; b. Detroit, June 24, 1929; s. Daniel Joseph and Helen Amelia (Sorenson) McC.; Dr. Podiatric Medicine, Baldwin Wallace Coll., Ohio Coll. Podiatric Medicine, 1954; B. Chem. Engring., Grace Theol. Sem., 1962, M.R.E., 1963; M.A., Ind. U., 1963; postgrad. Mich. State U., 1967, U. Windsor (Ont.), 1970-74; m. LaRene Ann Clark, Sept. 16, 1950; children—Thomas J., Timothy J., Daniel W., David M. Practice podiatric medicine, Manistee, Mich., 1954-59, Elkhart, Ind., 1959-63, Bay City, Mich., 1963-74; prof. devel. and microscopic anatomy Ill. Coll. Podiatric Medicine, Chgo., 1975—, chmn. dept., 1975—. Served with USNR, 1945-54. Recipient Amour award in research, 1972, Stickel Gold award, 1973. Mem. Electron Microscopic Soc. Am., Ill., Am. podiatric assns., Am. Med. Writers Assn., Optimists. Spl. editor pathology Jour. Am. Podiatry Assn., 1972—. Researcher histology, histochemistry, electron microscopy human skin. Home: 1246 Charleston Rd Cherry Hill NJ 08034 Office: 1001 N Dearborn St Chicago IL 60610

MC CARTHY, DONALD RUSSELL, credit union ofcl.; b. Elliott, Iowa, Apr. 20, 1906; s. Emmet C. and Clara E. (Hartman) McC.; A.B., Simpson Coll., 1927; M.A., U. Iowa, 1938; m. Irja W. Hasu, June 25, 1948; children by previous marriage—Duane R., Darlagene. Tchr., coach Toledo (Iowa) High Sch., 1927-28, Indianola, Iowa, 1929-41, William Penn Coll., 1941-42, Lyons High Sch., Clinton, Iowa, 1942-45, Hinsdale Twp. High Sch., 1945-69; treas., mgr. South Dupage Schs. Credit Union, Downers Grove, Ill., 1955—. Mem. Ill. Credit Union League (past pres. Aurora chpt.), Ill. Council Credit Union Execs. (treas. 1977, mgr. of year 1975), Downers Grove C. of C., Simpson Coll. Alumni Assn., Edn. Credit Union Council U.S., N.E.A. (life), Am. Council Consumer Interests, U.S. Track Coaches Assn., Nat. Ret. Tchrs. Assn., Phi Delta Kappa, Lambda Chi Alpha. Republican. Club: Hinsdale Kiwanis (treas.). Home: 436 Norfolk Ave Clarendon Hills IL 60514 Office: 5202 Washington St Downers Grove IL 60515

MC CARTHY, EDWARD ALBERT, fed. judge; b. Chgo., July 25, 1918; s. Edward A. and Anne (Golden) McC.; student DePaul U., 1937, U. Ill., 1938-39; J.D., John Marshall Law Sch., 1942; m. Agnes Page, July 5, 1941; 1 son, Edward Albert. Admitted to Ill. bar, 1942, Wis. bar, 1975; trial atty. Hartford Accident & Indemnity Co., Chgo., 1946-51; trial atty., sr. partner Epton, McCarthy, Bohling & Druth, Chgo., 1951-73; U.S. adminstrv. law judge, 1973—. Cons. Ill. Fair Plan, 1970—. Pub. mem. Water Pollution and Water Resources Commn. Ill., 1969—; mem. Flossmoor (Ill.) Zoning Bd. Appeals, 1966-68. Served to capt. USAAF, 1942-46; PTO. Decorated Bronze Star. Mem. Am., Chgo. bar assns., Ill. Trial Lawyers Assn., Trial Lawyers Club Chgo., Mil. Order World Wars. K.C. Home: 2205 Oakenwald Dr Long Beach IN 46360 Office: 230 S Dearborn St Chicago IL 60604

MC CARTHY, JOHN FRANCIS, civil engr.; b. St. Louis, May 5, 1920; s. John William and Helen Mary (McGinnis) McC.; B.S. in Civil Engring., U. Mo., 1948, M.S. in Civil Engring., 1950; m. Mariclare Ann Mohan, June 30, 1956; children—John, Ann, Thomas, Kathi, Maureen. Instr. civil engring. U. Mo., 1948-51; chief structural engr. Fruin-Colnon Co., 1951-52; chief structural engr. W.R. Bendy Co., 1953-54; asst. prof. St. Louis U., 1955-58, asso. prof., 1958-60, prof., 1961-69, chmn. dept. civil engring., 1956-69; supt. Met. St. Louis Sewer Dist., 1969—, tech. coordinator, 1975—. Chmn. St. Louis County Bldg. Code Review Com., 1961—. Served with AUS, 1941-45. Recipient Award of Merit, Engrs. Club St. Louis, 1971. Fellow ASCE; mem. Nat., Mo. socs. profl. engrs., Fed., Mo. water pollution control assns., Soc. Am. Value Engrs. Roman Catholic. Author: Fluid Mechanics Handbook, 1968. Home: 11756 Long Leaf Circle St Louis MO 63141 Office: 9200 S Broadway St St Louis MO 63125

MC CARTHY, JOSEPH MICHAEL, pub. relations co. exec.; b. Cin., Dec. 31, 1935; s. Joseph Lawrence and Alma Elizabeth (Dempsey) McC.; M.A., Xavier U., 1963, B.S., 1957; m. Phyllis Lynn Hotopp, Apr. 19, 1958; children—Teresa, Brian, Patrick. Tchr. pub. schs., Cin., 1957-58, 60-61; pub. relations staff Mead, Johnson & Co., Evansville, Ind., 1961-62; sr. pub. relations asso. Eli Lilly & Co., Indpls., 1962-66; pub. relations communications dir. Pillsbury Co., Mpls., 1966-68; dir. communications and pub. relations Dayton Hudson Corp., nat. retailer, Mpls., 1968-71; exec. v.p., gen. mgr. Northstar Pub. Relations, Inc., Mpls., 1971-74, pres., after 1975; pres. McCarthy Communications, Inc., 1976—; pres. ATM, Inc., Mpls., 1971—; dir. several small corps. Vice pres. Home and Sch. Assn., Wayzata, Minn., 1968-70. Served with AUS, 1958-60, 61. Recipient Silver Anvil award Pub. Relations Soc. Am., 1970; grad. fellowship Xavier U., 1957-58. Mem. Pub. Relations Soc. Am. (dir. 1971), Acad. Polit. and Social Sci. Clubs: Minnesota Press, Minneapolis Athletic (Mpls.); Wayzata Country. Contbr. articles to profl. pubs. Home: 307 Margaret Circle Wayzata MN 55391 Office: 1500 S Lilac Dr Minneapolis MN 55416

MC CARTHY, LEO ALBERT, lawyer; b. Titonka, Iowa, Oct. 29, 1936; s. Donald Charles and Marion Anna (Haan) McC.; B.S. in Bus. Adminstrn., Creighton U., 1959, J.D., 1963; m. Joy Katherine Westendorf, Apr. 20, 1963; children—Scott Albert, Ross Joseph, Jill Katherine. Admitted to Iowa bar, 1963, since practiced in Dubuque; partner firm Reynolds, Kenline, Brietbach, McCarthy & Clemens, 1966—. Legal counsel Iowa Jaycees, 1967; active Dubuque United Fund. Bd. dirs. Dubuque Community Sch. Dist., 1968-71, v.p., 1970-71; bd. dirs. Little Cloud council Girl Scouts, Dubuque Salvation Army, Dubuque Area Indsl. Devel. Corp.; mem adv. council Clarke Coll., Dubuque; adv. council, v.p. Loras Coll., Dubuque. Served with USAF, 1959. Recipient Distinguished Service award Dubuque Jaycees, 1968. Mem. Am., Iowa, Dubuque County bar assns., Dubuque C. of C. (pres. 1973-74, dir.), Alpha Sigma Nu. Democrat. Roman Catholic. K.C. (4 deg.). Home: 222 Southgate Dr Dubuque IA 52001 Office: 222 Fischer Bldg Dubuque IA 52001

MC CARTHY, LORRAINE CHAMBERS, painter; b. Detroit; d. Allan and Louise Heinrika (Swift) Chamber; student Stephens Coll., Wayne State U.; m. Howard J. McCarty; children—Allan Grant, Jean Louise, Jill McCarty Hartley, Read Swift. Exec. designer Internat. Women's Air and Space Mus., Oklahoma City, 1970-73; instr. Flint (Mich.) Inst. Arts, 1971—, Grosse-Point Meml. Inst., 1971—; artist-in-residence U. Liggett Schs., Grosse Pointe, Mich., 1974—; mem. Oakland County (Mich.) Cultural Council, 1975-78; aircraft pilot, 1960—, one-woman shows: Central Mich. U., 1976, Habatat Gallery, Dearborn, Mich., 1976, Midland (Mich.) Center Arts., 1976, Dayton Inst. Arts, 1978, Battle Creek Art Center, 1978; group shows include: Butler Mus. Am. Art, Youngstown, Ohio, 1967, 69, 71, 75, Detroit Inst. Arts., 1967, 69, Flint Mus. Arts, 1972, 75, 77, Battle Creek Art Mus., 1974, Grand Rapids Art Mus., 1973; represented in permanent collections: Fed. Aviation Agency, Bede Aircraft, Butler Mus. Am. Art, Detroit Mus. Art, No. Ill. U., Dow. Chem. Co. Recipient various awards for paintings. Mem. Mich., Associated arts councils, Mich. Acad. Arts, Scis. and Letters, Mich. Water Color Soc., Detroit Soc. Women Painters and Sculptors, Internat. Orgn. Women Pilots, Mich. Pilots, Mich. Aviation Hist. Soc. Club: Scarab (Detroit). Murals: Mich. Dept. Aviation, Internat. Women's Air and Space Mus. Home and Office: 1112 Pinehurst St Royal Oak MI 48073

MC CARTHY, MICHAEL CHARLES, lawyer; b. Farmington, Mo., Sept. 12, 1914; s. Charles Michael and Jessie Frances (Murphy) M.; A.A., U. Mo., 1935, J.D., 1939; m. Dorothy Margaret Hollman, Dec. 27, 1940; 1 son, Michael John. Admitted to Mo. bar, 1939, Neb. bar, 1946; practiced in Farmington, 1939-41, North Platte, Neb., 1946—; spl. agent FBI, 1942-44; mem. firms Damron & McCarthy, Farmington, 1939-41, Hollman & McCarthy, North Platte, 1946-77, McCarthy, McCarthy & Vyhnalek, North Platte, 1977—. Dir. Mutual Bldg. & Loan Assn., North Platte, 1949—. Chmn. North Platte Bd. Pub. Works, 1960-72; mem. North Platte Bd. Edn., 1957—, pres., 1959-60. Bd. dirs. North Platte Meml. Hosps., 1953-75. Served with O.S.S., 1944-45. Fellow Am. Coll. Probate Counsel; mem. Am., Neb., Lincoln County bar assns., C. of C. (dir. 1954-57), Phi Delta Phi, Kappa Alpha. Democrat. Presbyn. Elk, Mason, Rotarion (pres. 1955-56). Club: North Platte Country (dir. 1950-54). Home: 225 McDonald Ave North Platte NE 69101 Office: 121 W 2d St North Platte NE 69101

MC CARTNEY, RALPH FARNHAM, lawyer; b. Charles City, Iowa, Dec. 11, 1924; s. Ralph C. and Helen (Farnham) McC.; J.D., U. Mich., 1950; B. Sci., Iowa State U., 1972; m. Rhoda Mae Huxsol, June 30, 1950; children—Ralph, Julia, David. Admitted to Iowa bar, 1950; mem. firm Miller, Heuber & Miller, Des Moines, 1950-52, Frye & McCartney, Charles City, 1952—. Chmn., Iowa Republican Conv., 1972, 74; mem. Iowa Ho. of Reps., 1967-70, majority floor leader, 1969-70; mem. Iowa Senate, 1973—. Bd. regents U. Iowa, Iowa State U., U. No. Iowa, Iowa Sch. for Deaf, Iowa Braille and Sight Saving Sch. Served with AUS, 1942-45. Mem. Am., Iowa bar assns., Am. Judicature Soc., Civil War Round Table. Home: 200 Kelly St Charles City IA 50616 Office: 701 Blunt Pkwy Charles City IA 50616

MC CARTY, R(ALPH) LOWELL, county ofcl.; b. Peebles, Ohio, Feb. 15, 1927; s. Ralph Edgar and Inis Opal McCarty; B.S. in Civil Engring., Ind. Inst. Tech., 1951; m. Elizabeth Holland Dunlap, Dec. 8, 1968; children—Michael, Susan Joanne; (stepchildren) Robert Everson, Elizabeth Everson, David Everson. Sr. engr. Standard Oil Co. (Ohio), 1951-63; cons. engr., Hillsboro, Ohio, 1963—; dep. engr. Highland County, Ohio, 1965-69, engr., 1969—. Mem. exec. com. Highland County Planning Commn.; active Boy Scouts Am., Little League. Served with AUS, 1945-47. Mem. Profl. Land Surveyors Ohio, Ohio Soc. Profl. engrs. (pres. So. Ohio chpt. 1975), County Engrs. Assn. Ohio (dir.). Republican. Presbyterian (bd. deacons). Mason, Lion. Home: PO Box 391 Hillsboro OH 45133

MC CARTY, ROBERT FLOYD, labor union exec.; b. Sikes, La., Sept. 5, 1920; s. Rutherford and Mary Etta (Sensley) McC.; student Grambling Coll., 1936-38; m. Mattie L. Floyd, Oct. 1, 1953; Owner pvt. bus., Detroit, 1945-47; machine operator Budd Mfg., Detroit, 1947-66; mem. U.A.W., 1947—, trustee, 1951-60, delegated to Wayne County AFL-CIO Council, 1960-62, chief steward press shop, 1960-62, chmn. plant wide bargaining com., 1962-66, mem. intra corp. council, 1962-66, mem. Budd PAC election com., 1955-60; instr. basic edn., counselor U.A.W. On Job Tng. project, 1967—. Vice pres. Met. Detroit Community Assn., 1962-64. Coordinator, 13th Dist. Democratic Orgn., 1962-64. Served with USAAF, 1942-45. Mem. NAACP. Home: 7887 Sherwood St Detroit MI 48214 Office: 8000 E Jefferson Ave Detroit MI 48214

MC CARTY, THEODORE MILSON, mfg. co. exec.; b. Somerset, Ky., Oct. 10, 1909; s. Raymond Andrew and Jennie (Milson) McC.; Comml. Engr., U. Cin., 1933, postgrad., 1934-35; m. Elinor H. Bauer, June 14, 1935; children—Theodore F., Susan McCarty Davis. Asst. store mgr. Wurlitzer Co., Rochester, N.Y., 1936-38, mgr. real estate div., Cin. and Chgo., 1939-41, dir. procurement, DeKalb, Ill., 1942-45, mdse. mgr. retail div., Chgo., 1945-48; pres., gen. mgr., dir. Gibson, Inc., 1948-66; pres., treas., dir. Bigsby Accessories, Inc., Kalamazoo, 1966—; pres., dir. Flex-Lite, Inc.; v.p., dir. Command Electronics, Kalamazoo. Bd. dirs. Glowing Embers council Girl Scout U.S., 1968-74. Mem. Am. Music Conf. (pres. 1961-63, dir. 1956—, pres., adminstr. 1970-77), Guitar and Accessory Mfrs. Assn. (pres. 1954-56, life mem., dir. 1976—), Kalamazoo Symphony Soc. (pres. 1957-58), Alpha Kappa Psi, Alpha Tau Omega, Omicron Delta Kappa. Presbyterian (bd. dirs. 1957-60). Clubs: Masons, Rotary (pres. 1955-56), Kalamazoo Country (v.p. 1971-72, pres. 1972-73). Patentee in music field. Home: 2412 Bronson Blvd Kalamazoo MI 49008 Office: 3521 E Kilgore Rd Kalamazoo MI 49001

MC CAULEY, MICHAEL FREDERICK, editor; b. Chgo., Apr. 12, 1947; s. George Lawrence and Virginia Marie (Johnson) McC.; A.B. in English, Loyola U., 1969; m. Gabrielle Mary Goder, May 29, 1971; children—Megan Colleen, Maura Eileen. Tchr. of English, Woodlands Acad., Lake Forest, Ill., 1969-70; asst. editor Critic mag., Thomas More Assn., Chgo., 1970-73, book reviewer, 1971—, exec. editor newsletters including Overview, 1973—; book reviewer Commonweal mag., 1974—; author: A Contemporary Meditation on Doubting, 1976; editor: On the Run: Spirituality for the Seventies, 1974; The Jesus Book, 1978. Roman Catholic. Home: 146 N Taylor Ave Oak Park IL 60302 Office: 180 N Wabash Ave Chicago IL 60601

MC CAULEY, PHILIP CLAYTON, dentist; b. Akron, Ohio, May 24, 1926; s. Arthur James and Juna Ella (Ferguson) McC.; student U. Akron, 1944-45; D.D.S., Ohio State U., 1950; m. Edith Marion Seabolt, Apr. 7, 1951; children—Lyn Susan, Lee Steven, Laurie Kay. Practice dentistry, Akron, 1950—; dentist Summit County Health

Dept., Cuyahoga Falls, Ohio, part-time, 1951-53. Mem. Akron (editor 1953-56, pres. 1962-63), Chgo. (asso.) dental socs., Am. Endodontic Soc., Lambda Chi Alpha, Omicron Kappa Upsilon. Lutheran (librarian Christian edn. com. 1969—). Club: Optimist (pres. 1960) (West Akron). Home: 2521 Ridgewood Rd Akron OH 44313 Office: 2777 Copley Rd Akron OH 44321

MC CAULEY, PHILIP F., librarian; b. N.Y.C., May 28, 1931; s. Philip and Elizabeth Josephine (McBrien) McC.; student Tex. Tech., 1953, Tex. A. and M., 1953-55; B.A., U. Denver, 1964, M.A. in L.S., 1966; children—Kathleen (Mrs. R.L. Buck), Maureen (Mrs. D.E. Buck), Deborah, Michael. Dir. Devereaux Library S. D. Sch. Mines and Tech., Rapid City, 1968—. Mem. adv. council S.D. State Library Commn., 1970-72, chmn. spl. com. to survey state library operations, 1971; v.p., pres. Rocky Mountain Bibliog. Center for Research, Inc., 1971-72, mem. at large bd. trustees, 1970-74. Served with USAF, 1949-53. Mem. Spl. Libraries Assn., Am. Mgmt. Assn., Am. (ad hoc com. on flood damaged libraries 1972), S.D. (chmn. acad. sect. 1969-70), Mountain Plains (parliamentarian 1974-76) library assns. Episcopalian (jr. warden 1966-68, sr. warden 1975-76). Elk. Contbr. articles to profl. jours. Home: PO Box 2124 Rapid City SD 57709 Office: Devereaux Library SD Sch Mines and Tech Rapid City SD 57701

MC CAULEY, ROBERT WILLIAM, educator; b. Toronto, Ont., Can., July 8, 1926; s. Herbert and Mary (Mahaffy) M.; B.A., U. Toronto, 1950, M.A., 1955; Ph.D., U. Western Ont., 1962; m. Erika Augusta Hinz, May 19, 1956; children—Eva-Maria, Heidi, Friedrich. Asst. scientist Fisheries Research Bd. Can., 1956-62; research scientist Ont. Dept. Lands and Forests, Toronto, 1962-65; asso. prof. Wilfrid Laurier U., Waterloo, Ont., 1965—; cons. Ont. Hydro; adj. prof. U. Waterloo. Mem. Canadian Soc. Zoologists, Am. Fisheries Soc., Am. Inst. Biol. Scis., Assn. Southeastern Biologists. Lutheran. Contbr. articles to profl. jours. Home: 118 Forest Hill Dr Kitchener ON N2M 4G3 Canada Office: 75 University Ave Waterloo ON Canada

MC CHESNEY, KATHRYN MARIE (MRS. THOMAS DAVID MCCHESNEY), educator; b. Curwensville, Pa., Jan. 14, 1936; d. Orland William and Lillian Irene (Morrison) Spencer; B.A., U. Akron, 1962; M.L.S., Kent State U., 1965, postgrad., 1971—; m. Thomas David McChesney, June 12, 1954; 1 son, Eric Spencer. Tchr. English, Springfield Local High Sch., Akron, Ohio, 1962-63, librarian, 1963-64, head librarian, 1965-68; asst. to dean, instr. Kent (Ohio) State U. Sch. Library Sci., 1968-69, asst. dean, 1969-77, asst. prof., 1969—. Rep. Uniontown Community Council, 1964-66. Mem. Am., Ohio (chmn. Library Edn. Roundtable 1971-72, exec. council Div. VI Library Edn. 1972—) library assns., AAUP, Am., Ohio assns. sch. librarians, Beta Phi Mu, Phi Sigma Alpha, Phi Alpha Theta, Sigma Phi Epsilon. Club: Uniontown Jr. Womans (pres. 1965-66). Contbr. articles, book revs. to profl. periodicals. Home: 3611 Edison St NW Uniontown OH 44685 Office: Kent State U Kent OH 44242

MC CLAMROCH, LEMUEL PAUL, ins. assn. exec.; b. Crawfordsville, Ind., Mar. 30, 1902; s. Lemuel Ball and Mary Jane (Fordyce) McC.; student Wabash Coll., 1922-23; m. Elaine Podell, May 28, 1945; children—Tim, Ann, Kevin. Agt., Am. States Ins. Co., Indpls., 1926-29; claims mgr. Emmco Ins. Co., South Bend, Ind., 1942-44; spl. agt. Auto Owner Ins. Co., Lansing, Mich., 1945-67; exec. v.p. Ind. Ins. Agents Assn., Marion, 1967—. Pres. bd. dirs. Town of Swayzee, Ind., 1962-70. Mem. Nat. Soc. Assn. Execs., Ind. Soc. Assn. Execs. Republican. Methodist. Elk, Lion. Home: Rural Route 3 PO Box 635 Monticello IN 47960

MC CLANAHAN, LOWELL DALE, psychologist; b. Akron, Ohio, May 4, 1930; s. Earl A. and Bessie (Coberly) McC.; student Sophia U., Tokyo, 1954-55; B.S., Ohio U., 1957, Ph.D., 1973; M.A., U. Minn., 1963; m. Anne Holden, June 15, 1957; children—Sheila, Gloria, Kathryn. Employment mgr. Wellman Engring., Cleve., 1958-59; dir. guidance, tchr. North Royalton (Ohio) Bd. Edn., 1959-63; jr. high sch. counselor North Olmsted (Ohio) Bd. Edn., 1963-67; psychologist, mgmt. services div. Ernst & Ernst, Cleve., 1967-68; dir. research Athens (Ohio) Mental Health Center, 1971-76, program evaluation, 1977—; pvt. practice psychology, 1976—; lectr. psychologist Baldwin-Wallace Coll., Berea, Ohio, 1964. Chmn. mgmt. com. Snow Village Coop., Parma, Ohio, 1965-67; pres. Athens Community Choral Soc., 1975-76; v.p. Hocking Valley Arts Council, 1975—. Served with USAF, 1951-55. Mem. Am. Personnel and Guidance Assn., Soc. Psychotherapy Research, Southeastern Ohio, Midwestern psychol. assns., Phi Delta Kappa, Psi Chi. Unitarian (treas. Athens fellowship 1977—). Contbr. articles to profl. jours. Home: 8 Fort St Athens OH 45701 Office: Athens Mental Health Center Richland Ave Athens OH 45701

MC CLEAR, RICHARD VANCE, radio station exec.; b. Jersey City, N.J., Nov. 21, 1946; s. Vance Albert and Margaret (Brew) McC.; B.A. magna cum laude, St. Olaf Coll., 1968: M.A., U. Minn., 1975; m. Susan Anne Randall, June 10, 1968; children—Brian Boru, Kevin Seamus. Engr., Sta. WOR, N.Y.C., 1965-67; ops. mgr., pub. affairs dir. Sta. WCAL, St. Olaf Coll., Northfield, Minn., 1967-73; founder, pres. No. Community Radio, Grand Rapids, Minn., 1970—, program dir. Sta. KAXE-FM, 1976—. Bd. dirs. Com. for Open Media, 1974-75; active Grand Rapids Players. Recipient Minn. Edn. Assn. Best Ednl. Radio Program award, 1974, merit award for program series, 1974; Freedom fellow Seminar on Contemporary China for Sino and Am. Youth, Soochow U., Taipei, Taiwan, 1969. Mem. Nat. Assn. Ednl. Broadcasters, Assn. Minn. Pub. and Ednl. Radio Stas. (dir. 1974—), Grand Rapids C. of C., Phi Beta Kappa. Mem. Democratic-Farm-Labor Party. Exec. producer bicentennial series Minn.-States of the Union for Nat. Pub. Radio, 1976. Home: 737 Crystal Springs Rd Grand Rapids MN 55744 Office: Box 719 Grand Rapids MN 55744

MC CLEARY, GEORGE FRANKLIN, JR., cartographer, educator; b. Springfield, Ohio, Apr. 9, 1937; s. George F. and Mary Wilhelmina (Timmer) McC.; A.B., Yale U., 1959; M.S., U. Wis., 1963, Ph.D., 1969; m. Marilyn Baldwin, June 13, 1959; children—Joseph Franklin II, John Baldwin, George Franklin III. Pub. info. officer, U.S. Antarctic Projects Office, Washington, 1959-61; research asst. dept. geography U. Wis., Madison, 1961-66; asst. prof. Sch. Geography Clark U., Worcester, Mass., 1966-72, asso. prof., 1972-74, dir. Cartographic Lab., 1966-74; asso. prof. geography U. Kans., Lawrence, 1974—. Bd. dirs. Worcester Regional Environ. Council, 1970-71. Served with USNR, 1959-61. Recipient Library Map Prize, Yale U., 1959. Mem. Assn. Am. Geographers, Am. Congress Surveying and Mapping, Antarctican Soc. Home: 2514 Harvard Rd Lawrence KS 66044 Office: Dept of Geography Univ of Kansas Lawrence KS 66045

MC CLEARY, HENRY GLEN, geophysicist; b. Casper, Wyo., June 4, 1922; s. Raymond McCleary and Wyoma N. (Posey) McCleary Grieve; Geol. Engr., Colo. Sch. Mines, 1948; m. Beryl Tenney Nowlin, May 28, 1950; children—Gail, Glenn, Neil, Paul. Geophysicist to party chief seismic Amoco, various locations, 1948-53; exploration mgr. Woodson Oil Co., Fort Worth, 1953-60; resident mgr. NAMCO, Tripoli, Libya, 1961-62; chief geophysicist to geophys. asso. Amoco Internat. Oil Co., 1963—, Cairo, London and Buenos Aires, 1963-71, Chgo., 1971—. Served with USN, 1943-46. Mem. Soc. Exploration Geophysicists, Soc. Petroleum Engrs., AAAS, Sigma Alpha Epsilon, Theta Tau. Republican. Episcopalian. Club: Adventurers. Home: 2130 Lincoln Park W Chicago IL 60614 Office: 200 E Randolph Dr #5108 Chicago IL 60601

MC CLEARY, VIRGIL ARNOLD, optometrist; b. Warsaw, Ind., Feb. 13, 1914; s. Harvey D. and Bertha Della (Gragg) M.; A.B., Manchester Coll., 1936; D. Optometry, No. Ill. Coll., 1940; m. L. Lucille Hardin, May 14, 1938; children—Richard H., Jim E. Pvt. practice optometry, Warsaw, 1940—. Mem. city council, City of Warsaw, 1951-53; pres. Aeros. Com., Warsaw, 1961-69; 1st pres. Little League Club, Warsaw, 1951-54; mem. pres's. com. Grace Coll., Winona Lake, Ind., 1970—; mem. blood solicitation com. ARC, 1955-62; asst. covil def. dir. Kosciusko County. Precinct committeeman Warsaw Republican Com., 1949-54. Mem. Am., Ind. (pres. 1951-52) optometric assns., Ford Golf Course (sec., treas. 1960-68). Methodist (trustee 1953-59). Kiwanian (lt. gov. 1958-59, pres. 1943-45), Elk (state chaplin 1952-53). Home: Rural Route 2 Warsaw IN 46580 Office: 116 N Buffalo St Warsaw IN 46580

MC CLELLAN, WILLIAM DANIEL, clergyman; b. Columbia, Tenn., Nov. 16, 1937; s. Harry David and Dannie Ione (Robinson) McC.; student McNeese State Coll., Lake Charles, La., 1956-57, Henry Ford Community Coll., 1968; B.S.Ed., Wright State U., Dayton, Ohio, 1972; M.A. in Interpersonal Communications, Wheaton (Ill.) Coll., 1976; m. Barbara Nell Gay, Nov. 23, 1956; children—Jennifer Gay, William Daniel, David Lanis, Benjamin Ray, Timothy Ed. Ordained to ministry Ch. of Christ, 1960; minister Ch. of Christ, Stigler, Okla., 1960-61, Rapid City, S.D., 1961-64, Trenton, Mich., 1964-67; minister Huber Heights Ch. of Christ, Dayton, 1967-72; minister Ch. of Christ, Des Plaines, Ill., 1972—. Mem. adv. bd. York (Neb.) Coll., 1961—; mem. adv. com. Mich. Christian Coll., Rochester, 1966-72; teaching fellow Wheaton Coll., 1974-75; chaplain city council, Riverview, Mich., 1965-67; marriage and family counselor, 1972—. Served with USAF, 1955-60. Recipient Commendation, Mayor of Riverview, 1966; Edward M. Felsenfeld Distinguished Service award Wayne Township (Ohio), 1969. Mem. Am. Camping Assn., (dir. sect., chmn. com. membership 1969-72, camp visitor 1969-72), Am. Assn. Pastoral Counselors, Assn. Christian Marriage Counselors, Internat. Communications Assn., Civitan Club, Toastmasters (Toastmaster of Year 1963), Am. Assn. Marriage and Family Counselors, Nat. Council on Family Relations. Contbr. articles to religious mags. and edn. jours. Editor spl. issue Christian Bible Tchr., 1974. Home: 1403 Catalpa Ln Mount Prospect IL 60056 Office: 530 E Oakton St Des Plaines IL 60018

MC CLELLAND, ANN SAMONIAL (MRS. STEWART W. MCCLELLAND), educator, lectr.; b. Vincennes, Ind., Jan. 31, 1917; d. Charles Edward and Martha Ann (Love) Samonial; A.A., Vincennes U., 1936; B.S., Peabody Coll., 1938, M.A., 1941; postgrad. Vanderbilt U.; Litt.D. (hon.), Steed Coll., 1957; m. Stewart Winning McClelland, Aug. 2, 1947. Tchr. Bogalusa (La.) High Sch., 1938, Holmes High Sch., Covington, Ky., 1939-45; instr. Okla. Coll. Women, 1938-39; dean women Lincoln Meml. U., 1945-47; sponsor Dale Carnegie courses, Fla., Ind., 1947—; asso. with Mrs. Dale Carnegie in Dorothy Carnegie Courses Women, 1956—. Mem. women's com. Clowes Hall; mem. advisory bd. Pompeiiana. Fellow Royal Soc. Arts (London); mem. AAUW, Internat. Platform Assn., Indpls. Propylaeum (pres.), Wedgwood Internat. Seminar, DAR, Indpls. Museum Art Alliance, Kappa Kappa Kappa, Pi Gamma Chi. Republican. Roman Catholic. Affiliated with husband in Lincoln research; authority on Coin glass and Wedgwood, Lithophanes. Home: 730 Braeside Ct Indianapolis IN 46260

MC CLENAHAN, ANN CATHERINE, psychologist; b. Sioux City, Iowa, Apr. 17, 1932; d. Harold L. and Beatrice A. (Wilbur) McC.; B.A., U. S.D., 1953; M.Ed., S.D. State U., 1969; Ed.D., U. S.D., 1974. Tchr., Sioux Falls (S.D.) Pub. Schs., 1955-60; counselor/psychometrist Brandon Valley (S.D.) Schs., 1969-71; asst. prof. edn., psychology Dakota Wesleyan U., Mitchell, S.D., 1974-75; child psychologist Intercommunity Human Service Center, Mitchell, 1975-76; child psychologist Area Edn. Agy., Sioux Center, Iowa, 1976—; part-time pvt. practice psychology, Sioux Falls, 1977—. Mem. Am., S.D. psychol. assns., Iowa Sch. Psychologists Assn., Assn. Children with Learning Disabilities, Am. Personnel and Guidance Assn., Pi Beta Phi. Home: 2202 Pendar Ln Sioux Falls SD 57105 Office: 102 S Main Sioux Center IA 51250

MC CLENAHAN, JAMES WALLACE, dentist; b. Chgo., Nov. 23, 1942; s. John Paul and Johanna (Hibbler) McC.; D.D.S., Northwestern U., 1966; certificate periodontology U. Ill. Med. Center, 1971; m. Leslie Ann Phillips, July 31, 1971; children—Michelle Thomas, Paul David. Asso. Dr. Ronald Fabrick, Glenview, Ill., 1968-69; pvt. practice dentistry, Homewood, Ill., 1969—, specializing in periodontology, 1971—; asst. prof. periodontics Northwestern U. Dental Sch., 1971—; cons. periodontics U. Chgo. Hosp., 1976—. Mem. dental adv. bd. Prairie State Jr. Coll., 1971-72. Mem. Am. Dental Assn., Am. Acad. Periodontology, (regional dir. pub. relations 1975-77), Midwest Soc. Periodontology (co-chmn. pub. relations 1972-77). Rotarian. Home: 18645 Poplar Homewood IL 60430 Office: 2711 W 183d St Homewood IL 60430

MC CLENAHAN, RICHARD LEE, mgmt. cons.; b. N.Y.C., Aug. 9, 1903; s. Howard and Bessie (Lee) McC.; grad. cum laude Lawrenceville (N.J.) Sch., 1921; A.B., Princeton, 1925; m. Catherine Jane Hepburn, Mar. 30, 1943 (dec. 1966); children—Richard Lee (dec. 1966), Douglas S., Lorna, Helen Lee, Eben Lee; m. 2d, Rhea K. Knox, Sept. 5, 1974; 1 stepdau., Virginia K. Collins. Sales engr. N.J. Zinc Sales Co., 1925-30; v.p., treas. W. & J. Sloane, 1930-40; asst. dir. indsl. relations Fleetwings, Inc., 1941-42; asst. to resident mgr. The A.O.G. Corp., 1942-45; partner Donald Deskey Assos., N.Y.C., 1945-46; fin. v.p., asst. sec., treas., dir. Rand McNally & Co., Chgo., 1946-70; cons., 1970—; dir. Scot, Inc., 1957-76. Life mem. Chgo. Crime Commn. chmn. Chgo. chpt. SCORE. Village clk., Kenilworth, Ill., 1969-74. Active Boy Scouts Am. Trustee Allendale Sch. for Boys. Decorated Officier d' Academie, French Govt., 1938. Mem. A.I.M., Ill. St. Andrew Soc. (bd. govs.). Episcopalian. Rotarian. Clubs: Princeton (N.Y.C.); Glen View, Exmoor, University, Princeton (Chgo.). Author: Some Scottish Quaichs, 1955, 2d vol., 1968. Home: 91 Hazel Ave Highland Park IL 60035

MC CLINTOCK, JOHN STEPHEN, mfg. co. exec.; b. Mpls., Jan. 11, 1924; s. George Dunlop and Jesse Penelope (McCabe) McC.; B.A., Dartmouth Coll., 1946; m. Edith Sinclair Taylor, Mar. 17, 1945; children—Marney McClintock Toole, John Stephen, Todd C., Lon T., Corey. With Superior Separator Co., Hopkins, Minn., 1947-58; with Sheldahl, Inc., Northfield, Minn., 1958-77, corporate v.p., 1969-77; pres. Iron Works, Inc., Hopkins, Minn., 1977—; dir. Mchts. Bank, Rugby, N.D., 1953—; mem. industry sector adv. com. for Tokyo Round of Internat. Trade Negotiations, 1975—. Served with USAAF, 1943-45. Mem. Packaging Machinery Mfrs. Inst. (dir. 1966-73, pres. 1972). Republican. Home: 3342 Robinson's Bay Rd Wayzata MN 55391 Office: Iron Works Inc Hopkins MN

MC CLINTOCK, PETER LONGMIRE, geophys. co. exec.; b. Detroit, Nov. 28, 1941; s. Robert L. and June M. (McDonald) McC.; ed. high sch., Phoenix; m. Laura L. Nicholson, Apr. 30, 1965; 1 dau., Samantha. Seismic analyst Western Geophys. Co., Houston, 1968-69, Milan, Italy, 1969-72; mgr. data processing Seismograph Service Corp., Tananarive, Malagasy Republic, 1972-74, Alma, Mich., 1974—. Served with U.S. Army, 1960-63. Mem. Soc. Exploration Geophysicists. Rotary. Home: 727 Pine St Alma MI 48801 Office: PO Box 546 Alma MI 48801

MC CLINTON, JOHNNIE WAYNE, counselor; b. Limestone County, Tex., Dec. 18, 1938; s. Clyde Evans and Mattie Lou (Webb) McC.; B.A. in Math. Edn., Baylor U., 1962, M.S. in Edn. Counseling, 1970; Ph.D. in Student Personnel Services and Counseling Psychology, U. Mo., Columbia, 1972; m. Barbara Lee Bledsoe, Apr. 7, 1973; 1 son, Jay John. Tchr. math. and biology, coach Coolidge (Tex.) Ind. Sch. Dist., 1960-62; instr. math. Tex. State Tech. Inst., Waco, 1967-69; instr. psychology, counselor Longview Community Coll., Lees Summit, Mo., 1971—. Del. Tex. Democratic Conv., 1960; bd. dirs. Mental Health Assn. So. Jackson County, 1976—, 2d v.p., 1977—. Served with USAF, 1962-67. Decorated Air medal with 2 oak leaf clusters. Mem. Mo. Assn. Community and Jr. Colls. (bd. dirs. 1975-76, spl. service award), Am. Personnel and Guidance Assn., Am. Coll. Personnel Assn., Nat. Vocational Guidance Assn., Am. Counselor Educators Assn., Mo. Personnel and Guidance Assn., Mo. Psychol. Assn., VFW. Democrat. Baptist. Home: Route 2 Box 318A Pleasant Hill MO 64080 Longview Community Coll Lees Summit MO 64063

MC CLORY, ROBERT, congressman; b. Riverside, Ill., Jan. 31, 1908; s. Frederick Stephens and Catherine (Reilly) McC.; student L'Institut Sillig, Vevey, Switzerland, 1925-26, Dartmouth Coll., 1926-28; LL.B., Chgo.-Kent Coll., 1932; m. Audrey Vasey (dec. Sept. 1967); children—Beatrice (Mrs. Donald Etienne), Michael, Oliver; m. 2d, Doris S. Hibbard, Mar. 1969. Admitted to Ill. bar, 1932; practiced in Chgo. and Waukegan, Ill., 1932-62; mem. Ill. Ho. of Reps., 1951-52, Ill. Senate, 1952-62; mem. 88th-95th congresses from 13th Dist. Ill., mem. judiciary com., ranking Republican House Judiciary Com.; participant Ditchley Conf., London, 1966, mem. congl. del. Interparliamentary Union, 1964—, Environ. Conf., Stockholm, 1972. Mem. Am., Ill., Lake County bar assns., Navy League, Waukegan-North Chgo. C. of C., Phi Upsilon, Phi Delta Phi. Christian Scientist. Clubs: Chicago Law; Bath and Tennis (Lake Forest, Ill.); Capitol Hill (Washington). Home: 321 Constitution Ave NE Washington DC 20002 also 340 Prospect Ave Lake Bluff IL 60044 Office: Rayburn House Office Bldg Washington DC 20515 also Lake County Bldg Waukegan IL 60085 also 150 Dexter Ct Elgin IL 60098

MC CLOSKEY, DONALD NANSEN, economist; b. Ann Arbor, Mich., Sept. 11, 1942; s. Robert Green and Helen Louise (Stueland) McC.; B.A., Harvard U., 1964, Ph.D. in Economics, 1970; m. Joanne Marie Comi, June 19, 1965; children—Daniel Robert, Margaret Ann. Mem. faculty U. Chgo., 1968—, asso. prof. economics, 1973—; bd. editors Jour. Econ. History, Explorations in Econ. History. NSF grantee, 1974—. Mem. Am. Econ. History Assn., Am. Econ. Assn., English Economic History Soc. Author: Economic Maturity and Entrepreneurial Decline: British Iron and Steel, 1870-1913, 1973. Home: 5406 S Kimbark Ave Chicago IL 60615 Office: 1126 E 59th St Chicago IL 60637

MC CLUNEY, GREGORY DAY, advt. and pub. relations exec., publisher; b. Kansas City, Mo., Dec. 27, 1946; s. Glenn G. and Dorothy N. Boone McC.; B.S. in Journalism, U. Kans., Lawrence, 1970; postgrad. U. Mo.-Rolla, 1974; m. Anita L. Barnes, June 1, 1968. Advt. writer, TV producer Fremerman-Papin Advt., Kansas City, Mo., 1970-71; account exec. Valentine-Radford Advt., Kansas City, 1971—; founder, pres. NAS Advt. and Pub. Relations Inc., Overland Park, Kans. and Atlanta, Dallas, 1973-76; partner, exec. v.p. Am. Auto Systems, Inc., Overland Park; v.p., dir. Hudco Inc., Kansas City, 1973—, also dir.; v.p., treas. NAS Mktg. Inc., Overland Park, 1975—, also dir. Corp. chmn. spl. gifts Greater Kansas City chpt. Cancer Soc., 1969-70; promotional chmn. Greater Kansas City Vol. Action Center, 1971-72; co. chmn. Greater Kansas City United Fund, 1972-73; active Friends of Art Nelson Gallery and Mus. Hon. fellow Truman Library Inst., Independence, Mo., 1974-75. Promotional bd. Jr. Women's Philharmonic Assn. Kansas City, Mo., 1974—. Mem. Am. Advt. Fedn. (Addy award 9th Dist. 1972, 73, 75), Am. Bus. Writers Assn. (founding), Internat. Platform Assn., Assn. Indsl. Advertisers, Am. Mgmt. Assn., Advt. and Sales Execs. Club. Clubs: Kansas City, Leawood Country; Lakewood Country. Home: 9705 Lee Blvd Leawood KS 66204 Office: 300 Fox Hill Office Center 4550 W 109th St Overland Park KS 66211

MC CLURE, DAVID BOYD, dentist; b. Rawlings, Va., Apr. 20, 1926; s. Newman William and Maria Field (Tucker) McC.; B.S., Ind. U., 1950, D.D.S., 1953; m. Flora Helene Dixon, Oct. 28, 1948; children—David Craig, Jeffrey Steven, Douglas E. Individual practice pedodontics, Ind., 1953—; mem. teaching staff Riley Hosp., 1953—; mem. faculty Ind. U. Sch. Dentistry, 1955—, asso. prof. pedodontics, 1970—. Cons. Cerebral Palsy Assn., 1953—; vice chmn. Madison County Bd. Health, 1970—; mem. med. cons. bd. Madison County Cerebral Palsy Assn., 1968-70. Mem. exec. bd. local Boy Scouts Am., 1953—. Served with USNR, i943-46. Fellow Internat. Coll. Dentistry, Am. Acad. Pedodontics; mem. Am. (del. 1970-72, mem. jud. 1971—), Ind. (v.p. 1967-70, treas. 1968-70, sec. 1970—) dental assns., Ind. Soc. Dentistry Children (pres. 1964), Ind. Soc. Pedodontics (pres. 1965), Omicron Delta Kappa. Presbyterian (sec. 1971). Mason (Shriner). Contbr. articles to profl. jours. Home: 1907 W 10th St Anderson IN 46011 Office: 1415 Raible Ave Anderson IN 46001

MC CLURE, JAMES J., JR., lawyer; b. Oak Park, Ill., Sept. 23, 1920; s. James J. and Leslie (Baker) Mc C.; B.A., U. Chgo., 1942, J.D., 1949; m. Carolyn Phelps, Apr. 9, 1949; children—John Phelps, Julia Jean, Donald Stewart. Admitted to Ill. bar, 1950; asso. firm Hopkins Sutter Halls DeWolfe & Owen, Chgo., 1949-57; asso. Gardner Carton & Douglas, Chgo., 1957-62, partner, 1962—. Chmn. zoning amendment com. Village Oak Park, Ill., 1963-66, chmn. zoning com., 1969-73, mem. planning com., 1963-73; pres. Village of Oak Park, 1973—; exec. com. Cook County Council of Govts., 1973—. Pres. Oak Park River Forest Community Chest, 1967-69; legal counsel Thatcher Woods area council Boy Scouts Am., 1967—, v.p. council, 1970-74; pres. Erie Neighborhood House, Chgo., 1961-63, United Christian Community Services, 1967, 70-72; mem., chmn. intergovtl. relations com. Northeastern Ill. Planning Commn., 1974, pres., 1975-77; co-chmn. Bi-State (Ill.-Ind.) Commn., 1974-75. Bd. dirs. Presbyn. Home, Evanston, Ill., 1968-73; vice chmn. bd. trustees Christian Century Found., 1972—. Served with USNR, 1942-46, Recipient Distinguished Eagle Scout award, Silver Beaver award Boy Scouts Am. Mem. Order of Coif, Delta Upsilon. Presbyterian (ruling elder, moderator Presbytery Chgo. 1969). Club: University of Chgo. Home: 707 N Oak Park Ave Oak Park IL 60302 Office: 1 First Nat Plaza Chicago IL 60603

MC COLLEM, DONALD EARL, guidance counselor; b. Streator, Ill., Jan. 23, 1923; s. Richard Cray and Stella Athalina (Kosinske) McC.; B.S. in Edn., Ill. State U., Normal, 1961; M.S. in Edn., U. Ill., 1963; m. Mary C. Watson, Sept. 10, 1960; children by previous marriage—Donald Earl, Sean David; 1 dau., Kathleen; stepchildren—Mark, John and Bill Caplinger. Tchr. English, Crete-Monee, Ill., 1959-60, Oblong (Ill.) High Sch., 1961-62; counselor, tchr. English, Macon (Ill.) High Sch., 1963-64; guidance counselor Armstrong (Ill.) High Sch., 1964—. Served with USMC, 1943-45; PTO. Mem. Ill. Edn. Assn., NEA, Vermillion, North Vermillion (pres. 1968-69) tchrs. assns., Vermillion County Counselors Assn. (pres. 1975-76), Am., Ill. guidance and personnel assns. Home: Rural Route 1 Penfield IL 61862 Office: Armstrong High Sch Armstrong IL 61812

MC COLLEM, MARY CAROLYN WATSON, sch. counselor; b. McLean County, Bloomington, Ill., Nov. 10, 1925; d. William Francis and Estella B. (Kellogg) Watson; student Ill. Wesleyan U., 1944-47; B.S., Ill. State U., 1959; M.S., Purdue U., 1966; m. Donald McCollem, Sept. 10, 1960; children by previous marriage—Mark, John, Bill Caplinger; 1 dau., Kathleen McCollem; stepchildren—Don, Sean. Tchr. English, El Paso (Ill) High Sch., 1958-61, Oblong (Ill.) High Sch., 1961-62, Blue Mound (Ill.) High Sch., 1963-64, Mt. Pulaski (Ill.) High Sch., 1964-65; guidance counselor Normal (Ill.) Community High Sch., 1966-67; tchr. English, Univ. High Sch., Ill. State U., Normal, 1969-71; guidance counselor Potomac (Ill.) High Sch., 1973—. NDEA grantee, 1965-66. Mem. NEA, Ill. Edn. Assn., Am. Personnel and Guidance Assn., Am. Sch. Counselors Assn., D.A.R., Kappa Kappa Gamma. Democrat. Roman Catholic. Home: Route 1 Penfield IL 61862 Office: Route 136 Potomac High Sch Potomac IL 61865

MC COLLISTER, HOWARD RICHARD, oil co. exec.; b. Iowa City, Dec. 29, 1924; s. John Milton and Thelma Ruth (Yetter) McC.; B.A., U. Iowa, 1947; m. Marilyn Browning McCollister, Dec. 6, 1947 (dec. Aug. 1975); children—Howard M., Diane; m. 2d, Shirlee Lee Wallace Rushton, Feb. 14, 1976; stepchildren—Terri Rushton, Robin Rushton, John Rushton, Christine. Sales rep. IBM, Milw., 1947-54; v.p. McCollister Grease & Oil Corp., Omaha, 1954-65, Empak Industries, Omaha, 1965-72; pres. SW Grease & Oil Co. (Omaha), Inc., 1972—; v.p., SW Petro-Chem. Inc., Omaha, 1972—, also dir. Served with USNR, 1943-46. Mem. Ind. Oil Compounders Assn. (pres. 1964-66), Nebr. Amateur Golf Assn. (dir. 1964-67). Republican. Club: Happy Hollow (pres. 1975). Home: 10339 Broadmoor Ct Omaha NE 68114 Office: 6200 N 16th St Omaha NE 68110

MC COLLOUGH, FRED, educator; b. Crawfordsville, Ind., July 19, 1928; s. Fred and Dorothea Lucile (Weidner) McC.; A.B., Wabash Coll., 1950; M.S., U. Ill., 1952, Ph.D., 1955; m. Elizabeth Ruth Hall, Aug. 24, 1952; children—Bruce Stanley, Lynn Elizabeth. Research chemist, supr. Stauffer Chem. Co., Chgo., 1955-64; faculty MacMurray Coll., Jacksonville, Ill., 1964—, prof. chemistry, 1970—, chmn. dept. chemistry, 1969—. Bd. dirs. Presbyn. Day Care Center, 1972-75. Served to 1st lt. USAF, 1952-53. Mem. Am. Chem. Soc., Ill. Assn. Chemistry Tchrs. (regional v.p. 1973-74), Jacksonville Symphony Soc., Sigma Xi, Phi Beta Kappa. Presbyterian (elder, ruling elder 1970-73). Patentee in field. Home: 407 Sandusky St Jacksonville IL 62650

MC COLLOUGH, LUCILLE HANNA (MRS. CLARENCE LINDSAY MCCOLLOUGH), state legislator; b. Huron County, Mich., Dec. 30, 1905; d. William and Stella (Stover) Hanna; grad. Western Mich. U., 1923; m. Clarence Lindsay McCollough, June 16, 1925; children—Clarence, Marilyn McCollough Edwards, Patrick. Past tchr., sec., stenographer; mem. Mich. Ho. of Reps., 1955—. Active Dearborn Fedn. Civic Assns., N. Am. Benefit Assn., Citizens Traffic Safety Council, YWCA. Recipient Sr. Auto Worker award UAW Ret. Workers, 1964, citation for service Nat. Ret. Tchrs. Assn. and Am. Assn. Ret. Persons, 1965, certificate of appreciation Vets. World War I, 1966, citation VFW Mich., U.S., citation Allied Vets. Council, Dearborn, 1966, Outstanding Health Service award Mich. Med. Soc., 1969; named Bus. Woman of Year, Mich. Fedn. Bus. and Profl. Women, 1965, 68. Mem. Aviation Property Owners Assn., McDonald's Sch. Mother's Club, Navy Mother's Club, Ladies Aux. VFW, LWV, Nat. Order Women Legislators, Hist. Soc., Nat. Fedn. Bus. and Profl. Women. Democrat. Presbyterian. Club: Women of the Moose. Home: 7517 Kentucky Ave Dearborn MI 48126 Office: Mich State Capitol Ho of Reps Lansing MI 48901

MC COMBS, SHERWIN, oil and gas co. exec.; b. Sterling, Ill., Jan. 27, 1934; s. C. Vernon and Helen (Jennings) McC.; grad. Palmer Chiropractic Coll., 1956-60; m. Rita J. Page, Feb. 8, 1957; children—Kim, Kelly, Jeff, Terry. Owner McCombs Chiropractic Clinic, Sterling, Ill., 1960—, McCombs Petroleum Prodns., Sterling, 1966—; v.p., dir. Coyote Oil & Gas Corp., Casper Wyo., 1968-75, exec. v.p., dir., 1975—; v.p., dir. Coyote Assos., Inc., Ankeny, Iowa, 1970-72; pres., dir. Coyote Oil & Gas Programs, Inc., Ankeny, 1970-72; with McCombs-Conrad & Barrett Oil & Gas Properties, Sterling, Ill., 1972—. Served with USNR, 1952-54. Mem. Internat., Prairie, Whiteside County chiropractic assns., Internat. Chiropractic Honor Soc. Home: 1808 Thome Dr Sterling IL 61081 Office: 507 W 3d St Sterling IL 61081

MC CONAGHA, GLENN LOWERY, coll. spl. cons.; b. New Concord, Ohio, June 2, 1910; s. David Hawthorne and Lida (Taylor) McC.; A.B., Muskingum Coll., 1932; A.M., Ohio State U., 1934, Ph.D., 1941; postgrad. U. Pitts., 1936-37; m. Pearl Esther Hook, Apr. 8, 1939. Instr. social studies Aliquippa High Sch., Pa., 1934-38; asst. prof. edn., Muskingum Coll., summers 1935-38; instr. edn., Ohio State U. Columbus, 1939, 40; asst. dir. field service, 1941-42; classification and personnel cons. courses, Adj. Gen's. Sch., 1943; pre-induction classification officer, Huntington, W.Va., 1943; Sch. for Spl. Services, Lexington, Va., 1943; exec. officer U.S. Armed Forces Inst., Madison, Wis., 1944-45, comdt., 1945-49, ednl. dir., 1949-50, civilian dir., 1951-53; ednl. adviser to office of armed forces information and edn. Dept. of Def. exec. v.p. Muskingum Coll., 1953-62, pres., 1962-64; dean Blackburn Coll., Carlinville, Ill., 1964, pres., 1965-74, chancellor, 1974-77, spl. cons., 1977—. Former trustee Lincoln Acad. Ill. Served as maj. AUS, Res. Hon. mem. Brit. Royal Army Edn. Corps. Decorated Army Commendation Ribbon; recipient Assn. award, Columbia Scholastic Press. Mem. Presbyn. Coll. Union (pres. 1972-73), Higher Edn. Assn. Am., Am. Ednl. Research Assn., NEA, Mil. Order of World Wars, AAUP, Pi Gamma Mu. Alpha Phi Gamma, Phi Delta Kappa. Mason. Contbr. articles to profl. jours. Home: 10 Taggart Dr Carlinville IL 62626

MC CONNAUGHEY, GEORGE CARLTON, JR., lawyer; b. Hillsboro, Ohio, Aug. 9, 1925; s. George Carlton and Nelle (Morse) McC.; B.A., Denison U., 1949; J.D., Ohio State U., 1951; m. Carolyn Schlieper, June 16, 1951; children—Elizabeth, Susan, Nancy. Admitted to Ohio bar, 1951; asst. atty. gen. Ohio, 1951-54; partner firm McConnaughey & McConnaughey, Columbus, Ohio, 1954-57, McConnaughey, McConnaughey & Stradley, 1957-62, Laylin, McConnaughey & Stradley, 1962-67, George, Greek King, McMahon & McConnaughey, Columbus, 1967—. Dir., sec. Mid-Continent Telephone Corp.; dir. N.Am. Broadcasting Co. (WMNI Radio, Columbus), Newark Telephone Co. (Ohio), Mem. Upper Arlington (Ohio) Bd. Ed., 1962-70, pres., 1967-69; elector, Pres. U.S., 1956; chmn. Ohio Young Republicans, 1956. Trustee Buckeye Boys Ranch, Columbus. Served with AUS, 1943-45; ETO. Mem. Am., Ohio, Columbus bar assns., Columbus Town Meeting Assn. (pres. 1974-76), Sigma Chi, Phi Delta Phi. Presbyterian (elder). Mason. Clubs: Columbus, Columbus Athletic; Scioto Country (Columbus). Home: 1969 Andover Rd Upper Arlington OH 43212 Office: 100 E Broad St Columbus OH 43215

MC CONNELL, BERNIE ALLEN, dentist; b. Hartford, Conn., July 30, 1928; s. Harold Wilson and Harriet Virginia (Snyder) McC.; student Miami U., Oxford, Ohio, 1946-49; D.D.S., Ohio State U., 1953; m. Dona Mae Lowry, July 4, 1953. Practice pediatric dentistry, Canton, Ohio, 1953—; trustee, mem. exec. com. Delta Dental Plan of Ohio, Inc., Columbus. Cons., Stark County Cleft Palate Team, 1960—; mem. adv. bd. dental asst.'s vocational program Timken High Sch., 1965-68; mem. dean's adv. com. Ohio State U. Coll. Dentistry, 1976—. Pres. Council for Retarded Citizens of Stark County, 1963-65; chmn. dental div. United Way, 1960. Served with AUS, 1950. Recipient Certificate of Merit, Dental Soc. Guayas, Guayaquil, Equador, and U. Guayaquil, 1964, U. Nicaragua, 1966; Humanitarian Service award Ohio State Surg. Assn., 1965. Fellow Internat. Coll. Dentists, Acad. Dentistry for Handicapped (nat. pres. 1969-70); mem. Ecuadorian Nat. Dental Soc. (hon.), Pierre Fauchard Acad., Ohio Soc. Pedodontists (charter pres. 1966-67), Ohio Soc. Dentistry for Children (pres. 1965-66), Canton Dental Soc. (pres. 1956), Am. (nat. del. 1971-73, nat. alt. del. 1964, 69—), Ohio (state del. 1959—) dental assns., Stark County Dental Assn., Am. Acad. Pedodontics, Am. Soc. Dentistry for Children (nat. del. 1963-70), Phi Delta Theta, Psi Omega. Republican. Episcopalian. Home: 216 Lakecrest Ln NW Canton OH 44709 Office: Wells Profl Bldg 515 3d St NW Canton OH 44703

MC CONNELL, FORREST MATHEW, chem. processing co. exec.; b. Indpls., May 2, 1917; s. Forrest Mathew and Alice (Reynolds) McC.; B.A., Butler U., 1938; m. Marion Wolfe, Aug. 10, 1945. Sales mgr. Rite-Way Products Co., Chgo., 1938-48; v.p. sales Union Wadding Co., Pawtucket, R.I., 1948-58; pres., Koos, Inc., Kenosha, Wis., 1958—. Mem. library bd., Lake Forest, Ill., 1973-74. Served with AUS, 1942-44. Mem. Am. Vermiculite Assn. (dir. 1965—). Clubs: Knollwood (Lake Forest, Ill.); Curling (Chgo.); Town (Wilmette, Ill.). Home: 1826 Knollwood Rd Lake Forest IL 60045 Office: 4500 13th Ct Kenosha WI 53140

MC CONNELL, GLENN BRUCE, educator; b. Cavalier County, N.D., Mar. 10, 1901; s. William James and Ellen (Waddell) McC.; B.S., U.S. Mil. Acad., 1924; m. Agnes S. Buffington, June 2, 1932; 1 dau., Patricia Ellen. Commd. 2d lt. U.S. Army, 1924; advanced through grades to col., 1944; served in U.S., Hawaii, ETO, World War II; mem. mil. govt. Austria; ret., 1954; asst. prof. engring. graphics Iowa State U., Ames, 1956-71. Methodist. Rotarian. Home: 1425 Harding Ave Ames IA 50010

MC CONNELL, JOHN HENDERSON, steel co. exec.; b. New Manchester, W.Va., May 10, 1923; s. Paul A. and Mary Louise (Mayhew) McC.; B.A., Mich. State U., 1949; m. Margaret Jane Rardin, Feb. 8, 1946; children—Margaret Louise, John Porter. With blooming mill Weirton Steel Co. (W.Va.), 1941-43, with sales dept. 1950-52; with sales dept. Shenango Steel Co., Farrell, Pa., 1953-55; founder, chief exec. officer Worthington Steel Co. (Ohio) (name changed to Worthington Industries, 1971), 1955—; dir. Liebert Corp., Worthington, Exec. Jet Aviation, City Nat. Bank & Trust, Capital Equity Corp., Wendy's Internat., Columbus. Mem. Ohio State U. Zoning Commn.; mem. Ohio Gov.'s Devel. Advisory Council, also chmn. legis. sub-com. Bd. dirs. Pilot Dogs Inc., Columbus, Ohio. Served with USNR, 1943-46. Named Central Ohio Mktg. Man of Year, 1975. Mem. Columbus C. of C. (dir., chmn. aviation com., vice chmn. 1977), Columbus Indsl. Assn. (dir.), Mich. State U. Bus. Alumni Assn. (dir.). Republican. Presbyn. (past trustee). Mason (Shriner, 32 deg.). Clubs: Columbus Athletic, Columbus; The Golf (New Albany, Ohio); Brookside Country (Worthington); Muirfield Village Golf (Dublin, Ohio); Bob O' Link Golf (Chgo.); Sea Pines (Hilton Head, S.C.). Home: 244 Tucker Dr Worthington OH 43085 Office: 1205 Dearborn Dr Columbus OH 43085

MC CONNELL, ROBERT BRUCE, broadcasting exec.; b. Indpls., Apr. 17, 1921; s. Charles Bruce and Emma Lucile (Clemens) McC.; B.A., Ind. U., 1942; m. Frances Louise Hollingsworth, June 10, 1944; 1 dau., Sally Anne. Salesman radio sta. WISH, Indpls., 1944-47; v.p., gen. mgr. Universal Broadcasting Corp., Indpls., 1947-50; v.p. Ind. Broadcasting Corp., Indpls., 1950—; treas. Met. Ind. TV Assn., 1971-73. Pres., 500 Festival Assos., Indpls., 1966; mem. Greater Indpls. Progress Com., 1968—, pres., 1972; pres. Crossroads Rehab. Center, 1970—. Bd. dirs. United Way Indpls., 1965—. Served with USNR, 1941-45. Mem. Nat. (dir. 1975—), Ind. (dir. 1972-73) assns. broadcasters, Ind. (dir. 1976—), Indpls. (dir. 1972—) chambers commerce; Broadcasters Assn. (dir. 1972-73), Sigma Nu. Mason. Clubs: Columbia (pres. 1970), Indianapolis Athletic, Meridian Hills Country (Indpls.). Home: 8423 Overlook Pkwy Indianapolis IN 46260 Office: 1950 N Meridian St Indianapolis IN 46202

MC COOK, JOHN EDWARD, packaging co. exec.; b. Pitts., Jan. 4, 1936; s. John Ahl and Helen Patricia (McDavitt) McC.; B.A., Waynesburg Coll., 1959, postgrad., 1964; m. Rosemary Maraventano, June 30, 1962; children—John Ahl, Rosemary Frances. With Liberty Mut. Ins. Co., N.Y.C., 1961-62; salesman U.S. Envelope Co. div. Westvaco, N.Y.C., 1962-66; account exec. Mead Packaging, N.Y.C., 1966-71; nat. sales product mgr. Alton Box Board Co., Alton, Ill., 1971—; cons. N.Y. Small Businessmen Assn. Mem. exec. com. Cub Scouts; fund-raiser Khoury League; chmn. ch. bldg. fund. Served with U.S. Army, 1959-61. Mem. Sales and Mktg. Execs., Packaging Inst. (asso.). Clubs: West County Lawn Tennis Assn. (pres.), Forest Lake Tennis, River Bend Bath and Tennis. Home: 149 River Bend Dr Chesterfield MO 63017 Office: 401 Alton St Alton IL 62002

MC CORD, JOHN HARRISON, educator, lawyer; b. Oceanside, N.Y., Dec. 22, 1934; s. John Francis and Elsie (Powers) M.; A.B., Fordham Coll., 1957; J.D. (St. Thomas More fellow), St. John's U., 1960; LL.M., U. Ill., 1965; m. Maureen Ursula Maclean, Dec. 30, 1961; children—John F.X., Paul V., David G., Maureen E. Admitted to N.Y. bar, 1960, Ill. bar, 1964; atty. U.S. Dept. Justice, Washington, 1960-61; mem. faculty U. Ill. Coll. of Law, Champaign, 1964—, prof. law, 1965—. Acad. cons. Ill. Inst. on Continuing Legal Edn., 1968-72; vis. prof. law U. N.C., 1975, U. Hawaii, 1976. Served to capt. USAF, 1961-64. Mem. Am. (mem. com. on continuing legal edn. and chief reporter for study outline on buying, selling and merging businesses sect. fed. tax 1969-73; mem. com. estate and gift taxes 1973—, chmn. subcom. gross estate issues 1976—), Ill. (mem. exec. council fed. tax sect. 1966-73, chmn. sect. 1971-72), Chgo., Champaign County bar assns., Am. Judicature Soc., AAUP, Am. Arbitration Assn. (mem. nat. panel arbitrators 1969—), Eastern Ill. Estate Planning Council (pres. 1970-71), Assn. Am. Law Schs. (mem. fed. taxation roundtable council 1969-72), Order of Coif. Author: (with Keeton and O'Connell) Crisis in Car Insurance, 1967; Buying and Selling Small Businesses, 1969; (with O'Byrne) Deskbook for Illinois Estate Planners, 1969; Closely Held Corporations, 1971; (with Pedrick, Kirby, others) The Study of Federal Tax Law, 1972; (with O'Neill, Pearlman and Stroud) Buying, Selling and Merging Businesses, 1975; (with Lowndes and Kramer) Estate and Gift Taxes, 3d edit., 1974; (with McKee) Federal Income Taxation—A Summary Analysis, 1975; (with Kramer) Problems for Federal Estate and Gift Taxes, 1976. Editor: Dimensions of Academic Freedom, 1969; With All Deliberate Speed: Civil Rights Theory and Reality, 1969. Editor: Ill. Law Forum, 1965-69. Contbr. articles in field to profl. jours. Home: 15 Sherwin Dr Urbana IL 61801 Office: University Illinois College of Law Champaign IL 61820

MC CORMACK, MARK HUME, lawyer, corp. exec.; b. Chgo., Nov. 6, 1930; s. Ned Hume and Grace Catherine (Wolfe) McC.; B.A., William and Mary Coll., 1951; LL.B., Yale U., 1954; m. Nancy Breckenridge, Oct. 9, 1954; children—Scott Breckenridge, Todd Hume, Mary Leslie. Admitted to Ohio bar, 1958, since practiced in Cleve.; partner firm Arter & Hadden (and predecessor firm), Cleve. Pres., chmn. Internat. Mgmt. Group, mgrs. profl. athletes, Cleve., 1960—. Named to Sport Hall of Fame Coll. of William and Mary, 1971. Author: Arnie, The Evolution of a Legend, 1967; The World of Professional Golf, 1967-76; The Wonderful World of Professional Golf, 1973. Home: 2830 Lander Rd Cleveland OH 44124 Office: 1 Erieview Plaza Suite 1300 Cleveland OH 44114

MC CORMICK, BROOKS, mfg. exec.; b. Chgo., Feb. 23, 1917; s. Chauncey and Marion (Deering) McC.; grad. Groton Sch., 1936; B.A., Yale U., 1940; m. Hope Baldwin, 1940. With Internat. Harvester Co., 1940—, mfg. sales positions various locations U.S. and Gt. Britain, 1940-54, dir. mfg., 1954-57, exec. v.p., 1957-68, pres., 1968—, chief exec. officer, 1971—, also dir.; dir. 1st Nat. Bank, Chgo., Esmark, Inc., Commonwealth Edison Co.; adv. bd. internat. bus. Chem. Bank. Gen. chmn. Crusade of Mercy, 1961; bd. dirs. Community Fund of Chgo., 1960-77, pres., 1973-75; chmn. Nat. Safety Council, 1965-67. Life trustee Rush Presbyn. St. Luke's Med. Center; trustee Art Inst. Chgo., 1954—, Ill. Inst. Tech., 1962-75, Motor Vehicle Mfrs. Assn. (dir.), Chgo. Urban League (chmn. bus. adv. council 1967-76). Episcopalian. Clubs: Chicago, Commercial. Office: 401 N Michigan Ave Chicago IL 60611

MC CORMICK, HOPE BALDWIN (MRS. BROOKS MCCORMICK), Republican nat. committeewoman; b. N.Y.C., July 9, 1919; d. Alexander Taylor and Loise (Bisbee) Baldwin; student Ethel Walker Sch., Simsbury, Conn.; m. Brooks McCormick, June 26, 1940; children—Martha (Mrs. William O. Hunt, Jr.), Brooks II, Mark B., Abby D. (Mrs. Robert D. Stuart III). Mem. Ill. Ho. of Reps., 1965-67; mem. for Ill., Rep. Nat. Com., now vice-chmn. Past mem. women's bd. Children's Meml. Hosp., Lyric Opera; founder past pres. Ill. Epilepsy League; mem. women's bd. Rush-Presbyn.-St. Luke's Med. Center, Art Inst. of Chg., Field Mus. Natural History. Chmn. women's div. United Rep. Fund, 1957-61, bd. govs., 1957-65, now mem. exec. com. of bd. govs.; pres. Rep. Citizens Com. of 9th Congl. Dist., 1961-66; alternate del. Rep. Nat. Conv., 1968; now mem. exec. com. Ill. Fedn. Rep. Women. Trustee Ill. Children's Home and Aid Soc., Museum Sci. and Industry, MacMurray Coll., Chgo. Symphony Orch. Assn.; bd. govs. Rec. for the Blind; past dir. Chgo. Pub. Sch. Art Soc.; past trustee Chgo. Latin Sch.; past trustee, dir. Better Govt. Assn. Episcopalian. Address: 1530 N State Pkwy Chicago IL 60610

MC CORMICK, JOHN, hosp. adminstr.; b. New London, Conn., Mar. 29, 1943; s. John Donald and Gloria (Fernandez) McC.; M.H.A., Baylor U., 1969; m. Charlotte Anita Kearns, Apr. 2, 1965; children—Jacqueline Ann, John David. Asso. adminstr. Kelsey Seybold Clinic, Houston, 1971-74; project dir., dir. Robert Wood Johnson Found. grant Med. Group Mgmt. Assn., Denver, 1974-76; adminstr. Mayo Clinic, Rochester, Minn., 1976—. Served with AUS, 1965-71. Decorated Bronze Star. Recipient Glenn Ebersole award Assn. Western Hosps., 1968, Marshal Provost award Furman U., 1965. Mem. Am. Hosp. Assn., Med. Group Mgmt. Assn. Author: (with others) The Organization and Development of a Medical Group Practice, 1976; (with others) Medical Group Practice Management, 1977; the Management of Medical Practice, 1978. Home: 2303 Crest Ln SW Rochester MN 55901 Office: Mayo Clinic 200 First St SW Rochester MN 55901

MC CORMICK, MICHAEL DONALD, broadcasting exec.; b. Jeffersonville, Ind., Sept. 12, 1929; s. Patrick P. and May Theresa (Staton) McC.; m. Gay Dawn Medlin, Aug. 28, 1976; children—Timothy, Michele, Maureen, John, Kelly; student Ind. U., 1949-51. Vice pres., gen. mgr. KPLR-TV, St. Louis, 1966-70, WOR-TV, N.Y.C., 1970-72; pres. WTMJ, Inc., Milw., 1972—; v.p., dir. Journal Co., Milw.; mem. affiliates bd. NBC-TV. Bd. dirs. Milw. Internat. Summer Festival. Mem. Nat. Acad. Television Arts and Scis. (life mem., pres. St. Louis chpt. 1969-70). Home: 10848 N Pebble Ln Mequon WI 53092 Office: 720 E Capitol Dr Milwaukee WI 53201

MC CORMICK, ROBERT WILLIAM, educator; b. Venice, Ohio, Dec. 1, 1921; s. William A. and Rachel (Elmes) McC.; B.S., Ohio State U., 1948, M.S., 1956; Ph.D., U. Wis., 1959; m. Jean Schudel, Aug. 30, 1947 (dec. Mar. 13, 1969); children—Nicola Jo (Mrs. Rodney Myers), Christopher William; m. 2d, Virginia M. Evans, Oct. 7, 1972. Tchr., Union Twp. Schs., West Chester, Ohio, 1948-51; county extension agt. Ohio State U., 1951-54, instr., 1954-56, asst. prof., 1956-60, asso. prof., 1960-63, prof., 1963-77, prof. emeritus, 1977—, dir., asso. to v.p. Div. Continuing Edn., 1966-67, asst. v.p. for continuing edn., 1967-77. Served with AUS, 1943-45. Decorated Bronze Star. Kellogg Found. fellow, 1957-59. Mem. Adult Edn. Assn., Ohio Adult Edn. Assn. (dir.), Nat. U. Extension Assn., Am. Acad. Polit. and Social Sci., Am. Soc. Pub. Adminstrn., Phi Delta Kappa, Gamma Sigma Delta. Contbr. articles to profl. jours. Home: 1091 Morning St Worthington OH 43085 Office: Ohio State U Columbus OH 43210

MC CORMICK, ROGER DEAN, ednl. adminstr.; b. Logan County, Ohio, May 5, 1927; s. Paul Lister and Bernice Zenade (McPherson) McC.; B.S., Miami U., Oxford, Ohio, 1949; M.A., Ohio State U., 1957, Ph.D., 1969; m. Patricia Ann Green, Aug. 27, 1950; children—Paula, Michael, Mark, Mary Heather. Tchr., coach Martinsville (Ohio) Schs., 1949-53; dental technician Green Dental Lab., Dayton, Ohio, 1953-54; local supt. Martinsville Schs., 1954-60; tchr., coordinator Kettering (Ohio) City Schs., 1961-62, asst. prin. D.L. Barnes Jr. High Sch., 1962-65, supr. pupil personnel services, 1966-74, asst. supt. instructional services, 1974—; counselor Columbus (Ohio) City Schs., 1965-66; adj. asso. prof. guidance and counseling Wright State U., Dayton, 1968—; adj. asso. prof. Grad. Sch. Edn. U. Dayton, 1972—. Served with USNR, 1945-46. Mem. Am., Buckeye assns. sch. adminstrs., Am. Psychol. Assn., Am., Miami Valley (pres. 1971-72) personnel and guidance assns., Assn. Counselor Educators and Suprs., Assn. Supervision and Curriculum Devel., Am. Sch. Counselors Assn., Nat. Vocat. Guidance Assn., Council Exceptional Children, Ohio Assn. Children Learning Disabilities. (Pres. 1971-73), Ohio, Nat. edn. assns. Presbyn. Clubs: Optimists (pres. Dorwood 1971-72), Masons, Shriners, Order Eastern Star. Author: (with Herman Peters and Michael Shelley) Random House Elementary Guidance Program, 1966. Home: 4508 Drayton Ct Kettering OH 45440 Office: 3490 Far Hills Ave Kettering OH 45429

MC CORMICK, SCOTT, JR., educator; b. Evanston, Ill., June 4, 1929; s. Scott and Emma (Knuchell) McC.; B.A. summa cum laude, Davis and Elkins Coll., 1953; B.D., Union Theol. Sem., 1956, Th.M. (Moses D. Hoge fellow), 1957, Th.D., 1959; m. Mary Helen McLeod, June 2, 1956; children—Jane H., Scott III, Donald A. Ordained to ministry Presbyn. Ch., 1956; minister Tyler Meml. Presbyn. Ch., Radford, Va., 1958-65; prof. religion Washington and Jefferson Coll., Washington, Pa., 1965-70; Hastings (Nebr.) Coll., 1970—. Cons. to study commns. of the World and Nat. Council of Chs., 1966-72. Organizing chmn. Council on Human Relations, Radford, Va., 1963-64; chmn. the Human Relations Commn. of Washington, Pa., 1969-70. Chmn. bd. dir. United Fund, Radford, Va., 1961-63. Grantee United Presbyn. Ch., 1967-70. Mem. Am. Acad. Religion, Soc. of Bibl. Lit. Author: The Lord's Supper: A Biblical Interpretation, 1966. Contbr. articles in field to profl. jours. Home: 1120 Pleasant St Hastings NE 68901

MC CORMICK, WILLIAM EDWARD, assn. exec.; b. Potters Mills, Pa., Feb. 9, 1912; s. George H. and Nellie (Mingle) McC.; B.S., Pa. State U., 1933, M.S., 1934; m. Goldie Stover, June 6, 1935; children—John F., Kirk W. Tchr., Centre Hall (Pa.) High Sch., 1934-37; chemist Willson Products, Inc., Reading, Pa., 1937-43; indsl. hygienist Ga. Dept. Pub. Health, Atlanta, 1946; mgr. indsl. hygiene and toxicology B.F. Goodrich Co., Akron, Ohio, 1946-70, mgr. environ. control, 1970-73; mng. dir. Am. Indsl. Hygiene Assn., Akron, 1973—; exec. sec. Soc. Toxicology, 1976—. Mem. exec. com., rubber sect. Nat. Safety Council, 1955-73; mem. environ. health com. Chlorine Inst., 1968-73; mem. food, drug and cosmetic chems. com. Mfg. Chemists Assn., 1960-73, chmn., 1967-69, also mem. occupational health com., 1965-73; mem. adv. com. on heat stress U.S. Dept. Labor, 1973. Served to capt. USPHS, 1943-46. Mem. Am. Chem. Soc., Soc. Toxicology, AAAS, Am. Indsl. Hygiene Assn. (pres. 1964), Indsl. Hygiene Roundtable. Republican. Episcopalian. Mason. Contbr. articles to profl. jours. Home: 419 Dorchester Rd Akron OH 44320 Office: Am Indsl Hygiene Assn 475 Wolf Ledges Pkwy Akron OH 44311

MC COY, DONALD EDWARD, mgmt. cons.; b. Stanberry, Mo., Nov. 7, 1923; s. William Arthur and Gretchen Beulah (Frederick) McC.; B.A., U. Kansas City, 1946, M.A., 1948; AST fgn. area studies U. Calif. at Los Angeles, 1944; postgrad. U. Kans., 1947-49; Ph.D., U. Ill, 1952; m. Mary Sue Kearny, Aug. 31, 1946 (dec. 1967); children—Janet Sue, William Kearny, Barbara Anne; m. 2d, Ann Marie Barnes, Dec. 13, 1967; 1 dau., Tina Marie. Mem. faculty U. Kansas City, 1946-47, U. Kans., 1947-49, U. Ill., 49-52, 1956-61, U. Minn., 1952-56; prof. English, dir. summer sessions Principia Coll., Elsah, Ill., 1961-68; vis. prof. English U. Mo. at St. Louis, 1968-70; partner Higginbotham & McCoy, mgmt. cons., St. Louis, 1968-71; prin. D.E. McCoy Assos., ednl. and mgmt. cons., St. Louis, 1971—. Vice pres. Sales Dynamic Supply Inc. and Dynamic Prodns., St. Louis, 1971-75; pres. McCoy & Ross, Inc., communication resources assos., St. Louis, 1975-78; pres. Communication Centers Am., St. Louis, 1978—. Served with AUS, 1943-46; ETO; capt. USAF Res., ret. Fellow Internat. Inst. Arts and Letters (Geneva); mem. Am. Soc. Tng. and Devel., Internat. Platform Assn., Sigma Tau Delta. Club: Cadillac LaSalle. Author: Keys to Good Instruction, 1956, 58, 67; (with T.J. Kallsen) Rhetoric and Reading: Order and Idea, 1962. Editor Word Study, quarterly, 1958-70. Home: 1138 Westmoor Pl Saint Louis MO 63131 Office: 9600 Manchester Rd Saint Louis MO 63119

MC COY, E. JASON, JR., wholesale distbg. co. exec.; b. Canton, Ohio, July 5, 1923; s. Edgar Jason and Irene May (Stahl) McC.; B.A. magna cum laude, Kenyon Coll., 1944; M.B.A., Harvard U., 1947; m. Janet Ann Lynn, Mar. 3, 1945; children—Marjorie McCoy Mapes, Eric, Bradley. Sec., J.B. McCoy & Son Inc., Canton, Ohio, 1947-62, pres., 1962—. Bd. trustees YMCA, 1963—, internat. pres. Internat. Assn. of Y's, 1964; v.p. Buckeye Council Boy Scouts Am., 1976—; pres. Jr. Achievement, 1977-78; elder, former deacon Calvary Presbyn. Ch. Served to lt. comdr. USNR, 1943-46. Named Man of the Yr., Eastern Ohio Restaurant Assn., 1969. Mem. C. of C. (trustee 1972-76), Canton Wholesalers Assn. (past pres.), Nat. Candy Wholesalers Assn. (past dir.), Jr. Candy Execs. (past pres.), Phi Beta Kappa. Clubs: Rotary (pres. Canton chpt. 1974), Beta Theta Pi. Contbr. articles to trade mags. Home: 2923 Acacia Dr NW Canton OH 44718 Office: 1310 5th St NE Canton OH 44704

MC COY, FREDERICK JOHN, physician, surgeon; b. McPherson, Kans., Jan. 17, 1916; s. Merle D. and Mae (Tennis) McC.; B.S., U. Kans., 1938, M.D., 1942; m. Mary Bock, May 17, 1972; children—Judith, Frederick John, Patricia, Melissa, Steven. Intern Lucas County (Ohio) Hosp., Toledo, 1942-43; resident in plastic surgery U. Tex. Sch. of Medicine, Galveston, 1946; preceptorship in surgery, Grand Rapids, Mich., 1947-50; practice medicine specializing in plastic and reconstructive surgery, Kansas City, Mo., 1950—; mem. staff, chief plastic surgery Kansas City Gen. Hosp. and Med. Center, 1952—, Children's Mercy Hosp., 1954—, Research Hosp., 1950—, St. Luke's Hosp., 1951—, Baptist Hosp., 1958—, Meml. Hosp., 1950—; chmn. maxillo-facial surgery U. Kansas City Sch. of Dentistry, 1950-57; asso. prof. surgery Sch. of Medicine, U. Mo., Kansas City, 1964-69, clin. prof. surgery, 1969—. Served to maj. M.C., U.S. Army, 1943-46. Diplomate Am. Bd. Plastic Surgery (dir. 1973—). Mem. Am. Soc. of Plastic and Reconstructive Surgeons (dir. 1973-76, pres. 1976, chmn. bd. 1977), Pan-Pacific, Singleton (v.p. 1965) surg. socs., Am. Assn. of Plastic Surgeons, Am., Internat. socs. for aesthetic plastic surgery, Jackson County Med. Soc. (pres. 1964-65), Kansas City Southwest Clin. Soc. (pres. 1971), Mo. State Med. Assn. (v.p. 1975), AMA, A.C.S., Internat. Coll. of Surgeons (v.p. 1969), Kansas City C. of C., Conservation Fedn. of Mo., Natural Sci. Soc. (founder, chmn. 1973), Citizen's Assn. of Kansas City, Phi Delta Theta, Nu Sigma Nu. Republican. Mem. Christian Ch. Clubs: Mission Hills Country. Contbr. articles in field to profl. jours. and books; editor Year Book of Plastic and Reconstructive Surgery, 1971—. Home: 5814 Mission Dr Shawnee Mission KS 66208 Office: 4177 Broadway Kansas City MO 64111

MCCOY, JEANIE SHEARER, chemist; b. Mancelona, Mich., May 27, 1921; d. Theophilus R. and Goldie Margaret (Halladay) Schroeder; A.A., North Park Coll., 1941; B.S., Northwestern U., 1944; M.S., No. Ill. U., 1970; m. Theodore R. Shearer, June 14, 1958 (div. 1964); 1 son, Blair B.; m. 2d, George A. McCoy, July 23, 1966. Jr. analytical chemist Buick Motor div. Gen. Motors, Melrose Park, Ill., 1944-45; asst. research chemist Hodson Corp., Chgo., 1945-47; asst. analytical chemist Internat. Harvester Co., 1947-49, analytical chemist, 1949-63, prin. chemist, 1963-75, supr. metall. process control, testing labs., 1975—. Mem. Am. Chem. Soc., Am. Soc. Lubrication Engrs., Soc. Applied Spectroscopy, Soc. Automotive Engrs. Asso. editor Lubrication Engring. mag., 1976—. Home: 654 West Rd Lombard IL 60148 Office: International Harvester Co Melrose Park IL 60160

MC COY, JOHN GARDNER, banker; b. Marietta, Ohio, Jan. 30, 1913; s. John H. and Florence (Buchanan) McC.; A.B., Marietta Coll., 1935; M.B.A., Stanford U., 1937; LL.D. (hon.), Kenyon Coll., 1970; m. Jeanne Newlove Bonnet, Jan. 4, 1941; children—John B., Virginia B. With City Nat. Bank & Trust Co., Columbus, Ohio, 1937—, pres., 1958—, chmn. bd., 1968-77; pres. 1st Banc Group Ohio Inc., 1968—; chmn. Buckeye Steel Castings Co. now Buckeye Internat., Inc. Chmn. Devel. Com. for Greater Columbus, 1962-64. Bd. dirs. Franklin County chpt, ARC; trustee Marietta Coll. Served to lt. USNR, 1943-45. Mem. Assn. Res. City Bankers, Columbus Area C. of C. (past chmn.), Delta Upsilon. Clubs: Columbus, Columbus Country, Columbus Golf; University (Columbus and N.Y.C.); Hole in the Wall Golf, Royal Poinciana (Naples, Fla.); Little Harbor (Harbor Springs, Mich.); Muirfield Village Golf (Dublin, Ohio). Home: 11 Sessions Dr Columbus OH 43209 Office: 100 E Broad St Columbus OH 43215

MC COY, ROBERT CALVIN, mgmt. scientist, psychologist, educator; b. Detroit, Apr. 19, 1921; s. Reed Lawrence and Blanche Irene (French) McC.; A.B., Albion Coll., 1942; M.A., Wayne State U., 1947, Ph.D., 1966; m. Jean M. McCully, Apr. 8, 1944; children—Richard Paul, Mark David, Sally Jane. Indsl. and community relations mgr. Calumet & Hecla Inc., Detroit, 1947-61; dir. corp. personnel services Am. Motors Inc., Detroit, 1961-64; cons. psychologist William, Lynde & Williams, Detroit, 1964-68; orgn., personnel mgmt. cons. Ernst & Ernst, Detroit, 1968-72; asso. prof. mgmt. Coll. Bus., Eastern Mich. U., Ypsilanti, 1972—; corp. mem. Detroit Indsl. Mission, 1972—. Regional vice chmn. Detroit Citizens Adv. Com. Sch. Needs, 1958. Chmn. bd. mgmt. Detroit Western YMCA, 1953; dir. Detroit City Beautification campaign, 1955; v.p. Detroit Jr. Bd. Commerce, 1956-61; vice chmn. Detroit Indsl. Mission, 1970-72; mem. citizens for Mich. 1959-61. Trustee Albion Coll., 1968-77; bd. dirs. John C. Campbell Folk Sch., 1976—. Served from pvt. to capt., AUS, 1942-46. Mem. Internat. Communications Assn., Am. Psychol. Assn., Acad. Mgmt., Am. Mgmt. Assn., Am. Soc. Tng. and Devel. (pres. Mich. 1951-52), Audubon Soc., Detroit Employment Mgrs. Club, Phi Beta Kappa, Omicron Delta Kappa, Psi Chi, Delta Sigma Pi, Beta Gamma Sigma. Methodist (ch. lay leader). Mason. Contbr. articles mgmt., communications, corp. responsibility to profl. publs. Home: 3465 Woodland Rd Ann Arbor MI 48104 Office: Eastern Mich U Ypsilanti MI 48197

MC COY, ROBERT LEE, constrn. co. exec.; b. Whitley County, Ind., Dec. 25, 1924; s. Hubert O. and Edna M. (Schinbeckler) McC.; grad., Tri-State Coll., 1946; m. Donna Von Burns, Apr. 5, 1947; children—Michael L., Marcia A., Mark W. Pres., Heavy Constrn., Inc., Columbia City, Ind., 1961—. Served with AUS, 1944-46; ETO. Decorated 3 Bronze Clusters. Mem. Tri-State Alumni, Am. Legion. Roman Catholic. Clubs: Century (Columbia City, Ind.), Elks (ruler lodge, dist. ruler 1976-77), K.C. Home: Route 7 Columbia City IN 46725 Office: Route 7 Columbia City IN 46725

MC COY, ROBIN, ednl. adminstr.; b. Oklahoma City, Okla., Feb. 14, 1914; s. Frank Thomas and Virginia (Hightower) McCoy; A.B., Harvard U., 1935, A.M., 1940; B.A., Cambridge (Eng.) U., 1937, M.A., 1941; postgrad. U. Colo., 1937, U. Pitts., 1943-44. Tchr. Shattuck Sch., Faribault, Minn., 1937-39; instr. Okla. Agrl. and Mech. Coll., Stillwater, 1940-41; tchr. Milw. Country Day Sch., 1941-42, Phillips Exeter Acad., Exeter, N.H., 1942, 45, Milton (Mass.) Acad., 1944-46; founding head master, tchr. Thomas Jefferson Sch., St. Louis, 1946—. Served with USAAF, 1942-44. Mem. Soc. Italian Studies (Eng.), Classical Assn. New Eng. (hon.), Harvard Clubs Boston, N.Y.C., St. Louis. Contbr. articles to profl. publs. Address: 4100 S Lindbergh Blvd St Louis MO 63127

MC CRACKEN, DALE RUSSELL, mfg. co. exec.; b. Newark, Ohio, June 10, 1918; s. Henry Wilson and Jennie Blanche (Weakley) McC.; B.S. in Edn., Miami U. (Ohio), 1940; M.S., Purdue U., 1946; m. Jeannette Emma Seiss, Dec. 25, 1941; 1 son, Robert Dale. Training dir. Radio Corp. Am., Indpls., 1946-47; indsl. engr., Champion Spark Plug Co., Toledo, Ohio, 1947-65, dir., indsl. engring., 1965-67, dir. indsl. relations, 1967-72, dir. mfg. services, 1972-73, gen. mgr. mfg., 1973-74, v.p., gen. mfg. mgr., 1975—. Served with USN, 1943-46. Mem. Toledo Mgmt. Club (pres. 1952-53), Am. Inst. Indsl. Engrs., Sigma Chi. Home: 4753 Woodland St Port Clinton OH 43452 Office: 900 Upton St Toledo OH 43661

MC CRACKEN, HAROLD MACKENZIE, business exec.; b. Farmington, Mich., Feb. 3, 1904; s. Harry Norton and Isabella Florence (MacKenzie) McC.; A.B., Albion Coll., 1926; m. Helene Charlotte Sooy, June 10, 1933. Teller 1st Nat. Bank of Commerce Detroit, 1926-28; tax clk. Oakland County, Mich., 1928-29; treas. Gray Marine Motor Co., 1930-47; sec., treas., co-founder MP Pumps, Inc., Detroit, 1942-69, dir., 1942-75; past chmn. bd., co-founder, dir. Am. Community Mut. Ins. Co., 1938—; partner McBee Investors, 1943-76. Mem. Internat. Platform Assn., Ins. Inst. Am., Nat. Assn. Accountants, S.A.R., U.S. Power Squadron, Tau Kappa Epsilon. Presbyterian. Mason (K.T.), Rotarian. Clubs: Round Table (Plymouth, Mich.); Detroit Yacht, Economic (Detroit). Home: 295 Stephens Rd Grosse Pointe Farms MI 48236

MC CRACKEN, REGINALD LEO, elec. engr.; b. New Albany, Ind., Sept. 2, 1942; s. Herman Leo and Patricia (Parsons) McC.; B.S., Purdue U., 1965, M.S., 1967; m. Nancy Ann Merrill, Apr. 3, 1965; children—Nathanial Leo, Clayton Thor, Rebecca Dulcinea, Heidi Michelle. Elec. engr. Rotz Engring. Co., Indpls., 1971-73; pres. DM Engring. Co., Indpls., 1972—; county surveyor Morgan County (Ind.), 1973—. Mem. Morgan County Planning Commn., 1973—. Registered profl. engr., Ind., Ohio, Ky. Mem. Nat. Soc. Profl. Engrs. Republican. Baptist. Home: Box 439 Painted Hills St Martinsville IN 46151 Office: DM Engring Inc 6214 Morenci Trail Indianapolis IN 46268

MC CREERY, ROBERT HERMAN, metall. engr.; b. Muncie, Ind., Sept. 11, 1925; s. Herman and Margaret Allena (McKinley) McC.; student U. Ky., 1943, Ball State U., 1944-45; B.S. in Metall. Engring., Purdue U., 1948; m. Helen Brown, Dec. 21, 1947; children—Ann, Sarah. Metallurgist Internat. Harvester Corp., Evansville, Ind., 1948-51, prin. metallurgist, 1951-55; plant metallurgist Warner Gear div. Borg Warner Corp., Muncie, 1955-60; chief metallurgist Teledyne Portland Forge (Ind.), 1960-76; v.p. metall. engring. Teledyne, Portland Forge, 1976—. Fellow Am. Soc. Metals (nat. trustee 1969-71); mem. Nat. Soc. Profl. Engrs. Presbyterian (deacon, elder). Mason (32 deg.), Elk, Rotarian (pres. Portland 1964-65). Home: 321 E High St Portland IN 47371 Office: Teledyne Portland Forge PO Box 905 Portland IN 47371

MC CRONE, WALTER COX, research chemist; b. Wilmington, Del., June 9, 1916; s. Walter Cox and Bessie Lillian (Cook) McC.; B.Chemistry, Cornell U., 1938, Ph.D., 1942; m. Lucy Beman, July 13, 1957. With Ill. Inst. Tech. Research Inst., 1944-56; officer Walter C. McCrone Assos., Inc., Chgo., 1956—; pres. McCrone Research Inst., Inc., 1962—; dir. McCrone Research Assos., Ltd., London, McCrone Research Inst., Ltd., London; editor, pub. Microscope, London, 1962—; tchr. Ill. Inst. Tech., 1952—. Pres. bd. trustees Ada S. McKinley Community Services, Chgo. Recipient Benedetti-Pichler award Microchem. Soc., 1970. Mem. Am. Chem. Soc., Am. Phys. Soc., Royal, N.Y. (Ernst Abbe award), Ill. micros. socs., Am. Soc. Forensic Scientists, Midwest Soc. Electron Microscopists, Assn. Ofcl. Analytical Chemists, Sigma Xi, Phi Lambda Upsilon, Alpha Chi Sigma. Author books, chpts. in books; contbr. articles to profl. jours. Home: 501 E 32d St Chicago IL 60616 Office: 2820 S Michigan Ave Chicago IL 60616

MC CRORY, EDWARD LAWRENCE, ins. co. exec.; b. Grainola, Okla., June 29, 1921; s. William Lawrence and Jeanette Harriet (Matthews) McC.; B.J., U. Mo., 1949; m. Patricia Ann Curtis, Nov. 25, 1950; children—Bradley Lawrence, Linda Ann. Asst. editor Packer Publ. Co., Kansas City, Mo., 1949-51; supr. publicity Country Companies, Bloomington, Ill., 1951-59; dir. advt. and pub. relations Wolverine Ins. Co., Battle Creek, Mich., 1959-64, v.p., 1964; dir. advt. and pub. relations Fed. Life and Casualty Co., Battle Creek, 1959—; sr. v.p., People Home Life Ins Co. Ind., Battle Creek, 1970-78; sr. v.p. corporate communications Fed. Home Cos., 1978—. Bd. dirs. YMCA, Mich. Heart Assn., Calhoun County; mem. pub. relations com. Mich. Heart Assn., 1975—. Served with AUS, 1941-45. Mem. Pub. Relations Soc. Am., Life Ins. Advertisers Assn., Ins. Advt. Conf., Southwestern Mich. Adv. Roundtable (dir.), Alpha Delta Sigma. Republican. Presbyterian. Clubs: Battle Creek Country, Athelstan. Home: 27 Birch Hill Dr Battle Creek MI 48015 Office: 78 Michigan Ave W Battle Creek MI 49016

MC CROWEY, GEORGE ANTHONY, rehab. psychologist; b. Athens, Ga., Feb. 7, 1936; s. Scott and Mary Frances (Elder) McC.; B.A., Roosevelt U., 1967; M.S., Ill. Inst. Tech., 1973; m. Sherby Jean Harrell, Jan. 3, 1959; 1 son, George Christopher. Rehab. counselor, casework supr. Ill. Div. Vocat. Rehab., Chgo., 1967, rehab. facilities coordinator, service supr., 1972-74; asst. dir. Univ. Without Walls Chgo. State U., 1974-75; rehab. services program specialist HEW Rehab. Services Adminstrn., Chgo., 1975—. Pres. sch. bd. Holy Angels Catholic Sch., 1960-70; pres. Men's Club Holy Angels Catholic Ch., 1968-69; coordinator ARC Blood Drive for Cook County Region of Ill. Div. Vocat. Rehab., 1973. Served with U.S. Army, 1959-61. Research fellow rehab. psychology Ill. Inst. Tech., 1974-75; certified rehab. counselor Commn. Rehab. Counselor Certification, 1975. Mem. Nat. Rehab. Assn., Nat. Rehab. Counseling Assn. (bd. dir. 1975-77), Am. Personnel and Guidance Assn., Am. Rehab. Counseling Assn., Am. Mgmt. Assn., Ill. Rehab. Assn. (pres. 1974), Ill. Rehab. Counselors Assn. (pres. 1975). Clubs: K.C. Editor Ill. Rehab. Counseling Assn. Quarterly, 1972. Office: 300 S Wacker Room 1500 Chicago IL 60606

MC CRYSTAL, FRANK, psychiatrist; b. Belfast, No. Ireland, Sept. 3, 1920; s. Frank and Margaret (Donnelly) McC.; student Queens U., Belfast, 1936-48; M.D., Royal Coll. Physicians and Surgeons in Ireland, 1952; m. Maurita Kelly, June 30, 1961; 1 son, Frank III. Intern, Mercers Hosp., Dublin, 1952-53, Rotunda Hosp., Dublin, 1953; rotating resident Westminster Hosp., Victoria Hosp., St. Joseph's Hosp., London, Ont., Can., 1958-62; staff psychiatrist Ont. Hosp., St. Thomas, 1962-63; acting chief psychiatry VA Hosp., Perry Point, Md., 1963-65; practice medicine specializing in psychiatry, Kitchener, Ont., 1965—; cons. psychiatry St. Mary's Gen. Hosp.; sec.-treas. dept. psychiatry Kitchener-Waterloo Hosp. Served as comdt. Irish Army, 1939-45. U. Western Ont. fellow psychiatry, 1960-62. Diplomate Am. Bd. Psychiatry. Mem. Brit., Irish, Canadian med. assns., Am. Psychiat. Assn., Coll. Physicians and Surgeons of Ont. K.C. Clubs: Nat. Sporting (Belfast); Turf, Ont. Jockey. Home: 194 Mohawk Ave Waterloo ON N2L 2T4 Canada Office: 920 King St Kitchener ON N2G 1G4 Canada

MC CUBBREY, DAVID RAYMOND, surgeon; b. Canada, Dec. 15, 1928; s. David Dunlop and Ann (Zayots) McC.; came to U.S., 1929, naturalized, 1937; M.D., U. Mich., 1953; m. Claire Ward Lambert, Mar. 25, 1950; children—David, Douglas, Doris. Intern, Albany (N.Y.) Hosp., 1953-54; resident St. Joseph Hosp., Ann Arbor, Mich., 1957-61; practice medicine specializing in surgery, Plymouth, Mich., 1961—; mem. staff St. Joseph Hosp., Ann Arbor, St. Mary Hosp., Livonia, Mich. Served with AUS, 1955-57. Mem. A.C.S. Home: 505 McKinley St Plymouth MI 48170 Office: 221 Sheldon St Plymouth MI 48170

MC CUBE, ARTHUR LEE, chemist; b. Otsego, Mich., Dec. 18, 1937; s. Arthur Lee and Florence Gertrude (Mollison) McC.; student Kalamazoo Coll., 1956-58, Western Mich. U., 1958-59; m. Nancy Lee Smith, June 26, 1959; children—Janet Lee, William Arthur, Sherry Linn, Arthur Lee, Elizabeth Ann, Susan Faye. Asst. mgr. D & C Stores, Kalamazoo, 1959-60; asst. fleet supt. McNamara Motor Express Co., Kalamazoo, 1960-61; with Upjohn Co., Kalamazoo, 1961-63; chemistry technician Consumers Power Co., Kalamazoo, 1963-66, sr. chemistry technician, 1966-73, sr. radiation protection technician Palisades plant, Covert, Mich., 1973-74, chemistry supr., Palisades Nuclear Plant, 1974—. Dist. commr. Southwestern Mich. council Boy Scouts Am., 1973-74. Republican. Inventor in field. Home: R-3 PO Box 221 M-140 South Haven MI 49090 Office: R 2 PO Box 154 Blue Star Hwy Covert MI 49043

MC CUBE, BRIAN FRANCIS, physician; b. Detroit, June 16, 1926; s. Charles J. and Rosalie T. (Dropeske) McC.; B.S., U. Detroit, 1950; M.D., U. Mich., 1954; m. Yvonne L. Fecteau, Sept. 8, 1951; children—Brian F., Bevin E. Intern, Univ. Hosp., Ann Arbor, Mich., 1954-55; resident U. Mich. Med. Sch., 1955-59; practice medicine, specializing in otolaryngology and maxillofacial surgery, Iowa City, 1964—; cons. surgeon gen. USPHS, Iowa City VA Hosp.; prof., head dept. otolaryngology and maxillofacial surgery U. Iowa. Diplomate Am. Bd. Otolaryngology (dir. 1966). Mem. Am. Acad. Ophthalmology and Otolaryngology (sec. for otolaryngology), Am. Laryngol., Rhinol. and Otolaryngol. Soc., Am. Otol. Soc. (editor, librarian), Am. Laryngol. Soc. Otosclerosis Study Group, Galens Hon., Johnson County, Am., Iowa med. socs., Collegium Oto-Rhino-Laryngologicum Amicitiae Sacrum, Snipe Class Internat. Racing Assn., Nat. Amateur Yacht Racing Assn., DN Ice Yacht Racing Assn., Sigma Xi, Alpha Omega Alpha. Clubs: Centurion, Barton Boat, Hawkeye Sailing. Asso. editor Annals of Otology, Rhinology and Laryngology. Home: 237 Ferson St Iowa City IA 52240 Office: Univ Hosps and Clinics Iowa City 52242

MC CUE, JAMES JOSEPH, credit union exec.; b. Springfield, Ill., July 20. 1918; s. Peter W. and Mary (Brown) C.; B.S., DePaul U., 1941; m. Louise C. Wiesner, Oct. 21, 1944; children—Monica M., Michael J. Mgr., Am. Motors Credit Union, Milw., 1950-55; mgr. Collins Employees Credit Union, Cedar Rapids, Iowa, 1955-75, exec. v.p., 1975—; mem. Gov.'s Task Force Guaranteed Student Loans (Iowa), 1977—. Treas., Family Service Agy., 1975-76. Mem. Credit Union Execs. Soc. (dir., sec.-treas.), Iowa Credit Union League (dir.), Iowa League Corp. Central Credit Union (chmn. bd.), Nat. Accountants Assn. Club: K.C. Home: 3018 Leonard Terr NE Cedar Rapids IA 52402 Office: 1150 42d St NE Cedar Rapids IA 52402

MC CUEN, CHARLES ROBERT, savs. and loan exec.; b. Plano, Iowa, Sept. 19, 1927; s. Walter and Gladys Marie (Messerschmitt) McC.; B.A., Iowa Wesleyan Coll., 1950; m. Alice Jean Barnes, Sept. 10, 1950; children—Robert, David, Mary Lynn. With Capitol Savs. and Loan Assn., Mt. Pleasant, Iowa, 1950—, pres., 1967—; pres. United Service Corp., 1971—; dir. Iowa Investment Corp., Hawkeye Investment Co., Hawkeye Nat. Life Ins. Co., Capitol Mortgage Co., 1977—, United Service Corp., 1968—; dir. First Central Service Corp., chmn. bd., 1975, 76. Pres. Henry County ARC, 1958, Mt. Pleasant Community Sch. Bd., 1965; chmn. Radio Free Europe Fund, 1969, 70, 71; trustee, mem. exec. com. Iowa Wesleyan Coll., 1970—; bd. dirs. S.E. Iowa Symphony Orch., 1970—. Served with AUS, 1946-47. Recipient Distinguished Service award Mt. Pleasant Jaycees, 1958. Mem. Iowa Savs. and Loan League (vice chmn. 1975, chmn. 1977, dir.), Mt. Pleasant C. of C., Phi Delta Theta (alumni sec. 1954—). Clubs: Moose, Elks, Kiwanis (pres. 1960). Home: 807 Cherry Pl Mount Pleasant IA 52641 Office: 1 Washington St Mount Pleasant IA 52641

MC CUEN, HUBER MASON, dentist; b. Butler, Ohio, Sept. 20, 1917; s. Orvil Henry and Treva Estelle (Long) McC.; B.A. in Edn., Ashland Coll., 1941, B.S. in Edn., 1947; D.D.S., Ohio State U., 1952; m. Joanna Hess, June 7, 1942; children—Michael Hess (dec.), Joel Mason. Tchr., coach Ashland (Ohio) County Sch. System, 1941; golf coach Ashland Coll., 1946-47; instr. Ohio State U., Columbus, 1952; practice gen. dentistry, Ashland, 1952—; mem. staff Samaritan Hosp., Ashland, 1953—; dir. Parkwest Lanes Bowling Corp., 1966—. Mem. Ashland Bd. Health, 1960-64, pres., 1964. Served to lt. comdr. USNR, 1941-46. Mem. Am., Ohio dental assns., Ohio State U. Assn. (life), Young Men's Bus. Club (pres. 1964-65), Delta Sigma Delta (life), Alpha Psi Omega. Elk. Club: Country of Ashland. Home: 1643 Edgewood Ct Ashland OH 44805 Office: 58 W 2d St Ashland OH 44805

MC CULLOUGH, DOROTHEA GERBRACHT (MRS. S.K. MCCULLOUGH), editor; b. Hettinger, N.D.; d. John H. and Pearl (Rossiter) Gerbracht; student Dickinson State Coll., 1934-35; B.A., U. N.D., 1937; M.A., N.D. State U., 1962; m. S. K. McCullough, 1945 (dec. 1958); children—Paul Kenneth, Amoret McCullough Fish, Donald Starling. With various newspapers, 1933-42; grad. asst. dept. botany N.D. State U., Fargo, 1939, asst. agrl. editor, 1943-46, asso. agrl. editor, asst. prof. communications, 1957-73, asso. prof. communications, asst. publs. editor, 1973—, mem. Univ. senate, 1974-77; owner (with husband) drug store, Casselton, N.D., 1946-53. Mem. N.D., S.D., Cass County hist. socs., N.D., Minn. hort. socs., N.D. Acad. Sci. (editor 1975-77), Fargo-Moorhead Unitarian Fellowship (dir., sec. 1964-65, 67-68, pres. 1975-76), Fargo-Moorhead Audubon Soc. (corr. sec., editor), N.D. Natural History Soc., Minn. Ornithol. Union, LWV, Fargo-Moorhead Garden Soc. (v.p. 1962-63), Federated Womens Clubs (dist. and state history chmn. 1958-59), Epsilon Sigma Phi (annalist 1970—), N.D. Press Women. Club: Order Eastern Star. Editor N.D. Farm Research 1958—, N.D. Extension Rev., 1957-74. Home: 1114 College St Fargo ND 58102 also Route 5 Detroit Lakes MN 56501

MC CULLOUGH, GEORGE ELWOOD, lawyer; b. Coffeyville, Kans., Dec. 20, 1923; s. Harry Ermest and Gladys Margarite (Stoneking) McC.; B.A., Washburn Municipal U., Topeka, 1949, J.D., 1950; m. Vivian Austin, Oct. 7, 1967; children—George Elwood, Kristy L. Admitted to Kans. bar, 1950, U.S. Supreme Ct. bar, 1964; gen. counsel Kans. Fedn. Labor, AFL-CIO, also various local unions, 1952—; lectr. bar seminars; vis. lectr. Washburn Municipal U., 1973. Chmn. Topeka Urban Renewal Bd., 1975—. Served with USNR, 1943-46. Fellow Law-Sci. Acad., Law-Sci. Found.; mem. Am., Kans. bar assns., Am., Kans. trial lawyers assns., Am. Legion, V.F.W. Republican. Presbyterian. Mason (Shriner), Eagle, Elk. Club: Topeka. Home: 4336 SE 26th St Topeka KS 66605 Office: Box 1453 Topeka KS 66601

MC CULLOUGH, JOHN FRANCIS, heavy equipment mfg. exec.; b. Chgo., July 20, 1925; s. George J. and Elizabeth (McDonough) McC.; student Loyola U., Chgo., 1946-49, U. Ill., 1949-50, DePaul U., 1950-51; grad. Indsl. Engring. Coll., Chgo., 1952; m. Eileen R. O'Connell, Sept. 17, 1949; children—John Francis, Karen M., Diane C., Martin W., Brian E. Indsl. engr. Chgo. Carton Co. div. United Biscuit Corp. Am., 1951-53; methods engr. Ekco Products Co., Chgo., 1953-55; asst. to pres. W.C. Ritchie div. Stone Container Corp., Chgo., 1955-57; chief indsl. engr. Victor Mfg. & Gasket Co., Chgo., 1957-62; pres. John F. McCullough & Assos., mgmt. cons., Oak Park, Ill., 1962—; pres. Orton McCullough Crane Co., Oak Brook, Ill., from 1962, now chmn. bd. dirs.; dir. Athey Products Co., Raleigh, N.C. Bd. dirs. Am.-India Dispensary. Served with USCG, 1943-46. Mem. Indsl. Mgmt. Soc., A.I.M. (pres.'s council 1965—), Methods Time Measurement Assn. Standards and Research, World Trade Club, Western Rwy. Club, Maintenance of Way Club, V.F.W., Am. Legion. Home: 2925 S Meyers Rd Oakbrook IL 60521 Office: Oakbrook Executive Plaza 1211 W 22d St Oakbrook IL 60521

MC CULLOUGH, JOHN JEFFREY, physician, med. center adminstr., educator; b. Boston, Apr. 29, 1938; s. Joe Thompson and Mary Elizabeth (Brunner) McC.; B.A., Northwestern U., 1959; M.D., Ohio State U., 1963. Intern Vanderbilt U. Hosp., Nashville, 1963-64, resident in medicine, 1969-70; fellow dept. lab. medicine U. Minn. Hosps., Mpls., chief resident lab. medicine, 1968-69, dir. blood bank, 1970—; instr. dept. lab. medicine U. Minn., 1968-69, asst. prof., 1970-74, asso. prof. lab. medicine and pathology, 1974—; med. dir. St. Paul Regional ARC Blood Center, 1970-74, dir., 1974—; practice medicine specializing in clin. pathology; mem. blood program adv. com. to pres. ARC, 1976-78. Served with USPHS, 1964-67. Grantee ARC, 1972—, Nat. Heart Lung and Blood Inst., 1971—, Nat. Cancer Inst., 1975—. Recipient award Am. Cancer Soc., 1967. Mem. Am., Minn. (past pres.) assns. blood banks, AAAS, Minn. State Med. Assn. (com. on blood banks and labs. 1973—, Ramsey County Med. Soc. (chmn. com. on blood and blood banks 1972-76), Minn., Am. (council on immunohematology 1975—) socs. clin. pathologists, Acad. Clin. Lab. Physicians and Scientists, Am. Fedn. for Clin. Research, Am. Assn. Pathologists, Am. Assn. for Clin. Histocompatability Testing. Contbr. chpts. to med. books, articles to profl. jours. Home: 19 S 1st St Minneapolis MN 55401 Office: Box 198 Mayo U Minnesota Minneapolis MN 55455

MC CULLOUGH, JOSEPH, artist, inst. of art ofcl.; b. Pitts., July 6, 1922; s. Joseph Phillip and Margaret (List) McC.; diploma in painting, Cleve. Inst. Art, 1948; B.F.A., Yale, 1950, M.F.A., 1951; m. Florence Elizabeth Cramer, Mar. 31, 1945; children—Marjorie, Warren. Instr. art San Jose State Coll., 1948-49; asst. instr. Yale, 1949-51; asst. dir. Cleve. Inst. Art, 1952-55, dir., 1955-74, pres., 1974—; exhibited Cleve. Mus. Art, Butler Inst. Am. Art, Carnegie Mus. (Pitts.), Stanford, Oberlin Coll., Corcoran Gallery, Springfield (Mass.) Mus., U. Del., Akron Art Inst., U. Ill. Biennial. Addison Gallery Am. Art, Andover, Mass. Chmn. fine arts adv. com. City Planning Commn. Recipient prizes in painting, Pitts. Playhouse, Cleve. Mus. Art, Canton Art Inst., Ohio U., Asso. Artists Pitts., Butler Inst. Am. Art. Fellow Nat. Assn. Schs. Art (past pres.); mem. Cleve. Mus. Art (adv. bd.), Coll. Art Assn., Cleve. Art Assn. (sec.). Home: 2637 Wellington Rd Cleveland Heights OH 44118 Office: 11141 East Blvd Cleveland OH 44106

MC CUNE, DAVID WILLIAM, engr.; b. Columbus, Ohio, Apr. 27, 1950; s. Donald Ray and Virginia Mae (Strider) McC.; student Ohio State U.; m. Linda Marlene Trifonoff, July 9, 1977. Engr. Van de Graaff Nuclear Physics Lab., Ohio State U., 1974—. Home: 1075 Northridge Rd Columbus OH 43224 Office: 1302 Kinnear Rd Columbus OH 43212

MCCURDY, LARRY WAYNE, chems. co. exec.; b. Commerce, Tex., July 1, 1935; s. Weldon Lee and Eula Bell (Quinn) McC.; B.B.A., Tex. A. and M. U., 1957; m. Anna Jean Ogle, June 2, 1956; children—Michael, Kimberly, Laurie. Jr. accountant Tenneco Inc., Houston, 1957-60, sr. accountant Tenneco Oil Co., Houston, 1960-64, accounting supr. Tenneco Chems., Houston, 1964-69, div. controller, Saddle Brook, N.J., 1970-72, corp. controller, 1972-74, v.p. fin., 1974—, sr. v.p. fin. Tenneco Automotive, 1978—. Trustee Somerset County Coll., Somerville, N.J., 1974—; elder Liberty Corner Presbyn. Ch., N.J., 1973—. Served to capt. Air Def., USAR, 1958-66. Mem. Nat. Assn. Accountants, Fin. Execs. Inst. Office: Park 80 Plaza W 1 Saddle Brook NJ 07662

MC CURRY, DONALD REID, mktg. research exec.; b. Nashville, July 21, 1928; s. Ray Reid and Victoria Wanda (Stranz) McC.; B.A., Cornell U., 1950; m. Flora McKenzie, July 21, 1950; children—Diane, Kathryn, Laura. Research statistician A.C. Nielsen Co., Northbrook, Ill., 1955-56, asst. to pres., 1956-62, client service exec., 1962-67, v.p., 1967-74, exec. v.p., 1974—, also dir.; chmn. bd. Compumark, Inc., Coordinated Mgmt. Systems. Served with USAF, 1951-53. Mem. Am. Mktg. Assn. Club: Knollwood (Lake Forest, Ill.). Home: 1217 Everett Rd Lake Forest IL 60045 Office: Nielsen Plaza Northbrook IL 60062

MC CUTCHAN, NEIL JASON, educator; b. Evansville, Ind., Oct. 31, 1938; s. H. Jason and Laura (Swope) McC.; B.F.A., Coll. Conservatory Music Cin., 1960; M.A., U. Cin., 1972; m. Judith Katherine Grunow, Feb. 17, 1962; 1 son, Allen Neil. Asst. film dir. WKRC TV, Cin., 1958-61; prodn. asst. WTVW TV, Evansville, 1967-68; asst. prof. speech U. N.D., Grand Forks, 1976—. Served with USAF, 1961-67. Mem. Nat. Assn. Ednl. Broadcasters, Broadcast Edn. Assn., Speech Communication Assn., Internat. Communication Assn., Res. Officers Assn. Home: 1908 23d Ave S Grand Forks ND 58201 Office: Dept Speech Univ ND Grand Forks ND 58202

MC CUTCHEON, GEORGE BARR, educator; b. Chgo., Oct. 30, 1927; s. John T. and Evelyn (Shaw) McC.; grad. Milton Acad., 1944; A.B., Harvard U., 1948; Ed.M., Grad. Tchrs.' Coll. Winnetka, 1951; m. Paula Elisabeth Wilms, July 19, 1952; children—George Barr, III, Quentin, Corwen, Ian. Tchr. math. Chgo. Latin Sch., 1954-56; tchr. math. Francis W. Parker Sch., Chgo., 1949-54, 56—, chmn. math. dept., 1957—; faculty Pestalozzi-Froebel Coll., 1963-66, Roosevelt U., Chgo., 1965-67. Alderman, 43d Ward, 1967-71. Mem. Field Mus. Natural History, Art Inst. Chgo., Chgo. Hist. Assn. Clubs: Harvard, Saddle and Cycle. Author: From Chaos to Order, 1969; Fourteen Eggs Make a Dozen, 1969; The Power of Balance, 1969; The McCutcheon Mathematics Series, 7 vols., 1974. Home: 2236 N Lincoln Park W Chicago IL 60614 Office: 330 W Webster Chicago IL 60614

MC DANIEL, CHARLES WAYNE, chiropractor; b. Spencer, S.D., June 13, 1927; s. Wayne and Bertha (Duxbury) McD.; B.S., S.D. State U., 1950; D. Chiropractic, Nat. Coll. Chiropractice, Lombard, Ill., 1970; m. Florence Claussen, Mar. 21, 1949; children—David (dec.), James, Sharon McDaniel Zoellner, Susan. High sch. instr., Canova, S.D., 1950-52; with Soil Conservation Service, U.S. Dept. Agr., Milbank, Leola, Wessington Springs, S.D., 1952-65; chiropractic physician, Brookings, S.D., 1970—. Scoutmaster, mem. troup com. Boy Scouts Am., 1954-65. Served with Signal Corps, U.S. Army, 1945-46. Club: Kiwanis, Elks. Home: 1442 LeGeros Dr Brookings SD 57006 Office: 611 6th St Brookings SD 57006

MC DANIEL, DONALD NEAL, data processing mgr.; b. Osmond, Nebr., July 27, 1947; s. Arthur Edward and Beulah Unetta (Milne) McD.; programmers certificate Nettleton Bus. Coll., 1971; m. Vickie Jo Sowers, Oct. 7, 1966; children—Jeffery Neal, Jeremy Lynn. Computer operator Aaron Ferer & Sons, Omaha, 1970-72; accountant Kutak Rock Cohen Campbell Garfinkle & Woodward, Omaha, 1972-73, data processing mgr., 1973—. Mem. Macedonia Rescue Squad; past. sec. Macedonia Vol. Fire Dept. Served with USAF, 1966-70. Mem. Assn. for Systems Mgmt., Assn. of Accounting Machinery. Presbyterian. Clubs: Jaycees. Home: Box 253 Rural Route 5 Council Bluffs IA 51501 Office: Omaha Bldg 1650 Farnam St Omaha NE 68102

MC DANIEL, EDWIN CORR, urologist; b. Bloomington, Ind., Dec. 5, 1932; s. George Wesley and Mary Louise (Corr) McD.; A.B., Ind. U., 1954, M.D., 1957; m. Gloria Lee Harvey, Dec. 29, 1956. Intern, Fitzsimmons Army Hosp., Denver, 1957-58; resident Walter Reed Army Hosp., Washington, 1958-62; practice medicine specializing in urology, Indpls., 1967—; mem. staff Meth. Hosp., Winona Hosp., Community Hosp.; cons. Johnson County (Ind.) Meml. Hosp. Served to lt. col. M.C., U.S. Army, 1957-67. Diplomate Am. Bd. Urology. Fellow A.C.S.; mem. Am. Urol. Assn., Am., Ind. med. assns., Am. Legion, Res. Officers Assn. Address: 1815 N Capitol St Indianapolis IN 46202

MC DANIEL, JAMES AUSTIN, hosp. adminstr.; b. St. Louis, Apr. 5, 1915; s. Joseph Cleveland and Harriet Lunar (Hastings) McD.; student Southeast Mo. U., 1933-36; m. Helen Estelle Buscher, June 4, 1938; children—Fredrick Olin, John Paul, Philip Buscher. With Bonne Terre Farming & Cattle Co. (Mo.), 1936-46; accountant St. Joseph Lead Co., 1946-58; auditor, Mo., 1958-61; out supt. adminstrn. Mo. Div. Mental Health, 1961-71; adminstr. Perry County Meml. Hosp., Perryville, Mo., 1971—. Mem. Perry County ARC Blood Program; mem. adv. council St. Francis Mental Health Center; pres. Southeast Mo. Council. Leader Boy Scouts Am., 1938-58; Active local musical groups. Councilman, Bonne Terre, 1952-54. Served with USNR, 1944-46. Mem. Mo. Mental Health Assn., Assn. Mental Health Adminstrs., Am. Acad. Med. Adminstrs., Mo. Hosp. Assn. (treas., trustee), Perryville C. of C., Am. Legion, Soc. Preservation and Encouragement Barber Shop Quartet Singing in Am. (v.p.). Methodist (chmn. adminstrv. bd., choir dir.). Mason (Shriner), Lion, Rotarian. Clubs: Perryville Country. Home: Route 4 Perryville MO 63775 Office: Perry County Meml Hosp N West St Perryville MO 63775

MC DANIEL, JAMES EDWIN, lawyer; b. Dexter, Mo., Nov. 22, 1931; s. William H. and Gertie M. (Woods) McD.; A.B., Washington U., St. Louis, 1957, LL.B., 1959; m. Mary Jane Crawford, Jan. 22, 1955; children—John William, Barbara Anne. Admitted to Mo. bar, 1959; partner firm Barnard and Baer, St. Louis. Served with USAF, 1951-55. Mem. Am. Bar Assn. (ho. dels. 1976—, chmn. com. student loan fund), Bar Assn. Met. St. Louis (pres. 1972-73), Mo. Bar (gov. 1974—), Assn. Def. Counsel (pres. 1968), Legal Aid Soc. (treas., bd. dirs., 1965—), Mo. Savs. and Loan League (pres. attys. com. 1977-78), Phi Delta Phi. Congregationalist. (past moderator, chmn. bd. trustees). Home: 767 Elmwood Ave Glendale MO 63122 Office: 818 Olive St St Louis MO 63101

MC DANIEL, JOHN REDMOND, physician; b. Savannah, Mo., July 1, 1913; s. John and Ruth (Coffer) McD.; A.B., Central Coll., 1935; M.D., Harvard U., 1939; m. Mary Jane Chiles, Mar. 10, 1946; children—John Morton, James Alan. Intern, Mass. Gen. Hosp., Boston, 1939-41, resident, 1945-46; resident Boston City Hosp., 1941; practice medicine specializing in surgery, St. Joseph, Mo., 1947; chmn. sect. of surgery, surgeon Thompson Brumm & Knepper Clinic, 1947—, chmn. dept. surgery, 1956-60; asso. clin. dir., 1966-71; chmn. dept. surgery Mo. Meth. Hosp., St. Joseph, 1960-62, chmn. med. staff, 1961-62; chmn. dept. surgery St. Joseph Hosp., 1960-62. Dir. Thompson-Brumm-Knepper, Inc. Bd. dirs. St. Joseph Council of Churches, 1962-63, Community Concert Assn., 1963-68; trustee Meth. Hosp. and Med. Center; bd. of curators Central Coll., Fayette, Mo., 1958-70. Served to maj., M.C., AUS, 1942-45; ETO. Decorated Bronze Star medal; recipient Distinguished Alumnus award Central Meth. Coll, 1969. Diplomate Am. Bd. Surgery. Fellow A.C.S.; mem. Royal Soc. Medicine, AMA, Internat., Mo., Kansas City surg. socs., Pan Pacific Surg. Assn., Buchanan County (pres. 1962-63), Boyleston med. socs., Southwestern Surg. Congress, Alpha Omega Alpha. Democrat. Methodist. Mason (Shriner). Clubs: Benton; St. Joseph Country; Moila; Harvard (Kansas City). Home: 1808 N 29th Ave St Joseph MO 64506 Office: 902 Edmond St St Joseph MO 64501

MC DANIEL, ROBERT EDWIN, constrn. co. pres.; b. New Albany, Ind., Dec. 11, 1927; s. Alfred Edwin and Evelyn May (Jackson) McD.; B.S., U. Ky., 1950; m. June Haynes, Dec. 12, 1953; children—R. Stephen, Janet L. Vice pres. Am. Modulars Corp., Cin., 1963-68, pres., Dayton, 1968-76. Vice pres., treas. Eastern States Mortage Corp., Cin., 1963-68; pres. U.S. Steel Homes div., New Albany, Ind., 1972-75; sec.-treas. Remcraft Constrn., Inc., Dayton, 1976—; pres., treas. R.E. McDaniel Constrn. and Devel. Co., Dayton, 1976—; pres. Tri-Ohio Devel. Co., 1977—. Served with AUS, 1945-47. Mem. Home Builders Assn. Met. Dayton (pres. 1975—), Nat. Assn. Home Builders (dir. 1972-77), Ohio Home Builders Assn. (v.p.). Club: Masons. Home: 900 W Whipp Rd Dayton OH 45459 Office: 900 W Whipp Rd Dayton OH 45459

MC DANIEL, WILLIAM LESTER, dentist; b. Brewster, Wash., Feb. 14, 1918; B.S., Central Mich. Coll., 1941; D.D.S., Northwestern U., 1949, M. Dental Surgery, 1951; m. Laura Jane Cherry, June 26, 1943; children—George C., William C., Stewart C. Individual practice dentistry, Chgo., 1951—; asst. prof. clin. oral pathology Northwestern U., 1951-57; prof. periodontics, U. Ill., 1963—. Served to capt. USNR, 1942-46. Recipient anniversary award Central Mich. U., 1968. Diplomate Am. Bd. Endodontics. Fellow Am. Coll. Dentists, Internat. Coll. Dentists; mem. Am. Acad. Oral Pathology, Am. Acad. Periodontology, Am. Assn. Endodontics, Edgar Coll. Endodontic Study Club, Am. Legion (comdr. 1960-61, Delta Sigma Delta. Club: Germania (pres. 1971-73, dir. 1976—) (Chicago, Ill.). Home: 321 S Waiola Av LaGrange IL 60525 Office: 25 E Washington St Chicago IL 60602

MC DAVITT, ROBERT DUANE, veterinarian; b. Kansas, Ill., Sept. 24, 1940; s. John Notley and Velma Edna (Johnson) McD.; student Eastern Ill. U., 1958-61; B. Vet. Sci., U. Ill., 1964, D.V.M., 1965; m. Beverly Jeanne Boyd, Oct. 6, 1962; children—Kathleen, Kenneth, Bruce. Practice vet. medicine specializing in equine practice, Carmel, Ind., 1965-66, 66-68, Westfield, Ind., 1968—. Tchr. vet. sci. course 4H, Indpls. Mem. Am., Ind. (equine com. 1972—, chmn. 1977, program com. 1976, 77) vet. med. assns., Am. Assn. Equine Practitioners, Ind. Acad. Vet. Med. (charter), Ind. Reining Horse Assn. (pres. 1976), Am., Ind. (bd. dirs. 1970) quarter horse assns. Republican. Presbyn. Address: Rural Route 1 Box 255 Westfield IN 46074

MC DERMOTT, JOHN ANDREW, assn. exec.; b. Phila., June 12, 1926; s. John A. and Ellen (Plunkett) McD.; B.A., U. Villanova, 1948; diploma in pub. adminstrn. U. Pa., 1955; m. Marie Therese Hertel, June 27, 1964; children—John Andrew, Michael Francis, Matthew Justin. Dir. housing Phila. Commn. Human Relations, 1954-57; asso. dir. NCCJ, Phila., 1957-58; intergroup relations specialist FHA, N.Y.C., Washington, 1958-60; exec. dir. Cath. Interracial Council, Chgo., 1960-68; sr. project dir. Urban Inst., Washington, 1969-70; asso. dir. Community Renewal Soc., Chgo., 1970—. Chmn. Nat. Cath. Conf. Interrracial Justice. Served to ensign USNR, 1944-46. Lasker fellow Brandeis U., 1960. Editor, publisher The Chicago Reporter, 1972—. Home: 4811 S Kimbark Ave Chicago IL 60615 Office: 111 N Wabash Ave Chicago IL 60602

MC DEVITT, MICHAEL ROBERT, credit union adminstr.; b. Columbus, Ohio, July 18, 1942; s. John Edward and Esther Linda (Manhulter) McD.; student Ohio State U., 1960-61, Rio Grande Coll., 1962-64, Stark Tech. Coll., 1975-77; m. Virginia Lee McGuier, Nov. 22, 1969; children—Richard, Barbara, Michele. Lab technician Ohio State U. Hosp., Columbus, 1960-65; mgmt. trainee Nat. City Bank, Cleve., 1966; mgr. ITT Aetna Fin. Co., Cuyahoga Falls, Ohio, 1966-71; gen. mgr. Summit Fed. Credit Union, Akron, Ohio, 1971—; instr. Akron Bd. Vocat. Edn., 1973-76; lectr. in field. Mem. Credit Union Exec. Soc., Edn. Council Credit Unions, Credit Union Soc., Ohio Credit Union League. Office: 100 Wheeler St Akron OH 44311

MC DIVITT, JAMES A., astronaut, mfg. co. exec.; b. Chgo., June 10, 1929; s. James and Margeret (Maxwell) McD.; student Jackson Jr. Coll., 1948-50; B.S. in Aero. Engring., U. Mich., 1959, D. Astronautic Sci. (hon.), 1965; D.Sc. (hon.), Seton Hall U., 1969, Miami U., Ohio, 1970; LL.D. (hon.), Eastern Mich. U., 1975; m. Patricia Ann Haas; children—Michael A., Ann Lynn, Patrick W., Kathleen M. Joined U.S. Air Force, 1951, advanced through grades to brig. gen., 1972; served in Korean action; student Exptl. Test Pilot Sch., Edwards AFB, 1959-60, Aerospace Research Pilot Course, 1961; then exptl. flight test officer Edwards AFB; astronaut, 1962-69, command pilot Gemini IV spacecraft, 1965, comdr. Apollo IX, 1969; mgr. lunar landing operations, 1969; mgr. Apollo spacecraft program, 1969-72; exec. v.p. Consumers Power Co., 1972-75; v.p. Pullman Inc., Chgo., from 1975, subsequently pres. Mem. Soc. Exptl. Test Pilots, Am. Inst. Aeros. and Astronautics, Am. Astronaut. Soc. Office: Pullman Inc 200 S Michigan Ave Chicago IL 60604

MC DONALD, ANTHONY ALONZO EARL, computer specialist; b. Cleve., Feb. 19, 1945; s. Charles Morgan and Helen Loretta (Ballard) McD.; B.S. in Music Edn., Ind. State U., 1968. Music tchr. Chgo. Bd. Edn., 1968; systems engr. IBM, Chgo., 1968-73; systems rep. Burroughs Corp., Chgo., 1973-75; computer specialist GSA, Chgo., 1975—. Recipient certificate in data processing. Episcopalian. Home: 2901 S Michigan Ave Chicago IL 60616 Office: 230 S Dearborn St Chicago IL 60604

MC DONALD, BONNIE BELLE, educator; b. Quitman, Miss.; d. Daniel W. and Mattie B. (Irby) McDonald; B.S., Miss. State Coll. for Women, 1939; M.S., U. Tenn., 1949; Ph.D., Tex. Woman's U., 1969. Tchr. home econs. Pachuta (Miss.) High Sch., 1939-41; head homemaking dept. Sumrall (Miss.) High Sch., 1941-44, 46-48; grad. asst. nutrition U. Tenn., Knoxville, 1948-49, asst. prof. human nutrition, 1949-57; specialist in food and nutrition Agrl. Extension Service, U. Fla. and Fla. State U., Tallahassee, 1957-61; dietitian Emory U. Hosp., Atlanta, 1961-62; research asso. nutrition Med. Coll. Ga., Augusta, 1962-64; asst. prof. home econs. Wis. State U., Stevens Point, 1964-67, asso. prof., 1967-71, prof., dir. dietetics program, 1971—, program coordinator in foods and nutrition, 1973—. Cons. Head Start Project, 1966-72; grad. asst. Tex. Woman's U., Denton, 1967-69; co-chairperson Wis. Gov.'s Conf. on Nutrition for Health, 1974-75; cons. Community Services Program Wis., Stevens Point Commn. Aging. Served with WAVES, 1944-46. Fellow Royal Soc. Health; mem. Am., Wis. (mem. exec. bd. 1966-68), No. Wis. (pres. 1967-68) dietetics assns., Wis. Nutrition Council (charter mem., pres. 1973-74), Internat. Fedn. Home Econs., Am. (life), Wis. (chmn. research com. 1969-70) home econs. assns., NEA, AAAS, Am., Wis. pub. health assns., Nat. Council Aging, Nutrition Today Soc. (charter), Nutrition Edn. Soc. (charter), AAUW, Bus. and Profl. Women's Club, AAUP, Wis. Acad. Scis., Arts and Letters (life). Contbr. articles to publs. Home: 1609 4th Ave PO Box 525 Stevens Point WI 54481

MC DONALD, CLINTON GLEN, wood products mfg. co. exec.; b. Montgomery, Mich., Aug. 15, 1929; s. Elvyn Clyde and Wilma (Betts) McD.; B.A., Mich. State U., 1957; M.B.A., Central Mich. U., 1970; m. Irene Mary Kovachik, Apr. 4, 1951; children—Robert E., Larry J., Sharon G. Auditor, sr. accountant Price Waterhouse & Co., Detroit, 1957-64; v.p., controller, dir. DMH Co., St. Louis, Mich., 1964-71; asst. prof. accounting dept. Sch. Bus., Tex. A. and I. U., Kingsville, 1971-72; pres., treas., chmn. bd. Smithton Industries, Inc. (Mo.), 1972—. Active Boy Scouts Am., 1959-64. Served with USAF, 1948-52. C.P.A., Mich. Mem. Am. Inst. C.P.A.'s, Mich. Assn. C.P.A.'s. Home: Route 6 Sedalia MO 65301 Office: Corner Hwy W and US 50 Smithton MO 65350

MC DONALD, DONALD BURT, limnologist, educator; b. Salt Lake City, Mar. 5, 1932; s. Donald T. and Dorothea May (Miller) McD.; B.S. in Biology, U. Utah, 1954, M.S. in Zoology, 1956, Ph.D. in Limnology Microbiology, 1962; m. Joyce W. Weece, July 5, 1967 (dec. Sept. 1976); children—Barbara, Karen, Donald. Prof. energy engring., preventive medicine and environ. health U. Iowa, Iowa City, 1962—; research engr. Ia. Inst. Hydraulic Research, Iowa City, 1973—; pres. D.B. McDonald Research Inc., cons. ecologists, 1974—; cons. utilities. Served with USAF, 1951-52. Home: Box 129 Route 1 Iowa City IA 52240

MCDONALD, ELLIOTT RAYMOND, JR., lawyer; b. Peoria, Ill., Feb. 10, 1929; s. Elliott Raymond and Florence Valera (Cobb) McD.; B.A., U. Iowa, 1950, J.D., 1952; m. Mary Julienne Jensen, May 6, 1952; children—Beth, Elliott Raymond III. Admitted to Iowa bar, 1954—; practiced in Davenport, 1954—; mem. firm McDonald, McDonald & Stonebraker. Trustee, Davenport Pub. Library, 1972—, chmn. Served with USAF, 1952-54. Mem. Scott County Bar Assn. (pres. 1975-76). Home: 2800 E Locust St Davenport IA 52803 Office: 301 Northwest Tower Davenport IA 52806

MC DONALD, GEORGE JENNINGS, lawyer; b. Newark, Ohio, July 12, 1906; s. Benjamin Franklin and Maude Dorothy (Kendall) McD.; Ph.B., Denison U., 1928; J.D., Franklin Coll. Law, 1931; m. Isabelle Cooper, June 15, 1935; children—John Cooper, Sue (Mrs. Neil A. Bartley). Admitted to Ohio bar, 1931, since practiced in Newark; mem. firm McDonald, Robison, Spahr & Noecker, Newark, 1931—; dir. First Nat. Bank Newark, 1955—. Pres. alumni council Denison U., 1938-39. Asst. pros. atty., Licking County, Ohio, 1932-38; chmn. Licking County Dem. Exec. Com., 1934-38. Trustee Newark Pub. Library, 1953-75, pres., 1960-75. Served as lt. USNR, 1944-45. Mem. Am., Ohio, Licking County (pres. 1947-48) bar assns., Phi Delta Theta, Tau Kappa Alpha, Pi Delta Epsilon, Omicron Delta Kappa. Kiwanian, K.P. Club: Symposiarchs (Newark). Home: 681 Dogwood Ln Newark OH 43055 Office: 63 N 3d St Newark OH 43055

MC DONALD, SISTER GRACE, religious order adminstr.; b. Spokane, Wash., Nov. 26, 1917; d. John V. and Justine (Reimringer) McDonald; B.A., Viterbo Coll., 1946; M.A., Cath. U. Am., 1949, Ph.D., 1954. Joined Franciscan Sisters Perpetual Adoration, 1935; tchr. parochial schs., Wis., Ia., 1937-48; prin. St. Robert Sch., Halder, Wis., 1946-48; prof. history Viterbo Coll. La Crosse, Wis., 1952-70, dir. residence, 1952-60, pres. coll., 1960-70; pres. Franciscan Sisters of Perpetual Adoration, 1970—, treas., 1976—. Mem. nat. bd. Leadership Conf. of Women Religous, 1972—, treas., mem. exec. com., 1976—. Mem. Wis. Bd. Ethics, 1973—. Bd. dirs. La Crosse Citizens Planning Corp., Viterbo Coll. Mem. AAUW, Wis. Cath. Conf., Am. Cath. Hist. Assn., La Crosse County Hist. Soc., Greater La Crosse C. of C. (edn. com.), Pi Gamma Mu. Author: History of the Irish in Wisconsin in the Nineteenth Century, 1954. Address: 912 Market St La Crosse WI 54601

MC DONALD, JAMES ALEXANDER, physician; b. Wheaton, Ill., Dec. 22, 1916; s. William Alexander and Lucy Belle (Ott) McD.; B.S., Wheaton Coll., 1938; M.D., U. Ill., 1943; m. Alice L. McKelvey, Aug. 29, 1938; children—Bruce, Brian; m. 2d, Judith C. Crain, Mar. 29, 1975. Grad. fellow, athletic coach Wheaton Coll., 1938-40; with athletic dept. profl. schs. YMCA, Chgo., 1940-43; intern Cook County Hosp., Chgo., 1943-44; resident Community Hosp., Geneva, Ill., 1946-48; gen. practice medicine, Geneva, 1948—; mem. staff Community Hosp., Geneva, 1946—, pres. 1954-55. Med. adviser Selective Service Bd., St. Charles, Ill., 1949-73, for med. procurement Ill. Selective Service, 1950-72; twp. health officer, Geneva, 1952—. Mem. Mayor's Human Relations Commn., Geneva, 1964-65. Mem. sch. bd., Geneva, 1965-68. Bd. dirs. Community Chest, Geneva, 1958-61; Served with M.C., AUS, 1944-46. Mem. AMA, Ill. (house dels. 1969-73, vice speaker 1973, speaker 1975-77), Kane County med. socs., Nat. Geog. Soc., Smithsonian Instn. Republican. Presbyterian. Home: 515 Oakwood Dr Geneva IL 60134 Office: 13 S 2d St Geneva IL 60134

MC DONALD, JAMES JOHN, lawyer; b. Hayward, Wis., Oct. 28, 1886; s. Thomas and Hattie (McEvoy) McD.; B.A., U. Wis., 1912, LL.B., 1913; m. Grace A. Bogue, Nov. 25, 1915; 1 son, James B. Admitted to Wis. bar, 1913; practice law, Portage, Wis., 1913-14, Madison, Wis., 1915—; asst. dist. atty., Portage, 1913-14; mem. law firm McDonald, Purcell & Piper, and predecessor firm, Madison, 1962—; divorce counsel Dane County, Wis., 1943-47. Corp. bd. Meth. Hosp., Madison. Mem. Am., Wis., Dane County (past pres.) bar assns., Wis. Hist. Soc., Civil War Round Table, Madison Tech. Club, Badger State Folk Lore Soc. (pres. 1951-55), Phi Alpha Delta, Delta Sigma Rho. Mason (33 deg.), Optimist. Author: Paul Bunyon and The Blue Ox, 1931; If a Man Die, 1953. Conglist. Home: 733 Oneida Pl Madison WI 53711 Office: 122 W Washington Ave Madison WI 53703

MC DONALD, JAMES SMITH, aerospace co. exec.; b. Denver, Apr. 9, 1899; s. James Smith and Susan Belle (Hunter) McD.; B.S., Princeton U., 1921, LL.D., 1960; grad. A.A.C. Flying Sch. San Antonio, 1924; M.S. in Aero. Engring., Mass. Inst. Tech., 1925; E.D., U. Mo. at Rolla, 1957; D.Eng., Washington U., St. Louis, 1958, U. Ark., 1965; m. Mary Elizabeth Finney, June 30, 1934 (dec. 1949); children—James Smith III, John Finney; m. 2d, Priscilla Brush Forney, Apr. 1956; children—George David, Susan Brush (Mrs. Boyd), Priscilla Young (Mrs. Canny). Aero. engr., pilot Huff Daland Airplane Co., 1924; stress analyst, draftsman Consol. Aircraft Co., 1925; asst. chief engr. Stout Metal Airplane Co., 1925; chief engr. Hamilton Aero Mfg. Co., 1926-27; with McDonnell & Assos., 1928-30; v.p. Airtransport Engring. Corp., 1930-31; engr. test pilot Great Lakes Aircraft Corp., 1932; chief project engr. land planes Glenn L. Martin Co., 1933-38; founder, chmn. McDonnell Aircraft Corp., St. Louis, 1939-67, chmn. McDonnell Douglas Corp., 1967—. Hon. chmn. bd. St. Louis Country Day Sch. Recipient Daniel Guggenheim medal, 1963, Robert J. Collier trophy, 1966, Nat. Acad. Engring. Founders medal, 1967, Forrestal award, 1972. Fellow Am. Inst. Aeros. and Astronautics. Clubs: Old Warson Country, Noonday, University, Racquet, St. Louis Country, Missouri Athletic, St. Louis (St. Louis): Metropolitan (Washington); University (N.Y.C.); Bellerive Country. Home: PO Box 516 St Louis MO 63166 Office: McDonnell-Douglas Corp Lambert-St Louis Municipal Airport St Louis MO 63166

MC DONALD, JOHN CECIL, Republican nat. committeeman, lawyer; b. Lorimor, Iowa, Feb. 19, 1924; s. Cecil F. and Mary Elsie (Fletcher) McD.; student Simpson Coll., 1942, So. Ill. U., 1943; J.D., Drake U., 1948; m. Barbara Joan Berry, May 8, 1943; children—Mary Elisabeth (Mrs. Dell A. Richard), Joan Frances (Mrs. Andrew J. Ackerman), Jean Maurine. Admitted to Iowa bar, 1948, U.S. Supreme Ct. bar, 1956; practiced in Dallas Center, Iowa, 1948-71; sr. partner firm McDonald, Keller & Brown, 1971—; county atty., Dallas County, 1958-62, asst. county atty., 1963-69; city atty. Dallas Center, 1956—. Pres. alumni council Simpson Coll.; mem. nat. adv. com. Central Coll.; legal adviser Dallas Community Sch. Bd. Edn., 1953-69, pres., mem., 1968-76; chmn. Dallas County Republican Central Com., 1964-68, past finance chmn.; mem. Gov.'s Inaugural Com., 1969, 71, 73, 75; chmn. Rep. 7th Congl. Dist. Iowa, 1968-69; mem. Iowa Rep. Central Com., 1968—, chmn., 1969-75; mem. Rep. Nat. Com., 1969—, mem. exec. com., 1973; del. Rep. Nat. Conv., 1964, del., vice-chmn. del., 1972, chmn. com. credentials, del., 1976; chmn. Midwest Conf. Rep. State Chairman, 1973-75, Rep. State Chairmens Assn. U.S., 1973-75; nat. committeeman for Iowa, 1975—; chmn. com. on contests Rep. Nat. Com., 1976, mem. com. on arrangements, 1976. Trustee Dallas County Hosp., Perry, Iowa; bd. visitors USAF Acad., 1975—, chmn., 1977. Served Iowa USAAF, 1942-46, with USAF, 1951-52; now col. Res. Mem. Am., Iowa (past chmn. spl. com. mil. affairs), Dallas County (past pres.) bar assns., Am. Legion, Farm Bur., Blackfriars, Alpha Tau Omega, Delta Theta Phi, Alpha Psi Omega. Presbyn. Mason (32 deg., Shriner), Rotarian (past pres. Dallas Center). Clubs: Commercial (past pres.), Hillcrest Country (past pres.), Lincoln, Des Moines, Embassy. Home: 1507 Vine St Dallas Center IA 50063 Office: 502 15th St Dallas Center IA 50063

MC DONALD, JULIE J., author, journalist; b. Audubon County, Iowa, June 22, 1929; d. Alfred Julius and Myrtle Petra (Faurschou) Jensen; B.A., U. Iowa, 1951; LL.D. (hon.), St. Ambrose Coll., 1972; m. Elliott R. McDonald, Jr., May 6, 1952; children—Beth, Elliott R. Editor women's sect. Rockford (Ill.) Newspapers, 1951-52; feature writer, reviewer Quad-City Times, Davenport, Iowa, 1962—; lectr. journalism St. Ambrose Coll., Davenport, 1974—; writer-in-the-schs. Iowa Arts Council, 1974—; workshop leader Miss. Valley Writers Conf., 1974-75. Sec. Scott County Republican Central Com., 1957-74. Named Quad-City Writer of the Year, 1969; recipient Gov.'s Media in the Arts award, 1975. Mem. Iowa Arts Council (chmn. 1969-73), Nat. League Am. Pen Women, Authors Guild, Authors League Am., PEO, Questers Study Club, Bettendorf Community Band. Presbyterian. Author: Baby Black, 1960; Amalies Story, 1960; Pathways to the Present, 1977. Home: 2802 E Locust St Davenport IA 52803 Office: 124 E 2d St Davenport IA 52801

MC DONALD, MYRTIS BETHEL, judge; b. Midland, Mich., Aug. 4, 1913; d. Bernard C. and Ida E. (Howe) Madison; student pub. schs., Midland; m. Miles E. McDonald, Sept. 8, 1934; 1 son, Roy B. Clk., Probate Ct. Midland County (Mich.), 1935-46, sec. to children's worker, 1947-48, county juvenile agt., 1948, probate judge, 1949—. Sec. Midland chpt. ARC, also sec. to atty., 1946-47; treas. Child Welfare Service Fund, 1949—; chmn. case com. Mich. Soc. Crippled Children and Adults, 1953—; chmn. Youth Action Com. 1969—; pres. Vols. for Youth, 1970—; bd. dirs. Big Sister Orgn. Recipient Citizen of Year award Civitan Club, 1972, Outstanding Woman award Nat. Council Camp Fire Girls, Inc., 1972, certificate of merit U.S. Marine Corps, 1972; certificate of appreciation Midland C. of C., 1970, respect for law certificate morning Optimist Club, 1972, certificate of appreciation Big. Bros. Midland County, 1972. Mem. Internat. (life), Nat. (life) assns. probate judges, Am. Judicature Soc., Mich. Probate and Juvenile Ct. Judges Assn. (service certificate 1969), Nat. Council Juvenile Ct. Judges (award 1973, 74, 75). Methodist (service recognition 1945). Home: 1209 Baldwin St Midland MI 48640 Office: Courthouse W Main St Midland MI 48640

MC DONALD, NOEL, edni. adminstr.; b. Evansville, Ind., Jan. 24, 1937; s. Noah and Dorothy McD.; B.A., U. Evansville, 1962; M.S., Ind. U., 1965; m. Sandra Paceley, Apr. 7, 1963; children—Laura, Sarah. Elementary tchr. Evansville-Vanderburgh Sch. Corp., 1962-68, reading clinician, 1968-69, reading tchr., 1969-71, elementary sch. prin., 1971-75, jr. high sch. prin., 1975—; adj. instr. edn. Ind. State U., Evansville, 1972—. Served with AUS, 1958-61. Summer reading grantee Valparaiso U., 1966. Mem. Phi Delta Kappa. Mem. United Ch. Christ. Optimist. Home: 1273 Sheffield Dr Evansville IN 47710 Office: Lodge Elementary Sch 1400 E Riverside Dr Evansville IN 47714

MC DONALD, ROBERT DELOS, mfg. co. exec.; b. Dubuque, Iowa, Jan. 30, 1931; s. Delos Lyon and Virginia (Kolck) McD.; B.A. in Econs., State U. Iowa, 1952; m. Jane Locher, Jan. 16, 1960 (div.); children—Jean, Patricia, Maria, Sharon, Robert. Salesman A. Y. McDonald Mfg. Co., Dubuque, 1956-60, mgr. oil equipment sales, 1961-65, mgr. br., 1965-71, v.p., corporate sec., 1972—, also dir.; dir. Brock-McVey Co., Lexington, Ky., 1964—. Served with USNR, 1952-56. Mem. Am. Legion, Sigma Alpha Epsilon. Republican. Roman Catholic. Elk. Club: Dubuque (Ia.) Golf. Home: 3399 Roosevelt Rd Dubuque IA 52001 Office: 12th and Pine Dubuque IA 52001

MC DONALD, STANFORD LAUREL, clin. psychologist; b. Lincoln, Nebr., Mar. 14, 1929; s. Laurel C. and Irene V. (Frey) McD.; A.B., Nebr. Wesleyan U., 1956; M.A., U. Nebr., 1959; Ph.D., Fielding Inst., 1974; m. Shirley P. Peterson, Apr. 26, 1964; children—Stacia E.V., Jeffry J.S., Kathleen S., Patricia M. Intern, Nebr. Psychiatric Inst., Omaha, 1957-58; staff psychologist Presbyn. St. Luke's Hosp., Chgo., 1960-61; psychologist Chgo. Bd. Edn., 1961-65; supr. psychol. services Office Spl. Edn., Chicago Heights, Ill., 1965—; coordinator grad. extension program Nat. Coll. Edn., Evanston, Ill., 1969—; pvt. practice, Park Forest, Ill., 1967—; community prof. Govs. State U., 1975—; mem. faculty Ill. Sch. Profl. Psychology, 1977—; lectr. Ind. U., 1968-71. Mem. S. Suburban Human Services Coordinating Council, Park Forest South, Ill., 1974—. Served with USMC, 1950-52. Mem. Am. Orthopsychiatric Assn., Am., Midwestern, Ill. psychol. assns., Acad. Psychologists in Marriage and Family Therapy, Biofeedback Soc. Am., Biofeedback Soc. Ill. (pres.-elect), Zeta Psi, Phi Delta Kappa, Psi Chi. Home: 255 Rich Rd Park Forest IL 60466 Office: 1125 Division St Chicago Heights IL 60411

MC DONALD, WARD FULFER, lawyer, land title co. exec.; b. Decatur, Ill., Mar. 26, 1942; s. Carl Russell and Leona Doris (Fulfer) McD.; B.S., U. Ill., 1964, J.D., 1969; student U. So. Calif., 1964-65; m. Diana J. Pelc, Aug. 17, 1968; children—Aron Ward, Joel Colin. Admitted to Ill. bar, 1969; mem. staff Dept. Planning and Econ., Land Devel. Alcoa Properties Inc., Century City, Los Angeles, 1964-67; asso. law firm Hollerich & Hurley, LaSalle, Ill., 1969-70; exec. v.p. Attorney's Title Guaranty Fund, Inc., Champaign, Ill., 1970—. Div. chmn. Champaign County United Way, 1973-74; mem., sec. Pinetree Homeowners Assn., 1974—. Recipient Ill. State scholarship, 1960; Douglas County scholarship, 1960; Homebuilders Assn. Chicagoland scholarship, 1963, fellowship, 1964; James Scholar, 1960-63. Mem. Ill. State (mem., past chmn. real estate law sect. council 1971-77), Am. (mem. standing com. on lawyers title guaranty funds 1974—, chmn. young lawyers sect., membership com. Ill. div. 1971-74, regional vice-chmn. young lawyers sect., membership com. 1974-75, vice-chmn. young lawyers sect. com. on bar-related title ins. 1972-74, chmn. young lawyers sect. com. on real property practice 1974-75, chmn. com. title ins. 1976—), La Salle County, Champaign County, Chgo. (real property com.) bar assns., Nat. Conf. Bar-Related Title Insurers (pres. 1972-73, 75-77), Ill. Bd. Realtors, Am. Judicature Soc., Ill. State, Urbana, Champaign chambers commerce, Champaign County Bd. Realtors, U. Ill. Alumni Assn., Phi Gamma Delta (treas. 1974—). Republican. Mason, Rotarian. Home: 14 Pinetree RFD Seymour IL 61875 Office: 2408 Windsor Pl Champaign IL 61820

MC DONNELL, GERALD M., engring. co. exec.; B.S. in Civil Engring., U. Ill.; M.S. in Bus. and Pub. Adminstrn., U. Chgo. Engr. plant design and pollution control, project mgr., sr. civil engr., asso. and asst. civil engr. Met. San. Dist. of Greater Chgo., 1959-69; project mgr. design and constrn. mgmt. div. Roy F. Weston, Inc., 1969-76; v.p., dir. Snell Environmental Group, Lansing, Mich., 1976—. Diplomate Am. Acad. Environmental Engrs. Mem. ASCE (chmn. program com. Phila. sect., dir.), Water Pollution Control Fedn., Am. Pub. Works Assn. Contbr. tech. articles to profl. jours. Office: Snell Environmental Group 1120 May St Lansing MI 48906

MC DONNELL, ROBERT EDWARD, dentist; b. Oelwein, Iowa, Nov. 5, 1932; s. Edward James and Isabella Pauline (LaValette) McD.; student Coll. St. Thomas, 1950-52; B.S., U. Minn., 1954, D.D.S., 1956; m. Eileen Mary Coyne, June 30, 1956; children—Kathleen M. and Stephen R. (twins), Laura J., Caroline M., Timothy J., James E. Gen. practice dentistry, St. Paul, 1958—. Treas., dir. Delta Dental Plan Minn., 1969-72; mem. Minn. Bd. Dentistry, 1972—, sec.-treas., 1974—. Served with USAF, 1956-58. Fellow Internat. Coll. Dentists; mem. Am., Minn., St. Paul (exec. council 1965-71) dental assns., Minn. Acad. Gnathological Research (v.p. 1970-71, pres. 1973-74), Am., Minn. socs. dentistry for children, Pierre Fuachard Acad., Highland Park Dental Group (pres. 1966), Am. Assn. Dental Examiners, Central Region Dental Testing Service, Delta Sigma Delta (life). Roman Catholic. (chmn. parish sch. com. 1971-73). Home: 1705 Portland Ave St Paul MN 55104 Office: 542 S Snelling Ave St Paul MN 55116

MC DONOUGH, DAYLE CROCKETT, judge; b. Cameron, Mo., Dec. 14, 1891; s. William Edward and Mabel (Owen) McD.; LL.B. cum laude, U. Mo., 1912, J.D., 1969; m. Isabelle Mary Rickey, Jan. 20, 1949. Admitted to Mo. bar, 1912; gen. practice law, Kansas City, Mo., 1913-17; atty. Bur. of War Risk Ins., Treasury Dept., 1919; fgn. service officer U.S. Dept. State, 1919-51; probate judge, ex officio magistrate judge DeKalb County, Mo., 1957—. Mem. Am. Fgn. Service Assn., Dacor, Mo. Bar, Am. Legion. Order of Coif, Phi Delta Phi, Delta Sigma Rho. Democrat. Home: 608 S Water St Maysville MO 64469 Office: Court House Maysville MO 64469

MC DONOUGH, ISABELLE MARY RICKEY (MRS. DAYLE CROCKETT MCDONOUGH), clubwoman; b. Oskaloosa, Ia., Apr. 4; d. Lindsey Vinton and Heddy (Lundee) Rickey; B.A. in Govt., George Washington U., 1947, postgrad., 1947-49; m. Dayle C. McDonough, Jan. 20, 1949. Dep. tax assessor and collector Aransas Pass Ind. Sch. Dist., 1939-41; sec. to city atty., Aransas Pass, Tex., 1939-41; info. specialist U.S. Dept. State, Washington, 1942-48. Treas. Mo. Fedn. Women's Clubs, Inc., 1964-66, 2d v.p., 1966-68, 1st v.p., 1968-70, pres., 1970-72; bd. dirs. Gen. Fedn. Women's Clubs. Mem. steering com. Citizens Com. for Conservation; mem. exec. com. Missourians for Clean Water. Pres., DeKalb County Women's Democratic Club, 1964. Bd. dirs. DeKalb County Pub. Library, pres., 1966; bd. dirs. Mo. Girls Town Found. Mem. AAUW, Nat. League Am. Pen Women, DeKalb County Hist. Soc., Internat. Platform Assn., Zeta Tau Alpha, Phi Delta Delta, Phi Delta Gamma. Democrat. Episcopalian. Mem. Order Eastern Star. Clubs: Tri Arts, Shakespeare, Wimodausis, Gavel, Ledgers. Editor: Mo. Clubwoman mag. Home: 608 S Water St Maysville MO 64469

MCDONOUGH, JAMES J., urban transp. exec. Chmn., Chgo. Transit Authority. Address: care of Chicago Transit Authority Merchandise Mart PO Box 3555 Chicago IL 60654*

MC DOUGALL, ALLAN KERR, polit. scientist, educator; b. Montreal, Que., Can., Mar. 7, 1941; s. Allan Houliston and Elizabeth Ann (Kerr) McD.; B.A. with honors, McGill U., 1962; diploma in Pub. Adminstrn. Carleton U., Ottawa, Ont., 1966, M.A., 1967; Ph.D., U. Toronto (Ont., Can.), 1971; m. Barbara Lowery, May 21, 1966; children—Allan, Kathryn, Diana. Lectr. Erindale Coll., U. Toronto, 1969-70; asst. prof. polit. sci. U. Western Ont., London, 1970—. Resource person Task Force Policing Ont., 1974; mem. Ont. Council U. Affairs, 1976—. Chmn. steering com. Civic Election Group, London, 1972; pres. London South Progressive Conservative Assn. 1972-73. Served with Can. Army, 1959-65. Can. Council research grantee, 1971. Mem. Am. Soc. Criminology, Can. Polit. Sci. Assn. (program com. 1971-73), Inst. Pub. Adminstrn. Home: 673 Steeplechase Dr London ON N6J 3P3 Canada

MC DOUGALL, ALLAN NICHOL, physician; b. Grey County, Ont., Can., Nov. 23, 1936; s. Hubert Nicol and Margaret Maitland (Watson) McD.; M.D., U. Western Ont., 1962; m. Thelma Sarah Knisley, Aug. 13, 1960; children—Kelly Ann, Elizabeth Jean, Ian James. Intern, Toronto (Ont.) Western Hosp., 1962-64; propr. clinic, Chatsworth, Ont., 1964—; mem. staff Gen. Marine Hosp., Owen Sound, Ont., 1964—; coroner Grey County, 1969—; div. surgeon St. John's Ambulance Corp., Owen Sound, 1965-70; resident physician Lee Manor, Home for Aged. Bd. dirs. Owen Sound and Dist., Victorian Order Nurses. Mem. Coll. Family Physicians (pres. Grey-Bruce chpt. 1969-71). Mem. United Ch. Can. (chmn. bd. stewards). Club: Beaver Valley Ski (Kimberly, Ont.). Address: Chatsworth ON NOH IGO Canada

MC DOUGALL, WILLIAM CARL, JR., speech therapist, psychologist; b. St. Thomas, Ont., Can., Aug. 26, 1927; s. William Carl and Myrtle M. Eldert McD.; B.A., B.S., Bowling Green State U., 1953; M.E., Kent State U., 1959; postgrad. U. Cin., 1969—; m. Dorothy E. Hofer, Mar. 28, 1953; children—Kathleen, Sherri Lynn, Debbie Lee. Consumer rep. Scott Paper Co., Marinette, Wis., 1953-54; speech therapist Wadsworth (Ohio) City Schs., 1954-59; psychologist, dir. spl. edn. Wadsworth City Schs., 1959-61; psychologist Dayton City Schs., 1961-67, dir. spl. edn., 1967-73, speech therapist, 1973—; lectr. in field, cons. Chmn. Northmont Ednl. Citizens Assn., 1966-67. Bd. dirs. Tri County Mental Health Assn., 1958-61. Served with U.S. Mcht. Marine, 1948-50. Mem. Council for Exceptional Children (distinguished service award 1974), Am. Psychol. Assn., Ohio Sch. Psychologists Assn., Ohio Speech and Hearing Assn., Ohio, Nat. edn. assns. Home: 550 Imo Dr Apt 5 Dayton OH 45405 Office: Dayton City Schs Dayton OH 45402

MC DOWELL, DONALD NEWHALL, found. ofcl.; b. Montello, Wis., July 9, 1916; s. David P. and Nellie (McLane) McD.; B.S., U. Wis., 1938; m. Ardith Ellis, Aug. 28, 1937; children—Thomas D., Donna J. McDowell Beetsman, Bradley J., Mary E. Levan, Bonnie L. Sundal. Instr. vocat. agr. Spring Green (Wis.) High Sch., 1938-41, Waukesha (Wis.) High Sch., 1941-47; chief adminstrn. div. Wis. Dept. Agr., Madison, 1947-50, sec. agr., 1950-69; exec. dir. Nat. Future Farmers Am. Found., Madison, 1969—. Mem. Nat. Adv. Council on Vocat. Edn. Served with AUS, 1945. Home: 4829 Sheboygan Ave Apt

107 Madison WI 53705 Office: 310 N Midvale Blvd Madison WI 53705

MC DOWELL, JAMES, chem. products mfg. co. exec., mech. engr.; b. Belfast, N. Ireland, Sept. 16, 1929; s. Robert and Margaret (Kernaghan) McD.; came to U.S., 1957, naturalized, 1964; student Lurgan Tech. Jr. Coll., Ireland, 1948-49; B.S. in Mech. Engring., Belfast Coll., 1950-56; postgrad. Ill. Inst. Tech., 1958-59; m. Mildred Isabel McShane, July 17, 1954; children—Colwyn James, Craig Jay. Research engr., Scully Jones & Co., Chgo., 1957-59; dir. equipment research/devel. Diversey Corp., Chgo., 1959-65; dir. equipment mfg. ops. DuBois Chems., Cin., 1965—; tchr. math. and engring. tech. Lurgan Jr. Coll., Ireland, 1956-57. Commr. of youth soccer in Ohio, 1974-76; head soccer coach U. Cin., 1975—; chmn. of fin. and bldg. Methodist Ch., 1958-65. Recipient citation Materials in Design Engring. mag., 1962. Mem. ASME. Club: Golf. Author: ABC's of Soccer, 1975; contbr. articles on splty. chems. and equipment applications to profl. jours.; patentee in field. Home: 1620 Collinsdale Ave Cincinnati OH 45230 Office: DuBois Tower Cincinnati OH 45202

MC DOWELL, LAURA ELEANORA GILLIAM (MRS. GEORGE P. MCDOWELL), educator; b. Delphi, Ind., Nov. 30, 1913; d. Charles Ray and Delia (Cook) Gilliam; A.B., Ind. U., 1936; M.S., Purdue U., 1960; m. George P. McDowell, Oct. 27, 1942. Tchr., Royal Center (Ind.) High Sch., 1936-42, Rensselaer (Ind.) High Sch., 1942; employee counselor U.S. Army AC, Greensboro, N.C., 1942-46; tchr. Twin Lakes High Sch., Monticello, Ind., 1947—, chmn. English and speech depts., 1948—. Mem. NEA, Ind. Council Tchrs. English (v.p. 1962), Ind. High Sch. Forensic Assn. (Good Sportsmanship award 1961, mem. exec. bd. 1962-65), Nat. Forensic League (Diamond Pin award 1960, 65, dist. chmn. 1966-68; Gold Key award 1969, Bronze Plaque award 1973, parliamentarian Nat. Student Congress 1970, 72-74), Ind. High Sch. Speech Assn. (chmn. 1967-68), Internat. Platform Assn., Women's Soc. Christian Service (pres. 1968-71), Alpha Omicron Pi, Kappa Kappa Kappa (province officer 1973-75, state scholarship com. 1975-77, chpt. pres., asst. editor mag. 1977-79). Republican. Methodist (chmn. adminstrv. bd. 1968—, dist. location bd.). Home: 1250 Royal Oaks Dr Monticello IN 47960 Office: Twin Lakes High Sch Monticello IN 47960

MC DUFF, CHARLES ROBERT, microbiologist, lab. exec.; b. Austin, Tex., Nov. 17, 1929; s. Howard Lewis and Mildred (Lyles) McD.; student U. Tex., 1947-48; B.A., U. Miss., 1952; M.S. in Microbiology, U. Wis.-Madison, 1961; m. Caroline Mae Guinn, Feb. 19, 1955; children—Robert Blair, Margaret Ellen. Dir. govt. tech. affairs of research and devel. Econs. Lab. Inc., St. Paul, 1963—. Active PTA Mendota Sch., Mendota Heights, Minn.; bd. dirs. Bd. Edn. Ind. Sch. Dist. 197, St. Paul, 1974—, chmn., 1975—. Served to capt., Chem. Corps., AUS, 1955-63. Mem. Am. Soc. Microbiology, Soc. Indsl. Microbiology, Am. Pub. Health Assn., Nat. Environ. Health Assn., Nat. Mastitis Council, Internat. Assn. Milk, Food, Environ. Sanitarians, TAPPI. Contbr. articles to profl. jours. Patentee in field. Home: 651 S Freeway Rd Mendota Heights MN 55118 Office: Osborn Bldg St Paul MN 55102

MC EACHRAN, HUGH DOUGLAS, physician; b. Vermontville, Mich., Apr. 11, 1911; s. John and Mary (Fraser) McE.; M.D., U. Mich., 1936; m. Priscilla Becker, Feb. 20, 1935; children—John, David, Linda. Intern, Harpers Hosp., Detroit, 1936-38, resident, 1938-41; pvt. practice medicine specializing in eye, ear, nose and throat, Iron Mountain, Mich., 1946—; mem. staffs County Meml. Hosp. Cons. VA Hosp., Iron Mountain, Mich., 1950-73. Served to maj. M.C. AUS, 1942-44. Diplomate Am. Bd. Otolaryngology. Fellow Am. Acad. Ophthalmology and Otolaryngology; mem. Am. Assn. R.R. Surgeons, AMA, Am. Rhinol. Soc., Wis. Upper Mich. Eye, Ear, Nose and Throat Soc., Internat. Rhinol. Soc. Elk, Rotarian. Home: 401 E C St Iron Mountain MI 49801 Office: Commercial Bank Iron Mountain MI 49801

MC ELEANEY, DONALD ARTHUR, dermatologist; b. Clinton, Iowa, Dec. 28, 1924; s. Leo Patrick and Elsie Helen (Bonnemann) McE.; B.A., U. Iowa, 1948, M.D., 1951. Intern, Highland-Alameda County Hosp., Oakland, Calif., 1951-52; resident in dermatology U. Iowa Hosp., 1952-55; practice medicine specializing in dermatology, Cedar Rapids, Iowa, 1958—; preceptor family practice residency program Mercy and St. Luke's Hosps., Cedar Rapids. Served with U.S. Army, 1943-46. Fellow Am. Acad. Dermatology; mem. AMA, Iowa State, Linn County med. socs., Iowa Dermatol. Soc., N. Am. Clin. Dermatol. Soc., Internat. Soc. Tropical Dermatology. Roman Catholic. Club: Cedar Rapids Rotary. Home: 2222 1st Ave NE Apt 204 Cedar Rapids IA 52402 Office: 2720 1st Ave NE Cedar Rapids IA 52402

MC ELIN, THOMAS WELSH, physician; b. Janesville, Wis., Aug. 27, 1920; s. Bertrand James and Evelyn K. (Welsh) McE.; A.B. summa cum laude, Dartmouth Coll., 1942; M.D., Harvard U., 1944; M.S. in Obstetrics and Gynecology, U. Minn., 1948; m. Sylvia Dennison, June 30, 1945; children—Joan Dennison, Thomas Welsh. Splty. tng. Mayo Clinic, 1945-49, asso. attending staff, 1950; practice medicine specializing in obstetrics and gynecology, Evanston, Ill., 1950—; asso. in obstetrics and gynecology Northwestern U. Med. Sch., 1954-56, asst. prof., 1956-60, asso. prof., 1960-67, prof., 1967—, asst. chmn. dept. obstetrics and gynecology, 1974—; attending staff Evanston Hosp., 1952—, chmn. dept. obstetrics and gynecology, 1965—; attending gynecologist Mather Home, 1955—; courtesy staff St. Francis Hosp., Evanston, 1950—; chmn. dept. gynecology Presbyn. Home, Evanston, 1967—. Assoc. Examiner Am. Bd. Obstetrics and Gynecology. Fellow A.C.S. (gov. 1970—), Am. Coll. Obstetricians and Gynecologists (founding mem., mem. exec. bd. 1971—); mem. Central Assn. Obstetricians and Gynecologists (pres. 1970-71), Chgo. Gynec. Soc. (pres. 1969-70), Am. Assn. of Obstetricians and Gynecologists (exec. council 1974-76, pres. 1977-78), Endocrine. Soc., Soc. for Study Infertility, Central Travel Club of Obstetricians and Gynecologists (pres. 1967-68), North Am. Obstet. and Gynecol. Soc., Inst. Medicine Chgo., AMA, Am. Assn. Med. Colls., Phi Beta Kappa, Sigma Xi, Alpha Kappa Kappa. Clubs: Dartmouth, Harvard (Chgo.); Glen View (Golf, Ill.). Contbr. articles and monographs to profl. publs. Home: 560 Greenwood Ave Kenilworth IL 60043 Office: 2650 Ridge Ave Evanston IL 60201

MC ELROY, AUSTIN, ins. co. exec.; b. Columbus, Ohio, July 13, 1888; s. Frank Charles and Harriet (Bancroft) McE.; student Kenyon Coll., 1909, LL.D., 1964; student Cornell U., 1909; m. Elizabeth Spahr, Nov. 3, 1910 (dec. Oct. 1965); children—Mary Elizabeth (dec.), George, Ann (Mrs. Mark Follansbee); m. 2d, Lucia B. Despard, May 28, 1970. Co-owner, dir. emeritus McElroy-Minister Co., Columbus, 1907—. Pres., Community Chest, Columbus, 1930. Trustee emeritus Childrens Hosp., Grant Hosp., Kenyon Coll. Mem. Psi Upsilon. Clubs: Rocky Fork Hunt and Country, University; Columbus Country. Home: 1620 E Broad St Columbus OH 43203 Office: 141 E Town St Columbus OH 43215

MC ELROY, ELAM ERRETT, educator; b. Bell County, Tex., May 27, 1922; s. Emmett Holcomb and Gladys Lillian (Hicks) McE.; B.S., B.A., U. Okla., 1949, M.B.A., 1950; m. Granis Irene Belford, July 27, 1946; children—Randy, Mark. Mem. faculty Marquette U., Milw., 1950—, asso. prof. bus. statistics, 1958—; cons. Met. Milw. Assn. Commerce, 1952-70. Served with USCGR, 1942-45. Mem. Am. Inst. Decision Scis., Am. Statis. Assn., Wis. Bus. Econs. Assn., Beta Gamma Sigma. Author: Applied Business Statistics, 1971; also monographs, articles. Office: 606 N 13th St Milwaukee WI 53233

MC ELROY, JAMES ALBERT, metal mfg. co. exec.; b. Wadsworth, Ohio, Oct. 6, 1932; s. Marshall and Elva Mae (Hay) McE.; student Akron U., 1956-59; m. Marjorie Faye Pyle, June 8, 1968; children—David, Dennis, Yvonne. Prodn. mgr., OIC Corp., Wadsworth, 1957-59; gen. mgr., AMG Industries, Inc., Mt. Vernon, Ohio, 1959-61, v.p., 1961-62, pres., 1962-72, chmn. bd., 1972—; dir. First Knox Nat. Bank, Mt. Vernon. Bd. dirs. Mercy Hosp., Mt. Vernon, Mt. Vernon Area Devel. Found. Served with AUS, 1951-53. Mem. Mt. Vernon C. of C. (pres. 1971). Methodist (music dir.). Mason, Rotarian (pres. 1972-73), Lion. Home: 15324 Mansfield Rd Fredericktown OH 43019 Office: Commerce Dr Mt Vernon OH 43050

MC ELWAIN, JOHN ALLEN, printing co. exec.; b. Chgo., July 7, 1901; s. Frank and Bertha (Thompson) McE.; student Dartmouth Coll., 1920-22, Northwestern U., 1923; m. Jane Catherine McKenna. Apr. 3, 1926; children—Edward Frank, Phyllis Jane (Mrs. Richard Forward), John Allen IV. Tool draftsman Miehle Printing Press Corp., Chgo., 1923-24; rodman Chgo. North Shore & Milw. R.R., Chgo., 1924; circulation mgr. Toys and Novelties, Am. Artisan, Chgo., N.Y.C., 1925-27; sales engr. U.S. Gypsum Co., Chgo., 1927-33; owner John A. McElwain & Co., Chgo., 1933—. Trustee Hinsdale (Ill.) San. Dist., 1949—, pres., 1957—; chmn. DuPage County Drainage Com., 1955-56; precinct committman DuPage County Republican Com., 1940-60. John A. McElwain Water Reclamation Facility named in his honor. Mem. Ill. Assn. San. Dist. Trustees (pres. 1960-61), Chgo. Tennis Assn. (dir. 1942-52, pres. 1949), Kappa Sigma. Club: Hinsdale (Ill.) Golf. Home: 714 S Washington St Hinsdale IL 60521 Office: 133 N Jefferson St Chicago IL 60606

MC ENANY, GORDON EUGENE, mktg. exec.; b. Peoria, Ill., Sept. 11, 1930; s. Eldon Lewis and Ethel Mae (Baker) McE.; B.B.A., Northwestern U., 1968; m. Ethel Margaret Berlakovich, May 3, 1958; children-Brian F., Barton R., Blake J., Shana G. Asst. pub. relations mgr. Norge div. Borg Warner Corp., Chgo., 1954-58; account exec. Mayer & O'Brien, Chgo., 1959-61; writer Young & Rubicam, Chgo., 1961-63; advt. mgr. DeSoto, Inc., Des Plaines, Ill., 1964-68; mktg. communications mgr. United-DeSoto, Chgo., 1969-72; dir. advt. O'Brien Corp., South Bend, Ind., 1973-74; mktg. mgr. Fox Profl. Color Labs., Inc., South Bend, 1974—. Served with AUS, 1952-54. Home: 61545 Greentree Dr South Bend IN 46614 Office: 921 Louise St South Bend IN 46615

MC ENERNEY, JOHN JOSEPH, electric co. exec.; b. Elgin, Ill., Nov. 6, 1920; s. John Joseph and Virginia May (Henson) McE.; B.S., Washington U., St. Louis, 1942; m. Ellen L. Bakke, July 24, 1945; children—Mary McEherney Woolley, Michael T., Lawrence D. Credit mgr. Marshall Field & Co., Chgo., 1946-48; with Pioneer Electric & Research Corp., Forest Park, Ill., 1948—, pres., 1953—, dir., 1950—. Mem. pres.'s council Elmhurst Coll.; chmn. citizen's com. to investigate Chgo. Met. San. Dist., 1966-68; trustee Met. Crusade of Mercy, Chgo., 1967—, v.p., 1969-71, pres., 1973—; mem. Suburban Community Chest Council, 1965-71, v.p., 1968-69, pres., 1970-71; bd. dirs. Better Govt. Assn., 1964—, v.p., 1967-69, pres., 1970-72; bd. dirs. Elmhurst Community Chest, 1958-67, pres., 1965-67; trustee Union League Boys' Club Found., Chgo. Served to 1st lt. AUS, 1942-46. Mem. Glen Oak C. of C., Beta Theta Pi. Clubs: Foresters, Econ., Union League (dir. 1965-68, pres. 1973—) (Chgo.). Home: 155 Harbor Dr #1112 Chicago IL 60601 Office: 743 Circle Ave Forest Park IL 60130

MCENIRY, GLENN JOHN, assn. exec.; b. Lenox, Iowa, Nov. 28, 1916; s. John Joseph and Mary (Tracy) McE.; Ph.B., Creighton U., 1940, LL.B., 1948; m. Dorothy Arlene Mooney, Jan. 27, 1947; children—John Michael, Robert Francis. Mgr., Crete (Nebr.) C. of C., 1948-50; exec. v.p. Kearney (Nebr.) C. of C., 1950-62; exec. v.p. Nebr. Assn. Commerce and Industry, Lincoln, 1962—. Served to maj. USAAF, 1940-47. Mem. Nebr. State Bar Assn., Am. C. of C. Execs., Nebr. C. of C. Mgrs., Nebr. Assn. Comml. Orgn. Execs. (pres. 1951). Republican. Roman Catholic. Elk, K.C. Club: University (Lincoln). Home: 1720 Brookhaven Dr Lincoln NE 68520 Office: 147 N 9th St Lincoln NE 68501

MC ENTIRE, ESTHER MAXINE SHARP, educator, counselor; b. Oswego, Kans., Jan. 14. 1913; d. Henry Madison and Mary Esther (Miller) Sharp; B.S., Pittsburg (Kans.) State U., 1934; M.Ed., U. Kans., 1966; m. Richard B. McEntire, Dec. 9, 1944; children—Linda Basye McEntire Taylor, James Ralph. Tchr. math. Curtis Jr. High Sch., Roosevelt Jr. High Sch., Topeka, 1959, Topeka High Sch., 1960; tchr. math. Capper Jr. High Sch., Topeka, 1960, 65-76, counselor, 1965-76; tchr. math., counselor French Jr. High Sch., Topeka, 1976-77; counselor Jardine Jr. High Sch., Topeka, 1977—. Nat. Math. and Sci. Inst. grantee, 1961, 64. Certified guidance counselor, Kans. Mem. NEA, Am., Kans. personnel and guidance assns., Kans. Assn. Tchrs. Math., Nat. Council Tchrs. Math., DAR, Kappa Kappa Iota, Kappa Delta Pi, Kappa Mu Epsilon, Sigma Alpha Iota. Republican. Methodist. Club: Knife and Fork. Home: 1722 Medford St Topeka KS 66604 Office: 2600 W 33d St Topeka KS 66611

MC EVERS, ROBERT DARWIN, banker; b. Washington, May 18, 1930; s. John Henry and Beatrice (Holton) McE.; B.S. with distinction, U.S. Naval Acad., 1952; M.B.A. with distinction, Harvard U., 1958; m. Joan Manning, Mar. 29, 1954; children—Robert Darwin, Allison Holton. With First Nat. Bank of Chgo., 1958-61; spl. asst., exec. offices Trans Union Corp. (formerly Union Tank Car Co.), Chgo., 1961-64, gen. mgr. Canadian subsidiary, Toronto, Ont., 1964, asst. to pres., Chgo., 1964-65, v.p., gen. mgr. Tank Car div., 1965-70, pres., 1970-73; v.p. Trans Union Corp., 1965-73, dir., 1966-73; sr. v.p. 1st Nat. Bank, Chgo., 1973-75, head trust dept., 1974-77, exec. v.p., 1975—, head exec. dept., 1977—; pres Ft. Dearborn Income Securities, Inc., 1973-77; dir. Cooper Industries, Inc., Marquette Co. Bd. dirs. Central YMCA Community Coll., AMFUND, Civic Fedn. Served to 1st lt. USAF, 1952-56. Mem. Am. Mgmt. Assn., Chgo. Council Fgn. Relations, Newcomen Soc. N.Am., Beta Theta Pi. Clubs: Economic, Mid-Am., University (Chgo.); Army-Navy Country (Arlington, Va.); Kenilworth (Ill.); Indian Hill (Winnetka, Ill.). Home: 48 Kenilworth Ave Kenilworth IL 60043 Office: One First Nat Plaza Chicago IL 60670

MC FADDEN, MARY FRASER, personnel specialist; b. Victoria, Tex., Nov. 7, 1944; d. Edward S. and Elsie M. (Thomas) F.; B.A., No. Ill. U., 1967, M.A., 1976; m. Jack Donald McFadden, Mar. 9, 1974; children—Todd Fraser Morey, Thomas Harold Morey. Asst. dir., coordinator Admission Publ. No. Ill. U., DeKalb, Ill., 1971-73; mgr. corporate pub. relations DEKALB AgResearch, Inc., 1974-77; dir. personnel GTE Automatic Electric, Genoa, Ill., 1977—. Bd. dirs. United Way, 1977—; sec.-treas. DeKalb County Personnel Assn., 1976-77, 2d v.p., 1977—; mem. mktg.-mgmt. adv. bd. Kishwaukee Community Coll., 1976—. Mem. Pub. Relations Soc. Am., Indsl. Communications Council, Sigma Delta Chi. Office: 333 E 1st St Genoa IL 60135

MC FALL, ROBERT LLOYD, civil engr.; b. Pratt, Kans., Oct. 12, 1934; s. Harry Lloyd and Else Mabel (Day) McF.; B.S., Kans. State U., 1958; M.S., U. Idaho, 1959. Engr. State of Kans., Topeka, 1958-59; instr. U. Ill., Urbana, 1960-63; engr. C.E., Chgo., 1966-69; faculty La. State U., Baton Rouge, 1969; asst. chief engr. VA, Biloxi, Miss., 1970; cons. engr. Meurer-Serefini-Meurer, Denver, 1970; civil engr. Chgo. Sanitary Dist., 1971-74; hydrologist Gnosis Co., Evanston, Ill., 1974; civil engr. USAF, Chanute AFB, Ill., 1975. Served with AUS, 1954-56. Registered profl. engr., Ill. Mem. ASCE, Am. Geophys. Union, Am. Soc. Agrl. Engrs., Internat. Water Resources Assn., Water Pollution Control Fedn., Nat. Fedn. Fed. Employees, Amway Distbrs. Assn. Unitarian. Contbr. articles infield to prof. jours. Home: 2105 C Melrose Champaign IL 61820 Office: 3345 Civil Engr Squadron Chanute AFB IL 61868

MC FARLAND, CHARLES WARREN, chemist; b. Schenectady, N.Y., Jan. 24, 1942; s. George Leonard Jr. and Rosalind Kenway (Lewis) M.; A.B., Oberlin Coll., 1964; postgrad. N.Mex. State U., 1964-66; Ph.D., Case Western Res. U., 1971; m. Anne Southworth, June 9, 1964; 1 son, Michael Edward. Sr. research asst. biology dept. Case Western Res. U., Cleve., 1971-72, research asso., chemistry dept., 1972-73; postdoctoral research asso. Cuyahoga County Coroner's Office., Cleve., 1972-73; research chemist R.O. Hull & Co., Cleve., 1973-75, research mgr., 1975—; cons. in field. NASA trainee, 1965-66; NIH predoctoral research fellow, 1968-70. Mem. Am. Chem. Soc., Am. Electroplaters Soc., Am. Inst. Chemists, AAAS, Sigma Xi. Contbr. articles to profl. jours. Home: 2905 Scarborough Rd Cleveland Heights OH 44118 Office: 3203 W 71st St Cleveland OH 44102

MC GADY, DONALD LAWRENCE, elec. engr.; b. Chgo., July 22, 1947; s. David Lawrence and Irene Veronica (O'Connor) McG.; B.S. in Elec. Engring., Chgo. Tech. Coll., 1974; m. Joan May Bachman, Sept. 5, 1970; children—Jody Katherine, Donald Lawrence Carlson. Elec. supr. Mercy Hosp. and Med. Center, Chgo., 1969-73, mng. elec. engr., 1973-76, asst. dir. engring., 1976—. Mem. IEEE, Bio-med. Engring. Group, Industry Application Soc., Elec. Maint. Engrs., Ill. Fire Chiefs Assn., Internat. Assn. Elec. Inspectors, Kappa Sigma Kappa. Roman Catholic. Inventor in field of computerized monitoring, data logging and control system for hosp. sterilization equipment. Home: 7827 Pine Pkwy Darien IL 60559 Office: 2510 S King Dr Chicago IL 60616

MC GARY, THOMAS HUGH, lawyer; b. Milburn, Ky., Mar. 6, 1938; s. Ollie James and Pauline Elizabeth (Tackett) McG.; A.B., Elmhurst Coll., 1961; J.D., U. Chgo., 1964; m. Madalyn Maxwell, July 4, 1968. Admitted to Ill. bar, 1964; asst. atty. gen. State of Ill., 1965-67, supr. consumer credit, 1967-71; ind. practice law, Springfield, Ill., 1971—; v.p., dir. Citizens Bank of Edinburg (Ill.), 1971—, Bank of Kenney (Ill.), 1977—; dir. Schyler State Bank, Rushville, Ill., 1974—, Lincoln Savs. & Loan Assn., Mt. Zion, Ill., 1976—; instr. Lincolnland Coll., 1970-73. Mem. Ill. Spl. Com. on Uniform Credit Code, Springfield Art Assn., Springfield Symphony Assn. Mem. Am., Ill., Sangamon County bar assns., Am. Judicature Soc., 3d House, Sangamon County Hist. Assn., Chgo. Council on Fgn. Relations. Democrat. Episcopalian. Club: Sangamo (Springfield). Home: 1100 Orendorff Pkwy Springfield IL 62704 Office: 911 Ridgely Bldg Springfield IL 62701

MC GAUGHEY, ALBERT WAYNE, educator; b. Russellville, Ind., July 16, 1914; s. Walter Lee and Belvia Jane (Harbison) McG.; A.B., Wabash Coll., 1935; M.S., State U. Iowa, 1937; Ph.D., U. Cin., 1940; m. Margie Virginia Silverthorn, July 11, 1941; children—Stanley Wayne, Dennis Michael, Lynn (Mrs. David Kearney), Donna (Mrs. Russell Defenbaugh). Instr. math. Purdue U., Lafayette, Ind., 1940-41; faculty U.S. Naval Acad., Annapolis, Md., 1941-46; Westminster Coll., New Wilmington, Pa., 1946-48; faculty Bradley U., Peoria, Ill., 1948—, prof. math., 1953—, chmn. dept. math., 1971-77. AID cons. Summer Inst. High Sch. Tchrs. Math. Burdwan (India) U., 1966; asso. program dir. secondary edn. sect. NSF, Washington, 1968-69. Mem. Math. Assn. Am. (sec., treas. 1953-62), Phi Beta Kappa, Sigma Xi, Phi Kappa Phi. Mem. Christian Ch. (chmn. ofcl. bd. 1960-62, 75-76). Home: 2703 N Kingston Dr Peoria IL 61604 Office: Bradley University Peoria IL 61625

MCGAW, ROBERT WALTER, city ofcl.; b. Rockford, Ill., Apr. 9, 1923; s. James Lincoln and Loren (Lynch) McG.; B.S., No. Ill. U., 1950, M.S., 1966; m. Margaret Arlene Schindler, June 21, 1946; children—Marlis Jean McGaw Young, Roberta Sue, Raymond William. With Shabhona Pub. Sch., 1950-52; tchr. Harlem Consol. Schs., 1952-72, tchr., 1952-68, adminstr. Rock Cut Sch., Rockford, Ill., 1968-72; mayor of Rockford, 1972—. Chmn. bd. Park Tours, Inc., Rock Cut State Park, Ill., Alderman, City of Rockford, Ill., 1955-63; del. Democratic Conv. 1968, 72, county chmn., 1962-64, candidate lt. gov., 1960. Served with U.S. Army, 1942-46. Mem. Nat., Ill. edn. assn., V.F.W. Clubs: Masons (32 deg.), Shriners, Moose. Home: 2016 E State St Rockford IL 61108 Office: City Hall Bldg 425 E State St Rockford IL 61104

MCGEE, JAMES HOWELL, lawyer; b. Berryburg, W.Va., Nov. 8, 1918; s. Spanish and Perrie (Dalton) McG.; B.S., Wilberforce U., 1941; LL.B., Ohio State U., 1948; m. Elizabeth McCracken, Jan. 23, 1948; children—Annette, Frances. Admitted to Ohio bar, 1949, since practiced in Dayton. Pres., dir. Dayton br. NAACP, Dayton Urban League Commr. City of Dayton, 1967-70, mayor, 1970—. Served with U.S. Army, 1942-45; ETO. Mem. Alpha Phi Alpha. Home: 1518 Benson Dr Dayton OH 45406 Office: 1526 W 3d St Dayton OH 45407

MC GEE, MICHL THOMAS, accountant; b. Davenport, Iowa, Jan. 8, 1942; s. Arthur Thomas and Esther A. (Michl) McG.; B.A., St. Ambrose Coll., 1964; m. Ellen Ann Betts, Feb. 16, 1963; children—Scott, Todd, Doug, Tom, Anne, Erin, Adam, Dana, Kathryn. With McGladrey, Hansen, Dunn & Co., Clinton, Iowa, 1964—, partner, 1970—. Bd. dirs. United Way, Mercy Hosp. C.P.A., Iowa. Mem. Am. Inst. C.P.A.'s, Iowa Assn. C.P.A.'s. Clubs: Clinton Country, Rotary, Civitan. Office: 223 Wilson St Clinton IA 52732

MC GEE, RALPH EUGENE, automotive products co. exec.; b. Van Buren, Ark., Oct. 12, 1937; s. Robert E. Lee and Nellie Lea (Owens) McG.; B.S., San Jose State Coll., 1960; m. Merilyn Joan Kellogg, July 20, 1957; children—Steven, Colleen, Kathleen, Jennifer. Salesman, Masterson Bearing Co., Mountain View, Calif., 1960-62; salesman Am. Koyo Corp. subs. Boise Cascade Corp., 1962-63, regional mgr., 1963-68, sales mgr. Detroit Automotive Products Corp. div., Warren, Mich., 1968-69, gen. sales mgr., 1969-70, mgr. mktg. and sales, 1970-75, dir. sales and mktg., 1973—; lectr. Sch. Econs., Oakland U. Mem. Groveland Twp. Fire Bd., 1974; mem. com. Rochester Bd. Edn. Mem. Soc. Automotive Engrs. Republican. Mem. Community Ch. (chmn. bd. deacons 1974-76). Home: 691 Van Rd Holly MI 48442 Office: 11445 Stephens Dr Warren MI 48090

MC GEHEE, H. COLEMAN, JR., clergyman. Ordained to ministry Episcopal Ch.; formerly rector Immanuel Ch.-on-the-hill, Alexandria, Va.; elected bishop coadjutor of Mich., 1971-73, bishop of Mich., 1973—. Address: Episcopal Diocese of Michigan 4800 Woodward Ave Detroit MI 48201

MC GERVEY, JOHN DONALD, educator; b. Pitts., Aug. 9, 1931; s. Daniel Donald and Eleanor Antonia (Rogerson) McG.; B.S., U. Pitts., 1952; postgrad. (NSF fellow), U. Chgo., 1952-53; M.S., Carnegie Inst. Tech., 1955, Ph.D., 1961; m. Nancy Ruth Maher, July 6, 1957; children—Anne, Donald, Joan. Instr. math. Carnegie Inst. Tech., Pitts., 1957-60; asst. prof. physics Western Res. U., Cleve., 1960-65, asso. prof., 1965-67; asso. prof. physics Case Western Res. U., Cleve., 1967—; vis. scientist Kernforschungsanlage, Julich, W.Ger., 1972-73. Pres., Cath. Interracial Council of Cleve., 1969-72; pres. Project Equality of N.E. Ohio, 1970; exec. bd. Commn. on Cath. Community Action, Diocese of Cleve., 1968-72, 73—. Research grantee Air Force Office Sci. Research, 1960-62, AEC, 1962-65, NSF, 1974—. Mem. Am. Phys. Soc., Am. Assn. Physics Tchrs., AAUP, AAAS, Sigma Xi. Author: Introduction to Modern Physics, 1971. Home: 1819 Wilton Rd Cleveland Heights OH 44118

MC GETTIGAN, BRIAN JEROME, realtor; b. Darlington, Wis., May 10, 1937; s. William J. and Beryl (Mead) McG.; m. Josephine A. Palzkill, Sept. 27, 1958; 1 son, Kevin J. Br. mgr. Household Finance Corp., Madison, Wis., 1957-72; realtor Pyramid Realty Inc., Madison, Wis., 1971, v.p., gen. mgr., 1972-76, pres., 1976—, also dir. Group chmn. United Givers, 1963-66; pres. Cursillo Movement Diocese Madison, 1970; mem. council Parish, 1973-75, chmn. edn. commn., 1974-75, instr. religious edn. High Sch., 1968-75 Immaculate Heart of Mary Cath. Ch., Madison, also pres. Mens Club, 1969. Mem. Realtors Nat. Mktg. Inst. (co-chmn. Wis. 1976—), Greater Madison Bd. Realtors (dir. 1976, v.p. 1978), Wis. Realtors Assn. (dir. 1978—), Madison Builders Assn., Ws. Builders Assn., Nat. Assn. Home Builders, Nat. Assn. Realtors. Home: 3710 Valley Ridge Rd Middleton WI 53562 Office: 112 Washington Ave E Madison WI 53703

MC GHEE, ANDREW WHITE, container co. exec.; b. Pitts., Oct. 26, 1931; s. John Francis and Katherine (Easton) M.; B.S. in Indsl. Engring., Stanford U., 1953; m. Karen Janet Maxfield, May 1, 1954; children—Kristen Janet, Katherine Drew, Nancy Easton. Mem. prodn. staff Purex Corp., South Gate, Calif., 1956-62, plant mgr., East Chicago, Ind., 1962-65; sr. mgmt. cons. Cresap, McCormick & Paget, Chgo., 1965-68; mem. corporate mfg. staff Morton Salt Co., Chgo., 1968-71; v.p. ops. Packaging Systems Inc., Itasca, Ill., 1971-75, pres., 1975—; dir. Queen Ann Candy Co. Mem. fin. rev. com. Community Fund; chmn. Ill. com. Nat. Council on Crime and Delinquency, 1970-72; chmn. bd. trustees Latin Sch., Chgo., 1972-75. Served as lt. USNR, 1953-56. Mem. Plastic Bottle Inst., Soc. Plastics Industry. Republican. Clubs: Saddle and Cycle (dir., treas.), Racquet, Casino (Chgo.). Home: 27 E Scott St Chicago IL 60610 Office: Packaging Systems Inc 751 Hilltop Dr Itasca IL 60143

MC GHEE, JOHN EDWARD, biochemist; b. Gary, Ind., May 29, 1931; s. Willie Wesley and Margarett Eleanor (Dawson) McG.; B.S., Millikin U., Decatur, Ill., 1957; postgrad. Bradley U., Peoria, Ill., Ill. State U., Normal, U.S. Agrl. Research Grad. Sch., Peoria; m. Geraldine Augusta Winfrey, Jan. 30, 1960; children—Laurie Anne, John Wesley, Marcia Lynn, Steven Edward. Analytical chemist Agrl. Research Service No. Regional Research Center, Dept. Agr., Peoria, 1957-60, research biochemist, leader biochem. engring. project, 1960—; cons. to industry and govt. Counselor Boys Clubs of Peoria, Inc., 1965-70, Boy Scouts Am., 1971-77; Peoria area design for leadership officer Millikin U., 1976-77; mem. Peoria Area Air Pollution Adv. and Appeals Bd., 1974-77; judge Nat. Sci. and Engring. Sci. Fair, 1958-77. Recipient Internat. Sci. Competition award, 1974. Mem. Am. Oil Chemists Soc., Am. Assn. Cereal Chemists, Am. Translators Assn., Les Amis de la France (sec.-treas.), Mid-Am. Classical Guitar Soc. Contbr. articles to profl. jours., chpts. in books. French and German interpreter and translator in communication with fgn. scientists. Home: 2224 W Westport Rd Peoria IL 61614 Office: 1815 N University St Peoria IL 61604

MC GHEE, NOAH LAYNE, lawyer; b. Moline, Ill., Oct. 27, 1930; s. Rex Hammond and Velma Anna (Lewis) McG.; B.A., Augustana Coll., 1952; J.D., Northwestern U., 1955; m. Carolyn Marie Almer, June 26, 1954; children—Anne Carol, John Layne. Admitted to Ill. bar, 1958; portfolio mgr. Harris Trust & Savs. Bank, Chgo., 1955-59; sr. partner firm McGehee, Boling & Whitmire, Ltd., Silvis, Ill., 1959—; circuit magistrate, 1961-65; asst. atty. gen. State of Ill., 1969-72. Charter mem. Bi-State Met. Planning Commn., 1968, sec., 1970—. Vice chmn., bd. dirs. Illini Hosp., Silvis, 1968-72. Mem. Am., Ill., Rock Island County (bd. mgrs.) bar assns. Home: 1021 6th Ave Silvis IL 61282 Office: 105 7th St Silvis IL 61282

MC GHEE, PATRICIA LOUISE OHLSEN, educator; b. Monticello, Wis., Sept. 14, 1934; d. Michael Peter and Alicia Alma (Ellefson) Ohlsen; B.A., U. Ariz., 1956; M.A., Marquette U., 1958; postgrad. U. Wis-Madison, 1972-74; m. John Ferdinan; 2 children. Tchr. social studies pub. schs., Milw., 1960-62, Fox Point-Bayside (Wis.), 1963-67, Shorewood, Wis., 1971-72, Waukesha, Wis., 1974—; tchr. social studies Milw. Area Tech. Coll., 1968-74. Sec. Ozaukee County Democratic party, 1973. Taft fellow, 1975. Mem. Am. Hist. Assn., Hist. Assn., Historians Film Com., Soc. History Edn., U.S. Tennis Assn., Gamma Phi Beta, Pi Gamma Mu. Home: 12523 N Woodberry Dr Mequon WI 53092 Office: 2222 Michigan Ave Waukesha WI 53186

MC GIBBON, EDMUND LEAVENWORTH, lawyer, rancher; b. Grand Rapids, Mich., May 27, 1908; s. William and Franc (Leavenworth) McG.; A.B., Dartmouth Coll., 1929; J.D., Northwestern U., 1933; m. Catherine Jean Klink, Aug. 29, 1941; children—William, Catherine, Bonnie, Laurie. Admitted to Ill. bar, 1934, since practiced in Chgo; asso. firm Robertson, Crowe & Spence, 1934-38; partner Robertson & McGibbon, 1947-53, Williston, McGibbon & Stastny, 1953-66, Williston & McGibbon, 1966-71, Williston, McGibbon & Kuehn, 1971—. Chmn. bd. Santa Rita Ranch, Inc. Bd. govs. Scottish Old Peoples Home. Served from lt. to comdr. USNR, 1940-45, comdg. officer destroyer escort; capt. USNR. Mem. Am. Mgmt. Assn. (pres.'s council), Am., Ill., Chgo. bar assns., Nat. Rifle Assn. (life), Aircraft Owners and Pilots Assn., Ill. St. Andrew Soc. (past pres.), Phi Kappa Psi, Phi Alpha Delta. Republican. Episcopalian. Clubs: University, Chicago (Chgo.); Barrington Hills (Ill.) Country; Tucson Country, Old Pueblo (Tucson); Guadalajara (Mexico) Country. Home: Ridge Rd Barrington IL 60010 Office: 20 N Wacker Dr Chicago IL 60606 also 102 N Cook St Barrington IL 60010 also Santa Rita Ranch Box 647 Green Valley AZ 85614

MC GILL, JOHN WILLIAM, communications co. exec.; b. Cleve., July 5, 1944; s. William John and Harriet Gertrude (Phillips) McG.; B.S. cum laude, Dyke Coll., 1972; m. Diane Marie Klimkowski, Nov. 1962; children—Monica A., Jacqueline, Matthew, Tom, Steve. Western parts sales mgr. Hupp Corp., Cleve., 1963-68; asst. to chmn. The Finney Co., Bedford Heights, Ohio, 1968-71; chmn. bd. Tele-Communications Inc., Mayfield Village, Ohio, 1971—. Mem. Ohio Cable TV Assn., N. Am. Tel. Assn., Detroit C. of C. Republican. Club: Dyke Coll. Pres.'s. Home: 12036 Sperry Rd Chesterland OH 44026 Office: 600 Beta Dr Mayfield Village OH 44143

MC GILL, RALPH NORMAN, mech. engr.; b. Charlotte, N.C., Feb. 4, 1943; s. John McNeil and Edna Shirley (Morse) McG.; B.S., N.C. State U., 1965, M.M.E., 1968, Ph.D., 1969; m. Marianne Frances Raia, July 31, 1965; children—Norman, Kimberly. Asso. sr. research engr. Gen. Motors Research Labs., Warren, Mich., 1969—. NSF fellow, 1965-66, Ford Found. fellow, 1966-69. Mem. Soc. Automotive Engrs., ASME. Home: 53434 Heatherway Utica MI 48087 Office: 12 Mile and Mound Rds Warren MI 48090

MC GINNIS, CECIL GLENN, sch. adminstr.; b. Braddyville, Iowa, Jan. 4, 1913; s. D. Sherman and Mary Namatha (Morrow) McG.; A.B.; Tarkio Coll., 1941; M.Ed., U. S.D., 1949; postgrad. Westmar Coll., 1950, Drake U., 1968; m. Mary Ellen White, Dec. 12, 1942; children—Kathleen McGinnis Jennings, Glen Edward, Ellen Louise. Tchr. sci. Pickett High Sch., St. Joseph, Mo., 1941-42; tchr. sci., math, prin. Akron (Iowa) High Sch., 1946-54; prin. Belle Plaine (Iowa) High Sch., 1954-58, Carlisle (Iowa) High Sch., 1958-68; supt. Tri-County Community Schs., Thornburg, Iowa, 1968-72; supt. Murray (Iowa) Community Schs., 1972-78. Served with AUS, 1941, 42-46. Mem. Iowa Edn. Assn., Plymouth County Tchrs. Assn. (pres. 1947-48), Iowa Assn. Sch. Administrs., Phi Delta Kappa. Mason. Home: 923 Grant St Murray IA 50174 Office: PO Box 187 Murray IA 50174

MC GINNIS, CHARLES ALAN, psychologist; b. Como, Tex., Apr. 18, 1935; s. Thomas Edward and Madie Louise (Swindell) McG.; B.S., North Tex. State U., 1960, M.S., 1961; Ph.D. in Clin. Psychology, Heed U., Hollywood, Fla., 1977; m. Merilyn Sue Moody, Aug. 9, 1958; children—Merilyn Renee, Charles Alan, Stephen Gregory. Chief psychologist Wichita Falls (Tex.) State Hosp., 1960-62; clin. psychologist Fla. State Hosp., Chattahoochee, 1962-65; chief psychologist Bristol (Va.) Mental Health Clinic, 1965; chief psychologist, asst. dir. Adult Mental Health Clinic, Bay City, Mich., 1965-69, dir., 1969-70; community mental health cons. Alpena (Mich.) Mental Health Program, 1970-72; individual practice clin. psychology Salman Psychiat. Clinic and C & M Psychol. Cons., Bay City, 1970—. Instr. psychology Sullins Coll. for Women, Bristol, Va., 1965. Bd. dirs. Crisis Intervention-Hotline, Inc., Oscoda, Mich., Alcoholism Friendship House, Bay City. Served with AUS, 1953-55. Mem. Am., Mich. psychol. assns., Mich. Group Psychotherapy Assn., Nat. Assn. Applied Arts and Scis. Elk. Club: Midland (Mich.) Country. Home: 567 Woodcock Rd Midland MI 48640 Office: 2117 16th St Bay City MI 48706

MC GINNIS, CLAUDE PRESLEY, lawyer; b. Eldon, Mo., Apr. 24, 1926; s. Thomas Presley and Nellie Jane (Marriott) McG.; B.S., U. Mo., 1949; LL.B., U. Mo., Kansas City, 1961; m. Lucy Delilah Honeyfield, May 9, 1952; children—Claudia Lou, Suzanne René. Admitted to Mo. bar, 1961, Ia. bar, 1971; practiced in Kansas City, Mo., 1962; atty., sr. claims supr. Federated Ins. Co., Kansas City, 1962-71; corporate counsel Grinnell Mut. Reins. Co. (Iowa), 1971—; corporate sec. Big M Agy., Inc., 1974—, Grinnell Realty Co., 1976—. Police judge City of Lake Waukomis, Mo., 1967-71; v.p. South Platte Republican Club, 1971. Bd. dirs. Clay-Platte Children's House, Kansas City, 1966—; elder, trustee Presbyn. Ch. Served with AUS, 1944-46. Mem. Ia., Mo. bar assns., Fedn. Ins. Counsel. Home: 2010 Country Club Dr Grinnell IA 50112 Office: Hwy 146 at Interstate 80 Grinnell IA 50112

MC GINNIS, JAMES EDWARD, accountant; b. Oxford, Mass., July 31, 1917; s. John James and Jennie Catherine (Fenner) McG.; A.B., Youngstown (Ohio) Coll., 1950; m. Catherine Irene Cronk, July 12, 1941; children—Barbara McGinnis Cash II, Kathleen, Patricia McGinnis Vavrinak, James Brian, John Edward, Robert Michael. Accountant, W.L. Reali, Pub. Accountant, Youngstown, 1945-50; pvt. practice pub. accounting, Youngstown, 1950—; office mgr. Patterson Buckeye, Inc., North Lima, Ohio, 1950—, also dir.; partner McGinnis-Vavrinak Co., Austintown, Ohio, 1970—; income tax preparer; cons. state, county and local taxes. Chmn. Vets. Day Parade, Youngstown, 1970—, chmn. Meml. Day parade, 1971—; chmn. Mahoning County (Ohio) Grave Decorating Com., 1969-77, mem. Civic Day Com., 1970—; Ohio Bicentennial Com., 1974-75. Served to sgt. AUS, 1940-45; PTO. C.P.A., Ohio Mem. Amvets (past comdr.), V.F.W., 37th Div. Vets. Assn., United Vets. Council of Mahoning County (comdr. 1972), United Comml. Travellers, Nat. Soc. Pub. Accountants, Mahoning Valley Gaelic Soc., Youngstown U. Alumni Assn., Sigma Kappa Phi. Roman Catholic. K.C. (3 deg.). Home: 3821 Frederick St Youngstown OH 44515 Office: 550 W Pine Lake Rd North Lima OH 44452

MC GINNIS, LELAND BARNES, pipe organ technician and contractor; b. Sully County, S.D., June 13, 1910; s. Frank Adolphus and Lura (Wolff) McG.; B.S., Iowa State Coll., 1950; B.A., Buena Vista Coll., 1951; m. Marie Victoria Odquist, Dec. 25, 1937. Musician, traveling dance bands, 1929-41; music tchr. Fernald (Iowa) Consol. Sch., part-time 1946-50, Early (Iowa) Consol. Sch., 1951-52, Hayes Consol. Sch., Storm Lake, Iowa, 1952-56, Galva (Iowa) Consol. Sch., 1956-59; self employed pipe organ technician, 1959—. Mem. Karl King Band, 1946—. Served with AUS, 1941-45. Mem. Am. Fedn. Musicians, Am. Guild Organists, Am. Theatre Organ Soc., Mason. Performed with Karl King Band and Glee Club, Washington, 1976. Address: 510 Johnson St Alta IA 51002

MC GLINN, JOSEPH FRANCIS, realtor; b. Phila., Aug. 19, 1918; s. Michael Joseph and Marion Ann (Sweeney) McG.; student Villanova Coll., 1940; M.B.A., U. Dayton, 1967; m. Marjorie Kidnocker, June 21, 1947; children—Joan, Kathleen, Michael. Pres., Monarch Die Engring. Co., Dayton, Ohio, 1965-69; pvt. practice security analysis, Dayton, 1969-75; asso. Long Realty, Dayton, Ohio, 1976—; asso. S. Park Land Livestock Co., Inc.; bd. dirs. Monarch Die and Engring. Co.; cons. to bus. Chmn. bd. dirs. Catholic Charities, Dayton, 1960-65. Mem. Am. Mktg. Assn. (charter, Dayton chpt.), Dayton Tool and Die Assn. Roman Catholic. Clubs: Dayton Country, K.C. Home: 842 Revere Village Ct Centerville OH 45459 Office: 2090 Hewitt Ave Dayton OH 45440

MC GLYNN, GERALD EDWARD, JR., lawyer; b. Des Moines, June 15, 1929; s. Gerald Edward and Marjorie Louise (Brown) McG.; B.S. in Gen. Engring., Iowa State U., 1951; postgrad. Drake U. Law Sch., 1950-51; J.D. cum laude, George Washington U., 1956; m. Shayla Kathryn Skelley, June 16, 1951; children—Kathryn S., Mary Egan, Bridget, Gerald E. III, Meghan A., Daniel J. Admitted to Iowa bar, 1956, Mich. bar, 1957; patent atty. trainee and patent atty., Gen. Motors Corp. Patent Sect., Washington and Detroit, 1953-61; founder, partner, patent law firm McGlynn & Milton, Troy, Mich., 1961—. Mem. bd. control, Mich Technol. U., 1971—. Served with C.E., AUS, 1951-53; Korea. Decorated Army Commendation Ribbon with Medal Pendant. Mem. Am. Bar Assn., State Bar of Mich., Am., Mich. patent law assns., Am. Judicature Soc., Nat. Panel of Arbitrators, Am. Arbitration Assn. Home: 739 Hawthorne Dr Bloomfield Hills MI 48013 Office: 1650 W Big Beaver Rd Troy MI 48084

MC GOLDRICK, JAMES EDWARD, JR., historian; b. Phila., Jan. 5, 1936; s. James Edward and Bernardine Estelle (Glenn) McG.; B.S., Temple U., 1961, M.A., 1964; Ph.D., W.Va. U., 1974. Instr. history John Brown U., 1966-68, asst. prof., 1969-70; instr. W.Va. U., 1971-73; asst. prof. Cedarville (Ohio) Coll., 1973-74, asso. prof., 1974-75, prof., 1976—. Temple U. Hebrew award, 1961; named Faculty Mem. of Year, Cedarville Coll., 1977. Mem. Am. Hist. Assn., Am. Soc. Ch. History, Sixteenth Century Studies Conf., Am. Soc. Reformation Research, Conf. on Faith and History. Baptist. Home: 3812 Cheyenne Trail Jamestown OH 45335 Office: Box 617 Cedarville College Cedarville OH 45314

MC GOVERN, EARL ARTHUR, supt. schs.; b. Cleve., Dec. 14, 1928; s. Earl Michael and Evelyn (Spang) McG.; B.S. in Edn., Miami U., Ohio, 1951; M.Ed., Harvard U., 1955; Ed.D., Columbia U., 1959; m. Lila Barnes, June 16, 1956. Elementary tchr. Parma Park Sch., Parma, Ohio, 1953-54; elementary prin. Ridge Rd. Sch., Parma, 1955-58; research asst. Inst. Adminstrv. Research, Columbia Tchrs. Coll., 1958-59; asst. dir. adminstrv. research Ednl. Research Council Greater Cleve., 1959-62; adminstrv. asst. to supt., New Rochelle, N.Y., 1962-65; supt. schs. Lima, Ohio, 1965—; cons. legal and ednl. def. fund NAACP. Bd. dirs., pres. United Fund Greater Lima. Served with USMCR, 1951-53. Mem. NEA (life), Ohio Congress Parents and Tchrs (v.p.), Am. Assn. Sch. Adminstrs., Buckeye Assn. Sch. Adminstrs. (exec. com.), Am. Ednl. Research Assn., Lima Area C. of C., Phi Delta Kappa. Kappa Delta Phi. Presbyterian (elder). Clubs: Rotary, Elks. Editorial adv. bd. Croft Ednl. Services, Ednl. Service Bur. Home: 2351 W Spring St Lima OH 45805 Office: 515 S Calumet Ave Lima OH 45804

MC GOVERN, GEORGE STANLEY, senator; b. Avon, S.D., July 19, 1922; s. Joseph C. and Frances (McLean) McG.; B.A., Dakota Wesleyan U., 1945; M.A., Northwestern U., 1949, Ph.D., 1953; m. Eleanor Stegeberg, Oct. 31, 1943; children—Ann, Susan, Teresa, Steven, Mary. Prof. history and polit. sci. Dakota Wesleyan U., 1949-53; exec. sec. S.D. Democratic Party, 1953-56; mem. U.S. Ho. of Reps. from 1st dist. S.D., 85th-86th congresses, 1956-60; food-for-peace dir. Kennedy Adminstrn., 1960-62; mem. U.S. Senate from S.D., 1963—. Democratic candidate for Pres. U.S., 1972. Served as pilot USAAF, World War II. Decorated D.F.C. Mem. Am. Hist. Assn. Methodist. Mason (33 deg., Shriner), Elk, Kiwanian. Author: The Colorado Coal Strike, 1913-14, 1953; War Against Want, 1964; Agricultural Thought in the 20th Century, 1967; A Time of War A Time of Peace, 1968; (with Leonard Guttridge) The Great Coalfield War, 1972; An American Journey, 1974. Home: Mitchell SD 57301 Office: Senate Office Bldg Washington DC 20510

MC GOVERN, WILLIAM ALOYSIUS, med. supplies and services exec.; b. N.Y.C., Jan. 7, 1933; s. William Aloysius and Marie C. (Lynch) McG.; A.B., St. Peter's Coll., 1955; M.D., Johns Hopkins U., 1959; postgrad. U. Minn., 1962-64; m. Carol R. Yessak, May 8, 1965; children—William B., Laura Ann. Intern, U. Minn. Hosp., 1959-60, resident, 1962-64; practice medicine specializing in anesthesiology, St. Cloud, Minn., 1964-65; clin. investigator G.D. Searle & Co., Chgo., 1965-69, asso. dir. clin. research, 1969-70, dir. div. med. systems and instrumentation, 1970-76; dir. clin. research Ames Co. div. Miles Labs., 1976—. Served with USNR, 1960-62. fellow Am. Coll. Anesthesiologists, Soc. Advanced Med. Systems; mem. IEEE, Am. Soc. Clin. Pharmacology and Therapeutics, Am. Mgmt. Assn. Home: 1523 Ash Dr W Elkhart IN 46514 Office: 1127 Myrtle St Elkhart IN 46514

MC GOWEN, CHARLES HAMMOND, physician; b. Youngstown, Ohio, May 28, 1936; s. Keith Wellington and Frances Emily (Owen) McG.; A.B., Hiram Coll., 1957; M.D., Ohio State U., 1961; grad. USAF Sch. Aerospace Medicine, 1966; m. Kay Louise Umbel, Dec. 8, 1956; children—Wendy Kay, Charles Keith, Brenda Sue. Intern, Youngstown Hosp. Assn., 1961-62, resident in internal medicine, 1964-67; practice medicine specializing in internal medicine, Youngstown, 1967—; instr. residency-internship program, Youngstown Hosp. Assn., 1967—. Lectr., speaker pub. meetings, radio and TV, seminars on Creation vs. Evolution; bd. edn. Poland Local Sch. Dist., 1971—; mem. Christian Businessmen's Com. Internat. Evangel. Friends Ch. Served with M.C. USAF, 1962-64, with USAFR, 1964-69. Diplomate Am. Bd. Internal Medicine. Mem. Mahoning County Med. Soc., Ohio State Med. Assn., Creation Research Soc., Am. Diabetes Assn. Author: In Six Days, 1976; Where There's Smoke, 1977. Home: 16 Centennial Dr Poland OH 44514 Office: 1039 Boardman-Canfield Rd Youngstown OH 44512

MC GRATH, JOHN FRANCIS, printing co. exec.; b. Chgo., June 12, 1926; s. John Francis and Anna (Kinn) McG.; B.S., Loyola U., Chgo., 1946; m. Margaret Wilson, Apr. 19, 1952; children—Patrick, Janine. Salesman, Egry Corp. of Dayton (Ohio), 1946-47, Modern Bus. Forms, 1947-51; v.p. Am. Bus. Forms, Inc., Chgo., 1951-66; pres. Spectra Color, Inc., Chgo., 1961-66, now dir.; pres. Accurate Bus. Forms, Inc., Mundelein, Ill., 1966—. Mem. Mundelein C. of C., Printing Industry Am. Data Processing Mgrs. Assn. Moose, K.C. (4 deg.), Lion. Home: 637 Banbury Rd Mundelein IL 60060 Office: 279 Anthony St Mundelein IL 60060

MC GRATH, LAWRENCE EDWARD, banker; b. Clay Center, Kans., Sept. 30, 1927; s. Edward Lawrence and Rose (Mullen) McG.; B.S., U. Iowa, 1950; m. Johanna Judith Sivertson, Dec. 30, 1950; children—Mary Margaret, Catherine Ann, John Sivertson, David Kennedy. Bank examiner div. exam. FDIC, Washington, 1950-57; with City Nat. Bank, Cedar Rapids, Iowa, 1957-68; v.p., cashier Peoples Bank & Trust Co., Cedar Rapids, 1968—. Mem. 18th Jud. Dist. Nominating Commn., 1963-69; mem. Dubuque (Iowa) Archdiocesan Bd. Edn., 1975—; pres. United Way, 1970-73; chmn. Regis-LaSalle Found., 1977—. Served with AUS, 1946-47. Mem. Am. Inst. Banking. Democrat. Roman Catholic. Club: Elmcrest Golf and Country. Home: 1800 2d Ave SE Cedar Rapids IA 52403 Office: 101 3d Ave SW Cedar Rapids IA 52404

MC GRAW, DELFORD ARMSTRONG, process engr.; b. Keyrock, W.Va., May 13, 1917; s. Sidney Lott and Grace Leola (Stewart) McG.; A.B., Concord Coll., 1937; M.S., W.Va.U., 1939; postgrad. U. N.C., 1939-40; m. Elizabeth Ramsey, Mar. 13, 1941; children—Patrick A., Donald L. Ballistics engr. Hercules Powder Co., Wilmington, Del., 1941-45; with Owens-Ill. Inc., Toledo, 1945—, project engr., 1946-66, chief instrument sect., 1966-69, dir. engring. research, 1969-73, mgr. process and computer systems, 1973—. Recipient Soc. Plastics Engrs. award, 1950. Fellow Am. Ceramic Soc. (Forrest awards 1953, 59), Soc. Glass Tech. (Brit.); mem. Sigma Xi, Sigma Pi Sigma. Research in physics of glass-forming process. Patentee in field. Home: 3410 Chapel Dr Toledo OH 43615 Office: Owens-Ill Inc 1700 N Westwood St Toledo OH 43666

MC GRAW, ROBERT PAUL, dentist, corporate cons.; b. Miami, Fla., Feb. 8, 1929; s. Edward Walker and Mabel Bell (Pilster) McG.; A.A., Graceland Coll., 1948; student Washington U., St. Louis, 1948-49; B.A., U. Mo., 1954, D.D.S., 1955; m. Cicely Anne DeLapp, Nov. 25, 1949; children—Robert Paul, Steven Leslie, David Michael. Pvt. practice dentistry, Independence, Mo., 1957-63; R.P. McGraw Profl. Corp., Independence, 1963-65; pioneer 1st dental profl. corp. in Mo.; dentist Independence Dental Center, Inc., 1965—. Cons. corporate group practice, 1965—; asso. prof. Coll. Dentistry, U. Mo. at Kansas City, 1972—; lectr. med., dental, legal socs. on corporate practice in U.S., Europe, Mexico; adviser Med.-Legal Inst.; adviser to bd. dirs. L.D. Pankey Inst. Advanced Dental Research, Miami. Fla. Charter mem., dir. Commerce Bank Independence. Served with USAF, 1955-57. Mem. Am. Acad. Dental Practice Adminstrn. (chmn. speakers bur. 1972—), Am. Dental Assn., Am. Acad. Dental Group Practice (dir. 1973—), Sigma Delta. Author: Professional

Corporations-How to Succeed When Really Trying, 1974. Home: 3607 S Cottage St Independence MO 64055 Office: 11500 E 23d St Independence MO 64055

MC GREGOR, HARRISON EUGENE, entomologist; b. Cassoday, Kans., Aug. 30, 1918; s. Robert Lang and Jessie Bell (Newhall) McG.; B.S., Kans. State U., 1955, M.S., 1956; m. Dorothy Maye Knaus, Jan. 12, 1956. Research entomologist U.S. Dept. Agr., Manhattan, Kans., 1956—. Served with USCG, 1942-47. Mem. Entomol. Soc. Am., Am. Legion, V.F.W., Sigma Xi, Gamma Sigma Delta. Home: Route 1 Box 191 Riley KS 66531 Office: 1515 College Ave Manhattan KS 66502

MC GREGOR, LEE ROBERT, veterinarian; b. Salem, S.D., Aug. 5, 1923; s. Edwin Eugene and Myrna (Mabee) McG.; D.V.M., Iowa State U., 1951; m. Dorothy Mae Vogel, Feb. 18, 1951; children—Connie Lee, Nancy Ann, Marlene Jo. Practice veterinary medicine, Salem, 1951-57, Freeport, Ill., 1957—. Mem. Dist. 145 Sch. Bd., Freeport, 1967-74. Served with AUS, 1943-46. Mem. AVMA, Ill., N.W. veterinary med. assns. Republican. Methodist. Clubs: Masons, Shriners. Home: 1717 Sylvan Ct Freeport IL 61032 Office: 321 E South Freeport IL 61031

MC GREGOR, THOMAS HENRY, lawyer; b. Rayne, La., Sept. 25, 1903; s. Thomas Henry and Duffie (Willis) McG.; student U.S. Naval Acad., 1920-23, U. N.C., 1927, Georgetown U., 1923-24; J.D., George Washington U., 1928; m. Gladys Mae Alexander, July 7, 1941 (dec.); m. 2d, Wilma Proffitt Weibel, Jan. 27, 1965; children—Joan Alexandra, William Thomas, Admitted to N.C. bar, 1928, D.C. bar, 1929, Tenn. bar, 1944, Mo. bar, 1954; claim mgr. Nat. Surety Corp. of N.Y., Memphis, 1943-54; regional claim mgr. United Pacific Ins. Co., Tacoma, Wash., 1954-68; legal cons., Kansas City, Mo., 1968—. Mem. Am., Mo. bar assns. Presbyterian. Home: 12836 W 109th St Quivira Falls Overland Park KS 66210 Office: 1424 Commerce Tower Kansas City MO 64105

MC GUIGAN, JOHN ROBERT, univ. adminstr.; b. Phila., Dec. 16, 1923; s. John Joseph and Margaret Mary (Maher) M.; B.S., Washington U., St. Louis, 1959; m. Grayce Dorothy Rosegrant, Feb. 10, 1948; children—Cecilia Anne (Mrs. Yeager), Margaret Mary, A. John, Grayce Byrne. Systems mgr. UNIVAC, Washington, 1963-64; corporate systems mgr. Am. Motors Corp., Detroit, 1964-66, corporate dir. info. systems, 1966-75; dir. info. systems St. Louis U., 1975—. Served to maj. USMC, 1942-63. Decorated Bronze Star. Home: 3939 Canterbury Dr Pasadena Hills MO 63121 Office: 3690 W Pine St St Louis MO 63108

MC GUIGAN, ROBERT ALISTER, physician; b. St. Louis, Dec. 18, 1909; s. Hugh Alisterand Mabel (Leininger) McG.; B.S., Northwestern U., 1932; M.D., McGill U., 1937; m. Grace Catherine Podlesney, July 19, 1941; children—Robert Alister, Michael Alister, James Alister, Kathleen Alister. Intern, U. Ill., 1938-40; resident Chgo. Contagious Disease Hosp., 1939-40; resident in pediatrics Children's Meml. Hosp., 1940-41; individual practice medicine specializing in pediatrics, Winnetka, Ill., 1943—; staff Children's Meml. Hosp., Chgo., Evanston (Ill.) Hosp.; asst. prof. pediatrics Northwestern U. Served to comdr., USNR, 1941-45. Diplomate Am. Bd. Pediatrics. Fellow Am. Acad. Pediatrics. Mem. Chgo. Pediatrics Soc. Republican. Episcopalian. Home: 520 Orchard Ln Winnetka IL 60093 Office: 723 Elm St Winnetka IL 60093

MC GUIRE, RICHARD L., English scholar, educator; b. Parsons, Kans., June 10, 1940; s. Harold R. and Maxine (McEntire) McG.; A.B. (Henry J. Putnam Meml. scholar), Kans. State U., 1961, M.A., 1963; Ph.D., Rice U., 1968; m. Mary Jeane, May 28, 1961; children—Kevin, David. Instr. English, U. Southwestern La., 1963-65; teaching fellow Rice U., 1967-68; asst. prof. English, U. Wash., 1968-74; asso. prof. MacMurray Coll., 1974—. Mem. Phi Alpha Theta, Phi Kappa Phi. Presbyterian. Author: Passionate Attention: An Introduction to Literary Study, 1973. Office: Dept English MacMurray Coll Jacksonville IL 62650

MC GUIRE, RICK MICHAEL, broadcasting co. exec.; b. Pueblo, Colo., Aug. 12, 1953; s. Orville Thomas and Patricia Rayona (Nelson) McG.; B.A., Augustana Coll., 1975. Staff announcer WVIK-FM, Rock Island, Ill., 1971, news dir., gen. mgr., 1972-75; morning announcer, dir. spls. Sta. KIIK, Davenport, Iowa, 1976—. Methodist (pres. youth fellowship 1970-71). Home: 11719 1st St Milan IL 61264 Office: KIIK 805 Brady St Davenport IA 52808

MC GUIRE, ROBERT NICHOLAS, real estate broker; b. Evanston, Ill., Jan. 21, 1917; s. Walter John and Florence Ethel (Walsh) McG.; A.B., Beloit Coll., 1938; postgrad. John Marshall Law Sch., 1939-41; m. Diana Hill O'Neil, Oct. 23, 1971; 1 son, Robert Nicholas, Jr.; stepchildren—Joseph O'Neil III, Cyrus H. O'Neil, David G. O'Neil. With escrow dept. Chgo. Title & Trust Co., 1938-41; with McGuire & Orr, Inc., Evanston, 1946—, pres., 1960—; pres. Continental Real Estate, Inc., Evanston, 1971—. Instr., Ind. Realtor's Inst., 1971-72. Mem. Evanston Fair Housing Bd., 1967-71. Trustee Real Estate Group Ins. Trust, Nat. Assn. Realtors, Chgo. Served with USCGR, 1941-46; comdr. USNR, 1942-62; comdr. Res. ret. Named Ill. Realtor of the Year, Ill. Assn. Realtors, 1966; recipient 1st Realtor of Year award N. Shore Bd. Realtors, 1975. Mem. Nat. (dir., regional v.p. 1972—), Ill, (pres. 1959) assns. realtors, Realty Club Chgo., Sigma Chi, Lambda Alpha. Mason (Shriner). Clubs: University (Chgo.). Home: 1201 Elm St Winnetka IL 60093 Office: 518 Davis St Evanston IL 60201

MC GURR, ALOYSIUS WILLIAM, JR., city engr.; b. Akron, Ohio, Apr. 6, 1940; s. Aloysius William and Mildred Kathryn (Gunyan) McG.; B.C.E., Purdue U., 1962; m. Lynne A. Baldowsky, July 15, 1972. Office planning, cost engr. H.K. Ferguson Co., Cleve., 1966-68; city engr., City of Woodstock, Ill., 1968-70; municipal engr. City of Wheaton, Ill., 1970-72, city engr., 1972—. Served with AUS, 1962-65. Registered profl. engr., Ill. Mem. ASCE, Nat. Soc. Profl. Engrs., Ill. Soc. Profl. Engrs., Am. Pub. Works Assn., Am. Water Works Assn., Inst. Municipal Engrs. Home: 1002 N Stoddard Wheaton IL 60187 Office: PO Box 727 Wheaton IL 60187

MC HENRY, MARTIN CHRISTOPHER, physician; b. San Francisco, Feb. 9, 1932; s. Merl and Marcella (Bricca) McH.; student U. Santa Clara (Calif.), 1950-53; M.D., U. Cin., 1957; M.S. in Medicine, U. Minn., Mpls., 1966; m. Patricia Grace Hughes, Apr. 27, 1957; children—Michael, Christopher, Timothy, Mary Ann, Jeffrey, Paul, Kevin, William, Monica, Martin Christopher. Intern, Highland Alameda County (Calif.) Hosp., Oakland, 1957-58; resident, internal medicine fellow Mayo Clinic, Rochester, Minn., 1958-61, spl. appointee in infectious diseases, 1963-64; staff physician infectious diseases Henry Ford Hosp., Detroit, 1964-67; staff physician Cleve. Clinic, 1967-72, head dept. infectious diseases, 1972—. Asst. clin. prof. Case Western Res. U., 1970-77, asso. clin. prof. medicine, 1977—; asso. vis. physician Cleve. Met. Gen. Hosp., 1970—; cons. VA Hosp., Cleve., 1973—. Chmn. manpower com. Swine Influenza Program, Cleve., 1976. Served with USNR, 1961-63. Named Distinguished Tchr. in Medicine Cleve. Clinic, 1972. Diplomate Am. Bd. Internal Medicine. Fellow A.C.P., Am. Coll. Chest Physicians (chmn. com. cardiopulmonary infections 1975-77); mem. Am. Soc. Clin. Pharmacology and Therapeutics (chmn. sect. infectious diseases and antimicrobial agts., 1970-77, dir.), Am. Soc. Clin. Pathologists, Royal Soc. Medicine of Great Britain (asso.), Infectious Diseases Soc. Am., Am. Fedn. Clin. Research, Am. Soc. Microbiology. Contbr. 75 articles to profl. jours., also chpts. to books. Home: 2779 Belgrave Rd Pepper Pike OH 44124 Office: 9500 Euclid Ave Cleveland OH 44106

MC HOLLAND, JAMES DALE, clergyman, psychologist; b. Winchester, Ind., Mar. 9, 1936; s. James I. and Mildred G. (Knoelke) McH.; B.A., Ohio Wesleyan U., 1958; B.D., Garrett Theol. Sem., 1962; Ph.D., Northwestern U., 1965; m. Cassaline Tucker, July 16, 1959; children—Deborah, Cheryl, James David. Ordained to ministry Methodist Ch., 1963; pastor chs., Chgo., Wis., 1958-64; dir. counseling services Kendall Coll., Evanston, Ill., 1965-73; dir. Nat. Center Human Potential Seminars Services, Evanston, Ill., 1973—; nat. cons. motivation and human potential. Author texts in field. Home and Office: 2527 Hastings Ave Evanston IL 60201

MC HUGH, CHARLES THOMAS, physician, surgeon; b. Passaic, N.J., Dec. 5, 1937; s. Charles Patrick and Mary Gertrude (Kelly) McH.; A.B., Wesleyan U., Middletown, Conn., 1960; M.D., Albany (N.Y.) Med. Coll., 1964; m. Anne Ewing Jones, Sept. 7, 1974; 1 son, David Charles. Intern in surgery U. Chgo. Hosps., 1964-65; sr. asst. surgeon USPHS-Peace Corps, Tanzania, 1965-67; resident in surgery Northwestern U. Hosps., 1967-71; chief resident in surgery Columbus Hosp., Chgo., 1971-72; practice medicine specializing in surgery, Chgo., 1972—; v.p. med. edn. Columbus-Cuneo-Cabrini Med. Center, 1972—; asso. surgery Northwestern U. Med. Sch., 1972—; cons. continuing med. edn. Ill. Council Continuing Med. Edn. Bd. mgrs. Lathrop Chgo. Boys Club, 1973—; bd. dirs. Edn. Resource Center, Chgo., 1976—. Diplomate Nat. Bd. Med. Examiners, Am. Bd. Surgery. Fellow ACS; mem. Am. Acad. Family Physicians, AMA, Ill. (mem. council edn. and manpower, chmn. com. physician's assts. 1976—), Chgo. med. socs., Assn. Hosp. Med. Edn., Soc. Tchrs. Family Medicine, Inst. Medicine Chgo. Home: 3162 N Pine Grove Ave Chicago IL 60657 Office: 2520 N Lakeview Ave Chicago IL 60614

MC ILVAINE, CLIFFORD JAMES, mfg. exec.; b. St. Charles, Ill., Oct. 16, 1941; s. Oran T. and Nettie (Root) McI.; student Waubonsee Coll., 1969. Tech. engr. Energy Kontrols, Inc., Geneva, Ill., 1960-61; gen. mgr. Photo-Crystals Co., St. Charles, 1961-65, pres., 1965—; partner Electronic Products Co., 1964—; partner Mid-Valley Service Co., 1968—; owner, founder McIlvaine Electronic Security Systems, Inc., 1972—, McIlvaine Constrn. Co., 1975—. Radio officer St. Charles Civil Def. Corps, 1965-69. Home: 605 Prarie St St Charles IL 60174

MC ILVAINE, JOSEPH educator, psychologist; b. Hazelton, Pa., June 13, 1939; s. Joseph Francis and Margaret Mary (Lawler) McI.; m. Mary Joan Marsh, Apr. 28, 1962 (div.); children—Joseph Francis, III, Douglas William, Andrew Phillip; B.S., Pa. State U., 1961; M.S., Central Mo. State U., 1967; Ph.D., Ohio U., 1970. Instr. Central Mo. State U., Warrensburg, 1967; asso. dean of residence life Ohio U., Athens, 1969-70; asst. prof. edn. Kans. State U., Manhattan, 1970—; vis. prof. edn. Western Carolina U., Cullowhee, N.C., 1970; cons. USAF, 1970-71, U.S. Army, 1970-74, Kans. Human Relations Commn., 1970—, Am. Psychol. Assn., 1973—. Mem. Am., Southwestern psychol. assns., AAAS, Am. Personnel and Guidance Assn., Phi Delta Kappa, Delta Chi, Phi Kappa Phi, Kappa Delta Pi, Psi Chi, Elks. Home: PO Box 1288 Manhattan KS 66502

MC INNES, RALPH HARRY, real estate broker; b. Urbana, Ill., Aug. 25, 1910; s. Oliver Alexander and Elizabeth Hannah (Hadfield) McI.; grad. Worsham Coll. Mortuary Sci., Chgo., 1949; student real estate U. Ill., 1965-66, Champaign (Ill.) Comml. Coll., 1968; m. Wilma Kathryn Dunn, Feb. 21, 1934. Beekeeper, 1928-38; market gardener, 1930-36; florist, 1938-77; with Bauman Funeral Home, Monticello, Ill., 1949-72; real estate broker and builder, Monticello, 1950—. Pres. Ill. Pioneer Heritage Center, 4 museums, 1965—; treas. Monticello Community Chest, 1961-70, chmn., 1959; chmn. Monticello Salvation Army, 1971-75. Served with USNR, 1943-45. Scholar Funeral Dirs. Sch. Mgmt., 1950. Mason (Shriner), Rotarian (past pres. Monticello). Clubs: Monticello Toastmasters, Monticello Community (pres. 1960). Home: 210 W Main St Monticello IL 61856 Office: 315 W Main St Monticello IL 61856

MC INTEE, MICHAEL RAY, lawyer; b. Northgate, N.D., Aug. 5, 1921; s. Michael J. and Bernetta M. (O'Brien) McI.; B.S.C., U. N.D., 1943, J.D. with distinction, 1953; m. Marian Zerr, June 26, 1943; children—Rae, Jan, Michael, Geri. Supt. sch., 1946; with Montgomery Ward & Co., 1947-50; admitted to N.D. bar, 1953; practice law, Williston, N.D., 1953—; sr. partner McIntee & Whisenand, 1967—; state's atty., 1956-60. Pres. bd. dirs. Mercy Hosp. of Williston; chmn. bd. dirs. United Fund, 1970—. Mem. State Bar Assn. N.D. (pres. 1972-73), Am. Bar Assn., Judicature Soc., Am. Trial Lawyers, Am. Soc. Hosp. Attys., Assn. Bars Northwestern Plains and Mountains (chancellor 1974-75), Phi Alpha Delta, Am. Legion. K.C., Elk, Moose. Home: 1208 4th Ave E Williston ND 58801 Office: PO Box 1307 Williston ND 58801

MC INTOSH, HAROLD AUSTIN (MARC), advt. agency exec.; b. Olean, N.Y., July 2, 1921; s. Edgar Spencer and Bessie Irene (Patterson) McI.; B.F.A. in Visual Communications, Ohio State U., 1966; m. Betty Jane Rice, Aug. 7, 1954 (dec. Oct. 1967). With Crane Plumbing Co., Columbus, Ohio, 1954-60; salesman Cussins & Fearn No. Lights Center, Columbus, 1961-63; art dir. Charles E. Merrill Pub. Co., Columbus, 1966-69; with Lord, Sullivan & Yoder, advt., Marion, Ohio, 1969-70; sr. designer Follett Ednl. Corp., Chgo., 1970-73; account exec., art dir. Art Graphics, Inc., also David Stolz Assos., Columbus, 1973-76; owner-partner, art dir., treas. Adgraphix, Inc., Columbus, 1976—. Served with AUS, 1942-45; ETO. Mem. United Ch. of Christ. Mason; mem. Order Eastern Star. Home: 615 S LaZelle St Columbus OH 43206 Office: 632 City Park Ave Columbus OH 43206

MC INTOSH, WILLIAM CURRIE, mfg. exec.; b. Akron, Ohio, Jan. 28, 1926; s. William Bishop and Elizabeth (Currie) M.; B.A., U. Ariz., 1946; postgrad., U. Pa., 1951, U. Madrid, 1951-52. Pres. General Die Casters, Inc., Peninsula, Ohio, 1961—, W. McIntosh Internat., Ltd., Peninsula, 1961—, Moy Inc., Cleve., 1975—, Moy Internat. S.A., 1973—; partner firm Firestone-McIntosh Enterprises, Inc., 1961—; partner McIntosh Robinson, Inc., Akron, 1960—; pres. General Die Realty, Inc., Akron, 1961—. Mem. East India Sports and Pub. Sch. Club, Am. Film Inst., Soc. Die Casting Engrs. Republican. Clubs: Bath, Devonshire (London); Club Financiero (Madrid); Cleve. Athletic; Akron City; Portage Country; Sky, Atrium, El Morocco (N.Y.C.); Bluecoats of Ohio. Home: 1511 W Exchange St Akron OH 44313 also Villa Moy Torreblanca Fuengirola (Malaga) Spain

MC INTURF, FAITH MARY, thoroughbred harness racing exec., presch. edn. field exec.; b. Grand Ridge, Ill., Aug. 22, 1917; d. Lynne E. and Margaret (Garver) McInturf; grad. high sch. With The J.E. Porter Corp., Chgo., 1963-65, v.p., 1951-65, sec., 1951-65, also dir.; v.p., sec. Potomac Engring. Corp., 1941—; sec.-treas., dir. Chgo. Harness Racing Inc., also Balmoral Jockey Club, Inc., 1967-72, sec., dir., 1974—; sec., treas., dir. Balmoral Park Trot, Inc., 1969-72; sec., dir. Horse Racing Promotions, Inc., 1974—. Roman Catholic. Home: 1360 Lake Shore Dr Chicago IL 60610 Office: 664 N Michigan Ave Chicago IL 60611

MC INTYRE, DONALD GREGORY, dentist; b. Detroit, Mar. 23, 1933; s. Frank Daniel and Helen (McGregory) McI.; student Kalamazoo Coll., 1951-54; D.D.S., U. Mich., 1957; postgrad. Wayne State U., 1960-63. Practice gen. dentistry, Detroit, 1959—. Volunteer cons. Clinica Evangelica Pro-Salud, El Rancho, Guatemala, 1968-71, dental dept. Wanless Hosp., Miraj, India, 1973, dental dept. St. Luke's Hosp., Vengurla, India, 1974—; pres. Detroit chpt. Civitan Internat., 1966. Chmn. bd. dirs. Hannan br. YMCA, 1969; bd. dirs. Met. Detroit YMCA, 1969. Served to capt. Dental Corps, AUS, 1957-59; Germany. Mem. Delta Sigma Delta. Presbyterian (ruling elder 1969-71). Home: 532 Neff Ln Grosse Pointe MI 48230 Office: 3107 Book Tower Detroit MI 48226

MC INTYRE, FRANK JOSEPH, water and chem. treating lab. exec.; b. Columbus, Ohio, June 30, 1907; s. Edward Brown and Ula (Davis) McI.; grad. Ohio State U., 1930; m. Rebecca Jane Clark, Aug. 9, 1933; children—Daniel Allison, Louanne McIntyre Byrd. Chemist, Columbus, 1927-31; established Columbus Water and Chem. Testing Lab., 1931—; mem. Am. Council Ind. Labs. Councilman, Village of Riverlea, 1957-69. Registered profl. engr., Ohio. Mem. Am. Inst. Chemists, Am. Water Works Assn. (life), Water Pollution Control Fedn. (life), Nat., Franklin County socs. profl. engrs. Clubs: Masons, Shriners. Office: 4628 Indianola Ave Columbus OH 43214

MC INTYRE, RONALD LLEWELLYN, elec. engr.; b. Detroit, May 12, 1934; s. Nathaniel Francis and Cheaber (Hudson) Farmer; m. Amalia Leon, June 17, 1961; children—Carmen, Norman, Maritza, Yvonne, Carlos. B.S.E.E., Wayen State U., 1962, M.S.E.E., 1968. Registered profl. engr., Mich. With Detroit Edison Co., 1963—, instrumentation and controls engr., 1968-70, systems engr. Enrico Fermi 2 Nuclear Project, 1970-72, asst. project engr. Greenwood Nuclear Project, 1973-74, supr. power supply planning, 1974—. Pres. Gesu Parish Council, 1968-70. Mem. Instrument Soc. Am. (mem. exec. com., asso. dir. power div. 1968-73), IEEE, Am. Nuclear Soc., Engring. Soc. Detroit, Eta Kappa Nu. Home: 18015 Birchcrest St Detroit MI 48221 Office: Detroit Edison Co 2000 2d Ave Detroit MI 48226

MC INTYRE, THOMAS AQUINAS, mathematician; b. Attleboro, Mass., Oct. 20, 1940; s. John William and Margaret Ellen (Mc Brien) McI.; A.B. (Univ. scholar), Holy Cross U., 1962; M.A. (Univ. scholar), Ind. U., 1965; postgrad., U. Notre Dame, 1965-66, Ph.D. (Univ. scholar), 1971; m. Elizabeth Lou Grebb, June 25, 1966; children—Sean, Shannon, Heather. Asst. prof. St. Bonaventure U., Allegany, N.Y., 1966-68; vis. asst. prof. U. Notre Dame, Ind., 1971-73; asso. prof. mathematics, Tri-State U., Angola, Ind., 1973—; indsl. cons. in applied mathematics, 1976—; textbook cons., 1972-75. Organizer Little League, 1976-77; dir. Community Center, 1973; Housing Task Force, 1971-73. NSF research grantee summers, 1972, 71, 64, 57-58. Mem. Am. Math. Soc., AAUP. Democrat. Roman Catholic. Home: 304 S Washington St Angola IN 46703 Office: Mathematics Dept Tri-State Univ Angola IN 46703

MC IVER, LAWRENCE WALTER, dentist; b. Elbow Lake, Minn., July 31, 1914; s. Walter Thomas and Susanna Vebecca (Gryte) McI.; student Hamline U., 1932-34; D.D.S., U. Minn., 1937; postgrad. orthodontics U. Ill., 1946-48; m. Dorothy May Peterson, Nov. 29, 1941; children—Barbara Jean, Stephen John. Practice gen. dentistry, Mpls., 1937-42, specializing in orthodontics, Mpls., 1948—. Asst. prof. orthodontics U. Minn., 1948-55. Served with USNR, 1942-45. Mem. Internat. Coll. Dentists, Am. Assn. Orthodontists (pres. Minn. 1970), Edward H. Angle Soc. Orthodontia (pres. Midwestern component 1965), Omicron Kappa Upsilon. Home: 5301 Scenic Heights Ct Minnetonka MN 55343 Office: 1455 W Lake St Minneapolis MN 55408

MC KAY, BARBARA JOAN, psychologist, clergyperson; b. Chgo., Nov. 23, 1931; d. Benjamin Mark and Margaret June (Regan) Squires; B.S., Northwestern U., 1953, Ph.D., 1974; M.A., Garrett Theol. Sem., 1970; m. Lewis Anton Musil, May 3, 1973; children—James Robert, Deborah Lynn, Thomas Michael. Ordained to ministry United Methodist Ch., 1970; counseling minister Glenview (Ill.) Community Ch., 1971-76, dir. adult ministries, 1977—; pvt. practice psychologist, Winnetka, Ill., 1974—; psychologist Asso. Psychotherapists of Chgo., 1974-76, Asso. Mental Health Services of Chgo., 1976—; cons. Inst. for Christian Living, Winnetka, Ill., 1976—. Bd. dirs. LINKS North Shore Mental Health Services, Northfield, Ill., 1976-77. Mem. Am., Ill., psychol. assns., Chgo. Met. Assn. United Ch. Christ (mem. exec. council), Pi Lambda Theta, Gamma Phi Beta Alumna. Composer 3 musical comedies, 1 opera, 1 revue, 3 religious works, 6 piano suites, 1964-72. Author: The Unabridged Broad: A Guide to Growing up Female, 1976. Home: 1639 Elmwood Ave Wilmette IL 60091 Office: 525 Lincoln Ave Winnetka IL 60093

MC KAY, JOHN PAUL, real estate broker; b. Everett, Mass., Nov. 15, 1917; s. John Henry and Mary Agnes (Lillis) McK.; student Bus. Sch., Northwestern U., 1950, 52; m. Alma Antionette Baker, Oct. 25, 1967; children—John W., Janice A. (Mrs. Richard Mertlick). With Croname, Inc., Chgo., 1937-54, supr. prodn. control, 1936-54; partner McKay-Nealis, Realtors, Builders, Des Plaines, Ill., 1954—; chmn. bd., dir. Bristol Oaks Corp., Bristol, Wis., 1964—. Pres. N.W. Multiple Listing Service, 1965. Mem. Des Plaines Redevel. Planning, 1964-66. Served with USNR, 1940-45, 51. Mem. Ill. Assn. Realtors (dist. v.p. 1974), N.W. Suburban Bd. Realtors (dir. 1965-68, pres. 1970), Des Plaines C. of C. (dir. 1965), V.F.W. Elk, K.C. Clubs: Itasca Country; Bristol Oaks Country; Tamarac Country (Ft. Lauderdale, Fla.). Home: 205 W Dulles Rd Des Plaines IL 60016 Office: 1600 Oakton St Des Plaines IL 60018 also 1810 E Northwest Hwy Arlington Heights IL 60004

MC KAY, JOHN SANGSTER, educator; b. Farmer City, Ill., May 30, 1921; s. David Dea and Anna Josephine (Sangster) McK.; B.F.A., U. Ill., 1947; postgrad. Inst. Design, Chgo., 1948, U. Buffalo, 1950; m. Betty Jean Draper, Nov. 10, 1945; children—Candace Ann, John Gregory. Tchr. Albright Art Sch., Buffalo, 1947-54; prof., asst. dean Sch. Fine Arts, Washington U., St. Louis, 1954-68; prof. design U. Kans., Lawrence, 1968—, asso. dean visual arts, 1968-75. Cons. on accreditation concerns for Nat. Assn. Schs. Art and North Central Assn. Colls. and Secondary Schs., to schs. and univs., 1963—. Mem. Community Art Council, Lawrence, Kans., 1969-73. Served with AUS, 1942-46; PTO. Decorated Purple Heart, Bronze Star medal. Fellow Nat. Assn. Schs. Art (bd. dirs. 1961-75; pres. 1969-72); mem. Nat. Council Arts Edn. (bd. dirs. 1969-75), Patteran Soc. (pres. 1951-52), Delta Upsilon. Rotarian. Home: 742 Indiana St Lawrence KS 66044

MC KAY, NICHOLAS DOUGLAS, mfg. co. exec.; b. Glencoe, Ohio, Dec. 8, 1921; s. Mike and Minnie (Vucelich) Mikasinovich; B.S. in Elec. Engring., Tri-State Coll., 1948; m. Helen Steich, Feb. 14, 1952; children—Nancy Dee, William Douglas, Nicholas Douglas. Successively mining application engr., sales engr., br. sales mgr. Reliance Electric & Engring. Co., Cleve., 1948-59; pres., chief exec. officer Helmac Products Corp., Flint, Mich., 1959—; chmn. bd. Helmac S.A. Morainvilliers, France, 1963—, Helmac-Roth Ltd.,

Toronto, Ont., Can., 1963-71. Served with USNR, 1942-45. Inventor. Home: 9082 S Saginaw Rd Grand Blanc MI 48439 Office: 528 Kelso PO Box 73 Flint MI 48501

MC KAY, RICHARD HARRY, election cons., mfr. related supplies; b. Winnebago, Minn., June 30, 1928; s. Kenneth Hugh and Bessie Charlotte (Martin) McK.; B.S., U. Minn., 1950; m. Florine Mandel, Aug. 1, 1973; children from previous marriage—Richard Harry, Nan Louise. Sales rep. Welch Scientific Co., 1954-61; exec. v.p. Thornber Co., 1961-68; pres., chief exec. officer Frank Thornber Co., Chgo., 1968—, dir., 1961—; dir. Bank of Winfield (Ill.), 1969. Cons. county and township ofcls. Active Wheaton Little League. Bd. dirs. Wheaton Boys Baseball, Inc., exec. sec. 1962-65; bd. dirs. Frank Thornber Co. Employees Profit Sharing Trust; bd. govs. Central DuPage Hosp. Mem. Ill. C. of C., Township Ofcls. Ill., Friends of the Wheaton Library, Central DuPage Hosp. Men's Assn., Max McGraw Wild Life Found., U. Minn. Alumni Assn. Presbyterian. Mason (32 deg. Shriner, K.T.). Clubs: Union League (Chgo.), Lake Shore (Chgo.), Glen Oak Country (Glen Ellyn). Home: D301 Oak Brook Club Oak Brook IL 60521 Office: 161 W Harrison St Chicago IL 60605

MC KAY, ROBERT CLARK, pub. co. exec.; b. Chgo., May 14, 1926; s. Edward Franklin and Mary Agnes (Theobald) McK.; student U. Ill., 1949-51, Northwestern U., 1973; children—Scott Clark, Leslie McKay Parker. Circulation mgr. Am. Hosp. Assn., Chgo., 1949-54, Standard Rate & Data Service, Evanston, Ill., 1954-57; dir. circulation Putman Pub. Co., Chgo., 1957-64, publ. dir., 1974—; asso. pub. Modern Age, Chgo., 1964-67; dir. publ. ops. Lakewood Publs., Mpls., 1968-70; circulation mgr. Pit and Quarry Publs., Inc., Chgo., 1970-73. Served with USNR, 1944-46. Home: Terrace Manor D1 Fayetteville AR 72701 Office: 430 N Michigan Ave Chicago IL 60611

MC KAY, ROBERT STEPHENSON, II, paint mfg. co. exec.; b. Columbus, Ohio, Apr. 16, 1923; s. George W. and Hellen (Judy) McK.; A.B., U. Ala., 1945; m. Alice Daly, June 28, 1946; children—Virginia Alice, Mary Robin, Cynthia Ann, Robert Alan. With Dean & Barry Co., Columbus, 1945—, treas., 1948—, pres., 1951—. Active United Appeals; trustee Franklin County Crippled Children's Soc., 1961—, pres., 1968; mem. Franklin County Hosp. Commn., 1965—; trustee St. Anthony Hosp., Columbus, 1971—, chmn., 1972; trustee Ohio Blue Cross; trustee, treas. Amaranth Cemetery Assn., 1959—. Named Boss of Year Columbus chpt. Nat. Secs. Assn., 1960. Mem. Nat. Paint Varnish and Lacquer Assn. (regional v.p. 1958, 59, 60, dir. 1975—), Ohio, Columbus Area chambers commerce, Phi Beta Kappa, Pi Kappa Alpha. Clubs: Masons, Shriners, Rotary (past trustee), Columbus Athletic, Scioto Country, Zanesfield Rod and Gun. Home: 2285 Yorkshire Rd Columbus OH 43221 Office: 296 Marconi Blvd Columbus OH 43215

MCKEAG, WILLIAM JOHN, Canadian govt. ofcl.; b. Winnipeg, Man., Can., Mar. 17, 1928; s. George Hammill and Elizabeth (Biggar) McK.; B.Commerce, U. Man., 1949; m. Dawn Rue Ann Campbell, Dec. 28, 1950; children—Janis, Darcy, Kelly, Douglas. With Security Storage Co. Ltd., Winnipeg, 1949-56, gen. mgr., 1952-56; pres. McKeag-Harris Realty & Devel. Co. Ltd., Winnipeg, 1960—; lt. gov. Province of Man., 1970—. Dir. Canadian Motorways Ltd., M.E.P.C. Can. Properties Ltd. Chmn., Greater Winnipeg Election Com., 1967-70; councillor, Tuxedo, Man., 1966-70. Bd. regents United Coll., 1960-67; past mem. bd. govs. Balmoral Sch. for Girls. Hon. col. Fort Garry Horse; recipient Alumni Jubilee award U. Man., 1973. Mem. Winnipeg C. of C. (past dir.), Winnipeg Real Estate Bd. (past dir.), Zeta Psi. Home: 10 Kennedy St Winnipeg MB Canada Office: Legislative Bldg Winnipeg MB Canada

MC KEE, DONALD DARRELL, ins. and real estate broker; b. Highland, Ill., July 20, 1932; s. Earl Michael and Leta Evelyn (Dresch) McK.; grad. high sch.; m. Emma A. Becker, Aug. 28, 1956; children—Dale Michael, Gail Ann. Sales clk. C. Kinne & Co., Highland, 1952-63; salesman Lowenstein Agy., Inc., Highland, 1963-69, owner, 1970-77; owner Don McKee Realty, Highland, 1969-73. Tchr. real estate So. Ill. U., Edwardsville, 1974-77, Lewis and Clark Community Coll., Godfrey, Ill.; pres. Real Estate Inst., 1973-77; exec. officer Edwardsville-Collinsville Bd. Realtors, 1975-76. Mem. So. Ill. Tourism Council, 1969-77. Mem. So. Ill. Independent Ins. Agts. (pres. 1974-75), Edwardsville-Collinsville Bd. Realtors (pres. 1974), Nat., Ill. (v.p. dist. 1977) assns. realtors, Ill., East Side life underwriters, Ind. Ins. Agts. Ill., Ind. Ins. Agts. Am., Highland C. of C., Highland Hist. Soc. (dir.), Helvetia Sharpshooters Soc. Club: Highland Country. Contbr. articles to profl. jours. Home: 1403 Pine St Highland IL 62249 Office: 825 Main St Highland IL 62249

MC KEE, GEORGE MOFFITT, JR., cons. civil engr.; b. Valparaiso, Nebr., Mar. 27, 1924; s. George Moffitt and Iva (Santrock) McK.; student Kans. State Coll. Agr. and Applied Sci., 1942-43, Bowling Green State U., 1943; B.S. in Civil Engring., U. Mich., 1947; m. Mary Lee Taylor, Aug. 11, 1945; children—Michael Craig, Thomas Lee, Mary Kathleen, Marsha Coleen, Charlotte Anne. Draftsman, Jackson Constrn. Co., Colby, Kans., 1945-46; asst. engr. Thomas County, Colby, 1946; engr. Sherman County, Goodland, Kans., 1947-51; salesman Oehlert Tractor & Equipment Co., Colby, 1951-52; owner, operator George M. McKee, Jr., cons. engrs., Colby, 1952-72, spl. cons., 1972—; sr. v.p. engring. Contract Surety Consultants, Wichita, Kans., 1974—. Adv. rep. Kans. State U., Manhattan, 1957-62; mem. adv. com. N.W. Kans. Area Vocat. Tech. Sch., Goodland, 1967-71. Served with USMCR, 1942-45. Registered profl. civil engr., Kans., Okla. Mem. Kans. Engring. Soc. (pres. N.W. profl. engrs. chpt. 1962-63, treas. cons. engrs. sect. 1961-63), Kansas County Engr's. Assn. (dist. v.p. 1950-51), Northwest Kans. Hwy. Ofcls. Assn. (sec. 1948-49), Nat. Soc. Profl. Engrs., Kans. State U. Alumni Assn. (pres. Thomas County 1956-57), Am. Legion (Goodland 1st vice comdr. 1948-49), Colby C. of C. (v.p. 1963-64), Goodland Jr. C. of C. (pres. 1951-52). Methodist (chmn. ofcl. bd. 1966-67). Mason (32 deg., Shriner); Order Eastern Star, Elk. Club: Kansas State University Wildcat. Home: 785 N Illinois Wichita KS 67203 also North Range Ave Colby KS 67701 Office: 6500 W Kellogg Wichita KS 67209

MC KEE, JAMES ARDEN, physicist; b. Hays, Kans., May 29, 1925; s. Cecil William and Zita (Bissing) McK.; student U. Ga., 1943, Ft. Hays (Kans.) State Coll., 1954; B.S. in Physics, U. Wash., 1957, postgrad., 1958-60; postgrad. U. Ill., 1957-58. Owner Midway Enterprises, Hays, 1945-54; owner Mdse. Mart, Hays, 1945-50, pres., 1950-54; sec.-treas. central div. Nat. Credit Card, Inc., Hays, 1951-53; physicist applied physics lab. U. Wash., 1955-60; operations analyst ops. evaluation group Mass. Inst. Tech., 1960-61; sr. operations analyst Nat. Cash Register Co. (now NCR Corp.), Dayton, Ohio, 1961-62, sect. head ops. research, 1962-63, dept. head ops. evaluation, 1963-64, mgr. ops. evaluation, 1964-71, dir. ops. evaluations, 1971-74, cons. engring. and mfg., 1974—. Cons. physics, ops. research, mgmt. scis., behavioral sci. Served with AUS, 1943-45, 50-51. Mem. Am. Phys. Soc., Ops. Research Soc. Am., Inst. Mgmt. Scis., Am. Mgmt. Assn., Phi Beta Kappa. Lion. Contbr. tech. papers to tech. jours. Home: 1300 W Rahn Rd Dayton OH 45459 Office: NCR World Hdqrs Engring Mfg Group Dayton OH 45479

MC KEE, KEITH EARL, civil engr.; b. Chgo., Sept. 9, 1928; s. Charles Richard and Maude Alice (Hamlin) McK.; B.S., Ill. Inst. Tech., 1950, M.S., 1956, Ph.D., 1962; m. Lorraine Marie Cell, Oct. 26, 1951; children—Pamela Ann, Paul Earl. Civil engr. Swift & Co., Chgo., 1953-54; research engr. Armor Research Found., Chgo., 1954-63; dir. mech. design and product assurance Andrew Corp., Orland Park, Ill., 1963-68; dir. research, engring. mechanics IIT Research Inst., Chgo., 1968—; instr. civil engring. Ill. Inst. Tech., Chgo., 1957-62. Chmn. com. on hardening of materials for ground-based facilities for ballistic missile def. systems Nat. Acad. Sci., 1971-73; mem. com. on mech. rope and cable Nat. Material Adv. Bd., 1973-76, mem. ad hoc com. on structural ceramics, 1974-76; chmn. Symposium on Designing to Survive Disaster, 1973; co-chmn. Symposium on Automatic Inspection and Product Control, 1974, 2d Conf., 1976; chmn. Conf. Designing for Optimum Safety, 1977. Bd. dirs. Robot Inst. Am., 1974—. Served to capt. USMC, 1950-53. Mem. AAAS, Am. Concrete Inst., ASCE (sec. engring. mgmt. div.), ASME, Am. Def. Preparedness Assn. (chpt. dir. 1973—, pres. 1975—), Assn. U.S. Army, Soc. Am. Mil. Engrs., Navy League, Soc. Mfg. Engrs., Transp. Research Bd., Chgo. Armed Forces Council, Sigma Xi, Chi Epsilon, Tau Beta Pi. Contbg. editor: Shock & Vibration Digest, 1969—, Krybernetics, 1976—. Contbr. articles to profl. jours. Home: 608 Burns St Flossmoor IL 60422 Office: 10 W 35th St Chicago IL 60616

MC KEEN, CHESTER M., JR., helicopter co. exec.; b. Shelby, Ohio, Mar. 18, 1923; s. Chester M. and Nettie Ausuta (Fox) McK.; B.S., U. Md., 1962; M.B.A., Babson Coll., 1962; m. Alma Virginia Pierce, Mar. 1946; children—David Richard, Karin, Thomas Kevin. Enlisted U.S. Army, 1942, commd. 2d lt., 1943, advanced through grades to maj. gen., 1973; dir. procurement Army Materiel Command, Washington, 1972-75; cmdr. Tank Automotive Command, Warren, Mich., 1975-77, ret., 1977; dir. logistics Bell Helicopter Internat., Tehran, Iran, 1977—. Decorated Legion of Merit, D.S.M. Mem. Am. Def. Preparedness Assn. (adv. council), Assn. U.S. Army, Sigma Pi. Clubs: Masons, Potomac River Yacht Club Assn. Home: 1071 Clubview Blvd N Worthington OH 43095 Office: PO Box 44/163 Ave Jordan 10 Saba Str Tehran Iran

MC KELL, ROBERT, telephone co. exec.; b. Boston, July 30, 1923; s. William Scott and Estelle (Coward) McK.; B.S. in Elec. Engring., U. Colo., 1944; m. Amy Hardcastle Story, June 9, 1945; children—Phoebe Hardcastle (Mrs. Alfred P. Currier), Alice Lockwood (Mrs. Vernon J. Roden), Robin Story, William Scott. Asst. mgr. Chillicothe Telephone Co. (Ohio), 1946-50, v.p., asst. mgr., 1950-62, pres., 1962—; treas. Chief Logan Corp., Chillicothe, 1957—; pres. Chillicothe Telcom, Inc. 1964-74, Bus. Telephone Systems, Inc., Chillicothe, 1971-75; chmn. bd. Savs. Bank Co. (name now changed to Huntington Bank Chillicothe), Chillicothe, 1958-71, mem. exec. com., 1958—, also dir. Mem. Union-Scioto Bd. Edn., Chillicothe, 1960-71, pres., 1962-63; adv. bd. Salvation Army, Chillicothe, 1948-60, chmn. 1958; mem. Ohio Ednl. TV Network Commn., 1963-71, 75—, exec. com., 1968-71, 76—; dir. communications Ross County Civil Def., 1952-55; mem. Carver Center Human Resources Council, 1971—. Sec.-treas. regional council Ohio U.-Chillicothe. Served to 2d lt. Signal Corps, AUS, 1944-46. Recipient certificate of merit U.S. Jaycees, 1971. Mem. U.S. (broad-band services com. 1964—, dir. 1970—), Ohio (pres. 1964-65, dir. 1962-75, exec. com. 1967-72) Ind. telephone assns., Ind. Telephone Pioneers Assn. Episcopalian. Rotarian. Club: Cavalier (pres. 1953) (Chillicothe). Home: Route 3 Box 240 Chillicothe OH 45601 Office: PO Box 480 Chillicothe OH 45601

MC KELVEY, JOHN CLIFFORD, research inst. exec.; b. Decatur, Ill., Jan. 25, 1934; s. Clifford Venice and Pauline (Lytton) McK.; m. Susan Jean Echols, July 3, 1958; children—Sean, Kerry, Tara; B.A. in Social Sci., Stanford, 1956, M.B.A., 1958. Research analyst Stanford Research Inst., Palo Alto, Calif., 1959-60, indsl. economist, 1960-64; sr. economist Midwest Research Inst., Kansas City, Mo., 1964-66, asst. div. dir., econs. and mgmt. sci. div., 1966-69, dir., 1969-70, v.p. econ. and mgmt. sci., 1970-73, exec. v.p., 1973-75, pres., 1975—. Active, Urban League, Kansas City, Civic Council Greater Kansas City; parliamentarian 7th Ward Republican Club, 1964—; bd. dirs. YMCA, 1968-71; trustee Rockhurst Coll., Livestock Merchandising Inst., Oxford Park Acad., Avila Coll., Menninger Found., Blue Cross of Kansas City, Yellow Freight System, Inc. Mem. Nat. Assn. Bus. Economists, Travel Research Assn., Hammer and Coffin Soc., Alpha Kappa Lambda. Clubs: Stanford, Carriage, Mission Hills Country. Home: 210 W 53d St Kansas City MO 64112 Office: 425 Volker Blvd Kansas City MO 64110

MC KELVY, CHARLES LOCKHART, JR., banker; b. Toledo, Aug. 1, 1930; s. Charles Lockhart and Margaret (Gosline) M.; A.B., Williams Coll., 1956; m. Barbara B. McKelvy, July 27, 1974; children by previous marriage—Charles Lockhart, Taylor, Johnson. With Owens-Corning Fiberglas Corp., 1956-68, with personnel and rate structure areas, 1956-62, adminstrv. services mgr., 1962-64, asst. treas., 1964-65, treas., 1965-68; pres., chief exec. officer First Nat. Bank, Toledo, 1968—. Pres. bd. Maumee Valley Country Day Sch., Toledo, 1969—; trustee U. Toledo, Jr. Achievement Northwestern Ohio, Toledo Hosp., Toledo Mus. Art. Served with USAF, 1951-54. Mem. Downtown Toledo Assos. (pres. 1969—). Home: 28503 E River Rd Perrysburg OH 43551 Office: First National Bank PO Box 1868 Toledo OH 43604

MC KENNA, DONALD FREDERICK, hosp. adminstr.; b. Carson City, Mich., Oct. 22, 1919; s. Fred Thomas and Mary Theresa (McGraw) McK.; grad. high sch.; m. Mary Louise Tabor, Mar. 26, 1943; children—William Joseph, Susan Marie. Seed analyst Rockafellow Grain Co., Carson City, 1936-39; accountant Mich. Produce Co., 1939-42; adminstr. Carson City Osteopathic Hosp., 1946; dir. First Security Bank, Carson City. Chmn. practical nurses tng. program Montcalm Community Coll. Bd. dirs. Carson City Hosp. Served with USAAF, 1942-46. Fellow Am. Coll. Osteopathic Adminstrs.; mem. Am. (pres. 1968-69, award merit 1971, life), Mich. (pres. 1956—) osteopathic hosp. assns., Am. Legion (past post comdr.). K.C. (fin. sec. 1936-42). Home: Box 186 Route 1 Carson City MI 48811 Office: Carson City Osteopathic Hosp Elm at 3d St Carson City MI 48811

MC KENNA, GEORGE LAVERNE, mus. ofcl.; b. Detroit, Dec. 7, 1924; s. John LaVerne and Carolyn (Schwab) McK.; student U. Oreg., 1943-44; A.B. with distinction, Wayne State U., 1948, M.A., 1951; postgrad. U. Calif. at Berkeley, 1949, U. Chgo., 1950; m. Janice Ballinger, July 22, 1966. Registrar, Nelson Gallery-Atkins Mus., Kansas City, Mo., 1952—, editor Gallery News, 1953—, asst. curator prints, 1960-73, asso. curator prints, 1973—; asst. editor Gallery Handbook, 1973—; instr., Coll. St. Teresa, Kansas City, 1962; lectr. U. Mo. at Kansas City, 1966-75. Mem. visual arts adv. com. Mo. Council on Arts, 1971-74. Served with AUS, 1943-46. Mem. Am. Assn. Museums (chmn. registrar's sect., 1957). Home: 205 W 70th St Kansas City MO 64113 Office: Nelson Gallery Atkins Mus 4525 Oak St Kansas City MO 64111

MC KENNA, RICHARD HENRY, hosp. exec.; b. Covington, Ky., Dec. 19, 1927; s. Charles Joseph and Mary Florence (Wieck) McK.; B.S. in Commerce, U. Cin., 1959; M.B.A., Xavier U., 1963; children—Linda Ann, Theresa K., Joan Marie. Accountant, Andrew Jergens Co., Cin., 1947-55; treas., dir. Ramsey Bus. Equipment, Inc., Cin., 1955-59; with Oakley Die & Mfg. Co., also Electro-Jet Tool Co., Cin., 1959-60; pvt. practice accounting, No. Ky. and Cin., 1960-62; bus. mgr. St. Joseph Hosp., Lexington, Ky., 1962-66; asst. adminstr. finance U. Ky. Hosp., Lexington, 1966-70, St. Lawrence Hosp., Lansing, Mich., 1970—. Former mem. adv. com. to commr. of finance State of Ky.; chmn. cath. div. Oak Hills Bus. Com.; mem. speakers com. Oak Hill Sch. Dist. Served with U.S. Mcht. Marine, 1945-47, U.S. Army, 1948-51. C.P.A., Ohio, Ky. Mem. Hosp. Fin. Mgmt. Assn. (Follmer award, past dir. Ky. chpt.), Am. Mgmt. Assn., Am. Inst. C.P.A.'s, Ky. Soc. C.P.A.'s, Mich. Hosp. Assn. (former mem. com. on reimbursement), Delta Mu Delta, Alpha Sigma Lambda. Home: 1409 Wellington Rd Lansing MI 48910 Office: 1210 W Saginaw St Lansing MI 48914

MC KENNA, WALTER THOMAS, analytical chemist; b. Marietta, Ohio, Feb. 2, 1917; s. Jacob Edward and Dora May (Carver) McK.; student Marietta Coll., 1959-60; m. Opal Esta Grasley, Nov. 25, 1941; children—Michael Alan, Steven Douglas. Chief analyst Marietta Dyestuffs Co. (Ohio), 1937-41; control lab. supr. Calco div. Am. Cyanamid Co., Marietta, 1945-65, control and application lab. supr. parent co., Willow Island, W.Va., 1966—. Served with M.C. U.S. Army, 1942-45. Mem. Am. Chem. Soc., W.Va. Water Pollution Control assn., Ohio River Valley Water Sanitation Commn. Democrat. Baptist. Clubs: Cyanamid Suprs'., Masons; Shriners (Marietta). Author numerous analytical methods and procedures. Home: 113 Miller Ave Marietta OH 45750 Office: Am Cyanamid Co Willow Island WV 26190

MC KENZIE, LEON ROY, educator; b. Chgo., Mar. 20, 1932; s. Robert and Jeanette Cecilia (Welch) McK.; B.A., Glennon Coll., 1954; postgrad. Kenrick Sem., St. Louis, 1954-58, Kans. State Tchrs. Coll., summer 1958; M.A., Fordham U., 1968; Ed.D., Ind. U., 1973. Instr. St. Mary's Sch., Parsons, Kans., 1958-61, Cathedral H.S., 1961-65, Sacred Heart Coll., Wichita, Kans., 1966; asso. supt. Catholic schs., Wichita, 1966-67; asso. prof. adult edn. Ind. U., Bloomington, 1973—, also coordinator edn. Ind. U. Hosp. Cons. on group dynamics, lectr. Lilly fellow, 1972; Bergevin fellow, 1973. Mem. U.S., Ind. adult edn. assns. Editor: (with others) Diagnostic Process in Adult Education, 1973; Participation Training: A System for Adult Education, 1975. Contbr. numerous articles to profl. jours. Home: 4277 Woodsage Trace Indianapolis IN 46227

MC KENZIE, ROBERT SEATON, lawyer; b. Kansas City, Mo., Feb. 11, 1907; s. Abraham L. and Minnie E. (Seaton) McK.; student Kansas City Jr. Coll., 1924-26; A.B., U. Mo., 1930, LL.B., 1930; m. M. Evelyn Sherman, May 16, 1931; children—James B., Mary Kay (Mrs. Milton D. Skeens), William S. Admitted to Mo. bar, 1930; practiced in Kansas City, 1933—; mem. firm Stubbs, McKenzie & Stubbs, 1933-39, McKenzie, Williams, Merrick, Beamer & Wells, 1948—. Asst. pros. atty. Jackson County, Mo., 1946-47; sec. Kansas City (Mo.) Bd. Police Commrs., 1947-51. Mem. Am., Kansas City bar assns., Mo., Kansas City lawyers assn., Internat. Assn. Ins. Counsel, The Mo. Bar., C. of C., Kappa Sigma. Democrat. Presbyterian. Mason (Shriner). Contbr. to profl. publs. in field. Home: 205 W 114th Terr Kansas City MO 64114 Office: 2100 Bryant Bldg Kansas City MO 64106

MC KEOWN, MARY ELIZABETH, educator; b. Chgo., Nov. 26, 1921; d. Raymond Edmund and Alice (Fitzgerald) McNamara; B.S., U. Chgo., 1946; M.S., DePaul U., 1953; m. James Edward McKeown, Aug. 6, 1955. Supr. high sch. dept. American Sch., Chgo., 1948-68, high sch. prin., 1968—, mem. corp., 1972—, mem. exec. com., 1974—, trustee, 1975—. Mem. Nat. Council Tchrs. Math., Central States Assn. Sci. and Math. Tchrs., Adult Edn. Assn., League Women Voters, Nat. Assn. Secondary Sch. Prins. Home: 1469 N Sheridan Rd Kenosha WI 53140

MC KEWEN, GEORGE EARL, bus. exec.; b. Balt., Apr. 18, 1925; s. George Earl and Irene (Oler) McK.; B.S. in Elec. Engring., Mass. Inst. Tech., 1945, B.S. in Bus. Adminstrn., 1947; postgrad. in exec. program U. Chgo., 1970-71; m. Janice Louise Waller, Mar. 4, 1950; children—Glenn, Gary. Dist. mgr. dept. transformers Gen. Electric Co., Chgo., 1947-52; sales mgr. beta ray equipment Tracerlab. Inc., Waltham, Mass., 1952-57; indsl. sales mgr. vibration isolators Barry Wright Corp., Watertown, Mass., 1957-62; mgr. mktg. Westinghouse Air Brake Co., Sidney, Ohio, 1962-69; pres. Champion Pneumatic Machinery Co., Princeton, Ill., 1969—, also dir.; pres. Ludlow Industries, Des Plaines, Ill., 1971—, also dir.; pres. Internat. Metals & Machines Inc., Des Plaines, 1972—, also dir.; guest speaker Am. Mgmt. Assn., N.Y.C., 1965-67. Bd. dirs. Compressed Air and Gas Inst.; trustee Hodgman Mfg. Co., Columbia Research and Devel. profit sharing retirement trusts. Served with USNR, 1943-46. Mem. Ill. Mfrs. Assn., Theta Chi. Republican. Mem. Ch. of Christ (pres. council 1967-68). Mason (Shriner), Elk. Clubs: U. Chgo. Exec. Program, Bureau Valley Country. Home: 520 Harvey Dr Princeton IL 61356 Office: 2350 E Devon Des Plaines IL 60018

MC KIBBEN, ROBERT EARL, orthodontist; b. St. Cloud, Minn., Apr. 19, 1923; s. Harry Ernest and Anna (Edstrom) McK.; B.S., St. Olaf Coll., 1947; D.D.S., U. Minn., 1949, M.S. in Dentistry, 1967; m. Eunice M. Mikelson, June 13, 1948; children—Robert B., Patricia Ann, Susan Elaine, Mary Dru, Carol Lynn. Gen. practice dentistry, Valley City, N.D., 1949-65, specializing in orthodontics, 1967—. Mem. Valley City Sch. Bd., 1960-65. Served with AUS, 1943-45, 51-53; Korea. Diplomate Am. Bd. Orthodontists. Fellow Internat. Coll. Dentists; mem. Am., N.D. (pres. 1966), Minn., Clay County dental assns., Midwest Orthodontic Study Club, Am. Assn. Orthodontists, 40 and 8, Midwest Orthodontic Soc., U. Minn. Alumni Assn., Xi Psi Phi. Elk, Rotarian. Clubs: Legion (Valley City), Century (U. Minn.). Home: 3119 S River Shore Dr Moorhead MN 56560 Office: Holiday Mall Moorhead MN 56560

MC KILLIP, WILLIAM JOHN, data processing supply co. exec.; b. Chgo., Sept. 24, 1942; s. Hugh Anthony and Helen Jane (Graham) McK.; B.S.A., Walton Sch. Commerce, Chgo., 1962; m. Antonette Marie Wyrwicki, Nov. 12, 1966; children—Gwen, Sandra, Melissa, Vanessa. Sr. accountant Harry B. Bernfield and Co., C.P.A.'s, Chgo., 1962-67; corporate controller Pryor Corp. (formerly Info. Supplies Corp.), Chgo., 1967-77, corporate treas., 1977—. Mem. Am. Accounting Assn., Am. Inst. Corporator Controllers. Home: 112 E Woodland Rd Lake Forest IL 60045 Office: 400 N Michigan Ave Chicago IL 60611

MC KILLOP, ANDREW R., hosp. adminstr.; b. Forest Park, Ill., Mar. 30, 1931; s. John and Agnes (McGuinness) McK.; B.S., Elmhurst Coll., 1959; M.B.A., George Washington U., 1962; m. B. Ruth Corbin, July 28, 1964; children—Deborah R., Andrew R. Jr., William D., Michelle L. Adminstr. Emergency dept. Jackson Meml. Hosp., Miami, Fla., 1962-63; adminstr. Sun Ray Park Convalescent Center, Miami, 1963-64; adminstr. Brookwood Convalescent Center, Des Plaines, Ill., 1964-67; mgr. Provider Reimbursement dept. and Extended Care Facility coordinator Wis. Blue Cross, 1967-68; adminstr. United Care Center Nursing Home, Milw., 1968; asst. adminstr. Skokie Valley (Ill.) Hosp., 1968-70; adminstr. Rehab. Inst. Chgo., 1970-71, v.p. adminstrn., 1971-74; adminstr. Franklin Hosp.,

Benton, Ill., 1974-76; sr. v.p. Grant Hosp., Chgo., 1976—; instr. Northwestern U. Sch. Medicine, 1971—, also preceptor Grad. Sch. Mgmt.; adj. prof., preceptor Washington U. Sch. Hosp. Adminstrn., St. Louis. Pres. Health Careers Council, Benton; mem. Citizens Adv. Com. to Mayor, Benton. Served with AUS, 1952-54. Mem. Ill. Hosp. Assn. (chmn. ad hoc com. on medicare proposed guidelines for rehab. care 1971-72), Northwest Assos. for Health Resources (co-chmn. planning sub-com. 1969-70), Am. Hosp. Assn. (mem. governing council for rehab. facilities and chronic disease hosp. sect. 1972-75), Benton C. of C. Rotarian (dir.). Office: Grant Hosp 251 Grant Pl Chicago IL 60614

MCKINLAY, ROBERT TODD, ophthalmic surgeon; b. Chgo., Dec. 11, 1938; s. Robert Todd and Helen Elizabeth (Eaton) McK.; B.A., Yale U., 1960; M.D., U. Pa., 1964; m. Helen Elizabeth Ann Griffin, June 17, 1961; children—Kathleen, Lisa, Allyson, Elizabeth, Stephen. Commd. ensign U.S. Navy, 1963, advanced through ranks to comdr., 1973; gen. med. officer in ophthalmology Sta. Hosp., Danang, Vietnam, 1968-69; resident ophthalmology Nat. Naval Med. Center, Bethesda, Md., 1968-72; chief of ophthalmology Naval Hosp. Boston, Chelsea, Mass., 1972-74; ret., 1974; pres. Robert T. McKinlay, M.D., Inc., Marion, Ohio, 1975—; vice chmn. dept. surgery Marion Gen. Hosp., 1976—; asst. prof. ophthalmology Ohio State U. Coll. Medicine, 1974—. Decorated Navy Commendation medal with Combat V. Diplomate Am. Bd. Ophthalmology. Fellow Am. Acad. Ophthalmology and Otolaryngology; mem. Ohio Ophthalmologic Soc., Columbus EENT Soc., Am. Soc. Contemporary Ophthalmology, Soc. Mil. Ophthalmologists, AMA, Ohio Med. Assn., Marion Acad. Medicine (pres. 1977). Republican. Roman Catholic. Club: Yale. Home: 780 Loire Valley Dr Marion OH 43302 Office: 1130 Independence Ave Marion OH 43302

MC KINLEY, MARY CHERYL, counselor; b. Evergreen Park, Ill., Sept. 12, 1946; d. James Michael and Dorothy Grace (Shean) McK.; B.A., Loyola U. Chgo., 1968, M.Ed., 1974, Ph.D., 1978. Tchr. history Prosser Vocat. High Sch., Chgo., 1968-70; asst. dean students, also dir. activities Loyola U. Chgo., 1971-75, research asst. counseling, 1975-76, counselor, 1977—, co-therapist Sci. Anxiety Clinic; instr. psychology, counselor Oakton Community Coll., Chgo., 1975—; cons. in field. Univ. dissertation fellow, 1977-78. Mem. Am. Personnel and Guidance Assn., Ill. Group Psychotherapy Assn., Internat. Transactional Analysis Assn., Nat. Assn. Women Deans, Adminstrs. and Counselors. Home: 4980 N Marine Dr Apt 1035 Chicago IL 60640 Office: Loyola U Ednl Opportunity Program 6525 N Sheridan Ave Chicago IL 60626

MC KINNELL, ROBERT GILMORE, educator; b. Springfield, Mo., Aug. 9, 1926; s. William Parks and Mary Catherine (Gilmore) McK.; A.B., U. Mo., 1948; B.S., Drury Coll., 1949; Ph.D., U. Minn., 1959; m. Beverly Walton Kerr, Jan. 24, 1964; children—Nancy Elizabeth, Robert Gilmore, Susan Kerr. Research asso. Inst. for Cancer Research, Phila., 1958-61; asst. prof. biology Tulane U., New Orleans, 1961-65, asso. prof., 1965-69, prof., 1969-70; prof. zoology U. Minn., Mpls., 1970—, prof. genetics and cell biology, St. Paul, 1976—; vis. scientist Dow Chem. Co., Freeport, Tex., 1976. Mem. amphibian com. Inst. Lab. Animal Resources, NRC, 1970-73, mem. adv. council, 1974. Served to lt. USNR, 1944-47, 51-53. Research fellow Nat. Cancer Inst., 1957-58; Sr. Sci. fellow NATO, 1974. Mem. Am. Assn. Cancer Research, Am. Soc. Zoologists, Am. Inst. Biol. Scis., Soc. for Developmental Biology, Internat. Soc. Differentiation (mem. exec. com., secretariat 1975), Sigma Xi. Club: Gown-In-Town. Editorial bd. Differentiation, 1973. Contbr. articles to profl. jours. Home: 2124 Hoyt Ave W St Paul MN 55108 Office: Dept Genetics and Cell Biology U Minn St Paul MN 55108

MC KINNEY, BRYAN LEE, electrochemist; b. San Antonio, Jan. 2, 1946; s. Oscar Bryan and Mamye Maxine (Faubion) McK.; B.S., U. Tex. ar Arlington, 1968; Ph.D., U. Oreg., 1972; m. Susan Jane Northcutt, June 8, 1968; children—Samuel Bryan, Jennifer Rachel. Research electrochemist Battelle Meml. Inst., Columbus, 1973-77; staff electrochemist Gould Inc., Rolling Meadows, Ill., 1977—. Robert A. Welch postdoctoral fellow, Baylor U., 1972-73. Mem. Electrochemical Soc. (sec.-treas. Columbus sect. 1976), Am. Chem. Soc., Am. Electroplaters Soc. Democrat. Baptist. Home: 256 Hermitage Ct Hoffman Estates IL 60195 Office: 40 Gould Center Rolling Meadows IL 60008

MC KINNEY, DONALD LEE, author, clergyman, educator; b. Centerville, Ind., May 31, 1909; s. Andrew and Ida (Ebersole) McK.: M.A., Ball State U., 1949; m. Jan. 11, 1935; 1 dau., Carolyn. Ordained minister Religious Soc. Friends, 1933, minister Interfaith Apts., Richmond, Inc., 1970—; feature wrtier Richmond Palladium Item, 1933—; tchr. Wayne County (Ind.) Schs., 1945-65, prin., 1965-70; faculty Earlham Coll. extension Ind. U., 1970-74; tchr. adult edn. Richmond Hgih Sch., 1947—; asst. prin. Williamsburg (Ind.) High Sch., 1945-52; prin. Boston High Sch., 1965-70. Chmn. Centerville Bicentennial Commn., 1976—. Rector scholar DePauw U., 1928-32; named outstanding citizen Centerville Jaycees, 1970. Pres. Greater Centerville Inc., 1977—. Mem. Authors Guild, Soc. Children's Book Writers, Authors League Am. Club: Queen City Writers (pres. Cin. 1976—). Author: A Crooked Tree, 1973; Joy Begins with You, 1975; Living With Joy, 1976. Home: 6017 Nolansfork Rd Richmond IN 47374 Office: Box 91 Centerville IN 47330

MC KINNEY, JOSEPH KENT, psychiatrist; b. Muskogee, Okla., Feb. 21, 1932; s. Chester Curtis and Mary Belle (Anderson) McK.; B.A., Westminster Coll., 1954; M.D., Washington U., St. Louis, 1958; m. Barbara Maggison, June 14, 1958. Intern medicine Barnes Hosp., St. Louis, 1958-59, asst. resident psychiatry, 1959-61; asst. resident psychiatry U. Oreg., Portland, 1961-62; practice medicine specializing in psychiatry, St. Louis, 1964—; attending staff Mo. Bapt. Hosp., St. Vincents Hosp., St. Luke's Hosp., Jewish Hosp.; asst. psychiatrist Barnes and Affiliated Hosps.; instr. psychiatry Washington U. Sch. Medicine, St. Louis, 1964-74, asst. prof. clin. psychiatry, 1974—. Served to lt. USNR, 1962-64. Mem. AMA, Mo. Med. Assns., Am. Psychiat. Assn., Eastern Mo. Psychiat. Soc., St. Louis Med. Soc. Club: University (St. Louis). Home: 665 Oak Valley Frontenac MO 63131 Office: 777 S New Ballas Rd Suite 234E St Louis MO 63141

MC KINNEY, LORELLA A., educator; b. Lafayette, Ohio, June 7, 1925; d. Donovan Stanley and M. Lucile (Ewing) McK.; B.S. in Edn., Ohio No. U., 1947; M.A., Ohio State U., 1950; Ph.D., 1963; postgrad. Purdue U., 1954; Carnegie Inst. Tech., 1955, Case Inst. Tech., 1956. Tchr. math. Ohio No. U., Ada, 1947, Swanton (Ohio) High Sch., 1947-48, Ohio State U., 1949, Washington High Sch., Washington Court House, Ohio, 1950-52, Kenton (Ohio) High Sch., 1952-55, Wooster (Ohio) High Sch., 1955-57; adminstrv. asst. North High Sch., Willoughby, 1957, asst. prin., 1958-60, 63-65; instr. dept. secondary edn. Ohio State U., 1960-62; guest instr. dept. edn. Emory U., Atlanta summers, 1961-64, Oglethorpe Coll., Atlanta, summer 1965, asso. prof., dir. tchr. edn., 1965-67; asst. dir. edn. State U. Coll., New Palta, N.Y., 1967-68, asso. prof., asso. dir. edn., 1968-70, asso. dean edn., 1970-71; asst. dir. program devel. Comprehensive Career Edn. Model, Ohio State U., 1971-73, program dir. spl. projects, sr. research specialist, 1973—. Westminister Found. fellow, 1948-50; Gen. Electric fellow, 1954; Westinghouse fellow, 1955; Du Pont fellow, 1956. Mem. NEA (life), Ohio (life) edn. assns., Assn. Tchr. Educators, AAUP, Am. Assn. Sch. Adminstrs., World Council Curriculum and Instruction, Nat. Sch. Pub. Relations Assn., Comparative Edn. Soc., Nat. Soc. Profs. of Edn., N.Y. State Assn. Tchr. Educators, (exec. com., corr. sec.), Nat. Council Adminstrv. Women in Edn., Nat. Soc. Study Edn., Am. Ednl. Research Assn., Ednl. Facilities Planning Internat., Am. Vocat. Assn., Nat., Ohio assns. secondary sch. prins., Nat., N.Y. State (legis. com.), Ramapo-Catskill (rec. sec.) assns. supervision and curriculum devel., Internat. Platform Assn., Council Exceptional Children (dept. editor Career Devel. Exceptional Individuals Jour. 1977—) Faculty Assn. State Univ. N.Y., Assn. Higher Edn., Ohio No. U., Ohio State U. alumni assns., Delta Kappa Gamma, Pi Lambda Theta. Republican. Methodist. Club: Quota Internat. (v.p.). Author: (with others) Career Education Personnel Development: Ideas for University Planning, 1975. Contbr. articles to profl. jours. Research in staff utilization practices in pub. secondary schs. of Ohio. Home: 2853 Zollinger Rd Upper Arlington OH 43221

MC KINNEY, ROBERT LESTER, educator; b. Bolivar, Mo., Feb. 22, 1930; s. J. Albert and Katie Lucille (Cable) McK.; A.B., William Jewell Coll., 1952; M.Div., So. Baptist Theol. Sem., 1958; postgrad. Washington U., 1959-62, 69-70; m. Lavona Meekee Williams, June 7, 1951; children—Constance, Kathryn, Carrie, Kelly. Ordained to ministry Baptist Ch., 1951; minister, Lone Jack, Mo., St. Louis, Mo., Frankfort, Ky., 1951-59; prof. Mo. Baptist Coll., St. Louis, Mo., 1959-62; asso. prof. psychology William Jewell Coll., Liberty, Mo., 1962—, chmn. dept., 1962-73; sr. minister Birmingham Baptist Ch., Kansas City, Mo., 1967-71; pres. Residential Redevel. Co.; partner McKinney-Philpot Assos.; exec. dir. Counselors and Behavior Specialists. Minister of music South Liberty Bapt. Ch., 1972-75; asso. minister Independence Ave. Bapt. Ch., 1975—. Mayor, Village of Glenaire, Mo., 1974-76. Bd. dirs. United Community Services Clay and Platte Counties, Clay County Interaction Center, United Community Services Met. Kansas City, Mental Health Assn. Clay, Platte and Ray Counties, Midcontinent Psychiat. Hosp. Grantee J.McK. Cattell Fund, 1963, Kansas City Regional Council on Higher Edn., 1966, Am. Psychol. Assn., 1967. Mem. Am., Greater Kansas City psychol. assns. Baptist. Club: Sertoma (charter pres. 1968, chmn. bd. 1969) (Liberty). Home: 401 Smiley Rd Route 4 Liberty MO 64068 Office: William Jewell College Liberty MO 64068

MC KINNIE, CATO ALLEN, sch. counselor; b. Murphysboro, Ill., Oct. 20, 1932; s. Cato and Myrtle Eunice (Allen) McK.; B.S., Univ. Ill., 1955; M.A., Univ. Minn., 1966; one dau.—Karen Lynn. Quality control chemist Internat. Mfg. Co., Mpls., 1957-59; tchr. Mpls. pub. schs., 1959-60; biochemist, Univ. Minn., Mpls., 1960-62; secondary sch. counselor Mpls. Pub. Schs., 1962—; dir. Adult Basic Edn. Prog., Mpls., 1965—; cons. State Minn. Dept. Edn. Served in U.S. Army, 1955-57. Recipient Recognition Award, Div. Vocat. Rehab., 1968. Mem. Am. Personnel and Guidance Assn., Adminstrative Mgmt. Soc., Nat. Assn. Black Psychologists, Mpls. Counselors Forum, Phi Delta Kappa. Democrat. Christian Scientist. Club: Monitors. Contbr. articles in field to profl. jours. Home: 2480 S Highway 100 St Louis Park MN 55416 Office: South High School 3131 19th Ave So Minneapolis MN 55407

MC KINNON, DONALD WILLIAM, dentist; b. Oconomowoc, Wis., Dec. 19, 1930; s. Joseph J. and Irene G. (Knuth) McK.; student U. Wis., 1949-50; D.D.S., Marquette U., 1956; postgrad. U. Calif. at Los Angeles, 1958; m. Kathleen Ann McKevitt, June 29, 1957; children—Michael McKevitt, James Shawn, Daniel William, John Donald. Individual practice dentistry, Appleton, Wis., 1959—; mem. staff Appleton Meml., St. Elizabeth's hosps., Appleton, Theda-Clark Hosp., Neenah, Wis. Chmn., Outagamie County (Wis.) dental div. United Fund, 1968; pres. Jefferson PTA, Appleton, 1968-69; chmn. Outagamie Med.-Legal-Dental Charity Dance, 1969. Mem. Appleton area bd. Catholic Edn., 1974-76. Bd. dirs. Meadowview Manor Nursing Home, Sheboygan, Wis. Served to lt. comdr. USNR, 1956-59. Mem. Am. Dental Assn., Wis., Outagamie County (pres. 1969—) dental socs., Appleton C. of C., Marquette U. Alumni Assn. Roman Catholic. Home: 1603 Orchard Dr Appleton WI 54911 Office: 819 W Wisconsin Ave Appleton WI 54911

MC KNELLY, WILLIAM VON, JR., educator, psychiatrist; b. St. Louis, Aug. 23, 1929; s. William Von and Jennie (Todd) McK.; B.A., Westminster Coll., 1951; B.S., U. Mo., 1953; M.D., St. Louis U., 1955; m. Joyce Preis, June 13, 1954; children—Maureen, Michele, William Von III, Jennifer. Intern, St. Louis City Hosp., 1955-56; resident Barnes-Renard Hosps., St. Louis, 1956-57, 59-61; asst. psychiatry Washington U. Sch. Medicine, St. Louis, 1956-57, 59-61; instr. psychiatry Kans. U. Sch. Medicine, Kansas City, 1961-62, asst. prof., 1963-66, asso. prof., 1966—, dir. Univ. Affective Diseases Clinic, 1965—, dir. Univ. Methadone Clinic, 1966, dir. postgrad. psychiat. tng., dir. psychiat. cons. service U. Med. Center, 1961-68; psychiatrist VA Hosp., Kansas City, Mo., 1961—. Served to lt. USNR, 1957-59. Mem. AMA, Am. (pres. Western Mo. dist. br. 1972), Mo. (pres. 1973) psychiat. assns., Am. Coll. Psychiatrists, Jackson County Med. Soc., Phi Beta Pi, Phi Gamma Delta. Methodist. Office: Dept Psychiatry Univ Kansas Med Center 3900 Rainbow Blvd Kansas City KS 66103

MC KNIGHT, JOSEPH T(HOMAS), truck dealer; b. New Philadelphia, Ohio, June 13, 1931; s. Simon and Luella Julia (Korns) McK.; student schs. New Philadelphia; m. Shirley Harriet John, Dec. 6, 1952; children—Trudy, Julie, Thomas. Served with U.S. Navy, 1948-57; with Harry Humphries Ford, New Philadelphia, 1958-64, Harry Humphries Trucks, 1964-73; owner McKnight Trucks, Inc., New Philadelphia, 1973—. Chmn. Tuscarawas County United Way, 1976. Mem. Nat., Ohio (trustee) Automobile Dealers Assns., Ohio Trucking Assn. Clubs: Congress Lake (Hartville, Ohio), Union Country, Elks (Dover, Ohio), Atwood Yacht (Dellroy, Ohio). Home: Lodge Rd Sherrodsville OH 44675 Office: PO Box 523 New Philadelphia OH 44663

MC KNIGHT, VAL BUNDY, engring. cons.; b. Budapest, Hungary, Sept. 14, 1926; s. Valentine B. and Maria E. (Heray) Mariahegyi; came to U.S., 1966, naturalized, 1971; student Inst. Tech., Budapest; M.E.E., Tech. U. Budapest, 1954; m. Ruby P. Fulop, Aug. 3, 1947; children—Bela, Suzy. Mgr. engring. Ministry of Constrn. Industry, Budapest, 1955-57; supervising engr. Canadian Brit. Aluminum Co., Baie Comeau, Que., 1958-66; utilities cons. Caterpillar Tractor Co., Peoria, Ill., 1966—. Mem. Republican Nat. Com.; radio communication advisor Civil Def. System, 1969-76; nat. adv. bd. Am. Security Council, 1975-77; deacon Westminster Presbyterian Ch. Served to lt., Budapest Mil. Acad., 1954-55. Named Innovator of Yr., 1955; knighted, Order of Knights, 1942; registered profl. engr., Que. Mem. Am. Inst. Plant Engrs. (plant engr. of year 1976-77), Nat., Ill. socs. profl. engrs., Corp. of Profl. Engrs. of Que., IEEE, Illuminating Engring. Soc., Nat. Assn. Bus. Ednl. Radio, NAM (policy com.), Engring. Inst. Can., Assn. Energy Engrs. (joint indsl. council). Clubs: Masons, Shriners. Home: 6831 N Michele Ln Peoria IL 61614 Office: 100 NE Adams St Peoria IL 61629

MC LAIN, ALBERTON LAMSON, ret. fishery biologist; b. Stockton Springs, Maine, June 2, 1921; s. Llewellyn Percy and Lettie Emma (Lamson) McL.; B.S., U. Maine, 1949; m. Clara Mary Bubier, July 13, 1943; children—Llewellyn Roy, John Douglas. Fishery biologist U.S. Fish and Wildlife Service, Rogers City, Mich., 1950-53, Marquette, Mich., 1953-61; chief evaluation of sea lamprey control Bur. Comml. Fisheries, Marquette, 1961-65; investigation chief Lake Mich.-Huron fisheries Bur. Comml. Fisheries, Ann Arbor, 1966-70; Gt. Lakes coordinator U.S. Fish & Wildlife Service, Ft. Snelling, Twin Cities, Minn., 1970-77. Exec. sec. Internat. Gt. Lakes Fishery Commn., 1974—. Pres. Marquette Jr. Hockey Assn., 1960-64. Served with AAC, 1939-45. Co-recipient Dr. James Moffett Meml. award U.S. Fish and Wildlife Service, 1971, recipient spl. achievement award, 1974, Civil Servant of Yr. award Twin Cities staff, 1974; Meritorious Service award Dept. Interior, 1975. Mem. Am. Fishery Soc., Internat. Assn. for Gt. Lakes Research, Am. Inst. Fishery Research Biologists. Patentee in field. Home: 7327 Upper 139th St Apple Valley MN 55124 Office: Federal Bldg Fort Snelling Twin Cities MN 55111

MC LAIN, DAVID JOHN, JR., choreographer, educator; b. Brighton, Tenn., Dec. 29, 1931; s. John David and Elsie (Burt) McL.; B.S. in Edn., U. Ark., 1953; M.A., Wayne State U., 1962. Tchr., Am. Ballet Center, N.Y.C., 1962-63, Severo Ballet Sch., Detroit, 1957-62, Schwarz Sch. Dance, Dayton, Ohio, 1963-66; chmn. dance div., asso. prof. dance Conservatory Music U. Cin., 1966-71, prof., 1972—; asst. to artistic dir. Severo Ballet, Detroit, 1957-62; asst. to dir. Robert Joffrey Ballet Co., N.Y.C., 1962; ballet master Dayton Civic Ballet Co., 1963-66; artistic dir. Columbus (Ohio) Civic Ballet Co., 1965-66, Cin. Ballet Co., 1966—; founder, dir. David McLain Dance Theatre, Cin., 1969-70; guest artist, tchr. Chgo. Nat. Assn. Dance Masters, 1968-70; guest tchr. So. Assn. Dance Masters, Memphis, 1968-69, Ohio Dance Masters, Inc., Cleve., 1969; guest lectr. Wayne State U., 1962, Colo. State U., 1968; artist-in-residence Utah State U., summer 1970, Louisville Sch. Music, 1973-74. Named Outstanding Alumnus in Fine Arts U. Ark. Alumni Assn., 1962; recipient Cohen award for excellence in teaching U. Cin., 1971; Rosa F. and Samuel Sachs award Cin. Inst. Fine Arts, 1975; ofcl. Ark. Traveler, Ky. col. Mem. Am. Assn. Dance Cos. (dir. 1970-72), Phi Mu Alpha Sinfonia, Kappa Kappa Psi, Phi Delta Theta. Choreographer: Songs of Silence, commnd. for centennial dedication Conservatory Music U. Cin., 1967; The Nutcracker for premiere Cleve. Orch., Dayton Civic Ballet, 1963; Concerto and Romanza for premiere Cin. Symphony Orch., Cin. Ballet Co., 1969, Winter's Traces; Dilemmas Moderne Guitar Concerto, 1970; Clouds, 1971. Home: 854 Rue de la Paix Cincinnati OH 45220

MC LAIN, DONALD JOSEPH, coll. adminstr.; b. St. Louis, Sept. 15, 1935; s. Clyde J. and Genevieve C. (Dwyer) McL.; grad. Kenrick Sem., 1954; B.S., St. Louis U., i958; postgrad. Insts. Orgn. Mgmt., U. Santa Clara, 1969-70; m. Geraldine Peach, May 13, 1961; children—James P., Matthew J. With Anheuser-Busch, Inc., St. Louis, 1958-63; budget analyst United Fund of St. Louis, 1963-68; exec. dir. Am. Optometric Found., also exec. v.p. Optometric Progress Fund, Clayton, Mo., 1968-74; alumni relations dir. Washington U., St. Louis, 1974-77; v.p. devel. Maryville Coll., St. Louis, 1977—, sec. to bd. trustees, 1977—. Pres., Wedgwood Improvement Assn., Florissant, Mo., 1968-70; sec.-treas. Optometric Center of St. Louis, 1971-73. Served with AUS, 1965-66. Mem. Am. Soc. Assn. Execs. (Mgmt. award 1972), Internat. Assn. Optometric Execs., Nat. Soc. Fund Raisers, Nat. Council Philanthropy, U.S. C. of C. (assn. dept.), St. Louis Soc. Assn. Execs. Clubs: West County Rotary; Wedgwood Bath and Tennis (dir. 1970-71) (Florissant). Home: 2009 Long Gate Ct Chesterfield MO 63017 Office: Maryville Coll 13550 Conway Rd St Louis MO 63141

MC LAIN, JAMES MARION, educator; b. Atlanta, May 16, 1913; s. Elisha Alexander and Jessie (Starnes) McL.; B.A., U. Akron, 1940; M.A., Western Res. U., 1942; Ph.D., Ohio State U., 1959; m. Lela E. Howse, Feb. 27, 1940; children—James Thaden, Lela Elizabeth. Undergrad. asst. U. Akron, 1938-40; grad. asst. Western Res. U., 1941; instr. econs. U. Akron, 1946-53, asst. prof., 1953-69, asso. prof., 1969-77, prof., 1977—; asst. instr. Ohio State U., Columbus, 1950-52, lectr., 1968. Served to capt., inf. AUS, 1942-46. Decorated Bronze Star medal, Purple Heart. Mem. Am. Econ. Assn., Indsl. Relations Research Assn., AAUP. Contbr. to publs. in field. Home: 2192 Coon Rd Copley OH 44321 Office: U Akron Akron OH 44304

MC LAIN, STUART, nuclear cons. co. exec.; b. Tecumseh, Mich., Mar. 31, 1905; s. Henry and Mary (Elliot) McL.; Ph.D., U. Mich., 1933; m. Winifred Roberta Denman, Sept. 18, 1930; children—Neal Denman, Douglas Robert. Engr., U.S. Rubber Products, Detroit, 1933-35; asst. prof. chem. engring. U. Detroit, 1935-37, U. Ark., Fayetteville, 1937-41; prof. Wayne State U., Detroit, 1945-48; asst. dir. tech. div. Oak Ridge (Tenn.) Nat. Lab., 1948-49; project dir. Argonne (Ill.) Nat. Lab., 1949-58; prof. nuclear engring. Purdue U., Lafayette, Ind., 1960-65; pres. Nuclear Mgmt. & Mediatech Inc., Lafayette, Ind., 1972-77. Served with AUS, 1941-45. Mem. Am. Nuclear Soc. Home: 2323 S 9th St Lafayette IN 47905 Office: 601 N 4th St West Lafayette IN 47901

MC LANE, HELEN J., exec. search cons.; b. Indpls.; d. Alvin R. and Ethel (Ranck) McLane; B.S. with distinction, Northwestern U., 1951; M.B.A., 1965. Pub. relations writer Chgo. Assn. Commerce and Industry, 1952-53; press dir. Community Fund, Chgo., 1953-56; asso. Beveridge Orgn., Inc., Chgo., 1956-61, v.p., 1961-66; pub. relations cons. Internat. Harvester Co., Chgo., 1966-69, asst. to dir. pub. relations. 1969-70; asso. Heidrick & Struggles, Chgo., 1970-74, v.p., 1974—. Mem. Nat. Assn. Investment Clubs (dir. 1957-69, trustee 1969-72, adviser 1972—). Author: (with Patricia Hutar) The Investment Club Way to Stock Market Success, 1963. Home: 124 Robsart Rd Kenilworth IL 60043 Office: 125 S Wacker Dr Chicago IL 60606

MC LANE, WILLIAM BAYARD, engring. technician; b. Wilmington, Del., Jan. 5, 1945; s. William Leonard and Elizabeth Jane (Brown) McL.; Asso. Gen. Studies, Parkland Jr. Coll., 1975; m. Susan Joyce Von Linger, Aug. 27, 1971; children—Stacy Lynn, Stephanie Suzanne, Jennifer Kristen. Draftsman, Brown, Davis, Mullins & Assos., Champaign, Ill., 1971-72; designer Harold L. Fox & Assoc., Champaign, 1972-77; engring. technician Clark Dietz & Assos., Urbana, Ill., 1977—. Served with USNR, 1966—. Certified technician Inst. Certification Engring. Technicians. Mem. Am. Soc. Heating, Refrigerating and Air Conditioning Engrs., U.S. Naval Inst., Am. Soc. Plumbing Engrs., V.F.W. Republican. Lutheran. Home: 28 Cedric Dr Urbana IL 61801 Office: 211 N Race St Urbana IL 61801

MC LARNAN, JAMES CONARD, physician; b. Mount Vernon, Ohio, May 6, 1926; s. John Walter and Cora Marie (Conard) McL.; B.A., M.D., Ohio State U., 1951; m. Betty June Edwards, Dec. 17, 1949 (dec. Sept. 1971); 1 son, Patrick; m. 2d, Marthella Glover Andrews, June 3, 1972. Intern, Mercy Hosp., Toledo, 1951-52; practice medicine, gen. practice, Mount Vernon, 1952-57; resident anesthesiology Univ. Hosp., Columbus, Ohio, 1956-57; practice medicine specializing in anesthesiology and obstetrics, Mount Vernon, 1957-73, in anesthesiology, 1973—; mem. staff Mercy Hosp., Mount Vernon; mem. staff Bert W. Martin Meml. Hosp., Mount Vernon, chief of staff, 1961-65, exec. com., 1958-71; coroner Knox County (Ohio), 1957-69. Pres. Knox County Young Republican Club, 1957-58. Served with AUS, 1945-46. Mem. Ohio State Coroners Assn. (hon. life mem., pres. 1964-65), AMA, Am. Soc. Anesthesiologists, Ohio State Med. Assn. (dist. councilor 1969-75, dir. med. polit. action com. 1963—), Knox County Med. Soc. Clubs: Masons (32 deg.), Shriners, Old Homestead. Home: 312 Teryl Dr Mount Vernon OH 43050 Office: 307 Vernedale Dr Vernon OH 43050

MC LAUGHLIN, ALEXANDER CHARLES JOHN, oil co. exec.; b. N.Y.C., June 3, 1925; s. Alexander and Margaret (Percival) McL.; B.S., Va. Poly. Inst., 1946; postgrad. Columbia U., 1947-48; m. Joan Kosak, June 10, 1950; 1 dau., Jena Hilary. With Standard Vacumn Oil Co., N.Y.C., Shanghai, China, Hongkong, Yokohama, Japan, 1946-50; with Trans Arabian Pipeline Co., Turnaif, Saudi Arabia, 1951; with Andian Nat. Corp., Cartegena, Colombia, 1952-54; practice civil engring., N.Y.C., 1954-55; chief project engr. mktg. Am. Oil Co., N.Y.C., chief engr. South Atlanta, sr. head engr., Chgo., 1955-64; process engr. mfg. and mktg. Am. Internat. Oil Co., Europe, S.A., Asia, N.Y.C., 1964-66, sr. process engr. mfg. dept., Chgo., 1967-70, distbn. mgr., Singapore, 1970-73, offshore/onshore supr., Tehran, Iran, 1973—, staff engr. sr. grade, Chgo., 1974—. Vol. fireman Long Beach Fire Dept., 1955-63; tng. officer USCG Aux., 1962; scoutmaster, troop com. mem. Nassau County (N.Y.) council Boy Scouts Am., 1946-49. Decorated Order White Cloud. Fellow ASCE; mem. Nat. Assn. Corrosion Engrs., Nat. Soc. Profl. Engrs., Internat. Platform Assn., West Highland Bowling League, Mixed Bowling League Naperville, Omicron Delta Kappa. Republican. Moose. Clubs: Pathfinders (London, Eng.); Columbia Country (Shanghai); Singapore Petroleum, Singapore Swimming, American (Singapore); Pars American (Tehran); Mixers (Downers Grove, Ill.). Home: 37 Bluebird Ln Naperville IL 60540 Office: care Amoco Internat Oil Co PO Box 8368 MC4701 Chicago IL 60680

MC LAUGHLIN, EUGENE RAY, pharm. co. exec.; b. Aberdeen, S.D., Sept. 20, 1921; s. George Alfred and Marguerite (Lesh) McL.; student U. Minn., 1940-42, The Citadel, 1942, Rugers U., 1942-43, U. Manchester, Eng., 1945; B.S. in Pharmacy, N.D. State U., 1949; m. Marion Joan McCulloch, 1946; children—Joan M., Janet R., Julie A. Pharmacist, Schwankl Drug, Sauk Rapids, Minn., 1949-50, Hopkins (Minn.) Drug, 1950-51, Dunn Drug, Brainerd, Minn., 1951-54; gen. mgr. Service Drug Inc., Brainerd, 1954—; founder McLaughlin Enterprises, Brainerd, 1960, pres. bd., 1960—, dir. Marion Enterprises, 1960—; profl. cinematographer Sta. KSTP-TV, Mpls., 1955-59. Served with U.S. Army, 1942-46. Mem. Minn., Ariz. pharm. assns., Am. Defense Preparedness Assn., Nat. Writers Club, Associated Locksmiths of Am., Vets. Assn. Am. Legion, DAV, Nat. Rifle Assn. Republican. Presbyterian. Producer films: Helping Hands, 1961, 3 documentary movies, 1963-67, also TV news stories, 1963-69. Home: 218 W Washington St Brainerd MN Office: McLaughlin Enterprises PO Box 564 Brainerd MN 56401

MC LAUGHLIN, HARRY ROLL, architect; b. Indpls., Nov. 29, 1922; s. William T. and Ruth E. (Roll) McL.; student John Herron Art Sch., Indpls., 1936, 40, 41; m. Linda Hamilton, Oct. 23, 1954; 1 son, Harry Roll. Partner charge pub. relations, pres. James Assos., Architects and Engrs., Inc., Indpls., 1956—; sec., dir. James and Berger, Architects, Engrs., Planners, Economists, Inc., specializing in restoration of historic bldgs.; advisory bd. Pompeiiana Inc., Indpls. Mem. Mayor's Indpls. Progress Com., Arts and Culture Com., 1965—. Dir., Historic Landmarks Found., 1964—, pres., 1964-74, chmn. bd., 1974—; dir., past v.p. Marion County Hist. Soc.; past dir. Carmel Clay Ednl. Found.; nat. dir. Preservation Action; mem. archtl. adviser Historic Madison, Inc.; mem. adv. council Historic Am. Bldgs. survey Nat. Park Service, 1967-73; past adv. bd. Conner Prairie Mus., Pattrick Henry Sullivan Found.; past adviser Indpls. Historic Preservation Commn., New Harmony Historic Dist.; past mem. preservation com. Ind. U.; architect mem. state profl. adv. com. Nat. Register Nominations and State Inventory; architect mem. Indpls.-Meridian St. Preservation Commn., 1971—. Bd. dirs. Park Tudor Sch.; bd. dirs., hon. mem. Ind. Bicentennial Commn. Served with USNR, 1943-45. Recipient Town Crier award Zionsville C. of C., 1967; City of Indpls. Mayor's Citation for Outstanding Services to Community in Preservation, 1972; citations for design and environment in historic preservation Lockerbie Sq. Historic Dist., Indpls. Union Sta. Registered architect, Ind., Ohio, Ill., Va., Md., D.C., Alaska, Nat. Council Archtl. Bds. Fellow AIA (nat. com. historic bldgs., chmn. nat. historic resources com. 1970, state preservation coordinator); mem. Ind. Soc. Architects (preservation officer 1960—, 1st Design award 1972, Merit award 1972), Constrn. League Indpls. (dir. 1969-71), Nat. Trust Historic Preservation (past trustee, adv. bd., com. property mgmt. programs 1975—), Soc. Archtl. Historians (past dir.), Am. Assn. State and Local History, Indpls. Museum Art, Zionsville C. of C. (past dir.), U.S. Capitol Hist. Soc. (hon. trustee), Victorian Soc. Am. (adviser), Smithsonian Assos., East African Wildlife Soc., Conservation Council, Ind., Zionsville hist. socs., Navy League U.S. (life), Ind. State Museum Soc. (charter), Athenaeum Turners, Nat. Audubon Soc., English-Speaking Union (dir. Indpls. br.), Ind. Acad. Clubs: Portfolio, Amateur Movie, Athletic, Indpls. Literary, Woodstock (Indpls.). Restorations include: Old State Bank State Meml., Vincennes, Old Opera House State Meml., New Harmony, Old Morris-Butler House, Indpls., Market St. Restoration and Maria Creek Baptist Ch., Vincennes, Ind., Restoration of Present Benjamin Harrison House, Old James Ball Residence, Lafayette, Ind., Lockerbie Sq. Master Plan and Park Sch., Indpls., Knox County Court House, Vincennes, J.K. Lilly House, Indpls. Waiting Station Crown Hill Cemetery, Indpls., Crown Hill Cemetery Chapel, Glenn A. Black Mus. Archaeology at Ind. U., Angel Mounds Archeol. Site and Interpretative Center, Morgan County Courthouse, Martinsville, Ind., Indpls. City Market. Contbr. articles to jours. in field. Illustrator; Harmonist Construction. Home: 950 W 116th St Carmel IN 46032 Office: 2828 E 45th St Indianapolis IN 46205

MC LAUGHLIN, JERRY LOREN, educator; b. Coldwater, Mich., Oct. 14, 1939; s. Ralph Todd and Rosella (Shreve) McL.; B.S., U. Mich., 1961, M.S., 1963, Ph.D., 1965; m. Frances Jeanette Whitaker, July 15, 1960; children—Angie Lee, Andrew Todd. Asst. prof. pharmacognosy U. Mich., Ann Arbor, 1965-66, U. Mo., Kansas City, 1966-67; asst. prof. pharmacognosy U. Wash., Seattle, 1967-70, asso. prof., 1970-71; asso. prof. pharmacognosy Purdue U., West Lafayette, Ind., 1971-75, prof., 1975—, exec. adminstrv. asst., 1975—. Recipient Lederle Faculty Research award, 1969, 73. USPHS fellow, 1961-65, research grantee, 1965-66, 69-71, 74—; research grantee NSF, 1974-75. Mem. Am. Soc. Pharmacognosy (mem. exec. com. 1974-77), AAAS (life), Am. Pharm. Assn., Acad. Pharm. Sci., Soc. for Econ. Botany, Cactus and Succulent Soc., Sigma Xi, Kappa Psi, Phi Kappa Phi, Rho Chi, Phi Lambda Upsilon. Editor: (with M. Malone) Experiments in the Pharmaceutical Biological Sciences, 1973. Contbr. articles to profl. jours. Home: 2940 State Rd 26 W West Lafayette IN 47906 Office: Sch Pharmacy and Pharmacal Scis Purdue U West Lafayette IN 47907

MC LAUGHLIN, JOHN PATRICK, ins. exec.; b. Chgo., July 29, 1929; s. John A. and Mary (Duggan) McL.; B.S. in Bus. Adminstrn., Xavier U., 1951; m. Mariana Hagarty, Sept. 11, 1954; children—Mary Ellen, John Patrick, Patricia Anne, Timothy E., Nancy Ann, Martin J., Robert E., Eileen C., Carol S., Matthew T. With Marsh & McLennan, Inc., Chgo., 1953—, v.p., 1965-71, sr. v,p., 1971—, mgr. casualty dept., 1966-71, mgr. client services div., 1971-74, mgr. group II, 1974—. Lectr., Wash. U. Grad. Sch. Hosp. Adminstrn., 1964—; lectr. St. Louis U. Center for Hosp. Continuing Edn., 1968—; mem. profl. liability com. Am. Hosp. Assn., 1970—; mem. planning, finance coms. St. Joseph Hosp., Chgo., 1972—, mem. exec. adv. com., 1974—. Chmn., Hoffman Estates Police and Fire Commn., 1960-66. Served with AUS, 1951-53. Mem. Ill. Assn. Lloyd's Brokers (pres., dir. 1975—, chmn. 1974-75), Ill. Surplus Lines Assn. (dir. 1972, vice-chmn. 1974-75). Democrat. Roman Catholic. Clubs: Union League (Chgo.); Oak Park Country. Contbr. articles to profl. jours. Home: 321 S Courtland St Park Ridge IL 60068 Office: 222 S Riverside Pl Chicago IL 60606

MC LAUGHLIN, MARTIN JAMES, communications and pub. affairs exec.; b. Chgo., Nov. 16, 1944; s. Martin and Anne (Griffin) McL.; m. Kathleen Ann Meehan, May 11, 1974; children—Mark Kathleen, Bridget Anne; B.S., Loyola U., Chgo., 1967. Writer, reporter New World, 1962-67; adminstrv. asst. Ill. auditor pub. accounts, 1968-72; dir. communications Ill. sec. state, 1972-75, asst. sec., 1975-77; exec. v.p. Marett Assos., Chgo., 1977—. Chmn. Ann. St. Patrick's Day Queen Contest, 1973-77; area co-chmn. Friends of Channel 11, 1977; dir. Democratic Campaign for Sec. State in Chgo. Met. Area, 1972; coordinator Dem. Primary Campaign for Gov., 1976; bd. dirs. Carondelet Child Care Center of Chgo.; mem. exec. bd. St. Patrick's Day Parade Com. Mem. Pub. Relations Soc. Am., Am. Assn. Motor Vehicle Adminstrs. (vice chmn. pub. affairs com. Region 3, 1975-76), U.S. Navy League, Leo High Sch. Alumni Assn. (pres. 1973-74). Roman Catholic. Clubs: K.C. (4 deg., communications sec. Ill. 1970-72); Irish Fellowship (Chgo.). Home: 9911 S Hamilton St Chicago IL 60643 Office: Suite 1404 310 S Michigan Ave Chicago IL 60605

MC LAUGHLIN, WILLIAM GAYLORD, metal products mfg. co. exec.; b. Marietta, Ohio, Sept. 28, 1936; s. William Russell and Edna Martha (Hiatt) McL.; B.S. in Mech. Engring., U. Cin., 1959; M.B.A., Ball State U., 1967; m. Carrie Jones Weaver, Oct. 17, 1975; children by previous marriage—Debora, Cynthia, Leslie, Teresa, Kristin, Jennifer. Plant engr. Kroger Co., Marion, Ind., 1959-62; with Honeywell, Inc., Wabash, Ind., 1962-75, mgr. metal products ops., 1971-72, gen. mgr. ops., 1972-75; pres. MarkHon Industries Inc., Wabash, 1975—; dir. Frances Slocum Bank & Trust Co., Wabash. Pres. Wabash Assn. for Retarded Children, 1974-75; gen. chmn. United Fund Drive, 1971. Treas., Young Republicans., Wabash, 1968—. Bd. dirs. Youth Service Bur., Sr. Citizens, Jr. Achievement. Named Outstanding Young Man of Year, Wabash Jr. C. of C., 1972. Mem. Indsl. (pres. 1973—), Wabash Area (pres. 1976) chambers commerce, Am. Metal Stamping Assn. (vice chmn. Ind. dist.), Cincinnatus Soc. Rotarian (pres. 1970-71, dist. youth exchange officer 1974—). Methodist (mem. ofcl. bd. 1966—, pres. Methodist Men 1975—). Clubs: Wabash Country (v.p. 1972-76), Masons. Patentee design electronic relay rack cabinet. Home: 654 W Hill St Wabash IN 46992 Office: 200 Bond St Wabash IN 46992

MC LAURIN, HENRY JAMES, ins. agy. exec.; b. Sumter, S.C., Feb. 22, 1904; s. Henry James and Sara Frances (Paris) McL.; A.B., Presbyn. Coll. of S.C. 1925; m. Mildred Elaine Sederlin, Mar. 22 1939; 1 son, Henry James. With Equitable Life Ins. Co., Cin., 1925-27, asst. mgr., Detroit, 1927-39; gen. agt. Detroit Aetna Life Ins. Co., 1943-58; pres. G-M Underwriters, Inc., 1948—, also dir.; pres. McLaurin & Co., actuarial cons., dir. Detroit and Jacksonville, Fla., 1943—. Mem. Pres.'s Com. for Employment Handicapped, 1964—; mem. Gov.'s Comprehensive State Health Planning Adv. Council, 1968—; mem. state adv. bd. phase II, Econ. Stblzn. Program, 1972—. Pres., Burt Twp. Property Owners Assn., 1970—. Pres. Mich. chpt. Arthritis and Rheumatism Found., 1948-63, chmn. bd. dirs., 1967-70, vice chmn., 1971—; nat. dir., exec. com., 1958-68; mem. exec. com. Cheboygan Community Hosp., Brighton Hosp.; now v.p. The Arthritis Found., also hon. bd. dirs., 1969—. Trustee Brighton Hosp., 1968—; bd. dirs., v.p. Mich. United Fund; bd. dirs. Cheboygan Meml. Hosp., 1973—. Hon. consul of Guatemala, 1953—; named Gov.'s Distinguished Citizen of Mich., 1971. Mem. Mich. Life Underwriters (past pres.). Clubs: Detroit Athletic; Dearborn Country (Mich.); Seminole (Jacksonville, Fla.); Indian River (Mich.) Golf. Home: 4888 W Burt Lake Rd Brutus MI 49716 Office: 924 Mason St Dearborn MI 48124

MC LEAN, ARTHUR FREDERICK, mech. engr.; b. Bristol, Eng., Apr. 16, 1929; s. Frederick Robert and Edith (Hawkins) McL.; came to U.S., 1959; naturalized, 1966; Nat. and Higher Nat. degrees in Mech. Engring., Bristol Coll. of Tech., 1952; m. Oriole R. Robinson, Aug. 30, 1952; children—Mark F., Peter A. Sr. engr. aircraft control systems Bristol Aero (Eng.), Orenda Engines Can., 1954-59; sr. engr. power systems research Bendix Corp., Southfield, Mich., 1959-61; supervisor turbine systems sect. Ford Motor Co., Dearborn, Mich., 1961-66, mgr. turbine research and devel., 1967—. Served as engring. officer RAF, 1951-54. Mem. ASME (past chmn. vehicular com. and ceramics com.), Soc. Automotive Engrs. (past mem. turbine com.), Am. Ceramic Soc., Inst. Mech. Engrs. Patentee in field. Contbr. articles to profl. jours. Address: 860 Arlington Blvd Ann Arbor MI 48104

MC LEAN, GILBERT JAMES, editor; b. St. Louis, May 13, 1935; s. James Gilbert and Roseceille (Hary) McL.; B.A., Cardinal Glennon Coll., 1957; B.J., U. Mo., 1962; m. Joan Marie Castillon, Aug. 12, 1961; children—Patrick, Timothy, Brian, Terrence. State editor Defiance Crescent-News, Defiance, Ohio, 1962-65; bus. writer suburban editor, asst. sports editor Cin. Enquirer, 1965-68; editor State Underwriter, Nat. Underwriter Co., Cin., 1968—. Pres., NUCO Fed. Credit Union. Served with AUS, 1958. Mem. Inst. Study of Econ. Systems. Office: 420 E 4th St Cincinnati OH 45202

MC LEAN, MARTHA LOUISE, civic worker; b. Fordyce, Ark., July 15, 1923; d. Webb Smith and Myrle Essie (Jordan) Dean; ed. schs., Ark. Sec., Fordyce Lumber Co., 1942-45; chmn. speakers bur. Greene County (Mo.) Mansion Preservation, 1977-78; mem. edn. com., 1977—; pres. SW Mo. Museum Assos., 1975-76; sec. Mo. Mansion Preservation Bd., 1977-78; mem. Mus. Ozarks, Mo. Heritage Trust; city residential chmn. cancer drs., 1962, 63; pres. YWCA, Springfield, Mo., 1962, 63; active March of Dimes, 1950-60, St. John's Aux., Springfield, 1956-59; mem. bd. Campfire Girls, 1967-68, Easter Seals, 1970-71; mem. speakers bur. Bingham Sketches, Inc., 1975-76. Mem. Springfield C. of C. Republican. Baptist. Clubs: Hickory Hills Country, Saturday (Springfield); Mo. Federated Woman's. Address: 2459 Brentwood St Springfield MO 65804

MC LEAN, ROBERT WILLIAM, physician; b. Louisville, Feb. 17, 1924; s. Charles Ernest and Lois Lee (McKown) McL.; B.S., Bates Coll., 1949; M.D., Boston U., 1949; m. Margaret Ann O'Connor, Sept. 14, 1948;children—William, Robert, Patrick, Andrew, Molly, Eileen. Intern, S.I. Hosp., 1949-50, resident, 1950-51; gen. practice medicine, Hillsboro, N.D., 1952—; mem. staff Community Hosp., Hillsboro; asso. prof. family practice Med. Sch., U. N.D., 1975—, also mem. admissions com., 1974—. Dir. N.D. Blue Shield, 1960-69. Pres. Hillsboro Civic and Commerce, 1956, PTA, 1958; mem. Hillsboro Park Bd., 1956; Republican precinct committeeman; chmn. 20th Dist. Rep. Party, 1970. Served with USNR, 1941-46, 51-52. Mem. Am., N.D. acads. family practice, AMA, N.D. Med. Assn. (chmn. safety responsibility com. 1960—, ho. dels. 1956-60, sec. 1968, mem. council 1960-69, speaker of house 1970-73, 2d v.p. 1973-74, 1st v.p. 1974-75, pres. 1976-77), N. Central Med. Conf. (pres. 1973-74), Traill Steele Dist. Med. Soc. (pres. 1955, sec. 1956—), Internat. Platform Assn. Am. Legion. Conglist. (deacon 1953-59, 65-71). Elk, Kiwanian (pres. 1954). Home: Hillsboro ND 58045 Office: Hillsboro Clinic Hillsboro ND 58045

MC LELLAN, ADRIAN OSWALD, banker; b. Minto, N.D., July 25, 1914; s. Alexander and Oline (Sund) McL.; B.S., U. N.D., 1937, LL.B., 1939, J.D., 1969; m. Ada Thompson, June 8, 1938; children—Donn, Mary (Mrs. David Durham). With Mchts. Nat. Bank & Trust Co., Fargo, N.D., 1939-42, 46-65, trust officer, 1947-50, v.p., 1950-53, pres., 1953-65; spl. agt. FBI, 1942-45; pres., dir. First Nat. Bank of Gt. Falls, Mont., 1965-75; exec. v.p., dir. First Bank System, Mpls., 1975—; dir. First Computer Corp., St. Paul, Firs System Agys., Mpls., 1975—. State coordinator U.S. Savs. Bonds, 1973-74. Gt. Falls Credit Bur., United Fund Cascade County; past trustee Coll. of Gt. Falls, Heisey Found. Served with USNR, 1945-46. Mem. Am. Bankers Assn. (past pres. nat. bank div.), Gt. Falls C. of C. (past pres., dir., mem. exec. com.), Assn. Mil. Banks U.S. (past pres., dir.). Presbyn. Mason (Shriner). Clubs: Meadow Lark Country, Interlachen Country, Minneapolis (Mpls.); Minnesota (St. Paul). Home: 6800 Hillside Ln Edina MN 55435 Office: 1400 First Nat Bank Bldg Minneapolis MN 55480

MC LENDON, HENRY LEWELLYNN, real estate broker; b. Valdosta, Ga., Feb. 16, 1908; s. Henry Kirk and Lila (Sharp) McL.; student U. Miami, 1927, U. Ky., 1928-29; m. Mary Louise Plummer, May 27, 1938; children—Vicky Lu, Judy, James Clifford. Sec., treas. Zanesville Devel. Co., 1947—. Mem. Zanesville Exchange Club. Home: 804 Maple Ave Zanesville OH 43701 Winter: 615 Rabbit Rd Sanibel Island FL Office: 330 Main St Zanesville OH 43701

MC LENNAN, WILLIAM L., investment co. exec.; b. Lake Forest, Ill., Dec. 2, 1923; s. Donald R. and Katherine (Noyes) McL.; B.A., Yale U., 1945; m. Alice P. Warner, Aug. 27, 1945; children—William L., Katherine N. With Arthur Andersen & Co., 1946-48, Continental Ill. Nat. Bank & Trust Co., 1948-50, Chgo., Stockyards Compost Co., 1952-54; pres. North Woods Coffee Co., Chgo., 1955-63; pres. Pop-Ice Co., 1960-63; mgr. Brown Bros. Harriman & Co., 1963—; dir. First Nat. Bank Lake Forest, Ill., First Nat. Bank Lake Bluff, I.W. Colburn & Assos. Investment com. YMCA of Met. Chgo., 1955-77, Chgo. Presbytery, 1967—. Trustee Ravinia Festival Assn., 1973—. Served with USNR, 1942-46. Mem. Cradle Soc. (trustee 1954—). Presbyterian (investment com. bd. pensions 1965-74). Home: 963 Elm Tree Rd Lake Forest IL 60045 Office: 135 S LaSalle St Chicago IL 60603

MC LEOD, FREDERICK REINHARDT, educator; b. Sault Ste. Marie, Mich., Dec. 20, 1917; s. Donald Joseph and Helen (Reinhardt) McL.; B.A., Bowling Green State U., 1946; M.A., U. Detroit, 1950; postgrad. U. Mich. Teaching fellow English, U. Detroit, 1947-48, U. Mich., 1949-50; instr. English, Bowling Green State U., 1950-53; coll. editor World Pub. Co., 1953-57; prof. English, dir. freshman English, U. Mo., Kansas City, 1957—. Ednl. cons. World Pub. Co., Cleve., N.Y. Served with USAAF, 1942-45. Mem. Modern Lang. Assn., Nat. Council Tchrs. English, AAUP, Mo. Assn. Tchrs. English. Author: (with Roma A. King, Jr.) Modern American Writer, 1961; A Reader for Composition, 1962. Contbr. Webster's New World Dictionary of the American Language, 2d coll. edit., 1970. Home: 5911 Oak Kansas City MO 64113 Office: 5315 Holmes Kansas City MO 64110

MC LEOD, JAMES CURRIE, clergyman, educator; b. Buffalo; s. Dugald and Mary Holmes (Currie) McL.; B.S., Middlebury Coll., 1926, D.D., 1950; B.D., Yale U., 1929; D.D., Alfred U., 1941; m. Emily Louise Johnson, Aug. 24, 1929; children—Mary Louise (Mrs. James S. Aagaard), Adrienne (Mrs. Craig Heatley), James Currie. Ordained to ministry Presbyn. Ch. 1929; univ. (chaplain) Alfred (N.Y.) U., 1929-40; moderator Columbus Presbytery, 1942-43; minister to students Ohio State U., Columbus, 1940-43, univ. chaplain asso. prof. history and lit. of religion Northwestern U., 1946-50, prof., 1950—, dean students, 1952-67; guest preacher Presbytery of Glasgow, Scotland, 1950, also at Syracuse, Chgo., Rutgers, Lake Forest, Middlebury, Stanford, Howard, and others; research fellow Yale Div. Sch., 1964-65; vis. scholar Colgate-Rochester Div. Sch., 1967-68. Pres. bd. trustees Evanston (Ill.) Pub. Library. Served as lt. comdr., chaplain, USNR, 1943-46. Mem. Nat. Acad. Religion, Nat. Assn. Student Personnel Adminstrs. (pres. 1963-64), Religious Edn. Assn. (v.p. 1963-64), Presbytery of Chgo., Delta Upsilon (internat. pres. 1972-73). Republican. Mason, Rotarian (pres. 1964-65). Clubs: University (Evanston). St. Andrews Society (pres. bd. govs. 1974). Author: Fruits of Faith (symposium). Contbr. articles to various jours. Home: 1501 Maple Ave Evanston IL 60201

MC LEOD, JOHN DWIGHT, violinist, educator; b. N.Y.C., Mar. 9, 1947; s. Dwight Leon and Magdalene Margaret (Murphy) McL.; B.Mus., Manhattan Sch. Music, 1968, M.Mus., 1970; student State U. N.Y. at Binghamton, 1970-72; m. Marilyn Ann Raven, Sept. 19, 1968; 1 dau., Alison Marie. Performing violinist, mem. Manhattan String Quartet, 1969-73; in-residence Grinnell Coll., 1972-73; mem. Pro Arte String Quartet, 1973-74; asst. prof. music, Ohio Wesleyan U., 1974—, condr. Symphony Orch., 1974—. Mem. Am. Fedn. Musicians. Home: 564 Jefferson Dr Delaware OH 43015 Office: Sanborn Hall O Wesleyan U Delaware OH 43015

MC LOONE, EDWARD JAMES, newspaper pub.; b. New Ulm, Minn., Dec. 11, 1928; s. Edward A. and Helen Mae (Ernest) McL.; B.A., St. Mary's Coll., 1951; m. Mary Therese Finley, June 13, 1953; children—Patrick, J., Maureen A., Sheila M., Kathleen M., Bridget, John, Mary H., James J. Reporter, Hampton (Iowa) Times, 1953; news editor Hampton (Iowa) Times-Chronicle, 1954; news editor Blue Earth (Minn.) Post, 1955-56; pub. Stewartville (Minn.) Star, 1956-60; owner, pub. Lake Country Reporter, Hartland, Wis., 1960—, Focus, Hartland, 1960—, Sun, Sussex, Wis., 1963—, Dousman (Wis.) Index, 1969—, Mukwonago (Wis.) Chief, 1973—, Hartford Times Press, 1977—; pub. Hartland Lake Country Reporter, Hartland, 1960—; owner Monday Shopper, Hartland, 1977—; dir. State Bank of Hartland, Shinners Pubs., Brookfield; owner, pres. Integrity Travel, Hartland, 1975—; organizer, pres. DeVisser-McLoone Press, Inc., Hartland, 1976—. Adv. bd. Waukesha County Tech. Inst., 1967-68; pres. St. Charles Sch. Bd., Hartland, 1967-68. Served with USAAF, 1951-53. Mem. Wis. Newspaper Assn. (dir. 1971-74), C. of C., Southeastern Wis. Newspaper Assn., Nat. Newspaper Assn., Republican. Roman Catholic. Clubs: K.C., Moose. Home: 268 Hazel Ln Hartland WI 53029 Office: 122 Cottonwood Ave Hartland WI 53029

MC LUCAS, GRACE B., pub. relations exec.; b. Oak Park, Ill., Oct. 10, 1911; d. Charles Franklin and Leah (Van Blarcom) Beezley; B.A., Wellesley Coll., 1933; postgrad. Northwestern U., intermittently, 1939—, Moser Bus. Coll., 1933-34; m. Don Hamlin McLucas, Feb. 29, 1936 (div. 1961); children—Don Hamlin, Bruce Beezley, William Stoddard (dec.). Sec., research asst. to dir. econ. research Internat. Harvester Co., Chgo., 1934-36; office mgr. office of counselors Northwestern U., 1936-37, sec. grad. div. Sch. Commerce 1937-38; ofcl. rep. in Chgo. area Wellesley Coll., 1953-57; copy editor sch. map and book dept. Rand McNally & Co., Skokie, Ill., 1961; asst. editor Jour. Assn. Coll. Admissions Counselors, Evanston, 1962, Jour. Med. Edn., Assn. Am. Med. Colls., 1962; dir. pub. relations Vis. Nurses

Assn. Chgo., 1963-66; nat. program coordinator Council on Religion and Internat. Affairs, Evanston, Ill., 1967-68; dir. pub. relations YWCA Met. Chgo., 1969-74; v.p. Rathje and Assos., Chgo., 1975-77; dir. pub. relations Am. Assn. Med. Assts., 1977—. Mem. Pub. Relations Soc. Am. (asso.), Am. Soc. Assn. Execs., Chgo. Soc. Fund Raising Execs., Wellesley Alumnae Assn., Soc. Typog. Arts. Home: 314 Oxford Rd Kenilworth IL 60043 Office: One E Wacker Dr Chicago IL 60601

MC MAHAN, PARKER FRANK, JR., lawyer; b. Chgo., June 20, 1938; s. Parker Frank and Josephine (Anderson) McM.; B.A., Beloit Coll., 1960; J.D., Chgo. Kent Coll. Law, 1967; m. Anastasia Mary McMahon, Aug. 25, 1962; children—Anastasia Mary, Jolene Susan, Parker Frank III, Christopher Michael Charles. Admitted to Ill. bar, 1968; partner firm Parker F. McMahon Co., Chgo., 1960-68, law firm Brown, Stine, Cook & Hanson, Chgo., 1968-72; pvt. practice law, Chgo., 1972—; owner The Flying Fisherman, charter fishing yacht, Islamorada, Fla. Adviser, Parents Without Partners, 1971—; mem. Hanover Twp. Youth Commn., 1969-74, chmn., 1970-74; mem. Elgin (Ill.) Civic Symphony, 1954-62. Trustee Gail Borden Pub. Library Dist., Elgin, 1974—; bd. dirs. Family Service Assn. of Elgin, 1972-74; pres. Friends of Summit Sch., Dundee, Ill. Fellow Comml. Law Found.; mem. Am., Ill. bar assns., Comml. Law League Am., Internat. Game Fish Assn., Beta Theta Pi (Distinguished Alumni award 1970, 72). Home: 1010 Douglas Rd Route 1 Elgin IL 60120 Office: 208 S LaSalle St Chicago IL 60604

MCMAHON, JOHN ALEXANDER, med. assn. exec.; b. Monongahela, Pa., July 31, 1921; s. John Hamilton and Jean (Alexander) McM.; A.B. magna cum laude, Duke, 1942; student Harvard Bus. Sch., 1942-43, J.D., Law Sch., 1948; m. Betty Wagner, Sept. 14, 1947 (div. Mar. 1977); children—Alexander Talpey, Sarah Francis, Elizabeth Wagner, Ann Wallace; m. 2d, Anne Fountain Willets, May 1, 1977. Admitted to N.C. bar, 1950; prof. pub. law and govt., asst. dir. Inst. Govt. U. N.C., 1948-59; gen. counsel, sec.-treas. N.C. Assn. County Commrs., Chapel Hill, 1959-65; v.p. spl. devel. Hosp. Saving Assn., Chapel Hill, N.C., 1965-67; pres. N.C. Blue Cross and Blue Shield, Inc., Chapel Hill, 1968-72; pres. Am. Hosp. Assn., Chgo., 1972—. Mem. Chapel Hill Bd. N.C. Nat. Bank, 1967-72. Bd. govs. Blue Cross Assn., 1969-72. Mem. Orange County Welfare Bd., 1956-63; chmn. N.C. Comprehensive Health Planning Council, 1968-72; chmn. Health Planning Council of Central N.C., 1963-69; mem. President's Com. on Health Edn., 1971-72; mem. com. health services industry and health industry advisory com. Econ. Stablzn. Program, 1971-74; mem. advisory council Kate Bidding Reynolds Health Care Trust, 1971—; mem. advisory council Northwestern U.; mem. med. advisory com. VA.; mem. com. on nation's health care C. of C. U.S.; mem. commn. on cost med. care AMA Mem. Orange County Democratic Exec. Com., also chmn. Kings Mill Precinct, 1964-68. Chmn bd. trustees Duke, 1971—; bd. dirs. Research Triangle Found., Nat. Center for Health Edn.; bd. mgrs., mem. exec. com. Internat. Hosp. Fedn., London. Served with USAAF, 1942-46; col. Res. (Ret.). Mem. N.C. Bar Assn., N.C. State Bar, N.C. Citizens Assn. (dir. 1972), Duke Alumni Assn. (pres. 1968-70), Nat. Acad. Sci. (Inst. Med.). Presbyn. Clubs: Chapel Hill Country; Carlton (Chgo.). Author: North Carolina County Government, 1959; The North Carolina Local Government Commission, 1960. Editor N.C. County Yearbook, 1959-64. Contbr. articles to profl. jours. Home: 1150 N Lake Shore Dr Chicago IL 60611 Office: 840 N Lake Shore Dr Chicago IL 60611

MC MAHON, JOHN JOSEPH, cons. surveyor and community planner; b. Chgo., Oct. 6, 1910; s. James Joseph and Marie (Albert) McM.; student U. Detroit, 1929-32, U. Fla., 1954, Wayne State U., 1943-44; m. Janet Ruth Moffat, Apr. 3, 1937; children—Margaret B., Susan J., John Joseph. Engr. surveyor James McMahon cons., Detroit, 1938-53; surveyor, civil engr., community planner, sec., chmn. bd. McMahon Engring. Co., Detroit, 1953—; v.p., Mich. Engrs., Inc., 1960—; v.p. Lehner & Son cons. engrs., planners, Mt. Clemens, Mich., 1970—. Fellow Am. Congress Surveying and Mapping, Guild Surveyors London; mem. Mich. Soc. Registered Land Surveyors (life; surveyor of year state, 1970), Cons. Engrs. Council Mich., Engring. Soc. Detroit, Mich. Engrs. Soc., Nat. Council Engring. Examiners, Cons. Engrs. Council U.S. (recipient Excellence award). Mem. adv. bd. Mich. Hwy. Dept., 1958-62; meme., chmn. Mich. Bd. Registration for Land Surveyors, 1970—; mem., chmn. Mich. Bd. Registration for Architects, 1970—. Editor, publisher Mich. Surveyor Newsletter, 1965-71. Home: 20314 Webber Dr Harper Woods MI 48225 Office: 16058 E Eight Mile Rd Detroit MI 48205

MC MAHON, STANLEY JAHN, farmer, rancher; b. Webster County, Nebr., Mar. 29, 1929; s. Floyd Devere and Hazel Francis (Jahn) McM.; student U. Nebr., 1947-48; m. Janice Arnetta Schnuerle, Dec. 23, 1951; children—Craig, Brian. Farmer, rancher, Ayr, Nebr., 1954—. Mem. Adams County Extension Bd., 1954-58; mem. Bd. Edn. Hill Community Sch., Blue Hill, Nebr., 1973—. Served with AUS, 1952-54. Named Outstanding Young Farmer Adams County, Hastings (Nebr.) Jaycees, 1960. Mem. Old Reliable Hereford Assn. (pres. 1958-60), Nebr. Polled Hereford Assn. (pres. 1972—), Midwest Polled Hereford Assn. (v.p. 1971-77, pres. 1977—). Presbyterian (elder 1973—). Clubs: 4-H (leader 1960—); Adams County Sirloin (dir. 1962-66). Address: PO Box 111A Route 1 Ayr NE 68925

MC MANUS, BRUCE WILLIAM, correctional adminstr.; b. Mpls., July 4, 1934; s. William Michael and Violet (Dahlin) McM.; B.A., Carleton Coll., Northfield, Minn., 1956; M.A., Temple U., Phila., 1960; M.S.W., U. Minn., Mpls., 1969; m. Anne Grosvenor Hutchins, June 22, 1958; children—William, Stephen, Robert, Marianne Esperanza. Corrections officer Minn. State Prison, Stillwater, 1956-57, correction agt., 1960-61, social service supr., 1964-66, asso. warden, 1966-67, warden, 1971-76; project dir. high security facility Minn. Dept. Corrections, 1976—. Supr. Minn. Dept. Corrections, Stillwater, 1961-64; criminal justice planner Minn. State Planning Agy., St. Paul, 1968; dir. field services Minn. Dept. Corrections, St. Paul, 1969-71. Served with USCGR, 1957-60. Mem. Acad. Certified Social Workers, Minn. Corrections Assn., Am. Correctional Assn., Am. Assn. Wardens and Supts., West Central Wardens and Supts. Assn., Correctional Industries Assn., Nat. Assn. Social Workers, U. Minn. Sch. Social Work Alumni Assn. (dir. 1971-75). Lutheran (mem. ch. council). Lion. Home: 516 S 4th St Bayport MN 55003 Office: Minn Dept Corrections 430 Metro Sq Bldg St Paul MN 55101

MC MANUS, EDWARD JOSEPH, U.S. judge; b. Keokuk, Iowa, Feb. 9, 1920; s. Edward W. and Kathleen (O'Connor) McM.; student St. Ambrose Coll., 1936-38; B.A., U. Iowa, 1940, J.D., 1942; m. Sally A. Hassett, June 30, 1948; children—David P., Edward W., John N., Thomas J., Dennis Q. Admitted to Iowa bar, 1942; gen. practice law, Keokuk, 1946-62; city atty., Keokuk, 1946-55; mem. Iowa Senate, 1955-59; lt. gov. Iowa, 1959-62; U.S. judge No. Dist. Iowa, 1962—. Mem. Iowa Devel. Commn., 1957-59. Del. Democratic Nat. Conv., 1956, 60. Served as lt. AC, USNR, 1942-46. Home: Cedar Rapids IA Office: PO Box 4815 Cedar Rapids IA 52407

MC MANUS, ROBERT LEE, mktg. profl. services co. exec.; b. Carmi, Ill., Dec. 3, 1922; s. Merle LeRoy and Laura Marie (Dissman) McM.; B.A., U. Ill., 1950; children—Laurie Ann McManus Filanowicz, Katharine Sue, Bridgit Kathleen. Sales engr. James L. Lyon Co., Chgo., 1951-56; pres., R.L. McManus & Co., Peoria, Ill., 1956-65; dir. project devel. John Hackler & Co., architects, Peoria, Ill., 1966—. Pres., Greater Peoria (Ill.) Legal Aid Soc., 1972-74, Central Ill. Agy. on Aging, 1972-75; chmn. Comprehensive Geriatric Treatment Service, 1972-75; chmn. Mayor's Commn. on Aging, 1975—; pres., Sr. Citizens Found., Inc., 1972-75. Served with USAAF, 1941-43. Recipient Tech. Excellence in Specification Writing award Constrn. Specifications Inst., 1973. Mem. Constrn. Specifications Inst. (pres. Central Ill. chpt. 1973-75), U. Ill. Alumni Assn. Elk. Club: Creve Coeur (Peoria, Ill.). Home: 2408 W Pasmoso Unit 2 Apt 201 Peoria IL 61614 Office: 1 Commercial Nat Bank Bldg Peoria IL 61602

MC MEANS, EDWARD, data processing exec.; b. Portsmouth, Ohio, Sept. 9, 1928; s. Edward D. and Jessie I. (Fields) McM.; student Ohio U., 1949-50, U. Dayton (Ohio), 1957-59; m. Harriette Jean Jensen, May 31, 1952; children—Deborah, Lynne, Scott. Mgr. data processing dept. Eckert Packing Co., Troy, O., 1956-64; systems and programming analyst, software specialist McCall Info. Services, Dayton, 1964-69; systems project leader, adminstrv. analyst Monarch Marking Systems, Dayton, 1969-72; mgr. systems and programming Cin. Electronics, Evendale, Ohio, 1972—. Served with AUS, 1946-48. Mem. Data Processing Mgrs. Assn., Assn. Systems Mgrs. Lutheran (mem. council). Clubs: Lions, Fairfield Booster. Home: 921 Wesleyan Dr Fairfield OH 45014 Office: Cin Electronics Evendale OH 45241

MC MEEN, LEWIS CLYDE, lawyer; b. Burke, S.D., Feb. 21, 1942; s. Delbert Arthur and Dorothy (Erickson) McM.; LL.B., U. Iowa, 1967; m. Sharon Joan Ristau, Aug. 15, 1964; children—Kelly, Timothy. Admitted to Iowa bar, 1967; partner law firm Harned, McMeen & Steffes, Marengo, Iowa, 1967—. Iowa County atty., 1969-73; Iowa County chmn. U. Iowa Alumni Council, 1969-76. Mem. Iowa County, Iowa State, Am. bar assns. Mason. Kiwanian (pres. 1969). Home: W Main St Marengo IA 52301 Office: Vogler Bldg Marengo IA 52301

MC MILLAN, ERIC WILLIAM, environ. engr.; b. Phila., Apr. 7, 1946; s. William James and Florence (Meister) McM.; B.S., Del. Valley Coll., 1969; M.S. in Food Sci., 1974, Environ. Engring., 1975; m. Bonnie Stowell, June 14, 1969; one dau., Kimberly Michele. Technician quality control Dolly Madison Ice Cream Co., Phila., 1968, 69; grad. research fellow food sci. U. Ill., Urbana, 1969-70, 72-74, civil engring., 1974-75, research asst. food sci., 1975; environ. engr. Tee-Pak Inc., Danville, Ill., 1975—. Served with U.S. Army, 1970-72. Awardee Nat. Fruit and Syrup Mfrs. Assn., 1969; NSF trainee, 1969-70, USPHS trainee, 1974-75. Mem. Water Pollution Control Fedn., Am. Chem. Soc., Inst. Food Technologists, Am. Dairy Sci. Assn., Sigma Xi, Delta Tau Alpha, Gamma Sigma Delta. Office: Tee-Pak Inc Environ Assurance Dept 915 N Michigan Ave Danville IL 61832

MC MILLAN, ROBERT HAMILTON, field engr.; b. Greensboro, Ala., Sept. 3, 1937; s. William Hamilton and Marie (Day) McM.; m. Bessie Anita Wise, Aug. 24, 1957; children—William Robert, Cydell Anita; student U. Ala., 1969-72. Engring. aid Byrd L. Moore, Engrs., 1955-56, Ala. Hwy. Dept., 1956-57; mem. engring. dept. U.S. Steel Corp., 1957-69; field engr. Ala. Power Co., 1970-73; chief field engr. Daniel Internat. Corp., Fulton, Mo., 1973—. Mem. Ala. N.G. Pistol Team, 1957-66, recipient several awards for pistol competition. Registered land surveyor, Ala. Mem. Am. Congress on Surveying and Mapping. Mem. Christian Ch. Home: Route 1 Box 167 Holts Summit MO 65043 Office: PO Box 167 Fulton MO 65251

MC MILLAN, WILLIAM MARCUS, surgeon; b. Colville, Wash., May 22, 1899; s. Colin Riley and Sallie (Dicks) McM.; B.S., U. Chgo., 1922; M.D., Rush Med. Coll., 1926; m. Charlotte Jean Stenberg Mancini, May 17, 1969; children by previous marriage—William Griffith, Marcia Dicks (Mrs. Edward Hines). Intern, Washington Blvd. Hosp., Chgo., 1926-27; resident surgery Cook County Hosp., Chgo., 1927-28; postgrad. tng. Berlin, Germany, Vienna, Austria, 1929; sr. attending surgeon Chgo. Wesley Meml. Hosp.; cons. surgeon Highland Park Hosp.; prof. surgery Cook County Grad. Sch.; emeritus asst. prof. surgery Northwestern U. Diplomate Am. Bd. Surgery. Fellow A.C.S., Internat. Coll. Surgeons; mem. AMA, Chgo. Med. Assn., Ill. Surg. Soc. Clubs: Hillsboro (Pompano Beach, Fla.); University (Chgo.); Exmoor Country (Highland Park, Ill.). Home: 1500 Sheridan Rd Wilmette IL 60091 Office: 720 N Michigan Ave Chicago IL 60611

MC MILLEN, THOMAS DAVID, JR., assn. exec., lawyer; b. Syracuse, N.Y., Mar. 24, 1943; s. Thomas David and Elizabeth Clary (Neeley) McM.; B.S., Hobart Coll., 1965; J.D., Drake U., 1968; m. Linda Jean Smay, Oct. 10, 1970. Admitted to Ia. bar, 1968; with Gov.'s Office of Planning and Programming, Des Moines, 1968, Iowa Civil Rights Commn., 1968; legal counsel Asso. Gen. Contractors of Iowa, Des Moines, 1969-71; exec. dir. Am. Road Builders Assn. of Ia., Des Moines, 1971—; partner firm Austin, McMillen & Reed, Des Moines, 1976—; v.p. Pocket Fashions, Ltd., Des Moines, 1973-74; legal counsel Sheet Metal Contractors Assn. Ia., 1972—. Acting chmn. Law Enforcement Legis. Study Com., 1968; mem. joint constrn. com. Office Fed. Contract Compliance, U.S. Dept. Labor, 1973—; co-chmn. Joint Heavy-Hwy. Labor Councils Advancement Fund, 1974—. Chmn. bd. trustees Iowa Laborer Dist. Council Health and Welfare Fund, 1970—; sec.-treas. bd. trustees Teamsters Joint Council Health and Welfare Fund, 1972—, Iowa Operating Engrs. Apprenticeship Fund, 1972—. Recipient certificate of recognition Iowa Law Enforcement Acad., 1968, certificate of award Lawyers Coop. Pub. Co., 1967. Mem. Am. (Sta(state chmn. state and municipal law com. 1970-72), Iowa, Polk County bar assns., Assn. Trial Lawyers Iowa, Am. Judicature Soc., Iowa Soc. Assn. Execs., Greater Des Moines C. of C. Clubs: Embassy, Des Moines Racquet. Home: 2520 Camelot Dr Des Moines IA 50322 Office: 1490 NW 86th St Des Moines IA 50311

MC MULLEN, CHARLES HARSHA, physician; b. Polk, Ohio, July 24, 1923; s. Raymond Fay and Duanna (Harsha) McM.; student Ohio State U., 1941-43, M.D., 1950; student Hamilton Coll., 1944, U. N.H., 1943, L.I. Coll., 1945-46; m. Evelyn Genevieve Strutt, July 3, 1944 (div. 1974); children—Pamela Sue (Mrs. William Beachler), Cynthia, John L.; m. 2d, Maryellen Long Miefert, Feb. 22, 1975. Intern, Cin. Gen. Hosp., 1950-51; gen. practice medicine, Loudonville, Ohio, 1954—; mem. staff Kettering Hosp., Loudonville, Samaritan Hosp., Ashland, Ohio, 1971—, Mansfield (Ohio) Gen. Hosp. Pub., Loudonville Times. Mem. State Planning Com. Health Edn., 1970—; mem., vice chmn., chmn. joint com. on health problems in edn. NEA, AMA, 1968-73. Mem. Loudonville-Perrysville Exempted Village Bd. Edn., 1966-74, pres., 1968-74. Served with AUS, 1943-46, USAF, 1951-53. Recipient Distinguished Service award Loudonville and Greater Mohican Area Jr. C. of C., 1970. Fellow Am. Sch. Health Assn.; mem. AMA (medicine/edn. com. sch. and coll. health 1977), Am., Ohio acads. gen. practice, Ohio Med. Assn. (chmn. com. on sch. health 1956—), Ashland County Med. Soc. (pres. 1958), Am. Legion, Alpha Omega Alpha. Republican. Presbyn. (elder 1960). Mason (32 deg., Shriner), Rotarian (pres. 1967-68). Home: Box 89 RFD 2 Loudonville OH 44842 Office: Box 89 544 N Union St Loudonville OH 44842

MC MULLIN, EARL LAWRENCE, tool mfg. co. exec.; b. South Haven, Kans., Dec. 29, 1915; s. James Jason and Celia L. (Windsor) M.; student San Diego State Coll., 1942-44; m. Virginia Lucille Coggins, Sept. 21, 1935; children—Earlene (Mrs. Larry Baum), Earl W. Tool and die engr. Consol. Aircraft, San Diego, 1940-46; devel. engr. Narmco. Co., San Diego, 1946-50; chief engr., div. mgr. Orchard Industries, Hastings, Mich., 1950-59; with Hastings (Mich.) Fiber Glass Products, 1959—, pres., 1959—; dir. Hastings Mfg. Co., Hastings City Bank. Pres., Hastings (Mich.) Community Fund, 1973-74. Bd. dirs. YMCA, 1968, Pennock Hosp., 1973—. Presbyterian (chmn. bd. trustees 1968-71, elder 1960-66). Mason (Shriner, 32 deg.), Rotarian. Patentee in field. Home: 2496 Ottawa Trail Hastings MI 49058 Office: 770 S Cook St Hastings MI 49058

MC MULLIN, LEO FRANCIS, advt. agy. exec.; b. Paterson, N.J., Apr. 23, 1919; s. Edward P. and Abby (Martin) McM.; B.A. cum laude, Montclair State Coll., 1940; M.B.A., N.Y. U., 1949; m. Louise M. Willing, Apr. 26, 1947; children—Lawrence W., Amy Louise. Personnel tng. exec. bur. pub. debt U.S. Treasury Dept., Chgo., 1941-45; various positions Andrew Jergens Co., Cin., 1945-61; v.p., dir. media and research Stockton West Burkhart, Inc., Cin., 1961-75, exec. v.p., 1975—; adj. asso. prof. mktg. Xavier U., 1956—. Mem. Am. Mktg. Assn. (pres. Cin. chpt. 1959-60), Cin. Indsl. Advertisers, Am. Acad. Advt., Internat. Newspaper Advt. Execs., Am. Assn. Advt. Agys. (newspaper relations com. 1962-63, 67-76). Home: 211 Hill Top Ln Cincinnati OH 45215 Office: 212 E 3d St Cincinnati OH 45202

MC MURRIN, LEE RAY, supt. schs.; b. Ind., June 29, 1930; s. Albert R. and Mrytle E. (Brickley) McM.; m. Frances McMurrin, Aug. 19, 1956; children—Michelle, Marianne, Marshall; B.S. in Secondary Edn., Olivet Coll., Kankakee, Ill., 1952; M.Ed., U. Cin., 1955; postgrad. Miami U., Oxford, Ohio, 1955, Kent (Ohio) State U., 1957, Ohio State U., 1958-65; Ph.D., U. Toledo, 1971. Elementary tchr. Sharonville (Ohio) Local Schs., 1952-55; prin. elementary supr. Lectonia (Ohio) Exempted Village Schs., 1955-58; asst. supt. Dover (Ohio) City Schs., 1958-60, South-Western Ohio City Schs., 1960-65; asst. supt. Toledo Pub. Schs., 1965-71, dep. supt., 1971-75; supt. schs. Milw. Pub. Schs., 1975—. Active, Boy Scouts Am.; bd. dirs. Jr. Achievement of Southeastern Wis.; corporate bd. mem. Milw. Symphony Orch. Mem. Am., Buckeye assns. sch. adminstrs., Wis. Assn. Sch. Dist. Adminstrs., NAACP, Phi Delta Kappa, Rotary Club, Kiwanis Club. Home: 3435 N Lake Dr Milwaukee WI 53211 Office: 5225 W Vliet St PO Drawer 10K Milwaukee WI 53201

MC NAIR, DONALD WESLEY, pub. relations exec.; b. Dahlgren, Ill., May 8, 1938; s. Melvin Wesley and Ruth Leora McN.; B.S. in Bus., U. Evansville, 1961; m. Rita M. Hadley, Dec. 21, 1968; children—Gary, Amy, Scott. Asso. editor Baking Industry mag. Clissold Publs., Chgo., 1962-65, Constrn. Equipment Distbn. mag. Asso. Equipment Distbrs., Oak Brook, Ill., 1965-69; mng. editor Hardware Merchandising mag. Irving Cloud Publs., Lincolnwood, Ill., 1969-71; pub. relations sr. account exec. Burson-Marsteller, Chgo., 1971-77; pres. McNair Mkrg. Communications, Bloomingdale, Mich., 1977—. Mem. Glen Ellyn (Ill.) Capital Improvements Commn., 1976-77; sec. Ill. Sch. Dist. 41 PTA, 1972-74. Recipient Silver Anvil award Pub. Relations Soc. Am., 1972, Golden Trumpet award Publicity Club Chgo., 1972, 73, 75, certificate of merit Bus./Profl. Advt. Assn., 1975; named Top Ind. Coll. Cartoonist, Ind. Collegiate Press Assn., 1960. Mem. Am. Mktg. Assn. Home and Office: Route 1 Box 263F Bloomingdale MI 49026

MC NAIRY, PHILIP FREDERICK, bishop; b. Lake City, Minn., Mar. 19, 1911; s. Harry Doughty and Clara (Moseman) McN.; A.B., Kenyon Coll., Gambier, 1932, D.D. (hon.), 1951; B.D., Bexley Div. Sch., 1934; Dr. Laws and Letters, Lake Erie Coll., 1962; S.T.D., St. John's Coll., Winnipeg, Man., Can., 1963; D.D., Seabury-Western Sem., 1969; m. Cary Elizabeth Fleming, Nov. 29, 1935; children—Philip Edward, Judith, Patricia. Ordained to ministry Protestant Episcopal Ch., 1935; rector charge St. Andrew's Mission, Columbus, Ohio, and St. Stephen's Parish, Cin., 1934-40; rector Christ Ch., St. Paul, 1940-50; dean St. Paul's Cathedral, Buffalo, 1950-57; suffragan bishop Diocese Minn., 1958-68; bishop coadjutor Diocese Minn., 1968-71; bishop of Minn., 1971—. Exec. council Episcopal Ch., 1970-73; pres. Province VI, 1970-73. Pres. Buffalo Council Chs., 1954-55; protestant chaplain Buffalo Trades and Labor Assembly, 1955-57. Mem. St. Paul Community Chest Bd., 1947-50, hon. 1950; bd. dirs. Buffalo Community Chest, 1952-57. Named outstanding young man of St. Paul by Jr. C. of C., 1946. Mem. Sigma Pi. Mason. Author: Family Story, 1960. Contbg. author: Confirmation: History Doctrine and Practice, 1962. Home: 1820 Knox Ave S Minneapolis MN 55403 Office: 309 Clifton Ave Minneapolis MN 55403

MC NALLY, CRYSTAL ELAINE, ednl. adminstr.; b. Hiattville, Kans., Sept. 23, 1914; d. John and Mae Ann (Attkisson) McNally; B.S., Kans. State U., 1935; M.A., Columbia, 1954. Librarian, tchr. Bucklin (Kans.) High Sch., 1935-43; Plainview schs., Wichita Kans., 1943-49; dir. library media services Wichita schs., 1949—. Mem. Speakers Bur., P.T.A., Wichita, 1949—. Goodwill ambassador for UNESCO to Orleans, France, 1949. Mem. Am., Kans. library assns., Am., Kans. assns. sch. librarians, P.E.O., Kans. Authors. Delta Kappa Gamma. Methodist. Mem. Order Eastern Star. Editor Sch. Media Quar., 1953. Home: 119 S Estelle Wichita KS 67211 Office: 1847 North Chautauqua Wichita KS 67214

MC NALLY, THOMAS JOSEPH, author; b. Berlin, N.H., Mar. 8, 1923; s. Frank X. and Lena (Cassidy) McN.; B.S., Loyola Coll., Balt., 1949; m. Phyllis Gibson Brown, Dec. 31, 1949; children—Thomas Robert, Marc Francis. Mgmt. trainee Montgomery Ward & Co., Balt., 1949-52; outdoor editor Balt. Sun, 1952-56, Chgo. Tribune, 1956—; free-lance mag. writer, 1950—. Served with AUS, 1942-45. Mem. Outdoor Writers Assn. Am., Am. Fisheries Soc., Assn. Great Lakes Outdoor Writers. Club: Chicago Press. Author: Fishermen's Digest, 1958, 64; Fishing for Boys, 1961; Hunting for Boys, 1962; Ultra-Light Spinning, 1960; Tom McNally's Fishermen's Bible, 1970, 72; others. Midwest editor Field and Stream mag., 1972—. Home: 2506 Harrison St Glenview IL 60025 Office: Chgo Tribune 435 N Michigan Ave Chicago IL 60611

MC NAMAR, DAVID FRED, lawyer; b. Terre Haute, Ind., Mar. 26, 1940; s. Fred L. and Frances M. (Sachs) McN.; B.S., Purdue U., 1962; J.D., Ind. U., 1968; m. Ann Brewer, June 22, 1963; children—Richard Philip, Eric Christopher, Gregory David. Admitted to Ind. bar, 1968, U.S. Supreme Ct. bar, 1974; asso. Steers, Sullivan, McNamar & Rogers and predecessor, Indpls., 1968-70, partner, 1970—. Served to lt. comdr. USNR, 1961—. Mem. Am., Ind., Indpls. (bd. mgrs. 1977-78) bar assns., Nat. Health Lawyers Assn. Presbyterian (trustee 1973-75, elder 1973-75). Mason (Shriner). Home: 710 Fenster Court Indianapolis IN 46234 Office: 312 Union Fed Bldg Indianapolis IN 46204

MC NAMARA, BARTLETT WILLIAM, dentist; b. Hudson, Wis., July 1, 1932; s. Raymond Paul and Margaret Ruth (McAndrew) McN.; student Wis. State Coll., Stevens Point, 1950-52, Wis. State Coll., Eau Claire, 1952-53; D.D.S., Marquette U., 1957; m. Mary Katherine Michalke, July 9, 1955; children—Sheila, Tim, Kate, Pat,

Molly, Michael, Dan. Pvt. practice dentistry, Richfield, Minn., 1960, Edina, Minn., 1960—; cons. hosp. dentistry U. Minn., Mpls., 1966—. Mem. task force on health Republican party, 1972; alt. del. (precinct) Minn. Rep. party, 1972—; bd. dirs. Delta Dental Minn., 1968-69. Served with USNR, 1957-60. Fellow Acad. Gen. Dentistry; mem. Am. Soc. Preventive Dentistry (dir. 1974-77, treas. 1975-77), Am., Minn. (health care com. 1966-74, chmn. welfare com. 1975-76 del. and alt. 1965-76) dental assns., Am. Soc. Dentistry for Children, Acad. Gen. Dentistry, Am. Soc. Orthodontics for Gen. Practioners, Chgo. Dental Soc. (asso.), Sigma Phi Epsilon. Club: K.C. Home: 4629 Arden Ave Edina MN 55424 Office: 255 Southdale Medical Bldg Edina MN 55435

MC NAMARA, CAROLYN LEE, univ. adminstr.; b. Wayne, Mich., Oct. 16, 1944; d. Manuel Maurice and Virginia Lee (Tapp) Graddy; M.A., Purdue U., 1969, Ed.S., 1971; B.S., Murray State U., 1966. Family living editor, agrl. info. dept. Purdue U., W. Lafayette, Ind., 1969-72; residence complex dir. Ohio State U., Columbus, 1972-74; dir. residence life Capital U., Columbus, 1975—. Co-producer, co-host Concerns and Comments weekly pub. affairs TV show, 1976-77; vol. One to One, Columbus, 1976-77. Mem. Am. Personnel and Guidance Assn., Am. Coll. Personnel Assn., Nat. Assn. Student Personnel Adminstrs., Nat. Assn. Women Deans, Administrs and Counselors, Speech Communication Assn., Ohio Coll. Personnel Assn. (mem.-at-large), Alpha Omicron Pi, Lambda Iota Tau, Chi Delta Phi. Methodist. Home: 892H Chatham Ln Columbus OH 43221 Office: 110 Yochum Hall Capital Univ Columbus OH 43209

MC NAMARA, JOHN PATRICK, psychiatrist; b. Indpls., Sept. 28, 1919; s. Leo Carl and Ethel Louise (O'Connor) McN.; B.S., U. Notre Dame, 1941; M.D., St. Louis U., 1944; m. Mary Mason, Nov. 20, 1943; children—Kathleen Kelly (Mrs. Joseph Mucha), Mary Jane (Mrs. Robert Dircks), George Elliot, Timothy Wayne, John Patrick, Mary Ann (Mrs. Mary Ann Seanger), Elizabeth Ann, Christopher Michael, Erin Louise, Michaela Marie. Intern, St. Vincent Hosp., Indpls., 1944-45; resident Norways Found. Hosp., Indpls., 1952-53; gen. practice medicine, Indpls., 1945-52; resident psychiatry Menninger Found., Topeka, 1953-55, staff psychiatrist, 1955-57, psychoanalytic tng., 1954-58; clin. dir. Central Minn. Mental Health Center, St. Cloud, 1959-63, psychiatrist, 1975—; pvt. practice psychiatry, Rice, Minn., 1963—; lectr. psychology Washburn U., Topeka, 1955-57; cons. Crosier Sem., Onamia, Minn., 1961—, St. Benedict's Coll., St. Joseph, St. John's U., Collegeville, div. vocat. rehab. Minn. Dept. Edn. Served to capt. M.C., AUS, 1945-47. Fellow Am. Psychiat. Assn.; mem. St. Cloud C. of C. Club: Exchange (St. Cloud). Address: Rural Route 2 Rice MN 56367

MCNAMARA, JOSEPH DONALD, city ofcl.; b. N.Y.C., Dec. 16, 1934; s. Michael and Eleanor (Shepherd) McN.; B.S., John Jay Coll., 1968; M.P.A., John F. Kennedy Sch. Govt., Harvard U., 1971, D.Pub. Adminstrn., 1973; m. Rochelle Wall, Jan. 25, 1964; children—Donald, Laura, Karen. With N.Y.C. Police Dept., 1956-73; chief of police, Kansas City, 1973—. Tchr. police adminstrn. Northeastern U., Boston, 1970-71; adj. asso. prof. police adminstrn. John Jay Coll., N.Y.C., 1973-74; cons. Bolt, Beranek & Newman, Center for Criminal Justice, Harvard Law Sch. Criminal Justice fellow, 1969-70; Littauer fellow, 1971-72. Mem. Internat. Assn. Chiefs of Police, Acad. Police Sci. Contbr. articles on police work to mags. Office: 1125 Locust St Kansas City MO 64106

MCNARY, GENE, county ofcl.; b. Muncie, Ind., Sept. 14, 1935; s. Earl and Fern (Fisher) McN.; B.S. in Fin., Ind. U., 1957, J.D., 1960; m. Ina Louise Risch, Aug. 15, 1959; children—Mark Patrick Cole Christopher, Wade Douglas. Asso. firm Lashley, Lashley & Miller, St. Louis, 1961-63; asst. pub. defender St. Louis County, 1963-65, pros. atty., 1967-74, county supr., 1975—. Home: 10 Fox Meadows St Sunset Hills MO 63127 Office: 7900 Forsyth St Clayton MO 63105

MC NAUGHTON, WILLIAM FRANK, orientalist; b. Westboro, Mo., May 21, 1933; s. Frank and Ruth (Flanders) McN.; student U. Mo., 1951-53, Georgetown U., 1953-54; B.A., Bklyn. Coll., 1961; Ph.D. (Woodrow Wilson fellow), Yale U., 1965; m. Margaret Agnes Orminsky, Apr. 6, 1956 (div. Oct. 1971); 1 dau., Dorothy Ellen. Asst. prof. Chinese, Oberlin (Ohio) Coll., 1965-70, lectr. exptl. coll., 1970-71; vis. lectr. classics Denison U., 1972—; vis. lectr. Chinese, Bowling Green (Ohio) State U., 1973-74. Fulbright-Hays fellow, 1968-69, Nat. Translation Center fellow, 1967. Mem. Am. Oriental Soc., Assn. Asian Studies, Modern Lang. Assn. Author: Guerrilla War, 1970; The Taoist Vision, 1971; The Book of Songs, 1971; (with Lenore Mayhew) A Gold Orchid, 1972; Chinese Literature: an Anthology, 1974; The Confucian Vision, 1974; A Guide to Reading and Writing Chinese, 1977. Home: 172 Shipherd Circle Oberlin OH 44074

MC NEAL, R(ALPH) RICHARD, ins. cons.; b. Oakville, Iowa, Aug. 19, 1925; s. Ralph Vincient and Zella Barr (Wright) McN.; student U. Minn., 1943, Coll. St. Thomas, 1943-44; B.C.S., Drake U., 1948; m. Ruth Lucille Morgan, Aug. 31, 1947; children—Michael, Deborah McNeal Wood, Nancy McNeal Burtch. Mktg. rep. Aetna Life & Casualty Co., St. Louis, 1948-54; operator Kennew Land & Ins. Co., Atlanta, 1954-59; operator W. Lyman Case & Co., Columbus, Ohio, 1959-64; pres. R. Richard McNeal Assos., Co., Columbus, 1964—. Speaker to various mgmt. groups. Served with USNR, 1943-45. Recipient Young Man of Yr. award, Jr. C. of C., Cobb County, Ohio, 1958; Salesman of Yr. award Upper Arlington Civic Assn., 1972. Mem. Soc. of Ins. Research, Am. Assn. Risk Analysts (trustee 1969-74), Am. Mgmt. Assn. Young Bus. Men's Club. Lion. Clubs: Athletic (Columbus); Arlington (Upper Arlington, Ohio); Optimist (Atlanta). Contbr. articles to profl. jours. Home: 1880 Mackenzie Dr Columbus OH 43220 Office: Suite 2090 88 E Broad St Columbus OH 43215

MC NEAL, THOMAS RUSSELL, JR., hosp. adminstr.; b. Des Moines, Iowa, Feb. 27, 1926; s. Thomas Russell and Corrine Elizabeth (Conner) M.; B.A., Drake U., 1959, AC, SC, Air U., Maxwell AFB, 1962; m. Doris P. Grundon, Sept. 5, 1946; children—William M., Barbara J. Entered USAF, 1944, commd. 2d lt., 1949, advanced through grades to maj.; mil. aide, liaison officer UN Indo-China Truce Commn., 1954; asst. exec. to sec. Air Force, 1962-64; ret., 1966; personnel dir. Broadlawns Polk County Hosp., Des Moines, 1967-71; adminstr. Peoples Meml. Hosp., Ind., Iowa, 1971-75; adminstr. Methodist Hosp., Mitchell, S.D., 1975—; mem. Allied Health Adv. Council, Gov.'s Arbitration Panel, S.D. Com. on Malpractice; bd. dirs. N.E. Iowa Health Planning Council, 1971-75. Decorated D.F.C. with 2 oak leaf clusters, Purple Heart, Bronze Star (5), Presdl. Unit Citation. Mem. Am. Acad. Med. Adminstrs., Am. Hosp. Assn., Air Froce Aid Soc. (life). Roman Catholic. Home: 1311 N Kimball St Mitchell SD 57301 Office: 909 S Miller St Mitchell SD 57301

MC NEE, JOHN CALVIN, univ. adminstr.; b. Blairsburg, Iowa, Aug. 20, 1925; s. John Harve and Elsie Jane (Miller) McN.; A.B., Cornell Coll., 1950; M.L.S., U. Mich., 1951; M.S., Iowa State U., 1960; m. Dorothy Marilyn Law, Sept. 18, 1944. Instr., asst. reference librarian Iowa State U., Ames, 1951; instr., reference librarian charge phys. scis. reading room, 1951-53, asst. prof., circulation librarian, 1953-54, asst. prof., acting head circulation dept., 1954, asst. prof., head circulation dept., 1955-62, asso. prof., head circulation, 1962-69, prof., 1971—; asst. dir. pub. services, 1969—. Chmn. bd. J.D. Assos. Chmn. com. to locate and purchase bldg. for Black Cultural Center, 1969-70, bd. dirs., 1969-71; chmn. Story County Cancer Crusade, 1957; active Community Chest, Am. Heart Assn.; mem. Town and Gown Investment Group, pres., 1966, bd. dirs., 1962-65. Chmn. Martin Luther King scholarship fund, 1969. Served with AUS, 1944-46. Mem. AAUP (chmn. exec. com. 1966-67, chpt. pres. 1966-67), ALA (state chmn. for recruitment 1965-69), Iowa Library Assn. (chmn. legis. com. 1975—). Contbr. articles to profl. pubs. Home: 3511 Oakland St Ames IA 50010

MC NEELY, JAMES MICHAEL, publisher; b. Detroit, May 11, 1930; s. Edward and Mary L. (Sullivan) McN.; B.A., St. Norbert Coll., 1955; M.A., Wayne State U., 1960; m. Marialyce LaRock, Feb. 19, 1955; children—Mary Jo, Michael, Tim, Tom, Beth, Patti, Christopher. Pub. relations officer sta. WBAY-TV, Green Bay, Wis., 1953-55; tchr. Farmington (Mich.) Pub. Schs., 1955-62; dep. chmn. Oakland County (Mich.) Democratic Com., 1962-65; dep. chmn. Mich. Dem. State Central Com., 1968-69, chmn. 1969-73; dir. orgnl. devel. Citizens Conf. on State Legislatures, 1973; now owner, pub. Tex. Truck Trader. Exec. dir. Oakland County Commn. Econ. Opportunity, 1965-68. Served with AUS, 1951-53. mem. Mich., Nat. edn. assns., Am. Polit. Sci. Assn., NAACP. Roman Catholic. Home: 6081 Kinyon Dr Brighton MI 48116 Office: 4722 Broadway Kansas City MO 64112

MC NEESE, WOODROW FRANKLIN, silica co. exec.; b. Cowden, Ill., Jan. 3, 1918; s. Joseph Luther and Lutia Lenora (Cooksey) McN.; Stenographic Degree, Sparks Bus. Coll., Shelbyville, Ill., 1936; grad. Alexander Hamilton Inst., 1960, U.S. Army Command and Gen. Staff Coll., 1963, Indsl. Coll. Armed Forces, 1969; m. Helen Marguerite Mathias, Mar. 17, 1946; 1 son, Patrick Gail. Purchasing agt. Standard Silica Corp., Ottawa, Ill., 1939-55; engr. Ottawa Silica Co., 1955-60, operations mgr., 1960-62, plant mgr., 1962-63; gen. mgr. Am. Silica Sand Co., Ottawa, 1963-65; mgr. customer services Bellrose Silica Co., Ottawa, 1965—. Mem., sec., chmn. Bd. Fire and Police Commrs., City of Ottawa, 1952-71. Served to lt. col. Transp. Corps, AUS, 1942-46. Mem. Res. Officers Assn. U.S. (pres. LaSalle County chpt. 1953), Am. Legion. Methodist (chmn. bd. trustees 1970). Mason. Home: 748 Chambers St Ottawa IL 61350 Office: PO Box 460 Ottawa IL 61350

MC NELLY, FREDERICK WRIGHT, JR., psychologist; b. Bangor, Maine, Apr. 14, 1947; s. Frederick and E. Frances (Cutter) McN.; foster children—Joseph, Ronald, Michael. B.A. magna cum laude, U. Minn., 1969; M.A., U. Mich., 1971, Ph.D., 1973. USPHS trainee, 1969-70, 72. Research coordinator NSF project U. Minn., Morris, 1968-69, lab. instructor, 1969; teaching fellow psychology U. Mich., 1970-72; dir. psychol. services Children Devel. Center, Rockford, Ill., 1972—; lectr. Rock Valley Coll., Rockford, 1974-75. Active Boy Scouts Am.; chmn. spl. edn. regional advisory com. Bi-County Office of Edn., Rockford, 1976—. Registered psychologist Ill.; named U.S. Jaycees Outstanding Young Man of 1977. Mem. Am., Ill. No. Ill. (chmn. 1976-77) psychol. assns., Soc. Research in Child Devel., Nat., Ill. assns. retarded citizens, Am. Humane Assn. (children's div.), Nat., Ill. Foster parents assns. Contbr. articles to profl. jours. Home: 1141 Beverly Ln Belvidere IL 61008 Office: Childrens Devel Center 650 N Main St Rockford IL 61103

MC NERNEY, WALTER JAMES, assn. exec.; b. New Haven, June 8, 1925; s. Robert Francis and Anna Gertrude (Shanley) McN.; B.S., Yale U., 1947; M.H.A., U. Minn., 1950; m. Shirley Ann Hamilton, June 26, 1948; children—Walter James, Peter Hamilton, Jennifer Allison, Daniel Martin, Richard Hamilton. Research asst. Labor-Mgmt. Center, Yale U., 1947; instr. advanced math. Hopkins Prep. Sch., New Haven, 1947-48; adminstrv. resident R.I. Hosp., Providence, 1949-50; asst. to coordinator Hosp. and Clinics Med. Center, U. Pitts, 1950-53, instr., then asst. prof. hosp. adminstrn., asst. prof. hosp. and med. adminstrn., 1953-55; asso. prof., dir. program hosp. adminstrn. Sch. Bus. Adminstrn., U. Mich., 1955-58, prof., dir. Bur. Hosp. Adminstrn., 1958-61; pres. Blue Cross Assn., Chgo., 1961—. mem. Dept. Treasury Advisory Com. Pvt. Philanthropy and Pub. Needs; dir., mem. exec. com. Nat. Health Council, 1963—, pres., 1972-73; bd. dirs., mem. fin. and investment coms. Opportunity Funding Corp.; pres. Health Services Found., 1963—, bd. govs. Health Service, Inc., Chgo.; bd. dirs., mem. exec. com. Nat. Center for Health Edn., vice-chmn., 1972-73; dir. Group Health Assn. Am.; chmn. task force on medicaid and related programs HEW, 1969-70; mem. council mgmt. Internat. Fedn. Voluntary Health Service Funds, pres., 1970-72; charter mem. Inst. Medicine, Nat. Acad. Scis.; mem. adv. council on inst. health econs. U. Pa.; adv. council Grad. Sch. Mgmt., Northwestern U.; mem. undergrad. admissions com., chmn. maj. and spl. gifts com. Yale U.; bd. visitors U. Pitts. Grad. Sch. Pub. Health; bd. govs. VA Scholars Program. Served to lt. (j.g.), USNR, 1943-46. Named 1 of 100 most important young men and women in U.S., Life Mag., 1962; recipient Justin Ford Kimball award, 1967; Nuffield Provincial Hosps. Trust-King's Fund fellow, Eng., 1970. Fellow Am. Pub. Health Assn.; mem. Royal Soc. Health, Assn. Univ. Programs in Hosp. Adminstrn., Am. Hosp. Assn., Am. Coll. Hosp. Adminstrs., Assn. Tchrs. Preventive Medicine, Internat. Hosp. Fedn., Am. Mgmt. Assns. (trustee), Assn. Yale Alumni Mgmt. Execs. Soc., Sigma Xi, Delta Sigma Pi. Alumni, Clubs: Mid-Am., Whitehall, Chgo. (Chgo.); Yale (N.Y.C.); Cosmos (Washington). Author: Hospital and Medical Economics, 1962; Regionalization and Rural Health Care, 1962; contbr. articles to profl. jours. Home: 675 Blackthorn Rd Winnetka IL 60093 Office: 840 N Lake Shore Dr Chicago IL 60611

MC NULTY, ALFRED PETER, constrn. industry cons.; b. Patchogue, N.Y., Aug. 19, 1924; s. Raymond Peter and Alice (Roche) McN.; student Phillips Andover Acad., 1938-42; B.S., Princeton U., 1948, M.C.E., 1950; student Columbia U., 1959-62; m. Dorothy John, Apr. 23, 1960; children—Matthew, Peter, William. Structural designer J.G. White Engrs. and Constructors, N.Y.C., 1950-52; project engr., supt. Turner Constrn. Co., Ky., Conn., N.J., N.Y.C., 1952-62; project mgr. Diesel Constrn., N.Y.C., 1962-63; cons. Constrn. Mgmt. & Cost Control, N.Y.C., 1963-67, Cleve., 1969-76; founder APM Services, project mgmt., 1976; v.p. Hunkin Conkey Constrn. Co., Cleve., 1967-69; adj. lectr. Case Western Res. U.; active in developing a N.Y. Worlds Fair Pavilion for World Fedn. United Nations Assn., 1964. Bd. dirs. Glen Oak Sch. Served with AUS, 1943-45. Decorated Purple Heart medal, Bronze Star medal. Mem. ASCE. Roman Catholic. Rotarian (chmn. vocational service). Club: Cleve. Skating Club. Contbr. articles on constrn. mgmt. to mags. Home: 2923 Glengary Rd Shaker Heights OH 44120 Office: 614 The Arcade Cleveland OH 44114

MC NUTT, MRS. DOROTHY, librarian; b. Cin., Jan. 17, 1903; d. Dr. Milton G. and Emily (Thompson) Conger; A.B., Ohio Wesleyan U., 1926; m. Clyde D. McNutt July 3, 1928 (div. 1934). With Cin. Pub. Library, 1926-73, mem. library tng. class, 1926-27, asst. pub documents dept., 1934-36, asst. sci. and industry dept., 1927-34, 1936-52, head sci. and industry dept., 1952-73; library cons., 1973—. Mem. ALA, Ohio Library Assn. (editor bull. 1956-58; mem. exec. bd. 1956-57), D.A.R., Spl. Libraries Assn. (pres. Cin. chpt. 1958-59), Alliance francaise, Alpha Chi Omega. Methodist. Clubs: Soroptimist (Cin. pres. 1958-59), College, Bus. and Profl. Women, Monnett. Contbr. articles to profl. jours. and local newspapers. Home: 4239 Hamilton Ave Cincinnati OH 45223 Office: 28 Woodlawn Ave Fort Mitchell KY 41017

MC PHAIL, S(TANLEY) BRIAN, optometrist; b. Beinfeit, Sask., Can., Jan. 25, 1939; s. C.O. and Margaret (Beckwith) McP.; naturalized, 1957; Ph.B., U. N.D., 1961; Dr.Optometry, Ill. Coll. Optometry, 1964; m. Arlene Kay Mortenson, Aug. 5, 1962; children—Gregory Jon, Michael Sean. Practice optometry, New London, Wis., 1964—; pres. Profl. Procurement Corp., New London, 1970-71. Bd. dirs. New London Community Hosp., St. Joseph's Nursing Home. Mem. Wis. Optometric Assn. (Wis. vocat. guidance dir. 1967—), Am. Optometric Assn., Kappa Sigma, Omega Delta. Republican. Conglist. Lion (pres. 1971-72, cabinet sec.-treas. to dist. gov. 1972-73). Home: 806 Smith St New London WI 54961 Office: 303 N Water St New London WI 54961

MC PHEETERS, JAMES WALTER, III, hosp. adminstr.; b. Poplar Bluff, Mo., May 4, 1938; s. James Walter and Emma Louise (Ringo) McP.; B.S., U. Mo., 1961; M.H.A., Washington U., St. Louis, 1967; m. Sandra Kay Worley, Aug. 26, 1961; children—Elizebeth Louise, James Walter IV, Jonathan Wright. Adminstrv. resident Muskogee (Okla.) Gen. Hosp., 1966-67, asst. adminstr., 1967-69; asst. dir. exchange of med. info. program Okla. U. Med. Sch., Oklahoma City, 1969-71; adminstr. McCune-Brooks Hosp., Carthage, Mo., 1972—; instr. Okla. U. Sch. Medicine, 1969-71. Sponsor, Boy Scouts Am., 1975; chmn. Area Multiple Sclerosis, 1973; chmn. Ozark Gateway Home Health Care Task Force, 1974; bd. dirs. S.W. Mo. Health Systems Agy., Inc., 1976—, Carthage Area Sheltered Workshop, 1972-75; dir. Carthage Area United Fund, 1977. Served to lt. USN, 1962-65. Named Hon. Citizen of Yr., 1976; VA grantee, exchange of med. info. program, 1969-71. Mem. Am. Coll. Hosp. Adminstrs., Am., Mo. (mem. finance com., planning com. 1975, trustee 1978—) hosp. assns., S.W. Mo. Hosp. Council (pres. 1975), Ozark Gateway Health Planning Council, Washington U. Alumni Assn., Carthage C. of C. (dir. 1977—). Roman Catholic. Clubs: Rotary; Broadview Country (dir. 1973—) (Carthage, Mo.). Home: 1823 Wynnwood St Carthage MO 64836 Office: 627 W Centennial St Carthage MO 64836

MC PHERSON, EDWIN MALCOLM, engr.; b. Chgo., Sept. 28, 1917; s. Edwin M. and Lillian (Nason) McP.; A.B., U. of South, 1939; M.A., Vanderbilt U., 1951, postgrad. law sch., 1950-51; m. Mary Ann McCalla, July 5, 1941 (dec. 1968); children—Edwin Malcolm III, Elizabeth Nason, James Ramsey; m. 2d, Rita Teresa Malecki, July 11, 1970. Mgr. systems J. Shoneman, Inc., Balt., 1957-59, research dir., 1964-66; mgr. industry applications Electronic Data Processing Div., Camden Systems RCA, 1959-64; cons. Kurt Salmon Assos., 1966-72; chief engr. H.D. Lee Co., Inc., Shawnee Mission, Kan., 1972—; v.p. Lester B. Knight Assos., N.Y.C. Instr., George Peabody Coll. Tchrs. Mem. engring. adv. council Kans. State U. Served from ensign to lt. comdr. USNR, 1941-46, 51-52. Mem. Assn. Cons. Mgmt., Am. Econ. Assn., Econometric Soc., Philatelic Soc., V.F.W., Phi Delta Theta. Club: Chemist's (N.Y.C.). Contbr. numerous articles in field. Patentee clothing industry equipment. Home: 8924 W 101st Terr Overland Park KS 66212 Office: HD Lee Inc Shawnee Mission KS

MC PHERSON, EUGENE VIRGIL, media co. exec.; b. Columbus, Ohio, Aug. 29, 1927; s. Arthur Emerson and Emma (Scott) McP.; B.A., Ohio State U., 1950; m. Nancy Marie Clark, June 13, 1953; children—Lynne, Scott. Prodn. exec. WBNS-TV, Coumbus, 1952-62; exec. producer documentary unit WLWT-TV, Cin., 1962-64; dir. news and spl. projects WLWT-TV, Cin., 1964-66; v.p. news and spl. projects AVCO Broadcasting Co., Cin., 1966-69, v.p. programming, 1969-73; v.p., gen. mgr. WLWI-TV, Indpls., 1973-75; now pres. McPherson Media, Inc.; broadcast cons., 1975—. Served with AUS, 1946-47. Recipient creative writer producer award Alfred P. Sloan, 1966; Chris award Columbus Film Festival, 1960, 61, 62, 64, 71; Nat. Assn. TV Execs. Program award, 1968; Ohio State award, 1960, 63, 64; Freedom's Found. award, 1963. Mem. Broadcast Pioneers. Author: (with Bleum and Cox) Television in the Public Interest, 1961. Writer, producer, dir. films The Last Prom, 1963, Death Driver, 1968, Citizen, 1962, Birth by Appointment, 1960, Diagnostic Countdown, 1962, Veil of Shadows, 1961, Rails in Crisis, 1963. Office: Radio Tower Rd Box L Olney IL 62450

MC PIKE, J. DONALD, dentist; b. Muscatine, Iowa, Sept. 14, 1908; s. Cyrus William and Myrtle (Greiner) McP.; student Augustana Coll., 1926-27; D.D.S., U. Iowa, 1931; m. Barbara Louise Huizel, Dec. 25, 1932; children—J. Donald Jr., Richard Huizel. Intern oral surgery Mpls. Gen. Hosp., 1931-32; pvt. practice dentistry, Muscatine, Iowa, 1932-43, 1946—. Mem. Muscatine Plan and Zoning Commn., 1952-57, chmn. 1956-57; mem. Zoning Bd. Adjustment, 1958—, chmn., 1963, 68, 73; dir. Delta Dental Plan Iowa. Served with USNR, 1943-46. Fellow Am. Coll. Dentists, Internat. Coll. Dentists; mem. Iowa (pres. 1964-65, treas. 1967-72, named Dentist of Year 1975), Am. dental assns., Acad. Gen. Dentistry, Am. Prosthodontic Soc., Pierre Fauchard Acad., Am. Soc. Preventive Dentistry, VFW, Am. Rose Soc. Methodist. Mason (Shriner). Kiwanian (pres. 1936-37), Elk. Home and Office: 2601 Mulberry Ave Muscatine IA 52761

MC QUIGGAN, MARK CORBEILLE, physician; b. Detroit, May 15, 1933; s. Mark Ronald and Catherine Charlotte (Corbeille) McQ.; B.S., U. Mich., 1954, M.D., 1958; m. Carolyn Ann Brunk, Mar. 25, 1961. Intern, Univ. Med. Center, Ann Arbor, Mich., 1958-59, resident in urology, 1961-64; jr. clin. instr. U. Mich., Ann Arbor, 1959-64; asso. practice urology, Detroit, 1964-67; dir. med. edn. Providence Hosp., Southfield, Mich., 1967-69; practice medicine specializing in urology, Southfield, 1969—; sec. staff North Detroit Gen. Hosp., 1975—. Mem. A.C.S., Am. Urol. Assn., Oakland County Med. Soc. (dir.), Detroit Surg. Assn., Alliance Francaise (dir.). Republican. Methodist. Club: Detroit Sportsmen's Congress. Home: 29653 Club House Ln Farmington MI 48018 Office: 15901 W Nine Mile Rd Suite 320 Southfield MI 48075

MC QUILLAN, MARCY, pottery co. exec.; b. Elgin, Ill., July 12, 1919; d. Edmund Henry and Vera (Mills) Haeger; B.A., Beloit Coll., 1942; m. John McQuillan, Jr., Apr. 16, 1949 (dec. July 1976); children—John III, David, Phillip. Sec., Haeger Potteries, Inc., Dundee, Ill., 1943-50, editor of house organ, 1947-49; sec. Ruckels Potteries, Inc., White Hall, Ill., 1951—. Mem. AAUW (pres. 1965-67). Republican. Presbyterian. Clubs: P.E.O. (chpt. pres. 1965-67), Jacksonville Pi Beta Phi Alumnae (sec.-treas. 1955-61, pres. 1962-65). Home: 204 Massey Ln Jacksonville IL 62650 Office: PO Box 744 Jacksonville IL 62651

MC QUILLEN, MICHAEL PAUL, physician; b. N.Y.C., Sept. 9, 1932; s. Paul William and Dorothy Marian (Moore) McQ.; B.A. cum laude, Georgetown U., 1953, M.D., 1957; m. Louise Mary Devlin, May 25, 1957; children—Daniel, Thomas, Patrick, Kathleen. Intern, Royal Victoria Hosp., Montreal, Que., Can., 1957-58; resident Georgetown Med. Center, Washington, 1958-60; resident Johns Hopkins Sch. Medicine and Hosp., Balt., 1960-62, instr., 1962-65; mem. faculty U. Ky. at Lexington, 1965-74, asso. prof. neurology, 1968-72, prof., 1972-74; prof., chmn. dept. neurology Med. Coll. Wis. at Milw., 1974—; vis. scientist Inst. Neurophysiology, U. Copenhagen, 1971-72; mem. med. adv. com. Nat. Myasthenia Gravis Com., 1964—; mem. med. adv. com. Milw. Myasthenia Gravis

Found., 1974—, S.E. Wis. Multiple Sclerosis Found., 1974—. Diplomate Am. Bd. Psychiatry and Neurology. Fellow N.Y. Acad. Scis., Am. Neurol. Assn., Am. Acad. Neurology. Contbr. articles to profl. jours. Home: 5650 North Shore Dr Whitefish Bay WI 53217 Office: Dept Neurology Med Coll Wis 8700 W Wisconsin Ave Milwaukee WI 53226

MC QUISTON, JAMES STUART, internist; b. Pitts., May 27, 1904; s. Edward Curtis and Sophia B. (Irwin) McQ.; B.S., Allegheny Coll., 1926; M.D., U. Pa., 1929; M.S. in Medicine, U. Minn., 1934; m. Jean Dollman Kriz, Jan. 24, 1976; 1 son by previous marriage, Edward Conner. Intern, Western Pa. Hosp., Pitts., 1929-30; resident in internal medicine, Mayo Clinic, Rochester, Minn., 1930-34; practice medicine specializing in internal medicine, Cedar Rapids, Iowa, 1934-77, sr. partner five internists, 1974-77; attending staff St. Luke's Meth. Hosp., Cedar Rapids, Mercy Hosp., Cedar Rapids; cons. in internal medicine. Served to lt. col. M.C., AUS, 1942-46. Mem. AMA, Linn County (pres., 1950), Iowa State Med. Socs., Iowa Clin. Soc. (pres. 1940), Am. Heart Assn., A.C.P. Republican. Clubs: Cedar Rapids Country, Rotary (pres. Cedar Rapids, 1938), Masons. Contbr. articles to med. jours. Home: 2222 1st Ave NE Cedar Rapids IA 52402 Office: 1328 2d Ave SE Cedar Rapids IA 52403

MC QUISTON, RAYMER, univ. prof.; b. Kokomo, Ind., Nov. 6, 1892; s. John S. and Eleanor Frances (Raymer) M.; student Drake U., 1911-12, Kans. State Tchrs. Coll., 1913-14; A.B., Kans. U., 1916; M.A., Harvard U., 1922; m. Cathlene Rose Harris, June 9, 1919 (dec. Nov. 29, 1957); 1 son, Julian Raymer. Supt. schs. Fairview, Kans., 1916-18, Axtell, 1918-19; asst. prof. English, Ohio U., 1922-24, asso. prof., 1924-63, asso. prof. English emeritus, 1963—. Mem. Coll. English Assn. Ohio (past sec.), Modern Lang. Assn., Shakespeare Assn. Am., AAUP, Phi Beta Kappa (senator 1955-61), Delta Sigma Rho, Phi Delta Kappa, Tau Kappa Alpha. Author monograph on Ralph Waldo Emerson. Editorial bd. Key Reporter. Home: 50 Mill St Athens OH 45701

MC REE, EDWARD BARXDALE, hosp. adminstr.; b. Pauls Valley, Okla., Oct. 20, 1931; s. Henry Barxdale and Mary (Shumate) McR.; B.A., Okla. City U., 1953; student U. Okla., 1953; student Central State Coll., 1954-55; m. Jan Bryant, Aug. 23, 1953; children—Scott, Kent, Chad. Adminstr. Eaton Rapids (Mich.) Community Hosp., 1957-61; pres. Ingham Med. Center, Lansing, Mich., 1961—. Mem. Eaton Rapids (Mich.) Bd. Edn., 1964-71, treas., 1968-71. Pres., Tri-County Emergency Med. Services Council, 1974—, also mem. bd. dirs.; bd. dirs. Blue Cross Mich., 1974-75; bd. dirs. Hosp. Purchasing Service Mich., 1973—, pres., 1976-77; bd. dirs. Mid-Mich. Chtp. ARC, 1977—. Served with AUS, 1955-57. Mem. Mich. (v.p. 1965-68), Southwestern Mich. (pres. 1968) hosp. assns., Am. Coll. Hosp. Adminstrs., Am. Hosp. Assn., Lambda Chi Alpha. Beta Beta Beta. Methodist (mem. West Mich. Conf. Bd. Finance 1972—). Contbr. articles to profl. jours. Home: 201 S Center St Eaton Rapids MI 48827 Office: 401 W Greenlawn Ave Lansing MI 48910

MC REYNOLDS, JANIS GAY, educator, counselor; b. Omaha, Feb. 20, 1938; d. John Orthello and Caroline Augusta (Wittmuss) Cockerill; B.S., U. Nebr., Lincoln, 1958, M.E., 1966; M.S., Creighton U., 1976; m. James Edwin McReynolds, June 30, 1957; children—Jacy Lynn, Guy Cockerill. Tchr. bus. edn. Elkhorn (Nebr.) High Sch., 1958-60, Ashland (Nebr.) High Sch., 1960-61, Westside Community Schs., Omaha, 1967-72, instr. in psychology, leader growth group and assertiveness group Central Tech. Community Coll., Hastings, Nebr., 1976—. Leader Prairie Hills Council Girl Scouts U.S.A., 1960-64, 74; pres. Ashland Jr. Woman's Club, 1962-63; Nebr. chmn. Mrs. Jaycees Cancer Dr., 1970-71. Named Outstanding Mrs. Jaycee, Gretna (Nebr.) Mrs. Jaycees, 1966. Mem. Am., Nebr. personnel and guidance assns., Assn. Specialists in Group Workers, Am. Assn. Sex Educators, Counselors, Therapists, NEA, Nebr. Edn. Assn., P.E.O. Republican. Lutheran. Club: Rainbow Girls (life). Home: Box 574 803 Clay St Harvard NE 68944

MC ROBERT, LOWELL MAX, orthodontist; b. Memphis, Mo., Aug. 6, 1932; s. Leland and Irma LaRue (Burrus) McR.; B.A., Mo. U., 1954, D.D.S., 1961; m. Frances Louise Rossiter, Apr. 4, 1971; children—Michael Paul, Sally Ann. Practice dentistry specializing in orthodontics, Kansas City, Mo., 1963—. Served with AUS, 1954-56. Mem. ADA, Am. Orthodontists Assn. Club: Masons. Home: 5720 Wilson Blvd Kansas City MO 64118 Office: 7010 N Cherry St Kansas City MO 64118

MC ROY, PAUL FURGESON, broadcasting co. exec.; b. Carbondale, Ill., June 25, 1912; s. Robert D. and Ann Elizabeth (Furgeson) McR.; B.Ed., So. Ill. U., 1934; M.Philosophy, U. Wis., 1939; m. Mary Eleanor Helm, June 12, 1937; children—Paul, Ann (Mrs. Larry E. Meyer). Tchr., dir. audio-visual edn. Houston Sch. System, 1934-43; instr. U. Houston, 1940-43; owner, mgr. radio sta. WCIL-WCIL-FM, Carbondale, 1946—; developer Bonnie Brae Subdiv., 1964—, builder, owner Southgate Shopping Center, 1964— (both Carbondale); dir. Carbondale Savs. & Loan, 1947—, pres., 1962—; dir. Carbondale Indsl. Corp., 1967-73, pres., 1968-73. Dir. Holden Hosp., 1949-55, So. Ill. U. Alumni Found., 1959-65; chmn. United Fund, 1952; mem. Carbondale Grade Sch. Bd., 1949-55; scoutmaster Boy Scouts Am., 1952-53, adviser Explorer troop, 1953-54. Served to lt. comdr. USNR, 1943-46. U. So. Ill. Found. cum laude fellow, 1974. Recipient We All Made It award Boy Scout Philmont Sky Ranch, 1954. Mem. So. Ill. U. Mem. So. Ill. U. Alumni Assn. (pres. 1958), Flying Scot Sailing Assn. (gov. Midwest dist. 1967), Carbondale C. of C. (pres. 1956, Man of Year award 1973), So. Ill. Golf Assn., U.S. Golf Assn., N.Am. Yachting Union. Methodist (trustee 1950-56, chmn. 1956). Shriner, Rotarian (pres. Carbondale 1950). Clubs: Crab Orchard Lake Sailing (commodore 1957), Jackson Country. Home: 25 Bonnie Brae Carbondale IL 62901 Office: 211 W Main St Carbondale IL 62901

MC STEEN, HARRY CHIARO, lawyer; b. Chgo., Feb. 1, 1937; s. Harry J. and Angela (Chiaro) McS.; B.B.A., U. Notre Dame, 1958; J.D., Loyola U., Chgo., 1965; m. Eileen Moerschbaecher, July 25, 1959; children—Anne Marie, Harry, Mary Elizabeth, Raymond, Patrick, Michael. With Westlake Finance Co., Chgo., 1961-65; admitted to Ill. bar, Fed. bar, 1965; since practiced in Joliet, Ill.; mem. firm Galowich, Galowich, McSteen & Phelan. Lect. Central States Inst. Addictions, Chgo., 1971—. Pres., Easter Seal Soc. Will County, 1971—; mem. Drug Coordination and Info. Council, Joliet, 1970—; bd. dirs. Easter Seal Soc. Ill., 1975—. Served with USNR, 1958-61. Mem. Am., Ill., Will County bar assns. K.C. Home: Office: 57 N Ottawa St Joliet IL 60431

MC SWEENY, AUSTIN JOHN, physician; b. N.Y.C., Sept. 30, 1924; s. Austin John and Madelene (Jasmagy) McS.; student Queen's Coll., 1943, U. Ill., 1944; M.D., Loyola U., Chgo., 1949; m. Erna Eleanor DeSollar, June 10, 1945; children—Austin John, III, James Dennis, Catherine Lynn, Christopher Shawn, Terence Shane. Intern, E.J. Meyer Meml. Hosp., Buffalo, 1949-50; resident Buffalo (N.Y.) VA Hosp., 1950-51; fellow Mayo Clinic, Rochester, Minn., 1953-55; practice medicine specializing in psychiatry, Danville, Ill., 1955-57, Janesville, Wis., 1957—; clin. dir. Asso. Psychosomatic Cons., Janesville, 1973-77; mem. staffs Meml. Community Hosp., Edgerton, Wis., Mercy Hosp., Janesville. Served with U.S. Army, 1943-46, USAF, 1951-53. Recipient medal Acad. Psychosomatic Medicine, 1976. Mem. AMA, Biofeedback Research Soc., Internat. Soc. Hypnosis, Am. Soc. Clin. Hypnosis, Internat. Coll. Psychosomatic Medicine, Acad. Psychosomatic Medicine, A.C.P., Am. Med. Soc. of Vienna, Rock County Med. Soc. Contbr. articles in field to profl. jours. Home: 1311 Camden Sq Janesville WI 53545 Office: 415 Dodge St Janesville WI 53545

MC SWINEY, CHARLES RONALD, lawyer; b. Nashville, Apr. 23, 1943; s. James Wilmer and Jewell Allen (Bellar) McS.; A.B., Kenyon Coll., 1965; J.D., U. Cin., 1968; m. Jane Detrick, Jan. 2, 1970. Admitted to Ohio bar, 1968; partner firm Smith & Schnacke, Dayton, Ohio, 1968—. Presdl. interchange exec. Pres.'s Commn. on Personnel Interchange, 1972; program adviser EPA, 1972-73, recipient Bronze medal, 1973. Mem. Am., Ohio, Dayton bar assns. Presbyn. Clubs: Moraine Country. Home: 5922 Parkchester Pl Dayton OH 45459 Office: 2000 Courthouse Plaza NE Dayton OH 45401

MC TEE, LYLE PATRICK, coll. adminstr; b. North Platte, Nebr., May 26, 1951; s. Lyle Junior and Teresa Arlene (Lannin) M.; B.S., U. Nebr., 1974, M.S., 1977. Tchr. Lincoln (Nebr.) Pub. Schs., 1974-75; asst. coordinator for fraternities, sororities and cooperatives student affairs dept. U. Nebr., Lincoln, 1975-77; asst. dir. residential life Morningside Coll., Sioux City, Iowa, 1977—. Recipient Outstanding Service award Acacia Nat. Frat., 1972. Mem. Am. Personnel and Guidance Assn., Am. Coll. Personnel Assn., Nat. Assn. Student Personnel Adminstrs., Assn. Fraternity Advisors, U. Nebr. Alumni Assn. Republican. Roman Catholic. Club: Elks. Home: Box C-145 Morningside Coll Sioux City IA 51106 Office: 102 Lewis Hall Morningside Coll Sioux City IA 51106

MC TEER, THOMAS RANDOLPH, data processing exec.; b. Ridgeland, S.C., Apr. 12, 1942; s. Benjamin R. and Virginia T. (Thomas) McT.; student Furman U., 1957-61; B.A., Edison Coll., 1977; m. Jerrie Ann Alton, Jan. 11, 1964; children—Bradley Thomas, Heather Anne. Mgr. systems planning Whirlpool Corp., Evansville, Ind., 1966-73; mgr. tech. services White Motor Corp., Cleve., 1973-76, mgr. data processing services, 1976—; v.p. Libra Typographers, Inc., Louisville, Ky., 1977—. Chmn. bd. early childhood edn. 1st Baptist Ch., 1976-77. Mem. Assn. Systems Mgmt., Data Processing Mgmt. Assn. Club: Forest Hill. Home: 1454 Burlington Rd Cleveland Heights OH 44118 Office: 35129 Curtis Blvd Eastlake OH 44094

MC VEAN, DUNCAN EDWARD, pharm. chemist; b. Pontiac, Mich., June 8, 1936; s. Duncan and Vernice Adelaide (Bird) McV.; B.S., U. Mich., 1958; M.S., 1960, Ph.D., 1963; m. Virginia Jean Cibor, Aug. 13, 1960; children—Cynthia Lynn, Scott Duncan. Pharmacist, St. Joseph Hosp. and Village Apothecary, Ann Arbor, Mich., 1959-63; pharm. research chemist W.S. Merrell Co., Cin., 1965-70; head methods devel. sect., quality control dept. Merrell Nat. Labs., Cin., 1970-75, project asst. to v.p. quality ops., 1975-76, head chem. control sect., 1976—. Pres. PTA, elementary sch., Cin., 1969-71. Served to capt. USAF, 1963-65. Regents Alumni scholar, 1954-58; Upjohn fellow, 1959-62. Recipient Bristol award, 1958, Merit award Boy Scouts Am., 1971. Mem. AMA (asso.), Am. Pharm. Assn., Acad. Pharm. Sci., AAAS, Sigma Xi, Phi Sigma Kappa, Phi Delta Chi, Rho Chi. Presbyterian. (elder). Mason (32 deg.). Patentee in antifoam preparation. Home: 2447 Hunt Rd Cincinnati OH 45215 Office: 110 E Amity Rd Cincinnati OH 45215

MC VEY, FRANCIS DANIEL, aero. engr.; b. St. Louis, Jan. 19, 1929; s. Martin P. and Marguy J. (Boeckler) McV.; B.S. in Mech. Engring., Washington U., St. Louis, 1952, M.S., 1954; postgrad. Princeton U., 1955; m. Anna Elizabeth Moss, Nov. 26, 1958; children—Mark Andrew, Marguy Denise, Michael Sean. Instr. mech. engring. Washington U., St. Louis, 1954-55; group project engr. missiles engring. div. McDonnell Aircraft Co., St. Louis, 1955-58, asso. scientist research div., 1961-64, br. mgr. engring. tech. div., 1964-74, prin. staff engr., 1974—; chief aerodynamicist Cleve. Pneumatic Co., Washington, 1959-61. Lectr., St. Louis U., 1964-70, U. Mo., St. Louis/Rolla Extension, 1971. Panel mem. Navy Bur. Weapons Adv. Com. on Aeroballistics, 1957-72; mem. air breathing propulsion com. Joint Army, Navy, NASA, Air Force Propulsion Information Agy., 1970-73. Served with AUS, 1946-48. Recipient Lloyd R. Koenig prize in engring. Washington U., 1952. Asso. fellow Am. Inst. Aeros. and Astronautics (St. Louis sect. chmn. 1964-65, Service award 1967); mem. Am. Rocket Soc. (v.p. St. Louis chpt. 1962-63), Sigma Xi. Home: 7030 Delmar Blvd University City MO 63130 Office: PO Box 516 St Louis MO 63166

MC WAY, FRANCIS SULLIVAN, optometrist; b. St. Louis, July 9, 1918; s. Thomas Joseph and Mary Lillian (Blandford) McW.; O.D., No. Ill. Coll. Optometry, 1942; m. Irene Rose Bayer, Sept. 7, 1947; children—Francis Sullivan, Christine, Karen. Practice optometry, Clayton, Mo., 1947-49, Union, Mo., 1949—. Visual cons. Bull Moose Tube Co., 1966—; optometric vocat. guidance adviser, 1962—. Served with AUS, 1943-46; ETO, PTO. Mem. Vets. Bus. Mens Orgn. (pres. 1949), Am. Optometric Found., Am., Mo. optometric assns., Am. Legion, Phi Theta Upsilon. Republican. Roman Catholic. Lion (pres. Union 1950), Kiwanian (pres. St. Clair, Mo., 1967), Rotarian Union, Mo., (sec. 1955), K.C. (3 deg.). Home: 295 Lillian Ave Union MO 63084 Office: 18 S Washington Union MO 63084

MEACHAM, ESTHER ANNE, communications scientist; b. Acton, Ind., July 29, 1921; d. Oscar Frederick and Edna Irene (Neal) Meacham; B.S., Ind. U., 1947; M.A., Mich. State U., 1952; Ph.D., Ohio State U., 1962. Instr. textiles and clothing Mich. State U., East Lansing, 1951-55; asst. prof. textiles and clothing U. Nebr., Lincoln, 1955-58, asso. prof., 1958-60; asso. prof., chmn. textiles and clothing Ohio State U., Columbus, 1963-67, asso. prof. audiovisual materials, home econs., 1967-78, prof., 1973—. Gen. Foods fellow, 1961-62. Mem. Assn. Ednl. Communication Tech., Am. Home Econs. Assn., Nat. Assn. Ednl. Broadcasters, Phi Kappa Phi, Omicron Nu (nat. pres. 1973-75). Producer instructional TV series Clothing Design Analysis, 1962; producer films Clothing Techniques, 1968. Home: 3243 Mountview Rd Columbus OH 43221 Office: 1787 Neil Ave Columbus OH 43210

MEACHUM, HENRY JAMES, III, veterinarian; b. Benton Harbor, Mich., Dec. 22, 1932; s. Henry James and Helen Frances (Miska) M.; B.S., Mich. State U., 1955, D.V.M., 1957; m. Patsy Jean Moran, Oct. 27, 1953; children—Virginia Helen, Henry James, Patti Jo, Daniel Patrick. Asso. veterinarian Israel Animal Hosp., Bryan Ohio, 1957-58; head veterinarian Hartford (Mich.) Animal Hosp., 1958—, dir. clinic, 1970—. Trustee Hartford Twp., 1968-72, Fire Bd., 1973-77, Cemetery Bd., 1968-72. Mem. AVMA, Michiana (pres., treas., dir.), Southwestern Mich. veterinary med. assns. Republican. Methodist. Club: Elks. Home: Solid M Chateau R5 Dowagiac MI 49047 Office: Solid M Spread R1 Hartford MI 49057

MEAD, CLYDE FRANK, ret. educator; b. Gladstone, Ill., July 19, 1913; s. Clyde Twilley and Virgie Lincoln (Marsden) M.; B.Ed., Western Ill. U., 1940; M.A., U. Ill., 1946; Ed.D., Ind. U., 1954; m. Mary Isabel Foster, Feb. 14, 1942 (dec. May 1970); 1 dau., Mary Kay; m. 2d, Barbara Walpole, Sept. 4, 1971. Prin., Gladstone Grade Sch., 1938-41; tchr., coach Macomb (Ill.) Jr. High Sch., 1941-42; prin. Grinnell (Iowa) Jr. High Sch., 1946-49; tchr., Evansville, Ind., 1949-51; teaching fellow Ind. U., Bloomington, 1951-52; teaching fellow edn., U. Nev., Reno, 1952-56; faculty Western Ill. U., Macomb, 1956-75, prof. edn., 1961-75, found. bd., 1971-75; cons. aerospace edn.; dir. aerospace CAP workshops, evaluation teams for Office of Supt. Pub. Instrn., 1974—. Mem. housing com. for low-cost housing City of Macomb, 1968-69. Served with USNR, 1942-45. Mem. Nat. Elementary Prins. Assn., Aerospace Edn. Assn., V.F.W., Phi Kappa Phi, Phi Delta Kappa. Elk. Club: Macomb Country. Home: 720 Orchard Dr Macomb IL 61455

MEAD, GORDON STERLING, mgmt. co. exec.; b. Cleve., Nov 26, 1920; s. Sterling Victor and Grace (Cummingham) M.; student Fenn Coll., 1939-43, Western Res. U., 1943; B.S., Ohio State U., 1945, postgrad., 1946-47; postgrad. Capital U., 1957; m. Alice Jane Cox, Sept. 21, 1945; children—David Sterling, Richard Gordon, Jane Anne. Asst. prodn. mgr. Surface Combustion Corp., Columbus, Ohio, 1945-49; chief statistician Lustron Corp., Columbus, 1949; sales and advt. rep. Denison Engring. Co., Columbus, 1950-52; with Rockwell Internat. Corp., Columbus, 1952-73; pres. Mead's Bus. & Cons. Services, Columbus, 1950-60; pres. Mgmt. Services & Tng., 1973—; instr. Ohio U. Mem. Zoning Commn., Pickerington, Ohio, 1962-69; scoutmaster Boy Scouts Am., 1966-68, commr., 1958—; pres. Bd. Edn. Pickerington Sch. Dist., 1973—; mem. Pickerington Parks and Recreation Bd., 1973-76, chmn., 1975—. Treas. Ohio Gamma Co., 1954-63. Mem. Nat. (pres. Ohio Buckeye council, dir. Rockwell Internat. chpt.), Central Ohio (pres. 1975). Springfield mgmt. assns., Am. Soc. Tng. and Devel., Independent Profl. Cons. Assn., Soc. Automotive Engrs., Am. Inst. Indsl. Engrs. (pres. 1978), Property Adminstrn. Assn. Am. Def. Preparedness Assn. (chmn. exec. bd., indsl. preparedness div.), Nat. Soc. Profl. Engrs., Columbus Tech. Council (treas.), Ohio State Alumni Assn., Sigma Phi Epsilon. Methodist. Mason, Lion. Home: 310 Lorraine Dr Pickerington OH 43147 Office: 1166 Goodale Blvd Columbus OH 43212

MEADE, GEOFFREY BLAINE, advt. and pub. relations co. exec.; b. Niagara Falls, N.Y., July 13, 1948; s. Emil B. and Corinne M. (Stahl) M.; A.A., Cuyahoga Community Coll., 1970; student Cleve. State U., 1970—; m. Claudia Jean Ashby, Aug. 19, 1972. Inventory control coordinator Xerox Corp., Cleve., 1970-72; asst. treas. Ashby & Assos. Inc., Cleve., 1972-74, treas., 1975—. Active Heart Fund, United Torch Drive. Precinct rep. Republican party, 1974. Mem. Am. Assn. Advt. Agys., First Advt. Agy Network, Cleve. State Ski Club. Methodist. Mem. Order De Molay. Office: Ashby & Assos Inc 550 Terminal Tower Cleveland OH 44113

MEADOR, JIMMY CLAY, computer systems analyst; b. Lafayette, Tenn., Dec. 11, 1948; s. C.J. and Mabel Louise (Hawkins) M.; B.S., Miami U., 1970; m. Charlotte M. Galloway, Aug. 15, 1970; children—Michelle C., Jennifer L. Computer systems analyst Ohio Edison Co., Akron, 1970-73, sr. programmer analyst, 1973-75, sr. tech. systems analyst, 1977—; instr. Akron U. Home: 654 Dayton Akron OH 44310 Office: 76 S Main Akron OH 44308

MEADOR, JUDITH ELAINE, financial planning cons.; b. St. Louis, July 10, 1943; d. James Ruel and Marjorie Elaine (Holton) Meador; B.B.A., Northwestern U., 1965; M.B.A., Washington U., 1966; grad. Inst. Investment Banking, Wharton Sch. Finance and Commerce, U. Pa., 1971. Asst. v.p. A.G. Edwards and Sons, Inc., St. Louis, 1966-72, v.p., 1972-73; corp., financial planning cons., 1973—. Mem. adv. council Small Bus. Adminstrn., 1976—. Trustee St. Louis Council on World Affairs; mem. Northwestern Alumni Admission Council, Washington U. Bus. Sch. Century Club (program chmn. exec. com. 1970-74, pres. 1974-76), Washington U. Club (treas. 1974-76), Beta Gamma Sigma, Alpha Chi Omega. Contbr. article profl. jour. Home: 10330 Oxford Hill Dr St Louis MO 63141 Office: 10330 Oxford Hill Dr St Louis MO 63141

MEADORS, ALLEN COATS, govt. ofcl.; b. Van Buren, Ark., May 17, 1947; s. Hal Baron and Allene (Coats) M.; B.B.A., U. Central Ark., 1969; M.A. in Bus., U. No. Colo., 1974; M.P.A., U. Kans., 1975. Asst. adminstr. U.S. Air Force Clinic, Lowry AFB, Denver, 1972-73; asso. adminstr. U.S. Air Force Hosp., Forbes AFB, Topeka, Kans., 1972-73; asst. dir. health services devel. Kans. Blue Cross, Topeka, 1973-76; asst. dir. Kansas City (Mo.) Dept. Health, 1976-77; asst. prof., program dir. So. Ill. U., 1977—; tchr. health policy and pub. health adminstrn. Grad. Sch., U. Kansas; tchr. econs. and orgn. behavior Webster Coll.; cons. Region IV Center for Health Planning; cons. academic curriculum Med. Sch., U. Kans., preceptor univ. M.P.A. program. Bd. dirs. Civitan, 1975, Walden Homeowners Assn., 1976-77, Martin Luther King Hosp. Served to capt. USAF, 1969-73. Certified in health services adminstrn. Mem. Am. Hosp. Assn., Am. Coll. Hosp. Adminstrs., Assn. Mental Health Adminstrs. (dep. gov. region V), Am., Mo. pub. health assns., Assn. Mil. Surgeons U.S., Am. Assn. Health Planning. Methodist. Contbr. articles in field to profl. jours. Home: PO Box 15511 Kansas City MO 64106 Office: 414 E 12th St Kansas City MO 64106

MEAGHER, THOMAS FRANCIS, transport exec.; b. Chgo., July 19, 1930; s. Thomas F. and Marie B. (Brennan) M.; B. Bus. Sci., St. Mary's Coll., Winona, Wis., 1953; m. Mona L. Carens, June 20, 1953; children—Constance, Thomas, Michael, Terence. Mgmt. positions sales and customer service Am. Airlines, 1957-60; asst. to pres. Continental Air Transport Co., Inc., Chgo., 1960-63, v.p., 1963-70, pres., 1972—; pres. Chgo. Conv. and Tourism Bur., 1970-72, mem. exec. bd.; dir. Lakeside Bank, Fairfield Savs. & Loan Assn. Bd. dirs. Travelers Aid, Mercy Hosp., Chgo.; bd. dirs. Boy Scouts Am., chmn. growth program, 1969—. Served as capt. USMCR, 1953-57. Mem. Nat. Airline Ground Transp. Assn. (pres.), Econs. Club, Spl. Agts. Assn. (bd. dirs. 1965—), Chgo. Assn. Commerce and Industry (bd. dirs.). Clubs: Chgo. Athletic Assn., Hundred, Skaal, Tavern, Butterfield Country. Home: 848 Bruner St Hinsdale IL 60521 Office: 300 N Desplaines Chicago IL 60606

MEBUST, WINSTON KEITH, surgeon, educator; b. Malta, Mont., July 2, 1933; s. Hans G. and Anna C. (Leiseth) M.; student U. Wash., 1951-54; M.D., 1958; m. Lora June Peterson, Sept. 15, 1955; children—Leanne, Kevin, Kreg, Kari. Intern, King County Hosp., Seattle, 1958-59; resident Virginia Mason Hosp., Seattle, 1959-63; Kans. U. Med. Center, 1963-66; practice medicine specializing in urology, 1966—; instr. surgery and urology U. Kans. Med. Center, Kansas City, 1966-69, asst. prof., 1969-72, asso. prof., 1972-76, chmn. urology sect., 1974—, prof., 1977—; chief urology service VA Hosp., Kansas City, Mo., 1966—. Served with U.S. Army, 1961-63. Diplomate Am. Bd. Urology. Mem. Am. Cancer Soc., Am. Bd. Surgery, Kansas City Urol. Soc., Assn. for Acad. Surgery, Am. Urol. Assn., Wyandotte Med. Soc., Kans. State Med. Assn., Am. Coll. Surgeons, Soc. Univ. Urologists, Sigma Xi, Alpha Omega Alpha. Republican. Contbr. articles, chpts. to med. jours. and texts. Home: 309 Apache Trail W Lake Quivira KS 66106 Office: 39th and Rainbow Blvd Kansas City MO 66103

MEDAK, HERMAN, pathologist; b. Vienna, Austria, Apr. 26, 1914; s. Ignaz and Ella (Medak) M.; student U. Vienna, 1932-38, M.D., 1973; B.S., U. Toledo, 1943; D.D.S., Northwestern U., 1946, M.S., 1946; Ph.D., U. Ill., 1959; m. Vivian H. Fried, Dec. 24, 1945; children—Ruth Ellen, Joanne Marie, Susan Lee, Alan Walter. Came to U.S., 1939, naturalized, 1944. Med. technician lab. Flower Hosp., Toledo, 1939-43, Wesley Meml. Hosp., Chgo., 1943-47; research asst. U. Ill., 1948-51, instr. oral pathology, 1953-61, asso. prof., 1961-64, prof., 1964—, acting head dept. oral pathology, 1964-67, chief clin. oral pathology, 1967—, staff appointment, research and edn. hosp., prof. dept. preventive medicine and community health Coll. Medicine, 1966—; mem. staff Luth. Gen. Hosp.; practice dentistry, part-time, 1946—. Served with M.C., AUS, 1951-53. Diplomate Am. Bd. Oral Pathology. Mem. Am. Coll. Dentists, ADA, Internat. Assn. Dental Research, Am. Acad. Oral Pathology (chmn. com. continuing edn.), Internat. Coll. Dentists, AAAS, Am. Soc. Cytology, Omicron Kappa Upsilon, Sigma Xi. Author: Atlas of Oral Cytology, 1971. Research in oral radiation, cancer. Home: 6820 N Kostner Ave Lincolnwood IL 60646 Office: 801 S Paulina St Chicago IL 60680 also 5850 N Clark St Chicago IL 60660

MEDARIS, FLORENCE ISABEL, osteo. physician and surgeon; b. Kirksville, Mo.; d. Charles Edward and Nellie (Finley) Medaris; B.A., Coll. Wooster, 1932; D.O., Kirksville Coll. Osteopathy and Surgery, 1939; postgrad. U. Wis., Marquette U. Pvt. practice osteo. medicine and surgery, Milw., 1940—. Active YWCA, Milw. County Mental Assn., Multiple Sclerosis Soc., Milw. Art Center, Friends of Art. Mem. Mayor's Beautification Com., 1968—; co-chmn. Riverfront Beautification, 1969—. Bd. dirs. Zonta Manor, Inc., 1957-67; bd. dirs. Multiple Sclerosis-Milw. Soc., 1972—, med. bd. dirs., 1973—; dir. Brace Fund bd. of Advt. Women of Milw., 1958-64, pres. bd., 1962-63. Mem. Am. Osteo. Assn. (com. mental health 1964), Wis. Assn. Osteo. Physicians and Surgeons, Milw. Dist. Soc. Osteo. Physicians and Surgeons, Am. Coll. Gen. Practitioners, Applied Acad. Osteopathy, Am. Assn. U. Women, Inter-Group Council Women (pres. 1947-49), Wis. Pub. Health Assn., Photog. Soc. Am., Bookfellows, Inc. (mem. bd. 1968—), Delta Omega (nat. pres. 1952-53). Presbyn. Club: Zonta (dir. Milw. 1968-69). Home: 1121 N Waverly Pl Milwaukee WI 53202 Office: 161 W Wisconsin Ave Milwaukee WI 53203

MEDHUS, GLENN LOUIE, farm equipment mfg. co. exec.; b. Cedar Rapids, Iowa, June 19, 1928; s. Gerald B. and Bernice (Hansen) M.; B.S.C. in Accounting cum laude, State U. Iowa, 1950; m. Mary L. Flidr, May 28, 1955; children—Ann T., Thomas G. With John Deere & Co., 1950—, works mgr. John Deere Planter Works, Moline, Ill., 1964-66, gen. mgr., 1966-71, asst. gen. mgr. Plow and Planter Works, 1971-73, gen. mgr., 1973-76, dir. planning Deere & Co., 1976—. Gen. campaign chmn. United Way, 1972, v.p. campaign, 1973; v.p. finance Jr. Achievement, 1971, pres., 1973, also bd. dirs., vice chmn. Midwest region. Served to 1st lt. USAF, 1951-53. Mem. Nat. Assn. Accountants, Moline C. of C. (dir. 1972-75). Roman Catholic (trustee 1966-75). Rotarian. Club: Short Hills Country (East Moline). Home: 3528 52d St Moline IL 61265 Office: John Deere Rd Moline IL 61265

MEDIN, MYRON JAMES, JR., city mgr.; b. Ladysmith, Wis., July 8, 1931; s. Myron James and Mildred (Johnson) M.; B.A. in Sociology, St. Olaf Coll., 1954; M.P.A., U. Mich., 1959; m. Alice Louise Moholt, May 14, 1955; children—John Clare, Karen Elise, Anne Elizabeth. Adminstrv. aide city mgrs. office, Fond du Lac, Wis., 1959, adminstrv. asst. to city mgr., 1959-63; city mgr. New Ulm (Minn.), 1963-67; city mgr. Fond du Lac, 1967—; mem. Gov.'s Regionalism Task Force Adv. Com., 1969-70; sec.-treas. U. Wis. Center-Fond du Lac Citizens Adv. Council; mem. spl. com. on town govt. incorp. Wis. Legis. Council, 1974; mem. weights and measures adv. council Wis. Dept. Agr., 1975—; vice chmn. study com. on improved pub. purchasing Wis. Dept. Local Affairs and Devel., 1975—. Chmn., Fond du Lac City Planning Commn.; mem. Wis. Coalition Human Needs and Budget Priorities, 1973; mem. exec. com. Wis. Coalition for Action on Shared Taxes, 1971. Served as 1st lt. USAF, 1955-57. Mem. Internat. City Mgmt. Assn. (ann. conf. planning com. 1975, local govt. personnel com. 1977), Am. Soc. Pub. Adminstrn., Nat. League Cities (com. intergovtl. relations 1971-73, com. human resource devel. 1974-76), League Wis. Municipalities (dist. v.p. 1973-75, chmn. resolutions com. 1975, legis. com. 1976, 77), Wis. City Mgmt. Assn. (sec.-treas. 1973, v.p. 1974, pres. 1975), Wis. Alliance Cities (v.p., dir.), Western Govtl. Research Assn., Municipal Fin. Officers Assn., Fond du Lac County Hist. Soc., Nat. Trust Hist. Preservation, Nat. Wildlife Fedn., Sierra Club. Home: 528 Highland Ct Fond du Lac WI 54935 Office: City Hall Fond du Lac WI 54935

MEDLEY, MORRIS LEE, sociologist; b. Detroit, Sept. 16, 1942; s. Louis Morris and Katherine Lee (Alvis) M.; Asso. Sci., Vincennes U., 1962; B.S., Ind. State U., 1964, M.S., 1966; Ph.D., Purdue U., 1974; m. Janet Anne Gelb, Sept. 6, 1962; one dau., Cynthia Kay. Tchr. social sci. Lincoln High Sch., Vincennes, Ind., 1964-67; asso. prof. sociology Ind. State U., Terre Haute, 1967—. Mem. Am., N. Central sociol. assns., Nat. Council Family Relations, Ind. Council Family Relations, Ind. Acad. Social Sci. Editor: (with James E. Conyers) Sociology for the Seventies, 1972; (with Arthur F. Kline) Dating and Marriage: an Interactionist Perspective, 1973; contbr. articles and revs. to profl. jours. sociology, gerontology, edn. Home: 610 Monterey Ave Terre Haute IN 47803 Office: Indiana State Univ Dept Sociology Terre Haute IN 47809

MEDOW, WILLOTTE DALE, coll. dean; b. Seward County, Nebr., Apr. 6, 1936; s. Otto H. and Stella (Fillinger) M.; B.A., Nebr. Wesleyan U., 1957; M.Ed., U. Wyo., 1962; m. Jean Anne Asmus, Dec. 21, 1956; children—Gregory, Sheri, Brenda, Brian. Tchr., prin., pub. schs., Gurley, Nebr., 1957-61; dir. guidance, pub. schs., Geneva, Nebr., 1961-63, Norfolk, Nebr., 1963-69; dir. guidance Jr. Coll. Norfolk, 1963-69; dean students Northeastern Nebr. Coll., Norfolk, 1969-73, dean student services Northeast Tech. Community Coll., Norfolk, 1973—. NDEA fellow, 1960, 62. Mem. Nebr. Assn. Student Personnel Adminstrs. (pres.), Nebr. Personnel and Guidance Assn. (pres.), Nebr. Assn. Tech. Community Coll. Student Personnel Adminstrs., Phi Delta Kappa. Democrat. Methodist. Clubs: Shriners, Masons, Elks. Home: 609 Pierce St Norfolk NE 68701 Office: 801 E Benjamin St E Norfolk NE 68701

MEDZIHRADSKY, FEDOR, biochemist; b. Kikinda, Yugoslavia, Feb. 4, 1932; s. Miklos and Melanie (Gettmann) M.; M.S., Technische Hochschule Munich, Germany, 1961; Ph.D., 1965; m. Mechthild Westmeyer, Sept. 13, 1967; children—Sofia, Oliver. Instr. biochemistry U. Munich, 1965-66; asst. prof. biochemistry U. Mich. Med. Sch., Ann Arbor, 1969-73, asso. prof., 1973—, research asso. pharmacology, 1971-74, asso. prof., 1975—. Vis. asso. prof. pharmacology Stanford Med. Center, 1975-76. Postdoctoral fellow NIH, 1966-67, Nat. Inst. Neurol. Diseases and Blindness, 1967-69; Nat. Research Service grantee, 1975-76. Mem. Soc. German Chemists, Soc. Biol. Chemistry (Germany), Am. Soc. Neurochemistry, Am. Chem. Soc., Am. Soc. Biol. Chemists, Am. Soc. Pharmacology and Exptl. Therapeutics. Research neurochemistry, biochem. pharmacology, biol. transport. Home: 1615 E Stadium Blvd Ann Arbor MI 48104 Office: Dept Biological Chemistry Univ Michigan Medical School Ann Arbor MI 48109

MEE, JOHN F., educator; b. Ada, Ohio, July 10, 1908; s. R. Kirk and Helen F. (Hickernell) M.; A.B., Miami U., 1930, LL.D., 1964; A.M., U. Maine, 1932; Ph.D., Ohio State U., 1959; m. Muriel E. Collins, Apr. 5, 1941; children—Marcia Joan, Virginia Ann, Raymond Kirk. Teaching fellow U. Maine, 1930-32; dean Beal Coll., Bangor, Maine, 1932-34; placement dir. and instr. Ohio State U., 1934-39; asst. prof. and dir. placement Ind. U., 1939-41, 46—, prof. mgmt., 1946—, Mead Johnson prof. mgmt., 1961—, dean div. gen. and tech. studies, 1965, rep. Big Ten Conf., 1950-62; owner, operator livestock farms, 1950—; pres. Mee Farms, Inc., 1966—; mem. adv. Mgmt. Internat.; cons. personnel mgmt. and indsl. relations; cons. Exec. Office President U.S., 1950-52; exec. dir. Ind. Tax Study Commn.; staff dir. President's Com. on Presdl. Appointments, 1950, Ind. Study Commn. Intergovtl. Relations, 1954. Mem. arbitration panel of gov. Ind.; commr. Ind. Dept. State Revenue, 1948; gov.'s commn. State Hwy. Evaluation Survey; mem. sec. Navy Adv. Bd. Edn. and Tng., 1973. Chmn. Am. Mgmt. Seminar Team to France, 1952; pres. Council for Profl. Edn. for Bus., 1956-57; U.S. del. XIth Internat. Mgmt. Congress, 1957; adv. bd. Indsl. Coll. Armed Forces, 1956-59. Pres., Richard D. Irwin Found., 1975. Served as col. USAAF, 1941-46. Named Ky. col., Ind. Sagamore of the Wabash. Licensed psychologist, Ind. Mem. Soc. Advancement Mgmt. (v.p. research and devel. 1959, Taylor Key award 1972), A.I.M., Am. Psychol. Assn., Controllers Inst. Am., Inst. Mgmt. Scis. (edn. com.), Acad. Mgmt. (gov. 1959, Army adv. com.), Internat. Acad. Mgmt., S.A.R., Beta Gamma Sigma (nat. pres. 1970-72, Distinguished scholar 1973), Phi Beta Kappa, Phi Beta Kappa Assos. Club: Explorers. Author: Management Thought in a Dynamic Economy, 1963. Editor: Personnel Handbook, 1951; Irwin Industrial Engineering and Management Series; cons. editor Advanced Management, 1951-52; chmn. editorial bd. Bus. Horizons; co-editor Behavioral Sci. Bus. series; contbg. editor Ency. Mgmt. Home: 600 Soutar Dr Bloomington IN 47401

MEEK, EDWARD STANLEY, pathologist; b. Bristol, Eng., Oct. 9, 1919; s. Alfred Edward and Mary Ann Margaret (James) M.; M.B., Ch.B. cum laude, U. St. Andrews, Scotland, 1951, M.D., 1955; children—Pamela Ann, Patricia Susan. Intern, U. St. Andrews Hosps. and Clinics, Dundee, 1951-52; resident in pathology U. Bristol Hosps. and Clinics, Eng., 1952-56; practice medicine specializing in pathology U. Bristol, 1956-70; prof. microbiology U. Iowa, Iowa City, 1970—, prof. pathology, prof. ophthalmology, 1973—. Served with Brit. Army, 1940-46. Fellow Am. Acad. Microbiologists, Royal Coll. Pathologists, Inst. Biologists, Sigma Xi; mem. AMA, Am. Assn. Immunologists, Am. Soc. Microbiologists, Brit. Med. Assn., Path. Soc. Great Britain, N.Y. Acad. Scis. Author books and articles in field. Home: 614 E Jefferson St Iowa City IA 52240 Office: Dept Pathology U Iowa Iowa City IA 52242

MEEK, ROBERT LEE, cons. civil engr.; b. Greensburg, Ind., Sept. 2, 1903; s. Clyde Lester and Alice (Bird) M.; B.C.E., Purdue U., 1925, C.E., 1947; m. Carol Nelle Jerman, Dec. 25, 1925; children—Robert Lee Jr., John Jerman. Engr., W. & A. Smadbeck, Inc., Mo. also N.Y., 1925-26; dep. county engr., Decatur County, Ind., 1926-31; project engr. Ind. State Hwy. Commn., Greenfield, Seymore and Ft. Wayne dists., 1931-35; jr. engr. U.S. Dept. Agr., Ind., 1935-36; resident engr. Ulen Contracting Co., Lebanon, Ind., 1936-39; resident engr. Ind. Statewide REMC, Ind., 1939; resident engr. Putnam & Woolpert, Dayton, Ohio, 1939-40; engr. R.B. Moore Co., Indpls., 1940-42, chief resident engr., Ottumwa, Iowa, 1942-43; civil engr. Purdue U., 1944; chief civil engr. Moore & Owen, Indpls., 1944-49; asso. firm Mark B. Owen, Engrs., Indpls., 1949-50, partner, 1950; chief engr. Indpls. San. Dist., 1950-54; partner firm Hannan, Meek & Assos., Cons. Engrs., Indpls., 1954-65; pres. Architects-Engrs., Inc., Indpls., 1965-68; chmn. Meek & Hannan, Inc., Indpls., 1968—. Mem., chmn. Ind. State Bd. Registration for Profl. Engrs. and Land Surveyors, 1955—. Fellow ASCE (life mem.); mem. Nat. Soc. Profl. Engrs., Am. Cons. Engrs. Council, Water Pollution Control Assn., Indpls. Sci. and Engring. Found., Nat. Council Engring. Examiners, Alpha Tau Omega. Republican. Elk. Clubs: Greensburg Country, Columbia (Indpls.). Home: 332 N Franklin St Greensburg IN 47240 Office: 5440 E 38th St Indianapolis IN 46218

MEEKER, DAVID BOWYER, elec. equipment co. exec.; b. Troy, Ohio, Sept. 19, 1925; s. David Anderson and Laura (Bowyer) M.; B.A., Dartmouth Coll., 1948; M.B.A., U. Mich., 1950; m. Helen Sanders Nelson, June 30, 1948; children—David Nelson, George Nelson, Laura Jane, Susan Sanders. With Hobart Corp., 1949—, sales mgr. br. and agy. div., 1955-63, treas., 1963-66, v.p., treas., 1966-67, exec. v.p., 1967-68, pres., 1968—, chief exec. officer, 1970—, also dir.; dir. Phillips Petroleum Co., Armco Steel Corp., Winters Nat. Bank & Trust Co., Dayton, Ohio, R.R. Donnelley & Sons Co., Chgo., Dayton Power & Light Co., Huffy, Inc., Dayton, Trojan Farms, Inc., Troy. Trustee Hollins Coll., Roanoke, Engring. and Sci. Inst., Dayton, Nat. Inst. Food Service Industry, Chgo.; pres. Neil Armstrong Aerospace Mus., Wapakoneta, Ohio; bd. dirs. Jr. Achievement Dayton, Lincoln Community Center, Troy, Boy Scouts Am., Dayton. Served with USNR, 1943-46. Mem. NAM (chmn. 1975, life dir.), Ohio Mfrs. Assn. (v.p.), Newcomen Soc., Phi Delta Theta. Republican. Presbyterian. Clubs: Rotary, Dayton Racquet; Troy Country; Leland (Mich.) Country, Leland Yacht. Home: 420 S Market St Troy OH 45373 Office: World Hdqrs Bldg Troy OH 45374

MEEKER, DUANE B., agrl. engr.; b. Logansport, Ind., May 12, 1940; s. Clifford Eldo and Florence Louise (Eldridge) M.; student Mass. Inst. Tech., 1964; B.S., Purdue U., 1966; m. Kay Ann Purdy, Jan. 13, 1963; children—Karen, Barbara, James, Janet. Farmer, Logansport, Ind., 1966—; owner, founder Meeker Agrl. Cons., Logansport, Ind., 1967—, chief engr., 1970—. Cons. for The Heil Corp., Butler Mfg. Co., Beard Industries, Chief Industries, Huskee-Bilt, Agrl. Stablzn. and Conservation Service. Chief Clinton Twp. (Ind.) Volunteer Fire Dept., 1971-72; chmn. nominating com. Sch. Bd., Logansport, Ind., 1971-73. Bd. dirs. Cass County (Ind.) 4-H Fair, 1958-62. Recipient Am. Soc. Agrl. Engrs. honor award, 1966; Cass County Jr. C. of C. Outstanding Young Farmer award, 1975, Ind. State Jr. C. of C. Outstanding Young Farmer, 1975, Nat. Outstanding Young Farmer, 1975-76. Registered profl. engr., Ind. Standard Oil Co. Ind. scholar, 1961; NSF scholar, 1964. Mem. Cass County Livestock and Crop Improvement Assn. (pres. 1975), Cass County Beef Cattle Assn. (dir. 1975—), Top Farmer of Am. Assn., Profl. Farmers Am. Assn., Nat. Soc. Profl. Engr., Ind. Soc. Profl. Engrs., Am. Soc. Agrl. Engrs. (pres. 1972). Methodist (adminstrv. bd. 1970-75). Rotarian (dir. 1973-75), Mason. Home: Route 2 PO Box 157 Logansport IN 46947

MEEKS, LOUIS WALTER, orthopedic surgeon; b. Ann Arbor, Mich., July 4, 1937; s. A. James and Leona Frances (Gale) M.; B.A., Albion Coll., 1959; M.D., U. Mich., 1963; m. Berneda Slavik, May 21, 1970; children—Michelle, Louis, Jonathan, Laura. Intern, St. Joseph Mercy Hosp., Ann Arbor, 1963-64, asst. resident in gen. surgery, 1964-65; resident in orthopedic surgery U. Mich., 1965-66, 68-70; practice medicine specializing in orthopedic surgery, Ann Arbor, 1970—; mem. staff, chief dept. surgery Beyer Meml. Hosp., Ipsilanti, Mich.; vice chief dept. orthopedics St. Joseph Mercy Hosp.; clin. instr. in surgery U. Mich. Med. Center; cons. Wayne County (Mich.) Gen. Hosp., Wayne. Served as capt. M.C., U.S. Army, 1966-68. Voted Outstanding Instr. in Orthopedic Surgery sr. med. class U. Mich., 1974; diplomate Am. Bd. Orthopedic Surgery. Fellow AAUP, Internat. Coll. Surgeons, Am. Coll. Sports Medicine, A.C.S., Am. Acad. Orthopedic Surgeons; mem. Washtenaw County (Mich.), Mich. State med. socs., AMA, Mich. Orthopedic Soc., Beta Beta Beta. Contbr. articles to textbooks and profl. jours.; author sound slide program: Low Back Pain, 1976. Home: 3541 Windemere St Ann Arbor MI 48105 Office: 5305 E Huron River Dr Suite 3B100 Ypsilanti MI 48197

MEENGS, WILLIAM LLOYD, cardiologist; b. Zeeland, Mich., Dec. 23, 1942; s. Lloyd Stanley and Gertrude (Wyngarden) M.; A.B., Hope Coll., 1964; M.D., U. Mich., 1968; m. Helen Delores Van Dyke, June 10, 1964; children—Michelle Rene, William Lloyd, Lisa Ann. Intern in internal medicine Univ. Hosp., Ann Arbor, Mich., 1968-69, resident in internal medicine, 1971-73, fellow in cardiology, 1973-75; practice medicine specializing in cardiology, Petoskey, Mich., 1975—; cardiologist Burns Clinic Med. Center, Petoskey, 1975—; cardiologist Little Traverse Hosp., Petoskey, 1975—, dir. coronary care unit, 19—. Served as surgeon USPHS, 1969-71. Fellow Am. Coll. Cardiology; mem. A.C.P., Am. Heart Assn., Alpha Omega Alpha. Home: 1052 Lindell St Petoskey MI 49770 Office: Burns Clin Med Center 560 W Mitchell St Petoskey MI 49770

MEESE, ERNEST HAROLD, surgeon; b. Bradford, Pa., June 23, 1929; s. Ernest D. and Blanche (Raub) M.; B.A., U. Buffalo, 1950, M.D., 1954; m. Margaret Eugenia McHenry, June 4, 1952; children—Constance Ann, Roderick Bryan, Gregory James. Resident in gen. surgery Millard Fillmore Hosp., Buffalo, 1955-59; resident in thoracic surgery U.S. Naval Hosp., St. Albans L.I., N.Y., 1961-63; group practice thoracic and cardiovascular surgery, Cin., 1965—; asst. clin. prof. surgery Cin. Med. Center, 1972—; mem. staff Good Samaritan, St. Francis, St. George, Deaconess, Bethesda, Christ, Providence, Childrens, and St. Luke hosps., Cin. Pres. bd. dirs., chmn. service com. Cin.-Hamilton County unit Am. Cancer Soc.; trustee, exec. bd. Southwestern Ohio chpt. Am. Heart Assn. Served to comdr. M.C., USN, 1959-65. Diplomate Am. Bd. Surgery, Am. Bd. Thoracic Surgery. Fellow A.C.S., Soc. Thoracic Surgeons, Am. Coll. Chest Physicians, Am. Coll. Angiology, Cin. Surg. Soc., Am. Coll. Cardiology; mem. Gibson Anat. Hon. Soc., A.M.A., Am. Thoracic Soc., Assn. Mil. Surgeons U.S., Acad. Medicine Cin., Phi Beta Kappa, Phi Chi. Clubs: Bankers, Western Hills Country (Cin.). Contbr. articles to profl. jours. Home: 174 Pedretti Rd Cincinnati OH 45238 Office: 311 Howell Ave Cincinnati OH 45220

MEESE, WILLIAM GILES, utility co. exec.; b. Rugby, N.D., Aug. 27, 1916; s. William Gottlieb and Emma (LaPierre) M.; B.S., Purdue U., 1941, D.Eng. (hon.), 1972; m. Mary Edith Monk, Apr. 4, 1942; children—Elizabeth, Stephen, Richard. With Detroit Edison Co., 1941—, asst. v.p. constrn. and engring., 1967, v.p., 1967-69, exec. v.p. prodn., 1969-70, pres., 1970-75, chief exec. officer, 1971—, chmn. bd., 1975—, also dir.; dir. Mfrs. Nat. Bank, Mfrs. Nat. Corp., Eaton Corp., Edison Electric Inst., Ex-Cello Corp. Trustee New Detroit, Inc., Detroit Renaissance, Harper-Grace, United Hosps. Detroit, Rackham Engring. Found.; bd. dirs. United Found. Served to maj., F.A., AUS, 1941-45. Decorated Bronze Star medal; recipient Distinguished Alumnus award Purdue U., 1969; Internat. B'nai B'rith Humanitarian award, 1977; registered profl. engr., Mich. Fellow Engring. Soc. Detroit; mem. IEEE, Conf. Internationale des Grands Reseaux Electriques, Newcomen Soc. N.Am., Tau Beta Pi, Eta Kappa Nu. Clubs: Detroit, Detroit Athletic, Economic of Detroit (dir.). Home: 570 Rudgate Rd Bloomfield Hills MI 48013 Office: 2000 2d Ave Detroit MI 48226

MEETZ, JOHN EUGENE, assn. exec.; b. Newton, Kans., Nov. 10, 1944; s. Harry L. and Gladys (Koch) M.; B.S., Kans. State U., 1966, M.S., 1968; m. Margaret O'Bryan, Sept. 28, 1968; children—Carla Ann, Kelly Jo. Supr. market promotion programs Kans. Dept. Agr., 1967; instr. Western Ill. U., Macomb, 1968-70; exec. v.p. Kans. Livestock Assn., Topeka, 1970—. Pres., Com. Kans. Farm Orgns., 1974-75. Mem. Alpha Gamma Rho. Club: Cedar Crest Country. Home: Route 7 Topeka KS 66604 Office: 2044 Fillmore St Topeka KS 66604

MEFFERD, PAUL STENBERG, hydraulic cylinder co. exec.; b. nr. Pomeroy, Iowa, Sept. 28, 1915; s. Arthur Arvid and Anna Marie (Stenberg) M.; student grammar sch., nr. Pomeroy; m. Helen Dorothea Frykberg, Feb. 14, 1939; children—Patricia Eileen (Mrs. Kenneth D. Boughey), Thomas Arthur, Linda Helen (Mrs. Loren H. Gustafson), Paulette Marilyn (Mrs. Eduardo Reveiz), Kathleen Dorothy (Mrs. John M. Hinn), Margaret Janet (Mrs. Lawrence J. Beckman), Kristine Anne. Owner Paul's Garage, Pomeroy, 1930-37; chief tool and die maker Superior Mfg. Co., Albert City, Iowa, 1937-39; serviceman Burke Implement Co., Humboldt, Iowa, 1939-40; founder, owner Mefferd Mfg. Co., Albert City, 1940-41; founder, owner Twin Draulic, Laurens, Iowa, 1941-46, v.p., to 1951; founder, owner Mefferd Industries, 1951-71, inc. 1971, chmn. bd., 1959—; chmn. bd. Little Cedar Creek Game Farm, Laurens, 1957—. Mem. Dad's com. Stephens Coll., Columbia, Mo., 1969-70; mem. exec. council Boy Scouts Am. Named Outstanding Civic Leader Am., 1967. Mem. Laurens C. of C. Lutheran. Club: Sportman. Home: Seven Oaks Manor Laurens IA 50554 Office: 114 Rush Lake Rd Laurens IA 50554

MEFFERD, THOMAS ARTHUR, hydraulic cylinder mfg. co. exec.; b. Storm Lake, Iowa, July 31, 1941; s. Paul S. and Helen Dorothy (Frykberg) M.; student Gustavus Adolphus Coll., 1959-60, 61-62; B.S., Iowa State U., 1965; m. Bonnie L. Laidley, July 11, 1965; children—Shannon, Paul. Vice pres. Mefferd Industries, Inc., Laurens, Iowa, 1965-71, pres., 1971—, also sec.-treas.; owner, pres. TE Corp., Laurens, 1971-75. Treas., bd. dirs. Laurens Retirement Housing Corp., 1968—. Served with U.S. Army, 1960-61. Mem. Laurens C. of C. (pres. 1971, 72), Tau Beta Pi. Republican. Lutheran. Home: 526 N 1st St Laurens IA 50054 Office: Walnut St and Rush Lake Rd Laurens IA 50554

MEGOWEN, CHARLES GEYER, realty investment exec.; b. Toledo, Aug. 24, 1932; s. Carl Robert and Gladys (Geyer) M.; student Williams Coll., 1950-52; B.A., Ohio Wesleyan U., 1955; M.B.A., Ohio State U., 1965; m. Lita Soskin Zapata, July 6, 1974 (div. June 1975). Gen. adminstrv. trainee Owens-Ill., Inc., Toledo, 1955, 57-58, methods analyst trainee, 1961-62, procedures analyst, 1963-67, facilities coordinator, 1967-73, with realty investments, 1973—; partner Vertias Assos., Chgo., 1957-58. Presiding judge precinct 3, Lucas County Bd. Elections, Ottawa Hills, Ohio, 1965-76; v.p. Toledo Civic Playgoers, 1962—; pres. Found. for the Arts, 1967—; bd. dirs. Children's Theater Workshop of Toledo, 1964-75, pres., 1967-69; bd. dirs. Neighborhood Improvement Found. Toledo, 1971—; trustee Toledo Symphony Orch., 1964-74. Served with USAF, 1955-57. Mem. Alpha Tau Omega (alumni chpt. pres. 1964-65). Republican. Congregationalist. (deacon 1966-68, 74-76). Clubs: Toledo Country, Toledo. Home: Route 5 Box 338A Swanton OH 43558

MEGRAW, ROBERT ELLIS, clin. chemist; b. Phila., Feb. 10, 1930; s. John and Florence (Ellis) M. B.A., Fla. State U., 1956, M.S., 1960; Ph.D., Iowa State U., 1964; m. Clara Josephine Caccavale, Aug. 7, 1971; children—Jennifer, Timothy, Jason, Tobias, Jeremy. Postdoctoral fellow biochemistry Albert Einstein Med. Center, Phila., 1964-66; scientist dept. diagnostics research Warner Lambert Research Inst., Morris Plains, N.J., 1966-71; research chemist Sigma Chem. Co., St. Louis, 1971-73; mgr. Unitest chemistry Diagnostics div. Bio-Dynamics Inc., Indpls., 1973—. Served with USAF, 1948-52.

Mem. Am. Chem. Soc., Am. Assn. Clin. Chemists, AAAS, Soc. Exptl. Biology and Medicine, Central Ind. Clin. Biochem. Forum (dir.), Sigma Xi. Contbr. articles to profl. jours. Home: 8132 Teel Way Indianapolis IN 46256 Office: PO Box 50100 Indianapolis IN 46250

MEHAFFEY, JOHN ALLEN, journalist; b. Brainerd, Minn., Oct. 18, 1936; s. Scott Bailey and Belva LaVerne (Harris) M.; student Minn. Sch. Bus., 1954; m. Mary Jean Gaskins, Dec. 17, 1955; children—Mark Allen, Scott David, Chris Douglas. Sales and mgmt. service to various newspapers, 1955; editor, pub. Tioga Newspapers, Owego, N.Y., 1968-69; owner, editor, pub. Jefferson County Press Times, Crystal City, Mo., 1969-75; owner, pres. Communications Service Co., Crystal City. Lectr., William Allen White Sch. Journalism, U. Kans., and various seminars, workshops. Mem. Wabash Valley Assn., Ind., 1964-67; bd. dirs. Meramec Basin Assn., St. Louis, 1969—. Mem. Mo., N.Y., Hoosier, Inland Daily press assns., Sigma Delta Chi. Elk, Rotarian. Club: Press of Met. St. Louis. Home: Rural Route 6 Scenic Dr Festus MO 63028 Office: PO Drawer 133 Crystal City MO 63028

MEHAFFEY, JOHN RUSKIN, veterinarian; b. Zanesville, Ohio, Dec. 12, 1942; s. John Oscar and Frances Heloise (Hartley) M.; B.S. in Agr., Ohio State U., 1969, D.V.M., 1969; m. T'wana Lyna Watson, Jan. 27, 1977; 1 son, Jonathan Watson. With Paul E. Little Constrn. Co., Cambridge, Ohio, 1960-61, Fred Boggs' Riverby Farms Horse Training Center, Dublin, Ohio, part-time, 1963-65; with Timmons' Metal Products, Columbus, 1966-69; pvt. practice vet. medicine, Cambridge, Ohio, 1969-71, Pataskala, Ohio, 1971—; asso. Goldstein Vet. Hosp., Reynoldsburg, Ohio, 1971—. Recipient 1st pl. award slogan contest Nat. Mental Health Assn., 1978. Mem. Am., Ohio, Licking County vet. med. assns., Am. Assn. Equine Practitioners, Fifth Dist. Equine Practitioners Assn., Am., Ohio (winner state registered calf roping competition 1966) quarter horse assns., Nat. Reining Horse Assn. (amateur reining world champion 1967, 72), Am. Aberdeen Angus Assn. Assemblies of God. Address: 8883 National Rd SW Pataskala OH 43062

MEHBOD, HASSAN, nephrologist; b. Shiraz, Iran, Sept. 10, 1933; s. Mehdi and Homa (Anvar) M.; came to U.S., 1959, naturalized, 1969; M.D., Tehran U., 1958; m. Darlene Van Putten, June 6, 1964; children—William M., Diane H., Susan L. Intern, Bergen Pines County Hosp., Paramus, N.J., resident in internal medicine, 1960-61, 63-64; chief resident Goldwater Meml. Hosp., 1961-62; fellow Hahnemann Med. Coll. and Hosp., Phila., 1962-63, 64-65; pvt. practice medicine and nephrology, Dayton, Ohio; asso. clin. prof. medicine Ohio State U., Wright State U.; attending staff Good Samaritan, St. Elizabeth hosps. Diplomate Am. Bd. Internal Medicine. Fellow A.C.P.; mem. AMA, Ohio Med. Assn., Montgomery County Med. Soc., Am., Internat. socs. nephrology. Contbr. articles to profl. jours. Office: 2345 Philadelphia Dr Dayton OH 45406

MEHL, WARREN ROY, librarian, educator; b. St. Louis, Oct. 18, 1920; s. Roy John and Clara (Noeth) M.; B.B.A., U. Tex., 1946; B.D., Eden Theol. Sem., 1949; M.L.S., U. Okla., 1958; Ph.D., Ind. U., 1973; m. Lucy Ann Heitmann, June 7, 1948; children—David Edgar, Doris Jean. Ordained to ministry Evang. and Ref. Ch., 1949; pastor Zion Evang. and Reformed Ch. Mayview, Mo., 1949-51, Federated Ch., Kingfisher, Okla., 1951-57, First Presbyn. Ch., Purcell, Okla., 1957-58; cataloger Ridgley Library, Washington U., St. Louis, 1958-59; prof., dir. continuing edn., librarian Eden Theol. Sem., Webster Groves, Mo., 1959—. Served with USNR, 1942-46. Mem. Am. Theol. Library Assn. (treas. 1971-74), Soc. for Advancement Continuing Edn. for Ministry, Acad. Evangelism in Theol. Edn., Beta Gamma Sigma, Sigma Iota Epsilon, Beta Phi Mu. Home: 119 Bompart Ave Webster Groves MO 63119 Office: 475 E Lockwood Ave Webster Groves MO 63119

MEHLENBACHER, DOHN HARLOW, constrn. co. exec.; b. Huntington Park, Calif., Nov. 18, 1931; s. Virgil Claude and Helga (Sigfridson) M.; B.S. in Civil Engring., U. Ill., 1953; M.S. in City and Regional Planning Ill. Inst. Tech., 1961; M.B.A., U. Chgo., 1972; m. Barbara Ruth Stinson, Dec. 30, 1953; children—Dohn Scott, Kimberly Ruth, Mark James, Matthew Lincoln. Structural engr., draftsman Swift & Co., Chgo., 1953-54, 56-57, DeLeuw-Cather Co., Chgo., 1957-59; project engr. Quaker Oats Co., Chgo., 1959-61, mgr. constrn., 1964-70, mgr. real property, 1970-71, mgr. engring. and maintenance, Los Angeles, 1961-64; chief facilities engr. Bell & Howell Co., Chgo., 1972-73; v.p. design Globe Engring. Co., Chgo., 1973-76; project mgr. I.C. Harbour Constrn. Co., Oak Brook, Ill., 1976—. Served with USAF, 1954-56. Registered profl. engr., Ill., N.Y., Calif. Mem. Nat. Soc. Profl. Engrs., Am. Mgmt. Assn., ASCE, Constrn. Specifications Inst., Am. Arbitration Assn. Home: 2662 Sheridan Rd Highland Park IL 60035 Office: 615 W 22d St Oak Brook IL 60521

MEHLHAF, MILTON T., banker; b. Menno, S.D., May 7, 1926; s. Theodore and Emelia (Reiser) M.; B.S., U. S.D., 1949; m. Jacqueline Jean Waltner, Aug. 22, 1948; children—Mark S., Jan K. Coach basketball, baseball and track Lake Norden (S.D.) High Sch., 1949-53; v.p., dir. First Nat. Bank, Freeman, S.D. Counselor S.D. Boys State, 1952-57; treas. S.D. Amateur Baseball Assn., 1974—. Mem. Freeman Sch. Bd. Vice pres. bd. dirs. Freeman Jr. Coll.; trustee S.D. Fellowship Christian Athletes. Served with USNR, 1944-46. Mem. S.D. Bankers Assn. (chmn. edn. com. 1972), C. of C. (pres. 1962, sec.-treas. 1966), Am. Legion. Republican. Mem. Mennonite Ch. (chmn., tchr.). Home: 728 S Cherry St Freeman SD 57029

MEHLHOFF, MILBERT WARREN, realtor; b. Hosmer, S.D., Oct. 4, 1928; s. Emanuel and Magdelene (Heyne) M.; student Aberdeen Sch. Commerce, 1963; m. Vivian A. Schell, Oct. 3, 1954; children—Thomas, Nancy, Sharon, Timothy. With Taylor Music Co., Aberdeen, S.D., 1950-65, salesman, 1956-65; salesman Engel Agy. realty, Aberdeen, 1965-68; owner mgr. Mehlhoff Realty, Inc., Aberdeen, 1968—. Mem. City Planning Commn., 1967-69. Mem. mgmt. com. 1971-72. Named Realtor of Year, Aberdeen, 1971. Mem. Nat. Inst. Real Estate Bds., Nat. Assn. Realtors (pres. chpt. 1970, state dir. 1970-71). Lutheran. Elk. Club: Sertoma. Home: 806 17th Ave SE Aberdeen SD 57401 Office: 614 S Main St Aberdeen SD 57401

MEHLMAN, JEROME SAUL, internist; b. Chgo., Sept. 17, 1913; s. Benjamin and Bess (Bernstein) M.; A.B., Western Res. U., 1933; M.D., U. Ill., 1938; m. Felice P. Gottlieb, Jan. 7, 1940; children—Edward B., David J. Intern, Michael Reese Hosp., Chgo., 1938-39, resident, 1941; asst. in pathology Cook County Hosp., Chgo., 1937; practice medicine specializing in internal medicine, Chgo., 1942—; mem. staff Michael Reese Hosp., Weiss Meml. Hosp.; clin. prof. medicine U. Chgo., 1973—. Trustee Chgo. Coll. Jewish Studies, 1966-67, Bd. Jewish Edn. Met. Chgo., 1966-75. Served with AUS, 1943-46. Diplomate Am. Bd. Internal Medicine. Mem. Union Am. Hebrew Congregations (nat. bd. 1971, pres. Chgo. Fedn. 1972—). Jewish. Home: 5856 N Virginia Ave Chicago IL 60659 Office: 111 N Wabash Ave Chicago IL 60602

MEHMEL, PHILIP VINCENT, mental health dir.; b. Winnipeg, Man., Can., Sept. 16, 1927; s. Edward Oscar and Philipina (Rudolph) M.; came to U.S., 1958, naturalized, 1964; B.A., U. Man., 1948, M.A., 1950; Ph.D., Case Western Res. U., 1958; m. Norma Jeanne Gavette, July 25, 1952; children—Heidi Ann, Jennifer Jeanne, Gretchen Marie, Paula Victoria. Psychologist Psychiat. Services div. Dept. Pub. Health, Sask., 1951-58; area program dir. W. Central Community Services Center, Willmar, Minn., 1958—; instr. psychology Willmar (Minn.) State Jr. Coll., 1962-70, Mankato (Minn.) State Coll., 1972-73; mem. mental health services research review com. NIMH, 1973—; cons. Region 5, NIMH, 1971—. Pres. Willmar (Minn.) United Fund, 1964-65, campaign, dir., 1960-64. Bd. dirs. West Central Industries, Inc., Willmar, Minn., 1963-74, pres., 1963. Recipient Distinguished Service award, Willmar Jr. C. of C., 1961. Diplomate Am. Bd. Profl. Psychology. Mem. Am., Minn. psychol. assns., Am. Rehab. Assn. Lutheran. Elk, Lion. Club: Willmar Golf. Home: 815 E 4th St Willmar MN 56201 Office: 1125 E 6th St Willmar MN 56201

MEHN, W. HARRISON, surgeon; b. Monroe, Wis., Nov. 25, 1918; s. William Herman and Hedwig Gertrude (Butenhoff) M.; B.A., North Central Coll., Naperville, Ill., 1940; B.S., Northwestern U. Med. Sch., 1944, M.D., 1944, M.S. in Pathology, 1944; m. Jean Belle Dorr, Sept. 23, 1945; children—Mary Ann, Judith Susan. Intern, Passavant Meml. Hosp., Chgo., 1944, resident in surgery, 1947-50; resident in pathology Children's Meml. Hosp., Chgo., 1945, Alexian Bros. Hosp., Chgo., 1946-47, resident in surgery, Cook County Hosp., Chgo., 1949-53; clin. asst. dept. surgery Northwestern U., 1948-52, instr. in surgery, 1952-53, asso. in surgery, 1953-58, asst. prof. surgery, 1958-73, asso. prof., 1973-74, prof. clin. surgery, 1974—; practice medicine specializing in surgery, Chgo.; mem. staffs Passavant Meml. Hosp., VA Lakeside Hosp.; med. dir. Commonwealth Edison Co., Chgo., 1955—; mem. accident prevention com. Edison Electric Inst., N.Y.C., 1960—; participant profl. research task forces Electric Power Research Inst., Palo Alto, Calif., 1973—. Bd. dirs. Nat. Conf. Christians and Jews, 1968—; mem. bd. ruling elders Presbyn. Ch., Evanston, Ill., 1971—, bd. dirs. Presbyn. Home, Evanston. Served to lt. M.C. USN, 1945-46, to lt. comdr., 1953-55. Diplomate Am. Bd. Surgery. Mem. A.C.S. (mem. Chgo. Com. on Trauma 1970—), Chgo. Heart Assn., Chgo., Western surg. socs., Soc. Surgery Alimentary Tract, Collegium Internationale Chirurgiae Digestivae, Inst. Medicine, Chgo., Ill. State med. socs., AMA, Indsl. Med. Assn., Am. Trauma Soc., McGraw Wildlife Found., Sigma Xi, Pi Kappa Epsilon, Phi Beta Pi. Clubs: Westmoreland Country (Wilmette, Ill.) (pres.); Internationale, Anglers, Campfire (Chgo.); Bull Valley Hunt (Woodstock, Ill.). Contbr. articles to profl. publs. Home: 3033 Normandy Pl Evanston IL 60201 Office: 707 N Fairbanks Ct Chicago IL 60611

MEHR, JOSEPH JOHN, psychologist; b. Chgo., June 23, 1941; s. Peter Joseph and Elizabeth Alma (Gartner) M.; B.A., Bradley U., 1963, M.A., 1964; Ph.D., Ill. Inst. Tech., 1971; m. Nancy Claire Harrison, Apr. 4, 1970; 1 son, Ian Jason. Psychology intern Chgo. State Hosp., 1964-65; dir. family therapy program Elgin (Ill.) State Hosp., 1965-68, dir. fed. mental health tng. project, 1968-70, asst. dir. extended care program, 1970-74, dir. spl. programs, 1974-77, chief psychologist, dir. intensive behavior therapy program, 1977—; prof. psychology Northeastern Ill. U., 1971-74; adj. prof. No. Ill. U., 1973—; vice-pres., dir. Center for Human Potential, Inc., Elgin, Ill., 1974—. Registered Psychologist, Ill.; Certified Service Provider in Psychology, Council for Nat. Register of Health Service Providers in Psychology. Mem. Am., Ill. psychol. assns., Assn. Mental Health Adminstr. Co-author (with W. Fisher, P. Truckenbrod) Power, Greed and Stupidity in the Mental Health Racket, 1973; (with W. Fisher, P. Truckenbrod) Human Services: The Third Revolution in Mental Health, 1974; co-editor (with R. Agranoff, W. Fisher, P. Truckenbrod) Explorations in Competency Module Development: Relinking Higher Education and the Human Services, 1975. Contbr. articles to profl. jours. Home: 1028 N Spring St Elgin IL 60120 Office: 750 S State St Elgin IL 60120

MEHTA, TUSHAR MAGANLAL, elec. engr.; b. Porbunder, India, June 9, 1945; b. Maganlal J. and Bhanumati K. (Dhruva) M.; m. Traya R. Mahida, Aug. 18, 1968; came to U.S., 1968, naturalized, 1976; M.S., Ill. Inst. Tech., 1969; M.B.A., Loyola U., Chgo., 1971. Registered profl. engr., Iowa, Ind., Minn., Wis. Various positions to asst. project engr. White City Electric Co., 1968-72; with Austin Co., Des Plaines, Ill., 1972—, elec. constrn. supt., 1975-76, chief elec. engr., 1976—. Mem. Ill. Soc. Profl. Engrs., Assn. Master Bus. Adminstrs., Ill. Inst. Tech., Loyola U. alumni assns., Gujarat Cultural Assn. Office: Austin Co 2001 Rand Rd Des Plaines IL 60016

MEHURON, GEORGE CAROL, cons. elec. engr.; b. Lincoln, Nebr., July 12, 1925; s. George Gerald and Esther (Sundean) M.; B.S., U. Nebr., 1950; m. Mary Boylston, Sept. 16, 1950; children—Tamar Ann, Katie Marie. Constr. engr. C.E., 1951-57; design engr. D.B. Stevenson, Des Moines, 1957-59, Henningson, Durham & Richardson, Omaha, 1959-62; elec. cons. engr. specializing in meat packing plants, Omaha, 1962-72; prin. Mehuron & Assos., Inc., Omaha, 1973—. Served with AUS, 1943-47. Mem. IEEE, Nat. Soc. Profl. Engrs., Illuminating Engrs. Soc. (sect. chmn. 1971-72). Home: 5115 S 77th Ave Ralston NE 68127 Office: 606 S 75th St Omaha NE 68114

MEIER, ALLEN JOHN, state ofcl.; b. Napoleon, N.D., Aug. 20, 1929; s. John August and Eldora L. (Shafer) M.; student Cedar Rapids Bus. Coll., 1949, AFL-CIO Studies Center, 1969, U. Iowa, U. Wis., 1961, U. Mo., 1971; m. Dolores Ann Farrens, Mar. 3, 1952; children—Robert, Ronald, Rodney, Denise, Debbie, Pamala. Bus. mgr. Internat. Brotherhood Elec. Workers, Cedar Rapids, Iowa, 1959-67; legis. dir. Iowa Fedn. Labor, Des Moines, 1968-77; labor commr. State of Iowa, 1977—. Rev. commr. Occupational Safety Health Act, 1972-77. Mem. Gov.'s Com. on Transp., 1972; mem. Iowa Legis. Com. on Land Use, 1972; mem. Iowa Arts Council, 1974, 75. Mem. city planning commn., Cedar Rapids, 1963-68. Mem. Ia. Fedn. Labor (v.p. 1967-77). Democrat. Methodist. Home: 1831 Ellis Blvd Cedar Rapids IA 52405 Office: Bur Labor State Capitol Des Moines IA 50319

MEIER, AUGUST, educator; b. N.Y.C., Apr. 30, 1923; s. Frank A. and Clara (Cohen) M.; A.B., Oberlin Coll., 1945; A.M., Columbia U., 1949, Ph.D., 1957. Asst. prof. history Tougaloo (Miss.) Coll., 1945-49; research asst. to pres. Fisk U., 1953, asst. prof. history, 1953-56; asst., then asso. prof. history Morgan State Coll., Balt., 1957-64; prof. history Roosevelt U., Chgo., 1964-67; prof. history Kent (Ohio) State U., 1967-69, univ. prof., 1969—. Sec., Newark br. NAACP, 1951-52, 56-57; chmn. Balt. chpt. Ams. Democratic Action, 1960-61, mem. nat. bd. and exec. com., 1960-61; active Newark chpt. CORE, 1963-64, Balt. chpt. SNCC, 1960-63. Advanced grad. fellow Am. Council Learned Socs., 1952; Guggenheim fellow, 1971-72; Nat. Endowment for Humanities fellow, 1975-76; Center for Advanced Study in Behavioral Scis., 1976-77. Mem. Am., So. hist. assns., Assn. Study Afro-Am. Life and History, Orgn. Am. Historians. Unitarian. Author: Negro Thought in America, 1880-1915, 1963; (with Elliott Rudwick) From Plantation to Ghetto, 1966, 3d edit., 1976; CORE: A Study in the Civil Rights Movement, 1942-68, 1973; (with E. Rudwick) Along the Color Line, 1976; editor: (with Francis Broderick) Negro Protest Thought in the Twentieth Century, 1966; (with Elliott Rudwick) The Making of Black America, 1969; (with John H. Bracey, E. Rudwick) Black Nationalism in America, 1970; (with others) Black Protest Thought in the Twentieth Century, 1971. Gen. editor Atheneum Pubs. for Negro in Am. Life Series, 1966-74, U. Ill. Press Blacks in the New World Series, 1972—; editorial adv. bd. Integrated Edn., 1964—, Booker T. Washington Papers, 1967—, Civil War History, 1970—, Jour. Am. History, 1974-77. Home: 122 N Prospect St Kent OH 44240 Office: Dept History Kent State U Kent OH 44242

MEIER, JOHN DALE, cons.; b. St. Charles, Mo., Oct. 22, 1942; s. Hadley J. and Mildred M. (Muhm) M.; B.S. in Bus., SE Mo. State U., 1964, M.A. in Psychology, 1969; m. Lydia Ann Bunch, Apr. 5, 1969; 1 dau., Gayle Elizabeth. Profl. baseball player St. Louis Cardinals, 1964-68; tchr., counselor, coach pub. schs., Cape Girardeau, Mo., 1968-73; cons. Grant Cooper & Assos., St. Louis, 1973—. Served with Army N.G., 1966-72. Named Outstanding Young Educator Cape Girardeau, Mo., 1971. Mem. Indsl. Relations Assn. St. Louis, Am. Personnel and Guidance Assn., Nat. Vocat. Guidance Assn., Nat. Employment Counselors Assn. Methodist. Home: PO Box 26642 Kirkwood MO 63122 Office: 2388 Schuetz Rd Suite 40 Saint Louis MO 63141

MEIER, WILBUR LEROY, JR., educator; b. Elgin, Tex., Jan. 3, 1939; s. Wilbur Leroy and Ruby (Hall) M.; B.S., U. Tex. at Austin, 1962, M.S., 1964, Ph.D., 1967; m. Judy Lee Longbotham, Aug. 30, 1958; children—Melynn, Marla, Melissa. Planning engr. Tex. Water Devel. Bd., Austin, 1962-66; research engr. U. Tex. at Austin, 1966-67; asst. prof. Tex. A and M U., College Station, 1967-68, asso. prof., 1968-70, prof. indsl. engring., 1970-72; prof., asst. head dept., 1972-73; prof., chmn. dept. indsl. engring. Iowa State U., 1973-74; prof., head sch. indsl. engring. Purdue U., 1974—; cons. Computer Graphics Internat. Inc., Bryan, Tex., Tex. Water Devel. Bd., Austin, Tex. Gov.'s Office, Austin, Water Resources Engrs., Inc., Walnut Creek, Calif., Environments for Tomorrow, Inc., Washington, Kaiser Engrs., Inc., Oakland, Calif. Named Outstanding Young Engr. of Year, Travis chpt. Tex. Soc. Profl. Engrs., 1966. Mem. Am. Inst. Indsl. Engrs. (past editor newsletter, regional chmn., program chmn., div. dir., chpt. pres.), Operations Research Soc. Am., Inst. Mgmt. Scis. (past v.p. sect.), ASCE (past br. sec.-treas., com. chmn.), Tex. Soc. Profl. Engrs. (past chpt. dir.), Am. Soc. Engring. Edn. (past pres. chpt., vice chmn. div.), Sigma Xi, Tau Beta Pi, Alpha Pi Mu (regional dir.), Chi Epsilon, Phi Kappa Phi. Rotarian. Contbr. articles to profl. jours. Home: 368 Overlook Dr West Lafayette IN 47906

MEIER, WILLARD CHARLES, lawyer; b. Chgo., Sept. 22, 1914; s. Edward and Florence (Kindt) M.; B.A., Denison U., 1936; J.D., DePaul U., 1940; m. Judith H. Howes, June 10, 1947; children—Barbara (Mrs. Thomas S. Johnston), Willard Charles. Admitted to Ill. bar, 1940; mem. firm Scott, MacLeish & Falk, Chgo., 1945-51; atty. Bachmann Uxbridge Worsted Corp., Uxbridge, Mass., 1951-55; mem. firm Plunkett, Nisen, Elliott & Meier, Chgo., 1955—; dir. Johnson Bros. Metal Forming Co., Berkeley, Ill., NASH Industries, Inc., Chgo., Jack Denst Designs, Inc., Chgo., Woodbridge Ornamental Iron Co., Chgo. Mem. Wilmette (Ill.) Harmony Conv. Served with USNR, 1941-45. Mem. Am., Ill., Chgo., Fed. bar assns., Am. Judicature Soc. (mem. antitrust com. 1970—). Clubs: Carousel (pres. 1971, dir. 1965) (Winnetka, Ill.); Sheridan Shore Yacht (dir. 1965) (Wilmette); The Attic (Chgo.). Home: 2525 Thornwood Ave Wilmette IL 60091 Office: 1N LaSalle St Chicago IL 60602

MEIER, WILLIAM GEORGE, location and mgmt. cons.; b. Beacon, N.Y., June 24, 1915; s. William G. and Lillian A. (Newman); B.M.E., N.Y. U., 1937; m. Phyllis Elizabeth Friend. With N.Y. Quinine and Chem. Works, 1937-38, S.B. Penick & Co., 1938-39; engring. positions with various divs. Am. Home Products Co., 1939-52, chief engr. nutritional div., 1941-49; with Wyeth Internat., Ltd., 1949-52; supt. engring. Parke, Davis & Co., Detroit, 1952-53, asst. dir. engring., 1953-61, dir. prodn., engring., 1962-64, v.p., 1964-67, adminstrv. v.p., 1968-70, sr. group v.p., 1970-71; pres. William G. Meier Assos., location cons., Detroit, 1971—. Co-founder Found. for Exceptional Children, Inc.; hon. trustee Nat. Cystic Fibrosis Research Found.; bd. dirs. Mich. Epilepsy Center and Assn., Edward W. Sparrow Hosp., Mason Gen. Hosp. Corp. Registered profl. engr., N.Y., Mich. Clubs: World Trade, Boat, Athletic, Econ. (Detroit). Home: 400 E Elm St Mason MI 48854

MEISEL, JEROME, educator; b. Cleve., Aug. 9, 1934; s. David and Anne Irene (Meisel) Marmorstein; B.S.E.E., Case Inst., 1956, Ph.D., 1961; M.S.E.E., Mass. Inst. Tech., 1957; children—Denise Lauren, David Marc. Asst. prof. elec. engring. Case Inst., 1960-65; mem. tech. staff Bell Telephone Labs., Holmdel, N.J., 1965-66; asso. prof. elec. engring. Wayne State U., 1966-70, prof., 1970—; cons. in field. Union Carbide fellow; Mpls. Honneywell fellow. Mem. IEEE. Author: Principles of Electromechanical Energy Conversion, 1966. Contbr. articles in field to profl. jours. Home: 2190 W Lincoln St Birmingham MI 48009 Office: Department of Electrical Engineering Wayne State University Detroit MI 48202

MEISINGER, GEORGE FREDRICK, psychiatrist; b. Detroit, Nov. 6, 1915; s. Charles Edward and Bertha (Kuntz) M.; B.S., U. Detroit, 1938; M.D., Loyola U., Chgo., 1943; m. Lolita M. Lieske, Dec. 26, 1941; children—Patricia (Mrs. David W. Wirtz), Janice (Mrs. James Michels), Joann, Peter, James, Philip. Resident Danville (Pa.) State Hosp., 1947-48; cons. Wis. Dept. Div. Corrections, 1947-62; practice medicine specializing in psychiatry, Milw., 1949-62, Fond du Lac, 1962—; mem. staff St. Agnes Hosp., Fond du Lac, Wis.; dir. guidance clinics Dodge County and Fond du Lac County (Wis.), 1949—. Tchr., clin. prof. Marquette Med. Sch., 1948-49; instr. anatomy and physiology, Alverno Nursing Sch., Milw., 1948-62. Served with USNR, 1943-47. Mem. AMA, Wis., Fond du Lac (pres. 1970-71) med. socs., Am., Wis. (sec. north chpt. 1972-73) psychiat. assns., Wis. Assn. Child Guidance Clinics (pres. 1965-66). Home: Route 3 Box 233C Fond du Lac WI 54935 Office: 153 S Macy St Fond du Lac WI 54935

MEISSE, GUNTHER SAGEL, radio sta. exec.; b. Mansfield, Ohio, Nov. 28, 1942; s. Louis Albert and Barbara Marka (Sagel) M.; grad. high sch., Mansfield; m. Carol Lee McGinty, Mar. 9, 1963; children—Marka, Melinda, Gunther Sagel II, Robert. Salesman Service Audio Cons., 1956-61; part-time engring. radio stas. WMAN and WCLW, Mansfield, 1956-60; one of founders Johnny Appleseed Broadcasting Co. and radio sta. WVNO, Mansfield, 1961—, gen. mgr., v.p., 1962-74, pres., 1974-76; treas. Hi-Stat Mfg. Co., 1971—; mem. adv. bd. Richland Trust Co., 1972—. Bd. dirs. Planned Parenthood, 1973. Mem. Mansfield Area C. of C. (dir. 1970-75), Advt. Club (past dir.), North Central Ohio Marketing Club (past dir.), Nat. Assn. FM Broadcasters (dir. 1964-73, 75-76), FM Broadcast Pioneers (charter), Ohio Assn. Broadcasters (dir. 1975—, v.p. 1977-78). Rotarian. Home: Marion Ave Rd Mansfield OH 44903 Office: 2900 Park Ave W Mansfield OH 44906

MEISTER, RAYMOND ALBERT, indsl. engr.; b. Cleve., Sept. 23, 1938; s. Rudolph A. and Elizabeth (Glauche) M.; student Olivet Nazarene Coll., 1961-63; B.S., Ohio State U., 1968; M.B.A., Xavier U., 1973; m. Mary Jean Wilhoyte, Oct. 21, 1961; children—Raymond Albert, Michelle Rae, Maria Elizabeth. Draftsman Marquette Div., Cleve., 1957-59; design draftsman Towmotor Corp., Mentor, Ohio, 1959-61, John L. Fuller & Asso., Cleve., 1960-63, Hoist Equipment

Co., Bedford Heights, Ohio, 1963-64, Jervis B. Webb, Avon Lake, Ohio, 1964, CVI Corp., Hilliard, Ohio, 1965-66; indsl. engr. Alden E. Stilson & Assoc., cons. engrs., Columbus, Ohio, 1966-68, project mgr., 1968-73, asso., 1973-74; v.p. Robert S. Curl & Assos., cons. engrs., Columbus, 1974-76; engring. dir. Kuempel Co., Columbus and Cin., 1977—; pres. Innovative Devel. Unltd., Hilliard, 1973—. Adj. asst. prof. advanced mgmt. theory Xavier U., Cin., 1974—. Registered profl. engr., Ohio, Ky., Ind., W. Va., Calif., Pa., Mich. Mem. Am. Inst. Indsl. Engrs. (prodn. and quality control regional dir.), Nat., Ohio socs. profl. engrs., Am. Inst. Plant Engrs. (sec.), Profl. Engrs. Pvt. Practice, Internat. Platform Assn. Mem. Ch. of the Nazarene (chmn. bd. trustees, dir. Christian service tng., Sunday sch. supt.). Home and office: 3750 Smiley Rd Hilliard OH 43026

MEISTER, RICHARD THOMAS, editor, pub.; b. Cleve., Feb. 11, 1919; s. Edward George and Elsie (Giesen) M.; B.S., Cornell U., 1940; M.B.A., Harvard U., 1943; m. Lila Elizabeth Janes, Jan. 28, 1943; children—Cathy E., Linda S., Deborah D. Editor, Am. Fruit Grower Pub. Co., 1946-54; editorial dir., gen. mgr. Meister Pub. Co., Willoughby, Ohio, 1954—; dir. Lake County Nat. Bank, 1970—. Councilman, Village of Waite Hill, 1970-78. Served to capt. U.S. Army, 1943-46. Mem. Am. Soc. Hort. Sci., Ohio State Hort. Soc., Am. Agrl. Editors Assn., Chi Psi. Episcopalian. Club: Kirtland Country. Home: Hobart Rd RD 3 Willoughby OH 44094 Office: 37841 Euclid Ave Willoughby OH 44094

MEITNER, RAYMOND JOHN, realtor; b. Kansas City, Kans., July 27, 1918; s. John Rudolph and Frances Mary (Luebbert) M.; student Kansas City Jr. Coll., 1936-38; m. Barbara Pigg, Sept. 2, 1940; children—Barbara (Mrs. Timothy R. Emert), Phillip R., Raymond John II, John. Salesman, Jimmie Tank Realty, Kansas City, Kans., 1946-49; partner Meitner & Preston realtors, Shawnee Mission, Kans., 1949-59, prin. Ray Meitner & Co., 1959-76; prin. Ray Meitner & Co., Overland Park, Kans., 1969—, Century 21 Meitner Realtors, 1977—. Sec.-treas. M & P Constrn. Co., Shawnee Mission, 1949-59. Mem. Planning Commn., Kansas City, Kans., 1947-49, Roeland Park, Kan., 1958-60; mem. Planning Commn., Lenexa, Kans., 1971-74, chmn., 1974-75; mem. Westwood (Kans.) City Council, 1951-53. Served as pilot USAAF, 1944-46. Named Johnson County Realtor of Year, 1961, Kans. Realtor of Year, 1963. Mem. Johnson County Bd. Realtors (pres. 1953, Nat. Assn. Realtors nat. dir. 1966-67), Kans. Assn. Realtors (pres. 1967). Roman Catholic. Home: 12405 W 100th Pl Lenexa KS 66215 Office: 10063 Santa Fe Dr Overland Park KS 66212

MEJER, ROBERT LEE, artist, educator, gallery exec.; b. South Bend, Ind., Nov. 8, 1944; B.S., Ball State U., 1966; M.F.A., Miami U., Oxford, Ohio, 1968; postgrad. St. Mary's Coll., Notre Dame, summer 1968, Kent State U., summer 1973, Kalamazoo Inst. Art, summer 1975, Ox-Box Summer Sch. Art, summers 1976, 77; 1 child. Teaching asst. South Bend Art Center, 1960-62; instr. adult water color classes Muncie Artist's Guild, 1963; teaching asst. Ball State U., 1964-66, art gallery asst., 1962-66; instr. Ball State Art Workshop, summer 1966, 67; grad. teaching asst. Miami U., Oxford, 1966-68; asso. prof. art, gallery dir. Quincy (Ill.) Coll., 1968—; instr. Quincy Art Center, 1970-71, 76; vis. artist Twin Rivers Art League, Pittsfield, Ill., 1971; exhibited in one-man shows Womens Progress Club, South Bend, 1961, 68, St. Mary's Coll., 1964, 67, 70, Ball State Art Gallery, 1965, 67, Miami U., 1966, 67, 68, Quincy Coll., 1968, 69, Progressive Playhouse, Quincy, 1969-72, Culver Stockton Coll., Mo., 1970, 74, Ill. Spring Mus., Springfield, 1972, Western Ill. U., Macomb, 1971, Western Coll., Oxford, Ohio, 1968, David Strawn Art Gallery, Jacksonville, Ill., 1971, Limestone Coll., Gaffney, S.D., 1972, Anderson (Ind.) Fine Arts Center, 1973, Jane Shair Gallery, 1972, Tony's Art Gallery, 1973, Ill. Arts Council, Chgo., 1975; exhibited in group shows South Bend Art Center, 1960-62, Durban Art Gallery, Cape Town, South Africa, 1962, Karridene Gallery, Capetown, 1962, Johannesburg Library, Nappanee, Ind., 1962, Radecki Art Galleries, 1961, Muncie Artists Guild, 1963-64, Ball State U. Student Show, 1963, 64, 65, 66, Taylor U., 1964, Ball State Tchrs. Coll. Faculty Art Exhibit, 1964, Ball State Fine Arts Com. Gallery, 1964, Ball Art Center Gallery, 1965-67, Ball State Art Festival, 1965, Morris Civic Auditorium, 1966, Miami U. Faculty Show, 1967, Lima (Ohio) Art Center, 1967, Middletown (Ohio) Gallery, Miami Faculty Exhibit, 1968, Upstairs Gallery, South Bend, 1963-64, Ball State Exhbn., 1964, Oxford Art Center, 1967, Miami U. Union Gallery, 1968, Mother Seton High Sch., Chgo., 1968, Faculty Drawing Show Quincy Coll., 1968, 70, 72, 73, 74, 75, Wilberforce U., 1968, Lake Erie Coll., Parnesville, (Ohio), 1968, Butler Inst. Am. Art, Youngstown, Ohio, Wilmington (Ohio) Coll., 1968, Rio Grande, Ohio, 1968, Antioch Coll., Yellow Springs, Ohio, Findlay Coll., Ashland Coll., Malone Coll., Canton, Ohio, Equity Financial Corp., Hamilton, Ohio, Ball State U. 50th Anniversary Invitational Alumni Show, N.E. Mo. State Coll., 1973, Wabash Transit Gallery, 1972, Highland Park Gallery, 1972, Max 24-72 Nat. Painting Exhbn. Purdue U., 1972, Quincy Art Center Regional Exhbn., 1968-73, 27th Ill. Invitational Exhbn., Ill. State Mus., 1974, 28th Ill. State Fair Profl. Art Show, 1974, Western Ill. Watercolor Show, Galesburg, 1976, 31st Ill. State Fair Profl. Art Show, 1977, others. Recipient numerous awards including Outstanding Tchr. award Quincy Coll., 1974; 2d place watercolors 31st Ill. State Fair Profl. Art Show, 1977. Faculty devel. grantee, 1975, 76, 77. Mem. Nat. Art Edn. Assn., Ill. Art Edn. Assn. (exec. com.), Am. Fedn. Arts, Pratt Graphics Center, Internat. Platform Assn., N. Central Assn. Com., Delta Phi Delta. Contbr. articles to profl. jours. Two monoprints selected for inclusion in Smithsonian's Traveling Show: New American Monotypes, 1978-80. Office: Art Dept Quincy Coll Quincy IL 62301

MELAMED, LEO, lawyer, investment co. exec.; b. Bialystok, Poland, Mar. 20, 1932; s. Isaac M. and Fygla (Barakin) M.; came to U.S., 1941, naturalized, 1955; student U. Ill., 1950-52; LL.D., John Marshall Law Sch., 1955; m. Betty Sattler, Dec. 26, 1953; children—Idelle Sharon, Jordan Norman, David Jeffery. Admitted to Ill. bar, 1955; sr. partner firm Melamed, Kravitz & Verson, Chgo., 1956-66; pres. Dellsher Investment Co. Inc., Chgo., 1965—; chmn. Melamed, Wetterling & Fawcett, Inc., Chgo., 1977—. Mem. Chgo. Merc. Exchange, 1953—, gov., 1967—, sec. bd., 1967-69, 71-75, chmn. bd., 1969-71, 75-77; chmn. bd. Internat. Monetary Market, 1972-75; mem. Chgo. Bd. Trade, 1969—; mem. Chgo. Mayor's Council Manpower and Econ. Advisers, 1972—. Pres. North Suburban Yiddish Sch. Orgn., Skokie, Ill., 1967—. Named Man of Year, Israel Bonds, 1975. Mem. Am., Ill., Chgo. bar assns., Am. Judicature Soc., Am. Contract Bridge League (life master). Home: 350 Sunrise Circle Glencoe IL 60022 Office: 222 S Riverside Plaza Chicago IL 60606

MELCHER, MAURICE ARNOLD, mfg. co. exec.; b. Platte Center, Nebr., Jan. 26, 1930; s. Arnold Joseph and Sylvia Elizabeth (Langan) M.; A.A., Norfolk Jr. Coll., 1954; B.S., U. Nebr., 1957; m. Judith Marie Tylle, Oct. 28, 1961; children—Scott, Christine, Marin. Design engr. Kosch Co., Columbus, Nebr., 1957-69; pres. Indsl. Engring. Co., Columbus, 1970—. Served with USMC, 1948-52. Mem. ASME. Roman Catholic. Clubs: Optimists, K.C. Developer high speed tube cutting machine. Home: 2754 14th Ave E Columbus NE 68601 Office: Canal Industrial Park Columbus NE 68601

MELDMAN, ROBERT EDWARD, lawyer; b. Milw. Aug. 5; s. Louis Leo and Lillian (Gollusch) M.; B.S., U. Wis., 1959; LL.B., Marquette U., 1962; LL.M. in Taxation, N.Y. U., 1963; m. Sandra Jane Setlick, July 24, 1960; children—Saree Beth, Richard Samuel. Admitted to Wis. bar, 1962, U.S. Tax Ct., 1963, U.S. Supreme Ct. bar, 1970, U.S. Ct. Claims, 1971; practice tax law, Milw., 1963—; lectr. taxation U. Wis. at Milw. Mem. Am., Fed. (pres. Milw. 1966-67), Milw. (chmn. tax sect. 1970-71), bar assns., Wis. State Bar (dir. tax sect. 1964—, chmn. 1973-74), Marquette Law Alumni (dir. 1972-77), Phi Delta Phi, Tau Epsilon Rho (chancellor Milw. 1969-71, supreme nat. chancellor 1975-76). Jewish (trustee congregation). Mem. B'nai B'rith (Ralph Harris meml. award Century Lodge, 1969-70; trustee). Contbr. articles to legal jours. Home: 9015 N King Rd Milwaukee WI 53217 Office: 788 N Jefferson St Milwaukee WI 53202

MELENDY, EARLE RICHARD, musician, condr.; b. Brockton, Mass., May 26, 1925; s. Harold Arthur and Rose (Blum) M.; B.S., Wayne State U., 1947; Mus.M., Wayne State U., 1948; Ed.D., U. Va., 1955; m. Gene Phylus, Sept. 2, 1950; children—Lane, Leah, Lori, Luke. Concert violinist Detroit Symphony, 1948-50; violinist Mich. Opera, 1946-50; condr. Velvet Strings orch., 1946-50; condr., head string dept. Shenandoah Coll., 1950-52; condr., dir. music edn. U. Maine, 1954-57; concertmaster, soloist Terre Haute (Ind.) Symphony Orch., 1957—: dir. orchs., prof. music Ind. State U., Terre Haute, 1957—, founder, dir. Univ. Sinfonietta, 1957—; dir. mus. program TV series, 1957-68; soloist, guest condr. many high sch. instrumental programs; adjudicator, clinician in pub. schs. over country; mem. Performing Artist & Lecture Service, 1957—. Served with USAAF and Signal Corps, AUS, 1942-46; PTO. Decorated Bronze Star. Mem. AAUP, Fedn. Musicians, Nat. Sch. Orchs., Music Educators Nat. Conf., Mu Alpha Epsilon, Phi Delta Kappa, Phi Mu Alpha Sinfonia. Home: Box 186 9636 S 34th Pl Holly Hills Rural Route 22 Terre Haute IN 47802

MELHORN, J. JACK, ednl. adminstr.; b. York, Pa., Feb. 10, 1921; s. Bertus Jacob and Phebe (King) M.; B.A., Elizabethtown Coll., 1944, LL.D., 1965; B.D., Yale Div. Sch., 1947; M.A., U. So. Calif., 1956, Ph.D., 1967; m. Mary Louise Woody, June 6, 1948; children—John Mark, Linda Mary, Kent Edward. Instr., Arnold Coll., New Haven, 1945-47; asso. prof. LaVerne (Calif.) Coll., 1947-65; pres. prof. McPherson (Kan.) Coll., 1965-72; prof., chmn. sociology and anthropology Emporia (Kans.) State Coll., 1972—. Mem. Am., Midwest sociol. assns., Am. Assn. Higher Edn., Alpha Kappa Delta, Phi Delta Kappa. Home: 2189 Morningside Dr Emporia KS 66801

MELHORN, WILTON NEWTON, educator; b. Sistersville, W.Va., July 8, 1921; s. Ralph Wilton and Pauline (Jones) M.; B.S., Mich. State U., 1942, M.S., 1951; M.S., N.Y. U., 1943; Ph.D., U. Mich., 1955; m. Agnes Leigh Beck, Aug. 25, 1961; children—Kristina L., Kimberly M. Hydrogeologist, Mich. Geol. Survey, Lansing, 1946-49; hydrologist U.S. Weather Bur., Indpls., 1949-50; asst., asso. prof. engring. geology Purdue U., Lafayette, 1954-70, head dept. geoscis., 1967-70, prof., 1970—. Vis. prof. U. Ill., Urbana, 1960-61; vis. prof. U. Nev., Reno, 1971-72, adj. prof., 1973—; geol. cons. including Cook County Hwy. Commn., Chgo., 1955-56, Martin-Marietta Corp., Balt., 1964-66, Cal. Nuclear, Inc., Lafayette, 1966-68. Served to maj. USAAF, 1942-46. Fellow Geol. Soc. Am., A.A.A.S.; mem. Am. Assn. Petroleum Geologists, Soc. Econ. Geologists and Paleontologists, Speleological Soc., Ind. Acad. Scis., Mich. Acad. Arts, Sci. and Letters, Am. Meteorol. Soc., Clay Minerals Soc., Sigma Xi, Sigma Gamma Epsilon, Delta Chi. Contbr. articles to profl. jours. Home: 2065 S 9th St Lafayette IN 47905

MELICK, ROBERT LOUIS, accountant; b. Toledo, Dec. 8, 1931; s. Louis Lanning and Mary Alice (Swallow) M.; A.B., Princeton U., 1953; M.B.A., Harvard U., 1957; m. Katherine Jordan, July 11, 1964; children—Jordan Robert, Ariste Alice. With Price Waterhouse & Co., Detroit, 1957—, mgr., 1963—. Served to 1st lt. AUS, 1953-55. Club: Lochmoor. Home: 7 Carmel Lane Grosse Pointe Farms MI 48236 Office: 200 Renaissance Center Detroit MI 48243

MELLMAN, HARRY GEORGE, educator; b. St. Louis, Feb. 22, 1916; s. Jacob and Henrietta (Dobinsky) M.; A.B. with final honors, Washington U., St. Louis, 1935, A.M., 1936; Ph.D., U. Ill., 1940; m. Mildred Gendler, June 1, 1947; children—Robert E., Richard B., George S. Asst. in polit. sci. Washington U., 1934-35, asst. in history, 1936-37; instr. polit. sci. U. Ill., 1938-40; nat. field sec., dir. Met. N.Y., dir. U. Chgo. Hillel Found., 1940-43; recruiting rep. U.S. Civil Service Commn., 1943-44; adminstrv. asst. St. Louis Ordnance Dist., 1945; pres. Harry Mellman Co., St. Louis, 1945-66; dir. financial aids and found. relations Webster Coll., 1966-67; on assigment by pres. St. Louis U., 1968; dir. govtl. and community programs, Extension div. U. Mo., St. Louis, 1968-70, lectr. polit. sci., 1968—, lectr. administrn. justice, 1974-75, also adviser pre-law students. Lectr., St. Louis U., 1947-51. Commr. St. Louis Commn. Crime and Law Enforcement, 1970-73. Bd. dirs. Hillel Found. St. Louis, 1971-75, mem. exec. com., 1974-75. Recipient Distinguished Mfrs. Salesman award Nat. Toy Wholesalers Assn., 1962. Mem. Am. Polit. Sci. Assn., Nat. Municipal League, A.A.A.S., Am. Acad. Polit. and Social Scis., Am. Soc. Pub. Adminstrn. Jewish. Contbr. books revs. to profl. publs. Home: 7116 Waterman Ave University City MO 63130 Office: 8001 Natural Bridge Rd St Louis MO 63121

MELNICOFF, IRA LEE, rheumatologist, physician; b. Washington, Sept. 8, 1941; s. Ben Ivan and Iola Bernice (Elstein) M.; B.A., U. Va., 1963; M.S. in Cellular Physiology and Cell Biochemistry, W.Va. U., 1966; D.O., Chgo. Coll. Osteo. Medicine, 1970; m. Lorraine Janet Billowitz, June 19, 1965; children—Shara Byrne, Jared Benjamin. Intern Nassau County Med. Center, East Meadow, N.Y., 1970-71; resident in medicine Brown U.-R.I. Hosp., Providence, 1971-72; fellow in rheumatology and clin. immunology Roger Williams Gen. Hosp., Providence, 1972-74; research fellow bio-med. scis. Brown U., Providence, 1972-73, teaching fellow, 1973-74, research asso., 1973-74, instr. medicine, 1974; practice medicine specializing in rheumatology, Chgo., 1974—; chief rheumatology-clin. immunology Chgo. Osteo. Hosp., 1974—; asst. prof. medicine Chgo. Coll. Osteo. Medicine, 1974—; attending rheumatologist Luth. Gen. Hosp. Diplomate Nat. Bd. Med. Examiners, Am. Bd. Internal Medicine. Mem. R.I. Arthritis Found., New. Eng. Rheumatism Soc., A.C.P., Am. Rheumatism Assn., Chgo. Arthritis Found., Chgo. Rheumatism Soc., Chgo. Found. for Med. Care, Am. Soc. Internal Medicine, Chgo., Ill. med. socs., Am. Osteo. Coll. Rheumatology, Chgo. Soc. Internal Medicine. Contbr. articles to med. jours. Home: 3048 Moon Hill Dr Northbrook IL 60642 Office: 5200 S Ellis Ave Chicago IL 60615

MELOY, HAROLD H., lawyer; b. Waldron, Ind., Nov. 29, 1913; s. James Henry and Pearl (Haymond) M.; LL.B., Ind. U., 1939; m. Loretta Marie Schrader, Sept. 9, 1951. Admitted to Ind. bar, 1939; practice law, Shelbyville, Ind., 1939—; historian Mammoth Cave, 1960—; lectr. on history, legends and folklore of Mammoth Cave. Pros. atty. for 16th Jud. Circuit Ct. of Ind., 1945-50; city judge, Shelbyville, 1956. Bd. dirs. Maj. Hosp. Found., Shelbyville, pres., 1976—; mem. adv. bd. Shelbyville Salvation Army, chmn., 1971-72; Served with AUS, 1941-43. Fellow Nat. Speleol. Soc.; mem. Am. Spelean History Assn. (dir. 1968—), Shelby County Bar Assn. (pres. 1958), Cave Research Found., Mammoth Cave Nat. Park Assn. (dir. 1974—). Democrat. Methodist. Mason (Shriner). Elk. Author: Mummies of Mammoth Cave, 1968, 6th edit., 1977. Contbr. numerous articles on history of Mammoth Cave to various jours. Home: PO Box 454 Shelbyville IN 46176 Office: 302 Methodist Bldg PO Box 454 Shelbyville IN 46176

MELOY, LORETTA MARIE SCHRADER, lawyer; b. Shelbyville, Ind., Apr. 26, 1924; d. Conrad and Anna Elisabeth (Kranz) Schrader; B.S., Ind. U., 1946, J.D. (Wendell Willkie law scholar), 1968; m. Harold Meloy, Sept. 9, 1951. Admitted to Ind. bar, 1969; individual practice law, Shelbyville, 1969—; judge City Ct. Shelbyville, 1972-76. Address: PO Box 454 Shelbyville IN 46176

MELTON, ALTON RAY, mech. engr.; b. Lee County, Va., Oct. 10, 1931; s. Willie and Gladys (Lively) M.; B.S.M.E., U. Ky., 1954; m. Elizabeth Jean Richards, Jan. 29, 1950; children—Cynthia Rae, Tommy Ray. Plant mgr. Logan Long Co., Franklin, Ohio, 1958-65; asst. plant mgr. Philip Carey Mfg. Co., Lockland, Ohio, 1965-66; chief engr. Beckett Paper Co., Hamilton, Ohio, 1966—. Deacon Berea Baptist Ch., Middletown, Ohio. Mem. Paper Industry Mgmt. Assn., TAPPI. Home: 402 N Miami St Trenton OH 45067 Office: 400 Dayton St Hamilton OH 45011

MELVIN, CRUSE DOUGLAS, scientist; b. Emilee, Tex., June 5, 1942; s. Richard Sherman and Laura Ethel (Weaver) M.; student Lamar State Coll. Tech., 1960-62; B.S., Stephen F. Austin U., 1964, M.S., 1965; Ph.D., Tulane U., 1971; m. Sharron Baker, May 20, 1964. Instr. physics Stephen F. Austin U., Nacogdoches, Tex., 1965-66; asst. prof. physics Nichols State U., Thibodaux, La., 1966-70; sr. scientist, group leader sci. research staff Ford Motor Co., Dearborn, Mich., 1971-72, staff scientist, supr. engring. and research staff, 1972-77; asso. prof. physics Delta State U., Cleveland, Miss., 1977—. Presdl. scholar Electron Microscopy Soc. Am., 1970. Mem. Am. Assn. Physics Tchrs., Electron Microscopy Soc. Am., Sigma Pi Sigma. Baptist (chmn. deacons). Home: 1612 Terrace Rd Cleveland MS 38732 Office: PO Box 3255 Delta State U Cleveland MS 38732

MELVIN, PETER JOSEPH, math. astronomer, educator; b. Seattle, Mar. 12, 1944; s. William Leopold and Virginia (Stevens) M.; B.A., Western Wash. State Coll., 1965; M.S., U. Ill., Urbana, 1966, Ph.D., 1970; m. Alice Sue Pfiester, May 25, 1975. NASA trainee, 1966-68; instr. phys. sci. U. Ill., Urbana, 1970-72, asst. prof. phys. sci., liberal arts and scis. adminstrn., 1972—. Mem. Soc. Indsl. and Applied Math., Am. Math. Soc. Contbr. An International Symposium on Dynamical Systems, 1977; contbr. articles to profl. jours. Research on nonlinear ordinary differential equations, pulsation theory of variable stars.

MELVIN, RONALD MCKNIGHT, investment co. exec.; b. Regina, Sask., Can., Oct. 25, 1927; s. M. Gordon and Mary Gillespie (McKnight) M.; B. Commerce, U. B.C., 1949; m. Gwen Ellis, Apr. 30, 1955; children—Mary McKnight, Catharine Hastings. Came to U.S., 1953, naturalized, 1972. Various positions Powell River Co., Ltd., Vancouver, B.C., and Chgo. 1947-56; asst. to pres. Trans Union Corp., Chgo., 1956-58, mng. dir. subs. Procor Ltd., Toronto, Ont., Can., 1958-64; partner Blunt Ellis & Simmons, investment banking, Chgo., 1964-71 (firm inc. 1971), pres., 1972—; dir. Chef Pierre, Inc. Chmn. Chgo. adv. council Episcopal Ch. Found., 1974-76. Bd. govs. United Republican Fund Ill., 1972—; bd. dirs. Chgo. Old People's Home, 1977—. Mem. Securities Industry Assn. (chmn. Mid-Continental dist. 1977-78), Alpha Delta Phi. Episcopalian (vestryman 1970-74). Clubs: Racquet (bd. govs. 1965-71), Chicago, Casino (treas. 1971-73, Chgo.); Mill Creek Hunt (Wadsworth, Ill.); Attic. Home: 1143 N Green Bay Rd Lake Forest IL 60045 Office: 111 W Monroe St Chicago IL 60603

MELVOLD, ROBERT THOMSON, newspaper publisher; b. Cresco, Iowa, Aug. 22, 1918; s. Clarence T. and Mae Evelyn (Thomson) M.; B.A., U. Iowa, 1940; m. Frances Dale Elwood, Feb. 18, 1944; children—Douglas, Miriam, Janis, John, Annettee, Robert Brand. Editor-pub. Maquoketa (Iowa) Newspapers, 1946—; sr. partner, co-pub. DeWitt (Iowa) Observer, 1954—, Galena (Ill.) Gazette, 1961—, Stockton (Ill.) Herald-News, 1968—, Eldridge (Iowa) North Scott Press, 1968—; pres. Tri-State Graphics Co., Maquoketa, 1973—, Dubuque (Iowa) EconoPrint, 1974—, Cedar Rapids (Iowa) EconoPrint, 1976—; chmn. Jackson County Econ. Devel. Adminstrn., 1969-77; speaker, cons. in field. Served to lt. comdt. USNR, 1940-45. Mem. Nat. Newspaper Assn., Iowa Press Assn. (named Master Editor-Pub. 1970), Maquoketa C. of C. (chmn. indsl. devel. com. 1965-69), Sigma Delta Chi. Republican. Conglist. Clubs: Rotary, K.P. Home: Pershing Rd Maquoketa IA 52060 Office: 108 W Quarry St Maquoketa IA 52060

MENDELL, DONALD PRATT, chem. engr.; b. Bklyn., Dec. 29, 1933; s. Arthur W.P. and Helen M. (Clamp) M.; B.Chem. Engring., Rensselaer Poly. Inst., 1955; m. Ann C. Gregory, Oct. 15, 1960; children—Sarah, Thomas, Andrew. With M.W. Kellogg Co., South Plainfield, N.J., 1956-70, mgr. instrument and systems dept., 1965-70; asso. engr. control systems Mobil Oil Co., Princeton, N.J., 1970-71; dir. process engring. dept. Procon, Inc., Des Plaines, Ill., 1975-76, mgr. proposal dept., 1976—. Mem. Instrument Soc. Am. (pres. 1976-77), Am. Inst. Chem. Engrs. Methodist (trustee 1974-77). Home: 448 Eton Dr Barrington IL 60010 Office: 30 UOP Plaza Des Plaines IL 60016

MENDELSOHN, HARVEY JOSEPH, thoracic surgeon; b. Cleve., Sept. 14, 1911; s. Albert and Lena (Bernstein) M.; A.B., Western Res. U., 1933, M.D., 1936; m. Judith Agronsky, Oct. 19, 1947; children—Ruth, Michael, Daniel. Intern, resident in surgery Cleve. City Hosp., 1936-41, resident in thoracic surgery, 1946-47; practice medicine specializing in thoracic surgery, Cleve., 1947—; cons. thoracic surgery VA Hosps., 1951—; thoracic surgeon Univ. Hosps. Cleve., 1961—, Met. Gen. Hosps., Cleve., 1973—; prof. thoracic surgery Case Western Res. U., Cleve., 1972—. Served from lt. to maj. M.C., U.S. Army, 1941-45. Mem. AMA, Am. Assn. Thoracic Surgery, Soc. Thoracic Surgeons, Cleve. Acad. Medicine. Home: 29126 Bolingbrook Rd Pepper Pike OH 44124 Office: 2065 Adelbert Rd Cleveland OH 44106

MENDELSOHN, LAWRENCE VICTOR, physician; b. Detroit, Mich., Oct. 29, 1939; s. Max and Jean (Baron) M.; B.S., Mich. State U., 1961; M.D., U. Louisville, 1965; m. Jane Ellen Hessel, Mar. 20, 1966; children—Eva Rachel, David Joseph. Intern Detroit Gen. Hosp., 1965-66; resident in internal medicine Sinai Hosp. Detroit, 1966-68; fellow in endocrinology and metabolism, U. Pitts., 1968-69; chief endocrinology Brooke Gen. Hosp., Fort Sam Houston, Tex., 1969-71; clin. instr. U. Tex. Med. Sch., San Antonio, 1970; asst. attending physician Sinai Hosp. Detroit, 1971, asst. chief endocrinology, 1977—; asst. clin. prof. Waynee State U., Detroit, 1976—; practice medicine specializing in internal medicine, endocrinology and metabolism, Detroit, 1971—. Served with M.C., U.S. Army, 1969-71. Diplomate Am. Bd. Internal Medicine. Mem. AMA, Am. Diabetic Assn., Mich., Wayne County med. socs., Endocrine Soc. Contbr. articles to profl. jours. Address: 16500 N Park Dr Suite 101 Southfield MI 48075

MENDELSON, FRIEDA GARFINKEL, apparel co. exec.; b. Kansas City, Mo.; d. Jacob and Della (Baum) Bercu; m. Alec Mendelson; children—Arnold Garfinkel, Richard Garfinkel. Sec., Diamond Jewelry Co., Kansas City, 1940—; sec., bookkeeper Oppenstein Jewelry Co., Kansas City, 1972—; pres. Maurice Coat & Suit Co., Kansas City, 1964-70. Bd. dirs. Beth Shalom Synagogue, Jewish Community Center, Jewish Fedn. Mem. Jewish Geriatric Centers (life), Nat. Council Jewish Women (life), Brandeis Univ. Women (life), Menorah Med. Center (life). Home: 121 W 48th St W Kansas City MO 64112

MENDENHALL, ELWOOD HIRST, realtor; b. Winchester, Ind., Mar. 21, 1919; s. Arthur Monroe and Ella (Acker) M.; student Butler U., 1937-39; B.J., U. Mo., 1941; m. Mary Jane McDonnell, July 17, 1943; children—Richard Albert, Thomas Clark. Partner McDonnell Realty Co., Columbia, Mo., 1949-55, pres., 1955-64; pres. Boone Realty Corp., Columbia, 1964-74, chmn. bd., 1974—. Mem. exec. bd. Great Rivers council Boy Scouts Am., 1959—. Chmn. Boone County Welfare Commn., 1959—. Served to 1st lt. USAAF, 1943-45. Decorated D.F.C., Air medal with 13 oak leaf clusters. Recipient Silver Beaver award Boy Scouts Am., Realtor of Year award Columbia Bd. Realtors, 1969. Mem. Nat. Inst. Real Estate Brokers (bd. govs. 1969-73), Am. Legion, Phi Delta Theta. Kiwanian. Club: Pachyderm. Home: 705 Eastlake Dr Columbia MO 65201 Office: 15 E Broadway Columbia MO 65201

MENDHEIM, JOHN MURRAY, mgmt. cons. co. exec.; b. Berlin, May 24, 1926; s. Salli M. and Feodora (Weisshaus) M.; came to U.S., 1940, naturalized, 1943; B.A. in Psychology, Northwestern U., 1949, M.B.A., 1953; m. Stephanie LaCroix, May 3, 1976; 1 son, Justin; children by previous marriage—Kim, Michael. Corporate personnel dir. Solo Cup Corp., 1958-60, Griffith Labs., 1960-64; v.p. personnel Kitchens of Sara Lee div. Consol. Foods, Deerfield, Ill., 1964-68; v.p. employee relations Hardwicke Corp., N.Y.C., 1968-71; pres., chief exec. officer Mendheim & Assos., Inc., Chgo., 1968—; chmn. Post Mil. Career subs. Mendheim & Assos., Inc., 1969-73. Served with U.S. Army, 1942-45. Decorated Bronze Star, 5 battle stars. Mem. Am. Mgmt. Assn., Northwestern U. Alumni Assn., Urban League. Office: Mendheim and Assos Inc 6055 N Lincoln Ave Chicago IL 60659

MENGEL, ROBERT MORROW, educator, ornithologist, mus. curator; b. Glenview, Ky., Aug. 19, 1921; s. Charles C. and Mary A. (Kelly) M.; B.S., Cornell U., 1947; M.A., U. Mich., 1950, Ph.D., 1958; m. Marion Anne Jenkinson, Dec. 21, 1963; 1 dau., Tracy Lynn. Research asso. U. Kans., Lawrence, 1953-62, instr. and lectr. zoology, 1958-66, asso. prof. zoology, 1967, asso. prof. systematics and ecology, 1968-71, asso. curator in ornithology, 1968-71, prof. systematics and ecology, 1972—, curator Mus. of Natural History, 1972—. Exhibited paintings and water colors in one-man and group shows, Lawrence, Kans., 1973, 76, 77, Norman, Okla., 1974. Served with USAAF, 1942-46. Fellow Am. Ornithologists Union (editor jour. 1963-67, editor monographs series 1970-74, councillor 1972-74); mem. Cooper (councilor 1966-68), Wilson (asso. editor Bull. 1953-54), Kan., Ky. ornithol. socs., Soc. for the Study of Evolution, Am. Soc. Systematic Zoologists, Soc. Am. Naturalists, Brit. Ornithologists Union, Sigma Xi. Author and illustrator: The Birds of Kentucky, 1965. Author: The Ellis Collection of Ornithological Books in the University of Kansas Libraries, Vol. 1, 1972. Illustrator: Handbook of North American Birds, Vol. 1, 1962, Vols. 2, 3, 1976; contbg. illustrator: The Birds of Colorado (A.M. Bailey, R.J. Niedrach), 1965. Home: Route 4 Lawrence KS 66044 Office: Museum of Natural History Univ of Kansas Lawrence KS 66045

MENIER, VINCENT JOSEPH, coffee equipment mfg. co. exec.; b. Lakeside, Ohio, May 20, 1929; s. Vito James and Catherine Ida (Ruffa) M.; B.S. in Mech. Engring., U. Okla., 1953; m. Joan Sawyer, July 7, 1953; children—Mark, John, Patricia. Product mgr. Westinshouse Co., Dallas, 1955-65; mgr. mktg. GTE-Sylvania, Detroit, 1965-73; sr. v.p. Mr. Coffee, Bedford Heights, Ohio, 1973—. Mem. Bd. Health San Antonio, 1955-57. Served as pilot USAF, 1953-55. Mem. Am. Inst. Aeros. and Astronautics, Cleve. Engring. Soc., Air Force Assn., Res. Officers Assn., Aircraft Owners and Pilots Assn., Soc. Auto. Engrs., IEEE. Republican. Roman Catholic. Club: K.C. Home: 2 Pepper Creek Pepper Pike OH 44124 Office: 5433 Perkins Rd Bedford Heights OH 44146

MENK, LOUIS WILSON, r.r. ofcl.; b. Englewood, Colo., Apr. 8, 1918; s. Louis Albert and Daisy (Frantz) M.; student Denver U., 1937-38, Harvard Sch. Bus., 1953, Northwestern U. Transp. Sch., 1959; LL.D., Drury Coll., 1965, Denver U., 1966, Monmouth Coll., 1967; m. Martha Jane Swan, May 30, 1942; children—David Louis, Barbara Ann. Messenger, telegrapher U.P. R.R., Denver, 1937-40; with St.L. S.F. R.R., 1940-65, gen. mgr., 1956-58, v.p., gen. mgr., 1958-60, v.p. ops., 1960-62, pres., dir., 1962-65, chmn., 1964-65; pres., dir. Burlington Lines, 1965-66, No. Pacific Ry., St. Paul, 1966-70, Burlington No., Inc., 1970-71, chmn. bd., chief exec. officer, 1971—, also dir.; dir. Colo. & So. Ry. Co., Internat. Harvester Co., First Nat. Bank of Chgo., Gen. Mills, Inc., Am. Smelting & Refining Co., Minn. Mut. Life Ins. Co., Lemhi Telephone Co., No. Airmotive, Inc., 1st Bank System, Mpls. Mem. nat. exec. bd. Boy Scouts Am. Exec. com., adv. council Transp. Center, Northwestern U.; trustee U. Denver. Mem. Assn. Am. R.R.'s (dir.), Bus. Roundtable, Conf. Bd. Presbyterian (trustee). Clubs: Masons, Minn., Somerset Country (St. Paul); Transportation (Mpls., Chgo., St. Paul); Chicago (Chgo.). Home: 5904 S Robert Trail Route 10 South St Paul MN 55075 Office: Burlington No Bldg 176 E 5th St St Paul MN 55101

MENNEN, DOROTHY RUNK (MRS. HAROLD E. MENNEN), performing arts adminstr., educator; b. Marshfield, Wis., July 17, 1915; d. Jon Cleveland and Minnie Pearle (Walker) Runk; B.S. in Edn., Kent State U., 1938; M.A., Purdue U., 1964; m. Harold E. Mennen, Jan. 5, 1943; children—Ferol, Laurel (Mrs. Bruce Miller Robb). Tchr., choral dir. Twinsburg (Ohio) pub. sch., 1938-41; tchr. speech, English Aurora (Ohio) High Sch., 1941-42; tchr. Cuyahoga Falls (Ohio) High Sch., 1941-42; tchr. English, Wea High Sch., Tippecanoe County, Ind., 1951-53; tchr. vocal music West Lafayette (Ind.) pub. schs., 1957-60; asso. prof. theatre Purdue U., West Lafayette, Ind., 1964—, also vocal coach, 1964—. Contralto soloist, 1946—. Bd. dirs. Lafayette Symphony, 1958-60, Civic Theatre, Lafayette, 1972-73. Mem. Am. Theatre Assn. (nat. chairperson theatre, speech and voice 1968-71, 73-75; editor Directory Speech and Voice Specialists in Actor Tng. 1977-78), Nat. Assn. Tchrs. of Singing, Speech Communication Assn., AAUP, (chairperson com. W on Status of Women 1972-74, pres. chpt. 1974-75, 75-77), Women's Equity Action League, LWV. Democrat. Methodist. Home: 1804 Ravinia Rd West Lafayette IN 47906 Office: Theater Dept Creative Arts Stewart Center Purdue U West Lafayette IN 47907

MENNING, ARNOLD J., coll. dean; b. Alton, Iowa, Dec. 20, 1930; s. Bert and Nellie (Van Kley) M.; B.A., U. No. Iowa, 1952, M.A., 1956; Ph.D., S.D. State U., 1973; m. Thelma Marie Intveld, June 10, 1952; children—Jeri Ellen, Darrell Lee, Dale Robert, Carla Beth. Teacher, coach Hull (Iowa) Pub. Schs., 1955-61, Esterville (Iowa) Pub. Schs., 1961-65; dir. student personnel Iowa Lakes Community Coll., 1965-69; dir. gen. registration, dir. spl. student services S.D. State U., 1969-74, dean Coll. Gen. Registration, adminstr. career-academic programs S.D. State U., 1974—. Served with AUS, 1952-54. Mem. Am. Coll. Personnel Assn., Am. Personnel and Guidance Assn., Am. Assn. Higher Edn., Upper Midwest, Am. assns. collegiate registrar-admissions ofcls., Pi Gamma Mu, Gamma Sigma Delta, Kappa Delta Phi. Republican. Mem. Reformed Ch. Club: Am. Legion. Home: 1920 3d St Brookings SD 57006 Office: Adminstrn Bldg Room 128 SD State U Brookings SD 57007

MENNINGER, JEANETTA LYLE (MRS. KARL MENNINGER), editor; b. St. Louis; d. Edward Gerard and Jeanetta (Patterson) Lyle; A.B., Park Coll., 1923; postgrad. Columbia, 1930; m. Karl Menninger, Sept. 9, 1941; 1 dau., Rosemary. Prin. preparatory sch. Central Coll. for Women, 1925; reporter, feature writer Utica (N.Y.) Daily Press, 1925-30; with pub. relations dept. Columbia U., 1930; editorial worker, writer Menninger Clinic, Topeka, 1931; research asst. Carnegie Found. proj., Hollywood, Calif., 1937; freelance writer, 1937-41; editor Bull. of Menninger Clinic, Topeka, Kan., 1936-70, bd. editors, 1970—; dir. publs. Menninger Found., 1946-64; cons. editor Correctional Programs News, Clement and Jessie Stone Found., Chgo., 1971—; asso. editor Presbyn. Outlook, Richmond, Va., 1973—; exec. v.p. The Villages, Inc., 1976—. Active drives for A.R.C., Am. Cancer Soc., Multiple Sclerosis, Mental Hygiene, Art Center, others. Trustee Mulvane Art Center of Washburn Municipal U., 1954—, Family Service and Guidance Center, Topeka, 1957-70, The Villages, Inc., Topeka, 1969—, Park Coll., Parkville, Mo., 1970—, A.R.T. (prison art), Chgo., 1972; mem. women's com. Japan Internat. Christian U. Found., N.Y.C. Fellow Am. Med. Writers Assn.; mem. Kan. Press Women, Nat. Fedn. Press Women, Nat. Assn. Sci. Writers, YWCA, Women in Communications, Art Inst. Chgo. (life). Democrat. Presbyn. Author: (Collaborator with husband) in Love against Hate, 1942, and other books; contbr. numerous articles to profl. jours., various mags. Home: 1819 Westwood Circle Topeka KS 66604 Office: Menninger Found Box 829 Topeka KS 66601 also The Villages Inc Box 1695 Topeka KS 66601

MENNINGER, KARL AUGUSTUS, psychiatrist; b. Topeka, July 22, 1893; s. Charles Frederick (M.D.) and Flora (Knisely) M.; student Washburn Coll., 1910-12, Ind. U., summer 1910; A.B., U. Wis., 1914, M.S., 1915, D.Sc., 1965; M.D. cum laude, Harvard U., 1917; L.H.D., Park Coll., 1955, St. Benedict's Coll., 1963, Loyola U., 1972, DePaul U., 1974; LL.D., Jefferson Med. Coll. 1956, Parsons Coll., 1960, Kans. State U., 1962, Baker U., 1965, Pepperdine U., 1974; D.Sc., Washburn U., 1949, Oklahoma City U., 1966; m. Grace Gaines, Sept. 1916 (div. Feb. 1941); children—Julia Menninger Gottesman, Martha Menninger Nichols, Robert Gaines; m. 2d, Jeanetta Lyle, Sept. 1941; 1 dau., Rosemary Jeanette Karla. Chmn. bd. trustees, mem. ednl. com. Menninger Found.; prof. at large U. Kans.; distinguished prof. psychiatry Chgo. Med. Sch., Loyola U., Chgo., U. Cin.; vis. prof. U. Chgo.; cons. Ill. Dept. Mental Health, Ill. State Psychiat. Inst.; founder Menninger Sch. Psychiatry, 1946, dean, 1946-69; cons. Topeka VA Hosp., Topeka State Hosp., Stormont-Vail Hosp., Kans. Reception and Diagnostic Center, Kans. Neurol. Inst., Fed. Bur. Prisons, Office Vocat. Rehab., Dept. HEW, Pres.'s Task Force on Prisoner Rehab., 1969, Mt. Sinai Med. Center, Chgo., Com. on Penal Reform, Kans. Assn. Mental Health. Mem. spl. com. on psychiatry, OSRD, ETO, adv. to surgeon gen. U.S. Army, 1945; adviser Gov. Kans., 1966-75; mem. Nat. Council on Crime and Delinquency, Open Lands Project. Mem. Kans. Bd. Social Welfare; adv. bd. Am. Assn. Phys. and Mental Rehab., Adult div. Ill. Dept. Corrections, 1970-74, Ill. State Psychiat. Inst.; med. adv. council Gov. Ill.; mem. adv. coms. many other civic, govtl. orgns. Bd. overseers Lemberg Center for Study Violence, Brandeis U.; bd. dirs. Chgo. Boys Club, John Howard Assn. Chgo., Internat. Com. Against Mental Illness; trustee W. Clement and Jessie V. Stone Found., Chgo.; chmn. bd. dirs. Menninger Found., Villages, Inc., Topeka. Served as lt. (j.g.) USN, 1918-21. Recipient Isaac Ray award Am. Psychiat. Assn., 1962, Founders award, 1977; T.W. Salmon award N.Y. Acad. Medicine, 1967, Good Samaritan award Eagles Lodge, 1968, 69, Ann. Service award John Howard Assn., 1969, Good Shepherd award The Lambs, 1969, Golden AAPL award Am. Acad. Psychiatry and Law, 1974, Roscoe Pound award Nat. Council Crime and Delinquency, 1975. Life fellow Am. Psychiat. Assn. (1st distinguished service award 1965), Am. Coll. Psychiatrists (Bowis award 1973), Am. Med. Writers Assn.; master A.C.P., life mem. AMA, Am. Psychol. Assn., Chgo. Psychoanalytic Soc., Am. Orthopsychiat. Assn., Am. Psychoanalytic Assn. (pres. 1941-43); hon. mem. Am. Assn. Suicidology, Internat. Assn. for Suicide Prevention, Sigmund Freud Archives; charter mem. Central Neuropsychiat. Assn., Central Psychiat. Hosp. Assn., Med. Assn. for Research Nervous and Mental Diseases; mem. Am. Assn. for Child Psychoanalysis, Am. Soc. Criminology, Ill. Acad. Criminology, Assn. for Psychiat. Treatment Offenders, Royal Coll. Psychiatrists, Am. Acad. Psychiatry and Law, Am. Justice Inst. (adv. com. sponsors), Assn. Clin. Pastoral Edn., Ill. Com. on Family Law, Internat. Psychoanalytic Assn., Kans. Med. Soc. (trustee), Sigmund Freud Soc. Vienna, World Soc. Ekistics, Nat. Congress Am. Indians, Am. Hort Council, AAAS, ACLU, NAACP, Sierra Club, Chgo. Orchestral Assn. (gov.), Am. Assn. Bot. Gardens and Arboreta, Friends of the Earth, Am. Indian Center (Chgo. Grand Council) Aspen Inst. for Humanistic Studies (hon. trustee), Am. Humanics Found., Save the Tallgrass Prairie Inc. (chmn. nat. hon. bd.), others. Presbyterian. Clubs: Masons; Univ. (Chgo.); Country (Topeka), Author: (with others) Why Men Fail, 1918; The Human Mind, 1930, rev., 1945; (with others) The Healthy-Minded Child, 1930; Man Against Himself, 1938; (with others) America Now, 1938; (with Mrs. Menninger) Love Against Hate, 1942; A Guide to Psychiatric Books, rev. 3d edition 1972; Manual for Psychiatric Case Study, 1952; Theory of Psychoanalytic Technique, 1958, rev. with Dr. Philip Holzman, 1973; (selected papers) A Psychiatrist's World, 1959; The Vital Balance, 1963; The Crime of Punishment, 1968; Sparks, 1973; Whatever Became of Sin, 1973; also articles relating to field. Editorial bd. Bull. Menninger Clinic. Home: 1819 Westwood Circle Topeka KS 66604 Office: Menninger Found Box 829 Topeka KS 66601

MENNINGER, ROY WRIGHT, found. exec., physician; b. Topeka, Oct. 27, 1926; A.B., Swarthmore Coll., 1947; M.D., Cornell U., 1951; children—Heather, Ariel, Bonar, Eric. Intern, N.Y. Hosp., 1951-52; resident psychiatrist Boston State Hosp., 1952-53, Boston Psychopathic Hosp., 1953-56; from resident psychiatrist to asso. medicine in (psychiatry) Peter Bent Brigham Hosp., Boston, 1956-61; teaching and research fellow Harvard Med. Sch., 1956-61; staff psychiatrist C.F. Menninger Meml. Hosp., Menninger Found., Topeka, 1961-63, co-dir. div. sch. mental health, 1963-67; dir. dept. preventive psychiatry Menninger Found., 1965-67, pres. found., 1967—. Mem. sponsoring com. Inst. Am. Democracy, 1967—; adv. bd. Parents mag., 1966—; adv. group Horizons '76; adv. group Topeka Inst. Urban Affairs, 1967—, dir., 1969—; trustee Midwest Research Inst., 1967—, Baker U., 1968-72; vis. lectr. Fgn. Service Inst., State Dept., 1963-66; mem. Gov.'s Com. Criminal Adminstrn., 1971—; mem. social issues com. Group Advancement Psychiatry; bd. dirs. Goals for Topeka, 1969—, v.p., 1972—; mem. Task Force on Prevention Pres.'s Commn. Mental Health. Diplomate Am. Bd. Psychiatry and Neurology. Bd. dirs. Sex Info. and Edn. Council U.S., 1971-73, mem. edn. com, 1972—, mem. long-range planning com., 1972—; bd. dirs. A.K. Rice Inst., Washington. Asso. fellow A.C.P.; fellow Am. Psychiat. Assn. (joint info. service exec. com.); hon. mem. Northeastern Soc. Group Psychotherapy; mem. Am. Assn. Group Psychotherapy, Mass. Med. Soc., AAAS, Physicians Social Responsibility, Kans. Psychiat. Soc., Am. Orthopsychiat. Assn., Am. String Tchrs. Assn. Editorial cons. Continuing Edn. for Family Physicians; editorial bd. Clin. Psychiatry News. Office: PO Box 829 Topeka KS 66601

MENZ, WILLIAM WOLFGANG, research exec.; b. Zweibruecken, Germany, Mar. 2, 1917; s. Michael Rudolf and Rosel (Putzel) M.; B.S., U. Munich, 1937, M.S., 1939; postgrad. Ohio State U., 1949-50; m. Gertrude Weissman, May 17, 1941; children—Roberta (Mrs. John J. Suhrbier), Paul Fred. Came to U.S., 1939, naturalized, 1944. Br. chief intelligence dept. USAAF, Dayton, Ohio, 1946-50; editor USPHS, Cin., 1950-51; tech. info. analyst Gen. Aniline & Film Corp., Easton, Pa., 1951-52, Ethyl Corp., Detroit, 1952-57; sect. chief R.J. Reynolds Industries, Winston-Salem, N.C., 1957-70; v.p. research, exec. sec. Dairy Research Inc., Rosemont, Ill., 1970—. Served with USAAF, 1941-45. Mem. Am. Chem. Soc. (sect. chmn. 1962, nat. awards com. 1962-64), Soc. Tech. Writers and Editors (pres. 1960), Am. Dairy Sci. Assn., Inst. Aero. Scis., Sigma Xi. Home: 1515 E Central St Arlington Heights IL 60005 Office: 6300 N River Rd Rosemont IL 60018

MERAR, ERWIN JEROME, distbg. co. exec.; b. Green Bay, Wis., Jan. 19, 1924; s. Marcus C. and Sadye (Rosenberg) M.; student St. Norberts Coll., 1942-43, Bard Coll., 1943-44, U. Wis., 1945-47; m. Emma Lee Stern, Jan. 5, 1952; children—David L., Robert M. Advt. mgr. Humphrey Chevrolet Co., Milw., 1947-49; dir. advt. Samson Appliance Stores, 1949-54; v.p. Standard Electric Supply Co., Milw., 1954-70; pres. Merco Corp., Milw., 1970—; pres. Mid-Am. Acceptance Corp., 1960, Ader Corp., 1962, Summit Tower Corp., 1958. Served with AUS, 1942-45. Mem. Am. Legion, Elec. League Milw., Zeta Beta Tau Alumni Club. Mason (32 deg., Shriner). Club: Wisconsin (Milw.). Home: 7444 N Crossway Rd Milwaukee WI 53217 Office: 5500 W Douglas Av Milwaukee WI 53218

MERCER, VICTOR HAROLD, dentist, state ofcl., educator; b. Indpls., June 24, 1928; s. Harold Leslie and Helen Louise (Stevens) M.; student Wabash Coll., 1946-48, Butler U., 1948-49; B.S., Ind. U., 1950, D.D.S., 1953, M.S.D., 1963; m. Carolyn M. Favre, Feb. 6, 1954; children—Victor Harold, Diana Lee. Practice dentistry, Indpls., 1955—; asst. dir. div. dental Health Ind. Bd. Health, 1961—; asst. prof. preventive dentistry Ind. U. Sch. Dentistry, 1960—. Served to lt. USNR, 1953-55. Fellow Am. Coll. Dentists, Internat. Coll. Dentists; mem. Indpls. Dental Soc. (pres. 1973-74), Omicron Kappa Upsilon, Phi Delta Theta, Delta Sigma Delta. Contbr. numerous articles to profl. jours. Home: 6330 N Ewing Indianapolis IN 46220 Office: 1330 W Michigan Indianapolis IN 46220

MERCER, WILLIAM EARL, optometrist; b. Newark, Ohio, Apr. 11, 1907; s. Richard Lawrence and Lou Myrta (Johnson) M.; O.D., No. Ill. Coll. Optometry, 1931, D.O.S., 1932; m. Ethel Marie Sanders, Sept. 13, 1938; children—William Earl, Clara Jean (Mrs. Robert L. Shank). Practice optometry, Chgo., 1931-32; tchr. theoretic optics No. Ill. Coll. Optometry, 1931-32; mgr. optical dept. Lamson's, Toledo, Ohio, 1932-37; pvt. practice optometry, Toledo, 1937-77; owner Mercer Enterprises, Toledo, eyework instruments, 1970—. Mem. Omega Delta. Mason (Shriner), Kiwanian. Clubs: Toledo, Inverness Country (Toledo). Patentee in field. Home: 3121 Hopewell Pl Toledo OH 43606 Office: 306 Bell Bldg Toledo OH 43624

MERCHANT, FREDERICK TAYLOR, surgeon; b. Marion, Ohio, July 19, 1911; s. Harry J. and Hazel L. (Taylor) M.; A.B., Ohio Wesleyan U., 1933; M.D., Johns Hopkins U., 1937; m. Ethyl Irene Rush, June 29, 1940; 2 daus., Joan, Cathy. Intern in surgery Johns Hopkins Hosp., Balt., 1937-38; intern pathology Royal Victoria Hosp., Montreal, Que., Can., 1938-39, resident in surgery, 1940-42; instr. pathology McGill U., 1938-39, surgery, 1940-42; sr. intern in surgery Lakeside Hosp., Cleve., 1939-40; practice of surgery, Marion, Ohio, 1946—; attending surgeon Marion Gen. Hosp., 1946—, chief of staff, 1949-59, now chief of surgery, mem. bd. govs., 1959-65, 1968—; attending surgeon at the Wyandot Meml. Hosp., Morrow Co. Hosp., Mt. Gilead, Ohio, Community Med. Center Hosp., Marion; dist. surgeon Penn Central R.R., 1947-71. Dir. Marion County Bank. Mem. State Med. Bd. Ohio, 1957-72, pres., 1963, 69; mem. Nat. Bd. Med. Examiners, 1965-75, vice chmn., mem. exec. com.; mem. exec. com. Fdn. State Med. Bds. U.S., pres., 1970-71; gen. chmn. Fedn. Licensing Exam. Program, 1968—. Mem. exec. com. Rice Found. Premed. Edn., Ohio Wesleyan U. Gen. chmn. 1955 United Appeals. Served with AUS, 1942-45, chief surgeon thoracic surg. team, 1st aux. surg. group; disch. as lt. col.; recalled for spl. service as asst. chief, surg. cons. div. Office Surgeon Gen Army, Washington, 1950-51. Diplomate Am. Bd. Surgery. Fellow A.M.A., A.C.S.; mem. Ohio Med. Assn. (com. hosp. relations 1957-60, mem. profl. and jud. com. 1960-65, council 1964-68), Pan-Pacific Surg. Assn., C. of C. (dir. 1948-55, pres. 1950), Res. Officers Assn. (surgeon Ohio dept., pres. Marion area), Ohio Surg. Assn., Am. Legion, Assn. Mil. Surgeons U.S., Phi Gamma Delta, Nu Sigma Nu, Symposiarchs. Episcopalian. Contbr. articles to profl. jours. Home: 550 Virginia Ave Marion OH 43302 Office: 1051 Harding Memorial Pkwy Marion OH 43302

MEREDITH, BETTY JANE, guidance counselor; b. Flint, Mich., Sept. 18, 1919; d. Roy Willard and Nina (Cooley) Santee; B.S., So. Ill. U., 1967, M.S., 1970; m. Cameron William Meredith, Aug. 17, 1940; children—Cameron William, Marcia Ellen, Jane Elizabeth. Kindergarden tchr. Alton (Ill.) Pub. Sch., 1967-69; research asst. So. Ill. U., 1969-70; dir. pre-sch. and adjustment center Madison County Assn. Retarded Children, Edwardsville, 1970-73; elementary sch. counselor Alton Pub. Schs., 1973-74, primary sch. tchr., 1974-75, secondary sch. counselor, 1975—; marriage and family counselor Adlerian Counseling Assos., Alton, 1975—; pres. Alfred Adler Inst. St. Louis, 1977. Mem. Am., Ill. personnel and guidance assns., Am. Assn. Family and Marriage Counselors, Nat., Ill. edn. assns., AAUW, P.E.O., Kappa Delta Pi. Presbyterian. Address: 2010 Chapin Pl Alton IL 62002

MEREDITH, JAMES HARGROVE, judge; b. Wederburn, Oreg., Aug. 25, 1914; s. Willis H. and Ollie (Hargrove) M.; A.B., Mo. U., 1935, LL.B., 1937; m. Dorothy Doke, Sept. 7, 1937 (dec. Feb. 1972); 1 son, James Doke; m. 2d, Susan B. Fitzgibbon, 1977. Admitted to Mo. bar, 1937; practice law, New Madrid County, Mo., 1937-42, 46-49; spl. agt. FBI, 1942-44; partner firm Stolar, Kuhlman & Meredith, St. Louis, 1952-61, Cook, Meredith, Murphy and English, 1961-62, Stuart and Meredith, Washington, 1961-62; chief counsel Mo. Ins. Dept., Jefferson City, 1949-52; v.p., gen. counsel Nat. Underwriters, Inc., 1954-62; U.S. dist. judge Eastern Dist. Mo., 1962-71, chief judge, 1971—. Mem. Mental Health Commn. Mo., 1961-62; active Friend Mo. U. Library Assn. Served with USNR, 1944-46. Mem. Mo. Acad. Squires, Jud. Conf. U.S., Order Coif, Phi Delta Phi, Sigma Chi (Significant Sig award). Presbyterian. Mason (Shriner). Clubs: Mo. Athletic, Old Warson Country, University (St. Louis). Home: 108 Runnymede Dr St Louis MO 63141 Office: US Dist Court 1114 Market St St Louis MO 63101

MERICAS, VAN DIMOS, chiropractor; b. N.Y.C., Mar. 9, 1917; s. Dimos Evangelos and Aspasia (Saponjis) M.; D.C., Columbia Inst. Chiropractic, N.Y.C., 1940; D.C., Nat. Coll. Chiropractic, Chgo., 1947; postgrad. Wayne State U., 1947-50; m. Kristalia Poll, Dec. 28, 1947; children—Sia, Katherine. Practice chiropractics, Dearborn,

Mich., 1947—. Nat. adviser Jr. Am. Chiropractics Assn., 1968-69. Mem. City Beautiful Commn., Dearborn, 1958-67, chmn., 1962-64; councilman, Dearborn, 1967—, pres. city council, 1972; acting mayor of Dearborn, 1977; vice chmn. Com. Henry Ford Statue, Dearborn, 1968-75; v.p. William A. Ross Scholarship Found., Dearborn, 1975—; v.p. Found. for Chiropractic Edn. and Research, Des Moines, 1975—. Served with USCGR, 1941-45. Decorated Bronze Star with oak leaf cluster. Named Dearborn Father of Year East Dearborn Mchts. Assn., 1960. Fellow Internat. Coll. Chiropractors; mem. Mich. State, Am. (Mich. del. 1961-64) chiropractic assns., Council on Diagnosis and Internal Diagnosis (pres. 1972-74), Founders' Soc. Detroit Inst. Arts, Order of Am. Hellenic Ednl. Progressive Assn. (pres. chpts. 1940, 59). Greek Orthodox. Mason (Shriner), K.T., Kiwanian. Club: Fairlane Tennis, Fairlane Manor (Dearborn). Home: 23000 Hollander St Dearborn MI 48128 Office: 15608 Michigan Ave Dearborn MI 48126

MERILAN, CHARLES PRESTON, dairy husbandry scientist, educator; b. Lesterville, Mo., Jan. 14, 1926; s. Peter Samuel and Cleo Sarah (Harper) M.; B.S. in Agr., U. Mo., 1948, A.M., 1949, Ph.D., 1952; m. Phyllis Pauline Laughlin, June 12, 1949; children—Michael Preston, Jean Elizabeth. Instr. dairy husbandry U. Mo., Columbia, 1950-52, instr. bacteriology and preventive medicine, 1952-53, asst. prof. dairy husbandry, 1953-57, asso. prof., 1957-59, prof., 1959—, chmn. dept. dairy husbandry, 1961-62, asso. dir. Mo. Agrl. Expt. Sta., 1962-63, asso. investigator space sci. research center, 1964-74, exec. sec., dir. grad. studies physiology area, 1969-72, chmn. patent and copyright com., 1963—. Served with USMCR, 1944-45. Decorated Purple Heart. Mem. AAAS, Am. Chem. Soc., Am. Dairy Sci. Assn., Am. Soc. Animal Sci., IEEE (profl. group biomed. electronics), Soc. Cryobiology, Sigma Xi, Alpha Zeta, Gamma Sigma Delta, Phi Beta Pi. Research on biol. material preservation. Home: 1509 Bouchelle Ave Columbia MO 65201

MERITT, DENNIS ANDREW, JR., zoo dir.; b. Rochester, N.Y., May 17, 1940; s. Dennis Andrew and Mary (Gilbert) M.; B.S. in Biology and Psychology, U. Rochester, 1970; M.A. in Teaching of Biology, Northeastern Ill. U., 1976; m. Mary Gail Fitzpatrick, July 20, 1962; children—Laura, Jill. Research asst. depts. pharmacology, toxicology U. Rochester, 1962-67; zoologist Lincoln Park Zool. Gardens, Chgo., 1967-69, curator of mammals, 1969-76, asst. dir., 1976—; teaching asst. Northeastern Ill. U., 1974—. Mem. St. Athanasius Sch. Bd. Edn., Evanston, Ill., 1977—. Mem. Am. Assn. Zool. Parks, Aquariums (chmn. wildlife conservation and mgmt. 1976-78, dir. 1975-78, Presdl. award 1974, 75), Am. Mammalogists Soc., Smithsonian Assos., Nat. Geog. Soc., Field Museum Nat. History (asso.). Roman Catholic. Office: 2200 N Cannon Dr Chicago IL 60614

MERKEL, JAYNE SILVERSTEIN, art historian; b. Cin., Sept. 28, 1942; d. Elmore Herman and Ruth Dell (Feiler) Silverstein; B.S., Simmons Coll., 1964; postgrad. U. Mich., 1966-68; M.A., Smith Coll., 1968; m. Edward Wagner Merkel, Jr., Aug. 7, 1965; children—Mary Feiler, Jane Scranton. Curatorial asst. U. Mich. Mus. Art, 1965-68; curator Contemporary Arts Center, Cin., 1968-69; dir. edn. and pub. relations Taft Mus., Cin., 1969-73; adj. instr. art history Raymond Walters Coll. U. Cin., 1970-72; instr. art history Art Acad. of Cin., 1973—; columnist of archtl. criticism Cin. Enquirer, 1977—; cons. Space Design/Interior Architecture; judge AIA Awards, Cin., 1975, 77; speaker in field to civic and charitable groups. Recipient award for excellence in archtl. writing Cin. chpt. AIA, 1973. Mem. Coll. Art Assn. Author numerous mus. catalogues; contbr. articles to Art Jour., Cin. Mag., Cin. Enquirer, Quest 78. Home: 1908 Dexter Ave Cincinnati OH 45206 Office: Art Acad Cincinnati Eden Park Cincinnati OH 45202

MERKEL, KENNETH GAIL, mfg. engr.; b. St. Louis, Jan. 2, 1936; s. Frederick Paul and Lula Mae (Flowers) Spies; B.S. in Prodn. Mgmt., Washington U., St. Louis, 1960; M.B.A. in Fin., Case Western Res. U., Cleve., 1969, M.S. in Mgmt., 1975; B.S. in Accounting, Lake Erie Coll., Painesville, Ohio, 1976; m. Kathleen Marie Treacy, Nov. 28, 1957; children—Margaret Mary and Marie Michelle (twins), Kenneth Gail, II, Mary Kathleen, Mary Elizabeth, John Frederick, Ann Marie. With Gen. Electric Co., 1960—, project mgr. Ravenna (Ohio) Lamp Plant Project, 1967-70, shop ops. mgr., mgr. equipment design, mgr. quality control engring., mgr. mfg. engring., Cleve., 1970-77, specialist-logistics engring., 1978—; systems analyst McDonnell-Douglas Automation Center, St. Louis, 1965-66; instr. Washington U., St. Louis, 1965-66, Cuyahoga Community Coll., Cleve., 1968-69, Lake Erie Coll., 1972—. Mem. council Ch. of Gesu; active Heights Action Com. Served with USMC, 1953-54. Mem. Soc. Mfg. Engrs., Am. Mgmt. Assn., Am. Prodn. and Inventory Control Soc., Assn. U. Evening Colls. (asso.), Mensa, Tau Kappa Epsilon. Contbr. articles to profl. jours. Home: 3550 Cedarbrook Rd University Heights OH 44118 Office: 2000 Noble Rd East Cleveland OH 44112

MERKEL, WILLIAM KENNETH, steel foundry exec.; b. San Antonio, Feb. 27, 1926; s. Henry Christian Louis and Benita (Rehner) M.; student So. Methodist U., 1946-47; B.B.A., U. Tex., 1950; m. Jeanine Rae, Mar. 3, 1962; children—Pamela Ann, Paula Deneice, Dana Diane. With Tampo Mfg. Co., San Antonio, 1953-55, K.O. Steel Castings Co., 1955-64; with Burnside Steel Foundry Co., Chgo., 1964-72, v.p., 1968-72, also dir.; v.p. Morris Bean & Co., Yellow Springs, Ohio, 1972-75, also dir.; v.p. Westran Corp., Muskegon, Mich., 1975—. Active in fund raising Met. Crusade Mercy, YMCA, Boy Scouts Am. Served with USNR, 1944-46, USAF, 1951-53. Mem. Am. Foundrymen's Soc. (sect. chmn. 1957), Steel Founders' Soc. Am. (recipient Gustav Lillerquist award 1963, nat. tech. and operating com. 1963-64), Am. Soc. Metals, Aluminum Assn., ASME, Western Golf Assn. Clubs: Olympia Fields (Ill.) County; Muskegon (Mich.) Country. Home: 2121 Forest Park Rd Muskegon MI 49441 Office: 1148 W Western Av Muskegon MI 49443

MERMEL, MICHAEL GEORGE, lawyer; b. Chgo., June 2, 1951; s. Marion George and Ethel (Fuqua) M.; B.S., So. Ill. U., 1973; J.D., John Marshall Law Sch., 1976. Admitted to Ill. bar, 1976; asst. state atty. Cook County, Chgo., 1976—. Mem. Ill. State, Chgo. bar assns. Home: 20 Thorndale Ave Park Ridge IL 60068 Office: 5540 W Diversey Ave Chicago IL 60639

MERNER, R. WILLIAM, lawyer; b. Cedar Falls, Iowa, Jan. 11, 1931; s. Roland Frederick and Jane (Eccles) M.; B.A., U. Iowa, 1953; J.D., U. Mich., 1958; m. Shirley Ann Lechner, July 17, 1972; children—David William, Marci Lynn. Admitted to Iowa bar, 1958; partner firm Merner & Merner, Cedar Falls, 1958-65; partner firm Reed, Merner, Sindlinger, Baker & Sabbath, Cedar Falls, 1965-77, firm Reed, Merner, Sabbath & Strever, Cedar Falls, 1977—. Vice-pres. The Depot Ltd. Asst. county atty., Black Hawk County, Iowa, 1961-62, 1965. Served to lt. AUS, 1955-57. Mem. Am., Iowa, Black Hawk County bar assns., Cedar Falls C. of C. (dir. 1969-71), Sigma Alpha Epsilon (pres. U. Iowa br. 1951-52). Republican. Methodist. Clubs: Elks, Cedar Falls Lions. Home: 2802 Cottage Row Rd Cedar Falls IA 50613 Office: 3722 Cedar Heights Dr Cedar Falls IA 50613

MERNITZ, RICHARD JAMES, camp dir.; b. Chicago Heights, Ill., Sept. 27, 1922; s. Richard George Frederick and Magdalene Lydia (Klopsteg) M.; B.S., Elmhurst Coll., 1943; postgrad. Lafayette Coll., 1943, U. W.Va., 1944; m. Dorothy Louise Klick, Dec. 28, 1945; children—Scott, R. Craig, Mark K. Project engr. Battelle Meml. Inst., Columbus, Ohio, 1945-47; asst. to dir. research and devel. Am. Zinc Oxide Co., Columbus, 1947-52; partner, pvt. Iowa farm, Keota, 1952-55; resident exec. dir. Kroehler YMCA Camp and Lodge, Hayward, Wis., 1955—. Pres., Hayward All-Sports Booster Club. Bd. dirs. Hayward Civic Club, 1958-59. Served with AUS, 1943-45. Mem. Am. Camping Assn. (certified camp dir.), Assn. Profl. Dirs., Am. Water Ski Assn., Mt. Telemark Ski Assn. (dir. 1956-58). Mem. United Ch. of Christ (mem. ch. council 1966-76). Patentee in field. Address: Kroehler YMCA Camp and Lodge Route 6 Hayward WI 54843

MERRELL, JAMES LEE, clergyman, editor; b. Indpls., Oct. 24, 1930; s. Mark W. and Pauline (Tucker) M.; A.B. in Journalism, Ind. U., 1952; B.D., Christian Theol. Sem., Indpls., 1956; Litt.D., Culver-Stockton Coll., Canton, Mo., 1972; m. Barbara Jeanne Burch, Dec. 23, 1951; children—Deborah Lea Merrell Griffin, Cynthia Lynn, Stuart Allen. Ordained to minstry Disciples of Christ Ch., 1956; asst. editor World Call, internat. mag. Disciples of Christ Ch., Indpls., 1955-58, asso. editor, 1958-66, editor, 1971-73, editor The Disciple, 1973—; v.p. Christian Bd. Publ., 1976—; minister Crestview Christian Ch., 1966-71. Pres. Greenbriar PTA, 1968-69. Mem. Religious Pub. Relations Council, Asso. Ch. Press, Christian Theol. Sem. Alumni Assn. (pres. 1966-68, mem. adv. council 1968-72, Distinguished Alumnus award 1975), Sigma Delta Chi (award 1952), Theta Phi, Pi Kappa Alpha. Author: World Call-A Venture in Religious Journalism, 1956; They Live Their Faith, 1965; editor: The Power of One, 1976. Home: 5347 Warmwinds Ct Saint Louis MO 63129 Office: PO Box 179 Saint Louis MO 63166

MERRIHEW, VICTOR HUGO, owner lumber co.; b. Bethany, Mo., Nov. 28, 1901; s. William Earl and Josephine (Perkins) M.; grad. Chadron State Coll., 1925; m. Dorothy Ellen Patch, July 6, 1929; children—Walter Earl, Harry Bert. Tchr. pub. schs., Nebr., 1920-24; owner cattle ranch, Ashby, Nebr., 1926—, Ashby Lumber Co., 1962—. Pres., Panhandle Rural Electric, Alliance, Nebr., 1973-77. Pres. Grant County (Nebr.) Hist. Soc., Hyannis, Neb., 1960-75. Chmn. Republican county com., Grant County, 1954-62. Elk. Home and office: Box 103 Ashby NE 69333

MERRILL, DEAN ROGER, book pub. co. exec.; b. Los Angeles, Dec. 17, 1943; s. D. Raymond and Mary Lucille (Frantz) M.; Th.B., Chgo. Bible Coll., 1964; M.A., Syracuse U., 1970; m. Grace LaVonne Danielson, June 25, 1966; children—Nathan Dean, Rhonda Joy, Tricia Dawn. Asso. editor Campus Life mag., Wheaton, Ill., 1965-69, sr. editor, 1971-73; dir. univ. info. Oral Roberts U., Tulsa, Okla., 1970-71; exec. editor Creation House, Carol Stream, Ill., 1973-74; mng. editor books David C. Cook Pub. Co., Elgin, Ill., 1974—; mem. faculty communications Wheaton (Ill.) Coll., 1973-75. Mem. Evangelical Press Assn., Asso. Ch. Press. Author: The Way, 1972; Rock, Bach and Superschlock, 1972; Peace and Love, 1973; The Husband Book, 1977. Contbr. articles to religious publs. Home: 332 S River Rd Naperville IL 60540 Office: 850 N Grove Ave Elgin IL 60120

MERRILL, WILLIAM H., JR., lawyer; b. Indpls., Apr. 11, 1942; s. William H. and Jane (Robinson) M.; B.S., Butler U., 1965; J.D., Ind. U., 1967; m. Winifred Jane Baur, July 25, 1964; children—Michele Jane, Betsy Diane. Admitted to Ind. bar, 1967; trust officer Merchants Nat. Bank, 1965-69; gen. counsel Everett I. Brown Co., Indpls., 1969—; v.p., gen. counsel Landeco, Inc., 1970—; pres. Baumer, Inc., 1973—; pres. Bash Seed Co., 1975—. Mem. Carmel (Ind.) Town Plan Commn., 1975—. Mem. Am., Ind., Indpls. bar assns., Am. Judicature Soc. Club: Crooked Stick Golf. Home: Rural Route 2 Box 339A Carmel IN 46203 Office: 5406 W Bradbury Ave Indianapolis IN 46241

MERRIMAN, JOHN RILEY, surgeon; b. Williamsville, Ill., Mar. 31, 1894; s. Charles B. and Emma (Taylor) M.; B.S., U. Ill., 1916; M.D., Rush Med. Coll., 1918; m. Dorothy Carroll, Oct. 27, 1926. Intern and resident Presbyn. Hosp., Chgo.; practice medicine, surgery 1918-76. Mem. staff Northwestern Med. Sch.; surgeon, Evanston (Ill.) Hosp., St. Francis Hosp. Fellow Internat. Coll. Surgeons, Indsl. Med. Assn.; mem. A.M.A., Ill., Chgo. med. socs., Am. Assn. Ry. Surgeons, Chgo. Soc. Indsl. Medicine and Surgery, Central States Soc. Indsl. Medicine and Surgery, Internat. Soc. for Study Musculoskeletal Disabilities. Republican. Episcopalian. Clubs: Westmoreland Country; University of Evanston. Died Feb. 11, 1976. Home: 9447 Hamlin Ave Evanston IL 60203

MERRITT, ROBERT LLOYD, lawyer; b. N.Y.C., Sept. 24, 1919; s. Irving and Ida (Ellen) M.; B.S. cum laude, Coll. City N.Y., 1939; J.D. (James Kent scholar), Columbia U., 1942; m. Cynthia Lloyd, Feb. 17, 1952 (dec. June 1973); children—Ethan Allen, Andrew Lloyd, Elizabeth Ellen; m. 2d, Catherine Crowe Dickman, July 27, 1977. Admitted to N.Y. bar, 1942, Ohio bar, 1951; spl. atty. U.S. Dept. Justice, 1942; asso. Milbank, Tweed, Hope, Hadley & McCloy, N.Y.C., 1946-50; practiced in Cleve., 1951—; partner Guren, Merritt, Sogg & Cohen and predecessors, Cleve., 1958—. Dir., mem. exec. com. asst. sec. First Bank Nat. Assn., 1974—. Trustee Cleve. Pub. Library, 1968-74, pres., 1970-71, v.p., 1972-74; trustee Free Med. Clinic Greater Cleve., 1972—. Served with AUS, 1942-46. Mem. AAAS, Archaeol. Inst. Am., Soc. History Discoveries, Am., Cleve. (trustee 1968-71) bar assns., Phi Beta Kappa. Contbr. articles to profl. jours. Home: 2645 Fairmount Blvd Cleveland Heights OH 44106 Office: 650 Terminal Tower Cleveland OH 44113

MERRY, HENRY JOHN, educator; b. Pontiac, Mich., Sept. 28, 1908; s. Earl D. and Lillian (Eck) M.; A.B., U. Mich., 1931, J.D., 1936; M.A., Am. U., Washington, 1952; LL.M., Harvard, 1954; Ph.D., U. London, 1957; postgrad., Oxford, 1968-69; Admitted to Mich. bar, 1936, Ill. bar, 1937, D.C. bar, 1941, N.Y. State bar, 1944; with Arthur Andersen & Co., Chgo., 1937-41, U.S. Treasury Dept., Washington, 1941-44; with firm Milbank, Tweed, Hope & Hadley, N.Y.C., 1944-46; mem. excess profits tax council Bur. Internal Revenue, U.S. Govt. Washington, 1946-47, chmn., 1947-52; asst. controller Paris Regional Office, Mut. Security Agy., 1952-53; research asst. polit. sci. Mich. State U., 1957-58; legal analyst Legis. Reference Service, Library of Congress, Washington, 1958-60; asso. prof. polit. sci. No. Ill. U., 1960-62; asst. prof. polit. sci. Purdue U., Lafayette, Ind., 1962-65, asso. prof. Calumet Campus, 1965-74, prof. emeritus, 1974—. Recipient Ross Essay award Am. Bar Assn., 1954. Mem. Am. Polit. Sci. Assn., Am. Soc. Polit. and Legal Philosophy. Contbr. articles to profl. jours. Address: 555 E William St Ann Arbor MI 48108

MERSCHMAN, WILLIAM FRANCIS, seed and fertilizer co. exec.; b. St. Paul, Jan. 29, 1928; s. Henry Joseph and Agnes Wilhelmina (Rauenbuehler) M.; grad. high sch.; m. Bernice Elaine Mettenburg, Apr. 23, 1949; children—Kathleen, Jean, Joseph, Henry, George. Founder Merschman Seed & Fertilizer, Inc., West Point, Iowa, 1958, pres. and mgr., 1958—; mgr. farm, West Point, 1969—; pres. Midwest Research Corp.; pres., dir. Agriseed, Inc.; dir. Lec County Savs. Bank; dir. Iowa Mktg. Bd. Pres. sch. bd. Marquette Schs., Inc., 1971-73. Mem. Am. (nat. dir. 1966-68), Iowa (pres. 1966-68) soybean assns., Iowa Crop Assn. (dir., v.p. 1968-76), Iowa Seed Dealers Assn. (dir.), Iowa Fertilizer Council (chmn. 1971—). Democrat. Roman Catholic. Elk, K.C. Club: West Point Community. Home: Box 67 West Point IA 52656 Office: 2d St West Point IA 52656

MERSZEI, ZOLTAN, chem. co. exec.; b. 1922; student Fed. Poly. Inst., Zurich, Switzerland; LL.D., Northwood Inst.; married. With The Dow Chem. Co., Midland, Mich., 1949—, gen. sales mgr.-Europe, 1959-61, v.p. Dow Internat., 1961-65, pres., gen. mgr. Dow Chem. Europe S.A., 1965-71, corporate v.p., 1971-75, corporate exec. v.p., 1975-76, chmn. exec. com., pres., chief exec. officer, 1976—, also dir., corporate pres., chief exec. officer, 1976—; dir Handelsbank of Zurich, Dow Banking Corp., Zurich, Dow Corning Corp. Trustee Northwood Inst. Decorated Grand Cross Order Merit (Spain); comdr. Order Oranje Nassau (Netherlands). Office: Dow Chem Co 2030 Dow Center Midland MI 48640

MERTEN, ALAN GILBERT, educator; b. Milw., Dec. 27, 1941; s. Gilbert Ervin and Ruth Anna (Ristow) M.; B.S., U. Wis., 1963, Ph.D., 1970; M.S., Stanford U., 1964; m. Sarah Louise Otto, Jan. 28, 1967; children—Eric, Melissa. Asst. prof. indsl. and ops. engring. U. Mich., Ann Arbor, 1970-74, asso. prof. computer and info. systems, 1974—. Expert, UN devel. program, Budapest, 1974; cons. U.S. Navy, IBM, USAF. Served to capt. USAF, 1963-67. Mem. Assn. for Computing Machinery. Lutheran. Home: 1320 Cambridge St Ann Arbor MI 48104

MERTZMAN, ROBERT ARNOLD, ins. co. exec.; b. Dayton, Ohio, Dec. 13, 1948; s. Stanley Arthur and Sara Katherine (Culbertson) M.; M.A., Ohio U., 1969; C.Ph., Ind. U., 1972, postgrad., 1973; m. Janet Marie Schweller, Sept. 24, 1967; children—Tania Christine, Karina Allyne. Lectr. philosophy Ohio U., Athens, 1968-69; research fellow in philosophy of sci. Ind. U., Bloomington, 1969-72, Woodrow Wilson dissertation fellow, 1973; rep. Investors Trust Inc., Indpls., 1973-75, dist. dir., 1975, regional dir., 1975-76, tng. dir., 1976-77, state dir., 1977—. Pres., Save Hoosier Cts. Com., Bloomington, 1972-73. Mem. Am. Philos. Assn., Philos. Sci. Assn. Contbg. author: (with Nancy Woo): Studies in Linguistics, 1974. Home: 1095 Tennis Ct Circle Indianapolis IN 46260 Office: 107 N Pennsylvania St Indianapolis IN 46204

MERWICK, PATRICIA ANNE, physician; b. Chgo., Mar. 17, 1945; d. William Edward and Anna Veronica (Walsh) M.; B.S. magna cum laude, Loyola U., Chgo., 1967; M.D. with distinction, Northwestern U., 1971. Intern, Presbyn St. Lukes Hosp., Chgo., 1971-72; resident in internal medicine, Rush Presbyn. St. Lukes Hosp., 1972-74, chief resident, 1974-75, instr. internal medicine, 1974-76, asst. prof. internal medicine Rush Med. Coll., 1976—; gen. practice internal medicine, Elmhurst, Ill., 1975—. Recipient Roche Med. Book award, 1971; diplomate Am. Bd. Internal Medicine. Mem. Am. Coll. Physicians, Alpha Omega Alpha. Office: 135 Cottage Hill St Elmhurst IL 60126

MERWIN, HARMON TURNER, regional govt. ofcl.; b. Middlefield, Ohio, July 10, 1920; s. Harry Elverton and Ora (Turner) M.; B.Landscape Architecture, Ohio State U., Columbus, 1950; m. Eldred Louise Stahman, Apr. 10, 1954; children—Elaine, Brian, Kathy. Planner, then dir. Franklin County (Ohio) Regional Planning Commn., Columbus, 1951-69; dep. dir. Mid-Ohio Regional Planning Commn., Columbus, 1970-74, program mgr. spl. projects, 1975-76, program mgr. water related program, 1976—. Mem. bd. Ohio Planning Conf., pres., 1963-65; mem. bd. Columbus Met. Area Community Action Orgn., until 1976; mem. Franklin County environ. health subcom. and facilities com. Mid-Ohio Health Planning Fedn., until 1976. Served with USAAF, 1942-46. Mem. Am. Inst. Planners (pres. Ohio Valley chpt. 1963; chpt. award of merit 1966), Am. Soc. Landscape Architects. Methodist (ofcl. bd. 1960-64). Mason. Home: 2325 Lytham Rd Columbus OH 43220 Office: 514 S High St Columbus OH 43215

MESENBRINK, PHILIP EDWARD, cons. engr.; b. Lincoln, Nebr., Aug. 6, 1937; s. William Gregory and Dolores Elizabeth (Quinn) M.; B.S. in Civil Engring., U. Colo., 1962; M.S. in Civil Engring., Wayne State U., 1965; m. Joan Evelyn Erbecker, July 3, 1973; children—Thomas, Michael, Margaret; stepchildren—Christopher, Anne, Lisa. Designer, Colo. Dept. Hwys., Denver, 1957-58; sales engr. Internat. Pipe & Ceramics Corp., Denver, 1958-61, plant engr., Ada, Okla., 1961-62, prodn. control supt., Detroit, 1962-65; supr., maintenance and plant engr. LTV Aerospace Corp., Warren, Mich., 1965-68; asst. indsl. dept. head Giffels Assos., Detroit, 1968-73; mfg. div. dir. Smith, Hinchman & Grylls Assos., Detroit, 1973-77; pres. Mfg. Tech. Assos., Inc., Southfield, Mich., 1977—. Mem. bd. Com. to Incorporate Farmington Hills (Mich.), 1971. Registered profl. engr., Mich. Mem. Nat. Soc. Profl. Engrs., Am. Inst. Indsl. Engrs., ASCE, Internat. Materials Mgmt. Soc., Chi Epsilon. Republican. Roman Catholic. Club: Oakland Hills Country. Home: 1177 Chesterfield St Birmingham MI 48009 Office: 26011 Evergreen Rd Southfield MI 48076

MESKEN, LORRAINE ANN, counselor; b. San Francisco, Mar. 17, 1928; d. Harry Bennett and Prudence Viva (Stephens) Palmer; m. Charles Mesken, Aug. 8, 1972; children by previous marriage—Joe Donner, Mike Rybak, R.T. Rybak, Georgeann Rybak. Office mgr., Asso. Pipeline Welders, San Francisco, 1949-52; owner, mgr. Rybak Pharmacy, Mpls., 1964-67; dean girls Breck Sch., Mpls., 1967-74, dir. guidance, 1974—. Chmn. counseling Minn. Nat. Coll. Fair. Mem. Nat. Assn. Coll. Admissions Counselors, Cum Laude Soc., Minn. Assn. Coll. Counselors, Am. Personnel and Guidance Assn., Coll. Entrance Exam Bd., Am Legion Aux., Nat. Audubon Soc., Mpls. Inst. Arts, Smithsonian Instn. Republican. Episcopalian. Club: Order Eastern Star. Home: 2610 49th St W Minneapolis MN 55410 Office: 4200 River Rd W Minneapolis MN 55406

MESLER, RUSSELL BERNARD, educator; b. Kansas City, Mo., Aug. 24, 1927; s. James Elmer and Catheine Lena (Knaack) M.; B.S., U. Kans., 1949; M.S., U. Mich., 1953, Ph.D., 1955; m. Jenny-Lea Elizabeth McGowan, June 9, 1951; children—Diane Lee, Scott Owen, Douglas Bernard, Sandra Jeannine. Process engr. Colgate Palmolive Co., Kansas City, Kans., 1949-51; project engr. Ford Nuclear Reactor, Ann Arbor, Mich., 1955-57; asst. prof. chem. engring. U. Mich., Ann Arbor, 1955-57; asso. prof. U. Kans., Lawrence, 1957-61, prof., 1961-70, Warren S. Bellows prof., 1970—. mem. genrating bd. Berkeley Nuclear Labs., Eng., 1975-76. Served with USN, 1945-46. Danforth Asso., 1965-69. Mem. Am. Soc. M.E. (Robert T. Knapp award 1967), Am. Inst. Chem. Engrs., Am. Chem. Soc., Am. Nuclear Soc., Am. Soc. Engring. Edn., Sigma Xi. Lutheran. Contbr. articles to profl. jours. Home: 1629 Dudley Ct Lawrence KS 66044 Office: 102 Nuclear Reactor Center Lawrence KS 66045

MESLER, WILLIAM JOSEPH, III, auto mfg. co. exec.; b. Elizabeth, N.J., Sept. 19, 1942; s. William Joseph and Helen Irene (Arace) M.; Asso. in Mgmt. and Tech., Wayne State U., 1974; children from previous marriage—William Joseph IV, Jeffrey Allan. With Gen. Motors, Linden, N.J., 1960-68, Detroit, 1968—, gen. supr. engring. specifications and tech. data, 1970-73, sr. staff asst. process engring., 1973-77, engr.-in-charge process engring., 1977—. Served with USAR, 1960-67. Notary public, N.J., 1964-68, Mich., 1976—. Mem. Soc. Auto. Engrs., Standards Engrs. Soc. Roman Catholic.

Club: Optimist. Recipient Top Gen. Motors Employee Suggestion award, Linden, N.J., 1966. Home: 24466 Meadow Bridge Dr Mt Clemens MI 48043 Office: 30007 Van Dyke Rd Warren MI 48090

MESSANA, JOSEPH, ednl. adminstr.; b. Detroit, July 31, 1928; s. Frank Richard and Eleanor (Scaglione) M.; B.S., Wayne State U., 1951, M.Ed., 1957, Ed.D., 1968; m. Mary Jane Sasala, Sept. 18, 1954; children—Frank Stephen, Janet Lynn. Tchr., Clawson Pub. Schs., 1955-57; tchr. music and social studies Detroit Pub. Schs., 1957-63, counselor, work tng. coordinator, 1963-66, jr. adminstrv. asst. guidance and counseling, 1966-69; asst. dir. measurements and guidance Oakland Schs., Pontiac, Mich., 1969-72, dir., 1972—. Served with USAF, 1951-55. Recipient Certificate of Dedicated Service, Wayne State U. Edn. Alumni Assn., 1973. Mem. Am. (past senator, recipient Distinguished Service award 1968), Mich. (past pres., recipient Outstanding Service award 1973) personnel and guidance assn., Am. Sch. Counselors Assn., Assn. Counselor Edn. and Supervision, Nat. Vocat. Guidance Assn., Assn. Measurement and Evaluation in Guidance, Guidance Assn. Met. Detroit (past pres.), Oakland Area Counselors Assn., Phi Delta Kappa, Phi Mu Alpha. Contbr. articles in field to profl. jours. Home: 14432 Lakeshore Dr Sterling Heights MI 48078 Office: 2100 Pontiac Lake Rd Pontiac MI 48054

MESSERLI, JOHN HAIGH, edn. adminstr.; b. Monticello, Iowa, Sept. 11, 1923; s. John P. and Ethel (Haigh) M.; student So. Ill. U., 1943; B.A., U. No. Iowa, 1947; M.A., State U. Iowa, 1952, Ed.S., 1970; m. Lorna Caspers, Dec. 20, 1944; children—Douglas, David, Patricia. Tchr., high sch. prin. Ventural (Iowa) Consol. Sch., 1947-51; prin., supt. Newhall (Iowa) Consol. Sch., 1951-56; supt. schs. Marion (Iowa) Ind. Sch., 1956-65; coordinator Coop. Endl. Service Agy. No. 16, Waukesha, Wis., 1965-67; dir. instructional services Joint County Sch. System. Cedar Rapids, Iowa, 1967-70; supt. schs. Monticello (Iowa) Community Schs., 1970-74, Fairbault (Minn.) Pub. Schs., 1974—. Served with USAAF, 1942-45. Decorated Air medal (2). Fulbright grantee, 1963. Mem. Minn. Assn. Sch. Adminstrs., Am. Assn. Sch. Adminstrs., NEA, Phi Delta Kappa. Presbyterian (elder, deacon). Mason (32 deg.). Home: 700 St Paul Av Faribault MN 55021 Office: 2855 NW 1st Ave Faribault MN 55021

MESTEMAKER, ALBERT JOSEPH, JR., lawyer; b. Cin., Apr. 3, 1937; s. Albert Joseph and Jean Frances (Smith) M.; B.A., Xavier U., 1959; J.D., Salmon P. Chase Coll. Law, 1966; m. Sheryl F. Fiester, Sept. 5, 1964; children—Tonya, Michael. Investigator, IRS, 1960-66; admitted to Ohio bar, 1966; asso. firm Smith, Latimer, Doggett & Swing, 1966-71; partner firm Latimer & Swing, Cin., 1971—; asst. pros. atty. Hamilton County (Ohio), 1966-71; dir. Cin. Electric Equipment Co., 1967—, Pleasant Electric Co., 1967—; lectr. criminal law and criminal procedure Salmon P. Chase Coll. Law, 1969—. Served with AUS, 1959-60. Mem. Ohio, Cin. bar assns. Republican. Home: 1 Silo Farm Ln Cincinnati OH 45211 Office: 1014 Vine St Cincinnati OH 45202

METCALF, DORMOND EUGENE, physician; b. Burwell, Nebr., July 16, 1931; s. Earl Augustus and Geneva Eileen (Miller) M.; student Nebr. State Coll., 1956-59; B.S., M.D., U. Nebr., 1964; m. Bonnie Jean Powell, Oct. 24, 1954; children—Sheri Ann, Steven Douglas (dec.), Shelley Kay, Scott Dormond. Intern, Bryan Meml. Hosp., Lincoln, Nebr., 1964-65; practice medicine specializing in family practice, Gordon Clinic, Gordon, Nebr., 1965—; chief staff Gordon Meml. Hosp., asso. instr. sr. med. students in family practice, airman med. examiner; clin. asso. dept. family practice U. Nebr., 1972—. Chmn., Gordon Airport Authority, 1970-71; mem. bd. edn. Gordon Pub. Schs., 1975—; adminstrv. bd. United Methodist Ch., Gordon, 1977—; com. chmn. Cub Scouts. Served with USN, 1952-56. Fellow Am. Acad. Family Physicians; mem. Am., Nebr., N.W. Nebr. (sec.-treas. 1970, pres. 1974) med. socs., AMA (Physicians Recognition award 1977), Am. Acad. Gen. Practice, Aircraft Owners and Pilots Assn., Lambda Delta Lambda, Beta Beta Beta. Home: Box 303 Gordon NE 69343 Office: 807 N Ash St Gordon NE 69343

METCALFE, GRANT EMORY, psychiatrist; b. Albany, N.Y., July 21, 1906; s. Theodore Franklin and Elizabeth (Smith) M.; B.S., Hahnemann Med. Coll., 1928, M.D., 1930; postgrad. Columbia U., 1937, Chgo. Inst. for Psychoanalysis, 1948-53; m. Evelyn Steele, May 6, 1933; children—Benita (Mrs. Joseph Bernier), Grant Emory. Intern, Epworth Hosp., South Bend, Ind., 1930, Williamsport (Pa.) Hosp., 1930-31; resident Middletown State Hosp. (N.Y.), 1931-32; Gowanda State Hosp., 1936-37; practice gen. medicine and psychiatry, Brodheadsville, Pa., 1932-36, South Bend, 1939—; asst. outpatient dept. Edward J. Meyer Meml. Hosp., Buffalo, 1938-39; cons. neuro-psychiatry Children's Dispensary; attending staff Meml. Hosp., 1939-76, chief staff, 1960-63, 66-69; staff St. Joseph's Hosp., 1960-76; cons. psychiatrist Healthwin Hosp., 1939—, No. Ind. Children's Hosp., 1954-61; chief cons. psychiatrist Beatty Meml. Hosp., Westville, Ind., 1951-52; asst. prof. psychiatry Ind. U. Med. Sch., 1953-57, asso. prof., 1957—. Mem. Ind. Mental Health Study Com., 1969; adviser Juvenile Ct. Chmn. Ind. Mental Health Adv. Council, 1953-69. Named Sagamore of Wabash. Diplomate Am. Bd. Psychiatry and Neurology. Fellow Am. Psychiat. Assn. (life), Pan Am. Med. Assn., Royal Soc. Health; mem. Am. Assn. Med. Colls., Ill., Chgo. med. socs., AMA (Physician's recognition awards 1970-73, 73-76), No. Ind. Psychiat. Soc. (pres.), Nat., Ind. (v.p.), St. Joseph County (pres.) assns. for mental health, Am. Psychosomatic Assn., Acad. Religion and Mental Health, Assn. Am. Physicians and Surgeons, Med. Correctional Soc., AAUP, Ind., Mich. saddle horse assns., Alumni Assn. Ind. U. Presbyterian. Mason. Clubs: Michigan City Yacht; Indiana. Author articles in med. jours. Home: 101 S Conestoga Ln South Bend IN 46617 Office: Jefferson Medical Arts Bldg 919 E Jefferson Blvd South Bend IN 46622

METCALFE, RALPH H., congressman; b. Atlanta, May 30, 1910; s. Clarence and Marie (Attaway) M.; Ph.B., Marquette U., 1936; M.A., U. So. Calif., 1939; L.H.D., Ill. Coll. Pediatric Medicine, 1977; m. Madalynne Fay Young, July 20, 1947; 1 son, Ralph H. Track coach, instr. phys. edn. and polit. sci. Xavier U., New Orleans, 1936-42; dir. dept. civil rights Commn. on Human Relations, Chgo., 1945; commr. Ill. Athletic Commn., 1949-52; Democratic committeeman 3d Ward, Chgo., 1952-80, alderman, 1955-71; mem. 92d-95th Congresses from 1st Dist. Ill., also chmn. Panama Canal subcom. Com. on Mcht. Marine and Fisheries, mem. Com. Interstate and Fgn. Commerce, Com. P.O. and Civil Service; mem. Congl. Black Caucus. Dir. Ill. Fed. Savs. and Loan Assn. Mem. U.S. Olympic team, Los Angeles, 1932, Berlin, Germany, 1936; mem. Am. track team touring Europe, 1933, Far East, 1934; pres. Midwest chpt. U.S. Olympians; co-chmn. 3d Pan Am. Games, mem. organizing com., 1959. Mem. Helms Athletic Found., Plan Commn., 1964, Com. Urban Opportunities, 1964 (all Chgo.); pres. Joint Negro Appeal, 1963; convenor Concerned Citizens for Police Reform, Chgo.; bd. dirs. U.S. Olympic Com.; mem. Pres.'s Commn. on Olympic Sports, 1975. Mem. Democratic Steering and Policy Com., 1975—. Served from pvt. to 1st lt. AUS, 1943-45. Decorated Legion of Merit; set former World records for 220 yard dash around curve, 100 yard dash, 100 meter dash; named one of 100 influential blacks in Am., Ebony mag., 1976; recipient alumni award Marquette U., 1974; named to Black Athletes Hall Fame, 1974, U.S. Track and Field Hall Fame, 1974, Nat. Track and Field Hall Fame, 1975. Mem. Am. Vets. Com., Am. Legion, Amvets, Chgo. Urban League, N.A.A.C.P., Alpha Sigma Nu, Alpha Phi Alpha. Elk. Clubs: Masons, Varsity (Chgo.) (pres. 1962). Office: 2438 Rayburn House Office Bldg Washington DC 20515

METRO, PATRICK STEPHEN, oral surgeon; b. Cleve., Mar. 17, 1936; s. Stephen Edward and Caroline (Lombardo) M.; student John Carroll U., 1957; D.D.S., Western Res. U., 1961; m. Rosemary Donna Peakovic, Sept. 6, 1958; children—Jennifer Kay, Suzanne Patrice. Pvt. practice oral surgery, Cin., 1964-65, Cleve., 1965—; teaching staff U. Cin. Gen. Hosp., 1964-65; cons. to industry. Recipient Callaham Meml. award Western Res. Sch. Denistry, 1961. Diplomate Am. Bd. Oral Surgery. Fellow Am. Dental Soc. Anesthesiology; mem. Cleve. Dental Soc., Am. Soc. Oral Surgeons, Delta Sigma Delta. (J.D. Jungman award Lambda chpt. 1961). Club: Westwood Country. Contbr. articles in profl. jours. Home: 21584 Avalon Dr Rocky River OH 44116 Office: 3865 Rocky River Dr Cleveland OH 44111

METTE, ELDON R., savs. and loan exec.; b. Marion County, Mo., Oct. 30, 1936; s. Benjamin G. and Gladys E. (Hamilton) M.; grad. high sch.; m. Patricia Kay Still, Dec. 16, 1956; children—Susan, Vicki. Farmer, Marion County, 1954-58; partsman, salesman Vaughan & Burge, Palmyra, Mo., 1958-65; v.p. consumer loan dept. Palmyra State Bank, 1965-69; exec. v.p., mng. officer Palmyra Savs. & Bldg. Assn., 1969—. Mem. Palmyra (pres. 1976), Palmyra Jr. (charter, treas. 1964, pres. 1968, 76) chambers commerce, U.S. League Savs. Assns. (com. smaller assns. 1972-75, state legis. com. 1976), Mo. Savs. and Loan League (legis. com. 1974-75, 78). Lutheran (ch. sec., past pres. ch. P.T.A.). Kiwanian. Home: Route 2 Palmyra MO 63461 Office: 123 W Lafayette St Palmyra MO 63461

METZ, FLORENCE IRENE, phys. chemist; b. Willard, Ohio, Sept. 1, 1929; d. James A. Metz and Dorothy (Young Metz) Shockley; A.B., Western Res. U., 1951, M.S., 1956; Ph.D., Iowa State U., 1960. Mem. NACA (now NASA), Lewis Lab., Cleve., 1951-55; instr. U. Mo. at Kansas City, 1960-65; sr. chemist Midwest Research Inst., Kansas City, Mo., 1960-63, prin. chemist, 1963-67, sr. adviser for chemistry, 1967-68, head phys. and analytical chemistry, 1968-74, asst. dir. phys. scis. div., 1974-76, dir. chem. scis., 1976—. Director Germanium Info. Center, 1962-67. Mem. com. for community action Johnson County Jr. Coll., 1966-67. Bd. dirs. The Shamrocks, Prime Health. Mem. Am. Chem. Soc. (pub. relations, awards com.), AAAS, Research Soc. Am. (pres. 1970), Nat. Assn. Corrosion Engrs., AAUW (treas.), Zonta Internat. (local pres. 1968-70, chmn. Amelia Earhart fellowship 1968—), Iota Sigma Pi, Sigma Delta Epsilon (hon.). Episcopalian. Spl. contbr. Ann. Mining Rev., London, 1965-68. Contbr. articles to profl. jours. Home: 4927 Southridge Dr Shawnee Mission KS 66205 Office: 425 Volker Blvd Kansas City MO 64110

METZ, FLOYD A., social agy. exec.; b. Mainland, Pa., Dec. 7, 1933; s. Abram G. and Eva (Alderfer) M.; B.A. in Sociology, Goshen Coll., 1956; M.S.W., Wayne State U., 1962; m. Patricia Anne Harris, Aug. 23, 1958; children—Marcia Anne, Kevin Harris. Clin. social worker VA Mental Hygiene Clinic, Allen Park, Mich., 1962-63; sch. social worker Royal Oak (Mich.) Bd. Edn., 1963-65; exec. dir. Big Bros. Oakland County, Pontiac, Mich., 1965-73, chmn. Central region, 1970-72; exec. dir. Big Bros.-Big Sisters of Met. Detroit Area, 1973—. Chmn., Social Workers Forum, Detroit, 1964; treas. Mich. Vis. Tchrs. Assn., 1964-65; program chmn. Big Bros. Am., 1968-69; pres. Pontiac Area Execs. Council, 1971-73. Mem. Acad. Certified Social Workers, Wayne State U. Alumni Assn. (dir. 1964-66), Social Work Alumni Assn. (dir. 1965-66), Nat. Assn. Social Workers (exec. bd. Detroit 1964-68). Club: Detroit Press. Home: 18951 Rosemont Rd Detroit MI 48219 Office: 15800 W McNichols Detroit MI 48235

METZ, PATRICIA ANNE HARRIS, social worker; b. Detroit, May 10, 1936; d. Hugh and Frances (Alvord) Harris; B.A., Albion Coll., 1958; M.S.W., Wayne State U., 1960; m. Floyd A. Metz, Aug. 23, 1958; children—Marcia Anne, Kevin Harris. Caseworker, Family Service of Oakland County, Berkeley, Mich., 1958-59, Clinic for Child Study, Wayne County Juvenile Ct., Detroit, 1959-65, N.W. Wayne County Child Guidance Clinic, Garden City, Mich., 1965-67; exec. sec. Met. Detroit chpt. Nat. Assn. Social Workers, 1967-70; coordinator counseling Friends Sch. in Detroit, 1970-73. Dir. I.C. Harris, Inc., Detroit. Bd. dirs., mem. membership com. Children's Mus. Friends, 1975—; mem. comprehensive child care com. United Community Services, 1972-73; mem. Internat. Visitors Council Detroit; bd. dirs. Met. Detroit YWCA, 1967-74, asst. treas., 1971, treas., 1972-74; bd. dirs., chmn. vol. com. Travelers Aid Soc., 1974—; bd. dirs. Center for Urban Edn., 1975—. Mem. Nat. Assn. Social Workers (chpt. sec. 1966-67, chmn. fin. com. 1970-72, del. to nat. del. 1971, pres., 1976-77) Wayne State U. Sch. Social Work Alumni Assn. (dir. 1963-66, treas. 1964-66), Inkster Coop. Services Com. (sec. 1966-67), Acad. Certified Social Workers. Mennonite. Home: 18951 Rosemont St Detroit MI 48219

METZGAR, PATRICIA CATHERINE, mfg. co. exec.; b. Artesia, N.Mex., Jan. 17, 1912; d. John Francis and Margaret (Dooley) Hefferan; A.B., Western U., 1934; m. Robert Metzgar, Dec. 3, 1937; children—Robert, Mary. Field social worker Fed. Emergency Relief, Grand Rapids, Mich., 1934; tchr. McCabe Sch., Kent County, Mich., 1935; casework supr. categorical asst. State Welfare, Grand Rapids, 1936-46; dir. Metzgar Conveyor Co., Grand Rapids, 1954-62, pres., chief exec. officer, 1962—. Exec. mem. Diocesan Council Cath. Women, 1952; sec. Paulist Guild, 1969-71. Home: 2635 Cascade Rd Grand Rapids MI 49506 Office: 901 Metzgar St Comstock Park MI 49321

METZGER, JOHN DAVID, found. exec.; b. Columbus, Ohio, Feb. 28, 1924; s. Albert Columbus Delano and Anna (Huston) M.; USAAF trainee Eau Claire State Tchrs. Coll., 1942-43; B.F.A., Ohio U., 1947; m. Doris Jean Fahrbach, Sept. 14, 1946; children—John David, Daniel Virgil, Karla Ann, Marytha Jane. Founder, mgr. Sta. WOUB, Athens, Ohio, 1943, 46-47; announcer, writer, producer Sta. WCOL, Columbus, Ohio, 1947-49, Sta. WLW-C-TV, Columbus, Ohio, 1949-51; radio-TV dir. Byer & Bowman Advt. Agy., Columbus, 1951-64; sec., account exec. Joe Hill & Assos., Columbus, Ohio, 1965-66; dir. field services Central Ohio Ednl. TV Found., Inc., Columbus, 1967—. Served with USAAF, 1943-46. Mem. Nat. Acad. TV Arts Scis. (Founder Columbus Cin. Dayton chpt. 1962), Nat. Assn. Ednl. Broadcasters. Presbyterian. Home: 718 Grandon Ave Bexley OH 43209 Office: 2400 Olentangy River Rd Columbus OH 43210

METZGER, WILLIAM IRWIN, microbiologist; b. Peekskill, N.Y., Oct. 29, 1915; s. Harry Irwin and Sarah Fulton (Cramer) M.; B.S., Purdue U., 1937, M.S., 1939; Ph.D., U. Ill., 1946; m. Gertrude Agnes Konkel, July 14, 1941; children—Annettee (Mrs. Timothy J. Hagerty), Dennis. With Lederle Labs., Pearl River, N.Y., 1946-54; dir. microbiology Hektoen Inst. for Med. Research, Cook County Hosp., 1954—. Research asso. U. Ill. Coll. Medicine, 1960—; cons. St. Mary Nazareth Hosp., Chgo., 1966-73. Mem. Skokie Bd. Health (Ill.), 1958-62. Fellow Am. Acad. Microbiology, Am. Pub. Health Assn.; mem. Am. Soc. Microbiology, AAAS, I.S.M., Sigma Xi. Roman Catholic. Contbr. to profl. jours. Edit. bd. Applied Microbiology, 1968—, Jour. Clin. Microbiology, 1975—. Home: 1853 Pfingsten Rd Northbrook IL 60062 Office: 627 S Wood St Chicago IL 60612

MEUCH, VICTOR, comml. artist, educator, photographer; b. Mitterteich, Germany, May 23, 1945; s. Nickoli and Ewfrosina (Ichenko) M.; came to U.S., 1951, naturalized, 1963; student Prairie State Coll., 1963-66, Art Inst. Chgo., 1965; B.A. in Art, Greenville Coll., 1967; postgrad. Washington U., 1966-67, So. Ill. U., 1966, 70, Ill. State U., 1969-70, No. Ill. U., 1975-78; m. Beverly Zajicek, Aug. 17, 1968. Art instr. Kempton (Ill.) Consol. Schs., 1968-69, Marian Central Cath. High Sch., Woodstock, Ill., 1971-76; propr., dir. Masterpiece Gallery, Woodstock, Ill., 1973—, Bevick Photo Services, Woodstock, 1976—; tchr. art Spring Grove (Ill.) Sch., 1976-77; free-lance comml. artist, 1970—; artist photographer McHenry County (Ill.) Conservation Dist., 1977—; lectr. art history and travel, 1977-78; cinematographer for U.S. Youth Conservation Corps, 1977. comml. artist dept. parks and recreation City of Woodstock, 1976—; adjudicator arts and crafts div. McHenry County Fair, 1974—; organizer high sch. student trips to USSR, 1972, 76. Mem. Woodstock Town Square Players, 1975-76; camp counselor Corn Belt-Bloomington Council Boy Scouts Am., 1969; Sunday sch. tchr. Halford Chapel, Greenville, Ill., 1966-67. Recipient awards of Recognition, Chicago Heights Pub. Library, 1977, Woodstock Women's Club, 1975, Woodstock Fine Arts Assn., 1977. Mem. Nat. Art Edn. Assn., Around Chgo. Art Educators Assn., Profl. Photographers of Am. Assn., Nat. Assn. of Filmakers and Cinematographers, Ill. Art Edn. Assn. (McHenry county chmn. 1976—), Internat. Soc. of Artists, Northland Art League. Mem. Free Methodist Ch. Clubs: Kiwanis (recognition award 1975, 78); Woodstock Ski (dir.); Fort Dearborn Camera (Chgo.). Address: 840 N Seminary Ave Woodstock IL 60098

MEWISSEN, DIEUDONNE JEAN, radiobiologist, radiotherapist; b. Ans, Liege, Belgium, Oct. 25, 1924; s. Dieudonne Chretien and Renee Jeanne (Groven) M.; came to U.S., 1954; m. Marie Renee Breuls, Feb. 10, 1963; children—Evelyn, Mark William, Sophie; M.D., U. Liege, 1950, Ph.D., 1961. Resident, U. Liege Cancer Inst., 1950-53; sr. resident Erlanger Hosp., Chattanooga, 1954-55; resident physician Oak Ridge Inst. Nuclear Studies, Oak Ridge, Tenn., 1955-56; attending physician U. Liege Med. Sch., 1956-60; prof. radiology U. Chgo., 1969—; dir. Lab. Radiobiology, Free U. Brussels, 1960-68. Served with Belgian Army, 1945-46. Mem. Belgian Cancer Soc. (sec. gen.), Royal Soc. Medicine, Belgian Soc. Radiology, Belgian Soc. Biology, European Soc. Radiobiology, Radiation Research Soc., Belgian Soc. Radiobiology. Editor: (with J. H. Rust) Exposure of Man to Radiation in Nuclear Warfare, 1963. Home: 5530 S Shore Dr Chicago IL 60637 Office: Box 140 950 E 59th St Chicago IL 60637

MEYER, BARRY LAWRENCE, cardiologist, army officer; b. Bklyn., June 1, 1944; s. Louis and Tibbie (Kaplan) M.; B.A. with honors, U. Calif. at Santa Barbara, 1967; M.D., U. Kans., 1971; m. Earlynnda Louise Souza, Aug. 18, 1968. Intern, resident in internal medicine U. Kans., Kansas City, 1971-74, fellow in cardiology, 1974-76; chief cardiology Irwin Army Hosp., Ft. Riley, Kans., 1976—, chmn. intensive care unit, chmn. cardiopulmonary resuscitation com. Mem. Am. Coll. Cardiology, ACP. Democrat. Home: 2349 Bellehaven Rd Manhattan KS 66502 Office: Irwin Hosp Ft Riley KS 66442

MEYER, BETTY ANNE (MRS. JOHN ROLAND BASKIN), lawyer; b. Cleve.; d. William Henry and Monica (McSherry) Meyer; student Denison U., 1941-43; A.B., Flora Stone Mather Coll., Western Res. U., 1946, LL.B., 1947; m. John Roland Baskin, May 12, 1967. Admitted to Ohio bar, 1947; asst. to dean Adelbert Coll., Western Res. U., 1948-49; asso. firm Kiefer, Waterworth, Hunter & Knecht, Cleve., 1965-74; mem. firm Kiefer, Knecht, Rees, Meyer & Johnson, Cleve., 1974—. Mem. Alpha Phi. Home: 2679 Ashley Rd Shaker Heights OH 44122 also Key Largo FL also East Chop Martha's Vineyard MA Office: Terminal Tower Cleveland OH 44113

MEYER, CHARLES APPLETON, retail exec.; b. Boston, June 27, 1918; s. George von L. and Frances (Saltonstall) M.; B.A., Harvard U., 1939; m. Suzanne Seyburn, June 15, 1940; children—Brooke Meyer Franzgen, Nancy Meyer Hovey. With Sears, Roebuck & Co., 1939-69, 73—, v.p. corporate planning, 1973—, also dir. Sears subs., Bogota, Colombia, 1953-55, v.p., 1955-60, v.p., dir. Southwestern terr., Dallas, 1960-66, v.p., dir. Eastern terr., Phila., 1966-69; asst. sec. state for inter-Am. affairs Dept. State, Washington, 1969-73; dir. Dow Jones, Inc., Allstate Ins. Co., Homart Devel. Co., Gillette Co., Inter-Am. Found. Corp. Bd. dirs. Children's Meml. Hosp., Chgo., Lake Forest (Ill.) Coll. Served to capt. AUS, World War II. Clubs: Harvard, Brook (N.Y.C.); Racquet (Chgo.); Shoreacres (Lake Bluff, Ill.); Gulph Mills Golf; Onwentsia (Lake Forest, Ill.); Met. (Washington). Home: 1320 N Sheridan Rd Lake Forest IL 60045 Office: Sears Tower Chicago IL 60684

MEYER, DANIEL PATRICK, paper co. exec.; b. Marion, Wis., Dec. 19, 1927; s. Bernard E. and Rena N. (Horn) M.; B.S., U. Wis., 1951, m. Jeannine Forsmo, Jan. 19, 1952; children—Danielle, Robert, Richard, Christopher, Stephen. Adminstrv. asst. Consol. Papers, Inc., Wisconsin Rapids, Wis., 1951-56, dir. pub. relations, 1956-74, adminstrv. asst. to pres., 1966-71, adminstrv. asst. to chmn. bd., 1971-75, dir. pub. affairs, 1975—. Mem. Wis. Gov.'s Commn. Edn., 1969-70; vice-chmn., dir. Mid State Vocat. Tech. and Adult Edn. Dist., 1968—; pres. Wisconsin Rapids Area Bd. Catholic Edn., 1970-71; mem. exec. com. Wis. Clergy Econ. Edn. Conf., 1966-73; chmn. Wis. Occupational Alcoholism Task Force, 1973—; mem. Republican Exec. Com., Wood County, Wis., 1959—; trustee Western Mich. U. Paper Tech. Found., Inc., 1969-73; bd. dirs. Consol. Civic Found., Inc., 1967—, sec., 1974-77, pres., 1977—; bd. dirs. South Wood County Econ. Devel. Corp., 1967—, v.p., 1970—. Served with AUS, 1946-48. Recipient Distinguished Service award Wisconsin Rapids Jr. C. of C., 1963, Citizen of Year award Wisconsin Rapids Area C. of C., 1974. Mem. Am. Paper Inst. (pub. relations com. 1966—), Forest Industries Council (communications com. 1974—), Pub. Relations Soc. Am. (dir. Madison chpt. 1971-76), Theta Delta Chi. Roman Catholic. Home: 241 Shore Acres Dr Wisconsin Rapids WI 54494 Office: 231 1st Ave N Wisconsin Rapids WI 54494

MEYER, DOUGLAS OLIVER, lawyer; b. Port Clinton, Ohio, Apr. 8, 1939; s. Leslie Evan and Ada Marie (Schrock) M.; B.A., U. Mich., 1961, J.D., 1964; m. Janith Adele Ellithorpe, June 28, 1969; 1 dau., Adrienne Renee. Admitted to Ohio bar, 1964; since practiced in Port Clinton; partner firm True & Meyer, 1964-71, sole owner firm, 1971—; city solicitor City of Port Clinton, 1965-74. Dir., sec. Oak Harbor State Bank Co. (Ohio), 1971—. Bd. dirs., sec. George F. Lonz Found. Mem. Port Clinton C. of C. (dir. 1974), Ohio, Ottawa County (pres. 1966) bar assns., Phi Delta Phi, Sigma Nu. Republican. Episcopalian. Mason (Shriner, Jester), Rotarian (dir.). Clubs: U. Mich. (pres. Sandusky, Ohio); Playmakers Civic Theatre (dir. Port Clinton 1971); Port Clinton Yacht. Home: 1150 Lee Ave Port Clinton OH 43452 Office: 101 1/2 Madison St Port Clinton OH 43452

MEYER, DREW ALDEN, mktg. exec.; b. Hershey, Pa., Oct. 28, 1943; s. Ray Chester and Marian Jeanetta (Bomberger) M.; B.S., Pa. State U., 1965, M.S., 1966; m. Dixie Ruth Hollinger, Dec. 19, 1964; children—Kimberly Ann, Jennifer Anne. Market research analyst Vulcan Materials Co., Birmingham, Ala., 1966-67, 70-71, sr. market research analyst, 1971-72, mgr. market planning, Metals div., Sandusky, Ohio, 1972-75, bus. mgr. municipal metals, 1975-77; market devel. cons. Waste Mgmt. Inc., Oak Brook, Ill., 1977—. Adv.

council Perkins Citizens Com., Sandusky, 1974. Served to capt., AUS, 1967-70. Decorated Bronze Star medal, Army Commendation medal. Named Most Valuable Mem. Birmingham chpt. Am. Mktg. Assn., 1971-72. Mem. Am. Mktg. Assn. (chpt. v.p. 1972-73), Am. Inst. Mining, Metall. and Petroleum Engrs. Contbr. article to profl. jour. Home: 1803 Cliffside Ct Naperville IL 60540 Office: 900 Jorie Blvd Oak Brook IL 60521

MEYER, FRANK HENRY, educator; b. N.Y.C., July 11, 1915; s. Frank X. and Anna Helen (Wenzinger) M.; B.S., City Coll. N.Y., 1936; postgrad. Newark Coll. Engring., 1945-48; M.S., Poly. Inst. Bklyn., 1951; postgrad. Okla. State U., 1955-60, U. Wash., 1961-63; M.A., U. Minn., 1968; m. Winifred Josephine Duffy, Aug. 5, 1946; children—Frank, Vivian. X-ray crystallographer Textile Research Inst., Princeton, N.J., 1951-53; research physicist Continental Oil Co., Ponca City, Okla., 1954-60; research engr., project leader Kaiser Aluminum Co. Chem. Corp., Spokane, Wash., 1960-63; sr. research engr. Univac, Sperry Rand, St. Paul, 1963-65; asst. prof. physics and philosophy U. Wis., Superior, 1966—. Referee Am. Jour. Physics, 1972—. Dir. New Sci. Advocates, Inc. Dir. Lake Superior Spirit of '76 Forum, 1972-76. Am. Cancer Soc. grantee, 1948-51; U. Wis. grantee, 1970-75. Mem. Am. Phys. Soc., Am. Crystallographic Assn., Am. Assn. Physics Tchrs., A.A.U.P., Fedn. Am. Scientists, Common Cause, Soc. Physics Students, Sigma Pi Sigma. Unitarian Universalist. Editor: Reciprocity, 1971—. Patentee in field. Contbr. articles to profl. jours. Home: 1103 15 Ave SE Minneapolis MN 55414 Office: U Wis Physics Dept Superior WI 54880

MEYER, FRANK LOUIS, furnace co. exec.; b. Peoria, Ill., June 15, 1903; s. George F. and Lucia A. (Mueller) M.; student Bradley Acad., Peoria, 1917-21, U. Ill., 1921-23, 30; B.S. in Mech. Engring., Mass. Inst. Tech., 1927; m. Winifred Rogerson, Nov. 25, 1927; children—Winann (Mrs. William A. Rossetter), Frank Rogerson, Gregory Torrey. Draftsman Meyer Furnace Co., Peoria, 1923-24, engr., 1928-29, treas., dir., 1930-33, v.p., dir., 1933-40, pres., dir., 1941—; dir. Victor Foundry Co., Peoria, 1933-40; v.p., dir. Air Conditioning Finance Corp., Peoria, 1934-38; sec., dir. F. Meyer & Bro. Co., Peoria, 1940-57; pres., dir. F. Meyer Supply Co., 1964—; pres. Somerset of Gulfstream, Inc., Delray Beach, Fla., 1972-74. Mem. engring. bldg. adv. com. Bradley U., 1938-40. Bd. dirs. Children's Home, Peoria, Peoria YMCA. Mem. Peoria Assn. Commerce, Peoria Plan (v.p., dir., mem. exec. com.), Illinois Valley (dir., mem. exec. com., 1945-53), Ill. (mem. Congl. legis. com. 1950) mfrs. assn., Peoria (dir. 1948-49), ASME (life; chmn. Central Ill. sect. 1940-41), Am. Soc. Heating, Refrigeration and Air Conditioning Engrs. (life, mem. com. promotion research, com. rating heavy duty furnaces), Nat. Warm Air Heating and Air Conditioning Assn. (mem. finance com. 1950-58, chmn. research adv. council 1945-56, pres. 1956-58), Air Conditioning and Refrigeration Inst. (mem. planning com., dir. 1965-77), Gas Appliance Mfrs. Assn. (dir. 1948-56, chmn. gas house heating and air conditioning equipment div. 1948-49; chmn. furnace div. 1954-56), Am. Gas Assn. (mem. approval requirements com., mem. tech. adv. group heating and air conditioning research 1952-53), Phi Gamma Delta, Alpha Pi. Republican. Episcopalian (vestryman). Clubs: Peoria Country, Creve Coeur (Peoria); Gulfstream Bath and Tennis Little (Gulfstream, Fla.). Contbr. articles to profl. jours. Patentee in field. Home: 4304 Grandview Dr Peoria Heights IL 61614 Office: Meyer Furnace Co 1300 SW Washington St Peoria IL 61653

MEYER, FRED WILLIAM, meml. parks exec.; b. Fair Haven, Mich., Jan. 7, 1924; s. Fred W. and Gladys (Marshall) M.; A.B., Mich. State Coll., 1946; m. Jean Hope, Aug. 5, 1946; children—Frederick, Thomas, James, Nancy. Salesman Chapel Hill Meml. Gardens, Lansing, Mich., 1946-47; mgr. Roselawn Meml. Gardens, Saginaw, Mich., 1947-49; dist. mgr. Sunset Meml. Gardens, Evansville, Ind., 1949-53; pres., dir. Memory Gardens Mgmt. Corp., Indpls., Hamilton Meml. Gardens, Chattanooga, Covington Meml. Gardens, Ft. Wayne, Ind., Chapel Hill Meml. Gardens, Grand Rapids, Mich., White Chapel Meml. Gardens, Huntington, W.Va., Forest Lawn Memory Gardens, Indpls., Lincoln Memory Gardens, Indpls., Sherwood Meml. Gardens, Knoxville, Tenn., Chapel Hill Meml. Gardens, South Bend, Ind., Tri-Cities Meml. Gardens, Florence, Ala., Woodlawn Meml. Gardens, Paducah, Ky., White Chapel Meml. Gardens, Springfield, Mo., Floral Hills Meml. Gardens, Clarksburg, W.Va., Beverly Hills Meml. Gardens, Morgantown, W.Va., Mercury Devel. Corp., Indpls., Quality Marble Imports, Indpls., Quality Printers, Indpls., Am. Bronze Craft, Inc., Judsonia, Ark. Mem. C. of C., A.I.M., Nat. Assn. Cemeteries, Am. Cemetery Assn., Sigma Chi, Phi Kappa Delta. Elk. Clubs: Nat. Sales Executives, Athenaem Turners, Columbia, Meridian Hills Country. Home: 110 E 111th St Indianapolis IN 46280 Office: 3733 N Meridian St Indianapolis IN 46208

MEYER, HERBERT ALTON, III, editor, publisher; b. Kansas City, Mo., June 15, 1947; s. Herbert Alton, Jr. and Mary Janet (McDonald) M. B.S. in Bus. Adminstrn., U. Kans., 1969; m. Dorothy Dianne Eddins, June 3, 1969; children—Herbert Alton IV, Scott William. Courthouse reporter Lawrence (Kans.) Daily Jour.-World, 1969-71; editor, pub. Independence (Kans.) Daily Reporter, 1971—. Mem. Governmental Ethics Commn. State Kans., 1974—. Trustee William Allen White Found., U. Kans.; bd. dirs. Mercy Hosp., chmn., 1977; bd. dirs. Neewollah, Inc., Mid-Am., Inc. Served with AUS, 1969-70. Mem. Kans. Press Assn. (bd. dirs.), Independence C. of C. (dir.), Sigma Chi. Republican. Episcopalian. Elk, Rotarian. Home: 912 Birdie Dr Independence KS 67301 Office: 320 N 6th St Independence KS 67301

MEYER, HOWARD MAX, mech. engr.; b. Chgo., May 2, 1914; s. Max John and Nellie Dora (Dresher) M.; student Central YMCA Coll., Chgo., 1933-35; B.S.M.E., Ill. Inst. Tech., 1937; m. Miriam Hope Jack, Sept. 15, 1939; children—Jacqueline Ann, Betty Lou Meyer Barksdale. Engr., Danly Machine Corp., Cicero, Ill., 1937-45; engr. asst. to plant mgr. Rockola Mfg. Corp., Chgo., 1946-50; plant engring. project devel. supr. Ford Motor Co. aircraft engine div., Chgo., 1950-55, mfg. engr., gen. products div., Ypsilanti, Mich., 1955-59; competitive product analyst Chrysler Corp., Highland Park, Mich., 1959-66; mech. systems design engr. Hydra Matic div. Gen. Motors Corp., Ypsilanti, 1967—. Mem. indsl. drafting adv. bd. Washtenaw Community Coll., Ypsilanti, 1966-68. Registered profl. engr., Ill., Mich. Mem. Mich., Nat. socs. profl. engrs., Soc. Auto. Engrs., Soc. Mfg. Engrs., Am. Preparedness Def. Assn., Nat. Rifle Assn., Engring. Soc. Detroit, Ypsilanti Hist. Soc. Republican. Patentee conveyor for cylindrical parts, automated roller clutch assembly. Home: 510 Fairview Circle Ypsilanti MI 48197 Office: Hydra Matic Div Gen Motors Corp Willow Run Ypsilanti MI 48197

MEYER, IVAN HENRY, constrn. co. exec.; b. Adrian, N.D., July 21, 1930; s. Henry and Dorothy Mable (Wieck) M.; grad. high sch. Supt., estimator Wm. Collins & Sons, 1954-62; foreman Butler Constrn. Co., 1950-54; pres. Meyer Constrn. Co., Dickinson, N.D., 1962-70, 74—, Meyer Constrn. Co., 1970-73; owner Ivanhoe Inn, Dickinson; dir. Am. State Bank, Ramada Inn, O'Hearns (all Dickinson). Served with USNR, 1948-50. Mem. Asso. Gen. Contractors (bd. dirs. 1970-73, v.p. 1971-72, nat. dir. 1973—), Nat. Asphalt Pavement Assn. (gov. chpt. 1970), Am. Legion, C. of C. Clubs: Elks, Eagles. Home: Dickinson ND 58601 Office: Box 1035 Dickinson ND 58601

MEYER, JEROME HERBERT, surgeon; b. Butler, Pa., Sept. 6, 1910; s. Hyman Louis and Sarah (Shur) M.; B.A., Ohio State U., 1933, M.S., 1940, M.D., 1940; m. Florence Cohen, Feb. 22, 1931; children—David, Darlene. Intern, St. Luke's Hosp., Cleve., 1940-41, asst. resident, 1941-42; resident surgeon St. Joseph's Hosp., Milw., 1942; instr. surgery Marquette U., 1942; chief resident surgery, instr. sch. nursing Aultman Hosp., Canton, Ohio, 1946; chief aseptic surgery VA Brown Gen. Hosp., Dayton, Ohio, 1947-48; pvt. practice surgery, Dayton, 1948—; chief surgery Good Samaritan Hosp., 1966-70; asso. prof. clin. surgery Wright State U., Dayton, 1975—; sr. surgeon Barney Children's Hosp.; mem. staff Miami Valley, St. Elizabeth's, Kettering Meml. hosps.; cons. to surgeon gen. USAF, Wright Patterson AFB; med. adviser CAP. Bd. dirs. Jewish Home for Aged, 1954-65, pres., 1960-65; bd. dirs. Jewish Community Council, 1955-65; trustee Aviation Hall Fame, 1967—, curator. Served as maj. M.C., USAAF, 1943-45; ETO. Decorated Purple Heart; recipient Wright Aviation award, 1957; Jimmy Doolittle fellow award, 1977. Diplomate Am. Bd. Surgery, Internat. Bd. Surgery, Am. Bd. Abdominal Surgery. Fellow A.C.S., Internat. Coll. Surgeons; mem. AMA, Montgomery County, Ohio med. assns., Ohio, Dayton (pres. 1963-64) surg. socs., Air Force Assn. (dir. 1952-56), Silver Wings frat. (chmn. Ohio), World Wings Assn. (1st pres. 1976), OX 5 Aviation Assn. Author numerous articles in field. Home: 4237 Catalpa Dr Dayton OH 45405 Office: Fidelity Bldg 211 S Main St Dayton OH 45402

MEYER, JOHN ROLLIN, newspaper publisher; b. Lincoln, Nebr., July 22, 1932; s. Ralph Frank and Luemma Agnes (Bottorf) M.; B.A. with honors in Journalism, U. Iowa, 1954; m. Mary Helen Hanna, Dec. 28, 1952; children—Michael John, Kathleen Denise. Newsman sta. KCRG-TV, Cedar Rapids, Iowa, 1954-55; sports editor Oelwein (Iowa) Daily Register, 1956-57; sports reporter Cedar Rapids (Iowa) Gazette, 1958-60; news editor, bus. mgr. Denison (Iowa) Bull., 1960-63; pub. Detroit Lakes Tribune-Becker County Record, Lakes Pub., Detroit Lakes, Minn., 1963—; pres. Lakes Pub., 1970—, Lakeland Fed. Service Corp., 1972—. Co-founder Indsl. Corp., 1965; co-chmn. Centennial, 1972. Bd. dirs. Intra-Am. Student Founds., St. Mary's Hosp. Recipient Distinguished Service award, Detroit Lakes, 1968; named Boss of Yr., Detroit Lakes, 1969. Mem. Minn. Newspaper Assn. (pres. 1974-75), Am. Newspaper Reps. (pres. 1970-71), C. of C. (pres. 1970-71). Mason (Shriner), Elk, Eagle, Kiwanian. Home: Box 30 Route 5 Detroit Lakes MN 56501 Office: Box 826 Detroit Lakes MN 56501

MEYER, KENNETH MARVEN, seminary pres.; b. Chgo., Nov. 27, 1932; s. Kenneth Marven and Lorraine Barbara M.; student Greenville (Ill.) Coll., No. Baptist Coll., Wheaton (Ill.) Coll.; M.Div., Trinity Sem.; m. Carol Jean Ebner, June 12, 1953; children—Keith, Kevin, Caryn; Ordained to ministry Evang. Free Ch.; pastor Glenview (Ill.) Evang. Free Ch., 1954-60, Evang. Free Ch., Mpls., 1960-66; exec. dir. Christian edn. Evang. Free Ch., 1967-70; sr. pastor First Evang. Free Ch., Rockford, Ill., 1970-74; pres. Trinity Sem., Deerfield, Ill., 1974—; dir. Latin Am. Sem., Costa Rica, Lydia Childrens Home, Pioneer Girls Corp. Chmn. Leighton Ford Reachout. Mem. Nat. Assn. Evangelicals, Rockford Ministerial Assn. (chmn.), Police-Clergy Assn. (chmn. Rockford), Pres.'s Assn. AMA, Consortium Sem. Presidents, Crystal Municipal arbitrator. Home: 16 Reliance Ln Lincolnshire IL 60015 Office: 2045 Halfday Rd Deerfield IL 60015

MEYER, LEON JACOB, wholesale co. exec.; b. Chgo., Nov. 12, 1923; s. Joseph and Minnie (Lebovitz) M.; student Lake Forest Coll., 1941-43; B.S., U. Calif., Los Angeles, 1948; m. Barbara Gene Bothman, Oct. 17, 1948; children—Charles Scott, John Mark, Ellen Renee. Owner, operator Christopher Distbg. Co., Santa Monica, Calif., 1951-53; pres. J. Meyer & Co., Waukegan, Ill., 1953—, Western Candy & Tobacco Co., Carpentersville, Ill., 1970—, Ill. Briar Pipe & Sundry Co., Waukegan, 1963—; chmn. bd. Phillips Bros. Co., Kenosha, Wis., 1975—, Ill. Wholesale Co., 1976—. Served with U.S. Army, 1943-46; PTO. Named Sundry Man of Year, 1976. Mem. Nat. Assn. Tobacco Distbrs. (trustee), Ill. Assn. Candy-Tobacco Distbrs. (past chmn. bd.), Federated Merchandising Corp. (past pres.), Internat. Tobacco Wholesaler Alliance (v.p.), Nat. Automatic Merchandisers Assn., Nat. Candy Wholesalers Assn., Intercontinental Cons., U. Calif. (Los Angeles) Alumni Club, Waukegan/Lake County C. of C. Jewish. Clubs: Elks, Eagles. Home: 3444 University Ave Highland Park IL 60035 Office: 3055 Washington St Waukegan IL 60085

MEYER, LOUIS JON, agrl. products co. exec.; b. Sabetha, Kans. Dec. 7, 1948; s. Louis John and Mavis Louise (Strahm) M.; B.S. in Agronomy, Kans. State U., 1970, M.S. in Agronomy, 1972; m. Cathy Lavina Allison, Aug. 22, 1969; 1 dau., Nicole Ann. Research agronomist S.E. Kans. Expt. Sta., Mound Valley, 1972-75; mktg. devel. new products Monsanto Co., West Des Moines, Iowa, 1975-77, tech. mgr. mktg., 1977—. Mem. Am. Soc. Agrl. Engrs., Am. Soc. Agronomy, Weed Sic. Soc. Am., Am. Soybean Assn., Sigma Xi (Outstanding Sophomore award 1970), Alpha Zeta. Republican. Mem. Apostolic Christian Ch. Rotarian. Author: Determination of Fertilizer and Pesticide Compatibility, 1972; Development of Johnson Grass Control Systems in Southeast Kansas, 1975. Contbr. articles to profl. jours. Home: 647 Amberjack Ballwin MO 63011 Office: 800 N Lindberg St St Louis MO 63166

MEYER, MARLIN HENRY, supt. schs.; b. Watseka, Ill., Oct. 23, 1934; s. August J. and Ella (Rabe) M.; student Ill. State Normal U., 1952-54; B.S., U. Ill., 1955, M.Ed., 1959, Advanced Certificate in Ednl. Adminstrn., 1965; m. Jean Ellyn Leeseberg, Aug. 14, 1954; children—Judith Ann, Paul John, Mark John. Vocational agrl. tchr. Community Unit Dist. 1, Chatsworth, Ill., 1955-59, supt. schs., high sch. prin., 1959-66; supt. schs., elementary prin. Community Unit Dist. 205, Warren, Ill. 1966—. Mem. governing com. Northwest Div. Ill. Assn. Sch. Bds., 1968—; mem. Meridian Park Com., 1969-71; active Boy Scouts Am. Bd. dirs. JoDaviess County Ednl. Services Center, 1966-69, sec. 1968-69; exec. bd. JoDaviess-Carroll area Vocational Tech. Sch., 1970—, sec. pro-tem, 1970-71, chmn. exec. bd., 1972-73. Mem. Am., Ill. (ethics and welfare com. 1970-72) assns. sch. adminstrs., Livingston County Adminstrs. (pres. 1961-62), Vermillion Valley Athletic Conf. (pres., sec. 1960-66), Northwest Football Conf. (pres. 1967-68), U.S. Grant Conf. (pres. 1968-73), Chatsworth Lutheran Brotherhood, Warren C. of C. Lutheran (ch. council 1970). Lion (sec. 1964-65, pres. 1974-75). Home: 616 Galena Ave Warren IL 61087 Office: Warren IL 61087

MEYER, MAURICE WESLEY, educator; b. Long Prairie, Minn., Feb. 13, 1925; s. Ernest William and Augusta (Warnke) M.; B.S., U. Minn., 1953, D.D.S., 1957, M.S., 1959, Ph.D., 1961; m. Martha Helen Davis, Sept. 3, 1946; children—James Irvin, Thomas Orville. Teaching asst., U. Minn. Sch. Dentistry, 1954-55, research fellow, 1956-57, instr., 1960-61, asst. prof., 1961-64, asso. prof., 1964—; USPHS predoctoral research fellow dept. physiology, U. Minn., 1955-56, Nat. Inst. Dental Research postdoctoral research fellow, 1957-60, research fellow, 1958-61, lectr., 1961-73, asso. prof., 1973—, asso. prof. dept. neurology, 1974—; full mem. grad. faculty, 1973—. Nat. Inst. Dental Research research career devel. awardee, 1963-69; investigator Center for Research and Cerebral Vascular Disease, U. Minn., 1969—, dir. exptl. lab., 1975—; trainee, Inst. for Advanced Edn. in Dental Research, 1964; abstractor Oral Research Abstracts, 1966; cons. dental study sect. Nat. Inst. Dental Research, 1969, and Nat. Heart Lung Inst., 1973; vis. asso. prof., also vis. research fellow Dept. Physiology and Sch. Dentistry, Cardiovascular Research Inst., U. Calif., San Francisco, 1971. Served to col., Dental Corps, AUS, 1943-46, 46-50; comdr. 575 Moblzn. Designation Detachment (R&D), 1969—. Decorated Air medal with 3 oak leaf clusters, D.F.C. Fellow A.A.A.S.; mem. Am., Minn. dental socs., Internat. Assn. Dental Research (pres. Minn. sect. 1967-68), Soc. for Exptl. Biology and Medicine, Am. Physiologic Soc., Microcirculatory Soc., Am. Assn. Dental Schs. (chmn. 1972-73), Canadian Physiol. Soc., Sigma Xi, Omicron Kappa Upsilon. Mason. Contbr. to profl. publs. in field. Home: 560 Rice Creek Terrace Minneapolis MN 55432 Office: 424 Millard U Minn Minneapolis MN 55455

MEYER, RICHARD CARROLL, SR., civil engr.; b. St. Louis, Aug. 31, 1934; s. Edwin William and Ione (Roach) M.; B.C.E., U. Mo., 1957; m. Patricia Ann Woodworth, Sept. 8, 1956; children—Richard, Raymond, Tricia. Detailer, Riback Industries, Columbia, Mo., 1955-57; with U.S. Steel Corp., 1957—, plant engr., Waukegan, Ill., 1976—. Pres., Calumet Region (Ind.) Montessori Sch. Parents Group, 1968; pres. bd. dirs. Calumet Region Montessori Sch., Inc., 1969-72; active Boy Scouts Am. Served in U.S. Army, 1957-59. Registered profl. engr., Ind., Ill. Mem. Assn. Iron and Steel Engrs., Nat., Ill. socs. profl. engrs. Republican. Roman Catholic. Home: 1145 Weeping Willow Ln Libertyville IL 60048 Office: US Steel Corp PO Box 440 Waukegan IL 60085

MEYER, ROBERT SMITH, state ofcl.; b. Appleton, Wis., July 12, 1915; s. Jacob Cornelius and Alma Grace (Collins) M.; B.A., Beloit Coll., 1938; B.M. cum laude, Lawrence Coll., 1948; M.M., Northwestern U., 1954; M.S., U. Wis., 1968; m. Doris Elizabeth Pfaff, July 10, 1943; children—Lyndon, John, Lois. Br. underwriter, operating mgr. Allstate Ins. Co., Chgo., Phila., 1939-46; dir. music Escanaba (Mich.) Pub. Schs., 1949-59; program dir., bus. mgr. Christ Presbyn. Ch., Madison, Wis., 1959-63; sch. counselor, supr. guidance Madison (Wis.) Pub. Schs., 1965-71; state supr. career edn. Wis. Dept. Pub. Instruction, Madison, 1971—. Served with USNR, 1942-46. Certified sch. counselor, Wis.; licensed real estate and ins. salesman; certified instrumental music, music theory, social sci., exact sci. and French tchr.1,Mich. Mem. Am., Wis. personnel and guidance assns., Am. Vocat. Assn., Wis. Assn. of Vocat. and Adult Edn., Wis. Fedn. of Tchrs. Republican. Presbyterian. Contbr. articles to profl. edn., ch. and music jours. Home: 475 Presidential Ln Madison WI 53711 Office: 126 Langdon St Madison WI 53702

MEYER, STUART MELVIN, physician; b. Chgo., Ill., June 5, 1935; s. Martin and Sadie (Widdes) M.; B.S., Roosevelt U., 1956; M.D., Chgo. Med. Sch., 1960; m. Sandra Spak, June 17, 1956; children—Bonnie, Bruce, Stacy. Intern, Cook County Hosp., Chgo., 1960-61; resident St. Louis U. Hosps., 1961-65; practice medicine specializing in orthopedic surgery, Skokie, Ill., 1965; mem. staff Cook County (Ill.) Hosp., Chgo., Forest Hosp., Des Plaines, Ill., Skokie Valley Hosp., Skokie, Ill., Evanston-Glenbrook Hosp., Glenview, Ill.; attending surgeon Scoliosis Clinic, 1970—; asso. orthopedic surgery, Northwestern U., 1967—. Diplomate Am. Acad. Orthopedics. Fellow Am. Coll. Surgeons, Am. Acad. Orthopedics; mem. AMA, Chgo. Med. Assn. Ill. Med. Soc., ASTM. Home: 869 Peachtree Ln Glencoe IL 60022 Office: 9843 Gross Point Rd Skokie IL 60076

MEYER, WALTER, nuclear engr.; b. Chgo., Jan. 19, 1932; s. Walter and Ruth (Killoran) M.; B.Ch.E., Syracuse U., 1956, M.Ch.E., 1957; postgrad. (NSF, Sci. Faculty fellow) Mass. Inst. Tech., 1962; Ph.D., Oreg. State U., 1964; m. Jacqueline Miscall, May 8, 1953; children—Kim, Holt, Eric, Leah, Susannah. Prin. chem. engr. Battelle Meml. Inst., Columbus, Ohio, 1957-58; instr. chem. engring. Oreg. State U., Corvallis, 1958-64, asst. prof., 1964; research engr. Hanford Atomic Labs., Richland, Wash., 1959-60, Lawrence Radiation Lab., Livermore, Calif., 1964; asst. prof. nuclear engring. Kans. State U., Manhattan, 1964-66, asso. prof., 1966-68, prof., 1968-72; prof., chmn. nuclear engring. U. Mo.-Columbia, 1972—, Robert Lee Tatum prof. engring., 1974—; cons. Ga. Pacific Co., 1964, Kerr-McGee Co., 1966-67, Gen. Physics Corp., 1967-69, Union Carbide Corp., 1967-68, Argonne Nat. Lab., 1970, Boeing Co., Wichita, Kans., 1970—, Bendix Co., Kansas City, Mo., 1973, Mo. Pub. Service Commn., 1974, FTC, 1976-77; dir. summer insts. NSF-AEC, 1969, NSF, 1972; co-dir. summer inst. AEC, 1972, dir. workshop, 1973; dir. ERDA Workshops, 1975, 76, 77; mem. Columbia Coal Gasification Task Force, 1977. Mem. Manhattan Human Relations Orgn., 1966—; mem. Kans. Gov.'s Nuclear Energy Council, 1971-72; active Boy Scouts Am. NSF grantee, 1965-67, 73-75, 77—; AEC grantee, 1969-71, 73-74; Dept. Def. grantee, 1969-72; ERDA grantee, 1975, 77—. Mem. Am. Inst. Chem. Engrs. (chmn. nuclear engring. div. 1977-78), Am. Chem. Soc., Am. Nuclear Soc. (chmn. pub. info. com. 1975—; Nat. Spl. award 1974), Am. Soc. Engring. Edn. (exec. com. nuclear div. 1973-75, chmn. 1976-77, exec. com. 1977-78), Am. Wind Soc., Sigma Xi, Tau Beta Pi. Congregationalist. Contbr. articles to profl. jours. Patentee in field. Home: 206 Devine Ct Columbia MO 65201

MEYERHOFF, ARTHUR EDWARD, advt. agy. exec.; b. Chgo., Mar. 12, 1895; s. Emanuel and Jennie (Lewin) M.; student pub. schs., Chgo.; m. Madelaine H. Goldman, 1921; m. 2d, Elaine Clemens, Jan. 27, 1945; children—Jane, Arthur E., Joanne, William, Judith Lynn. With Hood Rubber Co., 1914-22; classified advt., circulation mgr. Wis. News, Milw., 1922-29; with Neisser & Meyerhoff, Chgo., advt. and merchandising, 1929-41; pres. Arthur Meyerhoff Assos., Inc., (formerly Arthur Meyerhoff & Co.), Chgo., 1941-65, chmn. bd., 1965—; organizer Gibraltar Industries, Inc., 1958; pioneered comic page advt.; dir. Santa Catalina Island Co., Chgo. Nat. League Ball Club, Inc.; developer Myzon products; Myzon, Inc. organized, 1951. Served with AEF, World I. Received 1st prize Marshall Field candid div., 6th ann., 3d internat. competition and salon, 1939; George Washington Honor Medal award Freedoms Found. at Valley Forge, 1967. Mem. Am. Assn. Advt. Agys., C. of C. Author: Strategy of Persuasion, 1965. Office: 410 N Michigan Av Chicago IL 60611

MEYERHOFF, RICHARD ARTELL, educator; b. Dunkerton, Iowa, Jan. 22, 1922; s. Leonard Julius and Alvina E. (Lamprecht) M.; B.A., U. No. Iowa, 1948; M.A., N.Y. U., 1951; m. Dorothy Gene Schoof, Dec. 17, 1944; children—Nancy Jean, Kay Lynn. Head driver edn. dept. Waterloo (Iowa) Schs., 1948-70; curriculum specialist Iowa driver edn. research and devel. project Iowa Dept. Pub. Instrn., Waterloo, 1971—. Mem. film adv. bd. Aetna Life, 1973. Served with USAAF, 1942-45. Mem. Nat., Iowa edn. assns., Am. Driver and Traffic Safety Assn., Iowa Driver Edn. Assn. (pres. 1951). Lutheran. Co-author: Drive Right, 1977. Contbr. articles to profl. jours. Home: 329 Colorado Rd Cedar Falls IA 50613 Office: Baltimore and Ridgeway Waterloo IA 50701

MEYERS, CHRISTINE LAINE, automobile co. exec.; b. Detroit, Mich., Mar. 7, 1946; d. Ernest R. and Eva L. (Laine) Meyers; B.A., U. Mich., 1968; m. Kenneth S. Adamski, Feb. 12, 1972. Editor indsl. relations Detroit Diesel div. Gen. Motors Corp., 1968; asso. editor Action Age, J.L. Hudson Co., Detroit, 1969-70, broadcast mgr., 1970-71, downtown store promotion mgr., 1971-72, mgr. internal sales promotion, 1972-73, dir. publicity, 1973-76; nat. advt. mgr.

Pontiac Motor div. Gen. Motors Corp., Pontiac, Mich., 1976—. Regional and state debate champion, 1964. Mem. Women's Economic Club (pres.), Women in Communications (2d v.p.), Women Who Move Detroit, Michigan Opera (chmn. bus. sect.), Founders Soc., Detroit Inst. of Arts, Women's Advt. Club, Adcraft, Pub. Relations Soc. of Am., First Soc. of Detroit (exec. com.), C. of C., Women for United Found., United Found., Internat. Assn. of Bus. Communicators, Mortarboard (past v.p.), Kappa Tau Alpha, Quill and Scroll. Home: 6729 Candlewood Trail West Bloomfield MI 48033 Office: 1 Pontiac Plaza Pontiac MI 48053

MEYERS, DONALD BATES, toxicologist; b. Cedar Rapids, Iowa, Jan. 30, 1922; s. Carl J. and Vera L. (Bates) M.; B.S., State U. Iowa, 1944, M.S. (Union Carbide and Carbon fellow), 1948; Ph.D., 1949; m. Evelyn M. Kudrna, Aug. 26, 1950; children—Donlyn, Ellyn, Beth, Darcy. Instr., State U. Iowa, Iowa City, 1948-49; asst. prof. Butler U., Indpls., 1949-53, asso. prof., 1953-59, prof., 1959-62; prof. U. Tex., Austin, 1962-63; sr. scientist Eli Lilly & Co., Greenfield, Ind., 1963-68, research scientist, 1968-71, research asso., 1971—; lectr. Grad. Coll., Butler U., 1965—. Mem. Ind. Drug Abuse Edn. Com., 1969-72. Recipient Distinguished Profs. award Baxter Found., 1958. Mem. Sci. Research Soc. Am., Acad. Pharm. Scis., Soc. Toxicology, Am. Pharm. Assn., AAAS, Sigma Xi. Republican. Methodist. Club: Masons. Contbr. articles to profl. jours. Home: 638 N State St Greenfield IN 46140 Office: Box 708 Greenfield IN 46140

MEYERS, FRANKLIN DAVID, state ofcl.; b. St. Joseph, Mich., Oct. 17, 1934; s. Henry David and Marie (Weinheimer) M.; B.S., Mich. Technol. U., 1957; postgrad. Wayne State U., 1960-65, Ga. Inst. Tech., 1965; m. Carole Ann Peterson, Nov. 6, 1954; children—David, Linda, Lori, Lisa, Donna. Field engr. Columbia So. Chem. Corp., Barberton, Ohio, 1957-60; prin. facility planner Detroit Met. Area Regional Planning Commn., 1960-63; chief planner Macomb County Planning Commn., Mt. Clemens, 1963-64; exec. dir. Inter-County Hwy. Commn. Southeastern Mich., Center Line, 1964—. Lectr. pub. transp. (Russia), Wayne State U., 1970. Chmn. Citizens Adv. Com. Warren Consol. Schs., 1968; mem. City of Warren Citizens Adv. Com. to Mayor, 1966-67. Mem. Macomb County Tax Allocation Bd., 1969-71; mem. Bd. Edn., Warren Consol. Schs., 1968-72, treas., 1971-72. Served to capt. C.E., AUS, 1957-58. Recipient Distinguished Service award Warren Edn. Assn., 1968, Distinguished Sec. award Nat. Exchange Clubs, 1972. Mem. Am. Soc. C.E. (Mich. pres. 1970-71), Am. Inst. Planners, Mich. Soc. Planning Ofcls., Am. Soc. Planning Ofcls., Pub. Works Assn. Club: Exchange (sec. Warren 1968-72, pres. 1973-74, dir. Mich. 1969-72) (Warren, Mich.). Methodist. Home: 11575 Helen Dr Warren MI 48093 Office: 24719 Van Dyke St Center Line MI 48015

MEYERS, JACK C(HARLES), real estate broker; b. Los Angeles, Dec. 10, 1922; s. Jack C(harles) and Georgia M. (Poulson) M.; student Kans. U., 1940; m. Dorothy L. Thompson, Dec. 11, 1958; stepchildren—Michael H. Stroth, Dennis L. Stroth; children by previous marriage—Susan M. (Mrs. Larry Wills), Donald C. Sales rep. Life Savers Corp., Mo. and Kans., 1941-42, 46-47; real estate salesman Start & Wilson Realtor, Mission, Kans., 1947-49, E.B. Mccormack Realty, Mission, 1950-54; owner Jack Meyers Realtor, Prairie Village, Kans., 1955—. Capt. disaster unit A.R.C., 1955-56. County finance chmn. Gov. Docking of Kans., 1966, 68. Served with AUS, 1942-46; ETO. Club: Optimist (local pres. 1956-57, zone lt. gov. 1966-67; award appreciation 1963, new bldg. club award 1967) (Mission). Home: 9331 Dearborn St Overland Park KS 66207 Office: 4500 W 90th Terrace Prairie Village KS 66207

MEYERS, VERYL NORBERT, lawyer; b. Cedar Rapids, Iowa, Sept. 29, 1923; s. Carl J. and Vera (Bates) M.; student U. Utah, 1943-44; B.S., U. Iowa, 1948; LL.B., U. Mich., 1951; m. Shirley J. English, Oct. 22, 1976; children—Robert, John, Margaret. Admitted to Mich. bar, 1951; asso. firm Clare J. Hall, Atty., Grand Rapids, 1951-58; asso. firm Sigmund S. Zamierowski, Grand Rapids, 1958-60; partner firm Mika, Meyers, Beckett & Jones, Grand Rapids, 1960—; dir. Petrotech, Inc. Mem. legal and legislative com. Mich. Oil and Gas Assn.; mem. oil and gas law com. State Bar Mich. Pub. adminstr. Kent County, Mich., 1959—. Served with AUS, 1943-46. Mem. Grand Rapids, Am. bar assns., State Bar Mich. Club: Peninsular Club (Grand Rapids). Author: Most Important Oil and Gas Lease Provisions, 1970; Conveying Interests in Oil and Gas, 1975. Home: O-3269 Lake Michigan Dr NW Grand Rapids MI 49504 Office: 500 Frey Bldg Ottawa Ave NW Grand Rapids MI 49503

MEYERS, WARD CARL, surgeon; b. Youngstown, Ohio, Oct. 10, 1915; s. Carl William and Louise Frederica (Wolf) M.; B.S., Northwestern U., 1936, M.B., M.D., 1940; M.S., U. Minn., 1947; m. Ruth Alice Groman, June 24, 1939; children—Mary Lou, Geoffrey G. Intern, Lankenau Hosp., Phila., 1940-42; fellow in surgery Mayo Grad. Sch. Medicine, Rochester, Minn., 1942-44, 47-48; practice medicine specializing in gen. surgery, Toledo, 1948—; dir. surgery St. Vincent Hosp. Med. Center, Toledo, 1967-71; asst. clin. prof. surgery Med. Coll. Toledo, 1962-71. Served to capt. M.C. AUS, World War II. Diplomate Am. Bd. Surgery. Fellow A.C.S.; mem. Toledo Surg. Soc. (pres.). Republican. Lutheran. Editor, staff procs. St. Vincent Hosp. Med. Center, 1966-71; contbr. articles to surg. jours. Office: 3100 W Central Ave Toledo OH 43606

MEYERSON, SEYMOUR, chemist; b. Chgo., Dec. 4, 1916; s. Joseph and Rena (Margulies) M.; B.S., U. Chgo., 1938; m. Lotte Strauss, May 22, 1943; children—Nancy, Phyllis. Chemist, research dept. Standard Oil Co. (Ind.), Whiting, 1946-61, research asso., research dept., Naperville, Ill., 1970-72, sr. research asso., 1972—; chemist, research and devel. dept. Am. Oil Co., Whiting, 1961-62, research asso., 1962-70. Served with AUS, 1943-46. Mem. Am. Chem. Soc., Am. Soc. Mass Spectrometry, ASTM (exec. bd. com. E-14 mass spectrometry 1962-64). Editorial adv. bd. Organic Mass Spectrometry, 1968—; contbr. to publs. in field. Patentee in field. Home: 650 N Tippecanoe St Gary IN 46403 Office: Box 400 Naperville IL 60540

MICALLEF, JOSEPH STEPHEN, lawyer; b. Malta, Oct. 19, 1933; s. John E. and Josephine (Brownrigg) M.; B.A., St. Thomas Coll., 1958; J.D., William Mitchell Coll. Law, 1962; m. Jane M. Yungers, Sept. 5, 1959; children—Lisa, Maura, Sara Lynn, Amy-Ann, Joseph Stephen, Jr. Pres. Fiduciary Counselling, Inc., St. Paul, 1973—; mem. trust com. Northwestern Nat. Bank St. Paul, 1972; dir. St. Paul Arts and Sci., 1971. Sec. Driscoll Found., St. Paul, 1968—; asst. sec., Weyerhaeuser Found., St. Paul, 1966—, asst. treas., 1971—; asst. sec., dir. E.W. and Catherine M. Davis Found., St. Paul, 1971—; hon. consul of Malta, St. Paul-Mpls. Bd. dirs. United Way St. Paul, Minn. Sci. Mus., 1974—, Minn. Mus. Art, 1974-77, Minn. Landmarks; trustee Gt. No. Iron Ore Trust, 1976—, Minn. Hist. Soc., 1975—; regent St. John's U., Collegeville, Minn. Served to capt. USAF, 1952-56, 61-62. Clubs: Minnesota, St. Paul Athletic (St. Paul). Home: 7 Montcalm Ct St Paul MN 55116 Office: Fiduciary Counselling Inc 2100 First Nat Bank Bldg St Paul MN 55101

MICAY, ARCHIE ROBERT, investment co. exec.; b. Winnipeg, Man., Can., Dec. 25, 1913; s. Morris and Rachel (Lockshin) Micanovsky; LL.B., U. Manitoba, 1937, LL.D. (hon.), 1977; m. Goldie Nepon, Aug. 13, 1939; children—Judith Micay Linhart, Marcia Micay Smithen, Leonard. Partner law firm Walsh Micay & Co., Winnipeg, 1942—; dir., sec. Edinburgh Fin. Advisers Ltd.; dir. Headway Corp. Ltd.; pres. Specialized Corporate Mgmt. Ltd., McAdam Investments, Alfred Investments Ltd., Portage Holdings Ltd., Elgin Investments Ltd.; lectr. on urban studies U. Man., 1960-73. Called to Man. bar, 1938; Queen's Counsel, 1957. Founder, 1st pres. Met. Election Com., 1968; pres. Jewish Welfare Fund, Winnipeg, 1956-57; chmn. United Jewish Appeal, Winnipeg, 1957; pres. YMHA Community Centre, Winnipeg, 1962-64; chmn. Civic Charities Endorsement Bur., Winnipeg, 1960-63; chmn. Winnipeg br. Technion U., Haifa, Israel, 1970-74, mem. internat. bd. govs.; pres. United Way of Winnipeg, 1973-74; exec. bd. Canadian Council of Christians and Jews, Manitoba br., 1966—; nat. dir., exec. com. Canadian Centennial Commn., 1965-68. Fin. chmn. Liberal Party of Man., 1966-68. Chmn. Hillel Advisory Bd., U. Man., 1952-55; bd. govs., exec. com., fin. com. Internat. Devel. Research Centre, Ottawa, Ont., 1973-77. Mem. Man. (pres. 1966-67), Canadian (provincial chmn. for Man. 1973-74) bar assns. Home: 402 Bower Blvd Winnipeg 29 MB Canada Office: 211 Portage Ave Winnipeg R3B 2A2 Canada

MICHAEL, GERALD DANTE, dentist; b. Memphis, July 23, 1924; s. Myer Gerty and Mollie (Dante) M.; D.D.S., U. Detroit, 1950; postgrad. Wayne State U., 1961-62; B.A., La. State U., 1961; m. Delores Rubin, Aug. 25, 1946; children—Margery Jean, Nancy Louise. Gen. practice dentistry, Clawson, Mich., 1950—. Asst. dir., instr. dental assts. program Highland Park (Mich.) Coll., 1964-69, Highland Park High Sch., 1967-69; adv. Downtown Dental Assts., Detroit, 1967-69; mem. med. staff Civilian Def. Program, 1952-55. Mem. City of Southfield (Mich.) Community Arts Council, 1971—. Served with AUS, 1943-46. Mem. Am. Dental Assn., Acad. Gen. Dentistry, Royal Soc. Health, Fedn. Dentaire Internationale, Am. Analgesia Soc., Internat. Acad. Orthodontics, Am. Endodontics Soc., Am. Soc. Clin. Research Dental Materials, U. Detroit Alumni Assn., Alpha Omega, Zeta Beta Tau, Phi Theta Kappa, Delta Psi Omega, Blue Key. Mem. Jewish. Mem. B'nai B'rith. Home: 27410 Bradford Lane Southfield MI 48076 Office: 17 S Main St Clawson MI 48017

MICHAEL, HAROLD LOUIS, educator, civil engr.; b. Columbus, Ind., July 24, 1920; s. Louis Edward and Martha (Armuth) M.; B.S. in Civil Engring., Purdue U., 1950, M.S. in Civil Engring., 1951; m. Betty Welch Williams, Dec, 12, 1954; 1 son, Edward; stepchildren—Betty Williams, Ellen Williams, Douglas Williams, Thomas Williams. Instr., grad. asst. Purdue U., 1950-51, research asst., 1951-54, asst. prof. hwy. engring., 1954-59, asst. dir. Joint Hwy. Research project, 1953-61, asso. prof. 1959-62, asso. dir. joint hwy. research project, 1961—, prof. hwy. engring., 1962—, head transp. and urban engring., 1966—. Chmn. Dept. Traffic and Operations, Hwy. Research Bd., 1964-70, West Lafayette Traffic Commn., 1956—, Group 3 Council Transp. Research Bd., 1970-73, Nat. Adv. Com. Uniform Traffic Control Devices, 1971-74; exec. com. Transp. Research Bd., 1975-76. Served from pvt. to capt., AUS, 1942-46. Decorated Bronze Star medal. Named Ind. Engr. of Year, Ind. Soc. Profl. Engrs., 1972. Registered profl. engr., Ind. Mem. Nat. Acad. Engring., Nat. Soc. Profl. Engrs. (nat. dir., past Ind. pres.), ASCE Inst. Transp. Engrs. (past Ind. pres., past nat. dir., past nat. sec.-treas., v.p. 1973-74, pres. 1975), Am. Ry. Engring. Assn., Engrs. Council Profl. Devel., Ind. Hwys. Survival (pres.), Soc. Am. Mil. Engrs., Am. Rd. and Transp. Builders Assn. (dir.), Am. Soc. Engring. Edn., Am. Pub. Works Assn., Sigma Xi, Tau Beta Pi, Chi Epsilon, Theta Xi (sec.-treas. Theta chpt.). Lutheran. Rotarian (pres. Lafayette 1973-74). Contbr. articles profl. jours. Home: 1227 N Salisbury St West Lafayette IN 47906 Office: Purdue U Civil Engring Bldg Lafayette IN 47907

MICHAEL, ROBERT CAMPBELL, dairy mfg. co. exec.; b. Glen Ellyn, Ill., Sept. 28, 1920; s. John William and Frances Lillian (Pound) M.; B.S. in Economics, U. Pa., 1942; m. Jo Ann Wright, Mar. 23, 1971; children—Robert Campbell, Brooks Cowles, Richard Preston. Floor mgr. J.C. Penney Co., Asheville, N.C., 1946-47; various positions Kraft Foods Co., N.C., S.C., Ga. and Fla., 1948-53; pvt. practice as distbr. Coble Dairy, Lexington, N.C., 1954, br. mgr., 1955-56; chief internal audit, 1956-59; part owner, mgmt. cons. Dairy Service Inc., Lexington, 1959-69; controller Wells Dairy Inc., Le Mars, Iowa, 1969—; dir. EDP div., Reiter Dairy, 1967-69; lectr. in field. Served with 492d Bomb Squadron, 20th Air Force, USAF, 1943-45. Republican. Episcopalian. Clubs: Rotary, Elks, Am. Legion. Home: 13 Linden St Armel Acres Le Mars IA 51031 Office: 121 2d Ave SE Le Mars IA 51031

MICHAELS, JOSEPH MAX, scrap iron and steel co. exec.; b. Chgo., Nov. 7, 1927; s. Joseph E. and Belle H. (Goldsmith) M.; B.A., U. Mich., 1950; m. Vicki A. Rosenfelder, Feb. 25, 1971; children—Beth Anne, Wendy Jo, Kimberly Joy. With Hyman-Michaels Co., Chgo., 1950-76, v.p. export, corp. sec., exec. v.p., 1974-76, also dir.; pres. Lakes Shipping & Trading, Chgo., 1970-76, Michaels Corp., 1976—; dir. Welcome Radio Inc., Cleve., 1965-70. Served with USN, 1946-48. Mem. Inst. Scrap Iron and Steel (chmn. transp. com. 1968-70, vice chmn. transp. com. 1971-74, chmn. 1975, v.p. chpt. 1968-70, 72-73, 74-75). Clubs: Westwood Country (St. Louis), Northmoor Country (Chgo.). Home: 399 Fullerton Pkwy Chicago IL 60614 Office: 55 E Monroe St Chicago IL 60603

MICHAELS, MITCH (RICHARD LOUIS SALCHOW), radio and television broadcaster; b. Cleve., Mar. 20, 1948; s. Louis F. and Shirley June (Myers) Salchow; student Kent State U., 1967-71; m. Lynn M. Julian, Aug. 25, 1967 (div.); children—Jennifer Lynn, Jeffrey Nathanial. Engr., WHFS Radio, Bethesda, Md., 1968-69, WGAR Radio, Cleve., 1969-70; broadcaster, air personality, prodn. dir. WNCR Radio, Cleve., 1970; broadcaster, air personality WMMS Radio, Cleve., 1971, WGLD Radio, Oak Park, Ill., 1971-72, WXRT Radio, Chgo., 1972, WDAI Radio, Chgo., 1972-75, WXRT Radio, Chgo., 1975-76, WKQX Radio, Chgo., 1976—, WDAI Radio, 1976—. Free-lance writer; producer, comml. recs. Bd. dirs. Easter Seals, 1977; vol. fund raiser Chgo. Lung Assn., Muscular Dystrophy, WTTW-TV. Recipient award for outstanding service Wilfox Internat. Pub. Corp., 1974; nominee Progressive Air Personality of Year Billboard mag., 1977. Contbg. editor JAM mag., 1974-75. Home: 430 S Wesley Oak Park IL 60302 Office: NBC Merchandise Mart Chicago IL 60154

MICHAK, HELEN BARBARA, nurse; b. Cleve., July 31; d. Andrew and Mary (Patrick) Michak; diploma Cleve. City Hosp. Sch. Nursing, 1947; B.A., Miami U., Oxford, Ohio, 1951; M.A., Case Western Res. U., 1960. Staff nurse Cleve. City Hosp., 1947-48; pub. health nurse Cleve. Div. Health, 1951-52; instr. Cleve. City Hosp. Sch. Nursing, 1952-56; supr. nursing Cuyahoga County Hosp., Cleve., 1956-58; pub. info. dir. N.E. Ohio Am. Heart Assn., Cleve., 1960-64; dir. spl. events Higbee Co., Cleve., 1964-66; exec. dir. Cleve. Area League Nursing, 1966-72; dir. continuing edn. nurses, adj. asso. prof. Cleve. State U., 1972—. Trustee N.E. Ohio Regional Med. Program, 1970-73; mem. adv. com. Dept. Nursing Cuyanoga Community Coll., 1967—; mem. long term care com. Met. Health Planning Corp., 1974-76; mem. policy bd. Center Health Data N.E. Ohio, 1972-73; mem. Rep. Assembly and Health Planning and Devel. Commn., Welfare Fedn. Cleve., 1967-72; mem. Cleve. Community Health Network, 1972-73; mem. nursing adv. com. Cleve. Maternal and Infant Care Project, 1972-73; mem. United Appeal Films and Speakers Bur., 1967-73; mem. adv. com. Ohio Fedn. Licensed Practical Nurses, 1970-73; mem. tech. adv. com. Tb and Respiratory Disease Assn. Cuyahoga County, 1967-74; mem. Ohio Commn. on Nursing, 1971-74; mem. Citizens com. nursing homes Fedn. Community Planning, 1973—; mem. com. on home health services Met. Health Planning Commn., 1973—. Mem. Nat. League Nursing (mem. com. 1970-72), Am., Greater Cleve. (joint practice com. 1973-74, trustee 1975—) nurses assns., Zeta Tau Alpha. Club: Zonta (Cleve.). Home: 4686 Oakridge Dr North Royalton OH 44133 Office: Cleve State U 2344 Euclid Ave Cleveland OH 44115

MICHEL, ROBERT HENRY, congressman; b. Peoria, Ill., Mar. 2, 1923; s. Charles and Anna (Baer) M.; B.S., Bradley U., 1948; m. Corinne Woodruff, Dec. 26, 1948; children—Scott, Bruce, Laurie, Robin. Adminstrv. asst. Congressman Harold Velde, 1949-56; mem. 85th to 95th Congresses, 18th Dist. Ill., house minority whip 94th and 95th Congresses. Vice pres. Towne House Inn, Inc. Del. Republican Conv., 1964, 68, 72, 76. Served with inf. AUS, World War II; ETO. Decorated Bronze Star Medal, Purple Heart; recipient Distinguished Alumnus award Bradley U., 1961. Mem. Am. Legion, V.F.W., D.A.V., Amvets, Cosmopolitan Internat. Home: 1029 N Glenwood St Peoria IL 61606 Office: Rayburn Office Bldg Washington DC 20515

MICHELICH, JOANNA KURDEKA, coll. dean; b. Twin Falls, Idaho, May 3, 1948; d. John Lawrence and Marjorie (Haight) Kurdeka; A.A., Cochise Coll., 1968; B.S., No. Ariz. U., 1969; M.Ed., U. Ariz., 1970; Ph.D., Wash. State U., 1977; m. John Joseph Michelich, July 22, 1972. Asst. dean women U. N.D., Grand Forks, 1970-71, dean women, 1971-72, asso. dean student devel., 1972-73; dean student personnel services West Shore Community Coll., Scottville, Mich., 1976—. Bd. dirs. Mason County Voluntary Action Center, 1976—. Named Most Outstanding Grad. Cochise Coll. 1964-77, Ariz. Bd. for Community Colls and Cochise Coll., 1977. Mem. Am. Personnel and Guidance Assn., Am. Coll. Personnel Assn., Nat. Assn. Student Personnel Adminstrs., Nat., Mich. assns. women deans, adminstrs. and counselors, Nat. Council Student Devel., Mich. Assn. Community Coll. Student Personnel Adminstrs. (exec. bd.), AAUW (exec. bd. 1971-73), Phi Kappa Phi, Phi Delta Kappa. Lutheran. Contbr. articles to profl. jours. Home: 402 Main St N Scottville MI 49454 Office: West Shore Community College Box 277 Scottville MI 49454

MICHELON, LENO C., investment co. exec.; b. Chgo., Aug. 25, 1918; s. Joseph and Elette Michelon; Ph.B. magna cum laude, DePaul U., 1939; M.E., Chgo. Tchrs. Coll., 1940; postgrad. Ill. Inst. Tech., 1941, Rensselaer Poly. Inst., 1942, Ind. Coll. Armed Forces, 1944, U. Chgo., 1946-48; m. Margaret Mary Devereaux; 1 dau., Cecilia Marie. Prof. indsl. mgmt. Purdue U., 1946-49; dir. mgmt. services, asst. prof. U. Chgo., 1949-52; mgmt. cons., Cleve., 1953-58; dir. pub. affairs and edn. Republic Steel Corp., Cleve., after 1958, pres. Republic Edn. Inst., 1967-76; chmn. Retirement Investment Co.; adj. prof. John Carroll U. U. Adviser, Center for Learning; cons. Assn. for Mgmt. Excellence; mem. Citizens Council for Ohio Schs. Served with USNR, 1942-46. Recipient gold medal Law-Sci. Acad., 1970. Mem. N.A.M. (pub. affairs cons.), U.S. C. of C. (pub. affairs adviser), Nat. Assn. Ind. Ednl. Cooperation. Author: Industrial Inspection Methods, 1942; Basic Economics, 1960; Modern Management Methods, 1967; (with Ernest Dale) Understanding Government and Understanding Politics, 1968; How to Be A Dynamic Conference Leader, 1968; (with Rueben Shlesinger) Understanding Basic Economics, 1968; Myths and Realities of Management, 1972; The Art and Science of Professional Supervision, 1972; The Secret of Making Things Happen, 1973. Home: 22307 Halburton Rd Cleveland OH 44122 Office: PO Box 6778 Cleveland OH 44101

MICHELS, EUGENE AUGUST, social worker; b. Detroit, June 2, 1934; s. August and Louise (St. John) M.; B.S., Wayne State U., 1963; M.S.W., U. Mich., 1967; postgrad. Walden U.; m. Coanne Johnson; children by previous marriage—Cynthia, Sean. Social worker Redford Union Sch., Detroit, 1965-77; dir. Redford Info. and Counseling Center, Detroit, 1969—. Pres. Western Wayne County Drug Alliance, 1971-72, CARE, 1973-75. Chmn. bd. dirs. Family Human Potential Services. Served with AUS, 1955-57. Mem. Mich. Soc. Group Psychotherapy (past pres.), Nat. Assn. Social Workers, Nat. Inst. Psychotherapists. Author manuals. Home: 23015 Inkster St Farmington Hills MI 48024 Office: 18499 Beech Daly Rd Detroit MI 48240

MICHELS, HUGH CONRAD, JR., finance co. exec.; b. Hugh Conrad and Dagmar Kristine (Iversen) M.; B.S. in Econs., U. Wis., 1955; postgrad. DePaul U. Law Sch., 1955-56; m. Evelyn Coogan, June 26, 1954; children—Cynthia Ann, Elizabeth Bermingham, Melissa Iversen, Jennifer. Dir. Old Colonial Ins. Agy., Inc., Chgo., 1962—, pres., 1971—; dir. Franklin Savs. Assn., 1963—, pres., 1963, chmn. bd., 1971; dir. Hugh C. Michels & Co., Chgo., v.p., 1957-69, pres., 1969—; dir. Mallers Bldg., Inc., pres., 1969—; dir. M & M Parking Co., v.p., 1957-69, pres., 1969—; pres. Winnetka (Ill.) Beach Estates, 1973, North Shore Inn, 1973—; dir. North Shore Hotels Corp., chmn. bd., pres., 1973—; dir. Susquehanna Corp., 1975. Chmn. No. div. Mental Health Soc. Greater Chgo., Inc., asst. chmn. Arthritis and Rheumatism Found. of Chgo., 1963; chmn. real estate and finance div. Chgo. Heart Assn., active Chgo. Real Estate Bd.; bd. dirs. Chgo. Eye, Ear, Nose and Throat Hosp., chmn. bd., 1971; bd. dirs. Chgo. Vision and Hearing Center, pres., 1962-69. Served to 1st lt., Transp. Corps, U.S. Army, 1955-57. Mem. Nat., Ill. assns. real estate bds., Am. Savs. and Loan Inst., Bldg. Mgrs. Assn. Chgo., U.S. Savs. and Loan League, Jr., Evanston-North Shore bds. realtors, Nat. League Insured Savs. Assns., Soc. Residential Appraisers, Chgo. C. of C. and Industry, Cook County Council Insured Savs. Assn., Am. Inst. Real Estate Appraisers, Exec. Club Chgo., Connoisseurs Internat., Anti-Superstition Soc. Chgo., Econ. Club Chgo. Roman Catholic. Clubs: Bull Valley Hunting; Pheasant Valley Hunting; Dairymen's Country; Chgo. Yacht, Mid-Day of Chgo., University (Chgo.); Michigan Shores; Admirals; Exmoor Country; United Airlines 100,000 Mile; Ocean of Fla.; TWA Ambassadors. Home: 473 Sheridan Rd Winnetka IL Office: Franklin Savs Assn 101 W Madison St Chicago IL 60602

MICHELS, LOUISE ANN, guidance counselor; b. Toledo, June 21, 1947; d. Leo Joseph and Margaret Mary (Kreuz) Michels; B.A., Mary Manse Coll., 1969; M.Edn., Bowling Green (Ohio) State U., 1976. Tchr., Our Lady of Perpetual Help Sch., Toledo, 1969-76; elementary guidance counselor Ashtabula (Ohio) Area City Schs., 1976-77; high sch. guidance counselor Tecumseh High Sch., New Carlisle-Bethel schs., New Carlisle, Ohio, 1977—. Sec. Maumee (Ohio) Civic Theatre 1973-76, bd. dirs., 1976-77. Mem. Am. Personnel and Guidance Assn., Am. Sch. Counselor Assn., Ohio School Counselor Assn., Nat., Ohio Edn. assns., Nat. Hist. Soc. Roman Catholic. Home: 842 Woodview Ct Vandalia OH 45377 Office: Tecumseh High Sch 9830 W National Rd New Carlisle OH 45344

MICHENER, CHARLES D(UNCAN), entomologist; b. Pasadena, Calif., Sept. 22, 1918; B.S., U. Calif., 1939, Ph.D. in Entomology, 1941; m. 1940; 4 children. Tech. asst. U. Calif., 1939-42; asst. curator lepidoptera and hymenoptera Am. Mus. Natural History, 1942-46, asso. curator, 1946-48; asso. prof. entomology U. Kans., 1948-50, prof., 1950-59, Elizabeth M. Watkins prof., 1959—, prof. systematics and ecology, 1969—, chmn. dept. entomology, 1949-61, 72-75; also curator Snow Entomol. Mus., 1949—, dir., 1974—; state entomologist south div. Kans., 1949-61. Guggenheim fellow, research prof. U. Paraná, 1955-56, Africa, 1966-67; Fulbright scholar U. Queensland (Australia), 1958-59. Fellow Am. Entomol. Soc. (hon.); mem. Nat. Acad. Sci., Soc. Study Evolution (pres. 1967), Am. Soc. Zoology, Soc. Systematic Zoology (pres. 1968), Am. Acad. Arts and Sci., Brazilian Acad. Scis. (hon., fgn.). Address: Div Biology U Kans Lawrence KS 66045

MICHNA, JAMES THOMPSON, librarian; b. Racine, Wis., May 19, 1934; s. Clarence Henry and Mildred (Thompson) M.; B.S., U. Wis., Milw., 1959; M.L.S., U. Wis., Madison, 1960; m. Mary Edna Blanchard, Aug. 27, 1960 (div. Mar. 1977). Reference librarian Kalamazoo Pub. Library, 1960-62; librarian U. Wis.-Green Bay Center, 1962-65; asst. dir. U. Wis. Center System Libraries, Madison, 1965-68; dir. Howard Colman Library, Rockford (Ill.) Coll., 1968—. Cons. Interior Space Design div. Perkins & Wills, Chgo. Pub. Library remodeling design competition. Explorer dist. chmn. Boy Scouts Am., 1968-71, committeeman-at-large, 1971-76, explorer adviser, 1971—. Served with U.S. Army, 1954-56. Mem. Rockford Profl. Mens Forum, AAUP, Beta Phi Mu, Phi Alpha Theta. Democrat. Elk. Editor: Quar. Am. Interprofl. Inst., 1974-76. Home: 4732 Ottawa Rd Rockford IL 61107 Office: 5050 E State St Rockford IL 61101

MICHNO, DOROTHY ANTONIA, counselor, editor; b. Chgo., July 31, 1945; s. Stanley Peter and Clara Ann (Rogusz) M.; B.S.Ed., Loyola U., Chgo., 1969, M.Ed., 1971. Auditor, Bankers Life & Casualty Co., Chgo., 1967-72; dir. guidance Queen of Peace High Sch., Burbank, Ill., 1972-74; counselor Sch. Dist. 59, Elk Grove Village, Ill., 1974—; editor Polish Museum of Am. Quaterly, 1974—. Program chmn. Community Services Orgn., Elk Grove Village. Grantee, Jagiellonian U., Krakow, Poland, summer 1974. Mem. Am. Personnel and Guidance Assn., Am. Sch. Counselors Assn., Ill. Sch. Counselors Assn., Ill., Chgo. guidance and personnel assns., Nat. Cath. Guidance Conf., Polish Am. Educators Assn. Democrat. Roman Catholic. Club: Polish Arts. Home: 5205 Henderson St W Chicago IL 60641 Office: 777 Elk Grove Blvd Elk Grove Village IL 60007

MICHOD, CHARLES LOUIS, lawyer; b. Chgo., Sept. 10, 1917; s. Charles L. and Else (Milner) M.; student Phillips Exeter Acad., 1932-35; A.B., U. Ill., 1939; LL.B., Harvard, 1942; m. Florence Wise, Jan. 31, 1942; children—Charles Louis, Richard E., Sally E. Admitted to Ill. bar, 1942; practiced in Chgo., 1942—; atty. Village River Forest (Ill.), 1953—. Dir. Sleepmakers, Inc., Chgo., Lauritzen & Co. Served to 2d lt. CIC, AUS, 1942-46. Mem. Delta Tau Delta. Republican. Presbyn. Contbr. articles to profl. jours. Home: 529 Keystone Ave River Forest IL 60305 Office: 115 S LaSalle St Chicago IL 60603

MICK, R. WYATT, JR., lawyer; b. Sturgis, Mich., Jan. 14, 1929; s. R. Wyatt and Maude (Essig) M.; B.B.A., U. Mich., 1950, J.D., 1953; m. Elaine Alice DeVries, Nov. 29, 1963; children—Laura Lynn, Andrew Wyatt. Admitted to Mich. bar, 1954, Ind. bar, 1959; law clk. to Hon. John D. Martin, U.S. Court Appeals, 6th Circuit, 1955-56, 58-59; practice law, Benton Harbor, Mich., 1956-58; pvt. practice law, Mishawaka, Ind., 1959—. Dep. pros. atty. St. Joseph County, Ind., 1963; atty. City of Mishawaka, 1964—; precinct committeeman Rep. Party, 1968-74. Mem. Ind. Commn. on Aging and the Aged, 1973—. Bd. dirs. Meals on Wheels, St. Joseph County, Ind., 1964—, pres., 1975; bd. dirs. Real Services of St. Joseph County, Inc., 1966—, pres., 1974-75. Served with AUS, 1953-55. Mem. Am., Fed., Ind., St. Joseph County bar assns., State Bar Mich. Episcopalian (sr. warden 1972-74, 77-78). Clubs: Mishawaka Garden (pres. 1971-72); Presbyterian Players; Mishawaka Lions. Home: 507 Edgewater Dr Mishawaka IN 46544 Office: 400 Lincoln Way E Mishawaka IN 46544

MICK, ROBERT KAY, dentist; b. Benton, Ill., Sept. 3, 1939; s. Herbert L. and Leota I. (Humphrey) M.; student So. Ill. U., 1957-60; D.D.S., U. Ill., 1964; m. Lois Jean Jackson, June 13, 1959; children—Robert Andrew, Angela Kay. Practice dentistry, Centralia, Ill., 1966—; mem. dental staff St. Mary's Hosp., chief staff, 1978. Guest lectr. dental assts. class Kaskaskia (Ill.) Jr. Coll., 1968-72, mem. dental adv. bd., 1968—; mem. Leonard S. Fodsick Dental Study Group. Mem. Mayors' Com. for Community Improvement, Centralia, 1973—; active Centralia Council Boy Scouts Am., 1972-74, dist. commr. Okaw Valley Council, 1977-78. Mem. Centralia Recreation Bd. Served with Dental Corps., USAF, 1964-66. Licensed high sch. assn. ofcl., Ill. Mem. Am. Dental Assn. (alternate del. 1973), Ill. (conciliation com.), So. Ill. (sec.-treas. 1971-73), Wabash River, Marion County (sec.-treas. 1970) dental socs., Khoury League (pres. Centralia, 1978, coordinator to Central Ill. dist. circuit council, dist. committeeman to bd.), Pierre Fauchard Acad., Alpha Phi Omega, Psi Omega. Baptist. Mason (Shriner), Elk. Club: Optimist. Home: 7 Orchard Dr East Centralia IL 62801 Office: 1519 E 2d St Centralia IL 62801

MICKELSON, ARNOLD, church exec.; b. Finley, N.D., Jan. 8, 1922; s. Alfred B. and Clara (Rust) M.; B.A., Concordia Coll., Moorhead, Minn., 1943, LL.D., 1972; m. Marjorie Arveson, June 8, 1944; 1 son, Richard. Owner, operator Luther Book Store, Decorah, Ia., 1946-48; credit supr. Gen. Motors Acceptance Corp., Fargo, N.D., 1948-53; mgr. Epko Film Service, Fargo, 1953-58; asst. to dist. pres. No. Minn. dist. Evang. Luth. Ch., Moorhead, Minn., 1958-61; asst. to dist. pres. No. Minn. dist. Am. Luth. Ch., Moorhead, 1961-66; gen. sec. Am. Luth. Ch., Mpls., 1967—; mem. U.S.A. nat. com. Luth. World Fedn., 1966—, sec. 1966-69, 72-75. Luth. Council in U.S.A. councilor, 1966—, sec., 1969-72, pres., 1973-76; sec. Consultation on Luth. Unity, 1970-73, chmn., 1974-76. Del. 4th Assembly, World Council Chs., Uppsala, Sweden, 1968, 5th Assembly, Nairobi, Kenya, 1975; chmn. Faith-in-Life Dialogue, Fargo-Moorhead, 1964; observer trainer Faith-in-Life Dialogue, Duluth, Minn., 1965. Mem. Town Meeting Council, Mpls.-St. Paul, 1968-70. Served with AUS, 1943-46. Recipient Civic Service award Eagles, 1965. Mem. Ch. Staff Workers Assn. (past pres.), Concordia Coll. Alumni Assn. (past pres.). Home: 6815 Harold Ave N Golden Valley MN 55427 Office: 422 S 5th St Minneapolis MN 55415

MICKELSON, GEORGE SPEAKER, lawyer, state legislator; b. Walworth, S.D., Jan. 31, 1941; s. George Theodore and Madge Ellen (Turner) M.; B.A., U. S.D., 1963, J.D., 1965; m. Linda Jane McCahren, Aug. 10, 1963; children—Mark, Amy, David. Admitted to S.D. bar, 1965; spl. asst. atty. gen. State S.D., 1967-68; partner McCann, Martin & Mickelson, Brookings, 1969—; mem. S.D. Ho. of Reps., 1974—, speaker pro tem, 1977-78. Spl. prosecutor for S.D. Atty. Gen., 1972—; states atty. Brookings County, 1970—. Chmn. Brookings County Rep. Central Com., 1970; chmn. com. to re-elect the Pres., 1972. Served to capt. AUS, 1965-67. Decorated Army commendation medal with oak leaf cluster. Mem. Brookings C. of C., Phi Delta Phi, Lambda Chi Alpha. Methodist (mem. commn. on missions, 1972—, mem. adminstrn. bd. 1972—). Mason (Shriner), Elk. Kiwanian. Bd. editors Univ. S.D. Law Review, 1964-65. Home: 1911 Lincoln Ln Brookings SD 57006 Office: 317 6th Ave Brookings SD 57006

MICKLEWRIGHT, JERROLD JOHN, constrn. co. exec.; b. Davenport, Iowa, May 6, 1934; s. Joseph Ralph and Elma (Endorf) M.; B.A., St. Ambrose Coll., 1960; m. Mary K. Lavery, Aug. 24, 1957; children—Mollie, Michele, Ann, Michael, Margaret. C.P.A., Peat Marwick & Mitchell, Omaha and Cedar Rapids, Iowa, 1960-62; systems analyst U.S. govt. agys., France, Germany and U.S., 1963-68; v.p. finance W.E. O'Neil Constrn. Co., Chgo., 1968—. Served with Armed Forces, 1954-56. C.P.A., Ill., Nebr. Mem. Am. Inst. C.P.A.'s, Ill., Nebr. socs. C.P.A.'s. Roman Catholic. Home: 153 Michigan St Highwood IL 60040 Office: 2751 N Clybourn St Chicago IL 60614

MICUN, RICHARD PETER, lawyer, educator; b. Chgo., Nov. 14, 1927; s. John Peter and Tekla (Marozas) M.; B.S., De Paul U., 1948, J.D., 1950, M.S. in Taxation, 1973; M.B.A., U. Chgo., 1958; m. Maureen M. Haggerty, Nov. 17, 1962; children—Thomas, Timothy, Terrence. Admitted to Ill. bar, 1950, U.S. Supreme Ct. bar, 1965; corp. atty. Brunswick Corp., Chgo., 1955-62; atty. Internat. Minerals & Chem. Corp., 1962-65; lectr. Chgo. City Jr. Colls., Colls., 1961-64, asst. prof., 1965-68, asso. prof., 1968-75, prof., 1975—. Served from 1st lt. to capt. AUS, 1950-55; col. J.A.G. Res. Decorated Bronze Star medal. Mem. Am., Fed., Chgo. bar assns. Home: 2647 W 94th Pl Evergreen Park IL 60642

MIDDEKE, ALBERT BERNARD, poultry and feed co. exec.; b. Breese, Ill., Jan. 14, 1932; s. Bernard and Mary Anna (Hellman) M.; student parochial schs.; m. Helen Lewies Adamson, Apr. 12, 1968; children by previous marriage—Alvina, Mary, Ann; 1 son, Albert Bernard. With Lincoln Mercury, St. Louis, 1955-58; prodn. mgr. Oslager Oil Co., Mt. Vernon, Ill., 1959-64; pres., mgr. Middeke Farm Feeds, Inc. and Middeke Pullets, Inc., Aviston, Ill., 1965—, pres. Holtkamp Feed, Inc., 1970—; v.p. Farm Constrn. Co., 1974—; dir. Highland Savs. & Loan Assn.; dir., officer Breese Farming, Inc., Breese Land Trust, Bows, Ltd.; bd. dirs. Ill. Egg Market Devel. Council. Dir. St. Rose Water Dist. Served with AUS, 1952-54. Roman Catholic. Club: K.C. Home: Box 98 Rural Route 1 Breese IL 62230 Office: PO Box 164 Aviston IL 62216

MIDDENDORF, DONALD FLOYD, research nutritionist; b. Templeton, Iowa, Feb. 26, 1931; s. Fred Henry and Johanna (Sanders) M.; B.S., Iowa State U., 1954; M.S., U. Md., 1958, Ph.D., 1959; m. Rose Marie Meyer, Aug. 24, 1962; children—Laura Jo, Janalee Kay, Lynn Alan. Research asst. U. Md., College Park, 1956-59; poultry research specialist Central Soya Co., Decatur, Ind., 1959-65, mgr. poultry Feeds, 1968-76, prin. scientist, 1976—; nutrition specialist Upjohn Co., Kalamazoo, Mich., 1967-68. Mem. Research Council Am. Dehydrators Assn., Poulty Sci. Assn., World's Poultry Sci. Assn., Animal Nutrition Research Council, AAAS, Am. Inst. Chemists, N.Y. Acad. Scis. Home: Route 4 Decatur IN 46733 Office: Central Soya Co Decatur IN 46733

MIDDENDORF, ROBERT WILLIS, cosmetic co. exec.; b. Akron, Ohio, Sept. 24, 1914; s. John Wienhold and Eva Belle (Foltz) M.; student pub. schs.; m. Olga Krist, Apr. 16, 1938; children—John Karl, Kathi (Mrs. Gerald Folden), Johanna (Mrs. Joseph Ogrin), Eric, Heidi. With Bonne Bell, Inc., Cleve., 1940—, salesman, 1940-50, sales mgr., 1950-60, v.p. sales, 1960-66, v.p. sales and mktg., 1966-70, sr. v.p., 1970-75, exec. v.p., 1975—, also dir. and chmn. exec. com. Vice chmn. Cleve. Better Bus. Bur., 1971—. Trustee Grad. Sch. of Sales Mgmt. and Mktg., Syracuse U. Mem. Cleve. Sales Marketing Execs. Club (pres. 1967-68), Sales Marketing Execs. Internat. (regional v.p. 1971, 72, 73, v.p. exec. edn. program). Mem. United Ch. of Christ (deacon). Mason (32 deg.). Club: Fairlawn Country (Akron). Home: 200 Schocalog Rd Akron OH 44313 Office: Bonne Bell Inc 18519 Detroit Ave Lakewood OH 44107

MIDDLEBUSH, CARL WESLEY, clin. psychologist; b. Urbana, Ill., Feb. 6, 1945; s. Carl Warren and Nellie Middlebush; B.S., Western Mich. U., 1967, M.A., 1969; specialist in gerontology U. Mich., 1974; Ph.D., Wayne State U., Detroit, 1974; m. Valerie Ann Ernest, Nov. 27, 1976. Sr. staff clin. psychologist VA Hosp., Battle Creek, Mich., 1969—; psychol. cons. Detroit Pub. Schs., 1973-74, Mich. Dept. Vocat. Rehab., 1975—; psychodiagnostic cons. Battle Creek (Mich.) Dept. Social Services, 1976—, Goodwill Industries, Battle Creek, D.A. Blodgett Homes for Children, Grand Rapids, 1977; pvt. practice adolescent and adult therapy, family and marriage counseling, 1976—. Served to capt. Intelligence Br. U.S. Army, 1970-71; Vietnam. Mem. Am., Southwestern Mich. psychol. assns. Address: 252 W Hamilton Ln Battle Creek MI 49015

MIDDLEKAUFF, GEORGE WILES, psychiatrist; b. Cleve., Mar. 5, 1944; s. Roger David and Ella Marie (Holan) M.; B.A., Northwestern U., 1966, M.S., 1970, Ph.D., 1971, M.D., 1971; m. Linda Jeanne Potts, Dec. 16, 1967; children—Cindy Kathleen, Andrew George. Intern, Evanston (Ill.) Hosp., 1971-72; resident in psychiatry U. Ill., 1972-75, fellow in child psychiatry, 1975-76, clin. instr., 1973-77, asst. prof., 1977—; staff psychiatrist VA West Side Hosp., Chgo., 1975—. Served to capt. USAR, 1971-77. Diplomate Am. Bd. Psychiatry Neurology. Mem. Ill., Am. psychiat. assns., AMA, Ill., Chgo. med. socs. Contbr. articles to profl. jours. Home: 736 S Taylor Ave Oak Park IL 60304 Office: 900 S Damen Ave Chicago IL 60612

MIDDLETON, DAN FRANK, ins. agy. exec.; b. Pitts., Sept. 15, 1930; s. Frank Riordon and Florence Anna Marie (Gross) M.; student Miami U., Oxford, Ohio, 1948-49, Ohio State U., 1951-54; m. Marilyn Joyce Calentine, Apr. 5, 1958; children—Timothy Irwin, Suzanne Marie. With Atkinson-Dauksch Agys., Columbus, Ohio, 1955—, asst. v.p., 1969-70, v.p., 1970—, dir., 1973—, mem. exec. com., 1974—, chmn. profit sharing plan adminstrn. com., 1970—. Active fund-raising Com. to Re-Elect Thomas Herbert, Judge of Supreme Ct. of Ohio, 1974. Served with USAF, 1951-52. C.P.C.U. (chpt. dir. 1967-68); asso. in risk mgmt. Mem. Ins. Bd. Columbus, Columbus Power Squadron, Cadillac-LaSalle Antique Car Club. Methodist. Clubs: Columbus Maennerchor, Executive (Columbus); Scioto Country. Home: 2410 Cambridge Blvd Upper Arlington OH 43221 Office: 50 W Broad St Columbus OH 43215

MIDDLETON, EDWARD KENT, adminstrv. broadcast engr.; b. Sacramento, Calif., Jan. 2, 1926; s. George Edward and Vivian (Grane) M.; B.F.A. in Broadcast Edn., Coll. Music, Cin., 1951; m. Lauretta Jean Fichter, Dec. 24, 1949; children—Dean Kent, Carol Lynn, Carla Jo Ann. Broadcast engr. Sta. WZIP, Covington, Ky., 1949-52, Sta. WKRC-AM, FM, TV, Cin., 1952-67; broadcast engr. Sta. WCET, Cin., 1966-67, dir. engring., 1967—; career adviser broadcast engring. U. Cin. Home: 468 Lenkenann Dr Cincinnati OH 45230 Office: 1223 Central Pkwy Cincinnati OH 45214

MIDDLETON, HARVEY NATHANIEL, JR., elec. engineer; b. Indpls., Oct. 14, 1949; s. Harvey N. and Easter G. M.; A.A.S., Vincennes U., 1971; student Purdue U., 1974—. Insp. quality control AVCO, Richmond, Ind., 1973; jr. elec. engr. technician Esterline Angus, Indpls., 1974—. Mem. Omega Psi Phi, NAACP. Home: 3828 Rockwood Ave Indianapolis IN 46208 Office: 1201 W Main St Speedway IN 46224

MIDDLETON, JAMES GAUTIER, counseler, educator; b. Kans. City, Mo., Feb. 7, 1932; s. Thomas E. and Francis E. M.; B.S. in Edn., Central Mo. State U., 1955, M.S. in Edn., 1956; Ed.D., U. Kans., 1976; m. Judith A. Krutz, Oct, 14, 1966; children—Anna, James, Joseph. Coordinator of counseling San Diego County Dept. Edn., Calif., 1965-68; asso. prof. edn. and psychology S.E. Mo. State U., Cape Girardeau, 1968-73; asst. prof. counseling Kearney (Nebr). State Coll., 1976—; cons. Stanford Research Inst., Palo Alto, Calif., 1968-73; ednl. cons., 1973—. Served with U.S. Army, 1953-55. Mem. Am. Personnel and Guidance Assn., NEA, Assn. Counselor Edn. and Supervision, Phi Delta Kappa. Contbr. articles in field. Home: 4007 Pony Express Rd Kearney NE 68847 Office: Kearney State Coll Kearney NE 68847

MIDDOUGH, WILLIAM VANCE, engring. exec.; b. Cleve., July 30, 1917; s. LeRoy Case and Cecilia (Loop) M.; B.S., Case Sch. Applied Sci., 1939; postgrad. Case Inst. Tech., 1941-42; m. Elisabeth June Heick, Sept. 5, 1942; children—Beverly Timothy, Daniel. Elec. supr. Arthur G. McKee & Co., 1940-47; head steel mill. elec. div. Osborn Engring. Co., Cleve., 1947-50; elec. cons. Lake Shore Electric Corp., Bedford, Ohio, 1950-51; pres. W. Vance Middough & Assos., Cleve., 1951—; v.p. Umbrella Heater Co.; dir. Technical Facilities Corp., Internat. Ventures Mgmt. Mem. Am. Inst. E.E., Soc. Naval Architects and Marine Engrs., Assn. Iron and Steel Engrs., Ohio Soc. Profl. Engrs., Eta Kappa Nu. Clubs: Propeller of U.S., Cleve. Athletic (Cleve.). Home: 3179 Ludlow Rd Shaker Heights OH 44120 Office: 1367 E 6th St Cleveland OH 44114

MIDELFORT, PETER ALBERT HANDE, surgeon; b. Eau Claire, Wis., Aug. 5, 1905; s. Hans Christian Ulrik and Margarita (Hande) M.; A.B. magna cum laude, Yale U., 1927; M.D. cum laude, Harvard U., 1931; m. Gerd Gjems, Mar. 29, 1941; children—Hans Christian Erik, Signe Louise Gjems, Elise Margrethe Gjems, Kristin Elsbeth. Intern, Peter Bent Brigham Hosp., Boston, 1931-33; resident in surgery Wis. Gen. Hosp., Madison, 1934-37, Wis. Orthopedic Hosp. for Children, Madison, 1934-35, Ullevaal Sykehus, Oslo, 1937-38; practice gen. surgery, Eau Claire, 1939-75; pres. Midelfort Clinic, Eau Claire, 1955-68; preceptor U. Wis. Med. Sch., Madison, 1939-68, chief preceptor, Eau Claire, 1946-67. Bd. dirs. Am. Cancer Soc., Eau Claire, 1970-75; Family Service Assn., Eau Claire, 1971-77. Served with U.S. Army, 1942-46. Decorated Bronze Star; recipient Max Fox Prize, 1970; U. Wis. Med. Alumni citation, 1977; Good Samaritan award Samaritan Club Luther Hosp., Eau Claire, 1977; diplomate Am. Bd. Surgery. Mem. AMA, Wis. Surg. Soc. (pres. 1960), A.C.S. (Gov. Wis., 1967-74), AAAS, Wis. Surg. Travel Club, Friday Discussion Club, Aesculapian Club, Phi Beta Kappa, Sigma Xi, Alpha Omega Alpha, Delta Kappa Epsilon. Lutheran. Club: Sunset View Golf. Contbr. articles to med. jours. Home: 321 Summit Ave Eau Claire WI 54701 Office: 733 W Clairemont Ave Eau Claire WI 54701

MIDELL, ALLEN IRWIN, surgeon, educator; b. Chgo., Oct. 11, 1934; s. S. D. and Helen (Rosen) Mittelpunkt; B.S., U. Ill., 1956; M.D., Northwestern U., 1960. Intern Cook County Hosp., Chgo., 1960-61, resident, 1961-65; resident Harvard V Surg. div. New Eng. Deaconess Hosp., Boston, 1966-68; fellow in cardiovascular surgery Baylor U., Houston, 1965-66; practice medicine specializing in cardiovascular and thoracic surgery, Chgo., 1968—; mem. staff Columbus Hosp., Chgo., chief cardiovascular surgery, 1971—; mem. staffs U. Chgo. Hosps. and Clinics, Augustana Hosp.; asst. prof. surgery U. Chgo., 1973—. Fellow A.C.S.; mem. Soc. Thoracic Surgeons, Am. Coll. Chest Physicians. Contbg. author: Operative Surgery, 1970. Contbr. numerous articles on cardiac surgery to profl. jours. Home: 1040 N Lake Shore Dr Apt 31D Chicago IL 60611 Office: 645 N Michigan Ave Chicago IL 60611

MIDGLEY, JOHN WILLIAM, civil engr.; b. Jackson, Mich., July 23, 1950; s. John Raymond and Beverly Ann (Houghtby) M.; B.S. in Civil Engring., Tri-State Coll., Ind., 1968-72; m. Diana Lynn Parrott, June 20, 1970; 1 dau., Kelly. Mem. staff Ind. Hwy. Commn., Indpls., 1972-73; engr. in tng. Mich. Dept. Hwys. Transp., Lansing, 1973-74, sr. instrumentman, 1974, asst. project engr., 1974-77, asst. r.r. crossing programs engr., 1977; asst. county hwy. engr. Jackson County (Mich.) Road Commn., 1977—. Registered profl. engr., Mich. Mem. ASCE, Nat., Mich. socs. profl. engrs. Home: 7961 Springport Rd Parma MI 49269 Office: 2400 Elm Rd Jackson MI 49201

MIDTLYNG, JOANNA, phys. edn. dir.; b. Deer Lodge, Mont., Oct. 5, 1927; d. Robert and Lottie (Nettle) Midtlyng; B.A., U. Mont., 1950; M.S., U. Wash., 1959; P.E.D., U. Ind., 1971. Swimming dir. and coach Deer Lodge (Mont.) Recreation Dept., 1948-50; phys. educator Custer County (Mont.) Jr. Coll. High Sch., 1950-52; supr. phys. edn. Deer Lodge (Mont.) City Schs., 1952-58; asst. prof. phys. edn., womens aquatic coordinator Ill. State U., Normal, 1958-66; asst. prof. phys. edn. Ball State U., Muncie, Ind., 1966-67, prof., asso. dir. aquatics, 1971—; asso. instr. phys. edn. U. Ind., Bloomington, 1967-71. Mem. Am. Alliance Health Phys. Edn. Recreation (chmn. aquatic council 1971-73, Outstanding Service award 1975-76). Author: Swimming, 1974: editor Aquatics Guide, 1973-75, Setting Pace in Sports, 1976. Home: 4501 N Wheeling Ave Muncie IN 47304 Office: Ball State Univ Muncie IN 47306

MIECHUR, THOMAS FRANK, union ofcl.; b. Martins Creek, Pa., Jan. 25, 1923; s. Adam and Sophia (Buczek) M.; student Princeton, 1943-44; m. Lorraine Wesolowski, Oct. 19, 1957. Dist. rep. United Cement, Lime and Gypsum Workers Internat. Union, Easton, Pa., 1957-59, asst. to pres., Chgo., 1959-71, pres., 1971—; mem. gen. bd. AFL-CIO, Exec. bd. indsl. union dept., maritime trades dept. Served with AUS, 1943-45. Mem. Indsl. Relations Research Assn., Chgo. Council Fgn. Relations, Smithsonian Assos. Democrat. Roman Catholic. K.C. Club: Moose. Home: 141 S Iroquois Trail Wood Dale IL 60191 Office: 7830 W Lawrence Ave Chicago IL 60656

MIEFERT, WILLIAM GERHARDT, III, dentist; b. Cin., Nov. 6, 1927; s. William Gerhardt and Irene Mildred (Robbins) M.; student Miami U., Oxford, Ohio, 1945-46; D.D.S., Ohio State U., 1955, M.S. in Orthodontics, 1974; m. Margot Anne Hoffman, Aug. 13, 1960; children—Michelle Lynne, Marlena Anne, Maria Jean. Practice dentistry, VanWert, Ohio, 1955-56; Marysville, Ohio, 1956—, Mansfield, Ohio, 1974—, practice ltd. to orthodontics, 1974—; cons. staff, Union Co. Meml. Hosp., Marysville, 1956-73. Pres. Col-Mar, Inc., Marysville, 1973—; sec. Deercreek Development Co., Mt. Sterling, Ohio, 1973—. Mem. Marysville Exempted Village sch. bd., 1969—. Served with USNR, 1946-48, with Ohio NG, 1950-60. Mem. Union County Acad. Dentistry (pres. 1963-66), Am., Ohio dental assns., Am., Gt. Lakes socs. orthodontists, central Ohio, Mansfield dental socs. Presbyterian (elder). Home: 417 Parkway Dr Marysville OH 43040 Office: 332 W 3d St Marysville OH 43040 also 391 Glessner Ave Mansfield OH 44903

MIGALA, LUCYNA, TV news producer; b. Krakow, Poland, May 22, 1944; d. Joseph and Estelle (Suwala) Migala; came to U.S., 1947, naturalized, 1955; student Loyola U., Chgo., 1962-63; student Chicago Conservatory Music, 1963-68; B.S. in Journalism, Northwestern U., 1966; m. Kazimierz Wieclaw, Nov. 27, 1971 (div. Jan. 4, 1978). Radio announcer, producer sta. WOPA, Oak Park, Ill., 1963-66; writer, reporter, producer NBC news, Chgo., 1966-69, 1969-71, producer NBC local news, Washington, 1969; producer, coordinator NBC Network news, Cleve., 1971—. Soloist, mgr. Lira Singers, Chgo., 1965—; mem., chmn. various cultural coms. Polish Am. Congress, 1970—. Washington Journalism Center fellow, spring

1969. Home: 10301 Lake No 703 Cleveland OH 44102 Office: 1403 E 6th St Cleveland OH 44114

MIHALOPULOS, GUS, JR., accountant; b. Christopher, Ill., July 17, 1937; s. Gus and Elizabeth (Urbain) M.; B.S., U. Ill., 1960; postgrad. U. Ala., 1964; m. Jacquelyn Fay Smith, Oct. 16, 1965; children—Michael Todd, Jennifer Elizabeth. With Laventhol & Horwath and predecessor firms, Carbondale, Ill., 1960—, partner, 1968—, dir., mem. nat. council, 1977—. Mem. council, chmn. finance com. St. Francis Xavier Ch., 1972-77. Mem. Hosp. Fin. Mgmt. Assn., Nat. Assn. Accountants, Am. Inst. C.P.A.'s, Ill. Soc. C.P.A.'s (treas. So. Ill. chpt. 1974-75). Clubs: Elks, K.C. Home: 500 Emerald Ln Carbondale IL 62901 Office: PO Box 2618 1116 W Main St Carbondale IL 62901

MIKAT, DOROTHY MARIE, pathologist, microbiol. dir.; b. Ann Arbor, Mich., Jan. 5, 1938; d. Nelson Irving and Dorothy Mary (Hopps) Rathburn; B.S., U. Mich., 1960; M.D., Med. Coll. Pa., 1964; m. Kurt Wolfgang Mikat, Aug. 23, 1958; children—Catherine, Richard, Daniel, Gregory, Allison, Jennifer. Intern, St. Francis Hosp., Evanston, Ill., 1964-65, resident in pathology, 1965-66; resident in pathology St. Joseph Hosp., Flint, Mich., 1966-69; pathologist Pontiac (Mich.) Gen. Hosp., 1969—, dir. microbiology, 1969—, chmn. infection control com., 1973—. Mormon. Author: A Clinician's Dictionary Guide to Bacteria, 1974; book reviewer Jour. Am. Med. Womens Assn. Office: Pontiac General Hospital Pontiac MI 48053

MIKELL, ARDELL, mfg. co. exec., minister; b. Prentiss, Miss., Apr. 23, 1927; s. Eline and Bertha (Weathersby) M.; grad. high sch.; m. Hattie Lee Williams, Jan. 22, 1946; children—Verastine (Mrs. Banjamine Wardlaw), Juanita (Mrs. William Paris II), Patricia (Mrs. Charles Chambliss), Arkenneth, Sharlette, Jeriel, Joel, Ezra, Alvin, Elizabeth. Die press operator Central Envelope and Lithograph, Forest Park, Ill., 1948-58, also machine operator Continental Envelope Co., Chgo., 1949-58; machine operator Gibralar Paper Corp., Chgo., 1958-67; owner United Envelope Co., Chgo., 1964—. Die press operator Outlook Envelope Co., Chgo., part time 1949-65; ordained to ministry Baptist Ch., 1955; pastor Little Mercy Seat Ch., 1958. Home: 7251 S Langley St Chicago IL 60619 Office: 525 W 76th St Chicago IL 60620

MIKESELL, JOHN PAUL, lawyer; b. Achilles, Kans., Nov. 26, 1899; s. Elihu A. and Sarah Catherine (Fleming) M.; student U. Kans., 1918-21; A.B., U. Mich., 1924, J.D., 1927; m. Ruth Elizabeth Zeiter, Aug. 1, 1936; children—Michael P., Sara Ann. Admitted to Mich. bar, 1927; asso. Bishop & Weaver, Detroit, 1927-29; claims atty. Hartford Accident & Indemnity Co., Detroit, 1929-30; individual practice, Detroit, 1931-57, 69—; mem. firm Mikesell & Young, 1931-57. Served with U.S. Army, World War I. Mem. Soc. Mayflower, Am., Mich., Detroit bar assns., Mich. Oil and Gas Assn. Mason (Shriner). Club: Detroit Athletic. Home: 17209 E Jefferson Ave Grosse Pointe MI 48230 Office: Penobscot Bldg Griswold & Fort St Detroit MI 48226

MIKESELL, SHARELL LEE, research and product devel. co. exec.; b. Coshocton, Ohio, Nov. 24, 1943; s. Forrest and Wilma Madeline (Axline) M.; A.B., Olivet Nazarene Coll., Kankakee, Ill., 1965; M.S., Ohio State U., 1968; Ph.D. (NDEA fellow), U. Akron, 1971. Chemist, Edmont-Wilson Co., Coshocton, Ohio, 1965; polymer chemist Gen. Electric Co., Coshocton, 1971-72, project mgr. polyester glass, 1972-74, mgr. market devel., 1974, mgr. indsl. product devel., 1975; lab. mgr. textile systems Owens-Corning Fiberglas, Granville, Ohio, 1976—. Mem. Am. Chem. Soc., Am. Assn. Textile Chemists and Colorists. Office: Owens-Corning Fiberglas Corp Technical Center Granville OH 43023

MIKHAIL, DAVID NAGIB, pathologist, clin. dir.; b. Cairo, Egypt, May 30, 1930; s. Nagib Mikhail and Mounira Daoud (Takla) Bishara; came to U.S., 1958, naturalized, 1970; M.D., Ain Shams U., Cairo, 1954; M.Sc. in Pathology, Temple U. Sch. Medicine, 1964; m. Samia Tawfik Saleh, Sept. 24, 1955; Teaching fellow pathology Temple U. Med. Sch., Phila., 1960-64; asso. pathologist Geisinger Med. Center, Danville, Pa., 1964-65; asst. clin. prof. pathology Temple U. Med. Sch., 1969-74; dir. pathology Evang. Community Hosp., Lewisburg, Pa., 1966-74; pathologist, dir. pathology Burns Clinic Med. Center, Petoskey, Mich., 1974—. Ruling elder United Presbyn. Ch. U.S.A., 1961—. Diplomate Am. Bd. Pathology. Fellow Royal Soc. Medicine, Royal Soc. Health, Coll. Am. Pathologists, Am. Soc. Clin. Pathologists, Assn. Clin. Scientists; mem. Internat. Acad. Pathology, Am. Assn. Blood Banks, AMA, Mich. Soc. Pathologists, Mich., No. Mich. med. socs., Christian Med. Soc. Republican. Home: PO Box 279 1289 North Shore Dr Walloon Lake MI 49796 Office: Burns Clinic Medical Center Petoskey MI 49770

MIKHAIL, GEORGE RIZK, dermatologist, clin. adminstr.; b. Cairo, Egypt, Dec. 6, 1914; s. Rizk and Chafikah (Girgis) M.; M.B., B.Ch., Cairo U., 1939; M.S. in Pathology (Univ. research fellow), Wayne State U., 1963; m. Elizabeth Noemie Duranti, May 19, 1955; children—Michael, Marianne. Practice medicine specializing in dermatology, Cairo, 1939-43; dermatologist, Ministry Pub. Health, Port Said, Egypt, 1943-61; dermatologist Henry Ford Hosp., Detroit, 1963—, head, chemosurgery clinic, 1969—, mem. teaching cons. staff, dept. dermatology, 1963—. Diplomate Am. Bd. Dermatology. Fellow Am. Acad. Dermatology, Am. Soc. Dermatopathology, Am. Coll. Chemosurgery (sec. treas. 1975—); mem. Am. Dermatol. Assn. Republican. Coptic Orthodox. Contbr. articles to med. jours. and chpts. to books. Office: Henry Ford Hosp 2799 W Grand Blvd Detroit MI 48202

MIKHAIL, RAMZY NAGUIB, surgeon; b. Cairo, Egypt, Mar. 19, 1933; s. Naguib Nicolas and Angele (Youssef) M.; came to U.S., 1959, naturalized, 1972; Baccalaureate in Scis., Coll. Ste. Famille, Cairo, 1950; M.B., Ch.B., Ain-Shams U., Cairo, 1957; m. Maryse Doss, Apr. 14, 1957; children—Francis, Nagwa, Laila, John. Sr. staff surgeon Am. Mission Hosp., Tanta, Egypt, 1965-67; surgeon Grant (Mich.) Community Hosp., 1968-70; practice medicine specializing in colon rectal surgery with spl. interest in colonscopic techniques, Toledo, Ohio, 1970—; v.p., sec. Drs. Blank and Mikhail, Inc., Toledo, 1971—; chief, sect. colon rectal surgery, St. Vincents Hosp. Med. Center, Toledo, 1973—; vice-chief sect. colon and rectal surgery St. Luke's Hosp., Maumee, Ohio, 1975—; active staff Toledo Hosp.; clin. asso. surgery, Med. Coll. Ohio, Toledo, 1971—. Diplomate Am. Bd. Surgery, Am. Bd. Colon Rectal Surgery. Fellow Am. Coll. Surgeons, Am. Soc. Colon Rectal Surgeons; AMA, Ohio Med. Assn., Toledo and Lucas County Acad. Medicine.

MIKRUT, JOHN JOSEPH, JR., labor arbitrator; b. Erie, Pa., Mar. 23, 1944; s. John Joseph and Helen Frances (Dorobiala) M.; B.S., Edinboro Coll., 1966; postgrad. U. Mass., 1966-68; Ed.D., U. Mo., Columbia, 1976; m. Lois Ann Leonard, Aug. 26, 1968. Intern edn. dept. United Steelworkers Am., Pitts., 1967-68; instr. labor studies Pa. State U., New Kensington, 1968-69; labor specialist, asst. prof. labor edn. U. Mo., Columbia, 1969—; mgmt. relations cons.; labor arbitrator. Trans World Airlines, Machinists Union; mem. labor arbitration panel Fed. Mediation Conciliation Service and Nat. Mediation Bd. Mem. City of Columbia Personnel Adv. Bd., 1976-80. Mem. Am. Arbitration Assn., (labor arbitration panel), Soc. Profls. Dispute Resolution, Iowa Pub. Employee Relations Bd., Univ. and Coll. Labor Edn. Assn., Indsl. Relations and Research Assn. Contbr. articles to profl. jours. Home: 2236 Country Ln Columbia MO 65201 Office: Dept Labor Edn Univ MO Columbia MO 65201

MIKS, GEORGE MARTIN, physician; b. Waukegan, Ill., Apr. 22, 1937; s. John George and Teresa Ursala (Svete) M.; B.S., Marquette U., 1959, M.D., 1963; m. Geraldine Marie Rosenberger, June 8, 1963; children—Laura Jean, George Edward, Susan Catherine. Intern, Cook County Hosp., Chgo., 1963-64, resident in gen. surgery, 1964-65; gen. practice medicine, Ely, Minn., 1965-66, Eveleth, Minn., 1966-67, East Range Clinic, Ltd., Aurora, Minn., 1967-74, Adams Clinic, Chisholm, Minn., 1975—; mem. staff Hibbing Gen. Hosp., Virginia (Minn.) Municipal Hosp., Chisholm Meml. Hosp.; clin. asst. prof. dept. family practice and community health U. Minn. Sch. Medicine, 1971—; asst. dep. med. examiner St. Louis County, Minn.; sr. med. examiner FAA. Precinct chmn. Republican Party, 1970-72, dist. legis. chmn., 1973-74. Diplomate Am. Bd. Family Practice. Mem. Am., Minn., Range acads. gen. practice, AMA, Minn., Range med. socs., Aircraft Owners and Pilots Assn., Canadian Owners and Pilots Assn., Am. Slovenian Catholic Union. Republican. Roman Catholic (pres. ch. council 1971-72). Club: Mesaba Country (Hibbing, Minn.). Home: 319 NW 6th Ave Chisholm MN 55719 Office: Adams Clinic Chisholm MN 55719

MIKSCHE, JEROME PHILLIP, research botanist; b. Breckenridge, Minn., June 11, 1930; s. Anthony F. and Clara C. (Braun) M.; B.S., Moorhead (Minn.) State Coll., 1954; M.S., Miami U., Oxford, Ohio, 1956; Ph.D., Iowa State U., Ames, 1959; m. Betty Jane Logan, May 23, 1953; children—Michael, Elizabeth, James. Instr. botany Iowa State U., Ames, 1958-59; postdoctoral fellow Brookhaven Nat. Lab., Upton, N.Y., 1959-61, mem. staff, 1961-65; asst. prof. botany C.W. Post Coll., N.Y.C., 1960-61; lectr. biology Adelphi Suffolk Coll., N.Y.C., 1962-65; research botanist Inst. Forest Genetics, Forest Service, U.S. Dept. Agr., Rhinelander, Wis., 1965—; cons. Life Books, 1963-64. Chmn. Headwaters Dist. Boy Scouts Am., 1970-72. Served with USMC, 1948-51. NIH fellow, 1960-61, NSF grantee, 1975-77. Fellow Royal Microscopical Soc.; mem. Nicolet Coll. and Tech. Inst. Found., Bot. Soc. Am., Am. Soc. Cell Biology, AAAS, Am. Soc. Plant Physiology, Sigma Xi, Gamma Sigma Delta, Phi Sigma. Contbr. articles to profl. publs. Home: 212 Grant St Rhinelander WI 54501 Office: Inst Forest Genetics N Central Forest Experiment Box 898 Rhinelander WI 54501

MIKSIC, BORIS ALEXANDER, research scientist; b. Yugoslavia, Oct. 11, 1948; s. Steven and Nina (Genrihsen) M.; came to U.S., 1974; B.S. in Mech. Engring., U. Zagreb, 1973; m. Olga Bonc, Nov. 26, 1972; children—Evonne Marie, Paul Richard. Sr. research scientist No. Instruments Corp., St. Paul, 1974—; pres. Cortec Corp., 1977—. Mem. Am. Chem. Soc., Nat. Assn. Corrosion Engrs. (chmn. internat. symposium volatile corrosion inhibitors 1976, chmn. task force T-3A-4 volatile corrosion inhibitors). Patentee in field; contbr. articles to profl. jours. Home: 21 Black Oak Rd North Oaks MN 55110 Office: Cortec Corp 366 Wacouta St Saint Paul MN 55101

MIKULA, EDWARD JOHN, art dir.; b. Chgo., Jan. 3, 1916; s. Joseph and Veronica (Komperda) M.; student Chgo. Art Inst., Evanston Art Center; m. Mae Strazzabosco, Apr. 13, 1947; 1 dau., Diane; 1 stepdau., Nancy (Mrs. Thornton Richardson). Illustrator, designer advt. art studios and agys., 1945-57; art dir. United Methodist Communications, Evanston, Ill., 1957—; exhibited group shows, London, Eng., Chgo. Served with AUS. Mem. Artist Guild Chgo., Art Inst. Alumni. Religious Pub. Relations Council, Asso. Ch. Press, Meth. Press Assn. Club: Polish Arts. Home: 208 N Gibbons St Arlington Heights IL 60004 Office: 1200 Davis St Evanston IL 60201

MIKVA, ABNER JOSEPH, congressman, lawyer, educator; b. Milw., Jan. 21, 1926; s. Henry Abraham and Ida (Fishman) M.; J.D. cum laude, U. Chgo., 1951; m. Zoe Wise, Sept. 19, 1948; children—Mary, Laurie, Rachel. Admitted to Ill. bar, 1951; law clk. to U.S. Supreme Ct. Justice Sherman Minton, 1951; partner firm Devoe, Shadur, Mikva & Plotkin, Chgo., 1952-68, D'Ancona, Pflaum, Wyatt & Riskind, 1973-74; faculty Northwestern U. Law Sch., Chgo., 1973-75; mem. Ill. Gen. Assembly from 23d Dist., 1956-66; mem. 91st-92d congresses, 2d Dist. Ill. 94th and 95th congresses from 10th Dist. Ill. Chmn. Ill. Bd. Ethics, 1973. Served with USAAF, World War II. Recipient Page One award Chgo. Newspaper Guild, 1964; Best Legislator award Ind. Voters Ill., 1956-66; named One of Ten Outstanding Young Men in Chgo., Jr. Assn. Commerce and Industry, 1961. Mem. Am. (com. on individual rights and responsibilities 1973), Chgo. (bd. mgrs. 1962-64) bar assns., Am. Civil Liberties Union, Phi Beta Kappa, Order of Coif. Democrat. Home: 1015 Sheridan Rd Evanston IL 60202 Office: 403 Cannon Bldg Washington DC 20515

MILANO, NICHOLAS PHILLIP, metallurgist; b. Milw., July 31, 1922; s. Lucas and Sarah (LaPorte) M.; student Ohio U., 1943-44; B.S. in Mech. Engring., Marquette U., 1950; M.S. in Metallurgy, U. Wis., 1954; m. Maxine R. Kulas, May 28, 1949; children—Dean, Paul, Mark, Steven, Phillip. Tool making apprentice Durant Mfg. Co., Milw., 1940-42; accounting clerk Internat. Harvester Co., Milw., 1942-43, cost accountant, 1946-48, asst. chief metallurgist, 1951-61, chief metallurgist, 1961-64, metals engr., Hinsdale, Ill., 1964-68, chief engr. metals, 1968-71; dir. mfg. Ill. Gear-Wallace Murray Corp., Chgo., 1971-73, dir. metallurgy, 1974—; cons. gear heat treat problems, Eng., France, Germany, 1965, 69. Water safety instr., disaster training instr., first aid instr. Am. Red Cross, 1946-75. Served with U.S. Army, 1943-46. Fellow Am. Soc. Metals (pres. 1977-78), Soc. Automotive Engrs. (certificate appreciation 1972), ASTM, Am. Welding Soc., Soc. Mfg. Engrs. Roman Catholic. Club: K.C. Contbr. articles on carburizing and carbonitriding to profl. jours. Home: 292 Oak St Glen Ellyn IL 60137 Office: 2108 N Natchez Ave Chicago IL 60635

MILBURN, SIDNEY EVERSTERN, veterinarian; b. Teche, La., Nov. 23, 1927; s. Curley and Alma (Rogers) M.; B.S., Southern U., Baton Rouge, 1950; D.V.M., Tuskegee Inst., 1957; m. Corinne N. Martin, June 14, 1952; children—Sidney E., Deborah A. Practice vet. medicine, Elk Point, S.D., 1957—; staff veterinarian Sch. Medicine, U.S.D., Vermillion, 1968—; S.D. state veterinarian, Park Jefferson, Sodrac Park, 1965—. Mem. Elk Point Republican Com., 1969—. Served with AUS, 1950-52. Decorated Purple Heart. Mem. Am., S.D. Vet. med. assns., C. of C. (past bd. dirs.), V.F.W., Am. Legion. Republican. Roman Catholic. K.C. Contbr. to profl. jours. Home: PO Box 456 108 Grant St Elk Point SD 57025 Office: PO Box 445 105 Douglas St Elk Point SD 57025

MILDER, MYRON HARRY, oil co. exec.; b. Omaha, Jan. 13, 1927; s. Hymie and Ella (Braunstein) M.; student U. Nebr., 1943-44, U. Idaho, 1946, George Washington U., 1946-47; B.S. in Edn., U. Omaha, 1948; m. Lois Rodin, Mar. 2, 1958; children—Myron Harry, Emily Idell. With Milder Oil Co., Omaha, 1948—, credit mgr., 1949-52, v.p., 1952-70, pres., chmn. bd., 1974—; cons. Research Grants Adv. Bd., Maternal and Child Health Service, HEW, 1970-72; bd. dirs. Eastern Nebr. Mental Health Assn., 1964-66; membership com. AKSARBEN, 1956-76; bd. mgmt. YMCA, 1967-69; Omaha pres. Jr. C. of C., 1950-57, Nebr. pres., 1959-60, v.p. internat. relations U.S., 1960-61; Easter seal chmn. Nebr. Soc. Crippled Children and Adults, 1964; nat. trustee World Refugee Orgn., 1962-63; mem. Omaha City Planning Comm., 1955-57; bd. dirs. Meyer Children's Therapy Center, 1962-66; active Republican polit. campaigns; del.-at-large Rep. Nav. Conv., 1968; del. various state and county Rep. convs.; nat. field dir. Com. to Re-Elect the Pres., 1972, Citizens for Ford, 1976. Served with USNR, 1945-46. Named Omaha's Outstanding Young Man, 1959. Mem. Nat., Nebr. oil jobbers confs., U.S., Omaha (dir. 1955-57) chambers commerce, Am. Legion (exec. com. 1953-54), U. Omaha Alumni Assn., Jewish War Vets., Omaha Magical Soc., Am. Polit. Items Collectors, Am. Philatelic Soc., Zeta Beta Tau. Clubs: Rotary, B'nai B'rith (Midwest adv. bd. Anti-defamation League 1954-72, local bd. dirs. 1953-55), Elks, Masons, Shriners, United Comml. Travelers, Highland Country, Capitol Hill, Fraternal Order Police. Home: 116 S 92 St Omaha NE 68114 Office: PO Box 3707 Omaha NE 68103

MILES, ALFRED LEE, educator; b. Eaton, Ohio, Aug. 4, 1913; s. James Sampson and Grace Blanche (Bittner) M.; student Ohio State U., 1930-33, Sinclair Coll., 1945, Miami-Jacobs Coll., 1954-56; m. Margaret Lucille Saul, Mar. 18, 1936 (div. Mar. 1949); children—Ronald Lynn, Walter Whitney; m. 2d, Virginia Null Engelman, Feb. 24, 1951; children—Victoria Ellen, Kimber Lee, Bethany Laine, Christopher Kent; stepchildren—Dianne Engleman (Mrs. M. Douglas Fogle), Norbert Nicholas Engelman, Jr. Instr. pvt. courses in real estate prins. and real estate law, Dayton, Ohio, 1949—; instr. short courses Spl. Sessions Div. U. Dayton. Violinist, Dayton Civic Orch., 1927-29, Ohio State U. Symphony, 1930-33, Columbus (O.) Symphony, 1930-33. Ky. Col. Mem. Nat. Assn. Realtors, Internat. Platform Assn. Republican. Methodist. Club: Cincinnati. Home: 1629 Far Hills Ave Dayton OH 45419 Office: 2185 S Dixie Ave Dayton OH 45409

MILES, JAMES SOUTHARD, ednl. technologist; b. Bellefontaine, Ohio, Sept. 22, 1916; s. Clarence Nash and Agnes Rebecca (Southard) M.; student Ohio State U., 1934-36; m. Elizabeth Evalyn Reber, June 7, 1940; 1 son, James Richard. Announcer, program dir. radio stations, Charleston, W.Va., Cin., Columbus, Dayton, Ohio, Fort Wayne, Ind., 1936-43; reading clk. Ohio Ho. of Reps., 1939, 41, 43; mgr. Sta. WBAA, W. Lafayette, Ind., 1943-60; dept. head airborne TV project Purdue U., W. Lafayette, Ind., 1960-62, dir. telecommunication center, 1962—; cons. AID, SE Asia, 1967, 69, 72, Pakistan, 1974. Mem. sch. bd., Klondike, 1955-62, Tippecanoe, 1964-70. Mem. Nat. Assn. Ednl. Broadcasters (exec. dir. 1951-53), Ind. Higher Ednl. Telecommunication System Council, Ind. Sch. Bds. Assn. (pres. 1967-68). Republican. Methodist. Club: Lions. Home: 1580 W State St West Lafayette IN 47906 Office: Telecommunications Center Purdue Univ West Lafayette IN 47907

MILFORD, WILLIAM EUGENE, dentist; b. Marion, Ind., Nov. 23, 1923; s. Lawrence M. and Amy (Duncan) M.; student Notre Dame U., 1941, Ind. U., 1942-43; B.S., St. Joseph's Coll., 1945; D.D.S., Wash. U., 1949; m. Patty Lou Sisson, Mar. 31, 1951; children—John B., Joseph B., Melissa M. Pvt. practice dentistry, Marion, 1949-51, 1953—. Dir. Superior Metal Products, Inc., 1957-72, chmn. bd. dirs., 1969—. Bd. dirs. Marion br. ARC. Served with USAF, 1951-53. Mem. Pierre Fauchard Acad. Dentists, Wabash Valley, Ind. State, Am. dental assns., Delta Sigma Delta. Republican. Clubs: Mecca, Columbia, Meshingomesia Country, Marion Aero. Home: 2610 Orchard Rd Marion IN 46952 Office: 315 N Western Ave Marion IN 46952

MILITZER, MARY ERIC, nun, ednl. TV programmer; b. Milw., Nov. 14, 1918; d. Erich Otto and Elizabeth Loretta (Roetto) Militzer; B.S. in Edn., Mt. Mary Coll., Milw., 1950; M.A. in Guidance and Counseling, Marquette U., Milw., 1968. Joined Sisters of Notre Dame, Roman Cath. Ch., 1938; tchr. prin. elementary schs., Wis., Ill., 1938-49; started 1st parochial schs., Guam, 1949-64; tchr. Latin, vice prin. Messmer High Sch., Milw., 1964-67; mem. instructional TV staff Roman Cath. Archdiocese Milw., 1968-74, dir., 1972-74; dir. religious and ednl. programming Cath. TV Network, Chgo., 1974—, program coordinator, 1976—; chmn. Southeastern Wis. Com. Full Utilization Instructional TV Fixed Service, 1972; mem. Wis. Broadcast Instructional Advisory Council, 1971-74; chmn. program dirs. Instructional TV Assos., 1971-77; mem. policy bd. Gt. Plains Nat. Instructional TV Library, 1975—; mem. ednl. TV commn. Ill. Bd. Higher Edn., 1976-77; mem. Ill. Broadcast Advisory Council, 1974—. Mem. UNDA (Cath. Assn. Radio TV), Nat. Assn. Ednl. Broadcasters, Assn. Ednl. Communications and Tech., Nat. Cath. Edn. Assn. Author: Chamorro Hymns, 1967. Home: 4910 N Menard St Chicago IL 60630 Office: 1 N Wacker Dr Chicago IL 60606

MILIVOYEVICH, MILORAD LJUBOMIR, project engr.; b. Beograd, Yugoslavia, Aug. 7, 1912; s. Ljubomir J. and Juliana G. (Georgevich) M.; came to U.S., 1962, naturalized, 1971; B.S. in Electro-Mech. Engring., Bundesgewerbe Schule, Vienna, Austria, 1932; m. Olga Varagich, Apr. 16, 1942. Chief Engr. Industria Colombiana de Rayon Barranquilla, Columbia, S.A., 1947-49; project engr. Chrysler-Dodge assembly plant Frederik Shnare Corp., Caracas, Venezuela, 1950; mech. engr. Internat. Gen. Electric, Caracas, 1950-52; chief engr. Corp. Venezolana de Fomento "Cadafe" branch Venezuela Govt. for Indsl. Devel., 1952-62; project engr. Nat. Can Corp., Chgo., 1964—. Recipient awards Corp. Venezolana de Fomento, Caracas, Venezuela, Nat. Can Corp., Chgo. Mem. ASME. Greek Orthodox. Interpreter U.S.-English Electrical Code to Spanish, 1955. Home: 3615 Central Rd Glenview IL 60025 Office: 8101 W Higgins Rd Chicago IL 60631

MILLAR, ALLEN ROBERT, coll. pres.; b. Ravinnia, S.D., Dec. 5, 1922; s. George Howard and Beulah (Wilhelm) M.; B.S., Chadron State Coll., 1947; M.A., Colo. State Coll., 1950; Ed.D., U. Neb., 1956; m. Edith C. Andrews, Dec. 22, 1943; children—Thomas Allen, Carolyn Edith. Tchr. sci. Chadron (Nebr.) pub. sch., 1947-48; asso. prof. sci., edn. Chadron State Coll., 1948-55; instr. U. Nebr., 1955-56; asso. prof. Mankato (Minn.) State Coll., 1956-62; pres. So. State Coll., Springfield, S.D., 1962-71, Dakota State Coll., Madison, S.D., 1971-72; prof. edn., asst. dir. Ednl. Research and Service Center, Sch. Edn., U. S.D., Vermillion, 1972-74; coll. and univ. programming counselor Gt. Plains Nat. Instrnl. TV Library, U. Nebr., Lincoln, 1974—. Served to 1st lt. C.E., AUS, 1943-46. Mem. NEA, Am. Assn. Sch. Adminstrs., Nat. Soc. for Study of Edn. Mason, Rotarian, Kiwanian; mem. Order Eastern Star. Home: 1701 No 50 Lincoln NE 68504

MILLAR, LEOLA FAUDREE (MRS. CHARLES J. MILLAR), librarian; b. Evansville, Ind., Dec. 4, 1905; d. Thomas Lee and Martha (Harris) Faudree; student Stephens Coll., 1923-25, Mo. Sch. Mines, 1926, U. Mo., summers 1951-53; m. Charles J. Millar, Dec. 25, 1925 (dec. Feb. 1955); children—Nancy Lee (Mrs. W.K. Mengel), James Bruce. Librarian Rolla (Mo.) High Sch., 1950-53, Rolla Free Pub. Library, 1954-75. Mo. exec. dir. Nat. Library Week, 1960. Mem. exec. bd. Mo. Arthritis Found. Mem. A.L.A., Mo. Library Assn. (sec. 1961-63, chmn. pub. libraries div. 1967—); P.E.O. Episcopalian. Home: 1400 Pine St Rolla MO 65401 Office: Box 1430 Rolla MO 65401

MILLARD, JOSEPH NESTER, SR., banker; b. St. Louis, May 18, 1937; s. Francis Earl and Dorothy (Nester) M.; B.S.B.A., Ill. Coll., 1959; m. Doris Donna, Oct. 21, 1961; children—Joseph Nester, Elizabeth Ann. Supt., Obear Nester Glass Co., East St. Louis, Ill., 1960-70; pres. Bankers Trust Co. Belleville, Ill., 1970—; dir. Bankers Trust Co., Bank of Belleville; sec. treas. Belleville Bancshares, Inc. Treas. Okaw Valley council Boy Scouts Am., 1971—; merit commr. St. Clair County, Ill., 1972—; trustee Blessed Sacrament Roman Catholic Ch., Belleville, 1971—. Served with AUS, C.E., 1959-60. Mem. Assn. Modern Banking, Ill. Bankers Assn., Am. Inst. Banking, Belleville C. of C. Club: St. Clair Country (sec., treas.). Home: 76 Country Club Pl Belleville IL 62223 Office: 6400 W Main St Belleville IL 62223

MILLER, ALICEMARIE MEYER, clin. psychologist; b. Evanston, Ill., Feb. 14, 1930; d. Charles H.Z. and Clara Frances (Bovee) Meyer; B.A., Northwestern U., 1950; M.A., U. Tex., 1952; postgrad. Washington U. Med. Sch., 1952-53; children—Jule P. III, Amanda B. Cons. clin. psychologist dept. psychiatry Mass. Gen. Hosp., Tufts Cleft Palate Inst., Boston, 1955-57; research asst. Austen Riggs Center, Stockbridge, Mass., 1957-58; pvt. practice, St. Louis, 1957-59, 74—; faculty Washington U., St. Louis, Lindenwood Coll., St. Louis, 1974-77. Pres. Dance Concert Soc., 1973-75; bd. dirs. New Music Circle, 1966-69, Opera Theatre, 1966-69. Certified sex educator, sex therapist. Mem. Am. Psychol. Assn., Soc. St. Louis Psychologists (chmn. speakers' bur. 1976-77), Assn. Sex Educators, Counselors and Therapists, Am. Personnel and Guidance Assn., Assn. Sex Therapists and Counselors. Episcopalian. Clubs: Jr. League. Home: 6932 Pershing Ave St Louis MO 63130 Office: 8011 Clayton Rd St Louis MO 63117

MILLER, ALVIN, ednl. adminstr.; b. Chgo., Dec. 23, 1928; s. Jacob and Dora (Shapiro) M.; student U. Ill. at Navy Pier, 1946-47; B.A., U. Chgo., 1949, M.A., 1951, postgrad., 1951-52; m. Marilyn J. Phillips, June 27, 1954; children—Michelle, Mark. Instr. social studies Herzl Jr. Coll., Chgo., 1954-62; tchr. history, chmn. history dept. Farragut High Sch., Chgo., 1954-62; prin. Tonti Sch., Chgo., 1962-67; prin. Judd Elementary Sch., Chgo., 1967—; instr. Chgo. Tchrs. Rev. Sch., 1955-60; mem. curriculum council Chgo. Pub. Schs., 1957-60. Mem. Jewish United Fund, Chgo., 1962—. Mem. Chgo. Prins. Assn., Phi Eta Sigma. Home: 6942 N Wolcott Chicago IL 60626

MILLER, ANDERSON (ANDY) FRANKLIN, designer, art cons.; b. Mayfield, Ky., Dec. 25, 1917; s. Nat L. and Edna (Herdy) M.; student Drury Coll., 1951-52; m. Juanita Russell, May 14, 1960; 1 son, Larry. Art and advt. mgr. Turner's Dept. Store, Springfield, Mo., 1947-54; art dir. Ralph Nelms Advt. Agy., Springfield, 1955-58; art dir. and set designer Ozark Jubilee, ABC-TV Network program, Springfield, Mo., 1959-61, Five Star Jubilee, NBC-TV, Springfield, Mo., 1962, Slim Wilson show sta. KYTV, Springfield, 1963-73; art and theme coordinator Craft and Theme Park, Silver Dollar City, Mo., 1964—; cons. for TV stations in Mo. and Ark., 1962—; judge for various art contests in schs. and museums, Mo., 1960-76; vis. tchr. of design and art Springfield Pub. Schs., also civic art groups. Guest speaker at various civic orgns., Springfield, Mo., 1960-64, Branson, Mo., 1964-78. Served with U.S. Army, 1941-45. Recipient awards for creative displays, 1955-64. Mem. Bonniebrook Hist. Soc. (dir. 1975—), Mo. Ad Club, Springfield Art Club. Democrat. Methodist. Club: Rose O'Neill. Designer of hist. bldgs. for theme parks. Home: SR-3 PO Box 18-C Mt Branson Branson MO 65616 Office: Theme Coordinator Silver Dollar City MO 65616

MILLER, CAROLE SEIFER, language pathologist; b. Chgo., Nov. 14, 1931; d. Joseph E. and Charlotte Rubin; B.S., Northwestern U., 1953, M.A., 1965; m. Robert A. Miller, Dec. 28, 1972; children—David Seifer, Frederic Seifer; stepchildren—Danny Miller, Julie Miller, Sarah Miller. Aphasia therapist Henner Hearing and Speech Center Michael Reese Hosp., Chgo., 1965-67; kindergarten cons. Latin Sch. of Chgo., 1970-73; aphasia cons. Chgo. Heart Assn. Stroke Rehab. Project Workshop, 1971-72; learning disabilities cons. Anshe Emet Day Sch., Chgo., 1973—; psycho-ednl. diagnosis Ill. Children's Home and Aid Soc., 1974-; lectr. in field. Certified learning disabilities tchr., Ill. Mem. Orton Soc., Am. Speech and Hearing Assn. (certificate clin. competence speech pathology), Ill. Speech and Hearing Assn. Jewish. Clubs: Saddle and Cycle. Home: 220 E Walton St Chicago IL 60611 Office: 700 N Michigan Ave Chicago IL 60612

MILLER, CARSON KEITH, mech. engr.; b. Cleve., Sept. 15, 1945; s. Carson Henry and Agnes (Singell) M.; A.A. in Sci., Stark Tech. Coll., 1966; B.S., Kent State U., 1968; M.S., U. Akron, 1977; m. Barbara Jean Feigum, July 16, 1966; children—Carson Scott, Doriann. Draftsman, Tyson div. SKF Industries, Massillon, Ohio, 1965-66; engring. technician Timken Co., Canton, Ohio, 1966-69, mech. engr., 1969-74; instr. mech. engring. tech. Stark Tech. Coll., Canton, 1974—, chairperson dept., 1977—. Active PTA. Served with USAF, 1969-73. Mem. ASME, Ohio Tech. Coll. Athletic Assn. (v.p.). Episcopalian. Author: Study Guide to Strength of Materials, 1976. Home: 1105 35th St NW Canton OH 44709 Office: 6200 Frank Ave NW Canton OH 44720

MILLER, CLARENCE E., congressman; b. Lancaster, Ohio, Nov. 1, 1917; hon. degree Rio Grande Coll.; m. Helen M. Brown; children—Ronald, Jacqueline (Mrs. Thomas Williams). Mem. City Council, Lancaster, 1957-63; mayor, Lancaster, 1963-65; mem. 90th to 95th congresses from 10th Ohio Dist. Bd. dirs. Fairfield County chpt. A.R.C., YMCA. Hon. mem. Ohio Valley Health Services Found.; hon. alumnus Ohio U. mem. coms. on appropriations. Republican. Methodist. Elk. Address: Cannon House Office Bldg Washington DC 20215

MILLER, CLIFFORD HARRY, dentist; b. Chgo., Dec. 9, 1932; s. James V. and Hazel M. (Smith) M.; D.D.S., Northwestern U., 1957; m. Ann F. Cannon, Mar. 29, 1974; 1 son, James Michael. Instr., Northwestern U., Chgo., 1959-61, asst. prof., 1961-64, asso. prof., 1964-66, prof. operative dentistry, 1966-69, prof., chmn. dept., 1969-72, asso. dean dental div., 1971—; cons. nat. bds. in operative ADA, 1968—. Served to lt. USNR, 1957-59. Fellow Am. Coll. Dentists, Internat. Coll. Dentists; mem. Am. Acad. Gold Foil Operators (pres. 1973-74), ADA, Ill., Chgo. dental socs., Odontographic Soc., Acad. Restorative Dentistry, Acad. Operative Dentistry, Internat. Assn. Dental Research, Omicron Kappa Upsilon. Editor Dental Student, 1968—, Bridge, 1972—; editorial bd. Foil Acad. jour., 1971—. Home: 4907 Farwell St Skokie IL 60076 Office: 311 E Chicago Ave Chicago IL 60611

MILLER, DANIEL MARTIN, surgeon, educator; b. Edmonton, Alta., Can., Dec. 16, 1917; s. David and Lena (Hurwich) M.; B.S. in Medicine, Creighton U., 1940; M.D., 1942; m. Harriet Rosen, Mar. 7, 1943; children—Neil R., Craig R., Alexander R. Intern, Michael Reese Hosp., Chgo., 1942-43; resident in surgery, 1946-49, Mass. Gen. Hosp., Boston, 1949-50; in charge surg. tumor clinic U. Nebr. Hosp., Omaha, 1954—, chmn. cancer com. dept. surgery, 1960—, asst. prof. dept. surgery; asso. prof. surgery U. Nebr. Med. Sch., 1967—, mem. oncology curriculum com.; chief investigator C.D.E. program Surg. Adjuvant Breast Program; chmn. dept. surgery Bishop Clarkson Meml. Hosp., Omaha, 1971-77, chmn. cancer com. and tumor registry; mem. Regional Adv. Group for Regional Med. Program, Nebr.; chmn. Cancer Task Force, State of Nebr. Served with USAAF, 1943-46. Diplomate Am. Bd. Surgery. Fellow A.C.S. (liaison fellow commn. on cancer, 1977—); mem. Am. Radium Soc., Pan-Pacific Surg. Assn., AMA, Pan Am. Med. Assn., James Ewing Soc., N.Y. Acad. Scis., Am. Fedn. Clin. Research, Douglas County Med. Soc., Am. Soc. Clin. Oncology, Am. Assn. for Cancer Research, Internat. Acad. Proctology, Soc. for Surgery Alimentary Tract. Contbr. articles to profl. jours. Home: 681 Hackberry Rd Omaha NE 68132 Office: Doctors Bldg Omaha NE 68131

MILLER, DON WILSON, engineer, educator; b. Westerville, Ohio, Mar. 16, 1942; s. Don P. and Rachel J. (Jones) M.; m. Mary Thompson, June 25, 1966; children—Amy, Stacy, Paul. B.S., Miami U., Ohio, 1964, M.S. in Physics, 1966; M.S., Ohio State U., 1970, Ph.D. in Nuclear Engring., 1971. Engr., N. Am. Aviation, Columbus, Ohio, 1964; teaching asst. physics dept. Miami U., Oxford, Ohio, 1964-66; research asso. Ohio State U., 1966-69, university fellow, 1970, teaching asso., 1971, asst. prof., 1971-74, asso. prof., 1974—, chmn. nuclear engring., dir. nuclear reactor lab., 1977—; dir. Cellar Lumber Co., 1972—; dir. Concord (Westerville) Drug Abuse and Crisis Center, 1974-76; bd. edn., Westerville, 1976—; tchr. Presbyn. Ch. Sch., Westerville, 1976-77. Mem. Am. Nuclear Soc., IEEE, Am. Soc. Engring. Educators, Instrument Soc. Am., Alpha Delta Phi, Hoover Yacht Club. Recipient Culler Prize, 1961. Contbr. articles to profl. jours.; patentee in field. Home: 172 Walnut Ridge Ln Westerville OH 43081 Office: 206 W 18th Ave Columbus OH 43210

MILLER, DONALD ANDERSON, surgeon; b. Youngstown, Ohio, Feb. 14, 1912; s. Ralph John and Florence Louise (Leonard) M.; A.B., Western Reserve U., 1933, M.D., 1937; M.S., U. Pa., 1942; m. Margaret V. Kaye; children—Gregory A., Lynne A. Intern, Youngstown Hosp. Assn., 1937-39; resident U. Pa., Phila., 1939-42; practice medicine, specializing in surgery, Warren, Ohio, 1947--; active staff chief surg. service Trumbull Meml. Hosp., Warren, 1954-74, chief of staff, 1974-76, also trustee; mem. active staff St. Joseph's Hosp., Warren; dir. 2d Nat. Bank, Warren. Pres., Am. Cancer Soc., 1967-69, campaign chmn., 1965-67, spl. gifts chmn. 1969-77. Served to col. MC AUS, 1942-47. Diplomate Am. Bd. Surgery, Pan Am. Surg. Soc. Fellow A.C.S.; mem. Am., Ohio med. assns., Trumbull County Med. Soc., Cleve. Surg. Soc. Episcopalian. Clubs: Ocean Reef (Fla.), Trumbull Country, Buckeye (both Warren, Ohio); Card Sound (Fla.) Golf. Contbr. articles to med. jours. Home: 6570 Mines Rd SE Warren OH 44484 Office: 2400 Niles Cortland Rd SE Suite 4 Warren OH 44484

MILLER, DONALD GEORGE, mech. engr.; b. Chgo., Jan. 1, 1929; s. John George and Cora Bell (Curran) M.; B.Engring. Sci., North Central Coll., 1952; postgrad. U. Calif. at Los Angeles, 1957-59; m. Rachel Beatrice Weeks, May 11, 1974; children—Sheila, Gordon. Sr. thermodynamics engr. Gen. Dynamics Co., Pomona, Calif., 1956-62; sr. design specialist Aerojet Gen., Sacramento, 1962-68; staff engr. Bell Comm Inc., Washington, 1968-71; sr. engr. Western Electric Co., Lee's Summit, Mo., 1971—. Mem. NASA team that participated in first landing on moon Apollo 11, 1969. Served with AUS, 1954-56. Mem. Am. Inst. Chem. Engrs., Combustion Inst. Mem. Ch. of Jesus Christ of Latter-day Saints. Home: 9808 Knox Dr Overland Park KS 66212 Office: 777 N Blue Pkwy Lee's Summit MO 64063

MILLER, DONALD MORTON, physiologist, biophysicist; b. Chgo., July 24, 1930; s. Harry Madison and Anna Loraine (Zeller) M.; A.B. in Zoology, U. Ill., Urbana, 1960, M.A. in Physiology, 1962, Ph.D. (NIH fellow), 1965; postgrad. U. Calif. at Los Angeles (NIH fellow), 1965-66; m. Joan Hempel, Mar. 9, 1963; 1 son, Tad Michael. Insp. Buick Jet div. Gen. Motors Corp., Willow Springs, Ill., 1953-55; sci. asst. Organic Chemistry Lab. U. Ill., 1960-62, counselor residence halls, 1960-63, teaching asst. physiology, 1960-64; asst. prof. physiology So. Ill. U., Carbondale, 1966-71, coordinator gen. biology, 1971-72, asso. prof. physiology Sch. Medicine, 1972-76, prof. physiology, 1976—; lectr. trauma edn. Ill. State Hwy. Div., So. Ill. Health Manpower Consortium, Critical Care Nurse program. Treas. Jackson County Red Cross Bd., 1973—; judge State of Ill. Jr. Acad. Sci.; active CAP. Served with USAF, 1955-59. USPHS summer trainee, 1962, 63; grantee NIH, 1968—, NASA, 1973—; Damon lectr., 1973-74. Mem. Am. Physiol. Soc., Biophys. Soc., Am. Microscopic Soc., Neurosci. Soc., Am. Soc. Zoologists, N.Y. Acad. Sci., Am. Soc. Photobiology (charter), Sigma Xi (pres. So. Ill. U. chpt. 1973), Chi Gamma Iota. Elk, Lion. Contbr. articles to profl. publs. Home: 2733 Kent Dr Carbondale IL 62901

MILLER, EARL EUGENE, food processing co. exec.; b. Manitowoc, Wis., May 7, 1913; s. Albert John and Julia (Mathieson) M.; grad. high sch.; m. Lucille Margaret Jagodinsky, May 28, 1938; children—Judith Ann, Michael John. Maintainence mechanic and machinist Lakeside Packing Co., Manitowoc, Wis., 1928-36, plant foreman, 1936-39, factory supt., 1939-50, plant mgr. factory and field ops., 1950-74, gen. mgr., 1974—; pres. Terra-Veg, Ltd., Manitowoc, 1969-74, gen. mgr., 1974—. Lutheran. Eagle, Elk. Home: 4103 Springhill Dr Manitowoc WI 54220 Office: 508 Jay St Manitowoc WI 54220

MILLER, EDWARD HENDERSON, orthopedic surgeon; b. Fort Worth, Tex., Sept. 16, 1935; s. Harry Jackson and Mary Elizabeth (Henderson) M.; B.S., Purdue U., 1957; M.D., U. Cin., 1961; m. Carol R. Roach, Sept. 7, 1957; children—Pamela Ann, Stephen Jackson, Edward Gaines Parker, Matthew Jersesen. Intern H.C. Moffitt Hosp., U. Cal. Med. Center, San Francisco, fellow orthopaedic surgery, 1964-65, resident orthopaedics, 1965-68; practice medicine specializing in orthopaedic surgery, Cin., 1968—; dir. orthopaedic surg. service U. Cin., 1968—, dir. dept. orthopaedic surgery, U. Cin. Med. Center; 1970—. Bd. dirs. Cin. Ballet Co., 1974—. Served with USAF, 1962-64. Diplomate Am. Bd. Orthopaedic Surgery. Mem. Am. Acad. Orthopaedic Surgeons, ASTM, Societe Internationale de Chirurgie Orthopaedique et de Traumatologie. Mason (Shriner). Home: 9795 Fox Hollow Cincinnati OH 45243 Office: U Cin Med Center Cincinnati OH 45267

MILLER, EUGENE, financial co. exec.; b. Chgo., Oct. 6, 1925; s. Harry and Fannie (Prosterman) M.; B.S., Ga. Inst. Tech., 1945; A.B. magna cum laude, Bethany Coll., 1947, LL.D., 1969; diploma Oxford (Eng.) U., 1947; M.S. in Journalism, Columbia, 1948; M.B.A., N.Y. U., 1959; m. Edith Sutker, Sept. 23, 1951 (div. Sept. 1965); children—Ross, Scott, June; m. 2d, Thelma Gottlieb, Dec. 22, 1965; stepchildren—Paul Gottlieb, Alan Gottlieb. Reporter, then city editor Greensboro (N.C.) Daily News, 1948-52; S.W. bur. chief Bus. Week mag., Houston, 1952-54, asso. mng. editor, N.Y.C., 1954-60; dir. pub. affairs and communications McGraw-Hill, Inc., 1960-63, v.p., 1963-68; v.p. pub. relations and investor relations, exec. com. N.Y. Stock Exchange, N.Y.C., 1968-70; sr. v.p., 1970-73; sr. v.p. CNA Fin. Corp., Chgo., 1973-75; v.p. U.S. Gypsum Co., 1977—; adj. prof. mgmt. Grad. Sch. Bus. Adminstrn., N.Y. U., 1963—; prof. bus. adminstrn. Fordham U. Grad. Sch. Bus. Adminstrn., 1969—; chmn., prof. finance Northeastern Ill. U., 1975—. lectr. econs. pub. relations to bus. and sch. groups; author syndicated bus. column, 1964—. Dir. Tabb, Inc., Ann Arbor, Mich. Cons. to sec. commerce, 1961-66. Alumni dir., trustee Bethany Coll.; mem. alumni bd. Columbia Sch. Journalism. Served to ensign USNR, World War II; comdr. Res. Mem. Am. Econs. Assn., Am. Finance Assn., Nat. Assn. Bus. Economists, Soc. Am. Bus. Writers, Pub. Relations Soc. Am., Newcomen Soc., Fin. Analyst Soc., Sigma Delta Chi, Alpha Sigma Phi. Clubs: Mid-Am. (Chgo.); Green Acres Country, N.Y.U. (N.Y.C.). Author: Your Future in the Securities Business, 1974; Barron's Guide to Graduate Business Schs., 1977. Contbg. editor: Public Relations Handbook, 1971. Home: 376 Sunrise Circle Glencoe IL 60022 Office: 101 S Wacker Dr Chicago IL 60606

MILLER, FLOYD GLENN, mech. engr., educator; b. Chgo., May 25, 1935; s. Harvey Roscoe and Alice Katherine (Koch) Shiffermiller; B.S. in Indsl. Engring., U. Ill., 1957, Ph.D. in Mech. Engring., 1961; m. Elizabeth Marie Hoffmann, Aug. 22, 1962; children—Liesl Katherine, Andrew George, John DeWitt. Tech. devel. mgr. 3M Co., Chgo., 1962-66; asst. mgr. and mgr. systems applications div. Northern Trust Co., Chgo., 1966-70; asst. prof. indsl. engring. U. Ill., Chgo., 1970-74, asso. prof., 1974—, asst. to dir. phys. plant, 1970—. Lectr. evening div. DePaul U., Chgo., 1970, 74—, also mem. faculty Sch. for Bank Adminstrn., 1969—. Assembly rep. 44th ward, Chgo., 1972-74. Recipient Teaching award Sch. for Bank Adminstrn., 1972. Mem. Am. Soc. M.E., Am. Soc. of Engring. Edn., Am. Inst. Indsl. Engrs., Assn. of Systems Mgmt. (Merit award 1973, Achievement award 1974), Assn. Phys. Plant Adminstrs. of Univs. and Colls. Lutheran (chmn. mission and service 1972-74). Contbr. articles on engring. and mgmt. to profl. publs. Home: 626 Wellington Chicago IL 60657 Office: Dept of Systems Engineering Univ of Illinois PO Box 4348 Chicago IL

MILLER, FRANCIS ALLEN, microbiologist; b. Indpls., May 3, 1917; s. Henry Eugene and Harriet Belle (Denison) M.; B.S., Ohio State U., 1941; M.S., U. Mich., 1947; m. Maudellen Chappell, May 16, 1943; children—Mark, Harriet Ione, Ross. Asst. research microbiologist Parke Davis & Co., Rochester, Mich., 1947-52, asso. research microbiologist, 1952-66, research microbiologist, 1966-76, sr. scientist, 1976—. Commr., Detroit dist. Boy Scouts Am., 1948-50; mem. planning com. Lake Orion Sch., 1968, v.p. P.T.A., 1960. Served with AUS, 1941-45. Mem. Am. Soc. Microbiology, Am. Acad. Microbiology. Mem. Christian Ch. (chmn. bd. elders). Contbr. articles to sci. jours. Home: PO Box 214 Lake Orion MI 48035 Office: Parkedale Rd Rochester MI 48063

MILLER, FRANK ELLIS, steel co. exec.; b. Elkhart, Ind., Jan. 26, 1914; s. Frank J. and Margaret (Ludwig) M.; student U. Mich., 1933, Ind. U., 1934; C.E., U. Ill., 1938; m. Kathryn Jane Frank, June 23, 1940; children—Linda (Mrs. Steven Wainwright), Jay Dudley. Sales mgr. Elkhart Bridge & Iron Co., 1940-42, v.p., asst. gen. mgr., 1942-46, v.p., 1946-52, pres., 1952—; pres. Miller Steel &Supply Co., 1952—, Miller Industries, 1959—; dir. 1st Nat. Bank Elkhart County. Mem. No. Side Bldg. Corp. Registered profl. engr., Ind. Mem. Young Pres. Orgn., ASCE, U. Ill. Alumni Assn. (dir. 1975). Clubs: City Elcona Country (Elkhart); Lake Shore (Chgo.). Elk, Lion. Home: 2123 Greenleaf Blvd Elkhart IN 46514 Office: 929 N Michigan St Elkhart IN 46514

MILLER, FREDERICK COLEMAN, newspaper exec., electronics co. exec.; b. Chgo., Jan. 3, 1923; s. Maxwell P. and Elizabeth (Burleson) M.; B.A., U. Chgo., 1947; m. Betty McAfee, Feb. 17, 1945; children—Lucy (Mrs. Steven J. Stanard), Elizabeth (Mrs. James F. Boyle), Fredrick Coleman, Marilyn, Fort. With Swift & Co., Chgo., 1947-49; mgr., sec., dir. Daily News-Tribune, Inc., LaSalle, Ill., 1949—; pres. Graphic Electronics, Inc., Ladd, Ill., 1960—; sec., dir. LaSalle County Broadcasting Corp. Served with USAAF, 1942-45. Home: 2222 Elmwood Rd Peru IL 61354 Office: Graphic Electronics Inc Lincoln and Locust Sts Ladd IL 61329

MILLER, GENEVIEVE, med. historian, educator; b. Butler, Pa., Oct. 15, 1914; d. Charles Russell and Genevieve (Wolford) M.; A.B., Goucher Coll., 1935; M.A., Johns Hopkins U., 1939; Ph.D., Cornell U., 1955. Asst. in history of medicine Johns Hopkins Inst. History of Medicine, 1943-44, instr. history of medicine, 1945-48; asst. prof. history of medicine Case Western Res. U. Sch. Medicine, Cleve., 1953-67, asso. prof. history of sci., 1967—; research asso. med. history Cleve. Med. Library, 1953-62; curator Howard Dittrick Mus. History of Medicine, 1962-67, dir., 1967—; mem. study sect. history life scis. NIH, Bethesda, Md., 1963-67. Recipient William H. Welch medal Am. Assn. History of Medicine, 1962. Trustee Goucher Coll., 1966-69. Mem. Am. Assn. History of Medicine (treas. 1942-43, chmn. Am. bibliography com. 1940-48, 54-65, mem. council 1960-63, sec.-treas. 1971-76, v.p. 1976-77, pres., 1978—, Fielding H. Garrison lectr. 1973), Soc. History of Tech., AAAS, Am. Hist. Assn., AAUP, Internat., Swedish, German, Spanish, Buenos Aires (corr.) socs. for history medicine, Am. Assn. Museums, Nat. Trust Historic Preservation, Soc. Archtl. Historians, History of Sci. Soc. (councilor 1948-51), Ohio Acad. Med. History (pres. 1959), Phi Beta Kappa. Author: William Beaumont's Formative Years: Two Early Notebooks 1811-1821, 1946; The Adoption of Inoculation for Smallpox in England and France, 1957; Bibliography of the History of Medicine of the U.S. and Canada, 1939-1960, 1964; Bibliography of the Writings of Henry E. Sigerist, 1966; asso. editor Bull. History Medicine, 1944-48, acting editor, 1948, mem. adv. editorial bd., 1960—; editor Bull. Cleve. Med. Library, 1954-72; mem. editorial bd. Jour. History Medicine and Allied Scis., 1948-65; contbr. articles to profl. publs. Home: 2235 Overlook Rd Cleveland Heights OH 44106 Office: Howard Dittrick Mus Hist Medicine 11000 Euclid Ave Cleveland OH 44106

MILLER, GREGORY ALBERT, elec. engr.; b. Highland, Ill., June 23, 1952; s. Albert Henry and Edna Josephine (Evans) M.; B.E.E., U. Mo., Rolla, 1974; m. Linda Marie Vidal, Feb. 21, 1976. Asst. to plant engr. Reilly Tar & Chem. Co., Granite City, Ill., summer 1974; elec. engr. Wis. Power & Light Co., Madison, 1974—. Adviser, Jr. Achievement, 1976. Mem. Nat., Wis. socs. profl. engrs., IEEE, Power Engring. Soc. (membership chmn. Madison sect. 1976-78), Alpha Phi Omega. Episcopalian. Club: DeMolay. Office: PO Box 192 222 W Washington St Madison WI 53701

MILLER, GREGORY ALLEN, rehab. counselor, educator; b. Grand Rapids, Mich., Apr. 6, 1919; s. Allen G. and Elsie (Shields) M.; B.A., Olivet Coll., 1941; M.A., Mich. State U., 1948, Ph.D., 1955; m. Gertrude Alma Mays, July 21, 1962; children—Linda Miller Rockey, Gregory Allen, David D. Psychologist, Traverse City State Hosp., 1941-42, 46-51; with Mich. Dept. Corrections, 1952-55; mem. faculty Mich. State U., East Lansing, 1955—, prof. edn., 1955—, coordinator rehab. counselor tng. program, 1955-76. Served with U.S. Army, 1942-46; PTO. Certified cons. psychologist Mich.; recipient Distinguished Alumni award Olivet Coll., 1976. Mem. Mich. Personnel and Guidance Assn. (Distinguished Leadership award 1973), Am. Rehab. Counseling Assn. (pres. 1970), Am. Psychol. Assn., Nat. Rehab. Assn., Mich. Counselors Assn. (exec. sec. 1962-70). Club: Hidden Valley. Home: 4103 Wagon Wheel Ln Lansing MI 48917 Office: Dept Counseling Personnel Service Educational Psychology Mich State Univ East Lansing MI 48824

MILLER, HALSEY WILKINSON, educator; b. Camden, N.J., July 1, 1930; s. Halsey Wilkinson and Carolyn Mulford (Borden) M.; A.B., Temple U., 1953; M.S., Yale, 1954; Ph.D., U. Kans., 1958; m. Carleen Sue Jones; children—Diana Lynn, Susan Paige, Susan Linda, Rhonda

Beth. Geologist, Kan. Geol. Survey, Lawrence, 1955-57; asst. prof. U. Ariz., Tucson, 1957-63; asso. prof. High Point (N.C.) Coll., 1963-67, Wake Forest U., Winston-Salem, N.C., summer 1967; asst. prof. Ft. Hays Kans. State Coll., 1967-69; prof. geology, dept. earth sci. So. Ill. U. at Edwardsville, 1969—. Mem. Paleontol. Soc., Am. Assn. Petroleum Geologists, A.A.A.S., Meteoritical Soc., Soc. Vertebrate Paleontologists, N.Y. Acad. Scis., Paleontological Research Inst., Sigma Xi (research award 1970). Elk. Author: The Fossil Origins of Man, 1972; The Earth and its Environment, 1973; Evolution: From Stellar Dust to Technological Society, 1975. Contbr. articles to profl. jours. Home: 3 Brookside Ct Edwardsville IL 62025 Office: Dept Earth Scis So Ill U Edwardsville IL 62025

MILLER, HARRY GEORGE, educator; b. Waukesha, Wis., Feb. 15, 1941; s. Harry Fricke and Ethel Ruth (D'Amato) M.; B.A., Carroll Coll., 1963; M.Ed., U. Neb., 1967, Ed.D., 1970; m. Mary Frances Shugrue, June 20, 1964; children—Alicia, Michael, Anne, Deirdre. Tchr., Westside Community Schs., Omaha, 1964-68; demonstration tchr. East Edn. Complex, Lincoln (Nebr.) Pub. Schs., 1967-68; instr. curriculum research Tchrs. Coll., U. Nebr., Lincoln, 1968-70; faculty So. Ill. U., Carbondale, 1970—, asso. prof. edn., dept. secondary edn., 1972-75, chmn. dept. secondard edn., 1973-75, prof., chmn. dept. ednl. leadership, 1975—. Cons. to various orgns. and instns., 1969-74. Mem. Ill. Migrant Council, 1974. Adv. bd. Evaluation and Devel. Center, Rehab. Inst., Carbondale, 1974-75. Mem. Pub. Adult and Continuing Edn. Assn., Rural Edn. Assn., Ill. Council for Social Studies (hon.), Greater Cleve. Council for Social Studies (hon.), Phi Delta Kappa, Kappa Delta Pi. Democrat. Roman Catholic. K.C. Author: Strong Confrontation as an Educational Technique, 1973; Drill Re-examined: A Taxonomy for Drill Exercises, 1975; Beyond Facts: Objective Ways to Measure Thinking, 1976; Adults Teaching Adults, 1977. Editorial bd. Tng., 1976. Home: 2908 W Kent Dr Carbondale IL 62901

MILLER, HARRY JOHNSON, internist, hematologist; b. Miles City, Mont., Feb. 19, 1926; s. Harry Garfield and Harriet Ruth (Wildish) M.; student U. Wis., 1946-48; B.S., Northwestern U., 1952, M.D., 1952; m. Lucia Fairchild Taylor, Dec. 31, 1947; children—Sally, Elizabeth, Katherine, Patricia, Blair. Intern, White Cross Hosp., Columbus, Ohio, 1952-53; resident in internal medicine Northwestern U., Chgo., 1955-58, fellow in hematology, 1958-59; practice medicine specializing in internal medicine and hematology, Evanston, Ill., 1959—; mem. staff Evanston Hosp., pres. staff, 1974-75; instr. medicine Northwestern U. Med. Sch., 1959-61, asso., 1961-70, asst. prof., 1970-76, asso. prof. clin. medicine, 1976—. Trustee Evanston Hosp., MaGaw-Northwestern Med. Center. Served with USAAF, 1944-46. Diplomate Am. Bd. Internal Medicine in hematology and internal medicine. Mem. AMA, AAAS, Ill., Chgo. med. socs., Am. Soc. Hematology, Chgo. Soc. Internal Medicine. Unitarian. Home: 136 Maple St Wilmette IL 60091 Office: 2500 Ridge St Evanston IL 60201

MILLER, HARRY JOSEPH, florist; b. Munhall, Pa., Oct. 12, 1908; s. Albert C. and Ida (Elicker) M.; student U. Pitts., 1926-27; m. Edith H. Rogers, Jan. 7, 1941; children—Barry R., Roger L. Owner, Harry Miller Flowers, Dearborn, Mich., 1938—, Fashion Fast Co., Dearborn, 1951—. Pres. Dearborn Boys Club, 1961-63; chmn. bd. Dearborn YMCA, 1954-56, Dearborn Tourist and Conv. Bur. Mem. Soc. Am. Florists (past pres.), Am. Acad. Florists (past chmn. trustees), Mich. Florist Assn. (dir., past pres.), Dearborn C. of C. (pres. 1947-48). Republican. Conglist. Rotarian. Clubs: Dearborn Country; Detroit Athletic. Patentee florist designer stand. Home: 2 Golfcrest Ct Dearborn MI 48124 Office: 14900 Michigan Ave Dearborn MI 48126

MILLER, J. CARTER, JR., fluid power mfr. exec.; b. Hammond, Ind.; s. J. Carter and Helen (Dillen) M.; B.A., Principia Coll., 1966; M.B.A., Ball State U., 1968. Vice pres. Carter Controls, Inc., Lansing, Ill., 1966—, also dir.; v.p. bd. Woodmar Realty Co., Hammond, Ind., 1972-74. Mem. Am. Soc. Lubrication Engrs. (vice chmn. hydraulics com. 1970-71), Fluid Power Soc., Profl. Photographers Am., Lansing C. of C. (indsl. dir. 1972-74), Lyric Opera Guild, Sarah Siddons Soc., Chgo. Symphony Soc., Chgo. Art Inst. Club: Woodmar Country (Hammond, Ind.). Home: 1315 Elliott Dr Munster IN 46321 Office: 3000 170th St Lansing IL 60438

MILLER, JAMES ALAN, chemist; b. Akron, Ohio, Oct. 27, 1939; s. Roy E. and Marie W. (Robinett) M.; m. Nancy L. Scott, June 25, 1965; children—Scott E., Mary L., Carol A. B.S. in Chemistry, U. Akron, 1964. Lab. technician Morgan Adhesives Co., Stow, Ohio, 1961-64, jr. chemist, 1964-68, plant chemist, 1968-70, research dir. graphic arts div., 1970-73, mgr. tech. service and devel., 1973—. Emergency coordinator Summit-Portage Counties (Ohio), 1972—; pres. Community Amateur Radio Services, Akron, 1972-74; disaster communications officer Summit County chpt. ARC, 1972—; trustee Community Amateur Radio Service, 1974—; elder Trinity United Ch. of Christ, Akron, 1976—. Mem. Cuyahoga Falls Amateur Radio Club, Am. Radio Relay League, Am. Chem. Soc., Akron Rubber Group, Cleve. Soc. Coatings Tech. Patentee in field. Home: 3057 Kent Rd Silver Lake Village Cuyahoga Falls OH 44224 Office: 4560 Darrow Rd Stow OH 44224

MILLER, JAMES NORMAN, social worker; b. nr. Somerset, Pa., Sept. 11, 1931; s. Harry E. and Luella (Shetler) M.; B.A., Goshen Coll., 1953; M.S.W., Ohio State U., 1955; m. Anna Marie Nofziger, Aug. 11, 1956; children—Daniel Geribo (foster son), Douglas, Stanley. Caseworker, Family and Children's Service of Montgomery County, Dayton, 1955-58; psychiat. social worker, instr. social work dept. psychiatry, Central Clinic, U. Cin. Sch. Medicine, 1958-60; asst. dir. Muskegon (Mich.) Children's Home, 1960-67; part-time instr. social work Hope Coll., Holland, Mich., 1962-67; exec. dir. Child and Family Service of Sangamon County, Springfield, Ill., 1967-73, Family Service Assn. of Indpls., 1973—; instr. sociology Lincolnland Community Coll., Springfield, part-time 1969-73; instr. social work Ind. U.-Purdue U. at Indpls., part-time, 1974—. Mem. Nat. Assn. Social Workers, Acad. Certified Social Workers, Family Service Assn. Am. (nat. bd. 1971-73). Methodist. Rotarian. Contbr. articles to profl. jours. Home: 6132 N Central Ave Indianapolis IN 46220 Office: 615 N Alabama St Indianapolis IN 46204

MILLER, J(AMES) ROSCOE, univ. chancellor emeritus; b. Murray, Utah, Oct. 26, 1905; s. Leroy Cromwell and Marjorie (Sidley) M.; B.A., U. Utah, 1925, LL.D., 1949; M.D., Northwestern U., 1930, M.S., 1931, LL.D., 1949; Sc.D., U. Ariz., 1951; LL.D., Williams Coll., 1950, Bradley U., 1950, Knox Coll., 1957, U. Mich., 1957, Ohio Wesleyan U., 1960, U. Notre Dame, 1964, U. Denver, 1964; L.H.D., Loyola U., Chgo., 1970; Litt.D., Jewish Theol. Sem. Am., 1974; m. Berenice Johannesen, Sept. 27, 1928; children—Roxelyn (Mrs. Richard S. Pepper), Jacquelyn (Mrs. Robert M. James), James Randall. Asst. dean Northwestern U. Med. Sch., 1933-41, dean 1941-49, asst. prof. medicine, 1938-41, asso. prof., 1941-49, prof., 1949-74, prof. emeritus, 1974—, pres. Northwestern U., 1949-70, chancellor, 1969-74, chancellor emeritus, 1974—. Dir. Am. Hosp. Supply Corp., 1st Nat. Bank & Trust Co., Evanston, Fidelity Life Assn., Fed. Kemper Life Assurance; Mem. Mayor's Com. Cultural Welfare, 1958. Trustee Northwestern Meml. Hosp., Field Mus. Natural History; bd. dirs. Mus. Sci. and Industry; bd. overseers Hoover Instn. War, Revolution and Peace; mem. Hosp. Research and Ednl. Trust Am. Hosp. Assn. Served with USNR, 1942-49, head med. br., profl. div. Bur. Med. and Surgery, 1944-45. Diplomate Am. Bd. Internal Medicine, Fellow A.C.P., Am. Heart Assn., Am. Coll. Cardiology (hon.), James IV Assn. Surgeons (hon.); mem. Central Soc. Clin. Research, A.M.A., Chgo. Med. Soc. (pres. 1948-49), A.A.A.S., Assn. Am. Med. Colls. (pres. 1948-49), Sigma Xi, Sigma Chi, Alpha Omega Alpha. Clubs: University (Chgo. and Evanston); Old Elm; Glenview (Golf, Ill.); Chicago, Chicago Economic, Executives, Commercial (Chgo.). Home: 2870 Sheridan Pl Evanston IL 60201 Office: 633 Clark St Evanston IL 60201

MILLER, JOE DAVID, assn. exec.; b. Smith Grove, Ky., Apr. 23, 1924; s. Paul S. and Rosa (Dillingham) M.; B.S. in Gen. Bus., U. Ky., 1949; m. Mary K. Kinnaird, June 6, 1948; children—Mary Margaret, David Gregory. Exec. dir. Ky. Tb Hosp. Commn., Frankfort, 1949-57; research asso., field rep. AMA, Chgo., 1957-61, exec. dir. polit. action com., 1961-68, dir. pub. affairs div., 1968-70, asst. exec. v.p., 1970-74, dep. exec. v.p., 1974-75, sr. v.p., 1975—; sec.-treas. AMA Services Inc., 1972—; dir. Am. Med. Assurance Co., 1975—. Dir. Pub. Affairs Council. Dir. Community Nursing Service, DuPage County, Ill., 1961-67; mgr. Wheaton (Ill.) Boys Baseball, 1962-68. Served with AUS, 1943-45; ETO. Decorated Purple Heart. Registered lobbyist U.S. Congress, 1969—. Mem. Am. Hosp. Assn., Am. Assn. Med. Soc. Execs.; Am. Coll. Hosp. Adminstrs. (affiliate), U.S. C. of C. (pub. affairs com. 1971—, task force on Powell memorandum 1972—), Kappa Sigma. Presbyn. Clubs: Capitol Hill (Washington); St. Charles Country. Home: 1534 S Gamon Rd Wheaton IL 60187 Office: 535 N Dearborn St Chicago IL 60610

MILLER, JOHN ALSTON, ins. co. exec.; b. Detroit, Jan. 23, 1935; s. George Earl and Laura Gladys (Palmer) M.; B.A., Mich. State U., 1958; m. Loraine Leah Trepagnier, Aug. 23, 1958; children—Michelle, Melinda. Rep. dept. mortgage loans Pacific Mut. Life Ins. Co., Chgo., 1958-59, supr., Cleve., 1959-61, mgr., Toledo, 1961-66; practice mortgage placement and appraising, Detroit, 1966-68; supr. dept. mortgage loans Northwestern Mut. Life Ins. Co., Detroit, 1968-73, asst. mgr., 1973—. Real estate appraiser. Served with AUS, 1961-62; France. Mem. Am. Inst. Real Estate Appraisers (vice chmn. chpt. com. profl. ethics 1973—, dir. chpt.), Delta Tau Delta. Club: Newburgh Swim (Livonia, Mich.). Home: 15423 Susanna Circle Livonia MI 48154 Office: Northwestern Mut Life Ins Co 26400 Lahser Rd Southfield MI 48034

MILLER, JOHN CHARLES, lawyer, farm equipment distbn. co. exec.; b. St. Nazianz, Wis., Nov. 17, 1942; s. Victor Andrew and Isabel (Grimm) M.; B.A., Marquette U., 1964; J.D., Georgetown U., 1967, LL.M., 1969; m. Katherine Bonafield, Nov. 8, 1969; children—Jeanne M., John W. Admitted to D.C. bar, 1967, Wis. bar, 1967; atty. office legal investment SBA, Washington, 1967-70; asso. with W. T. Stephens, Washington, 1970-72; partner firm Miller & Miller, St. Nazianz, 1972—; pres. John Miller Supply Co., Inc., St. Nazianz, 1974—; chmn. liaison com. Wis. Dept. Rev., 1975, chmn. agrl. tax com., 1973, 75; lectr. in field. Mem. Wis. Bar Found. (dir. 1977—), State Bar Wis. (dir. tax sect. 1975-79), Am. Bar Assn., Nat. Assn. Wholesalers (chmn. steering com. Wis. product liability task force). Club: St Nazianz Lions (pres. 1975). Contbr. articles to legal jours. Office: 107 W Main St Saint Nazianz WI 54232

MILLER, JOHN JOSEPH, mech. engr.; b. Cin., Mar. 16, 1942; s. John George and Claire Marie (Kuntz) M.; B.S. in Mech. Engring., U. Cin., 1965; m. Corisa Ann Poe, Aug. 24, 1968; children—Lisa Marie, Kimberly Lynn. Jr. engr. Am. Laundry Machinery Co., 1965-67, systems engr. 1967-68, project engr., 1968-73; sr. project engr. Stearns & Foster Co., Cin., 1973-75, sr. design engr., 1975—. Registered profl. engr., Ky., Miss., Ohio. Mem. ASME, Nat. Soc. Profl. Engrs., Pi Tau Sigma. Patentee in field. Home: 2871 Montana Ave Cincinnati OH 45211 Office: Williams and Wyoming Aves Cincinnati OH 45215

MILLER, JOHN LEWIS, accountant; b. Lebanon, Ohio, Dec. 9, 1934; s. Lester J. and Marie M. (Medley) M.; B.S., Miami U., 1957; m. Susan L. Bruere, Dec. 21, 1957; children—James, Stuart, Jennifer. Staff accountant Peat, Marwick, Mitchell & Co., Cleve., 1960-66, supr., 1966-68, mgr., 1968-70, partner, 1970—. Mem. Greater Cleve. Growth Assn., 1970—. Trustee Bay Village Health Fund; bd. mgrs. Central YMCA. Served to 1st lt. USAF, 1957-60. Gen. Electric scholar, 1956. C.P.A., Ohio. Mem. Am. Inst. C.P.A.'s, Ohio Soc. C.P.A.'s, Am., Ohio hosp. assns., Nat. Assn. Accountants, Hosp. Fin. Mgmt. Assn., Sigma Alpha Epsilon, Omicron Delta Kappa, Beta Gamma Sigma, Beta Alpha Psi. Clubs: Westwood Country, North Ridge Racquet, Cleve. Athletic, Westside Tennis. Home: 493 Walmar Dr Bay Village OH 44140 Office: 1400 Central Nat Bank Bldg Cleveland OH 44114

MILLER, JON CRISTOFER, data processing cons.; b. Los Angeles, July 24, 1938; s. Lorenzo Charles and Judith Virginia (Ransom) M.; B.A., Pomona Coll., 1959; M.A., U. Calif. at Los Angeles, 1961, Claremont Grad. Sch., 1968; m. Ngoc Lieng Dinh, Apr. 7, 1969; children—Jocelijn Hanh, Caralien Lan. With aerospace firms West coast, 1959-63; sr. mem. adv. staff Computer Sci. Corp., Los Angeles, 1964-71; dir. projects Programming Methods, Chgo., 1971-73; dir. ops. Plymouth Computer Systems, Chgo. and N.Y.C., 1973-74; analyst Montgomery Ward Co., Chgo., 1975; cons. Applied Info. Devel., Oak Brook, Ill., 1976-77; dir. Quijano Asso., data processing cons., Chgo., 1974—. Co-coordinator Vietnamese Am. Crisis Com., 1975-77; bd. dirs. Austin Neighborhood Housing Services, 1976-78; aldermanic candidate Chgo. 37th Ward, 1974-75; v.p. Central Austin Steering Com., 1973. George F. Baker scholar, 1955-59. Mem. Mensa. Democrat. Unitarian. Columnist, Tilting at Windmills, Chgo. News Jour. World, 1975—. Home: 5827 Race Ave W Chicago IL 60644

MILLER, JOSEPH IRWIN, mfr.; b. Columbus, Ind., May 26, 1909; s. Hugh Thomas and Nettie Irwin (Sweeney) M.; A.B., Yale, 1931, M.A. (hon.), 1959; M.A., Oxford (Eng.) U., 1933; LL.D., Bethany Coll., 1956, Tex. Christian U., 1958, Ind. U., 1958, Oberlin Coll., 1962, Princeton U., 1962, Hamilton Coll., 1964, Case Inst. Tech., 1966, Columbia U., 1968, Mich. State U. 1968, Dartmouth Coll., 1971, U. Notre Dame, 1972, Ball State U., 1972; Hum.D. (hon.), Manchester U., 1973, Moravian Coll., 1976; L.H.D., U. Dubuque, 1977; m. Xenia Ruth Simons, Feb. 5, 1943; children—Margaret Irwin, Catherine Gibbs, Elizabeth Ann Garr, Hugh Thomas II, William Irwin. With Cummins Engine Co., Inc., Columbus, Ind., 1934—, v.p., gen. mgr., 1934-42, exec. v.p., 1944-47, pres. 1945-51, chmn. bd. 1951—; pres. Irwin-Union Bank & Trust Co., 1947-54, dir., 1937—, chmn., 1954-75, chmn. exec. com., finance com., 1977—; dir. Am. Tel. & Tel. Co. Chmn., Pres.'s Spl. Com. East-West Trade Relations, 1965; mem. Pres.'s Commn. Postal Orgn., 1967-68, Com. Urban Housing, 1967-68; mem. Commn. Money and Credit, 1958-61, also Bus. Council; chmn. Nat. Adv. Commn. for Health Manpower, 1966-67; vice chmn. UN Com. Multinat. Corps., 1973-74; mem. advisory council Dept. Commerce, 1976-77. Pres. Nat. Council Chs. Christ in U.S.A., 1960-63. Mem. Nat. Indsl. Conf. Bd.; trustee Ford Found., Yale U., 1959-77. Fellow Branford Coll.; trustee Sloan Commn. Govt. and Higher Edn., 1977—. Served lt. USNR, aboard U.S.S. Langley, 1942-44. Mem. Phi Beta Kappa, Beta Gamma Sigma. Mem. Christian Ch. (elder). Clubs: Yale, Century, Links (N.Y.C.); Chicago; Indianapolis Athletic, Columbia (Indpls.). Home: 2760 Highland Way Columbus IN 47201 Office: 301 Washington St Columbus IN 47201

MILLER, JOSEPH KENNETH, med. adminstr.; b. Saginaw, Mich., Dec. 4, 1933; s. Joseph R. and Mary A. Shields M.; S.T.B., St. John's Sem., 1959; M.A., U. Detroit, 1970. Ordained priest Roman Catholic ch., 1960; asso. pastor, pastor, tchr. various chs., Saginaw/Bay area, Mich., 1960-70; staff psychologist Saginaw Mental Health Bd., 1970—; exec. dir. Saginaw County Drug Treatment Center Inc., 1971—; lectr. in field. Mem. Am., Mich., Mid-Mich. psychol. assns. Home: 2562 N Bond St Saginaw MI 48602 Office: 1422 E Genesee St Saginaw MI 48607

MILLER, KENNETH DUANE, real estate broker; b. Barry County, Mich., Apr. 1, 1926; s. Clifton Harvey and Edith Marian (Smith) M.; student Argubright Bus. Coll., 1946-47; m. Ruth Lorraine Marble, June 21, 1947; children—Stephen Duane, David Wesley, Jeffrey Owen. Staff mgr. Met. Life Ins. Co., Battle Creek, Mich., 1950-64; owner Ken Miller Ins. Agy., Hastings, Mich., 1964-72; owner Miller Real Estate, Hastings, 1964—; dir., treas. Barry Title Co., 1972-75. Mem. Hastings Planning Commn., 1970—. Bd. dirs. Barry County Agrl. Soc., 1971-74, Hastings YMCA, 1976—. Served with USAAC, 1944-46. Mem. Mich. Assn. Realtors (dir. 1975—), Battle Creek Assn. Life Underwriters (pres. 1957-58), Barry-Eaton-Ionia Bd. Realtors (pres. 1973; named Realtor of Year 1973), Hastings C. of C. (dir. 1968-70). Presbyn. (elder 1966-69). Clubs: Masons, Shriners, Kiwanis (pres. 1970-71, lt. gov. Mich. dist. 1976-77). Home: 505 N Taffee Dr Hastings MI 49058 Office: 137 W State St Hastings MI 49058

MILLER, KENNETH LAWRENCE, city ofcl.; b. Columbus, Ohio, May 9, 1910; s. William and Mary (Lucks) M.; grad. high sch.; m. Dorothy May Tapp, Nov. 25, 1937; children—Bonita Ann Miller Crawford, Don L. With Falkenbach Bros., Columbus, 1928-34; mechanic Metal Forge Co., Columbus, 1934-59; dept. mgr. Columbus Grant Hosp., 1959-75, asst. dir. bldgs. and grounds, 1960-75; mem. Village Council, Canal Winchester, Ohio, 1948-56, supt. streets, 1960-64, mayor, 1956-60, 64—. Active Boy Scouts Am., 1956—; vol. fireman Canal Winchester, 1941-73, sec.-treas., 1943-53; mem. Emergency Squad, Canal Winchester, 1946-73; chmn. Canal Winchester Planning Commn., 1964—. Mem. Canal Winchester Hist. Soc. Lutheran (past mem. ch. council). Home: 327 W Waterloo St Canal Winchester OH 43110

MILLER, KERMIT VINCENT, sch. adminstr.; b. McGregor, Iowa, May 14, 1921; s. Roy and Hildagard Elizabeth (Weller) M.; B.A., Iowa State Tchrs. Coll., 1951, M.A., 1954; postgrad. U. No. Iowa, 1957-64, U. Iowa, 1962; m. Lida Elizabeth Robison, Aug. 6, 1955; children—Melissa Ann, Beth Ellen, Marla Kay. Social sci. and agr. tchr., Andrew, Iowa, 1951-54; elementary tchr., prin. DeWitt, Iowa, 1954-55; high sch. prin. Waterville, Iowa, 1955-61; asst. supt. Clear Creek Community Schs., Oxford, Iowa, 1961-65; dist. adminstr. New Auburn (Wis.) area schs., 1965-69; dist. adminstr. Stanley-Boyd area schs., Stanley, Wis., 1969—. Served with USNR, 1945-46; PTO. Mem. Allamakee County Edn. Assn. (pres. 1959-60, 68-69, 70-71), Am. Legion. V.F.W., Iowa Edn. Assn., NEA, Nat. Sch. Dist. Adminstrs., Wis. Sch. Dist. Adminstrs. Clubs: Comml.; Conservation. Home: 600 Gilman St Stanley WI 54768 Office: 4th Ave Stanley WI 54768

MILLER, LARRY GENE, export co. exec.; b. Seymore, Iowa, May 25, 1938; s. Adrain W. and Helen A. (Johns) M.; student pub. schs., Walford, Iowa; m. Meredith Lee Clough, Nov. 9, 1957; children—Jody Lynn, Larry G., Jr., Michael S., Paloma M. Internat. traffic supr. Cherry Burrell Corp., Cedar Rapids, Iowa, 1956-67; dist. sales mgr. C.S. Green Co., Chgo., 1967-69; Iowa export mgr. Kwick-Way Internat., Inc., Cedar Rapids, 1969-74, Iowa asst. v.p., 1974—; tchr. internat. trade Kirkwood Coll., Drake U. Past chmn. Cedar Rapids Internat. Trade Bur., exec. com., 1977—. Mem. Cedar Rapids Am. Kennel Assn. (v.p.). Club: Greater Cedar Rapids Doberman Pinscher. Home: 1000 Clifton St NE Cedar Rapids IA 52402 Office: 500 57th St Marion IA 52302

MILLER, LARRY MICHAEL, EDP services co. exec.; b. Springfield, Ohio, Apr. 5, 1950; s. Harry W. and Virginia D. M.: B.B.A, Wright State U., 1974; m. Debra I. Hyden; children—Shawn M., Shanon M. Tech. specialist Reynolds & Reynolds Co., Dayton, Ohio, 1974-76, site mgr., Denver, 1976, EDP sales rep., Decatur, Ill., 1976—. Served with USAF, 1968-72. Mem. Am. Mktg. Assn., Am. Mgmt. Assn. Home: 1316 Hershey St Bloomington IL 61701

MILLER, LLOYD DANIEL, assn. exec.; b. Savannah, Mo., May 25, 1916; s. Daniel Edward and Minnie (Wiedmer) M.; B.S. in Agrl. Journalism, U. Mo., 1941; m. Mabel Gertrude Kurz, June 9, 1939; children—Sharon Gail (Mrs. A.E. Schumacher, Jr.), Donna Lynn (Mrs. Ronald L. Bodinson), Rosemary Rae, Jeffrey Lloyd. Reporter, feature writer, photographer, market editor Corn Belt Farm Dailies, Chgo., Kansas City, Mo., 1941-43; asst. agrl. editor U. Mo., 1946; dir. pub. relations Am. Angus Assn., Chgo., 1946-67, St. Joseph, Mo., 1967, asst. sec., dir. pub. relations, 1968, exec. sec., 1968—; bd. dirs. Am. Royal Livestock Show, Kansas City, Mo. Mem. U.S. Tech. Adv. Com. on Livestock and Livestock Products for Trade Negotiations. Bd. dirs. Mo. Western State Coll. Found. Served from pvt. to sgt. AUS, 1943-45. Recipient Silver Anvil award Pub. Relations Soc. Am., 1962; Faculty-Alumni award U. Mo.-Columbia, 1975. Mem. Pub. Relations Soc. Am., U.S. Beef Breed Council (pres. 1973-74, dir.), Am. Soc. Assn. Execs., World Aberdeen-Angus Secretariat (sec.-treas. 1973-75), Nat. Soc. Livestock Records Assns. (dir. 1976—), St. Joseph Area C. of C. (pres. 1969, dir. 1969-70), Sigma Delta Chi. Methodist (chmn. bd. dirs. 1959-60, chmn. adminstrv. council 1976-77). Mason (32 deg., Shriner), Kiwanian. Home: 3208 Miller Rd St Joseph MO 64505 Office: 3201 Frederick Blvd St Joseph MO 64506

MILLER, MARC EDWARD, psychologist; b. Lancaster, Ohio, Oct. 2, 1942; s. Walter F. and Elizabeth M. (Mowry) M.; B.A., Ohio U., 1967, M.Ed., 1969; postgrad. Nordenfjord U. (Denmark), Wright State U., 1970-72; Ed.D., Western Colo. U., 1976; m. Frances Lucille Levacy, Nov. 26, 1964; children—Kristina E., Marcy F. Tchr. developmentally disabled children pub. schs., 1964-69; therapist Ednl. Clinic, Inc., 1970-71; psychol. intern Wright State U., 1971-72; psychologist, coordinator programs Ednl. Clinic, Inc., Columbus, Ohio, 1972-75, asst. dir., psychologist, 1975—; instr. Capital U., 1973-74; cons. Columbus State Inst., Ohio Disability Determination Commn.; pvt. practice med. evaluation. Pres. St. Mary's Sch. Bd., Lancaster, 1977; v.p. Fairfield County Health Systems Council, 1976-77. Mem. Am., Ohio psychol. assns., Central Ohio Psychologists (pres.), Biofeedback Soc. Ohio (v.p. 1976-77), World Edn. Assn. Republican. Roman Catholic. Contbr. articles to profl. jours. Home: 3702 Stringtown Rd Lancaster OH 43130 Office: 3400 N High St Columbus OH 43202

MILLER, MARION SWANN, historian; b. E. Orange, N.J., Aug. 29, 1927; s. James Henry and Eva (Agutter) S.; B.A., Acadia U., 1948; M.A., U. Pa., 1953, Ph.D., 1965; m. June 13, 1959. Faculty, Wilson Coll., Chambersburg, Pa., 1957-63, Sweetbriar (Va) Coll., 1963-64, U.

Minn., Mpls., 1965-66; faculty Chgo. Circle campus U. Ill., 1967—, asst. prof. history, 1972—. Fulbright scholar Turin, Italy, 1954-55, Rome, 1955-56. Mem. Am. Hist. Assn., Soc. Italian Hist. Studies, Soc. French Hist. Studies, Instituto per la storia del Risorgimento. Centre Interuniversitaire d'Etudes Europeennes. Contbr. articles on 19th. century Italian Risorgimento to profl. publs. Home: 1804 55 W Chestnut St Chicago IL 60610

MILLER, MASON FERRELL, elec. engr.; b. Rockford, Nebr., Nov. 5, 1919; s. Martin Robertson and Bertha Luella (Story) M.; B.S., U. Nebr., 1940; M.S., Mass. Inst. Tech., 1941; m. Irene Elizabeth Westerman, Sept. 25, 1942; children—Paul Martin, James Mason, Marianne. Student engr. AT&T, N.Y.C., 1941; jr. engr. U.S. Navy, Bath, Maine, 1941; with NASA, Langley AFB, Va., 1941-51, aero. research scientist, 1948-51, Cleve., 1951-55; engr. specialist AiResearch Mfg. Co., Phoenix, 1955-57; preliminary design engr. Allison div. Gen. Motors Co., Indpls., 1957-61; sr. engring. specialist, supr. N. Am. Rockwell, Columbus, Ohio, 1961-69; performance engr. Gen. Electric Co., Aircraft Engine Group, Evendale, Ohio, 1969—; teaching advisor Gen. Motors Inst., 1960. Mem. Washington Twp. Sch. Planning Com., Indpls., 1961; asst. scoutmaster Boy Scouts Am., Berea, Ohio, 1954-55, pack treas., Phoenix, 1956-57, cubmaster, com. chmn., Indpls., 1959-61. U. Nebr. Regent's scholar, 1936; Mass. Inst. Tech. scholar, 1940; recipient NASA Merit Service award, 1948; Cleve. City and Plain Dealer award ARC program, 1953. Mem. Am. Def. Preparedness Assn., Pi Mu Epsilon, Sigma Tau. Presbyterian. Club: Order of DeMolay. Contbr. articles in field to profl. jours. Home: 10572 Hadley Rd Cincinnati OH 45218 Office: Gen Electric Co Cincinnati OH 45215

MILLER, MAX, physician; b. New Haven, June 22, 1910; s. Morris and Bessie (Shulim) M.; B.S., Yale, 1931, M.D., 1935; m. Barbara Ann Foster, June 29, 1940; children—Claire Louise, Eric Foster. Intern, Trudeau Sanatorium, 1934; intern New Haven Hosp., 1935-36, asst. resident, 1936-37; asst. in medicine Yale, 1936-37; teaching fellow in medicine Case-Western Res. U., Cleve., 1937-40, instr. in medicine, 1940-42, sr. instr., 1942-47, asst. prof. medicine, 1947-51, asso. prof. medicine, 1951-67, prof. medicine, 1967—, dir. clin. research center, 1962-72; physician Univ. Hosps., Cleve., 1967—. Mem. gen. medicine study sect. NIH, 1957-59; spl. cons. diabetes Nat. Inst. Arthritis and Metabolic Diseases, NIH, 1965—, mem. ad hoc. adv. com. diabetes, 1967—; cons. Nat. Eye Inst., 1971—, mem. policy adv. group of diabetic retinopathy study, 1972—; chmn. univ. group diabetes program NIH, 1959—; pres. Diabetes Assn. Greater Cleve., 1958-60; cons. metabolism VA Hosp., Cleve., 1963—; mem. spl. adv. com. to council Nat. Inst. Neurologic Disease and Blindness, 1968-71; spl. cons. diabetes and arthritis control program USPHS, 1963-66. Trustee Cleve. Chamber Music Soc., 1950—. Recipient Honor award Med. Mut. Cleve., 1972. Diplomate Nat. Bd. Med. Examiners, Am. Bd. Internal Medicine. Mem. Am. Soc. Clin. Investigation, Central Soc. for Clin. Research, N.Y. Acad. Scis., Am. Diabetes Assn., Soc. Exptl. Biology and Medicine, AAAS, Endocrine Soc., Am. Fedn. for Clin. Research, Cleve. Acad. Medicine, Soc. for Epidemiologic Research, Phi Beta Kappa, Sigma Xi, Alpha Omega Alpha. Contbr. articles to med. jours., also chpts. in textbooks. Editorial bd. Diabetes, 1955-70; editorial adviser Diabetes Literature Index, 1966—; co-editor Vol. 9 Advances in Metabolic Disorders: Internat. Studies in the Epidemiology of Diabetes, 1978. Research in epidemiology of diabetes, carbohydrate and intermediary metabolism. Home: 2288 Chatfield Dr Cleveland Heights OH 44106 Office: 2065 Adelbert Rd Cleveland OH 44106

MILLER, MERL KEM, textbook pub.; b. Cheyenne, Wyo., July 17, 1942; s. Walter Leroy and Margaret Ellen (Wissler) M.; B.S. cum laude in Indsl. Mgmt., U. Wyo., 1965; m. Patricia Ann Hayward, Oct. 2, 1976; children—Abigail, Susan, Merl Kem. Editor, Prentice-Hall, Englewood Cliffs, N.J., 1969-73, West Pub. Co., St. Paul, 1973-75; cons., 1975; pres. Matrix Pubs., Inc., Champaign, Ill., 1975—; partner Dilithium Press, Forest Grove, Oreg. Served with USMC, 1960-68. Decorated Navy Cross, Purple Heart. Mem. IEEE, Am. Soc. Engring. Edn., Am. Inst. Indsl. Engrs., Assn. Computing Machinery. Democrat. Episcopalian. Home: 3215 Kimberly St Champaign IL 61820 Office: 207 Kenyon Rd Champaign IL 61820

MILLER, MERLE MONROE, newspaper publisher; b. Belleville, Kans., Apr. 21, 1915; s. Alexander Quinn and Martha Lavina (Patterson) M.; F.S., Kans. State U., 1936; m. Erma Ann Schmedemann, Sept. 4, 1938; children—Monte M., Mark Luman, Margo Joanne. Pres., Telescope, Inc., Belleville, Kans., 1955—, Superior (Nebr.) Pub. Co., 1969—, Telegraphics, Inc., Baldwin City, Kans., 1973—, publisher of over 25 newspapers in rural Midwest, and various nat. publs.; pres. Kans. Press Assn., 1969-70. Pres., Pan Am. Hwy. Assn., 1967-74. Author newspaper editorials; polit. analyst; fgn. traveler and writer. Home: 2501 Sunset Dr Belleville KS 66935 Office: 1815 E Frontage Rd Belleville KS 66935

MILLER, MICHAEL ALLEN, advt. agency exec.; b. Bklyn., Apr. 3, 1938; s. Benjamin J. and Ruth (May) M.; B.B.A, Adelphi U., 1960; m. Lois E. Blumenfeld, June 10, 1961; children—Mark David, Kevin Scott. Asst. account exec. Benton & Bowles, Ltd., London, Eng., 1961-63; advt. mgr. Macrose, Inc., 1963-65; with Mktg. Evaluation, Inc., 1965-67; internat. product mgr. Chesebrough-Ponds, Inc., N.Y.C., 1967-68; internat. new product mgr. Shelton Inc., 1968-71; internat. nutritional products mgr. Miles Labs., Elkhart, Ind., 1972-75; part owner, mktg. dir., account exec. Markmakers, Inc., S. Bend, Ind., 1975—. Bd. dirs. YMCA, South Bend; bd. mgrs. Century Prodns.; mem. bd. Unitarian Ch., South Bend. Mem. Am. Marketing Assn. (dir.), Sales and Advt. Execs. Club. Home: 1426 E Wayne St South Bend IN 46615 Office: 322 W Washington St South Bend IN 46601

MILLER, MICHAEL JEFFREY, physician; b. Detroit, Dec. 12, 1944; s. Abraham and Thelma (Soller) M.; B.A., Wayne State U., 1965; M.D., Wayne State U., 1969; m. Sheila Ann Nusbaum, Dec. 23, 1967; children—Denise Ellyn, Brian Elliot. Intern, William Beaumont Hosp., Royal Oak, Mich., 1969-70, med. resident, 1970-73; practice medicine specializing in internal medicine, Southfield, Mich., 1973—; mem. attending staff dept. internal medicine William Beaumont Hosp., Royal Oak, Mich., 1973—. Diplomate Am. Bd. Internal Medicine. Mem. AMA, Mich., Oakland County (dir. 1977—) med. socs., Phi Beta Kappa. Editor Bulletin, Jour. Oakland County Med. Soc., 1976—. Office: 18161 W 13 Mile Rd Suite A-2 Southfield MI 48076

MILLER, MICHAEL LOUIS, environ. control adminstr.; b. Chgo., Mar. 6, 1948; s. Charles Robert and Marjorie Ann (Dolansky) M.; B.S. in Chem. Engring., Mich. State U., 1970; M.A. in Bus. Adminstrn., Sangamon State U., 1977; m. Toni K. Kohorst, Mar. 23, 1974; children—Michael John, Juliet Jacqueline. Nuclear engr. Mare Island Naval Shipyard, Vallejo, Calif., 1970-71; environ. engr., Ill. EPA, air pollution control, Springfield, 1972-73, program mgr., 1974—; process engr. Kaiser Agrl. Chemicals, Savannah, Ga., 1973-74. Advisory mem. Springfield-Sangamon County Regional Planning Commn. Registered profl. engr., Ill. Mem. Ill. Soc. Profl. Engrs., Evans Scholars Alumni Assn. Democrat. Roman Catholic. Home: 1031 N 6th St Springfield IL 62702 Office: 2200 Churchill Rd Springfield IL 62706

MILLER, MILFORD MORTIMER, lawyer; b. Evansville, Ind., Mar. 20, 1937; s. Milford Mortimer and Dorothy (Welborn) M.; A.B., Dartmouth Coll., 1959; J.D. with distinction, Ind. U. Sch. Law, 1962; m. Mary Elizabeth Patterson, Aug. 17, 1963; children—Milford Mortimer III, John Patterson, Calvert Sterling, Rebecca Welborn. Admitted to Ind. bar, 1962; asso. law firm Livingston, Dildine, Haynie & Yoder, Ft. Wayne, Ind., 1962-67, partner, 1967—. Bldg. chmn. Center of Performing Arts, Ft. Wayne, 1967-73. Pres., bd. dirs. Ft. Wayne Civic Theatre, 1963—; bd. dirs., mem. exec. com. Ft. Wayne Fine Arts Found.; pres. bd. dirs. Legal Aid of Ft. Wayne. Mem. Allen County (chmn. grievance com. 1970-72, mem. jud. selection and tenure com. 1968-74, trustee 1974-76, law med. rev. panel 1977—), Ind., Am. bar assns., Am. Judicature Soc., Assn. Am. Trial Lawyers, Def. Research Inst., Order of the Coif, Sigma Nu. Democrat. Presbyterian. Clubs: Dartmouth Alumni Club of Ft. Wayne, Ft. Wayne Country. Bd. editors Ind. Law Rev. Jour. Home: 4220 Old Mill Rd Ft Wayne IN 46807 Office: 425 Lincoln Tower Ft Wayne IN 46802

MILLER, NAN COURTNEY, pub. relations co. exec.; b. La Crosse, Wis., Jan. 22, 1925; d. Henry Daniel and Winifred (McMahon) Miller; B.A., Northwestern U., 1957, J.D., 1961. Pres., Nan Miller Prodns. & Theatrical Agy., Denver, 1945-53; pres., chief exec. officer Nan Miller & Assos., Inc., Pub. Relations, Chgo., 1963—; Intercomco Internat., Inc., Chgo., 1971—. Recipient Service to Youth award YMCA Camp Channing, 1968. Mem. Chgo. Assn. Commerce and Industry, Pub. Relations Soc. Am., Premium Industry Club, Small Industry Council, Presidents Club, Publicity Club of Chgo., Public Safety Council (crime prevention com.), Phi Beta Kappa, Alpha Lambda Delta. Club: Executives (Chgo.). Home: 1444 W Cullom Chicago IL 60613 Office: 55 E Washington St Chicago IL 60602

MILLER, NELSON BRUEGGEMANN, constrn. co. exec.; b. Fieldon, Ill., June 17, 1938; s. Ruby and Helen Pauline (Brueggemann) M.; student pub. schs., Jerseyville, Ill.; m. Nancy Sue Stark, Mar. 2, 1963; children—Mimi, Jennifer, Tammy. Pres., Jersey County Constrn., Inc. (Ill.), Jerseyville, 1965—, pres. J.C.C. Devel., 1975—, J.C.C. Rental & Supply, 1976—. Mem. Jersey County Democrat Precinct Com., 1966-74. Home: Rural Route 4 Jerseyville IL 62052 Office: Rural Route 3 Jerseyville IL 62052

MILLER, NORMAN JOHN, bacteriologist; b. Evansville, Ind., Apr. 14, 1905; s. I. and Carrie (Blount) M.; B.S., Iowa State Coll., 1930; Sc.D., Evansville Coll., 1959; m. Jeanne (Thomas) M., Feb. 25, 1938;children—Marcia Ellen (Mrs. Frank Holland). Bacteriologist, Mead Johnson & Co., 1930-35, asst. chief bacteriologist, 1935-51, dir. bacteriology control, 1951-60, cons., 1960-64. Mem. Soc. Am. Bacteriology (Ind. br. pres., 1944-45, nat. councilor 1946, 47, emeritus), Am. Dairy Sci. Assn. (hon.). Contbr. articles in field to sci. jours. Home: 850 Covert Evansville IN 47713

MILLER, NYLE H., historian; b. Anthony, Kans., Nov. 16, 1907; s. Alfred and Lulu Pearl (Blankinship) M.; student Friends U., Wichita, 1925-27; A.B., Coll. William and Mary, 1929; m. Esther Isbell Pennock, June 11, 1932; children—Virginia Ann, Nyle David, Janis Esther. Mem. staff Kans. State Hist. Soc., Topeka, 1931—, exec. dir., 1951-76, exec. dir. emeritus, 1977—; mng. editor Kans. Hist. Quarterly and all other Kans. Hist. Soc. publs., Topeka, 1939-76. Mem. Am. Assn. State and Local History, Western Hist. Assn., Native Sons Kan. (pres. 1944-45). Methodist. Co-author: Kansas: APictorial History, 1961; Kansas in Newspapers, 1963; Why the West Was Wild, 1963; Great Gunfighters of the Kansas Cowtowns—1867-1886, 1967. Author: Kansas—A Student's Guide to Localized History, 1965; Kansas: The 34th Star, 1976. Home: 1352 High St Topeka KS 66604 Office: 120 W 10th St Topeka KS 66612

MILLER, ORRIN DUANE, bus. developer; b. Randolph, Wis., Dec. 5, 1926; s. Otto Paul and Cecilia Angela (Sadowski) M.; B.A., U. Mich., 1947; m. Glenna June Douglas, Aug. 22, 1946; children—Daniel, Sharon, David. Field auditor Gulf Oil Corp., Toledo, 1946-49; fin. staff, internal auditor A.C. spark plug div. Gen. Motors Corp., Milw., 1949-55; fin. staff, internal auditor, dir. data processing Parker Pen Co., Janesville, Wis., 1955-65; treas. dir. Total TV Inc., Janesville, 1965—; treas. Lake County Cablevision, Leesburg, Fla., 1972—; gen. partner, treas. The Omega Co.; officer, dir. Total TV, Inc., Vumore TV Corp. Pres. Janesville (Wis.) City Council; dir. Big Bros. Janesville. Roman Catholic. Clubs: Serra Internat., Elks. Home: 417 Apache Dr Janesville WI 53545 Office: 839 Harding St Janesville WI 53545

MILLER, ORVILLE CROWDER, editor, poet, former educator, clergyman; b. Sullivan, Ill., Aug. 16, 1897; s. Earl Clyde and Della (Crowder) M.; diploma Curry Coll., Boston, 1917; student U. Chgo., 1920-21; A.B., Ind. U., 1925; postgrad. U. Wis., summers 1926, 44; M.A., U. Mich., 1928; postgrad. Columbia U., 1932-33, Northwestern U., summer 1938; Litt. D., L'Universite Libre Asie, 1968; m. Dorothy Marie Munns, August 29, 1925. Prof. pub. speaking, dept. chmn. Elon Coll., 1917-18; asso. prof. speech Willamette U., 1918-19, prof., chmn. dept., 1919-20; asso. prof. U. Pacific, 1925-27; instr. speech U. Mich., 1927-28; asst. prof. U. Ark., 1928-29; prof., chmn. dept. speech N.W. Mo. State Coll., 1929-34; acting prof. speech Vanderbilt U., 1934-36, asst. prof., 1936-42; instr., speech clinician Purdue U., 1942-45; licensed to ministry Christian Ch., 1942; minister Clay St. Christian Ch., Nashville, 1942, New Richmond, Ind., 1943-45, Hillsboro, Ind., 1945, Shelbyville, Ill., 1945-52, Oakwood, Ill., 1957-59, Arrowsmith, Ill., 1960, 1st Christian Ch., Atwood, Ill., 1961-63; field rep. Ill. Christian Advance of Disciples of Christ, 1953-56. Bd. dirs. Ill. Christian Missionary Soc., 1948-53, trustee permanent fund, 1950-52, chmn. bd. trustees, 1952-53; elder emeritus Disciples of Christ, 1956—; lectr. in field. Bd. dirs. Shelby County chpt. ARC, 1947-51. Recipient numerous awards for poetry Am., fgn. orgns., including Leonardo da Vinci Internat. Poetry award and gold medal for sonnet Tree of Paradise, Centro Studi e Scambi Internazionali, Italy; gold medal and Intercontinental Poet Laureate-Editor-Leader citation United Poets Laureate Internat.; gold medallion Pres. Republic Philippines; Poet of Mankind citation World Acad. Langs. and Lit., Brazil; citation Am. Poetry League, citation Hayden Library Ariz. State U.; (with wife) citation as Distinguished Couple in World Cultural Relations, Laureate trophy Philippine Com. Arts and Culture; diploma aureum honoris causa World Congress Poets; Bicentennial award Republic China; World Poetry award; citation Academia Pax Mundi, Israel; named life regent Internat. Hermetic Order Cosmosynthesis League, Australia. Life fellow Royal Soc. Arts; mem. Modern Poetry Assn., Am. Poetry League, Internat. Poets Shrine, Fedn. Am. State Poetry Socs., Ariz. State Poetry Soc., Ind. U. Alumni Assn. (life), U. Mich. Alumni Assn., Centro Studi e Scambi Internazionali, Accademia Internazionale Leonardo da Vinci, United Poets Laureate Internat., Societas Polyglottica Universalis, World Poetry Soc. Intercontinental (exec. chancellor 1968-70, v.p. 1970—, distinguished service editor-leader citation), AAUP (past pres. chpt.), Nat., Ill. (life) hist. socs., Nat. Trust Historic Preservation, Moultrie County Hist. and Geneol. Soc. (charter, patron, hon. life), Calif. Forensic Assn. (past pres.), Internat. Platform Assn., Nat. (exec. council), Internat. Platform Assn., Mo. (past pres.), Tenn. (past pres.) speech assns., So. Assn. Tchrs. Speech (past pres.), Tau Kappa Alpha, (past nat. v.p., province gov.), Delta Sigma Rho, Pi Kappa Delta (diamond rank), Theta Alpha Phi (founder Ind. U. chpt.), Alpha Psi Omega, Phi Delta Kappa, Kappa Delta Pi. Mason (32 deg.), Rotarian. Author: Sir Henry Irving, the Public Speaker, 1929; The Congress of Human Relations-A Technique of Public Discussion, 1938; Educational Debate and the Extension of the Classroom, 1932; The Conditioning of Personality by Speech Defects, 1932; Treasured Legacy (poems), 1967; Light Uplift Loaves (poems), 1971; Selected Nurture Poems, 1973. Editor: (with Della Crowder Miller, author) Abraham Lincoln-A Biographic Trilogy in Sonnet Sequence, 3 vols., 1965; co-editor pancontinental monthly Poet, 1968-73; founder, editor Tenn. Speech Jour., 1936-41; asst. editor So. Speech Jour., 1936-39; asso. contbg. editor Intercollegiate After-Dinner Speaking, 1937; adv. editor Quar. Speech Jour., 1942-45; editor Ill. Christian Advance, 1953-55; editor American University Poets Anthology, 1968; Anglo American Poets Anthology, 1969; Pancontinental Premier Poets Anthology, 1970; mem. editorial bd. Internat. Who's Who in Poetry. Contbr. articles and poetry to profl. jours., anthologies and mags. Home: 7 Montclair Rd Urbana IL 61801

MILLER, OTIS LOUIS, historian; b. Belleville, Ill., Aug. 8, 1933; s. Otis Louis and Viola (Neubarth) M.; B.A., So. Ill. U., 1956, M.S., 1963; Ph.D., St. Louis U., 1972; m. Sandra Jo Schilling, June 16, 1962; children—Deborah, Stacy. Tchr. Belleville Twp. (Ill.) High Sch., 1958-65; instr. history, polit. sci. Belleville Area Coll., 1965—, chmn. dept. social sci., 1967-73; instr. history, sociology McKendree Coll., Belleville, part-time 1975—; cons. in field. Mem. Ill. Ho. of Reps., 1961-62; alderman 7th ward City of Belleville, 1963—; mem. Belleville Pub. Library Bd., 1963-77, pres., 2 years; mem. SW Regional Planning Commn. Ill., 1976—; pres. Douglas Sch. PTA, 1975-77. Mem. Orgn. Am. Historians, Am. Hist. Assn., Ill., Ark., Mo. hist. socs., Am., St. Louis, Mo. numis. socs., Nat. Council Social Sci. Republican. Mem. United Ch. Christ. Clubs: Masons, Elks, Eagles, Moose. Home: 413 S Virginia St Belleville IL 62221 Office: 2500 Carlyle Ave Belleville IL 62221

MILLER, PEARSON L., supt. schs.; b. Clay City, Ind., Oct. 30, 1936; s. Raymond B. and Edith A. (Sinders) M.; B.S., Purdue U., 1958; M.S., Butler U., 1960, postgrad., 1961; m. Jeannine Ruth Boley, Sept. 15, 1957; children—Pearson Jon, Phillip Matthew. Asst. county agr. extension agt., Hancock County, Greenfield, Ind., 1958; tchr. pub. schs., Greenfield, Ind., 1960-63; prin. Mt. Comfort Sch., Fortville, Ind., 1963-70; prin. Lincoln Park Elementary Sch., Greenfield, 1970-72; supt. schs., Mt. Vernon Community Schs., Fortville, 1972—. Mem. Hancock County Health Bd., 1973—. Served to 1st lt. Transp. Corps, AUS, 1959. NSF study grantee, summer 1960. Mem. Ind. Assn. Pub. Sch. Supts., Phi Delta Kappa. Free Methodist (mem. bd. Christian edn. 1974, del. ann. Wabash conf. 1963—, del. gen. ch. conf. 1974). Lion (pres. 1972—). Home: Route 6 Greenfield IN 46140 Office: Rural Route 1 Fortville IN 46040

MILLER, RAY GLEN, lawyer, county judge; b. Elwood, Ind., Oct. 18, 1928; s. Jesse Everett and Edna Amanda (Merchant) M.; B.S., Ind. U., 1950; J.D., Ind. U. Sch. Law, 1954; m. Martha Ann Fergason, June 15, 1953; children—Leslie, Lisa. Admitted to Ohio bar, 1959; bond underwriter Ohio Farmers Ins. Co., Westfield Center, 1956-61; mem. firm Zinn, Cultice & Miller, Zanesville, Ohio, 1961—; asst. solicitor City Zanesville, 1962-68; county judge Muskingum County, Ohio, 1969—; dir. Grange Mut. Casualty Co., Columbus, Ohio. Instr. estate planning Ohio U., Zanesville, 1968; mem. law enforcement adv. com. Muskingum Area Tech. Inst., Zanesville, 1968—. Vice pres. Community Improvement Corp., 1973—. Bd. dirs. Girl Scouts Am., 1968-69, Boy Scouts Am., 1970-73; bd. dirs. United Way, 1968-77, mem. exec. com., 1968-77, pres., 1974, 77; trustee Muskingum Comprehensive Mental Health Center, 1972—. Pres. Muskingum County Young Republicans, 1964. Served to 1st lt. AUS, 1954-56. Mem. Zanesville Jr. C. of C. (sec. 1963-64; mem. bd. 1964-65), Am., Ohio, Muskingum County (pres.) bar assns., Ohio Judicial Conf., Ohio Assn. County Ct. Judges (pres. 1974), Delta Theta Phi. Methodist (lay leader 1969-73; pres. dist. Meth. Union 1971-75). Mason (Shriner), Rotarian. Club: Country (Zanesville). Bd. editors Ind. Law Jour., 1951-53. Home: 2739 W Ridgewood Circle Zanesville OH 43701 Office: 50 N 4th St Zanesville OH 43701

MILLER, RAYMOND LEE, supt. schs.; b. Chandlerville, Ill., Jan. 23, 1922; s. Abraham and Rachel (Masten) M.; B.S., Western Ill. State U., 1945; M.S., U. Ill., 1947, advanced certificate, 1961; Ed.D., No. Ill. U., DeKalb, 1973; m. Mavis Yvonne Remsburg, Apr. 4, 1946; children—Douglas Kent, Merridee Beth, Todd Randall. Tchr., coach Manito (Ill.) Grade Sch., 1942-44; tchr. Mason City (Ill.) High Sch., 1945-46; prin. Balyki High Sch., Bath, Ill., 1947-51; unit. supt. Delavan (Ill.) Com. Unit Schs., 1951-62; supt. schs. Lisle, Ill., 1962—. Bd. dirs. Spl. Edn. Coop. Mem. NEA, Ill. Edn. Assn. (dir., past pres. Peoria div.), Am., Ill. (legis. com.) assns. sch. adminstrs., West Suburban Supts. Assn. (pres.), Supts. Round Table No. Ill. (membership chmn.), County of DuPage Supts. (pres.), N. Central Assn. (chmn. evaluation team), Phi Delta Kappa. Methodist. Kiwanian (past pres.). Home: 5601 Westview Ln Lisle IL 60532 Office: 5211 Center Ave Lisle IL 60532

MILLER, RICHARD HAMILTON, lawyer, broadcasting co. exec.; b. Cleve., July 18, 1931; s. Ray Thomas and Ruth (Hamilton) M.; A.B., U. Notre Dame, 1953, J.D., 1955; m. Susan Elizabeth Klimcheck, June 27, 1953; children—James M., Suanne R., Elizabeth M., Judith K., William P., Matthew W. Admitted to Ohio bar, 1955; mem. firm Miller and Miller, Cleve., 1955—; asst. prosecutor Cuyahoga County, 1957-60; pres. Cleve. Broadcasting, Inc., 1966-70, Searles Lake Chem. Corp., Los Angeles, 1966-69, Miller Broadcasting Co., Cleve., 1970—, Hollywood Bldg. Systems, Inc., Meridian, Miss., 1974—; mng. partner Miller & Co., Cleve., 1974—; owner, dir. Cleve. Profl. Basketball Co., Cleve. Baseball, Inc. Gen. chmn. N.E. Ohio March of Dimes, 1971-73; mem. Cuyahoga Democratic exec. com., 1955-66; adv. council Catherine Horstman Home for Retarded Children, 1969-73. Served to capt., M.P., AUS, 1956-57. Mem. Ohio, Cleve., Cuyahoga County bar assns., Cleve. Citizens League. Clubs: K.C., Variety, Notre Dame (pres. 1964-65), Cleve. Athletic (dir. 1971-74) (Cleve.); Shaker Heights Country (Ohio). Office: 2021 Superior Bldg Cleveland OH 44114

MILLER, RITCHIE EUGENE, constrn. co. exec.; b. Yankton, S.D., Aug. 22, 1951; s. Gerald Eugene and Marjorie Ruth (Leise) M.; B.S., U. Nebr., 1973; m. Carol Ann Rager, Jan. 19, 1974. Salesman, Gerry Miller Implement Co., Hartington, Nebr., 1974; mgr. Gem Enterprises, Inc., Hartington, 1974—. Mem. Nat. Small Bus. Assn., Metal Bldg. Dealers Assn., Hartington C. of C. (sec. 1976-77), Kappa Sigma. Roman Catholic. Home and Office: Box 765 Hartington NE 68739

MILLER, ROBERT CARL, physicist; b. Chgo., Oct. 26, 1938; s. Carl and Violet (Nelson) M.; B.S. in Physics, Ill. Inst. Tech., 1961; M.S. in Physics, No. Ill. U., 1965, Certificate Advanced Study in Physics, 1972; m. Mary Kay Ball, Sept. 3, 1969. Researcher particle accelerator div. Argonne (Ill.) Nat. Lab., 1961-66, researcher high energy physics div., 1966—. Registered profl. engr., Ill. Mem. Am. Phys. Soc., Am. Nuclear Soc., IEEE, Nat. Soc. Profl. Engrs., Soc. Certified Data Processors, Instrument Soc. Am., Am. Inst. Aero. and Astronautics, Mensa, Internat. Soc. for Philos. Enquiry, Sigma Xi, Sigma Pi Sigma. Contbr. articles to profl. jours. Home: 1105 Elizabeth Ave Naperville

IL 60540 Office: High Energy Physics Div Argonne Nat Lab Bldg 362 Room G-216 9700 S Cass Ave Argonne IL 60439

MILLER, ROBERT ERNEST, research scientist; b. Des Moines, July 31, 1936; s. Howard Raymond and Kathaleen Gwendolyn (McGriff) M.; m. Kay Eloise Johnson, Aug. 11, 1957; children—Jeffrey David, Daniel Wayne, Stephanie Beth; B.S., Simpson Coll., 1958; M.S., Cornell U., 1961, Ph.D., 1963; postgrad. U. Calif., Berkeley, 1964-65. Plant pathologist-geneticist Campbell Soup Co., 1963-67, research asso. Pioneer Lab., 1967-70, research scientist, 1970-76, dir. pest mgmt., Napoleon, Ohio, 1976—; presented invitational sci. papers at Internat. Sci. Mushroom Congress, Eng., 1971, Japan, 1974. Candidate for Willingboro Twp. Council, 1973; Republican committeeman, 1970-74. Mem. Am. Phytopathol. Soc., Am. Soc. for Microbiology, Mycol. Soc. Am. Recipient Distinguished Service award N.J. Jr. C. of C., 1972.

MILLER, ROBERT FRANK, mech. seals and packing co. exec.; b. Chgo., Aug. 4, 1927; s. Frank and Anna P. (Petronis) M.; student Northwestern U., 1946; m. Deloris A. Glans, Sept. 1, 1951; children—Paul, Diana, Carol. With Crane Packing Co., Morton Grove, Ill., 1943—, br. mgr., 1968-76, regional mgr., Cedar Rapids, Iowa, 1976—. Served with AUS, 1946-47. Mem. Soc. Automotive Engrs., Am. Soc. Lubricating Engrs., Am. Legion, Izaak Walton League. Clubs: Dubuque Yacht, Elks.

MILLER, ROBERT FRANKLIN, banker; b. Canton, Ohio, Apr. 2, 1935; s. Robert Frank and Marie (Heid) M.; B.A., Principia Coll., 1957; m. Sarah Stevens, June 15, 1957; children—Marian Louise, Stephen Dana, Paul Franklin. Account exec. Griswold-Eshleman Co., Cleve., 1960-64; v.p. marketing Cleve. Trust Co., 1964—. Served to capt. USMCR, 1957-60. Trustee Brother's Brother Found., Cleve. Inst. Music, Planned Parenthood Assn.; bd. dirs. Cleve. chpt. A.R.C.; chmn. Waite Hill Planning and Zoning Bd.; exec. bd. N.E. Ohio council Boy Scouts Am.; pres. Trinity Day Care Center. Mem. Am. Inst. Banking, Pub. Relations Soc. Am., Cleve. Advt. Club (pres.), Urban League, Am. Mgmt. Assn., Lake County Bluecoats, Greater Cleve. Growth Assn., Bank Marketing Assn. (dir.). Club: Kirtland Country. Home: 6751 Eagle Rd Waite Hill Willoughby OH 44094 Office: Cleve Trust Co 900 Euclid Ave Cleveland OH 44101

MILLER, ROBERT HASKINS, state supreme ct. justice; b. nr. Columbus, Ohio, Mar. 3, 1919; s. George L. and Marian Alice (Haskins) M.; student Ohio State U., 1936-37; A.B., Kans. U., 1940; LL.B., 1942; grad. Nat. Coll. State Trial Judges, Phila., 1967; m. Audene Fausett, Mar. 14, 1943; children—Stephen F., Thomas G., David W., Stacey Ann. Admitted to Kans. bar, 1943; practiced law, Paola, Kans., 1946-60; judge 6th Jud. Dist., Paola, 1961-69, U.S. Magistrate Dist. Kans., Kansas City, 1969-75; justice Kans. Supreme Ct., 1975—. Served with U.S. Army, 1942-46. Mem. Kans., Shawnee County bar assns., Am. Judicature Soc., Am. Legion, Phi Gamma Delta, Phi Delta Phi. Presbyterian. Club: Masons. Author: (with others) Pattern (Civil Jury) Instructions for Kansas, 1966, 69. Home: 3440 Jardine Terr Topeka KS 66611 Office: Statehouse Topeka KS 66612

MILLER, ROBERT WILLIAM, cons. indsl. hygienist; b. Duluth, Minn., Aug. 11, 1945; s. William Washington and Lucylle (Johnson) M.; m. Claudia Schultz, July 10, 1976. B.A., U. Minn., 1967. Mem. indsl. hygiene tng. staff, occupat. safety health, Nat. Tng. Inst., Dept. Labor, Rosemont, Ill., 1972-74; owner, indsl. hygiene cons., product ling mgr., MDA Scientific, Inc., Park Ridge, Ill., 1974—; lectr. tng. courses Nat. Safety Council, OSHA Tng. Inst.; instr. first aid A.R.C., U.S. Bur. Mines. Ordained to ministry, 1969. Mem. Am. Indsl. Hygiene Assn., Am. Soc. Safety Engrs., Health Physics Soc., Soc. Plastic Engrs. (dir.). Contbr. articles in field to profl. jours. Home: 1260 Winwood Dr Lake Forest IL 60045

MILLER, ROY LAFETTE, II, psychologist; b. Alcoa, Tenn., Feb. 18, 1942; s. Roy L., Sr., and Nancy E. (Roberts) M.; M.S. in Clin. Psychology, Eastern Ky. U., 1971; Ed.S., Bowling Green State U., 1977; m. Dorothy Carol Lusby, Dec. 29, 1964; 1 dau., Nicole Leigh. Vocat. counselor Tenn. Div. Vocational Rehab., 1967-68; psychologist Tuscarawas Valley Mental Health Center, 1970-72; psychologist, dir. research and devel. Quadco Rehab. Center, Defiance, Ohio, 1972—; adj. prof. Defiance Coll. Licensed psychologist, Ohio. Mem. Am., Midwest, Ohio psychol. assns., Nat. Rehab. Assn., Profl. Assn. Retardation of Ohio. Home: 157 Cleveland Ave Defiance OH 43512 Office: 1055A Ralston Ave Defiance OH 43512

MILLER, RUTH RATNER, city ofcl.; b. Cleve., Dec. 1, 1925; d. Leonard and Lillian (Berntein) Ratner; student U. Wis., 1944; B.S., Cleve. Coll., 1969; Ph.D., Case Western Res. U., 1972; m. Samuel H. Miller, Aug. 10, 1946; children—Aaron, Richard, Gabrielle, Abraham. Counselor, Ednl. Devel. Center, Berea, Ohio, 1969-70, Caldonia Sch., East Cleveland, Ohio, 1970; grad. asst. dept. edn. Case Western Res. U., 1971, lectr., counselor, 1971-74; dir. City of Cleve. Dept. Pub. Health and Welfare, 1974-75, dir. Dept. Community Devel., 1976—. Mem. Mayor's Adv. Com. on Community Needs, 1976—; mem. Ohio Manpower Services Council; mem. manpower instl. adv. com. Oakland U.; trustee Nat. Housing Conf., 1977—. Recipient (with husband) City of Cleve. Real Estate award, 1976; named Fed. Woman's Program Women of Year, HUD, 1976; Brandeis Community Service award, 1977. Mem. Am. Humanist Assn., Gestalt Inst., Am. Soc. Adlerian Psychology, NOW, Greater Cleve. Growth Assn., Cleve. Mus. Art, Nat. Caucus on Black Aged, Am. Personnel and Guidance Assn., Council Jewish Women, Phi Delta Kappa. Jewish. Clubs: Women's City, WomenSpace. Home: 17220 Aldersyde Dr Shaker Heights OH 44120 Office: 777 Rockwell Av Cleveland OH 44114

MILLER, SAMUEL ELIAS, textile co. exec.; b. Chgo., Aug. 7, 1917; s. Benjamin Ted and Ida (Nisenfeld) M.; B.S., Northwestern U., 1940; m. Corinne Jansen Mosak, Mar. 4, 1973; children—David, Samuel E. II, Philip C. Plant mgr. J K Industries, 1940-42, Northwestern Mfg. Co., 1947-52, F.S. Tiger Co., 1952-58; v.p. in charge of devel. and mfg. QST Industries, Chgo., 1958—. Served with USAAF, 1942-46. Mem. Beta Gamma Sigma. Patentee in field. Home: 495 Sheridan Rd Winnetka IL 60093 Office: 300 W Congress Pkwy Chicago IL 60607

MILLER, SOL, research microbiologist, indsl. hygienist; b. Akron, Ohio, June 3, 1914; s. Phillip and Mollie (Drutz) M.; B.A., Akron U., 1936; M.S., Ohio State U., 1939; Ph.D., Sussex (Eng.) U., 1975; m. Rosalyn Raful, Dec. 28, 1937; children—Barbara Claire Miller Olschwang, Kenneth Arnold. Bacteriologist, Ohio Dept. Health, 1939-42; chief chemist Q.O. Ordnance Corp., Grand Island, Nebr., 1942-43; research asso. Children's Fund of Mich., Detroit, 1944-54; bacteriologist James Labs., Chgo., 1954-55; group leader, research bacteriologist IIT Research Inst., Chgo., 1955-72; corp. biohazard control, supr. indsl. hygiene Abbott Labs., North Chicago, Ill., 1972—; adj. instr. Chgo. Med. Sch., 1973; mem. exec. com. research and devel. sect. Nat. Safety Council, 1974—. Certified specialist Nat. Registry Microbiologists. Fellow Am. Inst. Chemists (hazard control mgr.); mem. Am. Inst. Biol. Scis., Am. Chem. Soc., Am. Soc. for Microbiology, Am. Soc. Profl. Biologists, Am. Assn. Clin. Chemists, Am. Indsl. Hygiene Assn., Sigma Xi. Mem. B'nai B'rith (past pres. Lodge 1455). Contbr. articles to profl. jours. Home: 2820 W Jarvis Ave Chicago IL 60645 Office: 1400 Sheridan Rd North Chicago IL 60064

MILLER, STEPHEN JOHN, social scientist; b. Secaucus, N.J., Sept. 11, 1936; s. George W. and Constance (Adamowicz) M.; B.S. in Sociology, St. Peter's Coll., 1958; Ph.D., St. Louis U., 1963; m. Roberta M. Brahm, Sept. 17, 1960; children—Andrew S., Rodney J., Jessica A. Resident sociologist Community Studies, Inc., Kansas City, Mo., 1962-64; asst. prof. social research Brandeis U., 1964-67, asso. prof. sociology Florence Heller Grad. Sch. for Advanced Studies in Social Welfare, 1967-72; asst. dir. Center for Community Health and Med. Care Med. Sch. and Sch. Pub. Health, Harvard, 1968-69, asso. dean for urban affairs Med. Sch., 1969-72, mem. pres.'s adv. com. on community relations, 1970-71, asso. dean admissions, 1970-74, asso. prof. preventive and social medicine, 1973-76; v.p. Affiliated Hosps. Center, Boston, 1972-76; asso. provost Northwestern U., 1976—, prof. community medicine Med. Sch., 1976—, mem. bd. McGaw Med. Center, 1976—, exec. com., 1977—; cons. River City Project, Chgo., 1976—, Assn. Am. Med. Colls., 1966-67, R.I. Dept. Pub. Assistance, 1967-69. Fellow Am. Sociol. Assn.; mem. Soc. for Study Social Problems, Midwest, Eastern sociol. socs. Author: A Division of Nursing Labor, 1965; Prescription for Leadership: Training for the Medical Elite, 1970. Dep. editor Jour. Health and Social Behavior, 1969-71. Address: Northwestern U Evanston IL 60201

MILLER, THEODORE WAYNE, mfg. co. exec.; b. Pitts., Sept. 5, 1930; s. Wayne Orlando and Geraldine (Brown) M.; student Ohio U., 1948-49; B.A., Coll. of Wooster, 1952; M.S., Case Western Res. U., 1954; m. Sanka Novovich, June 9, 1956; children—Bradford, William Todd, Stuart (dec.), Leslie Ann. Personnel adminstr. Salem China Co. (Ohio), 1954-55; with Whirlpool Corp., St. Joseph, Mich., 1957-69, dir. indsl. relations, 1965-69; dir. indsl. relations KDI Corp., Cin., 1969-74, v.p. indsl. relations, 1974—. Mem. adv. com. Mich. State U., S.W. Mich. Center, 1967-69. Mem. allocations com. United Appeal, Evansville, Ind., 1962. Served with AUS, 1955-57. Mem. Am. Psychol. Assn., Am. Soc. for Personnel Adminstrn., Am. Compensation Assn., Cin. Personnel Assn., Indsl. Relations Research Assn., Greater Cin. C. of C., Am. Mgmt. Assn. Unitarian. Rotarian. Home: 6801 Farmbrook Dr Cincinnati OH 45230 Office: 5721 Dragon Way Cincinnati OH 45227

MILLER, VICTOR ANDREW, lawyer; b. Manitowoc County, Wis., Aug. 27, 1916; s. John and Frances (Horneck) M.; B.S., Marquette U., 1938, J.D., 1940; m. Isabel Grimm, June 28, 1941; children—John C., Mary Miller Caldwell, Jane E., Margaret, Mark. Admitted to Wis. bar, 1940; pvt. practice law, St. Nazianz, Wis., 1940—. Lectr. on taxation, state and local groups; mem. nat. dealer council Internat. Harvester Co., Chgo., 1973-75; atty. gen. Wis., 1974—; dir. St. Nazianz (Wis.) State Bank, 1965—. Mem. Manitowoc County (Wis.) Mental Health Assn., 1970—; chmn. Wis. Adv. Com. on sml. bus., 1960-62; mem. consumer credit review bd. Wis. Dept. Banking, 1973—; legis. study com. Wis. Consumer Act, 1973-74; adv. bd. Wis. Dept. Revenue, 1970-73; regional adv. bd. Internal Revenue Service, Chgo., 1970—; Dem. del. Nat. Convs., 1948-60, 64. Bd. dirs. Big Bros., Manitowoc, Wis., 1970-71, Easter Seal Soc. for Wis., 1976—; bd. corp. mems. Silver Lake Coll.; J.F.K. Prep. Sch. Recipient Lions Service award, 1960; Man of Yr. award Notre Dame, 1976. Decorated Knight Equestrian Order St. Gregory Pope Paul VI, 1974. Mem. State Bar Wis. (pres. 1973-74, bd. govs. 1969-75), Am. Coll. Probate Counsel, Woolsack Soc., Am., Manitowoc County (pres. 1970) bar assns., Am. Bar Found., Marquette U. Law Sch. Alumni Assn. (bd. dirs. 1970-73), Wis. Sch. Bd. Atts. Assn., Sheboygan Economics Club (pres. 1973). Roman Catholic (bd. edn. 1969-74). Lion. Contbr. articles to profl. jours. Home: 106 Douglas Ct St Nazianz WI 54232 Office: 105 Main St St Nazianz WI 54232

MILLER, VINCENT ARVEL, tng. exec.; b. Evansville, Ind., Feb. 26, 1917; s. Marion Albert and Clara (Sitzman) M.; student U. Evansville, 1937-40; m. Ida Augusta Greif, Sept. 14, 1940; children—David, Catherine, Joseph, Mark. Tool and die maker Servel, Inc., Evansville, 1940-46, factory service supr., 1946-56; customer service engr. Whirlpool Corp., Evansville, 1956-60, gen. mgr. consumer affairs tng., Benton Harbor, Mich., 1960—. Pres., Lake Michigan Cath. Bd. Edn., 1969-70; mem. advisory council Mich. Bd. Edn., 1976—; pres. bd. trustees Evansville Redevel. Commn., 1959-60. Recipient Gordon M. Bliss award for most outstanding contbn. to tng. and devel. profession, 1975. Mem. Am. Soc. for Tng. and Devel. (dir. 1971—, pres. 1974, editor Internat. Newsletter), Internat. Fedn. Tng. and Devel. Orgn. (sec.-treas. 1973-75), Internat. Council for Adult Edn. (dir.), Council on Continuing Edn. Unit, Soc. for Tech. Communication. Clubs: K.C., Elks, Toastmasters Internat. (dist. gov. 1960). Editor: Guidebook for Internat. Trainers. Home: 923 State St Saint Joseph MI 49085 Office: Whirlpool Corp Benton Harbor MI 49022

MILLER, WALTER GORDON, water conditioning co. exec.; b. Havre, Mont., July 6, 1932; s. Walter Wesley and Vivian (Vagg) M.; B.A., Carleton Coll., 1954; M.S., Syracuse U., 1955; m. Gayle I. Highberg, Dec. 29, 1954; children—Peggy, Debby, David. Pres. Culligan Water Conditioning Co., Marlette, Mich., 1958—, Clean Water Corp., La Crosse, Wis., 1974—; dir. Wolverine State Bank; WQA Nat. Ins. Trust. Chmn. Sanilac County Mental Health Bd., 1971-76; v.p. Marlette Community Hosp., 1971—; sec. Sanilac County Bldg. Authority, 1972—. Recipient Key Man award, Internat. Water Quality Assn., 1976. Mem. Mich. Water Conditioning Assn. (founder, past pres.), Internat. Water Quality Assn. (past pres.), Mich. Culligan Assn. (past pres.), Marlette C. of C. (past pres.). Republican. Presbyterian. Clubs: Masons, Shriners. Home: 6623 Cooper Rd Marlette MI 48453 Office: 3099 Main St Marlette MI 48453

MILLER, WAYNE CHARLES, educator; b. N.Y.C., Nov. 3, 1939; s. Charles Henry and Florence Violet (Keenan) M.; B.A. magna cum laude (Rand McNally Centennial scholar), St. John's U., 1960; M.A. (N.Y. State Regents fellow), Columbia, 1961; Ph.D., N.Y. U., 1968; m. Patricia Clemens, Sept. 2, 1973; 1 son, Wayne Joshua; children by previous marriage—Alison Catherine, Heather Mary. Commd. 2d lt. U.S. Air Force, 1962, advanced through grades to capt., 1966, discharged, 1967; asst. prof. U.S. Air Force Acad., Colorado Springs, Colo., 1963-67; asso. prof. State U. N.Y., Oneonta, 1967-70; prof. dept. English, U. Cin., 1970—. Producer TV series WCET-TV, pub. broadcasting sta., Cin., 1973, 74, 75, 76, 77. State U. N.Y. fellow, 1969, U. Cin. fellow, 1971, Taft Found. fellow, 1972, Ohio Program in Humanities grantee, 1973, 74, 75, 76, 77. Mem. Modern Lang. Assn., Am. Acad. Polit. and Social Sci., Delta Kappa Tau. Author: An Armed America—Its Face in Fiction: A History of the American Military Novel, 1970; A Gathering of Ghetto Writers: Irish, Italian, Jewish, Black, & Puerto Rican, 1971; A Comprehensive Bibliography for the Study of American Minorities, 1976; A Handbook for the Study of American Minorities, 1976. Home: 343 Compton Hills Dr Cincinnati OH 45215

MILLER, WAYNE LOUIS, educator; b. Alexandria, La., Aug. 31, 1946; s. Jean Baptiste and Sophie Martha (Langlinais) M.; B.S., U. Mich., 1969; postgrad. U. Southwestern La., 1970; M.A., U. N.E. Mo., 1976; m. Lesley Carol Roost, Mar. 21, 1972; 1 dau., Sharon Lesley. Exhibitor 1970 Expo, Osaka, Japan; World Trampoline champion, 1966-70, trampoline demonstrator on tour, Eng., South Africa, 1970; tchr., coach trampoline, Rockford, Ill., 1971; dir. Gymnastics Club, Cedar Rapids, Iowa, 1972; tchr. phys. edn., intramural dir. Linn Mar High Sch., Marion, Iowa, 1972—. Dir. gymnastics program Marion YMCA, 1973—. Named U.S. Trampoline Coach of Year Amateur Athletic Union, 1971. Mem. Iowa High Sch. Gymnastics Coaches Assn. (pres. 1974-77), East Central Iowa Gymnastics Assn. (pres. 1975), Nat., Ia. State, Linn Mar edn. assns., U.S. Trampoline Assn. (editor jour. 1972), Amateur Athletic Union, Phi Delta Kappa. Mem. Christian Ch. Home: 364 Crandall Dr NE Cedar Rapids IA 52402 Office: N 10th St Marion IA 52302

MILLER, WAYNE STARR, surgeon; b. Logansport, Ind., Mar. 3, 1932; s. Charles A. and Alta (Starr) M.; A.B., Manchester Coll., 1955; M.D., Ind. U., 1957; m. Michele Bartels, Oct. 1973; children—Greg, Mona, Mark Brandon, Ashton. Intern Mercy Hosp., Springfield, Ohio, 1957-58; practice gen. medicine, Huntington, Ind., 1958-60; resident in surgery Hurley Hosp., Flint, Mich., 1960-64; practice medicine specializing in surgery, Huntington, Ft. Wayne, Ind., 1964—; dir. First Nat. Bank, Huntington. Bd. dirs. Allen County Med. Meml. Found. Mem. A.C.S., A.M.A., Ind., Huntington County med. socs. Office: 2828 Fairfield Ft Wayne IN 46807

MILLER, WILLIAM ANTON, mathematician, educator; b. Cedar, Mich., Apr. 16, 1935; s. William A. and Evelyn N. (Svoboda) M.; B.S., Mich. State U., 1956, M.A.T., 1961; M.A., U. Ill., 1963; Ph.D., U. Wis., 1968; m. Delores Ann Zamarron, Oct. 22, 1960; children—Sandra, William, Robert, Debra. Tchr., Sunfield (Mich.) Community Schs., 1956-60, Oak Park (Mich.) Community Schs., 1960-61, Waverly Schs., Lansing, Mich., 1961-62; asst. prof. math. Wis. State U., Whitewater, 1965-67, asso. prof., 1967-68; asso. prof. math., Central Mich. U., Mt. Pleasant, 1968-71, prof., 1971—. Mem. Mt. Pleasant Bd. Edn., 1971—, sec., 1972-76. Mem. Nat. Council Tchrs. Math., Math. Assn. Am., Nat. Sch. Bd. Assn., Sch. Sci. Math. Roman Catholic. Contbr. articles to math. edn. jours.; author instructional math. booklets. Home: 407 E Grand Ave Mt Pleasant MI 48858 Office: Central Michigan U 321 Pearce Hall Mt Pleasant MI 48859

MILLER, WILLIAM HALL, dentist; b. Akron, Ohio, June 14, 1931; s. William Dewey and Willa Marie (Hall) M.; student Ohio U., 1949-50; D.D.S., Ohio State U., 1955; m. Judith Ann Peavy, Feb. 16, 1957 (div. 1975); children—Nannette Elizabeth, Julie Marie; m. 2d, Patricia Ann Losee, 1975. Mem. staff Longview State Hosp., Cin., 1957-58; pvt. practice dentistry, Belpre, Ohio, 1958—; dir. Belpre First Fed. Savs. & Loan Assn., 1967—, v.p., 1977—. Bd. dirs. Parkersburg YMCA, 1967-69, Belpre United Appeals, 1965-69. Served with Dental Corps, AUS, 1955-57. Mem. Am. Dental Assn., Muskingum Valley Dental Soc. (pres. 1974-75), Belpre Area C. of C. (pres. 1970), Delta Sigma Delta. Moose, Lion (pres. local club 1962-63). Home: 1562 Gene St Belpre OH 45714 Office: 218 Maple St Belpre OH 45714

MILLER-TIEDEMAN, ANNA, ednl. adminstr.; b. Huntington W.Va., Sept. 21, 1934; d. Elmer and Pearl (Todd) Miller; B.B.A., Marshall U., 1963, M.A. in Sociology, 1967; Ph.D. in Guidance and Counseling, Ohio U., 1973; m. David V. Tiedeman, Jan. 6, 1973. Resident dir. Ohio U., Athens, 1967; human relations specialist Inst. for Regional Devel., Athens, 1968; housing specialist Action, Inc., Huntington, W.Va., 1969; real estate person Massey Realty Co., Huntington, 1968-71; writer, 1971-72; counselor P.J. Abbott Middle Sch., San Mateo, Calif., 1972-73; career guidance coordinator, counselor DeKalb High Sch., Dekalb, Ill., 1973—; asst. prof. career edn. No. Ill. U., DeKalb, 1974—; advisory bd. to villages, DeKalb, 1974—. Mem. Am., Ill. guidance and personnel assns., DeKalb Classroom Tchrs. Assn., NEA, Ill. Ednl. Assn. Contbr. numerous in personnel and guidance to profl. jours. Home: 807 Ridge Rd #1116 DeKalb IL 60115 Office: DeKalb High School Barb Blvd DeKalb IL 60115

MILLETT, STEPHEN MALCOLM, air force officer; b. N.Y.C., Feb. 22, 1947; s. John David and Catherine (Letsinger) M.; A.B., Miami U., Oxford, Ohio, 1969; M.A., Ohio State U., 1970, Ph.D., 1972; m. Patricia McBurney, Aug. 1, 1970; children—Jennifer Jane, Ann Elizabeth. Commd. 2d lt. USAF, 1971, advanced through grades to capt., 1976; asst. prof. humanities Air Force Inst. Tech., 1973-77; adj. asst. prof. U. Dayton, 1974-77; area mgr. Ohio Valley area Air Force Jr. ROTC, Columbus, Ohio, 1977—. Mem. Am. Hist. Assn., Orgn. Am. Historians, Soc. Historians Am. Fgn. Relations. Democrat. Methodist. Author: Selected Bibliography of American Constitutional History, 1975; American Diplomacy Before the Courts, 1977. Home: 180 W Cooke Rd Columbus OH 43214 Office: AFROTC/CC-OV Rickenbacker AFB OH 43217

MILLI, ROSE LYNN EILEEN, assn. exec.; b. Indpls., May 8, 1931; d. Oscar Burnett and Elsa Naomi (Lewark) Bunce; student Ind. U., 1949-53; children—Robert Wayne Albright, Gregory Layne Albright. Free lance comml. announcer, 1951-75 disc jockey, interviewer, 1958-59; creative dir. Paul Lennon Advt., 1964-69; pub. info., pub. relations and pub. health dir. Marion County Heart Assn., Indpls., 1969-77; mem. staff Wallis Advt., Mktg. & Pub. Relations, 1977—; pub. speaker; health agy. cons. Named pub. servant of the week Sta. WIFE, 1975. Mem. Soc. Heart Assn. Profl. Staff, Pub. Relations Soc. Am., Ind. Bus. Communicators. Baptist. Club: Indpls. Press. Author: (with Elsa Naomi Bunce) Echoes (poetry), in progress. Author column Letters to Lynn for Indpls. Gazette, 1958-59, series Take Time, articles in field. Composer 200 musical compositions, 7 commercially released. Home: 621 N Beville Ave Indianapolis IN 46201 Office: 6214 Morenci Trail Indianapolis IN 46268

MILLIGAN, FREDERICK JAMES, lawyer; b. Upper Sandusky, Ohio, Nov. 14, 1906; s. William G. and Grace (Kuenzli) M.; B.A., Ohio State U., 1928; LL.B., Franklin U., 1933; J.D., Capital U., 1966; m. Virginia Stone, June 30, 1934; children—Frederick James, David Timothy. Asst. nat. sec. Phi Delta Theta, 1928; asst. dean of men Ohio State U., 1929-33; admitted to Ohio bar, 1933; asst. atty. gen. State of Ohio, 1933-36; pvt. practice, Columbus, Ohio, 1937—; exec. sec. Adminstrv. La. Commn. of Ohio, 1940-42; exec. sec. to Gov. of Ohio, 1947; dir. commerce State of Ohio, 1948; sec. Louis Bromfield Malabar Farm Found., 1958-60. Pres. Central Ohio council Boy Scouts Am.; trustee Columbus Town Meeting; asst. dir. Pres.'s Commn. on Inter-govt. Relations, 1953; pres. Ohio Information Com., Inc., 1966—; chmn. Blendon Twp. Bicentennial Commn., 1974-77. Mem. athletic council Ohio State U., 1958-64; trustee Blendon Twp., 1971-78. Served from 1st lt. to maj. USAAF, 1942-45. Decorated Legion of Merit; recipient Silver Beaver award Boy Scouts Am., 1949; Ann. History award Franklin County Hist. Soc., 1957; D.A.R. Citizenship award, 1958; Distinguished Service citation Ohioana Library Assn., 1970. Mem. Am., Ohio, Columbus bar assns., Columbus Jr. C. of C. (hon. life mem.; pres. 1934), Ohio (trustee 1952-77, pres. 1963-65, Franklin County (pres. 1954-56) hist. socs., Ohio State U. Assn. (trustee 1952-55), Amvets (state comdr. 1949). Am. Legion, S.A.R., League of Young Republican Clubs of Ohio (pres. 1941-42). Presbyn. Clubs: University (trustee 1956-58), Ohio State U. Faculty (Columbus). Home: 3785 Dempsey Rd Westerville OH 43081 Office: 3791 Dempsey Rd Westerville OH 43081

MILLIGAN, ROBERT LEE, JR., computer co. exec.; b. Evanston, Ill., Apr. 4, 1934; s. Robert L. and Alice (Connell) M.; B.S., Northwestern U., 1958; m. Susan A. Woodrow, Mar. 23, 1957; children—William, Bonnie, Thomas, Robert III. Account rep. IBM, Chgo., 1957-66; sr. cons. L.B. Knight & Assos., Chgo., 1966-68; v.p. mktg. Trans Union Systems Corp., Chgo., 1968-73; v.p. sales Systems Mgmt. Inc., Des Plaines, Ill., 1973—; dir. Nanofast, Inc., Chgo., 1968—. Div. mgr. N. Suburban YMCA Bldg., 1967. Area chmn., Northfield Twp. Republican Party, 1965-71. Bd. dirs. United Fund, Glenview, Ill., 1967-69, Robert R. McCormick Chgo. Boys Club, 1974—; pres. bd. mgrs. Glenview Amateur Hockey Assn., 1974—, gen. mgr. Glenbrook South High Sch. Hockey Club; bd. dirs. Chgo. Boys Clubs, 1974—. Served with AUS, 1953-55. Mem. Data Processing Mgmt. Assn., Consumer Credit Assn. (bd. dirs., sec. 1969-70), Phi Kappa Psi. Presbyn. Clubs: Northwestern (dir. 1973-75) (Chgo.); Glen View (Ill.). Home: 702 Glendale Dr Glenview IL 60025 Office: 10400 W Higgins Rd Des Plaines IL 60018

MILLIGAN, ROBERT STIEPER, agri-bus. co. exec.; b. Omaha, Dec. 2, 1944; s. Harland Stieper and Evelyn Marie (Seivers) M.; B.S., U. Nebr., 1967; J.D., George Washington U., 1971; postgrad. finance Wharton Sch. U. Pa., 1976; m. Cynthia Wood Hardin, June 16, 1968; children—David Hardin, Catherine Seivers. Pres., Transamerican Carrier Co., Fremont, Nebr., 1966-69, also dir.; admitted to Nebr. bar, 1971, D.C. bar, 1975; trial atty. Dept. Justice, D.C., 1971-72; dir. spl. studies EPA, D.C., 1972-73; dep. asst. sec. for policy Dept. Commerce, D.C., 1973-76; chief exec. officer Centennial Corp., Lincoln, Nebr., 1977—, also dir.; dir. Cornbelt Elevator Co. City council, Hooper, Nebr., 1962-63; asst. regional dir. Republican presdl. campaign, Calif., Ind., Mich., Ohio, Wis., 1972. Served with U.S. Army, 1967-68. Mem. Am., Nebr., D.C. bar assns., Am. Law Inst., Am. Trucking Assn. Co-author: The American Economic System, and Your Part in It, 1975. Home: 2000 Pinedale Ave Lincoln NE 68520 Office: PO Box 5544 Lincoln NE 68505

MILLIKAN, LARRY EDWARD, dermatologist; b. Sterling, Ill., May 12, 1936; s. Daniel Franklin and Harriet Adeline (Parmenter) M.; B.A., Monmouth Coll., 1958; M.D., U. Mo., 1962; m. Jeanine Dorothy Johnson, Aug. 27, 1960; children—Marshall, Rebecca. Intern, Great Lakes (Ill.) Naval Hosp., 1962-63; housestaff in tng. U. Mich., Ann Arbor, 1967-69, chief resident, 1969-70; asst. prof. U. Mo., Columbia, 1970-74, asso. prof., 1974-77; cons. physician Ellis Fischel, VA Hosp., Student Health Service, Gunn Clinic. Served with USN, 1960-67. Nat. Cancer Inst. grantee, 1976—. Fellow ACP; mem. Am. Dermatol. Soc. for Allergy and Immunology (pres.), Soc. for Investigative Dermatology, Coll. Physicians Phila., AMA, Boone County Med. Soc. (pres.), Mo. State Med. Assn., AAAS, Mo. State Allergy Assn., Mo. State Dermatol. Assn., Internat. Soc. for Tropical Dermatology, Nat. Bd. Med. Examiners, Sigma Xi, Alpha Omega Alpha, Alpha Tau Omega. Contbg. editor pharmacology sect. Internat. Jour. of Dermatology, 1973—; contbr. articles to med. jours. Home: 203 Orchard Ct Columbia MO 65201 Office: M176 University Medical Center Columbia MO 65201

MILLIKEN, WILLIAM GRAWN, gov. Mich.; b. Traverse City, Mich., Mar. 26, 1922; s. James Thacker and Hildegarde (Grawn) M.; A.B., Yale U., 1944; m. Helen Wallbank, Oct. 5, 1945; children—Elaine, William Grawn. Pres., J. W. Milliken, Inc., dept. store, Traverse City, 1952-69; mem. Mich. Senate from 27th Dist., 1960-64, majority floor leader, 1963-64; lt. gov. Mich., 1965-68, gov., 1969—. Mem. Mich. Waterways Commn., 1947-55; pres. Scenic Trails council Boy Scouts Am., 1956; visited W. Ger. on intercultural exchange program Dept. State, 1953; chmn. Grand Traverse County Republican Com., 1948-54; trustee Northwestern Mich. Coll., 1957-60; bd. dirs. Greater Mich. Found., 1955—. Served with USAAF, World War II; ETO. Decorated Purple Heart. Mem. Traverse City C. of C. (past pres.). Club: Rotary. Home: 6103 Peninsula Dr Traverse City MI 49684 Office: State Capitol Bldg Lansing MI 48909

MILLIMET, CHARLES RAYMOND, psychologist; b. N.Y.C., May 17, 1941; s. Louis and Susan (Roisman) M.; m. Gloria Vivian Newmark, Aug. 27, 1967; children—Robert, Daniel. B.A., Hunter Coll., 1963; M.A., Miami U., 1965; Ph.D., Okla. State U., 1968. Asst. prof. dept. psychology U. Nebr., Omaha, 1968-72, asso. prof., 1972-77, prof., 1977—. Mem. Am., Midwestern psychol. assns. Club: Bella Vista Country. Author articles: Journal of Consulting and Clinical Psychology, Journal of Experimental Social Psychology, Journal of Personality Assessment, Stress and Anxiety, Vols. 1 and 4. Home: 1439 S 167th St Omaha NE 68127

MILLIRON, ALLISON INGHRAM, univ. adminstr.; b. Waynesburg, Pa., Mar. 17, 1933; s. William Clair and Carolyn (Allison) M.; B.A., Mich. State U., 1955; M.B.A., Bowling Green State U., 1976; m. Connie Anne Stormer, Aug. 1, 1954; children—Michael Robert, Eric William. Dir. food service Saga Food Service, Kalamazoo, Mich., 1957-58; dir. food service Bowling Green State U., 1951-65, dir. aux. services, 1965-76, dir. mgmt. support services, 1976—; pres., Design Mgmt., Inc. Active Boy Scouts Am. Served with AUS, 1956-57. Recipient Bowling Green State U. Spl. Achievement award, 1975. Mem. Nat. (pres. 1973), Central (pres. 1977) assns. aux. services, Central Assn. Coll. and Univ. Bus. Officers. Lutheran. Home: 871 Pearl St Bowling Green OH 43402 Office: 409 Administration Bldg Bowling Green State U Bowling Green OH 43403

MILLISER, STEPHEN CHARLES, psychologist, educator; b. Columbus, Ohio, Oct, 3, 1944; s. Russell V. and Mary Elizabeth (Goodrich) M.; B.A., Elmhurst Coll., 1967; M.A., Loyola U., Chgo., 1969, Ph.D., 1973; m. Sandra Ann Soroka, Apr. 15, 1967; children—Thomas Charles, Mary Elizabeth. Lectr., Loyola U., Chgo., 1961-71; asst. prof. psychology Gonzaga U., Spokane, 1971-75; asst. prof. Rockhurst Coll., Kansas City, Mo., 1975—. NSF trainee, 1967. Mem. Am., Midwestern, Western psychol. assns., Blue Key, Psi Chi. Home: 7820 103d Terr E Kansas City MO 64134 Office: 5225 Troost St Kansas City MO 64110

MILLMAN, RONALD BURTON, pub. relations agy. exec.; b. Chgo., Oct. 21, 1934; s. Boris I. and Pearl (Schwartz) M.; B.A., Roosevelt U., 1959; 1 son, Neil Roger. Publicity writer Victor Adding Machine Co., Chgo., 1959-60; asst. pub. relations mgr. Brunswick Corp., Chgo., 1960-63; pub. relations mgr. Bastian-Blessing Co., Chgo., 1963-66; pub. relations mgr. Nat. Video Corp., Chgo., 1966-67; sr. v.p., Harshe, Rotman & Druck, Chgo., 1967—. Served with AUS, 1954-57. Recipient Best in Industry award Financial World Annual Report Survey, 1967, 68, Certificate of Merit, Publicity Club Chgo., 1971, Golden Trumpet award Publicity Club Chgo., 1973, 74, 75, Addy award Am. Advt. Fedn., 1974. Mem. Pub. Relations Soc. Am. (acredited). Home: 4170 N Marine Dr Chicago IL 60613 Office: 444 N Michigan Ave Chicago IL 60611

MILLNER, ARNOLD JOHN, editor; b. N.Y.C., Oct. 10, 1920; s. Max Samuel and Bessie (Cohen) M.; B.J., U. Mo., 1949; m. Janice Lyle, June 1, 1948;children—John, Susan. Copy, telegraph editor Champaign (Ill.) News-Gazette, 1949-50; makeup editor, news editor Columbus (Ga.) Ledger, 1950-53; copy editor, picture editor St. Louis Globe-Dem., 1953-56; picture editor St. Louis Post-Dispatch, 1956-71, night city editor, 1971-73, asst. city editor, 1973-76, copy editor, 1976-77, met. editor, 1977—. Bd. dirs. Christian Hosp. N.E.-N.W., Florissant, Mo., 1972—. Served with inf. U.S. Army, 1938-45. Decorated Bronze Star medal, Purple Heart with two oak leaf clusters. Mem. Sigma Delta Chi. Mason (Shriner). Clubs: Press (St. Louis), Bogey Hills Country. Home: 11851 Cato Dr Florissant MO 63033 Office: 11700 Dunlap Industrial Blvd Maryland Heights MO 63043

MILLOY, FRANK JOSEPH, JR., physician; b. Phoenix, June 26, 1924; s. Frank Joseph and Ola (McCabe) M.; student Notre Dame U., 1942-43; M.S., Northwestern U., 1949, M.D., 1947. Intern, Cook County Hosp., Chgo., 1947-49, resident, 1953-57; practice medicine, specializing in surgery, Chgo., 1958—; asso. attending staff Presbyn.—St. Lukes Hosp.; mem. staff U. Ill. Research Hosp.; clin. asso. prof. surgery, U. Ill. Med. Sch.; asso. prof. surgery Rush Med. Sch. Cons. West Side Vet. Hosp. Served as apprentice seaman USNR, 1943-45; lt. M.C., USNR, 1950-52; PTO. Diplomate Am. Bd. Surgery and Thoracic Surgery. Mem. A.C.S., Chgo. Surg. Soc., Am. Coll. Chest Physicians, Soc. Thoracic Surgeons, Phi Beta Pi. Clubs: Metropolitan, University (Chgo.). Home: 10108 Old Orchard Ct Skokie IL 60076 Office: 122 S Michigan Ave Chicago IL 60603

MILLOY, PATRICK THEODORE, lawyer; b. Omemee, N.D., Feb. 17, 1909; s. Arthur and Elizabeth (Farrell) M.; LL.B., U. N.D., 1931, J.D., 1969; m. Lucille Ambrosich, June 15, 1936; children—John, Mary Jo (Mrs. Frank Lara), Paul, Eileen (Mrs. William Johnson), Ann (Mrs. Peter Ruddy). Admitted to N.D. bar, 1931; partner firm Johnson, Milloy, Johnson, Stokes & Robinson, Ltd., and predecessor firms, Wahpeton, 1933—, State's atty. Richland County, (N.D.), 1951-57. Served with AUS, 1944-45. Mem. 3d Jud. Dist. Bar Assn. (pres. 1958), Am. Legion (comdr. 1948, nat. exec. com. 1964-72). Home: 529 3d St N Wahpeton ND 58075 Office: 412 Dakota Ave Wahpeton ND 58075

MILLS, COLEY CLIFTON, editor, bus. analyst; b. Hope Hull, Ala., June 26, 1937; s. Coley Clifton and Mary Susan (Ward) M.; B.S., U. Chgo., 1959, postgrad., 1959-60. Editor, Sci. Research Assos., Inc., Chgo., 1962—, sr. editor, 1972-76, bus. mgmt. and product acquisitions analyst, mathematics and science, 1976—. Recipient Pres.'s Outstanding Achievement award, 1974. Mem. Am. Math. Assn., AAAS, Nat. Council Tchrs. of Math., Calif. Math. Council, Detroit Council Tchrs. of Math., Chgo. Council Fgn. Relations, Chgo. Symphony Soc. Editor: Advancing in Mathematics: Geometry, 1965; Elementary Functions, 1968; Today's Mathematics, 1971; Computapes (series), 1972-74. Home: 2815 N Orchard St Chicago IL 60657 Office: 155 N Wacker Dr Chicago IL 60611

MILLS, HOWARD SAMUEL, JR., food co. exec.; b. Indpls., Aug. 7, 1929; s. Howard Samuel and Bernice (Hadley) M.; B.A. in Economics, Earlham Coll., 1951; M.B.A., Ind. U., 1952; m. Alice Wolfe, Dec. 14, 1950; children—Deborah Mills Maximoff, Susan Elizabeth. With Maplehurst Farms, Inc., Indpls., 1956—, v.p., 1960-71, exec. v.p., 1971-76, pres., 1976—, exec. v.p. Maplehurst Deli-Bake, 1971—; v.p. Sr. Trust Corp., Indpls., 1971—; v.p. Studio P/R, Inc., 1966—. Mem. Indpls. Human Rights Commn., 1973-76. Mem. Indpls. C. of C. Quaker. Home: 5124 Mendenhall Rd Indianapolis IN 46241 Office: 3745 Farnsworth Indianapolis IN 46241

MILLS, JAMES MYRON, dentist; b. Cadiz, Ohio, Aug. 22, 1927; s. Edwin Lewis and Olive Jane (Moorhead) M.; student Denison U., 1945, Union Coll., 1946; B.B.A., Ohio State U., 1949; D.D.S. cum laude, 1957; m. Marilyn Joanne Mattern, June 20, 1959; children—Alison Jane, James Andrew, John Edwin, Meredith Lee. Pvt. practice dentistry, Cin., 1957-59, Marietta, Ohio, 1959—. Served with USNR, 1945-47. Mem. Am., Ohio, Muskingum Valley dental socs., Omicron Kappa Upsilon, Psi Omega, Delta Tau Delta. Republican. Presbyterian (deacon). Home: 148 Seneca Dr Marietta OH 45750 Office: 103 Seneca Dr Marietta OH 45750

MILLS, JAMES WILLIAM, realtor; b. Camden County, Mo., July 25, 1925; s. James Kelly and Mable (Cyrus) M.; student Drury Coll., 1963; m. Zella Mae Price, July 18, 1959; children—Douglas James, Michelle Jeanne. With Lebanon (Mo.) Coca Cola Bottling Co., 1941-43; parts mgr. Montgomery Motor Sales, Inc., Lebanon, Mo., 1947-69; br. mgr. Strout Realty, Lebanon, 1971—. Deacon First Baptist Ch., Lebanon, Mo., 1959—; city councilman, Lebanon, 1964, 66, 67, mayor pro-tem, 1967. Served with USNR, 1943-46. Recipient Pres.'s awards Strout Realty, also named to 5 Million Dollar Club; decorated Air medal. Mem. Nat., Mo. assn. realtors, Ozarks Bd. Realtors, C. of C. Club: Kiwanis. Home: 317 Sherman St Lebanon MO 65536 Office: 4th and Jefferson Sts Lebanon MO 65536

MILNER, WALKER WILSON, civil engr.; b. Tacoma, Sept. 10, 1907; s. William Wilson and Orabelle (Smith) M.; B.S., U.S. Mil. Acad., 1931; M.S., State U. Iowa, 1934; grad. Armed Forces Staff Coll., 1948, Army War Coll., 1951; m. Betty Maxine Miller, Dec. 27, 1934; 1 son, Robert Walker. Commd. 2d lt., C.E., U.S. Army, 1931, advanced through grades to col., 1944; chief tech. div. IV, Engr. Research and Devel. Labs., Ft. Belvoir, Va., 1942-44; exec. officer engring. sect. Pacific Air Command, 1944-45; chief staff engr. Hdqrs. Far East Air Forces, Manila and Tokyo, 1945-47; staff officer internat. br. Office Asst. Chief of Staff Plans and Ops., Dept. Army, Washington, 1948-50; chief standards br. Office Asst. Chief of Staff Logistics, 1951-54; U.S. Army attache, Australia, 1954-57; chief of staff Hdqrs. U.S. Army Engr. Tng. Center and Fort Leonard Wood, Mo., 1957-58; ret., 1958; asso. prof. civil engring. U. Mo.-Columbia, 1958-70, prof., 1970-73, prof. emeritus, 1973—. Pres. United Fund of Columbia, 1963, Parents Assn. of Westminster Coll., Fulton, Mo., 1971-72. Decorated Legion of Merit, Bronze Star, Commendation ribbon with oak leaf cluster; registered profl. engr., Mo. Fellow ASCE (pres. mid-Mo. sect. 1962-63); mem. Tau Beta Pi, Chi Epsilon, Phi Delta Theta. Republican. Presbyterian. Author: (with Harry Rubey) Construction and Professional Management, 1966, 2d rev. edit., 1971; (with others) The Engineer and Professional Management, 1970. Home: 201 W Ridgeley Rd Columbia MO 65201 Office: Dept Civil Engring U Mo Columbia MO 65201

MILONAS, CHARLES CONSTANTINE, dentist; b. Mar. 21, 1928; s. Elias and Maria (Vasiloudis) M.; B.S., Wayne State U., 1946-50; D.D.S., Northwestern U., 1954; postgrad. Walter Reed Army Med. Center, 1955, U. Detroit, 1960; m. Penelope Kleros, June 27, 1954; children—Maria, Louis. Night watchman Underwriters Labs., Chgo., 1952-54; gen. practice dentistry, Detroit, 1956-63, Mount Clemens, Mich., 1963—. Mem. Clintondale Bd. Edn., 1966-70, treas., 1968, sec., 1969; mem. Macomb Intermediate Sch. Dist. Bd. Edn., 1971—. Served with AUS, 1954-56. Mem. Am. Dental Assn., Acad. Gen. Dentistry, Am. Analgesia Soc., Internat. Platform Assn., Clinton Twp. Goodfellows, Hellenic Bd. Trade, Macomb Dental Soc., Am. Hellenic Ednl. Progressive Assn. (pres. 1962), Nat. Sch. Bd. Assn., Macomb Prosecutors Assn., Macomb Sch. Bd. Assn. Home: 36545 Little Mack St Mount Clemens MI 48043 Office: 21300 Fifteen Mile Rd Mount Clemens MI 48043

MILTON, JOHN RONALD, educator, author; b. Anoka, Minn., May 24, 1924; s. John Peterson and Euphamia Alvera (Swanson) M.; B.A., U. Minn., 1948, M.A., 1951; Ph.D., U. Denver, 1961; m. Leonharda Allison Hinderlie, Aug. 3, 1946; 1 dau., Nanci Lynn. Instr. English, philosophy, Augsburg Coll., Mnpls., 1949-57; asso. prof. English Jamestown (N.D.) Coll., 1957-60, also acting chmn., 1957-60, prof., 1961-63, chmn. English dept., 1961-63; prof. English U. S.D., Vermillion, 1963—, also editor S.D. Rev., 1963—, dir. writing program, 1965—, chmn. dept. English, 1963-65. Vis. prof. N.D. State U., summer, 1966, Ind. State U., Summer, 1966, Bemidji (Minn.) State Coll., 1969; chmn. Dakota Press, U. S.D., 1968—. Served with AUS, 1943-46; PTO. Wurlitzer Found. fellow, 1965. Hill Found. grantee, 1966, 69, 70, Whitney Found. grantee, 1970, 72, S.D. Arts Council grantee, 1969, 70, 74, 74, U. S.D. grantee, 1963, 64; Nat. Endowment for Arts writing fellow, 1976-77. Mem. Am. Studies Assn. (regional bd. 1957-59), Western Lit. Assn. (pres. 1971, editorial bd. 1966—), Western History Assn. Author: (poetry) The Loving Hawk, 1962, Western Plains, 1964, The Tree of Bones, 1965, This Lonely House, 1968, The Tree of Bones and Other Poems, 1973, The Blue Belly of the World, 1974; (novel) Notes to a Bald Buffalo, 1976; (biography) Oscar Howe, 1972, Crazy Horse, 1974; (interviews) Three West, 1970, Conversations with Frank Waters, 1971, Conversations with Frederick Manfred, 1974; (history) South Dakota: A Bicentennial History, 1977. Editor: The American Indian Speaks, 1969; American Indian II, 1971; The Literature of South Dakota, 1976. Conbr. numerous essays, stories and revs. to lit. publs. Home: 630 Thomas Vermillion SD 57069 Office: Box 111 University Exchange Vermillion SD 57069

MIN, TONY CHARLES, mech. engr., educator; b. Shanghai, China, Jan. 5, 1923; s. Tee and Wei-Inn (Huang) M.; came to U.S., 1949, naturalized, 1960; B.S. in Aero. Engring., Chaio Tung U., 1947; M.S. in Mech. Engring., U. Tenn., 1953, Ph.D. in Engring. Sci., 1969; NSF sci. faculty fellow U. Minn., 1961-63; m. Elsie H. Tan, Dec. 28, 1968; 1 son, Christopher. Mech. design engr. TVA, Knoxville, Tenn., 1951-54; research engr. ASHRAE Research Lab., Cleve., 1954-57; asso. prof. Auburn (Ala.) U., 1957-64; instr. engring. sci. and mechanics U. Tenn., Knoxville, 1964-68; prof. Mich. Tech. U., Houghton, 1968—, research engr. Argonne Nat. Lab., summer 1962, Oak Ridge Nat. Lab., 1963, 64 summers, Babcock & Wilcox Research Center, summer 1969; vis. scientist Argonne Nat. Lab., summer 1975, Beloit Research Center, summer 1976; cons. Oak Ridge Nat. Lab., 1963-68. Mem. Toastmasters Internat. (area gov. dist. 35 1974-75), ASME (tech. com. on fundamental solar energy div. 1975—), Am. Acad. Mechanics, Am. Phys. Soc., Am. Soc. Engring. Edn., N.Y. Acad. Sci., Am. Soc. Heating, Refrigeration and Air Conditioning Engrs., Soc. Engring. Sci., Combustion Inst., Sigma Xi, Phi Tau Phi (nat. v.p. 1974-76), Tau Beta Pi, Pi Tau Sigma. Contbr. numerous articles, revs., abstracts to engring. jours. Home: PO Box 354 Houghton MI 49931

MINASSIAN, DONALD PAUL, educator; b. N.Y.C., Dec. 8, 1935; s. George Diran and Lydia (Hartunian) M.; student Coll. Wooster, 1953-55, City U. N.Y., 1955-56; B.A., Fresno (Calif.) State U., 1957; M.A., Brown U., 1964; M.S., U. Mich., 1965, Ph.D., 1967; m. Elaine Shakay Garabedian, Aug. 15, 1964; children—Laura, Valerie. Asso. prof. math. Butler U., Indpls., 1967-73, prof., 1973—. Active Indpls. Symphonic Choir. Neshan Zovick and Univ. fellow U. Calif., 1957-59; Butler U. faculty fellow, 1973-74; NSF fellow Brown U., U. Mich., 1963-67. Mem. Math. Assn. Am., Soc. Indsl. and Applied Math., AAUP, Ind. Assn. C.P.A.'s, Econ. Club Indpls., Phi Beta Kappa, Phi Kappa Phi. Home: 410 Blue Ridge Rd Indianapolis IN 46208 Office: 4600 Sunset Ave Indianapolis IN 46208

MINDERMAN, JERALD PATRICK, psychiat. social worker; b. Sullivan, Ind., Sept. 13, 1945; s. Gerald Joseph and Mildred Mardelle (Mansell) M.; B.A., St. Meinrad Coll., 1967; M.S., Ind. State U., 1971; m. Donetta Ruth Jett, Apr. 8, 1972; children—Daniel Patrick, Ethan Marshall. Tchr.-counselor St. Vincent's Children's Orphanage, Vincennes, Ind., 1968-69; asst. dir. residence hall Vincennes U. Jr. Coll., 1969-73, dir. counseling services, 1973-76; psychiat. social worker Good Samaritan Hosp. Comprehensive Community Mental Health Center, Vincennes, 1977—; cons. human relations tng. Chmn. exec. bd. Knox County chpt. A.R.C., 1973—; pres. Knox County Mental Health Assn., 1974-76. Mem. Am. Personnel and Guidance Assn. Democrat. Roman Catholic. Home: 816 Harrison St Vincennes IL 47591 Office: Good Samaritan Hosp Comprehensive Community Mental Health Center Vincennes IN 47591

MINER, PAUL VIRGIL, ret. newspaper exec.; b. Kansas City, Mo., July 11, 1911; s. Charles Henry and Julia (Donelson) M.; A.B., U. Kans., 1933; m. Dorothy M. Wattenberg, May 11, 1935; children—Marilyn (Mrs. B. Ken Gray), Anne (Mrs. Terril H. Hart). With Kansas City (Mo.) Star, 1933-75, mng. editor, 1960-65, asst. to pres. and editor, 1965-66, exec. v.p., 1966-68, pres., 1968-75, chmn. bd., 1975-75. Vice pres. Kansas City, United Campaign Fund. Trustee Kansas City Assn. Trusts and Founds., Midwest Research Inst., U. Mo. at Kansas City, Boy Scouts Am., William Allen White Found., U. Kans., Greater Kansas City United Way Campaign, Nat. Coll.; hon. trustee Rockhurst Coll. Served with USNR, 1943-45. Recipient Hon. Am. Farmer degree Future Farmers Am., 1973, Matrix award Women in Communication, 1974, Distinguished Service citation U. Kans., 1974. Mem. Am. Newspaper Pubs. Assn., A.P. Mng. Editors (treas., dir.), Am. Soc. Newspaper Editors, Kansas City C. of C. (dir. downtown com.), Kansas City Man-of-Month Frat., Native Sons Kansas City, Jackson County Hist. Soc., Civic Council, Jr. Achievement, A.R.C., Kansas City Mus., Nelson Art Gallery Soc. Fellows Found., Friends of Art. Sigma Delta Chi. Mem. Christian Ch. Clubs: Kansas City Press, Woodside Racquet. Home: Wornall Plaza 4949 Wornall Rd Kansas City MO 64112

MINER, THOMAS HAWLEY, internat. cons.; b. Shelbyville, Ill., June 19, 1927; s. Lester Ward and Thirza (Hawley) M.; student U.S. Mil. Acad., 1946-47; B.A., Knox Coll., 1950; J.D., U. Ill., 1953. Admitted to Ill. bar, 1954; atty. Continental Ill. Nat. Bank & Trust Co., Chgo., 1953-55; pres. Harper-Wyman Internat. S.A., Venezuela and Mexico, 1955-58; pres. Hudson Internat. S.A., Can. and Switzerland, 1958-60; pres. Thomas H. Miner & Assos., Inc., Chgo., 1960—; pres., dir. Lakeside Travel; mng. dir. Intercontinental Mining Co. Ltd.; dir. Lakeside Bank; lectr. DePaul U., 1962-63, Northwestern U., 1960-63; vice chmn. Ill. dist. export council U.S. Dept. Commerce. Chmn. devel. com. Sch. Art Inst. Chgo.; former chmn. UN Assn. Chgo.; pres., founder Mid-Am. Com.; former bd. dirs. UNICEF; trustee 4th Presbyterian Ch., Chgo. Served with USNR, 1945-46; served to capt. AUS, 1946-47. Named One of Chgo.'s 10 Outstanding Young Men, 1962, Chicagoan of Year, Chgo. Assn. Commerce and Industry, 1968; hon. consul Republic of Senegal. Mem. Am. Mgmt. Assn., Chgo. Assn. Commerce and Industry, MidAm.-Arab C. of C. (dir.), Chgo. Bar Assn., Chgo. Com., Chgo. Council Fgn. Relations (past dir.), Council of Ams., Internat. Trade Club Chgo. (dir., past pres.), Japan-Am. Soc., Nat. Council U.S.-China Trade, English Speaking Union (dir.), U.S.-USSR Trade and Econ. Council, Newcomen Soc. N.Am., Phi Delta Phi, Phi Gamma Delta. Clubs: Chicago, Economic, Mid-Am., Rotary; Internat. (Washington). Home: 1350 Lake Shore Dr Chicago IL 60610 Office: 135 S LaSalle St Chicago IL 60603

MINETTI, ROBERT HUGO, univ. adminstr.; b. Torrington, Conn., Apr. 30, 1947; s. Hugo A. and Claire (Breen) M.; B.A., St. Michael's Coll., 1969; M.Ed., U. Vt., 1971; Ph.D., Mich. State U., 1977; m. Wendy L. Baker, Aug. 16, 1975. Area coordinator U. Vt., 1970-71; asst. dean of students St. Michael's Coll., 1971-73; adviser residence hall programs office Mich. State U., 1973-75, asso. dir. residence hall programs, 1975—. Mem. Am. Personnel and Guidance Assn., Am. Coll. Personnel Assn., Nat. Assn. Student Personnel Adminstrs. Club: Univ. of Mich. State U. Research on relationship between acad. tng. and assistantship experiences in student personnel adminstr. Home: 2926 Mount Hope Ave Okemos MI 48864 Office: 339 Student Services Mich State U East Lansing MI 48824

MINGLE, JOHN ORVILLE, engr.; b. Oakley, Kans., May 6, 1931; s. John Russell and Beulah Amelia (Johnson) M.; B.S., Kans. State U., 1953, M.S., 1958; Ph.D., Northwestern U., 1960; m. Patricia Ruth Schmitt, Aug. 17, 1957; children—Elizabeth Lorene, Stephen Roy. Tng. engr. Gen. Electric Co., Schenectady, 1953-54; instr. Kans. State U., Manhattan, 1956-58, asst. prof. nuclear engring., 1960-62, asso. prof., 1962-65, prof., 1965—, Black & Veatch Distinguished prof., 1973—, also dir. Inst. Computational Research in Engring.; instr. Northwestern U., 1958-59; vis. prof. U. So. Calif., 1967-68; cons. Gulf Gen. Atomic Corp., Wilson & Co. Engrs., So. Calif. Edison Co., Argonne Nat. Lab. Served to lt. AUS 1954-56. Registered profl. engr., Kans. Mem. Am. Nuclear Soc. (standards com. 1973—, pres. Mo.-Kans. sect. 1976-77), Am. Inst. Chem. Engrs. (nuclear heat transfer com. 1976—), Am. Soc. Engring. Edn., Nat. Soc. Profl. Engrs., Soc. Indsl. and Applied Math., Kans. Engring. Soc. (pres. Tri Valley chpt. 1973-74), Sigma Xi (chpt. lectr. Kans. State U., 1966-67, chpt. pres. 1969-70). Author: The Invarient Imbedding Theory of Nuclear Transport, 1973; contbr. articles to profl. jours. Home: 2408 Buena Vista Dr Manhattan KS 66502

MINGS, DWAIN EDWARD, ophthalmologist; b. Shelbyville, Ind., July 31, 1914; s. Ernest Mings and Hazel Mings Heck; B.S. Ind. U., 1938, M.D., 1940; married. Intern Wis. Gen. Hosp., Madison, 1940-41, asso. in eye, 1946-47; preceptor Davis & Neff Clinic, Madison, 1941-46; clin. asst. ophthalmology U. Wis.-Madison Hosp., 1941-46; mem. staff Columbia Hosp., Milw., 1947, St. Clare Hosp., Monroe, Wis., 1947—, Monroe Clinic, 1947—; asst. clin. prof. ophthal. surgery U. Wis. Sch. Medicine, Madison. Diplomate Am. Bd. Ophthalmology. Mem. A.M.A. (physician's Recognition award 1971, 74), Wis., Green County med. socs., Pan-Am. Med. Assn., Am. Acad. Ophthalmology and Otolaryngology, Am., Pan-Am. assns. ophthalmology, Assn. for Research in Ophthalmology, Milw. Ophthalmology Soc., Instituto Barraquer, Contact Lens Assn. Ophthalmologists, N.Y. Acad. Scis., Wis.-Upper Mich. Soc. Ophthalmology and Otolaryngology, Soc. Eye Surgeons. Home: Box 253 Monroe WI 53566 Office: 1515-10th St Monroe WI 53566

MINNESTE, VIKTOR, JR., electronic co. exec.; b. Haapsalu, Estonia, Jan. 15, 1932; s. Viktor and Alice (Lembra) M.; B.S. in Elec. Engring., U. Ill., 1960. Electronic engr. Bell & Howell Co., 1960-69, microstatics div. SCM Co., 1969-71, Multigraphics div. A-M Co., 1972-73; electronic engr. bus. products group Victor Comptometer Co. (merged with Walter Kidde Corp. 1977), Chgo., 1973-74, service mgr. internat. group, 1974-75, now with research group; pub. Motteid/Thoughts, 1962-68; chmn., Estonian-Ams. Polit. Action Com., 1968-72. Served with AUS, 1952-54. Home: 3134 N Kimball Ave Chicago IL 60618 Office: 3900 N Rockwell Chicago IL 60618

MINNICH, JOSEPH EDWARD, ch. adminstr.; b. Swanton, Ohio, Sept. 13, 1932; s. Charles Vincent and Leila Elizabeth (Gaiman) M.; student Gonzaga U., 1952, Eastern Wash. Coll. Edn., 1953, U. Toledo, 1956-58; m. Frances K. Minnich; children—Christopher, Susan, Teresa. With Toledo (Ohio) Trust Co., 1956-62, ops. mgr., 1961-62; ins. agt. Allstate Ins. Co., Toledo, 1962-63; ins. agt., asst. office mgr., partner Wright, Russell & Bay Co., Toledo, 1963-67; pres. Toledo Lake Erie & Western Ry., 1977—; ch. adminstr. St. Paul's Luth. Ch., Toledo, 1968—. Ch. mgmt. cons.; cons. on chapel mgmt. U.S. Air Force, 1974-76; exec. dir. St. Pauls Camp, Hillsdale, Mich., 1963-69; sec.-treas. Covenant House Inc., Toledo, 1969—; v.p. 8404 Corp., 1974—; Mich. dist. treas., mem. exec. com. Am. Luth. Ch., 1969-73; Toledo Conf. treas., mem. exec. com., 1968-72. Served with USAF, 1951-55. Fellow Nat. Assn. Ch. Bus. Adminstrs. (chpt. pres. 1973—, nat. sec. 1975—), Soc. for Religious Organizational Management; mem. Am. Camping Assn. Home: 200 Birchdale Dr Perrysburg OH 43551 Office: 428 N Erie St Toledo OH 43624

MINNICH, VIRGINIA, hematologist, educator; b. Zanesville, Ohio, Jan. 24, 1910; d. Rufus Humphrey and Ollie (Burley) Minnich; B.S. in Home Econs., Ohio State U., 1937; M.S. in Nutrition, Iowa State Coll., 1938; Sc.D. (hon.), William Woods Coll., 1972. Research asst. dept. medicine div. hematology Washington U. Sch. Medicine, St. Louis, 1939-54, research asso., 1954-58, research asst. prof., 1958-67, research asso. prof., 1967-74, prof. medicine, 1974—. Recipient Alumni award in home econs. Ohio State U., 1975; named St. Louis Woman of Achievement, Group Action Council, 1947; Fulbright-Hays research award, Turkey, 1964. Mem. Am. Fedn. for Clin. Research, Soc. for Exptl. Biology and Medicine, Internat., Am., socs. hematology, Sigma Xi, Omicron Nu, Phi Upsilon Omicron. Contbr. numerous articles to profl. jours. Home: 4501 Maryland Ave St Louis MO 63108

MINOR, WENDELL LAFAYETTE, rubber co. exec.; b. Brockway, Pa., Feb. 10, 1927; s. Wendell R. and Martha (Buehler) M.; B.S. in Elec. Engring., Carnegie Inst. Tech., 1948; grad. Advanced Mgmt. Program, Harvard U., 1971; m. Phyllis Milford Lankenau, Feb. 19, 1949; children—Wendell David, Paul Griffiths, Martha Lankenau. With Goodyear Tire & Rubber Co., Akron, Ohio, 1948—, v.p., 1972—. Served with USAAF, 1945-47. Mem. Soc. Automotive Engrs., Am. Mining Congress (bd. govs.), Constrn. Industry Mfrs. Assn. (bd. dirs.), Am. Rd. Builders Assn., Hwy. Users Fedn. for Safety and Mobility. Clubs: Country of Hudson; Portage Country. Home: 2371 Cambridge Dr Hudson OH 44236 Office: Goodyear Tire & Rubber Co Akron OH 44316

MINSHALL, DREXEL DAVID, automotive parts mfg. co. exec.; b. Bridgeport, Nebr., Nov. 1, 1917; s. Charles D. and Minnie C. (Nordell) M.; student Colo. U., 1934-38; m. Betty Jane Tesdell, Feb. 12, 1938 (dec. June 1971); children—Drexel David, Carol J. (Mrs. Michael L. Preston); m. 2d, Roylynn H. McAllister, Apr. 19, 1974. Sales mgr. Gates Rubber Co., Denver, 1939-61; v.p. marketing Perfect Circle Corp., Hagerstown, Ind., 1961-65; pres. Dana Parts Co. div. Dana Corp., Toledo, 1965-67, group v.p., from 1967, now sr. group v.p.; dir. Dana World Trade Corp., Toledo, Ludwig Motors Corp., N.Y.C., Corp. HZ, Caracas, Venezuela, Brown Bros. Ltd., Harlow, Eng. Bd. dirs. Community Chest, Nat. Inst. Automotive Excellence; trustee Boys Club, Toledo. Mem. Automotive Service Industries Assn. (pres. 1964-65), Automotive Old Timers, Automotive Acad., Automotive Pres.'s Council, Motor and Equipment Mfrs. Assn. (product v.p.), Toledo C. of C., Alpha Tau Omega. Mason (32 deg.). Clubs: Toledo; Sylvania Country. Contbr. articles to profl. pubis. Home: 4809 Carskaddon Ave Toledo OH 43615 Office: 4500 Dorr St Toledo OH 43697

MINSKER, ROBERT STANLEY, labor cons.; b. Pitts., Jan. 1, 1911; s. Theodore Kohene and Isabella Lavinia (Trumbor) M.; B.S., U. Ill., 1934; postgrad Pa. State U., 1938-39; m. Marion Elizabeth Warner, May 29, 1937; children—Norma (Mrs. Leo Jerome Brown II), Robert S., James D. With Owens-Ill., Inc., Alton, Ill., 1934-76, personnel dir. Clarion (Pa.) plant, 1936-40, personnel dir. Columbus (Ohio) plant, 1940-44, mgr. indsl. relations, Alton, 1945-72, adminstr. workmen's compensation, safety and health Ill. plants and pub. affairs, 1972-76; dir. Germania Fin. Corp., Germania Fed. Savs. & Loan Assn. Asso. faculty So. Ill. U., 1959-64; lectr., cons. Chmn. Madison County Savs. Bond Campaign, 1959-61; active Boy Scouts Am.; pres. Piasa Bird Council, 1949-51, mem. exec. bd., 1945—; mem. grievance com. panel State of Ill. Dept. Personnel, 1967—; vice chmn. Higher Edn. Coordinating Council Met. St. Louis, 1966-70; founder Board Pride, Inc., 1966—. Mem. Bd. Edn., 1957-70, pres. 1961-70. Bd. dirs., sec., exec. com. Alton Meml. Hosp., 1969—, Jr. Achievement, United Fund; bd. dirs. Community Chest, v.p., 1949-54, 61-66, gen. chmn., 1949-50; trustee Alton Found., sec., 1955—; trustee Lewis and Clark Community Coll., sec. bd., 1970-77. Recipient Silver Beaver award Boy Scouts of Am., 1951; recipient Achievement award U.S. Treasury Dept., 1951; Hall of Fame award Piasa Bird Council, 1969; Lewis and Clark Hall of Fame, 1977. Mem. Alton C. of C. (chmn. pub. relations 1951-54), Nature Conservation Assn. (a founder), Acacia, Alpha Phi Omega. Meth. Mason (32 deg., K.T., Shriner). Home: 2018 Chapin Pl Alton IL 62002

MINTER, JOHN B(ERNARD), project engr.; b. Chgo., Mar. 17, 1946; s. Fred P. and Estelle Ann (Schneider) M.; B.S.E.M., U. Ill., 1969; m. Janice M. Riegel, June 20, 1970; children—Brian, Jason. Mech. engr. U.S. Steel Corp., Chgo., 1968-70; mech. analyst Sargent & Lundy, Engrs., Chgo., 1970-73; plant engr. Park div. Jewel Co., Inc., Barrington, Ill., 1973-77; project engr. CFS Continental Inc., Chgo., 1977—; speaker Internat. Pollution Engring. Congress, Cleve., 1975. Supr. devel. Lake Forest Coll., 1976. Mem. ASME, U.S. Jaycees. Roman Catholic. K.C. Home: 329 Lewis St Wauconda IL 60084 Office: CFS Continental 2550 N Clybourn Ave Chicago IL 60614

MINTZER, OLIN WESLEY, III, civil engr.; b. Spokane, Wash., June 6, 1916; s. Olin W. and Ruth (Sugg) M.; B.C.E., U. Tenn., 1942; M.C.E., Purdue U., 1949; m. Marion Elizabeth Head, June 11, 1941; children—Elizabeth Wesley Mintzer Herron, Michael Olin, Patricia Ruthellen Mintzer Hopkins. Engring. aide TVA, Chattanooga, 1938-39, Paris, Tenn., 1940; instr. civil engring. Purdue U., Lafayette, Ind., 1947-49, asst. prof. hwy. engring., 1949-52, research engr., 1947-49; asst. prof. Case Inst. Tech., Cleve., 1952-56; prof. AID project in India, Punjab Engring. Coll., Chandigarh, India, 1956-58; asso. prof. civil engring. Ohio State U., Columbus, 1958-74, prof., 1974—; vis. prof. Escola Superior De Agricultura, U. Sao Paulo, Brazil, summer 1973. Asst. scoutmaster Central Ohio area council Boy Scouts Am., 1961-68; mem. bd. Trinity Meth. Ch., Columbus, Ohio, 1965-66. Served with C.E., U.S. Army, 1940-46. Decorated Legion of Merit; Deutscher Akademischer Austauschdienst fellow, 1970; registered profl. engr., Ohio, Ind.; registered profl. surveyor, Ohio. Mem. ASCE, Am. Soc. Engring. Edn., Nat. Soc. Profl. Engrs., Transp. Research Bd. of NRC, Res. Officers Assn., Am. Soc. Photogrammetry (citation 1972, 73), Sigma Xi, Chi Epsilon. Author: Manual of Highway Engineering Applications of Photogrammetry, 1959; (with others) Airphoto Interpretation of Soils and Rocks for Engineering Purposes, 1953; contbr. chpts. to profl. manuals, numerous articles on applications of aerial photography to civil engring. problems to profl. jours.; developed various terrain investigation techniques. Home: 2027 Indianola Ave Columbus OH 43201 Office: 2070 Neil Mall Columbus OH 43210

MINUI, MORTEZA, psychiatrist; b. Teheran, Iran, Mar. 12, 1927; s. Bagher and Khatoon Jan (Ahmadi) M.; came to U.S., 1952; B.S., Teheran U., 1945, M.D., 1951; m. Barbara Ann Alfie, Aug. 26, 1957; children—Marian, Nancy, Daria, Marty. Intern, Women's Hosp., Detroit, 1952-53; resident, in psychiatry Wayne County Psychiat. Hosp., Eloise, Mich., 1953-55, staff psychiatrist, 1958-62, dir., 1970—; resident in obstetrics and gynecology Sinai Hosp., Detroit, 1955-56; dir. Wayne County Mental Health Clinic, Detroit, 1963-70; practice medicine specializing in psychiatry, Westland, Mich., 1960—; asst. clin. prof. psychiatry, Wayne State U. Med. Sch., Detroit. Chmn. bd. dirs. Detroit Philos. Soc., 1970—. Diplomate Am. Bd. Psychiatry and Neurology. Fellow Am. Psychiat. Assn.; mem. AMA. Home: 1576 Kirkway St Bloomfield Hills MI 48013 Office: 33200 W Warren Rd Westland MI 48185

MIRACLE, GORDON ELDON, advt. specialist, educator; b. Olympia, Wash., May 28, 1930; s. Gordon Tipler and Corine Adriana (Orlebeke) M.; B.B.A., U. Wis., 1952, M.B.A., 1958, Ph.D., 1962; m. Christa Stoeter, June 29, 1957; children—Gary, Gregory, Glenn. Case officer, civilian intelligence analyst U.S. Army, Germany, 1955-57; instr. commerce Grad. Sch. Bus., U. Wis., Madison, 1958-60; instr. U. Mich., Ann Arbor, 1960-61, asst. prof., 1961-66; asso. prof. Mich. State U., 1966-70, prof. advt., 1970—, chmn. dept. advt., 1974—; vis. prof. marketing mgmt. N. European Mgmt. Inst., Oslo, Norway, 1972-73; cons. and lectr. in field. Served with U.S. Army, 1952-55. Am. Assn. Advt. Agencies fellow, 1967; Ford Found. fellow, 1964; Ford Found. fellow, 1961-62. Mem. Am. Acad. Advt. (editor Sharing for Understanding proc. ann. conf. 1977), Acad. Internat. Bus. (sec., exec. com. 1973-75), Am. Economic Assn., Am. Marketing Assn., Soc. Internat. Devel., Assn. Edn. in Journalism. Author: Instructor's Manual for International Marketing Management (with Gerald Albaum), 1971; Management of Internat. Advertising, 1966; Internat. Marketing Management, 1970 (with Gerald Album); editor: Marketing Decision Making: Strategy and Payoff, 1965; contbr. articles in field to profl. jours. Home: 1461 Cheboygan Rd Okemos MI 48864 Office: Dept Advt Mich State Univ East Lansing MI 48824

MIRALDI, FLORO DEO, physician; b. Lorain, Ohio, Mar. 21, 1931; s. John Baptista and Josephine Pia (DeArchangelis) M.; A.B., Coll. Wooster, 1953; S.B., Mass. Inst. Tech., 1953, S.M., 1955, Sc.D., 1959; M.D., Western Res. U., 1970; m. Nancy Ann Rufo, Jan. 19, 1957; 1 dau., Carla. Engr., Westinghouse Atomic Power div., Pitts., 1955; asst. prof. elec. engring. Purdue U., West Lafayette, Ind., 1959; asst. prof. nuclear engring. Case Inst. Tech., Cleve., 1964-70, prof. engring., 1970—; intern U. Hosps., Cleve., 1970-71, fellow, 1971-73, asst. prof. radiology, 1972-77, asso. prof., 1977—; chief nuclear medicine Cleve. Met. Gen. Hosp., 1973—. Mem. adv. com. on biotech. and human research NASA, 1963-65; cons. State Ohio, U.S. AEC, NASA, Argonne Nat. Lab., City of Cleve., Gen. Electric Corp., TRW Corp., Standard Oil Co. Mem. Soc. Nuclear Medicine, Am. Nuclear Soc. (pres. Cleve. chpt. 1963-64), Am. Soc. Engring. Edn., AAAS, AAUP, Cleve. Radiol. Soc., Sigma Xi. Roman Catholic. Club: Cleveland Skating. Contbr. articles to profl. jours. Patentee in field. Home: 3545 Lake Rd Sheffield Lake OH 44054 Office: Dept Radiology Univ Hosps Cleveland OH 44106

MIRENDA, JOSEPH JOHN, ednl. adminstr.; b. Milw., Jan. 30, 1935; s. John and Sarah Mirenda; B.S., U. Wis.-Milw., 1962, M.S., J 1966; Ph.D., U. Wis.-Madison, 1970. Former tchr. Whitefish Bay, Wis.; asso. dir. continuing edn. and summer sessions Marquette U., Milw.; now adult edn. program adminstr. Milw. Pub. Schs. Mem. Nat. Community Edn. Assn., Adult Edn. Assn. U.S., Milw. Council on Adult Learning, AAHPER, Phi Delta Kappa. Author: Mirenda Leisure Interest Finder, 1973; co-author: Leisure Counseling—The Milwaukee Model, A Practical Approach, 1975, The Milwaukee Leisure Counseling Model, 1975. Office: PO Drawer 10K Milwaukee WI 53201

MIRMAN, JOEL HARVEY, lawyer; b. Toledo, Dec. 3, 1941; s. Benjamin and Minnie (Pifko) M.; B.B.A., Ohio U., 1963; J.D., Ohio State U., 1966; m. Anne Mendelson; children—Lisa, Julie. Admitted to Ohio bar; partner firm Topper, Alloway, Goodman, DeLeone & Duffey, Columbus. Speaker Ohio Legal Center Inst., 1973, 74, 75, Ohio Jud. Conf., 1976. Mem. Ohio Elections Commn., 1976—. Republican. Jewish. Mem. B'nai B'rith. Address: care Topper Alloway Goodman DeLeone & Duffey 17 S High St Columbus OH 43215

MIROWITZ, LEO ISAAK, aerospace exec.; b. Mannheim, Germany, Dec. 11, 1923; s. Harry David and Golda (Schweitzer) M.; came to U.S., 1938, naturalized, 1944; B.S. in Elec. Engring., Washington U., St. Louis, 1944, M.S., 1957; m. Adele Shirley Levin, Oct. 12, 1947; children—Howard D., Sheldon P., Lisa S. Dynamics engr. McDonnell Aircraft Co., St. Louis, 1946-51, chief aeroelasticity group, 1951-54, project engr. structural dynamics, 1954-58, chief structural dynamics engr., 1958-64, mgr. advanced missiles programs, 1964-65, program mgr. Mars Lander-Voyager, 1965-68, dir. planetary programs, 1968-69; dir. advanced tech. McDonnell Douglas Astronautics Co., St. Louis, 1969-74, dir. diversification programs, 1974-75, v.p. corporate diversification, 1975—; pres. Vitek Systems, Inc., 1977—. Mem. Nat. Adv. Com. Aeros. subcom. vibration and flutter, 1957-60. Served to 1st lt. AUS, 1944-46. Asso. fellow Am. Inst. Aeros. and Astronautics (mem. spacecraft com. 1968-70; sect. chmn. 1958); mem. Aircraft Industries Assn. (mem. aeroelasticity panel 1954-64). Mem. B'nai B'rith (pres. 1957, council pres. 1963). Home: 40 Country Fair Creve Coeur MO 63141 Office: PO Box 516 St Louis MO 63166

MIRZA, DAVID BROWN, economist, educator; b. Dayton, Ohio, Feb. 28, 1936; s. Youel Benjamin and Althea (Brown) M.; A.B., Earlham Coll., 1958; Ph.D., Northwestern U., 1973; m. Leona Lousin, June 20, 1965; 1 dau., Sara Anush. Instr. econs. Dartmouth, 1961-63, Kalamazoo Coll., 1963-69; asst. prof. econs., dir. Inst. Futures Trading Loyola U., Chgo., 1969—; lectr. in field. Home: 795 Lincoln Av Winnetka IL 60093 Office: Loyola U 820 N Michigan Ave Chicago IL 60611

MISEMER, PAUL MAX, pharm. co. exec.; b. Springfield, Mo., Sept. 19, 1944; s. Beauford Lee and Georgia Maxine; B.S. in Bus. and Accounting, S.W. Mo. State U., 1966; m. Lucinda Irene, June 10, 1967; children—Todd Paul, Michael Loren. Salesman, Ayerst Labs., Inc., Columbia, Mo., 1969-71, Bomiseco Labs., Inc., Oklahoma City, Okla., 1971-76; v.p. ops. Bomiseco Labs., Inc., Springfield, 1976—, also dir; gen. partner Misemer and Assos., mgmt. and investment cons., Springfield; dir. Safe & Save Generics, Inc.; Drug Travelers Assn. (Okla., Mo.). Methodist. Home: 1732 E Carleton St Springfield MO 65807 Office: 1241 E Republic Rd Springfield MO 65807

MISHLER, ERNEST GERALD, dentist; b. Shipshewana, Ind., Apr. 8, 1919; s. Truman Jay and Nona (Yoder) M.; student Goshen Coll., 1937-38, 46-47; D.D.S., Northwestern U., 1951; m. Doris Laurine Unzicker, July 25, 1942; children—Judy (Mrs. W. David Otto), Julia, Jeffrey. Gen. practice dentistry, Greenwood, Ind., 1953—; dir. Greenwood Bldg. & Loan Assn. Bd. dirs. Crossroads Am. council Boy Scouts Am., 1969—, v.p., 1973-75, dist. chmn., 1970-72, advancement chmn., 1972, mem. exec. com., 1972—, mem. nat. council; bd. dirs. Johnson County United Fund, 1960-68, Johnson County Assn. Retarded Children, 1972, trustee Greenwood Pub. Library, 1966—, pres., 1970. Served with AUS, 1942-46, 50-53. Decorated Bronze Star medal, Commendation medal; recipient distinguished service award Greenwood C. of C., 1971, Greenwood Man of the Year award, 1972, Sagamore of the Wabash, 1972. Fellow Am. Coll. Dentists (section chmn. 1970); mem. Am., Ind., Indpls. dental assns., Am. Prosthodontic Soc., Ind. Acad. Dental Practice Adminstrn. (pres. 1966), John W. Geller Dental Research Group, Greenwood C. of C. (bd. dirs. i968-71). Am. Legion, Fraternal Order of Police, Psi Omega. Republican. Methodist (lay del. annual conf. 1967—, trustee 1960-64). Elk, Rotarian. Home: 284 Sunset Blvd Greenwood IN 46142 Office: 370 S Madison Ave Greenwood IN 46142

MISHRA, VISHWA MOHAN, educator; b. Hilsa, Patna, India, Nov. 12, 1937; s. Pandit Sheo Nath and Pandita Nitya (Rani) M.; came to U.S., 1956, naturalized, 1964; B.A. with honors, Patna U., 1954, M.A., 1956; M.A., U. Ga., 1958; Ph.D., U. Minn., 1968; m. Sally Schroeder, June 18, 1977; children—Aneil Kumar, Allan Kumar, Anand Kumar. Staff reporter, Hindusthan Samachar, Ltd., Patna, India, 1950-56; exec. dir. India for Christ, Inc., Mpls., 1960-64; research fellow, instr. Sch. Journalism and Mass Communication, U. Minn., 1964-68; asst. prof. U. Okla., 1968-69; asso. prof. Mich. State U., East Lansing, 1969—; dir. market and communication research Panax Corp., East Lansing, 1975-76; adminstrv. asst., research cons. to pres. Lansing (Mich.) Community Coll., 1976—. Recipient NSF award, 1969; Bihar Rastrabhasha Parishad Lit. award, 1st prize, 1954. Mem. Am. Mgmt. Assn., Am. Statis. Assn., Am. Pub. Opinion Research Council, Newspaper Research Council, Radio and TV News Dir.'s Assn., Assn. for Edn. in Journalism, Internat. Communication Assn., Am. Platform Assn., Smithsonian Instn. Assos., Kappa Tau Alpha, Sigma Delta Chi. Clubs: East Lansing Rotary, University. Author: Communication and Modernization in Urban Slums, 1972; The Basic News Media and Techniques, 1972; also monographs. Contbr. articles to scholastic jours. Home: 2176 Donovan Pl Okemos MI 48864 Office: Office of President Lansing Community Coll 419 N Capitol Ave Lansing MI 48901

MISKA, LEONARD FRANK, bus. exec.; b. Chgo., Sept. 19, 1921; s. Joseph L. and Rose (Grabinowski) M.; student Western State Coll., 1941-42, Inter-Am. Coll., Saltello, Mex., 1955, U. Chgo., 1956. Pres., Hartford Mortgage Corp.; former pres. Southtown Music Corp.; dir. 1st Nat. Bank Oak Lawn (Ill.). Pub., Continental Rev. Mag., Chgo., 1965-67; pres. Museum Publs. of Am., Inc. Chmn., Pan Am. Games, 1959; mem. S.W. Real Estate Bd., Chgo., 1965—, chmn. Chgo. housing com.; commr. Chgo. Commn. Human Relations, 1967—, chmn. health com., 1968—; commr. Police Study Com. Chgo., 1966; Chgo. Area chmn. S.W. Chgo. council Boy Scouts Am., 1968, 71; sponsor Lyric Opera Guild; chmn. Community Fund-ARC Appeal, 1958; mem. S. Side Planning Commn., 1961—; del. 6th Ill. Constl. Conv., 1969-70; bd. dirs. St. Joseph's Home of Friendless, Chgo., 1963, Richard J. Daley Coll., 1971, Ivy Cancer Research Found., 1971—, Adult Edn. Council Greater Chgo.; trustee St. Procopius Coll., Lisle, Ill., 1960—, Chgo. Youth Centers, 1967—; pres. Back-of-the-Yards Bus. Men's Assn., 1965—; chmn. Latin Am. Trade and Promotion Center, Chgo., 1967; mem. pres.'s adv. bd. DePaul U., 1966. Served with AUS, 1942. Decorated knight of St. John; knight Merit et Devouement Francais. Mem. Chgo. Council Fgn. Relations, Chgo. Chamber Commerce and Industry, Archer-Brighton Park Bus. Men's Assn., Hispanic Soc. (dir. Met. Chgo.), Alliance Française, Izaak Walton League Am., Balzekas Mus., English-Speaking Union, Chgo. Opera Studio, Art Inst. Chgo. (life mem.), Ill. Opera Guild, Am. Legion, Friends of Austria, Am. Knights Assn. (chancellor 1966—), Czechoslovak Savs. and Loan League. Democrat. Clubs: Elks,

Kiwanis, Lions, K.C., Chgo. Athletic, Chgo. Swedish, Chgo. Yacht, Belmont Yacht, South Shore Yacht, Variety, Barclay, Whitehall, Arts (Chgo.). Author: Police and Public—A Critique and a Program, 1967; contbg. editor Real Estate Advertiser. Home: 1925 W Garfield Blvd Chicago IL 60636 Office: 2108 W 51st St Chicago IL 60609

MISRA, PRABHAT KUMAR, food and feed co. exec.; b. Puri, India, Oct. 10, 1940; s. Nilakantha and Ashalata (Mohapatra) M.; came to U.S., 1963, naturalized, 1975; B.S. in Mech. Engring., Univ. Coll. Engring., 1962; M.S. in Indsl. Engring., Kans. State U., 1965, Ph.D. in Indsl. Engring., 1971; m. Nirmala Kumari Acharya, June 4, 1963; children—Sanjukta, Susan. Indsl. engr. St. Louis-San Francisco Ry., Springfield, Mo., 1965-67; sr. ops. research analyst Ralston Purina Co., St. Louis, 1967-68, cons., 1972-73, supr. mgmt. sci., 1974-76, mgr. planning systems, 1976—; asst. prof. bus. mgmt. Southwestern State U., Marshall, Minn., 1971-72, asso. prof., 1972-73, chmn. dept., 1972-73; asso. prof. Sch. Bus., U. Mo., St. Louis. Mem. adv. council Lindenwood Coll., St. Louis, 1975—; bd. dirs. S.W. Health Care Center, Marshall, Minn., 1972-73. HEW grantee, 1972-73. Mem. Am. Inst. Indsl. Engrs. (sr.), Inst. Mgmt. Sci., Planning Exec. Inst., Phi Kappa Phi, Alpha Pi Mu. Club: Ballwin Golf. Contbr. articles on invariant imbedding to profl. jours. Home: 6 Glenhaven Dr St Louis MO 63122 Office: Checkerboard Sq 4T St Louis MO 63188

MISRA, RAJENDRA KUMAR, psychologist; b. Delhi, India, Sept. 7, 1936; s. Chandra Bishal and Dharmeshwari Bai (Misra) M.; came to U.S., 1971; B.A. with honours, Lko U., 1957, M.A., 1958; D.Phil. in Psychology, Allahabad U., 1967; m. Alice Margaret Lyall, June 23, 1962; 1 dau., Anita. Research asst., then asst. prof. psychology Lko U., 1958-62; research officer Indian Internat. Center, New Delhi, 1962-63; lectr. psychology Allahabad U., 1963-67, Jodhpur U., 1967-69; research officer S.R. Center Indsl. Relations, New Delhi, 1969-71; dir. research and info. Community Action Against Addiction, Cleve., 1972-73; exec. dir. Glenville Community Mental Health Center, Cleve., 1973—; fieldwork supr. Cleve. State U.; mgmt. trainer, cons. psychologist. Mem. Am. Psychol. Assn., Internat. Assn. Applied Psychology, Internat. Assn. Cross-Cultural Psychology. Author: (in Hindi) Psychology Measurement, 1971; co-author Human Aspects of Shift Work (Escort Book award 1971), 1971. Home: 2007 E 115th St Cleveland OH 44106 Office: 900 E 105th St Cleveland OH 44108

MISTELSKE, EMERSON WARREN, cons.; b. Vergas, Minn., Feb. 11, 1924; s. Joe Albert and Anna Margaret (Trautner) M.; B.S., U. Minn., 1950, postgrad., 1967-71; m. Margene Marie Pekas, Oct. 13, 1950; children—John Michael, Mary Helen, Patrice Marie. Instr., U. Minn., Morris, 1950-53; plant mgr. Gedney Pickle Co., Chaska, Minn., 1953-55; tech. dir. Budlong Co., Jewel Tea Co., Chgo., 1955-62; research and devel. dir. Stoehmann Bros. Co., Williamsport, Pa., 1962-67; dir. engring. Land O Lakes, Mpls., 1968-72; partner, Environmental Process, Inc., Mpls., 1972—. Tchr. water safety, life guarding and swimming A.R.C., 1942-57. Served with USAAF, 1942-46; ETO. Mem. Am. Inst. Chem. Engrs., Reserve Officers Assn. Home: 1410 Hartford Ave St Paul MN 55116 Office: 1220 Glenwood Ave Minneapolis MN 55405

MITCHELL, A. BEN, lawyer; b. Mt. Vernon, Ill., June 15, 1941; s. Q.B. and Harriet A. (Young) M.; B.S., U. Tulsa, 1963; J.D., U. Ill., 1966; m. Cynthia Jane Glenn, Nov. 21, 1962; children—Jamie Denise, Mark Glenn. Admitted to Ill. bar, 1966; mem. firm Craig & Craig, 1966-77, partner, 1969-77; partner firm Campbell, Furnall, Moore & Jacobsen, Mt. Vernon, Ill., 1977—; dir. Edward E. Rue, Inc.; sec. Behimer & Kissner, Inc.; sec. Mitchell Energy Enterprises, Inc. Trustee 1st Meth. Ch., 1977—; dir. Meth. Children's Home; pres. Good Samaritan Hosp. Planning Bd., 1976-77; mem. Mt. Vernon Sch. Dist. Bd., 1972—, pres., 1977. Mem. Ill. State, Jefferson County bar assns., Mt. Vernon C. of C. (dir.). Clubs: Rotary, Elks. Home: 1801 Warren St Mt Vernon IL 62864 Office: 1007 Broadway Mt Vernon IL 62864

MITCHELL, ARNOLD MICHAEL, ophthalmologist; b. Cleve., Feb. 21, 1930; s. Irving and Elizabeth (Switky) M.; student Case Western Res. U., 1948-49; B.S., Ohio State U., 1952, M.S., 1954, M.D., 1957; m. Jean Ann Fuldauer, June 8, 1952; children—David, Richard. Intern Mt. Sinai Hosp., Cleve., 1957-58, now sr. attending ophthalmologist; resident in ophthalmology Univ. Hosp., Cleve., 1958-61, now asst. ophthalmologist; attending ophthalmologist VA Hosp., Cleve., Highland View Hosp., Hill Crest Hosp.; asst. clin. prof. ophthalmology Case Western Res. U. Sch. Medicine, Cleve. Served to capt. M.C. AUS, 1961-62. Diplomate Am. Bd. Ophthalmology. Fellow Am. Acad. Ophthalmology, Am. Coll. Surgeons; mem. A.M.A., Ohio Med. Assn., Cleve. Acad. Medicine, Cleve. Ophthal. Soc. (sec. 1968-69), Phi Delta Epsilon, Alpha Omega Alpha. Contbr. articles to profl. jours. Home: 5 Hunting Hollow Dr Cleveland OH 44124 Office: 5 Severance Circle Cleveland OH 44118

MITCHELL, CHARLES MONT, real estate broker; b. New Madrid, Mo., Dec. 21, 1924; s. Clay A. and Lucille P. (Proffit) M.; grad. high sch.; m. Mary Etta Cravens, Apr. 26, 1948; children—Mary Jane, Charles Mont, Jr., Theresa Carolyn. Owner, Charles M. Mitchell, Realtor, Sikeston, Mo., 1942-44; parts mgr. Mitchell-Sharp Chevrolet Co., Sikeston, 1944-62; owner, mgr. Sikeston Fruit & Produce Co., 1962-75; real estate broker, Sikeston, 1973—. Mem. Sikeston Planning and Zoning Commn., 1954-59; mem. Sikeston Housing Authority, 1959-75; sec., treas. Mo. Real Estate Polit. Action Com., 1971-75; chmn. Sikeston Pub. Housing Authority, 1972-75. Named Sikeston Jr. C. of C. Man of Year, 1956. Mem. Sikeston Bd. Realtors (pres. 1964-66), Mo. Real Estate Assn. (state v.p. 1970-73), Nat. Assn. Realtors, Nat. Inst. Real Estate Bd., Am. Inst. Real Estate Appraisers, Sikeston C. of C. (dir. 1967-68, man of year 1974). Democrat. Roman Catholic. Elk, Lion (dist. gov. 1965-66). Home: 116 W Wakefield St Sikeston MO 63801 Office: 305 Tanner St Sikeston MO 63801

MITCHELL, CHARLES RAYMOND, dentist; b. Chgo., Mar. 21, 1937; s. Charles R. and Rita (Cagney) M.; student St. Procopius Coll., 1954-57; D.D.S., Marquette U., 1961; m. Arlene Thollander, Sept. 6, 1958; children—Stephen, Edward, Cathy. Gen. practice dentistry, Downers Grove, Ill., 1963—; chmn. bd. Grove Dental Assos., P.C.; mng. partner Grove Enterprises, Grove Investments Nymits Enterprises; partner Mid-Continent Enterprises, Ltd.; pres. Arlu Enterprises, Inc.; v.p. Health Care Systems, Inc.; v.p., dir. Asso. Health Services, Inc.; v.p. Asso. Dental Consultants, Inc.; primary developer Greenbriar Center, Downers Grove, Bolingbrook (Ill.) Med. and Dental Center. dir. Am. Nat. Bank, Downers Grove. Chief dental staff Hinsdale (Ill.) Hosp., 1969-70; cons. Dental Care Plan Com. Mem. adv. com. Downers Grove Hosp., 1966-69; mem. pres.'s adv. council Ill. Benedictine Coll., 1971—; adv. com. Loyola U. Dental Sch., 1973-75; mem. vocat. adv. commn. High Sch. Dist. 99, 1971-72. Bd. dirs. Downers Grove Combined Community Appeal, 1969-71, Indian Boundary YMCA, 1970-72; vice chmn. Downers Grove Youth Devel. Service, 1973-74; chmn. bd. dirs., pres. Orchard Brook Home Assn., Downers Grove, 1969-70. Served to capt. USAF, 1961-63. Fellow Acad. Gen. Dentistry (v.p. Chgo. chpt. 1971-72, pres. Ill. chpt. 1972-74, nat. dir. 1975—); mem. Am. Dental Assn. (chmn. preventive dentistry 1975 gen. meeting), Ill., Chgo., West Suburban dental socs., Midway Acad. Dentists (pres. 1966-67), Am. Soc. Geriatric Dentistry, Am. Soc. Preventive Dentistry, Am. Acad. Hosp. Dentists, Far West Dental Study Club (pres. 1970-71), Fedn. Dentaire Internationale, Inst. for Advanced Dental Research, Am. (bd. dirs. 1973-75), North-Central (bd. dirs. 1974-75) acads. dental group practice, Ill. Dental Service Corp. (chmn. com. to study preventive dental programs), Legis. Interest Com. Ill. Dentists, Marquette U. Dental Sch. Alumni Assn. (class agt. 1971-73), Ill. Acad. Dental Practice Adminstrn., Pierre Fouchard Acad., Independents Dental Group Chgo., Downers Grove C. of C. (dir. 1969-72, sr. v.p. 1972-73), Psi Omega, K.C. Home: 3636 Quince Ct Downers Grove IL 60515 Office: 6800 Main St Downers Grove IL 60515

MITCHELL, DAVE CAMERON, educator; b. Licking, Mo., July 4, 1908; s. Phlander Eli and Jennie Belle (Cameron) M.; student U. Okla., 1960, S.W. Mo. State U., 1929-30, U. Mo., 1927-31; B.S., Lincoln U., 1967; m. Mabel Leon Kirkman, Oct. 22, 1931; children—Jane Mitchell McKinney, Sue Mitchell Steward, Terry. Tchr. Mooney Hollow, Mo., 1935-37; dep. clk. Recorder Office and timekeeper Workers Progress Assistance, Licking, 1937; pumper oil fields Coast Supply Co., Long Beach, Calif., 1937-42; independent ice dealer, Long Beach, 1942-47; farmer, cattleman Licking, 1953—; tchr. Plato R #5, Licking, 1953-72, prin., 1954-58. Vice pres., bd. dirs. Pub. Rural Water Dist. #4, Licking, 1967-73; county supt. Texas County (Mo.), 1974—, pub. adminstr., 1976—. Sherrill twp. committeeman 1968—, central com. treas., 1972—. Bd. dirs., Triple A., Houston, Mo., 1933-34. Mem. Texas County Tchrs. Assn. Mason. Address: PO Box 717 Licking MO 65542

MITCHELL, DELMER ROY, JR., lawyer; b. Johnston City, Ill., Sept. 21, 1941; s. Delmer Roy and Rose M. (Fletcher) M.; B.A., So. Ill. U., 1963; J.D., U. Ill., 1966; m. Barbara Jane Barham, Aug. 24, 1963; children—Stacy Lynn, Thomas Barham. Admitted to Ill. bar, 1966; law clk., investigator for John Alan Appleman, Urbana, Ill., 1964-66; mem. firm Meyer & Meyer, Belleville, 1966-69, Schmiedeskamp, Jenkins, Robertson & House, Quincy, 1969-71; partner Schmiedeskamp, Robertson, House, Neu & Mitchell, 1971—. Speaker, lectr. various civic and profl. orgns. Mem. adv. bd. project Youth and Soc. in Ill., Ill. Law Enforcement Commn., 1972—; volunteer atty. Acid Rescue, Inc., Quincy, Ill. Bd. dirs. Adams County Children and Family Services, Adams County Econ. Stabilization Com., Adams County Cancer Soc., 1969-72; adv. bd. Saukee Area council Explorers Scouts Am., 1971-74. Mem. Am., Ill. (mem. tort section council 1971—), St. Clair County (sec.-treas. 1967-69), Adams County (law day chmn. 1971-72) bar assns., Am., Ill. trial lawyers assns., Nat. Def. Inst., Nat. Legal Aid and Defenders Assn., Phi Alpha Delta. Mem. Christian Ch. Rotarian (com. chmn. 1972—). Club: Quincy Country. Home: 1 Briar Ln Quincy IL 62301 Office: 232 N 6th St Quincy IL 62301

MITCHELL, DOW PENROSE, artist; b. Winnipeg, Man., Can., Nov. 28, 1915; s. Frank Henry and Frances Fraser (Penrose) M.; B.F.A., Art Inst. Chgo., 1949; M.A., Bradley U., 1950. Jewelry designer, salesman Henry Birks & Sons, Vancouver, B.C., Can., 1934-42; prodn. illustrator Boeing Aircraft Canada, 1942-45; mem. faculty Bradley U., Peoria, Ill., 1950—, prof. art, 1969—, chmn. Sch. Art, 1969; founder art program Peoria State Hosp., 1958; group shows: Weyhe Gallery, N.Y.C., Gilman Gallery, Chgo.; represented in permanent collections: USIS cultural div., Library of Congress, Denison U., Granville, Ohio, U. Kans. Mus. Art, N.Y. State U. Coll. at Potsdam. Home: Box 65 Groveland IL 61535 Office: Dept Art Bradley Univ Peoria IL 61631

MITCHELL, FREDERICK JOSEPH, air force officer, scientist; b. Buzzards Bay, Mass., Jan. 7, 1937; s. George Herbert and Yvonne Rita (Barbeau) M.; B.S. in Bacteriology, U. Mass., 1959, M.S. in Microbiology, 1968. Commd. officer USAF, 1960, advanced through grades to lt. col.; stationed Nouasseur Air Base, Morocco, 1960-62, Whiteman AFB, Mo., 1963-66; mem. lunar quarantine team Apollos 11, 12, 13, 14 lunar receiving lab. Manned Spacecraft Center NASA, Houston, 1969-71; asso. prof. aerospace studies Tex. A. and M. U., College Station, after 1971; now configuration mgr. F-16 System Program Officer Wright-Patterson AFB. Contbg. author: Proc. of the Second Lunar Science Conference, vol. 3, 1971. Home: 515 Towncrest Dr Xenia OH 45385 Office: ASD/YPCB Wright Patterson AFB OH 45433

MITCHELL, GEORGE TRICE, physician; b. Marshall, Ill., Jan. 20, 1914; s. Roscoe Addison and Alma (Trice) M.; B.S., Purdue U., 1935, postgrad., 1935-36; M.D., George Washington U., 1940; m. Mildred Aletha Miller, June 21, 1941; children—Linda Sue, Mary Kathryn. Intern Meth. Hosp., Indpls., 1940-41; practice medicine, Marshall, 1946—; mem. courtesy staff Union, Regional hosps., Terre Haute, Ind.; clin. asso. Sch. Basic Med. Sci. U. Ill. Chmn. bd., dir First Nat. Bank, Marshall. Mem., pres. Marshall Community Unit Sch. Bd., 1955-67; coroners physician, Clark County, Ill., 1958—; mem. Bd. Health, 1946—; mem. City Planning Commn., 1953—; chmn. county med. adv. com. Ill. Dept. Public Aid, 1947-63, mem. state med. adv. com., 1965—. Mem. adv. council premedicine Eastern Ill. U., 1965-69. Alt. del. Republican Conv., 1968, del., 1972; trustee Lakeland Jr. Coll. Served from 1st lt. to lt. col., USAAF, 1941-45. Fellow Am. Acad. Family Physicians; mem. Clark County, Ill. med. socs., AMA, Aesculapian Soc. of Wabash Valley (pres. 1965), Clark County Hist. Soc. (pres. 1968-70). Republican. Methodist. Mason (32 deg., Shriner). Home: RFD 2 Marshall IL 62441 Office: 410 N 2d St Marshall IL 62441

MITCHELL, GEORGIA BONE, physician; b. Nashville; d. James Asbury and Ethel (Bell) Bone; B.A., Fisk U., 1947; M.A., Middlebury Coll., 1948; M.D., Meharry Med. Coll., 1958; student McGill U., Montreal, Que., 1947, U. Colo., 1966; spl. study internal medicine, Nairobi, Kenya, East Africa; m. William A. Mitchell, Aug. 23, 1952; 1 dau., Anne Elizabeth. Intern, St. Mary Mercy Hosp., Gary, Ind., 1958-59; practice medicine, Gary, 1959—; mem. staff St. Mary Mercy Hosp.; mem. staff, sec. Meth. Hosp. Asst. leader Girl Scouts U.S.A., Gary, 1964—. Bd. dirs. Gary Mental Health Center. Mem. AMA, Ind. State, Lake County med. assns., Am. Med. Womens Assn., Am. Assn. Family Practice, Jack and Jill of Am., Inc., Alpha Omega Alpha, Phi Beta Kappa, Delta Sigma Theta. Episcopalian. Home: 8733 Lake Shore Dr Gary IN 46403 Office: 1706 Broadway Gary IN 46407

MITCHELL, GLENFORD ECKLETON, assn. exec.; b. St. Elizabeth, Jamaica, W.I., Mar. 3, 1935; s. Hubert and Mabel (Shaw) M.; A.B., Shaw U., Raleigh, N.C., 1960; M.S. in Journalism, Columbia, 1962; m. Bahia Deloomy, June 27, 1972; 1 son, Denis Harrington. Reporter, The Carolinian, Raleigh, 1957-60; exec. sec. Maryknoll Book Club (N.Y.), 1962-63, also asst. editorial dir. publs., 1962-63; asst. editor Africa Report mag., Washington, 1963-67; instr. English, Howard U., 1966-67; dir. dept. youth and coll. activities Nat. Spiritual Assembly of Baha'i U.S., Wilmette, Ill., 1967-68, mng. editor World Order mag., 1967—, sec. Nat. Spiritual Assembly, 1968—; trustee Baha'i Pub. Trust, Wilmette, 1968—; instr. English, Upward Bound Program, Ind. State U., Terre Haute, summer 1967. Mem. Wilmette Human Relations Com., 1969—. Bd. dirs. Am. Nat. Inst. for Social Advancement. Mem. Chgo. Headline Club, Soc. Profl. Journalists Sigma Delta Chi, Alpha Kappa Mu. Rotarian. Author chpt. and editor: (with William Peace) The Angry Black South, 1962; (with Daniel C. Jordan) What Is Race, 1967. Home: 536 Sheridan Rd Wilmette IL 60091 Office: 112 Linden Ave Wilmette IL 60091

MITCHELL, HOBART THEOPHILUS, JR., real estate appraiser; b. Mpls., Sept. 2, 1927; s. Hobart Theophilus and Beulah Ethyl (VanHook) M.; student U. Minn., grad. LaSalle Sch. Med. Tech.; children—Hobart Theophilus III, Sharon, Annette, Jacqueline. Salesman, closer Hobart T. Mitchell Co., Realtors, Mpls.; ind. fee appraiser Hobart T. Mitchell Appraisal Service, Mpls. Mem. exec. bd. Urban Concerns Workshop; past pres. Women Helping Offenders; incorporater, bd. dirs. Minorities Appraisal Assn., Inc.; bd. dirs. New Way, Inc., Turning Point, Inc.; precinct chmn. 13th Precinct, 8th Ward, Republican party; vice-chmn. minorities div. Republican party; candidate for Minn. Ho. of Reps., 1974. Mem. NAACP (exec. bd. Minn. chpt., exec. bd. Mpls. br.), Urban League Task Force (Mpls. br.). Home: 3627 Nicollet Ave S Apt 301 Minneapolis MN 55407 Office: 4253 Nicollet Ave S Minneapolis MN 55409

MITCHELL, JAMES CURTIS, educator; b. Youngstown, Ohio, July 30, 1935; s. James C. and Mildred Elizabeth (Hohlock) M.; B.S., Ohio State U., 1957, M.S., 1959, Ph.D., 1962; m. Linda Milree Raborn, Dec. 17, 1976; stepchildren—Stephanie Noelle Raborn, John Craig Raborn. Asst. prof. psychology So. Ill. U., 1962-66; asso. prof. Kans. State U., Manhattan, 1966-72, prof., 1972—. NIH grantee, 1963-66. Mem. Am. Psychol. Assn., Midwestern Psycol. Assn., AAAS, Soc. Neuroscience, Psychomic Soc., Sigma Xi. Democrat. Contbr. articles to profl. jours. Home: 2220 Seaton St Manhattan KS Office: Dept Psychology Kans State Univ Manhattan KS 66502

MITCHELL, JAMES EARL, state ednl. adminstr.; b. West Frankfort, Ill., Dec. 26, 1932; s. Vertus and Esther (Edison) M.; B.S. with honors, Southeastern La. U., 1954; M.A. (NSF fellow), La. State U., 1960; Ph.D., Iowa State U., 1968; m. Patricia Lou Robertson, Aug. 16, 1958; children—David, Patricia. Tchr., coach Goode-Barren Twp. High Sch., Sesser, Ill., 1954-55, Christopher (Ill.) High Sch., 1957-59, Herrin (Ill.) High Sch., 1960-62; tchr., coach, adminstrv. asst. Salem (Ill.) Community High Sch., 1962-64; curriculum supr. Office of State Supt., Springfield, Ill., 1964-66; dir. Midwestern States Project Iowa Dept. Pub. Instrn., Des Moines, 1966-70, asso. state supt. in planning, research and computer center, 1970-76, dep. state supt., 1976—; cons. U.S. Office of Edn., Peat, Marwick & Mitchell for information systems, Bur. Research Memphis State U., Northwest Regional Lab. Bd. dirs., nat. chmn. Com. for Evaluation and Info. Systems, 1975. Served with AUS, 1955-57. U.S. Office Edn. grantee for 13-state project for information system. Mem. Am. Assn. Sch. Adminstrs., Assn. Sch. Bus. Ofcls., N.E.A., Assn. Ednl. Data Systems, Phi Delta Kappa. Contbr. articles on program budgeting and accounting; mgmt. information systems. Home: 8508 Ridgemont Dr Des Moines IA 50322 Office: Grimes Office Bldg Des Moines IA 50319

MITCHELL, JAMES VINCENT, JR., univ. dean; b. Chgo., Oct. 20, 1925; s. James Vincent and Amanda Bertha (Hansen) M.; B.A., U. Chgo., 1948, M.A., 1950, Ph.D., 1953; m. June Anne Frary, Jan. 14, 1950 (dec. Nov. 1971); children—Steven James, Keith Vincent; m. Margaret Mary Mattern, Jan. 6, 1973. Cons., dir. testing Quincy (Ill.) Youth Devel. Commn., 1953-54; asst. prof. edn. Sch. Edn., Miami, U., Oxford, O., 1954-57; asst. prof. edn. and psychology Purdue U., W. Lafayette, Ind., 1957-59; asso. prof. ednl. psychology Coll. Edn. U. Tex., Austin, 1959-62; prof. edn. Coll. Edn. U. Rochester (N.Y.), 1962-74, prof. psychology, 1972-74, asso. dean grad. studies, 1967-74; dean Tchrs. Coll. Ball State U., Muncie, Ind., 1974—; cons. Quincy (Ill.) pub. schs., 1953-54, Brighton (N.Y.) Pub. Schs., 1965-66; mem. advisory com. Ind. Supt. Pub. Instruction, 1975-77. Served with U.S. Army, 1944-45. Decorated Purple Heart. Recipient award Student Assn. U. Tex., 1962; award Television Bur. Advt., 1961; award Grad. Students Assn., Coll. Edn., U. Rochester, 1974; Walgreen fellow U. Chgo., 1951-52; Miami U. postdoctoral research fellow, 1957; Office Edn. grantee, 1965-67. Fellow Am. Psychol. Assn.; mem. Am. Assn. Higher Edn., Am. Ednl. Research Assn., Nat. Council on Measurement in Edn., Sigma Xi, Phi Delta Kappa. Home: 2908 University St Muncie IN 47304 Office: Tchrs Coll Ball State U Muncie IN 47306

MITCHELL, JERRY DAVID, broadcaster; b. Chgo., May 12, 1925; s. Richard L. and Cora (Dutton) M.; student Northwestern U., Chgo., 1947-51; m. Cyndi Howard, Dec. 7, 1974; 1 son by previous marriage, Mark David. Radio announcer WJOB, Hammond, Ind., 1948-50, radio farm dir., 1950-55, program mgr., 1955-59; newscaster, announcer WLS, Chgo., 1959-64; announcer NBC-WMAQ and WMAQ-TV, Chgo., 1964—, TV host, producer Town and Farm and Farm Forum, WMAQ-TV farm service dir., 1967-75. Served with USNR, 1943-46. Recipient Hoover Commn. nat. broadcasters award, 1951. Mem. A.F.T.R.A., Screen Actors Guild, Nat. Assn. Farm Broadcasters. Radio editor H.F. Henrichs Publs., 1952-74. Home: 642 Sheridan Rd Evanston IL 60202 Office: NBC Merchandise Mart Chicago IL 60654

MITCHELL, MARION BONNER, educator; b. Livingston, Tex., Nov. 28, 1929; s. Jewell Clarence and Verna Lorena (Bonner) Mitchell; B.A., U. Tex., 1949, M.A., 1951; postgrad. Sorbonne, Paris, 1951-52; Ph.D., Ohio State U., 1958. Prof. French and Italian, U. Mo., Columbia, 1958—; chmn. dept. romance langs., 1972-75. Served with AUS, 1952-54. Mem. Am. Assn. Tchrs. Italian, Modern Lang. Assn., Renaissance Soc. Am., Phi Beta Kappa. Author: Les Manifestes Litteraires de la Belle Epoque, Paris, 1966; (with ANdrew C. Minor) A Renaissance Entertainment, 1968; Rome in the High Renaissance, 1973. Home: 508 S Garth Columbia MO 65201

MITCHELL, MARION MIRANDA MCWILLIAMS, social work adminstr.; b. Elgin, Ill., Nov. 14, 1914; d. Henry Edgar and Ada (Young) McWilliams; B.A., U. Chgo., 1936, M.A., 1959; m. William Henry Mitchell, Jan. 11, 1941. Caseworker Chgo. Relief Adminstrn., 1938-41; library asst. Chgo. Pub. Library, 1941-42; caseworker Chgo. Orphan Asylum, 1943-44, caseworker spl. day care project, 1947-50; probation officer Juvenile Ct. of Cook County (Ill.), 1945-47; caseworker Chgo. Child Care Soc., 1950-54, supr. child placement and adoptions, 1954-74, dir. foster care and adoption, 1974—. Chmn. Chgo. chpt. Nat. Council on Illegitimacy, 1966-70; del. to Ill. Commn. on Children, 1970, mem. subcom. on adoption, 1972, mem. com. on rights of minors, 1975—, mem. com. youth and law, 1977—; adv. com. Project on Subsidy for Black Adoptions, 1971-75; chmn. Adoption Info. Service, 1974-77. Bd. dirs. Midwest Adoption Facilitating Service, 1971-77, Council on Unplanned Pregnancy, 1971-73. Mem. Ill. Welfare Assn. (mem. study course com. 1965-77, dir. 1972—), Nat. Assn. Social Workers, Acad. Certified Social Workers, Child Care Assn. Ill. (adoption sect. 1974—), Nat. Conf. Social Welfare. Home: 7552 S Wabash Ave Chicago IL 60619 Office: 5467 S University Ave Chicago IL 60615

MITCHELL, OTIS CLINTON, JR., educator; b. Spearville, Kans., Jan. 10, 1935; s. Otis Clinton and Joeanna Esther (Woodring) M.; A.B., Wichita U., 1957; M.A., Kans. State Coll., 1960; Ph.D., U. Kans., 1964; m. Darlene Foley, Aug. 20, 1966. Instr., Wichita State U. (Kans.), 1963-64; asst. prof. U. Cin., 1964-69, asso. prof., 1969-75, prof. history, 1975—. Dir. civic com., Hidden Valley Lake, Ind., 1975. Served with CIC, AUS, 1957-59. Taft fellowship fund grantee, 1969-74. Mem. Am. Hist. Assn., A.A.U.P., Phi Alpha Theta. Author:

(with Walter Langsam) The World Since 1919, 1971; Two Totalitarians, 1965; The Western Cultural Way, 1965; A Concise History of Western Civilization, 2d edit., 1976. Editor, contbr. Nazism and the Common Man, 1972. Home: RFD 2 Hidden Valley Lake Lawrenceburg IN 47025 Office: Dept History U Cin Cinnati OH 45221

MITCHELL, RAYMOND WILLIAM, mfg. co. exec.; b. Chgo., Jan. 31, 1935; s. Raymond-William and Eve Lynn (Minney) M.; grad. DeForest Tech. Inst., Chgo., 1951; m. Nancy J. Gallol, Apr. 11, 1953; children—Deborah, Terry, Tracy. Systems engr. Sperry Univac, Chgo., 1954-63, tech. specialist, 1963-67, customer engring. br. mgr., Mpls., 1967-69, br. mgr. customer engring., Indpls., 1969—. Chmn. employment com. Greater Indpls. Progress Com., 1976—, also Indpls. Human Relations Task Force; mem. Indpls. Employment and Tng. Adv. Council, Indpls. Contract Compliance Adv. Com.; mem. Gov.'s Youth Com. (Ind.); mem. career edn. coop. action com. Indpls. Pub. Sch. System; bd. dirs. Center for Leadership Devel., Indpls. Urban League. Served with USN, 1952-54. Mem. Indpls. C. of C. (vice chmn. urban affairs council), Soc. Advancement Mgmt. (exec. v.p. Indpls. chpt.), Urban League, World Future Soc., Indpls. Mus. Art, Acad. Polit. Sci., Nat. Soc. Lit. and Arts, Econs. Club Indpls. Home: 8022 Taunton Rd Indianapolis IN 46260 Office: 3500 W DePauw Blvd Suite 3020 Indianapolis IN 46268

MITCHELL, SAMUEL JOHNSON, real estate broker; b. Lansing, Mich., Oct. 4, 1934; s. James Lee and Katherine Kennedy (Johnson) M.; B.A., Mich. State U., 1958; m. Karen Francis Olson, Aug. 16, 1958; children—Linda, Samuel Johnson, Michael. With Chamberlain Co. real estate, Birmingham, Mich., 1959—, salesman real estate, 1959-64, mgr. br., 1964-67, gen. sales mgr., 1967-70, v.p., 1970—; guest speaker U. Mich. Real Estate Clinic, 1967. Candidate Certified Comml. Investment Program, 1974. Chmn. Birmingham Mich. Week, 1970; chmn. bd. mgmt. Birmingham YMCA, 1972. Served with AUS, 1954-56. Recipient Realtor of Year award Birmingham Bloomfield Bd. Realtors, 1971, Vol. Leadership award Gov. William G. Milliken, 1970. Mem. Birmingham Bloomfield C. of C. (pres. 1972), Gamma Psi, Sigma Chi. Methodist (bd. ofcls. 1967-70). Clubs: Mich. State U. Alumni of Oakland Country; Orchard Lake Country; Optimist (pres. Birmingham 1975). Home: 1001 Fairfax St Birmingham MI 48009 Office: 975 S Hunter Blvd Birmingham MI 48011

MITCHELL, STEPHEN CONNALLY, engr.; b. Albuquerque, Sept. 27, 1943; s. Claude Stephen and Alma Nelle (Cashion) M.; B.C.E., U. N.Mex., 1966, M.C.E., 1968; M.B.A., U. Chgo., 1974; m. Cynthia Eugenia McDonell, June 8, 1968; 1 son, Graham. Research asst. Civil Engring. Research Facility, N.Mex., 1964-68; engr. Inland Steel Co., East Chicago, Ind., 1968; sr. soils engr. Westenhoff & Novick, Cons. Engrs., Chgo., 1968; project mgr. Bauer Engring., Chgo., 1972-74, asst. dir. planning, 1974-75; mng. asso., mgr. bus. devel. Archtl./Engring. Group, Lester B. Knight & Assos., 1975—. Served to 1st lt. C.E., U.S. Army, 1969-72. Mem. ASCE, Soc. Am. Mil. Engrs., Sigma Tau. Home: 208 W St Paul St Chicago IL 60614 Office: 549 W Randolph St Chicago IL 60606

MITCHELL, STEPHEN KENT, banker; b. Evanston, Ill., June 16, 1945; s. Carroll Ray and Alma Edith (Wadsack) M.; B.S. in Finance, So. Ill. U., 1967; m. Nancy Jane Hill, Aug. 8, 1975; children—Donald Scott, Amy, Mark. Nat. Bank Examiner Washington, 1967-75; v.p. 1st. Nat. Bank Decatur (Ill.), 1975—; mem. com. Electronic Funds (Ill.). Republican. Presbyterian. Clubs: Decatur, S. Side Country, Racquet. Office: 130 N Water St Decatur IL 62523

MITCHELL, THELMA KATHERINE WOODLEY, coll. educator; b. Gloversville, N.Y., Sept. 22, 1931; d. Harold F. and Thelma Katherine (Goines) Woodley; B.S., Wayne State U., 1968; M.A. in Guidance, Counseling, Psychology, U. Mich., 1970, also postgrad.; m. Robert F. Mitchell, Aug. 25, 1951; children—Robert, Dana. Auditor, exec. offices, Singer Sewing Machine Co., Detroit, 1951-53; bookkeeper Douglas Gregory Inc. Detroit, 1954—; tchr. Detroit Bd. Edn., 1968-77; adj. prof. psychology Wayne County Community Coll., Detroit, 1977—; dir. St. Francis de Sales Sch. Hostess, Soc. Internat. Emergency Energy Crisis W. German Delegation; mem. Heartline Martin Luther King Found. Fund; chairperson Fine Arts Detroit Symphony Concert; treas. Links Inc. Recipient awards Mayor Coleman Young outstanding civic, culture contbn. to City of Detroit. Mem. U. Mich., Wayne State U. alumni assns., U. Detroit Parents Assn., NAACP, Am. Profl. Guidance Assn., U. Mich. Assn. Counselor Edn., Suprv. Vocat. Guidance Assn., Mich. Assn. Non White Concern (life), Nat., Mich. vocat. guidance personnel assns., Mich., Am. personnel & guidance assns. Clubs: Barrister's Wives (most outstanding achievement award 1976, dir. Central Regional Nat. Chapters), Archousa-Boule. Office: 515 W Larned St Detroit MI 48226

MITCHELL, THORAL J., phys. therapist; b. Bryan, Ohio, Dec. 22, 1931; s. Thoral T. and Marjorie Thompson (Kimpel) M.; B.S., Bowling Green State U., 1953; Frank E. Bunts phys. therapy certificate, 1955; M.S., Western Res. U., Cleve., 1959; m. Virginia Marie Rini, Dec. 27, 1958; children—Tracy Ann, Thoral David. Asst. chief phys. therapist St. Alexis Hosp., Cleve., 1956-57; dir. phys. therapy Mt. Sinai Hosp., Cleve., 1957-59; pres. Mitchell-Zoltowicz & Assos., Inc., Cleve., 1959—; cons. on phys. therapy nursing homes; tchr. Ohio Podiatry Coll., 1968-71. Fund raising chmn. Valley YMCA, 1973, bd. dirs., 1971-74. Served with AUS, 1953-55. Mem. Am. Phys. Therapy Assn. (dir. N.E. Dist. Ohio, treas. self-employed sect.). Mem. Christian Ch. Clubs: Pine Lake Trout, Rock Creek Raquet. Contbr. chpt. to book, 1971. Patentee arm therapist. Home: 34235 Sherbrook St Solon OH 44139 Office: 21100 Southgate Park Cleveland OH 44137

MITCHELL, WALTER ADRIAN, psychologist; b. Norwalk, Conn., Dec. 16, 1947; s. Joseph Lawrence and Eliza Jane (Smith) M.; B.A., Whitman Coll., 1971; M.A., Western Carolina U., 1974. Intern, Blue Ridge Community Mental Health Center, Ashville, N.C., 1973; clin. psychologist Northwest Community Mental Health Center, Lima, Ohio, 1974—, chmn. Utilization and Peer Rev. Com., 1976—. Mem. Am. Psychol. Assn., Biofeedback Soc. Ohio, Gestalt Inst. Cleve.

MITCHELL, WAYNE ANTOINE, educator; b. Tracy, Minn., Mar. 19, 1936; s. Lloyd Benton and Marie Susan (Antoine) M.; B.A., Augustana Coll., 1958; M.Mus., U. Colo., 1965; postgrad. U. Iowa, 1972-73, summers 1970-75; m. Miriam Allene Tollefson, June 21, 1959; children—Phillip Paul, David Kirk. High sch. choral dir. Tracy, Minn., 1958-66; asso. prof. Westmar Coll., LeMars, Iowa, 1966—, voice prof., 1966—, madrigal dir., 1966—, coll. chapel choir dir., 1966—. Concert artist, opera, recitalist, including Messiah, Brahms Requiem Sioux City Symphony, oratorios, numerous maj. opera roles, including La Traviata, The Consul, Magic Flute, Gianni Schichi, Mice and Men, Madame Butterfly, Amahl and the Night Visitors, The Crucible, Albert Herring, La Boheme, Die Fledermaus; premier as Christian in Cyrano de Bergerac; mus. dir. mus. theater and opera including Most Happy Fella, H.M.S. Pinafore, Marriage of Figaro, The Devil and Daniel Webster; baritone soloist 96th Messiah Festival, Bethany Coll., Lindsborg, Kans.; dir. Pub. Opera Co., Arts Councils NW Iowa; soloist oratorio Child of Our Time; lectr. on vocal pedagogy. Bd. dirs. LeMars (Ia.) Arts Council, 1973—. Ia. Arts Council grantee, 1974-75. Mem. A.A.U.P., Music Educators Nat. Conf., Nat. Assn. Tchrs. Singing, Am. Choral Dirs. Assn. Lutheran (bd. dirs. 1968-71). Rotarian (pres. 1970). Home: 40 8th St SW LeMars IA 51031

MITCHELL, WILLIAM HENRY, ret. state ofcl.; b. Macon, Ga., Mar. 18, 1913; s. Charles J. and Anna Mae (Smith) M.; B.A., Fisk U., 1941; m. Marion M. McWilliams, Jan. 11, 1941. Library asst. Chgo. Pub. Library, 1937-43; lab. asst. for atomic bomb Manhattan Dist. Project of Metall. Lab., U. Chgo., 1943-44, 46; supr. female record section Chgo. Health Dept., 1946; dep. Ill. Dept. Labor, Div. Unemployment Compensation, Chgo., 1946-54, dep. reviewer, 1954-55, adjudication supr., 1955-63, office mgr., Evanston, 1963-64, Elgin, Ill., 1964-68, Harvey, Ill., 1968-75. Served with USN, 1944-46. Mem. Ill. Unemployment Compensation Assn. Assn. (chpt. chmn. 1963-64), Internat. Assn. Personnel Employment Security (state treas. 1973-75), Am. Legion (comdr. 1974-75), Kappa Alpha Psi. Home: 7552 S Wabash Ave Chicago IL 60619

MITTELMANN, EUGENE, cons. electronics engr.; b. Bratislava, Czechoslovakia, May 29, 1903; s. Ludwig and Louise (Perlblum) M.; came to U.S., 1938, naturalized, 1942; E.E., Vienna Inst. Tech., 1927; Ph.D., U. Vienna, 1931; m. Gusta Davidsohn, Nov. 21, 1939. Dir. labs. Austrian br. ITT, 1931-36; ind. cons., Europe and U.S., 1936-41; biophys. researcher Rush Med. Coll., Chgo., 1939, Northwestern U., 1940-42; dir. electronic research Ill. Tool Works, 1942-46; cons. indsl. electronics, Chgo., 1946—; cons. to industry, Argonne Nat. Lab., Oak Ridge Labs. Recipient spl. award Am. Congress Phys. Therapy, 1938. Fellow IEEE (outstanding achievement award 1975), Instrument Soc. Am., AAAS; mem. N.Y. Acad. Scis., Sigma Xi. Editorial bd. Spectrum; contbr. articles tech. and sci. jours. Holder more than 100 U.S. and fgn. patents. Home: 1368 E Madison Park Chicago IL 60615 Office: 601 W Lake St Chicago IL 60615

MITTELSTADT, RUSSELL JAMES, lawyer; b. Eau Claire, Wis., Jan. 12, 1931; s. Frederick W. and Pearl H. (White) M.; B.S. (Rennebohm scholar), U. Wis., 1952, LL.B. (Wis. Law Alumnae scholar), 1960; student Command and Gen. Staff Coll., 1964-68, Nat. Judges Coll., 1969, Army War Coll., 1969-71, Indsl. Coll. Armed Forces, 1972-73, Nat. War Coll., 1973; m. Marlys L. Rudd, June 28, 1953; children—Mary Kathleen, Marcus James, Miles Steven. Admitted to Wis. bar, 1960; with firm Spohn, Ross, Stevens, & Pick, Madison, Wis., 1960-62; pvt. practice, 1962-66, 72—; county judge Dane County, Madison, 1966-72. Originator Madison Vols. in Probation. Bd. dirs. Dane County Republican Party 1963, 64, 65, treas., 1965. Bd. dirs. YMCA East, sec., 1972-73; bd. dirs. Jr. Achievement. Served to 1st lt. U.S. Army, 1951-57; col. Res. Mem. Am., Wis. bar assns., Am. Trial Lawyers Assn., Am. Judicature Soc., Wis. Bd. County Judges (hon. life), Wis., Wis. Law alumnus assns., Assn. U.S. Army, Res. Officers Assn. U.S. (nat. jr. v.p. army 1965, nat. exec. com. 1966-68, Wis. pres. 1966-67, nat. v.p. 1969-70, nat. councilman 1970-75), Internat. Res. Officers Assn., Mil. Order World Wars (comdr. Madison chpt. 1973—). Lutheran. Clubs: Madison, Exchange (past pres.). Home: 5219 Tonyawatha Trail Monona WI 53716 Office: 326 S Hamilton St Madison WI 53703

MITTEN, HORACE LEE, JR., machinery co. exec.; b. Millersburg, Ohio, May 9, 1919; s. Horace Lee and Martha Mae (Hummel) M.; B.S. in Agr., Ohio State U., 1942; M.S. in Engring., Mich. State U., 1949; m. Harriet Louise Franks, Oct. 24, 1942; children—Robert, John. Asst. prof. dept. dairy tech. Ohio State U., 1946-51; research engr. Crepaco, Inc., Chgo., 1951-56, asst. to v.p., 1956-60, dir. tech. sales, 1960-67, gen. sales mgr., 1967-69, dir. internat. ops., 1969-73, v.p. internat. ops., 1973-74, v.p. mktg., 1974—; dir. Creamery Package Mfg. Co. (Far East) Ltd., Tokyo, 1963—. Served with arty. AUS, 1943-46. Recipient Centennial award for Distinguished Service, Ohio State U., 1970. Mem. Am. Dairy Sci. Assn., Am. Soc. Agrl. Engrs., Internat. Assn. Food, Milk and Environ. Sanitarians, Gamma Sigma Delta, Tau Beta Pi. Methodist. Contbr. articles to profl. jours. Patentee in field of homogenizing valves. Home: 336 Kenilworth Ave Glen Ellyn IL 60137 Office: Crepaco Inc 8303 W Higgins Rd Chicago IL 60631

MIX, AMELIA EVANS, poet; b. Olden, Mo., Nov. 29, 1912; d. John Campbell and Edna (Clarkson) Evans; student Columbia Coll., 1930-31, U. Mo., 1933-34; m. Alva Leland Mix, Nov. 9, 1935; children—David, Carolyn, Marjorie, Amelia. Free-lance poet. Active Girl Scouts, U.S.A., 1957-67. Mem. Nat. League Am. Pen Women, Am. Poetry League, Mo. Writers Guild, Tri-Arts Federated Club, Nat. Bus. and Profl. Womens Club, Entre Nous Study Club. Methodist. Author: Scarlet Leaves, 1970; contbr. poetry to literary mags. and anthologies. Home: Harris St Rd Cameron MO 64429

MIXER, HARRY WEEBER, radiologist; b. St. Paul, Dec. 25, 1919; s. Walter Ritter and Winifred Mary (Weeber) M.; A.B., U. Minn., 1941, M.D., 1944, M.S., 1946; m. Delores Virginia Moline, Dec. 15, 1943; children—Sandra G. (Mrs. Glenn F. Ferguson), Bruce W., Todd H., Rachel L., Scott T. Intern, U. Minn. Hosp., 1944, resident in radiology, 1944-47; trainee Nat. Cancer Inst., 1946-47; fellow in radiology U. Minn., 1944-46, clin. asst. prof. radiology, 1947—; asso. radiologist Farview Hosps., 1947—; chief of staff Golden Valley Health Center, 1964, chief of radiology, 1950—; staff Mercy, Unity hosps.; sr. partner Suburban Radiol. Consultants, Mpls., 1966—; vis. staff cons. radiation therapy Vets. Hosp. Mem. Minnehaha Acad. Bd. Edn., 1968-73; bd. dirs. Colonial Acres Nursing Home, 1973—; trustee, vice chmn. bd. Brookdale Covenant Ch., 1965-75. Served to capt. M.C., AUS, 1953-55. Diplomate Am. Bd. Radiology, Nat. Bd. Med. Examiners. Fellow Am. Coll. Radiology (counselor); mem. Radiol. Soc. N.Am., Am. Roentgen Ray Soc., AMA, Christian Med. Soc., Minn. Med. Soc., Minn. Radiol. Soc., Mpls. Acad. Medicine, Phi Beta Kappa, Sigma Xi, Alpha Omega Alpha. Republican. Contbr. articles to profl. jours. Home: 166 Ardmore Dr Golden Valley MN 55422 Office: 606 24th Ave S Minneapolis MN 55406

MIYARES, MARCELINO, research and advt. exec.; b. Havana, Cuba, Mar. 23, 1937; s. Marcelino and Adela (Sotolongo) M.; came to U.S., 1962, naturalized, 1976; J.D., Villanova U., Havana, 1960; M.A., Georgetown U., 1966; Ph.D., Northwestern U., Evanston, Ill., 1974; m. Marta Clemente, Apr. 20, 1963; children—Marcelino Jose, Juan Antonio, Maria Isabel, Anne Marie. Chmn. polit. sci. dept., asso. prof. polit. sci. Ill. Benedictine Coll., Lisle, 1964-72; pres. Ops., Market, Advt. Research, Inc., Chgo., 1969—. Campaign dir., finance dir. Hispanic-Am. Com. for Re-election of Pres., 1972; bd. mem. Non-Partisan Com. Re-election Mayor Daley, 1974; mem. Ill. Bd. Edn., 1976—, parent's bd. Schs. Sacred Heart; bd. dirs. Chgo. Community Renewal Soc., 1976—; mem. Chgo. United. Named Pan-Am. Man of Year, Spanish TV Guide, 1974, Social Sci. Tchr. of Year, Ill. Benedictine Coll., 1967. Mem. Am. Polit. Sci. Assn., Am. Marketing Assn., Am. Research Found., Bus.-Profl. Advt. Assn., Am. Assn. Advt. Agys., Blue Key. Roman Catholic. Club: Internat. (Chgo.). Author: Models of Political Participation of Hispanic-Americans, 1974; Hispanic-American's Strategy for the Future, 1975; polit. sci. editor Cath. Book List, 1966-69. Office: 5525 Broadway Chicago IL 60640

MOAYAD, CYRUS, otolaryngologist; b. Iran, June 27, 1928; s. Dr. Mir and Mahbooba (Forouzan) M.; came to U.S., 1958; M.D., Geneva Med. Sch., 1957. Intern, Kingston-Gen. Hosp., Queens U., Can.; resident in otolaryngology Cleve. Clinic Found.; asst. prof. surgery Case-Western Res. U., to 1968; practice medicine specializing in otolaryngology and facial plastic surgery, Valparaiso, Ind., 1968—; staff Valparaiso, LaPorte hosps.; pres. Moayad E.N.T., Inc. Diplomate Am. Bd. Otolaryngology. Fellow A.C.S.; mem. AMA, Ind. Med. Assn., Am. Acad. Otolaryngology and Ophthalmology, Am. Acad. Facial Plastic Surgery, Am. Soc. Ophthalmology and Otolaryngology Allergy, Am. Soc. Study of Headache, Internat. Coll. Surgeons, Internat. Acad. Cosmetic Surgery. Author studies and articles about lost cities of the world. Home: MR 35 Box 158 Valparaiso IN 46383 Office: Moayad Clinic 1105 Glendale Blvd Valparaiso IN 46383

MOBLEY, GORDON ORVAL, retail exec.; b. Ottumwa, Iowa, Nov. 9, 1934; s. Orval S. and Loraine (Jessen) M.; student Drake U., 1953-57; m. JoAnn B. Baker, July 12, 1960; children—Christy, Cindy, Colleen. Store mgr., Spurgeon Mercantile Co., Centerville, Fort Madison, Iowa, 1960-67; owner, pres. The Villa Inc., Charles City, Iowa, 1967—, also dir. Mem. Planning Zoning Commn. City of Ft. Madison, 1966-67; treas. Lutheran Ch., 1966-67. Served with AUS, 1957-59. Mem. Charles City C. of C. (dir.), Iowa Retail Assn., Cedar Mall Assn. Republican. Club: Elks. Home: 120 Cedar Circle Charles City IA 50616 Office: 130 Cedar Mall Charles City IA 50616

MOCHA, FRANK, educator; b. Babice, Silesia, Poland, Feb. 18, 1921; s. Paul and Anna (Mandel) M.; came to U.S., 1951, naturalized, 1956; student U. London, 1946-48; B.Sc. magna cum laude, Columbia U., 1961, M.A. (Nat. Def. Fgn. Lang. fellow), 1963, Ph.D., 1970; m. Doreen Constance Hampson, Sept. 21, 1951; children—Paul Alexander, Jane Helena, Mark Henry. Proofreader, Retnak Press, N.Y.C., 1952-62; instr. U. Pitts., 1966-68, asst. prof., 1968-71; asso. editor Polish Rev., Polish Inst. Arts and Scis. in Am., 1972-75, chmn. lit. sect., 1974-77, dir., 1974—; asso. prof. slavic langs. and lits. U. Ill., Chgo. Circle, 1976—; lectr. on lang. Kosciuszko Found., 1963-64, on lit., 1975-76; adj. asst. prof. N.Y. U. Sch. Continuing Edn., 1974-76. Pres. Polish Arts Club of Chgo., 1977—; bd. dirs. Polish Am. Congress Ill. Div., 1977—. Served with inf. Polish Army, 1939-45. Internat. Research and Exchanges Bd. grantee, 1971-72; Kosciuszko Found. grantee, 1973, 74, 75. Mem. Modern Lang. Assn., Am. Assn. Advancement Slavic Studies, Am. Assn. Tchrs. Slavic, East European Langs., Phi Beta Kappa. Author: Poles in America: Bicentennial Essays, 1977; contbr. articles to profl. jours. Home: 730 S Carpenter St Chicago IL 60607 Office: U Ill-Chgo Circle Dept Slavic Langs and Lits Chicago IL 60680

MOCHON, MARION JOHNSON, anthropologist; b. Saratoga Springs, N.Y., June 6, 1929; d. James Moylan and Marion Elizabeth (Elliott) J.; B.A., U. Tex., 1950; M.A., U. Wis.-Milw., 1966, Ph.D., 1972; children—Michael Scott, Barbara, John. Asso. prof. anthropology, asst. vice-chancellor U. Wis.-Parkside, Kenosha, 1969-76; prof. anthropology, dean faculties Ind. U. N.W., Gary, 1976—; anthrop. cons. VISTA, 1968. Vice pres. Friends of Art, Milw. Art Center, 1960-62, sec., 1963. Am. Council on Edn. postdoctoral fellow U. Calif. at Irvine, 1974-75; grantee Wis. Alumni Found., 1972, Am. Philos. Soc., 1965. Fellow AAAS, Am. Anthrop. Assn., Soc. Applied Anthropology; mem. Soc. Am. Archeology. Contbr. articles to profl. jours. Home: 1037 52d Dr Merrillville IN 46410 Office: Ind U NW Gary IN 46408

MOCK, CHARLES JACKSON, surgeon; b. Chgo., June 13, 1917; s. Harry Edgar and Golda Murdoch (Taylor) M.; A.B. magna cum laude, Dartmouth Coll., 1938; M.D. with honors, Harvard, 1942; M.S., Northwestern U., 1951; m. Mary Joan Oltman, June 13, 1941; children—Penelope Ann, Charles J., Nicole Mock Donahoe, Peter Lawrence, Margot Mock McDonnell. Intern, Cook County Hosp., Chgo., 1942-43; grad. fellow anatomy and pathology Northwestern Med. Sch. and Cook County Hosp., Chgo., 1946; resident gen. surgery Hines (Ill.) VA Hosp., 1947-50; practice medicine, specializing in gen. and traumatic surgery, St. Luke's Hosp., Chgo., 1950-57, Presbyn. St. Luke's Hosp., Chgo., 1957-60; gen. surgeon Lenont-Peterson Clinic Ltd. and surgical staff Va. Municipal Hosp., Virginia, Minn., 1960—, chief staff, 1966-68, 71-72; instr. surgery Northwestern U. Med. Sch., Chgo., 1950-57, U. Ill. Med. Sch., Chgo., 1957-60. Chmn. Virginia (Minn.) Human Rights Commn., 1969—. Adv. bd. Salvation Army, Virginia, Minn., 1961—, pres., 1968-70, E. Range Fish, Virginia, Minn., 1968—, Virginia (Minn.) Meals-A-Moving, 1972-73, Virginia (Minn.) Community Action Council, 1971-72; mem. Adv. Com. on Chem. Dependency, 1975—; bd. dirs. Virginia (Minn.) United Fund, 1968-70. Served to capt., M.C., AUS, 1943-46; ETO. Recipient Virginia Jr. C. of C. Outstanding Citizen award, 1969. Diplomate Am. Bd. Surgery. Fellow A.C.S.; mem. Minn. League Human Rights Commns. (bd. dirs. 1972-76), Chgo., Minn. surg. socs., Range Med. Soc., Minn. Med. Assn., Am. Med. Assn., Am. Assn. Rwy. Surgeons, Am. Occupational Med. Assn., Phi Beta Kappa, Alpha Omega Alpha, Sigma Alpha Epsilon, Nu Sigma Nu. Republican. Episcopalian (sr. warden 1962-65, 68-71, dep. or alt. gen. conv. 1970, 73, 76). Kiwanian (dir. 1966-69). Contbr. articles to profl. jours. Home: 1805 11th Ave N Virginia MN 55792 Office: Lenont-Peterson Clinic Ltd Virginia MN 55792

MOCK, DONALD EUGENE, entomologist; b. Montrose, Colo., Dec. 30, 1938; s. Guy Eli and Rosetta (Paxton) M.; student Colo. State U., 1955-57; B.A., Western State Coll., Gunnison, Colo., 1959, postgrad., 1960, 66, 67; Ph.D., Cornell U., 1974; m. Patsy Elizabeth Noland, June 30, 1963; children—Donald Jeffrey, Linda Suzanne, William Patrick. Tchr. scis. and lang. arts pub. schs., Colo., Wyo., Iowa, 1961-69; asst. prof. Kans. State U., Garden City, 1973—. Leader, 4-H Club, Garden City, Kans., 1974-77. Served with Army Nat. Guard, 1959-65. Mem. Entomol. Soc. Am., Am. Inst. Biol. Sci., Central States Entomol. Soc. Contbr. articles to profl. jours., author extension publs. Home: 2318 B St Garden City KS 67846 Office: 1501 Fulton Terr Garden City KS 67846

MODE, RUTH (MRS. ARTHUR S. MODE), pub. relations counselor; b. Cin.; d. Louis and Amelia (Levy) Rosenthaler; B.S., Ohio State U., 1929; m. Arthur Sander Mode, Jan. 10, 1935; children—Arthur Sander, Robert L. Pub. relations writer Frederic W. Ziv, Inc., Cin., 1930-34; pub. relations writer Baer, Kemble & Spicer, Cin., 1955-57; dir. pub. relations Eli Cohan Co., Cin., 1958-61; dir. pub. relations Ted Menderson Co., Cin., 1962-74; free lance pub. relations counselor, Cin., 1974—; lectr. Writers Workshop, U. Cin., 1968-70; organizer Inst. for Communicators, Xavier U., 1976; mem. adv. bd. Continuing Edn. Program, No. Ky. U., 1976—. Chmn., Cin. Pub. Recreation Commn. Girls Week, 1950; mem. exec. com. Cin. chpt. Am. Jewish Com., 1964—, mem. steering com. Nat. Membership Cabinet, 1977—. Bd. dirs. Cin. Center for Developmental Disorders. Mem. Pub. Relations Soc. Am. (dir. Cin. chpt. 1964-68, sec. 1966-68), Women in Communications (pres. 1965-67). Club: Woman's City of Cin. Contbr. articles to Cincinnati mag., Enquirer mag., King Features Real World, also indsl., bus. publs. Home and office: 2444 Madison Rd Apt 502 Cincinnati OH 45208

MODIGLIANI, ANDRE, social psychologist; b. N.Y.C., May 21, 1940; s. Franco and Serena (Calabi) M.; A.B., Harvard Coll., 1962; Ph.D., U. Mich., 1966; m. Katherine Reed Horst, June 15, 1963;

children—Leah, Julia. Asst. prof. of social psychology Harvard Coll., 1967-72; asso. prof. sociology U. Mich., Ann Arbor, 1972—. Recipient Marquis award, 1966; NIMH research grantee, 1969-70. Mem. Am. Sociol. Assn., Am. Psychol. Assn., Soc. Study Social Issues. Peace Research Soc., Phi Beta Kappa. Author: (with William Gamson) Untangling the Cold War, 1970, Conceptions of Social Life, 1975. Home: 1616 Lincoln Ave Ann Arbor MI 48104 Office: 3516 LSA Dept Sociology U Mich Ann Arbor MI 48104

MODISETTE, BILLY RAY, behavioral scientist; b. Norphlet, Ark., Feb. 16, 1930; s. Clayton Stokes and Lillie Mae (Ware) M.; B.S., La. State U., 1951; B.A., U. Tex., 1955; M.S., Purdue U., 1958; postgrad. La. Poly. Inst., 1949, U. Colo., 1954. With System Devel. Corp., Santa Monica, Calif., 1958-70, sr. human factors analyst; behavioral scientist Am. Justice Inst., Marina del Rey, Calif., 1970-74; prin. scientist Angeles Research Co., Inglewood, Calif., 1974-75; sr. asso., dir. Planning Analysis and Research Inst., Santa Monica, Calif., 1975—; project mgr. System Devel. Corp., Santa Monica, 1977—; Former cons. Advanced Research Projects Agy., Office Sec. Def., Bell Telephone Labs., Italian Air Ministry, Criminal Justice Planning Inst., U. So. Calif., Am. Justice Inst., System Devel. Corp., Calif. Dept. Econ. Devel. Served to 1st lt. USAF, 1951-53. Mem. Am., Western psychol. assns., ACLU, Am. Justice Inst., Nat. Geog. Soc., Common Cause, Assn. for Criminal Justice Research, Human Factors Soc., Fortune Soc., World Future Soc., Phi Eta Sigma, Delta Sigma Pi, Kappa Alpha. Home: 2115 Ottawa St Apt 201-C Leavenworth KS 66048 Office: Bldg 802 Ft Leavenworth KS 66048

MODLY, ZOLTAN MARIA, research chemist; b. Budapest, Hungary, Sept. 21, 1928; s. Bela and Margit (Tahy) M.; came to U.S., 1950, naturalized, 1953; B.A., Coll. of St. Imre, Budapest, 1947; postgrad. U. Sci., Budapest, 1948; postgrad. Fenn Coll., Cleve., 1955-60; m. Doris Matherny, June 15, 1957; children—Charlotte, Thomas, Dora, Suzanne, Mira. Sr. lab. technician Ferro Corp. Color Research and Devel. Lab., Cleve., 1953-58; project leader research and devel. dept. Brookpark, Inc., Cleve., 1958-60; mgr. Plastic Pigment div. The O. Hommel Co., Pitts., 1961-62; sr. chemist pigment research central research and devel. dept. Harshaw Chem. Co., Cleve., 1962-76, group leader color dept., 1976—. Served with AUS, 1951-53. Mem. Fedn. Socs. for Coatings Tech. Patentee in field. Home: 3350 Chalfant Rd Shaker Heights OH 44120 Office: 1945 E 97th St Cleveland OH 44106

MOE, JOHN HOWARD, orthopedic surgeon; b. Grafton, N.D., Aug. 15, 1905; s. Hans Jacob and Gunhild (Loseth) M.; student U. N.D., 1923-25; A.B., Northwestern U., 1929, M.D., 1930; m. Mary Lou Kruger Wood, Aug. 1, 1976; children—Lawrence, Elizabeth; stepchildren—Kathleen Wood, Nancy Wood. Clin. instr. orthopedia surgery, U. Minn., Mpls., 1934-36, clin. asst. prof., 1942-57, clin. prof. and dir., 1957-64, prof., dir. div. orthopedic surgery, 1964-69, prof., head dept. orthopedic surgery, 1969-74, prof. emeritus, 1974—; dir. Twin Cities Scoliosis Center, Mpls., 1974—, instr. fellows in scoliosis; dir. Twin Cities Scoliosis Fund; mem. staff Fairview Hosp., hon. staff St. Mary's Hosp.; advisory bd. Medico; chief of staff Gillette State Hosp., 1958-73. Republican nat. com.; mem. Minnetonka Community Ch. Recipient Bernardo O'Higgins Medal, Chile, 1969, Sioux Award, U. N.D., 1968. Mem. AMA, Minn. Med. Assn., Am. Assn. Orthopedia Surgeons, A.C.S., Hennepin County Med. Assn., Chgo. Orthopedic Soc.; hon. mem. Orthopedic Socs. Brazil, Chile, Colombia, Peru, Argentina, Dominican Republic, Yugoslavia. Clubs: Interlachen Country, Normandale Sports and Health, Torsque Klubben, Gun Owners Am. Founder John H. Moe Scoliosis Fund, John H. Moe Scoliosis Fellowship, John H. Moe Endowment Fund; pioneer in study and research of scoliosis; author (with Walter Blount) The Milwaukee Brace in Scoliosis; contbr. writings on orthopedic surgery and scoliosis to profl. publs.; inventor surg. adaptations. Home: 6 Webster Place Hopkins MN 55343 Office: 606 24th Ave S Minneapolis MN 55454

MOE, WALTER WILLIAM, metal co. exec.; b. Milan, Minn., Jan. 28, 1913; s. Anton John and Sophie (Christopherson) M.; student St. Paul Vocat. Sch., 1934; m. Hazel Margaret Streed, Nov. 8, 1936; children—Arlene Jean (Mrs. Maurice Freeman), Gary. Farmer, Milan, 1934-43, Montevideo, Minn., 1943-47; owner Montevideo Mfg. & Metal Co., 1948—. Active Boy Scouts of Am. Treas. country sch. dist., 1944-46. Recipient Grand prize for hydraulic loader, Minn. Inventors Congress, 1969, grand prize for combination trailer and sled, 1970. Mem. C. of C. Eagle. Inventor: power driven post hole digger, 1942, corn stalk shredder, 1948. Patentee bolt gauge novelty, 1959, automotive air cleaner, hydraulic loader, truck hoist. Home: 502 S 12th St Montevideo MN 56265 Office: Wilking St Montevideo MN 56265

MOEHLENPAH, WALTER GEORGE, mfg. and distbn. co. exec.; b. Buffalo County, Wis., Jan. 1, 1908; s. Fred Ernst and Anna (Steyer) M.; B.E.E., Marquett U., 1936; m. Ardys May Ebert, Sept. 13, 1930; children—Jocelyn, Donn, Arlo. Tech. supr. Wis. Telephone Co., 1928-36; elec. engr., Milw. R.R., 1936-40; staff asst. to pres. Progressive Welder Co., 1940-42; founder, chmn., chief exec. officer Moehlenpah Engring., Inc., also Hydro-Air Engring., Inc., St. Louis, 1943—, Sacramento, Calif., Toronto, Can., Halesowen, Eng., Paris, Stockholm, Johannesburg, South Africa. Mem. Truss Plate Inst., Conf. Bd., UN Com., Am. Soc. Tool Mfg. Engrs., Am. Welding Soc. Clubs: Missouri Athletic, University, Masons. Patentee in field. Office: PO Box 7359 St Louis MO 63110

MOEHRKE, DON PAUL, computer systems co. exec.; b. Ishpeming, Mich., Aug. 6, 1940; s. Edward Herman and Mildred Leona (Lindberg) M.; B.S., Mass. Inst. Tech., 1962, M.S., 1963; m. Martha Sands Falk, Dec. 30, 1961; children—Scott Allen, Geoffrey Wahl, Christopher Don, Mark Joseph. Sr. systems analyst Cutler-Hammer, Inc., Milw., 1963-69; project leader data systems div. A.O. Smith Corp., Milw., 1969-70, supr. applications software, 1970-71, mgr. mfg. systems devel., 1971-72, mgr. automotive systems devel., 1973, product mgr.-cons., mfg., applications software, 1974—; adj. prof. bus. U. Wis., Milw., 1976-77. Mem. Kellett Commn. on Edn. in Wis., 1969-70; treas. Mayflower Congregational Ch., River Hills, Wis., 1970-71, chmn. bd. deacons, 1976, moderator, 1977—. Mem. Assn. for Computing Machinery (chmn. Milw. chpt. 1973-76, nat. vice chmn. bd. dirs. spl. interest group-mgmt. of data), IEEE (mem. computer soc.), Inst. Mgmt. Scis. (chmn. Milw. chpt. 1968-69), GUIDE Internat. Republican. Club: Town (Milw.). Contbr. articles to profl. jours. Home: 10312 N Versailles Ct Mequon WI 53092 Office: 8651 N Port Washington Rd Milwaukee WI 53217

MOELLER, THEODORE ALLEN, psychologist; b. Chgo., Nov. 3, 1946; s. Theodore Allan and Vivian Clair (Pondelicek) M.; B.A., Drury Coll., 1970; Ph.D. (Fellow), Nova U., 1973; m. Judith Clark, Aug. 16, 1969; children—Lee Abigail, Theodore Allen Clark. Intern, Wichita Collaborative Psychology Internship Program, 1973-74; dir. outpatient treatment Meml. Mental Health Center, Bismarck, N.D., 1974-75; chief psychologist dept. psychiatry Med. Sch. U. Kans., Wichita, 1975-78, subsequently asst. prof.; pvt. practice, 1978—; pres. bd. Parallax program drug treatment facility; v.p. bd. Wichita Council Drug Abuse; bd. dirs. Sedgwick County Mental Health Assn., Wichita Collaborative Psychology Internship Program. Mem. Am., Kans., Wichita psychol. assns. Unitarian. Home: 442 N Pershing St Wichita KS 67208 Office: Wichita Psychiatric Center 3101 E 9th St Wichita KS 67219

MOEN, JOSEPH EDWARD, radio broadcasting co. exec.; b. Beloit, Wis., Sept. 2, 1927; s. Thorey Ingwald and Olga Pauline (Ness) M.; student U. Wis., 1947; m. Eleanor Louise Grandholm, June 21, 1952; children—Gary Lee, Patricia Lynn. Salesman-announcer radio sta. WBEL, Beloit, 1948-50, sales mgr., 1950-55, sta. mgr., 1955-62, gen. mgr., 1962-73; corporate v.p. Salter Broadcasting Co., Beloit, 1973—; partner Moen-Salter Co., Beloit, 1970-75; dir. WIXN Radio, Dixon, Ill. Chmn. Equal Opportunity in Housing Commn., 1970; chmn. Greater Beloit Com., 1969-70; chmn. Greater Beloit Luth. Devel. Corp., 1972-73; mem. pres.'s council Beloit Coll., 1974-75. Bd. dirs. A.R.C., Beloit, Rock Valley Half-Way House, Adv. Council Wis., Am. Automobile Assn. Served with AUS, 1945-46. Recipient Distinguished Service citation Greater Beloit Assn. Commerce, 1971. Mem. Wis. Broadcaster's Assn., C. of C. (dir. 1960-65). Lutheran (mem. ch. council 1967-69). Mason, Elk, Lion. Home: 3543 Bee Lane Dr Beloit WI 53511 Office: 504 W Grand Ave Beloit WI 53511

MOEN, MERLIN ARVID, mfg. co. exec.; b. Madison, Wis., Apr. 1, 1926; s. Arvid Clarence and Esther Marie (Westby) M.; Asso. Arts and Scis., Wright Coll., 1948; student De Paul U., 1948-50; m. Lorraine Jean Moore, Oct. 22, 1944; children—Charlene Jean (Mrs. Gary Bockover), Larry A. With judgement dept. Chgo. Title & Trust Co., 1948-52; service mgr. South Town Refrigeration, Chgo., 1952-63; v.p., gen. mgr. Service Town Refrigerations, Chicago Heights, 1963-68; bd. mgrs. Town Refrigeration Group, Chgo., 1955-68; pres. Royal Oaks Recreation Center, 1968-77; pres. Royal Oaks Golf Club, dir. Royal Oaks Golf Camp, Waupaca, Wis., 1968-76; coordinator Central region Foremost-McKesson Co., Appleton, Wis., 1970-75, plant mgr., 1975-78, safety dir., 1976—, personnel mgr., 1977—. Committeeman Boy Scouts Am., Oak Lawn, Ill., 1957-58; solicitor United Fund, Appleton, 1971-73; adviser Jr. Achievement, Appleton, 1972; co. chmn. United Way, 1976-77. Served with USMCR, PTO, 1943-45. Decorated Purple Heart. Mem. U.S. Golf Assn., Am. Golf Found., Am. Camping Assn., Waupaca C. of C. Home: 1212 W Bell Ave Appleton WI 54911 Office: 935 E John St Appleton WI 54911

MOENICH, DANIEL MATTHIAS, metals co. exec.; b. Fremont, Ohio, Feb. 17, 1922; s. Matthias John and Mae Adelaide (Hanslik) M.; B.S., Fenn Coll.; certificate, Aviation Inst. Tech.; m. Genevieve H. Fisher, May 11, 1946; children—Daniel, Terence. Materials mgr. Cleve. Pneumatic Tool Co., 1948-59; plant mgr. John C. Virden Co., Cleve., 1960-64; asst. gen. mgr. Marquette Metal Products Co., Cleve., 1964-66; v.p. Rotor Tool div. Cooper Industries, 1966-70; pres. Apex Internat. Alloys, Inc., Des Plaines, Ill., 1970—. Faculty evening div. Fenn Coll., 1960-61. Served with USAF, 1942-45. Mem. Chgo. Assn. Commerce and Industry, Japan-Am. Soc. Chgo., U.S. Indsl. Council (bd. dirs.), Aluminum Recycling Assn. (past pres.), Independent Zinc Alloyers Assn. Club: Inverness Golf (Palatine, Ill.). Home: 352 Windsor Ln Barrington IL 60010 Office: 2340 Des Plaines Ave Des Plaines IL 60018

MOESTA, RODMAN CHARLES, lawyer; b. Detroit, Oct. 3, 1923; s. Waldemar Charles and Elvera Louise (Frederick) M.; student U. Mich., 1941-43; B.A., U. Detroit, 1946, LL.B., 1949; m. Mary B. Corcoran, June 8, 1944; children—Maureen (Mrs. John Bruce), Anne (Mrs. William Schultz), Elizabeth. Admitted to Mich. bar, 1949; since practiced in Detroit; partner Johnson, Campbell & Moesta, 1966—. Served with AUS, 1943-46. Decorated Bronze Star, Combat Inf. Badge. Mem. Am., Detroit bar assns., State Bar Mich., Fedn. Ins. Counsels, Def. Research Inst., V.F.W. Club: Beach Grove Golf & Country (Windsor, Ont., Can.). Home: 1148 Grayton St Grosse Pointe Park MI 48230 Office: 912 Buhl Bldg Detroit MI 48226

MOFFATT, EVA MAE, librarian; b. Oil City, Pa.; d. Francis Daniel and Mary (Finley) Moffatt; B.S., Ohio U.; M.A., Western U., 1958; postgrad. U. Va., U. Wis., U. Colo., Purdue U. Tchr., Woodsfield (Ohio) High Sch., 1931-53; head librarian Monroe County Library, Woodsfield, 1953—. Mem. Good Will delegation to Russia, 1968; treas. Woodsfield Arts and Crafts, 1968-69. Trustee Scholarship Found., Monroe County Hist. Soc. Mem. AAUW, Ohioana Library Assn., Hickory Hosp. Twig, Beta Phi Mu. Methodist. Mem. Order Eastern Star. Clubs: Women's Republican, Woodsfield Garden (sec. 1964). Home: 104 S Main St Woodsfield OH 43793 Office: 101 Court St Woodsfield OH 43793

MOFFETT, DONALD BAIRD, clergyman, coll. adminstr.; b. Plainfield, N.J., Mar. 8, 1932; s. Charles Leonard and Helen (Baird) M.; B.A., Maryville Coll., 1954; M.Div., Louisville Presbyn. Sem., 1957; m. Mildred Elizabeth Mowery, Aug. 20, 1955; children—Mark William, Rebecca Sue. Ordained to ministry Presbyn. Ch., 1957—; pastor chs., Salida, Colo., 1957-61, Pataskala, Ohio, 1961-66, Richland, Mich., 1966-69; asst. dir. admissions Beloit (Wis.) Coll., 1969-73, exec. asst. to provost, 1973-75, asso. dir. field placement and career counseling, 1975—. Mem. Coop. Edn. Assn., Am. Personnel and Guidance Assn., Am. Coll. Personnel Assn., Nat. Vocat. Guidance Assn., Milw. Presbytery. Home: 1835 Strong Ave Beloit WI 53511 Office: Beloit Coll Beloit WI 53511

MOFFETT, MAXINE ANDERSON, counselor, educator; b. Gary, Ind., Nov. 10, 1943; d. Herman Mac and Luciell (Lively) Anderson; B.S., Central State U., 1967; M.S., Purdue U., 1975; m. Mar. 29, 1971 (div.); 1 son, Danté Rick. Supr. park dept. City of Gary (Ind.), 1962-64; sec. to bursar Central State U., Wilberforce, Ohio, 1964-67; tchr., counselor Gary Community Schs., 1968—; counselor, monitor Neighborhood Youth Corps, Gary, 1971-74; peer counseling advisor, lang. arts cons. Gary Community Sch. Corp., 1975-77; coordinator peer counseling Gary Manpower, 1975-77; established Peer Helper/Listener Program; consumer fraud coordinator, Gary. Bd. dirs YWCA, 1976-79. Recipient Merit award Am. Fedn. Tchrs., 1973-77; Outstanding Leadership award YWCA, 1973-77, Roosevelt High Sch., 1976, Future Tchrs. Am., 1975, Future Bus. Leaders Am., 1975. Mem. Gary English Council, Am., NW Ind. (speaker) personnel and guidance assns., Central State U., Purdue U. alumni assns., Ind., Gary reading councils, NAACP, Am. Fedn. Tchrs., Ind. Assn. for Pub. Continuing Adult Edn., YWCA, Delta Sigma Theta (social action chairperson, journalist 1976-77). Democrat. Clubs: Y-Teens. Author drug and alcohol abuse programs for Gary Pub. Schs. Home: 1945 Burr St #308 Gary IN 46406 Office: Horace Mann High School 524 Garfield St Gary IN 46404

MOGDIS, FRANZ JOSEPH, research co. exec.; b. Hastings, Mich., Jan. 12, 1941; s. Joseph and Frances Lucille (Maurer) M.; student Northwestern U., 1959-60; B.A., U. Mich., 1970; m. Diane L. Fuller, July 16, 1977. Linguist, Nat. Security Agy., Ft. Meade, Md., 1962-64; dept. mgr. applied social sci. research Bendix Aerospace Systems div., Ann Arbor, Mich., 1964-74, gen. mgr. applied sci. and tech. div., 1974-75, gen. mgr. Energy, Environment and Tech. Office, 1975-76; pres. Chase-Mogdis Inc., 1976—; pres. Urban Adv. Group, Inc., Ann Arbor, 1973—. Lectr. Fgn. Service Inst., 1970-74. Mem. Mayor's Policy Com. on Circulation, 1973-75; mem. Ann Arbor Planning Commn., 1971-75; pres. Ann Arbor Tomorrow, 1974-77, bd. dirs., 1972—. Served with AUS, 1961-64. Mem. Am. Soc. Planning Ofcls., Am. Polit. Sci. Assn., Internat. Studies Assn., Am. Statis. Soc., AAAS. Home: 1220 Ferdom St Ann Arbor MI 48104 Office: 204 E Washington St Ann Arbor MI 48104

MOGNI, BEN JAMES, computer edn. co. exec.; b. Chgo., Aug. 28, 1935; s. Ben James and Grace Rose (Petersen) M.; B.S., Northwestern U., 1957, M.B.A. (Gen. Finance Corp. scholar), 1960; m. Renee A. De Smet, Aug. 19, 1961; children—Ben IV, James. With IBM, Chgo., 1960-67, dist. sales tng. mgr., 1966-67; pres. Corporate Computer Systems, data processing cons., Elmhurst, Ill., 1967-68; v.p. edn. Advanced Systems, Inc., Elk Grove Village, Ill., 1969-71, v.p. marketing, 1972-73, sr. v.p. adminstrn., 1974, sr. v.p. internat. mktg., 1975—; dir. VAI de Mex., Computer Resources Co., Australia. Pres. Hillsider Assn., Steamboat Springs, Colo., 1972-73; treas. Washington Sch. P.T.A., Elmhurst, 1968-70; chmn. Washington Sch. council Cub Scouts Am., 1972-75. Served to lt. (j.g.) USNR, 1957-59. Mem. Am. Marketing Assn., Am. Soc. Tng. Dirs., Data Processing Mgmt. Assn., Delta Tau Delta. Roman Catholic. Home: 493 Parkview St Elmhurst IL 60126 Office: 1601 Tonne Rd Elk Grove Village IL 60007

MOHAN, LALA SATISH, physician; b. India, Sept. 1, 1938; s. Ram Prasad and Sita Lal; came to U.S., 1965, naturalized, 1976; M.B., B.S., Patna U., 1961, M.Surgery, 1964; m. Usha Rani Sinha, June 18, 1961; children—Minni, Niraj, Ritu, Pankaj. Intern, St. Charles Hosp., Toledo, 1965-66, resident in surgery Maumee Valley Hosp., Toledo, 1966-67, resident in surgery Flower Hosp., Sylvania, Ohio, 1967-68, resident in family practice, 1970-71, asso. dir. med. edn., 1972-76, attending physician emergency dept., 1971—, dir. emergency med. services, 1976—; resident dept. accident emergency service Airedale Gen. Hosp., Eastburn, Keighley, Yorkshire, Eng., 1969, resident dept. orthopedic and traumatic surgery, 1969-70; clin. asso. Med. Coll. Ohio, Toledo, 1973—. Diplomate Am. Bd. Family Practice. Fellow Am. Acad. Family Physicians, Soc. Tchrs. Family Medicine; mem. AMA, Ohio State Med. Assn., Acad. Medicine of Toledo and Lucas County, Am. Coll. Emergency Physicians. Hindu. Home: 5246 Cambrian Rd Toledo OH 43623 Office: 5200 Harroun Rd Sylvania OH 43560

MOHARIB, NASSIF HABIB, urologist; b. Luxor, Egypt., Aug. 15, 1931; s. Habib and Ester (Moussa) M.; M.B., B.Ch., Cairo (Egypt) U. Med. Sch., 1954; m. Christine Anne Morris, Mar. 25, 1967; children—Nadia, Samia, Philip, Leila. Intern, Cairo U. Hosp., 1955-56, Crewe Meml. Hosp., U.K., 1957-58; resident urology Bridge of Earn Hosp., Gt. Britain, 1960-61, numerous others, 1961-66; sr. resident surgery East Hamm Meml. Hosp., London, Eng., 1967; urology resident U. Man. (Can.), 1968-69; practice medicine specializing in urology, Winnipeg, Man., 1970—; mem. active staff urology Misericordia Gen. Hosp., 1970—; active staff urology St. Boniface Gen. Hosp., 1970—. Fellow Royal Coll. Surgeons (Eng.), Royal Coll. Surgeons (Can.), Internat. Coll. Surgeons. Contbr. articles to profl. jours. Home: 150 Westgate Winnipeg MB R3C 2E1 Canada Office: 280 Memorial Blvd MB R3C 1V2 Canada

MOHINDRA, RAMESH KUMAR, physician; b. Nahan, India, Aug. 17, 1943; s. Sita Ram and Rattan Devi(Sahi) M.; came to U.S., 1967; F.Sc. Med. Degree, Mahendra Coll., Patiala, India, 1961; M.B.B.S., Delhi U., New Dehli, India, 1966; m. Hem Prabha Dausage, June 8, 1969; children—Amit, Arti. Intern, Irwin Hosp., New Dehli, 1966, McLaren Gen. Hosp., Flint, Mich., 1967-68; resident in internal medicine Mount Carmel Mercy Hosp., Detroit, 1968-71, fellow in hematology, 1971-72; fellow in oncology Wayne State U., Detroit, 1972-74, Detroit inst for Cancer Research, 1972-74; practice medicine specializing in oncology, Southfield, Mich., 1974—; asst. prof. oncology Wayne State U., 1974-75, clin. asst. prof., 1976—; chief oncology staff Mount Carmel Hosp., Detroit, 1976—; mem. staff United Hosps. Detroit, St. Joseph Mercy Hosp.; cons. in field. Recipient prizes for research papers Mount Carmel Mercy Hosp., 1970, 71. Diplomate Am. Bd. Internal Medicine, Am. Bd. Med. Oncology. Mem. A.C.P., Wayne County, Mich. med. socs. Contbr. articles to med. jours. Home: 6555 Spruce Dr Birmingham MI 48010 Office: 17320 W 12 Mile St Southfield MI 48076

MOHIUDDIN, SYED MAQDOOM, cardiologist; b. Hyderabad, India, Nov. 14, 1934; s. Syed Nizamuddin and Amat-Ul-Butool Mahmoodi; came to U.S., 1961, naturalized, 1976; M.B., B.S., Osmania U., 1960; M.S., Creighton U., Omaha, 1967; D.Sc., Laval U., Quebec, Can., 1970; m. Ayesha Sultana Mahmoodi, July 16, 1961; children—Sameena J., Syed R., Kulsoom S. Intern, Altoona (Pa.) Gen. Hosp., 1961-62; resident Creighton Meml. Hosp., St. Joseph Hosp., Omaha, 1963-65, now mem. staff; prof. adjoint Laval U. Med. Sch., 1970; practice medicine specializing in cardiology, Omaha, 1970—; asso. prof. Creighton U. Med. Sch.; cons. Omaha VA Hosp. Research fellow Med. Research Council Can., 1968, grantee, 1970; grantee NIH, 1973. Diplomate Am. Bd. Internal Medicine with subsplty. cardiovascular disease. Fellow A.C.P., Am. Coll. Cardiology, Council Clin. Cardiology of Am. Heart Assn.; mem. Am. Fedn. Clin. Research, Nebr. Heart Assn. (chmn. research com. 1974-76, dir. 1973—), Gt. Plains Heart Com. (Nebr. rep. 1976—, pres. 1977—). Democrat. Islam. Club: Omaha Tennis. Home: 12531 Shamrock Rd Omaha NE 68154 Office: 601 N 30th St Omaha NE 68131

MOHLENBROCK, ROBERT H(ERMAN), JR., botanist; b. Murphysboro, Ill., Sept. 26, 1931; s. Robert Herman and Elsie (Treece) M.; B.A., So. Ill. U., 1953, M.S., 1954; Ph.D., Washington U., St. Louis, 1957; m. Beverly Ann Kling, Oct. 19, 1957; children—Mark William, Wendy Ann, Trent Alan. With dept. botany So. Ill. U., Carbondale, 1957—, chmn. dept., 1966—. Trustee Ill. Nature Conservancy. Mem. Am. Fern Soc., Ill. Acad. Sci., Assn. Southeastern Biologists, So. Applachian Bot. Club. Author: A Flora of Southern Illinois, 1957; Plant Communities of Southern Illinois, 1963; Ferns of Illinois, 1967; Flowering Plants of Illinois, 2 vols., 1970; Grasses of Illinois, 2 vols., 1972, 73; Forest Trees of Illinois, 1973; Guide To The Vascular Flora of Illinois, 1975; Summer and Fall Wildflowers of Rand-Carlyle-Shelbyville Lakes, 1975; Sedges of Illinois, 1976. Contbr. articles to profl. jours. Home: 1 Bird Song Dr Carbondale IL 62901

MOHLER, EDWARD FRANCIS, JR., environ. engr.; b. Toledo, Ohio, Aug. 26, 1920; s. Edward Francis and Gertrude Dorothy (Aylward) M.; B.S., U. Toledo, 1943, M.S., 1959; student Columbia U., 1944, Balliol Coll. Oxford U. (Eng.), 1945, Drexel U., 1964; m. Dorothy Catherine Downey, June 21, 1947; children—Martin E., Carolyn M., Joan T., Claire P., Elizabeth A., Edward T., Margaret C., Steven F. With Sun Oil Co., Toledo, Ohio, 1943—, chemist, 1943-46, jr. analytical chemist, 1946-51, sr. analytical chemist, 1951-57, chem. foreman, 1957-66, asst. supt. operations, 1966-68, sr. staff asso., 1968-71, sr. environmental engr., 1971-77, environmental mgr., 1977—. Served with USNR, 1944-46. Registered Corrosion Engr. Mem. Ohio Petroleum Council (vice-chmn. air and water research com. 1973—), Nat. Mgmt. Assn. (nat. dir. 1976—, Midwest Area gov. 1977, 78), Am. Chem. Soc. (chmn. Toledo sect. 1957-58), Nat. Assn. Chem. Engrs., Am. Soc. Testing and Materials, Tech. Soc. Toledo, Sun Oil Tech. Soc., Sun Supervisory Assn., Am. Petroleum Inst., Am. Inst. Chem. Engrs., Air Pollution Control Assn., Water Pollution Control Assn., Ohio Water Pollution Control Conf. (F.H. Waring award 1971, J.W. Ellms award 1977, v.p. 1977-78), Toledo Mus. Art, Maumee Valley Hist. Soc., Nat. Geographic Soc., Toledo Area C. of

C. (environ. studies com.), Ohio C. of C. (environ. and energy policy com.). Roman Catholic. Clubs: Rosary Cathedral Holy Name Soc. (pres. 1965-66), Council Catholic Men. Contbr. articles to tech. jours. Patentee improvement in water treatment. Home: 315 Boston Pl Toledo OH 43610 Office: Sun Co PO Box 920 Toledo OH 43693

MOHLER, TERENCE JOHN, psychologist; b. Toledo, July 9, 1929; s. Edward F. and Gertrude A. (Aylward) M.; B.S. in Edn., Toledo U., 1955, M.Ed., 1968, Ed.S. in Psychology and Counseling, 1974; m. Carol B. Kulczak, Oct. 1, 1955; children—Renee, John, Timothy. Psychologist, Toledo Bd. Edn., 1968—; sr. partner Psychol. Assos., Maumee, Ohio, 1970—; asso. fellow Inst. for Advanced Study in Rational Psychotherapy, N.Y.C., Alfred Adler Inst., Chgo. Served with AUS, 1951-53; Korea. Licensed psychologist, Ohio. Mem. Am., Ohio, Northwestern Ohio psychol. assns., Soc. Behavioral Psychologists, Nat. Registry Mental Health Providers, Council for Exceptional Children, Kappa Delta Pi. Club: Rotary. Home: 1113 Winghaven Rd Maumee OH 43537 Office: 5757 Monclova Rd Maumee OH 43537

MOHLMAN, HAROLD JOHN, dentist; b. Platteville, Wis., Sept. 13, 1933; s. Harry Charles and Erma Anna (Popp) M.; student Platteville State Coll., 1951-52, U. Wis., 1952; D.D.S., Marquette U., 1957; m. Jeanne Anne Hosking, Aug. 31, 1957; children—Brian, Elizabeth, Barry, Gay. Practice dentistry, Battle Creek, Mich., 1959—; cons. med. hypnosis Western Mich. U., Kalamazoo, 1971—. Served with USAF, 1957-59. Named Outstanding Med. Service Officer, Air N.G., 1972. Mem. ADA, Soc. Clin. Hypnosis, N.G. Assn. Patentee dental amalgam mixing and delivery device. Home: 115 Wanondager Trail Battle Creek MI 49017 Office: 163 North Ave Battle Creek MI 49017

MOHR, HAROLD OLIVER, graphic arts products exec.; b. Chgo., Feb. 11, 1895; s. Charles Linder and Evelyn (Oliver) M.; grad. high sch. Janesville, Wis.; m. Alta Doty Fifield, Dec. 25, 1941. With Mohr Lino-Saw Co. (name now Mohr Enterprises), Skokie, Ill., 1919—, former pres., now chmn. bd. Served with AUS. Mem. Am. Legion. Mason. Editor: Le Journal des Exploits du Compagnie C, 1919. Home: 2306 Deerpass Rd Marengo IL 60152 Office: 8015 Ridgeway Ave Skokie IL 60076

MOHRLOCK, HOWARD ALLEN, indsl. security exec.; b. St. Louis, Apr. 21, 1927; s. Hugo F. and Hazel H. (Hill) M.; student pub. schs.; m. Dorothy C. Zimmermann, Aug. 25, 1951; children—Darla Fay Anna, John Castlen Hill. With Pinkerton's Inc., St. Louis, 1950—, mgr. St. Louis, 1957-60, div. mgr., 1960-61, asst. regional mgr., 1961-69, asst. v.p., regional mgr., Kansas City, Mo., 1969—. Mem. Mo. Peace Officers Assn., St. Louis Claim Mens Assn. Elk. Club: Toastmaster, Internat. Home: 1704 Wishingwell Dr St Louis MO 63141 Office: 7730 Carondelet St Louis MO 63105

MOISTER, MATTHEW ROBERT, JR., pharm. co. exec.; b. Bklyn., Aug. 26, 1941; s. Matthew Robert and Frances (Weaver) M.; B.A., Davis and Elkins Coll., 1963; postgrad. bus., N.Y. U., 1965-66. Sales rep. Procter & Gamble Co., N.Y.C., 1964-65; supr. sales forecasting Union Carbide Corp., N.Y.C., 1965-69; group product mgr. Schering-Plough Corp., Kenilworth, N.J., 1969-71, Memphis, 1971-76; dir. internat. bus. mgmt., consumer products Abbott Labs., North Chicago, Ill., 1976-77; dir. new products Searle Consumer Products, G.D. Searle Co., Chgo., 1977—. Bd. dirs. Bay Head Improvement Assn., 1967-69. Mem. Am. Mktg. Assn. Home: 289 Latrobe Ave Northfield IL 60093 Office: Box 5110 Chicago IL 60680

MOKLESTAD, NORMAN WALDIMAR, county ofcl.; b. Forest City, Iowa, Feb. 17, 1926; s. Peter Norman and Ruth Marian (Field) M.; student Waldorf Coll., 1948-50; B.S., Iowa State U., 1952; m. Mavis Jacobson, May 31, 1950; children—Nancy, Timothy, Mark, Teresa. Vocat. agr. instr. Wall Lake, Iowa, 1952-54, Dows, Iowa, 1954-55, Lake Mills, Iowa, 1955-61; county extension asso. Hancock County, Garner, Iowa, 1961-63; county extension dir. Humboldt, Iowa, 1963—. County fair judge; chmn. county corn and soybean yield contest, Humboldt, 1965—; mem. Humboldt County (Iowa) zoning bd., 1964-67, sec., 1964-67; county chmn. Coffee Day for Retarded Children, 1975—; treas. Humboldt County Hosp. Tree Fund, 1972—; pres. Winnebago County (Iowa) Fair Bd., 1960-61. Served with U.S. Army, 1946-47. Recipient Distinguished Service award for community service, Jr. C. of C., 1959. Mem. 4-H Club (hon. mem.), Vocational Agr. Assn. (dist. dir. 1957-58), Farm Bur., Iowa State U. Extension Assn., Nat. Assn. County Agrl. Agts. Lutheran (sec. ch. council 1968). Lion (pres. 1960). Contbr. articles to profl. jours. Home: 604 11th Ave S Humboldt IA 50548 Office: PO Box 158 Humboldt IA 50548

MOL, JACOB CORNELIUS, wholesale trade co. exec.; b. Grand Rapids, Mich., Mar. 30, 1934; s. John and Nellie (Wielhower) M.; student U.S. Armed Forces Inst., 1955-56, Dale Carnegie Inst., 1960, La. State U. extension, 1955, U. Mich. extension, 1957-59; m. Lois Verblaauw, June 2, 1955; children—Jacob Cornelius, Robert L., James H., Carol J. Accountant, R. G. Moeller Co., Grand Rapids, 1959-62; mgr. OK Tire Store, Grand Rapids, 1960-62; exec. v.p. Mfrs. Supply Co., Grand Rapids, 1962—, also dir.; exec. v.p. Wal-Vac Inc., Grand Rapids, 1962-72, pres., 1972—, also dir.; pres., treas., dir. Surplus Brokers Inc., Grand Rapids, 1975—; dir. Coastal Supply Co.; trustee Trust Funds, Wal-Vac, Mfrs. Supply Co. Served with AUS, 1954-57. Mem. Grand Rapids Assn. Purchasing Agts., Nat. Assn. Credit Mgmt., Built In Vac System Inst. (v.p. 1972—), Internat. Platform Assn., C. of C. Inventor. Home: 1086 Brookview St Grand Rapids MI 49505 Office: 2851 Buchanan St Grand Rapids MI 49508

MOLD, DOALD WILBUR, mfg. co. exec., engr.; b. Winnipeg, Man., Can., Apr. 7, 1921; s. John Frederick and Gertrude Emalaine (Hutchings) M.; came to U.S., 1924, naturalized, 1943; B.M.E., Lawrence Inst. Tech., 1957; m. Marjorie Elizabeth Clancy, June 16, 1942; children—Donald Frederick, Thomas Edward, Douglas William, Lawrence Clancy. Tool designer Ford Motor Co., Detroit, 1941, auto body draftsman, 1946-50; designer auto body structure/layout Briggs Mfg. Co., Detroit, 1950-51, Hudson Motor Car Co., Detroit, 1952-53, Packard Motor Car Co., Detroit, 1953-56, Ford-Mercury div., Detroit, 1956; project engr. auto body design/layout Young Spring & Wire Co., Detroit, 1957-59, project engr. refuse collection and compacting vehicle Daybrook div., Bowling Green, Ohio, 1959-62, chief engr. truck equipment line, Ottawa and Bowling Green, 1962-66; sales engr. City Auto Stamping div. Sheller Globe Corp., Toledo, 1966-70, coordinating engr.-engring. and mfg., 1971-77, chief engr., 1978—. Pres. bd. dirs. Designing Engrs. Credit Union, Detroit, 1958, 59. Served to 2d lt. USAAF, 1942-45, USAFR, 1950. Mem. Soc. Automotive Engrs., Am. Soc. Body Engrs. Republican. Lutheran. Clubs: Cooley Canal Yacht, Maumee Valley Hi-12 (charter), Twin Village Toastmasters (past pes., past area gov.), Masons (past master, past high priest). Patentee spl. hydarulic circuit for refuse vehicle packer. Home: 6622 Merritt St Whitehouse OH 43571 Office: Sheller-Globe Corp Lint and Dura Ave Toledo OH 43612

MOLDEN, ANNA JANE, ednl. adminstr.; b. Weeping Water, Nebr.; d. William Henry and Anna Amanda (Turner) M.; B.S., Schauffler Coll.; M.A., Princeton Theol. Sem. Dir. Community Outreach, Chgo.; campus minister Iowa State U., Ames, 7 yrs.; specialist high sch. program Am. Friends Service Com., Des Moines; dir. Willkie House, Congl. Chs. Nat. Speakers Bur.; dir. Community Outreach Met. Kansas City (Mo.); dir. Consortium Higher Edn. for Spl. Services, Des Moines, 1970—; human rights commr., Des Moines. Chmn. cross cultural relations bd. Des Moines Area Council of Chs. Mem. Am. Personnel and Guidance Assn., League Women Voters, Internat. Assn. Torch Clubs, Blacks in Mgmt., Delta Kappa Gamma. Democrat. Home: 3523 University Terr Apt 26-D Des Moines IA 50311 Office: 1200 Grandview Ave Des Moines IA 50311

MOLENDA, CHARLES ANTHONY, mktg. exec.; b. Cin., Dec. 23, 1939; s. Leonard Joseph and Wilma Ruth (Blackmore) M.; B.B.A., U. Tex., 1970; m. Petra Marina Deavours, Dec. 4, 1965; 1 son, David Christopher. Salesman, Dun & Bradstreet, Fort Worth, Tex., 1970-71; dist. sales mgr. Phila., 1971-72, regional mgr., St. Louis, 1972-75, regional v.p., Chgo., 1975—. Active Boy Scouts Am. Served with U.S. Army, 1960-68. Decorated D.F.C., Bronze Star, Air medal. Republican. Methodist. Club: Naperville Country. Home: 1933 Hansom Ct Naperville IL 60540 Office: 1211 W 22d St Oak Brook IL 60521

MOLENDA, MICHAEL HENRY, educator; b. S. Bend, Ind., Nov. 19, 1941; s. Henry Eugene and Helene Irene (Mendini) M.; B.A., Marquette U., 1963; M.S., Syracuse U., 1965, Ph.D., 1971; m. Carolyn Shockey, Aug. 17, 1968. Intern, NEA, Washington, 1965-66; asst. prof. U. N.C., Greensboro, 1968-72; asso. prof. instructional tech. Ind. U., Bloomington, 1972—; cons. univs., state and fed. agencies. NDEA fellow, 1963-67; recipient alumni award Marquette U., 1964; Fulbright lectr., Peru, 1976. Mem. Nat. Soc. Performance and Instrn., Assn. Ednl. Communications and Tech. (pres internat. div.). Contbr. articles profl. jours. Home: 1104 E 1st St Bloomington IN 47401 Office: Indiana University Bloomington IN 47401

MOLER, ROGER LEE, banker; b. Brookville, Ohio, Jan. 22, 1936; s. Edward D. and Ethel V. (Simmons) M.; Asso. Bus. Adminstrn., Miami Jacobs Coll., 1966; m. Janet L. Taggart, Feb. 2, 1957. Sect. head, equipment inventory dept., data processing sect. Nat. Cash Register Co., Dayton, 1956-62; pres., dir. Brookville Nat. Bank, 1962—. Served with U.S. Army, 1961-62, 68. Rotarian. Club: Optimists (Brookville). Home: 212 Villa Dr Brookville OH 45309 Office: 132 Market St Brookville OH 45309

MOLES, RANDALL CARL, orthodontist; b. Gary, Ind., Mar. 13, 1946; s. Ben and Sonia M.; D.D.S., Marquette U., 1970, M.S., 1974; m. Suzanne Katherine Schwan, Aug. 3, 1968; children—Brant Randall, Joelle Renae, Justin Hunter. Practice dentistry specializing in orthodontics, Racine, Wis., 1974—; asso. prof. clin. orthodontics Marquette U., 1976—. Served with USPHS, 1972-74. Mem. ADA, Wis., Greater Milw., Racine County dental assns., Am. Assn. Orthodontists, Omicron Kappa Upsilon. Home: 5044 Deerwood Dr Racine WI 53406 Office: 1300 Green Bay Rd S Racine WI 53406

MOLITOR, JOHN PARKER, stockbroker; b. Payne, Ohio, Oct. 1, 1926; s. John Frank and Ferne (Parker) M.; student Ind. State U., 1944-45, U. Ill., 1945; B.S. in Commerce, U. Notre Dame, 1949; m. Lois Mae Rodecap, July 18, 1948; children—John R., Nathalie A. Owner Kendallville Hardware Co. (Ind.), 1949-63; with DuPont Walston & Co., Inc., Ft. Wayne, 1964-74, v.p., 1967-74; br. mgr. Lamson Bros. & Co. stockbrokers, Ft. Wayne, 1974-75; br. mgr., v.p. A.G. Edwards & Sons, Inc., stockbrokers, Ft. Wayne, 1975—. Allied mem. N.Y. Stock Exchange. Mem. City Council, Kendallville, 1959-63; chmn. city Planning Commn., Kendallville, 1959-64, Bd. Zoning Appeals, Kendallville, 1959-64; chmn. Republican party, Kendallville, 1964-66. Served to lt. (j.g.) USNR, 1946-52. Mem. Am. Legion, V.F.W. Roman Catholic. Elk. Home: 5334 Century Ct Fort Wayne IN 46807 Office: Suite 225 5800 Fairfield Ft Wayne IN 46807

MOLL, EDWIN ALLAN, business exec.; b. Chgo., July 16, 1934; s. Maurice and Lillian (Lederman) M.; B.S., Loyola U., 1956; Ed.M., Northwestern U., 1960, Asso. in Police Sci., 1962; m. Natalie Kepner, Mar. 11, 1962; children—Kelli Lee, Dean Allan. Vice pres. Linnea Perfumes, Inc., 1950; owner, operator three restaurants, Chgo., 1952-56; producer, moderator radio shows This is Chgo., Grant Part Concert Rev., Fort Dearborn Concert, Chgo., 1957-65; bus. mgr. Chgo. Adler Planetarium, 1958-59; adminstrv. aide to mayor Chgo., 1959-63; pres. Edwin A. Moll Pub. Relations, Chgo., from 1963; pres. Profl. Adminstrv. Services Inc., 1975—, Profl. Service System, Inc., 1975—; chief ranger Cook County (Ill.) Forest Preserve, 1975-76; exec. Lee Optical Co., 1976—; chmn. bd. Profl. Med. Guidance Corp.; dir. Glenwood State Bank. Practice mgmt. cons. to professions; lectr. pub. relations and practice mgmt. Commr., Youth Welfare, Skokie, Ill., 1963-66. Exec. dir. mem. 40th ward Democratic Orgn., Chgo., 1948-68. Bd. dirs. Ill. Vision Services Corp., Nate Gross Found., Asthmacade. Recipient citation Red Cross, 1957. Mem. Am. Soc. Assn. Execs., Soc. Optometric Assn. Execs., Optometric Council for Polit. Edn. (exec. dir. 1968-69), Ill. Optometric Assn. (exec. sec. 1963-69, Optometric Layman of Year award 1967), Ill. Pub. Health Assn., Internat., Ill., West Suburban, South Suburban, North Suburban assns. chiefs of police, Ill. Police Assn., Internat. Platform Assn., Chgo. Forum Execs., Tau Delta Phi. Clubs: Illinois Athletic (Chgo.); President's (Washington). Author: Sell Yourself Big, 1966.

MOLL, VERDIN ATLEE, JR., architect; b. Dayton, Ohio, Apr. 5, 1923; s. Verdin Atlee and Ethel Maybell (Hammann) M.; student Ohio U., 1941-43; B.Arch., Ohio State U., 1950; m. Nancy Hartinger, Aug. 8, 1947 (dec. May 1976); children—Eric, Lance, Kirk. Self-employed as architect, Dayton, 1954-59; architect Hamilton Co., developers, San Juan, P.R. and Cin., 1959-60; partner Thomas & Moll, architects, Xenia, Ohio, 1961-70, Thomas, Moll & Klose, architects, Xenia, 1971-76, Thomas, Moll and Assos., Architects, Xenia, 1977—. Active local youth groups. Mem. Kettering (Ohio) Bd. Zoning Appeals, 1966-76, chmn., 1970-71, 75-76; mem. Kettering Bd. Constrn. Rev., 1970-76, chmn., 1971. Served to 2d lt. USAAF, 1943-45. Mem. A.I.A. (chpt. treas. 1963-71), Architects Soc. Ohio (trustee 1970-71), Colegio de Ingenieros Arquitectos y Agrimensores de P.R., Am. Legion, Beta Theta Pi. Rotarian. Home: 1420 Monroe Dr Xenia OH 45385 Office: 50 S Detroit St Xenia OH 45385

MOLLENHOFF, FRANCIS ANTHONY, rehab. center adminstr.; b. Webster City, Iowa, Aug. 19, 1939; s. Raymond Eldon and Margaret Pearl (Clark) M.; student Coll. St. Thomas, 1957-60; B.A. in Bus. Adminstrn., U. No. Iowa, 1967; m. Janice Elaine Ott, Aug. 5, 1961; children—Cynthia, Susan, David. Adminstrv. asst. Goodwill Industries of N.E. Iowa, Waterloo, 1960-69, exec. dir., 1969—. Mem. Gov.'s Com. on Archtl. Accessibility, 1970-76; bd. dirs. Easter Seal Soc., 1972—, Birthright of Black Hawk County, Inc., 1973—; mem., v.p. Area Edn. Agy. 7 Bd., 1972—; mem., v.p. Waterloo Community Sch. Dist. Bd. Edn., 1975—; chmn. Community Fin. Counseling Assn., 1973—; mem. parish council, fin. commn. Ch. of Blessed Sacrament; pres. Blessed Sacrament Bd. Edn., 1970—. Recipient Clayton Nodurft Meml. award Easter Seal Soc. for Crippled Children and Adults of Iowa, Inc., 1971; Outstanding Young Religious Leader award Waterloo Jr. C. of C., 1971; Service to Mankind award Waterloo Sertoma Club, 1974. Mem. Nat., Iowa (pres. 1974) rehab. assns., Iowa Assn. Rehab. Facilities. Home: 1233 Westland St Waterloo IA 50701 Office: 2640 Falls Ave Waterloo IA 50701

MOLLISON, CLARENCE LONGMAN, lawyer; b. West View, Ohio, May 31, 1906; s. Alexander D. and Maria (Knight) M.; student Cleve. Coll. of Western Res. U., 1924-26; J.D., Cleve.-Marshall Coll. Law, Cleve. State U., 1930, LL.M., 1932; m. Ethel Neoma Denman, Dec. 24, 1930 (div.); 1 dau., Marlene Joyce (Mrs. David Alan Baker); m. 2d, Charlotte Yorke, Dec. 9, 1969. Admitted to Ohio bar, 1930; mem. Payer, Bleiweiss, Crow and Mollison, 1931-51; asst. law dir. City of Cleve., 1945-51; mem. Hauxhurst, Sharp, Mollison & Gallagher, 1951—. Mem. Am., Ohio State, Cleve., Cuyahoga bar assns., Internat. Assn. of Ins. Counsel, Maritime Law Assn. of U.S., Am. Coll. Trial Lawyers (state chmn.), Citizens League Cleve., Iota Lambda Pi. Democrat. Baptist. Mason (32 deg., Shriner). Clubs: Shrine Luncheon of Cleveland, Lions (past pres.), (Cleve.). Author articles in field. Home: 762 Mentor Ave Painesville OH 44077 Office: 1501 Euclid Ave Cleveland OH 44115

MOLLISON, EARL DAVID, motor mfg. co. exec.; b. Cleve., Feb. 11, 1929; s. Earl Kenneth and Alvina Hedwig (Labuschef) M.; B.A., Ohio U., 1950; m. Eileen Francis Brooks, Sept. 1, 1956; children—Pamela Lee, Mark David. Inventory and prodn. control supr. Lear Siegler, Inc., Cleve., 1956-64, systems supr., 1965-68; materials mgr. Lamb Electric div. Ametek, Kent, O., 1969-71, systems and computer operations mgr., 1972—. Recipient award of Honor, Nat. Mgmt. Assn., 1966. Mem. Data Processing Mgmt. Assn. Republican. Baptist. Mason. Home: 1813B Higby Dr Stow OH 44224 Office: 627 Lake St Kent OH 44240

MOLLOY, PAUL GEORGE, journalist; b. St. Boniface, Man., Can., July 4, 1925; s. Thomas B. and Marie (Dubuc) M.; student U. Man., 1938-41; children—Paul, Georgia, Shonagh, Nelda, Marcia, Lisa, Barbara, Mark. Came to U.S., 1950, naturalized, 1956. With Montreal (Que., Can.) Herald, 1944; bur. mgr. U.P.I., 1946-50, Tulsa Tribune, 1950-51; staff writer Time Mag., N.Y.C., 1951-53; columnist Scripps-Howard morning paper in Memphis, The Comml. Appeal, 1953-56; columnist Chgo. Sun-Times, 1956-75; producer numerous radio and TV programs. Recipient Nat. Headliner award, 1960; Chicago's Outstanding Journalist, 1960, George Washington Honor medal, 1965, 72. Roman Catholic. Author: And Then There Were Eight, 1961; A Pennant for the Kremlin, 1964; All I Said Was . . .", 1966. Contbr. to Canadian and American mags. Address: care Madera del Rio Box 106 Mundelein IL 60060

MOLO, WALTER JOHN, JR., supt. schs.; b. Denver, Sept. 13, 1924; s. Walter J. and Kathryn V. (Spritzer) M.; B.S., U. Ill., 1948; M.S., 1949; Ed.D., Loyola U., 1970; m. Patricia Lee Preston, Nov. 1, 1952; children—Kathryn, Gayle, Jill. Dir. phys. edn. for boys, Rochelle (Ill.) High Sch., 1950-51; instr., coach Dist. 87, Berkeley, Ill., 1951-54; elementary prin. Eugene Field Sch., Berkeley, 1954-56, Whittier Sch., Northlake, Ill., 1956-62; supt. elementary schs. West Northfield Dist., Northbrook, 1962-73; unit supt. schs. Brentwood (Mo.) Pub. Schs., 1973-76; supt. Metropolis (Ill.) High Sch. Dist. 20, 1976—. Served with AUS, 1943-45. Mem. Ill. Edn. Assn., NEA, Am., Ill. assns. sch. adminstrs., Mo. Tchrs. Assn., No. Ill. Prins. Roundtable, No. Ill. Supts. Roundtable, Mo. Elementary Prins. Assn., Delta Theta Epsilon, Phi Epsilon Kappa, Phi Delta Kappa, Phi Kappa Psi. Home: 9 White Oak Ln Metropolis IL 62960 Office: 1004 Catherine St Metropolis IL 62960

MOMSEN, JOY JACQUELINE, speech pathologist; b. Grand Island, Nebr., Dec. 24, 1929; d. Melvin Chris and Frances (Woodman) Momsen; B.A., Morningside Coll., 1950; M.A., U. S.D., 1966; m. Charles William Corkhill, Jr., June 4, 1960; 1 dau., Helen Elizabeth Momsen. Tchr., Sioux City (Ia.) Leeds High Sch., 1963-64; head, speech hearing dept., Sioux City Community Schs., 1964-70; speech clinician Woodbury County, Ia., 1970-75; speech pathologist Area Edn. Agy., Sioux City, 1975—. Precinct and county rep., Republican Party, 1975-76. AAUW grantee, 1976. Mem. Am. Speech and Hearing Assn., Ia. Speech and Hearing Assn., Nat. Edn. Assn., Council for Exceptional Children, Ia. Edn. Assn., AAUW, Alpha Delta Kappa, Alpha Delta Pi. Republican. Conglist. Club: Order Easter Star. Home: 15 Gilman Terr Sioux City IA 51104 Office: 1520 Morningside Ave Sioux City IA 51106

MONACO, ANTHONY LOUIS, JR., corrections adminstr.; b. Cecil, Pa., Sept. 29, 1951; s. Anthony L. and Louise (Bogdewiecz) M.; B.A., Case Western Res. U., 1973; M.Ed., Kent State U., 1974; postgrad. Northwestern U., 1974—. Caseworker, Via House, Akron (Ohio) YMCA, 1974-76, casework supr., research asso., 1976, acting dir., 1976-77, dir., 1977—; lectr. in field. Certified rehab. counselor, workshop trainer, Ohio. Mem. Am. Personnel and Guidance Assn., Ohio Assn. Group Homes, Pub. Offender Counselor Assn., Phi Delta Kappa. Home: 2200 High St Apt 551 Cuyahoga Falls OH 44221 Office: 80 W Center St Akron OH 44308

MONACO, ATTILIO J., newspaper publisher; b. Warrenville, Ill., July 30, 1917; s. Giuseppe and Antionette (Coletta) M.; student Morgan Park Mil. Acad., Loyola U.; m. Rosemary A. Merhaut; children (by previous marriage)—Michael Stephen, Suzanne Lou, Stephen Attilio, Diane Alice, Alicia Janet. Field clk. Chgo. Dist. Generating Corp., Hammond, Ind., 1938-40; cost clk. Super Power Co. No. Ill., 1940-41; auditor Commonwealth Edison Co., 1941-45; v.p. Mitchell Serdiuk, Inc., 1945-47; pres., pub. Community Reporter, Inc., Chgo., 1947—; pres. C. F. Printing Service, 1964; chmn. bd. pres. M & M Printing and Pub. Co., Inc., 1965. Recipient citation of appreciation Boys' Club; award of merit. Cath. War Vets.; citation of appreciation, Infantile Paralysis; award for distinguished service, Am. Cancer Soc., 1951; plaque for outstanding community service from Citizens of Lawndale Crawford Community; hon. citizen Boy's Town; named Man of Yr., Chgo. Marshall Sq. Boys Club, 1970. Mem. 26th St. Area (dir.), Cermak Rd. chambers commerce. Lions. Club: Butterfield Country (dir.). Home: 4416 S Route 31 Crystal Lake IL 60014 Office: 4072 W 26th St Chicago IL 60623

MONACO, CARMEN FRANK, ins. co. exec.; b. Chgo., Mar. 9, 1942; s. Anthony Joseph and Lucille (Depa) M.; B.S., Marquette U., 1965; m. Eileen Mary McCarthy, Apr. 25, 1970; children—Christine Ann, Anthony Joseph. With Continental Assurance Co., Chgo., 1965—, asst. to nat. sales v.p., 1970-71, field profit loss specialist, 1971-72, financial mgmt. information mgr., 1972-75, asst. to sr. v.p., 1975—. Served with USMC, 1965-66. Mem. Am. Marketing Assn. (chpt. rec. sec., dir. 1971-72). Roman Catholic. Home: 4548 N Crab Orchard Dr Hoffman Estates IL 60195 Office: 310 S Michigan St Chicago IL 60604

MONAHAN, RAYMOND EDWARD, computer co. exec.; b. Mpls., Jan. 28, 1923; s. John Raymond and Edna Katherine (Norman) M.; B.Aero. Engring., U. Minn., 1944, B.S. in Ed., 1948; m. Pauline E. Ogden, Aug. 2, 1944; children—Donald, Barbara (Mrs. Martin Kaisto), Mary (Mrs. David Long), Diane (Mrs. Gary Fors), Karen (Mrs. Gregory Odash). Instr. engring. graphics U. Minn., Mpls., 1946-51; design engr. Minn. Engring. Co., Mpls., 1951-55; sr. devel. engr. FluiDyne Engring. Corp., Mpls., 1955-61; dir. documentation standards and services Control Data Corp., Mpls., 1961—. Pres., Richfield Girls Softball, 1962-68. Mem. Richfield Charter Commn., 1960-69. Served with USAAF, 1944-46. Recipient Distinguished Service award Richfield Jr. C. of C., 1957. Fellow Standards Engrs. Soc. (pres. 1972-74); mem. Minn. Soc. Profl. Engrs., U. Minn. Alumni

Assn., Am. Legion. Roman Catholic. Home: 7500 Cahill Rd Edina MN 55435 Office: 8100 34th Ave S Minneapolis MN 55440

MONAHAN, ROBERT HUGH, ophthalmologist; b. International Falls, Minn., Feb. 11, 1914; s. Robert Hugh and Elizabeth Ried (Stevens) M.; B.S., U. Minn., 1940, M.B., 1942, M.D., 1943; m. Marian Louise Willey, June 23, 1939; children—Robert Hugh, David Foster. Intern Miller Hosp., St. Paul, 1942-43; resident in ophthalmology U. Minn., Mpls., 1948-50; fellow ophthalmic pathology Harvard Med. Sch., 1950-51; partner Minn. Eye Clinic, St. Paul, 1952—; mem. staff, dir. ophthalmic pathology U. Minn. Hosp., 1952—; mem. staff, chmn. dept. ophthalmology St. Paul Ramsey Hosp. and Med. Center, 1959—, chief staff, 1964; mem. staff United Midway, Bethesda hosps., all St. Paul. Vol. physician Viet Nam, 1968—; mem. faculty U. Minn., 1952—, prof. ophthalmology, 1972—; cons. Minn. State Services for the Blind, St. Paul, 1970—, St. Paul Dept. Edn., 1967-76. Pres. Joint Commn. on Allied Health Personnel in ophthalmology, 1970-73, exec. v.p., 1973—; pres. Ednl. Study Assn., 1967-76, exec. v.p., 1976—; pres. Pre-Sch. Med. Survey of Vision and Hearing, 1959-60. Served from lt. to capt, M.C., AUS, 1942-45. Recipient Achievement award Minn. Alumni Assn., 1969. Mem. Minn. State Med. Assn. (chmn. ophthalmology com. 1961-73; vice speaker ho. dels. 1972-73), Am. Acad. Ophthalmology, Am. Assn. Ophthalmology (dir. 1972—), Minn. Soc. Prevention of Blindness (dir. 1968—, pres. 1977), Ramsey County Med. Soc. Lion, Mason. Club: Minnesota (St. Paul). Home: 999 W Nebraska Ave St Paul MN 55117 Office: 1573 University Ave St Paul MN 55104

MONASH, PETER ERNEST, mgmt. cons. co. exec.; b. Germany, Aug. 16, 1924; s. Alfred Otto and Hedwig (Mettke) M.; came to U.S., 1946, naturalized, 1952; student journalism U. Berlin; m. Dec. 23, 1957; 1 son, Curt Alfred. Exec. trainee Sears, Roebuck & Co., New Haven, Conn., 1947-49, Norwich, Conn., 1949-50, Lubbock, Tex., 1950-58, field positions, 1947-58, asst. nat. sales mgr. hardware, 1958-60; exec. v.p. Personal Dynamics Inc., Los Angeles, 1960-67; regional mgr. Interstate Dept. Stores-White Front, Los Angeles, 1967-76; v.p. Mgmt. Horizons Inc., Columbus, Ohio, 1976; sr. v.p. Doody Co., Columbus, 1976—. Pres. Council UN Lubbock, 1955; v.p. Lubbock Little Theater, 1953-56; v.p. YMCA Lubbock, 1955. Mem. Nat. Retail Mchts. Assn., Civitans (pres. Lubbock 1956). Democrat. Home: 2309 Haviland Rd Columbus OH 43220

MONDA, CORNELL PETER, SR., psychologist; b. Sibiu, Romania, July 27, 1911; s. Peter and Elena (Moldovan) M.; came to U.S., 1913, naturalized, 1923; B.S., Ohio U., Athens, 1942; M.A., Western Reserve U., Cleve., 1948; postgrad. Ohio State U., Columbus, 1951-52, Kent State U., 1954-55; m. Georgiana Buta, Dec. 28, 1941; children—Georgiana Elena, Cornell Peter and Michael John (twins). High sch. sci. tchr., Scio, Ohio, 1943-43, Canton South, Ohio, 1943-44, Norwalk, Ohio, 1944-46, Martins Ferry, Ohio, 1946-47, East Canton, Ohio, 1953-55; instr. psychol. subjects, supr. testing and guidance Kent State U., Canton, Ohio, 1947-51; psychiat. social worker Massillon (Ohio) State Hosp., 1950; sch. psychologist, Steubenville, Ohio, 1955-56, Cleve., 1956-58; sch. psychologist, dir. psychol. and guidance services Lisbon (Ohio) Schs., 1958-75; practice psychol. counseling, Lisbon, 1948—; cons. psychologist Bur. Vocat. Rehab., Columbiana County, Ohio, 1959-68, Head Start Program, 1967-68, East Liverpool Child Counseling Center, 1959-73. Pres., Columbiana County Muscular Dystrophy Assn., 1973, Lisbon Tchrs. and Community Scholarship Found., 1964-66; chmn. Lisbon Community Fund, 1962. Mem. Am. Assn. Retired Persons, Alliance Francaise, Am., Ohio, N.E. Ohio (pres. 1964-65, 72-73, 76-77) psychol. assns., Columbiana County Guidance Assn. (pres. 1965-66), Nat., Ohio, Columbiana County retired tchrs. assns., No. Columbiana County Community Hosp. Assn., Sch. Psychologists Ohio, Phi Delta Kappa, Tau Kappa Epsilon. Clubs: Nat. Travel, Kiwanis. Democrat. Romanian Orthodox. Home and Office: 425 W Lincoln Way Lisbon OH 44432

MONDALE, WALTER FREDERICK, Vice-Pres. U.S.; b. Ceylon, Minn., Jan. 5, 1928; s. Theodore Siguard and Claribel (Hope) M.; B.A. cum laude, U. Minn., 1951, LL.B., 1956; m. Joan Adams, Dec. 27, 1955; children—Theodore, Eleanor, William. Admitted to Minn. bar, 1956; practice law, 1956-60; atty. gen. Minn., 1960-64; U.S. senator from Minn., 1964-76; vice-pres U.S., 1976—. Served with U.S. Army, 1951-53. Named Outstanding Young Man of Year in Minn., 1960. Mem. Am., Minn., Hennepin County bar assns., Minn. Safety Council, Am. Assn. UN, Am. Legion, Minn. Jr. C. of C. Presbyterian. Moose, Eagle. Editorial bd. Minn. Law Rev., 1955-56. Office: Old Executive Office Bldg Washington DC 20501

MONICATTI, LAWRENCE ANGELO, aerospace co. exec.; b. Detroit, Nov. 18, 1934; s. Michael and Linda (Poli) M.; B.S. in Physics, Western Mich. U., 1957; B.S. in Aero. Engring., U. Mich., 1958; M.S. in Aerospace Engring., U. So. Calif., 1963; m. Kathleen Mary Maroney, Jan. 16, 1965; children—Kathryn, Matthew, Christian. Missile checkout technician Chrysler Missile Corp., Warren, Mich., 1957; structures engr. N.Am. Aviation, Los Angeles, 1958-63; program mgr. Vought Corp., Sterling Heights, Mich., 1963-77; program mgr. Honeywell Corp., Mpls., 1977—; past pres., treas., bd. dirs. Vought Mich. Fed. Credit Union. Pres. Lochmoor Hills Homeowners Assn., 1972; active YMCA; past chmn. Christian service commn. Roman Catholic Ch. Mem. Am. Inst. Aeros. and Astronautics, Aircraft Owners and Pilots Assn., Smithsonian Assos. Clubs: Men's Garden (Rochester, Mich.); Vought Mgmt., Elks. Home: 404 Pondridge Circle Wayzata MN 55391 Office: Honeywell Corp Defense Systems Div Minneapolis MN 55400

MONK, JOHN THOMAS, army officer, data systems adminstr.; b. Balt., Apr. 12, 1946; s. Galloway and Margaret (Fannan) M.; B.A., U. Okla., 1968; M.B.A., Ohio State U., 1975; M.D.P., Washington U., 1977; m. Susan Ann Sitorius, June 7, 1969; 1 son, Justin. Commd. 2d lt. U.S. Army, 1968; advanced through grades to capt., 1977; various command and staff positions in Europe and U.S., 1968-71; served combat tour in Kontun, Vietnam, 1971-72; project mgr. U.S. Army Automated Logistics Mgmt. Agency, St. Louis, Mo., 1975—. Chmn., Eureka Economic Devel. com.; pres. Eureka Khoury League Assn.; chmn., vice-chmn. Hilltop Villages Community Assn.; chmn. Eureka Town Meeting. Decorated Bronze Star medal, Cross of Gallantry with Palm; named Eureka Outstanding First Yr. Jaycee, 1976; U.S. Army grad. fellow, 1973-75. Mem. Data Processing Mgmt. Assn. , Assn. of the U.S. Army. Clubs: Delta Upsilon, Gamma Gamma, Jaycees. Home: 10 Muir St Eureka MO 63025 Office: USDARCOM ALMSA PO Box 1578 St Louis MO 63188

MONNINGER, ROBERT HAROLD GEORGE, ophthalmologist, educator; b. Chgo., Nov. 5, 1918; s. Louis Robert and Katherine (Lechner) M.; A.A., North Park Coll., 1939; B.S., Northwestern U., 1941, M.A., 1945; M.D., Stritch Sch. Medicine, 1953; Sc.D. (hon.), 1968; m. Anna Evelyn Turunen, Sept. 1, 1944; children—Carl John William, Peter Louis Philip. Intern St. Francis Hosp., Evanston, Ill., 1953-54; resident Presbyn.-St. Luke's, U. Ill. Research and Eye, VA hosps., 1954-57; instr. chemistry Lake Forest (Ill.) Coll., 1946-47; instr. biochemistry, physiology Loyola Dental Sch., 1948-49; clin. asso. prof. ophthalmology Stritch Sch. Medicine, Maywood, Ill., 1957-72; practice medicine specializing in ophthalmology, Lake Forest, 1957—. Guest lectr. numerous univs. med. centers U.S., Can., Europe, Central and S.Am., Orient; mem. panel Nat. Disease and Therapeutic Index; cons. Draize eye toxicity test revision Dept. Health, Edn. and Welfare; cons. research pharm. cos. Nat. asso. Smithsonian Instn. Bd. dirs. Eye Rehab. and Research Found.; postgrad. faculty Internat. Glaucoma Congress; cons. Nat. Acad. Sci.; advisory bd. Madera Del Rio Found. Served with USMCR, 1941-44. Recipient citation Gov. Bahamas, 1960, Ophthalmic Found. award, 1963, Sci. Exhibit award Ill. State Med. Soc., 1966, Franco-Am. Meritorious citation, 1967, Paris Post No. 1 Am. Legion award, 1967, citation Pres. Mexico, 1968, Sightsaving award Bausch & Lomb, 1968, exhibit award Western Hemisphere Congress Internat. Surgeons, 1968, Research citation Japanese Soc. Opthalmology, 1969; Barraquer Gold Medallion; Physician's Recognition award A.M.A. Catherine White Scholarship fellow, 1945-46. Fellow Internat. Coll. Surgeons (postgrad. faculty continuing edn.), Am. Coll. Angiology, Oxford Ophthal. Congress and Soc. (lectr. 1960-61), Royal Soc. Health, Internat. Acad. Cosmetic Surgery, Sociedad Mexicana Ortopedia (hon.), C. Puestow Surg. Soc.; mem. AAAS, Internat. Soc. Geog. Ophthalmology, Pan Am. Assn. Ophthalmology, Assn. for Research Ophthalmology, Am. Assn. Ophthalmology, Am. Soc. Contemporary Ophthalmology, Internat. Glaucoma Soc., Ill. Soc. for Med. Research, Internat. Soc. Clin. Electrophysiology of Vision (hon., lectr. 1978), Met. Opera Guild, Fedn. Am. Scientists, N.Y., Ill. acads. sci., AAUP, Nat. Soc. Lit. and Arts, Nat. Hist. Soc., Rush Med. Sch.-Presbyn. St. Luke's Alumni Assn., Internat. Platform Assn., Cousteau Soc., Sigma Xi, Sigma Alpha Epsilon, Phi Beta Pi, Theta Kappa Psi. Cons. author Textbook of Endocrinology. Editorial bd. Clin. Medicine, 1958—, EENT Digest, 1958—, Internat. Surgery, 1972—. Contbr. articles to profl. jours. Home: 734 S Oak Knoll Dr Lake Forest IL 60045 Office: 320 E Vine St Lake Forest IL 60045

MONROE, ALAN DOUGLAS, polit. scientist; b. Balt., Oct. 11, 1944; s. Robert Lloyd and Florence June (Pavey) M.; B.A. magna cum laude, Butler U., 1966; Ph.D. (NDEA fellow), Ind. U., 1971; m. Paula S. Conroy, Dec. 28, 1974; 1 dau., Melissa Ann. Asst. prof. polit. sci. Ill. State U., Normal, 1970-75, asso. prof., 1975—; cons. on survey research and polit. campaigning for local, state and nat. polit. candidates, 1970-76. Am. Polit. Sci. Assn. State and Local Govt. intern, 1968-69. Mem. Am., Midwest, So. polit. sci. assns. Republican. Author: Public Opinion in America, 1975. Home: 903 Broadway Normal IL 61761 Office: Dept Polit Sci Ill State U Normal IL 61761

MONROE, JOHN CLAYTON, JR., architect; b. Kansas City, Mo., Jan. 19, 1923; s. John Clayton and Virginia (McPherson) M.; B.S., U. Kans., 1949; m. Leona Wallenmeyer, Apr. 5, 1952; children—John Clayton III, Laurie K. Project architect Neville, Sharp and Simon, architects, Kansas City, Mo., 1949-53; architect, owner John C. Monroe, architect, 1953-55; pres. Monroe and Lefebvre Architects, Inc., Kansas City, 1955—; pres. Ten Seventeen Peen Co., Inc. Mem. Clay County Bd. Parks and Recreation, 1965, Kansas City Art Commn., 1960-63; chmn. Citizens Assn., 1959, City Central Exec. Com., 1960; mem. Kansas City Bd. Park Commrs., 1955-56; mem. Jud. Nominating Commn., Kansas City, Mo., 1965—; chmn. Clay County Park and Recreation Commn., 1970—. Bd. dirs. YMCA, 1959-64, Conv. and Visitors Bur., 1971-74; trustee Liberty Meml., 1970. Served with USMCR, 1943-45, 50-51. Mem. Mo. Assn. Registered Architects (pres. 1959), A.I.A., Constrn. Specification Inst. (pres. 1964). Democrat. Methodist. Clubs: University (pres. 1965), Vanguard, Mercury, Mission Hills Country. Home: 123 Greentree Ln Kansas City MO 64116 Office: 1021 Pennsylvania St Kansas City MO 64105

MONSALVATGE, RAYMOND FERNANDO, JR., lectr.; b. Savannah, Ga., Oct. 9, 1920; s. Raymond Fernando and Florence (Miller) M.; A.A., Armstrong State Coll., 1941; B.A., Birmingham So. Coll., 1943. Mgr. edn. Nat. Mgmt. Assn., Dayton, Ohio, 1948-58; vis. lectr. U. P.R. extension service, Rio Piedras, 1959; conv. keynoter, condr. spl. seminars, world wide, Dayton, 1959—. Trustee Dayton Soc. Natural History, 1954—. Served with USNR, 1943-45. Named Outstanding Speaker, Sales and Marketing Execs. Internat., 1968. Mem. Nat. Mgmt. Assn., Am. Assn. Museums, Internat. Brotherhood Magicians, Sierra Club, Nature Conservancy, Soc. Am. Magicians, Omicron Delta Kappa. Republican. Episcopalian. Clubs: Rotary, Engrs. (Dayton). Home: 401 Elmhurst Rd Dayton OH 45417 Office: 5327 F Salem Bend Dr Dayton OH 45426

MONSEES, RICHARD HENRY, real estate developer; b. Sedalia, Mo., Oct. 11, 1942; s. Dietrich G. and RubyLou (Bremer) M.; B.S., U. Mo., 1964; m. Janet Louise Hartin, Apr. 11, 1963; children—Richard Henry, Scott D., Robert M. Operator farm nr. Sedalia, 1964-69; exec. dir. Pettis County United Fund, Sedalia, 1964-65; pres. Monsees Realty Co., Sedalia, 1964—, Maplewood Service Co., pub. utility, Sedalia, 1974—, Brooking Park Geriatrics, Inc., Sedalia, 1974—; v.p., sec. A and R Industries, Ind., Sedalia; sec., treas. Monsees Devel. Corp., Sedalia. Mem. curriculum com. Smith-Cotton High Sch., Sedalia, 1972. Founder, pres. Pettis County Rep. Club, Sedalia, 1970; regional coordinator 4th Congl. Dist. Bond-for-Auditor Com., 1970, 4th Congl. Dist. Bond-for-Gov. com., 1972; mem. Pettis County Rep. Com., Sedalia, 1966—, chmn., 1974—. Mem. Nat. (mem. rural devel. com. 1974—), Mo. (chmn. rural devel. com. 1975) assns. home builders, Sedalia Bd. Realtors (pres. 1973), Nat. Inst. Real Estate Brokers, U. Mo. Alumni Assn., Sedalia C. of C. (dir. 1973-74), Mo. (community devel. chmn. 1966-67), Sedalia (dir. 1964-68) jr. chambers commerce, Alpha Kappa Psi. Methodist (bd. mem. 1965-68). Club: Walnut Hills Country (dir. 1969-73) (Sedalia, Mo.). Home: Hermosa Lake Route 2 Sedalia MO 65301 Office: 1609 S Limit St Sedalia MO 65301

MONSMA, STEPHEN VOS, state legislator; b. Pella, Iowa, Sept. 22, 1936; s. Martin and Marie (Vos) M.; A.B., Calvin Coll., 1958; M.A., Georgetown U., 1961; Ph.D., Mich. State U., 1965; m. Mary A. Carlisle, Dec. 19, 1964; children—Martin Stephen, Kristin Joy. Asst. prof. State U. Coll., Plattsburgh, N.Y., 1964-67; asst. prof. dept. polit. sci. Calvin Coll., Grand Rapids, Mich., 1967-69, asso. prof., 1969-73, prof., 1973-74, chmn. dept. polit. sci., 1969-74; mem. Mich. Ho. Reps., 1975—. Mem. Kent County Democratic Exec. Com., 1969—; chmn. 5th Dist. Kennedy for Pres. Com., 1968; bd. dirs. Center for Theology and Pub. Policy, 1976—. Served with AUS, 1960. Mem. Midwest Polit. Sci. Assn. (exec. council 1972-75), Grand Rapids Urban League (v.p. 1972-75). Mem. Christian Ref. Ch. Author: American Politics: A Systems Approach, 1969, 73, 76; The Unraveling of America, 1974; co-author: The Dynamics of the American Political System, 1972; co-editor: American Politics: Research and Readings, 1970; editorial bd. Am. Jour. Polit. Sci., 1973-75; contbr. articles to profl. jours. Home: 829 N Kent View Dr NE Grand Rapids MI 49505

MONSON, ROBERT JOSEPH, lawyer; b. Stillwater, Minn., June 10, 1924; s. Randolph Alvin and Mathilda (LaMere) M.; student St. Thomas Coll., 1945-48; B.S., St. Paul Coll., 1950, LL.B., 1952, J.D., 1969; student Miss. So. Coll., 1942-43; m. Lorraine Ann Pieruccioni, Aug. 3, 1946; children—Robert Joseph Jr., Michele L. Admitted to Minn. bar, 1952; mgr. collection dept. Income Tax div. Minn. Dept. Taxation, St. Paul, 1948-52; claims adjustor State Farm Mutual Automobile Ins. Co., St. Paul, 1952-53; pvt. practice law, St. Paul, 1953—; dir. Wm. F. Kopp Constrn. Co., St. Paul, 1955—; dir. Bostrom Sheet Metal Works Inc., St. Paul, 1961—; dir., sec. Equipment Supply Co., St. Paul; sec., dir. Dakota Improvement & Devel. Co., St. Paul, 1961—. Republican precinct chmn., 1958-63, regional chmn., 1963-70, vice-chmn. Dakota County, 1970—, del. to county and state conv., 1963-72, chmn. Dakota County for Nixon, 1968, mem. Minn. State Central Com., 1970-72; chmn. teenage activities St. Paul Winter Carnival, 1957. Served with USAAF, 1942-45. Mem. Am. (mem. standing com. on legislation 1967-70), Minn. (chmn. legislative com. 1959-74, mem. pub. relations com. 1955—, chmn. radio-TV-subcom. 1957-61), Ramsey County (chmn. legislative com. 1965-67, mem. exec. com. 1965-68, 74—, mem. ethics com. 1972—) bar assns., Am. Arbitration Assn., K. of C. (mem. council 1959—, advocate 1960-66, chancellor 1967), Minn. Hist. Soc., Phi Beta Gamma. Republican. Roman Catholic. Clubs: St. Paul Jaycees, Southview Country (dir. 1974, pres. 1976), St. Paul Athletic, Univ. (St. Paul). Home: 1018 Downing St Mendota Heights MN 55118 Office: 311 Degree of Honor Bldg St Paul MN 55101

MONTAG, THOMAS DALE, newspaper editor, poet; b. Ft. Dodge, Iowa, Aug. 31, 1947; s. Philip John and Oma Marie (Allen) M.; B.A., Dominican Coll., 1972; m. Mary Kathryn Whitford, 1969; children—Jenifer, Jessica. Editor, pub. Monday Morning Press, Milw., 1971-77, Margins, Milw., 1972—; asso. editor Fox River Patriot, Princeton, Wis., 1976—; dir. Boox, Inc., 1975-77; mem. lit. panel Wis. Arts Bd.; author: Wooden Nickel (poems), 1972; Measures (poems), 1972; To Leave This Place (poem), 1972; Making Hay (poem), 1973; Making Hay and Other Poems, 1975; 90 Notes (poem), 1976; Naming the Greeks (poem), 1976; Learning to Read Again (lit. criticism), 1976; Concerns (lit. criticism), 1977. Home and office: PO Box A Fairwater WI 53931

MONTEE, BENJAMIN MOHON, food vending co. exec.; b. Arcadia, Kans., Jan. 11, 1911; s. Clarence Mart and Sarah Catherin (Mohon) M.; m. Eunice Mae Hammett, Nov. 19, 1965. Mgr., Fox Midwest Theatres, 1930-50; pres. El Fran Theatres Inc., 1950-74; pres. Cater-Vend, Jacksonville, Ill., 1954—; pres. Jacksonville Coca-Cola Bottling Co., 1960-69; dir. Autoviable Services Inc.; Elliott State Bank, Jacksonville, Ill., St. Louis. Pres. Passavant Hosp., Jacksonville, 1958. Served with U.S. Army, 1943-46. Mem. Nat. Automatic Merchandising Assn. (chmn. bd. 1974), Ill. Automatic Merchandising Council (pres. 1968). Republican. Episcopalian. Clubs: Jacksonville Country, Elks. Home: 1905 Mound Rd Jacksonville IL 62650 Office: 320 S Main St Jacksonville IL 62650

MONTEITH, THOMAS WILSON, utility co. exec.; b. Port Huron, Mich., Jan. 6, 1919; s. Wilson Harvey and Laura May (Macdonald) M.; student Port Huron Jr. Coll., 1938-39, Lincoln Inst., 1951-52; m. Joyce Irene Jay, Oct. 15, 1939; 1 dau., Janet (Mrs. Ralph Douglas Bopra, Jr.). Prodn. control scheduler Mueller Brass Co., Port Huron, Mich., 1939-41; prodn. control mgr. Ainsworth Mfg. Co., Marysville, Mich., 1948-54; purchasing agt. Southeastern Mich. Gas Co., Port Huron, 1961—. Chmn. membership campaign YMCA, Port Huron, 1970, bd. dirs., 1970-76; sec. state council YMCA Mich., 1970-71. Served with AUS, 1942-45. Decorated Presidential Unit Citation. Mem. Am. Gas Assn. (mem. com. 1965-70), Nat. Assn. Purchasing Mgts., Am. Purchasing Soc. Presbyn. (elder 1968-71. Mason; mem. Order Eastern Star. Club: Blue Water Industrial (pres. 1967) (Port Huron). Home: 3210 Stone St Port Huron MI 48060 Office: 405 Water St Port Huron MI 48060

MONTES, PEGGY ANN, counselor; b. Chgo., Oct. 17, 1938; d. Thomas and Myrtle (Thomas) Booker; student Howard U., 1956-58; B.Ed., Chgo. State U., 1960; postgrad. Gov.'s State U., Chgo., 1973-74; m. Paul Joseph Montes, Dec. 17, 1960; children—Paul, Pia. Elementary tchr. Chgo. Bd. Edn., 1960-71, adjustment tchr.-counselor, 1971-74, coordinator counseling services dept. Percy Julian High Sch., 1975—; cons. in field. Pres. Profl. Aux. Provident Hosp., 1973—; bd. dirs. Harriet Harris YWCA, 1972—, Chgo. Area Planned Parenthood Assn., 1974-76. Named Woman of Year, Civic Aux. Planned Parenthood Assn., 1975. Mem. Am. Personnel and Guidance Assn., Council for Exceptional Children, Am. Assn. Supervision and Curriculum, League Black Women, Nat. Council Negro Women, Phi Delta Kappa, Phi Delta Kappa.

MONTESI, SUSAN JEAN, adminstrv. counselor, educator; b. Escanaba, Mich., Jan. 15, 1945; d. Ernest James and Jean Regina (Bichler) Vanlerberghe; B.S. in Chemistry, Ferris State Coll., 1966; M.A., in Guidance and Counseling, Central Mich. U., 1970, M.A. in Psychology, 1976; m. William A. Montesi, Apr. 16, 1966; children—Scott William, Aimee Danielle. Tchr., Rockford (Mich.) High Sch., 1966, Morley Stanwood High Sch., 1966-68, Adam Kolb Intermediate Sch., Bay City, Mich., 1968-70; tchr. Mich. Migrant Edn. Program, 1967-69; counselor Delta Coll., University Center, Mich., 1970—, chmn. dept., 1974—, evening asso. prof. psychology, 1972—; mem. advisory commn. on career edn. Mich. State Dept. Edn., 1976—. Recipient award local chpt. AAUP, 1975. Mem. Am. (dir. commn. 1975—), Mich. personnel and guidance assns., Am., Mich. coll. personnel assns., N.Central Guidance Assn., Nat. Council on Learning, Am. Psychol. Assn., Sex. Information and Edn. Council U.S. Co—author: Guidelines for Appointment, Reappointment, Promotion, Termination and Evaluation of Counselors, 1975. Home: 2080 Reppuhn Dr Bay City MI 48706 Office: K143 Delta College University Center MI 48710

MONTGOMERY, BURTIS EDGAR, physician; b. Princeton, Ind., July 14, 1898; s. Edgar Ernest and Etta (McCleary) M.; B.S., McKendree Coll., 1922; B.S., U. Ill., 1930, M.S., 1930, M.D., 1933; m. Kathleen Taylor, Dec. 19, 1924. Intern St. Lukes Hosp., Chgo., 1932-33, resident, 1933-34; practice medicine, specializing in internal medicine, Harrisburg, Ill., 1934—; mem. staff Doctors Hosp., chief med. staff, 1951, pres. bd. trustees, 1950-66; mem. staff Welborn Baptist Hosp., Evansville, Ind. Trustee Saline Valley Savs. & Loan, 1951—. Mem. Ill. Bd. Med. Examiners, 1951-66; chmn. Ill. Com. on Medicare, 1956-67; chmn. com. for Ill. med. care United Mine Workers of Am., 1956-67. Served with U.S. Army, 1917-18, comdr. USNR, 1942-46. Recipient Alumnus of Yr. award U. Ill. Med. Sch., 1966; Man of Yr. award Rotary Club, Harrisburg, 1970. Fellow A.C.P., Am. Acad. Family Practice; mem. Am. Soc. Internal Medicine, A.M.A. (life; chmn. bd. trustees), Saline-Pope-Hardin County (life), Ill. (life) med. socs., Am. Legion (life), V.F.W. (life), Sigma Xi. Methodist (trustee 1950-65). Mason (32 deg., Shriner), Elk, Rotarian. Alpha Omega Alpha. Home: 100 W Walnut St Harrisburg IL 62946

MONTGOMERY, JAMES WINCHESTER, clergyman; b. Chgo., May 29, 1921; s. James E. and Evelyn (Winchester) M.; B.A., Northwestern U., 1943; S.T.B., Gen. Theol. Sem., N.Y.C., 1949. Ordained to ministry Episcopal Ch., 1949; curate St. Luke's Ch., Evanston, Ill., 1949-51; rector St. John the Evangelist Ch., Flossmoor, Ill., 1951-62; dean Chgo.-South Deanery, Diocese of Chgo., 1955-62, mem. Diocesan Council, 1954—, dep. to General Convention, 1958, 61; suffragan bishop Episcopal Diocese of Chicago, 1962-65, bishop coadjutor, 1965-71, bishop, Chgo., 1971—. Served with USNR, 1943-46. Member Phi Beta Kappa, Delta Upsilon. Home: 1320 N State St Chicago IL 60610 Office: 65 E Huron St Chicago IL 60611

MONTGOMERY, JOHN OSBORN, automotive co. exec.; b. Detroit, Mar. 21, 1921; s. Henry Arthur and Bessie Ellen (Henderson) M.; B.S. in Agr., Mich. State U., 1950; m. Joy Evelyn Dunlop, Mar. 2, 1946; children—John Henry Earl, James Lawrence, Jeffrey Michael. Mem. editorial staff Detroit Times, 1937-40, columnist state capitol bur., 1946-49; owner, operator dairy farm, Howell, Mich., 1949-52; mem. pub. relations staff Chrysler Corp., Detroit, 1952-55, dir. pub. relations Chrysler div., 1955-60, corp. mgr. news relations, 1960-74, mgr. indsl. pub. relations, 1974—. Chmn. pub. relations com., bd. dirs. ARC, Detroit, 1971—; bd. dirs., chmn. pub. relations com. Wayne County unit Am. Cancer Soc., 1974—; chmn. pub. relations com. Boy Scouts Am., 1970—. Trustee Greater Detroit Council on Alcoholism, 1970-74. Served with AUS, 1940-46, PTO. Mem. Pub. Relations Soc. Am. (chpt. dir. 1962-64, pres. 1970, dir. 1971, Silver Anvil award, 1957). Mich. Press. Assn., Detroit Bd. Commerce, Detroit Hist. Soc., Founders Soc., Detroit Inst. Arts, St. Andrews Soc. Clubs: Detroit Press, Players, Crisis (Detroit). Home: 745 University Place Grosse Pointe MI 48230 Office: 12000 Oakland Ave Highland Park MI 48231

MONTGOMERY, REX, biochemist; b. Halesowen, Eng., Sept. 4, 1923; s. Fred and Jane (Holloway) M.; came to U.S., 1948, naturalized, 1963; B.Sc., U. Birmingham (Eng.), 1943, Ph.D., 1946, D.Sc., 1963; m. Barbara Winifred Price, Aug. 9, 1948; children—Ian, David, Jennifer, Christopher. Research asso. U. Minn., 1951-55; mem. faculty U. Iowa, Iowa City, 1955—, prof. biochemistry, 1963—, asso. dean Coll. Medicine, 1974—; cons. Gen. Mills, Inc., 1964-69, NRC Can., 1973; mem. study sect NIH, 1968-72, mem. drug devel. contract rev. com., 1975—; vis. prof. Nat. Australian U., 1969-70. Postdoctoral fellow Ohio State U., 1948-49; Sugar Research Found. fellow, U.S. Dept. Agr., 1949-51. Mem. Nat. Acad. Scis. (chmn. com. biol. chemistry 1961-64). Author: Chemical Production of Lactic Acid, 1949; Chemistry of Plant Gums and Mucilages, 1959; Quantitative Problems in the Biochemical Sciences, 1969, 2d edit., 1976; Biochemistry-A Case-Oriented Approach, 1974, 2d edit., 1977; editorial bd. Carbohydrate Research, 1968—; contbr. articles to profl. jours. Home: 5 Princeton Ct Iowa City IA 52240 Office: Office Dean Coll Medicine U Iowa Iowa City IA 52242

MONTGOMERY, ROBERT MAX, dentist; b. Topeka, Nov. 27, 1918; s. Simpson K. and Ella Mae (Roberts) M.; Asso. Sci., Kemper Mil. Sch., 1938; B.S., U. Mo. at Kansas City, 1943, D.D.S., 1943; m. Nola K. Sannaman, May 28, 1958; children—Mindy Sue, Tammy Kay. Dentist, Clay Center, Kans., 1946—. Mem. U.S. Assay Commn., 1971. Served to lt. (s.g.), USNR, 1943-46. Mem. Am. Numis. Assn. (life), Clay Center C. of C., Kans., Am. dental assns. Republican. Elk. Home: 1801 6th St Clay Center KS 67432 Office: 712 6th St Clay Center KS 67432

MONTGOMERY-SHORT, RUTH GERTRUDE (MRS. JOSEPH C. SHORT), physician; b. Denison, Kans., July 7, 1910; d. Raymond F. and Freda D. (Banaka) Montgomery; B.S. magna cum laude, Washburn U., 1932; M.D., U. Kans., 1937; m. Joseph C. Short, June 21, 1936; children—Marian L. (Mrs. Randle K. Hope), Martha J. (Mrs. Ronald G. Merritt), Marilyn R. (Mrs. Aron G. Strange). Intern North Hudson Hosp., Weehawken, N.J., 1937-38, Margaret Hague Maternity Hosp., Jersey City, 1937; staff physician Student Health Service, Kans. State U., Manhattan, 1938-42; preceptorship in ear, nose, throat, Wichita, Kans., 1942-45; practice medicine specializing in ear, nose and throat, Wichita, 1945-50; ear, nose, throat staff Hertzler Clinic, Halstead, Kans., 1950—; ear, nose, throat staff Halstead Hosp., 1950—, pres. med. staff, 1971. Mem. Gov.'s Commn. on Status of Women, 1965-67. Trustee Sterling (Kans.) Coll., 1972-78. Mem. AMA; Am. Med. Women Assn., Pan Am. Med. Women's Alliance (sec. 1967-77), Pan Am. Assn. Otorhinolaryngology and Bronchoesophagology, Am. Assn. Ry. Surgeons, Kans. (pres. ear, nose, throat sect. 1963-64, 69-70), Harvey, Sedgwick County med. socs., Kansas City Soc. Otorhinolaryngology, Dental Aux., Tau Delta Pi, Phi Kappa Phi, Alpha Epsilon Iota (pres. 1935-36). Presbyterian (elder). Clubs: Soroptimist (pres. 1967-68 Wichita, Opti-Mrs. Contbr. articles to profl. jours. Home: 1019 W 50th St N Wichita KS 67204 Office: 327 Chestnut St Halstead KS 67056

MONTIEGEL, BERNARD ALBERT, educator; b. Saginaw, Mich., Mar. 21, 1951; s. Albert E. and Kathryn L. (Ward) M.; B.S., No. Mich. U., 1973, M.A. in Edn., 1976; m. Jeri Lynn Corey, Apr. 7, 1972; children—Joseph Paul, Kathryn Rose. Instr., Baraga Twp. Schs./Keewenaw Bay Ojibwé Tribal Council, Baraga, Mich., 1975, Mathias Twp. Sch., Trenary, Mich., 1975—. Center for History of Am. Indian fellow, 1975. Mem. Am. Hist. Assn., Am. Studies Assn., Orgn. Am. Historians, Soc. History Edn., Phi Alpha Theta. Liberal Democrat. Lutheran. Home: 903 N 4th St Marquette MI 49855 Office: PO Box 210 Trenary MI 49891

MONUS, NATHAN HARLOW, wholesale grocery co. exec.; b. Youngstown, Ohio, Oct. 14, 1921; s. Frank and Sarah (Lebov) M.; student Va. Mil. Inst., Lexington, 1939-40; grad. Ohio State U., 1942; m. Frances Tamarkin, June 16, 1946; children—Michael Ira, Susan Beth. Owner dairy equipment and supply firm, 1946-50; with Tamarkin Co., Youngstown, 1950—, now corporate financial exec. Bd. dirs. Jewish Fedn., 1972-73. Served with AUS, 1943-46. Mem. Nat. Assn. Wholesale Grocers Assn. (bd. govs. 1973—), Phi Sigma Delta (pres. 1942). Jewish (bd. dirs. temple 1972-73). Rotarian pres. Austintown club 1972-73. Club: Squaw Creek Country (pres. 1963-64). Home: 1380 Virginia Trail Youngstown OH 44505 Office: 375 Victoria Rd Youngstown OH 44515

MOODY, BLAIR, JR., state supreme ct. justice; b. Detroit, Feb. 27, 1928; s. Blair and Mary (Williamson) M.; B.A., U. Mich., 1949, LL.B., 1952; m. Mary Lou Kennedy, Aug. 18, 1951; children—Diane Marie, Blair III, Susan Beth, Brian Thornton, Peter Kennedy. Reporter, Detroit News, summers 1949-50; reporter Washington Post, 1952; admitted to Mich. bar, 1952; practiced in Detroit, 1953-65; mem. firm Sullivan, Eames Moody & Petrillo, 1953-65; judge Circuit Ct. Wayne County, Detroit, 1966-76; justice Mich. Supreme Ct., 1977—. Mem. Citizens Com. for Equal Opportunity, 1966—. Democratic precinct del., 1954-62; chmn. Citizens for Kennedy Wayne County, 1960. Served with USAF, 1952-53. Mem. Phi Delta Theta, Phi Delta Phi. Presbyterian. Clubs: Detroit Press, Economic. Home: 69 Willow Tree Pl Grosse Pointe Shores MI 48236 Office: 1425 Lafayette Bldg Detroit MI 48226

MOODY, G. WILLIAM, aerospace mfg. co. exec.; b. Cleveland Heights, Ohio, Nov. 6, 1928; s. John Walter and Anna Barbara (Keck) M.; student Ohio U., 1948-49; B.S. in Civil Engring., Mich. State U., 1952; m. Loisjean Kanouse, Sept. 17, 1955; children—Elizabeth Jean, Cynthia Ann, G. William. Sales engr. Rich Mfg. Corp., Battle Creek, Mich., 1952-55; chief engr. Air Lift Co., Lansing, Mich., 1955-61; product engr. Aeroquip Corp., Jackson, Mich., 1961-62, chief engr. Barco div., 1962-68, v.p., gen. mgr., 1968-72, v.p., ops. mgr. AMB div., 1972-74, v.p., gen. mgr. aerospace div., 1974—, dir. Aeroquip Aerospace S.A.; sr. design engr. Clark Floor Machine Co., Muskegon, Mich., 1962. Gen. campaign chmn. Jackson County United Way, 1976; mem. planning commn. North Barrington, Ill., 1967-72; chmn. Joint Com. for an Area Hosp., Barrington, 1969-72. Served with U.S. Army, 1946-48. Mem. Soc. Automotive Engrs., ASME, Am. Mgmt. Assn., Jackson C. of C. Lutheran. Clubs: Jackson Country, Jackson County Sportsman's. Patentee in field. Home: 612 S Bowen Jackson MI 49203 Office: 300 S East Ave Jackson MI 49203

MOODY, JOSEPH PALMER, physician; b. Toronto, Ont., Can., Nov. 2, 1919; s. William and Jennie (Sommerville) M.; M.D., Western U., 1946; m. Viola Olive Barrick, Nov. 3, 1942; children—Gloria May (Mrs. John Pelchat), Robert, Mary, Richard. Med. officer Canadian Govt., Chesterfield Inlet East Arctic, 1946-50, North Battleford, Sask., 1950-52, Manitoulin Island, Ont., 1952-57; med. dir. Elliot Lake (Ont.) Clinic, 1957—; field med. officer Rio-Algom Mines, Elliot Lake, 1959—. Mem. Med. Assn. Can., N.Y. Acad. Scis., Coll. Family Physicians of Can., Am. Thermographic Soc. Progressive Conservative. Participant Arctic Mercy Flights - stopped great polio epidemic of the Arctic, 1948-49; spl. research work for Am., Can. Armies in Arctic, 1948. Home: 47 Axmith Elliot Lake ON Canada Office: 60 Hillside Dr Elliot Lake ON Canada

MOODY, ROBERT ADAMS, neurosurgeon; b. Swampscott, Mass., Oct. 1, 1934; s. George F. and Florence P. Moody; B.A., U. Chgo., 1955, B.S., 1956, M.D., 1960; m. Clara Mae Emerson; children—Robert Adams, II, Cathy, Paul, Lisa, Sherri. Intern, Royal Victoria Hosp., Montreal, 1960-61; resident U. Vt. Affiliated Hosps., 1961-66; fellow Lahey Clinic, 1963-64; asst. prof. neurol. surgery U. Chgo. Med. Sch., 1966-71; sr. clin. instr. Tufts U. Med. Sch., Boston, 1972, asst. clin. prof., 1973-74; prof. neurosurgery Abraham Lincoln Med. Sch., U. Ill., Chgo., 1975—; chmn. div. neurosurgery Cook County Hosp., Chgo., 1974—, asso. chmn. dept. surgery, 1976—. USPHS fellow, 1957-58. Mem. ACS, Am. Assn. Neurol. Surgeons, Central Neurosurg. Soc. (v.p. 1977-78), Assn. Acad. Surgery, Interurban Neurosurg. Soc., Alumni Assn. Lahey Clinic Found. Contbr. articles to med. jours. Office: 1825 W Harrison St Chicago IL 60612

MOODY, TOM, mayor; b. Columbus, Ohio, Nov. 26, 1929; B.S. summa cum laude, Ohio State U., 1954; J.D., Franklin U., 1956; m. Jean Watson, Sept. 9, 1949; children—Todd, Trent, Paula Jean. Admitted to Ohio bar, 1956; pvt. practice law, Columbus, 1956-63; judge Franklin County (Ohio) Municipal Ct., 1963-67; judge Common Pleas Ct. Franklin County, 1969-71; mayor, Columbus, Ohio, 1971—; counsel firm Crabbe, Newlon, Potts, Schmidt, Brown & Jones, Columbus, 1971—. Lectr. in torts Law Sch., Franklin U., 1958-60; lectr. in evidence Captial U., Franklin Law Sch., 1968-70. Mem. city council, Columbus, 1961-63; mem. 28th Ward Republican Com., 1958-63. Past pres., bd. dirs. Franklin County chpt. Muscular Dystrophy Assn. Am.; chmn. membership drive South Side YMCA; mem. legal div. United Appeals; mem. exec. bd. Central YMCA. Mem. Am., Ohio State, Columbus bar assns., Ohio Jud. Conf., Ohio Municipal Judges Assn. (past v.p.), Am. Legion, Kappa Sigma. Lutheran. Clubs: Barristers, Lawyers, Mason (Shriner). Home: 945 Stoney Creek Rd Columbus OH 43085 Office: City Hall 90 W Broad St Columbus OH 43215

MOON, BYUNG SOO, engring. analyst; b. Korea, Feb. 10, 1944; s. Chong Shik and Mac Nam (Park) M.; came to U.S., 1966, naturalized, 1977; B.S. in Physics, Utah State U., 1969; M.S. in Mathematics, U. Ill., 1970, Ph.D. in Math., 1974; m. Kyung Mee Cho, July 12, 1973; 1 dau., Annie. Engring. analyst Sargent & Lundy Engrs., Chgo., since 1974. Mem. Am., Korean math. socs. Home: 1330 Rockcove Ct Hoffman Estates IL 60172 Office: 55 E Monroe St Chicago IL 60603

MOON, CHARLES REDMAN, lawyer; b. St. Anthony, Idaho, Nov. 21, 1913; s. C. Redman and Elsa (Haass) M.; student Dartmouth, 1931-33; A.B., U. Mich., 1935, J.D., 1937; m. Miriam G. Robertson, Oct. 14, 1939 (dec. 1967); children—Charles R. III, William R. m. 2d, Janet Faden Crow, Feb. 8, 1969; stepchildren—Allen F., Stephen L., Jeffrey L. Admitted to Mich. bar, 1937, since practiced in Detroit; asso. Dickinson, Wright, McKean, Cudlip & Moon, 1937-48, partner, 1948—; dir. Douglas & Lomason Co.; justice of peace, Pleasant Ridge, Mich., 1949-60. Served as lt., USNR, 1942-46; PTO. Mem. Am., Mich., Detroit bar assns., Am. Judicature Soc., Order of Coif, Mil. Order World Wars, Kappa Sigma, Phi Delta Phi. Clubs: Century (Muskegon, Mich.); Barristers, Detroit Athletic (dir. 1977—), Bond, Country of Detroit, Renaissance, Detroit (Detroit). Presbyterian. Home: 224 Vendome Rd Grosse Pointe Farms MI 48236 Office: First National Bldg Detroit MI 48226

MOON, GEORGE DONALD, JR., chem. engring. cons.; b. Dayton, Ohio, Apr. 15, 1927; s. George Donald and Ruth Isabelle (Drake) M.; B. Chem. Engring., U. Dayton, 1949; m. Nancy Green, Dec. 19, 1953; children—Nancy Margaret, George Donald III, Ruth Marie, Joseph Hughes. Asst. prof. chem. engring. U. Cin., 1951-65, asso. prof., 1965-73; sr. process engr. Raphael Katzen Assos., chem. cons., Cin., 1954—. Mem. Am. Inst. Chem. Engrs., Am. Chem. Soc., Am. Soc. Engring. Edn., Triangle (Service award 1973), Sigma Xi, Phi Lambda Upsilon, Alpha Chi Sigma, Tau Beta Pi, Omega Chi Epsilon. Presbyn. (deacon). Mason (32 deg.). Patentee multiphase contacting apparatus and method. Home: 1181 Hawkstone Dr Cincinnati OH 45230 Office: Raphael Katzen Assos 1050 Delta Ave Cincinnati OH 45208

MOON, HAROLD EUGENE, banker; Middletown, Ohio, June 11, 1934; s. Harold Eugene and Sarah (Leaf) M.; student Miami U. (Ohio), 1952, 54-56; B.S., Xavier U., 1958; M. in Banking, Rutgers-The State U., 1968; m. Marylyn Danford, June 21, 1958; children—Kathryn Heather, Fred Danford, Suzanne Shearman, Elizabeth Anne. With Fifth Third Union Trust Co., Cin., 1958-69, asst. cashier, 1963-65, asst. v.p., 1965-69; v.p. Ind. Nat. Bank, Indpls., 1969-73; v.p., corporate banking group mgr. Beverly Bank, Chgo., 1973-76; chief exec. officer State Bank of Lombard (Ill.), 1976-77; exec. v.p. So. Ohio Bank, Cin., 1977—. Scoutmaster, Boy Scouts Am., 1963-66, dist. commr., 1967-69, dist. chmn., 1972-73, council exec. bd., 1970—, lodge lay adviser, 1973-74, Wood badge, 1969, Vigil honor, 1967, Silver Beaver, 1969. Served with U.S. Army, 1953-55. Mem. C. of C., Soc. Colonial Wars (gov. Ind. soc. 1973). Republican. Episcopalian. Mason. Clubs: University, Miami (Cin.). Home: 7579 Montridge Ct Cincinnati OH 45244 Office: 515 Main St Cincinnati OH 45202

MOON, JESSE MORRIS, JR., lawyer; b. Wichita, Kans., Nov. 15, 1918; s. Jesse Morris and Edna (Clarke) M.; student Butler County Jr. Coll., 1936-38; B.S. in Bus., U. Kans., 1940, J.D., 1946; m. Shirley Johnson, Dec. 20, 1941; children—Jesse III, Marilyn, Robert, David, Richard. Admitted to Kans. bar, 1946; asst. atty. Butler County, El Dorado, Kans., 1946-51, county atty., 1951-55; atty. City Augusta, Kans., 1962—. Dir. Prairie State Bank, Augusta, and several other corps. Trustee Flossie E. West Meml. Trust. Served to lt. (j.g.) USCGR, 1942-45. Mem. Kans. Bar Assn. (chmn. title standards com.), City Atty.'s Assn. Kans. (past pres.), County Atty.'s Assn. Kans. (past pres.), Augusta C. of C. (past pres.), Am. Legion. Republican. Methodist. Elk, Mason, Rotarian. Home: 1917 Meadowlake Dr Augusta KS 67010 Office: 103 E 5th Ave Augusta KS 67010

MOON, MARCUS ARTHUR, painter; b. Middletown, Ohio, Apr. 6, 1923; s. Virgil and Mary Elizabeth (Ingalls) M.; student Applied Art Acad., Akron, Ohio, 1945-48; m. Mary Lou Pathbun, Oct. 6, 1945; children—Lou Ann, Beverly Jean, Lawrence Michael. One man shows: Akron (Ohio) Art Inst., 1963, Canton (Ohio) Art Inst., 1965, Columbia (S.C.) Mus. Art, 1967; group shows include: Toledo Art Inst., Canton Art Inst., Columbia Mus., Charles and Emma Frye Mus., Seattle, Norfolk (Va.) Mus. Art, Charleston (W.Va.) Art Gallery; represented in permanent collections: Massilon (Ohio) Art Mus., Springfield (Mo.) Art Inst., Canton Art Inst., Columbia Mus., Richmond (Va.) Mus.; tchr. figure drawing and design Applied Art Acad., Akron, 1948-54, owner, dir., 1954-60; owner, mgr. Applied Art Supply, Akron, 1954-60; Owner, mgr. Marc Moon Studio, Cuyahoga Falls, Ohio, 1960—; tchr. watercolor workshops Sarasota, Ft. Myers and Miami, Fla., Dallas, Huntington, W.Va., Charlotte, N.C., Southport, N.C., Greenwich, Conn., Akron and Canton, Ohio. Recipient Best Watercolor award, Canton Art Inst., 1963, 66, 1st prize watercolor, 62, 63, 67, purchase award, 1962, 63, Honor award, 1966; 1st prize water color Va. Beach Art Show, 1965, 66, 70, Best in Show, 1964, 1st prize pastel, 1965; Hudson Valley Art Assn. 1st prize watercolor, 1968; Mario Cooper Award, 1970. Mem. Am. Watercolor Soc., Salamagundi Club. Club: Rotary. Home: 505 W Portage Trail Cuyahoga Falls OH 44223

MOON, ROBERT ALLEN, dentist; b. Atlantic, Iowa, May 1, 1933; s. Clarence Allen and Effie (Berry) M.; B.S., Ind. U., 1955, D.D.S., 1958; m. Janice Lilian Hahn, Sept. 5, 1954, (div. May 1972); children—Robert, Mark, David, Kevin, Jeff, Gregory, Susan; m. 2d Donna June Busse, Oct. 21, 1972. Individual practice dentistry, Hobart, Ind., 1961—; instr. Ind. U. Northwest. Lake County dir. March of Dimes, 1971-72. Served with USAF, 1958-61. Mem. Northwest Dist. Dental Soc. (pres. 1968-69, editor newsletter), Ind. Dental Assn. (trustee 1970—, dir. ann. session programs 1976), Internat. Coll. Dentists, Acad. Gen. Dentistry, Am. Dental Assn., Res. Officers Assn., Pierre Fauchard Acad., Phi Delta Kappa, Delta Sigma Delta, Acacia. Methodist. Club: Rotary (pres. 1966-67). Home: 566 Harrison St Valparaiso IN 46383 Office: 904 W Ridge Rd Hobart IN 46342

MOON, WILLIAM, JR., counselor; b. Cleve., Dec. 23, 1920; s. William and Annie Frances (Daniels) M., Sr.; B.S., Kent State U., 1957, M.Edn., 1972; M.F.A., Carnegie Mellon U., 1971; m. Ruth Naomi Black, July 22, 1945; children—Marjorie Ann, Joyce Lucile, William Franklin, Madonna Louise. Mail clerk U.S.P.O., Cleve., 1947-57; tchr. vocal and instrumental music, Cleve. Bd. Edn., 1957-73, guidance counselor, 1973—; instr. instrumental music, Karamu House, Cleve., 1958-62. Lay leader United Methodist Men, Cleve., 1962-70; precinct committeeman, Cleve., 1960-65; leader Boy Scouts Am., Cleve., 1958-60. Served with U.S.N. band, 1942-45. Recipient Martha Holden Jennings award Cleve. Bd. Edn., Carnegie Mellon U., Pitts., 1963, Carnegie Mellon fellowship, 1969; certified instrumental music, guidance, secondary sch. admnstrs., supervisers, Ohio. Mem. Am., Ohio personnel and guidance assns., Phi Mu Alpha Sinfonia. Methodist. Home: 449 E 112th St Cleveland OH 44108 Office: 6809 Franklin Ave Cleveland OH 44102

MOON, WILLIAM ISHAM, truckstop services co. exec.; b. Cook County, Ill., Dec. 13, 1932; s. William Isham and Nellie Ethyl (Carrol) M.; B.S., S.W. Mo. Coll., 1958; grad. Harvard Bus. Sch., 1977; m. Carolyn Blanch Cusac, Nov. 5, 1961; children—William Isham III, Adelia Ann, Carolyn Jill. Sales engr. Standard Oil Co., Wichita, Kans., 1958-60; mgr. Truckstop Standard Oil Co., Kansas City region, 1960-65; pres. Iowa 80 Truckstop Inc., Walcott, 1965—. Served with inf. AUS, 1952-54; Korea. Mem. Nat. Truckstop Operators Assn. (J.L. Schaffer award outstanding truckstop operator, 1974), Am. Truck Hist. Soc. (dir. 1974-77, treas. 1977). Methodist. Home: 403 Main St N Walcott IA 52773 Office: Interstate 80 & 40 Walcott IA 52773

MOORE, CATHERINE GILBERT, research adminstr.; b. Evanston, Ill., Mar. 17, 1936; d. Lewis W. and Marie (Kennedy) Gilbert; A.A., Stephens Coll., 1955; student Northwestern U., 1956-57, Art Inst. Chgo., 1957-58; m. Stanley E. Moore, June 14, 1968; 1 son, Michael G. Roman. Staff, House Beautiful mag., Chgo., 1957-58, Tom O. Moles & Assos., Chgo., 1964-65; staff Newspaper Advt. Bur., Chgo., 1965—, research coordinator, 1968—. Democrat. Unitarian. Home: 5000 N Marine Dr Chicago IL 60640 Office: Newspaper Advt Bur 400 N Michigan Ave Chicago IL 60611

MOORE, CHARLES EDWIN, state justice; b. Des Moines, Aug. 2, 1903; s. William Henry and Metta Mae (Davis) M.; LL.B., Drake U., 1927; m. Iva Mae Barton, Aug. 2, 1930 (dec. June 1959); 1 dau., Marilyn Mae; m. 2d, Margaret Lillian Sundberg, June 23, 1962. Admitted to Iowa bar, 1927; gen. practice, Des Moines, 1927-34; asst. county atty. Polk County, 1934-36; judge Des Moines Municipal Ct., 1936-43, 9th Jud. dist. Iowa Dist. Ct., 1942-62; justice Iowa Supreme Ct., 1962—, now chief justice; part-time instr. Drake U. Law Sch., 1941-62. Mem. Am., Iowa, Polk County bar assns. Republican. Methodist. Mason (33 deg., Shriner). Home: 1540 Guthrie Ave Des Moines IA 50316 Office: State House Des Moines IA 50316

MOORE, CLARA EVELYN MITCHELL, counselor; b. Newark, Aug. 20, 1935; d. James Hugo and Pattie Evelyn (Booker) Mitchell; student Clark U., 1952-54; A.B., Boston U., 1956; M.A., Columbia U., 1957; Ph.D., Case Western Res. U., 1973; children by previous marriage—Tanya Monique, Lance Randall. Tchr. English, Cleve. Bd. Edn., 1957-66; coordinator Schs. Neighborhood Youth Corps, Cleve., 1966-68; tchr. Work Study Program, Cleve., 1968-71; tutor-counselor Case Western Res. U., 1971-73; counselor adult edn. div. Cleve. Bd. Edn., 1973—; mem. faculty dept. ednl. specialists Cleve. State U., 1975—. Chmn. friendly town project Mt. Zion Congl. Ch., 1977, sec. bd. Christian edn., 1976. Mem. NEA, Ohio, Cleve. edn. assns., North East Ohio Tchrs. Assn., Northeast Ohio, Am. personnel and guidance assns., Am. Sch., Ohio sch. counselors assns., Nat. Assn. Women Deans, Adminstrs. and Counselors. Home: 8907 Columbia Ave Cleveland OH 44108 Office: 4966 Woodland Ave Cleveland OH 44104

MOORE, CLARENCE EUGENE MC DANIEL, psychiatrist; b. Des Moines, Oct. 18, 1934; s. Martin F. and Harriett (McDaniel) M.; B.S., State U. Iowa, 1956, M.D., 1964; m. Linda Jean Kemmerer, June 13, 1964; children—Anne Marie, Jill Christine. Intern, Iowa Meth. Hosp., Iowa City, 1964-65; resident State Psychopathic Hosp., Univ. Hosps. U. Iowa, Iowa City, 1965-68; practice medicine specializing in psychiatry, 1968—; chief staff children's cons. service Winnebago (Wis.) State Hosp., 1968-74; cons. psychiatrist Fond du Lac County Hosp., 1969—; Tomorrow's Children, Residential Treatment Facility, Waupaca Wis., 1973—, Tomorrow's Youth, 1973-76; chief internal medicine St. Agnes Hosp., Fond du Lac, Wis., 1976—. Served with U.S. Army, 1956-58. Diplomate Am. Bd. Psychiatry and Neurology in psychiatry. Mem. AMA, Am. Psychiat. Assn., Am. Assn. Automotive Medicine, Motor Racing Safety Soc., Sports Car Club Am., League Am. Wheelmen. Republican. Congregationalist. Contbr. article to med. jours. Home: Route 6 Fond du Lac WI 54935 Office: 153 S Macy St Fond Du Lac WI 54935

MOORE, DAN TYLER, writer; b. Washington, Feb. 1, 1908; s. Dan T. and Luvean Jones (Butler) M.; B.S., Yale U., 1931; m. Elizabeth Valley Oakes, Mar. 12, 1932; children—Luvean O. (Mrs. Owens), Elizabeth Oakes (Mrs. Thornton), Harriet (Mrs. Clements), Dan Tyler, III. Asst. to pres. Intercontinental Hotels Corp., Istanbul, Turkey, 1948-50; pres. Middle East Co., Cleve., China Co., Cleve.,

1946-48; former nat. fgn. corr. in Middle East, N.Am. Newspaper Alliance. Pres. Greater Cleve. Muscular Dystrophy Assn., 1952-65. Mem. exec. com. Cuyahoga County Democratic Party, 1951-70, mem. state exec. com., 1962-65; commr. Ohio Fed. Jury, 1961-68. Trustee Cleve. Museum Natural History; bd. dirs. Near East Rehab. Center, Near East Coll. Assn., Karamu Theatre, Cleve., Cleve. Mus. Natural History. Served with AUS as chief counterintelligence for OSS in Cairo, 1942-44. Mem. Internat. Platform Assn. (chmn. bd., dir. gen). Author: Cloak and Cipher, 1962, The Terrible Game, 1957; Wolves Widows and Orphans, 1966; Lecturing For Profit, 1967. Contbr. articles to popular mags. in U.S. and fgn. countries. Home: 2564 Berkshire Rd Cleveland Heights OH 44106

MOORE, DAVID LOWELL, dentist; b. Hartshorne, Okla., Apr. 3, 1930; s. David Lee and Zula (Winslow) M.; B.S., Okla. State U., 1949; M.S., U. Mo., 1964, M.A., 1964, D.D.S., 1955; m. Mary Janell Stewart, Sept. 7, 1962; children—David Lee, Andrew Stewart. Asst. prof. U. Mo., Kansas City, 1958-61, teaching fellow, 1961-63, asso. prof., 1963-64, prof., chmn. dept. operative dentistry, 1964—; dental cons. U.S. Army, Ft. Leonard Wood, Mo., VA Hosp., Leavenworth, Kans., Topeka, Kansas City and Columbia, Mo. Served with USAF, 1955-58. Mem. ADA, Omicron Kappa Upsilon, Phi Kappa Phi, Omicron Delta Kappa, Psi Omega. Baptist (deacon). Contbr. articles to profl. jours.; chpt. dental textbook. Home: 10705 W 52d Circle Shawnee KS 66203 Office: 650 E 25th St Kansas City MO 64108

MOORE, DEAN ARLIN, telephone co. exec.; b. Hiawatha, Kans., Jan. 22, 1931; s. George Washington and Marion Ennis (Jones) M.; student Railway Communications Training Sch., 1949-50, Southeastern Signal Sch., 1951-52, Dakota Bus. Coll., 1954-59; m. Lois Lovelle Stogdill, Sept. 14, 1973; children—Deborah M., Sheryl D., Julie A., Margo L., Bradley D. Agt., Great No. R.R., Minot, N.D., 1951-61; gen. mgr. Rainbow Telephone Coop., Everest, Kans., 1961-68; gen. mgr. Citizens Mutual Telephone Co., Bloomfield, Iowa, 1968-77; gen. mgr. W. Iowa Telephone Co., 1977—; dir. Kans. Telephone Assn., 1964-68; dir. Rural Iowa Ind. Telephone Assn., 1968-71, pres., 1971-72; dir. Iowa Telephone Assn., 1972—; mem. Lightning Protection Com., Nat. Fire Protection Assn., Nat. Safety Council. Bd. dirs. Bloomfield Indsl. Devel. Comm. Served with U.S. Army, 1951-53. Recipient Certificate of Appreciation, Nat. Safety Council. Mem. Ind. Telephone Pioneers of Am., Southeast Iowa Pioneer Club, Remsen C. of C. (dir.). Democrat. Methodist. Clubs: Lions, VFW, Masons, Co-inventor Pedestal Integrity Guard. Home: Rural Route 2 Remsen IA 51050 Office: 302 Fulton St Remsen IA 51050

MOORE, DENNIS FREDERIC, hematologist, onocologist; b. Kansas City, Mo., Apr. 10, 1936; s. Frederic D. and Rhetta L. (Dowling) M.; B.A., Westminster Coll., 1958; M.D., Tulane U., 1962; m. Mary Jane O'Malley, Sept. 3, 1960; children—Dennis Frederic, Thomas Allen, Timothy Joseph, Michael Christopher. Intern, St. Francis Hosp., Wichita, Kans., 1962-63; resident VA Hosp., Wichita, 1963-66; chief out-patient services USPHS Hosp., Galveston, Tex., 1966-67, dep. chief med. service, 1967-68, advanced sr. fellow M.D. Anderson Hosp., Houston, 1968-69; practice medicine specializing in hematology and oncology, 1969—; clin. instr. medicine U. Tex., Galveston, 1968; clin. asso. Kans. U., Wichita State Branch, 1973-76, clin. asst. prof. 1977—; mem. staffs. St. Joseph Med. Center, Wesley Med. Center, St. Francis Med. Center, Osteopathic Hosp., VA Hosp., Wichita; Central Kans. Med. Center, Great Bend, Kans., Hadley Regional Med. Center, Hays, Kans.; clin. investigator SW Oncology Group., Wichita, 1971—. Active ARC, Wichita, 1975—; cubmaster Quivira council Boy Scouts Am., Wichita, 1972-75; trustee Leukemia Soc. Am., 1974—. Served with USPHS, 1966-68. Diplomate Am. Bd. Internal Medicine. Fellow Am. Coll. Physicians; mem. Am. Med. Assn., Internat. Cancer Congress, Am. Soc. Hematology, Am. Fedn. Clin. Research, Am. Soc. Clin. Oncology, Kans., Sedgwick County med. socs., Nat. Pilots Assn. Republican. Club: Wichita Country. Contbr. articles to med. jours. Home: 7439 Tanglewood Ln Wichita KS 67206 Office: Suite 265 1035 N Emporia Wichita KS 67204

MOORE, GERALD LOUIS, food service exec.; b. Muscatine, Iowa, Apr. 4, 1934; s. William Francis and Carllena (Diercks) M.; student Muscatine Jr. Coll., 1952-53, State U. Iowa, 1953-55; B.S., U. Denver, 1957. Mgr., Cleaves Food Service Corp., Silver Spring, Md., 1960-63, personnel dir., 1963-65; personnel dir. Progressive Cafeterias, Inc., Chgo., 1965, asst. to pres., 1966-68; food systems supr. Kitchens of Sara Lee, Deerfield, Ill., 1969-71, nat. accounts mgr., 1972, sales promotion mgr., 1973-75, advt. and sales promotion mgr., 1975—; dir. Menu Marketers Inc. Served with AUS, 1957-60. Mem. Duck Woods Improvement Assn. (pres. 1977-78, trustee 1978), Delta Sigma Pi. Republican. Episcopalian. Club: Lions. Home: 618 Oakwood Duck Lake Woods Ingleside IL 60041 Office: 500 Waukegan Rd Deerfield IL 60015

MOORE, HARLAN EDGAR, bldg. materials co. exec.; b. Mt. Sterling, Ill. Sept. 28, 1885; s. Joseph and Josephine (Gerrish) M.; student public schools; m. Theresa E. Travis; children—Audrey A., Charles E. Asso. with Munsell & Co., 1900-06, Johns Manville Co., 1912-50; pres. Harlan E. Moore & Co., Champaign, Ill., 1950—; partner Roofing & Insulation Supply Co., 1933-50; owner Fisher Lumber Co., Fisher, Ill., 1951—; grain and livestock farming, nr. Farmer City, Ill., 1933—. Treas. Champaign County Urban League, 1961—; pres. Harlan E. Moore Heart Research Found., 1972—. Mem. Nat. Bldg. Materials Distbg. Assn., Unitarian-Universalist Assn. Mason. Kiwanian. Home: 908 W Healey St Champaign IL 61820 Office: 24 E Green St Champaign IL 61820 also 15 E John St Champaign IL 61820

MOORE, HARWOOD BARROWS, mfg. co. exec.; b. Providence, Mar. 9, 1928; s. Philip Mitchenson and Lois (Barrows) M.; B.S.E.E., U. Buffalo, 1953; M.B.A., U. Chgo., 1973; m. Marie Estelle White, Oct. 22, 1949; children—Donna, David, Diane, Duane, Daryl, Derek. Design engr. Gen. Electric Co., Lynn, Mass., Hendersonville, N.C., 1953-58, devel. engr., Utica, N.Y., 1958-61, product planner, 1961-63, mgr. advanced engring., 1963-65, mgr. engring., 1965-70; v.p. engring. Hammond Organ, Chgo., 1970-73, v.p. operations, 1973-75; pres., chief exec. officer Lawndale Industries, Aurora, Ill., 1975—; dir. E.I. Ltd., Hammond Organ Europe, Alpha Omega Inc. Active Boy Scouts Am. Served with USNR, 1946-48, 51-52. Registered profl. engr., N.Y., Ill. Mem. Porcelain Enameling Inst. (dir.). Patentee in field. Home: 4010 Picardy Dr Northbrook IL 60062 Office: 821 N Russel Rd Aurora IL 60507

MOORE, HOWARD DENIS, editor, publisher; b. St. Louis, July 22, 1939; s. Howard Stanley and Dorothy Ola (Woltjen) M.; student U. Mo., 1957-60, Nikon Sch. Photography, 1971, 73; m. Mary Jean Brauch, June 1, 1963; children—Michael Anthony, Mark Denis. Newsboy, St. Louis Globe Democrat, 1948-52; with St. Clair Chronicle, 1953-57; advt. editor Tri County News, Sullivan, Mo., 1960-63, editor, 1963—, publisher, 1970—. Vice pres. sec. Moore Enterprises, Inc., Sullivan, Mo., 1966—; also dir. Founding pres. Sullivan Indsl. Devel. Corp., 1973-74; v.p. Sullivan Community Betterment, 1963-72, pres., 1972—. Police commr. Sullivan, 1974-76; treas. Crawford County Citizens and Friends for Meramec Park Lake, 1977-78; pres. Sullivan United Republican Club, 1972-73; bd. dirs. Meramec Basin Assn., 1977—. Recipient Leadership award Mo. Gov., 1972. Mem. Nat. Newspaper Assn., Mo. Press Assn., C. of C. (pres. 1973), Sigma Tau Gamma. Republican. Roman Catholic. Rotarian (pres. 1972-73). Home: 650 Crestview Dr Sullivan MO 63080 Office: 226 W Main St Sullivan MO 63080

MOORE, HUGH TRAVIS, dentist; b. Kansas City, Mo., Jan. 10, 1925; s. Hugh Coleman and Neva Maurine (Grimes) M.; student Washington U., St. Louis, 1941-43; D.D.S., U. Mo. at Kansas City, 1946; m. Clarabeth Whyte, Feb. 11, 1956; children—Maribeth, Patricia, Susan, Thomas. Practice dentistry, Kansas City, Mo., 1948—. Instr. U. Mo.-Kansas City Sch. Dentistry. 1948-62, asst. clin. prof., 1974. Served to comdr. USNR. Mem. U. Mo. at Kansas City Alumni Assn. (pres. 1955), Omicron Kappa Upsilon. Presbyn. (elder). Clubs: Carriage, Dental Clinic (pres. 1959) (Kansas City). Office: Plaza Pkwy Bldg Kansas City MO 64112

MOORE, JACK FAY, labor union ofcl.; b. Springfield, Mo., Feb. 19, 1927; s. Elba Fay and Stella (Inmon) M.; student Drury Coll., 1959; m. Betty Lou Johnston, Dec. 29, 1950; children—Thomas Joseph, Deborah (Mrs. Michael Stephen Mills), Marilyn Faye. Electrician, Aton-Luce Electric Co., Springfield, 1946-58; bus. mgr. Local 453 Internat. Brotherhood Elec. Workers, Springfield, 1958-76, mem. exec. council, 1966-76, internat. v.p., 1976—. Labor mem. Mo. Bd. Mediation, 1971-75; pres. Springfield Labor Council, 1958-76; mem. exec. bd. State Com. on Polit. Edn., 1964-76. Mem. Springfield Park Bd., 1962-68. Served with USNR, 1944-46, 50-51. Mem. Mo. Elec. Workers (pres. 1960—). Democrat. Mem. Ch. of Christ. Home: 1300 Cozy St Springfield MO 65804 Office: 300 S Jefferson Ave Springfield MO 65806

MOORE, JAMES EDWARD, city ofcl.; b. Cleveland, Tenn., Aug. 12, 1945; s. William Monroe and Myrtle (Upton) M.; B.A., Grand Valley State Coll., 1967; M.A., Mich. State U., 1974; m. Geraldine J. Jackson, Dec. 18, 1971; 1 dau., Jami Marchelle; 1 dau. by previous marriage, Gina Marie. Social welfare worker Dept. Social Services Los Angeles County (Calif.), 1967; youth and edn. dir. Grand Rapids (Mich.) Urban League, 1969-72, program dir., 1972-77, counselor, 1972-77, staff supr., 1976-77; exec. dir. Aurora (Ill.) Urban League, 1977—; adviser to Minority Tradesmen Assn., 1972-77; mem. Grand Rapids Area Manpower Planning Council, 1972-77. Served with U.S. Army, 1967-69; Viet-Nam. Mem. Am. Personnel and Guidance Assn., Nat. Vocat. Guidance Assn., Nat. Employment Counselors Assn., Assn. Non-White Concerns in Personnel and Guidance, Am. Legion, Mich. State, Grand Valley alumni assns., Aurora C. of C. (employment com. 1977), Nat., Ill. exec. dirs. councils. Baptist. Club: Rotary. Columnist Grand Rapids Times newspaper, 1969-72. Home: 1364 Monomoy St Aurora IL 60506 Office: 20 S Lincoln Ave SE Aurora IL 60506

MOORE, JAMES STUART, JR., radiologist; b. Mpls., Oct. 7, 1941; s. James Stuart and Evangeline Pauline (VanHoose) M.; A.B., U. Minn., 1963, M.D., 1967; m. Sally Ruth Brown, Aug. 6, 1966; children—Anne Elizabeth, James Stuart III, John Alexander. Intern in internal medicine U. Ill., Chgo., 1968; resident in radiology U. Minn., Mpls., 1971-73, fellow in neuroradiology, 1973-74, instr. dept. radiology, 1974-75; dir. neuroradiology Mpls. VA Hosp., 1974; practice medicine specializing in radiology, St. Paul, 1974—; mem. staffs St. Jospeh's Hosp., United Hosps., St. John's Hosp.; clin. asst. prof. radiology U. Minn. Served with USPHS, 1969-71. Diplomate Am. Bd. Radiology. Mem. AMA, Am. Soc. Neuroradiology, Am. Coll. Radiology, Radiol. Soc. N.Am., Minn. Med. Assn., Ramsey County Med. Soc., Minn. Soc. Neurol. Scis., Minn. Radiol. Soc., Clin. Club St. Paul, St. Paul Med. Assembly. Clubs: St. Paul Athletic, Minnesota. Contbr. numerous papers to confs. and publs. Home: 645 Montcalm Pl Saint Paul MN 55116 Office: 69 W Exchange St Saint Paul MN 55102

MOORE, JEAN DOLORES, hide processing co. exec.; b. Madison, Wis., Mar. 1, 1926; d. Sidney Dayre and Mary Ethel (Lowry) Kuykendall; grad. high sch.; children—Dyann Dayre Ellsworth, Jay J. Jensen, Beau R. A. Moore. Free-lance photographer, 1947-53; legal sec., Rockford, Ill., 1958-65; br. mgr. finance corp., 1965-71; corporate sec. and comptroller Rockford Quality Pak (formerly Rockford Hide & Fur Co.), 1973-75, exec. v.p., 1976-77, pres., 1977—; v.p. Hidebound, Inc., Rockford, 1973; dir. Rockoil, Inc. Mem. library bd. Mem. Nat. Hide Assn., Tanners Council, LWV, Cousteau Soc. Home: 425 Calvin Park Blvd N Rockford IL 61107 Office: 2009 Kishwaukee St Rockford IL 61101

MOORE, JOAN WELLS, veterinarian; b. Columbus, Wis., June 17, 1949; d. Russell Robert and Jane Wells (Pratt) Moore; student U. Wis., Madison, 1967-70; D.V.M., Iowa State U., 1974; m. William Daniel Bolton Jr., Aug. 24, 1974. Intern Colo. State U., Ft. Collins, 1974-75; veterinarian Barnes Bone Animal Hosp., Chgo., 1975—. Mem. Am. Animal Hosp. Assn., Am., Ill., Chgo., Women's vet. med. assns., Iowa State U. Alumni Assn. Mem. United Ch. of Christ. Home: 147 N Elmwood St Palatine IL 60067 Office: 3631 N Elston Ave Chicago IL 60618

MOORE, JOHN NEWTON, natural scientist, educator; b. Columbus, Ohio, Apr. 2, 1920; s. Lawrence Newton and Grace C. (Jones) M.; A.B., Denison U., 1941; M.S., Mich. State U., 1943, Ed.D., 1952; m. Wilma Marie Proctor, Aug. 30, 1941; children—Douglas Warren, Donald Norman. Grad. asst. botany Mich. State U., East Lansing, 1941-43, instr. math., 1943-44, instr., asst. prof. biol. sci., 1946-52, asst. prof. natural sci., 1952-59, asso. prof., 1959-70, prof., 1970—; vis. prof. edn. Tenn. Temple Coll., summer 1974. Bd. dirs. Creation Research Soc. 1963—. Served to lt. (j.g.) USN, 1944-46. Mem. Nat. Assn. Biology Tchrs., Assn. for Edn. of Tchrs. in Sci., Nat. Assn. Geology Tchrs., Assn. Gen. and Liberal Studies, Soc. Study Evolution, Creation Research Soc., Nat., Mich. sci. tchrs. assns., Lambda Chi Alpha, Beta Beta Beta. Editor (with Harold S. Slusher) Biology: A Search for Order in Complexity, high sch. textbook, 1970, rev. edit., 1974; Questions and Answers on Creation/Evolution, 1976. Mng. editor Creation Research Soc. Quar. 1965-77. Home: 1158 Marigold Ave East Lansing MI 48823

MOORE, JOSEPH JOHN, steel co. exec.; b. Youngstown, Ohio, Jan. 4, 1912; s. Joseph Francis and Mary Ann (Mulvey) M.; B.S. in Mech. Engring., Case Inst. Tech., 1934, M.S. in Indsl. Mgmt., 1940; m. Catherine Cecelia Shea, Feb. 18, 1939; 1 dau., Mary Louise (Mrs. Roger K. West). Asst. to pres. Case Inst. Tech., 1937-40; asst. purchasing agt. Rohm & Haas Co., Phila., 1940-48; asst. purchasing agt. A.G. McKee Co., Union, N.J., 1948-50; dist. sales mgr. G.O. Carlson Co., Cleve., 1950-53; v.p. Viking Steel Co., Cleve., 1953—; v.p. Case Investors Corp., 1950-73. Pres. Cleve. chpt. Steel Service Inst. Team capt. fund raising Jr. Achievement, 1965-68. Trustee Cleve. Internat. Program, 1973—. Mem. Council on World Affairs, Catholic Bus. and Profl. Mens Club, First Friday Club, Case Inst. Tech. Alumni Assn. (v.p.), Phi Delta Theta. Rotarian. Club: Shaker Heights (Ohio) Country. Home: 3691 Rawnsdale Rd Shaker Heights OH 44122 Office: 16700 St Clair Ave Cleveland OH 44110

MOORE, KENNETH EDWARD, biologist, electron microscopist; b. Sheridan, Wyo., Jan. 24, 1939; s. Kenneth Scott and Nellie Ruby (Hamer) M.; B.S. in Edn., Nebr. State Coll., Chadron, 1960; postgrad. St. Louis U., 1966-67; m. JoAnn Marie Rewerts, Nov. 4, 1971. Research asst. U. Nebr. Med. Center, Omaha, 1960-65; research asst., tech. supr. St. Louis U., 1965-67; supr. electron microscopy, research asst. Jewish Hosp., St. Louis, 1967-71; research biologist, electron microscopist VA Hosp., Omaha, 1971-76; research asst. depts. microbiology and pathology U. Nebr. Coll. Medicine, 1976—. Instr. Washington U., St. Louis, 1968-71; cons. in electron microscopy. Mem. Electron Microscope Soc. Am. Contbr. articles to profl. jours. Home: 6211 Poppleton St Omaha NE 68106 Office: 42d and Dewey Sts Omaha NE 68105

MOORE, MICHAEL, gas distbn. co. exec.; b. Liberal, Kans., May 8, 1940; s. John Walter and Margaret (Colvin) M.; student U.S. Mil. Acad., 1958-62; m. Penny Lou Sparks, May 8, 1977. Mgr. Liberal Gas Co. (Kans.), 1968-70, exec. v.p., 1970-74, pres., 1974—. Served with U.S. Army, 1962-68. Decorated D.F.C., Bronze Star, Air medal; Vietnamese Cross of Gallantry. Mem. Midwest Gas Assn. Republican. Clubs: Country, Elks. Home: 1820 N Calhoun St Liberal KS 67901 Office: 18 W 3d St Liberal KS 67901

MOORE, PAULINE RUYLE, lawyer; ed. MacMurray Coll., George Washington U., Am. U., Washington Coll. Law; m. J. Cordell Moore, July 29, 1939. Adminstrv. sec. to Ill. Congressman James M. Barnes 1939-42; adminstrv. work Democratic Nat. Com., 1945-47; chief clk. and counsel Dem. Policy Com., U.S. Senate, 1948-70; now practice law, Washington; admitted to Tenn. bar, U.S. Supreme Ct. Mem. Phi Alpha Delta. Home and Office: 2304 Bates Ave Springfield IL 62704

MOORE, RALPH CORY, radiologist; b. Omaha, Nov. 23, 1911; s. John Clyde and Lura (Daggett) M.; B.Sc., U. Nebr., 1932, M.D., 1937; m. Dorothy Jean Keech, Apr. 13, 1946; children—Virginia, John, Barbara, David. House officer internal medicine Peter Bent Brigham Hosp., Boston, 1937-39, asst. resident radiology, 1940-41; radiologist Nebr. Meth. Hosp., Omaha, 1946—, Childrens Meml. Hosp., Omaha, 1949—; prof. radiology U. Nebr. Coll. Medicine, 1957—. Served with AUS, 1941-46; PTO. Fellow Am. Coll. Radiology; mem. Radiol. Soc. N.Am., Am. Roentgen Ray Soc., AMA. Republican. Conglist. Contbr. articles on arteriography, decelleration trauma to profl. jours. Home: 2017 S 107th St Omaha NE 68124 Office: 8303 Dodge St Omaha NE 68114

MOORE, RAY DELOSS, JR., sch. adminstr.; b. North Baltimore, Ohio, Dec. 20, 1931; s. Ray D. and Dora L. (Slaughterbeck) M.; B.S., Ind. U., 1954, M.S., 1955; postgrad. Ind.-Purdue U., Ft. Wayne, 1967-73; m. Nancy L. Rosenberger, Aug. 17, 1952; children—Denise, Pamela, Sherill. Tchr., coach, drama dir. Muncie (Ind.) Burris Exptl. Sch., 1955-56, Laketon (Ind.) High Sch., 1956-58, Columbia City (Ind.) High Sch., 1958-68; Ft. Wayne (Ind.) Community Sch., 1968-69; asst. prin. Northwood Jr. High Sch., Ft. Wayne, 1969-71; prin. Franklin Jr. High Sch., Ft. Wayne, 1971—. Recipient Educator of Year award Columbia City Jr. C. of C., 1966. Mem. N.E.A., Nat. Assn. Secondary Sch. Prins., Ft. Wayne Prins. Assn., Ind. U. Alumni Assn., Phi Delta Kappa, Phi Epsilon Kappa. Republican. Methodist. Mason (Shriner). Home: 5423 Brook Farm Pl Fort Wayne IN 46815

MOORE, RICHARD, educator; b. Los Angeles, Jan. 19, 1927; s. Dennis Albert and Marjorie (Kahn) M.; student Deep Springs (Calif.) Jr. Coll., 1944-46; B.S., U. Mo., 1949; Ph.D., U. Rochester, 1956; D.Sc., George Washington U., 1970; m. Lillian Elizabeth Karska, Apr. 5, 1969; children—Peter, Don Andrew, Ann. Marie. Engr. Radiol. Health program USPHS, Washington, 1955-57; scientist NIH, Bethesda, Md., 1957-60, mem. data logging com., 1959-60; chief biophysics sect. Research Lab. Am. Nat. Red Cross, Washington, 1960-69; asso. prof. U. Minn., 1969—; cons. div. biophysics Walter Reed Army Inst. of Research, Washington, 1960-65; vis. prof. Howard U., 1958-66; vis. prof. George Washington U., 1968-69; cons. St. Paul chpt. A.R.C., 1969-71. Served to maj. USPHS, 1955-60. AEC Grad. fellow, 1950-52; NIH Research grantee, 1965-69. Registered profl. engr., Minn.; diplomate Am. Bd. Radiology. Fellow AAAS, Soc. Advanced Med. Systems; mem. Washington Area Biophysics Soc. (mem. council 1968-69), Am. Heart Assn. (council cardiovascular radiology), Am. Coll. Radiology, Soc. Gen. Physiologists, Soc. Exptl. Biology and Medicine. Unitarian. Asso. editor Pattern Recognition, Computers in Biology and Medicine; cons. editor Med. Electronics and Data. Contbr. numerous sci. articles to profl., sci. jours. Home: 2190 Fowell St St Paul MN 55108 Office: Box 701 Mayo Bldg U Minn Minneapolis MN 55455

MOORE, RICHARD HOFFMAN, guidance counselor; b. Wooster, Ohio, Apr. 11, 1945; s. Robert H. and Sara Margret (Craig) M.; B.S. in Edn., Ashland Coll., 1967; M.Ed., Xavier U., Cin., 1972; m. Sandra Jayne Longacre, July 29, 1967; children—Amy Christine, Kristen Renee. Tchr. Wooster Twp. Schs. Dist., Wooster, 1967-68, coach basketball, track, 1967-68; Centerville City (Ohio) Schs., 1968-73; counselor Kettering (Ohio) City Schs., 1973—; cons. Beechwood (Ohio) City Schs., 1969. Mem. Nat., Ohio edn. assns., Am., Miami Valley personnel guidance assns., Am., Ohio sch. counselors assns., Kettering Classroom tchrs. Assn. Home: 3155 Sandywood Dr Kettering OH 45440

MOORE, RILEY AMBROSE, trade co. exec.; b. Dayton, Ohio, Oct. 6, 1949; s. Lonnie and Mary D. (Ferrell) M.; B.S., U. Dayton, 1972; postgrad. Northwestern Sch. Law, 1972-74. Owner, operator Riley Moore & Co., Chgo., 1974—, Bargain Barns Store Outlets, Chgo., 1977—. Mem. 47th. St. Businessmen's Council. Republican. Club: Porsche. Home: 1 E Schiller St Apt 22B Chicago IL 60610 Office: 78 E 47th St Chicago IL 60653

MOORE, ROBERT HENRY, JR., mfg. co. exec.; b. Bluefield, W.Va., Apr. 17, 1923; s. Robert Henry and Margaret Huston (St. Clair) M.; B.A., Washington and Lee U., 1944, Certificate in Commerce, 1947; M.B.A., Harvard, 1951; J.D. Cleve. State U., 1963; m. Patricia Hewittson-Fisher, Dec. 5, 1960; children—Diana, Robert Henry III, Turner Cronin. Salesman, Pitts. Consolidation Coal Co., 1951-54; security analyst, asst. to pres., sec., asst. treas., dir. Otis & Co., Cleve., 1954-64; with Aquarium of Niagara Falls, Inc., 1964-71, chmn. exec. com., dir., 1969-71; pres., treas., dir. Aquarium Systems, Inc., Eastlake, Ohio, 1964-72; pres., treas., dir. Mystic Aquarium, Inc., 1971-72; mng. partner Pocahontas Mining Co.; chmn. bd. Aqualife Research Corp., Marathon, Fla. Served to lt. (j.g.) USNR, 1942-46. Mem. Am. Bar Assn., Cleve. Soc. Security Analysts. Republican. Presbyn. Clubs: Union, Cleveland Skating (Cleve.); Army and Navy (Washington); Harvard (N.Y.C.). Home: 2530 Fairmount Blvd Cleveland Heights OH 44106

MOORE, ROBERT PITTMAN, lawyer; b. Anderson, Ind., Dec. 19, 1904; s. Harry Edgar and Eva (Pittman) M.; student U. Pa., 1924-25; B.A., Ohio State U., 1928; LL.B., U. Cin., 1931; m. Helen Demorest, Apr. 4, 1929 (dec. Jan. 1949); children—Robert Pittman, Donald C., David P., Sara Helen (Mrs. Michael Peter Scheu); m. 2d, Sarah Spence, Dec. 31, 1955. Admitted to Ohio bar, 1932, practiced in Cin., 1931—; mem. firms Woeste & Quinn, 1932-39, McIntosh, Moore & Katz, 1948-54; partner Moore, Moore & Moore, Cin., 1964—. Gen. counsel, dir. Cherry Grove Savs. & Loan Co., Cin., 1942—, v.p., 1946—; gen. counsel, sec. Mariemont Laundry, Inc., Cin., 1950—. Silver Hat Mining Inc., Ophir, Colo., 1961-63; sec. Matthes Enterprises, Inc., Cin., 1965-73. Charter mem. adv. bd. Ohio Deposit Guarantee Fund. Charter mem. bd. dirs., gen. counsel Cin. Musicians

Assn., Cin. Summer Opera, 1932-57. Mem. Am., Ohio, Cin. bar assns., Fedn. Ins. Counsel, Ky. Civil War Round Table, Ky. Hist. Soc., Phi Kappa Tau, Delta Theta Phi. Clubs: Cincinnati Lawyers; Terrace Park Country. Author: The Medical Practice, Bona Fide-Mala Fide, 1978. Home: 6902 Woodsedge Dr Cincinnati OH 45230 Office: 7168 Beechmont Ave Cincinnati OH 45230

MOORE, THOMAS EDWARD, environ. chemist; b. Bowling Green, Ohio, Sept. 19, 1951; s. Zenas H. and Genevieve M. (Roberts) M.; B.S., Bowling Green State U., 1972; J.D., U. Dayton, 1978; m. Isabel Marie Suydam, Feb. 16, 1974. Environ. chemist, supr. field services Pollution Control Sci. Inc., Miamisburg, Ohio, 1973-75; cons. in field. Mem. Am. Bar Assn., Phi Alpha Delta. Home: 334 Blackwood Ave Apt 5 Dayton OH 45403

MOORE, THOMAS HUGH, assn. exec.; b. Morrilton, Ark., Jan. 13, 1929; s. James Thomas and Annie (Van Marion) M.; student Hendrix Coll., 1947-48; B.A., Ark. State Tchrs. Coll., 1951; m. Clara Jean Jackson, Nov. 18, 1950; children—Melanie Anne, Stephanie Suzanne, James Van. Dir. pub. relations Ark. State Electric Coop., Inc., North Little Rock, 1957-61; exec. v.p. Assn. Ill. Electric Coops., Springfield, 1961—. Pres. Ill. Farm Electrification Council; bd. dirs. Farm Electrification Council, 1962-64. Bd. dirs. Ill. 4-H Club Found. Served to lt. USNR, 1951-57. Mem. Rural Electric Statewide Mgrs. Assn. (pres.), Ill. Fedn. Consumers (pres.), Springfield Assn. Execs. Methodist. Mason (Shriner). Home: 2117 Kenwood Dr Springfield IL 62704 Office: PO Box 3787 Vice 1180 Springfield IL 62708

MOORE, WILLIAM ARTHUR, chemist; b. Middletown, Ohio, May 22, 1920; s. Arthur Wright and Thelma Louise (Robison) M.; A.A., U. Cin., 1951, Ph.B., 1959; m. Herta Emma Luise Liebschwager, Apr. 8, 1944; children—Karla Emilie Luise, Ingrid Ilse Herta, Lisa Anna Marie. Jr. metallurgist Wright Aero. Co., Cin., 1942-44; chemist Armco Steel Co., Middletown, Ohio, 1944—, spl. analytical chemist, spectroscopist, 1962—; guest lectr. in indsl. chemistry Miami U., Oxford, Ohio, 1973. Treas. Butler County (Ohio) Bicentennial Commn., 1974-77, chmn., heritage div., 1974-77. Served with Ordnance Corps U.S. Army, 1942. Recipient certificate of appreciation U.S. Grant Sespuicentennial Commn., 1972, Butler County Bicentennial Commn., 1976, Middletown Bicentennial Commn., 1976, Fairfield (Ohio) Bicentennial Commn., 1976, Hamilton Altrusa Club, 1976; Mil. Order World Wars, 1971. Mem. Am. Def. Preparedness Assn. (life), Butler County (pres. 1967-70), Middletown (founder 1967) hist. Socs., Hamilton Civil War Round Table (co-founder 1967), Deutscher Hausverein. Clubs: Hamilton City, Am. Legion (Hamilton). Contbr. ethnic and hist. essays to Hamilton Jour. News, 1965—. Home: 346 Marcia Ave Hamilton OH 45013 Office: Armco Steel Corp Metallurgical Dept Curtis St Middletown OH 45042

MOORE, WILLIAM LYLE, lawyer; b. Alta., Can., Dec. 6, 1912; s. John Carlyle and Ethel (Piche) M.; student Royal Mil. Coll., 1934; grad. Osgoode Hall Law Sch., 1938; m. Elinor Mary Adams, Feb. 2, 1940; 1 dau., Georgia Nadine. Admitted to Ont. bar, 1938; gen. practice law, Orillia, Ont., Can., 1938-70; city solicitor City of London, Ont., 1970-77, counsel, 1977—. Dir. Victoria & Grey Trust Co. Chmn. reference bd. Orillia Hosp., 1946-70; chmn. Orillia Library Bd., 1960-69; mem. adv. bd. Salvation Army, Orillia, 1950-70. Served to lt. comdr. Royal Canadian Navy, 1940-45. Mem. Power Squadron, Royal Canadian Legion (pres. 1949-51), Royal Canadian Mil. Inst. Clubs: Masons, London. Home: 815-52 Wellington St London ON Canada Office: 200 Queen's Ave London ON Canada

MOORHEAD, JOHN BEKINS, livestock farmer; b. Sioux City, Iowa, Feb. 16, 1937; s. Park W. and Edna (Bekins) M.; B.A., Cornell Coll., Mt. Vernon, Iowa, 1959; m. Anita Kalskett Moorhead, July 16, 1960; children—Mary Elizabeth, Ann Louise. Mgr., Moorhead Stock Farms (Iowa); dir. Moorhead Co-op., 1971-73; mem. farm adv. group to Rep. Berkley Bedell of Iowa, 1976-77. Mem. Iowa Livestock Feeders Assn. (sec.-treas. 1970-71), Iowa Beef Industry Council (chmn. 1973-74), Am., Iowa cattlemen's assns. Club: Masons. Home: Moorhead IA 51558

MOORHEAD, PHILIP DARWIN, research pathologist; b. Pratt, Kans., Nov. 21, 1933; s. William Darwin and Josephine Marye (Hastings) M.; B.S., D.V.M., Kans. State U., 1957; M.S., Purdue U., 1964, Ph.D., 1966; m. Patricia Jean Wollner, July 22, 1956; children—Jennifer Lynne, Amy Jo, Matthew Duane. Self-employed veterinarian, Palestine, Ill., 1957-62; NIH postdoctoral fellow Auburn (Ala.) U., 1962-63; instr. veterinary medicine Purdue U., West Lafayette, Ind., 1963-66; asso. prof. veterinary sci. Ohio Agrl. Research and Devel. Center, Wooster, 1966—; cons. vet. pathology. Mem. AVMA, Am. Assn. Avian Pathology, Assn. Comparative Pathologists. Clubs: Masons, Elks, Lions. Contbr. articles on avian diseases, pathology to profl. publs. Home: 816 Quinby St Wooster OH 44691

MOORJANI, GULAB ISSARSING, computer service co. exec.; b. Khairpur, India, Nov. 7, 1937; s. Issarsing Revasing and Mevibai (Ramchandani) M.; came to U.S., 1967, naturalized, 1977; B.S. in Elec. Engring., U. Toledo, 1970; m. Zubeida Gulab, Mar. 18, 1966; children—Sunil, Deepak. Contract engr., Haughton Elevators div. Reliance lectric Co., Toledo, 1970-73; instrumentation engr. in charge, Finkbeiner Pettis & Strout Ltd. cons. engrs., Toledo, 1973-75; chief engr. Energystic Inc., Toledo, 1975; dir. mktg. Internat. Computer Service, Toledo, 1975—. Mem. IEEE, Instrument Soc. Am. Club: Jamaican Social. Adviser, Jr. Achievement. Home: Villa Riviera 500 Riverside Dr Rossford OH 43460 Office: International Computer Service Box 393 Toledo OH 43691

MOOS, MALCOLM CHARLES, author, educator; b. St. Paul, Apr. 19, 1916; s. Charles John and Katherine Isabelle (Grant) M.; A.B., U. Minn., 1937, M.A., 1938; Ph.D., U. Calif., 1942; LL.D., Ohio No. U., 1960, U. N.D., 1968, Georgetown U., 1968, Johns Hopkins U., 1969; Litt.D., Coll. of St. Thomas, 1970, U. Notre Dame, 1973; m. Margaret Tracy Gager, June 29, 1945; children—Malcolm, Katherine, Grant, Ann, Margaret. Teaching fellow U. Minn., 1938; research asst. League Minn. Municipalities, 1938-39; teaching fellow U. Calif., 1939-41; research asst. U. Ala., 1941-42; asst. prof. polit. sci. U. Wyo., 1942; asst. prof. polit. sci. Johns Hopkins, 1942-46, asso. prof., 1946-52, prof., 1952-61, 63; pres. U. Minn., 1967-74; pres. Fund for the Republic, 1974-75, Center for Study Democratic Instns., 1974-75; cons. White House Office, 1957-58, adminstrv. asst. to Pres., 1958-60, spl. asst., 1960-61; adviser on pub. affairs to the Messrs. Rockefeller, 1961-63; mem. President's Commn. on campaign costs, 1961-62; vis. prof. U. Mich., 1955, Columbia, 1963-65; asso. editor Balt. Eve. Sun, 1945-48. Dir. policy and planning Ford Found., 1964-66; dir. Office Govt. and Law, Ford Found., 1966-67; cons. Pub. Broadcast Lab.'s Polit. Affairs Project, 1967-75; mem. Commn. Presdl. Scholars, 1969-74, Pres.'s Task Force on Priorities in Higher Edn., 1969—. Alternate del. Rep. Nat. Conv., 1952, del., 1956; chmn. Rep. State Central Com. Balt., 1954-58; mem. Balt. City Jail Commn., 1953-55, Prisoner's Aid Soc., 1952-58; cons. Md. Commn. Orgn. State Govt., 1952-54; dir. research com. on Govt. and Higher Edn., 1957-60; mem. com. on plans and objectives for higher edn. Am. Council on Edn., 1968-70, chmn. higher edn. adv. com. wages and prices, 1971—, dir., 1971-74; mem. adv. council pres.' Assn. Governing Bds. Univs. and Colls., 1968-71. Bd. dirs. Harry S. Truman Library Inst., 1967-74, Govtl. Affairs Inst., Overseas Devel. Council; trustee Citizen's Research Found., Inst. for the Future, Ednl. Testing Service; trustee Carnegie Found. for Advancement of Teaching, 1969-77, mem. exec. com., 1971-73; trustee Pub. Adminstrn. Service; mem. Brit.-N.Am. Com.; mem. nat. adv. panel Computer Data Banks, Nat. Acad. Scis.; chmn. Midwest Univs. Consortium for Internat. Activities, 1969-74; mem. bd. Nat. Book Com.; mem. Theodore Roosevelt Award Jury, Nat. Collegiate Athletic Assn.; mem. adv. council Pioneer Found., Brooking-Instn. Mem. Am. Polit. Sci. Assn., Polit Economy Club, Century Assn., Minn. Hist. Soc. (mem. exec. council 1968-71), Am. Antiquarian Soc. (mem. exec. com. Worcester, Mass.), Nat. Assn. State Univs. and Land-Grant Colls. (vice chmn. fed. relations com. 1970-72, mem. com. on urban problems 1970—, com. on voluntary support 1971-74, com. problems and issues), Minn. Newspaper Assn. (mem. Minn. Press Council 1971-74). Phi Beta Kappa. Author: State Penal Adminstrn., in Ala., 1942; Politics, Presidents and Coattails, 1952; A grammar of American Politics (with Wilfred E. Binkley), 1949; State and Local Government (with Wilfred E. Binkley), 1952; Presidential Nominating Politics in 1952 (with Paul T. David), 1954; Power Through Purpose: The Bases of American Foreign Policy (with Thomas I. Cook), 1954; The Republicans: A History of the Party, 1956; (with Francis Rourke) The Campus and the State, 1959; (with Stephen Hess) Hats in the Ring, 1960; Dwight D. Eisenhower, 1964. Home: 79 Western Ave N St Paul MN 55102

MOOSBRUGGER, MARY COULTRIP, mktg. exec.; b. Urbana, Ill., Sept. 1, 1947; d. Donald Lyle and Charlotte Carol (Barber) Coultrip; B.A., U. Ill., 1969; m. John Robert Moosbrugger, Apr. 24, 1971; 1 son, Peter John. Research analyst Leo Burnett Co., Chgo., 1969-72; research cons., study dir. Booz Allen & Hamilton, Chgo., 1972-73; research supr. Quaker Oats Co., Chgo., 1974-75; mgr. mktg. research Kitchens of Sara Lee, Deerfield, Ill., 1975-77; pres. Moosbrugger Mktg. Research, LaGrange Park, Ill., 1977—. Mem. Am. Mktg. Assn. (guest speaker Midwest research conf. 1975). Roman Catholic. Address: 934 N Brainard Ave LaGrange Park IL 60525

MORAGNE, RUDOLPH, physician; b. Evanston, Ill., Feb. 5, 1933; s. Joseph and Linnie (Lee) M.; B.S., U. Ill., 1955; M.D., Meharry Med. Sch., 1959; m. Kathlyn Elaine Lawrence, June 15, 1958; children—Donna Kaye, Diana Patrice, Lisa Michelle. Intern, Cook County Hosp., Chgo., 1960-61, resident in obstetrics, gynecology, 1963-66; practice medicine specializing in obstetrics, gynecology, Chgo., 1966—; instr. U. Chgo., 1966—; attending physician U. Chgo. Lying In Hosp., 1967—, Columbus Hosp., Chgo., 1966—, Woodlawn Hosp., Chgo., 1967—; dir. South Side Bank, Chgo. Mem. Chgo. Urban League, 1969—, Operation Push, 1970—. Served to capt. USAF, 1961-63. Mem. A.C.S., Am. Coll. Obstetricians and Gynecologists, A.M.A., Ill., Chgo., Nat. med. socs., Cook County Physicians, N.A.A.C.P., Chgo. Jr. C. of C., Chi Delta Mu, Alpha Phi Alpha. Author: (with Lenore Moragne Champion) Our Baby's Early Years, 1974; Beautiful People, 1975. Home: 5036 S Ellis Ave Chicago IL 60615 Office: 8044 Cottage Grove Chicago IL 60619

MORALES, MILTON FRANCIS, real estate cons.; b. Leavenworth, Kans., Dec. 26, 1914; s. Francis Eldon and Myrtle Mary (Bacon) M.; A.B., William Jewell Coll., Liberty, Mo., 1938; M.Sc. in Pub. Adminstrn., Mo. U., 1963; LL.D., SW Bapt. Coll., Bolivar, Mo., 1977; m. Virginia Avery Harland, Dec. 9, 1938; children—Linda Morales Dix, David, Marilyn Morales Jones, Paul. Chief supply equipment Dept. Agr., Dallas, 1938-42; tng. dir. City of Kansas City, Mo., 1945-47; personnel mgr. Puritan Compressed Gas Corp., Kansas City, Mo., 1947-48; exec. sec. Mo. Baptist Found., Kansas City, 1948-50; self-employed contractor, Kansas City, Mo., 1950-60; asst. city mgr., Kansas City, Mo., 1960-66; regional dir. Fed. Housing Adminstrn., Kansas City, 1967-70; cons. real estate devel. and investment, Independence, Mo., 1970—; dir. Chrisman Sawyer Bank; mem. faculty U. Mo., Kansas City, 1967-68, William Jewell Coll., 1976—. Pres. Jackson Council United Funds and Council, 1957-58; bd. dirs. Kansas City Area council Boy Scouts Am., 1952-68; v.p. bd. trustees Starlight Theatre, Kansas City, 1963—; pres., trustee Baptist Meml. Hosp., Kansas City, 1973-75; pres. Mo. Bapt. Conv., 1976-77; trustee Mid-Continent Libraries, Inc. Served to lt. USNR, 1942-45. Decorated Commendation medal; recipient Achievement award William Jewell Coll., 1977. Mem. Am. Soc. Pub. Adminstrn. (past dir.). Club: Rotary. Address: 14608 E 44th St Independence MO 64055

MORAN, EDWARD MARTIN, wholesale co. exec.; b. Chgo., Sept. 25, 1912; s. Patrick J. and Margaret (Prendergast) M.; B.C.S., U. Notre Dame, 1934; postgrad. Washington and Jefferson Coll., 1943; m. Arlene Bransley, Dec. 28, 1954; children—Marcia, Renee, Edward Martin. Pres., Moran Supply Co., Chgo., 1946—; v.p. Plumbing and Heating Wholesale Credit Bur., 1977. Pres., Com. to Make Ireland Our 51st State, 1960-61, Better Heating Cooling Council Chgo., 1962-64, Ezzard Charles Trust Fund; chmn. Ezzard Charles Appreciation Night Dinner, 1968, Universal Notre Dame Night, 1965, 68, 69; co-chmn. Com. to Make St. Patrick's Day Legal Holiday, 1972; 1st pres. Immaculate Conception Grammar Sch. Parent's Club, Elmhurst, Ill.; mem. senate U. Notre Dame. Served to lt. USAAF, 1943-46. Named Man of Year, Mayomen's Assn. Chgo., 1969, Notre Dame U., 1970, Notre Dame Club, 1970. K.C. Clubs: U. Notre Dame (v.p., hon. pres. 1972) (Chgo.); National Monogram (Notre Dame). Home: 210 Elm Park Ave Elmhurst IL 60126 Office: 2501 N Central Ave Chicago IL 60639

MORAN, JAMES HERBERT, elec. and automotive products mfg. co. exec.; b. Saginaw, Mich., May 19, 1938; s. Leo Lewis and Marie Katherine M.; B.A., U. Notre Dame, 1960, B.S.M.E., 1961; m. Mary Etta MacPherson, June 25, 1960; children—Tracey Marie, Michael William, James Lewis. Engr., Detroit Edison Research Lab., 1961-63; instrumentation engr. Saginaw steering gear div. Gen. Motors Co., 1963-64, asst. lab. supr., 1964-66, sr. project engr., 1966-68, asst. staff engr., 1968, asst. staff engr. Buick Motor div., Flint, Mich., 1968-72; chief sales engr. Quality Spring Products div. Kuhlman Corp., Troy, Mich., 1972-75, mgr. new bus. devel. div., 1975—. Active Greater Flint Youth Hockey Assn. and Eastern Mich. Hockey Assn., 1972-77. Mem. Soc. Automotive Engrs., Engring. Soc. Detroit, Tau Beta Pi. Republican. Roman Catholic. Clubs: Warwick Hills Golf and Country, Elks. Home: 4393 E Cook Rd Grand Blanc MI 48439 Office: 2565 W Maple St Troy MI 48084

MORAN, JOHN VINCENT, lawyer; b. Detroit, Oct. 8, 1913; s. Edward J. and Margaret (Quigley) M.; A.B., U. Detroit, 1935; LL.B., U. Mich., 1938; m. Ellen Thompson, July 5, 1943; children—John T., Edward T. Legal research asst. Mich. Supreme Court, 1938-39; transp. bus., Detroit, 1939-40; practice in Detroit, 1940-43, 46—; dir. McCormick Industries, Inc. Served from pvt. to capt. AUS, 1943-46. Mem. Cath. Lawyers' Soc. (dir., past pres.), Mich. State Bar Assn. (dist. chmn. character and fitness com.), Alpha Sigma Nu. Author articles in field. Home: 292 Merriweather Rd Grosse Pointe Farms MI 48236 Office: 3263 City National Bank Bldg Detroit MI 48226

MORAN, PATRICIA ANNE, nun, clin. psychologist; b. Seattle, Mar. 9, 1940; d. James Lawrence and Anna Patricia (Laub) Moran; A.B., Fontbonne Coll., 1962; M.S., St. Louis U., 1969, Ph.D., 1972. Joined Sisters of St. Joseph of Carondelet Roman Cath. Ch., 1957; elementary tchr. Sacred Heart Sch., Indpls., 1962-64, St. Thomas of Aquin Sch., St. Louis, 1964-68; clin. intern St. Louis U., 1970-71; staff psychologist 22nd Jud. Circuit of Mo. Juvenile Div., St. Louis, 1971-72, supervising psychologist, 1972-74, chief psychologist, 1974—; mem. profl. advisory com. St. Louis State Hosp.-Youth Center, 1976—; cons. St. Louis U. Dept. Psychology, 1977. Mem. Am., Mo. (certified clin. psychologist) psychol. assns., Am. Assn. Correctional Psychologists, Am. Psychology-Law Assn., Nat. Registere Health Service Providers Psychology, Psi Chi. Home: 1413 S 10th St Saint Louis MO 63104 Office: 920 N Vandeventer St Saint Louis MO 63108

MORAN, PAUL ROBERT, lawyer; b. Cin., Sept. 4, 1933; s. Robert Leo and Margaret (Burns) M.; B.A., U. Cin., 1957; LL.B., U. Va., 1959; m. Barbara Neuss, June 24, 1967; children—Robert Lee, Paul Robert. Admitted to Ohio bar, 1959; asso. firm Taft, Stettinius & Hollister, Cin., 1963-67; partner firm Cors, Hair, & Hartsock, 1968—. Served to capt. USAF, 1960-63. Mem. Am. (mem. sect. labor relations law), Ohio, Cin. bar assns., Indsl. Relations Research Assn., The Greyton H. Taylor Wine Mus., Sigma Chi, Phi Alpha Delta. Clubs: Coldstream Country (trustee 1972—), Cin. Athletic. Home: 1161 Edwards Rd Cincinnati OH 45208 Office: 1700 Carew Tower Cincinnati OH 45202

MORAN, PHILIP ANTHONY, banker; b. Morrisonville, Wis., Dec. 1, 1939; s. Ted Herbert and Francis Ruth (Mielkie) M.; student U. Wis., 1957-58, Grad. Sch. Banking, 1972-75; m. Susanna Lucille Darcy, June 18, 1966. With Burroughs Corp., Chgo., 1963-65; systems analyst 1st Bank of Oak Park (Ill.), 1965-68; v.p. data processing Mt. Prospect (Ill.) State Bank, 1968—. Served with USAF, 1958-62. Mem. Am. Inst. Banking, Bank Adminstrn. Inst. Club: Shriner. Home: 111 Regency Dr W Arlington Heights IL 60004 Office: 111 Busse Ave Mount Prospect IL 60056

MORAN, S. JOSEPH, pub. relations exec.; b. Chgo., Oct. 4, 1929; s. Samuel Joseph and Lillian Rose M.; A.B., U. Iowa, 1955; m. Colette Catherine Murphy, June 18, 1955; children—Mindy, Mark, Monica, Melissa, Joe, Michael. Account exec. E.R. Hollingsworth & Assos., Rockford, Ill., 1960-62; sr. account supr. Burson Marsteller Assos., Chgo., 1962-67; v.p. Aaron D. Cushman & Assos., Chgo., 1967-69; v.p. Hoffman, York, Baker & Johnson, Inc., Milw., 1969—. Bd. dirs. Ozaukoo Hockey Assn., Inc., 1974-76. Served with USN, 1950-54. Recipient Golden Trumpet awards Publicity Club Chgo. Mem. Pub. Relations Soc. Am. (dir. 1977—). Home: W55N816 Cedar Ridge Dr Cedarburg WI 53012 Office: 2300 Mayfair Rd N Milwaukee WI 53226

MORANKAR, SUDHAKAR DATTATRAY, machine devel. engr.; b. India, Oct. 10, 1944; s. Dattatray V. and Sulochana (Dattatray) M.; came to U.S., 1968; M.S. in Indsl. Engring., Okla. State U., 1969, M.S. in Mech. Engring., 1971; m. Vijaya Mahadeo Shukla, Oct. 8, 1971; children—Anand, Madhavi. Tool designer Crane Packing Co., Morton Grove, Ill., 1971-72, machine devel. engr., 1972—. Co-chmn. Smithsonian on Tour-India, India League Am., Chgo., 1976. Mem. ASME (sec.-treas. Skokie Valley subsect.), Maharashtra Mandal of Chgo. (sec. 1975-76, v.p. 1977-78). Home: 7809 N Avers St Skokie IL 60076 Office: 6400 W Oakton St Morton Grove IL 60053

MORASON, ROBERT HENRY, dentist; b. Toledo, Jan. 30, 1938; s. Henry and Jenniveve M.; A.B., Miami U., Oxford, Ohio, 1960; D.D.S., Ohio State U., 1964; m. Peggy Jean Kappelman, May 3, 1963; children—Cathrine, Robert Todd. Individual practice dentistry, Toledo, 1964—. Mem. N.W. Ohio Cancer Planning Network; adviser diversified health occupations. dept. Sylvania (Ohio) Schs. Served with USAF, 1966; now maj. USAF Res. Decorated Air Force Commendation medal. Mem. Am., Ohio dental assns., Toledo Dental Soc. (chmn. peer rev. com. 1977—), Acad. Gen. Dentistry, Mil. Surgeons Assn. U.S., Res. Officers Assn. U.S., Sigma Alpha Epsilon. Home: 4835 Rudgate Blvd Toledo OH 43623 Office: 3030 Sylvania Ave Toledo OH 43613

MORDECAI, BENJAMIN, theatre dir.; b. N.Y.C., Dec. 10, 1944; s. Allen Lewis and Florence (Goldman) M.; B.A., Buena Vista Coll., 1967; M.A., Eastern Mich. U., 1968; postgrad. Ind. U., 1968-70; m. Sherry Lynn Morley, July 20, 1974. Costumer; co-founder, producing dir. Ind. Repertory Theatre, Indpls., 1972—. Cons. Found. for Extension and Devel. Am. Profl. Theatre, 1974—. Bd. dirs. Hosp. Audiences, Inc., Indpls., 1974—, pres., 1975; pres. Profl. Cultural Alliance, Indpls., 1976—. Mem. Am. Theatre Assn., League Resident Theatres (chmn. children's theatre com. 1974—, exec. com. 1976—). Producer, dir. Am. premiere: Bird in the Hand, 1975. Home: 5255 N New Jersey St Indianapolis IN 46220 Office: 411 E Michigan St Indianapolis IN 46204

MORDUE, HOWARD WILBUR, diversified industry exec.; b. Hillsdale, Mich., June 10, 1930; s. Howard Wilbur and Helen Clare (Brasch) M.; student U. Mich., 1948-50; B.S., Detroit Inst. Tech., 1956; m. Patricia Alice, June 10, 1967; children—Howard, Marc. Pres., Drug Industries Co., Inc., Detroit, 1958—; pres. H.P. Corp, Detroit, 1972—; pres. Detroit Med. Arts, Inc., 1956—; v.p. 13700 Woodward Corp., Detroit, 1956—. Mem. Highland Park City Planning Commn., 1958—; chmn. Highland Park Gen. Hosp., 1967. Served with USCGR, 1950-51. Mem. Am. Pharm. Assn., Wayne County Med. Soc., Am. Soc. Hosp. Pharmacists. Methodist. Clubs: Commander's (Lansing, Mich.); Bayview Yacht (Detroit); Mackinaw Yacht (Mackinaw Island, Mich.). Home: 930 Lakeshore Grosse Pointe Shores MI 48236 Office: 13700 Woodward St Highland Park MI 48203

MOREFIELD, WILLIAM MERRITT, nursing home adminstr.; b. Chgo., July 7, 1937; s. Clarence Odell and Dorothy Jo (Merritt) M.; student Monmouth (Ill.) Coll., 1956-57; m. Judy Marie Weeks, Aug. 17, 1967; 1 son, William Derik. Asst. adminstr. Monmouth Nursing Home, 1961-65; adminstr. Mercer County Nursing Home, Aledo, Ill., 1965-68; adminstr. Valley Hi Nursing Home, Woodstock, Ill., 1969—. Chmn. nurse's aide adv. com. McHenry County Jr. Coll., 1973—. Chmn. Welfare Services Com. McHenry County, Ill., 1970—; chmn. adv. bd. McHenry County Dept. Pub. Aid, 1970—. Mem. County and Non Profit Nursing Home Assn. (sec. 1974, dir.). Home: 2406 Hartland Rd Woodstock IL 60098

MOREHOUSE, LAWRENCE GLEN, veterinarian, ednl. adminstr.; b. Manchester, Kans., July 21, 1925; s. Edwy O. and Ethel (Glenn) M.; B.S. in Biol. Sci., Kans. State U., 1952, D.V.M., 1952; M.S. in Animal Pathology, Purdue U., 1956, Ph.D., 1960; m. Georgia Ann Lewis, Oct. 6, 1956; children—Timothy, Glenn Ellen. Veterinarian, County Vet. Hosp., St. Louis, 1952-53; supr. Brucellosis labs. Purdue U., Lafayette, Ind., 1953-60; staff veterinarian lab. services U.S. Dept. Agr., Washington, 1960-61; discipline leader in pathology and toxicology, animal health div. Nat. Animal Disease Lab., Ames, Iowa, 1962-64; prof., chmn. dept. veterinary pathology Coll. Vet. Medicine, U. Mo., Columbia, 1964-67, dir. Vet. Med. Diagnostic Lab., 1968—; cons. to U.S. Dept. Agr., Miss. State U., St. Louis Zoo Residency Tng. Program, Miss. Vet. Med. Assn. Served with USN, 1943-46, U.S. Army, 1952-53. Recipient Outstanding Service award U.S. Dept. Agr., 1959. Fellow Royal Soc. Health, London; mem. Am., Mo. vet.

med. assns., Nat. Assn. Fed. Veterinarians, Am. Assn. Vet. Lab. Diagnosticians (E.P. Pope award 1976, chmn. lab. accreditation bd. 1972—), U.S. Animal Health Assn., Am. Assn. Lab. Animal Medicine, Mo. Soc. Microbiology, Am. Assn. Avian Pathologists. Presbyterian. Co-editor: Mycotoxic Fungi, Mycotokins, Mycotoxicoses - An Encyclopedic Handbook, 3 vols., 1977. Contbr. numerous articles on diseases of animals to profl. jours. Home: 916 Danforth St Columbia MO 65201 Office: Veterinary Med Diagnostic Lab Univ of Missouri Columbia MO 65201

MORELAND, KENNETH ORMAN, educator; b. Eureka, Ill., Mar. 26, 1915; s. Harper Richard and Carrie (Street) M.; B.S., Ill. State U., 1947, M.S. in Edn., 1954; advanced certificate edn. U. Ill., 1966; m. Harriet Virginia Allin, June 1, 1947; children—Kristan Marie (Mrs. Lloyd Nash), Kenneth Allin. Tchr. elementary schs., Secor, Ill., 1939-41, El Paso, Ill., 1941-43; supt. McLean (Ill.) Community Consol. Sch., 1947-55, McLean-Waynesville (Ill.) Community Unit Sch. Dist. 12, 1955-64; asst. prof. elementary edn. Ill. State U., Normal, 1964—. Chmn. McLean (Ill.) Centennial Assn., 1955. Served with AUS, 1943-46. Mem. N.E.A., Nat. Soc. Study Edn., Assn. Tchr. Educators. Home: 107 William Dr Normal IL 61761

MORELAND, WILLIAM JOHN, real estate broker; b. Chgo., Feb. 21, 1916; s. James C. and Izora M. (McCabe) M.; A.B., U. Ill., 1938; student Northwestern U., 1937. With James C. Moreland & Son, Inc., real estate and home building, Chgo., 1938—, pres., 1952—; pres. Moreland Realty, Inc., Chgo., 1952-72. Builder, operator Howard Johnson Motor Lodge, Chgo., 1960-72. Helped develop model housing community, El Salvador, Central Am., 1960's. Presidential appointment to commerce com. for Alliance for Progress, 1962-64. Served to lt. USNR, 1941-46. Mem. Home Bldrs. Assn. Chicagoland (pres. 1961-62), Chgo. Assn. Commerce and Industry, Chgo., N.W. real estate bds., N.W. Bldrs. Assn., Nat. Assn. Home Bldrs. (hon. life dir. 1972—), Chi Psi. Republican. Roman Catholic. Office: 5717 Milwaukee Ave Chicago IL 60646

MORELLO, VICTOR SALVATORE, chem. engr.; b. Clairton, Pa., Oct. 5, 1915; s. Salvatore and Anna (Junek) M.; B.S., Carnegie-Mellon U., 1938, M.S., 1947, D.Sc., 1949; m. Carolyn Skapik, June 15, 1948; 1 dau., Carol Ann. With Dow Chem. Co., Midland, Mich., 1938-46, 49—, process cons., 1968—. Served with C.E. U.S. Army, 1941-46. Decorated Bronze Star medal. Consol. Coal Co. fellow, 1947-49. Mem. Am. Chem. Soc., Am. Inst. Chem. Engrs. Presbyterian. Club: Kiwanis. Contbr. articles in field to profl. jours. Home: 1811 Sylvan Lane Midland MI 48640 Office: Dow Chem Co 256 Bldg Midland MI 48640

MORENCY, ROBERT JOSEPH, archtl. woodwork co. exec.; b. Oak Park, Ill., July 13, 1930; s. George Anthony and Florence (Tourtelot) M.; ed. DePaul U.; m. Doris Marie Lohorne, Mar. 27, 1954; children—Paula, Claire, Steven, Kenneth, Patricia, Thomas. With Bedard & Morency Mill Co., Elgin, Ill., 1954—, v.p., 1961-64, pres., 1964—. Commr., River Forest Park Dist., 1971-73; trustee Village of Sleepy Hollow, 1975—, also chmn. police comm., 1975—. Bd. dirs. Oak Park-River Forest Community Chest, 1967-68; bd. dirs. Summit Sch., East Dundee, Ill., 1974—, chmn., 1976—; trustee Oak Park Hosp., 1968—. Served with USNR, 1950-54. Decorated Purple Heart with oak leaf cluster. Mem. Archtl. Woodwork Inst. (dir. 1967-72, v.p. 1971-73, pres. 1973-74), Chgo. Woodworkers Assn. (pres. 1963-64, treas. 1965-68), Sleepy Hollow Service Club (pres. 1974-75). Clubs: Oak Park (pres. 1968-69); Midday (Chgo.). Home: 230 Rainbow Dr Sleepy Hollow IL 60118 Office: 1100 Davis Rd Elgin IL 60120

MORENO, FRANKLYN HENRY, urban planner; b. Chgo., Feb. 10, 1938; s. Paul Peter and Irene Margaret (Kwaitkowski) M.; student U. Ill., 1955-57; B.S., So. Ill. U., 1960, M.S., 1962; m. Nancy Ann Dukes, Mar. 3, 1962; children—Mark A., Cynthia L., Deborah A., Paula M. Owner Independent Design Studio, Carbondale, Ill., 1959-62; planning intern Village of Western Springs (Ill.), 1960; community devel. intern So. Ill. U., Carbondale, 1961-62; planner Greater Egypt Regional Planning Commn., Carbondale, 1962-66; exec. dir. Greater Egypt Regional Planning and Devel. Commn., Carbondale, 1966—. Vis. lectr., instr. So. Ill. U., intermittently 1967—. Mem. Nat. Assn. Regional Councils (mem. adv. council 1972—), Nat. Assn. Devel. Orgns. (dir. 1968-72), Ill. Planning and Conservation League (dir. 1972-74), Am. Inst. Planners (dir. Ill. chpt. 1970—, pres. 1971-73, nat. chmn. met. and regional planning dept. 1975-77). Editor, pub. Parallax mag., 1961-64. Home: 1212 W Schwartz Carbondale IL 62901 Office: 608 E College St Carbondale IL 62901

MORETSKY, LEWIS ROBERT, sales exec.; b. Bklyn., Aug. 25, 1940; s. Samuel and Shirley (Wexelbaum) M.; B.S. in Pub. Accounting, N.Y. U., 1963; M.A. in Bus., Central Mo. State U., 1971; m. Judith Goodman, June 27, 1965; children—Susan Faye, David Michael. Treas. United System Supply, Inc., Westwood, Kans., North Electric Co., Lenexa, Kans.; mgr. sales Original Equipment Mfg., 1971-73, eastern regional mktg. mgr., 1973-75, nat. accounts sales rep., 1975-77, mgr. retail sales, 1977—. Served to capt. USAF, 1963-68. Home: 1020 W 69th St Kansas City MO 64113

MOREY, WALTER THOMAS, lawyer, savs. and loan exec.; b. Decatur, Ill., Aug. 2, 1918; s. Henry H. and Helen E. (Devlin) M.; B.S., U. Ill., 1940; J.D., Harvard U., 1947; m. Dorothy P. Huff, Nov. 3, 1945; children—Madelyn, Cynthia, Marcia. Admitted to Ill. bar, 1948; house counsel A.E. Staley Co., 1948-55; individual practice law, Decatur, 1955—; pres. Security Savs. and Loan Co., Decatur, 1967—; chmn. bd. Soy Capital Bank, 1955—. City councilman, Decatur, 1959-65; mem. Decatur Housing Authority, 1964-67. Served with AUS, 1940-46, Korea, 1950-52. Decorated Legion of Merit, Bronze Star, Croix de Guerre. Mem. Am., Ill. bar assns. Clubs: Country Decatur, Union League (Chgo.). Home: 275 Park Pl Decatur IL 62522 Office: 243 S Water Decatur IL 62523

MORF, THEODORE FERDINAND, former govt. ofcl., cons. civil engr.; b. Chgo., Feb. 13, 1908; s. Paul Frederick and Louise E. (Paulus) M.; B.S., Northwestern U., 1930; m. Gertrude Elizabeth Sweeney, Jan. 26, 1932; children—Catherine Darrow (Mrs. Robert Edward Morrison), Paul Frederick. With Ill. Div. Hwys,., 1930-70, in charge research and planning work, 1955-63, dep. chief hwy. engr., Springfield, Ill., 1963-70; cons. civil engr., Springfield, 1970—. Mem. Nat. Acad. Scis. (transp. research bd.), Am. Assn. Hwy. and Transp. Ofcls., Nat. Soc. Profl. Engrs., Ill. Assn. Hwy. Engrs., Sangamon County Hist. Soc., Springfield Art Assn., Order St. Gambrinus, Nat. Trust for Hist. Preservation, Phi Delta Theta. Presbyn. (elder). Mason. Clubs: Sangamo (Springfield), Springfield 35 Camera, Island Bay Yacht (past commodore). Home and office: 73 Glen Aire Dr Springfield IL 62703

MORGAN, BARBARA ELLEN, ednl. adminstr.; b. Milw., May 10, 1944; d. Lyman Almond and Grace Emma (Erion) M.; B.S., U. Wis., 1967, M.S., 1971. Residence hall dir. U. Wis., Whitewater, 1969-72, fin. aids counselor, Madison, 1972-74; counselor Ind. U. SE, New Albany, 1974-75, coordinator student devel. center, 1976—. Bd. dirs. League of Women Voters, So. Clark County, 1975-77. Mem. Am. Personnel and Guidance Assn., Am. Coll. Personnel Assn. Home: 4127 Reas Ln New Albany IN 47150 Office: 4201 Grant Line Rd New Albany IN 47150

MORGAN, COBURN, designer; b. Letcher County, Ky., Jan. 29, 1922; s. Jesse and Ethel (Stamper) M.; B.A. in Architecture, U. Ky., 1954; m. Laura Jean Cooper, Oct. 16, 1941; children—Pamela Anne, Rodney Jesse. Self-employed Comml. Art and Design Studio, 1954-59; instr. U. Ky., 1954-59, instr. archtl. design, 1953-57; cons. product design Tectum, 1959-62; indsl. and interior designer, Columbus, Ohio, 1962—. Served with USMC, 1942-49, 50-52. Decorated Letters of Commendation. Recipient Design award Beaux Art, (7), also grphic instn. and city plan awards. Mem. Marine Corps Res Officers Assn., Am. Soc. Interior Designers, Internat. Profl. Designers. Baptist. Home: 3445 Wenwood Ave Columbus OH 43220 Office: 2043 Arlingate Ln Columbus OH 43228

MORGAN, DAVID BASIL, dermatologist; b. Emporia, Kans., Sept. 19, 1911; s. David Lloyd and Luella Winifred (Morris) M.; student Coll. of Emporia, 1929-30, U. Kans., 1930-33; B.S., Northwestern U., 1935, B.M., 1937, M.D., 1938; postgrad. in dermatology U. Pa., 1938-39; m. Elsie Catharine Cairns, Aug. 15, 1941; children—Ann Ashton, Marjorie Warren, David Lloyd, Thomas Sidney, Robert Price. Intern, Kansas City Gen. Hosp., 1937-38; preceptee in dermatology and syphilology Charles C. Dennie, M.D., 1939-42; practice medicine specializing in dermatology, Kansas City, Mo., 1945—; asso. clin. prof. medicine U. Kans. Med. Center, 1965—; lectr. dermatology U. Mo., Kansas City, 1972. Served to maj. M.C., AUS, 1941-45; ETO. Diplomate Am. Bd. Dermatology. Fellow Am. Acad. Dermatology; mem. AMA, Mo. Med. Assn., Jackson County Med. Soc., Mo. Dermatol. Soc. (pres. 1977-78), Kansas City Dermatol. Soc. (past pres.), Beta Theta Pi, Nu Sigma Nu. Republican. Presbyterian. Club: Indian Hills Country. Contbr. articles to profl. jours., chpts. in books. Home: 6513 Jefferson St Kansas City MO 64113 Office: 4620 J C Nichols Pkwy Kansas City MO 64112

MORGAN, GEORGE HENRY, mfg. co. exec.; b. St. Louis, July 23, 1935; s. George Nathaniel and Helen Henrietta (Weiss) M.; B.S. in Mech. Engring., La. State U., 1958; M.S. in Mech. Engring. (Mineral Studies grantee), U. Mo., 1959; postgrad. Rice Inst. (fellowship and teaching asst.), 1959, Purdue Extension, 1962, Notre Dame, 1962, Mich. State U., 1966, Ind. U., South Bend, 1970; m. Janis S. Leinenbach, Aug. 11, 1962; children—George D., Christopher D., Robert A., Anne M., James P., Thomas H. Project engr. Uniroyal, Mishawaka Ind., 1962-66; devel. engr. Bendix Corp., South Bend, 1966-69; brake engr. Auto Spltys. Mfg. Co., St. Joseph, Mich., 1970-73, marketing mgr. brake div., 1973—; dir. Builders United Enterprises, Inc., South Bend, 1972-73; partner All Am. Mfg. Co., South Bend, 1971-75. Commr., South Bend (Ind.) Pub. Housing Authority, 1967-72. Served with AUS, 1953-55. Registered profl. engr., Mich., Ind., Ky., La. Mem. Soc. Mfg. Engrs., Soc. Automotive Engrs., Pi Tau Sigma, Tau Beta Pi. Roman Catholic. Patentee in field. Address: 1217 Diamond Ave South Bend IN 46628

MORGAN, HOWARD KNIGHT, mini—conglomerate co. exec.; b. McConnellsville, O., Jan. 14, 1917; s. Carleton Calvin and Gladys (Knight) M.; B.A., Kenyon Coll., 1938; M.B.A., Harvard U., 1939; m. Barbara Jean Sprow, Sept. 6, 1941; children—Hannah Knight, Christopher Carleton, Howard Knight, William James. With Halsey, Stuart & Co., N.Y.C., 1939-41; asst. mgr., treas. Diamond Fertilizer Co., Sandusky, Ohio, 1945-62; chmn., pres. Wallace Expanding Machines, Inc., Indpls., 1962-72; chmn. STI Corp., Sandusky, O., 1962—; dir. Western Security Bank, Consol. Chems. Inc., Dist. Petroleum Products, Inc., Wagner Quarries Co. Trustee Firelands council Boy Scouts Am., 1955-62, Providence Hosp., 1955-62. Served from ensign to lt. comdr. USNR, 1941-46. Recipient Distinguished Service award Kenyon Coll., 1975. Mem. Beta Theta Pi. Republican. Episcopalian. Clubs: Meridian Hills (Indpls.); Plum Brook Country (pres. 1956)(Sandusky, O.); Longboat Key Golf (Sarasota, Fla.); Bradenton (Fla.) Country; Elks. Home: 3913 Hilltop Dr Huron OH 44839 Office: PO Box 2393 Sandusky OH 44870

MORGAN, JAMES ROBERT, govt. cons.; b. Oshkosh, Wis., June 13, 1926; s. Richard William and Caroline (Vogtmann) M.; student Oshkosh State U., 1946-48; B.S., U. Wis., 1950, LL.B., 1952, postgrad. in pub. adminstrn., 1954-57; m. Evonne M. Kellerman, Jan. 28, 1950; children—William, Jonathan, Carrie, James, Ann. Admitted to Wis. bar, 1952; research atty. Wis. Taxpayers Alliance, Madison, 1953-64, exec. v.p., 1971-75, pres., 1975—; sec. Wis. Dept. of Revenue, 1965-71. Cons., Wis. Blue Ribbon Tax Study Com., 1959. Wis. Gold Ribbon Com., 1963; mem. Gov.'s Medicare Task Force, 1966, Commn. on Interstate Cooperation 1966-70; vice chmn. Gov.'s Task Force on Local Government Finance and Orgn.; chmn. Legislative Council Spl. Com. on County Home Rule; mem. spl. legislature com. Taxation of Agr. Land; mem. Gov.'s Commn. on State-Local Relations and Fin.; mem. Spl. Legis. Com. on Occupational Licensing; chmn. State Personnel Bd. Past pres. Diocesan Council of Madison. Served with USAAF, 1944-46. Mem. Am. Soc. for Pub. Adminstrn. (past pres. Madison chpt.), Midwest Assn. Tax Adminstrs. (past pres.), Nat. Assn. Tax Adminstrs. (past pres). Home: 216 Virginia Terr Madison WI 53705 Office: 335 W Wilson St Madison WI 53702

MORGAN, JOHN DERALD, educator; b. Hays, Kans., Mar. 15, 1939; s. John Baber and Avis Ruth (Wolf) M.; B.S. in Elec. Engring., La. Tech. U., 1962; M.S. in Elec. Engring., U. Mo., Rolla, 1965; Ph.D., Ariz. State U., 1968; m. Elizabeth June McKneely, June 23, 1962; children—Laura Elizabeth, Kimberly Ann, Rebecca Ruth. Elec. engr. Tex. Eastman div. Eastman Kodak, 1962-63; instr. elec. engring. U. Mo., Rolla, 1963-65; instr. Ariz. State U., 1965-68; asso. prof. elec. engring. Alcoa Found., U. Mo., Rolla, 1968-72, prof. elec. engring., 1972-75, asso. dir. Center for Internat. Programs, Emerson Electric prof. elec. engring., 1975—; cons. Ariz. Pub. Service, Westinghouse, Electric Power Research Inst., Union Electric Co., A. B. Chance Co., Hames, Ris & Wood, Fane, Britt & Browne, Black & Veatch, Emerson Electric, Mobil. Pres. bd. trustees First Meth. Ch., 1971-73; v.p. bd. adminstrn. People to People, 1976; bd. dirs., cubmaster Ozarks dist. Boy Scouts Am., 1968—, asst. dist. commr., 1971-73; active Partners of the Americas. Recipient Scouters Key award Ozarks council Boy Scouts Am., 1971; T. H. Harris scholar, 1959-61, John H. Horton scholar, 1961-62; registered profl. engr., Mo. Mem. IEEE (chmn. internat. practices subcom. 1972—, chmn. ednl. resources subcom. 1973—), Am. Soc. Engring. Edn., Nat., Mo. socs. profl. engrs., Engrs. Club St. Louis, (mem. awards and recognition com. 1971—, mem. edn. com. 1970—), Sigma Xi, Tau Beta Pi, Eta Kappa Nu, Omicron Delta Kappa, Phi Kappa Phi. Author: Power Apparatus Testing Techniques, 1969; Computer Monitoring and Control of Electric Utility Systems, 1972; Control and Distribution of Megawatta Through Man-Machine Interaction, 1973; contbr. articles to profl. jours. Home: Route 4 Box 31 Rolla MO 65401 Office: U Mo Rolla MO 65401

MORGAN, JUNE JACK (MRS. JOHN E. MORGAN), former educator; b. Elkader, Iowa; d. S. V. and Grace (Powell) Jack; B.A., State U. Iowa, 1917, M.A., 1925, Ph.D., 1928; m. John E. Morgan, Oct. 29, 1932 (dec. Oct. 1962). Grad. asst. State U. Iowa, 1924-28, instr., 1928-29; prof., head English dept. Sterling Coll., Kans., 1929-30; asso. prof. English, Kans. State Tchrs. Coll., Emporia, 1930-32, asst. prof., 1960-62, asso. prof., 1962-66, prof., 1966-70; prof., head English dept. Emporia (Kans.) Coll., 1970-73. Mem. AAUP, AAUW (past pres. Emporia br.), D.A.R. (past regent), Daus. Am. Colonists (past state registrar), N.E.A, Modern Lang. Assn., Coll. English Assn., Nat. Council Tchrs. English, Midwest Modern Lang. Assn., Kans. Coll. Tchrs. English, Internat. Arthurian Soc., Am. Comparative Lit. Assn., Shakespeare Assn. Am., English Speaking Union, Bus. and Profl. Women (past pres. Emporia), Pi Lambda Theta, Sigma Kappa. Conglist. Mem. Order Eastern Star. Home: PO Box 602 Emporia KS 66801

MORGAN, LEE LAVERNE, tractor co. exec.; b. Aledo, Ill., Jan. 4, 1920; s. L. Laverne and Gladys (Hamilton) M.; B.S., U. Ill., 1941; m. Mary Harrington, Feb. 14, 1942. With Caterpillar Tractor Co., Peoria, Ill., 1946—, mgr. sales devel., 1954-61, v.p. charge indsl. div., 1961-65, exec. v.p., 1965-72, pres., 1972-77, chmn., 1977—, also dir.; dir. Comml. Nat. Bank, Central Ill. Light Co., Peoria, 1st Chgo. Corp., 1st Nat. Bank of Chgo., Minn. Mining & Mfg. Co. Bd. dirs. Monmouth Coll., Proctor Community Hosp. Served to maj. AUS, 1941-46. Mem. Bus. Roundtable, C. of C. of U.S. (dir.), Ill. C. of C., Soc. Automotive Engrs., Engine Mfrs. Assn. (past pres.) Presbyn. Mason. Clubs: Peoria Country, Creve Coeur; Chicago, Union League (Chgo.); Augusta Nat. Golf; Tucson Nat. Golf. Home: 7510 N Edgewild Dr Peoria IL 61614 Office: Caterpillar Tractor Co Peoria IL 61629

MORGAN, LEWIS V., JR., judge; b. Elmhurst, Ill., Dec. 17, 1929; s. Lewis V. and Meta (Schmidt) M.; B.A., DePauw U., 1951; J.D., U. Chgo., 1954; m. Marilyn F. Sherman, Nov. 17, 1950; children—Barbara Anne Burkey, Lewis V. III, Diane Marie Reilly; m. 2d, Alice E. Phillips, May 8, 1971; m. 3d, Linda L. Holmes, Mar. 31, 1978. Admitted to Ill. bar, 1954; mem. law firm Locke & Locke, Glen Ellyn, Ill., 1956-59; practice law, Wheaton, Ill., 1959-75; partner law firm Redmond, Morgan, Mraz & Bennorth, 1965-70, Morgan & Wilkinson, 1972-74, Morgan & Van Duzer, 1974-75; asso. circuit judge 18th dist., DuPage County, Ill., 1975—; asst. state's atty., DuPage County, Ill., 1958-61; mem. Ill. Ho. Reps., 1963-71, chmn. elections com., 1967, 69, majority leader, 1969-71. Chmn. Milton Twp. Republican orgn., DuPage County, 1961; precinct committeeman Rep. party, 1957-66, 69-73. Chmn. Ill. Commn. on Atomic Energy, 1966-71; mem. County Bd. Sch. Trustees, DuPage County, 1973-75. Trustee Wheaton Pub. Library. Served with AUS, 1954-56. Mem. Acad. Matrimonial Lawyers (bd. mgrs. Ill. chpt.), Ill., DuPage County bar assns., Ill. Trial Lawyers Assn. (former dir.), Sigma Nu. Contbg. author: DuPage Discovery, 1776-1976. Home: 1333 S Lorraine Rd Apt 201 Wheaton IL 60187 Office: DuPage County Courthouse Wheaton IL 60187

MORGAN, MARSHAL CHARLES, physician; b. Akron, Ohio, July 18, 1925; s. Marshall Chalmers and Hazel Edna (Dice) M.; B.S., Ohio State U., 1945, M.D., 1948; m. Patricia Gay Billow, Jan. 22, 1949; children—Julie Elizabeth, John Marshal, James Billow, Jeffrey Lyle. Intern, Akron City Hosp., 1948, sr. staff, 1959—, chief of family practice, 1977; family practice medicine, Akron, 1951—; pres. Med-Mor Inc.; chief family practice Akron Gen. Hosp., 1967-72, sr. staff, 1958—, mem. med. council, 1967-72. Dir. Permanent Fed. Savs. & Loan, Akron, Billow Co. Trustee Akron Child Guidance, pres., 1964; trustee United Services for Handicapped, 1965, pres., 1967; exec. bd. United Fund Summit County, 1963, United Community Council, 1964-65, hon. trustee, 1971. Served as capt. AUS, 1949-50. Diplomate Am. Bd. Family Practice. Mem. A.M.A., Am., Ohio acads. family practice, Summit County Acad. Family Practice, A.M.A., Ohio Med. Assn., Summit County Med. Soc. (council 1958-62), Phi Chi, Beta Theta Pi. Episcopalian. Mason. Clubs: Portage Country (dir. 1971-74, v.p. 1974) (Akron); Ruggles Yacht (Ruggles Beach, O.). Home: 2324 Ridgewood Rd Akron OH 44313 Office: 750 W Market St Akron OH 44303

MORGAN, MELANIE MC KENZIE, heavy equipment mfg. co. exec.; b. Chgo., Apr. 1, 1950; d. Robert H. and Olive (McKenzie) Satkowski; B.S.J., Northwestern U., 1972, M.S.J., 1973; m. Alan J. Morgan, June 23, 1973. With Internat. Harvester Corp., Chgo., 1973—, project coordinator, 1974-76, planning coordinator export advt., 1976-77, agrl. program coordinator N.Am. ops., supr. comml. prodn. and scheduling U.S. Farm Report weekly TV program, 1977—. Mem. Am. Mktg. Assn. Club: Seafans Scuba Diving. Home: Wilmette IL 60091 Office: 401 N Michigan Ave N Chicago IL 60611

MORGAN, MICHAEL FITZGERALD, dentist, b. Provo, Utah, Sept. 3, 1939; s. Ralph William and Elizabeth (Fitzgerald) M.; B.S., Brigham Young U., 1961; D.D.S., Case Western Res. U., 1966; m. Mary Lee Thatcher, Sept. 1, 1961; children—Michelle, Christine, Tamara, Deborah, Michael, David. Gen. practice dentistry, Zanesville, Ohio, 1966—. Mem. Am., Ohio dental assns., Pierre Fauchard Acad., Toastmaster Club (chapt. pres.). Mem. Ch. Jesus Christ Latter-Day Saints (bishop ward, pres. stake). Home: 2670 Eva Circle Zanesville OH 43701 Office: 2927 Bell St Zanesville OH 43701

MORGAN, MICHAEL SPEER, photographer; b. Carthage, Mo., Jan. 19, 1950; s. Claude D'Val and Margaret Lynne (Speer) M.; student Mo. So. Coll.; B.F.A. in Photography, S.W. Mo. State U., 1971; M.A., Kans. State Coll., 1972. Grad. asst. Kans. State Coll. at Pittsburg, 1971; exhibited in one man show at S.W. Mo. State U. at Springfield, 1971; exhibited in group shows at Spiva Open, Joplin, Mo., 1968, Delta Phi Delta Open, Springfield, 1969, Springfield Art Mus., 1971, Kans. State Coll., Smoky Hill Exhibition, Hayes, Kans., 1972, Profl. Photographers Am., St. Louis, Profl. Photographers Ozarks, Fayetteville, Ark., 1974; photographer Morgan Studio & Frame Shop, Carthage, 1972—. Past bd. dirs. Sunshine Childrens Home. Recipient Excellence award Mo. Profl. Photographers Assn., Profl. Photographers Ozarks, 1974, Best in Show award-Profl. Photographers Ozarks, Spring 1975, 76. Mem. Profl. Photographers Am., Profl. Photographers Ozarks (v.p. 1977-78). Club: Rotary. Home: 117 W 4th St Carthage MO 64836 Office: Morgan Studio & Frame Shop 340 Lyon St Carthage MO 64836

MORGAN, RICHARD LEE, med. and optical co. exec.; b. Morgantown, W.Va., Aug. 20, 1938; s. Kenneth I. and Wilma Josephine (Hines) M.; B.S. in Chemistry, W.Va. Wesleyan U., 1962; m. Beth Brown, Aug. 28, 1960; children—Jill, Michael Andrew. Tech. rep. silicones div. Union Carbide Co., Cleve., Akron, Ohio, Indpls., 1964-65; byproduct salesman Slab Ford Coal Co., Cherry Hill, N.J., 1964-65; sales mgr. Preiser Scientific Co. Ohio, 1965-69; v.p. Morgan Instruments, Cin., 1969—; pres. Cin. Med. Equipment. Democrat. Jewish. Office: 11484 Rockfield Ct Cincinnati OH 45241

MORGAN, ROBERT DALE, judge; b. Peoria, Ill., May 27, 1912; s. Harry Dale and Eleanor (Ellis) M.; A.B., Bradley U., 1934; J.D., U. Chgo., 1937; m. Betty Louise Harbers, Oct. 14, 1939; children—Thomas Dale, James Robert. Admitted to Ill. bar, 1937; practiced in Peoria, 1937-42, 46-67, Chgo., 1946-50; partner firm Morgan, Pendarvis & Morgan, Peoria, 1946-57, Davis, Morgan & Witherell, Peoria, 1957-67; U.S. judge So. Dist. Ill., Peoria, 1967—, now chief judge. Mayor, Peoria, 1953-57. Bd. dirs., YMCA, Peoria, 1940-72, pres., 1947-53. Trustee Bradley U. Served from 1st lt. to maj., AUS, 1942-46. Mem. Am., Ill., Peoria County bar assns., Am. Judicature Soc. Presbyterian. Clubs: Rotary (pres. 1962-63), Creve

Couer, Country (Peoria). Contbr. articles to law revs. Home: 4943 N Grand View Dr Peoria IL 61614 Office: Fed Bldg Peoria IL 61601

MORGAN, STANLEY LEINS, pharm. co. exec.; b. Sandyville, Ohio, Jan. 28, 1918; s. Eben T. and Nora (Leins) M.; B.S. in Chem. Engring., Case Inst. Tech., 1939; m. Eloise Morkel, Feb. 22, 1941; children—Susan, Patricia, Ann. Chem. engr. Ben Venue Labs., Inc., Bedford, Ohio, 1940-42, mgr. blood plasma lab., 1942-44, gen. mgr., chief engr., 1944-61, v.p., 1961-63, exec. v.p., 1963—, also dir. Registered profl. engr., Ohio. Fellow Am. Inst. Chemists; mem. AAAS, Am. Chem. Soc., Am. Inst. Chem. Engrs., N.Y. Acad. Sci., Cryobiology Soc., Parental Drug Assn., Cleve. Engring. Soc., Assn. Ofcl. Racing Chemist. Methodist. Clubs: Acacia Country (Cleve.) Home: 31051 Northwood Dr Pepper Pike OH 44124 Office: 270 Northfield Rd Bedford OH 44146

MORGAN, WILLIAM DEWITT, advt. exec.; b. Williamstown, W.Va., Feb. 4, 1924; s. Douglas Davidson and Emma (Cotton) M.; student Butler U., 1950-51, Chgo. Acad. Fine Arts, 1951-52; m. Elizabeth Muterspaugh, Feb. 27, 1949; children—David Allen, Dennis Ray, Dale Eugene. Supr., Remington Rand Microfilm, Chgo., 1946-54; advt. sales Chgo. Daily News, 1955-60; dir. advt. sales promotion Watland, Inc., Blue Island, Ill., 1961-69; dir. advt. Whiting Corp., Harvey, Ill., 1969-70, William Morgan Advt., 1970—. Mem. Bd. Edn. Hoover-Schrum Schs., Calumet City, Ill., 1965-68, Thornton Fractional N. and S., Calumet City and Lansing, Ill., 1968-77; Calumet City C. of C. Kiwanian (corr. sec. 1968-71, v.p. 1975, pres. 1976-77). 311 166th St Calumet City IL 60409 Office: 311-166th St Calumet City IL 60409

MORGAN, WILLIAM PERCY, III, artist; b. St. Louis, Jan. 12, 1937; s. William Percy and Mary (Noland) M.; B.F.A. (Skowhegan Sch. fellow), Washington U., St. Louis, 1958; M.F.A., U. Colo., 1960; postgrad. (univ. fellow) Ohio State U., 1960-64. Mem. faculty Wis. State U., Superior, 1964—, asst. prof. fine arts, 1967-70, asso. prof., 1970—. Exhibited in 80 one-man shows, including St. Mary of Springs, Columbus, Ohio, 1962, Episcopal Theol. Sem., Cambridge, Mass., 1963, Hiram (Ohio) Coll., 1963, Basil's Art Gallery, Duluth, Minn., 1966-67, galleries in St. Paul, Eau Claire, Wis., Milw., 1968, also Ft. Worth, also J. Hunt Gallery, Mpls., Charybdis 2 Gallery, Mpls., 1976-77. Exhibited in group shows including Skowhegan Alumni Show, N.Y.C., 1967, 68, Mo. Show, St. Louis Art Mus., 1956, St. Louis Artists Guild (2d prize), 1956, Mead Corp. Art Across Am., 1965; represented in permanent collections U. Colo., St. Louis U., Coll. St. Mary of Springs, Otterbein Coll., Westerville, also pvt. collections U.S., fgn. countries, Wis. State Tchrs. fellow Kansai U., Japan, 1972. Recipient Gold award Duluth Art Inst., 1967, Dean Fine Arts Ann. award, 1977; named Tchr. of Yr. award U. Wis., Superior, 1976-77. Designer covers Mary Today Mag., No. 6, 1966, No. 1, 1967, 70, also Luth. Forum Mag., 1968-71, Retrospectives, 1973, front page designs Christmas issue Cath. Newspapers of Wis., full page designs Christmas issue Superior Evening Telegram. Home: 602 E 9th St Superior WI 54880

MORGAN, WILLIAM RICHARD, plastic surgeon; b. Oahu, Hawaii, July 21, 1934; s. William Richard and Margaret (Eckhout) M.; B.S., U. Okla., 1955, M.D., 1958; m. Janice J. Kelly, Aug. 6, 1960; children—Amy Marie, Michael Christopher, Patrick Brian, Leigh Kathleen, Katherine Kelly. Intern, Cin. Gen. Hosp., 1958-59; gen. surgery resident, U. Okla., Oklahoma City, 1959-63; practice medicine specializing in gen. surgery, Yuma, Ariz., 1965-71; resident in plastic surgery Kans. U., Kansas City, 1971-73; practice medicine specializing in plastic surgery, Kansas City, Mo., 1973—. Served with USN, 1961-63. Diplomate Am. Bd. Surgery, Am. Bd. Plastic Surgery. Fellow A.C.S.; mem. AMA, Mo. State Med. Assn., Jackson County Med. Soc., Am. Soc. Plastic and Reconstructive Surgeons. Roman Catholic. Home: 9500 Russell St Overland Park KS 66212 Office: 1010 Carondelet Dr #440 Kansas City MO 64141

MORGANSTERN, RAMON JEROME, lawyer; b. St. Louis, Dec. 14, 1932; s. David Martin and Elsie (Merkadeau) M.; A.B., Washington U., 1955, J.D., 1957; m. Lois Elaine Levin, July 25, 1965; children—Denise Holly, Julie Faith. Admitted to Mo. bar, 1957; asso. atty. Husch, Eppenberger, Donohue, Elson & Cornfeld, St. Louis, 1959-65; pvt. practice, St. Louis, 1965-69; partner Schramm & Morganstern, Clayton, 1970-76, Gallop, Johnson, Godiner, Morganstern & Crebs, 1976—. Pres., Good Shepherd Sch. for Spl. Children Parents Assn., 1972-73; pres., rep. Wash. U. dept. neurology to St. Louis Met. Council Developmental Disabilities, 1971—. Bd. dirs. St. Louis Assn. for Retarded Children, 1975—. Served to 1st lt. AUS, 1957-59. Mem. Am., Mo., St. Louis County, St. Louis bar assns., Jewish Fedn. St. Louis (mem. leadership devel. council 1971-74), Phi Beta Kappa, Pi Sigma Alpha, Phi Delta Phi, Sigma Alpha Mu. Democrat. Mason. Home: 1328 Benbush Dr St Louis MO 63141 Office: 7733 Forsyth Blvd Clayton MO 63105

MORGENSTERN, JACK ARNOLD, dir. mental health center; b. Cleve., Dec. 18, 1934; s. Morris and Rose Ruth (Lowry) M.; B.S. cum laude, Washington and Lee U., 1956; M.D., Case Western Res. U., 1960; M.S., U. Calif. at Los Angeles, 1966, M. Social Psychiatry, 1968; m. Mary Geraldine Hotchkiss; children—Steven, Margaret, Michael, Daniel. Asst. prof. psychiatry Sch. Medicine, U. Calif. at Los Angeles, 1966-71, dir. child tng., 1969-71, dir. community liaison and evaluation programs, 1969-71; exec. dir. Columbus Area Community Mental Health Center and Franklin County Comprehensive Drug Treatment Program, 1971—. Clin. asso. prof. psychiatry Ohio State U., Columbus, 1971—; cons. NIMH, Columbus State Hosp., Dept. Social Work Capital U. Bd. dirs. Maryhaven Alcoholism Program. Served to capt. USAF, 1961-63. Recipient Merit award Columbus Police Dept. Fellow Am. Psychiat. Assn.; mem. Ohio Psychiat. Assn. (exec. com., sec.), Neurospsychiat. Soc. Central Ohio (pres.). Club: Torch. Office: 1515 E Broad St Columbus OH 43205

MORGENSTERN, JUNE RUTH, psychologist; b. Cleve.; d. Irving and Molly (Sobul) Siegel; A.B., Western Res. U., 1957, M.S., 1960, postgrad. 1960-63; postgrad. Nova U., Ft. Lauderdale, 1974-76; m. David Morgenstern, May 30, 1940 (div. 1970); children—Jeffry David, Kirk Laurence. Ballet tchr., dance therapy, Cleve., 1940-65; grad. student tng. psychology research services Western Res. U., 1957-58, clin. psychology intern, 1959-60; rehab. counselor State of Ohio, Cleve., 1960-62; clin. psychologist Cleve. Center on Alcoholism, 1963, Cuyahoga Co. Criminal Ct., 1966-76; asst. prof. psychology Cuyahoga Community Coll., 1963-68, asso. prof. psychology, 1968-75, prof., 1975-76, ednl. area specialist, 1975-76; also curriculum coordinator for social sci. div. Night Sch. Mem. Am., Ohio, Cleve. psychol. assns., Internat. Transactional Analysis Assn., Phi Beta Kappa (pres. Phi Soc., 1965-66), Phi Sigma Iota, Tau Delta Alpha. Died Oct. 19, 1976. Home: 28749 Jackson Blvd Orange Village OH 44022

MORGENTHALER, DAVID TURNER, investment co. exec., b. Chester, S.C., Aug. 5, 1919; s. Henry W. and Elizabeth (Taylor) M.; B.M.E. and M.M.E., Mass. Inst. Tech., 1941; m. Lindsay Anne Jordon, May 17, 1945; children—David T., Gary J., Todd W., Gaye Elizabeth. Vice pres., dir. sales Delavan Mfg. Co., Des Moines, 1950-57; pres. Foseco, Inc., Cleve., 1957-68; chmn. bd. Foseco Technik Ltd., Birmingham, Eng., 1964-68; chmn. bd. API Instruments Co., 1968-70, dir., 1963-70; chmn. bd. Mfg. Data Systems, Inc., Ann Arbor, Mich., 1969—; chmn. exec. com., dir. LFE Corp., Waltham, Mass., 1970—; sr. partner Morgenthaler Assos.; dir. E.F. Hauserman Co., Cleve., Space Comfort, Inc., Cleve., Ohio Industries, Inc., Cleve., Dynamet, Inc., Pitts., Modular Computer Systems, Inc., Ft. Lauderdale, Fla., Vlasic, Inc., Lathrup Village, Mich., Doweave, Inc., Phila. Trustee High Blood Pressure Research Council, Project Yardstick. Served to capt., AUS, 1941-45. Mem. Chief Execs. Forum (dir., former pres.), Nat. Venture Capital Assn. (dir.). Clubs: Westwood Country, Clevelander, Mid-Day. Home: 13904 Edgewater Dr Cleveland OH 44107 Office: 1033 Nat City Bank Bldg Cleveland OH 44114

MORGILLO, MARY ELIZABETH DU BRY, counselor, psychometrist; b. Monroe County, Mich., Apr. 29, 1934; d. Earl Alfred and Clara Cecelia (Dressel) DuBry; B. Ed., U. Toledo, 1970, M. Ed., 1974, postgrad. 1974—; certificate in psychometry Boston Coll., 1974; m. Constantine Vincent Morgillo, June 20, 1953; children—Vincent, Sharon, Robert. Tchr. Good Shepherd Parochial Sch., Toledo, Ohio, 1966-70, guidance counselor, 1970-72; tchr. math. Libbey High Sch., Toledo, 1972-76; grad. asst., coordinator student personnel U. Toledo, 1976-78; counselor-psychometrist Cath. Social Services, Toledo, 1976—. Mem. Am. Personnel and Guidance Assn., Nat. Assn. Specialists in Group Work, Nat. Cath. Guidance Conf., U. Toledo Alumni Assn., Kappa Delta Pi, Pi Lambda Theta. Phi Kappa Phi. Contbr. articles to profl. publs. Home: 913 Wardell St Toledo OH 43605 Office: 1933 Spielbusch St Toledo OH 43624

MORGISON, F. EDWARD, investment broker; b. Clay Center, Kans., Oct. 4, 1940; s. Fred and Lena Edna (Chaput) M.; B.A. in Math., Emporia State U., 1963; M.S. in Bus. Adminstrn., U. Mo., Columbia, 1964; m. Karen Lorene Herdman, Nov. 21, 1964; 1 dau., Diana Michelle. Computer programmer U. Mo. Med. Center, Columbia, 1964-65; adminstrv. and budget analyst Urban Renewal Project, Independence, Mo., 1965-66; account exec., bank broker Stifel Nicolaus & Co., Kansas City, Mo., 1966-73; pres., chief exec. officer Will-Mor Investment Systems, Kansas City, Mo., 1973-75; br. mgr. Edward Jones & Co., 1975; editorial and exec. asst. to Morgan Maxfield, candidate for U.S. Congress, Kansas City, 1976; sr. account exec., merger and acquisitions specialist R. Rowland & Co., Kansas City, Mo., 1976-77; chmn. bd., pres., chief exec. officer Mo. Securities Inc., Kansas City, 1977—; sec., treas., dir. several Kansas City corps. Recipient Bausch and Lomb Sci. award, 1959; Sci. award Lambda Delta Lambda, 1962; registered account exec. N.Y. Stock Exchange, Am. Exchange, registered securities agt., Mo., Kans., Ill. Mem. U. Mo. (life), Emporia State U. (life) alumni assns., Nat. Rifle Assn. (life), U.S. Chess Fedn. (life), Mensa (life). Home: 1000 NE 96th Terr Kansas City MO 64155 Office: Walltower Bldg 9th and Walnut Kansas City MO 64106

MORIARTY, MICHAEL DAVID, lawyer; b. Indpls., Nov. 14, 1950; s. David John and Agnes LaVonne (Slick) M.; B.S. in Fin., Ind. U., 1972, J.D., 1978; m. Kimberly Ann Schmalz, June 8, 1974. Sr. corp. lending analyst, Am. Fletcher Nat. Bank, Indpls., 1972-73; v.p. Fidelity Bank of Ind., Carmel, 1973, v.p. and cashier, 1973-74, v.p. and trust officer, 1974-78; asso. firm Locke, Reynolds, Boyd & Weisell, Indpls., 1978—. Mem. allocation subcom. Greater Indpls. United Way. Mem. Beta Theta Pi (asst. gen. sec. nat. frat.). Roman Catholic. Clubs: Ind. U. Alumni Assn., Ind. U. Indpls. Men's Club Assn., K.C. Home: 829 Hickory Dr Carmel IN 46032

MORITZ, MICHAEL EVERETT, lawyer; b. Marion, Ohio, Mar. 30, 1933; s. Charles Raymond and Elisabeth Bovie (Morgan) M.; B.S., Ohio State U., 1958, J.D. summa cum laude, 1961; m. Lou Ann Yardley, Sept. 12, 1959; children—Ann Gibson, Jeffrey Connor, Molly Elisabeth, Catharine Morgan. Admitted to Ohio bar, 1961; asso. firm Dunbar, Kienzle & Murphey, Columbus, Ohio, 1961-65, partner, 1966-72; partner firm Moritz, McClure, Hughes & Hadley, 1972—; dir. Cardinal Foods, Inc., Pharmacy Systems, Inc., and others. Adj. prof. Capital U. Law Sch., 1969-70; lectr. Ohio Legal Center Inst., 1967. Chmn. legal div. United Appeal of Franklin County (Ohio), 1964. Pres. The Capital City Young Republican Club, 1966; mem. Franklin County Rep. Exec. Com., 1966—. Trustee Omicron Deuteron Assn. 1964-71, pres., 1970. Served with USNR, 1954-56. Recipient Distinguished Service award Columbus Jr. C. of C., 1966; named Outstanding Young Republican, Capital City Young Rep. Club, 1966. Mem. Am., Ohio, Columbus bar assns., Am. Judicature Soc., Order of Coif, Beta Gamma Sigma, Phi Gamma Delta. Clubs: Athletic of Columbus, Presidents of Ohio State U., Ohio State U. Faculty, Lawyers, Scioto Country. Home: 1110 Kingsdale Terr Columbus OH 43220 Office: 155 E Broad St Columbus OH 43215

MORLEY, GEORGE WILLIAM, obstetrician, gynecologist, clin. dir.; b. Toledo, Ohio, June 6, 1923; s. Frank and Florence (Sneider) M.; B.S., U. Mich., 1944, M.D., 1949, M.S., 1955; m. Marcheta Frye; children—Beverly Ann, Kathryn Bel, George W. Intern, Univ. Hosp., Ann Arbor, Mich., 1949-50, resident in obstetrics and gynecology, 1950-52, clin. instr., 1952-54; practice medicine specializing in obstetrics and gynecology, Ann Arbor, Mich., 1956—; with U. Mich. Med. Center, Ann Arbor, 1956—, prof. obstetrics and gynecology, 1970—, chief gynecology service, 1973—, acting chmn. dept. obstetrics and gynecology, 1973-74, dir. gynecology oncology, 1974—. Elder, 1st Presbyn. Ch., Ann Arbor, 1972—; bd. dirs. United Fund and Community Services Greater Ann Arbor, 1965-69. Served to capt. M.C., U.S. Army, 1954-56. Recipient Speculummaward U. Mich. Med. Center, 1974. Diplomate Am. Bd. Obstetrics and Gynecology. Fellow A.C.S., Am. Coll. Obstetricians and Gynecologists (dist. vice chmn. 1975—, mem. nat. com. on maternal health, 1967-71); mem. Soc. Gyncecologic Oncologists (pres. 1976), N.Y. Acad. Scis., N.D. Soc. Obstetrics and Gynecology (hon.), Washtenaw Obstetrical and Gynecologic Soc. (past pres.), Central Assn. Obstetricians and Gynecologists, Mich. Soc. Obstetricians and Gynecologists (past pres.), A.M.A., Norman Miller Gynecologic Soc. (pres. 1968-69), Galens Hon., Victor Vaughan Hon., Washtenaw County (pres. 1976), Mich. State (mem. Ho. of Dels. 1974—) med. socs., Internat. Soc. for Study Vulvar Diseases, Soc. Pelvic Surgeons, Am. Gynecological Soc., Am. Assn. Obstetricians and Gynecologists, Am. Fedn. Clin. Oncologic Socs., Sigma Chi (bd. dirs., pres. 1972-73, pres. Ann Arbor chpt. 1971-73), Ann Arbor Amateur Hockey Assn. Clubs: Univ. (bd. dirs. 1973), U. Mich., Ann Arbor Golf and Outing. Contbr. articles to med. jours. Office: Univ Michigan Medical Center Ann Arbor MI 48104

MORLEY, JAMES QUINCY, civil engr.; b. Knox County, Ind., Oct. 23, 1941; s. Warren and Dorothy Mae (Clark) M.; A.S. in Engring., Vincennes U. Jr. coll., 1962; B.S. in Civil Engring., Tri-State Coll., 1965; m. Joan Marie Stoelting, June 23, 1963; children—Janet Marie, Darlene Ann, James Edward. Coop. student-work program Ind. Hwy. Dept., 1962-65; asst. project engr. Ind. Hwy. Dept., 1965-67; asst. prof. sci. and engring. Vincennes (Ind.) U. Jr. Coll., 1967-70; chief civil engr. Biagi-Hannan & Assoc., Inc., Evansville, Ind., 1970-76; pres. Morley & Assos., Inc., 1976—. Registered profl. engr., Ind., Ky. Registered land surveyor, Ind. Mem. Am. Soc. C.E. (state pres. 1974), Ind. Soc. Profl. Land Surveyors. Methodist. Editor: Ind. Civil Engr. Engring. works include unique swimming pool designs, Newburgh and Evansville, Ind., 1971; oily wastewater treatement system Farm Bur. Refinery, Mt. Vernon, Ind., 1972; Beverly Heights Urban Renewal Area, Evansville, Ind., 1973; Barren River Lake Recreation Facilities, Ky., 1973; cons. civil engr. Evansville-Vanderburgh Levee Authority. Home: 6608 Kembell Dr Evansville IN 47710 Office: 312 NW 7th St Evansville IN 47708

MORRELL, DAVID BERNARD, novelist, educator; b. Kitchener, Ont., Can., Apr. 24, 1943; s. Clarence and Beatrice (Markel) Bamberger; B.A., U. Waterloo (Ont., Can.), 1966; M.A., Pa. State U., 1967, Ph.D., 1970; m. Donna Maziarz, Oct. 11, 1965; children—Sarie, Matthew. Instr., Am. Literature, Pa. State U., 1969-70; asst. prof. Am. Literature, U. Iowa, Iowa City, 1970-74, asso. prof., 1974-77, prof., 1977—; novelist: First Blood, 1972 (Distinguished Recognition award Friends Am. Writers); Testament: 1975; Last Reveille, 1977; author: John Barth: An Introduction, 1976. Home: 1805 W Benton St Iowa City IA 52240 Office: Univ Iowa English Dept Iowa City IA 52240

MORRELL, DAVID LA DUE, elec. products co. exec.; b. Evanston, Ill., Oct. 28, 1930; s. Louis C. and Marian (LaDue) M.; student Ripon Coll., 1948-50; B.S. in Physics, Ill. Inst. Tech., 1953; m. Bernice Ellen Johnson, June 20, 1953; children—Edward LaDue, Louise Ellen, Paul David. With Zonolite Co. Research Labs, Evanston, 1952-56, Controls Co. of America, Schiller Park, Ill., 1956-58, Burgess-Manning Co., Chgo., Libertyville, Ill., 1958-61; pres., treas., chmn. bd. Acoustics Devel. Corp., Northbrook, Ill., 1961—; chmn. bd. Geeco, Inc., St. Joseph, Mo.; pres. Auto Classics, Inc., Rockford, Ill.; v.p. Med. Environ. Devices, Inc., Wheeling, Ill. Mem. Acoustical Soc. Am., Theta Chi, Alpha Omega Alpha. Episcopalian. Home: 1867 W Crescent Ave Park Ridge IL 60068 Office: 1810 Holste Rd Northbrook IL 60062

MORRICE, GEORGE, physician; b. St. Johns, Mich., Aug. 21, 1919; s. George and Ruth (Lung) M.; A.B., Andrews U., Berrien Springs, Mich., 1941; M.D., Loma Linda (Calif.) U., 1945; m. Svea Vernette Nord, Sept. 28, 1944; children—George Erik, Ruth-Ann Lenore Gallagher, Bryce Ian, Elena Kay Valerie. Intern, Henry Ford Hosp., Detroit, 1944-45; resident internal medicine and cardiology Henry Ford Hosp., Detroit, 1945-46, 48-51; practice medicine, specializing in internal medicine and cardiology, Columbus, Ohio, 1952-66, Newark, Ohio, 1966—; dir. cardiology div. Licking Meml. Hosp., 1966—; clin. asso. prof. medicine Ohio State U. Vice pres. North Central region Am. Heart Assn., 1974-75. Served to lt. (j.g.) USNR, 1946-47. Fellow A.C.P., Am. Coll. Cardiology, Council Clin. Cardiology; mem. Ohio (past pres.), Central Ohio (past pres.) heart assns. Home: 1689 Bryn Mawr Dr Newark OH 43055 Office: 1320 W Main St Newark OH 43055

MORRILL, WALTER DUNLAP, coll. librarian; b. Pitts., Jan. 11, 1936; s. Allen Conrad and Eleanor (Dunlap) M.; A.B., Monmouth Coll., 1957; M.S., U. Ill., 1960; m. Marcia Lou Simpson, Aug. 18, 1957; children—Allen Simpson, Matthew Richard, Stephen Conrad. Rhetoric instr. U. Ill., 1957-59, asst. catalog librarian, 1959-60, binding librarian, 1960-61; coll. librarian Muskingum Coll., 1961-65; asst. dir. libraries Kent State U., 1965-66; dir. libraries Hanover (Ind.) Coll., 1966—. Adminstrv. cons. Library Service Center of Eastern Ohio, 1965-66; mem., also chmn. adv. council Ind. Library and Hist. Bd. Mem. ALA, AAUP, Ind. Library Assn. (pres. 1974-75), Assn. Coll. and Research Libraries, Beta Phi Mu, Sigma Omicron Mu, Pi Delta Kappa, Theta Chi. Republican. Presbyn. (elder). Rotarian. Contbr. articles to profl. jours. Home: Box 53 Hanover IN 47243

MORRIS, ARLENE JANET ROBERTS, clin. psychologist; b. Moline, Ill., Apr. 7, 1926; d. Alexander Watt McCoy and Della Mae (Bishop) Roberts; B.A., U. Iowa, 1948; M.A., Drake U., 1967; m. James Braddie Morris, Jr., Mar. 29, 1948; children—James Bradford III, William Stephen, Robert Virgil. Clin. psychologist, Broadlawns Hosp. Psychiat. Clinic, Des Moines, 1967—. Sec. Des Moines Planned Parenthood Com., 1955; mem. Know Your Neighbor panel, 1960-70; mem. Des Moines Mayor's Sign Com., 1966-67; sec. Iowa Children's and Family Service Bd., 1966-67; bd. dirs. Des Moines YWCA, 1956. Licensed psychologist Iowa. Mem. Central Iowa, Iowa, Am. psychol. assns., Psi Chi, Alpha Kappa Alpha. Methodist. Home: 1600 Hickman Rd Des Moines IA 50314 Office: 1800 Hickman Rd Des Moines IA 50314

MORRIS, DONALD, educator; b. Chgo., Oct. 13, 1945; s. Donald Charles and Cathleen (Lautner) M.; B.A., Calif. State U. at Los Angeles, 1968; M.A., DePaul U., 1971; Ph.D., So. Ill. U., 1978; m. Linda Susan Yeager, Dec. 26, 1966; children—Keith Anthony, Sarah Kathryn. Caseworker, Cook County Dept. Pub. Aid, Chgo., 1968; employment counsellor Ill. Dept. Labor, Chgo., 1969-71; instr. Waubonsee Community Coll., Sugar Grove, Ill., 1970-71; instr. philosophy, coordinator humanities dept. John A. Logan Coll., Carterville, Ill., 1971—. Mem. Am. Philos. Assn., Ill. Philosophy Conf. Home: 603 Glenview Carbondale IL 62901 Office: Dept Humanities John A Logan College Carterville IL 62918

MORRIS, DONALD FISCHER, art gallery exec.; b. Detroit, Apr. 12, 1925; s. Walter George and Margaret Elizabeth (Fischer) M.; student N.Y. U., 1943, U. Detroit, 1946-47; B.A., Wayne State U., 1950; m. Florence Marie Alper, Apr. 6, 1950; children—Steven Alan, Mark Christopher. Owner, Park Gallery, Detroit, 1958-66; pres. Donald Morris Gallery, Inc., Detroit, 1966—. Mem. visual arts com. Mich. Council for the Arts, 1966—. Mem. community edn. com. Cranbrook Acad. Art, 1969-70. Served with AUS, 1943-46. Mem. Art Dealers Assn. Am., Detroit Art Dealers Assn. (pres. 1971-73, v.p. 1973—), Am. Assn. Dealers in Ancient, Oriental and Primitive Art. Home: 25915 Salem Rd Huntington Woods MI 48070 Office: 105 Townsend St Birmingham MI 48011

MORRIS, EDWARD LOUIS, investment banker; b. Belleville, Ill., Oct. 17, 1942; s. Edward Henry and Virginia Nelda (Jung) M.; B.A., Washington U., 1964; M.B.A., U. Pa., 1970; m. Ann Nicklas Bottger, June 18, 1966; children—Edward Louis, Nicklas C. Asso., Reinholdt & Gardner, St. Louis, 1970-73, ltd. partner, 1973-74, gen. partner, 1974—; dir. Artronix, Inc., EAC Corp.; lectr. St. Louis U., 1970—. Mem. adv. bd. St. Louis YMCA, 1975—. Served to lt. USN, 1965-68. Chartered fin. analyst, Mo. Mem. St. Louis Soc. Fin. Analysts, Beta Gamma Sigma. Congregationalist. Club: Media. Home: 119 S Gore St St Louis MO 63119 Office: 506 Olive St St Louis MO 63101

MORRIS, ELIZABETH MAY, ednl. adminstr.; b. Indpls., Oct. 15, 1922; d. Herbert and Helen Salena (Leftridge) Morris; B.A., Mich. State Normal Coll., 1951; M.A., Eastern Mich. U., 1958. Tchr., supr. N.P.I. and Childrens Psychiat. Hosp., Univ. Hosp. Sch., Ann Arbor, Mich., 1951-56; dir. spl. edn. Hawthorn Center, Northville, Mich., 1956—; vis. instr. Eastern Mich. U., U. Mich.; cooperating prin. for tchr. tng. program of 6 Mich. univs. Mem. Council for Exceptional Children, Mich. Assn. TchRs. Emotionally Disturbed Children (past pres.), Mich. Assn. for Emotionally Disturbed Children, Delta Sigma Theta. Home: 755 Dellwood Dr Ann Arbor MI 48103 Office: Hawthorn Center 18471 Haggerty Rd Northville MI 48167

MORRIS, EUGENE, ins. co. exec.; b. Promise City, Iowa, Sept. 27, 1918; s. William Harley and Ethel (Enright) M.; student pub. schs., Promise City; m. Helen Eloise McCart, Sept. 27, 1938; 1 son, Elgin

Eugene. Farmer nr. Corydon, Iowa, 1938-47; ins. insp. Grinnell Mut. Re-Ins. Co. (Iowa), 1947-49; parts man Forest City Motor Co. (Iowa), 1949-50; owner, real estate broker Eugene Morris Ins. and Realty, Forest City, 1950—. Dir. Forest City Devel. Inc., 1960—. Mem. city council Forest City, 1964-76, mayor, 1976—; gen. chmn., local pageant dir. Miss Forest City Pageant, 1975-77. Mem. Ind. Ins. Agts. Assn., Nat., Iowa real estate assns., Forest City C. of C. (past pres.), Iowa Numis. Assn. (pres. 1975-76). Clubs: Lions (dist. gov. 1959-60, 63-64, Key of Nations award 1967, local Mr. Lion award 1970, also 4 dist. awards), Odd Fellows (past local noblegrand). Home: 234 Riverview Dr PO Box 467 Forest City IA 50436 Office: 234 N Clark St Forest City IA 50436

MORRIS, GARY JAY, lawyer; b. St. Louis, Sept. 7, 1936; s. Sidney and Sybil (Samuel) M.; A.B., Washington U., St. Louis, 1958, J.D., 1960; m. Barbara Joyce Weissman, Aug. 31, 1958; children—Marjorie Ann, David Joel. Admitted to Mo. bar, 1960; practice law, Clayton, Mo., 1961-67; partner firm Carp and Morris, Clayton, 1968—; gen. counsel, exec. dir. Coin Machine Operators Assn. Inc., Clayton, 1968—. Mem. leadership devel. council Jewish Fedn. St. Louis, 1968—; active Clayton United Fund Campaign, 1972. Served with AUS, 1960-61; capt. Res. Mem. Bar Assn. Met. St. Louis, St. Louis County, Am., Mo. Bar assns., Am. Trial Lawyers Assn., Jr. C. of C., Res. Officers Assn., Sigma Alpha Mu. Mason (32 deg., Shriner). Club: Creve Coeur Racquet. Home: 200 Brooktrail Ct Creve Coeur MO 63141 Office: 225 S Meramec Ave Clayton MO 63105

MORRIS, HUGH IRVIN, electronic systems mfg. co. exec.; b. Indpls., Dec. 28, 1924; s. Irvin and Lillian (Berryman) M.; student Purdue U., 1945-47. Pres., Communications Equipment Co., Inc., Glen Arbor, Mich., 1955—; pres. Glenwood Corp., Glen Arbor, 1964—. Dir. Citizens Council of Sleeping Bear Dunes Area, Inc., 1971—; chmn. Glen Arbor Twp. Fire Dept., 1969-73. Served with USAF, 1943-46. Mem. Accoustical Engring. Soc., Am. Radio Relay League, Soc. Mfg. Engrs., IEEE. Home: PO Box 700 Glen Arbor MI 49636 Office: 6443 Western Av Glen Arbor MI 49636

MORRIS, JACK ALLEN, banker; b. Hammond, Ill., June 22, 1932; s. Agnes Lelia (Gharst) M.; student Brown's Bus. Coll., 1950, 58, 61.; m. Marlene Davey, Dec. 24, 1953; children—Harold W., Jack Aaron. Customer service supr. Ill. Nat. Bank, Springfield, 1955-63; with Pleasant Palins (Ill.) State Bank, 1963—, subsequently exec. v.p., also dir. Served with U.S. Army, 1952-54. Methodist. Clubs: Am. Legion, Methodist Men's. Home: 213 E Main St Pleasant Plains IL 62677 Office: 106 W Main St Pleasant Plains IL 62677

MORRIS, JOHN MICHAEL, phys. plant engr.; b. Chester, Pa., Aug. 31, 1949; s. John Arthur and Joan Ann (O'Hara) M.; B.A., U. of Parkside, 1975; B.A., Chapman Coll., 1976; M.A., Calif. State U., 1977; certificate Milw. Sch. Engring., 1977; m. Lois Ann Rouleau, Apr. 18, 1970; children—Tracy Noel, Andrew Stephen. Served with USN, 1968-76, leading petty officer aboard warship, 1971-74, night dir. bldgs. and grounds, Great Lakes, Ill., 1974-76; asst. dir. phys. plant Waukesha County Tech. Inst., Pewaukee, Wis., 1976-77; phys. plant dir. Monroe County Community Coll., Monroe, Mich., 1977—; cons. in field. Certified in supervision of people Dunn & Bradstreet; certified counselor Lake City Probation Dept.; certified in hydronics specialties, Morton Grove, Ill., in air controls, Milw. Mem. Am. Sociol. Assn., Am. Hist. Soc., Am. Inst. of Maintenance, Nat. Assn. Power Engrs., Assn. Phys. Plant Adminstrs. Roman Catholic. Home: 1517 Stewart Apt 347 Monroe MI 48161 Office: MCCC 1555 S Raisinville Rd Monroe MI 48161

MORRIS, MARTIN AZELLE, JR., bank ofcl.; b. Birmingham, Ala., Dec. 21, 1941; s. Martin Azelle and Mary Elizabeth (Doolittle) M.; student U. Ala., 1961-69, U. Miss., 1962-67; B.S. in Mathematics, Ind. State U., 1971; m. Linda Mae Carpenter, May 27, 1961; children—Douglas Wayne, Deborah Lynn. Programmer, U.S. Pipe and Foundry Co., Birmingham, 1968-69; systems analyst, programmer Columbia House Div., Terre Haute, Ind., 1969-72; systems analyst Chain Store Systems, Burlington, Iowa, 1972-73; unit mgr. 1st Nat. Bank of Chgo., 1973—. Served with USAF, 1961-68. Certified data processor. Mem. Assn. of Computer Programmers and Analysts (chmn. bd., Merit award 1975, 76), Inst. for Certification of Computer Profls. (sec. 1976). Contbr. articles in field of data processing, data base mgmt. to profl. jours. Office: 1 N Dearborn 13th Floor Chicago IL 60670

MORRIS, RALPH WILLIAM, educator; b. Cleveland Heights, Ohio, July 30, 1928; s. Earl Douglas and Viola Minnie (Mau) M.; B.A., Ohio U., 1950, M.S., 1953; Ph.D., U. Iowa, 1955; m. Virginia Myrtha Lynn, June 4, 1955; children—Christopher Lynn, Kirk Stephen, Timothy Allan and Todd Andrew (twins), Melissa Mary. Research fellow in pharmacology U. Iowa, 1952-53, teaching fellow, 1953-55; instr. pharmacology U. Ill. at Chgo., 1955-56, asst. prof., 1956-63, asso. prof., 1963-69, prof., 1969—; adj. prof. edn. U. Ill.-Chgo. Circle, 1976—. Contract writer, 1961—; drug cons. to state and city agys., colls., sch. dists., legal assns., jour. referee; adviser to Mayor of Palatine; mem. adv. com. on first aid and safety Midwest chpt. Am. Nat. Red Cross, Chgo.; mem. adv. coms. on youth and drug abuse. Trustee Palatine Pub. Library, 1967-72, pres. bd. trustees, 1969-70; bd. dirs. North Suburban Library System, 1968-72, pres. 1970-72, mem. long range planning com., 1975—. Recipient Golden Apple for teaching Coll. Pharmacy, U. Ill., 1966, Palatine certificate merit, 1972. Mem. AAAS, Am. Assn. Coll. Pharmacists, Am., Ill. pharm. assns., Internat. Soc. for Chronobiology, Am. Soc. Pharmacology and Exptl. Therapeutics, Drug Info. Assn. Internat. Platform Assn., Am. (mem. action devel. com. 1969-73), Ill. (v.p. 1970-72, dir. 1969-72) library trustee assns., Sigma Xi, Rho Chi, Gamma Alpha. Episcopalian (sr. warden 1969-72, vestry 1965-72). Contbr. articles to profl. and sci. jours., lay mags., books. Home: 901 Arrowhead Dr Palatine IL 60067

MORRIS, ROBERT B(ARRETT), city ofcl.; b. Mankato, Minn., Mar. 1, 1922; s. Albert Barrett and Della (Mathews) M.; B.S., U. Minn., 1942, M.A. in Pub. Adminstrn., 1948, postgrad.; grad. study Northwestern U.; certificate Inst. Tng. Municipal Adminstrn., 1948; m. Louise Spaeth, Oct. 10, 1948; children—Sandra Lockwood, Rolf Barrett, Paul Spaeth, Jane Louise. Research asst. Municipal Reference Bur. U. Minn., 1946-47; asst. to city mgr. Albert Lea (Minn.), also field rep. League of Minn. Municipalities, Mpls., 1947-48; staff Internat. City Mgrs. Assn., 1948-49; asst. village mgr. Glencoe (Ill.), 1949-51, village mgr., 1951—; instr. Inst. Tng. Municipal Adminstrn., 1953—; lectr. Traffic Inst., Northwestern U., 1953-56; lectr. polit. sci. Roosevelt U., Chgo., 1965—; mem. community service and continuing edn. council Ill. State Bd. Higher Edn., 1967-72. Exec. bd. N. Shore area council Boy Scouts Am., 1961-64, Family Counseling Service of Glencoe, 1961-66; exec. bd. Ill. Local Govt. Law Enforcement Officers Tng. Bd., 1974—, chmn., 1976—. Served in USAAF, 1943-46. Mem. Internat. Personnel Mgmt. Assn., Internat. City Mgmt. Assn. (pres. Chgo. Met. chpt. 1957, v.p. Ill. 1962-64, pres. 1964-65, Midwest v.p. 1965-67, L.P. Cookingham Career Devel. award 1969), Acad. Profl. Devel., Am. Soc. Planning Ofcls., Am. Soc. Pub. Administrn. (pres. Chgo. chpt. 1966-67). Club: Rotary (pres. 1962-63). Contbr. to profl. publs. Home: 250 Park Ave Glencoe IL 60022 Office: 675 Village Ct Glencoe IL 60022

MORRIS, VIRGIL DIXON, clergyman; b. Little Rock; s. Luther Walter and Hattie (Dixon) M.; B.A., Hendrix Coll., 1929; B.D., Th.M., So. Meth. U., 1931; D.D., Centenary Coll., 1954; postgrad. Candler Sch. Theology, Emory U., St. Paul Sch. Theology, Perkins Sch. Theology, Iliff Sch. Theology, Garrett Sch. Theology; m. Fannie Elizabeth Emmerich, Sept. 6, 1930 (dec. 1953); children—Ouida Fae, Virgil Dixon; m. 2d. Marjorie Marie Minkler, Nov. 28, 1954. Ordained to ministry Meth. Ch., 1929; minister, Douglasville and Geyer Springs, Ark., 1927-29, Elm Ridge and Rhea Mills, Tex., 1929, Tioga and Gunther, Tex., 1930, Delta Circuit, La., 1931-32, Chalmette and Gentilly, New Orleans, 1932-34, Columbia, La., 1934-39, 1st Ch. Lafayette, La., 1939-42, 1st Ch. Homer, La., 1942-44, 1st Ch. Alexandria, La., 1948-52; dist. supt. Baton Rouge dist. Meth. Ch., 1944-48, New Orleans dist. Meth. Ch., 1952-58; pastor Trinity Ch., Ruston, La., 1958-60, Istrouma Meth. Ch., Baton Rouge, 1960; exec. dir. South Central Jurisdiction, United Meth. Ch., 1961-73; pastor, Linfield, New South Wales, Australia, 1974-75; New Life missioner Bd. Discipleship, 1975—. mem. gen. commn. structure Methodism overseas, 1956-72. Bd. trustees Meth. Seashore Assembly, Biloxi, Miss., 1952-60, Meth. Gulfside Assembly, Waveland, Miss., 1972-73 La. ann. conf. Meth. Ch., 1951-60; commr. The Ark.-La. Meth., Little Rock, 1950-60; del. gen. confs. Meth. Ch., 1944-60, jurisdictional conf., 1944-60; alternate del. Meth. Ecumenical Conf., Oxford, 1951; del. World Meth. Conf., Oslo, 1961, Conf., London, Eng., 1966, Denver, 1971, Dublin, Ireland, 1976, World Meth. Family Life Conf., London, 1966. Trustee Centenary Coll., 1949-61, Meth. Children's Home, Ruston, 1958-60, Meth. Home Hosp., New Orleans, 1961-73, St. Paul Sch. Theology, Kansas City, Mo., 1961-73, Lydia Patterson Inst., El Paso, Tex., 1958-73, Mt. Sequoyah Meth. Assembly, 1961-73. Mason (Shriner, K.T.). Co-founder, asso. editor The La. Meth., 1949-50. La. Conf. trustee New Orleans Christian Advocate files, 1950—. Home: 505 Albright Ct Marionville MO 65705 Office: 205 S College St Marionville MO 65705

MORRIS, WILLIAM EMERSON, JR., welding supply co. exec.; b. Toledo, Mar. 5, 1949; s. William E. Morris; student Bus. Sch. Toledo U., 1967-70. With Welders Needs Inc., Toledo, 1967—, salesman, 1970-72, purchasing agt., 1972-75, v.p., 1975-76, pres., 1976—. Mem. Am. Welding Soc., Nat. Welding Supply Assn., C. of C. Club: Kiwanis. Home: PO Box 3632 Station D Toledo OH 43608 Office: 1219 Expressway Dr N Toledo OH 43608

MORRIS, WILLIAM LEWIS, savs. and loan exec.; b. Elyria, Ohio, June 6, 1937; s. William Lewis and Ruth Elanor (Barton) M.; student Fenn Coll., 1963-64, John Carroll U., 1965, Inst. Fin. Edn., Ohio Savs. and Loan Acad., 1963-67; m. Jill Maureen O'Leary, Dec. 24, 1975; children—Jill Marie, William Lewis III. Teller savs. dept. Lorain County Nat. Bank, Lorain, Ohio, 1954-56; mgr. Beneficial Finance Co., Cleve., 1958-63; with Shaker Savs. Assn., Shaker Heights, Ohio, 1963—, v.p. ops., 1975—; pres. Shaker Data Corp. subs. Shaker Savs. Assn. Mem. Ohio Electronic Funds Transfer Com. Served with USCGR, 1956-58. Mem. Mortgage Servicing Soc. Northeastern Ohio (past pres.). Home: 5879 N Oval St Solon OH 44139 Office: 29169 Euclid Ave Wickliffe OH 44092

MORRIS-JONES, DANA Z., cons. human relations; b. Milw., Sept. 21, 1949; d. Norman E. and Winifred June (Rosenberg) Zimmerman; B.S., U. Wis.-Milw., 1972; postgrad. U. Wis.-Madison, 1973—; m. Donald R. Morris-Jones, Jan. 3, 1976. Project asst./supr. student tchrs. U. Wis.-Madison, 1972-74, program asst. human relations certification program, 1974-75, research asst. research and guidance lab., 1975—; cons. human relations Beloit and Sheboygan (Wis.) pub. schs., 1974—. Adv. bd. group programs YWCA, Madison. Mem. Am. Personnel and Guidance Assn., Am. Psychol. Assn. (student), Pi Lambda Theta, Phi Delta Kappa. Office: Dept Counseling and Guidance Research and Guidance Lab U Wis Madison WI 53706

MORRISON, CHARLES, social anthropologist; b. London, Sept. 7, 1929; s. Charles and Christina M.; came to U.S., 1956, naturalized, 1962; B.A. magna cum laude, U. Minn., 1960; M.A., U. Chgo., 1962, Ph.D., 1965; spl. courses S. Asian langs. U. Calif. at Berkeley, U. Wis.-Madison; m. Mary Louise Hutcherson, Sept. 9, 1962; children—Leila Christina, Ian Hugh. Journalist, Lincolnshire Echo and Birmingham Evening Dispatch, Eng., 1950-56; asst. prof. social anthropology U. Rochester (N.Y.), 1965-72; asso. prof. anthropology Mich. State U., East Lansing, 1972-76, prof., 1976—; cons. in field. Served with Brit. Army, 1948-49. Ford Found. fellow, India, 1963-64; NSF grantee, 1967-68; Faculty research fellow Am. Inst. Indian Studies, 1967-68; postdoctoral fellow Am. Inst. Pakistan Studies, 1976. Mem. Phi Beta Kappa. Contbr. articles to profl. jours. Home: 429 Kensington Rd East Lansing MI 48823

MORRISON, CHARLES JOHN, assn. exec.; b. Chgo., Dec. 22, 1944; s. Glen Bryant and Katherine Louise (Hendry) M.; B.S. with honors, Bradley U., 1967; M.S. in Edn., No. Ill. U., 1971; postgrad. Northwestern U., 1972—; m. Mary Jean Lenzini, June 7, 1968; children—Kelleen Marie, Patrick Sean. Tchr., North Chicago High Sch. (Ill.), 1967-70, asst. prin., 1970-72; dir. edn. Inst. Real Estate Mgmt., Chgo., 1972-76, v.p. edn. and admissions, 1976—; lectr., cons. in field; mem. task force industry HUD, 1977—. Campaign mgr. Republican polit. campaigns, Lake County, Ill., 1972—. Recipient Harvard Book award, 1962. Mem. Nat. Sch. Pub. Relations Assn. (pres. Ill. chpt. 1972—), Am. Soc. Assn. Execs., Am. Soc. Tng. and Devel., Community Assns. Inst., Omicron Delta Kappa. Roman Catholic. Club: Toastmasters (pres. N. Shore 1971). Home: 635 Byron Ct Deerfield IL 60015 Office: 430 N Michigan Ave Chicago IL 60611

MORRISON, DAVID LEE, chemist, research inst. exec.; b. Butler, Pa., Jan. 25, 1933; s. Charles R. and Mildred (McFadden) M.; B.S., Grove City Coll., 1954; M.S., Carnegie Mellon U., 1960, Ph.D., 1961; m. Carole J. White, July 31, 1954; children—Scott, Karyn. Chemist, Callery Chem. Co. (Pa.), 1954; with Battelle Meml. Inst., Columbus, Ohio, 1961-77, mgr. environ. systems and processes sect., 1970-74, mgr. energy and environ. programs office, 1974-75, asso. dir., 1975-77; exec. v.p., dir. IIT Research Inst., Chgo., 1977—; mem. industry adv. com. AEC, cons. adv. com. on reactor safeguards. Mem. exec. staff Ohio Citizens Environ. Task Force. Served with USAF, 1954-57. Mem. Am. Nuclear Soc., Am. Chem. Soc., Internat. Solar Energy Soc., AAAS, Ohio Acad. Sci., Sigma Xi, Omicron Delta Kappa. Contbr. articles to profl. jours. Office: IIT Research Inst 10 W 35th St Chicago IL 60616*

MORRISON, DAVID RICHARD, physician; b. Jerusalem, Palestine, Sept. 21, 1924; s. Maurice and Ruth (Whiting) M.; came to U.S., 1937;; B.S., Monmouth Coll., 1947; M.D., Loyola U., 1951, postgrad., 1958-60; m. Joan M. Moore, July 26, 1952; children—Timothy Francis, Anne Elizabeth, Martha Marie, Daniel Matthew, Mark Anthony, James Phillip, Thomas Patrick, Joseph Michael, Mary Joan, Rebecca Ruth, Margaret Anne, Cecilia Marie, Steven Paul, Michael David. Intern, St. Francis Hosp., Evanston, Ill., 1951-52, pediatric residency, 1952-53; pvt. practice medicine specializing in gen. practice, W Chgo., 1953-58, 60-71; former mem. staffs Delnor Hosp., St. Charles, Ill., Community Hosp., Geneva, Ill.; pres. staff Delnor Hosp., St. Charles, 1966-68; dir. student health Kans. State Coll., 1971-72; staff physician, asso. prof. Student Health Service, Kans. State U., Manhattan, 1972-75; med. dir. Hilton-Davis Chem. Co. div. Sterling Drug Corp., Cin., 1975—; asso. staff Christ Hosp., Cin. Bd. dirs. YMCA, pres., 1969-70. Served with U.S. Army, 1944-46. Mem. Am., Western Ohio occupational med. assns., Phi Beta Pi. Roman Catholic. Home: 7740 Hopper Rd Cincinnati OH 45230 Office: Med Dept Hilton Davis Chem Co 2235 Langdon Farm Rd Cincinnati OH 45237

MORRISON, DONALD THOMAS, lawyer; b. Chgo., Sept. 7, 1928; s. Donald T. and Stella (Brokamp) M.; B.S.L., Northwestern U., 1950, LL.B., 1955; m. Catherine E. Mariga, Aug. 18, 1956 (dec. July 1975); children—Joseph T., Sheila M., Mary E., Kathleen A., Eileen T., Margaret J., Frances C., Donald J.; m. 2d, Georgeann G. Daly, Aug. 14, 1977. Admitted to Ill. bar, 1955; asso. law firm Morgan, Halligan & Lanoff, Chgo., 1955-61; practice law, Highland Park, Ill., 1961-62, Waukegan, Ill., 1962-64; partner firm Morrison & Nemanich, Waukegan, 1964—; dir. Deerfield (Ill.) State Bank, 1970-73. Spl. asst. atty. gen. Ill. for Condemnation, 1961-68. Comml. pilot, 1972—. Served with USNR, 1951-54. Fellow Am. Coll. Trial Lawyers; mem. Am., Ill. (sec. specialization com.), Lake County (pres. 1977—) bar assns., Theta Xi, Phi Delta Phi. Democrat. Roman Catholic. Club: Bob-O-Link Country (Highland Park). Author: Condemnation Trial Technique, Illinois Eminent Domain Practice, 1971, 75; Investigation and Development of the Product Liability Case, 1974. Home: 645 Westgate Deerfield IL 60015 Office: 325 Washington St Waukegan IL 60085

MORRISON, DWIGHT EDWARD, lawyer; b. Boone, Iowa, Nov. 19, 1919; s. Wayland H. and Lulu May (Latham) M.; B.S., Iowa State U., 1942; A.M., Columbia, 1944, Ph.D. (Lydia Roberts fellow, DuPont fellow), 1946; J.D., Ind. U., 1968; m. Martha Louise Holmes, June 19, 1948; 1 son, Wayne Holmes. With Eli Lilly & Co., Indpls., 1945—, sr. organic chemist, 1945-62, patent technician, 1962-67, patent agt., 1967-68, patent atty., 1968—; admitted to Ind. bar, 1968. Mem. Ind., Am. bar assns., Sigma Xi, Alpha Chi Sigma, Phi Lambda Upsilon, Phi Kappa Phi, Pi Mu Epsilon. Methodist (past trustee). Home: 250 Williams Dr Indianapolis IN 46260 Office: 307 E McCarty St Indianapolis IN 46206

MORRISON, EDWARD JAMES, pub. co. exec.; b. Morris, Minn., Apr. 18, 1920; s. James Crossett and Edna Pearl (Murphy) M.; B.A., U. Minn., 1941; m. Helen Jane Stevenson, Sept. 21, 1941; 1 son, James Steven. With Morris (Minn.) Tribune, 1932—, partner, 1946—; owner Morris Sun, 1947—; a founder and pres. Quinco Press, Inc., Lowry, Minn., 1969—; part owner Lake Region Echo, Lake Region Press, Alexandria, Minn., 1970—, Staples (Minn.) World, 1969—, Wadena (Minn.) Pioneer-Jour., 1974—, Holibrook, Inc., Brookings, S.D., 1971—; pres. Leawood Corp., Hobbs, N.Mex., 1963—; pres. First Fed. Savs. and Loan Assn., 1969—, also dir.; dir. Morris Community Indsl. Devel. Corp. Chmn. Morris Planning Commn., 1961; founder West Central Ednl. Devel. Assn., pres. 1963-64; bd. dirs. Minn. Good Roads, Inc., 1973—; chmn. bldg. com. Stevens County Meml. Hosp., 1974-75. Served to lt. USNR, 1943-46. Recipient Commendation award Soil Conservation Soc. Am., 1967. Mem. Minn. Newspaper Assn. (pres. 1957), C. of C. (v.p. 1947), Am. Legion, VFW. Clubs: Masons, Lions (pres. 1947), Minn. Press (Mpls). Home: 5 Circle Pines Morris MN 56267 Office: 108 East 6 St Morris MN 56267

MORRISON, FRANCIS ARTHUR, chiropractor; b. Wheatland Township, Mich., Dec. 5, 1921; s. John Henry and Genevieve Ellen (Kerr) M.; D.C., Palmer Coll. Chiropractic, 1947, postgrad., 1947-48; m. Margaret Elizabeth Woodward, July 28, 1956; children—Shaun F., Craig K., Tyler F., Rebecca E. Elec. truck operator div. parts Chrysler Corp., Marysville, Mich., 1942—, accountant, 1950-60; dir. Morrison Marysville Chiropractic Center, 1957—; practice chiropractics, Marysville, 1957—, acupuncutурist, 1974—. Mich. Chiropractic Council Roentgenology, 1975-76. Bd. dirs. Goodwill Industries. Mem. Chiropractic Research Found., 1960—. Served to cpl., Mil. Police, AUS, 1942-45. Mem. St. Clair County (Mich.) (pres. 1964, 76), Am. (council on roentgenology 1970-76) chiropractic assns., Acupuncture-Ryodoraku Assn. (v.p. 1975, 76, dir.), Am. Metapyschiat. Assn. (charter). Episcopalian (jr. warden 1974-75, sr. warden 1976, lay reader, 1976, sec. com. bldg. 1966, 75). Mason (32 deg., Shriner), Rotarian (chpt. pres.-elect 76, dir. 1974-75), Moose. Home: 1404 Pennsylvania Ave Marysville MI 48040 Office: 212 14th St Marysville MI 48040

MORRISON, FRANK ALBERT, JR., mech. engr.; b. Greensburg, Pa., Feb. 6, 1943; s. Frank Albert and Millicent Elizabeth (Morgan) M.; B.M.E., Carnegie Inst. Tech., 1963, M.M.E., 1964, Ph.D., 1966; m. Louise Oklin, Oct. 26, 1963; children—Joshua Evan, Benjamin Bartlett. NSF postdoctoral fellow U. Cambridge (Eng.), 1966-67; asst. prof. mech. engring. U. Ill., Urbana, 1967-70, asst. dean engring., 1970-71, asso. prof., 1970-74, prof., 1974—; cons. Lawrence Livermore Lab. Corning fellow, 1963-64; NSF fellow, 1964-66. Mem. ASME, AAAS, Soc. Petroleum Engrs., Sigma Xi, Phi Kappa Phi, Tau Beta Pi, Pi Tau Sigma. Contbr. articles to tech. jours. Office: Mech Engring Dept U Ill Urbana IL 61801

MORRISON, HARRIET BARBARA, educator; b. Boston, Feb. 23, 1934; d. Harry and Harriet (Hanrahan) Morrison; B.S. in Edn., State Coll. at Boston, 1956, M.Ed., 1958; Ed.D., Boston U., 1967. Tchr. pub. elementary schs., Arlington, Mass., 1956-67; asst. prof. edn. No. Ill. U., DeKalb, 1967-71, asso. prof., 1971—. Mem. Am. Fedn. Tchrs., Assn. Supervision and Curriculum Devel., Ill. Assn. Supervision and Curriculum Devel., Philosophy Edn. Soc., Midwest Philosophy Edn. Soc., Soc. Profs. Edn., Pi Lambda Theta. Home: 314 W Sunset Pl DeKalb IL 60115

MORRISON, JAMES FRANK, optometrist; b. Colby, Kans., Apr. 11, 1942; s. Lloyd Wayne and Catherine Louise M.; student U. Kans., 1960-64, then postgrad.; B.S., then O.D., So. Coll. Optometry, 1964-67; m. Karen Jean Carr, Aug. 25, 1963; children—Mike, Jeffrey, Scott. Partner optometric practice, Garden City, Kans., 1967-69; individual practice, Colby, 1969—; founder, chief staff N.W. Kans. Ednl. Diagnostic and Referral Center for Children, Inc., Colby; cons. numerous schs.; lectr. in field. Cub master Cub Scout pack, Colby, 1970—, committeeman troop Boy Scouts Am., 1971—; mem. adv. bd. Colby Good Samaritan Home, 1971—. Fellow Am. Acad. Optometry, Coll. Optometrists in Vision Devel (asso); mem. Kans. Optometric Assn. (dir. extension program, com. grad. edn.), Kans. (founder, pres. 1970-71), N.W. Kans. (v.p. 1970-72) Assns. children learning disabilities, Thomas County Assn. Retarded Children. Methodist (mem. bd.). Lion (chmn. signt com. 1970-72; chmn. com. children and youth 1971—), Kiwanian (pres. 1971-72), Mason. Office: 180 W 6th St Colby KS 67701

MORRISON, LEWIS EVERETT, physician; b. Indpls., Jan. 18, 1918; s. Donald Ambrose and Edna (Krauss) M.; B.S., Purdue U., 1940; M.D., Ind. U., 1943; m. Dorothy Miller Andrew, May 15, 1942; children—Florence (Mrs. John Stanton), Amy (Mrs. Arthur Thadeus Perry), Andrew Lewis, John Joseph, Louise (Mrs. Alexander J. Baer). Intern, Marion County Gen. Hosp., Indpls., 1943-44, resident, 1944-45; pvt. practice medicine, specializing in otorhinolaryngology, Indpls., 1948—; mem. staff Community Hosp., Meth. Hosp., Winona Hosp., St. Vincent Hosp., Ind. U. Hosp., Wishard Meml. Hosp.; asst. prof. Ind. U. Med. Sch., 1958-70, asso. prof., 1972—. Chmn. com.

odor control Civic Air Pollution Control Bd., Indpls., 1971-72. Served with AUS, 1945-48; now col. Res. ret. Mem. Am., Ind. med. assns., Am. Council Otolaryngology (dir. 1968—), Am. Rhinologic Soc. (bd. dirs. 1962-64), Marion County Med. Soc., Am. Soc. Ophthalmologic and Otolaryngologic Allergy (pres. 1969), Am. Bronchoesophagological Assn., Am. Laryngol., Rhinol. and Otol. Soc., Am. Bd. Otolaryngology, Am. Acad. Ophthalmology and Otolaryngology, Internat. Rhinologic Soc., Ind. Acad. Ophthalmology and Otolaryngology (pres. 1967), Am. Acad. Facial Plastic and Reconstructive Surgery, Indpls. Ophthalmology and Otolaryngology Soc., A.C.S., Internat. Acad. Metabology, Inc., Am. Legion (comdr. 1969), Junto of Indpls. (pres. 1973). Presbyn. (elder 1960—). Mason (Shriner), Rotarian. Club: Winter (pres. 1969-72), (Indpls.). Contbr. articles to profl. publs. Home: 7501 Mohawk Lane Indianapolis IN 46260 Office: Suite A-56 Riley Hosp 1100 W Michigan Ave Indianapolis IN 46202

MORRISON, MICHAEL CHARLES, educator; b. Osage, Iowa, Aug. 21, 1946; s. Mitchell W. and Maxine L. (Stockdale) M.; A.A., Austin State Jr. Coll., 1966; B.A., U. Minn., 1968, M.A., 1970; m. Patricia A. Keefe, Sept. 16, 1967; children—Scott Michael, Melanie. Tchr. Imlay (Mich.) City Community Schs., 1968-70; faculty N.D. State Sch. Sci., Wahpeton, 1970-77, chmn. dept. social scis., 1975-77, dir. devel., 1977—. Mem. Edn. Commn. of The States, 1975—. Mem. N.D. Higher Edn. Assn. (pres. 1974-75), N.D. Edn. Assn. (bd. dirs. 1974-75), Am. Sociol. Assn. Elk. Author: Man in Modern Society, 1974. Home: 1305 14th Ave N Wahpeton ND 58075 Office: N College St Wahpeton ND 58075

MORRISON, RICHARD DONALD, dentist, educator; b. Kansas City, Mo., Aug. 5, 1927; s. Robert Donnell and Gladys Vivian (Crump) M.; A.B., Washington U., St. Louis, 1949, D.D.S., 1954; m. Virginia Mae Rives, Dec. 29, 1955; 1 dau., Nancy. Instr. operative dentistry and pharmacology, Washington U., 1954-58, asst. prof. operative dentistry, 1960-66, asso. prof. restorative dentistry, 1969-71, asst. dean, 1971-72, prof. community and preventive dentistry, 1971—; pvt. practice dentistry Pacific, Mo., 1973—; dental cons. Shriners' Hosp. for Crippled Children, St. Louis Juvenile Detention Center, Herbert Hoover Boys' Club, St. Louis. Served with USNR, 1945-47. USPHS tchr. tng. fellow, 1958-59; Fulbright-Hays vis. prof. U. Baghdad, Iraq, 1966-67; USPHS grantee, 1963-65. Mem. Am., Mo. dental assns., Greater St. Louis Dental Soc., Omicron Kappa Upsilon, Xi Psi Phi, Sigma Alpha Epsilon, Delta Sigma Theta (hon.). Home: Nolands Point Ocie MO 65719

MORRISON, THOMAS HERRING, oil co. exec.; b. Louisville, Aug. 3, 1941; s. Thomas Jefferson and Emma Elizabeth (Herring) M.; B.B.A., U. Miami (Fla.), 1963; m. Jean Bowman Linn, Oct. 24, 1962; children—Thomas Herring, Jeffrey Scott. Sales rep. Scott Paper Co., Nashville, 1964-65; mgr. Southside Realty Co., Louisville, 1965-66; with Valvoline Oil Co. div. Ashland Oil Corp., 1966-74, dist. mgr., Chgo., 1969-70, div. mgr., 1970-74, div. mgr. Mac's Inc. div., Cin., 1974—. Adviser Jr. Achievement, Nashville. Ky. col. Mem. Phi Delta Theta (v.p.). Republican. Methodist. Home: 8024 Blair House Dr Cincinnati OH 45244 Office: 5246 Wooster Rd Cincinnati OH 45226

MORRISSEY, ROBERT EMMETT, display co. exec.; b. Madison, Wis., Jan. 20, 1913; s. Francis Patrick and Margaret (O'Keefe) M.; student U. Wis., 1931-32; m. Marie Dorothy Ripp, Sept. 26, 1938; children—Kathleen Ann, Timothy Robert. Owner, Manor Dairy, Madison, 1935-40, Borden Dairy, Madison, 1940-44; store mgr. Firestone Tire & Rubber Co., Milw., 1943-45; pres. Frank Mayer & Assos., Graftn, Wis., 1945—. Mem. Point of Purchase Advt. Ins. (-chmn. bd. 1974-75), Madison Jr. C. of C. (past pres.), Milw. Sales Execs. Club (dir. 1950-52). Roman Catholic. Home: 713 Grand Ave Thiensville WI 53092 Office: 1975 Wisconsin Ave Grafton WI 53024

MORROW, GEORGE WILLIAM, JR., internist; b. Rock Island, Ill., Nov. 13, 1925; s. George William and Ruth E. (Carter) M.; A.B., U. Ill., 1948, B.S., 1950, M.D., 1952; M.S., U. Minn., 1957; m. Jean Plambeck, Aug. 26, 1950; children—Jill, George, Janet, Sandra. Intern, Cook County Hosp., Chgo., 1952-53; resident in internal medicine Mayo Clinic, Rochester, Minn., 1953-57, cons. internal medicine, 1957—, chmn. div. community medicine, 1970—; asso. prof. medicine Mayo Med. Sch., 1974—; trustee St. Marys Hosp., 1968-76. Chmn. Southeastern Minn. chpt. A.R.C., 1966-67; mem. adv. bd. Rochester Community Coll., 1971-77; mem. com. on physicians Am. Hosp. Assn., 1970-75. Served with USNR, 1944-46; PTO. Diplomate Am. Bd. Internal Medicine. Fellow A.C.P.; mem. AMA, Minn. Med. Assn., Zumbro Valley Med. Soc., Am. Assn. Med. Colls., Sigma Xi, Alpha Omega Alpha. Methodist. Editorial adv. bd. Hosp. Med. Staff, 1970-75. Office: 200 1st St SW Rochester MN 55901

MORROW, JERRY LEE, journalist; b. Toledo, Oct. 5, 1933; s. Walter Spencer and Jennie Catherine (Criss) M.; B.A., U. Toledo, 1959, Ph.D., 1971; M.S. (Earl Godwin Meml. fellow), Columbia U., 1961; m. Elizabeth E. Gross, Dec. 1973. News writer WSPD-Radio, Toledo, 1957-62; dir. info. services U. Toledo, 1962—, instr. journalism, 1962-71, asst. prof., 1971—, dir. univ. relations, 1964-73; v.p. Morrow Plating Co., Toledo, 1968—, also dir.; pres. J & J Plating Co., Toledo, 1975—. Vice pres. Commn. on Publicity and Efficiency, City of Toledo, 1963-65, pres., 1966-68. Served with USAF, 1951-55. Mem. Soc. Profl. Journalists, Pub. Relations Soc. Am., Columbia, Toledo alumni assns., Toledo Press Club, Mensa, Pi Kappa Alpha, Phi Delta Kappa, Sigma Delta Chi. Lutheran. Home: 4430 Sheraton Rd Toledo OH 43615 Office: U Toledo Toledo OH 43606

MORROW, MARY JO, speech pathologist; b. Hastings, Nebr., Apr. 1, 1936; d. Lawrence James and Leta Mae (Ritchie) McCune; B.S., U. Nebr., 1958; M.A. (Office Vocat. Rehab. trainee), Northwestern U., Evanston, Ill., 1963; m. Gordon S. Morrow, Aug. 21, 1965; children—J. Ritchie, Robert G., Kathryn L. Speech clinician Omaha Pub. Schs., 1958-59, Kearney (Nebr.) Pub. Schs., 1959-62, 63-64; instr. speech pathology U. Nebr., Lincoln, 1964-65, Kearney State Coll., 1965—; coordinator, dir. neonatal audiometric testing program, Kearney, 1968—. Organizer, 1st pres. Friends of Kearney Pub. Library; exec. sec. Kearney United Way, 1974-77. Mem. Am., Nebr. (pres.) speech and hearing assns., Gamma Phi Beta. Republican. Presbyterian. Clubs: Nebr. (pres.), Kearney Mrs. jaycees. Editor, Nebr. Speech and Hearing Jour., 1964-68. Home: 1507 W 36th St Kearney NE 68847 Office: Kearney State Coll Kearney NE 68847

MORROW, ROBERT CHARLES, feedlot equipment marketing co. exec.; b. Early, Iowa, July 25, 1926; s. James A. and Emily Stuart (Patterson) M.; B.S. in Agrl. Engring., Iowa State U., 1952; m. Myrna Jeanne Simmons, Sept. 13, 1952; children—William A., Ann Louise, Robert S. Dist. mgr. Massey Ferguson, 1952-57; chief engr. Am. Planter Co., 1957-59, v.p. marketing, 1959-60; mgr. feedlot planning A.O. Smith Harvestore Products, Inc., 1960-64, area mgr., 1964-71; salesman Mich. Glass Lined Storage, Inc., Sturgis, 1971—; owner, operator cattle feeding farm, Sturgis, Mich., 1958—. Served with USN, 1944-47. Recipient 1st Place award Alcoa Aluminum Nat. Design Contest, 1951. Mem. Am. Soc. Agrl. Engrs., Am. Farm Bur. Mason. Author: Dairy Feedlot Planning, 1962; Beef Feedlot Planning, 1963. Home: Rural Route 5 Sturgis MI 49091

MORSE, C. DWAYNE, state ofcl., pub. health adminstr.; b. Kewanee, Ill., Nov. 26, 1939; s. Carl C. and Anna M. (Cole) M.; B.S. in Microbiology, Ariz. State U., 1966; M.P.H., U. of N.C., 1973, Dr. P.H., 1975; m. Susan Virginia Simon, Apr. 30, 1966; children—Matthew Carl, Jeremy Dwayne, Bridget Kathryn. Microbiologist Maricopa County Health Dept., Phoenix, 1966-72; br. lab. dir. Ariz. State Dept. of Health, Tucson, 1972; research asst. U. of N.C., Chapel Hill, 1972-74, Center for Disease Control, Atlanta, 1974-75; dep. dir. Office of Labs. and Research, Kans. Dept. of Health and Environment, Topeka, 1975-76, dir., 1976-78; dir. Div. Pub. Health Labs. Minn. Dept. Health, Mpls., 1978—; adj. asst. prof. of microbiology U. Kans., 1977-78. Served with USN, 1957-60. USPHS grantee, 1972. Mem. Am. Soc. for Microbiology, Am. Pub. Health Assn., Kans. Pub. Health Assn., Conf. Pub. Health Lab. Dirs., Kans. Soc. of Pathologists, Kans. Acad. Sci., Assn. State and Territorial Pub. Health Lab Dirs., Sigma Xi. Roman Catholic. Club: Lake Shore Swim. Contbr. articles in field to profl. jours. Office: Minn Dept Health 717 Delaware St SE Minneapolis MN 55414

MORSE, H. CLIFTON, IV, publishing co. exec., indsl. engr.; b. Chgo., Sept. 3, 1924; s. Henry Clifton III, and Augusta (Metz) M.; B.A., U. Ala., 1942; M.F.A., Brown U., 1944. Mem. planning staff Howard Hughes, Culver City, Calif., 1958-60; asst. to gen. mgr. Aircraft Engine div. Ford Motor Co., Chgo., 1955-60; pres. Wyatt & Morse, Inc., mgmt. cons., Chgo., 1960-66; pres. Morse Assos., Chgo., 1966—. Pres., Chgo. Chamber Orch. Assn., 1960-62; chmn. Better State and Local Govt. Bus. Practices Bur., Chgo., 1960-66. Bd. dirs. Wesley Found., 1961-62. Served with USNR, 1942-45. Recipient TV Author's award Television Acad. Arts and Scis., 1949. Mem. Inst. Mgmt. Scis. (pres. Chgo chpt. 1959-61, nat. chmn. 1962), Operations Research Soc. (charter mem.), Am. Mgmt. Assn., Systems Procedures Assn. Am., Nat. Assn. Advancement Sci., Chgo. Urban League. Club: Union League (Chgo.). Author: Machinery Replacement Analysis, 1955; Operations Research for Nontechnical Management, 1956; Organization-Function Guide for Manufacturers, 1957; Numerically Controlled Machine Tools, 2d edit., 1971; Cost Reduction Guide for Manufacturing Management, 2d edit., 1978; Autofacturing, 1965. Editor: Profit Improvement and Cost Reduction Newsletter, 1960-78; Morsels-Humor Anthology, 1978. Home: 345 Fullerton Pkwy Chicago IL 60614 Office: 203 N Wabash Ave Chicago IL 60601

MORSE, ROBERT KENNETH, cons. found. engr.; b. Bloomington, Ill., Sept. 21, 1919; s. Edwin Blaine and Hazel (Maloney) M.; B.S., Rose Poly. Inst., 1950; M.S. C.E., Bradley U., 1954; Ph.D., U. Ill., 1961; postgrad. Purdue U., Ill. State U., U. Tenn.; m. Gladys Moore, Aug. 29, 1940; children—Martha Ann (Mrs. John D. Kiefer), Edwin William, Walter John, Marilyn Sue (Mrs. Michael S. Detherage). Civil engr. Ill. Div. Hwys., 1941-46, J.J. Woltmann, Bloomington, 1946-48; contractor, 1948-51; teaching soil mechanics Bradley U., Peoria, Ill., 1958; research on groundwater recharge Ill. Water Survey, Peoria, 1951-53; cons. found. engr.-engring. geologist, El Paso, Ill., 1942—; pres. Geotech. Engring. Assos.; chmn. bd. Morse Enterprises, Inc. Mem. exec. com. Am. White Water Affiliation. Served to capt. USMCR, 1943-46. Mem. Geol. Soc. Am., Am. Soc. C.E., Soc. Am. Mil. Engrs., Am. Soc. for Testing and Materials, Nat. Soc. Profl. Engrs., Internat. Soc. Soil, Mech. and Found. Engrs., Am. Quaternary Assn. Contbr. articles to profl. jours. Home: US 51 S El Paso IL 61738

MORTENSEN, ROBERT HENRY, landscape architect; b. Jackson, Mich., June 9, 1939; s. Henry and Charlotte Marie (Brown) M.; B.Landscape Arch., Ohio State U., 1961; M.Landscape Arch., U. Mich., 1965; div. Sept. 1974; children—Phillip, Paul, Susan, Julia; m. 2d, Meta Jane Hearne Blakely, Nov. 1975; stepchildren—Laura and Kathryn Blakely. Landscape architect Miller Wihry & Lantz, Landscape Architects, Engrs., Louisville, 1960, 61-63, State of Ohio Div. Parks, Columbus, 1960-61, Arthur Hills & Assos., Landscape Architects, Toledo, 1963, 65-67; pvt. practice landscape architecture, Ann Arbor, Mich., 1963-65; partner Mortensen, Meyers & Assos., 1967-69, prin. Mortensen, Meyers, Squire & Smith, Inc., 1969-73, Collaborative, Inc., Architects, Engrs., Landscape Architects, 1973—(all Toledo); asso. prof. U. Mich. Am. Grad. Sch., 1973; vis. lectr. Ohio State U., 1965—, Bowling Green (Ohio) State U., 1969—, U. Mich., Purdue U., 1971—, Mich. State U., 1973—; lectr. civic, social, pvt. groups, 1966—. Mem. Ohio Bd. Unreclaimed Strip Mined Lands, 1973-76; mem. Lucas County facilities rev. com. Health Planning Assn. N.W. Ohio, 1972-76, chmn. maternal and child health subcom., 1972-74, recipient Distinguished Service award 1973; mem. archtl., environ. rev. com. Ohio Arts Council, 1974—. Mem. Am. (registration com. 1962-63, chmn. pvt. practice com. 1970-72, 76-77, council profl. practice 1973-74, nat. pub. relations com. 1974-75, officer Ohio chpt. 1968-74, pres. 1972-74, trustee 1977—), Ohio (pres. 1969-71) socs. landscape architects, Am. Soc. Planning Ofcls., Toledo C. of C. (chmn. sts. hwys. transit com. 1972-73), Sigma Phi Epsilon. Roman Catholic. Club: Toledo Editor: Handbook Professional Practice, 1972. Home: 834 Louisiana Ave Perrysburg OH 43551 also 387 W Broad St Falls Church VA 22046 Office: 1647 South Cove Blvd Toledo OH 43606

MORTON, JOSEPH LEWIS, radiologist; b. New Vienna, Ohio, Dec. 13, 1912; s. Lyle George and Helen Vashti (Hull) M.; M.D., Ohio State U., 1936; m. Mary Frances Boone, June 14, 1937; children—Joseph Lewis, John Arthur. Intern, Cleve. City Hosp., 1936-37, resident, 1937-41; practice medicine specializing in radiology, 1941—; radiologist Paris (Ill.) Clinic, 1941—; asst. prof. radiology Ohio State U., 1946-47, asso. prof., 1947-54; radiologist Hurley Hosp., Flint, Mich., 1954-55, St. Vincent Hosp., Indpls., 1955—; asst. clin. prof. radiology Ind. U., 1957—. Dir. Little Red Door, Marion County, 1965-71. Served with Am. Vol. Service, 1942-46. AEC research grantee, 1946-54. Fellow Am. Coll. Chest Physicians, Am. Coll. Radiology, Am. Coll. Nuclear Medicine; mem. AMA, Soc. Nuclear Medicine, Am. Soc. Theraputic Radiologists, Radiol. Soc., Radiol. Soc. N. Am., AAAS, AAUP. Republican. Presbyterian. Club: Masons. Home: 3272 W 42d St Indianapolis IN 46208 Office: 2001 W 86th St Indianapolis IN 46260

MORTON, PHILIP GOODRICH, psychotherapist; b. Rawlins, Wyo., Sept. 16, 1911; s. Leonard Joseph and Marie C. (Carlson) M.; B.A., U. Utah, 1940; M.A., Bowling Green State U., 1976; m. Beatrice K. Kerr, Sept. 14, 1936; children—David, Rebecca, Penelope. Hwy. surveyor Bur. Reclamation and Pub. Rds., 1930-40; cost accountant Am. Smelting & Refining, Salt Lake City, 1940-42; asso. prof. sculpture and contemporary jewelry U. Minn., 1948-61; licensed land surveyor, Jackson Hole, Wyo., 1961-65; dir. Working Hand Craft Center, Bowling Green, Ohio, 1968-74; pvt. practice psychotherapy, Chgo., 1977—; exhbns. and awards in sculpture, painting, etching and contemporary jewelry. Mem. Am. Soc. Engrs. and Surveyors, N.Am. Goldsmiths, Am. Personnel and Guidance Assn., Nat. Rehab. Counseling Assn. Author: Contemporary Jewelry, rev. ed., 1976; editor Pioneer of Contemporary Jewelry, 1946—; contbg. editor The Working Craftsman, 1970-77; contbr. articles to profl. jours. Home: Apt 270 525 W Arlington St Chicago IL 60614

MORTON, STEPHEN DANA, chemist; b. Madison, Wis., Sept. 7, 1932; s. Walter Albert and Rosalie (Amlie) M.; B.S., U. Wis., 1954, Ph.D., 1962. Asst. prof. chemistry Otterbein Coll., Westerville, Ohio, 1962-66; postdoctoral fellow water chemistry, pollution control U. Wis., Madison, 1966-67; water pollution research chemist WARF Inst., Madison, 1967-73, head environ. quality dept., 1973-76, mgr. quality assurance, 1977—. Served to 1st lt. Chem. Corps, AUS, 1954-56. Fellow Am. Inst. Chemists; mem. Am. Chem. Soc., Am. Water Works Assn., Am. Soc. Limnology and Oceanography, Water Pollution Control Fedn., AAAS. Author: Water Pollution—Causes and Cures, 1976. Home: 1126 Sherman Ave Madison WI 53703 Office: PO Box 7545 Madison WI 53707

MORTON, TERRY LEE, financial exec.; b. Hammond, Ind., Oct. 11, 1944; s. Hugh James and Mae Catherine (Meyers) M.; B.B.A. in Accounting with high honors (Univ. Leadership scholar), U. Wis.-Madison, 1969, M.S. in Accounting and Quantitative Analysis, 1971; m. Karen Ann Beerkircher, Oct. 26, 1963; children—Terry Lee, Melinda Mae. Cost analyst Oscar Mayer & Co., Madison, Wis., 1968-69; accountant firm Arthur Andersen & Co., Milw., 1971-75; asst. corp. controller Congoleum Corp., Milw., 1975—. Instr. accounting U. Wis., 1969-70. Chmn. com. Potawatom I Area Council Boy Scouts Am., 1973-74. Served with arty., AUS, 1963-66. C.P.A., Wis. Mem. Am. Inst. C.P.A.'s. (Elijah Watts Sells award 1971), Am. Accounting Assn., Beta Alpha Psi (v.p. 1968), Beta Gamma Sigma. Episcopalian. Home: 2505 Parkside Dr New Berlin WI 53151 Office: 777 E Wisconsin Ave Milwaukee WI 53201

MORTON, THOMAS JESSE, JR., corp. exec.; b. Hartford, Ky., Feb. 25, 1900; s. Thomas Jesse and Lucy Caroline (Townsend) M.; B.S., Purdue U., 1920; H.L.D., U. Evansville, 1977; m. Edna Noelle Morton, May 5, 1973; children—Thomas Rand, Susan Elizabeth Morton Reitz, James Townsend. Sec., mgr. Star Foundry, Evansville, Ind., 1922-28; pres., mgr. Hoosier Lamp and Stamping Corp., Evansville, 1928-44; pres. Hoosier Cardinal Corp., Evansville, 1944—; chmn. bd. Fiberfil, Inc., 1956-67; dir., chmn. exec. com. Old Nat. Bank, Evansville, 1936—; dir. Credithrift Fin. Corp., Internat. Steel Co., Hotel McCurdy Bldg. Co.; chmn., dir. Benerson Corp., 1959-69; pres., dir. Warrick Corp., 1935-69. Trustee U. Evansville, 1969—, Purdue U., 1954-57, Welborn Baptist Hosp., 1972—, Welborn Baptist Hosp. Found., 1973—. Mem. Am. Saddle Horse Breeders Assn. (pres., dir.), Am. Horse Shows Assn. (dir.), Am. Horse Council (trustee), Nat. Assn. Mfrs. (past dir.), Nat. Metal Trades Assn. (past pres.), Evansville Mfrs. and Employers Assn. (past pres.). Clubs: Evansville Petroleum; Union League (Chgo.); Elks. Home: Old Stone House Newburgh IN 47630 Office: PO Box 487 Newburgh IN 47630

MORTON, WILLARD LEMUEL, radio sta. exec.; b. Cody, Nebr., Dec. 18, 1922; s. Lemuel Aaron and Elizabeth Katherine (Minarick) M.; student Chadron (Nebr.) State Coll., 1941. Tchr. pub. schs., 1940-41; with KMMJ Radio, Grand Island, Nebr., 1946—, mgr., stockholder, 1967—. Treas. Grand Island United Fund, 1958, co-chmn. initial gifts div., 1961; Treas. Hall County Republican Central Com., 1965. Chmn. adv. bd. Grand Island Salvation Army, 1966-68; adv. council Grand Island Area Hosp., 1968-73. Served with U.S. Army, World War II. Mem. Grand Island C. of C., Kansas City Advt. Club, V.F.W., Am. Legion, Sigma Delta Chi. Methodist. Clubs: Masons, Shriners, Kiwanis (sec. Grand Island 1968), Elks, Omaha Press. Home: 1615 S Blaine St Grand Island NE 68801 Office: 205 S Cedar St Grand Island NE 68801

MOSBAUGH, PHILLIP GEORGE, physician; b. Noblesville, Ind., Jan. 15, 1938; s. Ward Conrad and Frances Jean (Weaver) M.; A.B., Ind. U., Bloomington, Ind., 1960, M.D., 1963; m. Vera A. Deganutti, Jan. 21, 1962; children—Anne Ruth, Virginia Greer. Intern Orange County (Calif.) Gen. Hosp., Orange, 1963-64; resident surgery Ind. U., 1964-65, resident urology, 1965-68, asst. clin. instr. urology, 1971—; practice medicine specializing in urology, Indpls., 1971—; mem. staff Meth. Hosp., Indpls., mem. kidney transplantation team, 1971—; mem. staffs St. Vincents Hosp., Indpls., Winona Meml. Hosp., Indpls. Mem. med. adv. bd. Ind. chpt. Kidney Found., 1971—; cons. Westview Osteo. Hosp., Indpls., Riverview Hosp., Noblesville, Clinton County (Ind.) Hosp., Frankfort. Served to lt. comdr., M.C., USNR, 1969-70. Diplomate Am. Bd. Urology. Fellow A.C.S.; mem. Marion County (Ind.), Ind. State med. socs., A.M.A., Am. Urol. Assn., Am. Fertility, Sterility Soc., Urologist's Correspondence Club. Home: 623 Round Hill Rd Indianapolis IN 46260 Office: 1633 N Capitol Ave Indianapolis IN 46202 also 2010 W 86th St Indianapolis IN 46260

MOSBAUGH, RICHARD KARL, oral surgeon; b. College Corner, Ohio, Nov. 28, 1916; s. Robert Pierce and Nina Gertrude (Pentecost) M.; A.B., Miami U., Oxford, O., 1938; D.D.S. cum laude (Psi Omega scholar), Ohio State U., 1942; m. Florabel Hain, June 28, 1943; children—Carl Douglas, Allen Lee, Dale William. Intern Fitzsimmons Gen. Hosp., Denver, 1942-43; individual practice dentistry specializing in oral surgery, Cin., 1946—; mem. staff Deaconess Hosp., Christ Hosp., Good Samaritan Hosp., Bethesda Hosp. Chmn. com. statewide fluoridation Ohio Fluoridation Law, 1969. Mem. Cin. Bd. Health, 1969-71. Served with AUS, 1943-46. Fellow Am. Coll. Dentists, Internat. Coll. Dentists, Acad. Internat. Medicine and Dentistry; mem. Am. (mem. council legislation 1966-72, chmn. 1971-72), Ohio (pres. 1964-65, spl. award 1969) dental assns., Cin. Dental Soc. (pres. 1957), Ohio Delta Dental Plan (dir. 1965-71), Am. Soc. Oral Surgeons, Internat. Assn. Oral Surgeons, Omicron Kappa Upsilon. Rotarian. Club: Torch. Home: 2981 Werk Rd Cincinnati OH 45211 Office: 2563 Eden Ave Cincinnati OH 45219

MOSBY, DEWEY FRANKLIN, art historian, mus. curator; b. San Augustine, Tex., Jan. 2, 1942; s. Dewey and Jessie Evelyn (Jones) M.; Ph.D. (Grand Prize fellow), Harvard U., 1974; m. Evelyne vanNes, Mar. 23, 1967; children—Christophe D., Veronique J. Asst. curator J. Paul Getty Mus., Malibu, Calif., 1967-70; asst. prof. art history State U. N.Y., Buffalo, 1973-74; vis. prof. fine arts Harvard U., Cambridge, Mass., 1974; curator European art Detroit Inst. Arts, 1974—; mem. arts com. New Detroit, Inc., 1976—. Cited in Mich. Senate Resolution, 1977. Mem. Midwest Art History Soc. (univ. museums relations com. 1975—). Author: Alexandre-Gabriel Decamps (1803-1860), 1977; arranger internat. art exhbns.; contbr. articles to art history jours. Home: 18273 Fairfield St Detroit MI 48221 Office: 5200 Woodward Ave Detroit MI 48202

MOSBY, DORIS VIRGINIA PERRY, clin. psychologist, educator; b. Starkville, Miss., Mar. 11, 1940; d. Martin James and Maydella (Watson) Perry; A.B., Washington U., St. Louis, 1960, Ph.D. (Univ. fellow), 1965; m. Wilbert Lee Mosby, Sept. 29, 1962; children—Krista Joi, Jay Jourard. Clin. psychologist Jewish Hosp. of St. Louis, 1964-65, 66-68, St. Louis Bd. Edn., 1965-66; asst. prof. psychology, clin. psychologist U. Mo., St. Louis, 1968-71; asso. prof. Ga. State U., 1971-72, Webster Coll., 1972-74, Washington U., 1974-77; coordinator psychology St. Louis State Sch. and Hosp., 1977—; vis. prof. Mich. State U., 1978—; pvt. practice clin. psychology, St. Louis, 1974—; cons. in field; v.p. home health care advisory bd. St. Louis Comprehensive Health Center, 1973-75. Recipient award of appreciation for vol. services King-Fanon Mental Health Center of St. Louis Assn. Black Psychologists, Inc., 1976; USPHS trainee, 1960-64. Mem. Am. (vis. psychologists program 1974-75), Mo. psychol. assns., Assn. Black Psychologists Nat., St. Louis Assn. Black Psychologists (co-chmn. 1969-70, sec. 1974-75), Phi Beta Kappa, Alpha Lambda Delta, Sigma Gamma Rho. Baptist. Contbr. articles to profl. publs.

Home: 6328 Emma Ave Saint Louis MO 63136 Office: 10695 Bellefontaine Rd Saint Louis MO 63137

MOSELEY, RAY (BENJAMIN) F(RANKLIN), real estate broker; b. Kansas City, Mo., Jan. 17, 1898; s. Rev. George E. and Mary Helen (Rose) M.; student pub. schs.; m. Lavinia Tobener, Sept. 2, 1919; children—Ray F., Frank W. Began business career as office boy, 1911; salesman Chamberlin Weatherstrip Co., 1915-18; sec. Schoenberg Realty & Investment Co., 1918-22; founder-pres. Moseley-Comstock Realty Co., 1923-30; pres. Moseley & Company, Kansas City, Mo., 1930-58, chmn. bd., 1958—; pres. Greater Kansas City Indsl. Parks, Inc. Dir. Kansas City Crime Commn., Christian Bus. Mens Com.; mem., past dir. Kansas City Council of Chs.; frequent lay-preacher in various Protestant chs.; founder, pres. Ray F. Moseley Charities Fund; past pres. City Union Mission, Am. War Dads. Trustee, a founder, past pres. Baptist Meml. Hosp.; past pres. Bapt. Found. Mo. Mem. C. of C. Kansas City (past dir.), U.S. C. of C., Real Estate Bd. Kansas City, Nat. Assn. Real Estate Bds., Nat. Inst. Real Estate Brokers, Soc. Indsl. Realtors, Mo. Real Estate Assn. Native Sons Kansas City. Baptist. Mason (32 deg., Shriner); mem. Legion Honor, Order De Molay. Clubs: Kansas City, Automobile (Mo.); TWA Ambassadors; Airways, Inc.; Rockhill Tennis. Home: 438 W 56th St Kansas City MO 64113 Office: 1111 Grand Ave Kansas City MO 64106

MOSER, HANNAH SCHLESINGER, audiologist; b. Vienna, Austria, Apr. 22, 1921; d. Isidor and Emilie (Wirz) Schlesinger; came to U.S., 1949, naturalized, 1955; B.A., Hunter Coll., 1954; M.A., Northwestern U., 1956; m. John B. Moser, Mar. 6, 1954; 1 dau., Barbara Elizabeth. Teaching asst. audiology Northwestern U., Evanston, Ill., 1955-56; tchr., supr. edn. for deaf, dir. auditory tng. Chgo. Pub. Schs., 1956-75; audiologist Whitney Young Magnet High Sch., Chgo., 1975—; lectr. No. Ill. U., 1970, Northwestern U., 1970, 73; audiologist Centro para la Salud del Pueblo, Chgo., 1972. Mem. Am. (certified in audiology), Chgo. speech and hearing assns., Chgo. Tchrs. of Hearing Impaired (pres. 1972-74), A.G. Bell Assn., Zeta Phi Eta. Home: 415 Audubon Rd Riverside IL 60546 Office: 211 S Laflin St Chicago IL 60607

MOSER, ROBERT LEE, civil engr.; b. Bern, Kans., Apr. 15, 1933; s. Aaron and Hulda (Giesel) M.; B.S., Finlay Engring. Coll., Kansas City, Mo., 1960; m. Norma Jean Williams, Dec. 15, 1957; children—Bradley Scott, Leslie Ann. Land surveyor Kans. Hwy. Commn., 1955-57; civil engr. Ill. Hwy. Dept., Dixon, 1960-64; civil engr., mgr. Kans. Engrs., Newton, 1964-67; civil engr., owner Moser & Assos., Engrs., Architects & Planners, Newton and Hiawatha, Kans., Lee's Summit, Mo., 1967—; owner Scottan Constrn. Co.; owner Anscot Homes, Inc. Cons. Northview Opportunity Center for Retarded Children, 1968; mem. Southcentral Kans. Health Planning Council, 1968, Newton Housing Authority; chmn. County United Fund, 1971. Bd. dirs. Community Chest, 1971. Served with USAF, 1951-55. Registered profl. engr., Kans., Mo., Okla., Iowa, Nebr., Ark., Colo., Ill. Mem. Nat. Soc. Profl. Engrs., Kans. Engring. Soc., Profl. Engrs. in Pvt. Practice, Newton C. of C., Am. Legion. Methodist. Elk, Optimist, Eagle. Club: Toastmasters International (past v.p. Newton). Home: 1401 Terrace Newton KS 67114 Office: 500 1/2 Main St Newton KS 67114

MOSER, ROBERT PEABODY, educator; b. Elmwood, Wis., Apr. 26, 1917; s. Robert and Blanche Elizabeth (Peabody) M.; B.S., U. Wis., 1939; M.S., 1940; Ph.D., U. Chgo., 1957; m. Alice Emma Schwake, May 23, 1942; children—Mary Alice (Mrs. Richard Prosise), Robert Philip, Thomas Alan, Timothy John. Prin. high sch., Chilton, Wis., 1940-42, supt. schs., 1946-49; supt. schs., Columbus, Wis., 1949-55; staff asso. Midwest Adminstrn. Center U. Chgo., 1955-57; adminstr. Whitnall Sch. dist., Hales Corners, Wis., 1957-61; supt. schs. Fond du Lac, Wis., 1961-67; prof. ednl. adminstrn. U. Wis., Madison, 1967—. Bd. dirs. Marian Coll. Found., Fond du Lac, 1970—. Served with AUS, 1942-46: CBI. Mem. A.A.U.P., Future Homemakers Am. (hon.), Am. Assn. Sch. Adminstrs., Wis. Secondary Sch. Adminstrs. Assn., Wis. Elementary Sch. Prins. Assn., Assn. Supervision and Curriculum Devel., Wis. Assn. Sch. Dist. Adminstrs. Contbr. articles to profl. jours. Home: 2317 Regent St Madison WI 53705

MOSES, HAROLD ALTON, educator; b. Flippin, Ark., Dec. 20, 1926; s. William J. and Mae (Hampton) M.; B.S., S.E. Mo. State U., 1955; M.A., U. Mich., 1960; Ed.D. (Rehab. Services Adminstrn. fellow), U. Mo., 1965; m. Martha L. Hopkins, Mar. 3, 1950; children—Randall H., Joe M. Tchr., counselor Hazelwood (Mo.) Sch. Dist., 1955-65; asst. prof. edn. U. Ill., Urbana, 1965-70, asso. prof., 1970—. Served with AUS, 1943-45. NDEA fellow, 1959-60. Mem. Am. Psychol. Assn., Phi Theta Kappa, Phi Alpha Theta, Kappa Delta Pi, Phi Delta Kappa. Baptist. Mason. Author: (with J.S. Zaccaria) Facilitating Human Development through Reading, 1968. Sr. editor: Readings in Rehabilitation Counseling, 1971; Research Readings in Rehabilitation, 1973; Student Personnel Work in General Education, 1974. Contbr. articles to profl. jours. Home: 804 Stratford Dr Champaign IL 61820 Office: Dept Education Univ Illinois Urbana IL 61801

MOSES, KENNETH LEE, ins. co. exec.; b. Allentown, Pa., Dec. 7, 1924; s. Jacob Meyer and Alice Katie (Ritter) M.; student Mass. Inst. Tech., 1943-44, Tufts Coll., 1944; B.S. in Elec. Engring., Lehigh U., 1948; m. Jean Elizabeth Kulp, Aug. 31, 1946; children—Robert Kenneth, Barbara Jean. Insp. Fact. Mut. Engring. div., Chgo., 1948-52; fieldman Protection Mut. Ins. Co., Chgo., 1952-54, Detroit, 1954-60, Chgo., 1960-64, v.p., chief engr., Park Ridge, Ill., 1964—. Served with USNR, 1943-46. Mem. Nat. Fire Protection Assn., Soc. of Fire Protection Engrs., Aircraft Owners and Pilots Assn., Newcomen Soc., Theta Chi. Republican. Lutheran. Mason. Home: 1404 W Arlington Ln Schaumburg IL 60193 Office: 300 S Northwest Hwy Ridge IL 60068

MOSHER, GEORGE ALLAN, retail furniture co. exec.; b. Detroit, June 21, 1939; s. Carroll Leonard and Susan (Harris) M.; A.B., Harvard, U., 1961, M.B.A., 1963; m. Julie Ann Zaber, Dec. 31, 1966; children—Karen Susan, Holly Lynn. Sales promotion staff Look mag., N.Y.C., 1963-65; pres. Bus. and Instl. Furniture, Milw., 1965-75; pres. Nat. Bus. Furniture, Milw., 1975—. Bd. dirs. Milw. Pub. Affairs Council, 1976—, sec. treas., 1977-78. Mem. Harvard Bus. Sch. Club Milw. (pres. 1976), Harvard Club Wis. (dir. 1976-77, sec. treas., 1977-78. Republican. Club: Kiwanis. Home: 998 East Circle Dr Whitefish Bay WI 53217 Office: 222 Michigan St E Milwaukee WI 53202

MOSHER, KENNETH EDWARD, dentist; b. Sterling, Colo., Sept. 14, 1925; s. James Owen Mosher; B.S., U. Denver, 1951; D.D.S., St. Louis U., 1959; m. Sandra Jeanne McKinney, Sept. 6, 1958; children—Pamela Kerry, Kenneth Edward. Gen. practice dentistry, St. Louis, 1959—. Served with USNR, 1944-46. Mem. Am. Dental Assn., Mo., Greater St. Louis dental socs., Am. Dental Soc. Anesthesiology (pres. Mo. chpt. 1964). Mason (Shriner). Home: 258 Ridgetrail Rd Chesterfield MO 63017 Office: 8938 St Charles Rock Rd St Louis MO 63114

MOSIER, C. FRED, constrn. co. exec.; b. Muncie, Ind., Apr. 16, 1930; s. Claude F. and Ethel (Tussey) M.; student Chgo. Tech., 1949-50; m. Natalie Joan Milhollin, June 4, 1950; children—Linda Kay (Mrs. Chris Thrope), Daniel R., Robert J. Owner, C. Fred Mosier, bldg. contractor, Muncie, 1950-65; pres. Mosier Constrn., Inc., Muncie, 1965—. Cub scoutmaster Boy Scouts Am., 1965-67. Pres. bd. dirs. Muncie Mission, 1969-70, trustee, 1970—; bd. dirs. Ind. Masonic Home & Hosp., 1965-67. Mem. Nat. Home Builders Assn., Asso. Gen. Contractors Am., Muncie Contractors Assn. (pres. 1973—). Mason; mem. Order Eastern Star. Home: R#1 Box 200A Ridgeville IN 47380 Office: 4309 S Madison St Muncie IN 47302

MOSKOP, ROY LORENZ, telephone co. exec.; b. St. Louis, Aug. 12, 1921; s. Peter G. and Emma C. (Kuhs) M.; B.J., U. Mo., 1942; m. Helen F. Baxter, Oct. 6, 1945; children—Kerry P., Randall S., Nancy C. Advt. asst. Southwestern Bell Telephone Co., St. Louis, 1946-48, gen. advt. asst., 1948, info. supr., 1948-50, info. mgr., 1950-52, gen. advt. supr., 1952-54, area information mgr., 1954-59, gen. information mgr., 1959-61, asst. v.p. information, 1961-66, asst. v.p. pub. relations, 1966—. Served to capt. F.A., U.S. Army, 1942-45; ETO. Decorated Bronze Star medal. Mem. Pub. Relations Soc. Am. (pres. St. Louis chpt. 1965-66), Journalism Alumni Assn. U. Mo. (pres. 1968-70), St. Louis Press Club, Mo. Athletic Club, Young Audiences (v.p. St. Louis chpt. 1977), Kappa Sigma. Presbyterian. Home: 1387 Thornwick Dr Manchester MO 63011 Office: 1010 Pine St Saint Louis MO 63101

MOSKOVIC, JACOB LEON, psychiatrist; b. Berehovo, Czechoslovakia, Oct. 22, 1933; s. Josef Majer and Dora (Selmanovic) M.; came to U.S., 1964, naturalized, 1969; M.D., U. Buenos Aires, Argentina, 1962; postgrad. psychiatry Ill. State Psychiat. Inst., 1965-68; m. Brenda J. Moskovic; children—Alexander, Jori, Joshua. Intern Mt. Sinai Hosp., Chgo., 1964-65; psychiat. resident Ill. State Psychiat. Inst., Chgo., 1965-68, asst. chief outpatient dept., 1968-70; practice medicine specializing in psychiatry Arlington Heights, Ill., 1969—; liaison psychiatrist Community Mental Health program, 1968-70; clin. instr. psychiatry U. Ill., Chgo., 1972-73, clin. asst. prof., 1973—; cons. psychiatry, staff mem. Northwest Community Hosp., Arlington Heights, 1972—, chief psychiatry, 1975—; staff mem. Forest Hosp., Des Plaines, Ill., 1969—, Skokie Valley Hosp., Skokie, Ill., 1976—; med. dir. Northwest Mental Health Center, Arlington Heights, 1970-72. Mem. A.M.A. (award for continued med. edn. 1970—), Ill., Chgo. med. socs., Am. Psychiat. Assn., Am. Soc. Clin. Hypnosis, Ill. Psychiat. Home: 3019 Washington Ave Wilmette IL 60091 Office: 2010 S Arlington Heights Rd Arlington Heights IL 60025

MOSS, DAVID MAC BETH, III, clergyman, psychotherapist; b. St. Louis, Jan. 12, 1943; s. Harry Nichols and Helen Josephine (Miller) M.; B.A., Wash. U., 1966; M.Div., Western Theol. Sem., 1969, S.T.M., 1970; Ph.D., Northwestern U., 1974; postgrad. Rutgers U., 1971, Family Inst. Chgo., 1973, Chgo. Inst. for Psychoanalysis, 1975; m. Faryl Evan Sims, Aug. 17, 1968. Chaplain intern Fla. Alcoholic Rehab. Center, Avon Park, summer 1967; ordained to ministry Episcopal Ch., 1970; asst. rector St. Chrysostom's Ch., Chgo., 1969-73; pastoral counselor Lutheran Gen. Hosp., Park Ridge, 1970-75; mem. clin. and teaching staffs Center for Religion and Psychotherapy, Chgo., 1975—; asso. chaplain Canterbury House, Northwestern U., Chgo., 1975—; clin. supr. Christian Outreach to Handicapped, 1976—; field edn. supr. Seabury-Western Theol. Sem., 1969-73. Fellow Am. Assn. Pastoral Counselors; mem. Am. Assn. Marriage and Family Counselors (clin.), Am. Psychol. Assn., Ars Moriendi, Conseil International sur les Problemes de l'Alcoholisme. Club: Racquet of Chgo. Editorial bds. Jour. Religion and Health, Pilgrimage, Jour. Pastoral Psychotherapy, 1973-77. Contbr. articles and poetry to profl. jours. Home: 2815 Girard St Evanston IL 60201 Office: 7 Dearborn St Chicago IL 60603

MOSS, HENRY S., mgmt. cons.; b. N.Y.C., Oct. 11, 1926; s. Louis John and Bryna (Finegold) M.; B.M.E., Columbia, 1948, M.I.E., 1950; M.S., L.I. U., 1955; m. Barbara Janet Lieberman, Aug. 28, 1949; children—Philip, Lawrence, David, Boris. Mgr. film and kinescope operations RCA Corp., N.Y.C., 1953-59; mgr. systems and data processing, Moorestown, N.J., 1959-64; mgr. mgmt. services Touch Ross & Co., C.P.A.'s, Chgo., 1964-67; partner firm Altschuler, Melvoin & Glasser, C.P.A.'s, Chgo., 1967—. Vis. lectr. U. Ill., DePaul U.; automation com. Mt. Sinai Hosp., Chgo. Mem. automation com. Jewish Fedn. Met. Chgo., 1968—. Served with AUS, 1945-46. C.P.A., 1965. Mem. Am. Inst. C.P.A.'s (standards com. 1970—), Ill. Soc. C.P.A.'s (chmn. mgmt. adv. services com. 1972), Am. Inst. Indsl. Engrs. (treas. Chgo. chpt. 1973). Clubs: Ravinia Green Country, Standard of Chgo. Author: Guidelines to Data Processing Management, 1966; Guidelines to the Administration of Management Advisory Services, 1970. Home: 1160 Pelham Rd Winnetka IL 60093 Office: 69 W Washington St Chicago IL 60602

MOSS, ROBERT HENRY, chemist; b. N.Y.C., July 26, 1922; s. Jacob S. and Bessie (Scheindlinger) M.; B.S., U. N.H., 1943; M.S., U. Ark., 1948; Ph.D., U. Conn., 1955; m. Mary Jean Lee, Oct. 4, 1952; children—Joanne, Rebecca, Nancy, David. Research asst. indsl. engring. engring. erpt. sta. U. N.H., Durham, 1943-46; grad. asst. U. Ark., Fayetteville, 1946-48; grad. asst., research asst. U. Conn., Storrs, 1948-54, asst. instr., 1954-55; prin. chemist Mine Safety Appliances Co., Pitts., 1955-56; engr. Westinghouse Elec. Corp., Pitts., 1956-58, sr. engr., 1958-64; sr. scientist solid state research lab. Harshaw Chem. Co., Cleve., 1964-69, sect. head purification sect. crystal and electronic parts dept., 1969—. Served with USNR, 1945. Mem. Am. Chem. Soc., Electrochem. Soc. Home: 3018 E Overlook Rd Cleveland Heights OH 44118 Office: Crystal and Electronic Parts Dept Harshaw Chemical Co 6801 Cochran Rd Solon OH 44139

MOSS, WALTER GERALD, historian; b. Cin., Apr. 20, 1938; s. Walter Benjamin and Alvina Josephine (Meibers) M.; B.S., Xavier U., Cin., 1960; Ph.D., Georgetown U., Washington, 1968; m. Nancy Sue Pierce, Sept. 7, 1963; children—Jennifer, Thomas, Daniel. Instr., Wheeling (W.Va.) Coll., 1967-68, asst. prof., 1968-70; asst. prof. history Eastern Mich. U., Ypsilanti, 1970-74, asso.prof., 1974—; project dir. Southeastern Mich. Consortium on Gerontology and the Humanities, 1973-75; exec. dir. Presdl. Commn. on Future of Eastern Mich. U., 1975-76; cons. gerontology and humanities projects; panelist, cons. Nat. Endowment for Humanities Div. Pub. Programs, 1976—. Mem. adv. bd. Washtenaw County Ret. Citizens Sr. Vol. Program, 1974. Served to 1st lt. arty. AUS, 1960-62. Georgetown U. grad. fellow, 1962-65; recipient Nat. Endowment for Humanities grant, 1973-75, Case Western Res. U. grant, 1975-76. Mem. Am. Assn. Advancement Slavic Studies, AAUP, Am. Hist. Assn. Author narrator TV tape: Aging and the American Experience, 1974; editor: (with Gordon E. Moss) Growing Old, 1975; Humanistic Perspectives on Aging, 1976; contbr. to Ageing and the Elderly in press. Home: 208 Doty St Ann Arbor MI 48103 Office: History and Philosophy Dept Eastern Michigan University Ypsilanti MI 48197

MOSSBAUER, LOUIS, optometrist; b. Bavaria, Germany, Mar. 1, 1902; s. Karl and Margaret (Meister) Mossbauer; student Fortbildungsschule and Musikschule. Bavaria: postgrad. Hosp. and Med. Sch., Chgo., 1945; Dr. Optometry, Monroe Coll. Optometry. 1946; m. Alice Harkness, Nov. 15, 1947; 1 son, Louis Carl. Came to U.S., 1927, naturalized, 1937. Dir. United Artists Conservatories Music, Balt., 1928-40; practice optometry Chgo. Elmhurst. Ill., 1946—; pres. Midwestern Sch. Optics, 1946-52, pres. German-Am. Contact Lens Mfg. Co., Elmhurst. Founder, Internat. Contact Lens Specialists. Mem. Am., Ill. (trustee 1959-61) optometric assns., N.E. Ill. Optometric Soc. (rec. sec. 1953-56, 59-63, pres. 1957-58, 64-65), Ednl. Council Optometry (past sec.), Am. Pub. Health Assn. (vision com.), Better Vision Inst., Ill. Soc. for Prevention Blindness, Ill. Coll. Optometry Alumni Assn., Tomb and Key. Kappa Phi Delta. Rotarian (past dir. Elmhurst). Research in fitting and mfg. latest types corneal contact lenses. Home: Elmhurst IL 60126 Office: 191 Addison Ave Elmhurst IL 60126

MOSSE, GEORGE L., historian, educator; b. Berlin, Sept. 20, 1918; s. Hans Lachmann and Felicia M.; B.S., Haverford Coll., 1941; Ph.D., Harvard U., 1946; D. Litt. (hon.), Carthage Coll., 1973. Instr., asst. prof., asso. prof. history U. Iowa, 1944-55; asso. prof. U. Wis., Madison, 1955-60, prof., 1960—, Bascom prof. history, 1964—; vis. prof. Stanford U., 1963, Hebrew U. Jerusalem, 1969, 72, 74, 76, 78, Jewish Theol. Sem. Am., 1977. Mem. bd. dirs. Wiener library, London. Recipient Harbison award Danforth Found, 1970; Sr. fellow Australian Nat. U., 1972. Mem. Am. Soc. Ch. History (council 1970-73), Am. Soc. Reformation Research (pres. 1962-62). Author: The Struggle for Sovereignty in England, 1950; The Reformation, 1953; The Holy Pretence, 1957; The Culture of Western Europe, 1961; The Crisis of German Ideology, 1964; Nazi Culture, 1966; Germans and Jews, 1971; The Nationalisation of the Masses, 1975; Intervista Sul Nazismo, 1977; Toward the Final Solution: a History of European Racism, 1978; (with H. Koenigsberger) Europe in the Sixteenth Century, 1968; co—editor Jour. Contemporary History, 1966—. Home: 36 Glenway St Madison WI 53705 Office: Dept History Univ Wis Madison WI 53706

MOTA, CARLOS ROBERTO, surgeon; b. Jalapa, Veracruz, Mexico, Feb. 6, 1919; s. Victor and Victoria (Aguirre) M.; came to U.S., 1950, naturalized, 1958; M.D., U. Mexico, 1942; m. Elizabeth Pauline Jakovac, June 6, 1952; children—Hector, Kevin, Karen, Mario, Laurence, Alan. Intern, Juarez Hosp., Mexico City, 1940-41; intern Henry Ford Hosp., Detroit, 1951-52, resident gen. and thoracic surgery, 1952-58, asso. thoracic surgery, 1958; research physician Wesley Hosp., Oklahoma City, 1958-60; sr. surg. resident VA Hosp., Wadsworth, Kans., 1960-61; staff surgeon Omaha VA Hosp., 1961-63, asst. chief surg. service, 1963-67; chief surg. service Lincoln (Nebr.) VA Hosp., 1968—. Asst. prof. surgery U. Nebr. Coll. Medicine, 1968—; asst. prof. pathology U. Nebr. Coll. Dentistry, 1968—. Diplomate Am. Bd. Surgery, Am. Bd. Thoracic Surgery. Fellow A.C.S., Am. Coll. Chest Physicians. Address: 600 S 70th St Lincoln NE 68510

MOTEN, CHAUNCEY DONALD, ednl. adminstr.; b. Kansas City, Kans., July 2, 1933; s. Eugene D. and Estella M. (Jackson) M.; B.A., Tex. Coll., 1955; M.A., Vandercook Coll. of Music, 1959, U. Mo., 1968; Ph.D. (Mott fellow), U. Mich., 1972; m. Barbara Jean Brooks, Aug. 16, 1959; children—Allison Kaye, Dion Brett. Tchr., Kansas City pub. schs., 1965-68; dir. New Careers Tng., U. Mo., Kansas City, 1968-70, dir. of Ethnic Awareness Center, 1971-73; exec. asst. to chancellor Met. Community Colls., Kansas City, Mo., 1974—; cons. to Kans. and Mo. bds. of edn., 1972—, CBS Network News, 1974, Kansas City Regional Commn. on Higher Edn., 1976—, HEW, 1976, Univ. Research Corp., Washington, 1977, others, nat. rev. panelist HEW, 1977. First vice pres. Boys' Clubs of Am., Greater Kansas City chpt., 1977—; bd. dirs. Kansas City Assn. for the Blind, 1977—, Black Archives of Mid-America, 1974-77, Charlie Parker Meml. Found., 1977-78, Vols. Intervening for Equity, 1977-78, A.M. Roundtable Urban League, 1977-78, Greater Kansas City Assn. Affirmative Action, 1977-78, others. Served with U.S. Army, 1955-57. Recipient Affirmative Action award Urban League of Kansas City, 1976, Pub. Relations award Sta. KPRS, 1977. Rockefeller fellow, 1973-74. Mem. Am. Assn. for Affirmative Action, NAACP. Democrat. Baptist. Home: 10616 E 98th St Terr 2B Kansas City MO 64134 Office: 560 Westport Rd Kansas City MO 64111

MOTLEY, LARRY LEE, real estate investor; b. Acmar, Ala., Sept. 28, 1944; s. A.G. and Helen (Jones) M.; student Wayne County Community Coll., Detroit, 1973; B.A. in Psychology, Shaw Coll., Detroit, 1976; m. Wyanetta Cowart, Dec. 3, 1964; children—Larry Lee, Michelle Y., Juanda P., Tamara C., Carmel. With Hydra-Matic div. Gen. Motors Corp., 1963-67; salesman Nat. Life Ins. Co., 1967-68; mgr. Montgomery Ward & Co., 1968-69; mgr. Wright Mut. Ins. Co., 1969-70; pres. Tamara Mgmt. & Investment Co., Inkster, Mich., 1970—. Pres. Internat. Black Devel. Assn., 1975—. Mem. Assn. Social Sci. (pres. 1976-77), Smithsonian Assos., African Heritage Studies Assn. Home: 4057 Fox St Inkster MI 48141 Office: 3648 Inkster Rd Inkster MI 48141

MOTTL, RONALD MILTON, congressman; b. Cleve., Feb. 6, 1934; s. Milton and Anna (Hummel) M.; B.S., U. Notre Dame, 1956, LL.B., 1957; m. Debra Mary Budan; children—Ronald Milton, Ronda Ann, Ronald Michael. Admitted to Ohio bar, 1957; gen. practice law; asst. dir. law city of Cleve., 1958-60; councilman from 2d Ward, Parma City Council, 1960-61, pres. council, 1961-67; mem. Ohio Ho of Reps. from 51st Dist., 1967-69, Ohio Senate from 24th Dist., 1969-75; mem. 94th-95th Congresses from 23d Ohio dist., chmn. Spl. Investigating Subcom. of House Vet. Affairs Com., mem. House Edn. and Labor Com., House Vet. Affairs Com. Served with U.S. Army, 1957-58. Democrat. Home: 7713 Wake Robin Dr Parma OH 44130 Office: Room 1233 Longworth House Office Bldg Washington DC 20515

MOTTON, ROSITA ELORISE, chemist, editor; b. Orange, Tex., May 31, 1947; d. Robert Edward and Altha Burnham (Hoyt) Pettaway; B.S., Tenn. State U., 1970; m. Leroy Motton, Dec. 29, 1970; 1 son, LeSean Eric. Jr. chemist Dow Corning Co. Midland, Mich., 1969; jr. chemist electrokinetics group Standard Oil Co. of Ohio, Cleve., 1970-71, chemist petroleum research group, 1971-73, analytical services and gas chromatography, 1973-76, asst. editor Sohio Test Methods, 1976—; chemistry tutor for coll. students. Mem. Am. Chem. Soc., Tenn. State Alumni. Democrat. Baptist. Clubs: Desk and Derrick of Cleve. (charter, 2d v.p. 1973), Toastmasters. Inventor in field. Home: 20610 Selfridge Pkwy Warrensville Township OH 44128 Office: 4440 Warrensville Center Rd Warrensville Heights OH 44128

MOTTS, WARREN EARL, photographer; b. Brice, Ohio, Nov. 10, 1940; s. Wilbur E. and Mabel M. (Rawn) M.; student Still Photog. Sch., 1960; m. Daisy Nell Blair, July 1, 1962; children—Wayne Earl, Lori Lynn. Lab. technician Battelle Meml. Inst., Columbus, Ohio, 1960-61; med. photographer asst. U. Hosp., Columbus, 1962-64; chief photog. asst. Columbus & So. Ohio Electric Co., Columbus, 1964-66; photographer Clyde Williams & Co., Columbus, 1966; comml. and advt. photographer Columbus Art, 1968-69; photographer, v.p. Charles Moor Photo., Inc., Columbus, 1969-72; pres., propr. Motts Photog. Center, Inc., Columbus, 1972—, photographer for Am. Freedom Train Found. Commemerative program, 1975. Lectr. Ohio Presbyn. Homes, 1971, Daguerre Club of Ind., 1974. Pres. Columbus Civil War Roundtable, 1967. Recipient Bronze medallion Am. Freedom Train, 1976. Mem. Profl. Photographers of Ohio (ct. of honor award 1968, 1970, dir. 1968—, pres. 1977), Columbus Soc. of Communicating Arts (pres. 1975), Profl. Photographers of Central

Ohio (pres. 1972), Profl. Photographers of Am. (councilman 1972—, photog. craftsman 1976, M. Photography 1977), Columbus Advt. Club (trustee 1973-74). Methodist (dir. 1974—). Home: 5761 Ebright Rd Groveport OH 43125 Office: 1461 Gerrard Columbus OH 43212

MOTTWEILER, JACK HUGO, clergyman; b. Danville, Ill., May 4, 1927; s. Vernon Hugo and Mildred Ann (Martin) M.; A.B., Greenville Coll., 1947; Th.M., Asbury Theol. Sem., 1950; M.S. in Edn., Ind. U., 1976; m. Evelyn Lucile Marston, May 31, 1948; children—Marston Hugo, Ann Lucile Mottweiler Truesdell. Ordained to ministry Free Methodist Ch., 1947; pastor St. Francisville, Ill., 1950-52, Redlands, Calif., 1956-66, Los Angeles, 1966-71; Western regional youth dir. Free Methodist Ch., 1952-56, dir. adult ministries, Winona Lake, Ind., 1971-76, dir. dept. spl. ministries, 1976—. Sec., trustee bd. Azusa Pacific Coll., 1965-71; chmn. bd. trustees Pacific Christian High Sch., 1966-71; bd. adminstrn. Nat. Assn. Evangelicals, 1974—. Recipient Azusa Pacific Coll. Recognition Plaque, 1971. Mem. Nat. Assn. Evangelicals, Nat. Council Family Relations. Author: (with others) Blueprint for Sunday Schs., 1971. Contbr. articles to religious, profl. jours. Home: 516 School Ave Winona Lake IN 46590 Office: PO Box 368 Winona Lake IN 46590

MOULDER, JAMES EDWIN, civil engr.; b. Roach, Mo., Aug. 29, 1926; s. Cyrus B. and Lela (Morgan) M.; B.S. in Civil Engring., U. Mo., 1953, M.S., 1955; m. Eldora Rhodes, Dec. 19, 1954; children—Robin Edwin, Bradley James. Structural engr. Boeing Airplane Co., Wichita, Kans., 1953; research engr. U. Mo., Columbia, 1953-56; cons. engr. Smith & Gillespie, Engrs., Jacksonville, Fla., 1956-60; cons. engr. Booker Assos., Inc., St. Louis, 1961—, dir., v.p., 1963-66, sec., dir., v.p. 1966-68, exec. v.p., dir., 1968-73, pres., 1973-77, chmn. bd., pres., dir., 1977—; dir. Mark Twain O'Fallon Bank N.A., O'Fallon, Mo. Mem. adv. com. Coll. Engring., U. Mo. at Columbia. Served with USMC, 1945-46; served with AUS, 1950-52. Mem. ASCE, Nat. Assn. Housing Redevel. Ofcls., Nat., Mo. soc. profl. engrs., Mo. Planning Assn., Cons. Engrs. Council Mo. (pres. 1975-76), So. Indsl. Devel. Council, Nat., Mo. parks and recreation assns., Hwy. Engrs. Assn. Mo., Alliance of Alumni Assns., U. Mo. at Columbia Alumni Assn. (pres. engring. div.). Club: Rotary. Home: 93 Rue Grand Lake St Louis MO 63367 Office: 1139 Olive St St Louis MO 63101

MOULTRIE, JOHN WESLEY, JR., state ofcl.; b. Marion, S.C., May 23, 1904; s. John Wesley and Missouri (Crockett) M.; A.B., Allegheny Coll., Meadville, Pa., 1927; postgrad. Harvard Law Sch., 1927-28, U. Mich. Law Sch., 1929-30, U. Minn., 1935-36, 38-39; M.A., Roosevelt U., 1967; m. Alice Gibson, Oct. 1, 1939 (dec. Nov. 1962); children—John Wesley III, Stanton Randolph. Prin. rural sch., Jacksonville, Fla., 1932-33; editor-in-chief The Spotlight, Chgo., 1934-35; dir. Consumer Center, Phyllis Wheatley House, Mpls., 1941-42; interviewer, unit supr. Minn. State Employment Service, Mpls., 1942-54; interviewer, counselor Gen. Indsl. Office, Ill. State Employment Service, Chgo., 1959-65, counseling supr., 1965-69, program coordinator, 1969—; real estate broker, Chgo., 1955—, ins. broker, Chgo., 1956—. Mem. Am. Personnel and Guidance Assn., Nat. Employment Counselors Assn., Ill., Chgo. guidance and personnel assns. Methodist (pres. ch. credit union). Home: 4354 S Martin Luther King Dr Chicago IL 60653 Office: Ill State Employment Service 4314 S Cottage Grove Ave Chicago IL 60653

MOUNTFORD, RICHARD DEAN, educator; b. Kansas City, Kans., Oct. 28, 1937; s. George Allen and Margarite Marie (Edwards) M.; student Bethany Nazarene Coll., 1955-58; B.Mus.Edn., U. Kans., 1960, M.Mus.Edn., 1963; Ph.D., Ohio State U., 1977; m. Marjorie (Gentz), Aug. 23, 1957; children—Roxanne Denise, Janelle Rene. Instrumental, vocal music tchr. Basehor (Kans.) pub. schs., 1960-67; asso. prof. music Malone Coll., Canton, Ohio, 1967—; research asst. Ohio State U., Columbus, 1974-75; bass trombonist Canton Symphony Orch., 1968. Recipient award Ohio Fedn. Music Clubs, 1975. Mem. Ohio Music Edn. Assn., Music Educators Nat. Conf., Am. Fedn. Musicians, Coll. Band Dirs. Nat. Assn. Mem. Religious Soc. Friends. Editor: Jour. of Grad. Music Students, 1974-75. Contbr. articles to profl. jours. Home: 1113 29th St NE Canton OH 44714

MOUNTZ, LOUISE CARSON SMITH (MRS. GEORGE EDWARD MOUNTZ), librarian; b. Fond Du Lac, Wis., Oct. 20, 1911; d. Roy Carson and Charlotte Louise (Scheurs) Smith; student Western Coll., Oxford, Ohio, 1929-31; A.B., Ohio State U., 1933; M.A., Ball State U., 1962; postgrad. Manchester Coll., 1954, Ind. U., 1960-61; m. George Edward Mountz, May 4, 1935 (dec. Oct. 1951); children—Peter Carson, Pamela Teeters (Mrs. George Edmund McDonald). Tchr. high sch., Monroeville, Ind., 1953-54, Riverdale High Sch., St. Joseph, Ind., 1954-55; tchr., librarian high sch., Avilla, Ind., 1955-58; head librarian Penn High Sch., Mishawaka, Ind., 1958-67, Northwood Jr. High Sch., Fort Wayne, 1967-69, McIntosh Jr. High Sch., Auburn, Ind., 1969-74; dir. Media Center DeKalb Jr. High Sch., Auburn, 1974—. Cons. media center planning Penn Harris Madison Sch. Corp., Mishawaka, 1966—. Bd. dirs. DeKalb County chpt. ARC, 1938-42, 51-53, DeKalb County Heart Assn., 1946-52, DeKalb County Community Concert Assn., 1946-58, Am. Field Service chpt., Mishawaka, 1960-67. Mem. AAUW, ALA, World Confedn. Orgns. Teaching Professions, Nat. Council Tchrs. English, NEA, Ind. Sch. Librarians Assn. (dir. 1963-67), Internat. Assn. Sch. Librarianship, Ind. Assn. Ednl. Communication and Tech., Ind. Tchrs. Assn., Ind., Garrett, DeKalb County, Allen County hist. socs., Nat. Trust for Historic Preservation, Delta Kappa Gamma (charter mem., v.p. Beta Beta chpt. 1960-62), Kappa Kappa Kappa (state officer 1941-45, pres. Alpha Chi chpt. 1938-40), Delta Delta Delta (house pres.), Epsilon Sigma Omicron, Garrett Community Hosp. Women's Aux. Methodist. Mem. Order Eastern Star. Club: Athena (hon. mem.)(Garrett, Ind.). Author: Biographies for Junior High Schools. Contbr. articles to profl. jours. Home: 412 E King St Garrett IN 46738

MOUREK, ANTON PETER, building contractor, indsl. land developer; b. Chgo., Oct. 19, 1908; s. Anton and Anna Josefa (Prucha) M.; student Northwestern U., 1926-27; m. Margaret J. Walsh, Sept. 7, 1935; children—Anthony John, James Otto, Michael Thomas. Partner, A. Mourek & Son, Westchester, Ill., 1929-46, pres., 1946—, also chmn. bd.; dir. J.A.M. Inc., Amtex Inc., Lincoln Fed. Savings and Loan, 1948—, founder, dir. Bank of Elmhurst, 1970-76; trustee, Ill. Benedictine Coll., 1967—. Sec., Cicero Library Bd., 1936-42. Served with U.S. Army, 1943-46. Recipient hon. Sc.D., Ill. Benedictine Coll., 1977. Roman Catholic. Clubs: Riverside Country, Key Biscayne Yacht, Knights of Columbus, Elks. Address: 970 N Oaklawn Ave Elmhurst IL 60126

MOUW, EDWARD WAYNE, lawyer; b. Madison, Wis., Nov. 12, 1935; s. Gerritt E. and Margaret Elizabeth (Dodero) M.; B.B.A., U. Wis.-Whitewater, 1960; J.D., U. Wis.-Madison, 1966; m. Diana Jo Olson, July 10, 1965 (dec. Dec. 1970); children—Elizabeth, Peter; m. 2d, Annabelle J. Meyer, Aug. 3, 1972; children—Tamara, Rebecca. Admitted to Wis. bar, 1966; asso. firm Arthur, Tomlinson & Gillman, Madison, 1966-69; asso. Korth, Rodd & Sommer, 1969-71; mem. Korth, Rodd, Sommer & Mouw, Rhinelander, Wis., 1972—. Instr. Nicholet Coll. and Vocational Sch. 1969, 74. Mem. adv. com. Oneida County (Wis.) Dept. Social Services, 1970; chmn. civic affairs com. Oneida County Assn. Retarded Children, 1970-71; mem. Sch. Bd. Sch. Dist. of Rhinelander, 1976—. Served to 1st lt. USMCR, 1960-63. Mem. Am., Wis., Oneida-Vilas-Forest (pres. 1973-74) bar assns. Conglist. (deacon 1972-74). Rotarian. Home: 1850 Larsen Dr Rhinelander WI 54501 Office: First National Bank Bldg Rhinelander WI 54501

MOUZAKEOTIS, THEODORE CONSTANTINE, surgeon; b. Chgo., July 13, 1906; s. Constantine John and Catherine (Kozialis) M.; B.S., U. Ill., 1930, M.D., 1933; m. Helen Karedes, Jan. 28, 1940; children—Kathy (Mrs. Clayton E. Whiting, Jr.), Teddy (Mrs. Plato Foufas), Sonia (Mrs. Stuart Leventhal), Theodore Constantine. Intern Cook County Hosp., Chgo., 1933-34; instr. surgery and cardiology Rush Med. Sch., U. Chgo., 1934-39; instr. phys. diagnosis U. Ill. Coll. Medicine, 1939-43, instr. obstetrics and gynecology, 1943-46, clin. instr. obstetrics and gynecology 1946-62; practice medicine specializing in surgery, Chgo., 1935—; asso. in obstetrics and gynecology Chgo. State Hosp., 1947-49; mem. staff Columbus, Ill. Masonic, Cuneo hosps., Chgo; mem. att. staff Research and Edn. Hosp., Chgo., 1943-61, Weiss Meml. Hosp., Chgo., 1954-57. Dir. Howard Savs. & Loan, Evanston, Ill. Former explorer troop chmn. Boy Scouts Am. Trustee Roycemore Sch., Evanston, Ill., 1951-53, exec. com., 1951-53. Mem. AMA, Ill., Chgo. med. socs., AHEPA, Phi Sigma Epsilon (founder, hon. pres.). Clubs: Saddle and Cycle (Chgo.); Point Of Woods Country (Benton Harbor, Mich.). Contbr. articles profl. jours. Home: 7 Woodley Rd Winnetka IL 60093 Office: 55 E Washington St Chicago IL 60602

MOVCHAN, JULIAN GEORGE, physician, journalist; b. Zorokiv, Ukraine, Feb. 19, 1913; s. George John and Olga O. (Kolomijec) M.; student Ukrainian Inst. Journalism, 1932-35; M.D., Kharkiv and Iviv Med. Colls., 1943; m. Helen Skibicka, Sept. 3, 1949; children—Ola Movchan Ivanicki, Lida Movchan Plesh. Came to U.S., 1949, naturalized, 1956. Corr. staff several Ukrainian newspapers, 1932-37; intern Alexian Bros. and Elizabeth hosps., N.J., 1949-53; practice medicine specializing in internal and gen. medicine, Oakwood and Macedonia, Ohio, mem. staff Bedford (O.) Municipal Hosp., 1960—. Vice pres. Paulding County (Ohio) Bd. Health, 1957-60. Mem. Ohio Med. Assn., Summit County Med. Soc. (award 1964). Author: How to Cure Oneself and Others in Emergency Cases, 1946; Things Worth Knowing, 1966; Doctor's Notes, 1970. Contbr. articles to med. lit. Home and office: 10115 Valley View Rd Macedonia OH 44056

MOWERY, ALBERT SAMUEL, ednl. adminstr.; b. Mowersville, Pa., Oct. 15, 1915; s. Norman Gochenour and Dora Myrtle (Hollar) M.; B.S., Pa. State U., 1939, M.S., 1949, Ph.D., 1957; A.A. (hon.), Lake Mich. Coll., 1977; m. Dorothy Virginia McBride, May 3, 1936; children—Albert Samuel, Alan Wayne, Thomas McBride, Carol Keen (Mrs. Sheldon Frye), Jean Foering (Mrs. Richard Block). Tchr., Mechanisburg (Pa.) High Sch., 1939-46; asso. prof. agrl. engring. Pa. State U., 1946-52; field rep. Douglas Fir Plywood Assn., Tacoma, Wash., 1952-56; div. sales promotion mgr., div. sales engr., gen. mgr. agrl. sales U.S. Plywood Corp., N.Y.C., 1959-62; regional dir. Upper Peninsula Mich. State U., Marquette, 1962-66; dir. grad. center Mich. State U., Benton Harbor, 1966—, prof. continuing edn., 1966—, regional dir. continuing edn., 1966—; guest lectr. Middle Atlantic Lumberman's Assn., 1953-56; cons. Upper Peninsula Crafts Council, 1962-66; cons., adv. com. Upper Peninsula Com. Area Progress, 1962-66. Pres., Upper Peninsula Field Services Com., 1963-64; pres. Twin Cities Community Forum Bd., 1968-69; adv. Future Farms Am., 1939-46; active Boy Scouts Am., 1946-52; exec. dir. Berrien County Bicentennial Commn., 1974—; chmn. bd. dirs. Berrien County Bicentennial Pageant, 1975—. Trustee, Twin Cities Symphonic Soc., 1966—, pres., 1969-71; parent adv. council Dickinson Coll., Carlisle, Pa., 1964-66. Recipient 1st prize James F. Lincoln Arc Welding Nat. Contest, 1950. Mem. Mich. Adult Edn. Assn. (pres. 1972-73, dir. 1970-75), Adult Edn. Assn. U.S., Am. Soc. Agrl. Engrs., Nat. U. Extension Assn., Alpha Zeta, Delta Theta Sigma, Alpha Tau Alpha. Episcopalian. Mason. Co-inventor or developer many labor saving devices in agrl. field. Author: Farm Shop Skills in Mechanized Agriculture, 1955. Contbr. to profl. publs. in field. Home: 3030 Lakeshore Ave Benton Harbor MI 49022 Office: 777 Riverview Dr Bldg B Benton Harbor MI 49022

MOWERY, JOHN HENRY, psychologist; b. Cin., Jan. 22, 1920; s. John Henry and Minna Henrietta (Hageman) M.; B.A., Bowling Green State U., 1950; M.A., Kent State U., 1951; m. Carolyn Rubel, June 4, 1960. Clin. psychologist Ind. Mental Health Div., Indpls., 1952; personnel psychologist Aero Mayflower Transit Co., Indpls., 1952-55; personnel adminstr. Am. Legion Nat. Hdqrs., Indpls., 1955-56; psychologist Am. Legion State Hdqrs., Indpls., 1956; asst. personnel dir. Hook Drugs Inc., Indpls., 1956-60; staff psychologist Psychol. Service Center, Toronto, Ont., Can., 1960-62; pvt. practice clin. psychologist, Mpls., 1963—; cons. psychologist Lutheran Social Service Minn., 1970—. Served with USAAF, 1942-46. Mem. AAAS, Am., Minn. psychol. assns. Methodist. Clubs: Mason, Statesman's, Regency. Home: 400 Groveland Ave Minneapolis MN 55403

MOWRER, ERNEST RUSSELL, educator; b. Lost Springs, Kans., Aug. 18, 1895; s. James Theodore and Anna (Smith) M.; B.A., U. Kans., 1918; M.A., U. Chgo., 1921, Ph.D., 1924; m. Harriet C. Rosenthal, Oct. 12, 1924. Asst. prof. sociology Coe Coll., Cedar Rapids, Iowa, 1922-23; asst. prof. sociology Ohio Wesleyan U., Delaware, 1924-25; research sociologist Wieboldt Found., Chgo., 1926-28; asst. prof. sociology Northwestern U., Evanston, Ill., 1928-32, asso. prof., 1932-43, prof., 1943-63, prof. emeritus, 1963—; vis. prof. sociology Mich. State U., East Lansing, 1940, U. Chgo., 1948, U. Ariz., Tucson, 1964. Served with U.S. Army, 1918-19. Social Sci. Research Council fellow, 1925-26, grantee, 1933. Mem. Am. Sociol. Assn. (sec.-treas. 1947-49), Sociol. Research Assn., Am. Assn. Univ. Profs., Nat. Council on Family Relations, Alpha Kappa Delta. Contbg. editor Social Sci. Abstracts, 1928-33. Mng. editor Am. Sociol. Review, 1947-49. Editor Crofts Sociol. Series, 1940-50. Author: Family Disorganization, 1927, 2nd. edit. 1939; The Family, 1932; Disorganization Personal and Social, 1942. Author: (with Harriet R. Mowrer) Domestic Discord, 1929; (with William Dobriner) The Suburban Community, 1958; (with E.W. Burgess and Donald Bogue) Contributions to Urban Sociology, 1964. Contbr. articles to profl. jours. Home: 4037 Fairway Dr Wilmette IL 60091

MOWRY, DAVID DEE, educator; b. Fairfield County, Ohio, Oct. 21, 1936; s. David William and Betty Madge (Mericle) M.; B.Sc. in Bus. Adminstrn. Ohio State U., 1958, B.Sc. in Edn., 1960; M.Ed., Ohio U., 1969; m. Kathy Suzanne Beavers, Sept. 7, 1975. Tchr. Lancaster (Ohio) City Schs., 1960-63, sci. supr., 1963-69; asst. prin. Lancaster High Sch., 1969-70; asst. prof. zoology Ohio U., Lancaster, 1970—. Bd. dirs. Fairfield County Heart Assn.; ruling elder Bremen United Presbyterian Ch., Bremen, Ohio, 1974—. Fellow Ohio Acad. Sci.; mem. AAUP, AAAS, Ohio Edn. Assn., World Population Soc., Ohio Coll. Biology Tchrs. Assn., Population Reference Bur., Phi Delta Kappa. Republican. Clubs: Mason, Shriner, Kiwanian. Home: 146 Mulberry St Bremen OH 43107 Office: 1570 Granville Rd Lancaster OH 43130

MOWRY, JOHN L., lawyer; b. Baxter, Iowa, Dec. 15, 1905; s. William and Grace (Conn) M.; B.A., U. Iowa, 1929, J.D., 1930; student Ohio State U., 1926-27; m. Irene E. Lounsberry, Oct. 9, 1941; 1 dau., Madelyn E. (Mrs. Stephen R. Irvine). Admitted to Ia. bar, 1930, N.Y. bar, 1945; spl. agt. F.B.I., 1930-34; mem. staff firm Thomas E. Dewey, N.Y.C., 1935-36; mem. exec. dept. N.Y. State, 1946; pvt. practice law, Marshalltown, Iowa, 1936-41, 1947—; owner Evans Abstract Co., also G.M.K. Inc., Marshalltown, 1950—. County atty. Marshall County (Iowa), 1939-41; mayor City of Marshalltown, 1950-55; rep. Iowa Gen. Assembly, 1956-68, majority floor leader, 1963-65; senator Iowa Gen. Assembly, 1968-72; del. Republican Nat. Conv., Miami, Fla., 1972. Served with USAAF, 1941-45. Mem. Soc. Former Spl. Agts. FBI (nat. pres. 1945), Marshall County, Ia. bar assns., Marshall County Hist. Soc. Republican. Presbyn. Mason (Shriner), Elk. Home: 503 W Main St Marshalltown IA 50158 Office: 25 N Center St Marshalltown IA 50158

MOYER, DAVID EMERSON, chemist; b. Goshen, Ind., Apr. 4, 1946; s. Stanley Emerson and Eileen Lois (Naylor) Moyer; m. Alma Jean Breneman, Aug. 23, 1968; children—Chadwick, Andrea. B.A., Goshen Coll., 1968. Project chemist Ill. Water Treatment Co., Rockford, Ill., 1971-74, chief chemist, 1974-76, sr. research chemist, 1976—. Mem. Am. Chem. Soc., AAAS, Soc. Applied Spectroscopy, Nat. Space Inst., Am. Soc. Testing and Materials. Home: 2620 Burrmont Rd Rockford IL 61107 Office: 4669 Shepherd Trail Rockford IL 61105

MOYER, LAWRENCE NOEL, educator; b. Lancaster, Ohio, Jan. 28, 1924; s. Harl Wayne and Lois Catheran (Miller) M.; B.A., Ohio State U., 1959, M.A., 1960, Ph.D., 1963; m. Janet Lee McClure, Nov. 25, 1967; children—Lawrence Noel II, Indira Renee, Karima Noel, Alexander Noel. Teaching asst. Ohio State U., Columbus, 1960-61, asst. instr., 1962-63; asst. prof. U. N.D., 1963-65, chmn. dept. sociology, 1964-65; asso. prof. sociology U. Toledo, 1965-69, prof., 1969—, acting chmn. dept. sociology, 1966-67; adj. prof. Med. Coll. Ohio, Toledo, 1971—. Cons. numerous orgns. and agys. Served with USNR, 1941-45. Mem. Am. Sociol. Assn., Ohio Valley Sociol. Assn., AAUP, AAAS, Mensa, Alpha Kappa Delta. Contbr. articles to profl. jours. Home: 4226 Corey Rd Toledo OH 43623

MOYER, MARY SUZANNE, recreation dir.; b. Atascadero, Calif., June 23, 1939; d. John Leslie and Helen Ethel (Pemble) Moyer; B.A., U. Calif., 1963; M.A., U. Tenn., 1967; postgrad U. Minn., 1975—. Tchr. Esparto (Calif.) High Sch., 1963-65; tchr. Esparto Elementary Sch., 1965-66; instr. edn. U. Tenn., 1966-67; instr. phys. edn. Randolph Macon Womans Coll., Lynchburg, Va., 1967-68, Wis. State U., 1968-70; program mgr. City of Duluth, Minn., 1971-76, asso. dir. recreation, 1976—. Vol., Light House for Blind, Duluth, Minn., 1971-73; bd. dirs. ARC, Duluth, 1976-77, Girls Club of Duluth, 1974-77; mem. budget review and priorities review panel United Way, Duluth, 1976-77. Mem. Nat., Minn. recreation and parks assns., Am. Alliance of Health, Phys. Edn. Recreation. Pi Lambda Theta. Republican. Presbyterian. Clubs: Altrusa Internat. Home: 718 W 3d St Duluth MN 55806 Office: Office: 208 City Hall Duluth MN 55802

MOZDZIERZ, GERALD JOHN, psychologist; b. Chgo., Sept. 7, 1940; s. Felix Vincent and Genevieve (Lacic) M.; B.S., Loyola U., Chgo., 1961, Ph.D., 1965; certificate psychotherapy Alfred Adler Inst. Chgo., 1975; m. Charlene Mae Greco, Sept. 14, 1963; children—Kimberly, Krista, Pamela, Andrea. Intern, Hines VA Hosp., W. Side VA Hosp., Chgo., 1964-66; staff clin. psychologist VA Hosp., Hines, 1966—; cons. community mental health program St. Josephs Hsp., Chgo., 1968—; asst. clin. prof. psychiatry Loyola Med. Sch., 1967-72; vis. prof. U. Louvain (Belgium), 1973. Certified psychologist, Ill.; NDEA fellow, 1961-64; diplomate Am. Bd. Profl. Psychology. Mem. Am. Soc. Adlerian Psychology (del.), Alfred Adler Inst. Chgo., Am., Ill. psychol. assns., Am. Soc. Clin. Hypnosis. Contbr. articles to profl. jours. Home: 5608 Lawn Dr Western Springs IL 60558 Office: VA Hospital Mental Hygiene Clinic Hines IL 60141

MRAVA, GENE LOUIS, mech. engr.; b. Cleve., Aug. 7, 1935; s. Louis and Mary Carolyn (Lorenz) M.; B.S. in Mech. Engring., Rose Poly. Inst., 1957; M.S., Case Inst. Tech., 1962; children from previous marriage—Diane Marie, James Louis. Prin. engr., TRW In., Cleve., 1957-67; chief engr., dir. biomedical engring. Cleve. Clinic Found., 1967-72; dir. tech. opns. North West Ohio Clin. Engring. Center, Toledo, 1972-73; v.p. research and devel. V. Mueller div. Am. Hosp. Supply Corp., Chgo., 1973—. Served with C.E. U.S. Army, 1958. Walter Charman scholar, 1953-57; recipient Leadership medal S.A.R., 1957; certified market mgmt. program Columbia U., 1976; registered profl. engr., Ohio. Mem. ASME, Am. Soc. Artificial Internal Organs, Assn. Advancement Med. Instrumentation, Nat. Rose Tech. Clubs (chmn. 1969-70), Blue Key. Tau Beta Pi. Roman Catholic. Club: Woodfield Racquet. Patentee in field. Contbr. articles to profl. jours. Home: 4600 Morning Hill Ct Midlothian VA 23113 Office: 7280 Caldwell Ave Chicago IL 60648

MUCCIOLI, ANNA MARIA, artist; b. Detroit, Apr. 23, 1922; d. Anthony and Josephine (Coccardi) Di Pascale; student Soc. Arts Crafts, 1970-75; m. Joseph E. Muccioli, Dec. 26, 1942; children—Ronald, Nathan, Edward, James. One-woman shows of water color paintings include: Verve Gallery, Detroit, 1965, Left Bank Gallery, Flint, Mich., 1969, Univ. Liggett Sch., Grosse Pointe Farms, Mich., 1961-77; group shows include: Ford Motor Co., Dearborn, Mich., 1965, 70, 71, 73, 76, 77, Scarab Club, Detroit, 1965, 70, 71, 76, 77, Ann Arbor St. Art Fair, Ann Arbor, Mich., 1966, 67, Oakland (Mich.) Community Coll., 1967, Detroit-Windsor Internat. Freedom Festival, 1968, Mich. Water Color Soc., Detroit, 1970, Am. Water Color Soc., N.Y.C., 1970, Nat. Art Club, N.Y.C., 1971, Birmingham (Ala.) Mus. of Arts, 1971, Detroit Inst. of Arts, 1976, Battle Creek Civic Art Center, Battle Creek, Mich., 1974, Carrol Reece Mus., Johnson City, Tenn., 1974, Gallery One, Petoskey, Mich., 1970; group show exhibit of sculpture includes: Scarab Club, 1971, 73, 76; represented in permanent collection: rental gallery Detroit Inst. Art; propr., dir. Muccioli Studio Gallery, Grosse Pointe Farms, Mich., 1973—. Recipient numerous awards Ford Motor Co., 1961-77, Watercolor award Lafayette Park Community Assn., 1967. Mem. Mich. Watercolor Soc. Roman Catholic. Home: 16194 Sprenger East Detroit MI 48021 Gallery: 85 Kercheval Ave Grosse Pointe Farms MI 48236

MUCHEMORE, RUTH JEANINE, hosp. adminstr., nurse; b. Blair, Nebr., Nov. 5, 1931; d. David Ziegler and Lois Lorraine (Seltz) Mummert; R.N., Clarkson Hosp. Sch. Nursing, Omaha, 1953; B.S. Nursing, U. Nebr., Omaha, 1968, M.S. in Counseling and Guidance, 1976; children by previous marriage—Kevin, Kelly, Karin. Mem. faculty in med.-surg. nursing Clarkson Hosp., Sch. Nursing, 1969-76; psychiat. nursing adminstr. VA Hosp., Omaha, 1976—; cons. gerontology, pre-retirement counseling. Del., Nebr. Republican Conv.; bd. dirs. Planned Parenthood, Omaha, 1970, Legal Aid, Omaha, 1971. Mem. Nat. League Nursing, Nat. Gerontol. Soc., Am. Personnel and Guidance Assn. Republican. Home: 2521 Brookside Ave Omaha NE 68124 Office: 4101 Woolworth St Omaha NE 68105

MUCHOW, ROBERT LOUIS, mgmt. cons. co. exec.; b. Sioux City, Iowa, Aug. 3, 1917; s. Frank Henry and Ella May (Peterson) M.; student U. S.D., 1936-37, U. Minn., 1937-38; B.B.A., U. Chgo., 1939; m. Helen Lucille Frisch, Feb. 28, 1942; children—David Allen, James Louis. Auditor, Arthur Andersen & Co., Chgo., 1939-41; prodn. mgr. Automatic Electric Co., Northlake, Ill., 1941-59; exec. v.p. Malco-Mandex Mfg. Co., Chgo., 1959-62; exec. v.p. Graphic Mgmt. Services, Elmhurst, Ill., 1962—, also dir.; dir. Control-O-Gram Bldg.

Corp., Elgin Sweeper Co., Templeton-Kenly Co. Asst. dir. communication equipment div. War Prodn. Bd., Washington, 1944; dist. chmn. United Appeal, Northlake, Ill., 1948-49; chmn. bldg. com. N.W. Community Hosp., Rolling Meadows, Ill., 1958-59. Mem. Nat. Assn. Cost Accountants, Nat. Soc. Pub. Accountants, Prodn. Control Mgmt. Assn. Republican. Lutheran. Clubs: Inverness Golf, Plum Grove, Meadow. Contbr. articles to profl. jours. Home: 377 E Briarwood Ln Palatine IL 60067 Office: 102 Haven Rd Elmhurst IL 50126

MUCKERMAN, DAVID KEVIN, city engr.; b. St. Louis, July 11, 1953; s. William V. and Annabel (Rubottom) M.; B.S. in Civil Engring., U. Mo., Rolla, 1975, postgrad. civil engring., 1978—; m. A. Catherine Seidler, Sept. 13, 1975. With City of Dodge City, Kans., 1975—, asst. city engr., 1975—. Mem. ASCE, Ducks Unltd. Roman Catholic. Clubs: Ford County Sportsman's, Southside Conservation. Home: #4 Southbrook Rolla MO 65401

MUDGE, WILLIAM ALBERT, JR., physician; b. Mpls., Nov. 23, 1917; s. Dr. William Albert and Elizabeth (Martins) M.; B.S., Northwestern U., 1940; M.D., Med. Coll. Wis., 1944; m. Faith MacDade, Sept. 6, 1956; children—Jane, Mary, Ann, Susan, William Albert III. Resident, Hines (Ill.) VA Hosp., 1949-53; sec. pres., dir. Physicians Park, Inc., 1958—; asso. clin. prof. medicine Marquette U., Milw., 1959-72; adj. prof. clin. medicine No. Mich. U., 1975—; staff Milwaukee County Gen. Hosp., 1959-72. Mem. cancer study group Wis. Regional Med. Program, 1969-72; mem. Wis. Gov.'s Task Force on Edn., 1970-71; mem. exec. com. and bd. United Migrant Opportunity Service, Inc., 1964-68; mem. north central regional adv. com. Upper Peninsula Health Systems Agy., Inc., 1977—; mem. Marquette City Commn. on Aging, 1977—. Served as capt. M.C., USAAF, 1945-47. Mem. Wis. Heart Assn., Kenosha Anti Tb Assn. (v.p. 1958-60, dir. 1957-62), A.M.A., Mich., Marquette med. socs., Upper Peninsula Areawide Comprehensive Health Planning Assn. (dir. 1975), Am. Soc. Internal Medicine, Am. Coll. Physicians (asso.). Episcopalian (vestryman 1963-66, 74-77). Rotarian (pres. 1958-59). Home: 419 E Arch St Marquette MI 49855

MUDIE, HERBERT CLARK, coll. dean; b. New Haven, Apr. 20, 1941; s. James McAsh and Eleanor North (Holt) M.; A.B. in History, St. Lawrence U., Canton, N.Y., 1963; postgrad. N.Y.U., 1964, Harvard U., U. Maine, Orono; m. Betsy Marie Parrish, Aug. 2, 1975. Tchr., coach Jonathan Law High Sch., Milford, Conn., 1963-64; asst. dir. admissions Waynesburg (Pa.) Coll., 1964-66; asst. dir. admissions and financial aid Yale U., 1966-67; dir. admissions, then dean admissions Randolph-Macon Women's Coll., Lynchburg, Va., 1970-75; mem. faculty Inst. Coll. Admissions, Harvard U., summer 1972; dean admissions and financial aid Stephens Coll., Columbia, Mo., 1975—; instl. tester Ednl. Testing Service, Coll. Entrance Exam. Bd.; bd. dirs. Coll. Bound, Inc., 1970—; mem. bd. higher edn., adv. com. admissions and recruiting United Methodist Ch., 1973-75. Pres. Forest Brook II Homeowners Assn., 1975; bd. dirs. Family Service Columbia, 1976-77. Served with AUS, 1967-70. Decorated Army Commendation medal. Mem. Nat. Assn. Coll. Admissions Counselors (chmn. sch. and coll. conf. com. 1971-72, chmn. nat. coll. day 1973, chmn. spl. interests sessions 1975), Am. Assn. Collegiate Registrars and Admissions Officers, Am. Assn. Higher Edn., Am. Personnel and Guidance Assn., Am. Coll. Personnel Assn., Nat. Assn. Prins. Schs. Girls (chmn. sch. and higher edn. com. 1974-75), Nat. Assn. Ind. Schs., European Council Internat. Schs. (chmn. com. coll. entrance 1976-78), Am. Assn. Univ. Adminstrs., Women's Ind. Colls. (treas. 1972—), Nat. Assn. Fgn. Student Affairs. Episcopalian. Club: Lions Home: 10 Westwood Ave Columbia MO 65201 Office: Box 2121 Stephens Coll Columbia MO 65201

MUEHRCKE, ROBERT CARL, physician, educator; b. Cin., Aug. 4, 1921; s. Bernhard and Otelia (Drazdik) M.; M.S., M.D., U. Ill.; postgrad. U. London (Eng.); m. JoAnn A. Madenwalt, June 18, 1972. Intern, Cin. Gen. Hosp., 1952-53; resident in internal medicine U. Ill., 1953-55; faculty Rush Med. Coll., Chgo., 1972—, prof. medicine, 1976—; practice medicine specializing in internal medicine, Chgo., 1956—; attending physician West Suburban Hosp.; cons. Presbyn.-St. Luke's; cons. in field. Served with 96th. inf. div. U.S. Army, World War II. Decorated Combat Inf. Badge, Purple Heart with 3 oak clusters, Bronze Star with clusters. Diplomate Am. Bd. Internal Medicine, Am. Bd. Nutrition. Mem. Chgo. Med. Soc. (pres. Aux Plaines br. 1972-73), Chgo. Soc. Internal Medicine (v.p. 1976-77), A.C.P. (chmn. 54th. ann. session Chgo. 1973). Author books: contbr. articles to profl. publs. Home: 12 Croydon Ln Oak Brook IL 60521

MUELLER, BRUCE ANTHONY, employee benefits adminstr.; b. LaSalle, Ill., Jan. 6, 1947; s. Joseph William and Sally Marie (Lesczyinski) M.; B.B.A., Loyola U., Chgo., 1968, M.B.A., 1974; m. Genevieve T. Molinari, Dec. 16, 1967; children—Margaret, Kristen. Systems analyst Johnson & Johnson, Chgo., 1968-69, Hammond Organ Co., Chgo., 1969-70; sr. mgr. EDP and telecommunications Blue Cross Assn., Chgo., 1972-73, dir. adminstrv. services, 1973-75, sr. dir. nat. employee benefit adminstrn., 1975-77; dir. employee benefits financing G.D. Searle & Co., 1977—; v.p., dir. Plum Grove Non-Profit Orgn.; instr. Harper Coll., Palatine, Ill. Mem. Assn. Systems Mgmt. Clubs: Plum Grove Tennis and Swim, Arlington Park Tennis. Home: 1099 King Charles Ct Palatine IL 60067 Office: Box 1045 Skokie IL 60676

MUELLER, DON SHERIDAN, sch. adminstr.; b. Cleve., Nov. 4, 1927; s. Don P. and Selma Christina (Ungericht) M.; B.S., Mt. Union Coll., 1948; M.A., U. Mich., 1952; Ed.S., Mich. State U., 1968; Ph.D., Am. Internat. U., 1977; m. Vivian Jean Santrock, Aug. 27, 1947; children—Carl Frederick, Cathy Ann. Tchr., Benton-Harbor and Fair Plain (Mich.) Schs., 1947-52; dir. music edn. Okemos (Mich.) Pub. Schs., 1952-64; jr-sr. high prin. Dansville (Mich.) Schs., 1964-68; prin. DeWitt (Mich.) High Sch., 1968-73; supt. Carsonville-Port Sanilac Schs., Carsonville, Mich., 1973—. Recipient Community Leader of Am. award, 1968, 72, 73-74; Acad. Am. Educators award, 1973-74. Mem. Am., Mich. assns. sch. adminstrs., Mich. Assn. Sch. Bds., NEA, Assn. Supervision and Curriculum Devel., Clinton Prins. Assn. (pres. 1972-73), Ingham Prins. Assn. (pres. 1967-70), Mich. Sch. Band/Orch. Assn. (sec. 1962-63, pres. dist. 5 1958-60), Okemos Edn. Assn. (pres. 1962-63). Contbr. article to profl. jour. Home: 188 S High St Carsonville MI 48419 Office: 100 N Goetze Carsonville MI 48419

MUELLER, HERBERT A., clergyman; b. Lone Elm, Mo., June 2, 1914; s. John H. and Anna (Vetter) M.; grad. Concordia Coll., Milw., 1934, Concordia Sem., St. Louis, 1938, D.D., 1976; LL.D., Concordia Coll., Seward, Nebr., 1966; m. Elfrieda Rische, May 20, 1939; children—Susanne (Mrs. Leslie Engstrom), Thomas Mueller, Joanne. Ordained to ministry Luth. Ch., 1940; pastor Trinity Luth. Ch., Lombard, Ill., 1940-43. Bethlehem Luth. Ch., Dundee, Ill., 1943-69. Sec. No. Ill. Dist., Luth. Ch.-Mo. Synod, 1951-65; sec. Luth. Ch.-Mo. Synod, 1965—. Vice pres. Luth. Council in the U.S.A., 1973-76, sec., 1976—, consultation on Luth. Unity, 1972-75. Mem. bd. for higher edn., 1960-65, bd. dir., 1965—, mem. commn. on constl. matters, 1965—. Bd. dirs. Community Chest, 1962-69. Home: 6219 Alamo St Louis MO 63105 Office: 500 N Broadway St Louis MO 63102

MUELLER, HERBERT RODD, optometrist; b. Lakewood, Ohio, July 20, 1927; s. Robert Ernest and Anita Virginia (Rodd) M.; student Wayne State U., 1945-47; O.D. cum laude, Northern Ill. Coll. Optometry, 1949; m. Rebecca J. O'Toole, Nov. 29, 1952; children—Gregory, Marcia, Valerie. Practice optometry, Lansing, Mich., 1951-56, Lowell, Mich., 1956—; pres. Glide-eez Mfg. Co., 1962-68; pres. Mich. Optometric Realty Exploration, Inc., 1969-75. Councilman, mayor pro-tem, Lowell, 1970-75. Chmn. Barrier Free Design Bd. State of Mich., 1974—; bd. dirs. Royal Residential Center, 1977—. Mem. Am., Mich. (treas. 1963-68, Keyman award 1968) optometric assns., Cherry Home Assn. (dir. 1968-72), Tomb and Key, Beta Sigma Kappa. Lion (past pres.). Home: 216 Riverside Dr Lowell MI 49331 Office: 1125 W Main St Lowell MI 49331

MUELLER, JOHN CARL, found. exec.; b. Toropy, Rio Grande de Sol, Brazil, Nov. 9, 1911; s. Reinhold John and Natalie (Boettcher) M.; came to U.S., 1913; A.B., Valparaiso U., 1935; M.A., Ind. U., 1942; m. Lillian Oetting, Apr. 30, 1938; children—Ann Elizabeth (Mrs. Thomas W. Lees), Todd Arnold, Jean Louise (Mrs. Thomas M. Nelson), Marilyn Flora. Asst. probation officer Juvenile Ct., Indpls., 1941-43, 47-48; field dir. A.R.C., Ft. Knox, Ky., 1943-44; dir. Marion County (Ind.) Welfare Dept., 1948-51; asst. dir. San Diego County (Calif.) Dept. Pub. Welfare, 1951-52, acting dir., 1952, dir., 1952-57; with Equitable Life Assurance Soc., San Diego, 1957-59; social service dir. Bethesda Luth. Home for Mentally Retarded, Watertown, Wis., 1959-63; exec. dir. Beverly Farm Found., home and tng. center for mentally retarded, Godfrey, Ill., 1963—; asso. prof. San Diego State U., 1956-57. Chmn. nat. commn. for mentally retarded Luth. Ch.-Mo. Synod, 1970. Chmn. bd. Salvation Army, Alton-Wood River, Ill., 1971-73; bd. dirs. YMCA, Alton, Ill., 1970-71. Served to lt. USNR, 1944-46. Mem. Madison County Assn. Retarded Children (chpt. v.p. 1975), Nat. Assn. Pvt. Residential Facilities for Mentally Retarded (dir. 1975, chmn. awards com. 1975), Am. Assn. Mental Deficiency. Lion. Home: 516 Summit St Alton IL 62002 Office: Beverly Farm Humbert Rd Godfrey IL 62035

MUELLER, ROLAND FREDERICK, surgeon; b. St. Joseph, Mo., Aug. 29, 1905; s. Charles Frederick and Elizabeth (Krebs) M.; A.A., Kansas City (Mo.) U., 1925; student Kans. U., 1926; M.D. cum laude, Washington U., 1929; m. children—Nancy (Mrs. Robert H. Pecha), Judith (Mrs. Roger W. Hall), Kathryn Lucile. Intern, resident surgery Barnes Hosp., St. Louis, 1929-33; instr. surgery Washington U., 1930-33; practice surgery, Canton, Mo., 1933-37; chief surgeon Two Harbors (Minn.) Hosp., 1937-46, also asso. chief surgeon Duluth, Mesabi & Iron Range R.R., 1937-46; practice surgery, Lincoln, Nebr., 1949—; attending surgeon St. Elizabeth's Hosp., Bryan Meml. Hosp.; prof. surgery Creighton U.; cons. surgeon U.P.R.R., VA Hosp., Lincoln; pres. Lincoln Community Blood Bank, 1976. Pres. States Oil Royalty Co. U.S. del. 7th Inter-Am. Congress Surgery, Peru, 1950. Recipient 25 Year Faculty award Creighton U. Fellow A.C.S.; mem. Central Surg. Assn., Southwestern Surg. Congress, Internat. Soc. Surgery, Peruvian Acad. Surgery (hon.), Am. Thyroid Assn., AMA, Nebr. State, Lancaster County (pres. 1977) med. assns., Phi Beta Pi, Alpha Omega Alpha. Clubs: University (Lincoln); Washington University (St. Louis). Contbr. articles to profl jours. Home: 1000 Fall Creek Rd Lincoln NE 68510 Office: 5440 South St Suite 1700 Lincoln NE 68506

MUELLER, WILLYS FRANCIS, JR., pathologist; b. Detroit, July 15, 1934; s. Willys Francis and Antoinette Frances (Stimac) M.; M.D., U. Mich., 1959; m. Dolores Mae Vella, Aug. 25, 1956; children—Renee Ann, Willys Francis, Paul E., Mark A., Maria D., Beth M., Matthew P. Intern, Providence Hosp., Detroit, 1959-60, resident, 1960-62; resident Wayne County Gen. Hosp., Eloise, Mich., 1962-64; asst. pathologist Grace Hosp., Detroit, 1964; asso. pathologist Hurley Hosp., Flint, Mich., 1964-66, Hurley Med. Center, Flint, 1968—; chief dep. med. examiner Genesee County, Mich., 1971—; pres. Pathology Assos. Inc.; asst. clin. prof. Coll. Human Medicine, Mich. State U. Served with M.C., U.S. Army, 1966-68. Fellow Am. Soc. Clin. Pathologists, Coll. Am. Pathologists, Am. Acad. Forensic Scis.; mem. AMA (Physician's Recognition award 1974-77), Genesee County, Mich. State med. socs., Mich. Soc. Pathologists, Nat. Assn. Med. Examiners. Republican. Roman Catholic. Club: K.C. Editor: Bulletin of the Genesee County Medical Society. Home: 13335 Pomona Dr Fenton MI 48430 Office: Dept Pathology Hurley Med Center Flint MI 48502

MUFFLY, ROBERT BENTON, psychiatrist, educator; b. Lincoln, Nebr., Feb. 2, 1928; s. Harold Benton and Madge May (Boyce) M.; B.A., Nebr. Wesleyan U., 1949; M.D., U. Nebr., 1952; m. Margaret Anne Cleary, Jan. 15, 1977; children—Kirk, Karl, Kimberly, Kathleen. Intern, U. Tex. Med. Br., Galveston, 1952-53; resident in psychiatry Nebr. Psychiat. Inst., Omaha, 1953-58; instr. to asso. prof. psychiatry U. Nebr., Omaha, 1959—, asso. prof. internal medicine, 1967—; practice medicine specializing in psychiatry, Omaha, 1971—; mem. Health Advisory Bd. Nebr. Dept. Motor Vehicles. Served to capt. M.C., U.S. Army, 1955-57. Diplomate Am. Bd. Psychiatry and Neurology. Fellow Am. Psychiatric Assn. (del., mem. exec. com.); mem. AAAS, Am. Psychosomatic Soc., Central Neuropsychiat. Assn., Nebr. Soc. Neurology and Psychiatry (sec.-treas. 1961-65), Nebr. Mental Health Assn. (dir. 1971-74), Nebr. State Med. Assn. (mem. com. on mental health, mental retardation), Omaha-Douglas County Med. Soc. (mem. peer rev. com. 1971—). Episcopalian. Contbr. articles in field to profl. jours. Home: 8707 William St Omaha NE 68124 Office: 8300 Dodge St Suite 220 Omaha NE 68114

MUGALIAN, ROBERT HAIG, dentist; b. Chgo., Apr. 4, 1922; s. Levon Bedros and Grace (Bynderian) M.; B.S., Northwestern U., 1944, D.D.S., 1949; m. Lillian Najarian, June 9, 1956; 1 son, Brian Pearce. Individual practice dentistry, Chgo., 1949-76, Evanston, Ill., 1977—; mem. faculty Northwestern U. Dental Sch., 1951-53; research cons. dept. research Mercy Hosp. and Med. Center, Chgo., 1974—, mem. human research com., 1976—; mem. asso. staff St. Francis Hosp., Evanston. Served to lt. (j.g.) USNR, 1943-46. Fellow Ill. Dental Soc.; mem. Chgo. Dental Soc., Am. Dental Assn., Community Renewal Soc., G.V. Black Soc., Delta Sigma Delta (asst. dep. supreme grand master 1952-61). Congregationalist (chmn. bd. deacons 1953-55). Contbr. articles to profl. jours. Home: 3118 Big Tree Lane Wilmette IL 60091 Office: 800 Austin St Evanston IL 60202

MUGFORD, ALFRED GEORGE, machine co. exec.; b. Everett, Mass., Sept. 7, 1928; s. James and Emmie (Boone) M.; B.S., Bentley Coll., 1950; m. Dorothy E. Yetman, July 16, 1949; children—Janet Anne Sprague, Nancy Anne, George Edward. With Jerguson Gage & Valve Co., Burlington, Mass., 1947-63, controller, 1963-64; treas., controller Sarco Co., Inc., Allentown, Pa., 1964-66; v.p. fin. Whitin Machine Works, Whitinsville, Mass., 1966-67, vice pres.-gen. mgr., 1967-68, corp. staff, 1968; with White Consol. Industries, Cleve., 1963—, corp. staff, div. v.p., group v.p., 1969-76, exec. v.p., 1976—; v.p. Aetna-Standard, Pa., Blaw-Knox Equipment, Pa., Duraloy Blaw-Knox, Pa., Copes-Vulcan, Inc., Pa., Blaw-Knox Co., others; dir. Fundicion Nodular, S.A., Spain, Wirz Y Machuca, S.A., Mex., Duraloy Blaw-Knox, Scottdale, Pa. Chmn. Burlington Fin. Bd., 1958-62, New Bldg. and Capital Fund Raising Com., 1960-63. Mem. Burlington Jr. C. of C. (charter mem., v.p. 1956-58). Presbyterian (chmn. bd. trustees fellowship 1961-63). Clubs: Lions; Avon Oaks Country (pres.) (Ohio); Duquesne (Pitts.). Home: 30529 Ednil Dr Bay Village OH 44140 Office: 11770 Berea Rd Cleveland OH 44111

MUHN, ROBERT ALAN, automotive engr.; b. Auburn, Ind., Nov. 14, 1942; s. Pery Arthur and Anna Manerva (Zimmerman) M.; B.S., Purdue U., 1968; m. Susan Kay Korn, June 25, 1966; 1 dau., Tami Ann. With Gen. Electric Co., Ft. Wayne, Ind., 1961-69; mgmt. trainee Internat. Harvester Co., Ft. Wayne, 1969; asst. chief engr. Superior Ball Joint Co., New Haven, Ind., 1969-72; chief engr. Superior Linkage, New Haven, 1972-77; dir. engring. Gripco Co. div. Mite Corp., South Whitley, Ind., 1977—. Bd. dirs. Soap Box Derby, Ft. Wayne, 1972-73. Mem. Ft. Wayne Jaycees (Key Man award 1975, pres. 1975-76), Ft. Wayne C. of C., Soc. Mfg. Engrs., Soc. Automotive Engrs. Republican. Lutheran. Clubs: Filmm Stock, Purdue Alumni, Acacia. Contbr. articles in field to profl. jours. Home: 918 Reed Rd Fort Wayne IN 46815 Office: PO Box 97 Montpelier IN 47359

MUHRER, MERLE EDWARD, biochemist, educator; b. Clark County, Mo., Aug. 5, 1913; s. Henry Victor and Elizabeth Belle (McLaughlin) M.; B.S., N.E. Mo. State U., 1935; M.A., U. Mo.-Columbia, 1940, Ph.D., 1944; m. Madaline Acklie, Feb. 4, 1939; children—Verle, Darryl, Merlin, Henry. Tchr. high sch. sci., Kahoka, Mo., 1935-39; asso. prof. chemistry N.W. Mo. State U., Kirksville, 1941-43; mem. faculty U. Mo.-Columbia, 1943—, prof. biochemistry, 1950—, chmn. dept., 1954-67, cons. to univ. dir. research, 1967—. Pres. Columbia Community Improvement Assn., 1969-72. Friends of Rocheport Hist. Soc., 1972-73; 4-H Club project leader, 1950-65. Mem. Strawn Bd. Edn., 1946-68; pres. Boone County Sch. Bd., 1956-68. Bd. dirs. Pachyderms, Columbia YMCA, Nat. Thrombosis Council. Recipient Grim award N.E. Mo. State Coll., 1935. Curators scholar, 1936; Markle grantee, 1944. Mem. Am. Chem. Soc. (past pres. Mo. div.), Gamma Sigma Delta (past pres.). Mem. United Ch. of Christ (pres. men's club 1970). Kiwanian. Club: U. Mo.-Columbia Faculty. Contbr. articles to profl. jours. Co-author: Zinc Metabolism, 1966. Patentee in field. Home: 3009 I-70 Dr NW Columbia MO 65201

MUIRHEAD, VINCENT URIEL, aerospace engr., educator; b. Dresden, Kans., Feb. 6, 1919; s. John Hadsell and Lily Irene (McKinney) M.; B.S., U.S. Naval Acad., 1941; B.S. in Aero. Engring., U.S. Postgrad. Sch., 1948; Aero. Engr., Calif. Inst. Tech., 1949; postgrad. U. Ariz., 1962, 64, Okla. State U., 1963; m. Bobby Jo Thompson, Nov. 5, 1943; children—Rosalind, Jean, Juleigh. Midshipman, U.S. Navy, 1937, commd. ensign, 1941, advanced through grades to comdr., 1951; nav. officer U.S.S. White Plains, 1945-46; comdr. Fleet Aircraft Service Squad, 1951-52; with Bur. Aeros., Ft. Worth, 1953-54; comdr. Helicopter Utility Squadron 1, Pacific Fleet, 1955-56, chief staff officer Comdr. Fleet Air, Philippines, 1956-58; exec. officer Naval Air Tech. Tng. Center, Memphis, 1958-61; ret., 1961; asst. prof. U. Kans., Lawrence, 1961-63, asso. prof. aerospace engring., 1964-76, prof., chmn. dept., 1976—; cons. Black & Veatch, cons. engrs., Kansas City, Mo., 1964—. Decorated Air Medal. Mem. Am. Inst. Aeros. and Astronautics, Am. Soc. Engring. Edn., N.Y. Acad. Scis., Sigma Gamma Tau. Mem. Ch. of Christ (elder). Author: Introduction to Aerospace, 1972; Thunderstorms, Tornadoes and Building Damage, 1975. Research on aircraft, tornado vortices, shock tubes and waves. Home: 503 Park Hill Terr Lawrence KS 66044

MUKHERJEE, SUBHASH CHANDRA, psychologist, mental health center adminstr.; b. Baraut, India, June 10, 1940; s. Panchanand and Susen (Roy) M.; came to U.S., 1965, naturalized, 1977; B.A., Rajasthan U., Jaipur, India, 1960; M.A., DePaul U., 1967; Ph.D., Ill. Inst. Tech., 1971; m. Bharoti Choudhury, May 20, 1964; children—Sunit, Sonjit. Psychologist, Jacksonville (Ill.) State Hosp., 1967-68; psychologist, chief of services Chgo. Read Mental Health Center, 1968-74; psychologist Madden Zone Center, Hines, Ill., 1974-75; exec. dir. Greene County Guidance Center, Xenia, Ohio, 1975—; asst. prof. psychology Triton Coll., River Grove, Ill., 1972-75; asst. clin. prof. Wright State Med. Sch., Dayton, Ohio, 1975—; cons. dept. psychiatry VA Hosp., Dayton, 1977—; mem. advisory bd. Dayton Mental Health Center, 1976—; mem. Greene County Health Planning Council, 1976—, Miami Valley Higher Edn. Consortium. Registered psychologist, Ill.; lic. psychologist, Ohio; diplomate Am. Bd. Profl. Psychology. Mem. Am., Ohio, psychol assns., Ohio Mental Health Adminstrs. Assn., Nat. Register of Health Service Providers in Psychology. Hindu. Author: Five Years Report of S.S.L.M. Institute, 1962; co-author: Munesh, 1963, Prabhu, 1964. Address: 1336 De Quincy Dr Xenia OH 45385

MUKHERJI, SANJIB KUMAR, environ. scientist; b. Calcutta, India, May 13, 1938; s. Ram Ch. and Anima (Bhattacharya) Mukhopadhyay; came to U.S., 1962, naturalized, 1976; B.Engring. (State Merit scholar), U. Calcutta, 1960; M.S. in Engring., 1965; Ph.D., Colo. State U., 1974; m. Jeanette Marie Kruse, June 8, 1968; children—Suneepa, Sudeepto. Engring. asst. AID, N. Delhi, India, 1961-62; project engr. JFB Research Center, Gen. Mills Co., Mpls., 1965-68; group leader air pollution control div. State of Ind., Indpls., 1974-75, chief program support br., air pollution control div., 1975—. Served with Nat. Cadet Corps, India, 1956-60. Registered profl. engr., Colo., Ind. Mem. ASME, Air Pollution Control Assn., Am. Inst. Aeros. and Astronautics, Sigma Xi. Hindu. Editor Engring. Jour. Calcutta U., 1959; contbr. articles in field to profl. jours. Home: 16 Northbrook Circle Westfield IN 46074 Office: 1330 W Michigan St Indianapolis IN 46206

MUKHOPADHYAY, ALPANA, physician. Lab. dir. Merry Thompson Hosp., Chgo.; instr. dept. pathology U. Ill. Abraham Lincoln Sch. Medicine. Fellow Coll. Am. Pathology; mem. Am. Soc. Clin. Pathology, Internat. Acad. Pathology, Chgo. Pathol. Soc., Am., Ill., Chgo. med. assns. Office: 140 N Ashland Ave Chicago IL 60607

MULARZ, STANLEY LEON, credit info. services exec.; b. Chgo., Apr. 11, 1923; s. Stanley A. and Frances (Baycar) M.; A.B., St. Louis U., 1944; M.A., De Paul U., 1956; M.B.A., U. Chgo., 1960; Ed.D. Loyola U., Chgo., 1971; m. Lillian M. Kammerer, Apr. 10, 1948; children—James P., Thomas E., Geraldine E., Joanne F., John F., Paul S., Donna M. Tchr., Benedictine Jr. Coll., Savannah, Ga., 1945-46, Grant Community High Sch., Fox Lake, Ill., 1946-47; fgn. corr. Continental Ill. Nat. Bank, 1947-48; tchr., adminstr. Morgan Park Mil. Acad. and Jr. Coll., 1948-51; mgr. Spiegel, Inc., 1951-52; regional credit mgr. Aldens, Inc., Chgo., 1952-54, ops. mgr., 1954-67, mgr. indsl. relations, 1967-68, credit div. group mgr., 1968-69; pres. Credit Info. Services Corp., 1969—; v.p. Trans Union Systems Corp., Chgo., 1972—. Chgo. Lectr., adviser on consumer edn. Mem. Gov.'s Commn. Schs./Bus. Mgmt. Task Force; chmn. State Info. Systems com., 1974—. Mem. Internat. Consumer Credit Assn. (pres. Dist. V 1975—), Mchts. Research Council (dir., treas. 1975—), Soc. Certified Consumer Credit Execs. (dir.), Am. Statis. Assn., U. Chgo. Exec. Program Club, Phi Delta Kappa (pres. chpt. 1970-71). Office: 444 N Michigan Ave Chicago IL 60611

MULCRONE, RICHARD THOMAS, state govt. ofcl.; b. St. Paul, May 23, 1934; s. Emmett Edward and Gertrude Julia (Macauley) M.; student St. Thomas Coll., St. Paul, 1952-53, 56; m. Mary Ann I. Carlin, May 10, 1958; children—Timothy S., David P., Susanna C., Dean T., Vaughn F., Perry R. Park Police patrolman, St. Paul, 1953;

roving gang worker, St. Paul, 1956-57; probation officer Carver and Scott counties, Minn., 1957-63, dir. ct. services, 1963-67, family ct. referee, 1967-73; ct. adminstr. Scott County, 1973; chmn. Minn. Corrections Authority, 1973—. Pres. Minn. Assn. County Probation Officers, 1961-63, Minn. Polygraph Assn., 1973. Del. Minn. Democratic Farm Labor Party Conv., 1962-72. Bd. dirs., pres. Catholic Athletic Assn., 1972. Served with AUS, 1953-55. K.C. Mem. Minn. Corrections Assn. (pres. 1974). Contbr. articles to profl. jours. Home: 1043 S Main St Shakopec MN 55379 Office: Suite 238 Metro Square Bldg St Paul MN 55101

MULLAN, JOSEPH DELBERT, automotive co. exec.; b. Washington, Ind., Oct. 17, 1920; s. Willis Holman and Minnie Irene (Hastings) M.; B.S., Ind. U., 1941, M.C.S., 1947; m. Jean Good, Nov. 9, 1943; children—James David, John Walter. Bus. tchr. Washington (Ind.) High Sch. and Arsenal Tech., Indpls., 1941-43; instr. accounting Ind. U., Bloomington, 1946-48; controller R.C. Graham & Sons, Washington, Ind., 1948-51; accountant George S. Olive & Co., Indpls., 1952; pvt. practice accounting, Washington, Ind., 1953; with Ford Motor Co., Dearborn, Mich., 1953—, spl. order sales mgr. Ford div., 1972—. C.P.A., Ind. Mem. Am. Inst. C.P.A.'s, Ind. Assn. C.P.A.'s, Am. Accountants Assn., Am. Inst. Mgmt., Beta Gamma Sigma, Kappa Delta Pi, Pi Gamma Mu, Pi Omega Pi, Blue Key. Club: Dearborn Country. Methodist. Home: 1060 S Gulley Rd Dearborn Heights MI 48125 Office: PO Box 1504-A Dearborn MI 48121

MULLEN, HENRY ANDREW, metallurgist; b. Adena, Ohio, June 14, 1943; s. Raymond Andrew and Ermma Gayle (Worner) M.; B.Sc., Colo. Sch. Mines, 1970. Tech. supt. refinery dept. smelting div. St. Joe Lead Co., Herculaneum, Mo., 1970-71, asst. refinery supt., 1971-73, refinery supt., 1973-75, supt. operation and maintenance air pollution control equipment Acid Plant and Baghouses, 1975—. Served with USN, 1961-66. Mem. Metall. Soc., Am. Inst. Mining, Metall. and Petroleum Engrs., Am. Soc. Metals, Am. Inst. Chem. Engrs., Colo. Sch. Mines Alumni Assn. Presbyn. Home: PO Box 657 Herculaneum MO 63048 Office: St Joe Lead Co Herculaneum MO 63048

MULLEN, JANUARIUS ARTHUR, mfg. co. exec.; b. O'Neill, Nebr., June 18, 1905; s. Arthur Francis and Mary Theresa (Dolan) M.; Ph.B., Creighton U., 1928, LL.B., 1930, LL.D., 1970; m. Exilona Luisa Hamilton, June 5, 1935; children—Francis Hamilton, Michael Ann, Mary Luisa. Admitted to Nebr. bar, 1930, D.C. bar, 1933; mem. firm Mullen & Morrisey, Omaha, 1930-34; legal adviser, asst. U.S. State Dept., Washington, 1934-35; v.p., dir. Standard Accident & Ins. Co., Detroit, 1936-64; founder Glenvale Product Corp., Detroit, 1939-51; pres. Project Constructors of Mich., Detroit, 1951-60; chmn., pres., dir. Sheller Mfg. Co., Detroit, 1961-64; chmn. bd. Sheller-Globe Corp., Detroit, 1964-72, dir., cons., 1972—. Bd. dirs, trustee, v.p. United Found., 1950-77; bd. dirs., v.p. United Community Services, 1951-61; bd. dirs. United Way of Mich., 1952—; pres. United Health Orgn., 1967-69; pres. bd. dirs. Rehab. Inst. Detroit, 1968, chmn., 1971; trustee Detroit Med. Center, 1968—; bd. dirs., vice chmn. Southeastern Mich. Transp. Authority, 1970—. Served with U.S. Army, 1942-46. Mem. Am., Nebr., D.C. bar assns., Alpha Sigma Nu. Roman Catholic. Clubs: Detroit, Recess, Country, Econ., Athletic (Detroit); Grosse Pointe, Bloomfield Hills Country; Chevy Chase (Md.); Everglades, Country of Fla. Home: 45 Dyar Ln Grosse Pointe Farms MI 48230 Office: 1641 Porter St Detroit MI 48216

MULLEN, JOHN LAWRENCE, appliance repair parts mfg. co. exec.; b. N.Y.C., Nov. 8, 1938; s. John Lawrence and Frances Catherine (Cooke) M.; B.S., magna cum laude, L.I. U., 1970; m. Constance Marie Williams, Mar. 13, 1960; children—John Lawrence, Coleen, Michael. Mem. quality assurance staff Republic Aviation Co., Farmingdale, N.Y., 1959-64, Grumman Aviation Co., Bethpage, N.Y., 1964-66; dir. purchasing Crest Mfg. Co., Syosset, N.Y., 1966-70; dir. purchasing P-G Assco, Huntington Station, N.Y., 1970—, gen. mgr. N.Y. div., 1973-75, corp. v.p., gen. mgr. Detroit div., Ferndale, Mich., 1975—. Served with USN, 1956-59. Mem. Purchasing Mgmt. Assn. Detroit, Alpha Sigma Lambda, Delta Mu Delta. Republican. Lutheran. Club: Pine Lake Country. Home: 3974 Inverness Ln West Bloomfield MI 48033 Office: 1395 Jarvis St Ferndale MI 48220

MULLEN, WILLIAM STANLEY, JR., pump co. exec.; b. Forest Hills, N.Y., Jan. 14, 1924; s. William Stanley and Kathryn Eugenia (Cumisky) M.; B.M.E., Brown U., 1944; m. Barbara E. Needels, Sept. 9, 1950; children—Priscilla Ann, Jeanne Ellen. Engr., Morris Machine Works, Baldwinsville, N.Y., 1944-46; founder, chmn. bd. Mullen Pump & Supply Co., Detroit, 1946—; dir. Chemineer, Inc., Dayton, Ohio. Mem. Birmingham (Mich.) Bd. Zoning Appeals, 1976-77, chmn., 1968, 69, 77-78. Bd. dirs. Birmingham Park Improvement Assn., 1965—; charter bd. govs. Marion High Sch., Birmingham, 1963-68. Mem. Engring. Soc. Detroit, Water Pollution Control Assn. Home: 136 Linden Rd Birmingham MI 48009 Office: 4252 N Woodward Ave Royal Oak MI 48072

MULLENDORE, JAMES MYERS, educator; b. Fort Wayne, Ind., Aug. 15, 1919; s. Harvey and Edith Aileen (Myers) M.; B.S., Northwestern U., 1941, M.A., 1942, Ph.D., 1948; m. Edith Elaine Gregg, June 6, 1942; children—Lauren G., James Myers, Richard H., Nancy E. Instr. Northwestern U., Evanston, Ill., 1944-45; asst. prof., founder, dir. Speech and Hearing Center, U. Va., Charlottesville, 1945-50, asso. prof., 1950-61; prof., chmn. div. audiology and speech pathology Vanderbilt U. Sch. Medicine, Nashville, 1961-63, dir. Bill Wilkerson Hearing and Speech Center, 1961-63; prof., coordinator speech pathology and audiology W.Va. U., Morgantown, 1963-67; prof., dir. Sch. Speech and Hearing Scis., Bradley U., Peoria, Ill. 1967-77, dean Coll. Health Scis., 1978—; ednl. cons. State Farm Mut. Ins. Co., Charlottesville, 1956-61. Bd. dirs. Va. Easter Seal Soc., 1959-61, W.Va., 1965-67. Republican city chmn., Charlottesville, Va., 1946-49. Founder Camp Woodrow Wilson Speech Camp, 1949, Camp Easter Seal, Morgantown, W.Va., 1964; co-founder Va. Hearing and Speech Found., Inc., 1958. Recipient Distinguished Service award Va. Jr. C. of C., 1952. Fellow Speech and Hearing Assn. Va. (life, co-founder 1959—, 1st pres. 1959-60), Am. Speech and Hearing Assn. (mem. legis. council 1970, 72, ethical practices bd. 1974-78); mem. Va. Jr. C. of C. (nat. dir. 1951-52; state pres. 1952-53), W. Va. Speech And Hearing Assn. (pres. 1965-66), Ill. Speech and Hearing Assn. (mem. exec. com. 1968-72, pres. 1973-74), Speech Assn. Eastern States (exec. council 1955-57), Sigma Alpha Epsilon, Phi Kappa Phi. Rotarian. Contbr. articles to profl. jours. Home: 203 W Northgate Peoria IL 61614 Office: Coll Health Scis Bradley U Peoria IL 61625

MULLER, HERMAN JOSEPH, historian; b. Cleve., Apr. 7, 1909; s. Joseph John and Julia (Zwilling) M.; Lit.B., Xavier U., Cin., 1932; M.A., Loyola U., Chgo., 1936, Ph.D. in History, 1950; S.T.L., St. Louis U., 1942. Joined S.J., Roman Cath. Ch., 1928, ordained priest, 1941; instr. history Xavier U., 1943-47, Loyola U., Chgo., 1950-52; asst. prof. John Carroll U., Cleve., 1952-56; mem. faculty U. Detroit, 1956—, prof. history, since 1963, chmn. dept., 1959-67; centennial historian, 1976-77; vis. lectr. Univ. Coll., Dublin, 1968-69, 71-72, Univ. Coll., Cork, 1974-75. Grantee Chgo. province S.J., 1947-50. Mem. Am. Hist. Assn., Am. Cath. Hist. Assn., Mich. Acad. Arts Scis., Phi Alpha Theta, Alpha Sigma Nu. Club: Town and Country (Detroit). Author: The University of Detroit, 1877-1977, A Centennial History, 1976; also articles, revs. Address: Univ Detroit 4001 W McNichols Rd Detroit MI 48221

MULLER, JOHN BARTLETT, educator; b. Port Jefferson, N.Y., Nov. 8, 1940; s. Frederick Henry and Estelle May (Reeve) M.; A.B., U. Rochester, 1962; student Westminster Sem., 1962-63; M.S., Purdue U., 1968, Ph.D., 1975; m. Barbara Ann Schmidt, May 30, 1964 (dec. Sept. 1971). Asst. prof. psychology, dir. research, div. chmn. Roberts Wesleyan Coll., Rochester, N.Y., 1964-65, 67-70; vis. asst. prof. Wabash Coll., Crawfordsville, Ind., 1970-71; research asso. Ind.-Purdue U., Indpls., 1971-72; asso. prof. psychology, div. chmn., dir. instl. research Hillsdale Coll. (Mich.), 1972—, v.p. for academic affairs, 1976—. NIMH fellow, 1963-64; Townsend fellow, 1962. Mem. A.A.A.S., Assn. Instl. Research, Am. Sci. Assn., Am. Assn. Higher Edn., Phi Beta Kappa, Phi Kappa Phi. Contbr. articles to profl. jours. Home: 133 Lake Pleasant Rd Osseo MI 49266 Office: Hillsdale Coll Hillsdale MI 49242

MULLER, SIGFRID AUGUSTINE, dermatologist; b. Panama City, Panama, Feb. 20, 1930; s. Luis and Marciana (Espino) M.; came to U.S., 1932, naturalized, 1967; A.B., Pepperdine U., 1949; M.D., St. Louis U., 1953; M.S., Mayo Grad. Sch. Medicine, 1958; m. Jane Barbara Zierden, Dec. 28, 1964; children—Sigfrid Augustine, Stephen, Scott, Maria. Intern, Gorgas Hosp., Canal Zone, 1953-54; resident Indpls. Hosp., 1954-55, Mayo Grad. Sch. Medicine, 1955-58; practice medicine, specializing dermatology, Rochester, Minn., 1961—; cons. dermatology Mayo Clinic, Rochester, Minn., 1961—; asst. prof. dermatology U. Panama, 1958-60; prof. dermatology Mayo Clinic Med. Sch., Rochester, Minn., 1972—. Dir. task force for genetics Nat. Program for Genetics, 1969; bd. dirs., treas. Found. for Internat. Dermatologic Edn., 1976—. Recipient Pres.'s award, Pepperdine U., 1973. Fellow A.C.P.; mem. Am. Dermatological Assn, Am. Acad. Dermatology, Soc. of Investigative Dermatology, Am. Soc. Human Genetics, Am. Soc. Dermatopathology, AAAS, AMA, Am. Fedn. Clin. Research, Minn. Dermatological Soc. (pres. 1972-73), Soc. Dermatologic Genetics (pres. 1972-73), Noah Worcester Dermatologic Soc. (pres. 1972-73), Internat. Soc. Tropical Dermatology (v.p. 1974—). Contbr. articles to profl. jours. Asst. chief editor Archives of Dermatology, 1972-74. Editorial bd. Archives of Dermatology, 1974—; Medicina Cutanea, 1968—; Internat. Bull. Psoriasis, 1973—. Home: 24 Skyline Dr Rochester MN 55901 Office: 200 1st St SW Rochester MN 55901

MULLIGAN, BARBARA E., coll. adminstr.; b. Grand Rapids, Mich., June 25, 1927; d. Raymond Christopher and Gertrude (Moran) Mulligan; B.A., Marquette U., 1962, M.A., 1964. Instr. polit. sci., asst. dir. continuing edn. Alverno Coll., Milw., 1966-68, dir. continuing edn., 1968-71, asst. dean, 1971-72, co-dir. Research Center on Women, 1970-72; asst. dir. Div. Continuing Edn. Marquette U., 1972-74, asso. dir. Div. Continuing Edn. and Summer Sessions, 1974—. Mem. Govs. Commn. Status of Women, 1967-71; govs. appointee Wis. Ednl. Approval Bd., 1968-71. First vice chmn. Wis. Women's Republican Club, 1964-68. Bd. dirs. Greater Milw. chpt. ARC, 1973-74, also personnel com., community services programs com. Mem. Adult Edn. Assn. Wis. (dir. 1969-71, 75-77), Wis. Polit. Sci. Assn., (treas. 1970-72), Milw. Council Adult Learning, Wis. Soc. Health and Tng., Nat. Univ. Extension Assn., Marquette U. Alumni Assn., AAUW, Am. Assn. Univ. Adminstrs. (dir. Delta chpt. 1975-76), Am. Assn. Higher Edn., Nat. Trust Historic Preservation, Smithsonian Assos., Phi Delta Kappa. Home: 2703 N Hackett Ave Milwaukee WI 53211

MULLIGAN, THOMAS JAMES, ednl. adminstr.; b. Aurora, Ill., June 25, 1932; s. Thomas Francis and Clare Magdalene (Mateas) M.; B.A., St. Ambrose Coll., 1953; m. Frances Mildred Moore, Dec. 31, 1960; children—Michael Thomas, Mary Frances. Reporter Davenport (Iowa) Times, 1956; dir. news, asso. dir. devel. St. Ambrose Coll., Davenport, 1956-60; dir. devel. Chaminade Coll. Honolulu, 1960-65; dep. dir. pub. info. East-West Center, Honolulu, 1965; dir. devel. St. Procopius Coll., Lisle Ill., 1966-67, St. Dominic Coll., St. Charles, Ill., 1967-68, Univ. Sch. Milw., 1968-76, Pembroke Country Day Sch., Kansas City, Mo., 1976—. Membership com. Central YMCA, Milw., 1973-76. Served with AUS, 1954-56. Recipient George Washington Honor Medal, Freedoms Found., 1964. Mem. Council for Advancement and Support of Edn., Pub. Relations Soc. Am., Nat. Soc. Fund Raisers, Indsl. Editors Hawaii (pres. 1965). Roman Catholic (mem. parish council 1973-76, pres. 1975-76, adv. bd. Cath. Social Service, Honolulu, 1962-65). Moose. Home: 4405 W 78th St Shawnee Mission KS 66208

MULLIKEN, ROBERT SANDERSON, educator; b. Newburyport, Mass., June 7, 1896; s. Samuel Parsons and Katherine (Mulliken) M.; B.S., Mass. Inst. Tech., 1917; Ph.D., U. Chgo., 1921; Sc.D. (hon.), Columbia, 1939, Marquette U., Cambridge U., 1967, Gustavus Adolphus Coll., 1975; Ph.D. (hon.), Stockholm U., 1960; m. Mary Helen von Noé, Dec. 24, 1929 (dec. Mar. 1975); children—Lucia Maria (Mrs. John P. Heard), Valerie Noé. Research on war gases, Washington, 1917-18; tech. research with N.J. Zinc Co., 1919; research on separation isotopes, 1920-22; researches on molecular spectra and molecular structure, 1923—. Nat. research fellow U. Chgo., 1921-23, Harvard, 1923-25; asst. prof. physics Washington Sq. Coll. (N.Y. U.), 1926-28; asso. prof. physics U. Chgo., 1928-31, prof. physics, 1931-61, Ernest DeWitt Burton Distinguished Service prof., 1956-61, Distinguished Service prof. physics and chemistry, 1961—; Distinguished Research prof. chem. physics Fla. State U., 1965-71. Baker lectr. Cornell U. 1960; vis. prof. Bombay, 1962, Indian Inst. Tech., Kanpur, 1962; Silliman lectr. Yale, 1965; Jan Van Geuns vis. prof. Amsterdam U., 1965. J.S. Guggenheim fellow for European study, 1930, 32; leave of absence, 1942-45, as dir. information div. Plutonium Project at Chgo.; editor Plutonium Project Record in Nat. Nuclear Energy Series. Fulbright research fellow for research at Oxford, 1952-53; vis. fellow St. John's Coll., Oxford, 1952-53; sci. attaché Am. embassy, London, 1955. Served with C.W.S., U.S. Army, 1918. Recipient medal U. Liege, 1948; Gilbert N. Lewis medal Calif. sect. Am. Chem. Soc., 1960, Theodore W. Richards medal Northeastern sect., 1960, Peter Debye award Am. Chem. Soc., 1963, J.G. Kirkwood award New Haven sect., 1964, Willard Gibbs medal Chgo. sect., 1965; Nobel prize for chemistry, 1966. Fellow Am. Phys. Soc. (chmn. div. chem. physics 1951-52), A.A.A.S.; hon. fellow Indian Nat. Acad. Sci., London Chem. Soc.; mem. Nat. Acad. Scis., Am. Philos. Soc., Am. Chem. Soc., Internat. Acad. Quantum Molecular Sci., Am. Acad. Arts and Scis., Royal Soc. (fgn. mem.), Soc. de Chimie Physique (hon.), Royal Soc. Sci. of Liège (corr.), Royal Irish Acad. (hon.), Chem. Soc. Japan (hon.), Gamma Alpha. Clubs: Quadrangle; Cosmos (Washington). Home: 5825 S Dorchester Ave Chicago IL 60637

MULLIN, KENNETH RAY, architect; b. Kenosha, Wis., Oct. 6, 1936; s. Wilbur Aaron and Ella H. (Lockwitz) M.; B.Arch., Iowa State U., 1959; m. Shirley Marie Meyers, May 11, 1963; children—Matthew John, Amanda Michels. Architect Holabird & Root, Chgo., 1959, Skidmore Owings & Merrill, Chgo., 1960-69, participating asso., 1964; project mgr. Metz Train Olson & Youngren, Inc., Chgo., 1969—, asso., 1970-74, prin., 1974—. Lectr. Dept. Architecture, U. Ill., Urbana, 1971; dir. Chgo. Bldg. Congress, 1977-80; Chmn. constrn. div. Chgo. Heart Fund, 1972-73. Profl. adv. bd. Dept. Architecture, Iowa State U., Ames, 1971—, chmn., 1972—. Served to capt. C.E., AUS, 1959-60. Mem. Am. Inst. Architects, Ill Hosp. Assn., Am. Hosp. Assn., Alpha Tau Omega, Chgo. Athletic Assn. Home: 110 Joyce Pl Park Ridge IL 60068 Office: 1 E Wacker Dr Chicago IL 60601

MULLIN, PATRICIA EVELYN, lawyer; b. Dubuque, Iowa, Aug. 13, 1926; d. Cornelius Edward and Isabelle Julia (Healey) Mullin; B.A., Clarke Coll., 1948; J.D., DePaul U., 1959. Admitted to Iowa bar, 1960, Ill. bar, 1960; with Bankers Life & Casualty Co., Chgo., 1961—, corporate and litigation atty., 1962—; sec. Datronics, Inc., Brookshore Co., Mailers, Inc., Precision Dynamics Corp., Rondat, Inc., Nat. Drilling Co.; treas. Simi Valley Devel. Corp.; dir. Ponderosa Ga. Corp., Ponderosa Fibres Am., Inc., Ponderosa Tenn. Corp., B.J. Fibres, Inc. Chmn. com. to select outstanding supervisory employee of yr. Chgo. Fed. Exec. Bd., 1971. Mem. Women's Bar Assn. Ill. (pres. 1970-71), Cath. Lawyers Guild Chgo. (gov. 1971). Office: 4444 W Lawrence Ave Chicago IL 60630

MULLINS, RICHARD AUSTIN, chem. engr.; b. Seelyville, Ind., Apr. 22, 1918; s. Fred A. and Ethel (Zenor) M.; B.S. in Chem. Engring., Rose Poly. Inst., 1940; postgrad. Yale, 1942-43; m. Margaret Ann Dellacca, Nov. 27, 1946; children—Scott Alan, Mark Earl. Chemist, Ayrshire Collieries Corp., Brazil, Ind., 1940-49; chief chemist Fairview Collieries Corp., Danville, Ill., 1949-54; preparations mgr. Enos Coal Mining Co., Oakland City, Ind., 1954-72, Enoco Collieries, Inc., Bruceville, Ind., 1954-62; mining engr. Kings Station Coal Corp.; mgr. analytical procedures Old Ben Coal Corp., 1973—. Am. Mining Congress cons. to Am. Standards Assn. and Internat. Orgn. for Standards, 1960-74; mem. indsl. cons. com. Ind. Geol. Survey, 1958-72; mem. organizing com. 5th Internat. Coal Preparation Congress, Pittsburgh, 1966. Mem. exec. bd. Buffalo Trace council Boy Scouts Am., also mem. speakers bur. Bd. dirs. Princeton Boys Club. Served with AUS, 1942-46; ETO. Decorated Medaille de la France Liberee (France); recipient Eagle Scout award, Boy Scouts Am., 1935, Silver Beaver award, 1962, Wood Badge Beads award, 1960; Outstanding Community Service award Princeton Civitan Club, 1964; Engr. of Year award S.W. chpt. Ind. Soc. Profl. Engrs., 1965. Registered profl. engr., Ind., Ill. Mem. Am. Inst. Mining, Metall. and Petroleum Engrs., Am. Soc. for Testing and Meterials, Nat. Soc. Profl. Engrs., Ind., Ill. mining insts., Ind. Coal Soc. (pres. 1958-59), Am. Mining Congress (chmn. com. coal preparation 1964-68), Am. Legion, 40 and 8, Ind. Soc. Profl. Land Surveyors, Rose Tech. Alumni Assn. (pres. 1976-77), Sigma Nu. Methodist (lay speaker). Mason, Elk. Contbr. articles to profl. jours. Home: 8 Circle Dr Princeton IN 47670 Office: Old Ben Coal Co div Sohio Oakland City IN 47660

MULLINS, ROBERT PAUL, health center adminstr.; b. Cin., Dec. 28, 1945; s. Robert Perry and Leola Margaret M.; B.A., Western Ky. U., 1968; M. Div., Eden Theol. Seminary, 1971; M.S., Wright State U., 1974; m. Nancy Claire Virus, Aug. 3, 1968. Ordained to minstry, 1971; pastor 1st. United Ch. of Christ Piqua, Ohio, 1971-74; exec. dir. Miami County Big Bros. Assn., 1971-72; clin. counselor S. Community Mental Health Center Kettering, Ohio, 1974—. Mem. Am. Personnel and Guidance Assn., Am. Orthopsychiatric Assn. Club: Masons. Home: 4234 W Franklin St Bellbrook OH 45305 Office: 5777 Far Hills Dayton OH 45429

MULVANEY, RONALD, bank assn. exec.; b. Bklyn., July 26, 1933; s. Martin Vincent and Jean Catherine (Zabinski) M.; B.A., Marquette U., 1960; m. Joan M. Helget, June 6, 1958; children—Therese, Sharon, Janet, Daniel, David, Susan. Asso. editor Mid-Western Banker Mag., Milw., 1960-65; asst. cashier Midland Nat. Bank, Milw., 1965-66; exec. dir. Engrs. & Scientists of Milw., Inc., 1966-71; asso. dir. Wis. Bankers Assn., Madison, 1971—, also editor Bank Notes; organizer Midtown State Bank, Milw., 1967. Pres. Coop. West Side, Inc., 1964; chmn. 10th Dist. Wis. Democratic Com., 1965; treas. 5th Congl. Dist. Wis. Dem. Com., 1966. Served with USMC, 1953-56. Roman Catholic. Club: Toastmasters. Home: 17540 Sierra Ln Brookfield WI 53005 Office: 16 N Carroll St Madison WI 53703

MULVANEY, WILLIAM PETER, urologist, clin. dir.; b. Cin., Mar. 28, 1921; s. William Peter and Elsie Marie (Heil) M.; B.S., Xavier U., Cin., 1943; M.D., Loyola U., Chgo., 1946; postgrad. U. Minn., 1949-52; m. Pauline Dwenger, 1970; children—Mary Kathleen, Sharon, William P., James Foley, Terence M. Practice medicine specializing in urology, Cin., 1952—; asst. prof. urology U. Cin., 1953-68, laser researcher, 1970-74; dir. urology Good Samaritan Hosp., 1952-72, dir. urol. research, 1974—; cons. Eaton Labs.; dir. Camargo Manor Nursing Home; cons. Com. Establishment Care Standards Nursing Homes Midwest. Recipient Sci. Exhibits awards Am. Urol. Soc., 1973-75; diplomate Am. Bd. Urology. Fellow ACS; mem. Pan-Pacific Surg. Assn., Internat. Soc. Laser Surgeons. Inventor first topical solvent for kidney bladder stones; oral drug for preventing and dissolving cystine kidney stones. Home: 687 N Meadowcrest Cr Cincinnati OH 45231

MULVIHILL, DONALD FERGUSON, educator; b. Chgo., Mar. 12, 1911; s. William Frank and Emma May (Hubbard) M.; B.S., U. Ill., 1933, M.S., 1940; M.A., U. Chgo., 1937, Ph.D., 1954; m. Ruth Cope, Dec. 22, 1934; children—Ann (Mrs. Burke H. Webb), William Cope. Editor Lake View Bull., Chgo., 1933-37; instr. U. Ill., 1937-40; from instr. to prof. mktg. U. Ala., 1940-62; prof. mktg. Kent (Ohio) State U., 1962—, chmn. dept., 1962-72; cons. in field, 1940—. Served with AUS, 1942-46. Grantee Gulf Oil Corp., 1958; fellow Ford Found., 1965, Regional Council Internat. Bus., 1969. Mem. Midwest Bus. Adminstrn. Assn. (pres. 1970-71), Am. Mktg. Assn. (dir. 1959-62), A.A.A.S., Nat. Def. Transp. Assn. (charter), Acad. Internat. Bus., Beta Gamma Sigma, Alpha Kappa Psi. Kiwanian. Author: Geography, Marketing and Urban Growth, 1970; also articles, monographs. Editor: Guide to the Qualitative Age, 1966; Domestic Marketing Systems Abroad, 1967; Price Policies and Practices, 1967. Home: 450 Bowman Dr Kent OH 44240

MUMA, JACK WESLEY, ins. exec.; b. Villa Grove, Ill., Jan. 5, 1927; s. Wilbert W. and Maxine L. (Wood) M.; B.S.C.E. in Structural Engring., Wayne State U., 1950; m. Dolores M. Power, June 24, 1950; children—Michael W., Lindsay A., Margaret E., Andrew J., David P. Fire protection engr. Homer Warren & Co., Detroit, 1950-54; adminstrv. asst., jr. partner Grow, Sumner, Englebert, Detroit, 1954-58; v.p. Hudson & Muma, Inc., Southfield, Mich., 1958-66, pres., 1966-70; pres., chief exec. officer Guardian Nat. Corp., Royal Oak, Mich., 1970-73; pres., chief operating officer, mem. exec. com. Fin. Guardian Group, Inc., Fin. Guardian Ins. Agy., Inc., Fin. Compensation Cons., Inc., Fin. Guardian Services, Inc., World-surance, Inc., 1973—; vice chmn. bd., mem. exec. com. Risk Adminstrn. Services, Inc., Fin. Guardian Ins. Agy. Inc. of Colo., Stockyards Ins. Agy., Inc., Worldsurance Ins. Brokers, Inc. Pres. Detroit Homeowners Assn., 1962-64. Served with USNR, 1945-71; PTO, CBI; comdr. Res. ret. Mem. Nat. Assn. Casualty and Surety Agts., Mo. Assn. Ind. Ins. Agts., Nat. C. of C., Alpha Sigma Phi (treas. alumni 1951-59). Home: 11815 Pennsylvania Ave Kansas City MO 64114 Office: 3100 Broadway Kansas City MO 64111

MUNCASTER, EDWARD HAMPTON, pub. relations co. exec.; b. Chgo., Feb. 27, 1933; s. Edward James and Lennie Grace (Williams) M.; B.A., Northwestern U., 1955; postgrad. U. Chgo., 1965. With A. G. Becker & Co., Chgo., 1955-62; dir. mgmt. devel. programs U. Chgo., 1962-66; v.p. Gardner, Jones-Hill & Knowlton, Inc., Chgo., 1966—. Bd. dirs. Bishop Hill (Ill.) Heritage Assn. Served to lt., USNR, 1955-57. Western Golf Assn. Evans scholar. Mem. Western Golf Assn., Assn. for Corporate Growth, Nat. Trust for Hist. Preservation, Nat. Investor Relations Inst. (chpt. pres., dir.), Pub. Relations Soc. Am., Bureau Valley C. of C. Club: The Attic (Chgo.). Contbr. articles to profl. jours. Home: 516 5th St Wilmette IL 60091 Office: 111 E Wacker Dr Chicago IL 60601

MUNDA, RINO UMBERTO, surgeon; b. Rome, Feb. 19, 1943; s. Salvador and Marina M.; came to U.S., 1967; M.D., Universidad Nacional Mayor de San Marcos, Lima, Peru, 1960; B.S., Facultad de Medicina Cayetano Heredia, Lima, 1966; m. Margarita Landra, Nov. 19, 1968; 1 son, Sergio. Intern, Mt. Sinai Hosp., Elmhurst, N.Y., 1967-68, jr. asst. resident, 1968-70; with N.Y. Med. Coll., 1970-71, sr. asst. resident in surgery, 1971-72, chief resident, 1972-73, fellow in vascular surgery, 1973-74; practice medicine specializing in surgery, 1974—; mem. staffs Christ Hosp., Cin., 1975, Cin. Gen. Hosp., 1974; instr. in surgery N.Y. Med. Coll., 1972-73; asst. prof. research surgery U. Cin., 1974-75, asst. prof. surgery, 1975—. Diplomate Am. Bd. Surgery. Mem. Surg. Soc. N.Y. Med. Coll., Soc. Academic Surgery, Am. Soc. for Transplant Surgeons, Cin. Surg. Soc. Contbr. articles to med. jours. Home: 3859 Middleton Ave Cincinnati OH 45220 Office: 234 Goodman St Cincinnati OH 45267

MUNDELL, JUNIUS LEE, farmer, civic worker; b. Linn County, Mo., Aug. 13, 1928; s. James N. and Garnet Pearl (Kimbrough) M.; student N.E. Mo. State U., 1947-51; m. Lou Ann Edmundson, Oct. 6, 1951; children—Brenda Jo, Anthony Clark. Tchr. elementary sch. Linn County (Mo.) schs., 1948-56; asst. cashier Citizens Savings Bank, Browning, Mo., 1967-68; livestock and grain farmer, Browning, 1953—; carpenter, furniture craftsman, 1951—. Dir. Farmer's Mutual Ins. Co. Linn County, Mo., Meadville, Mo., 1971—. Pres. Linn County pub. schs., Meadville, 1970-75; Dem. committeeman, Jackson, Twp., Mo., 1968—. Adv. bd. to dean agr. U. Mo., Linneus, 1974—. Served with U.S. Army, 1951-53. Named Outstanding Linn County Farmer, Spotlight on Agr., 1974; recipient Distinguished Agr. Appreciation award Gov. of Mo., 1974. Mem. Mo. Farmers Assn. (dir. 1970-75; champion corn grower 1955), Mo. Cattleman's Assn. (state dir. 1977—). Methodist (lay leader 1965-75, chmn. trustees 1968-75). Address: Browning MO 64630

MUNDELL, WILBUR LEWIS, assn. exec., producer; b. Waltersburg, Pa., Mar. 12, 1928; s. Clyde Sterling and Mary Audrey (Boord) M.; B.S. in Edn., Waynesburg (Pa.) Coll., 1953; M.A., George Washington U., 1966; m. Elva Jean Cannon, Aug. 25, 1948; children—Douglas, Deborah (Mrs. Robert Ray), Gregory, Laura. Commd. officer U.S. Marine Corps, 1953, advanced through grades to capt.; ret., 1966; tchr. Am. history, analysis of teaching in secondary schs., dir. continuing edn. Ohio U., Chillicothe, 1966-70; exec. v.p. Scioto Soc., Inc., cultural, hist. and ednl. econ. devel., Chillicothe, 1970-73, pres., 1973—; writer Wild Kingdom TV series, 1973; cons. Inst. Outdoor Drama, U. N.C., Chapel Hill, 1973—. Mem. Chillicothe/Ross County Bicentennial Commn., 1974—. Pres. Chillicothe Bd. Edn., 1972-73. Recipient Ohio Statehood Achievement award, 1973. Mem. New Eng., Southeastern theatre confs., Ohio Travel Council, Symposiarchs (v.p. 1968), Nat. Tour Brokers Assn., Smithsonian Assos., Rotarian (chmn. music com. Chillicothe 1975). Home: 792 Cliffside Dr Chillicothe OH 45601 Office: PO Box 73 Chillicothe OH 45601

MUNDIE, DONALD ROBERTSON, pediatrician; b. N. Tonawanda, N.Y., Apr. 13, 1923; s. Franklin Warren and Mildred (Robertson) M.; M.D., Duke U., 1947; m. Elizabeth Champion, June 3, 1947; children—Donna, Gregory, Catherine, Benjamin, Patricia, Jennifer, Ian. Temporary county health officer Miss. State Health Dept., 1948; intern Meyer Meml. Hosp., Buffalo, 1948-49; resident in pediatrics Duke Hosp., Durham, N.C., 1949-50, Chelsea Naval Hosp., Boston, 1950-51; practice medicine specializing in pediatrics, Northbrook, Ill., 1954—; asso. in pediatrics Northwestern U., Chgo., 1956—; chmn. pediatrics St. Francis Hosp., Evanston, Ill., 1970—; pediatric cons. Vis. Nurses Assn., 1970—; dir. Infant Welfare program City of Evanston, 1972—. Served with M.C., USN, 1950-54. Diplomate Am. Bd. Pediatrics (fellow). Mem. AMA, Chgo. Med. Soc., Am. Acad. Pediatrics. Baptist. Home: 2040 Orrington Ave Evanston IL 60201 Office: 1775 Walters Ave Northbrook IL 60062 also 636 Church St Evanston IL 60201

MUNDY, DANIEL L., printing co. exec.; b. Ireland, Ind., Apr. 15, 1948; s. Ben D. and Frieda Mundy; student Automation Tng. Inst., 1966; m. Theresa Herzog, Aug. 9, 1969; children—Aaron, Chad, Ben. Mgr. data processing United Cabinet Corp., Jasper, Ind., 1967-71; mgr. data processing St. Meinrad Arch Abbey, St. Meinrad, Ind., 1972—; pres. Mundy's Inc., hardware, 1976—. Dir. Spencer County Ambulance Service, Inc. Asst. fire chief Santa Claus (Ind.) Vol. Fire Dept. Mem. Mchts. Assn. Democrat. Roman Catholic. Clubs: K.C., Optimist. Home: PO Box 81 Santa Claus IN 47579 Office: Abbey Press St Meinrad IN 47577

MUNDY, MELVIN DUANE, metals co. material mgr.; b. Indpls., Dec. 2, 1943; s. Kenneth Clark and Martha Jane (Shelley) M.; B.S. in Bus. Adminstrn., Ball State U., 1966; m. Marilyn Kay Snodgrass, Aug. 15, 1965; children—Clark Edward, Adam Zachary. With Gen. Telephone of Ind., 1966-67; with Superior Linkage div. Tuthill Pump Co., New Haven, Ind., 1967—, various positions including purchasing agt., traffic mgr., data processing mgr., sales coordinator, 1967-73, prodn. mgr., 1973—. Active Catholic Youth Orgn. Mem. Am. Prodn. Inventory Control Soc., Beta Theta Pi. Baptist. Home: Rural Route 3 Grabill IN 46741 Office: 11102 Edgerton Rd New Haven IN 46774

MUNEIO, FRANK RAYMOND, JR., savs. and loan, ins. exec.; b. Chgo., Nov. 1, 1915; s. Frank R. and Evelyn M. (Johnson) M.; student U. Ill., 1936, LaSalle Extension U., 1939; grad. Am. Savs. and Loan Inst., 1949; postgrad. U. So. Calif., 1969; children—Linda (Mrs. Howenstein), Sally (Mrs. Daniel E. Booth), Pamela, Frank Raymond, Susan, Jared, Jennifer. With accounting dept. Cudahy Packing, Chgo., 1936-40; accountant Oak Park (Ill.) Fed. Savs. & Loan Assn., 1940-45, v.p., sec., 1946-53; asst. v.p. St. Paul Fed. Savs. and Loan Assn., 1953; exec. v.p., sec. First Fed. Savs. & Loan Assn., Aurora, Ill., 1954-60, pres., chmn. bd., 1961-77; pres., chmn. bd. Aim Agy., Inc., Aurora; exec. v.p. Forecee Corp., 1977—. Mem. Aurora Hist. Soc., Aurora Found. Moose, Lion, Elk (exalted ruler 1962-63). Home and Office: 111 N Rosedale Ave Aurora IL 60506

MUNOZ, RODRIGO ALBERTO, psychiatrist, med. service adminstr.; b. Popayan, Colombia, Mar. 21, 1939; s. Cesar E. and Livia (Barragan) M.; came to U.S., 1964, naturalized, 1974; M.D., U. Cauca, Colombia, 1963; m. Marilyn Barnett, Sept. 9, 1968; children—Rodrigo Alberto, Lisa Ann, Julie Ann. Intern Mental Hosp., Medellin, Colombia, 1962-63; resident Fairfield Hills Hosp., Newton, Conn., also Washington U., St. Louis, 1964-67; practice medicine specializing in psychiatry Sheboygan, Wis., 1970—; supr. emergency service Malcolm Bliss Mental Health Center, St. Louis, 1967-69; instr. psychiatry Washington U., St. Louis, 1969-70; med. dir. Olive Schaeffer Home, Sheboygan, 1972; staff physician Sheboygan Meml. Hosp., 1970—, St. Nicholas Hosp., Sheboygan, 1970—; staff psychiatrist Sheboygan County Comprehensive Mental Health Center, Sheboygan Falls, Wis., 1970—; psychiat. cons. to Holiday House, Manitowoc, Wis., 1970, Rocky Knoll Sanitorium, Sheboygan, 1970. Diplomate Am. Bd. Psychiatry and Neurology. Mem. A.M.A. (physicians recognition award 1969), Am., Wis. psychiat. assns., State Med. Soc. Wis., Sheboygan County Med. Soc., Acad. Psychosomatic Medicine, Royal Coll. Psychiatrists, Am. Sch. Health Assn., Nat. Rehab. Counseling Assn., Am. Geriatrics Soc., Am. Gerontological Soc., A.A.A.S., Soc. Clin. Psychiatrists. Contbr. articles on psychopathological disorders to med. jours. Home: 721 Birch Tree Rd Sheboygan WI 53081 Office: 1226 N 8 St Sheboygan WI 53081

MUNRO, (HARRIET) BERNICE, mathematician, educator; b. Detroit, June 17, 1916; d. George Thomas and Viola Banghart (McCormick) Proctor; B.A., Mich. State U., 1938; M.Ed., Wayne State U., Detroit, 1961; m. Donald McAlpine Munro, Oct. 23, 1942; children—Douglas Roy, David McAlpine. Tchr. pub. schs., Detroit, Clare, Mich., 1940-63; NSF aide, instr. Applied Mgmt. Tech. Center, Wayne State U., 1960-68; tchr. Ann Arbor (Mich.) pub. schs., 1963-71, math. coordinator, 1971—; cons. in field. Mem. Nat., Mich. (past pres.), Detroit (past pres.) councils tchrs. math., Math. Assn. Am., Nat. Council Suprs. Math., Kappa Delta, Delta Kappa Gamma, Alpha Delta Kappa. Clubs: Ann Arbor Women's City, Order Eastern Star. Editor Math Mots, 1971-77. Home: 1950 Longshore Dr Ann Arbor MI 48105 Office: 2555 S State St Ann Arbor MI 48104

MUNSON, CARL EDWARD, transp. cons.; b. Sterling, Ill., May 15, 1926; s. August William and Loretta Lucile (Fagan) M.; grad. Coll. of Advanced Traffic, 1949; m. Darda Helena Lubben, Sept. 15, 1946; children—Carol (Mrs. M.E. Frommelt), William, James, Mark, Brian, Christopher, Kevin. Rate clk. C. B.& Q. R.R., Sterling, 1945-48, rate analyst, Rock Island, Ill., 1949-50; Carstensen Freight Lines, Inc., Clinton, Iowa, 1948-49; rate analyst Dohrn Transfer Co., Rock Island, Ill., 1950-55; mgr. Dubuque (Iowa) Traffic Assn. cons. Carl E. Munson Assos., Dubuque, 1965—, also propr., 1965—. Mem. United Fund of Dubuque, chmn. transp. div., 1956-59. Served with U.S. Army, 1944-45. Mem. Iowa Indsl. Traffic League (pres. 1966-67), Nat. Assn. Freight Transp. Consultants (v.p. 1973—), Assn. ICC Practitioners, Alumni Assn. Coll. Advanced Traffic, Nat. Travel Club. Democrat. Roman Catholic. K.C., Kiwanian (dir. 1973-75, chmn. vocat. guidance com. 1972-75). Home: 934 University St Dubuque IA 52001 Office: 469 Fischer Bldg Dubuque IA 52001

MUNSON, HOWARD ROGER, educator; b. Red Wing, Minn., May 14, 1923; s. Arthur Morris and Ruth Edith (Edstrom) M.; B.S. in Biology, U. Minn., 1948, postgrad., 1949; postgrad. U. Colo., 1950; M.Ed., Macalester Coll., 1953; Ed.D., Wash. State U., 1959; certificate postdoctoral study N.Y. U., 1969; m. Dolores Ilene Johnson, June 18, 1948; children—Bruce Howard, Beth Ann (Mrs. John Prorok), Daniel Keith. Tchr. biology, Alexandria, Minn., 1948-52, sci., Albert Lea, Minn., 1954-55; faculty Winona (Minn.) State Coll. Lab. Sch., 1955-57, prin., dir., 1956-68, asst. prof. edn. Winona State Coll., 1955-59, asso. prof., 1959-62, prof., 1962—. Cons. Coronet Learning Films, 1970, D.C. Heath & Co., Pubs., 1970-71, Little, Brown & Co., 1976-77. Bd. dirs. Winona Day Activity Center for Handicapped; mem. Minn.-Wis. Boundary Area Commn. Served with AUS, 1943-46; ETO. N.Y. U. Tri-Univ. Project fellow, 1968; Fulbright grantee pilot project Fed. Republic Germany for ednl. experts, 1974. Mem. Nat. Sci. Tchrs. Assn., Assn. Educators Tchrs. in Sci. (regional chmn. 1969-70), Inter-Faculty Orgn., Winona State Coll. Faculty Assn. (treas. 1956-57), Phi Delta Kappa. Democrat. Lutheran. Mason (32 deg.). Author: Science with Simple Things, 1972. Contbr. articles to profl. jours. Home: 502 Westdale St Winona MN 55987

MUNTZ, ERNEST GORDON, historian, ednl. adminstr.; b. Buffalo, Nov. 15, 1923; s. J. Palmer and Laura Estelle (Wedekindt) M.; B.A., Wheaton Coll., 1948; Ph.D. (grad. teaching fellow, So. Fellowships Fund fellow 1955), U. Rochester, 1960; m. Marjorie Corrine Wilson, June 29, 1948; children—Carolyn Odell, Deborah Lynn, Howard Gordon. Asst. prof. social sci. Blue Mountain (Miss.) Coll., 1954-56; asst. then asso. prof., then prof. history Union U., Jackson, Tenn., 1956-61; asso. prof. then prof. history U. Cin., 1961—, asst. dean Raymond Walters Gen. and Tech. Coll., 1966-69, dean, 1969—; cons., evaluator N. Central Coll. Assn. Served with USAAF, 1943-46. Mem. Am. Hist. Assn., AAUP, Pi Gamma Mu, Phi Alpha Theta. Presbyterian. Clubs: The Literary (Cin.), Cincinnatus Assn. Home: 6 Dexter Pl Cincinnati OH 45206 Office: 9555 Plainfield Rd Cincinnati OH 45236

MUNTZ, MARJORIE CORINNE, univ. ofcl.; b. Glenville, N.C., Oct. 22, 1925; d. Lyman Lynn and Bertie Mae (Moore) Wilson; B.A., Wheaton Coll., 1946; M.Ed., U. Cin., 1964, Ed.D., 1971; m. Ernest Gordon Muntz, June 29, 1948; children—Carolyn Odell, Deborah Lynn, Howard Gordon. Instr. English, Union U., Jackson, Tenn., 1958-61; mem. faculty U. Cin., 1962—, asst. prof. English, 1970-72, asso. prof., 1972—, asst. dean Summer Sch., 1972-74, asst. dir. Office Continuing Edn. and Met. Affairs, 1974—. Chmn. women's com. on colls. and univs. Cin. May Festival, 1973; chmn. com. on colls. and univs. and com. for Saturday sales Cin. Symphony Orch., 1974-76; trustee Ohio Commn. on Status of Women, 1975-76. Mem. AAUP, Am. Assn. Higher Edn., Nat. Assn. Women Deans, Adminstrs. and Counselors, Am. Personnel and Guidance Assn., Adult Personnel Assn., Assn. for Women Adminstrs. (founder, 1st pres. 1974-75), Alphu Mu Sigma (hon.). Presbyterian. Clubs: College (gov.), Cin. Woman's (exec. bd.), Zonta (exec. bd.) (Cin.). Home: 6 Dexter Pl Cincinnati OH 45206 Office: U Cin Cincinnati OH 45221

MUNTZ, MARVIN EUGENE, systems analyst; b. Defiance, Ohio, Mar. 1, 1945; s. Clifford Herman and Mary Elizabeth (McLaughlin) M.; B.S. in Agrl. Engring., Ohio State U., 1969; postgrad. indsl. tech., Central Mich. U., 1971—. Computer systems analyst, cost analyst Ideanamics, Columbus, Ohio, 1974; asst. mgr. Muntz-McLaughlin Co., Holgate, Ohio, 1974-76; computer systems programming dir., chief of data systems Symo-Life, Millersburg, Ohio, 1976—. Served with USAF, 1970-74. Mem. Am. Soc. Agrl. Engrs. Contbr. articles to profl. jours. Home: Route 3 Barnhart's Ct Apt 6 Millersburg OH 44654

MURACO, WILLIAM ANTHONY, educator; b. Cleve., Dec. 23, 1940; s. Anthony Samuel and Elvera Ann (Broncaccio) M.; B.S., Ohio State U., 1964, M.A., 1966, Ph.D., 1971; m. JoAnn Bidwell, Dec. 15, 1962; children—Ronald Anthony, Brenda Ann. Teaching and research asso. Ohio State U., Columbus, 1964-68; instr. Wright State U., Dayton, Ohio, 1968-71; asso. prof. U. Toledo, 1971—. Cons. to NASA, 1974-75, Community Research Assos., Inc., 1971-75, Ohio Real Estate Commn., 1974-75. Recipient Pace Setters award, Ohio State U., 1966. NSF fellow, 1966-67. Mem. Assn. Am. Geographers, Regional Sci. Assn., Ohio Acad. Sci., Pi Gamma Mu, Delta Sigma Phi. Contbr. articles to profl. jours. Home: 136 Birchcrest Dr Perrysburg OH 43551 Office: Dept Geography U Toledo Toledo OH 43606

MURASKEVICS, JOHN, JR., material handling equipment distbg. co. exec.; b. Latvia, May 17, 1939; s. John and Anna (Rullits) M.; came to U.S., 1950, naturalized, 1962; student Data Processing Inst., Ind., 1959; computer programming course U. Colo., 1964. Gen. mgr. parts ops. Morrison Co., Cleve., 1965—. Active in restoration project Akron (Ohio) Civic Theater, 1970—. Trustee Community Hall Found., Inc., Akron Civic Theater, 1973—, v.p., 1974-76. Served with U.S. Army, 1963-65. Mem. Akron Civic Theater Organ Guild (founding pres. 1973), Theater Hist. Soc., Am. Theater Organ Soc. Home: 11800 Edgewater Dr Lakewood OH 44107 Office: Morrison Co 5415 Schaaf Rd Cleveland OH 44131

MURATA, KAZUNAO, bank exec.; b. Tsu-city, Miye Pref, Japan, Nov. 1, 1929; s. Jiun and Yoshiko (Suzuoki) M.; M.B.A., U. Mass., 1962-63; m. Akiko Miyatake, Oct. 12, 1959; children—Yoichi, Junko. With The Sanwa Bank Ltd., Osaka, Japan, 1950—, asst. mgr., 1961-66, asst. gen. mgr. corp. banking hdqrs., Tokyo, 1976, gen. mgr. Chgo. br., 1976—. Mem. Japanese C. of C. of Chgo., Japanese-Am. Soc. Chgo., Ill. Bankers Assn. Author: An Electronic and Credit System (in Japanese), 1969. Clubs: Exec., Internat. Trade. Home: 445 Country Ln Glenview IL 60025 Office: 39 S La Salle St Chicago IL 60603

MURDOCK, CHARLES KENNEDY, radio broadcasting co. exec.; b. Lakeland, Fla., Sept. 15, 1932; s. Charles K. and Ethel B. (Brinson) M.; B.A., U. Fla., 1954; m. Helen Stephenson, June 28, 1968; children—Martha, Randy, Tara, Merri, Bree Ann. Announcer radio sta. WRUF, Gainesville, Fla., 1950-54; disc jockey, sports dir. radio sta. WRVA, Richmond, Va., 1956-57; program dir., ops. mgr. radio sta. WQAM, Miami, 1957-65; gen. mgr. WSAI, Cin., 1965-67; sr. v.p. radio Avco Broadcasting and gen. mgr. WLW, Cin., 1967-76; pres. WLW Radio, Inc., 1976—. Bd. dirs. Cin. Conv. Bur., Cancer Family Care, Kidney Found. Served with AUS, 1954-56. Mem. Platform Speakers Assn., Nat., Ohio assns. broadcasters, Sales and Mktg. Execs. Club (pres. 1971-72), Ad Club (pres. 1969), Cin. C. of C. Baptist. Kiwanian. Home: 6500 Wyman Ln Cincinnati OH 45243 Office: 901 Elm St Cincinnati OH 45202

MURFIN, ALLEN EUGENE, assn. exec.; b. Kirksville, Mo., Sept. 29, 1938; s. John Larkin and Lois Pauline (Epperson) M.; grad. high sch.; m. Evelyn Marie Rottinghaus, May 25, 1963; children—Christina Marie, Jo Ann Renee, Marcie Lynn. With Davis Paint Co., Kansas City, Mo., 1956-58; various positions Massey Ferguson, Inc., Kansas City, Kans., 1962-68; office mgr. real estate co., 1968-70; pres. Mo. Jr. C. of C., Sedalia, 1970-71; v.p. U.S. Jr. C. of C., Tulsa, 1971-72, dir. regional office, Marlboro, Mass., 1972-74; tng. officer U.S. Jaycees, Tulsa, 1974-76; exec. v.p. Columbia (Mo.) C. of C., 1975—. Mem. City Planning Commn., Gladstone, Mo., 1966-70; mem. City Zoning Bd. of Adjustments, Gladstone, 1970-72. Bd. dirs. Wonder Land Camp Found., 1969-71. Served with USAR, 1956, USMC, 1958-62. Elk. Home: 40 Victoria Dr Columbia MO 65201 Office: 123 S 8th St Columbia MO 65201

MURNEY, JOSEPH ANTHONY, physician; b. Springfield, Mo., May 27, 1920; s. William B. and Genevieve (Glynn) M.; B.S., St. Louis U., 1949; M.D., 1953; m. Jean M. Pinnell, Oct. 15, 1975; children—Anne Theresa, Deirdre Glynn. Intern, Fitzsimons Gen. Hosp., Denver, 1953-54; resident in gen. surgery DePaul Hosp., St. Louis, 1954-55; resident thoracic surgery Wilford Hall Air Force Hosp. and San Antonio TB Hosp., 1957-61; practice medicine specializing in surgery, Washington, Mo., 1964—; asst. clin. prof. surgery St. Louis U. Med. Sch., 1974—; dir. emergency dept. St. Francis Mercy Hosp., 1976—; mem. staff St. Francis Mercy Hosp., Washington, Mo., Sullivan Community Hosp. Served with USAAF, 1955-63, USAF, 1963-64. Diplomate Am. Bd. Surgery, Am. Bd. Thoracic Surgery. Fellow A.C.S., Am. Coll. Chest Physicians; mem. St. Louis Surg. Soc., AMA, Mo. Med. Soc. Home: 1360-3 South Winds St Washington MO 63090 Office: 201 Elm St Washington MO 63090

MUROGA, SABURO, computer scientist, elec. engr., educator; b. Numazu, Japan, Mar. 25, 1925; s. Teiji and Kenko (Abe) M.; came to U.S., 1960; Gakushi degree in Elec. Engring., Tokyo U., 1947, Ph.D., 1958; m. Yoko Nakamura, Feb. 5, 1956; children—Eisuke, Edith Rie, David Kenji, Judith Lisa. Mem. research staff Nat. Ry. Pub. Corp., Tokyo, Japan, 1947-49; engring. staff Radio Regulatory Commn. Japanese Govt., Tokyo, 1950-51; mem. research staff Elec. Communication Lab., Nippon Tel. & Tel. Pub. Corp., Tokyo, 1951-60, IBM Research Center, Yorktown Heights, N.Y., 1960-64; prof. computer sci., U. Ill., Urbana, 1964—. Mem. IEEE, Assn. Computing Machinery, Info. Processing Soc. Japan, Inst. Elec. Communication Engrs. Japan (Inada award 1955). Designer Parametron computer Musashino-1, 1954-60. Author: Threshold Logic and Its Application, 1971. Contbr. articles to profl. publs. on info. theory, threshold logic, switching theory. Home: 703 Brighton Dr Urbana IL 61801

MURPHY, ALAN CHARLES, accountant; b. Frederic, Wis., July 20, 1937; s. Edward Lester and Irene Margaret (Rogers) M.; B.B.A., U. Wis., 1959. Timekeeper, Stokely-VanCamp, Inc., Milltown, Wis., 1955-59; partner Touche Ross & Co., Mpls. and St. Paul, also Dayton, Ohio, 1960—. Served with AUS, 1959-60. C.P.A., Wis., Minn., Ohio, S.D., La., N.C. Mem. Am. Inst. C.P.A.'s, Minn., Wis., Ohio socs. C.P.A.'s, Inst. Internal Auditors, Nat. Assn. Accountants for Co-ops. Clubs: Sycamore Creek Country (Springboro, Ohio); Racquet (Dayton). Home: 4719 Wilmington Pike Kettering OH 45440 Office: 1700 Courthouse Plaza NE Dayton OH 45402

MURPHY, CECIL PATRICK, ednl. adminstr.; b. Wichita, Kans., Nov. 7, 1949; s. Darold Dean and Wanda May (Carruthers) M.; B.A., Wichita State U., 1976, postgrad. European Mil. History, 1975—; Asst. dir. vet. services, office vet. Mil. Services, Wichita State U., 1976—. Served with Hosp. Corps, USN, 1967-71. Mem. Emergency Med. Technician Assn. Central Kans. (chmn. pub. com. 1976-77), Wichita Scale Aircraft Modelers Assn., U.S. Naval Inst. Home: 1559 N Emporia St Wichita KS 67214 Office: Box 105 Wichita State U Wichita KS 67208

MURPHY, DANIEL MICHAEL, civil engr.; b. Rochester, N.Y., Nov. 3, 1947; s. Daniel James and Mary Kathleen (Kobryn) M.; B.S. in Civil Engring., U. Mich., 1969, M.S. in Civil Constrn. Engring., 1970; m. Deborah Jane Stevens, June 12, 1970; children—Doreen Michelle, Danielle Melissa. Design and inspection engr. N.Y. State Dept. Transp., Rochester, 1968; design and project coordination engring. Xerox Corp., Webster, N.Y., 1969; estimator, supt. M & B. Equipment Co., Warren, Mich., 1969-70; scheduling engr., Owens-Corning Fiberglas Co., Toledo, 1970-72, constrn. engr., 1972-74, constrn. mgr., 1974-75, facilities engr., 1975-76, reinforced concrete products engr., 1976—. U. Mich. Grad. Sch. fellow, 1969-70; registered profl. engr., N.Y. Mem. ASCE, Am. Concrete Inst., Nat. Concrete Masonry Assn. Roman Catholic. Home: 6585 Tennyson Dr Ottawa Lake MI 49267 Office: Fiberglas Tower #E8 Toledo OH 43659

MURPHY, DARYL EMERSON, communications co. exec.; b. Sterling, Kans., Nov. 14, 1935; s. Clyde Emerson and Alice Mae (Burke) M.; student Kans. State Tchrs. Coll. Emporia, 1953-54, Sterling Coll. 1955-57; m. Kathleen Jane Minter, Dec. 28, 1964; 1

dau., Kelley Maureen. TV prodn. staff sta KCKT-TV, Gt. Bend and Oberlin, Kans., 1957-60; staff artist Record Stockman, Denver, 1960-62; staff TV prodn., promotion and programming Sta. KSLN-TV, Salina, Kans., 1962-65; merchandising mgr. marketing div. Cessna Aircraft Co., 1965-72; mktg. mgr. Impala Industries Inc., Wichita, 1972-75; pres. Creative Marketing, Wichita, 1975—; lectr. in field. Republican. Episcopalian. Home: 1000 S Woodlawn St Apt 708 Wichita KS 67218 Office: 1000 S Woodlawn St #703 Wichita KS 67218

MURPHY, GLENN, educator; b. Boulder, Colo., Jan. 17, 1908; s. Peter Francis and A. Myrtle (Eggleston) M.; B.S. in Civil Engring., U. Colo., 1929, M.S., 1930; M.S. in Civil Engring., U. Ill., 1932; Ph.D., U. Iowa, 1935; C.E., U. Colo., 1937, Sc.D. (hon.), 1973; m. Frances Pearce, Aug 18, 1934 (dec. 1976). Spl. research asst. U. Ill., 1930-32; instr. Iowa State U., 1932-34, asst. prof., 1934-38, asso. prof., 1938-41, prof., 1941-56, sr. engr. Inst. for Atomic Research, 1948-63, Anson Marston distinguished prof. engring., 1956—, head dept. aero. engring., 1952-55, head dept. theoretical and applied mechainics, 1955-60, head dept. nuclear engring., 1959-73, coordinator engring. edn. projects office, 1972—. Fellow Royal Soc. Arts, AAAS, N.Y. Acad. Scis., mem. Iowa Engring Soc., Am. Soc. M.E., Am. Soc. Engring. Edn. (George Westinghouse award 1951, Lamme award 1972, council 1946, 54, v.p. central divs., 1957-59, pres. 1962-63, v.p. projects operating unit 1965-68), Am. Soc. C.E., Am. Nuclear Soc., Royal Aero. Soc., Am. Inst. Aeros. Astronautics. Author: Properties of Engineering Materials, 1957; (with Gilkey and Bergman) Materials Testing, 1941; Mechanics of Fluids, 1942; Advanced Mechanics of Materials, 1946; Mechanics of Materials, 1950; Similitude in Engineering, 1950; Elements of Nuclear Engineering, 1975; Elementos de Ingenieria Nuclear, 1962; (with Shippy and L) Engineering Analogies, 1962. Contbr. articles to profl. jours Home: 2129 Ashmore Dr Ames IA 50010 Office: Sweeney Hall Iowa State Univ Ames IA 50011

MURPHY, JAMES WILLIAM, state senator, ins. co. exec.; b. St. Louis, July 2, 1936; s. William John and Evelyn Margaret (Hirbe) M.; student St. Louis U., 1957-58; m. Marilyn R. Ban, July 4, 1958; children—Timothy, James, Robert, Barbara, Margaret. With Western Electric Co., 1958-69; with Northwestern Nat. Life Ins., St. Louis, 1969-72, Am. Family Life Ins., St. Louis, 1972-73, Gen. Am. Life Ins., St. Louis, 1973-74; v.p. Futures Cons., Inc., St. Louis, 1974—. Democratic committeeman 12th Ward, St. Louis, 1972—; constable 6th dist., St. Louis, 1975—; mem. Mo. Senate, 1976—. Served with AUS, 1958-59. Mem. Hiberians, Haven Club, Judge Dowd Soccer League (pres. 1960-63). Roman Catholic. Lion, Elk. Club: Carondelet Sunday Morning. Home: 3942 Upton St St Louis MO 63116 Office: 7733 Forsyth Suite 850 St Louis MO 63105

MURPHY, JOHN ARTHUR, tobacco and brewing co. exec.; b. N.Y.C., Dec. 15, 1929; s. John A. and Mary J. (Touhey) M.; B.S., Villanova U., 1951; LL.B., Columbia, 1954; m. Carole Ann Paul, June 28, 1952; children—John A., Kevin P., Timothy M., Kellyann, Robert B., Kathleen. Admitted to N.Y. bar, 1954, since practiced in N.Y.C.; partner firm Conboy, Hewitt O'Brien & Boardman, 1954-62; asst. gen. counsel Philip Morris Inc., N.Y.C., 1962-66, v.p., 1967-76, exec. v.p., 1976—, also dir.; asst. to pres. Philip Morris Internat., 1966-67, exec. v.p., 1967-71; pres., chief exec. officer Miller Brewing Co., Milw., 1971—, also dir. Mem. Am., N.Y. State bar assns. Dir. J.A. of Southeastern Wis. Inc., M & I Marshall & Ilsey Bank. Pres., dir. Miller High Life Found., Inc. Bd. dirs. Milw. County Council Boy Scouts Am., Greater Milw. Com., U.S. Brewers Assn.; trustee Alverno Coll., 1976—, Milw. Boys Club, 1977—; trustee, campaign cabinet Marquette U. Mem. Met. Milw. Assn. Commerce (bd. dirs. 1976—). Home: 7624 North Beach Dr Fox Point WI 53217 Office: 3939 W Highland Blvd Milwaukee WI 53201

MURPHY, JOHN THOMAS, ins. co. exec.; b. Detroit, Dec. 18, 1928; s. Herbert F. and Edna (Gallier) M.; B.S. cum laude, U. Notre Dame, 1950; M.B.A., Harvard, 1952. Services trainee Allstate Ins. Co., Chgo., 1954-55, office supr., Detroit, 1955-56, operation div. supt., 1956-57, pub. relations mgr., Milw., 1957-63, pub. affairs mgr., Skokie, Ill., 1963-71, state and community relations dir., Northbrook, Ill., 1971—, exec. dir. Allstate Found., 1971—. Chmn. Milw. County Heart Assn. Bd. dirs. Wis. Council Safety, Chgo. chpt. U.S.O., Skokie Valley United Fund; bd. dirs., mem. finance com. Nat. League Nursing, N.Y.C. Served to 1st lt. USAF, 1952-54. Mem. Skokie C. of C. (pres.), Pub. Relations Soc. Am., Milw. Assn. Commerce. Clubs: Press (Milw.); University (Milw. and Detroit); Chicago Athletic Assn., Chicago Press (Chgo.). Home: 111 E Chestnut 41G Chicago IL 60611 Office: Allstate Plaza Northbrook IL 60062

MURPHY, LESTER FULLER, JR., lawyer; b. East Chicago, Ind., Nov. 28, 1936; s. Lester FUller and Angelique (Molloy) M.; B.Arts and Letters, U. Notre Dame, 1959, J.D., 1960; children—John Justin, Angelique, Lester Fuller III, Christopher, Colleen, Bridget. Admitted to Ind. bar, 1960, since practiced in East Chicago; asso. mem. firm Murphy, McAtee, Murphy & Constanza and predecessor firms, East Chicago, 1960-64, partner, 1965—. Dir. R.T. Skewes Freight Lines, Inc., East Chicago, 1965-74; trust officer First Nat. Bank East Chicago, 1963—; partner M & O Cattle Co., St. Clairsville, Ohio, 1973-74; arbitrator Am. Arbitration Assn., 1973—. Mem. Ind. Legislature and Gov.'s Ind. Trust Code Study Commn., 1965-71; mem. World Peace Through Law Confs., 1967—. Mem. Am. (mem. exec. council young lawyers sect. 1965-68), East Chicago, 7th Jud. Circuit, Ind. (bd. mgrs. 1964-65) bar assns. Contbr. articles to profl. jours. Office: 720 W Chicago Ave East Chicago IN 46312

MURPHY, MARY BORREDELL DALTON (MRS. JIM GORDON MURPHY), librarian; b. Lawrence, Kans., Dec. 31, 1917; d. William B. and Margery (Bowersock) Dalton; A.B., U. Kans., 1939; B.S., Columbia U., 1940; m. Jim Gordon Murphy, June 20, 1941 (dec. June 5, 1977); children—Michael Sean, Donald Evan, Neil Gordon. Acquisitions asst. U. Kans. Library, Lawrence, 1940, periodicals librarian, 1941; hdqrs. librarian Johnson County Library, Shawnee Mission, Kans., 1961-66, dir. in-service tng. 1966-68; reference librarian Lawrence Pub. Library, 1968—; reference librarian, cons. N.E. Kans. Library System, Lawrence, 1968—. Mem. ALA, Kans., Mountain Plains library assns., LWV, Gamma Phi Beta. Conglist. Home: Lake Dabinawa McLouth KS 66054 Office: 707 Vermont St Lawrence KS 66044

MURPHY, MARY EDITH FOX, food mfg. co. exec.; b. Catasauqua, Pa.; d. Henry Howard and Bessie Violetta (Flemming) Fox; student Boston U., 1937-38. With Sta. WSAN, Allentown, Pa., 1936-37, Kraftco, N.Y.C., 1939-48, Ted Bates Advt. Agy., N.Y.C., 1948-57; mem. pub. relations dept. plans bd., mgr. product publicity Borden, Inc., N.Y.C., 1957-71, mgr. product info. Borden Foods, Columbus, Ohio, 1971—; appeared in TV pub. relations films For Your Information, 1963-64. Recipient Outstanding Contbr. to Food Industry award Food Industry Assocs. of Lehigh Valley, 1963. Mem. Pub. Relations Soc. Am. (accredited), Am., Ohio home econs. assns., Am. Women in Radio and TV, Women in Communications, Home Fashions League, Publicity Club N.Y. (pres. 1955-56). Republican. Methodist. Home: 1000 Urlin Ave Columbus OH 43212 Office: 180 E Broad St Columbus OH 43215

MURPHY, MARY THERESA, counselor; b. Winthrop, Mass., Jan. 5, 1951; d. Lawrence John and Edna Louise (Lavery) Murphy; B.A., U. Mass., Boston, 1974; M.Ed., Suffolk U., Boston, 1975. Counselor, psychometrist Counseling Service Center, Woburn, Mass., 1974-76; counselor Booth Meml. Home, Boston, 1976; asst. dir. student affairs Lyman Briggs Coll., Mich. State U., East Lansing, 1976-77, asso. dir. student affairs, 1977—; cons. in field, condr. workshops. Mem. Am. Personnel and Guidance Assn., Nat. Catholic Guidance Conf. Researched and developed death edn. program for grades K-12. Home: 181E Holmes Hall Mich State Univ East Lansing MI 48824

MURPHY, MAX RAY, lawyer; b. Goshen, Ind., July 18, 1934; s. Loren A. and Lois (Mink) M.; B.A., DePauw U., 1956; J.D., Yale Law Sch., 1959; student Mich. State U., 1960; m. Judith Helen French, Sept. 11, 1957; children—Michael Lee, Chad Woodrow. Admitted to Mich. bar, 1960; legal asso. Glassen, Parr, Rhead & McLean, Lansing, Mich., 1960-67; instr. Lansing Bus. U., 1963-67; partner firm Boter, Dalman Murphy and Bidol, Holland, Mich., 1967—. Democratic candidate for Ingham County (Mich.) Pros. Atty., 1962, 1964; asst. pros. atty. Ottawa County, Mich., 1967-70. Mem. Ottawa County, Ingham County, Am. bar assns. Clubs: Holland Country, Michigan Jaycees. Home: 4941 174th Ave Holland MI 49423 Office: 274 E 8th St Holland MI 49423

MURPHY, MORGAN F., Congressman; b. Chgo., Apr. 16, 1932; B.S., Northwestern U., 1955; LL.B., DePaul U., 1962, J.D.; m. Charlene D. Jurgensen, 1959; children—Morgan, Michelle, Constance. Admitted to Ill. bar, 1962; practice law, 1962-70; mem. 92d-95th congresses from 2d Ill. Dist. Served as officer USMC. Mem. Sigma Chi, Am., Ill., Chgo. bar assns., Am., Ill. trial lawyers assns. Trustee Morgan Park Acad. Office: Room 2436 Rayburn House Office Bldg Washington DC 20515*

MURPHY, MORGAN F., congressman; b. Chgo., Aug. 22, 1905; s. Morgan and Johanna (Nolan) M.; student DeLaSalle Inst., Northwestern U.; LL.D. honoris causa, St. Xavier Coll., 1960; m. Anne Burns, Aug. 18, 1928; children—Mary (Mrs. R. F. Stump), Morgan, Carol (Sister Carol Ann R.S.M.), Jane (Mrs. R.J. Holmes), John, Bernard. With Chgo. Rapid Transit Co., 1924; sec. to pres. Pub. Service Co. of No. Ill., 1935-43, asst. to pres., 1943-47, v.p. since 1947; v.p. Commonwealth Edison Co., 1952-62, exec. v.p., 1962-64, chmn. exec. com., 1964-68; mem. 91st-95th congresses from 2d dist. Ill.; dir. Central Nat. Bank Chgo., Talman Fed. Savs. and Loan Assn. Chgo. Mem., v.p. Chgo. Police Bd.; v.p. U. Chgo. Cancer Research, Found. Life trustee St. Xavier Coll. for Women; dir. Cath. Charities, Archdiocese of Chgo.; mem. citizens bd. Loyola U.; trustee Ill. Inst. Tech., Cardinal Stritch Youth Guidance Found., St. Joseph's Coll., Rensselaer, Ind.; mem. provincial bd. regents Sisters Mercy; mem. lay bd. consultors Mercy Hosp. Pres., dir. Washington Park Trotting Assn.; dir. Western Golf Assn. Vice pres., dir. 100 Club Cook County. Knight of St. Gregory. Clubs: Commercial, Chicago Athletic Association, Irish Fellowship of Chgo. (past pres.) (Chgo.); Beverly Country; Chicago. Home: 2440 W 113th St Chicago IL 60655

MURPHY, PATRICK HENRY, mfg. co. exec.; b. Nokomis, Ill., Oct. 26, 1941; s. Patrick Henry and Elizabeth Bessie (Durbin) M.; certificate Coll. Advanced Traffic, 1965-67; certificate transp. law, 1968; certificate bus. adminstrn. Millikin U., 1970; B.S., Lindenwood Coll., 1974; m. Constance J. Kunel, June 12, 1965. Traffic supr. Allis Chalmers Mfg. Co., Springfield, Ill., 1963-66; with Muss Co., Decatur, Ill., 1966-71; with Debron Corp., St. Ann, Mo. 1971—, mgr. purchasing and transp., 1971—. Served with AUS, 1960-63. Mem. Am. Soc. Traffic and Transp., Delta Nu Alpha. Clubs: Traffic (dir. 1973-75); World Trade. Home: 21 San Carlos Dr St Charles MO 63301 Office: PO Box 1007 St Ann MO 63074

MURPHY, PAUL LLOYD, historian, educator; b. Caldwell, Idaho, Sept. 5, 1923; s. Paul and Anna Ruth (Weltner) M.; B.A., M.A., Coll. Idaho, 1947, LL.D.(hon.), 1976; Ph.D., U. Calif., Berkeley, 1953; m. Helen W. Chase, Aug. 9, 1946; children—Patricia Anne, Karen Diane. Asst. prof. history Colo. State U., 1953; instr. history Ohio State U., 1953-57; asst. prof. history U. Minn., Mpls., 1957-60, asso. prof., 1960-70, prof., 1970—; vis. asst. prof. history Northwestern U., 1958; Robert Lee Bailey vis. prof. history U. N.C., Charlotte, 1977; vis. prof. history U. Colo., 1961, Stanford U., 1966; research fellow Center History of Liberty Harvard U., 1961-62. Bd. dirs. Twin City Internat. Program, 1969-72, ACLU, Minn., 1962-67. Guggenheim fellow, 1965-66; sr. Fulbright lectr. U. Lagos (Nigeria), 1971-72; Danforth fellow, 1973. Mem. AAUP (chpt. pres. 1972-73), Phi Beta Kappa. Author: The Constitution in Crisis Times, 1918-1969, 1972; The Meaning of Freedom of Speech: First Amendment Freedoms from Wilson to FDR, 1972 (Gavel award Am. Bar Assn.); Political Parties in American History, 1974; The Passaic Textile Strike, 1974; contbr. articles to hist. jours. Home: 2159 Folwell St Falcon Heights MN 55108 Office: Dept History 614 Social Science Bldg Minneapolis MN 55455

MURPHY, ROBERT EDWARD, real estate broker; b. Chgo., Oct. 9, 1930; s. George J. and Margaret (Crogan) M.; B.A., U. Miami, 1955; m. Elizabeth Margaret Shedd, June 18, 1966; children—Margaret, Suzanne. Account exec. Gen. Outdoor Advt. Co., 1955-59, CBS, 1959-60, Sta. WLS, ABC, Chgo., 1960-67; gen. sales mgr. Sta. WCFL, Chgo., 1967-68; real estate broker, 1968—; v.p. in charge marketing, dir. Bank of Dwight, Ill. Served with USMCR, 1947-52. Club: Ill. Athletic. Home: 1501 Tower Rd Winnetka IL 60093

MURPHY, ROBERT THOMAS, surgeon; b. Chgo., July 6, 1917; s. Harold Francis and Lelah Ray (Massie) M.; A.B., Albion Coll., 1939; M.D., U. Mich., 1942; m. Joan Louise Hartrick, July 3, 1941; children—Jean E., Paul G., Michael R. Intern, U. Mich. Hosp., 1942; resident in surgery U. Mich., 1942-45, teaching asst. in pathology, 1943; surgeon Harper Hosp., Detroit, 1945-55; chief resident Huron Rd. Hosp., Cleve., 1957, staff surgeon, 1958—, asso. chief surgery, 1968—, dir. surg. dept., 1977—. Bd. dirs. Great Lakes Shakespeare Theatre, 1977. Served to maj. USAF, 1955-57. Recipient certificate in pathology U. Mich. Sch. Postgrad. Medicine, 1943. Diplomate Am. Bd. Surgery. Fellow A.C.S.; mem. Royal Coll. Physicians London (asso.), AMA (Merit certificate, 1969), Ohio Med. Assn., Acad. Medicine Cuyahoga County, Cleve. Surg. Soc., Irish Am. Cultural Soc. Republican. Methodist. Clubs: Canterbury Golf, Rowfant. Editor column in New Physician mag., 1960-70; contbr. surg. articles to profl. jours. Home: 2812 Brainard St Cleveland OH 44124 Office: Huron Rd Hosp 13951 Terrace Rd East Cleveland OH 44112

MURPHY, THOMAS A., automotive co. exec.; b. Hornell, N.Y., 1915; B.S., U. Ill., 1938. With Gen. Motors Corp., 1938—, v.p. and exec.-car and truck group, 1970-72, vice chmn. bd., 1972-74, chmn., chief exec. officer, dir., 1974—. Home: 1761 Huntingwood Ln Bloomfield Hills MI 48013 Office: 3044 W Grand Blvd Gen Motors Bldg Detroit MI 48202*

MURPHY, THOMAS BERNARD, ins. co. exec.; b. Brockton, Mass., Aug. 30, 1927; s. John Joseph and Anna Madeline (Mackin) M.; B.S., Boston Coll., 1950; M.S., U. Mich., 1953; m. Jacquelyn Mackenzie, Dec. 8, 1957; children—Thomas, Mark, Robert, Elizabeth, Michael. Exec. v.p. Boston Mut. Life Ins. Co., Canton, Mass., 1963-70; v.p. Maccabees Mut. Life Ins. Co., Southfield, Mich., 1970-72; chmn., chief exec officer George Washington Corp., Jacksonville, Fla., 1976; chmn., chief exec. officer TOP Inc., Troy, Mich., 1977—, also dir. Served to 1st lt. AUS, 1951-53. Fellow Soc. Actuaries; mem. Internat. Assn. Actuaries, Am. Acad. Actuaries. Roman Catholic. Club: Birmingham Country. Home: 4683 Brightmore St Bloomfield Hills MI 48013 Office: 363 W Big Beaver St Troy MI 48084

MURPHY, THOMAS VINCENT, leasing co. exec.; b. Phila., Oct. 12, 1928; s. James Frances and Mary Magdeline (McLaughlin) M.; bus. certificate Columbia Bus. Coll., 1948; student Temple U., 1948-49, 49-50, Alexander Hamilton Bus. Mgmt., 1954-59; m. Patricia Ann Martin, Apr. 26, 1952; children—Thomas Vincent, John M., Richard G., David G. With Nat. Cash Register Co., Phila., 1949-50, Stewart Equipment Co., Phila., 1950-60; with Bell Equipment Corp. (now Tiger Equipment Services), leasing engineered equipment to petroleum industry, N.Y.C., 1960—, exec. v.p., Los Angeles, 1968—, dir., 1972—; pres. Bell Worldwide, Inc., Chgo., 1973—; dir. Tiger Equipment & Services Ltd., Tiger Equipment & Services (London) Ltd., Tiger Equipment & Services NV, Curacao, Soon Douglas (Pte.) Ltd., Singapore. Cons. Quebec Iron & Titanium, Tin and Asso. Minerals, Royal Dutch Shell, Alyeska Pipeline Service Co. Bd. dirs. United Fund, Allentown, Pa., 1950-51. Judge of elections State of Pa., Springfield, 1953-54. Served with AUS, 1944-46. Decorated Purple Heart. Mem. Am. Mgmt. Assn., Am. Material Handling Soc. Inc., Franklin Inst. Mech. Arts, Smithsonian Instn. Clubs: Sleepy Hollow Country (Scarsborough, N.Y.); 21 Club Soc. (London, Eng.); Vesper (Phila.); Metropolitan (Chgo.). Contbr. to profl. pubs. Patentee in field. Home: 854 W Deerpath Lake Forest IL 60045 Office: 222 S Riverside Plaza Chicago IL 60606

MURPHY, WILLIAM VALENTINE, health systems exec.; b. Bronx, N.Y., Feb. 14, 1937; s. William Francis and Bridget Josephine (Morahan) M.; B.E.E., Manhattan Coll., 1959; M.S., Adelphi U., 1964; M.B.A., N.Y. U., 1970; m. Roberta Jean Ritter, Apr. 19, 1969. Design engr. Def. Contractors, 1959-64; mgr. airborne computer systems Grumman Aircraft Co., 1964-69; sr. v.p. systems ops. Telemed Corp., Hoffman Estates, Ill., 1969—. Mem. Am. Mgmt. Assn., IEEE, Assn. Computing Machinery, Assn. Advancement Med. Instrumentation. Home: 1580 Lake Shore Dr S Barrington IL 60010 Office: 2345 Pembroke St Hoffman Estates IL 60195

MURRAY, BEVERLY ANN, psychotherapist, educator; b. Atlantic, Iowa, Jan. 27, 1939; d. Ernest Wayne and Martha Louise (Storie) Shaw; B.A., U. No. Iowa, 1961; M.Ed., Fitchburg State Coll., 1973; M.A. in Counseling, Sangamon State U., 1978; m. L. W. Murray, Sept. 3, 1960 (div. May, 1977); children—Brenda Lea, Jennifer Lyn, Laurena Ann. Tchr. pub. schs., Cedar Falls, Iowa, 1961-63, Charles City, Iowa, 1964-67; clin. instr. student tchrs. Clark U., Worcester, Mass., 1972-73; reading specialist, therapist Baumann Clinic, Springfield, Ill., 1974—; remedial reading tchr. Washington Middle Sch. Dist., Springfield, 1975—; tchr. nutrition edn., counselor women infants children program adult edn. Springfield Urban League, 1976—. Active Civic Nu-Comer Group. Mem. Nat., Ill., Springfield edn. assns., Central Ill. Reading Council, Internat. Reading Assn., Am. Personnel and Guidance Assn., Sigma Alpha Iota. Episcopalian. Home: Rural Route 3 Crows Mill Lane Springfield IL 62707 Office: Washington Sch 2300 E Jackson St Springfield IL 62703 also Baumann Clinic 725 S 2nd St Springfield IL 62703

MURRAY, CHARLES JOHN, bldg. and constrn. exec.; b. Oak Park, Ill., July 25, 1934; s. Harold James and Evelyn (Stephens) M.; student Tex. Mil. Inst., 1951-53; B. in Bus. Adminstrn., So. Meth. U., 1958; m. Christl Reitinger, May 16, 1960; children—Mark F., Linda M., Katherine A. Field projects engr. Mellish & Murray Co., Chgo., 1960-62, projects capt., 1962-63, projects coordinator, 1963-65, constrn. mgr., 1965-68, treas., 1968-71, sec., treas., 1971—, also dir. Instr. Dale Carnegie courses Mid-West Inst., Chgo., 1969—. Mem. exec. bd. Horace Mann Sch. P.T.A., Oak Park, Ill., 1968—; pres. Near Northwest Civic Com., Inc., Chgo., 1969—. Trustee Granco Trust, Chgo., Pension Fund Local 73 Sheet Metal Worker Internat. Assn. Served with AUS, 1958-60. Mem. Am. Soc. Heating, Refrigerating and Air-Conditioning Engrs. (chmn. scholarship and edn. com. Ill. chpt. 1972), Ventilating and Air Conditioning Contractors Assn. Chgo. (mem. air test and balance com. 1970), U.S. Power Squadron, Chgo. Assn. Commerce and Industry. Home: 931 Forest Ave Oak Park IL 60302 Office: 1720 Fulton St Chicago IL 60612

MURRAY, DANIEL GARDNER, marketing exec.; b. Troy, N.Y., Apr. 13, 1934; s. Daniel George and Theressa Eleanor (Riley) M.; A.A. Sci., State U., N.Y., 1953; B.S., U. Ga., 1962, M.S., 1963; m. Patricia ann Hollis, Nov. 24, 1956; children—Timothy F., Daniel Steven. Supr., Nat. Starch and Chem., Plainfield, N.J., 1963-67; mgr. product devel. Grain Processing Corp., Muscatine, Ia., 1967-69, mgr. food tech. services, 1969-73; marketing dir. Amoco Foods Co., Chgo., 1973—. Chmn. low rent housing commn., Muscatine, Ia., 1971-73; Republican committeeman, county central com. Muscatine, 1970-73. Served with USAF, 1954-59. U. Ga. grad. fellow, 1962; recipient Distinguished Service award for community service, C. of C., 1972. Mem. Research and Devel. Assn. (bd. dirs. 1975-77), Inst. Food Technologists (exec. com. 1977-79), Am. Marketing Assn., Am. Assn. Cereal Chemists, Am. Meat Inst., U.S. Air Force Acad. Republican. Episcopalian. Patentee in field. Home: 1205 Clyde Dr Naperville IL 60540 Office: 200 E Randolph Dr Chicago IL 60601

MURRAY, DONALD RICHARD, educator; b. Youngstown, Ohio, Sept. 29, 1931; s. Paul Burnett and Mary Louise (James) M.; B.Sacred Music., Vennard Coll., 1954; student William Penn Coll., 1951; postgrad. Am. Conservatory Music, 1955-56; M.Mus., Ind. U., 1965; m. Dorothy May Grenfell, June 5, 1953; children—Deborah May, Donald Richard, David Paul. Faculty Vennard Coll., University Park, Iowa, 1954-55, Bethel Coll., Mishawaka, Ind., 1955-58, Olivet Nazarene Coll., Kankakee, Ill., 1958-67; faculty Malone Coll., Canton, Ohio, 1967—, prof. music, chmn. Div. Fine Arts. Guest lectr. various subjects; minister music First Friends Ch., Canton, 1968—; minister music Presbyn. Ch., 1958-63, Nazarene Ch., 1963-67. Pres. Arts Council, Stark County, Ohio, 1973-76. Program com. Canton Cultural Center, 1970—. Mem. Nat. Ch. Music Fellowship (treas. 1969-70), Music Educators Nat. Conf., Coll. Music Soc. Home: 359 19th St NW Canton OH 44709

MURRAY, GORDON NICHOLAS, educator; b. Chgo., Mar. 22, 1917; s. Alfred Nicholas and Edna (Schmidt) M.; B.S., Northwestern U., 1939, M.S., 1948; diploma Army Vet. Sch. Army Med. Center, Washington, 1941, Med. Field Service Sch., 1942; postgrad. Punahou U., Oahu, Hawaii, 1944, U. Ill., 1951-52, Washington and Lee U., 1945; m. Leda A. Johnson, Dec. 15, 1945; children—Robert Nicholas, Susan Carolyn (Mrs. Thomas A. Neill), Nancy Jean (Mrs. Jeffrey D. Dunlap), Alfred Nicholas II. Cons. camp leadership, counselor tng. course Northwestern U., 1940; asst. prof. biology U. Tenn., 1946-50; asso. prof. biology and microbiology City Colls. Chgo., 1950-69, prof., 1969—; microbiologist Grant Hosp. Sch. Nursing, Chgo., 1958-63, Evang. Hosp. Sch. Nursing, Chgo., 1961-62; prof. med. terminology, anatomy and physiology Augustana Hosp., Columbus Hosp., St. Joseph Hosp., Chgo., 1973-77. Instl. rep., merit badge counselor com. chmn. N.E. Ill. council Boy Scouts Am.; founding mem. Bethesda

Nat. Found.; nat. adv. bd. Am. Security Council. Served from pvt. to capt. Med. Adminstrv. Corps, U.S. Army, 1940-46. NSF grantee, 1964. Mem. Chgo. Art Inst., AAUP, Bot. Soc. Am., Am., Ill. socs. microbiology, Ill. (tchr. tng. com.), Chgo. acads. scis., AAAS (life), Am. Inst. Biol. Scis., Ill., Chgo. edn. assns., Am. Forestry Assn., Nat. Wildlife Fedn., Ill. Audubon Soc., Nat. Parks Assn., Ill. Assn. Classroom Tchrs., Council Basic Edn., Higher Edn. Assn., Field Mus. Chgo., Adler Planetarium, Nat. Assn. Biology Tchrs., Chgo., Lincoln Park zool. socs., Am. Mus. Natural History, Nat., Ill. Audubon socs., Wilderness Soc., Isaak Walton League Am., Am., Ill. assns. higher edn., Nat. Geog. Soc., Internat. Oceanographic Found., Oceanic Soc. (charter), NEA, Internat. Platform Assn., Smithsonian Assos., U.S. Olympic Soc., Lambda Chi Alpha. Republican. Presbyterian (Christian edn. council; exec. bd. deacons). Home: 1016 Harvard Terr Evanston IL 60202 Office: 1145 W Wilson Ave Chicago IL 60640

MURRAY, HARRY LEE, microbiologist; b. Covington, Ind., June 6, 1922; s. Lee Alexander and Marjorie Caroline (Carnahan) M.; A.S., Vincennes (Ind.) U., 1942; A.B. in Biology, U. Evansville (Ind.), 1954; m. Mary Claire Theriac, Oct. 9, 1949; children—Thomas, Richard, Janet, Susan. Office asst. Vincennes Sun-Comml. Newspaper, 1939-40; pharmacist apprentice Duesterberg Drug Store, Vincennes, 1940-42; head lab. technician, X-ray technician Clearview Hosp., Evansville, 1953, Hillcrest Hosp., Vincennes, 1949-56; sr. scientist Mead Johnson & Co., Evansville, 1954—, instr. speech, 1972—; speaker in field. Instr. speech Dale Carnegie Internat., Evansville, 1958. Served with USNR, 1942-44, USMCR, 1944-46. Mem. Am. Soc. Microbiology, Dale Carnegie Alumni Assn., Internat. Platform Assn., Toastmasters Internat. (Russel Caray award 1969, award Humorous Speech Contest 1969, chmn. area consumers rights 1972), Debater, Amateur Writers, Sigma Xi. Author: Blooeyflum, 1970. Contbr. articles to profl. jours. Home: 2368 E Walnut St Evansville IN 47714 Office: 2404 W Pennsylvania St Evansville IN 47721

MURRAY, JUDSON THRASH, state adminstr.; b. Shreveport, La., Dec. 26, 1918; s. Louis E. and Seabelle (Thrash) M.; A.B., Wiley Coll., 1940; postgrad. Howard U., 1940-41, John Marshall Law Sch., 1949-51, DePaul U., 1959; m. Julia B. Johnson, Sept. 8, 1945; children—Joyce A., Jacqueline T. Caseworker Pub. Aid Dept. Cook County (Ill.), Chgo., 1947-51, resources cons., 1951-68, tech. adviser, 1968, asst. chief Bur. Resources and Legal Services, 1969-75; asst. regional dir., region IV, Pub. Aid Dept. Ill., Chgo., 1975—. Mem. Com. Cts. and Justice, 1970—. Served with AUS, 1942-45. Mem. Chgo. Urban League, NAACP, Omega Psi Phi. Presbyterian. Club: City (Chgo.). Home: 7304 S Eberhart Ave Chicago IL 60619 Office: Illinois Pub Aid Dept 840 E 87th St Chicago IL 60619

MURRAY, J(ULIAN) RONALD, sales exec.; b. Mpls., June 9, 1916; s. Douglas Ronald and Flora (Marot) M.; B.S. in Mech. Engring., Purdue U., 1938; postgrad. U. Mich., 1943-44; m. Marilynn R. Miller, Apr. 12, 1947; children—William R., James S. With Babcock & Wilcox Co., 1938—, sales engr. Chgo. office, 1946-62, dist. sales mgr., 1962-66, regional sales mgr., 1966—. Vestryman St. Matthews Episcopal Ch., 1955-58, warden, 1958-60; vestryman Holy Comforter Episc. Ch., 1974-77. Served to capt. ordnance dept. U.S. Army, 1942-45. Mem. ASME, Western Soc. Engr., Am. Nuclear Soc., Chgo. Assn. Commerce and Industry. Clubs: Union League, Monroe, Westmoreland Country, Masons, Shriners. Patentee. Home: 228 Leicester Rd Kenilworth 60043 Office: 29 S LaSalle St Chicago IL 60603

MURRAY, KERMON, govt. research engr.; b. Lowmansville, Ky., Dec. 20, 1921; s. Arby and Eva (Castle) M.; B.A., Wittenberg U., 1953; m. Blanche Elaine Angus, July 31, 1965; children—Cheryl (Mrs. Gary Farmer), Larry, Terry, Valerie, Daniel, Gary. Chemist Air Force Materials Lab., Wright-Petterson, AFB, Ohio, 1953-54, materials engr., 1964—. Served in USN, 1941-45, 50-51. Mem. Am. Chem. Soc., Am. Soc. Lubrication Engrs., Southern Ohio Rubber Group, Navy Enlisted Reserve Assn. (pres. Dayton chpt. 1972—). Baptist. Home: 68 Skyline Dr Enon OH 45323 Office: Air Force Materials Lab Wright-Patterson AFB OH 45433

MURRAY, MERRILL R., ednl. adminstr.; b. New Castle, Ind., Aug. 3, 1917; s. Arthur Gray and Mary (Dixon) M.; student Hanover Coll., 1935-36, Kent State U., 1943; B.S., Ball State U., 1949, M.S., 1951; Ed.D., Ind. U., 1960; m. Eva Jean Yergin, Mar. 30, 1940; 1 son, Michael Russell. Math. tchr. high sch., New Castle, Ind., 1949-51, 53-54; dir. USAF Dependents Schs., Burtonwood, Eng., 1952-53; prin. high sch., Ridgeville, Ind., 1954-56; research asso. Ind. U., Bloomington, 1956-58; dean of students Tri-State U., Angola, 1958-59; dean specialized edn. div. Ferris State Coll., Big Rapids, Mich., 1959-65, asst. dean Sch. Gen. Edn., 1965-69, asso. dean, 1969—, asso. dean Coll. Optometry, 1977—; dir. Central Mich. Bank & Trust. Bd. dir. Area Crippled Childrens Soc. Served with USAAF, 1943-45, USAF, 51-53; col. Res. Mem. Nat. U. Extension Assn. (div. chmn.), Mich. Coordinating Council Continuing Higher Edn. (pres.), Am. Soc. for Tng. and Devel., Am. Personnel and Guidance Assn., Am. Assn. Sch. Adminstrs., Air Force Assn., Mich. Assn. Schs. and Colls., Res. Officers Assn., Am. Assn. Higher Edn., Mecosta Pilots Assn. (pres.), Phi Delta Kappa, Kappa Delta Phi, Sigma Mu Sigma. Presbyn. (elder). Mason, Rotarian (pres. 1964-65). Home: Route 1 Box 50 Chula Vista Dr Big Rapids MI 49307 Office: 901 S State St Big Rapids MI 49307

MURRAY, MICHAEL RUSSELL, banker; b. New Castle, Ind., Oct. 20, 1953; s. Merrill Russell and EvaJean (Yergin) M.; B.S. in Bus. Adminstrn., Central Mich. U., 1975; M.B.A., Ball State U., 1976. Grad. asst. Ball State U., Muncie, Ind., 1975-76; personnel officer Central Mich. Bank & Trust, Big Rapids, Mich., 1976—. Mem. Am. Mktg. Assn., Me-La-Wex-Ola, Mich. (personnel com.) bankers assns. Democrat. Clubs: Order of DeMolay, Rotary. Home: Route 1 Chula Vista Dr Big Rapids MI 49307 Office: 101 N Michigan Ave Big Rapids MI 49307

MURRAY, MICHAEL THOMAS, finance co. exec.; b. Ft. Francis, Ont., Can., May 4, 1949; s. Joseph Thomas and Edna Mary (Sanders) M.; came to U.S., 1960; B.S., U. Wis., 1971; m. Gwen Mary Kapitan, Dec. 22, 1975. Dir. finance Guardian Internat. Inc., Mpls., 1972-74; pres., dir. Nat. Investment Consultants, Mpls., 1974—, C.F.M. Enterprises Minn. Inc., Mpls., 1976—; dir. Nat. Investment Corp., Internat. Commodity Consultants Miami. Mem. Inst. Certified Bus. Counselors, Minn., Fla. real estate exchangors. Home: 16 Birnamwood Dr Burnesville MN 55337 Office: 800 S Gate Office Plaza Minneapolis MN 55437

MURRAY, RICHARD DEIBEL, physician; b. Youngstown, Ohio, Dec. 25, 1921; s. Thomas Henry and Olive (Deibel) M.; B.S., U. Notre Dame, 1942; M.D., Georgetown U., 1946; M.S., U. Pa., 1953. Intern, Youngstown Hosp. Assn., 1946-47, mem. attending staff, chief of plastic surgery service; resident in plastic surgery Kings County Hosp. Bklyn., 1952-54; practice medicine specializing in plastic surgery, Youngstown, 1955—; mem. courtesy staff St. Elizabeth Hosp.; mem. cons. staff Salem City Hosp.; plastic surgery cons. Hosp. of Our Lady of Maryknoll, Kowloon, Hong Kong, Louis Guerrera Meml. lectr. Santo Tomas U., Manila, Philippines, 1964. Served to lt. (j.g.), M.C., USNR, 1947-49. Recipient Frank Purnell award for outstanding contributions to the Youngstown Community. Executed marble Orpheus fountain, Youngstown, other sculptures. Exhibited in group shows at Am. Physicians Art Assn., Butler Art Inst., Am. Soc. Cleft Palate Rehab. Pres. Youngstown Symphony Soc. Decorated Order St. John of Jerusalem. Mem. Am. Soc. Plastic and Reconstructive Surgery, Robert Ivy Soc. Phila., Ohio Valley Plastic Soc., Kings County Soc., A.M.A., Ohio, Mahoning County med. socs. Elk. Clubs: Youngstown Country, Rotary (Youngstown); N.Y. Athletic. Author: The Rise and Fall of the State, 1967; The Key to Nostradamus, 1975. Contbr. articles to sci. jours. Home: 171 Newport Dr Youngstown OH 44512 Office: 2125 Glenwood Ave Youngstown OH 44511

MURRAY, ROBERT EUGENE, coal co. exec.; b. Martins Ferry, Ohio, Jan. 13, 1940; s. Albert Edward and Mildred Etheline (Shepherd) M.; B.Engring., Ohio State U., 1962; postgrad. Case Western Res. U., 1968-70; m. Brenda Lou Moore, Aug. 26, 1962; children—Sherri Sue (dec.), Robert Edward, Jonathan Robert. Asst. to mgr. indsl. engring. and coal preparation N.Am. Coal Corp., 1961-63, sect. foreman, plant foreman, gen. mine foreman, Ohio div., 963-64, asst. supt., 1964-66, supt. 1966-68, asst. to pres., Cleve., 1968-69, v.p. operations, v.p. eastern div., 1969-74, pres. Western div., 1974—; pres. Coteau Properties Co., Falkirk Mining Co.; mining engring. departmental asst. Ohio State U., 1960-62; pres. N.D. Lignite Council. Mem. exec. bd., v.p. dist. ops. No. Lights council Boy Scouts Am.; bd. dirs. United Way of Bismarck. Registered profl. engr., Ohio. Mem. Am. Mining Congress, Mining Electro-Mech. Assn. (pres. Ohio Valley br. 1967-68), Pitts. Coal Mining Inst. Am., Am. Inst. Mining, Metall. and Petroleum Engrs. (chmn. underground mining com., exec. com. coal div.), Rocky Mountain Coal Mining Inst. (v.p., program chmn.), Ohio (pres. east Ohio chpt. 1966-67), Nat. socs. profl. engrs., Ohio Engrs. in Industry (mem. bd. govs. 1966-67), Ill. Mining Inst., N.D. Water Users Assn. Republican. Methodist (mem. adminstrv. bd. 1968-69, lay speaker, tchr.). Mason (32 deg., Shriner). Home: 1230 W Highland Acres Rd Bismarck ND 58501 Office: Kirkwood Office Tower Bismarck ND 58501

MURRAY, RUTH ELAINE, psychologist; b. Litchfield, Ill., June 3, 1942; d. Hugh Rice and Norma Marie (Eden) Murray; M.S. in Psychology, So. Ill. U., 1974. Tchr. Marquette High Sch., Alton, Ill., 1964-65; coordinator testing and evaluation service So. Ill. U., Edwardsville, 1965—, adj. instr. psychology. Mem. Am., Midwestern Psychol. Assns., Psi Chi. Contbr. articles to profl. publs., paper to psychol. conv. Home: 769 Condit St Wood River IL 62095 Office: Student Devel Services Southern Ill Univ Edwardsville IL 62026

MURRAY, WALTER ALLAN, JR., lawyer; b. Washington, Mo., May 6, 1942; s. Walter Allan and Ruth Estora Sullivan M.; A.B., Central Methodist Coll., 1964; J.D., Washington U., St. Louis, 1967; m. Monica Louise Klekamp, Aug. 5, 1972; children—Walter Allan III, Andrew Todd. Admitted to Mo. bar, 1967; legal clk. Strubinger, Wion & Burke, St. Louis, 1966-67; asso. firm Wion, Burke & Boll, Clayton, Mo., 1968-69; pvt. practice law Union, Mo., 1969—; asst. pros. atty. Franklin County (Mo.), 1970—, city atty. City of Union, 1973—. Adv. bd. Profl. Counseling Center, New Haven, Mo., 1972—. Treas. Franklin County Republican Central Com., 1970—. Mem. Franklin County Youth Fair Bd., 1969-72, treas., 1971; bd. dirs. Profl. Health Services, Inc., New Haven. Mem. Union Jaycees (Region legal council 1971-72, presl. award 1970), Mo. Bar Assn., 20th Jud. Dist. Bar Assn., Union C. of C., Mo. Municipal Attys. Assn., Sigma Alpha Chi, Phi Delta Phi. Presbyn. (clk. session). Rotarian (pres. Union 1972). Home: 12 Valley Dr Union MO 63084 Office: 17 S Oak St Suite 200 Union MO 63084

MURRAY, WILLIAM FRANCIS, clergyman, clin. psychologist; b. Rochester, N.Y., Sept. 15, 1926; s. Jeremiah John and Gertrude (L'Huillier) M. B.A., U. Toronto, Canada, 1948; Ph.D., U. St. Thomas, Rome, 1961; M.S., Ind. State U., 1975. Registered psychologist, Ill. Intern, VA Hosp., Canadaigua, N.Y., 1972-73, Gibault Sch. for Boys, Terre Haute, Ind., 1975; dir. Douglas County (Ill.) Mental Health Center, Tuscola, 1975—. Mem. Am. Psychol. Assn., Am. Catholic Philos. Assn., Am. Soc. Clin. Hypnosis (asso.), K.C. Home: PO Box 102 Tuscola IL 61953 Office: 120 W Sale St Tuscola IL 61953

MURRAY, WILLIAM FREDERIC, banker; b. Ft. Dodge, Iowa, Sept. 19, 1912; s. Alvin Ellis and Anne (Hartigan) M.; B.S., U. Ill., 1934; m. Dorothy Ann Bailly, June 12, 1940; children—Jean, Marilyn, Timothy. With Harris Trust & Savs. Bank, Chgo., 1934—, asst. cashier, 1947-49, asst. v.p., 1949-51, v.p., 1951-64, sr. v.p., 1964-68, pres., after 1968, now chmn., chief exec. officer; dir. Empire Dist. Electric Co., Joplin, Mo. Bd. dirs. U. Ill. Found. Served with USNR, 1943-46. Mem. Phi Delta Theta. Clubs: Westmoreland Country (Wilmette, Ill.); Chicago, University, Economic, Bankers (Chgo.). Home: 105 Woodley Rd Winnetka IL 60093 Office: 111 W Monroe St Chicago IL 60690

MURRELL, PETER CHARLES, dentist; b. Glasgow, Ky., May 14, 1920; s. Samuel Clem and Nellie Murrell; B.S., Ky. State Coll., 1941; D.D.S., Marquette U., 1947; postgrad. U. Wyo., 1952; m. Eva Ruth Greenlee, Sept. 28, 1947; children—Peggy Joyce, Peter Charles, Linda Jean, James Arthur. Instr. prosthodontia Howard U. Coll. Dentistry, Washington, 1947-48; practice gen. dentistry, Milw., 1948-51, 53—. Mem. Comprehensive Health Planning Agy. Southeastern Wis., Inc. Mem. We-Milwaukeans Civic Com., 1963—; bd. dirs. Childrens' Service Wis., 1962—, treas., 1972-74; bd. dirs. Northside YMCA, 1947—, chmn., 1949-51; bd. dirs. Greater Milw. Survey Social Welfare and Health Services, Inc., 1972-73. Served with USAAF, 1943-44, with Dental Corps, USAF, 1951-53. Recipient plaque for profl. excellence Community Pride Expo, 1975; Decade of Service award North Central YMCA, 1975. Service award Opportunities Industrialization Center Greater Milw. 1971. Mem. Am., Nat., Wis., Greater Milw. (sec. 1974-75, v.p. 1975-76) dental assns., Am. Soc. for Preventive Dentistry, Am. Acad. Gen. Practice, Greater Milw. Dental Soc. (dir. 1969-72, librarian 1972-73, treas. 1973-74, pres. 1977-78), Garfield Found., Alpha Kappa Mu, Alpha Phi Alpha (chpt. pres. 1953-57). Baptist. Home: 1302 W Capitol Dr Milwaukee WI 53206 Office: 2545 N Teutonia Ave Milwaukee WI 53206

MURRELL, TURNER MEADOWS, lawyer; b. Greensboro, N.C., Feb. 5, 1923; s. James Robert and Sallie Frances (Page) M.; B.A., Washburn U., 1948, J.D., 1949; children—Gregory S., Leslie Ann, Todd G.; m. 2d, Patricia L. Shortall, Dec. 4, 1975; stepchildren—John J., Janis L., Kathleen A. and Lisa M. Shortall. Admitted to Kans. bar, 1949, since practiced in Topeka; partner Murrell, Corrick & Coleman, 1969—; chmn. bd. Nat. Investment Corp., Inc., 1968—; chmn., pres., dir. Am. Investors Life Ins. Co., Inc., 1973—; chmn. bd. dirs. Internat. Investors Life Ins. Co., Inc., 1969—; pres., dir. Am. Option and Equity Fund, Inc., 1969—. City judge, Topeka, 1953-57; mem. Kans. Ho. of Reps., 1957-61, majority leader, 1959-61. Served with USNR, 1943-46, 51-52. Recipient Distinguished Service award City of Topeka, 1967, Young Man of Year award U.S. Jr. C. of C., 1957. Mem. Delta Pheta Phi. Clubs: Masons, Country (Topeka). Home: 421 Danbury Ln Topeka KS 66606 Office: 3301 Van Buren St Topeka KS 66611

MURRY, CHARLES EMERSON, adj. gen. N.D.; b. Hope, N.D., June 23, 1924; s. Raymond Henry and Estelle Margarete (Skeim) M.; m. Donna Deane Kleve, June 20, 1948; children—Barbara, Karla, Susan, Bruce, Charles; B.S., U. N.D., 1950, J.D., 1950. Admitted to N.D. bar, mem. firm Nelson & Heringer, Rugby, 1950-51; dir. N.D. Legis. Council, 1951-75; adj. gen. N.D., Bismarck, 1975—; cons. Council State Govts. Vice pres. Missouri Slope Lutheran Home, Bismarck. Mem. Am., N.D. bar assns., NG Assn., Nat. Legis. Conf. (past chmn.), Adjs. Gen. Assn., Commrs. on Uniform State Laws. Clubs: Masons; Elks; Exchange of Bismark (past pres.). Recipient Sioux award U. N.D., Gov.'s Nat. Leadership award. Contbr. articles to profl. jours. Home and office: PO Box 1817 Bismarck ND 58505

MURRY, EDWARD JAMES, physicist, research co. exec.; b. Freeport, Mich., July 18, 1925; s. John Edward and Catherine Mary (Wiegand) M.; B.A., Wayne U., 1939; M.S., Ill. Inst. Tech., 1953; Ph.D., U. Chgo., 1964; m. Jeannette Celine Verdoncq, June 4, 1947; 1 stepson, Alain A. Chief electronic services USAF, U.S., Far East, Europe, 1946-53; lab. chief, head research and devel. I.I.T.R.I., Chgo., 1954-63; with Fibra Sonics Inc., Chgo., 1964—, exec. v.p., 1966—; lectr., cons. in field. Served with U.S. Army, 1940-45, to lt. col. USAF, 1946-48. Mem. IEEE, Ultrasonics Industries Assn. (dir. 1965—), AAAS, Am. Nat. Standards Inst., Assn. Advisors Med. Instns. Presbyterian. Author books, contbr. articles to profl. publs.; over 100 inventions. Home: 9223 W 119th St Palos Park IL 60464 Office: 4626 N Lamon Ave Chicago IL 60464

MURTONEN, DONALD JOHN, optometrist; b. Laurium, Mich., Jan. 28, 1939; s. David John and Florence Tyne (Liimatta) M.; student U. Mich., 1956-58; B.S., D. Optometry, Ill. Coll. Optometry, 1961; m. Helen Marlene Hartje, Apr. 18, 1968; children—Jason David, Aaron Henry, Heidi Erika. Practice optometry, Calumet, Mich., 1966—, Hancock, Mich., 1970—; pres. Redjacket, Inc., 1977—. Served to capt. USAF, 1961-66. Pres. Coppertown USA Devel. Corp., 1974-76, Coppertown Fund, 1975—, v.p. Calumet Theatre Bd., 1974-76; mem. Copper Country Council for Arts, 1976—. Mem. Am., Mich. (pres. local soc. 1968-70) optometric assns., Am. Optometric Found., North Central States Optometric Conf. (cabinet mem. 1970-72), Calumet C. of C. (pres. 1972-74, chmn. exec. bd. 1972-75), Copper Country Chorale (pres. 1968). Elk, Lion (pres. 1970-71). Clubs: University of Michigan (pres. 1970-76), University (pres. 1970-72). Home: 1167 Calumet Ave Calumet MI 49913 Office: Box 468 Calumet MI 49913 also Box 639 Hancock MI 49930

MUSCA, ALBERT ANTHONY, physician and surgeon; b. Cleve., Aug. 16, 1935; s. Anthony John and Amelia Molly (Tambascio) M.; B.S. in Natural Sci., John Carroll U., 1957; M.D., Case-Western Res. U., 1961; m. Sandra Ann Ward, Aug. 4, 1962; children—Albert Michael, Daniel Girard, Julie Ann, John Jude. Intern, Cleve. Met. Gen. Hosp., 1961-62, resident in gen. surgery, 1962-67; resident in pathology Wadsworth VA Hosp.; West Los Angeles, Calif., 1969-72; forensic pathologist Coroner's Office of Los Angeles, 1972-73; plant med. dir. U.S. Steel Co., Cleve., 1973-74; practice medicine, Cleve., 1974-77; corporate med. dir. Rockport Med. Center, Cleve., 1977—. Served to lt. comdr., USNR, 1967-69. Recipient outstanding surgical research award Cleve. Surg. Soc., 1963. Mem. Cleve. Acad. Medicine, Ohio Med. Assn., AMA. Roman Catholic. Home: 22647 Meadowhill Ln Rocky River OH 44116 Office: 13355 Lorain Ave Cleveland OH 44111

MUSCHENHEIM, CARL ARTHUR, architect; b. N.Y.C., Apr. 23, 1933; s. William and Elisabeth (Bodanzky) M.; B.Arch., U. Mich., 1956; m. Gunhild G. Voege, Dec. 28, 1958; children—Mark William, Kenton Ernst, Nana Elisabeth. Designer Skidmore, Owings & Merrill, Chgo., summer, 1956, sr. architect, 1959-62; sr. designer Apel & Beckert Architekton, Frankfurt, Germany, 1962-64; project coordinator Skidmore, Owings & Merrill, Chgo., 1964—, asso. partner, 1974—. Second v.p. Evanston (Ill.) Recreation Bd., 1972-74, 1st v.p. 1974, pres., 1975. Served with AUS, 1956-58. Mem. AIA (edn. com. 1968-69), Nat. Council Archtl. Registration Bd. Clubs: Arts, University (Chgo.). Author: Guide to Chicago Architecture, 1962, 65. Home: 1010 Asbury St Evanston IL 60202 Office: Skidmore Owings and Merrill 30 W Monroe St Chicago IL 60603

MUSCHENHEIM, WILLIAM EMIL, educator; b. N.Y.C., Nov. 7, 1902; s. Frederick Augustus and Elsa (Unger) M.; student Williams Coll., 1919-21, Mass. Inst. Tech., 1921-24; M.Arch., Behrens Master Sch. Architecture, Acad. Fine Arts, Vienna, Austria, 1929; m. Elizabeth Marie Bodanzky, Nov. 29, 1930; children—Carl Arthur, Anna Elizabeth Muschenheim Arms. Archtl. designer Joseph Urban, architect, N.Y.C., 1929-33; prin. William Muschenheim, architect, N.Y.C., Ann Arbor, Mich., 1934—; prof. architecture U. Mich., Ann Arbor, 1950-74, now emeritus. Recipient Horace H. Rackham research travel grant, 1958, 64, 72. Fellow AIA (edn. com. 1959-61, fgn. relations com. 1963-64); mem. Assn. Collegiate Schs., Architecture, (edn. com. 1961-63, fgn. relations com. 1964-66), AAUP. Author: Elements of the Art of Architecture, 1964. Contbr. articles to profl. pubs. Home: 1251 Heatherway Ann Arbor MI 48104

MUSCHEWSKE, ROBERT CHARLES, mgmt. cons.; b. Waukegan, Ill., Dec. 17, 1941; s. Charles Louis and Gwendolyn Marie (Grams) M.; A.B., Carthage Coll., 1963; M.A., U. Nebr., 1966, Ph.D., 1969; m. Sandra Ruth Britton, June 10, 1966; children—Scott Robert, Shauna Suzanne. Dir. orgn. and mgmt. devel., Hay Assos., Chgo., 1974—. Served to capt. U.S. Army, 1968-74. Mem. Am. Psychol. Assn. Home: 2012 N Kennicott St Arlington Heights IL 60004 Office: 1 E Wacker Dr Chicago IL 60601

MUSEGAAS, JAN, food co. exec.; b. Semarang, Indonesia, May 22, 1924; s. Frederik and Johanna Jacoba (Van Schijndel) M.; student Nyenrode, bus. coll., The Netherlands, 1946-48; student numerous seminars and schs. data processing; m. Rose De Keyser, Aug. 21, 1951; children—Margaret (Mrs. John Posten), Karen (Mrs. Ron Abileah), Gwendolyn, Phillip. Came to U.S., 1951, naturalized, 1957. With Consular Service, Netherlands State Dept., London, Eng., 1948-50, Antwerp, Belgium, 1950-51; accountant, retail controller Hallmark Cards, Kansas City, Mo., 1951-67; mgr. data processing Seaboard Allied Milling Corp., Kansas City, Mo., 1967—. Served with Netherlands Corps Interpreters, 1944-46. Decorated Netherlands War Cross with combat bar. Mem. Nat. Retail Mchts. Assn. (chpt. pres. 1965-66), Nat. Accountants Assn. (dir. 1970-72), Data Processing Mgmt. Assn. (dir. 1970-72). Home: 429 W 57th St Kansas City MO 64113 Office: PO Box 19148 Kansas City MO 64141

MUSGRAVE, OLIE LEE, banker; b. Jonesboro, Ill., Feb. 15, 1934; s. Willis E. and Irula E. (Edmonds) M.; ed. Draughan's Bus. Coll., spl. banking courses So. Ill. U., U. Wis., Am. Inst. Banking, bus. adminstrn. Harvard U., 1974; m. Betty June McNail, Nov. 1, 1956; 1 son, Jon Manning. Asst. mgr. Household Fin. Corp., Indpls., 1954-59; pres., dir. Bank of Marion (Ill.), 1960—; instr. banking courses John A. Logan Jr. Coll., Carterville, Ill., Southeastern Ill. Jr. Coll., Harrisburg. Former mem. bd. dirs. Marion Meml. Hosp.; former advisor Shawnee Resources Conservation and Devel. Project; chmn. Williamson County Savs. Bond. Com.; former treas. Williamson County Salvation Army; bd. dirs., v.p. So. Ill., Inc. Served with AUS, 1956-58. Mem. Marion C. of C. (bd. dirs., past pres., man of year award), Bank Adminstrn. Inst. (past pres. So. Ill.). Republican.

Baptist. Club: Marion Rotary (sec., dir.). Home: 204 Boswell Rd Marion IL 62959 Office: 300 Tower Square Plaza Marion IL 62959

MUSGROVE, VIRGINIA MARGARET, poet, writer; b. Middlesex County, Va., Jan. 21, 1915; d. George Edward and Virginia Thomas (Hibble) Sibley; A.A., Oceanside-Carlsbad Coll., 1964; postgrad. Palmer Writer's Sch., Mpls., 1966; m. James Carrigan Musgrove, May 10, 1941; 1 dau., Patricia Musgrove Robinson. Vocat. nurse Bapt. Home Md., Balt., 1937-39, Balt. Nurses Exchange, 1937-39; vol. social welfare worker Navy Relief Soc., Camp Pendleton, Calif., 1952-58; free-lance poet, writer, 1957—. Active Calif. Humane Soc., 1958-68. Recipient Meritorious Service award Navy Relief Soc., 1955; Clement Hoyt Meml. award for Poetry, 1975; winner 1st prize Internat. Poetry Inst., 1977. Mem. Internat. Platform Assn., Internat. Poetry Inst., Internat. Biographical Assn., Am. Poets Fellowship Soc., Humane Soc. U.S., Acad. Am. Poets, Internat. Assn. Born-Again Christians. Author: Raindrop in a Dust Pool, 1971; Sonnets and other Poems, 1971; To Color the Echo, 1973. Home and office: Route 2 Box 198 Hartville MO 65667

MUSINSKI, DONALD LOUIS, physicist; b. Winsted, Conn., Mar. 29, 1946; s. Louis Edward and Dorothy Elisabeth (Shaw) M.; B.S., Trinity Coll., 1968; M.A., U. Rochester, 1970, Ph.D., 1973; m. Jean Elisabeth Abramson, June 12, 1971. Research asso. Cornell U., Ithaca, N.Y., 1973-75; research scientist KMS Fusion, Inc., Ann Arbor, Mich., 1975—. Mem. Am. Phys. Soc. Office: S Industrial Hwy Ann Arbor MI 48104

MUSSELMAN, BARBARA LYNN, educator; b. Dayton, Ohio, Sept. 7, 1947; d. Anthony Edward and Ruth Marie (Stumbo) Musselman; B.A., Wright State U., 1969, M.A., U. Cin., 1971, Ph.D., 1975. Vis. instr. dept. history Tex. Tech. U., 1974; instr. dept. humanities Ohio Coll. Applied Sci., 1974-75; asst. prof. labor edn. and research U. Ala., 1975-76; asst. prof. labor edn. and research service Ohio State U., 1976—; cons. in field. Commr. Cin. Human Relations Commn., 1977—. Nat. Endowment for the Humanities grantee, 1975-76. Mem. Am. Hist. Assn., Orgn. Am. Historians, Univ. and Coll. Labor Edn. Assn., Coalition of Labor Union Women, Phi Alpha Theta. Home: 2680 Lehman Rd Cincinnati OH 45204 Office: 1015 Vine St Suite 706 Cincinnati OH 45202

MUSSELMAN, LARRY LEE, chem. engr.; b. Erie, Pa., Aug. 16, 1947; s. Lloyd Harvey and Lyda M.; student (Scholar) Malone Coll., 1966-67; B.S. in Chem. Engring. magna cum laude (scholar), Akron U., 1971, M.S. in Engring., 1972; m. Marilyn Ann Musselman, Nov. 25, 1966; children—Cheri Ann, Jason Lawrence. Sr. research engr. Alcoa Co., Alcoa Center, Pa., 1971—; mem. tech. adv. com. Ohio Legislature. Mem. ASME (sect. dir.), Am. Soc. Lubrication Engrs., Am. Soc. Metals, Sigma Tau, Alpha Chi Sigma. Patentee bearing. Home: 1208 Vincent St NW North Canton OH 44720 Office: PO Box 2371 North Canton OH 44720

MUSSER, JOSEPH ELDER, dentist; b. Augusta, Kans., Sept. 4, 1922; s. Howard Elder and Pansy Armanda (Henderson) M.; student Wichita State U., 1940-41, Friends U., 1941-43; D.D.S., U. Mo., Kansas City, 1947; m. Alyce Virginia Berry, June 7, 1947; children—Howard Joseph, William Allen. Practice dentistry, Wichita, Kans., 1947-51, 53-73; sr. staff dentist VA Hosp. Dental Clinic, 1973—. Cons. dental product companies. Served to lt. USNR, 1951-53. Fellow Internat. Coll. Dentistry; mem. Kans. Dental Assn. (pres. 1973-74), Wichita Dist. Dental Soc. (pres. 1960), Pierre Fauchard Acad., A.A.A.S., U. Mo. Kans. City Sch. Dentistry Alumni Assn. (trustee 1966—), Psi Omega. Republican. Episcopalian. Mason, Lion (pres. S.E. Wichita chpt. 1968-69). Recipient Grand award Kans. State Dental Conv., 1963. Home: 3407 E Clark St Wichita KS 67218 Office: 5500 E Kellogg St Wichita KS 67218

MUSSER, ROBERT DANIEL, JR., hotel exec.; b. Circleville, Ohio, Apr. 29, 1932; s. Robert Daniel and Elizabeth (Woodfill) M.; B.A., Dartmouth, 1955; m. Amelia Epler, Nov. 30, 1957; children—Robin Epler, Margaret Stewart, Robert Daniel, III. Asst. mgr. Grand Hotel, Mackinac Island, Mich., 1957-61, pres., gen. mgr., 1961—; bd. overseers Hanover (N.H.) Inn, 1973—, chmn. bd. overseers, 1976—. Mem. Mich. Travel Commn., 1976—. Served with AUS, 1956-57. Mem. Mackinac Island C. of C. (v.p. 1963—), Am. Hotel and Motel Assn., Hotel Sales Mgmt. Assn., Alpha Delta Phi. Republican. Episcopalian. Club: Mackinac Island Yacht. Home: 424 S Ridge Rd Lake Forest IL 60045 Office: 222 Wisconsin Ave Lake Forest IL 60045 summer Grand Hotel Mackinac Island MI 49757

MUSSON, VICTORIA LELAND, guidance counselor; b. Detroit, May 19, 1917; d. Frederick H. and Mary Ann (Meida) L.; B.S., Wayne State U., 1939; M.A., U. Mich., 1965; m. Richard Woodrow Musson, Dec. 19, 1942; children—Marilyn Ann, Warren Richard. Social studies tchr. Detroit Pub. Schs., 1941-43, 49-52, 65-66; mem. staff Laredo Army Air Force Civilian Personnel, 1944-45; kindergarten tchr. Detroit Pub. Schs., 1960-65; guidance counselor Tri-Area Integration Project, Detroit, 1966-68, Cass Tech. High Sch., Detroit, 1968—; mem. secondary sch. com. Mich. ACT Council, 1976—, exec. com., 1977—. Mem. Dearborn (Mich.) Com. to Promote Young Peoples Concerts, 1952-58. Mem. Am., Mich. personnel and guidance assns., Guidance Assn. Met. Detroit, AAUW, U. Mich. Alumni Assn. Episcopalian. Home: 26440 Westphal Dr Dearborn Heights MI 48127 Office: 2421 2d Blvd Detroit MI 48201

MUTHARIKA, ARTHUR PETER, lawyer; b. Malawi, July 18, 1940; s. Ryson Thom and Ellen (Chingwalu) M.; came to U.S., 1971; LL.B., U. London, 1965; LL.M., Yale U., 1966, J.S.D., 1969; m. Christophine Griffin, Apr. 6, 1968; children—Monique, Moyenda, Mahopela. Admitted to Tanzania bar, 1970; lectr. law U. Dar-es-Salaam, Tanzania, 1968-71; lectr. internat. law and diplomacy to fgn. service officers from Asia and Africa, U. Makerere, Kampala (Uganda), summer 1969; vis. lectr. law Haile Selassie U., Ethiopia, 1970; adj. prof. Rutgers U., 1972; mem. faculty Washington U. Law Sch., St. Louis, 1972—, prof. law, since 1977. Internat. Law fellow UN, 1971. Mem. Am. Soc. Internat. Law, Internat. Law Assn., World Peace Through Law Center. Author: The Regulation of Statelessness Under International and National Law, 1977; The International Law of Development, 4 vols., 1978. Home: 6634 Pershing Ave St Louis MO 63130 Office: Washington Univ Sch Law St Louis MO 63130

MUTZABAUGH, JAMES CHARLES, project engr.; b. Perth Amboy, N.J., May 5, 1950; s. Benjamin Charles and Florentine Barbara (Lakomski) M.; B.S. in Elec. Engring., Northwestern U., 1973; m. Mary Ann Domzalski, Apr. 30, 1977. Design engr. Riley Co., Skokie, Ill., 1973-76, sr. project engr., 1976, 77—; project engr., instrumentation supr. Alnor Instrument Co., Niles, Ill., 1976-77; cons. in field. Mem. Des Plaines (Ill.) Emergency Service and Disaster Agency. Served with U.S. Army, 1968-70. Registered Emergency Med. Technician, Ill. Mem. Instrument Soc. Am. Roman Catholic. Home: 10022 Holly Ln Apt 2S Des Plaines IL 60016 Office: 7401 N Hamlin Skokie IL 60076

MUZIK, EDWARD JOHN, educator; b. Lorain, Ohio, Nov. 28, 1922; s. Wesley James and Catherine (Nemecek) M.; B.A., U. Mich., 1948, M.A., 1952; Ph.D. (William Randolph Hearst fellow), Northwestern U., 1960; m. Carol Vlasaty, June 24, 1950; children—Edward John, Susan Melody. Chmn. div. history and social sci. So. State Coll., Springfield, S.D., 1955-66; prof. history U. Wis., Eau Claire, 1966—. Exec. sec. Assn. Univ. of Wis. Faculties, 1973—. Served with USAAF, 1943-46. Mem. Am. Hist. Assn. (life), Orgn. Am. Historians (life), N.E.A., (life), Czechoslovak Soc. Am., Phi Kappa Phi. Conglist. Home: 3105 Patton St Eau Claire WI 54701 Office: 139 W Wilson St Madison WI 53703

MYCUE, DAVID JOHN, historian, archivist; b. Niagara Falls, N.Y., Oct. 4, 1935; s. John Powers and Ruth Agnes (Delehant) M.; B.A., N. Tex. State U., 1964; M.A. (Fellow), U. Ill., Champaign, 1973, M.S., 1976; m. Elena De Los Santos, June 13, 1964; children—Alfredo, Victoria, Marcelo. Instr. history N. Tex. State U., Denton, 1966-67; tchr. high schs., Irving, Tex., 1964-65, San Antonio, 1967-68; historian, mil. airlift command Office of Chief Staff USAF, Scott AFB, Ill., 1968-71; instr. history U. Ill., Champaign, 1972-75; archivist Ill. State Archives, Office of Sec. State, Springfield, 1976—. Served with Security Agy. U.S. Army, 1958-61. Recipient Donald G. Wing award Sch. Library Sci. U. Ill., 1976. Mem. Assn. Govt. Historians Archivists (sec. 1969-71), ALA. Contbr. articles to library jours. Home: 1110 S Walnut St Springfield IL 62704 Office: Illinois State Archives Springfield IL 62704

MYERHOLTZ, RALPH W., JR., chemist; b. Bucyrus, Ohio, July 29, 1926; s. Ralph and Vera (Kirkland) M.; B.S., Purdue U., 1950; Ph.D. in Organic Chemistry, Northwestern U., 1954; m. Lois Ellen Congram, June 24, 1951; children—Carl Alan, Lynn Elaine. Project chemist Standard Oil Co. (Ind.), Whiting, 1954-58; group leader Amoco Chems. Corp., Whiting, 1958-60, 60-66, research asso., 1966-69, dir. polymer properties div., Naperville, Ill., 1969—. Radio officer Naperville Civil Def., 1971—; active Boy Scouts. Served with AUS, 1944-46. Mem. Am. Chem. Soc., Soc. Plastics Engrs., Am. Radio Relay League, Sigma Xi, Phi Lambda Upsilon, Sigma Delta Chi, Pi Kappa Phi. Contbr. articles to profl. jours. Patentee in field. Research in preparation and characterization of synthetic high polymers and catalytic processes. Home: 232 S Charles St Naperville IlL60540 Office: Amoco Chem Corp PO Box 400 Naperville IL 60540

MYERS, EDDIE EARL, psychologist; b. Ardmore, Okla., Nov. 24, 1937; s. Finis Weldon and Fern Durrel (Johnson) M.; B.S., Tex. Christian U., 1958; M.Ed., N. Tex. State U., 1967, Ed.D., 1969; m. Ineta June Moore, July 2, 1955; children—Richard Weldon, Ronald Leland, Marilyn June, Rebecca Jean. Machinist Chance Vaught Aircraft, Grand Prairie, Tex., 1957-58; tchr., coach Ft. Worth (Tex.) Christian schs., 1958-59; tchr. Corpus Christi (Tex.) pub. schs., 1959-60; ordained to ministry, Ch. of Christ, 1960; youth, religious edn. minister Norton St. Ch. of Christ, Corpus Christi, Tex., 1960-61; minister Ch. of Christ, Cameron, Tex., 1961-63; youth, music, religious edn. minister Procter St. Ch. of Christ, Port Arthur, Tex., 1963-65; high sch. English tchr. Christian Schs., Inc., Dallas, 1965-66; psychology instr. Tex. Women's U., Denton, 1968-69; acting dir. Child-Ednl. Psychology and Preventive Psychiatry Dept., Ednl. Research Council Am., Cleve., 1972-74, dir., 1974-76, asst. dir., 1972-74, sr. research asso., 1969-72, dir. evaluative research and psychology, 1976—. Faculty Dept. Counseling and Guidance, U. Oreg., workshop, Frankfurt, Germany, Aug. 1972; vis. prof. Cleve. State U., 1970-71, adj. prof., 1975—; workshop dir. Dept. Edn., State U., Kans., Fort Hays, 1973; human behavior and teaching workshop dir. Murray State U., Murray, Ky., July 1974, Central Mich. U., 1974, Cleve. State U., 1974. Mem. Ohio Dept. Edn. adv. com. on drug edn. efforts, 1974-76; mem. adv. bd. Cleve. Clearinghouse for Drug Edn., 1974-76; mem. mental health project com. Cleve. Fedn. for Community Planning, 1970—, chmn. mental health steering com., 1977—; mem. Eastern U.S. drug abuse task force Am. Social Health Assn., 1971-73; mem. drug. edn., prevention com. Cuyahoga County (Ohio) Mental Health and Retardation Bd., 1972-75; mem. alcoholism project planning com. Cleve. Met. Health Planning Commn., 1972-73; chmn. drug abuse and alcoholism task force Cleve. Fedn. Community Planning, 1970-71. NIMH grantee, 1974—. Mem. Am. Psychol. Assn., Am. Ednl. Research Assn., Phi Delta Kappa. Author: Handy Asks the Psychologist, A Mini Course in the Psychology of Understanding Children, 1974; The New Model Me, An Operators Guide to Coping with Frustration and Aggression, 1974; Social Isolation and Personality, 1973, others. Contbr. articles to profl. jours. Home: 2430 Woodmere Dr Cleveland Heights OH 44106 Office: Rockefeller Bldg Cleveland OH 44113

MYERS, FRANK KENNETH, JR., mfg. co. exec.; b. Muncie, Ind., June 2, 1928; s. Frank Kenneth and Ethel Vune (Dick) M.; student Coll. William and Mary, 1958, Old Dominion Coll., 1959-60, U. Va., 1961, Ind. U.-Purdue U., 1969-70; m. RosaLea Byall, Apr. 6, 1948; children—Steven K., Sharon (Mrs. Stuart Downhour), Richard A., Ronald L. Asst. treas. Colonial Finance Corp., Norfolk, Va., 1952-66; transp. mgr. duplicating and paper products div. 3M Co., Hartford City, Ind., 1967—; owner cons. firm F.K. Myers Assos., 1965—, Leisur-Lea Charters Ltd., charterboats, 1971—; owner Fran Lea Kennels, 1975—. Pres. Blackford County Football League, 1968-69, chmn., 1970-71, award of merit, 1969, 70. Served as officer U.S. Mcht. Marine, 1945-49. Mem. Asso. Investors (pres. 1964-65), Nat. Assn. Accountants (v.p. 1965). Home: Rural Route 2 Montpelier IN 47359 Office: PO Box M Hartford City IN 47348

MYERS, GEORGE ELLIOTT, educator; b. Blackpool, Eng., Mar. 22, 1916; s. Ernest and Emily (Elliott) M.; B.D.S., U. Manchester (Eng.), 1939; F.D.S., Royal Coll. Surgeons, Eng., 1951; M.S., U. Mich., 1952, D.D.S., 1956; m. Merle Robinson, Oct. 23, 1940; children—Elizabeth, Nicholas, Charlotte, Caroline. Came to U.S., 1955, naturalized, 1961. Lectr., Sch. Dentistry, U. Liverpool, Eng., 1946-53; sr. lectr. U. London, 1953-55; prof. chmn. dept. fixed prosthodontics U. Mich. at Ann Arbor, 1961—. Mem. dental rev. panel FDA, HEW, 1972-76; cons. VA Hosp., Ann Arbor. Served with Royal Army Dental Corp., 1941-46. Recipient Jerome Schweitzer Research award The Greater N.Y. Acad. Prosthodontics. Fellow Am. Coll. Dentists, Am. Dental assn. (chmn. council dental materials and devices 1972-74), Brit. Dental Assn., Internat. Assn. Dental Research. Author: Textbook of Crown and Bridge Prosthodontics, 1969. Contbr. to profl. publs. in field. Editorial bd. Jour. Oral Rehab., 1972—. Home: 1339 Pomona St Ann Arbor MI 48107

MYERS, GEORGE VINCENT, petroleum co. exec.; b. Townsend, Mont., May 21, 1916; s. Arthur Elmer and Mabel (Etnoyer) M.; B.A., U. Chgo., 1936; m. Christine MacGregor, Aug. 13, 1949; children—Susan, Janet, Nancy. Staff accountant Haskins & Sells, 1936-40; spl. agt. FBI, 1940-41; asst. controller, then controller Westinghouse Air Brake Co., 1946-53; dir., financial v.p. Stanolind Oil & Gas Co., 1953-56; dir., gen. mgr. prodn. Standard Oil Co. (Ind.), 1956-58, v.p. prodn., 1958-59, exec. v.p., 1959-74, also dir., pres., 1974—. Served as lt. USNR, 1942-46. C.P.A., Pa. Mem. Controllers Inst., Am. Petroleum Inst., Phi Beta Kappa. Clubs: Longue Vue (Pitts.); Chicago. Home: 600 Glenayre Dr Glenview IL 60025 Office: 200 E Randolph Dr Chicago IL 60601

MYERS, HAL HANAUER, mfg. co. exec.; b. Karlsruhe, Ger., Aug. 9, 1930; s. David Nathan and Inez Marcella (Pink) M.; came to U.S., 1941, naturalized, 1951; B.S. in Chem. Engring., Case Inst. Tech., 1953; m. Linda Chesney, June 12, 1960; children—Robert, Andrew. Engr., Byerlyte Corp., Cleve., 1957-62; mgr. Cook United Co., Syracuse, N.Y., 1962-66; plant mgr., Cleve. area mgr., Koppers Co., 1966-72; gen. mgr. Lake Erie Asphalt Co., Cleve., 1972-74; mfg. mgr. Mameco Internat., Cleve., 1974—, dir. Mameco Europe, 1976—. Trustee Bur. Jewish Edn.; active Jewish Welfare Fedn.; mem. exec. com. Heights Area Project; chmn. Bur. Transp. System. Served to capt. USAF, 1953-57. Mem. ASTM, Am. Chem. Soc., Am. Inst. Chem. Engrs., Am. Assn. Asphalt Paving Technologists. Democrat. Home: 3329 Stockholm Rd Shaker Heights OH 44120 Office: 4470 E 175th St Cleveland OH 44128

MYERS, HOWARD, chem. physics cons.; b. N.Y.C., Jan. 27, 1928; s. Howard Gould and Sally Ann (Kline) M.; Ph.B., U. Chgo., 1948, B.S. in Math, 1950, M.S. in Chemistry, 1958; m. Joan Cerwin, May 29, 1976; 1 dau., Sally Joy. children from previous marriage—Susanna, William. Project scientist, Jupiter orbiter probe project McDonnel Douglas Co., St. Louis, 1969—; mem. tech. staff TRW, Redondo Beach, Calif., 1966-68; program mgr. Aerospace Corp., El Segundo, Calif., 1961-66; tech. specialist Douglas Aircraft Co., Santa Monica, Calif., 1957-61; mem. tech. staff Research Labs. Hughes, Culver City, Calif., 1954-57; pres. CPRL, St. Louis, 1968—. Fellow Am. Inst. Chemists; mem. Am. Astronom. Soc., Am. Chem. Soc., Am. Geophys. Union, Am. Inst. Aeros. stronautics, Am. Phys. Soc., Sigma Xi. Democrat. Unitarian. Contbr. articles to profl. jours. Home: 1232 Wissmann Dr Manchester MO 63011 Office: PO Box 516 St Louis MO 63166

MYERS, JAMES RUSSELL, educator; b. Middletown, Ohio, June 17, 1933; s. Edward Franklin and Edna Catherine (Fravel) M.; B.S., U. Cin., 1956; M.S., U. Wis., 1957; Ph.D., Ohio State U., 1964. Research tech. Research Labs., Armco Steel Corp., Middletown, 1952-56; materials engr. Air Force Materials Lab., Wright-Patterson AFB, Ohio, 1957-60; sr. materials engr. X-20 System Project Office, Aeronautical Systems Div., Wright-Patterson AFB, 1960-62; prof. metallurgy Air Force Inst. Tech., Wright-Patterson AFB, 1962—. Corrosion cons. to Air Force Civil Engring., 1967—. Served to 1st lt., USAF, 1957-59. Inland Steel Co. fellow, 1956-57; registered profl. engr., Calif. Mem. Nat. Assn. Corrosion Engrs., Am. Soc. Metals, Am. Inst. Metall. Engrs., Corrosion Soc. Japan, British Inst. Corrosion Sci. and Tech., Tau Beta Pi, Sigma Xi, Phi Lambda Upsilon. Mason (Shriner). Contbr. articles to profl. jours. Home: 4198 Merlyn Dr Franklin OH 45005 Office: Civil Engring School Air Force Inst Tech Wright Patterson AFB OH 45433

MYERS, JEROME M., restaurateur; b. Mpls., July 23, 1917; s. Michael David and Goldie (Meyer) M.; student Northwestern U., 1935-41; m. Dorothy Stein, Sept. 20, 1956; 1 son, Michael David. Owner, operator Jerry's Food & Liquors, Chgo., 1948—; pres. Galaxy Growth Fund, Chgo., 1969—. Mem. P.T.A., Anshe Emet Day Sch., Chgo., 1969—. Served to capt. AUS, 1941-45. Decorated Purple Heart, Bronze Star medal; Croix de Guerre (France). Mem. United World Federalists, SANE, U.N. Assn. Mem. B'nai B'rith. Home: 3200 Lake Shore Dr Chicago IL 60657 Office: 215 E Grand Ave Chicago IL 60611

MYERS, JOHN CLEMENT, JR., bus. cons.; b. Ashland, Ohio, Jan. 31, 1918; s. John C. and Alice (Mould) M.; B.A., Rollins Coll., 1942; m. June Reinhold, May 31, 1942; children—John Clement, Paul Reinhold. Vice pres. charge pub. and indsl. relations F.E. Myers & Bro. Co., Ashland, Ohio, 1952-61; pres. F.E. Myers & Bro. Co. Ltd., Kitchener, Ont., Can., 1956-61; bus. cons., 1961-65; v.p. mgmt. devel. services Myers Enterprises, Ashland, 1963-69; pres. Mytowne Inc., Ashland, 1969—, Topper Assos., Ashland, 1969—, Myers Enterprises, Ashland, 1969—; v.p. Myco Corp., Ashland, 1969—, Jefco Corp., Ashland, 1969—. Vice pres. Johnny Appleseed Council, Mansfield, Ohio, 1968—; alumni bd. Rollins Coll., 1967-70; adv. bd. Ashland Coll., 1960—; trustee Cheboygan (Mich.) Hosp., 1956-59; bd. dirs. Ashland YMCA, 1948-49; bldg. com. Lutheran Ch., Ashland, 1947-53. Served to capt. U.S. Army, 1942-46. Decorated Bronze Star medal; named Rollins Coll. Alumnus of Year, 1965. Mem. Am. Mgmt. Assn., Personnel Adminstrs. Assn., Ashland, U.S. chambers commerce. Lutheran. Clubs: Ashland Country (pres. 1967-70), Univ. (Man of Year 1975), Country of Ashland, Birchwood Farms, Hidden Valley, Sawgrass, Ponte Vedra Golf, Mullet Lake Country, Wequetonsing Golf. Home: 1730 Upland Dr Ashland OH 44805 Office: PO Box 528 Ashland OH 44805

MYERS, JOHN THOMAS, congressman; b. Covington, Ind., Feb. 8, 1927; s. Warren E. and Myra (Wisher) M.; B.S., Ind. State U., 1951; m. Carol Carruthers, May 30, 1953; children—Carol Ann, Lori Jan. Farmer Covington, 1951—; with Fountain Trust Co., Covington, 1952—; mem. 90th-95th Congresses from Ind. 7th Dist. Served with AUS, 1944-46; ETO. Home: 921 2d St Covington IN 47932 Office: Rayburn Bldg Washington DC 20515

MYERS, KENNETH E., hosp. adminstr.; b. Battle Creek, Mich., Jan. 1, 1932; s. Orlow J. and Kathryn (Brown) M.; B.B.A., U. Mich., 1956, M.B.A., 1957; m. Nancy Lee Lindgren, June 9, 1956; children—Cynthia, Anne, Thomas, Susan. With Burroughs Corp., Detroit, 1957-66, successively econ. and financial analyst, facilities planner Burroughs Finance Corp., Def. and Space Group, Internat. div.; with Touche Ross & Co., 1966; controller William Beaumont Hosp., Royal Oak, Mich., 1966-68, asso. dir., 1968-69, dir., 1969-76, exec. v.p., hosp. dir., 1976—. Served to 2d lt. AUS, 1951-53. Mem. Am., Mich. hosp. assns., Greater Detroit Area Hosp. Council, Comprehensive Health Planning Council Southeastern Mich. Presbyn. Home: 5085 Lake Bluff Rd West Bloomfield MI 48033 Office: William Beaumont Hosp 3601 W 13 Mile Rd Royal Oak MI 48072

MYERS, MICHAEL JOHN, educator; b. Scotland County, Mo., Aug. 4, 1934; s. Michael B. and Ida (Witte) M.; B.S. in Agr. Bus., U. Mo., 1955; B.S. in Edn., Northeast Mo. State U., 1959, M.A., 1960; Ed.D. (Anderson fellow 1964-66), N.Y. U., 1966; m. Callie Hicks, Aug. 4, 1957. Tchr. Epping (N.D.) High Sch., 1955-56, Eldon (Iowa) High Sch., 1956-58, Elmer (Mo.) High Sch., tchr. 1958-60; Grant Jr. High Sch., Springfield, Ill., 1960-62, adminstrv. asst. 1962-64; dir. research and community information Dist. 186, Springfield, 1966-67; dir. research Dist. 11, Alton, Ill., 1967-69; asst. supt. for curriculum Dist. 207, Park Ridge,Ill., 1969—. Active various youth groups including YMCA, Drug Control Councils. Served with AUS, 1957-63. Recipient Curators award U. Mo., 1951. Founders Day award N.Y. U., 1966, Phi Delta Kappa (chpt. pres. 1962-63). Rotarian. Home: 2619 Irwin Ave Park Ridge IL 60068 Office: 1131 S Dee Rd Park Ridge IL 60068

MYERS, NORMA JANE MCKAY, psychologist; b. Springfield, Mass., Aug. 27, 1928; d. Claude Carson and Norma Alice (Scott) McKay; student Heidelberg Coll., 1945-47; student Bliss Bus. Coll., 1947-48; B.S., Bowling Green State U., 1960, M.S., 1963; m. W. Howard Myers, Sept. 15, 1947 (div. 1969); children—Virginia (Mrs. Jerry Stidham), Carl. Tchr. elementary schs. Port Clinton, Ohio, 1955-63; reading specialist Elyria (Ohio) City Schs., 1964-65; intern sch. psychologist Tiffin (Ohio) City Schs., 1965-66; sch. psychologist Fremont (Ohio) City Schs., 1966—. Tchr. in child devel. and psychology Michael J. Owens Tech. Coll., Perrysburg, Ohio, 1972-77. cons. to sch. systems in reading and psychology. Bd. dirs. Sandusky County Mental Health Assn., 1972—. Mem. NOW, Fremont Bus. and

Profl. Women (v.p. 1972-73), Maumee Valley Sch. Psychologist Assn. (pres. 1970-71), Nat., Ohio assns. sch. psychologists, NEA (life), Ohio Edn. Assn. (life), Delta Kappa Gamma. Home: 1139 N Byrneal Dr Port Clinton OH 43452 Office: 211 S Park Ave Fremont OH 43420

MYERS, ROBERT HARRY, educator; b. Muncie, Ind., May 19, 1919; s. Robert Henry and Clyda (Weikel) M.; A.B., Kenyon Coll., 1941; M.B.A., Ind. U., 1948, D.B.A., 1952; m. Joan Stevens Miller, Nov. 1944; children—Robert Miller, Stephanie Jo, Michael Joseph, Susan Elizabeth. Instr. marketing Miami U., Oxford, Ohio, 1949-50, asso. prof., 1952-60, prof., 1960—, dir. bur. bus. research, 1963-65, dir. middle mgmt. seminar, 1964-74, dir. div. research, asso. dean Sch. Bus. Adminstrn., 1968-73. Bus. cons. dept. stores, advt. agys., trade assns., financial instns., real estate devel. firms; econ. cons. county and municipal govts. Chmn., Butler County Econ. Devel. Com.; v.p. Community Improvement Corp. Butler County. Sec. bus. adv. council Miami U. Recipient Outstanding Service award Oxford Community Improvement Corp., 1965, Alumni award Miami chpt. Alpha Delta Phi, 1968. Served to 1st lt. Med. Service Corps, AUS, 1942-46. Mem. Phi Beta Kappa (pres. Miami chpt.), Beta Gamma Sigma (pres. Miami chpt.), Omicron Delta Kappa, Delta Sigma Pi. Episcopalian. Clubs: Masons, Rotary (past pres., dir.) (Oxford); Torch (Butler County, Ohio). Contbr. articles to profl. jours. Home: 5295 Hillcrest Dr Oxford OH 45056

MYERS, ROBERT HENRY, banker; b. Findlay, Ohio, Jan. 21, 1894; s. Robert and Charlotte (Drewett) M.; M.A. in Polit. Sci., U. Chgo., 1951, Ph.D., 1955; m. Clyda Alice Weikel, Nov. 22, 1917; 1 son, Robert Harry. With Mchts. Nat. Bank of Muncie, 1914-54, successively asst. cashier, asst. to pres., v.p., 1914-46, v.p., dir., 1946-54; vice chmn. Commn. for Financial Instns., State of Ind., 1941; hon. dir. Am. Nat. Bank & Trust Co., Muncie; lectr. in bus. and fin. Ball State U., 1956-73. Served from pvt. to capt. U.S. Army, 1917-19; maj. to col. AUS, 1941-45. Mem. Am., Ind. (past pres.) bankers assns., Am. Legion, Ret. Officers Assn., Disabled Officers Assn., U. Chgo. Alumni Assn., Delta Sigma Pi, Phi Beta Lambda, Alpha Delta Phi. Episcopalian. Mason, Rotarian. Clubs: The Muncie, Columbia (Indpls.). Author numerous articles in field. Editor, co-author Beneficence, 1972. Home: Westminster Village Muncie IN 47305

MYERS, VICTOR IRA, research engr.; b. Casa Blanca, N.Mex., June 8, 1921; s. John Preston and Mary Ada (Alford) M.; B.S., U. Idaho, 1949, M.S., 1955; m. Dorothy Jean Christensen, Apr. 20, 1940; children—Gary Allen, Douglas Richard, Wayne Victor. Agrl. engr. U.S. Dept. Agr.-Agrl. Research Service-Soil and Water Conservation, Weslaco, Tex., 1960-68, project mgr., 1960-68, research investigations leader in remote sensing, 1963-68; dir. Remote Sensing Inst. S.D. State U., Brookings, 1969—. Cons. on Egyptian Remote Sensing Project Acad. Scientific Research and Tech., Cairo; cons. Mexico Nat. Water Plan and Remote Sensing Tech.-World Bank; cons. UN Desert Studies in S.Am. and S.W. Asia, 1976, 77. Served with USAF, 1944-45. Mem. Am. Geophys. Union, Am. Soc. Photogrametry, Am. Soc. C.E., Am. Soc. Agrl. Engrs., Sigma Xi. Rotarian. Contbr. Remote Sensing, 1970; also articles. Home: 440 Dakota Ave Brookings SD 57006

MYERS, WARREN ERWIN, ret. county ofcl.; b. Greenville, Ill., May 30, 1912; s. John J. and Evelyn W. (Wise) M.; student Eastern Ill. U., 1930-31; B.S., U. Ill., 1938; postgrad. U. Colo., 1952, 70, 72, U. Ariz., 1970, 73; m. Sarah Elizabeth Kelly, May 2, 1940; children—Patricia Ann Myers Johnson, Phyllis Elizabeth Myers Wilson, Ronald E. Elementary sch. tchr. Greenville, Ill., 1931-35; vocat. agr. tchr. Mazon (Ill.) High Sch., 1938-42, 45-46; owner Bush feed and hatchery business, Dwight, Ill., 1942-45; farm adviser, Coop. Extension Service, Toulon, Ill., 1946-50, Decatur, Ill., 1950-75; cons. Archer Daniels Midland Co., corn and soybean processors, 1975—; cons. Richland Jr. Coll., Decatur, Ill., 1975—. County chmn. United Way Dr., Decatur, Ill., 1975; mem. action programs on war and poverty, Decatur, Ill., 1969-72, mem. traffic safety com., 1968, com. mem. civil def., 1970-72. Bd. dirs. Ill. 4-H Found., 1964-65, County 4-H Found., 1968-75. Mem. Nat. Assn. County Agrl. Agts., Ill. Assn. Farm Advisers. Baptist (vice-chmn. bd. deacons 1956-58). Mason, Lion. Home: 793 Apache Dr Decatur IL 62526

MYERS, WILLIAM CLAUDE, JR., lawyer; b. Monett, Mo., Mar. 30, 1921; s. William Claude and Helen Elizabeth (Hardy) M.; LL.B., U. Mo., 1949; m. Carlyn Merryman, July 5, 1947; children—Lisa Merryman, Lynn Elizabeth, Leslie Reese, Gretchen Hardy, Ann Catherine. Admitted to Mo. bar, 1949; labor relations officer U.S. C.E., 1940-41; practice law, Webb City, Mo., 1949—, mem. firm Myers, Perry, Ossman & Copeland, 1949—; 1949—; pros. atty. Jasper County, Mo., 1956-60. Mem. Gov.'s Com. on Mo. Reorganization. Mem. Mo. Gen. Assembly, 1954-56; chmn. Mo. Republican Legis. Com., 1956. Past pres. bd. curators U. Mo., mem. bd., 1965-75; bd. dirs. Oak Hill Hosp., Joplin, Mo. Served with USAAF, 1941-45. Decorated Air medal with four oak leaf clusters. Mem. Am., Mo. bar assns., Assn. Trial Lawyers of Am., Am. Judicature Soc., U.S., Webb City (past pres., dir.) chambers commerce, Mo. Trial Lawyers Assn. (gov. 1960-68, pres. 1968), Am. Legion, V.F.W., Phi Alpha Delta. Presbyterian (elder, trustee). Home: 16 S Pennsylvania St Webb City MO 64870 Office: 112 N Webb Webb City MO 64870

MYERS, WILLIAM OSGOOD, thoracic and cardiovascular surgeon; b. Hastings, Nebr., Aug. 19, 1929; s. Joy Uberto and Lena C. (Osgood) M.; B.A., Hastings Coll., 1951; M.D., Northwestern U., 1955; m. Lois Mae Payne, Dec. 26, 1952; children—Jessica, Wendell, Inez, John, Michael. Intern, City Detroit Receiving Hosp., 1955-56, resident in anesthesiology, 1956-57; gen. practice medicine, Blue Hill, Nebr., 1959-62; cons. in anesthesia, anesthesiologist, Mary Lanning Meml. Hosp., Hastings, Nebr., Webster County Hosp., Red Cloud, Nebr., and Smith County Hosp., Smith Center, Kans., 1963-65; surg. resident Sacred Hosp., Yankton, S.D., 1962-65; instr. anatomy U. S.D. Med. Sch., Vermillion, S.D., 1963-65; resident in gen. surgery U. Kans. Med. Center, Kans. City, 1965-66; fellow thoracic and cardiovascular surgery U. Kans. Med. Center, 1966-68; cardiovascular surgeon Marshfield Clinic, Marshfield, Wis. and St. Joseph's Hosp., Marshfield, 1968—, chmn. sect. thoracic and cardiovascular surgery, 1972-76, chmn. dept surgery, 1974—. Active Boy Scouts Am.; mem. respiratory therapy adv. com. Midstate Tech. Inst., Marshfield, 1975—; mem. finance com. 1st Presbyn. Ch., Marshfield, 1974—. Served with USAF, 1957-59. Diplomate Am. Bd. Surgery, Am. Bd. Thoracic Surgery. Mem. Wis., Wood County med. socs, AMA, Wis. Surg. Soc., A.C.S., Am. Thoracic Soc., Am. Assn. Thoracic Surgery, Frederick A. Coller Surg. Soc., Central Surg. Assn. Contbr. articles to profl. jours. Home: 1110 Balsam Ave Marshfield WI 54449 Office: 1000 N Oak Ave Marshfield WI 54449

MYHRE, HAROLD GORDON, lawyer; b. Argyle, Minn., Jan. 8, 1928; s. Joseph G. and Inga (Hendrickson) M.; B.S., U. N.D., 1950; LL.B., J.D., 1955; m. Evangeline Anderson, Nov. 5, 1956; children—Gretchen, Justin, Christopher, Erik, Joseph. Admitted to Minn. bar, 1955; practiced in Warren, 1955—; mem. firm Myhre, Jorgenson & Drenchkakn, 1970—. Marshall County Atty., 1968—. Trustee, Marshall County Hist. Soc. Served with AUS, 1950-52. Mem. Am., Minn., 14th Dist. (pres. 1968-69) bar assns., Am. Trial Lawyers Assn., Nat. Dist. Attys. Assn., Minn. County Attys. Assn., Warren C. of C. (pres. 1962-63). Lutheran (trustee 1969-72). Mason (Shriner), Elk, Lion (pres. 1964-65). Home: 705 E Fletcher St Warren MN 56762 Office: 423 N Main St Warren MN 56762

MYLER, BERNARD JAMES, banker; b. Muskegon, Mich., July 10, 1926; s. Harry M. and Theresa M. (Vandreumel) M.; B.A., U. Tulsa, 1949; postgrad. U. Mich., 1956, U. Wis., 1963; m. Anne J. Wright, Feb. 15, 1947; children—David J., Stephen J. Supr., ops. mgr. Mich. Nat. Bank, Grand Rapids, 1950-58; v.p., dir. Security Nat. Bank, Manistee, Mich., 1958-61; pres., dir. Empire Nat. Bank, Traverse City, Mich., 1961-66; pres. Union Nat. Bank & Trust Co., Marquette, Mich., 1966-76, Ludington (Mich.) Bank & Trust Co., 1976—; dir. Marquette, Lake Superior and Ishpeming R.R. Mem. adv. com. No. Mich. U. Sch. Banking, 1968-74. Bd. dirs. Operation Action Up Marquette Devel. Corp., Marquette Gen. Hosp. Served with USNR, 1944-46. Mem. Am., Mich. bankers assns., Marquette (dir. 1966-68), Mich. State (dir. 1970-74), Ludington (dir. 1976—) chambers commerce. Club: Rotarian. Home: 306 S Ferry St Ludington MI 49431 Office: One Financial Plaza Ludington MI 49431

NABER, EDWARD CARL, nutritionist, educator; b. Fond du Lac, Wis., Sept. 12, 1926; s. Alfred F. and Edna (Kluenner) N.; B.S., U. Wis., 1950, M.S., 1952, Ph.D., 1954; m. Marie Anne Peterson, June 20, 1953; children—Thomas E., Diane M. Asst. nutritionist Clemson U., 1954-56; asst. prof. Ohio State U., Columbus, 1956-59, asso. prof., 1959-63, prof., 1963-69, prof., chmn. dept., 1969—; vis. prof. U. Wis., Madison, 1964-65. Mem. poultry nutrition subcom. NRC, 1966-71, 74-77, mem. animal nutrition com., 1973-77. Served with USNR, 1944-46. Mem. Am. Inst. Nutrition, Am. Chem. Soc., Poultry Sci. Assn. (exec. com. 1970-72, 74-78, pres. 1976-77), Am. Inst. Biol. Scis., A.A.A.S., World's Poultry Sci. Assn., Sigma Xi, Gamma Alpha, Phi Kappa Phi, Phi Sigma, Gamma Sigma Delta, Alpha Zeta, Alpha Gamma Rho. Lutheran (deacon 1968-74). Club: Faculty. Contbr. articles to profl. jours. Editor: (asso.) Poultry Sci., 1963-69. Home: 3600 Clearview Ave Columbus OH 43220

NABER, FAITH, librarian; b. Miltonvale, Kans., Sept. 27, 1920; d. Peter Gombert and Mary Orilla (Grise) Naber; A.A., Kendall Coll., Evanston, Ill., 1942; A.B., Otterbein Coll., 1944; postgrad. Hartford Sem., 1949-50; M.L.S., Ball State U., 1970; postgrad. Ill. No. U.; m. Frank E. Robinson, Sept. 5, 1943 (div. 1976); children—Paul David, Mary (Mrs. Larry Howard), John Timothy, Faith (Mrs. David Gluckman), Frank Eric. Ednl. missionary Meth. Ch., Philippines, 1950-55; tchr. Mississinawa Valley Schs., Union City, Ohio, 1957-60, librarian Ansonia (Ohio) High Sch., 1962-65, Wayne local schs., Waynesville, Ohio, 1965-67, Middletown, Ohio, High Sch., 1967-69, Middletown Freshman Sch., 1969-70, Bluffton (Ohio) Pub. Library, 1970-71, H.H. Conrady Jr. High Sch., Hickory Hills, Ill., 1971—; library cons. to faculty mem. Chgo. State U., Orchard Hill Farm Sch., Tinley Park, Ill. Leader, Buckeye Trails council Girl Scouts U.S., 1955-56, Wapahani council, 1957-62. Mem. ALA, NEA, Am. Sch. Library Assn., AAUW (recipient 3d prize short story, 1970), Methodist. Author 2 primers, also articles. Home: 14924 Riverside Dr Harvey IL 60426 Office: 97th and Roberts Rd Hickory Hills IL 60457

NADESAN, ALEXANDER GOVIND, polit. scientist, educator; b. Medan, Sumatra, Indonesia, Nov. 10, 1935; LL.B., Islamic U. N. Sumatra, 1956; B.A., Gustavus Adolphus Coll., 1958; postgrad. U. Minn., 1961 M.A.; Ph.D., Am. U. Sch. Internat. Service, Washington, 1968; m. Ardell Pogatchnik, Dec. 28, 1960; children—Grace Nadesan, Alexander G. Nadesan. Came to U.S., 1956, naturalized, 1967. Cons. U.S. Dept. State, Washington, 1963-64; vis. lectr. polit. sci. Wartburg (Iowa) Coll., 1965; faculty Bemidji (Minn.) State U., 1965—, prof., chmn. dept., 1972—. Named Smith Mundt Scholar, 1956. Mem. AAUP, Am., Minn. (dir. 1972-73) polit. sci. assns., Am. Soc. Internat. Law, Minn. Acad. Sci. (chmn. polit. sci. sect. 1970), Pi Sigma Alpha. Home: 403 Lincoln Ave Bemidji MN 56601

NAEGELE, ROBERT ARTHUR, engineer; b. Chgo., Aug. 17, 1934; s. Arthur Vincent and Miriam Anna (Marthens) N.; student U. Mich., 1952-55; M. Engring., Chgo. Tech. Coll., 1965; m. Lela Ann Beck, Apr. 27, 1957; children—Mary Lou, George Robert, Thomas Lee. Toll testman Mich. Bell Tele. Co., Monroe, 1955-60; engr. J.E. Watkins Co., Maywood, Ill., 1960-70; project engr. Austin Co., Des Plaines, Ill., 1970—. Active Boy Scouts Am., 1970-73; pres. Yorkfield Civic Assn., 1972-74. Mem. Am. Soc. Heating, Refrigeration and Air Conditioning Engrs. (pres. Chgo. chpt. 1976-77). Patentee solid state refrigerant level control. Home: 15W780 Fillmore St Elmhurst IL 60126 Office: 2001 Rand Rd Des Plaines IL 60016

NAFFZIGER, DEWEIN HAVEN, bus. co. exec.; b. Manito, Ill., Jan. 23, 1931; s. Arthur John and Golda Mildred (Hanes) N.; B.S. in Metall. Engring., Purdue U., 1953; m. Mary Germaine Clark, May 2, 1953; children—Audrey Denise, Patricia Lee, Deborah Ann, Andrey Dewein, Michael Anthony. Engr. electrometall. div. Union Carbide Corp., Marietta, Ohio, 1953; supr. Metal Casting Devel. Delco Remy div. G.M.C., Anderson, Ind., 1956-60; melting sales mgr. Ajax Magnethermic Corp., Warren, Ohio, 1961-68; pres., Advance Achievement Systems Inc., Warren, 1969—; cons. tng. metalcasting industry, partnership Admeltco., Waukesah, Wis., 1977. Served with U.S. Army, 1953-55. Registered profl. engr., Ind., Ohio, Mass., Mich. Mem. Soc. Die Casting Engrs. (chairperson, Ind., 1960-61), Am. Foundrymen's Soc., Am. Soc. Metals, Am. Soc. Tng. and Devel., Foundry Ed. Found. (alumni), Phi Eta Sigma, Sigma Gamma Epsilon, Tau Beta Pi. Roman Catholic. Lodge: B.P.O. Elks. Editor, publisher: High Frequency Induction Furnace Training Program, 1976; author: Induction Furnace Training Program, 1970; Metalcasting Orientation and Training Program, 1974; patentee in field. Home: 2925 Crescent Dr NE Warren OH 44483 Office: PO Box 1029 Warren OH 44483

NAGAR, ARVIND KUMAR, mech. engr.; b. Achheja (Ghaziabad), India, July 4, 1939; s. Kaley Singh and Risalo (Bhati) N.; came to U.S., 1960, B.S. in Mech. Engring., Okla. State U., 1969; M.M.E., Midwest Coll. Engring., Lombard, Ill., 1978; m. Sampat Dhabhai, June 5, 1971; children—Anil, Sunil. Mech. engr. Xerox Corp., Webster, N.Y., 1969-71; mech. designer Multigraphics div. A.M. Corp., Mt. Prospect, Ill., 1972-73; mech. engr. All Steel, Inc., Aurora, Ill., 1973—. Registered profl. engr., Ill. Mem. Nat., Ill. socs. profl. engrs., ASME, Altrusa Salutes, Toastmasters Internat. (certificate of merit), Pi Tau Sigma, Sigma Pi Sigma. Club: Flying Aviation. Asst. editor, bus. mgr., contbr. Engring. Coll. mag., 1960-63. Home: 1221 Coventry Pl Aurora IL 60506 Office: All Steel Inc Route 31 Aurora IL 60507

NAGEL, JON ALAN, mgmt. cons.; b. Cin., Nov. 8, 1950; s. Arthur R. and Marie Ann (Vollmer) N.; B.A., U. Cin., 1972, M.A., 1975; M.B.A., Columbia U., 1973; postgrad. Emory U. Law Sch., Harvard U., Oxford (Eng.) U. Mgmt. cons., Cin. and N.Y.C., 1975—; dir. ARNCO, Inc., 1972—; chmn. Prepco Intercontinental Inc., 1977—. Mem. Am. Econ. Assn., Young Men's Merc. Library Assn. Cin., Phi Alpha Delta. Clubs: Atrium, Doubles, El Morocco, Met., Met. Opera, St. Bartholomew's (N.Y.C.). Author: World Trade, 1973; Multinational Corporations in World Politics: Ecopolitics and Nation-State Responses, 1975. Home: 2875 Montana Ave Cincinnati OH 45211 also One E 60th St New York City NY 10021 Office: PO Box 11336 Cincinnati OH 45211 also Citicorp Center 153 E 53d St New York City NY 10022

NAGERA, HUMBERTO, psychiatrist; b. Havana, Cuba, May 23, 1927; B.Sc., U. Havana, 1945; M.D., Havana Med. Sch., 1952; m. Gloria Maria Hernandez, Sept. 8, 1952; children—Lisette Maria, Humberto Felipe, Daniel. Intern, resident in psychiatry Havana U. Hosp., 1950-55; sr. staff, chmn. research Anna Freud's Clinic, London, 1958-68; prof. psychiatry U. Mich., Ann Arbor, 1968—, chief youth services, 1973—. Mem. Internat., Am. psychoanalytic assns., Mich. Psychoanalytic Inst. (pres. 1975-77), Brit. Psychoanalytic Soc., Am. Assn. Child Psychoanalysis, Cuban Med. Assn. in Exile, Center for Advancement Psychoanalysis. Author: Early Childhood Disturbances, the Infantile Neurosis, and the Adulthood Disturbances, Problems of Developmental Psychoanalytic Psychology, 1967; Basic Psychoanalytic Concepts on the Libido Theory, 1969; Basic Psychoanalytic Concepts on the Theory of Dreams, 1969; Basic Psychoanalytic Concepts on the Theory of Instincts, 1970; Basic Psychoanalytic Concepts of Metaphysiology Conflicts, Anxiety, and Other Subjects, 1970; Female Sexuality and the Oedipus Complex, 1975; Obsessional Neurosis: Developmental Psychopathology, 1977. Contbr. articles to profl. jours. Home: 1421 Crawford Ln Ann Arbor MI 48105 Office: Children Psychiatric Hosp Univ Med Center Ann Arbor MI 48109

NAGEY, TIBOR FRANZ, mfg. co. exec.; b. Nagyvarad, Hungary, Apr. 4, 1922; s. Stephan and Charlotte (Rosette) N.; came to U.S., 1924, naturalized, 1936; student Northwestern U., 1939, Miami U., Oxford, Ohio, 1940-42; B.S., Case Inst. Tech., 1944; postgrad. Cleve. Coll., 1944-45, Western Res. U., 1949-50; m. Patricia Ann Griffin, Feb. 8, 1947; children—David A., Robert C., Barbara F. Researcher, thermodynamics and physics NACA, Cleve., 1944-53; mgr. nuclear div. Martin Co., Balt., 1953-58; dir. research for aircraft engines and transmission Allison div. Gen. Motors Corp., Indpls., 1958-60; dir. passenger car turbine devel., engring. staff Gen. Motors Corp., Warren, Mich., 1960-74, dir. research and devel., transp. systems div., 1974—. Mem. com. on nuclear power plants NASA, 1956-66; lectr. Ind. U. Sch. Medicine, Indpls., 1965-69; lectr. bioengring. Duke U. Sch. Medicine, Durham, N.C., 1972—. Chmn. Citizens Tb Eradication Com., 1965-66; chmn. Greater Detroit Hosp. Assn., 1972, 74. Trustee Marion County Gen. Hosp. Corp., 1968-69. Named Ind. Engr. of Yr., Soc. Profl. Engrs., 1963. Fellow N.Y. Acad. Sci.; mem. Sigma Xi, Phi Delta Theta. Contbr. articles to profl. jours. Patentee in field. Home: 2202 Bordeaux Dr West Bloomfield MI 48033 Office: GM Transportation Systems Div Gen Motors Tech Center Warren MI 48090

NAGI, MOSTAFA HELMEY, social scientist, educator; b. Samalig, Egypt, June 15, 1934; s. Faried and Hamida Ahmed (Shenishen) N.; came to U.S., 1964, naturalized, 1975; B.Sc. in Agr., Cairo (Egypt) U., 1958; M.A. in Sociology, Bowling Green (Ohio) State U., 1966; Ph.D. in Sociology and Demography, U. Conn., 1970. Specialist on social devel. Higher Council Pub. Services Govt. Egypt, Basandila, 1958-60, agr. specialist Ministry Agr. Syria, Latakia, 1962-64; agr. specialist Ministry of Agr. of Egypt, Zefta, 1960-62; grad. asst. Bowling Green State U., 1964-66, instr. sociology, 1969-70, asst. prof., 1970-71, asso. prof., 1972-77, prof., 1977—; grad. research asst. U. Conn., Storrs, 1966-69. Adv. participant on population, environment and social gerontology to confs., coms.; cons. Govt. Iraq, 1974-75, Arab Projects and Devel. Inst., Beirut, Lebanon, 1974-75, Arab Labor Orgn., Cairo, 1975. Mem. Am. Sociol. Assn., Population Assn., Gerontol. Soc., A.A.A.S., Rural Sociol. Soc., Ohio Acad. Sci., Am. Pub. Health Assn., Arab-Am. Univ. Grads. Author: Labor Force and Employment in Egypt, 1971. Contbr. articles to profl. jours. Home: 1722 Spruce Dr Bowling Green OH 43402

NAGLER, LA RUE (LARRY) HAMILTON, cons. automotive engr.; b. Hastings, Mich., June 30, 1903; s. John G. and Helen (Moore) N.; B.S. with honors in Mech. Engring., Mich. State U., 1925; m. Emma J. Erny, Aug. 23, 1930; children—Loraine (Laurie) Alice, Marlene Ruth. With research lab. of Gen. Motors Corp., Detroit, 1925-29, automotive testing engr. Oldsmobile Div., Lansing, Mich., 1929-37, adminstrv. engr. Product Engring. Dept., Eastern Aircraft Div., Linden, N.J., 1942-43, project engr. Detroit Transmission Div., 1943-45; liaison for engring. activities J.I. Case Co., Racine, Wis. and exec. engr. Tractor Div., 1939-42; tech. adviser Nash Motors, Detroit, 1948-50, coordinator of govt. regulations in Nash-Kelvinator central office, 1951-52, staff and safety engr. Nash and Am. Motors Corp., 1953-67, dir. New Devices Sect., 1956-67; automotive engring. cons., 1967—. Mem. Soc. Automotive Engrs. (auto council, v.p. passenger car activity), mem. safety com. 1961-67), Am. Assn. Automotive Medicine, Internat. Assn. Accident and Traffic Medicine, Automobile Mfrs. Assn. (vehicle safety com. 1956-67, chmn. 1960-62, lighting research com. 1963-67), Engring. Soc. Detroit, Am. Standards Assn. (automotive glazing com. 1960-70), Am. Automobile Assn., Automobile Orgn. Team, Am. Assn. Ret. Persons, Tau Beta Pi. Club: Kiwanis. Contbr. numerous articles on automotive engring. and safety to profl. jours.; editor Indsl. Power mag., 1937-39; tech. editor Motor Mag., 1945-48. Address: 35627 Heritage Ln Farmington MI 48024

NAGY, DENES, cons. engr.; b. Budapest, Hungary, Oct. 19, 1929; s. Denes and Margit (Lukacs) N.; came to U.S., 1957, naturalized, 1962; student Hungarian Comml. Inst. of Pest, 1950; B.A., Tech. U. Budapest, 1954, B.S. in Mech. Engring., 1954, M.S. in Mech. Engring., 1954; m. Margarita Penaherrera, Jan. 13, 1968. Design engr. Gebr. Van Swaay, Mij., engrs. and constructors, The Hague, Holland, 1956-57; project engr., design engr. Walter Scholer & Assos., Inc., architects and engrs., Lafayette, Ind., 1957-65; project engr. Dalton-Dalton Assos., Inc., architects and engrs., Cleve., 1965-67; pres., dir., chief engr. Environ. Engring. Corp., Chgo., 1967-72; pres., dir. Martin-Nagy-Tonella Assos., Inc., cons. engrs., Chgo., 1972-76; partner, dir. MNT Internat., Quito, Ecuador, 1975—; owner, pres. Denes Nagy Assos., Ltd., Chgo. Registered profl. engr., Ind., Ill., Wash., Wis., Mass., N.Y., Calif., W.Va. Mem. Am. Soc. M.E., Am. Soc. Heating, Refrigerating and Air-Conditioning Engrs., Internat. Dist. Heating Assn., Nat., Ill. socs. profl. engrs., Nat. Fire Protection Assn., Constrn. Specifications Inst., Air Pollution Control Assn., Automated Procedures for Engring. Cons. (trustee 1968-71), Soc. Am. Value Engrs., Am. Cons. Engrs. Council, Cons. Engrs. Council Ill., Ill. Architect-Engr. Council (mem. exec. com.), U.S. Power Squadron, Internat. Visitors Center, Chgo. Council on Fgn. Relations. Home: 505 N Lake Shore Dr Apt 2604 Chicago IL 60611 Office: 201 E Ohio St Chicago IL 60611

NAGY, THOMAS FRANCIS, psychologist; b. Newton, Mass., Sept. 6, 1945; s. Laszlo James and Paula Christina (Schneider) N.; A.B., Hamilton Coll., 1967; M.Ed., U. N.H., 1968, certificate advanced grad. study, 1969; Ph.D. in Counseling Psychology, U. Ill., Urbana, 1972; m. Kären Nani Lingrell, Mar. 25, 1972. Counseling psychologist Univ. High Sch., Urbana, 1969-72, Cleve. State U., 1972; staff psychologist Loyola U., Chgo., 1972—; pvt. practice, 1973—. Lectr. in field. Mem. Am., Midwest, Ill. psychol. assns., Am. Psychol.-Law Soc., Soc. Clin. and Exptl. Hypnosis, Chgo. Psychol. Club, Am. Soc. Psychologists in Pvt. Practice, Kappa Delta Pi. Co-author: Counseling-Preparation, Supervision and Assessment, 1971. Home: 2313 Thayer St Evanston IL 60201 Office: Suite 409 636 Church St Evanston IL 60201

NAIDEN, JAMES, journalist, poet; b. Sept. 24, 1943; student Seattle U., U. Iowa. Poet, critic lit. jours., 1968—; journalist newspapers, jours., U.S., Europe, 1968—; author: Asphyxiations/1-40 (poetry), 1978. Recipient Guillaume Apollinaire Prix, La Nuit Blanche, 1968. Mem. Coordinating Council Lit. Mags., Plains-Distbn. Service, Com. Small Mags., Editors and Pubs., Poetry Soc. Am. Contbr. articles to lit. jours.; editor North Stone Rev., 1971—. Address: Univ Station 14098 Minneapolis MN 55414

NAINES, JOSEPH BENJAMIN, JR., mgmt. co. exec.; b. Chgo., Feb. 28, 1928; s. Joseph Benjamin and Margaret Elizabeth (Soderstrom) N.; B.S., Northwestern U., 1950, M.S., 1953, Ph.D., 1965; m. Angelajo Barbagallo, June 14, 1952; children—Monica, Maribeth. Project engr., Northwestern U., Evanston, Ill., 1951-55, chief engr. analog div., 1955-57, chief engr. design div., 1957-60, chief engr. systems div., 1960-63; cons. Spaceonics, Inc., Geneva, Ill., 1962, University Patents, Inc., Chgo., 1965-67; mgr. econ. research Whirlpool Corp., Benton Harbor, Mich., 1967-69, mgr. mktg. econs., 1970-72, corp. economist, mgr. mktg. info., 1973-77; econ. cons. Mgmt. Horizons, Inc., Worthington, Ohio, 1977—. Chmn. consumer survey com. Assn. Home Appliance Mfrs., 1971-77. Mem. adv. council econ. edn. Olivet Coll., 1972—; sec. St. Joseph Sch. Bd., 1975—; vice chmn. Council on Econ. Evaluation in Mich., 1977—. Registered profl. engr., Ill. Mem. Am. Econ. Assn., Nat. Assn. Bus. Economists, Ops. Research Soc. Am., IEEE, Nat. Soc. Profl. Engrs., Navy League, Nat. Econ. Club Washington, Am. Def. Preparedness Assn., Sigma Xi, Tau Beta Pi, Pi Mu Epsilon, Eta Kappa Nu, Pi Tau Sigma. Patentee in field. Home: 314 Murphy Ct St Joseph MI 49085

NAJARIAN, JOHN SARKIS, surgeon; b. Oakland, Calif., Dec. 22, 1927; s. Garabed Lazarus and Siranoush (Demerjian) N.; A.B. with honors, U. Calif., Berkeley, 1948, M.D., 1952; m. Arlys Viola Mignette, Apr. 27, 1952; children—Jon, David, Paul, Peter. Intern, U. Calif. Med. Sch., San Francisco, 1952-53, resident in surgery, 1955-60; spl. NIH research fellow U. Pitts. Med. Sch., 1960-61; NIH sr. fellow and asso. Scripps Clinic and Research Found., La Jolla, Calif., 1961-63; asst. prof. surgery, dir. surg. research labs., chief transplantation service U. Calif. Dept. Surgery, San Francisco, 1963-66, prof. surgery, vice chmn. dept., 1966-67; prof. surgery, chmn. dept. U. Minn. Health Scis. Center, Mpls., 1967—; spl. cons. clin. research tng. com. Inst. Gen. Med. Scis., USPHS, NIH, 1965-69; lectr. in field. Served with USAF, 1953-55. Recipient Calif. Trudeau Soc. award, 1962; Markle scholar, 1964-69; named Football Alumnus of Yr., U. Calif., 1967, Alumnus of Yr., 1974, 77; diplomate Am. Bd. Surgery. Fellow A.C.S.; mem. AAAS, AMA, Am., Central surg. assns., Am. Assn. for Lab. Animal Sci., Am. Assn. Immunologists, Am. Heart Assn., Am. Diabetes Assn., Am. Council Exptl. Pathology, Internat., Am. (council mem. 1972) socs. nephrology, Am. Soc. Transplant Surgeons (pres. 1976), Assn. for Academic Surgery (pres. 1969), Council on Kidney in Cardiovascular Disease, Hagfish Soc., Halsted, Howard C. Naffziger, Minn., Mpls., St. Paul surg. socs., Minn., Hennepin County med. socs., Italian Surg. Research Soc. (correspondent mem.), Internat. Soc. Surgery, Minn. Acad. Medicine, Minn. Med. Assn., Minn. Med. Found., Soc. for Exptl. Biology and Medicine, Soc. Clin. Surgery, Soc. Surg. Chmn., Soc. Univ. Surgeons, Surg. Biology Club, Transplantation Soc., Sigma Xi, Alpha Omega Alpha. Lutheran. Author: Transplantation, 1972. Editor: Am Jour. Surgery, 1967—, Annals of Surgery, 1972—, Jour. Surg. Oncology, 1968—, Jour. Surg. Research, 1968—, Surg. Techniques Illustrated, 1973—, World Jour. Surgery, 1976—, Yearbook of Surgery, 1970—; asso. editor Surgery, 1971—. Home: 4345 E Lake Harriet Blvd Minneapolis MN 55409 Office: U Minn Hosps Minneapolis MN 55455

NAKRA, NARESH KUMAR, energy and environ. engring. adminstr.; b. Delhi, India, Jan. 8, 1946; s. Tilak Raj and Bimla Kumari (Kalra) N.; came to U.S., 1969, naturalized, 1977; M.S., U. Iowa, 19—, Ph.D., 1975; m. Kavita Gopal, Aug. 16, 1971; children—Neal, Navin. Asst. plant engr. Sriram Chems., Kota, India, 1967-69; research asst. U. Iowa, Iowa City, 1969-71, instr., 1971-73; asso. engr. Quaker Oats Co., Cedar Rapids, Iowa, 1973-74, engr., 1974-77, sr. process engr., 1977—. Registered profl. engr., Iowa. Mem. Nat. Soc. Profl. Engrs., Iowa Engring. Soc., ASME (organizing mem. food processing and prodn. com. 1977). Home: 433 Philadelphia Ave Westmont IL 60559 Office: Merchandise Mart Plaza Chicago IL 60654

NALIPINSKI, RUDOLPH EDWARD, naval equipment mfg. co. exec.; b. St. Paul, Sept. 23, 1912; s. Casimir Leon and Frances (Preble) N.; m. Ann Violet Antoinette Lucky, May 28, 1938; children—Annette J. Stenger, Rudolph L., David A., Elena M. Morehead. Supr. splty. work Twin City Iron and Wire Co., Mpls., 1929-40; assembly work No. Ordinance div., F.M.C. Corp., Mpls., 1940-45, group leader finishing and sizing hydrolic parts, 1945-52, supr. lapping, 1952—. Roman Catholic. Clubs: K.C., Twin City Suprs., F.M.C. Suprs. Home: Rural Route 2 Cedar Lake New Richmond WI 54017 Office: 4800 Marshall St Minneapolis MN 55421

NAMEN, ROBERT MARVIN, civil engr.; b. Cleve., June 23, 1930; s. Maurice and Dorothy Frances (Marvin) N.; B.S.C.E., U. Mich., 1952, M.S.C.E., 1956; children—Kimberlee, Kristin, Kathryn. Structural engr. NASA, 1952-53; structural designer, The Osborn Engineering Co., Cleve., 1956-63, asst. chief structural engr., 1963-72, dir., 1968-73, sec., 1970-71, treas., 1971-72, exec. v.p., 1973—. Served with U.S. Army, 1953-55. Registered profl. engr., Ohio, Ill., Mich., W.Va., N.J., Pa., Ky., N.Y., Calif., Ga., Ark., Tenn., Okla., Tex. Mem. Am. Soc. C.E., Nat. Soc. Profl. Engrs., Cons. Engrs. Ohio, Chi Epsilon. Methodist. Club: National Exchange (Cleve.) (dir.). Design works include D.C. stadium, San Juan stadium, Kent State stadium, numerous indsl. and comml. facilities. Home: 6805 Mayfield #303 Mayfield Heights OH 44124 Office: 666 Euclid Ave Cleveland OH 44114

NAMMACHER, THOMAS JOHN, pub. co. exec.; b. Oconomowoc, Wis., Oct. 31, 1931; s. T. H. and Rose E. (Mantell) N.; student Oberlin Coll., 1950-51; B.B.A., U. Wis., 1954; m. J. Joan Weismantel, Dec. 19, 1954; children—Scott A., Mark T., Jeffery S., Carrie J., Susan L. Chmn. Lakewood Pubs., Inc., Mpls., 1961—; pres. Pathfinder Village, Inc., Mpls., 1973—. Served with USAF, 1954-57. Mem. Am. Bus. Press (bd. dirs. 1972-74), Phi Gamma Delta. Author: Guide to Governmental Purchasing, 1972. Office: 731 Hennepin Ave Minneapolis MN 55403

NANCE, EARL WALTON, elec. engr.; b. Collinsdale, W.Va., Mar. 3, 1921; s. Edgar Joseph and Elizabeth May (Peppers) N.; B.S.E.E., Duke, 1954; m. Ruth Bresenham, July 30, 1950; 1 dau., Jerri Ruth. Elec. engr. Union Carbide Chems. Co., South Charleston, W.Va., 1954-62; elec. engr. U.S. Indsl. Chems. Co., Tuscola, Ill., 1962-67; chief elec. engr. Monsanto Enviro-Chem Co., Chgo., 1967-71; asso. Consoer Townsend & Assos., cons. engrs., Chgo., 1971-77; head elec. dept. Harza Engring. Co., cons. engrs., Chgo., 1977—. Served with AUS, 1944-46. Mem. Nat., Ill. socs. profl. engrs. Mason (32 deg.). Home: 7516 Baimbridge Dr Downers Grove IL 60515 Office: 150 S Wacker Dr Chicago IL 60606

NANEY, ALVA PAUL, physician; b. St. Louis, Sept. 15, 1918; s. Paul and Dora (Horn) N.; student U. Ill., 1936-39; M.D., Washington U., St. Louis, 1943; m. Janis Lorraine Hayes, June 8, 1942; children—Alan Paul, Robert Hayes. Intern, Presbyn. Hosp., Chgo., 1943; postgrad. in pathology Washington U. Sch. Medicine, St. Louis, 1946-47; resident in internal medicine VA Hosp., McKinney, Tex., 1947-49; practice medicine specializing in internal medicine, Flora, Ill., 1949—. Mem. bd. edn. Flora Twp. High Sch., 1952-64. Served with M.C., U.S. Army, 1943-45. Diplomate Am. Bd. Internal Medicine. Fellow A.C.P., Am. Coll. Cardiology, Council Clin. Cardiology; mem. Am. (dir. 1967-70), Ill. (dir. 1951—, pres. 1960-61) heart assns., AMA, Ill. Med. Soc. Home: 3 Circle Dr Flora IL 62839 Office: 433 E 7th St Flora IL 62839

NANSEN, EVERETT JAMES, ret. rubber co. salesman; b. Mpls., Apr. 20, 1910; s. Edward Jonas and Alma (Lindskoog) N.; student Armour Tech., 1928-34; m. Katherine O'Brien, Feb. 8, 1942; children— Arlene Donna (Mrs. Charles Knowles), Everett James, Katie Flo, Pam Mary. Indsl. engr. G. & W. Electric Specialty, Chgo., 1934-38, Am. Steel Foundry, Indiana Harbor, Ind., 1938-44, Gates Rubber Co., Denver, 1945-49; salesman Ohio Rubber Co. div. Eagle Picher Industries, Inc., Conneautville, Pa., 1949-75. Served with USNR, 1944-45. Mem. Am. Soc. Agrl. Engrs. Home: Box 146 Coal Valley IL 61240

NAP, KIMBEL ANTON, lab. adminstr.; b. Milw., Sept. 27, 1949; s. Anton Peter and Lucille Margart (Klann) N.; diploma United Tech. Inst., 1968; A.A.S. in Engring., Milw. Sch. Engring., 1971, B.S. in Bus., 1972; postgrad. No. Ill. U., 1973-74. Market devel. cons. Motorola, Inc., Schaumburg, Ill., 1972-74; gen. mgr. Knight Systems, Milw., 1974-76; v.p., dir. Draco Labs., Inc., Milw., 1976—; tchr. Milw. Sch. Engring., Milw. Area Tech. Coll. Mem. Sales and Marketing Execs. Clubs: Milw. Yacht, Metro Flying. Home: 1920 W Marne Ave Milwaukee WI 53209 Office: 2010 W Bender Rd Milwaukee WI 53209

NAPADENSKY, HYLA SARANE, engr.; b. Chgo., Nov. 12, 1929; d. Morris J. and Minnie D. (Litz) Siegel; student Ill. Inst. Tech., 1946-48; B.S., U. Chgo., 1950, M.S., 1952; m. Arnaldo Napadensky, Aug. 26, 1956; children—Lita Lynn, Yafa Lea. Design analysis engr. Internat. Harvester Co., Chgo., 1952-57; engring. advisor, mgr. fire and safety research Ill. Inst. Tech. Research Inst., Chgo., 1957—, part-time instr. dept. mechanics, 1964-66. Mem. com. on hazardous materials Nat. Acad. Scis.; chmn. risk analysis com. Joint Army Navy NASA Air Force Working Group on Safety and Environ. Protection. Mem. System Safety Soc. (pres. North Central chpt.), Combustion Inst., Am. Nuclear Soc., Sigma Xi. Adv. bd. Jour. Accident Analysis and Prevention, 1969-76. Contbr. articles to profl. jours. Home: 650 Judson Ave Evanston IL 60202 Office: 10 W 35th St Chicago IL 60616

NAPHIN, FRANCIS JOSEPH, lawyer; b. Chgo., Jan. 17, 1907; s. Patrick Henry and Margaret Agnes (Brennan) N.; A.B., Loyola U., Chgo., 1927; J.D., Northwestern U., 1930; m. Isabel Mary Byrne, Feb. 22, 1938; children—Isabel Mary, Francis Joseph, Martha Ann (Mrs. John J. O'Toole), Mary M. (Mrs. Allan J. Frenzel), Rosemary B., Catherine E. Admitted to Ill. bar, 1930; asso. firm Alden, Latham & Young, Chgo., 1930-39, Pruitt & Grealis, Chgo., 1939-55; partner firm Grealis & Naphin, Chgo., 1955-60, Grealis, Naphin, Sullivan & Banta, 1960-61; sr. partner firm Naphin, Sullivan & Banta, Chgo., 1961-69, Naphin, Banta & Cox, 1969—. Mem. Am., Ill., Chgo. bar assns. Roman Catholic. Home: 210 Broadway St Wilmette IL 60091 Office: 105 W Adams St Chicago IL 60603

NARCONIS, ROMAN JOSEPH, JR., electron microscopist, educator; b. Scranton, Pa., Apr. 25, 1946; s. Roman Joseph and Jean E. (Yusczyk) N.; A.A., State U. N.Y., Buffalo, 1964-68; diploma, lab. mgmt. program Buffalo Gen. Hosp., 1971; m. Susan J. Tarbox, June 28, 1969. Sr. electron microscopist, instr. clin. pathology Buffalo Gen. Hosp., also State U. N.Y., Buffalo, 1969-70; sr. electron microscopist, instr. pathology Sch. Medicine, St. Louis U., 1971—. Cons. Grand Island Biol. Co. (N.Y.). Served with M.C., AUS, 1972. Mem. Am. Soc. Clin. Pathologists, Electron Microscopy Soc. Am., Central States, N.Y. State electron microscopy socs., Am. Soc. Physics Affiliate, Amateur Athletic Union. Contbr. articles to profl. jours. Home: 8045 Paterson St Berkeley MO 63134 Office: Pathology Dept St Louis U 1402 S Grand Ave St Louis MO 63104

NARDINE, FRANK EDWARD, educator; b. Claremont, N.H., Nov. 21, 1935; s. Leo J. and Eleanor H. (Wells) N.; A.B., Dartmouth Coll., 1957; Ed.M., Harvard, 1958, Ed.D., 1965; m. Elisabeth Steiwer McElvenny, Aug. 11, 1962; children—Jennifer Talbot, Timothy McElvenny. Research asst. Harvard, Cambridge, Mass., 1961, teaching fellow, 1962-64, research asso., 1965, asst. prof., 1966-68; research asso. ednl. research council, Washington U., St. Louis, 1969-72; asso. prof., chmn. dept. ednl. psychology U. Wis., Milw., 1972—. Cons. Mass., Va., Pa., Mo. Peace Corps, U.S. State Dept., 1968. Mem. steering com. Mayor's Action Council, Cleve., 1969. Mem. Am. Psychol. Assn., Am. Edn. Reserve Assn., Phi Delta Kappa. Clubs: Dartmouth, Harvard. Home: 4901 N Oakland Whitefish Bay WI 53217

NASBY, CHARLES LELAND, JR., constrn. supply co. exec.; b. Mpls., Dec. 11, 1928; s. Charles Leland and Esther (Fjeldstad) N.; B.A., St. Olaf Coll., 1951; postgrad. U. Minn., 1951-52; m. Patricia Ann Ree, July 18, 1953; children—Gregory Charles, Timothy Arthur. With The Ceco Corp., Mpls., 1953-70, asst. mgr., 1965-70; pres., treas., dir. Charles Nasby Assos., Inc., Mpls., 1970—, Span-Dock, Inc., Mpls., 1977—. Vice chmn. bd. dirs. Ebenezer Soc., Mpls., 1968—; bd. dirs. Mpls. Builders Exchange, 1976—. Served with USNR, 1953-56. Registered profl. engr., Minn. Mem. Am. Soc. C.E., Minn. Soc. Profl. Engrs., Constrn. Specifications Inst., Comml. Constrn. Industries, Nat. Exchange. Republican. Lutheran. Clubs: Edina Country; Torske Klubben. Patentee in field. Home: 4624 Bruce Ave Minneapolis MN 55424 Office: 5100 Eden Ave Minneapolis MN 55436

NASH, EDWARD MERL, indsl. engr.; b. Van Buren County, Mich., Aug. 28, 1927; s. Aubrey J. and Lena M. (Phillips) N.; student U. Notre Dame, 1949-50, Alexander Hamilton Inst. Bus., 1963-64, Purdue U. Extension, 1965-66; m. Shirley A. Long, Sept. 11, 1948; children—Dennis M., Barry A., Kathleen M., Cynthia A. Mgr. indsl. engring. Studebaker Corp., South Bend, Ind., 1957-64; corp. mgr., indsl. automotive engr. Maremont Corp., Chgo., 1964-66; v.p., gen. mgr. Automotive Seating div. Young Spring & Wire Corp., Chgo., 1966-69; exec. v.p. Paramount Fabricating-Swift Mfg. Co., Detroit, 1969-71; pres. Hawthorne Paper Co., Kalamazoo, 1971-73; mgmt. cons., 1973—; pres. container group Triangle Corp., 1973—; dir. Hamlett Engring., Farmington, Mich. Tchr. indsl engring. South Bend Coll. Commerce, 1953—. Served with AUS, 1945-47. Mem. Am. Inst. Indsl. Engrs., Indsl Mgmt. Assn. Elk. Clubs: Beacon, Elk's Country (Kalamazoo); Long Beach (Ind.) Country. Home: 2711 Floral Trail Long Beach Michigan City IN 46360 Office: 127-131 W Taylor Grant Park IL 60940

NASH, JOHN PRITCHARD, lawyer; b. Manitowoc, Wis., Dec. 29, 1908; s. Archie Lyman and Mary (Pritchard) N.; student Lake Forest Acad., 1925; grad. Lawrenceville Sch., 1927; B.A., Princeton, 1931; LL.B., Harvard, 1934; m. Ruth Chapelle, Nov. 3, 1951; children—Barbara Pritchard, James Lyman. Admitted to Wis. bar, 1934, Fed. Dist. Ct., Eastern Dist. Wis., Western Dist. Wis., 7th U.S. Ct. Appeals bars; practice law Manitowoc, 1934—, with Nash & Nash, 1934-36, partner Nash & Nash (now Nash, Spindler, Dean & Grimstad), 1936—; dir. A.M. Richter Sons Co., The Manitowoc Co., Inc., Manitowoc Indsl. Devel., Inc., Richter Vinegar Corp. Chmn. fund raising Manitowoc County unit Am. Cancer Soc., 1954-56; active Manitowoc Community Fund, 1940-60; mem. adv. council Boy Scouts Am., 1972—. Chmn. Manitowoc County com. Higher Edn., 1960-64; chmn., Wis. Commn. Higher Ednl. Aids, 1967-69; mem. state adv. council Fed. Higher Edn. Act., 1965—, vice chmn., 1966—; mem. citizens adv. council U. Wis.-Green Bay, 1969—; mem. Gov.'s Commn. Edn., 1969-71. Bd. dirs. Holiday House, Rahr-West Fund Bd., Manitowoc Meml. Hosp., Manitowoc Day Care Center, YMCA; bd. advisers Salvation Army. Served to major, AUS, 1942-46. Decorated Bronze Star medal. Recipient Certificate Merit Manitowoc, 1967, award of merit U. Wis., 1972. Mem. Am., Wis., Manitowoc County (pres. 1958-59) bar assns. Manitowoc C. of C. Presbyn. (trustee 1957-60, elder 1965-68; trustee Wis. Synod 1969-72). Rotarian (pres. 1959-60). Clubs: B and B, Branch River Country (Manitowoc); University (Milw.). Home: 819 N 14th St Manitowoc WI 54220 Office: 926 S 8th St Manitowoc WI 54220

NASON, HOWARD K., research exec.; b. Kansas City, Mo., July 12, 1913; s. Eber James and Florence (King) N.; student, Kansas City Jr. Coll., 1929-32; A.B., U. Kan., 1934; post grad. Washington U., 1937, Harvard Grad. Sch. Bus. Adminstrn., 1950; m. Phyllis Maddock. Chief chemist Anderson-Stolz Corp., Kansas City, 1935-36; with Monsanto Chem. Co., St. Louis, 1936—, research chemist, 1936-39, asst. dir. research plastics div., 1939-44, asso. dir., div. central research dept., 1944-50, asst. to v.p., 1950-51, research dir. Organic Chems. div., 1951-56, v.p., gen. mgr. Research and Engring. div., 1956-60; pres. Monsanto Research Corp., 1960-76, IRI Research Corp., 1976—; dir. Carboline Co. Mem. adv. com. isotopes and radiation devel. AEC, 1964-68; mem. Atomic Energy-Labor-Mgmt. Adv. Com., 1965—; mem. Pres.' Comm. on Patent System, 1965-68, St. Louis Planetarium Commn., 1966—, Aerospace Safety Adv. Panel, 1972—; mem. patent adv. com. U.S. Patent Office, 1968-72; mem. Nat. Acad. Engring. materials adv. bd. com. on materials sci. application and coordination, 1972-76; exec. fellow Rensselaer Inst., 1977. Trustee-at-large Univs. Research Assn.; trustee Charles F. Kettering Found., 1973—; chmn. bd. St. Louis Research Council, 1971-73; mem. St. Louis County Fin. Com., 1976—; exec. com., v.p. Atomic Indsl. Forum, Inc., 1971-73. Mem. Soc. Chem. Industry (Am. sect. exec. com.), Am. Inst. Chem. Engrs., N.Y. Acad. Scis., Am. Chem. Soc., Am. Inst. Aeros and Astronautics, Soc. Rheology, AAAS, ASTM (dir.), Inst. Aero. Scis., Am. Mineral. Soc., Sci. Research Soc. Am., Am. Nuclear Soc., Washington U. Faculty Conf. Center Assn., Nat. Rifle Assn., St. Louis Regional Commerce and Growth Assn. (bd. dirs., exec. com. 1971-74), U.S. C. of C. (com. sci. and tech. 1968-71), Mfg. Chemists Assn. (nuclear com.), Am. Inst. Chemists. Clubs: Quiet Birdmen; Cosmos (Washington); St. Louis. Author articles profl. jours. Holds one fgn. and ten U.S. patents. Office: 7800 Bonhomme St Louis MO 63105

NASSER, STEPHEN CHARLES, chiropractor; b. Terre Haute, Ind., Sept. 15, 1938; s. Nasser George and Ethel Jane (Malooley) N.; B.A. in Zoology, Ind. U., 1962, postgrad. Sch. Medicine, 1962-64; D.C. summa cum laude, Lincoln Coll. Sch. Chiropractic, 1970. Pharm. rep. Abbott Labs., Terre Haute, 1965-68; practice chiropractics, Terre Haute, 1970—. Instr. Lincoln Coll. Sch. Chiropractic, 1969-70; mem. Nat. Bd. Chiropractic Examiners, 1970. Diplomate Nat. Bd. Chiropractic Examiners. Mem. Am., Ky. chiropractic assns., Ind. Chiropractic Physicians Assn., Ind. State U. 200 Club for Athletics, Wabash Valley Quarterback Club, Strawberry Hill Cannoneers of Terre Haute, Phi Delta Theta (v.p. 1957-62), Alpha Epsilon Delta, Delta Tau Alpha. Republican. Mem. Orthodox Ch. Clubs: Masons, Shriners, Kiwanis. Home: 24 S 23d St Terre Haute IN 47807 Office: 1407 Ohio St Terre Haute IN 47807

NATHAN, KENNETH SAWYER, lawyer; b. Oshkosh, Wis., Feb. 8, 1906; s. Abraham and Jennie (Blumenthal) N.; student U. Chgo., 1923-26; J.D., DePaul U., 1930; m. Jean Hollander, Dec. 31, 1932 (div. June 1962); children—Anthony R., Meryl; m. 2d, Doris Jean Kahn, Sept. 26, 1962; 1 son Kenneth; 1 stepson, Jeffery Preucil. Admitted to Ill. bar, 1930; mem. staff Chgo. Crime Commn., 1928-29; arbitrator state Ill., 1940-41; asst. U.S. atty. No. Dist. Ill., 1943-46; partner law firm Nathan & Klafter, Chgo., 1954—. Mem. Am., Fed., Ill., Chgo. bar assns., Am. Judicature Soc., Trial Lawyers Assn., 7th Dist. Bar Assn., Pi Gamma Mu, Zeta Beta Tau. Elk, Moose. Office: 39 S LaSalle St Chicago IL 60603

NATIONS, GUS ORVEL, lawyer; b. St. Louis, Sept. 16, 1927; s. Gus Orvel and Mabel (Sackmann) N.; A.B., Washington U., 1950, J.D., 1952; m. Virginia Lee Meroney, Sept. 2, 1955; children—Kimberly, Thomas, Jeffrey and Laura (twins), Gus O. III, John, Kathryn Maurine. Admitted to Mo. bar, 1952, asso. firm Lashly, Lashly and Miller, St. Louis, 1952-57; practiced in Clayton, Mo., 1957—; partner firm Nations and McSweeney, Clayton, 1957-64, firm Nations and Yocum, 1964-68, Nations & Muelle, 1968—. City councilman and mayor pro-tem, Webster Groves, 1958-60, mayor, 1960-66. Mem. St. Louis County Civil Rights Commn. Chmn. St. Louis County Bd. Police Commrs., 1973—. Bd. dirs., vice chmn. St. Louis chpt. Nat. Found., Salvation Army. Named Young Man of Yr. Webster Groves Jr. C. of C., 1962. Served with AUS, 1946-47. Mem. Am., Mo., St. Louis County bar assns., Mo. (dir.), St. Louis County (pres. 1963-64) leagues municipalities, St. Louis C. of C. (dir.), Sigma Chi, Phi Delta Phi. Mason (master 1961, dist. dep. grand master, 33 deg., Shriner). Mem. Christian Ch. (deacon). Clubs: Clayton, John Marshall, Mo. Athletic. Home: 448 W Swon Ave Webster Groves MO 63119 Office: 130 S Bemiston Clayton MO 63105

NAUMAN, DELBERT ARNOLD, chemist; b. Frankfort, Kans., Nov. 22, 1932; s. Irving Agustus and Hazel (Arnold) N.; B.S. in Chemistry, Kans. State U., 1955; postgrad. U. Wichita, 1957, U. Ala., 1964, Purdue U., 1969-72; m. Joanne Alberta Lindeen, May 29, 1952; children—Jo Deaun, Mark Arnold. Chemist, Dowell, Inc., Tulsa, 1955-56; engr. Boeing Co., Wichita, Kans., 1956-62; sr. engr. Chrysler Corp., Huntsville, Ala. and Cape Canaveral, Fla., 1962-69, Western Elec. Co., Indpls., 1969—, chief chemist, 1972—. Mem. Soc. Applied Spectroscopy, Microbeam Analysis Soc. Republican. Lutheran. Club: Moose. Home: 2434 Constitution St Indianapolis IN 46229 Office: 2525 Shadeland Ave Indianapolis IN 46206

NAUMANN, WILLIAM LOUIS, mfg. co. dir.; b. Desloge, Mo., Nov. 20, 1911; s. Jules L. and Barbara (Eichenlaub) N.; ed. pub. schs., Ill.; m. Emma H. Bottin, June 1, 1934; children—William C., Virginia L. With Caterpillar Tractor Co., Peoria, Ill., 1929—, mgr. Joliet plant, 1952-56, mgr. Peoria plant, 1956-60, v.p. charge direction domestic plants, 1960-63, v.p. charge mfg., purchasing quality control and traffic, 1963-66, exec. v.p., 1966-72, vice chmn. bd., 1972-75, chmn. bd., 1975-77, now dir.; dir. Pekin Nat. Bank (Ill.), Jefferson Trust & Savs. Bank of Peoria, Internat. Exec. Service Corps, Abex Corp., IC

Industries, Inc., Helmerich & Payne, Inc. Mem. adv. bd. St. Francis Hosp., Peoria; trustee Ill. Wesleyan U., Bloomington, Ill. Home: 8307 Bramberry Lane Peoria IL 61614 Office: Caterpillar Tractor Co 100 NE Adams St Peoria IL 61629

NAUSS, LEE AUGUST, anesthesiologist; b. Estherville, Iowa, Mar. 28, 1932; s. Albert August and Avis B. (Cole) N.; student Iowa State Tchrs. Coll., 1955; diploma Allen Meml. Hosp. Luth. Sch. Nursing, 1958, Mayo Clinic Sch. Anesthesia for Nurses, 1960; student La Sierra Coll., 1965-66, Little Rock U., 1966-67; M.D., U. Ark., 1971; m. Maria Rosenau, June 7, 1958. Anesthetist, Juneau (Alaska) Clinic, 1960-65, Children's Hosp., Little Rock, 1966-67; intern U. Ark. Med. Center, Little Rock, 1971-72; resident anesthesiology Virginia Mason Clinic, Seattle, 1972-73, Mayo Grad. Sch., Rochester, Minn., 1973-74; anesthesiologist, cons. pain clinic and anesthesiology Mayo Clinic, Rochester, 1974—. Instr. anesthesiology Mayo Clinic Med. Sch., 1974—. Served with M.C., AUS, 1952-53. Mem. Internat. Anesthesia Research Soc., Am. Soc. Anesthesiologists, Alpha Omega Alpha. Lutheran (sec. ch. council 1964-65). Home: 410 6th Ave SW Rochester MN 55901 Office: 200 1st St SW Rochester MN 55901

NAVARRO, ANNA MARIA, chem. co. exec.; b. Havana, Cuba, Mar. 1, 1947; d. Eugene and Maria (Castro) Navarro; naturalized, 1962; B.A., New Coll., 1967; M. Pub. Affairs, Princeton U., 1969. Project dir. Independent Research Assos., Inc., 1969-70; dir. polit. polling Muskie Presdl. campaign, 1970-72; pres. Navarro Opinion Research Co., St. Louis, 1972-76; v.p. Fleishman-Hillard Inc., St. Louis, 1972-76; dir. corp. social responsibility Monsanto Co., St. Louis, 1976—. Mem. St. Louis Conv. and Tourist Bd. Commn.; staff mem. Women's Counseling Center; bd. dirs. Conf. on Edn., New City Sch. Home: 4402 McPherson St Apt 9W Saint Louis MO 63108 Office: Monsanto Co 800 W Lindbergh Blvd Saint Louis MO 63166

NAYDEN, JOHN MICHAEL, radiologist; b. Canton, Ill., Mar. 25, 1938; s. John Joseph and Frances Lucille (Champlin) N.; B.S., U. Ill., 1960, M.D., 1964; m. Carol Jean Siegfried, Dec. 28, 1963; children—J. Michael, Mark Howard, Max Edward, Catherine Lynn. Intern, Ill. Central Hosp., Chgo., 1964-65; resident in radiology U. Ill. Hosp., Chgo., 1968-71, instr. Abraham Lincoln Sch. Medicine U. Ill., 1968-73, asst. prof., 1973—; radiologist, S. Suburban Hosp., Hazelcrest, Ill., 1971—, pres. med. staff, 1975—. Served as flight surgeon M.C. USAF, 1965-68. Diplomate Am. Bd. Radiology, Am. Bd. Nuclear Medicine. Republican. Home: 684 Brookwood Dr Olympia Fields IL 60461

NAYLOR, GEORGE LEROY, lawyer, r.r. exec.; b. Bountiful, Utah, May 11, 1915; s. Joseph Francis and Josephine Chase (Wood) N.; student U. Utah, 1934-36; student George Washington U., 1937; J.D. (Bancroft Whitney scholar, 1950-51, 52), U. San Francisco, 1953; m. Maxine Elizabeth Lewis, Jan. 18, 1941; children—Georgia (Mrs. Ralph E. Price), RoseMaree (Mrs. Glenn B. Hammer), George LeRoy II. Admitted to Calif. bar, 1954, Ill. bar, 1968; v.p., sec., legis. rep. Internat. Union of Mine, Mill & Smelter Workers, CIO, Dist. Union 2, Utah-Nevada, 1942-44; examiner So. Pacific Co., San Francisco, 1949-54, chief examiner, 1955, asst. mgr., 1956-61; carrier mem. Nat. R.R. Adjustment Bd., Chgo., 1961-71 chmn., 1970-77; atty. Village of Fox River Valley Gardens, Ill., 1974-77; gen. counsel for Can-Veyor, Inc., Mountain View, Calif., 1959-64. Served with AUS, World War II. Mem. Am. Bar Assn. Mem. Ch. of Jesus Christ of Latter Day Saints. Author: Defending Carriers Before the NRAB and Public Law Boards, 1969, Choice Morsels in Tax and Property Law, 1966, Underground at Bingham Canyon, 1944. Home: 128 Center St Barrington IL 60010

NAZETTE, RICHARD FOLLETT, lawyer; b. Eldora, Iowa, July 27, 1919; s. Hilmer H. and Genevieve A. (Follett) N.; B.A., U. Iowa, 1942, J.D. with distinction, 1946; m. M. Joan Chehak, June 20, 1942; children—Ronald D., Randall A. Admitted to Iowa bar, 1946; practice law Cedar Rapids, Iowa, 1946—; asst. atty. Linn County, Iowa, 1951-56, county atty., 1957-63; dir. United State Bank, Cedar Rapids, Iowa, 1968—, chmn., 1976—; dir. State Surety Company, Des Moines, 1966—. Bd. dirs. Linn County Health Center, 1968-73, chmn., 1968-69. Served with AUS, 1942-44. Fellow Am. Bar Found.; mem. Iowa (bd. govs. 1972-76), Linn County (pres. 1963) bar assns., Iowa County Attys. Assn. (pres. 1959), Cedar Rapids Law Club (pres. 1954), Iowa Acad. Trial Lawyers (pres. 1964), Sigma Phi Epsilon. Republican. Presbyterian. Clubs: Elks, Masons, Shriners, Jesters, Optimist (internat. v.p. 1955), Cedar Rapids Country (pres. 1975). Home: 2224 Country Club Pkwy SE Cedar Rapids IA 52403 Office: 200 1st St SW Cedar Rapids IA 52404

NEAL, CHARLOTTE ANNE, ednl. adminstr.; b. Hampton, Iowa, May 8, 1937; d. Sebo and Marion Bradford (Boutin-Clock) Reysack; B.A., U. No. Iowa, 1958; M.Ed., DePaul U. (Chgo.), 1966; postgrad. No. Ill. U.; m. Paul Gordon Neal, Mar. 29, 1969; children—Rachel Elizabeth, Kory Bradford. Tchr., 4th grade, Des Moines Ind. Sch. Dist., 1958-59; tchr., 3d grade Glenview (Ill.) Pub. Schs., 1959-61, tchr. 3d grade, psychol. ednl. diagnostic Schaumburg Dist. Schs., Hoffman Estates, Ill., 1961-69; supr. learning disabilities and behavior disorders Springfield (Ill.) Pub. Schs., 1969-73; psycho-ednl. diagnostician Barrington (Ill.) Sch. Dist. 220, 1973—; ednl. cons. Spl. Edn. Dist. Lake County, Gurnee, Ill., summer, 1968. Certified K-14 teaching and supervising in guidance, counseling, elementary supervisory K-9, elementary K-9 teaching, spl. K-12 learning disabilities. Mem. NEA, Barrington, Ill. ednl. assns., Delta Kappa Gamma. Republican. Mem. United Ch. of Christ. Author: Handbook for Learning Disabilities Tchrs., 1971. Home: 1102 Sunset Dr Parkersburg IA 50665

NEAL, MARK WAYNE, paper co. mktg. exec.; b. Ottumwa, Iowa, Sept. 29, 1942; s. Ronald Wayne and Mary Grace (Cawley) N.; student St. Thomas Coll., St. Paul, 1960-62; B.S., Iowa State U., 1967; m. Susan June Halmrast, June 20, 1964; children—Timothy Mark, Julia Christine. Designer packaging Mead Containers Co., Ft. Dodge, Iowa, 1965-67, editor house organ, 1965, field salesman, 1967-74, mgr. field sales, 1974—. Instr. Tobin Bus. Coll., Ft. Dodge, 1962-63. Campaign worker Democratic Party, 1967-68. Co-recipient Bronze award Fiber Box Assn., 1967. Mem. Am. Meat Sci. Assn. (profl.). Roman Catholic. Clubs: Sertoma Sundowners (dir., v.p. programs 1976-77, pres. elect 1977), Fort Dodge Country, Elks (officer). Inventor in field. Home: 3072 12th Ave N Fort Dodge IA 50501 Office: 1142 SW 14th St Fort Dodge IA 50501

NEAL, PAUL EDWIN, research scientist; b. Oilton, Okla., Apr. 4, 1924; s. George Bradford and Estella Bernadine (Baker) N.; student Stevens Inst. Tech., 1944, Mass. Inst. Tech., 1944-45; B.Aero.Engring., Rensselaer Poly. Inst., 1947, B.Mech. Engring., 1949; postgrad. W.Va. U., 1951-52, Ohio U., 1953-51, U. Buffalo, 1956-58; m. Dana Lorine Cooper, July 1, 1972; 1 son by previous marriage, Bradford Carl. Mathematician, Consol. Vultee Aircraft, Fort Worth, 1947-48; sr. process engr. Corning Glass Works (N.Y.), 1950-56; sr. engr. Carborundum Co., Niagara Falls, N.Y., 1956-58; mgr. spl. projects Lawrence Radiation Lab., Mercury, Nev., 1959-64; div. mgr. Aerojet Gen. Corp., Sacramento, 1964-71; asso. lab. dir. Argonne Nat. Lab. (Ill.), 1971—. Served with USNR, 1943-46. Registered profl. engr., Calif. Mem. Am. Nuclear Soc., Am. Inst. Aeros. and Astronautics, Combustion Inst. Democrat. Methodist. Home: 7722 Stevens St Darien IL 60559 Office: 9700 S Cass Ave Argonne IL 60439

NEAL, PAUL GORDON, social worker; b. Exra, Ill., Nov. 5, 1933; s. Clyde Edward and Thelma (Turner) N.; B.A., So. Ill. U., 1960; M.S., U. Mo., 1963; m. Charlotte Anne Reysack, Mar. 29, 1969; children—Rachel Elizabeth, Kory Bradford. Social work supr. Elgin (Ill.) State Hosp., 1963-64; adminstr. marital clinic Forest Hosp., Des Plaines, Ill., 1964-66; chief social worker McHenry (Ill.) Mental Health Clinic, 1966-68; supervising social worker Sch. Dist. 54, Schaumburg, Ill., 1968-69; psychiat. social worker Springfield (Ill.) Mental Health Clinic, 1969-73; psychiat. social worker Maine Twp. High Sch., Park Ridge, Ill., 1973-77, Area Edn. Agy. 7, Cedar Falls, Iowa, 1977—; practice of psychiat. social work, Palatine, Ill., 1963-69. Group treatment cons., Arlington Heights, Ill., 1968-69; social work cons. Clembrook Center for Retarded, 1966-67. Served with USAF, 1952-56. Mem. Nat. Assn. Social Workers, Acad. Certified Social Workers, Am. Orthopsychiat. Assn., Am. Assn. Marriage Counselors. Research in firesetting syndrome in children. Home: 1102 Sunset Dr Parkersburg IA 50665 Office: 3712 Cedar Heights Dr Cedar Falls IA 50613

NEALE, GARY LEE, corp. planning cons.; b. Lead, S.D., Mar. 3, 1940; s. Vearl J. and Gladys M. (Trenkle) N.; B.A. in Econs., U. Wash., 1962, M.B.A., 1965; m. Sandra C. Lovell, June 16, 1962; children—David G. Neale, Julie C. Loan examiner Wells Fargo Bank, San Francisco, 1964-68; sr. financial analyst Kaiser Cement & Gypsum Co., Oakland, Calif., 1968-69; with On Line Decisions Inc., Berkeley, Calif., 1969-71, Chgo., 1971—, v.p., 1970-73, regional mgr. for Midwest and West Coast, 1971-73, pres., chief exec. officer, 1973—; pres., chief exec. officer Planmetrics Inc., Chgo.; chmn. bd. Energy Mgmt. Assos., Atlanta; dir. Modine Inc. Served to lt. (j.g.), USNR. Mem. Planning Execs. Inst., Corp. Planners Assn., Am. Inst. Mgmt. Clubs: Chgo. Economics; Racine Yacht. Lectr. in field. Home: 1414 North Ave Bannockburn IL 60015 Office: 233 S Wacker St Chicago IL 60606

NEBLETT, THOMAS RANDOLPH, clin. microbiologist; b. Lexington, Ky., June 4, 1928; s. Thomas Walter and Deborah Jewell (Eades) N.; B.A., Mich. State Coll., 1951; postgrad. U. Louisville, 1951-52; M.S., Wayne U., 1955; Ph.D., Mich. State U., 1957; m. Nancy Ellen Glunz, Feb. 27, 1960. Asso. in charge Serology Lab., Dept. Pathology, Henry Ford Hosp., Detroit, 1957-66, head Bacteriology-Serology div., 1966—, chief microbiologist, 1976—; adj. asst. prof. microbiology Wayne State U., 1975—, Mich. State U., 1974-75. NIH research grantee antinuclear factors, 1968-69. Mem. U.S. Power Squadron (Dist. 9 chmn. advanced grades 1972—), Am. Soc. Microbiology, South Central Assn. Clin. Microbiology (area dir. 1973-75), Sigma Xi, Phi Kappa Tau. Clubs: Detroit Yacht, Detroit Navigators. Researcher fluorescent antibody detection of antinuclear factors, serum complement, serological tests syphilis, urinary tract bacteriology, anaerobic bacteriology. Home: 22455 Walsingham Dr Farmington Hills MI 48024 Office: 2799 W Grand Blvd Detroit MI 48202

NECHIN, HERBERT BENJAMIN, lawyer; b. Chgo., Oct. 25, 1935; s. Abraham and Zelda (Benjamin) N.; B.A. with distinction and honors in History, Northwestern U., 1956; LL.B., Harvard U., 1959; m. Susan Zimmerman (div.); 1 dau., Jill Rebecca; m. 2d, Roberta F. Aronfeld, Oct. 24, 1976; 1 stepson, Stefan E. Aronfeld. Admitted to Ill. bar, 1960; partner Brown, Fox & Blumberg, Chgo., 1967-74; prin. Taussig, Wexler & Shaw, Ltd., Chgo., 1974—. Bd. dirs. Jewish Vocational Service, Chgo., 1970—, sec., 1974-75, treas., 1975-76; trustee Harris Sch., Chgo., 1972-75; pres. young peoples div. Jewish Fedn. Met. Chgo., 1967-68. Served with AUS, 1960-66. Mem. Am., Ill., Chgo. bar assns., Phi Beta Kappa. Home: 399 Fullerton Pkwy Chicago IL 60614 Office: Suite 3225 180 N LaSalle St Chicago IL 60601

NEDERLANDER, CAREN ELAINE, psychologist; b. Detroit, July 25, 1942; d. Morris and Janet Ruth (Sloman) Berman; B.F.A., U. Mich., 1971, M.A., 1974, Ph.D., 1976; m. Robert Elliott Nederlander, June 17, 1962; children—Robert Elliott, Eric Arthur. Dir. behavior therapy Franklin Center for Behavior Change, Southfield, Mich., 1974—; lectr. dept. psychiatry U., also coordinator human sexuality sequence Mich. Docent Detroit Inst. Arts, 1965-76. Mem. Am. Art Therapy Assn. (registered art therapist), Am. Assn. Sex Educators, Counselors and Therapists (certified sex therapist), Assn. Advancement Behavior Therapy, Am. Assn. Marriage and Family Counselors, Am. Psychol. Assn., Soc. Sci. Study of Sex. Author: New Sexual Awareness-Self-Help for Females, 1976; A Sex Education Program for Females Incorporating Graphic Expression in the Modification of Sexual Behavior, 1976. Home: 4616 Private Lake Dr Birmingham MI 48010 Office: 29260 Franklin Rd Suite 117 Southfield MI 48034

NEDERLANDER, ROBERT ELLIOTT, lawyer; b. Detroit, Apr. 10, 1933; s. David T. and Sarah (Applebaum) N.; B.A., U. Mich., 1955, J.D., 1958; m. Caren Elaine Berman, June 17, 1962; children—Robert Elliott, Eric Arthur. Admitted to Mich. bar, 1958; since practiced in Detroit; partner, Fenton, Nederlander, Dodge & Ritchie, P.C., Detroit, 1960—; exec. v.p. Nederlander Theatrical Corp., 1960-73; part-owner N.Y. Yankees, Baseball Club, 1973—; dir. Mich. Nat. Bank, Detroit. Regent, U. Mich., 1969—; V.P. Muscular Dystrophy Assn. Am.; pres. Muscular Dystrophy Assn. SE Mich. Home: 4616 Private Lake Dr Birmingham MI 48010 Office: 1930 Buhl Bldg Detroit MI 48226

NEDERVELD, TERRILL LEE, mktg. exec.; b. Hudsonville, Mich., Jan. 26, 1934; s. Fred and Clara (DeGroot) N.; student Purdue U. 1952, U. Mich. 1976, in profl. sales mgmt. W.Mich. U. 1975; m. Ruth E. Schut, June 6, 1952; children—Courtland Lee, Valerie Lynn Nederveld Heisey, Darwin Frederick. Design mgr. Packaging Corp. of Am., Lancaster, Pa. 1959-67, mkt. coordinator 1967-73, mgr. mkt. coordination Grand Rapids, Mich. 1973-74, mktg. mgr. 1974-76, corp. mktg. mgr. 1976—; lctr. Mich. State U. Sch. of Packaging, East Lansing, 1977-78. Recipient silver award for outstanding package development Fibre Box Assns. 1966. Mem. Sales Mktg. Execs. (1st v.p. 1976-77, pres. 1978-79), U.S. Power Squadron, Soc. of Packaging and Handling Engrs., Pi Sigma Epsilon. Mem. Presbyterian Ch. (deacon). Clubs: Nat. Campers and Hikers, Caravan Shrine, Mason, Shriner. Inventor in field of packaging; holder 6 U.S. patents in field. Office: 470 Market St SW Grand Rapids MI 49502

NEDZI, LUCIEN NORBERT, congressman; b. Hamtramck, Mich., May 28, 1925; s. Alexander and Estelle (Wojszko) N.; A.B. in Econs., U. Mich., 1948, J.D., 1951; postgrad. U. Detroit, 1949; m. Margaret Kathleen Garvey, Jan. 28, 1952; children—Lucien Alexander, Bridget Kathleen, Brendan Thomas, Gretchen Teresa, Eric Francis. Admitted to Mich. bar, 1952, practiced in Hamtramck, 1952—, pub. adminstr., Wayne County, Mich., 1955—; mem. 87th-88th Congresses, 1st Dist. Mich.; mem. 89th-95th Congresses, 14th Dist. Mich. Neighborhood commr. Boy Scouts Am., 1957; commr. United Community Services, 1957; treas. Wayne County com. Democratic party, 1956-58, chmn. 1st dist. orgn., 1958—, del. Dem. Nat. Conv., 1960. Served with AUS, 1944-46, 51. Decorated Bronze Star. Mem. Am., Mich., Detroit, Hamtramck (pres.) bar assns., Am. Judicature Soc. Roman Catholic. Clubs: Advocates of Detroit, National Advocates. Home: 19421 Conley St Detroit MI 48234 Office: 2930 Holbrook Hamtramck MI 48212 also 2418 Rayburn House Office Bldg Washington DC 20025

NEE, WILLIAM JOSEPH, advt. agy. exec.; b. Evanston, Ill., Apr. 20, 1925; s. Patrick Joseph and Ruby Henrietta (Bacus) N.; B.A., U. Minn., 1950; m. Kay Bonner, Apr. 19, 1947; children—Christopher, Nicole, Lisa, Rachel. Radio producer WTCN Radio, Mpls., 1948-50; pub. relations dir. Hamline U., St. Paul, 1950; radio-TV dir. Bozell Jacobs Advt., Mpls., 1951, Erwin Wasey Advt., Mpls., 1952-55; prin., exec. v.p. Pederson, Herzog & Nee, Mpls., 1955—. Councilman City of Fridley (Minn.), 1960-63, 73-74, mayor, 1963-66, 75—; trustee North Suburban Sanitary Sewer Dist., Fridley, 1962-66; mem. Gov.'s Commn. on Water Resources, State of Minn., 1964-65. Served with AUS, 1943-46. Decorated Purple Heart. Democrat. Home: 219 Logan Pkwy Fridley MN 55432 Office: 401 2d Ave S Minneapolis MN 55401

NEECE, ROBERT FREDERIC, investment co. exec.; b. St. Louis, Nov. 8, 1936; s. Robert Vissering and Helen Avada (Barnett) N.; B.A. in Speech, Mich. State U., 1957; M.A., U. Mich., 1958; m. Gavin Grey Freund, Aug. 29, 1968; children—Elizabeth, Bradford, Catherine, Craig, Nancy. Owner, dir. Frederic Industries, St. Louis, 1957—, Tali Corp., St. Louis, 1967—; dir. Wayfair Internat., St. Louis, Airport Courtesy Services, St. Louis, Danbury Bancshares, Padanaram, Mass., Legasi Corp., Los Angeles. Councilman, City Ladue (Mo.), 1972-74. Trustee Neece Family Trust, 1961—, Carter Trust, 1969—; bd. dirs. TV Program Conf.; Los Angeles, 1966-70, 76-78, Strauss Found. Mem. Young Presidents Orgn., Nat. Assn. Broadcasters, Nat. Assn. TV Program Execs., Phi Kappa Psi (vice chmn. membership com. 1960-65). Clubs: St. Louis, Old Warson Country; Brookhaven Country (Dallas). Patentee in field. Home: 13 Maryhill Dr Ladue MO 63124 Office: PO Box 12733 St Louis MO 63141

NEEDELS, RICHARD EUGENE, ret. air force officer, food co. exec.; b. Toledo, Apr. 28, 1928; s. Forrest Emery and Bernice Lucille (Gerhart) N.; grad. Bucyrus (Ohio) High Sch., 1947; m. Donna Carol Moore, June 24, 1963; children—Peggy, Richard Lee. Enlisted U.S. Air Force, 1950, commd. air crew mem., advanced through grades to master sgt., 1969; served weather squadron, Mobile, Ala., 1950, various assignments; Korea, 1951, instr. N.G., Memphis, 1952, flight instr. AFB, Ardmore, Okla., 1953, squadron leader, Wright-Patterson AFB, 1954, 64, various assignments, Turkey, 1963, instr. Sheppard AFB, 1967, various assignments, Vietnam, 1969, ret., 1970; v.p. No. div. Shur Good Biscuit Co., Cin., 1970—. Decorated 17 medals. Mem. Am. Legion, VFW, Dayton Food Assn., Cin. Food Brokers, Ky. Col. Assn. Home: 377 Tanglewood Dr Dayton OH 45440 Office: 5035 Winton Rd Cincinnati OH 45232

NEEDHAM, GEORGE, JR., distbg. co. exec.; b. Lafayette, Ind., May 3, 1921; s. George G. and Nellie (Collins) N.; student Purdue U., 1939-40; m. Helen R. Lowther, May 4, 1941; children—G. Ronald, Gordon R., Douglas C. Contractor 1940-43; pres. Biggs Pump & Supply, Inc., Lafayette, Ind., 1946—; dir. Lafayette Bank & Trust Co. Chmn. steering com. Tippecanoe County Home, 1967—. Served with USNR, 1944-46. Mem. Central Supply Assn. (pres. 1962-63), Am. Supply Assn. (v.p. 1970-72), Quiet Birdman. Mason. Home: 1028 State St Lafayette IN 47905 Office: Rd 52 Bypass Lafayette IN 47902

NEEPER, RALPH ARNOLD, cartographer; b. Toledo, Sept. 29, 1940; s. Guy Enoch and Alice Elizabeth (Arnold) N.; B.S., Purdue U., 1963, M.S., 1972; m. Nancy Diane Smith, Sept. 15, 1973; 1 dau., Rachel Claudine. Mathematician, Def. Mapping Agy., St. Louis, 1969-73, cartographer, 1973—. Mem. Democratic Precinct Com., Toledo, 1965-69; chmn. worship com. Holy Trinity Luth. Ch., 1977. Mem. AAAS, Am. Math. Soc., Math Assn. Am., Am. Def. Preparedness Assn., Am. Soc. Photogrammetry, Am. Congress Surveying and Mapping, Am. Numismatic Assn. Soc. St. Louis South Camp, Gideons Internat., 1975-77. Home: 216 Kingston St Apt B St Louis MO 63125

NEETZEL, RAYMOND JOHN, transp. analyst; b. St. Paul, Minn., Apr. 2, 1937; s. John R. and Alyce I. (Berge) N.; m. Marlene F. Jezerski, 1974; children—John, Michael, Thomas. B.A., U. Wis., Green Bay, 1973; certificate urban transp. planning, 1976. Free-lance photographer, St. Paul, 1955-72; planning cons. City of Green Bay (Wis.), 1972-73; transit analyst Met. Transit Commn., St. Paul, 1973-76, sr. transit analyst, 1977—; lectr., U. Aston, Birmingham, Eng., 1972, U. Wis., Green Bay, 1973; panelist Nat. Transp. Research Bd., 1977. Sec. Neenah (Wis.) Planning Commn., 1967-69. Mem. Nat. Inst. Transp. Engrs., Alpha Phi Omega. Contbr. research papers in field. Office: Metropolitan Transit Commission American Center Bldg St Paul MN 55101

NEFE, CLEMENS RALPH FRANK, landscape architect; b. Frankenmuth, Mich., Dec. 19, 1922; s. Albert Joseph and Alma Gertrude (Frank) N.; B.S., Mich. State U., 1951; m. Madeline Margaret Lange, July 31, 1948; children—Barbara (Mrs. William Belden), Erick, Gregory. Lathe operator Universal Engring. Co., Frankenmuth, 1941-43; landscape architect Lambert Landscape Co., Dallas, 1951-53, Consumers Power Co., Jackson, Mich., 1953—. Cons. landscape architect area residence, chs., pub. bldgs., 1951—. Served with USAAF, 1943-47. Recipient Plant Am. award Am. Assn. Nurserymen, Traverse City, Mich., 1960. Mem. Am. Soc. Landscape Architects. Lutheran (officer). Club: Consumers Employees (trustee 1962). Prin. works include: Traverse City Service Center, 1957; Big Rock Plant, Charlevoix, Mich., 1962; Grand Rapids (Mich.) Service Center, 1968; Consumers Power Co. Gen. Offices, Jackson, 1973; Palisades Plant, South Haven, Mich., 1974; Ludington (Mich.) Pumped Storage, 1974. Home: 2709 Glendale Rd Jackson MI 49203 Office: 212 W Michigan Ave Jackson MI 49203

NEFF, KENNETH D., realtor; b. Montpelier, Ind., Oct. 19, 1929; s. Clyde A. and Cora I. (Neff) N.; B.S., Ball State U., 1953; postgrad. Purdue U. Extension, 1974; student Ford Motor Marketing Inst., 1965, Indsl. Coll. of the Armed Forces, 1972; m. Nancy Sue Stiffler, Dec. 26, 1951; children—David K., Susan L. Neff Edwards, Julie A., K. Bradley. Propr., mgr. C.D. Neff & Son Ford Agy., Montpelier, Ind., 1956-75; v.p. Brookside Cemetary Assn., Montpelier, 1965—; propr. Thunderbird Rental Mgmt., Montpelier, 1968—; propr. Kenneth D. Neff Realty, Montpelier, 1976—, Williamsburg Manor Apts., 1977—; partner Fairlane Fin. Co., Montpelier, 1966-72. Regional vice chmn. Ind. Criminal Justice Planning Agy., 1969—; asst. dir. Sagamore council Boy Scouts Am., 1977—; projects chmn. Montpelier Bicentennial Com., 1975-77; chmn. Montpelier Planning and Zoning Bd., 1964-70. Served with USAF, 1953-55, 61-62; served to base commdr. Ind. Air N.G., 1974-77. Recipient Montpelier Jaycee Pub. and Civic award, 1965; Ford Dealer's Distinguished Achievement award, 1965; Indiana Beautiful award, 1966; Auto Dealer's Traffic Safety Council award, 1965; Auto Dealers Nat. and State Assn. awards; Ind. Commendation awards (2). Mem. Soc. Real Estate Appraisers (asso.), Montpelier C. of C. (pres. 1959, 60-66, Citizen of Year award 1963), N.G. Assn. of Ind., N.G. Assn. of U.S., Am. Legion. Methodist. Clubs: Kiwanis (pres. 1964-68), Masons. Author: Indiana Air National Guard History Book, 1969. Home: 129 S Washington St Montpelier IN 47359 Office: 109 W Huntington St Montpelier IN 47359

NEFF, RAY ALLEN, educator; b. Bristow, Va., Jan. 23, 1924; s. Charles Edward and Mary Elizabeth (Runion) N.; B.A., Bridgewater Coll., 1950; postgrad. Med. Coll. Va., 1954; M.S., Jefferson Med. Coll., 1960; Ed.D., Ball State U., 1975; m. Augusta Mae Kossman, Dec. 19, 1948; children—Charles Frederick, Robert Allen. Food cons. Commonwealth Va. Dept. Health, Richmond, 1950-54; analyst FDA, U.S. Dept. Health, Edn. and Welfare, 1955; sr. analyst Smith, Kline & French Labs., Phila., 1956-58; Walter G. Karr research fellow Jefferson Med. Coll., Phila., 1958-60; health officer Cape May County (N.J.) Dept. Health, 1960-67; asst. prof. dept. health and safety Ind. State U., Terre Haute, 1967—. Vice pres., dir. research and devel. Visu-Phonics, Inc., Terre Haute, 1968—, also dir.; cons. Served with USNR, 1944-45. Fellow Soc. Mil. Historians. Am. Pub. Health Assn.; mem. Ind. Pub. Health Assn., N.J. Health Officers Assn., Royal Soc. Health (Gt. Britain). Pub., Abraham Lincoln Lithographs, 1968; Pawn of Traitors, 1969. Patentee solvent extractor, aircraft proximity device. Home: 514 N 8th St Marshall IL 62441 Office: Ind State U Parsons Hall Terre Haute IN 49809 also Visu-Phonics Inc 2216 Twickingham Dr Muncie IN 47304

NEFF, RICHARD GEORGE, contractor; b. Columbus, Ohio, Aug. 22, 1935; s. George Frederick and Grace Elenore (Robbins) N.; student pub. schs. Columbus; m. Yvonne Eileen Everett, June 11, 1955; children—Kenneth George, Jerold Richard, Jonathan Frederick. With G.F. Neff Co., Columbus, 1953—, owner, pres., 1965—. Chmn. trustees mem. budget and bldg. coms. Columbus West Ch. of God; coach Little League Baseball, 1969—. Served with AUS, 1954-56. Mem. Nat. Fedn. Ind. Bus. Republican. Home and Office: 491 Powell Ave N Columbus OH 43204

NEFF, ROBERT MARSHALL, mfg. co. exec.; b. New Orleans, June 28, 1941; s. Marshall Snow and Viola Ruth (Hall) N.; B.S., Fla. State U., 1963; postgrad. Stetson U., 1968, U. No. Colo., 1970; m. Jessie Doll McCain, Nov. 28, 1971; children—Robert Marshall, Richard Roy, Dianne Melaine. With Gen. Electric Co., Phoenix, 1964-69, supr. cost accounting, 1968-69; internal auditor Samsonite Corp., Denver, 1969-70; controller Buehner Schokbeton Co., Denver, 1970-71; corporate controller North Star Concrete Co., Mankato, Minn., 1971-72, divisional v.p., gen. mgr., 1972-73; mgmt. cons. Gulf & Western, Southfield, Mich., 1973-74, div. controller, Danville, Ill., 1974—. Scout master Boy Scouts Am., Phoenix, 1968-69. Mem. Am. Nat. accounting assns., Am. Inst. Corporate Controllers, Fin. Mgmt. Assn., Beta Alpha Psi. Republican. Baptist. Home: 37 Shorewood Dr S Danville IL 61832 Office: care Bohn Heat Transfer Div Gulf and Western Mfg Co 1625 E Voorhees St Danville IL 61832

NEIBEL, OLIVER JOSEPH, JR., med. services exec.; b. Kansas City, Mo., Apr. 17, 1927; s. Oliver Joseph and Eula Lee (Durham) N.; LL.B., U. Va., 1952; B.S., U. Ariz., 1949; m. Patricia Helen O'Keefe, June 24, 1950 (div. 1971); children—Oliver Joseph III, Deborah Sue. Instr., U. Washington, 1952-53; admitted to Wash. bar, 1952, Ill. bar, 1961, Nebr. bar, 1973; practiced in Seattle, 1953-57; asst. atty. gen. State of Wash., 1957-61; legislative atty. A.M.A., Chgo., 1961-63; exec. dir., gen. counsel Coll. Am. Pathologists, Chgo., 1963-72; v.p., gen. mgr. Physicians Lab., Omaha, 1973—. Justice of peace, Mountlake Terrace, Wash., 1955-57. Served with USNR, 1945. Mem. Am. Wash., Nebr., Ill. bar assns., Med. Group Mgmt. Assn., Phi Kappa Psi (chpt. pres. 1948-49), Delta Theta Phi, Alpha Kappa Psi, Delta Sigma Rho. Mason, Elk, Rotarian. Clubs: Wash. Athletic (Seattle); Tavern (Chgo.); Omaha Press, University (Nebr.). Home: 806 N 93d St Omaha NE 68114 Office: 105 N 37th St Omaha NE 68131

NEIDENBACH, JOHN JOSEPH, equipment distbg. co. exec.; b. Chgo., Mar. 16, 1916; s. Joseph Peter and Theresa Mary (Thierjung) N.; grad. Freight Traffic Inst., 1941, various home study, specialized courses; m. Carol Lee Sheehan, Feb. 13, 1943; children—Joseph, Susan, Mary Henzler, Judy Cramer, Nancy, Peter, Barbara, Thomas. Sales mgr. Empire Equipment Co., Sioux Falls, S.D., 1946-51, Rosholt Equipment Co., Mpls., 1952-55, Sheehan-Bartling Equipment Co., Sioux Falls, 1955-57; owner John J. Neidenbach Equipment Co., Oklahoma City, 1957-58; engr.-examiner Chgo. Com. Finance, 1958-61; pres. Schuster Equipment Co., Chgo., 1961—, also dir., trustee profit sharing plan and trust; treas. S.N.S. Inc., 1963—. Civil def. dir. Am. Legion, Sioux Falls, 1946-60; instl. rep. Boy Scouts Am., Mpls., 1952-55. Served to maj. USAAF, 1941-46. Fellow AIM (pres.'s council 1969); mem. Asso. Distbrs. Equipment, Am. Pub. Works Assn. (asso.). Office: 4101 S Morgan St Chicago IL 60609

NEIDERHISER, FLOYD JOHN, educator; b. Stahlstown, Pa., Aug. 3, 1902; s. Albert M. and Mattie (Kimmel) N.; A.B., Findlay Coll., 1927; M.A., Columbia, 1931; postgrad. Ohio State U., summer 1949; m. Fae Ileau Rader, June 19, 1923; children—Marilyn (Mrs. Robert E. Wenig), Harry. Tchr., Centralized High Sch., McComb, Ohio, 1927-36, prin., 1936-41, acting supt., 1942; supt. Damascus Local Sch., McClure, Ohio, 1943-65. Pres., dir. Polio Assn., 1948-50; pres. Tb Assn., 1951-53; 65—, dir. 1951—; clk. McClure Town Council, 1948-52; sec. McClure Civic Club, 1955-56; mem. Henry County Bd. Edn., 1966—, Henry County Retardation Bd. Chmn. Jake Love Meml. Scholarship Fund, 1947—; pres. 4 County Br., Kellogg Found. Mem. Nat. Soc. for Study Edn., N.E.A., Ohio Edn. Assn., Northwestern Ohio Tchrs. Assn., Henry County Tchrs. Assn. (pres. 1944-45), Henry County Ret. Tchrs. Assn. (pres. 1969), Northwestern Ohio Sch. Adminstrs. Assn. Republican. Mem. Evang. U.B. Ch. Mason (32 deg.). Club: Henry County (pres. 1958, 69). Home: McClure OH 43534

NEIDERT, ANDREW REINHARDT, savs. and loan exec.; b. Akron, Ohio, June 10, 1925; s. Andrew and Lena Margaret (Haas) N.; B.S., Miami U., 1947; postgrad Ind. U., 1959; m. Ruth Purdy, Apr, 3, 1948; children—Gerald Andrew, Judith Ann, Jeffrey Alan, James Arthur. Salesman, Allen & Hartzell, Inc., Wadsworth, Ohio, 1949-52; asst. v.p. Akron Savs. &Loan Co., 1952-61; exec. v.p. First Fed. Savs. and Loan Assn., Akron, O., 1961-65; pres. Standard Fed. Savs. and Loan Assn., Cin., 1965—, also dir.; pres. Standard Financial, Inc., Cin., 1970—, also dir.; dir. Fed. Home Loan Bank of Cin.; adv. com. Fed. Home Loan Mortgage Corp., 1973; mem. Fed. Savs. and Loan Adv. Council, 1974-76, chmn, agenda com., 1975; mem. UN and devel. com. Internat. Union Bldg. Socs. and Savs. Assns.; instr. Am. Savs. Loan Inst., 1960-73. Mem. Real Estate Bd., Cin., 1965—; active Boy Scouts Am. Mem. Parents Council, Lincoln (Ill.) Coll., 1969, 70; trustee Savs. and Loan Found., Inc., Washington, 1969-73. Mem. Soc. Real Estate Appraisers (chpt. pres. 1961-62, sr. residential appraiser), Am. Savs. and Loan Inst. (chpt. pres. 1962-63), Savs. and Loan League of South Western Ohio (pres. 1971-72), C. of C. (dir.), Home Builders Assn. Greater Cincinnati, Phi Mu Alpha, Delta Kappa Epsilon. Mason (Shriner). Clubs: Cincinnati, Maketewah Country, Bankers, Queen City (Cin.); Statesman's Internat. (chmn. bd., dir., Los Angeles). Home: 3310 Lamarque Dr Cincinnati OH 45236 Office: 525 Vine St Cincinnati OH 45202

NEIL, EUGENE, utility co. exec.; b. Two Harbors, Minn., Sept. 25, 1921; s. Johan Elis and Wilhelmina (Pesonen) N.; B.A., U. Minn., 1968; m. Elizabeth Midtlyng, June 18, 1949; children—Bette, Warren, Kathleen, Nancy, Marcella, Mary, Kurt. Contract clk. Link Belt Co., Chgo., 1939-40; with inventory control dept. Kelley-How-Thomson Co., Duluth, Minn., 1941-42; with Co-op. Light & Power Assn., Two Harbors, 1946—, office mgr., asst. to gen. mgr., 1951—. Mem. Lake Superior Sch. Bd. Dist. 381, Two Harbors, 1969—, treas. 1970-71, clk., 1972, chmn. 1973; bd. dirs. Minn. Sch. Bds. Assn., 1976—. Served with AUS, 1943-46. Mem. Nat. Assn. Accountants, Nat. Soc. Pub. Accountants, Am. Legion. Home: 623 8th Ave Two Harbors MN 55616 Office: PO Box 69 Two Harbors MN 55616

NEIL, JAMES WELLINGTON HARRY, veterinarian; b. London, Ontario, Can., July 24, 1926; s. Harry and Pearl (Whiteford) N.; D.V.M., Ontario Veterinary Coll., 1951; m. Janyce Martin, Nov. 17, 1950; children—CherokeeAnn and Martin James. Asso. veterinarian, R. C. Patterson, Ottawa, Ill., 1951-53; pvt. practice Elgin Veterinary Clinic, St. Thomas, Ontario, Can., 1953-54; pvt. practice Ottawa Veterinary Hosp.(Ill.), 1954—; cons. Diamond Lab., Des Moines, 1965-65. Served with Can. Infantry and Paratroopers, 1945-46. Mem. Am. Veterinary Med. Assn., Ill. Veterinary Med. Assn., Am. Animal Hosp. Assn., Chgo. Veterinary Med. Assn., No. Veterinary Med. Assn. Republican. Anglican. Clubs: Masons, Elks, Shriners. Home: 907 Evans St Ottawa IL 61350 Office: R 2 Ottawa IL 61350

NEIL, RANDOLPH LANING, assns. exec.; b. Kansas City, Mo., Dec. 16, 1941; s. Randolph Steele and Elizabeth Floyd (Laning) N.; B.S. in Journalism, U. Kans., 1966; m. Debra Kay Panknin, Oct. 4, 1974; 1 dau., Merritt Angeline. Founder, exec. dir. Internat. Cheerleading Found., Inc., Shawnee-Mission, Kans., 1964—, exec. dir., chmn., 1976—, editor Cheerleading, 1973—; founder, pres. Nat. Film Soc., Shawnee-Mission, 1975—, editor Am. Classic Screen mag., 1976—, chmn. bd., 1977—. Mem. exec. com. Muscular Dystrophy Assn. of Hawaii; vice chmn. Johnson County (Kans.) Democratic Party; mem. Dem. State Com. of Kans. Named Good Will Ambassador, U.S. Savings Bonds div. Treasury Dept., 1967; honored for guiding preservation of heritage of industry of motion pictures Women of Motion Picture Industry, 1977. Mem. Am. Soc. Assn. Execs., Nat. Trust Hist. Preservation, So. Poverty Law Center, Nat. Collegiate Athletic Assn., Am. Film Inst., Overland Park C. of C. Episcopalian. Club: Rockhill Tennis (Kansas City, Mo.). Author books on cheerleading, including: You Can Become A Cheerleader, 1974; The Encyclopedia of Cheerleading, 1975. Home: 3005 W 83d St The Cloisters Leawood KS 66206 Office: The Neil Bldg 7800 Conser Pl Shawnee-Mission KS 66204

NEIMAN, LIONEL JOSEPH, educator, sociologist; b. Cleve., May 23, 1921; s. Lionel and Essie (Nyman) N.; A.B., Ind. State U., 1943; M.A., 1946; postgrad. Ind. U., 1947-52; m. Edith Blanche Grossman, Dec. 26, 1943. High sch. tchr., 1943-46; dir. Monroe County Welfare Dept., Bloomington, Ind., 1952-60; parole officer Ind., 1952-56; faculty Ball State U., Muncie, Ind., 1962—, prof. sociology, 1975—, coordinator criminal justice and corrections, 1973-76, chmn. dept. criminal justice and corrections, 1976—. Lectr., Ind. U., 1972—; cons. in field. Grantee Ind. Criminal Justice Planning Agy., 1970-73, Law Enforcement Assistance Adminstrn., 1970—, Lilly Endowment, 1974. Mem. Am., Ind. (Distinguished Service award 1974, pres. 1978) correctional assns., Am. Sociol. Assn., AAUP, Ind. Conf. Social Welfare, Am. Judicature Soc., Nat. Council Crime and Delinquency, Acad. Criminal Justice Scis., Am. Soc. Criminology, ACLU.

NEIMAN, SIMON (S.I.), pub. relations, advt. counsel; b. Scranton, Iowa, Mar. 28, 1904; s. Elias and Eva (Balaban) N.; student Drake U., Des Moines, 1923-24, U. Iowa, 1924-25; m. Vera Rothschild, Feb. 21, 1934; children—Robert Ellis, Joan Carol (Mrs. R.E. Ordahl). Reporter Des Moines Register-Trib., 1923-24; joined Internat. News Service 1926, becoming successively mem. N.Y. staff, asst. mgr. Pitts. bur, 1927, mgr. Central Pa. bur. 1928, regional mgr. Pa., Ohio, W.Va., 1929; gen. bus. rep. King Features Syndicate, 1930-35; gen. mgr., propr. Feature Sales Syndicate, Chgo.; gen. mgr. Ernest, Frank & Neiman, Chgo., 1937-42; dir. pub. relations U.S. Army Signal Corps, 1942-46; pres. Pub. Relations Affiliates, Chgo.; exec. sec. Radar-Radio Industries of Chgo., Inc.; pres. Internat. Sight and Sound Expn., Inc., Electronics Information Bur., Chgo. Editorial Service; gen. mgr. High Fidelity Shows, Chgo.; adminstrv. sec. High Fidelity Council, Inc.; dir. Lerner Communications, Chgo. Gen. mgr. Electronic Merchandising mag. Nat. chmn. All-Industry Electronics Conf. Pres. Highland Park (Ill.) Civic Assn. Decorated ASF meritorious service ribbon, 1945. Mem. Soc. Midland Authors, Civil War Round Table, Confederate Hist. Soc. (Gt. Britain), Army Navy Pub., Publicity Club of Chgo., Armed Forces Communications Assn., Signal League, Nat. Hist. Soc., Sigma Delta Chi, Pi Lambda Phi, Phi Beta Delta. Author books: contbr. to trade and profl. publs. Home: 891 Pleasant Ave Highland Park IL 60035 Office: 11 E Adams Chicago IL 60603

NELLEN, JAMES WILLIAM, physician; b. Madison Wis., Dec. 2, 1913; s. Anthony F. and Alice A. (Gannon) N.; B.S., U. Wis., 1936, M.D., 1940; m. Ruth R. McClung, Feb. 23, 1946; children—James, Mary-Beth, Suzanne, Richard. Orthopedic surgeon, Green Bay, Wis., 1940—. Bd. dirs., Green Bay Packers, 1960—. Regent, U. Wis., 1965—, pres. 1970. Served to lt. comdr. USNR, 1941-46. Diplomate Am. Bd. Orthopedic Surgery. Mem. A.C.S., Am. Acad. Orthopedic Surgery. Home: Old Plank Rd De Pere WI 54115 Office: 118 N Monroe Ave Green Bay WI 54301

NELLESSEN, ALFRED HENRY, cons. chem. engr.; b. St. Paul, June 13, 1918; s. Peter Henry and Elizabeth Willomena (Wolking) N.; B.Chem.Engring., U. Minn., 1949; m. Ruth V. Nimlos, Aug. 13, 1955; children—James Edward, Jeanne Marie, Marita Lee. Product devel. supr. reflective products 3M Co., St. Paul, 1954-68, chem. engring. specialist recreation and athletic products, 1968-73, sr. research specialist Comml. Tape div., 1973—. Served to cpl. AUS, 1943-46. Mem. Am. Inst. Chem. Engrs., Am. Chem. Soc., Fedn. Socs. for Paint Tech. Club: K.C. Patentee on reflection and adsortion of light and energy. Home: 411 S Owasso Blvd Saint Paul MN 55113 Office: 3M Co 3M Center Saint Paul MN 55101

NELMS, GEORGE EDWARD, biomed. engr.; b. Chgo., Jan. 28, 1937; s. John Williams and Ana Lee (Cheatem) N.; B.S. in E.E., U. Ill., 1962; P.R.D., U. Minn., 1977; m. Noella Delaine Berg, Apr. 23, 1966; children—Christopher John, Michael Raymond. Engr., Astro-Electronic div. RCA, Princeton, N.J., 1963; devel. engr. Honeywell, Inc., 1963-67; new product mgr. Medtronics, Inc., Mpls., 1967—. Certified profl. ski instr. Mem. IEEE, Assn. Advancement Med. Instrumentation, Internat. Soc. Hybrid Microelectronics, NAACP. Patentee in field. Home: 3908 Abbott Ave S Minneapolis MN 55410 Office: 6120 Earle Brown Dr Minneapolis MN 55430

NELSON, BRUCE KERN, educator; b. Marquette, Mich., Nov. 13, 1915; s. George Henry and Margaret (Kern) N.; A.B., No. Mich. U., 1936; M.A., U. Mich., 1944, Ph.D. (Burke Aaron Hinsdale fellow), 1953; D.Sc., Cleary Coll., 1966; m. Agnes June Johnson, June 17, 1939 (dec. May 25, 1949); 1 dau., Jill (Mrs. David Becker); m. 2d, Frances Louise Stakel, Apr. 10, 1950; children—John K., Scott B., David C., Nancy L. Tchr. gen. sci. Hulst Jr. High Sch., Iron Mountain, Mich., 1936-37; tchr. grade sch. Central Grade Sch., Negaunee, Mich., 1937-39, tchr. biology, 1939-44, elementary prin., 1946-47, high sch. prin., 1947-50; Horace H. Rackham spl. fellow U. Mich., 1950-52; gen. secondary cons. Battle Creek (Mich.) Pub. Schs., 1952-53; asst. supt. Lorain Pub. Schs. (Ohio), 1953-54; supt. Lincoln Consol. Sch., Eastern Mich. U., Ypsilanti, 1954-55, dean instrn., 1956-57, v.p. instrn., 1957-75, prof. ednl. leadership, 1975—. Vice chmn. Mich. commn. United Ministries in Higher Edn., Presbyterian Ch., 1977—. Served to lt. (j.g.) USNR, 1944-46. Recipient Distinguished Alumni award No. Mich. U., 1973. Mem. Classroom Tchrs. Assn. (state v.p. 1944), NEA, Nat. Assn. Coll. and Univ. Adminstrn. (dir. 1969-73, pres. 1971-72), Mich. Edn. Assn., Mich. Higher Edn. Assn. (pres. 1971), Mich. Schoolmasters Club (pres. 1968-69, dir. 1968-71), Phi Kappa Phi (chpt. pres. 1977-78), Phi Delta Kappa (Outstanding Educator award Delta Gamma chpt. 1975), Gamma Theta Upsilon. Home: 215 Hillcrest St Ypsilanti MI 48197

NELSON, CHARLES EDMUND, cons.; b. Oak Park, Ill., June 21, 1922; s. Stanley Luther and Helen (Smith) N.; certified in advanced mgmt., U. Chgo., 1957; m. Mary P. Milosits, May 31, 1947; children—Charles Edmund, Mark T. Indsl. engr. Bell & Howell Co., Chgo., 1948-51; sr. indsl. engr. Admiral Corp., 1952-55; from staff mfg. mgr. to ops. mgr. Avon Products Inc., Chgo., 1956-67; pres., dir. Beeline Fashions, Inc., Bensenville, Ill., 1968-72; v.p., mem. exec. com. Fuller div. Consol. Foods, 1972-73; cons. nat., internat. bus. and industry, 1972—; former dir. Goulder, Inc., N.Y.C., Climax Spltys., Inc., Allentown, Pa.; vice chmn. Isochronics, Bensonville, 1971-72; exec. in residence No. Ill. U., 1972—. Past pres., dir. Work Factor Assos. Midwest, Community chmn. local ARC, 1962-63; mem. UN Com. for UN Day, 1968-71; mem. Dept. Commerce sponsored Trade Mission to Europe, 1970; bd. advisers U. Minn. Exec. Program; mem. coordinating com. Bus. World Ahead Confs., State of Ill.; mem. White House Conf. Planning for Bus. World Ahead, 1972. Served to maj. AUS, World War II. Recipient No. Ill. U. Found. Pres.'s award for outstanding service, 1972. Mem. Chgo. Assn. Commerce and Industry (govt. affairs council), Ill. C. of C. (legis. com.), Nat. Assn. Direct Selling Cos. (dir., chmn. finance com., pres. council). Author articles. Home: 14 Dukes Ln Lincolnshire Woodlands Deerfield IL 60015

NELSON, CHARLES WEGO, educator; b. Mohall, N.D., Aug. 12, 1915; s. Henry and Katherine (Smith) N.; m. Dorothea Davidson, Sept. 20, 1939; children—Michael, William, James. B.S., U. Oreg., 1940; M.A., Wash. State U., 1942; Ph.D., U. Chgo., 1949. Registered psychologist, Ill. Dir. leadership research and program evaluation Indsl. Relations Center U. Chgo., 1949-56; exec. dir. Mgmt. Research Assos., Chgo., 1956-68; ednl. cons. Mid-Continent Regional Ednl. Lab., Kansas City, Mo., 1968-70; prof. sociology Ind. State U., Terre Haute, 1968—; vis. prof. U. Wash., Seattle, 1975-76. Vice-pres. Promotion Park Forest (Ill.) Community Aquacenter, 1955-58. Mem. Acad. Mgmt., Am. Psychol. Assn., Am. Sociol. Assn., Indsl. Relations Assn. (program chmn. 1956-58), Alpha Kappa Delta. Author: Survey of Leadership Practices, 1949; Leadership and Communication Series, 1955; Survey of Management Perception, 1956; Multiple Purpose Self-Trainer, 1951; producer film: Learning Through Inquiry, 1970; contbr. articles to profl. jours. Home: Rural Route 25 Box 26 Terre Haute IN 47802 Office: Dept Sociology Ind State U Terre Haute IN 47809

NELSON, DALE ALLEN, architect; b. Kansas City, Mo., Sept. 14, 1926; s. Robert Wayne and Ester (Koch) N.; Asso. Sci., Kansas City Jr. Coll., 1947; B.S., U. Kans., 1950; m. Lorraine E. Hennigin, Feb. 28, 1952; 1 dau., Mary Elizabeth. Chief draftsman Tanner-Mitchell, Inc., Sunflower, Kans., 1950-56; project architect, mgr. drafting room E.W. Tanner & Asso., Kansas City, Mo., 1956-60; in-house architect Bennett Constrn. Co., Inc., Kansas City, 1956-60, Vick-Lintecum Gen. Contractors, Inc., North Kansas City, Mo., 1968; staff architect Herbert E. Duncan Architect, Inc., Kansas City, 1969-71; staff architect Marshall & Brown, Inc., Kansas City, 1972; mgr. engring. and constrn. dept., corporate architect Western Auto Supply Co., Kansas City, 1972—. Served with AUS, 1945-46. Mem. A.I.A. (chmn. tours com. 1974—), Constrn. Specifications Inst., Mo. Council Architects, Midwest Concrete Industry Bd. (co-founder 1958, pres. 1969), Constrn. Industry Affairs Council (co-founder 1970, dir. 1970-72), Am. Arbitration Assn. (regional comml. panel 1977), U. Kans. Alumni Assn. Mem. Christian Ch. Mason. Clubs: Woodside Racquet, Jacomo Sailing, Perry Yacht. Home: 5109 Cambridge St Kansas City MO 64129 Office: 2107 Grand Ave Kansas City MO 64108

NELSON, DALLAS LEROY, veterinarian, toxicologist; b. Clay Center, Kans., Oct. 4, 1928; s. Herbert Leroy and Rosalie (Jenkins) N.; B.S., Kans. State U., 1953, D.V.M., 1953, M.S., 1958, Ph.D., 1963. m. Evelyn Nona King, Aug. 12, 1951; children—Cathy Lynn, Douglas Leroy. With Vet. Corps, U.S. Army, Omaha, 1953-55; pvt. practice vet. medicine, Clay Center, 1955-56; faculty Sch. Vet. Medicine, Kans. State U., Manhattan, 1956-64; mgr. toxicology research Chemagro div. Mobay Corp., Kansas City, Mo., 1964—. Mem. Am., Kans. vet. med. assns., Am. Coll. Vet. Toxicologists, Soc. Toxicology, Am. Assn. Vet. Parasitologists, Gamma Sigma Delta. Clubs: Acacia, Masons. Contbr. articles to profl. jours. Home: 1013 Lennox Dr Olathe KS 66061 Office: PO Box 4913 Hawthorne Rd Kansas City MO 64120

NELSON, DAVID JOE, paint mfr.; b. Cherokee, Iowa, Apr. 28, 1942; s. Joe George and Ruth (Jones) N.; A.B., Harvard U., 1964, M.B.A., 1968; m. Jean Vaughan Wells, Nov. 25, 1965; children—Joe Heaps, Anne Vaughan, William David. Loan officer trainee Irving Trust Co., N.Y.C., 1964-66; v.p., sec.-treas. Mid-Am. Foods, Inc., Humboldt, Iowa, 1968-73; fin. v.p., treas. Iowa Paint Mfg. Co., Inc., Des Moines, 1973—; fin. and investment cons. Del., Polk County Republican. Conv., also Iowa State Statutory Conv., 1976. Mem. Assn. M.B.A. Execs. Mem. United Ch. of Christ. Clubs: Des Moines; Harvard (N.Y.C.). Home: 109 SW 42d St Des Moines IA 50312 Office: Box 1417 Des Moines IA 50305

NELSON, DAVID LEONARD, process mgmt. co. exec.; b. Omaha, May 8, 1930; s. Leonard A. and Cecelia (Steinert) N.; B.S., Iowa State U., 1952; m. Jacqueline J. Zerbe, Dec. 26, 1952; children—David John, Nancy Jo. Marketing adminstr. Ingersoll Rand, Chgo., 1954-56; systems engr. Indsl. Nucleonics Corp., Columbus, O., 1956-58, sales engr., 1958-61, area sales mgr., 1961-64, mgr. corporate planning and devel., 1964-65, mgr. new product devel. dept., 1965-66, v.p. operations, 1966, exec. v.p., gen. mgr., 1967, pres., 1967—, chief exec. officer, 1970—, also dir.; dir. Indsl. Nucleonics Corp., Herman Miller, Inc., Beverage Mgmt., Inc. Bd. dirs. N.C. Pulp and Paper Found., The Cardinal Fund, Inc., Western Mich. Paper Tech. Found. Served to capt. USMCR, 1952-54. Mem. I.E.E.E., Instrument Soc. Am., Am. Mgmt. Assn., Newcomen Soc. N.Am., Young Pres.'s Orgn., Tau Beta Pi, Phi Kappa Phi, Phi Eta Sigma, Delta Upsilon. Patentee in field. Office: 1768 Millwood Dr Columbus OH 43221

NELSON, DAVID TORRISON, educator; b. Decorah, Iowa, May 16, 1927; s. David Theodore and Esther Caroline (Torrison) N.; B.A., Luther Coll., 1949; M.A., U. Rochester, 1955; Ph.D., Iowa State U., 1960; m. Betty Jane Rikansrud, Apr. 20, 1957; children—Elise Marie, Andrea Kathleen, Kathryn Renee, Stephen David. Instr. Luther Coll., Decorah, 1954-57, asst. prof., 1960-63, asso. prof., 1963-67, prof. physics, 1967—, chmn. dept. physics, 1972—; research asst. Iowa State U., Ames, 1958-60; vis. prof. engring. Ariz. State U., 1974. Owner, Oneota Fotos, Decorah; v.p., dir. O. Torrison Co., Manitowoc, Wis. Chmn. Winneshiek County Rep. Central Com., 1963-66; mem. Decorah City Council, 1972-74, mayor Decorah,

1978—. NSF Sci. Faculty fellow Stanford U., 1967-68. Mem. Am. Phys. Soc., Am. Assn. Physics Tchrs. (chmn. Iowa sect. 1964-65), Internat. Solar Energy Soc., Optical Soc. Am., Acoustical Soc. Am., Iowa Acad. Sci., Norwegian-Am., Iowa hist. socs., Luren Singing Soc., Sigma Xi. Lutheran. Home: 215 High St Decorah IA 52101

NELSON, DEANE DALE, cons. psychologist; b. Brooten, Minn., June 20, 1937; s. Dale G. and Myrtle (Jacobson) N.; B.S., Gustavus Adolphus Coll., 1959; M.A., Coll. St. Thomas, 1964; Ed.D., U. S.D., 1968; m. Lois Florence Anderson, Aug. 19, 1961; children—Brian, David. Tchr., counselor pub. schs., Richfield, Minn., 1960-66; dir. counseling, prof. U. S.D., 1967-69; dir. Counseling Center, prof. Moorhead (Minn.) State U., 1969-74, prof. edn., 1975-78; cons. psychologist, corporate trainer, 1978—; nat. teaching fellow Mt. Marty Coll., Yankton, S.D., 1974-75. Mem. Clay County Mental Health Bd. Mem. Am., Minn. psychol. assns., Am. Personnel and Guidance Assn., Nat. Vocat. Guidance Assn., Phi Delta Kappa. Contbr. articles to profl. jours. Address: 89 N 22d Ave N Fargo ND 58102

NELSON, ESTHER LOUISE HILEY, counselor; b. Washington, Aug. 29, 1935; d. Eugene Walter and Frances Case (Culverwell) Hiley; B.E., Chgo. State U., 1957; M.A., Northwestern U., 1967; postgrad. U. Ill., 1973, Ind. U., 1974; m. Paul Augustus Nelson, Mar. 19, 1955; children—Paul Augustus, David Walter, Elizabeth Jean, Margaret Frances. Career guidance coordinator West Chgo.-Winfield Community Dist. #94, 1967—; instr. parent and child relationships Adult Edn., Coll. DuPage, 1977. Chmn. edn. and local govt. Wheaton LWV, 1960-62. Mem. Christian Assn. Psychol. Studies, Nat. Assn. Marriage and Family Counselors, Am. Personnel and Guidance Assn., Assn. Measurement and Evaluation in Guidance, Nat. Vocat. Guidance Assn., DuPage Counselors Assn., NEA (life), Ill. Edn. Assn., West Chicago Community Tchrs. Assn., New Eng. Hist. and Gnealogical Soc., N.J., Ill. geneal. socs., Palatines to Am. Soc., DAR. Republican. Mem. Glen Ellyn Covenant Ch. Home: 1352 S Main St Wheaton IL 60187 Office: 326 Joliet St West Chicago IL 60185

NELSON, EUGENE WILLIAM, photographer; b. Baudette, Minn., Sept. 28, 1937; s. Robert William and Elsie Margaret (Fausher) N.; certificate of completion, Gale Tech. Inst., 1957; B.S., U. Minn., 1967; m. Shirley Amanda Ludemann, June 27, 1964; children—Marc Christopher, Michell Christine. Railroad telegrapher Northern Pacific, Mpls., 1957-67; comml. photographer, Mpls., 1965-67; owner Gene's Studio 1, Inc., Mora, Minn., 1967—. Councilman, City of Mora (Minn.), 1971—, mem. planning commn., 1971—. Mem. Profl. Photographers Am., Profl. Photographers Minn., Minn. Profl. Photographers Assn. (mem. council 1977—). Home: 611 Carol Ave Mora MN 55051 Office: 200 E Forest Ave Mora MN 55051

NELSON, FRED ERNEST, army officer; b. Chgo., Sept. 21, 1929; s. Ernest George and Anna Caroline (Hinze) N.; B.S., Ill. State U., 1952; M.A., U. Chgo., 1954; m. Delores June Webb, Feb. 16, 1952; children—Kim Lorraine, Jill Marie, Tyler Scott. Commd. 1st lt. U.S. Army, advanced through grades to lt. col., 1968; chief social worker child guidance clinic Walter Reed Army Med. Center, Washington, 1957-60; chief social worker mental hygiene clinic Ft. Eustis, Va., 1960-63; chief med. social worker Brooke Army Med. Center, San Antonio, 1963-66; dir. social work services, adminstr. dept. psychiatry 97th Gen. Hosp., W.Ger., 1966-69; mental health and social work cons. European Med. Command, W.Ger., 1969-70; dir. social work services Brooke Army Med. Center, 1970-74; mental health and social service cons. U.S. Army Health Services Command, San Antonio, 1974-75; dir. profl. services Wabash Valley Hosp. Mental Health Center, West Lafayette, Ind., 1976—. Mem. Nat. Assn. Social Workers (v.p. S. Tex. chpt. 1973-75, v.p. European chpt. 1968-70), Am. Group Psychotherapy Assn. Presbyterian (elder). Club: Optimist. Home: 1317 Palmer Dr West Lafayette IN 47906 Office: Wabash Valley Hosp Mental Health Center West Lafayette IN 47906

NELSON, GAYLORD ANTON, U.S. senator; b. Clear Lake, Wis., June 4, 1916; s. Anton and Mary (Bradt) N.; grad. San Jose State Coll., Cal., 1939, U. Wis. Law Sch., 1942; m. Carrie Lee Dotson, Nov. 14, 1947; children—Gaylord, Cynthia, Jeffrey. Admitted to Wis. bar, 1942; practiced in Madison, 1946—; mem. Wis. Senate, 1948, 52, 56, Democratic leader, 1948-52; gov. Wis., 1958-63; U.S. senator from Wis., 1963—, mem. fin. com., chmn. finance subcom. on social security, mem. human resources com., chmn. subcom. on employment, poverty and migratory labor, chmn. select com on small bus., chmn. monopoly subcom., chmn. select com. on small bus. Served as 1st lt. AUS, World War II. Mem. Am. Legion, VFW, State Bar Assn. Wis. Home: 618 Bordner Dr Madison WI 53705 Office: Senate Office Bldg Washington DC 20510

NELSON, HERBERT CECIL QUINTEN, dentist; b. Sidney, Nebr., Mar. 18, 1921; s. Edward Marius and Verda Jeanette (Glassburn) N.; student Chadron State Coll., 1941-42; B.A., U. Nebr., 1950, B.S., 1950, D.D.S., 1952; m. Dorothy Olive Roberts, July 6, 1942; children—Lyndell, Laurence, Gayle. Pvt. practice dentistry, Sidney, 1952—. Mem. external adv. council Nebr. Coll. Dentistry, 1972—. Mem. dental staff Meml. Hosp., 1958—. Mem. bd. edn., Sidney, 1956-68, pres., 1960-62; mem. Ednl. Service Unit, 1966-73, sec., 1970-73; mem. Nebr. coordinating commn. Tech. Community Colls., Nebr. coordinating commn. post-secondary edn., 1975—; mem. Cheyenne County Democratic Central Com., 1958-68; bd. dirs. United Fund, Sidney; area bd. dirs., pres. Western Nebr. Tech. Community Coll., 1973-75; mem. state bd. Tech. Community Colls., 1975; trustee U. Nebr. Found., 1975—. Served with AUS, 1942-45. Mem. Acad. Gen. Dentistry, Am., Nebr. (trustee 1966-69, 70-73, pres. 1977), West Dist. (pres. 1963) dental assns., Sidney C. of C., Nebr. Coll. Dentistry Alumni Assn. (dir. 1968-70). Presbyterian (trustee 1954-57). Clubs: Masons, Elks, Lions. Home: 2616 El Rancho Rd Sidney NE 69162 Office: 1116 10th Ave Sidney NE 69162

NELSON, HERBERT LOU, cons.; b. Marietta, Ohio, Aug. 26, 1924; s. Herbert Louis and Grace Agnes (Gerber) N.; B.S., Marietta Coll., 1950; M.S. in Bus. Adminstrn., Bowling Green State U., 1951; Ps.D., Coll. Divine Metaphysics, 1969; m. Betty Ruth Dawson, Aug. 26, 1948; 1 dau., Diana Jeanne. Sales mgr. Master Pneumatic Tool Co., Cleve., 1951-54; financial analyst Cleve. stamping plant Ford Motor, Co., 1954-60; prin. cons. Trundle Cons., Inc., Cleve., 1960—. Active Friends of Solon Library. Chmn. bd. dirs. Solon (Ohio) Drug Abuse Center, 1971-72. Served with USAF, 1942-45. Decorated Bronze Star (6); licensed psychologist, Ohio. Mem. Am. Mktg. Assn., Am. Mgmt. Assn., Inst. Mgmt. Cons., Assn. to Advance Ethical Hypnosis, Lambda Chi Alpha, Early Settlers Assn. Western Res., Solon Hist. Soc. Home: 6923 Highland Dr Solon OH 44139 Office: 5500 S Marginal Rd Cleveland OH 44103

NELSON, IVAN LLOYD, agrl. engr.; b. Boone, Iowa, Aug. 14, 1921; s. Lloyd Franklin and Ethel (Gustafson) N.; student Boone Jr. Coll., 1939-40, Miss. State Coll., 1944; B.S., Iowa State U., 1948, postgrad., 1961-65; m. Frances Naomi Mathson, Aug. 7, 1948; children—Audrey Marie, Kathleen Ann, Joyce Elise. With John Deere Des Moines Works, 1948-71, jr. engr., 1949-55, engr., 1956-58, sr. engr., 1959-71; dir. engring. So. Iowa Mfg. Co., Osceola, 1971—. Pres. Madrid (Ia.) Community Sch. Bd., 1965-66. County del. Republican Conv., 1964, 68, 74, 76, treas. Clarke County Rep. Central Com. Bd. dirs. Evang. Free Ch. Home for Aged, 1956-62, 71—. Served with U.S. Army, 1943-46. Mem. Am. Soc. Agrl. Engrs. Evang. (deacon 1964-72). Home: 217 W Fayette St Osceola IA 50213 Office: Box 448 Osceola IA 50213

NELSON, JAMES NELS, psychiatrist; b. Tulsa, Okla., Nov. 3, 1930; s. Melvin Nels and Ruth Ann (Stierwalt) N.; student Northwestern U., 1948-50; B.A., U. Kans., 1952, M.D., 1959; m. JoAnne E. Wellman, June 23, 1956; children—James N., Nancy JoAnne, Eric Joseph. Intern, Detroit Gen. Hosp., 1959-60; resident in neurology Wayne State U., Detroit, 1960-62; resident in psychiatry Menninger Clinic, Topeka, Kans., 1962-65, asst. dir. div. indsl. mental health Menninger Found., 1967-70; chief, child study unit Kans. Neurol. Inst., Topeka, 1965-66; sr. psychiatrist Topeka Med. Center, 1970—; chmn. staff Stormont Vail Hosp., 1975-77; pres. staff, trustee Topeka Meml. Hosp., 1976—. Mem. exec. com. Goals for Topeka, 1969-70; chmn. citizens advisory com. Topeka Bd. Edn., 1975-76. Diplomate Am. Bd. Psychiatry and Neurology. Contbr. chpt. to med. textbook. Office: 918 W 10th St Topeka KS 66604

NELSON, JOHN ARTHUR, psychologist; b. Goodman, Miss., Oct. 23, 1946; s. Virge and Lenzell (Story) N.; B.A., Jackson State U., 1974; M.A., Washington U., 1976. Drug counselor Narcotics Service Council, St. Louis, 1976-77; diagnostic cons. Municipal Ct. Services, St. Louis, 1976; psychol. examiner Wellston Sch. Dist., Halter High Sch., St. Louis, 1975-76; counselor Malcolm Bliss Mental Health Center, St. Louis, 1976—, King-Fanon Mental Health Center, 1975-77; Mo. Dept. Mental Health. Served with AUS, 1966-69. Mem. Nat. Council Minority Health, Black Psychologists Assn. St. Louis, Drugs and Substance Abuse Council, Am. Personnel and Guidance Assn. Home: 7432E Parktowne St Louis MO 63136 Office: 724 N Union St Louis MO 63108

NELSON, LEONARD NECOLAI, adhesives co. exec.; b. Duluth, Minn., July 7, 1925; s. Albert Theodore and Myrtle Ingeborg (Nelson) N.; B.A., U. Minn., 1948; m. Joan Colleen Henjum, Sept. 9, 1951; children—Nancy Leigh, David Christopher. Marketing exec. John Morrell & Co., 1948-65; exec. v.p., pres. Cosco Industries, 1965-71; group v.p., Morgan Adhesives Co., Stow, Ohio, 1971—. Pres. Rockland Co. United Fund, 1970—. Served to lt. comdr., USNR, 1942-46, 51-53. Mem. Am. Mgmt. Assn., Sales and Mktg. Execs. Internat. Lutheran (chmn.). Rotarian. Club: Hudson (Ohio) Country. Home: 75 Atterbury Blvd Hudson OH 44236 Office: 4560 Darrow Rd Stow OH 44224

NELSON, LEROY ELBURN, veterinarian; b. Arlington, Wash., June 5, 1926; s. Carl S. and Francis Viola (Eidem) N.; D.V.M., Iowa State U. 1949; student U. Minn., 1944-45; m. Julia Jeanne McAllister, Jan. 1, 1950; children—Julia, Paul, Nancy. Practice veterinary medicine, Bricelyn, Minn., 1949-71; veterinary med. officer U.S. Dept. Agr., Albert Lea, Minn., 1971—. Mem. Sch. Bd., Bricelyn, 1965-72, Volunteer Fire Dept. 1951-77; treas. Volunteer Relief Assn., 1967-69; pres. Band Parents Assn., 1972. Mem. AVMA, Minn., South Central (pres. 1957), So. Minn. (pres. 1970) veterinary med. assns., Am. Assn. Food Hygiene Veterinarians, No. Iowa Veterinary Med. Assn., Nat. Assn. Fed. Veterinarians (Minn. rep. 1973-77). Trustee Bricelyn Luth. Ch., 1974-77. Home: Box 365 Bricelyn MN 56014 Office: Bricelyn MN 56014

NELSON, MARY BERTHA RING, pub. relations dir.; b. Mpls., Aug. 26, 1921; d. Charles and Edna (Wrabek) Ring; student U. Minn., 1939-41; m. Roger A. Nelson, Jan. 4, 1941; children—Barbara L. (Mrs. Earl Jasper), Judith A. (Mrs. Thomas Ptasienski), Ward A. Columnist, reporter Minn. Daily, 1936-41; columnist Argus Publs., Mpls., 1949-57; feature writer, reporter Suburbanite newspaper, Oak Lawn, Ill., 1959-61; feature writer, columnist S.W. Messinger Press, Midlothian, Ill., 1961-69, also dir. pub. info. Moraine Valley Community Coll., Palos Hills, Ill., 1968—; tchr. group dynamics and leadership Moraine Valley Community Coll., 1969—. State dir. Ill. PTA, 1963-68; hon. nat. life mem. PTA; pres. Dr. Batho Award Fund, 1967-77; dir. Evergreen Park chpt. Am. Field Service, 1961-69; sec. Evergreen Park Scholarship Bd., 1959-69; mem. Jr. Coll. Planning Com. for Ill. Suburbs, 1961-67; dir. South Suburban Homemakers, 1967-69; dir., mem. bd. mgrs. Child and Family Services, 1967-76; sec. pub. relations Evergreen Park Community Chest, 1959—; chmn. Mothers March of Dimes, 1967-68; sec., dir. Family Service of S.W. Cook County, 1967—; exec. sec. pub. relations pub. edn. program Bds. of Edn., 1967; bd. dirs. Southwest YMCA, 1974—. Mem. Am., Ill. (pres.) coll. pub. relations assns., Community Relations Roundtable Ill., Pub. Relations Workshop Assn., League Women Voters, Council for Advance Secondary Edn. Home: 9940 Spaulding Ave Evergreen Park IL 60642 Office: 10900 S 88th Ave Palos Hills IL 60465

NELSON, NANCY JANE, guidance counselor; b. Jefferson, Iowa, May 7, 1945; d. Orman and Helen May (Shearman) Nelson; student Drake U., 1963-65; B.A., U. Iowa, 1967; M.S., Iowa State U., 1976. Tchr. Springfield, Mo., 1967-68, Augusta, Kans., 1968-69, Ames, Iowa, 1969-76; elementary guidance counselor Manning, Iowa, 1976—; lectr. in field. Sr. high sch. Sponsor Meth. Ch., Manning, 1977-78. Mem. Manning, Iowa, Nat. edn. assns., Iowa, Am. personnel and guidance assns., Am. Sch. Counselor Assn. Home: 38 May St Manning IA 51455 Office: Manning Community Sch Manning IA 51455

NELSON, ORVILLE KENNETH, real estate broker; b. Cedar Mills, Minn., Sept. 27, 1906; s. Alex Albert and Marie Agnes (Nelson) N.; student Carleton Coll., 1925-26; m. Laura Winifred Childs, Sept. 22, 1934; children—David Eugene, Sally Corrine Nelson Bronski. Reporter Dodge Reports, Mpls., 1926-28; bldg. contractor Superior, Wis., 1929-31; mfrs. rep. Kohler Co., Mpls., 1931-35; archtl. examiner Fed. Housing Adminstrn., Mpls., 1939-42; constrn. analyst War Prodn. Bd., Mpls., 1943-45; gen. bldg. contractor, Mpls., 1937-39, 45-58; realtor asso., broker, appraiser Bermel-Smaby Realty Co., Mpls., 1958-76, Century 21 Goodyear Realty, Mpls., 1976—. Instr. U. Minn., Mpls., 1950-62. Mem. Minn. State Housing com., 1945; mem. Mayor's Housing Com., Mpls., 1946. Mem. Mpls. Builders Assn. (pres. 1946, dir. 1946-48), Minn., Mpls. Real Estate Bds., Nat. Real Estate Bd., Richfield C. of C. (bd. dirs. 1974-76). Congregationalist (trustee 1950-52). Home: 5636 Harriet Ave Minneapolis MN 55419 Office: 6620 Penn Ave S Richfield MN 55423

NELSON, REGINALD DAVID, research info. scientist; b. Water Glen, Alta., Can., Nov. 27, 1924; s. Carl Hjalmer and Agnes Emelia (Bjorkgren) N.; B.Sc. magna cum laude, U. Alta., 1946; Ph.D., Iowa State U., 1951; m. Mae Clara Ericson, July 16, 1950; children—Janet, Daniel, Karen, Kristen. Instr. gen. chemistry Iowa State U., Ames, 1950-52; asst. prof. Bethel Coll., St. Paul, 1952-55, asso. prof., head chemistry dept., 1955-56; asst. editor Chem. Abstracts Service, Ohio State U., Columbus, 1956-59, asso. editor, 1959-62, sr. asso. editor, 1963-64, staff cons., 1965, 67-69, head organic index editing dept., 1966, sr. info. scientist, 1970—. Mem. Am. Chem. Soc., Am. Soc. Info. Sci. Home: 535 Longfellow Ave Worthington OH 43085 Office: Chemical Abstracts Service PO Box 3012 Columbus OH 43210

NELSON, RICHARD E., psychologist; b. Wichita, Kans., Nov. 4, 1936; d. Roy and Blanche Allgood) N.; B.S. Emporia State U., 1959, M.S., 1962; Ph.D., U. Mo., Columbia, 1975; m. Barbara Ann Johnson, Sept. 1, 1957; children—Jeffery Scott, Jay Dee, Jody Marie. Tchr., Tonovay High Sch., Eureka, Kans., 1959-60; counselor Cirlce High Sch., Towanda, Kans., 1960-65, Sherman Jr. High Sch., Hutchinson, Kans., 1965-68; ednl. specialist Kans. Dept. Edn., Topeka, 1968-72; asst. prof., psychologist U. Kans., Lawrence, 1975—. Mem. Kans., Am. personnel and guidance assns., Kans. (pres. elect 1977-78), Nat. vocat. guidance assns., Kans. Assn. Suprs. and Counselor Educators. Methodist. Club: Elks. Home: 3005 Yellowstone Dr Lawrence KS 66044 Office: Bailey Hall Univ Kansas Lawrence KS 66045

NELSON, RICHARD HAROLD, civil engr.; b. Indpls., June 24, 1925; s. Harold Jennings and Helen Fern (Sutherlin) N.; B.S.C.E., Purdue U., 1950; m. Linda Ann Hartley, June 22, 1968; children—Rikki Lin, Benjamin Richard. Vice pres. Henry B. Steeg & Assos., Inc., Indpls., 1950-73, dir. mktg. environ. engring. services, Howard Needles, Tamen & Bergendof, 1973—. Served to 1st lt., AUS, 1950-53, to sgt., inf., 1943-46. Decorated Bronze Star medal. Fellow ASCE; mem. Cons. Engrs. Ind. (pres. 1966-68, dir. 1976-77), Am. Cons. Engring. Council U.S. (dir. 1971-73), Am. Pub. Works Assn. (section dir. 1966-68), Indpls. C. of C., Ind. Water Pollution Control Assn., Am. Water Works Assn., Water Pollution Control Fedn., Chi Epsilon. Presbyn. (deacon 1972-75, elder 1976—). Clubs: Columbia (Indpls.); Yacht and Racquet (Ponta Gorda, Fla.). Home: 5540 E 75th St Indianapolis IN 46250 Office: 3333 Founders Ln Indianapolis IN 46268

NELSON, ROBERT EDDINGER, mgmt. and devel. cons. co. exec.; b. Mentone, Ind., Mar. 2, 1928; s. Arthur Irven and Tural Cecile (Eddinger) N.; B.A., Northwestern U., 1949; L.H.D., Iowa Wesleyan Coll., 1969; m. Carol J., Nov. 24, 1951; children—Janet K. Nelson Callighan, Eric P. Asst. dir. alumni relations Northwestern U., Evanston, Ill., 1950-51, 54-55; v.p. and dir. pub. relations Iowa Wesleyan Coll., Mt. Pleasant, 1955-58; vice chancellor for devel. U. of Kansas City, 1959-61; v.p. instl. devel. Ill. Inst. of Tech., Chgo., 1961-68; pres. Robert Johnston Corp., Oak Brook, Ill., 1968-69, Robert E. Nelson Assos., Inc., Elmhurst, Ill., 1969—; dir. Chautauqua Workshop in Fund Raising and Instl. Relations, 1970-74, Snelling & Snelling, Inc., 1974—; nat. conf. chmn. and program dir. Am. Coll. Pub. Relations Assn., 1961; trustee, Iowa Wesleyan Coll., 1962-68; faculty mem. Ind. U. Workshops on Coll. and Univ. Devel., 1963-65, Lorretto Heights Summer Inst. for Fund Raising and Pub. Relations, 1964-68; mem. Pub. Review Panel for Grants Programs, Lilly Endowment, Inc., 1975. Served with U.S. Army, 1951-54. Mem. Council on Fin. Aid to Edn. (bd. dirs. 1957-63), Pub. Relations Soc. of Am., Nat. Soc. of Fund Raisers, Inc., Nat. Small Bus. Assn., Chgo. Soc. of Fund Raising Execs. Methodist. Clubs: Execs. Club of Chgo., Economic Club of Chgo., Union League Club of Chgo., Delta Tau Delta, Hon. Blue Key, Masons. Author chpt. in Handbook of Coll. and Univ. Adminstrn., 1970. Home and Office: 5 Oak Brook Club Dr N101 Oak Brook IL 60521

NELSON, ROY JAY, educator; b. Pitts., July 27, 1929; s. Roy J. and Ruth Brown (Bainbridge) N.; AB. summa cum laude, U. Pitts., 1951; M.A., Middlebury Coll., 1952; Ph.D., U. Ill., 1958; m. Anita Lee Chandler, Aug. 16, 1954; children—Wendy Anne, Barbara Jay. Instr. French, U. Mich., Ann Arbor, 1957-60, asst. prof., 1960-65, asso. prof., 1965-72, prof., 1972—, acting chmn. dept. Romance langs., 1977. Fulbright scholar, 1951-52; U. Ill. non resident fellow, 1955-56; Rackham summer fellow, 1964, research grantee, 1967-68. Mem. Modern Lang. Assn., Am. Assn. Tchrs. French, Amitié Charles Péguy. Author: Péguy, poète du sacré, 1960. Office: Dept Romance Langs Univ Mich Ann Arbor MI 48109

NELSON, STANLEY R., hosp. adminstr.; b. Wis., Aug. 12, 1926; s. Newell N. and Signe (Roe) N.; B.S. in Econs., U. Minn., 1948, M.H.A., 1950; m. Virginia Rifenbary, June 18, 1949; children—Mark, Janet. Asst. adminstr. Butterworth Hosp., Grand Rapids, Mich., 1950-52; asst. adminstr. Parkview Hosp., Ft. Wayne, Ind., 1952-55, adminstr., 1955-61; adminstr. Northwestern Hosp., Mpls., 1961-68, pres., 1968-70; pres. Abbott-Northwestern Hosp. Corp., Mpls., 1970-71; former exec. dir. Henry Ford Hosp., Detroit, 1971-76; exec v.p., 1976—. Chmn. adminstrv. com. Mpls. Med. Center, 1969-71; mem. Study Commn. Accreditation of Selected Health Ednl. Programs, 1971-72. Bd. dirs. Mpls. chpt. A.R.C., 1968-71, Minn. Blue Cross, 1970-71. Served with USNR, 1944-45. Mem. Am. Coll. Hosp. Adminstrs., Am. (chmn. com. on licensure of health personnel 1970-71, chmn. Council on Financing 1975—), Minn. (pres. 1969-70) hosp. assns., Am. Pub. Health Assn., Hosp. Adminstrs. Study Soc. Clubs: Detroit; Bloomfield Hills Country; Interlachen Country. Home: 4580 Lahser Rd Bloomfield Hills MI 48013 Office: 2799 W Grand Blvd Detroit MI 48202

NELSON, THOMAS EUSTIS, JR., educator; b. Sharon, Mass., May 3, 1922; s. Thomas Eustis and Mary Elise (Piguet) N.; A.B., Antioch Coll., 1947; student Denison U., 1943-44 (USNR-V12); M.S., U. So. Calif., 1951, Ph.D., 1956; m. Marjory Miller, June 23, 1947; children—Deanna Elise, Nancy Evelyn, Penelope Lynne. Instr., research asso. U. So. Calif. Sch. Medicine, Los Angeles, 1956-57; asst. prof. pharmacology Sch. Med. Dentistry, U. P.R., San Juan, 1957-60, asso. prof., acting chmn., 1960-61; asst. prof. U. Colo. Sch. Medicine, Denver, 1961-68; asso. prof. pharmacology, U. Tex. Dental Br., Houston, 1968-70; prof. pharmacology, chmn. dept. biomed. scis. So. Ill. Sch. Dental Medicine, Edwardsville, 1970—. Served with USNR, 1943-46. Los Angeles County Heart Assn. fellow, 1953; NIH grantee, 1964-67, 66-69, 72-73. Mem. Am. Soc. Pharmacology and Exptl. Therapeutics, Western Pharmacology Soc., Am. Physiol. Soc., Soc. for Exptl. Biology and Medicine, Microcirculatory Soc., IEEE, Am. Assn. Dental Schs., Internat. Assn. Dental Research, AAAS, Sigma Xi. Contbr. articles to profl. jours. Home: 12 Ouatoga Bluff Godfrey IL 62035 Office: Dept Pharmacology Sch Dental Medicine So Ill U Edwardsville IL 62025

NELSON, WARREN DONALD, pub. relations exec.; b. Milw., June 15, 1924; s. Carl Edwin and Gunda (Dahl) N.; student Am. Sch. of Law, 1949-52; m. Barbara Mosher, Sept. 30, 1960; 1 dau., Elisabeth Carol. Motion picture editor USPHS, Atlanta, 1948-52; motion picture editor-film librarian U.S. Dept. of Agrl., Washington, 1952-53; motion picture editor, writer, dir., Sam Orleans & Asso., Knoxville, Tenn., 1953-55; motion picture editor-dir. Atlas Film Corp., Oak Park, Ill., 1955-59; motion picture editor Wilding Inc., Chgo., 1960-64; communications dir. of Lutheran services Lutheran Ch. in Am., Chgo., 1964-68; dir. devel., pub. relations Resurrection Hosp., Chgo., 1968—. Mem. exec. com., bd. mgrs. Communications Commn., Nat. Council Churches, N.Y., 1965—. Served with USN Air Corps, 1943-45. Mem. Pub. Club of Chgo. (Distinguished Service award 1965, dir. 1972-74), Chgo. Hosp. Pub. Relations Soc. (pres. 1973-74; past pres. award 1974), Chgo. Soc. of Fund Raising Execs., Hon. Order of Ky. Cols., Chgo. Religious Pub. Relations council, Inc., (pres., 1966-67). Clubs: Chgo. Press, Kiwanis (pres., 1973-74; recipient Layman's award, 1974). Writer TV film prodn. "Come Sweet Death", 1953. Home: 1219 Woodford Pl Arlington Heights IL 60004 Office: 7435 W Talcott Ave Chicago IL 60631

NEMEC, STANLEY S., physician; b. Yugoslavia, June 16, 1911; s. Adolf and Josefina (Koblizek) N.; M.D., St. Louis U., 1936; m. Katherine M. Vidakovich Barr, June 15, 1940; children—Edward S., Mary K., Charles S., Robert S., Louise K., Dorothy K., Barbara K. Gen. med. practice, 1936-43; radiologist, St. Louis City Hosp., 1943-46; practice medicine specializing in radiology, 1946—; cons. radiologist Wabash R.R. Woodland Hosp., Moberly, Mo.; radiologist St. Charles Clinic, Marian Hosp.; asst. in radiology St. Louis U. Sch. Medicine. Diplomate Am. Bd. Radiology, Nat. Bd. Med. Examiners, Fellow Am. Coll. Radiology; mem. Radiology Soc. N.A., A.M.A., So. Med. Assn., St. Louis Med. Soc., St. Louis Soc. Neurology and Psychiatry. Author: History of the Croatian Settlement in St. Louis, 1931; Yugoslav Sokol Almanac, 1933. Editor: Sokol Magazine, 1931-34, The Koch Messenger, 1939. Contbr. articles to profl. jours. Home: 2870 S Lindbergh Blvd Huntleigh Village St Louis County MO 63131 Office: Suite 1 6500 Chippewa St St Louis MO 63109

NENCKA, HELEN (ANN), writer; b. Thorp, Wis., May 1, 1908; d. Stanislaus J. and Ann (Knapik) Kujawski; student Milw. Area Tech. Coll., 1926-29; m. Walter Nencka, Apr. 22, 1931; children—Sue Nencka Lugviel, Walter D. Sec., Robert A. Johnston Co., Milw., 1926-29, Underwriters Casualty Co., Milw., 1929-31; comml. poet Redwood Park, Crescent City, Calif., 1939-47; artist-poet Reminiscence in Rhyme, radio program, Hartford, Wis., 1951-53; partner, co-operator Alpine Retreat, restaurant, Hubertus, Wis., 1950-70; author Tender Conscience column Hartford Times Press, 1954—; author: Island Seed, 1954, To My Love, 1957, The Christmas Tree Story, 1965; contbr. poems to Ideal Mag., Pen Woman, numerous anthologies; translator Polish, Spanish poetry. Asst. leader 4-H Club, Hubertus, 1946-51; chmn. Com. for Local Sch. Control Hubertus, 1971-76. Recipient numerous awards including Liberty award Congress of Liberty, 1976; Wis. Woman's Day award, 1976. Mem. Nat. League Am. Pen Woman (nat. historian 1974-76, br. historian 1960—), Nat. Writers Club (award for Tender Conscience column 1958, award 1971), Stella Woodall Poetry Soc. (hon.), Council Wis. Writers, Wis. Fellowship Poets, Wis. Regional Writers, Wis. Acad. Scis., Arts, West Bend Fine Arts Soc. Roman Catholic. Club: Statesman's of Wis. Home and Office: 1400 Friess Lake Rd Hubertus WI 53033

NEPHEW, ALBERT HENRY, II, educator; b. Detroit, Oct. 20, 1940; s. Albert Henry and Julia Alexandra (Keturi) N.; B.A., Gonzaga U., 1962; Ph.D., Marquette U., 1970; m. Elizabeth Anne Hilber, Aug. 3, 1963; children—Elizabeth Joan, Julia Anne, John Albert, James Thomas. Teaching asst., lectr. Marquette U., Milw., 1965-66; instr. Alverno Coll., Milw., 1966-69, asst. prof., 1969-70; asst. prof. Coll. St. Scholastica, Duluth, Minn., 1970-73, asso. prof., 1973—, chmn. dept. philosophy, 1970—, chmn. div. humanities, 1971-76, dir. Montessori Program, 1976—; faculty Nat. Humanities Series, Midwestern Center, Madison, Wis., 1975, Grad. Theol. Edn. Program Concordia Coll. and Luther Sem., 1973—. Bd. dirs. Childbirth Edn. Assn. N.E. Minn., 1971-74. NDEA fellow, 1962-65; Carnegie grantee, 1972. Mem. AAUP, Am. Cath. Philos. Assn., Am., Minn. philos. assns., Hegel Soc. Am., Inst. for Soc. Ethics and Life Scis., Internat. Soc. Metaphysics, Metaphys. Soc. Am. Author: (with others) Educator's Thesaurus of the Lake Superior Basin and Region, 1975; Transportation and Distribution Economics of the Lake Superior Region, 1975. Home: 1532 E 8th St Duluth MN 55812

NEPOTE, HAZEL ELLEN, bank ofcl.; b. Robinson, Ill., Oct. 5, 1921; d. Henry Elmer and Effie Mae (Matheny) York; B.A. in Edn., U. Ill., 1942; m. Peter A. Nepote, Dec. 26, 1942; children—Peter Anthony, John Lynn. Sec., Keokuk C. of C. (Iowa), 1958-61; real estate officer Keokuk Savs. Bank & Trust Co., 1964—, personnel mgr., 1973—, trust officer, 1974—. Mem. Keokuk Personnel Forum, 1975—; bd. dirs. Lee County (Iowa) Mental Health Assn. Named Woman of Yr., Keokuk, 1967. Mem. Nat. Assn. Bank Women (treas. 1977, sec. 1978), Iowa Realtors Assn., Beta Sigma Phi. Republican. Roman Catholic. Club: Soroptomists. Home: 2819 Middle Rd Keokuk IA 52632 Office: 501 Main St Keokuk IA 52632

NERLINGER, JOHN WILLIAM, corp. exec.; b. Detroit, June 22, 1920; s. John W. and Bessie Prudence (Beith) N.; student Detroit Bus. Inst., 1938-39; B.A., Detroit Inst. Tech., 1950; m. Pearl Pauline Procup, Nov. 4, 1943; children—John Charles, Ruth Marie (Mrs. Richard Paul Blazevich). Bus. mgr. Retail Gasoline Dealers Assn. of Mich., Detroit, 1939-51, exec. sec., 1951-63; exec. sec. Nat. Congress of Petroleum Retailers, Detroit, 1951-63; asst. exec. v.p. Automotive Service Industry Assn., Chgo., 1963-73; exec. v.p., 1973—; adviser Nat. Highway Users Fedn. Served AUS, 1942-45; PTO. Recipient Petroleum "Man of Year" award, Gasoline News, 1961, Automotive Replacement Edn. award Northwood Inst., 1975; Distinguished Service award Automotive Orgn. Team, 1978. Mem. Am. (mem. edn. com.), Chgo. socs. assn. execs., Automotive Old Timers, Automotive Booster Clubs Internat., Automotive Acad., Chgo. Assn. Commerce and Industry (mem. govt. relations com.), Nat. Assn. Wholesalers-Distbrs. (exec. com.), Automotive Orgn. Team (v.p.). Lutheran. Clubs: Mid Am., Michigan Ave (Chgo.), Masons, Shriners. Home: 601 E Fairview Arlington Heights IL 60005 Office: 444 N Michigan Ave Chicago IL 60611

NESBITT, ARTHUR WALLACE, mail order and mfg. co. exec.; b. Enon Valley, Pa., July 29, 1927; s. William and Frances (Gilmore) N.; B.S., Pa. State U., 1950; children—Warren children—Warren P., David G.; m. 2d, Donna Saviers Fox, Aug. 19, 1967; stepchildren—Marsha, Marilyn, William, Leann, Sandra. Asst. county agt. Agr. Extension Service Pa. State U., Clarion, 1950-51; exec. sec. Pa. Holstein Assn., State College, 1952-59; sales mgr. Nasco, Ft. Atkinson, 1959-63; v.p., sales, 1963-71; v.p. Nasco Internat., Inc., 1971-72, exec. v.p., 1972-74, pres., 1974—; also dir. Bank of Ft. Atkinson. Bd. dirs. World Dairy Expo. Served with AUS, 1945-46. Mem. Am. Dairy Sci. Assn., Internat. Assn. Milk and Food Sanitarians, Holstein-Friesian Assn. Am., Dairy Shrine Club (sec. treas.), Dairy and Food Industries Supply Assn. (bd. dirs. 1973—), Delta Theta Sigma (pres.). Kiwanian (past pres.) Home: 711 Blackhawk Dr Fort Atkinson WI 53538 Office: 901 Janesville Ave Ft Atkinson WI 53538

NESMITH, LESLIE WALLACE, ophthalmologist, retinal surgeon; b. Lawrence, Kans., Sept. 7, 1940; s. Dean D. and Norma Roy (Wallace) N.; B.S., U. Kans., 1962; M.D., Kans. U., 1966; m. Elizabeth Ann Duley, Nov. 23, 1968; children—Trent L. W., Brooke L.W., Seth L.W., Britt L.W., Cade L.W. Intern Kans. U. Med. Center, Kansas City, 1966-67, resident, 1969-72; retinal fellowship Mass. Eye and Ear Infirmary, Harvard U., and Retina Found., Boston, 1972-73; practice medicine specializing in ophthalmology and retinal surgery, Wichita, Kans., 1974—. Served with USAF, 1967-69. Diplomate Am. Bd. Ophthalmology. Fellow A.C.S.; mem. Am., Kans., Sedgwick County med. assns., Am. Acad. Ophthalmology and Otolaryngology. Contbr. articles to med. jours. Home: Rural Route 3 Box 161-C Augusta KS 67010 Office: 3333 E Central Suite 504 Wichita KS 67208

NESPECA, GLENN ALDO, civil engr.; b. Youngstown, Ohio, Apr. 15, 1950; s. Aldo and Vita Marie (Miceli) N.; B.S. in Civil Engring., U. Akron, 1973, M.S. in Civil Engring., 1976; m. Gabrielle Nameth, Sept. 10, 1973; 1 dau., Natalie. Asst. engr. City of Barberton, Ohio, 1973-77; engr. soils and found. Burgess & Niple, Ltd., Columbus, Ohio, 1977—. Registered profl. engr., Ohio. Mem. ASCE, Nat. Soc. Profl. Engrs. Democrat. Roman Catholic. Home: 2164 Tuliptree Ave Columbus OH 43229 Office: 5085 Reed Rd Columbus OH 43220

NESS, ORDEAN GERHARD, educator; b. Buxton, N.D., Oct. 4, 1921; s. Ole Thomas and Gerda (Johnson) N.; B.A., U. N.D., 1942; M.A., U. Wis., 1947, Ph.D. (fellow 1949-50, 52-53), 1953. Instr., Syracuse U., 1947-49; asst. prof. Pa. State U., 1953-55; asst. prof. U. Wis., Madison, 1955-59, asso. prof., 1959-61, prof. communication arts, theatre and drama, 1961—, asso. chmn. dept. speech, 1964-70; asso. dir. articulated instructional media program, 1964-66, prof., chmn. dept. theatre and drama, 1973-75, chmn. dept. communication arts, 1975—, chmn. faculty div. humanities, 1976—; free-lance stage and radio actor-dir. Vice pres. Dutch Hollow Property Owners Assn.; bd. dirs. Madison Civic Repertory Theatre. Served to 1st lt. AUS, 1942-46, capt., 1950-52. Mem. Speech Communication Assn., Nat. Collegiate Players, Nat. Assn. Ednl. Broadcasters, Broadcasting Edn. Assn., AAUP, Am. Film Inst.; Central States Speech Assn., Wis. Hist. Soc., Wis. Acad. Scis., Letters and Arts, Am., Wis. theatre assns., Wis. Speech Communication Assn., U. Wis., U. N.D. alumni assns., Bascom Hill Soc., Nature Conservancy, Friends of Channel 21, WHA Radio Assn., Phi Beta Kappa, Delta Sigma Rho, Blue Key, Phi Eta Sigma, Phi Beta (hon. patron). Author: (with A.T. Weaver) The Fundamentals and Forms of Speech, 1957, 1963; An Introduction to Public Speaking, 1961. Deptl. editor Speech Tchr., 1955-63. Contbr. articles in field to profl. jours. Home: 4715 Sheboygan Ave Madison WI 53705

NESSE, ANTON STEPHAN, radiologist; b. Bergen, Norway, Apr. 25, 1938; s. Harold and Esther (Stephansen) N.; came to U.S., 1957, naturalized, 1962; B.S. (Med. Research fellow), U. Minn., 1961, M.D. in Radiology, 1963; children—Brian Scott, Dawn Michelle. Intern, Hennepin County Gen. Hosp., Mpls., 1963-64; resident radiology U. Minn., Mpls., 1966-70 clin. instr. radiology, U. Minn.-Mpls. VA Hosp., 1970—; radiologist Suburban Radiologic Cons. Ltd., Mpls., 1970—; staff Unity, Mercy hosps., Mpls., 1970—. Served as flight surgeon USAF, 1964-66. Mem. AMA, Alpha Omega Alpha, Phi Rho Sigma, Theta Chi. Home: 7541 Van Buren St NE Fridley MN 55432 Office: 6600 France Ave S Minneapolis MN 55435

NESSE, HAROLD, dentist; b. Borgund, Sogn, Norway, Nov. 15, 1904; s. Anders I. and Anna Sofie (Husum) N.; D.D.S., U. Minn., 1929; m. Esther Stephansen, Oct. 24, 1931 (div); children—Einar, Anton Stephan; m. 2d, Lizzie Katherine Olsen, July 23, 1954. Came to U.S. 1953, naturalized, 1957. Gen. practice dentistry, Bergen, Norway, 1929-52, Mpls., 1953, Foley, Minn., 1954-55, Jordan, Minn., 1956-77. Lectr. to various clinics and orgns. in Norway and Denmark, 1933-51; mem. dental adv. com. Scott County, 1963-75. Mem. City Council, Jordan, Minn., 1964-71. Bd. dirs. Norwegian Am. Mus., Decorah, Iowa, 1960—; pres. Nat. Sognalag of Am., 1958-62, 66, 68, 72-74. Served with Norwegian Air Force, 1949. Mem. Am., Minn. dental assns., Mpls. Dist. Dental Soc., Internat. Fedn. Norsemen, Norwegian Am. Hist. Soc., Sons of Norway. Lutheran. Club: Lions (v.p. 1972-73). Contbr. articles to profl. jours. Home: 305 Hillside Dr Jordan MN 55352 Office: 224 Broadway Jordan MN 55352

NESTERENKO, DIMITRI A., structural engr.; b. Kiev, Ukraine, USSR, May 23, 1909; s. Atanazy and Maria (Mikulinski) N.; C.E., Tech. State U., Warsaw, Poland, 1935; m. Herta Reichardt, Oct. 22, 1939;children—Elizabeth, Alexander. Came to U.S., 1948, naturalized, 1954. Field engr. City of Sochaczew, Poland, 1935-36; city engr., Otwock, Poland, 1936-44; structural design specialist Stanley Cons., Inc. (formerly Stanley Engring. Co.), Muscatine, Iowa, 1948-55, prin., chief structural engr., 1955—, v.p., 1972—. Registered profl. engr., Iowa, Mo., Ky., Wis., Alaska, Ohio; structural engr., Ill. Mem. Nat. Soc. Profl. Engrs., Am. Concrete Inst., Iowa Engring. Soc. Mem. Greek Orthodox Ch. Author math. work pub. by Stanley Engring. Co., also numerous tech. articles. Home: 206 W 4th St Muscatine IA 52761 Office: Stanley Bldg Muscatine IA 52761

NETSER, JAMES RAYMOND, radio supply co. exec.; b. Washington County, Iowa, Feb. 25, 1928; s. Ira D. and Ethel Belle (Glanz) N.; student U. Iowa, 1962-65; m. Carol Ann Shimerda, June 20, 1954; children—Julie, Lisa. Salesman, Gifford Brown Inc., Cedar Rapids, Iowa, 1951-60; v.p., buyer, salesman Iowa Radio Supply Co., Cedar Rapids, 1960-63, 65-77, owner, mgr., 1977—. Congregationalist. Home: 301 Hilltop Rd Marion IA 52302 Office: 719 Center Point Rd Cedar Rapids IA 52402

NEU, ARTHUR ALAN, lt. gov. Iowa, lawyer; b. Carroll, Iowa, Feb. 9, 1933; s. Arthur N. and Martha (Frandsen) N.; B.S., Northwestern U., 1955, J.D., 1958; LL.M., Georgetown U., 1960; m. Mary Naomi Bedwell, Apr. 4, 1964; children—Arthur Eric, Mary Martha, Towle Harold. Admitted to Iowa bar, 1958, since practiced in Carroll; mem. firm Minnich and Neu, 1963—; mem. Iowa senate, 1967-73; lt. gov. Iowa, 1974—. Served with JAG, AUS, 1958-62. Mem. Am., Iowa bar assns. Presbyterian. Club: Rotary. Home: 801 N Adams St Carroll IA 51401 Office: State Capitol Des Moines IA 50319

NEUBAUER, CHARLES FREDERICK, journalist; b. Elmhurst, Ill., Feb. 13, 1950; s. Fred Charles and Dolores Jeanne (Pries) N.; B.S. in Journalism, Northwestern U., 1972, M.S., 1973; m. Sandra Carol Bergo, Oct. 4, 1975. Investigator, Better Govt. Assn., Chgo., 1971-73; investigative reporter Chgo. Today, 1973-74, Chgo. Tribune, 1974—. Co-recipient Pulitzer prize for local investigative reporting, 1976. Home: 813 Dobson St Apt 1 Evanston IL 60202 Office: Chgo Tribune 435 N Michigan Ave Chicago IL 60611

NEUENSCHWANDER, FREDERICK PHILLIP, bus. exec.; b. Akron, Ohio, Mar. 19, 1924; s. Willis Lee and Esther (Mayer) N.; student Franklin and Marshall Coll., 1942-43, U. Akron, 1946-48; m. Mary Jane Porter, Mar. 19, 1948; children—Carol, Frederick Philip, Lynn, Dean, Richard. Chief insp. Retail Credit Co., Akron, 1948-55; exec. v.p. Wadsworth (Ohio) C. of C., 1955-62, Wadsworth Devel. Corp., 1955-62, Wooster (Ohio) C. of C., 1962-63, Wooster Expansion, Inc., 1962-63; dir. devel. dept. State of Ohio, Columbus, 1963-71; exec. v.p. James A. Rhodes & Assos., Columbus, 1971-74; prin. F.P. Neuenschwander & Assos., Columbus, 1975—. Mem. adv. council Small Bus. Adminstrn. Exec. dir. Wadsworth United Fund, Inc., 1956-62; pres. Templed Hills, Inc.; pres. Central Ohio exec. bd. Boy Scouts Am.; vice-chmn. Ohio Water Commn., Ohio Expns. Commn.; chmn. Ohio Water and Sewer Rotary Fund Commn.; mem., past chmn. Midwest Gov.'s Adv. Council; sec. Ohio Devel. Council, Ohio Devel. Finance Commn. Adv. council Rio Grande Coll.; 1st chmn. bd. trustees Ohio Transp. Research Center. Served with AUS, 1943-46. Named Outstanding Young Man of Year, Wadsworth Jr. C. of C., 1958; recipient SIR award for directing outstanding state indsl. devel. program N. Am., 1966, 68, Ohio Gov.'s award 1967. Mem. Am., Gt. Lakes indsl. devel. councils, C. of C. Execs. of Ohio, Huguenot Soc. Am., Am. Legion, Ohio Soc. N.Y. (res. v.p.). Mem. United Ch. of Christ (property mgmt. com. Ohio Conf.). Home: 1155 Clubview S Worthington OH 43085 Office: 50 W Broad St Columbus OH 43215

NEUGENT, DAVID SMITH, ins. co. exec.; b. Green Bay, Wis., June 1, 1925; s. Joseph and Alma (Smith) N.; student U. Wis., 1942, N.D. Agr. Coll., 1943, U. Paris (France), 1945, Marquette U., 1948; m. Marie A. Neary, Jan. 11, 1947; children—Dennis Joseph, Timothy Lawrence, Gerard David, Kevin James. Dir. hosp., physician, pub. relations Blue Cross of Wis., 1959-63, v.p. mktg., 1963-72, sr. v.p., 1972; with Office Chief Execs. Blue Shield of Iowa, 1973—, pres. Blue Cross of Iowa, 1972—, Iowa Pharmacy Service Corp., 1972—, Delta Dental of Iowa, 1974— (all Des Moines); mem. plan performance com. Blue Cross Assn., 1973—, nat. employee benefits com., 1973-77. Vice chmn. Health Planning Council Central Iowa, 1973-77; mem. exec. com. Office Comprehensive Health Planning Com., State of Iowa, 1973—. Mem. Polk County Commn. for County Correction, 1977—. Bd. dirs. State Health Coordinating Council, 1976—, Better Bus. Bur., 1977—, Chem. Dependency Agy., 1977—, Iowa Crime Prevention Coalition, 1976—, Kidney Found. Iowa, 1974—. Served with AUS, 1942-45. Decorated Purple Heart. Named Man of Year, South Milwaukee Jr. C. of C., 1956, Cath. War Vets, S. Milw., 1956. Mem. Des Moines C. of C. (chmn. urban affairs com. 1974—). Roman Catholic (chmn. fin. adminstrn. com. ch. 1974—, vice chmn. bishop's study com. on Des Moines diocesan council 1974—). Club: Rotary. Home: 2807 Wolcott St Des Moines IA 50321 Office: Blue Cross of Iowa 636 Grand Ave Des Moines IA 50307

NEUMANN, AUGWILL WALTER, corp. exec.; b. Milw., June 26, 1914; s. Walter Frederick and Katherine M. (Heyer) N.; architecture student, U. Ill., 1938-42; M.B.A., Harvard, 1943; m. Ann Jo Woodward, Dec. 25, 1943; children—Barbara Simmonds, David, Stephen. Supt. constrn. W.F. Newmann & Sons, Milw., 1936-38; asst. to exec. v.p. The Willett Co., Chgo., 1946-71, exec. v.p., 1971-74, also dir.; exec. v.p., dir. Willett Transports, Inc., 1971-74, exec. v.p. corp. affairs parent co. Willett, Inc., 1974—; gen. mgr. Willett Truck Leasing Co., 1959-65, pres., 1965—, dir.; pres., dir. Nat. Truck Leasing System; sec., dir. Nat. Lease Purchasing Corp.; designer buildings and homes; dir. The Hooven & Allison Co., Xenia, Ohio, Jefferson Corp., Chgo.; farm agt. Homestead Farm, Xenia, 1976—. Mem. Gov.'s Adv. Com. on Fleet Vehicle Mgmt., Ill. Vehicle Adv. Com., 1969; active Boy Scouts Am.; adviser Chgo. Jr. Achievement. Bd. dirs. Barbereux Sch., Evanston, Ill.; v.p., bd. dirs. Hilltop Sanatorium, Lake Bluff, Ill.; bd. dirs., v.p., treas. Howard L. Williett Found., Inc., 1972—. Served to capt. Q.M.C. AUS, 1943-46. Mem. Am. Trucking Assn. (chmn. engring., equipment and policy com.). Automotive Transp. Suprs. Assn., A.I.M., Nat. Def. Transp. Assn. Am. Ordnance Assn., Soc. Automotive Engrs., Soc. Advancement Mgmt., Pvt. Truck Council Am. (dir., chmn. equipment and maintenance com.). Christian Scientist. Rotarian. Clubs: University (Chgo.): Westmoreland Country, Michigan Shores (Wilmette, Ill.). Author articles and profl. papers. Home: 2928 Indian Wood Rd Wilmette IL 60091 Office: 700 S Desplaines St Chicago IL 60607

NEUMANN, FORREST KARL, hosp. adminstr.; b. St. Louis, Oct. 7, 1930; s. Metz Earl and Ruth Estelle (McGhee) N.; B.S., Roosevelt U., 1953; M.S. in Hosp. Adminstrn., Northwestern U., 1955; m. Erika S. Turkl, Feb. 11, 1955; children—Tracey Lee, Karen Ruth, Scott Forrest, Lisa Kay. Adminstrv. resident Louis A. Weiss Meml. Hosp., Chgo., 1954-55; asst. dir. Edward W. Sparrow Hosp., Lansing, Mich., 1958-61, asso. dir., 1961-62, dir., 1962-71, pres., trustee, 1971—; pres., dir. Mason Gen. Hosp., 1973—. Dir. Am. Bank and Trust Co., 1973—. Pres., Southwestern Mich. Hosp. Council, 1969-70, trustee, 1968-73; mem., vice chmn. Mich. Arbitration Adv. Com., 1975. Chmn. budget steering com. United Way, Lansing, 1970-71, bd. dirs., mem. exec. com., 1969-75; bd. dirs. Grad. Med. Edn., Inc., 1971—, pres., 1972-73, treas., 1973—. Served as 1st lt. Med. Services Corps, USAF, 1955-58. Fellow Am. Coll. Hosp. Adminstrs.; mem. Am., Mich. (trustee 1969—, 1st v.p. 1972-73, treas. 1974—, chmn. 1976-77) hosp. assns. Rotarian (dir. Lansing 1974-76). Contbr. articles profl. jours. Office: 1215 E Michigan Ave Lansing MI 48909

NEUSCHEL, ROBERT PERCY, mgmt. cons.; b. Hamburg, N.Y., Mar. 13, 1919; s. Percy J. and Anna (Becker) N.; B.A., Denison U., 1941; M.B.A., Harvard U., 1947; m. Dorothy Virginia Maxwell, Oct. 20, 1944; children—Kerr Anne Ziprick, Carla Becker, Robert Friedrich. Indsl. engr. Sylvania Electric Products Co., Inc., 1947-49; with McKinsey & Co., Inc., 1950—, sr. partner, dir., 1967—; dir. Butler Mfg. Co., Combined Ins. Co. Am., Norfolk & Western Ry. Co.; lectr. in field. Mem. McKinsey Found. Mgmt. Research, Inc. Pres. bd. edn., Lake Forest, Ill, 1965-70. Trustee N. Suburban Mass Transit; bd. dirs. Chgo. Boys Club, Boy Scouts Am., Nat. Center for Voluntary Action; mem. citizens bd. Loyola U., Chgo.; chmn. Lake Forest Symphony, 1973. Served to capt. USAAF, World War II. Mem. Ry. Systems and Mgmt. Assn., Transp. Assn. Am., Inst. Mgmt. Consultants (dir., trustee). Methodist (trustee). Clubs: Harvard Bus. Sch. (pres. 1964-65), Econ., Exec., Chicago, Mid America (Chgo.); Onwentsia (Lake Forest, Ill.). Contbr. articles to profl. jours. Home: 890 Larchmont Ln Lake Forest IL 60045 Office: Two First Nat Plaza Chicago IL 60670

NEVIN, TIMOTHY WILLIAM, research immunologist; b. Bellefonte, Pa., Apr. 5, 1948; s. Charles S. and Myra Minton (King) N.; student Eastern Ill. U., 1966-67; B.S., Ill. State U., 1973, postgrad., 1973-74. Immunologist pediatric research Michael Reese Med. Center, Chgo., 1975—, teaching asst., 1976-77. Served with USAF, 1967-71. Mem. Am. Soc. Microbiology, Ill. State U. Soc. Med. Tech. (charter pres.). Presbyn. Home: 5121 Mackie Pl Downers Grove IL 60515 Office: 501 Cummings Michael Reese Med Center 29th and Ellis Ave Chicago IL 60616

NEW, JACK L., state ofcl.; grad. Ind. U., 1948; m.; four children. Research dir. Ind. Democratic State Central Com., 1948-51; dep. dir., acting dir. Ind. Office Price Stblzn., 1951-53; operator office furniture co., 1953—; former exec. sec. to gov. Ind.; treas. State of Ind., 1965-67, 71—. Democrat. Methodist. Office: State Capitol Bldg Indianapolis IN 46204

NEWBANKS, JAMES ALLAN, broadcast engr.; b. Effingham, Ill., Apr. 25, 1939; s. Voris William and Ruby M. N.; A.S. in Electronic Tech., So. Ill. U., Carbondale, 1967, B.S. in Occupational Edn., 1974; m. Alice Joan Antrim, Nov. 25, 1956; children—Cathy Jo, James Allan, II, Robert Patrick. Announcer, chief engr. Sta. WCRA, Effingham, 1955-57; broadcast engr. Sta. WCIA, Champaign, Ill., 1958-62; broadcast engr. Sta. WSIU-TV-FM, So. Ill. U., 1962-67, asst. chief engr., 1967-74; dir. engring. Sta. WSSR, Sangamon State U., 1974—; radio technician Ill. Police Radio Bur., Urbana, Ill., 1959-62. Mem. Soc. Broadcast Engring., Soc. Motion Picture and TV Engring., Nat. Assn. Ednl. Broadcasters, Phi Kappa Phi. Lutheran. Club: Elks. Home: 109 Stony Creek Chatham Office: Sta WSSR Sangamon State U Springfield IL 62708

NEWBURY, DAVID NORMAN, pub. sch. adminstr.; b. Sunbury, Pa., Aug. 9, 1931; s. Charles Edward and Priscilla Allen (Persing) N.; B.S., Bloomsburg State Coll., 1953; M.S., Bucknell U., 1956; Ed.D., Wayne State U., 1967; m. Nancy Joan Stephens, Nov. 21, 1956; 1 son, Stephen. Tchr. jr. high sch., Hazel Park, Mich., 1956-59, sci. coordinator elementary and secondary schs., 1959-63, curriculum coordinator elementary and secondary schs., 1963-67, asst. supt. for instrn. and personnel, 1967—. Mem. faculty grad. sch. Oakland U., 1969-75, Eastern Mich. U., 1968-69; cons. Wayne State U., 1968-69;

vis. lectr. Mott Community Edn. Leadership Program, 1969-75. Mem. adv. bd. Warren (Mich.) Salvation Army, 1971—; mem. Hazel Park (Mich.) Commn. on Drug Abuse, 1972—; chmn. City Youth Protection Com., 1972—. Bd. govs. Wayne State Coll. Edn. Alumni; bd. dirs. Try, Inc. Served with AUS, 1953-55. Recipient Outstanding Service award Oakland County Curriculum Council, 1970; Gold Key award Bloomsburg State Coll. Mem. Assn. for Supervision and Curriculum Devel. (dir.), Mich. Assn. for Supervision and Curriculum Devel. (dir. 1964-65, 69-70, 73-75, sec. 1974-75, pres.-elect 1976-77), Mich., Nat. community sch. edn. assns., Am. Assn. Sch. Adminstrs., Mich. Assn. Sch. Adminstrs., Phi Delta Kappa. Rotarian. Author: Teacher Negotiations: A Guide for Bargaining Teams, 1970. Contbr. articles to profl. jours. Home: 4852 Iowa Dr Warren MI 48092 Office: 23136 Hughes Ave Hazel Park MI 48030

NEWBY, GERALD CAPPER, city ofcl.; b. Sterling, Kans., Aug. 29, 1912; s. Clarence Garfield and Edna Pearl Rose (Smisor) N.; grad. high sch.; m. Jennie Josephine White, July 4, 1941; children—Jerene Ann, Ben Clare. Houseman Warren Hotel, Liberal, Kans., 1931-33; deliveryman Carey Ice Co., Sterling, 1933-34; clk. Wheeler Grocery, Sterling, 1934-40; servicemen City Sterling, 1940-41, dep. city clk., 1947-49, city clk., 1949-65, city mgr., 1965—. Bd. trustees bldg. com. Girl Scouts U.S., 1962—. Bd. dirs. Community Chest, Sterling, 1965—; chmn. bd. Salvation Army, Sterling, 1965—. Served with AUS, 1941-46. Decorated Purple Heart, Bronze Star. Mem. Kans. Assn. City Clks., Kans. Assn. City Mgrs., League Kans. Municipalities, Kans. Municipal Utilities, Am. Legion. United Presbyterian (chmn. bd. trustees 1970-71, trustee 1961-64, 65-71, treas. Sunday sch. 1962-72). Club: Sterling Quarterback. Home: 330 N Broadway Sterling KS 67579 Office: 114 N Broadway Sterling KS 67579

NEWBY, JOHN MELVIN, coll. ofcl.; b. Westfield, Ind., Jan. 31, 1928; s. James Edwin and Mary Augusta (Williams) N.; diploma Union Bible Sem., 1948; A.B., LaVerne Coll., 1952; M.S., U. So. Calif., 1958; Ph.D., Mich. State U., 1972; m. Rebecca Jean Hall, Apr. 15, 1949; children—Sharon Jean, Karen Jane, Becky Lynette, John Melvin. Ordained to ministry Pilgrim Holiness Ch., 1951; minister Pilgrim Holiness Ch., San Dimas and Pasadena, Calif., 1950-59; instr. music Upland (Calif.) Coll., 1951-52; mgr. of schs. Pilgrim Holiness Ch., Zambia, Africa, 1959-63, acting field supr. and edn. sec., 1963-64; registrar, instr. Owosso (Mich.) Coll., 1964-66, dir. bus. affairs, 1966-67, registrar, 1967-68; registrar Spring Arbor (Mich.) Coll., 1968-73, dir. instl. research and planning, 1972—, acting dean acad. affairs, 1973-74, v.p. adminstrv. affairs, 1974—; mem. Free Methodist Ch., 1974—, minister music Spring Arbor Free Meth. Ch., 1970-73; examiner N. Central Assn. Colls. and Schs., 1977—. Sec. Owosso Library Bd., 1966-68; bd. dirs. David Livingston Tchr. Tng. Coll., Zambia, 1963-64; trustee Western Pilgrim Coll., sec., 1951-58; trustee Mich. Library Consortium; bd. dirs. Mich. Heart Assn. Mem. Assn. for Instl. Research, Council for Advancement Small Colls. (chmn. student learning outcomes task force and student attrition task force, 1975—), Nat. Assn. Evangelicals (sec. 1956-58), Am. Assn. for Affirmative Action, Am. Assn. Higher Edn., Phi Delta Kappa, Phi Kappa Phi. Republican. Club: Rotary (dir. 1966-71). Home: 3736 Chapel Rd Spring Arbor MI 49283 Office: care Spring Arbor College Spring Arbor MI 49283

NEWBY, RICHARD PROUTY, clergyman; b. Des Moines, Apr. 13, 1923; s. James Moore and Bertha (Prouty) N.; B.A., William Penn Coll., 1945; m. Doris Prignitz, June 1, 1945; children—Darlene Ann, James Richard, John Charles. Pastor Soc. of Friends Ch.; pastor, Pleasant Plain, Iowa, 1945-47, Mpls., 1947-58, Muncie (Ind.) Friends Ch., 1958-67, University Friends Ch., Wichita, Kans., 1967-73, College Ave. Friends Ch., Oskaloosa, Iowa, 1973-74, Friends Meml. Ch., Muncie, 1974—. Presiding clk. Iowa Yearly Meeting of Friends, 1955-58; chmn. bd. on Christian edn. Friends United Meeting, 1955-66; pres. Delaware County Council Chs., 1965-66, Wichita Council Chs., 1970-71. Chmn. Muncie Mayor's Com. on Human Relations, 1962-63. Bd. dirs. Am. Friends Service Com., 1960-64; trustee William Penn Coll., 1955-58, Earlham Coll., 1962-67, 77—, Friends U., Wichita, 1970-74; bd. advisers Earlham Sch. Religion, 1976—. Recipient award of merit William Penn Coll., 1957. Mem. Delaware County Ministerial Assn. (pres. 1961-62). Home: 605 S Rambler Rd Muncie IN 47304 Office: Friends Memorial Ch Adams and Cherry Sts Muncie IN 47305

NEWCOMB, WARD CRAWFORD, dentist; b. Kearney, Nebr., Aug. 23, 1921; s. Wayne Kenneth and Leta Mabel (Crawford) N.; B.A., Kearney State Tchrs. Coll., 1943; D.D.S., U. Nebr., 1951; m. Juanita Elaine Fisher, Feb. 19, 1944; children—Ward Melvin, Timothy Kenneth, Michael Scott. Instr. sci., coach Wood River (Nebr.) High Sch., 1946-47; instr. U. Neb., Lincoln, 1949-51; practice dentistry, Chappell, Nebr., 1951—. Founder, pres. Bovine Crowns, Inc., Chappell, 1959—. Bd. regents Deuel County, 1953-68; service chmn. Am. Red Cross Home, 1956-66; chmn. Deuel County Pub. Health, 1960—; vice chmn. bd. dirs Deuel County Hosp. and Rest Home, 1973—. Served to 1st lt. USMC, 1943-46. Decorated Purple Heart. Mem. Am., Nebr., dental assns., Am. Endodontic Soc., Am. Legion, D.A.V., Delta Sigma Delta. Republican. Methodist. Mason, Lion (pres. 1956—). Home: 1081 5th St Chappell NE 69129 Office: 279 Matlock Ave Chappell NE 69129

NEWCOMER, DAVID WILLIAM, III, funeral dir.; b. Kansas City, Mo., Mar. 19, 1911; s. David William and Margaret Anna (Zahner) N.; A.B., U. Kans., 1932; postgrad. U. Mo., 1933-34; m. Pamela Kinney, Apr. 26, 1941; children—David William IV, Douglas Barry. Vice-pres. Mo. Casket Co., 1933-35; partner D.W. Newcomer's Sons, Kansas City, Mo., 1936—, pres., 1971—; pres. D.W. Newcomer's Sons Funeral Home Diversified and Combined, Kansas City, 1965—, Tech. and Profl. Services, Kansas City, 1971—, D.W. Newcomer's Sons Found., 1965—, Tech. & Profl. Services, 1965—, Meml. Heritage Corp., 1965—, Johnson County Meml. Gardens, Overland Park, Kans., 1965—; Heart of Am. Investment Services, Kansas City, 1971—; v.p. Central Nat. Finance Co., 1970—. Pres. Greater Kansas City Community Chest, 1964-65, Kansas City Red Cross Chpt. 1957-58, Greater Kansas City chpt. Am. Cancer Soc., 1959-60. Bd. dirs. YMCA, Boy Scouts Am., Traveler's Aid, Crippled Children's Nursery, Rehab. Inst., Assn. for the Blind; trustee Kansas City Philharmonic, Kansas City Museum, Pembroke Country Day Boy's Sch., U. Mo., Kansas City. Served as lt. comdr. USNR, 1942-46. Mem. Sigma Nu. Roman Catholic. Clubs: Mission Hills Country; University, Mercury (pres. 1970) (Kansas City); Homestead (Prairie Village, Kans.). Home: 6537 High Drive Shawnee Mission KS 66208 Office: 1331 Brush Creek Kansas City MO 64110

NEWELL, PINKNEY JANIORY, JR., state ofcl.; b. Chaffee, Mo., June 21, 1925; s. P. J. and Sarah (Crites) N.; B.Ed. S.E. Mo. State, 1947; M.Ed., U. Mo., 1951; m. M. Marjorie McGee, May 26, 1945; children—M. Judith (Mrs. Paul Wylie), Pinkney W., John K. Tchr., Kennett (Mo.) High Sch., 1947-49; supt. schs. Grandin, Puxico, Kahoka, Wellsville and Farmington, Mo., 1949-65; asst. commr. edn. Mo. State Dept. Edn., Jefferson City, 1965—. Served to lt. (j.g.) USNR, 1943-46. Mem. Am. Assn. Sch. Adminstrs., Mo. Assn. Sch. Adminstrs., Mo. Tchrs. Assn., Phi Delta Kappa. Home: 2303 Livingston Jefferson City MO 65101

NEWELL, VIRGINIA SHAW, ret. educator; b. Eau Claire, Wis., Jan. 15, 1901; d. La Forrest and Caroline (Wingen) Newell; student Eau Claire Normal Sch., 1919-21; B.A., U. Wis., Madison, 1924, postgrad., 1964-68; postgrad. Northwestern U., 1941; M.A., Catholic U. Am., 1951. Tchr., Eau Claire Sr. High Sch., 1924-43; tchr., drama dir. Adams-Friendship High Sch., Adams, Wis., 1951-54; tchr. English and speech Westfield (Wis.) High Sch., 1954-55; tchr. English Medford (Wis.) High Sch., 1955-57; tchr., drama dir. Marinette, Wis., 1957-63; tchr., dir. forensics, dir. contest plays Adams-Friendship High Sch., 1963-66; free-lance writer. Vol. Adams County unit Am. Cancer Soc., 1972-75, crusade chmn., 1975, bd. dirs., 1975-77; pres. Adams County Assn. Republican Women, 1969-73; publicity chmn. Adams County Rep. Party, 1973-76; vice chairperson, 1975-76; coordinator congressman's re-election campaign, 1972; sponsor Nat. Rep. Congressional Com., 1976. Served to lt. Women's Res., USCG, 1943-46. Ann. fellow Intercontinental Biog. Assn.; mem. Res. Officers Assn. U.S., AAUW, Winnebago County Ret. Tchrs. Assn., Wis. Tchrs. Assn. (life), Nat. Ret. Tchrs. Assn., Cath. U. Am. Alumni Assn., Internat. Platform Assn. (admissions control com. 1972), Nat. Travel Club, Roche-A-Cri Recreation, Inc., Delta Kappa Gamma. Roman Catholic. Author: (radio play) Charity, Inc., 1941; asst. editor: Stories and Poems from the First Grade through the Eighth, 1924; contbr. articles to profl. jours. Home: 200 Merritt Ave Apt 202 Oshkosh WI 54901

NEWEY, PAUL DAVIS, lawyer, investigator; b. Mpls., July 4, 1914; s. Paul S. and Mary (Yonan) N.; A.A., Central YMCA, 1935; J.D., John Marshall Law Sch., 1940; A.B., Detroit Inst. Tech., 1947; diploma U.S. Treasury Dept. Law Enforcement Sch., 1943; spl. courses U.S. Govt. and Mil. Intelligence Schs., 1951-53; m. Viola W. Raymond, Dec. 16, 1943; children—Paul Sarkhoshe II, Davis Raymond, Dean Alan, Arthur Tyler. Admitted to Ill. bar, 1946; squad leader Bur. Census, Dept. Commerce, 1940; officer Uniformed Force U.S. Secret Service, 1940-42; agt. Bur. Narcotics Treasury Dept., 1942-47; pvt. practice law, real estate, ins. broker, Chgo., 1948-51; spl. rep. CIA, 1951-57; asst. state's atty.-investigator, County of Cook, Ill., 1957-58, asst. state's atty.-chief investigator, chief of state's atty.'s police, 1958-60; pvt. practice law, Chgo., 1961-65; spl. investigator, Chgo., 1961—; partner law firm Adamowski, Newey & Adamowski, Chgo., 1965—. Sec., dir. Master Fishing Gear, Inc., 1956-57. Served as pvt. AUS, 1941; 1st lt., CIC, 1949-54. Recipient Medal of Merit and elected to Hall of Fame, Nat. Police Officers Assn. Am., 1960; Distinguished Citizen award Assyrian-Am. Welfare Council, 1970; citation merit John Marshall Law Sch., 1970. Mem. Am., Ill., DuPage, Chgo. bar assns., Internat. Assn. Investigators and Spl. Police (chmn. bd. dirs. 1963—), N. Am. Inst. Police Sci. (dir. 1961—), N. Am. Detective Agy. (dir. 1961—), Spl. Agts. Assn. (Chgo. chpt.), U.S. Treasury Agts. Assn. (pres. 1970-71), John Marshall Law Sch. Alumni Assn. (dir. 1968—, treas. 1973-75), Internat. Assn. Chief Police, Am. Judicature Soc., Chgo. Assn. Commerce and Industry, Ill. Assn. Chiefs Police. Mem. United Ch. of Christ. Mason (32 deg., Shriner). Clubs: Chicago Congregational (pres. 1963-64, dir. and trustee 1962-65); Starcraft. Home: 1034 W Altgeld St Chicago IL 60614 Office: 11 S LaSalle St Chicago IL 60603

NEWHOUSE, EUGENE JOSEPH, photographer; b. Rockwell City, Iowa, July 7, 1905; s. Lehr and Hannah Myrtle (Parsons) N.; B.S., Iowa State U., 1935. Free lance photo journalist, 1935-37; owner, operator Newhouse Studio, Rockwell City, 1937-64. Served with USAAF, 1942-45. Mem. Iowa Local Hist. and Mus. Assn. (regional v.p. 1967-77), Iowa Soc. Preservation of Historic Landmarks (bd. dirs. 1972—), Calhoun County Hist. Soc. (curator 1961—), Alpha Phi Omega. Odd Fellow. Home: North First St Rockwell City IA 50579

NEWLIN, JOSEPH EDWARD, lawyer; b. Middletown, Ohio, Jan. 11, 1943; s. Harry Edward and Mabel Martha (Tope) N.; A.B., Wittenberg U., 1965; J.D., Case Western Res. U., 1968; m. Lillian Christine Rogers, June 19, 1965; children—John Edward, Sarah Christine, David Rogers. Admitted to Ohio bar, 1968; with legal dept. Armco Steel Corp., summer 1967; practice law, Hamilton, Ohio, 1969-72, Middletown, 1972—; mem. firm Randolph, Thomas, Froelke & Newlin, 1969-72, firm Newlin, Green & Weinrich, L.P.A., Inc., 1974-76, Newlin & Weinrich Co., L.P.A., Inc., 1976—; solicitor Village Monroe, Ohio, 1972-74; agt. Chgo. Title Ins. Co. Served with AUS, 1968. Mem. Am., Ohio, Middletown, Butler County bar assns. Clubs: Masons, Shriners. Home: 4401 Nelson Rd Middletown OH 45042 Office: 3925 Roosevelt Blvd Middletown OH 45042

NEWMAN, LOUIS EDWARD, III, veterinarian, educator; b. Schenectady, N.Y., Nov. 14, 1930; s. Louis Edward and Ruth (Sensenbrenner) N.; B.S. in Agr., U. N.H., 1952; D.V.M., Cornell U., Ithaca, N.Y., 1956; M.S. in Pathology, Mich. State U., East Lansing, 1975; m. Leslie Williams, June 9, 1955; children—Lise, Kathryn, Janet, Tracy, James, Richard; m. 2d, Jane Anne Yarhouse, Jan. 2, 1972; 1 adopted dau., Elaine. Practice vet. medicine, Worland, Wyo., 1956-57; founder, owner, operator Glasgow (Mont.) Vet. Clinic, Glasgow Vet. Supply & Flying N Ranch, 1957-69; extension project leader dept. large animal surgery and medicine Coll. Vet. Medicine, Mich. State U., 1969—. Cons. herd health Miss. State U., Starkville, 1975-76. Mem. adv. bd. Valley County (Mont.) Devel. Council, Glasgow, 1966-69; chmn. LeRoy Twp. (Mich.) Zoning Bd., Webberville, 1975-76, Planning Commn., 1976—, Zoning Bd. Appeals, 1976—. Trustee Williamston (Mich.) Community Schs. Bd. Edn. Mem. Mich. State U. Extension Specialists Assn. (dir.), Nat. Mastitis Council (dir., chmn. com. coliform mastitis research 1975-76), Am., Mich. vet. med. assns., Am. Vet. Soc. for Study Breeding Soundness (chmn. bd. 1966), Am. Assn. Bovine Practitioners, Am. Assn. Vet. Clinicians, Am. Assn. Vet. Nutritionists, Am. Assn. Extension Veterinarians, Soc. Theriogenology, Alpha Zeta, Phi Zeta, Epsilon Sigma Phi. Research on neonatal calf mortality, intestine of gnotobiotic calves, role of sawdust bedding in etiology of coliform mastitis in dairy cattle. Home: 2762 E Grand River Williamston MI 48895 Office: Vet Clinic Mich State U East Lansing MI 48824

NEWMAN, M. W., editor; b. N.Y.C., 1917; B.A. in Journalism, U. Wis., 1938; m. Nancy Newman. Formerly with Indpls. Times, Greensboro (N.C.) Daily News, Hoboken (N.J.) Observer; joined Chgo. Daily News as copyreader, 1945, successively, rewrite man, gen. assignment reporter, book editor, 1971—, editor arts and amusements dept. and Panorama mag., 1973—; editor Inland Architect mag., 1969—. Address: c/o Daily News 401 N Wabash Chicago IL 60611

NEWMAN, MERLE EDWARD, business exec.; b. Guthrie County, Iowa, Sept. 24, 1934; s. Clarence Elmer and Martha Josephina Carolina (Guttenfelder) N.; student sales and mgmt. Drake U., 1961-64; m. Gwendolyn May Dutler, Sept. 13, 1957; children—Ronald Wayne, Roger Merle, Richard Lane. Vice pres. Casey's Gen. Stores, Inc., Des Moines, 1970—; pres. Consol. Bldg. Systems, Inc., Des Moines, 1971—; owner E.T. Systems, Des Moines, 1975—; tchr. constrn. estimating and specification writing, archtl. div. Des Moines Area Community Coll. Patentee heat pump and heat recovery system. Home: 6897 2d Ave Des Moines IA 50313 Office: 1277 E Broadway Des Moines IA 50313

NEWMAN, MURIEL KALLIS STEINBERG, art collector; b. Chgo., Feb. 25, 1914; d. Maurice and Ida (Nudelman) Kallis; Art Inst. Chgo., 1932-36, Ill. Inst. Tech., 1940, U. Chgo., 1950; m. Albert H. Newman, May 14, 1955; 1 son, Glenn D. Steinberg. Painter, 1930's and 1940's; dir. 20th Century Painting and Sculpture Com. of Art Inst. Chgo., 1955-78, also mem. com. for purchasing, 1955-78; governing mem. of Art Inst. Chgo., 1955—, benefactor, 1976—; pioneer collector of Am. abstract expressionist art, 1949—. Mem. bd. govs. Landmarks Preservation Council, Chgo., 1966-78; mem. U. Chgo. Woman's Bd., 1960-78, Art Inst. Chgo. Woman's Bd., 1953—; trustee Chgo. Sch. of Architecture Found., Mus. of Contemporary Art, Chgo. Recipient Scroll Recognition of Pub. Service, U.S. Dept. of State, 1958. Mem. Chgo. Hist. Soc., Antiquarian Soc. of Art Inst. Chgo. Club: Casino (Chgo.). Address: 179 E Lake Shore Dr Chicago IL 60611

NEWMAN, NANCY BLITZSTEN, pub. relations exec.; b. Chgo.; d. Harry and Alice Eleanor (Karno) Blitzsten; student Cape Cod Theatre Sch.; B.A., B.S., U. Chgo. Coll.; m. M.W. Newman, Apr. 21, 1962. Former editor nat. directory safety films editor Nat. Safety Council, Chgo.; later staff writer Chgo. Sun-Times and Chgo. Daily News; then pub. relations staff writer U. Chgo. Hosps. and Clinics; former asst. dir. pub. relations Michael Reese Hosp. and Med. Center, Chgo.; later pub. relations dir. Ravenswood Hosp. Med. Center, Chgo.; account supr. Manning, Selvage & Lee, Chgo., 1973—. Bd. dirs. Urban Gateways, 1975-77. Mem. Publicity Club Chgo., Pub. Relations Soc. Am., Am. Soc. Hosp. Pub. Relations, Am. Hosp. Assn., Arts Club Chgo. Cookbook and food columnist Chgo Daily News; gourmet cooking writer. Home: 433 W Briar Pl Chicago IL 60657 Office: 333 N Michigan Ave Chicago IL 60601

NEWMAN, RALPH GEOFFREY, bookseller, author, cons.; b. Chgo., Nov. 3, 1911; s. Henry and Dora (Glickman) N.; Litt.D., James Milliken U. (Lincoln Coll.), 1950, Knox Coll.; LL.D., Iowa Wesleyan Coll.; Litt.D., Rockford Coll.; m. Estelle Hoffman (div.); children—Maxine (Mrs. Richard G. Brandenburg), Carol Jacqueline Parry; m. 2d, Patricia L. Simon. Founder, pres. Abraham Lincoln Book Shop, Inc., Chgo., 1933—; owner Americana House, pubs., 1947—; pres. Lincoln's New Salem Enterprises, Inc., 1952-75, Ralph Geoffrey Newman, Inc., Chgo., 1967—; appraiser, cons. rare manuscripts and archives. Pres. bd. dirs. Chgo. Pub. Library; pres. Urban Libraries Council; mem. library council U. Notre Dame; former pres. Adult Edn. Council Greater Chgo.; trustee Lincoln Meml. U., Lincoln Coll. Served with USNR, 1944-45. Recipient diploma of honor Lincoln Meml. U., 1952; Am. of Year award Independence Hall Assn., 1958; Nevins-Freeman award for Civil War history, 1975. Fellow Royal Soc. Arts London; mem. Civil War Round Table Chgo. (founder 1940), Abraham Lincoln Assn. (dir.), Ulysses S. Grant Assn. (pres.), Stephen A. Douglas Assn. (pres.), Am., Ill., Iowa, Kans., Chgo. hist. socs., Am. Legion, Am. Booksellers Assn., Bibliog. Soc. Am., Lincoln Fellowship of So. Calif., Pa., Wis., Phi Alpha Theta. Clubs: Caxton, Press, Arts; Sangamo (Springfield, Ill.). Author: (with Otto Eisenschiml) The American Iliad, 1947. Editor: The Diary of a Public Man, 1945; The Railsplitter, 1950; (with Otto Eisenschiml and E.B. Long) The Civil War, 1956; The Abraham Lincoln Story (radio series), 1958-59; Lincoln for the Ages, 1960; (with Otto Eisenschiml) Eyewitness, 1960; (with E.B. Long) The Civil War Digest, 1960; Pictorial Autobiography of Abraham Lincoln, 1962; Abraham Lincoln, An Autobiographical Narrative, 1970; Abraham Lincoln: His Story in His Own Words, 1975. Home: 175 E Delaware Pl Chicago IL 60611 Office: 18 E Chestnut St Chicago IL 60611

NEWMAN, TERRY KAY, counselor; b. St. Louis, Nov. 7, 1950; d. Frank Harris and Dorothy Mildred (Selig) Newman; B.S. in Edn., U. Tex., 1972; M.S.W., Washington U., St. Louis, 1976, M.A. in Edn., 1976. Tchr. Austin (Tex.) Ind. Sch. Dist., 1972-74: elementary sch. counselor Normandy Sch. Dist., St. Louis, 1977—; problem pregnancy counseling Reproductive Health Services; participant Masters and Johnson and Virginia Satir seminars. Mem. Am. Personnel and Guidance Assn., St. Louis Suburban Guidance Assn., NEA, Mo. Nat. Edn. Assn., St. Louis Suburban, Normandy tchrs. assns., Nat. Assn. Social Workers. Democrat. Jewish. Home: 8360 Delmar St Apt 3S St Louis MO 63124 Office: 6815 Robbins Ave St Louis MO 63133

NEWMAN, WILSON LANDESS, former psychologist, adminstr.; b. West Point, N.Y., May 30, 1905; s. William and Jean (Holman) N.; B.A., Vanderbilt U., 1926; M.A., Peabody Coll., 1928; postgrad. (Noyes scholar) U. Chgo., 1931-37; m. Helen Moore Cook, Aug. 24, 1937; children—Alice Jean (Mrs. Jay F. Mulberry), Edith, Mary. Tchr., Phillips High Sch., Birmingham, Ala., 1928-30; instr. psychology U. Chgo., 1933-42; psychologist Ill. State Employment Service, 1939-40, 42-46; instr. Englewood Evening Coll., 1941-46; supervising psychologist State Prison, Joliet Ill., 1938, 46-53; psychologist, tchr. Chgo. Bd. Edn., 1953-60; psychologist Psychol. Lab., Chgo., 1960; asst. mgr. Am. Arbitration Assn., Chgo., 1962-63; adminstrv. sec. Continental Assn. Funeral and Meml. Socs., 1965-67; mng. dir. Forty Plus of Chgo., 1961; vice-chmn. South Side Coop.-Condominium Owners Assn., 1972-73; mem. Hyde Park-Kenwood Community Conf. Founder, 1st pres. Am. Assn. Correctional Psychologists, 1951-53. Mem. Am., Ill. psychol. assn., Chgo. Psychol. Club (sec. 1935-38, chmn. program com., 1945-46, archivist 1974—). Home: 1534 E 59th St Chicago IL 60637

NEWMYER, ELDON LEE, chiropractor; b. Willard, Ohio, June 21, 1946; S. Al H. and Minta Ora (Waters) N.; student Findlay Coll., 1964-66; Dr. Chiropractic, Palmer Coll. Chiropractic, 1969; postgrad. Palmer Jr. Coll., 1969-70; m. Ardyth Alma Koeppe, Nov. 1, 1969; 1 son, Troy Michael. Practice sci. of chiropractic, Middleville, Mich., 1972-75, Kentwood, Mich., 1975—. Mem. Parker Chiropractic Research Found., 1972—. Served with AUS, 1970-71. Diplomate Nat. Bd. Chiropractic Examiners. Mem. Sacral Occipital Research Soc. (pres. Mich. chpt. 1974-75), Grand Valley Chiropractic Soc. (pres. 1977—), Middleville C. of C. (sec. 1973). Episcopalian. Home: 408 Charles St Middleville MI 49333 Office: 1500 44th St SE Kentwood MI 49508

NEWNUM, RAYMOND LAVERN, internist; b. Kingman, Ind., June 18, 1925; s. Robert P. and Sylvia Grace (Alward) N.; student Purdue U., 1943-44; B.S. in Anatomy and Physiology, Ind. U., Bloomington, 1948, M.D., 1951; M.Sc., U. Minn., 1958; m. Betty Lou Coffing, Dec. 20, 1944; children—Kathleen Sue Newnum Roetzer, Janice Marie Newnum Sbrocchi, Betsy Rae, Paul Douglas, Lisa Dawn. Rotating intern Ind. U., 1951-52; gen. practice medicine, Hagerstown, Ind., 1952-55; resident in internal medicine Mayo Found., Rochester, Minn., 1955-58; cons. in internal medicine Carle Clinic, Urbana, Ill., 1958-61; practice medicine specializing in internal medicine, Evansville, Ind., 1961-75; founder, pres. Tri-State Internal Medicine, Inc., Evansville, 1975—; pres. staff St. Mary's Hosp., 1970-71, chief of medicine, 1965-67, clin. instr. medicine, 1973-77, cons. internal medicine, 1961-77. Served with USNR, 1943-47. Diplomate Am. Bd. Internal Medicine. Fellow A.C.P. (life); mem. AMA, Ind., Vanderburgh County med. socs., Evansville (pres.), Ind., Am. socs. internal medicine. Mem. Ch. Christian Fellowship. Home: 6710 Washington Ave Evansville IN 47715 Office: 801 Saint Marys Dr Evansville IN 47715

NEWPHER, JAMES ALFRED, JR., mgmt. cons.; b. New Brighton, Pa., Nov. 14, 1930; s. James Alfred and Olive Myrtle (Houlette) N.; B.S., U. Pa., 1952; M.B.A., Wharton Sch. U. Pa., 1957; m. Mildred Taylor, Aug. 23, 1953. Indsl. engr., Corning Glass Works (N.Y.), 1957-58, plant supr., 1958-60, prodn. supt., 1960-61, plant mgr., 1961-63, dept. mgr. advance products, 1963-64; asso. Booz, Allen & Hamilton, Inc., Chgo., 1964-69; v.p., mng. officer Lamalie Assos., Chgo., 1969-73; pres., chief exec. officer Newpher-Baas & Co., Inc., Chgo., 1973—; dir. D.B. Corkey Co., The Selden Co. Served with USN, 1951-56. Decorated Purple Heart. Mem. Naval Res. Assn., Inst. Mgmt. Cons., Res. Officers Assn. Presbyn. Club: Metropolitan Chgo. Home: 1655 We-Go Trail Deerfield IL 60015 Office: 55 E Monroe St Chicago IL 60603

NEWTON, BARRY NEAL, research chemist.; b. Springfield, Ky., July 19, 1944; s. Joseph Franklin and Francis (Mattingly) N.; B.S., Campebbsville Coll., 1966; Ph.D., Purdue U., 1971; m. Michelin D. Newton; children—Sulayne Elizabeth, Matthew Neal. Teaching asst. Purdue U., 1966-69; dir. organic synthesis Lafayette (Ind.) Pharmacal. Inc., 1972—. Active Boy Scouts Am. Mem. Am. Chem. Soc., Acad. Pharmaceutical Scis., Pharmaceutical Mfgrs. Assn. Contbr. articles to profl. jours.; patentee in field. Home: 212 S 9th St Lafayette IN 47901 Office: 522 N Earl Ave Lafayette IN 47904

NEWTON, GEORGE, musician; b. Kankakee, Ill., Jan. 18, 1908; s. George Andrew and Helen Hall (Coy) N.; A.B., Princeton U., 1929; postgrad. (sch. fellow) Juilliard Sch. Music, 1929-33; m. Melba Florence Nesbit, Dec. 26, 1946; 1 dau., Lucy Park. Solo singer in recital and oratorio, 1930—; instr. voice Ball State U., 1936-74; pvt. tchr. singing, Indpls., 1933—; dir. ch. choir; lectr., lecture-recitalist at convs., workshops, 1950—. Fellow Am. Inst. Vocal Pedagogy; mem. Nat. Assn. Tchrs. Singing (regional gov., nat. dir., founder Indpls. chpt.), Music Tchrs. Nat. Assn., Am. Musicol. Soc. Republican. Presbyterian. Clubs: Indpls. Athletic, Portfolio, Parrhesian. Contbr. numerous articles on singing and composers, translations to profl. jours. Home: 747 N Graham Ave Indianapolis IN 46219 Studio: 319 N Pennsylvania St Indianapolis IN 46204

NEWTON, JOHN MARSHALL, mfg. co. exec.; b. Popejoy, Iowa, May 20, 1913; s. George and Fannie P. (Dixon) N.; student Ellsworth Jr. Coll., 1931-33; B.S., Iowa State U., 1936, Ph.D., 1941; grad. Advanced Mgmt. Program, Harvard, 1959; m. Irene E. Vogt, Apr. 29, 1941; children—Beth L. Newton Savage, Steven M., Martha S. Research fellow Iowa State U., Ames, 1937-41; research chemist Clinton (Iowa) Corn Processing Co., 1941-43, asst. research dir., 1943-50, dir. tech. service, 1951-63, tech. asst. to v.p. sales, 1964-74, market research and planning, 1974-77, mgr. regulatory compliance, 1977—. Active Community Fedn., Clinton, 1941—; active Boy Scouts Am. Mem. Am. Chem. Soc., Inst. Food Technologists, Am. Assn. Cereal Chemistry, Am. Assn. Textile Chemists and Colorists, TAPPI, AAAS, Iowa Acad. Sci., Assn. Food and Drug Ofcls. U.S. Clubs: Chemist; Clinton Engineers. Contbr. articles to profl. jours. Home: 1425 7th St NW Clinton IA 52732 Office: PO Box 340 Clinton IA 52732

NEYHART, LOUISE ALBRIGHT (MRS. CARL NEYHART), author, tchr.; b. Amboy, Ill.; d. Frederick Stuyvesant and Lillian Marie (Fitchner) Albright; student Lake Forest Coll., 1922-24; diploma Nat. Coll. Edn., 1925; m. Carl Herbert Neyhart, Sept. 24, 1927; 1 son, Frederick Albright. Tchr. Freeport (Ill.) Pub. Schs., 1925-28, substitute tchr., 1928-55; author: Henry's Lincoln, 1945; Henry Ford Engineer, 1950 (published in ten languages by U.S.I.A.); Giant of the Yards, 1952. Trustee Highland Community Coll., 1966-70; bd. dirs., charter mem., v.p. Highland Community Coll. Found., 1963—; bd. dirs. Ill. Community Coll. Bd., 1970-75, recipient plaque, 1975; trustee Freeport Pub. Library, 1965—, pres., 1972-74; mem. citizens com. U. Ill., 1970—; mem. ednl. TV commn. Ill. Bd. Higher Edn., 1976-77. Recipient Alumni Achievement award Nat. Coll. Edn., 1972; Hon. resolution Ill. Community Coll. Presidents, 1975; plaque and hon. membership Ill. Community Coll. Trustees Assn., 1975. Mem. P.E.D., Beta Sigma Phi (hon life). Home: 1309 W Lincoln Blvd Freeport IL 61032

NICHOL, FRED JOSEPH, U.S. judge; b. Sioux City, Iowa, Mar. 19, 1912; s. Ralph Edwin and Florence (Young) N.; A.B., Yankton Coll., 1933; J.D., U. S.D., 1936; LL.D. (hon.), Dakota Wesleyan U., 1975; m. Evelyn Parrish, June 2, 1939; children—Allan H., Janet M. Admitted to S.D. bar, 1936; mem. firm Hitchcock, Nichol & Lasegard, Mitchell, 1938-58; mem. S.D. Ho. of Reps. from Davison County, 1951-52, 57-58; state's atty. Davison County, 1947-51; circuit judge 4th Jud. Circuit S.D., 1959-65; U.S. dist. judge for S.D., 1965-66, chief judge, 1966—. Mem. exec. com. Legis. Research Council, 1951; S.D. del. Nat. Trial Judges Conv., 1962, 63, 64. Mem. sch. bd. and library bd., Mitchell, 1958-64; del. White House Conf. on Aging, 1961. Sec. S.D. delegation Dem. Nat. Conv., 1956. Mem. corp. bd., also trustee Yankton Coll., 1954—. Served to lt. USNR, World War II. Mem. Am. Bar Assn., Am. Judicature Soc., Phi Delta Phi. Conglist. (past chmn.). Elk, Mason (32 Shriner, K.T.), Rotarian. Home: 1100 Tomar Rd Sioux Falls SD 57105 Office: US Court House Sioux Falls SD 57101

NICHOL, IRA WESLEY, machinery co. exec.; b. Lawrence, Mass., Feb. 21, 1923; s. Wesley Ivan and Ethel Mae (Annis) N.; B.S.M.E., U. R.I., 1947; M. Automotive Engring., Chrysler Inst. Engring., 1949; m. Joan Ayer Sweeney, Aug. 3, 1946; children—Martha (Mrs. John Arthur McCallister), Jeffrey D., Bruce W., Melanie A., Margaret A. Project engr. Chrysler Corp., Detroit, 1949-51; chief engine and power train br. research and devel., Detroit Tank Arsenal, 1951-54; engring. mgr. gas turbines, Continental Aviation and Engring. Corp., 1954-63, dir. engring., Continental Motors Corp., Detroit, 1963-65, v.p. govt. mktg. Teledyne Continental Motors, 1966-70, v.p. engring. and mktg., 1970-72, v.p. and asst. gen. mgr., Gen. Products div. Teledyne Continental Motors, Warren, Mich., 1972-75. Instr. engring. Lawrence Inst. Engring., Detroit, 1948-50. Cubmaster Boy Scouts Am., 1959-60, community commr. Detroit Area council, 1960-61. Served with USNR, 1944-45. Mem. Assn. U.S. Army (pres. Detroit chpt., dir. nat. council advisers), Am. Ordnance Assn. (dir. Mich. chpt., chmn. fighting vehicle sect.), Jr. Sci. and Humanities Symposia (mem. nat. adv. com.), Engring. Soc. Detroit. Roman Catholic. Home: 910 Hawthorne St Grosse Pointe Woods MI 48236

NICHOLAS, CLEMENS, architect; b. St. Louis, Mar. 6, 1897; s. Paul and Amanda (Busch) N.; B.Arch., Wash. U., 1920; m. Elizabeth Reel Lemmon, Aug. 1, 1959; children (from previous marriage)—Nancy (Mrs. Charles H. Baumann), Jan (Mrs. J. Roger Nelson), Sue (Mrs. John A. Morrow). Architect, partner Ferrand and Fitch, St. Louis, also Dallas, 1922-29; partner Hawkins and Nicholas, Springfield, Mo., 1929-31; partner Fitch & Nicholas, St. Louis, 1945-65; artist, 1930—; one man show Monday Club, St. Louis, 1970, Mus. Sci. and Natural History, St. Louis, 1970. Chmn. architecture O'Fallon Tech. Sch., St. Louis, 1931-67. Mem. A.I.A., Ozark Artist Guild (pres. 1930-31), St. Louis Artist Guild, Acad. Profl. Artists, Soc. Independent Artists of St. Louis, Scarab, (nat. pres. 1922-23). Patentee in art field. Prin. archtl. works include University City High Sch., 1937, United Hebrew Temple 1928, Tower Grove Baptist Ch. 1960-64, St. Louis. Author: Blueprint Reading for the Building and Machine Trades. Home: 801 Sudbury Dr Clayton MO 63105

NICHOLAS, DAVID M., historian; b. Knoxville, Tenn., Oct. 11, 1939; s. David M. and Iris (Ward) N.; A.B., U. N.C., Chapel Hill, 1961; A.M., U. Calif., Berkeley, 1963; Ph.D., Brown U., 1967; m. Karen Schroeder, July 2, 1967; children—Keith, Jennifer. Mem. faculty U. Nebr., Lincoln, 1967—, prof. history, 1976—. Research tng. fellow Social Sci. Research Council, 1966; fellow younger scholars Nat. Endowment Humanities, 1969-70. Mem. Am. Hist. Assn., Mediaeval Acad. Am. Author: Town and Countryside: Social, Economic and Political Tensions in Fourteenth-Century Flanders, 1971; Stad en Platteland in de Middeleeuwen, 1971; The Medieval West, 400-1450; a Preindustrial Civilization, 1973; also numerous articles. Home: 3501 Mohawk St Lincoln NE 68510 Office: Dept History Univ Nebr Lincoln NE 68588

NICHOLAS, DIMITRI PAUL, lawyer, bus. exec.; b. Montreal, Que., Can., Aug. 18, 1914; s. Nicholas Dimitri and Margaret Emilia (Kestner) Manoilovich; came to U.S., 1919, naturalized, 1925; B.A., Washington Square Coll., N.Y.C., 1937; J.D., N.Y. U., 1940; m. July 1937; children—Colombe (Mrs. Frank Bucalo), Nicole (Mrs. Roger Greenwald), Camille, Greta, Dimitri. Admitted to Ohio bar, 1958; with Sperry Gyroscope, Lake Success, N.Y., Diehl Mfg. Co., Finderner, N.Y.; v.p., gen. mgr. B.V.D. Co., Piqua, O., 1945-60; practice law, Piqua, 1960-64; owner, chmn. bd. Orr Felt Co., Piqua, 1964—; owner, chmn. bd. Trojan Container Co., Piqua, 1974; owner, chmn. bd. Dart Internat. Group Inc., N.Y.C., 1973—. Mem. Alumni Council on Admissions for Ohio N.Y. U., 1968—. Candidate for rep. to Congress, 4th Congl. Dist., O., 1972, 74. Named Hon. Col. N.G. La., 1953. Mem. Am., Ohio State, Miami County (O.) bar assns., UN Assn. U.S., Piqua C. of C., Social Register Assn. N.Y.C., Nat. Rifle Assn., Skeet Shooting Assn., Amateur Trap Shooting Assn. Elk. Clubs: Poinciana, Beach, Palm Beach (Fla.) Yacht (Palm Beach); Dayton Racquet; Piqua Country. Home: 10789 Hardin Rd Piqua OH 45356 Office: 750 S Main St Piqua OH 45356 also 417 E 50th St New York City NY 10022 also 150 S Ocean Palm Beach FL

NICHOLAS, GEORGE WALLACE, meteorologist; b. Vienna, W.Va., Oct. 18, 1927; s. Hosea Howard and Tina Jamima (Duncan) N.; B.S. in Mathematics magna cum laude, Fairmont State Coll., 1960; M.S. in Meteorology, Pa. State U., 1962; m. Elizabeth Ann Walters, June 7, 1958; children—Michael George, Neal Thomas. Research meteorologist lab. for atmospheric and biol. scis. NASA Goddard Space Flight Center, Greenbelt, Md., 1962-65; project mgr. HRB-Singer, Inc., Rome, N.Y., 1965-67; research meteorologist, computer programmer Control Data Corp. Research Div., Mpls., 1967-72; supervising meteorologist environ. div. Sargent and Lundy, Engrs., Chgo., 1972-74; asso., cons. environ. div. atmospheric services Dames & Moore, Park Ridge, Ill., 1974—. Served with USN, 1945-48. Recipient Outstanding Student award of Am. Legion, Fairmont State Coll., 1960; Univ. Corp. fellow, 1960-61. Mem. Am. Meteorol. Soc. (certified cons. Meteorologist), Air Pollution Control Assn., Am. Nuclear Soc., (chmn. standards working group), Nat. Council Indsl. Meteorologists (nat. sec.-treas.), Sigma Xi. Eastern Orthodox. Contbr. articles to profl. jours. Home: 822 Highview Ave Glen Ellyn IL 60137 Office: 1550 Northwest Hwy Park Ridge IL 60068

NICHOLAS, ROBERT LEON, educator; b. Lebanon, Oreg., Dec. 10, 1937; s. Elmer Leon and Luella Lillian (Haberling) N.; B.A., U. Oreg., 1959, M.A. (NDEA fellow), 1965, Ph.D., 1967; postgrad. U. Calif., Los Angeles, summer 1961, U. Madrid, 1963-64; m. Carole Ann Roberts, June 11, 1967; children—Scott Allen, Paul Elliot. Tchr., Pacoima (Calif.) Jr. High Sch., 1960-61; teaching asst., fellow U. Oreg., 1961-65; instr. U. Wis., Madison, 1965-67, asst. prof. Spanish, 1967-71, asso. prof., 1971-76, prof., 1976—, chmn. dept. Spanish and Portuguese, summers 1973-75, 77. U.Wis.-Madison Grad. Sch. grantee, 1969, 75. Mem. Modern Lang. Assn., Am. Assn. Tchrs. Spanish and Portuguese. Democrat. Unitarian. Author: El mundo de hoy, 1971; The Tragic Stages of Antonio Buero Vallejo, 1972; (with Eduardo Neale-Silva) En Camino!, 1977, Adelante!, 1977. Home: 2126 Chadbourne Ave Madison WI 53705 Office: Dept Spanish and Portuguese U Wis Madison WI 53706

NICHOLS, RONALD LEE, surgeon; b. Chgo., June 25, 1941; s. Peter Raymond and Jane Eleanor (Johnson) N.; M.D., U. Ill., 1966, M.S., 1970; m. Elsa Elaine Johnson, Dec. 4, 1964; children—Kimberly Jane, Matthew Bennett. Intern U. Ill. Hosp., Chgo., 1966-67, resident surgery, instr., 1967-72; asst. prof. surgery U. Ill. Med. Sch., 1972-75; asso. prof. U. Health Scis. Chgo. Med. Sch., 1975-77, dir. surg. edn., 1975-77; Henderson prof. surgery Tulane U. Sch. Medicine, New Orleans, 1977—; attending surgeon Tulane Med. Center Hosp., Charity Hosp. La.; cons. surgeon VA Hosp., Alexandria, Va., Huey P. Long Hosp., Pineville, La., Louie Kemp Charity Hosp., Independence, La. Mem. exec. bd. Westminster House, Chgo., 1974—. Recipient Med. Council Teaching award U. Ill. Med. Sch., 1972; Bd. Trustees award for research U. Health Scis./Chgo. Med. Sch., 1977, Clin. Prof. of Year award, 1977. Diplomate Am. Bd. Surgery, Nat. Bd. Med. Examiners. Fellow A.C.S.; mem. Central, Midwest surg. assns., Ill., Chgo. surg. socs., AMA, Assn. VA Surgeons, N.Y. Acad. Sci., Inst. Medicine of Chgo., Soc. Surgery Alimentary Tract, Assn. Acad. Surgery, Collegium Internationale and Chirurgiae Digestivae, Warren H. Cole Soc., Sigma Xi. Lutheran. Mem. editorial adv. bd. Guidelines to Antibiotic Therapy; editorial bd. Rev. Surgery. Contbr. chpts. to med. books, articles to med. jours. Home: 1521 7th St New Orleans LA 70115 Office: Dept Surgery Tulane Med Sch 1430 Tulane Ave New Orleans LA 70112

NICHOLS, RUTH ANNETTE, artist, educator; b. Columbus, Ohio, Jan. 21, 1919; d. Robert O. and Annette L. (Wells) Nichols; B.F.A., Ohio State U., 1941; postgrad. Northwestern U., 1946-48, Columbia, 1949, Ohio No. U., 1955-56, 62, John Herron Art Inst., 1960, U. Toledo, 1957-65, 67. Asst. childrens librarian Hoyt Pub. Library, Saginaw, Mich., 1941-42; free lance artist, 1941-45; cartographer Pure Oil Co., Saginaw, 1942-46, jr. geologist, Chgo., 1946-48; med. sec. Kenton (Ohio) Physicians Group, 1951-55; art supr. Exempted Village Schs., Tipp City, Ohio, 1955-56; tchr. Ohio history, girls health Ellis Jr. High Sch., Kenton, 1956-57; tchr. art Findlay (Ohio) City Schs., 1957—, Tobe art cons. jr. high schs., 1970-71; exhibited in group shows Ohio State Fair, Columbus, 1937, So. Hotel Galleries, Columbus, 1940, Hayes Hall Gallery, Columbus, 1940, 41, Women's Club, Saginaw, 1942, Harriet McCormick YWCA, Chgo., 1946, Little Gallery Tchrs. Coll. Columbia, 1949, Findlay High Sch. Gallery, 1964, Findlay Art League at Imperial Motel, 1966, 67, Lima (Ohio) Art Assn., 1967. Co-chmn. Ohio Council Human Resources. Mem. Ohio Fedn. Republican Womens Orgns. Mem. Nat., Ohio, Findlay, Donnell (past sec.-treas.) edn. assns., Nat. Western, Ohio art edn. assns., Am. Soc. Aesthetics, Internat. Soc. for Edn. through Art, Brit. Soc. Aesthetics, Hardin County Hist. Soc., Inst. for Study Art in Edn., Lima Art Assn., Toledo Mus. Art, Ohio State U. Alumni Assn., Hardin County State U. Assn. (past sec.), AAUW, Delta Kappa Gamma. Methodist. Mem. Order Eastern Star (pres. Past Matron Assn. Kenton, past trustee, matron Latham chpt.). Club: Minerva (past treas., program chmn. Kenton). Contbr. to Creative Year Book Ohio State U., 1941. Home: 235 Rector Ave Findlay OH 45840 Office: 200 W Main Cross St Findlay OH 45840

NICHOLS, THEODORE GEORGE, hosp. engr.; b. Chgo., July 27, 1927; s. Michael Feodor and Sophia (Lewandowski) N.; student Wright Jr. Coll., 1950-53, Ill. Inst. Tech., 1956-61: m. Barbara McKillip, Mar. 14, 1975; children by previous marriage—Michael J., Julie Ann, Theodore George. Supt., Paschen Contractors, Ill. and Ind., 1947-56; dir. phys. plant Ill. Inst. Tech. Research Inst., Chgo., 1956-69; dir. engring. Rush Presbyn. St. Luke's Med. Center, Chgo., 1969—. Deacon, sec. council St. Andrews Ch., 1966-68; com. chmn., instl. rep. Chgo. Area Council Boy Scouts Am., 1967-68. Mem. Am. Hosp. Assn., Inst. Plant Maintenance, Western Soc. Engrs., Chgo. Supts. Assn. Supervised constrn. 1st indsl. nuclear reactor, 1955. Home: 111 Fernwood Dr Glenview IL 60025 Office: 1753 W Congress Pkwy Chicago IL 60612

NICHOLS, THOMAS HOGAN, steel fabricating co. exec.; b. Kansas City, Mo., Feb. 14, 1926; s. Harold F. and Bess V. (Hogan) N.; B.S., Ind. U., 1950; B.S. in Metallurgy, Purdue U., 1959; bus. certificate U. Chgo., 1962; m. Patricia A. Young, June 7, 1952; children—Patricia J., Susan T. Salesman, U.S. Steel Corp., Chgo., 1950-53; quality control supr. Taylor Forge & Pipe Co., Gary, Ind., 1953-55; asst. supt. prodn. control Youngstown Steel Co., East Chicago, Ind., 1955-70; exec. v.p. Sherman-Reynolds Co., Chgo., 1972—; dir. 240 Venture Land Devel. Co. Adviser Jr. Achievement, Chgo.; cons. Dawson Skill Center, Chgo.; bd. dirs. Chgo. State U.; mem. Joint Hosp. Fund Com. Lake County (Ind.), 1972-74. Served with U.S. Army, 1944-46. Recipient Boss of Yr. award Hammond (Ind.) Jr. C. of C., 1964; certificate of merit Jr. Achievement, Chgo., 1960. Mem. Am. Iron and Steel Inst., Ind. U. Alumni Club, Midwest Alumni Club U. So. Calif., Parents Club U. So. Calif. Republican. Presbyterian. Clubs: Masons, Shriner. Home: 5455 Taney Pl Merrillville IN 46410

NICHOLS, WILLIAM CURTIS, JR., marital therapist, psychologist; b. Fayette, Ala., Apr. 16, 1929; s. William Curtis and Eva (Hargett) N.; A.B., U. Ala., 1953; Ed.D., Columbia U. Tchrs. Coll., 1960; NSF fellow, U. Colo., summer 1963; postdoctoral fellow Merrill-Palmer Inst., Detroit, 1963-64; m. Alice Louise Mancil, May 29, 1954; children—Alice Camille, William Mancill, David Paul. Mem. faculty U. Ala., Birmingham, 1960-63, Samford U., Birmingham, 1963-65, Merrill-Palmer Inst., 1965-69, Advanced Behavioral Sci. Center, Grosse Pointe, Mich., 1969-72; pvt. practice psychology and marriage counseling, Grosse Pointe, 1969-73; prof. home and family life Fla. State U., Tallahassee, 1973—; lectr. Eastern Mich. U., Ypsilanti, 1970-71; mem. mental health com. Mayor Detroit Commn. Children and Youth, 1966-68, mem. health com., 1968-69. Served with AUS, 1948-49. Recipient Service award Ala. Assn. Mental Health, 1962. Fellow Am. Assn. Marriage and Family Counselors (spl. award 1976), Am. Orthpsychiat. Assn.; mem. Am. Psychol. Assn., Nat. Council Family Relations (dir., exec. com., pres. 1976-77), Am. Sociol. Assn., AAAS. Presbyn. Editor: Marriage and Family Therapy (A Reader), 1974; The Family Coordinator, 1970-75, Jour. Marriage and Family Counseling, 1974-76. Home: 405 North Fox Hills Bloomfield Hills MI 48013 Office: Suite 379 30400 Telegraph Rd Birmingham MI 48010

NICHOLSON, GARY LEWIS, physician; b. Clovis, N.Mex., Aug. 8, 1945; s. Alvin Lewis and Marcelene (Powell) N.; A.B., Miami U., Oxford, Ohio, 1967; M.D., U. Ky., 1971; m. Shirley Jean Hooper, Dec. 20, 1969; children—David Scott, Jennifer Dawn. Intern, resident in internal medicine Charles F. Kettering Med. Center, Dayton, Ohio, 1971-74; fellow in med. oncology M.D. Anderson Hosp. and Tumor Inst., Houston, 1974-76, faculty asso., 1976-77; practice medicine specializing in oncology, Dayton, 1977—; asst. prof. medicine Wright State U. Med. Coll., Dayton, 1977—; instr. Kettering Med. Center, St. Elizabeth Hosp., Dayton. Am. Cancer Soc. fellow, 1974; diplomate Am. Bd. Internal Medicine. Mem. AMA, Ohio Med. Assn., Montgomery County Med. Soc., Dayton Soc. Internal Medicine, Dayton Oncology Club. Methodist. Home: 2264 Berry Creek Dr Dayton OH 45440 Office: 2600 Far Hills St Dayton OH 45429

NICHOLSON, NANCY VIOLA SNIDER, educator; b. Lachine, Mich., May 28, 1923; d. John William and Edna (Mills) Snider; B.A., U. Mich., 1946, M.A., 1947, Ph.D., 1962; m. Fred Nicholson, May 24, 1967 (div. Oct. 1968). English instr. Iowa State Tchrs. Coll., Cedar Falls, 1947-48; instr. Alpena (Mich.) Community Coll., 1953-54; asst. prof. U. N.Y. State Tchrs. Coll., Cortland, N.Y., 1955-56; instr. supr. Columbia Thcrs. Coll., Afghanistan, 1956-57; instr. Tufts U., Medford, Mass., 1957-60; asso. prof. Clarion State Coll., Clarion, Pa., 1963-66; asso. prof. Wis. State U., LaCrosse, 1966-67; lectr. Eastern Mich. U., Ypsilanti, 1967-69; prof. English, So. U., Baton Rouge, 1969-71; research on folklore, Lachine, Mich., 1971-74; lectr. U. Isfahan (Iran), 1974-76; vis. prof. grad. studies U. Paraiba (Brazil), 1976—. Seminar dir. Ford Found., U. Pitts. summer 1964. Founded library in South India, 1954, social work in India, 1954. Mem. Hindustani Assn., U. Mich. (pres. 1954), Modern Lang. Assn., Coll. English Assn., AAUW, AAUP, League of Women Voters. Contbr. articles in field to profl. jours. Home: Lachine MI 49753

NICKEL, THOMAS BERNARD, publishing co. exec.; b. Chgo., June 20, 1925; s. Thomas August and Sylvia (Gruelich) N.; student Hampden Sydney Coll., 1943, Cornell U., 1944; B.S., Northwestern U., 1948; postgrad. U. Chgo., 1958; m. Vivian F. Nannenborn, May 6, 1950;children—Thomas E., Robert J., James E. Salesman, Curtiss Candy Co., 1948-50; salesman Rand McNally & Co., Chgo., 1951-65; pres. Baldwin Cooke Co., Chgo., 1956-75, chmn. bd., 1975—, dir., 1957—; v.p., dir. Saber Mgmt. Systems, Alhambra, Cal.; pres. Knobbs Corp., Milw., 1966-75, chmn. bd., 1975—; chmn. Tex. High Reach Equipment Co., Dallas. Served to lt. (j.g.) USNR, 1943-46. Mem. Direct Mail Advt. Assn., Mail Advt. Club Chgo., Advt. Splty. Assn., Phi Kappa Sigma. Clubs: Lake Forest (dir.), Metropolitan (Chgo.). Home: 1044 E Walden Ln Lake Forest IL 60045 Office: 5714 W Dempster St Morton Grove IL 60053

NICKELSON, HARRY EDWARD, mktg. research co. exec.; b. Spring Lake, Wis., Sept. 24, 1915; s. Emil J. and Ellen C. (Christensen) N.; student Pere Marquette Normal, 1933-34, U. Mich., 1934-36, LaSalle Extension U., 1936-39; m. Ruth G. Faust, Dec. 26, 1941; 1 dau., Jacqueline. Accountant George Rossiter & Co., Public Accounting, 1937-38; landscaping Nickelson Bros., Ludington, Mich., 1938-39; v.p., dir. Universal Farm Sales Inc., Saginaw, Mich., 1952—; exec. v.p., dir. A.C. Nielsen Co., Chgo., 1941—. Mem. Am. Mktg. Assn. Club: McHenry (Ill.) County. Home: 1041 Timber Ln Lake Forest IL 60045 Office: Nielsen Plaza Northbrook IL 60062

NICKERSON, MAX ALLEN, mus. ofcl.; b. Maryville, Mo., July 18, 1938; s. Ivan James and Ruby (Wineinger) N.; A.B., Central Coll., 1960; postgrad. U. Tex., 1962-63; Ph.D., Ariz. State U., 1968; m. Carolyn Yvonne Bartee, Aug. 6, 1960; 1 dau., Cheryl Anne. Teaching asst. Ariz. State U., Tempe, 1960-61, 61-62; faculty Ark. State U., State University, 1968-70, U. Wis., Milw., 1973-77; head vertebrate div. Milw. Pub. Mus., 1971—, chmn. scientific staff, 1971-73. Ariz. State U. grantee, 1965-67, 68-71; Ariz. Acad. Sci. grantee, 1966-67; Friends of Mus. grantee, 1971-72, 77, Fred Ott Research Fund grantee, 1971-72; James L. Kuehn Research Fund grantee, 1973, 74, Stiemke Found. grantee, 1976, Karl Schmidt Research Fund grantee, 1976. Fellow Am. Inst. Chemists; mem. A.A.A.S., Am. Inst. Biol.

Scis., Soc. for Study of Amphibians and Reptiles (sec. 1971-73, bd. dirs. 1971-74, chmn. 1977), Wis. Herpetological Soc. (pres. 1972—), Internat. Platform Assn., Internat. Soc. Toxicology, Am. Soc. Ichthyologists and Herpetologists, Herpetologists League, Southwestern Assn. Naturalists, Am. Assn. Zool. Parks and Aquaria, Southwestern Herpetological Soc., Ecol. Soc. Am., Phila. Herpetological Soc., Am. Soc. Zoologists, Md., Ky. St. Louis herpetological socs., British Soc. Herpetologists, Am. Assn. Zoo Veterinarians, Kan. Acad. Sci., N.Y. Herpetological Soc., Am. Inst. Chemists, Chgo. Herpetological Soc., Beta Beta Beta, Sigma Xi. Contbr. articles to profl. jours. Originator TV series on Mo. Wildlife, KDRO-TV, 1956, Zoo World, KOMU-TV, 1964-65, series on animal ecology, KY-TV, 1965, Desert Denizens, KAET-TV, 1966. Editor Herpetological Review, 1974—. Home: 4622 S 20th St Milwaukee WI 53221 Office: Milw Mus Milwaukee WI 53233

NICODEM, HAROLD ERNEST, ins. co. exec.; b. Darjeeling, India, May 8, 1926; s. Frank and Ruby Clarissa (Fairchild) N.; student Wheaton Coll., 1947-50; m. Margery P. Knecht, Dec. 18, 1946; children—Phyllis (Mrs. John Dovgin), Carolyn, Janet (Mrs. Kent Smith), Leslie, Harold Ernest. Agt.-mgr. Prudential Ins. Co., Chgo., 1950-54; mgr. Servicemaster Inc., Lyle, Ill., Ill. broker mgr. Southland Ins., 1961-65; brokerage mgr. Continental Assurance Co., Chgo., 1965-68: exec. v.p. Central Security Ins. Co., Rolling Meadows, Ill., 1968-71, pres., 1971-77; exec. v.p. No. Ill. Farmers Ins. Co. Arlington Heights, Ill., 1977—; dir. Bank Rolling Meadows, Bond Safeguard Ins. Co., Glenview, Ill., United Bus. and Profl. Services, Elmhurst, Ill.; chmn. Interlink Inc., Wheaton, Ill. Bd. dirs., treas. Timberlee Christian Center Wis., East Troy. Served with USMCR, 1943-46. Club: Lions. Home: 165 Harbor Rd Barrington IL 60010 Office: 2120 E NW Hwy Arlington Heights IL 60004

NICOL, SHELDON SPENCER, physician; b. Decatur, Ill., Dec. 18, 1942; s. Melvin James and Zona Zae (Nicol) N.; B.A. with honors, Ill. Wesleyan U., 1964; M.D., Washington U., St. Louis, 1968; m. Susan Antoinette Hjort, Nov. 14, 1970; 1 dau., Diana Renee. Fellow, St. Thomas Hosp., London, Eng., 1967; intern Alameda County Hosps., Oakland, Calif., 1968-69, mem. staff, 1969; resident in internal medicine Abington (Pa.) Hosp., 1972-74; specialist in internal medicine Joliet (Ill.) Internists, 1974—; mem. staff Silver Cross Hosp., St. Joseph's Hosp. Served to capt. M.C., U.S. Army, 1969-71. Decorated Bronze Star, Army Commendation medal. Diplomate Am. Bd. Internal Medicine. Mem. AMA, Am. Coll. Physicians, Will-Grundy County Med. Soc., Phi Kappa Phi, Beta Beta Beta. Republican. Office: 58 E Clinton St Joliet IL 60431

NICOLETTE, ANTHONY ORLAND, coach, assn. exec.; b. Leetonia, Ohio, Feb. 17, 1902; s. Guliano Anthonio and Maria Michele (Ricci) N.; B.P.E., Am. Coll. Phys. Edn., 1926; postgrad. Northwestern U., 1930, U. Ill., 1960; m. Rose Anna Skaloud, Jan. 28, 1928; children—Robert Lane, John Anthony. Dir. playground Chgo. Bd. Edn., 1923-24; phys. edn. tchr., coach Chgo. parochial schs., 1925-60; chmn. track and field ofcls. certification com. Central AAU, Chgo., 1972—, pres., 1974—. Coach, dir. various capacities Chgo. Boys Clubs, 1924-68, dean phys. edn., 1935-60; mem. nat. com. health and phys. edn. Boys Clubs Am., 1957-60; mem. Sullivan Award Com., 1974-75, panel Pres.'s Commn. on Olympic Sports, 1975-76; mem. Pres.'s Conf. Fitness Am. Youth; ofcl. numerous nat. and internat. track meets. Mem. adv. com. recreation aide, Coll. DuPage, 1969—. Recipient Citizens Greater Chgo. award, 1957; Distinguished Service award Kiwanis Club, Chgo., 1960; Humanitarian Service award Boys Clubs Am., 1962; Fred Steers Meml. award Central AAU, 1977; numerous other awards. Mem. Nat. Amateur Athletic Union (life, Golden Service award, nat. exec. com. 1975-76, certificate of appreciation 1977), AAHPER, Am. Camping Assn., Phi Epsilon Kappa. Club: Kiwanis (hon. pres. Logan Sq. 1965-77). Home: 325 W 41st St Downers Grove IL 60615 Office: CAAU 205 W Wacker Chicago IL 60606

NIEBLER, CHESTER JOHN, lawyer; b. Milw., Jan. 5, 1915; s. John J. and Margaret (Burkard) N.; Ph.B. summa cum laude, Marquette U., 1937; J.D. magna cum laude, 1939; m. Lorraine M. Millmann, Mar. 30, 1940; children—John H., Anne N. (Mrs. James McNamara), Joseph C., Paul F. Admitted to Wis. bar, 1939; practiced in Milw., 1945-69, Menomonee Falls, 1969—; ct. commr., 1961—; dir. numerous corps.; lectr. legal aspects profl. archtl. and engring. liability. Bd. govs. St. Thomas More Soc. Mem. Wis., Milw., Waukesha, bar assns., Am. Trial Lawyers Assn., Am. Judicature Soc., Woolsack Soc. (sec. 1966, dir. 1966-67), Marquette Law Alumni Assn. (dir. 1963-70), Alpha Sigma Nu, Delta Sigma Rho, Sigma Nu Phi. Club: Kiwanis (dir. 1956-58). Co-editor Marquette Law Rev., 1938-39. Home: N94 W21825 Schlei Rd Menomonee Falls WI 53051 Office: PO Box 444 Menomonee Falls WI 53051

NIEBYLSKI, LEONARD MARTIN, physicist; b. Detroit, Nov. 11, 1925; s. Joseph M. and Sophia (Kalenchuk) N.; B.S., Wayne State U., 1949, M.S., 1952; postgrad. U. Mich., 1953-54, U. Calif. at Los Angeles, 1961, Harvard, 1972; m. Jeannette S. Horozaniecki, July 31, 1950; children—David, Richard, Margaret, Bruce, Mary, Roger, Charles, Mark, Amy. Research physicist Pioneering Research div., Ethyl Corp., Ferndale, Mich.; 1950-67, asso., 1967-71, sr. research asso., 1971—. Served with USAAF, 1944-46. Mem. Am. Soc. Testing and Materials, Electron Microscopy Soc. Patentee in field. Contbr. articles to profl. jours. Home: 32365 Robinhood St Birmingham MI 48010 Office: 1600 W 8 Mile Rd Ferndale MI 48220

NIEDERHAUSER, DALE RAY, airline exec.; b. Marshalltown, Iowa, July 20, 1946; s. Glen Truman and Esther Lillian (Farr) N.; student pub. schs., Cedar Falls, Iowa; m. Sandra Kay Billman, Feb. 27, 1965; children—Christopher Dale, Robert Craig, Michael Glen. Linesman, Niederhauser Airways, Waterloo, Iowa, 1964-65, line chief, 1966-67, chief pilot, gen. mgr., 1968-70, v.p., 1970-73, pres., 1974—. Mem. citizen adv. council Iowa Dept. Transp.; pres. Softball Assn., 1974-75. Mem. Pilots Internat. Assn., Aircraft Owners and Pilots Assn., Air Force Assn., Nat. Fedn. Ind. Bus., Nat. Aviation Trades Assn., Quiet Birdmen. Clubs: Sertoma (pres. 1971-72), Porky's Red Carpet, U. No. Iowa Athletic (v.p. 1977-78, pres. 1978-79). Home: 3014 Vally High Dr Cedar Falls IA 50613 Office: Box 2127 Waterloo IA 50705

NIEHAUS, WILLIAM ROGER, newspaper exec.; b. Cin., June 10, 1932; s. George Anthony and Lorine Rosemary (Bennett) N.; B.S. in Physics Xavier U., 1954; M.S. in Physics (Univ. fellow), St. Louis U., 1956; m. Marian Camille Martinson, Oct. 21, 1961; children—Theodore, David, Jennifer, Thomas, Juliet, Natalie. Engring. cons. Allstates Design & Devel. Co., Cin., 1959-61; engring. physicist Thompson-Ramo-Wooldridge Co., Cleve., 1961; head of aerothermodynamics systems analysis Aeronca Mfg. Corp., Middletown, Ohio, 1961-65; engring. cons. Belcan Corp., Montgomery, Ohio, 1965-70; research dir. E.W. Scripps Co., Cin., 1970—. Bd. dirs. Montgomery Baseball Assn., 1972—. Served as 1st lt. ordnance U.S. Army, 1956-58. Mem. Am. Inst. Aeros. and Astronautics, Am. Inst. Indsl. Engrs., Internat. Newspaper Promotion Assn., Am. Newspaper Printing Assn., Nat. Rifle Assn. (life), Sigma Xi. Republican. Roman Catholic. Patentee. Home: 10240 Pendery Dr Cincinnati OH 45242 Office: 1100 Central Trust Tower Cincinnati OH 45202

NIELANDER, RUTH MARIE, librarian; b. Lansing, Iowa, Jan. 27, 1912; d. Harry Carl and Elsie (Hufschmidt) Nielander; B.S., U. Minn., 1933. Supr. Mayo Clinic, Rochester, Minn., 1936-43; reference librarian Nat. Safety Council, Chgo., 1943-51; librarian Kemper Ins. Cos., Long Grove, Ill., 1951-76. Mem. Spl. Libraries Assn. (pres. Ill. chpt. 1950-52, consultation chmn. 1962—; mem. nat. nominating com. 1951-52, 61-62, chmn. nominating com. 1969-70, chpt. liaison officer 1956-60, dir. 1965-68, Hall of Fame award 1976), Am., Chgo. (mem. bd. 1950-52) assns. law librarians, P.E.O., Delta Zeta. Presbyterian. Co-author: Special Libraries; A Guide for Management. Home: 1206 N Dale Ave Arlington Heights IL 60004

NIELD, JOHN B., counselor educator; b. Montpelier, Idaho, Feb. 23, 1941; s. LaVar B. and Rhena Emily (Wilkes) N.; B.A., Idaho State U., 1967, M.A., 1969, Ed.D., 1976; m. Karla Anne Nelson, July 5, 1963; children—Kip J., Tani Kim, Suzette. Counselor Snake River Jr. High Sch., Blackfoot, Idaho, 1968-69; sch. psychologist White Pine County Schs., East Ely, Nev., 1969-70; dir. child devel.-family counseling, also instr. psychology No. Nev. Community Coll., Elko, 1970-74; asst. prof. psychology, counseling edn. Pittsburg (Kans.) State U. 1976—; cons. in field Bd. dirs. Head Start, Elko, 1973-74. Mem. Am., Kans. personnel and guidance assns., Assn. Counselor Edn. and Supervision, Kans. Assn. Counselor Edn. and Supervision, N.Am. Soc. Adlerian Psychology (state rep. 1976—). Mem. Ch. Jesus Christ of Latter-Day Saints. Home: 401 W Quincy St Pittsburg KS 66762 Office: Room 134 Russ Hall Pittsburg State U Pittsburg KS 66762

NIELSEN, ANNA FRANCES NIELSEN (MRS. ERNEST DAVID NIELSEN), church worker; b. Chgo.; d. Niels Peter and Jensine (Thomsen) Nielsen; B.A., Carthage Coll., 1927; m. Ernest David Nielsen, June 22, 1930; children—Ernest Wismar, Paul Christian, Brian David. Tchr. English, Chgo. Luth. High Sch., 1927-30; study supr. North Park Acad., Chgo., 1945-46; instr. English Grand View Coll., Des Moines, 1964-72. Mem. Bd. of World Missions, Luth. Ch. Am., 1964-76; mem. Am. Bd. of Santal Mission, 1948-72, mem. exec. com., 1953-64; mem. Council Ecumenical Studies, 1956-60; mem. gen. assembly Nat. Council Chs. of Christ in U.S.A., 1954-58; mem. bd. mgrs. United Ch. Women, 1955-64, bd. dirs. Des Moines council 1957-65, pres. Des Moines council, 1962; bd. dirs. Iowa United Ch. Women, 1960-65; mem. com. on world missions Joint Commn. on Luth. Unity, 1957-62, mem. com. Women's Work Joint commn., 1957-62; bd. dirs. Luth. Women's Service Fedn., Des Moines, 1953-66, pres. bd., 1957; bd. dirs. Iowa Luth. Ch. Women, 1962-66, pres. Central dist., 1974-76. Mem. Gov.'s Com. for UN Day Observance in Iowa, 1964-67; active various community drives. Mem. AAUW, P.E.O., Pi Kappa Delta. Republican. Club: Des Moines Women's. Contbr. to Luth. Ency. Home: 7312 Madison Ave Urbandale IA 50322

NIELSEN, ARTHUR CHARLES, business exec.; b. Chgo., Sept. 5, 1897; s. Rasmus and Harriet Burr (Gunn) N.; B.S. in E.E., U. Wis., 1918, D.Sc. (hon.), 1974; m. Gertrude B. Smith, June 15, 1918; children—Arthur Charles, Margaret Ann, Philip Robert, Barbara Harriet, Virginia Beatrice. Elec. engr. The Isko Co., Chicago, 1919-20; engr. H.P. Gould Co., Chgo., 1920-23; pres. A.C. Nielsen Co., 1923-57, chmn., 1957-75, chmn. exec. com., 1976—, mktg. research and bus. services, operators of the Nielsen Retail Index Services, TV Index Services, Nielsen Coupon Clearing House, others; chmn. A.C. Nielsen Internat., Inc., A.C. Nielsen Co., Can., Ltd., A.C. Nielsen Pty., Ltd. Australia and New Zealand, A.C. Nielsen Co. (Pty.) Ltd., Johannesburg, S. Africa, A.C. Nielsen (Nederland) B.V., A.C. Nielsen (Argentina) S.A., A.C. Nielsen Co., G.m.b.H., Germany, A.C. Nielsen Mgmt. Services Switzerland, A.C. Nielsen S.A., Switzerland, A.C. Nielsen Co., France, A.C. Nielsen Company, Japan, A.C. Nielsen Co., Ges. M. B.H. Austria, A.C. Nielsen Prodn. S.A., Switzerland, A.C. Nielsen Co., Italy, A.C. Nielsen Co., Spain, A.C. Nielsen Co. Mexico, A.C. Nielsen Co. Portugal; dir. A.C. Nielsen Co. Ltd. (Oxford), A.C. Nielsen Co. (Belgium) S.A., A.C. Nielsen of Ireland, Ltd. Served as ensign USNRF, World War I. Awarded 1936 Silver Medal, Ann. Advt. Awards Com.; award by Chgo. Federated Advt. Club, 1941; Paul D. Converse award, 1951, award, 1970, both Am. Marketing Assn., Hall of Fame in Distribution, 1953; knight Order Dannebrog, 1961; Parlin Meml. award, 1963; Internat. Advt. Assn.'s annual award, 1966; elected to Hall of Fame in Tennis, 1971. Mem. Tau Beta Pi, Eta Kappa Nu, Sigma Phi. Clubs: West Side Tennis (Forest Hills, L.I., N.Y.); University (N.Y.); Indian Hill (Winnetka). Home: 720 Ardsley Rd Winnetka IL 60093 Office: A C Nielsen Co Nielsen Plaza Northbrook IL 60062

NIELSEN, ARTHUR CHARLES, JR., marketing research exec.; b. Chgo., Apr. 8, 1919; s. Arthur Charles and Gertrude (Smith) N.; Ph.B., U. Wis., 1941; m. Patricia McKnew, June 24, 1944; children—Arthur Charles III, John Christopher, Elizabeth Kingsbury. With A.C. Nielsen Co., Chgo., 1945—, adminstrv. v.p., 1950-53, exec. v.p., 1953-57, pres., 1957-76, chmn., 1976—; dir. Gen. Binding Corp., Walgreen Co., Harris Trust & Savs. Bank, Hercules, Inc., Motorola, Inc., Marshe Plehennan Co. Dir. Fair Campaign Practices Com. Cons., U.S. Govt. mission to Italy, 1952, OEEC, France, 1953, Japan, 1955, Israel, 1958, India, 1960, Middle East, 1961; mem. nat. marketing adv. com. U.S. Dept. Commerce; mem. Pres.'s Com. on Health Edn.; nat. adv. council Peace Corps; pres. Adv. Council for Minority Enterprise; chmn. adv. com. on privacy and confidentiality U.S. Census Bur.; mem. U.S. Adv. Commn. on Info. Bd. dirs. Ill. Children's Home and Aid Soc., Northwestern Meml. Hosp., Alliance to Save Energy, Jr. Achievement, Chgo., Advt. Council, Advt. Research Found., Nat. Health Council; trustee U. Chgo.; mem. bus. adv. council Grad. Sch. Bus., Northwestern U., U. Wis. Served to maj., C.E., AUS, 1941-45. Mem. Nat. Planning Council, Mgmt. Exec. Soc., U. Wis. Alumni Assn., Phi Eta Sigma, Phi Kappa Phi, Beta Gamma Sigma, Sigma Phi. Clubs: Chicago, Commonwealth, Economic (past pres.), Casino, Indian Hill, Racquet, Commercial (Chgo.). Home: 1122 Pelham Rd Winnetka IL 60093 Office: AC Nielsen Co Nielsen Plaza Northbrook IL 60062

NIELSEN, CHARLES PAUL, woodlands exec.; b. Sault Ste Marie, Mich., Jan. 31, 1926; s. Paul Jorgeson and Agnes (Thornhill) N.; B.S., Mich. Tech. U., 1950; m. Nancy Ann Wandler, Mar. 20, 1948; children—Bruce, Charlene, Gunnar. Forester aid U.S. Forest Service, Colo., 1950; scaler Nat. Container Corp., 1951-52, camp supt., 1952-53, woodyard supt., 1953-54, woodlands mgr., 1954-58; v.p., gen. mgr. Owens-Ill., Bahama Islands, 1960-65, v.p., gen. mgr. woodlands, Toledo, O., 1966-74, v.p., gen. mgr. Kraft Mill Operations, Toledo, 1975—. Bd. dirs. Wis. Valley Improvement Co. Served with USMCR, 1943-46; PTO. Recipient Silver medal Mich. Tech. Bd. Control, 1971. Mem. Am. Pulpwood Assn. (dir. 1970—), Am. Forest Inst. (trustee 1972—), Soc. Am. Foresters, Fourdineer Kraft Inst. (chmn. wood conservation div. 1972—), Toledo C. of C., Phi Kappa Phi. Home: 5325 Carlingfort Dr Toledo OH 43623 Office: PO Box 1035 Toledo OH 43666

NIELSEN, HOWARD NORBERT, motor equipment mfg. co. exec.; b. Decatur, Ind., Feb. 27, 1935; s. Herman F. and Bertha (Haar) N.; student Valparaiso U., 1953-54; B.S., Ohio State U., 1958; m. Norita Jane Kitter, June 14, 1958; children—Kathryn Jean, Steven Robert. Accountant on staff Cassel, Groneweg, Rohlfing, and Clark, C.P.A.'s Dayton, Ohio, 1958-62; internal auditor Magnavox Co., Ft. Wayne, Ind., 1962-63; plant controller Warner Gear div. Borg Warner Corp., Muncie, Ind., 1963-72, div. controller Hydraulics div., Wooster, Ohio, 1972—. Active Boy Scouts Am., Jr. Achievement, P.T.A. Served with AUS, 1954-56. C.P.A., Ohio, Ind. Mem. Nat. Assn. Accountants, Am. Inst. C.P.A.'s, Ohio, Ind. socs. C.P.A.'s. Lutheran. Lion. Home: 1823 Christmas Run Blvd Wooster OH 44691 Office: Hydraulics Div Borg Warner Corp Old Mansfield Rd Wooster OH 44691

NIELSEN, KATHY ANN, clin. social worker; b. Owatonna, Minn., Dec. 14, 1949; d. Stanley Kristen and Shirley Mae (Engle) Nielsen; B.A., George Peabody Coll., 1972; postgrad. Wake Forest U., 1974-75, Xavier U. Asst. psychometrist U. Minn. Hosps., Mpls., 1970; research asst. Evaluation Survey and Health Research, Nashville, 1972-73; vocat. counselor, evaluator Goodwill Industries, Winston-Salem, N.C., 1973-75; clin. social worker Comprehensive Care Corp., Newport Beach, Calif. at St. Francis Hosp., Cin., 1975—; lectr. in field. Mem. Am., Cin. personnel and guidance assns., Am. Rehab. Counseling Assn., Nat. Inst. Alcoholism and Alcohol Abuse, Assn. Specialists in Group Work. Democrat. Lutheran. Office: 1860 Queen City Ave Cincinnati OH 45214

NIELSON, JOSEPH FINLEY, educator; b. Bristol, Penn., Nov. 10, 1925; s. John Niels and Sarah Estella (Bechtold) N.; A.B. in Philosophy Olivet Nazarene Coll., 1949; Keyon Coll. Seminary, 1949-51; M.A. in Sociology, Mich. State U., 1965 Ph.D. in Social Sci., 1972; m. Esther Jeanette Morse, June 16, 1949; children—Rebecca Sue, Joseph Mark. Ordained minister Ch. of the Nazarene, 1949; minister Fredericktown, O., 1949-51; minister Bucyrus, O., 1951-58; minister Saginaw, Mich., 1958-61; minister Mason, Mich., 1961-69; prof. sociology and anthropology, Olivet Nazarene Coll., Kankakee, Ill., 1969—, chmn. Dept. of Sociology, (developer Social Welfare Program, 1973), 1969-75; cons. Dept. of Children Family Services, Kankakee, 1974-75; in service tng. Kankakee State Hosp. Nursing Tng. and tip top mgmt. in businesses, 1973-74. Bd. dir. Com. Chest, Mason, Mich., 1966-68, Mason Gen. Hosp., 1967-68, Kankakee County Tng. Center for Disabled, 1971—; bd. dir. A.R.C., Bucyrus, O., 1954-56, YMCA, Bucyrus, 1955-57. Served with AUS, 1943-46. Tchr. of the Year award, Olivet Nazarene Coll., 1974. Mem. Am., Ill. social. assns. Mem. Ch. of Nazarene (Dist. Young Peoples Pres., 1953-58, dir. Youth Camp, 1953-58, cons. for ministers groups, 1969-75. Founder "Seminar on Poverty", 1971; community organizer Medics for Mason, Mich., 1966-68. Address: 450 S Cleveland Bourbonnais IL 60914

NIEMAN, CHARLES EBERSOL, lawyer; b. McComb, Miss., Jan. 22, 1907; s. Arthur Roy and Marion (Ebersol) N.; B.A., Beloit Coll., 1928; J.D., U. Wis. Law Sch., 1937; m. Dorothy Anne Murphy, Sept. 7, 1935; children—Stephen C., Nancy Dale. Admitted to Minn. bar, 1937; asso. firm Doherty Rumble & Butler, St. Paul, 1936-44; asst. gen. mgr., corp. counsel Farmers Union Grain Terminal Assn., St. Paul, 1944-46; practice in Mpls., 1947—; sr. partner Nieman & Bosard, Mpls., 1948—. Lectr. William Mitchell Coll. Law, St. Paul, 1939-46; prof. law U. Minn. Law Sch., Mpls., 1947-48; spl. asst. atty. gen. State Minn., 1955-58. Bd. dirs. Minn. Unity Settlement Assn., 1951-66, pres., 1957-61; trustee Beloit (Wis.) Coll., 1955-58, 60—. Recipient Distinguished Service citation Beloit Coll., 1973. Mem. Am., Minn., Hennepin County bar assns., Assn. ICC Practitioners, Tau Kappa Epsilon (dir. 1939-44; nat. pres. 1942-44). Contbr. articles to various publs. Home: 6730 Vernon Ave Apt 320 Edina MN 55436 Office: 1110 Northwestern Bank Bldg Minneapolis MN 55402

NIEMAN, TIMOTHY ALAN, analytical chemist; b. Cin., Dec. 31, 1948; s. Everett Orville and Emma (Hoffmeier) Nieman; m. Sandra Toth, Aug. 29, 1970. B.S., Purdue U., 1971; Ph.D., Mich. State U., 1975. Grad. asst. in chemistry Mich. State U., 1971-75; asst. prof. chemistry U. Ill. at Urbana-Champaign, 1975—. Mem. Am. Chem. Soc., Optical Soc. Am., Alpha Chi Sigma, Phi Beta Kappa, Phi Lambda Upsilon. Mich. State U. Chemistry Dept. fellow, 1971-74; Eastman Kodak fellow, 1973-74; Am. Chem. Soc. Analytical Div. fellow, 1974-75. Contbr. articles to Analytical Chemistry jour. Home: 204 E McHenry St Urbana IL 61801 Office: Sch Chem Scis U Ill Urbana IL 61801

NIEMEYER, GLENN ALAN, coll adminstr.; b. Muskegon, Mich., Jan. 14, 1934; s. John T. and Johanna F. (Walhout) N.; B.A., Calvin Coll., 1955; M.A., Mich. State U., 1959, Ph.D., 1962; m. Betty Sikkenga, July 8, 1955; children—Kristin, Alexis, Sander. Social scis. tchr. Grand Haven (Mich.) Christian Sch., 1955-58; teaching asst., asst. instr. Mich. State U., 1958-63; asst. prof. history Grand Valley State Colls., Allendale, Mich., 1963-66, asso. prof., 1966-70, prof., 1970, dean Coll. Arts and Scis., 1970-73, v.p. colls., 1973-76, v.p. acad. affairs, 1976—; cons., evaluator commn. instns. higher edn. North Central Assn. Colls. and Schs. Trustee Calvin Coll. Mem. Am. Assn. Higher Edn., Am. Council on Edn., Am. Hist. Assn., Orgn. Am. Historians, Mich. Council State Coll. Pres.'s and Acad. Officers. Mem. Christian Ref. Ch. Author: The Automotive Career of Ransom E. Olds, 1963. Contbr. articles and book reviews to profl. jours. Office: Grand Valley State Colleges Allendale MI 49401

NIEMEYER, MAXINE BREWER, ins. exec.; b. Detroit, Jan. 14, 1920; d. Daniel Frederick and Ella (Case) Niemeyer; student Detroit Coll. Bus., 1938-39, Exec. Sec. Asso. (hon.), 1960; grad. Dale Carnegie course, 1946; student Wayne U., 1958, Wayne State and U. Mich. Extension Schs., 1961-64, 65—. Gen. office clk. Hart Sewing Machine Supplies Co., Detroit, 1938-39; cashier, sec. N.Am. Life Assurance Co., Detroit, 1939-41, office mgr., 1942-43; office mgr. L.A. Walden & Co., Detroit, 1943-46; asst. office mgr. Dr. Ralph H. Pino, Ophthalmologist, Detroit, 1946-48; registrar Leadership Tng., Inc., Detroit, 1948-50; sec. to mgr. market analysis and dealer orgn. dept. Sales div. Chevrolet Motor Co., Detroit, 1950-56; office mgr., sec. to Walter R. Cavanaugh, C.L.U., 1956—, corp. sec. 1958—, mgr. policyholders service and sales promotion, 1966; staff mgr. Phoenix Mutual Life, also owner M.B. Niemeyer Clu & Assos., 1966—; advanced underwriting cons., agt., surplus lines mgr. Phoenix Cos.; registered rep. Phoenix Equity Planning Corp. Named Detroit Sec. of Year Detroit chpt. Nat. Secs. Assn. Internat., 1960, One of Top Ten Working Women Central Bus. Dist. Assn., Detroit, 1965, Man of Yr., Phoenix Detroit Agy., 1969, 71. C.L.U. Mem. Nat. Secs. Assn. (pres. Detroit chpt. 1962-64), Nat., Detroit (sec. 1970-72, pres. 1974-75) assns. life underwriters, Am. Soc. C.L.U.'s (treas. 1970-71, sec. 1971-72, v.p. 1972-73, pres. Detroit chpt. 1973-74), Am. Soc. Pension Actuaries, Internat. Assn. Fin. Planners, Women Leaders Round Table Life Underwriters, Alpha Iota Internat. (chpt. pres. 1944). Presbyn. Club: Soroptimist (pres. 1972—), Lochmoor (Grosse Pointe, Mich.). Home: 1792 Vernier Rd Grosse Pointe Woods MI 48236 Office: 385 Advance Bldg Southfield MI 48075

NIESSE, JOHN EDGAR, materials engr.; b. Indpls., Nov. 30, 1927; s. John Leo and Jessie Louise (Pohlig) N.; B.S., U.S. Naval Acad., 1950; M.S., Mass. Inst. Tech., 1956, Sc.D., 1958; m. Elaine Corinne Morin, Dec. 27, 1958; children—John A., Ann L. With textile dept. Carborundum Co., Niagara Falls, N.Y., 1966-67, mgr., 1961-66; sect. mgr. metals and ceramics AVCO Corp., Lowell, Mass., 1967-72; sr. research group leader Monsanto Co., Durham, N.C., 1972-75, engring. supt., St. Louis, 1975—. Served with U.S. Navy, 1950-55; capt. Res. Registered profl. engr., Mo. Mem. Am. Ceramic Soc., Nat.

Assn. Corrosion Engrs., Am. Soc. Metals. Author tech. papers. Home: 424 Glan Tai Dr Manchester MO 63011 Office: Monsanto Co 800 N Lindbergh Blvd Saint Louis MO 63166

NIEUBUURT, JOHN EDWARD, realtor; b. Chgo., Mar. 27, 1931; s. Edward John and Minnie (Riemersma) N.; student U. Wyo., 1953; grad. Realtors Inst., 1970; m. Beatrice T. Tallackson, Feb. 2, 1957; children—Pamela, John Edward. Asso. Edward J. Nieubuurt Realtor, Chgo., 1949-52; partner Nieubuurt Realtors, Evergreen Park and Tinley Park, Ill., 1956-74; dir. state and urban affairs Nat. Assn. Realtors, Chgo., 1974—. Pres. bd. dirs. Holland Home for Aged, Chgo., 1966-68. Chmn. real estate examining com. Ill. Dept. Registration and Edn., 1971-73. Served with USAF, 1952-56. Mem. Nat., Ill. (dist. v.p. 1968) assns. real estate bds., Nat. Assn. Ind. Fee Appraisers (chpt. treas. 1970), Chgo.'s South Side Real Estate Bd. (pres. 1968), Southwestern Suburban Bd. Realtors (pres. 1966-67), Home: 12243 S 69th Ct Palos Heights IL 60463 Office: 430 N Michigan Ave Chicago IL 60611

NIGHTINGALE, EDMUND ANTHONY, educator, cons. transp. economist; b. St. Paul, July 17, 1903; s. Edmund Alexander and Katherine Ellen (Eagan) N.; B.B.A., U. Minn., 1933, M.A., 1936, Ph.D., 1944; m. Lauretta A. Horejs, June 5, 1937; children—Edmund Joseph, Paul Lawrence. With operating dept. various railroads, 1920-33; teaching asst. econs. U. Minn., 1933-36, instr. in econs., transp., 1936-44, asst. prof., 1944-47, asso. prof., 1947-52, prof., 1952-72, prof. emeritus, 1972—, dir. insts. in rail transp., 1948-49. Cons. to Mpls. Mayor's Citizen Adv. Com. on streetcar and bus matters, 1952-54; cons. transp. economist. Editorial statistician Minn. State Planning Bd., 1936; prin. indsl. specialist, prin. transp. economist WPB, Washington, 1942-43; cons. transp. economist to Minn. Resources Commn., Minn. Iron Range Resources and Rehab. Commn., 1941-48; cons. to dir. mil. traffic service Office Sec. Def., Washington, 1950-53; cons. Minn. Legis. Interim Com. to Study R.R. and Warehouse Commn., 1956-57; mem. Transp. Research Adv. Com., U.S. Dept. Agr., 1960-63, mem. adv. com. mktg. research and service programs, 1963-66; mem. Gov.'s Transit Authority Study Com., 1964-69; research cons. Mid-Am. Gov.'s Transp. Council, 1965-72; cons. Minn. Pub. Service Commn., 1965-72, U.S. Dept. Transp., 1969-70. Mem. Gov's Transp. Adv. Com., 1968-72. Chmn. Highlands dist. Indianhead council Boy Scouts Am., 1955-58, mem.-at-large, exec. bd., 1958-74. Recipient diploma of honor internat. prize jury VIII Pan-Am. Congress, Washington, 1953; St. George award, Cath. Com. Scouting Archdioces St. Paul, 1960. Registered practitioner ICC. Mem. Am. Soc. Traffic and Transp., Transp. Club Mpls. and St. Paul, AAUP, Am. Econ. Assn., Am. Agr. Econ. Assn., Assn. ICC Practitioners (pres. chpt. 1957-58; regional v.p. 1961-63, chmn. com. edn. for practice 1971-73), Internat. Assn. Assessing Officers, Nat. Tax Assn. (com. on taxation pub. utility and transp. 1971—), Midwest Econs. Assn., Royal Econ. Soc., Nat. (legis. com. 1969—), N.W. (mem. legislative com. 1952-69, chmn. 1960-67) assns. shippers adv. bds., Asso. Traffic Clubs Am. (v.p. edn. and research 1958-62, v.p. W. N. Central States 1962-63; Distinguished Transp. Educator, 1966), Transp. Research Forum, Beta Gamma Sigma, Beta Alpha Psi, Alpha Kappa Psi. Clubs: Transp., Campus (Mpls.). Co-author: Aviation in Minnesota, 1952; Foreign Trade via the St. Lawrence Seaway, 1965; Transportation Problems and Policies in the Trans-Missouri West, 1967. Contbr. to Freight Traffic Management at Installations of the Military Depts., Dept. of Defense, rev. edit., 1952. Contbr. articles econs., taxation, transp. jours. Home: 2120 Niles Ave St Paul MN 55116 Office: Grad Sch Bus Adminstrn University of Minn Minneapolis MN 55455

NIGHTINGALE, EDMUND JOSEPH, clin. psychologist; b. St. Paul, Jan. 10, 1941; s. Edmund Anthony and Lauretta Alexandria (Horejs) N.; student Nazareth Hall Prep. Sem., 1959-61; A.B., St. Paul Sem., 1963; A.B. magna cum laude, Cath. U. of Louvain (Belgium), 1965, M.A., 1967, S.T.B. cum laude, 1967; postgrad. U. Minn., 1971; M.A., Loyola U., Chgo., 1973, Ph.D. in Clin. Psychology, 1975. Pastoral appointments Cath. Archdiocese of St. Paul and Mpls., 1967-73; intern in clin. psychology Michael Reese Hosp. and Med. Center, Chgo., 1973-74, W. Side VA Hosp., Chgo., 1974-75; staff psychologist, student counseling center, Loyola U., Chgo., 1975; staff psychologist and clin. coordinator of inpatient unit, drug dependency treatment center, Hines (Ill.) VA Hosp., 1975—; mem. personnel bd. Archdiocese of St. Paul and Mpls., 1968-70; lectr. psychology, Loyola U., Chgo., 1975; asst. professorial lectr. psychology, St. Xavier Coll., Chgo., 1976—; adj. asst. prof. psychology in psychiatry, Abraham Lincoln Sch. Medicine, Med. Center U. Ill., Chgo., 1977—. Registered psychologist, Ill.; certified Nat. Registry of Health Service Providers in Psychology. Mem. Am. (clin. psychology and psychotherapy divs.), Ill. (clin. psychology and acad. sects.) psychol. assns. Assn. for Advancement of Psychology. Founding editor: Louvain Studies, 1966. Home: 436 N Harvey St Oak Park IL 60302 Office: Hines VA Hosp 116C Hines IL 60141

NIKISHIN, IGOR FEDOR, surgeon; b. Kharkov, Russia, Dec. 25, 1917; s. Fedor F. and Maria A. (Dikarev) N.; came to U.S., 1949, naturalized, 1954; A.B., French Lyceum Prague, Czechoslovakia, 1936; M.D., Charles U., Prague, 1941; children—Nina, Alexander, Michael, Igor. Intern, George August U. Med. Sch., Goettingen, Germany, 1941-42, resident, 1942-46; chief surgeon 326th Res. Detachment Mil. Govt. Hosp., Brit. Army of the Rhine, 1945-47, sr. med. officer hdqrs. 509, 1947-48; sr. med. officer 609 Hdqrs. Control Commn. Germany, 1948-49; chmn. dept. surgery, sr. attending surgeon Aultman Hosp., Canton, Ohio, 1970—; asst. prof. surgery George August U., Goettingen, Germany, 1943-47; sr. attending surgeon Timken Mercy Hosp., Canton, 1959—. Pres., Canton Symphony Assn., 1964-68, East Central Heart Assn., 1965-67; bd. dirs. Am. Cancer Soc., 1976; bd. dirs. AmDoc., Santa Barbara, Calif., 1965-69. Diplomate Am. Bd. Surgeons, Am. Bd. Abdominal Surgeons. Mem. AMA, Am. Soc. Abdominal Surgeons, ACS, Am. Coll. Angiology, Am. Geriatrics Soc., Ohio State Med. Assn., Ohio State Surg. Assn., N.Y., Ohio acads. scis., Med. Educators Assn. N.E. Ohio, Stark County Med. Soc. Club: Canton. Contbr. articles to profl. jours. Home: 3405 20th St NW Canton OH 44708 Office: 214 Dartmouth Ave SW Canton OH 44710

NIMMERFROH, CLARENCE LEO, city ofcl.; b. Mpls., May 23, 1916; s. Charles and Mary C. (Cummings) N.; grad. high sch.; m. Eunice Uhler, Aug. 18, 1972; children by previous marriage—Barbara (Mrs. Neil Hanson), Janet (Mrs. John Palmer), Charles. Mem. Fire Service, Mpls., 1943—, captain, 1954-62, dist. chief, 1962-71, chief officer, 1971—. Bd. dirs. Mpls. Aquatennial. Served with AUS, 1944-45. Mem. U.S. Power Squadrons, Mpls. C. of C. Home: 5840 Clinton Minneapolis MN 55419 Office: 200 Grain Exchange Bldg Minneapolis MN 55415

NIMS, CHARLES FRANCIS, clergyman, egyptologist; b. Norwalk, Ohio, Oct. 19, 1906; s. Joel Benjamin and Grace (Wildman) N.; student U. Toledo, 1924-25; A.B., Alma Coll., 1928; B.D., McCormick Theol. Sem., 1931; Ph.D., U. Chgo., 1937; m. Myrtle Eileen Keillor, Apr. 18, 1931. Ordained to ministry Presbyn. Ch., 1931; pastor, First Ch., Eldorado, Ill., 1940-43; research asst. Oriental Inst., 1934-40; staff Sakkarah Expdn., Egypt, 1934-36; staff Epigraphic Survey, 1937-39; egyptologist Epigraphic Survey, 1946-63, field dir., 1964-72; research asso. dept. Oriental lang. U. Chgo., 1948-67, faculty mem., 1960-61, asso. prof., 1967-70, prof., 1970-72, emeritus, 1972—; staff mem. Chgo. Archeol. Expdn., Tolmeita, Libya, 1954, 56, 57, 58; lectr. adult edn. Field Mus. Natural History, 1976. Mem. Found. Egyptologique Reine Elizabeth, Egypt Exploration Soc., Soc. Bibl. Lit., Am. Oriental Soc., Am. Photog. Soc. Am Schs. Oriental Research, Mil. Chaplains Assn. U.S., AAUP, Am. Research Center in Egypt, L'Association Internationale pour l'Etudé du Droit Pharaonique (hon. pres.); ordinary mem. Deutsches Archaologisches Instut; asso. mem. L'Institut d' Egypte. Served as chaplain (capt.) U.S. Army, 1943-46. Author: (with H.H. Nelson et al) Medinet Habu IV, 1940; (with Prentice Duell) Mastaba of Mereuka, 1938; (with G.R. Hughes) Reliefs and Inscriptions in Karnak, III, 1954; Medinet Habu V-VIII (with G.R. Hughes), 1957-70; Thebes of the Pharoahs, 1965; The Tomb of Khereuf (with E.F. Wente), 1978. Contbr. profl. jours. Home: 5540 Blackstone Ave Chicago IL 60637 Office: Oriental Inst U Chgo Chicago IL 60637

NINKE, ARTHUR ALBERT, cons. accountant; b. Coloma, Mich., Aug. 20, 1909; s. Paul F. and Theresa Grace (Warskow) N.; student accounting Internat. Bus. Coll., 1928; diploma commerce Northwestern U., 1932; m. Claudia Wagner, Sept. 13, 1930; children—Doris (Mrs. Leroy Hart), Donald, Marion, George, Arthur Albert, Thomas, Mark, Albert. Auditor, Arthur Andersen & Co., C.P.A.'s, Chgo., 1929-36, St. Louis, 1950-55, Midwest Stock Exchange, 1936-41, SEC, 1942-45; expense controller Butler Bros., Chgo., 1946-49; office mgr. Hargis Electronics, 1956-59; auditor HUD, Detroit, 1960-64; owner Urban Tech. Staff Assos., cons. urban renewal projects and housing devel., Detroit, 1965—. Controller, Lake Superior Research and Devel. Inst., Munising, Mich., 1973-76; pres. Luth. Friendship Homes, Inc., 1975—; controller S.E. Mich. Billy Graham Crusade, 1976-77. Mem. Nat. Soc. Pub. Accountants, Nat. Assn. Housing and Redevel. Ofcls. (treas. Mich. 1973-75), Luth. Center Assn. (treas. 1975—, dir. 1975—), Internat. Luth. Laymen's League (treas. S.E. Mich. 1971-75, dir. 1976—), Am. Mgmt. Assn. Author: Family Bible Studies. Developer simulated machine bookkeeping system. Home: 12937 Santa Clara St Detroit MI 48235 Office: 18415 James Couzens Blvd Detroit MI 48235

NINOMIYA, JACK SADAO, environ. engr.; b. Koshien, Japan, Nov. 24, 1935; s. Yasuo and Ruth Toshiko (Hayakawa) N.; came to U.S., 1951, naturalized, 1960; B.S. in Chemistry, Wayne State U., 1961, M.S. in Chemistry, 1966; m. Alexandra Bogumila Twarkowski, Oct. 16, 1959; children—Mark, Timothy, Christopher. With Ford Motor Co., Dearborn, Mich., 1961—, research engr. sci. research lab., 1966-70, research planner, tech. liaison for Ford/govt. interchanges, automotive emissions office, 1970—; speaker on vehicle emissions to pub. schs., univ. groups, profl. meetings; tech. reviewer EPA, 1976. Recipient certificate of recognition EPA, 1976. Mem. Soc. Automotive Engrs., Air Pollution Control Assn. (chmn. mobile source com. 1973-77), Air Pollution Research Adv. Council, Motor Vehicle Mfrs. Assn. Contbr. articles to profl. jours. Office: Ford Motor Co Room 221 WHQ Dearborn MI 48121

NIRO, RAYMOND PARDO, lawyer; b. Pitts, Dec. 6, 1942; s. Pardo and Adeline (DeCesare) N.; B.S. in Chem. Engring. with high honors, U. Pitts., 1964; J.D. with honors, George Washington U., 1969; m. Judith L. Heil, Sept. 12, 1964; children—Dean, Raymond, Brian. Admitted to Ill. bar, 1970; chem. engr. Shell Chem. Co., Houston, 1964-65; patent agt. E.I. DuPont de Nemours & Co., Washington, 1966-69; asso. firm Hume, Clement, Brinks, Willians, Olds & Cook, Chgo., 1969-73, partner, 1973-76; partner firm Hosier, Niro & Deleiden, Chgo, 1976—. Mem. Am., Chgo., N.W. Suburban, Ill. bar assns., Am., Chgo. Patent law assns., Phi Eta Sigma, Omega Chi Epsilon, Delta Theta Phi. Roman Catholic. Home: 1005 N Arlington Heights Rd Arlington Heights IL 60004 Office: 135 S La Salle St Chicago IL 60603

NISSEN, CARL ANDREW, JR., govt. ofcl.; b. Manhattan, Kans., June 26, 1930; s. Carl Andrew and Bernice Lydia (Varney) N.; B.A. in History, Ohio State U., 1960; postgrad. Grad. Sch. Theology, Oberlin, Ohio, summer 1959, Berkeley (Calif.) Bapt. Div. Sch., 1960-61; student def. basic procurement mgmt. Army Logistics Mgmt. Center, Ft. Lee, Va., 1964, def. advanced procurement mgmt., 1970. Student pastor Bapt. chs. in Ohio, 1959-60; student campus pastor San Francisco State Coll., 1960-61; clk. Univ. Bookstore, Ohio State U., 1958-60, 61, 62-63; adminstrv. technician Ohio Air NG, Springfield, 1961-62; contract asst. Def. Electronics Supply Center, Dayton, Ohio, 1963-64, procurement asst., 1964-65, procurement agt., 1965-66, contract negotiator, 1966—. Served with AUS, 1950-53. Recipient George Washington Honor medal Freedoms Found., 1972. Mem. Am. Def. Preparedness Assn. (life), Nat. Rifle Assn. (life), Ohio State U. Alumni Assn. (life), S.A.R. (pres. Richard Montgomery chapt.), Air Force Sgts. Assn. (life), Co. Mil. Historians, Ohio Hist. Soc., Ohio Geneal Soc., Soc. Mayflower Descendants, Alpha Phi Omega. Mason. Baptist. Home: 727 W Riverview Ave Dayton OH 45406 Office: Def Electronics Supply Center Dayton OH 45444

NISSIMOV, NORBERT J., allergist; b. Sofia, Bulgaria, Feb. 27, 1922; s. Joseph and Emilia (Koyuumdjiiski) N.; came to U.S., 1970, naturalized, 1977; M.D., U. Sofia, 1950; m. Florence Kostov, Jan. 1, 1950; children—Aliza, Joseph, Dan, Raphael, Ronen, Talli. Research fellow in allergy immunology U. Colo., Denver, 1970-72; practice medicine specializing in allergy, Chillicothe, Ohio, 1972—. Diplomate Am. Bd. Allergy and Immunology. Mem. Ohio Med. Assn., Am. Acad. Allergy, Am. Assn. Certified Allergists. Jewish. Office: 39 W Main St Chillicothe OH 45601

NISSING, BURTON JOHN, accountant, educator; b. Marthasville, Mo., July 3, 1927; s. Alex W. and Clara A. (Brakemeyer) N.; B.S. in Bus. Adminstrn., U. Mo., 1949; M.S. in Commerce, St. Louis U., 1959, Ph.D., 1976; m. Mary Ann Gatchell, May 24, 1958; children—Douglas Frederic, Angela Kay. With C.F. Jacobs & Co., St. Louis, 1949-52, Ralph F. Curry, C.P.A. and atty., St. Louis, 1952-59, John J. Lang & Co., C.P.A.'s, St. Louis, 1959-62, L. Ray Schuessler & Co., C.P.A.'s, St. Louis, 1962-64; pvt. practice accounting, Webster Groves, Mo., 1964—; asst. prof. accounting So. Ill. U., 1965-75; asso. prof. accounting St. Louis U., 1976—. Served with USNR, 1945-46. C.P.A. Mem. Am. Inst. C.P.A.'s, Mo. Soc. C.P.A.'s, Nat. Assn. Accountants, Am. Accounting Assn., Alpha Kappa Psi, Beta Gamma Sigma. Home: 360 Oakwood Ave Webster Groves MO 63119

NISWONGER, C(LIFFORD) ROLLIN, educator; b. Pitsburg, Ohio, Mar. 24, 1907; s. Clifford O. and Edith Rose (Vance) N.; S.B., Miami U., 1929, LL.D., 1973; S.M., U. Ill., 1931; Ph.D., Ohio State U., 1950; m. Sue Janes, Aug. 22, 1938; children—Cynthia Sue, Thomas Rollin. Asst. instr. accounting, U. Ill., 1929-31; instr. accounting State U. Wash., 1931-35; asst. prof. accountancy Miami U., 1935-41, asso. prof., 1941-47, chmn. dept., 1947-66, prof., 1947-72, emeritus, 1972—, asst. dean sch. bus. adminstrn., 1940-56, acting dean, 1954-55, dir. summer session, 1946-48; cons. office U.S. Comptroller Gen., 1955-58; accounting exec. OPA, 1943. Served as lt. Supply Corps, USNR, cost inspection service, 1944-46. C.P.A., Washington, Ohio. Mem. Am. Inst. C.P.A.'s, Financial Execs. Inst., Am. Accounting Assn. (pres. 1958), Ohio Soc. C.P.A.'s, Phi Beta Kappa, Sigma Chi, Beta Gamma Sigma, Beta Alpha Psi (nat. pres. 1962-63), Delta Sigma Pi, Omicron Delta Kappa. Author (with others) Federal Tax Accounting, annually, 1940-46; Income Tax Procedure for Individuals, 1942; Income Tax Procedure, annually, 1947-67; Accounting Principles, 6th-12th edit., 1953-77. Contbr. to jours. Home: 8 Robin Ct Oxford OH 45056

NISWONGER, PHILIP GORDON, counselor; b. Phila., Feb. 3, 1945; s. Eugene Franklin and Esthyre Pauline (Hoffman) N.; B.A. in Philosophy and Anthropology, Queen of Apostles Coll., Dedham, Mass., 1967; M.A. in Edn. and Psychology, Catholic U. Am., 1972. Tchr., coach Marian High Sch., Mishawaka, Ind., 1972-76; camp dir. Wood Lake Scout Reservation, Jones, Mich., summers 1975, 76; counselor Bur. Employment and Tng., South Bend, Ind., 1976—; cons., adviser in field. Dist. commr. Kankakee dist. Boy Scouts Am., 1973-74, dist. chmn. St. Joseph County, Ind., 1974-75; mem. choir St. Joseph Roman Cath. Parish, South Bend, 1972—, rep. parish council, 1974—; referee, coach Cath. Youth Orgn., 1970, 72-74; bldg. rep. CATCH, 1975-76; sec. social justice commn. NE Neighborhood Center, 1976-77. Named Outstanding Cath. Layman, K.C., 1976; recipient numerous scouting awards. Mem. Am. Personnel and Guidance Assn., Nat. Vocat. Guidance Assn., Nat. Employment Counselor Assn., Assn. Non-White Concerns in Personnel and Guidance, Pub. Offender Counselor Assn., Ind. Employment Counselors Assn., Marian Tutors Assn. Club: K.C. (3 deg.). Author manuals. Home: 1428 Wall St South Bend IN 46615 Office: CETA Manpower Office County-City Bldg South Bend IN 46601

NITSCHKE, CHARLES ALBERT, architect; b. Columbus, Ohio, July 15, 1928; s. Andrew Gunning and Carrie (Fiedler) N.; B.Arch., Ohio State U., 1951; m. Sally Moore, Nov. 29, 1953; children—Christopher Moore, Caren, David Rathburn. Designer Tully & Hobbs, Columbus, 1953-55; partner Downie W. Moore-Charles A. Nitschke, architects, Columbus, 1955-60; prin. C. Nitschke & Assos., Columbus, 1960-72; partner Nitschke Godwin Bohm, architects, Columbus, 1972-76; prin. Nitschko Assos., Columbus, 1976—. Instr. architecture Ohio State U., Columbus, 1955-60; v.p., dir. Columbus Properties, Inc., 1970—; v.p. Nitschke Bros., Inc., Columbus, 1972—; occasional lectr. architecture, city planning and redevel. econs. Ohio State U., U. Wis., others. Founding bd. dirs. Columbus Landmarks Found., 1977. Served with USNR, 1951-53. Recipient Plan awards, Jr. League of Columbus, 1966, 68. Mem. Columbus C. of C. (mem. downtown action com. 1972—), Volunteers Am. (v.p., dir. 1972—), AIA (bd. dirs. 1967-74, pres. 1973), Urban Land Inst., Nat. Trust Historic Preservation, Am. Inst. Planners (asso.), Alpha Tau Omega. Episcopalian (lay reader). Clubs: Ohio State U. Faculty, University (Columbus). Contbr. articles to profl. jours. Home: 6570 Plesenton Dr Worthington OH 43085 Office: 31 E Gay St Columbus OH 43215

NIU, STANLEY HSIEN P., engr.; b. Nanking, China, June 20, 1935; s. Z.K. and Yin Hwa (Wei) N.; came to U.S., 1959, naturalized, 1972; B.S., Cheng Kung U., Taiwan, 1957; M.S., U. Wis., 1962, Ph.D., 1967; m. Yolande Tiao, June 19, 1965; children—Tina, Mark. Engr., C.F. Murphy Assos., Architects and Engrs., Chgo., 1962; asst. prof. civil engring. S.D. Sch. of Mines, Rapid City, 1966-69; asst. prof. gen. engring. U. Mo., Kansas City, 1969-73, asso. prof. engring., 1973—; cons. in field. Bd. dirs. Midwest Children's Center, Kansas City, Mo., 1971-73. Mem. ASCE, ASME, Am. Assn. Engring. Edn., AAUP, Tau Beta Pi. Methodist. Contbr. articles to profl. jours. Home: 10013 Briar St Overland Park KS 66207 Office: 1122 E 48th St Kansas City MO 64110

NIVEN, ALEXANDER CURT, historian, educator; b. Vienna, Austria, Dec. 25, 1920; s. Stefan Otto and Hedda (Beck) N.; came to U.S., 1952, naturalized, 1963; M.A., Washington U., St. Louis, 1954, M.A., 1970; Ph.D., Occidental U., 1973; m. Joan Pauline Garnett, Aug. 1964; 1 son, Alexander Stefan Edward. Grad. asst. lectr. Washington U., St. Louis, 1953-59; chmn. history dept. St. Louis Priory Sch., 1959-62; lectr. history St. Louis Country Day Sch., 1963-68; prof. history Meramec Community Coll., Kirkwood, Mo., 1968—; pres. Occidental (open) U., Clayton, Mo.; exec. dir. Internat. Inst. for Advanced Studies, Inst. for Civil War Studies, Clayton. Recipient Goldstein Prize Am. Civil War History, Washington U., 1955; named hon. col. Ala. Fellow Royal Geog. Soc.; mem. Am., So. hist. assns., Orgn. Am. Historians, Oriental Inst., Confederate High Command Internat., Am. Security Council. Clubs: Masons, Shriners. Author books on Serbo-Croatian lang., grammar; contbr. numerous articles to profl. jours. Home: 1121 Timberlane Dr Warson Woods MO 63122 Office: 11333 Big Bend Blvd Kirkwood MO 63122

NIXON, DON LEWIS, real estate broker; b. Ann Arbor, Mich., Jan. 3, 1918; s. Lewis and Myrtie L. (Forshee) N.; A.B., U. Mich., 1940, postgrad., 1941. Mgr. personal real estate, Ann Arbor, 1941-43; sales rep. Am. Airlines, Inc., Detroit, 1946-50; dist. mgr. Bur. Nat. Affairs, Inc., Detroit, 1950-59; v.p., partner Silloway & Co., Detroit, 1960-76, also dir.; pres. Don L. Nixon, Realtor, 1976—. Fund raiser spl. gifts City of Detroit United Found., 1967, U. Mich., 1968. Served to lt., USNR, 1943-46. Mem. Alumni Assn. U. Mich. (exec. com. class officers council 1960-64), Soc. Indsl. Realtors, Chi Phi. Home: 830 St Clair Ave Grosse Pointe MI 48230

NIXON, R(ICHARD) ROY, radiologist; b. St. Louis, May 11, 1932; s. Roy A. and Clara (Neuman) N.; student U. Notre Dame, 1950-53; M.D., Loyola of Chgo., 1957; m. Inalee M. Lapert, Sept. 20, 1958; children—James, Thomas, Robert. Intern, Little Co. of Mary Hosp., Chgo., 1957-58; resident in radiology Cook County Hosp., Chgo., 1960-63; dir. dept. radiology St. Joseph Hosp., Concordia, Kans., 1964—; cons. Republic County Hosp., Mitchell County Hosp., Marysville Community Hosp., 1969—; preceptior radiology U. Kans. Med. Sch., 1972—. Dir. regional med. program North Central Kans., 1972-74. Served to capt. USAF, 1958-60. Diplomate Am. Bd. Radiology. Mem. Am. Coll. Radiology, Kans. Med. Soc., Radiol. Soc. N. Am. Republican. Roman Catholic. Club: Elks, Concordia Country. Founder, Sch. Radiologic Technology St. Josephs Hosp., Concordia, 1968. Home: 1530 Highland Dr Concordia KS 66901 Office: 519 Washington St Concordia KS 66901

NOACK, HELMUT OTTO, material handling co. exec.; b. Bad Freiewalde, Germany, June 5, 1938; s. Werner and Gerda (Baehre) N.; came to U.S., 1976; doctorate, U. Berlin, 1966; m. Gudrun Matthaei, May 26, 1966; children—Karoline, Isabell, Dorothee. Asst. prof. bus. adminstrn. Technische Universitaet Berlin, 1966-70; controller Rhone-Poulenc, France, 1970-75; internat. controller Demag Material Handling Corp., W.Ger., 1975-76, v.p. fin. Cleve., 1976—. Mem. Am. Mgmt. Assn. Club: Rotary. Author: Der Aufbau eines EDV-Systems, 1969. Home: 5850 Briar Hill Dr Solon OH 44139 Office: 29201 Aurora Rd Solon OH 44139

NOBES, LEON DURRELL, educator; b. Muskegon, Mich., Apr. 9, 1911; s. Leon G. and Ruby (Travis) N.; B.A., magna cum laude, Western Mich. U., 1964, M.A., 1966. Dir. priorities Continental Aviation & Engring. Corp., Muskegon, 1944-46; prodn. engring. div. supr. Navy Dept., Detroit, 1952-57; tchr. Muskegon High Sch., 1965; instr. dept. communication arts and scis. Western Mich. U., Kalamazoo, 1966-71, asst. prof., 1971—, dir. Resource Center, 1966-68; founder Center for Internat. Security Studies, Boston, Va. Mem. Am. Acad. Polit. and Social Sci., Am. Security Council (adv. bd.), U. Profs. for Acad. Order, Phi Theta Kappa, Delta Psi Omega,

Phi Rho Pi, Theta Alpha Phi, Kappa Delta Pi, Pi Gamma Mu, Alpha Kappa Psi. Clubs: Republican Capitol Hill, Republican Congl. (charter), U.S. Senatorial (founding mem.). Office: Dept Communication Arts and Scis Western Mich U Kalamazoo MI 49001

NOBLE, ELLSWORTH GLENN, writer; b. Sioux City, Iowa, Sept. 2, 1902; s. Lincoln and Zada Belle (Gardner) N.; B.A., Coe Coll., 1927; postgrad. U. Iowa, 1927, U. Nebr., 1932-33; m. Lillian Peterka, June 8, 1933. Reporter, Morning Republican, Findlay, Ohio, 1922-23, 25, Mankato (Minn.) Free Press, 1924; partner drug store, Table Rock, Nebr., 1928-29; area circulation mgr. Omaha Bee-News, 1929-30; interviewer, then field rep. Nat. Reemployment Service, 1934-37; area mgr. Nebr. Employment Service, Nebraska City, 1937-67; dir. Wildwood Center, cultural center, mus., arts-crafts facility, Nebraska City, 1967-76, mem. bd., 1967—. Mem. Nebr. Writers Guild (v.p. 1956), Nebraska City C. of C., Brownville (charter, dir. 1956-62, pres. 1962, editor quar. 1956-60), Nebr., Kans. hist. socs. Author: Colorful Old Brownville, 3d edit., 1970; John Brown and the Jim Lane Trail, 1977. Home: 502 N 17th St Nebraska City NE 68410

NOBLE, HOWARD BATES, orthopaedic surgeon; b. Pocatello, Idaho, Aug. 3, 1939; s. Wallace Bert and Melrhea (Parker) N.; B.A., U. Wash., 1961; M.D., Bowman Gray Med. Sch., 1965. Intern, Passavant Meml. Hosp., Chgo., 1965-66; resident Northwestern U., 1968-72; practice medicine specializing in orthopaedic surgery, Chgo., 1972; attending physician Northwestern Meml., Children's Meml., Grant hosps.; team physician U. Ill., Chgo. Circle.; instr., mem. exec. com. Center Sports Medicine, Northwestern U. Med. Sch.; cons. Peoples Gas Co. Served with USNR, 1966-68. Travelling fellow James IV Soc. Surgeons, 1975. Diplomate Am. Bd. Orthopaedic Surgery. Fellow A.C.S., Am. Acad. Orthopaedic Surgeons; mem. AMA, Am. Assn. Ry. Surgeons, Ill., Chgo. med. socs. Address: 233 E Erie St Chicago IL 60611

NOBLE, ROBERT RAY, educator; b. Oakville, Iowa, Oct. 6, 1920; s. Arthur Joseph and Addie Mae (Lamb) N.; B.A. (honor scholar), Coe Coll., 1942; M.A., U. Nebr., 1948, Ph.D. (Johnson grad. fellow), 1950; postgrad. U. Wis., summer, 1949; m. Leora Darleen Rath, Mar. 17, 1946; children—Kent Rath, Karen Rae. Instr. sociology U. Nebr., Lincoln, 1946-50; asst. prof. sociology Kans. State Coll., Pittsburg, 1950-56, asso. prof., 1956-59, prof., 1959—. Cons. Crawford County (Kans.) Juvenile Ct., 1965-75, Crawford County Children's Ct. Center, 1973-75, Gov.'s Com. on Criminal Adminstrn., 1974-75. Chmn. Crawford County chpt. A.R.C., 1955-61; pres. Crawford County Mental Health Assn., 1961-62. Cb. dirs. Elm Acres Youth Homes, 1955-66, pres., 1955-56. Served with USAAF, 1942-45. Decorated Bronze Star medal. Mem. Nat. Council on Family Relations (dir. 1958-59), Am., Midwest sociol. assns., Nat. Council on Crime and Delinquency, Kans. Council on Crime and Delinquency (dir. 1972—), Kans. Family Life Assn. (pres. 1958-59), Kans. Council on Children and Youth (pres. 1965-66), Kans. Council Social Welfare (dir. 1966-70). Kiwanian. Contbr. to publs. in field. Home: 1511 S College St Pittsburg KS 66762

NOBLE, WILLIAM JAMES, JR., maintenance adminstr.; b. Portland, Oreg., June 5, 1952; s. William James and Bernice (Scott) N.; B.S.E.E. (Kaiser scholar, Boeing scholar), Oreg. State U., 1974; M.B.A. (Commonwealth Edison fellow), U. Chgo., 1976; m. Anita Jo Paden, June 21, 1975. Asso. engr. Pacific N.W. Bell Co., Portland, Oreg., 1971, 72, plant service supr., 1973; engr. trainee Commonwealth Edison Co., Chgo., 1974, 75; fin. analyst Owens-Ill. Co., Toledo, Ohio, 1976—, elec. maintenance supr., 1977—; owner, operator investment services firm. SEC registered investment advisor. Mem. Am. Mgmt. Assn., Inst. of Mgmt. Accounting of Nat. Assn. of Accountants. Democrat. Methodist. Home: 2366 Cheyenne Blvd Apt 12 Toledo OH 43614 Office: PO Box 1035 Toledo OH 43666

NOCON, JAMES JEFFREY, perinatologist; b. Cleve., Mar. 18, 1946; s. Stanley James and Anita Marie (Enki) N.; B.A., LaSalle Coll., 1967; M.D., Jefferson Med. Coll., 1971; m. Barbara Muratore, June 8, 1966; children—Jennifer Alyssa. Intern, Jefferson Med. Coll., Phila., 1971-72, resident, 1972-75; asst. prof. obstetrics-gynecology U. Wis. Sch. Medicine, Milw., 1975—; dir. perinatology, residency dir. Mt. Sinai Med. Center, Milw., 1975—. Mem. Med. Commn. on Human Rights, 1969. Fellow Nat. Bd. Med. Examiners; mem. Aerospace Med. Assn., AMA, Am. Coll. Obstetrics-Gynecology, Wis., Milw. med. socs., Milw. Gynecologic Soc. Roman Catholic. Club: Jefferson Rugby Football. Contbr. articles to profl. jours. Home: 1915 E Glendale St Milwaukee WI 53211 Office: 950 N 12th St Milwaukee WI 53233

NOE, DONALD ARDEN, stock broker; b. Columbus, Ohio, Nov. 19, 1923; s. Leo A. and Bertha (Yank) N.; grad. Franklin U., 1946, U. Pa., 1967; m. Ellabelle Redman, Jan. 24, 1946; children—Penny Sue (Mrs. Thomas Miller Kelsey), Bonita Lynne. With Bache, Halsey, Stuart, Inc., Columbus, 1942—, sr. v.p. Ohio, Ky., Pa. and W.Va. offices, 1971—. Bd. dirs. Goodwill Industries of Central Ohio, 1962—, pres., 1967; bd. dirs. Six Pence Sch., YMCA Columbus, 1953-56; mem. nominating com. United Community Council of Franklin County, 1970—. Mem. Investment Bankers of Am. (dir. 1959-69), Nat. Assn. of Securities Dealers, Inc. (com. chmn. 1967-68), Soc. for Financial Counselling Ethics, Inc., Mutual Fund Council Million Dollar Producers, C. of C. (mem. downtown area com. 1968-73). Methodist (sec. ofcl. bd. 1958, chmn. financial drives 1959, 62). Mason (33 deg.). Clubs: Columbus Stock and Bond (dir. 1952-55, pres. 1956); Athletic Club; Columbus Sales Execs.; Execs. Club of Columbus; Columbus Maennerchor. Home: 3459 Inverness Way Columbus OH 43221 Office: 41 S High St Columbus OH 43215

NOE, FRANCES ELSIE (MRS. ROBERT DAVIES), physician; b. Beacon Falls, Conn., May 23, 1923; d. Alfred and Edith (Carlson) Noe; B.A., Middlebury Coll., 1944; M.N., Yale, 1947; M.D., U. Vt., 1954; m. Robert Davies, June 16, 1956; children—Kenneth Roger, Ralph Eric. Intern, Mary Hitchcock Meml. Hosp., Hanover, N.H., 1954-55; fellow cardiovascular research Mich. Heart Assn., 1955-56; resident Henry Ford Hosp. Pulmonary div., Detroit, 1956-57; fellow cardiopulmonary research Wayne State U. Coll. Medicine, 1957-58, instr. anesthesia dept., 1958-61, asst. clin. prof. anesthesia dept., 1961-65, 76—; asso. staff, div. research Sinai Hosp. of Detroit, 1965-70, chief pulmonary physiology sect., div. research, 1970—. Mem. Am. Soc. Anesthesiologists, Sigma Xi. Contbr. articles in field to profl. jours. Home: 1601 Kirkway Bloomfield Hills MI 48013 Office: Sinai Hosp Detroit MI 48235

NOEL, CLAUDE BERT, mfg. co. exec.; b. Fairfield, Iowa, July 21, 1919; s. Claude Bert and Etta (Allred) N.; grad. high sch.; m. Lucelle E. Floyd, Nov. 30, 1939; children—Charles, Thomas, Michael. With Interstate Oil Co., 1939-41; engaged in automotive repair, 1945-48; office mgr. City of New London (Iowa), i948-49, U.S. Govt. Transp., 1949-52; transp. mgr. Mason, Hangen, Silas Mason Co. Inc., Burlington, Iowa, 1952—. Mem. New London City Council, 1946-48, New London Sch. Bd., 1959-61, Burlington Airport Adv. Com., 1970. Served with AUS, 1941-45. Decorated Purple Heart. Mem. Contractors Traffic Mgrs. Assn. (chmn. 1969), V.F.W., Am. Legion (past post comdr.). Eagle. Home: 210 Orchard Lane New London IA 52645 Office: PO Box 561 Burlington IA 52601

NOEL, DONALD, TV producer; b. Omaha, Mar. 28, 1947; s. Timothy and Eleanor Bonnie (Edson) Parks; B.A., U. Nebr., Omaha, 1970; m. Selga Ritums, June 21, 1970; 1 son, Justin Donald. Prodn. asst. Sta. KVON-TV, U. Nebr., Lincoln, 1965-67; prodn. asst. Sta. KYNE-TV, U. Nebr., Omaha, 1967-70, dir., producer, 1972—; dir. Sta. KETV, Omaha, 1970-72; dir. summer workshops in broadcasting, Omaha, 1972-76. Mem. Nat. Assn. Ednl. Broadcasters (award). Democrat. Episcopalian. Home: 101 N 69th St Omaha NE 68132 Office: 60th and Dodge St Omaha NE 68101

NOETH, CAROLYN FRANCES, speech, language, and hearing clinician; b. Cleve., July 21, 1924; d. Sam Falco and Barbara Serafina (Loparo) Armaro; A.B. magna cum laude (Univ. Scholar 1962-63), Western Res. U., 1963; M.Ed., U. Ill., 1972; postgrad. Nat. Coll. Edn., 1975—; m. Lawrence Andrew Noeth, June 29, 1946; children—Lawrence Andrew, Barbara Marie Noeth Kukura. Speech therapist Chgo. Pub. Schs., 1965; speech, language and hearing clinician J. Sterling Morton High Schs., Cicero-Berwyn, Ill., 1965—, Title I Project tchr., summers 1966-67, lang. disabilities cons., summers 1968-69, in-service tng. cons., summer 1970, dir. Title I Project, summers 1973-74, learning disabilities tchr. W. Campus of Morton, 1971-75, chmn. Educable-Mentally Handicapped-Opportunities Tchrs. Com., 1967-68, spl. edn. area and in-sch. tchrs. workshops, 1967—. Precinct elections judge, 1953-55; block capt. Mothers March of Dimes and Heart Fund, 1949-60; St. Agatha's rep. Nat. Catholic Women's League, 1952-53; collector for charities, 1967. First recipient Virda L. Stewart award for Speech, Western Res. U., 1963, recipient Outstanding Sr. award, 1963. Mem. Am. (certified), Ill. speech and hearing assns., Council Exceptional Children (div. for children with learning disabilities, chpt. spl. projects chmn., exec. bd. 1976—), Assn. Children with Learning Disabilities, Kappa Delta Pi, Delta Kappa Gamma. Roman Catholic. Clubs: St. Norbert's Women's (Northbrook, Ill.), Case-Western Res. U., U. Ill. Alumni Assns., Lions (vol. Northbrook, 1966—). Chmn. in compiling and publishing Student Handbook, Cleve. Coll., 1962; contbr. lyric parodies and musical programs J. Sterling Morton High Sch. West Retirement Teas, 1972—. Home: 1849 Walnut Circle Northbrook IL 60062 Office: 2400 S Home Ave Berwyn IL 60402

NOETH, RICHARD JEROME, psychologist; b. N.Y.C., Sept. 24, 1944; s. William Henry and Helen Josephine (Jerome) N.; B.A. in History, Coll. Holy Cross, Worcester, Mass., 1966; M.S. in Counselor Edn., St. John's U., Jamaica, N.Y., 1970; Ph.D. in Counseling and Personnel Services, Purdue U., 1972; m. Patricia Eileen O'Byrne, Aug. 16, 1969; children—Kristyn Marie, Erinn Kyle. Counselor, caseworker St. Mary's Home, Syosset, N.Y., 1967; grad. research asst. dept. counselor edn. St. John's U., 1968, supr. testing Community Counseling and Testing Center, 1968-70; guidance counselor, history tchr. St. John the Bapt. High Sch., West Islip, N.Y., 1968-70; grad. asst. Purdue U., 1970-72, counselor office admissions, 1970-71, counselor adminstrv. asst. dean of students' office, 1971-72, counseling supr. dept. counseling and personnel services, 1972; research psychologist div. research and devel. Am. Coll. Testing Program, Iowa City, Iowa, 1972—; guest lectr. U. Iowa Dept. Counselor Edn, 1973—; cons. in field. Purdue U. Office Admissions summer research grantee, 1971; NSF grantee, 1975-76. Mem. Am. Personnel, Guidance Assn. (Nat. Research award 1975), Assn. Counselor Edn. Supervision (Commn. Counselor Preparation in Career Devel. 1974—), Assn. Measurement, Evaluation in Guidance, Am. Coll. Personnel Assn. (Commn. on Career Counseling and Commn. on Assessment for Student Devel. 1974—), Nat. Vocat. Guidance Assn., Am. Sch. Counselor Assn., Am. Ednl. Research Assn., Am. Psychol. Assn. Author: (with Harold B. Engen and Dale J. Prediger) Exploring: You and your Career, 1974; (with John D. Roth and Dale J. Prediger) Handbook for the ACT Career Planning Program, Grades 8-12, 1974; A Guide to increasing student career development, 1974; contbr. articles to profl. jours. Home: 712 Normandy Dr Iowa City IA 52240 Office: Am Coll Testing PO Box 168 Iowa City IA 52240

NOFFSINGER, DONALD ALLEN, pub. co. exec.; b. Defiance, Ohio, Apr. 18, 1929; s. Obert M. and Mazie V. (Etter) N.; B.S. in Commerce, Internat. Coll., 1949; postgrad. U. Calif. at San Diego, 1959-61, Anderson Coll., 1964, Ball State U., 1967-72; m. Birdie F. George Smith, May 21, 1955; 1 son, Mark A.; stepchildren—Gregory L. Smith, Ronald D. Smith, Randall G. Smith. With dist. accounting office Burroughs Corp., Chgo., 1949-50; accounting supr. Gen. Motors Corp., Defiance, 1950-59; in charge financial forecasting Convair astronautics div. Gen. Dynamics Corp., San Diego, 1959-61; sec.-treas., sr. v.p. Warner Press, Inc., Anderson, Ind., 1961-74, exec. v.p., 1974, pres., 1975—, also dir.; partner Orange Blossom Gardens Devel. Co., Anderson, 1964—; dir., mem. exec. com. Laymen Life Ins. Co., Anderson; dir. Comml. Service Co., Asso. Cos., Inc., Anderson. Mem. City Council, Defiance, 1958-59, pres. pro tem, 1958-59; mem. Redevel. Commn., Anderson, 1968-70, v.p., 1968-69, pres., 1969-70; dir. Wilson Boys Clubs, Inc.; mem. exec. council Ch. of God. Bd. dirs. Nat. Bd. Ch. Extension and Home Missions, Ch. of God, Anderson, Ind., Community Hosp. Anderson and Madison County, Jr. Achievement of Madison County, Inc., Anderson YMCA. Served with AUS, 1948-55. Mem. Am. Mgmt. Assn., Nat. Assn. Accountants, Am. Accounting Assn., Presidents Assn., Protestant Ch. Owned Publishers Assn. (v.p., dir.), Anderson C. of C., Urban League. Clubs: Anderson Country, Optimist (v.p. 1965-66, pres. 1971-72, lt. gov. 1972-73) (Anderson), Masons. Home: 240 Graceland Ave Anderson IN 46012 Office: PO Box 2499 Anderson IN 46011

NOFZIGER, TERRY LEE, physician; b. Wauseon, Ohio, Sept. 6, 1945; s. Roy E. and Lucille A. (Frey) N.; B.A. cum laude in Chemistry, Goshen Coll., 1967; M.D., Ind. U., 1971; m. Mary Helen Liechty, Dec. 24, 1965; children—Anne, Matthew, Mary Elizabeth. Intern, Methodist Hosp. of Indpls., 1971-72, resident in family practice (recipient Mead-Johnson award), 1972-74, chief resident, 1973-74; practice medicine specializing in family practice, Paoli, Ind., 1974—; mem. staff Orange County Hosp. Treas. Paoli Mennonite Fellowship. Diplomate Am. Bd. Family Practice. Robert Wood Johnson Found., HEW grantee for devel. rural health care, 1976—. Fellow Am. Acad. Family Physicians; mem. Ind. Acad. Family Physicians, Ind., Mennonite med. assns., Orange County Med. Soc., Alpha Omega Alpha. Home: Rural Route 2 Paoli IN 47454 Office: Hospital Rd Paoli IN 47454

NOGAJ, RICHARD JOSEPH, cons. environ. engr.; b. Chgo., Feb. 17, 1938; s. Joseph John and Loretta Elizabeth (Kowalczyk) N.; B.S. in Civil Engring., Ill. Inst. Tech., 1960, M.S. in San. Engring., 1963; m. Barbara Ann Fitzmaurice, Aug. 22, 1959; children—Debra, Thomas, John. Civil engr. Met. San. Dist. Greater Chgo., 1960-61; mgr. engring. Clow Corp., Melrose Park, Ill., 1961-70; dir. engring. Keene Corp., Aurora, Ill., 1970-73; head dept. san. engring. Harza Engring. Co., Chgo., 1973-75; pres. RJN Environ. Assos., Wheaton, Ill., 1975—. Bd. dirs. Marion Park, Inc., 1977—, Du Page County (Ill.) Health Systems Agy., 1977—. Registered profl. engr., Ill. Mem. Water Pollution Control Fedn., ASCE, Nat., Ill. socs. profl. engrs. Roman Catholic. Club: Wyncliff Swim. Contbr. articles on wastewater treatment to tech. publs. Patentee wastewater treatment process equipment. Home: 27W147 Fleming Dr Winfield IL 60190 Office: 213 S Wheaton Ave Wheaton IL 60187

NOGLE, TIMOTHY FENTON, dentist; b. Hamilton, O., Feb. 24, 1940; s. Fenton and Ruby V. (Pierson) N.; D.D.S., Ohio State U., 1965; m. Leslie Nelson, Oct. 16, 1971; children—Tara Lynn, Matthew Timothy. Individual practice dentistry, Kettering, O., 1967—. Cons., Dayton (O.) Sch. System, 1972—, Greene County Health Commn., 1972—. Served with Dental Corps, USNR, 1965-67. Mem. Nat., Ohio State dental assns., Dayton (mem. council 1973), Chgo. dental socs., Dayton Suburban Dental Study Club, Delta Sigma Delta. Republican. Episcopalian. Optimist. Home: 5971 Bunnell Hill Rd Lebanon OH 45036 Office: 3809 Wilmington Pike Kettering OH 45429

NOLAN, CAROLE RITA, broadcasting co. exec.; b. Chgo., Jan. 28, 1932; d. Martin Francis and Caroline Rita (Alton) N.; B.A., DePaul U., 1954, M.A., 1961. Tchr. Chgo. pub. schs., 1954-61, sci. cons., 1961-66, dir. instructional TV, 1966-71; dir. bur. telecommunications and broadcasting, mgr. WBEZ-FM, Chgo., 1971—. Faculty Northeastern U., 1964-65, De Paul U., 1975—; cons. Comptons Ency., 1964-65, Chgo. Area Sch. TV, 1964-72, Ill. TV Adv. Council, 1969. Mem. Nat. Assn. Ednl. Broadcasters, Ill. Assn. Supervision and Curriculum, Nat. Pub. Radio, Japan Am. Soc., DePaul Univ. Alumni Assn., Delta Kappa Gamma. Home: 1031 Meadow Rd Glencoe IL 60022 Office: 228 N LaSalle Chicago IL 60601

NOLAN, DAVID P., civil engr.; b. Euclid, Ohio, Mar. 26, 1953; s. Michael J. and LaVerne A. (Pepper) N.; B.S. in Civil Engring., Ohio No. U., 1975. Civil engr. Osborn Engring. Co., Cleve., 1975-77, Medusa Corp., Cleve., 1977—. Mem. ASCE, Tau Beta Pi, Omicron Delta Kappa, Alpha Phi Gamma. Clubs: Mayfield Village Racquet. Home: 151 Bell St Chagrin Falls OH 44022 Office: Lee and Monticello Blvds Cleveland Heights OH 44101

NOLAN, RICHARD, congressman; b. Brainerd, Minn., Dec. 17, 1943; s. James Henry and Mary Jean (Aylward) N.; student St. John's U., 1962; B.A., U. Minn., 1966; postgrad. U. Md., 1967; m. Marjorie C. Langer, June 13, 1964; children—Michael, Leah, John, Katherine. Ednl. staff asst. to Senator Walter Mondale of Minn., 1966-68; dir. Project Headstart, Minn., 1968; curriculum coordinator adult basic edn. Little Falls (Minn.) Sch. Dist.; tchr. social scis., Royalton, Minn., 1968-69; project coordinator Center Study Local Govt. St. John's U., Collegeville, Minn., 1971; adminstrv. asst. to sr. v.p. Fingerhut Corp., 1973-74; mem. 94th Congress from 6th Minn. dist. Mem. Minn. Ho. of Reps., 1969-73. Roman Catholic. Home: Waite Park MN 56387 Office: 214 Cannon House Office Bldg Washington DC 20515

NOLAND, MARION SEYMOUR, nutritionist; b. Claresholm, Alta., Can., Feb. 2, 1930; d. Ferdinand Brown and Lucy Mary (Hart) Seymour; came to U.S., 1956, naturalized, 1964; B.S. in Home Econs., U. Man., 1952; M.S. in Dietetics, Ohio State U., 1954; M.A. in Counseling, U. Mo., Kansas City, 1969; m. Norman Asbury Noland, Feb. 2, 1964. Instr. Sch. Home Econs. U. B.C., Vancouver, Can., 1953-55; asst. prof. Sch. Nursing U. Tex. Med. Branch, Galveston, 1956-60; asso. prof. dept. dietetics and nutrition U. Kans. Med. Center, Kansas City, 1960-66; counselor Franklin Smith Elementary Sch., Blue Springs, Mo., 1969-71, 1974-76; pvt. practice cons. nutritionist and counselor, Blue Springs, 1976—. Recipient U. Man. Home Econs. award, 1952; Singer Co. award, 1952; certified profl. counselor Profl. Counselors Assn., 1968. Mem. Am. Dietetic Assn. (registered dietitian), Am. Personnel and Guidance Assn., Mo. State Tchrs. Assn., Am. Mental Health Counselors Assn., Cons. Nutritionists Groups, AAUW (v.p. 1974-76), Blue Springs Community Educators Assn., Tex. League for Nursing, League of Women Voters, Beta Sigma Phi (chpt. pres.), Sigma Delta Epsilon. Mem. Unity Sch. of Christianity Ch. Clubs: Lake Tapawingo Women's (v.p. 1971-73). Author, pub. Nutrition and Special Diet Helpletter, 1977—. Contbr. articles to Jour. Home Econs., Am. Jour. Clin. Nutrition, Jour. Am. Dietetic Assn., 1955-65. Home and Office: Route 2 Box 108 Blue Springs MO 64015

NOLEN, GRANVILLE ABRAHAM, biologist; b. Richmond, Ky., Apr. 21, 1926; s. Granville and Bettie Mae (Dyehouse) N.; A.B., Miami U., Oxford, Ohio, 1950; m. Dolores Larrison, Nov. 10, 1950; children—Melanie Ann, Pamela Sue, Timothy Granville, Melissa Kay, Jonathan Ryan. Chief animal technician Miami Valley Labs., Proctor & Gamble Co., Cin., 1955-65, staff researcher in nutrition and teratology, 1965-70, sr. biologist, 1970—. Lectr. toxicology and animal sci. U. Cin., 1970-76. Bd. dirs. Soc. Crippled Children and Adults of Butler County, 1971-76, sec. 1972. Served with USAAC, 1944-45. Mem. Am. Inst. Nutrition, Am. Teratology Soc., AAAS, Am. Assn. Lab. Animal Sci., Congenital Anomalies Research Assn. Japan. Home: 316 Erickson Dr Oxford OH 45056 Office: PO Box 39175 Cincinnati OH 45247

NOLING, MICHAEL STEPHEN, mgmt. cons.; b. Rockford, Ill., June 22, 1938; s. Martin Norman and Elizabeth Helen (Sipple) N.; student Purdue U., 1956-57; B.S. in Mech. Engring., U. Wis., 1960, M.B.A., 1961; m. Elizabeth Charlotte Ketchum, June 11, 1960; children—Elizabeth Susan, Calvin Paul, Jill Marie. Partner adminstrv. services div. Arthur Andersen & Co., Milw., 1961-71, partner-in-charge, 1972—; White House fellow Office of Mgmt. and Budget, Exec. Office of Pres., Washington, 1971-72. Mem. Wis. Gov.'s Commn. on Edn., 1969-70; pres. Greater Milw. Survey Health and Social Services, 1974—. Bd. dirs. Milw. Met. Girl Scouts U.S.A., 1973—; treas. United Way Greater Milw., 1975—; trustee Citizens Govtl. Research Bur., 1974—. C.P.A., Wis. Mem. Inst. Mgmt. Sci. (chmn. 1969-70), Am. Prodn. and Inventory Control Soc., Sigma Chi. Unitarian (pres. bd. trustees 1968-70). Home: 2701 E Shorewood Blvd Milwaukee WI 53211 Office: 777 E Wisconsin Ave Milwaukee WI 53202

NOLTE, HENRY R., JR., lawyer; b. N.Y.C., Mar. 3, 1924; s. Henry R. and Emily A. (Eisele) N.; B.A., Duke, 1947; LL.B., U. Pa., 1949; m. Frances Messner, May 19, 1951; children—Gwynne Kippe, Henry R. III, Jennifer, Suzanne. Admitted to N.Y. bar, 1950, Mich. bar, 1967; asso. firm Cravath, Swaine & Moore, N.Y.C., 1951-61; asso. counsel Ford Motor Co., Dearborn, Mich., 1961, asst. gen. counsel, 1964-67, 69-71, asso. gen. counsel, 1971-74, v.p., gen. counsel, 1974—; v.p., gen. counsel, sec. Philco-Ford Corp., Phila., 1961-64; v.p., gen. counsel, sec. Ford Europe, Inc., Warley, Brentwood, Essex, Eng., 1967-69. Trustee Cranbrook-Kingswood Schs., Bloomfield Hills, Mich., 1974—; pres.'s asso. Duke U., 1976; vice chmn. adv. bd. Internat. and Comparative Law Center, Southwestern Legal Found. Served to lt. USNR, 1943-46; PTO. Mem. Am. (com. on corp. law depts. 1974—), Mich. bar assns., Assn. Bar City of N.Y., Assn. Gen. Counsel, Am. Judicature Soc. Episcopalian. Clubs: Country (Orchard Lake, Mich.); Hunters Creek (Metamora, Mich.), Cranbrook Tennis (Bloomfield Hills). Office: American Rd Dearborn MI 48121

NOONAN, MELVIN ARTHUR, pedodontist; b. Detroit, Sept. 14, 1918; s. John Henry and Tillie (Wieck) N.; student Eastern Mich. U., 1936-37, 39-40; D.D.S., U. Detroit, 1943; M.S., U. Mich., 1949; m. Laurene Elizabeth Scriven, Sept. 25, 1943; children—Timothy, Brian, Thomas. Pvt. practice dentistry, Detroit, 1946-47; pvt. practice pedodontics, Birmingham, Mich., 1949—. Asso. dir. children's clinic U. Detroit Sch. Dentistry, 1949-54; profl. adviser Birmingham (Mich.) Sch. System Fluoride Program, 1955-72. Served with Dental Corps, AUS, 1943-46. Diplomate Am. Bd. Pedodontics. Fellow Internat.,

Am. colls. dentists; mem. Am. (pres. 1967-68), Mich. (organizer, 1st pres. 1974) acads pedodontics, Kenneth A. Easlick Grad. Soc. (1st pres. 1957-59), Mich. Soc. Dentistry for Children (pres. 1952-53), Oakland County Dental Soc. (pres. 1961-62), Omicron Kappa Upsilon, Phi Kappa Phi. Club: Birmingham (Mich.) Country (dir. 1976—). Home: 32380 Mayfair St Birmingham MI 48009 Office: 630 N Woodward St Birmingham MI 48011

NOONAN, THOMAS CLIFFORD, architect; b. LaSalle, Ill., July 7, 1900; s. James Henry and Ellen (Pillion) N.; student U. Ill., 1920-21; B.A. in Architecture, U. Notre Dame, 1924; m. Ethel Jennett, Sept. 5, 1925; children—Jean (Mrs. Don Faulkner), James, Edward, Thomas Clifford. Desginer Graham, Anderson, Probst and White, Architects-Engrs., Chgo., 1924-40, chief architect, 1940-55, v.p., 1955-68, sr. v.p., 1968-75; project dir. Naval Ammunitiion Depots, Hastings, Nebr., Seal Beach, Calif., Camden, Ark., 1941-45; dir. planning, New State Dept. Bldg., Washington, State of Ind. Bldg., Indpls., Am. Dental Assn. Hdqrs. Bldg., Chgo., Morton Salt Co., Chgo., Loyola U. Sci. Bldg., Chgo., Motorola Complex, Chgo., Honeywell, Inc., Chgo., St. Joseph Mercy Hosp., Aurora, Ill. Bd. dirs. Catholic Charities, Chgo.; mem. citizens bd. Loyola U., Chgo. Registered profl. engr. Ill.; registered architect, Ill., Washington, Ariz. Mem. A.I.A., Ill. Soc. Architects (past dir.), Chgo. Assn. Commerce and Industry, Execs. Club. Roman Catholic. Clubs: Executive, University, Economic (Chgo.); Michigan Shores (Wilmette, Ill.). Home: 1414 Hinman Ave Evanston IL 60201 also Redondo Towers 8 Paseo Redondo Tucson AZ 85705 Office: 600 Davis St Evanston IL 60201 also 376 S Stone Tucson AZ 85702

NOPPER, RALPH JACOB, civil engr.; b. Toledo, O., July 5, 1916; s. Charles Joseph and Martha Elizabeth (Rippel) N.; B.Engring., U. Toledo, 1939; m. Roberta R. Newcomb, July 31, 1943; children—Linda E. (Mrs. Kenneth J. Keiser). Structural engr. A. Bentley & Sons Co., Toledo, O., 1937-38; constrn. engr. E.B. Badger & Sons Co., Boston, 1938-39; engr., H.C. Baker Co., Toledo, 1939-40; chief maintenance engr. Libbey-Owens-Ford Co., Toledo, 1940—; self-employed as cons. engr., Toledo, 1940—. Registered profl. engr., Ohio. Mem. Am. Soc. C.E. (pres. Toledo sect. 1954), Nat., Ohio, Toledo (pres. 1953) socs. profl. engrs., Toledo Tech. Council (pres. 1952-53). Home: 3710 Harley Rd Toledo OH 43613

NORA, PAUL FRANCIS, surgeon; b. Chgo., Aug. 14, 1929; s. Ernest Greeley and Margaret Helen (Coughlin) N.; M.D., Loyola U., Chgo., 1952; M.S. in Surgery, Northwestern U., 1964, Ph.D., 1968; m. Valerie Nortob, Aug. 18, 1956; children—Suzanne, Stephanie, Paul, Peter, Michelle. Intern, Cook County Hosp., Chgo., 1953, resident in surgery, 1959; surg. fellow Lahey Clinic, Boston, 1960; practice medicine specializing in surgery, Chgo., 1960—; attending surgeon VA Research Hosp., 1962—; chmn. dept. surgery Columbus-Cuneo-Cabrini Med. Center, 1964—; asso. prof. Northwestern U. Med. Sch.; trustee Commn. Profl. and Hosp. Activities. Served to lt. USNR, 1953-55. Mem. A.C.S. (chmn. com. operating room environment), Illuminating Engring. Soc. Editor: Operative Surgery, Principles and Techniques. Address: 2520 N Lakeview Ave Chicago IL 60614

NORDBY, JACK SOGGE, lawyer; b. Windom, Minn., Feb. 10, 1941; s. Elvin R. and Loraine (Sogge) N.; A.B. magna cum laude, Harvard, 1964, LL.B., 1967; postgrad. U. Minn., 1967-68; m Gudrun Elisabeth Einenkel, June 10, 1963; children—Andrea Elisabeth Loraine, Christopher Jack. Admitted to Minn. bar, 1967; since practiced in St. Paul; asso. firm Douglas W. Thomson, 1968-70; partner firm Thomson, Wylde & Nordby, 1970-72, Thomson, Wylde, Nordby, Friedberg & Rapoport, St. Paul, 1973—. Mem. Nat. Assn. Criminal Defense Lawyers, Am. Judicature Soc., Minn. State Bar Assn. Home: 15526 S Afton Hills Dr Afton MN 55001 Office: Suite 1530 55 E 5th St St Paul MN 55101

NORDBY, NORMAN EDWARD, ednl. adminstr.; b. Strathcona, Minn., Sept. 13, 1908; s. Carl Hanson and Anna Louise (Gustavson) N.; B.S., No. State Coll., 1940; M.A., U. S.D., 1941; m. Mary Alice Baker, Apr. 13, 1935; children—Daniel, John, Richard. Tchr. secondary schs., S.D., 1932-38; tchr. pub. sch., Timber Lake, S.D., 1938-39; tchr. counselor, prin. secondary sch., Rapid City, S.D., 1941-43, 46-74, ret. Chmn., Gov.'s Com. to Re-write State Sch. Standards, 1959. Served with AUS, 1943-46. Mem. Nat., S.D. assns. secondary prins., Nat. Secondary Prins., Am. Legion, S.D., Rapid City (pres. 1947) tchrs. assns., Phi Delta Kappa. Lutheran. (bd. govs. 1971-74). Kiwanian (pres. 1950, dist. officer 1952). Club: Beadle (hon.). Address: 1905 9th Ave Rapid City SD 57701

NORDEEN, DALE ARRON, financial assn. exec.; b. Madison, Wis., Dec. 23, 1927; s. Frank Edward and Pearl (Day) N.; B.A. in Accounting with honors, U. Wis., 1950; m. Nora Ellen Haley, Aug. 26, 1950; children—Kathy, Chris, Andy. Bus. trainee Gen. Electric, Madison, 1950-52; auditor Ernst & Ernst, C.P.A.'s, Madison, 1952-55; mgr. Hill Farms Devel. U. Wis., 1956-58; clk. First Fed. Savs. & Loan, 1948-49, auditor, 1955, asst. treas., 1956-60, v.p., treas., 1960-61, dir., 1961, pres., 1962—; dir. Wis. Devel. Corp., 1967-70; vice-chmn., dir. Fed. Home Loan Bank of Chgo., 1974. Chmn. Wis. Housing Finance Authority, 1974-75; mem. Equal Opportunities Commn. Housing Com. Bd. dirs. Jr. Achievement, 1969—; bd. dirs., treas. Methodist Hosp., 1973—. Served with USNR, 1945-46. Mem. U.S. (chmn. internal ops. com.), Wis. (pres., Outstanding Service award 1974) savs. and loan leagues. Home: 4206 Yuma Dr Madison WI 53711 Office: 202 State St Madison WI 53703

NORDLIE, ROBERT CONRAD, educator; b. Willmar, Minn., June 11, 1930; s. Peter Conrad and Myrtle (Spindler) N.; student Gustavus Adolphus Coll., 1948-49; B.S. in Edn., St. Cloud (Minn.) State Coll., 1952; M.S., U. N.D., 1957, Ph.D. (NIH fellow), 1960; m. Sally Ann Christianson, Aug. 23, 1959; children—Margaret, Melissa, John. Teaching and research asst. biochemistry U. N.D. Med. Sch., Grand Forks, 1955-60, Hill research prof. biochemistry, 1962-74, Chester Fritz distinguished prof. biochemistry, 1974—; NIH fellow Inst. Enzyme Research, U. Wis., 1960-61; mem. biochemistry study sect. NIH. Cons. enzymology Oak Ridge, 1961—. Mem. research com. N.D. Tb and Respiratory Disease Assn., 1966—, chmn. Grand Forks County, 1964—. Served with AUS, 1953-55. Mem. Am. Soc. Biol. Chemists, Am. Chem. Soc., AAAS, Internat. Union Biochemists, Am. Soc. for Microbiology, Soc. for Exptl. Biology and Medicine, Nat. Inst. Nutrition, Sigma Xi. Editorial bd. Biochimica et Biophysica Acta. Research, publs. on enzymology relating to metabolism of various carbohydrates in mammalian livers. Home: 162 Columbia Ct Grand Forks ND 58201

NORDLING, BERNARD ERICK, lawyer; b. Nekoma, Kans., June 14, 1921; s. C.R. Ebben and Edith (Freeburg) N.; A.B., McPherson Coll., 1947; student George Washington U., 1941-43; LL.B., Kans. U., 1949; m. Barbara Ann Burkholder, Mar. 26, 1949; children—Karen, Kristine, Leslie, Erick, Julie. Clerical employee FBI, 1941-44; admitted to Kans. bar, 1949; practiced in Hugoton, Kans., 1949—; mem. firms Kramer & Nordling, 1950-65, Kramer, Nordling, Nordling & Fay, 1966—; city atty., Hugoton, 1951—; county atty. Stevens County (Kans.), 1957-63. Sec., Raycolor, Inc., Hugoton, 1968—; exec. sec. S.W. Kans. Royalty Owners Assn., 1968—; Kans. mem. legal com. Interstate Oil Compact Commn., 1969—, mem. supply tech. adv. com. Nat. Gas Survey, FPC, 1975—; mem. Kans. Energy Adv. Council, 1975—, exec. com., 1976—. Mem. Hugoton Sch. Bds., 1954-68, pres. grade sch. bd., 1961-66; pres. Stevens County Library Bd., 1957-63. Trustee McPherson Coll., 1971—, mem. exec. com., 1975—; bd. govs. Seward County (Kans.) Community Jr. Coll. Devel. Found., 1971—. Served with AUS, 1944-46. Mem. Nat. Honor Soc., Order of Coif. Home: 218 N Jackson St Hugoton KS 67951 Office: 209 E 6th St Hugoton KS 67951

NORDLING, LELAND EBBEN, lawyer; b. Nekoma, Kans., Sept. 13, 1924; s. C.R. Ebben and Edith (Freeburg) N.; B.S., McPherson Coll., 1949; J.D., Washburn U., 1950; m. Janet Owen, Aug. 15, 1948; children—Katherine Lea, Melanie Edith, Ebben Lee, Swen Erick. Admitted to Kans. bar, 1950; practice law, Johnson, Kans., 1950-66; partner Kramer, Nordling, Nordling & Fay, Hugoton, Kans., 1966—; county atty. Stanton County, Johnson, Kan., 1951-61. Gov.'s rep. Pub. Land Law Rev. Commn., 1965-66; chmn. Stanton County Unification Bd., 1964; mem. pub. lands com. Interstate Oil Compact Commn., 1965-66. Served with AUS, 1943-46; ETO. Mem. S.W. Kans. Royalty Assn. (asst. sec. 1967—). Am., Kans., S.W. Kans. bar assns., V.F.W., Hugoton C. of C. (pres. 1969-70). Rotarian (pres. Johnson 1961), Odd Fellow. Home: 1202 S Main St Hugoton KS 67951 Office: 209 E 6th St Hugoton KS 67951

NORDMAN, JOHN CARLTON, chemist; b. Mace, Ind., July 17, 1917; s. John and Fannie May (Peterman) N.; A.B., Wabash Coll., 1939; postgrad. Ind. U., 1940-41; m. Margaret Alice Riley, Dec. 25, 1939; children—Mark Allen, Karl Thomas. With Allison div. Gen. Motors Corp., Indpls., 1940-43, Wright Aeronautical, Cin., 1943, World Bestos div. Firestone Tire & Rubber, New Castle, Ind., 1946-66; chemist friction materials research and devel. Chem. div. Chrysler Corp., Trenton, Mich., 1966-70, mgr. friction materials research and devel. lab., 1971—. Served with USAAF, 1943-45. Recipient Silver Beaver award, Boy Scouts Am., 1963. Mem. Am. Chem. Soc., Soc. Automotive Engrs. Author: Resume: Friction, Friction Materials and Automotive Brake Fundamentals, 1969 (tng. manual). Home: 2305 Norwood Ct Trenton MI 48183 Office: 5437 W Jefferson Ave Trenton MI 48183

NORDMARK, TORBERG PEDER, clin. psychologist; b. Fairview, Mont., Nov. 20, 1936; s. Torberg P. and Aziel E. (Fladmoe) N.; m. Joan Stedronsky, Aug. 11, 1960; children—Lisa, Eric, Julie. B.A., Concordia Coll., 1957; B.S., Luther Theol. Sem., 1961; M.A., U. N.D., 1964, Ph.D., 1968. Intern N.D. State Hosp., Jamestown, 1966-67, staff psychologist, 1967-69; clin. psychologist Marshfield (Wis.) Clinic, 1969—; instr. part time Jamestown Coll., 1968-69; U. Wis., Marshfield Wood County campus, 1969-70; lectr. U. Wis., Green Bay, 1975-76. Active PTA, 1974-75; pres. Faith Luth. Ch., 1974-75. Licensed psychologist, Wis. Mem. Am., Wis. psychol. socs., Psi Chi, Sigma Xi (asso.). Contbr. articles to profl. jours. Home: 1012 W Blodgett St Marshfield WI 54449 Office: Marshfield Clinic Marshfield WI 54449

NORDSTROM, CARL CLIFFORD, assn. exec.; b. Topeka, Mar. 5, 1916; s. Edward and Betty (Holcomb) N.; A.B., Washburn U., 1938; m. Virginia Hamm, Apr. 2, 1943; children—Carla (Mrs. Randy Hearrell), Mary (Mrs. Fred Foster), Mark. Mem. staff research dept. Kans. Legislative Council, 1938-42, 45-46; research dir. Kans. C. of C., 1946-54, asst. mgr., 1954-70; exec. v.p., gen. mgr. Kans. Assn. Commerce and Industry, Topeka, 1970—. Served to lt. USNR, 1942-46. Mem. Am., Kans. socs. assn. execs., Kans. C. of C. Execs. (v.p. 1958-59, pres. 1959-60). Home: 813 Oakley St Topeka KS 66606 Office: 500 First Nat Tower Topeka KS 66603

NORDYKE, HOLLIS JUDSON, newspaper publisher; b. Villisca, Iowa, Mar. 13, 1908; s. Harold Hastings and Grace Elva (Mayhew) N.; B.S., Simpson Coll., 1930; m. Garnette Winifred Rogers, Feb. 14, 1931; children—Linda Ann (Mrs. John Shortridge), John Rogers. With advt. sales dept. Des Moines Register & Tribune, 1930-32; bus. and advt. mgr. Creston (Iowa) News Advertiser, 1932-35; bus. mgr. Ames (Iowa) Daily Tribune, 1935-59, pub., 1959—. Lectr., Sch. Journalism, Iowa State U., 1948-49. Recipient Distinguished Service award Ames Jr. C. of C., 1940; Ames Boss of Yr. award, 1965, Master Editor-Pub. award Iowa Press Assn., 1967. Mem. Am. Newspaper Pubs. Assn., Nat. Newspaper Assn., Iowa Daily Press Assn. (past pres.), Iowa Press Assn., Internat. Newspaper Advt. Execs. (dir. 1956), Inland Daily Press Assn. (dir. 1964-67), Ames C. of C. (pres. 1951), Alpha Tau Omega, Sigma Delta Chi. Republican. Mem. United Ch. of Christ. Mason, Elk, Rotarian. Home: 1519 13th St Ames IA 50010 Office: 317 Fifth St Ames IA 50010

NORMAN, ELVA PAULINE KUYKENDALL (MRS. ISAAC DANIEL NORMAN), pub. relations, writer; b. Waxahachie, Tex., Jan. 18, 1911; d. Thomas Calvin and Laura (Martin) Kuykendall; B.J., Mary Hardin-Baylor Coll., 1930; postgrad. U. Mo., St. Louis, 1964-66; m. Isaac Daniel Norman, Aug. 30, 1931; children—John Kuykendall, Eric Jesse, Thomas Daniel. Publicity dir. St. Louis YWCA, 1944-64; pub. relations dir. St. Louis County Library, 1955-64; editor The Suburban Educator, 1964-72; asst. exec. sec., pub. relations dir. St. Louis Suburban Tchrs. Assn., 1964-72; writing tchr. Pattonville Evening Sch., 1973; St. Louis pub. relations rep. Mo. Tchrs. Assn., 1973. Nat. pub. relations chmn. Nat. Fedn. Garden Clubs Conv., St. Louis, 1959; local press relations chmn. Nat. Library Assn. Conv., St. Louis, 1964; mem. state com. Nat. Library Week, 1965; mem. communications adv. bd. University City schs., 1973—; vol. various local social agys. Bd. dirs. University City Youth Center, Wigwam, 1957, University City Adult Evening Sch., 1950-72; bd. mgrs. Washington U. Campus YM-YWCA, 1972—; mem. Friends of University City Library; chmn. Theta Sigma Phi scholarship com. St. Louis Journalism Found., 1968-72. Recipient awards for mag. editing Mo. Press Women, 1965, 66, 68, 69, 70, 71, 72; award for news story Ednl. Press Assn., 1966, news series, 1969, mag. editing, 1971; Nat. Press Women award, 1968, 70; St. Louis Indsl. Press Assn. award, 1969, 71, 72. Mem. Nat. Sch. Pub. Relations Assn., Nat. Press Women, Mo. Press Women, Pub. Relations Soc. Am. (accredited mem.), Delta Kappa Gamma (hon.), Theta Sigma Phi (pres. St. Louis chpt. 1937, 47, 53-56, nat. pub. relations dir. 1959-61), Pi Gamma Mu. Baptist. Club: St. Louis Press. Author: Biography of a Church, 1978. Contbr. articles to newspapers, also to various publs. Home: 7407 Melrose Ave University City St Louis MO 63130 Office: 7209 Delmar Blvd St Louis MO 63130

NORMAN, FORREST ALONZO, lawyer; b. Renton, Pa., Nov. 21, 1929; s. Forrest Alonzo and Nellie Elizabeth (Corley) N.; B.B.A., Case Western Res. U., 1952, J.D., 1954; m. Christine Dende, July 5, 1954; children—Sally, Forrest Alonzo III, William. Admitted to Ohio bar, 1954; Mem. firm Gallagher, Sharp, Fulton, Norman & Mollison and predecessor firms, Cleve., 1956—. Served with AUS, 1955-56. Mem. Internat. Soc. Barristers, Def. Research Inst. Inc. (v.p. 1973-75, dir.), Fedn. Ins. Counsel (v.p. 1974-75, dir.), Nat. Assn. R.R. Trial Counsel, Order of Coif, Delta Theta Phi. Clubs: Shaker Heights Country, Union, Masons. Home: 2977 Courtland Blvd Shaker Heights OH 44122 Office: 630 Bulkley Bldg Cleveland OH 44115

NORMAN, JOHN WILLIAM, oil co. exec.; b. Harrisburg, Ill., Sept. 4, 1910; s. Walter Jacob and Clarissa May (Bush) N.; student pub. schs., Saline County, Ill.; m. Marcella Mary Souheaver, July 2, 1937. Dist. mgr. Martin Oil Co., 1936-54; with Am-Bulk Oil Co. (name changed to Norman Oil Co., 1960), Lisle, Ill., 1949—, pres., 1960—; dir. 1st Ogden Corp., Bank Hinsdale, Bank Lisle, Bank Lockport. Served with USNR, 1943-44. Mem. VFW, Am. Legion. Home: 4333 Main St Lisle IL 60532 Office: 1018 Ogden Ave Lisle IL 60532

NORMAN, RONALD VICTOR, library adminstr.; b. Venice, Calif., July 10, 1929; s. Victor Stephen and Violet B. (Aughton) N.; B.A. (NROTC scholar), U. N.Mex., 1953; M.Div., Lutheran Sch. Theology, Chgo., 1960; M.A. in Library Sci., U. Denver, 1970; m. Anita Louise Redstrom, June 5, 1953; children—Ronald Stephen, Jennifer Lynn, Mark Andrew. Ordained to ministry Lutheran Ch., 1960; pastor Trinity Luth. Ch., Dalton, Nebr., 1960-64, Messiah Luth. Ch., Broadwater, Nebr., 1962-64, St. Paul Luth. Ch., Auburn, Nebr., 1964-69; reference librarian Iliff Sch. Theology, Denver, 1969-70; telecommunications coordinator Tex. State Library, Austin, 1970-71; dir. library Kearney Pub. Library, Kearney, Nebr., 1971—. Served with USN, 1953-56. Mem. Am., Nebr. (pres. 1974-75), Mt.-Plains library assns., Am. Soc. for Info. Sci., Sci. Fiction Research Assn. Democrat. Home: 3607 6th Ave Kearney NE 68847 Office: 2020 1st Ave Kearney NE 68847

NORMAN, WAYNE ANDREW, real estate investment mgmt. cons.; b. Dubuque, Iowa, Jan. 1, 1920; s. Wayne Albert and Mildred Harrison (Galliart) N.; B.S., Iowa State U., 1942; m. Edith Stuart, Aug. 29, 1942; children—Wayne, Andrew, Beth. Dir. research Caradlo, Inc., Dubuque, 1946-55, exec. v.p., gen. mgr., 1955-69; owner Julien Dubuque Co., 1975—; dir. First Nat. Bank, Dubuque. Cons. Expansion Arts panel Nat. Endowment for the Arts, Washington, 1975—; chmn. Iowa Arts Council, 1975—; bd. dirs. YMCA, Dubuque, U. Dubuque, 1969-75, Finley Hosp., Dubuque. Served with USAAF, 1942-46. Named Man of Year, Nat. Mgmt. Assn., 1970; recipient First Citizen of Dubuque award, 1973. Mem. Nat. Woodwork Mfg. Assn. (pres. 1969), Nat. Forest Products Assn. (mem. exec. com. 1970—), Nat. Assn. State Arts Agys. (v.p. 1973-75), Phi Kappa Phi, Tau Beta Pi, Tau Sigma Delta, Phi Gamma Delta. Presbyn. (elder). Home: 1525 Douglas St Dubuque IA 52001 Office: PO Box 717 Dubuque IA 52001

NORMOYLE, JOHN LOUIS, pub. relations exec.; b. Chgo., Mar. 27, 1922; s. John Joseph and Catherine Henrietta (Shroede) N.; grad. Morton Jr. Coll., 1947; B.S., Northwestern U., 1952; m. June Rose Bastlin, Sept. 8, 1947 (div. Sept. 1969); children—Janice, Judy, Joyce, Jennifer. Asso. editor Brick and Clay Record mag., Chgo., 1950-53; publicity supr. Allstate Ins. Co., Skokie, Ill., 1953-60; account exec. Philip Lesly Co., Chgo., 1960-62; pub. relations dir. Alberto Culver Co., Chgo., 1963; exec. v.p. Compass 4 Pub. Relations, Chgo., 1964-67; dir. press info. Bonsib Advt., Fort Wayne, Ind., 1968-69; mng. editor Lab. Medicine mag., Chgo., 1969-77; dir. pub. info. Am. Soc. Clin. Pathologists, Chgo., 1977—. Dir. Intercomco, Inc., Chgo., 1972—; guest lectr. pub. relations and journalism Mich. State U., East Lansing, 1965-66, Columbia Coll., Chgo., 1961, YMCA Central Coll., Chgo., 1970-71, U. Ill., 1973, Chgo. Med. Coll., 1974-75, Northwestern U., 1976, Sangamon Coll., Springfield, Ill., 1977. Served with AUS, 1942-45. Decorated Bronze Star medal, Purple Heart with oak leaf cluster. Recipient Honor award for best feature writing, Publicity Club of Chgo., 1962, award for best continuing pub. relations campaign, 1964. Mem. Publicity Club Chgo. (bd. dirs. 1958-66), Pub. Relations Soc. Am., Chgo. Press Club, Mensa. Author: The News Release Format, 1956. Contbr. articles to profl. jours. Home: 1216 W Lunt Ave Chicago IL 60626 Office: 2100 W Harrison St Chicago IL 60612

NORRICK, WAYNE COLEMAN, real estate developer; b. Winslow, Ind., July 5, 1927; s. Claude Bryan and Edith Ione (Coleman) N.; B.S. in Edn., U. Evansville, 1948; postgrad. Oakland City Coll., 1948-50, Ind. State U., 1952-53; m. Elaine Wood, Aug. 18, 1951; children—Cindy, Kim, Scott. Tchr., coach, Ft. Branch, Ind., 1951-57; partner fast-food drive-ins, So. Ind. and Ill., 1954-59; salesman Dog n Suds, Inc., Champaign, Ill., 1959-61, sr. v.p., 1961-69; partner Norrick & Morrow, realtors, Champaign, 1970—. Mem. UN Day Com., 1975. Served with USNR, 1945-46. Clubs: Masons, Shriners, Kiwanis (head So. Ind. Key clubs 1954-55). Home: 2111 Noel Dr Champaign IL 61820 Office: 8 Henson Pl Champaign IL 61820

NORRIS, G. KENNON, realty co. exec.; b. Kearney, Nebr., Apr. 16, 1929; s. George E. and Mable S. (Nieman) N.; B.A., Kearney State Coll., 1950; m. Margaret M. Schlagel, May 20, 1951; children—Deborah, Sandra, Jennifer, Kyle. Sch. tchr., coach, Woodston, Kans., 1950-51; divisional sales mgr. Hybrid Seed Corn Co., Spencer, Iowa, 1953-63; with Spencer Realty, 1963—, pres., 1974—. Pres. YMCA, Spencer, 1977—. Mem. Nat. (C.R.S.), Iowa (asso. v.p. 1970) assns. realtors, Nat. Mktg. Inst., Spencer C. of C., Iowa Great Lakes Bd. Realtors (pres. 1970-71). Served with AUS, 1951-53. Home: 2107 W 11th St Spencer IA 51301 Office: 1823 Hwy Blvd Spencer IA 51301

NORRIS, JAMES LAWRENCE, coll. ofcl.; b. Lancaster, Pa., Dec. 12, 1918; s. James Arthur and Luella (Walton) N.; B.S., Franklin and Marshall Coll., 1948; A.M., U. Pa., 1949; m. Gertrude G. Weaver, Oct. 17, 1942; children—G. Nicia, Kendra Lu. Asst. bus. mgr. Millersville (Pa.) State Coll., 1949-51; exec. dir. alumni assn. Franklin and Marshall Coll., Lancaster, 1951-54; comptroller Lake Erie Coll., Painesville, Ohio, 1954-60; bus. mgr., 1960-70, treas., 1970-74, v.p., 1974—. Instr. transp. Cleve. U.S. Army Res. Sch., 1954-66. Served to capt., ordnance corps AUS, 1942-46; lt. col. Res., ret. Mem. Eastern Assn. Coll. and U. Bus. Officers, Coll. and U. Personnel Assn., Nat. Assn. Ednl. Buyers, Delta Sigma Phi, Alpha Delta Sigma. Republican. Presbyn. Home: 9431 Smith Rd Waite Hill Village Willoughby OH 44094 Office: 391 W Washington St Painesville OH 44077

NORRIS, PAUL NATHAN, auditor, fin. co. exec.; b. St. Paul, Minn., Nov. 18, 1937; s. Walter N. and Margaret Florence (Weyh) N.; B.A., Macalester Coll., 1964; postgrad. U. Minn., 1968-69, bus. adminstrn. Mankato State U., 1974—; m. Carol Ann Barker, July 25, 1963; children—Jonathan Walter, Georgine Ann, Jane Margaret. Internal traveling auditor Great No. Ry., 1964-65, computer system designer, St. Paul, 1965-67, cons. to McKinsey & Co., Spokane, 1967, asst. to auditor, St. Paul, 1968-70; asst. to dir. internal audit Burlington No., Inc., St. Paul, 1970-73, mgr. internal audit dept., 1973—; guest lectr. U. Minn., 1975-77; instr. Inst. Internal Auditors, Cadmus Edn. Found., 1974—. Bd. dirs. Ry. Employees Cafeteria Assn., pres., 1976-77; trustee EDP Auditors Found. Edn. Research, 1977—. Served with M.C., U.S. Army, 1958-61. Certified Internal Auditor. Mem. Am. Assn. Railroads, EDP Auditors Assn. (pres. 1974-75, dir. 1976—), Inst. Internal Auditors, Nat. Assn. of Accountants (dir. 1976—). Presbyterian. Club: St. Paul Athletic. Contbr. articles on control of computer systems, mng. internal audit, and auditing to tech. publs. Home: 1066 Fairmount Ave St Paul MN 55105 Office: 176 E 5th St St Paul MN 55101

NORRIS, ROBERT MIRANDA, physician; b. Oviedo, Spain, Sept. 3, 1923; s. Theodore F. and Lillian (Norris) Miranda; B.A., U. Oviedo, 1942; M.D., U. Madrid (Spain), 1949, U. Havana (Cuba), 1951; m. Maruja Gonzalez, Nov. 18, 1951; children—Robert, Josephine. Came to U.S., 1957, naturalized, 1962. Gen. practice medicine, Havana, 1951-57; intern Passavant Meml. Hosp., Chgo., 1957-58; basic ophthalmology U. Ill. Med. Sch., 1958-59; resident ophthalmology City Hosp. Center, N.Y.C., 1959-61; with Canfield Clinic, Rockford, Ill., 1961—, asso. med. dir., chief ophthalmology, 1973—; asso. prof. ophthalmology Rockford Sch. Medicine. Diplomate Am. Bd. Ophthalmology. Fellow Am. Acad. Ophthalmology, A.C.S., Royal Soc. Health, Soc. Eye Surgeons; mem. A.M.A. Club: Rockford Country. Home: 3510 Val Mark Terrace Rockford IL 61107 Office: 1215 N Alpine Rd Rockford IL 61107

NORTH, VICTOR, physician; b. Kansas City, Kans., Jan. 2, 1918; s. Peter and Nell (Zemait) N.; A.B., U. Kans., 1939, M.A., 1940, M.D., 1947; postgrad. George Washington U., 1942-44; m. Doris Griffin Nov. 2, 1940; children—James, Daniel, Frederick. Inst. U. Pitts., 1940; chemist geol. survey U.S. Dept. Interior, Washington, 1941-44; intern Wesley Hosp., Wichita, 1947-48; resident Sedgewick County Hosp., 1948-49; gen. practice medicine, Wichita, Kans., 1948—; mem. staff St. Joseph Hosp., Wichita, 1949—, staff pres., 1973, bd. dirs., 1972-73, mem. med. exec. com., 1972-76. Served with USN, 1944-47, 50-52. Diplomate Am. Bd. Family Practice. Mem. AMA, Kans. (hosp. reps. del. 1975—), Sedgewick County (dir. 1975—) med. socs., Am. Acad. Family Practice, Phi Beta Kappa, Alpha Omega Alpha. Home: 1105 Perry Ave Wichita KS 67203 Office: 1148 S Hillside Wichita KS 67211

NORTH, WILLIAM STANLEY, mfg. co. exec.; b. Chgo., May 1, 1911; s. Francis Stanley and Julia (Morgan) N.; B.S. in Mech. Engring., Harvard, 1934, postgrad., 1935; m. Sarah Jackson, 1934; children—Sarah Randolph, Elizabeth Holmes; m. 2d, Patricia Cathcart Armstrong, Mar. 20, 1958; 1 stepson, James Cathcart Armstrong. With Union Spl. Corp., Chgo., 1935—, successively engr. and salesman, personnel dir., 1941-44, v.p., 1944-47, asst. gen. mgr., 1947-52, pres., gen. mgr., 1952-76, chmn. bd., chief exec. officer, 1976—; dir. Signode Corp., Portec Inc. Adv. bd., past pres. Ill. Mfrs. Assn.; bd. dirs., past chmn. Lawson YMCA (Chgo.); past chmn., bd. dirs., past pres. Allendale Sch. for Boys; bd. dirs., pres. Chgo. Lyric Opera. Mem. Lake Forest Open Lands Assn. (dir., treas.), U.S. Seniors Golf Assn., Midwest Indsl. Mgmt. Assn. (past pres.). Republican. Episcopalian (sr. warden). Clubs: University, Harvard, Campfire, Casino, Commonwealth (past pres., treas.); Commercial (Chgo.); Onwentsia, Old Elm (former dir.), Winter (Lake Forest, Ill.); Tin Whistles (Pinehurst, N.C.); Pine Valley Golf (Clementon, N.J.); Gulf Stream Bath and Tennis (dir.), Gulf Stream Golf (Delray Beach, Fla.); Mill Reef (Antigua, W.I.). Home: 1490 N Green Bay Rd Lake Forest IL 60045 Office: 400 N Franklin St Chicago IL 60610

NORTHROP, GORDON DOUGLAS, educator, anthropologist; b. Illion, N.Y., Oct. 31, 1919; s. Elmer Daniel and Mina Caroline (Utter) N.; A.B., Wheaton (Ill.) Coll., 1942; B.D., Eastern Baptist Sem., Phila., 1944; A.M., U. Mich., Ann Arbor, 1961; Ph.D., Mich. State U., Lansing, 1970; m. Shirley Ann Blakely, Aug. 6, 1944; children—Gordon Daniel, Deborah Ann, Priscilla Elizabeth, Timothy Douglas. Teaching asst. U. Mich., 1960-61; mem. faculty Wayne State U., Detroit, 1962-65, 70-72; mem. faculty Henry Ford Community Coll., Dearborn, Mich., 1965—, prof. anthropology, 1973—; spl. research contemporary Indian Am. Bd. dirs. Southeastern Mich. Ethnic Heritage Assn. Fellow Am. Anthrop. Assn., A.A.A.S.; asso. Current Anthropology; mem. Central State Anthrop. Assn., Am. Ethnol. Soc., Mich. Acad. Arts and Scis., Am. Assn. Coll. and Univ. Profs., N. Am. Indian Assn. Detroit (hon.). Author: The Effects of White Contact on Crow Culture Through the Period of the Great American Fur Trade to 1870, 1944; The Rise of Phonecian Baalism and its Diffusiin into Palestine, 1944; Pan-Indianism in the Metropolis: A Case Study of an Emergent Ethnosyncretic Revitalization Movement, 1970. Home: 36335 Grand River Rd Farmington MI 48024 Office: 5101 Evergreen Rd Dearborn MI 48128

NORTHROP, STUART JOHNSTON, mfg. co. exec.; b. New Haven, Oct. 22, 1925; s. Filmer Stuart and Christine (Johnston) N.; grad. Phillips Acad., 1943; B.A. in Physics, Yale U., 1948; m. Cynthia Daniell, Feb. 23, 1946; children—Christine Daniell, Richard Rockwell Stafford. Indsl. engr. U.S. Rubber Co., Nangatuck, Conn., 1948-51; head indsl. engring. dept. Am. Cyanamid Co., Wallingford, Conn., 1951-54; mfg. mgr. Linear, Inc., Phila., 1954-57; mgr. mfg. and quality control Westinghouse Electric Co., Pitts., 1957-58; prodn. supt. SKF Industries, Phila., 1958-61; v.p. Am. Meter div. Singer Co., 1961-70, v.p., gen. mgr. water resources div., 1970-72; pres., dir. Huffman Mfg. Co., Dayton, 1972—. Mem. Delaware Valley Investors Assn., Delta Kappa Epsilon. Clubs: Moraine, Racquet (Dayton); Elihu (New Haven); Interlocutors (Phila.). Home: 3732 Blossom Heath Rd Dayton OH 45419 Office: Byers Rd Dayton OH 45401

NORTHRUP, ARTHUR HARRY, lawyer, economist; b. Indpls., June 3, 1920; s. Leonard Everett and Margaret (Couden) N.; B.A. in Econs. with honors, Harvard U., 1942, M.B.A., 1946; J.D., U. Mich., 1949; m. Anne Mary Holmes, July 31, 1948; children—Arthur Harry, Nancy Anna Northrup Eastman, m. 2d, Deborah Lee Norris, Sept. 19, 1969; children—Heather Lynn, Christopher A., Holly Margaret; m. 3d, Joan Dearmin Finney, Jan. 2, 1977; 1 stepson, Mark D. Finney. Quality control engr. Wright Aero. Corp., 1943-44; admitted to Ind. bar, 1949; since practiced in Indpls.; mem. firm Gregg, Fillion, Hughes & Northrup, 1951-70, firm Martz, Beattey, Hinds & Wallace, 1970—; lectr. econs. Earlham Coll., 1949, Butler U., 1950-57, 59-76; asst. city atty., Indpls., 1951-54, 68-76; mem. Ind. Ho. of Reps., 1969-70; gen. counsel Ind. Consumer Finance Assn., 1954-74, Ind. Restaurant Assn., 1951-56, sec., dir. Carbob, 1957—, S.E. Drey and Co., 1973—. Sec. Ind. Corps. Survey Commn., 1958-77. Pres. Washington Twp. Republican Club, 1966-68; sec. bd. dirs. Summer Mission for Sick Children. Served with USNR, 1944-46. Mem. Am., Seventh Circuit, Ind. (chmn. probate trust and real estate sect.), Indpls. bar assns., Am. Legion (past post comdr.), S.A.R. (pres. Ind. 1956). Republican. Episcopalian. Clubs: Century (pres. 1960), Ind. Harvard (pres. 1954), Harvard Bus. Sch. (pres. 1955), U. Mich. (pres. Indpls. alumni 1975-77) (Indpls.). Editor: Forms for Indiana Corporations, 1966, 77. Contbr. articles on trusts, income tax and other tax laws to profl. jours. Home: 7770 N Pennsylvania Indianapolis IN 46240 Office: 130 E Washington St Indianapolis IN 46204

NORTON, CLIFFORD RAYMOND, JR., civil engr.; b. Mpls., Sept. 30, 1926; s. Clifford Raymond and Dorothy M. (Knowles) N.; student Coe Coll.; B.Civil Engring., U. Minn., 1949; m. Mary Joan Towey, Nov. 19, 1949; 1 son—Thomas C. Civil engr. Bur. Reclamation, Sheridan, Wyo., 1949-51, estimating engr., Billings, Mont, 1951-52; cons. engr. Consoer, Townsend & Asso., Greencastle, Ind., 1952-58, asso. in charge of br. office, 1958—; cons. engr. City of Greencastle, 1960—. Mem. Greencastle Plan Commn. 1960—, pres., 1975—; mgr. Little League, 1960-70; sec., treas. Pee Wee Football, 1972-73. Served with USAF, 1945. Mem. ASCE, Nat., Ind. socs. profl. engrs., Cons. Engrs. Ind. (dir.), Am. Arbitration Assn., Am. Legion. Roman Catholic. Clubs: Elks, Moose. Home: 529 N Arlington St Greencastle IN 46135 Office: 19 E Franklin St Greencastle IN 46135

NORTON, JOHN PHILEMON, engring. mgr.; b. Galesburg, Ill., Oct. 12, 1930; s. Edward Joseph and Violet Rose (West) N.; B.S.E.E., Ohio State U., 1960; m. Jane Ann Kurth, May 16, 1953; children—John, Pamela, David. Project engr. Armstrong Furnace Co., Columbus, Ohio, 1958-62, Am. Air Filter Co., St. Louis, Mo., 1962-64, mgr. research and devel., 1964-68, mgr. design and devel., 1968-71, mgr. engring., 1971—. Pres., local PTA; active Boy Scouts Am. Troop Council, 1965-76. Mem. Am. Soc. of Heating and Refrigeration and Air Conditioning Engrs., Am. Inst. of Aero. and Astronautics. Clubs: Elks. Holder 8 patents on Combustion Tech. and Rankine Cycle Systems. Home: 3 Gandy Dr Creve Coeur MO 63141 Office: 1270 N Price Rd St Louis MO 63132

NORTON, ROBERT PILGER, savs. and loan exec.; b. East Orange, N.J., July 23, 1933; s. Frank Robert and Ruth E. (Pilger) N.; B.S., Purdue U., 1955, M.S., 1957; m. Beverly Ruth Martin, Sept. 10, 1955; children—Robert Lyle Pilger, Rebecca Ann Marie, Jonathan Van Ness. Rep., Walley Agrl. Service, Ft. Wayne, Ind., 1957-59; loan counselor First Fed. Savs. & Loan Assn., Ft. Wayne, 1960-67, asst. sec., 1965-67, asst. v.p. research and devel., 1967-73, sec., 1970—, v.p., 1973—; v.p., sec., dir. N. Central Enterprises, Inc.; sec., dir. North Eastern Ins. Agy., Inc., Ft. Wayne. Past pres. St. Joseph Twp. Civic Assn., Maysville Rd. Suburban Assn.; vice chmn. Allen County Bd. Zoning Appeals; bd. dirs. Allen-Wells chpt. ARC. Mem. Am. Savs. and Loan Inst. (pres. Ft. Wayne chpt. 1969), Ft. Wayne Bd. Realtors (affiliate), Ft. Wayne Home Builders Assn. (affiliate), Dutch Settlers Soc. Albany (N.Y.), Greater Fort Wayne C. of C. (chmn. local govt. com.), Nat. Hist. Soc. (founding mem.). Presbyterian. Club: Masons. Editor Flash, 1968—. Home: 8861 Lake Lane Fort Wayne IN 46815 Office: 719 Court St Fort Wayne IN 46801

NOSAL, CHESTER WALTER, lawyer; b. Chgo., July 12, 1944; s. Chester and Frances (Winclechter) N.; B.S. in Commerce, DePaul U., 1966, M.B.A., 1967; J.D., Georgetown U., 1970; m. Kathleen Waehler, Sept. 4, 1971. Admitted to D.C. bar, 1970, Ill. bar, 1970; asst. to sec.-treas. automotive parts div. Borg Warner, Inc., Chgo., 1967; tax law specialists, Office Internat. Ops., IRS, Washington, 1968; gen. staff atty. Office of the Sec., U.S. Dept. Treasury, Washington, 1969; partner firm Winston & Strawn, Chgo., 1970—; mem. franchise advisory bd. Ill. Sec. State, 1975-77; commr. Cook County (Ill.) Bd. Corrections, 1973—; mem. planning com. Health Systems Agency, City of Chgo., 1976—; mem. Ill. State Health Coordinating Council, 1976—; Pace Inst. Com. of 100; T Group trainer Upper Kenmore Devel. Project, Chgo., 1965-67; mgmt. con. Appalachian Study Center, 1965-67; bd. dirs. Ill. Coop. Health Data System, Inc., 1977—. Exec. editor Law & Policy in Internat. Bus., 1966-67; recipient Am. Civil Liberties Commendation, 1975; Arthur Young Award, 1965. Mem. Am., Ill., Chgo. bar assns., AM. Correction Assn., Am. Soc. Internat. Law, Beta Gamma, Sigma, Delta Mu Delta, Deta Alpha Psi. Clubs: Racquet, Executive (Chgo.). Home: 1320 N State Parkway Chicago IL 60610 Office: 1 1st Nat Plaza Chicago IL 60603

NOSE, YUKIHIKO, physician; b. Hokkaido, Japan, May 7, 1932; s. Minoru and Haru (Murakami) N.; M.D., U. Hokkaido, 1957, Ph.D., 1962; came to U.S., 1962; m. Bonnie Jean Mac Donald, Mar. 15, 1965; children—Kimi Willhemina, Ken William, Kevin Scott. Rotating intern, U. Hokkaido, 1957-58, resident in surgery, 1958-62; fellow dept. surgery Maimonides Med. Center, Bklyn., 1962-64; grad. fellow dept. artificial organs Cleve. Clinic, 1964-66; asso. staff dept. artificial organs Cleve. Clinic Found., 1966-67, head staff Artificial Organs Research Lab., 1967-70, head dept. artificial organs, 1971—. Adj. prof. biomed. engring. Case Western Res. U., Cleve., 1973—. Chmn. bd. trustees Kolff Found., 1974—. Fellow N.Y. Acad. Scis.; mem. Am. Coll. Cardiology, Am. Coll. Angiology, Internat. (sec.), Am. socs. artificial internal organs, AAAS, IEEE, Instrument Soc. Am. (sr.), ASTM. Editorial bd. Jour. Biomed. Materials Research, Artificial Organs, Jour. Biomaterials, Med. Devices and Artificial Organs. Contbr. articles to profl. jours. Home: 2864 Fairmount Blvd Cleveland Heights OH 44118 Office: 9500 Euclid Ave Cleveland OH 44106

NOTCH, HERBERT LAWRENCE, psychologist; b. Melrose, Minn., Oct. 27, 1933; s. Al Henry and Clara (Tabatt) N.; B.A., Pontificial Coll., 1956; M.S., S.D. State U., 1967; Ph.D., U. Iowa, 1973; m. Diane Kay Rife, June 8, 1966. Ordained priest Roman Catholic Ch., 1960; priest Diocese St. Cloud, Minn., 1960-66; clin. psychologist Clarida (Iowa) Mental Health Inst., 1967-68; exec. dir., clin. psychologist Jasper County Mental Health Center, Newton, Iowa, 1968—. Pvt. practice, cons. psychologist, Des Moines, 1968—. Mem. Gov's. Adv. Com. on Alcoholism Iowa, 1972; Iowa rep. Council Advancement Psychol. Professions and Scis., 1972; mem. Iowa Drug Treatment Licensing Bd., Iowa Bd. Examiners in Profl. Psychology. Bd. dirs. Community Mental Health Centers Assn. Iowa, Des Moines Community Youthline. Law Endorcement Assistance Adminstrn. grantee, 1971-72. Mem. Am. Assn. Marriage and Family Counselors, Am., Iowa (pres. 1973-74) psychol. assns., C. of C. (mem. edn. com.). Home: 905 1st St Newton IA 50208 Office: 2009 1st Ave E Newton IA 50208

NOTZ, JOHN KRANZ, JR., lawyer; b. Chgo., Jan. 5, 1932; s. John Kranz and Elinor (Trostel) N.; B.A., Williams Coll., 1953; J.D., Northwestern U., 1958; m. Janis Lee Wellin, Apr. 23, 1966; children—Jane Elinor, John Wellin. Admitted to Ill. bar, Fla. bar; mem. law dept. First Nat. Bank Chgo., 1956; asso. firm Gardner, Carton & Douglas, Chgo., 1960-66, partner, 1967—; dir. Edward Hines Lumber Co., So. Mineral Corp., Albert Trostel & Sons Co. Served to capt. USAF, 1957-60. Mem. Am., Ill., Chgo., Fla. bar assns. Republican. Episcopalian. Clubs: Economic, Racquet, Mid-Day (Chgo.). Home: 399 Fullerton Pkwy Chicago IL 60614 Office: 4600 One First National Plaza Chicago IL 60603

NOVAK, EDWIN DANIEL, nuclear engr.; b. Chippewa County, Wis., Sept. 4, 1942; s. Ed and Bernice Lulu (Richard) N.; B.A., U. Wis., 1965, M.S., 1966; m. Marilyn Adriane Smith, July 13, 1963; children—Daniel, Thomas, Keith, Kyle, John. Nuclear engr., Knolls Atomic Power Lab., Schenectady, 1966-68; nuclear engr. Wis. Pub. Service Corp., Green Bay, 1968-73, nuclear fuel supr., 1973—. Mem. Am. Nuclear Soc. Republican. Lutheran. Home: 2785 Pamela Dr Green Bay WI 54302 Office: 700 Adams St N Green Bay WI 54301

NOVAK, JAMES F., elec. engr.; b. Oak Park, Ill., Sept. 5, 1926; s. James and Mary (Bartunek) N.; B.E.E., Ill. Inst. Tech., 1952; m. Lorraine Waisnor, Aug. 16, 1952; children—Ann Marie, James Edward. With Jensen Mfg. Co., Schiller Park, Ill., 1952—, chief engr. Jensen Sound Labs. div. Pemcor, Inc., 1969-74, v.p. engring., 1974—. Served with USNR, 1944-47. Audio Engring. Soc. fellow. Mem. IEEE (sr.), Acoustical Soc. Am. Club: Moose. Research loudspeaker enclosure design. Patentee in field. Contbr. articles to profl. jours. Office: 4136 N United Pkwy Schiller Park IL 60176

NOVAK, MICHAEL PAUL, educator, writer; b. Cicero, Ill., July 6, 1935; s. Joseph Francis and Mae Barbara (Killian) N.; B.A., Catholic U. Am., 1957; M.F.A., U. Iowa, 1962; m. Julia A. Callanan, July 12, 1958; children—Brian, Christina. Instr. English, Ill. State U., Normal, 1961-63; asso. prof. English, St. Mary Coll., Leavenworth, Kans., 1963—, chmn. dept. English, 1972-76; Harcourt, Brace fellow U. Colo. Writers' Conf., 1966. Bd. dirs. St. Joseph Sch., Leavenworth, 1967-69, pres., 1967-69; del. Kans. Democratic Conv., 1972, 76; Democratic precinct committeeman, Leavenworth, 1976—. Served with U.S. Army, 1958-60. Recipient award for poems Kans. City (Mo.) Star, 1969, 70, poetry award Kans. Quar., 1974, Outstanding Educator award St. Mary Coll., 1970. Democrat. Roman Catholic. Author: (poetry) The Leavenworth Poems, 1972; Sailing By The Whirlpool, 1978; poems and book revs. Home: 1816 Cherokee St Leavenworth KS 66048 Office: St Mary Coll Leavenworth KS 66048

NOVAK, RICHARD FRANCIS, pathologist, educator; b. Chgo., May 4, 1932; s. Frank S. and Marie L. (Kawula) N.; B.S., Loyola U., Chgo., 1953, M.D., 1957; m. Rose J. Ippolito, June 23, 1956; children—Catherine Ann, Richard Francis, James I. Intern, Madison (Wis.) Gen. Hosp., 1958, resident, 1959; resident Cook County Hosp., Chgo., 1959-62; asst. pathologist Swedish-Am. Hosp., Rockford, Ill., 1962-63; clin. instr. pathology Coll. Medicine, U. Ill., 1962-63; asso. dir. labs. St. Anthony Hosp., Rockford, 1963-69; asst. dir. No. Ill. Blood Bank, Rockford, 1963-69; dir. clin. lab., dir. program for med. tech. Loyola U. Hosp., Chgo., 1969-72; asst. prof. pathology Stritch Sch. Medicine, Loyola U., Chgo., 1969-72; prof. pathology Rockford Sch. Medicine, U. Ill., 1972—; pathologist Rockford Meml. Hosp., 1972-77, chmn. dept. pathology, v.p. med. affairs, 1977—; cons. blood bank program Ill. Dept. Health, 1972—. Diplomate Am. Bd. Pathology. Fellow Coll. Am. Pathologists, Am. Soc. Clin. Pathologists; mem. AMA, Am., Ill. (sec.-treas. 1970-74) assns. blood banks, Ill. Soc. Pathologists (pres. 1976-77), Ill. Pathology Soc., Ill. Med. Soc., Winnebago County Med. Soc. Roman Catholic. Contbr. artilces in field to profl. jours. Home: 3292 Andover Dr Rockford IL 61111 Office: 2400 N Rockton Ave Rockford IL 61103

NOVAK, ROBERT JOHN, physician; b. Oak Park, Ill., Oct. 16, 1930; s. Albert J. and Bohumila T. Novak; B.S., St. Procopius Coll., Lisle, Ill., 1952; M.D., Loyola U., Chgo., 1959, M.S. in Anatomy, 1956; m. Marjorie Ann Licar, June 7, 1958; children—Mary, Catherine, Elizabeth, John, Robert. Intern, resident in family practice MacNeal Hosp., Berwyn, Ill.; gen. practice medicine, Riverside, Ill., since 1961; chmn. dept. gen. practice MacNeal Hosp., 1968, chief staff, 1973-74, chmn. div. family practice, 1977, exec. bd., 1967—; pres., chmn. bd. Windsor Med. Assos., Riverside, 1976—; clin. asst. prof. Abraham Lincoln Sch. Medicine, U. Ill. Diplomate Am. Bd. Family Practice. Mem. Am. Acad. Family Practice (chpt. pres. 1977), AMA, Am. Assn. Physicians and Surgeons, Ill., Chgo. med. socs. Republican. Roman Cath. Home: 221 Shenstone St Riverside IL 60546 Office: 3722 S Harlem Ave Riverside IL 60546

NOVAK, ROBERT LEE, educator; b. Olney, Ill., Sept. 4, 1933; s. Ed and Beulah (Nichols) N.; A.B., Wabash (Ind.) Coll., 1955; M.A., U. Okla., 1957, Ph.D., 1972. Mem. faculty Purdue U., Ft. Wayne, Ind., 1960-76; asso. prof. English, Ind. U., Ft. Wayne, 1976—. Mem. Modern Lang. Assn. Episcopalian. Author: (poetry) Machines for Loving, 1973, Shoes, 1975; Writing Haiku From Photographs, 1977. Editor: The Windless Orchard, quar. jour. contemporary poetry and photography, 1970—. Home: 6718 Baytree Dr Fort Wayne IN 46825 Office: English Dept Indiana Univ Fort Wayne IN 46805

NOVICK, DAVID, cons. engr.; b. N.Y.C., May 14, 1926; s. Harry and Charlotte (Menzin) N.; B.S., C.E., Columbia U., 1948, M.S., 1954; m. Minna Sommer, Aug. 28, 1953; children—Martha, Linda, Emily. Founds. and soils engr. Tippetts-Abbett-McCarthy-Stratton, N.Y.C., 1948-54; found. and structural engr., exec. v.p. Goodkind & O'Dea, Inc., Hamden, Conn., Chgo., 1954-60; pres. Westenhoff & Novick, Inc., Chgo., 1960-77; vis. prof., asso. dir. Urban Systems Lab., U. Ill. at Chgo. Circle, 1977; sr. v.p. Lester B. Knight & Assos., Chgo., 1977—; adj. prof. systems engring. U. Ill., Chgo., 1977—; lectr. hwy. engring. Ill. Inst. Tech. Bd. consultants Lake Michigan Airport, 1968-70; sec., mem. Ill. Structural Engring. Examining Bd., 1970-75. Active United Settlement Appeal, 1963-74; vice chmn. engring. div. Met. Crusade Mercy, Chgo., 1967-68; mem. Chgo. exec. com. Anti-Defamation League. Trustee N. Suburban Mass Transit Dist., 1970-74. Served with AUS, 1944-46. Registered profl. engr., N.Y., Ill., Conn., Ky., Iowa, Ind., Mo., Wis., Wash., Ohio, Mich., Fla., Md., Kans. Fellow ASCE (nat. dir. 1977—, pres. Ill. sect., mem. nat. pub. affairs com.), Am. Cons. Engrs. Council; mem. Am. Ry. Engring. Assn., ASTM, Nat., Ill. (past v.p., com. chmn.) socs. profl. engrs., Nat., Western (trustee) socs. engrs., Internat. Soc. Bridge and Structural Engrs., Internat. Soc. Soil Mechanics and Found. Engrs., Columbia U. Alumni Assn., Am. Arbitration Assn. (panel arbitrators, regional bd.). Jewish. Clubs: Univ. (Chgo.); Princeton of N.Y. Contbr. articles to profl. jours. Home: 2275 Sheridan Rd Highland Park IL 60035 Office: 549 W Randolph Chicago IL 60606

NOVICK, MARVIN, accounting co. exec.; b. N.Y.C., July 16, 1931; s. Joseph and Anna (Leichter) N.; B.B.A., Coll. City N.Y., 1952; M.B.A., N.Y. U., 1955; m. Margaret A. Blau, Apr. 9, 1960; children—Jeffrey, Stuart, Barry. Accountant, Marks & Grey, N.Y.C., 1954-56; sr. accountant Kalish, Rubinroit and Co., N.Y.C., 1956-59; supr. financial Ford Motor Co., Dearborn, Mich., 1959-62; v.p. finance, chief financial officer Mich. Blue Shield, 1962-70; v.p. finance, chief financial and adminstr. officer Meadowbrook, Inc., Southfield, Mich., 1970-72, also dir.; partner mgmt. services J.K. Lasser & Co., 1972-77; partner Touche Ross & Co., 1977—; dir. Pub. Loan Co., Detroit. Mem. Oak Park Sch. Bd., 1966—; v.p. Oak Park Bd. Edn., 1968-69, pres., 1969-70; mem. exec. com. Human Relations Com. Oak Park, 1964—; nat. mem. Health Care Com. Pres. Democratic Club Oak Park, Huntington Woods and Pleasant Ridge, 1971, dir., 1964—; chmn. 18th Congl. Dem. Dist., 1960-70, 73—; mem. exec. com. Oakland County Dem. Orgn., 1971. Bd. dirs., v.p. Mich. Assn. Emotionally Disturbed Children; trustee Family Trust Fund; sec., trustee, chmn. fin. com., sec. Providence Hosp., 1974—; pres., trustee Temple Beth El, 1976—; v.p., bd. dirs. United Hebrew Sch., 1975-77. Served with AUS, 1952-54. Named Oak Park Man of Year, 1967; one of Outstanding Young Men U.S., 1968. Mem. Am. Inst. C.P.A.'s, Mich. Assn. C.P.A.'s, Processing Mgmt. Assn., N.Y. Assn. C.P.A.'s, Am. Statis. Assn., Am. Mgmt. Assn., Assn. Computing Machinery, Mich. Assn. Pub. Health, Assn. for Children's Edn. Mem. B'nai B'rith (v.p. 1968-69). Club: Economic (Detroit).

NOVOTNY, VLADIMIR, civil engr., educator; b. Olomouc, Czechoslovakia, Aug. 30, 1938; s. Vladimir and Frantiska (Havrankova) N.; came to U.S., 1969; diploma in Engring., Tech. U. Brno (Czechoslovakia), 1963, Candidate of Sci., 1968; Ph.D. in Environ. Engring., Vanderbilt U., 1971; m. Lynn E. Braasch, June 14, 1975. Research engr., Hydraulic Research Inst., Brno, Czechoslovakia, 1962-69, acting head Inst., 1966-67; research engr. Vanderbilt U., Nashville, 1969-71; sr. cons. engr. Asso. Water & Air Resources Engrs., Nashville, 1971-73; asso. prof. dept. civil engring. Marquette U., Milw., 1973—; cons. in water pollution control and mgmt. to various govtl. agys. and industries, 1972—. Internat. Joint Commn. for Great Lakes grantee, 1975-77; registered profl. engr., Wis. Mem. ASCE, Water Pollution Control Assn., Internat. Assn. on Water Pollution Research, Assn. Environ. Engring. Profs., Am. Water Resources Assn., Am. Automobile Assn. Clubs: Nashville Ski; Ski of Milw., Sokol (Milw.). Contbr. numerous articles on water quality mgmt. to profl. jours. Home: W 132 N11589 Forest Dr Germantown WI 53022 Office: 1515 W Wisconsin Ave Milwaukee WI 53233

NOWELL, LAWRENCE ALEXANDER, clin. psychologist; b. Detroit, Nov. 22, 1944; s. Alexander Stanley and Charlotte Beatrice (Mikulski) Nowosielski; B.A., U. Mich., 1967; M.A., U. Detroit, 1972. Instr., Detroit Bd. Edn., 1967-68; social worker Mich. Wayne County Dept. Social Services, Detroit, 1968-71; sch. psychologist

Lakeview Pub. Schs., St. Clair Shores, Mich., 1971-76; clin. psychologist Eastwood Community Clinic, Detroit. 1974—. Certified psychological examiner, social worker, sch. psychologist, Mich. Mem. Am. Psychol. Assn., Mich. Psychol. Assn., Macomb County Psychol. Assn., Mich. Assn. Sch. Psychologists, Nat. Assn. Sch. Psychologists, Am. Orthopsychiatric Assn., Nat., State edn. assns., Psy Chi. Roman Catholic.

NOYES, RONALD TACIE, engr.; b. Leedey, Okla., Jan. 4, 1937; s. Johnny Lyle and Anna Madeline (Allen) N.; B.S. in Agrl. Engring., Okla. State U., 1961, M.S. in Agrl. Engring., 1964; postgrad. Purdue U., 1965-68; m. Zona Gail McMillen, Apr. 16, 1960; children—Cynthia Gail, Ronald Scott, David Eric. Extension agrl. engr., dept. agrl. engring. Purdue U., Lafayette, Ind., 1964-68; chief engr. Beard Industries, Frankfort, Ind., 1968—. Served as 1st lt. C.E., AUS, 1961-63. Registered profl. engr., Ind., Ill., Iowa. Mem. Am. Soc. Agrl. Engrs. (vice-chmn. Ind. sect. 1970, 71, chmn. 1973, Young Designer award 1975), Aircraft owners and Pilots Assn., Blue Key, Sigma Tau, Farm House Soc. Frat., Alpha Zeta. Presbyterian (chmn. deacons 1976). Clubs: Kiwanis, Toastmasters. Patentee automatic grain dryer. Home: 901 Eastwood Dr Frankfort IN 46041 Office: St RD 28 W Frankfort IN 46041

NUCCITELLI, SAUL ARNOLD, civil engr.; b. Yonkers, N.Y., Apr. 25, 1928; s. Agostino and Antoinette (D'Amicis) N.; m. Concetta Orlandi, Dec. 23, 1969; children—Saul A. B.S., N.Y. U., 1949; M. of Civil Engring., 1954; D. in Civil Engring., Mass. Inst. Tech., 1960. Registered profl engr., N.Y., Mo., Colo., Conn., Mass.; licensed land surveyor, Mo., Colo., Conn., Mass. Asst. civil engr. Westchester County Engrs., N.Y.C., 1949-51, 53-54; project engr. H.B. Bolas Enterprises, Denver, 1954-55; asst. prof., research engr., U. Denver, 1955-58; mem. staff Mass. Inst. Tech., 1958-60; asst. prof. engring. Cooper Union Coll., N.Y.C., 1960-62; pvt. practice consulting engring., Springfield, Mo., 1962—; dir. Bell Savings & Loan Assn., Springfield. Bd. dirs. YMCA, Springfield. Served with C.E., U.S. Army, 1951-53. Mem. Nat., Mo. socs. profl. engrs., ASCE, Boston Soc. Civil Engrs., Am. Concrete Inst., Am. Inst. Steel Construction, Am. Welding Soc., ASTM, Am. Mil. Engrs., Springfield C. of C. (dir.). Named Mo. Consulting Engr. of the Year, 1973. Contbr. articles in field to profl. jours. Home: 2919 Brentmoor Ave Springfield MO 65804 Office: 306 McDaniel Bldg Springfield MO 65806

NUN, EDWARD WALTER, ins. and financial exec.; b. Ohiowa, Nebr., Sept. 23, 1911; s. Anton and Anna (Sieber) N.; diploma Lincoln (Nebr.) Sch. Commerce, 1930; m. Lucile M. Bartels, Jan. 30, 1940; children—Catherine, Richard, Jane. Bookkeeper, Nat. Bank Commerce, Lincoln, 1930-31; postal clk., Ohiowa, 1932-36; bookkeeper Lytton (Iowa) Savs. Bank, 1936-37; with Pioneer Credit Corp., Fairmont, Minn., 1937-40; cashier, exec. officer 1st Nat. Bank, Wilmont, Minn., 1940-43; rent div. inspector Office of Price Adminstrn., 1943; with Ute (Iowa) State Bank, 1946—, cashier, exec. officer, 1946-68, pres., 1969—. Mem. Iowa State Banking Bd., 1957-61. Mem. Monona County (Iowa) Planning and Zoning Commn., 1971—; city clk., Ute, 1947-63; Democratic committeeman, St. Claire Twp., 1957—. Served with AUS, 1943-46; PTO. Mem. Am. Legion, V.F.W., Ute Comml. Club. Democrat. Lutheran. Address: Ute IA 51060

NUNEMAKER, WESLEY, grain and livestock rancher, utility assn. exec.; b. Langdon, Kan., July 9, 1919; s. Joseph J. and Gladys Mary (Kabler) N.; student Southwestern Coll., Winfield, Kans., 1937-38, Kan. State U., 1938-39; m. Twila Virl Reece, Aug. 22, 1937; children—Marcia (Mrs. Jack Castleberry), Wayne Wesley. Farm, ranch mgr., operator, Langdon, Kans., 1940—. Dir. Ark. Valley Electric Co-op. Assn., Inc., 1955-61, 73—, chmn., 1959-61. Dist. bd. chmn. Lerado Cemetery, 1952-58; mem. Reno County Extension Council, 1949-53, chmn., 1951-53; active United Fund and Christian Rural Overseas Program drives Bell Twp., 1959-62; twp. committeeman Agrl. Stablzn. and Conservation Service, 1960-66; mem. Reno County Spl. Edn. Bd. of Control, 1973. Bd. dirs. Local High Schs., 1952-73; trustee Hutchinson Community Jr. Coll., 1959—, chmn., 1959-60, 67-68, 73-74; bd. dirs. Central Kans. Area Vocat. Tech. Sch., 1975—, v.p., 1976—; trustee Kans. Electric Power Coop., 1976—. Recipient Kans. Master Farmer award, 1973. Mem. Kans. Farm Bur., Kans. Wheat Growers Assn., Kans. Farm. Mgmt. Assn., Top Farmers Am. Assn., Reno County Bankers Soil Conservation (mem. awards selection com. 1953), Kans. Master Farmer Assn. (pres. 1976—). Christian Ch. (elder 1971—, Sunday sch. supt. 1941-46). Home: Langdon KS 67549

NUNN, JOE RICHARD, rancher, utility assn. exec.; b. Lakin, Kans., Dec. 3, 1933; s. Pete and Genieva Grace (Barber) N.; student Colo. State U., 1951-54; m. Patricia Marie Corbin, Sept. 24, 1953; children—Connie Jo, Thomas Evans, Barbara Sue, Neil Allen, Richard Faye. Partner, mgr. Pete Nunn & Son Ranch, Harrison, Nebr., 1956—. Dir. Niobrara Electric Assn.; state dir. Nebr. Rural Electric Assn., 1970—. Mem. Sioux County Fair Bd., 1966—, pres., 1968-74; mem. Sioux County Extension Bd., 1960-64; adv. bd. Panhandle Sta., U. Nebr., 1966—. Bd. dirs. Nebr. High Sch. Rodeo Assn., 1963-69, sec., 1967-69. Recipient 4-H Alumni award, 1971. Mem. Future Farmers Am. (hon.), Nebr. Stockgrowers Assn. (exec. bd. 1970-72, vice chmn. labor com.), Tau Kappa Epsilon. Republican. Methodist. Club: Harrison Mens Community. Home: Box 426 Harrison NE 69346

NUPEN, HARLAN CLARENCE, air force officer, counseling service dir.; b. Hudson, S.D., Oct. 30, 1936; s. Clarence Harry and Honore Hilde (Benjamson) N.; B.S., S.D. State U., 1958; m. Colleen Rose Brown, June 29, 1958; children—Valerie, Monae, Amber. Commd. 2d lt. U.S. Air Force, 1958, advanced through grades to lt. col., 1975; flight officer, 1958-67; instr. flight leader in helicopter gunships, Vietnam, 1967-68; staff officer Hdqrs. 13th AF, Pil., 1968-70; operations officer Helicopter div. Ellsworth AFB, S.D., 1973-75, war plans operations officer, 1975-76, comdr. 28th Bomb Wing Hdqrs. Squadron, 1975-76, wing exec. officer, 1976—; dir. Black Hills Counseling Service; bd. dirs. Midwest Assn. Christian Counselors; mil. cons. equal employment opportunity activities Ellsworth AFB, 1975-77. Lay minister Wesleyan Ch., trustee, 1972-75, mem. ch. bd., 1972-77, v.p. ch. bd., 1977—; firearms instr. 4-H Clubs, Boy Scouts Am. Decorated D.F.C. with oak leaf cluster, Air Medal with 13 oak leaf clusters, AF Commendation Medal with 2 oak leaf clusters; certified marriage counselor, personal and family counselor, firearms instr.; qualified expert high power and smallbore rifle competition. Mem. Am. Numismatic Assn. (life, edn. award), S. African Numismatic Soc., Nat. Rifle Assn., S.D. Shooting Sports Assn., Midwest Assn. Christian Counselors, Nat. Assn. Christian Marriage Counselors. Club: Cosmopolitan. Research on numismatics of Edward VIII of Eng. Home: 4602 Baldwin St Rapid City SD 57701 Office: 429 Kansas City St Rapid City SD 57701

NUSSEL, EDWARD JOSEPH, educator; b. Detroit, Apr. 14, 1932; s. Edward and Emily (Pearman) Nussel; m. Lorraine Rita Varana, Oct. 10, 1953; children—Jay, Gregory, Philip. B.Ed., U. Detroit, 1953; M.Ed., Wayne State U., 1957, Ed.D., 1964. Tchr., Detroit Pub. Schs., 1953-64; asst. prof. U. Toledo, 1964-66, assoc. prof., 1966-68, prof. edn., 1968—, dir. div. founds. and edn., 1971-75, asso. dean Coll. Edn., 1975—; vis. prof. Bowling Green State U., 1967, U. Pacific, 1971, Miami U., 1973, U. Richmond, 1975; vis. scholar U. Calif. at Riverside, 1977. Mem. Toledo Diocesan Sch. Bd., 1968-73, pres., 1970-73; chmn. bd. Lourdes Coll., 1976-78. Mem. AAUP (pres. Toledo chpt. 1968-69), Am. Ednl. Research Assn., Assn. for Individually Guided Edn., Phi Kappa Phi (pres. 1977-78), Phi Delta Kappa. Author: An Introduction to the Foundations of Education, 1966, 68; The Teacher and Individually Guided Education, 1976. Contbr. articles to profl. jours. Home: 3309 Cheltenham St Toledo OH 43606 Office: Coll Edn U Toledo Toledo OH 43606

NUTTER, ERVIN JOHN, diversified industry exec.; b. Hamilton, Ohio, June 26, 1914; s. Ervin F. and Carrie V. (McDavid) N.; B.S.M.E., U. Ky., 1943, LL.D., 1974; m. Zoe Dell Lantis, Dec. 30, 1965; children—Kenneth E., Joseph L., Robert W. Chief test br. Wright AFB, Dayton, Ohio, 1943-51; founder, chief exec. officer Elano Corp., Xenia, Ohio, 1950—, Enzo Realty, Enlo, Inc., precision lost wax foundry, 1970—, KBJ Ranch, beef cattle breeding, 1953—, Acme Screw Products, Xenia, 1965—; dir. Citizens First Nat. Bank, Xenia. Mem. nat. exec. com. Boy Scouts Am., 1967—; former mem. and chmn. Beavercreek Zoning Commn.; former mem. Greene County Regional Airport Authority. Chmn. fellows com. U. Ky. Past mem. Ohio Republican Finance Com., 1964, chmn. Greene County Rep. Com., 1964-65. Trustee, pres. Aviation Hall of Fame; bd. dirs. Leukemia Soc. Dayton.; adv. council Coll. Engring., U. Ky., 1969—. Recipient numerous commendations and awards USAF, Navy, AEC; Distinguished Service award U. Ky., 1972; Man of the Year award Beavercreek C. of C., 1971. Mem. Shikar Safari Club Internat., Headhunters Ohio, League Ohio Sportsman, Game Conservation Internat., African Wildlife Soc., Soil Conservation Soc. Am., Aircraft Owners and Pilots Assn. Methodist. Clubs: Walnut Grove Country (Dayton); Old Port Cove Yacht (North Palm Beach, Fla.), Masons, Shriners, K.P. Patentee in field. Home: 986 Trebein Rd Xenia OH 45385 Office: 2455 Dayton-Xenia Rd Xenia OH 45385

NUTTER, GENE DOUGLAS, physicist; b. Columbus, Tex., June 9, 1929; s. William F. and Susie M. (Baker) N.; B.S., U. Nebr., 1951, M.S., 1956; m. Mary Ann Souder, June 9, 1956; children—John William, Kathleen Annette. Physicist, Nat. Bur. Standards, Washington, 1952-54; engring. supr. Atomics Internat., Canoga Park, Calif., 1956-67; asst. dir. Instrumentation Systems Center, U. Wis.-Madison, 1967—. Cons. in radiation thermometry; UNESCO cons. metrology Govt. of South Korea, 1968. Mem. ASME (com. temperature measurement), Instrument Soc. Am. (sr.), IEEE (sr.), Precision Measurement Assn. (dir. 1973—), ASTM (chmn. subcom. on radiation thermometers 1973—). Democrat. Unitarian. Mason. Contbr. articles to profl. jours. Home: 1610 Gateway St Middleton WI 53562 Office: Instrumentation Systems Center 1500 Johnson Dr Madison WI 53706

NUTTLE, DANIEL EDWARD, real estate broker; b. Flint, Mich., June 20, 1936; s. Earl and Myrtle Anna (Pushel) N.; student Morningside Coll., 1954-55, Eastern Mich. U., 1955-56; B.S., Western Mich. U., 1960; postgrad. U. Mich., 1967-70; m. Carolyn K. Nicholson, July 25, 1975; children by previous marriage—Steven E., Susan E. With R.J. Den Herder Asso., Inc., Jackson, Mich., 1966—, v.p., sales mgr., 1975—; promotion mgr. Paka Plaza Mchts. Assn., Jackson, 1966-72; owner Nuttle Ins. Agy., Jackson, 1967-71. Bd. dirs. Mich. Space Center Bd., 1974-75. Mem. Real Estate Alumni of Mich. (dir. 1973—), Jackson Bd. Realtors (asso. dir. 1971). Republican. Club: Jackson County. Home: 806 S Webster St Jackson MI 49203 Office: 760 W Franklin Jackson MI 49201

NUZMAN, CARL EDWARD, hydrologist; b. Topeka, Aug. 5, 1930; s. Loren Manuel and Lorraine Lillian (Bowler) N.; B.S. in Agrl. Engring., Kans. State U., 1953; M.S. in Water Resources Engring., U. Kans., 1966; m. Janet Ruth Steck, Aug. 23, 1952. Engr. div. water resources Kans. Bd. Agr., Topeka, 1957-65; hydrologist Kans. Water Resources Bd., Topeka, 1965-66; hydrology supr., sales engr. Layne-Western Co., Inc., Shawnee Mission, Kans., 1967—. Treas. local sch. bd., 1958-59. Served to 1st lt. USAF, 1953-56. Registered profl. engr., Kans., Mo. Mem. Am. Soc. Agrl. Engrs., ASCE, Am. Geophys. Union, Kans. Engring. Soc. (sec.-treas. 1965-68, Outstanding Young Engr. award Topeka chpt. 1965), Nat. Soc. Profl. Engrs., Alpha Kappa Lambda, Sigma Tau, Steel Ring. Elk. Contbr. articles to profl. jours. Home: Route 1 Silver Lake KS 66539 Office: PO Box 1322 Mission KS 66222

NYE, CHARLES NEAL, bus. exec.; b. Shakopee, Minn., Nov. 24, 1941; s. Benjamin Franklin and Marien Alice (Murphy) N.; B.S., U. Minn., 1964; M.B.A. (Continental Grain fellow), Wharton Sch. U. Pa., 1975; m. Barbara Faye Gilliland; children—Scott Charles, Julie Marie. Dir. planning S.W. Forest Industries, 1969-72; corp. fin. dir. Stern, Frank, Meyer & Fox, Los Angeles, 1972; v.p., div. mgr. Continental Western Industries, Des Moines, 1972-74; dir. corporate planning and devel. Apache Corp., Mpls., 1975-77; v.p. planning and devel. Turbodyne Corp., 1977—; instr. mgmt. St. Thomas Coll., 1976—; guest lectr. Wharton Sch., 1976. Served with USMCR, 1963-69. Mem. Am. Mktg. Assn., Fin. Execs. Inst., Soc. Fin. Analysts, Mensa, Tau Kappa Epsilon, Club: Athletic (Mpls.). Home: 18225 24th Ave N Wayzata MN 55341

NYGAARD, LOYD DANIEL, innkeeper; b. St. Francis, Kans., Feb. 14, 1952; s. Olav and Goldie (Halligan) N.; B.S., Fort Hays State Coll., 1975; m. Brenda L. Harbaugh, Mar. 8, 1975. With Ramada Inn, Hays, Kans., 1971—, club mgr., asst. gen. mgr., 1974-76, gen. mgr., 1977—; asst. gen. mgr. Canterbury Inn, Wichita, 1976—. Mem. Nat. Fed. Ind. Businessmen, Am. Hotel and Motel Assn., Hays Jr. C. of C. Republican. Methodist. Clubs: Elks, Masons. Home: 116 37th St W Hays KS 67601 Office: Box 336 Hays KS 67601

NYHUS, LLOYD MILTON, surgeon, educator; b. Mt. Vernon, Wash., June 24, 1923; s. Lewis Guttorm and Mary (Shervem) N.; B.A., Pacific Lutheran Coll., 1945; M.D., Med. Coll. Ala., 1947; m. Margaret Sheldon, Nov. 25, 1949; children—Sheila Margaret, Lief Torger. Intern, King County Hosp., Seattle, 1947-48, resident in surgery, 1948-50, 54, 55-56; USPHS research fellow U. Wash., 1952-53; practice medicine specializing in surgery, Seattle, 1956-67, Chgo., 1967—; instr. surgery U. Wash., Seattle, 1954-56, asst. prof., 1956-59, asso. prof., 1959-64, prof., 1964-67; Warren H. Cole prof. surgery U. Ill., Chgo., 1967—, head dept. surgery, 1967—; surgeon-in-chief U. Ill. Hosp., Chgo.; sr. cons. surgeon Cook County Hosp., West Side VA Hosp., Hines VA Hosp.; cons. in field. Served with M.C., USNR, 1943-46, 50-52. Guggenheim fellow, 1955-56. Recipient M. Shipley award So. Surg. Assn., 1967. Diplomate Am. Bd. Surgery (chmn. 1974-76). Fellow A.C.S., Royal Soc. Medicine, Assn. Surgeons Gt. Britain and Ireland (corr.), Brazilian Coll. Surgeons (corr.), German Surg. Soc. (corr.), Academie de Chirurgie; mem. Am. Gastroent. Assn., A.M.A., Am. Physiol. Soc., Am., Pacific Coast, Western, Central So., surg. assns., Chgo. (past pres.), Seattle surg. socs., Central Soc. Clin. Research, Illingworth Surg. Club, Inst. for medicine Chgo., Internat. Soc. Surgery, Collegium Internat. Chirurgiae Digestivae (past pres. III World Congress), Soc. Surgery Alimentary Tract (past pres.), Soc. Clin. Surgery, Soc. Surg. Chmn., Soc. Univ. Surgeons (past pres.), Surg. Biol. Club, Warren H. Cole Soc., Sigma Xi, Alpha Omega Alpha, Phi Beta Pi. Author: Surgery of the Stomach and Duodenum, 1962, 2d edit. 1969, 3d edit., 1977; Hernia, 1964; Abdominal Pain, 1969; Manual of Surgical Theraputics, 1969, 2d edit., 1972, 3d edit., 1975; Surgery Annual, 1970—; Treatment of Shock, 1974—. Editor-in-chief: Rev. of Surgery, 1967—; asso. editor Quar. Rev. Surgery, 1958-61; mem. editorial bd. Am. Jour. Digestive Diseases, 1961-67, Scandinavian Jour. Gastroenterology, 1966—, Am. Surgeon, 1967—, Jour. Surg. Oncology, 1969—, Archives of Surgery, 1977—. Contbr. numerous articles to profl. jours. Home: 310 Maple Row Northbrook IL 60062 Office: 840 S Wood St Chicago IL 60612

OAKAR, JAMES LOUIS, lawyer; b. Cleve., Oct. 7, 1936; s. Joseph M. and Margaret Mary (Ellison) O.; B.B.A., John Carroll U., 1958; J.D., Georgetown U., 1962; m. Loretta Ann Coleman, Jan. 11, 1964; children—Kathleen, Patricia, James T., Mary Ellen, Ann. Admitted to Ohio bar, 1962, U.S. Supreme Ct. bar; law clk. to U.S. Dist. Ct. chief judge, Cleve., 1963-64; trial atty., pros. atty. Cuyahoga County (Ohio), Cleve., 1964-65; trial atty. Dept. Justice, Cleve., 1965-69; partner firm Zidar, Morgan, Oakar & Burns, Cleve., 1969-71; individual practice law, Cleve., 1972—; spl. counsel to atty. gen. Ohio, 1971—; asst. law dir., prosecutor City of Bedford Heights (Ohio), 1972—, City of Richmond Heights (Ohio), 1974—. Trustee Cath. Charities Corp.; ward chmn. Am. Cancer Soc., 1964. Served as capt. U.S. Army, 1958-59. Mem. Cath. Lawyers Guild (treas.), Nat. Assn. Criminal Def. Lawyers, Ohio, Cleve., Cuyahoga County bar assns., Am. Arbitration Assn. (panel arbitrators), Holy Name Soc. Democrat. Roman Catholic (parish trustee). Club: K.C. Home: 9617 Stoney Creek Ln Parma Heights OH 44130 Office: One Erieview Plaza Cleveland OH 44114

OAKAR, MARY ROSE, congresswoman; b. Cleve.; B.A., Ursuline Coll., Cleve., 1962; M.A., John Carroll U., Cleve., 1966; postgrad. Columbia U., 1967—. Clk., Higbee Co., 1956-58; long distance operator Ohio Bell Telephone Co., 1957-62; instr. English and drama Lourdes Acad., Cleve., 1963-70; asst. prof. English, speech and drama Cuyahoga Community Coll., 1968-75; mem. 95th Congress from 20th Ohio Dist. Ward leader Cuyahoga County Democratic Com., 1972-76; mem. Cleve. City Council, 1973-76; state central committeewoman 20th Congl. Dist., 1974; trustee Fedn. for Community Planning, Health and Planning Commn., Community Info. Service, Soc. for Crippled Children, Nationalities Services Center, YWCA. Recipient Outstanding Service award OEO, 1973-75, Community Service awards Am. Indian Center, 1973, Nationalities Service Center, 1974, Club San Lorenzo, 1976. Home: 1892 W 30th St Cleveland OH 44113

OAKES, KENT ALLEN, forensic chemist; b. LaPorte, Ind., Sept. 24, 1943; s. George Reed and Marie (Stehr) O.; m. Susan VanMarter, Aug. 15, 1970; 1 son, Courtney. Student Reed Coll., 1962-63; B.A., Lawrence U., 1966; Ph.D., U. Wash., 1972. Re search asst. Argonne (Ill.) Nat. Lab., 1965; research asst. research and devel. Minn. Mining Mfg. Co., St. Paul, 1966; instr. gen. chemistry U. Wash., 1972; forensic chemist Wash. Patrol Crime Lab., Seattle, 1972-74; head trace analyst Wis. Regional Crime Lab., New Berlin, 1974—. Mem. Am. Chem. Soc., NW Assn. Forensic Scientists, Phi Beta Kappa. Recipient Outstanding Sr. Chemist award Am. Chem. Soc. Lawrence U., 1966. Contbr. articles to chem. and forensic jours. Home: 1711 South East Ln New Berlin WI 53151

OAKLEY, BRICE CASE, lawyer; b. Washington, Iowa, Feb. 4, 1937; s. Robert M. and Helen L. (Case) O.; B.A., U. Iowa, 1958, J.D., 1961; m. Bette Jeanne Machael, Sept. 7, 1957; children—Kristin, Kathlyn, Robert. Admitted to Iowa bar, 1961; asst. atty. gen. State of Iowa, 1961-63; partner Johnson & Oakley, Clinton, 1963—; mem. Iowa Ho. of Reps., 1973-77; Pres. Clinton Assn. for Handicapped Children, 1963-66, Community Action Program, 1965-68; mem. Clinton Sch. Bd., 1968-71, Iowa Energy Policy Council, 1974-76; chmn. State Coll. Young Republicans, 1960-61; mem. Rotary Group Study Exchange Program to Norway, 1969. Recipient award of merit Clinton Community Sch. Dist., 1971; named Outstanding Young Man of Year, Clinton, 1966. Mem. Am., Iowa, Clinton County (pres. 1970) bar assns., Clinton C. of C. (dir.). Methodist. Clubs: Masons, Shriners, Rotary. Home: 1 Heather Lane Clinton IA 52732 Office: 601 S 3d St Box 749 Clinton IA 52732

OATS, CHARLES SAMUEL, accountant; b. Pekin, Ill., May 17, 1931; s. Ernest Michael and Ollie May (Hakes) O.; student pub. schs.; m. Barbara Jean Evans, Feb. 23, 1951; children—Kenneth Dale, Charles Clifford. Bookkeeper, Internat. Harvester, Indpls., 1953-55; accountant Clark Crawford & Co., C.P.A., Indpls., 1955-58; field examiner Ind. Bd. Accounts, 1958-65; owner C.S. Oats, C.P.A., Lebanon, 1965—, Crawfordsville, Ind., 1973—. Pres. Lebanon Boys Club, 1970-71, v.p., 1971-72; swim coach YMCA, Montgomery County, Lebanon chambers commerce, mem. membership drive com., 1970-71, mem. finance com., 1970-71. Bd. dirs. Boone County United Fund, 1968-70, treas., 1968-70, drive vice chmn., 1969-71; bd. dirs. 4th of July Com., 1967-69, v.p., 1969-70, pres., 1970-71; past pres. Acton (Ind.) Vol. Fire Dept. Served with USMCR, 1949-52. Named Jaycee of Year, Lebanon Jr. C. of C., 1966; recipient Region C Key Man award Ind. Jr. C. of C., 1966; Outstanding Service award Boys Club, 1970. C.P.A., Ind. Mem. Am. Inst. C.P.A.'s, Ind. Assn. C.P.A.'s (mem. pres.'s adv. bd., dir. 1971-74, chmn. relations with govt. agys., chmn. ad hoc com. instl. advt. and influence outside forces on practice of pub. accounting, coordinator com. activities), Airplane Owners and Pilots Assn., Montgomery County, Lebanon Chambers Commerce. Republican. Baptist (ch. financial sec. 1965-66, mem. adv. bd. 1965-66). Club: Ulen Country (Lebanon). Contbr. to Taxation for Accountants. Home: 422 Glendale Dr Lebanon IN 46052 Office: 312 Heflin Bldg Lebanon IN 46052 also 313 Ben Hur Bldg Crawfordsville IN 47933

OBAYASHI, ALAN WALTER, civil engr.; b. San Diego, Calif., Feb. 24, 1946; s. Walter H. and Michiko (Shiraishi) O.; B.S., San Diego State Coll., 1967; M.S., Stanford U., 1968; Ph.D., Okla. State U., 1972; m. Bobbie Jane Kida, Feb. 17, 1965; children—Keith Alan, Derek Thomas. Project mgr. wastewater treatment research Met. Sanitary Dist. Greater Chgo., Cicero, Ill., 1972—; instr. Ill. Inst. Tech., Chgo., 1974—. NASA trainee, 1968; Environ. Protection Agy. trainee, 1970. Mem. Water Pollution Control Fedn., Internat. Assn. Water Pollution Research, ASCE, Sigma Xi, Chi Epsilon. Contbr. articles to profl. jours. Home: 1918 Springside Dr Naperville IL 60540 Office: 5901 W Pershing Rd Cicero IL 60650

OBER, DAVID LAWRENCE, design engr.; b. Kansas City, Mo., Oct. 2, 1936; s. David Wendell and Maude Pearl (Ferguson) O.; A.Sci., Kansas City Jr. Coll., 1957; B.S.C.E., Finlay Engring. Coll., 1963; m. Carol Enola Gohres, Apr. 4, 1958; children—Daniel Gregory, Cynthia Lynn, Steven Christopher. Design engr. Lloyd T. Thorp, Cons. Engr., Prairie Village, Kans., 1962-65; design engr. Black & Veatch, Cons. Engrs., Kansas City, Mo., 1965-66, asso. planner, 1966-68, project planner, 1968-71, design engr., 1971-77, project coordinator, 1977—. Volunteer worker Heart of Am. United Way campaign, Kansas City, 1972-74; dir. Post Oak Farm Homeowners Assn., Lenexa, Kans., 1974—; asst. scoutmaster Boy Scouts Am., Lenexa, Kans., 1971—, troop chaplain, 1972-73, named to Order of Arrow Honor Camping Soc., 1974. Recipient Honor award, Frontiersmen Drum and Bugle Corps, 1973; Certificate of Merit, YMCA, 1967. Christian Ch. (elder 1974-77, chmn. deacons

1970). Home: 7900 Noland Rd Lenexa KS 66215 Office: 1500 Meadowlake Pkwy Kansas City MO 64114

OBERDIECK, WILLIAM HUBERT, fruit grower; b. Muelheim-Ruhr, Ger., Aug. 3, 1922; s. Hubert and Antonie (Kotermann) O.; came to U.S., 1950, naturalized, 1955; student schs. Germany; m. Adele Heffels, Nov. 11, 1947; children—Laurine A., Wilma L., Richarda A. Mgr., Kimmel Orchard, Nebraska City, Nebr., 1950-64, owner, operator, 1964—. Served with German Afrikakorps, 1941-43. Mem. Nebr., Iowa, Mich., Wash. State hort. socs. Club: Elks. Home and Office: Route 2 Nebraska City NE 68410

OBERHAMER, DOUGLAS ROY, trade assn. exec.; b. St. Paul, Apr. 22, 1949; s. Roy Raymond and Hulda Wilhemina (Gens) O.; grad. high sch. Sales mgr. Hilton Hotels Corp., St. Paul, 1969-71; adminstrv. asst. to exec. v.p. Water Conditioning Assn. Internat., Wheaton, Ill., 1971-74; exec. dir. Water Quality Assn., Lombard, Ill., 1974—; dir. Water Quality Research Council, Ground Water Council, 1976-77, Water Quality Improvement Standards and Certification Council. Served with USAF, 1969-71. Recipient award for youth Optimists, 1967; Distinguished Service award ARC, 1967; certified assn. exec. Mem. Am., Chgo. socs. assn. execs., European Water Conditioning Assn. (dir.). Republican. Home: 19W151 Rue Royal Oak Brook IL 60521 Office: 477 E Butterfield Rd Lombard IL 60148

OBERHART, JACK CHARLES, ednl. adminstr.; b. Oak Park, Ill., Aug. 29, 1919; s. John Lyle and Anne Josephine (Durschmidt) O.; B.Ed., Chgo. Tchrs. Coll., 1946, M.Ed., 1964; D.Ed., U. Sarasota (Fla.), 1977; m. Mary Lu McGeoghegan, July 2, 1949; children—Jack Charles, Anne, Michael, Ellen. Elementary and high sch. tchr., then sch. counselor Chgo. pub. schs., 1947-64; pupil personnel supr. Chgo. Bd. Edn., 1964-67, dir. sch. attendance, 1967—; adj. prof. psychology Ill. Inst. Tech.; mem. Ill. Gov.'s Task Force Edn.; vocat. cons. to industry. Chmn. sch. bd. adv. com. Dist. 36, Wheaton, Ill., 1962, chmn. sch. bd. mem. selection com., 1963. Served with AUS, 1943-45. Mem. Am., Ill. (pres. 1972) personnel and guidance assns., Nat. Vocat. Guidance Assn., Internat. Assn. Pupil Personnel Workers (pres. 1977), Ill. Vocat. Assn. (pres. 1975), Nat. Assn. Industry-Edn. Coop., Epsilon Pi Tau, Phi Delta Kappa. Club: Cliff Dwellers (Chgo.). Contbr. to profl. publs. Home: 25 W 617 Geneva Rd Wheaton IL 60187 Office: 228 N LaSalle St Chicago IL 60601

OBERHOLTZER, JOHN CLAYTON, lawyer; b. Cleve., Sept. 11, 1942; s. Clayton J. and Winefred E. (Graham) O.; grad. Coll. of Wooster, 1964; LL.B., Western Res. U., 1967; m. Janet L. Bartter, June 20, 1965; children—Julie, John Jacob. Admitted to Ohio bar, 1967; partner Oberholtzer & Oberholtzer, Medina, 1967—; county commr. Medina County, 1971—, pres. bd. commrs., 1975-77. Pres., Minn. Title Agy. of Medina, Inc.; Chmn. housing com. NE Ohio Area Co-ordinating Agy., 1972-73; former mem. Five County Mass Transp. Study Adv. Com.; mem. Tri County Manpower Consortium. Bd. dirs. Medina County United Appeal; trustee United Fund, United Torch Drive. Mem. Am., Ohio, Medina County bar assns., Comml. Law League of Am. Methodist. K.P., Kiwanian (pres. Medina 1974-75). Home: 875 Damon Dr Medina OH 44256 Office: 120 W Washington St Medina OH 44256

OBERLE, KEVIN RAY, pub. relations adminstr.; b. Columbus, Ohio, Nov. 24, 1948; s. Raymond Zeigler and Kathern Viola (Hickerson) O.; B.S. in Communication (Zousmer Meml. award), Ohio U., 1971. Broadcast technician Sta. WLWC-TV, Columbus, 1971; prodn. asst. Sta. WSTV-TV, Steubenville, Ohio, 1972; dir. Sta. WTVN-TV, Columbus, 1972-74; broadcast technician Sta. WLWC-TV, Columbus, 1974; community relations dir. Goodwill Industries of Central Ohio, Inc., Columbus, 1974-77, pub. relations cons. Goodwill Industries Am., Inc., Washington; regional field rep. St. Jude Childrens Research Hosp., Columbus, Ohio, 1977—. Mem. spl. events com. United Way Franklin County. Served with Signal Corps, U.S. Army, 1971-72. Mem. Pub. Relations Soc. Am., Nat. Acad. TV Arts and Scis., Columbus Advt. Fedn. Club: Kiwanis. Home: 933-A Forest Creek Dr E Columbus OH 43223 Office: 5150 E Main St Suite 217 Columbus OH 43213

OBERMAN, MOISHE DAVID, mag. pub.; b. Springfield, Ill., Mar. 3, 1914; s. Harry and Ida (Guralnik) O.; student St. Louis Coll. Pharmacy, 1931-33; m. Bobbye Friedman, Oct. 8, 1939; children—Michael Alan, Martin Jay, M.H. William, Marjorie Ann. Scrap metals broker, Springfield, 1937-41; founder Scrap Age Mag., 1944, Mill Trade Jour., 1963, Waste Age Mag., 1969, Encyclopedia of Scrap Recycling, 1976; pres., editor, pub. 3 Sons Pub. Co., Niles, Ill., 1944; pres. Emde Realty Devel. Corp., Springfield, 1957-63; exec. sec. Midwest Scrap Dealers Assn., Springfield, 1941; treas. North Shore Investments, Highland Park, Ill., 1968; exec. dir. Springfield Area Devel. and Tourist Commn., 1963-68; mem. Ill. Inst. Environ. Quality Solid Waste Task Force Com., 1971. Pres. Ill. Assn. Jewish Centers, 1934-40; editor congregation publs., treas. North Suburban Synagogue Beth El. Mem. War Production Bd., 1942-44. Recipient Meritorious Service award for outstanding contbns. to iron and steel industry St. Louis Steel Assn., 1961. Mem. Nat. Solid Waste Mgmt. Assn., Am. Pub. Works Assn. (solid waste mgmt. task force), Execs. Inc. (pres. 1963-67), Am. Soc. Assn. Execs., Internat. Platform Assn., Nat. Press Club, Springfield Jr. C. of C. (pres. 1946-47), Springfield Assn. Execs., Springfield Assn. Commerce and Industry. Jewish. Club: B'nai B'rith (sec. 1935-39, pres. 1942-45). Home: 857 Stonegate Dr Highland Park IL 60035 Office: 6311 Gross Point Rd Niles IL 60648

OBERMILLER, STANLEY MATHEW, retail trade co. exec.; b. Norman County, Minn., Dec. 1, 1914; s. Frank and Josephine (Rubash) O.; student Marquette U., 1936-37, N.D. State U., 1940-41; m. Elaine Bursch, Jan. 26, 1946; children—Michael, Karen. Dep. county auditor Mahnomen County, Minn., 1937-40; sales exec. Ford Motor Co., Fargo, N.D., 1945-49; propr., mgr. Elaine's Store, Thief River Falls, Minn., 1949-52; propr., mgr. Palette Shop, Milw., 1953—; dir. Nat. Art Industries, Inc., 1971—. Bd. dirs. Milw. Sch. of the Arts. Served with USAAF, 1942-45. Recipient Hall of Fame award Nat. Art Materials Trade Assn., 1977. Mem. Milw. Soc. of Communicating Arts, Wis. Rural Artists Assn., Milw. Advt. Club, Milw. Assn. of Commerce, Illustrators and Designers of Milw., Nat. Art Materials Trade Assn. (dir. 1958-67, pres. 1963-65), Wis. Painters and Sculptors. Roman Catholic. Club: K.C. (past grand knight) Columnist. Art Material Trade News, 1971—. Home: 4332 W Grace Ave Mequon WI 53092 Office: 409 E Michigan St Milwaukee WI 53202

OBERROTMAN, ALAIN MAURICE, mgmt. cons.; b. Paris, France, Mar. 17, 1951; s. Joseph and Janine (Binder) O.; came to U.S., 1955, naturalized, 1961; B.S. in Accounting cum laude, U. Ill., 1972; M.B.A. cum laude, U. Chgo., 1974. Mgmt. cons. to MARCOR, Chgo., 1972-74, to Touche Ross & Co., Chgo., 1974—; research cons. to N.Y. U., dept. of accounting, N.Y.C., 1974—. Guest lectr. U. Chgo., 1975-76, Northwestern U., Loyola U., Milliken U., 1976. Recipient Bronze medal for sabre fencing Israel World Games, 1973. C.P.A., Ill. Mem. Nat., Am. accounting assns., Am. Inst. Certified Public Accountants, Ill. Soc. Certified Public Accountants, Am. Finance Assn. Author: SEC Replacement Cost Accounting: A Guide to Implementation. Home: 1953 N Cleveland Chicago IL 60614 Office: 111 E Wacker Dr Chicago IL 60601

OBERST, BYRON BAY, physician; b. Omaha, Mar. 15, 1923; s. Byron Bay and Claire Matilda (Healy) O.; B.A., U. Omaha, 1943; M.D., U. Nebr., 1946; m. Mary Catherine Nadolny, Dec. 27, 1945; children—Byron Joseph, Terrence Martin, Matthew Robert. Intern, U. Nebr. Hosp., Omaha, 1946-47, resident in pediatrics, 1947-48; resident Henry Ford Hosp., Detroit, 1950-51; practice medicine specializing in pediatrics, Omaha, 1951—; instr. pediatrics Wayne U. Sch. Medicine, Henry Ford Hosp. Sch. Nursing, Detroit, 1950-51, Creighton Coll. Medicine, 1951-54, St. Catherine's Sch. Nursing, Omaha, 1952-55; faculty U. Nebr. Coll. Medicine, 1951—, asso., 1954—, asso. prof., 1969—, dir. adolescent clinic, 1960-63, clin. prof. pediatrics, 1977—; adj. prof. psychology Bellevue (Nebr.) Coll., 1966-68; staff mem. Children's Meml. Hosp., 1951—, treas. staff, 1958, dir. adolescent clinic, 1967-70, pres. staff., 1968-70; clinician in charge nursery, mem. infection control com. Nebr. Meth. Hosp., 1957-60; asst. clinician for heart diseases Nebr. Services for Crippled Children, 1953-60; pediatrician in charge pediatrics, newborns Bishop Clarkson Meml. Hosp., 1963-76; pediatrician in chief Archbishop Bergan Mercy Hosp., 1965-66; guest lectr. civic orgns., ch. young people's groups, schs., tchr. groups. Bd. dirs. Operation Bridge, Suburban Youth Guidance Counselling Service, 1968-73; active Boy Scouts Am., 1951-67, troop scoutmaster, 1960-67; founder, bd. dirs. Omaha STAAR Program for Sch. Learning Disabilities, 1968—; mem. com. on health planning Health Planning Council of Midlands, 1976—; hon. life mem. PTA. Served to capt. M.C., AUS, 1948-50. Sch. Health Physicians fellow, 1970-73. Fellow Am. Acad. Pediatrics (chmn. Nebr. chpt. 1976—, chpt. chmn. com. on med. practice 1971-76); mem. AMA, (Recognition award 1969, 73, 76), Nebr. (com. on mental health 1971), Omaha-Douglas County (com. on edn. 1971), Pan Am. med. socs., NW, Nebr. (pres. 1958) pediatric socs., Midwest Clin. Soc. (chmn. sect. pediatrics 1957), Soc. for Adolescent Medicine (charter, mem. com. on med. practice 1971—), Soc. for Computer Medicine (chmn. com. on standards 1974-77), Gt. Plains Orgn. for Perinatal Health Care, Nat. Assn. Children's Learning Disabilities (hon. life). Republican. Roman Catholic. Author: Practical Guidance for Pediatric and Adolescent Office Practice, 1973; contbr. articles to profl. jours. Home: 307 S 93d St Omaha NE 68114 Office: 3925 Dewey Ave Omaha NE 68105

OBERST, DANIEL C., civil engr.; b. Ind., June 25, 1942; B.S.C.E., Tri-State U., Angola, Ind., 1970; m. Wanda Rebber, Oct. 1972; children—Lawrence Keith, Dealia Ann. Dep. county surveyor, Steuben County, Ind., 1961-62; land surveying technician C.B. Wood & Assos., Angola, 1969-70; with Ind. State Hwy. Commn. Grad. Engr. Tng. Program, 1971-72, asst. materials research engr., div. materials and tests, 1972-74, engr. phys. tests, 1974, asst. dist. engr. materials and tests, 1974—; dir. Hayden Rural Water Co. Served with U.S. Army, 1966-69. Recipient Gov.'s citation for inventing Core Lifter, 1975. Registered profl. engr. and land surveyor, Ind. Mem. ASCE, Ind. Soc. Profl. Engrs. (dir. EADS chpt.). Lutheran. Clubs: Masons; Elks. Home: Rural Route 4 North Vernon IN 47265

OBERSTAR, JAMES L., congressman; b. Chisholm, Minn., Sept. 10, 1934; s. Louis and Mary (Grillo) C.; B.A. summa cum laude, St. Thomas Coll.; postgrad. in French, Laval U., Que., Can.; M.A. in Govt. (scholar), Coll. Europe, Bruges, Belgium; postgrad. in govt. Georgetown U.; m. Marilynn Jo Garlick, Oct. 12, 1963; children—Thomas Edward, Katherine Noelle, Ann-Therese, Monica Rose. Adminstrv. asst. to Congressman John A. Blatnik, 1963-74; adminstr. Pub. Works Com., U.S. Ho. of Reps., 1971-74; mem. 94th-95th Congresses from 8th Minn. Dist. Mem. Am. Polit. Sci. Assn. Home: 317 NW 9th St Chisholm MN 55719 Office: 323 Cannon House Office Bldg Washington DC 20515

OBEY, DAVID ROSS, congressman; b. Okmulgee, Okla., Oct. 3, 1938; s. Orville John and Mary Jane (Chellis) O.; B.S. in Polit. Sci., U. Wis., 1960, M.A., 1962; m. Joan Therese Lepinski, June 9, 1962; children—Craig David, Douglas David. Mem. Wis. Assembly from Marathon County, 1963-69, asst. minority leader, 1967-69; mem. 91st-95th Congresses from 7th Dist. Wis., mem. Democratic steering com., vice chmn. house Dem. study group, mem. appropriations com., house budget com., subcoms. on labor, HEW and fgn. ops., chmn. commn. adminstrv. rev. Mem. adminstrv. com. Wis. Democratic Party, 1960-62. Named Edn. Legislator of Year rural div. NEA, 1968; recipient Legis. Leadership award Eagelton Inst. Politics, 1964. Home: 831 Dunbar St Wausau WI 54401 Office: Rayburn House Office Bldg Washington DC 20515

OBLAK, ROBERT OTTO, plastic mfg. co. exec.; b. Akron, Ohio, Nov. 4, 1941; s. Otto Joseph and Mary Angela O.; B.B.A., Kent State U., 1966, M.B.A., 1972; m. Patricia Ann McDonald, Mar. 28, 1964; children—Amy, Terry. Mfg. analyst, cost estimator Terex div. Gen. Motors Corp., Hudson, Ohio, 1966-69; supr. mfg. analysis Geauga Industries Co., Middlefield, Ohio, 1969-72; mgr. mfg. George J. Meyers Co., Akron, 1972-74; v.p., gen. mgr. Plasti-Chain Corp., Hebron, Ill., 1974—. Democrat. Presbyterian. Home: 205 Abbey Springs Dr Fontana WI 53125 Office: PO Box 267 Hebron IL 60034

OBLINGER, JOSEPHINE KNEIDL HARRINGTON (MRS. WALTER L. OBLINGER), state ofcl.; b. Chgo., Feb. 14, 1913; d. Thomas William and Margaret (Kneidl) Harrington; B.S., U. Ill., 1933; J.D., U. Detroit, 1968; L.H.D., Sioux Empire Coll., 1966; m. Walter L. Oblinger, Apr. 27, 1940; 1 son, Carl D. Tchr. Lanphier High Sch., Springfield, Ill., 1951-62; clk. Sargamon County, assessor Capital Twp., Springfield, 1962-69; asst. dir. Ill. Dept. Registration and Edn., Springfield, 1970—; exec. dir. Gov.'s Com. on Voluntary Action, 1970-73; asst. to pres. Lincoln Land Community Coll., 1973-77; dir. Ill. Dept. on Aging, 1977—. Sec. Springfield and Sangamon County Community Action, 1965-70 pres., 1970-74; mem. finance com. Child and Family Service, Springfield, 1965-70; mem. Nat. Com. for Day Care of Children, 1960—; pres. Springfield Fedn. Tchrs. AFL-CIO, 1957-59, Ill. Fedn. Tchrs. AFL-CIO, 1959-63; mem. adv. com. to Gov.'s ACTION Office; mem. Planning Consortium for Services to Children in Ill. Officer Repulican Women's Luncheon Club, 1959—, pres., 1963-67; chmn. Sangamon County Rep. com., 1965—; pres. Ill. Fedn. Rep. Women. Del. to White House Conf., 1960. Bd. dirs., pres. Sangamon-Menard County Council on Alcoholism and Drugs, Nat. Center Vol. Action; mem. bd. Sangamon County Salvation Army, Ret. Sr. Vol. Program. Mem. Ill. Assn. County Clks. and Recorders (pres.), Am. Bus. Women's Assn., Am., Ill., Sangamon County bar assns., Am. Assn. Vol. Services Coordinators (dir., chmn. pub. policy com.), N.A.A.C.P. (exec. bd.), Urban League, U. Ill. Alumni Assn., Nat. Assn. Counties, Nat. Assn. Recorders and Clks., Sangamon County Hist. Soc., P.E.O., Kappa Delta Pi, Sigma Delta Pi, Delta Delta Delta. Clubs: Springfield Women's; Altrusa (pres. 1968-70, dir.) (Springfield). Home: Rural Route 1 Sherman IL 62684 Office: 2401 W Jefferson Springfield IL 62706

O'BLOCK, FRANK ROBERT, psychologist, educator; b. Greenford, Ohio, July 4, 1932; s. Frank Ernest and Barbara Louise (Mikicic) O'B.; B.S., Youngstown (Ohio) U., 1959; M.S., Bowling Green U., 1962; Ed.D. (NIMH fellow), U. Ill., 1967. Draftsman, Delta Power Tool Div., Leetonia, Ohio, 1950-52; tchr. Austin-Fitch Pub. Sch., Austintown, Ohio, 1959-60; psychologist pub. sch., Urbana, Ill., 1965-69; asso. prof. psychology Chgo. State U., 1969—; testing cons. Operation Headstart, Urbana, 1966, dir. Project Upgrade, 1967. Certified psychologist and sch. psychologist, Ill. Mem. Nat. Assn. Sch. Psychologists (chartered), Am., Ill. psychol. assns. Roman Catholic. Contbr. articles to psychol. publs. Home: 2236 N Racine Ave Chicago IL 60614

O'BRIEN, CHARLES RICHARD, JR., educator; b. Boston, Nov. 10, 1934; s. Charles R. and Dorothy Margaret (DeBesse) O'B.; B.A., St. John's U., Boston, 1956; M.S., N.D. State U., 1968; Ed.D., U. Wyo., 1972. Dir. religious edn., Framingham, Mass., 1963-66; dir. of guidance Cardinal Muench Sem., Fargo, N.D., 1966-69; asst. prof. edn. N.D. State U., Fargo, 1969-73; asso. prof. of counselor edn. Western Ill. U., Macomb, 1974—; pastoral adviser Norfolk County (Mass.) Hosp., 1960-63, Waltham (Mass.) Hosp., 1973-74; guidance cons. Diocese of Fargo, 1966-73, Newman Found., Ill., 1974; vis. lectr. Fitchburg State Coll., Fitchburg, Mass., 1973-74; teaching cons. Office of Employment Security, N.D., 1972-72. Mem. Am., Midwestern psychol. assns., Am. Coll. Personnel Assn., Am. Personnel and Guidance Assn., Phi Delta Kappa, Phi Kappa Phi, Kappa Delta Pi. Roman Catholic. Contbr. 30 articles on counseling to profl. jours. Home: 204 Shannon Dr Macomb IL 61455 Office: 127 Sherman Hall Western Illinois Univ Macomb IL 61455

O'BRIEN, FRANCIS DAVID, energy engr.; b. Jamacia, N.Y., Aug. 31, 1939; s. Francis Aloysius and Margaret Eugenia (Stabler) O'B.; B.S., St. Peter's Coll., 1961; m. Ann McCaffrey, Apr. 20, 1963; children—David, Marita Anne, Mary Margaret, Daniel, Maureen. Project engr. Westinghouse Electric Corp., Monroeville, Pa., 1966-72; project mgr. Houston Lighting & Power Co., 1972-74; dir. regulatory and industry services Fluor Pioneer Inc., Chgo., 1974—. Served with U.S. Army, 1962-66. NSF fellow, 1962; registered profl. engr., Tex., Ill., Pa. Mem. Project Mgmt. Inst. (nat. pres.), Nat. Assn. Environ. Profls. (pres. Midwest chpt., nat. v.p.), Am. Nuclear Soc. (dir. environ. scis. div.), Nat. Soc. Profl. Engrs., Americans for Energy Independence. Republican. Roman Catholic. Contbr. articles to profl. jours. Home: 860 Harvard Dr Palatine IL 60067 Office: 200 W Monroe St Chicago IL 60606

O'BRIEN, GEORGE HERBERT, mech. engr.; b. Rawlins, Wyo., Mar. 5, 1917; s. George Higginbotham and Hazel Beatrix (Johnston) O'B.; B.S. Mech. Engring., Kans. State U., 1940; postgrad. bus. adminstrn. Ind. U., 1968; m. Mary Elizabeth Kerr, Oct. 7, 1944; children—Kathy Ann, Jean Marie. Engr., Wright Aero. Corp., 1940-47; field research engr., Cummins Engine Co., Columbus, Ind., 1940-53, area service mgr. and tech. service mgr., 1953-66, service tool engring. mgr., tech. specialist salvage, 1966—. Mem. Soc. Auto. Engrs. Republican. Roman Catholic. Home: 2564 Pearl St Columbus IN 47201 Office: 1000 5th St Columbus IN 47201

O'BRIEN, GEORGE MILLER, congressman; b. Chgo., June 17, 1917; s. Matthew J. and Isabel (Hyde) O'B.; A.B., Northwestern U., 1939; J.D., Yale U., 1947; m. Mary Lou Peyla, Sept. 6, 1947; children—Caryl Isabel O'Brien Bloch, Mary Deborah O'Brien Pershey. Admitted to Ill. bar, 1947; sr. partner O'Brien, Garrison, Berard, Kusta & DeWitt, Joliet, 1966—; mem. 93d-95th Congress from 17th Dist. Ill., mem. armed services com. Chmn. Will County chpt. ARC, 1957-58; pres. Joliet-Will County Community Chest Program; mem. Will County Bd. Suprs., 1956-64; mem. Legis. Adv. Com. to Northeastern Ill. Planning Commn., 1971-72; mem. Ill. Ho. of Reps., 1970-72, mem. exec. and judiciary II coms. Served to lt. col. USAAF, 1941-45. Recipient Distinguished Service award Joliet Boys' Club. Mem. Am., Ill., Chgo., Will County bar assns., Trial Lawyers Assn. Ill., Am. Legion, VFW, Phi Beta Kappa. Roman Catholic. Clubs: Elks, Rotary, Union League (Chgo.). Office: 434 Cannon House Office Bldg Washington DC 20515

O'BRIEN, GREGORY MICHAEL ST. LAWRENCE, univ. dean; b. N.Y.C., Oct. 7, 1944; s. Henry Joseph and Mary Agnes (McGoldrick) O'B.; B.A. with honors, Lehigh U., 1966; M.A., Boston U., 1968, Ph.D., 1969; m. Mary Kathleen McLaughlin, Dec. 28, 1968; children—Jennifer Jane, Merideth Kathleen. Asso. in psychiatry Lab. Community Psychiatry, Harvard, Cambridge, Mass., 1969-70; evaluation research cons. Human Relations Lab., Boston U., N.Y.C., 1969-70; dir. Human Services Design Lab., Sch. Applied Social Sci., Case Western Reserve U., Cleve., 1970-74, asst. prof., 1970-71, asso. prof., 1971-74; dean, prof. Sch. Social Welfare, U. Wis., Milw., 1974—; teaching fellow social psychology Boston U., 1967-68. Chmn. Milwaukee County Human Services Project. Bd. dirs. Friends of Channel 10, Milw., 1974—, treas., 1975—. NIMH fellow, 1968-69. Mem. Eastern Psychol. Assn., Am. Pub. Health Assn., Am. Pub. Welfare Assn., Council on Social Work Edn., Nat. Assn. Social Workers, Nat. Conf. on Social Welfare, Soc. for Gen. Systems Research. Editorial adviser Adminstrn. in Mental Health, 1967-73. Contbr. articles to profl. jours. Home: 2637 E Beverly Rd Milwaukee WI 53211

O'BRIEN, JOHN PATRICK, educator; b. Rice Lake, Wis., Oct. 18, 1916; s. James Vincent and Bridget (Higgins) O'B.; B.S., U. Wis., 1939, M.S., 1954; m. Dolores Kramschuster, June 24, 1946; children—Peggy O'Brien Nehring, Dorothy O'Brien Antoine, Maureen, Peter, Patricia. Coach, tchr. Chippewa Falls (Wis.) High Sch., 1939-41, Marmion Mil. Inst., Aurora, Ill., 1946-48, Ladysmith (Wis.) High Sch., 1948-61; faculty Barron County Tchrs. Coll., Rice Lake, 61-66; faculty U. Wis. Center-Barron County, Rice Lake, 1966—, athletic dir., coach, asso. prof., 1974—. Mem. Ladysmith (Wis.) City Council, 1958-61; mem. Rusk County (Wis.) Bd., 1958-61; Barron County (Wis.) rep. to U.S. Draft Bd., 1962-66; exec. com. Barron County Dems., 1972—. Served with USAAF, 1941-45. NSF grantee, 1960. Mem. Barron County Campus Found., Rice Lake Scholarship Found., Ambassadors Club. Democrat. Roman Catholic. Clubs: K.C., Elks. Address: 408 Hatten St Rice Lake WI 54868

O'BRIEN, WILLIAM PATRICK, warehousing exec.; b. Chgo., May 25, 1921; s. William Patrick and Mary Agnes (Brennan) O'B.; B.S., Loyola U., Chgo., 1943; postgrad. U. Chgo., 1946-47; m. Monica Mary Cummingham, Nov. 17, 1951; children—William E., Margaret L., Mary Patricia, Robert G., Barbara Ann. Chief accountant Madigan Brothers, 1946-49; sr. accountant Burlingame & Co., C.P.A.'s, 1949-51; auditor Minute Maid Corp., 1951-56, distbn. mgr., 1956-57; comptroller E.A. Aaron Bros., 1957, pres., 1957-59; v.p. Continental Freezers of Ill., Chgo., 1959—. Sec.-treas. Total Distbn. Plan for Am., Inc.; pres. Lafayette Refrigerated Services, Inc. (Ind.). Mem., finance chmn. St. Cletus Sch. Bd., 1971—. Chmn. bd. Interfaith Council of La Grange. Served to lt. (j.g.) USNR, 1943-46; PTO. Decorated Commendation medal. Mem. Midwestern Frozen Food Assn. (pres. 1970-71, bd. mgrs.), Am. Frozen Food Inst. (allied industries bd.). Club: Lafayette Country. Home: 411 S Spring Ave La Grange IL 60525 Office: 4220 S Kildare Ave Chicago IL 60632

OCEPEK, ANTHONY STEVEN, broadcasting exec.; b. Barberton, O., Aug. 3, 1938; s. Anthony and Josephine Helen (Jastraub) O.; B.S., Kent State U., 1960; m. Marcia Tamplin, Aug. 4, 1960; children—Beth, Mark, Paul. With Westinghouse Broadcasting Co. KYW-TV, Cleve. and Phila., NBC-WKYC-TV, Cleve.; pres. WPVL, Painesville, O., 1970—; pres. Capital Communications, Inc.; v.p. Lake Cable TV, Inc., WHOK, Inc.; dir. Citizens Savs. & Loan Co., Lake County Nat. Bank. Bd. dirs. Lake County Hist. Soc., Holden Arboretum, Lake County Devel. Council. Mem. Nat., Ohio assns. broadcasters, Painesville Area C. of C. (dir.). Rotarian. Home: 9045

Baldwin Rd Kirtland Hills OH 44060 Office: 1 Radio Pl Painesville OH 44077

O'CONNELL, DANIEL CRAIG, univ. pres.; b. Sand Springs, Okla., May 20, 1928; s. John Albert and Letitia Rutherford (McGinnis) O'C.; A.B., St. Louis U., 1951, Ph.L., 1952, A.M., 1953, S.T.L., 1960; Ph.D., U. Ill., 1963. Tchr. high sch. Campion Jesuit High Sch., Prairie du Chien, Wis., 1953-55; NSF postdoctoral fellow Harvard U., 1963-64, 65-66; asst. prof. psychology St. Louis U., 1964-67, asso. prof., 1967-72, prof., 1972—, pres., 1974—, trustee, 1973—. Bd. dirs. Council Fin. Aid to Edn., 1975—, St. Louis Council on World Affairs, 1975-77; bd. dirs., edn. chmn. St. Louis chpt. United Way, 1976-77. Recipient Nancy McNeir Ring award St. Louis U., 1969; NSF fellow, 1961, 63, 65, 68; Humboldt fellow Free U. Berlin, 1968, Humboldt grantee, 1973. Fellow Am., Mo. psychol. assns.; mem. Psychologists Interested in Religious Issues, Psychonomic Soc., Soc. Sci. Study Religion, AAUP, N.Y., Mo. acads. scis., Midwestern, Southwestern, Eastern psychol. assns., Phi Beta Kappa, Alpha Sigma Nu. Roman Catholic. Contbr. articles to profl. jours. Home: 3601 Lindell Blvd St Louis MO 63108 Office: 221 N Grand Blvd St Louis MO 63103

O'CONNELL, MARVIN RICHARD, historian; b. Mpls., July 9, 1930; s. Richard C. and Anna Mae (Kelly) O'C.; B.A., St. Paul Sem., 1952, M.A., 1955; Ph.D., U. Notre Dame, 1959. Instr. history Coll. St. Thomas, 1958-59, asst. prof., 1959-63, asso. prof., 1963-72; asso. prof. history U. Notre Dame, 1972-77, prof., 1977—, chmn. dept. history, 1974—. Lingard fellow, 1956-58; Hill fellow, 1964. Mem. AAUP, Am. Hist. Assn. Roman Catholic. Author: Thomas Stapleton, 1964; The Oxford Conspirators, 1969; The Counter Reformation, 1974. Contbr. articles to profl. jours. Home: 15625 Hearthstone Dr Mishawaka IN 46544 Office: 347 O'Shaughnessy Hall U Notre Dame Notre Dame IN 46556

O'CONNELL, WILLIAM JAMES, educator; b. Lima, Ohio, May 22, 1924; s. Daniel and Mary (Boda) O'C.; student John Carroll U., 1942-44; B.Arch., Cath. U. Am., 1949; M.Arch., U. Calif. at Berkeley, 1966; m. Dorothy Jean Lynch, Apr. 10, 1950; children—Daniel, Janice, Thomas. Archtl. trainee, 1949-56; architect O'Connell & Swing, Chgo., 1956-57; with John Carl Warnecke and Leo A. Daly, San Francisco, 1957-59; prof. architecture U. Ill. at Urbana, 1959—; pvt. practice of architecture, part-time, 1959—. Mem. Ill. Gov.'s Adv. Council, 1969. Served with USNR, 1943-46. Mem. Nat. Council Archtl. Registration Bds., A.A.U.P., Assn. Collegiate Schs. Architecture. Author: Standard Format for Architectural Working Drawings, 1966; Graphic Communications in Architecture, 1972. Home: 1607 Oxford Dr Champaign IL 61820 Office: Dept Architecture U Ill Urbana IL 61801

O'CONNELL, WILLIAM THOMAS, financial exec.; b. Oak Park, Ill., Dec. 23, 1922; s. William T. and Agnes (Draehn) O'C.; B.S., U. Ariz., 1948; postgrad. Grad. Sch. Credit and Fin., Stanford U., 1967-69; m. Drinette M. Slatten, May 28, 1949; children—Carole A., Joan M., George L., Celia L., Richard S. With Dun & Bradstreet, Inc., 1948—, mgr., Phoenix, 1953-64, dist. mgr., Portland, Oreg., 1964-69, Chgo., 1969-71, Milw., 1971-74, regional mgr., Chgo., 1974-75, v.p., 1975—. Active United Fund, Salvation Army. Served with USAAF, 1942-45. Mem. Chgo. Assn. Commerce and Industry, Nat. Assn. Credit Mgmt. Clubs: Rotary; Union League, Execs. (Chgo.); Glen Oak Country (Glen Ellyn, Ill.). Home: 1767 Marion Ct Wheaton IL 60187 Office: 300 W Adams St Chicago IL 60606

O'CONNOR, CARL BERNARD, dentist; b. Daviess County, Ind., July 27, 1922; s. Matt and Corine (Arvin) O'C.; A.S., Vincennes U., 1949; D.D.S., St. Louis U., 1953; m. Betty Wade, Aug. 18, 1944; children—Julia (Mrs. Tom Brewer), James, Patrick, Mark, Janice, Lori. Pvt. practice dentistry, Washington, Ind., 1953—; mem. med. staff Daviess County Hosp. Chmn. bd. S.M.O.W. Shopping Center, Washington. Mem. Ind. Bd. Dental Examiners, 1974—. Bd. dirs. Daviess County YMCA, chmn. bd., 1968-73. Served to capt. USMCR, 1942-46. Recipient Outstanding Service award Jaycees, 1957; Laetare award K.C., 1966, named Father of the Year, 1966. Mem. Ind. Acad. Practice Adminstrs. (pres. 1966), 1st Dist. Dental Soc. (pres. 1969-70), Roman Catholic (trustee 1962-65). K. C. (faith navigator 1963-67, 4 deg.). Home: 309 N Meridian St Washington IN 47501 Office: 300 NE 4th St Washington IN 47501

O'CONNOR, CHARLES, JR., city ofcl.; b. Sioux City, Iowa, Oct. 21, 1922; s. Charles and Juanita (Cage) O'C.; B.C.S., Drake U., 1943. Jr. accountant Peat-Marwick-Mitchell & Co., Des Moines, 1943-46; accounting supr. Bankers Life Co., Des Moines, 1946-58; adminstrv. asst. to city mgr., Des Moines, 1959-64; city finance dir., Des Moines, 1964—. Served with USNR, 1943-46. C.P.A., Iowa. Fellow Life Mgmt. Inst.; mem. Am. Inst. C.P.A.'s, Iowa Soc. C.P.A.'s, Municipal Finance Officers Assn., Internat. City Mgrs. Assn., Am. Soc. Pub. Adminstrn., Delta Sigma Pi. Democrat. Roman Catholic (ch. trustee). Home: 2309 N Union St Des Moines IA 50316 Office: City Hall E 1st and Locust Sts Des Moines IA 50309

O'CONNOR, CHARLES GARRY, dentist; b. Hamilton, Ont., Can., Dec. 11, 1942; s. Charles Henry and Madeline (Burley) O'C.; student Kilgore Coll., 1961-63, 64-65, Stephen F. Austin State U., 1965; D.D.S., Marquette Dental Sch., 1969; M.S., Case Western Res. U., 1969-71; m. Elizabeth Christine Brett, July 24, 1965; 1 dau., Candace Deirdre. Came to U.S., 1952, naturalized, 1970. Practice dentistry, La Crosse, Wis., 1971—. Recipient award of Excellence in Periodontics, Am. Acad. Periodontics, 1969. Fellow Royal Soc. Health; mem. Am. Soc. Preventive Dentistry, ADA, Am. Assn. Periodontics, Am. Dental Soc. Anesthesiology, Am. Soc. Hosp. Dentists. Club: Serra (La Crosse). Home: 513 1/2 Johnson St La Crosse WI 54601 Office: Gunderson Clinic 1836 S Ave La Crosse WI 54601

O'CONNOR, CLAUDE LINDBERGH, real estate broker; b. Tarkio, Mo., Mar. 2, 1927; s. Claud F. and Bessie (White) O'C.; student Fairbury Jr. Coll., 1945-46; postgrad. Mo. Auction Sch., 1967, Grad. Real Estate Inst., 1969-71; m. Betty L. Mooren, Feb. 23, 1950; children—Claudia Kay (Mrs. Stephen Robinson), Donald S. Mgr., Terrill's Grocery, Fairbury, Nebr., 1946-57; mgr. Sherwin-Williams Paint Store, Columbus, Nebr., 1957-66; owner-mgr. Armor Realty, Inc., Columbus, 1966—. Pres., Columbus Bd. Realtors, 1970-71. Bd. dirs. Mid Am. council Boy Scouts Am. Served with AUS, World War II. Recipient award of merit Boy Scouts Am., 1971, Silver Beaver award, 1974; named Optimist of Year, 1971-72. Mem. Nebr. Real Estate Assn. (gov.), Nebr. C. of C., P.T.A. (life), Am. Legion. Methodist. Elk. Club: Optimist (pres., v.p., lt. gov.). Home: 307 Pershing Rd Columbus NE 68601 Office: 2815 13th St Columbus NE 68601

O'CONNOR, DAVID, assn. exec.; b. Worcester, Mass., Mar. 6, 1926; s. Michael Joseph and Lucy Margaret (Dowd) O'C.; B.S. in Pub. Relations, Boston U., 1950; m. Beverley Ruth Hallberg, Jan. 12, 1950; children—Brian, Andrew, Timothy, Jenny. With Nat. Screw & Mfg. Co., Cleve., 1950-67, dir. pub. relations, 1960-67; pub. relations dir. Constrn. Employees Assn., Cleve., 1967—. Exec. sec. Greater Cleve. Roofing Contractors Assn., 1969—, Insulation Contractors Assn. Cleve., SMACNA of N. Central Ohio, Acoustical and Interior Contractors Assn. Cleve. Mem. nat. alumni council Boston U., 1960—. Served with USNR, 1944-46; comdr. Res., ret. Recipient George Washington medal Freedoms Found., Valley Forge, Pa., 1959, 60, 61, 62, 63. Mem. Pub. Relations Soc. Am. (nat. assembly del. 1970, 71), No. Ohio Indsl. Editors Assn. (pres. 1961), Cleve. Soc. Assn. Execs. Home: 35665 Chardon Rd Willoughby Hills OH 44094 Office: 1801 E 12th St Cleveland OH 44114

O'CONNOR, JAMES IGNATIUS, educator; b. Chgo., July 30, 1910; s. James Francis and Margaret (Quealy) O'C.; Litt.B., Xavier U., 1934, M.A., 1935; Ph.L., West Baden Coll., 1938, S.T.L., 1944; J.C.B., Cath. U. Am., 1946; J.C.L., Gregorian U. (Rome), 1948, J.C.D., 1950. Ordained priest Roman Catholic Ch., 1943; mem. S.J., 1930—; prof. canon law and rites West Baden Coll. (Ind.), 1948-64, Bellarmine Sch. Theology, Chgo., 1964-73, Jesuit Sch. Theology, Chgo., 1973-75, prof. emeritus, 1975—; lectr. U. Detroit, 1949, St. Mary's Coll., Notre Dame, 1949, Loyola U., Chgo., 1951, 53, Xavier U., 1953, 56-65, Mundelein Coll.; 1964-65; many others; cons. Cath. Hosp. Assn., St. Louis, 1953—; chaplain St. Mary of the Lake Sem., Mundelein, Ill., 1976—. Mem. Canon Law Soc. Am., Canon Law Soc. Gt. Britain and Ireland, Canadian Canon Law Soc. Contbr. articles to New Cath. Ency., profl. jours. and books. Home: Saint Mary of the Lake Sem Mundelein IL 60060

O'CONNOR, JAMES JOHN, utility exec.; b. Chgo., Mar. 15, 1937; s. Fred James and Helen Elizabeth (Reilly) O'C.; B.S., Holy Cross Coll., 1958; M.B.A, Harvard U., 1960; J.D., Georgetown U., 1963; m. Ellen Louise Lawlor, Nov. 24, 1960; children—Fred, John, James, Helen. Admitted to Ill. bar, 1963; with Commonwealth Edison Co., Chgo., 1963—, asst. to chmn. exec. com., 1964-65, comml. mgr., 1966, asst. v.p., 1967-70, v.p., 1970-73, exec. v.p., 1973—; dir. Talman Fed. Savs. & Loan Assn. Bd. dirs. Chgo. unit Am. Cancer Soc., chmn. bd., 1971-73; bd. dirs. Chgo. Boys' Clubs, v.p., 1970—; bd. dirs. Leadership Council for Met. Open Communities, v.p., 1976—; bd. dirs. Lyric Opera Chgo.; trustee Adler Planetarium, Ill. Children's Home and Aid Soc., Sprague Meml. Inst., Sta. WTTW, Michael Reese Med. Center, Field Mus.; chmn. bd. Chgo. Conv. and Tourism Bur.; bd. dirs., treas. Chgo. Urban League; mem. exec. bd. Boy Scouts Am.; v.p. adv. bd. Mercy Hosp.; chmn. bd. Citizenship Council Met. Chgo.; mem. pres.'s adv. council Chgo. State U. Served with USAF, 1960-63. Named One of Chgo.'s 10 Outstanding Young Men, Chgo. Jr. Assn. Commerce and Industry, 1970. Mem. Am., Ill., Chgo. bar assns. Roman Catholic. Clubs: Comml., Econ., Chgo., Chgo. Commonwealth, Met. (Chgo.). Home: 9549 Monticello Ave Evanston IL 60203 Office: PO Box 767 One First Nat Plaza Chicago IL 60690

O'CONNOR, JEROME WILLIAM, broadcasting co. exec.; b. Pitts., Aug. 23, 1923; s. Thomas Lee and Bertha Marie (Bortell) O'C.; student U. Ala., 1941, 42, U. Miami (Fla.), 1943, 44, Northwestern U., 1946; m. Dorothy June Conover, Dec. 22, 1944; children—Kerby William, Maureen Dee, Kathleen Dawn, Valerie Dodds, Clinton Anthony. With WGN Radio and Television, Chgo., 1946-50, Storer Broadcasting Co., Miami, Fla., 1950; ind. producer, announcer WCFL, WIND, WBKB-TV, WGN-TV, WMAQ, WENR, Chgo., 1951-65; pres. WCVS, Springfield, Ill., 1958-66, WBOW, Terre Haute, Ind., WHUT, Anderson, Ind., 1958-70; pres., gen. mgr. WCIU-TV, Chgo., 1965—; dir. Weigel Broadcasting Co., Chgo., WRAC Broadcasting Co., Racine, Wis. Served with USNR, 1942-46. Mem. Broadcast Pioneers, Chgo. Press Vets., Nat. Assn. Television Arts and Scis., Phi Gamma Delta. Club: Key Biscayne Yacht (Fla). Home: 660 Winnetka Mews Winnetka IL 60093 Office: Bd Trade Bldg 141 W Jackson Blvd Chicago IL 60604

O'CONNOR, MICHAEL DAVID, educator; b. Oconto, Wis., June 6, 1918; s. William S. and Stella (Picard) O'C.; student U. Wis., 1935-36, Kansas City Conservatory Music, 1938, 40-41, Rockhurst Coll., 1946-47; B.S., M.A., U. Mo., Kansas City, 1956-60; m. Betty Ann Wagner, June 25, 1949; children—David, Patrick, Diane, Brian, Jean Marie. Instr., Rockhurst Coll., Kansas City, Mo., 1947-51, asso. prof. psychology, chmn. dept. psychology, 1962-77, prof., 1977—, chmn. div. psychology and edn., 1971—. Pvt. practice psychol. counseling, 1947—; staff psychologist Upward-Bound, 1965—; cons. field of hypnosis, bio-feedback, electrosleep. Bd. dirs. City Coll. Kansas City. Served with USMCR, 1942-45; PTO. Mem. Greater Kansas City Soc. Clin. Hypnosis (pres. 1967-69). Home: 8817 Ford Ave Kansas City MO 64138

O'CONNOR, MICHAEL DENNIS, editor, publisher; b. Kankakee, Ill., Nov. 7, 1947; s. William Alex and Berdell M. (Crawley) O'C.; B.S., No. Ill. U., 1969; m. Linda Kay Murney, Sept. 6, 1969; children—Timothy Michael, Erin Elizabeth. Reporter, Rockford Register-Republic (Ill.), 1969-70, Rockford Morning Star, 1971-72; editor, pub. Mendota (Ill.) Reporter, 1972—. Bd. dirs. Mendota Devel. Commn. Mem. No. Ill. (pres. 1975-76), Nat. newspaper assns., Ill. Press Assn., Soc. Profl. Journalists, Mendota Area C. of C. (pres. 1976), Internat. Soc. Weekly Newspaper Editors, Ill. Press Photographers Assn. Roman Catholic Elk. Served with U.S. Army, 1970-71. Decorated Bronze Star; Newspaper Fund. editing scholar, 1968. Home: 605 7th Ave Mendota IL 61342 Office: 702 Illinois Ave Mendota IL 61342

O'CONNOR, SARA ANDREWS, theater exec.; b. Syracuse, N.Y., Apr. 5, 1932; d. Harlan Francis and Ethel (Hoyt) Andrews; m. Boardman O'Connor, Aug. 26, 1955 (div. 1969); children—Ian, Douglas; B.A. with high honors, Swarthmore Coll., 1954; M.A. in Drama, Tufts U., 1955. Asso. producer Co. of the Four, 1959-65; asso. producer Theatre Co. of Boston, 1965-68, producer, 1969-71; pub. relations dir. Repertory Theatre, New Orleans, 1968-69; gen. mgr. Cherry County Playhouse, summer, 1970; mng. dir. Cin. Playhouse, 1971-74, Milw. Repertory Theater, 1974—; v.p. League Resident Theatres; bd. dirs., mem. exec. com. Theatre Communications Group; bd. dirs. Theatre X; cons. Found. for Extension and Devel. Am. Profl. Theatre. Mem. Actors Equity Assn., Wis. Theatre Assn. Office: 929 N Water St Milwaukee WI 53202

O'CONNOR, TIMOTHY EDMUND, chemist; b. Cork, Ireland, Dec. 5, 1925; m. 1932; 6 children; came to U.S., 1950, naturalized, 1958; B.S., Nat. U. Ireland, 1947, M.Sc., 1948, Ph.D., 1951. Fellow, Mayo Found., 1950-51, U. Wis., 1951-52; chemist E.I. duPont de Nemours & Co., Wilmington, Del., 1952-60, research scientist, 1960-61; Spl. research fellow NIH, USPHS, 1961-63, chemist Nat. Cancer Inst., 1963-75; dir. div. biol. and med. research Argonne (Ill.) Nat. Lab., 1975—. Office: Argonne Nat Lab 9700 S Cass Ave Argonne IL 60439

ODEBRECHT, A. RICHARD, real estate appraiser, mortgage banker; b. Columbus, O., Dec. 11, 1926; s. Asbury Leonce and Elva (Linton) O.; B.S., Ohio State U., 1950; m. Shirley Ruth Keller, Aug. 6, 1955; children—James, Virginia, Laurance. Div. mgr. mortgage and real estate investment dept. Equitable Life Assurance Soc. U.S., Columbus O., Baltimore, St. Louis, 1953-67; v.p. Real Estate Research Corp., St. Louis, 1967-76; v.p. Nationwide Real Estate Services, Inc., Columbus, 1976—. Dir. Chartwell on the Severn Community Assn., Severna Park, Md., 1964-65. Mem. Am. Inst. Real Estate Appraisers (chpt. treas. 1974, sec. 1975, pres. elect 1977), Phi Delta Theta. Clubs: Cherry Hills Country (St. Louis), Masons, Shriners. Office: One Nationwide Plaza Columbus OH 43216

O'DELL, FREDERICK CHARLES, JR., surgeon; b. Bad Axe, Mich., Sept. 23, 1924; s. Frederick Charles and Charlotte (Herrington) O.; A.B., U. Mich., 1946, M.D., 1949; m. Deborah Lincoln, Oct. 29, 1955; children—Winnifred Charlotte, Catherine Hobbs, Mary Lincoln. Intern U. Mich. Hosp., 1949-50, resident 1949-55; registrar in surgery St. Bartholomews Hosp., London, 1955-56; practice medicine specializing in surgery, Alpena, Mich., 1956—; mem. staff Alpena Gen. Hosp. Pres. Alpena Community Concert Assn., 1976—; trustee Alpena Community Found., 1974—. Served with USN, 1951-53. Mem. AMA, Midwest Surg. Assn., ACS, Frederick A. Coller Sur. Soc. Episcopalian. Home: 445 Island View Dr Alpena MI 49707 Office: 615 W Chisholm St Alpena MI 49707

O'DELL, LYNN MARIE LUEGGE (MRS. NORMAN D. O'DELL), librarian; b. Berwyn, Ill., Feb. 24, 1938; d. George Emil and Helen Marie (Pesek) Luegge; student Lyons Twp. Jr. Coll., La Grange, Ill., 1957; student No. Ill. U., Elgin Community Coll., U. Ill., Coll. of DuPage; m. Norman D. O'Dell, Dec. 14, 1957; children—Jeffrey, Jerry. Sec., Martin Co., Chgo., 1957-59; librarian Carol Stream (Ill.) Pub. Library, 1964—; exec. com. Du Page County Library System, 1967, 68, 71—. Active Carol Stream unit Central DuPage Hosp. Aux. Named Woman of Year, Wheaton Bus. and Profl. Woman's Club, 1968. Mem. ALA, Carol Stream Hist. Soc. (v.p.). Club: Carol Stream Woman's (sec. 1968, 1st v.p. 1969). Lutheran (organist). Home: 182 Yuma Ln Carol Stream IL 60187 Office: 616 Hiawatha Dr Carol Stream IL 60187

O'DELL, RICHARD FREDERICK, historian; b. Lansing, Mich., Oct. 16, 1914; s. George Maywood and Edna Blanche (Spindler) O'D.; B.A., Mich. State U., 1935; M.A., U. Mich., 1939, Ph.D. in History, 1948; m. Louise Sprau, Jan. 26, 1940; children—Dorothy Louise O'Dell Clore, Richard Frederick. Tchr., Mt. Morris (Mich.) Jr. High Sch., 1939-40, prin. sr. high sch., 1940-41; instr. Navy V-12 Program, U. Mich., 1943-46; asso. prof. history Evansville (Ind.) U., 1947-48; asso. prof. history No. Mich. U., Marquette, 1949-52, prof., 1952-74, head dept. history, 1957-63, prof. emeritus, 1975—; pres. Upper Peninsula Child Guidance Clinic, Marquette, 1962-65. Chmn., Upper Peninsula Mental Health Planning Com., 1964-65. Alfred H. Lloyd fellow, 1948-49. Mem. Am. Hist. Assn., Hist. Soc. Mich. (trustee 1949-52, v.p. 1951-52), AAUP, Marquette County Hist. Soc. (trustee 1950—, pres. 1956-59), Phi Kappa Phi, Alpha Phi Omega. Home: 321 E Hewitt Ave Marquette MI 49855 Office: Dept of History Northern Mich Univ Marquette MI 49855

ODER, DONALD RUDD, financial exec.; b. Gibbon, Okla., Sept. 16, 1931; s. Lowell Burgess and Bessie Sarah (Rudd) O.; B.S., Wichita State U., 1956; m. Roberta Pauline Sallee, Aug. 2, 1958; children—Joseph Rudd, Jennifer Susan, Karl Lyndon. Audit mgr. Arthur Andersen & Co., Chgo., 1956-66; with Rush-Presbyn.-St. Luke's Med. Center, Chgo., 1966—, v.p.-fin., 1966-75, treas., 1970—, sr. v.p., 1975—; asst. prof. Rush U. Coll. of Health Scis., 1972-77, asso. prof., 1977—. Served with USA, 1950-53. C.P.A., Ill. Fellow Hosp. Fin. Mgmt. Assn. (pres. 1st Ill. chpt. 1974-75; mem. Am. Inst. C.P.A.'s, Ill. C.P.A. Soc., Am., Ill. (trustee 1977—) hosp. assns., Am. Coll. Hosp. Adminstrs., William G. Follmer award 1974), Alpha Kappa Psi. Home: 1280 Warwick Ct Deerfigld IL 60015 Office: 1753 W Congress Pkwy Chicago IL 60612

O'DILLON, RICHARD HILL, physician; b. Watkinsville, Ga., Dec. 11, 1934; s. Herman Thomas and Elizabeth (Hill) O'D.; B.S., U. Ga., 1956; M.D., Med. Coll. Ga., 1960. Intern, Athens (Ga.) Gen. Hosp., 1960-61; resident Grady Meml. Hosp., Atlanta, 1963; practice medicine, specializing in clin. investigation, Rochester, N.Y., 1964—; asst. med. dir. Strasenburgh Labs., 1964-65, asso. med. dir., 1966; group dir. product devel., clin. research Merrell-Nat. Labs., Cin., 1966-75, group dir. gastrointestinal clin. research, 1975—. Served as capt. USAF, 1961-62. Mem. AMA, So. Med. Assn., N.Y. Acad. Scis., Am. Acad. Dermatology, Ohio Med. Assn., Acad. Medicine Cin., AAAS, Gamma Sigma Epsilon, Phi Eta Sigma, Alpha Epsilon Delta, Delta Phi Alpha. Home: 1203 Firewood Dr Cincinnati OH 45215 Office: 110 E Amity Rd Cincinnati OH 45215

ODITA, FLORENCE CHINYERE UWANDU, psychologist; b. Owerri, Nigeria, Sept. 11, 1942; d. Douglas Uzegbu and Nwanna (Ohaegbulem) Uwandu; m. E. Okechukwu Odita; children—Donald, Peggy, Betsy, Eric. B.S., Ind. U., 1968; M.S., Ind. State U., 1969; Ph.D., Ohio State U., 1972. Sec., Ahmadu Bello U., Nigeria, 1959-62, Ministry of Agriculture, Enugu, Nigeria, 1962-63; tchg. asso. Ind. State U., Terre-Haute, 1968-69; research asso. Ohio State U., Columbus, 1969-71, research specialist, 1972-73; chief Bureau of Research & Statistics, Ohio Dept. Public Welfare, Columbus, 1973—. Teen leader, YWCA, Enugu, Nigeria, 1962-63. Mem. Am. Psychol. Assn., Internat. Congress of Cross-cultural Psychology, Internat. Assn. Survey Statisticians. Recipient certificate for high scholastic achievement, Ind. U., 1968. Editor: Public Welfare Statistics, 1975—; author numerous articles in field. Home: 3155 Wareham Rd Columbus OH 43221 Office: 30 E Broad St 32nd Floor Columbus OH 43215

ODLAND, LYNN V., accountant; b. Britton, S.D., Mar. 25, 1939; s. Virgil S. and Lucille V. (Foster) O.; student S.D. U., 1958-61; m. Linda Lee Kostboth, Nov. 22, 1959; children—Amy Lynn, Carrie Lee, Paul Tom. Asst. accountant Haskins & Sells, Denver, 1961-62, semi-sr. accountant, 1962-64, sr. accountant, 1964-68; prin., Mpls., 1969—, partner, 1974—; dir. Tamay Corp. Chmn. Edina (Minn.) Human Rights Commn., 1970—. Republican precinct chmn. Frenzel for Congress, 1962-65, campaign mgr., i973. C.P.A., Minn., Colo. Recipient Distinguished Service award Village of Edina, Minn., 1971. Mem. Am. Inst. C.P.A.'s, Minn. Soc. C.P.A.'s, (chmn. publs. and accounting prins. com.), Land of Lakes Accountants and Statisticians, Edina Jr. C. of C. (bd. dirs. 1966-69). Lutheran (treas., deacon). Clubs: Rotary (treas. 1976-78, pres. 1978), Optimists. Home: 6301 Cherokee Trail Edina MN 55435 Office: Suite 210B NW Financial Center Bloomington MN 55431

ODOM, JOHN EDWARD, ednl. adminstr.; b. McPhee, Colo., Dec. 11, 1941; s. Henry Hicks and Mildred Helen (Phillips) O.; student Ft. Lewis Coll., 1962-64; B.S., Mankato State Coll., 1968, M.A., 1969; m. Ellen Elaine Jensen, Sept. 28, 1963; children—Deborah Marie, Constance Helen. Programmer analyst Mankato (Minn.) State Coll., 1967-69, asst. prof. computer sci. dept., 1969-75; dir. elementary, secondary and vocat. edn. Region V, Mgmt. Info. Services Coop., Rochester, Minn., 1975—. Dir. So. Minn. Sch. Computer Project, 1969-74, dir. NSF Inst., 1971-72. Served with USN, 1959-62. Mem. Assn. for Ednl. Data Systems, Minn. Assn. for Ednl. Data Systems (past pres.), Phi Delta Kappa. Lutheran. Club: Masons. Home: 926 1st Ave NW Byron MN 55920 Office: 334 16th St SE Rochester MN 55901

O'DONNELL, BERNARD, ednl. assn. exec.; b. Teaneck, N.J., July 26, 1929; s. James Edward and Mabel Rosemund (Kelly) O'D.; B.S., St. Peters Coll., 1956; M.A., Columbia U., 1957; Ed.D., Harvard U., 1963; m. Holly Fiebelkorn; children—Kelly, Colleen, Erin, Padriac, Erich. Instr. dept. English, W.Va. U., 1957-59; asst. prof. U. Iowa, 1965-67; dir. Ednl. Resources Info. Center Clearinghouse on Teaching of English, Nat. Council Tchrs. English, Urbana, Ill., 1967-72, Clearinghouse on Reading and Communication Skills, 1972—; vis. prof. dept. English, U. Ill., 1970-72. Bd. dirs. Champaign

County (Ill.) Opportunities Industrialization Center, 1968-73. Served with AUS, 1951-53. Mem. Nat. Council Tchrs. of English, Modern Lang. Assn., Nat. Conf. Research in English, Am. Dialect Soc., Phi Delta Kappa. Roman Catholic. Author: An Analysis of Prose Style to Determine Authorship, 1970. Home: 121 W Franklin St Urbana IL 61801 Office: 1111 Kenyon Rd Urbana IL 61801

O'DONNELL, DAVID RICHARDSON, civil engr.; b. Bishop, Calif., June 2, 1937; s. Herbert Preston and Elizabeth Menerva (Richardson) O.; A.A., Am. River Community Coll., 1959; B.S., U. Idaho, 1961; children—Derek T., Irene Denise. Jr. civil engr. Calif. Dept. Water Resources, Sacramento, 1962-67; hydraulic engr. Pioneer Service & Engring. Co., Chgo., 1969-72; hydraulic structures engr. Harza Engring. Co., Chgo., 1973-75; chief engring. dept. Urban Planning Consultants, Inc., Chgo., 1975—. Served with U.S. Army, 1961-62. Registered profl. engr., Del., Pa., N.J., Ill., Ind., Iowa. Mem. ASCE, Am. Water Works Assn., Water Pollution Control. Fedn., Nat., Ill. socs. profl. engrs., Parents Without Partners (chpt. dir.). Republican. Home: PO Box 7 Bolingbrook IL 60439 Office: 612 N Michigan Ave Chicago IL 60611

O'DONNELL, THOMAS MICHAEL, financial exec.; b. Cleve., Apr. 9, 1936; s. John Michael and Mary L. (Hayes) O'D.; B.B.A., U. Notre Dame, 1959; M.B.A., U. Pa., 1960; m. Nancy A. Dugan, Feb. 4, 1961; children—Christopher and Colleen (twins), Julie A. Research analyst Saunders Stiver & Co., Cleve., 1960-65; with McDonald & Co., Cleve., 1965—, partner corp. finance dept., 1968—; dir. Hauserman, Inc., Cleve., Seaway Food Town, Toledo, Overmyer Corp., Winchester, Ind., Hancor Inc., Findlay, Ohio, Mc Neil Corp., Akron, Ohio. Trustee Cath. Charities Corp. Cleve.; trustee, treas. St. John's Hosp., Cleve., 1969—. Clubs: Mid-Day, Union (Cleve.); Westwood Country (Rocky River, Ohio). Office: Central Nat Bank Bldg Cleveland OH 44114

O'DONOVAN, CORNELIUS JOSEPH, pharm. co. exec.; b. Bridgeport, Conn., Nov. 3, 1920; s. Patrick and Margaret (Farrelly) O'D.; A.B., Dartmouth Coll., 1942; M.D., N.Y. U., 1945; m. Margaret Rose Kane, Dec. 27, 1943; children—James David, Margaret Anne, Brendan Richard, Terence Roch, Liam Lawrence. With USPHS, 1947-51; asst. med. dir. Armour Labs., Chgo., 1951-53; sr. staff physician Upjohn Co., Kalamzoo, 1953-60; med. dir. Merck, Sharp & Dohme, West Point, Pa., 1960-63; v.p. research and med. affairs Ames Co. div. Miles Labs., Elkhart, Ind., 1963-68; v.p. med. affairs Miles Labs., Elkhart, 1968—. Served with M.C., U.S. Army, 1946-47. Recipient Upjohn award, 1958. Mem. AMA, Ind. Med. Soc., Am. Diabetic Assn., Am. Fedn. for Clin. Research, AAAS, N.Y. Acad. Scis. Developed oral antidiabetic therapy in U.S. Home: 2308 Broadmoor Dr Elkhart IN 45614 Office: 1127 Myrtle St Elkhart IN 45614

ODVARKA, ROBERT CHARLES, dentist; b. Omaha, Jan. 5, 1926; s. V.L. and Helen (Stenicka) O.; B.S., U. Nebr., 1951, D.D.S., 1953; m. Arlene Mae Fayman, Aug. 16, 1947; children—Sandra Odvarka Weeder, Robert Scott, Scott Brian. Gen. practice dentistry, Clarkson, Nebr., 1953—. Vice pres. Clarkson Bd. Edn., 1961-64. Served with AUS, World War II. Mem. ADA, Acad. Gen. Dentistry, Am. Legion, VFW, Internat. Platform Assn. Republican. Presbyterian. Home: Drawer F 523 Pine St Clarkson NE 68629 Office: Drawer F 244 Pine St Clarkson NE 68629

OEHMKE, THOMAS HAROLD, urban economist, lawyer; b. Detroit, Nov. 13, 1947; s. Harold W. and Elizabeth A. (Ryerse) O.; Ph.B., Wayne State U., 1969, J.D., 1973; children—Theodore, Jason, Admitted to Mich. bar, 1973, U.S. Supreme Ct. bar, 1977; tchr. St. Edward Sch., Detroit, 1967-69, Stephenson (Mich.) High Sch., 1969-70; labor relations cons. Employers Assn. Detroit, 1970-73; urban economist New Detroit, Inc., 1973—; individual practice law, Detroit, 1973—. Mem. Council on Urban Econ. Devel., State Bar Mich., Am., Detroit bar assns., Commercial Panel Arbitrators, Am. Arbitration Assn., Soc. Profl. in Dispute Resolution, Am. Judicature Soc., Indsl. Relations Research Assn. Author: Sex Discrimination in Employment; Michigan Incorporation Manual; Master Guide to Civil Litigation. Home: 13548 Tacoma Ave Detroit MI 48205 Office: 1010 Commonwealth Bldg Detroit MI 48226

OEHMLER, DONALD CLIVE, purchasing exec.; b. Toledo, O., July 31, 1922; s. Clive R. and Millie O.; B.S., Ohio State U., 1948; postgrad. Cleve. State U., 1961-68, Marquette U., 1956-57. Prodn. trainee TRW Inc., Cleve., 1949-50, buyer, 1950-53, prodn. buyer, 1953-57, 57-65, purchasing mgr., 1965-67; dir. purchases and traffic Lester Engring. Co., Cleve., 1967-70; mgr. purchases and traffic Hewitt-Robins, Columbia, S.C., 1970-71; corporate dir. purchases and traffic Am. Hoist & Derrick Co., St. Paul, 1971—. Lectr. Cleve. State U., 1961-68, Lester Engring. Co., Cleve., 1967-69; cons. to industry; guest speaker Nat. Assn. Purchasing Mgmt. Seminars, 1968-69. Served with U.S. Army, 1943-46. Mem. Minn. World Trade Assn., Nat. Assn. Purchasing Mgmt., Twin City Purchasing Mgmt. Assn., Nat. Indsl. Traffic League, Twin City Transp. Club Am., Twin City Transp. Club, Purchasing Agts. Assn., Ohio State Alumni Assn., St. Paul Athletic Club, Delta Tau Delta. Mason (32 deg., Shriner). Guest author Midwest Purchasing mag., 1966, 67, The Conn. Purchaser, 1968-69. Home: 2485 Londin Lane Maplewood MN 55119 Office: 63 S Roberts St St Paul MN 55107

OELJEN, SIEGFRIED CARL GEORGE, ophthalmologist; b. Waseca, Minn., July 9, 1903; s. Frederick and Katherine (Reul) O.; B.S., U. Minn., 1929, M.D., 1932; postgrad. U. Vienna (Austria), 1938; m. Adele E. Tiede, June 24, 1941; children—Carl G., Richard J. Intern, St. Lukes Hosp., Duluth, Minn., 1931-32; resident U. Vienna, 1938; practice gen. medicine, Waseca, 1932-37, specializing in ophthalmology, Waseca, 1939—. Mem. Waseca Bd. Edn., 1949-67; mem. Selective Service Bd., 1940-46. Diplomate Nat. Bd. Med. Examiners, Am. Bd. Ophthalmology. Fellow A.C.S., Am. Acad. Ophthalmology and Otolaryngology; mem. AMA, Minn., Waseca County med. assns., Alpha Omega Alpha. Lutheran. Home: 331 N State St Waseca MN 56093 Office: 329 N State St Waseca MN 56093

OESTREICH, KARL LYNN, paint co. exec.; b. Two Rivers, Wis., Oct. 7, 1942; s. Karl E. and Sally (Beitzel) O.; B.S., U. Wis., 1965; m. Jeanenne LaMarsh; children—Karl Lynn, Nicole Marie. Systems analyst Firestone Tire & Rubber Co., Akron, 1965-68; prodn. control supr. Baxter Labs., Morton Grove, Ill., 1968-71; gen. prodn. mgr. Intercraft Industeis, Chgo., 1971-73; corp. materials mgr. Rust-Oleum Corp., Evanston, Ill., 1973—. Mem. exec. bd. North East Ill. council Boy Scouts Am., 1975—; trustee Village of Morton Grove, 1975-77; Republican precinct capt.; chmn. Morton Grove Police and Fire Com., Morton Grove Traffic and Safety and Civil Def. Com. Mem. Assn. Protection Adopted Triangle (dir., treas.), Am. Prodn. Inventory Control Soc., Am. Mgmt. Assn., No. Ill. Indsl. Assn. Republican. Home: 7409 Davis St Morton Grove IL 60013 Office: 2301 Oakton St Evanston IL 60204

OETJEN, ROBERT ADRIAN, univ. dean; b. Detroit, Mar. 31, 1912; s. Frederick Tobias and Vida Pearl (Au) O.; B.A., Asbury Coll., Wilmore, Ky., 1936; M.S., U. Mich., 1938, Ph.D., 1942; m. Dorothy Mae Myers, June 3, 1936; children—Barbara (Mrs. Lawrence Miller), Charlene (Mrs. Richard Gordon), Margaret (Mrs. William K. Williams III), Charles, Marilyn Ruth (Mrs. Edward Philipp). Chemist, Mellon Inst. Inds. Research, 1936-37; physicist Texaco Research Labs., Beacon, N.Y., 1941-46; mem. faculty Ohio State U., 1946-70, prof. physics, 1957-70, asso. dean Coll. Arts and Scis., 1960-62, 64-67, 69-70, acting dean, 1967-69; dean Buchtel Coll. Arts and Scis., U. Akron (Ohio), 1970-77; acting v.p. for acad. affairs, dean advance programs Malone Coll., Canton, Ohio, 1977—; asst. to dir. Ohio State U. Research Found., 1953-55. Chief scientist Tokyo office NSF, 1962-64; mem. U.S. del. Internat. Commn. Optics, 1965-70. Trustee Malone Coll., Canton, Ohio, 1970-77; dir. Japan Internat. Christian U. Found. Fulbright grantee, 1955-57. Fellow Optical Soc. Am.; mem. Am. Phys. Soc., Am. Assn. Physics Tchrs., Physics Soc. Japan, Applied Physics Soc. Japan, Korean Phys. Soc., Japan Soc., Asia Soc., Am. Conf. Acad. Deans (dir.). Home: 1231 Carol St NE North Canton OH 44720 Office: Malone Coll Canton OH 44709

OFFENHISER, ANDREW BREWSTER, business exec.; b. Palo Alto, Calif., May 28, 1926; s. Paul Lloyd and Edith (Wise) O.; student U. Ill., 1943-44, 1946-47; A.B., Colby Coll., 1949; M.B.A., Stanford U., 1955; m. Helen Louise Forker, Nov. 1, 1952; 1 dau., Nancy Louise. Passenger dept. Burlington R.R., 1950, Pa. R.R., 1951, supr. service Pa. R.R., 1951-53; div. head traffic dept. J.C. Penney Co., N.Y.C., 1956-60; asst. traffic mgr., 1960, civic affairs co-ordinator, pub. relations dept., 1961-64, regional pub. relations co-ordinator, 1964-73, regional pub. relations mgr., 1973-76; with Gen. Growth Mgmt. Corp., Des Moines, 1976—. Mem. solicitations panel, adv. com. on solicitations Nat. Better Bus. Bur., mem. adv. com. contbns. execs. United Community Funds and Councils Am. Served with USNR, 1944-46. Mem. Am. Retail Fedn. (state orgn. com.), SAR, United Way Am. Corporate Assos., Soc. Mayflower Descs., Sigma Alpha Epsilon. Republican. Episcopalian Club: Bohemian. Home: 7848 Harbach Blvd Des Moines IA 50311 Office: 1111 E Army Post Rd Des Moines IA 50315

OFFINGER, WALTER EUGENE, JR., assn., exposition and trade show mgmt. co. exec.; b. Zanesville, Ohio, Oct. 6, 1942; s. Walter E. and Margaret O. (Owens) O.; student Muskingum Coll., 1963; B.A. in Business, Denison U., 1964; m. Sarel Duberstein, May 5, 1973; Personnel planning and service mgr. F & R Lazarus Co., Columbus, Ohio, 1964-68; pres., owner Offinger Mgmt. Co., Zanesville, 1968—. Served with USAF, 1964-70. Recipient Nat. Assn. Exposition Mgrs. Certificate of Outstanding Scholastic Achievement in Expn. Professionalism, 1975. Mem. Am. Soc. Assn. Exec., Nat. Assn. Expn. Mgrs., Mid-Am. Craft Hobby Assn., Columbus Conv. Bur., Nat. Craft Assn., Hobby Industry Am. (life), Nat. Rifle Assn., Am. Forestry Assn., Nat. Audubon Soc., Ducks Unlimited. Republican. Lutheran. Clubs: Masons, Shrine, Rotary, Zanesfield Rod and Gun. Home: 475 W Highland Dr Zanesville OH 43701 Office: 1100 Brandywine Blvd PO Box 2188 Zanesville OH 43701

OFTEDAHL, EVERETT JOHN, plastics co. exec.; b. Oak Park, Ill., Mar. 1, 1926; s. John and Wanda (Soma) L.; grad. high sch.; m. Elaine D. Van Horn, May 24, 1947; children—Glen Frank, Laura Ruth. Developer, Roll-on-Sealer Co., 1946-51; pres. Frostee Foam Co., Inc., Antioch, Ill., 1952—, Expanda-Foam, Inc., Antioch, 1963—; dir. State Bank of Antioch. Mem. Antioch Rescue Squad, 1947-48, capt. 1960-65. Bd. dirs. Soc. Plastics Industry. Served with USNR, 1943-46. Recipient citation County A.R.C., 1968. Lutheran (pres. council 1958-62, 65—). Mason (Shriner). Patentee portable tape dispenser. Lion (sec. 1961). Home: 505 Hwy 173 Antioch IL 60002 Office: 181 Ida St Antioch IL 60002

OGDEN, MERLENE ANN, educator; b. Lincoln, Nebr., June 10, 1929; d. Edwin B. and Virginia (Rees) Ogden; B.A., Union Coll., 1950; M.A., U. Nebr., 1954, Ph.D., 1964. Instr. English, Platte Valley Acad., Shelton, Nebr., 1951-54; asst. prof. English, Andrews U., Berrien Springs, Mich., 1955-60; grad. teaching asst. U. Nebr., Lincoln, 1961; prof. English, Andrews U., 1962—, dir. honors program, 1969—, asst. dean Coll. Arts and Scis., 1976—; vis. prof. Loma Linda U., 1970. Exec. sec.-treas. Upper Midwest Honors Council, 1975—. Mem. Twin Cities Symphony Orch., St. Jospeh, Mich., 1969—. Bd. dirs. Upper Midwest Honors Council; mem. Nat. Collegiate Honors Council. Recipient Tchr. of Year award Andrews U., 1966; named Outstanding Educator in Am., 1970. Mem. Nat. Council Tchrs. English, Modern Lang. Assn. Home: 740 Timberland St Berrien Springs MI 49104

OGDEN, RUSSELL LEE, educator; b. Isabel, Ill., Nov. 10, 1923; s. Clarence Haney O.; B.S., Eastern Ill. U., 1947; M.A., U. No. Colo., 1952, Ed.D., 1964; m. Marianne Johnson, Feb. 9, 1951; children—Sally Jo Ogden Rudolph, James Russell, Suzanne Marie. Tchr., Kansas (Ill.) Community Unit Sch. Dist. No. 3, Kansas High Sch., 1947-55; supr. student tchrs. Eastern Ill. U., Kansas (Ill.) High Sch., 1953-55; asst. prof. dept. bus. Eastern Mich. U., Ypslianti, 1956-63, asso. prof. Coll. Bus., 1964-67, prof., 1967—, undergrad. academic adviser, 1966-69, freshman and transfer admissions, 1967-69, faculty senator at large, 1971-74, del. at large faculty council, 1975-77. Pres. Parent Tchrs. Orgn. Roosevelt Campus Sch., Eastern Mich. U., 1964-65; trustee Ypsilanti Bd. Edn., 1976—, also v.p.; mem. West Jr. High Parent Adv. Group, Ypsilanti, 1965-66; cons. low income counselors dept. housing and urban devel. State of Mich., 1973; cons. Consumer Edn. Council, Ypsilanti, 1973-76, Sci. Research Assos., State of Mich., 1975. Served with AUS, 1943-47. Recipient Outstanding Service citation Eastern Mich. U. chpt. Phi Sigma Epsilon, 1974. Mem. Nat., Mich. (asst. editor Bull. 1957-58) bus. edn. assns., AAUP (treas. chpt. 1975-77), Phi Delta Kappa, Delta Pi Epsilon, Alpha Kappa Psi (Outstanding Educator in Coll. Bus. 1969-70, 75, 25 Year Service citation 1974), Pi Omega Pi, Psi Kappa Alpha. Club: Mich. Schoolmasters (chmn. bus. edn. div. 1958-59) (Ann Arbor). Editorial cons. Introduction to Modern Business (Musselman, Hughes), 1958, Personal Finance Textbook, 1977. Home: 1206 Grant St Ypsilanti MI 48197

O'GEARY, DENNIS TRAYLOR, contracting and engring. co. exec.; b. Waverly, Va., Feb. 20, 1925; s. King William and Mary Virginia (Traylor) O'G.; surveying degree Tri-State U., 1943; B.S. in Civil Engring., Ill. Inst. of Tech., 1947; m. Alice Stuart Baum, Aug. 3, 1947; children—Dennis Patrick, Mary Alice O'Geary Burton, Elizabeth Christina. Resident engring. trainee Va. Hwy. Dept., Richmond, 1947-50; civil engring. supt. Wiley Jackson Co., Roanoke, Va., 1950-57; engr., asst. estimator, project mgr., v.p. and asst. to area mgr. S.J. Groves & Sons Co., Mpls. and Springfield, Ill., 1957—. Served with USNR, 1943-46. Mem. ASCE, Am. Concrete Inst., Soc. Am. Mil. Engrs., Internat. Oceanographic Found., Cousteau Soc. Methodist. Home: Rural Route 2 Rochester IL 62563 Office: 1104 W Reynolds St Springfield IL 62705

OGILVIE, BRUCE CAMPBELL, ins. agy. exec.; b. N.Y.C., Apr. 1, 1944; s. Bruce Crossan and Martha Marie (Campbell) O.; student No. Ill. U., 1962-63; A.A., Kendall Coll., 1965; B.A., Monmouth Coll., 1968; postgrad. Seabury-Western Theol. Sem., 1972—; m. Rebecca Jane Reedy, June 12, 1967; children—Anne Christy, Kathryn Leigh. Salesman, mem. editorial devel. staff Little, Brown & Co., Coll. Div., Boston, 1968-71; mem. sales and editorial devel. staff Coll. Mktg. Group Inc., Reading, Mass., 1971-72; spl. agt. Northwestern Mut. Life Ins. Co. Milw., Evanston, Ill., 1972—; partner Hardy-Ogilvie Assos., Evanston, 1973-75; asso. John O. Todd Orgn., Inc., Evanston, 1976—. Publicity dir. Republican party candidate Ill. legis. dist., 1970. Named jr. asso. of year Gen. Agts. and Mgrs. Assn. Chgo., 1973; C.L.U. Mem. Kendall Coll. Alumni Assn. (pres. 1971-73), Monmouth Coll. Alumni Assn. (dir. 1974—, v.p. 1976—), Nat., Chgo. (officer, dir. 1976—) assns. life underwriters, Ill. St. Andrew Soc. (bd. govs. 1977—), Assn. Am. Geographers, Sigma Alpha Epsilon (life). Episcopalian (vestryman.). Office: 1578 Sherman Ave Evanston IL 60204

O'GRADY, LILLIAN MARY QUINLAN (MRS. VALENTINE M. O'GRADY), social worker; b. Chgo.; d. Norbert A. and Lillian (Johnson) Quinlan; A.B., St. Xavier Coll., 1937; M.S.W., Loyola U., Chgo., 1943; postgrad. U. Chgo., 1954-56, 68—, U. Ill., 1958-64, U. No. Ill., 1965—; m. Valentine M. O'Grady, Aug. 30, 1939; children—Thomas J., John J., Mary Jo. Sr. caseworker Chgo. Welfare Dept., 1938-39, Ill. Pub. Aid, 1939-40; sr. interviewer, tng. dir. Ill. Employment Service, 1940-42; sr. social worker Municipal Ct. Chgo., 1948-50; sr. social worker Blue Island (Ill.) Pub. Schs., 1953-62, 63—; social work cons. Park Lawn Sch. for Retarded Children, 1965—; supr. social work Chgo. Foundlings Homes, 1962-63; pvt. practice social work, Chgo., 1963—. Program dir. Blue Island Area Youth and Family Council, 1953—, So. Area Counselors, 1961-63; speaker, chmn. Worth Twp. Tchrs. Inst., 1959-60; sect. del. White House Conf. on Children, 1960; chmn. Ill. Inst. for Sch. Social Workers, 1961-62; mem. human service aids adv. bd. Morain Valley Community Coll., recipient award of merit, 1969. Licensed real estate broker, Ill. Mem. Acad. Certified Social Workers, Nat. Assn. Social Workers (chmn. sch. council sect. 1966-68), State Inst. Sch. Social Workers (chmn. 1967-73), Nat., Ill. edn. assns., Ill. Welfare Assn., St. Xavier Coll., Loyola U. alumnae, AAUW. Contbr. articles to profl. jours. Home: 2941 W 102d Pl Chicago IL 60642 Office: 2515 W 123rd St Blue Island IL 60406

OH, BONNIE BONGWAN CHO, historian; b. Seoul, Korea, Aug. 15, 1934; d. Pyong-chae and Yun-soo (Koo) Cho; came to U.S., 1956, naturalized, 1971; B.A., Barnard Coll., 1959; M.A., Georgetown U., 1964; Ph.D., U. Chgo., 1974; m. John Kie-chiang, Sept. 5, 1959; children—Jane Junghwa, Marie Jaehwa, James Jaeyong. Lectr. U. Wis., Milw., 1973-74, 76-77, Mt. Mary Coll., Milw., 1973-76; asst. prof. Marquette U., Milw., 1976-77, prof. Loyola U., Chgo., 1977—. Recipient Internat. fellowship, AAUW, 1961; Grad. fellowship for Women, Danforth Found., 1965-70; NDEA Title VI award, 1965; U. Chgo. Dissertation grantee, 1972; Nat. Endowment for the Humanities fellow, 1976. Mem. Assn. for Asian Studies, Am. Hist. Assn., Milw. County Hist. Assn., Soc. for Values in Higher Edn., Internat. History Honor Soc., Phi Alpha Theta. Roman Catholic. Home: 2231 W Apple Tree Rd Glendale WI 53209 Office: 6525 N Sheridan Rd Chicago IL 60626

O'HAGAN, JAMES JOSEPH, lawyer; b. Chgo., Dec. 29, 1936; s. Francis J. and Florence A. (Dychowski) O'H.; B.S., DePaul U., 1958, J.D., 1962; m. Suzanne E. Wiegand, June 28, 1958; children—Timothy, Karen, Peggy, Kevin. Admitted to Ill. bar, 1963; law clk. Querrey, Harrow, Gulanick & Kennedy, Chgo., 1958-62, asso., 1963-65, partner, 1965—, mng. partner, 1972—. Mem. Trial Lawyers Club Chgo., Am., Ill., Chgo. bar assns., Ill. Def. Counsel. Club: Park Ridge Country. Home: 2131 Manor Ln Park Ridge IL 60068 Office: 135 S LaSalle St Suite 827 Chicago IL 60603

O'HARA, DELMAR T., lawyer, bus. exec.; b. Wellsville, Ohio, Nov. 10, 1916; s. Delmar T. and Blanche (Mylar) O'H.; A.B., Ohio Wesleyan U., 1938; J.D., Western Res. U., 1948; m. Becky Janet Savage, June 24, 1944 (dec. 1975); children—Terrence, Timothy, Kathleen, Becky Jane, Patrick. Admitted to Ohio bar, 1948; individual practice law, Wellsville, Ohio. Chmn. bd. W.C. Bunting Pottery Co., East Liverpool, O. Mem. Ohio Far Eastern Trade Mission, 1967; del. Meth. World Council, London, Eng., 1966, Meth. Gen. Conf., Atlanta, 1972; pres. Young Republican Club, 1950-53; state rep. from Columbiana County, 1951-55; chmn. Pub. Welfare Com., 1953-55; city solicitor, Wellsville, 1966-68. Trustee Nat. Assn. Coll. Stores, 1956-58, United Methodist Found. Served as officer AC, USNR, 1941-44. Mem. C. of C. (pres. 1955), Greater Wellsville Assn. (pres. 1960-65), Ohio Mfrs. Assn., Ohio Hwy. Patrol Aux., Am., Ohio, Columbiana and Carroll County bar assns., Ohio Trial Lawyers Assn., Am. Legion (post comdr. 1957-58), DAV, Grange, Fraternal Order of Police Assos. (pres. 1973), Beta Theta Pi, Delta Theta Phi. Republican. Methodist. Clubs: Elks, Moose, Odd Fellows, Kiwanis (pres. 1959), Rotary (pres. 1975), Ohio Order Commodores, Columbiana County; East Liverpool Country; Columbus Athletic; Cap and Whip; Atwood Yacht; Carroll County Vets. Home: 2023 Fargo Rd SW Sherrodsville OH 44675 Office: 125 3d St Wellsville OH 43968

O'HARA, FRANCIS ANTHONY, nuclear engr., educator; b. Dayton, Ky., Dec. 11, 1941; s. Frank Anthony and Florence Philomena (Eichhorn) O.; A.B. (scholar), Thomas More Coll., 1963; M.S., U. Ky., 1965; Ph.D., U. Cin., 1971; m. Mary Margaret Feldhues, May 31, 1965; children—Kathleen, Michael, Daniel, Steven. Grad. research asst. U. Ky., Lexington, 1963-65; research physicist Monsanto Research Corp., Mound Lab., Miamisburg, Ohio, 1963-69, sr. physicist, 1969-72, specialist nuclear waste mgmt., 1972-74; asst. prof. nuclear engring. program Ohio State U., Columbus, 1974—; cons. Battelle Meml. Inst., Argonne Nat. Lab., Ford, Bacon & Davis, Ohio Edison Co., Sci. Applications, Inc.; mem. Nuclear Fuel Cycle Edn. Com. 1975—. Mem. Am. Nuclear Soc. (chmn. S.W. Ohio sect. 1976-77), AAAS, Inst. Nuclear Materials Mgmt., Am. Soc. Engring. Edn., Arms Control Assn., Am. Nat. Standard Inst. (task force chmn. 1971—). Contbr. articles to profl. jours. Home: 2620 Henthorn Rd Upper Arlington OH 43221 Office: 206 W 18th Ave Columbus OH 43210

OHL, HAZEL MCNITT, librarian; b. Trent, Mich., May 23, 1910; d. George Edward and Effie (Nelson) McNitt; student Hiram Coll., 1928-32; m. Wayne Clifford Ohl, Feb. 10, 1934. Librarian, Moses Cleaveland Jr. High Sch., Cleve., 1936-37; asst. librarian Portage County (Ohio) Pub. Library, Hiram, 1938-40, 45-46, librarian, 1940-44; asst. librarian bookmobile, 1949-56; librarian Breaden br. Youngstown (Ohio) Pub. Library, 1957-61; librarian Struthers (Ohio) Pub. Library, 1961-66; head gen. reference div. Youngstown Pub. Library, 1967—. Dir. Project NOLA, 1972-73. Mem. Ohio Library Assn. (coordinator div. VII, 1976—), Soc. Ohio Archivists, Pub. Librarians Assn. Youngstown. Home: 6116 Glenwood Ave Youngstown OH 44512 Office: 305 Wick Ave Youngstown OH 44503

OHLSON, DONALD ERNEST, architect; b. Evanston, Ill., Mar. 6, 1931; s. Sven A. and Inga M. (Jensen) O.; B.Arch., U. Ill., 1957. With Skidmore, Owings & Merrill, Chgo., 1957—, asso. partner, 1965—. Design critic U. Ill. Grad. Sch. Design, Urbana, 1963. Served with USNR, 1950-52. Mem. A.I.A. (chpt. sec. 1969), Gargoyle Soc. Club: Arts (Chgo.). Designer 600 Bldg., Lake Meadows, Chgo., 1959, nat. hdqrs. A.C.S., Chgo., 1961, library U. Ill.-Chgo. Circle, 1963; project mgr. Fermi Inst.-Lab. for Space Research, 1968, Joseph Regenstein Library, 1966 (both U. Chgo.); dormitory, 1959, academic bldg., 1966 (both Lake Forest (Ill.) Acad.); phys. edn. bldg., athletic field devel. Grinnell (Ia.) Coll., 1972; St. Matthew's Meth. Ch., Chgo., 1972; nat. hdqrs. U.S. Geol. Survey, Reston, Va., 1972; Winnebago Children's Home, Neillsville, Wis., 1973; New Town Community devel. center, golf and tennis club, Poinciana, Fla., 1973-74; concept master plan vehicle service bldg. Ohio Transp. Research Center, East Liberty, 1974, class room pavilions, library, sci. bldg., commons at Montgomery Coll., Selby Pub. Library, Sarasota, Fla., sch. art, east entry, auditorium, McKinlock Ct. galleries of Art Inst., Chgo. Home: 482 Sheridan Rd Evanston IL 60202 Office: 30 W Monroe St Chicago IL 60603

OHLSON, EDWARD LA MONTE, psychologist, clin. dir., educator; b. Norfolk, Nebr., Apr. 8, 1944; s. Carl LaMonte and Mary Olea (Oriski) O.; B.A., U. Alta. (Can.), 1965; M.Ed., U. Mont., 1967; Ed.D., U. Okla., 1970; Ph.D., Am. Internat. U., St. Louis, 1976; m. Rose Ellen Blake, Aug. 2, 1969; children—Blake LaMonte, Jason Edward, Sansanee Joelene. Dir. psychol. services Nevada County (Calif.), 1970-71; mem. faculty psychology U. Calif. (Davis), 1970-71; exec. dir. mgmt. Continental Child Care, Inc., Denver, 1971-73; mem. staff psychology Mosca (Calif.) Med. Clinic, 1971-72; mem. faculty psychology U. No. Colo., Greeley, 1971-73; Ohio State U., Columbus, 1973-75, Case Western Res. U. Sch. Medicine, Cleve., 1975—; dir., Learning Disabilities/Exceptional Children Clinic Cleve. Met. Gen. Hosp., 1975—; cons. Dept. Armed Forces, HEW, Midco Edn. Research Assos. Recipient recognition Sexual Dysfunctioning Research, Assn. Research Sexual Dysfunctioning, 1976; lic. psychologist, Ohio, Ariz., Alta. (Can.). Mem. Nat. Register Health Service Providers. Author: An Overview of Basic Statistics, 1976; Etiology of Learning Dysfunctions, 1977; researcher child devel., learning disabilities, homosexuality, fetal alcoholism. Home: 101 Anglers Dr Chagrin Falls OH 44022 Office: #209 Lowman Dept Psychiatry Case Western Reserve Univ 3395 Scranton Rd Cleveland OH 44109

OHMAN, JOHN HAMILTON, forestry research adminstr.; b. Detroit, Jan. 26, 1931; s. Elmer Walter and Mabel Terese (Anderson) O.; B.S. in Forestry, U. Minn., 1957, M.S., 1958, Ph.D. in Plant Pathology, 1961; m. Jacquelyn Marie Jensen, May 1, 1954; children—Jack H., James M. Research asst., fellow U. Minn., 1957-61; plant pathologist, research project leader U.S. Forest Service, Marquette, Mich., 1962-67; asst. chief forest disease research, Washington, 1968-70, asst. dir. Northeastern Forest Expt. Sta., Upper Darby, Pa., 1971, dir. North Central Forest Exptl. Sta., St. Paul, 1972—; instr. forest pathology Mich. State U. at Marquette, 1966-67. Vice chmn. Fed. Exec. Bd., Twin Cities, 1974. Served with AUS, 1951-54. Decorated Bronze Star; recipient award of Excellence, Weed Soc. Am., 1964. Fellow agrl. sci., Caleb Dorr; mem. Soc. Am. Foresters, Am. Forestry Assn., Soil Conservation Soc. Am., Internat. Union Forestry Research Orgns., Am. Phytopath. Soc., Sigma Xi, Xi Sigma Pi, Alpha Zeta. Author publs. in field. Office: North Central Forest Expt Sta Folwell Ave Saint Paul MN 55101

OHNO, MITSUGI, glassblower; b. Tochigi, Japan, June 28, 1926; s. Shigeo and Tsuya (Ohgane) O.; came to U.S., 1961, naturalized, 1970; m. Kimiyo Nagayama, Oct. 13, 1953; children—Tsutomu, Hiroko, Julie. Glassbower, U. Tokyo, 1947-61, Kans. State U., Manhattan, 1961—; works include: USS Constitution (at Eisenhower Museum), 1971, Independence Hall (at White House), 1972, U.S. Capitol (at Smithsonian), 1975, and others. Home: 2808 Nevada St Manhattan KS 66502 Office: Dept Physics Cardwell Hall Kansas State Univ Manhattan KS 66506

O'HORA, JAMES BALDWIN, childrens home adminstr.; b. Binghamton, N.Y., Nov. 1, 1939; s. James Kenneth and Helen Marjore (Baldwin) O'H.; B.A., U. Dayton, 1962; M.S.W., Ohio State U., 1964; m. Judith Ann Kruskamp, June 8, 1963; children—Kelly Michele, James Michael. Psychiat. social worker Lsalle Sch. for Boys, Albany, N.Y. 1964-66; caseworker Cath. Social Services, Binghamton, N.Y., 1965-66; with Susquehanna Valley Home, Binghamton, 1967-72, asst. dir., 1969-71, exec. dir., 1971-72; exec. dir. St. Joseph Home for Children, Dayton, Ohio, 1972—. Mem. U. Dayton Alumni Assn. (v.p. 1974—), Nat. Assn. Social Workers, Acad. Certified Social Workers, Nat. Conf. Cath. Charities, Ohio Mental Health Assn., Ohio Assn. Child Care Agencies. K.C. Home: 6340 Seven Pines Dr Dayton OH 45499 Office: 650 St Paul Av Dayton OH 45410

O'KEEFE, BETH EGAN, psychologist; b. Springfield, Ill., Aug. 27, 1945; d. James Michael and Margaret M.L. (Kuhn) Egan; A.B., Mt. St. Scholastica Coll., Atchison, Kans., 1967; M.S., St. Louis U., 1970, Ph.D., 1971; m. Rip L. O'Keefe, June 27, 1969; 1 dau., Kelly Egan. Psychology intern Alton (Ill.) State Hosp., 1968; trainee VA Hosp., Jefferson Barracks, Mo., 1968-70, John Cochran VA Hosp., St. Louis, 1970-71; staff psychologist Comprehensive Community Mental Health Center, Rock Island, Ill., 1971-72, coordinator psychol. services, 1972—; adj. asst. prof. St. Ambrose Coll., Davenport, Iowa, 1976-77. Bd. dirs. Neighborhood Health Center, Rock Island, Ill., 1973-77; mem. budget com. United Way of Rock Island and Scott Counties, 1977; mem. mental health subcom. Illowa Health Systems Agency, Davenport, 1976—. Mem. Am., Ill., Upper Miss. Valley psychol. assns., Irish Setter Club Am., Irish Setter Club Greater Davenport. Home: 12514 106th Ave Coal Valley IL 61240 Office: 2701 17th St Rock Island IL 61201

O'KEEFE, JAMES L., lawyer; b. Chgo., Jan. 8, 1910; s. Raymond T. and Sadie (Monahan) O'K.; student Northwestern U., 1931-35; J.D., Chgo.-Kent Coll., 1936; m. Josephine Killian, June 19, 1933; children—James L., William J., Dennis M. Asst. state's atty. Cook County (Ill.), 1933-37; partner O'Keefe, Ashenden & Lyons, 1937—; master in chancery Circuit Ct. Cook County, 1942-62; pub. adminstr., Cook County, 1961-70; dir. Nat. Blvd. Bank Chgo., Chessie System Inc., Chesapeake & Ohio Ry., Daniel Woodhead Co., C. & O. R.R., Brink's, Inc., Peterson Howell & Heather. Chmn. host com. Democratic Nat. Convs., 1952, 56, del.-at-large, 1952, 56, 60, 64, exec. mem. fin. com., 1960; vice chmn. Chgo. Non-Partisan com. 1960 Rep. Nat. Conv.; trustee Chgo.-Kent Coll. Law, Evans Scholars Found. Mem. Ill. C. of C., Am. (commn. nat. system of justice, co-chmn. host com.), Ill., Chgo. bar assns., Chgo. Assn. Commerce and Industry, Chgo. Conv. Bur., Chgo. Dist. (pres. 1966-67), Western (pres. 1955-56), U.S. (exec. com. 1968-69) golf assns., Law Club, Newcomen Soc. Clubs: Chgo., Mid-day (trustee), Met., Northwestern U. (past pres.) (Chgo.); Evanston (Ill.) Golf; Ocean, Delray (Fla.) Yacht, Country of Fla. Home: 1420 Sheridan Rd Wilmette IL 60091 Office: 1 First Nat Plaza Chicago IL 60670

O'KEEFE, THOMAS JOSEPH, metall. engr.; b. St. Louis, Oct. 2, 1935; s. Thomas and Hazel (Howard) O.; B.S., Mo. Sch. Mines, 1958; Ph.D., U. Mo., Rolla, 1965. m. Jane Gilmartin, Aug. 31, 1957; children—Thomas, Kathleen, Matthew, Daniel, Margaret Mary. Process control engr. Dow Metal Products, Madison, Ill., 1959-61; asst. prof. metall. engring. U. Mo., Rolla, 1965-68, asso. prof., 1968-72, prof., 1972—; research technologist NASA, Houston, Tex., summer 1965; research metall. engr. Ames Lab. (Iowa), 1966-67; research metall. engr., cons. Cominco Ltd., Trail, B.C., Can., 1970-71. Mem. Am. Inst. Mining and Metall. Engrs. (dir. 1976-77), Am. Electroplating Soc., Can. Inst. Metallurgy, Alpha Sigma Mu, Sigma Xi, Tau Beta Pi, Phi Kappa Theta (dir. 1965-77). Recipient certificate of commendation Phi Kappa Theta, 1970; named one of Outstanding Young Men of Am., U. Mo., Rolla, 1970, recipient Alumni Merit award, 1971. Home: 5 Crestview Dr Rolla MO 65401 Office: Material Research Center Univ Mo Rolla MO 65401

OKULITCH, PETER VLADIMIR, clin. psychologist; b. Vancouver, B.C., Can., Apr. 9, 1946; s. Vladimir Joseph and Susan (Kouhar) O.; m. Judy Schuerman, Dec. 28, 1974. B.A., U. B.C., 1969; M.A., U. Wis., 1971, Ph.D., 1973. Chief psychology Regional Med. Center, Abbotsford, B.C., 1974-76; staff psychologist Mt. Sinai Med. Center, Milw., 1976—; asst. clin. prof. psychiatry and mental health scis. Med. Coll. Wis., 1977—. Licensed psychologist, Wis. Mem. Am., Wis. psychol. assns., AAAS, Waukesha Flying Club. Contbr. articles to profl. jours. Home: 2014 E Jarvis St Shorewood WI 53211 Office: Mt Sinai Med Center 950 N 12th St Milwaukee WI 53233

O'LANE, JOHN MICHAEL, obstetrician, gynecologist, educator, clin. adminstr.; b. Vallejo, Calif., Jan. 13, 1934; s. John Michael and Gene Levi (Stephenson) O'L.; B.S. in Basic Med. Scis., U. Wash., 1955, M.D., 1958; m. Phyllis Marie Wait, Jan. 3, 1953 (dec.); children—John, Thomas, Howard, Sally, Alan, Mary, Kevin, Karen. Intern, King County Hosp., Seattle, 1958-59; resident in obstetrics and gynecology USN Hosp., San Diego, 1961-64; asst. prof. obstetrics and gynecology, dir. obstetrics div. Temple U. Sch. Medicine, Phila., 1967-69; practice medicine specializing in obstetrics and gynecology, Ridgecrest, Calif., 1969-73; chief, obstetrics and gynecology Ridgecrest Community Hosp., 1969-73; chief, obstetrics and gynecology St. John Hosp., Detroit, 1974—; asso. prof. gynecology and obstetrics Wayne State U., Detroit, 1974—; med. dir. Jefferson-Chalmers Free Clinic, Detroit, 1977—; mem. med. advisory bd. Planned Parenthood Detroit; bd. dirs. Desert Counseling Service, pres., 1970-73. Advisory bd. Calif. State Coll., Bakersfield, 1973. Served with M.C. USN, 1959-67. Diplomate Am. Bd. Obstetrics Gynecology. Fellow Am. Coll. Obstetricians Gynecologists. Contbr. articles to med. jours. Home: 281 University Pl Grosse Pointe MI 48230

OLD, ROBERT LEE, agrl. chems. co. exec.; b. St. Louis, Jan. 9, 1930; s. Ed Lee and Mary Elizabeth (Townzen) O.; B.A., Washington U., St. Louis, 1950, M.B.A., 1960; m. Jean Gilbert Voohers, Nov. 22, 1948; children—Robert Lee, Richard W., Mary Jill, Nancy J., John E. Mktg. research mgr. Emerson Electric Co., St. Louis, 1950-64; v.p. mktg. Amphenol sales div. Bunker Ramo Corp., Chgo., 1964-71; v.p. planning Koss Corp., Milw., 1971-72, sr. v.p., 1972-75; exec. v.p. Nitragin Co., Milw., 1975—. Bd. mgrs. YMCA, 1956-58; committeeman Boy Scouts Am., 1959-62; adviser Jr. Achievement, 1958-59. Served with AUS, 1947-48. Mem. Am. Mgmt. Assn., Am. Mktg. Assn., Nat. Assn. Bus. Economists, Midwest Planning Assn. Home: 730 E Carlisle Ave Whitefish Bay WI 53217 Office: 3101 W Custer Ave Milwaukee WI 53209

OLDAM, PAUL BERNARD, mfg. co. exec.; b. Newark, Aug. 20, 1934; s. Paul Andrew and Katherine Ann (Kraft) O.; B.S. in Econs. and Finance, Georgetown U.; m. Margaret M. Henne, Oct. 6, 1956; children—Katherine, Christine, Mary. Financial mgmt. trainee Gen. Electric Co., 1956-57; asst. v.p. comml. lending div. Pitts. Nat. Bank, 1961-67; v.p. ops. Allis-Chalmers Credit Corp., 1967-71, asst. treas., then treas., 1972—; treas., v.p. Allis-Chalmers Corp., Milw., 1976—. Served with USAF, 1957-61. Mem. Nat. Assn. Credit Mgrs., Am. Inst. Mgmt., Nat. Investor Relations Inst. (v.p. chpt.), Financial Execs. Inst. Home: 7837 Mary Ellen Pl Wauwatosa WI 53213 Office: PO Box 512 Milwaukee WI 53201

OLDEG, HARRY WILLIAM, JR., aerospace mfg. co. exec.; b. St. Louis, Sept. 20, 1919; s. Dr. Harry William and Mildred (Mozer) O.; B.S., St. Louis U., 1941; m. Eliabeth Theresa Pohrer, Mar. 31, 1951; children—Margaret, Carol, Joan. Auditor, C.E., U.S. Army, 1941-43; cost estimator McDonnell Douglas Corp., St. Louis, 1942-43, contract adminstr., 1946-51, contract mgr., 1951-61, v.p. fiscal mgmt., 1968—; dir. Powercraft Corp. Bd. dirs. Met. St. Louis YMCA, 1973. Served to lt. comdr. USNR, 1943-46; PTO. Mem. Nat. Contract Mgmt. Assn., St. Louis U. Alumni Assn. Roman Catholic. Club: Forest Hills Country (St. Louis). Home: 1508 Azalea Dr Saint Louis MO 63119 Office: PO Box 516 Saint Louis MO 63166

OLDENBURGER, DEREK, internist; b. Chgo., May 19, 1946; s. Rufus and Eleanor (Wolf) O.; B.S., Purdue U., 1967; M.D., U. Calif., Los Angeles, 1971; m. Norma Hoggarth, Jan. 17, 1975. Intern, U. Wis., Madison, 1971-72; resident in medicine U. N.Mex., Albuquerque, 1972-74; mem. dept. internal medicine Mid Dakota Clinic, Bismarck, N.D., 1974—; staff physician St. Alexius, Bismarck hosps.; clin. asso. U. N.D.; pub. health officer Kidder County, N.D., 1977. Diplomate Am. Bd. Internal Medicine. Mem. A.C.P., AMA, Alpha Omega Alpha. Presbyterian. Office: 9th St and Rosser Ave Bismarck ND 58501

OLDESCHULTE, BURTON LAWRENCE, bus. services co. exec.; b. Detroit, June 27, 1922; s. Burton Lawrence and Agnes Catherine (Steinlaughly) O.; m. Rosemary Carnagie, Aug. 25, 1945 (div. 1963); 7 children; m. 2d, Hattie Marks, June 20, 1964. Various positions Hamtramck (Mich.) plant Chrysler Corp., 1946-76; owner, operator Service Landscape & Snow Removal Co., Warren, Mich., since 1976—; first aid instr. Red Cross, Southeastern Mich.; lectr. in field. Served with USMC, 1942-46, 52-66. Clubs: Eagles, Masons. Home and office: 8115 Orchard St Warren MI 48089

OLDHAM, HOWELL G., supt. schs.; b. Atoka, Okla., Jan. 31, 1925; s. Jack V. and Mildred D. (Surrell) O.; Asso. Sci., Cameron State Coll., Okla., 1948; B.A., Hastings Coll., 1950; Mus.M. (Ak-Sarben scholar), U. Nebr., 1958, Ed.D., 1966; m. Mary Ann Hitchler, Aug. 11, 1945; children—Jack E., Suzanne Oldham Gallagher, Jeffrey Lynn, Gregg A. Tchr., music dir. Gibbon (Nebr.) Pub. Schs., 1950-54; music specialist Grand Island (Nebr.) Pub. Schs., 1954-60, coordinator instrumental music, 1960-69; supt. Gothenburg (Nebr.) Pub. Schs., 1969—; dir., mgr. Grand Island Municipal Band, 1961-69; mem. music com. Nebr. Centennial, 1964-65; music cons. Nebr. State Arts Council, 1966-70; guest dir., contest judge various Nebr. dists., 1967-74. Mem. Gov.'s Council on Nebr. Cultural Resources, 1965. Served with USAAF, 1943-44. Inst. Devel. Ednl. Activities fellow, 1970, 72, 74, 75; Danforth/NASE fellow, 1976; recipient Rotary award for Outstanding Teaching Grand Island Rotary Club, 1956. Mem. Am. Assn. Sch. Adminstrs., Nebr. Council Sch. Adminstrs. (legis. com. 1970-74), Am. Legion, Gothenburg C. of C., Phi Theta Kappa, Phi Delta Kappa, Pi Kappa Lambda, Central Nebr. Musicians Assn. (sec. 1961-69). Clubs: Elks, Kiwanis, Gothenburg Service. Home: 803 13th St Gothenburg NE 69138 Office: 1415 Ave G Gothenburg NE 69138

OLDHAM, LOWELL TINCHER, dentist; b. Moberly, Mo., Sept. 29, 1910; s. Rufus Kent and Lula (Tincher) O.; D.D.S., U. Ia., 1933, Cert. Orthodontics, 1934, M.S., 1934; m. Wyntrice Earwood, Apr. 15, 1934; 1 son, Thomas E. Research asst. U. Ia., 1933-34, research asst. Child Welfare Sta. U. Ia., 1933-34; pvt. practice dentistry, specializing in orthodontics, Mason City, Iowa, 1934—. Served with AUS, 1943-45. Mem. Iowa State Dental Assn. (past pres. North Central dist.), Iowa State Orthodontic Soc. (past pres.), Am. Dental Assn., Midwestern Soc. Orthodontists, Am. Bd. Orthodontics, Omicron Kappa Upsilon. Clubs: Elks, Euchre & Cycle, Masons, Shriners. Home: B-101 Ambassador East II 502 S Ohio Mason City IA 50401 Office: 307-10 Brick & Tile Bldg Mason City IA 50401

O'LEARY, CARL THOMAS, banker, state ofcl.; b. Russell, Kans., Apr. 25, 1909; s. Thomas J. and Mary (Fox) O'L.; grad. U. Wis., 1954; m. Christina Hays, Sept. 21, 1936; children—Mont Thomas, Bridget (Mrs. Paul Piper). With Baxter State Bank, Baxter Springs, Kans., 1946—, pres., 1967—. Bank commr. Kans., 1971-75. Mem. Kans. C. of C. Home: 1312 Cleveland Ave Baxter Springs KS 66713 Office: PO Box 69 Baxter Springs KS 66713

O'LEARY, FRANCIS BERNARD, librarian; b. N.Y.C., Oct. 6, 1926; s. Bernard and Bridget (O'Sullivan) O'L.; B.S., Manhattan Coll., N.Y.C., 1949; M. L.S., Columbia U., 1952; m. Antoinette M. Walbroel, Sept. 26, 1964; 1 son, Paul. Zoology-botany librarian Columbia U., 1949-53, asst. librarian for natural scis., 1953-57; librarian Inst. Tech., U. Minn., 1957-60; librarian Med. Center, St. Louis U., 1960—; project dir. Med. Library Network Bistate Regional Med. Program, 1970-73. Mem. Grand Jury, Bronx County, N.Y., 1956-57; rep. Assn. Coll. and Reference Libraries to 4th Nat. Conf. on Health in Colls., N.Y.C., 1953. Mem. Spl. Libraries Assn. (pres. Greater St. Louis chpt. 1963-64), AAUP, Med. Library Assn. (chmn. med. schs. sect. 1968-69), AAAS, U.S. Naval Inst. Club: Naval Records. Author articles in field. Editor: Science Reference Notes (Columbia), 1954-57. Home: 5865 Delor St Saint Louis MO 63109 Office: 1402 S Grand Blvd Saint Louis MO 63104

O'LEARY, JOSEPH AUGUSTINE, state ofcl.; b. Lawrence, Mass., Mar. 6, 1908; s. Laurence J. and Carolyn (Carpenter) O'L.; student Philips Acad., 1924-25; A.B., Dartmouth, 1929; M.B.A, Boston U., 1941; postgrad. Am. U., 1946, Loyola U., Chgo., 1947-51, Mich. State U., 1959-60; m. Marguerite Virginia Mudd, Nov. 4, 1934. Various hotel operations, 1929-42; with OPA, Washington, 1942-43, 46; asso. prof. accounting Loyala U., Chgo., 1947-52; asst. prof. hotel and restaurant accounting Mich. State U., East Lansing, 1952-58; supr. financial planning Mich. Dept. State Hwys., Lansing, 1958—; with OPS, Washington, 1951; accountant C.P.A. firms, Chgo., 1950-52. Lectr., tchr. spl. accounting courses, 1947—; instr. govtl. accounting part time Lansing (Mich.) Community Coll., 1967-73. Served from lt. (j.g.) to lt. comdr. USNR, 1942-46. C.P.A., Ill. Mem. Am. Inst. C.P.A.'s, Ill. Soc. C.P.A.'s, Mich. Assn. C.P.A.'s, Am. Accounting Assn., Nat. Assn. Accountants, State Govtl. Accountants Assn. Mich. (pres. 1966-67). Author booklets. Contbr. accounting articles to publs. Home: 1369 E Jolly Rd Okemos MI 48864

O'LEARY, VIRGINIA ELIZABETH, psychologist, educator; b. Washington, July 3, 1943; d. John H. and Stella V. (Frizzell) Fisher; B.A. in Psychology, Chatham Coll., 1965; M.A., Wayne State U., 1967, Ph.D. in Social Psychology, 1968; m. David M. Stonner, May 1, 1976; 1 son, Sean Morgan. Teaching asst. dept. psychology Wayne State U., Detroit, 1965-68; lectr. psychology in nursing U. Mich., 1968-69; research asso. Wayne State U., 1968-69, sr. research asso. Center for Urban Studies, 1969-70, adj. asst. prof. dept. psychology, 1969-70; asst. prof. dept. psychology Oakland U., Rochester, Mich., 1970-76, asso. prof. psychology, 1976—; panelist NSF Grant Rev., 1974, 76; guest lectr. various colls., 1974—. Mem. Am., Midwestern, Mich. psychol. assns., Assn. Women in Psychology, Mich. Women's Research Assn., Soc. Study Psychol. Issues, Sigma Xi. Democrat. Unitarian. Author: Toward Understanding Women, 1977. Ad hoc editorial cons. to various jours on psychology, 1974—. Contbr. articles in psychology of women, social psychology to profl. jours. Home: 3960 Mystic Valley Dr Bloomfield Hills MI 48013 Office: Dept of Psychology Oakland Univ Rochester MI 48063

OLEGARIO, GIL FORTUNATO SEVILLA, pathologist, nuclear physician; b. Lingayen, Pangasinan, Philippines, Oct. 18, 1933; s. Fortunato Garcia and Agripina Marino (Sevilla) O.; came to U.S., 1958, naturalized, 1968; A.A. in Pre-medicine, U. Santo Tomas, Manila, Philippines, 1952, M.D., 1957; m. Rosario Velasco Gatchalian, Apr. 18, 1958; children—Gilda Ruby, Gil Francis. Extern, adjunct gen. practice resident, Pangasinan Provincial Hosp., Dagupan City, Philippines, 1957-58; rotating intern, Bklyn. Hosp., N.Y., 1958-59, 1959-60, resident in pathology, 1960-61; practice medicine specializing in gen. practice, Mangatarem, Pangasinan, Philippines, 1961-62; resident in pathology, Bklyn-Cumberland Hosp. Med. Center, Bklyn., 1963-65, Beth Israel Med. Center, N.Y.C., 1965-66; asst. pathologist, Maimonides Med. Center, Bklyn., 1966-67, 1969-70, asst. dir. labs., 1970-72, asso. pathologist, 1971-72; asso. pathologist, Manhasset (N.Y.) Med. Center, 1967-69; asso. pathologist, Beyer Meml. Hosp., Ypsilanti, Mich., 1973-75, Annapolis Hosp., Wayne, Mich., 1975—; clin. instr. pathology, U. Santo Tomas, Manila, 1962-63, State U. N.Y., Downstate Med. Center, Bklyn., 1969-72. Served from lt. to capt. M.C. Res., Armed Forces of Philippines, 1962-63. Diplomate Am. Bd. Pathology, Am. Bd. Nuclear Medicine. Fellow Am. Soc. Clin. Pathologists, Coll. Am. Pathologists; mem. AMA, N.Y., Kings County med. socs., N.Y. Pathol. Soc., Pathologists Club, Am. Soc. Cytology, Washtenaw County, Mich. State med. socs. Roman Catholic. Home: 3031 Warwick Rd Ann Arbor MI 48104 Office: Annapolis Hosp 33155 Annapolis Ave Wayne MI 48184

OLEJAR, MARIE CELINE, nun, counselor; b. Youngstown, Ohio, Apr. 23, 1914; d. Michael and Anna (Hudak) Olejar; B.S. in Edn., St. John Coll., 1947; M.A., Cath. U. Am., 1957. Joined Ursuline Sisters, Roman Catholic Ch., 1927; tchr. St. John Baptist Sch., Campbell, Ohio, 1930-37, Holy Name Sch., Youngstown, 1937-47; tchr. Ursuline High Schs., Youngstown, 1947-57, dean of girls, 1957-60, dir. guidance, 1960—. Pres. Youngstown Diocesan Guidance Council, 1964-68, treas., 1972-74. Recipient Outstanding Contribution to Guidance in Cath. Schs. award, Nat. Cath. Guidance Council, 1975. Mem. Am. Personnel and Guidance Assn., Am. Sch. Counselors Assn., Nat. Vocational Guidance Assn., Nat. Cath. Guidance Assn. Contbr. articles and reviews to profl. jours. Home: 745 Bryson St Youngstown OH 44502 Office: 740 Wick Ave Youngstown OH 44505

OLEJNICZAK, DOMINIC, realtor, football exec.; b. Green Bay, Wis., Aug. 18, 1908; s. John A.B. and Victoria (Marshall) O.; ed. U. Wis., U. Chgo.; m. Regina Bettine, Nov. 24, 1938; children—Thomas, Mark. Owner realty firm, Green Bay, 1955—; pres. Green Bay Packer Football Corp., 1958—. Mem. Gov.'s Comm. on Mass Urban Transp., 1953-54; mem. City Council, Green Bay, 1936-44, mayor, 1945-55. Mem. Land Bank Assn. (past sec.), Wis. League Municipalities (past pres.). Roman Catholic (treas. congregation 1944—). Elk. Home: 1736 Carriage Ct Green Bay WI 54304 Office: 1265 Lombardi Ave Green Bay WI 54305

OLEKSY, STANLEY PETER, ophthalmologist; b. Jackson, Mich., May 1, 1916; s. Peter and Catherine (Czarnecki) O.; B.A., U. Mich., 1938, M.D., 1941, M.S. in Ophthalmology, 1955; m. June Maxine White, Sept. 13, 1962; children—Nancy E. Oleksy Grosso, Daniel D. Intern, Mercy Hosp., Jackson, 1941-42; gen. practice medicine, Jackson, 1942-50; resident in ophthalmology U. Mich., Ann Arbor, 1951-53; practice medicine specializing in ophthalmology, Jackson, 1953—; mem. staff Mercy, Foote Meml. hosps. Served with USAF, 1943-46. Diplomate Am. Bd. Ophthalmology. Mem. Mich., Jackson County med. socs., Am. Assn. Ophthalmology, Am. Acad. Ophthalmology, Internat. Implants Club, Am. Intraocular Implant

Soc. Club: Country. Home: 5904 Joymont St Jackson MI 49201 Office: 306 W Washington St Jackson MI 49201

OLESON, CLARA RODRIGUEZ, lawyer; b. Bklyn., Mar. 7, 1942; d. Antonio and Elena (Diaz-Zawisttowska) Rodriguez; B.A., St. Joseph's Coll., 1964; postgrad. U. Pa., 1965; J.D., U. Iowa, 1976. Adminstrv. asst., tech. writer Coll. Pharmacy, U. Iowa, 1966-72, legal research asst., 1975-76, teaching asst. Center for Labor and Mgmt., Coll. Bus. Adminstrn., 1975-76; bartender Lazy Leopard Lounge, Iowa City, 1972-74; admitted to Iowa bar, 1976; partner firm Oleson & Eikleberry, Iowa City, 1976—; conf. coordinator Women and Work, U. Iowa, 1971; co-dir. Nat. Endowment for Humanities grant, 1972. workshop leader Conf. Urban Research Corp., Chgo., 1973; mem. steering com. 7th Nat. Conf. on Women and the Law, Temple U., Phila., 1975-76. Founder, Johnson County Council on Status of Women, 1971; mem. Johnson County Democratic Central Com., 1972-74, Iowa Womens Polit. Caucus, 1973—. Recipient Internat. Womens Year award Fed. Regional Council, Dept. Labor, Midwest Region, 1975. Mem. Iowa Bar Assn., Nat. Womens Polit. Caucus, Bus. and Profl. Womens Club (hon.). Author: (with Mildred Lavin) Women and Public Policy, 1973. Home: 208 6th St Coralville IA 52241 Office: Suite 6 Paul-Helen Bldg Iowa City IA 52240

OLESON, GEORGE BOWEN, auditor; b. Fargo, N.D., Mar. 10, 1917; s. George Henry and Violet Jane (Bowen) O.; B.A., Moorhead State Coll., 1958. Self-employed as auditor, Fargo, 1958—. Treas., N.D. Assn. Blind, 1968—. Served with AUS, 1942-46; ETO. Mem. Am. Legion, VFW, Philalethes Soc., Nat., N.D. socs. pub. accountants. Methodist. Mason (Shriner). Club: Bridge. Address: 119 8th St Fargo ND 58102

OLIN, HAROLD BENNETT, trade assn. exec.; b. Chgo., Feb. 17, 1930; s. Benjamin S. and Ruth (Nudelman) Oleinick; B.Arch., Ill. Inst. Tech., 1954; m. Joan Claire Berc, Aug. 21, 1954; children—Ruth, Jeffrey, Susan. Supervising architect H.T. Fisher & J.D. Randall, architects, Chgo., 1958-60; asso. architect John D. Randall & Assos., architects, Chgo., 1960-61; partner Olin & Kosover, architects, Chgo., 1961-66; asst. dir. archtl. and constrn. research U.S. League Savs. Instns., Chgo., 1966-72, dir. archtl. and constrn. research, 1972—; instr. bldg. constrn. Central YMCA Community Coll., Chgo., 1967—, mem. continuing edn. curriculum com., 1969-76; mem. sec.'s adv. commn. Ind. Dunes Nat. Lakeshore, U.S. Dept. Interior, 1969-72; mem. presdl. adv. panel Office of Tech. Assessment, U.S. Congress, 1977—; dir. Lake Mich. Region Planning Council, 1970-73, v.p., 1977—; pres. Lake Mich. Fedn., 1971-74, mem. exec. council, 1974—; v.p. Save-the-Dunes Council, 1970-73, dir., 1970-76. Mem. AIA (chmn. housing com. 1968, 69), Constrn. Specifications Inst., Am. Soc. Testing and Materials, Izaak Walton League (chpt. pres. 1968, 69, chpt. dir.). Jewish. Author: (with J.L. Schmidt and W.H. Lewis) Construction Lending Guide, 1966, Construction: Principles, Materials and Methods, 1970, 72, 75. Home: Box 115 Beverly Shores IN 46301 Office: US League Savings Assns 111 E Wacker Dr Chicago IL 60601

OLINGER, DAVID DUANE, accountant; b. Warsaw, Ind., May 8, 1947; s. Robert Eugene and Betty Alice (Krichbaum) O.; grad. Internat. Bus. Coll., Fort Wayne, Ind., 1967. Jr. accountant Ramsey, King, McBride & Horn, Warsaw, 1968-74; accountant Ray E. Plummer, C.P.A., Warsaw, 1974-75; comptroller Skystream Airlines, Inc., Chgo., 1975-77; accountant Leon W. Horn, P.A., Warsaw, Ind., 1977—. Mem. Internat. Newspaper Collectors, Am. Soc. Notaries, Nat. Wildlife Fedn. Home: 635 N Harrison St Warsaw IN 46580

OLIVE, ROGER OSWALD, psychologist; b. El Paso, Tex., Oct. 22, 1919; s. Henry and Christine Olive; B.A., Hope Coll., 1949; M.A., Mich. State U., 1962, Ph.D., 1966; m. Charlotte Kammeraad, Sept. 28, 1942; 1 dau., Eileen (Mrs. John Robert Mooney). With New Riverside Center (Mich.) Psychiat. Facility, 1952—, dir. psychology, 1963—. Asso. prof. Central Mich. U., Mt. Pleasant, 1969-72. Exec. sec. Community Chest of Greater Ionia, 1953—. Served with USCG, 1941-46. Mem. Mich. Psychol. Assn. Presbyn. (elder 1954). Rotarian. Home: 1770 Nottingham Trail Ionia MI 48846 Office: New Riverside Center 4000 N Michigan Dimondale MI 48821

OLIVER, SYLVIA ELLEN BASSETT (MRS. WILLARD CHELSEA OLIVER), librarian; b. South Bend, Ind., Mar. 24, 1921; d. Clark and Lillian (Geer) Bassett; B.S., S.W. Tex. U., 1942; M.L.S., U. Mo., 1969; m. Willard Chelsea Oliver, Jan. 10, 1942; children—Jeffrey David, Jill Jeanette (Mrs. James Pilkington). Tchr., Moberly (Mo.) Jr. High Sch., 1954-55, Westran High Sch., Huntsville, Mo., 1955-58, Springfield Twp. Jr. High Sch., Michigan City, Ind., 1958-59; dir. Little Dixie Regional Library, Moberly, 1962-73; librarian Moberly Area Jr. Coll., 1973—. Founder, mem. exec. com. Randolph County Social Agys., Moberly, 1973—. Bd. dirs. Randolph County United Fund. Mem. Am. (councilor 1974—), Mo. (exec. bd. pub. relations com. 1970-73, exec. bd. outreach round table 1971-73) library assns., Mo. Assn. Social Welfare (bd. dirs. E. Central div. 1973—). Baptist. Clubs: Lioness (pres. Huntsville, Mo. 1973-74); Altrusa (pres. Moberly, Mo. 1974-75). Home: Route 2 Huntsville MO 65259

OLIVIA, LAWRENCE ANTHONY, assn. exec.; b. 1933; m.; four children; B.S., Pa. State U., 1959, M.S., 1970. With Sterling Hotel Corp., Wilkes-Barre, Pa., summers 1957-58; steward, banquet mgr. Wilson Lodge, Wheeling, W.Va., 1958-59; asst. food and beverage mgr. Nittany Lion Inn, State College, Pa., 1959-64; supr. coll. food service ops. Instl. Food Research and Services, Pa. Dept. Pub. Instrn. and Pa. State U., 1964-67, instr. food service and housing adminstrn., 1967-70; adminstr. dept. habitational resources U. Wis., Stout, 1970-75; dir. program devel. Ednl. Inst., Am. Hotel and Motel Assn., East Lansing, Mich., 1975—; project dir. Food and Nutrition Services, Dept. Agr.; adviser Cahners Books, Inc.; lectr. numerous profl. orgns. Recipient H.B. Meek Hospitality Educator of Year award, 1976. Mem. Am., Mich., Lansing (chmn. Nutrition Week 1976) dietetic assns., Am., Mich. home econs. assns., Am. Assn. Housing Educators, Am. Assn. Ret. Persons, Travel Research Assn., Travel Industry for Environment, Am. Vocat. Assn. (asso.), Nat. Assn. Profl. Industry Trainers, Council on Hotel, Restaurant and Instl. Edn. (past dir.), Pa. State Hotel and Restaurant Soc. (pres.), Pa. State Alumni Assn., Coll. Human Devel. Alumni Assn. (past dir.). Contbr. articles to profl. jours. Address: 1039 Fox Hills Dr East Lansing MI 48823

OLMSTEAD, WILLIAM EDWARD, educator; b. San Antonio, June 2, 1936; s. William Harold and Gwendolyn (Littlefield) O.; B.S., Rice U., 1959; M.S., Northwestern U., 1962, Ph.D., 1963; m. Jo-Ann Irene Hopkins, June 7, 1971; children—William Harold, Randell Edward. Mem. research staff S.W. Research Inst., San Antonio, 1959-60; Sloan Found. postdoctoral fellow Johns Hopkins U., 1963-64; prof. applied math. Northwestern U., Evanston, Ill., 1964—, chmn. com. on applied math., 1972—; vis. mem. Courant Inst. Math. Scis., 1967-68; regional lectr. Soc. Indsl. and Applied Math., 1972-73. Mem. Am. Phys. Soc., Soc. Indsl. and Applied Math., Am. Math. Soc., Sigma Xi, Tau Beta Pi, Sigma Tau. Contbr. articles to profl. jours. Home: 141 Lockerbie Ln Wilmette IL 60091 Office: Tech Inst Northwestern U Evanston IL 60201

OLNEY, ROBERT CARROL, advt. exec.; b. Bklyn., Aug. 19, 1926; s. H.M. and Martha (Otten) O.; A.B., Cornell U., 1946; postgrad. N.Y. U., 1946-48; m. Wanda Gasch, July 17, 1948; children—Robert Carrol, Thomas, Douglas. Salesman, Minn. Mining & Mfg. Co., Minn. and Fla., 1948-51, spl. service rep., Chgo., 1951-52, sales mgr. N.E. div., Chgo., 1952-55, regional sales mgr., Chgo., 1955-57; field sales mgr. Minn. Mining & Mfg. Co. Nat. Advt. Co., Chgo., 1957-58, gen. sales and mktg. mgr., Chgo., 1958-69, mktg. dir., Chgo., 1969-74, gen. mgr., 1974—, v.p., 1976—, also dir. Served with USNR, 1943-45. Mem. Discover Am. Travel Orgn., Am. Petroleum Inst. Clubs: St. Paul Athletic; Cornell, Mid-America (Chgo.); Hinsdale (Ill.) Golf. Home: 707 E 7th St Hinsdale IL 60521 Office: 6850 S Harlem Ave Argo IL 60501

OLSEN, ARTHUR ROBERT, educator; b. Bklyn., Dec. 1, 1910; s. Martin and Clara Anita (Hansen) O.; student Potsdam Tchrs. Coll., 1935; B.S., N.Y. U., 1939, A.M., 1940, Ed.D., 1942; m. Helen M. Fehleisen, June 25, 1938; 1 dau., Karen Marie. With auditing div. Equitable Life Assn. Soc., N.Y.C., 1933-35; statistician Rayonier, Inc., N.Y.C., 1944-47; prin. Elwood Sch., L.I., N.Y., 1935-37; asst. prin. and instr. soc. sci., N. Merrick Sch., 1937-43; instr. geography, Pratt Inst. (both N.Y.C.) 1943-44; asso. prof. to prof. econs. Western Ill. U., 1947, prof. emeritus, 1970—; now economist-author South Western Pub. Co.; del. 7th Nat. Conf., U.S. Nat. Commn. for UNESCO; economist S.W. Mo. Council on Econ. Edn.; econ. cons. Macomb City Planning Commn.; dir. Ill. Council Econ. Edn. Fellow Joint Council Econ. Edn.; mem. Nat. Geog. Soc., AAUP, NEA (life), Ill. Edn. Assn., Am. Econ. Assn., Higher Edn. Assn., Phi Delta Kappa, Kappa Delta Pi, Omicron Delta Epsilon. Lutheran. Clubs: Masons (33 deg.). Author: Economic Institutions (Nat. Protestant Council Chs.); Readings on Marriage and Family Relations, 1953; co-author econs. textbook; contbr. articles to profl. jours. Home: 1 Cedar Dr Macomb IL 61455

OLSEN, DOUGLAS ALFRED, engring. co. exec., scientist; b. Mpls., Oct. 10, 1930; s. Alfred Julius and Lydia Victoria (Strand) O.; B.A., Gustavus Adolphus Coll., 1953; M.S., U. Iowa, 1955, Ph.D., 1960; m. Jeanne Marie Lindberg, Aug. 16, 1958; children—Victoria, Elliot, Valerie. Devel. chemist Bemis, Inc., Mpls., 1955-57; sr. research scientist Honeywell, Inc., Hopkins and Mpls., 1959-63; project leader Archer Daniels Midland Co., Mpls., 1963-67; dept. head Litton Systems, Inc., Mpls., 1967-70; v.p., treas. Bio-Medicus, Inc., Minnetonka, Minn., 1970-75, dir., 1970-76; pres. PMD, Inc., Eden Prairie, Minn., 1975—, also dir. Research asso. biochemistry U. Minn., 1973-76; vis. prof. Tech. U. Denmark, 1974. Mem. Citizens League, 1973—. Served with Chem. Corps, AUS, 1956. Registered profl. engr., Minn. Mem. Am. Chem. Soc., AAAS, Am. Soc. Artificial Internal Organs, AAUP, Sigma Xi, Alpha Chi Sigma, Phi Lambda Upsilon. Episcopalian. Adv. editor Progress in Surface and Membrane Sci., 1969-77; editorial cons. Polymer Digests, 1969-70. Contbr. articles to profl. jours. Patentee in field. Home: 4106 Linden Hills Blvd Minneapolis MN 55410 Office: 12985 Pioneer Trail Eden Prairie MN 55344

OLSEN, EDWARD HAROLD, JR., physician; b. Milw., Jan. 16, 1930; s. Edward Harold and Geraldine Elizabeth (Pugh) O.; student Marquette U., 1952, M.D., 1955; children—Sue, Anne, Thomas, Daniel, Theodore. Intern, Phila. Gen. Hosp., 1955-56; psychiat. resident dept. psychiatry U. Wis. Med. Sch., Madison, 1966-69; gen. practice medicine, West Bend, Wis., 1958-66; asst. prof. psychiatry, dir. grad. edn. Med. Coll. Wis., 1969-72, asso. prof. psychiatry, dir. grad. edn., 1972-73, asso. clin. prof. psychiatry, 1973—; coordinator psychiat. services Columbia Hosp., Milw., 1973—; cons. psychiatry VA Hosp., Wood, Wis., 1969—, Waukesha (Wis.) Meml. Milw. Children's hosps., 1970—, Milw. Psychiat. Services, 1970—, St. Charles Boys Home, 1971—. Served to capt. USAF, 1956-58. Diplomate Am. Bd. Psychiatry and Neurology. Mem. Am. Assn. Dirs. Psychiatry Residencies, Am., Wis. (com. on continuing edn. 1972—) psychiat. assns., Phi Chi. Home: 6609 N Lake Dr Milwaukee WI 53217 Office: 3321 N Maryland Ave Milwaukee WI 53211

OLSEN, JAMES GEORGE, furniture co. exec.; b. Milw., Dec. 12, 1924; s. James Burton and Clara (Krueger) O.; grad. high sch.; m. Mary Jean Burns, July 12, 1952; children—James, Richard, Jane. With Cudahy Trading Post Co., 1946-50, Capitol Lumber Co., 1950-51, Standard Millwork Co., 1951-52; salesman Butter Hardware Co., Milw., 1952-65; pres. Berlin Seating, Inc., Waupun, Wis., 1965-72, pres., 1972—, also dir. Served with USNR, 1943-46. Mem. Nat. Sch. Supply and Equipment Assn. (chmn. bleacher sect. 1967—, chmn. backstop sect. 1969-70), Oshkosh Power Squadron (lt. comdr. 1973-75). Mason (Shriner). Club: Amity Hunting (Oshkosh). Home: 1643 Algoma Blvd Oshkosh WI 54901 Office: 1050 S Watertown Rd Waupun WI 53963

OLSEN, PAUL DAVID, data processing mgr.; b. Evergreen Park, Ill., Mar. 5, 1945; s. Thomas Jacob and Dorothy Marie (Bensen) O.; B.S., Ill. Inst. Tech., 1967, postgrad., 1967-71; m. Karin Ruth Swearingen, Apr. 16, 1977. Teaching asst. Ill. Inst. Tech., 1970-71; dir. Christian edn. Bethel Bible Ch., Evergreen Park, 1971-72; data processing mgr. Inst. in Basic Youth Conflicts, Oak Brook Ill., 1973—. Baptist. Home: 7324-6 Winthrop Way Downers Grove IL 60515 Office: Box 1 Oak Brook IL 60521

OLSEN, ROBERT ALLEN, microbiologist, environ. scientist; b. Mt. Vernon, Wash., Jan. 11, 1931; s. Christopher Gunerius and Minnie Delia (Danielsen) O.; B.S., Wash. State Coll., 1952, M.S., 1954; Ph.D., U. Wash., 1958; postgrad. U. Cin., 1965; m. Donna Mae Decker, Apr. 7, 1952; children—Stephen, Debra, Carrie, Kristen. Staff microbiologist foods div. Procter & Gamble Co., Cin., 1958-64, project leader food product devel., 1964-72, environ. scientist/microbiologist indsl. chems. div., 1972, mem. profl. and regulatory staff, govt. tech. liaison, 1972—. Bd. mem., sec. Community Sch. Athletic Assn., 1965-67; bd. dirs. Community Sch. Boosters Assn., 1968-73, pres., 1971-72; active Greater Cin. United Appeal. NSF fellow, 1954. Mem. Am. Soc. Microbiology, Inst. Food Technologists, Sigma Xi. Lutheran. Clubs: Private Pool Swim (sec. 1975-77), Scandinavian Soc. Cin. (pres. 1975-76). Patentee in field. Home: 8495 Foxcroft Dr Cincinnati OH 45231 Office: 11530 Reed Hartman Hwy Cincinnati OH 45240

OLSEN, W(ILHELM) F., food co. cons.; b. nr. Alberta, Minn., Oct. 5, 1902; s. Rev. Engel O. and Gunda (Lund) O.; student Luther Coll., 1921-24; m. Maria Fiala, Aug. 8, 1928; children—Mary Reiss, Karen Rogers. Clk. Chgo. Norfolk Western Coal Co., Chgo., 1924-25, Western Electric Co., Cicero, Ill., 1926; clk., buyer purchasing dept. Curtiss Candy Co., Chgo., 1926-41, gen. purchasing agt., 1941-53, v.p., exec. com., 1953-57; dir. Central Enterprises Inc.; owner Keeline Co., food brokers, 1957-69; gen. cons. Keeline Co. div. Enzer Payne Co., Chgo., 1969—, Bend Southall-McBratnie, Inc., sugar brokers, 1974—; mem. adv. com. Sec. of Agr., 1953; mem. Commn. for Hoover Report, 1952-53. Mem. Republican Club; chmn. Chgo. devel. bd. Luther Coll., Decorah, Iowa, co-chmn. Vanguard program, 1971-72, Distinguished Service award, 1972. Mem. Nat. Confectioners Assn., Nat. Sugar Brokers Assn., Nat. Peanut Council, Luther Coll. Alumni Assn., Sons of Norway, Internat. Norsemen's League. Lutheran. (former deacon). Clubs: Pioneer, Norske (past pres.), Lake Shore, Execs. (Chgo.). Home: 1326 Chicago Ave Evanston IL 60201 Office: 5475 Milwaukee Ave Chicago IL 60630

OLSHAVSKY, RICHARD WILLIAM, psychologist; b. Portage, Pa., Feb. 21, 1941; s. Michael and Helen (Manchak) O.; m. Jill Edwards, June 22, 1967; B.S. in Mech. Engring., Carnegie-Mellon U., 1963, M.S. in Psychology, 1965, Ph.D., 1967. Instr., Carnegie-Mellon U., 1966; asst. prof. psychology Ga. Inst. Tech., 1967-70; asso. prof. mktg. Ind. U., Bloomington, 1970—; cons. NSF. Mem. Am. Psychol. Assn., Am. Mktg. Assn., Assn. for Consumer Research, Beta Gamma Sigma, Delta Sigma Pi. Author: No More Butts-A Psychologists Approach to Quitting Cigarettes, 1977; contbr. articles to profl. jours. Home: 2978 Ramble Rd E Bloomington IN 47401

OLSON, ALEC GEHARD, lt. gov. Minn.; b. Mamre Twp., Minn., Sept. 11, 1930; s. Axel Gehard and Florence Romonia (Hoglund) O.; grad. high sch.; student U.S. Dept. Agr., 1967; m. Janice Ruth Albrecht, July 3, 1957; children—Alan, Dennis, Deron, Eric. Farmer, Pennock, Minn., 1948-55; ins. rep. Nat. Farmers Union Service Corp., 1955-62; mem. 88th-89th congresses from 6th Minn. Dist., 1963-67; asst. to sec. U.S. Dept. Agr., 1967; account exec. Kelly & Morey, 1969; mem. Minn. Senate, 1969-77; lt. gov. Minn., 1976—; farmer, Spicer, Minn. Chmn., Democratic-Farmer-Labor Party of Kandiyohi County, 1954-57; del. Dem. Nat. Conv., 1960, 64, 68. Lutheran. Home: Route 1 Spicer MN 56288 Office: State Capitol Saint Paul MN 55155*

OLSON, ALLEN INGVAR, atty. gen. N.D.; b. Rolla, N.D., Nov. 5, 1938; s. Elmer Martin and Olga (Sundin) O.; m. Barbara Benner, Aug. 29, 1964; children—Kristin, Robin, Craig; B.S. in Bus. Adminstrn., U. N.D., 1960, J.D., 1963. Admitted to N.D. bar, U.S. Supreme Ct. bar; asst. dir. N.D. Legis. Council, 1967-69; partner firm Conmy, Rosenberg, Lucas & Olson, 1969-72; atty. gen. N.D., 1972—; chmn. N.D. Law Enforcement Council; bd. dirs. Bank of N.D. and State Mill and Elevator, N.D. Indsl. Commn. Vice pres. Dakota Zool. Soc. Mem. N.D. Bar Assn., Masons, Elks, Exchange Club. Named Man of Year, Am. Religious Town Hall Found., 1977. Home: Star Route 2 Bismarck ND 58501 Office: Office Atty Gen State Capitol Bismarck ND 58501

OLSON, BARBARA FORD, physician; b. Iowa City, June 15, 1935; d. Leonard Augustine and Anne (Swanson) Ford; B.A., Gustavus Adolphus Coll., 1956; M.D., U. Minn., 1960; m. Robert E. Olson, Mar. 21, 1959 (div. Oct. 1973); children—Katherine Anne, Eric Ford, Julie Marie. Intern, St. Paul-Ramsey Hosp., St. Paul, 1960-61; resident anesthesia Western Res. U. Hosps., 1961-62, U. Minn. Hosps., 1962-63; practice anesthesia St. Luke's, St. John's, Divine Redeemer hosps., St. Paul, 1963-67, Mercy Hosp., Mpls., 1967-73; staff anesthesiologist Hennepin County Gen. Hosp., Mpls., 1973-74; sr. staff physician Glen Lake State Sanatorium, Mpls., 1974—. Diplomate Am. Bd. Family Practice. Fellow Am. Coll. Anesthesiologists; mem. Minn., Ramsey County med. socs., AMA, Am., Minn. socs. anesthesiologists, Alpha Epsilon Iota. Home: 7001 Mark Terr Dr Minneapolis MN 55435 Office: Glen Lake State Sanatorium Minnetonka MN 55343

OLSON, CLITUS WILBUR, surgeon; b. Omaha, Oct. 20, 1916; s. Enock and Nellie Ingeborg (Rotsten) O.; A.B., Municipal U. Omaha, 1939; M.D., U. Nebr., 1948; m. Dorothy Mae Nord, Mar. 20, 1948; children—Paul Edward, Eleanor Louise Olson Bowman, Barbara Jean Olson Molina, Joan Elaine. Intern, Jefferson-Hillman Hosp., Birmingham, Ala., 1948-49; gen. resident Mercy Hosp., Des Moines, 1949-50; student Inst. Tropical Medicine, Antwerp, Belgium, 1951; med. missionary Mission Evangelique de l'Ubangi, Karawa, Kinshasa, and Kisangani, Belgian Congo, 1951-59, Dem. Republic of Congo and Republic of Zaire, 1964-71; resident in surgery Univ. Hosp., Omaha, 1959-63, asst. surgeon, 1963-64; staff surgeon VA Hosp., Hot Springs, S.D., 1971-73; practice medicine specializing in surgery, Goodland, Kans., 1973—; mem. staffs M.E.U., Karawa, I.M.E., Kimpese, VA Hosp., Hot Springs, S.D., and NW Kans. Med. Center; dean faculty of medicine Free U. of Zaire (later Nat. Univ.), 1970-71. Mem. A.C.S., AMA, N.W. Kans. Med. Soc., Royal Soc. Tropical Medicine, Hygiene, Alpha Omega Alpha. Mem. Evang. Covenant Ch., United Methodist. Club: Kiwanis. Home: 610 Harrison St Goodland KS 67735 Office: 520 Main St Goodland KS 67735

OLSON, DAVID HERMAN, educator; b. Albert Lea, Minn., Oct. 11, 1940; s. Milton G. and Marvyl (Johnson) O.; B.A., St. Olaf Coll., 1962; M.A., Wichita State U., 1964; Ph.D., Pa. State U., 1967. Research asst. Pa. State U., University Park, 1964-65, vocat. rehab. fellow, 1965-67; fellow Family Study Center, U. Minn., Mpls., 1967-68; co-dir. longitudinal study early marriage and family devel. Child Research Br. NIMH, Bethesda, Md., 1968-71; asso. prof., research coordinator family and community devel. U. Md., College Park, 1968-72; prof. family studies U. Minn., St. Paul, 1972—; psychologist, marital and family therapist. Mem. Am. Psychol. Assn., Am. Sociol. Assn., Nat. Council Family Relations, Am. Assn. Marriage and Family Counselors, Soc. Research in Child Devel., Groves Conf. on Family, Sigma Xi, Psi Chi, Alpha Kappa Delta. Author: Treating Relationships, 1976; (with R.C. Cromwell) Power in Families, 1975; contbr. articles to profl. jours.; asso. editor: (with N. Dahl) Inventory of Marriage and Family Literature: 1973-74, vol. III, 1975, vol. IV, 1977. Home: 825 W Montana Saint Paul MN 55117 Office: 217 North Hall U Minn Saint Paul MN 55108

OLSON, DEAN ALAN, engr., mfr.; b. Rockford, Ill., Nov. 10, 1918; s. Otto H. and Florence (McCauley) O.; B.M.E., U. Ill., 1941; postgrad. corp. pres. course Harvard U., 1958; m. Nancy Nichols, June 24, 1942; children—Dean Alan, Julie Ann, James Nichols, Nobel Dean. Engr., Barber-Colman Co., Rockford, 1941-49; pres., founder Die Max Products Co., Rockford, 1952—, also pres. Rockford Acromatic Products Co., 1949—; chmn. bd. Aircraft Gear Corp., 1965—, pres., 1966—; chmn. bd. D.J. Stewart & Co., Rockford, 1972—; dir. Barrett Electronics Corp., Barrett Cravens Co., Ill. Nat. Bank & Trust Co., Howard H. Monk & Assos., Inc.; instr. engring. U. Ill., 1945-46. Mem. nat. council Boy Scouts Am., 1959-62, mem. exec. com. region 7; founding dir. Rockford Jr. Achievement, 1958; mem. AID Mission to Peru, 1965; mem. spl. adv. com. U.S. Dept. State, 1970—; mem. Ill. Gov.'s Adv. Council, 1970—; corporate mem. Ill. Council Econ. Edn., 1970—; mem. Sec. Navy's Adv. Bd. on Edn. and Tng., 1973—; trustee D.A.O. Found., 1960—, Rockford Acromatic Products Co. Trust, 1960—, Young Pres.' Orgn. Found., Winnebago County Republican Fund, 1970—; pres., chmn. bd. Winnebago-Boone County Jr. Coll.; bd. dirs. Nat. Center for Responsible Enterprise, Inc., U.S. Indsl. Council; chmn. bd. trustees Aircraft Gear Corp.; trust adv. bd. Center Strategic and Internat. Studies, 1970—. Served with ordnance, AUS, 1941-44; PTO. Mem. World Bus. Council, Am. Mgmt. Assn., Young Pres. Orgn., U.S. C. of C., NAM, Brit. Inst. Dirs., Alpha Tau Omega, Beta Gamma Sigma. Congregationalist (deacon). Clubs: Rotary, Union League (Chgo.). Home: 3318 Brookview Rd Rockford IL 61107 Office: 611 Beacon St Rockford IL 61111

OLSON, DONAEBILL GLEN, social agy. exec.; b. Sacred Heart, Minn., Dec. 27, 1941; s. Glen Herman and Angeline Thyra (Knigge) O.; student U. Minn., 1959-60; B.A., Augsburg Coll., 1964; M.S., Eastern Wash. State Coll., 1967; m. Harriet Bernice Huseby, June 20, 1964; children—Kara Sue, Christopher Glen. Corrective therapist

Cambridge (Minn.) State Hosp., 1964-66, 67-68; exec. dir. Robert Milton Home for Mentally Retarded, Redwood Falls, Minn., 1968-77; exec. dir. Home for Creative Living, Windom, Minn., 1977—. Former mem. Minn. State Adv. Bd. for Licensure of Mental Retardation Facilities, Redwood Falls Bicentennial Com.; mem. Minn. Adv. Council on Mental Retardation and Physically Handicapped; former bd. dirs. Service Industries, Inc. Sheltered Workshop. Mem. Am. Corrective Therapy Assn. (accreditation council 1977 past pres.), Cottonwood County Assn. Retarded Children, Am. Assn. Mental Deficiency, Minn. Assn. Residencies of Retarded, Internat. Racquetball Assn., Redwood Falls C. of C. (past dir.). Home: 775 20th St Windom MN 56101 Office: 108 9th St Windom MN 56101

OLSON, EDWARD LOUIS, instl. exec.; b. Glenfield, N.D., Apr. 24, 1924; s. Edward Gustav and Julia (Person) O.; student North Park Coll., Chgo., 1942-43, Kans. State U., 1943-44; B.A., U. Wash., 1949; M.S., Northwestern U., 1959; m. Doris Lorraine Swedenburg, Apr. 25, 1951; 1 son, Stephen Edward. Accountant, Wash. Natural Gas Co., Seattle, 1949-53; accountant Kennedy & Coe, C.P.A.'s, Salina, Kans., 1953-54; dir. purchasing Swedish Covenant Hosp., Chgo., 1954-59, asst. adminstr., 1959-62, asso. adminstr., 1962-65, adminstr., 1965-75, v.p. Covenant Benevolent Instns., 1975—, also dir.; mem. exec. com., chmn. nominating com. Hosp. Laundry Services, Inc., Chgo.; preceptor faculties Grad. Sch. Mgmt., Northwestern U., Grad. Sch. Bus. Adminstrn., U. Chgo. Bd. dirs. Chgo. North Side Commn. on Health Planning, North River Commn., Chgo. Served with AUS, 1943-46. Decorated Combat Inf. badge. Mem. Am. Coll. Hosp. Adminstrs., Hosp. Purchasing Agts. Assn. Met. Chgo. (pres. 1956-57), Nat. Assn. Hosp. Purchasing Mgrs. (v.p. 1957-58), Am., Ill., Am. Protestant (del., com. chmn., trustee) hosp. assns., Chgo. Assn. Commerce and Industry, Friends of North Park Coll., Chgo. Hosp. Council, Northwestern U. Grad. Sch. Mgmt. Alumni Assn., Field Mus. Natural History, Nat. Geog. Soc. Mem. Evang. Covenant Ch. Clubs: Kiwanis, Svithiod (Chgo.). Home: 2050 Valencia Dr Northbrook IL 60062 Office: 5145 N California Ave Chicago IL 60625

OLSON, EVERETT ATLEY, JR., lawyer; b. Joplin, Mo., Jan. 11, 1938; s. Everett Atley and Anna Marie (Dobson) O.; A.B., U. Mo., 1958, LL.B., 1961; m. Sandra Jean Stroud, Apr. 1, 1960; children—Christine Marie, David Atley, William Everett. Admitted to Mo. bar, 1961; partner firm Shook, Hardy & Bacon, Kansas City, Mo., 1961-67, partner, 1968—. Served with USNG, 1954-60. Mem. Am., Mo., Kansas City bar assns., Lawyers' Assn. Kansas City, Phi Delta Phi. Republican. Methodist. Clubs: Woodside Racquet. Bd. editors U. Mo. Law Rev., 1960-61. Home: 822 W 57th Terr Kansas City MO 64113 Office: 19th Floor Mercantile Tower 1101 Walnut St Kansas City MO 64106

OLSON, FREDERICK IRVING, historian; b. Milw., May 30, 1916; s. Frank and Clara Sophie (Hansen) O.; A.B., Harvard U., 1938, M.A., 1939, Ph.D., 1952; m. Jane Marian Correll, June 8, 1946; children—David Frederick, Donald Frank, Roger Alan. Faculty, U. Wis.-Milw. and predecessor instns., 1946—, prof. history, 1956—, chmn. dept. history, 1960-62, 67-70; asso. dean Extension, 1960-68, asso. dean. Coll. Letters and Sci., 1971-76, acting dean Sch. Library Sci., 1977—; vis. prof. history U. Wis.-Madison, 1957; dir. Wauwatosa State Bank (Wis.). Bd. dirs. Milw. County Hist. Soc., 1947—, pres. 1953-57, 71-74; trustee Milw. Pub. Mus., 1951-52; bd. curators Wis. Hist. Soc., 1961—; mem. Milw. Landmarks Commn., 1964-71; chmn. Milwaukee County Landmarks Com., 1976—. Served with U.S. Army, 1942-45. Recipient award of merit Milwaukee County Hist. Soc., 1963, distinguished service award U. Wis.-Extension, 1969. Mem. Am. Hist. Assn., Orgn. Am. Historians, AAUP, Nat. Trust Historic Preservation, Am. Assn. State and Local History, Phi Beta Kappa, Phi Alpha Theta, Phi Kappa Phi. Lutheran. Club: North Hills Country (Menomonee Falls, Wis.). Contbr. articles, revs. to profl. publs. Home: 2437 N 90th St Wauwatosa WI 53226 Office: Dept History U Wis-Milw PO Box 413 Milwaukee WI 53201

OLSON, GORDON EVERETT, city mgr.; b. Des Moines, Sept. 21, 1916; s. John Albin and Thelma (Nystrom) O.; B.C.S., Drake U., 1938; M.S.P., Purdue U., 1948; m. Mary Grace Zimmerman, Dec. 28, 1940; children—Kathleen, Nancy, Douglas, Dennis, Carolyn. City mgr. North St. Paul, Minn., 1951-57, Berkeley, Mo., 1957-62; cons. bus. and govt., city planning, Midwest, 1962-65; exec. dir. St. Louis County Urban Rd. System, Olivette, Mo., 1965-69; cons. bus. and govt., city planning, 1962-65, 69—. Served with AUS, 1943-46. Mem. Internat. City Mgrs. Assn., Am. Soc. for Pub. Adminstrn., Delta Sigma Pi. Home: 8837 Santa Bella Dr Hazelwood MO 63042 Office: 6130 Madison St Louis MO 63134

OLSON, GORDON WIN JUM, agrl. engr.; b. Brookings, S.D., July 27, 1922; s. Orrin Odel and Clara A. (Win Jum) O.; B.S., S.D. State U., 1947; m. Dorothy Mae Olson, June 1, 1947; children—Larry, James, Steven. Asst. test engr. Tractor Test Lab., U. Nebr., Lincoln, 1947-50; sr. engr. John Deere Dubuque Works (Iowa), 1950—. Pres. Martin Luther Home Corp., Dubuque, 1965—; active 4-H, Dubuque, 1963—. Served with USAAF, 1943-46. Mem. Am. Soc. Agrl. Engrs., Soc. Automotive Engrs. Home: 913 Liberty St Dubuque IA 52001

OLSON, HARRIET ANN HOWARD, guidance counselor, actress; b. Pitts., Mar. 25, 1931; d. Ralph Murch and Harriet Howard (Tucker) Whitehouse; B.Music Edn., Northwestern U., 1956; postgrad. Western Mich. U., 1955-56; M.S., U. Nebr., Omaha, 1978; m. Melvin Donald Olson, Jan. 3, 1952; children—Christine Frances, Erica Marie. Tchr., Ill., Mich., Wis., 1953-60; free-lance radio-TV-film performer, 1957—; profl. actress, 1959—; women's dir., on camera hostess KMTV, Omaha, 1962-69; graphoanalysis cons., lectr., 1969—; guidance counselor, 1977—; counselor, groups facilitator Women's Resource Center, U. Nebr., Omaha, 1977—, also with gerontology program; bd. dirs. Project Equality Nebr./Iowa, 1968-73; charter mem. Mayor's Commn. on Status of Women; sec. support com. Miriam Center (Rehab. Women Offenders), 1977—. Recipient several service awards KMTV. Mem. Am., Nebr. personnel and guidance assns., Internat. Graphoanalysis Soc., Am. Sch. Counselors Assn., Actors Equity Assn., Met. Actors Guild, Common Cause, Nat. Panel of Am. Women, Delta Zeta, Sigma Alpha Iota. Democrat. Methodist. Home: 322 E 54th St Omaha NE 68132

OLSON, JAMES JOHN, mining researcher; b. Granite Falls, Minn., Oct. 5, 1938; s. Curt Arnold and Christina Johnson (Bogle) O.; student Gustavus Adolphus Coll., 1956-58; B.S. with honors, U. Minn., 1961; M.S., 1963; m. Sandra Ellen Olsen, Mar. 30, 1963; children—Melissa Ann, Jon Peter, Christine Ellen. Research asso. U. Minn., Mpls., 1961-63; researcher Alaska and Antarctic, geophysicist U.S. Bur. Mines, Mpls., 1963-70, mining engr., 1970-74, research supr., 1974—. Mem. Am. Inst. Mining, Metall. and Petroleum Engrs. Presbyterian (ruling elder). Club: Masons. Contbr. articles on vibration, rock damage from underground blasting, rapid excavation, long wall mining and in situ mining to profl. publs. Home: 1241 Delaware Ave Mendota Heights MN 55118 Office: PO Box 1660 Minneapolis MN 55111

OLSON, LINDA KATHRYN, counselor; b. Wisconsin Rapids, Wis., Aug. 26, 1947; d. Samuel Ellsworth and Lillian (Dvorak) Olson; B.S., U. Wis. at Stevens Point, 1969, teaching certificate, 1970, M.S.T., 1972; postgrad. U. Wis. at Madison, 1969-70; M.S., U. Wis. at Whitewater, 1975; Ed.S., U. Wis.-Stout, 1978. Clk., Univ. Counseling Center, U. Wis., Stevens Point, 1965-69; elementary sch. tchr., Wisconsin Rapids, 1970-76, sch. counselor, 1976—. Active Wisconsin Rapids Hosp. Aux.; sec. PTA. Mem. NEA, Wisconsin Rapids Edn. Assn., Am. Personnel and Guidance Assn., Am. Sch. Counselor Assn., AAUW. Mem. Moravian Ch. Club: Hosp. Aux. Women's. Home: 1011 16th St S Wisconsin Rapids WI 54494 Office: Howe Elementary Sch 8th St S Wisconsin Rapids WI 54494

OLSON, MELVIN DONALD, choral condr.; b. Janesville, Wis., Dec. 24, 1930; s. Francis and Ethel Amanda (Christeson) O.; B. Music Edn., Northwestern U., 1954; M.Mus., Westminster Choir Coll., Princeton, N.J., 1960; m. Harriet Ann Howard Whitehouse, Jan. 3, 1952; children—Christine Frances, Erica Marie. Music tchr. pub. schs., Nebr. and Ill., 1952-54; dir. choral music, Kalamazoo, 1954-58; dir. choral ensembles U. Nebr., Omaha, 1960-63; minister music Dundee Presbyn. Ch., Omaha, 1963-73; dir. ministry music First United Meth. Ch., Omaha, 1973—; founder, artistic dir. Voices of Mel Olson, 1965—, Young People's Choir of Midlands, 1973—; mem. faculty Saratoga/Potsdam (N.Y.) Choral Inst., also Choral Assos. workshops in N.Y., Wash., Ariz. and Nebr.; pres. bd. dirs. Concert Halls Series, Inc.; clinician, adjudicator music festivals; music dir. community theatres, choruses, choral activities Omaha Symphony, Omaha Opera Co. Grantee Nebr. Arts Council, 1969—; recipient profl. and pub. service certificates. Mem. Am. Choral Dirs. Assn. (chmn. nat. standing coms. community choruses and ch. music), Music Educators Nat. Conf., Nebr. Arts Council (advisory com.), Assn. Profl. Vocal Ensembles (charter), Am. Fedn. Musicians, Met. Arts Council, Nebr. Choral Dirs. Assn., Common Cause, Chi Phi, Phi Mu Alpha (hon.). Club: Omaha Press (hon.). Home: 322 S 54th St Omaha NE 68132 Office: 6906 Cass St Omaha NE 68132

OLSON, MELVIN JOYCE, automotive engr.; b. Rochelle, Ill., Sept. 19, 1912; s. Charles and Mabel Josephine (Quitno) O.; grad. LaSalle Extension U., 1939; student Bradley U., 1956, U. Wis., 1968; m. Zori G. Gasway, Dec. 18, 1947; children—Melinda Joy, Melvin Jay. Contractor, Rochelle, 1930-33; with Douglas Guardian, Rochelle, 1933-36; engr. Whitcomb Locomotive Co., Rochelle, 1936-51 specification engr. Fairbanks Morse & Co., Beloit, Wis., 1951-54; layout designer Letourneau-West Co., Peoria, Ill., 1954-58; engine application engr. NW Engring. Co., Green Bay, Wis., 1958—; cons. in field. Mem. Soc. Automotive Engrs. Republican. Presbyterian. Clubs: Washington (Ill.) Presbyn. Men's (pres. 1956), Beloit (Wis.) Presbyn. Men's, Masons, Shriners. Home: 831 Laverne Dr Green Bay WI 54302 Office: 201 W Walnut St Green Bay WI 54305

OLSON, ORVILLE BERNARD, mfg. co. exec.; b. Ellsworth, Wis., Aug. 27, 1926; s. Oscar J. and Selma (Dahl) O.; student Dunwoody Inst., 1948-50; M.E., U. Minn., 1954; m. Annabell V. Mattson, May 31, 1947; children—Debra, Janice. Tool designer Precision Products, Mpls., 1945-48; salesman R.C. Duncan, Mpls., 1948-51; with Grain King Industries, St. Paul, 1952-63, pres., gen. mgr., dir. 1958-63; dist. mgr. Barnard & Leas, Cedar Rapids, Iowa, 1963-64; with Haban Mfg. Co., Racine, Wis., 1964—, v.p. sales, 1970—, dir., 1970—. Mem. Am. Soc. Agrl. Engrs. (chmn. PM 52 sect. 1975). Patentee in field. Home: 3806 Carter St Racine WI 53402 Office: 2100 Northwestern Ave Racine WI 53404

OLSON, O(SCAR) WILLIAM, transp. co. exec.; b. Oak Park, Ill., Feb. 1, 1927; s. Oscar William and Eudora (Landstrom) O.; A.B., DePauw U., 1949; J.D., John Marshall Law Sch., 1953; m. Margaret Greiner; children—Peter W., Stephen W., Martha L. Admitted to Ill. bar, 1953; partner Brandel, Olson, Johnson & Erickson, Chgo., 1969—; chmn. bd. Safeway Precision Products, Pompano Beach, Fla., 1968—, Intercontinental Steel Corp., Chgo., 1965—; chmn. bd., pres., chief exec. officer South Suburban Safeway Lines, Inc., Harvey, Ill., 1970—; chmn. bd. Safeway Enterprises, Inc., Chgo.; pres. Barr Industries, Inc., Intercontinental Sales, Ltd., Intercontinental Services, Ltd., Illectric Industries, Inc., Dahltron Corp. (all Chgo.). Served with USAAF, 1944-46: ETO. Mem. Am., Ill., Chgo. bar assns. Clubs: Monroe, Union League, Swedish, Chgo. Athletic Assn., Execs., Nordic Law (Chgo.); Edgewood Valley Country (LaGrange, Ill.). Home: 15W121 81st St Hinsdale IL 60521 Office: 111 W Washington St Room 1035 Chicago IL 60602

OLSON, PRISCILLA MAE, educator, counselor; b. Eau Claire, Wis., Nov. 14, 1936; d. Forrest Howard and Laura Mae (Archer) Mewhorter; B.S., Hamline U., 1961; M.A., U. Wis. at River Falls, 1971; postgrad. St. Thomas Coll.; m. Gordon Olson, July 27, 1957; children—Maylin K., Glenna J. Tchr. pub. schs., St. Paul, 1961-63, S. St. Paul, 1968—; tchr., adminstr. pvt. sch. St. Paul Park, 1963-67; remedial reading tchr., dist. reading coordinator, tchr., counselor; individual practice counseling, reading tutoring adults; discussion leader Great Books. Mem. Am., Minn. personnel and guidance assns., Am. Sch. Counselors Assn., Dakota County Counselors Assn., Minn. Reading Assn., Twin-City Reading Assn. Contbr. articles to profl. jours. Research in field. Home: 1300 Chicago Ave South Saint Paul MN 55071 Office: 357 9th St South Saint Paul MN 55075

OLSON, RAYMOND ROY, transp. co. exec.; b. Chgo., Aug. 28, 1913; s. Raymond Roy and Margaret (Crowley) O.; student U. Ill., 1931-35; m. Marjorie Ruth Stafford, Jan. 11, 1941; children—Patience Olson Tressler, Allan R., Gloria (dec.). Prodn. mgr. Kropp Forge Co., Chgo., 1945-58; v.p. C.D. Gammon Co., Chgo., 1958-63, Willett Co., Chgo., 1963—; v.p. Solar Liquid Heating Co., Chgo., 1965-69, pres., 1969—; sales mgr. Willett Truck Leasing Co., Chgo., 1963-70, v.p., 1970—; sales mgr. Willett Transports, Inc., Chgo., 1963-70, v.p., 1970—; v.p. Willett Motor Coach Co., 1973—. Mem. Chgo. Assn. Commerce and Industry, Shrine Transp. Club (v.p. 1969-70), Piggyback Assn. Chgo. Presbyterian. Clubs: Masons, Shriners, Exec., Traffic, Press (Chgo.). Patentee drip proof bottle, window, solar distillation apparatus. Home: 635 N Ridgeland Oak Park IL 60302 Office: 700 S Desplaines Chicago IL 60607

OLSON, RAYMOND STANLEY, educator; b. Sandstone, Minn., Jan. 13, 1929; s. Olaf Raymond and Minnie (Vork) O.; A.A., Ellsworth Coll., 1957; B.A., U. No. Iowa, 1959; M.A., State U. Iowa, 1960; Ed.D., U. No. Colo., 1973; m. Lois Marie Below, Dec. 20, 1952; 1 dau., Jan Michele. Mgr. service sta., Hubbard, Iowa, 1953-55; tchr. Abbottsford (Wis.) Pub. Schs., 1959-62; faculty, coach Black Hawk Coll., Moline, Ill., 1962—. Served with AUS, 1951-53. Mem. AAHPER, Phi Epsilon Kappa. Home: 3328 41st St Moline IL 61265

OLSON, RICHARD GOTTLIEB, nuclear, computer sci. elec. engr.; b. Terre Haute, Ind., Dec. 17, 1922; s. Gottlieb W. and Lucille (Clifton) O.; B.S. in Elec. Engring., Rose Poly. Inst., 1941-47; M.S. in Nuclear Engring., U. Mich., 1955; postgrad. Wayne State U., 1950-53; m. Virginia Ann Abbinett, June 22, 1947; children—Stephen P., Mary Ann. Instr. Rose Poly. Inst., 1947-48; elec. engr., nuclear engr., sr. sci. analyst, sr. engring. analyst in computer sci. Detroit Edison Co., 1948—, systems specialist tng. coordinator tech. systems planning dept., 1969-73, work leader nuclear and design group, 1973—; staff mem. Atomic Power Devel. Assn., Detroit, 1954-60, Power Reactor Devel. Co., 1960-65; instr. Wayne State U., 1950-75; cons. nuclear engr., 1958—. Mem. Dearborn Citizens Edn. Adv. Com. Served with AUS, 1943-46. Mich. Meml. fellow, 1954-55. Mem. Assn. for Computing Machinery, AAUP, Am. Nuclear Soc., IEEE, Am. Mgmt. Assn., Engring. Soc. Detroit, Instrument Soc. Am. Contbr. articles to profl. jours. Home: 1505 Venice Ave Dearborn MI 48124 Office: 2000 2d Ave Detroit MI 48226

OLSON, ROBERT CLAUDE, brush mfg. co. exec.; b. Mpls., Sept. 10, 1915; s. Claude Robert and Alice Augusta (Anderson) O.; student U. Minn., 1933-37; m. Eva Elizabeth Johnson, Apr. 15, 1939; children—Bruce R., William C., Kathleen A. (Mrs. Donald B. Wood), Lawrence W. With Flo Pac Corp., Mpls., 1937—, exec. v.p., 1937-77, pres., 1977—, also dir.; pres., dir. Flour City Brush Co., Mpls., 1937—; pres., dir. Pacific Coast Brush Co., Los Angeles, 1940—; sec., dir. Twenty-Thirty E. 7th St. Corp., Los Angeles, 1957—; pres., dir. Southeastern Brush Co., Decatur, Ga., 1966—, Olson Corp., Mpls., 1963—. Bd. dirs., sec. Big Bros. of Mpls., 1975—. Mem. Asso. Industries Mpls. (dir. 1974—), Delta Chi. Republican. Lutheran. Mason (Shriner). Club: Optimist. Home: 124 Ardmore Dr Minneapolis MN 55422 Office: 918 N 3d St Minneapolis MN 55401

OLSON, RUE EILEEN (MRS. RICHARD L. OLSON), librarian; b. Chgo., Nov. 1, 1928; d. Paul H. and Martha M. (Fick) Meyers; student HerzlColl., 1946-48, Northwestern U., 1948-50, Ill. State U., 1960-64; m. Richard L. Olson, July 18, 1964; children—Catherine, Karen. Accountant Ill. Farm Supply Co., Chgo., 1948-59; asst. librarian Ill. Agrl. Assn., Bloomington, 1960-66, librarian, 1966—. Mem. area Com. Nat. Library Week, 1971, area steering com., 1972; mem. adv. council of librarians Grad. Sch. Library Sci. U. Ill., 1976—. Mem. Am., Ill., McLean County (pres. 1970-71) library assns., Spl. Libraries Assn. (pres. Ill. 1977-78), Internat. Assn. Agrl. Librarians and Documentalists, Am. Soc. Information Sci., Am. Mgmt. Assn. Home: 103 Radliff Rd Bloomington IL 61701 Office: 1701 Towanda Ave Bloomington IL 61701

OLSON, VICTOR EDWARD, banking co. exec.; b. Mpls., Nov. 18, 1927; s. Edwin Albin and Martha Agnes (Von Speecken) O.; m. Ann Esther Jakupciak, Sept. 23, 1950; children—Marcia Ann, Michael Edwin, Marnee Suzanne, Marcus Edward. Sec., Olson's Baker and Gourmet, Inc., Wayzata, Minn., 1945-72, pres., 1972—. Served with C.E., U.S. Army, 1946-48, 50-51. Mem. Minn. Bakers Assn. (pres. 1972-77, dir. 1978), Retail Bakers Am., Am. Soc. Bakery Engrs., Midwest Chef Soc., Am. Culinary Fedn. Lutheran. Club: Rotary. Home: 2301 Linner Rd Wayzata MN 55391 Office: 726 E Lake St Wayzata MN 55391

OLSON, WESLEY WILLIAM, dentist; b. Sioux Falls, S.D., Nov. 28, 1927; s. William Orvile and Louise (Schultz) O.; D.D.S., Creighton U., 1954; m. Clara June Sohl, Sept. 9, 1950; children—Mark William, Claire Dorene. Tchr. dentistry Creighton U., 1954-55; gen. practice dentistry, Lennox, S.D., 1955-75; tchr. prosthetic dentistry Creighton U., Omaha, 1975—. Vice pres. Lennox Sch. Bd., 1965; bd. advisors Inst. for Latin Am. Concern. Served with Hosp. Corps, USN, 1946-48. Mem. ADA, Nebr., Omaha dental assns., Am. Acad. Gen. Dentists, Am. Soc. Dentistry for Children, Am. Soc. Preventive Dentistry, Internat., Am. assns. for dental research. Republican. Lutheran (past pres.). Clubs: Masons, Order Eastern Star, Kiwanis. Home: 114 S 51st St Omaha NE 68132

OLSON, WILLIAM HOWARD, dentist; b. La Crosse, Wis., July 24, 1939; s. Turnie and Agnes Marvel (Bakke) O.; student St. Olaf Coll., 1957-59; B.S., U. Minn., 1963, D.D.S., 1963; m. Jeanine Bernice Lundahl, June 21, 1969; children—Jennifer Ann, Steven Paul. Dental intern USPHS Hosp., San Francisco, 1963-64; USPHS dentist Winnebago (Nebr.) Indian Reservation, Flandreau (S.D.) Indian Sch., 1964-66; pvt. practice dentistry, Pipestone, Minn., 1966—; chmn. dental staff Pipestone County Hosp., 1972—; v.p., dir. Sypo Corp., 1967-69. Bd. dirs. Pipestone Area Devel. Corp., 1972-75, sec.-treas., 1973-75; bd. dirs. Hiawatha Concert Assn., 1968-71, pres., 1969-70; v.p. Pipestone Community Club, 1969-70; chmn. acad. affairs com. bd. regents Augustana Coll., Sioux Falls, S.D., 1971-77. Served to lt. comdr. USPHS, 1963-66. Mem. Am., Minn. (del. 1976) dental assns., So. Dist. Dental Soc. (exec. com. 1975—), Western Minn. Dental Study Club, Omicron Kappa Upsilon. Lutheran (chmn. bd. deacons, pres. congregation). Club: Pipestone Country (past pres., dir.). Home: 910 3d Ave SW Pipestone MN 56164 Office: 101 2d St SE Pipestone MN 56164

OLSTON, MARY KAY, sch. psychologist; b. Milw., Oct. 27, 1949; d. Gordon Rhodes and Mary Anne (Popp) Olston; B.A., Carroll Coll., 1970; M.S., U. Wis. at Milw., 1971. Asso. sch. psychologist Milw. Pub. Schs., 1971-74, sch. psychologist, 1974—; research asst. U. Wis. at Madison, 1973—. Mem. Am. Psychol. Assn., Wis. Sch. Psychol. Assn., Milw. Pub. Schs. Adminstrs. and Suprs. Council, Milw. Pub. Schs. Adminstrv. Women's Assn., Milw. Pub. Schs. Psychologists Assn. (mem. exec. bd. 1971-72, 76-77). Home: 10541 W Woodward Ave Wauwatosa WI 53222 Office: 5225 W Vliet St Milwaukee WI 53201

O'MAHONEY, MICHAEL TERRENCE, psychologist; b. Chgo., May 7, 1943; s. James Fanahan and Mary Terese (Roche) O'M.; B.S., Ill. Inst. Tech., 1969, M.S., 1970, Ph.D., 1972; m. Linda Ann Bliznik, May 30, 1967; children—Jean Marie, Michael T., Maura Elizabeth. Research scientist Inst. for Juvenile Research, Chgo., 1968-72; instr. psychology Ill. Inst. Tech., Chgo., 1972-75; dir. research and evaluation Mental Health Center of LaSalle County, Ottawa, Ill., 1974-75; vis. prof. St. Xaviers Coll., Chgo., 1975; asst. prof. psychiatry U. Ill. Med. Sch., 1973-75; asst. dir. psychol. services Cook County Sch. Nursing, Chgo., 1972-75; asso., dept. psychiatry Northwestern U. Med. Sch., Chgo., 1975—; treatment coordinator, out-patient dept. Inst. of Psychiatry, Northwestern Meml. Hosp., Chgo., 1975—. Served with U.S. Army, 1964-67. Mem. Am., Ill. psychol. assns. Home: 296 Hagans St Elmhurst IL 60126 Office: 320 E Huron St Chicago IL 60611

O'MALLEY, KENNETH GERALD, clergyman, librarian; b. Detroit, Oct. 30, 1936; s. John Peter and Winifred Lucy (McCarthy) O'M.; ed. Mother Good Counsel Coll., Normandy, Mo., 1954-56, House Philosophy Holy Cross Province, 1957-60, House Theology, Louisville, 1960-64, Loyola U., Chgo., summer 1964, U. Detroit, 1964-65; A.M. in L.S., U. Mich., 1968; postgrad. St. Louis U., 1965-68, U. Ill., 1974—. Entered Congregation of the Passion, 1957; ordained priest Roman Catholic Ch., 1964; case worker Cath. Social Services, Detroit, 1964-65; tchr.-librarian Mother of Good Counsel Sem., Warrenton, Mo., 1965-69; co-dir. library Cath. Theol. Union, Chgo., 1969-70, dir. library, 1971—. Week-end chaplain Ft. Leonard Wood, Mo., 1965-68; convenor Chgo. Cluster Theol. Schs. Librarians, 1970-71. Mem. ALA, Am. Theol., Cath. (chmn. sem. sect. 1970-72, chmn. No. Ill. unit 1974—), Ill. library assns., Ind. Voters Ill., Ams. Dem. Action, New Dem. Coalition, Conscience of Am., Nat. Cath. Edn. Assn., Nat. Council Chs. Christ, Intersem. Faculties Union. Address: 5401 S Cornell Ave Chicago IL 60615

O'MALLEY, WILLIAM PAUL, II, dentist; b. Perry, Iowa, Nov. 29, 1905; s. William Paul and Margaret Elizabeth (Tiernan) O'M.; D.D.S., Creighton U., 1929; m. Esther Emily Morrow; 1 son, William Paul III.

Practice dentistry, Merna, Nebr., 1930-37, Oshkosh, Nebr., 1937—. Mem. dist. council Boy Scouts Am., 1950-54. Mem. Am., Nebr. dental assns., U.S., Nebr. chambers commerce, Psi Omega. Roman Catholic. Rotarian. Club: Oshkosh Country. Home: 374 W 3d St Oshkosh NE 69154 Office: 304 Main St Oshkosh NE 69154

O'MEARA, JOHN THOMAS, advt. photographer; b. Delmar, Iowa, Sept. 9, 1929; s. Patrick Austin and Elizabeth Agnas (Costello) O'M.; B.A., St. Ambrose Coll., 1958; m. Donna Patricia Figle, Aug. 6, 1955; children—John Thomas, Paul Patrick, Elizabeth Marie. Interior-exterior decorator, Delmar, 1953-54; photojournalist Davenport (Iowa) Newspapers Inc., 1958-59; advt. photographer Deere & Co., Moline, Ill., 1959—. Served to capt. AUS, 1948-53. Recipient 1st pl. internat. photography Soc. Tech. Writers and Artists, 1971. Mem. Profl. Photographers Am. (nat. prizes 1964, 69), Am. Fedn. Musicians. Home: 4516 14th Ave Rock Island IL 61201 Office: John Deere Rd Moline IL 61265

O'MEARA, MARK THOMAS, surgeon; b. West Bend, Wis., June 23, 1918; s. Joseph Martin and Caroline Ann (Thoma) O'M.; B.S., Marquette U., 1939, M.D., 1942; m. Mary Elizabeth King, May 1, 1948; children—John K., Mark T., Margaret, Daniel, Mary, Jane, Joe. Intern, Milw. County Hosp., 1942-43, resident surgery, 1946-49; practice medicine, specializing in gen. surgery, LaCrosse, Wis., 1949—; pres. Skemp-Grandview Clinic, LaCrosse, Wis., 1969-74; staff, St. Francis Hosp., LaCrosse; asso. preceptor Wis. State Med. Bd. Examiners, 1973. Pres. LaCrosse Bd. Health, 1966-72. Served to capt., M.C., USNR, 1943-46. Diplomate Am. Bd. Surgery. Fellow A.C.S.; mem. Wis. Surg. Soc., LaCrosse C. of C., Phi Chi, Alpha Sigma Nu. Democrat. Roman Catholic. Clubs: Elks, Lions, K.C., LaCrosse Country (dir. 1965-68). Editor-in-chief Marquette Med. Rev., 1941-42. Home: 2536 Madison Pl LaCrosse WI 54601 Office: 815 S 10th St LaCrosse WI 54601

O'MEARA, THOMAS FRANCIS, lawyer, b. West Bend, Wis., Dec. 29, 1911; s. Thomas Francis and Emma A. (Pick) O'M.; B.A., U. Notre Dame, 1933; LL.B., U. Wis., 1935; m. Agnes Raiss, Jan. 18, 1941; children—Elizabeth (Mrs. Robert Threlkild), Virginia, Thomas, Mary Frances (Mrs. Phillip Eckert), Agnes (Mrs. John Pier), Patricia, Shelia, Colleen. Admitted to Wis. bar, 1935; since practiced in West Bend; partner firm O'Meara & O'Meara, 1935—; chmn. bd., dir. West Bend Mutual Ins. Co.; dir. West Bend Marine Bank, Moraine Mutual Ins. Co. City atty. City of West Bend, 1941-70; village atty. Village of Germantown (Wis.), 1962—. Bd. dirs. West Bend Meml. Found. Served to lt. comdr. USNR, 1942-45. Fellow Am. Coll. Trial Lawyers, Am. Coll. Probate Counsel; mem. Internat. Assn. Ins. Counsel, Am. Judicature Soc., Am. Legion, VFW, Am., Wis. (mem. bd. govs. 1964-68), Washington County (pres. 1955-56) bar assns., Sigma Chi, Phi Delta Phi. Roman Catholic. K.C. Clubs: Athletic (Milw.); West Bend Country. Home: 915 Walnut St West Bend WI 53095 Office: 622 Elm St PO Box 348 West Bend WI 53095

OMER, SHIRLEY JEAN, newspaper publisher; b. Sanborn, Iowa, Sept. 22, 1927; d. Samuel Milham and Minnie Floy (Finchum) Omer; grad. high sch. Various positions, 1945-50; partner Omer's Cafe, Sanborn, 1950-55; with O'Brien County Bell Newspaper, Primghar, Iowa, 1955—, owner, editor, 1967—; pub. Peterson (Iowa) Patriot, 1966—; co-owner, dir. N.W. Iowa Publishers, Inc., 1974—; instr. linotype operation Iowa Vocat. Rehab., 1960-65. Mem. Primghar Town Council, 1972—; savs. bond chmn. O'Brien County, 1975—. Recipient award for promoting soil conservation in state, Mississippi Valley Assn., 1960. Mem. Nat. Newspaper Assn., Iowa Press Assn., Primghar C. of C. (pres., dir.), Paullina Womens Bowling League (v.p. 1969-71, pres. 1967-69), Baum-Harmon Hosp. Aux. Home: 620 12th St Primghar IA 51245 Office: 612 15th St Primghar IA 51245

OMINSKI, JULIAN MARION, JR., architect; b. Kansas City, Kans., Jan. 16, 1942; s. Julian Marion and Josephine Mary (Mikinski) O.; student Kansas City Jr. Coll., 1959-60; B.Arch. (scholar Univ.), Kans. U., 1964; m. Mary Patricia Imming, Sept. 22, 1964; children—Paula Kay, Jennifer Lynn, Craig Steven. Asso., Angus McCallum & Assos., architect, Kansas City, Mo., 1964-69, Lund/Balderson, architects, Overland Park, Kans., 1969-72; architect, designer Duncan Architects, Inc., 1972—. Recipient 1st Pl. Design award Kans. Masonry Assn., 1962; Thayer Medal award Kans. U., 1964. Mem. AIA (dir. Kansas City chpt. 1974-76, chmn. historic resources 1977, Allied Arts award Kansas City chpt. 1977), Prairie Ridge Homes Assn. (dir. 1970-73), Indian Heights Athletic Assn. (chmn. 1976-77). Democrat. Roman Catholic. Clubs: Cosmopolitan (pres. Shawnee Mission, Kans. 1970-71); Belton Bits and Spurs Saddle. Home: 9912 Wayne St Kansas City MO 64131 Office: 2440 Pershing Rd Crown Center Kansas City MO 61112

OMMODT, DONALD HENRY, dairy co. exec.; b. Flom, Minn., July 7, 1931; s. Henry and Mabel (Kvidt) O.; student Interstate Bus. Coll., 1949-50; m. Evelyn Blilie, June 15, 1957; children—Linette, Kevin, Lee Ann, Jodi. With Farmers State Bank, Waubun, Minn., 1950-53; with Cass-Clay Creamery, Inc., Fargo, N.D., 1953—, gen. mgr., 1965—; mem. N.D. Dairy Products Promotion Commn. Pres., Messiah Lutheran Ch., 1976—; trustee Blue Cross N.D. Mem. N.D. Dairy Industries Assn. (pres., 1970, dir.), Moorhead Area C. of C. (past dir.), N.D. Dairy Assn. (dir.). Home: 1328 Oak St Fargo ND 58102 Office: 200 20th St N Fargo ND 58102

ONDREY, JOSEPH THOMAS, printing co. exec.; b. Cleve., May 15, 1923; s. Joseph Jacob and Elizabeth Gertrude (Feld) O.; B.S., Miami U., Oxford, Ohio, 1946; M.B.A., Case Western Res. U., 1972; m. Teri Tatary, Jan. 10, 1948; children—Carol, David, Thomas, James. Vice-pres. sales promotion William Feather/Printers, Cleve., 1948-61; pres. Mueller Printing Co., Cleve., 1961-71; pres. J.T. Ondrey Assos., Inc., Chagrin Falls, Ohio, 1971-75. Res. Lithograph Co., Cleve., 1975—; editor/pub. Gt. Lakes Jour., Cleve., 1962—; pub. Children's Playmate mag., Cleve., 1961—; dir. Hosp. Computing Corp., Toledo. Councilman, City of Orange (Ohio), 1955-64, pres., 1967-68. Served to capt., USAAF, 1943-45. Decorated Air Medal with 2 clusters. Mem. Printing Assn. Am., Printing Assn. No. Ohio, Am. Angus Assn., League Am. Wheelmen. Club: Chagrin Valley Country. Golden Keys awardee Club Printing House Craftsmen N.Y., 1967. Home: 17444 Ravenna Rd Chanticleer Farm Burton OH 44021 Office: 2342 E 9th St Cleveland OH 44115

O'NEAL, DAVID CORTLAND, lt. gov. Ill.; b. Belleville, Ill., Jan. 24, 1937; s. Floyd Cortland and Edna Ruth (Barrow) O'N.; student McKendree Coll., 1955-56; B.S., St. Louis Coll. Pharmacy, 1962; m. Sandra Finley, Dec. 26, 1958; children—Allison, Kelly. Pres., Westown Pharmacy, Inc., Belleville, 1962-70; sheriff St. Clair County, 1970-76; lt. gov. Ill., 1977—. Mem. adminstrn. justice task force East West Gateway Council, 1971—; mem. Ill. Law Enforcement Commn., 1971-73; chmn. Tech. Advisory Com. on Aging, abandoned mines land reclamation council; chmn. Gov.'s Spl. Commn. on State Mandated Programs; chmn. Ill. Senior Citizens Legis. Forum. Mem. bd. trustees McKendree Coll. Mem. Young Republicans, Mens Rep. Club. Bd. dirs. Okaw Valley council Boy Scouts Am., St. Clair County Health and Welfare Council, Metro-East Health Council. Served with USMC, 1956-59. Recipient Distinguished Service award Belleville Jaycees, 1971; named Outstanding Young Reps., 1971, Humanitarian of the Year, 1973, Outstanding Young Rep. of Nation, 1975. Mem. Belleville C. of C., Madison-St. Clair Profl. Pharmacy Assn. Address: 40 Signal Hill Blvd Belleville IL 62221 Office: Office of Lt Gov State House Springfield IL 62706

O'NEIL, DANNY, entertainment prodn. and mktg. cons.; b. Birmingham, Ala., Dec. 12, 1923; s. William Michael and Nancy Louise (Rule) O'N.; student Ga. Inst. Tech., 1940; m. Patricia Geraghty, Jan. 2, 1953; children—William Michael, Danna, Thomas Michael, Kathleen, Patricia. Mem. staff CBS, N.Y.C., 1943-48, NBC, Los Angeles, 1948-50; pres. Video Advt., Chgo., 1950-56; pres. Gaelic Prodns., Chgo., 1950-56; pres. O'Neil Automatic Corp., Chgo., 1956-63; v.p. Commissary, Inc., Chgo., 1963-66; host-performer ABC-TV, 1967; v.p. Nightingale-Conant Corp., Chgo., 1968-74; chmn. bd., pres. Danny O'Neil Prodns. and Cons. Services, Inc., 1974—; pres. Pro-Sport Mktg. Group, 1975—. Bd. dirs., sec. Chgo. Conv. Bur., Back of Yards Council, Chgo., Little Flower Soc., Chgo., Internat. Livestock Exposition, Chgo. Served with USNR, 1940-42. Decorated Purple Heart. Mem. Nat. Assn. Broadcasters, Nat. Assn. TV Program Execs., Nat. Acad. TV Arts and Scis., Internat. Platform Assn., Bank Mktg. Assn. Clubs: Medinah (Ill.) Country (dir. 1960-63); Oak Park (Ill.) Country; Irish Fellowship (exec. com., dir.) (Chgo.). Home: 518 N East Ave Oak Park IL 60302 Office: 711 South Blvd Oak Park IL 60302

O'NEIL, JACK WILHELM, heating and cooling co. exec.; b. Milw., Mar. 5, 1927; s. Sylvestor Henry and Ora Adeline (Wilhelm) O'N.; B.S. in Journalism, Northwestern U., 1950; m. Mary Alice McManus, Sept. 8, 1949; children—Connie Anne, Eileen Alice. Asst. advt. mgr. Skil Corp., Chgo., 1950-53; advt. and pub. relations mgr. C.A. Dunham Co. div. Signal Oil Co., Chgo., 1953-56; asst. advt. and pub. relations mgr. Am. Air Filter Corp., Louisville, Ky., 1956-59, div. pub. relations and advt. mgr., 1959-63, asst. mktg. mgr., 1963-69, mgr. advt. and pub. relations, 1969-72; pub. relations and advt. mgr. Nat. Can Corp., Chgo., 1972-74; dir. advt. and pub. relations fluid handling div. ITT, Skokie, Ill., 1974—; cons. Steam Heating Mfrs. Assn., 1956-59. Served to 1st lt. USAF, 1943-46. Decorated Air medal. Mem. Pub. Relations Soc. Am. (accredited), Bus./Profl. Advertisers Assn. (dir. Chgo. chpt.), Am. Mktg. Assn. Roman Catholic. Contbr. articles to profl. advt. and pub. relations mags. Home: 627 Clinton Pl Evanston IL 60201 Office: 4711 Golf Rd Skokie IL 60076

O'NEILL, C. WILLIAM, chief justice; b. Marietta, O., Feb. 14, 1916; s. Charles Thompson and Jessie (Arnold) O'N.; A.B., Marietta (O.) Coll., 1938, LL.D. (hon.), 1953; J.D., Ohio State U., 1942; LL.D., Defiance Coll., 1953, Ohio U., 1957, Wilberforce U., 1958, W.Va. U., 1957, Miami U., 1957, Steubenville Coll., 1957, Heidelberg Coll., 1958, Bowling Green State U., 1958, Capital U., 1971, Dickinson Sch. Law, 1975; L.H.D., Bethany Coll., 1971; D.C.L., Ohio Wesleyan U., 1973; D. Pub. Service, Ohio No. U., 1973; m. Betty Estelle Hewson, July 29, 1945; children—Charles William, Peggy Elizabeth. Admitted to Ohio bar, 1942; practiced in Marietta, 1946-50; instr. Marietta Coll., 1949-50; atty. gen. State Ohio, 1951-57, gov., 1957-58; prof. pub. affairs Bethany Coll., 1959-60; asso. justice Supreme Ct. Ohio, 1960-70, chief justice, 1970—. Mem. Spl. Com. on Legal Edn. in Ohio. Mem. Ohio Ho. Reps., rep. Washington County, 1939-50, speaker, 1947-48, minority leader, 1949-50. Vice pres. Nat. Center State Cts., 1977—; chmn. Nat. Conf. Chief Justices, 1977. Trustee Harding Hosp., Worthington, O.; trustee, treas. Riverside Meth. Hosp., Columbus. Served from pvt. to sgt. AUS, 1943-46; ETO. Named one of ten outstanding young men of Am. Jr. C. of C. U.S., 1950, Most Outstanding State Appellate Ct. Judge in U.S., Assn. Trial Lawyers Am., 1974; recipient Centennial Achievement award Ohio State U., 1970; medal Ohio Bar Assn., 1971; Ohio Gov.'s award, 1972; Columbus award Columbus Area C. of C., 1974; Citizen of Year award Kiwanis Club Columbus, 1974; Nat. Criminal Justice award Am. Soc. for Pub. Adminstrn., 1975; Christopher Columbus award Columbus-Day USA Assn., 1975. Mem. Am., Ohio, Washington County, Columbus bar assns., Am. Judicature Soc. (Herbert Harley award 1975), Alumni Assn. Ohio State U. Law Sch. (pres. 1966-67), Ohio State U. Alumni Assn. (pres.), Am. Legion, VFW, Soc. Benchers, Garfield Soc., Phi Beta Kappa, Order of Coif, Delta Upsilon. Republican. (chmn. state conv., 1948). Baptist. Mason (33 deg., K.T., Shriner). Club: University of Columbus (pres. 1967). Home: 1290 Fountaine Dr Columbus OH 43221 Office: State Office Tower Columbus OH 43215

O'NEILL, DANIEL CLARKE, pub. relations exec.; b. Detroit, Feb. 21, 1934; s. Gerald Raphael and Julie Sorrel (O'Dea) O'N.; B.B.A., U. Detroit, 1964; m. Mary Frances Starks, June 29, 1957; children—Daniel, Mary, Patricia, James. Gen. reporter Windsor (Ont.) Daily Star, 1956-58; asst. advt. mgr. Traffic Transport Engring., Inc., Dearborn, Mich., 1958-61; asst. advt. and sales promotion mgr. Ditzler Color div. Pitts. Plate Glass Co., Detroit, 1961-64; pub. relations supr. Detroit Free Press, 1964-66; account supr. A.M. Franco, Inc., Detroit, 1966-67; pub. relations mgr. Shatterproof Glass Corp., Detroit, 1967-69, George Bilson & Assos., Inc., Plymouth, Mich., 1969; communications coordinator Detroit-Wayne County Community Mental Health Bd., 1969—. Served to sgt. USMCR, 1954-56. Mem. Pub. Relations Soc. Am., Nat. Pub. Relations Council Health and Welfare Services, Amvets (dist. comdr. 1967), Sad Sacks, Delta Sigma Pi. Club: Bombay Bicycle. Home: 6131 Cambourne Rd Dearborn Heights MI 48127 Office: 10th Floor Book Bldg Detroit MI 48226

O'NEILL, JOSEPH THOMAS, JR., lawyer; b. St. Paul, Nov. 13, 1931; s. Joseph Thomas and Marie Agnes (O'Connell) O'N.; B.A., U. Notre Dame, 1953; LL.B., U. Minn., 1956; m. Marianne Kenefick, Sept. 11, 1954; children—Kathleen M., Joseph E., Maureen P., Thomas M., John P., Michael D., Kevin D., Shelagh M. Admitted to Minn. bar, 1956; mem. firm Firestone, Fink, Krawetz, Miley & O'Neill, St. Paul, 1959-67, O'Neill, Burke, O'Neill & Dickstad, Ltd., 1968—. Pres., Legal Assistance of Ramsey County, Inc., 1966-68. Chmn. gen. bus. div. St. Paul United Fund. Mem. Minn. Ho. of Reps., 1966-70; mem. Minn. Senate, 1970—, mem. various coms., 1970—. Trustee St. Joseph's Hosp. Served with USAF, 1956-59. Recipient various service awards. Mem. Minn. (chmn. legal aid 1964-71), Ramsey County (mem. exec. council 1967-70) bar assns., St. Thomas Alumni Assn. (pres. 1971-72), Notre Dame Alumni Assn. (city pres. 1959-60; nat. dir. 1968-72). Home: 1381 Summitt Ave St Paul MN 55105 Office: 60 W 4th St St Paul MN 55102

O'NEILL, MICHAEL STEVEN, psychologist; b. Oakland, Calif., Dec. 10, 1944; s. Francis Carroll and Ellen Geraldine (Harper) O'N.; B.S., Brigham Young U., 1965; M.A., U. Utah, 1968, Ph.D., 1974; m. Claudia Moss, Jan. 11, 1964; children—Timalyn, Malachi Merritt, Morggan Patrick. Asso. psychologist, Childrens Center, Salt Lake City, 1969-71; dir. children services Med Nebr. Community Mental Health Center, Grand Island, 1971-74, clin. dir., 1974-75; pvt. clin. practice specializing in children and adolescents, Grand Island, 1975—; advisor cons. mental health, tng. office, Nebr. Head Start, 1973—. Bd. dirs. Childrens Village Grand Island, 1973-75, YMCA, Grand Island, 1975—. USPHS fellow, 1965. Mem. Mem. Am., Midwestern, Rocky Mountain, Oreg., Nebr. psychol. assns., Applied Psychologists Assn. Nebr., Am. Soc. Psychologists in Pvt. Practice, Assn. Children with Learning Disabilities, Nat. Soc. Autistic Children, Sigma Xi. Home: 1603 Gretchen Ave Grand Island NE 68801 Office: 706 1st St W Grand Island NE 68801

O'NEILL, RICHARD BURNS, savs. and loan co. exec.; b. Graceville, Minn., May 11, 1918; s. Richard C. and Gracia M. (Burns) O'N.; student St. Thomas Coll., 1936-37; B.B.A., U. Minn., 1942; m. Mary Alice Mast, June 5, 1943; children—Margaret (Mrs. J.T. Beaulieu), William Bernard, Richard Thomas. Accountant, Morris, Minn., 1946-63; pres. Morris Realty, Inc., Morris, 1946-67; sec., treas. 1st Fed. Savs. & Loan of Morris, 1956-67, dir., 1956-67; exec. sec., treas. 1st Fed. Savs. & Loan of Hastings, Minn., 1967—, dir., 1967—; pres. S & L Agy., Inc., Hastings, 1967—; dir. Hastings Indsl. Devel. Corp., 1972—; pres. Citizen Devel. Corp., Morris, 1956—. Served from 2d lt. to maj., Transp. Corps, AUS, 1942-46. Mem. Morris Civic and Commerce Assn. (chmn. indsl. devel. com. 1956-67), West Central Devel. Assn., Minn. Ind. Ins. Agts. Assn. (regional sec. 1952-53), Hastings Ins. Agts. Assn. (pres. 1973), Am. Legion, VFW, U. Minn. Alumni Assn. Lion (pres. Morris chpt. 1963-64, pres. Hastings chpt. 1973-74), K.C. (grand knight 1974-75). Club: Hastings Country Club. Home: 1120 Bahls Dr Hastings MN 55033 Office: 122 E 2d St Hastings MN 55033

O'NEILL, WILLIAM JAMES, leasing and transp. exec.; b. Cleve., Sept. 21, 1906; s. Hugh and Louise (Berchtold) O'N.; A.B., U. Notre Dame, 1928; m. Dorothy Kundtz, May 28, 1932; children—William James, Dorothy (Mrs. John Donahey), Kathleen (Mrs. William France), Molly (Mrs. George Sweeney), Timothy. Operating mgr. Superior Transfer Co., 1928-30, Motor Express, Inc., 1928-30; v.p., chief operating officer over-the-road carrier subsidiaries. U.S. Truck Lines, Inc. of Del., 1930-37; founder, owner, pres., chief exec. officer Niagara Motor Express, Inc., 1938-59; chmn. bd. Lease Plan Internat. Corp., N.Y.C., 1959-61; pres., chief exec. officer Leaseway Ltd. (Can.), 1959-75; founder, pres., chief exec. officer Leaseway Transp. Corp., 1961-69, chmn. bd., chief exec. officer, 1969-75; chmn. bd., founder, chief exec. officer Leaseway Intercontinental (LEASECO) S.A., Zug, Switzerland, 1962-72; partner N.Y. Yankees; dir. Portec, Inc. Trustee, pres. O'Neill Bros. Found.; trustee, mem. distbn. com. The Cleveland Found.; trustee Sherwick Found.; 1st lay pres. Gilmour Acad., Gates Mills. Ohio. Mem. Newcomen Soc. N.Am. Clubs: Metropalitan (N.Y.C.); The Country, Pepper Pike Country; Chagrin Valley Hunt (Gates Mills); Union (Cleve.). Home: Clanonderry Ct 33917 Hackney Rd Daisy Hill RD 3 Chagrin Falls OH 44022 Office: Two Commerce Park Sq 23200 Chagrin Blvd Cleveland OH 44122

O'NEILL, WILLIAM JAMES, JR., transp. co. exec.; b. Cleve., Aug. 28, 1933; s. William James and Dorothy (Kundtz) O'N.; B.S. cum laude, Georgetown U., 1955; J.D., Harvard U., 1958; m. Deborah J. Baker, Oct. 22, 1966; children—Alec M., Sara L., Jessie A., Laura E. Admitted to Ohio bar, 1958; gen. counsel Leaseway Transp. Corp. and subs.'s, 1961-67, East coast group head, Phila, 1967-68; v.p. East coast group, 1968-69, sr. v.p., Cleve., 1969-74, pres., chief operating officer, 1974—, also dir. Mem. Dyke Coll. Corp., Cleve.; trustee O'Neill Bros. Found., Gilmour Acad., Bluecoats, Inc. (all Cleve.). Served to capt. USAF, 1958-61. Recipient Air Force Commendation medal with oak leaf cluster; named Man of Year, Gilmour Acad., 1974. Mem. Am. Bar Assn. Roman Catholic. Clubs: Hunting Valley Gun, Country, Cleve. Polo. Home: 2735 Cranlyn Rd Shaker Heights OH 44122 Office: 21111 Chagrin Blvd Cleveland OH 44122

ONG, JOHN DOYLE, rubber products co. exec.; b. Uhrichsville, O., Sept. 29, 1933; s. Louis Brosee and Mary Ellen (Liggett) O.; B.A., Ohio State U., 1954, M.A., 1954; LL.B., Harvard, 1957; m. Mary Lee Schupp, July 20, 1957; children—John Francis Harlan, Richard Penn Blackburn, Mary Katherine Caine. Admitted to Ohio bar, 1958; asst. counsel B.F. Goodrich Co., Akron, 1961-66, group v.p., 1972-73, dir., 1973—, exec. v.p., 1973-74, vice chmn. bd., 1974-75, pres., 1975—; asst. to pres. Internat. B.F. Goodrich Co., Akron, 1966-69, v.p., 1969-70, pres., 1970-72; dir. Cooper Industries, Kroger Co. Vice pres. exploring Gt. Trail council Boy Scouts Am., 1974—; bus. adv. com. Transp. Center, Northwestern U. Trustee St. John's Home for Girls, Painesville, 1969-71, Western Res. Acad., Hudson, O., 1975— Kent State U. Found., 1974-76, Bexley Hall Sem., Rochester, N.Y., 1974—; nat. trustee Nat. Symphony Orch., 1975—; adv. bd. Blossom Music Center. Served with Judge Adv. Gen.'s Corps, AUS, 1957-61. Mem. Ohio Bar Assn. (corp. counsel sect. bd. govs. 1962-73, chmn. 1970), Rubber Mfrs. Assn. (dir.), Hudson Library and Hist. Soc. (pres. 1971-72, trustee) Phi Beta Kappa, Phi Alpha Theta. Episcopalian. Clubs: Akron City, Portage Country (Akron); Links, Union League (N.Y.C.); Union (Cleve.); Country of Hudson (O.); Georgetown (Washington). Home: 230 Aurora St Hudson OH 44236 Office: 500 S Main St Akron OH 44318

ONGARO, MARIO PETER, psychologist, clergyman; b. Verona, Italy, Apr. 7, 1926; s. Giuseppe and Julia (Bonfante) O.; came to U.S., 1947, naturalized, 1958; B.A., Athenaeum of Ohio, 1951; M.A. in Ednl. Guidance, Xavier, U., Cin., 1961, postgrad. sch. psychology, 1968-70; M.A. in L.S., U. Mich., 1964; Ordained priest Roman Catholic Ch., 1951; instr. philosophy, classical langs. Sacred Heart Sem., Monroe, Mich., 1952-56; pastoral ministry with Indians, San Diego County, Calif., 1956-58; instr. classical langs. Sacred Heart Sem., Cin., 1958-61, philosophy and classical langs., Monroe, 1961-64, sch. counselor, Cin., 1964-68; psychologist in pvt. practice, Cin. Mem. Am., Ohio psychol. assns., Am. Orthopsychiat. Assn., Soc. for Personality Assessment. Address: 8108 Beechmont Ave Cincinnati OH 45230

ONOFRIO, ANGELO MICHAEL, counseling psychologist; b. Chgo., June 26, 1947; s. Angelo M. and Lucille Marie (Bagnolia) O.; B.A. with distinction, U. Ill., 1969; M.A. in Counseling Psychology, Roosevelt U., 1974. Tchr. of reading and English, Hyde Park High Sch., Chgo., 1970-71; tchr. St. Joseph High Sch., Westchester, Ill., 1971-72; grad. asst. Coll. of Edn., Roosevelt U., Chgo., 1972-74; reading therapist and counselor Student Counseling Service, U. Ill., Chgo., 1974; English tutor Alexander-Smith Acad., Chgo., 1974-75; counselor Morton Coll., Cicero, Ill., 1975—, also instr. English, 1975—. Mem. Am., Ill. personnel and guidance assns., Nat. Council Tchrs. of English, Nat. Vocat. Guidance Assn., U. Ill., Roosevelt U. alumni assns. Democrat. Roman Catholic. Home: 1135 S Clinton Ave Oak Park IL 60304 Office: 3801 S Central Ave Cicero IL 60650

OOST, STEWART IRVIN, educator; b. Grand Rapids, Mich., May 20, 1921; s. Jacob John and Bessie Ola (Stewart) O.; A.B., U. Chgo., 1941, M.A., 1947, Ph.D., 1950; postgrad. Yale U., 1943-44. Tchr., Starr Commonwealth for Boys, Albion, Mich., 1941-42; instr. history So. Methodist U., 1948-50, asst. prof., 1950-54, asso. prof., 1954-59; asso. prof. ancient history U. Chgo., 1959-64, prof., 1965—. Served with U.S. Army, 1942-46. Ford Fellow, 1955-56. Mem. Am. Hist. Assn., Am. Philol. Assn., Classical Assn. Middle West and South, Phi Beta Kappa. Republican. Methodist. Club: Quadrangle. Author: Roman Policy in Epirus and Acarnania in the Age of the Roman Conquest of Greece, 1954; Galla Placidia Augusta: A Biographical Essay, 1968. Mem. editorial bd. Classical Philology, 1959—; cons. Ency. Britannica. Contbr. articles to profl. jours. Home: 9652 S Seeley Ave Chicago IL 60643 Office: 1050 E 59th St Chicago IL 60637

OPDAHL, KEITH MICHAEL, educator; b. Cook County, Ill., Nov. 4, 1934; s. Olaf Solomen and Florence Hilda (Holmquist) O.; B.A., Denison U., 1956; M.A., U. Ill., Champaign, 1957, Ph.D., 1961; m. Martha Ines Donovan, June 6, 1965; children—Michael, Cristina. Teaching asst. U. Ill., 1957-61; asst. prof. English, U. Wis., Madison,

1961-67; asst. prof. DePauw U., 1967-69, asso. prof., 1969-77, prof., 1977—. U. Ill. grantee, 1959-60; U. Wis. grantee, 1962-65; DePauw U. grantee, 1968-71; Fulbright grantee, 1971-72. Mem. AAUP, Modern Lang. Assn. Author: The Novels of Saul Bellow, 1967. Home: 714 Highridge St Greencastle IN 46135 Office: 304 Asbury Hall DePauw U Greencastle IN 46135

OPENSHAW, CALVIN REYNOLDS, surgeon; b. Salt Lake City, Nov. 4, 1921; s. Clarence Roy and Elna Dehlin (Shipp) O.; B.S., U. Utah, 1942, M.D., 1944; M.S., U. Minn., 1953; m. Blanche Hiley, Dec. 11, 1948; children—Calvin Reynolds, Susan Beaver, Michael Browne; m. 2d, Evelyn Constance Miller, Dec. 19, 1973. Intern, Salt Lake County Gen. Hosp., 1944-45; resident, research fellow surgery U. Utah, Salt Lake City, 1946-47; fellow in surgery Mayo Found., 1948-51, fellow in thoracic surgery, 1951-53; chief thoracic surgery VA Hosp., Fort Douglas, Utah, 1955-56; practice medicine specializing in surgery, Med. Center, Hutchinson, Kans., 1957—, pres. center, 1976-77; asst. clin. prof. surgery U. Utah, 1955-56. Served with USN, 1945-46, 53-54; PTO. Mem. AMA, A.C.S., Southwestern Surg. Congress, Am. Legion. Republican. Congregationalist. Club: Elks. Home: 1824 N Main St Hutchinson KS 67501 Office: 1100 N Main St Hutchinson KS 67501

OPP, PAUL FRANKLIN, JR., hosp. adminstr.; b. Fairmont, W.Va., Feb. 10, 1937; s. Paul Franklin and Helen Katherine (Crawford) O.; student W.Va. U., 1955-56; B.S. in Bus. Adminstrn., Fairmont State Coll., 1960; M.Bus. and Hosp. Adminstrn., Xavier U., 1963; m. Paulette Elizabeth Hogan, Aug. 16, 1969; children—Richard Patrick, Paul Elliott, Ian Charles Crawford. Evening adminstr. Michael Reese Hosp.-Med. Center, Chgo., 1967-69, asst. adminstr., asst. to med. dir., 1969-71; asst. adminstr. St. Bernard Hosp., Chgo., 1971-73, 73-75, acting adminstr., 1973; adminstr. Edgewater Hosp., Chgo., 1975-76, S. Suburban Hosp., Hazel Crest, Ill., 1976—. Served to 1st lt., Med. Service Corps, USAF, 1964-67. Mem. Chgo. Area Healthcare Safety Assn. (co-founder, dir.), Nat. Safety Council (co-founder, hosp. and healthcare sect., chmn. disaster planning com. 1970-71, region 5 chmn. 1971-74, exec. com. 1970—), Am. Hosp. Assn., Am. Pub. Health Assn., Nat. Fire Protection Assn., Chgo. Assn. Commerce and Industry, Nat. Rifle Assn., Sigma Alpha. Contbr. articles on hosp. safety, disaster planning, areawide disaster planning to profl. jours. Home: 4211 W 175th Pl Country Club Hills IL 60477 Office: S Suburban Hosp 178th St and Kedzie Ave Hazel Crest IL 60429

OPPENHEIM, BERNARD EDWARD, radiologist, educator; b. Chgo., July 5, 1937; s. Michael Robert and Mae (Greenwald) O.; B.S. in Math., U. Ariz., 1959; M.D., U. Chgo., 1963; m. Renee Lee Roth, June 9, 1963; children—Stephen Barry, David Jeffrey, Sharon Beth, Daniel Howard. Intern, Michael Reese Hosp., Chgo., 1963-64; resident radiology U. Chgo.-Hosps., 1964-67, instr. radiology, 1970-71, asst. prof., 1971-75, asso. prof., 1975-76, asst. dir. nuclear medicine, 1971-74, acting dir., 1974-76; asso. prof., asst. dir. nuclear medicine Ind. U. Sch. Medicine, Indpls., 1976—; cons. Nat. Cancer Inst. Served to maj. M.C., AUS, 1967-70. James Picker scholar radiol. research, 1972-74. Mem. Soc. Nuclear Medicine, Radiation Research Soc., Phi Beta Kappa, Phi Kappa Phi, Pi Mu Epsilon. Discoverer statis. method for motion correction in liver scanning; investigator biases in studies fetal irradiation; pioneer three-dimensional reconstrn. from incomplete views. Office: 2033 Whitewood Ct Indianapolis IN 46260

ORANDI, AHMAD, urologist; b. Rafsenjan, Iran, Dec. 26, 1931; s. Reza and Roack-sara (Orandi) O.; came to U.S., 1956, naturalized, 1969; B.S., Am. Alborz Coll., Tehran, Iran, 1950; M.D., Tehran U., 1957; m. Ruth L. Ott, Aug. 18, 1962; children—Margaret, Susan, Linda. Intern, City Hosp., Binghamton, N.Y., 1958-59; resident Bellevue Hosp., Cornell U. div., N.Y.C., 1959-64, fellow in research, Cornell Div. Urology, 1964, asso. dir., 1965; practice medicine specializing in urology, Fergus Falls, Minn., 1966—; instr. urology, U. Minn., 1967; cons. St. Mary's Hosp., Detroit Lakes, Minn., St. Francis Hosp., Breckenridge, Minn.; mem. Minn. Med. Peace People-to-People delegation, Europe, 1969, S. Am., 1971. Recipient honors achievement award, Purdue Found., N.Y.C., 1965, F.C. Valentine fellow, N.Y. Acad. Medicine, 1965, His Majesty Shah of Iran's Royal award for one of 10 Outstanding Iranian students abroad, 1961, 1st place sci. exhibits award, Am. Urological Assn., 1971. Moslem. Office: 615 Mill St S Suite 125 Fergus Falls MN 56537

ORANDI, MEHDI, pathologist; b. Iran, Nov. 29, 1929; s. Reza and Rokh Sarah Orandi; came to U.S., 1958, naturalized, 1964; M.D., U. Tehran, 1955; m. Katherine Shirley Wilcox, Aug. 1, 1959; children—Maryam, Yasmin, Shirene, Sarah, Adam. Intern, Binghamton (N.Y.) Gen. Hosp., 1958-60; resident anatomic pathology McGill U., Montreal, Que., Can., 1960-61; resident clin. pathology Med. Coll. Ga., Augusta, 1961-63; dir. City Hosp., Rafsenjan, Iran, 1957-58; dir. labs. Lake Region Hosp., Fergus Falls, Minn., 1963—; cons. Tricounty Hosp., Wadena, Minn., 1963—; adv. bd. St. Paul ARC Blood Bank. Served to lt. M.C., Iranian Army, 1955-57. Diplomate Am. Bd. Pathology. Fellow Am. Soc. Clin. Pathology, Coll. Am. Pathologists; mem. AMA, Minn. Med. Assn., Minn. Coroners and Med. Examiners Assn. (pres. 1977-78). Contbr. to med. jours. Home: 2614 Lakeview Dr Fergus Falls MN 56537 Office: 712 S Cascade Ave Fergus Falls MN 56537

ORCHARD, EDGAR LEE, corrugated box mfg. co. exec.; b. St. Louis, Apr. 20, 1926; s. Herman Charles and Ethel (Winner) O.; B.S., Purdue U., 1950; m. Donna Lee Arenson, Feb. 5, 1957; children—Laura Ellen, Barri Louise, Caroline Courtney. With Orchard Paper Co., St. Louis, 1950-64; v.p. Tobey Fine Papers, St. Louis, 1965; v.p. Ajax Corrugated Paper Co., St. Louis, 1966; pres. Orchard Container Corp., 1967-77, Orchard Consol. Industries, Inc., 1977—. Mem. St. Louis Repertory Theater, 1962-64, 64—; mem. Gateway Theater, 1964-67, v.p., 1965-67; mem. St. Clair Crime Control Commn., 1968; mem. St. Louis Art Mus., St. Louis Philharmonic Assn., Nelson Mus., Kansas City, St. Louis Asian Art Soc.; founding mem., chmn. bd. rev. St. Louis Eagle Scout Bd., 1969—; bd. dirs. Loretto Hilton Repertory Theater, Jewish Relations council Boy Scouts Am., Mo. C. of C., Edn. Council Adminstrv. Com. (chmn.). Served with USNR, 1944-46. Mem. Conservation Fedn. Mo., Fibre Box Assn., Purdue Alumni Assn., Am. Def. Preparedness Assn., Assn. Ind. Corrugated Converters (v.p., dir. 1974—), Nat. Eagle Scout Assn., Sigma Alpha Mu. Jewish (treas. temple 1970-73). Clubs: Masons (32 deg.), Shriners, Mo. Athletic, Pike County Country. Home: 1 Robindale Dr Saint Louis MO 63124 Office: 8230 Forsyth Blvd Clayton MO 63105

ORDINACHEV, MILES DONALD, educator; b. St. Louis, Oct. 23, 1926; s. Delmar Marko and Ann Louise (Allen) O.; B.S., Wash. U., St. Louis, 1968, postgrad. computer sci., 1975; children—Linda, Jean. With Midwest Pipe & Supply Co., St. Louis, 1944-47, Bailey Tech. Sch., St. Louis, 1950-53; dir. instr. Mo. Tech. Sch., St. Louis, 1953-63; instruction programmer Perceptual Devel. Labs., St. Louis, 1963-66; tchr., chmn. indsl. electronics dept. South County Tech. High Sch., Sunset Hills, Mo., 1966—. Mem. Am., Mo. vocat. assns., Spl. Sch. Dist. Community Tchrs. Assn. (pres. 1969-70), Mo., Greater St. Louis tchrs. assns., Midwest Soc. Individual Psychology, Assn. Supervision and Curriculum Devel. Clubs: Mason, Shriner, Computer. Home: 9541 Avila Dr Affton MO 63123 Office: 12721 W Watson Rd Sunset Hills MO 63127

ORE, DONALD EUGENE, pedodontist; b. Harvey, Ill., Jan. 26, 1934; s. Carl Victor and Elizabeth (Webb) O.; B.S., U. Ill., 1957, D.D.S., 1960, M.S., 1960; m. Audrey Roberta Talpa, Sept. 1, 1956; children—Cathy Lynn, Cheryl Beth, David Henry. USPHS research fellow U. Ill., 1959, instr., 1963, asst. prof., 1964-67, asso. prof., 1967; pvt. practice dentistry, Homewood, Ill., 1964-75, Chicago Heights, Ill., 1975—, specializing in pedodontics, 1968—; mem. cons. staff Ill. Masonic Med. Center. Chmn. adv. bd. Prairie State Coll., Chicago Heights, Ill., 1972. Served to capt. Dental Corps, U.S. Army, 1960-63. Fulbright prof. to Brazil, 1968. Fellow Am. Coll. Dentists; mem. Sigma Xi, Omicron Kappa Upsilon. Club: Masons. Contbr. articles to profl. jours. Home: PO Box 161 Flossmoor IL 60422 Office: 165 W 10th St Chicago Heights IL 60411

O'REILLY, CLARENCE JOSEPH, physician; b. Chgo., Dec. 29, 1922; s. Clarence Michael and Anna Loretta (Curtis) O'R.; student pre-med. studies Loyola U., Chgo., 1940-42, M.D., 1946; m. Geraldine Ann Silha, Feb. 26, 1949; children—Michael, William, Daniel, Mary, Maura, David. Intern, Cook County Hosp., Chgo., 1946-47; resident in internal medicine Hines VA Hosp., Maywood, Ill., 1950-52; practice medicine specializing in internal medicine, Palos Heights, Ill., 1950—; sr. mem. med. staff Little Co. Mary Hosp., Evergreen Park, Ill., 1950—, pres. med. staff, 1972, trustee, 1972—; mem. med. staff Palos Community Hosp., Palos Park, Ill., 1972—. Served to capt. M.C., U.S. Army, 1948-50. Recipient Caritas award J.P. Kennedy Sch. Retarded Children, Palos Park, 1975; Service award Little Co. Mary Hosp., 1975; diplomate Am. Bd. Internal Medicine. Mem. AMA, A.C.P., Am. Soc. Internal Medicine, Cook County Hosp. Alumni Assn. Roman Cath. Home: 12344 S Oak Park Ave Palos Heights IL 60463 Office: 12150 S Harlem Ave Palos Heights IL 60463

O'REILLY, DONALD EUGENE, research scientist; b. Chgo., Mar. 22, 1930; s. Eugene C. and Winifred M. (Gallagher) O'R.; B.S. in Chem. Engring., Purdue U., 1951; M.S., U. Chgo., 1952, Ph.D. in Chem. Physics (U.S. Rubber Co. fellow, DuPont fellow), 1955; m. Joan T. Clark, July 26, 1952; children—Patricia Marmitt, Susan, Thomas, Donald, Jane, Roger, John. Research scientist Gulf Research & Devel. Co., Pitts., 1955-60; sr. scientist Argonne (Ill.) Nat. Lab., 1960—. Fellow Am. Inst. Chemists; mem. Phys. Club Chgo. (pres. 1970-71), Am. Phys. Soc., Am. Chem. Soc. Contbr. articles to sci. jours. Home: 7930 Woodglen Ln Downers Grove IL 60515 Office: 9700 S Cass Ave Argonne IL 60439

O'REILLY, FRANCIS JUSTUS, oil refining co. exec.; b. Girard, Kans., Oct. 27, 1912; s. Patrick Arthur and Harriet Elizabeth (Peak) O'R.; B.S. in Chem. Engring., Kansas State U., 1935; M.B.A., U. Tulsa, 1971; m. Flossie Mae Smith, Oct. 3, 1937; children—Flossie Kathleen O'Reilly Bales, Larry James. With Skelly Oil Co., 1935-73, spl. asst. to v.p. mfg., Tulsa, 1941-46, refinery supt., El Dorado, Kans., 1946-61, engring., Tulsa, 1961-63, mem. tech. services, 1963-65, project devel., 1965-73; co-owner, v.p., gen. mgr. Mid Am. Refining Co., Inc., Chanute, Kans., 1973—, also dir.; dir. Nuclear Fuel Services. Deacon First Baptist Churches, El Dorado, Tulsa, Chanute, 1937-77; bd. trustees Ottawa Kans. U., 1954-77; pres. Kans. Baptist Conv., 1961. Mem. Am. Inst. Chem. Engrs., Eastern Kans. Oil and Gas Assn., Independent Petroleum Assn. Am., Kansas Assn. Bus. and Industry, Am. Petroleum Inst., Am. Petroleum Refiners Assn. (pres. 1977), Nat. Petroleum Refiners Assn. (dir. 1973-77). Republican. Club: Rotary. Home: 1114 S Tennessee St Chanute KS 66720 Office: PO Box 31 Chanute KS 66720

O'REILLY, ROBERT CLYDE, educator; b. Girard, Kans., Dec. 17, 1928; s. Patrick Arthur and Harriet Elizabeth (Peak) O'R.; B.S., Kans. State Coll., 1951; M.A., U. Wyo., 1956; Ed.D. (Univ. fellow), U. Kans., 1962; m. Marjorie Ione Newell, May 29, 1954; children—Daniel, Timothy, Megan. Tchr., admnstr. Robinson (Kans.) Pub. Schs., 1953-60; asso. prof. edn., dir. evening div. Morningside Coll., Sioux City, Iowa, 1961-64; asso. prof. edn., asso. dean grad. studies, dir. grants and research U. Nebr. Omaha, 1964-73, prof. ednl. adminstrn., 1973—. Mem. Ralston (Nebr.) Bd. Edn., 1972—; trustee MidContinent Regional Ednl. Lab., 1966-71. Served with AUS, 1951-53. Mem. Am. Ednl. Research Assn., Nat. Orgn. Legal Problems of Edn. Phi Delta Kappa. Club: Lions. Home: 5141 S 83d St Ralston NE 68127 Office: Coll Edn U Nebr at Omaha 60th and Dodge Omaha NE 68101

O'REILLY, ROGER KEVIN, lawyer; b. Chgo., Nov. 8, 1934; s. Eugene Carolan and Winifred Marguerite (Gallagher) O'R.; B.S., Notre Dame U., 1956; J.D., Chgo. Kent Law Sch., 1959; m. Dorothy Isabel Mukenschnabl, Apr. 28, 1962; children—Margaret Mary, Kevin, Molly, John, Kathleen. Admitted to Ill. bar, 1959; atty. Askow, Stevens & Hardy, Chgo., 1960; atty. George Miller, Chgo., 1961-64; atty. Baker & McKenzie, Chgo., 1964-65; atty., partner O'Reilly & Quetsch, Wheaton, Ill., 1965—; asso. prof. John Marshall Law Sch., 1963-65. Mem. Sch. Bd., St. Petronille-Glen Ellyn, Ill., 1972—, pres., 1974-75. Served with U.S. Army, 1959-60. Mem. Ill., Chgo., DuPage bar assns., Ill. Def. Counsel, Am., Ill. trial lawyers assns., Am. Assn. Trial Lawyers, Fedn. Ins. Counsel, Am. Arbitration Assn., Phi Alpha Delta. Home: 1528 Gamon Rd Wheaton IL 60187 Office: 200 E Willow St Wheaton IL 60187

ORF, DOUGLAS JAMES, air pollution specialist; b. Dayton, Ohio, Feb. 3, 1948; s. James Joseph and E. Jewell (Hurt) O.; B.S., U. Dayton, 1970; m. Gemma Natalie Massa, May 22, 1971; 1 dau., Angelique Marie. Environmentalist, Bur. Environmental Health, City of Dayton, 1970-71; environmentalist Montgomery County Combined Gen. Health Dist., Dayton, Ohio, 1971-72; air pollution specialist, Engring. Services Unit, Regional Air Pollution Control Agy., Dayton, Ohio, 1972—, working supr. motor vehicle emissions testing program, agy. expert on energy, motor vehicle emissions, sulfur dioxide, fuels. Mem. Soc. Automotive Engrs. Home: 2199 Vemco Dr Bellbrook OH 45305 Office: 451 W 3d St Dayton OH 45422

ORFANOS, MINNIE, librarian; b. Hinsdale, Ill., Dec. 10, 1921; d. Antonious George and Catherine (Lekatsos) Orfanos; Ph.B., Northwestern U., 1954; M.A. in L.S., U. Mich., 1958. Library clk. Chgo. Pub. Library, 1940-43; library asst. Dental Sch. Library, Northwestern U., Chgo., 1943-45, asst. librarian, 1945-50, acting librarian, 1950-52, librarian, 1952—. Sec. governing bd. Midwest Regional Med. Library, 1971-72, vice chmn., 1973, pres., 1974; cons., surveyor for Assn. Canadian Faculty of Dentistry, 1970-72; mem. grant rev. com. NIH, 1974; mem. Northwestern U. Library Council, 1975—; cons. dental libraries. Recipient Merit award for distinguished service to dentistry Am. Coll. Dentists, 1967. Mem. Med. Library Assn. (dental group chmn. 1952, sec. Midwest regional group 1957, pres. 1968; exchange com. 1964, chmn. exchange com. 1965—, exec. com. midwest group 1965—, cons. to coms., fin. trustee 1976-77), Am. Assn. Dental Schs., Sigma Phi Alpha. Roman Catholic. Contbr. articles to profl. publs. Compiler list of textbooks for dental curriculum Acad. Ednl. Devel., 1977. Home: 45 Wilmette Ave Glenview IL 60025 Office: 311 E Chicago Ave Chicago IL 60611

ORGLER, RUDOLPH JOHN, architect; b. Breslau, Germany, Aug. 22, 1910; s. Ernst and Lilly (Friedmann) O.; came to U.S., 1938, naturalized, 1948; Architect, Tech. Univs. Breslau and Berlin (Germany), 1933; m. Oneta F. Fisher, Jan. 2, 1977. Pvt. practice architecture, Cleve., 1948—. Instr. Cleve. Engring. Inst., 1945-52. Mem. Cleve., Nat. socs. profl. engrs. Jewish. Club: Mason. Home: 14004 Watt Rd Novelty OH 44072 Office: 23366 Commerce Park Rd Beachwood OH 44122

ORLAND, FRANK J., oral microbiologist, educator, historiographer; b. Little Falls, N.Y., Jan. 23, 1917; s. Michael and Rose (Dorner) O.; A.A., U. Chgo., 1937, M.S., 1945, Ph.D., 1949; B.S., U. Ill., 1939, D.D.S., 1941; m. Phyllis Therese Mrazek, M.D., May 8, 1943; children—Frank R., Carl P., June R., Ralph M. With U. Chgo., 1941—, beginning as intern Zoller Meml. Dental Clinic, 1941-42, successively Zoller fellow and asst. in dental surgery, 1942-49, instr., asst. prof., asso. prof., prof. dental surgery, 1949—, instr., asst. prof., asso. prof. microbiology, 1950-58, research asso. (prof.), 1958-64; attending dentist Country Home for Convalescent Children, 1942-45; dir. W.G. Zoller Meml. Dental Clinic of U. Chgo., 1954-67; spl. cons. NIH (Nat. Inst. Dental Research), USPHS, Bethesda, Md. Panel mem. on dental drugs The Nat. Formulary; mem. Com. Instnl. Coop. among M.W. Univs. (representing U. Chgo. on dental subcom.). Past chmn. adv. council Forest Park (Ill.) Bd. Edn.; mem. Forest Park Citizens Com. for Better Schs.; past pres. Garfield Sch. P.T.A., 1953-55; founding pres. Hist. Soc. Forest Park, 1976—. Recipient Research Essay award Chgo. Dental Soc., 1955. Diplomate Am. Bd. Microbiology. Fellow Am. Coll. Dentists, Inst. Medicine Chgo. (chmn. sub-com. publ. communications), Am. Acad. Microbiology, A.A.A.S.; mem. Internat. Assn. Dental Research (past pres., past councillor Chgo. sect.; past dir., past chmn. publs. com., chmn. com. on history, internat. pres. 1971-72), Am. Dental Assn. (past chmn. council dental therapeutics), Am. Assn. Dental Schs. (past chmn. conf. oral microbiology, past chmn. com. on advanced edn.), Am. Assn. Dental Editors, Am. Assn. U. Profs., Ill. Soc. Med. Research, Fedn. Dentaire Internat., Am. Acad. History Dentistry (pres.), Am. Forestry Assn., Sigma Xi, Gamma Alpha. Clubs: Quadrangle, Chicago Literary. Author: The First Fifty Year History of the International Association for Dental Research, 1974. Editor: Journal Dental Research, 1958-69. Home: 521 Jackson Blvd Forest Park IL 60130 Office: 950 E 59th St Chicago IL 60637

ORLAND, HENRY, composer, condr., coll. adminstr.; b. Saarbruecken, Germany, Apr. 23, 1918; s. Theodor and Hedwig (Weill) O.; came to U.S., 1939, naturalized, 1944; certificat d'etudes U. Strasbourg (France); B.Mus., Northwestern U., 1949, M.Mus., 1950, Ph.D., 1959. Acting dean, prof. St. Louis Inst. Music, 1960-63; chmn. music dept. Florissant Valley Coll., St. Louis, 1963—; music dir., condr. St. Louis String Ensemble, 1961-66, Maplewood-Richmond Heights Symphony Orch., St. Louis, 1964—; artistic dir., condr. Midwest Chamber Ensemble, St. Louis, 1965—; guest condr. Südwestfunk Baden-Baden and Studio Kaiserslautern, Germany, 1973; dir. Eden Choral Soc., St. Louis, 1974—; music, lit. critic St. Louis Post-Dispatch, 1964-69, St. Louis Globe-Democrat, 1971—; lit. critic Music and Man, 1970—; editorial adviser Focus, 1964-76; broadcaster KFUO-FM AM, St. Louis, 1961-71; chmn. applications and judging com. Artist Presentation Soc. St. Louis, 1968-74. Served with AUS, World War II. Decorated Purple Heart; recipient award for composition Chgo. Music Critics, 1951; Delius Assn. prize for Composition, 1973; MacDowell Found. resident composer fellow, 1972. Mem. ASCAP, Fedn. Musicians, Am. Musicological Soc., Pi Kappa Lambda. Home: 21 Bon Price Terr Olivette Saint Louis MO 63132

ORLAND, PHYLLIS THERESE MRAZEK (MRS. FRANK J. ORLAND), physician; b. Oak Park, Ill., Apr. 11, 1919; d. Rudolph G. and Lilliam (Mikota) Mrazek; B.A., U. Ill. at Urbana, 1939; B.S., U. Ill. at Chgo., 1943, M.D., 1943; m. Frank J. Orland, May 8, 1943; children—Frank R., Carl P., June R., Ralph M. Intern U. Ill. Research and Edn. Hosp., Chgo., 1943-44, resident in pediatrics, 1944-45; resident pediatrics Children's Meml. Hosp., Chgo., 1946, staff mem., 1946-64; mem. staff MacNeal Meml. Hosp., 1951—, Oak Park Hosp., 1971—; pvt. practice medicine specializing in pediatrics, Berwyn, Ill., 1946-54, Forest Park, Ill., 1954—; pediatrician Oak Park (Ill.) Infant welfare, 1952—, Stickney (Ill.) Well Baby Clinics, 1956—; instr. U. Ill. at Chgo., 1944-45; clin. asso. in pediatrics Abraham Lincoln Sch. Medicine, 1972—. Mem. adv. council to Bd. Edn. Forest Park Pub. Sch. Dist. 91, 1962-64. Diplomate Am. Bd. Pediatrics. Fellow Am. Acad. Pediatrics; mem. A.M.A., Chgo. Med. Soc., Am. Med. Women's Assn., Chgo. Pediatric Soc., Forest Park C. of C., Alpha Omega Alpha, Alpha Epsilon Iota. Author articles profl. jours. Home: 521 Jackson Blvd Forest Park IL 60130 Office: 519 Jackson Blvd Forest Park IL 60130

ORLIN, LOUIS LAWRENCE, educator; b. Bayonne, N.J., Nov. 7, 1925; B.A., U. Mich., 1949, M.A., 1950, Ph.D., 1960; children—Leslie, David, Hugh, Celia. Mem. faculty U. Mich., Ann Arbor, 1955—, prof. ancient Near Eastern history and lit., 1961—, dir. residential coll., 1973—. Active Ann Arbor Symphony Orch. Served with inf. U.S. Army, 1943-45. Decorated Bronze Star, Purple Heart. Recipient E. Harris Harbison award Danforth Found., 1966; Distinguished Service award U. Mich., 1961. Mem. Am. Hist. Assn., Am. Oriental Soc., Am. Inst. Archaeology, Assn. Ancient Historians, Internat. Platform Assn., Phi Kappa Phi. Author: (TV series) The City of Time, 1964; Ancient Near Eastern Literature: A Bibliography, 1969; Assyrian Colonies in Cappadocia, 1970. Editor: Janus: Essays in Ancient and Modern Studies, 1975; Michigan Oriental Studies in Honor of George G. Cameron, 1975. Home: 1331 Culver Rd Ann Arbor MI 48103 Office: 3084 Frieze Bldg Ann Arbor MI 48109

ORMAN, ALLAN DONALD, sociologist; b. Mpls., Nov. 23, 1931; s. Benjamin B. and Esther (Landy) O.; B.A., U. Minn., 1952, M.A., 1953; Ph.D., U. Wis., 1958; m. Marilyn Cheminrow, Aug. 23, 1953; children—Ashley, Sarah, Rebecca, Spencer, Seth, Rachel. Asst. prof. rural sociology Iowa State U., 1958-61; mgr. new products market research Pillsbury Co., Mpls., 1961-69; v.p. Tastest, Mpls., 1969-75; pres. Orman Guidance Research Inc., Mpls., 1975—. Mem. Am. Sociol. Assn., Inst. Food Technologists, Am. Mktg. Assn., Am. Soc. Testing and Materials. Home: 4617 Chatelain Terr Golden Valley MN 55422 Office: 715 Southgate Office Plaza Minneapolis MN 55437

ORMOND, BETTY LOU (HAYDEN), employment agency exec.; b. LaPlata, Mo., Dec. 31, 1932; d. Laurice P. and Cecil J. (Whitfield) Hayden; ed. high sch.; m. Walter James Ormond, Apr. 12, 1952; children—Becky Sue, John Joseph. Various secretarial, clerical positions, Ill., 1949-59; specialist consumer relations Audio Products div. Gen. Electric Co., Decatur, Ill., 1959-69; mgr. Kelly Services, Decatur, 1969—; owner, mgr. Betty Ormond Personnel, Decatur, 1972—; lectr. in field. Chairperson membership Decatur Convs. and Tourism Bur., 1975—; bd. dirs. Jr. Achievement Decatur; mem. Macon County Zoning Bd. Appeals, Decatur, 1977—. Mem. Decatur C. of C. (dir. 1976-78), Nat., Ill. (dir. 1977—, pres. downstate chpt. 1976-77) employment assns., Nat. Personnel Assos. Presbyterian. Clubs: Altrusa Women's, Women's Aux. Moose. Home: 4654 Hale Dr Decatur IL 62626 Office: 1204 W Grand St Suite 1 Decatur IL 62522

ORMSETH, ROBERT OWEN, radio broadcaster; b. Detroit Lakes, Minn., Jan. 25, 1950; s. Earl Owen and Mildred (Haberer) O.; B.A., U. Minn., 1976. Announcer copywriter KDLM, Detroit Lakes, 1966-70; music dir., announcer, transmitter engr. KOVC, Valley City, N.D., 1968; dir. newscaster, news photographer KTHI-TV, Fargo, N.D., 1970-71; radio announcer, asst. chief engr. KFGO, Fargo, N.D., 1970-75; announcer, reporter KUOM radio U. Minn., Mpls., 1976-77; anchorman, news producer, reporter KDAL Radio/TV, Duluth, Minn., 1977—. Asst. scoutmaster Boy Scouts Am., 1967-69; pres. Trinity Luth. Luther League, Detroit Lakes, 1967-68. Mem. Cousteau Soc., Profl. Assn. Diving Instrs., Pi Kappa Delta. Home: 516A3 E 1st St Duluth MN 55805

O'ROURKE, PETER EDWARD, lawyer; b. Detroit, Nov. 14, 1933; s. Randall Michael and Alice Ellen (White) O'R.; B.A., Wayne State U., 1955; J.D., Detroit Coll. Law, 1958; m. Susan Ellen Gehrke, Sept. 30, 1968; children—Kathleen Ann, Peter Edward. Admitted to Mich. bar, 1958; practiced in Detroit, 1961—; partner firm Porritt, Hegarty & O'Rourke, 1964-67; sr. partner firm Elsman, Young & O'Rourke, 1967-75; partner firm O'Rourke, Fitzgerald, Kazul & Rutledge, 1975—. Chmn. Mich. Employment Security Appeal Bd., 1969-72; mem. Regional Export Expansion Council, 1971-74, Gov.'s Spl. Commn. on Energy, 1972-74. Republican candidate for Mich. Senate, 1966, U.S. Congress, 1968. Comdr. USCG Res., 1958—. Mem. Mich., Detroit bar assns., Mich. C. of C., Am. Judicature Soc. Roman Catholic. Clubs: Mackinac Island (Mich.) Yacht (commodore); Grosse Pointe Yacht (dir.). Home: 241 Lewiston Rd Grosse Pointe Farms MI 48236 Office: 2000 First Federal Bldg Detroit MI 48226

O'ROURKE, RANDALL MICHAEL, physician; b. St. Paul, Jan. 3, 1900; s. Francis Henry and Mary Agnes (McDonnell) O'R.; student St. Thomas Coll., 1918-20; B.S., U. Minn., 1922, M.B., 1925, M.D., 1926; m. Alice Ellen White, May 23, 1931; children—Randall, Peter, Patrick, Timothy, Terrence, Alice O'Rourke Faber, Sheila, Mary Ellen. Intern, Ancker Hosp., St. Paul; resident Jackson Meml. Hosp., Miami, Fla., 1926-27, St. Francis Hosp., Miami Beach, 1927; practice medicine, Detroit, 1927—; med. dir. U.S. Army Tank Automotive Command, Warren, Mich., 1961—. Served with U.S. Army, World War I. Mem. AMA, Mich. State, Wayne County med. socs. Roman Catholic. Club: Detroit Golf. Author: Thoughts of a Catholic Doctor, 1948. Home: 8465 Kennedy Circle Warren MI 48093 Office: US Army Tank Automotive Command Warren MI 48090

ORR, BRUCE ALAN, real estate co. exec.; b. Des Moines, Jan. 3, 1948; s. Delbert Vernon and Betty Jean (Brown) O.; B.B.A., U. Iowa, 1970, postgrad., 1975-76. Mgmt. intern civil service Washington, 1970; nat. dir. youth affairs VA, Washington, 1971-72; coordinator ambulatory clinics Iowa City VA Hosp., 1972-73, asst. chief staff, 1973-76; gen. partner Medivestments Co., Iowa City, 1976—; pres. Orr Corp., Iowa City, 1976—; pres. Melrose Corp., Iowa City, 1977—; cons., lectr. in field. Mem. Nat. Small Bus. Assn. Home: 300 Samoa Ct Iowa City IA 52240 Office: 321 E Market St Iowa City IA 52240

ORR, EARL LAWTON, obstetrician-gynecologist; b. Savannah, Ga., July 12, 1934; s. Alfonso and Geneva Zenobia (Marks) O.; B.S., N.C. U., 1955; M.D., Meharry Med. Coll., 1960; m. Suzanne M. Harwood, Aug. 21, 1969 (dec. Aug. 1974); children—Alfonso, Rhonda, Vanessa, Andrea. Intern, Wilford Hall Hosp., San Antonio, 1960-61; resident Huron Rd. Hosp., Cleve., 1962-65, St. Vincent Hosp., Toledo, 1965-66; practice medicine specializing in obstetrics and gynecology, Chgo., 1967—; chief cons. gynecologist Louise Burg Hosp., 1969—; cons. Chgo. Bd. Health, 1969—; dir. obstetrics-gynecology Martin L. King Health Center, Chgo., 1968-74, Tabernacle Hosp., Chgo., 1974—; sr. attending St. Francis Cabrini Hosp., Chgo., 1976—; clin. asso. Chgo. Med. Sch., 1967-74. Fellow A.C.S., Internat. Coll. Surgeons, Am. Coll. Obstetrics and Gynecology, Am. Fertility Soc.; mem. AMA, Ill. Med. Assn., Chgo. Med. Soc. (profl. orientation com. 1972-74), Am. Assn. Gynecologic Laparoscopists. Roman Catholic. Home: 2825 S Michigan Ave Chicago IL 60616 Office: 3233 Martin L King Dr Chicago IL 60616

ORR, GORDON DICKSON, JR., architect; b. Meriden, Conn., May 16, 1926; s. Gordon Dickson and Eunice May (Stadtmiller) O.; B.Arch., Rensselaer Poly. Inst., 1950; M.A., U. Wis., 1971; m. Elayne Mercedes Soley, Sept. 20, 1952; children—Blair Dickson, Keith Gordon. Architect, William H. MacKay, Meriden, 1950; designer Henry A. Pfisterer, New Haven, 1951; sr. architect Walter J. Douglas Assos., West Hartford, Conn., 1952, 54-55, Harold H. Davis, New Haven, 1952-54; pvt. practice architecture, Wallingford, Conn., 1955-60; partner, Tuttle & Orr, architects, Winter Park, Fla., 1960-63; architect Wis. Bur. Engring., Madison, 1963-65; campus architect U. Wis., Madison, 1965—; lectr. archtl. history U. Wis., 1968-69, 71. Chmn. Wallingford Bd. Bldg. Commrs., 1957-60; mem. Citizens Adv. Com. for Civic Improvement, Orlando, Fla., 1962-63; mem. Urban Design Commn., Madison, Wis., 1970-74, Landmarks Commn., 1974—, Wis. State Historic Preservation Rev. Bd., 1973—; pres. Taychopera Found., Inc., 1970, Historic Madison, Inc., 1974, Conn. chpt. Nat. Multiple Sclerosis Soc., 1957-60. Served with USNR, 1944-46; PTO. Mem. AIA (chpt. exec. bd. 1972-74, nat. com. on historic resources 1972—), Assn. Preservation Tech., Nat. Audubon Soc., Wilderness Soc., Nat. Panel Arbitrators, Am. Arbitration Assn., Soc. Archtl. Historians, Sigma Xi, Tau Beta Pi. Home: 2729 Mason St Madison WI 53705

ORR, JOAN, state senator; b. Cedar Rapids, Iowa, Feb. 10, 1923; d. Joseph Urvin and Gail Helen (Gauby) Yessler; B. Music Ed., Oberlin Coll., 1946; postgrad. Chgo. Tchrs. Coll., U. Iowa, 1949-51; m. Carl Orr, Nov. 26, 1947. Former tchr., Chgo., Cedar Rapids; operator dairy, Grinnell, Iowa, until 1966; mem. Iowa Senate, 1970, 73—, chmn. Edn. Com. Commr. Edn. Commn. of the States. Mem. League Women Voters. Address: 10 Merrill Park Circle Grinnell IA 50112

ORR, SISTER MARY MARK, librarian; b. Beattie, Kans., Mar. 1, 1900; d. Thomas John and Julia (Kraemer) Orr; A.B., U. Kans., 1928, M.A., 1931; B.S. in L.S., U. Ill., 1933; postgrad. Universidad Nacional de Mexico, 1944; workshop in archival mgmt. Truman Library, Independence, Mo., 1959. Tchr. rural schs., Marshall County, Kans., 1918-22; prin. pub. sch., Home, Kans., 1922-24; tchr. Annunciation High Sch., Denver, 1928-30, Immaculata High Sch., Leavenworth, Kans., 1930-32; asst. librarian, St. Mary Coll., Leavenworth, Kans., 1933-36, head librarian, 1936-72, spl. collections librarian, 1972—, chmn. program and exhibits ann. Bible Weeks, 1943—, Presdl. grantee, 1968, 69. Mem. Am., Kan., Mt. Plains, Cath. (citation as founder, organizer, 1st chmn. Midwest unit 1960) library assns., NEA, Cath. Bibl. Assn., Met. Opera Guild, Delta Epsilon Sigma, Phi Alpha Theta. Contbr. chpt. to The Beattie Story, 1970. Book editor Poise, 1943-44; contbr. to profl. jours. Home: St Mary Coll Leavenworth KS 66048

ORR, RICHARD TUTTLE, newspaperman; b. Springfield, Ill., Feb. 19, 1915; s. Thomas E. and Maude (Tuttle) O.; B.S., U. Ill., 1937; m. Lois Marie Hollesen, June 3, 1939. Reporter, City News Bur., Chgo., 1941-42; reporter Chgo. Tribune, 1942-49, farm editor, 1949-72, editorial writer, 1961-72, editor rural affairs, 1972—. Served with USAAF, 1943-46. Recipient Edward Scott Beck award, 1962; J.S. Russell Meml. award, 1965; Oscar in Agr. award, 1969, Pfizer Agrl. Communications award, 1969. Mem. Newspaper Farm Editors Am. (past pres.), Chgo. Press Club (past pres.), Chgo. Press Vets. Assn. (past chmn.). Home: 2933 Sheridan Rd Chicago IL 60657 Office: 435 N Michigan Ave Chicago IL 60611

ORR, VICTOR DARRYL, engr.; b. Poplar Bluff, Mo., Aug. 17, 1944; s. Charles Victor and Jewell Elizabeth (Eavenson) O.; m. Linda Jarell, Sept. 6, 1969; 1 son, David. B.S., U. Mo., Rolla, 1970, M.S., 1971. Registered profl. engr., Mo. Co-owner, engr. Trotter Assos., Dexter, Mo., 1971—, pres., 1977—; city rep. Bootheel Regional Planning Commn., 1973—; mem. Dexter Planning and Zoning Commn., 1973—. Mem. Nat., Mo. (Outstanding Young Engr. of Yr. 1977), socs. profl. engrs., Profl. Engrs. in Pvt. Practice, Water Pollution Control Fedn., Am. Water Works Assn., Dexter C. of C., Water and Sewerage Conf., Phi Kappa Phi, Chi Epsilon. Recipient Outstanding Young Engr. of Yr., SE Mo. chpt. Mo. Soc. Profl. Engrs., 1977; contbr. articles to profl. jour. Home: Route 3 Orchard Lake Subdivision Dexter MO 63841 Office: 100 Ridgetop Dr Dexter MO 63841

ORR, WENDELL EUGENE, educator, musician; b. Gilman, Ill., July 23, 1930; s. Lloyd William and Ruth Louise (Bireline) O.; B.S., Lawrence Coll., 1952, Mus.B., 1955; M.Mus., U. Mich., 1957; pvt. study Rome, London, Edinburgh, Scotland, student Chase Baromeo, Giovanni Manurita, Josef Blatt, Pierre Bernac; m. Nancy Lynn Brannan, June 11, 1952; children—Patricia Ellen, Douglas Bennett. Opera appearances in concert, on TV, radio, New Eng., Eastern Seaboard, Midwest, 1950—; instr. voice, opera, chorus Wis. State Coll., Stevens Point, 1958-63; instr. voice, opera Kans. State Tchrs. Coll., Emporia, 1963-64; asst. prof. voice, opera, men's chorus U. N.H., Durham, 1964-69; asst. prof. voice, men's chorus Youngstown (Ohio) State U., 1969-77, asso. prof., 1977—; dir. music 1st. Christian Ch., Youngstown, 1969—; bass Lyric Opera Quartet, Youngstown, 1969—; appearances with Boston Pops, 1965, 67-69; founder Opera Workshop U. N.H., 1964. Mem. Poland Optimist Club (sec. 1973), Nat. Assn. Tchrs. Singing, Am. Choral Dirs. Assn., Internat. Platform Assn., Nat. Trust Historic Preservation, Central Opera Service, Pi Kappa Lambda. Episcopalian. Home: 7197 Elmland St Poland OH 44514 Office: 410 Wick St Youngstown OH 44555

ORTEGA, CARLOTA AYALA, sch. counselor; b. Piedras Negras, Mex. (parents Am. Citizens); d. Jose Angel and Antonia (de Hoyos) Ayala; B.A. summa cum laude, Saginaw Valley State Coll., 1974; M.A., Central Mich. U., 1975, Guidance and Counseling Edn. Endorsement, 1977; m. Guadalupe F. Ortega, Apr. 11, 1942; children—Yvonne Ortega Tutunjian, David R., Joseph G. Ct. interpreter U.S. Narcotics and Immigration Authorities, 1944-47; sec. Saginaw (Mich.) Planned Parenthood, 1967-70; employment interviewer Mich. Employment Security Commn., Saginaw, 1970-74; secondary sch. tchr., Saginaw, 1974; Sch. Counselor Saginaw Pub. Schs., 1974—; supr. Mid-Mich. Bilingual Bicultural Program at Saginaw Valley State Coll. for Bay City Sch. Dist., 1978—; field reader HEW Office Edn.; cons. tchrs. inservice tng. Bd. dirs. United Migrant Opportunities, 1960-61; commr. Saginaw Human Relations Commn., 1970-74; mem. La Raza Citizens Adv. Com. to State Bd. of Edn., 1974-75. Mem. Am., Mich. personnel and guidance assns., Mich. Assn. for Specialist in Group Work, North Central Guidance Assn. of Mich., Nat. Assn. Bilingual Edn. Am. Legion, League Women Voters, Alpha Mu Gamma. Home: 1842 Coolidge St Saginaw MI 48603

ORTHWEIN, WILLIAM COE, mech. engr.; b. Toledo, Jan. 27, 1924; s. William Edward and Millie Minerva (Coe) O.; B.S., Mass. Inst. Tech., 1946; M.S., U. Mich., 1957, Ph.D., 1959; m. Helen Virginia Poindexter, Feb. 1; children—Karla Francid, Adele Diana, Maria Theresa. Aerophysicist, Gen. Dynamics Co., Ft. Worth, 1951-52; research asso. U. Mich., 1952-59; adv. engr. IBM Corp., Owego, N.Y., 1959-61; dir. Computer Centers, U. Okla., Norman, 1961-63; research scientist Ames Lab., NASA, Moffett Field, Calif., 1963-65; mem. faculty So. Ill. U., Carbondale, 1965—, prof. engring., 1967—; cons. in field. Pres. Jackson County (Ill.) Taxpayers Assn., 1976. Served with AUS, 1943-46. Registered profl. engr., Ill., Ind., Ky. Mem. ASME (Outstanding Service award 1972), Ill. Soc. Profl. Engrs. (chmn. salary and employment com. 1974, chmn. ad hoc com. continuing edn. 1975), Soc. Exptl. Streess Analysis. Tensor Soc., Soc. Mining Engrs., Am. Gear Mfrs. Assn., Am. Acad. Mechanics, Nat. Rifle Assn., Aircraft Owners and Pilot Assn., Sigma Xi. Mormon. Author papers, revs. Home: PO Box 3332 Carbondale IL 62901 Office: So Ill Univ Carbondale IL 62901

ORTINO, LEONARD JAMES, mfg. exec.; b. Seneca Falls, N.Y., May 31, 1919; s. V. Michael and Florence (Campeggio) O.; B.S.M.E., Carnegie-Mellon U., 1950; postgrad. U. Mich., 1964-68; m. Evangeline Canellos, Apr. 1, 1945; children—Evangeline L., Stephanie J. Engr. group leader, Westinghouse Electric Co., Pitts., 1940-50; engr. mgr. IBM, Poughkeepsie, N.Y., 1950-54; chief mech. engr. Beckman Instruments, Fullerton, Calif., 1954-60, Magnavox Co., Ft. Wayne, Ind., 1960-64; asst. gen. mgr. Buhr Machine Tool Co., Ann Arbor, Mich., 1964-68; pres. Indsl. Mgmt. Council, Denville, N.J., 1969-71; v.p. Athlone Industries, Parsippany, N.J., 1972-73; v.p., gen. mgr. Mich. Dynamics div. AMBAC Industries, Garden City, Mich., 1973—; instr. Ordnance Sch., Aberdeen, Md., 1944-46; cons. Small Bus. Admin., 1969-73; instr. IBM Tng. Sch., 1950-53, Fullerton Jr. Coll., 1955-58; indsl. arbitrator Am. Arbitration Assn., 1955—. Dist. chmn. Boy Scout Am., 1954-60, pres. Forest Hills Civic Assn., 1948-49. Served with U.S. Army, 1944-46. Certified engr., 1950. Mem. ASME (Instrument div. chmn., 1958, Mid-Hudson chpt. chmn., 1953), Am. Mgmt. Assn., Indsl. Wire Cloth Inst., C. of C. Republican. Roman Catholic. Clubs: Newman (pres. 1942-44), Rotary, Elks. Author: Optical Instruments, 1950. Home: 3535 Sturbridge Ct Ann Arbor MI 48105 Office: 32400 Ford Rd Garden City MI 48135

ORTIZ, JOSE DENNIS, audiologist, educator deaf; b. Capulin, Colo., Mar. 18, 1934; s. Jose Fidel and Genoveva (Chacon) O.; B.S., Coll. Santa Fe, 1956; M.S., U. Kans., 1957; children—Anna Marie, Rachelle M., Matthew J., Antoinette G. Tchr., counselor Kans. Sch. Deaf, Olathe, 1958-60; adminstr., audiologist Greater Kansas City (Mo.) Hearing and Speech Center, 1960-69, Mich. Assn. Better Hearing and Speech, East Lansing, 1970—; cons. Commn. Accreditation Rehab. Facilities, HEW occupational safety and health. Served with AUS, 1957-58. Mem. Nat. Assn. Hearing and Speech Action (dir.), Am. Speech and Hearing Assn., Coll. Adminstrs. in Hearing and Speech, Conf. Am. Instrs. of Deaf, Profl. Rehab. Workers with Adult Deaf. Home: 3640 Bayou Pl Holt MI 48842 Office: 724 Abbott Rd East Lansing MI 48823

ORTMAN, FRANK J., lawyer; b. Cullom, Ill., Dec. 6, 1899; s. Frank A. and Annie (Maloney) O.; A.B., U. Mich., 1923, J.D., 1925; m. Marcella Gfell, June 24, 1926; children—John R., James F., William A. Admitted to Mich. bar, 1925, since practiced in Detroit; dir. Larson Clay Pipe Co., Uhrichsville, Ohio. Mem. Am. Judicature Soc., Am., Detroit, 40th Jud. Circuit (past pres.) bar assns., State Bar Mich., Alumni Assn. U. Mich. (dir., past pres.), Lawyers Club, Am. Legion, Am. Coll. Probate Counsel. Clubs: K.C., Detroit Athletic, Lapeer (Mich.) Country, Cardinal. Home: 971 Waddington Rd Birmingham MI 48009 also 3507 Lippincott Rd Lapeer MI 48446 Office: 2238 Commonwealth Bldg Detroit MI 48226

ORTMAN, WILLIAM ANDREW, SR., lawyer; b. Detroit, Mich., Mar. 22, 1934; s. Frank J. and Marcella Pauline (Gfell) O.; B.A., Wayne State U., 1958; grad. Bus. Sch. U. Mich., 1960; J.D. (regional outstanding student 1962, scholarship certificate and key, jurisprudence awards), U. Detroit, 1963; m. Lavina Mae Ladson, June 29, 1957; children—William A., Nancy Lee, Merrie Jo, Kristy Ann, Keira Therese. Radio sta. mgr., 1953-56; para-legal Ortman Co., 1956-60, real estate broker, co-partner, 1956—; indsl. relations analyst FoMoCo, 1960-62; pub. info. specialist Dept. Def., Detroit, 1962-63; admitted to Mich. bar, 1963, Ohio Fed. bar, 1963; sr. atty. firm Ortman & Ortman, Detroit, 1964—; polit. campaign specialist, 1968—; real-estate, mortgage broker, 1956—; cons. pub. relations and advt., 1962—; lectr. St. Joseph Comml. Coll., 1961-62. Bd. govs., past dean Detroit Metro. Alumni Senate; councilman, Farmington Hills area, 1968-75; nominee Mich. Supreme Ct., 1972. Served with AUS, 1953-56. Mem. Am., Mich., Oakland, 40th Jud. bar assns., Delta Theta Phi, Alpha Kappa Delta. Roman Catholic. Clubs: Detroit Athletic, German-Am. Cultural Center, Elks. Contbr., author and editor of nat., State and local legal jours. Home: 28010 S Harwich Dr Farmington Hills MI 48018 Office: 2238 Commonwealth Bldg Detroit MI 48226

ORTMEIER, EVELYN J., chem. co. exec.; b. Chattanooga, Jan. 1, 1922; d. Fred L. and Inez Lillian (Love) Dickson; student U. Chattanooga, 1947-48, now William Rainey Harper Coll.; m. Ernest C. Ortmeier, Jr., Mar. 7, 1946; children—Timothy M., David C. Sec. Am. Nat. Bank, Chattanooga, 1940-44; teller Fla. Nat. Bank, Jacksonville, Fla., 1944-45; supr. stenographic pool So. Railway System, Chattanooga, 1945-54; sec. archtl. and steel div. TVA, Chattanooga, 1954-55; v.p., treas. Ortmeier Machinery Co., Inc. and Airdraulics, Inc., 1955-65; sec. to pres. Chgo. Coatings and chem. div., 1965-66, sec. to dir. purchases, 1966-73, asst. mgr. purchases and adminstrv. services, 1973-76, mgr. purchases and adminstrv. services, 1976—. Mem. Purchasing Mgmt. Assn. Chgo., Chgo. Paint and Coatings Assn. Republican. Lutheran. Home: 8544 W Rascher Chicago IL 60656 Office: 2629 S Dearborn St Chicago IL 60656

ORVIS, ALAN LEROY, med. physicist; b. Cleve., May 2, 1921; s. Harvey Willard and Helen Louise (Gerlach) O.; B.S., Westminster (Pa.) Coll., 1944; certificate meteorology U. Calif. at Los Angeles, 1943; M.S., Case Inst. Tech., 1949; Ph.D., U. Tex., 1952; m. Jennie Morgan, Aug. 30, 1947; children—James Alan, Joan Morgan. Grad. asst. physics Case Inst. Tech., 1946-48, instr., 1948-49; teaching fellow physics U. Tex., Austin, 1949-50, instr., 1950-52; instr. biophysics Mayo Grad. Sch. Medicine, U. Minn., Rochester, 1956-59, asst. prof., 1959-67, asso. prof., 1967—; cons. in biophysics Mayo Clinic, Rochester, 1952—, radiol. safety officer, 1954—; mem. Adv. Com. Radiation Safety, Minn. State Bd. Health, 1960—, chmn., 1964-69; mem. Biomed. Users Group, Los Alamos, Meson Prodn. Facility, 1969—. Served to capt. USAAF, 1943-46. Mem. Am. Assn. Physicists in Medicine, Am. Geophys. Union, Soc. Nuclear Medicine, Health Physics Soc. (dir. chpt. 1968-71, pres. 1971-72), AAAS, Am. Assn. Physics Tchrs., Minn. Soc. Radiologic Technologists (hon.), Minn. Radiol. Soc., Minn. Acad. Sci., Sigma Xi, Sigma Pi Sigma. Author sci. publs. in field; contbr. chpts. to several books. Home: 2512 Crest Ln SW Rochester MN 55901 Office: Curie Pavilion Mayo Clinic Rochester MN 55901

ORYSHKEVICH, ROMAN SVIATOSLAV, physician, dentist; b. Olesko, Ukraine, Aug. 5, 1928; s. Simeon and Caroline (Deneszczuk) O.; came to U.S., 1955, naturalized, 1960; D.D.S., Ruperto-Carola U., Heidelberg, Germany, 1952, M.D., 1953; Ph.D. cum laude, U. Heidelberg, 1955; m. Oksana Lishchynsky, June 16, 1962; children—Martha, Mark, Alexandra. Research fellow in cancer Exptl. Cancer Inst., U. Heidelberg, 1953-55; rotating intern Coney Island Hosp., Bklyn., 1955-56; resident in diagnostic radiology N.Y. U. Bellevue Med. Center and Univ. Hosp., 1956-57; resident, fellow in phys. medicine and rehab. Western Res. U. Highland View Hosp., Cleve., 1958-60, in orthopedic surgery Met. Gen. Hosp., Cleve., 1959; asst. chief rehab. medicine service VA West Side Hosp., Chgo., 1961-74, chief, 1974—; dir. integrated residency tng. program U. Ill. Affiliated Hosp., 1974—; clin. instr. U. Ill., 1962-64, asst. clin. prof., 1965-69, asst..prof., 1970-74, asso. clin. prof., 1975—. Diplomate Am. Bd. Phys. Medicine and Rehab. Fellow Am. Acad. Phys. Medicine and Rehab.; mem. Assn. Acad. Physiatrists, AAUP, Am. Assn. Electromyography and Electrodiagnosis, Am. Congress Rehab. Medicine, Ill. Soc. Phys. Medicine and Rehab. (trustee), Ukrainian Med. Assn. No. Am. (state pres. Ill. 1977—; dir.; adminstr., fin. mgr. 17th med. conv. and congress, Chgo. 1977), World Fedn. Ukrainian Med. Assns. (co-founder 1977, 1st exec. sec. gen. of sci. 1977—), Internat. Rehab. Medicine Assn., Rehab. Internat. U.S.A., Nat. Assn. VA Physicians, AAAS, Assn. Med. Rehab. Dirs. and Coordinators, Nat. Rehab. Assn., Nat. Assn. Disability Examiners, Nat. Rehab. Counseling Assn., Nat. Congress on Rehab. Homebound and Institutionalized Persons, Am. Acad. Manipulative Medicine, Assn. Am. Med. Colls. (individual mem.), Am. Med. Writers Assn., Pan Am. Med. Assn., Biofeedback Research Soc. Am. Ukrainian Catholic. Contbr. articles profl. jours. Home: 1819 N 78th Ct Elmwood Park IL 60635 Office: 820 S Damen Ave Chicago IL 60612

OSBORN, CHARLES HOWARD, mech. engr.; b. Phoenix, Dec. 12, 1937; s. Howard Hillstrom and Fern Inez O.; B.S. in Mech. Engring., U. Ariz., 1962; m. Priscilla Fern Keith, Feb. 2, 1969; children—Billie-Ann, Amber Lynn. Mech. engr. Gen. Electric Corp., Phoenix, 1962-64; design engr. North Electric Co., Galion, Ohio, 1964-66; chief engr. snowmobiles Rupp Industries, Inc., Mansfield, Ohio, 1966-73; chief engr. research and devel. Gorman Rupp Corp., Mansfield, 1973—. Served with USAF, 1955-59. Mem. ASME, Soc. Mfg. Engrs. (sr.). Methodist. Home: 1837 Grace Ave Ontario OH 44906 Office: 305 Bowman St Mansfield OH 44902

OSBORN, DONALD DEAN, elec. engr.; b. Villisca, Iowa, Apr. 5, 1922; s. Ned Cecil and Blanche (Winter) O.; student State U. Iowa, 1943-44, U. Mo. 1946-47; B.S. in Elec. Engring., Iowa State U., 1949; m. Emogene Faye Strausbaugh, Nov. 26, 1949; children—Larry Jay, David Lee, Melvin Randall, Patricia Ann. With Stanley Cons., Inc., Muscatine, Iowa, 1949—, head elec. design dept., 1962-70, head elec. systems group, 1970-77, v.p., 1972—, head transmission and distbn. group, 1977—, specializing in design electric power transmission lines, substas.; mem. Am. Nat. Standards Com. on Wood Poles; mem. ICA engring. team studying feasibility of electric power system for Republic of Liberia, W. Africa, 1958. Served as pfc. 83d Inf. Div., U.S. Army, 1943-46; ETO. Registered profl. engr., Iowa, Ill., Ky., Colo., Ariz., S.D., Alaska, Ala., Ohio, Wis. Mem. IEEE (sr.), Power (towers, poles and conductors subcom., chmn. task group on wood structures), Iowa engring. socs., Nat. Soc. Profl. Engrs., Iowa Geneal. Soc. Republican. Presbyn. Mason. Designer 1st maj. transmission line in permafrost region of Alaska, 1965. Home: Rural Route 4 Box 134 Muscatine IA 52761 Office: Stanley Cons Inc Stanley Bldg Muscatine IA 52761

OSBORN, FRANCIS HOWARD, JR., ednl. pub.; b. Cleve., Mar. 27, 1933; s. Francis Howard and Thelma (Foster) O.; A.B. (scholar), Case Western Reserve U., 1955, M.A. (scholar), 1957, Ph.D., 1970. Various positions in Cleve. Pub. Schs. including tchr., dept. chmn., asst. prin., research asso., 1956-70; editor, sr. editor McGraw-Hill Films McGraw Hill Book Co., N.Y.C., 1970-75; dir. social studies and career edn. Singer Soc. Visual Edn., Chgo., 1975-77, v.p. product devel., 1977—; author radio programs and curriculum guides Cleve. Bd. Edn., 1958, 59, 62, 63; instr. Bir Zeit (Jordan) Coll., 1965; instr. Univ. Sch., Shaker Heights, Ohio, summer 1967; chmn. curriculum com. N.Y. State Council for Social Studies, 1972-74; mem. house of dels. Nat. Council for Social Studies, 1973; bd. dirs. Lake View Acad., Chgo., 1976—. Coordinator Project Talent Search, Cedar Branch YMCA, Cleve., 1967-70. Recipient scholarship Boston U. Summer Human Relations Inst., 1957, Ohio State U. Summer Human Relations Inst., 1958, Audubon Camp of Maine Summer Inst., 1959, Soc. Friends Internat. Volunteer Service program, Sweden, 1960; named Volunteer of the Yr., Cedar Branch YMCA, 1970. Mem. Am. Mgmt. Assn., DuSable Museum of African-Am. History, Peoria (Ill.) Art Guild, Ill., Nat. councils for social studies, Phi Delta Kappa. Democrat. Presbyterian. Compiler: Resource Handbook in Human Relations, 1959; producer films The New Deal (Chris award Columbus Film Festival), 1972; The Am. People in WW II (Chris award, Ill. Dept. Edn. Film Festival award), 1974; producer filmstrip Slavery (Learning Mag. award), 1976. Home: 655 W Irving Park Rd Apt 3713 Chicago IL 60613 Office: 1345 Diversey Pkwy Chicago IL 60614

OSBORN, LAURA (MRS. HENRY P. ZUIDEMA), lawyer, educator; b. Detroit; d. Francis Conrad and Laura (Freele) Osborn; studied opera in Italy, 1927; B.S., Vassar Coll., 1927; LL.B., Detroit Coll. of Law, 1934, J.D., 1935; m. Henry P. Zuidema, June 15, 1940. Admitted to Mich. bar, 1935; pvt. practice, Detroit, 1935—; concert singer, 1929-40; tchr. Spanish high schs., Detroit, 1930-34; dir. student activities Wayne U., 1930-34, dir. alumni relations, instr. Spanish, 1934-43, asso. prof., 1943—; supr. Inter-Am. and world studies Detroit pub. schs., 1943-65. Producer ednl. sound, color, motion pictures including Sons of Montezuma; Land Under The Sea; The Three Perus and others. Mem. Am. Assn. for UN (pres. Greater Detroit chpt. 1952-54), Detroit Sci. Mus. Soc. (dir. 1956—, treas. 1956—), NEA, Mich. (chmn. bldg. internat. goodwill sect. 1949-58), Detroit edn. assns., Am., Mich., Detroit bar assns., Fine Arts Soc. Detroit, Tuesday Musicale of Detroit, Internat. Platform Assn., Internat. Fedn. Women Lawyers, Founders Soc. Detroit Inst. Arts, Pro Musica, Sigma Alpha Iota. Club: Women's City. Home: 130 Lawrence Ave Detroit MI 48203 Office: Wayne State U Detroit MI 48202

OSBORN, MYRON WALLACE, III, patient care evaluation cons.; b. Oak Park, Ill., Feb. 26, 1946; s. Myron Wallace and Audrey Fern (Secrest) O.; B.S., Ohio State U., 1971, M.A., 1972; m. JoEllen Gegenheimer, Sept. 28, 1975. Exec. dir. Quad River Found. for Med. Care, Joliet, Ill., 1975-77; patient care evaluation cons. Ill. Hosp. Assn., Oak Brook, 1977—; bd. dirs. Region IX Health Systems Agy., 1976-77; mem. data element com. Ill. Coop. Health Data Systems, Inc., 1976-77. Served with U.S. Army, 1966-69. Mem. Am. Assn. Profl. Standards Rev. Orgn., Am. Mktg. Assn., Am. Soc. Pub. Adminstrn., DAV, Am. Soc. Assn. Execs., Beta Gamma Sigma. Home: 1360 S Finley Rd Apt 3G Lombard IL 60148 Office: 1200 Jorie Blvd Oak Brook IL 60521

OSBORNE, ARTHUR ELLSWORTH, JR., dept. store exec.; b. Chgo., May 21, 1920; s. Arthur Ellsworth and Esther Irene (Harrison) O.; student, Grinnell (Iowa), 1942; m. Barbara Jane Rupp, May 21, 1943; children—Arthur Ellsworth III, Richard Harrison, David Charles. Asst. to dir. personnel Marshall Field & Co., 1945-46, group mgr. fine jewelry, 1947-65, v.p. women's apparel, 1966-71, v.p., gen. mgr., 1972-75, sr. v.p., 1975—, dir., 1976—, pres., 1977—; dir. Upper Ave. Nat. Bank. Chmn. Chgo. crusade Am. Cancer Soc., 1975, vice chmn. Chgo. chpt., 1976—; chmn. State St. Council 1972-73; bd. dirs. Evanston Hosp., 1974—, United Cerebral Palsy; trustee Ill. Children's Home and Aid Soc. Served to capt. USAAF, 1942-45. Decorated D.F.C., Purple Heart, Air medal, Presdl. Citation. Mem. Nat. Retail Merchants Assn. (exec. com. 1973), Chgo. Hist. Soc. (trustee 1977). Episcopalian (vestry). Clubs: Chicago, Glen View, Mid-America, Carlton. Home: 935 Woodland Dr Glenview IL 60025 Office: 111 N State St Chicago IL 60690

OSBORNE, NEWELL YOST, coll. librarian; b. Jewett, O., Nov. 10, 1914; s. Thomas Newell and Augusta (Yost) O.; A.B., Mount Union Coll., 1936; Litt.M., U. Pitts., 1939; B.L.S., Western Res. U., 1940; m. Mary E. Carson, Sept. 9, 1939; 1 dau., Nancy Jane (Mrs. Thomas Michael Fox). Librarian, Mount Union Coll., Alliance, O., 1940—. Served with AUS, 1943-46. Mem. A.L.A., Alpha Tau Omega. Methodist. Author: A Select School; A History of Mount Union College and an Account of a Unique Educational Experiment, 1967. Home: 3210 Beechwood St Alliance OH 44601

OSBORNE, ROBERT VANDERVOORT, hardware mfg. co. exec.; b. Racine, Wis., Oct. 16, 1916; s. William Vandervoort and Adele (Gianella) O.; B.S., Northwestern U., 1937; m. Mary Lois Marcal, June 22, 1953; children—Consuela, Robert Vandervoort, Beatriz, David. Engr., Carnegie Ill. Steel Corp., 1937-41; v.p. Lakeside Malleable Castings Co., Racine, 1941-62; pres. Ridgeway Mfg. Corp., Racine, Wis., 1962—. Mem. Am. Foundrymens Soc. (past pres.), Malleable Founders Soc. (past dir.), SAR (pres.), Caledonian Soc. Wis. (dir.). Republican. Episcopalian. Clubs: Univ. of Milw., Racine Country, Mason. Home: 3624 Gifford Rd Franksville WI 53126 Office: PO Box 1226 Racine WI 53405

OSENBERG, WARREN ERWIN, ins. agt.; b. De Kalb, Ill., June 23, 1926; s. Erwin and Celia (Ellithorpe) O.; student Beloit Coll., 1943-46; m. Arlene Whittenberg, June 10, 1950; children—Craig, Camille. Field rep. Md. Casualty Co., Chgo., 1948-49, Peoria, Ill., 1949-50; ins. mgr. No. Ins. Agy., No. Ill. Fin. Corp., De Kalb, 1950-55; v.p. William F. Wiltberger Co., De Kalb, 1955—; dir. De Kalb Forge Co.; Ins. agt. mem. Gov.'s Spl. Com., Med. Malpractice Commn. Ill., 1976; ins. producer mem. Products Assistance Commn., 1977; cons. in field. Mem. De Kalb Library Bd., 1968-72, De Kalb County Bd., 1966-70; pres. De Kalb Devel. Corp., 1975—; bd. dirs. Pine Acres Inc. Named Ins. Agt. of Year Comml. Union Ins. Cos., Nat., 1969. Mem. Ind. Ins. Agts. Ill. (pres. 1974), De Kalb C. of C., VFW, Am. Legion. Republican. Lutheran. Clubs: Lions, Elks. Home: 1212 Stafford St De Kalb IL 60115 Office: 231 S 2d St PO Box 399 De Kalb IL 60115

OSIPOW, SAMUEL HERMAN, educator, psychologist; b. Allentown, Pa., Apr. 18, 1934; s. Louis Morris and Tillie (Wolfe) O.; B.A., Lafayette Coll., 1954; M.A., Columbia U., 1955; Ph.D., Syracuse U., 1959; m. Sondra Beverly Feinstein, Aug. 26, 1956; children—Randall A., Jay I., Reva S., David S. Lectr., U. Wis., Madison, 1961; psychologist, asst. prof. Pa. State U., University Park, 1961-67; asso. prof. psychology Ohio State U., Columbus, 1967-69, prof., 1969—, chmn. dept., 1973—; vis. prof. Tel-Aviv (Israel) U., 1972; vis. research asso. Harvard U., 1965; cons. govt. agys. Served to 1st lt. AUS, 1959-61. Fellow Am. Psychol. Assn. Author: Theories of Career Development, 1973; Strategies in Counseling for Behavior Change, 1970; Behavior Change in Counseling, 1970; editor Jour. Vocat. Behavior, 1970-75, Jour. Counseling Psychology, 1975—. Home: 575 Enfield Rd Columbus OH 43209

OSMANSKI, WILLIAM THOMAS, dentist; b. Providence, Dec. 29, 1915; s. Alexander and Elizabeth Rose (Venitskis) O.; B.S., Holy Cross Coll., Worcester, Mass., 1939; D.D.S., Northwestern U., 1943; m. Mary Gavin, Feb. 15, 1947; children—Mary Osmanski Ferlic, William Thomas, John, Katherine, Stephen, Robert. Mem. Chgo. Bears Pro Football Team, 1939-47, backfield coach, 1947; head football coach Holy Cross Coll., Worcester, 1948-49; pvt. practice dentistry, Chgo., 1946—; pres. Dura Plaque Laminating Co., Chgo., 1963—; sec.-treas., dir. sav. Rogers Park (Ill.) Prudential Bank, 1972-72; lecture staff Northwestern U., 1958-64; mem. Ill. Bd. Dental Examiners, 1969—, chmn., 1974-75; mem. staff St. Francis Hosp., Evanston, Ill. Masonic Hosp., Chgo. Chmn. alumni fund dr. Holy Cross Coll., 1966-72; bd. dirs. Northwestern U., 1963—, mem. exec. com., 1958—; trustee Nat. Hemophilia Found. Served to lt. USNR, 1943-46; capt. Res. Recipient Most Valuable All Star trophy Chgo. Tribune, 1940, Silver Anniversary All Am. award Sports Illustrated mag., 1963, Man of Year award Evanston K.C., 1960, Man of Year award City Hope, 1970, George award Nat. Hemophilia Found., 1965; inducted to Nat. Football Found. and Hall of Fame, 1973; Distinguished Am. award Nat. Football Found., 1973. Mem. ADA (del. 1949-67), Internat. Coll. Dentists, Ill. (legis. com. 1958-62), Chgo. (br. pres. 1952, br. bd. dirs. 1954-58) dental socs., Am. Acad. Gen. Dentistry, Am. Equilibration Soc., Dental Research Group, Midwest Seminar Dental Group, Dental Arts Club, Navy Res. Assn., U.S. Naval Inst., Navy League U.S., Chgo. Bears Alumni Assn. (v.p. 1952), Polish Roman Cath. Union, Lithuanian C. of C., Polish Nat. Alliance. Roman Catholic. Clubs: Chgo. Athletic Assn., Chgo. Sportsman, Exec., Anvil. Contbr. to profl. pubIs. in field. Home. 920 Ramona Rd Wilmette IL 60091 Office: 25 E Washington St Chicago IL 60602

OSMON, ROBERT VANCE, educator, ednl. psychologist; b. Washington, Ind., Jan. 28, 1928; s. Roy Cletus and Hazel Anna (Mendenhall) O.; B.A. in Zoology, Ind. U., 1950, M.S., 1954, Ed.D., 1959; m. Carla J. Elliott, Dec. 21, 1952; children—Robert Vance, Jullianna, Charles Elliott. Faculty, N. Tex. State U., Denton, 1957-65; asst. prof. U. Mo., St. Louis, 1965-67, asso. prof., 1967-70; prof. ednl. psychology Western Ill. U., Macomb, 1967—; pres. adv. council Caribbean Ednl. Research Inst., 1976; cons. St. Louis Pub. Schs., 1965-67. Mem. Republican Central Com. Denton County, 1962-65. Served with AUS, 1945-47. Named Danforth Asso., 1960. Mem. Ill. Psychol. Assn., Ill. Assn. Higher Edn. (pres. Western Ill. U. 1972), AAUP (pres. univ. 1966-67, Am. Ednl. Research Assn., Internat. Platform Assn., Phi Delta Kappa (pres. N. Tex. State U. 1962-65, Western Ill. U., 1970). Clubs: Masons, Kiwanis. Author: The Improvement of Secondary Teaching, 1962; Strategies for the Complete Teacher, 1969; A Preformance-Based Module on Evaluation, 1974; contbr. articles to profl. jours. Home: 1590-4 Riverview Macomb IL 61455

OSMOND, JOHN DEXTER, JR., radiologist; b. Cleve., Nov. 14, 1913; s. John Dexter and Nellie A. (Pratt) O.; A.B., Denison U., 1935; M.D., Western Res. U., 1939; m. Jean M. Lindstrom, June 15, 1937; children—John Dexter III, Jean L. Osmond Schneider, Charles D., Mark W. Intern, resident in obstetrics and gynecology and radiology Cleve. City Hosp. and Univ. Hosp., 1939-41, Cleve. Clinic Found., 1945-47; asso. radiologist Univ. Hosps., Cleve., 1947, Drs. Hill and Thomas Radiology Group, 1948—; dir. radiology Euclid Gen. Hosp. (Ohio), 1947-71; asso. clin. prof. radiology Case Western Res. U. Bd. trustees Cleve. Health Edn. Mus., 1961—, pres., 1965-74, chmn. bd., 1974—. Served from 1st lt. to maj. M.C., AUS, 1941-45. Decorated 2 Bronze Stars; recipient Alumni citation Denison U., 1966; Distinguished Alumnus award Case Western Res. U. Sch. Medicine, 1972; Order of Merit, Boy Scouts Am., 1965, Silver Beaver award, 1966. Diplomate Am. Bd. Radiology. Fellow Am. Coll. Radiology; mem. Acad. Medicine Cleve. (pres. 1961-62), Cleve. Med. Library Assn. (trustee 1965-68), Ohio Med. Assn., AMA, Cleve., Ohio radiol. socs., Radiol. Soc. N.Am., Am. Roentgen Ray Soc., Eastern Radiol. Soc. (pres. 1976—), Phi Beta Kappa, Omicron Delta Kappa. Republican. Presbyterian. Clubs: Cleve. Country, Cleve. Skating. Contbr. articles to profl. jours. Home: 32899 S Woodland Rd Cleveland OH 44124 Office: 101 E 185th St Euclid OH 44119

OSNESS, JOHN M., quality control mgr.; b. Cambridge, Iowa, Mar. 31, 1917; s. John Lars and Randi Carrie (Fatland) O.; student Iowa State U., 1940-42, Ill. Inst. Tech., 1942; m. Lois Grace Boller, July 6, 1947; children—Nick Alan, Randi Sue, April Ann. Bd. marker Lamson Bros., and Goodbody & Co., Des Moines, 1935-41; civilian materials insp., Chgo. Ordnance Dist. U.S. Army, Waterloo, Iowa, 1942-45; with Chamberlain Mfg. Corp., Waterloo, Iowa, 1945—, engr., 1945-47, chief insp., 1947-61, mgr. quality control, 1961—; dir. employees credit union, 1949-55, 58—, chmn., 1969—. Mem. Iowa Chess Assn. (officer, tournament dir, 1957-76), U.S. Chess Fedn. (U.S. open tournament dir. 1975), Iowa Ornithologists Union (pres. 1971-73). Editor pub. Iowa Chess En Passant, 1961-74; collaborator Official Rules of Chess, 1974. Home: 320 Columbia Circle Waterloo IA 50701 Office: Chamberlain Mfg Corp E 4th & Esther Sts Waterloo IA 50703

OSNESS, WAYNE HANS, univ. adminstr.; b. Merrill, Wis., July 11, 1933; s. Leonard H. and Marion J. (Fisher) O.; B.S., U. Wis., 1956, Ph.D., 1966; m. Donna L. Murray, June 15, 1951; children—Patrick, Karen, Cinda, Deena, Lynne. Tchr. sci., math., phys. edn. Marion (Wis.) High Sch., 1956-57, West High Sch., Madison, Wis., 1957-64; faculty exercise physiology U. Kans., Lawrence, 1966-72, chmn. dept. health, phys. edn. and recreation, 1972—; cons. VA Hosp., Leavenworth, Kans. Recipient Honors award Kans. Assn. Health, Phys. Edn. and Recreation, 1972, Honor award Medicine Dello Sport, Rome. 1974; NDEA fellow, 1964-66. Mem. Am., Kans. (pres.) assns. health, phys. edn. and recreation, Nat. Assn. Sport and Phys. Edn. (nat. council 1972-77, pres. 1977-78), Central Dist. Assn. for Health, Phys. Edn. and Recreation (Honor award 1976), Assn. Coll. Sports Medicine, Nat. Coll. Phys. Edn. Assn. Men, C. of C. Clubs: Masons, Shriners, K.T., Kiwanis (pres. 1973, chmn. found., 1973-74). Editor phys. edn. Kans. Assn. Health, Phys. Edn. and Recreation; contbr. articles to profl. jours. Home: 1654 University Dr Lawrence KS 66044 Office: 108 Robinson U Kans Lawrence KS 66045

OSSENBERG, ROBERT DEAN, communications co. exec.; b. Evansville, Ind., Dec. 2, 1927; s. William Arnold and Kathryn (Weber) O.; A.B., Evansville Coll., 1955; m. Myra Glenda Roberts, Mar. 8, 1963; children—Karen Kay, Elizabeth Dean, Jeffrey Marshall. City clk., City of Evansville, 1952-55; account exec. Evansville TV, Inc., sta. WTVW, 1956-59, gen. sales mgr., 1959-68; v.p. ops. Telesis Corp., Evansville, 1968—, dir., 1975—. Mem. Evansville Bicentennial Steering Com., 1975-76; v.p. Evansville Freedom Festival Found., 1973-77; bd. dirs. Cath. Ednl. Found., 1976-78; trustee Evansville-Vanderburgh Sch. Corp. Served with U.S. Army, 1946-48. Mem. Evansville Met. C. of C. (dir. 1974-77), Evansville Advt. Club, Am. Legion, VFW, U. Evansville Alumni Assn. (Achievement award 1972), Sigma Alpha Epsilon. Republican. Roman Catholic. Home: 5618 Spring Lake Dr Evansville IN 47710 Office: 1018 Lincoln Ave Evansville IN 47714

OSSIP, KENNETH IRWIN, optometrist; b. N.Y.C., Oct. 22, 1924; s. Harry and Fannie (Wolin) O.; B.S., Ohio State U., 1948; m. Joan Kramer, Jan. 27, 1951; children—Eric, Gregg, Sharon. Pvt. practice optometry, Indpls., 1952—. Nat. bd. dirs. Nat. Fedn. Temple Brotherhoods, v.p., 1974—; bd. dirs. Jewish Chautauqua Soc., 1968—. Served with USAAF, 1943-46; ETO. Mem. Am. (mem. com. on optometric practice 1972-73, com. on assistance to undergrads. and grads. 1974-75, exec. com. adminstrv. div. 1975—), Ind. (chmn. vision care of aging 1969-73, chmn. practice mgmt. com. 1976—) optometric assns., Central Ind. Optometric Soc. (pres. 1967), Greenbriar Civic Assn. (pres. 1962). Mem. B'nai B'rith (pres. Indpls. 1961). Club: Ripple-Dale Optimist (pres. 1974-75) (Indpls.). Home: 8035 Claridge Rd Indianapolis IN 46260 Office: 840 Broad Ripple Ave Indianapolis IN 46220

OSTAND, PAUL RAYMOND, mech. engr.; b. Cin., July 2, 1939; s. Saul and Lillian (Tenenholtz) O.; Asso. Sci., Ohio Coll. Applied Sci., 1959; B.S., U. Cin., 1969; m. Lois Barbara Wilner, Dec. 15, 1963; 1 dau., Traci Lynn. Design engr. Littleford Brothers, Inc., Cin., 1962-68; project engr. OPW div. Dover Corp., Cin., 1968—. Registered profl. engr., Ohio, Ky. Patentee in field. Mem. ASME. Home: 7243 Scottwood Ave Cincinnati OH 45237 Office: 9393 Princeton-Glendale Rd Cincinnati OH 45240

OSTBY, DONALD HAROLD, environ. engr.; b. Muskegon, Mich., Feb. 17, 1927; s. Ernest Harold and Evelyn (Roberts) O.; B.S., M.E., U. Wash., Seattle, 1951; m. Mary E. Shaw, Feb. 14, 1951; children—Michael Lee. Vice pres. engring. Lakey Foundry Corp., Muskegon, 1951-70; engring. cons. Nat. Chinese Govt., 1970-71; chief engr. East Muskegon Roofging & Sheet Metal Co., Muskegon, 1972-73; environ. engr Sealed Power Corp., Muskegon, 1973—. Served with USN, 1944-48. Decorated Purple Heart. Mem. Am. Foundry Soc., Plant Engrs. Soc. Patentee air pollution control equipment. Home: 838 Forest Ave E Muskegon MI 49442

OSTEN, DONALD WALTER, marketing co. exec.; b. Bklyn., Mar. 20, 1923; s. Walter Charles and Paula (Osten) Gigerich; A.B., Clark U., 1947, M.A., 1948; postgrad. Am. U., 1950-52; m. Eleanor Louise Beckley, Aug. 31, 1946; children—Richard Donald, David Walter. Media and research dir. Larrabee Asso., advt., Washington, 1953-56; asst. marketing dir., asso. media dir. Gardner Advt. Co., St. Louis, 1956-63; media dir. plans review com. BBD&O, Chgo., 1963-65; founder, pres. Media/Marketing Service Center, Western Springs, Ill., 1965—, chmn. bd. 1968—. Lectr. marketing and advt. Roosevelt U., Chgo., 1968—. Mem. steering com. Western Springs (Ill.) Bicentennial Commn., 1974-76; dep. coordinator emergency services, Western Springs, 1976—; scoutmaster Boy Scouts Am., Western Springs, Ill., 1972—, recipient Vigil Honor, Order of the Arrow. Served with USMCR, 1942-43, USNR, 1943-46. Mem. Am. Mgmt. Assn. Republican. Presbyn. Club: Broadcast Advt. Home: 4106 Clausen Ave Western Springs IL 60558 Office: 901 Burlington Western Springs IL 60558

OSTENDORF, EDGAR LOUIS, JR., real estate co. exec.; b. Cleve., July 30, 1934; s. Edgar Louis and Mary Martha (McConnell) O.; B.S. Bus Adminstrn., John Carroll U., 1957; m. Joan Marie Donahue, Feb. 10, 1962; 1 dau., Mary E. Salesman real estate Ostendorf-Morris Co., Cleve., 1959-68; pres. First Commerce Realty Co., Mentor, O., 1968-70; owner Ostendorf Assos., Cleve., 1970—. Mem. Citizens League, 1964—, speakers com. United Appeal, 1966-70; occupational planning com. Welfare Fedn., 1965-67; mem. council smaller enterprises Cleve. Growth Assn., 1973—, v.p. 1974-76. Served with U.S. Army, 1957-59. Mem. Real Estate Securities and Syndication Inst. (pres. Ohio chpt. 1976), Nat., Ohio, Cleve. bds. realtors, Nat. Assn. Real Estate Appraisers, Nat. Inst. Real Estate Brokers. Clubs: Chagrin Valley Hunt, Union. Home: 3425 Roundwood Rd Chagrin Falls OH 44022 Office: 28349 Chagrin Blvd Cleveland OH 44122

OSTERKAMP, WAITE ROBERT, hydrologist; b. Clayton, Mo., Nov. 7, 1939; s. Clifton Grover and Constance Elizabeth (Waite) O.; B.A.Geology, U. Colo., 1961, B.A. in Chemistry, 1963; M.S. (B.S. Butler scholar), U. Ariz., 1970, Ph.D., 1976; m. Marilynn Spear Bowie, June 15, 1963; children—Jeffrey Mark, Laurel Alyce. Chemist, U.S. Geol. Survey, Denver, 1965, Helena, Mont., 1966-68, hydrologist, Tucson, 1971-73, Lawrence, Kans., 1974—; research asst. U. Ariz., Tucson, 1969, teaching asso., 1970. Mem. AAAS, Am. Geol. Soc., Nat. Water Well Assn., Sierra Club, Sigma Gamma Epsilon. Contbr. articles to profl. jours. Home: 2628 Bardith Ct Lawrence KS 66044 Office: 1950 Ave A Capus West U Kans Lawrence KS 66044

OSTERLUND, RUSSELL GAYLORD, cons. engr.; b. Lawrence, Mich., Nov. 15, 1922; s. Carl August and Bertha (Hackonson) O.; B.S., U. Mich., 1950; m. Joyce Dolores Brown, Feb. 11, 1950 (div. Apr. 1970); children—Russell Gaylord, Robert Girard, Lynnette Gail. Supr., Parke Davis & Co., Detroit, 1950-55; sales engr., mgr. Fisher Sci. Co., Pitts., 1955-62; cons. engr. R. G. Osterlund & Assos., Pitts., 1962-64; project engr., mgr. The Austin Co., Detroit, 1964-66, Des Plaines, Ill., 1966-70; design engr. Williams & Works, Grand Rapids, Mich., 1970-72; project engr., mgr. Roy F. Weston, Inc., Wilmette, Ill., 1972-76; project mgr. Murphy Engrs., Inc., Chgo., 1976—. Mem. Oak Park (Ill.) Concert Tour Assn., 1973—. Served with U.S. Army, 1943-46. Registered profl. engr., Ill., Mich., Pa., N.Y., Ind., Wis., Minn., Iowa. Mem. Am. Inst. Chem. Engrs., Nat. Soc. Profl. Engrs. Home: 179 N Lombard St Oak Park IL 60302 Office: 224 S Michigan Ave Chicago IL 60604

OSTFELD, ALEXANDER MARION, advt. agy. exec.; b. St. Louis, Feb. 13, 1932; s. Simon and Margaret (Fishmann) O.; B.S., Washington U., St. Louis, 1953; postgrad. St. Louis U., 1953-56. Mktg. mgr. lighting div. Emerson Electric Co., St. Louis, 1955-59; dir. research and media Frank Block Assos., St. Louis, 1959-61; research and media supr. Compton Advt., Chgo., 1961-65; media and mktg. supr. Leo Burnett Advt., Chgo., 1965-68; dir. mktg. and account planning, v.p. McCann-Erickson, Chgo., 1968-72, Kenyon & Eckhardt, Chgo., 1972; now dir. Canadian and internat. ops. A. Eicoff & Co., Chgo. Cons. Am. Assn. Advt. Agys. Mem. Am. Mktg. Assn. (sec. St. Louis 1956-57), Internat. Platform Assn., Broadcast Advt. Club, Am. Research Found. Clubs: Chgo. Exec.; Hadlock Hunt (Cary, Ill.). Home: 391 Poplar Ave Elmhurst IL 60126 Office: 520 N Michigan Ave Chicago IL 60611

OSTLUND, ARTHUR CLAYTON, accounting firm exec.; b. Mpls., June 7, 1920; s. Carl Oscar and Eleanor Rachael (Boquist) O.; B.B.A. with distinction, U. Minn., 1948, M.A., 1949; m. Virginia Eileen Rapacz, Aug. 12, 1948; children—Suzanne (Mrs. E. Marshall Fisher), Eileen. With firm Touche Ross & Co., Mpls., 1949-65, exec. office, Chgo., 1965—, partner, 1963—. Leader courses for profl. devel. programs, Ill., Iowa bd. dirs. Western Springs (Ill.) Library Bd., 1971-77, pres., mem. planning com., 1975-77. Served to maj. AUS, 1941-46. C.P.A., Minn., Ill. Mem. Nat. Assn. Accountants, Am. Accounting Assn., VFW, Am. Inst. C.P.A.'s (editorial bd. Jour. Accountancy 1969-71, accountants legal liability com. ethics div. 1970-74, chmn. com. behavioral standards 1973-76, mem. exec. com. 1972—, chmn. exec. com. 1976—, mem. council 1975—), Ill. (trustee found., pres. soc. and found. 1976—), Minn. Soc. C.P.A.'s, Beta Gamma Sigma, Beta Alpha Psi. Clubs: Edgewood Valley Country, Mid-America, Executive. Home: 5208 Clausen Ave Western Springs IL 60558 Office: 111 E Wacker Dr Chicago IL 60601

OSTLUND, LEONARD ALEXANDER, educator; b. Bronx, N.Y., July 1, 1910; s. Charles and Bertha Christina (Sandstrom) O.; B.A. magna cum laude, Colgate U., Hamilton, N.Y., 1948; M.Ed., Clark U.,

1949; Ph.D., Kans. U., 1953; m. Anna Lisa Frideborg Hanson, June 4, 1938. Instr. psychology Colgate U., 1949-50; asst. prof. psychology, sch. examiner Okla. State U., Stillwater, 1953-56; asst. prof. psychology, counselor Psychology Clinic Kent (O.) State U., 1956-60; asso. prof. human relations Ohio U., Athens, 1960-67, prof. guidance and counseling, 1967—. Fulbright vis. prof. psychology U. de Rennes, France, 1968, U. de Bordeaux, 1959; cons. NSF, 1956-61, HEW, 1955—, NDEA Inst., 1960, Goodwill Industries, 1960-66, Bur. Vocat. Rehab., 1960-66, Athens (O.) City Schs., 1960—, Good Samaritan Hosp., Zanesville, O., 1963-64, Wright-Patterson AFB, 1964. Bd. dirs. YMCA, 1956-60. Served with USNR, 1944-46; ETO. Mem. AAAS, AAUP, Am. Personnel and Guidance Assn., Am., Ohio, S.E. Ohio psychol. assns., Assn. Coll. Educators and Suprs., Nat. Vocat. Guidance Assn., Am. Rehab. Counselors Assn., Am. Coll. Personnel Assn., Phi Beta Kappa, Sigma Xi, Phi Delta Kappa. Contbr. numerous articles and book revs. to profl. jours. Home: Route 6 Box 83 Coolville Ridge Athens OH 45701

OSTRAND, JANET LOUISE, psychologist; b. Highland Park, Ill., May 25, 1945; d. Walter August and Lucille Louise (Gerken) Ostrand; B.S., U. Ill., 1968, M.A., 1970, Ph.D., 1973; m. Thomas Hubert Plaisance, Apr. 24, 1976. Intern, Chgo. Read Mental Health Center, 1971; asst. supr. to counseling practicum U. Ill., Urbana, 1972; psychotherapist, Rehab. Center U. Ill., Urbana, 1973; psychologist, counseling service U. Ill., Chgo. Circle, 1973—; pvt. practice, Chgo., 1976—; mem. council Nat. Register Health Service Providers in Psychology. Mem. Am. Psychol. Assn., AAUP, Kappa Delta Pi. Contbr. articles to profl. jours. Office: University Hall Univ Ill Chicago IL 60680

OSTROM, KAY ANN, speech pathologist; b. Belleville, Ill., Aug. 10, 1948; d. Robert George and Dorothy Matilda (Wlasak) Fritz; B.S., So. Ill. U., 1970, M.S., 1972; m. Donnie Charles Ostrom, Aug. 21, 1971; 1 son, Nels Patrick. Speech therapist intern Jewish Hosp., St. Louis, 1971; speech therapist Kaskaskia Spl. Edn. Dist., Centralia, Ill., 1971—. Mem. Am., Southwestern Ill. speech and hearing assns. Democrat. Mem. United Ch. of Christ. Home: 203 Bel Air Dr Mascoutah IL 62258 Office: 308 N Washington Trenton IL 62293

OSTROM, SUSAN MC WHIRTER, realtor, newspaper columnist, civic worker, clubwoman; b. Greencastle, Ind., Aug. 28, 1888; d. Felix T. and Luella (Smith) McWhirter; student Vassar Coll., 1907-08; A.B., De Pauw U., 1909; m. Henry Evan Ostrom, Apr. 29, 1910 (div. Apr., 1951); children—Ethel Mary (Mrs. Theodore Clay Pilcher), Henry Felix. With Clyde Realty Co., Indpls., 1948—; sec. Ostrom Realty and Constrn. Co., Indpls., 1912-50; columnist Indpls. News, 1913-63; dir. pub. relations and information div. Ind. Dept. Pub. Instrn., 1942-47. Sec., Indpls. Council Federated Ch. Women, 1931-35; charter mem. Meth. Hosp. White Cross Guild, 1933—; hon. mem. commn. ecumenical mission and relations United Presbyn. Ch. U.S., 1966; chmn. Marion Co. women's div. Ind. War Finance Com., 1942-47; vice-chmn., incorporator Monument Circle Easter Sunrise Carol Service, 1935-61; mem. Indpls. Anti-Crime Crusade. Del., Ind. Republican Conv., 1946; bd. dirs. Indpls. Women's Rep. Club, 1963-64. Recipient Frances Wright award outstanding contbn. to journalism 1958, Women in Communications, Gold medallion 50 yrs.-in-journalism, 1963; awards (2) Ind. Fedn. Women's Clubs, 1963; Distinguished Service certificate of honor Gen. Fedn. Women's Clubs, 1972; 50 year service pin Indpls. Newspapers, Inc., 1963. Mem. Ind. Fedn. Clubs (adv. council 1913-63; hon. mem. state officers clubs 1958—), Nat. W.C.T.U. (adv. bd. 1913-20), Nat. League Am. Pen Women (v.p. Indpls. br. 1960-62), Soc. Ind. Pioneers (publicity chmn. 1963-65), Ind. Hist. Soc., Ind. Vassar Alumnae Club (sec. 1935-37), DePauw U. Alumni Assn., Indpls. Women's Dept. Club (charter mem. 1912, dir. 1965-67, recognition award 1973), Woman's Press Club Ind. (charter mem. 1913, sec. 1921-23, emblem locket 1973), D.A.R., Epsilon Sigma Omicron, Kappa Alpha Theta (pres. Indpls. alumnae chpt. 1918-19). Presbyn. (sec. ch. circle 1965-67). Address: 3777 N Meridian St Apt 304 Indianapolis IN 46208

OSUCH, LEONARD JOHN, mech. engr., electronic designer; b. Chgo., Nov. 19, 1918; s. Louis Stanley and Anna Mary (Orzada) O.; student Chgo. Tech. Coll., 1942-46; m. Bernice Louise Kiernoski, Sept. 27, 1942; children—James, Barbara, Robert, Annette. Asst. chief of engrs., then mgr. aircraft div. H.M. Harper Co., Morton Grove, Ill., 1952-57; founder, pres. Osuch Bros. Tool Co., Chgo., 1953—; founder, operator, cons., advisor Osuch Ceramic Co., Niles, Ill., 1963—; pvt. practice mech. engring., elec., electronic designing, Niles, Ill., 1948—. Mem. ASME, Soc. Mfg. Engrs., Am. Soc. Metals. Democrat. Roman Catholic. Clubs: Holy Name Soc. (past pres.), K.C. (4th deg.), Great Central Ceramic League (past pres.), Chicagoland Ceramic Circle (treas. 1975-77). Patentee automatic kiln firing, 1974. Home: 3077 N Elbridge Ave Chicago IL 60618 Office: 7430 N Milwaukee Ave Niles IL 60648

O'SULLIVAN, JOHN FRANCIS, constrn. co. exec.; b. Pawtucket, R.I., Aug. 2, 1918; s. John F. and Mary (Taylor) O'S.; B.S. in Civil Engring., U. R.I., 1950; M.S. in Engring., U. Fla., 1951; m. Helen Ethyl Halipos, Dec. 29, 1942; children—John Francis, James T., Jay D., Jacqueline. Enlisted U.S. Army, 1940, commd. capt., 1947, resigned, 1947; design engr. Charles A. Maguire & Assos., Boston, 1950-51, Keyes & Holroyd, Troy, N.Y., 1953, Metcalf & Eddy, Boston, 1953-56; chief san. engr. East Providence (R.I.), 1951-53; project engr. Wilhelm Constrn. Co., Indpls., 1956-59; chief engr., sec.-treas. Joe R. Norman Contractor, Inc., Indpls., 1960-71, Indpls. Rentals, Inc., 1960-71; chief engr., v.p. Eagle Valley Constrn. Corp., Clermont, Ind., 1971—; sec.-treas. Frash, Inc., 1972—. Decorated Silver Star medal, Bronze Star medal, Purple Heart. Registered profl. engr., R.I., Ky. Mem. Soc. Profl. Engrs., Aircraft Owners and Pilots Assn., Res. Officers Assn., Sigma Nu. Episcopalian (jr. warden 1966, 67). Club: Greenfield (Ind.) Country. Home: 5908 Karen Dr Indianapolis IN 46239 Office: 20222 Hague Rd Noblesville IN 46060

O'SULLIVAN, JOHN LEWIS, physician; b. Cwm, Monmouthshire, Eng., Mar. 24, 1932; s. Florance and Eileen (Lewis) O'S.; student Cambridge U., 1949-52; M.A., M.B., B.Chir., Westminster Hosp. Med. Sch., 1955; m. Elizabeth Brewis, Oct. 30, 1956; children—Timothy, Clare (dec.), James, Anne. Intern, Addenbrooke's Hosp., Cambridge, Eng., 1955-56; resident Royal Ipswich and East Suffolk Hosp., Eng., 1956-57; med. officer, Uganda, 1959-62; gen. practice medicine, Emo, Ont., Can., 1964—; dir. Falcon Holidays Ltd., County Kerry, Ireland. Coroner, Dists. of Kenora and Rainy River, 1964—; mem. Emo Red Cross Hosp. Com., 1966—; mem. Ad Hoc Health Council, Rainy River Dist., 1972—. Served with M.C., Brit. Army, 1957-59. Mem. Harrow Assn., Brit. Med. Assn., Coroners Assn. Ont. Club: Sidney (Cambridge). Address: Box 116 Emo ON POW 1E0 Canada

OTANI, YOSHIHIKO, educator; b. Fukui, Japan, Jan. 10, 1938; s. Shigeki and Fumiko (Adachi) O.; B.A., Kobe U., 1960; Ph.D., U. Minn., 1969; m. Junko Amaike, Oct. 22, 1969; 1 son, Atsuhisa. Researcher, Shell Oil Co., Japan, 1960-65; asst. prof. econs., U. Minn., 1969-70; asst. prof. Purdue U., Lafayette, Ind., 1970-74, asso. prof., 1974-76; asso. prof. U. Kans., Lawrence, 1976—. Woodrow Wilson dissertation fellow, 1968-69. Mem. Am. Econ. Assn., Econometric Soc., Soc. Indsl. and Applied Math. Home: 507 Arizona St Lawrence KS 66044 Office: Dept Econs Univ Kansas Lawrence KS 66045

OTIS, JAMES CORNISH, judge; b. St. Paul, Mar. 23, 1912; s. James Cornish and Winifred (Brill) O.; B.A., Yale U., 1934; LL.B., U. Minn., 1937; m. Constance S. Dillingham, Apr. 6, 1974; children by previous marriage—Emily T., James D., Todd H. Admitted to Minn. bar, 1937; partner firm Otis, Faricy & Burger, St. Paul, 1937-48; municipal judge City St. Paul, 1948-54; judge 2d Dist. Ct. Minn., St. Paul, 1954-61; asso. justice Supreme Ct. Minn., 1961—. Trustee Hamline U., Amherst Wilder Found., Minn. Nature Conservancy. Mem. Inst. Jud. Adminstrn., Am., Minn. bar assns., Am. Judicature Soc., Nat. Council Crime and Delinquency, Phi Delta Phi. Unitarian. Home: 7 Crocus Hill St Paul MN 55102 Office: 230 State Capitol St Paul MN 55155

OTIS, JAMES JOHN, physician; b. Ann Arbor, Mich., Oct. 22, 1913; s. Lloyd M. and Barbara (Audritsh) O.; A.B., Denison U., 1935; M.B., U. Cin., 1939, M.D., 1940; m. Betty Hammel, Oct. 9, 1944; children—Sharon Otis Gray, Vicki Lynn, James Lloyd, Jean Ellen. Intern, Christ Hosp., Cin., 1939-40; resident in obstetrics Toledo Hosp., 1940; practice medicine, specializing in obstetrics and gynecology, Celina, Ohio, 1940—; adminstr. Otis Hosp., Inc., Celina, 1953—. Pres., Mercer County Heart Assn., 1958-68, 73; med. dir. Mercer County Red Cross, 1968-73; trustee, pres. bd. Otis Hosp., Inc.; trustee Central Ohio Heart Assn.; mem. devel. fund Ohio State U., 1970—. Mem. Ohio State Med. Assn., AMA, Am. Assn. Family Practice, Mercer County Med. Assn. (polit. activity com. 1968-73), Nu Sigma Nu, Sigma Chi. Methodist (chmn. fin. 1973). Clubs: Masons, Shriners, Jesters. Home: 3150 Maple Dr Celina OH 45822 Office: 111 N Walnut St Celina OH 45822 also 441 E Market St Celina OH 45822

OTIS, ROBERT CHARLES, prodn. engr., power supply mfg. co. exec.; b. Missouri Valley, Iowa, Mar. 12, 1932; s. Joseph Charles and Lucille Frances (Lahman) Otis; student Alexander Hamilton Inst., 1965-67, Milw. Area Tech. Coll., 1971-72; m. Charlene Utech, Oct. 30, 1953; children—Joseph, Vickie, Randall, Susan, Steven, Robert. Vice pres., gen. mgr. Coiltronics, Inc., Harlen, Iowa, 1961-62; exec. v.p. Coils, Inc., Omaha, 1962-66; pres. Otis Industries, Omaha, 1962-66; pres. Brubo Industries, Mpls., 1969—; prodn. engr. Ault, Inc., Mpls., 1974—. Clubs: Masons, Eagles. Patentee automatic grease filter for instnl. cookers. Home: 1523 S Timber Ridge Fridley MN 55432 Office: 1600 H Freeway Blvd Minneapolis MN 55430

OTIS, ROBERT EDWARD, educator; b. Bellingham, Wash., Mar. 16, 1943; s. Robert Burns and Veda Irene (Sills) O.; B.A., Western Wash. State Coll., 1965; M.A., 1968, Mich. State U., Ph.D., 1972; m. Barbara Ann Boike, May 18, 1968. Psychology technician VA Hosp., Battle Creek, Mich., 1966-73; research asso. dept. pathology Mich. State U., 1972-73; instr. U. Wis., Fond du Lac, 1974-75; asst. prof. psychology Ripon (Wis.) Coll., 1973—. Bd. dirs. Ripon Area Service Center. Mem. Am., Midwestern psychol. assns., Animal Behavior Soc., AAAS, others. Contbr. articles to profl. jours. Home: Union St Ripon WI 54971 Office: Dept Psychology Ripon College Ripon WI 54971

O'TOOLE, JEANNE MARIE, hosp. educator; b. Chgo., Sept. 18, 1924; d. Dennis Joseph and Eleanor Marie (Fleming) O'Toole; B.A., Mt. Mary Coll., 1946; M.A., St. Xavier U., 1966; Ph.D., Loyola U., Chgo., 1972. Supr., Hartford Accident and Indemnity Co., Chgo., 1946-53; supr. personnel Carson Pirie Scott & Co., Chgo., 1953-57; tchr. Evergreen Park Sch. Dist., 1957-69; dir. edn. Meml. Hosp., Elmhurst, Ill., 1975—; lectr., Loyola U., Chgo., 1969—. Chmn. ednl. planning Beverly Area Planning Assn., 1973—; mem. finance com. Christ the King Sch. Bd., 1973—, pres. bd., 1974—; mem. exec. adv. bd. Loyola U., Chgo., 1972—, chmn. grad. sch. fund raising drive, 1973, pres. Chgo. Alumnae Assn., 1975. Recipient Fellowship, Loyola U., 1970. Mem. PTA (life), AAUP, Am. Hosp. Assn., Council Basic Edn., History Edn. Soc., Delta Kappa Gamma, Phi Delta Kappa. Republican. Roman Catholic. Club: Big Sand Lake (Phelps, Wis.). Home: 9636 S Oakley St Chicago IL 60643

OTRICH, GEORGE HAMILTON, supt. schs.; b. Jonesboro, Ill., Aug. 26, 1918; s. Charles O. and Mabel (Hileman) O.; student Wofford Coll., 1944; B.S., So. Ill. U., 1947, M.S., 1950, Ed.S., 1956, postgrad., 1956-60; postgrad. Washington U., 1959; Ph.D., So. Ill. U., 1965; m. Mildred Adams, July 26, 1939; 1 dau., Janet Marie. Tchr. Jonesboro Elementary Sch., 1941-47; tchr. social studies, coach, athletic dir., asst. prin. Anna (Ill.) Jr. High Sch., 1947-59; supt. schs. Union County, Ill., 1959—. Chmn. edn. com. for Union County, White House Conf. Children and Youth, 1960. Bd. dirs. Stinson Meml. Library, 1959—. Served from pvt. to 2d lt. U.S. Army, 1942-45. Mem. NEA, Ill. Assn. County Supts. Schs. (pres. 1973), Sch. Masters Club, Am., Ill. assns. sch. adminstrs., Rural Edn. Assn., Am. Legion, Phi Delta Kappa. Democrat. Baptist. Contbr. chpts. in books; also articles to profl. jours. Home: 206 Walnut St Jonesboro IL 62952 Office: 311 N Market St Jonesboro IL 62952

OTT, JERRY D., painter; b. Albert Lea, Minn., July 31, 1947; s. Elmer and Erma (Bratsch) O.; student Mankato (Minn.) State Coll., 1965-69, U. Minn., 1971; m. Lynn Townsend, July 29, 1972. One man shows: Meisel Gallery, N.Y.C., 1973, 75, Gallery 118, Mpls., 1973, Morgan Gallery, Kansas City, 1977, Monte Carlo, Monaco, 1974; group shows include: Walker Art Center, Mpls., 1968; Tokyo Biennial, 1974; N.Y. Cultural Center, N.Y.C., 1975. Home: 210 County Rd B2 East St Paul MN 55117

OTT, MELVIN DALE, leasing co. exec.; b. Manistique, Mich., Oct. 8, 1936; s. Dale D. and Helen (Johnson) O.; grad. certificate Am. Inst. Banking, 1963; m. Mary Louise Edwards, Aug. 27, 1966; 1 stepdau., Paula MacKenzie. Head teller Detroit Bank & Trust Co., 1955-58; collection mgr. Bank Dearborn (Mich.), 1958-63, asst. br. mgr., 1963-64; v.p. Consol. Acceptance Corp., Detroit, 1964-65; ops. mgr., asst. sec. Internat. Leasing Corp., Detroit, 1964-66; ops. mgr., controller Robert Smith Leasing, Grand Rapids, Mich., 1966-68; v.p., gen. mgr. Vandenberg Leasing, Inc., Holland, Mich., 1968—. Sec.-treas. Dearborn (Mich.) Inter-Service Club Council, 1960; divisional membership chmn. Dearborn YMCA, 1961; treas. Dearborn Coordinating Com. for new Constitution, 1958; adviser Jr. Achievement Southeastern Mich., 1956-58. Served with Mich. N.G., 1957. Recipient Key Man award Dearborn Jr. C. of C., 1963. Mem. Nat. Assn. Fleet Adminstrs., Am. Fleet and Leasing Assn., Car and Truck Rental and Leasing Assn. (v.p. Mich. chpt.). Clubs: Eagles, Elks, Rotary, Optimists (dir. 1972-73), Country (Holland, Mich.). Home: 694 Marylane Holland MI 49423 Office: 1191 S Washington St Holland MI 49423

OTT, RICHARD HERBERT, automobile co. exec.; b. Muskegon, Mich., Nov. 24, 1937; s. Herbert Lawrence and Minnie Irene (Poe) O.; student Muskegon Community Coll., 1958; B.S., Mich. Tech. U., 1960; m. Barbara Jean Nauta, Sept. 2, 1960; children—Kathleen Ann, Richard Herbert, Kelly Sue, Karen Jean. Process engr., project engr., maintenance and prodn. supr. Anaconda Wire & Cable Co., Muskegon, Mich., 1960-67; plant engr. A W & C Co., LaGrange, Ky., 1967-69; supt. maintenance and constrn. Badische Anilin and Soda Fabrik-Wyandotte, Wyandotte, Mich., 1969-71, supt. works engring., 1971-72; mgr. plant engring. Milw. body plant Am. Motors Co., 1972-74, mgr. mfg. engring., 1974—. Patentee in field. Home: 12147 W Belmar Dr Hales Corners WI 53130 Office: 3880 N Richards St Milwaukee WI 53201

OTT, ROGER ARTHUR, surgeon; b. Dubuque, Iowa, Aug. 12, 1930; s. Arthur William and Gertrude (Manders) O.; B.S. magna cum laude, Loras Coll., 1951; M.D., Loyola U., Chgo., 1955; m. Luanus McDermott, June 11, 1955; children—Roger Arthur, Lezlie Erin, Judson William, Kristin Feeley, Jennifer Alane, Stefanie Ann, Sarah Lynn, Alison Suzanne. Intern, Cook County Hosp., Chgo., 1955-56, resident surgery, 1959-63; clin. instr. surgery U. Ill., 1960-62; surgeon Med. Assos., Dubuque, 1963—; mem. staff Mercy Hosp., 1963—, chief of staff, 1967; mem. staff Finley, Xavier Hosps. Served to capt. M.C., AUS, 1956-58. Recipient Bruno Epstein Achievement award Cook County Hosp., 1956. Diplomate Am. Bd. Surgery. Fellow A.C.S.; mem. A.M.A., Iowa, Dubuque County med. socs., Midwest, Western surg. assns., Karl Meyer Surg. Soc., Iowa Acad. Surgeons, Am. Med. Soc. Vienna, Phi Chi. Home: 300 Fremont St Dubuque IA 52001 Office: 1000 Langworthy St Dubuque IA 52001

OTTE, KARL HENRY, research engr., educator; b. Chgo., Feb. 20, 1904; s. Paul C. and Mileta (Olbert) O.; B.S., Armour Inst. Tech., 1926, M.E., 1933; S.M., Mass. Inst. Tech., 1928; m. Maxine Muriel Roehl, June 10, 1950. Mech. engr. F.J. Littell Machine Co., 1926-27; mech. engr. on foundry devel. Hawthorne Plant, Western Electric Co., 1928-32; sr. indsl. engr. supr. devel. improved methods E.J. Brach & Sons, 1933-41; mech. engr. on research in printing equipment R. R. Donnelley & Sons, Inc. (all Chgo.), 1942; bldg. process engr. supervising process engring. dept. Milw. (Wis.) Ordnance Plant U.S. Rubber Co., 1942-43; mech. engr. supervising engring. research and devel. equipment Purity Bakeries Service Corp., Chgo., and its successor Am. Bakeries Co., 1943-63; asst. prof. mech. engring. U. Ill., Chgo.; lectr. in machine design Lewis Inst. Bd. dirs. St. Paul's House (home for aged). Registered profl. engr., Ill. Fellow Am. Soc. M.E.; mem. Nat. Soc. Profl. Engrs., Am. Mgmt. Assn., Western Soc. Engrs., Am. Foundrymen's Soc., Am. Soc. Engring. Edn. Clubs: University, Massachusetts Institute Technology (Chgo.). Patentee. Home: 1005 S Knight Ave Park Ridge IL 60068 Office: University of Ill Chgo Circle Chicago IL 60680

OTTEN, KENNETH HARRY, lawyer; b. Springfield, Ill., Mar. 17, 1918; s. Harry and Almuth E. (Raman) O.; B.S., U. Chgo., 1940; M.S., U. Okla., 1943; LL.B., U. Mich., 1954; m. Dorothy M. Wilson, Apr. 12, 1952; children—Gregory P., Gretchen E. Personnel technician Ill. CSC, Springfield, 1946-51; admitted to Ill. bar, 1955; since practiced in Springfield. Chmn., Springfield Zoning Bd. Appeals, 1956-60. Served with USAAF, 1943-46. Mem. Am., Ill. State (chmn. pub. utilities sect. 1971-72), Sangamon County (pres. 1969-70) bar assns. Republican. Congregationalist (moderator 1972-73). Clubs: Masons (32 deg.), Shriners, Lions (pres. 1973-74). Home: 1215 Ivywood Dr Springfield IL 62704 Office: 916 Illinois Bldg Springfield IL 62701

OTTENFELD, MARSHALL, mktg. research exec.; b. Chgo., Jan. 15, 1937; s. Leo and Sadie (Patt) O.; B.A., U. Chgo., 1959; M.A., Roosevelt U., 1968; m. Gloria Jean Zilke, Dec. 28, 1960; children—David Joel, Jonathan Lawrence, Jennifer Lynn, Heather Anne. Study dir. Chgo. Tribune, 1962-64; project dir. Gardner Advt. Co., N.Y.C., 1964-65; research asso. Advt. Research Found., N.Y.C., 1965-66, Abbott Labs., Waukegan, Ill., 1966-70; sr. v.p. mktg. research D'Arcy-MacManus & Masius, Chgo., 1970—, pres. subs. Mid-Am. Research Assos., Chgo., 1970—; lectr. mktg. Roosevelt U. Active Boy Scouts Am. Served with U.S. Army, 1960-61. Mem. Am. Mktg. Assn., Am. Acad. of Polit. and Social Sci., Am. Assn. of Advt. Agencies (equal employment opportunity com.), Zeta Beta Tau. Jewish. Home: 1050 Summit Dr Deerfield IL 60015 Office: 200 E Randolph St Chicago IL 60015

OTTINGER, DENISE CATHERINE, coll. adminstr.; b. Wyandotte, Mich., Dec. 28, 1952; d. William D. and Catherine M. (Franks) Ottinger; B.S., Bowling Green State U., 1975, M.A., 1976. Asst. to asst. dean Firelands campus Bowling Green State U., Huron, Ohio, 1975-76; asst. coordinator campus life Ashland (Ohio) Coll., 1976-77, dir. residence hall staff and programs, 1977—. Task force Ashland Alcoholism Center, 1977—. Mem. Am. Personnel and Guidance Assn., Am. Coll. Personnel Assn., Kappa Delta. Home: Myers Hall Ashland Coll Ashland OH 44805 Office: 213 Founders Hall Ashland Coll Ashland OH 44805

OTTMAR, CLINTON RAYMOND, lawyer; b. nr. Wishek, N.D., Nov. 17, 1928; s. John O. and Katie (Ackerman) O.; Ph.B., U. N.D., 1951, J.D., 1955; m. Grace Bertha Gackle, Dec. 25, 1951; children—Timothy J., Mark D., Thomas C., Gail G. Admitted to N.D. bar, 1955; asso. firm Hjellum, Weiss, Nerison & Ottmar, Jamestown, 1955-62; individual practice, Jamestown, N.D., 1962-64; partner Ottmar & Nething, Jamestown, 1965-74, Ottmar, Nething & Pope, 1974-76, Ottmar & Pope, 1976—, states atty. Stutsman County, 1964-69; spl. asst. atty. gen. N.D., 1966—; city atty. Jamestown, 1974—. Merit badge counselor Red River council Boy Scouts Am., 1960-73; mem. Bd. Adjustments, City of Jamestown, 1969-74. Served to 1st lt. inf., U.S. Army, 1951-53. Decorated Combat Inf. badge, Commendation medal. Mem. Am., N.D. (past exec. com., past chmn. title standards com., pres. elect 1975, pres. 1976), 4th Jud. Dist. (past pres.), Stutsman County (past pres.) bar assns., N.D. States Attys. Assn. (past sec., dir.), Assn. Bars Northwestern Plains and Mountains (vice chancellor 1977-78), Am. Legion (past judge adv.), Jamestown C. of C. (past dir.). Republican. Methodist (chmn. trustee bd. N.D. conf.). Clubs: Masons, Elks, Rotary. Home: 509 1st Ave N Jamestown ND 58401 Office: 223 1st Ave N Jamestown ND 58401

OTTO, PATRICIA RUTH, counselor; b. St. Louis, Jan. 17, 1932; d. Loren Joel and Esther Ruth Helen (Hoge) LaMore; B.A., Central Meth. Coll., 1953; M.Ed., U. Mo., 1965; m. Robert J. Otto, Jan. 31, 1953. Tchr., Elsberry (Mo.) Schs., 1953-55, Kirkwood (Mo.) Schs., 1955-65; counselor Sch. Dist. of Clayton (Mo.), 1965—; mem. Supts. Juvenile Facilities of St. Louis County. Mem. St. Louis County Decent Lit. Commn. Mem. Am., St. Louis (treas.) personnel and guidance assns., Kirkwood Community Tchrs. Assn. (pres.), St. Louis English Tchrs. Assn. (pres.), St. Louis Suburban Guidance Assn. (pres.), St. Louis Met. Middle Sch. Assn. (pres.), St. Louis Suburban Tchrs. Assn. (sec.), Mo. Guidance Assn., Nat. Assn. Pupil Personnel Adminstrs., Pi Lambda Theta. Editorial bd. Elementary Guidance and Counseling Jour., 1974-77. Contbr. articles to profl. jours. Home: 9869 Musick Rd Affton MO 63123 Office: 6500 Wydown Blvd Clayton MO 63105

OTTO, ROSWELL D., antique dealer; b. Mpls., June 29, 1920; s. Henry C. and Hildur T. (Linton) O.; A.B., U. Minn., 1943, A.M., 1945, grad. study, 1951—. Announcer, actor, writer, producer, KUOM, Mpls., 1943—; became asst. prof. speech, dir. radio programs Gustavus Adolphus Coll., 1947; instr. gen. studies, speech U. Minn., 1953-60; antique dealer, St. Cloud, Minn., 1969—. Mem. U. Minn. Radio Guild, theatre workshop, Alpha Epsilon Rho, Delta Phi Lambda, Speech Assn. Am. Club: Canterbury. Home: 324 3 Ave S St Cloud MN 56301

OTTO, WAYNE RAYMOND, educator; b. Fremont, Wis., Oct. 22, 1931; s. Henry F. and Edna A. (Wohlt) O.; B.S., U. Wis., 1953, M.S., 1959, Ph.D., 1961; m. Shirley J. Bergen, Oct. 13, 1953; 1 dau., Eleni.

Asst. prof. U. Oreg., 1961-64; asso. prof. U. Ga., 1964-65; prof. U. Wis., Madison, 1965—, prin. investigator, asso. dir. Wis. Research and Devel. Center, 1965—, chmn. dept. curriculum and instrn., 1972-76; cons. Time-Life Video, Am. Insts. for Research, CEMREL, Inc., Bur. for Edn. of Handicapped, also pub. schs.; edn. collaborator Coronet Ednl. Films. Served with USMCR, 1953-55. Mem. Internat. Reading Assn., Nat. Reading Conf. (dir.). Am. Ednl. Research Assn., Am. Psychol. Assn., Nat. Council Research in English. Author: (with others) Teaching Adults to Read, 1967, Administering the School Reading Program, 1970, Wisconsin Design for Reading Skill Development, 1972, Corrective and Remedial Teaching, 1973, Focused Reading Instruction, 1974, Merrill Linguistic Reading Program, 1975, Objective Based Reading, 1976, Speedway: The Action Way to Speed Read, 1975; co-editor: Remedial Teaching, 1969; Reading Problems: A Multidisciplinary Approach, 1977; exec. editor Jour. Ednl. Research, 1969—. Home: 4161 Cherokee Dr Madison WI 53711 Office: 1025 W Johnson St U Wis Madison WI 53706

OTTOLINI, JAMES LOUIS, physician; b. Herrin, Ill., Apr. 18, 1939; s. Mario Alex and Mary Alice (Doyle) O.; B.A., So. Ill. U., 1961; M.D., St. Louis U., 1965; m. Barbara Lee Reber, June 18, 1966; children—Elisabeth, James, Alice. Intern, John Mercy Med. Center, St. Louis, 1965, resident in obstetrics and gynecology, 1966-69, asst. dir. dept. obstetrics and gynecology, 1972—, also dir. ultrasound lab.; practice medicine specializing in obstetrics and gynecology, St. Louis, 1970—; mem. staff St. John's Mercy Hosp., St. Mary's Hosp., sec. Met. Obstet. Gynecol., Inc., 1971—. Served to capt. USAF, 1969-71. Fellow A.C.S., Am. Fertility Soc., Am. Coll. Obstetrics and Gynecology; mem. St. Louis Gynecologic Soc., Am. Inst. Ultrasonic Medicine. Roman Catholic. Club: Elks. Home: 12523 Trammell St Creve Coeur MO 63141 Office: 621 S New Ballas Rd Creve Coeur MO 63141

OTTOW, ORVILLE CHARLES, mfg. co. exec.; b. Chgo., Oct. 23, 1921; s. Fred C. and Marie B. (Dumke) O.; B.A., Loyola U., 1954; m. Ann Marovich, Jan. 30, 1943 (dec. 1970); children—Patricia Ottow Galen, Dan, David; m. 2d, Beverly Parker, Oct. 2, 1971. Asst. mgr. Triangle Paper Box, 1953-56; sales mgr. Triangle Container, 1956-59; sales mgr. display div. Menasha Corp., Chgo., 1959-64; v.p. display div. Tri-Pack Corp., Chgo., 1964—, also Western Tri. Pack, San Francisco. Sec. Niles, Ill. Zoning Bd. and Planning Commn., 1968—; chmn. bd. Point of Purchase Advt. Inst., 1976-77. Served to capt. AUS, 1942-46. Mem. Fibre Box Assn., Lithographers Club Chgo., Am. Legion. Home: 8555 W Clara Dr Niles IL 60648 Office: 2828 S Lock St Chicago IL 60608

OTWAY, FRANK HAMILTON, bakery co. exec.; b. St. George, B.W.I., Mar. 1, 1923; s. Claude Hamilton and Verna Claire (Hughes) O.; came to U.S., 1926, naturalized, 1941; B.S., Rider Coll., 1951; m. Isabel Thorburn, Feb. 6, 1942; children—Dale Hamilton, Gary Scott, Christine C. (Mrs. James Cline), Lyris A. (Mrs. Robert Woodruff), Robert David. Asst. div. sales mgr. Wesson Oil Co., Bayonne, N.J., 1952-56; regional sales mgr. Joe Lowe Corp., N.Y.C., 1956-59; v.p. sales Cooper-Mattei Corp., Chgo., 1959-64; with Schaefers Bakery, Inc., Springfield, O., 1964—, pres., 1964—, dir. 1973—; dir. First Nat. Bank of Springfield, Sweet Mfg. Co., Springfield, O. Mem. exec. com. United Way of Clark County, Springfield, O., 1971—, campaign chmn. 1973, pres., 1975; mem. exec. com. Tecumseh Council, Boy Scouts Am., 1970. Bd. dirs. Jr. Achievement, 1968-75, pres. 1970-71; mem. bd. dirs. Springfield Symphony, 1968-72. Served to sgt. USMC, 1943-46. Mem. Ohio Bakers Assn. (dir. 1968—, pres. 1971), Am. Soc. Bakery Engrs. (exec. com. 1975—), Springfield C. of C. (pres. 1972), Tri State Bakers Club (pres. 1972). Presbyn. (mem. bd. trustees 1968—). Rotarian. Home: 1700 Fairfield Pike Springfield OH 45502 Office: 508 W Main St Springfield OH 45504

OUGHTON, JAMES HENRY, JR., bus. exec., farmer; b. Chgo., May 14, 1913; s. James H. and Barbara (Corbett) O.; student Dartmouth Coll., 1931-35; m. Jane Boyce, Jan. 23, 1940; children—Diana (dec.), Carol Oughton Biondi, Jr., Pamela Oughton Powell, Deborah. Pres., dir. L.E. Keeley Co., Dwight, Ill., 1936—, Nev. Corp.; past adminstr. The Keeley Inst., Dwight, 1938—; v.p., dir 1st Nat. Bank of Dwight, 1946—, Ill. Valley Investment Co.; farmer, farm mgr., livestock feeder, Ill.; sec., dir. Dwight Indsl. Assn.; past mem. Ill. Ho. of Reps. Co-chmn. 1st Indsl. Conf. on Alcoholism, 1948; chmn. Midwest Seminar on Alcoholism for Pastors, 1957, 58, 59, 60; chmn. adv. bd. Ill. Dept. Corrections; chmn. Gov.'s Task Force on Mental Health Adminstrn., 1971-72; chmn. adv. bd. Ill. Dept. Mental Health; dir., mem. exec. bd., Corn Belt council Boy Scouts Am. Served as lt. (j.g.) USNR, 1944-46; PTO. Republican. Episcopalian. Clubs: Univ., Union League (Chgo.). Address: 103 W South St Dwight IL 60420

OUGHTON, RICHARD CORBETT, banker; b. Chgo., July 10, 1919; s. James Henry and Barbara I. (Corbett) O.; grad. Lake Forest Acad., 1937; student Dartmouth Coll., 1937-39, U. Va., 1939-40; m. China Robbins Ibsen, Apr. 2, 1945; children—China (Mrs. David Ayer), John Richard, Michael Corbett. With First Nat. Bank of Dwight (Ill.), 1940-42, 57—, pres., 1966-71, chmn., 1972—, also dir.; self employed as family real estate mgr., 1946-57; treas., dir. Dwight Indsl. Assn., 1967—, Ill. Valley Investment Co., 1971—; treas. Dwight Continental Manor, Inc., 1972—. Mem. Dwight High Sch. Bd. Edn., 1955-68, pres., 1962-68. Served to maj. USMCR, 1942-46. Decorated Air medal. Mem. Livingston County Bankers Fedn. (pres. 1964). Rotarian. Clubs: Dwight Country; Racquet, Saddle and Cycle, Casino (Chgo.). Home: 404 Old Morris Rd Dwight IL 60420 Office: 122 W Main St Dwight IL 60420

OUIMET, ALFRED JOSEPH, JR., editor; b. Wilmington, N.C., Apr. 7, 1931; s. Alfred Joseph and Eleanor Gertrude (Mulrooney) O.; B.A., U. Conn., 1953, Ph.D., 1962; m. Louise Jacqueline Proulx, Sept. 11, 1954; children—Jeanine M., Peter C., Jacqueline L. Products applications research chemist Esso Research & Engring. Co., Linden, N.J., 1962-66; sr. asso. editor Chem. Abstracts Service div. Am. Chem. Soc., Columbus, Ohio, 1966—. Served to 1st lt. USAF, 1954-55. Mem. Am. Chem. Soc., Sci. Research Soc. N.Am., Sigma Xi, Sigma Pi Sigma, Phi Lambda Upsilon. Patentee in field. Home: 1655 Doone Rd Columbus OH 43221 Office: Chem Abstracts Service Ohio State U Columbus OH 43210

OUZTS, DALE KEITH, broadcasting exec.; b. Miami, Fla., Aug. 26, 1941; s. Jacob Clinton and Edna Pearl (Sloan) O.; tech. certificate So. Bus. U., 1960; B.A. in Journalism, U. Ga., 1965, M.A. in Mass Communication, 1966; m. Judith Susan Olcott, June 11, 1964; children—Dale Keith, Karen Jacy. Prodn. mgr. Sta. WSJK-TV, Knoxville, Tenn., 1966-67, sta. mgr., 1967-69; exec. v.p., gen. mgr. sta. KPTS-TV, Wichita, Kans., 1969-72; dir. broadcast services-radio and TV, gen. mgr. univ. sta. WSSR (FM), Sangamon State U., Springfield, Ill., 1972-78, asst. prof. communications, 1974-78; sr. v.p. for representation Nat. Pub. Radio, Washington, 1978—; cons. Sta. WTVP, Peoria, Ill., 1974, Western Ill. U., 1974-75, Ohio State U., 1976, Augustana Coll., 1977; Mem. nat. radio devel. com. Corp. Pub. Broadcasting, 1974-77, nat. radio task force long range planning, 1975; pres. Pub. Radio in Mid-Am., 1976-77, bd. dirs., chmn. membership by-laws com., Nat. Pub. Radio, 1977—. Bd. dirs. Jr. Achievement, 1975—, Big Bros., Big Sisters, 1975—, YMCA, 1976—; mem. Springfield Family Service Center; pres. Abraham Lincoln Unitarian Universalist Fellowship. Named One of 5 Outstanding Young Men of Year, Wichita Jaycees, 1972; recipient Outstanding Contbns. to Edn. award Wichita Edn. Assn., 1971, Service to Coll. award Lincoln Land Community Coll., 1977; Distinguished Service award Pub. Radio in Mid-Am., 1978; nat. award Corp. Pub. Broadcasting, 1971, Outstanding Broadcaster award Kappa Mu Psi, 1970, others. Mem. Springfield Ednl. Communications Assn. (pres. 1973-77), Nat. Assn. Ednl. Broadcasters, Ill. Broadcasters Assn., Sigma Delta Chi, Kappa Tau Alpha, Di Gamma Kappa, Phi Kappa Tau, Phi Kappa Phi. Club: Rotary (chmn. community services com. Springfield 1974-75, chmn. pub. relations com. 1975-76). Home: 1240 Cherry Rd Springfield IL 62704

OVERBERG, PAUL JOSEPH, actuary; b. Toledo, Feb. 25, 1926; s. Frank and Frieda (Bohnett) O.; B.B.A., U. Toledo, 1948; M.A., U. Mich., 1950; m. Lottie Marie Modlinski, Apr. 3, 1948; children—Cynthia Ann, Debra Denise, David Paul. Asst. actuary, actuarial student Pan Am. Life, New Orleans, 1950-54; asst. actuary Am. United, Indpls., 1954-57; group actuary Security Mut., Binghamton, N.Y., 1959-61, asso. actuary, 1957-59; actuary Allstate Life Ins. Co., Northbrook, Ill., 1961-63, chief actuary, 1963—, v.p., 1964-74, sr. v.p., 1974—, also dir.; v.p. Cross-Country Life Ins. Co.; actuary Allstate Life Ins. Co. Can., 1964—; asst. sec. Allstate Ins. Co., 1963-76. Served as aviation cadet USAAF, 1944-45. Fellow Soc. Actuaries; mem. Ill. C. of C., Am. Acad. Actuaries, Nat. Assn. Securities Dealers (gov.), Canadian Inst. Actuaries, Chgo. Actuarial Club. Republican. Roman Catholic. Clubs: Lake Forest; Execs. Chgo. Home: 1223 W Inverlieth Ra Lake Forest IL 60045 Office: Allstate Plaza Northbrook IL 60062

OVERGAARD, BJORN, physician; b. Goteborg, Sweden, May 16, 1927; s. Thomas Elsasser and Ammy Elin Sofia (Holmgren) O.; M.D., Kungl. Karolinska Medico-Kirurgiska Inst., Stockholm, Sweden, 1957; m. 2d, Margareta Karin Setterberg, Feb. 11, 1971; children—Hans, Malin, Niklas, Carl. Resident in surgery Univ. Hosp., Goteborg, Central Hosp., Karlstad, Sweden, 1957-66; clin. fellow in surgery Royal Victoria Hosp., Montreal, Que., Can., 1960-61; asst. chief surg. service County Hosp., Kungalv, Sweden, 1966-71; intern Iowa Lutheran Hosp., Des Moines, 1971-72; staff physician VA Hosp., Des Moines, 1973—. Served as comdr. M.C., Royal Swedish Navy, 1966. Merck, Sharp & Dohme research fellow, McGill U., 1960-61. Recipient AMA physicians recognition awards 1974, 77. Mem. Assn. VA Surgeons, Nordic, Swedish surg. socs., Polk County Med. Soc., Swedish Med. Assn., Nat. Assn. VA Physicians. Lutheran. Club: Rotary. Contbr. articles to profl. jours. Home: 3000 Grand Ave Apt 310 Des Moines IA 50312 Office: VA Hosp 30th & Euclid Sts Des Moines IA 50310

OVERHOLSER, RONALD LEE, actor, scriptural character impressionist; b. Washington, Ind., June 25, 1942; s. James Ora and Jewel Emily (Wise) O.; pvt. voice lessons Mrs. John Sellman and Roger Nye of Bowdoin Coll. (Maine); student Johnson Bible Coll., Knoxville, 1964, Cin. Bible Coll., 1968-70. Various clerical and manual positions, 1963-66; narrator The Good Life, N.Am. Christian Conv., Cin. Riverfront Stadium, 1972; has portrayed numerous Bibl. characters for schs., chs. and colls. including: Messiah, Paul of Tarsus, 12 disciples; designer 14 costumes for portrayals; interpreter Miami Purchase Assn. Mem. ARC, Friends of Cin. Parks. Served with USN, 1960-63. Winner, Internat. Platform Conv. Talent Previews, Washington, 1974. Fellow Intercontinental Biog. Assn.; mem. Internat. Platform Assn., Am. Soc. Distinguished Citizens, Smithsonian Inst. (nat. asso.). Mem. Christian Ch. Home: 5104 Hawaiian Terr Cincinnati OH 45223

OVERHOLT, ROBERT EUGENE, dentist; b. Petoskey, Mich., Aug. 4, 1932; s. Leon Noel and Esther Mae (Adams) O.; B.S., U. Mich., 1955, D.D.S., 1961; m. Dorothy Ruth Samuelson, June 26, 1954; children—Leigh Anne, Brad R. Gen. practice dentistry, Ludington, Mich., 1961—. Dir. Ludington Bank & Trust Co. Sec., bd. dirs., editor Newsletter, Jr. C. of C., 1961-68; dist. chmn. Boy Scouts Am., 1971—; mem. Ludington Bldg. Authority, 1972—. Mayor, Ludington, 1968-70. Chmn. adv. bd. Salvation Army. Served with U.S. Army, 1955-57. Mem. Am. Dental Assn., F.B. Vedder Crown and Bridge Club, Omicron Kappa Upsilon. Republican. Mem. Ch. of Jesus Christ of Latter-day Saints. Home: 903 Seminole St Ludington MI 49431 Office: 921 E Tinkham St Ludington MI 49431

OVERHOLT, ROBERT LESLIE, dentist; b. Ada, Mich., Aug. 15, 1920; s. Clyde Walter and Mary Zoe (Collar) O.; B.S., Mich. State U., 1943; D.D.S., U. Mich., 1945; m. Frances Virginia Lostutter, Dec. 31, 1949; children—Robert Peter, Nancy Jane, David Charles. Gen. practice dentistry, Detroit, 1947-48, Lansing, Mich., 1948-51, East Lansing, Mich., 1951—; acting dir. dental dept. Mich. State U. Hosp.; v.p. Delta Dental Plans Mich., 1975—; del. Mich. Health Council; treas. Mich. Dental Service Corp., 1961-62; chmn. health div. Community Service Council, 1955-56. Active fund drives YMCA, Boy Scouts Am.; bd. dirs. Highfield's Boys Opportunity Camp and Home, Mich. Delta Dental Plans. Served to lt. Dental Corps, USNR, 1945-47; ETO. Fellow Internat., Am. colls. dentists, Acad. Internat. Dentistry, Pierre Fauchard Acad.; mem. ADA (chmn. council on dental care programs 1971-72), Mich. Dental Assn. (chmn. group purchase program com. 1964-66), Central Dist. Dental Soc. (past pres.), Mich Soc. Dentistry for Children, R.W. Bunting Periodontal Study Club, F. Vedder Crown and Bridge Prosthesis Study Club, Alpha Chi Sigma, Xi Psi Phi. Episcopalian. Clubs: Masons, Kiwanis. Home: 5050 Country Dr Okemos MI 48864 Office: 6020 N Hagadorn Rd East Lansing MI 48823

OVERHOLT, WILLIAM ALVIN, univ. adminstr.; b. Elkins, W.Va., May 23, 1917; s. Gilbert Henry and Ethel Mae (Beall) O.; B.A., Davis and Elkins Coll., 1937; M.A., Boston U., 1941, Ph.D., 1951; m. Dorothea Carolyn Donenwirth, May 12, 1944; children—William H., Carolyn Overholt Talbot. With YMCA, Canton, Ohio, 1937-40, state extension sec., Charleston, W.Va., 1947-49, nat. student staff, Mpls., 1949-54; protestant chaplain, asst. prof. religion in higher edn. Boston U., 1954-70, asso. dean student affairs, 1970-73; dean student affairs U. Ill. Med. Center, Chgo., 1973—; leader, U.S.-USSR, student exchanges, 1961, 66, 77; sabbatical prof. Central Philippine U., 1963-64. Served with USAAF, 1943-46. Mem. Nat. Assn. Student Personnel Adminstrs., AAUP, Am. Coll. Personnel Assn., Inst. of Soc., Ethics and the Life Scis., Soc. for Health and Human Values, Am. Assn. for UN, Phi Delta Kappa. Methodist. Contbr. articles in field to profl. jours.; editor: Exploring Humanistic Health Science Education, 1977; Fostering Ethical Values in the Education of Health Professionals, 1976. Home: 5149 Riverview Dr Lisle IL 60532 Office: 1737 W Polk St Chicago IL 60612

OVERTON, GEORGE W., lawyer; b. Hinsdale, Ill., Jan. 25, 1918; s. George Washington and Florence Mary (Darlington) O.; A.B., Harvard U., 1940; J.D., U. Chgo., 1946; m. Jane Vincent Harper, Sept. 1, 1941; children—Samuel Harper, Peter Darlington, Ann Vincent. Admitted to Ill. bar, 1947; prin. Overton, Schwartz & Yacker, Ltd., Chgo.; dir. River Oaks Bank & Trust Co., Hyde Park Fed. Savs. and Loan Assn. Bd. dirs. Open Lands Project, Chgo. Bar Found. Mem. Am., Ill., Chgo. bar assns., Assn. Bar City N.Y. Home: 1368 E 57th St Chicago IL 60637 Office: 105 W Adams St Chicago IL 60603

OVERTON, JANE VINCENT HARPER, educator; b. Chgo., Jan. 17, 1919; d. Paul Vincent and Isabel (Vincent) Harper; A.B., Bryn Mawr Coll., 1941; Ph.D., U. Chgo., 1950; m. George W. Overton, Jr., Sept. 1, 1941; children—Samuel, Peter, Ann. Research asst. U. Chgo., 1950-52, asst. prof. biology, 1952-64, asso. prof., 1964-72, prof. biology, 1972—. NIH and NSF research grantee, 1965-76. Contbr. articles to profl. jours. Research embryology and cell biology. Home: 1368 E 57th St Chicago IL 60637

OVIATT, CHARLES DIXON, ednl. adminstr.; b. Washington, Penn., Dec. 24, 1924; s. Howard Jones and Nellie Eltha (Dixon) O.; B.A., Tarkin Coll., 1947; M.A., Ohio State U., 1949, Ph.D., 1954; m. Esther Isabelle Gifford, June 16, 1948; children—Mary Elizabeth, Charles Gifford, Sarah Phyllis, Judith Ellen, Howard Scott. Prof. chemistry Tarkio (Mo.) Coll., 1949-57; editor McGraw-Hill Ency. Sci. and Tech., Charlottesville, Va., 1957-60; editor in chief Webster div. McGraw-Hill Book Co., N.Y.C., 1961-63, St. Louis, 1963-72; dir. Mo. Statewide Assessment Project, Dept. Elementary, Secondary Edn. Jefferson City, 1974—; cons. in field. Served with USN, 1943-46. Mem. Am. Chem. Soc., AAAS, Nat. Sci. Tchrs. Assn., Am. Inst. Biol. Scientists, Phi Delta Kappa. Author: Health and Safety for You, 1975, People, Concepts, and Processes, 1974. Home: Route 1 PO Box 34 Vienna MO 65582 Office: PO Box 480 Jefferson City MO 65101

OWEN, BRUCE WILMOT, fin. and engring. cons.; b. Perry County, Pa., Nov. 26, 1922; s. Wilmot Ayres and Margaret Katheryn (Wilson) O.; B.S. in Mech. Engring., Lehigh U., 1948; M.B.A., Case Western Res. U., 1956; m. Lois Jean Tedrow, Oct. 18, 1968; children—Kimberley, Gail, Cynthia, Connie. Engr. NACA, Cleve., 1948-50; Bryant Heater Co., Cleve., 1950-52; estimator Wean Equipment Co., Euclid, Ohio, 1952-54; engr. Addressograph-Multigraph Corp., Euclid, Ohio, 1954-64; prin. cons. engr. Latech Cons., Willowick, Ohio, 1965—; pres. Latech Developers, Willoughby, Ohio, 1975—; v.p., Problem Solvers, Inc., Beechwood, Ohio, 1972—; rep. Herman Realty, Beechwood, 1977—; Sec. Ocen Assos., Inc., Willoughby, 1974—. Served with USAAF, 1942-45. Decorated Air Medal, D.F.C. Mem. Nat., Ohio, Cleve. East socs. profl. engrs. Presbyterian. Home: 30410 Thomas St Willowick OH 44094 Office: PO Box 907 Willoughby OH 44094

OWEN, JOHN ELLIOT, educator; b. Bay City, Mich., Oct. 4, 1939; s. Dale Hawley and Wilmay Jeannette (Sidney) O.; student George Williams Coll., 1958-60; A.B., B.S., Central Mich. U., 1964, postgrad., 1966—; m. Elizabeth Margaret Mexicotte, Nov. 13, 1965 (div. Feb. 1977); 1 dau., Lisa Marie. Youth worker Lawson YMCA, Chgo., 1959-60; tchr. TV dept. Bridgeport (Mich.) High Sch., 1964-68, All Saints High Sch., Bay City, 1968—. Self-employed portrait photographer, Bay City, 1970—. Pres., All Saints Edn. Found., 1974—; co-chmn. Pub. Schs. Millage campaign, 1974. Trustee Bay City Bd. Edn., v.p., 1975-76, pres. 1976. Mem. Profl. Photographers Am., Bay Area Council on Edn. Episcopalian. Elk. Home: 1828 W Norfolk Dr #6 Essexville MI 48732 Office: 217 S Monroe St Bay City MI 48706

OWEN, MARGARET FRANCES RICHARDS (MRS. GEORGE EARLE OWEN), clergyman, civic worker; b. nr. Winchester, Va., Sept. 29, 1912; d. Boyd Ross and Mary (Shryock) Richards; student Goucher Coll., 1929-30; diploma George Washington U., 1932; B.S., Columbia, 1939, M.A., 1940; B.D. cum laude, Union Theol. Sem., 1944; Ed.D., Columbia, 1952; m. George Earle Owen, May 23, 1936; children—Mary Devon (Mrs. Gordon Covert O'Brien), Anne Franklin (Mrs. Alvin Marcus Fountain II), Margaret Earle (Mrs. Gerald Daniel Clark, Jr.), Deborah Elizabeth. Ordained to ministry Christian Ch., Disciples of Christ, 1943; missionary United Christian Missionary Soc., 1943-54; prof. O.T., Facultad Evangelica de Teologia, Buenos Aires, Argentina, 1944-48; instr. religious edn., psychology of religion Union Theol. Sem., Manila, Philippines, 1951-54; chmn. family life com. Ch. Fedn. Greater Indpls., 1955-59. Chmn. Indpls. Family Life Clinic, 1956-58; chmn. Missionary Edn. Inst., Ch. Women United, Indpls., 1961, 62; mem. Inter-profl. adv. com. preparation for Christian marriage Ch. Fedn. Greater U. Indpls., 1958-64; mem. womens planning com. Japan Internat. Christian Univ. Found., 1958—; mem. Commn. on Theology of Mission, 1958-63; bd. dirs. Aux. to Community Hosp., Indpls., 1963-66; v.p. Marion County Children's Guardian Home Guild, 1963-64. Bd. dirs. Marion County Mental Health Assn., 1969-72; bd. dirs. Irvington Hist. Landmarks Found. Inc., v.p., 1969-74, pres., 1974—. Recipient Distinguished Service award Disciples of Christ Chs. in Tagalog Area, Philippines, 1954; Distinguished Service award Ch. Fedn. Greater Indpls., 1958. Mem. Ind. (pres. 1970-72), Nat. councils on family relations, Indpls. Mus. Art, Art League Irvington (pres. 1969-70), Irvington Union of Clubs (pres. 1963-65), Irvington Hist. Soc., Irvington Coterie (sec. 1969-70, pres. 1972-73), Benton House Assn. (pres. 1969-71), Family Service Assn., Indpls. Council on World Affairs, Alpha Delta Pi. Mem. Christian Ch. (chmn. bd. 1974-75). Clubs: Irvington Woman's (pres. 1972-73), Contemporary (bd. mem. 1969-70), Friday Social (pres. 1969-70). Author: Created Male and Female, 1971. Contbr. articles to pubis. Home: 5354 Julian Ave Indianapolis IN 46219

OWEN, MICKEY, real estate, constrn. and devel. co. exec.; b. Evansville, Ind., Mar. 10, 1939; s. Lloyd Nelson and Margaret Marie (Gonterman) O.; B.S.M.E., Evansville Coll., 1957-63; student Ind. U. Sch. of Law, 1963; m. Ruth Ann Stephan, Feb. 21, 1959; children—Marc Allen, Christina Marie, Bryan Keith. Designer heating and air conditioning George Koch Sons, Inc., Evansville, Ind., 1959-63; project engr. U.S. Naval Avionics Facility, Indpls., 1963-67; design group supr. Emerson Electric, St. Louis, 1967-70; group engr. McDonnell Douglas, St. Louis, 1970-72; owner, pres. Owen Real Estate, Constrn., Investment and Devel. Co., St. Charles, Mo., 1972—; owner, pres. King Line Products, Inc., pres. O.S.T. Devel. Co.; owner Owen Farms, Williamsburg, Mo.; exec. v.p. Pickett, Ray and Silver, Inc., Civil Engrs., Land Surveyors. Mem. Nat. Assn. Realtors, St. Charles County Bd. Realtors (sec. 1974), St. Charles Home Builders (pres.), St. Louis Home Builders Assn., Nat. Inst. Farm and Land Brokers, Am. Polled Hereford Assn., St. Louis Real Estate Exchange Group. Patentee in field. Home: 3344 Ridgeway Dr St Charles MO 63301 Office: 1411 Harvester Rd St Charles MO 63301

OWEN, RICHARD CLEMENT, JR., mfg. co. exec.; b. Norfolk, Va., Dec. 29, 1921; s. Richard Clement and Judith Ferebee (Berkley) O.; B.S., U. Richmond 1943; postgrad. Wharton Sch. Fin., U. Pa., 1943-44; m. Claire Elizabeth Gibson, June 2, 1949; children—Betsy Owen Graham, Richard Clement. Advt. mgr. Nestle-LeMur Co., N.Y.C., 1946-50; advt. mgr. B.T. Babbitt Inc., N.Y.C., 1950-55; account supr. Batten, Barton, Durstine & Osborn, Inc., N.Y.C. and Cleve., 1955-62; v.p., account group supr. Meldrum & Fewsmith, Inc., Cleve., 1962-69; mgr. advt. and sales promotion Revere Copper and Brass Inc., N.Y. and Clinton, Ill., 1969—. Served with U.S. Army, 1943-46. Mem. Phi Kappa Sigma, Omicron Delta Kappa. Methodist. Home: 3691 E Hardy St Decatur IL 62521 Office: PO Box 250 Clinton IL 61727

OWEN, ROBERT CARROLL, real estate broker; b. Hermitage, Ark., June 22, 1915; s. Robert Franklin and Mimmie Mae (Roark) O.; teaching certificate Ark. A. and M. U., Monticello, 1936; m. Lois Margaret Clanton (div. Aug. 1966); children—David C., Nancy K.

(Mrs. Vince Driski), Randi J. (Mrs. Wally Jones); m. 2d, Marjorie G. Gaylord, Feb. 11, 1967. Tchr., Hermitage High Sch., 1936-40; insp., chief tax sect., chief storekeeper Gaugers, Bur. Internal Revenue, 1940-51; realtor Bob Owen & Co., Inc., Overland Park, Kans., 1951—; dir. Hedrick Title Co., Bob Owen Co. Chmn. Johnson County Multiple Listing Service, 1968; pres. Johnson County Bd. Realtors, 1969. Named Realtor of Year Johnson County, 1971. Baptist. Clubs: Brook Ridge Country, Wolf Creek. Home: 6832 W 100th St Overland Park KS 66212 Office: 7121 W 79th St Overland Park KS 66204

OWENS, DOROTHY ELIZABETH, secondary sch. counselor; b. St. Louis, Feb. 9, 1920; d. Hillery and Gladys (Peterson) Owens; B.S. (Nat. Coll. Women's Club scholar 1937), Lincoln U., 1941; M.A. (work-study fellow 1942-44), Fisk U., 1944; M.S. (Vocat. Rehab. Adminstrn. scholar 1967-68), U. Ill., Urbana, 1968; M.Ed. (Parson scholar 1973), Mo. U., St. Louis, 1975; m. Winston C. Hurley, July 21, 1950. Social worker in Anniston, Ala. and St. Louis, 1944-48; tchr. St. Louis Roman Cath. Archdiocesan schs., 1948-49; tchr. phys. edn. and health St. Louis pub. schs., 1949-67, spl. edn. tchr., 1968-72, secondary sch. counselor, 1972—; part-time counselor Forest Park Community Coll., St. Louis, 1976—. cons. in field. Active local Girl Scouts. Mem. Am. Personnel and Guidance Assn., Nat. Vocat. Guidance Assn., Mo. Tchrs. Assn., Nat. Honor Soc., Alpha Kappa Alpha. Democrat. Roman Catholic. Author curriculum materials. Home: 4840 Northland Ave St Louis MO 63113 Office: 3125 S Kingshighway Blvd St Louis MO 63139

OWENS, DWIGHT RAY, microbiologist; b. Hickory Creek, Tex., Nov. 15, 1942; s. Sim Francis and Kathleen (Butler) O.; B.S., East Tex. State U., 1964, M.S., 1965; m. Linda Kay Vandiver, June 3, 1969; 1 dau., Shari. Microbiologist, Ark. Livestock and Poultry Commn., Little Rock, 1966-68; microbiologist U. Mo., Coll. of Vet. Medicine, Columbia, 1968—. Mem. Am. Soc. Microbiology, Am. Acad. Microbiology, Soc. for Applied Microbiology, Am. Assn. of Lab. Animal Sci., Sigma Xi. Democrat. Clubs: Masons, Shriners. Contbr. numerous articles in field to sci. jours. Home: 2623A Summit Rd Columbia MO 65201 Office: Univ of Missouri Veterinary Medical Diagnosis Lab Columbia MO

OWENS, FREDERICK MITCHUM, JR., surgeon; b. St. Paul, Feb. 21, 1913; s. Frederick Mitchum and Eloise Durkey (Morley) O.; A.B., Princeton, 1935; M.D., U. Chgo., 1939; m. Lucy Proctor Trumbull, Sept. 12, 1942; children—Lucy Owens Smith, Sally M. Owens Palmer, Helen Proctor. Intern, U. Chgo. Hosps., 1939-40, resident in surgery, 1940-43; asst. prof. surgery U. Chgo. Med. Sch., 1946-49; mem. faculty U. Minn. Med. Sch., 1949—, clin. prof. surgery, 1972—; practice medicine specializing in surgery, St. Paul, 1951—; dir. Dakota County State Bank. Chmn. Dist. 197 Sch. Bd. Dalota County, 1953-54. Served to maj. M.C. U.S. Army, 1943-46. Decorated Army Commendation medal. Diplomate Am. Bd. Surgery. Mem. A.C.S. (gov. 1969-75), Western (dir. 1974-77), Central surg. assns., Soc. Univ. Surgeons, Internat., Minn., St. Paul surg. socs. Episcopalian. Clubs: Rotary, Gyro, Somerset Country, Minnesota. Contbr. articles to med. publns. Home: 2455 Delaware Ave St Paul MN 55118 Office: 920 Lowry Medical Arts Bldg St Paul MN 55102

OWENS, HORACE GORDON, diversified indsl. products co. exec.; b. Homerville, Ga., Oct. 20, 1940; s. John Ellis and Catherine (Hodges) O.; A.B., Dartmouth Coll., 1962; M.B.A., Northwestern U., 1972; m. Karen Sue Brodahl, Dec. 30, 1961; children—Horace Gordon, Eric Christopher. Systems analyst Container Corp. Am., Chgo., 1963-66; mgr. info. systems Stone Container Corp., Chgo., 1966-76; dir. mgmt. info. systems The Richardson Co., Melrose Park, Ill., 1977—. Served with USNR, 1963. Mem. Sigma Nu. Club: Lake Bluff Yacht (dir.). Home: 359 Hirst Ct Lake Bluff IL 60044 Office: 2701 W Lake St Melrose Park IL 60160

OWENS, JAMES HAMILTON, JR., structural engring. cons.; b. N.Y.C., Dec. 17, 1913; s. James H. and Olga (Von Hartz) O.; student Mass. Inst. Tech., 1935-37; B.S., Johns Hopkins U., 1953, M.S., 1958; m. Helen Purdy Nixdorff, May 3, 1938: children—Helen Pierpont, James Hamilton, Alan Schuyler, Alexander Hamilton. Engr. and draftsman Faisant & Kooken Consulting Engrs., Balt., 1945-49; asso. engr. City of Balt. Dept. Pub. Works, 1949-50; sr. stress analyst, group engr. Martin Co., Balt., 1950-59; sr. stress analyst Fairchild Stratos Corp., Hagerstown, Md., 1959-62; staff engr. Bendix Corp., Ann Arbor, Mich., 1962-72; structural designer, analyst AM Gen. Corp., Detroit, 1972-74; sr. engr. Aeronca Corp., Middletown, Ohio, 1976-77; cons. structural design and analysis to various machine mfg. cos., 1972—; lectr. flight structures aerospace engring. dept. U. Mich., Ann Arbor, 1963-65. Mem. Am. Inst. Aeros. and Astronautics. Democrat. Club: Kiwanis. Author: (with D.C. Chang) Belleville Springs Simplified, 1970. Home and Office: 1859 Country Club Rd Ann Arbor MI 48105

OWENS, LYELL GARY, educator, philosopher; b. Balt., May 22, 1948; s. Thomas Lyell and Ruth Charlotte (Markel) O.; B.S., Towson State Coll., 1970; M.A., Kans. State U., 1971; Ph.D., Purdue U., 1977; m. Ivy Jane Lucy Patterson, May 23, 1970. Lectr. philosophy Ind. U.-Purdue U., Indpls., 1972—. Mem. Am., Mountain-Plains philos. assns., Modern Lang. Assn. Editor Eros, 1972—. Home: 131-14 Nimitz Dr West Lafayette IN 47906 Office: 925 W Michigan St Indianapolis IN 46202

OWINGS, MALCOLM WILLIAM, packaging co. exec.; b. Cin., Feb. 5, 1925; s. William Malcolm and Margaret (Benvie) O.; B.S. in Bus. Adminstrn., Miami U., Oxford, Ohio, 1950, LL.D. (hon.), 1976; m. Margie M. Gehlker, Sept. 4, 1948; children—Lynn A., Sandra S., Wendy K., Cheryl M. With Continental Can Co., 1950—, sales rep., Milw., 1950-58, dist. sales mgr., Mpls., 1959-61, Milw., 1963-66, div. product sales mgr., Chgo., 1961-63, asst. gen. mgr. sales, Chgo., 1966-67, gen. mgr. sales, Chgo., 1967-69, gen. mgr. So. metal div., Atlanta, 1969-71, v.p., gen. mgr. gen. packaging div., Chgo., 1971-73, v.p., gen. mgr. beverage div., 1973-76, v.p. pub. affairs and bus. devel., 1976—; dir. Control-Dyne, Mpls. Village trustee Thiensville (Wis.), 1956-59; mem. alumni council Miami U., 1958-65, pres.'s devel. council, 1965-75; bd. dirs. Barrington Area Devel. Council. Served with USNR, 1942-44; N. Africa, ETO. Recipient certificate of meritorious service Miami U., 1967, named Alumnus of Year, 1970; 1st Am. recipient Order of Apteryx, Earth Awareness Found., 1971. Mem. Miami U. Alumni Assn. (nat. pres. 1964-65), Master Brewers Am., Sales Mgmt. Execs., Ill. State C. of C. (dir. 1976—), Omicron Delta Kappa, Sigma Chi, Delta Sigma Pi. Clubs: Cherokee Town and Country (Atlanta); Barrington (Ill.) Hills Country. Home: 115 Old Oak Dr Barrington IL 60010 Office: O'Hare Plaza Chicago IL 60631

OWLEY, GORDON THOMAS, psychologist; b. Waukesha, Wis., Mar. 25, 1947; s. Carl Gordon and Lillian Catherine (Heinzelman) O.; A.B., Coll. St. Thomas, 1969; Ph.D., Marquette U., Milw., 1976; m. Candice Marian Ades, Feb. 14, 1970; children—Eric Jennings, Jessica Noel, Nathan Kristian. Teaching asst. Marquette U., 1970-76, also psychometrist Milw. Pub. Schs., 1972-76; psychologist Milw. Pub. Schs., 1976—; cons. Internat. Personnel Services, Milw., 1975—. NSF trainee, 1971. Mem. Am., Midwest psychol. assns., Phi Delta Kappa, Psi Chi. Research on patterns of intellectual performance as function of socio-econ. status and sex, devel. of child's concept of ecology. Home: 2845 N 50th St Milwaukee WI 53210 Office: 5225 W Vliet St Milwaukee WI 53208

OWNBY, PAUL DARRELL, educator; b. Salt Lake City, Nov. 9, 1935; s. Paul William and Isabel Hope (Pearson) O.; B.S., U. Utah, 1961; M.S. (Kaiser Aluminum & Chem. Co. fellow), Mo. Sch. Mines and Metallurgy, 1962; Ph.D. (Kennecott Copper fellow), Ohio State U., 1967; m. Nina Rose Mugleston, Aug. 31, 1961; children—Melissa, Heather, Kirsten, Shannon, Paul William, Evan Darrell, Martha. Research ceramist Battelle Meml. Inst., Columbus, Ohio, 1963-68; asst. prof. U. Mo., Rolla, 1968, asso. prof., 1969-74, prof. ceramic engring., 1974—; vis. scientist Max Planck Institut fur Werkstoff Wissenschaften, Stuttgart, Germany, 1974-75; dir. Rinco, Inc., Rolla, Mo., 1972-77; cons. Battelle Meml. Inst., Columbus, 1968-70, Dynasil Corp. Am., 1969-74, Eagle Picher Industries, Inc., 1970—, McDonnell Douglas Astronautics Co., 1974-76. Neighborhood commr. Central Ohio dist. Boy Scouts Am., 1966-67, instl. rep., 1970, 73-74, troop com., 1961-62, 70-74, chmn., 1973. Battelle Meml. Inst. fellow, 1973. Mem. Am. Ceramic Soc., Am. Vacuum Soc., Ceramic Edn. Council, Keramos, Sigma Xi. Republican. Mem. Ch. Jesus Christ of Latter-day Saints. Inventor in field. Home: 8 Burgher Dr Rolla MO 65401 Office: U Mo Rolla MO 65401

OXLEY, JOSEPH HUBBARD, tech. engr., labs. exec.; b. Akron, O., Aug. 3, 1929; s. Joseph Charles and Helen Margaret (Harmon) O.; B.S., Carnegie Inst. Tech., 1952, Ph.D., 1956; m. Margaret Carolyn Steward, Aug. 25, 1951; children—Linda M., Carolyn B., Joan C., Joseph S., James H., Laura M. Prin. engr. Battelle Meml. Inst., Columbus, O., 1956-58; asst. div. chief Battelle Devel. Corp., Columbus, 1958-66, tech. adminstr., 1966-67; asso. mgr. Battelle Columbus Labs., 1967-69, mgr., 1969-72, sect. mgr., 1972—. Dir. Wirand Concrete Spltys., Inc., 1967-69. Coach Little League Football, 1962-72. Mem. Am. Inst. Chem. Engrs., Am. Chem. Soc., Electrochem. Soc., Am. Inst. Mining, Metall. and Petroleum Engrs., Licensing Execs. Soc., Nat. Council U. Res. Adminstrs., Columbus C. of C. (named 1 of 10 outstanding young men), Sigma Xi. Co-author Vapor Deposition. Patentee in field. Home: 298 Brevoort Rd Columbus OH 43214 Office: 505 King Ave Columbus OH 43201

OXLEY, LORIN EARL EVERETT, writer; b. West Liberty, Iowa, July 17, 1903; s. Henry White and Lena Leota (Siders) O.; student pub. schs.; m. Doris Dorothy Nusbaum, July 24, 1929; children—Donald E., Robert L., Marilyn Jean (Mrs. John Hamilton). Farmer, purebreed breeder, showman Hampshire hogs, Iowa City, 1919-36, West Liberty, 1936-55; office mgr. Pella (Iowa) Farm Service, 1968-69; freelance writer pamphlets, 1942—. Founder laymen's commn. Am. Council Christian Chs., 1964-69; founder, nat. chmn. Am. League Christian Voters, 1975. Co-author Am. party platform, Louisville, 1972, nat. central committeeman Dallas, 1972, Wichita, Kan., 1973, Chgo., Memphis, 1974; Am. party nominee U.S. Senate, 1974. Hon. mem. Congress of Freedom, 1969. Elder Tipton Bible Ch., 1957-66. Address: Tipton Sr Park Apt E4 Tipton IA 52772

OXTOBY, ROBERT BOYNTON, lawyer; b. Huron, S.D., May 8, 1921; s. Frederic Breading and Frieda (Boynton) O.; B.A., Carleton Coll., 1943; J.D., Northwestern U., 1949; student Ill. Coll., 1939-40; m. Carolyn Bartholf, Feb. 25, 1956; children—Michael, Thomas, Susan. Admitted to Ill. bar, 1949, since practiced in Springfield, mem. firm Van Meter, Oxtoby & Funk; asst. U.S. Atty., 1953-57; spl. asst. atty. gen., 1957-61, 69—; dir. Ill. Nat. Ins. Co., Springfield, N.H. Ins. Co., Manchester, Ill. Nat. Bank Springfield, Downtown Park. Bd. dirs. Ill. Coll.; chmn. bd. Meml. Med. Center; mem. Ill. Capital Devel. Bd. Served to 1st lt. USMCR, 1942-46; PTO. Mem. Am., Ill., Sangamon County bar assns. Republican. Presbyterian. Clubs: Sangamo (dir., pres. 1965), Illini Country. Home: 1933 Outer Park Dr Springfield IL 62704 Office: INB Center 1 N Old Capitol Plaza Springfield IL 62705

OZAR, MILTON BERNARD, urologist; b. Kansas City, Mo., Sept. 14, 1924; s. Simon Jacob and Sadie (Friedman) O.; B.S. in Pharmacy, U. Mo., 1944; M.D., Kans. U., 1949; m. Marilyn Brand, June 29, 1947; children—Stuart, Judy, Donna. Intern, Kans. U. Med. Center, 1949-50, resident in urology, 1951-54; resident Menorah Med. Center, 1950-51; practice medicine specializing in urology, Kansas City, 1954—; active attending staff Menorah Med. Center; active staff Bapt. Meml. Hosp., 1960—, pres. med. staff, 1969-70; courtesy staff Research Hosp.; cons. Truman Med. Center, Mercy Hosp.; asst. clin. prof. urology U. Kans. Sch. Medicine; lectr. medicine U. Mo. at Kansas City Med. Schs.; dir. Rockhill Med. Bldg. Corp., Broadway Nat. Bank, Kansas City; area med. rep. Mid American Comprehensive Health Planning Agy. Mem. 16th Circuit Ct. Jud. Commn., 1969-74. Served to capt. USAF, 1955-57. Diplomate Am. Bd. Urology. Fellow A.C.S., Internat. Coll. Surgeons; mem. Am. Urol. Soc., Am. Fertility Soc., AMA, So., Mo. med. assns., Kansas City Urol. Soc. (past pres.), Fedn. Mo. Urologists (past pres.), Jackson County Med. Soc. Jewish. Club: B'nai Brith. Home: 1206 W 62d St Kansas City MO 64113 Office: 6700 Troost St Kansas City MO 64131

OZINGA, JAMES RICHARD, educator; b. Grand Rapids, Mich., Mar. 6, 1932; s. James and Esther Ruth (Van Houten) O.; A.B., Calvin Coll., 1956; B.D., Calvin Sem., 1959; postgrad. U. Mich., 1959-60; A.B., Western Mich. U., 1962, M.A., 1964; Ph.D. (NDEA fellow), Mich. State U., 1968; m. Suzanne Willard, Dec. 31, 1959; children—James Michael, Kurt Stephen, Karen Sue. Faculty polit. sci. Oakland U., Rochester, Mich., 1967—, asso. prof., 1974—. Served with USAF, 1951-53. Mem. Am. Polit. Sci. Assn., Internat. Soc. Systems Research, Mich. Council Internat. Edn. (v.p. 1973-74, pres. 1974-76). Author: Communism-A Tarnished Promise, 1975. Contbr. articles to profl. jours. Home: 62 Bellarmine St Rochester MI 48063

PABST, THEODORE SHUSTER, lawyer; b. Chgo., Mar. 24, 1917; s. Theodore Shuster and Mary Margaret (Hudson) P.; student U. Ill., 1935-37; B.A., U. Chgo., 1938, J.D., 1940; m. Virginia E. Shaw, Nov. 23, 1953; children—Theodore III, Tracie Elizabeth. Admitted to Ill. bar, 1940; practiced in Evergreen Park, Ill., 1946—; dir. various corps. Served to 1st lt. U.S. Army, 1942-46. Mem. Ill., Chgo., South Side (pres. 1963) bar assns., Amvets (comdr. post 1957), Am. Legion (adjutant 1953), Chi Psi. Mem. Christ Ch. Home: 802 S Bruner St Hinsdale IL 60521 Office: Capitol Fed Bldg 3960 W 95th St Evergreen Park IL 60642

PACE, JULIAN HUGHES, librarian; b. Abilene, Tex., Dec. 11, 1938; s. Julian Henry and Ruby (Hughes) P.; B.A., Baylor U., 1961; postgrad. U. Tex., 1961-62; M.L.S., U. Okla., 1963; postgrad. Kans. State U., 1968; m. Elizabeth Anne Mitchell, Aug. 25, 1962; children—Julian Hughes, Emily Suzanne. Page, Waco (Tex.) Pub. Library, 1954-57, night page, 1960-61; serials page Baylor U. Library, Waco, 1958-60; asst. in Bass collection bus. history U. Okla. Library, Norman, 1962-63; adminstrv. librarian S.W. Bapt. Coll., Bolivar, Mo., 1963-72; asst. to librarian S.W. Mo. State U., 1972—; mem. adv. com. to Mo. State Librarian on Title III of Library Services and Constrn. Act, 1967. Mem. ALA, Mo., Greater Springfield library assns., Mo. Assn. Coll. and Research Librarians (sec. 1968-69, vice chmn. 1969-70, chmn. 1970-71), Nat. Geog. Soc. Baptist. Home: 535 E Lindon St Bolivar MO 65613

PACHMAN, DANIEL J., physician; b. N.Y.C., Dec. 20, 1911; A.B., U. N.C., 1931; M.D., Duke U., 1934; m. Vivian Allison Futter, Nov. 8, 1935; children—Lauren Merle, Grace Allison. Intern dept. pediatrics U. Chgo., 1934-35, N.Y. Hosp., 1935-36; resident pediatrics, attending pediatrician Duke Hosp., Durham, N.C., 1936-37; instr. pediatrics Duke U. Med. Sch., 1936-37, U. Chgo., 1937-40, Northwestern U., 1940-42, clin. asst. prof. pediatrics U. Ill., 1950-59, clin. asso. prof., 1960-67, clin. prof. pediatrics, 1967—; attending pediatrician Ill. Research and Edn. Hosp., 1950—; cons. pediatrician Presbyn.-St. Luke's Hosp., Chgo., 1962—; cons. South Shore Hosp., 1955—; cons. dept. pediatrics Ill. Central Hosp., 1962—, chmn. 1962-70; attending pediatrician South Chgo. Hosp., 1971—; prof. pediatrics Rush Med. Coll., 1971—; active staff Children's Meml. Hosp., 1971—; courtesy staff Chgo. Lying-in Hosp.; med. cons. Bd. Edn., South Shore High Sch., 1954—; mem. adv. com. on sch. health Bd. Health, 1962—, Bd. Edn., 1962— (all Chgo.); mem. Ill. State Adv. Commn. Revision of Rules for Control of Disease, 1973—; pediatric cons. Ill. Council for Mentally Retarded Children, 1960—; chmn. subcom. on sch. health Chgo. Med. Sch.; mem. Mayor's Com. on Sch. Bd. Nominations; chmn. Ill. Pediatric Coordinating Council, 1969—; mem. com. rights of minors Ill. Commn. on Children, 1974-76. Served to lt. col. M.C., AUS, 1942-46. Diplomate Nat. Bd. Med. Examiners, Am. Bd. Pediatrics. Fellow Am. Acad. Pediatrics (exec. com. Ill. chpt. 1961—), rep. to adv. council on child health Nat. Congress Parents and Teachers, chmn. sci. exhibits com., 1964-72, pres. Ill. chpt. 1968-71), Am. Cancer Soc. (pub. edn. com. Chgo.), Inst. Medicine (mem. at large joint com. on sch. services 1961—); mem. Chgo. Med. Soc. (chmn. child health com. 1958-62), Chgo. Pediatric Soc. (Archibald L. Hoyne award 1977), AMA, Duke Pediatric Soc. (pres. 1954—), N.Y. Acad. Scis., Phi Beta Kappa, Sigma Xi. Club: Quadrangle (dir.) (Chgo.). Contbr. articles to med. jours. Home: 1212 N Lake Shore Dr Chicago IL 60610 Office: 2315 E 93d St Chicago IL 60617

PACK, DENNIS HARVEY, broadcasting exec.; b. Salt Lake City, Mar. 16, 1938; s. Eugene Grant and Lucile Clara (Payne) P.; B.S., U. Utah, 1967, certificate internat. relations, 1967; M.A., Northwestern U., 1973; m. Carol Bickerstaffe, Sept. 20, 1968; children—John Lee, Robert James. Cameraman, producer-dir. Sta. KUED-TV, Salt Lake City, 1962-69; program mgr. Sta. KESD-TV, Brookings, S.D., 1969-74; dir. programming S.D. Pub. TV Network, 1974—. Instr. speech S.D. State U., Brookings, 1969—. Served with USCG, 1956-60. Mem. Pi Sigma Alpha, Kappa Tau Alpha, Alpha Epsilon Rho. Home: 1031 9th Ave Brookings SD 57006 Office: KESD-TV 116 Solberg Hall SD State U Brookings SD 57006

PACKARD, MARTIN THEODORE, psychotherapist; b. Washington, July 26, 1941; s. Julius David and Lillian (Weiner) P.; B.A. cum laude, State U. N.Y. at Buffalo, 1963; Ph.D., Ind. U., 1971; m. Sandra Podolin, Aug. 2, 1964; children—Dawn, Shana. Psychologist, Monroe County (Ind.) Mental Health, 1967, Goodwill Industries, Indpls., 1968, E.J. Meyer Hosp., Buffalo, 1971; founder, dir. Project Pathway, Buffalo, 1971-73; coordinator div. community services Niagara Falls Community Mental Health Center, Buffalo, 1973-74; dir. Middletown (O.) Mental Health Clinic, 1974-75. Cons. Lackawanna Community Health Center; clin. instr. psychiatry State U. N.Y. at Buffalo, 1971-74; adj. prof. Miami U., Oxford, O. Mem. Ohio Psychol. Assn., Sigma Xi. Jewish. Home: 3617 Pamajera Dr Oxford OH 45056 Office: 312 S Breiel St Middletown OH 45042

PADANILAM, GEORGE JOSEPH, physician; b. Kerala, India, July 12, 1939; s. Joseph Chacko and Aleyamma Joseph (Padanilam) P.; came to U.S., 1967; M.B.B.S., Med. Coll., Trivandrum, S.India, 1962; m. Mariamma Padanilam, July 5, 1964; children—Thomas, Joseph, Jimmy. Intern, Riverside Hosp., Toledo, Ohio, 1967-68; resident in surgery Med. Coll. Ohio, Toledo, 1968-72; practice medicine specializing in gen. surgery, 1972—; mem. staff Fostoria (Ohio) City Hosp. Fellow Royal Coll. Surgeons Can., A.C.S.; mem. Seneca County Med. Soc., Toledo Surg. Soc. Roman Catholic. Club: Rotary. Home: 1719 N Walnut St Fostoria OH 44830 Office: 504 Van Buren St Fostoria OH 44830

PADBERG, DANIEL LEE, educator; b. St. Louis, Jan. 8, 1937; s. Edwin Louis and Lyda Fay (Ruffin) P.; student Mo. U., 1956-58; B.S., S.E. Mo. State Coll., 1961; M.A., No. Ill. U., 1965; postgrad. U. Ill., 1969-70; m. Anna Ruth Pavell, June 19, 1976; dau. by previous marriage—Cheryl Lynn. Tchr. English, speech, drama High Sch. Dist. 214, Arlington Heights, Ill., 1961-66; tchr. speech, drama High Sch. Dist. 207, Park Ridge, Ill., 1966-69; asst. prof. communication and creative arts Purdue U., Calumet campus, Hammond, Ind., 1969-76; asst. prof. speech, dramatic arts, also dir. theatre Drury Coll., Springfield, Mo., 1976—. Co-producer, mng. dir., prodn. dir. Twin Towers Playhouse, Merrillville, Ind., 1974-75. Bd. dirs. New-In-Town Players, Lowell, Ind., 1973-75, Springfield Little Theatre, 1977—; dir. Am. div. Familienverband Padberg. Mem. AAUP, ANTA, Am. Theatre Assn., Speech Communication Assn., Nat. Geneal. Soc., Ind. Speech Assn., Hammond Saengerbund-Fidelia, Mo. Speech and Theatre Assn., Tau Kappa Epsilon. Episcopalian. Home: 1354 S Ventura Springfield MO 65804 Office: Drury Coll Springfield MO 65802

PADGETT, KATHARINE LONG, counselor; b. Balt., Dec. 19, 1927; d. Malcolm A. and Amy L. (Fahrney) Long; B.S., Juniata Coll., Huntington, Pa., 1950; M.A., U. Mich., 1970; m. Jack F. Padgett, Dec. 21, 1949; children—Deborah, Stephen, Susan, Thomas. Co-dir. women's programs Albion (Mich.) Coll., 1971-73, counselor Counseling Center, also instr. psychology, 1971-73, dir. career planning and placement, 1973—, instr. human services, 1977—. Mem. Coll. Placement Council, Midwest Coll. Placement Assn., Am. Personnel and Guidance Assn., Am., Mich. Coll. personnel assns., Nat., Mich. assns. women deans adminstrs. counselors, AAUW, PEO. Author articles. Home: 1206 E Michigan Ave Albion MI 49224 Office: Albion Coll Albion MI 49224

PAETZKE, ROY WARREN, accountant; b. Lidgerwood, N.D., Feb. 25, 1925; s. Harry George and Sabine Amalie (Falber) P.; B.S. in Edn., Valley City (N.D.) State Coll., 1953; M.A. in Accounting, U. N.D., 1957; m. Doris Karin Kristensen Kjelland, Feb. 3, 1967; stepchildren—Debra Kjelland, Lisa Kjelland, Mark Kjelland, Erik Kjelland. Tchr. pub. schs. Duerr Twp. (N.D.), Lidgerwood, 1943-48; tchr. Alsen (N.D.) Jr. High Sch., 1949-52; tchr. Alsen High Sch., 1954-55, prin., 1955-58; chief accountant N.D. Pub. Service Commn., Bismarck, 1958—. C.P.A., N.D. Mem. NEA, Am. Accounting Assn., Internat. Brotherhood Magicians, Sons of Norway. Home: 416 W Turnpike Bismarck ND 58501 Office: Capitol Bldg Bismarck ND 58501

PAFFRATH, LESLIE, found. exec.; b. N.Y.C., May 10, 1915; s. John and Alice (Gray) P.; student Mercersburg (Pa.) Acad. 1931-35; A.B., Union Coll., 1939; student Inst. World Affairs, Geneva, 1939; L.H.D. (hon.), U. Cin.; m. Adrianne Marcia Knight, June 26, 1954; children—Marytha, Mark, Elise, Rebecca. Mem.-in-tng. staff Inst. Pub. Adminstrn., N.Y.C., 1939-40; spl. asst. N.H. State Comptroller's Office, 1940; acting exec. dir. N.H. State Council Civilian Def., 1941; sr. adminstrv. asst. U.S. Regional Office Civilian Def. (New Eng.), 1941-42; dir. N.H. State Planning and Devel. Commn., 1943-46, exec. office, 1946-49; sec. Carnegie Endowment for Internat. Peace, 1950-59; pres.

The Johnson Found., Racine, Wis., 1959—; mem. Commn. to Study Orgn. of Peace; mem. internat. affairs com. and mem. gen. com., dept. internat. affairs. Nat. Council Chs. of Christ in U.S.A.; sec. gen. Internat. Convocation on Pacem in Terris, 1965; mem. spl. com. UN Internat. Environment Year; accredited rep. UN Econ. and Social Council Albert Schweitzer Fellowship, pres., 1965-68, chmn., 1968-72; a founding mem. World Assembly for Human Rights, 1968; mem. U.S. del. 4th Dartmouth Conf. Leningrad., 1964, 5th Dartmouth Conf., Rye, N.Y., 1969; mem. adv. com. on internat. orgns. Dept. State, 1972-74; mem. Wis. Humanities Com., 1973-75, Wis. Arts Bd., 1973-76; mem. health and sci. affairs com. Nat. Kidney Found., 1975—. Bd. advisers Prairie Sch., 1971—; vis. com. div. Social Scis. U. Chgo., 1977—; adv. council Med. Coll. Wis., 1976—. Commd. ensign, U.S. Navy, 1942; advance base liaison officer Panama Sea Frontier; spl. liaison officer Brit., French, and Netherlands Naval units, Phila.; lt. comdr. Supply Corps, USNR, 1948-62. Recipient citation Extension dir. U. Wis., 1970. Mem. UN Assn. U.S. (dir.), Council Fgn. Relations, Wis. Acad. Scis., Arts and Letters (citation 1970), Alpha Delta Phi. Episcopalian. Contbr. chpt. to The Quality of Urban Life. Home: 1632 College Ave Racine WI 53403 Office: The Johnson Found 33 E Four Mile Rd Racine WI 53402

PAGANO, SALVATORE JOHN, dentist; b. St. Louis, June 27, 192i; s. Salvatore and Angelina (Tocco) P.; D.D.S., St. Louis U., 1946; m. Crucifix Mary Bono, Sept. 1, 1946; children—Salvatore, Peter, Paul, Christopher, Joseph. Pvt. practice dentistry, St. Louis, 1946—. Tchr. operative dentistry St. Louis U. Sch. Dentistry, 1946, 48-53; mem. staff Faith Hosp.; mem. Vitale Med. Found. Bd. dirs. Greater St. Louis Dental Soc. Found.; trustee Faith Hosp. Served to 1st lt. AUS, 1946-48. Mem. Pierre Fauchard Acad., Am. Soc. Dentistry for Children, Am., Mo. (gov. 1963-66, 3d v.p. 1972-73) dental assns., Greater St. Louis Dental Soc. (pres. 1970), N. Dist. Dentists (pres. 1955), St. Louis Dental Soc. Golf Assn. (pres. 1960-61, dir. 1959-61, 67-69), Unico Nat., Am. Vets. service orgns., St. Louis U. Dental Alumni Assn. (pres. 1956), St. Apollonia Guild Cath. Dentists, St. Louis Soc. Dental Sci., Delta Sigma Delta (pres. 1958). K.C. (4 deg.). Home: 225 Ladue Lake Dr St Louis MO 63141 Office: 1040 N Mason Rd St Louis MO 63141

PAGE, ALFRED PERCY, chiropractor; b. Barrington, N.J., Nov. 13, 1932; s. Alfred Percy and Ellen Elizabeth (Dean) P.; A.A., Temple U., 1954; B.S. summa cum laude, Lincoln Chiropractic Coll., 1967, D.C., 1969; M.A.T., DePauw U., 1975; m. Delores Ann Murphy, July 21, 1971; children—Patricia, Craig. Practice chiropractic medicine, Greencastle, Ind., 1969—. Capt. fire dept. Hadden Heights, N.J., 1950-60; instr. first aid ARC, 1955—; Sunday sch. supt. Ch. of God; hon. fire chief Madison Twp. Fire Dept. Recipient Community Service award Gov. Ind., 1974; Humanity award ARC; named Man of Year Jaycees, 1965; master firefighter, 1st class instr. Ind. Fire Service Edn. Mem. Am., Internat. chiropractic assns., Putnam County Firemen's Assn. (chmn. bd. dirs. 1974-75, sec.-treas. 1977-78). Club: Putnam Country. Home: Route 1 Greencastle IN 46135 Office: Route 1 Greencastle IN 46135

PAGE, DOZZIE LYONS, educator; b. Tiptonville, Tenn., Apr. 13, 1921; d. Lessie LeRoy and Carrie (Oldham) Lyons; B.S.Ed., Chgo. Tchrs. Coll., 1968; M.S.Ed., Chgo. State U., 1976; m. Eugene Page, Dec. 22, 1973; children—Rita, Gerald. Cashier receptionist Unity Mut. Life Ins. Co., Chgo., 1939-47; sec. United Transport Service Employees Union, Chgo., 1947-51; sec. to dir. YMCA West Side, Chgo., 1951-53; sec., office mgr. Joint Council Dining Car Employees AFL CIO, Chgo., 1957-59; sr. stenographer Chgo. Police Dept., 1962-65; tchr. office practice Manpower Devel. Tng. Act, Chgo. Bd. Edn., 1965-67; tchr., coordinator distributive edn. Dunbar Vocational High Sch., Chgo., 1968—. Mem. Office Occupations Club, Distbr. Edn. Club, Chgo. Urban League, Chgo. Bus. Tchrs. Assn., Ill., Am. personnel and guidance assns., Phi Delta Kappa. Home: 6120 Justine St S Chicago IL 60636 Office: 3000 ML King Dr Chicago IL 60616

PAGE, EDWIN RICHARD, ednl. adminstr.; b. Battle Creek, Mich., May 24, 1932; s. Frank Clement and Josephine Marie (Giroux) P.; B.A., Western Mich. U., 1960; M.A., Ohio U., 1962, Ph.D., 1970; m. Michaelyn Ann Wheeler, Aug. 16, 1961; children—Lisa Ann, Thomas. Asst. prof. speech pathology Indiana (Pa.) State Coll., 1963-64, W.Va. U., Morgantown, 1964-66; research speech pathologist Plymouth Center for Human Devel., Northville, Mich., 1966-70; dir. pupil personnel services Plymouth-Canton Community Schs., Plymouth, Mich., 1970—; vis. prof. speech pathology Madonna Coll., Livonia, Mich., 1967—, Eastern Mich. U., Ypsilanti, 1967—. Served with USN, 1952-56; Korea. NDEA fellow, 1960-63. Mem. Am. Speech and Hearing Assn., Am. Assn. Mental Deficiency, Assn. Children with Learning Disabilities, Council for Exceptional Children, Mich. Assn. Adminstrs. in Spl. Edn., Kappa Delta Pi, Phi Delta Kappa. Club: Lions (pres. Plymouth 1971-72, zone chmn. 1972-73). Author: A Parent's Handbook for the Handicapped, 1976. Contbr. articles on spl. edn., sch. adminstrn., handicapped to profl. pubs. Home: 11000 McClumpha Rd Plymouth MI 48170 Office: 454 S Harvey St Plymouth MI 48170

PAGE, ELEANOR (MRS. FRANK E. VOYSEY), journalist; b. Chgo.; d. Edwin and Elsie (Bell) Page; m. Norman W. MacDonald, Feb. 27, 1936; children—Elsie Anne, Bruce Alexander, Malcolm Cameron; m. 2d, Frank E. Voysey, Nov. 18, 1972. Reporter soc. dept. Chgo. Tribune, 1933-42, soc. editor, 1942—. Sustaining mem. Jr. League of Chgo., Inc. Clubs: Saddle and Cycle, Arts. Home: 427 W Roslyn Pl Chicago IL 60614 Office: Chgo Tribune 435 N Michigan Ave Chicago IL 60611

PAGE, HOWARD KELSEY, elec. mfg. co. exec., realtor; b. Duluth, Minn., July 9, 1926; s. Sidney Howard and Helen Laura (Kelsey) P.; B.A. cum laude in Economics, Brown U., 1950; m. June J. Whelan, Jan. 7, 1951; children—Kelsey, Kathy, Julie, Beth. Exec. trainee Ford Motor Co., Dearborn, Mich., 1950-51; asst. to pres. Bond Internat., Detroit, 1951-53; partner, pres. Cooper Page Co., Mpls., 1953-67; pres. Crest Electronics Inc., Dassel, Minn., 1967—; pres. Greenwood Enterprises, Inc., Dassel, 1968—; dir. University Apts., Inc. Dir. Dassel Lakeside Home, 1974—; del. Meeker County (Minn.) Repuplican Party, 1974—. Served with U.S. Army, 1944-45. Mem. N. Central Electric League, N. Central Mfg. Club, Dassel Comml. Club. Republican. Methodist. Club: Masons. Home: 460 William Ave E Dassel MN 55325 Office: Simon at 3d St Dassel MN 55325

PAGE, ROBERT WRIGHT, dentist; b. Mpls., Sept. 6, 1913; s. Wright Benton and Ethel Irene (Farnham) P.; D.D.S., U. Minn., 1936; m. Eleanor Josephine Affeldt, June 23, 1940; children—Nancy Page Burns, Barbara Page Tieso, Roger A., Douglas R. Pvt. practice dentistry, Mpls., 1936-40, Anoka, Minn., 1946—; mem. dental staff Mercy Hosp., Coon Rapids, Minn., 1966—. Chmn. Anoka Republican Com., 1963-64, del. state conv., 1963, 64, 65. Served to col. Dental Corps, AUS, 1940-46. Mem. Am., Minn State dental assns., Mpls. Dist. Dental Soc., Anoka C. of C., Pearl Harbor Survivors Assn., Theta Delta Chi. Lutheran (trustee 1956-59). Club: Kiwanis. Home: 1410 3d Ave S Anoka MN 55303 Office: 1829 5th Ave S Anoka MN 55303

PAGE, WALTER SHARP, JR., assn. exec.; b. Columbus, Ohio, July 16, 1917; s. Walter Sharp and Esther (Johnson) P.; student Denison U., 1934-35; B.A., M.A., Ohio State U., 1939; m. Eva Johnson, Mar. 1, 1941; children—Frances Johnson, Walter Sharp. Community sec. Winston-Salem (N.C.) YMCA, 1939-40; field rep., state campaign dir. N.C. Tb Assn., 1940-42; exec. sec. Passaic County (N.J.) Tb and Health Assn., 1947-49; program cons. Am. Heart Assn., 1949-50; exec. dir. Ohio affiliate Am. Heart Assn., Columbus, 1952—. Mem. Gov.'s Task Force on Environ. Protection, 1971. Served to maj. AUS, 1942-46, 50-52. Decorated Bronze Star with 2 oak leaf clusters. Mem. Staff Soc. Heart Assns. (pres. 1958-59), Ohio Pub. Health Assn. (chmn. vol. health agy. sec. 1966-68, pres. 1971-72), Phi Delta Theta. Methodist. Clubs: Rotary, Univ. (Columbus). Home: 1544 Guilford Rd Columbus OH 43221 Office: 10 E Town St Columbus OH 43215

PAGE-EL, EDWARD, physician; b. South Bend, Ind., Apr. 25, 1928; s. Joseph and Pearl (Davenport) Page-El; B.S. cum laude, Va. Union U., 1953; M.D., Meharry Med. Coll., 1959; m. Ann Burns, June 4, 1959; children—Kim, Peter, Brett. Intern, G.W. Hubbard Hosp., Nashville, 1959-60, resident pediatrics, 1960-63; instr. pediatrics Meharry Med. Coll., Nashville, 1963-64; NIH fellow neurology U. Ill., 1964-67; practice medicine specializing in pediatric neurology, Chgo., 1967—; mem. staff U. Ill. Hosps., Chgo., Rush-Presbyn. Hosp.; asst. prof. pediatrics and neurology U. Ill., 1967—, Rush-Presbyn. Med. Sch., 1971—; dir. out-patient dept. Ill. State Pediatric Inst., Chgo., 1968—; cons. Ill. Hosp. Sch., Chgo., Ridgeway Sch. Emotionally Disturbed Children. Bd. dirs. Garfield Community Hosp., Chgo., Julius Levinson Found. Retarded Children. Served with U.S. Army, 1946-48. Mem. Am. Acad. Neurology, Am. Assn. Mental Disease, Child Neurology Soc., Nat. Med. Assn., Phi Beta Sigma, Beta Kappa Chi. Mem. Moslem religion. Editorial cons. Mental Retardation, 1971—. Home: 401 E 32d St Chicago IL 60616 Office: 1640 W Roosevelt Rd Chicago IL 60608

PAGEL, RICHARD FREDERICK, metallurgist; b. Beckingen, Germany, May 28, 1920; s. Richard and Paula A. (Roth) P.; m. Frieda H. Stallinger, Sept. 28, 1952; children—Carmen L., Ricarda L. B.S. in Metall. Engring., U. Idaho, 1949. Research metallurgist Cerro de Pasco Corp., LaOroya, Peru, 1949-52; plant metallurgist Am. Zinc Co., Dumas, Tex., 1952-55; research engr., Sauget, Ill., 1955-71, chief metallurgist, 1973—. Mem. Moose. Patentee electrolytic zinc refining, wastewater treatment; contbr. articles to profl. jours. Home: Belleville IL 62221 Office: AMAX Zinc Co PO Box 2347 East St Louis IL 62202

PAGEL, WILLIAM RUSH, labor relations exec., author, lectr.; b. Egan, S.D., Nov. 4, 1901; s. William Rienhart and Carrie E. (Rush) P.; B.A. cum laude, U. Wis., 1924; m. Dorothy L. Johnsen, Aug. 19, 1939; children—William Kingston, Diane Lynette Pagel Harsh. With Ill. Bell Telephone Co., Chgo., 1924-67, comml. results supr., 1932-43, comml. personnel supr., 1943-67; cons. labor relations and arbitration. Speaker, U. Wyo. Old Time Ranch Tour, 1961. Mem. Telephone Pioneers Am., Soc. Mayflower Descs. (bd. assts. Ill. 1968-71, gov. Kans. 1975—), Sons and Daus. Pilgrims, Descs. Colonial Clergy, Soc. Colonial Wars, Huguenot Soc. (dir. 1964-67, v.p. 1965-67), Union Vets. of Civil War, Descs. Colonial Govs., SAR (founding mem. George Rogers Clark chpt., Ill. historian 1960-61, Ill. sec. 1961-63, state v.p. 1963-68, Nat. Distinguished Service award 1963, 64, 65, 66, Patriot medal 1966), Heart of Am., Johnson County (founding mem.) geneal. socs., Moody County Hist. Soc. Republican. Lutheran (council 1948-55). Club: Aztec. Author: A Mayflower Lineage of Twelve Generations; George Morgan, American Hereford Pioneer. Geneal. research on early Am. and early Western families. Home: 5208 W 96th St Shawnee Mission KS 66207

PAGEN, JOHN, supt. schs.; b. Port Huron, Mich., Dec. 27, 1926; s. Nick and Katherine (Boncheff) P.; B.S., Ferris State Coll., 1956; M.S., Wayne State U., 1958, Ed.D., 1967; m. Mary Lou White, June 5, 1954; children—John Robert, Mary Katherine. Math. and sci. tchr. Harper Woods (Mich.) High Sch. and Jr. High Sch., 1956-59; prin., Beacon Elementary Sch., Harper Woods, Mich., 1959-65; asst. supt., gen. adminstr., chief negotiator Waterford Sch. Dist., Pontiac, Mich., 1966-67; dir. Individual Communications System Project, Computer Assisted Instrn., Waterford Sch. Dist., 1967-69, supt., 1969—. Sec.-treas. Detroit Met. Bur. Sch. Studies, 1971-72, vice-chmn., 1972-75, chmn., 1975—. Mem. exec. bd. Clinton Valley council Boy Scouts Am., 1972—. Served with USNR, 1944-46. Mott fellow Wayne State U., 1965-66. Mem. Nat. Acad. Sch. Execs., Internat. Platform Assn., N.E.A. (life), Am. Ednl. Research Assn., Nat. Community Sch. Assn., Am., Mich. assns. sch. adminstrs., Nat., Mich. assns. ednl. data systems, Phi Delta Kappa. Clubs: Masons, Shriners, Kiwanis, Rotary. Home: 463 Berrypatch St Pontiac MI 48054 Office: 6020 Pontiac Lake Rd Pontiac MI 48054

PAGTAKHAN, REYNALDO DALUZ, physician; b. Manila, Jan. 7, 1935; s. Victor N. and Fabiana G. (Daluz) P.; B.S., U. Philippines, 1960, M.D., 1961; M.S. in Physiology, U. Man., 1969; m. Gloria Ll. Visarra, Oct. 31, 1964; children—Reynaldo Ishmael, Adriel Vincent, Sherwin Mendel. Intern, Philippine Gen. Hosp., Manila, 1960-61, research asso. in pediatrics, 1961-63; resident pediatrician Childrens Hosp., Washington U., St. Louis, 1963-65, fellow pediatric cardiology, 1965-67; practice medicine, specializing in pediatric respirology, Winnipeg, Man., Can., 1971—; fellow pediatric respirology Childrens Hosp., U. Man., 1968-71, also asso. dir. sect. pediatric respirology, 1971—, dir. Cystic Fibrosis Center; 1972—; asso. prof. pediatrics U. Man. Recipient First Prize award for basic research Manila Med. Soc., 1963. Diplomate Am. Bd. Pediatrics. Fellow Am. Coll. Chest Physicians; mem. Canadian Physiol. Assn., Am., Canadian thoracic socs., Man. Med. Assn. Contbr. chpts. to Kendig's Pulmonary Disorders, 1972, 77; Kagan and Gellis Current Pediatric Therapy, 1973. Home: 6 Sandee Bay St Vital Winnipeg MB R2M 1Z1 Canada Office: 685 Bannatyne Ave Winnipeg MB R3E 0W1 Canada

PAINE, CARLTON BENTLEY, clin. psychologist; b. Lincoln, Nebr., Nov. 4, 1939; s. Charles Bentley and Hazel Marie (Beechner) P.; B.A., Nebr. Wesleyan U., 1962; M.A., U. Mo., 1964, Ph.D., 1971; m. Judith Anne Umberger, June 21, 1963; children—Liza Anne, Heather Lynne, Jennifer Leigh. Intern, Greater Kansas City (Mo.) Mental Health Found. and U. Mo. Sch. Medicine, 1966-67; psychologist, dir. Day Center, Western Mo. Mental Health Center, Kansas City, 1967-71; psychologist, program dir. Lincoln-Lancaster Mental Health Center, Lincoln, 1971-77; dir. outpatient and emergency services Community Mental Health Center, Lancaster County, 1977—; sch. clin. psychologist Nebr. Wesleyan U., Lincoln, 1973—. Instr. psychiatry U. Mo. Sch. Medicine, Kansas City, 1967-71; cons. Otoe County Mental Health Clinic, Nebraska City, Nebr., 1971-73; asso. clin. psychology U. Nebr., Lincoln, 1971—; profl. adviser Lancaster County Assn. Mental Health, 1974-76, USPHS trainee, 1964-65. Mem. Am., Nebr. psychol. assns., Zeta Psi, Psi Chi. Democrat. Unitarian. Contbr. articles to profl. jours. Home: 201 Carolyn Ct Lincoln NE 68510 Office: 134 S 13th St Lincoln NE 68508

PAINE, CHARLES BENTLEY, lawyer; b. Grand Island, Nebr., May 1, 1905; s. Bayard Henry and Grace Newcomb (Bentley) P.; A.B., Nebr. Wesleyan U., 1927; J.D. cum laude, U. Nebr., 1929; postgrad. Judge Adv. Gen. Dept. Sch., 1942, Command and Gen. Staff Coll., 1944; m. Hazel Marie Beechner, Oct. 29, 1932; children—Elizabeth Ann Paine Dillon, Carlton Bentley. Admitted to Nebr. bar, 1929; Fed., Tax and Mil. Cts.; practiced in Lincoln, 1929-41, Grand Island, 1946—; partner firm Paine & Paine, 1946-75, Paine, Paine & Huston, 1975—. Pres., Grand Island Land Co., 1951—; sec., bd. dirs. Grand Island Parking Corp., 1967-76. Pres. Lincoln chpt. Wesley Found.; trustee Nebr. Wesleyan U., 1947-55, 58-65, So. Meth. U., 1952-65. Served to lt. col., Judge Adv. Gen. Dept., U.S. Army, 1941-46; PTO. Decorated Bronze Star medal. Mem. Am., Nebr., Hall County (past pres.) bar assns., Res. Officers Assn. (past pres. Lincoln chpt.), Grand Island C. of C. (past dir.), Am. Legion, Judge Adv. Gens. Assn., Blue Key, Order Coif, Phi Kappa Phi, Pi Kappa Delta, Pi Gamma Mu. Republican. Methodist. Clubs: Masons, Kiwanis, Liederkranz. Home: 2316 W Anna St Grand Island NE 68801 Office: 108 N Locust St Grand Island NE 68801

PAINTER, MILTON MCFARLAND, mfg. co. exec.; b. Friars Point, Miss., Dec. 6, 1920; s. Milton McFarland and Ernestine (Cobb) P.; B.A., La. State U., 1942; m. Frances Elwanda Groves, Apr. 4, 1955; children—Michael Cobb, Cynthia Lee, Judy Frances. Creative dir., merchandising dept. Walgreen Drug Stores, Chgo., 1946-50; account exec. Chek-Chart Corp., 1950-53; asst. dir. advt. and sales promotion Ency. Brit., Inc., 1953-56; advt. supr., canned meat div. and frozen food div. Libby, McNeil & Libby, 1956-66; account exec. Young & Rubicam, Inc., 1966-68; advt. and sales promotion mgr. Westclox div. Gen. Time Corp., LaSalle, Ill., 1968-72; advt. and sales promotion mgr. Republic Molding Corp., Chgo., 1972—. Served to lt. col. USAFR, 1946-72. Mem. Smithsonian Assos., Res. Officers Assn., Daggers, Sigma Alpha Epsilon. Home: 881 Darlington Ln Crystal Lake IL 60014

PAINTER, SYDNEY SHAW, III, chemist; b. Phila., Sept. 21, 1934; s. Sydney Shaw, Jr., and Margurite Eleanor (Hurleman) P.; m. M. Julie Eberhart, Aug. 4, 1956; children—Suzanne, Stephen, Lynne. Student, Mass. Inst. Tech., 1952-56. Research chemist, Pecora, Inc., Phila. and Garland, Tex., 1956-62, J.W. Mortell, Kankakee, Ill., 1962-63; sr. research chemist, Helene Curtis, Chgo. and Dayton, Ohio, 1963-66; chief chemist, Gibson-Homans Co., Cleve., 1966-76, v.p. research, 1976—. Mem. Am. Chem. Soc., Am. Soc. for Testing and Materials (chmn. sub-com., mem. at large of exec. sub-com.), AAAS, Nat. Paint and Coatings Assn. (chmn. roof coatings tech. sub-com.), Canadian Govt. Specifications Bd. Com. on Caulking and Sealing Compounds, Am. Contract Bridge League. Named Man-of-Year, ASTM, 1975, also named to their Sealants Hall of Fame, 1975; contbr. article in field. Home: 17-2 Meadowlawn Dr Mentor OH 44060 Office: 2366 Woodhill Rd Cleveland OH 44106

PAISLEY, DENNIS LEE, physicist; b. Macomb, Ill., May 16, 1942; s. Lyle H. and Clarice K. (Ward) P.; B.S. in Physics, Western Ill. U., 1965; M.S. in Physics, Xavier U., 1973; m. Daisy I. Fernetti; 1 son, Dennis Lyle. Physics instr. Scioto (Ill.) High Sch., 1964-65; engr. div. hyws. State of Ill., Peoria, 1965-67; sr. research physicist Mound Lab. Monsanto Research Corp., Miamisburg, Ohio., 1967—; cons. in ultra-high speed photography, laser photography, streak photography, hydro diagnostics, explosives, shock and detonation phenomena. Mem. Soc. Motion Picture and TV Engrs, Lions. Author publs. in field. Home: 708 St Dunstan Ct Dayton OH 45449 Office: Mound Lab Monsanto Corp Miamisburg OH 45342

PAJIC, SVETOMIR, veterinarian; b. Obrenovac, Yugoslavia, Nov. 24, 1932; s. Ljubomir and Paulina (Vukajlovic) P.; D.V.M., U. Hannover (Germany), 1964; postgrad. Fed. Veterinary Inst., Hannover, 1964, U. Chgo., 1965; m. Gerda M. Hanschmann, 1960; 1 dau., Renata. Came to U.S., 1963, naturalized, 1968. Veterinary practice, Obrenovac, 1958-59; cons. meat industry, Germany, 1959-60; veterinary ins. in charge, Osijek, Yugoslavia, 1960-62; veterinary practice, Lensahn, W.Ger., 1962-63; veterinary meat insp. U.S. Agr. Dept., 1964-68, supervisory veterinary med. officer, 1968—. Mem. AVMA, Nat. Assn. Fed. Veterinarians, Am. Pub. Health Assn., Internat. Platform Assn. Clubs: Lions; Chess (St. Charles). Home: 1702 Jay Ln Saint Charles IL 60174 Office: 309 W Nebraska St Elburn IL 60119

PAKIS, VAL, engring. mgr.; b. Cleve., Sept. 22, 1924; s. Val and Mary (Hribar) P.; B.S. in Elec. Engring., Mont. State Coll., 1950; m. Therese Molinski, Jan. 31, 1948; children—Val, Fred, Laura. With Illuminating Co., Cleve., 1948-51, Reliance Electric Co., Cleve., 1951, Austin Co., 1951-55; with W.W. Clark Corp., Cleve., 1955—, engring. mgr., 1973—. Mem. City Planning Commn., Willowick, Ohio, 1974-76. Served with Paratroops, U.S. Army, 1943-46. Decorated Bronze Star, Purple Heart. Mem. Cleve. Engring. Soc., IEEE, Internat. Assn. Elec. Insps. Republican. Home: 377 Clarmont Rd Willowick OH 44094 Office: 1251 E 286 St Euclid OH 44132

PAKYZ, LAWRENCE JOSEPH, dentist; b. Chgo., Feb. 9, 1943; s. Izydor Joseph and Dorothy Ida (Frederickson) P.; D.D.S., Marquette U., 1967; m. Carol M. Potvin, Aug. 25, 1965; children—Christopher, Troy. Dental intern St. Anthony's Hosp., Oklahoma City, 1967-68; practice dentistry Drs. Wagner & Pakyz Dental Group, Prairie du Sac, Wis., 1968—; mem. staff Sauk-Prairie Meml. Hosp. Recipient First Pl. Table Clinics award Okla. State Dental Soc., 1968. Mem. ADA, Am. Endodontic Soc., Nat. Assn. Profession, Wis. State, Sauk-Juneau County (pres. 1975-76) dental socs., Prairie du Sac C. of C. Clubs: Lions, Optimist (pres. 1970-71). Home: RFD 2 Box 282 Sauk City WI 53583 Office: 335 Galena St Prairie du Sac WI 53578

PALBYKIN, DONALD JOHN, aviation exec.; b. Oak Park, Ill., Oct. 11, 1929; s. Albert Alfred and Cecilia Mary (Keiper) P.; student pub. and parochial schs.; m. Elizabeth Mae Perry, May 29, 1948; children—Stephen, Alan, Martin, Julie, Debra, Susan, Ann Marie. Laborer, Studebaker Corp., 1948-56; chief pilot Stockert Flying Service, 1956-59; asst. pres. Wheel Horse, 1959-66; pres. Skystream, Inc., Plymouth, Ind., 1966—; pres. Ecco, Inc., Palbykin Enterprises. Club: Plymouth Country. Home: 310 N Michigan St Penthouse 500 Plymouth IN 46563 Office: Plymouth Bldg Plymouth IN 46563

PALENCHAR, ROBERT EDWARD, diversified industry exec.; b. Detroit, Apr. 8, 1922; s. John Peter and Irene Ann (Repicky) P.; A.B. in Econs. and Personnel Adminstrn., U. Notre Dame, 1942; postgrad. U. Mich., 1943; m. Ethel Lindsay, Sept. 10, 1942; children—Patricia Ann (Mrs. Richard K. Atchinson), James Lindsay. With Ex-Cell-O Corp., Detroit, 1949-62, dir. indsl. relations, 1962; v.p. employee relations automotive div. Budd Co., Detroit, 1962-66; v.p., dir. employee relations Sunbeam Corp., Chgo., 1966-69; v.p. personnel and pub. relations Esmark, Inc., 1969-77, v.p. corp. affairs and personnel, 1977—. Served with U.S. Army, 1943. Mem. Chgo. Bd. Commerce, N.A.M., Notre Dame Alumni Assn., Am. Mgmt. Assn., Conf. Bd. Clubs: Recess (Detroit); Mid-America (Chgo.). Home: 64 Joyce Ct Glen Ellyn IL 60137 Office: 55 E Monroe St Chicago IL 60603

PALERMO, ANTHONY, JR., elec. engr.; b. Cleve., Sept. 22, 1926; s. Anthony and Sblendora (Palange) P.; m. Margaret Theresa Packer, July 28, 1951; children—Thomas, David, Patricia, Steven, Nancy, James, Jeanne. Student U. Dayton, 1944, U. Ind., 1945; B.S.E.E., Case Inst. Tech., 1949. Engr., Picker Corp., Cleve., 1949-58, sr. engr., 1959-62, chief engr. indsl. products group, 1962-64, engring. mgr.

indsl. products group, 1964-72, cons. engr., 1972-75, engring. mgr. x-ray generators spl. systems group, 1975—; profl. musician, 1949—. Active Boy Scouts Am., 1961-62; publicity chmn., mem. speakers bur. S. Euclid Hist. Soc., 1972—, pres., 1977—. Mem. Am. Nat. Standards Inst., Am. Soc. for Metals, Little Red Schoolhouse Hist. Soc., Cleve. Musicians Union, Theta Chi. Clubs: Lander Haven Country, Pioneer Investment. Contbr. articles, chpts. to profl. jours., texts; author: Our Own Little Red Schoolhouse, 1976; holder numerous patents. Home: 1715 Biltamy Blvd South Euclid OH 44121 Office: 600 Beta Dr Mayfield OH 44143

PALIA, CHARLES CANTARDO, ednl. adminstr.; b. Spring Valley, Ill., Sept. 5, 1923; s. Cantardo and Mary Lou (Barto) P.; B.S. in Zoology, So. Ill., 1950; M.S., No. Ill.U, 1960; m. Enise M. Nanni, Aug. 2, 1947; children—Charles, David Damian. Tchr. math. and sci. Spring Valley Elementary Schs., 1950-60; prin. Lincoln Sch., Spring Valley, 1960-64; supt. schs., Spring Valley, 1964—. Post adviser Explorer Scouts; active civil def., Salvation Army, A.R.C., Tri-County Humane Soc. Bd. dirs. Spring Valley Assn. City Library, 1965-71; pres. adult bd. Spring Valley Youth Center. Served with USNR, 1942-45. Recipient Silver Beaver award Boy Scouts Am., 1971. Mem. Ill. Assn. Mental Health, Ill. Assn. Sch. Adminstrs., Bur. County Adminstrs., Ill. Sch. Bd. Assn., Am. Legion, Bqr.-Marshal-Putnam Tri-County Spl. Ednl. Coop. (chmn. 1971—), Am. Sch. Food Service Assn. Clubs: K.C., Rotary (pres. Spring Valley 1974-75). Home: 325 W Minnesota St Spring Valley IL 61362 Office: 800 N Richard Ave Spring Valley IL 61362

PALLMANN, MARGOT SIMONS, mathematician; b. Stolberg, W. Germany, Dec. 13, 1927; d. Hubert J. and Bernadette (Waleffe) Simons; came to U.S., 1963; B.A., U. Cologne, 1953, M.A., 1955; M.A., Washington U., 1971, Ph.D. (NDEA grad. fellowship), 1975; m. Albert J. Pallmann, June 26, 1958; 1 son, Thomas R. Instr., City-Gymnasium, Cologne, W. Germany, 1955-57; instr., head physics div. Private Coll. Prep. Sch., Cologne, 1957-59; prof., chmn. dept. physics U. de El Salvador, Central Am., 1961-63; instr., U. Mo., St. Louis, 1965-68; instr. mathematics Washington U., St. Louis, 1973-77, lectr. math., 1977—; asst. prof. math. Harris-Stowe Coll., St. Louis, 1977—. Mem. Am. Math. Soc., The Math. Assn. of Am. Home: 9 Middlesex Dr St Louis MO 63144

PALM, ERNEST THEODORE, surgeon; b. Missoula, Mont., Apr. 2, 1922; s. Ernest A. and Edith Anna (Cling) P.; B.A., Gustavus Adolphus Coll., 1942; B.S., U. Minn., 1944, M.B., 1945, M.D., 1946; m. Muriel Charlotte Larson, June 5, 1947; children—Augusta Jane, David, Barbara, William. Intern, Hahnemann Med. Sch. and Hosp., Phila., 1945-46; resident in surgery Swedish-St. Barnabas Hosp., Mpls., 1963-67; mem. staff Met. Med. Center, Fairview-Southdale Hosp., Meth. Hosp., Mpls. Diplomate Am. Bd. Surgery. Recipient Ross award for sci. lit., 1964. Fellow A.C.S., mem. AMA, Minn. State, Hennepin County med. socs., Minn., Mpls. surg. socs., Am. Physicians Art Assn. Lutheran. Contbr. articles in field to med., surg. jours., yearbooks. Home: 144 W Minnehaha Pkwy Minneapolis MN 55419 Office: 1202 Metropolitan Med Bldg Minneapolis MN 55404

PALMER, AGNES MAE HIGH (MRS. DANIEL DAVID PALMER), sculptress, clubwoman; b. Lancaster, Pa.; d. David and Elizabeth (Futerer) High; D.C., Palmer Coll., 1938; m. Daniel David Palmer, June 27, 1943; children—Bonnie Joan (Mrs. Thomas McCloskey), Jenny Wren (Mrs. Kermit Sutton), Vickie Anne. Pvt. practice as chiropractor, West Chester, Pa., 1938-43. Sculptress, 1967—; important works include portraits Robert Kennedy, D.D. Palmer I, D.D. Palmer II, Bonnie, Jenny, Vickie, Philip D. Adler. Performer Music Clubs Davenport; writer, dir., producer children's play McKinley Sch., Davenport, 1961. Life mem. aux. Naples (Fla.) Community Hosp., Mercy Hosp., Davenport, St. Luke's Hosp., Davenport. Former mem. Daus. of Nile, Tri-City Symphony Assn., Internat. Chiropractors Assn., Iowa Fedn. Music Clubs (life), Sigma Phi Chi (supreme kiatrus). Clubs: Saint Katherine's Mothers (pres.), Town (Davenport), Music Students, Etude (past pres.), Davenport, Davenport Country, Union League (Chgo.), Naples Garden, Naples Music, Eldorado Country, Royal Poinciana Golf, Rock Island Arsenal Golf, Davnport Country, Crow Creek Country. Home: 5 Forest Rd Davenport IA 52803

PALMER, CLOYCE DEAN, engring. and mfg. co. exec.; b. Washington, Iowa, May 31, 1933; s. Harold Samuel and Alice Elizabeth (Herr) P.; B.S., Iowa State U., 1954; M.B.A., Drake U., 1971; m. Nelda Peryl Williams, Oct. 15, 1954; children—Kimberly Dan, Lori Alise, Leslie Lane. With Pamco, Oskaloosa, Iowa, 1957-73, v.p. mktg., 1970-73; pres. Fairfield Engring. and Mfg. (Iowa), 1973—; dir. Capital Resource Corp., 1969-72; pres. Jefferson Industries, 1974—, Keota Mfg. Co., 1974—, Van Buren Mfg. Co., 1976—. Mem. Airport Commn., Fairfield, 1973-75. Served with U.S. Army, 1954-57. Mem. Am. Feed Mfrs. Assn., Sales Mgmt. Execs. Republican. Methodist. Club: Shriners. Home: 502 Fairway Pl Fairfield IA 52556 Office: 601 W Kirkwood Fairfield IA 52556

PALMER, DANIEL DAVID, coll. pres.; b. Davenport, Iowa, Jan. 12, 1906; s. Bartlett Joshua and Mabel Sarah (Heath) P.; B.S., Wharton Sch. Fin. and Commerce, U. Pa., 1929; D.C., Palmer Coll. Chiropractic, 1938, Ph.C., 1941; grad. Advanced Mgmt. Program, Harvard U., 1958; LL.D., Parsons Coll.; m. Agnes High, June 27, 1943; children—Bonnie Joan, Jenny Wren, Vickie Anne. Pres. Palmer Coll. Chiropractic, Davenport, 1961—, chmn. bd. trustees, 1973—; pres. Palmer Jr. Coll., 1964—, chmn. bd. trustees, 1975—; pres. Palmer Broadcasting Co., 1961—. Past chmn. Scott County chpt. ARC; past pres. YMCA, Davenport and Scott County; past pres. United Fund of Scott County, Jr. Achievement of Davenport, Tri-City Symphony Orch. Assn.; past v.p. Civic Music Assn.; bd. dirs. United Community Services Scott County. Recipient Distinguished Service award C. of C., 1960, Quad-Cities Sales Execs., 1960; Quad City Man of Year, B'nai B'rith, 1967. Mem. Broadcast Pioneers (dir.), Davenport Jr. (a founder, past pres.), Davenport chambers commerce (past pres.), NCCJ (trustee nat. bd., dir. Davenport chpt.), Delta Tau Delta, Delta Sigma Chi. Episcopalian. Clubs: Masons, Shriners; Rotary, Davenport Country, Davenport, Crow Valley Golf (Davenport); Rock Island Arsenal Golf; Lake Shore, Union League (Chgo.; Harvard (Boston); Des Moines, Embassy (Des Moines); Hole-In-The-Wall Golf, Royal Poinciana Golf, Naples Yacht (Naples, Fla.); Eldorado Country (Palm Desert, (Calif.); Town; Knife and Fork (past pres.); Racquet (Palm Springs, Calif.). Office: 1000 Brady St Davenport IA 52803

PALMER, DENNIS LEE, accountant; b. Rockford, Ill., Oct. 25, 1942; s. Paul Leroy and Jeanette Carline (Rose) P.; student U. Omaha, 1963, Rock Valley Coll., 1965-66, 74; m. Patricia Ann Murphy, Sept. 8, 1962; 1 son, Michael Edward. Mem. engring. dept. Ill. Water Treatment Plant, Rockford, 1964-65, Woodward Gov. Co., Rockford, 1965-69; accountant Gibbs-Beach-Palmer & Assos., Rockford, 1969—, v.p., 1972-77, pres., 1977—. Served with USAF, 1960-64. Mem. Nat. Soc. Pub. Accountants, Ind. Accountants Ill. Baptist. Office: 2409 Broadway St Rockford IL 61108

PALMER, DONALD CURTIS, clergyman, fgn. missions adminstr.; b. Nelson, Minn., Oct. 8, 1934; s. Roy A. and Cora (Bergner) P.; student U. Minn., 1952-55; diploma Briercrest Bible Inst., 1958; M.A. in Missions, Trinity Evang. Div. Sch., 1972; m. Dorothy Mae Nordquist, Mar. 16, 1962; children—Jean, John. Ordained to ministry Conservative Bapt. Ch., 1959; missionary Gospel Missionary Union, Colombia, S.Am., 1959-71, coordinator evangelism, 1970-71, area sec. Latin Am., Kansas City, Mo., 1971-72, dir. field affairs Latin Am., 1973—, mem. evang. com. Latin Am., 1975—, bd. dirs., 1976—. Author: Explosion of People Evangelism, 1974; contbg. author Dynamic Religious Movements, 1978. Home: 6111 N Woodland St Kansas City MO 64118

PALMER, EDWARD HENRY, cons. and devel. exec.; b. Riverside, Ill., Feb. 12, 1932; s. Brian Charles and Catherine (Roemanker) P.; A.B., Hanover Coll., 1955; S.T.B., Berkeley Div. Sch., 1956; student Yale U., 1957-58, Northwestern U., 1960-63; m. Virginia Van Name, Oct. 5, 1960. Staff asst. Inst. Human Relations, Yale U., 1956—; youth worker St. Paul's Ch., New Haven, 1957-58, asst. rector, 1958-60; community and tenant relations Chgo. Housing Authority, 1960-62; exec. dir. Trumbull Park Community Center, Chgo., 1962-64; exec. dir. Hyde Park-Kenwood Community Conf., Chgo. Mem. Commn. on Human Relations, Chgo., 1964-66; pres. Real Estate Data Co. and Social Planning Assos., 1966-75; pres. SPA/REDCO, Inc., Palmer, France, Green & King, 1975—; chmn. bd., pres. Mark VII Corp., 1972-75. Mem. Phi Gamma Delta. Clubs: Univ., Cliff Dwellers, Carlton, Quadrangle, Chicago City. Home: 2206 Orrington Ave Evanston IL 60201 Office: 1 E Wacker Dr Chicago IL 60601

PALMER, HARRISON ROWE, clin. psychologist; b. Hamilton, Ala., Jan. 23, 1920; s. Clover McKinley and Cora Lee (Goodson) P.; certificate elementary teaching Florence (Ala.) State Tchrs. Coll., 1940; B.S. in Psychology, U. Ala., 1951, M.A. in Clin. Psychology, 1953; postgrad. clin. psychology La. State U., 1953-56; m. Margaret E. Witty, July 11, 1942; children—Coralie Harriet (Mrs. John Paul Mincey), Margaret Claire (Mrs. James D. Ferguson), Charlotte Anne (Mrs. Richard A. Podsednik, Jr.), Robert Leslie, William Edward. Fellow clin. psychology S.E. La. State Hosp., Mandeville, 1955-56; staff clin. psychologist Porterville (Calif.) State Hosp., 1956-60; chief clin. psychologist Riverside (Calif.) State Mental Hygiene Clinic, 1960-66; clin. psychologist Calif. Rehab. Center Narcotics, Corona, 1966-70, Gulf Coast Mental Health Center, Gulfport, Miss., 1970-72, part-time pvt. practice clin. psychology, Porterville, Calif., 1956-60, Riverside, Calif., 1960-70; coordinator adult out-patient program Good Samaritan Community Mental Health Center, Dayton, O., 1975—. Instr. psychology U. So. Miss., Gulfport, 1971. Served to 2d lt., communications officer, USAAF, 1941-45. Mem. Am., Miss. psychol. assns., Internat. Transactional Analysis Assn., Inland So. Cal. Soc. Clin. Psychologists. Clubs: Rotary, Gulf Coast Wheelers Assn. Home: 922 Wheatley Ave Apt #4 Dayton OH 45405 Office: Good Samaritan Community Mental Health Center 2222 Philadelphia Dr Dayton OH 45406

PALMER, JOHN LEWIS, lawyer, plumbing equipment mfg. co. exec.; b. Milw., Nov. 22, 1921; s. John Lewis and Florence Margaret (Schneider) P.; B.A., Beloit Coll., 1947; J.D., U. Wis., 1949; m. Virginia Frances Smith, July 15, 1944; children—Michael J., Steven P. Admitted to Wis. bar, 1949; mem. law firm Whyte & Hirschboeck, Milw., 1949-71; with Bradley Corp., Menomonee Falls, Wis., 1971—, exec. v.p., 1972—, gen. counsel, 1971—, sec., 1971—, dir., 1969—; dir. Eilcar Corp., Alpha Cellulose Corp., KSM Industries, Inc., Pelton Casteel, Inc., Kieckhefer Assos., Inc. Served to capt. USMCR, 1943-46. Mem. Am., Wis. (chmn. taxation sect. 1962-63), bar assns., Beloit Coll. Alumni (trustee 1971-74), Phi Beta Kappa, Order of Coif, Phi Kappa Psi, Phi Delta Phi. Republican. Congregationalist. Clubs: Milw. Country; Tucson Nat. Golf. Home: 780 E Ravine Ln Milwaukee WI 53217 Office: PO Box 446 Menomonee Falls WI 53051 also 7939 N Tuscany Dr Tucson AZ 85704

PALMER, MARGARET LOUISE, speech and lang. pathologist; b. Flint, Mich., Sept. 18, 1935; s. Frederick William and Sylvia Elvira (Mattsen) P.; B.A., Mich. State U., 1959, M.A., 1967. Speech and lang. pathologist Ingham Intermediate Sch. Dist., Mason, Mich., 1959—; cons. Ednl. Consultation Center. Mem. Am. Speech and Hearing Assn. (certificate of clin. competence), Council of Exceptional Children, Mich. Speech and Hearing Assn., Phi Kappa Phi. Clubs: Bonsai Soc. Mich., (dir. 1974, librarian 1975). Home: 408 Durand St East Lansing MI 48823 Office: 2630 W Howell Rd Mason MI 48854

PALMER, MICHAEL A., mfg. co. exec.; b. Spiske Vlache, Czechoslovakia, May 20, 1920; s. Alex R. and Regina (LIttman) P.; came to U.S., 1923, naturalized, 1928; B.S., Ill. Inst. Tech., 1943; M.B.A., Northwestern U., 1954; m. Harriet Margolis Palmer, June 3, 1950; children—David Jay, Deborah Lynn. Staff engr. Dravo Corp., Pitts., 1943-45; chief indsl. engr. Cummins Bus. Machines, Chgo., 1947-49; chief indsl. engr. Rauland Corp., Chgo., 1949-54; mgmt. cons. Barcus Orgn., 1954-56; self employed, Chgo., 1956-59; dir. mfg. Am. Photocopy Equipment Co., Evanston, 1959-65; founder, owner Michael Palmer & Assos., 1965-67; plant mgr. Rauland Corp. (now Rauland div. Zenith Radio Corp.), Melrose Park, Ill., 1967-71; v.p. mfg. Asso. Mills, Inc., Chgo., 1971—; lectr. Northwestern U., 1954—, Loyola U., 1973—; instr. Midwest Indsl. Mgmt. Assn., 1969—. Active Cub and Boy Scouts Am.; del. Wilmette Sch. Bd. Caucus. Served with USNR, 1945-46. Mem. Soc. Advancement Mgmt. (pres. 1972-74, regional v.p. 1974-76); Am. Mgmt. Assn., Skokie Valley Indsl. Assn., Tau Beta Pi, Pi Tau Sigma. Jewish (dir. congregation). Home: 3131 Nina St Wilmette IL 60091

PALMER, PAIGE (MRS. ARTHUR FREEMAN), television personality; b. Akron, Ohio, Jan. 17; d. Paul and Katharine (Grisbraun) Rohrer; degree in Phys. Edn., U. Akron, postgrad. in fashion and home econs.; m. Arthur Freeman, Apr. 18, 1964; children—Richard Rohrer Roush, Paul Allen Roush, Perry Nelson Brown. Asst. dir. Richard Hudnut Success Sch., N.Y.C., 1942; dir. teen cosmetic line Tene, Helena Rubenstein, 1943; dir. retail promotion Cohn-Hall-Marx, N.Y.C., 1944; mng. dir. Dorothy Ferrier Sch. Fashion and Modeling Beverly Hills, Calif., San Francisco, Los Angeles, San Diego, 1946, also fgn. fashion editor California Mag., 1946; presented 1st woman's program on fashions and fabric, exptl. television N.Y.C., 1947; originator 1st women's television program WEWS, Cleve., 1948—, presently women's dir. Syndicated columnist Fashion 'n Figure, 1970—; travel writer World Wide Travel Advice, Traveling Times. Bd. dirs. Goodwill Industries, Cleve., Highlandview Hosp. Shop. Recipient numerous awards, including FRANY Fashion award, Nat. Golden Slipper award, A.F.T.R.A. award, Best of Industry award Cleve. Press Club, Patroness of Arts award Cleve. Artists, Nat. Arthritis and Rheumatism Found. award, March of Dimes award, Nat. Heart Assn. award, Meritorious Service award Goodwill Industries, Service award Salvation Army; mentioned in Congl. Record for work in phys. fitness; decorated Lion medal Premier Nickolai Bulganin, 1957, Confrerie des Compagnons de Bordeaux, Confrerie du Diament Noire et du Vin de Cahors, Confrerie de St. Vincent, French govt, 1970. Mem. Am. Women in Radio and TV (pres. Western Res. chpt. 1968—), Overseas Press Club, Fashion Group, Acad. TV Arts and Scis., Nat. Trust, Western Res., Bath hist. socs., Cleve. Press Club. Author: Fitness Is A Family Affair; Woman and Her Concerns for Being a Woman; A Pain in the Back and How To Get Rid of It. Home: 2750 N Revere Rd Bath OH 44210 Office: PO Box 255 Bath OH 44210

PALMER, RALPH VINCENT, fin. co. exec.; b. Omaha, Dec. 2, 1943; s. Louis and Mary (Falconeri) P.; B.A., U. Nebr., Omaha, 1968; m. Paulette Haley, June 13, 1969. With Comml. Fed. Savs. & Loan Assn., Omaha, 1970—, asst. v.p., 1974-77, v.p., 1977—; speaker various bus. groups, 1975—. Mem. United Community Services Drive, Omaha, 1971-74, Coll. of St. Mary's Drive, Omaha, 1974; mem. United Negro Coll. Drive, 1974, 75. Served with U.S. Army, 1968-70. Recipient Five Times Quota Buster award YMCA, 1975. Mem. Nebr. Mortgage Assn. (dir. 1976—), Young Mortgage Bankers Assn. (sec. 1972-73, v.p. 1974-75), Am. Savs. and Loan Inst., Rho Epsilon. Club: Optimist (pres. 1973-74, dir. community services 1974-75). Columnist Omaha World Herald, 1974-77. Home: 14517 R St Omaha NE 68137 Office: 4501 Dodge St Omaha NE 68132

PALMER, RAY GREENLEAF, lawyer; b. Fairmont, Minn., Feb. 19, 1900; s. John Earl and Winnifred (Ibertson) P.; A.B. summa cum laude, Hamline U., 1922; LL.B., Harvard U., 1925; m. Ruby Dell Wilson Dec. 23, 1930 (dec. Mar. 1966). Admitted to Minn. bar, 1925; practiced in Duluth, Minn., 1925—, mem. firm Hunt & Palmer, 1924-28, firm Hunt, Palmer & Hood, 1938-52, firm Hunt, Palmer, Hood & Crassweller, 1952-55, firm Palmer, Hood, Crassweller & McCarthy, 1955—. Mem. Duluth Bd. Edn., 1938-41; pres. Duluth YMCA, 1944-52. Mem. Minn. State (past bd. govs.), Duluth (pres. 1955-56) bar assns. Phi Beta Kappa. Club: Kitchi Gammi. Home: 831 E Superior St Duluth MN 55802 Office: First Nat Bank Bldg Duluth MN 55802

PALMER, ROBERT GERALD, educator; b. Phillips, Wis., May 25, 1936; s. Albert Gerald and Leona Marjorie (Hill) P.; diploma Hiwassee Coll., 1956; B.S., U. Tenn., 1960, M.S., 1962; Ph.D., Iowa State U., 1967; m. Doris Leah Denton, Jan. 25, 1957; children—Wesley Rene, Robert Gerald, Virginia Denise. Instr. soils Iowa State U., Ames, 1964-66; asst. prof., extension soil mgmt. specialist Okla. State U., Stillwater, 1966-68; tech. advisor on AID/India program U. Tenn., 1968-70; asso. prof. soils and conservation Western Ill. U., Macomb, 1970—; specialist in soil conservation So. Ill./FAO/UN program Fed. U. Santa Maria, Brazil, 1975-76; v.p., treas. Key Agrl. Services, Inc., Macomb, 1977—; sec.-treas. Steering Com. for Lamoine River Watershed Conservancy Dist., 1971—; sec.-treas. steering com. Prairie Hills Resource Conservation and Devel. Project, 1972-75; mem. adv. com. to bd. dirs. Ill. Fertilizer and Chem. Assn., 1970—. Mem. Soil Conservation Soc. Am. (service award 1972), Soil Sci. Soc. Am., Am. Soc. Agronomy, Nat. Geog. Soc. Club: Kiwanis. Author: (with Frederick Troeh) Fundamentals of Soil Science, 1966, 2d edit., 1977. Home: 30 Steven Ct Macomb IL 61455

PALMER, SUZANNE JENNIFER, ednl. cons.; b. Ottumwa, Iowa, May 18, 1938; s. James Anthony and Eunice Frances (Phillips) Williams; B.A., Central Coll., Pella, Iowa, 1960; M.A., State U. Iowa, 1961; postgrad Drake U., 1974—; m. John Mathiew Palmer, June 9, 1962; 1 dau., Catherine Ann. Tchr. social studies, secondary schs., Wausau, Wis., 1961-65, Merrill, Wis., 1966-67, Albia, Iowa, 1969-75; ednl. cons. Area Edn. Agy. 15, Ottumwa, 1975—. Trustee, Monroe County Hosp., 1969—, chmn., 1976—; mem. Monroe County Republican Com., 1974—; bd. dirs. Monroe County Day Care Bd., 1975—. Mem. Assn. Supervision and Curriculum Devel., Nat. Council Social Studies, Am. Hist. Assn., State U. Iowa Alumni Council, Beta Sigma Phi. Episcopalian. Home: 234 N 11th St Albia IA 52531 Office: Area Education Agy 15 Box 498 Bldg 40 Ottumwa Industrial Airport Ottumwa IA 52501

PALMITER, HARRY ALVA, editor; b. Edgerton, Wis., Dec. 14, 1922; s. Louis Orsamus and Carrie Eliza (Thompson) P.; B.S., U. Wis., 1950; m. Marjory E. Roeber, Dec. 16, 1950; children—Lynn E., Steven Jay. Mem. editorial staff Olsen Publ. Co., Inc., Milw., 1950; asst. editor, 1951, mgr. spl. services div., 1953-58; promotions chief, markets div. Wis. Dept. Agr., Madison, 1958-62; with Cheese Reporter, Madison, 1962—, editor, pub., 1962—. Active Boy Scouts Am., Madison, 1971-76. Served with AUS, 1943-46. Mem. Internat. Milk and Food Sanitarians, Wis. Dairy Tech. Soc., Alpha Gamma Rho. Presbyterian (elder 1966—). Home: 917 Lorraine Dr Madison WI 53705 Office: 115 W Main St Madison WI 53703

PALMORE, JULIAN IVANHOE, III, mathematician, educator; b. Balt., Sept. 26, 1938; s. Julian I. and Josephine Keith (Shellman) P.; B. in Engring. Physics, Cornell U., 1961; M.A. in Mathematics, U. Ala., 1964; M.S. in Aerospace Sci., Princeton U., 1965; M.S. in Astronomy, Yale, 1966, Ph.D., 1967; Ph.D. in Mathematics. U. Calif., Berkeley, 1973; m. Barbara Bland Hawkins, May 27, 1967; children—Andrew Hanson, Rebecca Keith. Asso. staff mem. Boeing Co., Seattle, 1966; research asso. U. Minn., Mpls., 1967-68; vis. fellow Princeton (N.J.) U., 1968; instr. mathematics Mass. Inst. Tech., Cambridge, 1973-75; vis. asst. prof. dept. mathematics U. Mich., Ann Arbor, 1975—77; asst. prof. mathematics U. Ill., Urbana, 1977—; lectr. in various univs. including Purdue U., 1976, U. Chgo., 1976, Brown U., 1973; participant NSF regional conf., u.n.c., Chapel Hill, 1976. Served with USN, 1961—64. Lilly Teaching fellow, 1974—75; USF grantee, 1974—77. Fellow Royal Astronomical Soc.; mem. Am. Math. Soc., Sigma XI. Contbr. articles on research in mathematics and celestial mechanics to sci. jours. Office: Math Dept Univ of Illinois Urbana IL 61801

PAMBOOKIAN, HAGOP SARKIS, educator; b. Kerek-Khan, Turkey, Dec. 18, 1932; s. Sarkis and Tamom (Karageuzian) P.; came to U.S., 1961, naturalized, 1971; diploma in Pedagogy, Melkonian Ednl. Inst., Nicosia, Cyprus, 1953; B.A., Am. U. Beirut, Lebanon, 1957; M.A., Columbia Tchrs. Coll., 1963, postgrad., 1963-64; Ph.D., U. Mich., 1972. Tchr., Armenian Evang. Coll., Beirut, 1957-60, Melkonian Ednl. Inst., 1960-61; instr. psychology Adirondack Community Coll., Hudson Falls, N.Y., 1964-66; asst. prof. psychology State U. N.Y., Potsdam, 1966-70; teaching fellow U. Mich. Sch. Edn., Ann Arbor, 1971-72, research asso. Center for Research on Learning and Teaching, 1974; asst. prof. ednl. psychology Marquette U., Milw., 1974—. Mem. N.Y. chpt. Armenian Gen. Benevolent Union Jr. League, corr. sec. 1962, pres. Milw. chpt., 1975—; adviser, mem. exec. com. Tekeyan Cultural Assn., Detroit, 1972-74; chmn. Armenian Genocide Com., Wis. rep., 1975; mem. Milw. Ednl. Resources Coordinating Com., a task force chmn., 1975-76; mem. program com. Internat. Inst. Milw., 1976—; mem. St. John Armenian Ch., Greenfield. Mem. Am. Psychol. Assn., Am. Ednl. Research Assn., Nat. Assn. Armenian Studies and Research, Internat. Platform Assn. (Red Carpet chmn. for greeting VIPs, 1974—, bd. govs. 1976—), U. Mich. Alumni Assn., Phi Delta Kappa. Contbr. articles to profl. jours. Home: 3210 W Wells St Milwaukee WI 53208

PAN, ALEXANDER KEE SUI, physician; b. Swatow, China, Jan. 30, 1932; s. Tsoh-Chen and Mary (Chow) P.; M.D. with honors, U. Man., 1958; m. Eudora Pan, July 19, 1970; children—Janice Mabel, James Alexander. Intern Winnipeg (Man., Can.) Gen. Hosp., 1958-59; resident St. Boniface Gen. Hosp., Winnipeg, 1959-60, 61, 62, Winnipeg Gen. Hosp., 1960-61, Mayo Clinic, 1962-64; practice medicine specializing in internal medicine, Winnipeg, 1964—; mem. staff St. Boniface Gen., Victoria Gen. hosps., Winnipeg. Asst. prof., faculty of medicine U. Man., 1966—. Fellow Am. Coll. Chest Physicians, Royal Coll. Physicians and Surgeons Can.; mem. Canadian, Man. med. assns., A.C.P., Coll. Physicians and Surgeons

Man., Ont., Mayo, U. Man. alumni assns., Nat. Assn. Photog. Art, Can. Nature Fedn., Can. Wildlife Fedn. Mem. United Ch. Can. (elder 1966—). Home: 13 Bittersweet Bay Winnipeg MB R2J 2E5 Canada Office: 219 Marion St Winnipeg Manitoba R2H 0T5 Canada

PAN, JAMING, physicist, educator; b. Fukien, China, Dec. 9, 1929; s. Chung-ling and Mei-Wu (Wu) P.; came to U.S., 1957, naturalized, 1967; M.S., Northwestern U., 1960; Ph.D., Ill. Inst. Tech., 1971; m. Clara Ching-ching Sung, Aug. 26, 1961; children—Wilbur J., Hubert B., Wileen C. Mem. faculty Purdue U., Hammond, Ind., 1960—, asso. prof. physics, 1967—, head dept., 1970; vis. research faculty Argonne (Ill.) Nat. Lab., 1975—. Mem. Sch. Bd. Dist. 153 Ill., 1973-75; v.p., bd. dirs. Chinese Am. Ednl. Found., 1974-75. AEC summer fellow, 1962, 63; NSF summer fellow, 1961; Argonne Lab. fellow, 1975; recipient grant Cancer Research Inst., 1977. Mem. Am. Phys. Soc., Am. Assn. Physics Tchrs.-IEEE, Nat. Sch. Bd. Assn. Contbr. articles to profl. jours. Home: 2848 MacHeath Crescent Flossmoor IL 60422 Office: Dept Physics Purdue U Hammond IN 46323

PANCERO, JACK BLOCHER, restaurant exec.; b. Cin., Dec. 27, 1923; s. Howard and Hazel Mae (Blocher) P.; student, Ohio State U., 1941-44; m. Loraine Fielman, Aug. 4, 1944; children—Gregg Edward, Vicki Lee. Partner, Howard Pancero & Co., Cin., 1948-66; stockbroker Gradison & Co., Cin., 1966-70; real estate asso. Parchman & Oyler, Cin., 1970-72; v.p. Gregg Pancero, Inc., Kings Mills, Ohio, 1972—. Methodist. Clubs: Western Hills Country, Cincinnati, Engrs. Table, Masons, Shrine. Home: 5730 Pinehill Ln Cincinnati OH 45238 Office: Kings Island Columbia Rd Kings Mills OH 45034

PANDE, SHARAD CHANDRA, radiologist; b. Ujjain, M.P., India, Dec. 5, 1937; s. Badriprasad and Dwarkabai (Joshi) P.; M.B., B.S., M.D., Gajra-raja Med. Coll., Gwalior M.P., India, 1958. Intern, Resurrection Hosp., Chgo., 1964-65; resident Mt. Sinai Hosp., Chgo., 1964; instr. Northwestern U., Chgo., 1965-66; radiologist Selkirk Mental Hosp., Selkirk, Man., Can., 1969—. Fellow Royal Coll. Physicians and Surgeons (Can.); affiliate mem. Royal Soc. Medicine (Eng.). Home: Selkirk Mental Hosp Selkirk MB R1A 2B5 Canada

PANEC, ALBER ELDON, broadcasting exec.; b. Pawnee City, Nebr., July 4, 1934; s. Albert and Thelma Irene (Sebring) P.; student York Coll., 1952-54, Westmar Coll., 1954-55, U. Mich., 1956, Coll. William and Mary, 1958-59; B.A., U. Nebr., 1965; m. Mildred Lucille Shinn, June 6, 1954; children—Albert Robert, William Joseph, Dawn Marie. With Cooper's Feed Mills, Humboldt, Nebr., 1951-52; TV technician Norgren's Sporting Goods and TV, York, Nebr., 1952-54; electronics technician stas. KOLN-TV, KGIN-TV, Lincoln-Grand Island, Nebr., 1961-63, news dir. KGIN-TV, Grand Island, 1963—; dir., treas. Panec Farms, Du Bois, Nebr. Pres. bd. YMCA, Grand Island, 1966-72; pres. Sertoma, 1967, gov., 1968-69; v.p. bd. St. Frances Hosp. Home Health Care, 1968—; bd. dirs. Overland Trails council Boy Scouts Am., Nebr. Hearing and Speech Bd. Served with USNR, 1955-61. Recipient outstanding Sertoma award, 1966, service award Grand Island C. of C., 1969. Mem. Western Bohemian Assn., Fellowship Christian Athletes (pres. 1974-75), Nat. Rifle Assn., Nebr., Nat. press photographers assns., Comensky Club. Methodist (pres. bd. trustees). Home: 2523 W Charles St Grand Island NE 68801 Office: Box 1069 Grand Island NE 68801

PANEC, WILLIAM JOSEPH, lawyer; b. Pawnee City, Nebr., June 22, 1937; s. Albert and Thelma I. (Sebring) P.; B.S., U. Nebr., 1962, J.D., 1965; m. Carolyn R. McVitty, Aug. 17, 1963. Admitted to Nebr. bar, 1965, since practiced in Fairbury; county judge Jefferson County (Nebr.), 1965-70, county atty., 1973-75; mem. Nebr. Jud. Qualifications Commn., 1968-70; organizer Nebr. Jud. Reform; chmn. Region XIV Crime Commn., 1969-71, cons. on law enforcement and criminal justice, 1971—; cons. Regions VIII, IX and XIV Regional Jail Study, 1972; profl. instr. Nebr. Law Enforcement Adv. Council, 1972—; village atty. Diller (Nebr.), 1975—; chmn. law day Jefferson County, 1972, 73. Served with AUS, 1955-56. Mem. Am., Nebr., Jefferson County bar assns., Nebr. County Judges Assn. (v.p., pres.), Am. Judicature Soc., Nebr. Assn. Trial Attys., Assn. Trial Attys. Am., Internat. Footprint Assn., U. Nebr. Alumni Assn., Delta Theta Phi. Methodist (trustee). Clubs: Masons, Elks. Author: Probate Procedures and the Uniform Probate Code. Home: 1529 G St Fairbury NE 68352 Office: 610 D St Fairbury NE 68352

PANG, JOSHUA KEUN-UK, trade co. exec.; b. Chinnampo, Korea, Sept. 17, 1924; s. Ne-Too and Soon-Hei (Kim) P.; came to U.S., 1951, naturalized, 1968; B.S., Roosevelt U., 1959; m. He-Young Yoon, May 30, 1963; children—Ruth, Pauline, Grace. Chemist, Realemon Co. Am., Chgo., 1957-61; chief-chemist chem. div. Bell & Gossett Co., Chgo., 1961-63, Fatty Acid Inc., div. Ziegler Chem. & Mineral Corp., Chgo., 1963-64; sr. chemist-supr. Gen. Mills Chems. Inc., Kankakee, Ill., 1964-70; pres., owner UJU Industries Inc., Broadview, Ill., 1971—, also dir. Bd. dirs. Dist. 92, Lindop Sch., Broadview, 1976—; chmn. Proviso Area Sch. Bd. Assn., Proviso Twp., Cook County, Ill., 1976-77. Mem. Am. Chem. Soc., Am. Inst. Parliamentarians, Internat. Platform Assn., Ill. Sch. Bd. Assn., Chgo. Area Parliamentarians. Toastmaster (dist. gov. 1970). Home: 2532 S 9th Ave Broadview IL 60153 Office: PO Box 351 Broadview IL 60153

PANGILINAN, NESTOR STA CRUZ, psychiatrist; b. Manila, Philippines, May 10, 1940; s. Felixberto Ocampo and Consuelo Del Barrio (Sta Cruz) P.; A.A., U. East, Manila, 1959; M.D., U. East, Quezon City, Philippines, 1964; m. Janet Jordan, Aug. 31, 1968; children—Faith, Scott, Todd. Came to U.S., 1965, naturalized, 1974. Intern, St. Mary's Hosp., Waterbury, Conn., 1965-66; resident Fairfield Hills Hosp., Newtown, Conn., 1966-68; practice medicine, specializing in psychiatry; staff psychiatrist Trenton (N.J.) Psychiat. Hosp., 1969-72; asst. chief adult services Mental Health Inst., Independence, Iowa, 1972-74, dir. outpatient services, 1974—. Diplomate Am. Psychiat. Assn. Mem. AMA, Buchanan County Med. Soc. (pres. 1975-76). Rotarian. Home: Box 111 Independence IA 50644

PANOSH, RICHARD LOUIS, scientist; b. Berwyn, Ill., May 25, 1943; s. Carl Martin and Hermina Lillian (Rosenberg) P.; B.S. in Physics and Math., St. Procopius Coll., Lisle, Ill., 1966. Co-owner, operator C. & R. Panosh TV, Lisle, 1961-70; sci. asso. alloy properties group, material sci. div. Argonne (Ill.) Nat. Lab., 1966-71, actinide group, 1971—; cons. med. products Stoelting Co., Chgo., 1976—. Roman Catholic. Clubs: Argonne Amateur Radio, McGraw-Hill Engrs. Book. Patentee automatic fluid skimmer. Home: 717 Front St Lisle IL 60532 Office: 9700 S Cass Ave D-212 Argonne IL 60439

PANSCH, FRANK NORMAN, obstetrician, gynecologist; b. Oshkosh, Wis., May 2, 1910; s. Frank Christian and Emma Anna (Wentzel) P.; student Oshkosh Tchrs. Coll., 1928-29; B.S., U. Wis., 1934; B.M., Northwestern U., 1937; M.D., Mayo Found., 1940; m. Marie Konrad, Sept. 14, 1935; children—Robert F., Donald J., James N., Jane M. Intern, Ancker Hosp., St. Paul, 1936-37; resident in obstetrics and gynecology Mayo Clinic, Rochester, Minn., 1937-40; gen. practice medicine, Appleton, Wis., 1941-43; obstetrician, gynecologist U.S. Naval Dispensary, Washington, 1943-46; practice medicine specializing in obstetrics and gynecology, Neenah, Wis., 1946—; founder Twin City Clinic, Nicolet Clinic, Service Corp.; dir. Elpa Corp.; chief of staff Theda Clark Meml. Hosp., also chief dept., mem. exec. com. Served to lt. comdr., USNR, 1943-47. Diplomate Am. Bd. Obstetrics Gynecology. Fellow A.C.S., Internat. Coll. Surgeons, Am. Coll. Obstetricians Gynecologists; mem. Am. Soc. Abdominal Surgeons, Wis. Soc. Obstetrics-Gynecology, AMA, Wis., Winnebago County med. socs., Am. Soc. Obstetricians Gynecologists. Clubs: Kiwanis, Elks, Masons. Home: 730 Congress Pl Neenah WI 54956 Office: PO Box 525 Neenah WI 54956

PANSEGRAU, DUANE FRANCIS, surgeon; b. Sioux City, Iowa, Nov. 26, 1930; s. Adolph and Ruth Lillian (Barker) P.; student Morningside Coll., 1948-50; B.A., State U. Iowa, 1952, M.D., 1956; m. Cynthia Lois Johnson, Aug. 10, 1956; children—Paul, Susan, Rebecca. Intern, Broadlawns Hosp., Des Moines, 1956-57; resident VA Hosp., Iowa City, Iowa, 1957-58, U. Iowa Hosps., Iowa City, 1963-65; practice medicine specializing in surgery, Karlstad, Minn., 1960-63, Marshfield, Wis., 1965-66, Grand Forks, N.D., 1966—; mem. staff Grand Forks Clinic, 1966—, pres., 1976-77, also dir.; mem. staffs United Hosp., Med. Center Rehab. Hosp.; clin. prof. surgery U. N.D. Bd. dirs. Sunset West Inc., United Fund, Grand Forks. Diplomate Am. Bd. Surgery. Fellow A.C.S.; mem. AMA, N.D. State, 3d Dist. med. socs., Grand Forks C. of C. (med. liaison), Whipple Soc., Soc. Surg. Chmn., Phi Beta Kappa, Alpha Omega Alpha. Republican. Lutheran. Clubs: Rotary, Lions. Home: 3010 W Elmwood Dr Grand Forks ND 58201 Office: 1000 Columbia Rd Grand Forks ND 58201

PANTER, IRWIN, lawyer; b. Chgo., Apr. 16, 1914; s. Philip and Mollie (Bender) P.; A.B., U. Chgo., 1935, J.D., 1937; m. Ruth Schwartz, June 18, 1950; children—Michael Richard, Deborah Lynn, Janet Phyllis. Admitted to Ill. bar, 1937, since practiced in Chgo.; sr. partner firm Panter Nelson & Bernfield, 1966—; dir. Crawford Enterprises, Inc., Hinsdale, Ill., Guardian Leasing, Inc., Hinsdale, Wesley-Jessen, Inc., Chgo., Nat. Clothier Corp., Chgo. Mem. adv. com. high sch., Oak Park, Ill., 1965-66, jr. coll., Oak Park, 1963-64; bd. dirs. Nat. Eye Research Found., Vision Found. for Blind Youth. Served to capt. U.S. Army, 1941-45. Recipient grand honors Nat. Eye Research Found., 1966. Mem. Am., Ill., Chgo. bar assns., Decalogue Soc., Chgo. Art Inst., Chgo. Assn. Commerce (govtl. affairs counsel 1961-71), Village Mgrs. Assn. Oak Park. Club: Mid-Day. Home: 1300 Lake Shore Dr Chicago IL 60610 Office: 33 N Dearborn St Chicago IL 60602

PANTOJA, ENRIQUE, radiotherapist; b. Morovis, P.R., Oct. 14, 1932; s. Enrique and Inocencia (Marrero) P.; B.S. in Chem., U. P.R., 1954, M.D., 1958; m. Carmen Gloria Nieves, June 30, 1956; children—Yazmin, Enrique, Benjamin. Intern, Mercy Hosp., Toledo, 1958-59, U.S. Army Med. Corps, 1959-61; resident in radiology, Bronx VA Hosp., 1961-64; asst. radiologist Queens Gen. Hosp., N.Y.C., 1964-66; chief radiotherapy Jewish Hosp., Bklyn., 1966-70, Oncologic Hosp., San Juan, P.R., 1970-75, St. Peter's Hosp., Albany, N.Y., 1975-76; commd. lt. col., USAF, 1976-77; chief radiology USAF Hosp., Offutt AFB, Nebr., 1976-78, chief radiotherapy USAF Med. Center, Wright Patterson AFB, Ohio, 1978—; clin. asst. prof. Radiology, State U. N.Y., 1967-70, U. Nebr., 1977; clin. asso. prof. radiology Wright State U., 1978. Served in U.S. Army, 1959-61. Mem. Am. Roentgen Ray Soc., Am. Coll. Radiology, Radiological Soc. N. Am., Am. Soc. Therapeutic Radiologists, Inter-Am. Coll. Radiology. Contbr. articles to profl. jours. Home: 207 DuPont Way Wright Patterson AFB OH 45433 Office: USAF Medical Center Wright Patterson AFB OH 45433

PANTZER, KURT FRIEDRICH, JR., lawyer; b. Indpls., May 24, 1928; s. Kurt Friedrich and Katharine Hunter (Ferriday) P.; B.A., Yale U., 1950; J.D., Harvard U., 1955; m. Elizabeth Elliott Kennedy, Aug. 25, 1951; children—Elizabeth E., Katharine H., Kurt Friedrich III, Julia F. Admitted to Ind. bar, 1955; practiced in Indpls., 1955—; partner Royse, Travis, Hendrickson & Pantzer, 1966—; dir., sec. Aircraft and Electronic Specialties, Inc., Avon, Ind., 1961—; pres. Ind. Neuromuscular Research Lab., Inc., 1970—. Pres. Estate Planning Council Indpls., 1977-78. Treas., 11th Congl. Dist. Republican Central Com., 1964-66. Bd. dirs. Marion County Muscular Dystrophy Found., 1958—, pres., 1960-62; bd. dirs. Greater Indpls. chpt. The Myasthenia Gravis Found., 1970-77, chmn., 1970-72; bd. dirs. Eisenhower Meml. Scholarship Found., Park Tudor Sch.; bd. dirs. Booth Tarkington Civic Theatre, Indpls., pres., 1977—. Served to 1st lt. U.S. Army, 1951-53. Decorated Bronze Star. Fellow Am. Coll. Probate Counsel; mem. Am., Ind., Indpls. bar assns. Presbyn. (deacon). Clubs: Columbia, Dramatic (sec. 1963-64), Players, Lambs (dir. 1962—). Author: Documentary Evidence, 1961; Unauthorized Practice of Law, 1962; Pre-Nuptial Agreements, 1973; Probate Fees, 1976; Orphans' Deduction, 1977. Co-editor: Trusts, Wills, Estate Adminstration and Taxes, Parts 1 and 2, 1963. Home: 9801 Springmill Rd Indianapolis IN 46260 Office: 500 American Fletcher Bldg Indianapolis IN 46204

PANWAR, KRIS, anesthesiologist; b. Indore, India, Feb. 7, 1933; s. Manohar and Kesho (Parmar) P.; M.D., U. Bombay (India), 1955; m. Irene LaRicheliere, Nov. 27, 1965; 1 son, Manu. Intern, Mt. Sinai Hosp., Milw., 1957-59; resident, Montreal, Ont., Can., 1961-64; practice medicine, specializing in anesthesia, Sarnia, Ont., 1965—; chief dept. anesthesia St. Joseph's Hosp., 1965—. Cons. anesthesiologist CEE Hosp., Petrolia, Ont. Diplomate Am. Bd. Anesthesiology. Fellow Am. Coll. Anesthesiologists, Royal Coll. Physicians (Can.); mem. Am. Soc. Anesthesiologists, Canadian Anesthesists Soc., Internat. Anesthesia Research Soc., Canadian, Ont. med. assns. Mason (Shriner). Home: 1740 Notre Dame St Sarnia ON Canada Office: PO Box 2222 Sarnia ON Canada

PANZICA, JOSEPH SALVATORE, realtor, businessman; b. Urbana, Ill., Oct. 31, 1934; s. Charles Cosimo and Margaret Elizabeth (Dattilo) P.; student Ind. U., 1952-56; m. Sandra Kay MacCarroll, Sept. 12, 1964; children—Lisa Marie, Terri Ann, Maria Michelle, Joseph. Sales rep. Studebaker Corp., 1959-61; state mgr. Gallo Wine Co., 1961-63; owner Miami Plaza Liquor Mart, South Bend, Ind., 1963—; partner Panzica Realty, South Bend, 1966—; dir. Pancir Enterprise, Inc. Served with U.S. Army, 1956-58. Mem. Ind. Package Liquor Dealers. Republican. Roman Catholic. Clubs: K.C., Elks, Four Lakes Country, Kensington. Home: 6124 York Rd South Bend IN 46614

PAO, YOH-HAN, communications tech. co. exec.; b. Kiukiang, China, July 17, 1922; s. Wei-Deh and Annie (Lo) P.; matriculated London U., 1941; B.S., Henry Lester Inst. Tech. Edn., 1945; Ph.D., Pa. State U., 1952; m. Helen Chung-Ying Koo, Dec. 26, 1948; children—John Desire, Victor Emil, Robin Aimee. Came to U.S., 1947, naturalized, 1962. Research scientist, supr. physics research E.I. duPont de Nemours & Co., Wilmington, Del., 1954-61; sr. research physicist Lab. Applied Sci., U. Chgo., 1961-62; mem. tech. staff Bell Telephone Labs., Murray Hill, N.J., 1962-67; prof. engring. Case Western Reserve U., Cleve., 1967-69, head dept. elec. engring., 1969—; pres., Laser Communications, Inc., Cleve., 1970—. NATO sr. sci. fellow U. Edinburgh, 1973. Fellow IEEE, Optical Soc. Am.; mem. Am. Phys. Soc., Acad. Scis. N.Y., Sigma Xi. Editor Quantum Electronics Series, Acad. Press, 1972—. Patentee in field. Home: 2721 Scarborough Rd Cleveland Heights OH 44106 Office: 10900 Cedar Ave Cleveland OH 44106

PAPADAKIS, CONSTANTINE NICHOLAS, hydraulic engr.; b. Athens, Greece, Feb. 2, 1946; s. Nicholas and Rita (Mashiotti) P.; came to U.S., 1969, naturalized, 1972. diploma Nat. U. Athens, 1969; M.S., U. Cin., 1970; Ph.D., U. Mich., 1973; m. Eliana Apostolides, Aug. 28, 1971. Hydraulics cons. Commonwealth Assos., Jackson, Mich., James F. MacLaren Ltd., Willowdale, Ont., 1973-74; postdoctoral scholar U. Mich., Ann Arbor, 1973-74; add. asst. prof. George Washington U., Washington, 1975-76; vis. asso. prof. Mich. State U., 1978; hydraulics and hydrology engring. mgr. Bechtel, Inc., Ann Arbor, Mich., 1974—; adj. asst. prof. U. Mich., 1976—; teaching fellow U. Mich., 1971-73, U. Cin., 1969-71. Horace W. King grantee civil engring. dept. U. Mich., 1971-73; registered profl. engr., Mich., Va., Greece. Mem. ASCE, ASME, Internat. Assn. Hydraulic Research, Am. Mgmt. Assn., Tech. Chamber Greece, Am. Water Resources Assn., Am. Geophys. Union, Sigma Xi, Tau Beta Pi, Chi Epsilon. Greek Orthodox. Author: (with J. Kiourtzoglou) Problems on Strength of Materials, 1968, Sewer Systems Design, 2d edit., 1969; Solutions to Problems in Fluid Mechanics, 1975; contbr. 20 tech. articles to profl. jours. Home: 1420 Bardstown Trail Ann Arbor MI 48105 Office: 777 E Eisenhower Pkwy PO Box 1000 Ann Arbor MI 48106

PAPANDREA, JAMES JOHN, dentist; b. Chgo., July 26, 1941; s. Louis and Nancy Ann (Amidie) P.; B.S., U. Wis., 1963; D.D.S., Loyola Dental Sch., 1968; m. Nancy Carol Kennedy, Aug. 6, 1962; children—James, Ricky. Pvt. practice dentistry, West Allis, Wis., 1970—; mem. staff West Allis Meml. Hosp., 1975—; tchr. Chgo. Dental Sch. of Nursing, 1967-68. Cons. Mt. Sinai Hosp., Milw., 1970—. Served with U.S. Army, 1968-70. Mem. Am., Milw., Chgo. dental assns. Home: 2947 S Root River Pkwy West Allis WI 53227 Office: 10202 W Hayes Ave West Allis WI 53227

PAPAY, ANDREW GEORGE, chem. engr.; b. K. Achaia, Greece, Oct. 10, 1924; s. George P. and Martha (Paparodis) P.; B.S., Athens U., 1951; M.S. (grad. fellow 1957-58), Colo. Sch. Mines, 1959; Eng.D., Athens Tech. U., 1974; came to U.S., 1957, naturalized, 1966; m. Vasso Skiadas, Dec. 12, 1960; children—Martha, Tinna. Sr. research engr. Mobil Oil Research & Decel. Co., Paulsboro, N.J., 1959-69; supr. Stauffer Chem. Co., Dobbs Ferry, N.Y., 1969-71; asso. dir. technology Edwin Cooper Inc., St. Louis, 1971—. Mem. Soc. Automotive Engrs., Coordinating Research Council, Am. Soc. Lubrication Engrs. (chmn. St. Louis), ASTM. Greek Orthodox. Patentee in field. Contbr. articles to profl. jours. Asso. editor Lubrication Engring., 1977—. Home: 897 Rusticmanor Circle Manchester MO 63011 Office: 125 Lafayette Ave St Louis MO 63104

PAPER, CHARLES, hide and fur co. exec.; b. Fargo, N.D., July 16, 1918; s. Samuel Ephraim and Bertha (Lesk) P.; student N.D. State Coll., 1936-39; m. Bernice L. Hartman, June 30, 1946; children—Richard, Stephen, Thomas. Owner, operator Wadena Hide & Fur Co., Wadena, Minn., 1946—. Pres., Wadena C. of C., 1967; dir. Wadena Indsl. Devel. Corp., 1969-75; mem. Wadena City planning commn., 1970—, chmn., 1973-76. Served with U.S. Army, 1942-46. Decorated Purple Heart; named Man of the Yr., C. of C., 1966. Mem. Minn. Auto Truck Salvage Dealers Assn., Nat. Hide Assn. (pres. N.W. chpt. 1954), Am. Iron Steel Inst. Jewish. Clubs: Rotary, Am. Legion, DAV, VFW, Elks, Shriners. Home: 815 3rd St S W Wadena MN 56482 Office: Box 207 Wadena MN 56482

PAPEZ, DONALD WESLEY, marketing exec.; b. Albion, Nebr., June 21, 1923; s. John S. and Olive (Maricle) P.; student Doane Coll., 1941-42, Colo. Coll., 1943-44; B.S., U. Nebr., 1947; grad. Inst. Internat. Studies, Geneva, Switzerland, 1949; m. Simone Girod de Boeck, Dec. 6, 1947; children—Ronald, Chantal. Staff mem. UN Secretariat Econ. Commn. for Europe, Geneva, Switzerland, 1949-53; sr. econ. and marketing research analyst Matson Navigation Co., San Francisco, 1954-64; v.p. Ceco Marketing Research Inc., San Francisco, 1964-68; v.p. Transam. Research Corp., San Francisco, 1968-70; dir. eastern Can., Wm. Wrigley Jr. Co., Ltd. Toronto, Ont., 1971-74; dir. marketing research, Chgo., 1975—. Served to lt. (j.g.) USNR, 1943-46. Mem. Am. Marketing Assn. (bd. govs., nat. dir. 1967-69), Econ. Round Table San Francisco (pres. 1950). Episcopalian. Club: University (Chgo.). Home: 1120 N Lake Shore Dr Chicago IL 60611 Office: 410 N Michigan Ave Chicago IL

PAPIER, DAVID, chemist, bacteriologist, engr.; b. Columbus, Ohio, Aug. 14, 1915; s. Jacob and Blanche (Masoie) P.; B.S., Ohio State U., 1938, postgrad., 1940-42. children—Stephen, Larry. Certified in fishery adminstrn. and limology Am. Fisheries Soc.; in san. engring. Taft San. Engring. Center, Cin. Partner, Control Lab., Cleve., 1940-46; with Ohio Div. Conservation and Nat. Resources, Columbus, 1946-60; liaison chemist, chem. cons. Ohio Dept. Health, Div. San. Engring., Columbus, 1960-69; chief water quality, research coordinator Ohio Dept. Natural Resources, 1969-77. Mem. Am. Fisheries Soc., Lymnol. Soc., Pollution Control Fedn., Wildlife Mgmt. Assn., League Ohio Sportsmen (Outstanding Conservationist award 1970), Ohio Conservation Congress. Contbr. articles in field to profl. jours. Home: 2451 Stafford Rd Columbus OH 43209 Office: Fountain Sq Bldg E Columbus OH 43224

PAPIN, LAWRENCE EDWARD, constrn. co. exec.; b. Bonne Terre, Mo., Aug. 26, 1913; s. Almah Lawrence and Mary (Krodinger) P.; B.Arch., Washington U., 1940; postgrad. St. Louis U., 1964; m. Frances Marion Kergo, Aug. 7, 1943. Draftsman, builder trainee A. L. Papin, Master Builder, 1932-40, partner, 1940-42; partner Papin Builders, Inc., 1946-58, v.p., chmn. bd., Sappington, Mo., 1958—. Served with USAAF, 1942-46. Registered architect, Mo. Mem. Mo. Assn. Registered Architects, Cath. Holy Name Soc., Scarab. Patentee concrete forming device. Home: 11864 Doverhill Ct Saint Louis MO 63128 Office: 11420 Gravois Rd Saint Louis MO 63126

PAPLAUSKAS, LYNN ELLEN, hosp. ofcl.; b. Montreal, Que., Can., Dec. 22, 1944; d. Clarence Peter and Frances Ellen (Dixon) Verhoeven; B.A., St. Xavier Coll., 1965; m. Leonard Paul Paplauskas, Nov. 25, 1972. Research technician Stritch Sch. Medicine, Maywood, Ill., 1965-66; electron microscopy technologist U. Ill., Chgo., 1966-68; scientist Alpha Research and Devel. Co., Blue Island, Ill., 1968-71; electron microscopist Nalco Chem. Co., Chgo., 1972; researcher So. Ill. U., Carbondale, 1972-74; chief electron microscopy Cook County Hosp., Chgo., 1974—; v.p. Infi-Tek Assos., Chgo., 1976—. Mem. Am. Soc. Electron Microscopy, Ill. Microscopical Soc., Midwest Soc. Electron Microscopists, Defenders of Wildlife, Audubon Soc., Nat. Wildlife Fedn. Baptist. Contbr. articles in field to profl. jours. Home: 5606 Crestwood Rd Matteson IL 60443 Office: 627 S Wood St Chicago IL 60612

PAPLOW, JOHN EDWARD, hosp. adminstr.; b. Buffalo, Dec. 28, 1918; s. Edward Louis and Elsie (Putnam) P.; B.S. with highest distinction, Northwestern U., 1947, M.H.A.; 1949; m. Marguerite Klobe, Feb. 15, 1943; children—David Steven, Michael Jeffrey, Peter Allan. Office staff Buffalo Gen. Hosp., 1939-42; instr. U. Calif. at Berkeley, 1948; adminstrv. resident Herrick Meml. Hosp., Berkeley, Calif., 1948-49; asst. adminstr. Santa Barbara (Calif.) Cottage Hosp., 1949-50, adminstr., 1950-57; exec. dir. Lima (O.) Meml. Hosp., 1957-75, pres., chief exec. officer, dir., 1975—. Active United Fund. Past mem. bd. dirs. Lima Symphony Orch.; bd. dirs., treas. Hosp. Service of Lima (Blue Cross), 1959-72; bd. dirs., treas. United

Cerebral Palsy Lima and Allen County; bd. dirs., exec. com., fiscal officer Northwestern Ohio Regional Med. Program; bd. dirs., past pres. Comprehensive Health Planning Assn. Greater Ottawa Valley; health adv. com. Lima Tech. Center; adv. council Ohio Bd. Nursing Edn. and Registration, 1968-75, mem. bd. Allen County chpt. A.R.C., 1972-75. Served from 2d lt. to capt., Med. Adminstrv. Corps, U.S. Army, 1942-46. Recipient Malcolm T. MacEachern award, 1949. Pres. Hosp. Council of So. Cal., 1956-57. Fellow Am. Coll. Hosp. Adminstrs.; mem. Am. Hosp. Assn., Ohio Hosp. Assn. (mem. ins. com., com. vol. health planning, health adv. com.), Alpha Delta Mu (nat. pres. 1953), Beta Gamma Sigma, Delta Mu Delta. Republican. Presbyn. (elder, past trustee). Clubs: Masons, Elks, Rotary, Shawnee Country. Home: 1411 Crayton Rd Lima OH 45805 Office: Lima Meml Hosp Linden and Mobel Sts Lima OH 45804

PAPO, MICHAEL, family practitioner; b. Sarajevo, Yugoslavia, July 26, 1925; s. Albert and (Tolentino) P.; came to U.S., 1951, naturalized, 1956; student U. Rome, 1946-51; B.S. cum laude, Wayne State U., 1953; M.D., U. Mich., 1957; m. Madeleine B. Vallier, Feb. 25, 1956; children—Michele, Rene. Intern, St. Joseph Hosp., Ann Arbor, Mich., 1957-58, mem. staff, 1958—; family practice medicine, Chelsea (Mich.) Med. Clinic, 1958—, med. dir., 1958—; dir. Chelsea Med. Center, Inc., 1969-71; dir. Chelsea Community Hosp., 1970-73; instr. in anatomy, Dental Sch. U. Mich., 1954; dir. sr. preceptorship program, Med. Sch., U. Mich., med. dir. Chelsea Med. Clinic, Ltd., 1958—, chief preceptorship program, 1969—; mem. Washtenaw County Blue Shield Liaison Com., 1971-73; med. advisor Youth for Understanding, 1956. Bd. dirs. Washtenaw County Red Cross, 1959-74; chmn. Chelsea Community Chest Fund, 1959-63, chmn. recreation council, 1960-63. Recipient Chelsea Man of Year award, 1973. Diplomate Am. Bd. Family Practice (charter). Fellow Am. Acad. Family Practice; mem. AMA (physician's recognition award, 1970, 74, 77), Am. Coll. Cardiology, Am. Coll. Emergency Room Physicians, Am. Hosp. Assn., Am. Assn. Med. Clinics (legis. adv. com., 1972-74), Mich. State (com. on legal affairs, 1972), Washtenaw County Med. Socs., Mich. Acad. Family Physicians (dir., 1970-72, 73-75, econ. com., 1970-77), Mich. Chpt. Arthritis Found., Mich. Heart Assn., Soc. Tchrs. of Family Medicine, Pan. Am. Med. Assn., Royal Soc. Health, Washtenaw County Obstetrics and Gynecology Soc. Contbr. presentation to U. Mich. Pharmacy Lectures, 1968, articles to med., pharm. publs. Home: 19345 Bush Rd Chelsea MI 48118 Office: 775 S Main St Chelsea MI 48118

PAPPAJOHN, JOHN GEORGE, financial cons.; b. St. Luke's, Greece, July 31, 1928 (parents Am. citizens); s. George and Maria (Zanios) P.; B.Sc., U. Iowa, 1952; m. Mary Limberis, Sept. 10, 1961; 1 dau., Ann. Agent, Aetna Life Ins. Co., Mason City, Iowa, 1953-58; gen. agt. Occidental Life Ins. Co., Mason City, 1958-63; co-founder, exec. v.p. Guardsman Life Ins. Co., Des Moines, 1963-69; pres. Ins. Investors, Inc., Des Moines, 1963-69, Guardsman Ins. Investors, Inc., Des Moines, 1965-69, Jo-Tel-So, Inc., Mason City, 1966—, Equity Dynamics Inc., John Pappajohn & Assos. Inc., Equimatics, Inc., Evia Ltd., Fedinco, Inc., Jay Barmish Loan Co., Agrl. Bus. Credit Corp. (all Des Moines); v.p. State St. Investments Corp., Mason City; dir. Key Labs., San Diego, Sentinel Electronics, Mpls., Edko, Inc., Des Moines, Curries Mfg., Mason City, Am. Trencher Inc., Delhi, Iowa, Iowa Gateway Inc., Keokuk, Shirlamar Inc., Des Moines, ISCO, Inc., Cin., Mid-Continent Industries, Inc., Des Moines; gen. partner Growth Equities Ltd. Trustee, treas. Des Moines Art Center; bd. dirs., sec. Big Bros. Am.; chmn. Iowa Citizens for Arts. Mem. Internat., Nat. assns. merger and acquisition consultants, Nat. Assn. Life Underwriters, Soc. Fin. Analysts, Soc. Advancement Mgmt., Nat. Assn. Life Cos., Investment Bankers Assn., Consultants Com. of 100, U. Iowa Alumni Assn., Order of Ahepa, Phi Gamma Delta. Republican. Orthodox. Clubs: Masons, Shriners, Des Moines, Univ., Embassy, Country (Des Moines). Home: 7301 Benton Dr Des Moines IA 50322 Office: 2116 Financial Center Des Moines IA 50309

PAPPAS, APHRODITE MEZILZOGLOU (MRS. PETER PAPPAS), pedodontist; b. 40 Churches, Greece, June 29, 1914; d. Theodore and Lukia (Gounaris) Mezilzoglou; D.D.S., U. Athens (Greece), 1939; D.D.S., Northwestern U., 1948; postgrad. U. Ill., 1954-55; m. Peter Pappas, Apr. 30, 1949; children—Lucia, Theodore. Came to U.S., 1947, naturalized, 1952. Pvt. practice dentistry, Athens, Greece, 1939-47; interc. orthodontics Michael Reese Hosp. Med. Center, 1965-66, preventive dentistry Walter Reed Hosp., 1969; instr. operative dept., 1955, U. Ill. Coll. Dentistry, children's clinic, 1955-61; practice pedodontics, Oak Park, Ill., 1957—. Recipient certificates sci. contbrns. to convs. Mem. Am. Dental Assn., Internat. Research Assn., Am. Soc. Dentistry for Children, Hellenic Dental Soc., Soc. Preventive Dentistry, Upsilon Alpha. Greek Orthodox. Office: 1011 Lake St Oak Park IL 60301

PARADOSKI, EDWIN ANDREW, accountant; b. St. Louis, Apr. 9, 1912; s. Andrew and Frances (Sadowski) P.; grad. certificate St. Louis U., 1939; m. Mary Elizabeth Gates, Apr. 26, 1941. Partner, Paradoski, Vogt & Co. C.P.A.'s, Clayton, Mo., 1946—; asst. prof. accounting St. Louis U., 1946-48. Served with AUS, 1943-46. C.P.A., Mo., Ill. Mem. Am. Inst. C.P.A.'s, Mo. Soc. C.P.A.'s (council 1970—), Nat. Assn. Accountants, Clayton C. of C. (fin. com. 1968—), Mo., Carondelet hist. socs., Mil. Hist. Soc. St. Louis, Civil War Round Table, Landmarks Assn. St. Louis, St. Louis Westerners. Clubs: Rotary, Mo. Athletic; Clayton. Home: 7344 Melrose Ave University City MO 63130 Office: 222 S Meramec Ave Clayton MO 63105

PARANJPE, SURESH CHINTAMAN, mech. engr.; b. Indore, India, Oct. 7, 1940; s. Chintaman Savala ram and Vimal (Mone) P.; came to U.S., 1967; B.S., Birla Inst. Tech., 1962; Ph.D., U. Windsor, Ont., Can., 1973; m. Sheela Shamsunder Kanitker, July 31, 1969; children—Jay, Arvin. Asst. engr. Heavy Engring. Corp., Ranchi, India, 1962-64, Canadian Nat., Montreal, 1966-67; mech. engr. Bell Aerospace, Buffalo, 1967-69; sr. analytical engr. United Aircraft, Dayton, Ohio, 1972-74; successively project engr., mgr. reliability group, mgr. high resolution dept. Mead Corp., Dayton, 1974—; research and teaching fellow U. Windsor, 1969-72. Mem. ASME. Club: India of Met. Dayton (treas.). Editor: (with others) Soc. Automotive Engrs. Applied Thermodynamics Manual, 1974—. Contbr. articles to profl. jours. Patentee in field. Home: 433 Towncrest Dr Xenia OH 45385 Office: 1368 Research Park Dr Dayton OH 45432

PARDO, MANUEL POLICARPIO, educator; b. Manila, Philippines, Apr. 24, 1935; s. Leopoldo Gonzales-Pardo and Catalina Tianco (Policarpio) P.; B.A., U. Santo Tomas, Manila, 1957, M.D., 1962; m. Lillian Gonzalez, June 20, 1964; children—Manuel, Lillian Elizabeth, Patrick Edward. Intern, North Gen. Hosp., Manila, 1962; resident in psychiatry U. Kans. Med. Center, Kansas City, 1963-66, asst. prof. psychiatry, 1970—; treas., Assos. in Psychiatry, Inc., Kansas City, Kans., 1972—. Mem. environ. control com. City of Prairie Village, Kans., 1973-75; pres., Philippino Assn. Greater Kansas City, 1972. Bd. dirs. Country Side East Homes Assn., Prairie Village, Kans., 1972-74. Mem. Am. Psychiat. Assn., AMA, Philippine Soc. Psychiatry and Neurology, Inc. (pres. 1971), Kans. Med. Soc. Home: 6316 Ash St Prairie Village KS 66208 Office: U Kans Med Center Kansas City KS 66103

PAREDES, AUGUST VICTOR, cardiologist; b. Arequipa, Peru, Apr. 16, 1929; s. Carlos Augusto and Rosa Amelia (Alvarez) P.; came to U.S., 1955, naturalized, 1960; M.D., U. San Marcos, Lima, Peru, 1955; m. Margaret Connor, Jan. 19, 1956; children—Mark, Nancy, Christopher, Anne Marie, Patrick, Jacquelyn, Michael, Peggy. Intern, Michael Reese Hosp., Chgo., 1955-56, resident, 1956-58, fellow in cardiology, 1958-60; practice medicine specializing in cardiology, 1961—; mem. staff Ingalls Meml. Hosp., Harvey, Ill., 1961—, dir. cardiology, 1968; mem. staff Michael Reese Hosp., Chgo.; dir. Mobile Intensive Care Network S. Cook County, 1975; pres. S. Suburban Cardiology, Ltd., 1971—; chmn. Mobile Intensive Cardiac Care Com., Chgo. Heart Assn., 1975—. Served with Peruvian Navy, 1953-54. Recipient Meritorious Service award Chgo. Heart Assn., 1975. Fellow Am. Coll. Cardiology, Inst. Medicine Chgo.; mem. Peruvian Soc. Cardiology, Am. Soc. Internal Medicine, Michael Reese Alumni Assn., AMA, Ill. State, Chgo. med. socs., Am. Heart Assn. Home: 783 Brookwood Olympia Fields IL 60461 Office: 71 W 156th St Harvey IL 60426

PARENT, DAVID JOSEPH, author, educator; b. Hamlin, Maine, May 31, 1931; s. Patrick David and Yvonne Marie (Violette) P.; B.A., Marist Coll., 1953; M.A., U. Cin., 1965, Ph.D., 1967; m. Ana Maria Ferran, May 2, 1970; children—David Alberto, Michael Joseph, Robert Raphael. Instr. German, Coll. Mount St. Joseph, Cin., 1963-66; instr., asst. prof. German, Boston Coll., 1966-68; prof. German, Ill. State U., Normal, 1968—; author: Werner Bergengruen's Das Buch Rodenstein, 1974; Werner Bergengruens Ungeschriebene Novelle, 1974; translator: Philosophical Anthropology (M. Landmann), 1974; Reform of the Hebrew Alphabet (M. Landmann), 1976; Entry into Matter: Modern Literature and Reality (Juan Garcia Ponce), 1976; The Intellectual and Moral Challenge of Mass Society (Jorge Millas), 1977; Philosophy: Its Mission and Its Disciplines (M. Landmann), 1977; For Socialism (Gustav Landauer), 1978; editor Applied Lit. Press, 1976—. Served with U.S. Army, 1953-56. Mem. Am. Assn. Tchrs. of German, Modern Lang. Assn. Home: 1422 Hanson Dr Normal IL 61761 Office: Foreign Language Dept Illinois State Univ Normal IL 61761

PARENT, JOSEPH DOMINIC, cons.; b. Boston, Aug. 4, 1910; s. Joseph Emile and Mary Brigid (Smyth) P.; B.S. in Chem. Engring., Cath. U. Am., 1929; M.S., Rensselaer Poly. Inst., 1931; postgrad. U. Md., 1931-32; Ph.D. in Chem. Engring., Ohio State U., 1933; m. Margaret Mary Madden, Feb. 15, 1941; children—J. Dennis, Mary M. (Mrs. Joseph Warnemuende), Margaret (Mrs. Anthony Knapp), Gerard T., Ellen (Mrs. Gregory Caputo), Mary T. (Mrs. Robert Essig), Christine (Mrs. Francis Zeman), Joan. Asst. prof. chemistry Loyola U., Chgo., 1935-42; asso. prof. chem. engring., Kans. State U., Manhattan, 1942-43; dean students Inst. Gas Tech., Chgo., 1943-53, cons., 1972—; cons. The Peoples Gas Light & Coke Co., Chgo., 1953-72. Mem. Am. Chem. Soc., Am. Inst. Chem. Engrs., Am. Gas Assn., Sigma Xi, Alpha Delta Gamma, Phi Lambda Upsilon, Alpha Chi Sigma. Elk. Home: 614 Linden Ave Wilmette IL 60091 Office: 3424 S State St Chicago IL 60616

PARISE, RONALD JOSEPH, chem. co. exec.; b. Westport, Conn., Aug. 21, 1949; s. Frank and Frances (Kirik) P.; B.M.E., Ga. Inst. Tech., 1972; m. Terri Gail Ottinger, June 22, 1974. Design engr. Syntex Rubber Co., Bridgeport, Conn., 1973-74; maintenance engr. Stauffer Chem. Co., Gallipolis Ferry, W.Va., 1974-75, mech. engr., 1975-77, engring. supt., 1977—, plant energy coordinator, 1974—. Registered profl. engr., W.Va. Mem. ASME, Soc. Automotive Engrs., Central Engring. Soc. Home: 536 Jackson Pike Apt 64 Gallipolis OH 45631

PARISI, JOSEPH ANGELO, assn. exec.; b. Paterson, N.J., Aug. 13, 1916; s. Joseph Angelo and Elizabeth (Folco) P.; student in Bus. Adminstrn., U.S. Armed Forces Inst., 1942-45; m. Dorothy Louise Beimer, Oct. 12, 1944; 1 son, John Joseph. Clk. law firm Berry & Adleman, Paterson, 1933-38; asst. dir. plant protection Air Assos., Bendix, N.J., 1938-42; cartographer for county surveyor, Kalamazoo, Mich., 1947-51; clk., Kalamazoo, 1951-57; exec. dir. Mich. Twps. Assn., Lansing, 1957—. Lectr. polit. sci. Western Mich. U., Mich. State U., various high schs., 1957—. Chmn., Kalamazoo Recreation Commn., 1956-57; commr. Kalamazoo Twp. Police Dept., 1951-57; mem. Mich. Commn. Inter-govtl. Relations, 1956-57; mem. Continuity of Govt. Commn., 1959-60. Gov.'s Study Commn. on Met. Problems, 1958-60. Pres., Kalamazoo County Fedn. Young Reps., 1948-49; exec. com. Kalamazoo County Rep. Com., 1950—. Bd. dirs. Keep Mich. Beautiful, bd. Kalamazoo County Tb Assn. Served from pvt. to capt. U.S. Army, 1942-47; ETO, MTO; col. Res. ret. Decorated Legion of Merit (U.S.); Order Crown of Italy, Order St. Maurice and Lazarus (Italy). Mem. Res. Officers Assn. U.S. (past pres.), Am. Legion (past chmn. un-Am. activities com.), Kalamazoo Cardinals Soft-Ball Team (bus. mgr.), Mich. Tb. Assn., Internat. Platform Assn., DAV, VFW, Am. Vets. World War II, Kalamazoo County Humane Soc. Club: Optimist (Kalamazoo). Author: A Handbook for Township Officials, 1957; A Manual for Township Officials, 1963; A Manual for Township Government. Home: 1609 Cambridge Dr Kalamazoo MI 49001 Office: 6667 W Michigan Ave PO Box 226 Oshtemo MI 49077

PARK, CHAN HYUNG, physician, educator; b. Seoul, Korea, Aug. 16, 1936; s. Chung Suh and Yoon Sook (Yuh) P.; came to U.S., 1964, naturalized, 1976; M.D., Seoul Nat. U., 1962, M.S., 1964; Ph.D., U. Toronto, 1972; m. Mary Hyungrok Kim, Apr. 16, 1966. Intern, St. Francis Gen. Hosp., Pitts., 1964-65; resident in medicine U. Miami and Jackson Meml. Hosp., Miami, Fla., 1966-68; fellow in oncology-hematology Brown U. and Roger Williams Gen. Hosp., Providence, 1972-74; practice medicine specializing in med. oncology, Kansas City, Kans., 1974—; asst. prof. medicine Kans. U. Med. Center, Kansas City, 1974—. Mem. Soc. Nuclear Medicine, Am. Fedn. Clin. Research, Internat. Soc. Exptl. Hematology, Cell Kinetics Soc. Home: 9137 Grandview Dr Overland Park KS 66212 Office: 39th and Rainbow Sts Kansas City KS 66103

PARK, JOHN LIONEL, govt. ofcl.; b. Virden, Ill., Sept. 1, 1922; s. John H. and Lena D. (Westfall) P.; student U. Ill., 1941-42, Chgo. Tech. Coll., 1943; m. Margaret J. Maher, May 29, 1942; children—John R., Greg W. (dec.). Cartographer, chief draftsman Ill. Div. Hwys., Springfield, 1943-71; adminstrv. asst. Ill. Dept. Transp., 1971—. Mem. Inst. for Certification Engring. Technicians (trustee 1968-72, chmn. bd. trustees 1972-74), Am. Soc. Engring. Edn. (steering com. tech. inst. council 1964-65), Ill. Soc. Profl. Engrs., Am. Soc. Certified Engring. Technicians (pres. 1965-67, chmn. bd. dirs. 1967-68, adviser to bd. dirs. 1976—), Ill. Assn. Hwy. Engrs. (sec. bd. dirs. 1954). Methodist. Clubs: Anchor Boat, Masons, Elks. Home: 200 Twin Oaks Dr Rochester IL 62563 Office: 2300 S 31st St Springfield IL 62706

PARK, JOHN NELSON, educator; b. Rochester, Minn., Aug. 29, 1930; s. John Callaway and Marjorie Antoinette (Nelson) P.; B.A., U. Ariz., 1952; postgrad. Union Theol. Sem., 1952-54, Yale U., 1954, 56; M.A., U. Kans., 1961, Ph.D., 1964. Asst. prof. psychology State U. N.Y., Cortland, 1964-65, Mont. State U., Bozeman, 1965-66, DePaul U., Chgo., 1966-68; research scientist Human Resources Research Office, Fort Bliss, Tex., 1968-69; asst. prof. psychology Mankato (Minn.) State U., 1969-72, asso. prof., 1972-76, prof., 1976—, dept. chmn., 1975—. Phelps-Dodge fellow, 1952-53; NIMH fellow, 1958-60, grantee, 1966-67. Mem. Am., Midwestern Psychol. assns., AAUP, AAAS, Phi Beta Kappa, Phi Kappa Phi. Address: Psychology Program Mankato State U Mankato MN 56001

PARK, KEIL-SOON, educator; b. Pusan, Korea, June 6, 1941; s. Sung-Sul and Myung-Yae (Chung) P.; came to U.S., 1968; naturalized, 1974; B.Sc. in Phys. Edn., Korean Yudo Coll., 1963; M.P.E., Slippery Rock State Coll., 1975; m. Suk-Yeun Choi, Aug. 15, 1970; children—Eu-Gene, Hae-Jhin. Instr., Korean Judo Coll., Seoul, 1963-68, Korean Transp. Co., Seoul, 1964-67, Seoul Police Sta., 1963-68, Seoul YMCA, 1962-67; instr. judo Kent (Ohio) State U., 1969—, Slippery Rock (Pa.) Coll., 1973-74; owner Park's Judo and Karate Sch., Akron, Ohio, 1970—. Recipient award Outstanding Achievement in Phys. Edn., Pusan, Korea, 1966, award Outstanding Athlete of Year Korean AAU, 1966, Ministry Edn. Korea, 1966, Seoul Newspaper, 1967; recipient Bronze medal Fourth World Judo Championship, Brazil, 1965, Silver medal Fifth World Judo Championship, Utah, 1967; named Korean Nat. Judo Champion, 1963, 64, 65, 66, 67. Mem. Lake Erie Amateur Athletic Union (chmn. Judo Promotion 1973-74), Lake Judo Assn. (pres. Lake Erie chpt. 1973-74). Home: 3405 Elgin Dr Akron OH 44313 Office: 3223 Copley Rd Copley OH 44321

PARK, U. YOUNG, nuclear engr.; b. Seoul, Korea, Oct. 12, 1940; s. M.W. and D.C. (Chang) P.; m. Linda Rugh, Nov. 9, 1975; 1 dau., Terra. B.S., Seoul Nat. U., 1963; M.S., U. Cin., 1970. Licensed profl. engr., Ohio. Nuclear engr. Ohio Power Siting Commn., Columbus, 1975—. Mem. Am. Nuclear Soc., Nat., Ohio socs. profl. engrs., Nat. Assn. Underwater Instrs. Club: Adventurers Yacht and Sailing Club. Home: 2826 Zollinger Rd Columbus OH 43221 Office: PO Box 1735 Columbus OH 43216

PARK, YONG HWA, surgeon; b. Chung-Nam, Korea, Jan. 3, 1934; s. Young Woo and Ok Kum (Son) P.; came to U.S., 1966, naturalized, 1977; grad. in pre-med. Seoul U., 1952, M.D., 1958; m. Chung Suk Kim, Apr. 24, 1965; children—Sung Nan, Samuel Yong, Susan Denice. Intern, Jon-Ju Presbyterian Med. Center, Jon-Buk, Korea, 1958-59; chief resident gen. surgery Crawford W. Long Meml. Hosp., Atlanta, 1970; sr. resident thoracic and cardiovascular surgery Wayne State Univ. Affiliated Hosps., Detroit, 1972; practice medicine specializing in surgery, Howell, Mich., 1972—. Deplomate Am. Bd. Surgery. Fellow ACS, Royal Coll. Surgeons Can. Contbr. articles to med. jours. Home: 514 Aberdeen Way Howell MI 48843 Office: 620 Byron Rd Howell MI 48843

PARKER, BEVERLY ANN, guidance counselor; b. Durham, N.C., Dec. 7, 1948; d. Leroy Arthur and Odessa (Turrentine) Parker; B.A., Defiance Coll., 1970; M.A., Bowling Green U., 1971; Ph.D., Mich. State U., 1978; Adviser residence halls Defiance (Ohio) Coll., 1969-70; asst. dir. residence halls/counselor Bowling Green (Ohio) U., 1970-71; asst. to asso. dean students Western Mich. U., Kalamazoo, 1971-75; grad. asst. counseling Mich. State U., East Lansing, 1975—; cons. in field. NIMH fellow, 1975-78. Mem. Am. Personnel and Guidance Assn., Assn. Black Psychologists, Assn. Non-White Concerns, Am. Assn. Marriage and Family Counselors. Baptist. Home: 2317-14 E Jolly Rd Lansing MI 48910 Office: W-37 Owen Hall Mich State U East Lansing MI 48823

PARKER, CHARLES WALTER, JR., equipment co. exec.; b. nr. Ahoskie, N.C., Nov. 22, 1922; s. Charles Walter and Minnie Louise (Williamson) P.; B.S. in Elec. Engring., Va. Mil. Inst., 1947; m. Sophie Nash Riddick, Nov. 26, 1949; children—Mary Parker Hutto, Caroline Davis, Charles Walter III, Thomas Williamson. With Allis-Chalmers Corp., 1947—, dist. mgr., Richmond, Va., 1955-57, Phila., 1957-58, dir. sales promotion industries group, Milw., 1958-61, gen. marketing mgr. new products, 1961-62, mgr. marketing services, 1962-66, v.p. marketing services and pub. relations, 1966-70, v.p., dep. group. exec., 1970-72, staff group exec., 1972—; dir. Inland Heritage Corp. Gen. chmn. United Fund Greater Milw. Area, 1975; mem. exec. bd. Boy Scouts Am., Jr. Achievement Milw. Trustee Milw. Univ. Sch., Carroll Coll.; bd. regents Milw. Sch. Engring. Served to capt. U.S. Army, 1943-46; ETO. Decorated Bronze Star. Mem. Wis. C. of C. (pres.), IEEE (asso.), Sales and Mktg. Execs. Internat. (pres., chief exec. officer 1974), Am. Mktg. Assn. (dir. 1976—), Pi Sigma Epsilon, Kappa Alpha. Home: 2907 E Linnwood Ave Milwaukee WI 53211 Office: PO Box 512 Milwaukee WI 53201

PARKER, CLYDE WENDEL, dentist; b. nr. Chrisney, Ind., May 16, 1923; s. Walter Adam and Thelma Anna (Barton) P.; student U. Ky., 1943; D.M.D., U. Louisville, 1947; m. Nina Lee Abshire, Oct. 21, 1944; children—Karin Lee, Carol Lynn. Pvt. dental practice, Evansville, Ind., 1948—. Cons., Ind. State U., 1970, part time instr. admissions com. chmn., 1971—. Mem. Ind. Comprehensive Health Planning Commn., Dental Health Task Force, 1969-75, vice-chmn., 1969-75; mem. regional Ind. Comprehensive Dental Health Planning Com., 1970—, dental div. Allied Health Program, Ind. State U., Evansville, 1971—. Chmn. council ministries Methodist Ch., 1972-75, chmn. evangelism commn., 1976-79. Mem. Internat. Coll. Dentists, Ind. Dental Assn. (pres. 1968, cons. council on dental care 1977—), 1st Dist. (trustee 1957-63), Evansville (pres. 1952) dental socs., Pierre Fauchard Dental Acad., Ind. Acad. Dental Practice Adminstrn. (pres. 1978—), ADA, Acad. Gen. Dentistry, Am. Soc. Psychosomatic Dentistry and Medicine, Met. Evansville C. of C., Fellowship of Christian Athletes, Ind. U. Alumni Assn. (affiliate), Delta Sigma Delta, Omicron Kappa Upsilon. Clubs: Rolling Hills Country, Masons, Shriners. Home: 4222 Lincoln Ave Evansville IN 47715 Office: 5200 Washington Ave Evansville IN 47715

PARKER, DARYL MCCOID, ophthalmologist; b. Whittier, Calif., Mar. 17, 1904; s. Harry Coleman and Nina (McCoid) P.; A.B., Occidental Coll., 1926; M.D., Northwestern U., 1933; postgrad. U. Pa., 1940-41; m. Martha B. Neiderhiser, June 27, 1932; children—Donald Lee, Robert Lynn, Jean Anne Parker Smith, Carol Rae Parker Staggs. Intern, Evanston (Ill.) Gen. Hosp., 1932; resident Meth. Hosp., Indpls., 1941-42; med. missionary, Shansi, China, 1933-40, 46-49, Castaner, P.R., 1942-46; pvt. practice medicine, specializing in ophthalmology, New Madison, Ohio, 1949-77; mem. cons. staff Wayne Hosp., Greenville, Ohio, 1949—; eye cons. Brethren Home, Greenville, 1949—; surg. cons. Garkida and Lassa hosps., Jos, Nigeria, 1967-73. Fellow A.C.S., Ohio Med. Assn. Mem. Ch. of the Brethren (social action com. 1968-78). Home: 750 Chestnut St Greenville OH 45331 Office: Medical Center Greenville OH 45331

PARKER, DONALD LA RUE, leisure activities co. exec.; b. Montgomery, Ala., Jan. 13, 1935; s. Ernest Jefferson and Dorothy (McGee) P.; B.A., Southwestern U., Memphis, 1957; M.Div., Yale U., 1960; certificate U. Geneva, Switzerland, 1964; m. Alice Limperis, June 3, 1966; 1 dau., Allison Cay. Ordained to ministry Presbyterian Ch., 1960; minister, Old Hickory, Tenn., 1960-63; epidemiologist, information and edn. specialist USPHS, Detroit, 1964-66; mgmt. tng. specialist, supr. marketing mgmt., orgn. devel. Gen. Motors Inst. and Gen. Motors Corp., Flint, Mich., and Detroit, 1966-70; mgmt. devel. specialist, dir. orgn. development, sr. dir. marketing and operations, tng. and devel. Pan Am World Airways, N.Y.C., 1970-74; successively dir. tng., corporate task force dir., v.p. planning and devel., sr. v.p. planning and adminstrn. Playboy Enterprises, Inc.,

Chgo., 1974—. Mem. Am. Mgmt. Assn., Am. Marketing Assn., Acad. Mgmt., Planning Execs. Inst., Fgn. Relations Assn. Clubs: Yale (N.Y.C.); Chgo. Forum. Home: 2920 N Commonwealth Ave Chicago IL 60657 Office: 919 N Michigan Ave Chicago IL 60611

PARKER, EDWIN LYNCH, sporting goods mfr.; b. Torrington, Conn., Feb. 4, 1908; s. Lucien Eliphaz and Cornelia (Lynch) P.; student pub. schs., Wadsworth, Ohio; m. Ruth Elizabeth Edis, Sept. 21, 1940; children—Michael, Steven, Jill, James. Profl. tennis coach, 1926-38; mgr. sporting goods dept. M.S. Long Co., Akron, Ohio, 1926-29; prodn., prodn. control Ohio Match Co., Wadsworth, 1929-36; mgr. sporting goods dept. Central Hardware Co., Akron, 1936-38; sales Seiberling Rubber Co., Akron, 1939-41, mgr. home and auto supply dept., 1941-43; div. mdse. mgr. Firestone Tire & Rubber Co., Akron, 1943-48; v.p. Blazon Assos., Inc. (became Akron Mercantile Co., 1956), Akron, 1948-56, pres., dir., 1956; v.p., treas., dir. Blazon Internat. Can., Ltd., Akron, also Montreal, Can.; pres., dir. Jamestown Machine & Mfg. Co. (Pa.), 1950-56; v.p., dir. Sampson Mfg. Co., Akron, 1948-56; exec. v.p. A.G. Spalding Bros., Inc., Chicopee, Mass., 1956-58, pres., dir., 1958-69; v.p. mktg. Excel Mfg. Corp., 1969-74; adv. bd. Old Phoenix Nat. Bank, Wadsworth; cons., writer, lectr. Methodist. Author weekly column White Hook News. Club: Lions (dir.). Home: 271 Deepwood Dr Wadsworth OH 44281

PARKER, ETHEL MAX (MRS. CEDRIC M. PARKER), journalist; b. Sheboygan, Wis.; d. Mayer and Jennie (Zion) M.; B.A., U. Wis., 1928, M.A., 1951; m. Cedric M. Parker, Aug. 19, 1951. Tchr. elementary sch., Cudahy, Sheboygan, 1921-25; columnist-feature writer Capital Times, Madison, Wis., 1926-33; secondary and adult edn. tchr. Sheboygan, 1934-49; pub. info. dir. ARC, Madison, 1952-66; vol. pub. info. cons. Southwestern Wis. Combined Service Ter. ARC, 1967-72; vol. publicity cons., chmn. coordinating council Wis. Capital div. ARC, 1976—. Chmn. pub. policy com. for establishment Wis. Child Treatment Center, Wis. Mental Health Assn., 1958-59; pres. Madison Profl. Theta Sigma Phi, 1961-63. Mem. Wis. Acad. Scis., Arts and Letters, AAUW, Wis. Alumni Assn., Pi Lambda Theta. Home: Box 320 Route 3 Madison WI 53711 Office: Box 603 Madison WI 53701

PARKER, FRANK PARISH, JR., shopping center developer; b. Harrisburg, Ill., Nov. 29, 1928; s. Frank Parish and Helen (Robb) P.; student Wentworth Mil. Acad., 1947, Murray State Coll., 1948; m. Mary Ann Murphy, Feb. 6, 1954; children—Frank Parish II, Charles P., Mary Helen, Colleen. Pres., Parker Shopping Plaza, Harrisburg, 1968—; dir. Harrisburg Nat. Bank, First Trust Assn. Served with USMCR, 1950. Mason (32 deg., Shriner), Kiwanian. Home: 101 S Webster St Harrisburg IL 62946 Office: PO Box P Route 45 S Harrisburg IL 62946

PARKER, FRANK RALPH, state ofcl.; b. Beloit, Wis., May 31, 1935; s. Ralph Johnson and Charlotte (Livick) P.; student Beloit Coll., 1953-55; B.S., U. Wis., 1960, LL.B., 1965; m. Patricia Ann Ramsfield, Apr. 4, 1964; children—Samuel James, Benjamin Alan. Admitted to Wis. bar, 1965; asst. dist. atty. Dane County, Madison, Wis., 1965-66; asst. family ct. commr. Dane County, Madison, 1966-68, family ct. commr., 1968—. Served with AUS, 1957-59. Mem. Am., Dane County bar assns., State Bar Wis., Wis. Family Ct. Commrs. Assn. (pres. 1969). Home: 4217 Wanetah Trail Madison WI 53711 Office: City-County Bldg Madison WI 53709

PARKER, GERALD EDMUND, educator; b. Huron, S.D., Oct. 11, 1937; s. Gerald Edmund and Grace Alicia (Conway) P.; B.S. in Commerce, Notre Dame U., 1959; M.S. in Commerce, St. Louis U., 1961; Ph.D. in Bus. Adminstrn., 1972; certificate in Asian Studies, Sophia U., European Studies, Coll. Europe, 1964; m. Judith Koehler, Dec. 30, 1964; children—James Edmund, Gerald Michael. Jr. cost analyst Mo. Pacific R.R., 1964-65; instr. mgmt. St. Louis (Mo.) U., 1966-69, asso. prof. mgmt. scis., 1975—; instr. engring. mgmt. U. Mo., Rolla, 1969-72. Cons. mgmt. Human Resources. Mem. Indstl. Relations Assn. Greater St. Louis, Alpha Sigma Nu, Beta Gamma Sigma, Alpha Kappa Psi. K.C.

PARKER, JACK DARWIN, advt. agy. exec.; b. Saginaw, Mich., Sept. 6, 1916; s. William Harold and Catherine (Smith) P.; student Flint Jr. Coll., 1933-34, Mich. State Coll., 1934-36, 38-39, U. Mich., 1936-37; m. Elizabeth Hamilton, Apr. 12, 1939; children—William H., Phillip Scott. Writer, reporter, fgn. corr., 1938-52; combat war corr. ETO, NBC-ABC, 1944-45; writer, producer radio programs, N.Y.C., 1945-47; covered Canadian uranium strikes, coronation Queen Elizabeth II, Arctic DEWline; spl. events and feature commentator WJR, Detroit, 1962—; chmn. bd. Parker, Willox, Fairchild & Campbell, Inc., Saginaw. Pres., Mich. Advt. Industry Alliance. Active various community drs.; bd. dirs. Saginaw Osteo. Hosp. Mem. Saginaw C. of C., Radio Pioneers. Clubs: Masons (32 deg.); Saginaw, Saginaw Bay Yacht (fleet capt.); Great Lakes Cruising (rear commodore); Germania. Home: 115 Gratiot Ct Saginaw MI 48602 Office: 808 N Michigan Saginaw MI 48602

PARKER, JAMES MITCHELL, mktg. co. exec.; b. Chgo., Sept. 3, 1931; s. Robert Barnett and Bonnie (Mitchell) Chidester; student Wilson Jr. coll., 1949-51; B.S., U. Ill., 1955; M.B.A., U. Chgo., 1969; 1 dau., Ginger. Asso. producer Lee Parker Productions, Chgo., 1955-59; sales exec. Borg-Warner Corp., Chgo., 1959-65; account supr. Perrin & Assos., Chgo., 1966-69; pres. Parkton Corp., Ellsworth, Kans., 1969-72; v.p. Dynamark Corp., Chgo., 1972-77; pres. United Mktg. Corp., Chgo., 1977—. Served to lt. U.S. Army, 1951-53. Mem. Exec. Club, Exec. Program Club. Clubs: Chgo. Athletic; Flossmoor Country. Patentee improved lawn mower. Home: 1117 Leavitt Ave Flossmoor IL 60422 Office: 35 E Wacker Dr Chicago IL 60601

PARKER, RAYMOND LEROY, bus. machines co. exec.; b. Detroit, Oct. 8, 1924; s. Peter and Kornelia (Gosky) P.; B.S. in Elec. Engring.)Bomber scholar), U. Mich., 1950; m. Dorothy Cieslak, Aug. 2, 1947; children—Constance, Margaret, Barbara. Design engr. Burroughs Corp., Detroit, 1951, asst. supt., 1955-57, supt., 1957-66, supt. assembly ops. Downington (Pa.) plant, 1966-68, quality control mgr., 1968-71, cons. Croydan (Eng.) plant, 1972, product assurance mgr. Plymouth (Mich.) plant, 1974—. Bd. dirs. Nat. Home Respiratory Care Center S.E. Mich., 1977—. Served with USNR, 1943-46. Mem. Am. Soc. for Quality Control, IEEE. Roman Catholic. Home: 36817 Rayburn St Livonia MI 48154 Office: 41100 Plymouth Rd Plymouth MI 48170

PARKER, RICHARD HENDERSON, psychiatrist; b. Regina, Sask., Can., July 9, 1919; s. Samuel Rutherford and Elizabeth Riddell (Henderson) P.; student Regina Normal Sch., 1940; M.D., U. Man., 1948; postgrad. U. Leeds, 1954; m. Helen Nora Roberta Carter, Mar. 26, 1949; children—Susan May, Catherine Hellen, David Rutherford McDonald. Sr. intern Winnipeg (Man.) Gen. Hosp., 1947-48; house physician in psychiatry East Riding Mental Hosp., Beverley, Yorkshire, Eng., 1948; asst. psychiatrist West Riding Mental Hosp., Menston nr. Leeds, Eng., 1948-52; psychiatrist The Retreat, York, Eng., 1952-60; dir. Adult Outpatient Child Guidance Clinic, Brandon, Man., Can., 1960-62; dir. guidance clinic Mental Health Centre, Brandon, 1962—; cons. Brandon Gen. Hosp., Childrens Aid Western Man., Canadian Assn. Mentally Retarded. Mem. adv. com. Jeff Umphrey Research Centre Retardation of Brandon. Served with Royal Canadian Corps Signals, 1940-42. Mem. World, Canadian, Man. psychiat. assns., Royal Coll. Psychiatry, Canadian, Man. med. assns., Royal Canadian Legion, Delta Upsilon. Anglican. Home and office: Mental Health Centre #2 Harley Dr Box 420 Brandon MB R7A 5Z5 Canada

PARKER, WAYNE FREDERICK, heat processing equipment exec.; b. Sylvania, Ohio, Nov. 10, 1927; s. Harry Costello and Edna Johanna (Kubitz) P.; student U. Toledo, 1946-53; m. Martha M. McQuade, Sept. 21, 1973; 1 dau., by previous marriage—Sharon L.; stepchildren—Deborah L. Kelley Weisbrod, David M. Kelly, Vicki L. Kelley, Kathye A. Kelley, Bryan J. Kelley. With Surface div. Midland-Ross Corp., Toledo, 1944—, beginning as draftsman, insp., successively elec. designer, elec. engr. and safety coordinator, estimator, product engr., project elec. engr., tech. service specialist, systems supr., mgr. quality assurance, 1944-77, mgr. product assurance, 1977—; lectr.; cons. product liability laws, codes, standards and interpretations. Former pres. Redeemer Lutheran Ch. Served with AUS, 1946-48. Recipient youth leadership outstanding award Jr. Achievement, 1971. Mem. Indsl. Heating Equipment Assn., Nat. Fire Protection Assn., Am. Nat. Standards Inst., Am. Gas Assn. (Hall of Flame 1975), Am. Soc. Quality Control. Clubs: Anthony Wayne Toastmasters (pres. 1965), Heather Downs Country (Toledo), Masons. Contbr. articles to trade jours. Home: 2156 Chadbury Ln Toledo OH 43614 Office: 2375 Dorr St Toledo OH 43691

PARKHURST, EDWIN WALLACE, JR., hosp. cons.; b. Waukegan, Ill., June 17, 1943; s. Edwin Wallace and Marie Violet (Wolf) P.; B.A., Carthage Coll., 1965; M.B.A., U. Chgo., 1968; m. Grace Ann Dovemuehle, July 6, 1963; children—John Edward, Janet Lynn, Jeanine Marie, Julie Ann. Adminstrv. trainee West Allis Meml. Hosp. (Wis.), 1965-66; research asso. Herman Smith Assos., hosp. cons., Hinsdale, Ill., 1967-68; asst. dir., asst. prof. U. Mo. Med. Center, Columbia, 1968-71; prin. Herman Smith Assos., hosp. cons., Hinsdale, Ill., 1971-75, partner, 1975—; guest lectr. U. Mo., 1971—, U. Chgo., 1971—. Active Boy Scouts Am.; pres. Health Issues Study Soc., 1975-76. Fellow Am. Assn. Hosp. Cons.; mem. Am. Hosp. Assn., Health Issues Study Soc., Am. Coll. Hosp. Adminstrs., Am. Assn. Hosp. Planning, Beau Bien Homeowners Assn. (dir. 1973-76). Home: 4517 Waubansie Ln Lisle IL 60532 Office: 120 E Ogden Ave Hinsdale IL 60521

PARKIN, EVELYN HOPE, ret. med. social worker; b. Owatonna, Minn., d. Wilbur L. and Verta (Cowles) P.; B.A., Carleton Coll., 1931; postgrad. U. Minn., 1939-41. Pediatric social worker, instr. field work U. Minn. Hosps., 1941-45; pediatric med. social worker, supr. Med. Social Service Dept., Mayo Clinic, Rochester, Minn., 1946-53, dir. Med. Social Service Dept., 1953-75, voting mem., 1972-75, emeritus staff, 1975—. Bd. dirs. Minn. Heart Assn., 1959-64; mem. nat. com. Am. Heart Assn., 1958-62; treas. Young Republican League Rochester, 1962; sec. Olmsted County Rep. Com., 1953-55; bd. dirs. YWCA, Rochester, 1953-54; sec. bd. dirs. Mayo Clinic Credit Union, 1958-65, 65-68. Mem. Nat. Assn. Social Workers (exec. com. Minn. sect. 1964-65), Minn. Welfare Conf. (sec. 1954), AAUW (asst. treas. 1953-54), Am. Hosp. Assn. Presbyterian. Clubs: Mayo Clinic Women's (pres. 1950-52), Carleton Coll. Alumni. Home: 502 15th Ave SW Rochester MN 55902 Office: Mayo Clinic Rochester MN 55902

PARKINSON, GEORGE AMBROSE, ednl. adminstr.; b. Columbus, Ohio, Jan. 22, 1899; s. Daniel Homer and Cynthia Catherine (English) P.; B.S., Ohio State U., 1922, M.A., 1923; postgrad. U. Chgo., 1930; Ph.D., U. Wis., 1929; m. Mildred Jane Smith, June 17, 1920 (dec.); children—Virginia Jane, George (dec.), Daniel Smith; m. 2d, Myrtle Volger, June 20, 1975. Prin., Parkinson High Sch., Zanesville, Ohio, 1916-17, Ripley High Sch., Greenwich, Ohio, 1917-18; instr. math. Worthington (Ohio) High Sch., 1921-23; instr. engring. math. U. Wis., 1923-27; asst. prof., chmn. dept. math. Milw. extension div. U. Wis., 1927-29, asso. prof., 1929-40, asst. dir. in charge evening classes, 1934-40, dir., prof., 1945-56; vice provost, dir. bus. affairs, prof. U. Wis., Milw., 1956-58; dir. Milw. Area Tech. Coll., 1958-68, dir. emeritus, cons. to bd., 1968—; cons. on evaluation manpower programs GAO, 1969—, Am. Assn. Jr. Colls.; chmn. Albert S. Puelicher Meml. Scholarship Com., 1969—. Trustee, Midwestern Ednl. TV, Inc., 1961—, v.p., 1964—; mem. policy bd. Great Plains Nat. Instructional TV Library, 1962—. Served with USN, 1918-19, 40-45. Recipient Meritorious Service award Students Milw. Tech. Coll., 1968, award of honor Wisdom Soc., 1970. Mem. SAR (bd. govs. Wis. soc. 1953—, Gold medal 1959, Patriot's medal 1972), Am. Tech. Edn. Assn. (nat. trustee 1962—), Navy League (dir. Milw. council 1947—), Am. Math. Soc., Math. Assn. Am. (chmn. Wis. sect. 1935-36), Adult Edn. Assn. U.S.A., Am. Vocat. Assn., Am. Soc. Engring. Edn., Am. Vocat. Edn. Research Assn., Assn. Pub. Sch. Adult Educators U.S., Wis. Assn. Vocat. and Adult Edn. (citation 1968), Sigma Xi, Phi Eta Sigma, Phi Delta Kappa, Pi Mu Epsilon, Gamma Alpha, Alpha Kappa Psi, Phi Theta Kappa. Presbyterian. Clubs: Univ., Press (life, Headliner award 1968), Statesmen's (Milw.); Univ. (life) (Madison, Wis.); Masons (supreme council), Shriners. Author: Vocational and Technical Education in a Decade of Change, 1974; A Brief Introduction to Analytic Geometry, 1944; (with D.S. Parkinson) Education, Man and Society, 1952; contbr. articles to profl. jours. Home: Rural Route 2 Box 662 Oostburg WI 53070 Office: 1015 N 6th St Milwaukee WI 53203

PARKINSON, LEONARD CURTIS, tool co. exec.; b. Medford, Wis., Feb. 9, 1919; s. Elmer Curtis and Lillie (Holtzmann) P.; grad. eve. tech. sch.; m. Norma M. Larsen, Aug. 1, 1958; children—David, Dale, Daniel. With Kearney & Trecker Corp., 1939-56, proposal engr., 1945-56; mfg. engr. Kempsmith Machine Co., 1956-60; shop supt. Precision Machine Alignment Co., 1960-62; maintenance planner Falk Corp., 1962-64; design engr. Baush Machine Tool Co., West Allis, Wis., 1964-69, v.p., 1969—. Founder, Prescriptive Teaching Center, West Allis, 1969, inc., 1969—, also bd. dirs.; bd. dirs. United Assn. for Retarded Citizens, 1970—, pres., 1974-75; bd. dirs. Soc. For Brain Injured Children, 1969-70. Lutheran (mem. ch. council 1968-70). Home: 5047 S 65th St Greenfield WI 53220 Office: 6810 W National Ave West Allis WI 53214

PARKINSON, WILLIAM CHARLES, educator; b. Jarvis, Ont., Can., Feb. 11, 1918; s. Charles Franklin and Euphemia Alice (Johnston) P.; came to U.S., 1925, naturalized, 1941; B.S.E., U. Mich., 1940, M.S., 1941, Ph.D., 1948; m. Martha Bennet Capron, Aug. 2, 1944; children—Martha Reed, William Reid. Physicist, Johns Hopkins U., Applied Physics Lab., Silver Springs, Md., 1942-46; physicist Office Sci. Research and Devel., Europe, 1943-44; instr. U. Mich., Ann Arbor, 1947-48, asst. prof. physics, 1948-53, asso. prof., 1953-58, prof., 1958—, dir. Cyclotron Lab., 1962—; cons. Oak Ridge Nat. Lab., 1955-60, Ramo-Woolridge Corp., 1955-56, Los Alamos Lab., 1958-60, Argonne Nat. Lab., Physics Rev. Com., 1959-63; mem. subcom. on nuclear structure NRC, 1959-68; mem. adv. panel for physics NSF, 1966-69; cons. grad. sci. facilities NSF, 1968; cons. deptl. sci. devel. program NSF, 1968, cons. ad hoc accelerator panel, 1968, chmn. postdoctoral fellowship evaluation panel, 1969; mem. nuclear physics sub panel on mgmt. and costs nuclear program NRC, 1969-70. Recipient USN Ordnance Devel. award, 1946; Fulbright research scholar Cavendish Lab., Cambridge U., 1952-53. Fellow Am. Phys. Soc.; mem. N.Y. Acad. Scis., Sigma Xi, Phi Kappa Phi, Kappa Kappa Phi. Patentee in field. Home: 1600 Sheridan Dr Ann Arbor MI 48104

PARKS, JAMES DALLAS, artist; b. St. Louis, Aug. 25, 1907; s. John Henry and Katie (Cannon) P.; B.S., Bradley U., 1927; M.A., State U. Iowa, 1943; m. Florence E. Wright, Nov. 17, 1934; 1 son, James Peter. Asst. prof. art Lincoln U., Jefferson City, Mo., 1927-58, asso. prof., 1958-69, prof., 1969-76, head dept. art, 1927-76, prof. emeritus, 1976—; one-man shows include: W.Va. State U., 1959, Savannah State U., 1967, So. Univ., New Orleans, 1968, Bradley U., 1972; group shows include: Joslyn Mus., 1946, St. Louis Art Mus., 1948, Rockhill Nelson, 1951; represented in permanent collections: Lincoln U., Dunbar Sch., Kansas City, Mo., Tex. So. U., Houston; cons. Va. State Coll., 1976, U. Ark., Pine Bluff, 1977. Mem. Nat. Art Edn. Assn., Coll. Art Assn. Am., Mo. Coll. Art Conf., Alpha Phi Alpha. Democrat. Mem. African Methodist Episcopal Ch. Art editor Sphinx Mag., 1926-50. Home: 923 E Dunklin St Jefferson City MO 65101

PARKS, JAMES WILLIAM, motor club exec.; b. Wabash, Ind., Jan. 17, 1929; s. George Lewis and Mildred Gertrude (Smith) P.; B.S., Ball State U., 1951, M.A., 1956; m. Joyce Arlene Lillibridge, June 27, 1949; children—Kimberly, James William II, Jeffrey. Tchr., prin. pub. schs., Wabash, Ind., 1954-57; prin. sch. North Manchester, 1957-60, Met. Sch. Dist. Washington Twp., Marion County, 1960-66; exec. v.p. Hoosier Motor Club, Indpls., 1966—. Mem. Washington Twp. Vocational Bldg. Bd., 1970—. Served with AUS, 1951-53. Named Outstanding Young Man of Am., U.S. Jr. C. of C., 1965. Rotarian, Elk. Home: 5521 Vin Rose Ln Indianapolis IN 46226 Office: 40 W 40th St Indianapolis IN 46208

PARKS, LYMAN STARLING, clergyman, city ofcl.; b. Princeton, Ind., Mar. 12, 1917; s. Madison Lyman and Minnie (Roundtree) P.; student Ind. State U., 1936-37; A.B., Wilberforce (O.) U., 1944; B.D., Payne Theol. Sem., 1944; m. Cleo I. Sweat, June 25, 1944; children—Linda (Mrs. Dock Miller), Larry, Leo, Lana (Mrs. Parks Dixon), Londa, Lyman Starling, Lawana. Ordained pastor African M.E. Ch., 1943; pastor, Marion, Ind., 1944-47, Richmond, Ind., 1947-54, Ann Arbor, Mich., 1954-65, River Rouge, Mich., 1964-66, Grand Rapids, Mich., 1966—; city commr. Grand Rapids, 1967-71, mayor protem, 1971-72, mayor, 1972-75. Mem. Ind. Gov.'s Commn. on Youth, Richmond, 1951-52, Ann Arbor Human Relations Commn., 1952-64, Criminal Justice Com., 1972-74, Hist. Commn., 1976—, Sports Hall of Fame, 1976—; mayor's citizens adv. com. Office Econ. Opportunity, River Rouge, 1964-66, Grand Rapids, 1966-68; treas. Henry Sch. P.T.A., 1967-69. Sec., Grand Rapids and Kent County Council Chs., 1966-69; mem. relocation com. Urban Renewal Legislative Com., Mich. Council Chs., 1966—; mem. bd. religious affairs com. U. Mich., Ann Arbor, 1952-64. Mem. NAACP, Alpha Phi Alpha. Clubs: Masons, Kiwanis. Home: 530 Madison Ave SE Grand Rapids MI 49503 Office: 500 James Ave SE Grand Rapids MI 49503

PARKS, MURRILL DOUGLAS, veterinarian; b. Chickasha, Okla., Mar. 28, 1931; s. Murrill Douglas and Dora Mae (Baker) P.; student Okla. U., 1948-49, Oklahoma City U., 1950, Oklahoma State U., 1950-51; B.S., Colo. State U., 1956, D.V.M., 1961; m. Shirley Ann Singleton, July 4, 1960; children—Douglas Craig, Bellamy Ann, James Gregory. Research and mgmt. biologist Alaska Fish and Wildlife Service, 1955-59; gen. practice veterinary medicine, Ogallala, Nebr., 1959—. Mem. Ogallala Planning Commn., 1970-71. Served with U.S. Army, 1951-54. Decorated Korea medal with 4 Bronze Stars. Mem. Am., Nebr. vet. med. assns., Beta Beta Beta, Am. 1st Day Cover Soc. Democrat. Methodist. Clubs: Rotary, Elks. Home and Office: 303 E 9th St Ogallala NE 69153

PARKS, SHERWOOD RACE, radio sta. exec.; b. Eureka, Kans., Feb. 12, 1924; s. Race and Hazel Marie (Carrithers) P.; student Port Arthur Coll., 1942; m. Madge Lewis, Feb. 13, 1945; children—Lewis, Biffton. Program dir. KWHK Radio, Hutchinson, Kans., 1946-48; asst. mgr. KVGB Radio, Great Bend, Kans., 1948-55; sales mgr. KFH Radio, Wichita, Kans., 1955; pres., gen. mgr. KVOE Radio, Emporia, Kans., 1955-57; sales mgr. KVGB Radio, Great Bend, Kans., 1957-62; gen. mgr. KGNO Radio, Dodge City, Kans., 1962-70; pres., gen. mgr. KINA Radio, Salina, Kans., 1970—; dir. Salina Radio, Inc. (Kans.). Bd. dirs. Salina (Kans.) Pub. Library, Salina (Kans.) Community Theatre. Served with USAAF, 1943-46. Named Boss of Year, Sunflower Am. Bus. Women's Assn., 1972, Salina Jr. C. of C., 1974. Mem. Broadcast Pioneers, Nat. Assn. Broadcasters, Kans. Assn. Broadcasters (pres. 1971-72), Am. Legion, VFW, Dodge City (pres. 1968), Salina Area (pres. 1975) chambers commerce. Clubs: Masons, Shriners, Elks. Home: 661 Rockview Rd Salina KS 67401 Office: PO Box 778 Salina KS 67401

PARKS, TERRY EVERETT, ednl. adminstr.; b. Satanta, Kans., Feb. 20, 1941; s. Everett Clayton and Margaret Irene (Teeter) P.; B.S., Emporia State Coll., 1961, M.S., 1965; postgrad. Temple U., 1966-69; Ph.D., Brown U., 1971; postgrad. Cornell U., 1970-71; m. Dianne Dennis, Dec. 23, 1961; children—Glenn Parks, Mary Beth. Tchr., Shawnee Mission (Kans.) High Sch. Dist., 1961-66, gen. dir. basic services Unified Sch. Dist. No. 512, 1972-75, K-12 math. specialist and supr. fed. projects, 1975—; predoctoral fellow Temple U., 1966-69, Brown U., 1969-70; postdoctoral fellow Cornell U., 1970-71; pres. New Chem., Inc., Shawnee Mission, 1972—; cons. design Shawnee Mission Unified Sch. Dist. No. 512, 1971-72; adj. prof. Emporia (Kans.) State Coll., 1972, Kans. State U., 1974-75. Bd. dirs. Asbury Day Sch., Shawnee Mission, 1972-75; mem. Kans. State Metric Edn. Task Force, 1974-76. Mem. Am. Chem. Soc., Nat. Council Tchrs. Math., U.S. Metric Assn., Assn. Supervision and Curriculum Devel., Sigma Xi. Clubs: Optimists, Masons, Brown (co-chmn. 1974-76) (Kansas City, Kans.). Home: 6114 Noland Rd Shawnee KS 66216 Office: 7235 Antioch St Shawnee Mission KS 66216

PARKS, THOMAS AQUINAS, mfg. co. exec.; b. Cleve., Nov. 4, 1929; s. Jonathan B. and Marian Mae (Campbell) P.; B.A., State U. Iowa, 1954; postgrad. U. Ill., 1965; m. Judith Fausch; children—David Jonathan, Sandra Anne. Dept. head internat. sales div. Collins Radio Co., Cedar Rapids, Iowa, 1954-58; asst. export sales mgr. Amana Refrigeration, Inc. (Iowa), 1958-62; export sales mgr. Cedar Rapids Engring. Co., 1962-64, gen. sales mgr., 1964-65, v.p. sales, dir., 1966-68, pres., 1968—; pres. Kwik-Way Industries, 1969—; pres. Kwik-Way Ltd. (Can.), 1969—; chmn., dir. Line-O-Tronics Inc., 1972—; chmn. bd. Material Products Co., Rock Island, Ill., 1972—. Fgn. affairs speaker Speakers Bur., Cedar Rapids C. of C., 1958—, chmn. Fgn. Trade Bur., 1956-62, bd. dirs., 1974-77; council v.p. Boy Scouts Am., 1976—; trustee Cedar Rapids Children's Home, 1974—, Coe Coll., 1977—; bd. dirs. Cedar Rapids Symphony Assn., 1975-77. Served with USAF, 1951-53. Republican. Club: Cedar Rapids Country. Home: Timberlake Estates Swisher IA 52338 Office: 501 American Bldg Cedar Rapids IA 52401

PARKS, WILLIAM ROBERT, univ. adminstr.; b. Lincoln County, Tenn., Oct. 13, 1915; s. Benjamin N. and Minnie A. (Taylor) P.; B.A., Berea Coll., 1937, LL.D. (hon.), 1966; M.A., U. Ky., 1938, D.Sc. (hon.), 1973; Ph.D., U. Wis., 1948; LL.D., Drake U., 1968; L.H.D., Westmar Coll., 1968; m. Ellen R. Sorge, July 1, 1940; children—Andrea, Cynthia. Economist bur. agrl. econs. Dept. Agr.,

1940-48; prof. govt. Iowa State Coll., 1948-56; prof. agrl. econs. U. Wis., 1956-58; dean of instrn. Iowa State U., 1958-61; v.p. academic affairs, 1961-65, pres., 1965—. Cons. TVA, part-time 1956-57, also Dept. Interior; dir. Northwestern Bell Telephone Co., Central Life Assurance Co. Trustee Coll. Retirement Equity Fund, U. of Mid-Am. Served to lt. (j.g.) USNR, 1943-46. Mem. Assn. Am. Univs. (pres. 1977, chmn. 1978), Mid-Am. State Univs. Assn. (pres. 1965), Nat. Assn. State Univs. and Land Grant Colls. (pres. 1973). Contbr. articles to profl. jours. Home: The Knoll Iowa State U Ames IA 50010

PARKS, WILLIAM WILSON, transp. equipment co. exec.; b. Oak Park, Ill., Dec. 11, 1921; s. Paul Brownlee and Margery Eulalie (Rohan) P.; B.S., Ill. Inst. Tech., 1944; M.B.A., U. Chgo., 1959; m. Mary Patricia Gagan, Sept. 19, 1959; 1 dau., Julia. Structural designer Swift & Co., Chgo., 1946-47; devel. engr. Vapor Corp., Chgo., 1947-50, chief research engr., 1950-55, chief engr. Vap-Air div., 1956-62, chief engr. Vapor Corp., 1962-66, v.p., gen. mgr. Transp. Systems div., 1966-76, sr. v.p., gen. mgr. vapor div., 1976—. Bd. dirs. Ronald Knox Montessori Sch., 1964-66; trustee Ill. Inst. Tech., 1973—. Served as lt. (j.g.) C.E., USNR, 1943-46. Mem. Am. Soc. M.E., Am. Pub. Transit Assn. (dir. 1972-76), Instrument Soc. Am., Internat. Star Class Yacht Racing Assn. (mem. governing com. 1965—, pres. 1974—), Ill. Inst. Tech. Alumni Assn. (pres. 1972-73). Episcopalian. Club: Chicago Yacht (dir. 1960-72). Patentee in field. Home: 1724 E Ridgewood Lane Glenview IL 60025 Office: 6420 W Howard St Chicago IL 60648

PARKUS, PAUL PHILLIP, dentist; b. Balt., Feb. 20, 1924; s. Julius and Bertha (Richman) P.; student Johns Hopkins U., 1947-49; D.D.S. (Univ. grantee 1953), U. Mich., 1955; m. Carolyn Jane Shurts, July 8, 1953; children—Barbara, Richard, William. Practice gen. and restorative dentistry, Ann Arbor, Mich., 1955—; teaching staff Dental Sch., U. Mich., Ann Arbor, 1955-57; treas. bd. dirs. Adaptive Devices, Inc., Ann Arbor, 1971-72. Served with AUS, 1944-46. Mem. Am., Mich. dental assns., Mich. Assn. Professions (charter), Ann Arbor Power Squadron. Home: 1401 Russell Rd Ann Arbor MI 48103 Office: 1817 W Stadium St Ann Arbor MI 48103

PARKYN, JOHN DUWANE, nuclear engr.; b. La Crosse, Wis., Feb. 20, 1944; s. Lionel Eric and Florence Katrina (Klum) P.; student Wis. State U., 1962-64, U. N.Mex., 1968-69; B.S. in Nuclear Engring. and Physics, U. Wis., 1972; m. Betty Christine Tarnutzer, Aug. 13, 1966; children—Christine Peggy, Sarah Katherine. Asst. plant engr. Ohio Med. Products Co., 1966-67; party chief U.S. Geol. Survey, Madison, Wis., 1971-72; asst. operations group Point Beach Nuclear Plant, Two Rivers, Wis., 1972-74; operations engr. La Crosse Boiling Water Reactor, Genoa, Wis., 1974—. Mem. Two Rivers City Council, 1974, Vernon County Bd. Suprs., 1976—; assessor Bergen Twp. (Wis.), 1976-77, Sterling Twp. (Wis.), 1977—; chmn. Vernon County Library Com. and Bd. Equalized Values, 1976—. Served with U.S. Army, 1967-69. Certified assessor, Wis.; lic. sr. reactor operator. Mem. Am. Nuclear Soc., Nat. Assn. of Former Youth Govs., Am. Legion. Mem. United Ch. of Christ. Club: Mason. Home: Pleasant Valley Stoddard WI 54658 Office: La Crosse Boiling Water Reactor Route 1 Genoa WI 54658

PARMAN, LARRY VANCE, investment banker; b. Bethany, Mo., July 17, 1947; s. Vance Edgar and Avis Jean (Ruckman) P.; B.S. in Pub. Adminstrn., U. Mo., Columbia, 1969; J.D., U. Mo., Kansas City, 1974; m. Frances Darlene Trammell, Aug. 16, 1969; 1 dau. Alexandra Trammell. Teller Commerce Bank of Columbia (Mo.), 1968-69, loan anaylst, 1971-72; with United Mo. Bank., Kansas City, 1972—, municipal bond underwriter, 1973-74, asst. v.p., 1974-76, v.p., 1976—; chmn. bd. Farmers Nat. Bank, Ridgeway, Mo., 1977—; dir. Bank of Gallitin (Mo.); instr. Avila Coll., 1975-76. Served as lt. U.S. Army, 1972. Mem. Pi Omicron Sigma, Kansas City Municipal Bond Club. Home: 440 W 67th St Kansas City MO 64113 Office: PO Box 226 Kansas City MO 64141

PARMELEE, DAVID FREELAND, educator; b. Oshkosh, Wis., June 20, 1924; s. Gale Freeland and Helen Dale (MacNaughton) P.; B.A., Lawrence U., 1950; M.S., U. Mich., 1952; Ph.D., U. Okla., 1957; m. Jean Marie Peterson, Dec. 4, 1943; 1 dau., Helen Gale. Grad. asst. U. Okla., Norman, 1952-56, instr., 1956-58; asst. prof. Kans. State Tchrs. Coll., Emporia, 1958-60, asso. prof., 1960-64, prof. biology, 1964-70; prof. ecology and behavioral biology, chmn. field biology program U. Minn., Mpls., 1970—; dir. field ops. for bird virus and parasite research studies U. Okla. Med. Center, NIH, 1963-65; program dir. U. Minn. Forestry and Biol. Sta., Lake Itasca, Cedar Creek Natural History Area, Anoka and Isanti Counties, Minn., 1970—. Served with USMCR, 1943-46. U.S. Antarctic Research Program NSF grantee, 1972—, Canadian Arctic Research Programs, NSF, Arctic Inst. N.Am., Nat. Mus. Can. research grantee, 1953-71; recipient Conservation Edn. award Kans. Wildlife Fedn., Sears-Roebuck Found., 1965. Mem. Orgn. Inland Biol. Field Stas., Nature Conservancy, Cooper's Ornithol. Soc., Wilson's Ornithol. Club. Home: 1595 Northrop St Saint Paul MN 55108 Office: 349 James Ford Bell Mus Natural History U Minn Minneapolis MN 55455

PARMER, DAN GERALD, veterinarian; b. Wetumpka, Ala., July 3, 1926; s. James Lonnie and Virginia Gertrude (Guy) P.; student Los Angeles City Coll., 1945-46; D.V.M., Auburn U., 1950; m. Florence Kellogg, July 30, 1970; 1 dau. by previous marriage—Linda Leigh; stepchildren—Allison, Lynda Shaw. Gen. practice vet. medicine, Galveston, Tex., 1950-54, Chgo., 1959—; staff veterinarian Chgo. Commn. Animal Care and Control, 1974—; tchr. Highlands U., 1959. Served with USNR, 1943-45; PTO; served as staff veterinarian and 2d and 5th Air Force veterinarian chief USAF, 1954-59. Recipient Veterinary Appreciation award U. Ill., 1971. Mem. Ill. (chmn. civil def. and package disaster hosps. 1968-71), Nat., Chgo. (bd. govs. 1969-72, 74—), South Chgo. (pres. 1965-66) veterinary med. assns., Am. Animal Hosp. Assn. (dir.), Ill. Acad. Vet. Practice, Nat. Assn. of Professions, Am. Assn. Zoo Veterinarians, Am. Assn. Zool. Parks and Aquariums, VFW. Democrat. Clubs: Masons, Shriners, Kiwanis, Midlothian Country, Valley Internat. Country. Discoverer Bartonellosis in cattle in N.Am. and Western Hemisphere, 1951; co-developer bite-size high altitude in-flight feeding program USAF, 1954-56. Address: 7953 S Cicero Ave Chicago IL 60652

PARRIS, PORTER P., hotel exec.; b. Gilliland, Tex., Aug. 7, 1917; s. Samuel B. and Gertrude (Collier) P.; student North Tex. State Coll., 1934; grad. Tex Technol. Coll., 1938; m. Mary Ross Edwards, Nov. 5. Various positions Hilton Hotels, 1935—, including El Paso, Tex., Long Beach, Calif., Lubbock, Tex., 1935-43; asst. mgr. Roosevelt Hotel, N.Y.C., 1943-44; gen. mgr. Dayton-Biltmore Hotel, Dayton, Ohio, 1949-51; resident mgr. Conrad Hilton Hotel, Chgo., 1951-53, gen. mgr., 1962-68; gen. mgr. Hotel Plaza, N.Y.C., 1954-55; v.p., gen. mgr. Shamrock Statler Hilton, Washington, 1968-69, Boston, 1969-70; mng. dir. Shamrock Hilton, Houston, 1970-74; v.p., gen. mgr. Palmer House, Chgo., 1974—. Bd. dirs. Greater Houston Conv. and Visitors Bur. Served as sgt. maj. inf., AUS, 1944-46. Mem. Hotel Assn. Washington, Am. Hotel-Motel Assn. (dir. 1972), Houston Hotel-Motel Assn. (pres.). Address: Palmer House Chicago IL 60690

PARRISH, DONALD GRAHAM, cons. elec. engr.; b. Homer, N.Y., Apr. 18, 1926; s. Donald Graham and Ethel May (Maddock) P.; B.S. in Physics and Math., Baldwin-Wallace Coll., Berea, Ohio, 1949; B.S. in Elec. Engring., Mass. Inst. Tech., 1951; m. Estela Mejia, June 7, 1952; 1 dau., Sandra Luz Parrish Wilson. Tech. engr. Procter & Gamble Co., Cin., 1951-57; asst. engring. mgr., engr. Davison chem. div. W.R. Grace & Co., Cin., 1957-60; key engr. Processes Research, Inc., Cin., 1960-62; asso. prof. elec. engring. Ohio Coll. Applied Sci., Cin., 1962-64; prin. Aero Tech Cons., Cin., 1964—; lectr. Cin. Tech. Coll., 1974-75, U. Cin., 1974—; arbitrator Am. Arbitration Assn., 1969—. Bldg. commr., Evendale, Ohio, 1965-71; bd. dirs. Hub Services, Inc., Model Cities agy., 1972—, treas., 1973—; adv. bd. Pilot Cities Health Center, 1975—, sec., 1976-77. Served with AUS, 1944-47. Registered profl. engr., Ohio, Ky. Club: Clinton Hills Swim. Home: 3989 Beechwood Ave Cincinnati OH 45229 Office: 1125 Walnut St Cincinnati OH 45210

PARRISH, JAMES HILLIARD, librarian; b. Nashville, May 23, 1926; s. Joseph Warren and Katherine (Cooper) P.; B.S., Middle Tenn. State U., 1953; M.L.S., George Peabody U., 1955. Spl. student asst. Vanderbilt U. Med. Library, Nashville, 1953-55; circulation, reference librarian U. Tenn., Martin br., 1955-57; reference librarian Air U., Maxwell AFB, Ala., 1957-60, Sch. Aerospace Medicine, San Antonio, 1960-63; head library services NASA Tech. Library, Houston, 1963-64; asst. med. librarian U. Ky., Lexington, 1964-66; acting dir. Falk Library, U. Pitts., 1967-68, asst. librarian, 1966-67; librarian Hawaii Med. Library, Honolulu, 1969-71; prof., coordinator for extramural programs U. Ill. Med. Center, Library of Health Scis., Chgo., 1971—. Served with USNR, 1944-46, 50-52. Mem. Spl. Libraries Assn., Med. Library Assn. Home: 4235 N Keeler St Apt 1C Chicago IL 60641 Office: 1750 W Polk St Chicago IL 60612

PARRISH, JOHN BISHOP, economist, educator; b. Decatur, Ill., June 11, 1911; s. Roy C. and Frances Effie (Wayne) P.; B.A., U. Ill., 1934, Ph.D., 1939; m. Anne D'Nelle Bullock, Aug. 31, 1940; children—Adrianne Parrish Casey, John Gregory. Sr. economist War Manpower Commn., Washington, 1941-42; prin. economist Nat. War Labor Bd., Washington, 1942-44; regional dir. U.S. Bur. Labor Statistics, Chgo., 1944-47; asso. prof. econs. U. Ill., Urbana, 1947-55, prof., 1956—; mem. edn. adv. com. NAM, ednl. adv. com. Am. Mgmt. Assn. Bd. visitors Mary Baldwin Coll., Staunton, Va., 1974—. Recipient Distinguished Service award social scis. Phi Gamma Mu; Rodney D. Chipp award Soc. Women Engrs., 1974. Mem. Am., Midwest econ. assns., Phi Beta Kappa, Phi Eta Sigma, Kappa Zeta Psi. Author: (with Carroll R. Daugherty) The Labor Problems of American Society, 1952. Home: 1801 Pleasant Circle Urbana IL 61801

PARRISH, JOHN EDWARD, judge; b. Lebanon, Mo., June 10, 1940; s. Folie and Thelma (Osborn) P.; B.S. in Bus. Adminstrn., U. Mo., 1962, J.D., 1965; m. Claudia Kathleen Barbee, Sept. 1, 1962; children—Mark Everett, Michael Brett. Staff accountant Arthur Andersen & Co., St. Louis, 1965-66; admitted to Mo. bar, 1965; mem. firm Phillips & Parrish, Camdenton, 1968-73; pros. atty. Camden County, Camdenton, 1969-73; judge 26th Jud. Circuit Mo.; pres. MBJ, Inc., Camdenton, 1971—; mem. Lake of Ozarks Region XVI Law Enforcement Assistance Council. Bd. dirs. Lake of Ozarks Gen. Hosp.; bd. dirs., v.p. Camdenton Civic Assn., 1969-72, Camdenton Dist. Bd. Edn., 1973-76. Served to capt. arty. AUS, 1966-68. Decorated Army Commendation medal. Mem. Mo. Bar (council young lawyers sect. 1973-75), Mo. Council Juvenile Ct. Judges, Mo. Trial Judges Assn., Beta Gamma Sigma. Clubs: Rotary, Lake Valley Golf and Country (Camdenton). Home: Route 2 Box 81E Camdenton MO 60520 Office: Camden County Court House Camdenton MO 65020

PARRISH, MATTHEW DENWOOD, mental health adminstr.; b. Washington, Apr. 1, 1918; s. Forrest Denwood and Alice Lorena (Flynn) P.; B.A., U. Va., 1939; M.D., George Washington U., 1950; children—Denwood, John, Stephen. Intern, Letterman Gen. Hosp., San Francisco, 1951; psychiat. resident Walter Reed Gen. Hosp., Washington, 1954; commd. officer U.S. Army, advanced through grades to col., 1967; div. psychiatrist, Korea, 1954-55, U.S. Army Dispensary, Yokohama, 1955-56; chief psychiatrist, Ft. Belvoir, Va., 1956-60; asst. chief psychiatrist Office Army Surgeon Gen., 1960-62; chief psychiat. service U.S. Army Hosp., Frankfurt am Main, 1962-65; chief psychiatry dept. Walter Reed Army Inst. Research, Washington, 1965-67; chief psychiatrist for combat theatre, Viet Nam, 1967-68; chief psychiatrist Office Army Surgeon Gen., Washington, 1968-70; psychiat. cons. Blackman's Devel. Center, Washington, 1969-72; cons. Md. Drug Abuse Program, Va. Dept. Vocat. Rehab., Fairfax, 1969-72; tng. program exec. Ill. Dept. Mental Health and Developmental Disabilities, Chgo., 1972—; supt. Singer Zone Center, Rockford, Ill., 1974—. Clin. prof. psychiatry Abraham Lincoln Sch. Medicine, U. Ill., Chgo., 1973—; cons. Ch. of Jesus Christ of Latter-day Saints, Potomac Stake, Washington, 1969-75. Mem. governing bd. Family Services, Alexandria, Va., 1959-62. Served with U.S. Army, 1941-45. Decorated Air medal with oak leaf, Legion of Merit with oak leaf. Fellow Am. Psychiat. Assn.; mem. Am. Soc. Group Psychotherapy and Psychodrama, Assn. Mil. Surgeons. Editor-in-chief U.S. Army Vietnam Med. Jour., 1967-68. Home: 4817 Alpine Park Dr Rockford IL 61108 Office: 4402 N Main St Rockford IL 61103

PARRISH, ORVILLE STANLEY, ret. die casting co. exec.; b. Woodstock, Ill., June 3, 1916; s. William A. and Augusta W. (Ohlrich) P.; grad. high sch.; m. Edith Mae Gronow, May 21, 1938; children—Thayer W., Kathleen N., Gary A. Engr., Auto Lite Die Casting Co., Woodstock, Ill., 1935-46, Odel Die Casting Co., Detroit, 1946-48; supt., Ind. Die Casting Co., Elwood, 1948-50; v.p., gen. mgr. Aluminum Foundry and Aluminum Die Cast Foundry, Winchester, Ind., 1950-62; pres., chmn. bd. The Top Die Casting Co., Marengo, Ill., 1964-74, ret., 1974, now dir. Mem. Soc. Die Cast Engrs., U.S. C. of C. Elk. Clubs: Abbey Yacht (Fontana, Wis.); Woodstock (Ill.) Country; Anvil (Dundee, Ill.). Home: 7226 W Hillside Rd Crystal Lake IL 60014 Office: Route 23 N Marengo IL 60152

PARRISH, RUFUS HERALD, psychiatrist; b. Donora, Pa.; s. Rufus and Mary Elizabeth (Wright) P.; B.S. magna cum laude, St. Augustine's Coll., 1938; M.D. with honors, Meharry Med. Coll., 1944; m. Alma Elizabeth Marion, Nov. 24, 1957. Intern, Harlem Hosp., N.Y.C., 1945; resident N.Y.C. Cancer Inst., 1945-47, Wayne County Gen. Hosp., Eloise, Mich., 1961-63; practice medicine specializing in psychiatry, Detroit, 1964—; staff psychiatrist Wayne County Gen. Hosp., Eloise, Mich., 1964-68, asst. dir. psychiat. service, 1969-73; dir. Wayne County Mental Health Clinic, Detroit, 1973—; instr. Wayne State U. Med. Coll., Detroit, 1969—. Diplomate Am. Bd. Psychiatry-Neurology. Mem. Am. Psychiat. Assn., AMA, Mich. Soc. Psychiatry-Neurology, Mich. State, Wayne County med. socs., Kappa Alpha Psi. Episcopalian. Clubs: Masons (32 deg.), Shriners, Nat. Guardsmen (Detroit). Home: 19525 Roslyn Rd Detroit MI 48221

PARROTT, DEAN ALLEN, clergyman; b. Cass City, Mich., Aug. 24, 1922; s. Earl Watts and Anna Lura (Smith) P.; A.B., Adrian Coll., 1953; Th.B., Owosso Bible Coll., 1957; M.A., Mich. State U., 1960; postgrad. Wayne State U., 1960-63, Western Mich. U., 1967-68; m. Ione Elizabeth Kneeshaw, Apr. 18, 1942; children—Jean Parrott Dunsford, Keith, Dale. Ordained to ministry Free Meth. Ch., 1944; asst. pastor, Ovid, Mich., 1943-44; supply pastor Hillman and Pleasant Valley, Mich., 1944; pastor, Rose City, Mich., 1944-45; dir. pastoral services, Grace Chapel, Greenville, Ill., 1945-46; pastor, Sandusky, Mich., 1946-50, Adrian, Mich., 1950-53, Hillsdale, Mich., 1953-59, Lincoln Park, Mich., 1959-66, Kalamazoo Free Meth. Ch., 1966-76, Westland (Mich.) Free Meth. Ch., 1976—. Counselor, religious instr., chaplain Girl's Tng. Sch., Adrian, 1950-53; chaplain intern Harper Hosp., Detroit, 1960; counselor Christian Enterprise Inc., Detroit, 1959-61, Christian Leadership Tng., 1961-64, Christian Found. for Emotional Health, Detroit, 1964-66; dean Mich. Bible Inst., Detroit, 1964-66; marriage and family counselor, del. Conf. on Prophecy, Jerusalem, Israel, 1971, Gen. Conf. Free Meth. N.Am., Winona Lake, Ind., 1974; host daily radio broadcast Question Hour, WKPR, Kalamazoo, 1966-72. Mem. Lincoln Park (Mich.) Mental Health Council, 1960-66; mem. pastor's adv. bd. Planned Parenthood, Detroit, 1963-66; mem. community relations bd. City of Kalamazoo, 1969-71. Mem. Kalamazoo Ministerial Assn. (pres. 1971-73), Wesleyan Theol. Soc., Am. Psychol. Assn., Nat. Council Family Relations, Acad. Religion and Mental Health, Am. Inst. Family Relations, Christian Assn. Psychol. Studies. Author: Arnold's Commentary, 1968; Light from the Word, 1971. Home and office: 1421 Venoy Westland MI 48185

PARROTT, ROGER LEE, dentist; b. Sumner, Ill., Feb. 22, 1927; s. Omar F. and Charlotte (Pauley) P.; student Vincennes U., 1947-49, postgrad. 1953-54; D.D.S., Washington U., 1953; m. Joanne Stansfield, May 5, 1951; children—Dennis, Nancy, David, Beth. Clin. instr. pedodontics, St. Louis County Health Dept., 1953-55; pvt. practice dentistry specializing in dentistry for children, St. Louis, 1954—; clin. instr. Washington U. Dental Sch., 1957-63. Bd. dir. YMCA. Served with AUS, 1945-46. Fellow Am. Coll. Dentists; mem. Greater St. Louis Dental Soc. (sec., treas. 1968-73), Am. Soc. Dentistry for Children (pres. Mo. 1961), St. Louis Soc. Dental Sci., ADA (del. 1971), Am. Coll. Dentists, Am. Acad. Pedodontists, Omicron Kappa Upsilon, Delta Sigma Delta. Methodist (bd. dirs.). Home: 101 Calverton Rd St Louis MO 63135 Office: 7440 W Florissant Ave St Louis MO 63136

PARSON, DAVID, lawyer; b. Dubuque, Iowa, Feb. 26, 1924; s. Morris and Lillian (Rotman) P.; A.B. maxima cum laude, Loras Coll., 1944; J.D., U. Chgo., 1947; m. Barbara Meyers, Dec. 15, 1954; children—Mary, Julie, Ann. Admitted to Ill. bar, 1947; practiced in Chgo., 1947-62, 65—; mem. Kirkland & Ellis, 1947-62, partner, 1955-62; partner firm Goldberg, Weigle, Mallin, Gittles & Parson and predecessor firms, 1965-69; dep. gen. counsel USIA, Washington, 1962-65. Pub. mem., sec. Ill. Commn. Low Income Housing, 1965-67; chmn. Bd. Police and Fire Commrs., Winnetka, Ill., 1973-76; vice chmn. Caucus, Winnetka, 1974-75; trustee Drexel Home for Aged, 1965-77, Village of Winnetka, 1976—. Mem. Fed., Am., Chgo. bar assns. Club: Standard. Home: 1138 Tower Rd Winnetka IL 60093 Office: 55 E Monroe St Chicago IL 60603

PARSONS, AUGUSTINE CHAPMAN, librarian, assn. exec.; b. Ripley, W.Va., Apr. 30, 1922; s. Harry Paul and Mary (McGrew) P.; B.S. in Edn., W. Va. U., 1949; M.S. in Library Sci., Western Reserve U., 1950; postgrad. Inst. Orgn. Mgmt. Syracuse U., 1966; m. Elizabeth Eloise Hall, Aug. 30, 1947; children—Gary Chapman, Terry Leland (twins), Sherilyn Sue, Marilyn Ann. Instr. dept. library sci. W.Va. U., summers 1954-58; librarian Gallia County (Ohio) Dist. Library, Gallipolis, 1952-56, Alliance (Ohio) Pub. Library, 1956-62, Rodman Pub. Library, Alliance, 1962-64. Mem. ALA Ohio rep. council, 1960-63, 68-72, mem. legislation com. 1973-76, chmn. membership com. Ohio, 1960-63, mem. com. orgn. library adminstrn. div., 1961-64; chmn. Pub. Library Assn., 1965-66, chmn. com. promotion standards, 1966-69, mem. coms. architecture standards, 1961-64, mem. council, 1969—; exec. dir. Ohio Library Assn., 1964—, mem. recruitment com., bus. mgr. Bull. publ., 1958-64; exec. v.p. Ohio Library Found., 1964—; exec. dir. Ohio Library Trustees Assn., 1964—; pres. Council Library Assn. Execs., 1975—; past pres. Stark County (Ohio) Library Assn. Chmn. pub. service div. Alliance United Fund, 1957-60; mem. Stark County Tech. Inst. Survey Com., 1962-64. Served with USNR, 1942-46. Mem. Stark County (bd. dirs. 1960-64), Alliance (bd. dirs. 1958-64) hist. socs., U.S., Ohio chambers commerce, Am. Soc. Assn. Execs., Ohio Geneal. Soc. Ohio Hist. Soc., Ohio Ednl. Media Assn. Methodist. Rotarian (sec. 1959-64). Clubs: University, Press (Columbus); Wranglers (sec. Alliance 1962-64). Author: Ohio Libraries: A Growth Industry. Editor: Ohio Library Assn. Bull., Ohio Library Trustee. Home: 6886 Clydeway Ct Worthington OH 43085 Office: 40 S 3d St Columbus OH 43215

PARSONS, DANA LEE, lawyer; b. Sedalia, Mo., Feb. 4, 1941; d. Gilbert Leroy and Erna Verna (Steiner) Parsons; B.A., U. Mo., Kansas City, 1963, M.A., 1965, J.D., 1976; 1 son, Charles Dana. Admitted to Mo. bar, 1977; faculty Kans. State U., Pittsburg, 1965-66, Kennedy Coll., Wahoo, Nebr., 1967-68, U. Nebr., Omaha, 1968-71; tchr. Kansas City (Mo.) Sch. Dist., 1977—; individual practice law, Kansas City, 1977—. Mem. Fed., Mo., Kansas City bar assns., AAUW, NOW, Kansas City Assn. Women Lawyer, League Women Voters. Home and Office: 409 W 90th St Kansas City MO 64114

PARSONS, DONALD JAMES, bishop; b. Phila., Mar. 28, 1922; s. Earl and Helen (Drabble) P.; B.A., Temple U., 1943; B.D., Phila. Div. Sch., 1946, Th.D., 1953; D.C.L., Nashotah (Wis.) House, 1973; m. Mary Russell, Sept. 17, 1955; children—Mary Helen, Rebecca, Bradford. Ordained as deacon and priest Episcopal Ch.; prof. N.T., Nashotah House, 1950-63, pres., 1963-73; bishop Diocese of Quincy, Peoria, Ill., 1973—. Author: Lifetime Road to God, 1965; In Time—With Jesus, 1973. Home: 3900 Hawthorne St Peoria IL 61614 Office: 3601 N North St Peoria IL 61604

PARSONS, FREDERICK AMBROSE, educator; b. Mpls. Feb. 21, 1916; s. Olof and Volborg (Anderson) P.; B.E., St. Cloud State Coll., 1939; postgrad. Colo. U., 1941; M.A., U. Minn., 1947, Ed.S., 1970; m. Margaret C. Anderson, June 20, 1943; children—Gretchen, Mark, Christine. Tchr., Delano (Minn.) High Sch., 1940-43, prin., 1943-47; supt. schs. Delano, 1947—. Mem. century council U. Minn. Mem. Am., Minn., assns. sch. adminstrs., Met. Supts. Assn., U. Minn. Alumni Assn., Tau Kappa Alpha, Kappa Delta Pi, Phi Delta Kappa. Mason. Address: Delano MN 55328

PARSONS, GAMALIEL LEROY, JR., pediatrician; b. Duluth, Ga., Jan. 31, 1921; s. Gamaliel Leroy and Emma Mae (Poole) P.; student Fisk U., 1940-44; M.D., Meharry Med. Coll., 1947; m. Reva Young, May 1, 1946; children—Patricia Ann, Gamaliel Leroy, Paulette. Intern, Provident Hosp., Chgo., 1947-48, resident, 1948-50, attending physician dept. pediatrics, 1950—, pres. med. staff, 1968-71, chmn. pediatrics, 1968—; practice medicine specializing in pediatrics, Chgo., 1950—; asst. attending physician Children's Meml. Hosp., Chgo., 1957—; founding pres. Daniel Hale William Neighborhood Center, Chgo., 1970-71, dir., 1970—. Served with M.C., AUS, 1951-53. Mem. AMA, Nat. Med. Assn., Ill. State, Chgo. med. socs., Chgo. Pediatric Soc. Congregationalist (asst. treas. 1967—). Clubs: Saracens, Inc.; 1st Tee Golf; Exec. (Chgo.). Home: 7817 S Wabash Ave Chicago IL 60619 Office: 3507 S King Dr Chicago IL 60653

PARSONS, JAMES BENTON, fed. judge; b. Kansas City, Mo., Aug. 13, 1911; s. James Benton and Maggie (Virgia) P.; A.B., James Millikin U., 1934; M.A., U. Chgo., 1946, LL.D., 1949; also hon. degrees; m. Amy Maxwell, Dec. 24, 1952 (dec.); 1 son, Dieter K. Faculty, Lincoln U. Mo., 1934-40, asst. to dean of men, instr. polit. sci., acting head music dept., 1938-40; supr. pub. schs., Greensboro, N.C., 1940-42; faculty John Marshall Law Sch., Chgo.; asst. corp. counsel City of Chgo., 1949-51; asst. U.S. atty., Chgo.; judge Superior Ct. of Cook County, Ill., 1960-61; judge U.S. Dist. Ct., No. Dist. of Ill., Chgo., 1961—, chief judge, 1977—. Active Boy Scouts Am., mem. nat. exec. bd., mem. adv. bd. Reading Research Found.; mem. citizens com. U. Ill., Champaign; mem. pres.'s council St. Ignatius Coll. Prep. Sch., Chgo.; mem. centennial anniversary com. Loyola U., Chgo.; hon. chmn. Chgo. Conf. on Religion and Race and Tri-Faith Employment Ser.; exec. bd. Chgo. Community Music Found.; adv. bd. Ill. Masonic Hosp., Chgo. Trustee Millikin U., Decatur, Ill., Ada S. McKinley Community Sers.; bd. dirs. Harvard-St. George Sch., Chgo., Leukemia Research Found., Chgo., Mercy Halfway House Corp., Chgo.; nat. bd. trustees Nat. Conf. Christians and Jews. Home: 2801 King Dr Chicago IL 60616 Office: US Dist Ct US Courthouse 219 S Dearborn St Chicago IL 60604

PARSONS, M(ELVIN) GODFREY, mgmt. cons.; b. St. Louis, Apr. 25, 1924; s. Melvin Godfrey and Aline Helen (Gruber) P.; B.S., U. Mo., 1949, M.S., 1950; m. Marie Marguerite Lambert, Aug. 5, 1949; 1 son, Robert Gerald. Mgmt. analyst U.S. Govt., Rantoul, Ill., 1950-53; mktg. analyst Eli Lilly & Co., Indpls., 1953-54; prof. U. Ill., Urbana, 1954-64, U. Mo., Columbia, 1964-67; prof., dir. bur. bus. research Eastern Mich. U., Ypsilanti, 1967-71; sr. partner MNO Programs Internat., mgmt. and mktg. cons. tng. and research, Ypsilanti, Mich., 1971—; dir. Lenise Cosmetics, Champaign, Ill., Domino Pizza, Ypsilanti, Mich. Bd. commrs. City of Ypsilanti Bldg. Authority, 1971—; dist. chmn. Arrowhead council Boy Scouts Am., 1962-64, dist. commr. 1956-60, dist. commr. Wolverine council, 1967-70, mem. exec. com., 1967-69. Served with USAAF, 1942-43. Mem. Nat. Council Small Bus. Mgmt. Devel. (pres. 1971-72), Washtenaw Sales and Mktg. Execs. (pres. 1972-73), Am. Mktg. Assn. (dir. 1961-63), Am. Econ. Assn., AAUP, Internat. Platform Assn., Delta Sigma Pi. Kiwanian (pres. 1975-76). Address: 1471 Gregory St Ypsilanti MI 48197

PARSONS, PETER PEABODY, automobile co. exec.; b. Lock Haven, Pa., Aug. 3, 1930; s. Frederick Henry and Elizabeth Tracy (Peabody) P.; B.M.E., Lehigh U., 1953; postgrad. (Sloan program fellow) Stanford U., 1968: m. Antoinette Frances Schultes, June 5, 1971; 1 son, Jeffrey Michael; children by previous marriage—Janet Elizabeth, Sally Mary, Diane Jean. With Fisher Body div. Gen. Motors Corp., Warren, Mich., 1953—, sr. engr. in charge, 1977—. Mem. Soc. Automotive Engrs., Am. Soc. Body Engrs. Republican. Home: 2459 Chelsea Ln Troy MI 48084 Office: 30001 Van Dyke St Warren MI 48090

PARSONS, SAMUEL DALE, agrl. engr.; b. Brazil, Ind., Sept. 4, 1939; s. Ray Edison and Vera Pauline (Ames) P.; B.S., Purdue U., 1961; M.S., Cornell U., 1964; Ph.D., Mich State U., 1975; m. Jane Ann Evans, June 11, 1961; children—Samuel Dale, William E. Design engr. Cummins Engine Co., Columbus, Ind., 1961-63; extension agr. engr. Purdue U. and Coop. Extension Service, Lafayette, Ind., 1964—, asso. prof. dept. agrl. engring., 1975—; cons. various agrl. equipment firms. Mem. Am. Soc. Agrl. Engrs., Tau Beta Pi, Gamma Sigma Delta, Epsilon Sigma Phi. Office: Agrl Engring Dept Purdue U Lafayette IN 47905

PARTAIN, CARL STANLEY, optometrist; b. Harrisburg, Ill., May 16, 1942; s. Carl and Mary Agnes (Stanley) P.; student U. Ill., 1960-62; O.D., Ill. Coll. Optometry, 1965; m. Judith Ann Lawson, Oct. 29, 1967; children—Joe, Jonathan, Jill. Practice optometry, Flora, Ill., 1965-66, Hoopeston, Ill., 1970—. Served with AUS, 1967-68. Mem. Am., Ill., Eastern Ill. (pres. 1973) optometric assns., Hoopeston C. of C., Hoopeston Jr. C. of C. (dir. 1971). Home: 827 E Maple St Hoopeston IL 60942 Office: Rural Route 3 851 E Orange St Hoopeston IL 60942

PARTEE, CECIL A., city ofcl.; b. Blytheville, Ark., Apr. 10, 1921; s. Charles C. and Bessie (Dupree) P.; B.S., Tenn. State U., 1944, J.D., Northwestern U., 1946; m. Paris Bradley, Dec. 23, 1955; children—Paris Irene, Cecile. Partner firm Partee & Green, Chgo.; asst. state's atty., Ill., 1948-56; mem. Ill. Ho. of Reps., 1957-66; mem. Ill. Senate, 1967—, pres. pro tem, 1971-73, minority leader, 1973-75, pres., majority leader, 1975-77; commr. human services City of Chgo., 1977—. Active various community drives. Mem. N.A.A.C.P. Address: 640 N La Salle St Chicago IL 60610

PARTINGTON, PHILIP FRANKLIN, surgeon; b. Orange, N.J., Dec. 19, 1909; s. James and Lucy May (Gatts) P.; B.S. magna cum laude, Yale U., 1931; M.D., Harvard U., 1935; m. Gertrude Else Mehling, Apr. 2, 1938; children—Michael, Anne, Constance, Jonathan. Intern, Huntington Meml. Hosp., Boston, 1935-36, Lakeside Hosp., Clevel, 1936-38; resident in surgery N.Y. Presbyn. Hosp., 1939-41; chief of surgery Cleve. VA Hosp., 1946-50, also sr. cons. surgery; practice medicine specializing in surgery, Shaker Heights, Ohio, 1950—; chmn. gen. surgery St. Luke's Hosp., 1963-74; asso. clin. prof. surgery Case Western Res. U. Served to maj. M.C. AUS, 1942-45. Decorated Bronze Star. Diplomate Am. Bd. Surgery. Fellow A.C.S.; mem. AMA, Central Surg. Assn. Republican. Episcoplaian. Clubs: Pasteur, Profl. Men's. Home: 24000 Hazelmere Shaker Heights OH 44122 Office: 3461 Warrensville Center Rd Shaker Heights OH 44122

PARUK, WALTER ADAM, judge; b. Hamtramck, Mich., July 9, 1925; s. Anthony and Lucy (Klimsza) P.; J.D., U. Detroit, 1950; m. Phyllis M. Lesinski, May 8, 1955; children—Anthony, Steven, Paul, Mary, James, Carolyn. Admitted to Mich. bar, 1951; partner Lesinski & Paruk, Hamtramck, 1951-60, Paruk & Miller, Hamtramck, 1961-73; municipal judge City of Hamtramck, 1961—. Bd. dirs. Jud. Research Found., 1968-72, treas., 1972-74; bd. dirs. Nat. Polish Sports Hall Fame, St. Francis Hosp. Served with USNR, 1943-46. Mem. N.Am. Judges Assn. (gov. 1969-72), Mich. Assn. Municipal Judges (pres. 1967), Advocates Bar Assn. (pres. 1972, sec., editor 1973—). Home: 11609 Lumpkin St Hamtramck MI 48212 Office: 11445 Conant Ave Hamtramck MI 48212

PASCH, DOROTHY FRANCES, ret. ednl. adminstr.; b. Toledo, March 28, 1907; d. Albert F. and Mary (Helwig) P.; student Toledo U., 1924-25; A.B., Ohio State U., 1928; A.M., Northwestern U., 1938. Tchr. elementary schs., Toledo, 1929-39, tchr. high sch., 1939-42; dir. Toledo Nursery and Extended Sch. Services, 1942-45; dir. spl. edn. Toledo Bd. Edn., 1945-66, project dir. Children's Assessment, Placement and Instruction Center, 1966-67, dir. ednl. innovations and planning Toledo Pub. Schs., 1967-70; vis. lectr. U. Cin., summer 1951; summer sch. staff Ohio State U.; staff summer sch. Southbury (Conn.) Tng. Sch., 1955; dir. summer sch. Rainier State Sch. for U. Wash., 1957-59; staff mem. Western Interstate Conf. Higher Edn., U. Colo., summer 1961; summer guest instr. Colo. State Coll., 1962-65; pres. Nat. Council Adminstrs. Spl. Edn. in Local Sch. Dists. U.S., 1956-57. Past bd. dirs. Toledo Day Nursery; sec. Northwestern Ohio Lung Assn.; past trustee Toledo Hearing and Speech Center. Fellow Am. Assn. Mental Deficiency (v.p., chmn. com. edn., mem. planning bd.); mem. Ohio Dirs. Spl. Edn. (pres.), Council Exceptional Children, NEA, AAUW, Zeta Tau Alpha. Clubs: Zonta, Toledo. Author monograph; contbr. Contbr. chpt. to bull. Home: Executive Towers #701 1920 Collingwood Blvd Toledo OH 43624

PASCHAL, WILLIAM BARRON, mech. engr.; b. Chgo., Feb. 26, 1948; s. William Kiernan and Sophie Marie (Kaczmar) P.; B.S. in Mech. Engring., U. Ill., Chgo., 1971; m. Rosanne A. Pancerz, May 27, 1972. Project engr. heating, ventilating and air conditioning Sherwin Stenn Engrs. Inc., Chgo., 1969-76, Sargent and Lundy Engrs., Chgo., 1976—; cons. on bldg. design and constrn. to architects and owners. Registered profl. engr., Ill. Mem. ASME, Am. Soc. Heating, Refrigerating, Air Conditioning Engrs., Am. Soc. Plumbing Engrs., Ill. Soc. Radiologic Technologists. Roman Catholic. Home: 4224 Saratoga St Apt J310 Downers Grove IL 60515 Office: 55 E Monroe St Chicago IL 60603

PASCHALL, HOMER DONALD, educator; b. Clarksville, Tenn, Aug. 29, 1926; s. Homer Stoddard and Beulah Elma (Dawdy) P.; A.B., Trevacca Nazarene Coll., 1948; B.S., Austin Peay State U., 1950; M.A., George Peabody Coll. Tchrs., 1950; Ph.D., Iowa State U., 1963; m. Martha Jean Reding, June 2, 1950; children—Donald Paul, Linda Gail, David Wayne, Brenda Kay. Tchr. sci., math. Greenbrier (Tenn.) High Sch., 1948-49, Fort Campbell (Ky.) Elementary Sch., 1950-51; instr. math., biology Bethany Nazarene Coll., (Okla.), 1951-55; prof. physiology and health sci. Ball State U., Muncie, Ind., 1955—. Served with USNR, 1944-46. Recipient fellowship NSF, 1959-60. Mem. Nat. Assn. Biology Tchrs., Am. Sci. Affiliation, Ind. Acad. Sci., AAAS, Sigma Xi, Phi Delta Lambda, Sigma Zeta. Mem. Ch. of Nazarene. Home: 3013 W Twickingham Dr Muncie IN 47304 Office: Ball State U Muncie IN 47306

PASCOE, PERCY WILLARD, JR., editor; b. Little Rock, Jan. 31, 1930; s. Percy Willard and Oma Mae (Grizzle) P.; student pub. schs., Little Rock, St. Louis; m. Delma Lucille Huff, Sept. 27, 1967. Founder editor Cuba (Mo.) Free Press, 1960—; mem. advisory bd. Sta. KUMR, U. Mo., St. Louis. Served with USAF, 1951-55. Recipient Tilghman Cloud Meml. Editorial award Mo. Press Assn., 1975, Best Editorial Page award, 1975; Best Advt. Idea award Met. Newspaper Services, 1975. Mem. Mo. Press Assn. (Blue Ribbon Newspaper award 1968, 72), Mo. Ad Mgrs. (pres. 1976-77), Nat. Newspaper Assn. (Blue Ribbon award 1975, 76, 77). Democrat. Mem. Ch. of Christ. Home: Route 2 Cuba MO 65453 Office: 110 S Buchanon St Cuba MO 65453

PASEK, MICHAEL ANTHONY, computer technologist; b. Duluth, Minn., Sept. 5, 1951; s. Antone William and Helene (Tunsky) P.; ed. pub. schs., tech. schs. and colls. Operator, Bd. Pensions, Lutheran Ch. in Am., 1973-75; corporate mgr. Microtex Corp., Cloquet, Minn., 1975—; systems programmer Comten, Inc., 1977—; mem. Data Communications Adv. Panel. Club: Comten Hobbyists. Home: 5020 Washington St NE Minneapolis MN 55421 Office: 208 Ave C Cloquet MN 55720

PASSAGE, MICHAEL JOHN, personnel cons.; b. Mount Vernon, Wash., Mar. 22, 1946; s. Richard James and Alice Elizabeth (Dopps) P.; B.A., U. Wash., 1968; M.B.A., Harvard U., 1972. Asst. dir. internat. tchrs. program Harvard U., Boston, 1970-72; asst. to pres., dir. mgmt. info. systems Levinson Corp., St. Louis, 1972-74; v.p. fin. LinClay Corp., St. Louis, 1975-76; pres. Passage & Assos., St. Louis, 1976—; dir. LinClay Corp. Am., Corp. Staffing Cons., N. Am. Cons. Served with Army Nat. Guard, 1970. Mem. Harvard Club, Harvard Bus. Sch. Club (v.p. St. Louis chpt. 1974). Home: 665 S Skinker St St Louis MO 63105 Office: 7701 Forsyth St Suite 1354 St Louis MO 63105

PASSI, RONALD BERNHART, physician, educator; b. Sudbury, Ont., Can., Jan. 11, 1936; s. John A. and Viola S. (Palo) P.; M.D., U. Western Ont., 1960; m. Nancy M. Hanninen, Aug. 16, 1958; children—Sharon J., Norman R., Eric J. Intern, Victoria Hosp., London, Ont., 1960-61, resident surgery, 1961-62, 64, mem. teaching staff, 1968—; resident physiology U. Western Ont., 1962-63; resident surgery St. Joseph's Hosp., 1963-64, Westminster Hosp., 1965, pathology, 1965; instr. surgery Ohio State U. Hosp., 1966-67; asst. prof. U. Western Ont., 1968-75, asso. prof., 1975—; pvt. practice medicine, London, Ont. Recipient J.B. Campbell Meml. prize in medicine, 1960; Samuel McLaughlin Found. traveling fellow, 1966. Fellow Royal Coll. Surgeons, Med. Council Can., A.C.S.; mem. Canadian, Ont. med. assns., Assn. Acad. Surgery, Soc. Surgery Alimentary Tract, Canadian Assn. Clin. Surgeons, Sigma Xi, Alpha Omega Alpha. Club: London Hunt and Country. Home: 82 Normandy Gardens London ON N6H 4A9 Canada Office: University Hosp London ON Canada

PASSMAN, RICHARD HARRIS, educator; b. Providence, Sept. 22, 1945; s. Carl and Ruth Ilse (Oberlander) P.; m. Jane Aline Horvitz, June 22, 1969; B.A., Brown U., 1967; M.A., Temple U., 1970; Ph.D., U. Ala., 1972; intern clin. psychology U. Minn., 1972. Instr. psychology U. Ala., Tuscaloosa, 1971; asst. prof. psychology U. Wis.-Milw., 1972—; dir. psychol. services Head Start, Pawtucket, R.I., 1968; psychol. cons., staff child psychology instr. Head Start, Providence, 1969; dir. psychol. services Head Start, East Providence-Bristol County, R.I., 1969; staff psychologist U. Ala. Psychology Clinic, 1971. Bd. dirs. Milw. Mental Health Assn. USPHS fellow U. Ala., 1969-71, NIMH fellow U. Minn., 1971-72; U.Wis. Grad. Sch. research grantee, 1972-74. Mem. Am., Midwestern psychol. assns., Soc. Research in Child Devel. Contbr. articles to profl. jours. Home: 310 E Calumet Rd Fox Point WI 53217 Office: Psychology Dept U Wis Milwaukee WI 53201

PASTIN, MARK JOSEPH, educator; b. Ellwood City, Pa., July 6, 1949; s. Joseph and Patricia Jean (Caminite) P.; B.A. summa cum laude, U. Pitts., 1970; A.M., Harvard U., 1972, Ph.D., 1973; m. JoAnne Marie Reagle, May 30, 1970. Teaching fellow Harvard U., Cambridge, Mass., 1972-73; asst. prof. philosophy Ind. U., Bloomington, 1973-76, asso. prof., 1976—; vis. asst. prof. philosophy Wayne State U., Detroit, 1975; vis. asso. prof. philosophy U. Mich., Ann Arbor, 1978. NSF fellow, 1970-73, Nat. Endowment for Humanities fellow, summer 1975, 76-77. Mem. Am. Philos. Assn., Soc. Exact Philosophy, Internat. Phenomenological Soc., Philosophy of Sci. Assn., Ind. Philos. Assn., Harvard Grad. Sco., Phi Beta Kappa, Phi Eta Sigma. Home: 1921 E 3d St Bloomington IN 47401 Office: Dept Philosophy Sycamore 026 Ind U Bloomington IN 47401

PATCHAK, RUSSELL GEORGE, accountant; b. Chgo., Oct. 10, 1924; s. Joseph E. and Wilhelmina (Washack) P.; B.S. in Bus. Adminstrn., Northwestern U., 1949; C.P.A., U. Ill., 1951; m. Mary Ann Koler, Apr. 26, 1947; children—Randall Richard, Debra Sue. With George W. Peterson & Co., C.P.A.'s, Chgo., 1949-51, Peter Shannon & Co., C.P.A.'s, Chgo., 1951-55; pvt. practice as accountant, Chgo. and Homewood, Ill., 1955—; partner Milano-Patchak & Co., C.P.A.'s, Chgo., 1963-65, Ash Investments, Flossmoor, 1963—; dir. various corps. Served with AUS, 1943-46. Mem. Am. Inst. C.P.A.'s, Ill. Soc. C.P.A.'s, C.P.A.'s of So. Cook County (pres. 1963-64), Computer Accountants Assn. Home: 12634 London Ln Palos Heights IL 60463 Office: Profl Arts Bldg 18227 Harwood Ave Homewood IL 60430

PATEL, ARUN KANTILAL, chem. engr.; b. India, Aug. 9, 1947; s. Kantilal Purushottam and Sushilaben (Kantilal) P.; came to U.S., 1969, permanent resident, 1976; B.E. in Chem. Engring., M.S. Univ., India, 1969; Ph.D. in Chem. Engring., Iowa State U., 1974; m. Hema R. Desai, Apr. 25, 1974. Product devel. engr. Chems. div. U.S. Steel Corp., Ironton, Ohio, 1974-75, process engr., 1975-77, plant engr., 1977—; cons. Mem. Soc. Plastics Engrs., Am. Inst. Chem. Engrs., Phi Kappa Phi, Phi Lambda Upsilon. Club: Lions. Patentee in field. Home: 2701 Edmond Dr Rt 1 Wheelersburg OH 45694 Office: PO Box 127 Ironton OH 45638

PATEL, JAYANT AMBALAL, pharmacist; b. Indore, India, May 23, 1935; s. Ambalal Jeshingbhai and Hiraben Ambalal P.; came to U.S., 1959, naturalized, 1973; B.S. in Chemistry, U. Saugor, 1957, in Pharmacy, 1958; M.S., U. Mich., 1961, Pharm.D., 1966; m. Kala Jashbhai, May 28, 1954; children—Visha, Neeta, Rita, Manish. Pharmacist, Ernest Labs., India, 1958-59, U. Mich., Ann Arbor, 1961; pharmacist, dir. drug analysis lab. Univ. Hosp., Ann Arbor, 1964—. Recipient grant Roche Co., 1969, Achievement award Am. Soc. Hosp. Pharmacists Research Edn. Found., 1976; registered pharmacist, Mich. Mem. Am. Soc. Hosp. Pharmacists (contbg. editor jour.), AAAS, Rho Chi. Hindu. Home: 474 Larkspur St Ann Arbor MI 48105 Office: 1601 Ann St Ann Arbor MI 48109

PATEL, LOK NATH, metall. and materials engr.; b. Kuntara, India, June 1, 1943; s. Kamal Lochan and Khatkuri (Nayak) P.; came to U.S., 1969, naturalized, 1977; B.S., Utkal U., 1965; B.S., Indian Inst. Tech., 1968; M.S., U. Tenn., Knoxville, 1977; M.S., Va. Poly. Inst., 1973; m. Basanti Patel, Jan. 9, 1969; 1 dau., Veena. Materials and processes engr., nuclear power generation div. Babcock & Wilcox Co., Lynchburg, Va., 1973-75; materials and metal. engr. John Deere & Co., Moline, Ill., 1977—. ASG Glass Industries fellow, 1971-73; Nat. Merit scholar, 1961-68. Mem. Am. Soc. Metals, Am. Inst. Mining Metall. Engrs., Am. Welding Soc., Am. Ceramic Soc. Contbr. articles to profl. jours. Home: 3614 25th St Moline IL 61265 Office: John Deere Co 501 3d Ave Moline IL 61265

PATEL, MADHU, architect; b. Adalaj, India, Oct. 25, 1941; s. Ottambhai Shanabhai and Chanchalben Lallubhai P.; came to U.S., 1968, naturalized, 1977; diploma in fine arts Govt. Gujrat (India), 1965; B.Arch., Maharaja Sayajirao U. of Baroda, 1966; M.S., Ill. Inst. Tech., 1969; m. Ludinila Bustamante, Mar. 14, 1971; 1 child, Nigam Madhusudan. Designer, Warwick Electronics, Chgo., 1969-70, Zenith Radio Corp., Chgo., 1971-74; tech. advisor Ill. Dept. Transp., 1976-77; also co-dir. Gov.'s Info. Center for Asian Assistance; designer R.J. MacDonald Internat. Corp., Skokie, Ill.; cons., lectr. in field. Mem. bd. advisors Asian Am. Community Legal Aid Clinic, Chgo., 1976—. Mem. Indian Inst. Architects (asso. 1966-69), Gujrat Cultural Assn. (Chgo.). Home: 920 Lakeside Pl #2401 Chicago IL 60640

PATEL, PRAVINCHANDRA VALLABHBHAI, microbiologist; b. Ahmedabad, India, Sept. 1, 1935; d. Vallabhbhai Lallubhai and Sakerben Vallabhbhai P.; came to U.S., 1970; B.S. in Microbiology, Gujarat U., India, 1957, M.S. in Indsl. Microbiology, 1959; Ph.D. in Applied Microbiology, U. Stratchclyde, Glasgow, Scotland, 1968; m. Jotilaben Patel, Feb. 2, 1964; children—Hitashvi, Preya. Microbiologist, Baroda, India, 1959-65; research fellow McMaster U., Hamilton, Ont., Can., 1969-71; bacteriologist No. Ohio Med. Lab., Cleve., 1972-74; clin. microbiologist Woman's Gen. Hosp., Cleve., 1974—. Can. NRC research fellow, 1969-71. Mem. Am. Soc. Microbiology, Am. Acad. Microbiology, Soc. Indsl. Microbiology. Home: 1632 Joann Dr Parma OH 44134

PATEL, RAMESH BALDEVBHAI, architect-urbanist; b. Sandakan, North Borneo, Sept. 24, 1937; s. Baldevbhai Mathurbhai and Chanchalben (Baldevbhai) P.; B.Arch., Maharaja Sayajirao U., Baroda, India, 1961; M.Arch., Yale, 1964; postgrad. Harvard; m. Ranjana Purushottamdas, June 14, 1966; children—Neesha, Neeshad. Architect, Vastushilpa, India, 1961-63; designer Perry, Dean, Hepburn & Stewart, Boston, 1964-66; sr. designer Richardson Assos., Seattle, 1966-71; chief designer The Cannon Partnership, Buffalo, 1971-72; design architect John Portman & Assos., Atlanta, 1972-74; dir. design and planning P.C., Inc., Atlanta, 1974—; asso. Paul Rudolph and Kenzo Tange, 1963, 66. Tchr., Sch. Arch., Ahmedabad, India, 1962-63; active Vista, Washington, Bd. Profl. Personnel UN. Mem. Royal Inst. Brit. Architects, AIA, AIP, Nat. Council Archtl. Registration. Recipient award Tourist Center competition, Ahmedabad; runner up Art Center competition, Berkeley, Calif. Contbr. designs to nat. and internat. publs. Home: 5369 Bahama Terr #10 Cincinnati OH 45223

PATEL, VIRENDRA CHATURBHAI, engineer; b. Mombasa, Kenya, Nov. 9, 1938; s. Chaturbhai S. and Kantaben N. (Rai) P.; came to U.S., 1969; naturalized 1975; B.Sc., with honors, Imperial Coll., London, 1962; Ph.D., Cambridge (Eng.) U., 1965; m. Manjula Patel, May 29, 1966; children—Sanjay, Bindiya. Sr. asst. in research Cambridge U., 1965-69; vis. prof. Indian Inst. Tech., Kharagpur, India, 1966; cons. Lockheed Ga. Co., Marietta, 1969-70; asst. prof. energy engring. U. Iowa, Iowa City, 1971-72, asso. prof., 1972-75, prof., 1975—, chmn. div. energy engring., 1976—, research engr. Iowa Inst. Hydraulic Research, 1971—; cons. in field; mem. Iowa Gov.'s Science Adv. Council, 1977—. Mem. Am. Inst. Aeros. and Astronautics, ASME, Sigma Chi. Author: Three Dimensional Turbulent Boundary Layers, 1972; contbr. articles to profl. jours. Home: 1212 Teg Dr Iowa City IA 52240 Office: Div Energy Engring Univ Iowa Iowa City IA 52242

PATHAK, DEV S., mktg. analyst, educator; b. Ahmedabad, India, Nov. 18, 1942; s. Shankerlal C. and Champa S. (Raval) P.; came to U.S., 1965, naturalized, 1975; LL.B., Gujarat U., India, 1965; M.S. in Econs., So. Ill. U., 1966; M.B.A. in Mktg., Mich. State U., 1969, D.B.A., 1972; m. Diane L. Dallas, Nov. 21, 1970; 1 son, Jay Ryan. Instr. Saginaw Valley Coll., University Center, Mich., 1970-71, asst. prof., 1971-73; asst. prof. Phila. Coll. of Textiles and Sci., 1973-74, also dir. Inst. for Research in Textile Mktg., 1973-74; asso. prof. Appalachian State U., Boone, N.C., 1974-76, asso. dir. Bur. Econ. and Bus. Research, 1975-76; asso. prof. pharmacy adminstrn. dept. Ohio State U., Columbus, 1976—; mktg. cons. Fla. Internat., Whirlpool, Inc., Second Nat. Bank of Saginaw, Walgreen Drug Stores, Health Info. Design, Inc. Mem. Am. Collegiate Retailing Assn., Acad. of Mgmt., Assn. for Consumer Research, Am. Mktg. Assn., Am. Assn. Colls. of Pharmacy, Am. Inst. for Decision Scis. (acad. affairs com. 1975-77). Author: Student Involvement Guide to Accompany Marketing Principles: The Management Process, 1977; contbr. articles on mktg., mgmt. and consumer research to profl. publs. Home: 912 Middlebury Dr Worthington OH 43085 Office: College of Pharmacy Ohio State Univ Columbus OH 43210

PATHE, ANTONE PETER, mfg. co. exec.; b. Lorain, Ohio, Apr. 23, 1929; s. Anton and Veronica (Torma) P.; A.B., Miami U., Oxford, Ohio, 1951; B.B.A., Bowling Green State U., 1956; M.B.A. (Sears Roebuck fellow), U. Chgo., 1957; m. Geraldine M. Vargo, Dec. 30, 1950. Supr. data processing Westinghouse Electric Corp., Lima, Ohio, 1957-61, mgr. data processing, Cleve., 1961-65; dir. fin. services Whitehead & Kales Co., Detroit, 1965—. Dist. commr. Boy Scouts Am., 1970, dist. vice chmn., 1971-72. Served with AUS, 1952-54.

Mem. Am. Mgmt. Assn., Assn. Systems Mgmt. (Distinguished Service award 1977; div. dir. 1971-73, internat. membership chmn. 1972-73, internat. dir. 1973-76), Tau Kappa Epsilon, Sigma Gamma Epsilon. Roman Catholic. Clubs: K.C., Woodmen of World. Home: 739 John Daly Rd Dearborn Heights MI 48127 Office: 58 Haltiner St River Rouge MI 48218

PATRICK, DANIEL RAY, dentist; b. Hope, Mich., Mar. 1, 1940; s. Burton Edward and Ardieth Louise (Patterson) P.; A.B., Ind. U., 1963, D.D.S., 1967, postgrad., 1967-69; m. Jacquelyn Sue Ray, Oct. 14, 1960; children—Michael Ray, Sean Ray. Instr. crown and bridge dept. Ind. U. Sch. Dentistry, Indpls., 1967-69; practice dentistry, Brownsburg, Ind., 1969-73, Kokomo, Ind., 1969—. Mem. Am., Ind. dental assns., Wabash Valley Dist., Howard County dental socs., Am. Acad. Gen. Dentistry, Internat. Coll. Oral Implantology, Am. Acad. Implant Dentistry, Acad. Dentistry for Handicapped, Kokomo C. of C., Omicron Kappa Upsilon. Clubs: Kokomo Y's Men, Elks, Kokomo Country. Home: 5601 4 Mile Dr Kokomo IN 46901 Office: 3423 A S LaFountain St Kokomo IN 46901

PATRICOSKI, THOMAS STANLEY, physician; b. Mt. Carmel, Pa., May 8, 1932; s. Peter Paul and Elien (De Manincor) P.; B.S., St. Vincent Coll., 1959; M.D., Jefferson Med. Coll., 1963; m. Marie L. Andruscauage, Oct. 24, 1953; children—Paul, Michael, Ann, Christopher, Matthew, Amy, Joseph, Eve, Joy. Intern, Little Co. of Mary Hosp., Evergreen Park, Ill., 1963-64; practice medicine specializing in family medicine, Chgo., 1974—; sr. attending physician Little Co. Mary Hosp., 1964—, chmn. dept. family practice, 1972-77, pres.-elect staff, 1978-79; sr. attending mem. dept. family practice St. George Hosp., Chgo., 1969-72, Palos Community Hosp., Palos Heights, Ill., 1972—. Served to 1st lt. Med. Service Corps, U.S. Army, 1952-57. Diplomate Am. Bd. Family Practice. Fellow Am. Acad. Family Physicians; mem. AMA, Ill., Chgo. (pres. Calumet br. 1971) med. socs., Cath. Physicians Guild, Ill. Acad. Family Physicians (pres. Beverly chpt. 1974—), N.W.T. Med. Assn., A. Louis Rosi Med. Soc. (Guadalajara, Mex.). Club: Salmon Unltd. Home: 12210 S 86th Ave Palos Park IL 60464 Office: 11110 Sawyer Ave Chicago IL 60655

PATTEN, THOMAS HENRY, JR., educator; b. Cambridge, Mass., Mar. 24, 1929; s. Thomas Henry and Lydia Mildred (Lindgren) P.; A.B., Brown U., 1953; M.S., Cornell U., 1955, Ph.D., 1959; m. Jule Ann Nichols, Aug. 27, 1972. Dir. program planning Ford Motor Co., Dearborn, Mich., 1957-65; prof. mgmt. and sociology U. Detroit, 1965-67; prof. orgnl. behavior and personnel mmgt. Sch. Labor and Indsl. Relations Mich. State U., 1967—; cons. in field. Served with USMC, 1946-48. Mem. Indsl. Relations Research Assn. (pres. chpt. 1970-71), Am. Soc. Tng. and Devel. (chmn. orgn. devel. div. 1972), Am. Sociol. Assn., Internat. Personnel Mgmt. Assn., Inst. Applied Behavioral Sci., Acad. Mgmt., Am. Compensation Assn. Clubs: Fourth Estate (Boston); Mich. State U. Faculty. Author: The Foreman: Forgotten Man of Management, 1968; Manpower Planning and the Development of Human Resources, 1971; OD-Emerging Dimensions and Concepts, 1973; A Bibliography of Compensation Planning and Administration, 1960-1974, 1975; Pay: Employee Compensation and Incentive Plans, 1977. Home: 4423 Wausau Rd Okemos MI 48864

PATTERSON, CHARLES WARD, physician; b. Santa Monica, Calif., June 3, 1939; s. Charles Everett and Martha Frances (French) P.; B.S., Calif. State Poly. U., 1962; M.D., U. Louisville, 1966; m. Elizabeth Wall, June 4, 1966 (div. May 1976); children—Charles Michael, Laura Elizabeth; m. 2d, Janet Sue Beatty, Aug. 5, 1977. Intern, Bethesda Hosp., Cin.; psychiat. resident Rollman Psychiat. Inst., Cin., 1967-70; practice medicine specializing in psychiatry, Middletown, Ohio, 1970—; mem. staff Middletown Hosp., dir. psychiat. services, 1976—; asst. clin. prof. psychiatry Wright State U., 1975—. Mem. Butler County (Ohio) Republican Exec. Com., 1974—. Served to capt., M.C., USAFR. Recipient Continuing Edn. award AMA, 1972, 75, Distinguished Alumni award Calif. State Poly. U., 1972. Mem. Am. Psychiat. Soc., Am. Soc. Social Psychiatry, Ohio State, Butler County (chmn. legis. com. 1973-74) med. socs. Home: 1807 N Briel Blvd Middletown OH 45042 Office: Suite 505 Cin Gas and Electric Co Bldg Middletown OH 45042

PATTERSON, GLORIA JEAN, counselor; b. Toledo, Nov. 18, 1941; d. Joseph Bankert and Wilhelmina (Pistole) Sprinkle; B.A., Olivet Nazarene Coll., 1965; M.Ed. in Counseling, U. Toledo, 1975; m. Charles Leon Patterson, Oct. 1, 1966. Tchr., Toledo Pub. Schs., 1963-64, substitute tchr., 1970-75; tchr. Mason (Mich.) Consol. Schs., 1964-66; job developer Concentrated Employment Program, Toledo, 1968-70; counselor St. Joseph Central Catholic High Sch., Fremont, Ohio, 1976—. Adviser sr. scouts Maumee Valley council Girl Scouts U.S.A. Mem. Am., Ohio personnel and guidance assns., Am. Sch. Counselor Assn., NAACP. Methodist. Club: Bay View Yacht. Home: 3134 Kimball Ave Toledo OH 43610 Office: 702 Croghan St Fremont OH 43420

PATTERSON, HARLAN RAY, educator; b. Camden, Ohio, June 27, 1931; s. Ernest Newton and Beulah Irene (Hedrick) P.; B.S., Miami U., 1953, M.B.A., 1959; Ph.D., Mich. State U., 1963; m. Carol Lee Reighard, July 31, 1970; children—Kristan Lee (previous marriage), Leslie, Nolan Gene. Asst. prof. finance U. Ill. at Urbana, 1962-66; asso. prof. finance Ohio U., Athens, 1966-77, prof., 1977—. Research projects for Bank of Am., Morgan Guaranty Trust, Am. Investment Corp., City Pub. Service Bd. of San Antonio. Chmn. Athens adv. bd., Ohio State scholarship com. of Rainbow for Girls. Served with USN, 1953-56. Stonier fellow, 1961; Found. Econ. Edn. fellow, 1965, 67, 69, 71; vis. prof., fellow Chgo. Merc. Exchange, 1971. Mem. Phi Beta Kappa, Beta Gamma Sigma, Phi Eta Sigma, Omicron Delta Epsilon, Pi Kappa Alpha, Alpha Kappa Psi. Republican. Mason (32 deg., Shriner). Contbr. articles in field to profl. jours. Home: 17 LaMar Dr Athens OH 45701

PATTERSON, JAMES MCCOY, oil co. exec.; b. Shanghai, China, Nov. 25, 1915 (parents Am. citizens); s. Lorenzo Dow and Annie Clark (McCoy) P.; B.S., Birmingham So. Coll., 1936; M.A., Emory U., 1937; postgrad. Columbia U., 1938-39; m. Naomi Comstock, May 16, 1941; children—James McCoy, William Comstock, David Bain, John Scott. Asst. to dir. research and statistics Nat. council Boy Scouts, N.Y., 1937-40, field scout exec., Atlanta, 1940-42; supr. youth and ednl. activities Standard Oil Co., Chgo., 1946-51, mgr. field services, 1951-58; dir. pub. relations Am. Oil Co., N.Y., 1958-61, Chgo., 1961-63, 65-73, spl. assignment mktg. dept., Eau Claire, Wis., 1963-65; mgr. pub. affairs services Standard Oil Co. (Ind.), Chgo., 1973—. Mem. Rich Twp. Bd. Edn., 1949-58, 67—, pres., 1956-58; mem. Ill Gov.'s Adv. Council, 1968-73; mem. pub. relations com. Nat. council Boy Scouts Am., 1963—, mem. area council exec. bd., 1961—, v.p. Calumet Area council, 1969-76, recipient Silver Beaver award, 1972. Mem. Ill. Election Laws Commn., 1975—; bd. regents Ill. Colls. and Univs., 1972—. Served to lt. comdr. USNR, 1942-46. Recipient citation and medal U.S. Dept. Agr., 1955. Mem. Am. Petroleum Inst., Pub. Relations Soc. Am., Ill C. of C., Chgo. Assn. Commerce and Industry. Republican. Methodist. Club: Olympia Fields (Ill.) Country. Home: 401 Brookwood Terr Olympia Fields IL 60461 Office: 200 E Randolph St Chicago IL 60601

PATTERSON, LAWRENCE THOMAS, II, cons. economist; b. Cin., Aug. 8, 1937; s. Lawrence Thomas and Helen Adelaid (Wintering) P.; B.S. cum laude, Miami U. Oxford, Ohio, 1957; postgrad Wharton Sch. U. Pa., 1958; M.B.A., U. Mich., 1959; m. Diessla Stauffer, Aug. 8, 1966; children—Page Patrick, Lawrence Thomas III, Blake Shannon. Sec.-treas. P-G Products, Inc., 1959-60; with Arrington Van Pelt Mgmt. Cons., 1960-61; founder, pres. Patterson Internat. Corp., Cin., 1964-75, Am. Youth Mktg. Corp., Cin., 1969-75; publisher, estate planning cons. L.T. Patterson Strategy Letter, Cin., 1974—. Chmn., Center for Fin. Freedom, 1977—. Served with USAF, 1961-62: Berlin. Mem. Internat. Assn. Fin. Planners (life), Am. Numis. Assn. (life), Com. for Monetary Research and Edn., Phi Beta Kappa, Phi Eta Sigma. Publisher: Freedom Fighter Index, 1975; The Conspiracy Theory Catalog, 1975. Author: Swiss Real Estate and How to Retire in Switzerland, 1977. Home: 6785 East Beechlands Dr Cincinnati OH 45237 Office: Box 37432 Cincinnati OH 45237

PATTERSON, LUCILLE JOAN, author, lyricist, educator; b. Chgo.; d. William Leon and Hortense Adele (Brooks) Washington; B.A., DePaul U., 1962; M.A., Northeastern Ill. U., 1973; m. Owen J. Patterson II, June 17, 1956 (div.); children—Karin Janine, Owen Jeremiah III. Tchr. English, speech, Spanish, journalism and Afro-Am. lit. Chgo. Pub. Schs., 1962-66, 68—, Cook County Dept. Pub. Aid, 1966-68; Upward Bound tchr. Barat Coll., Lake Forest, Ill., 1976, Loyola U., Chgo., 1977; chairperson dept. English, Carver Area High Sch., 1977-78; instr. Chgo. Sun-Times Tchr. Inst., 1974-76; dir., founder Young Peoples Writers Workshop. Recipient award for contbns. to arts and letters Nat. News Media Women, 1974, award for contbns. to journalism Loyola U. Upward Bound Program, 1977. Mem. Nat. council Tchrs. of English, Ill. Speech and Theatre Assn., Assn. Study of Afro-Am. Life and History. Episcopalian. Club: English of Greater Chgo. Author: Sapphire (poetry), 1972; Moon in Black (poetry and short stories), 1974. Songwriter for Curtis Prince Jazz ensemble. Daughter of the Hawk, 1975; Windy City Rhythms, 1975; Raindrops and Mud Puddles, 1977. Home: 8555 S Prairie Ave Chicago IL 60619 Office: 13100 S Doty Ave Chicago IL 60627

PATTERSON, MICHAEL MILTON, educator; b. Muscatine, Iowa, Mar. 17, 1942; s. Harvey Milton and Vivienne Doris Ann (Bridgeman) P.; B.A., Grinnell Coll., 1964; postgrad. (teaching and research asst.) Ind. U., 1964-66; Ph.D. (Nat. Inst. Mental Health fellow), U. Iowa, 1969; m. Janice Pauline Ficke, June 11, 1966; children—Michael Shane, Shad Milton. Research instr., also NIMH postdoctoral fellow U. Calif. at Irvine, 1969-71; asst. prof. Calif. State Coll., Dominguez Hills, 1970, 71; asst. prof. physiology Kirksville (Mo.) Coll. Osteo. Medicine, 1971-75, asso. prof., 1975-77, cons. to dean for preclin. scis. and research, 1972-75; dir. research, asso. prof. psychology and osteo. medicine Coll. Osteo. Medicine, Ohio U., Athens, 1977—; editorial cons. Behavior Research Methods and Instrumentation, 1971—, Physiology and Behavior, 1972—, Physiol. Psychology, 1973, Animal Learning and Behavior, 1973—; grant reviewer NIH, NSF, 1970—. Mem. Am. Inst. Biol. Scis., Am., Midwestern psychol. assns., Psychonomic Soc., Interam. Soc. Psychology, Soc. for Neuroscis., Sigma Xi. Republican. Mem. Disciples of Christ. Club: Kiwanis. Editor: (with Richard F. Thompson) Recording of Bioelectric Potentials, 1973; contbr. articles on psychology and psychobiology to profl. jours. Home: 88 Wonder Hills Dr Athens OH 45701 Office: Coll of Osteo Medicine Ohio Univ Athens OH 45701

PATTERSON, RICHARD GEORGE, engring. co. exec.; b. Cascade, Iowa, May 26, 1928; s. George Samuel and Mary Anna (Heffernen) P.; B.S. in Elec. Engring., Purdue U., 1949, M.S. in Elec. Engring., 1950; m. Jeanne Lundberg, Oct. 10, 1953; children—Christa, Courtney. Project engr. Honeywell Inc., Mpls., 1956-66, sec. head, 1966-68, engring. mgr., 1968-72, sec. head, 1972-74, engring. mgr. 1974—. Mem. Am. Inst. Aeronautics and Astronautics, Tau Beta Pi, Eta Kappa Nu. Roman Catholic. Patentee autothrottle, servo loop synchronizer. Home: 4336 Avondale Rd Minneapolis MN 55416 Office: 2600 Ridgway Pkwy Minneapolis MN 55413

PATTERSON, RICHARD HENRY, psychiatrist; b. Milw., June 15, 1931; s. Richard John and Gertrude (Biegel) P.; B.S., Marquette U., 1953, M.D., 1956. Intern, St. Joseph's Hosp., Milw., 1956-57; psychiat. resident Colo. Psychopathic Hosp., Denver, 1957-58, The Asso. Psychiat. Tng. Program Milw., 1960-62; staff psychiatrist Milw. Sanitarium Found.; practice medicine specializing in psychiatry, Milw., 1962—; sec., treas. Philstan Corp., health care study group; cons. Social Security Adminstrn., Bur. Hearings and Appeals, 1966—. Served to capt. M.C., USAF, 1958-60. Diplomate Am. Bd. Psychiatry and Neurology. Mem. AMA, Am., Wis. (chmn. 3d party payments com.; mem. peer standards rev. com. Milw. chpt., pres.-elect) psychiat. assns., Med. Soc. Milw. County (surg. care operating com. Blue Shield Plan). Home: 13145 Dunwoody Dr Elm Grove WI 53122 Office: 111 E Wisconsin Ave Milwaukee WI 53202

PATTERSON, SHIRLEY LOUISE, counselor, educator; b. Rankin, Tex., July 22, 1933; d. William Fush and Mary Emma (Cunningham) P.; B.A., N. Tex. State U., 1955; M.A., McCormick Theol. Sem., 1957; M.S.W., U. Kans., 1964; postgrad. U. Wis., 1969-71. Social worker Kan. State Reception and Diagnostic Center, Topeka, 1964-65; dir. Cross Lines Family Counseling Center, Kansas City, Kans., 1965-66; faculty U. Kans. Sch. Social Welfare, Lawrence, 1966—, asso. prof., 1975—; cons. Topeka VA Hosp., 1971-72, Prairie View Mental Health Center, 1971, NIMH Research Project, 1969-71. Mem. Nat. Assn. Social Workers, Acad. Certified Social Workers, Gerontol. Soc., AAUP, Council on Social Work Edn. Contbr. articles to profl. jours. Home: 1320 NW Menninger Rd Topeka KS 66618

PATTERSON, THELMA K. (MRS. JOHN E. PATTERSON), polit. worker; ed. Grand Rapids, Mich.; m. John E. Patterson; children—Maureen (Mrs. George E. Phillips), Sharon (Mrs. Philip F. Burns), Kathleen (Mrs. Ronald L. Gulch), Dennis B. Engaged in real estate bus., 1951—; with Arlan Ley Realtors, Grand Rapids, 1962—. Pres., Kent County Democratic Womens Club, 1959-60, 1966-67, also sec., dir., mem. exec. bd.; past mem. exec. bd. Fifth Congl. Dist. Orgn.; past mem. Mich. Dem. Central Com.; mem. North Kent Dem. Club; del. numerous county and state Dem. convs.; campaign mgr. in various state and nat. elections; vice chmn. Kent County Bd. Election Canvassers, 1963—. Pres., Claudian League for Crippled Children of St. Mary's Hosp., 1962-63, 65-66, treas., 1968-69; trustee Claudian League for Crippled Children of Indian Trails Camp, 1970-72; past v.p. So. Deanery Council Catholic Women. Bd. dirs. Indian Trails Camp for Crippled Children. Mem. Mich. Real Estate Assn. (asso.), Nat. Realtors Assn., Internat. Platform Assn., Nat. Assn. for Female Execs., Nat. Bus. Womens Assn., Smithsonian Assos., Grand Rapids Real Estate Bd. Roman Catholic (past co-chmn. St. Anne's Circle, mem. Womens Guild, Home and Sch. Assn.). Mem. Elks Aux. Address: 500 SE Glenwood Ave Grand Rapids MI 49506

PATTERSON, TOMMY WAYNE, clin. psychologist; b. Frederick, Okla., Sept. 12, 1931; s. Walter R. and Dena Belle (Adams) P.; B.A., U. Okla., 1953, M.S., 1956; Ph.D., U. Nebr., 1963; m. Naomi Ann Bruey, Jan. 22, 1961; children—David Wayne, Carol Sue. Asst. psychologist Lincoln (Nebr.) State Hosp., 1962-63; asso. prof. psychology Colo. State U., Ft. Collins, 1963-71; chief psychology service VA Hosp., Topeka, 1971—; pvt. practice psychology, 1965—; adj. prof. psychology Washburn U., U. Kans.; bd. dirs. Colo. Assn. Mental Health, 1967-69; pres. Larimer County Mental Health Assn., 1968-69. Chmn. Larico Village, 1969-70. Served with AUS, 1953-55. Recipient superior performance award VA, 1975; Vocational Adminstrn. grantee; NIH biol. sci. support grantee; Faculty Improvement grantee; licensed psychologist, Colo. Diplomate Am. Bd. Profl. Psychology; certified psychologist, Kans. Mem. Am., Southwestern psychol. assns., Psi Chi. Club: Masons. Cons. editor Profl. Psychology, 1976—, Jour. Personality Assessment, 1972—; contbr. articles to profl. jours. Home: 2015 Birchwood Ln Topeka KS 66604 Office: Veterans Administration Hospital 2200 Gage Blvd Topeka KS 66622

PATTERSON, VIRGINIA NORRELL, physician; b. Dallas, Sept. 23, 1917; d. Leiland Augustus and Marie Elnore (Hilliard) Norrell; A.B., Tex. State Coll. Women, 1939; B.S., U. Ill., 1947, M.D., 1949; m. John V. Patterson, Dec. 20, 1952 (div. Oct. 1961); 1 son, John V. III. Intern, St. Barnabas Hosp., Mpls., 1949-50; practice medicine, Brunswick, Ga., 1953-55; resident radiology DePaul Hosp., Norfolk, Va., 1955-57; resident U. Ill. Hosp., 1958, asst. radiologist, 1959-65, asso. radiologist, 1965—, chief nuclear medicine sect., 1959; asso. prof. radiology U. Ill., after 1965, prof. clin. radiology, 1976-77, ret., asso. radiologist, dir. sect. nuclear medicine, 1959-77; cons. radiologist Chgo. State Tb Sanitorium, 1962-63; cons. nuclear medicine Delnor Hosp., St. Charles, Ill., 1973—, diagnostic radiology, 1977—. Served to lt. USNR, 1950-53. Diplomate Am. Bd. Radiology, Am. Bd. Nuclear Medicine. Mem. Am. Coll. Nuclear Medicine (charter), Soc. Nuclear Medicine, Am. Coll. Radiology, A.M.A., Am. Med. Women's Assn., D.A.R. Nat. Geneal. Soc., New Eng. Hist. Geneal. Soc., Alpha Omega Alpha. Baptist (trustee 1967-70). Home: 1111 E Illinois St Wheaton IL 60187

PATTERSON, WARD LAMONT, clergyman, writer, artist; b. Killbuck, Ohio, Dec. 26, 1933; s. Raymond Floyd and Florence May (Crosby) P.; A.B., Cin. Bible Sem., 1956, M.A., 1958; M.S., Ft. Hays (Kans.) State Coll., 1959. Ordained to ministry Christian Ch., 1958; instr. Ft. Hays State Coll., 1959-60; asso. minister 1st Christian Ch., Springfield, Ohio, 1955; minister Antioch Christian Ch., Montgomery, Ind., 1956-58, Hays (Kans.) Christian Ch., 1959-60; Rotary student exchange fellow U. Melbourne (Australia), 1960-61; asso. minister Ind. U. Campus Christian Ministry, 1974-75, minister, 1976—; instr. speech Ind. U., 1974-75; travel lectr. Knife anf Fork Clubs. Author: Yesterday/Today, 1974; Struggle, Crisis and Victory, 1976; At the Testing Tree, 1977; contbr. articles to religious jours.; developer technique for doing rubbings of archaeol. designs; exhibitor art shows. Home: 4166 Belle Ave Bloomington IN 47401 Office: 707 E 8th St Bloomington IN 47401

PATTERSON, WILLIAM JAMES, real estate broker; b. Columbus, Ohio, Aug. 26, 1934; s. Merle B. and Margaret Ethel (Lynn) P.; B.S., Ohio State U., 1956; postgrad. Wright State U., 1960; m. Linda Sue Bower, May 24, 1958; children—Jeffrey Alan, Cheryl Lynn, Steven Todd. With mktg. dept. Ohio Bell Telephone Co., Toledo, 1959-61, long distance ops. dept., Dayton, 1961-66, long distance ops. dept., Springfield, 1966-67, mem. comptroller's staff, Cleve., 1967-70; asst. dir. property mgmt. Multicon Properties, Inc., Columbus, 1970-74; pres. Patterson Merkle & Assos., Inc., property mgmt. and real estate, Columbus, 1974—. Adviser 4-H Clubs, 1972-75; mem. sponsoring com. All Am. Youth Horse Show, 1972-76. Served as 1st lt. U.S. Army, 1957-59. Certified property mgr. Mem. Nat., Ohio, Columbus bds. realtors, Inst. Real Estate Mgrs., Columbus Apt. Assn. (dir.), Ohio State U. Alumni Club, Am. Horse Show Assn., Am., Ohio quarter horse assns., Fellowship Christian Athletes. Clubs: River Ridge Riding, Chatham. Home: 2179 Fairfax Rd Columbus OH 43221 Office: 941 Chatham Ln Suite 100 Columbus OH 43221

PATTERSON, WILLIS CHARLES, bass; b. Ann Arbor, Mich., Nov. 27, 1930; s. James (stepfather) and Kathleen (Gulley) P.; m. Frankie Audreymae Bouyer, June 21, 1958; children—Sharon Lynelle, Kevin Charles, Shelia Kathleen; B.Mus., U. Mich., 1958, M.Mus., 1959. Instr. music So. U., Baton Rouge, 1959-61; asst. prof. music Va. State Coll., Petersburg, 1962-68; prof. music U. Mich., Ann Arbor, 1968-71, prof. music, dir. Mens Glee Club, 1970-75, prof. music, chmn. voice dept., 1976—; profl. bass soloist with orchs. throughout U.S.; song recitalist. Mem. Ann Arbor Citizens Recreation Adv. Com., 1970-76, State Council of Arts Music Adv. Com., 1974—. Mem. Nat. Assn. Tchrs. Singing, Nat. Assn. Negro Musicians, NAACP, Alpha Phi Alpha, Rotary Club. Recipient Marian Anderson award for singers, 1959; Fulbright grantee, 1965-66; Author: Anthology of Art Songs of Black American Composers, 1977. Home: 2906 Brandywine Blvd Ann Arbor MI 48104

PATTIS, S. WILLIAM, publisher; b. Chgo., July 3, 1925; s. William Robert and Rose (Quint) P.; B.S., U. Ill., 1949; postgrad. Northwestern U.; m. Bette Z. Levin, July 16, 1950; children—Mark Robert, Robin Lynn. Exec. v.p., pub. United Bus. Publs., 1949-59; pres. The Pattis Group, 1959—, Nat. Textbook Co., Skokie, Ill., 1961—; dir. Bank of Highwood (Ill.), New Century Bank, Mundelein, Ill.; v.p. Pattis-Hirsch Internat., Miami, Fla.; pres. Wartell-Pattis Co., N.Y.C. Mem. Pres.'s Council Youth Opportunity, 1968-70; bd. dirs. Photography Youth Found., Expt. Internat. Living; Chgo. bd. dirs. Brandeis U. Served with C.E., AUS, 1943-46; ETO. Recipient human relations award Am. Jewish Community, 1971. Clubs: Standard, Monroe (Chgo.); Northmoor Country (Highland Park, Ill.); N. Shore Racquet (Northbrook, Ill.); Tennis (Palm Springs, Calif.). Home: 195 Elder Ln Highland Park IL 60035 Office: 4761 W Touhy Ave Lincolnwood IL 60646

PATTISHALL, BEVERLY WYCKLIFFE, lawyer; b. Atlanta, May 23, 1916; s. Leon Jackson and Margaret Simkins (Woodfin) P.; B.S., Northwestern U., 1938; J.D., U. Va., 1941; m. Nancy Jane Hansen, Sept. 13, 1947 (div. Nov. 1974); children—Margaret Ann Arthur, Leslie Hansen, Beverly Wyckliffe, Paige Terhune, Woodfin Underwood. Admitted to Ill. bar, 1941, D.C. bar, 1971, practiced in Chgo., 1941—; mem. firm Pattishall, McAuliffe & Hofstetter, 1969—; U.S. del. Diplomatic Confs. on Trademark Treaty, Geneva and Vienna, Austria, 1970-73. lectr. trademark, trade identity and unfair trade practices law Northwestern U. Sch. Law. Bd. dirs. Juvenile Protective Assn. Chgo., 1946—, pres., 1961-63; bd. dirs. Vol. Interagy. Assn., 1975—, sec., 1977—; bd. dirs. Chgo. Bar Found., 1977—. Served to lt. comdr. USNR, 1941-46; PTO, ETO, comdr., ret. Fellow Am. Coll. Trial Lawyers; mem. Internat. Patent and Trademark Assn. (pres. 1935-57, exec. com. 1953—), Am. (chmn. sect. patent, trademark and copyright Law 1963-64, Internat., Ill., Chgo. bar assns., U.S. Trademark Assn. (dir. 1963-65). Clubs: Legal, Law, Econ., Univ., Mid-America (Chgo.); Fox River Valley Hunt. Author: (with Hilliard) Trademarks, Trade Identity and Unfair Trade Practices, 1974; contbr. articles to profl. jours. Home: 505 N Lake Shore Dr Chicago IL 60611 Office: Pattishall McAuliffe & Hofstetter Suite 3500 Prudential Plaza Chicago IL 60601

PATTISON, JEFFRY ALAN, chem. co. exec.; b. Ashtabula, Ohio, Jan. 15, 1950; s. Roy Brown and Lucylle Edith (Thompson) P.; B.S., Capital U., 1972; m. Kathy Lee Peaspanen, June 13, 1970. Chemistry lab. instr. Capital U., Columbus, Ohio, 1972-73; mgr. analytical services Borden Chem. Co., Columbus, 1973-75; v.p. research

Digicolor Inc., Columbus, 1975-76, pres., 1976—, also dir.; dir. Solecon Co.; cons. Century Systems Corp. Mem. adminstrv. bd. Bexley United Methodist Ch. Mem. Am. Chem. Soc., ASTM, Am. Indsl. Hygiene Assn., Ambassadors Nat. Home: 755 Stelzer Rd Box 64 Columbus OH 43219 Office: 3110 N High St Columbus OH 43202

PATTON, AUDLEY EVERETT, ret. bus. exec.; b. Eve, Mo., Nov. 9, 1898; s. Charles Audley and Letitia Virginia (Earhart) P.; B.S. in Indsl. Adminstrn., U. Ill., 1921, M.S. in Bus. Orgn. and Operation, 1922, Ph.D. in Econs., 1924; m. Mabel Dickie Gunnison, Aug. 5, 1930 (dec. Feb. 1976); 1 dau., Julie Ann Patton Watson; m. 2d, Mary Ritchie Key, June 24, 1977. Auditor, Mfg. Dealers Corp., Cambridge, Mass., 1921; instr. econs. pub. utilities U. Ill., Champaign-Urbana, 1924-25, asst. prof. econs. Coll. Commerce and Bus. Adminstrn., 1925-26; asst. to pres. Chgo. Rapid Transit Co., Chgo. South Shore & South Bend R.R. Co., Chgo. North Shore & Milw. R.R. Co., Chgo. Aurora & Elgin R.R. Co., 1926; asst. to pres. Pub. Service Co. No. Ill., Chgo., 1926-43, sec., 1928-52, asst. treas., 1928-44, v.p., 1943-53; v.p., dir. No. Ill. Gas Co., 1953-54; v.p. Commonwealth Edison Co., Chgo., 1952-63, ret., 1963; asst. to pres. Presbyn-St Luke's Hosp., Chgo., 1963-65; former v.p., dir. Big Muddy Coal Co.; past dir. Chgo. & Ill. Midland Ry. Co., Allied Mills, Inc., Am. Gage & Machine Co., Elgin, Ill.; dir. HMW Industries, Inc., Stamford, Conn., 1975—. Bd. dirs. Am. Cancer Soc. Ill. div., 1948-76, pres., 1957-59, chmn. bd., 1959-62, mem. fin. com., 1970-76; bd. dirs. Civic Fedn., 1945-63, v.p., 1954-63; bd. dirs. South Side Planning Bd. Chgo., 1950-58; trustee Christine and Alfred Sonntag Found. for Cancer Research, 1965—. Recipient Am. Cancer Soc. medal, 1951. Mem. U. Ill. Found., U.S. Men's (dir. 1958-62, v.p. 1960-65), Midwest (dir. 1956-60) curling assns., Beta Gamma Sigma, Phi Eta, Delta Sigma Pi, Phi Kappa Phi, Delta Chi. Episcopalian. Clubs: Univ. (dir. 1944-46, treas. 1945-46), Tower (Chgo.); Exmoor Country (Highland Park, Ill.); Chgo. Curling (pres. 1956-57) (Northbrook, Ill.). Contbr. articles to profl. jours. Home: 375 East Oakdale Ave Lake Forest IL 60045

PATTON, EARL DEAN, ednl. adminstr.; b. Eldorado, Ill., Oct. 3, 1922; s. Ernest H. and Lola A. (Overton) P.; certificate So. Ill. Normal U., 1940; B.S. in Edn., So. Ill. U., 1947, M.S. in Edn., 1952; Ed.D., U. Ill., 1962; m. Catherine Gaynelle Dent, Dec. 25, 1948; children—James Kevin, John Brian. Tchr., elementary prin. Gallatin and Saline County Schs., Ill., 1940-43; grad. asst., instr. history So. Ill. U. at Carbondale, 1947-48; supt. schs. City of Shawneetown, Ill., 1948-50; supr. elementary schs., Virginia, Ill., 1950-51; prin. elementary and jr. high sch., Salem, Ill., 1951-53; dir. instrn., asst. supt. and acting supt. schs., Kankakee, Ill., 1953-57; research asso. U. Council Tchr. Edn., U. Ill. at Urbana, asso. dir. Ill. Curriculum Program, Office of Ill. Supt. Pub. Instrn., Springfield, 1957-59; gen. asst. supt. schs., Champaign, Ill., vis. lectr. U. Ill. at Urbana, 1959-63; supt. schs. Culver City (Cal.), Unified Sch. Dist., 1963-69; supt. schs. Dist. 186, Springfield, Ill., 1969-73; adj. prof. ednl. adminstrn. Western Ill. U., Macomb, 1972—; asst. state supt. edn. Ill. Office of Edn., Springfield, 1973-75; head Office of Ombudsman, Ill. Office Edn., Springfield, 1975—. Vis. prof. adminstrn. Sangamon State U., Springfield, 1973—. Mem. instrn. resources councils, equal ednl. opportunity com. Ill. State Supt. of Pub. Instrn., 1962-70, mem. gen. adv. coms., 1962—; research cons. U. Wis. at Milw., 1963, North Central Assn. Colls. and Secondary Schs., 1964. Sacramento County (Calif.) Schs., 1964, Nuclear Sci. Curriculum Project, Calif., 1967, Project Capital, Springfield, 1970-72. Bd. dirs. United Fund, Boy Scouts Am., YMCA, Urban League, Mental Health Assn. Served to capt. AUS, 1943-46. Decorated Bronze Star; named Distinguished Citizen Kankakee C. of C., 1955; recipient Pub. Relation award Sch. Mgmt., Rutgers U., 1961; Distinguished Ednl. Service awards Copley Press, City of Culver City, Los Angeles County Bd. Suprs., 1969; Citizen of Year award Frontiers Internat., 1972-73, Distinguished Service award Ill. Curriculum Council, 1975; Mentor Graham award Ill. Ednl. Consortium, 1977. Mem. NEA, Am. Assn. Sch. Adminstrs., Ill. Sch. Adminstrs. Assn. (pres. 1973, Citation 1974), Nat. Soc. Study of Edn., U. Ill., So. Ill. U. alumni assns., Phi Delta Kappa, Kappa Delta Pi. Mason (32 deg.). Rotarian, Elk. Home: 49 Inverness Rd Springfield IL 62704 Office: 100 N First St Springfield IL 62777

PATTON, HAROLD PRESTON, fine arts cons.; b. Calgary, Alta., Can., Nov. 9, 1929; s. William Lawrence and Ida (Mackey) P.; student Banff Sch. Fine Arts (Alta.), 1948, Vancouver (B.C.) Sch. Fine Art, 1945-50, U. B.C., 1950; m. Eleanor Smith, Sept. 25, 1953; children—Fiona Marri-Margaret, Isabelle Carol-Ann. Came to U.S., 1966. Asst. dir. Calgary Allied Arts Center (Alta., Can.), 1958-60; dir. Vincent Price Gallery, Chgo., 1966-69, London Arts, Detroit, 1970-71; designer theater sets; works exhibited Alta. Soc. Artists, 1960-65, Calgary, 1953, traveling shows, 1960-64; one man shows Vancouver Art Gallery, 1950, Calgary Allied Arts, 1953, Bowness, Alta., 1957; music editor Chicagoland Omnibus, 1967-70, Birmingham Eccentric; lectr. in field; cons. fine arts to architects, industry, museums, 1971—; art cons. S.S. Kresge Internat. Hdqrs., Troy, Mich., Smith Hinchman & Grylls Assos., Architects, A. Kahn & Assos., Architects, City Nat. Bank Detroit, Nat. Bank Detroit, McDowell Gallery, Toronto, Ont.; music reviewer Impressario Mag.; lectr., cons. Haverford (Pa.) Coll., U. Windsor (Ont., Can.); tchr. cultural resources dept. U. Alta. (Can.), Banff, 1973—. Recipient Visual Presentation award Alta. Drama Festival, 1959. Mem. Alta. Soc. Arts, Canadian Mozart Soc. (founder 1956). Author: Correspondence with a Sculptor, 1973. Contbg. columnist Can. newspapers, 1961-66. Home: 51 Holmcrest Trail West Hill ON M1C 1V5 Canada

PATTON, JAMES THOMAS, ednl. cons.; b. Manchester, N.H., Aug. 15, 1923; s. Hugh and Bernice (Jackman) P.; Ph.D., U. Chgo., 1946, M.A. with honors, Oriental Inst., 1952; postgrad. U. Edinburgh (Scotland), 1952-53; m. Dorothy Elizabeth Reinke, July 25, 1947; 1 son, Peter Mark. Research dir. Maine Council of Chs., 1942; minister youth All Souls Congl. Ch., Bangor, Maine, 1941-42, 1st Congl. Ch., Oak Park, Ill., 1944-45, Bryn Mawr Community Ch., Chgo., 1946; minister Crawford Congl. Ch., Chgo., 1947-51; founder with Dr. J. Archie Hargraves, West Side Christian Parish, Chgo., 1952; instr. humanities Chgo. City Coll., 1954-57; asst. to pres. Charles R. Feldstein & Co., Inc., Chgo., 1958-59; asst. to pres., dir. devel. Houston Mus. Natural Sci., 1959-61; regional dir. Alumni Capital Gifts Program, Carleton Coll. Devel. Program, Chgo., 1961-63; dir. central dist. Program for Harvard Medicine, Harvard Med. Sch., 1963-65; cons. St John's Coll., Santa Fe, 1966-67, Crane Found. and Mus. N.Am. Indian, Marathon, Fla., 1967—; asso. dir. Ill. div. ACLU, 1968-72; asso. dir. Roger Baldwin Found., 1968-72; dir. devel. Nat. Coll. Edn., Evanston, Ill., 1972-74; pres. Patton Assos., 1974—; minister congl. chs., Maine, summers 1943-45; lectr. USIS, Edinburgh, Scotland, 1952-53, also with French Priest Workers Movement, Paris, France. Bd. dirs. Planned Parenthood Assn., Chgo. Recipient Certificate of Excellence, 27th Ann. Exhbn., Art Dirs. Club Chgo., 1963; Certificate of Excellence, 36th Ann. Design in Chgo. Printing Exhbn., 1963; Certificate for Services to Harvard Medicine, Harvard Med. Sch., 1965. Mem. Internat. Platform Assn., British Pelargonium and Geranium Soc., Vt. Hist. Soc., Chgo. Soc. Fund Raising Execs., Iron Mask, Delta Upsilon. Conglist. Clubs: Columbia U. (N.Y.C.); Lake Shore, Cliff Dwellers (Chgo.). Home: 222 E Chestnut St Chicago IL 60611

PATTON, NOEL THOMAS, mfg. co. exec.; b. Fort Wayne, Ind., Dec. 16, 1945; s. Bennie Noel and Marcella (Branstrator) P.; B.Philosophy with honors, Ind. U., 1969; postgrad. Harvard Bus. Sch., 1977. Salesman Patton Electric Co., Inc., Fort Wayne, 1967-69, sales mgr., 1969-70, exec. v.p., 1970-73, pres., chmn., 1973—. Chmn. Ind. Students for Robert Kennedy, 1968; campaign dir. Students and Faculties for Birch Bayh, 1968. Rhodes scholar candidate, 1967. Mem. Le Club (N.Y.C.); Eagle (Gstaad, Switzerland); Ferarri. Patentee electric fans. Home: 8227 Westridge Rd Fort Wayne IN 46825 Office: PO Box 128 New Haven IN 46774

PATTON, PETER CLYDE, computer system engr.; b. Wichita, Kans., June 11, 1935; s. Claude and Beryl Inez (Jones) P.; A.B., Harvard U., 1957; M.A., U. Kans., 1959; Dr.Ing., Stuttgart U., 1966; m. Naomi Julia Lawson, Aug. 30, 1957; children—Peter, Claudia, Theresa, Richard, Phillip. Engr., Boeing Aircraft, 1957-58; research engr. Midwest Research Inst., 1958-61; prin. programmer UNIVAC, St. Paul, 1961-62; sci. cons. UNIVAC Internat., Lausanne, Switzerland, 1962-67; mgr. system design UNIVAC, St. Paul, 1967-68; sr. cons. Analysts Internat. Corp., 1969-71; dir. univ. computer center, asso. prof. computer sci., ancient studies, asso. dir. Center for Ancient Studies, U. Minn., 1971—. Fellow Inst. Math. and Its Applications (Eng.); mem. IEEE Computer Soc. (sr.), Assn. Computing Machinery, Am. Inst. Archaeology, Am. Oriental Soc. Contbr. articles to profl. jours.; author: (with K.J. Thurber) Data Structures and Computer Architecture. Home: 3471 Churchill St Saint Paul MN 55112 Office: Univ Computer Center U Minn Minneapolis MN 55455

PATTOU, BRACE, press relations mgr.; b. Chgo., Nov. 18, 1923; s. Albert Brace and Mardo Alice (Peck) P.; A.B., U. Chgo., 1945; m. Suzanne Pirie, July 1, 1964; 1 dau., Edith. Reporter, Chgo. Jour. Commerce, 1944-45, Wis. State Jour., Madison, 1945-47; news editor ABC Radio, Chgo., 1947-51; account exec. Curtis Billings & Assos., Chgo., 1951-56; owner, operator Brace Pattou & Assos., Chgo., 1956-74; mgr. press relations Harris Bank, Chgo., 1974—. Mem. Publicity Club Chgo. (dir. 1977—, Distinguished Service award 1977). Episcopalian. Home: 1448 Lake Shore Dr Chicago IL 60610 Office: 111 W Monroe St Chicago IL 60690

PATTYN, REMI CEASAR, utility co. exec.; b. Chatham, Ont., Can., Jan. 12, 1922; s. Achille J. and Marie (Simoens) P.; brought to U.S., 1927, naturalized, 1932; student Coll. of Wooster, 1944, U.N.C., 1945, Wright Jr. Coll., Chgo., 1947; B.S. in Indsl. Engring., Ill. Inst. Tech., 1950; M.B.A., U. Chgo., 1954; postgrad. Ind. U. Law Sch., 1961; m. Mary Devine, Nov. 10, 1945; children—John Martin, Drew Remi, Lynn Mary, Diane Marie, Carol Ann, Neal Remi. Methods engr. Internat. Register Co., Chgo., 1939-44; acting dir. adminstrn. Chgo. Housing Authority, 1950-52; mgmt. cons. Booz, Allen & Hamilton, Chgo., 1952-56; asst. sec. personnel dir. Chgo. Aerial Industries, Inc., Barrington, Ill., 1956-58; v.p., personnel relations Pub. Service Co. of Ind., Inc., Plainfield, 1958-74, v.p. adminstrv. services, 1974-77, v.p. ops., 1977—. Asso. faculty Ind. U., Purdue U., 1965—; lectr. Ind. Med. Sch., 1967—, Bus. Roundtable, 1970—. Chmn. coordinating com. Ind. Constrn.-Anti-Inflation Roundtable, 1970-76; mem. Nat. Labor Relations Council, State Chambers Commerce, 1971—; mem. 3 Gov.'s Spl. Task Forces, chmn. Ind. Council Econ. Edn., 1973-75. Past bd. dirs. Ind. div. Am. Cancer Soc.; chmn. Ind. fund campaign Ind. Mental Health Assn., 1977—. Served with USNR, 1944-47. Recipient Outstanding Indsl. Engr. Alumnus award Ill. Inst. Tech., 1970, Alumni award of merit, 1976. Mem. Personnel Assn. of Indpls., Ind. Electric Assn. (past pres., indsl. relations adv. council), Am. Soc. Personnel Adminstrn. (pres. Indpls. chpt. 1973-74, chmn. president's nat. council 1977—), Ill. Inst. Tech. Alumni Assn. (dir., pres. Indpls. 1963—), Edison Electric Inst. (past chmn. personnel relations com.), Ind. C. of C. (indsl. relations com.), Delta Lambda Xi. Republican. Roman Catholic. Club: Executive program (Chgo.); Rivera (Indpls.). Home: 728 Round Hill Rd Indianapolis IN 46260 Office: 1000 E Main St Plainfield IN 46168

PAUL, EILEEN SUSAN, brewing co. exec.; b. El Paso, Tex., Nov. 30, 1943; d. Ralph Dewey and Bettie Jane (Payne) P.; B.A., Coll. of Mt. St. Vincent, 1967; postgrad. U. Wis., 1976—. Nat. tng. mgr. Manpower, Inc., Chgo., 1969-71, dir. ops., 1971-73; sales promotion coordinator Miller Brewing Co., Milw., 1973-75, asst. brand mgr., 1975—. Mem. United Fund Speakers' Bur., 1974-76. Mem. Am. Mktg. Assn. (pres. 1975-76, census adv. com. 1977—), Nat. Mgmt. Assn., Tempo. Clubs: Milw. Advt., Toastmasters, Miller Brewing Co. Mgmt. (dir. 1977—). Home: 5305 N Lovers Ln Rd Milwaukee WI 53225 Office: 3939 W Highland Blvd Milwaukee WI 53201

PAUL, ELMER WILLIAM, hosp. cons.; b. Harvard, Ill., July, 20, 1901; s. Harry William and Myrtle May (Maxon) P.; B.A., U. Kans., 1923; M. Hosp. Adminstrn., Northwestern U., 1946; m. Ruth Linnea Sederberg, June 19, 1924. Accountant, real estate broker, property mgr., Chgo., 1930-48; adminstr. Flower Hosp., Toledo, 1949-54, Meth. Hosp., Lubbock, Tex., 1954-55, Burge Hosp., Springfield, Mo., 1956-66; hosp. cons., Springfield, 1966-69; adminstr. Springfield Gen. Osteo. Hosp., 1969-73; hosp. cons., 1973—; instr. hosp. adminstrn. U. Toledo, 1952. Pres., Lucas County (Ohio) unit Am. Cancer Soc., 1952-54; bd. dirs. Springfield chpt. ARC, 1966-72. Recipient Malcolm T. MacEachern award Northwestern U., 1946. Fellow Am. Coll. Hosp. Adminstrs.; mem. Mo. Hosp. Assn. (pres. 1964-65), Am. Protestant Hosp. Assn. Republican. Methodist. Clubs: Masons, Shriners (32 deg.), Kiwanis (pres. 1966), Exec. Dinner (pres. 1962), Univ., Twin Oaks Country (Springfield, Mo.); Union League (Chgo.). Home and Office: 2250 S Cedarbrook Ave Springfield MO 65804

PAUL, GABRIEL (GABE), baseball exec.; b. Rochester, N.Y., Jan. 4, 1910; s. Morris and Celia (Snyder) P.; ed. pub. schs., Rochester; m. Mary Frances Copps, Apr. 17, 1939; children—Gabriel, Warren, Michael, Jennie Lou, Henry. Reporter, Rochester Democrat and Chronicle, 1926-28; publicity mgr., ticket mgr. Rochester Baseball Club, 1928-34, traveling sec., dir., 1934-36; publicity dir. Cin. Baseball Club, 1937, traveling sec., 1938-48, asst. to pres., 1948-49, v.p., 1949-60, gen. mgr., 1951-60; v.p., gen. mgr. Houston Baseball Club, 1960-61; gen. mgr. Cleve. Baseball Club, 1961-63; pres., treas., gen. mgr. Cleve. Indians, Inc., 1963-72; pres., treas. Cleve. Soccer, Inc., 1967-68; pres., partner N.Y. Yankees, 1973-77; pres. Cleve. Indians, 1978—. Trustee various bus., civic and charitable instns. Served with inf. U.S. Army, 1943-45. Named Major League Exec. of Year, Sporting News, 1956, 74, United Press Exec. of Yr., 1976, Sports Exec. of Year, Gen. Sports Time, 1956, Baseball Exec. of Yr. Boston Baseball Writers Assn., 1974, 76; recipient J. Lewis Comiskey Meml. award Chgo. chpt. Baseball Writers Assn. Am., 1961, Bill Slocum award N.Y. chpt., 1976, Emil Fuchs award Boston Baseball Writers Assn., 1968, 76 Sports Touch of Learning award, 1976. Clubs: Skyline Country (Tucson); Palma Ceia Country (Tampa, Fla.). Home: 2012 Acacia Park Dr Beachwood OH 44122 also 3700 Mariner Dr Tampa FL 33609

PAUL, HOWARD ALEX, engring. co. exec.; b. Bismarck, N.D., Oct. 29, 1932; s. Howard Allinson and Alma Mae (Kersten) P.; student N.D. Sch. Forestry, 1950-52; B.S., N.D. State U., 1956; m. Donna DeVonne Dennis, July 25, 1954; children—Stephen, Deborah. Engr., Scott Engring. Co., Watertown, S.D., 1956-57; asst. city engr. City of Bismarck (N.D.), 1957-61; city engr. City of Huron (S.D.), 1961-62; with Schmucker, Paul, Nohr & Assos., Mitchell, S.D., 1962—, pres., 1973-75; prin., treas. R.F. Sayre & Assos., cons. engrs., Sioux Falls, S.D., 1968—; dir. Mitchell Indsl. Devel. Corp., 1972-77. Bd. dirs. YMCA, Mitchell, S.D., 1965-71, 74-76; mem. bd. commrs. S.D. Housing Devel. Authority, 1973-77, chmn., 1973-77. Registered profl. engr. N.D., S.D., land surveyor, S.D. Mem. Nat. Soc. Profl. Engrs., Am. Pub. Works Assn. (chpt. pres. 1969), Nat. Assn. Housing and Redevel. Ofcls., S.D. Engring. Soc., Greater S.D. Assn. (dir. 1972-76), Am. Cons. Engrs. Council (chmn. nat. rural com. 1976—), Cons. Engrs. Council S.D. (pres. 1970, nat. dir. 1974-76). Club: Elks. Home: 211 S Harmon Dr Mitchell SD 57301 Office: 620 N Lawler St Mitchell SD 57301

PAUL, JUSTUS FREDRICK, historian, educator; b. Boonville, Mo., May 27, 1938; s. Firdel W. and Emma L. (Frankenfeld) P.; A.B., Doane Coll., 1959; M.A., U. Wis., 1960; Ph.D., U. Nebr., 1966; m. Barbara Jane Dotts, Sept. 10, 1960; children—Justus, Rebecca, Ellen. Tchr., Wausau (Wis.) High Sch., 1960-62; instr. history U. Nebr., 1963-66; asst. prof. history U. Wis., Stevens Point, 1966-69, asso. prof., 1969-72, prof., 1973—, chmn. dept. history, 1969—. State of Wis. grantee, 1974-76; Am. Assn. State and Local History grantee, 1968-69. Mem. Am. Hist. Assn., Orgn. Am. Historians, Hist. Soc. Wis., Nebr. Hist. Soc., Assn. U. Wis. Faculty. Mem. United Ch. Christ. Author: Senator Hugh Butler and Nebraska Republicanism, 1976; contbr. articles in field to profl. jours. Home: 2001 Country Club Dr Stevens Point WI 54481 Office: Dept History Univ Wisconsin Stevens Point WI 54481

PAUL, MORTON MALCOLM, constrn. co. exec.; b. Chgo., Nov. 25, 1923; s. George and Sophia (Marshak) P.; B.C.E., Ill. Inst. Tech., 1944; m. Helen Lorraine Herron, Jan. 26, 1947; children—Warren Joel, Gloria Georgeanne, Julie Frances. Stress analyst Douglas Aircraft Co., Santa Monica, Calif., 1944-45; sewers designer City of Chgo., 1945-47; With E.J. Albrecht Co., Chgo., 1948—, corporate sec., 1967-75, pres., 1975—, also dir. Registered profl. and structural engr., Ill. Fellow ASCE; mem. Soc. Am. Mil. Engrs. Club: B'nai Brith. Jewish. Developer heavy concrete counterbalance for bridges. Home: 1640 E 50th St Chicago IL 60615 Office: 2626 W 26th St Chicago IL 60608

PAUL, OGLESBY, physician; b. Vilianova, Pa., May 3, 1916; s. Oglesby and Laura Little (Wilson) P.; A.B., Harvard U., 1938, M.D., 1942; m. Marguerite Black, May 29, 1943; children—Marguerite, Rodman. Intern, Mass. Gen. Hosp., Boston, 1942, resident, 1946-48; practice medicine specializing in cardiology, Chgo., 1948—; mem. staff Presbyn. St. Lukes Hosp., Northwestern Meml. Hosp.; J. Roscoe Miller prof. medicine Northwestern U., Chgo., 1974—; chmn. steering com. Multiple Risk Factor Intervention Trial, Nat. Heart Lung and Blood Inst., 1972—. Served with M.C., USNR, 1943-46. Fellow ACP, Am. Coll. Cardiology; mem. Royal Soc. Medicine (London), Am. Clin. and Climatological Soc., Am. Epidemiological Soc., Am. Heart Assn. (pres. 1960-61). Episcoplaian. Clubs: Commercial, University (Chgo.); Indian Hill (Winnetka, Ill.). Home: 1012 Westmoor Rd Winnetka IL 60993 Office: 222 E Superior St Chicago IL 60611

PAUL, PROSPER FREDERICK, hotel-motel exec.; b. Mansfield, Mass., July 31, 1932; s. Alexander J. and Blanche (Dion) P.; B.S., U. Mont., 1954; m. Mary Ellen F. Truckner, Nov. 7, 1964; children—Kevin, Jeffrey Mark. Asst. mgr. Hotel Florence, Missoula, Mont., 1957-59, gen. mgr., 1959-63; gen. mgr. Abbey Resort, Lake Geneva, Wis., 1963-64; innkeeper Holiday Inn, Jackson, Mich., 1964-77, Elk Grove Village, Ill., 1977—. Served to 1st lt. AUS, 1955-57. Mem. Am. Hotel and Motel Assn. (dir. 1961-63), Mich. Hotel and Motor Hotel Assn. (treas. 1972-73, pres. 1974-75). Rotarian. Home: 107 Stacy Ct Glenview IL 60025 Office: 1000 Busse Rd Elk Grove Village IL 60007

PAULISSIAN, ROBERT, educator, anesthesiologist; b. Kermanshah, Iran, Mar. 8, 1935; s. Babajan and Asnat (Oshana) P.; M.D. 1st rank, U. Tehran (Iran), 1960; m. Martha Nazar Begian, Mar. 17, 1973; 1 dau., Belit Victoria. Rotating intern U. Tehran Hosps., 1959-60; missionary physician Christian Am. Hosp., Hamadan, Iran, 1961-63; rotating intern Wheeling (W.Va.) Hosp., 1963-64; resident anesthesiology U. Pitts. Health Center Hosps., 1964-66; fellow, asst. instr., 1966-67; instr. U. Chgo. Pritzker Sch. Medicine, 1967-70, asst. prof., 1971-73, asso. prof., 1973—; clin. asso. prof. anesthesiology Abraham Lincoln Sch. Medicine, U. Ill., Chgo., 1977—; head anesthesia for cardio-thoracic surgery U. Chgo. Hosps. and Clinics, 1969-74; attending physician dept. anesthesiology Ill. Masonic Med. Center, Chgo., 1974—. Diplomate Am. Bd. Anesthesiologists. Fellow Am. Coll. Anesthesiologists; mem. Am., Pan Am., Ill., Chgo med. assns., Am., Ill. socs. anesthesiologists. Co-author: Acute Aortic Dissections; contbr. chpt. to med. textbook. Home: 3017 Margo Ln Northbook IL 60062 Office: Dept Anesthesiology Ill Masonic Med Center 836 W Wellington Ave Chicago IL 60657

PAULL, DONALD, lawyer, psychologist, educator; b. Chgo., Nov. 22, 1928; s. William and Tilva (Cohen) P.; m. Marva Weisler, Mar. 7, 1976; children—Michael, Richard. B.S., U. Ill., 1949, A.M., 1951; B.A., Roosevelt Coll., 1950; Ph.D. in Psychology, Ill. Inst. Tech., 1954; J.D., Chgo. Kent Coll. Law, 1974; postdoctoral clin. psychology trainee Downey and W. Side VA Hosps., Chgo., 1956-57. Registered profl. psychologist, Ill.; admitted to Ill. bar, 1974. Staff psychologist Westside VA Hosp., Chgo., 1958-63; chief psychologist Forest Hosp., Des Plaines, Ill., 1963; pvt. practice psychology, Skokie, Ill., 1964-65; asst. prof. Northeastern Ill. State U., Chgo., 1966; asso. prof. Chgo. State U., 1967-70, Chgo. City Colls., 1970-72; staff psychologist Psychiat. Inst. Circuit Ct. Cook County, 1973-74, asst. Cook County Pub. Defender, 1974—; lectr. John Marshall Law Coll., 1975—; mem. Ill. Dangerous Drug Adv. Council, 1976—. Mem. Am., Midwestern, Ill. psychol. assns., Am., Ill., Chgo. bar assns., Ill. Pub. Defenders Assn., Am. Psychology-Law Soc., Am. Bd. Profl. Psychology (diplomate), Sigma Xi, Psi Chi. Contbr. articles to profl. jours. Home: 2940 W Gregory St Chicago IL 60625 Office: 2600 S California Ave Chicago IL 60608

PAULS, RICHARD DAYTON, bank exec.; b. Madison, Wis., May 26, 1940; s. Dayton Frank and Margaret Florence (Stetzer) P.; B.A., Amherst Coll., 1962; M.B.A., Columbia U., 1964; m. Lois Ethel Ewalt, Feb. 13, 1965; children—Rebecca, Amanda, Andrew. Banking officer Citibank Nat. Assn., N.Y.C., 1964-67; with Citizens Bank of Sheboygan (Wis.), 1967—, sr. v.p., 1974—; sr. v.p. Citizens Bancorporation, Sheboygan, 1974—; chmn. Citizens Mortgage Co., Sheboygan, Citizens Equipment Financing Corp., Sheboygan; instr. Ind. U. Grad. Sch. Bus. Loan Seminar. Treas. Sheboygan Arts Found., Inc., 1967-69, 72-77, pres., 1969-72; trustee Kohler (Wis.) Trust for Arts and Edn., 1977—. Mem. Wis. Bankers Assn., Robert Morris Assos. Congregationalist. Clubs: Shehobgan Country, Milw., Rotary. Home: 110 Timberlake Rd Sheboygan WI 53081 Office: 636 Wisconsin Ave Sheboygan WI 53081

PAULSEN, FAYETTA MAE, univ. adminstr.; b. Muskegon, Mich., Sept. 9, 1925; d. Alfred and Gladys May (Irish) Paulsen; B.S., Western Mich. U., 1947; M.S., Mac-Murray Coll., Jacksonville, Ill., 1948. Asst. prof. phys. edn. St. Olaf Coll., Northfield, Minn., 1948-52; dir. phys. edn. women Augustana Coll., Rock Island, Ill., 1952-53; dean women, asso. prof. psychology Luther Coll., Decorah, Iowa, 1955-63; asst. vice provost Bowling Green (Ohio) State U., 1963—. Mem. AAUW, Am., Ohio coll. personnel assns., Am. Personnel and Guidance Assn., Nat., Ohio assns. women deans adminstrs. counselors, Mortar Bd., Alpha Lambda Delta, Pi Lambda Theta, Alpha Xi Delta. Democrat. Methodist. Club: Bowling Green Country. Home: 1001 Boone Ct Bowling Green OH 43402 Office: 425 Student Services Bldg Bowling Green State Univ Bowling Green OH 43402

PAULSEN, HAROLD MAURICE, advt./pub. relations exec.; b. Sioux Falls, S.D., Mar. 5, 1927; s. Harold William and Dorothy Grace (Clark) P.; B.S., U. Idaho, 1948; postgrad. Yale U., 1948-49; m. Carolyn Jean Knight, Aug. 14, 1954; children—Cynthia, Thane Eric, William. Advt. mgr. Donahue Furniture Co., Sioux Falls, 1949-51; founder, pres. Maurice Paulsen Advt., Inc., Sioux Falls, 1951—. Bd. dirs. Lifeline, Inc., Madison, S.D.; pres. Keep Faith Com., 1964. Served with USN, 1945-48. Recipient Silver Medal award S.D. Advt. Fedn., 1972. Mem. Delta Tau Delta. Baptist. Home: 4411 S Cliff Ave Sioux Falls SD 57103 Office: 3015 S Phillips St Sioux Falls SD 57105

PAULSEN, RICHARD WALLACE, data processing mgr.; b. Blue Island, Ill., Aug. 9, 1945; s. Richard Wallace and Betty Lucille (Frobish) P.; student Carson Coll., 1966-67; B.S. in Bus. Adminstrn., U. Nev., 1972, M.B.A., 1978; student law DePaul U., 1975-76; m. Mildred Stephenson Baker, July 16, 1964 (dec. Jan. 1977); children—David Charles, John Stanley, Claire Jane, Kristen Irene. Materials and testing engr. State of Nev. Dept. Hwys., 1964-69, computer programmer, analyst, 1969-72; computer systems analyst Nev. Dept. Employment Security, 1972-74; systems officer, sr. project mgr. corp. lending Continental Bank, Chgo., 1974—; computerized systems designer; initiated EDP rehab. program Nev. State Prison-Nev. Employment Security Dept., 1972-74. Recipient Outstanding Grad. award State of Nev., 1969; certified data processor. Mem. Soc. Mgmt. Info. Systems, Am. Inst. Banking, Omicron Delta Epsilon, Beta Gamma Sigma. Unitarian. Home: 4716 Lee Ave Downers Grove IL 60515 Office: 231 S LaSalle St Chicago IL 60690

PAULSON, BELDEN HENRY, educator; b. Oak Park, Ill., June 29, 1927; s. Henry Thomas and Evelina (Belden) P.; A.B., Oberlin Coll., 1950; M.A., U. Chgo., 1955, Ph.D., 1962; m. Louise D. Hill, Jan. 9, 1954; children—Eric, Steven. With Italian service mission, Naples, 1950-53; organizer Homeless European Land Program, Sardinia, 1957-59; with UN High Commn. for Refugees, Rome, Italy, 1960-61; prof. polit. sci. U. Wis. at Milw., 1962—, chmn. Center for Urban Community Devel., 1967—. Served with USNR, 1945-46. Social Sci. Research Council grantee, 1967-68. Mem. Am. Polit. Sci. Assn., Soc. Internat. Devel., Adult Edn. Assn. U.S.A., Latin Am. Studies Assn., AAAS, AAUP. Author: The Searchers, 1966. Contbr. articles to profl. jours. Home: 2602 E Newberry Milwaukee WI 53211

PAULSON, LOUISE HILL (MRS. BELDEN HENRY PAULSON), author; b. Summit, N.J., May 19, 1928; d. William Scott and Mary Elizabeth (Dietrich) Hill; student Vassar Coll., 1946-48; B.A., Oberlin Coll., 1950; m. Belden Henry Paulson, Jan. 9, 1954; children—Eric Belden, Steven Benjamin. Dir. admissions Expt. in Internat. Living, Putney, Vt., 1950-52; social worker Casa Mia Social Center, Naples, Italy, 1952-53; head student employment, counselor U. Chgo. Personnel Office, 1954-56; writer, researcher, corporate sec. Psy-Bionics Center, 1971-74; v.p. Psy-Bionics Ednl. and Research Found., 1975—. Cellist, Milw. Civic Symphony Orch., 1962—; bd. mem. High Wind Assn., 1977—. Danforth fellow, 1975. Mem. U. Milw. Women's League (chmn. modern dance group 1969—), Wis. Soc. Psychial Research (dir. 1972-73). Congregationalist. Author: (with Belden Henry Paulson) The Searchers, 1966. Home: 2602 E Newberry Blvd Milwaukee WI 53211

PAULSON, MONROE BURTON, dentist; b. Corsica, S.D., May 11, 1922; s. Theodore Martin and Bertha Irene (Kirkeby) P.; B.A. magna cum laude, Augustana Coll., 1943; D.D.S. with highest honors, State U. Iowa, 1947; m. Darlene Mae Dorothy, June 20, 1944; children—David, Karen, John, Mark, Mary, Julie. Pvt. practice dentistry, Sioux Falls, S.D., 1947—. Dental missionary Country of Madagascar, 1968. Served with M.C., AUS, 1943-44, 52-54. Mem. Am., S.D. dental assns., Sons of Norway, Omicron Kappa Upsilon. Lutheran (past chmn. congregation 1971-73). Home: 1102 S 2d Ave Sioux Falls SD 57105 Office: 1908 S Minnesota Ave Sioux Falls SD 57105

PAULSON, WILLIAM L., state supreme ct. justice; b. Valley City, N.D., Sept. 3, 1913; s. A.P. and Inga G. Paulson; B.A., Valley City State Tchrs. Coll., 1935; J.D. U. N.D., 1937; m. Jane E. Graves, Sept. 8, 1938; children—John T., Mary (Mrs. Mikal Simonson). Admitted to N.D. bar, 1937; practiced in Valley City, 1937-66; state's atty. Barnes County, 1941-50, 59-66; asso. justice N.D. Supreme Ct., 1967—. Mem. N.D. Combined Law Enforcement Council, 1969; mem. nat. awards jury Freedoms Found., Valley Forge, Pa., 1969, 71, 77. Mem. alumni adv. bd. U. N.D., 1971—. Mem. Am., N.D. (ex officio mem. com. unified court system) bar assns., N.D. States Attys. Assn. (pres. 1964), Nat. Dist. Attys. Assn. (state dir. 1963-65), Valley City Jr. C. of C. (pres. 1943, Outstanding Jaycee award 1945, dist. v.p. 1945-46), Valley City C. of C. (dir. 1960, 61). Episcopalian (chancellor N.D. 1965—). Clubs: Masons, Shriners, Elks, Eagles, K.P. Home: 1009 E Highland Acres Rd Bismarck ND 58501 Office: Supreme Ct State Capitol Bismarck ND 58505

PAULUS, PETER VIRGIL, chemist; b. Newark, Feb. 14, 1914; s. James and Helen (Pateas) P.; student Carnegie Inst. Tech., 1931-33; A.B., Ohio State U., 1937; M.A., U. Cin., 1939, Ph.D., 1941; m. Sara Josephine Thompson, Mar. 13, 1943; 1 dau., Marsha Lynn. Research chemist Mine Safety Appliances Co., Pitts., 1941-46; pres., gen. mgr. Paulus, Inc., Connellsville, Pa., 1946-53; with Standard Products Co., Port Clinton, Ohio, 1953—, tech. dir., 1953-55, chief engr., 1955-60, factory mgr., 1960-64, asst. gen. mgr., 1964-67, corp. dir. research and devel., 1967-72, v.p. product devel., Dearborn, Mich., 1972—; dir. ADCO Corp., Jackson, Mich. Mem. adv. bd. Bowling Green State U.; chmn. Ahepa Ednl. Found. Bd. dirs. Boy Scouts Am. Candidate for U.S. Congress, 1958; chmn. Ottawa County (Ohio) Democratic campaign, 1960. Mem. Nat. Forensic League (hon.), Order of Ahepa (internat. v.p.), Sigma Xi, Phi Lambda Upsilon. Kiwanian (pres.). Research and devel. in elastomers, plastics, adhesives. Home: 859 Cliffs Dr Ypsilanti MI 48197 Office: 2401 S Gulley Rd Dearborn MI 48124

PAVELKA, ELAINE BLANCHE, mathematician, educator; b. Chgo., Feb. 4, 1934; d. Frank Joseph and Mildred Bohumila (Seidl) P.; B.A., Northwestern U., 1955, M.S., 1956; Ph.D., U. Ill., 1974. Mathematician, Northwestern U. Aerial Measurements Lab., Evanston, Ill., 1956; instr. Leyden Community High Sch., Franklin Park, Ill., 1956-57; prof. math. Morton Coll., Cicero, Ill., 1957—. Mem. Am. Ednl. Research Assn., Am. Math. Assn. of Two-Year Colls., Am. Math. Soc., Mensa, Assn. Women in Math., Canadian Soc. History and Philosophy of Math., Ill. Council Tchrs. of Math., Ill. Math. Assn. for Community Colls., Math. Assn. Am., Math. Action Group, Ga. Center for Study of Learning Teaching Mathematics, Nat. Council Tchrs. of Math., Sch. Sci. and Math. Assn., Spl. Interest Group Research in Math. Edn., Soc. Indsl. and Applied Math., Northwestern U., U. Ill. alumni assns., Pi Mu Epsilon, Sigma Delta Epsilon. Home: 1900 Euclid Ave Berwyn IL 60402 Office: Morton Coll 3801 S Central Ave Cicero IL 60650

PAVLIC, ROBERT STEPHEN, obstetrician, gynecologist; b. Milw., Oct. 24, 1929; s. Victor Charles and Pauline Catherine (Magenheim) P.; B.S., Marquette U., 1951, M.D., 1954; m. Mary Elizabeth Zilg, Nov. 6, 1954; children—Kathryn, Robert, Terence, Pamela, Patricia. Intern, St. Joseph Hosp., Milw., 1954-55; resident in obstetrics and gynecology Loyola U., Chgo., 1957-60; practice medicine specializing in obstetrics and gynecology, Brookfield, Wis., 1960—; founder Brookfield Profl. Suite, 1967; chief obstetrics-gynecology Elmbrook Meml. Hosp., 1969-75; clin. instr. obstetrics-gynecology Med. Coll. Wis., Milw., 1961—; dir. Regency Nat. Exchange Bank. Pres. adv. bd. Milw. Cath. Family Life Program, 1970-72; bd. dirs. Rosalie Manor, 1970—. Served with USAF, 1955-57. Recipient Outstanding Young Man award Brookfield Jr. C. of C., 1965. Mem. A.C.S., Am. Coll. Obstetricians and Gynecologists, Am. Fertility Soc., Fitzgerlad Obstetrics-Gynecology Soc., Milw. Gynecol. Soc. Republican. Roman Catholic. Clubs: Milw. Athletic, Chenequa Country. Contbr. articles to profl. jours. Home: 15800 Sky Cliff Dr Brookfield WI 53005 Office: 17000 W North Ave Brookfield WI 53005

PAWL, RONALD PHILLIP, physician; b. Chgo., July 26, 1935; s. Phillip Joseph and Ruby Helen (Graham) P.; B.S., Loyola U., Chgo., 1957, M.D., 1961; m. Mary Margaret Rohner, July 11, 1959; children—Mary, Linda, Diane, Julie, Matthew, Michael. Intern, Resurrection Hosp., Chgo., 1961-62; resident in surgery VA Hosp., Hines, Ill., 1962-63; resident in neurosurgery U. Ill., 1962-66, asst. prof. neurosurgery, 1969-73, asso. prof., 1973—; practice medicine specializing in neurosurgery, Chgo., 1968—, Lake Forest, Ill., 1974—; mem. staff Ill. Masonic Med. Center, pres. staff, 1974-75; mem. staff Lake Forest Hosp. Hon. trustee Ill. Masonic Med. Center, 1975—. Served with AUS, 1966-67. Diplomate Am. Bd. Surgery. Fellow A.C.S.; mem. Central Neurosurg. Soc. (past pres.), Ill. Neurosurg. Soc. (sec.-treas. 1975-77), AMA, Am. Assn. Neurol. Surgeons, Congress Neurol. Surgeons, Chgo. Neurol. Soc. Roman Catholic. Club: Lake Forest. Home: 1221 Loch Ln Lake Forest IL 60045 Office: 912 Wood St S Chicago IL 60612

PAWLEY, RAY LYNN, zoo curator; b. Midland, Mich., Nov. 7, 1935; s. Lynn R. and Alice M. (Skelton/Pike) P.; student Mich. State U., 1958; m. Ethel Marie Condon, Feb. 19, 1955 (div. 1974); children—Ray Allyn, Shanna Sue Pawley Bielski, Cynthia Ann, Dawn Marie, Brandon Earl, Dareen Joy. Asst. curator, lectr. Black Hills Reptile Gardens, Rapid City, S.D., 1952-53; animal collection mgr. Fairyland Zoo, Custer, S.D., 1955; biochem. lab. asst. Dow Chem. Corp., Midland, Mich., 1956; owner Devil's (Reptile) Garden, St. Ignace, Mich., 1958-60; mgr. Beniteau Bird Corp., Detroit, 1961; devel. mgr. Animal Land of Fla., Ormond Beach, 1961; zoologist Lincoln Park Zoo, Chgo., 1961-64; curator birds and reptiles Brookfield (Ill.) Zoo, Brookfield, Ill., 1964—; mem. Ill. Endangered Species Protection Bd., 1976—; cons. and lectr. on care of animals, animal behavior; tech. cons. animal filming for TV. Mem. Am. Assn. Zool. Parks and Aquariums (awards 1969, 73, chmn., editor editorial com. 1972, chmn. antivenin com. 1969, 76), Am. Assn. Zoo Keepers, Am. Soc. Ichthyologists and Herpetologists, Internat. Wild Waterfowl Assn., Internat. Union for Conservation, Chgo. Herpetological Soc. (hon., pres. 1969, 71, 72), Soc. Study Amphibians and Reptiles, Herpetologists League, Am. Soc. Mammalogists. Contbr. articles to jours. Home: 15W506 W 63d Hinsdale IL 60521 Office: Brookfield Zoo Brookfield IL 60513

PAWLOWSKI, HARRY MICHAEL, water purification engr.; b. Chgo., Oct. 30, 1929; s. Thomas Joseph and Marie Bonaventure (Gasiorowski) P.; B.C.E., Ill. Inst. Tech., 1952, M.S., 1960; m. Elizabeth Bielski, Aug. 20, 1960; children—Cynthia, Catherine, Cheryl, Harry Michael. Hydraulic engr. U.S. Geol. Survey, Champaign, Ill., 1952; civil engr. Chgo. Depts. of Subways and Superhwys. and Pub. Works, 1952-61; chief san. engr. Chgo. Dept. Water and Sewers, 1961-76, engr. water purification, 1977—. Served with AUS, 1948-49. Mem. ASCE (treas. 1967-68), Am. Pub. Works Assn. (chpt. v.p. 1975, pres. 1976-77), Am. Water Works Assn., Internat. Assn. Great Lakes Research, Holy Name Soc. Roman Catholic. Home: 6717 N Keota Ave Chicago IL 60646 Office: 1000 E Ohio St Chicago IL 60611

PAXTON, GEORGE BENJAMIN, JR., ednl. adminstr.; b. Harrisburg, Pa., Aug. 3, 1927; s. George B. and Mary Elizabeth (Canning) P.; B.A., Maryville Coll., 1950; M.A., U. Tenn., 1951; postgrad. U. Mo., 1953-57; m. Anne Catherine Gates, May 30, 1950; children—Catherine Anne, Mary Elizabeth, Judith Lynn, Amy Susan. Announcer, Sta. WEXL, Royal Oak, Mich., 1945, Sta. WGAP, Maryville, Tenn., 1947-51; tech. dir. U. Tenn. Theatre, Knoxville, 1950-51; announcer, news dir. Sta. WMBD, and Sta. WTVR, Havens & Martin Inc., Richmond, Va., 1951-53; announcer Sta. KOMU-TV, Columbia, Mo., 1953-57; instr. U. Mo., Columbia, 1953-57; asst. prof. speech dept. Creighton U., Omaha, 1957-65; mem. faculty Ill. State U., Normal, 1965—, mgr. Sta. WGLT-FM, 1965—; mem. advisory council Ill. Office Edn., 1966-69. Served with USN, 1945-46. Mem. Nat. Assn. Ednl. Broadcasters, Pub. Radio in Am., Ill. Council Telecommunications (pres. 1968-70). Presbyterian. Home: 805 Richland Ave Normal IL 61761 Office: Station WGLT Illinois State Univ Normal IL 61761

PAYAN, HUSHANG MOFAKHAM, pathologist; b. Iran, Jan. 1, 1925; s. Ali M. and Bel M. P.; came to U.S., 1952, naturalized, 1960; M.D., U. Teheran, 1951; m. Irene Ruszkowski; children—Leila, John. Intern, Jewish Meml. Hosp., N.Y.C., 1953; resident Queens Gen. Hosp., N.Y.C., 1954-58; practice medicine specializing in pathology, 1960—; asst. pathologist Booth Meml. Hosp., N.Y.C., 1958-60; dir. labs. VA Hosp., Clarksburg, W.Va., 1965-68; dir. labs. Bell Meml. Hosp., Ishpeming, Mich., 1968—; asst. prof. pathology N.Y. Med. Coll., N.Y.C., 1960-65; asso. prof. pathology U. W.Va., 1965-68; clin. asst. prof. pathology U. Wis., Madison, 1968—. Diplomate Am. Bd. Pathology. Mem. AMA, Mich. State, Marquette County med. socs., Am. Coll. Pathologists, Soc. Clin. Pathologists, Internat. Acad. Pathologists, Am. Soc. Exptl. Pathologists, N.Y. Acad. Scis. Contbr. articles to med. jours. Home: 681 Mather Ave Ishpeming MI 49849 Office: Bell Meml Hosp Ishpeming MI 49849

PAYANT, VITAL ROBERT, judge; b. Iron Mountain, Mich., June 25, 1932; s. Vital and Anna (Freele) P.; B.S. in English, Marquette U., 1954, LL.B., 1956; m. Virginia Henneberry, June 23, 1956; children—Margaret Mary, Thomas More, Mary Adele, Edmund, Robert Vital. Agt., Pub. Expenditure Survey, Madison, Wis., 1956, Milw., 1958-59; admitted to Mich. bar, Wis. bar, 1956; mgr. Iron Mountain C. of C., 1957; practice law, Iron Mountain, 1959—; judge probate Dickinson County Mich., 1963-68; dist. judge 95th Dist., 1969—. Lectr., Inst. Continuing Legal Edn.; lectr. Nat. Coll. of State Judiciary, 1972—; chmn. Community Mental Health Clinic. Mem. Mich., Wis. bar assns., United Comml. Travelers, Dickinson Area C. of C. (dir.), Mich. Dist. Judges Assn. (pres.), Alpha Sigma Nu, Delta Sigma Rho, Sigma Tau Delta. Republican. Clubs: K.C. (advocate), Rotary (pres.). Contbr. articles to Sunday news mags. Home: 1114 Carpenter St Iron Mountain MI 49801 Office: Ct House Iron Mountain MI 49801

PAYNE, FREDERICK JOHN, banker; b. L'Anse, Mich., Aug. 11, 1932; s. John F. and Emma (Hendersickson) P.; B.A. in Mktg., Ferris State Coll., 1957; B.A. in Econs., Mich. State U., 1958; postgrad. U. Houston, 1959, Western Mich. U., 1962; grad. Grad. Sch. Banking, U. Wis., 1969; m. Emma M. Olson, May 27, 1956; children—Thomas Frederick, James Walter. Credit trainee Tex. Nat. Bank, Houston, 1959-62; asst. v.p. Security 1st Bank & Trust Co., Grand Haven, Mich., 1962-67; exec. v.p. Charlevoix County (Mich.) State Bank, 1967-69, 1st Nat. Bank of Ironwood (Mich.), 1969-76; pres. Deerfield (Ill.) State Bank, 1976—; pres. Ironwood Indsl. Devel. Co.; dir. Northwood Call Newspaper, Charlevoix; tchr. Am. Inst. Banking, Ironwood. Mem. Spring Lake Bd. Trustees, 1967, Downtown Adv. Com., Deerfield, 1977. Certified comml. loan officer. Mem. Am. Inst. Banking, Am., Ill. bankers assns., Am. Mktg. Assn., Ill. Comml. Bankers Assn. Clubs: Masons (32 deg.), Kiwanis of Deerfield (pres. elect). Home: 960 Summit Dr Deerfield IL 60015 Office: 700 Deerfield Rd Deerfield IL 60015

PAYNE, JAMES LEROY, fin. exec.; b. Carthage, Mo., Oct. 8, 1936; s. Leonard Wilson and Faye Emma (Brooks) P.; B.S., U. Mo., 1958; m. Virginia Marlene Cowan, Aug. 11, 1957; children—Robert James, Catherine Marlene. Tab supr. Southwestern Bell Telephone Co., St. Louis, 1959-60; sr. accountant Peat, Marwick Mitchel & Co., Kansas City, Mo., 1960-63; controller Kansas City (Mo.) Star Co., 1963—. Served with arty. AUS, 1958-59. C.P.A.; certified data processor. Mem. Nat. Assn. Accountants (asso. dir. Kansas City chpt. 1965-66, 69-70), Data Processing Mgmt. Assn. (dir. Kansas City chpt. 1966-68), Kansas City C. of C., Beta Gamma Sigma. Republican. Baptist. Home: 3801 Canterbury St Independence MO 64055 Office: 1729 Grand St Kansas City MO 64108

PAYNE, NELLIE MARIA DE COTTRELL, zoologist, entomologist; b. Cheyenne Wells, Colo., Dec. 11, 1900; d. James Edward and Mary Emmeline (de Cottrell) P.; B.S., Kans. State Coll., 1920, M.S., 1921; Ph.D., U. Minn., 1925; student U. Vienna, 1930-31. Asst. entomologist Kans. State Coll., 1918-21; asst. instr. entomology U. Minn., 1923-25; instr. math. and chemistry Lindenwood Coll., St. Charles, Mo., 1921-22; fellow NRC, 1925-27; mem. biol. abstracts sci. staff, Phila., 1927-33; lectr., fellow U. Minn., 1933-37; asst. research entomologist Am. Cyanamid Co., Stamford, Conn., 1937-44, biologist, 1944-57; lit. chemist Velsicol Chem. Corp., Chgo., 1957-70; cons. entomology and agrl. chem. lit., 1970—; with Marine Biol. Lab., Woods Hole, Mass., summers; Marine Biol. Lab., Plymouth, Eng., 1930; guest investigator Biologisches Versuchsantait, Berlin-Delhem, Germany, 1931. Co-founder, Stamford (Conn.) Cath. Library, endowment trustee, 1974—. Fellow AAAS, Entmol. Soc. Am.; mem. N.Y. Acad. Sci., Am. Soc. Zoologists, N.Y. Entomol. Soc., Am. Chem. Soc. (counselor 1972—), Am. Documentation Inst., Marquis Biog. Library Soc., Sigma Xi, Phi Kappa Phi, Iota Sigma Pi (nat. v.p. 1966-72), Sigma Delta Epsilon. Republican. Roman Catholic. Contbr. tech. jours. Home: 2908 W Fletcher St Chicago IL 60618

PAYNTER, DONALD G., psychologist; b. Detroit, Feb. 26, 1923; s. William Patrick and Sarah (Cook) P.; B.A., Mich. State U., 1950, M.A., 1953; m. Ellen C. Case, Aug. 22, 1959; 1 son, Donald G. Pres. Donald G. Paynter & Assos., cons. psychologists, Grosse Pointe, Mich., 1953—. Instr., Wayne State U. Mem. Am., Mich. psychol. assns., Mich. Soc. Cons. Psychologists, AAAS, Psi Chi. Club: Torch. Home: 20383 Sunningdale Park Grosse Pointe Woods MI 48236 Office: Suite 112 22811 Greater Mack Ave Saint Clair Shores MI 48080

PAYNTER, LAWSON, pub. relations cons.; b. Bklyn., Mar. 1, 1909; s. Frank Webb and Edith Matilda (Lawson) P.; B.A., Columbia U., 1931. Reporter Long Island Daily Press, Jamaica, N.Y., 1931-33; asst. city editor Bklyn. Daily Eagle, 1933-35; free-lance script writer of network programs for advt. agys., 1934-39; radio copy chief McCann-Erickson, Inc., N.Y.C., 1939-43, TV-radio bus. mgr., 1943-50; TV copy chief Erwin, Wasey & Co., Inc., N.Y.C., 1950-53; mgr. TV-radio production, N.Y. office Ewell & Thurber Associates, Toledo, Ohio, 1953-55; TV radio bus. mgr. Campbell-Ewald Co., Detroit, 1955-63; pub. relations writer James P. Chapman, Inc., Detroit, 1963-65; dir. of communications Am. Presidents Life Ins. Co., Detroit, 1965-69; pub. relations staff Alexander Hamilton Life Ins. of Am., Farmington Hills, Mich., 1970-73; pub. relations cons. and free lance writer, 1973—. Mem. publicity com. First Congl. Ch. of Detroit, 1975—. Mem. Pub. Relations Soc. Am., Internat. Assn. Bus. Communicators (Ernie Rowland award 1971), Detroit Alumni Assn., Phi Kappa Psi. Republican. Mem. Congregational Ch. Club: Columbia of Mich. Author animated cartoon: Cheers for Chubby, 1950. Address: 7800 E Jefferson Ave Detroit MI 48214

PEABODY, SYLVIA ROCKWOOD, health agy. exec.; b. Chester, Vt., June 12, 1919; d. Arthur Cochrane and Gladys Ina (Davis) P.; student Wellesley Coll., 1937-40, Children's Hosp. Sch. Nursing, 1940-43; B.S., Columbia U., 1946; M.S., Simmons Coll., 1954; postgrad. Harvard U. Sch. Bus., 1974. Staff nurse Vis. Nurse Service of N.Y., 1944-46, Barry County (Mich.) Health Dept., 1946-49; cons. Mich. Crippled Children's Commn., 1949-50; instr. Children's Hosp. Sch. Nursing, Boston, 1950-53; supr., nurse coordinator, asst. dir. Vis. Nurse Assn. Met. Detroit, 1954-64, exec. dir., 1964—; mem. bd. dirs. Nat. Council for Homemaker-Home Health Aide Services; mem. program rev. com. Nat. Cancer Inst.; lectr. U. Mich., 1970-77. Active LWV; trustee Comprehensive Health Planning Council Southeastern Mich., 1970-78. Fellow Am. Pub. Health Assn. (v.p. 1968-69); mem. Nat. League Nursing (pres. 1977—), Am. Nurses Assn., Mich. League Human Services, Sigma Theta Tau. Contbr. chpt. to The Nursing Audit, 1976; contbr. articles, commentaries, editorials to profl. mags. Home: 1989 Hyde Park Dr Detroit MI 48207 Office: Vis Nurse Assn Office 4421 Woodward Ave Detroit MI 48201

PEAK, WILBUR JAMES, cons. pub. relations; b. Quincy, Ill., Mar. 6, 1907; s. Roy Thomas and Violetta (Lay) P.; B.S., Knox Coll., 1928; m. Ruth Visny, Aug. 28, 1937; children—Kathy Ann Peak Miller, Thomas J. Accountant, Ill. Bell Telephone Co., 1928, supr., 1936, supr. tng., 1938, employee info. supr., 1942, pub. relations supr., 1945, demonstrations supr., 1945, gen. info. mgr., 1949, asst. v.p., 1955-71; cons. pub. relations, 1971—; dir. State Bank of Geneva (Ill.). Recipient Achievement award Knox Coll., 1968. Mem. Telephone Pioneers Am., Ill. C. of C., Chgo., Chgo. Jr. (life mem., pres. 1942-43) assns. commerce and industry, Pub. Relations Clinic, Pub. Relations Soc. Am. (pres. 1963). Methodist. Clubs: Masons, Press, Lake Shore (pres. 1963-64), Publicity (pres. 1955-56), Tavern, Headline, Econ., Knox Alumni (pres. 1950) (Chgo.), Lions, Kiwanis. Home: 301 Charles St Geneva IL 60134

PEARCE, HARRY JONATHAN, lawyer; b. Bismarck, N.D., Aug. 20, 1942; s. William Ridgely and Jean Katherine (Murray) P.; B.S., USAF Acad., 1964; J.D., Northwestern U., 1967; m. Katherine Bruk, June 19, 1967; children—Shannon Paula, Susan Jean, Harry Mark. Commd. 2d lt. USAF, 1964, advanced through grades to capt., 1967; asst. staff judge adv. Chanute AFB, Ill., 1967-68; staff judge adv. High Wycombe Air Sta., Eng., 1968-69; judge adv. Camp New Amsterdam, Netherlands, 1969-70; admitted to N.D. bar, 1967; municipal judge City of Bismarck, 1970-76; U.S. magistrate U.S. Dist. Ct., 1970-77; partner firm Pearce, Anderson, Thames & Durick, Bismarck, 1970—; mem. Jud. Planning Com., 1977—. Trustee Bismarck Hosp. Mem.

Am., Fed., N.D., Burleigh County bar assns., Am. Judicature Soc., Assn. Grads. USAF Acad., Am. Legion. Republican. Roman Catholic. Clubs: Elks, Rotary. Home: 824 Ave B West Bismarck ND 58501 Office: PO Box 400 Bismarck ND 58501

PEARCE, JOHN LAWRENCE, paper co. exec.; b. St. Paul, Jan. 18, 1926; s. Seth William and Priscilla Mary (Nolan) P.; B.A., St. Thomas Coll., St. Paul, 1949; m. Irene Mathilda Warner, June 5, 1948; children—John, Mary, Mark, Gregg, Joan, David, Michael, James. Tchr., Balaton (Minn.) High Sch., 1949-50; mktg. rep. Great No. Burlington No. R.R., St. Paul, Fargo, Duluth, Minn., 1951-71; mgr. transp. Blandin Paper Co., Grand Rapids, Minn., 1971—; treas. No. Central Paper Traffic Conf., N.W. Shippers Adv. Bd. Pres. St. Joseph's Sch. Bd., Grand Rapids, 1972-76; bd. dirs. Health Systems Agy. Western Lake Superior, Duluth; mem. parish council St. Joseph's Ch. Served with AUS, 1943-46. Decorated Purple Heart, Bronze Star medal. Republican. Roman Catholic. Clubs: Superior-Duluth Transp., K.C. Home: 1309 Fraser Dr SW Grand Rapids MN 55744 Office: 115 SW 1st St Grand Rapids MN 55744

PEARL, IRWIN ALBERT, chemist; b. Seattle, Dec. 25, 1913; s. Louis and Lena (Stusser) P.; B.S., U. Wash., 1934; M.S., 1935, Ph.D., 1937; m. Lillian Aronin, Dec. 24, 1938; children—Cheryl Pearl Rubin, Hugh Stuart. Supr. labs. Wash. Dept. Conservation and Devel., 1938-40; research asso. U. Wash., 1940-41; sr. research asso. Inst. Paper Chemistry, Appleton, Wis., 1941-76; cons. in chemistry, Appleton, 1977—. Bd. dirs. Moses Montefiore Congregation, Appleton, 1950-69, chmn., 1955; chmn. United Jewish Charities, 1951-55. Fellow N.Y. Acad. Scis.; mem. TAPPI (chmn. wood chemistry div. 1971), Forest Products Research Soc. (chmn. wood conversion div. 1960), Am. Chem. Soc. (exec. com. cellulose and wood chemistry div. 1964), Phytochem. Soc. N.Am., Outagami Philatelic Soc. (past pres.), Wis. Fedn. Stamp Clubs (past pres.), Am. Philatelic Soc., Brit. Assn. Palestine and Israel Philatelists, Soc. Israel Philatelists. Club: B'nai Brith. Author: Chemistry of Lignin, 1967. Contbr. articles on wood chemistry and related subjects to profl. jours. Home: 2115 N Linwood Ave Appleton WI 54911

PEARSALL, HARRY JAMES, dentist; b. Bay City, Mich., Apr. 12, 1916; s. Roy August and Gladys Agnes (Tierney) P.; B.S., Marquette U., 1937, D.D.S., 1939; m. Betty Almina Dahlke, Oct. 5, 1946; 1 son, Paul Roy. Dentist, Couzens Fund for Children, 1940; gen. practice dentistry, Bay City, 1946—. Mem. Bay City Charter Revision Commn., 1965-66. Bd. dirs. Downtown Bay City, 1962-73. Served with Dental Corps, AUS, 1940-44, USAAF, 1944-46; PTO. Mem. Am. Coll. Dentists (past pres.), Detroit, Chgo., Bay County (past pres.), Saginaw Valley (past pres.) dental socs., Am., Mich. (past pres.) dental assns., Internat. Coll. Dentists, Am. Legion, Psi Omega, Alpha Sigma Nu. Roman Catholic. Elk. Home: 304 Hill St Bay City MI 48706 Office: Shearer Bldg Bay City MI 48706

PEARSALL, THOMAS EDWARD, prof. Rhetoric; b. N.Y.C., Oct. 28, 1925; s. Lewis and Anna V. (Farrell) P.; A.B. magna cum laude, Colgate U., 1949; M.A., U. Tex., 1956; Ph.D., U. Denver, 1960; m. Anne K. Chimato, Sept. 1, 1946; children—Mark, Susan, Morgan, David. Asso. prof. English USAF Acad., Colo., 1959-69; prof. Tech. Communication U. Minn., St. Paul, 1969—; cons. to Minn. Dept. Transp. Served in USAF, 1949-69. Named Twin Cities Tech. Communicator of the Yr., 1975; recipient Distinguished Tech. Communication award Soc. for Tech. Communication, 1974. Mem. Modern Lang. Assn., Nat. Council Tchrs. English, Council Programs in Tech. and Scientific Communication (pres. 1974-78), Soc. for Tech. Communication (program chmn. internat. tech. communication conference 1978). Co-author: Reporting Tech. Info., 1st edit. 1968, 2d edit. 1973, 3d edit. 1977, Better Spelling, 1971, How to Write for the World of Work, 1977; author: Teaching Tech. Writing, 1975, Audience Analysis for Tech. Writing, 1969. Home: 2098 Folwell St St Paul MN 55108 Office: Dept of Rhetoric University of Minnesota St Paul MN 55108

PEARSON, HELEN R. (MRS. RUSSELL S. PARKS), author, educator; b. Amboy, Ind.; d. T. Carelton and Olive (Resler) Pearson; A.B., Ind. U., 1926, M.A., 1931; postgrad. U. Chgo., 1938-42; m. Russell S. Parks. Tchr. math. Arsenal Tch. High Sch., Indpls., 1942-61; head math. dept. Arlington High Sch., Indpls., 1961-65; lectr. Purdue U., 1965-68. Named Outstanding Woman Educator, Indpls. Pi Lambda Theta, 1956. Mem. Nat. Council Tchrs. Math., Central Assn. Sci. and Math. Tchrs., NEA, Phi Beta Kappa, Pi Lambda Theta (nat. treas. 1952-56), Delta Kappa Gamma (Ind. corr. sec.). Club: Ind. Sch. Women's. Author math. text books. Home: 6246 N Olney St Indianapolis IN 46220

PEARSON, JAMES BLACKWOOD, U.S. senator; b. Nashville, May 7, 1920; s. John W. and Lillian (Blackwood) P.; LL.B., U. Va., 1950; m. Martha Mitchell, Sept. 7, 1946; children—James, Thomas, William, Laura Alice. Admitted to Kans. bar, 1950, since practiced in Shawnee Mission; city atty., Westwood, Fairway and Lenexa, 1950-61; asst. county atty. Johnson County, 1952-54, probate judge, 1954-56; mem. Kans. Senate from 10th Dist., 1956-60; mem. U.S. Senate from Kans., 1962—. Chmn. Kans. Republican Com., 1960—. Served as pilot USNR, 1943-46. Home: 5219 W 68th St Shawnee Mission KS 66208 Office: Dirksen Office Bldg Washington DC 20510

PEARSON, JOHN SUMNER, psychologist; b. Hatton, N.D., June 26, 1922; s. John Edward and Hazel Alva (Olson) P.; m. Jacqueline Anderson, Aug. 14, 1943 (div. 1976); children—John K., Scott G., Kristine A. Pearson Bohlig, Linnea H.; m. 2d, Ruth Carlson, Aug. 18, 1976. B.A., Gustavus Adolphus Coll., 1944; Ph.D., U. Minn., 1954. Certified psychologist, Minn., Kans. Clin. psychol. supr. Minn. Dept. Pub. Welfare, 1949-58; asst. to asso. prof. psychology Mayo Grad. Sch. Medicine, 1959-69; cons. Wichita (Kansas) Clinic, 1969—. Pres. Minn. Human Genetics League, 1956-60; pres. Minn. Council for the Gifted, 1955-57; cons. Mayo Clinic, 1958-69; mem. Rochester (Minn.) Bd. Edn., 1961-69. Mem. Am., Southwestern psychol. assns., Behavior Genetics Assn., World Fedn. of Neurology, Rotary. Author: A User's Guide to the Mayo Clinic Automated MMPI Program, 1967; An MMPI Source Book: Basic Item, Scale, and Pattern, 1973; contbr. articles in field to profl. jours. Home: 232 S Pinecrest St Wichita KS 67218 Office: Suite 230 1035 N Emporia Wichita KS 67214

PEARSON, LOUISE MARY (MRS. NELS K. PEARSON), mfg. co. exec.; b. Inverness, Scotland, Dec. 14, 1919 (parents Am. citizens); d. Louis Houston and Jessie M. (McKenzie) Lenox; grad. high sch.; m. Nels Kenneth Pearson, June 28, 1941; children—Lorine (Mrs. Ronald Walters), Karla (Mrs. John Rapp). Dir. Wauconda Tool & Engring. Co., Inc., Algonquin, Ill., 1950—. Reporter Oak Leaflet, Crystal Lake, Ill., 1944-47, Sidelights, Wilmette, Ill., 1969-72. Active Girl Scouts U.S.A., 1955-65. Recipient award for appreciation work with Girl Scouts, 1965. Clubs: Antique Automobile of Am. (Hershey, Pa.); Veteran Motor Car (Boston); Classic Car of Am. (Madison, N.J.). Home: 125 Dole Ave Crystal Lake IL 60014

PEARSON, MARTHA ELIZABETH MITCHELL (MRS. JAMES B. PEARSON), U.S. senator's wife; b. Kansas City, Mo., Apr. 16, 1921; d. James Bourne and Alice (Morrison) Mitchell; A.A., Bradford Jr. Coll., 1940; A.B., U. Mo., 1942; m. James B. Pearson, Sept. 7, 1946; children—James B., Thomas W., William C., Laura A. Mem. Kansas City Jr. League, Phi Beta Kappa, Kappa Kappa Gamma. Home: 5219 W 68th St Shawnee Mission KS 66208

PEARSON, NELS KENNETH, mfg. co. exec.; b. Algonquin, Ill., May 2, 1918; s. Nels Pehr and Anna (Fyre) P.; student pub. schs.; m. Louise Mary Houston Lenox, June 28, 1941; children—Lorine Marie Pearson Walters, Karla Jean Pearson Rapp. Assembler, Oak Mfg. Co., Crystal Lake, Ill., 1936-38, machine operator, assembly line foreman, 1938-43, apprentice tool and die maker, 1946-50; co-founder, pres. Wauconda Tool & Engring. Co., Inc., Algonquin, 1950—; co-founder, treas. Kenmode Tool & Engring. Co., Inc., Algonquin, 1960-72. Mem. McHenry County Edn. and Tng. Com., 1961—, treas., 1961—. Served with AUS, 1943-46. Mem. Am. Soc. Tool and Mfg. Engrs. Clubs: Moose, Antique Auto, Classic Car, Vet. Motor Car, Horseless Carriage. Home: 125 Dole Ave Crystal Lake IL 60014 Office: Huntley Rd Algonquin IL 60102

PEARSON, NORMAN, town planning cons., author; b. Stanley, County Durham, Eng., Oct. 24, 1928; s. Joseph and Mary (Pearson) P.; came to Can., 1954; B.A. with honors in Town and Country Planning, U. Durham (Eng.), 1951; m. Gerda Maria Josefine Riedl, July 25, 1972. Cons. to Stanley Urban Dist. Council, U.K., 1946-47; planning asst. Accrington Town Plan and Bedford County Planning Survey, U. Durham Planning Team, 1947-49; planning asst. to Allen and Mattocks, cons. planners and landscape designers, Newcastle upon Tyne, U.K., 1949-51; adminstrv. asst. Scottish Div., Nat. Coal Bd., Scotland, 1951-52; planning asst. London County Council, U.K., 1953-54; planner Central Mortgage and Housing Corp., Ottawa, Ont., Can., 1954-55; planning analyst City of Toronto Planning Bd., 1955-56; dir. of planning Hamilton Wentworth Planning Area Bd., Hamilton, Ont., Can., 1956-59; dir. planning for Burlington (Ont.) and Suburban Area Planning Bd., 1959-62, also commr. planning, 1959-62; pres. Tanfield Enterprises Ltd., London, Ont., Can., 1976—; cons. in planning, 1962—; mem. U.S. Com. for Monetary Research and Edn., 1976—; spl. lectr. in planning McMaster U., Hamilton, 1956-64, Waterloo (Ont.) Luth. U., 1963-67; asso. prof. geography U. Guelph (Ont.), 1967-72; prof. polit. sci. U. Western Ont., London, 1972-77; mem. Social Scis., Econ. and Legal Aspects Com. of Research Adv. Bd. Internat. Joint Commn., 1972-76; cons. to City of Waterloo, 1973-76, Province of Ont., 1969-70; adviser to Georgian Bay Regional Devel. Council, 1968-72; real estate appraiser, province of Ont., 1976—. Pres. Unitarian Ch. of Hamilton, 1960-61. Served with RAF, 1951-53. Fellow Royal Town Planning Inst. (Bronze medal award 1957), Royal Econ. Soc.; mem. Internat. Soc. of City and Regional Planners, Am., Canadian insts. planners, Canadian Polit. Sci. Assn. Clubs: Masons, Empire; Ontario, University. Author: (with others) An Inventory of Joint Programmes and Agreements Affecting Canada's Renewable Resources, 1964. Editor, co-author (with others) Regional and Resource Planning in Canada, 1963, rev. edit., 1970; editor (with others) The Pollution Reader, 1968. Contbr. numerous articles on town planning to profl. jours. and chpts. in field to books. Home: 223 Commissioners Rd East London ON N6C 2S9 Canada Office: PO Box 4362 Station C London ON N5W 5J2 Canada

PEARSON, PETER ROBB, film dir.; b. Toronto, Ont., Can., Mar. 13, 1938; s. Charles Todd and Dorothy (Robb) P.; B.A. in Polit. Sci., U. Toronto, 1961; postgrad. Centro Sperimentale di Cinematografia, Rome, 1963; m. Suzanne Nicole Vachon, June 15, 1974; 1 son, Louis-Charles de Beauce. Producer, dir.: This Hour Has Seven Days, CBC, 1964-66; dir. Nat. Film Bd., Montreal, Que., Can., 1966-68; free-lance producer, dir., writer, 1968—; films include: Best Damn Fiddler From Calabogie to Kaladar, 1969 (Canadian Film of Yr. 1969), Paperback Hero, 1973 (3 Canadian Film awards 1973), Along Theses Lines, 1975 (Best Theatrical Short 1975); author screenplay: The Insurance Man from Ingersoll, 1977 (Best Original Screenplay ACTRA Awards 1977); mem. advisory com. Canadian Sec. State, 1972-75; mem. Toronto Arts Council, 1974-76. Named Best Dir., Canadian Film Awards, 1969, Best Producer, 1973. Mem. Dirs. Guild Can. (pres. 1972-75), Council Canadian Filmmakers (chmn. 1973-75). Home: Rural Route 3 Mansfield ON L0N 1M0 Canada

PEARSON, PHILLIP THEODORE, univ. dean; b. Ames, Iowa, Nov. 21, 1932; s. Theodore B. and Hazel C. (Christianson) P.; D.V.M., Iowa State U., 1956, Ph.D., 1962; m. Mary Jane Barlow, Aug. 28, 1954; children—Jane Catherine, Bryan Theodore, Todd Wallace, Julie Ann. Intern Angell Meml. Animal Hosp., Boston, 1956-57; instr. Coll. Vet. Medicine, Iowa State U., 1957-59, asst. prof., 1959-63, asso. prof., 1963-64, prof. vet. clin. scis. and biomed. engring., 1965-72, dean Coll. Vet. Medicine, 1972—; prof. Sch. Vet. Medicine, U. Mo., 1964-65. Bd. dirs. Iowa State Meml. Union, 1970—, v.p., 1977—. Recipient Riser award, 1956; distinguished Tchr. award Norden Labs., 1962; Gaines award Gen. Foods Corp., 1966, Outstanding Tchr. award Iowa State U., 1968. Mem. Am., Iowa vet. med. assns., Am. Animal Hosp. Assn., Am. Assn. Vet. Clinicians, Am. Coll. Vet. Surgeons (bd. regents 1972, chmn. bd. regents 1978), Sigma Xi, Phi Kappa Phi, Phi Zeta, Alpha Zeta, Gamma Sigma Delta. Kiwanian (bd. dirs., pres. Ames 1966-67). Home: 621 Carr Dr Ames IA 50010

PEARSON, ROBERT EDWIN, psychiatrist; b. Toledo, Apr. 29, 1923; s. Albin Lawrence and Elizabeth Genevieve (Christ) P.; B.S., Wayne State U., 1949, M.D., 1952; m. Katherine Lee Gerrie, Oct. 15, 1955; children—Robert, Michael, Barbara, Eric, Brian, Katherine. Intern, Highland Park (Mich.) Gen. Hosp., 1952-53; gen. practice medicine, Boyne City, Mich., 1953-66; resident in psychiatry Traverse City (Mich.) State Hosp., 1966-69, chief receiving service, 1969-71, asst. dir. psychiat. edn., 1971—; asst. clin. prof. psychiatry Mich. State U., 1971—. Served with U.S. Army, 1941-45. Decorated D.F.C., Air medals (13). Fellow Am. Soc. Clin. Hypnosis (ann. award 1972, past pres.), Soc. Clin. and Exptl. Hypnosis; mem. Am. Soc. Clin. Hypnosis Ednl. and Research Found. (chmn. 1976-77, ann. award 1976), AMA, Am. Psychiat. Assn., Am. Psychol. Assn., Mich. State Med. Soc. Contbr. articles to profl. jours. Home and Office: Box C 1001 W 11th St Traverse City MI 49684

PEASE, DONALD JAMES, congressman; b. Toledo, Sept. 26, 1931; s. Russell Everett and Helen Mary (Mullen) P.; B.S. in Journalism, Ohio U., Athens, 1953, M.A. in Govt., 1955; Fulbright scholar Kings Coll., U. Durham, (Eng.), 1954-55; m. Jeanne Camille Wendt, Aug. 29, 1953; 1 dau., Jennifer. Mem. Ohio Senate, 1965-66; mem. Ohio Ho. of Reps., 1969-74; mem. Ohio Senate, 1975-76; mem. 95th Congress from Ohio. Chmn., Oberlin Pub. Utilities Commn., 1960-61; mem. Oberlin City Council, 1961-63. Served with U.S. Army, 1955-57. Home: 285 Oak St Oberlin OH 44074

PEAVLER, ROBERT J., educator; b. Whittington, Ill., Feb. 15, 1924; s. Olin L. and Hazel (Meredith) P.; B.A., So. Ill. U., 1947; M.S., U. Ill., 1949; Ph.D. (research fellow 1950-52), Purdue U., 1953; m. Dorothy Kathryn Schreiner, May 18, 1957; children—Robert David, Emily Ruth, James Thomas. Engr., Westinghouse Electric Corp., Pitts., 1952-59; instr. chemistry Carnegie Inst. Tech., Pitts., 1957-59; head chemistry dept., Ottawa U., 1959-62; physicist Midwest Research Inst., Kansas City, Mo., 1962-64; prof. physics Northeast Mo. State Coll., Kirksville, 1964—. Served with Signal Corps, AUS, 1943-46. Mem. Am. Chem. Soc., Am. Crystallographic Assn., Am. Inst. Chemists, Sigma Xi. Republican. Baptist. Mason. Contbr. articles to profl. jours. Home: Route 4 Kirksville MO 63501

PECARO, DANIEL THOMAS, radio and TV sta. exec.; b. Chgo. Jan. 24, 1926; s. William and Rose Catherine Kopke P.; B.S., DePaul U., 1950; m. Nancy Jean Mihills, Apr. 15, 1950; children—Timothy Scott, Daniel Drew. Tchr., sports coach Chgo. Pub. Schs., 1950-55; radio producer, dir., writer WGN radio, Chgo., 1955-57, prodn. supr., 1957-58, asst. program mgr., 1958-60, program mgr., 1960-62, program mgr. WGN-TV, 1962-65, group P program mgr. WGN-TV, KDAL-TV, KWGN-TV, 1965-66, v.p., group program chmn., 1966-67, v.p., gen. mgr. WGN-TV, 1967-72, exec. v.p., gen. mgr., 1972-74, exec. v.p., gen. mgr., dir. WGN Continental Broadcasting Co., 1974-75, pres., chief exec. officer, 1975—; pres. WGN Colo. Inc., also dir.; dir. KDAL Inc., WGN Continental Sales Co. Mem. program policy adv. com. Catholic TV Network, Archdiocese Chgo., 1975—; bd. dirs. Chgo. Boys Clubs, 1976—. Served with Amphibious Corps USNR. Mem. Nat. Assn. Broadcasters (TV bd. dirs.). Clubs: Oak Park Country, Lake Shore Athletic, Metropolitan. Home: 2955 N Oak Park Ave Chicago IL 60634 Office: 2501 W Bradley Pl Chicago IL 60618

PECINA, RICHARD WAYNE, chem. and indsl. engr., cons. co. exec.; b. Cedar Rapids, Iowa, Mar. 2, 1935; s. Milo Stanley and Emma Valentine (Hartl) P.; B.S. in Chem. Engring., State U. Iowa, 1956, M.S. in Chem. Engring., 1957, Ph.D. in Indsl. Engring. and Mgmt., 1962; m. Joan Doris Steffenson, June 10, 1956; children—Julia Ann, Kristin Marie, Jennifer Lynn. Plant mgr., Abbott Labs., N. Chgo., Ill., 1968-72; v.p. sci. affairs, Respiratory Care, Inc., Arlington Heights, Ill., 1972-75; pres. Richard W. Pecina and Assos., Inc., Waukegan, Ill., 1975—. Mem. Soc. Plastic Engrs., Am. Inst. Profl. Conss., Sigma Xi, Tau Beta Pi, Pi Lambda Upsilon. Lutheran. Contbr. articles to jours., book chpt. to Remmington Pharmaceutical; patentee med. devices. Home and Office: 2348 N Lewis St Waukegan IL 60085

PECK, GLENN MACKEY, optometrist; b. Detroit, June 7, 1915; s. Cecil Wyckoff and Treva Marie (Mackey) P.; D.Optometry, No. Ill. Coll. Optometry, 1936; m. Martha Harriet Sullivan, June 6, 1937; children—Terry Jo (Mrs. Jack A. Gile), Larry Don. Asso. practice optometry with Dr. Wayne Gettman, Sioux City, Iowa, 1936, with Dr. Arthur P. Wheelock, Des Moines, 1936-37; practice optometry, Ft. Madison, Iowa, 1937-42; optometrist Vision Center, Ft. Madison, 1942—. Mem. Indsl. Devel., 1968—; membership chmn. Dad's Club Wentworth Mil. Acad., 1970; chmn. Gov.'s campaign Lee County, 1969-71. Mem. Am., Iowa optometric assns., Pres. Club Ill. Coll. Optometry (life), C. of C., Omega Delta, Beta Sigma Kappa. Methodist. Elk, Mason (Shriner, K.T.), Lion. Home: 1102 Ave A Ft Madison IA 52627 Office: 716 Av G Ft Madison IA 52627

PECK, JOHN W., judge; b. Cin., June 23, 1913; s. Arthur M. and Marguerite (Comstock) P.; A.B., Miami U., 1935; LL.D., 1966; J.D., U. Cin., 1938, LL.D., 1965; LL.D., Chase Coll. Law, 1971; m. Barbara Moeser, Mar. 25, 1942; children—John Weld, James H., Charles E. Admitted to Ohio bar, 1938; partner Peck, Shaffer & Williams, Cin., 1938-61; judge Ct. Common Pleas, Hamilton County, Ohio, 1950-51, 54; tax commr. Ohio, 1951-54; judge Supreme Ct. of Ohio, 1959-60, U.D. Dist. Ct., So. Dist. Ohio, 1961-66; circuit judge 6th Circuit Ct. Appeals, 1966—; exec. sec. Frank J. Lausche, gov. Ohio, 1949-50; lectr. U. Cin. Coll. Law, 1948-70, Salmon P. Chase Coll. Law, 1949-51. Mem. Ohio Unemployment Study Commn., 1951; mem. Princeton City Sch. Dist. Bd. Edn., 1958-63, pres. bd., 1963-69; mem. com. adminstrn. criminal law Jud. Conf. U.S., 1971—; trustee Miami U., 1958-59, trustee emeritus, 1975—; bd. dirs. Cin. chpt. ARC. Served to capt. JAGC, AUS, 1942-46. Mem. Cincinnatus Assn., Queen City Assn., Beta Theta Phi, Phi Delta Phi. Club: Cincinnati Literary. Home: 165 Magnolia Ave Glendale Cincinnati OH 45246 Office: US Post Office and Court House Cincinnati OH 45202

PECK, LEE BARNES, metalsmith, educator; b. Battle Creek, Mich., Sept. 21, 1942; s. Edwin Lee and Ruth Catherine (Morley) P.; A.A., Kellogg Community Coll., Mich., 1963; B.S. in Art Edn., Western Mich. U., 1965; M.F.A., U. Wis., 1969; m. Naomi Greenburg, May 9, 1971; children—Jonathan Michael, Joel David. Jeweler and metalsmith, Sycamore, Ill., 1969—; asso. prof. art No. Ill. U., De Kalb, 1970—; lectr. in jewelry Rosary Coll., River Forest, Ill., 1972—; lectr. jewelry and metalsmithing Ill. Art Edn. Assn. Conv., De Kalb, 1971, Fox Valley Art League, Fox Valley Ill., 1972, State U. Coll. at Buffalo, 1973, Sioux Falls (S.D.) Civic Art Center, 1974, Western Mich. U., Kalamazoo, 1974, Fine Arts Soc., Peoria, Ill., 1975, Grand Valley State Coll., Allendale, Mich., 1975, Rosary Coll., River Forest, Ill., 1975, Kishwaukee Valley Art League, De Kalb, Ill., 1975, Ellwood House Hist. Mus., De Kalb, 1976, Kellogg Community Coll., Battle Creek, Mich., 1976; group shows jewelry and metalwork include (juried) Renwick Gallery, Smithsonian Instn., Washington, 1970, 74, Ill. State Mus., Springfield, 1971, 73, 77, Western Colo. Center for Arts, Grand Junction, 1971, 73, 75, 77, Milw. Art Center, 1971, 72, 74, 75, Tex. Tech. U., 1973, 75, 77, Columbus (Ohio) Gallery Fine Arts, 1973, 75, 77, Marietta (Ohio) Coll., 1974, Valley City (N.D.) State Coll., 1975, 77, Colo. State U., Ft. Collins, 1975, U. Ariz. Mus. Art, Tucson, 1977, (invitational) Art Gallery Ont., Toronto, 1971, Dallas Contemporary Gallery Fine Arts, 1973, State U. Coll. Brockport, N.Y., 1974, Bowling Green (Ohio) State U., 1975, Calif. State U., Fullerton, 1976, Mont. State U., Bozeman, 1976, Middle Tenn. State U., Murfreesboro, 1977, Humboldt State U., Arcata, Calif., 1977; represented in permanent collections: Detroit Inst. Art, Kalamazoo (Mich.) Art Center, Minn. Mus. Art, St. Paul, Carnegie Inst. Mus. Art, Pitts., Mus. Contemporary Crafts, N.Y.C., Oak Park River Forest (Ill.) Pub. Sch. System. Recipient Top Jury award Corning Mus. of Glass, 1968; Purchase prize, merit award Renwick Gallery, 1974; Merit award Phoenix Art Mus., 1977; 1st prize Cooperstown Art Assn., 1977. Mem. Soc. N.Am. Goldsmiths, Am. Crafts Council, Wis. Designer/Craftsman. Research into formation of jewelry and hollowware by process of copper electroforming. Home: 121 Mason Ct Sycamore IL 60178 Office: 402 VAB Northern Illinois Univ De Kalb IL 60115

PECK, MARTHA HARRIET SULLIVAN (MRS. GLENN MACKEY PECK), optometrist; b. Hamburg, Iowa, June 16, 1915; d. Terry Dennison and Trecie Adeline (Barger) Sullivan; student Pa. State Coll. Optometry, 1933-35; D.Optometry, No. Ill. Coll. Optometry, 1936; m. Glenn Mackey Peck, June 6, 1937; children—Terry Jo (Mrs. Jack Andrew Gile), Larry Don. Practice optometry, Shenandoah, Iowa, 1936-37, Mt. Pleasant, Iowa, 1947-49, Ft. Madison, Iowa, 1960—; mem. adv. bd. Iowa Soc. Prevention of Blindness, 1966—; mem. Nat. Eye Research Found., 1969—; chmn. Iowa Bd. Optometry Examiners. Trustee Bd. Acad. Corrective Optometry. Mem. TTT Soc. (pres. 1956, 60, 77), Ft. Madison C. of C., Daus. of the Nile, Kings Daus. and Sons (pres. 1972), P.E.O., Phi Beta Rho, Pi Kappa Rho. Republican. Methodist. Mem. Order Eastern Star. Club: Fort Madison Country (dir.). Home: 1102 Ave A Fort Madison IA 52627 Office: 716 Ave G Fort Madison IA 52627

PECK, WILLIAM ARNO, physician, educator; b. New Britain, Conn., Sept. 28, 1933; s. Bernard Carl and Molla (Nair) P.; m. Nancy Wade Jones, July 24, 1961; children—Catherine, Edward Pershall, David Nathaniel; A.B., Harvard U., 1955; M.D., U. Rochester (N.Y.), 1960. Intern, Barnes Hosp., St. Louis, 1960-61, resident, 1961-62; asst. prof. medicine U. Rochester, 1966-69, asso. prof., 1969-73, prof. medicine and biochemistry, 1973-76, head endocrinology and metabolism, 1969-76; John E. and Adaline Simon prof., co-chmn.

dept. medicine Washington U. Sch. Medicine, St. Louis, 1976—; physician in chief Jewish Hosp. St. Louis, 1976—. Served as med. officer USPHS, 1963-65. Mem. Am. Soc. Biol. Chemists, Am. Physiol. Soc., Am. Soc. Clin. Investigation, Am. Fedn. Clin. Research, Am. Diabetes Assn., Orthopedic Research Soc., Sigma Xi, Alpha Omega Alpha. Recipient Mosby Book award, 1960, Dorah J. Stephens award, 1960, Lederle Med. Faculty award, 1967-70, NIH Career Program award, 1970-75. Contbr. articles to profl. jours. Home: 4635 Maryland Ave Saint Louis MO 63108 Office: Sch Medicine Washington U Saint Louis MO 63130

PECK, WILLIAM HENRY, art historian; b. Savannah, Ga., Oct. 2, 1932; s. William Henry and Mildred Elizabeth (Bass) P.; student Ohio State U.; B.F.A., Wayne State U., Detroit, 1960, M.A., 1961; m. Elsie Holmes Peck, 1967; children—Alice Ann, Sarah Louise, William Henry, IV. Mem. staff Detroit Inst. Arts, 1960—, curator ancient art, 1968—; lectr. art history Cranbrook (Mich.) Acad. Art, 1963-65, bd. govs., 1974—; vis. lectr. classics U. Mich., 1970—; adj. prof. art history Wayne State U., 1966—; archaeol. field work, Egypt, 1964-67, 71, Bklyn. Mus. Theban Expedition, 1978. Served with U.S. Army, 1953-55. Travel grantee Ford Motor Co. Eng., 1962, Smithsonian Instn., 1975; fellow Am. Research Center in Egypt, 1971. Mem. Am. Assn. Museums, Archaeol. Inst. Am. Episcopalian. Author Drawings from Ancient Egypt, 1978, also articles in field. Home: 1901 Orleans St Detroit MI 48207 Office: 5200 Woodward Ave Detroit MI 48202

PECKENPAUGH, DONALD HUGH, supt. schs.; b. East Chicago, Ind., Aug. 11, 1928; s. George M. and Thelma (Anderson) P.; Ph.B., U. Chgo., 1948, A.M., 1954, Ph.D., 1968; m. Marifran Dreesen, Sept. 9, 1950; children—Ann, Eve. Placement worker Lake County (Ind.) Dept. Pub. Welfare, 1948-50; psychologist Gary (Ind.) Pub. Schs., 1950-58; various adminstrv. positions Munster (Ind.) Pub. Schs., 1958-64; adminstrv. asst. Pitts. Pub. Schs., 1966-67; supt. schs., West Bend, Wis., 1967-69, Duluth, Minn., 1969-72, Birmingham, Mich., 1972—. Served with adj. gen. corps AUS, 1952-54. Mem. Am. Assn. Sch. Adminstrs., Phi Delta Kappa. Author: School Systems Role in Social Renewal, 1966. Home: 412 Berwyn Rd Birmingham MI 48009 Office: 550 W Merrill Birmingham MI 48012

PECKHAM, CHARLES WESLEY, social service adminstr.; b. West Lima, Wis., Nov. 18, 1923; s. Leo E. and Isabelle E. Carmack P.; B.A., Ind. Central U., 1951; M.Div., United Theol. Sem., 1954, S.T.M., 1962; Ed.D., U. Cin., 1971; m. Arline B. Beason, July 3, 1953; children—Deborah, Charles Wesley, Mark, Elizabeth. Ordained pastor United Methodist Ch., 1954; pastor Trinity Ch., San Bernardino, Calif., 1954-56, 1st Ch., Kenosha, Wis., 1956-58, 1st Ch., Dayton, Ohio, 1958-66; pastor-program dir. Otterbein Home, Lebanon, Ohio, 1966-72, asst. adminstr. program and social service, Lebanon, 1972—; adj. prof. gerontology, ministering to aged United Theol. Sem., Dayton, 1972—; lectr. in field. Active United Appeal, Common Cause; first chairperson Warren County Community Action Com., 1967-70; pres. bd. dirs. Warren County Council on Aging, 1976—; Pres. bd. trustees Community Action Agy., 1976—; mem. Ohio Council Chs. Task Force Poverty and Nat. Health Ins., 1973-75. Served with AUS, 1945-46; Korea. Mem. Nat. Assn. Health and Welfare Ministries United Methodist Ch., Ch. and Soc. W. Ohio United Methodist Ch. (dir. 1970-75), Phi Delta Kappa. Home: 689 N St Route 741 Lebanon OH 45036 Office: Otterbein Home Lebanon OH 45036

PECKINPAUGH, PHILIP EARL, water conditioning co. exec.; b. Muncie, Ind., June 5, 1946; s. Robert Ephraim and Audrey Vivian (Rawlings) P.; A.B., U. Cin., 1968; M.B.A., Ind. U., 1972; m. Janet Lee Bartchy, Jan. 25, 1969. Dir. spl. edn. Perry Sch. Dist., Massillon, Ohio, 1968-70; mgr. internat. personnel dept. Borg-Warner Corp., Chgo., 1972-73; v.p., Servisoft Inc., Canton, Ohio, also gen. mgr. Peck Water Conditioning Co., Canton, 1973—, asst. chmn. bd. Servisoft Inc., 1970—. Bd. dirs. Canton Urban League, 1977. Certified water conditioning specialist. Mem. Canton Jaycees (dir. 1974), Ohio (pres. 1977), U.S. water quality assns., Canton C. of C. Presbyterian. Rotary. Home: 8640 Foxglove Ave NW Clinton OH 44216 Office: 1434 Cleveland Ave NW PO Box 9006 Canton OH 44711

PEDERSEN, MARLIN ANTHONY, educator; b. Pierre, S.D., Oct. 31, 1937; s. Lauritz Elmer and Helen Marie (Lindskov) P.; B.S., S.D. State U., 1959, M.Ed., 1963; m. Sharon Ann DeVaney, Aug. 11, 1967; children—Mary Jane, Anne, Matthew. Tchr. instrumental music Volga (S.D.) Pub. Schs., 1959-63, Gregory (S.D.) Pub. Schs., 1963—. Mem. Nat. Band Assn., S.D. Bandmasters Assn., Am. Sch. Band Dirs. Assn., Jaycees (pres. 1963), Phi Beta Mu (state pres. 1976-77). Lion (pres. 1972-74, sec.-treas. 1974-75), K.C. Home: 1321 N Main St Gregory SD 57533 Office: 717 Rosebud St Gregory SD 57533

PEDERSON, DAVID DAVIS, psychologist, psychic; b. Duluth, Minn., Oct. 30, 1933; s. Charles and Leila M. (Davis) P.; B.A., U. No. Iowa, 1976, M.A., 1977; Ph.D., U. Sussex (Eng.), 1976; m. Lorena Collmann, Jan. 14, 1953; children—David C., Derek C. Television news dir. KIFI-TV, Idaho Falls, Idaho; news anchorman KGLO-TV, Mason City, Iowa; pvt. practice psychol. counseling, hypnotherapy, Mason City, 1971—; profl. psychic; lectr. in field; dir. Midwestern Inst. Parapsychology, 1967-73. Counselor in adult edn. program North Iowa Area Community Coll., 1976—. Served with U.S. Army, 1949-56. Decorated Purple Heart, Silver Star; recipient Pub. Service award USAF, 1974. Mem. Am. Personnel and Guidance Assn., Ia. Assn. Life Long Learning, SEARCH of Minn., VFW, Am. Legion, Assn. for Ethical Hypnosis. Republican. Author: The Heroic Thieves, 1955; Sunday Is a Day of . . ., 1956. Home: 1200 Meadowbrook Dr Mason City IA 50401 Office: PO Box 262 Mason City IA 50401

PEDERSON, ROBERT MURWIN, communication exec.; b. Jamestown, N.D., June 23, 1951; s. Murwin James and Jane Margaret (Schwartz) P.; B.A., No. Ill. U., 1973, M.A. in Speech Communications, 1975; m. Phyllis Lynn Paxton, Aug. 26, 1972; children—Jennifer Diane, Nicholas R. Sales mgr. Media Masters Inc., DeKalb, Ill., 1972-73; TV prodn. mgr. No. Ill. U., DeKalb, 1973-76; dir., writer Sta. WREX-TV, Rockford, Ill., 1976; writer, producer State Farm Ins. Cos., Bloomington, Ill., 1976—; photographer E. & L Trucking, Palos Heights, Ill., 1975—. Vol. worker United Way, DeKalb, 1975. Mem. Assn. Ednl. Broadcasters (mem. producer's council 1975-77, mgr.'s council 1975-77). Methodist. Author: Claim Investigation Workbook, 1977. Home: 2204 Clearwater Bloomington IL 61701 Office: One State Farm Plaza Bloomington IL 61701

PEDIGO, HOWARD KENNETH, steel fabricating co. exec.; b. Charleston, Ill., Aug. 5, 1931; s. Clarence and Cecil (Elliot) P.; B.S. in Civil Engring., Rose Poly. Inst., 1953; M.B.A., Ohio State U., 1963; m. Doris Dean Mullins, Mar. 21, 1954; children—Susan Kay, John Jay. Stress analyst Bendix Corp., South Bend, Ind., 1955-61; project engr. Wright Field, Dayton, Ohio, 1961-63; project mgr. TRW Corp., Cleve., 1963-64; v.p. prodn. Universal Tank & Iron Co., Indpls., 1964—. Chmn., United Way Hendricks County (Ind.), 1973; bd. dirs. United Way Greater Indpls., 1975—. Served to 1st lt. U.S. Army, 1953-55. Registered profl. engr., Ala., Ill., Ind., N.J., Ohio, Tenn., Wis. Mem. ASCE, Am. Water Works Assn. (steel tank com.), Steel Plate Fabricators Assn., Rose Tech. Alumni (class agt. 1971-73), Lambda Chi Alpha. Methodist. Club: Elks. Home: 633 Elm Dr Plainfield IN 46168 Office: 11221 Rockville Rd Indianapolis IN 46231

PEDLEY, GRACE BALDWIN, civic worker; b. Omaha; d. William Arthur and Elizabeth (Bratt) B.; A.B., U. Nebr., 1932; m. William Harold Pedley, June 26, 1933; children—Helen Elizabeth (Mrs. Lyman J. Cass), Patricia May (Mrs. Michael S. Milroy). Mem. State Central Com. Republican Party, Neb., 1950; republican chmn. Kearney County, Minden, Nebr. 1958; charter mem. Minden City Recreation Bd., 1949-59. Chmn., County Heart Fund, 1965—. Mem. AAUW, Native Sons and Daus. Nebr., Kearney County Hist. Soc. (dir.), Nebr. Art Assn., Nebr. Alumnae Assn., Alpha Phi (chmn. Nebr. Alumnae 1961-66), P.E.O. (pres. 1951-53; reciprocity pres. 1952). Presbyn. (pres. Women's Assn. 1962, treas. Platte Presbyterial Neb. 1963-67). Home: 105 S Nance St Minden NE 68959

PEDRAJA, RAFAEL RODOBALDO, food scientist; b. Sagua la Grande, Cuba, Oct. 21, 1929; s. Jesus M. and Ursula H. (Dulzaides) P.; came to U.S., 1953, naturalized, 1962; B.S., Superior Sch. Arts and Trades (Havana), 1947; M.S., U. Havana, 1950, Ph.D., 1952; m. Gladys Hortensia Ochoa, Jan. 23, 1954; children—Ralph Kelvin, Amy Ann. Auditor chemist Chas. Martin Co., Havana, Cuba, 1953; chemist, bacteriologist Specialty Products div. Borden Co., Elgin, Ill., 1953-56; research chemist Griffith Labs., Inc., Chgo., 1956-62; tech. dir. Am. Dry Milk Inst., Chgo., 1962-65; tech. dir. Food Products div. Superior Tea & Coffee Co., Chgo., 1965-67; v.p. research devel. and quality assurance Booth Fisheries div. Consol. Foods Corp., Chgo., 1967—; lectr. sci. and tech. topics related to food industry; mem. U.S. del. to Codex Alimentarius Commn., sponsored by FAO and WHO of UN, 1972—; spl. hon. tech. councilor to Chamber of Fisheries of Nicaragua, 1972—; mem. food sci. and tech. indsl. adv. bd. U. So. Miss., 1974; judge Putnam Food awards Food Processing mag., 1971—. Mem. Am. Chem. Soc., AAAS, Am. Dairy Sci. Assn., Am. Assn. Cereal Chemists, Inst. Food Tech., Am. Soc. Microbiology, Nat. Fisheries Inst. (mem. tech. com. 1970—), Nat. Shrimp Breeders and Processors Assn. (mem. tech. com. 1968—), Am. Soc. Heating, Refrigeration and Air Conditioning Engrs. (mem. tech. com. 1972—). Contbr. articles to sci. jours. Mem. editorial adv. bd. Food Processing mag., 1971—. Home: 2804 White Pine Dr Northbrook IL 60062 Office: 2 N Riverside Plaza Chicago IL 60606

PEEBLES, CARTER DAVID, lawyer; b. Chgo., July 9, 1934; s. Carter Davis and Vera Virginia (Howd) P.; A.B., DePauw U., 1956; M.A., U. Stockholm (Sweden), 1955; J.D., U. Chgo., 1959; m. Donna Ruth Hostetter, Aug. 3, 1957; children—John Carter, Mary Elizabeth, Sarah Anne. Admitted to Ind. bar, 1959; partner firm Peebles, Thompson, Rogers & Hamilton, Ft. Wayne, 1976—. Faculty labor relations Purdue U. Regional Campus; U.S. commr., 1961-71; U.S. magistrate, 1971—; dir. Keystone Bldg. Products Corp. Bd. dirs. Antioch Found., Religious Instrn. Assn., Religious Heritage of Am. Mem. Am., Ill., Ind., Allen County bar assns., Phi Delta Phi. Mason (Shriner, Jester), Kiwanian. Author: Model Business Corporation Act, 3 vols., 1960; Indiana Bankruptcy Handbook, 1968, rev. edit., 1976; Business Practice Under the UCC, 1970; (with Daniel E. Johnson) Indiana Uniform Commercial Code, Forms and Comment, 2 vols., 1970; Indiana Legal Business Forms, 2 vols., 1967. Home: 137 W Lexington St Ft Wayne IN 46807 Office: 201 Commerce Bldg Ft Wayne IN 46802

PEEL, MALCOLM LEE, educator; b. Jeffersonville, Ind., June 12, 1936; s. Frank Peyton and Ella (Ditsler) P.; A.B. (Merit scholar), Ind. U., 1957; B.D. (W.K. Patterson fellow in N.T. Greek), Louisville Presbyn. Sem., 1960; M.A., Yale U., 1962, Ph.D. (United Presbyn. grad. fellow), 1966; postgrad. U. Claremont, 1967-69, Harvard U., 1970, Utrecht (Netherlands), 1972, U. Chgo., 1975, (Univ. House fellow), U. Iowa, 1977; m. Ruth Ann Nash, June 18, 1960; children—Noel Carol, Drew George. Asst. in instrn. Yale Divinity Sch., New Haven, Conn., 1960-62; mem. faculty Lycoming Coll., Williamsport, Pa., 1965-69, asst. prof. religion, 1965-69; asst. prof. religion Coe Coll., Cedar Rapids, Iowa, 1969-71, asso. prof. religion, 1972—, chmn. dept. religion and philosophy, 1970-71, 72—, chmn. core course, 1973-75; dir. Center for Computer-Oriented Research in Bibl. and Related Ancient Langs. and Lit., 1970-72; mem. Iowa Educators' Task Force on Teaching about Religion in Pub. Schs.; ordained ministry Presbyn. Ch., 1960; minister interim parishes So. Ind., Southeastern Alaska, Conn., Pa. Recipient Grafton trophy in homiletics, 1960; Research awards Am. Philos. Soc., 1967, 68, 69; Younger Humanist fellow Nat. Endowment for Humanities, 1971; Patterson fellow in Bibl. theology, 1960; Guggenheim fellow, 1972; Fulbright Travel grantee, 1972; Newberry Library fellow, 1974. Mem. Soc. Bibl. Lit., Inst. for Antiquity and Christianity, AAUP, Eta Sigma Phi. Author: The Epistle to Rheginos: A Valentinian Letter on the Resurrection, 1969; (with Carsten Colpe) Yale Gnosticism Seminar, 1963; (with Jan Zandee) The Teachings of Silvanus: A Critical Commentary, 1975. Contbr. articles and book revs. to profl. publs. Mem. research team translating Nag Hammadi Coptic Gnostic Library, 1967—. Home: 3918 Wenig Rd NE Cedar Rapids IA 52402

PEES, RANDALL WILLIAM, lawyer; b. McComb, O., Sept. 5, 1942; s. William Miller and Vera Mae (Prater) P.; B.A., Ohio State U., 1964, J.D., 1967; m. Mary Jane Mills, Aug. 26, 1967; children—William E., Ann E. Admitted to Ohio bar, 1967, also U.S. Supreme Ct. bar; instr. English, Liberty Center, Ohio, 1967-69; asso. firm Waldman, Sperling & Pazol, Youngstown, Ohio, 1969-71; mem. firm Volkema, Post & Pees, Columbus, Ohio, 1971-73, Volkema & Pees, 1973-74, Volkema, Pees & Snevel, 1974-77, Volkema, Pees & Sara, 1977—; asso. local counsel ACLU, 1970-71. Mem. Ohio, Columbus (ct. appeals com. 1974—, govtl. agys. com. 1976—, ad hoc com. on med. malpractice 1975, lectr. trial practice 1977) bar assns., Assn. Trial Lawyers in Am., Ohio (sec. standing com. legis. liaison 1973, mem. standing com. negligence law 1974-76, membership com. 1977—, lectr. jury argument 1977), Franklin County (officer 1974—, pres. 1976-77, editor lawyers monthly newsletter 1973-74, chmn. spl. projects com. 1973-74) acads. trial lawyers, Am. Arbitration Assn. (panel arbitrators), Ohio, Franklin County Dem. attys. assns. Democrat. Office: 88 E Broad St Columbus OH 43215

PEHLKE, ROBERT DONALD, educator; b. Ferndale, Mich., Feb. 11, 1933; s. Robert William and Florence Jenny (McLaren) P.; B.S.E., U. Mich., 1955; M.S., Mass. Inst. Tech., 1958, Sc.D., 1960; student Tech. Inst., Aachen, Germany, 1956-57; m. Julie Anne Kehoe, June 2, 1956; children—Robert Donald, Elizabeth Anne, David Richard. Asst. prof. dept. materials and metall. engring. U. Mich., 1960-63, asso. prof., 1963-68, prof., 1968—, chmn. dept., 1973—; cons. metall. industries. Registered profl. engr., Mich.; NSF fellow, 1955-56; Fulbright fellow, 1956-57. Mem. Iron and Steel Soc. of Am. Inst. Metall. Engrs. (chmn. process tech. div. 1976-77, Sci. award Gold medal extractive div. 1976), Am. Soc. Metals, Iron and Steel Soc. (London), Iron and Steel Soc. (Japan), Soc. Iron and Steel (Germany), Am. Foundrymans Soc., Am. Soc. Engring. Edn., N.Y. Acad. Sci., Sigma Xi, Tau Beta Pi, Alpha Sigma Mu (nat. pres. 1977). Author: Unit Processes of Extractive Metallurgy, 1973. Contbr. articles to sci. jours.; chmn. editorial bd. AIME Monograph series on Basic Oxygen Steelmaking. Home: 9 Regent Dr Ann Arbor MI 48104 Office: 2026 E Engring Bldg U Mich Ann Arbor MI 48109

PEIKOFF, LOUIS ARNOLD MENDEL, lawyer, real estate, ins. broker; b. Russia, Feb. 2, 1906; s. Mendel and Sarah Deborah (Orloff) P.; student U. Man. (Can.), 1923-25, LL.B., 1929; m. Katharine Fichter, June 6, 1947; 1 son, Mark Jerome. Admitted to Man. bar, 1929; practiced in Winnipeg, Man., 1929—; real estate and ins. broker, Winnipeg. Mem. Family Planning Assn. Man. Served with RCAF, 1943-45. Mem. Man. Soc. Criminology, Royal Can. Geog. Soc., Hist. and Sci. Soc. Man., Canadian, Man. Bar Assn., Man. Medico-Legal Soc., Tourist and Conv. Assn. Man., Royal Can. Legion, Alumni Assn. U. Man., Canadian Nature Fedn., Heritage Can. Eagle. Club: Canadian (Winnipeg). Home: Box 184 B Route 5 Winnipeg MB R2C 2Z2 Canada Office: 209-309 Hargrave St Winnipeg MB R3B 2J8 Canada

PEIRCE, THOMAS SEELEY, constrn. co. exec.; b. Toledo, Nov. 29, 1939; s. Richard Howell and Elizabeth (Seeley) P.; B.A., DePauw U., 1961; m. Deborah DeSilva, July 20, 1968; children—Michael, David, Paige, Lara, Patricia; step-children—Christopher, Carin. Purchasing agt. Peirce Constrn Co., Toledo, 1961, v.p., dir., Holland, Ohio, 1968—; v.p. Bellevue Trucking Corp., Holland, 1962-63, pres., 1964-67; pres. Peirce Distbg. Co., Toledo, 1968-71; sec., dir. Combined Distbn. Center Greater Toledo, Inc., 1969-71. Trustee Ohio Operating Engrs. Health and Welfare Plan, 1971—, Ohio chpt. Nat. Found. Iletis and Colitis, 1972—. Mem. Ohio Contractors Assn. (labor exec. bd. 1971-76, chmn. heavy hwy. sect. 1975, chmn. 1976, dir. 1976—, mason's negotiating com. 1972, legis. com. 1973, teamsters negotiating com. 1974, operating engrs. negotiating com. 1975, 77, chmn. safety com. 1977, chmn. Toledo chpt. 1974), U.S. Indsl. Council (dir. 1975—). Home: 6528 Abbey Run Sylvania OH 43560 Office: 1049 S McCord Rd Holland OH 43528

PEIRICK, ELYSE MACH, pianist, educator; b. Chgo., Jan. 12, 1941; d. Theodore August and Minna Louise (Holz) Machnek; B. Mus. Edn., Valparaiso U., 1961; Mus.M., Northwestern U., 1962, Ph.D., 1965; m. John Edward Peirick, Aug. 14, 1971; children—Sean Rogers, Aaron Thomas. Mem. faculty Northeastern Ill. U., Chgo., 1964—, asso. prof. music, 1970-74, prof., 1974—; piano soloist Gary Symphony Orch., 1958, NBC Symphony Orch., 1964, Netherlandische Omkoerst Orch., 1966, Netherlandisiche Symphony Orch., 1968; recitals: Switzerland, Germany, Holland, 1958-68. Recipient 1st prize Farwell Piano Competition, 1962. Mem. Am. Liszt Soc. (exec. sec. 1970-77), Internat. Liszt Centre (US. rep. 1972—), English Liszt Soc., Ill. Music Tchrs. Assn., Chgo. Fedn. Musicians. Author: The Liszt Studies, 1973; Contemporary Class Piano, 1976; Pianorama, 1977; contbr. articles to profl. jours. Home: 6551 Waukesha Ave N Chicago IL 60646 Office: Dept Music Northeastern Ill Univ Chicago IL 60625

PEKAREK, ROBERT CHARLES, psychologist; b. Cleve., Sept. 9, 1938; s. Thomas and Johanna (Miller) P.; B.S., Purdue U., 1963, M.S., 1967, Ph.D. (fellow), 1969; m. Mary Ann Hulburt, Nov. 29, 1969; children—Kristina Lynn, Brian, Robert. Dir. activities and orgns. Fla. State U., Tallahassee, 1967-69; pvt. practice marriage and family counseling, 1969-73; dir. White House Conf. on Children and Youth, Fla. Bur. of Planning, Tallahassee, 1970-71; nat. follow-up dir. White House Confs. on Children and Youth, Washington, 1971-72; psychologist Medina & Thompson Inc., Chgo., 1973—; dir. N.Am. Biologicals, Miami, Fla., 1976-77. Served as 1st lt. USAF, 1963-65. Mem. Am. Psychol. Assn., Alpha Tau Omega, Kappa Delta Pi, Phi Delta Kappa. Presbyterian. Author: Florida's Children and Youth, 1971. Home: 1220 Wild Rose Ln Lake Forest IL 60045 Office: 100 South Wacker Dr Chicago IL 60606

PELANDA, KATHERINE BRAZAR, speech pathologist; b. Canton, Ohio, Aug. 29, 1931; d. Paul and Anna (Matasich) Brazar; B.S. in Edn., Kent State U., 1953, M.Ed. (Elks grantee), 1964; m. Raymond V. Pelanda, Apr. 25, 1953; children—Raymond P., Kevin L., Melanie A., Kenneth B. Adminstrv. dir. Community Rehab. Clinic, Canton, 1952-56; speech therapist Massillon (Ohio) Pub. Schs., 1956-57, Jackson Local Schs., Massillon, 1961-63, Alliance (Ohio) Pub. Schs., 1964-66; grad. asst. Kent State Child Study Center, 1962-63; mem. faculty, drama and speech dept. Mt. Union Coll., Alliance, 1963-64, 67-68; dir. developmental programs Kent State U., Salem (Ohio) campus, 1964—; supr. Stark Speech and Hearing Clinic, Canton. Bd. dirs. Stark County Mental Health Assn., 1960-75, chmn. speakers bur., 1962-70, program chmn., 1970-72; sec. Stark County Ecumenical Assn., 1971-72; chmn. lease and contracts com. Stark County Bd. Mental Health and Retardation, 1975—, sec., 1977—; mem. Stark County Developmental Disabilities Treatment Task Force, 1977—: chmn. sesquicentennial year St. John The Baptist Roman Catholic Ch., 1974. Mem. Am. Speech and Hearing Assn. (certificate of clin. competance), Kappa Delta Pi, Gamma Phi Beta. Author: (with K. Ward) Speak Your Piece, 1976. Home: 915 24th St NE Canton OH 44714 Office: Kent State U Salem Campus Salem OH 44460

PELISSIER, RENE EMILE, newspaper editor; b. N.Y.C., Aug. 6, 1917; B.A., N.Y. U., 1941; M.A., Mich. State U., 1970; m. Halina Nagorka, June 9, 1951; children—Ann Michele, Steven Rene. With St. Albans (Vt.) Messenger 1941, Waterbury (Conn.) Republican-Am., 1943-47; with Grand Rapids (Mich.) Press, 1947—, city editor, 1966-71, editor for pub. affairs, 1971—. Served with AUS, World War II. Mem. Sigma Delta Chi. Home: 1129 Idema Dr SE Grand Rapids MI 49506 Office: Grand Rapids Press Press Plaza Grand Rapids MI 49502

PELLEGRIN, JOSEPH, JR., supt. schs.; b. Fairmont, W.Va., June 7, 1933; s. Joseph and Laura (Julian) P.; B.A., Fairmont State Coll., 1954; M.S., Stout State Coll., 1957; Ph.D. (Wis. Assn. Sch. Adminstrs. scholar), U. Wis., 1970; postgrad. U. Minn., 1958-60, W.Va. U., 1962-63, Marquette U., 1961-63; m. Ellen Margaret Stienhoff, Aug. 10, 1957; children—Elizabeth Ann, Mary Ellen, Anthony Joseph. Instr. Fairmont State Coll., 1956; tchr. Carlisle (Ohio) Pub. Sch., 1957-59; instr. Western Mich. U., 1959-60; tchr. Milw. Pub. Schs., 1960-62, Grafton (Wis.) Pub. Schs., 1962-65; supt. schs., Bloomington, Wis., 1965-67, Markesan, Wis., 1967-69, Germantown, Wis., 1970-72, Oshkosh, Wis., 1972—. Cons. Ednl. Curriculum Devel. 1961-63; mem. State Steering Com. for Trade Industry in Wis., 1964-65; mem. Wis. Adv. Council to Vocat. Edn., 1968—; mem. career edn. adv. bd. Stout State U.; mem. steering com. Carrer Info. Center Lakeshore Tech. Inst., 1969-70; adv. com. Sch. Edn. U. Wis.-Oshkosh, 1973—. Mem. Planning Commn., Grafton, Wis., 1964-65. Mem. Library Bd., Bloomington and Markesan, Wis., Oshkosh Library Bd.; bd. dirs. Oshkosh Boys Club; adv. bd. United Way, Oshkosh. Served with AUS, 1954-56. Inst. Devel. Ednl. Activities, 1966; recipient scholarship, Wis. Assn. Sch. Adminstrs., Mem. Wis. (chmn. vocat. com. 1965-70), Nat. assns. sch. dist. adminstrs., Holy Name Soc. (pres. 1965), Phi Delta Kappa, Epsilon Pi Tau. Roman Catholic (mem. parish council 1967-69). Rotarian. Contbr. articles to profl. publs. Developer tri-mester curriculum for Wis. schs. Home: 1728 Jefferson Ave Oshkosh WI 54901 Office: 215 S Eagle St Oshkosh WI 54901

PELLEGRINI, NORMAN ROY, broadcasting exec.; b. Chgo., July 18, 1929; s. Paul and Mamie (Mary) Mascione; student U. Chgo., 1947-48; B.Speech, Columbia Coll., Chgo., 1950. With radio sta. WOAK, Chgo., 1950-51; with radio sta. WFMT, Chgo., 1951—, program dir., 1953—, host Midnight Spl., 1954—; producer, commentator Chgo. Symphony Orch. Transcription Service, 1965-69, 76—; v.p. WFMT, Inc., 1969—; host Chgo. Festival series

WTTW-TV, Chgo. 1967-68. Home: 1501 N State Pkwy Apt 14-C Chicago IL 60610 Office: 500 N Michigan Ave Chicago IL 60611

PELLETIER, ALCID MILTON, psychologist; b. Bridgeport, Conn., Aug. 27, 1926; s. Alcid L. and Mary Jane (Auger) P.; A.A., Graceland Coll., 1951; B.A. in Psychology, U. Mo., Kansas City, 1971; M.A. in Psychology, Western Mich. U., 1972, Ed.D., 1975; m. 2d, Linda Arnold, May 23, 1973; children—Paulette, Alcid Milton, Lionel, Debra, Jon, Jacques, Teresa, Melanie, William, Scott, Angelique. Ordained to ministry, Reorganized Church of Jesus Christ of Latter Day Saints, 1951, assigned to transfers, Ont., Can., Ill., Pa., Mo., Mich., 1951-72; chief forensic psychology, Kent County Jail, Grand Rapids, Mich., 1972-74; asst. to med. dir., clin. coordinator, chief psychologist, chief admissions officer, Kent Oaks Hosp., Grand Rapids, 1974-78; adminstr. Mich. Med. Weight Control Clinics, Grand Rapids, Lansing, Kalamazoo, 1978—; pvt. practice, cons., Grand Rapids; cons. Family Services Assn., Grand Rapids, 1972-74; instr. Calhoun County Juvenile Ct., 1974-77, Grand Valley State Colls., 1975, Western Mich. U., 1974; instr. nursing Butterworth Gen. Hosp., 1974; instr. New Clinic for Women, 1974, 77. Condr. workshops for Mich. Supreme Ct., annually 1973—, probate cts., Mich. Dept. Social Services, 1977, 78. Mem. sheriff's adv. com., 1976—; mem. Human Devel. Assn., Mt. Vernon, Ill., 1959, Kent County Mental Health Assn., Mich. Soc. for Mental Health. Served with U.S. Army, 1945-46. Recipient certificate of appreciation Western Mich. U., 1974; certified psychologist, Mich., also certified rehab. counselor. Mem. Am., Mich. psychol. assns., Am., Mich. personnel and guidance assns., Assn. Counselor Edn. and Supervision, Am. Rehab. Counselors Assn., Mich., Am. socs. clin. hypnosis, Am. Coll. Hosp. Adminstrs., Internat. Assn. Clin. and Exptl. Hypnosis. Republican. Contbr. articles to profl. jours., speeches to confs. in fields of use of hypnosis as treatment. Home: 2951 Vineland NE Grand Rapids MI 49508 Office: 1500 44th SE Grand Rapids MI 49508

PELLETT, KENT LOUIS, editor; b. Salem, Mo., Feb. 12, 1904; s. Frank Chapman and Ada Eugenie (Neff) P.; B.S., Iowa State Coll., 1928; m. Marie Summerbell, June 23, 1929; children—Franklin, David, Susan Pellett Penn. Partner, Pellett & Porter, Printers, Hamilton, Ill., 1921-24; co-owner, co-editor Lehigh (Iowa) Valley Argus, Ft. Dodge (Iowa) Independent, 1929-35; freelance writer Ft. Dodge, 1935-42; mng. editor Soybean Digest, Hudson, Iowa, 1942-67, editor, 1967-73; editor Co-Op-Co News, Hudson, 1943-67; editor Soybean Blue Book, 1947-73; editor Late News, Newsletter, 1953-72. Mem. Hudson Comml. Club (sec. 1943), Iowa State Ames Commons Club (pres. 1926). Mem. Community Ch. (dir., chmn. 1959-60). Club: Lions (pres. 1964-65). Author: Pioneers in Iowa Horticulture, 1941; Livestock Feeding, 1952. Home: PO Box 126 Hudson IA 50643

PELOZA, STANLEY JOSEPH, hosp. ofcl.; b. Vele Mune, Yugoslavia, May 16, 1919; s. John and Anna (Zadkovic) P.; came to U.S., 1928, naturalized, 1928; student St. Louis U., 1946-48, Duquesne U., Pitts., 1957-58, Ind. U., 1963-64; m. La Rita Inez Russell, Feb. 28, 1941; 1 dau., Stana Jo Peloza Bowman. Enlisted in USMCR, 1937, advanced through ranks to sgt. maj., 1961; service in China, Hawaii and U.S., Philippines, Okinawa, South Vietnam; br. sgt. maj., acting div. sgt. maj. 3d Marine Div., Fleet Marine Force Far East, 1964-65; 2d Force Service Regt., Camp Lejeune, N.C., 1966-67; ret., 1967; mem. mgmt. staff Wishard Meml. Hosp., Indpls., 1968—, supt. bldgs., 1968—, also mem. infection control and safety coms., 1969—; bd. dirs. United Hosps. Service, Inc., Indpls., 1975—, chmn. stadardization com., 1975-76. Mem. Nat. Exec. Housekeepers Assn., Am. Inst. Maintenance, Naval Fleet Res. Assn., Marine Corps Assn., Croatian Fraternal Union. Roman Catholic. Clubs: Elks, K.C. (4 deg.). Home: 4340 Ashbourne Ln Indianapolis IN 46226 Office: Wishard Meml Hosp 1001 W 10th St Indianapolis IN 46202

PEMBAUR, BERTOLD JOSEPH, physician; b. Salzburg, Austria, Aug. 24, 1919; s. Friedrich Paul and Berta (Radauer) P.; M.D., U. Innsbruck (Austria), 1945; came to U.S., 1951, naturalized, 1961; m. Joan Elizabeth Bruder, Oct. 2, 1954; children—Odilie, Berthold, Robert, Derrick, Lisa. Intern, Univ. Hosp., Innsbruck, 1948-51; resident in medicine Deaconess Hosp., Cin., 1951-52, mem. attending staff, 1967—; resident in medicine/surgery St. Francis Hosp., Cin., 1953-54; practice medicine, Cin., 1954—; asso. attending staff Good Samaritan Hosp.; courtesy staff Providence Hosp., Cin.; med. dir. Rockdale Med. Center; clin. instr. dept. family medicine Coll. Medicine U. Cin. Mem. task force Avondale Task Force Planning Team, 1976-77. Recipient Hon. award Am. Acad. Gen. Practice-Cancer Control br. USPHS, 1968. Diplomate Am. Bd. Family Practice. Fellow Am. Acad. Family Physicians (charter); mem. AMA, Austrian Acad. Medicine, Am., Ohio acads. family physicians, Ohio Med. Assn., Southwestern Ohio Soc. Family Physicians, Cin. Acad. Medicine. Republican. Roman Catholic. Club: Bankers. Office: 430 Rockdale Ave Cincinnati OH 45229

PENCE, LELAND HADLEY, research chemist; b. Kearney, Mo., Oct. 1, 1911; s. Samuel Anderson and Rose Louise (Reid) P.; student Stanford U., 1928; B.S., U. Fla., 1932; M.S., U. Mich., 1933, Ph.D., 1937; m. Mary Ellen Elliott, Aug. 6, 1938; children—Jean, Daniel, Elizabeth. Research chemist Biochem. Research Found. of Franklin Inst., Phila., 1937-39; instr. chemistry Reed Coll., 1939-42, asst. prof., 1942-45; sr. scientist Difco Labs., Inc., Detroit, 1945—; research chemist Mayo Found., Rochester, Minn., summer 1940; research fellow Cal. Inst. Tech., spring 1943. Fellow AAAS; mem. Am. Chem. Soc., Tissue Culture Assn., Am. Soc. Microbiology, Sigma Xi. Republican. Presbyn. (trustee 1969-75, 78—). Research on carcinogens, estrogens, bile acids, steroids, cardiolipin, lecithins, serological reagents, fluorescent antibodies, phytohemagglutinin, mitogens, chromosome reagents, lectins, immunochemistry. Home: 972 Alberta Ave Ferndale MI 48220 Office: 920 Henry St Detroit MI 48201

PENDLETON, DON, author; b. Little Rock, Dec. 12, 1927; s. Louis Thomas and Drucy (Valentine) P.; student pub. schs.; m. Marjorie Williamson, Feb. 4, 1946; children—Stephen, Gregory, Rodney, Melinda, Jennifer, Derek. R.R. telegrapher, 1948-52, 54-57; controller FAA, 1958-61; aerospace engr., 1961-67; novelist, 1967—; author: 32 Executioner novels, 1969-76; Revolt!, 1968; The Olympians, 1969; Cataclysm, 1969; Population Doomsday, 1970; Guns of Terra 10, 1970; (under pseudonym of Dan Britain) Civil War II and the Godmakers, 1971; also novels under pseudonym of Stephan Gregory, 1961-67. Served with USNR, 1942-47, 52-54. Mem. Authors Guild, Authors League Am., Internat. Platform Assn., Brown County Metaphys. Soc. Office: care Scott Meredith Lit Agy 845 Third Ave New York City NY 10022

PENDLETON, THELMA BROWN, ret. physical therapist; b. Rome, Ga., Jan. 30, 1911; d. John Oliver and Alma (Ingram) Brown; diploma Provident Hosp. Sch. of Nursing, 1931; certificate Loyola U., Chgo., 1942, Northwestern U., 1946; m. George Winston Pendleton, Mar. 2, 1946; 1 son, George William. Pediatric nurse, Rosenwald Found., Chgo., 1931-32; staff nurse Vis. Nurse Assn., Chgo., 1932-45; chief phys. therapist Provident Hosp., Chgo., 1946-55; cons. in phys. therapy Parents Assn., Inc., Chgo., 1956-60, United Cerebral Palsy of Greater Chgo., 1970-75; dir. Physical Therapy Services, LaRabida Children's Hosp. and Research Center, Chgo., 1964-75; mem. nat. com. Joint Orthopedic Nursing Advisory Service, 1947-55; clin. supr. and instr. of programs in phys. therapy Northwestern U., Med. Sch., Chgo., 1947-55; lectr. on cerebral palsy to Japanese Service Com., 1970; mem. Ill. Phys. Therapy Examining Com., 1952-62. Dir., Pipers Portal Sch., 1963-64. Recipient Certificate of Commendation, Civil Service Commn. of Cook County (Ill.). Mem. Nat. League for Nursing, Am. Phys. Therapy Assn., Provident Hosp. Nurses Alumni Assn., Northwestern U. Phys. Therapy Alumni Assn., NAACP, Loyola Alumni Assn. Democrat. Author: Low-Budget Courmet, 1977; contbr. articles on nursing and phys. therapy to profl. pubis. Address: 3001 S Michigan Ave Chicago IL 60616

PENICK, JAMES LAL, JR., educator; b. Charleston, S.C., Aug. 22, 1932; s. James Lal and Annie Cecelia (Sheedy) P.; B.A., Coll. William and Mary, 1957, M.A., U. Calif. at Berkeley, 1959, Ph.D., 1962; m. Barbara Sue Perlmutter, June 20, 1959; children—Michael Andrew, Katherine Leona. Intermediate instr. Calif. State Poly. Coll., San Luis Obispo, 1963-65; asst. prof. Loyola U., Chgo., 1965-68, asso. prof., 1968-72, prof. history, 1972—. Served with USN, 1951-54. Archbishop Riordan scholar, 1959-60; grantee Am. Council Learned Socs., 1968. Mem. Orgn. Am. Historians. Author: Progressive Politics and Conservation: The Ballinger-Pinchot Affair, 1968; The Politics of American Science, 1939 to the Present, 1972; The New Madrid Earthquakes of 1811-1812, 1976; contbr. articles to profl. jours. Home: 923 Wesley Ave Evanston IL 60202 Office: 6525 N Sheridan Rd Chicago IL 60626

PENKAVA, ROBERT RAY, radiologist; b. Virginia, Nebr., Jan. 30, 1942; s. Joseph Everet and Velta Mae (Oviatt) P.; A.B., B.S., Peru State Coll., 1963; M.D., U. Nebr., 1967; m. Mary Kathryn Secrest, Apr. 6, 1973. Intern, Lincoln (Nebr.) Gen. Hosp., 1967—68; resident Menorah Med. Center, Kansas City, Mo., 1968—71; asso. radiologist Deaconess Hosp., Evansville, Ind., 1973—. Served to maj. U.S. Army, 1971—73. Recipient Sci. Tchr. of Year award Lewis and Clark Jr. High Sch., 1963. Mem. AMA. Am. Coll. Radiology, N.A.M., Bluegrass, Tri-State (sec.) radiol. socs., Evansville Med. Radiol. Assn. (v.p.), Ind. State, Vanderburgh County med. socs. Office: 611 Harriett St Evansville IN 47710

PENMAN, ALLEN STUART, cons. psychologist; b. Williston, N.D., June 16, 1920; s. Roy R. and Daisy M. (Huntington) P.; B.S., U. Ill., 1947, M.S., 1948, Ph.D., 1951; m. Jean M. Kron, Dec. 28, 1946; children—Geoffrey, Steven, Patricia. Chief psychologist VA Hosp., St. Cloud, Minn., 1951-57; cons. psychologist Rohrer, Hibler & Replogle, Detroit, 1957-58, mng. partner, Toronto, Ont., Can., 1958-66, gen. partner, Chgo., 1966-68, sr. partner, 1968-73, chmn., chief exec. officer, 1973—, also dir.; dir. Rohrer, Hibler & Replogle Internat. (Europe), Rohrer, Hibler & Replogle Inst., 1st Fed. Savs. & Loan Assn. Chgo. Bd. dirs. Hinsdale (Ill.) Community House, 1971, Robert Crown Center for Health Edn.; bd. mgrs. Chgo. Met. YMCA; trustee 1st. Fed. Found., Found. U. Ill. Served with USAAF, 1942-45. Mem. Am., Ill. psychol. assns., Chgo. Sunday Evening Club (trustee), Newcomen Soc., Execs. Club Chgo. Republican. Lutheran (chmn. ch.). Clubs: Met., Monroe (Chgo.); Ruth Lake Golf and Country. Editor, contbg. author Managing Through Insight, 1968. Home: 530 Princeton Rd Hinsdale IL 60521 Office: 55 E Monroe St Chicago IL 60602

PENNELL, JOHN SPEAR, lawyer; b. Jackson, Mich., Jan. 7, 1916; s. Henry R. and Stella (Spear) P.; A.B., U. Mich., 1938, J.D., 1940; m. Era Northcutt, Nov. 30, 1946; children—William, Jeffrey, Patricia. Admitted to Mich. bar, 1940, Ill. bar, 1941; asso. in law U. Mich. Law Sch., 1940-41; asso. McDermott, Will & Emery, Chgo., 1941-51, partner, 1951—; cons. fed. income tax project Am. Law Inst.; lectr. various tax insts. Tulane U. Tax Inst., N.Y.U. Tax Inst., U. Miami Tax Conf. (adv. com. 1964—), U. Chgo. Fed. Tax Conf., Mid-Am. Tax Conf., Ark. Fed. Tax Inst., Ky. Inst. Fed. Taxation, Ala. Ann. Fed. Tax Clinic, So. Fed. Tax Inst., Inst. Fed. Taxation U. So. Calif., Hawaii Tax Inst. Served to capt. AUS, 1942-46. Decorated Order Cross of Italy. Mem. Am. (chmn. com. on partnerships tax sect. 1965-68, council sect. taxation 1970-73, vice chmn. sect. 1971-73, chmn. elect sect. 1976—), Ill. (chmn. sect. on fed. taxation 1958-59, vice chmn. adv. council Inst. on Continuing Edn. 1962-69, chmn. 1969-71), Chgo. (chmn. com. on fed. taxation 1974-75) bar assns., State Bar Mich. Clubs: Union League (pres. 1976-77), Metropolitan, Executive (Chgo.); Midday; Westmoreland Country. Co-editor partnership dept. Jour. Taxation. Home: 1030 Romona Rd Wilmette IL 60091 Office: 111 W Monroe St Chicago IL 60603

PENNER, DAVID, physician; b. Altona, Man., Can., May 1, 1930; s. David D. and Agneta (Peters) P.; certificate Man. Tech. Inst., 1951; M.D., U. Man., 1963; D.P.H., U. Toronto, 1968; m. Margaret Andres, Sept. 2, 1956; children—Randolph, Carol, Peter, Philip. Intern St. Boniface Hosp., Winnipeg, Man., 1963-64; with Dr. Bryson Murray, Winnipeg, 1964-65; practice medicine, 1965-66; med. dir. Man. Dept. Health and Social Devel., 1966—, med. dir. Virden Health unit, 1966-67, Kildonan St. Paul Health unit, 1968, So. Health unit, 1969-71, No. Health Services, The Pas, Man., Can., 1971—; mem. courtesy staff St. Boniface, Concordia, Misericordia, Winnipeg Gen., St. Anthonie's hosps. Mem. Coll. Family Physicians of Can., Man. Med. Assn., Alumni U. Man., Alumni U. Toronto. Mennonite. Home: 330 Verendrye The Pas MB R9A 1M5 Canada Office: Provincial Bldg The Pas Man R9A 1M5 Canada

PENNER, LORNE WILFRED, physician; b. Morris, Man., Can., Nov. 5, 1929; s. Abram Warkentine and Katharine Hiebert (Ens) P.; grad. Briercrest Bible Inst., 1951; M.D., U. Man., 1958; m. Jean Tomlinson, June 5, 1957; children—Catherine, Kevin, Reginald, Jennifer, Geoffrey, Gretchen. Intern St. Paul's Hosp., Vancouver, B.C., Can., 1958-59; practice medicine, Steinbach, Man., 1959-60; med. missionary Middle East Gen. Mission, Ethiopia, 1960-68; practice medicine, Steinbach, Man., 1969-77; pres. med. staff Bethesda Hosp., 1972; mem. med. staff Moose Jaw (Sask.) Union Hosp., Providence Hosp., Moose Jaw, 1977—. Chmn. Canadian council Middle East Christian Outreach, 1976—; bd. dirs. Briercrest Bible Inst., 1973—. Mem. Canadian, Man. med. assns. Mem. Evang. Free Ch. Home: Box 362 Caronport SK S0H O5O Canada Office: 318 Hammond Bldg Moose Jaw SK Canada also Caronport Med Clinic Caronport SK S0H O5O Canada

PENNER, WILLIAM ARNOLD, JR., bank and trust co. exec., lawyer; b. Sault Ste. Marie, Mich., May 18, 1937; s. William Arnold and Kathryn Jeanette (Hopkins) P.; A.B., U. Mich., 1959; J.D., Wayne State U., 1966; m. Kathleen Beth Mitchell, June 16, 1961; children—William Edward, Stephen Michael. Admitted to State bar of Mich., 1966; trust adminstr. Detroit Bank & Trust Co., 1963-67, trust officer, Birmingham, 1967-71, v.p., 1971—; mem. firm Franklin, Penner & Franklin, Troy, Mich., 1967. Dir. Rip's Ba Restaurant, Pontiac, 1967-71. Mem. Detroit Financial and Estate Planning Council, 1970—. Team capt. Lawyers' Solicitation for United Found. Drive, 1968-69. Bd. dirs. Met. Soc. Crippled Children and Adults, 1973—. Served with AUS, 1960-62. Mem. State Bar of Mich., Am. Bar Assn., Am. Bankers Assn. Presbyn. Rotarian. Home: 611 Hendrie Blvd Royal Oak MI 48067 Office: 188 N Woodward St Birmingham MI 48011

PENNINGROTH, ROBERT PAUL, psychiatrist, mental health adminstr., educator; b. St. Petersburg, Fla., Aug. 3, 1939; s. Paul William and Mary Persis (Carney) P.; B.A., State U. Ia., 1960; M.D., U. Iowa, 1964; m. Kathryn Elizabeth Erwin, June 16, 1961; children—Cynthia Lynn, Ann Persis, Ellen Kay, Kathryn Lea, Paige Allison. Intern, Marion County Gen. Hosp., Indpls., 1964-65, resident in psychiatry, 1965-68; asst. prof. U. Iowa Coll. Medicine, Iowa City, 1970-72, asst. clin. prof., 1972—; mem. staff VA Hosp., Iowa City, 1971-72, acting chief psychiatry service, 1971-72, dir. drug dependency unit, 1971-72; dir. Linn County Psychiat. Clinic, Cedar Rapids, Iowa, 1973—, Linn County Dept. Mental Health Services, Cedar Rapids, 1973—; pvt. practice psychiatry, Iowa City, 1972—; mem. staff Mercy, St. Luke's Meth. hosps., Cedar Rapids, 1972—; cons. in field; owner Penningroth Apts., Iowa City, 1962—. Pres. Area X Drug Abuse Council, 1971-73; chmn. comm. human sexuality U. Iowa, 1972; mem. Pres.'s Club, U. Iowa Found., 1973—; trustee Penningroth Found., 1962-73. Served to maj. AUS, 1968-70. Mem. Am. Psychiat. Assn., Iowa Psychiat. Soc., AMA, Iowa Med. Soc., AAUP. Home: 916 12th Ave Coralville IA 52241 Office: 400 3d Ave SE Cedar Raoids IA 52401

PENNINGTON, EUNICE CATHERINE RANDOLPH (MRS. DANIEL DOUGLAS PENNINGTON), librarian; b. Fremont, Mo., Feb. 16, 1923; d. Charley Albert and Hattie (Pritchard) Randolph; B.S. in Edn., Ark. State Coll., 1963; M.L.S., George Peabody Coll., 1967; m. Daniel Douglas Pennington, Aug. 29, 1942; children—Mary Ann (Mrs. Kenneth McDowell), Albert Joe. Tchr. pub. schs., Carter and Shannon counties, 1940-63; free-lance writer, 1945-55; librarian Current River Regional Library, Van Buren, Mo., 1963—, Pres. Carter County Save the Children Fedn. Mem. A.L.A., Mo., Carter County hist. socs., Am. Legion Aux. (post historian 1955—), Eugene Poetry Soc. (hon. life). Author: History of Carter County, 1959; History of Ozarks, 1963; Perry, the Pet Pig, 1966; Ozark National Scenic Riverways, 1967; Master of the Mountains, 1971; Ladybird Mystery, 1974. Home: Fremont MO 63941 Office: Current River Regional Library Van Buren MO 63965

PENNINGTON, LEA GIBLYN, psychologist; b. Freeport, N.Y., June 9, 1935; d. Leo Frederick and Edna (Decker) Giblyn; B.A. in Sociology, Hofstra U., 1957; M.S. in Sch. Pshchology, U. Wis., 1960; m. Leonard W. Pennington, Jr., Dec. 26, 1969; 1 son, Christopher Leonard. Playground asst. Freeport Pub. Schs., 1951-52, playground instr., 1953-57, tchr., 1957-59, psychologist, 1960-61; tchr. Madison (Wis.) Pub. Schs., 1961-63, psychologist, 1963—, psychologist spl. lang. clinic, summers 1967-72. Mem. Nat., Wis. edn. assns., Nat., Wis. assns. sch. psychologists, Madison Tchrs. Assn., Alpha Delta Kappa, Pi Delta Epsilon, Phi Epsilon. Home: 6309 Landfall Dr Madison WI 53705 Office: 545 W Dayton St Madison WI 53703

PENNINGTON, LEONARD WILLIAM, JR., psychologist; b. Washington, Apr. 14, 1930; s. Leonard William and Selma Nina (Lackey) P.; B.S., Richmond Profl. Inst., Coll. William and Mary, 1952, M.S., 1954; postgrad. U. Wis., 1958—; m. Lea Giblyn Kroll, Dec. 26, 1969; 1 son, Christopher Leonard; children by previous marriage—Scott William, Pamela Ann. Psychologist, Wis. Dept. Health Social Services, Madison, 1956-63; sch. psychologist Madison Pub. Schs., 1963-68; supr. sch. psychol. services Wis. Dept. Pub. Instruction, Madison, 1968—; instr. emotional health and curriculum U. Wis.; staff psychologist Wis. Diagnostic Center; cons. Minn. Dept. Pub. Instrn.; pvt. practice psychology; mem. Gov's. Commn. Status Women, Wis. Bd. dirs. Family Services Soc., Madison. Served with M.I., AUS, 1954-56. Mem. Nat. Assn. Sch. Psychologists (co-chmn. accreditation, credentialing and tng. com.), Am., Wis., Dane County (Wis.) psychol. assns., Wis. Sch. Psychologists Assn. Episcopalian. Contbr. articles in field to profl. jours. Home: 6309 Landfall Dr Madison WI 53705 Office: 126 Langdon St Madison WI 53702

PENRY, RICHARD EARL, surgeon; b. Belgrade, Nebr., June 10, 1912; s. John William and Minnie Frances (Peters) P.; B.S., U. Nebr., 1941, M.D., 1941; m. Martha Ann Pfingsten, Mar. 31, 1941; children—Kandis Lynn Penry Haggstrom, Deborah Ann Penry Lewis, John Jay (dec.). Intern, Immanuel Deaconess Inst., Omaha, 1941-42; resident in gen. surgery Ft. Campbell, Ky., 1942-43, 136th Evacuation Hosp. U.S. Army, 1943-45, Ft. Jackson, S.C., 1945-46; individual practice medicine, specializing in gen. surgery, Hebron, Nebr., 1945—; chief of staff Thayer County Meml. Hosp., Hebron, 1975—. Mem. bd. Hebron Municipal Airport, 1950-60; bd. edn. Hebron Pub. Schs., 1960-67. Served as surgeon, U.S. Army, 1941-46. Mem. Nebr., S. Central med. socs., Am. Acad. Family Practice, Am. Soc. Abdominal Surgeons, Internat. Bd. Proctology, Nat. Assn. Legions Honor. Republican. Lutheran. Clubs: Masons, K.T., Shriners, Rotary (pres. Hebron 1955-56). Home: 534 N 4th St Hebron NE 68370 Office: Bryan Bldg Hebron NE 68370

PENSLER, ALVIN VICTOR, dentist; b. Detroit, Jan. 17, 1928; s. Max Elliot and Irene Sarah (Eisenman) P.; B.A., Wayne State U., 1949; D.D.S., U. Detroit, 1959; m. Joanne Aran, Aug. 31, 1960; children—Elizabeth, Karen, Michele (dec.), Catherine. Practice dentistry, Garden City (Mich.) Diagnostic Center, 1959—; cons. Kerr Mfg. Co., Gen. Elec. Co.; lectr.; pres. Heritage Equity Corp. Citizen advisor Southfield (Mich.) Bd. Edn., 1966. Served to capt. USAF, 1953. Fellow Royal Soc. Health, Acad. Gen. Dentistry; mem. ADA, Detroit Dist. Dental Soc. Club: K.P. Contbr. articles to profl. jours. Developer combined bite impression technique. Home: 21759 Independence St Southfield MI 48076 Office: 6255 N Inkster Rd Garden City MI 48135

PENTECOSTE, JOSEPH CLARENCE, educator; b. Selma, Ala., July 30, 1918; s. Joseph C. and Georgia A. (Watson) P.; A.A., Wilson Jr. Coll., 1950; B.A., Roosevelt U., 1954; M.A., Northeastern Ill. State Coll., 1968; postgrad. Chgo. State U., 1977; Ph.D., Purdue U., 1972; children—Joseph, Maria Faith. Dir. publicity and edn. United Farm and Metal Workers Union, 1941-52; chmn. fair employment practices commn. Farm-Equipment Elec. Workers, 1952-54; publicity dir. Nat. Negro Labor Council, 1946-50; dir. counseling Warehouse Workers Union Local 500, 1954-59; asso. Hall & Brock Research Assos. and Accountants, 1959-63; counselor, youth worker Victor Oleander Boys Club, Chgo., 1966-67; asst. psychologist to psychologist in pvt. practice, Chgo., 1967-68; research dir. Better Boys Found., Chgo., 1968-70; asst. prof. inner city studies Northeastern Ill. State Coll., 1969-72, asso. prof., 1972—; chmn. dept. Afro-Am. studies Ind. U. N.W., Gary, 1972—; cons. in field. Mem. Am., Midwest psychol. assns., Soc. Psychol. Study of Social Issues, Assn. Black Psychologists, Am. Edn. Research Assn., AAUP, Assn. Study of Afro-Am. Life and History, Assn. Social and Behavioral Scientists, Council Advancement of Psychol. Professions and Scis., Psi Chi, Phi Delta Kappa, Kappa Alpha Psi. Author: The Systems of Poverty, 1977; contbr. articles to profl. jours. Office: 3400 Broadway Gary IN 46408

PENZEL, CARL LINUS, constrn. co. exec.; b. San Antonio, Sept. 21, 1908; s. Linus Robert William and Mathilda Emma (Kies) P.; student Washington U., St. Louis, 1927, Central Wesleyan Coll., 1928, RCA Insts., 1929, S.E. Mo. State Coll., 1929-30; m. Mettie Jane Killian, Apr. 19, 1931; children—Carl Gene and Carol Jane (Mrs. Donald Ellington) (twins). Supt. Linus Penzel, Jackson, Mo., 1930-37; partner Penzel Constrn. Co., Jackson, 1937-54, owner, 1954-59, pres., 1959—; dir. Jackson Exchange Bank. Mem. Jackson Sch. Bd.,

1939-48; treas. Cape Girardeau County (Mo.) Park and Recreation Commn., 1969-70; mem. Jackson Library Bd., 1969—; bd. dirs. SE Mo. Hosp., 1965-71, 76—, SE Mo. Hosp. Found., 1977—; trustee Blue Cross, Mo., 1968-72. Mem. Mo. C. of C. (mem. bd. 1962-67, 69-70), Mo. Good Roads Assn. (mem. bd. 1958—), SE Mo. Contractors Assn. Republican. Mem. United Ch. of Christ (state bd., 1971—, bd. social action 1973-76). Mason. Home: 1118 Shady Ln Jackson MO 63755 Office: PO Box 329 Jackson MO 63755

PEPER, CHRISTIAN B(AIRD), lawyer; b. St. Louis, Dec. 5, 1910; s. Clarence F. and Christine (Baird) P.; A.B. cum laude, Harvard, 1932; LL.B., Washington U., St. Louis, 1935; LL.M. (Sterling fellow), Yale, 1937; m. Ethel C. Kingsland, June 5, 1935; children—Catherine K., Anne C., Christian B. Admitted to Mo. bar, 1934, since practiced in St. Louis; partner Peper, Martin, Jensen, Maichel & Heflage; lectr. Washington U. Law Sch., 1943-63, St. Louis U. Law Sch., 1954-55; partner A.G. Edwards & Sons, 1945-67; pres. St. Charles Gas Corp., 1953-72; chmn. Hydraulic Press Brick Co., St. Louis Steel Casting, Inc. Trustee St. Louis Art Mus. Mem. Am., Mo., St. Louis bar assns., Order of Coif, Phi Delta Phi. Roman Catholic. Clubs: Noonday, Harvard, University (St. Louis); East India, Devonshire (London, Eng.). Contbr. articles various jours. Home: 1454 Mason Rd St Louis MO 63131 Office: 720 Olive St Louis MO 64101

PEPINSKY, PAULINE NICHOLS, psychologist; b. Baton Rouge, June 17, 1919; d. Irby Coghill and Pauline (Wright) Nichols; B.A., La. State U., 1939, M.A., 1941; Ph.D., U. Minn., 1949; m. Harold B. Pepinsky, Aug. 27, 1943; 1 son, Harold E. Acting asst. prof. psychology Mich. State U., 1946-48, Wash. State U., 1949-51; research asso., psychology, personnel research bd. Ohio State U., Columbus, 1952-61, sr. research asso., psychology, Mershon Center, 1970—. Rosenwald fellow, 1945-46; Fulbright scholar, Tech. U., Norway, 1961-62; certified psychologist, Ohio. Mem. Am., Ohio psychol. assns., Soc. Psychol. Study Social Issues, NAACP, Sigma Xi, Phi Kappa Phi, Chi Omega, Mortar Bd. Author: (with Harold B. Pepinsky) Counseling: Theory and Practice, 1954; contbr. collected papers; author articles in field to profl. jours. Home: 519 Evergreen Circle Worthington OH 43085

PEPPER, HENRY CORNELIUS, educator; b. Wyaconda, Mo., Jan. 10, 1901; s. Jesse James and Mary Minerva (Koontz) P.; A.B., U. Mo., 1922, A.M., 1924; postgrad. Stanford U., 1925; Ph.D., U. Iowa, 1932; m. Paula Freda Henry, Aug. 25, 1924 (div. 1945); 1 dau., Henria Paula; m. 2d, Mary Elizabeth Martin, Dec. 11, 1945. Instr., Columbia (Mo.) Coll., 1922-24; asst. prof. U. Ark., Fayetteville, 1926-28; research asst. Colo. A. and M. Coll., Ft. Collins, 1931-32; prof. Paducah (Ky.) Jr. Coll., 1932-35; sec. Paducah (Ky.) C. of C., 1935-36; prof. Georgetown (Ky.) Coll., 1936-39; field rep. Kiwanis, Chgo., 1939-45; prof. Mo. Valley Coll., Marhsall, 1949-51; prof. Ga. State U., Atlanta, 1951-68, dir. hosp. adminstrn. program, 1952-54; prof. S.E. Mo. State U., Cape Girardeau, 1968-70; faculty Shawnee Coll., Ullin, Ill., 1970—. Recipient numerous citations for work with Ga. Hosp. Adminstrn., Ga. Legislature. Mem. Am. Polit. Sci. Assn., AAUP, Nat. Geog. Soc., Nat. Wildlife Assn., Audubon Soc., Smithsonian Center. Clubs: Masons, Shriners, Order Eastern Star, Kiwanis (pres. Georgetown 1938). Author: County Government in Colorado, 1934; Handbook for Georgia Sheriffs, 1953; Handbook for County Commrs. Georgia, 1955; The Legislative Process in Georgia, 1955; editor legis. service Ga. Gen. Assembly, 1952, 53, 54; Fulton County Ann. Report, 1953-58; contbr. articles to profl. jours. Home: 2525 Lynwood Dr Cape Girardeau MO 63701 Office: Shawnee Coll Ullin IL 62992

PEPPING, RAYMOND AUSTIN, aerospace industry exec.; b. St. Louis, Nov. 8, 1918; s. Fred W. and Beatrice M. (Murray) P.; B.S., Washington U., 1941, M.S., 1942; m. Sue S. Sheffield, Jan. 21, 1950; children—Janet Ellen, Eric Philip. With McDonnell Douglas Corp., St. Louis, 1946—, v.p. space programs, 1974—. Served with USAAF, 1942-46. Mem. flutter sub-com. NACA, 1951-55; mem. research adv. com. on missile and space vehicle aerodynamics NASA, 1961-65. Mem. Aircraft Industries Assn. (mem. aircraft research and testing com. flutter sub-com. 1947-55).

PEPPLER, HENRY JAMES, microbiologist; b. Hussenbach, Russia, Nov. 29, 1911; s. Jacob and Anne Elizabeth (Streck) P.; came to U.S., 1912, naturalized, 1937; B.S., U. Wis., 1936, M.S., 1937, Ph.D., 1939; m. Genevieve Lindert, Aug. 12, 1939; children—James Henry, Mark Steven. Teaching asst. bacteriology U. Wis., Madison, 1936-37; research asst. Wis. Alumni Research Found., Madison, 1937-39; instr. bacteriology Kans. State U., Manhattan, 1939-42; research asso. microbiology, asst. dir. Carnation Co. Research Lab., Milw., 1946-51; dir. biochemistry research lab. Red Star Yeast & Products Co., Milw., 1951-53, asst. dir. research, 1954, mgr. research, 1954-60; mgr. research and devel. Universal Foods Corp., Milw., 1960-70, sci. dir., 1971—. Trustee, sec.-treas. Milw. Sci. Ednl. Found., 1966—. Served to maj. AUS, 1942-46; ETO. Mem. Am. Soc. Microbiology (br. pres. 1959-60), Am. Acad. Microbiology, Am. Dairy Sci. Assn., AAAS, Am. Chem. Soc. (div. sec.-treas. 1959-65, Sect. award 1966, Distinguished Service award 1972, councilor 1973—), Inst. Food Technologists (councilor 1965-67), Wis. Assn. Milk and Food Sanitarians, The Chemists Circle (pres. 1959-61), Internat. Union Pure and Applied Chemistry, Sigma Xi, Alpha Zeta, Phi Kappa Phi, Phi Sigma, Phi Eta Sigma. Contbr. articles to profl. jours. Patentee in field. Office: 433 E Michigan St PO Box 737 Milwaukee WI 53201

PEQUIGNOT, STANLEY EDWARD, lawyer; b. Warsaw, Ind., Dec. 31, 1942; s. Edward Louis and Hildreth Elouise (Stump) P.; B.S., Ind. U., 1965, J.D., 1968; m. Diana Lynn Bisig, June 12, 1966; children—Tyler Stanley, Todd Eric. Admitted to Ind. bar, 1968; partner Rockhill, Kennedy, Pinnick, Sand, Bent & Pequignot, Warsaw, 1968—; city atty. Warsaw, 1977—; dir. Pierceton State Bank (Ind.). Chmn. orgn. and extension Kosciusko County Boy Scouts Am., 1969-70; bd. dirs. United Fund of Kosciusko County, 1970—, v.p., 1973, pres., 1974, chmn. bd., 1975; pres. Kosciusko County Sheriff's Merit Bd., 1977—. Mem. Am., Ind., Kosciusko County (pres. 1975-77) bar assns., Ind. Def. Lawyers Assn. Club: Rotary. Home: Rural Route 2 Southwood Warsaw IN 46580 Office: 1st National Bank Bldg Warsaw IN 46580

PERAINO, CARL, biochemist; b. Passaic, N.J., Mar. 10, 1935; s. George Carl and Elizabeth (Piazza) P.; B.S., Lebanon Valley Coll., 1957; M.S., U. Wis., 1959, Ph.D., 1961; m. Nancy Gibson, June 18, 1958; children—Suzanne, Judith. Instr. oncology U. Wis., 1964-65; biochemist Argonne (Ill.) Nat. Lab., 1965—; adj. asso. prof. No. Ill. U., 1972—. Nat. Cancer Inst. Research fellow, 1961-64. Mem. Fedn. Am. Socs. Exptl. Biology, Am. Assn. Cancer Research, Am. Inst. Chemists. Research on mechanisms liver carcinogenesis. Home: 4632 Seeley St Downers Grove IL 60515 Office: Biology Div Argonne Nat Lab Argonne IL 60439

PERCIVAL, WORTH HARRIS, mech. engr.; b. Des Moines, Dec. 28, 1919; s. Worth Hemenway and Esther June (Riggs) P.; student Drake U., 1938-39; B.S., Iowa State U., 1942; M.S., Mass. Inst. Tech., 1947; m. Madelin M. Lucas, May 3, 1952; children—Lawrence Scott, Lisa Cathryn. Indsl. research engr. Indsl. Liaison div. Sloan Lab., Mass. Inst. Tech., 1947; with research labs. Gen. Motors Corp., Warren, Mich., 1947-73, supervisory engr., 1953-57, asst. dept. head, 1957-67, dept. head, 1968-73; engring. cons., Manchester, Mo., 1973—. Served with USAAF, 1942-45. Mem. Soc. Automotive Engrs., ASME, Sigma Xi, Tau Beta Pi, Phi Kappa Psi. Christian Scientist. Patentee in field. Contbr. to profl. publs. Home: 707 Barham Down Manchester MO 63011

PERCY, CHARLES HARTING, U.S. senator; b. Pensacola, Fla., Sept. 27, 1919; s. Edward H. and Elisabeth (Harting) P.; A.B., U. Chgo., 1941; LL.D., Ill. Coll., 1961, Roosevelt U., 1961; H.H.D., Willamette U., 1962, LL.D., Lake Forest Coll., 1962, Bradley U., 1963; L.H.D., Nat. Coll. Edn., 1964; m. Jeanne Valerie Dickerson, June 12, 1943 (dec.); children—Valerie Jeanne (dec.) and Sharon Lee (Mrs. John D. Rockefeller IV) (twins), Roger; m. 2d, Loraine Diane Guyer, Aug. 27, 1950; children—Gail, Mark. Sales trainee, apprentice Bell & Howell, 1938, mgr. war coordinating dept., 1941-43, dir., 1942-66, asst. sec., corp. sec., 1946-49, pres., 1949-61, chmn., chief exec. officer, 1961-63, chmn. bd., 1963-66; sales promotion Crowell-Collier Pub. Co., 1939; mem. U.S. Senate from Ill., 1967—. Dir., Nat. Recreation and Park Assn.; co-chmn. NCCJ, Chgo., 1951, 54; mem. Bus. Adv. Council; spl. ambassador and personal rep. Pres. U.S. to presdl. inauguration ceremonies in Peru and Bolivia, 1956. Past chmn. Fund for Adult Edn., Ford Found.; trustee U. Chgo.; mem. citizens bd., bd. dirs. alumni found., Cal. Inst. Tech., until 1967. Chmn. Republican Com. on Program and Progress, 1959, Rep. Platform Com. Nat. Conv., 1960. Served as lt. USNR, 1943-45. Named one of 10 outstanding young men of 1949, U.S. Jr. C. of C., Business Man of Year, Saturday Review, 1962, Alumnus of Year, U. Chgo. Alumni Assn., 1962, Father of Year, Nat. Father's Day Com., 1973; recipient World Trade award, World Trade Award Com., 1955; Nat. Sales Execs. Mgmt. award, 1955; French Legion of Honor, 1961, Statesmanship award Harvard Sch. Assn., Chgo., 1962, Abraham Lincoln Centre award for humanitarian service, 1962. Mem. Phi Delta Phi, Alpha Delta Phi. Clubs: Chicago, Economic (past dir.), Executives (past dir.), Commercial (Chgo.). Author: Growing Old in the Country of the Young, 1974; I Want to Know about the United States Senate, 1976. Home: Wilmette IL 60091 Office: Senate Office Bldg Washington DC 20510

PERESS, MAURICE, symphony condr.; b. N.Y.C., Mar. 18, 1930; s. Haskell Ben Ezra and Elka (Tygier) P.; B.A., N.Y. U., 1951, postgrad. (Millicent James fellow) Grad. Sch. Musicology, 1955; postgrad. (Coll. scholar) Mannes Coll. Music, 1955-57; m. Gloria Vando, July 2, 1955; children—Lorca Miriam, Paul Avram, Anika Tygier. Asst. condr. Mannes Coll. Music, 1957-60; music dir. N.Y. U., 1958-61; asst. condr. N.Y. Philharmonic, 1961-62; music dir. Corpus Christi (Tex.) Symphony, 1961-74, Joffrey Ballet, 1966, Austin (Tex.) Symphony, 1970-72, Kansas City (Mo.) Philharmonic, 1974—; dir. Bur. Indian Affairs pilot project Communications Through Music, 1968; mem. faculty N.Y. U., 1957-61, Queens Coll., 1969-70, U. Tex., 1970-72; mus. dir. world premiere Bernstein Mass., J. F. Kennedy Center, Washington, 1971. Served with AUS, 1953-55. Recipient Beethoven medal German Consul Gen., 1969; named Arts Council Artist of Year, 1969. Mem. ASCAP. Jewish. Pub. orchestrations: Tocatta and Ritornelli from Orfeo (Monteverdi); West Side Story Overture (Bernstein); Black Brown and Beige Suite (Ellington); author: Some Music Lessons for American Indian Youngsters, 1968; contbr. articles to profl. jours. Home: 627 E 46th St Kansas City MO 64110 Office: 210 W 10th St Kansas City MO 64105

PEREZ, CARLOS A., radiologist, educator; b. Colombia, Nov. 10, 1934; came to U.S., 1960, naturalized, 1970; B.S., Universidad de Antiquia, Medellin, Colombia, 1952, M.D., 1960; m. Blanca; children—Carlos S., Bernardo, Edward P. Rotating intern Hosp. Universitario Saint Vincente de Paul, Medellin and Caldas, Colombia, 1958-59; resident in radiology Hosp. Universitario del Valle, Cali, Colombia, 1959-60; resident in radiology Mallinckrodt Inst. Radiology, Washington U. Sch. Medicine, 1960-63, instr. in radiology, 1964-66, asst. prof. radiology, 1966-67, asso. prof., 1967-72, prof., 1972—, dir. div. radiation oncology, 1976—; fellow in radiotherapy M.D. Anderson Hosp. and Tumor Inst., U. Tex., Houston, 1963-64; chmn. task force on cancer of lung, chmn. membership com., mem. exec. com. Radiation Therapy Oncology Group; chmn. com. on radiation therapy, mem. exec. com. Southeastern Cancer Study Group; mem. adv. com. div. cancer treatment Nat. Cancer Inst.; mem. written exam. com. Am. Bd. Radiology. Mem. Internat. Assn. Study Lung Cancer, Am. Soc. Clin. Onco- logy, Am. Radium Soc., Am. Assn. Cancer Research, Am. Assn. Cancer Edn., Am. Coll. Radiology, Radiol. Soc. N.Am., Brit. Inst. Radiology, Assn. Univ. Radiologists, AAAS, AMA, Mo. Radiol. Soc., Mo. Acad. Sci., Mo., St. Louis med. socs., Greater St. Louis Soc. Radiologists, Radiation Research Soc., Soc. Surg. Oncologists, Am. Soc. Therapeutic Radiologists. Contbr. articles to profl. publs.; editorial bd. Yearbook of Cancer, 1973—; asso. editor, mem. editorial bd. Internat. Jour. Radiation Oncology, Biology and Physics, 1975—. Home: 3 Layton Terr Saint Louis MO 63124 Office: Div Radiation Oncology 4511 Forest Park Blvd Saint Louis MO 63108

PERK, RALPH JOSEPH, mayor of Cleve.; b. Cleve., Jan. 19, 1914; s. Joseph Charles and Mary (Smirt) P.; evening student Cleve. Coll. of Western Res. U., 1942-43, 54-55, St. Johns Coll., 1959; certificate Bethany Coll., 1960; LL.B., Ill. Benedictine Coll., 1974; m. Lucille Gagliardi, May 4, 1941; children—Virginia (Mrs. Cecil Bowers), Ralph Joseph, Kenneth, Thomas, Michael, Allen, Richard. Staff mem. of Atty. Gen. of Ohio, 1950-53; mem. City Council, Cleve., 1953-63; county auditor Cuyahoga County (Ohio), 1963-71; mayor Cleve., 1971—. Mem. Greater Cleve. Growth Bd., 1964—; mem. Pres.'s Adv. Com. on Pub. Opinion, 1970—; v.p. Greater Cleve. Safety Council, 1971—; mem. NCCJ; founder, chmn. Am. Nationalities Movement Ohio; chmn. Cleve. Conv. and Visitors Bur.; chmn. Chmn. Ohio Electoral Coll., 1968, 72; del. to Republican State Convs., 1940—, Rep. Nat. Conv., 1972, 76. Recipient Outstanding Citizenship award VFW, 1957; named Cath. Man of Year of Cleve. Diocese, 1955. Mem. U.S. Conf. Mayors (adv. bd.), Nat. Conf. Rep. Mayors (chmn.), Nat. League Cities, Citizens League Greater Cleve., Cleve. Inst. Music, Cleve., No. Ohio opera assns. Kiwanian. Home: 3421 E 49th St Cleveland OH 44127 Office: 601 Lakeside Ave Cleveland OH 44114

PERKIN, ETHEL MURPHY (MRS. FRANK SCOTT PERKIN), clubworker; b. Chgo., July 21, 1916; d. John F. and Ethel (Howden) Murphy; sutdent Highland Park Jr. Coll., 1935-37; A.B. in English Edn., Wayne U., 1939; m. Frank Scott Perkin, Feb. 27, 1942 (dec. Nov. 1973); children—Linda Josephine, John Francis, Sandra Ethel. Tchr. elementary English, lit., gen. lang., Detroit, 1941-45; personnel counselor women Plymouth plant Chrysler Corp., Detroit, 1943; asst. sec., dir. Murphy Ventures Corp., Grosse Pointe, Mich., 1956—. Chmn. membership Harper Hosp. Aux., Detroit, 1951, chmn. publicity, 1961; treas. Maire Sch. P.T.A., Grosse Pointe, 1960-62, mem. P.T.A. Council, 1960-62; mem. bd. Mich. Humane Soc.; 2d v.p. Women's City Club of Detroit, 1969-71, bd. dirs., 1964—, nominating com., 1972—; mem. women's aux. Wayne County Med. Soc., 1942—; mem. women's com. Grosse Pointe Symphony Orch.; life mem. Women's assn. Detroit Symphony Orch.; mem. women's div. Project Hope. Mem. Detroit Hist. Soc. (life) Internat. Platform Assn., Art Founders' Soc., Archives Am. Art, Detroit, Friends Pub. Library, Grosse Pointe, AAUW, Detroit Rev. Club (pres. 1974-75), Liggett Sch. Parents Assn. (bd. 1965-66), Alpha Gamma Delta. Club: Colony Town (asst. rec. sec. 1975-78). Address: 1709 Shore Club Dr St Clair Shores MI 48080

PERKINS, EDWARD HOWARD, JR., mfg. co. exec.; b. Flint, Mich., May 2, 1927; s. Edward Howard and Bertha Katherine (Talbot) P.; A.B., U. Mich., 1948, B.S., 1950; m. Elaine Wagley, Dec. 28, 1955; children—Jeffrey Perry, Edward Howard III. Trainee, sales engr. Aluminum Co. Am., Jackson, Mich., 1950-51; sales engr. Brooks & Perkins, Inc., N.Y.C., 1952-53, v.p., dir., Detroit, 1955, exec. v.p., 1960-61, pres., 1961-67, chief exec. officer, 1963-67, chmn. bd., pres.,1967—; dir. Wall Colmonoy Corp., Douglas & Lomason Co., City Nat. Bank Detroit, No. States Bancorp. Bd. govs. Cranbrook Inst. Sci., 1967—. Served with AUS, 1954-55. Mem. Magnesium Assn. (pres. 1961-62, dir. 1961—), Employers Assn. Detroit (v.p. 1969—, dir. 1966—, chmn. 1973), World Bus. Council, Am. Soc. Metals. Presbyterian. Clubs: Detroit; Orchard Lake (Mich.) Country; Bloomfield Hills (Mich.) Country; Hidden Valley; Mill Reef (Antigua, W.I.). Home: 381 Keswick Rd Bloomfield Hills MI 48013 Office: 17515 W Nine Mile Rd Southfield MI 48075

PERKINS, FREDERICK GARLAND, III, photog. equipment mfg. co. exec.; b. Jersey City, Apr. 5, 1932; s. Frederick Garland and Gertrude Shields P.; B.A., U. Wis., 1954; M.B.A., Harvard U., 1961; m. Caroline Trefry, Aug. 28, 1976; children—Frederick G., IV, John Robert, Diane Frances. Staff cons. Price Waterhouse & Co., Chgo., 1962-64; sales mgr. Hitemp Inc., Northlake, Ill., 1964-67; pres. Revco, Inc., W. Columbia, S.C., 1967-69; v.p., Guerdon Industries, Louisville, Ky., 1969-71, pres., 1971-72; pres. Perkins & Assos., Columbia, S.C., 1972-73; pres. Calumet Scientific Inc., Elk Grove Village, Ill., 1973—; dir. Helados 33. Served with USAF, 1954-59. Club: Harvard Bus. Sch. Home: 175 E Delaware Pl Chicago IL 60611 Office: 1590 Touhy Ave Elk Grove Village IL 60007

PERKINS, JOHN HAROLD, banker; b. Chgo., Aug. 28, 1921; s. Harold Reed and Roschen (Baker) P.; B.S., Northwestern U., 1943; m. Len Welborn, June 24, 1944; children—John H., Robert G., Reed F. With Continental Ill. Nat. Bank & Trust Co., Chgo., 1946—, asst. cashier, 1949-52, 2d v.p., 1952-56, v.p., 1956-65, sr. v.p., 1965-68, exec. v.p., dir., 1968-71, vice chmn., 1971-73, pres., 1973—; pres. Continental Ill. Corp., 1973—; dir. Continental Bank Internat., Continental Ill. Overseas Service Corp., Continental Internat. Fin. Corp., Pillsbury Co.; chmn. Continental Ill. Venture Corp.; lectr. Sch. Banking, Baton Rouge, 1954-58, Madison, Wis., 1956—; instr. fin. dept. Northwestern U., 1950-54; bd. govs. Midwest Stock Exchange; Bd. dirs. Community Fund; trustee Northwestern U.; trustee Chgo. Symphony Orch., Episcopal Diocesan Found., Underwriters Labs., Michael Reese Hosp. and Med. Center. Served with USNR, 1943-46. Mem. Econ. Club, Assn. Res. City Bankers, Am. Bankers Assn. (dir., mem. governing council), U.S. C. of C. (policy com.), Phi Beta Kappa, Delta Tau Delta. Clubs: Wall St. (N.Y.C.); Indian Hill (Winnetka, Ill.); Met. (Chgo. and Washington); Bankers, Little La Salle St., Econ., Chgo., Univ., Carlton, Comml., Bond (Chgo.); Old Elm (Ft. Sheridan, Ill.). Office: Continental Bank 231 S LaSalle St Chicago IL 60693

PERKINS, JOHN ROBERT, advt. exec., musician; b. Schenectady, Mar. 7, 1938; s. John R. and Catherine (Brown) P.; B.S., U. Ky., 1960; M. Sacred Music, So. Bapt. Coll., 1964; m. Sharon Lynn Cook, Aug. 24, 1958; children—Karon E., Laura L., Melissa A. Asst. research met. Bethlehem Steel Co., Lackawanna, N.Y., 1960; dir. research, account exec. Jayme Orgn., Cleve., 1960-65; asso. media dir.-indsl. products Meldrum & Fewsmith, Cleve., 1965-67; supr. marketing services Taylor-Winfield Corp., Warren, Ohio, 1967-68, mgr. promotion and mktg., 1968-69; account exec. Campbell-Ewald Co., 1969-74, account supr., 1974-76; copy chief Delco Remy div. Gen. Motors Corp., Anderson, Ind., 1976—. Fellow AAAS; mem. Am. Inst. Mining and Metall. Engrs., Assn. Indsl. Advertisers, Ky. Soc. Profl. Engrs. Clubs: Masons, K.T., Shriners, Edgewood Country, Detroit Adcraft. Contbr. articles to profl. jours. Composer, arranger, condr. sacred music, French hornist various local orchs., 1960—. Home: 3422 Berkeley Rd Anderson IN 46011 Office: 2401 Columbus Ave Anderson IN 46011

PERKINS, MARVIN DEUANE, real estate broker; b. Hoyt, Kans., Nov. 5, 1934; s. David Elmer and Gladys Lucille (Vaught) P.; B.A.I.S., Columbia Coll., 1975; m. Virginia Lee Hoyt, Sept. 9, 1956; children—Bradley Allen, Trudy Lynn, Tracy Scott. Sales mgr. George B. Emery Jr., real estate and ins., Topeka, 1963-64, Gerlach Marcy Co., realtors, Topeka, 1965-67; owner M.D. Perkins Agy., real estate, Topeka, 1967-68, 70-74; partner Coin-op. Laundry P & W Enterprises, Topeka, 1963-76; v.p. Thomas E. Crosley & Assos., realtors, Topeka, 1975-76; appraiser-broker Griffith & Blair, Inc., Topeka, 1976—; lectr. in field; treas. Topeka Bd. Realtors, 1972. Pres., Tecumseh Sch. Parent-Tchr. Orgn., 1973-74; trustee Topeka Twp., 1977—; clk., 1965-68, justice of peace, 1973-74; chmn. Topeka Bd. Equal Opportunity in Housing Com., 1975; bd. govs. Kans. Grad. Realtors Inst., 1975—, dean, 1977. Served to maj. AUS, 1968-69; Vietnam; to lt. col. Res., 1969—. Decorated Bronze Star; certified rev. appraiser, real estate counselor. Mem. Eastboro Mchts. Assn. (dir. 1974-75), Shawnee Heights Boosters Club (dir. 1975—), Assn. U.S. Army (dir. 1970-72), Topeka Housebuilders Assn. (v.p. 1963), Topeka Real Estate Bd., Kans. (v.p. zone 1, 1978), Nat. assns. realtors, Nat. Inst. Real Estate Brokers, Nat. Guard Assn. Kans. and U.S., Ind. Fee Appraisers, VFW, Am. Legion. Methodist (adminstrv. bd.). Clubs: Optimists (v.p. Shawnee Heights 1974), Toastmasters (edn. v.p. Topeka chpt. 1963), Masons, Shriners, Lake Shore Country (pres. 1973). Research new methods appraisal. Home: 2426 SE 37th St Topeka KS 66611 Office: Griffith & Blair Inc 2222 W 29th St Topeka KS 66611

PERKINS, WILLIAM H., JR., financial co. exec.; b. Rushville, Ill., Aug. 4, 1921; s. William H. and Sarah Elizabeth (Logsdon) P.; ed. Ill. Coll.; m. Eileen Margaret Nelson, Jan. 14, 1949; 1 son, Gary Douglas. Legis. rep. CNA Fin. Corp., Chgo., 1949—. Mem. Nat. Armed Forces Mus. Adv. Bd. of Smithsonian Instn., 1964—; mem. Ill. AEC, 1963—, sec., 1970—; mem. Ill. Traffic Safety Adv. Council; sgt.-at-arms Dem. Nat. Conv., 1952, 56, del.-at-large, 1964, 68, 72; spl. asst. to chmn. Dem. Nat. Com., 1960; mem. Presdl. Inaugural Com., 1961, 65, 69, 73. Served with AUS, 1944-46; aide to prime minister and Brit. ambassador at founding of UN, 1945. Mem. Internat. Platform Assn., Ill. C. of C. (chmn. legis. com. 1971), Ins. Fedn. Ill. (pres. 1965—, also dir.), Ins. Econs. Soc. Am. (treas. 1970—), Chgo. Assn. Commerce and Industry (legis com.), Health Ins. Assn. Am. Methodist. Clubs: Masons, Shriners; Ill. Athletic (Chgo.); Sangamo (Springfield, Ill.); Riverside (Ill.); Fed. City (Washington). Home: 52 N Cowley Rd Riverside IL 60546 Office: CNA Plaza Chicago IL 60685

PERKINS, WILLIAM SWAIN, lawyer; b. Springfield, Mo., July 15, 1945; s. William Winthrop and Lena (Swain) P.; B.S., Ark. State U., 1967; J.D., U. Ark., 1971; m. Karen Gay Carhart, Mar. 11, 1972. Legal analyst Ark. Legis. Council, Little Rock, 1970-71; admitted to Mo. bar, 1971; asso. Patrick O. Freeman Jr., Thayer, Mo., 1971-73; pvt. practice law, Alton, Mo., 1973—; pros. atty. Oregon County, Mo., 1973—. Atty., City of Thayer, Mo., 1973-74, City of Koshkonong, Mo., 1973, City of Birch Tree, Mo., 1974. Committeeman, Dem. party, 1973. Mem. 37th Jud. Dist. (v.p. 1974-75, pres. 1975—), Am., Mo. bar assns. Mason (K.T.). Home: Box 455 Koshkonong MO 65692 Office: Box 304 Alton MO 65606

PERLMAN, DANIEL HESSEL, univ. adminstr.; b. Chgo., Sept. 24, 1935; s. Henry B. and Dorothy (Zimmerman) Perlman; m. Suzanne Meyer, June 30, 1966; children—Julia, David. B.A., Shimer Coll., 1954; B.A., U. Chgo., 1955, M.A., 1956, Ph.D., 1971. Registered Psychologist, Ill. Psychol. counselor Roosevelt U., 1961-64, asst. to pres., 1965-70, dir. govt. relations and planning, 1970-72, sec. bd. trustees, 1965—, prof. edn., 1974—, dean adminstrn., 1972—. Spl. asst. to the dep. commr. for higher and continuing edn. U.S. Dept. Health, Edn., Welfare, 1977-78. Bd. dirs. Congregation K.A.M. Isaiah Israel, 1970-75. Mem. Am. Assn. Higher Edn., AAUP, Am. Assn. Univ. Adminstrs., Am. Ednl. Research Assn., Nat. Council Univ. Research Adminstrs., Soc. Coll. and Univ. Planning. Recipient Distinguished Alumnus award Shimer Coll., 1972; sr. Fulbright-Hays lectr., Philippines, 1975; Am. Council on Edn. fellow, 1972-73. Contbr. articles to profl. jours. Home: 413 Grove St Evanston IL 60201 Office: 430 S Michigan Av Chicago IL 60605

PERLMAN, EDWARD, housewares distbg. co. exec.; b. Chgo., May 29, 1927; s. Nathan Hyman and Leona (Levin) P.; B.S., U. Ill., 1950; m. Roberta Cohen, Mar. 10, 1951; children—David, Rachel, Daniel. Exec. v.p. Handy Button Machine Co., Chgo., 1950-65; asst. sec., treas. Gordon-Burke Steel Co., Chgo., 1965; pres. Internat. Metals Co., Chgo., 1965-66; registered rep. H. Hentz & Co., Chgo., 1966-71; pres. Mars Housewares Inc., Evanston, Ill., 1971—. Asso. bd. Nat. Conf. Christians and Jews, 1958-65, Mt. Sinai Hosp., 1963-67. Served with USNR, 1945-46. Mem. Am. Research Merchandising Inst. Home: 133 Timber Ln Glencoe IL 60022 Office: 1000 Grey Ave Evanston IL 60202

PERLMUTTER, MARION A., psychologist; b. N.Y.C., Sept. 2, 1948; d. Frank and Eleanor (Lifshutz) P.; B.A., Syracuse U., 1970; M.S., State U. N.Y., Albany, 1971; Ph.D., U. Mass., 1976. Asst. prof. psychology U. Minn., Mpls., 1976—. Mem. AAAS, Am. Psychol. Assn., Gerontol. Soc., Soc. Research Child Devel. Contbr. articles to profl. jours and chpts. to books. Home: 1600 S 6th St Minneapolis MN 55454 Office: Inst Child Development Univ Minn Minneapolis MN 55455

PERLOFF, RICHARD MARK, educator; b. July 28, 1951; A.B. with distinction, U. Mich., 1972; M.S. in Communications, U. Pitts., 1975; Ph.D. candidate, U. Wis., 1977. VISTA vol., N.Y.C., 1972-73; interviewer Am. Inst. for Research, Palo Alto., Calif., 1974; teaching asst., dept. speech and theatre arts, U. Pitts., 1974-75; teaching asst. sch. journalism and mass communication, U. Wis., Madison, 1976—, sci. writer Univ.-Indsl. Research Program, 1976. Campaign worker Robert F. Kennedy for Pres., Ind., 1968; George McGovern for Pres., 1972. Mem. Assn. for Edn. in Journalism (student mem.), Internat. Communication Assn., Am. Psychol. Assn. (asso.). Contbr. articles in field to newspapers and profl. jours. Home: 815 Saint James St Pittsburgh PA 15232 Office: Mass Communications Research Center 5050 Vilas Hall Univ Wis Madison WI 53706

PERLOW, S. JAMES, steel co. exec.; b. Chgo., June 10, 1945; s. Roland Leo and Mildred (Glassman) P.; B.S., U. Wis., 1967; J.D., Northwestern U., 1970; m. Marjorie Rose Gordon, May 1, 1976. Vice pres. R.L. Perlow Steel Corp., Chgo., 1970—; dir. Al-Per Bldg. Corp.; cons. Dante Co.; admitted to Ill. bar. Recipient Pres.'s award Assn. Steel Distbrs., Elk's Youth Leadership award. Mem. Am., Ill., Chgo. bar assns., Assn. Steel Distbrs. (nat. bd. dirs.), U.S., Ill., Chgo. S. (dir. 1976, pres. young men's bus. com. 1975). Jewish. Home: 1440 N State Pkwy Chicago IL 60610 Office: 933 E 95th St Chicago IL 60619

PERNER, DENNIS MAX, banker; b. Pittsville, Wis., Jan. 19, 1913; s. Bruno M. and Selma W. (Daemmrich) P.; student Spencerian Coll., Milw., 1931-32; m. Luella S. Goodwin, Oct. 16, 1937; children—Dorothy M. (Mrs. Eugene M. Raatz), Shirley L. (Mrs. Charles W. Beckman), Marjorie E. (Mrs. Roy E. Carlson), Suzanne R. (Mrs. John C. Husmoc), Loretta J. Free-lance ct. reporter, Wis., 1932-33; co. clk. Civilian Conservation Corps, Wis., 1933-36; parts dept. mgr. Hall Garage Corp., Wausau, Wis., 1936-37; stenographer Wis. State Legislature, 1937; reporter Div. Consumer Credit Wis. Banking Dept., 1937-57; v.p. First Am. State Bank, Wausau, 1957-59; cashier Community State Bank, Eau Claire, 1959-63; cashier People's State Bank, Wausau, 1963—; instr. Am. Inst. Banking, 1964. Treas. Wausau Area Taxpayers League, 1969—. Bd. dirs. Wausau chpt. Muscular Dystrophy Assn. Am., Inc., 1969—. Recipient plaque and citation merit Muscular Dystrophy Assn. Am., Inc., 1970-71. Mem. Am. Inst. Banking, Chippewa-Eau Claire County Bankers Assn. (sec.-treas. 1962). Home: 1022 S 5th Ave Wausau WI 54401 Office: 1905 W Stewart Ave Wausau WI 54401

PEROS, ALEX GEORGE, acupuncturist, chiropractor; b. Pretoria, S. Africa, Jan. 17, 1934; s. George and Irene (Tsolas) P.; came to U.S., 1954, naturalized, 1962; student Witwatersrand Tech. Coll., 1950-52, Britzuis Bus. Coll., 1952-53; D. Chiropractic, Los Angeles Coll. Chiropractic, 1960; m. Cheryl Ann Robinson, Aug. 26, 1971; children—Diane, Darlene, Dean, Dale, Brian, Trina, Andrew. Asst. to Ray La Fontaine, D. Chiropractic, Eureka, Calif., 1960; pvt. practice chiropractic, Eureka, 1961-64, Watseka, Ill., 1964-67, Crescent City, Ill., 1967-70, Fairbury, Ill., 1970—; pres. Peros Acupuncture Center, Fairbury, 1975—. Precinct committeeman, exec.-sec. Iroquois County Republican party, 1964-68. Mem. Eureka (v.p. 1962-64, Keyman award community devel. 1963), Internat. (senate 1963-75) jr. chambers commerce, Acad. Chinese Medicine (charter), Internat. Chiropractic Physicians Acupuncture Assn. (dir. 1975-76), Nev. Assn. Chinese Medicine (hon.). Clubs: Masons, Moose. Office: 310 S 7th St Fairbury IL 61739

PERPICH, RUDY G., gov. Minn.; b. Carson Lake, Minn., June 27, 1928; s. Anton and Mary (Vukelich) P.; A.A., Hibbing Jr. Coll., 1950, D.D.S., Marquette U., 1954; m. Delores Helen Simic, Sept. 4, 1954; children—Rudy George, Mary-Susan. Lt. gov. of Minn., 1971-76, gov., 1976—. Mem. Hibbing (Minn.) Bd. Edn., 1956-62. Mem. Minn. Senate, 1962-70. Served with AUS, 1946-47. Roman Catholic. Address: State Capitol Bldg St Paul MN 55155

PERRET, MAURICE EDMOND, educator; b. La Chaux-de-Fonds, Switzerland, May 19, 1911; s. Jules Henri and Henriette Marie (Leuba) P.; Bac. es Lettres, U. Zurich (Switzerland), 1930; License es Lettres, U. Neuchatel (Switzerland), 1940; M.A. (Internat. House fellow 1940-42), U. Calif. at Berkeley, 1942; Doctorat es Lettres, U. Lausanne (Switzerland), 1950. Tchr., Petropolis and Lycee Francais, Rio de Janeiro, Brazil, 1935-37; asst. consulate Switzerland, San Francisco, 1942-43; del. internat. com. Red Cross, Washington, 1943-45; del. Aid to Arab Refugees, Palestine, 1949-51; asst. Internat. Telecommunication Union, Geneva, Switzerland, 1951-52; librarian La Chaux-de-Fonds, Switzerland, 1953-54; asst. Oltremare, Rome, Italy, 1955-56; prof. Avenches, Switzerland, 1957-63; prof. geography, map librarian U. Wis., Stevens Point, 1963—. Curator Roman Mus., Avenches, Switzerland, 1960-63. Mem. city council Avenches, Switzerland, 1961-63. Served with Swiss Army, 1939-40. Mem. Assn. Am. Geographers, Nat. Council Geog. Edn., Am. Geog. Soc., Wis. Acad. Scis., Arts and Letters, Societe vaudoise de geographie (v.p. 1960-63), Fedn. Swiss Geog. Socs. (v.p. 1961-63). Editorial com. Atlas Switzerland, 1960-63. Contbr. articles to profl. jours. Home: 1711 Jefferson St Stevens Point WI 54481 Office: Geography Dept U Wis Stevens Point WI 54481

PERROTTO, LARRY JAMES, publisher; b. Oil City, Pa., Apr. 16, 1938; s. James Vincent and Ann (Bagnato) P.; student Allegheny Coll., 1955-56; B.S., Edinboro State Coll., 1959; m. Jill Gisewhite, Sept. 21, 1956; children—James, Mark, John. Announcer, news reporter WMGW Radio, Meadville, Pa., 1953-59; sales mgr. WPIC Radio, Sharon, 1959-63; sta. mgr. WLSV Radio, Wellsville, N.Y., 1963-64, gen. mgr., 1964—; gen. mgr. WWGO Radio, Erie, Pa., 1964-67; pub. Daily Am. Newspaper, West Frankfort, Ill., 1967—; treas., dir. Am. Daily Pub. Corp., West Frankfort, 1968—; sec., dir. Marion Pub. Co. (Ill.), Carmi Times Pub. Co. (Ill.), Hartford City News-Times Co. (Ind.), Barber Mine Timber Co. (Ill.). Chmn. adv. bd. Smith Negro Welfare Assn., Erie, Pa., 1965-67. Bd. dirs., treas. West Frankfort Community Council, 1971—; bd. dirs. So. Ill., Inc., Franklin Hosp., Benton, Ill. Mem. Ill. Daily Press Assn., Nat. Assn. Broadcasters, West Frankfort C. of C. (dir.). Roman Catholic. K.C. Home: 47 Frankfort Dr West Frankfort IL 62896 Office: 111 S Emma St West Frankfort IL 62896

PERRY, ESTHER MARY IZZO (MRS. PETER PERRY), librarian; b. Chgo., Jan. 31, 1917; d. Ralph Anthony and Louise (Picerno) Izzo; student Wilson Jr. Coll., 1934; m. Peter Perry, June 24, 1939; children—Peter, Daniel, Christine. Maintenance clk. Teletype Corp., Skokie, Ill., 1938; cataloguer, Northlake (Ill.) Pub. Library, 1958-62, dir., 1962—, head cataloger, 1972—. Sec., PTA, 1960. Mem. Am., Ill. library assns., Library Adminstrs. Conf. No. Ill., Suburban Library System. Club: Garden (Northlake). Home: 36 East Dr Northlake IL 60164 Office: 231 N Wolf Rd Northlake IL 60164

PERRY, GEORGE WILLIAM, communications co. exec.; b. Central City, Ill., Sept. 23, 1925; s. George and Florence May (Gott) P.; B.S.C., Northwestern U., 1955; m. Elaine Lois Berezin, Jan. 13, 1951; children—Robin A., Eric T. Freelance actor, announcer, radio, TV, recordings, film, vaudeville, theatre, Chgo., 1938-53; orders and service mgr. RCA Rec. Studios, Chgo., 1951-53; asst. dir. radio and TV, Nat. Safety Council, Chgo., 1953-61, mem. pub. info. conf., 1961-76; exec. sec. Chicago Unlimited Inc., 1961—; charter mem., treas. Joseph Jefferson Awards Com., 1969-73; bd. advisers Bedside Network, 1972—; mem. steering com. Midwest Seminar Videotape and Film, Chgo., 1974-75. Publicity dir. Oakton Cub Scouts, Evanston, 1968. Served with USAAF, 1943-45. Mem. Nat. Acad. TV Arts and Scis. (exec. dir. Chgo. chpt. 1961-73), Goodman Sch. Drama Alumni Assn. (exec. sec. 1977—). Editor: CU Directory, CU Digest, Weekly, 1961—. Office: 203 N Wabash Ave Suite 1020 Chicago IL 60601

PERRY, GLENN EARL, polit. scientist, educator; b. Tedders, Ky., Jan. 28, 1940; s. Tollie and Mazie Pearl (Taylor) P.; A.B., Union Coll., 1960; Ph.D., U. Va., 1964; postdoctoral Princeton, 1967-68; m. Eleanor Rose Hypes, Aug. 13, 1963; children—Barbara, Glenn, Jr., Catherine, Lucy, Alexander. Instr. polit. sci. Union Coll., Barbourville, Ky., 1960; asst. prof. polit. sci. U. SW La., Lafayette, 1963-66; asst. prof. Ind. State U., Terre Haute, 1966-68, asso. prof., 1970-77, prof., 1977—; vis. asst. prof. Am. U., Cairo, Egypt, 1968-70. Woodrow Wilson fellow, 1960-61; NDEA fellow, 1960-63; Nat. Def. Fgn. Lang. fellow, 1967-68; Fulbright grantee, 1965. Fellow Middle East Studies Assn. N.Am.; mem. Middle East Inst., Am. Polit. Sci. Assn. Contbr. articles to profl. jours. and books. Home: 2913 Crawford St Terre Haute IN 47803 Office: Dept Polit Sci Ind State U Terre Haute IN 47809

PERRY, HAROLD, radiation therapist; b. Hamtramck, Mich., June 26, 1924; s. James Arthur and Ida B. (Hill) P.; student Wayne State U., 1941-43, Cornell U., 1944; M.D., Howard U., 1948; m. Agnes Marie Barnes, June 12, 1948; children—Harold Arthur, Karen Fanchon, Michael Elliott. Intern, Freedmen's Hosp., Washington, 1948-49, resident in radiology, 1949-52; resident in radiation therapy Meml. Hosp. for Cancer and Allied Diseases, N.Y.C., 1952, 55, Olin-Squibb Sr. fellow, 1964; Kress fellow in radiation therapy Meml. Hosp., dept. biophysics Sloan-Kettering Inst., N.Y.C., 1956-57; asst. prof. radiology U. Cin., 1957-63, asso. prof., 1963-66; clin. asso. prof. radiology Wayne State U., 1966-68, adj. asso. prof., 1969-73, clin. asso. prof., 1973—; pvt. practice medicine specializing in radiation therapy, Detroit, 1966—; asso. mem. staff S.W. Oncology Group, Detroit, 1976—; mem. staffs Sinai, Detroit VA hosps., S. Macomb Hosp., Warren, Mich.; dir. radiation therapy Abraham and Anna Srere Radiation Therapy Center, Sinai Hosp., Detroit, 1966—; bd. dirs. Mich. Cancer Found., Detroit, 1968—; mem. hosp. adv. council S.E. Mich. Regional Med. Program, 1969—, mem. radiation therapy adv. council, 1969—; mem. exec. com. Mich. Cancer Found., 1970—, co-dir. radiation therapy network Met. Detroit Cancer Control Program, 1974—, chmn. radiation therapy adv. panel, 1976—, vice chmn. bd., 1976—. Served with AUS, 1942-46, as capt. M.C., USAF, 1953-55. Diplomate Am. Bd. Radiology. Fellow Am. Coll. Radiology; mem. AAAS, N.Y. Acad. Scis., Am. Radium Soc., Radiol. Soc. N.Am., Am. Soc. Therapeutic Radiologists (chmn. com. on edn. 1968-69), AMA, Wayne County (Mich.) Med. Soc., Mich. Radiol. Soc. (pres. 1977—), Mich. Soc. Therapeutic Radiologists, Detroit Cancer Club, Nat. Med. Assn., Kappa Pi. Contbr. articles to profl. jours. Home: 287 Orange Lake Dr Bloomfield Hills MI 48013 Office: 6767 W Outer Dr Detroit MI 48235

PERRY, IRVING CHESTER, III, real estate broker; b. Phila., Jan. 18, 1943; s. Irving Chester and Erma (McNeil) P.; B.A., Lake Forest Coll., 1965; m. Dayanne Schurecht, Aug. 27, 1966; 1 son, London Schade. Sr. mgmt. trainee Brit. Overseas Airways Corp., London, 1968-69; founder, owner ITEC Internat. Ltd., Barrington, Ill., 1969—, pres. 1970—, chmn. bd. dirs., 1970—; pres. ITEC Trading Co., Ltd., Barrington; tchr. local courses in fin. and real estate; mem. O'Hare Group for Industry and Bus., 1972—. Served with AUS, 1965-68. Decorated Air medal, Purple Heart, Army Commdation medal. Mem. Barrington Bd. Realtors (dir. 1974—), Barrington C. of C., Chgo. Real Estate Bd., Internat. Real Estate Fedn., Nat. Inst. Farm and Land Brokers, Nat. Inst. Real Estate Brokers, Kappa Sigma. Mem. Religious Soc. Friends. Club: Barrington Bath and Tennis. Home: 200 Coolidge St Barrington IL 60010 Office: 111 North Ave Barrington IL 60010

PERRY, JAMES EDWARD, food franchising co. exec.; b. St. Louis, Aug. 5, 1949; s. Louis Claude and Ora Louise (Gothard) P.; B.S. in Marketing, St. Louis U., 1972, M.B.A. in Marketing, 1974; m. Sandra Lee Hammond, Aug. 20, 1977; Purchasing v.p. Louis C. Perry Co., St. Louis, 1974—; media planner and buyer D'Arcy MacManus and Masius Advt., St. Louis, 1972-74; media dir. Total Communications Advt., St. Louis, 1974-76; dir. field marketing Arthur Treacher's Fish & Chips, Columbus, O., 1976—. Membership chmn. St. Louis Young Republicans Club, 1968; judge for Emmy award for pub. service campaigns Acad. TV Arts and Scis., 1976. Mem. Am. Marketing Assn., Am. Mgmt. Assn., Columbus Advt. Fedn., Columbus C. of C. Roman Catholic. Home: 3170 Cranston St Dublin OH 43017 Office: 1328 Dublin Rd Columbus OH 43215

PERRY, JIMMY DALE, trade co. exec.; b. Gilbert, W.Va., Aug. 7, 1944; s. Troy Edward and Marjorie Kathleen (Beanblossom) P.; student W.Va. U., 1962-66, U. Nebr. at Omaha, 1977, Bellevue Coll., 1977—; m. Lois Faye Lasley, Dec. 26, 1971. Parts mgr. Truesdell Distbg. Corp., Omaha, 1976—; instr. electronics parttime Met. Tech. Community Coll., Omaha, 1976—; electronics field service engr. Ohio Nuclear Inc., Omaha, 1975-76. Served with USN, 1966-75; Vietnam. Decorated Vietnamese Gallantry Cross. Home: 7203 Chandler Hills Dr Omaha NE 68147 Office: 6009 Center St Omaha NE 68106

PERRY, MILTON FREEMAN, found. exec.; b. Ahoskie, N.C., Aug. 14, 1926; s. Rosville Westley and Etta May (Holloman) P.; B.A., Coll. William and Mary, 1950, postgrad., 1951; m. Barbara Lee Posivak, Apr. 7, 1949; children—Carolyn (Mrs. Charles Vellar), Julia (Mrs. John Bakos), Linda. Instr. history Coll. William and Mary, 1951; asst. to dir. Craft Shops, Coll. Williamsburg, 1951-52; curator Fort Macon State Park, N.C., 1952-53; curator history West Point Mus., N.Y., 1953-58; mus. curator Harry S. Truman Library and Mus., Independence, Mo., 1958-76; dir. history Historic Kansas City (Mo.) Found., 1976—; mus. cons. Jackson County (Mo.) Parks, Joseph Smith Properties, Nauvoo, Ill., Jackson County (Mo.) Hist. Soc., World Hdqrs., Saints Ch., Wornall House Restoration, Kansas City, Mo., 35th Div. Hist. Assn., George C. Marshall Library, Ft. Leavenworth Mus.; instr. mus. appreciation Penn Valley Coll.; mem. Mo. Adv. Council on Historic Sites and Bldgs., 1969—; mem. council Mo. Heritage Trust, 1976—. Served with USAF, 1945-47. Mem. Am. Assn. Museums Council, Mo. Museums Assos. (pres. 1971-73), Midwest Museums Conf. (v.p. 1967-72, regional rep. 1972—), Museums Council Mid-Am. (chmn. 1968—), Mountain-Plains Museums Conf. (sec. 1971-72). Author: Infernal Machines: The Story of Confederate Submarine and Mine Warfare 1861-1865, 1965; co-author (with Barbara W. Parke): Patton and His Pistols, 1957; (with James A. Ryan, Gayle Eggen, Patricia Hardy): Mulkey Square 1869-1973, 1973. Home: 1005A Quality Hill Towers 817 Jefferson St Kansas City MO 64105 Office: 20 W 9th St Bldg Kansas City MO 64105

PERRY, NEVA SABBAGH, personal counselor; b. West Lafayette, Ind., Mar. 4, 1934; d. Elias Morshed and Waded Kathryn (Corey) Sabbagh; B.S.H.E., Purdue U., 1955, M.S., 1973, postgrad., 1973—; children by former marriage—Steven David, Michael Andrew. Mng. editor The Purdue Alumnus, Purdue U., West Lafayette, 1956-61; tchr. home econs. North Jr. High Sch., Randolph, Mass., 1968-72; guidance counselor Frankfort (Ind.) Jr. High Sch., 1974-76; counselor Title XX social services and child welfare units Dept. Pub. Welfare, Lafayette, 1976—; pvt. practice individual, family, marriage and divorce counseling, divorce adjustment groups, workshops for singles, Lafayette, 1976—. Program-edn. dir., discussion-workshop facilitator Lafayette chpt. Parents Without Partners, 1973-76; vol. counselor Crisis Center Lafayette, 1973-74; participant, facilitator workships in human relations, common skills, non-verbal, Gestalt, 1972-77. Mem. Am. Personnel and Guidance Assn., Am. Mental Health Counselors Assn., Assn. Specialists in Group Work, Gestalt Inst. Cleve. Home: 2550 Yeager Rd West Lafayette IN 47906 Office: Tippecanoe County Office Bldg 20 N 3d St Lafayette IN 47901

PERRY, OSCAR L., SR., clergyman; b. Blytheville, Ark., Apr. 9, 1935; s. Will and Lettie (Lewis) P.; D.D. (hon.) in Religious Sci. and Art, 1975; m. Dariene Burgess, Feb. 14, 1954; children—Oscar L., Brenda K. Ordained to ministry Pentecostal Ch., 1954; asst. pastor Power House Ch. God in Christ, 1955-69; pastor Mt. Sinai Ch., Indpls., 1969—; plant mgr. Carter Indsl. Service, Anderson, Ind., 1976—; v.p. Inst. of Religious Sci., Inc., Gary, Ind., 1975-77. Mem. Am. Hort. Soc. Home: 2121 Brentwood Dr Anderson IN 46011 Office: PO Box 2739 Anderson IN 46011

PERRY, RICHARD PALESE, dentist; b. Chgo., Apr. 7, 1940; s. Robert Palese and Gertrude Katherine (Hyman) P.; B.S., Roosevelt U., 1963; D.D.S., U. Ill., 1968; m. Eleanor Theresa Bruni, Aug. 21, 1966; children—Katherine, Sara, Teresa. Gen. practice dentistry, Chgo., 1968—; asst. prof. operative dentistry U. Ill., 1970—; dental cons. Schwab Rehab. Hosp., Park House Nursing Center, Belhaven Nursing Home. Pres. Western Polk Neighborhood Assn., 1969-70. Mem. Am. Soc. Preventive Dentistry, Am. Soc. Dentistry for the Handicapped, Chgo. (pres. West Side br. 1975-76, sec. 1973-74), Ill. dental socs., ADA, Acad. Gen. Dentistry, Am. Soc. Geriatric Dentistry, Am. Endodontic Soc., Am. Assn. Dental Schs., Acad. Operative Dentistry, U. Ill. Dental Alumni, Delta Sigma Delta (asst. dep.). Home: 854 S Kenilworth Ave Oak Park IL 60304 Office: 752 S Western Ave Chicago IL 60612

PERRY, ROBERT JOSEPH, lawyer; b. Glenford, Ohio, Nov. 19, 1932; s. Elmer L. and Claudia (Vinson) P.; B.A., Ohio State U., 1955, J.D., 1961; postgrad. U.S. Fgn. Service Inst., 1957; children—Scott Warren, Elaine Marie, Karen Elizabeth. Vice consul, 3d sec. Am. embassy, Mexico, 1957-59; admitted to Ohio bar, 1962; practiced in Columbus, 1962—; asso. DeVennish & Hague, 1962; asst. atty. gen. State of Ohio, 1963-65; asso. Fontana, Ward & Kaps, 1965-70; partner Fontana, Ward, Kaps & Perry, 1970—. Asst. scoutmaster Boy Scouts Am., 1968-73; pres. Ohio State U. Law Sch. Republican Club, 1961. Served with USAF, 1951-53. Mem. Am., Ohio (chmn. prepaid legal services com. 1975-76), Columbus (chmn. prepaid legal services com. 1972-75, lawyers referral coms. 1971-72, bd. govs. 1975-77) bar assns., Franklin County Trial Lawyers Assn., Ohio Assn. Attys. Gen., Order Demolay (Legion of Honor), Delta Sigma Phi, Phi Delta Phi. Republican. Presbyterian. Club: Masons. Home: 244 E Beck St Columbus OH 43206 Office: 50 W Broad St Columbus OH 43215

PERRY, ROGER LAWRENCE, printing co. exec.; b. Ironwood, Mich., Apr. 3, 1923; s. Lawrence E. and Bessie (Thompson) P.; B.B.A., U. Wis., 1948; m. Ellen Schwandt, June 28, 1947; children—Pamela, Allison. Sales mgr. Hamilton Mfg. Co., Two Rivers, Wis., 1949-56; pres. Perry Printing Corp., Waterloo, Wis., 1956—; dir. Milw. Jour. Mem. City Council, 1958; bd. dirs. Manitowish Waters Alliance. Served with USN, 1941-45. Named Man of Year, C. of C., 1964. Mem. Mag. Printers Am. (pres. 1977—), Printing Industries Am. (pres. 1968-71, dir. 1971—), Printing Industries Wis. (dir. 1971—, Man of Year 1972, pres. 1973), Young Pres.'s Orgn., 49'ers. Clubs: Cambridge (Wis.) Country, Masons. Home: 513 Indian Hills St Waterloo WI 53594 Office: 240 Madison St Waterloo WI 53594

PERRY, THEODORE EDWARD, ednl. adminstr.; b. Cleve., Nov. 14, 1929; s. Calvin K. and Hanna E. (Kloetzer) P.; B.S., Kent State U., 1952, M.A., 1963; postgrad. John Carroll U., 1966-70; m. Carolyn Susanne Kendig, Dec. 22, 1962; children—Melissa Susanne, James Edward Kirkpatrick. Sci. instr., guidance counselor Mentor (Ohio) Pub. Schs., 1955-65, dir. adult edn., 1966-68, guidance counselor, chmn. guidance dept. Meml. Sch., 1965—. Chmn. Mentor chpt. Am. Field Service, Ams. Abroad, 1972—. Mem. Am. Personnel and Guidance Assn., NEA, Nat. Soc. Study Edn., Ohio Acad. Sci., Ohio Edn. Assn., Kappa Delta Pi, Phi Alpha Theta, Gamma Theta Upsilon. Republican. Mem. Friends Ch. Contbr. articles on entomology, others to profl. publs. in field. Home: River Rd Gates Mills OH 44040 Office: 8979 Mentor Ave Mentor OH 44060

PERRY, VICTOR EDWARD, pilot, airline co. exec.; b. Saranac, N.Y., Dec. 30, 1921; s. Edward Joseph and Sara Theresa (Gonyea) P.; student Dannemora (N.Y.) Pub. Schs.; m. Rita Barabra Kaseman, May 29, 1950; 1 dau., Mary Ann. Chief pilot Postal Finance Co., Sioux City, Iowa, 1965—; pres. Northwestern Flyers Inc., Sioux City, 1971—. Served to maj. USAF, 1942-65; PTO. Decorated D.F.C., Air medal. Mem. Nat. Pilots Assn., Am. Legion, Small Business Assn.

Republican. Roman Catholic. Club: K.C. Office: PO Box 765 Sioux City Muni Airport Sergeant Bluff IA 51054

PERSKY, SEYMOUR HOWARD, lawyer; b. Chgo., May 22, 1922; s. Joseph E. and Bertha (Solomon) P.; A.A. magna cum laude, City Coll., Chgo., 1949; B.A., Roosevelt U., 1952; J.D., DePaul U., 1952; postgrad. Northwestern U., 1961-62; m. Beverly M. Lipsky, July 8, 1962; children—Jonathan E., Abbe Joan. Admitted to Ill. bar, 1952, U.S. Supreme Ct. bar, 1965; resident counsel Mid-West Loan Co., Chgo., 1953-58; sr. partner firm Persky, Phillips & Berzock, Chgo., 1961-63; practiced in Chgo., 1963—; pub. defender Narcotics Ct., Municipal Ct. of Chgo., 1964—; lectr. Truman Jr. Coll.; mem. Mid Am. Commodity Exchange, Internat. Monetary Market (Chgo. Merc. Exchange). Vice pres. Peoples Rehab. Found., Yiddish Theater Assn.; bd. govs. Israel Bonds of Greater Chgo., chmn. young peoples div., 1970-72, chmn. lawyers div., 1973-74; bd. dirs. Hillel Torah North Suburban Day Sch., Skokie, Ill. 1973, Arie Crown Day Sch., 1977—, Skokie Valley Synagogue, 1977—; partner DePaul U. Coll. Law; mem. endowment bd. DePaul U. Served with USAAF, 1941-44. Mem. Am., Ill. (chmn. subcom. unauthorized practice law com. 1962), Chgo. (criminal law com., def. prisoners com.) bar assns., Ill. Acad. Criminology, Decalogue Soc., Def. Lawyers Assn., Am. Trial Lawyers Assn., Nat. Trust for Historic Preservation, Lex Legio DePaul U., Soc. Fellows DePaul U., DePaul U. Alumni Assn (pres. class 1952), Nu Beta Epsilon. Clubs: City, Covenant of Ill. (vice chmn. library com.), Execs., Lincoln Park Builders (Chgo.). Home: 8939 Lincolnwood Dr Evanston IL 60203 Office: 105 W Madison St Chicago IL 60602

PERSON, EARLE GEORGE, JR., dentist; b. Mt. Vernon, Ill., Apr. 28, 1928; s. Earle G. and Willie Claude (Bryant) P.; B.S., U. Ill., 1950; D.D.S., Creighton U., 1958; m. Estelle McCraty, Dec. 30, 1960. Individual practice dentistry, Omaha, 1958—. Instr., Creighton U., 1959-62; cons., Child and Youth Project, Omaha, 1969-72; pres. Comprehensive Health Assn., Omaha, 1973—. Mem. state steering com. McGovern for Pres., 1971-72; black coordinator Nebr. McGovern structure, 1971-72; pres. Urban League Nebr., 1965-68; state chmn. del. Nat. Black Polit. Conv., 1972; del. Nat. Democratic Conv. Miami, 1972; assemblyman Nat. Black Assembly, Nat. Black Polit. Conv., 1972—. Trustee Nebr. Goodwill Industries, 1965-71; pres. Community Plaza for Human Resources, 1977. Served to 1st lt. AUS, 1950-53. Recipient service award Owlers, 1966, Distinguished Service award Urban League, 1967. Fellow Internat. Coll. Dentists; mem. ADA, Nebr. Dental Soc., Ill. Soc. Microbiologists, Omicron Kappa Upsilon, Alpha Sigma Nu, Alpha Phi Alpha. Contbr. articles to profl. pubs. Home: 3212 Myrtle Ave Omaha NE 68131 Office: 3707 N 24th St Omaha NE 68110

PERSON, MARJORIE PERRY, educator; b. Mound City, Mo., Sept. 14, 1917; d. David Clinton and Nelle Katherine (Yous) Perry; B.S. in Edn., NW Mo. State U., 1940; M.B.A., Ind. U., Bloomington, 1956, D.B.A., 1965; m. Paul Manning Person, May 23, 1940 (dec. 1943); 1 son, William Paul. Tchr. Mound City Pub. Schs., 1946-54; instr. bus. NW Mo. State U., 1954-55; asst. prof. bus., 1956-62; asso. prof. bus. adminstrn. Idaho State U., Pocatello, 1963-65; asst. prof. bus. adminstrn., Ind. U. at Fort Wayne, 1965-69, asso. prof., 1969—; vis. prof. mktg. U. Nev., Las Vegas, 1972-73; cons., bd. dirs. Arnolt Corp., Warsaw, Ind., 1968-72; exec. v.p., dir. JMB Enterprises, Inc., Fort Wayne, 1968-72. Nonservice fellow Ind. U., Bloomington, 1961-62; Summer Faculty fellow, Ind. U. Fort Wayne, 1972; named Outstanding Educator, Alpha Delta Kappa, Fort Wayne, 1972; recipient Distinguished Teaching award Ind. U., Fort Wayne, 1970. Mem. Am. Mktg. Assn., Fort Wayne Advt. Club, Pi Omega Pi, Delta Pi Epsilon, Beta Gamma Sigma, Alpha Sigma Alpha. Republican. Club: Eastern Star. Co-editor: The Challenge of Change, Marketing Readings, 1974; contbr. articles in field to profl. jours. Home: 1206 3 Rivers Apts N Fort Wayne IN 46802 Office: Ind Univ-Purdue Univ Fort Wayne IN 46805

PERSONS, WALLACE R., mfg. exec.; b. Cleve., July 23, 1909; s. Wallace Ransom and Jeanette (Morrison) P.; M.S., Case Inst. Tech., 1932; m. Helen Robinson, Sept. 29, 1935; 1 dau., Barbara. With Lincoln Electric Co., Cleve., sales engr., dist. mgr., v.p., dir., 1934-53; pres., chief exec. officer, dir. Emerson Electric Co., St. Louis, 1954-65, chmn. bd., 1966-74, also chmn. exec. and finance coms.; dir. First Union Corp., Anheuser-Busch, Inc., Diamond-Shamrock Corp., First Nat. Bank, St. Louis, Inforex, Inc., Boston, St. Louis Baseball Cardinals, St. Louis Union Trust Co. Mem. St. Louis Crime Commn., Civic Progress, Inc., St. Louis; adv. com. Community Chest; bd. dirs. St. Louis Symphony Soc., Whitfield Sch., Boy Scouts Am., United Fund Greater St Louis; trustee Barnes Hosp., David Ranken Jr. Sch., St. Louis Govtl. Research Inst. Mem. Nat. Elec. Mfrs. Assn., Sigma Xi. Clubs: Links (N.Y.C.); Racquet, Mayfield Country (Cleve.); Gulf Stream Golf (Delray, Fla.); Madison (Ohio) Country; St. Louis Country, Cuivre, Log Cabin (St. Louis). Home: 24 Upper Ladue Rd Saint Louis MO 62134 Office: 8100 W Florissant Ave Saint Louis MO 63136

PESCH, LEROY ALLEN, physician, educator, hosp. cons.; b. Mt. Pleasant, Iowa, June 22, 1931; student State U. Iowa, 1948-49, Iowa State U., 1950-52; M.D. cum laude, Washington U., St. Louis, 1956; 3 children. Intern Barnes Hosp., St. Louis, 1956-57; research asso. biochemistry NIH, Bethesda, Md., 1957-59; asst. resident medicine Grace-New Haven Community Hosp., 1959-60; clin. fellow medicine Yale, 1960-61, instr. medicine, 1961-62, asst. dir. liver study unit, 1961-63, asst. prof., 1962-63; asso. prof. Rutgers U., 1963-64, prof., chmn. dept. medicine, 1964-66; asso. dean, prof. medicine Stanford U., 1966-68; dean, dir. Univ. Hosps., prof. medicine State U. N.Y. at Buffalo, 1968-71; pres. Michael Reese Med. Center, Chgo., 1971-76; pres. L.A. Pesch Assos., Inc., Chgo., 1976—; prof. div. biol. scis. and medicine U. Chgo., 1972-77; prof. Northwestern U. Sch. Medicine, Chgo., 1977—; cons. in field. Mem. Am. Assn. Study Liver Diseases, Am. Fedn. Clin. Research, AAAS, Am. Soc. Biol. Chemists, Assn. Am. Med. Colls., Buffalo, N.Y. acads. medicine, Sigma Xi, Alpha Omega Alpha, Contbr. articles to profl. jours. Address: LA Pesch Assos Inc 303 E Ohio St Chicago IL 60611

PESCHIERA, ANTONIO WENCESLAO, physician; b. Chincha Alta, Peru, Aug. 31, 1940; s. Pablo and Yolanda (Marchand) P.; came to U.S., 1967; M.D., Cayetano Heredia Peruvian U., 1967; m. Aida Maria Peschiera, June 22, 1967; children—Pablo, Andrea. Intern Brit. Am. Hosp., Lima, Peru, 1966-67, attending pediatrician, pediatric cardiologist, 1972-73; resident pediatrics Montefiore Hosp., N.Y.C., 1967-68; resident pediatrics Hosp. for Sick Children, Toronto, Ont., Can., 1968-70, fellow in cardiology, 1970-72; attending pediatric cardiologist Montefiore Hosp., N.Y.C., 1973-74; asst. prof. pediatrics Albert Einstein Med. Sch., N.Y.C., 1973-74; pediatric cardiologist, Kalamazoo, 1974—; mem. staff Borgess, Bronson hosps., Kalamazoo. Diplomate Am. Bd. Pediatrics. Fellow Royal Coll. Physicians Can., Am. Acad. Pediatrics; mem. AMA. Home: 6333 Liteolier St Kalamazoo MI 49002 Office: 1631 Gull Rd Suite 211 Kalamazoo MI 49001

PESHKIN, SAMUEL DAVID, lawyer; b. Des Moines, Oct. 6, 1925; s. Louis and Mary (Grund) P.; B.A., U. Iowa, 1948, J.D., 1951; m. Shirley Isenberg, Aug. 17, 1947; children—Lawrence Allen, Linda Ann. Admitted to Iowa bar, 1951, since practiced in Des Moines; partner Bridges & Peshkin, 1953-66, Peshkin and Robinson, 1966—; chmn. Iowa Bd. Law Examiners, 1970-76. Bd. dirs. Sch. Religion, U. Iowa, U. Iowa Old Gold Devel. Fund, 1955—, Iowa Meml. Union, 1957—, State U. Iowa Found., 1957—. Served with USNR, 1943-45. Fellow Am. Bar Found., Internat. Soc. Barristers; mem. Internat., Inter-Am., Am. (bd. govs. 1973—, ho. of dels. 1968—, chmn. standing com. on membership 1959—), Iowa State (pres. jr. bar sect. 1958-59, bd. govs. 1958-59, chmn. com. on ann. meeting 1953—, award of merit 1974), Polk County bar assns., Am. Law Inst., Am. Judicature Soc., State U. Iowa Alumni Assn. (pres. 1957—, dir., 1951—). Home: 3000 Grand Ave Apt 613 Des Moines IA 50312 Office: 1010 Fleming Bldg Des Moines IA 50309

PESKE, PATRIC O., psychologist; b. Akron, Ohio, Sept. 21, 1942; s. Robert Wilhelm and Eileen Michele (Doherty) P.; B.A., Akron U., 1968, M.A., 1972; postgrad. Case Western Res. U., 1969, Temple U., 1971-72, U. Chgo., 1975; m. Nancy Lee Pokorosky, Nov. 20, 1967. Sr. asst. to dir. personality research Hay Exec. Mgmt., Phila., 1970-72; intern child study psychologist Wadsworth-Rittman (Ohio) Edn. Systems, 1972-73; pvt. practice psychiatric cons., Phila., 1970-72, Akron, 1972-73; child study psychologist Genesee Intermediate Edn. System, Flint, Mich., 1973—; lectr. psychology Gen. Motors Inst., Flint, 1973—; instr. psychology and modern life Mott Community Coll., Flint, 1977—; internat. lectr. psychol. and Rorschach techniques. Exec. dir. Rorschach Seminars, Workshops for Advanced Profl. Edn., Workshops for Tchrs. Mem. Internat. Congress for Sci. Study Rorschach and other Projective Methods, Internat. Congress Study Art and Psychopathology, Am. Assn. Learning Disabilities, Nat., Internat. assns. sch. psychologists, Am. Psychol. Assn. (ethics com., child advocacy com.), Internat. Rorschach Soc. (chmn., U.S. del.), Soc. Personality Assessment, Psi Chi. Author charter of childrens rights proposals and books and articles in field. Home: PO Box 7149 Flint MI 48507 Office: 2203 and 2413 W Maple Ave Flint MI 48507

PETACQUE, ARTHUR MARTIN, journalist; b. Chgo., July 20, 1924; s. Ralph David and Fay Nora (Brauner) P.; student U. Ill., 1941-42; m. Regina June Battinus, Dec. 10, 1944; children—Susan Wendy (Mrs. James Bradley Leshin), William Scott. Investigative reporter, columnist Chgo. Sun-Times, 1943—. Cons. World Book Ency. Recipient Pulitzer prize for local investigative reporting, 1973; Jacob M. Scher award Northwestern U., 1964; Marshall Field award, 1968; Nat. Big Story awards NBC; numerous awards A.P., U.P.I.; named outstanding journalist Villa Scalabrini, Little Flower; Prime Minister of Israel medal, 1976. Mem. Sigma Delta Xi, Sigma Alpha Mu. Jewish. Home: 4075 Chase Lincolnwood IL 60646 Office: 401 N Wabash St Chicago IL 60611

PETCHENIK, EDWARD M., surgeon; b. Clinton, N.Y., Dec. 25, 1919; s. Patrick and Bridget (McCabe) P.; grad. sch., Plattsburgh, N.Y.; student Plattsburgh Normal Sch.; M.D., Albany Med. Coll., 1944; post-grad. work, Postgrad. Med. Sch. and Hosp., and N.Y. Polyclinic; m. Nora Loomis, Oct. 15, 1950. Practice medicine, Kingston, N.Y., 1950; chief of staff, Augustana Hosp.; chmn. clinics County Com. for Prevention Tb; chmn. County Pub. Health Co. Bd. mgrs. Training Sch. for Boys, Hudson; now v.p., bd. mgrs. Tb Hosp. Democrat. Clubs: K.C., Elks. Home: 335 Lincolnwood Rd Highland Park IL 60035

PETERHANS, LOUIS RAYMOND, JR., aluminum products mfg. co. exec.; b. Evanston, Ill., Oct. 14, 1949; s. Louis R. and Rosemary (Rudersdorf) P.; B.A., St. Thomas Coll., 1971; M.B.A., Loyola U., Chgo., 1972; m. Mary Carol Toebber, June 1, 1974. Fin. planning mgr. Nichols-Homeshield, Aurora, Ill., 1977—; instr. quantitative methods St. Thomas Coll., St. Paul, 1969-71. Served with USAF, 1973-77. Mem. Assn. of M.B.A. Execs., Am. Def. Preparedness Assn. Home: 214 N Lincoln St Batavia IL 60510 Office: 1470 Farnsworth Ave Aurora IL 60507

PETERS, ALVERA KAE, savs. and loan exec.; b. Washington, Mo., Aug. 24, 1951; d. Allen Robert and Vera Schulte (Kriete) P.; B.S. cum laude, SW Mo. State U., 1973. Savs. counselor, loan clk. Prudential Savs. & Loan Assn., Union, Mo., 1973-74, area coordinator community relations, 1974—. Publicity chmn. City of Union Bicentennial Celebration, 1976. Mem. AAUW (treas. Franklin County br. 1975-76), Am. Mktg. Assn., Am. Legion Aux., Franklin County Hist. Soc. Republican. Mem. United Ch. Christ. Home: PO Box 135 Union MO 63084 Office: 100 Locust St Union MO 63084

PETERS, FARNSLEY, assn. exec.; b. Louisville; B.S. in Econs., U. Wis., 1952; m. 1 son, 1 dau. Exec. v.p. Rockford Area C. of C. (Ill.). Mem. bd. regents No. Central Inst. Organizational Mgmt. Mem. Ill. Assn. C. of C. Execs. (past pres.), Am. C. of C. Execs. (dir.), Ill. Indsl. Council (pres.). Club: Nat. W. Home: 5875 Old Millstone Rd Rockford IL 61111 Office: 815 E State St Rockford IL 61101

PETERS, FRANK LEWIS, JR., music editor; b. Springfield, Mo., Oct. 19, 1930; s. Frank Lewis and Mary (Frissell) P.; B.A., Drury Coll., 1951; postgrad. State Iowa U., 1953-54; m. Alba Manciani, Jan. 20, 1963; children—Carl Nathaniel, Adrian Frissell. Copy editor Ark. Gazette, Little Rock, 1958-59, Springfield (Mo.) Newspapers Inc., 1959-61; mng. editor Daily American, Rome, Italy, 1961-64; music critic St. Louis Post-Dispatch, 1965—, music editor, 1967—. Served with AUS, 1951-52. Recipient Pulitzer prize for distinguished criticism, 1972. Mem. S.A.R., Lambda Chi Alpha. Home: 1400 S Rock Hill Rd St Louis MO 63119 Office: 1133 Franklin Ave St Louis MO 63101

PETERS, FRED HAROLD, welding supply co. exec.; b. Chgo., Dec. 28, 1934; s. Fred and Evelyn (Fasse) P.; student U. Ill.; m. Phyllis Jane Lincke, Sept. 3, 1955; children—Fred Harold, Cynthia Lynn, Gregg, Walter, Heidi, Ann. Asst. sec. Fred Peters Welding Supply Co., Chgo., 1955-58, v.p., 1958—, also dir. Vice chmn. Kiwanis Council Crippled Children, 1962, chmn., 1963-64-67; adv. bd. Salvation Army Settlement vice chmn., 1964-69, chmn., 1970-71; com. chmn., instnl. rep. Cub Scout troop, 1965. Mem. Am. Welding Soc., Nat. Welding Supply Assn., Ill. C. of C., Palos-Orland Swim Assn. (pres. 1973-75), Sigma Phi Epsilon. Republican. Presbyn. (elder, trustee, steward). Mason (32 deg., Shriner), Kiwanian (pres. S. Central Club 1960). Club: Builders Tee. Home: PO Box 278 Palos Park IL 60464 Office: 2335 W Cermak Rd Chicago IL 60608

PETERS, GEORGE DAVID, educator; b. Evansville, Ind., Aug. 30, 1942; s. Ralph H. and Mary (Hilliard) P.; B. Music Edn., U. Evansville, 1964; M.S., U. Ill., 1965, Ed.D., 1973; m. Jean G. Wolter, Dec. 27, 1964; children—Lisa, Ian. Band dir., brass instr. Tex. So. U., Houston, 1965-69; prof. music U. Ill., Urbana, 1970—; Mem. Music Educators Nat. Conf., Ill. Music Educators Assn., Coll. Band Dirs. Nat. Assn., Nat. Bandmasters Assn., Assn. Devel. Computer-Based Instruction Systems, Nat. Consortium Computer-Based Music. Instruction, Academic Affairs Adminstrs. Conf., Am. Fedn. Musicians, Phi Mu Alpha. Home: 1113 W Union St Champaign IL 61820 Office: College Fine Applied Arts Univ Illinois Urbana IL 61801

PETERS, IRA BUFORD, JR., utility co. exec.; b. Roanoke, Va., July 20, 1920; s. Ira Buford and Etta L. (Hylton) P.; student Roanoke Coll., U. Va.; m. Doris Lucile Trout, Sept. 3, 1949; children—Ira Gregory, Dawn Peters Wilkerson. With Appalachian Power Co., Roanoke, 1940—, div. asst. supr. personnel, 1964-68, wage and salary asst., 1968-76, personnel supr. Roanoke div., 1976—. Pres. Family Service Assn. of Roanoke, 1976; treas. Blue Ridge unit Indsl. and Commercial Ministries, 1977—. Served with U.S. Navy, 1942-45. Mem. Roanoke C. of C. Mem. Ch. of the Brethren (chmn. gen. bd. 1970-74, moderator elect, 1976-77, moderator, 1977—). Club: Kiwanis. Home: 3215 Troy Ave Roanoke VA 24012 Office: 40 Franklin Rd SW Roanoke VA 24016

PETERS, JEROME FRANK, credit union exec.; b. Milw., June 14, 1917; s. Jerome Michael and Meta A. (Pinz) P.; student pub. schs., Chgo.; m. Armella L. Dapper, Jan. 13, 1940; children—Jerome Frank, Susan T. Treas., gen. mgr., dir. Am. United Cab Assn. Credit Union, Chgo., 1953-56; field rep. Ill. Credit Union League, Chgo., 1956-57; treas., gen. mgr., dir. East Moline (Ill.) Works Credit Union, 1957-65, State Capitol Credit Union, St. Paul, 1965—; dir. Minn. On-Line, Inc. Mem. Credit Union Execs. Soc., Minn. League Credit Unions (dir. 1968-69, Distinguished Leadership award), North Star Chpt. Credit Unions (pres. 1969-71). Recipient citation for meritorious service rendered on behalf of entire Credit Union Movement, 1971, Fin. Stblzn. award, 1975; registered profl. engr., Ill. Home: 222 Wentworth St West Saint Paul MN 55118 Office: 95 Sherburne Ave Saint Paul MN 55103

PETERS, JOSEPH HARLAN, savs. and loan exec.; b. Coffeyville, Kans., Feb. 21, 1920; s. Phillip John and Florence (Harris) P.; A.A., Coffeyville Jr. Coll., 1940; A.B., Baker U., 1942; m. Geraldine Carr, Feb. 8, 1947; children—Susan Jo, Julie Lynn. With Blue Valley Fed. Savs. & Loan Co., Kansas City, Mo., 1946—, successively clk., asst. sec., 1946-52, v.p., 1952-61, dir., 1955—, pres. mng. officer, 1961—; dir., sec. Am. Insurers Agy., Inc., Kansas City, Mo., 1958—; dir. United Mo. Bank of Blue Valley, Kansas City, Mo.; mem. Fed. Savs. and Loan Adv. Com., Washington. Mem. Independence Bd. Edn., 1966-72; treas., trustee Jackson County 4-H Found.; trustee Baker U., Baldwin City, Kans., Mt. Washington Cemetery; bd. dirs. Assn. for Indsl. Devel. of Independence, Kansas City Bd. Realtors. Served with USNR, 1943-46. Recipient Distinguished Service award Independence Jr. C. of C., 1954; hon. fellow Harry S. Truman Library Inst. (life). Mem. Mil. Order World Wars (life), Am. Savs. and Loan Inst. (chpt. pres. 1948), Mo. (pres.), Kansas City (chpt. pres. 1965-66), savs. and loan leagues, Kansas City Real Estate Bd., Kansas City, Independence chambers commerce, Blue Valley Mfrs. and Bus. Mens Assn. (pres. 1966-67), Am. Royal Assn. (gov. 1974—), Am. Legion, Delta Tau Delta (Nat. Achievement award 1976). Democrat. Presbyterian (elder). Club: Masons. Home: 673 Red Rd Independence MO 64055 Office: 6515 Independence Ave Kansas City MO 64125

PETERS, NATHANIEL ASHBY, III, educator, psychologist; b. Kansas City, Mo., Mar. 29, 1941; s. William Ashby and Nina Muriel (Ottman) P.; B.A., U. Kans., 1963; M.A., Columbia U., 1966; Ph.D., U. Wis., 1971; postgrad. in family therapy dept. psychiatry Georgetown U., 1976—; m. Juanita Inez del Regato, June 17, 1967; children—Christopher William Ashby, Charles Andrew Ottman. Tchr., N.Y. Philanthropic League, N.Y.C., 1964-66, Kansas City, Mo., 1966-68; research asso. Wis. Research and Devel. Center for Cognitive Learning, Madison, 1968-70; asst. dir. reading and lang. center Oakland Schs., Pontiac, Mich., 1970—; cons. Oakland County Community Mental Health Bd., 1973—; ednl. cons. Pontiac Urban League, 1972; adj. prof. Marygrove Coll., Detroit, 1971—. NDEA fellow, 1963; Elk's Club Found. grantee, 1964-65. Mem. Am., Mich. psychol. assns., Assn. for Children with Learning Disabilities, Internat. Reading Assn., Nat., Mich. assns. sch. psychologists, Mich. Reading Assn., Nat. Reading Conf., Orton Soc., Internat. Neuropsychology Soc., Phi Delta Kappa. Author: (with others) Reading Problems: A Multidisciplinary Perspective, 1977. Contbr. articles to profl. jours. Home: 2498 Pineview Dr West Bloomfield MI 48033 Office: 2100 Pontiac Lake Rd Pontiac MI 48054

PETERS, RONALD ROSS, orthodontist; b. Dayton, Ohio, Feb. 13, 1943; s. Donald Wright and Bernice Arnell (Ross) P.; student (Athletic scholar) U. Mo., Columbia, 1961-65, D.D.S., Kansas City, 1969, degree in grad. orthodontics, Kansas City, 1974; m. Laura Margaret Emanuelson. With Cody Dental Group, Denver, 1971-72; pvt. practice orthodontics, Kansas City, Mo., Blue Springs, Mo., 1974—; clin. instr. Sch. Dentistry U. Mo., Kansas City. Served with Dental Corps USN, 1969-71. Mem. Am., Mo., Kansas City dental assns., Mo., Kansas City orthodontic socs., Am. Assn. Orthodontists, Midwestern Soc., Eastern Jackson County Dental Group, Blue Springs C. of C. Methodist. Clubs: Lions, Greater Kansas City Track. Home: 1202 Quail Creek Independence MO 64055 Office: 1212 S Luttrell St Blue Springs MO 64015 also 4140 Blue Ridge Blvd Kansas City MO 64133

PETERSEN, DIETRICH LINDE, mfg. co. exec.; b. Pana, Ill., Sept. 3, 1933; s. Alfred C. and Gladyce E. (Anderson) P.; B.S., Millikin U., 1955; M.Litt., U. Pitts., 1959, Ph.D., 1968; m. Marjorie J. Beatty, Aug. 27, 1955; children—Erich K., Kurt F., Krista M., Heidi A. Sr. staff engr. and supr. Westinghouse Air Brake Co., Pitts., 1955-65; mgr. advt. materials Allis-Chalmers, West Allis, Wis., 1965-67; asst. prof. Sch. Bus. Adminstrn. Marquette U., Milw., 1967-69; research staff mem. Inst. for Def. Analysis, Washington, 1969-70; mgr. mfg. services Fiat-Allis Co., Chgo., 1970-75; v.p. and dir. of mfg. Perkins Diesel Corp., Canton, Ohio, 1975-78; pres. Perkins Diesel Corp., 1978—; lectr. Sangamon State U., Springfield, Ill., 1972-74, Stark Tech. Coll., 1977. Mem. advisory bd. of Malone Coll., Canton, Ohio, 1977—. Mem. Canton C. of C. (mem. edn. subcom. 1977-78). Methodist. Club: Congress Lake. Contbr. articles on econs. to profl. jours. Home: 1209 Briarview NW North Canton OH 44720 Office: 515 11th St SE Canton OH 44711

PETERSEN, DONAL CHRISTIAN, physician; b. Escanaba, Mich., Dec. 26, 1920; s. Arthur Christian and Gertrude Marie (Deasy) P.; B.S., U. Notre Dame, 1942; M.B., Northwestern U., 1945, M.D., 1946; m. Elaine Anne Browne, Sept. 18, 1943; children—Barbara, Susan, Donal A., Bernard. Intern, U.S. Naval Hosp., Corona, Cal., 1945-46; resident anesthesia U. Ia., 1948-49; practice medicine, specializing in anesthesiology, Burlington, Ia., 1949—; mem. staff Meml. Hosp., pres. staff, 1962. Bd. dirs. Mercy Hosp., Burlington, 1953-68, Burlington Art Guild, 1967-68. Served with USNR, 1945-47. Diplomate Am. Bd. Anesthesiology. Mem. A.M.A., Am. Soc. Anesthesiologists, Ia., Des Moines County (pres. 1966) med. socs., Ia. Anesthesia Soc. Club: Golf (Burlington). Home: 113 Orchard Pl Burlington IA 52601 Office: F & M Bank Bldg Burlington IA 52601

PETERSEN, DONALD EUGENE, automobile co. exec.; b. Pipestone, Minn., Sept. 4, 1926; s. William L. and Mae (Pederson) P.; B.S. in Mech. Engring., U. Wash., 1946; M.A. in Bus. Adminstrn., Stanford, 1949; m. Jo Anne Leonard, Sept. 12, 1948; children—Leslie Carolyn, Donald Leonard. Various positions in product planning Ford Motor Co., Dearborn, Mich., 1949-63, dir. forward mktg. plans, 1963-65, asst. to v.p. N.Am. ops., 1965-66, car product planning mgr., 1966-69, exec. dir. adminstr., engring. and indsl. design, 1969, v.p. car planning and research, 1969-71, v.p., gen. mgr. truck and recreation products ops., 1972-75, exec. v.p. diversified products ops., 1975-77, internat. automotive ops., 1977—. Active Ednl. Community,

Bloomfield Hills, Mich. Trustee Cranbrook 1973-75. Served with USMCR, 1946-47, 51-52. Mem. So. Automotive Engrs., Engring. Soc. Detroit, Mensa, Phi Beta Kappa, Sigma Xi, Tau Beta Pi. Episcopalian. Clubs: Fairlane; Bloomfield Hills Country; Otsego Ski. Home: 1318 Country Club Dr Bloomfield Hills MI 48013 Office: American Rd Dearborn MI 48121

PETERSEN, EDWARD SCHMIDT, assn. exec., physician; b. Chgo., Nov. 19, 1921; s. William F. and Alma C. (Schmidt) P.; student Harvard U., 1943, M.D., 1945; m. Zoe A. Bakeeff, June 11, 1944; children—Catherine B. Petersen Mack, Edward B. Rotating intern St. Luke's Hosp., Chgo., 1945-46; residency medicine U. Chgo., 1948-51; pvt. practice, Chgo., 1951-53; mem. staff Northwestern Med. Sch., Chgo., 1953-72; asst. dir. dept. undergrad. med. edn. AMA, Chgo., 1972-76, dir., 1976—, co-sec. liaison com. med. edn., 1976—; asso. prof. medicine Northwestern U., Chgo., 1964-72, asso. dean, 1960-72, lectr., 1972—; chmn. Com. Hosps. and Clinics, Ill. Dept. Pub. Aid, 1961-70; v.p. Inst. Medicine, Chgo., 1971-74, pres., 1975-76. Bd. dirs. Hull House, 1962-70; exec. com. health div. Welfare Council Chgo., 1956-62. Served with M.C., AUS, 1946-48. Diplomate Am. Bd. Internal Medicine. Recipient Danielson award hist. writing, 1972. Fellow A.C.P.; mem. Assn. Am. Med. Colls. (chmn. Midwest Group on student affairs 1967-69), Civic Assn. Lake Geneva (Wis.) (v.p. 1972-76), Chgo. Soc. History Medicine, (dir. 1974-77), Westerners Chgo. (dir. 1972—). Clubs: Lake Geneva Yacht, Lake Geneva Country; Racquet (Chgo.). Contbr. articles diabetes, med. edn., med. history to profl. publs. Home: 1350 Astor St Chicago IL 60610 Office: 535 N Dearborn St Chicago IL 60610

PETERSEN, ROLAND FREDERICK, editor, pub.; b. Chgo., Aug. 3, 1930; s. Frederick Christian and Elizabeth (Kutzik) P.; student Sioux Falls (S.D.) Coll., 1948-50; B.A. in Sociology, Roosevelt U., Chgo., 1955; M.S. in Indsl. and Labor Relations, Loyola U., Chgo., 1960; m. Esther Sypek, Nov. 11, 1954 (dec. July 1970); children—Grant Charles, Mark Vaughn; m. 2d, Madeline Porter Coyne, Mar. 1, 1975. Indsl. engr. Western Elec. Co., Chgo., 1956-64, labor relations investigator, 1964-66; personnel mgr. St. Regis Paper Co., Chgo., 1966-67; employment mgr. John Plain & Co., Chgo., 1967-68; sales rep. Digest Publs., Inc., Chgo., 1968-74, pres., treas., dir., 1974—, pub. Police Digest. Served with USMC, 1952-53. Mem. Chgo. Police Lts. Assn. (hon.). Republican. Baptist. Home: 3400 N Lakeshore Dr Chicago IL 60657 Office: 2234 W Irving Park Rd Chicago IL 60618

PETERSEN, SUSAN ROSE, counselor; b. Ontario, Calif., Jan. 19, 1946; d. Donal Christian and Elaine (Browne) Petersen; B.A. in Psychology, St. Louis U., 1968; M.A., U. Mo., St. Louis, 1976. Supr., Project, Inc., St. Louis, 1968-70, evaluator, 1970-72, chief counselor, 1972-77, coordinator rehab., services, 1977—; guest lectr. U. Mo., St. Louis, 1970—. Mem. Am. Personnel Guidance Assn., Nat. Rehab. Assn., Mo. Rehab. Assn., Vocational Evaluation and Work Adjustment Assn. (pres. elect 1977-78). Roman Catholic. Home: 481 Brightspur Ln Ballwin MO 63011 Office: 6301 Manchester St Louis MO 63139

PETERSON, ALPHONSE, dentist; b. St. Louis, Sept. 9, 1926; s. Alphonse Herman and Pearl (Green) P.; B.S., Howard U., 1948; D.D.S., Meharry Med. Coll., 1954; m. Jessie Clark, Dec. 16, 1951; children—Alphonse, Alan Clark, Alex Ira. Pvt. practice dentistry, St. Louis, 1957—; asst. prof. clin. oral diagnosis and radiology Washington U. Sch. Dental Medicine, St. Louis, 1972—. Served with USAF, 1955-57. Fellow Royal Soc. Health (Eng.); mem. Kappa Alpha Psi. Mason, Lion. Contbr. articles to profl. publs. Home: 3001 Norwood Dr W St Louis MO 63115 Office: 3737 N Kingshighway Blvd St Louis MO 63115

PETERSON, ARTHUR LAVERNE, educator; b. Glyndon, Minn., June 27, 1926; s. John Martin and Hilda (Moline) P.; A.B., Yale, 1947; M.S., U. So. Calif., 1948; Ph.D., U. Minn., 1962; m. Connie Lucille Harr, June 14, 1952; children—Jon Martin II, Rebecca Ruth, Donna Harr, Ingrid Bliss. Mem. Wis. Assembly, 1951-55; prof. polit. sci. Wis. State Univ., 1955-60, Ohio Wesleyan U., 1961-65; pres. Am. Grad. Sch. Internat. Mgmt., Phoenix, 1966-70; prof., chmn. politics and govt. Ohio Wesleyan U., 1970—, dir. Ben A. Arneson Inst. Practical Politics, Ohio Center for Edn. in Politics, 1970—; vis. prof. Novin Inst. Polit. Sci., Tehran, Iran, fall 1973. Chmn. Ohio Civil Rights Commn., 1963-66, Delaware Civil Service Commn., 1972—. Asst. to nat. chmn. Republican party, 1960-61; chief adminstrv. asst. to Rep. nat. chmn., 1965-66; chief-of-staff platform com. Rep. Nat. Conv., 1968, 72, 76; mem. Ohio Ethics Commn., 1976—; chmn. Ohio UN Day, 1975-77; trustee Robert A. Taft Inst. Govt., Am. Grad. Sch. Internat. Mgmt. Served with USNR, 1944-46; served to capt. USMCR, 1951-52. Mem. United Ch. of Christ (lay minister, 1958—). Mason. Author: (with Daniel Ogden) Electing the President, 1964, rev. edit., 1968; (with William Lonthan) Republicans and Democrats: Similarities and Differences, 1976. Address: Ohio Wesleyan U Delaware OH 43015

PETERSON, ARTHUR THEODORE, lawyer; b. Mizpah, Minn., Feb. 6, 1906; s. Fred Bernard and Ragnhild (Otterstad) P.; student St. Cloud State Coll., 1924-26; LL.B., U. Minn., 1936; m. Sylvia Fisher, June 30, 1938; 1 dau., Ardyce Peterson Jarvis. Admitted to Minn. bar, 1936, since practiced in Walker; jr. partner DeLury & Peterson, 1936-51; individual practice, 1951-53; sr. partner Peterson & Renner, 1953-68, Peterson, Tupper & Smith, 1969—; instr. adult classes Am. Inst. Banking; Torrens title examiner for counties of Beltrami, Cass, Clearwater and Hubbard; village counsel Walker, 1946-52, village atty., 1952-71. Mem. 15th Jud. Dist., Minn. bar assns. Republican. Mem. United Ch. Christ (trustee). Clubs: Masons, Rotary; Tianna Country. Home: 705 Cleveland Blvd Walker MN 56484 Office: Walker MN 56484

PETERSON, CALVIN CLIFTON, tractor mfg. co. exec.; b. Pochahontas, Iowa, Sept. 23, 1924; s. Clifton William and Elsie Margaret (Brodersen) P.; B.A., Augustana Coll., Rock Island, 1948; m. Carol Louise Johnson, June 8, 1946; children—Bruce M., Thomas C. and Leland D. (twins). With Deere & Co., various locations, 1952—, works mgr., Mannheim, Germany, 1968-72, Waterloo, Iowa, 1972-74, ops. mgr., 1974, gen. mgr., 1974—; dir. Waterloo Savs. Bank. Pres., Schoitz Meml. Hosp., 1976; bd. dirs. Wartburg Coll., Waverly, Iowa, Jr. Achievement Black Hawk Land, Black Hawk Area Med. Edn. Found., Met. Improvement Services. Served to sgt. USMC, 1943-46. Mem. Am. Mgmt. Assn., Waterloo Indsl. Devel. Assn. (dir.), Am. Def. Preparedness Assn. (dir.). Lutheran. Clubs: Sunnyside Country, Elks, Rotary, Symposium. Home: 100 Woodstock Rd Waterloo IA 50701 Office: PO Box 270 Waterloo IA 50704

PETERSON, CHARLES ROLAND, farm supplies co. exec., feedlot operator; b. Amelia, Nebr., Sept. 21, 1935; s. Charley Warren and Della Ernestine (Palmer) P.; grad. Graceland Jr. Coll., 1955; m. Shirley Ann Kaiser, Jan. 1, 1953; children—Barbara, Brenda, Belinda, Charles Roland II, Clifton, Blythe. Established P & P Farms and Farm Supply, Atkinson, Nebr., 1960-70; pres. Nat. Alfalfa Dehydrating and Milling Co., 1970-74, Shawnee Mission, Kans., 1970—. Mem. Am. Dehydrators Assn. (dir. 1971-73). Home: Amelia NE 68711

PETERSON, CHESTER, JR., publisher, photographer, writer; b. Salina, Kans., Mar. 24, 1937; s. Chester and Erma (Reed) P.; B.S., Kans. State U., 1959, B.S., 1960, M.S., 1960; m. 2d, Nancy Anne Bowden, June 5, 1970; 1 son, Eugene Ragnar; children by previous marriage—Joy, Nels, Erik. Asst. editor, asso. editor Successful Farming, Des Moines, 1960-64; creative contact exec. Gardner Advt. Co., Inc., St. Louis, 1964; photographer-writer, Lindsborg, Kans., 1965—; pub. Beef Digest, Hog Digest; pub., editor Simmental Shield; pres. Falun State Bank (Kans.), Shield Pub. Co., Inc., STDA, Inc., Sunshine Unltd., Inc. Mem. Am. Soc. Photographers in Communication, Photographers of Am. Contbr. articles to profl. jours. Home: PO Box 71 Lindsborg KS 67456

PETERSON, DONALD CURTIS, entrepreneur, bus. exec.; b. Seattle, Feb. 27, 1931; s. Arthur Oscar and Agnes V. (Erickson) P.; A.A., North Park Coll., 1950; m. Marilyn J. Weiberg, June 21, 1952; children—Bruce, Mark, Daryl, Debra. Parts distbn. and fgn. operations Internat. Harvester Co., Chgo., 1950-54; product mgr. Uarco, Inc., Barrington, Ill., 1954-66, also account rep., dist. mgr.; group v.p. sales Victor-Comptometer Corp., Lincoln, Nebr., 1966-68; pres. Nationwide Bus. Forms Inc., Nationwide Data Forms Inc., Wheeling, Ill., 1968-71; chmn., pres. Alpha Internat., Sawyer, Mich., 1971-75; chmn. Omega Enterprises Ltd., 1975—. Mem. Data Processing Mgmt. Assn., Nat. Assn. Cost Accountants, Am. Mgmt. Assn. Republican. Baptist. Office: Lock Box 157 Sawyer MI 49125

PETERSON, DONALD GEORGE, wholesale trade exec.; b. Milaca, Minn., May 1, 1925; s. Louis Theodore and Anna Olive (Peterson) P.; student U. Cin., 1943; B.B.A., U. Minn., 1948; m. Oral Edith Ortquist, Sept. 17, 1948; children—Stephen, Jeffrey, Michael. Office mgr. Northland Electric Supply Co., Mpls., 1948-59, v.p., asst. treas., 1960-67, exec. v.p., 1969-76; v.p., gen. mgr. So. Minn. Supply (name changed to S.M. Supply Co.) Mankato, 1967-69, pres. S.M. Supply Co., Makato, Rochester, Eau Claire, Wis., 1969-76, Northland Electric Supply Co. of St. Cloud, 1972-76; pres., treas. Progressive Electric Supply Co., Plymouth, Minn., 1976—; dir. Outdoor News, Mpls. Served to capt. USAF, 1943-46. Mem. Nat. Assn. Elec. Distbrs. (gov. 1970-74, Distinguished Service award 1977), North Central Electric League. Mason. Home: 2405 Jewell Ln N Wayzata MN 53391 Office: 2050 E Center Circle Plymouth MN 55441

PETERSON, DONALD ROBERT, chem. engr.; b. Ogallala, Nebr., Nov. 28, 1929; s. John Edward and Bessie Iona (Miller) P.; m. Mary Louise Forney, Dec. 28, 1958; children—Kirstin, Eric. B.Sc., U. Nebr., 1961, B.Ch.E., 1961. Staff chemist Dale Electronics, Inc., Columbus, Ohio, 1961-63, sr. materials engr., 1963—, mgr. chemistry lab., 1965—. Chmn., Columbus City Republican Party, 1968; chmn. Platte County Republican Party, 1972-73; mem. Columbus (Nebr.) City Council, 1974—; police commnr., City of Columbus, 1974—. Mem. Am. Electroplaters Soc. (sec., treas., v.p. Nebr. Iowa br. 1972-77), Platte County Hist. Soc., C. of C., Masons (Shriner), Rotary Club, Pawnee Shrine Club, Delta Sigma Phi, Elks Club, Pawnee Motor Patrol. Home: 1870 25th Av Columbus NE 68601 Office: Dale Electronics Inc PO Box 609 Columbus NE 68601

PETERSON, DUANE MALCOLM, lawyer; b. Duluth, Minn., Sept. 18, 1929; s. Martin Joseph and Catherine Sarah (Thompson) P.; student U. Minn. at Duluth, 1947-49; LL.B. cum laude, St. Paul Coll. Law, 1953; m. Patricia C. Hart, Aug. 9, 1952; children—Mark, Daniel, Joan, Paul, Nora. Admitted to Minn. bar, 1953; practice law, St. Paul, 1955-57; asso. Plunkett & Plunkett, Austin & Rochester, 1957-59; partner Peterson, Delano & Thompson, and predecessors, Winona, Minn., 1959—; judge Minn. Tax Ct., 1972—. Chmn. Winona County Dem. Farm Labor Party, 1961-64, chmn. 1st Dist., 1965-69; mem. Winona City Charter Commn., 1965-71; chmn. Winona Merit Bd., 1968-76; bd. dirs. Cancer Soc., 1962-66, Winona Community Chest, 1967-69. Served with USMCR, 1953-55. Named Outstanding Young Man, Winona Jr. C. of C., 1965. Mem. Minn., Winona County (pres.) bar assns., Am. (state committeeman), Minn. (pres.) trial lawyers assns. Roman Catholic. Club: Winona Country. Home: 418 Hiawatha Blvd Winona MN 55987 Office: 1st Nat Bank Bldg Winona MN 55987

PETERSON, EDWARD NORMAN, historian; b. St. Joseph, Mo., Aug. 27, 1925; s. Roscoe Dillon and Rachel Bernice P.; student St. Joseph Jr. Coll., 1943, 48; B.A., U. Wis., Madison, 1950, M.A., 1951, Ph.D., 1953; m. Ursula Martha Schmidt, Aug. 29, 1946; children—John Edward, Michael Paul. Asst. prof. Eastern Ky. State Coll., Richmond, 1953-54; mem. faculty U. Wis., RiverFalls, 1954—, asso. prof. history, 1954-61, prof., 1961—, chmn. social sci. dept., then history, 1962—. Treas., Pierce County Hist. Assn.; sec., pres. Upper Midwest Hist. Assn. Served with U.S. Army, 1944-47. Decorated Combat Infantry Badge; Alexander von Humboldt fellow, 1963-64; recipient grants U. Wis., 1963-64, Nat. Endowment Humanities, 1969-70, Social Sci. Research Council, 1970-71. Mem. Am. Hist. Assn., Conf. Group on German Politics. Author: Hjalmar Schacht For and Against Hitler, 1954; Limits of Hitler's Power, 1969; Retreat to Victory, 1978; asst. editor Pierce County Heritage, 1971—. Home: 936 Maple St W River Falls WI 54022 Office: Dept History Univ Wis River Falls WI 54022

PETERSON, FREDDIE-NADINE, surgeon; b. Varna, Ill., June 26, 1911; d. Enoch Fred and Edna Munn (Ledwith) P.; B.S., Northwestern U., 1933, M.B., 1939, M.D., 1940; 1 adopted dau., Valerie Anne. Intern, Milw. County Gen. Hosp., 1939-40; surg. resident Passavant Meml. Hosp., Chgo., 1940-41, Milw. Children's Hosp., 1941-43; plastic surgery, preceptor Milw., 1943-47; resident Milw. Children's Hosp., 1955-56; practice medicine, specializing in plastic and reconstructive surgery, Milw., 1947-53, also specializing in pediatrics, Wayland, Mass., 1959—; med. fellow Children's Med. Center, Boston, 1956-58; instr. oral medicine Marquette U. Dental Sch., Milw., 1945-50; pediatric investigator NIH maternal infant health program Boston Lying-In Hosp., 1958-64; head civilian def. program for physicians Milwaukee County Med. Soc., 1947-53; founder, mgr. DuPont Creche and Youth Centre for Fgn. Missions, Kingston, Jamaica, B.W.I., 1954-55; mem. staff, dir. pediatric emergency service Newton-Wellesley Hosp.; mem. staff lying-in div. Boston Hosp. for Women, Boston Children's Med. Center Oconomowoc (Wis.) Meml. hosps.; physician Wayland Pub. Schs., 1962-68 pediatrician, surgeon Hartland (Wis.) Clinic, 1968—. Served as sr. surgeon, med. dir. USPHS Res., 1965. Diplomate Am. Bd. Plastic Surgery, Am. Bd. Pediatrics; mem. AMA, Wis., Milwaukee County med. socs., New Eng. Pediatric Soc., Wayland LWV, Delta Delta Delta. Republican. Clubs: Alumni of Boston, Children's Hosp.; Milw. Athletic; Wayland Swimming and Tennis; Nashoba Valley Hunt (Pepperell, Mass.); Yankee Appaloosa. Home: 6151 Sand Beach Rd Oconomowoc WI 53066 Office: Oconomowoc Meml Hosp Oconomowoc WI 53066

PETERSON, HARRY EDWARD, packaging co. exec.; b. Chgo., Aug. 13, 1921; s. Palmer and Florence (Skedd) P.; student Ill. Inst. Tech., 1939; B.S. in Chemistry, DePaul U., 1943; m. Elaine Meyer, May 26, 1944; children—Pamela Jewel, Liane, Kevin E., Daryl M., Niel E. Chemist research dept. Continental Can Co., Chgo., 1937-47, Sect. chief indsl. products, 1941-47; founder Continental Filling Corp., 1947, v.p. gen. mgr., 1947-53, pres., 1953-55, dir., 1947-55; pres., dir. Peterson/Puritan, Inc., 1955—, chmn. bd., 1974—; dir. Bank of Danville, Dutch Pantry. Mem. Sci. Manpower Conservation Com., 1950-59; conservation com. WPB, World War II. Adv. bd. St. Elizabeth Hosp., Danville, Ill., 1954-65, pres., 1955; bd. dirs. United Hosp. Fund, Inc. of Danville, vice chmn. budget com.; bd. dirs. Piankeshaw council Boy Scouts Am. Mem. Am. Am. Chem. Soc., Soc. Cosmetic Chemists, Packaging Inst., Compressed Gas Assn., Chem. Specialties Mfg. Assn. (chmn. aerosol div. 1948-51, gov. 1952-53, pres. 1957, bd. govs. 1958-62, mem. finance com.), Ill. Danville C.'s of C. Elk. Club: Danville Country. Home: 1511 N Vermillion St Danville IL 61832 Office: Hegeler Ln Danville IL 61832

PETERSON, HARRY WALTER, electronics co. exec.; b. Chanute, Kans., May 13, 1923; s. Harry Joe Samuel and Bertha (Buford) P.; grad. high sch.; m. Kathryn Elizabeth Boggs, Jan. 10, 1942; children—Donna (Mrs. Calvin Duane Waller), Jerry Ronnell. Various positions, 1942-56; mem. Lincoln (Nebr.) Police Dept., 1956-66; with King's Food Host U.S.A., Lincoln, 1966-76, area supr., 1970-76; safety, security and tng. supr. Hy-Gain Electronics, Lincoln, 1976—. Chmn. Human Rights Com., Lincoln, 1962—; vice chmn. city council, Lincoln, 1971-73; mem. adv. com. Head Start, Lincoln, 1967-70; mem. state selection com. Nat. ROTC Scholarships, 1970-71; mem. Gov.'s Adv. Council on Alcoholism, 1973—; counsellor vols. in probation Lincoln Juvenile Ct., 1973—. Bd. dirs. Lincoln (Neb.) Gen. Hosp., Nebr. chpt. ARC; pres. Nebr. Human Resources Found. Served with AUS, 1943-46. Recipient Outstanding Pub. Service award Kiwanis Club, 1970, Good Govt. award Jr. C. of C., 1972. Mem. C. of C. Republican. Methodist (trustee). Clubs: Masons, Kiwanis, Squires. Home: 2621 S 40th St Lincoln NE 68506 Office: 8601 NE Hwy 6 Lincoln NE 68510

PETERSON, JOHN MARSILJE, architect, educator; b. Holland, Mich., July 21, 1935; s. Walter John and Helen Jane (Bosman) P.; B. Arch., N.C. State U., 1958; M. Arch., Mass. Inst. Tech., 1959; m. Mary Pledge, Aug. 17, 1957. Asso. Leif Valand and Assos. Architects, Raleigh, N.C., 1955-57; with Kendall Taylor and Co., Inc., Architects, Cambridge, Mass., 1958-59; archtl. cons., 1964—; painter, sculptor, 1963—; critic Boston Archtl. Center, 1958-59; asst. prof. architecture U. Cin., 1959-66, mem. grad. faculty, 1964, asso. prof. architecture, 1966-71, prof., 1971—; lectr. in field. Affiliate psychology and arts div. Am. Psychol. Assn. Mem. A.I.A., Architects Soc. Ohio, Assn. Collegiate Schs. Architecture, Design Methods Group, Am. Soc. Aesthetics, Environmental Design Research Assn., AAAS, Computer Art Soc. Home: 495 Howell Ave Cincinnati OH 45220

PETERSON, LLOYD RICHARD, educator; b. Mpls., Oct. 1, 1922; s. Theander and Teckla (Tacktor) P.; B.A., Gustavus Adolphus Coll., 1944; M.A., U. Minn., 1951, Ph.D., 1954; m. Margaret Jean Lowther, Dec. 28, 1953; children—Laryn, Bruce, Celia. Faculty, Ind. U., Bloomington, 1955—, prof. dept. psychology, 1964—. Mem. Am., Midwestern psychol. assns., AAAS, Psychonomic Soc. Home: 2200 E Maxwell Ln Bloomington IN 47401 Office: Indiana Univ Psychology Dept Bloomington IN 47401

PETERSON, MARILYN ANN (MRS. RICHARD FAY PETERSON), educator; b. Holdrege, Nebr., July 22, 1933; d. Claude F. and Esther (Soderholm) Whitney; B.A., Kearney State Coll., 1955; M.A., U. No. Colo., 1963; m. Richard Fay Peterson, June 17, 1956. Tchr., Gothenburg (Nebr.) High Sch., 1955-56, pub. schs., Kearney, Nebr., 1956-57, Cozad, Nebr., 1957-60, Wheat Ridge, Colo., 1960-62, Eustis, Nebr., 1962-64; asso. prof. Midland Coll., 1964—. Mem. Nat. Council Coll. Publs. Advisers (state chmn. 1970-72, 76-77, nat. awards chmn. 1973-74, exec. bd. 1973-75), Nat. Council Tchrs. English, Asso. Collegiate Press, Nebr. High Sch. Press Assn., Nat. Press Photographers Assn., AAUW (state cultural interests chmn. 1970-72, pres. 1975-76), Nebr., Dodge County hist. socs., Women's Soc. Christian Service (v.p.), Kearney State Coll. Alumni (dir., treas. 1970-72), Altrusa (v.p. 1971-73, pres. 1973-75), Delta Kappa Gamma (pres. 1974-76), Soc. for Collegiate Journalists, Kappa Delta Pi, Delta Omicron. Methodist. Republican. Home: Fontanelle Oaks Nickerson NE 68044

PETERSON, MARTHA ELIZABETH, coll. pres.; b. Jamestown, Kans., June 22, 1916; d. Anton R. and Gall (French) Peterson; A.B., U. Kans., 1937, M.A., 1943, Ph.D., 1959; postgrad. Northwestern U., Columbia U., L.H.D., Chatham Coll., 1968, Med. Coll. Pa., 1970, Molloy Coll., 1971, Mundelein Coll., 1972, Pace Coll., 1974, U. Wis., Madison, 1975, Temple U., 1975; D. Letters and Laws, Columbia, 1968. Douglas Coll., 1968; LL.D., Hofstra U., 1969, Austin Coll., 1972, Hamilton Coll., 1974, Drury Coll., 1975, W.Va. Wasleyan Coll., 1976, Dr. Pedagogy, R.I. Coll., 1975. Instr. U. Kans., 1942—46, asst, dean women, 1946—52, dean women, 1952—56; dean women U. Wis., 1956—63, asst. to pres., 1963, univ. dean students, 1963—67; pres. Barnard Coll., also dean in Columbia U., 1967—75; pres. Beloit Coll., 1975—. Dir. Met. Life Ins. Co., Exxon Corp., First Wis. Corp., United Banks Ill., R.H. Macy & Co. Mem. exec. com. commn. Ind. colls. and univs.; mem. Pres.'s Commn. White House Fellowships, Rhodes Scholarship Com. Wis.; trustee U. Notre Dame, Chatham Coll., Pitts., 1965—; mem. Com. Econ. Devel.; bd. dirs, Council Fin. Aid to Edn. mem. vis. com. Am. Council Learned Socs. Recipient Charles Evans Hughes award, 1975, Spirit of Achievement award Albert Einstein Coll. Medicine, 1975; named to U. Kans. Women's Hall Fame, 1972. Mem. Am. Council Edn. (student personnel commn. 1956—59, commn. acad. affairs 1970—, chmn. exec. com. 1971—), Nat. Assn. Women Deans and Counselors (exec. bd. 1959—61, pres. 1965—67), Nat. Assn. Ind. Colls. and Univs. (dir. 1976—77), Intercollegiate Assn. Women Students (nat. adviser 1953—55, 59—61), Am. Arbitration Assn. (dir.), Phi Beta Kappa, Sigma Xi, Mortar Bd., Pi Lambda Theta, Phi Kappa Phi. Office: Beloit Coll Beloit WI 53511

PETERSON, MILDRED OTHMER, lectr., writer, librarian, photographer, civic leader; b. Omaha, Oct. 19, 1902; d. Frederick George and Freda Darling (Snyder) Othmer; student U. Nebr., U. Iowa, U. Chgo., Northwestern U.; m. Howard R. Peterson, Aug. 25, 1923 (dec. Feb. 1970). Asst. Central High Sch. Library, Omaha, 1915-19; asst. Tech. High Sch. Library, 1919-20; asst. purchasing agt. Met. Utilities Dist., 1920-21; asst. U. Nebr. library, 1921-23; tchr. piano, dir. choir, Harlan, Iowa, 1924-26; dir. pub. relations and gen. asst. Des Moines Pub. Library, 1928-35; broadcaster weekly book programs WHO and other Iowa radio stas.; columnist, writer Mid-West News Syndicate, Des Moines Register and Tribune, editor Book Marks, 1929-35; writer for Drug Topics, Drug Trade News and others, for No. Ill., 1935; editor Adelphean of Alpha Delta Pi, 1938-39; writer and spl. asst. ALA, 1935—, Chgo. Tribune, 1941—, Hyde Park Herald, 1974—; lectr. on travel, fgn. jewelry and internat. relations, 1940—; lectr. S.S. Rotterdam of Holland Am. Line, 1971. Del. 1st Assembly Librarians of Ams., Washington, 1947. Chgo. chmn. India Famine Relief, 1943. A founder, pres. Pan. Am. Bd. Edn., 1955-58, Internat. Visitors Center, 1954-58; rep. Chgo. at State Dept. Founding Conf. on Community Services to Fgn. Visitors, Washington, 1957; mem. Mayor's Com. on Chgo. Beautiful; mem. chancellor's com. U. Nebr. Cited by Chgo. Sun and Ill. Adult Edn. Council; recipient scholarship in Latin-Am. field U. Chgo. and Coordinator Inter-Am. Affairs, U.S. Govt., 1943; world understanding merit award Chgo. Council Fgn. Relations, 1955; named Woman of Year for U.S. and Can. by Alpha Delta Pi, 1955; recipient Distinguished Service award Hospitality Center, 1958; Distinguished Service medal U.

Nebr., 1963, Distinguished Achievement award, 1975; Ambassador of Friendship award Am. Friendship Club, 1963; Merit award YWCA, Distinguished Service award, 1975; Civic Salute WMAQ Radio, Chgo., 1965; Distinguished Service award Pan-Am. Bd. Edn., 1966, also Founders award, 1968; Laura Hughes Lunde Meml. award Citizens of Greater Chgo., 1968; Uruguayan Medal, 1952; Internat. Eloy Alfaro medal, 1952, medal Order of Carlos Manuel de Cespedes, 1956 (Cuba); medal Order of Vasco Nunez de Balboa (Panama), 1956; Internat. Friendship award Girl Scouts of Philippines, 1971; Outstanding Service award OAS, 1971; Distinguished Service award Internat. Travelers Assn., 1971, Fedn. Latin Am. Orgns., Chgo., 1976; named a Woman of Year Friends of Chgo. Schs. and Workshop for Retarded, 1974; recipient award Mayor Bilandic and Internat. Visitors Center, 1977, Nat. Council Community Services to Internat. Visitors, 1977. Fellow Am. Internat. Acad. (life mem.); mem. Nat. Council Women U.S., Pan-Am. Bd. Edn., U.S. Capitol, Ill., Nebr., Chgo., Hyde Park hist. socs., Chgo. Natural History Mus., Citizenship Council Met. Chgo., Oriental Inst., Internat. Relations Library (consular ball com.), Am. Heritage Council, Am., Ill. library assns., Soc. Woman Geographers, Council Fgn. Relations (speakers bur.), Ill. Partners of Ams. (gov.'s com. Saõ Paulo, Brazil-Ill.), Friends Chgo. Pub. Library, Chgo. Opera Guild, Chgo. Hort. Soc., Marquis Biog. Soc., Am. Security Council, Chgo. Zool. Soc., Mus. Contemporary Art, Crossroads Student Center, Hyde Park Neighborhood Club, Hyde Park-Kenwood Community Conf., Internat. House Assn. (dir., v.p.), Japan-Am. Soc., Pan Am. Council (a founder, distinguished service award 1966), U. Nebr. Alumni Assn. (past pres. local chpts. and zones), U. Nebr. Found., Chgo. Art Inst., U. Chgo. Service League (dir.), Am. Legion Aux. (mem. state bds. Iowa and Ill.), AAUW, League Women Voters, Children's Benefit League, United Negro Coll. Fund Bd., Renaissance Soc., Peruvian Arts Soc., Hispanic Soc. Chgo., Chgo. Acad. Scis. (woman's bd.) Chgo. Chamber Orch. Assn., John G. Shedd Soc., Internat. Platform Assn., English Speaking Union, Japan-Am. Soc., U.S.-China Friendship Assn., Alpha Delta Pi (past pres. local alumnae chpts., nat. dir.), Xi Delta. Clubs: South Shore Country, College, Quadrangle, Ill. Athletic, U. Chgo. Dames, Iowa Authors; Pan Am Airways Clipper; Lakeside Lawn Bowling, Hyde Park Neighborhood, Order Eastern Star. Contbr. to newspapers, periodicals, encys. and yearbooks. Visited and photographed with husband and alone 125 fgn. countries, including China; lectr. on fgn. countries; unofcl. attendant numerous internat. confs. Address: 5834 Stony Island Ave Chicago IL 60637

PETERSON, PAUL JEROME, agrl. co. exec.; b. Omaha, Jan. 25, 1931; s. Arthur Herman and Gladys Eileen (Malmrose) P.; student Wayne State Coll., 1949-51; B.S., Kans. State U., 1956; m. Ruby Levene Smith, May 28, 1953; children—Krista, Douglas, Rebecca. Mgmt. trainee Ralston Purina, Iowa Falls, Iowa, 1956-58; ingredient buyer Supersweet Feeds, New Ulm, Minn., 1958-61, procurement mgr., 1961-66, asst. dir. procurement, Mpls., 1966-68, dir. procurement, 1968-69, gen. procurement mgr., 1969-70; sales ter. mgr. Dawes Labs., Minnetonka, Minn., 1970-73; dir. procurement Doane Products Co. Inc., Joplin, Mo., 1973—. Pres. PTA, 1968-69. Bd. dirs. Joplin Area Sheltered Workshop, 1973—. Served with AUS, 1952-54; ETO. Presbyn. Club: Toastmasters (pres. 1962) (New Ulm, Minn.). Address: 2801 Ohio Joplin MO 64801

PETERSON, RALPH HENRY, lawyer; b. Hunter, N.D., Aug. 26, 1922; s. Henry R. and Ella C. (Peterson) P.; B.S., U. Minn., 1945, J.D., 1947; m. Marjorie C. Youngquist, Sept. 25, 1948; children—Charlotte, Patricia, Carol, Anita. Admitted to Minn. bar, 1947, since practiced in Albert Lea; mem. firm Sturtz, Peterson, Chesterman, Erickson, Anderson & Hareid, and predecessor firms, 1947—; dir. Jobs, Inc., 1st Nat. Bank of Albert Lea, 1st Nat. Bank of Emmons (Minn.). Mem. Minn. Bd. Edn., 1967-75, pres., 1971-72; supr., Town of Albert Lea, 1954-58; chmn. Freeborn County Republican Com., 1956-57; chmn. bd. trustees Lea Coll. Mem. Am., Minn., 10th Jud. Freeborn County bar assns., Albert Lea C. of C. (past com. chmn.), Gamma Eta Gamma. Lutheran. Rotarian. Asso. editor: Minn. Law Rev., 1946. Home: 929 Lakeview Blvd Albert Lea MN 56007 Office: 402 S Washington Ave Albert Lea MN 56007

PETERSON, RICHARD M., newspaper editor and pub.; b. Minot, N.D., Oct. 24, 1941; s. Hans G. and Emma M. (Heupel) P.; A.A., Lake Region Jr. Coll., 1961; B.A., U. N.D., 1963. Editor, pub. Benson County Farmers Press, Minnewaukan, N.D., 1963-67, 70—, Devils Lake (N.D.) World, 1973—; dir. Prairie Press, Inc., New Rockford, N.D., 1973—, pres., 1975-77. Served to 1st lt. Inf. U.S. Army, 1967-70. Decorated Bronze Star medal. Mem. N.D. (dir. 1973-74, 76—), Nat. newspaper assns., N.D. Hist. Soc. of Germans from Russia, Devils Lake Civic Assn., Sigma Delta Chi. Clubs: Elks, Eagles, Masons, Am. Legion, VFW, Minnewaukan Country (pres. 1970-77), Devils Lake Town and Country, Minnewaukan Comml. (sec.). Home: Minnewaukan ND 58351 Office: 4318 B Ave Minnewaukan ND 58351

PETERSON, ROBERT AUSTIN, mower mfg. co. exec.; b. Sioux City, Iowa, July 5, 1925; s. Austen W. and Marie (Mueller) P.; B.S., U. Minn., 1946, B.A., 1947; m. Carol May Hudy, May 17, 1952; children—Roberta, Richard, Thomas, Bruce. Credit mgr. New Holland Machine div. Sperry Rand Corp., Mpls., 1952-61; credit mgr. Toro Co., Mpls., 1961-68, treas., 1968-71, v.p. finance, after 1971, now v.p., treas., internat. finance officer; dir. State Bond & Mortgage, State Bonding Co., Auto Turf Care, Darlington, Eng., Norton Corp., Phoenix, Clapper Corp., Boston. Chmn., Prior Lake Spring Lake Watershed Dist., 1970—; chmn. mem. bd. dirs. Prior Lake Bd. Edn., 1965-71; chmn. Scott County Republican Party, 1969-70. Bd. dirs. Scott Carver Mental Health Center, 1969-73. Served to ensign USNR, 1943-46. Mem. Financial Execs. Inst. Clubs: Prior Lake Yacht (dir.); Decathlon Athletic (Mpls.) Mpls. Home: 14956 Pixie Point Circle SE Prior Lake MN 55372 Office: 8111 Lyndale Ave S Minneapolis MN 55420

PETERSON, RODNEY KELLER, physician; b. LaCrosse, Wis., Sept. 12, 1917; s. Alvin Benjamin and Bessie Viola (Keller) P.; B.S., U. Wis., 1938, M.D., 1940; m. Janet Maud Nelson, June 20, 1942 (dec. Feb. 1964); children—Deni Ellen Peterson Svendsen, Mark F., Brett J., Shelley J. Peterson Gladowski, Jill E. Peterson Hagar; m. Frances Louise Gumble Keller, June 24, 1965; stepchildren—Joan L. Roche, Gail F. McMahan, James H., Ann L. Bjoin. Intern Med. Coll. of Va., Richmond, 1940-41; resident Navy Aviation Med. Sch., Pensacola, Fla., 1941-42, U.S. Naval Sch. Medicine, Washington, 1941-42, U.S. Naval Sch. Tropical Medicine, 1942; practice medicine, Stoughton, Wis., 1947—; mem. staff Stoughton Hosp., chief staff, 1971—; cons. physician Uniroyal Co., Stoughton, 1952—. Served with M.C., USNR, 1941-47. Fellow Am. Acad. Family Physicians; mem. Am., Wis., Dane County med. assns., Am. Legion, Phi Beta Pi. Clubs: Stoughton Country, Masons. Home: Route 5 Box 155 Stoughton WI 53589 Office: 314 S Division St Stoughton WI 53589

PETERSON, ROGER DEAN, dentist; b. Feb. 1, 1936; s. Fred C. and Myrle (Sindt) P.; B.S., Creighton U., 1957; D.D.S., U. Tenn., 1965; m. Carolyn Gutschenritter, Feb. 7, 1959; children—Michelle Marie, Jacqueline Kay, Roger Dean, Patricia Ann, Edward Fredrick. Gen. practice dentistry, Omaha, 1965—. Chmn., Citizens for Ednl. Freedom, 1968—; com. chmn. Leawood Homeowners Assn., 1972-73. Served as 2d lt., arty. AUS, 1958. Mem. Millard Jr. C. of C., Gretna Jr. C. of C. (charter, 2d v.p. 1966-67), Am., Nebr. dental assns., Omaha Dist. Dental Soc., Acad. Gen. Dentistry, Nebr. Soc. Dentistry for Children, Holy Name Soc., Psi Omega. Clubs: Oak Hills Country (charter), West Omaha Wine Study (charter). Home: 6226 S 118th Plaza Omaha NE 68137 Office: 11836 Elm St Omaha NE 68144

PETERSON, ROGER MARSHALL, mgmt. cons.; b. Chgo., Mar. 6, 1936; s. Marshall Carl and Lorene Jennie (Horn) P.; B.S. in Bus. Adminstrn., Northwestern U., 1958, M.B.A., 1959; m. Grace Gayle Younger, Oct. 10, 1959; children—Todd Marshall, Scott Edward. With Bell & Howell Co., Chgo., 1959-64, salesman Cedar Rapids, Iowa, 1961-62, asst. gen. sales mgr. Rochester (N.Y.) film div., 1962-64; asst. to pres. Stebbins Hardware Co., Chgo., 1964; mgmt. cons. A.T. Kearney Inc., Chgo., 1964—; faculty Am. Mgmt. Assns. Inc., 1967—. Pres. New Trier Young Republican Orgn., 1967-68; mem. panel arbitrators Am. Arbitration Assn. Mem. Sales and Mktg. Execs. Assn. Chgo. (dir. 1970-76, pres. 1973-74), Sales and Mktg. Execs. Internat. (dir. 1975—), Econ. Club Chgo. Presbyterian. Clubs: Sunset Ridge Country (dir. 1974-77); Univ., Execs. (Chgo.). Contbr. articles profl. publs. bus. mgmt., lectr. in field. Home: 430 Sheridan Rd Kenilworth IL 60043 Office: 100 S Wacker Dr Chicago IL 60606

PETERSON, ROY EDWIN, water resources planner; b. Jamaica, N.Y., Dec. 6, 1928; s. Albert Hendix and Ethel (Belles) P.; B.S., N.Y. U., 1953, M.S., 1956; m. Donna Mae Bradbury, June 30, 1956; children—Brad Aldon, Kevin Royce. Prin. sci. Gen. Mills Electronics Div., Mpls., 1955-62; operations analyst Honeywell, Mpls., 1962-63; mgr. ops. research and systems analysis Litton Applied Sci. Div., Mpls., 1963-66, mgr. advanced planning, 1967-69; sr. prin. scientist Honeywell, 1966-67; pres. Creative Research Services, Inc., 1969-74; study dir. Upper Mississippi River Basin Commn., 1974—. Mem. Richfield Charter Commn., 1962-68, Richfield Planning Commn., 1971-75. Served with USAAF, 1946-49. Mem. Am. Meterol. Soc., Ops. Research Soc. Am. (asso.). Contbr. articles to profl. jours. Address: 6324 Russell Ave S Minneapolis MN 55423

PETERSON, RUSSELL ARTHUR, clergyman, educator; b. Mpls., July 11, 1922; s. Oscar Arthur and Henrietta (Schroeder) P.; student Augsburg Coll., Mpls., 1940-42; B.A., Augustana Coll., Sioux Falls, S.D., 1944; M.A., U. Iowa City, Iowa, 1950; postgrad. Luther Theol. Sem., N.Y.C., 1947, Union Theol. Sem., N.Y.C., 1946, Columbia U., 1946; Ph.D., U. N.D., 1959; postgrad. Oxford (Eng.) U., 1958, 72-75; m. Thelma B. Renning, Oct. 19, 1947; children—Ann, Jan, Karen, Barry. Ordained to ministry Am. Lutheran Ch., 1947; librarian designate Luther Theol. Sem., St. Paul, 1947-49; sr. pastor Flandreau (S.D.) Luther Parish, 1949-51; exec. dir. Luth. Home for Children, Fergus Falls, Minn., 1951-54; pres. Dakota Luth. Acad., Minot, N.D., 1954-57; adminstrv. asst. U. N.D., Grand Forks, 1960-65, asso. prof. higher edn., 1965-67, prof., 1967—, chmn. dept. edn., 1971-72, prof. intellectual founds., 1972—; examiner N. Central Assn., 1964—; cons. in field. Recipient Distinguished Service award U.S. Jr. C. of C. for work with mentally retarded children, 1953, B.C. Gamble Distinguished Service award, 1972. Author: Luther for Today, 1948; Lutheranism and the Educational Ethic, 1950; The Size of Death, 1951; How Love Will Help, 1953; God and I, 1958; Existentialism and the Creative Teacher, 1970; Counseling Tips for the Beginning Teacher, 1970; translator: The Modern Message of the Psalms, 1948; Children's Tales from Norway, 1950; The God That Job Had, 1951; The Synoptic New Testament, 1951. Home: 802 Boyd Dr Grand Forks ND 58201 Office: U ND Dept Edn Grand Forks ND 58201

PETERSON, VERNON JEROME, radiologist; b. Elkhorn, Iowa, Feb. 20, 1942; s. Alva Raymond and Gladys Tena May (Johnson) P.; student Union Coll., 1960-62; B.S. in Chemistry, Denver U., 1964; M.D. with honors, Loma Linda U., 1968; m. Beverly Jo Owen, July 29, 1962; children—Tamara Lynn, Scott Allen. Intern, Riverside County and Univ. Teaching Hosp., 1968-69; resident in radiology U. Mo., Columbia, 1969-73; diagnostic radiologist Radiology and Nuclear Medicine Profl. Assn., Topeka, 1974—; instr. radiology U. Mo., 1973-74; active staff Stormont-Vail, St. Francis, Meml. hosps. Served to capt. M.C., AUS, 1970-72. Named Outstanding Intern Riverside Hosp., 1968-69. Diplomate Am. Bd. Radiology. Mem. Am. Coll. Radiology, Radiol. Soc. N.Am., Kans., Shawnee County med. socs., AMA, Alpha Omega Alpha. Republican. Seventh-day Adventist. Home: 4730 Brentwood St Topeka KS 66606 Office: 310 Medical Arts Bldg 10th and Horne Sts Topeka KS 66604

PETERSON, WILLIAM MC CLURE, machine tool mfg. co. exec.; b. Detroit, Feb. 14, 1930; s. Signor and Frances Elizabeth (McClure) P.; student Lawrence Inst. Tech.; m. Carol Lynn Straub, June 20, 1975; children—Shelly Frances, Carl Eric, Paul David, Mark Edward, Stephen Alan. Prodn. mgr. Cargill Detroit Corp., 1951-59; v.p. Olsen Mfg. Co., Inc., Royal Oak, Mich., 1959-68, dir., 1960—; v.p., dir. Hydramet Amm., Inc., Royal Oak, Mich., 1968—; mem. task com. guarding power presses Cemented Carbide Producers Assn. Served with USMCR, 1948-50. Mem. Soc. Mfg. Engrs. (sr.), Am. Ceramic Soc., Am. Nuclear Soc., Soc. Carbide and Tool Engrs., Am. Def. Preparedness Assn., Nat. Wildlife Fedn., Nat. Audubon Soc., U.S. Power Squadron, Boat Owners Assn. U.S. Republican. Club: Elks. Patentee lubricating devices, method for compacting powders. Home: 1153C Kirts St Troy MI 48084 Office: 4605 Delemere St Royal Oak MI 48073

PETKE, FREDERICK EDWARD, chem. co. exec.; b. East Paterson, N.J., July 8, 1913; s. Edward and Frieda (Schumacher) P.; B.S. magna cum laude, Bates Coll., 1934; M.A., Clark U., 1935; m. Marie Elizabeth Wisseman, June 8, 1940; children—F. David, Kenneth E., Richard A. Chemist, Calco Chem. Co., 1935-39; asso. chem. dir. Hilton Davis Chem. Co., Cin., 1940-48; v.p. research Ander Chem. Co., Cin., 1948-60; resin dir. Columbian Carbon Co., Cin., 1960-62; mgr. color, resin, varnish lab. Cities Service Co., Cin., 1962-74; tech. dir. colors and chems. div. Borden Chem. div. Borden Inc., Cin., 1974—. Active Boy Scouts Am. Mem. Cin. Dayton Indpls. Columbus Soc. Paint Tech., Nat. Printing Ink Research Inst., Dry Color Mfrs. Assn., Am. Chem. Soc. Methodist (trustee). Lectr., patentee in field. Home: 6743 Camaridge Pl Cincinnati OH 45243 Office: Borden Chem Div Borden Inc 630 Glendale-Milford Rd Cincinnati OH 45215

PETRE, HARVEY ALVIN, dentist; b. Milw., Feb. 20, 1921; s. Joseph Edmund and Helen (Walezak) Pietruszynski; B.Sc., Marquette U., 1942, D.D.S., 1944; m. Adeline Niedzwiecki, Dec. 2, 1944; children—Judith Petre Krawczyk, Gary R., Susan M., Mark S., Gail A., Richard J., Timothy S., Greg A., Donald J. Individual practice dentistry, Milw., 1946—; mem. dental staff St. Francis Hosp., 1959—, chief dental staff, 1959-62; clin. instr. Marquette U. Dental Coll., 1946-48. Active Boy Scouts Am., 1959-76; dental chmn. United Fund, 1965. Served with USNR, 1942-46; now lt. comdr. Res. ret. Mem. Greater Milw. Dental Assn. (dir. 1964-76, pres. 1975), Am. Acad. Orthodontics Gen. Practitioner (pres. 1965-66), Polish Nat. Alliance, St. Vincent de Paul Soc. (dental chmn. 1966-76). Holy Name Soc. (pres. 1946-48). Home: 8240 Fairmont Ln Greendale WI 53129 Office: 924 W Oklahoma Ave Milwaukee WI 53215

PETRI, HENRY LAW, mfg. co. exec.; b. Brookline, Mass., Nov. 9, 1914; s. Gunther Hector Petri and Gertrude Dennison (Bement) Petri Dennison; grad. Gov. Dummer Acad., 1935; m. Avalo Brown, Mar. 23, 1943; children—Pamela Dennison, Stephanie Petri Lord. With Filene's, Boston, 1936-40; with United Carr Fastener (later merged with TRW), Cambridge, Mass., 1940-45, sales engr., Detroit, 1945-57, dist. sales mgr. Ucinite div., 1957-72, mgr. customer relations and sales rep. Carr div. TRW, Southfield, Mich., 1972—. Mem. Am. Soc. Body Engrs., Soc. Automotive Engrs. Episcopalian. Club: Country of Detroit. Home: 97 Handy Rd Grosse Pointe Farms MI 48236 Office: 21311 Civic Center Dr Southfield MI 48075

PETRI, KENNETH MILLER, lawyer, banker, savs. and loan exec.; b. Galion, Ohio, Aug. 27, 1907; s. Edward W. and Lillian M. (Miller) P.; student Ohio Wesleyan U., 1925-26, also Spencerian Coll. Accounting and Fin., Cleve. State U.; LL.B., John Marshall Sch. Law, 1931, LL.M., 1933; m. Hazel Marie Nichols, Mar. 6, 1938. Admitted to Ohio bar, 1931; practiced in Galion, 1931—; mem. firm Petri, Hottenroth & Garverick, 1965—; counsel, chmn. bd. Buckeye State Bank, Galion, 1951—; counsel, dir., 1st v.p. First Fed. Savs. & Loan Assn. Galion, 1953—. Mem. Galion Bd. Edn., 1951-52; mem. Ohio Ho. of Reps., 1932-38, chmn. bank com., 1934-36, mem. taxation com., sec. ho. judiciary com., 1936-38; del. to Democratic Nat. Conv., 1956; bd. dirs., sec. Family Service N. Central Ohio, Galion; mem. Crawford County Draft Adv. Bd. Fellow Ohio Bar Found.; mem. Am. (corp. banking and bus. law sect. 1963-73), Ohio (exec. com. 1963-66, also sub-coms.; chmn. legis. screening com. 1964-65; mem. council dels. 1963-66), Galion, Crawford County (pres. 1936, 39, 73, 74, 75) bar assns., Am. Judicature Soc., N.Y., Am. trial lawyers assns., Ohio Acad. Trial Lawyers, Galion Hist. Soc., Am. Legion, Delta Theta Phi. Lutheran (pres. congregation 1943-53; mem. ch. council 1943-53, 72-73, 74-75; pres. Brotherhood 1935-36; pres. Ohio dist. Luther League 1932-33). Club: Elks. Home: 1084 Bucyrus Rd Galion OH 44833 Office: 126 S Market St Galion OH 44833

PETRIE, BRUCE INGLIS, lawyer; b. Washington, Nov. 8, 1926; s. Robert Inglis and Marion McClurg (Douglas) P.; B.B.A., U. Cin., 1948, J.D., 1950; m. Beverly Ann Stevens, Nov. 3, 1950; children—Laurie Ann, Bruce Inglis, Karen Elizabeth. Admitted to Ohio bar, 1950; asso. firm Kunkel & Kunkel, Cin., 1950-51; asso. firm Graydon, Head & Ritchey, Cin., 1951-56, partner, 1957—. Mem. Ohio Ethics Commn., 1974-75; mem. bd. Charter Com. Greater Cin., 1952-76; mem. Green Areas adv. com. Village of Indian Hill, Ohio, 1969—, chmn., 1976—; mem. Bd. Edn. Indian Hill Exempted Village Sch. Dist., 1964-67, pres., 1967; mem. adv. bd. William A. Mitchell Center, mental health center, 1969—; mem. sta. WGUC-FM Community Bd., 1974—, chmn., 1974-76; bd. dirs. Murray Seasongood Good Govt. Fund. Served with USMCR, 1944-46. Recipient Young Man of Year Distinguished Service award Jr. C. of C., 1959; Pres.'s award for Excellence, U. Cin., 1976. Fellow Ohio State Bar Assn. Found., Am. Bar Found.; mem. Am., Ohio State (modern cts. com. 1965—, chmn. 1977—, council dels. 1976, dir. OBAR Automated Research Corp. 1974-77), Cin. (exec. com., 2d v.p. 1977—), bar assns., Cin. Lawyers Club, Am. Judicature Soc. (dir., Herbert Lincoln Harley award 1973), Cincinnatus Assn. (exec. com. 1972-75), U. Cin. Law Sch. Alumni (chmn. 1974-75), Order of Coif, Lit. Club Cin., Sigma Chi. Presbyterian (elder, trustee, deacon). Clubs: University (gov. 1972-75), Cincinnati Country (Cin.). Home: 5940 Crabtree Ln Cincinnati OH 45243 Office: 5th 3d Center 511 Walnut St Cincinnati OH 45202

PETRIE, GEORGE ROLLO, obstetrician, gynecologist; b. Cadillac, Mich., Aug. 27, 1934; s. George Rollo and Nan Marie (Brown) P.; A.B., U. Mich., 1956, M.D., 1960; children— George Jeffrey, John Marshall, Matthew Cooper. Intern, St. Joseph Mercy Hosp., Pontiac, Mich., 1960-61; resident Grace Hosp., Detroit, 1961-64; practice medicine specializing in obstetrics and gynecology, Parma, Ohio, 1966—; mem. staff Deaconess Hosp., Cleve., Parma Community Hosp. Served with U.S. Army, M.C., 1964-66. Diplomate Am. Bd. Obstetrics and Gynecology. Fellow Am. Coll. Obstetrics and Gynecologists; mem. Choyamoga County Med. Soc., Ohio State, Am. med. assns., Cleve. Soc. Obstetricians and Gynecologists, Sierra Club, Wilderness Soc., Nat. Wildlife Fedn., New Eng. Hist. and Geneaological Soc. Republican. United Ch. Christ. Home: 6814 Rosemont Dr Brecksville OH 44141 Office: 6681 Ridge Rd Parma OH 44141

PETROCHUK, KONSTANTIN, artist, filmmaker; b. Wurzach, W. Ger., Apr. 30, 1947; s. Nick and Lillian (Darvinski) P.; came to U.S., 1951, naturalized, 1973; B.F.A., Kent State U., 1971, M.A., 1975. Filmmaker, photographer; faculty art dept. U. Akron (Ohio), 1976—; films shown: Ann Arbor Film Festival, 1976, Mus. Modern Art, N.Y.C., 1977, others; tchr. Kent State U., 1973-74; curator art gallery, 1974-75. Cleve. Area Arts Council Film grantee, 1977. Address: 437 Lake St Kent OH 44240

PETROS, SOPHIE KARIPIDES (MRS. THOMAS S. PETROS), home economist, dir. pub. relations; b. Canton, O., Nov. 4, 1932; d. Constantine N. and Martha (Sideropoulos) Karipides; student Ohio State U., 1950-52; B.S. in Journalism, Northwestern U., 1954; m. Thomas S. Petros, Jan. 10, 1960; 1 son, Dean. Tchr. home econs. St. Charles Borromeo Environment House, Chgo., 1958; publicity-promotion asst. Toni Co., Chgo., 1954-55; TV account exec. Yardis Advt. Co., Phila., 1955-56; TV writer, demonstrator Crestline Co., Chgo., 1957; home service rep. Peoples Gas Light & Coke Co., Chgo., 1957-62; dir. pub. relations and advt., sec. Dial On Corp., Milw., 1962—; condr. gourmet cooking show WISN-TV, Milw., 1971—; free-lance food demonstrator; free-lance television commls., 1956—. Chmn., Hope for Hope Fund, Canton, 1954. Recipient debate award Nat. Forensic League, 1950. Mem. Am. Fedn. Television and Radio Artists, Am. Home Econs. Assn., Home Econs. in Bus., Northwestern U. Alumni Assn., Theta Sigma Phi, Alpha Xi Delta. Mem. Greek Orthodox Ch. Author: Sophie Kay's Step-by-Step Cook Book, 1972; Sophie Kay's Family Cookbook, 1974; International Menu Cookbook, 1976; Junior Chef Cookbook, 1977; Sophie Kay's Yogurt Cookery, 1978. Home: 15325 Westover Rd Elm Grove WI 53108 Office: 4747 S Howell Ave Milwaukee WI 53207

PETROSKI, CATHERINE ANN GROOM, author; b. St. Louis, Sept. 7, 1939; d. Robert John and Mary Louise (Stirling) Groom; B.A., MacMurray Coll., Jacksonville, Ill., 1961; postgrad. Breadloaf Sch. English, Vt., 1961; M.A., U. Ill., Urbana, 1961; m. Henry J. Petroski, July 15, 1966; children—Karen, Stephen. Instr. English, Belleville (Ill.) High Sch. and Area Coll., 1962-65, U. Ill., Urbana, 1965-67; writer, editor Nat. Council Tchrs. English, 1967-68; reviewer Austin (Tex.) Am. Statesman, also freelance writer, 1969-75; freelance author, writer-in-residence Ill. Arts Council, 1976—; author short fiction, poetry, essays, articles and revs. in mags. and quars.; mem. bd. Friends of Downers Grove (Ill.) Pub. Library, 1977—; vol. leader writing workshop Downers Grove pub. schs., 1977. Recipient Berlin prize MacMurray Coll., 1961; Fiction prize Sou'wester mag., 1974; Best Short Story prize Tex. Inst. Letters, 1976; Bridgman scholar, 1974; Nat. Endowment for Arts fellow, 1978. Mem. Ill. Writers. Address: 4628 Main St Downers Grove IL 60515

PETROSKI, HENRY RAYMOND JOSEPH, mech. engr.; b. N.Y.C., Feb. 6, 1942; s. Henry Frank and Victoria Rose (Grygrowych) P.; B.M.E., Manhattan Coll., 1963; M.S., U. Ill., 1964, Ph.D., 1968; m. Catherine Ann Groom, July 15, 1966; children—Karen Beth, Stephen James. Instr. theoretical and applied mechanics U. Ill., 1965-68; asst. prof. engring. mechanics U. Tex., 1968-74; mech. engr. Argonne (Ill.) Nat. Lab., 1975—. NSF grantee, 1973; recipient Sigma Xi Paper award, 1968; Ill. Arts Council Poetry award, 1976. Registered profl. engr., Tex. Mem. Am. Acad. Mechanics, ASME, Soc. Natural Philosophy, History Sci. Soc., Sigma Xi. Contbr. articles in field to profl. jours., also poetry to literary mags. Home: 4628 Main St Downers Grove IL 60515 Office: Argonne National Laboratory Argonne IL 60439

PETROSKY, J(OHN) DALE, dental surgeon; b. Detroit, Mar. 24, 1935; s. John N. and Corinne T. (Drollinger) P.; student Mich. State U., 1952-55; D.D.S., U. Detroit, 1959; m. Edith E. Ebel, July 7, 1957; children—Nina Ellen, Norman Eric, Wendy Stephenson. Practice dentistry, St. Clair Shores, Mich., 1961—; pres., chmn. bd. Petrosky Investments Inc., Grosse Pointe, Mich., 1968—; owner Fino Yacht Co. Pres. Inner City Community Clinic, Detroit, 1964-68, Riverside Civic Fund, 1967—. Served with USNR, 1959-61. Recipient Riverside Community Service Award, 1966. Mem. Am., Mich. dental assns., Aircraft Owners and Pilots Assn., Psi Upsilon, Psi Omega, Omicron Kappa Upsilon. Home: 578 Heather Lane Grosse Pointe Woods MI 48236 Office: 23915 Jefferson St St Clair Shores MI 48080

PETROVICH, MIODRAG BOZIDAR, educator; b. Zemun, Yugoslavia, Sept. 29, 1933; s. Bozidar V. and Nadezda M. (Zivanovic) P.; came to U.S., 1956, naturalized, 1965; student U. Ljubljana, Yugoslavia, 1953-54; B.A., Shepherd Coll., 1960; M.A., U. Chgo., 1965, Ph.D., 1974; m. Joyce Hope Grim, Sept. 29, 1962. Translator, tech. editor Research Internat. Assos., Washington, 1960-61; escort officer, interpreter U.S. State Dept., Washington, 1961-66; asst. prof. history, dir. Balkan areas studies program Hope Coll., Holland, Mich., 1966-74, asso. prof. history, 1976—; asso. prof. history and internat. relations, Internat. Studies Inst., Grand Valley State Colls., Allendale, Mich., 1974-76; reader group projects abroad HEW, 1972, 77, mem. Fulbright panel, 1974-75, mem. Title VI panel, 1976-77; cons. Am. Council on Edn., 1973; moderator The Great Decisions 1975 television program, Grand Rapids, Mich., 1975-77. Recipient Outstanding Polit. Sci. Student award, Shepherd Coll., 1960; Internat. Research and Exchanges Bd. fellow, 1971. Mem. Am. Assn. Advancement Slavic Studies, Am. Polit. Sci. Assn., World Affairs Council, Acad. Polit. Sci., Phi Sigma Epsilon, Phi Alpha Theta. Clubs: Serbian Academic (Chgo.), Holland (Mich.) Country. Home: 90 W 14th St Holland MI 49423 Office: Dept History Hope Coll Holland MI 49423

PETRUCCI, ANTHONY, pub. relations exec.; b. McComas, W.Va., Sept. 1, 1932; s. Joseph and Amelia (Giacobbi) P.; A.A., Henry Ford Community Coll., 1954; B.A., Wayne State U., 1961; m. Patricia Ann Weir, Aug. 18, 1956; children—Susan, Lauren, Paul. Journalist, Dearborn (Mich.) Independent, 1958-60; with Hoskins Mfg. Co., Detroit, 1960-64, Ex-Cell-O Corp., Detroit, 1964-67, Fed. Mogul Corp., Detroit, 1967-68, Diversified Pub. Relations Services, Southfield, Mich., 1969-73; pub. relations counselor McMaster Assos., Pub. Relations, Detroit, 1973-76; speechwriter Rockwell Internat., Troy, Mich., 1976—. Adviser congl. and municipal candidates. Served with AUS, 1956-58. Mem. Pub. Relations Soc. Am. (accredited), Pub. Relations Counselors, Detroit Press Club. Home: 26448 Morley Dr Inkster MI 48141 Office: 720 Free Press Bldg Detroit MI 48226

PETRULIS, JOHN BRUNO, SR., savs. and loan assn. exec.; b. Vilkaviskis, Lithuania, Sept. 28, 1944; s. Pius and Magdalena (Maila) P.; came to U.S., 1949; naturalized, 1966; B.A. (Procopian Recognition scholar), Ill. Benedictine Coll., 1966; grad. certificate N.Y. Inst. Finance, 1969; M.B.A., Loyola U., Chgo., 1973; J.D. with honors, Lewis U., 1978; m. 1967 (div. 1973); children—Donna Michelle and Dora Marie (twins), John Bruno, Paul Vincent. Trust trainee 1st Nat. Bank of Chgo., 1966-67; outfielder in minor leagues Atlanta Braves Baseball Club, 1966-67; tchr. Chgo. Bd. Edn., 1967-68; stockbroker, adminstrv. asst. Harris Upham & Co., Chgo., 1968-73; exec. v.p., dir. Sauk Prairie Savs. & Loan Assn., Frankfort, Ill., 1973—, also dir. Mem. Frankfort, Lithuanian-Am. c's. of c. Roman Catholic. Home: 212 Venetian Way Orland Park IL 60462 Office: 28 Kansas St Frankfort IL 60423

PETTENGILL, ROSCOE ROBERT, concrete and gravel co. exec.; b. Rock Rapids, Iowa, Mar. 8, 1918; s. Sylvester Harry and Christena (Guyan) P.; student, Dunwoody Inst., 1939; m. Nadene Campbell, Oct. 27, 1946; children—Peter E., Leslie Lois. Employee Pettengill Concrete & Lumber (name changed to Pettengill Concrete & Gravel, Inc., 1962), Rock Rapids, 1937-45, partner, 1945—, pres., 1959—; pres. Pettengill Concrete & Gravel Inc., 1962—. Pres. Rock Rapids Air Port Commn., 1969—. Served with AUS, 1941-45. Decorated Purple Heart. Mem. Rock Rapids Devel. Commn., Rock Rapids C. of C., Am. Legion, V.F.W. Methodist (trustee 1969-74). Kiwanian (pres. Rock Rapids 1968-75). Home: Route 2 Rock Rapids IA 51246 Office: North Boone Rock Rapids IA 51246

PETTIPIECE, CLAYTON LLOYD, psychiatrist; b. Rusville, Nebr., Feb. 25, 1929; s. Clarence Lloyd and Vivian Gertrude (Reinohl) P.; student Chadron State Coll., 1948-49, 52-54; B.S., U. Nebr., 1956, M.D., 1958; m. JoAnne Elizabeth Shea, Mar. 13, 1971; children—Kim Anne, Kurt R., Jay R., Julianne, Jannette, Jeannine. Intern, Bishop Clarkson Meml. Hosp., Omaha, 1958-59; resident psychiatry Nebr. Psychiat. Inst., Omaha, 1967-70; practice medicine, Sidney, Iowa, 1959-63, Shenandoah, Iowa, 1963-67; fellow child psychiatry Nebr. Psychiat. Inst., 1969-71; dir. outpatient dept. Immanuel Community Mental Health Center, Omaha, 1971-72, dir. 1972—; dir. Blair (Nebr.) Mental Health Center, 1972—, Fremont (Nebr.) Mental Health Center, 1973—; instr. U. Nebr. Coll. Medicine, Omaha, 1970—; pvt. practice medicine specializing in psychiatry, Omaha, 1977—. Pres., Nebr. Assn. Community Mental Health Centers, 1972-74; rep. Nat. Council Community Mental Health Centers, 1973—. Served with AUS, 1950-52. Mem. Am. Acad. Child Psychiatrists, Am., Sioux psychiat. socs., Nebr., Douglas County med. socs., Nebr. Assn. Mental Health, Am. Legion, Phi Rho Sigma. Republican. Home: 3507 N 111th Plaza Omaha NE 68164 Office: 6901 N 72d St Omaha NE 68122

PETTIS, EUGENE ERNEST, social worker; b. Detroit, Sept. 29, 1931; s. Louis James and Gladys (Walker) P.; B.A. in Sociology, Wayne State U., 1961, M.S.W., 1962; m. Olga Jean Granberry, June 20, 1953; children—Eugene Ernest, Kara Simone, Erica Nicolle. Social case worker Dept. Pub. Welfare Detroit, 1957-64; clin. social work dir., outpatient dept. Plymouth State Home and Tng. Sch., Northville, Mich., 1964-71; with U. Mich. Inst. for Study Mental Retardation and Related Disabilities, 1971—; social work cons. Child Appraisal Center, Wyandotte (Mich.) Gen. Hosp., 1968—; part-time instr. sociology Wayne County Community Coll., Detroit, 1969—, Schoolcraft, Community Coll., Livonia, Mich., 1967—; dir. Detroit East Mental Health Center, 1975—. Bd. dirs. Wayne Center for Retarded and Developmentally Disabled, Housing for Exceptional People. Served with USNR, 1954-56. Mem. Nat. Assn. Social Workers, Acad. Certified Social Workers, Am. Assn. Mental Deficiency, Mich. Welfare League, Plymouth Assn. Retarded Children, Internat. Afro-Am. Mus., Nat. Conf. on Social Welfare. Home: 31499 Harlo St Madison Heights MI 48071 Office: 7737 Kercheval St Detroit MI 48214

PETTIT, MARLIN HAZEN, design and furnishings co. exec.; b. Oskaloosa, Iowa, Sept. 14, 1942; s. Hazen C. and Rhea Ferne (Shultz) P.; S.B., Mass. Inst. Tech., 1964; student law, U. Va., 1965-66; M.B.A. (Stein, Roe fellow 1967), Harvard U., 1968; m. Maureen T. Kelly, Aug. 8, 1970; children—R. Mark, K. Nicole. Internat. fin. specialist, corp. treas.'s office Chrysler Corp., Detroit, 1968-70; pres. Cimarron Corp., Detroit, 1970-71; sr. fin. analyst J.L. Hudson Co., Detroit, 1971, gen. mgr. contract div., 1972-75; pres., treas., chief exec. officer Contract Interiors, Inc., Detroit, 1975—. Active Citizens Research Council of Detroit, Jaycees, Big Bros. Recipient Beaver Key, Mass. Inst. Tech., 1964; Geyer's Grand award for office and showroom design, 1976. Mem. Nat. Office Products Assn., Knoll Dealer Council, Detroit, Downriver C.'s of C. Roman Catholic. Clubs: Econ. of Detroit, Rotary, Harvard. Office: 511 Woodward Ave Detroit MI 48226

PETTIT, ROBERT CECIL, curator; b. Lincoln, Nebr., Sept. 10, 1936; s. Cecil Ernest and Clara Ann (Umland) P.; B.A., U. Nebr., Lincoln, 1958, postgrad., 1958-60. Part-time mus. asst. Nebr. State Hist. Soc., Lincoln, 1957-62, mus. asst., 1965, curator collections, 1965—. Served with AUS, 1962-65. Mem. Am. Assn. State and Local History, Mountain-Plains Museums Conf., Nebr. Mus. Conf. Home: 3748 C St Lincoln NE 68510 Office: 1500 R St Lincoln NE 68508

PETTY, ELIJAH EDWARD, oil processing exec.; b. Terre Haute, Ind., June 12, 1920; s. Curtis and Bonnie Belle (Reed) P.; M.E., U. Ariz., 1943; B.S. in Chem. Engring., U. Okla., 1947; m. Nelda Morris, Nov. 8, 1942; children—Montie Curtis, Vicki Ann. Mgr., Anderson Clayton Edible Oil Plant, Sao Paulo, Brazil, 1959-62, Armour Edible Oil Plant, Kankakee, Ill., 1963-66; supt. refineries Archer Daniels Midland Co., Decatur, Ill., 1966-68; v.p. M. Neumonz & Son, N.Y.C., 1968-73; pres. Petco Internat., Mt. Zion, Ill., 1973—; pres. I. & I. Co., Ltd.; chmn. bd. I. & I. Co., Ltd. (Ireland); tech. dir. AGRIMA (Rio de Janeiro). Cons. oil seed processing FAO, UN Indsl. Devel. Orgn., Am. Soybean Assn., Fgn. Agr. Service, U.S. Dept. Agr., numerous fgn. cos. and govts. Adv. com. Jacksonville (Ill.) Sch. Bd. Adv. Com.; chmn. Jacksonville Community Chest. Served to sgt., AUS, 1943-46. Registered profl. engr., Tex. Mem. Am. Oil Chemists Soc. Democrat. Patentee continuous hydrogenation. Home: Rosewood Acres Mount Zion IL 62549 Office: PO Box 209 Mount Zion IL 62549

PETZKE, ALFRED JULIUS, elec. engr.; b. South Bend, Ind., Mar. 14, 1927; s. Julius and Anna (Schultz) P.; Asso. Sci., Valparaiso Tech. Inst., 1949; m. Georgiann May Grabner, May 20, 1950; children—Gregory, Janice, Karl, Mark, Kathleen. Transmitter engr. sta. WSBT, South Bend, Ind., 1949-50, Sta. WJOB, Hammond, Ind., 1950-53; TV engr. Sta. WTVO, Rockford, Ill., 1953-54, asst. chief engr., 1954-60, chief engr., 1960-74; dir. engring., cons. Harry and Elmer Balaban Corp., Chgo., 1974—. Served with U.S. Army, 1945-46. Mem. Assn. of Fed. Communications Cons. Engrs., IEEE, Rock River Valley Electric Assn. Lutheran. Office: 1917 N Meridian Rd Rockford IL 61105

PETZOLD, FRITZ HERBERT, transit adminstr.; b. Freital, Germany, Feb. 21, 1937; s. Walter Bruno and Charlotte C. P.; came to U.S., 1953, naturalized, 1958; student Wright Jr. Coll., 1961-65; B.S., U. Ill., 1970; m. Karen J. Schmutte, June 23, 1973; children—Brian, Patrick, Erika. Operator printing press Chippewa Paper Products Co., Chgo., 1953-59; bus operator Chgo. Transit Authority, 1959-65, project mgr. engring. dept.-capital improvements transp., 1974—; mech. engr., project engr. dept. aviation Chgo. Pub. Works, 1970-74. Mem. ASME. Office: Chgo Transit Authority Room 7-169 Mdse Mart PO Box 3555 Chicago IL 60654

PETZOLD, RUDOLF HEINRICH, pub.; b. Millington, Mich., Mar. 26, 1933; s. Gustav Paul and Helen (Woelzlein) P.; B.A., Mich. State U., 1955. Mng. editor Tuscola County Advertiser, Caro, Mich., 1958-65, pres. Tuscola County Advertiser, Inc., 1965—; pres. Vassar Pioneer-Times, 1966—; pub. Mich. Lutheran, 1972—; v.p. TV 3, Inc., 1975—; dir. Presto Art Caro, Mich., 1965—, State Savs. Bank Caro; sec., treas. Thumb Web Offset, Inc. Sec. Caro Planning Commn.; chmn. Tuscola County Republican Com., 1962-63; del. Rep. conv., 1962; bd. dirs. Catholic Family Service, Bad Axe. Served with AUS, 1956-58. Mem. Tuscola County Fair Assn., Caro C. of C. (dir.), Sigma Delta Chi. Republican. Lutheran. Home: 344 N State St Caro MI 48723 Office: Caro MI 48723

PEW, STEPHEN ELIOT, real estate broker; b. Detroit, June 17, 1939; s. Frederic Cline and Gladys (Duffy) P.; B.A., Denison U., 1961; m. Kathryn Deger Boles, Dec. 22, 1961; children—Stephen F., Scott C. With Max Broock, Inc., Realtors, Birmingham, Mich., 1964—, pres., 1975—. Adj. prof. Sch. Bus. Adminstrn., U. Mich., Ann Arbor, 1970—. Chmn., Parks and Recreation Bd., Birmingham, 1968—. Served with USMCR, 1961-64. Named Distinguished Citizen of Birmingham, Birmingham Jr. C. of C., 1972; named Realtor of the Year, Birmingham Bd. Realtors, 1973. Mem. Mich. Assn. Realtors (dir. 1970—), Met. Detroit Alumni Assn. Denison U. (pres. 1968-73), Village Players (pres. 1975-76) St. Dunstan's Guild. Club: Birmingham Athletic. Home: 563 Lakeview St Birmingham MI 48009 Office: 300 S Woodward Ave Birmingham MI 48011

PEYRONNIN, JOSEPH FELIX, III, television producer; b. Chgo., Aug. 3, 1947; s. Joseph Felix and Dorothy Ethel (Hargraves) P.; B.S. in Communications, Columbia Coll., Chgo.; M.B.A., Roosevelt U., 1978. Radio announcer WLSU, Baton Rouge, 1967-68, WEXI-FM, Arlington Heights, Ill., 1969-70; prodn. asst., assignment editor, news producer, asst. assignment mgr. WBBM-TV, Chgo., 1970-76; asso. producer CBS News, Chgo., 1976—. Mem. Chgo. Press Club. Recipient Emmy award as producer WBBM-TV news coverage of transit train crash in Chgo., 1976. Home: 1400 N Lake Shore Dr Chicago IL 60610 Office: 630 N McClurg Ct Chicago IL 60611

PEYSER, JOSEPH LEONARD, educator; b. N.Y.C., Oct. 19, 1925; s. Samuel and Sadye (Quinto) P.; B.A., Duke U., 1947; M.A., 1949, profl. diploma, Columbia, 1955; etudes superieures, Universite de Nancy (France), 1949-50; Ed.D., N.Y. U., 1965; m. Julia Boxer, May 30, 1948; children—Jay Randall, Jan Ellen. Tchr., chmn. fgn. langs. pub. schs. Nancy, France, 1949-50, Monroe, N.Y., 1951-54, Uniondale, N.Y., 1954-61; asst. prin. high sch. Plainview, N.Y., 1961-63; asst. prof. Hofstra U., Hempstead, N.Y., 1963-66, asso. prof., 1966-68, asst. dean Sch. Edn., 1964-66, asso. dean, 1966, interim dean, 1966-68; dean for acad. affairs, prof. French and edn. Dowling Coll., Oakdale, N.Y., 1968-70, v.p. for acad. affairs, dean of faculty, 1970-73; prof. edn. and French, Ind. U., South Bend, 1973—, dean of faculties, 1973-75; vis. asst. prof. N.Y. U., N.Y.C., 1964-66; adj. asst. prof. L.I. U., 1961-63; cons. Pathescope Ednl. Films, Inc., 1960-71, N.Y. State Edn. Dept., 1966-68. Scoutmaster, neighborhood commr., eagle scout bd. rev., dean merit badge counselors, mem. exec. bd. No. Ind. council Boy Scouts Am.; mem. alumni admissions com. Duke U., 1969-73. Served with USNR, 1943-46. Teaching fellow French Ministry Edn., 1949-50. Recipient N.Y. U. Founders Day award, 1966. Mem. AAUP, NEA, Phi Delta Kappa, Kappa Delta Pi, Pi Delta Phi. Editor: Pathescope-Berlitz Fgn. Lang. Series, 1960; Israel, Crossroads of History, 1971. Contbr. articles. Office: 1825 Northside Blvd South Bend IN 46615

PFABE, BRUCE YETTER, banker; b. Cleve., Dec. 5, 1946; s. Edsel H. and Betty S (Snyder) P.; B.B.A., Bowling Green State U., 1969; grad. Ohio Bankers Nat. Sch. Real Estate Fin., Ohio State U., 1972; m. Christine Lynne Townley, May 16, 1970. Mgmt. trainee Lake County Nat. Bank of Painesville (Ohio), 1969-70, installment loan adminstr., 1970, asst. mgr. Willoughby (Ohio) Office, 1970-71, br. mgr. Mentor Shore br., 1971-72, mortgage loan adminstr., Painesville, 1972, adminstrv. officer mortgage loan dept., 1972-74, adminstrv. officer, mgr. Willo Plaza Office, Willoughby, 1974-76, asst. v.p. comml. loan dept., Painesville, 1976—. Treas., Lake County Kidney Found., 1971-72, pres., 1972-74, 75; chmn. campaign publicity United Way of Lake County, 1973, 74, mem. publicity com., 1973-74, chmn. bus. solicitation div., 1975-76, chmn. loaned exec. program, 1977; br. solicitor Central and Eastern United Fund, 1971-72, treas., 1973-75; solicitor Heart Fund, 1971-72, Muscular Dystrophy, 1971-72; solicitor, agy. rep. Western Lake County Greater Torch Assn., 1971-72, 74, 75; instr. C.P.R., Am. Heart Assn., 1976—; bd. dirs. Lake County unit Am. Cancer Soc., 1972—, 2d v.p., 1974-75, 1st v.p., 1975, campaign chmn., 1975, pres., 1976—; trustee Kidney Found. Ohio, Inc., 1972-75. Mem. Robert Morris Assos., Lake Erie Wheelers. Roman Catholic. Clubs: Madison (Ohio) Country, Lions (dir. Willoughby 1971—, 1st v.p. 1974-75, pres. 1975, zone chmn., dist. cabinet 1976—). Home: 145 Overlook Rd Painesville OH 44077 Office: 30 S Park Pl Painesville OH 44077

PFAENDER, LAWRENCE VERNON, mech. engr., mfg. co. exec.; b. Toledo, Jan. 13, 1927; s. Vernon Herman and Ada Margaret (Cousino) P.; student U. Mich., 1947; B.M.E., U. Toledo, 1950; m. Donna Marie Coy, June 24, 1950; children—Michael, James, Amie, Lynn, Beth. Process devel. engr. Glass Fibers Inc. (now Johns Manville Corp.), Waterville, Ohio, 1950-52; indsl. engr. Rossford Ordnance Depot, U.S. Army, Toledo, 1952-53; devel. engr. Owens Ill. Inc., Toledo, 1953-65, mgr. glass processing, consumer div., 1965-75, chief display panel mfg. engring., Perrysburg, Ohio, 1975-77, sr. scientist adminstrn. div., 1977—; dir. Noble Metal Co., Inc., Toledo. Treas., Corey Woods Property Owners Assn., 1964-77. Served in USN, 1945-46. Mem. Am., N.W. Ohio ceramic socs. Republican. Roman Catholic. Patentee in field (20). Home: 4525 Carskaddon St Toledo OH 43615 Office: 1700 N Westwood Ave Toledo OH 43551

PFAFFENBACH, HERBERT EMIL, dentist; b. Watertown, Wis., Mar. 5, 1920; s. Emil Louis and Ella (Strattman) P.; D.D.S., Marquette U., 1944; teaching certificate Stout State U. and Whitewater State U., 1970; m. Mary Jane Byington, June 26, 1943 (dec. 1975); children—Mary Ellen Pfaffenbach Sarko, Myra Jane. Intern, Eastman Dispensary, Rochester, N.Y., 1944; practice dentistry, Stoughton, Wis., 1946—; instr. Madison Area Tech. Coll., 1968—; research asso. dept. biol. materials Northwestern U. Dental Sch., Chgo., 1975—. Mem. Stoughton Planning Commn., 1960-75. Served with USNR, 1944-46, USMCR, 1953; Mem. ADA, Wis., Dane County (pres. 1966, trustee 1961-67) dental socs. Lutheran. Home: 404 Grant St Stoughton WI 53589 Office: 221 S Water St Stoughton WI 53589

PFAFFMANN, GEORGE DAVID, mfg. co. exec.; b. Detroit, Feb. 13, 1928; s. George Oswald and Anna (Ubel) P.; student Mich. Coll. Mining and Tech., 1945-46; B.E.E., U. Mich., 1951; m. Shirley Zolotoff, Oct. 29, 1955; children—Lori Lea, Leslee Lyn. Elec. engr. Gt. Lakes Engring. Works, River Rouge, Mich., 1951-52; service engr. TOCCO div. Park-Ohio Industries, Inc., Madison Heights, Mich., 1952-53, comml. engr., 1953-56, dist. engr., 1956-57, engring. rep., 1957-61, dist. mgr., 1961-76, regional mgr., 1976—. Bd. dirs. Kimberly Homeowners Assn., 1973-74; bd. dirs., v.p. Michawye Owners Assn., 1975-78. Served with U.S. Army, 1945-46. Mem. Am. Soc. Metals, Soc. Metall. Engrs., Soc. Automotive Engrs. Patentee in field (6). Home: 30021 Pipers Ln Farmington Hills MI 48018 Office: 30100 Stephenson Hwy Madison Heights MI 48071

PFAHL, STANNARD BAIRD, JR., ophthalmologist; b. Harrisburg, Pa., Sept. 9, 1933; s. Stannard Baird and Sara Snow (McAdams) P.; A.B., Harvard U., 1955; M.D., U. Pitts., 1959; postgrad. Ohio State U., 1960-63; m. Phyllis Faye Bolman, June 12, 1959; children—Scott, Douglas, Daniel, Todd. Intern, Western Pa. Hosp., Pitts., 1959-60; resident Ohio State U. hosps., 1960-63; practice medicine specializing in ophthalmology, Sandusky, Ohio, 1965—; mem. active and cons. staff Good Samaritan Hosp., Sandusky, pres. staff, 1973-75; mem. cons. staff Providence, Sandusky, Bellevue hosps. Bd. dirs. Mental Health Assn., 1967-69. Served with USNR, 1963-65. Diplomate Am. Bd. Ophthalmology. Fellow Am. Acad. Otolaryngology and Ophthalmology; mem. Ohio Ophthal. Assn. (dir. 1967-69), Am., Ohio (dist. councilor), Erie County med. assns. Presbyterian. Clubs: Rotary (pres. 1972-73); Plum Brook Country (Sandusky). Home: 416 Newport Dr Huron OH 44839 Office: 521 W Perkins Ave Sandusky OH 44870

PFALLER, MARK A(RTHUR), architect; b. Milw., Sept. 23, 1921; s. Mark Frank and Mary Ann (Rechner) P.; B.Arch., U. Notre Dame, 1942; m. Elizabeth Rae Campbell, May 25, 1946; children—Mark Frank II, Jeffrey J., Christopher J., Patrick C. With Mark F. Pfaller Assos., Milw., 1946-50, partner, 1950-59; partner Mark F. Pfaller Assos., Inc., 1959-71, pres., 1965—; chmn. In de'x, Inc. Mem. Elm Grove (Wis.) Planning Commn., 1955-58, Elm Grove Bldg. Bd., 1972-76; trustee Kiwanis Children's Center of Curative Workshop; corp. bd. St. Charles Boys Home, Fellow AIA (pres. Wis. chpt. 1965, mem. jury fellows 1973-75, mem. nat. com. architecture for health 1973-74, mem. nat. documents bd. 1976—); mem. Nat. Council Archtl. Registration Bds., Constrn. Specification Inst. (dir., past pres. Milw. chpt.). K.C., Kiwanian. Clubs: Wisconsin, Notre Dame of Milw. Pres., Wis. Architect mag., 1968-69. Contbr. articles to profl. and trade jours. Prin. works include Elmbrook Meml. Hosp., Brookfield, Wis., 1969, St. Michael Hosp., Stevens Point, Wis., 1971, Washington High Sch., Milw., 1970, St. Michael Hosp., Milw., 1973, Residential Care Treatment Center, Union Grove, Wis., 1976, Rufus King High Sch. addition, 1977. Home: 2275 Michelle Ct Brookfield WI 53005 Office: 3112 W Highland Blvd Milwaukee WI 53208

PFARNER, GERALD CHARLES, elec. engr.; b. Buffalo, Nov. 4, 1945; s. Earl William and Martha Clara (Miller) P.; B.E.E., Rensselaer Poly. Inst., 1970; M.B.A., U. Chgo., 1977; m. Jane Carol Manly, Nov. 25, 1967; children—Preston Manly, Kerry Elizabeth. TV engr. Gen. Electric Co., Schenectady, 1967-70; mgr. electronic equipment Sprague Electric Co., Wichita Falls, Tex., 1970-72; applications engring. mgr. Teradyne Co., Des Plaines, Ill., 1972-75; sr. mem. tech. staff Interdata, Arlington Heights, Ill., 1975-77; area support mgr. Honeywell Info. Systems, Schiller Park, Ill., 1977—; owner, mgr. Mu-Tronics, Roselle, Ill., 1967—. Pres. bd. dirs. Ventura 21 Inc. homeowners assn., 1975—. Recipient Hon. Sci. award Bausch & Lomb, 1963; N.Y. State Regents scholar, 1963-67; Rensselaer Poly. Inst. scholar, 1963-64. Mem. IEEE, Assn. Computing Machinery, Mensa, Nat. Aeros. Assn., Rensselaer Poly. Inst. Alumni Assn., U. Chgo. Alumni Assn. Lutheran. Home: 580 Lakeview Ct E Roselle IL 60172 Office: 4849 Scott St N Schiller Park IL 60176

PFAU, MICHAEL JOHN, lawyer; b. Detroit, Feb. 21, 1939; s. Ray H. and Mary Ann (Devaney) P.; B.S., Marquette U., 1961, J.D., 1964; m. Nancy M. Wendlandt, Dec. 28, 1963; children—Michael, Patrick, Susan. Admitted to Wis. bar, 1964; asso. firm Kluwin, Dunphy, Hankin & Hayes, Milw., 1964-70; partner Kluwin, Dunphy, Hankin & McNulty, 1971—. Mem. Am., Milw. County (mem. jud. selection com., joint bench and bar com. 1970-73) bar assns., State Bar Wis. (mem. grievance com. 1970—, vice chmn. 1974-75, chmn. sect. 3 dist 2, 1972-73), Milw. Jr. Bar Assn. (mem. exec. bd. 1967-69; treas. 1968-69), Internat. Assn. Ins. Counsel, Def. Research Inst. (state chmn. 1976—), Ins. Trial Counsel Wis. (treas. 1973-74), Am. Judicature Soc., Delta Sigma Pi, Phi Delta Phi. Club: Highlander Park Indoor Tennis. Home: 2759 N 118th St Wauwatosa WI 53222 Office: 1100 W Wells St Milwaukee WI 53233

PFEFFER, ROBERT IRVING, obstetrician, gynecologist; b. New Haven, July 31, 1923; s. George Henry and Maude Louise (Fowler) P.; student Miami U., 1943-46; M.D., Washington U., 1950; m. Marie Bebe Aran, Dec. 24, 1948; children—Robert Irving, Anne Elizabeth, Laura Marie. Intern, St. Louis County Hosp., Clayton, Mo., 1950-51, resident in obstetrics gynecology, 1954-56; resident in obstetrics gynecology, St. Louis Maternity Hosp., 1953-54; practice medicine specializing in obstetrics gynecology Thompson-Brumm-Knepper Clinic, Inc., St. Joseph, Mo., 1956—; dir. Am. Group Practice Assn. Pres., St. Joseph Mental Health Assn., 1960-64. Served with USN, 1941-45; U.S. Army, 1950-53. Diplomate Am. Bd. Obstetrics and Gynecology. Fellow Am. Coll. Obstetrics and Gynecology; mem. Mo. State, Buchanan County med. socs., Central Assn. Obstetrics and Gynecology. Presbyn. Clubs: St. Joseph Country, Shriners. Contbr. articles in field to profl. jours. Home: 1915 N 29th St St Joseph MO 64506 Office: 902 Edmond St St Joseph MO 64502

PFEIL, RICHARD JOHN, elec. mfg. co. exec.; b. Niles, Mich., Oct. 6, 1932; s. John and Marie J. (Metzger) P.; B.S., Mich. State U., 1954; M.B.A., Ind. U., 1956; m. Elaine C. Vance, Aug. 10, 1954; children—Mary, Laura, John. Teaching asso. Ind. U., 1954-56; with RCA, 1955-56; with Koontz-Wagner Electric Co., South Bend, Ind., 1956—, pres., chief exec. officer, 1963—, also dir.; dir. First Bank & Trust Co., South Bend, FBT Bancorp. Pres. South Bend Park Bd., 1969-77; chmn Mayor's Fin. Commn., 1964; pres. Jr. Achievement, 1966-68; bd. dirs. South Bend Civic Center Authority, 1973-74; mem. adv. bd. Ind. U., South Bend. Recipient South Bend Man of Year award Jaycees, 1966. Mem. Am. Mgmt. Assn., C. of C. (dir. 1971—, pres. elect 1978), Tau Beta Pi, Eta Kappa Nu. Republican. Roman Catholic. Club: Summit (South Bend). Home: 1203 Avondale Rd South Bend IN 46614 Office: 3801 Voorde Dr South Bend IN 46628

PFEILER, THOMAS ADAMS, lawyer; b. Waukesha, Wis., Nov. 4, 1929; s. Reuben Valentine and Lula Marie (Horne) P.; student Carroll Coll., 1947-49; B.S., U. Wis., 1952, LL.B., 1957; postgrad. U. Chgo., 1966-67; m. Annamae Busse, Aug. 27, 1955; children—Elizabeth, Mary. Admitted to Wis., Ill. bars, 1957; atty. law div. Chgo. Title & Trust Co., 1957-59; asso. counsel U.S. League of Savs. Assns., Chgo., 1959—; instr. Chgo. chpt. Inst. Fin. Edn., 1960-65. Served with Fin. Corps, AUS, 1953-55. Mem. Internat., Am. (vice chmn. savs. and loan law com. 1974—), Chgo. bar assns., Nat. Lawyers Club, Phi Delta Phi. Episcopalian (vestryman). Club: Lake Forest. Contbr. articles to profl. jours. Home: 1824 Hackberry Ln Lake Forest IL 60045 Office: 111 E Wacker Dr Chicago IL 60601

PFENING, FREDERIC DENVER, JR., mfg. co. exec.; b. Columbus, Ohio, Mar. 29, 1925; s. Frederic Denver and Isadora (Wells) P.; student Ohio State U., 1943-48; m. Lelia R. Bucher, May 30, 1947; children—Frederic Denver, Timothy Daniel. Pres., Fred D. Pfening Co., Columbus, Pfening & Snyder, Pfening Properties, Inc., Indsl. Aluminum Foundry, Inc., Columbus, Personal Records, Ltd., Frederic Advt. Assos.; dir. Dollar Savs. Assn. Bd. dirs. Central Ohio council Boy Scouts Am., 1959-61, Circus World Museum, Baraboo, Wis., 1958—, Buckeye Boy's Ranch, 1972—, Franklin County Crippled Children's Soc., 1970—, Ohio Soc. for Crippled Children, 1976—; trustee Six Pence Sch., 1974—; mem. Friends Ohio State U. Libraries. Mem. Bakery Equipment Mfg. Assn., (dir. 1977—), Am. Soc. Bakery Mgrs., Chief Execs. Forum (nat. sec. 1977—), Nat. Fedn. Ind. Businessmen, Newcomen Soc. N. Am., Young Bus. Men's Club, Circus Fans Assn., Circus Hist. Soc. Clubs: Rotary; Scioto Country, Columbus, Ohio State U. Faculty (Columbus). Author: History of Col. Tim McCoy Wild West, 1955; History of Cristiani Bros. Circus, 1958; History of Beatty-Cole Circus, 1960; editor Bandwagon mag., 1961—; contbr. articles to various publs. Home: 2515 Dorset Rd Columbus OH 43221 Office: 1075 W 5th Ave Columbus OH 43212

PFETTSCHER, EARL ERNEST, sch. prin.; b. Evansville, Ind., Sept. 9, 1939; s. Earl Henry and Helen Louise (Daum) P.; B.A. Elementary Edn., Evansville Coll., 1964; M.S., Ind. U., 1966; m. Darlene E. Kissel, Aug. 22, 1964; children—Jill Anne, Rebecca. Comml. pilot, flying instr. Skylane Flying Service, Evansville, Ind., 1957-64; tchr. Evansville-Vanderburgh Sch. Corp., 1964-69; elementary prin. Warrick County Sch. Corp., Boonville, Ind., 1969—. Vice pres. Warrick County CD Adv. Bd., 1977. Named Outstanding Educator service in Warrick County, Jaycees, 1974. Mem. Nat., Ind. Assns. Elementary Sch. Prins., NEA (life), Warrick County Assn. Sch. Adminstrs. (pres. 1972-74), Phi Delta Kappa. Roman Catholic. Club: Kiwanis. Home: Rural Route 2 Box 676 Telephone Rd Newburgh IN 47630 Office: Chandler Elementary School 401 S Illinois St Chandler IN 47610

PFISTER, PAUL JAMES, real estate broker; b. Terre Haute, Ind., Sept. 15, 1920; s. Joseph Ben and Emma Catherine (Welte) P.; B.S. with high distinction, Ind. U., 1947; m. Marjorie J. Engstron, Jan. 29, 1944 (dec. Jan. 1971); children—Paul James, Donald R., Mary Caye, David H., Margaret Ann. Therese Jane; m. 2d Betty J. Pfister, Apr. 19, 1974; stepchildren—Karen, Debra, Cathy, Marcia. Pres., J.B. Pfister Co., Inc., Terre Haute, 1969—; Distinguished faculty mem. Sch. Bus., Ind. U., 1963—. Pres., Terre Haute Bd. Realtors. Mem. Area Planning Commn. Bd. dirs., past pres. Taxpayers Assn. Vigo County. Served to lt. USNR, 1942-46. Decorated Air medal; named Outstanding Young Man of Year, Terre Haute Jr. C. of C., 1955. Mem. Nat., Ind. assns. realtors, Internat. Real Estate Fedn., Soc. Indsl. Realtors (v.p., dir., chmn. ednl. com.), Nat. Inst. Real Eastate Brokers, Ind. Mortgage Bankers Assn. (pres., dir.), Urban Land Inst., Ind., Terre Haute chambers commerce, Am. Mgmt. Assn., Am., Gt. Lakes States Indsl. Council (past pres., dir.), Ind. Devel. Council, Omega Tau Rho, Beta Gamma Sigma. K.C. (4 deg.), Elk, Silent Men. Club: Terre Haute Country. Home: 3047 N 9th St Terre Haute IN 47804 Office: 662 Ohio St Terre Haute IN 47808

PFLANZER, RICHARD GARY, educator; b. Ashland, Wis., June 16, 1940; s. Raymond Glenn and Alice Elizabeth (Ryskey) P.; A.B., Ind. U., 1964, Ph.D. Med. Physiology, 1969; m. Diane Kathleen Kelly, Aug. 29, 1964; children—Mark Alan, Kelly Ann. Asso. prof. physiology Ind. U., Indpls., 1969—; cons. John Wiley & Sons, Inc., N.Y.C., 1972—, William C. Brown Co., Dubuque, Iowa, 1975—. Active Boy Scouts Am. NIH fellow, 1965-68; NASA grantee, 1971. Mem. AAAS, Am. Inst. Biol. Scis., AAUP, (pres. local chpt. 1975-76), Ind. Acad. Sci., Nat. Rifle Assn., Nat. Muzzle Loading Rifle Assn., Nat. Model Railroaders Assn., Sigma Xi, Phi Delta Theta. Author: Basic Experimental Physiology, 1974; Experimental and Applied Physiology, 1977; contbr. chpt. to med. textbook, articles to profl. jours. Home: 742 Leisure Ln Greenwood IN 46142 Office: Dept Physiology Sch Medicine Ind U CA325 925 W Michigan St Indianapolis IN 46202

PFLEIDERER, FLORIZEL A., clergyman; b. Claypool, Ind., Aug. 13, 1901; s. David Henry and Maude (Minear) P.; A.B., Ashland Coll., 1923; B.D., McCormick Theol. Sem., 1925; D.D., Hanover Coll., 1947; m. Edna Hoyt, May 20, 1925; children—David Hoyt, Stephen Douglas. Ordained to ministry of Presbyn. Ch., 1925; pastor Kelvyn Park Ch., Chgo., 1925-27, Rossville (Ind.) Ch., 1927-29, Sutherland Ch., Indpls., 1929-46; adminstrv. dir. Weekday Religious Edn., 1946-53, exec. dir., 1953-71; exec. dir. Weekday Religious Edn. Found., 1955-73; fund raising cons., 1973—. Chmn. united promotion Presbytery of Indpls.; chmn. Synod com. on United Promotion, 1938-44; trustee Presbytery of Indpls., 1951-69, pres. bd. trustees, 1958-69. Rotarian. Club: Columbia. Author textbooks on religious edn. Editor: Ind. Presbyn., 1939-46. Home and office: 4011 Forest Manor Ave Indianapolis IN 46226

PFLUEGER, CHARLES ALLEN, market analyst; b. Cleve., Mar. 15, 1949; s. William and Betty Jane (Ager) P.; B.A. in History, Cleve. State U., 1971; M.B.A., Baldwin-Wallace Coll., 1976; m. Kathleen Jean Wasson, June 3, 1972; 1 son, Bradley Christopher. Mgmt. devel. program trainee Nat. City Bank, Cleve., 1971-73, adminstrv. asst., 1973-76; mkt. analyst Gumout div. Pennzoil Co., Cleve., 1976—. Served with USNG, 1971-77. Mem. Am. Mktg. Assn. Baptist. Home: 3798 Merrymound Rd South Euclid OH 44121 Office: 2686 Lisbon Rd Cleveland OH 44104

PFLUG, FRED LOUIS, telephone co. exec.; b. Lincoln, Nebr., June 6, 1928; s. Louis Henry and Suzanne Marie (Limbeck) P.; B.A., U. Nebr., 1950; m. Elizabeth Anne Reese, Nov. 24, 1950; children—Anne Pflug Dana, Thomas, John, James. Outside rep. Northwestern Bell Telephone Co., Omaha, 1953-55, mgr., McCook, Nebr., 1955-58, asst. dist. mgr., Omaha, 1959, gen. mktg. mgr., 1960-62, gen. comml. mgr., 1962-63, chief statistician, 1964, asst. v.p. pub. relations, 1964—. Pres., Family and Child Service of Omaha, 1970-72, Visiting Nurse Assn., 1972-74, St. Mark Luth. Ch., 1975—; dir. Midwest region NCCJ; dir. Omaha Sister City Assn., 1975—. Served to 1st lt. USAF, 1951-53. Accredited, Pub. Relations Soc. of Am. Mem. Nebr. Telephone Assn. (dir. 1962), Pub. Relations Soc. of Am., Phi Beta Kappa. Republican. Home: 1700 S 108th St Omaha NE 68144 Office: 100 S 19th St Omaha NE 68102

PFUNDSTEIN, KEITH LAWRENCE, heavy equipment mfg. co. exec.; b. Erie, Ill., Sept. 20, 1917; s. Bert Lederer and Valentine (Dickinson) P.; B.M.E., U. Ill., 1940; m. Mary Jane Hetrick, Aug. 27, 1945; children—Donald Keith, Kathy Joan. Tech. sales rep., research engr. Ethyl Corp., Denver, St. Louis and Detroit, 1940-44, with tech. service div., 1944-65, mgr. div. agrl. engring. dept., Detroit, 1953-65; with Deere & Co., Moline, Ill., 1965—, mgr. product safety dept., 1966—; lectr., seminar instr. product safety and product liability U. Wis., Mich. State U., U. Ill., Soc. Automotive Engrs., Am. Soc. Agrl. Engrs., Am. Soc. Quality Control. Bd. dirs. Nat. Safety Council; v.p. bd. dirs. Forsberg Community Retirement Center. Mem. Am. Soc. Agrl. Engrs. (chmn. power and machinery div. 1972-73), Soc. Automotive Engrs. (pub. affairs com. 1970-73), Farm and Indsl. Equipment Inst. (safety policy com. 1969—), Triangle Frat. Methodist (trustee 1972—). Club: Rotary (dir. 1970-72). Contbr. articles on product safety and liability. profl. publs. Home: 3714 44th St Rock Island IL 61201 Office: Deere & Co Moline IL 61265

PHAIR, GRETCHEN MUELLER, speech pathologist; b. Marinette, Wis., Jan. 19, 1913; d. George Anton and Margarethe Louisa (Uecke) Mueller; B.S., U. Wis., Madison, 1944, M.S., 1946; m. George Milton Phair, Sept. 7, 1946. Tchr., Marinette County, Wis., 1930-39; speech therapist Madison (Wis.) Pub. Schs., 1944-46; supr. speech therapy Bur. for Handicapped Children, Dept. Pub. Instrn., State of Wis., Madison, 1946-74; pvt. practice speech therapy; cons. Cleft Palate program U. Wis. Med. Sch.; instr. U. Utah summer sessions, 1954, 56. Chmn. bd. dirs. Friend of the Waisman Center, 1975-77; tutor, Lauback Literacy program. Fellow Am. Speech and Hearing Assn.; mem. Council for Exceptional Children, Wis. Speech and Hearing Assn. (honors 1955, 74), Am. Cleft Palate Assn., Friends of Channel 21, Zeta Phi Eta (Distinguished Service award, 1971), Sigma Alpha Eta. Clubs: West Side Garden, Friends of Arboretum, Friends of Waisman Center. Coordinator movies Wis. Cleft Palate Story (Golden Reel award), 1955; M.R. Mental Retardation, 1967; author chpt. in Voice and Speech Disorders, 1962; contbr. articles in field to profl. jours. Home: 306 Westmorland Blvd Madison WI 53705

PHALEN, THOMAS FRANCIS, JR., lawyer; b. Waterbury, Conn., June 27, 1938; s. Thomas Francis and Helen Theresa (Farrell) P.; B.S., Coll. of Holy Cross, 1960; LL.B., J.D. (Legal fellow), Catholic U. Am., 1967; m. Mary Anne Imwalle, Aug. 31, 1963; children—Thomas Francis III, Timothy Joseph, Helene Marie, Brian Christopher. Admitted to Ohio bar, 1967, U.S. Supreme Ct. bar, 1973, also Ohio Supreme Ct., U.S. Dist. Ct. So. Dist. Ohio, No. Dist. Ohio, 6th Circuit Ct. Appeal, U.S. Ct. Appeal bars; atty. NLRB, Cin., 1967-69, law clk. trial examiner div., 1966; partner Knee, Synder & Parks, Dayton, Ohio, 1969-73; partner Latimer & Swing Co., Cin., 1973—; tchr. union leadership tng. courses Wright State U., also Edgecliff Coll., 1970-71. Mem. Hamilton County Democratic Central Com., 1972—. Served to 1st lt. USAF, 1961-64. Mem. Am. (union counsel, developing labor law subcom. on strikes and picketing), Dayton, Cin. (chmn. labor law com. 1977—), Ohio (gov. labor law sect. 1977—) bar assns., Indsl. Relations Research Assn. K.C. Home: 6377 Grand Vista Ave Cincinnati OH 45213 Office: Latimer & Swing Co 2312 Kroger Bldg Cincinnati OH 45202

PHEGLEY, RICHARD DEAN, real estate and ins. co. exec.; b. Rensselaer, Ind., Oct. 29, 1937; s. Raleigh Heath and Martha Irene (Keister) P.; student Ind. U., 1964, Bill Miller's Coll. Sch. Real Estate, 1968; m. Bonnie Sue DeWees, Mar. 8, 1959; children—Terry Dean, Timothy Lee. With Smith Realty Co., Rensselaer, 1968-77; ins. agt. Blue Agy., Inc., Rensselaer, 1964-70; agt. Consol. Ins. Agy., Rensselaer, 1970—; owner Phegley Real Estate, Rensselaer. Sec.-treas. Levee Plaza Skate Bd. Park, W. Lafayette, Ind.; deacon, First Christian Ch., Rensselaer, 1976—; Past pres., past state dir. Jaycees. Mem. Nat., Ind. assns. realtors, Independent Ins. Agts. Ind. Clubs: Eagles (past pres.), Rensselaer Central Sch. Bomber Booster (pres.). Home: 455 Emmett Ave Rensselaer IN 47978 Office: 116 S Van Rensselaer St Rensselaer IN 47978

PHELAN, J. J., physicist; b. San Francisco; s. James and Mary (O'Donnell) P.; B.S. in Physics and Math., U. San Francisco, 1959; Ph.D. in Physics, St. Louis U., 1967; m. Nancy J. Hull, 1962; children—James K., Christopher J., Maureen L. Physicist, Rutherford High Energy Lab., Berkshire, Eng., 1968-72, Argonne (Ill.) Nat. Lab., 1972—. Democrat precinct committeeman. Mem. Am. Phys. Soc., Sigma Xi. Contbr. profl. jours. Address: Argonne Nat Lab Bldg 362 9600 S Cass Ave Argonne IL 60439

PHELAN, JOHN DENSMORE, ins. co. exec.; b. Kalamazoo, Aug. 31, 1914; s. John and Ida (Densmore) P.; B.A. magna cum laude, Carleton Coll., 1935; m. Isabel McLaughlin, July 31, 1937; children—John Walter, William Paul, Daniel Joseph. With Hardware Muts., Stevens Point, Wis., 1936-45; with Am. States Ins. Co., Indpls., 1945—, chmn., also of subsidiaries Am. States Life Ins. Co., Am. Economy Ins. Co., Am. States Ins. Co. Tex., Am. Union Ins. Co. of N.Y., Preferred Ins. Co.; dir. Lincoln Nat. Corp., Ft. Wayne, Ind., Indpls. Power & Light, Mchts. Nat. Bank and Trust Co., Mchts. Nat. Corp., Indpls. Past pres. Marion County Assn. for Mental Health; bd. dirs. United Way Greater Indpls. Mem. C.P.C.U. Soc. (nat. past pres.), C.L.U. Soc., Ind. C. of C. (dir.), Am. Inst. Property and Liability Underwriters (dir.), Phi Beta Kappa. Presbyterian. Clubs: Indpls. Athletic; Woodland Country; 100 of Indpls. Author: Business Interruption Primer, 1st edit., 1949; contbr. articles profl. trade publs. Home: 307 Woodland Ln Carmel IN 46032 Office: 500 N Meridian St Indianapolis IN 46206

PHELAN, WILLIAM HENRY, internist; b. Albany, N.Y., Sept. 15, 1926; s. Thomas William and Helen (Rausch) P.; B.S. magna cum laude, Coll. of Holy Cross, 1949; M.D., Albany Med. Coll., 1953; m. Evlyn Dereen May, Jan. 18, 1958; children—John M., William H., Jr., Thomas W., Julie Anne, Elizabeth M. Rotating intern Albany Hosp., 1953—54; resident in internal medicine Presbyterian Hosp., Chgo., 1954-56, chief resident, 1957, attending staff, 1957—, advisory com. dept. of medicine, 1975—; instr. in medicine U. Ill., 1956—64, clin. asst. prof., 1964—69, clin. assn. prof., 1969—71; assn. prof. medicine Rush Med. Coll., 1971—, mem. faculty council, 1973—76; practice medicine specializing in internal medicine, cardiology, Chgo., 1957—. Bd. dirs. Chgo. Heart Assn., 1969—75. Served with USN, 1945—46. Diplomate Am. Bd. Internal Medicine, Nat. Bd. Med. Examiners. Fellow A.C.P., Am. Coll. Chest Physicians; mem. Am. Heart Assn., N.Y. Acad. Sci., Am., Chgo. secs. internal medicine, AMA, Ill., Chgo. med. secs., Alpha Omega Alpha. Club: Northbrook Racquet. Contbr. articles in field. Home: 1620 Blackthorn Dr Glenview Il 60025 Office: 122 S Mich Ave Chicago IL 60603

PHELPS, BETTY JEANE POTTENGER (MRS. CHARLES PUTERBAUGH PHELPS), civic worker, writer; b. Warsaw, Ind., Oct. 20, 1921; d. Royal and Erba Ermal (Hinkson) Pottenger; A.B., Manchester Coll., 1943; registered Occupational Therapist, Washington U., St. Louis, 1952; m. Charles Puterbaugh Phelps, June 5, 1955; children—Carl James, Rebecca Susan. Tchr., Richland Center Sch., Rochester, Ind., 1943-44, Lakewiew Sch., Tulia, Tex., 1944-45; staff therapist, student supr. Indpls. Gen. Hosp., 1953; dir. occupational therapy James O. Parramore Hosp., Crown Point, Ind., 1954-55. Vol. worker Meals-onWheels, 1972-73; active fund-raising drives United Fund, March of Dimes, Cancer Fund; local contact person Hoosiers for Equal Rights Amendment. Mem. Am. Occupational Therapy Assn., Universal Esperanto Assn., Esperanto League N.Am., World Federalists, UN Assn., Ole Olsen Community Players, Common Cause. Democrat. Presbyn. Home: 18 E 2d St Peru IN 46970

PHELPS, EDWIN RICE, coal co. exec.; b. Leavenworth, Kans., Jan. 12, 1915; s. Edwin Rice and Thekla (Wulfekuhler) P.; B.S., Kans. U., 1937; postgrad. Mass. Inst. Tech., 1942; m. Yvonne White, June 18, 1938; children—Edwin Rice, Janet L. Phelps Karr), Jonathan F., William Bruce. Engr., Southwestern Ill. Coal Co., Percy, 1937-42; supt. constrn. Constant Constrn. Co., Lawrence, Kans., 1946-48; gen. supt. Pittsburg and Midway Coal Mining Co. (Kans.), 1948-51, v.p. ops., 1951-59, pres., 1959-60; chief engr. Peabody Coal Co., St. Louis, 1960-62, v.p. engring., 1962-68, sr. v.p. ops., 1968-71, pres., chief exec. officer, 1971—; dir. Bank of St. Louis; mem. Am. Team Coal Experts, Poland, 1957, India, 1960; mem. coal adv. com. Dept. Interior, 1976; mem. adv. com. World Energy Conf., 1976, 77; mem. adv. com. Sch. Engring. Kans. U., 1958-62. Served to lt. comdr. USNR, 1942-46. Registered profl. engr., Kans., Ky. Mem. Am. Inst. Mining, Metall. and Petroleum Engrs. (Eavenson award 1972), Nat. Indsl. Pollution Control Council, Nat. Coal Assn. (chmn. 1974-75, dir. 1972—, chmn. exec. com. 1972-73, chmn. ad hoc exec. com. surface mining 1973—), Am. Mining Congress (dir. 1971—), Bituminous Coal Operators Assn. (dir. 1971—, exec. com.), Nat. Soc. Profl. Engrs., Kans. U. Alumni Assn. (dir. 1957-60), U.S. C. of C. (natural resources com. 1959-60), Sigma Tau, Phi Delta Theta. Home: 12000 Heatherdane St Saint Louis MO 63131 Office: 301 N Memorial Dr Saint Louis MO 63102

PHELPS, NAN DEE HINKLE (MRS. ROBERT PHELPS), artist; b. London, Ky.; d. John W. and Lula May (Weaver) Hinkle; ed. Cin. Art Acad. m. Robert Phelps, Apr. 9, 1927; children—Alma (Mrs. Norman Lamb), Wilmarie (Mrs. Robert P. Gfroerer), Donna (Mrs. Hans Beer), Paul R., Robbie, John Robert. One man shows at Galerie Etienne, N.Y.C., Cin. Mus.; exhibited in group shows at Paula Insen, N.Y.C., Galerie St. Etienne, Copley Soc., Bos., Pallette Club, Lynn Katler Gallery, N.Y.C., Hamilton, Ohio, Trinidad, Lima, Peru, numerous others Ohio area; executed 17 murals in chs., homes, instn.; represented in permanent collections at Ford Motor Co., Pulaski (Va.), Lincoln Sch., Hamilton, Ohio, other schs., numerous pvt. collections; executed murals in churches and residences. Mem. Copley Soc. Club: The Brush Easel (Hamilton, O.). Address: 1721 Green Wood Ave Hamilton OH 45011

PHELPS, WILLIAM CUNNINGHAM, lt. gov. Mo.; b. Nevada, Mo., Apr. 5, 1934; s. Dean Henry and Julia Irene (Myers) P.; A.B., U. Mo., 1956, J.D., 1959; m. Joanne Ronchetto, July 22, 1972. Admitted to Mo. bar; partner firm Morrison, Hecker, Cozad, Morrison & Curtis, Kansas City, 1959-73; mem. Mo. Ho. of Reps., 1961-73; lt. gov. Mo., 1973—. State chmn. YMCA's youth in govt. program, 1966—; mem. Jackson County Charter Transition Commn. Pres. Mo. Assn. Republicans, 1963; vice chmn. Midwest region Nat. Lt. Govs. conf., chmn. aging com., mem. exec. com; chmn. Govs. conf. edn., 1976; hon. dir. Rockhurst Coll.; trustee Kansas City Philharmonic Orch.; bd. govs. Citizens Assn. Kansas City. Served as capt. U.S. Army, 1957. Mem. Mo. Bar Assn., Beta Theta Pi, Phi Delta Phi. Episcopalian. Rotarian. Home: 5016 Grand Kansas City MO 64112 Office: 327 State Capitol Jefferson City MO 65101

PHENICIE, MARLOND DEAN, mech. contractor; b. Champaign County, Ill., Mar. 11, 1930; s. Chester Leo and Gertrude Claudia (Steele) P.; ed. parochial schs., spl. courses; m. Blanche E. Seymour, July 6, 1953. Gen. foreman Colwell Pub. Co., 1952-55; sales mgr. Chief Heating & Air Conditioning Co., Urbana, Ill., 1956-60, pres., 1961—. Served with AUS, 1949-51; Korea. Recipient tech. achievement award Carrier Corp., 1976, Select dealer award Janitrol Corp., 1962-70. Mem. Asso. Builders and Contractors. Republican. Home: Rural Route Seymour IL 61875 Office: 703 S Glover St Urbana IL 61801

PHETTEPLACE, BETTY HELENA (MRS. JOSEPH ARTHUR PHETTEPLACE), curator; b. Sterling, Ill., Dec. 24, 1916; d. Thomas and Oral (Leland) Shelkey; grad. high sch.; m. Joseph Arthur Phetteplace, June 25, 1936; 1 adopted son, Larry Charles. Curator, Phetteplace Mus., Wauzeka, Wis., 1956—. Lapidary tchr. State Youth Camp, Lomira, Wis., 1949-54. Mem. Midwest Fedn. Mineralogical and Geol. Socs. Methodist. Home: Wauzeka WI 53826 Office: Phetteplace Museum 115 Inlay Ave Wauzeka WI 53826

PHIBBS, CLIFFORD MATTHEW, surgeon; b. Bemidji, Minn., Feb. 20, 1930; s. Clifford Matthew and Dorothy Jean (Wright) P.; B.S., Wash. State U., 1952; M.D., U. Wash., 1955; M.S., U. Minn., 1960; m. Patricia Jean Palmer, June 27, 1953; children—Wayne Robert, Marc Stuart, Nancy Louise. Intern, Ancker Hosp., St. Paul, 1955-56; resident in surgery U. Minn. Hosps., 1956-60; practice medicine specializing in surgery, Oxboro Clinic, Mpls., 1962—; mem. staff St. Barnabas Hosp.; mem. staff Fairview-Southdale Hosp., 1965—, chief of surgery, 1970-71, sec.-treas., 1971-72, chmn. intensive care unit, 1973-76; clin. asst. prof. U. Minn., Mpls., 1975—. Bd. dirs. Bloomington (Minn.) Bd. Edn., 1974—, treas., 1976—; mem. adv. com. for jr. coll. study City of Bloomington, 1964-66, mem. community facilities com., 1966-67, adv. youth study commn., 1966-68; vice chmn. bd. Hillcrest Meth. Ch., 1970-71; mem. Bloomington Adv. and Research Council, 1969-71; bd. dirs. Bloomington Symphony Orch., 1976—; dir. bd. mgmt. Minnesota Valley YMCA, 1970-75; bd. govs. Mpls. Met. YMCA, 1970—. Served to capt. M.C., U.S. Army, 1960-62. Diplomate Am. Bd. Surgery. Mem. AMA (Physician's Recognition awards 1969, 73-76, 76—), Minn. Med. Assn., Minn., Mpls. surg. socs., Hennepin County Med. Soc., Pan-Pacific Surg. Assn., A.C.S. Club: Jaycees. Contbr. articles to med jours. Home: 9613 Upton Rd S Minneapolis MN 55431 Office: 9820 Lyndale Ave S Minneapolis MN 55420

PHILGREEN, IRVING AXENE, clergyman, religious assn. exec.; b. Kansas City, Mo., Apr. 10, 1934; s. George I. and Evelyn V. (Josephson) P.; B.A., Bob Jones U., 1956; postgrad. North Park Theol. Sem., 1964-66; m. Yvonne Ann McInnis, July 13, 1956; children—Daniel I., Deborah Joy. Ordained to ministry Central Bible Ch., 1957; asso. dir. Youth for Christ, Kansas City, Mo., 1956-60, dir., Toledo, 1960-61, Muskegon, Mich., 1961-65; youth coordinator P.S. Profile, Hinsdale, Ill., 1966; exec. dir. Short Terms Abroad, missionary recruiting, Downers Grove, Ill., 1967—; dir. stewardship Scripture Press Ministries, Glen Ellyn, 1970-73; registered rep. Westamerica Financial Corp., Downers Grove, 1970-75; pastor First Bapt. Ch., Downers Grove, 1975—; dir. Scripture Press Employees Credit Union, 1971-73, chmn., 1973—. Pres., treas. Southeast Asia Found. Edn., 1970-77; service rep. Nat. Heritage Found., 1973—; mem. steering com. DuPage County Bd. Chmn.'s Prayer Breakfast, 1973-77; bd. dirs. Pace Inst., Chgo., 1967-72, sec., 1968-70, pres., 1971-72. Mem. Muskegon (Mich.) Pastors Conf. (sec. 1962-63), Aircraft Owners and Pilots Assn. Baptist (deacon 1969-73, chmn. bd. deacons 1973-74, ch. moderator 1975). Club: Hinsdale (Ill.) Flying. Editor: Opportunities 1973, 1970-73. Home and office: 1604 Jefferson St Downers Grove IL 60515 also Short Terms Abroad PO Box 575 Downers Grove IL 60515

PHILION, JAMES ROBERT, car rental co. exec.; b. Glens Falls, N.Y., Jan. 3, 1944; s. Robert Francis and Margery Madeline (Streeter) P.; student Tex. A. and M. U., 1961-63, Arlington State U., 1963-64; m. Sharon Sue McGinness, Dec. 4, 1965; children—Robert Barton, Tami René. Ticket agt./sales rep. Central Airlines, Dallas, 1963-66; account exec. Hertz Corp., Houston, 1966-67; dist. sales mgr. Nat. Car Rental Systems, Inc., 1967-68, Los Angeles, 1968-69, regional sales mgr. western region, Los Angeles, 1969-70, nat. accounts mgr., Mpls., 1970-71, dir. sales, 1971, v.p. sales, 1971—. Mem. Nat. Passenger Traffic Assn. (Account Exec. of Year 1970), Traffic Clubs Internat., Am. Soc. Travel Agts., Sales and Mktg. Execs. Home: 7361 Longview Circle Chanhassen MN 53317 Office: 5501 Green Valley Dr Minneapolis MN 55437

PHILIPPS, LOUIS EDWARD, hosp. data system mfg. co. exec.; b. Duluth, Minn., Feb. 7, 1906; s. Carl Frederick Ferdinand and Sarah Marguerithe (Mortenson) P.; student Duluth pub. schs.; m. Gladys Victoria Monsen, Nov. 13, 1930. Engr., Cleve. Radioelec. Co., 1946-48; v.p., gen. mgr. Radio Systems, Inc., Cleve., 1948-50; v.p., gen. mgr. Royal Communications, Inc., Cleve., 1950-56; dir. engring. Auth Elec. Co., N.Y.C., 1956-59; chief engr. Hosp. Products div. Motorola-Dahlberg Co., Mpls., 1959-63; founder, pres., chmn. bd. Medelco, Inc., Schiller Park, Ill., 1964-74; founder, chmn. bd. DATX Corp., Chgo., 1975—. Named Father of the Hosp. Systems Industry, Am. Hosp. Assn., 1974. Mem. IEEE (sr.). Republican. Presbyterian. Clubs: Anvil (East Dundee, Ill.), Eastern Star, Masons, Shriners. Patentee in field. Office: 303 E Ohio St Chicago IL 60611

PHILIPSON, WILLARD DALE, educator, univ. adminstr.; b. Sleepy Eye, Minn., Mar. 18, 1930; s. Walter and Alice Anna (Rasmussen) P.; B.S., U. of Minn. 1953, M.A. 1959, Ph.D. 1967; m. Sylvia Eileen Olson, Sept. 26, 1953; children—Andrew Will, Jennifer Dale, Pamela Elizabeth. Instr. agri. engring. U. of Minn. at Morris, 1959; audio visual materials advisor Audio Visual Edn. Service, Mpls., 1960-63; asst. prof., head ednl. film library N. Ill. U., DeKalb, 1963-66; asso. prof., dir. audio visual library services U. of Minn., Mpls. 1966—. Active mem. Commn. on Minn. Civil Service Exec. Mgmt. Tng., St. Paul, 1969-71, Troop 401, Boy Scouts of Am., St. Paul, 1972-75; chmn. fund dr. 1974-75; mem. Citizens for Libraries, Legis. Com., St. Paul, 1976—. Served with USN 1953-58. Decorated Nat. Service medal, Naval Reserve medal, Armed Force Campaign ribbon; recipient Adult Educator of Yr. award Sears, Roebuck & Co., St. Paul, 1972; service award Gov. LeVander, Minn. 1969. Mem. Naval Reserve Assn., Assn. Ednl. Communicatons and Tech., Adult Edn. Assn., Minn. Ednl. Media Orgn., Alpha Tau Alpha. Editor Audio-Visual Jour., 1966—. Home: 3020 N Chatsworth St St Paul MN 55113 Office: 3300 University Ave SE Minneapolis MN 55414

PHILLIAN, HARRY EDGAR, architect, educator; b. Delaware, Ohio, Feb. 17, 1914; s. Walter H. and Mary (Bird) P.; B.A., Ohio Wesleyan U., 1936; B.Arch., Ohio State U., 1939; m. Nadine Beatty, Aug. 20, 1940; 1 dau., Jody Ann. Faculty, Ohio State U., Columbus, 1948—, prof. architecture, 1957-77, emeritus, 1977—; pvt. practice architecture, Ohio, Fla., Ariz. and other states, 1940—; cons. numerous archtl. firms and corps. Bd. dirs. Crippled Children Soc. Served with USAAF, 1942-46. Mem. AIA (trustee 1952), Architecture Alumni Assn. Ohio State U. (pres.), Sigma Chi. Presbyn. (trustee). Mason (32 deg., Shriner). Club: Ohio Country (Columbus). Prin. archtl. works include Fine Arts and Union bldgs. Bowling Green U., Clintonville (Ohio) Fed. Bank, Fibre Glass Tower Toledo, Cincinnati Center. Address: 259 Village Dr Columbus OH 43214 also 9 N Birch Rd Fort Lauderdale FL 43214

PHILLIP, LEE (MRS. WILLIAM J. BELL), TV performer; b. Chgo.; d. James A. and Helen Phillip; B.S., Northwestern U., 1950; m. William J. Bell, Oct. 23, 1954; children—William J., Bradley P., Lauralee Kristen. Under contract CBS-TV, Chgo., 1954—, appearing currently on WBBM-TV shows, Lee Phillip Show. Mem. Mayor's Spl. Com. for a More Beautiful City, 1957—, Chgo. Maternity Center, United Cerebral Palsy; mem. Def. Adv. Com. for Women in Service, 1970—, chmn. pub. relations com., 1972. Trustee Chgo. Northwestern U. Hosp. Named outstanding woman of radio and TV, McCalls mag., 1957, 58, 64; voted top favorite feminine personality TV Guide Poll, 1956; award Top Woman's TV Show, Chgo. Federated Advt. Club, 1956; Chgo. Emmys for best performer female, best sales person 1960, 61, 62, 63, 64, 65, 66; Media Person of Year, 1960; 1 of Chgo.'s 10 best dressed women, 1960; One of World's 10 Best Coiffured Women, Helene Curtis Guild, 1967; Golden Mike award Am. Women In Radio and TV, 1968; I Will award City Chgo., 1971; TV Broadcaster of Year, 1972; DuPont-Columbia award for Rape of Paulette, 1973; Ill. Med. Soc. award, 1973; Cambridge U. award, 1973. Mem. Fashions Group, Am. Women in Radio and TV, Chgo. Unlimited, Nat. Acad. TV Arts and Scis. (Outstanding achievement award 1971-72), Delta Delta Delta. Home: 209 E Lake Shore Dr Chicago IL 60602 Office: 630 N McClurg Ct Chicago IL 60611

PHILLIPS, BERTRAND DOUGLASS, painter, photographer; b. Chgo., Nov. 19, 1938; s. Alfred and Doesrous L. (Thurman) P.; B.F.A., Art Inst. Chgo., 1961; M.F.A., Northwestern U., 1972. Instr., Elmhurst (Ill.) Coll., 1970-72; asst. prof. Northwestern U., 1971—; one-man shows: Valparaiso (Ind.) U.; Infinity Gallery, Gov.'s State U., Park Forest S., Ill., The Darkroom, Chgo.; group shows include: Bergman Gallery, U. Chgo., 1972; Herbert F. Johnson Mus. Art, Ithaca, N.Y., 1974; Mus. Science Industry, Chgo., 1976; Artists Guild Chgo., 1976, Dulin Gallery, Knoxville, Tenn., 2d St. Gallery, Charlottesville, Va., Eastern Mich. U.; represented in permanent collections: DuSable Mus. African Am. History, Chgo., Gov.'s State U., Park Forest S., Ill. Home: 6617 S Perry St Chicago IL 60621 Office: 216 Kresge Hal Northwestern U Evanston IL 60201

PHILLIPS, CAROLE ANN, educator; b. Princeton, Ill., Nov. 1, 1936; d. Ward Elwood and Anna Victoria (West) Birkey; B.S., Ill. State U., 1961; M.Ed., Macalester Coll., 1970; M.S. of Ed., No. Ill. U., 1975; m. Bobby Elwood Phillips, Aug. 15, 1963; children—Keith Robert. Tchr., Walnut (Ill.) Pub. Schs., 1956-57, Wyanet (Ill.) Pub. Schs., 1958-60, Princeton (Ill.) Elementary Schs., 1960-63, Batavia (Ill.) Pub. Schs., 1963-71; with Hinsdale (Ill.) Health Mus. (now Robert Crown Center for Health Edn.), 1972-74; guidance counselor Aurora (Ill.) Central Cath. High Sch., 1974—; cons. to Region V HEW, Chgo., 1972-74; lectr. in field. NSF grantee, 1969-70. Mem. NEA, Am. Guidance and Personnel Assn., Nat. Vocational Guidance Assn. Mem. United Ch. of Christ. Contbr. articles in field to profl. jours. Home: 1212 N Brandywine Circle Batavia IL 60510 Office: Aurora Central Catholic High Sch 157 N Root St Aurora IL 60505

PHILLIPS, CHANDLER ALLEN, physician, educator; b. Los Angeles, Dec. 21, 1942; s. Chandler Arza and Ann (Lloyd) P.; A.B., Stanford U., 1965; M.D., U. So. Calif., Los Angeles, 1969. Intern, Hosp. Good Samaritan, Los Angeles, 1969-70; research physician U. Dayton (Ohio) Research Inst., 1972-74; asst. prof. physiology and engring., program mgr. bio med. engring. Wright State U., Dayton, 1975—; cons. physician Dayton VA Hosp.; research asso. Miami-Valley Heart chpt. Am. Heart Assn., 1973-76. Served to capt. USAF, 1970-72; Vietnam. Diplomate Nat. Bd. Med. Examiners; registered profl. engr. Mem. Am. Soc. Engring. Edn., IEEE (chmn. engring. in medicine and biology Dayton sect. 1976-77), AAAS, Biomed. Engring. Soc., Instrument Soc. Am., Ohio Acad. Sci. Office: Wright State U Dept Engring Dayton OH 45431

PHILLIPS, ENOS LESLIE, lawyer; b. Urbana, Ill., Feb. 18, 1896; s. John Andrew and Sally (Lee) P.; ed. pub. schs., and law office of Henry I. Green; m. Sarah May Connour, May 26, 1917; 1 dau., Elizabeth Jane Phillips Knox. Admitted to Ill. bar, 1921, practiced with Henry I. Green, Urbana; mem. firm Phillips, Phebus, Tummelson & Bryan; chmn. bd. dirs. emeritus Busey First Nat. Bank; dir. emeritus Comml. Savs. & Loan Assn.; chmn. Community Plan Commn.; past pres. Urbana Library Bd. Mem. Am., Ill., Champaign County bar assns., Am. Judicature Soc., Urbana Assn. Commerce, Ill. C. of C. Republican. Methodist. Clubs: Masons, Elks, Rotary, Univ.; Union League (Chgo.). Home: 801 W Vermont St Urbana IL 61801 Office: 136 W Main St Urbana IL 61801

PHILLIPS, JOHN MILTON, lawyer; b. Kansas City, Mo., Dec. 16, 1915; s. John and Atha (Dennis) P.; A.B., U. Kans., 1937; J.D., Harvard, 1940; m. Mary Hamilton Bracken, Aug. 29, 1942; children—Mary Bracken, Patricia Ann, Jean Hamilton, John Milton, Daniel Dennis. Admitted to Mo. bar, 1940; asso. firm Stinson, Mag, Thomson, McEvers & Fizzell, 1940-46, partner, 1946—; dir. Southtown Motors Co., Byron Shutz Co. Trustee Philharmonic Assn. of Kansas City, pres., 1965-67; former v.p. dir. Am. Symphony Orch. League 1965-67; bd. dirs. Kansas City chpt. ARC; mem. Soc. Fellows William Rockhill Nelson Art Gallery. Served from pvt. to capt. AUS, 1942-46. Mem. Citizens Assn. Kansas City (past pres.), Kansas City Council on Edn. (past pres.), Am. Judicature Soc., Internat., Am., Mo., Kansas City bar assns., Acad. Social and Polit. Sci., SR, Mil. Order of World Wars, Phi Gamma Delta, Delta Sigma Rho. Republican. Episcopalian. Clubs: Kansas City, Harvard. Home: 311 W 99th St Kansas City MO 64114 Office: 2100 Ten Main Center Kansas City MO 64105

PHILLIPS, JOSEPH JAMES, diversified industry co. patent agent; b. Youngstown, Ohio, Apr. 13, 1917; s. James and Erminia (Bellino) P.; B.A., Ohio State U., 1953; postgrad. Ind. U. Law Sch., 1964-65; m. Josephine E. Molli, Mar. 11, 1939; children—Joseph, Louis, Michael, Christina Ann. Metall. research Battelle Meml. Inst., Columbus, Ohio, 1942-53; tech. editor, patent engr. Union Carbide Corp., Kokomo, Ind., 1953-70; registered patent agt. legal div. Cabot Corp., Kokomo, 1970—; lectr. Purdue U., 1965-77. Mem. Creative Arts Council, Kokomo, 1966-76; active Sagamore council Boy Scouts Am., chmn. explorer com., 1973. Recipient award U.S. Office Sci. Research and Devel., 1947. Mem. Nat. Soc. Profl. Engrs., Am. Soc. Metals, Engring. Soc. Kokomo, Soc. Tech. Writers and Editors, Spl. Libraries Assn., Ohio State U. Assn. (life). Home: 513 Holly Ln Kokomo IN 46901 Office: 1020 W Park Ave Kokomo IN 46901

PHILLIPS, JOSHUA, mgmt. cons.; b. N.Y.C., Dec. 15, 1936; s. Eli and Hilda (Peters) P.; B.A. in Chemistry, Williams Coll., 1957; M.B.A., Wharton Grad. Sch. of Fin. and Commerce, 1959; m. Rheva Betensky, Dec. 24, 1961; 1 son, Jason. Comml. devel. rep. The Nat. Cash Register Co., Dayton, Ohio, 1959-60; corp. bus. devel. specialist Nalco Chem. Co., Chgo., 1960-67; mgmt. cons. A.T. Kearney & Co., Inc., Chgo., 1967-71; exec. v.p., dir. Environ. Recreation Systems, N.Y.C. and San Juan, P.R., 1971-72; asst. to the pres. Pioneer & Conco Mortgate Co., Chgo., 1973-74; pres. J. Phillips & Assos., Highland Park, Ill., 1974—; lectr. Am. Mgmt. Assn., Chgo., 1968-71. Active Cub Scouts Am., 1973-75. Served with U.S. Army, 1959-61, 61-62. Mem. Am. Chem. Soc., Comml. Devel. Assn., Chem. Mktg. Research Assn., Midwest Chem. Mktg. Assn., Williams, Wharton Grad. Sch. alumni assns., Phi Sigma Kappa. Clubs: Deer Creek Racquet (Highland Park). Address: 1725 Northland Ave Highland Park IL 60035

PHILLIPS, LLOYD JAMES, dentist; b. Lykens, Pa., Feb. 27, 1922; s. James J. and Mary Margaret (Uhler) P.; B.S. with high honors, Ind. U., 1951, D.D.S. with high honors, 1954; m. Barbara Jean Brown, Apr. 7, 1944; children—Pamela Thiesing, Timothy, Cathy Sue. Practice gen. dentistry, Waterloo, Iowa, 1954-55, Indpls., 1955—; asst. prof. periodontics Ind. U., 1968—. Dir. Ind. Blue Cross-Blue Shield, 1971—. Mem. Ind. Health Council, 1954—, pres., 1971; dir. Ind. div. Am. Cancer Soc., 1968—, pres. Marion County unit, 1967—. Served with USNR, 1942-46. Mem. Am. (trustee), Ind. (sec. 1964-70) dental assns., Indpls. Dist. Dental Soc., Am. Acad. Periodontology, Am. Prosthodontic Soc., Internat. (regent), Am. colls. dentists, Internat. Assn. Dental Research, Pierre Fauchard Acad., Indpls. C. of C., Psi Omega, Omicron Kappa Upsilon. Mason, Rotarian. Club: Indianapolis Athletic (Indpls.). Contbr. articles to profl. jours. Home: 9540 Kenwood Ave Indianapolis IN 46260 Office: 842 Consolidated Bldg 115 N Pennsylvania St Indianapolis IN 46204

PHILLIPS, MARGARET JOSEPHINE, educator; b. Sandusky, Ohio, Mar. 19, 1943; d. Armenio and Lidia (Arduini) Phillips; B.S., Bowling Green State U., 1965; M.A., George Washington U., 1969; postgrad. Firelands Coll., part-time. Tchr. 6th grade Randolph Village Elementary Sch., Landover, Md., 1965-68, tchr. learning disabilities, 1968-69; tchr. 6th grade Bataan Elementary Sch., Port Clinton, Ohio, 1969-70; tchr. learning disabilities Portage Elementary Sch., Gypsum, Ohio, 1970-77; tchr. english Port Clinton (O.) High Sch., 1977—. Mem. governing bd. Tri-County Vol. Counselors, Inc., trustee Vol. Probation Officers, Inc. Mem. Port Clinton (exec. bd. 1970—), N.W. Ohio, Ohio edn. assns., George Washington U. Gen. Alumni Assn., Council for Exceptional Children, Ohio Assn. for Children with Learning Disabilities, Bowling Green State U. Found., Delta Kappa Gamma. Democrat. Roman Catholic. Home: 311 11th St Port Clinton OH 43452 Office: Port Clinton High Sch 821 Jefferson St Port Clinton OH 43452

PHILLIPS, MARGARET NADENE, univ. residence hall dir.; b. Bowen, Ill., June 28, 1934; d. Glenn Ramey and Frances Carlene (McGinnis) Phillips; B.S. in Edn., Western Ill. U., Macomb, 1955; M.Ed., U. Ill., Urbana, 1964. Vocat. home econs. tchr. Annawan (Ill.) High Sch., 1955-57, Carthage (Ill.) High Sch., 1957-63, Grant Community High Sch., Fox Lake, Ill., 1963-66; residence hall dir. Neptune Halls, No. Ill. U., DeKalb, 1966—. Mem. Am. Personnel Assn., Am. Coll. Personnel Assn., Alpha Delta Kappa, Delta Zeta. Methodist. Clubs: DeKalb-Syramore Altrusa (corr. sec. 1976-77), Eastern Star. Home and Office: West Neptune Hall Northern Illinois University DeKalb IL 60115

PHILLIPS, MICHAEL JOSEPH, poet, educator; b. Indpls., Mar. 2, 1937; s. Hayes A. Hollibaugh and Bernice Rebecca (Farmer) P.; B.A. cum laude, Wabash Coll., 1959; M.A., Ind. U., 1964, Ph.D. (grantee), 1971; C.A., Oxford U., 1971. Coll. traveler Bobbs-Merrill, 1964-65; lectr. U. Wis. Milw., 1970-71; tchr. pub. schs., Indpls., 1972-73; lectr. Ind.-Purdue U., Indpls., 1973-76; vis. fellow Harvard U., 1976—; poetry reader Nat. Endowment for the Arts, 1969-71; poet-in-the schs-State of Ind., 1974-75. Mem. Modern Lang. Assn., Midwest Modern Lang. Assn., Ind. Coll. English Assn., Am. Comparative Lit. Assn., Nat. Council Tchrs. English. Author: Indiana Sesquicentennial Poets, 1967; Poëzie in Fusié, 1968; Imaged Words and Worded Images, 1970; Visual Poetry Anthology, 1975. Contbr. poetry to 495 mags., jours., and books. Home: 109 N Clark St Apt 2 Bloomington IN 47401

PHILLIPS, MICHAEL KEITH, lawyer, state legislator; b. Huntingburg, Ind., Sept. 2, 1943; s. Lowell T. and Ida Ruth (Kelley) P.; B.A., DePauw U., 1965; J.D., Ind. U., 1969; m. Julie Mahon, June 8, 1963; children—Mark, Jennifer, Stephanie, Jeffrey, Emily. Admitted to Ind. bar; with firm Rideout & Phillips, Boonville, Ind., 1969-73, Michael K. Phillips Law Office, Boonville, 1973—. Adminstr. asst. to state chmn. Ind. Democratic Central Com., 1965-69; asst. voter registration chmn. Dem. Nat. Com., 1968; mem. Ind. Ho. of Reps., 1970-72, 74—, majority leader, 1974-77, minority leader, 1977—. Mem. Am., Ind., Warrick County bar assns., Am. Trial Lawyers Assn., Boonville Jr. C. of C., Boonville C. of C., Beta Theta Pi. Mason, Kiwanian, Lion, Elk. Home: 1441 S 1st St Boonville IN 47601 Office: 117 W Main St Boonville IN 47601

PHILLIPS, PAUL RICHARD, sch. exec.; b. Harvey, Ill., July 31, 1924; s. William Robert and Rose Belle (Kuykendall) P.; student U. Rochester, 1942-43, U. Chgo., 1945-46; m. Mary Louise Bakke, May 18, 1946; children—Barbara, Frederick, Joan, Richard. Media dir. Erwin Wasey Advt. Agy., Chgo., 1947-49; v.p. fin., part owner, dir. Knox Reeves Advt. Agy., Mpls., 1949-66; mktg. mgr., sr. v.p., dir. Art Instrn. Schs., Mpls., 1966—. Founder, dir., treas. Mount Olivet Rolling Acres, 1965—. Served with USAAF, 1943-45. Clubs: Advertising, Wayzata Country (Mpls.). Home: 2160 County Rd 6 Long Lake MN 55356 Office: 500 S 4th St Minneapolis MN 55415

PHILLIPS, RICHARD BRACEWELL, physician; b. Des Moines, Aug. 5, 1928; s. Russell S. and Elsie (Wright) P.; B.A., Cornell Coll., 1948; M.D., U. Iowa, 1952; m. Lois Harsch, June 6, 1953; children—William R., Joanne I., Jill W. Intern, Lankenau Hosp., Phila., 1953; resident Albuquerque VA Hosp., 1955-59; practice medicine, specializing in surgery, Barnesville, Ohio, 1959—; mem. staff Barnesville Gen. Hosp., trustee; cons. in surgery U.S. Dept. State, Nat. Health Service Corps. Pres., Appalachian Realty Corp., Barnesville, Ohio, 1967—, Barnesville Med. Center, Inc. Trustee Martins Ferry Housing Authority. Served to capt. USAF, 1953-55. Mem. Belmont County Med. Soc. (pres. 1969-70). Republican. Clubs: Masons (32 (deg.), Shriners. Contbr. articles on research in intestinal obstruction, abdominal surgery to profl. jours. Home: Route 3 Barnesville OH 43713 Office: PO Box 369 Barnesville OH 43713

PHILLIPS, RICHARD MILES, machine tools co. exec.; b. Akron, Ohio, May 11, 1935; s. Wilmer Miles and Thelma Evelyn (Cooper) P.; student U. Akron, 1957-58, Pierce Coll., 1964-65; m. Merida M. Vough, July 4, 1953; children—Steven Miles, Michael Richard. Pres., chmn. bd. Ward-Riddle Co., Ravenna, Ohio, 1971—, Three/Phase Electronics Corp., Kent, Ohio, 1975—, Phillips Indsl. Properties Inc., Kent, 1974—, Software & Computer Service Inc., Ravenna, 1975—, MSM Leasing & Sales, Stow, Ohio, 1975—. Chmn., Republican Party City of Stow, Ohio, 1972-73. Served with AUS, 1952-56. Mem. Stow Jaycees (pres. 1957-58), Am. Soc. Metals, Am. Soc. Tool Mfg. Engrs. Home: 3247 Patty Ann St Stow OH 44224 Office: PO Box 191 6168 Woodbine Ave Ravenna OH 44266

PHILLIPS, SARAH VIRGINIA CYRUS (MRS. DONALD RAY PHILLIPS), real estate exec.; b. Louisa, Ky.; d. W. Raymond and Isabelle Evelyn (Johnson) Cyrus; student pub. schs.; m. Donald Ray Phillips, Mar. 20, 1954; children—Donald Bruce, David Brian. Dep. circuit court clk. Lawrence County, Louisa, 1952-53; sec. Nationwide Ins. Co., Columbus, Ohio, 1953-56; jr. accountant Nationwide Mortgage Co., Columbus, 1957-63; gen. clk. Ohio State Life Ins. Co., Columbus, 1963-64; clk. council city clk., Whitehall, Ohio, 1964-71; adminstrv. asst. City of Columbus, 1972-76; realtor asso. Sparks Real Estate of Century 21, 1976—. Publicity chmn. Whitehall Boys Baseball Assn., summers 1965-68; sec., publicity chmn. Whitehall Boys' Basketball; mem. Ohio Commn. on Status Women; pres. Downtown Women's Republican Club, 1974-75; Whitehall Rep. Com., 1977; mem. Rep. Central Com., 1974-77; mem. Whitehall City Council, 1977—; trustee, sec.-treas. Whitehall Devel. Corp.; bd. dirs. Columbus Area Women's Polit. Caucus, 1977—. Mem. Central Ohio Mayors and Municipal Officers Council (exec. sec.-treas.), Ohio Municipal Clks. Assn. (trustee, v.p. 1971), Whitehall Civic Celebrations Assn. (sec., trustee 1968-71), League Women Voters, Ohio Hist. Soc., Internat. Toastmistress Club (Woman of Influence 1976, 77). Mem. Ch. of Christ (bd. dirs., treas., mem. youth com.). Home: 1010 S Yearling Rd Whitehall OH 43227 Office: 826 S Yearling Rd Whitehall OH 43213

PHILLIPS, WALLY, radio announcer; ed. Schuster-Martin Sch. Drama; children—Holly, Todd, Jennifer. TV, radio personality stas., WJEF, Grand Rapids, Mich., 1947, WSAI, Cin., 1948-50, WCPO,

Cin., 1950-52, WLW, Cin. 1952-56, WGN, Chgo., 1956—. Served with USAAF, World War II. Office: 2501 Bradley Pl Chicago IL 60618

PHILLIPS, WENDELL LEROY, retail exec.; b. Conrad, Iowa, May 23, 1919; s. Ralph Sylvester and Ada Faye (Brown) P.; grad. Central Iowa Bus. Coll., 1938; m. Eva B. Klinefelter, June 5, 1940; children—Wendy Phillips Taylor, Jr., Bonnie Phillips Zimmer. With Wellman Savs. Bank (Iowa), 1938-49, cashier, 1946-49; owner Gen. Ins. Agy., Skelgas L.P. Gas, Wellman, 1949—, Ross Severt Accounting & Tax Service, 1956—, Trio Gas Inc., 1960—; dir. Trio Gas. Mem. Washington Magistrate Bd., 1972—, Wellman City Council, 1952-60, Washington County Health Bd., 1969—. Mem. Nat. Soc. Pub. Accountants. Republican. Methodist. Clubs: Masons, Shriners, Rotary; Wellman Community. Home: 107 11th St NE Wellman IA 52356 Office: 248 8th Ave Wellman IA 52356

PHIPPS, JAY LAWRENCE, media center coordinator; b. Vancouver, B.C., Can., July 13, 1947; s. Donald and Lois Gertrude (Gillis) P.; B.A., U. B.C., 1971; diploma B.C. Inst. Tech., 1972; m. Blanche Yvette Marie Gagne, Dec. 26, 1972; children—Darcy Richard, Nicole Jacquelyn. Program coordinator B.C. Dept. Edn., Vancouver, 1972-73; master tchr., ITV producer Humber Coll. Applied Arts, Toronto, 1973-75; coordinator Media Centre, Ryerson Poly. Inst., Toronto, 1975—; instr. Sony of Can., Ltd.; pres., chief exec. officer TJ Communications Group, Ltd. Served to acting sub-lt., Royal Canadian Navy, 1967. Mem. Assn. Media and Tech. in Edn. in Can. (award of merit), Assn. Ednl. Communications and Tech., Soc. Motion Picture and TV Engrs., Internat. Indsl. TV Assn. Home: 48 Merrylynn Dr Richmond Hill ON L4C 5A9 Canada Office: Media Centre Ryerson Polytechnical Institute 350 Victoria St Toronto ON M5B 1E8 Canada

PIASCIK, PETER KENNETH, mgmt. cons.; b. Providence, R.I., Aug. 24, 1946; s. Stephen and Helen Josephine (Borowicz) P.; B.S., U. R.I., 1969, M.B.A., 1972; M.S., Ariz. State U., 1970; m. Rosanne Gorey (div.); 1 dau., Jennifer Marie. Systems analyst Burroughs Corp., Detroit, 1972-75; asso. mgmt. cons. Touche Ross & Co., Detroit, 1975-76, sr. mgmt. cons., 1976—. Served with AUS, 1972. Mem. Am. Inst. Indsl. Engrs., Am. Mgmt. Assn. Home: 35948 N Valley Ct #39103 Farmington Hills MI 48018 Office: 1300 First Nat Bldg Detroit MI 48226

PIATT, WILLIAM MAC-A-CHEEK, curator; b. West Liberty, Ohio, Sept. 12, 1914; s. John MacA Cheek and Kathryn (Sullivan) P.; student U. Dayton, 1947-48; m. Frances Monahan, Apr. 6, 1942; children—William Mac-a-Cheek II, Margaret (Mrs. P.J. Eckert). With State Capitol Ins. N.C., 1946-47, Gen. Foods Corp., Dayton, Ohio, 1947-48; curator, co-owner Piatt Castle, West Liberty, 1948—. Co-chmn. Ohio Sesquicentennial for West Liberty, 1953, Sesquicentennian, 1967. Served with M.C., AUS, 1938-46. Decorated Bronze Star, Purple Heart. Mem. DAV, Am. Legion (post service officer), VFW, Ohio Travel Council (charter mem., dir.), Tecumseh Tourist Council (founding pres. 1971), Logan County Tourist Assn. (founder 1971), West Liberty Bus. Assn., Bellefonatine C. of C. (dir. tourist div. 1965-71), Discover Am. Travel Orgn., 40 and 8. Roman Catholic. Clubs: K.C. (4 deg.), Lions. Address: RD 2 West Liberty OH 43357

PIAZZA, COSMO CHARLES, realtor; b. Chgo., Sept. 12, 1921; s. Carlo and Virginia (Guardinia) P.; student Roosevelt U., 1958-62; 1 son, Carl Frank. With A.F. Keeney Co., Chgo., 1958-63; staff appraiser Oak Park (Ill.) Fed. Savs. & Loan Assn., 1964-73; owner, mgr. Cosmo C. Piazza Realty, Palatine, Ill., 1973—. Sr. mem. Soc. Real Estate Appraisers. Office: 246 N Schubert St Palatine IL 60067

PIAZZA, JAMES FREDERICK, bus. exec.; b. Detroit, Aug. 6, 1951; s. Julius and Jane A. (Gade) P.; A.B., Saginaw Valley State Coll., 1976. Owner, exec. v.p. Luigi's Inc., Saginaw, Mich.; bd. dirs. Luigi's Inc. Del. to Rep. state conv., 1976; mem. Greater C. of C., Saginaw. Roman Catholic. Contbr. poetry to coll. mag. Home: 5386 Lessandro St Saginaw MI 48603 Office: 1518 S Michigan St Saginaw MI 48602

PICKENS, ROBERT BRUCE, bus. exec.; b. Uniontown, Pa., May 20, 1926; s. Joseph Abraham and Margaret Gertrude (Brown) P.; B.S. in Bus. Adminstrn., Waynesburg Coll., 1950; m. Mary Ellen Evans, Sept. 9, 1950; children—Laura Gail Pickens Martin, Rachel Diane, David Bruce. Vice pres., dir. Home Bottle Gas Corp., Uniontown, Pa., 1950-51; jr. accountant Tenney & Co., Uniontown, 1951-52, sr. accountant, 1952-56; mgr. of reports budgets and procedures Hosp. Service Assn. Western Pa., Pitts., 1956-57; auditor and analysis officer U. Pitts., 1957-58; sr. accountant Eugene A. Conniff Co., Pitts., 1958-59; mgr. Sheppard & Co., Pitts., 1959-63; supr. Alexander Grant & Co., Chgo., 1963-65; asst. to the treas. CTS Corp., Elkhart, Ind., 1965, gen. auditor, 1965-66, controller, 1966—. Served with AC U.S. Army, 1944-45. C.P.A., Pa., Ill., Ind. Mem. Accounting Research Assn., Am., Pa. insts. C.P.A.'s, Ill. Soc. C.P.A.'s Ind. Assn. C.P.A.'s. Republican. Presbyterian. Home: 3322 Calumet Ave Elkhart IN 46514 Office: 905 N West Blvd Elkhart IN 46514

PICKETT, DAVID FRANKLIN, JR., chemist; b. Littlefield, Tex., May 3, 1936; s. David Franklin and Dottie Ardell (Britton) P.; B.S. in Chemistry, U. Tex., 1962, M.A., 1965, Ph.D., 1970; m. B. Christine Klop, Aug. 21, 1971. Research chemist Am. Magnesium Co., Snyder, Tex., 1969-70; chemist/chem. engr. USAF Aero Propulsion Lab., Wright-Patterson AFB, Ohio, 1970—. Served with USN, 1955-57. Mem. Am. Chem. Soc., Electrochem. Soc., AAAS. Contbr. articles to profl. jours. Patentee in field. Home: 3116 Don Quixote Dr Dayton OH 45431 Office: AFAPL POE 1 Wright Patterson AFB OH 45433

PICKFORD, THOMAS MICHAEL, steel co. exec.; b. Hammond, Ind., Nov. 20, 1929; s. Jerome M. and Marguerite (Brennan) P.; B.S. in Civil Engring., Purdue U., 1952; m. Patricia V. White, Oct. 3, 1953; children—Mollie W., Peggy A., Thomas M., Timothy W. Civil engr. McWilliams Dredging Corp., New Orleans, 1955; sales engr. Armco Steel Corp., St. Louis, 1956-62, regional engr., Topeka, 1962, dist. engr., 1963-65, dist. mgr., 1965—. Mem. Nat. Res. Policy Bd. USMC, 1965—. Served to col. USMCR, 1952-55; Korea. Registered profl. engr., Kans. Mem. Nat. Soc. Profl. Engrs., ASCE, Nat. Soc. Mil. Engrs., Am. Water Works Assn., Kans. Engring. Soc. (chmn. profl. engrs. in industry), Kans., Topeka chambers commerce. Club: Shawnee Country (pres.). Home: 6761 Sherwood Ct Topeka KS 66614 Office: Commerce Plaza Bldg Topeka KS 66611

PICKING, ROBERT BOYD, architect, engr.; b. Somerset, Pa., Oct. 21, 1914; s. Jay Sylvester and Ruey Florence (Boyd) P.; B.A., Lehigh U., 1936; M.Arch., Yale, 1940; student Duke, Tech. U., Stockholm, Sweden, 1939; adopted children—Erich Alexander, Isabella Maria. Asst. project mgr., planner housing project Ernst Grönwald SAR, Stockholm, 1939; prin. Robert Picking, architect/engr., Somerset, Pa., 1940-42; sr. designer Skidmore, Owings & Merrill, architects and engrs., Chgo., 1946-48; pres. Boyd Britton Assos. Inc., 1949—; prin. Robert Picking, architect, planner, engr., 1952—; dir. bus. devel., promotion, pub. relations Consoer & Morgan, architects, Chgo., 1974-76; prin. Design Mgmt., 1976—; past pres. Two Pennsylvania Corp.; lectr. in field. Served with USNR, 1941-45. Mem. AIA (chmn. planning and pub. relations com. Chgo. chpt., mem. nat. pub. relations, urban planning and design com., Merit awards in design), Iktinos, Kappa Sigma. Presbyn. Clubs: Onwentsia (Lake Forest, Ill.); Rolling Rock (Ligonier, Pa.); Arts (Chgo.); Bath and Tennis (Lake Bluff, Ill.). Patents and trademarks in field. Contbr. articles to jours. Office: 105 Green Bay Rd Lake Bluff IL 60044

PIEPMEIER, ROBERT BRANOM, electronics co. exec.; b. St. Louis, Oct. 17, 1946; s. Francis Harmon and Mildred Elizabeth (Branom) P.; B.A., Northwestern U., 1968; M.S., Purdue U., 1971; m. Christine Fay Cummins, June 20, 1969; children—Jeffrey Robert, Jeremy Ross. Pres., Info. Analysts, Inc., Evanston, Ill., 1968-70; sr. analyst, product mgmt. adminstr. RCA Corp., Indpls., 1971—; dir. Info. Analysts, Inc.; lectr. Butler U. Coll. Bus. Adminstrn. Econs. advisor Republican Party Central Com., Marion County, Ind., 1974-75, precinct capt. 1976. Mem. Am. Production and Inventory Control Soc. (chpt. v.p. for edn. and research), Am. Statis. Assn., World Future Soc. Baptist. Clubs: Toastmasters (v.p. chpt.). Author: Interactive Business Planning Systems, 1972; Models of Conflict, 1967. Home: 5271 Brendon Park Dr Indianapolis IN 46226 Office: 600 N Sherman St Indianapolis IN 46201

PIERARD, RICHARD VICTOR, historian, educator; b. Chgo., May 29, 1934; s. John Perkins and Diana (Russell) P.; B.A., Calif. State U., 1958, M.A., 1959; Ph.D., U. Iowa, 1964; m. Charlene Burdett, June 15, 1957; children—David Edward, Cynthia Kay. Instr., U. Ia., Iowa City, 1964; asst. prof. history Ind. State U., Terre Haute, 1964-67, asso. prof., 1967-72, prof. history, 1972—; vis. lectr. German Bible Sch., Seeheim, Germany, spring, 1971; vis. prof. Greenville (Ill.) Coll., 1972-73; vis. lectr. Regent Coll., Vancouver, B.C., Can., summer 1975; dir. The Word Christian Bookstore, Terre Haute, 1976; sec.-treas. Conf. on Faith and History, 1967. Mem. planning com. Ind. Gov.'s Conf. on Libraries and Information Services, 1978. Served with U.S. Army, 1954-56. Fulbright scholar, U. Hamburg (Germany), 1962-63, research fellow U. Aberdeen (Scotland), winter-spring 1978. Mem. Am. Hist. Assn., Soc. for Preservation and Encouragement of Barbershop Quartet Singing in Am., Phi Alpha Theta. Democrat. Baptist. Author: Protest and Politics, 1968; The Unequal Yoke, 1970; The Cross and the Flag, 1972; Politics: A Case for Christian Action, 1973; Twilight of the Saints, 1978; contbr. articles in field to profl. jours. Home: 1101 Maple Ave Terre Haute IN 47804 Office: Dept History Ind State U Terre Haute IN 47809

PIERCE, DANIEL MARSHALL, lawyer, state legislator; b. Chgo., Mar 31, 1928; s. Hyman A. and Thelma (Udwin) P.; A.B., Harvard U., 1949, LL.B., 1952; m. Ellen Morel Field, June 27, 1953; children—Andrew, Anthony, Theodore. Admitted to Ill. bar, 1952; asso. Ross, McGowan, Babcock & O'Keefe, Chgo., 1954-59; partner Stebbins & Pierce, Chgo., 1959-66; partner Altheimer & Gray, Chgo., 1966—; mem. Ill. Ho. of Reps., 1964—, now chmn. Revenue com. Mem. Ill. Reapportionment Commn., 1963. Democratic state central committeeman, 1962-66, 70—. Bd. dirs. Cove Sch., Evanston, Ill. Served to 1st lt. USAF, 1952-54. Mem. Am., Ill., Chgo. bar assns. Club: Harvard of Chgo. Home: 1923 Lake Ave Highland Park IL 60035 Office: 1 IBM Plaza Chicago IL 60611

PIERCE, DANNY PARCEL, artist; b. Woodlake, Calif., Sept. 10, 1920; s. Frank Lester and Letitia Francis (Parcel) P.; student Chouinard Art Inst., 1940, 46-47, Am. Art Sch., 1947-48, Bklyn. Mus. Art Sch., 1950-53; B.A., U. Alaska, 1963; m. Julia Ann Rasmussen, July 19, 1943; children—Julia Ann, Mary, Danny L., Duane Nels. Free-lance illustrator, 1948-53; instr. art Hunter Coll., N.Y.C., 1952-53, Burnley Sch. Profl. Art, Seattle, 1954-59; artist in residence U. Alaska, 1959-63, chmn. dept. art, 1960-63; guest instr. art U. Wis., Milw., 1965, asso. prof., 1971—; chmn. dept. art Cornish Sch. Allied Arts, Seattle, 1965-66. Served with Inf. U.S. Army, 1942-45. Decorated Purple Heart, Bronze Star, Combat Inf. badge. Recipient several grants to study art. Mem. Artist Equity Assn., Am. Colorprint Soc. Author, artist: Little No Name, 1959; The Bear That Woke Too Soon, 1964; Little Ezukvuk, 1965; Washington's Dilemma: Sack Cloth and Butternut 1775-83, 1973; Edge of the Sea, 1974; Cattle Drive 76, 1977. Home: 3548 N Murray Ave Shorewood WI 53211

PIERCE, DONALD NORMAN, mech. engr., educator; b. Lincoln, Nebr., Oct. 30, 1921; s. Tracy Augustus and Lucy Isabelle' (Keith) P.; B.M.E., U. Nebr., 1948, M.M.E., 1954; m. Lela Ruth Lyne, Oct. 10, 1943; children—David Alan, Marilyn Pierce Edwards. Instr. dept. engring. mechanics U. Nebr., Lincoln, 1948-55, asst. prof., 1955-61, asso. prof., 1961—; engr. Aircraft Gas Turbine div. Gen. Electric Co., Evendale, Ohio, 1952, 53; test engr. Aero. div. Mpls. Honeywell Corp., Mpls., 1955, 56. Served to capt. AUS, 1943-47. NDEA scholar U. Colo., 1964-65. Mem. Am. Soc. Engring. Edn., ASME, AAAS, Am. Acad. Mechanics, Nebr. Engring. Soc. (pres. 1963), Sigma Xi. Author: (with D.I. Cook) Engineering Mechanics: Statics and Dynamics, 1961. Home: 2501 N 46th St Lincoln NE 68504

PIERCE, DOUGLAS JOHN, architect; b. Gary, Ind., Apr. 21, 1944; s. Kenneth Ray and Lenore May (Shuster) P.; B.S. in Architecture, U. Cin., 1968. Architect, GSA, N.Y.C., 1964-66, Skidmore, Owings & Merrill, Chgo., 1966-67, Wildermuth & Bone, Portage, Ind., Design Orgn., Valparaiso, Ind., 1971—. Bd. dirs. Porter County Arts Commn., 1972-76, pres. bd., 1972, 73; bd. dirs. Porter, Starke Mental Health Center, 1973-75, Valparaiso Found., 1973—, Fairview Youth Treatment Center, 1974-77, No. Ind. Health Systems Agy., Ind. Statewide Health Coordinating Council. Served with AUS, 1969-71. Mem. AIA, Nat. Com. Architecture for Health, Ind. (exec. bd., dir. 1974—), Porter County (pres. 1973, 74) Mental Health assns., Assn. Artists and Craftsmen Porter County, Valparaiso Profl. Businessmen's Assn., Valparaiso C. of C. (dir. 1974-77). Clubs: Rotary, Moose, Elks. Major works include: Porter-Starke Mental Health Center, Hobart (Ind.) Library, Court Restaurant, Southlake County Mental Health Center. Office: 103 E Indiana Ave Valparaiso IN 46383

PIERCE, JAMES GRAY, milk products mfg. co. exec.; b. Columbus Junction, Iowa, Feb. 13, 1915; s. Chester Earl and Marian Edith (Gray) P.; B.A., Iowa Wesleyan Coll., 1937; postgrad. Iowa State U., 1935; certificate meteorology U. Chgo., 1942-43; m. Elizabeth Newsome, June 12, 1943; children—Jane Anne (Mrs. David Scott Finch), James Newsome. Researcher, salesman Western Condensing Co., whey processing, San Francisco, 1937-38; asst. state chemist Iowa Dept. Agr., Des Moines, 1939-41; chief chemist Nat. By-Products, Inc., 1941-52; dir. quality control Walnut Grove Products Co., Atlantic, Iowa, 1952-64; mgr. govt. compliance, agrl. chems. group W.R. Grace & Co., feed, fertilizer and agrl. chems., Atlantic, St. Louis and Memphis, 1965-70; v.p. Milk Spltys. Inc., Dundee, Ill., 1970—. Served with USAAF, 1942-46, USAF, 1951-52. Recipient Spl. service award Nat. Feed Ingredients Assn., 1972. Mem. Am. Chem. Soc., Am. Oil Chemists Soc., Am. Assn. Cereal Chemists, Am. Feed Mfrs. Assn. (mem. feed control relations com. 1963—), Nat. Feed Ingredients Assn. (chmn. govt. relations com. 1967—), Am. Assn. Feed Microscopists (chmn. 1956-65). Methodist. Lion (pres. 1967); Toastmaster (pres. 1963-64). Contbr. to profl. publs. in field. Home: 148 Linden St Dundee IL 60118 Office: Box 278 Dundee IL 60118

PIERCE, LAMBERT REID, architect; b. Evanston, Ill., Apr. 12, 1930; s. Ellsworth Reid and Jessie (Lambert) P.; B.S., Northwestern U., 1953, postgrad., 1955; m. Julia Ellen Sellers, Nov. 20, 1948; children—Kenneth Reid, Rebecca June, Wendy Lynn. Archtl. draftsman Rader & Co., builders, Skokie, Ill., 1949-58; asso. architect Richard E. Dobroth & Assos., Deerfield, and Glenview, Ill., 1958-67; v.p. Richard E. Dobroth & Assos., Inc., Glenview, 1967-71; owner Lambert R. Pierce Architect AIA, Glenview, 1971—; del. First Internat. Congress on Religion, Architecture and Visual Arts, N.Y.C., 1967. Commr. United Christian Community Services, Chgo., 1968-69; bd. dirs. Beacon Neighborhood House, Chgo., 1966-69, pres., 1968. Mem. AIA (mem. Chgo. chpt. housing com., govt. affairs com.), Glenview C. of C. (dir. 1972—, v.p. 1976-77, pres. 1978). Presbyterian (elder 1962-68, 71-76, mem. program cabinet Presbytery of Chgo. until 1976). Prin. archtl. works include Pelican Cove Beach Club, St. Croix, U.S. Virgin Islands, 1967-70; Queen's Quarter Hotel, St. Croix, U.S. Virgin Islands, 1964-70, Golden Dragon, Glenview, Ill., 1976. Home: 503 Briarhill Rd Glenview IL 60025 Office: 1865 Grove St Glenview IL 60025 also 27 Queen's Quarter Circle PO Box 770 Christiansted St Croix VI 00820

PIERCE, RALPH, cons. engr.; b. Chgo., Apr. 14, 1926; s. Charles and Fay (Reznik) P.; B.E.E., Northwestern U., 1946; m. Marion R. Aaron, Nov. 10, 1946; children—Marc Fredrick, Deborah Ann, Elizabeth Allison. Test engr. Am. Elec. Heater Co., Detroit, 1946-47; sr. asso. engr. Detroit Edison Co., 1947-52; sec., chief utility engr. George Wagschal Assos. Detroit, 1952-58; partner Pierce, Yee & Assos., Engrs., Detroit, 1958-71; mng. partner Harley Ellington Pierce Yee Assos., 1971—; mem. Dept. Commerce Mission to Yugoslavia. Served to ensign USNR, 1944-46; comdr. Res. ret. Registered profl. engr., Mich., Ind., Ill., Ohio, Ky., N.Y., Washington, Fla., Ont. (Can.). Mem. Nat. Council Engring. Examiners, Nat. Soc. Profl. Engrs., Engring. Soc. Detroit, IEEE, Illuminating Engring. Soc., Mich. Soc. Architects (asso.). Designer major airport and outdoor lighting systems, power systems, utility systems. Home: 5531 Pebbleshire Rd Birmingham MI 48010 Office: 26111 Evergreen Rd Southfield MI 48076

PIERCE, RICHARD, exec. recruiter; b. Chgo., Oct. 19, 1938; s. Ben L. and Carrah M. (Elam) P.; B.B.A., U. Iowa, 1962; m. Susan C. Kaspar, Sept. 2, 1961; children—Richard S., Edward M., Lauren S. Research analyst CNA Corp., Chgo., 1962-65; asso. research dir. Kenyon & Eckhardt Advt., Chgo., 1965-67; with First Nat. Bank of Chgo., 1967-74, mktg. research mgr., 1970-74; dir. mktg. Harris Trust & Savs., Chgo., 1974-76; v.p. Russell Reynolds Assos., Chgo., 1976—. Mem. Am. Mktg. Assn., Bank Mktg. Assn. (mem. direct electronic funds transfer com. 1968-72, mem. research council 1972—, co-chmn. research conf. 1973), Kappa Sigma. Author: How to Conduct a Psychographics Study, 1972. Home: 633 S Bruner St Hinsdale IL 60521 Office: 230 W Monroe Chicago IL 60606

PIERRE, KENNETH JEROME, psychologist, clergyman; b. St. Paul, Jan. 16, 1937; s. Willard Joseph and Leona Marie (Welter) P.; B.A., St. Paul Sem., 1959, M.A., 1964; M.A., Fordham U., 1968; Ph.D., Loyola U., Chgo., 1971. Ordained priest Roman Catholic Ch., 1963; asso. pastor Nativity Parish, St. Paul, 1963-64; chancery ofcl. Archdiocese St. Paul, 1964-66; rector St. John Vianney College Sem., St. Paul, 1971—, dir. consultation services center, 1971—. Mem. Am., Minn. psychol. assns. Home and Office: 2115 Summit St St Paul MN 55105

PIERSOL, LAWRENCE LEROY, lawyer; b. Vermillion, S.D., Oct. 21, 1940; s. Ralph Nelson and Mildred (Millette) P.; student U. Nebr., 1958-59; B.A., U. S.D., 1952, J.D. summa cum laude, 1965; m. Catherine Vogt, June 30, 1962; children—Leah, William, Elizabeth. Admitted to S.D. bar, 1965; asso. Davenport, Evans, Hurwitz & Smith, Sioux Falls, 1968-69, partner, 1970—; mem. State Jud. Council, 1971-75; mem. S.D. Ho. of Reps., 1970-74, minority whip, 1970-71, majority leader, 1972-74; del. Democratic Nat. Conv., 1972, 76; mem. Dem. Nat. Com. Commn. on Del. Selection, 1973—; chmn. S.D. Citizen's Commn. Exec. Reorgn., 1971-75. Mem. adv. bd. Head Start, 1969-70; bd. dirs. Sioux Falls Civic Fine Arts Assn., treas., 1972—; mem. State Planning Commn., 1971-74; bd. dirs. Sioux Falls chpt. ARC, 1968-72, chmn., 1970; mem. S.D. Bd. Environ. Protection, 1975—; mem. sch. bd. O'Gorman High Sch., 1974—; bd. dirs. Sioux Falls Human Relations Commn., 1971-74, E. River Legal Services Corp., 1975—. Served to capt. AUS, 1965-68. Mem. Am., S.D. (chmn. revision mental health laws com. 1969-71), Minnehaha County bar assns., S.D. Trial Lawyers Assn. Roman Catholic (dir. ch. 1972-75). Club: K.D. Home: 103 S Duluth Sioux Falls SD 57104 Office: Nat Res Bldg Sioux Falls SD 57102

PIERSON, EDWIN KENNETH, JR., physician; b. North Platte, Nebr., Feb. 17, 1921; s. Edwin Kenneth and Nancy Carolyn (Coggins) P.; B.S. in Edn., Kearney (Nebr.) State Coll., 1943; B.S. in Medicine, U. Nebr., 1945, M.D., 1947; m. Margaret Kathryn Downing, June 16, 1946; children—Susan Pierson Hoppel, Eric, Karen, Nancy Pierson Christatos. Intern, Kings Daus. Hosp. Temple, Tex., 1947-48; with Cowling Clinic, Ada, Okla., 1948; gen. practice medicine, Kearney, 1948-50; resident in surgery Detroit Receiving Hosp., 1950-52; practice medicine, specializing in surgery, Neligh, Nebr., 1952—; mem. staff Antelope Meml. Hosp., Neligh, 1952—, pres. staff, 1967-68; city health officer Neligh, 1964-69; health officer Antelope (Nebr.), 1964-69. Scoutleader, Boy Scouts Am.; mem. Neligh Sch. Bd., 1968-70, sec., 1969-70. Served to maj., M.C., AUS, 1957-59; ETO. Recipient Soil Conservation award Sioux City (Iowa) C. of C., 1956. Fellow Royal Soc. Health, Internat. Biog. Assn., Internat. Acad. Proctology (affiliate); mem. AMA, Nebr. Hist. Soc., Sierra Club, Alpha Kappa Kappa. Methodist. Club: Alaska Husky (organizer, pres.). Address: Box 22 Neligh NE 68756

PIERSON, FRITZ ARTHUR, JR., dentist; b. Lincoln, Nebr., July 10, 1920; s. Fritz Arthur and Alberta Vincent (Blanchette) P.; B.S., U. Nebr., 1942, D.D.S., 1944; m. Charlotte Maxine Smith, Nov. 14, 1948; children—Patricia Dee, David Arthur. Pvt. practice dentistry, Lincoln, 1946—; mem. dental adv. com. to sec. HEW, 1970-72. Bd. dirs. Lincoln YMCA, 1954-56, Nebr. Dental Service Corp., 1971—. Served with AUS, 1944-46. Mem. Am. (mem. council relief 1970-75, chmn. 1974-75), Nebr. (chmn. council legislation 1961—, chmn. com. constn. and by-laws 1970-72), Am. Coll. Dentists. Mason (Shriner, Jester). Home: 3601 Country Club Blvd Lincoln NE 68502 Office: 1112 Lincoln Benefit Life Bldg Lincoln NE 68508

PIERSON, LORRAINE JOSEPHINE, tool and engring. co. exec.; b. Glenwood City, Wis., Sept. 17, 1928; s. Percy Floyd and Clara A. (Spaeth) Fansler; student Bemidji State U., 1971; m. Neil Pierson, Dec. 23, 1948; children—Robert, Keith, Richard, Michael. Home demonstrator Decor Co., Mpls., 1962-63; sec., bookkeeper Progressive Tool & Engring. Co., Roseau, Minn., 1964—. Active Boy Scouts Am.; pres. Luth. Ch. Women, 1976-77; ambassador Minn. Soc. Crippled Children and Adults. Mem. Minn. Hort. Soc., Women's Internat. Bowling Congress, Lady Slipper Garden Club (sec. 1976-77). Republican. Home and Office: PO Box 98 Roseau MN 56751

PIERSON, PAUL SANFORD, JR., architect; b. Lawton, Okla., Mar. 12, 1928; s. Paul Sanford and Ica J. (Lewis) P.; student Tex. A. and M., 1945-46, U. Colo., 1948-52; m. Mary L. O'Donnell, Dec. 23, 1953; children—John L., William S. (dec.), Susan, Caroline. Asso. with various archtl. firms, Colo., 1952-59; pvt. practice, Denver,

1959-67; sr. architect USPHS, Boston, 1967-68; dir. div. design and constrn. Am. Hosp. Assn., Chgo., 1969-73; v.p., dir. health facilities projects Perkins & Will, Architects, Chgo., 1973—; sr. v.p. Perkins & Will, Internat., Inc., Chgo.; vis. lectr. U. N.H., 1971-72. Bd. advisers Sch. Architecture, Tex. A. and M. U. Served with USAF, 1946-47. Registered profl. engr., Colo. Mem. AIA (nat. com. on architecture for health 1969-73), Am. Assn. Hosp. Planning (dir.), Am. Hosp. Assn., Nat. Fire Protection Assn. (com. on hosps. 1969-73, com. on safety to life 1977—). Home: 518 Rosewood Ave Winnetka IL 60093 Office: 309 W Jackson Blvd Chicago IL 60606

PIETROFESA, JOHN JOSEPH, educator; b. N.Y.C., Sept. 12, 1940; s. Louis John and Margaret (Proietti) P.; B.E. cum laude, U. Miami, 1961, M.Ed., 1963, Ed.D., 1967; m. Diana Pinto, June 8, 1963; children—John, Paul. Counselor, Dade County (Fla.) pub. schs., 1965-67; faculty Wayne State U., Detroit, 1967—, prof. edn., 1974-77, div. head theoretical and behavioral founds., 1977—; cons. to various schs., hosps. and univs. Served to 1st lt. Mil. Police Corps, AUS, 1963-65. Mem. Am. Psychol. Assn., Am., Mich. personnel and guidance assns., Assn. Counselor Edn. and Supervision, Phi Delta Kappa. Author: The Authentic Counselor, 1971; School Counselor as Professional, 1971; Counseling and Guidance in the Twentieth Century, 1971; Elementary School Guidance and Counseling, 1973; Career Development, 1975; Career Education, 1976; College Student Development, 1977; Counseling: Theory Research and Practice, 1978; editorial bd. Counseling and Values, 1972-75. Home: 2437 Clawson Royal Oak MI 48073 Office: 319 Education Wayne State U Detroit MI 48202

PIGATTI, EUGENE RUDOLPH, lawyer; b. Rockford, Ill., Jan. 12, 1930; s. Eugene V. and Dina E. (Malvesti) P.; Ph.B., Marquette U., 1951, J.D., 1956; m. Margaret Mary O'Brien, Jan. 15, 1955; children—Diane, Deborah, Eugene Richard III, Mary, John, Ann. Admitted to Wis. bar, 1956, Ill. bar, 1957; gen. practice, Rockford, Ill., 1957—; partner Cannariato & Pigatti, 1962—. Bd. dirs. St. Elizabeths Community Center, 1960-70, pres., 1965-70. Served with CIC, U.S. Army, 1953-55. Mem. Am., Wis., Ill., Winnebago County bar assns., Ill. Trial Lawyers Assn., Delta Theta Phi, Alpha Phi Omega. Club: Serra Internat. (dist. gov., past pres.). Home: 1212 Garrison Ave Rockford IL 61103 Office: 324 Chestnut St Rockford IL 61101

PIKAART, LEN, mathematician, educator; b. Nutley, N.J., Jan. 4, 1933; s. Leonard Gascoigne and Janette Theodora (Hendricks) P.; student U.S. Naval Acad., 1952-55; B.A. with distinction, U. Va., 1959, M.Ed., 1960, Ed.D., 1963; m. Constance Natalie Headapohl, Nov. 6, 1954; children—Leonard Frederick, William Edward, Lori Janette, Lucinda Corinne. Tchr. math. jr. and sr. high schs., Arundel County (Md.), 1955-56; sr. research asst. and instr. div. ednl. research U. Va., Charlottesville, 1960-62, instr. div. math. Sch. Engring., 1962-63; asst. prof. math. edn. U. Ga., Athens, 1963-67, head dept. math. edn., 1966-69, asso. prof. math. edn., 1967-71, prof. math. edn., 1971-74, dir. Ednl. Profl. Devel. Act Program for math. suprs., 1969-70, program for doctoral study in math. edn., 1964-74; Robert L. Morton prof. math. edn. Ohio U., Athens, 1974—; cons. to Center for Internat. Math. Edn. Info., U. Chgo., 1968, E.L. Kizziah Co., Rome, Ga., 1965-74, U.S. Office of Edn., 1969-74; participant First Internat. Congress in math. edn., Lyon, France, 1969. Served to sgt. with arty. U.S. Army, 1956-58. Post Doctoral fellow N.Y. U., 1970-71. Mem. Math. Assn. Am. (cons. com. undergrad. program in math. 1968), Am., Nat., Ohio, Ga. (pres. 1972-73) councils tchrs. math., AAUP, Am. Ednl. Research Assn. (steering com. spl. interest group for research in math. edn. 1968-69), Phi Delta Kappa (pres. U. Ga. chpt. 1967-68, del. biennial council 1967, 69). Kiwanian. Author: (with K. J. Travers) Mathematics Teaching, 1977; asst. editor The Arithmetic Tchr., 1967-70; contbr. articles on edn. in math. to profl. publs. Home: 18 Angela Dr Athens OH 45701 Office: McCracken Hall Ohio U Athens OH 45701

PIKARSKY, MILTON, transp. ofcl.; b. N.Y.C., Mar. 28, 1924; s. Abraham J. and Celia (Kaufman) P.; B.C.E., Coll. City N.Y., 1944; postgrad. Ill. Inst. Tech., 1947-56, M.S. in Civil Engring., 1969; postgrad. DePaul U., 1959-60; m. Sally Nesel, Aug. 9, 1947; children—Joel Jay, Amy Jo. Asst. engr. N.Y.C R.R., Chgo., 1944-57; cons. civil engr., Chgo., Gary, Ind., Dearborn, Mich., 1955-60; engr. Dept. Pub. Works, Chgo., 1960-64, commr., 1964-73; chmn. Chgo. Transit Authority, 1973-75; chmn. Regional Transit Authority (RTA), Chgo., 1975—; mem. faculty Northwestern U.; adj. prof. U. Ill.; mem. steering com. Nat. League of Cities' Com. on Transp. and Communication, 1968; mem. steering com. Urban Mass Transp. Adv. Council, U.S. Dept. Transp.; mem. Engrs. Joint Council Panel on Tech. Assessment, 1973; mem. transp. adv. com. Fed. Energy Adminstrn., 1976; nat. adv. com. Inst. Aviation, U. Ill., 1976; mem. adv. com. basic transp. research studies Mass. Inst. Tech. Center Transp. Studies. Trustee Children's World Montessori Sch. Park Ridge; mem. indsl. adv. com. Coll. Engring., U. Ill. Named Chicagoan of Year in Architecture and Engring., Chgo. Jr. Assn. Commerce and Industry, 1967; Outstanding Engring. award for Chgo. Central Filtration Plant, Nat. Soc. Profl. Engrs.; named One of Top 10 Pub. Works Men-of-Year, 1969; Townsend Harris medal City Coll. N.Y., 1969; Chgo.'s Outstanding Leader in Transp. award Soc. of Little Flower, 1969. Fellow ASCE (Civil Govt. award 1973); mem. Nat., Ill. socs. profl. engrs., Am. Ry. Engring. Assn., Am. Road Builders Assn. (chmn. council urban mass transp.), Inst. for Rapid Transit (com. on govt. affairs), Western Soc. Engrs. (past pres.), Transp. Research Bd. (exec. com., chmn.), Nat. Acad. Engring. (BART impact com., com. pub. engring. policy), Am. Pub. Transit Assn., Chi Epsilon, Lambda Alpha. Clubs: Economic, Chicago Engineers, Ground Hog (pres.). Home: 5878 N Lacey Ave Chicago IL 60646 Office: PO Box 3858 Chicago IL 60654

PIKE, JOHN RAYMOND, advt. co. exec.; b. Albany, N.Y., Aug. 6, 1929; s. John Raymond and Laura Elizabeth (Craft) P.; B.A., Emerson Coll., 1950; postgrad. Columbia, 1950; M.A., Boston U., 1952; m. Harriet Loewenstein, Dec. 4, 1955; children—Laura Michelle, Karen Virginia. Copy contact J. Walter Thompson Co., N.Y.C., 1952-54, copychief, Miami, 1954-56, creative dir. Mexico City, 1956-58, sr. writer, producer, N.Y.C., 1958-60, creative dir., Mexico City 1960-63; v.p., asso. dir. broadcasting Campbell-Ewald, Detroit, 1965-69; v.p., asso. creative dir. Kenyon & Eckhardt, N.Y.C., 1969; v.p., asso. creative dir. D'Arcy, MacManus & Masius, Bloomfield Hills, Mich., 1969—. Mem. West Bloomfield Citizens Adv. com. to Sch. Bd., 1969-71. Bd. dirs. Orchard Lake Shore Property Owners Assn. Recipient 17 awards and 6 Clios, Am. Tv. Comml. Festival, 1965-75, 4 TV awards N.Y. Art Dirs. Club, 1965-67, 12 awards Hollywood Advt. Club, 1964-76, award Venice Film Festival, 1968, award Cork Film Festival, 1966, 18 awards N.Y. Internat. Film and TV Festival, 1968-76, 5 awards Detroit Art Dirs. Club, 1964-66, merit award Advt. Writers Assn. N.Y., 1964, 8 "100 Best" awards Advt. Age, 1973-76, 1st award to comml. Film Adv. Bd., 1976, citation for Save the Eagle campaign Nat. Wildlife Fedn., 1976. Home: 4150 Pontiac Trail Orchard Lake MI 48033 Office: Long Lake Rd Bloomfield Hills MI 48013

PIKE, ROBERT ALLEN, pub. relations co. exec.; b. Austin, Minn., Mar. 1, 1946; s. Luverne Carl and Evelyn Marie (Johnson) P.; student Upper Ia. Coll., 1966, U. No. Iowa, 1966-68; m. Ann Hanson, Aug. 1, 1968. Printer, photoengraver Lithocraft Co., Grundy Center, Iowa, 1968-69; graphic artist Bob Pike Studio, Grundy Center, 1969-71; artist, art dir. Waldbillig & Besteman Advt. & Pub. Relations Co., Madison, Wis., 1971—. Bd. dirs. Grundy Center Devel. Corp., 1970-71. Home: 5317 Burnett Dr Madison WI 53705 Office: 810 University Bay Dr Madison WI 53705

PIKUNAS, JUSTIN, psychologist, educator; b. Alytus, Lithuania, Jan. 7, 1920; s. Baltrus and Anele (Radzius) P.; Ph.B., Vytautas the Great U., Lithuania, 1943; Ph.D., U. Munich (Germany), 1949; postgrad. U. Paris (France), 1949-50; m. Regina Liesunaitis, Aug. 8, 1953; children—Justas, Kristina, Ramona. Came to U.S., 1950, naturalized, 1956. Asst. prof. psychology U. Detroit, 1952-56, asso. prof., 1956-61, prof., 1961—, dir. sch. psychology program, 1970-75, dir. Children's Psychodiagnostic Center, 1972—, chmn. dept. psychology, 1974—, mem. faculty senate, 1972—. Pres Lithuanian Cath Fedn. Ateitis, 1967-73. Research grantee NIMH, 1960, NSF, 1962. Mem. AAAS, Nat. Soc. Study Edn., Am. Psychol. Assn. Author: Fundamental Child Psychology, 1957, rev. edit., 1965; Psychology of Human Development, 1961; Human Development: A Science of Growth, 1969; Human Development: An Emergent Science, 3d rev. edit., 1976. Home: 8761 W Outer Dr Detroit MI 48219 Office: Dept Psychology U Detroit Detroit MI 48221

PILDITCH, WALTER EDWARD, ednl. adminstr.; b. Chgo., Apr. 30, 1931; s. Howard Tallet and Edith Margaret (Boisselier) P.; A.A., Wilson Jr. Coll., 1951; B.Ed., Chgo. Tchrs. Coll., 1953; M.A., Northwestern U., 1957; postgrad. U. Chgo., 1957-62; m. Eleanor Joyce Howard, Apr. 15, 1966; children—Ruth Ann, Kenneth Eric, Matthew Edward. Tchr., Herman Felsenthal Elementary Sch., Chgo., 1953-54, 56-60, acting asst. prin., 1960; adminstrv. intern Chgo. Pub. Schs., 1960-62, staff mem., supr., Bur. Human Relations, Central Office, 1962-69; prin. Joseph Jungman Elementary Sch., Chgo., 1969—. Instr. community leadership tng. Crane Jr. Coll., Chgo., 1962-69; instr. human relations courses for tchrs. and staff mems. Chgo. Pub. Schs., 1963—. Scoutmaster, Boy Scouts Am., 1958-66, troop committeeman, 1966—, troop treas., 1970-77, recipient Order of Arrow, 1947; bd. dirs. Beverly Improvement Assn., Chgo., 1968—, sec., 1971-73, v.p., 1973-75, pres., 1975-77. Served with AUS, 1954-56. Kellogg Found. fellow in ednl. adminstrn., 1960-62; Nat. Edn. fellow, 1963-69. Mem. Chgo. Prins. Assn. (sec. dist. 1971-74), Phi Delta Kappa, Theta Alpha Phi. Mem. Protestant Ch. (treas., trustee, supt. Sunday sch., elder finance chmn.). Club: George Howland (treas. 1971-75, pres. 1975-77). Co-editor filmstrip evaluation articles Ednl. Screen and Audio-Visual Guide, 1956-58; editor Child Psychology Guide for Television, Channel 11, Chgo., 1963-65; asst. Guide for Teaching Non-English Speaking Children, 1970. Research in sch. community relations, human relations in schs. Home: 9409 S Leavitt St Chicago IL 60620 Office: 1746 S Miller St Chicago IL 60608

PILGRIM, MARY JANE, social worker; b. Youngstown, Ohio; d. Frederick Henry and Geneva (Jones) Pilgrim; student Wittenberg U., 1938-40; B.S., Western Res. U., 1942; M.A., Ohio State U., 1949; postgrad. Boston U., 1954-55. Social worker Youngstown Family Service and Youngstown Community Corp., 1950-52; dir. social services Mahoning County Tb Sanitarium, Youngstown, 1952-54; social worker Youngstown Child Guidance Center, 1955-58, dir. social services 1964-69; chief specialized services child and Adult Mental Health Center, Youngstown, 1970-74; asso. dir. adult services North Central Mental Health Center, Columbus, Ohio, 1974—. chief social worker Athens County Mental Health Center, Athens, Ohio, 1958-59; social work supr. Family Service, Warren, Ohio, 1959-61; chief social worker Norfolk (Va.) Mental Health Center, 1961-62, Athens Mental Health Center, 1962-64. Cons. home sch. visitation program, 1966—; guest lectr. Youngstown State U., 1967. Mem. adv. bd. Soc. for Blind, Youngstown, 1969-70. Mem. Nat. Assn. Social Workers (vice chmn. 1967-68, sec.-treas. 1951-53), Acad. Certified Social Workers, Ohio Mental Health Forum, Kappa Delta Alumni Assn. Baptist. Club: Quota. Home: 92 Buena Vista Ave Youngstown OH 43512

PILLER, HEINAR FRIEDRICH, stage and film dir.; b. Vienna, Austria, Apr. 23, 1939; s. Rudolf Ernest and Maria (Rieder) P.; student U. Toronto, 1963-66, m. Clare Elena Mazzoleni, May 16, 1971; children—Erika, Christiaan; came to Can., 1960, naturalized, 1966. Freelance actor, producer, stage and film dir.; appeared with Barn Players, Coach House Theatre, German Theatre, Ryerson Studio, 1960-63, Hart House Theatre, U. Toronto, 1963-65; prodn. asst. Canadian Opera Co., 1965, asst. dir., 1967, 69; resident dir., tour mgr. Neptune Theatre, Halifax, N.S., 1966-67, artistic dir., 1968-71; artistic dir. Theatre London (Ont.), 1971-76; pres. Errant Prodns., Ltd., London and Toronto, 1976—. Mem. Canadian Actors Equity Assn., Arts and Letters Club, Toronto. Recipient award Canadian U. Drama League Festival, 1965; Ford of Can. Centennial scholar; Can. Council grantee, 1971. Home: PO Box 46 Delaward ON N0L 1E0 Canada Office: 651 Yonge St Toronto ON M4Y 1Z9 Canada

PILLIOD, CHARLES JULE, JR., rubber co. exec.; b. Cuyahoga Falls, Ohio, Oct. 20, 1918; s. Charles Jule and Julia (Sullivan) P.; student Muskingum Coll., 1937-38, Kent State U., 1938-40; m. Marie Elizabeth Jacobs, June 15, 1946; children—Christine Marie, Charles Jule III, Mark Alan, Stephen Matthew, Renee Elizabeth. With prodn. squadron Goodyear Tire & Rubber Co., 1941; salesman Goodyear Internat. Corp., 1945-47, mgr., dir. Panama, field rep., Costa Rica, 1947-51, field rep., Chile, Bolivia, Peru, 1951-53, asst. sales mgr., Peru, 1953, sales mgr., Colombia, 1954-56, comml. mgr., Brazil, 1956-59, mng. dir., Brazil, 1959-63, sales dir., Eng., 1963-64, mng. dir., Eng., 1964-66, dir. ops., Akron, Ohio, 1966-67, v.p., 1967-71, pres., 1971—; v.p. Goodyear Tire & Rubber Co., 1971, exec. v.p., dir., 1971-72, pres., 1972, pres., chief exec. officer, 1973, chmn., chief exec. officer, 1973—; dir. CPC Internat., Inc. Trustee Akron Community Trusts, Com. for Econ. Devel., Nat. Urban League, Akron City Hosp.; bd. dirs. Nat. Merit Scholarship Corp., Internat. Road Edn. Found.; trustee U. Akron, Mt. Union Coll., Alliance, Ohio. Served to capt. USAAF, 1942-45. Mem. Rubber Mfrs. Assn. (dir.), U.S.-Mexico C. of C. (dir.); Bus. Roundtable (policy com.), Conf. Bd., Internat. C. of C. (trustee U.S. council). Home: 311 Ely Rd Akron OH 44313 Office: 1144 E Market St Akron OH 44316

PILLON, NANCY HARGIS BACH, educator; b. Jackson, Ky., July 28, 1917; d. Grannis and Evelyn (Crawford) Bach; student Lees Jr. Coll., 1934-36; B.A., Western Ky. State U., 1939; M.S. in Library Sci., U. Ky., 1957, Ed.D., 1967; m. Richard Walsh Pillon, Oct. 6, 1950 (div.); 1 son, Richard Crawford. Librarian Breathitt County High Sch., Jackson, Ky., 1939-42, tchr., librarian, 1952-60; instr. library sci. No. Ill. U., Dekalb, 1960-65; asst. prof. library sci. U. Ky., Lexington, 1965-69; asso. prof. library sci. Ind. State U., Terre Haute, 1969—, acting chmn. dept. library sci., 1971, 77. Chmn. conf. Indian Sch. Library Suprs., 1969-73; former mem. Ind. State Com. Certification Sch. Librarians, 1971—; dir. inst. tng. sch. librarians Higher Edn. Act, 1969. Served with USNR, 1942-46, USN, 1946-50. Mem. ALA, Am. Assn. Library Schs., D.A.R. (chpt. regent 1958-60). Democrat. Presbyterian. Home: 2375 Ohio St Terre Haute IN 47803

PILLOW, THOMAS MASTIN, chiropractor; b. Houston, June 29, 1932; s. Will G. and Janette H. (Gill) P.; student Tex. Tech. U., 1951, Tex. A. & I. U., 1956; D.C., Logan Coll. Chiropractic, 1968; children—Thomas L., Caron R., Bruce W., David G., Brian S. Pres. Multi Products, Inc., Houston, 1957-63; practice chiropractic medicine, St. Charles, Mo., 1968—; mem. faculty Logan Coll. Chiropractic St. Louis, 1968-71. Treas. St. Charles Sr. Citizens Corp., 1973-76; dir. Youth in Need, 1975-77; chmn. bd. dirs. Salvation Army, St. Charles, 1973-76. Served with USNR, 1952-56. Named Chiropractor of Year, State of Mo., 1973. Mem. Am., Mo. (chmn. ins. com. 1969-77) chiropractic assns. Club: Kiwanis (St. Charles). Home: 26 Park Charles St Charles MO 63301 Office: 1148 S Benton St St Charles MO 63301

PILLSBURY, GEORGE STURGIS, state senator; b. Crystal Bay, Minn., July 17, 1921; s. John S. and Eleanor (Lawler) P.; A.B., Yale U., 1943; m. Sally Whitney, Jan. 4, 1947; children—Charles Alfred, George Sturgis, Sarah Kimball, Katharine Whitney. Pres., Sargent Mgmt. Co.; mem. Minn. Senate; dir. Whitney Land Co., Pillsbury Co., Fiduciary Trust Co., N.Y.C. Mem. Smithsonian Assos. (nat. dir.). Clubs: Woodhill, Minnetonka Yacht, Mpls. Athletic, Mpls.; Minnesota (St. Paul); River (N.Y.C.); Seminole Golf (Palm Beach, Fla.). Home: 1320 Bracketts Point Rd Wayzata MN 55391 Office: 930 Dain Tower Minneapolis MN 55402

PILLSBURY, JOHN SARGENT, JR., ins. co. exec.; b. Mpls., Oct. 28, 1912; s. John Sargent and Eleanor (Lawler) P.; B.A., Yale U., 1935; LL.B., U. Minn., 1940; m. Katharine Harrison Clark, June 11, 1936; children—John Sargent, Donaldson Clark, Lynde Harrison, Katharine Pillsbury Wood. Various positions Pillsbury Mills, Inc., 1936-37; admitted to Minn. bar, 1940; asso. Faegre & Benson, Mpls., 1940-45, partner, 1946-56; pres. Northwestern Nat. Life Ins. Co., 1956-69, chmn., 1969—, chief exec. officer, 1969-77, also dir.; dir. NW Bell Telephone Co., Boise Cascade Corp., Pillsbury Co., Minn. Title Fin. Corp., Northwestern Nat. Bank Mpls., NW Bancorp. Life dir. Minn. Orchestral Assn.; trustee Dunwoody Indsl. Inst.; founding trustee Twin Cities Pub. TV. Served from lt. (j.g.) to lt. comdr., air combat intelligence, USNR, 1942-45. Mem. Am., Minn., Hennepin County bar assns., Phi Delta Phi, Order of Coif. Republican. Congregationalist. Clubs: Minneapolis, Minnetonka Yacht, Woodhill Country (Mpls.); Yale (N.Y.C.). Home: 315 Woodhill Rd Wayzata MN 55391 Office: 20 Washington Ave S Minneapolis MN 55440

PILLSBURY, KATHARINE C. (MRS. JOHN S. PILLSBURY, JR.), civic worker; b. New Haven, May 23, 1916; d. Donaldson and Katharine (Harrison) Clark; student pvt. schs.; m. John S. Pillsbury, Jr., June 11, 1936; children—John S. III, Donaldson C., L. Harrison, Katharine Wood. Chmn. home service dept. A.R.C., 1948-50; dir. Minn. Human Genetics League, 1954-71, Minn. Mental Health Soc., 1957-61, Family and Children's Services, 1958-61; woman's chmn. Community Chest drive, 1957; dir. Community Chest and Council, 1958-65; pres., dir. Hennepin County Rep. Workshop, 1953-56; pres. Nat. Council of Rep. Workshops, 1957-59; docent Mpls. Inst. Arts, 1964—; adv. com. Kennedy Center for Performing Arts, 1970-73; trustee Mpls. Inst. Fine Arts, 1974—, Med. Found., 1973-76, Woodhill Country Club, 1974—. Pres. Friends Art Inst., 1964-67. Mem. Colonial Dames of Am. Conglist. (trustee ch.). Home: 315 Woodhill Rd Wayzata MN 55391

PILOT, ISADORE, physician; b. Chgo., Oct. 15, 1895; s. Israel and Ida (Guss) P.; B.S., U. Chgo., 1918; M.D., U. Ill., 1917; m. Anna B. Glick, July 2, 1922; children—Saralee Pilot Hurwitch, Martin L. Intern Cook County Hosp., Chgo., 1917-18, resident, 1919-20; asso. prof. pathology and medicine U. Ill., Chgo., 1923-65; practice medicine specializing in internal medicine, Chgo., 1929—. Pres. Phi Delta Epsilon Found. Chgo., 1954-74. Served with U.S. Army, World War I, World War II. Mem. AMA, Am. Rheumatic Assn., Am. Coll. Allergists, Am. Assn. Pathology, Soc. Microbiology, and others, Sigma Xi, Alpha Omega Alpha. Home: 300 N State St Chicago IL 60610 Office: 185 N Wabash Ave Chicago IL 60601

PINCE, BRUCE WAYNE, cons. co. exec., educator; b. Chgo., Dec. 7, 1927; s. Otto Charles and Ann (Greenwald) P.; B.S., Northwestern U., 1949; M.S., U. Ill., 1950; postgrad., 1951-54; m. Betty Louise Svitak, July 24, 1954; children—David Samuel, Jane Ellen. Mgr. systems research and devel. Gen. Motors Corp., Warren, Mich., 1961-62; v.p. research Space/Def. Corp., Birmingham, Mich., 1962-70, also dir.; gen. mgr. cons. div. Comar Corp., Birmingham, 1970-72; also dir.; v.p. systems group Sandy Corp., Detroit, 1972—; prof. indsl. engring. Wayne State U., Detroit, 1965-67; guest lectr. U. Calif. at Los Angeles, 1960, Tulane U., New Orleans, 1971. Bd. dirs. Am. Documentation Assn., 1965-66, Engring. Index, 1965-74, Kresge-Hooker Sci. Found., Detroit, 1965-68, Wayne State U. Center for Application of Sci. and Tech., 1963-67. Served with USAF, 1954-61. Fellow Aerospace Med. Assn. (asso.), Am. Inst. Aeros. and Astronautics (asso.); mem. Aerospace Indsl. Life Scis. Assn. (founder 1962, pres. 1972), AAAS, N.Y. Acad. Scis., Sigma Xi, Beta Theta Pi. Clubs: Cranbrook Tennis (pres. 1975), Cranbrook Indoor Tennis (founder 1972, pres. 1976). Author: The Response of Squirrel Monkey to High Accelerative Forces, 1965; contbr. articles to profl. jours. Home: 210 N Glenhurst St Birmingham MI 48009 Office: 16025 Northland Dr Southfield MI 48075

PINDER, ALBERT JOSEPH, newspaper publisher; b. E. Pitts., Pa., Feb. 21, 1920; s. Stanley and Gizella (Boca) P.; student U. Pa., 1937-42; diploma commerce Northwestern U., 1948; m. Dorothy Jeanne Watt, Feb. 19, 1949; children—Joe, Peg, Jeanne, Ann, Larry, Martha. Accountant, Westinghouse Electric Co., Lester, Pa., 1939-43, Truax-Traer Coal Co., Chgo., 1946-49; reporter Grinnell (Iowa) Herald-Register, 1949-56, bus. mgr., 1956-62, mng. editor, 1962-74, publisher, 1974—; leader people-to-people newspaper group to Europe and Russia, 1976; dir. Grinnell Fed. Savs. & Loan, 1976—; pres. Greater Grinnell Devel., Inc., 1966—. Participant Wilton Park Conf., Sussex, Eng., 1972, Canadian-Am. Assembly, Toronto, Ont., Can., 1969, Am. Assembly, Arden House, N.Y., 1972; delegation host People to People trip to Russia, 1976; past pres. bd. trustees Grinnell Gen. Hosp. Served to chief warrant officer U.S. Army, 1943-46. Mem. Iowa Press Assn. (dir. 1971—). Republican. Episcopalian. Club: Grinnell Country. Home: 1714 Country Club Dr Grinnell IA 50112 Office: 813 5th Ave Grinnell IA 50112

PINDERA, JERZY TADEUSZ, mechanics scientist, educator; b. Czchow, Poland, Dec. 4, 1914; s. Jan Stanislaw and Natalia Lucia Knapik P.; came to Can., 1965, naturalized, 1975; B.S. in Mech. Engring., Tech. U., Warsaw, 1936; M.S. in Aero. Engring., Tech. Univs. Warsaw and Lodz, 1947; D. Tech. Scis., Polish Acad. Scis., 1959; D. Habil. in Applied Mechanics, Tech. U. Cracow, 1962; m. Aleksandra-Anna Szal, Oct. 29, 1949; children—Marek Jerzy, Maciej Zenon. Asst. Lot Polish Airlines, Warsaw, 1947; lab. head Aero. Inst., Warsaw, 1947-52, Inst. Metallography, Warsaw, 1952-54; dep. prof., head lab. Polish Acad. Scis., Warsaw, 1954-59; head lab. Bldg. Research Inst., Warsaw, 1959-62; vis. prof. mechanics Mich. State U., East Lansing, 1963-65; prof. mechanics U. Waterloo (Ont., Can.), 1965—; cons. in field; vis. prof. France, Germany. Served with Polish Army, 1939. Registered profl. engr., Ont. Mem. Can. Soc. Mech. Engring., Gesellschaft fuer angewandte Mathematik und Mechanik, Soc. Exptl. Stress Analysis, ASME, Société Française des Mécaniciens, Assn. Profl. Engrs. Province Ont. Chmn. Internat. Symposium Exptl. Mechanics U. Waterloo, 1972. Editorial adv. bd. Mechanics Research Communications, 1974—. Author, contbg.

author books, contbr. articles profl. publs. exptl. mechanics. Home: 310 Grant Crescent Waterloo ON N2K 2A2 Canada Office: Dept Civil Engring 200 University Ave Waterloo ON N2L 3GI Canada

PINE, SHIRLEY ANN, sch. counselor; b. Kansas City, Mo., Oct. 30, 1942; d. Carl Ferrel and Mae E. (Maxville) Brandon; B.S. cum laude in Edn., Mo. Western State Coll., 1972; M.S. in Edn., N.W. Mo. State U., 1976; m. Ronnie B. Pine, Nov. 24, 1960; children—Kelly Sue, Randy Scott. Bookkeeper, Commerce Trust Co., Kansas City, 1960; cosmetologist Platte Beauty Shop, Platte City, Mo., 1966-68; tchr. social sci. Mid-Buchanan High Sch., Faucett, Mo., 1972-74, Barry Middle Sch., Platte City, 1974-76; elementary counselor Platte County Schs. Reorganized Dist., 1976—. Mem. Mo. State Tchrs. Assn., Mo. Greater Kansas City guidance assns., Am. Personnel and Guidance Assn., Mo. Western State Coll. Alumni Assn., Bus. and Profl. Women's Club (1st v.p. 1977—). Club: Pilots Internat. (bd. dirs. local chpt. 1977—). Home: 800 2d St Platte City MO 64079 Office: Platte County R III Schs Platte City MO 64079

PINEDA, ELIZA LAOANG (MRS. BERNARDO G. PINEDA), psychiatrist; b. Camiling, Tarlac, Philippines, Feb. 9, 1930; d. Julio C. and Marciana (Concepcion) Laoang; M.D., U. Santo Tomas, 1955; m. Bernardo G. Pineda, Jan. 21, 1956; children—Grace Lynn, Michelle, Duane. Intern, St. Clare's Hosp., Schenectady, 1957-58; resident in psychiatry Traverse City (Mich.) State Hosp., 1959-63; practice medicine specializing in psychiatry, Manila, Philippines, 1963-66, Burlington, Iowa, 1969—; tchr. health edn. and guidance and counseling Nat. Tchrs. Coll., Philippines, 1964-66; staff psychiatrist Mental Health Inst., Mt. Pleasant, Iowa, 1966-69; med. dir. Henry County Mental Health Center, Mt. Pleasant, 1971; mem. med. staff Meml. Hosp. Burlington, Iowa, Mem. Des Moines County Med. Soc., Women's Aux. Med. Soc. Burlington. Rotary Ann. Club: Golf (Burlington). Home: 2917 Garden St Burlington IA 52601 Office: Reipe Peterson Bldg Burlington IA 52601

PINGATORE, ROSARI ANTOINETTE FOTI (MRS. ANTHONY PINGATORE), educator; b. Westfield, N.Y., June 4, 1921; d. Salvatore Paul and Margaret (Lotempio) Foti; B.E., State U. Coll. Fredonia, 1942; spl. edn. certificate Kent State U., 1970; M.S., St. John Coll., 1972; postgrad. John Carroll U.; m. Anthony Pingatore, Sept. 22, 1951; children—Frances, Toni-Marie. Tchr. rural schs., N.Y. State, 1942-44; tchr. Charlotte Sidway Sch., Grand Island, N.Y., 1944-47; mgr. Childcraft div. Field Enterprises, Pitts., 1947-52; tchr. trainable retarded Cuyahoga County, Cleve., 1962; supr. trainable classes Murray Hill Sch., also William Brett Schs., Cleve., 1964-67; tchr. intermediate class educable mentally retarded Mayfield (Ohio) Center, 1970-71; tchr. primary educable mentally retarded Mayfield Sch. Dist., 1971; elementary cons. educable mentally retarded Lake and Geauga Counties, 1971-72; tchr. children with learning disabilities and behavior disorders Mapledale Sch., Wickliffe, Ohio, 1972—. Leader Girl Scouts, 1966-68; mem. Ohio Citizens Com. for Spl. Edn., 1972—; mem. adv. com. Explorer Troop of Retarded Children, 1973—; pres. Greater Cleve. Friends and Parents of Slow Learners, 1963-65, Garfield Heights Friends and Parents of Slow Learners; v.p. Hillcrest Friends of Library, 1970-71; mem. adv. bd. spl. edn. dept. Notre Dame Coll., Cleve., 1972—; advisory bd. Lake Geauga Spl. Edn. Service Center. Named Wickliffe Tchr. of Year, 1976-77. Mem. Council Exceptional Children, N.E. Ohio (mem. bd.), Cleve. assns. children with learning disabilities, Ohio PTA (hon.). Home: 6756 Bonnie View Rd Mayfield Village OH 44143

PINGRY, CHARLES WARREN, real estate co. exec.; b. Riceville, Iowa, Oct. 17, 1928; s. Gary William and Erma Ethyln (Frazer) P.; B.S., Iowa State U., 1947-51; m. Arlene Mae Johnson, Jan. 24, 1954; children—Gregory, Charlene, Brian. Asst. exptl. farm mgr. J.R. Watkins Co., Winona, Minn., 1953-54; farm mgr. Green Giant Co., Vinton, Iowa, 1954-56, field supt., Blue Earth and Montgomery, 1956-64, plant supt., Blue Earth, 1965-72; partner, pres. Anchor Realty & Devel. Inc., Blue Earth, Minn., 1972—; v.p. Blue Earth Indsl. Service Co., 1972—, sec.-treas., 1973-75. Treas. Blue Earth Sch. Bd. Edn., 1968—. Served with AUS, 1952-54. Mem. Faribault Martin Jackson Bd. Realtors, Am. Legion, VFW. Presbyterian (elder). Clubs: Masons, Shriners, Lions. Home: 212 Oak Knoll Ct Blue Earth MN 56013 Office: 121 N Main St Blue Earth MN 56013

PINKELTON, NORMA BERTHA HARRIS, nurse, educator; b. Phila., Oct. 15, 1927; d. Robert Reynolds and Olivia (Gilbert) Harris; grad. Lincoln Sch. for Nurses, N.Y.C., 1950; B.S.N., U. Cin., 1963, M.S.N., 1965, Ed.D. (NDEA fellow), 1976; m. Monroe Pinkelton, May 20, 1967. Nurse phychiat. med. and surg. unit Bellevue Hosp., N.Y.C., 1950-53; staff nurse surgery, Mt. Sinai Hosp., N.Y.C., 1953-56; pvt. and semi-pvt. nurse Luth. Hosp., N.Y.C., 1955-56; pub. health nurse Pub. Health Dept., Phila., 1956-57; labor and delivery nurse, Chestnut Hill Hosp., Phila., 1957-58; supr., staff nurse Cin. Gen. Hosp., 1958-61; counselor research project, Cin., 1965-67; asst. prof. Coll. of Nursing and Health, U. Cin., 1967—; adj. prof. Afro-Am. Studies, U. Cin.; pvt. practice family marriage and individual counseling, Cin.; bd. trustees Children's Hosp. Med. Center, Cin.; bd. mem. Mental Health, Mental Retardation-Children's Services. Mem. Am. Nurses Assn., Nat. League for Nurses, Council for Exceptional Children, Child Health Assn., Mental Health Assn., AAUP, Black Faculty Assn., Black Nurses Assn., Sigma Theta Tau. Episcopalian. Home: 3808 Dunloe Ave Cincinnati OH 45213 Office: Proctor Hall 3110 Vine St Univ Cincinnati Cincinnati OH 45219

PINKENBURG, CHRISTOPHER ALBERT, chiropractor; b. Saline County, Kans., Oct. 20, 1919; s. Albert Conrad and Mollie Theresa Bieber P.; D. Chiropractic, Palmer Coll. Chiropractic, 1959; m. Mary Frances Komarek, Apr. 11, 1968. Pvt. practice chiropractic, La Junta, Colo., 1960-63, Lyons, Kans., 1963-66, Hoisington, Kans., 1966—; mem. research com. Found. Chiropractic Edn. and Research, 1970—. Served with AUS, 1942-46; ETO. Fellow Internat. Coll. Chiropractors; mem. Am. Council Chiropractic Technic (pres. 1969-71), Am. (Meritorious Service award 1976, Kans. del. 1972-77), Kans. chiropractors assns., European Chiropractors Union (asso.). Unitarian. Home and Office: 254 W 1st St Hoisington KS 67544

PINKERTON, RICHARD LADOYT, univ. dean; b. Huron, S.D., Mar. 5, 1933; s. Abner Pyle and Orral Claudine (Arneson) P.; B.A. (La Verne Noyes scholar), U. Mich., 1955; M.B.A., Case Western Res. U., 1962; Ph.D. (Nat. Assn. Purchasing Mgmt. fellow), U. Wis., 1969; m. Sandra Louise Lee, Aug. 28, 1965; children—Elizabeth, Patricia. Sr. market research analyst Harris-Intertype Corp., Cleve., 1957-61; mgr. sales devel. Triax Co., Cleve., 1962-64; coordinator mktg. programs Mgmt. Inst., U. Wis., 1964-67, dir. exec. programs Grad. Sch. Bus., asst. prof. mktg., 1969-74; prof. mgmt., dean Grad. Sch. Adminstrn., Capital U., Columbus, Ohio, 1974—; cons. dep. asst. sec. USAF, Washington, 1972-76; cons. House of Vision, Chgo., Control Products div. Amerace Corp., Union, N.J., United Shoe Machinery, Boston, Union Carbide Corp., N.Y.C., Westinghouse, Pitts., Ansul Co., Marinette, Wis., Esna, Ltd., Toronto, Ont., Can.; mem. Wis. Gov.'s Exec. Conf. on Mktg. and Research and Devel., 1969-70. Bd. govs. Hannah Neil Home for Children, Columbus. Served as 1st lt. USAF, 1955-57; now lt. col. Res. Mem. Am. Mktg. Assn. (chpt. pres. 1972-73; bd. publs. 1973—), Nat. Assn. Purchasing Mgmt. (nat. vice chmn. profl. devel.), Sales Mktg. Execs. Internat., Air Force Assn., Res. Officers Assn. U.S., Bus. and Econ. Forum Wis. (program dir. 1972-73), Beta Gamma Sigma, Alpha Kappa Psi, Phi Gamma Delta. Club: Athletic (Columbus). Author: (with K. Lawyer) Small Business Success: Operating and Executive Characteristics, 1963; Curriculum for Purchasing, 1969; also articles. Home: 200 S Chesterfield Rd Columbus OH 43209

PINKERTON, ROBERT JOHN, newspaper publisher; b. Madison, Nebr., July 28, 1932; s. John Lowell and Vesta Evelyn (Cronin) P.; B.A. with certificate in journalism, U. Nebr., 1954; m. Carol Jean Patterson, July 24, 1954; children—Becky Nan, Pamela Jean, Linda Marie, Cheryl Lynn. Editor, Western Nebr. Observer, Kimball, 1954, 56-62, owner, pub., 1962—. Pres., Kimball Sch. Bd., 1964-72. Served to 1st lt. USAF, 1954-56. Recipient 1st place awards Nat. Newspaper Assn., 1970, 71. Mem. Nebr. Press Assn. (dir. 1966-73, v.p. 1971, pres. 1972), Sigma Delta Chi, Kappa Alpha Mu (past pres.). Home: 19 Dowd Ct Kimball NE 69145 Office: 118 E 2d St Kimball NE 69145

PINKERTON, VERNON THEODORE, JR., aquatic center exec.; b. Huntington, Ind., July 8, 1923; s. Vernon Theodore and Eva Louise (Sutton) P.; B.S.Ed., Huntington Coll., 1950; bus. certificate Ashland (Ohio) Coll., 1963; M.Ed., Bowling Green (Ohio) State U., 1975; m. D. Marianne Specker, Sept. 3, 1949; children—Julie Ann (Mrs. Peter Lune Roth), Barry, Brian. Tchr.-coach pub. schs., La Rue, Ohio, 1951-52; sales mgr. Armour Agr. Chem. Co., Sandusky, Ohio, 1953-63; sales mgr. Allied Chem. Co., Ashland, 1963-65; tchr.-coach pub. schs., Sandusky, 1966-70; exec. dir. Lorain (Ohio) Aquatic Center, 1970-73; dir. C. T. Branin Natatorium, Canton, Ohio, 1973—. Youth dir. Salvation Army, Ashland, 1958-65; youth dir. Ashland YMCA, 1955-65; bd. dirs. YMCA, Pinkerton Assos. Served with USMCR, 1943-45. Decorated Purple Heart, Gold Star. Named Salesman of Year Armour & Co., 1956, 60, 61, 62, 63, Coach of Year Ohio Swimming Coaches Assos., 1968. Mem. Ohio Health, Phys. Edn., and Recreation Assn., Ohio Tchrs. Assn., Ohio Coaches Assn., Nat. Swimming Coaches Assn., Smithsonian Assos., Lake Erie Assn., AAU (commr. 1973-75, dir. aquatics 1973-75, v.p. Lake Erie 1977), Lorain C. of C. (chmn. mem. relations 1971-72), Am. Legion, DAV, Nat. Rifle Assn., Canton Aquatic Assn. Methodist. Mason. Home: 4891 Echo Valley NW North Canton OH 44720 Office: 1815 Harrison Ave NW Canton OH 44708

PINKUS, CRAIG ELDON, lawyer; b. Indpls., Feb. 8, 1943; s. Seymour and Virginia M. (Schwartz) P.; A.B. magna cum laude, Butler U., 1965; J.D., Harvard U., 1968; 1 son, Aaron. Admitted to Ind. bar, 1968, U.S. Supreme Ct. bar, 1971; asso. firm Barnes, Hickam, Pantzer & Boyd, 1968-69; exec. dir. Ind. Civil Liberties Union, Indpls., 1969-71; chief counsel Legal Services Orgn., Indpls. Inc., 1971-72; partner firm King, Pinkus & Beeler, Indpls., 1972—; host, writer program Family and Consumer Law, Ind. Higher Edn. TV Service, 1974; chief counsel Marion County (Ind.) Prosecutor, 1976—; dir. Consol. Productions Inc. Mem. Am. (Silver Gavel award 1975), Ind., Indpls. bar assns., Bar Assn. of 7th Circuit. Democrat. Jewish. Club: Indpls. Athletic. Home: 1337 D Racquet Club N Dr Indianapolis IN 46260 Office: 1530 Market Square Center Indianapolis IN 46204

PINNELL, WILLIAM GEORGE, univ. ofcl.; b. Clarksburg, W.Va., Sept. 6, 1922; s. George Mason and Anna (Wagner) P.; A.B., W.Va. U., 1950, M.A., 1952; Dr. Bus. Adminstrn., Ind. U., 1954; m. Dortha Elizabeth Graham, June 25, 1946; 1 dau., Georgia Pinnell Stowe. Asst. dean Ind. U. Sch. Bus., 1954-56, became asso. dean, 1956, acting dean, 1959, dean Sch. Bus., 1963-71, v.p., treas., 1971-74, exec. v.p., 1974—, chmn. Grad. Sch. Savs. and Loan, 1958—; dir. Kroger Co., Bus. and Real Estate Trends, Inc., Bus. and Community Services, Inc.; trustee Am. Fletcher Mortgage Investors. Research dir. Ind. Post High Sch. Edn. Study Commn.; mem. Task Force on Area Redevel.; former mem. adv. com. Air Force Inst. Tech.; mem. exec. advisers Ind. Limestone Inst. Am. Former bd. dirs. Council for Internat. Progress in Mgmt., Ind. U. Found. Served to lt. (j.g.) USNR, 1942-47. Mem. Am., Midwest econ. assns., Am. Finance Assn., Ind. Acad. Social Scis. Am. Assn. Collegiate Schs. Bus. (chmn. standards com.), Internat. Bus. Edn. Assn., Midwest Bus. Adminstrn. Assn., Regional Sci. Assn., Beta Gamma Sigma, Beta Alpha Psi, Sigma Iota Epsilon, Alpha Kappa Psi. Methodist. Club: Bloomington Country (dir.). Author: An Analysis of the Economics Base of Evansville; co-author Case Study of a Depressed Area. Mem. editorial bd. Business Horizons, 1959—. Contbr. articles to profl. jours. Home: 2700 Pine Lane-Bittner Woods Bloomington IN 47401

PINSKY, MARK ALLAN, mathematician, educator; b. Phila., July 15, 1940; s. Harry A. and Helen V. (Marker) P.; B.A., Antioch Coll., 1962; Ph.D., Mass. Inst. Tech., 1966; m. Joanna K. Leff, Dec. 23, 1963; children—Seth, Jonathan, Lea. Instr., Stanford U., 1966-68; asst. prof. math. Northwestern U., Evanston, Ill., 1968-72, asso. prof., 1972-76, prof., 1976—, dir. Integrated Sci. Program, 1977—; prof. associe Universite Paris, Paris, 1972-73. Fellow Inst. for Math. Statistics; mem. Am. Math. Soc., Math. Assn. Am., AAUP. Home: 1223 Grant St Evanston IL 60201

PINSKY, STEVEN MICHAEL, radiologist, educator; b. Milw., Feb. 2, 1942; s. Leo Donald and Louise Miriam (Faldberg) P.; B.S., U. Wis., 1964; M.D., Loyola U., Chgo., 1967; m. Sue Brona Rosenzweig, June 12, 1966; children—Mark Burton, Lisa Rachel. Resident in radiology and nuclear medicine U. Chgo., 1968-70, chief resident in diagnostic radiology, 1970-71, asso. prof. radiology and medicine, 1973—; dir. nuclear medicine Michael Reese Med. Center, Chgo., 1973—; dir. nuclear medicine tech. program Triton Coll., River Grove, Ill., 1974—. Served to maj., M.C., U.S. Army, 1971-73. Am. Cancer Soc. research fellow, 1969-70. Mem. Am. Coll. Nuclear Physicians. (Ill. del.). Contbr. articles on nuclear medicine to med. jours. and chpts. to books. Home: 90 Ferndale St Deerfield IL 60015 Office: Michael Reese Med Center 2929 S Ellis Ave Chicago IL 60616

PINSOF, NATHAN, advt. agy. exec.; b. Havana, Cuba, July 16, 1926; s. Oscar and Rose (Newman) P.; came to U.S., 1928, naturalized, 1952; student City Jr. Coll., Chgo., 1944-46; M.B.A., U. Chgo., 1949; m. Barbara Cohn, Oct. 28, 1956; children—Ellen, Diane. Asst. controller Stineway Drugs, 1949-51; mgr. media dept. Weiss & Geller, 1953-60; sr. v.p., media dir. Edward H. Weiss & Co., 1960-67; v.p., mgr. media dept. J. Walter Thompson, 1967-69; exec. v.p., dir. media, adminstr. fin. Grey-North, Inc., Chgo., 1969—. Mem. pub. relations com. Jewish United Fund, 1968-71. Bd. dirs. Off the Street Club. Served with AUS, 1951-53. Mem. Broadcast Advt. Club, Mental Health Assn., Art Inst. Jewish (trustee congregation). Mem. B'nai B'rith. Home: 445 Sunset Lane Glencoe IL 60022 Office: Merchandise Mart Chicago IL 60654

PINTAR, MILAN MIK, physicist, educator; b. Celje, Yugoslavia, Jan. 17, 1934; s. Richard and Milena (Kovac) P.; B.Sc., U. Ljubljana, 1958, M.Sc., 1964, Ph.D., 1966; m. Sandra Dawn Burt, Nov. 7, 1974; children—Richard, Katarina. Research fellow Inst. J. Stefan, Ljubljana, 1957-66; postdoctoral fellow McMaster U., Hamilton, Ont., Can., 1966-67; asst. prof. physics U. Waterloo (Ont., Can.), 1967-69, asso. prof., 1969-75, prof., 1975—; chmn. Internat. Summer Sch. Nuclear Magnetic Resonance, 1969—; cons. Ont. Cancer Found. Recipient Nat. award Sci., B. Kidric, Ljubljana, 1965, Student Research award Presern, Ljubljana, 1956; NRC grantee, 1967—; NIH grantee, 1973-76; Med. Research Council grantee, 1973-74. Mem. Can. Assn. Physicists, Am. Phys. Soc., Ampere Soc. Editor: NMR Introductory Essays, 1976. Home: 134 Dunbar S Waterloo ON Canada Office: Dept Physics U Waterloo ON N2L 3G1 Canada

PINTO, MICHAEL, mech. and indsl. engring. exec.; b. Thomas, W.Va., May 4, 1909; s. Carmelo and Isabel (Duca) P.; student Potomac State Coll., 1929; B.S. in Mech. Engring., Lawrence Inst. Tech., Detroit, 1936, M. Mech. Engring., 1957; student Harvard Bus. Sch., 1958; m. Jenny L. Brackett, 1963; children—Michael Loren and Marla Louise. Tool and die maker Bower Roller Bearing Co., 1930-36, Briggs Mfg. Co., 1936-38, Motor Products Corp., 1938-39; insp. Packard Motor Co., 1939-40, Pioneer Engring. & Mfg. Co., Detroit, 1941-43, pres., treas., 1952—, chmn. bd., 1952-62. Registered profl. engr., Mich. Mem. Chief Execs. Forum (v.p. 1962), Young Pres. Orgn., Am. Soc. Mfg. Engrs. (chmn. Detroit chpt. 1953), Soc. Am. Value Engrs. (chmn. Detroit chpt. 1963), Nat. Inst. Indsl. Engrs., Am. Soc. Automotive Engrs., Engring. Soc. Detroit, Mich. Assn. Profl. Engrs., Am. Inst. Indsl. Engrs., Am. Soc. Body Engrs., N.A.M. Republican. Clubs: Plum Hollow Golf and Country (Detroit); Lost Lake Woods Country (Lincoln, Mich.). Home: 1195 Burnham Rd Bloomfield Hills MI 48013 Office: 2500 E Nine Mile Rd Warren MI 48091

PINZARRONE, PAUL F., artist; b. Grand Rapids, Mich., Nov. 19, 1951; s. Joseph J. and Theresa M. (Ferruggia) P.; B.F.A. with Highest Honors, U. Ill., 1973; m. Rebecca Downing, Dec. 27, 1975. One-man shows of paintings include: Gilman Galleries, Chgo., 1974, Joy Horwich Gallery, Chgo., 1975, 76, Louisville (Ky.) Art Center, 1975, Ill. Arts Council, Chgo., 1975, Gloria Luria Gallery, Miami, Fla., 1977; group shows include: Beloit (Wis.) Juried Exhbn., 1974, 75, 77, Ill. State Invitational Exhbn., Springfield, 1975, New Horizons Art, 1975, 76, Art Independent, Lake Geneva, Wis., 1977, Gloria Luria Gallery, 1977; represented in permanent collections: Ill. State Mus., Springfield, Kemper Ins. Collections, Long Grove, Ill., Butler Inst. Am. Art, Youngstown, Ohio, Container Corp., Ill. Address: 103 Paris St Rockford IL 61107

PIPER, WILLIAM ARCHIBALD, plastic surgeon; b. Montserrat, B.W.I., Apr. 13, 1935; s. Charles L. and Mildred L. P.; came to U.S., 1973; M.D., Dalhousie U., Can., 1966; M.S. in Surgery, McGill U., Can., 1969. Intern, Victoria Gen. Hosp., Halifax, N.S., Can., 1965-66; resident Montreal (Que., Can.) Gen. Hosp., McGill U. Teaching Hosp., 1967-72; practice medicine specializing in plastic surgery, Flint, Mich., 1974—; mem. staff Hurley Med. Centre, McLaren Hosp.; asst. prof. surgery Mich. State U. Fellow A.C.S., Royal Coll. Surgeons (Can.); mem. AMA, Mich. State Med. Soc., Mich. Acad. Plastic Surgery, Flint Acad. Surgery, Am. Assn. Plastic Surgery. Home: 1180 River Valley Dr Flint MI 48504 Office: 2710 W Court St Flint MI 48503

PIPITONE, PHYLLIS LUIS (MRS. S. JOSEPH PIPITONE), psychologist, educator; b. Chgo.; d. Max and Julia Antionette (Walkey) Luis; student Chgo. Conservatory Music, Chgo. Tchrs'. Coll., Peabody Conservatory Music, So. Meth. U.; B.A., U. Akron, M.A.; Ph.D. (NIMH grantee), Kent State U.; children—Guy, Daniel, Paul. Pvt. practice psychologist, Akron, Ohio, 1967-72; psychologist, instr. Kent (Ohio) State U., 1970—. Instr. piano and theory Music Acad., Chgo. Mem. Council for Exceptional Children, Am. Psychol. Assn., Am. Soc. Psychologists Assn., Am. Soc. for Psychical Research, Kent PSI Research Group, Mensa, Tuesday Mus. Club, Weathervane Theatre Women's Bd. Home: 560 Winslow Ave Akron OH 44313

PIRLOT, FRED, pub. relations exec.; b. Escanaba, Mich., Nov. 26, 1950; m. Fred and Rose Marie (Meyette) P.; B.S., No. Mich. U., 1972. Creative writer in comml. production for sta. WLUC-TV, Marquette, Mich., 1972-73, account exec., 1973-75; pub. relations dir. Selins Furniture Co., Marquette, Mich., 1975—; media cons. sta. WDMJ, 1976—. Recipient 2d pl. Nat. Retail Advertiser of Year, 1977. Mem. Am. Mktg. Assn., Phi Kappa Theta. Home: 912 Northland Dr Marquette MI 49855 Office: Selins Furniture Hwy US 41 West Marquette MI 49855

PIRRUNG, CLIFFORD MARK, brewery exec.; b. St. Louis, Dec. 7, 1950; s. Gilbert Robinson and Joan Dorothy Harrisson (Burgess) P.; B.A. cum laude, U. Va., 1973; postgrad. Washington U., St. Louis, nights 1974—. Media supr. Gardner Advt., St. Louis, 1974-77; asst. to v.p. mktg. Anheuser-Busch Inc., St. Louis, 1977—. Chmn. polo game Muscular Dystrophy, 1976, 77; vol. United Fund, 1977. Mem. Jacques Cousteau Soc., Assn. Nat. Advertisers. Clubs: Racquet of St. Louis; Little Harbor (Harbor Springs, Mich.). Home: 29 Westmoreland Pl St Louis MO 63108 Office: 2800 S 9th St St Louis MO 63118

PIRTLE, BARBARA BETHEA, counselor; b. Washington, July 28, 1947; d. Edwin Allen and Virginia Ann (Boyd) Bethea; B.A., Howard U., 1970, M.Ed., 1973; postgrad. St. Louis U., 1975—; m. James David Pirtle, July 23, 1973; 1 son, James David. Librarian, cataloger Library Congress, Washington, 1967-73, ednl. research, 1970-72, copywright examiner, 1972-73; counselor, instr. reading State Community Coll., East St. Louis, 1973—; asso. partner Psychol. Testing and Services, Inc., St. Louis, 1974—. Mem. Howard U. Alumni Club (pres. St. Louis 1976-77), Am. Personnel and Guidance Assn., Am. Coll. Personnel Assn., Assn. Non-White Concerns in Guidance and Counseling, AAUP, Am. Assn. Higher Edn. Adminstrn., Internat. Reading Assn., Mo. Personnel and Guidance Assn., Adult Student Personnel Assn., Am. Assn. Community and Jr. Colls., Alpha Kappa Alpha. Democrat. Episcopalian. Home: 1138 Birchgate Trail Ferguson MO 63135 Office: State Community Coll 417 Missouri Ave East St Louis IL 62201

PISANI, ALBERT LOUIS, pediatrician; b. Shamokin, Pa., Feb. 8, 1924; s. Louis and Catherine (Mirachi) P.; B.S. magna cum laude, Duquesne U., 1950; M.D., Loyola U., 1954; m. Ellen Marie Murry, Nov. 4, 1961; children—Albert Louis, James Andrew, Paul, Daniel. Intern, Cook County Hosp., Chgo., 1954-55; rotating resident Mercy Hosp., Chgo., Loyola U. Clinics, 1955-57; practice medicine specializing in pediatrics, Chgo., 1957—; cons. pediatrician Cook County Hosp.; mem. staff Hinsdale Sanitarium & Hosp., Community Meml. Hosp., LaGrange, Ill., Loyola U. Hosp.; clin. asso. prof. pediatrics U. Ill. Coll. Medicine, Loyola U. Served with AUS, 1943-46. Diplomate Am. Bd. Pediatrics. Fellow Am. Sch. Health Assn., Am. Acad. Pediatrics (pres. Ill. chpt.), Am. Pub. Health Assn., Am. Coll. Chest Physicians; mem. Ambulatory Pediatric Assn., AAAS, N.Y. Acad. Scis., Inst. Medicine, Chgo. Pediatric Soc. (past pres.), AMA, Duquesne Alumni Assn. (past pres. Chgo. chpt.). Roman Catholic. Clubs: Order Sons Italy, Moose. Contbr. articles in field to med. jours. Home: 430 69th St Darren IL 60559 Office: 40 S Clay St Hinsdale IL 60521

PISARCHICK, SALLY ELLEN, ednl. adminstr.; b. Pitts., Mar. 28, 1934; B.S. in Secondary Edn., Youngstown State U., 1965; M.S. Edn. Profession Devel. Act grantee, Kent State U., 1970, Ph.D., 1975; m. Regis Joseph Pisarchick, May 21, 1952; children—Tom, Darlene, Mark, Brad. Tchr. spl. edn. Springfield Local High Sch., Mahoning County, Ohio, 1962-69; instr. Youngstown State U., 1968-71; cons. supr. spl. edn. Columbiana County, Ohio, 1969-71; temporary instr.

Kent State U., 1971-73, teaching fellow, 1972-75; coordinator Instructional Resource Center, East of Cuyahoga Spl. Edn. Service Center, South Euclid, Ohio, 1973—; grant reader Bur. Edn. for Handicapped; adj. prof. Notre Dame Coll., Cleve.; instr. Case Western Res.U.; cons. in field. Mem. Council Exceptional Children (founder, pres. chpts. Columbiana County 1968, South Euclid 1974), Council Adminstrs. in Spl. Edn., Am. Guidance and Personnel Assn. Author tng. materials. Home: 13067 Cedar Rd Cleveland Heights OH 44118 Office: IRC-East 4300 Bayard Rd South Euclid OH 44121

PISCHKE, FRANK JOHN, otolaryngologist; b. Chgo., July 7, 1936; s. Frank Joseph and Edith Jeanette (Godar) P.; B.S., Rockhurst Coll., 1958; M.D., Kans. U., 1962; m. Elsa Mendez, Aug. 21, 1965; children—Mark, Andrew, Rebecca. Intern USPHS, Hosp., S.I., 1962-63; resident Kans. U. Med. Sch., 1965-69; practice medicine specializing in otolaryngology, Kansas City, Kans., 1969—; mem. staff Bethany Hosp., chief otolaryngology, 1970; mem. staff Providence-St. Margaret Hosps., asst. chief otolaryngology, 1970 (both Kansas City); instr. otolaryngology Kans. U. Med. Sch., 1969—. Served with USPHS, 1962-65. Fellow A.C.S.; mem. A.M.A. Home: Lake Quivira Kansas City KS 66106 Office: 255 Brotherhood Bldg Kansas City KS 66101

PISCOPO, JOSEPH ANTHONY, sci. co. exec.; b. Marysville, Calif., Sept. 1, 1944; s. John Michael and Marjorie Maxine (Sadler) P.; B.S., U. Ill., 1965; m. Mary Lou Vecchiollo, Nov. 29, 1969; children—Philip Joseph, Thomas Alan. Programmer U.S. Army Ammunition Plant, Joliet, Ill., 1965-66; lead programming mgr. Montgomery Ward & Co., Chgo., 1966-68; v.p. tech. research and devel. Consumer Systems Corp., Oak Brook, Ill., 1968-69; pres. Pansophic Systems Inc., Oak Brook, Ill., 1969—, also dir. Certificate in data processing. Mem. Software Industry Assn. (dir. 1971-73), Am. Mgmt. Assn., Data Processing Mgmt. Assn., Assn. Computing Machinery, Clubs: Execs. Chgo.; Butler Nat. (Oak Brook). Research software, computer sci. Office: 709 Enterprise Dr Oak Brook IL 60521

PISZCZEK, EDWARD ANDREW, physician; b. Peru, Ill., May 20, 1908; s. Andrew Henry and Louise (Kwiatek) P.; B.S., Loyola U., Chgo., 1931, M.D., 1933; M.P.H., Harvard U., 1939; m. Dorothy Bobrytzke, Aug. 22, 1936; children—Agnes Louise, Margaret Ann (Mrs. Thomas Kloempken), Mary Susan (Mrs. Larry McPartlin), Dorothy Judith (Mrs. James Caliendo). Intern, St. Anthony's Hosp., Chgo., 1932-33; resident Municipal Contagious Disease Hosp., Chgo. Health Dept., 1934, asst. med. supr., 1934-38, epidemiologist, syphilis and gonorrhea sect., 1939-40; dir. Cook County Dept. Pub. Health, 1940-49; field dir. Suburban Cook County Tb Sanitarium Dist., Forest Park, Ill., 1949—; practice medicine specializing in preventive medicine and pub. health, Cook County, Ill., 1934—; mem. staff Cook County, St. James, Columbus, McNeal hosps.; asst. prof. preventive medicine, acting chmn. dept. Loyola U. Stritch Sch. Medicine, 1941-48, asso. prof., chmn. dept., 1949-59, clin. prof., chmn., 1959-65, clin. prof., chief sect. on pub. health, 1966—; asso. prof. preventive medicine and community health U. Ill. Coll. Medicine, 1942—; clin. asso. prof. preventive medicine and community health Abraham Lincoln Sch. Medicine, U. Ill., Chgo., 1970—, clin. asso. prof. epidemiology Sch. Pub. Health, 1972—. Diplomate Am. Bd. Preventive Medicine. Fellow Am. Coll. Preventive Medicine, Am. Pub. Health Assn., Am. Acad. Pediatrics, Am. Coll. Chest Physicians; mem. AMA (chmn. Ill. del. 1975—, mem. council environ., occupational and pub. health 1974-76), Ill. (pres. 1964-65), Chgo. (exec. com. 1975—) med. assns., Ill. Pub. Health Assn. (sec.-treas. 1946-62, pres. 1947-48), Am. Coll. Preventive Medicine (sec.-treas. 1966-70), Assn. Tchrs. Preventive Medicine, Am. Thoracic Soc., Inst. Medicine of Chgo. Home: 6410 N Leona Ave Chicago IL 60646 Office: 7556 W Jackson Blvd Forest Park IL 60130

PITCHER, ROBERT WALTER, educator; b. Grand Rapids, Mich., Oct. 26, 1918; s. Harry Lewis and Mable Louise (Morrison) P.; A.B. summa cum laude, Alma Coll., 1946; M.R.E., No. Bapt. Sem., 1949; Ph.D., U. Mich., 1953; m. Adretta Katherine Atchinson, Aug. 21, 1943; children—James Robert, Judith Kay (Mrs. William J. Gelvin). Asst. prof. psychology Baldwin Wallace Coll., Berea, Ohio, 1952-56, asso. prof., 1956-64, prof., 1964—, chmn. dept. psychology, 1955-59, 77—, dean students, 1959-66, v.p. student affairs, 1966-69, dir. ednl. devel. center, 1963—; dir. Cleve. Cons., Council Advancement Small Colls. Mem. Am. Psychol. Assn., Am. Personnel and Guidance Assn. Methodist. Author: (with Babette Blaushild) Why College Students Fail, 1970. Home: 55 Barrett Rd Apt 437 Berea OH 44017

PITCHFORD, WILLIAM MYRON, photographer; b. Berkeley, Calif., Sept. 8, 1912; s. Harold Ivan and Gladys Ogier (Stanford) P.; student U. Calif., 1930-31, U. Calif. at Berkeley, 1931, U. Mo., 1968-69; children—Stanford, Dean, James, Patricia. Chief photographer research dept. Dole Corp., Hawaii, 1943-62; chief photographer and photo coordinator Hawaii Press Newspapers, Honolulu, 1963; regional photographer FAA Central Region, Kansas City, Mo., 1964-72, Great Lakes Region, Des Plaines, 1972—; lectr. photography U. Hawaii, 1955-58. Served with USNR, 1941-44. Recipient Gold medal Photographers Hawaii, 1954. Mem. Soc. Photog. Scientists and Engrs., Photog. Soc. Am. (Service medal 1956), Profl. Photographers Assn. Am. (elector Photog. Hall Fame 1975), Kansas City Profl. Photographers Assn. Contbr. photographs to Cleared to Land, The FAA Story (Frank Burnham), 1977, also to profl. jours. and popular mags. Home: 936M Jefferson Sq Elk Grove IL 60007 Office: FAA 2300 E Devon Ave Des Plaines IL 60018

PITT, GEORGE, lawyer; b. Chgo., July 21, 1938; s. Cornelius George and Anastasia (Geocaris) P.; B.A., Northwestern U., 1960, J.D., 1963; m. Barbara Lynn Goodrich, Dec. 21, 1963; children—Elizabeth Nanette, Margaret Leigh. Admitted to Ill. bar, 1963; asso. firm Chapman and Cutler, Chgo., 1963-67; partner firm Borge, Leiter & Pitt, 1968-69, Borge and Pitt, 1969—. Served to 1st lt. AUS, 1964. Mem. Am., Ill., Chgo. bar assns., Phi Delta Phi, Phi Gamma Delta. Home: 872 Burr Ave Winnetka IL 60093 Office: 120 S LaSalle St Chicago IL 60603

PITTS, JAMES WILLIAM, coll. adminstr.; b. East St. Louis, Ill., Aug. 7, 1941; s. James D. and Alene F. (Gerstenecker) P.; B.A., McKendree Coll., 1964; M.Ed., U. Ill., 1967; postgrad. So. Ill. U., 1971-75, U. Minn., 1972, U. Ind., 1974—; m. Patricia L. Hefferly, May 2, 1964; children—Laura Lee, Lisa Kay, Leslie Marie. Tchr., Waterloo (Ill.) High Sch., 1964-67; asst. provost Black Hawk Coll., Kewanee, Ill., 1967-71; dir. student activities Lewis and Clark Community Coll., Godfrey, Ill., 1971—. Mem. Ill. Coll. Personnel Assn., U. Ill. Alumni Assn., Sportsman's Club, Phi Delta Kappa. Home: 5216 Shannon Dr Godfrey IL 62035 Office: Godfrey Rd Godfrey IL 62035

PITZER, ERRINGTON ELWOOD, dentist; b. Cooksville, Ill., Oct. 15, 1911; s. Errett Swiney and Essie Matilda (Williams) P.; student Ill. Wesleyan U., 1930-34, U. Ill., 1935-37; D.D.S., Loyola U., 1944; m. Opal Irene Hotchkiss, Dec. 17, 1938; children—John Errett, James Errington. Pvt. practice dentistry, Decatur, Ill., 1947—. Served with AUS, 1943-46. Mem. Blue Key, Gideons Internat., Delta Sigma Delta, Omicron Kappa Upsilon, Acacia. Presbyterian. Club: Masons (32 deg.). Home: 228 N Woodlawn St Decatur IL 62522 Office: 1349 N Jasper St Decatur IL 62521

PIZER, IRWIN HOWARD, librarian, educator; b. Wellington, New Zealand, Oct. 16, 1934; s. Harry and Cecelia (Cohen) P. (parents Am. citizens); B.S., Antioch Coll., 1957; M.S., Columbia U., 1960. Librarian, asso. prof. med. history Upstate Med. Center, State U. N.Y., Syracuse, 1964-69, dir. biomed. communication network, 1966-70; asso. dir. libraries, State U. N.Y., Buffalo, 1969-71; univ. librarian, prof. library adminstrn. U. Ill. Med. Center, Chgo., 1971—. Bd. dirs. Ranch Triangle Conservation Assn., Chgo., 1971-74, pres. 1973; bd. dirs. Lincoln Park Conservation Assn., 1972-73. Mem. Med. Library Assn. (Murray Gottlieb prize 1964, continuing edn. com. 1963-66, sr. adviser 1967-68, mem. goals and structure com. 1969-73, dir. 1975-78), Spl. Libraries Assn., Upstate N.Y.-Ont. Med. Library Assn. (hon.), Sigma Xi. Contbr. articles to profl. jours. Home: 1875 N Fremont St Chicago IL 60614 Office: 1750 W Polk St Chicago IL 60612

PLACK, HAROLD JOSEPH, III, museum adminstr.; b. Peoria, Ill., Dec. 25, 1948; s. Harold Joseph and Bettie Jean (Delong) P.; B.S., Ill. State U., 1970; M.B.A., Roosevelt U., 1976; m. Katha B. Fahey, Aug. 1, 1970. Program adminstr. Ill. State U., Normal, 1970; adminstrv. mgr. U.S. Govt., Fort Sheridan, Ill., 1972-74; asst. to v.p. adminstrv. affairs Art Inst. Chgo., 1974—. Served with U.S. Army, 1970-72. Mem. Sports Hall of Fame Ill. State U., 1976. Mem. Ill. High Sch. Ofcls. Assn., Restaurant Food Buyers Assn. (dir. Chgo.), Nat. Assn. Accountants, Inst. Internal Auditors, Amateur Athletic Union. Lutheran. Clubs: Lions. Home: 412 Cumnor Ct Deerfield IL 60015 Office: Art Institute Michigan at Adams Sts Chicago IL 60603

PLANK, RAYMOND, corp. exec.; b. Mpls., May 29, 1922; s. Raby and Maude (Howe) P.; B.A., Yale U., 1944; m. Louise Benz Cobb, Mar. 19, 1976; children by previous marriage—Katherine, Michael, Pamela, Roger, Dana. Founder, partner Plank and Somekawa, accounting, Mpls., 1946-53; founder, pres., chief exec. officer Apache Corp., 1954—; dir. St. Paul Cos., Questor Corp., Fabri-Tek, Inc. Bd. dirs. Boys' Clubs Mpls., 1960—; trustee U. Minn. Found., 1971—, Carleton Coll., Northfield, Minn. Served to 1st lt. USAAF, 1943-46. Clubs: Mpls., Woodhill (Minn.) Country. Home: 550 E Long Lake Rd Wayzata MN 55391 Office: Foshay Tower Minneapolis MN 55402

PLANT, MARCUS LEO, educator; b. New London, Wis., Nov. 10, 1911; s. George Henry and Margaret (McGinty) P.; B.A., Lawrence Coll., 1932, M.A., 1934; J.D., U. Mich., 1938; m. Geraldine Hefter, Dec. 27, 1944; children—Margaret Ann, Elizabeth, Mark, Nancy. Admitted to Wis. bar, 1939, N.Y. bar, 1946, Mich. bar, 1949; pvt. practice Miller, Mack & Fairchild, Milw., 1938-44, Cahill, Gordon, Zachry & Reindel, N.Y.C., 1944-46; prof. law U. Mich., 1946—. Rep. of U. Mich. in Intercollegiate Conf. of Faculty Reps., 1955—, sec., 1956—; mem. U.S. Olympic Com., 1969-72; trustee Lawrence U., 1972—. Mem. Nat. Collegiate Athletic Assn. (pres. 1967-69), Delta Tau Delta, Order of Coif, Tau Kappa Alpha. Author: Cases on the Law of Torts, 1953; (with Burke Shartel) The Law of Medical Practice, 1959; (with Wex S. Malone) Cases and Materials on Workmen's Compensation, 1963; (with W.S. Malone, Joseph W. Little) Cases and Materials on the Employment Relation, 1974. Home: 2311 Woodside St Ann Arbor MI 48104

PLANTE, JULIAN GERARD, educator; b. St. Paul; s. Roland Joseph and Marion Magdalen (Herold) P.; M.A., Fordham U., 1963, Ph.D., 1972. Asst. to pres. Elmer R. Davis & Assos. mgmt. cons., N.Y.C., 1964-66; asst. prof. classics City Coll., City U. N.Y., 1964-66; research prof. classics, dir. Hill Monastic Manuscript Library, St. John's U., Collegeville, Minn., 1966—; guest prof. Manchester Coll. (Ind.), 1972; cons. reorgn. library Augustinian Hist. Inst., N.Y.C., 1967-68. Decorated Lalibela cross Patriarch Ethiopian Orthodox Ch., 1973. Mem. Minn. (exec. bd. 1971-74), St. Cloud Area geneal socs., Stearns County (Minn.) Hist. Soc., AAUP, Am. Philol. Assn., Mediaeval Acad. Am., Vergilian Soc., Am. Papyrological Soc., Conseil Internat des Archives, Soc. Internat. des Papyrologistes. Club: Moose. Contbr. articles to profl. jours. Home: 111 Park Ave S Saint Cloud MN 56301 Office: Hill Monastic Manuscript Library Saint Johns U Collegeville MN 56321

PLANTINGA, ALVIN CARL, educator; b. Ann Arbor, Mich., Nov. 15, 1932; s. Cornelius A. and Lettie G. (Bossenbroek) P.; A.B., Calvin Coll., 1954; A.M., U. Mich., 1955; Ph.D., Yale, 1958; m. Kathleen Ann DeBoer, June 16, 1955; children—Carl, Jane, Harry, Ann. Instr., Yale, 1957-58; asst. prof. Wayne State U., Detroit, 1958-60, asso. prof., 1960-63; prof. philosophy Calvin Coll., 1963—; adj. prof. U. Notre Dame, 1973—; vis. prof. Harvard, 1963-64, U. Calif. at Los Angeles, 1972, Boston U., 1970, U. Ind., 1971. Lectr., Council for Philos. Studies Summer Inst., 1968, 73; dir. Nat. Endowment for Humanities Summer Seminar, 1974, 75. Guggenheim fellow, 1971-72; fellow Center for Advanced Study in the Behavioral Scis., 1968-69; sr. fellow Nat. Endowment for Humanities, 1975-76; vis. fellow Balliol Coll., Oxford (Eng.) U., 1975-76. recipient E. Harris Harbison award Danforth Found., 1968. Fellow Am. Acad. Arts and Scis. Mem. Christian Ref. Ch. Author: God and Other Minds, 1967; The Nature of Necessity, 1974; God, Freedom and Evil, 1974. Home: 2200 Heather St Grand Rapids MI 49506 Office: Calvin Coll Grand Rapids MI 49506

PLASS, HERBERT FITZ RANDOLPH, internist; b. Newark, July 17, 1912; s. Herbert Edmond and Rae Fitz (Randolph) P.; S.B., Mass. Inst. Tech., 1934, S.M., 1935; M.D., Harvard U., 1939; m. Beverly Wright, Dec. 28, 1974; children—Penelope Jean, Edward Fitz Randolph. Intern, House Good Samaritan, Boston, 1939, U.S. Marine Hosp., Boston, 1939-40, Lakeside Hosp., Cleve., 1940-41; resident Pratt Diagnostic Hosp., Boston, 1941-42, U. Minn. Hosp., 1945-46; practice medicine specializing in internal medicine, Mpls., 1947—; mem. staff Abbott, Northwestern, Hennepin County Gen., U. Minn. hosps., Mpls.; clin. prof. internal medicine U. Minn., 1973—. Served with USAAF, 1942-46; ETO. Diplomate Am. Bd. Internal Medicine. Fellow A.C.P., Am. Coll. Chest Physicians, Royal Soc. Health; mem. AAAS, AAUP, Minn. (exec. com. 1957-59), Mpls. acads. medicine, Minn., Mpls. (pres. 1952-53) socs. internal medicine, Hennepin County (pres. 1954-55), Minn. (chmn. med. service com. 1955-56) med. socs. Club: Mpls. Contbr. articles to profl. jours. Home: 1916 Knox Ave S Minneapolis MN 55403 Office: Med Arts Bldg Minneapolis MN 55402

PLATT, BRAINARD WINDELL, newspaper columnist, editor; b. Louisville, Jan. 19, 1913; s. Brainard and Rachael (Heffernan) P.; student Hanover Coll., 1931-32, U. Louisville, 1932-33; m. Jane Rice Young, Oct. 21, 1933; children—Brainard, Stephen Young. Courthouse reporter, polit. writer, rewrite man Louisville Courier-Jour., 1933-43; editorial writer, sports editor Dayton (Ohio) Jour., 1943-45; pub. relations Nat. Cash Register Co., Dayton, 1945-47; newspaper columnist, bus. editor Dayton Jour. Herald, 1947—. Club: Walnut Grove Country; Am. Business. Home: 1317 Robert Dickey Pkwy Dayton OH 45409 Office: 4th and Ludlow Sts Dayton OH 45401

PLATT, DORIS HUBBARD, historian; b. Elgin, Ill., Aug. 14, 1914; d. Frank James and Georgia May (Hubbard) Platt; B.A., Beloit (Wis.) Coll., 1935; M.A., U. Wis., 1945, Ph.D., 1947. Ad writer Chgo. Daily News, 1935-37; tchr. French and English Mooseheart (Ill.) High Sch., 1937-41; tchr. Freeport (Ill.) High Sch., 1941-44; instr. English U. Wis., 1947-48; research asso. State Hist. Soc. Wis., Madison, 1948-55, editor Badger History mag., 1955-62, dir. sch. services, radio and TV coordinator, 1961-65, supr. mus. edn., 1965—, curator of interpretation, 1978. Recipient Golden Mike award, 1976. Mem. Am. Assn. State and Local History, Wis. Council for Social Studies (v.p. 1973-77), Nat. Assn. Ednl. Broadcasters, State Hist. Soc. Wis., Am. Hist. Assn., Orgn. Am. Historians, Am., Wis. councils for better broadcasts; Wis. Acad. Sci. Arts and Letters, Nat., Madison (sec. v.p. 1972-74) audubon socs., Internat. Crane Found. Democrat. Mem. United Ch. of Christ. Author: Wisconsin Reader, 1960; Wisconsin, A Student's Guide to Localized History, 1965; contbr. articles in field to profl. jours. Home: 4723 Sheboygan Ave Madison WI 53705 Office: 816 State St Madison WI 53706

PLATT, GEORGE JARVIS, elec. products co. exec.; b. Manitowoc, Wis., June 4, 1912; s. Edward Marcellus and Alida King (Hoskinson) P.; student Mass. Inst. Tech., 1931-32; m. Constance Crafts, Jan. 7, 1939 (div. 1943); 1 son, George C.; m. 2d, B. Dorcas Cameron, May 23, 1945; children—Dorcas Platt Wagenknecht, Cameron K., Robert L., Barbara T. With Paragon Electric Co., Manitowoc, 1932—, plant mgr., v.p., dir., 1946-59, pres., 1959-61 (name changed to Paragon Electric Co., Inc. div. Am. Machine & Foundry, 1961), pres., 1961-69, chmn., 1970—; dir. First Nat. Bank, Gen. Telephone Co. of Wis., Aluminum Specialty Co., Lapcor Plastics, Uni-Trol, Inc., Manitowoc Motor Hotel. Bd. dirs., pres. Meml. Hosp., Manitowoc. Mem. Northeast Wis. Indsl. Assn. (dir., pres. 1955-71), Power Squadron, Coast Guard Aux., Delta Tau Delta. Episcopalian (exec. bd. 1954-55, conv. del. 1955). Clubs: Masons, Shriners, Rotary, Elks; Sturgeon Bay Yacht, Branch River Country. Home: 601 N 6th St Manitowoc WI 54220 Office: 1600 12th St Two Rivers WI 54241

PLAXTON, KENNETH DEAN, lawyer; b. Port Huron, Mich., July 29, 1921; s. Harry A. and Elizabeth E. (Reid) P.; student U. N.D., 1943; A.B., Alma Coll., 1947; J.D., U. Mich., 1948; m. Katherine F. Peshke, Mar. 6, 1945; children—Thomas S., Janet K. Admitted to Mich. bar, 1948; partner Netzorg & Plaxton, Alma, 1948-59, Fortino, Plaxton & Moskal, 1959—; dir. Whitman Industries, Inc.; asso. prof. speech Alma Coll., 1969-73; pros. atty. Gratiot County (Mich.), 1951-56; city atty. Alma, 1959—. Mem. Alma Pub. Schs. Bd., 1966-71; trustee Alma Coll. Served with USAAF, 1941-46. Mem. Mich. Bar Assn. (chmn. criminal jurisprudence com. 1954-56). Presbyterian (elder 1960—). Republican. Clubs: Masons, Kiwanis (pres. 1954). Home: 1060 Riverview Dr Alma MI 48801 Office 175 Warwick Dr Alma MI 48801

PLAYE, MARGARET L. BERG (MRS. GEORGE L. PLAYE), educator; b. Pitts.; d. Ragnar and Margaret (Peacock) Berg; A.B., U. Pitts., 1940, M.Lett., 1942; postgrad. McGill U., summer 1941, U. Ill., 1942-46; m. George L. Playe, July 9, 1943; children—Marcia Gail (Mrs. Stephen Jon Bittner), Stephen Jan. Instr. French, Geneva Coll., Beaver Falls, Pa., 1940-42; grad. asst. U. Ill., Urbana, 1942-46; lectr. French, Calumet Center of Ind. U., East Chicago, 1953-61; instr. French, N.W. Campus Ind. U., Gary, 1961-66, asst. prof., 1966-73, asso. prof. French, 1973—, chmn. dept., 1966-71, chmn. dept. modern langs., comparative lit. and linguistics, 1971—. Mem. Am. Assn. Tchrs. French, Modern Lang. Assn., Ind. Fgn. Lang. Tchrs. Assn., N.W. Ind. Lang. Assn., AAUP. Home: 18233 Center Ave Homewood IL 60430 Office: 3400 Broadway Gary IN 46408

PLETCHER, DAVID MITCHELL, historian, educator; b. Faribault, Minn., June 14, 1920; s. Nuba Mitchel and Jean (Hutchinson) P.; B.A., U. Chgo., 1941, M.A., 1941, Ph.D., 1946. Asst., U. Chgo., 1943; instr. history U. Iowa, 1944-46; asso. prof. history Knox Coll., Galesburg, Ill., 1946-56; asso. prof. Hamline U., St. Paul, 1956-63, prof., 1963-65; prof. history Ind. U., 1965—. Recipient Albert J. Beveridge award, 1957; McKnight Found. award, 1962; Social Science Research Found. grantee, 1950-51, 62-63; Nat. Archives Research grantee, 1972; Fulbright Sr. Research fellow, 1953-54. Mem. Am. Hist. Assn., Soc. for Historians of Am. Fgn. Relations. Author: Rails, Mines, and Progress, Seven American Promoters in Mexico, 1867-1911, 1958; The Awkward Years, American Foreign Relations under Garfield and Arthur, 1962; The Diplomacy of Annexation, Tex., Oreg., and the Mexican War, 1973. Home: 509 N Fess Ave Bloomington IN 47401 Office: Dept History Ballantine Hall Ind U Bloomington IN 47401

PLETCHER, KENNETH E., physician, ret. air force officer, ins. co. exec.; b. Pacific, Mo., Nov. 26, 1909; s. John W. and Blanch (Close) P.; A.B., Central Methodist Coll., 1932; M.D. cum laude, Washington U., St. Louis, 1936; m. Muzette Martin, Dec. 23, 1932; children—Peggy, Suzanne, John. Intern, St. Lukes Hosp., St. Louis, 1936-37, resident, 1937-39; commd. 1st lt. U.S. Air Force, 1939, advanced through grades to lt. gen., 1967; asst. air attache, London, 1950-54; surgeon SAC, 1965-66; surgeon gen., Washington, 1967-70, ret., 1970; v.p., asso. med. dir. Mut. of Omaha Ins. Co., 1970—. Decorated D.S.M., Legion of Merit with oak leaf cluster, Air Force Cross with oak leaf cluster; diplomate Am. Bd. Preventive Medicine. Fellow Am. Coll. Physicians, Am. Coll. Preventive Medicine, Am. Coll. Chest Physicians, Aerospace Med. Assn.; mem. AMA, Nebr. Med. Assn. Clubs: Met. (Washington); Masons. Home: 505 Martin Dr Bellevue NE 68005 Office: 33d and Dodge Sts Omaha NE 68131

PLINKE, JOHN FREDERICK, educator; b. Lancaster, Ohio, Sept. 19, 1927; s. George Walter and Mary M. (Dyson) P.; B.S., Bowling Green State U., 1950; M.Ed., Kent State U., 1955; D.Phys. Edn., Ind. U., 1966; m. Barbara Anne Israel, Aug. 17, 1952; children—Kristen Diane, Kurt Frederick, Gretchen Louise, Eric John. Coach, Brush High Sch., South Euclid, Ohio, 1950-56, Lancaster High Sch., 1956-62; instr. Ohio U., 1962-63; teaching asso., fencing coach Ind. U., 1963-65; prof. phys. edn., basketball coach Wis. State U., Whitewater, 1965-71; athletic dir., chmn. dept. phys. edn. Capital U., Columbus, Ohio, 1971-77; chmn. health, phys. edn. and recreation Wilmington (Ohio) Coll., 1977—. Served with AUS, 1946-47. Mem. AAHPER, Nat. Coll. Phys. Edn. Assn., Nat. Assn. Basketball Coaches, Book and Motor, Sigma Chi, Omicron Delta Kappa, Phi Delta Kappa, Phi Epsilon Kappa. Club: Kiwanis (pres. 1959-61). Home: 783 Mitchell Rd Wilmington OH 45177

PLODZIEN, RICHARD JOHN, personnel cons. co. exec.; b. St. Louis, Aug. 6, 1947; s. Joseph Frank and Evelyn Margaret (Bailey) P.; student Florissant Valley Community Coll., St. Louis, 1966-70, So. Ill. U., 1970-71. Prodn. control planner Reynolds Metals Co. div. Reynolds Aluminum Corp., St. Louis, 1966-69; cons. firm J. C. Bonner & Assos., St. Louis, 1969-70; exec. v.p. Profl. Career Devel. Inc. St. Louis and Kansas City, 1970—, also dir.; dir. Cycle Shoppes Ltd. Mem. Nat. Assn. Accountants (vol. cons. for minority bus.), Lake St. Louis Community Assn., Data Processing Mgmt. Assn., Am. Accounting Assn. Roman Catholic. Clubs: K.C., Quarterback. Home: 6567 W Foxridge Dr Shawnee Mission KS 66202 Office: Profl Career Devel Inc 7777 Bonhomme Saint Louis MO 63105

PLOESER, WALTER CHRISTIAN, ins. cons., diplomat; b. St. Louis, Jan. 7, 1907; s. Christian D. and Maud Elizabeth (Parr) P.; student City Coll. of Law and Fin., St. Louis; LL.D., Norwich U., 1948; Dr. hon. causa, Nat. U. Asuncion, Paraguay; m. Dorothy Annette Mohrig, Aug. 17, 1928; children—Ann Ploeser Bergan, Sally Ploeser Chapel III. In ins. bus., St. Louis, 1922—; founder firm

Ploeser, Watts & Co., 1933, organized subs. Marine Underwriters Corp., 1935, former pres.; now cons.; founder Ins. Inst. Mo., 1938, pres., 1938-40; past pres. Grant, Ploeser & Assos., Inc., nat. and internat. pub. relations, offices in Mexico City, Washington, St. Louis, South Bend, Ind.; pres. Walter C. Ploeser Co.; dir. Webster Groves Trust Co.; U.S. ambassador to Republic of Paraguay, 1957-59; ambassador to Costa Rica, 1970-72. Mem. Mo. Legislature, 1931-32; chmn. 5th dist. com. fin. and budget Rep. Nat. program Com., 1937-39; mem. 77th, 78th, 79th and 80th Congresses from 12th Mo. dist.; mem. appropriations com., Rep. steering com., chmn. select com. on small bus. chmn. subcom. on govt. corps.; mem. econ. adv. com. U.S. Senate com. on banking and currency, 1953-54; Rep. nat. committeeman for Mo., 1964-66; chmn. bd. Salvation Army, 1967-70; trustee Shriners Hosp. for Crippled Children, St. Louis, Scottish Rite Found.; Mo. DeMolay Ednl. Fund; chmn. Scottish Towers Residence Found. Recipient Nat. Religious award Ams. United, 1976; Freedoms Found. award, 1949; decorated Grand Cross Republic of Paraguay, 1959. Mem. Miss. Valley Assn. (pres. 1955, chmn. bd. 1956) DeMolay Legion of Honor, Ins. Bd. St. Louis, St. Louis C. of C. (chmn. nat. affairs com. 1964-66), C. of C. Met. St. Louis (dir.). Republican. Clubs: Masons (33 deg.), Shriners; Order of DeMolay (supreme council, grand master internat. 1952; Sovereign grand insp. gen. Scottish Rite in Mo.); Mo. Athletic, St. Louis Triple A Golf (dir.). Home: 275 Union Blvd Saint Louis MO 63108 Office: 3633 Lindell Blvd Saint Louis MO 63108

PLOTNICK, HAROLD, dermatologist; b. Detroit, Aug. 14, 1925; s. Myer M. and Freda (Willis) P.; A.B., Dartmouth Coll., 1946; M.D., Wayne U., 1949; m. Evelyn Weisberg, Sept. 3, 1961. Intern, Cin. Jewish Hosp., 1949-50, resident pathology, 1950-51; resident dermatology Cin. Gen. Hosp., 1953-56; practice medicine specializing in dermatology, Detroit, 1957—; mem. staff Harper, Sinai, Detroit Meml., Detroit Gen. hosps.; asso. prof. dermatology Wayne State U., 1971. Served with USAF, 1951-53. Mem. Mich. Dermatol. Soc. (pres. 1972-73), Noah Worcester Dermatol. Soc. (sec.-treas. 1971-76, pres. 1977-78). Author: Clinical Dermatology, 1972. Home: 31960 Mountain View Ln Franklin MI 48025 Office: 1150 David Whitney Bldg Detroit MI 48226

PLUCKER, ORVIN LOWELL, supt. schs.; b. Emery, S.D., July 18, 1922; s. John E. and Johannah (Olthoff) P.; student Sioux Falls Coll., 1940-41; B.A. cum laude, Augustana Coll., 1943; M.Ed., U. S.D., 1948; Ed.D., U. Colo., 1951; m. Mavis Appleton, Mar. 3, 1945; 1 dau., Mary Kathryn. Tchr. pub. schs., Alexandria, S.D., 1943-44, Canton, S.D., 1944-48; dir. curriculum pub. schs., Yankton, S.D., 1948-49; instr. U. Colo., Boulder, 1949-51; dir. instrn., Independence, Mo., 1951-54, supt. schs., 1954-62; pres. Kansas City (Kans.) Jr. Coll., 1962-66; supt. schs., Kansas City, Kans., 1962—; educator in residence U. Kans., 1973; dir. Anchor Savs. & Loan Co., Kansas City, Kans. Bd. dirs. Mid-continent Ednl. Lab., Kansas City, Mo., 1965—, v.p., 1967, pres., 1968—; mem. Kan. Gov.'s Commn. Sch. Finance, 1968; bd. dirs., exec. com. West Central Area YMCA, Kansas City, Kans., pres., 1964, sec., 1966-69; dir., v.p. YMCA of Rockies, Estes Park, Colo.; bd. dirs. Mid-Am. region YMCA; bd. dirs. Urban League, Kansas City, Mo., Sci. Fair, Kansas City, Mo., Heart Assn., Kansas City, Kans., United Fund, Kansas City, Kans., Central Bapt. Sem., Kansas City, Kans. Recipient Distinguished Service award Jr. C. of C., Independence, Mo., 1958; YMCA Distinguished Service award, 1964, Man of Year award, 1972. Mem. C. of C. (dir. 1976-79), Am. Assn. Sch. Adminstrs., Kans. Assn. Sch. Adminstrs. (dir.), Wyandotte County Council Govts. (founder, pres. 1967—), Met. Sch. Supts. Assn. Kansas City (charter mem. bd. dirs.), United Sch. Adminstrs. of Kans. (dir. 1970—, pres. 1973-74), Horace Mann League, Kans. Sch. Masters (pres. 1973-74), Conf. Sch. Supts. in Cities with Populations over 100,000 (chmn. exec. com. 1976—), Phi Delta Kappa. Baptist (deacon). Clubs: Masons (32 deg.), Shriners, Rotary (pres. Kansas City 1968-69, dir. 1968—; chmn. internat. group study exchange com. 1967-69). Home: 2235 Washington Blvd Kansas City KS 66102 Office: 625 Minnesota St Kansas City KS 66101

PLUGGE, DALE LAVERN, mech. engr.; b. Columbus, Nebr., Nov. 29, 1928; s. Alfred and Mathilda (Korte) P.; B.S., U. Nebr., 1951; m. Betty Ann White, Dec. 29, 1952; children—Julie Ann, Greg Lavern. Mech. engr. Fleischer-Schmid Corp., Columbus, Nebr., 1949-50; co-owner Overland Constrn. Co., Columbus, 1951-58; project engr. Behlen Mfg. Co., Columbus, 1951-59, chief mech. engr., 1960-68, engring. mgr., 1968-71; sec.-treas. Evans-Plugge Co., Inc., Columbus, 1957-71, pres., 1971—; dir., pres. Westside Indsl. Corp., Columbus, 1969—, Tran-Tec Corp., Columbus, 1971—; dir. TLC Ednl. Corp. (KTLX) Radio. Registered profl. engr. Mem. ASME, Am. Soc. Agrl. Engrs., Soc. Plastics Engrs., IEEE, Nat. Soc. Profl. Engrs. Lutheran. Elk. Patentee in field. Home: 1920 28th St Columbus NE 68601 Office: Box 1044 Columbus NE 68601

PLUMB, JOSEPH CHARLES, JR., lectr., author; b. Gary, Ind., Nov. 3, 1942; s. Joseph Charles and Margery Ruth (Stanford) P.; B.S. in Engring., U.S. Naval Acad., 1964; m. Patrica Anne Swarts, July 1, 1977. Commd. ensign, U.S. Navy, 1960, advanced through grades to lt. comdr., 1972; mem. fighter squadron, S.E. Asia, 1966-67; prisoner N. Vietnam, 1967-73, res., 1974—; lectr., 1973—; pres. Inform, Inc., Mission, Kans., 1974—, Globemaster Travel, Mission, 1975—. Chmn. Kans. Cerebral Palsy Fund, 1975; chmn. Vets. for Ford/Dole Campaign, 1976—; mem. Citizens Advisory Bd. for Kans., 1976. Decorated Silver Star, Bronze Star, Purple Heart, Air Medal, Navy Commendation Medal; named Distinguished Citizen, Boy Scouts Am., 1975. Mem. Nat. Speakers Assn., DAV, Antique Aircraft Assn. Author: I'm No Hero, 1973; The Last Domino, 1975; Stand Up Speak Out and Win, 1977. Contbr. articles to mags. Office: 6950 W 105th St Overland Park KS 66212

PLUMMER, ROBERT EUGENE, data processing exec.; b. Perry, Kans., Nov. 26, 1928; s. Maurice Robert and Dorothy Lucille (McNerney) P.; student U. Kans., 1946, Washburn U., 1948-49; m. Nancy ops. Mar. 11, 1960; children—Jennie Colleen, Mary Elizabeth. Adminstrv. asst. doctor-hosp. relations Kans. Blue Cross—Blue Shield, Topeka, 1953-67; v.p. EDP, Security Benefit Life Ins., Topeka, 1967—. Dir. Shawnee County (Kan.) Farm Bur., 1971-74. Served with USAF, 1949-52. Mem. EDP Mgmt. Assn. (dir. 1969-70, sec. Kaw Valley chpt. 1971-72), Assn. Systems Mgmt., Am. Angus Assn., 1976—. Asso. Topeka, Phi Delta Theta. Republican. Methodist. Clubs: Capital City Rifle Pistol (pres.), Johnson County Outdoor Soc., Shawnee Yacht, Bass Anglers Sportsman Soc., Kans. Profl. Bass Anglers, Kans. Trails Council. Home: 8141 SE 29th St Tecumseh KS 66542 Office: 700 Harrison St Topeka Ave 66603

PLUNKETT, CHARLES WALTER, ry. exec.; b. Franks, Mo., May 2, 1926; s. Charley Amos and Ethel M. (Rockey) P.; grad. high sch. With Rock Island R.R., Chgo., 1943-58, supr. signal dept., 1959-62; ops. mgr., sales engr. Matisa Equipment Corp., Chicago Heights, Ill., 1962-67; asst. chief engr. Mo. Pacific R.R., St. Louis, 1967-68; gen. mgr. sales Jackson Vibrators, Inc., Chgo., 1969-70, v.p. r.r. sales, 1970, exec. v.p. r.r. products, 1970—; owner, pres. Comml. Quality Feed Center, Lebanon, Mo., 1970—; pres. Comml. Quality Feed, Inc., 1970—; pres., dir. Materials Consultants Inc., Butte, Mont., 1975—; pres., chmn. bd. Agr. Assos. Mont., Inc., 1977—. Served with USAAF, 1944-46. Decorated Purple Heart, D.F.C., Air medal. Club: Union League (Chgo.); Optimist (Lebanon). Home: Apt 5 Washington Apts Lebanon MO 65536 Office: 274 W Pierce St Lebanon MO 65536

PLUNKETT, JAMES GARDNER, architect; b. Milw., Jan. 31, 1933; s. Henry Philip and Jenette Gardner (Rossbach) P.; B.Arch., Cornell U., 1956; m. Gwendolyn K. Gienke, July 12, 1959; children—Karen, Robert, Katherine, Laura. Partner Plunkett, Keymar, Reginato, Architects, Milw., 1960—; pres. PKR Assos., Inc., Milw., 1960—, Design Research, Inc., Milw., 1965—. Bd. dirs. Bel Canto Chorus, Milw., 1968—, United Performing Arts Fund, Milw., 1970—, Milw. Symphony Orch., 1970—; mem. adv. bd. Booth Meml. Hosp., Milw., 1968-77; mem. Southeastern Wis. Health Systems Agy., 1976—, Citizens Govtl. Research Bur., 1976—, Schlitz Audubon Center, 1976—, Riveredge Nature Center, 1969—, Milw. Art Center Friends of Art, 1976—, Friends of Museum, 1977—. Served to 1st lt. AUS, 1959-60. Mem. AIA (regional committeeman 1973—), Am. Arbitration Assn. (arbitrator). Clubs: Rotary, Univ., Cedar Lake Yacht. Important works include Luth. Hosp. Milw., Milwaukee County Med. Complex-Ambulatory Care Facility, Mt. Sinai Med. Center, Milw., others. Home: 8500 N River Rd Milwaukee WI 53217 Office: 6830 W Villard Ave Milwaukee WI 53218

POAGE, GEORGE RICHARD, historian; b. Gallatin, Mo., July 25, 1914; s. George Naylor and Linda Lane (Doolin) P.; student Harvard U., 1932-33; B.A. summa cum laude, U. No. Iowa, 1951; M.A., U. Iowa, 1952, Ph.D., 1954; m. Patricia Ann Lowe, May 20, 1946; 1 dau., Susan Kathleen. Cryptanalist, War Dept., Washington, 1941-42; instr. history, U. Iowa, 1952-53, univ. fellow, 1954-55, vis. prof. German history, 1966-67; asst. prof. history U. No. Iowa, 1954-59, asso. prof., 1959-65, prof., 1965—; dir. Iowa High Sch. Model UN, 1965—; bd. dirs. Iowa div. UN Assn., 1965—, Council on Internat. Relations and UN Affairs, 1967-73, UN Assn. of U.S.A., 1973—; chmn. Gov. Iowa's Com. on UN, 1976—. Served with Signal Corps, U.S. Army, 1942-45; MTO. Decorated Silver Battle Star; recipient citation for outstanding service Gov. Iowa, 1975. Mem. Am. Hist. Assn., Conf. Group for Central European History, AAUP (pres. U. No. Iowa chpt. 1957). Democrat. Presbyterian. Club: Masons. Home: 1421 W 18th St Cedar Falls IA 50613 Office: 309 Sabin Hall U of No Iowa Cedar Falls IA 50613

POCKRAS, LAURENCE MALVIN, structural and civil engr.; b. Bklyn., Aug. 12, 1927; s. Harry and Sue (Elias) P.; B.S., U. Cin., 1950, C.E., 1952; m. Sarah Lou Curtis, Apr. 10, 1949; children—Philip, Sarah, Charles, Laurence. Draftsman, Am. Bridge Co., Gary, Ind., 1950-51; engr. A.M. Kinney, Inc., Cin., 1951-62, dep. dir. civil engring., 1962-76, dir. structural engring., 1976—. Mem. ASCE, AISC, Chi Epsilon. Republican. Presbyn. (elder 1970-73, deacon 1966-69). Home: 8459 Fernwell Dr Cincinnati OH 45231 Office: 2900 Vernon Pl Cincinnati OH 45231

PODDAR, SHRIKUMAR, direct mail marketing co. exec.; b. Calcutta, West Bengal, India, Sept. 11, 1940; s. Shirishchandra and Rukmani (Makharia) P.; came to U.S., 1959; B.A., Mich. State U., 1964, 66, M.B.A., 1968; m. Mayurika Sheth, June 28, 1963. Draftsman, Chrisman Constrn. Co., Lansing, Mich., 1960; copyboy Lansing (Mich.) State Jour., 1961; chmn. Ednl. Subscription Service, 1961—; pres. Zip Code Publs., 1967—. Founder, vice chmn. Ams. for Peace, 1969-71. Nat. dir. direct mail fund-raising McGovern for Pres., 1971, McCarthy for Pres., 1968, 76. Mem. Am. Com. Rehab. Cyclone Victims in India, 1978. Bd. dirs. India Found., Emergency Relief Fund, Washington Watch, India Devel. Soc. (founder), Indians for Democracy (founding mem.). Mem. Hindu religion. Editor: Saral Bhautic Shashtra, 1956. Home: 2601 Cochise Lane Okemos MI 48864 Office: 3308 S Cedar St Lansing MI 48910

PODELL, RALPH JACK, judge; b. Milw., Mar. 25, 1913; s. Jacob M. and Ida (Zhartsky) P.; J.D. cum laude, Marquette U., 1934; m. Della M. Nickoll, Jan. 1, 1977; children—James J., Richard J. Admitted to Wis. bar, 1934; practiced law, Milw., 1934-72; judge County Ct., Milwaukee County, Wis., 1972, circuit judge, 1972—; faculty Nat. Coll. State Judiciary, 1976—; mem. subcom. on marriage, div. and annulment certificates U.S. HEW, 1972-75; instr. family law Wis. Jud. Coll., 1973—. Fellow Am. Bar Found.; mem. Am. (chmn. family law sect. 1971-73, family law sect. spl. com. on bill of rights for children 1974), Wis. (chmn. family law sect. 1962-71, bd. govs. 1969-72, dir. family law sect. 1961—), Milw. bar assns., Am. Judicature Soc., Am. Acad. Matrimonial Lawyers (bd. govs. 1969—). Clubs: Masons, Shriners, Eagles. Asso. editor domestic relations Law Notes, 1967—. Home: 1610 N Prospect Ave Milwaukee WI 53202 Office: Ct House Milwaukee WI 53233

PODOLSKY, B(ERTHA) POLLY EDELMAN, writer, educator; b. Wales; d. Joshua and Esther (Soloman) Edelman; came to U.S., 1937, naturalized, 1941; m. Boris Podolsky, Aug. 3, 1937 (dec. Nov. 1966); 1 son, Robert Earl. Editorial asso. Writer's Digest Mag., 1964-71; lectr. journalism U. Cin., 1968-73; free lance writer short stories and articles in various publs. including Harper's Bazaar (British and German), Ellery Queen Mystery Mag., Columbia, Mystery Writers' Am. Anthology; classical readings recorded for McGraw-Hill Co.; spl. lectr. creative writing Xavier U., 1967-69. Mem. Mystery Writers Am., Soc. Authors (London). Contbr. to Cin. Enquirer, Nat. Enquirer. Home: 222 Senator Cincinnati OH 45220

PODREBARAC, CHARLES MATTHEW, dentist; b. Kansas City, Kans., May 26, 1926; s. Matthew Daniel and Barbara (Macan) P.; D.D.S., Creighton U., 1952; m. Mary Jean McKinney, July 26, 1952; children—Rebecca, Marya, Charles, Pierre, Gina. Practice dentistry, Kansas City, Kans., 1952—; dir. Gibralter Savs. and Loan Assn. Bd. dirs. Mental Health and Guidance; hon. bd. dirs. Rockhurst Coll. Served with USNR, 1944-46. Fellow Internat. Coll. Dentists; mem. Am., Kans. dental assns., Fedn. Dentaire Internationale, Wyandotte Dental Soc. (pres. 1962-63), Creighton U. Dental Alumni (adv. bd. 1968—), Catholic Laymen Conf. (pres. 1967-68), Alpha Sigma Nu, Jesuit Honor Soc., Omicron Kappa Upsilon, Pierre Fauchard Acad. K.C. (4 deg.). Clubs: Terrace, Victory Hills Country, Kaw Valley Study. Home: 8012 Washington Ave Kansas City KS 66112 Office: 316 Brotherhood Bldg Kansas City KS 66101

PODRUCH, LOUIS LEO, JR., dentist; b. Wausau, Wis., Jan. 27, 1921; s. Louis Leo and Catherine A. (Molter) P.; student U. Notre Dame, 1938-40, U. Minn., 1940; D.D.S., Marquette U., 1943; m. Alice Ann Sniegoski, Sept. 18, 1948; children—Mary Therese, LeeAnn, Paul Louis, Lucy Catherine. Pvt. practice dentistry, Wausau, Wis., 1946—; dir. Franklin Savs. & Loan, Wausau, Wausau Profl. Center, Inc.; instr. dental sci. St. Mary's Hosp., Wausau, Wis., 1947-50. Bd. dirs. 7th Area Comprehensive Health Planning, 1971-73; bd. dirs. Wis. Health Care Review, Inc., Madison, 1971—. Served with AUS, 1943-46. Fellow Internat. Coll. Dentists; mem. Marquette U. Parents Orgn. (mem. bd. 1972—), Am. (council 1973—), Wis. (trustee 1962-69, 75—), Central Wis. (pres. 1960-61), Marathon County dental assns., Pierre Fauchard Acad. Dentistry, Serra Internat., Delta Sigma Delta. K.C., Kiwanian. Clubs: Wausau Country; Maple Hills Golf (Wittenberg, Wis.). Home: 1239 Washington St Wausau WI 54401 Office: 110 S 2d St Wausau WI 54401

POE, OSCAR AUGUST, constrn. co. exec.; b. nr. Carrollton, Mo., Apr. 6, 1914; s. Benjamin Franklin and Laura Francis (Bahr) P.; grad. Chillicothe Bus. Coll.; m. Mabel Marie Lightfoot, May 3, 1936; children—Grace (Mrs. Clyde Justice), Raymond F., Doris E. Manual laborer, various cos., Mo., Kans., Nebr., 1930-39; laborer Armco Steel Metal Products div., constrn., 1940-45, foreman, 1945-52, asst. constrn. mgr., 1952-60; v.p., supt. Hansen Tunneling, Inc., Columbus, Ohio, 1960-61, gen. mgr., v.p. constrn., 1961-71, v.p., co-owner Capitol Tunneling, Inc., 1971-73, pres., treas., co-owner, 1973—. Mason (32 deg.). Home: 1651 McCoy Rd Columbus OH 43220 Office: 1165 W 3d Ave Columbus OH 43212

POE, WAYNE ALAN, shopping center exec.; b. Washington, Oct. 15, 1941; s. Leslie Alfred and Marilynn Lois (Juergensmeier) P.; student Mich. State U., 1970; m. Nancy Lynn Stevens, Oct. 24, 1946; 1 dau., Coleen Noell. Mem. mgmt. staff J.C. Penney & Co., Mayfield Heights, Ohio, 1961-67; promotion dir. Southland Shopping Center, Cleve., 1967-70; gen. mgr. Westland Mall, Columbus, Ohio, 1970-72, Fashion Sq. Mall, Saginaw, Mich., 1972-74, Southlake Mall, Merrillville, Ind., 1974-76, Euclid Sq. Mall, Euclid, Ohio, 1976—. Mem. Internat. Council Shopping Centers, Shelby Owners Assn., Corvette Club Am. Home: 9545 Fairmount Rd Novelty OH 44072 Office: 100 Euclid Sq Mall Euclid OH 44132

POE, WEYLAND DOUGLAS, educator; b. Wilburton, Okla., Apr. 3, 1915; s. John and Edna Porter (Smith) P.; student Eastern Okla. Jr. Coll., 1931-32; B.S., Okla. A. and M. Coll., 1939; Ph.D., Ind. U., 1959; m. Betty Ruth Bobbitt, Nov. 25, 1948; children—Weyland Douglas, Patricia Gail. Clk., Fed. Emergency Relief Adminstrn., Wilburton, 1933-35; various clerical and adminstrv. positions Tide Water Asso. Oil Co., Tulsa, 1936-37, 39-42, 46; editor, publisher of various weeklies and semi-weeklies, Okla. and Tex., 1948-56; faculty Ill. State U., Normal, 1959—, prof. econs., 1968—. Trustee Town of Normal, 1964-68. Served to capt. AUS, 1942-46. Recipient Good Govt. award Jr. C. of C., 1965; Certificate of Honor Ill. Credit Union Assn., 1973. Mem. AAUP, Sigma Alpha Epsilon, Pi Gamma Mu, Omicron Delta Epsilon. Author: Local Sales Taxation in U.S. and Canada; Tax Alternatives for Illinois. Home: 410 Normal Ave Normal IL 61761 Office: Economics Dept Ill State U Normal IL 61761

POELKER, JOHN HENRY, mayor St. Louis; b. St. Louis, Apr. 14, 1913; s. John G. and Anna (Bongner) P.; student St. Louis U., 1930-34; m. Ruth Cambron, Oct. 19, 1940; children—John S., Susan M., Kathy M. Sales corr., asst. to div. sales mgr. Nat. Ammonia div., E. I. duPont de Nemours Co., Inc., St. Louis, 1930-42; spl. agt. FBI, 1942-53; city assessor St. Louis, 1953-56, city comptroller, 1957-73, mayor, 1973—. Mem. Internat. Assn. Assessing Officers, Municipal Finance Officers Assn., Nat. Assn. Accountants. Democrat. Home: 4555 Dryden St Saint Louis MO 63115 Office: City Hall 12th and Market Sts Saint Louis MO 63103

POGRUND, SHERWIN IVAN, lawyer; b. Chgo., Sept. 4, 1934; s. Carl and Belle (Wax) P.; student U. Ill., 1951-53; B.A., Roosevelt U., 1955; J.D., Northwestern U., 1957; postgrad. U. Oxford, 1955; m. Toby Urkov, June 16, 1957; children—David, Debra. Admitted to Ill. bar, 1957; partner Stone, Pogrund & Korey, Chgo., 1958—; gen. counsel Profl. Remodelers Assn. Greater Chgo., 1962—. Asso. Talmud Torah United Jewish Fund, 1970—; bd. dirs. N.W. Jewish Fedn., Skokie Valley Traditional Synagogue. Served with Ill. Nat. Guard, 1957-58. Recipient Man of Year award Skokie Valley Traditional Synagogue, 1976. Mem. Am., Ill., Chgo. bar assns., Home Improvement Council Greater Chgo. (award of merit 1968, 74), Profl. Remodelers Assn. Greater Chgo. (man of year award 1971), Tau Epsilon Ro. Club: B'nai B'rith. Home: 9121 Kedvale St Skokie IL 60076 Office: 221 N LaSalle St Chicago IL 60601

POHL, KENNETH ROY, electronics co. exec.; b. Beloit, Wis., Nov. 11, 1941; s. Walter John and Ruth Margret (Wieck) P.; student Wis. State Coll., Whitewater, 1959-60, Milton Coll., 1963-66; m. Deloris Jean Harris, Sept. 22, 1970. With Beloit Corp., 1960-63; mgr. trainee Faimly Fin. Corp., 1966; with Chrysler Corp., 1966-67; owner, operator bowling alley and lounge, 1967-68; with Automatic Electric Co., Genoa, Ill., 1968-69; buyer Fox Corp., Janesville, Wis., 1969-70; materials mgr. Clinton Electronic Corp., Loves Park, Ill., 1970-72, import-export mgr., supr. sales adminstrn., 1972—; cons. internat. transp.; mem. Midwest Shippers Adv. Fed. Maritime Commn. Founder, exec. dir. Tri-State All Star Bowling Assn. Mem. Am. Prodn. and Inventory Control Soc. Lutheran. Clubs: Lions, Rock River Valley Traffic; World Trade (charter mem.) (Nortren, Ill.). Home: 100 W Webb St Davis 61019 Office: 6701 Clinton Rd Box 2277 Loves Park IL 61113

POHLMAN, KENNETH LOUIS, telephone and utility co. exec.; b. Niles, Mich., June 15, 1921; s. Louis Ernest and Louise Alice (Williams) P.; student Ind. Bus. Coll., 1939-41; B.S., Ind. U., 1949; m. Doris A. Schulte, Aug. 9, 1952; children—Craig, Diane, Eric. Accountant, Arthur Andersen & Co., 1949-55, asst. to controller, 1955-56, controller, 1956-69; sec.-treas. Central Telephone & Utilities Corp., Lincoln, Nebr., after 1969, v.p., after 1973. Served with USNR, 1942-46. C.P.A., Ill. Mem. Beta Gamma Sigma. Lutheran (treas. 1956-60). Elk, Optimist. Home: 444 Signal Hill Rd Barrington IL 60010 Office: 5725 E River Rd Chicago IL 60631

POINDEXTER, CLIFFORD EDWARD, entomologist; b. Covington, Okla., Jan. 8, 1935; s. George Clifford and Goldy E. (Woodring) P.; B.S., Clemson U., 1966, M.S., 1968; m. Ann Adell Hales, Dec. 26, 1955; children—Michael Scott, Annadell. Entomologist, U.S. Dept. Agr., Rosenberg, Tex., 1968-72; consumer safety officer EPA, Kansas City, Mo., 1972-75; extension coordinator pesticides Kans. State U., Manhattan, 1975—. Recipient Alpha Tau Alpha award 1966. Mem. Am. Registry Profl. Entomologists, Entomol. Soc. Am. Club: Masons. Home: 1800 Willow Brook Dr Blue Springs MO 64015 Office: Kans State U Manhattan KS 64106

POINDEXTER, HENRY PRATT, security exchange exec.; b. Kansas City, Mo., July 3, 1921; s. Harry Keller and Elizabeth Brereton (Pratt) P.; student Kansas City U.; m. Carol Ann Milnes, Feb. 23, 1946; children—Elizabeth (Mrs. Frank Martin), Harry Milnes, Diane Adele, Donald Pratt. Salesman, H.T. Poindexter & Sons Mdse. Co., Kansas City, Mo., 1946-48, buyer, 1948-51, mdse. mgr., v.p., 1951-62, pres., chmn. bd., 1962-64; account exec. Dean Witter & Co., Inc., Kansas City, 1964—. Mem. personnel bd., Kansas City, 1954-60. Mem. Bd. Edn., Kansas City, 1960-73; trustee, Kansas City Pub. Library, 1960-73. Served with USAAF, 1942-45. Decorated Air medal. Mem. Mo. Sch. Bd. Assn. (bd. dirs. 1968), Nat. Sch. Bd. Assn. (assembly del. 1969-71). Republican. Episcopalian (vestryman 1970-72). Home: 1227 W 66th St Kansas City MO 64113 Office: Dean Witter & Co Inc 10 Main Center Kansas City MO 64105

POINSETT, ALEXANDER CAESAR, journalist; b. Chgo., Jan. 27, 1926; s. Alexander A. and Adele Leola (Prindle) P.; B.S. in Journalism, U. Ill., 1952, M.A. in Philosophy, 1953; postgrad. U. Chgo., 1953-54; m. Norma Ruth Miller, Aug. 24, 1951; children—Pierrette Mimi, Alexis Pierre. Asso. editor Jet Mag., Chgo., 1954-61, Ebony Mag., Chgo., 1961-67, sr. staff editor, 1967—. Served with USNR, 1944-47. Recipient Penny-U. Mo. journalism award. Unitarian (past ch. trustee). Author: Common Folk in an Uncommon

Cause; Black Power: Gary Style. Home: 8532 S Wabash Ave Chicago IL 60610 Office: 820 S Michigan Ave Chicago IL 60616

POINSETTE, DONALD EUGENE, bus. exec., value mgmt. cons.; b. Fort Wayne, Ind., Aug. 17, 1914; s. Eugene Joseph and Julia Anna (Wyss) P.; student Purdue U., 1934, Ind. U., 1935-37, 64; m. Anne Katherine Farrell, Apr. 15, 1939; children—Donald J., Eugene J., Leo J., Sharon (Mrs. Stacy Smith), Irene (Mrs. Dennis Snyder), Cynthia, Maryanne, Philip J. With various cos., 1937-39; metall. research and field sales cons. P.R. Mallory Corp., 1939-49; dist. sales mgr. Derringer Metall. Corp., Chgo., 1949-50; plant engr. Cornell-Dubilier Electric Corp., Indpls., 1950-53; with Jenn-Air Corp., Indpls., 1953-74, purchasing dir., 1953-71, mgr. value engring. and quality control, 1969-74; bus. mgmt. cons. Mays and Assos., Indpls., 1974-76; treas. Poinsette Lawn & Garden Equipment, Inc., Indpls. Named to U.S. Finder's List, Nat. Engrs. Register, 1956. Pres., Marian Coll. Parents Club, Indpls., 1969-70; com. mem. Boy Scouts Am. Nat trustee Xavier U., 1972-73, Dad's Club, Cin. Mem. Nat. Assn. Purchasing Mgmt., Indpls. Purchasing Mgmt. Assn., Soc. Am. Value Engrs. (certified value specialist; sec.-treas. S.A.V.E. Central Ind. chpt. 1972-73), Soc. Ret. Execs. Indpls. C. of C., Ind. U., Purdue U. alumni assns., Columbian (pres. 1972-73), Triad choral groups, Internat. Platform Assn., Tau Kappa Epsilon. K.C. (4 deg.). Club: Devon Country. Home: 5760 Susan Dr E Indianapolis IN 46250

POIRIER, BROOKE ELIZABETH, mgmt. cons.; b. San Luis Obispo, Calif., Aug. 12, 1942; d. Vincent Brian and Jane Elizabeth (Strosnyder) Curran; B.A., Washburn U., 1966; M.B.A., U. Mo., Kansas City, 1976; m. Constant John Poirier, III, Apr. 19, 1969; 1 son, Desmond Constant. Reporter, Topeka Capital-Jour., 1965-67; fin. reporter, asst. to bus. editor Kansas City Star, 1968-69; pub. affairs officer Model Cities Dept., City of Kansas City, Mo., 1969-72; coordinator media relations Am. Nurses Assn., Kansas City, Mo., 1972-75; pres. MarCom, Inc., Kansas City, 1976—. Founding pres. Dimensions Unlimited, 1972. Mem. Pub. Relations Soc. Am., Beta Gamma Sigma. Episcopalian. Home and Office: 654 W 69th Terr Kansas City MO 64113

POIRIER, CURTIS RAYMOND, advt. printing exec.; b. Montevideo, Minn., Sept. 11, 1934; s. Raymond Martin and Fay A. (Tagart) P.; grad. high sch.; m. Gail Poirier, Aug. 17, 1957; children—Mark, Steven, Beth. Pub. Daily Reminder, Montevideo; also job printer. Mem. Montivideo C. of C. (dir.). Clubs: Masons, Shriners. Home: 1336 Ridgeview Dr Montevideo MN 56265 Office: 309 N 1st St Montevideo MN 56265

POLAKOFF, DONALD MILES, assn. exec.; b. Shelbyville, Ind., Dec. 7, 1933; s. Maurice Howard and Helen Elizabeth (Behrendt) P.; B.S., Ind. U., 1956; m. Jackie Lou Hawkins, Mar. 8, 1958; children—Susan, Jennifer. Indsl. relations dir. Shelby Mfg. Co., Shelbyville, 1958-61, plant mgr., 1962-68; v.p. Ind. Mfrs. Assn., Indpls., 1968—; instr. suprs. inst. Ind. Central Coll., Indpls., 1968—; mem. adv. council Vocat. Tech. Services Center, Ind. State U., Terre Haute, 1975—; mem. research adv. com. Ind. Bd. Vocat. Tech. Edn., 1975—; mem. Ind. Manpower Planning Council, 1973, Ind. Manpower Devel. Council, 1974-76, Ind. Adv. Com. on Day Care Services, 1969, Ind. Manpower Devel. Council, 1974-76; chmn. Hoosier State Apprenticeship Conf., 1973, 75, 77; mem. curriculum adv. com. Vincennes U., 1975—; area rep. Youth for Understanding, Exchange Student Program. 1975—. Served with CIC, AUS, 1956-58. Mem. Ind. Personnel Assn. (dir.), Personnel Assn. Indpls. (dir.), Ind. Manpower Research Assn. Republican. Jewish. Clubs: Elks, Eagles, Moose. Home: PO Box 178 Shelbyville IN 46176 Office: 115 N Pennsylvania St Indianapolis IN 46204

POLAN, JEANNE WARSAW FOX, bus. co. exec., camp adminstr.; b. Chgo., Oct. 31, 1927; d. Herman Irving and Jessie (Warsaw) Fox; B.S., U. Ill., 1948; m. Julius Polan, Sept. 6, 1948; children—David Jay, Jeri Deborah, Greg Charles. Tchr. modern dance U. Ill., Champaign, 1947; secondary tchr. Chgo. Bd. Edn., 1948-51, 52, 59-62; co-dir. Illini Day Camp, 1949-63; co-owner, dir. Kiddie Kampus Nursery Sch., 1951-60; owner, dir. Kiddie Klass Pre-sch., 1956-60; co-owner, dir. Burr Oaks Camp for Girls, Mukwonago, Wis., 1964—; sec.-treas., dir. Northtown Bus. Co., Lincolnwood, Ill., 1958—. Brownie troop leader Girl Scouts U.S.A., Glenview, Ill., 1963-65; awards chmn. N.W. Suburban council Boy Scouts Am., Skokie, 1960, den mother, Glenview, 1965-67; rep. Dist 209 Sch. Bd., 1971—. Chpt. rec. sec. Am. Med. Center, Denver, 1963. Recipient Vol. Service award VA, 1947, 63. Mem. Am. Camping Assn. (mem. standards com.), Assn. Pvt. Camps, Nat. Rifle Assn., Nat. Horsemanship Assn., Camp Archery Assn., Am. Skiing Assn., Lake Beulah Preservation and Conservation Assn., Hadassah (chpt. 1st v.p. 1956), Jewish War Vets. Assn. (chpt. pres. 1951-52). Mem. B'nai B'rith. Home: 2522 W Harrison St Glenview IL 60025 Office: 2640 W Golf Rd Glenview IL 60025 also Route 3 Box 193 Mukwonago WI 53149

POLAND, ANNE SPELLMAN, counselor; b. Woodward, Iowa, June 13, 1922; d. Martin Edward and Margaret Corinne (Geneser) Spellman; B.S., Marycrest Coll., 1942; M.Ed., Drake U., 1970; m. Philip H. Poland, July 26, 1947; children—Margaret, Mary, Suzanne, Patricia, John, Christopher, Eileen, Mark, George, Martha, Stephen, Peter. Home economics tchr. Westside (Iowa) Community Sch., 1942, Minburn (Iowa) Community Sch., 1943; extension home economist Carroll County, Iowa, 1944-47; elementary tchr. Carroll (Iowa) Community Sch., 1966-74, guidance counselor, 1974—. Active Carroll County Democratic Central Com., 1970—. Mem. Nat., Iowa, Carroll edn. assns., Am., Iowa personnel guidance assns. Roman Catholic. Home: Rural Route 2 Carroll IA 51401 Office: Fairview Sch 18th Grant Rd Carroll IA 51401

POLASKY, FRANK MARTIN, lawyer; b. Detroit, Oct. 17, 1926; s. Harry G. and Rose (Schiff) P.; certificate of merit Mich. State U., 1945; B.A., U. Mich., 1948; J.D., Detroit Coll. Law, 1950; postgrad. Wayne U., 1951; m. Betty A. Goldstone, Aug. 29, 1948; children—Wendy R., Diane H., William M. Clk., Kroger Co., Saginaw, Mich., 1940-44; ins. salesman Polasky Ins. Co., Saginaw, 1946-48; real estate salesman, broker O.B. Hart, Detroit, 1948-50; admitted to Mich. bar, 1951; since practiced in Saginaw; field agt. IRS, Detroit, 1950-51; sr. partner Polasky, Meisel, Rosenbaum & Meyer, Saginaw, 1952—; fin., sec., officer Tri-City Acoustical, Saginaw, King Nursing Home, Houghton Lake, Mich., Houghton Lake Snow Bowl (Mich.), Henderson Bros. Constrn., Cheboygan, Mich., Magline Corp., Pinconning, Mich., First State Bank, Saginaw, Garber Buick, Bay City, Mich. Pres. Saginaw Jewish Welfare Fedn., 1965-68; bd. dirs. Saginaw Jewish Community Center; trustee Lurie-Polasky Found., Saginaw; bd. dirs. Martin Luther King Found., Saginaw. Served with CAP, 1942-44, AUS, 1944, USAAF, 1945. Mem. Am. Judicature Assn., Am., Fed., Mich., Saginaw bar assns., Am. Legion, Tau Epsilon Rho. Jewish (dir. temple 1956—). Clubs: B'nai B'rith, Saginaw Country. Home: 49 Benton Rd Saginaw MI 48602 Office: 141 Harrow Ln Saginaw MI 48603

POLCAR, GERTRUDE ELIZABETH, judge; b. Cleve., Oct. 10, 1916; d. Martin and Gertrude (Jirele) Polcar; A.B. in Law, U. Chgo., 1938, J.D., 1940. Admitted to Ohio bar, 1941; pvt. practice law, Cleve., 1942-44, 50-56, 60-72; asst. atty. gen. Ohio, 1945-49, 1957-59; city councilman, Parma, Ohio, 1960-69; mem. Ohio Ho. of Reps., Dist. 51, 1969-72; judge Parma Municipal Ct., 1972— presiding and adminstrv. judge, 1976—. Mem. Ohio, Cleve., Cuyahoga County bar assns., Women Lawyers Club Cleve. Mem. Ladies Oriental Shrine N.A.; mem. Order Eastern Star. Home: 7060 Ridge Rd Parma OH 44129 Office: 5750 W 54th St Parma OH 44129

POLEN, THOMAS MORRIS, bank exec.; b. Cleve., Feb. 14, 1935; s. Harry and Dora (Chesler) P.; B.S.J. cum laude, Ohio U., 1956; m. Mary Louise Sipser, Jan. 29, 1961; children—Debora, Michelle, Gary. Line mgr. Am. Greetings Corp., Cleve., 1959-64; account exec. Cleve. Overseas Corp., 1964-69; advt. mgr. Craftint Mfg. Co., Cleve., 1969-73; v.p. mktg. Lake County Nat. Bank, Painesville, Ohio, 1973—. Mem. Path. Assn. Cleve., 1970—; co-chmn. Communicators for Peace, Cleve., 1970; vol. mem. Big Bros. Cleve. Block leader Democratic Senate Campaign in Ohio, 1970. Bd. dirs. Lake County Mental Health Assn., Citizens League of University Heights. Served with AUS, 1956-58. Mem. Bank Mktg. Assn., Cleve. Advt. Club, Consumers League of Ohio, Phi Sigma Delta. K.P. Club: Suburban Investment. Home: 4202 Bushnell Rd Cleveland OH 44118

POLIAN, HAROLD, investment banker; b. Omaha, Oct. 14, 1893; s. John Albert and Ida Louise (Brandt) P.; LL.B., Creighton U., 1921; m. Gladys L. Fessenden, 1921; children—Virginia Avalon, Maxine Lenore. With Peters Trust Co., Omaha, 1921-26; investment banker Smith Polian & Co., Omaha, 1927—; chmn. bd. So. Calif. Water Co., Los Angeles, Edison Sault Electric Co., Sault Ste. Marie, Mich.; pres. Smith Polian Co. Mem. Nebr. Investment Bankers Assn. (past pres.), Omaha C. of C., Am. Legion. Clubs: Union League (Chgo.); Omaha, Happy Hollow. Home: 2527 Country Club Ave Omaha NE 68104 Office: 1623 Farnam St Suite 700 Omaha NE 68102

POLICASTRO, ANTHONY JOSEPH, mech. engr.; b. Elizabeth, N.J., Mar. 5, 1946; s. Anthony George and Etta (Gigante) P.; B.S., Columbia U., 1966, M.S., 1967, Eng. Sc.D. (NASA fellow), 1970; m. Laurie Marie Zeman, June 13, 1976. San. engr. N.Y.C. Health Dept., summer 1966; engr. Argonne (Ill.) Nat. Lab., 1970—; cons. Swedish Meteorol. and Hydrol. Inst., 1976, Rudjer Boskovic Inst. and Boris Kidric Inst., Yugoslavia, 1976; adj. asso. prof. Southern Ill. U. at Cardondale, 1976—; cons. Internat. Atomic Energy Agency, 1978; Grantee Nuclear Regulatory Commn., 1976, Electric Power Research Inst., 1977. Mem. Internat. Center for Heat and Mass Transfer, Am. Inst. Aeros. and Astronautics, ASME, Internat. Assn. Great Lakes Research. Roman Catholic. Contbr. articles to profl. jours. Home: 1260 Andrus Ave Downers Grove IL 60515 Office: 9700 Cass Ave S Argonne IL 60439

POLICH, JOHN EDMUND, environ. cons. co. exec.; b. Sturgeon Bay, Wis., Oct. 12, 1945; s. John J. and Frieda A. (Krueger) P.; B.S., U. Wis., 1968; m. Mary A. Gibson, Aug. 26, 1972; children—Joshua, Sarah. Project engr. Cities Service Co., East Chicago, Ind., 1968-70, Borg Warner Co., Parkersburg, W. Va., 1970-71; pollution control engr., asst. to head enforcement Met. San. Dist. Chgo., 1971-72; mgr. environ. services div. Erickson Chem. Co., Chgo., 1972-73; asso., prin. Gabriel & Assos., Chgo., 1973—, also founder. Mem. Chgo. Indsl. Water, Waste and Sewage Group (sec. 1974-75). Address: 1439 W George St Chicago IL 60657

POLK, GLORIA HARRIS, speech pathologist; b. Norfolk, Va., Aug. 27, 1944; d. E-lis James and Annie Gertrude (Smith) Harris; B.A., Hampton (Va.) Inst., 1966; M.A., Western Mich U., 1967; m. Silas William Polk, III, Mar. 26, 1971; children—John Elder, Audra Alise. Speech and lang. pathologist Elkhart (Ind.) County Assn. for Retarded, Elkhart, 1968-69; mgr. speech, lang. and audiology dept. Wyandotte (Mich.) Gen. Hosp., 1969-77; v.p. Speech, Lang. and Audiology Programs, Inc., Cons., Detroit, 1976—. Chmn. improvement com. Hartwell-Grove Block Club, Detroit, 1976-77. Mem. Am., Mich. (v.p. community and hosp. services 1975-77) speech and hearing assns., Mich. Speech Pathologists in Clin. Practice. Mem. United Ch. Christ. Club: Sunday Bridge. Contbr. articles to profl. confs. Home: 16502 Hartwell St Detroit MI 48235 Office: 2333 Biddle Ave Wyandotte MI 48192

POLK, RICHARD THADDEUS, equipment co. exec.; b. Cleve., Dec. 17, 1930; s. Joseph B. and Henrietta C. (Schwind) P.; student Western Reserve U., 1949-51; B.S., B.A., John Carroll U., 1960; m. JoAnne E. Uht, Apr. 5, 1952; children—Daniel, Ronald, Jerome, Judith. Asst. mgr. Wright Sales Co., Cleve., 1953-56; dist. sales engr. Bellows-Valvair Co., Cleve., 1957-67; v.p. Techno Truck Mfg. Co., Cleve., 1967—; pres., Polk Equipment Co., Gates Mills, Ohio, 1976—; cons. physical distbn. in food industry. Active Cub Scouts, 1969-71; mem. sch. athletic com., 1970-73; pres. Nocturnal Adoration Soc., 1970-74. Served with AUS, 1951-53. Mem. Food Distbn. Research Soc. Republican. Roman Catholic. Home: PO Box 34 Gates Mills OH 44040 Office: Techno 20850 St Clair Ave Cleveland OH 44117

POLK, ROTHWELL CONWAY, surgeon, pharm. co. research exec.; b. Lakeland, Fla., Apr. 11, 1921; s. Robert Henry and Roberta Eggleston (Conway) P.; A.B., Emory U., 1942; M.D., Med. Coll. Ga., 1945; m. Jacqueline Dew, Aug. 31, 1946; children—Beverly Polk Henke, Rothwell Conway, Richard L., Michael D. Intern, Duval Med. Center, Jacksonville, Fla., 1945-46, resident in gen. surgery, 1948-52; practice medicine specializing in gen. surgery, Jacksonville, 1952-56, 58-65; fellow in surgery Lahey Clinic, Boston, 1956-58; dir. profl. info. med. dept. Searle Labs., Chgo., 1965-69, asst. dir. clin. research, 1969-74, dir. gen. medicine and neuropsychiatry clin. research, 1974-77, dir. med. research, 1977—; chmn. Ill. Interagy. Council on Smoking and Disease, 1970-72, 74-75; mem. safety commn., Northfield, Ill., 1975—; chmn. Midwest Com. on Drug Investigation, 1975-76. Bd. dirs. North Shore unit Ill. div. Am. Cancer Soc., 1965-75, chmn., 1967-69, bd. dirs. Ill. div., 1969-75, 1st v.p., 1976-77, pres., 1977—, mem. exec. com., 1976—. Served with AUS, 1945-46. Diplomate Am. Bd. Surgery. Fellow A.C.S. Episcopalian (sr. warden 1963-64, 73-74). Home: 186 Riverside Dr Northfield IL 60093 Office: Searle Labs PO Box 5110 Chicago IL 60680

POLKING, KIRK, ednl. adminstr.; b. Covington, Ky., Dec. 21, 1925; d. Henry and Mary (Hull) Polking; student U. Cin., 1943—, Xavier U., 1944—. Editorial asst. Modern Photography mag., Cin., 1948-50; circulation mgr. Farm Quarterly mag., Cin., 1952-57; freelance writer, 1957-62; editor Writer's Digest, Cin., 1963-73; dir. Writer's Digest Sch. Lectr. U. Cin., Ind. U., U. Calif. and numerous writers workshops in U.S. Recipient Nat. Headliner award Theta Sigma Phi, 1970. Mem. Nat. League Am. Pen Women (state pres. 1972—), Author's League. Roman Catholic. Author: Let's Go With Lewis and Clark, 1963; Let's Go With Henry Hudson, 1964; Let's Go See Congress at Work, 1966; Let's Go To An Atomic Energy Town, 1968; The Private Pilot's Dictionary and Handbook, 1974. Editor: The Beginning Writer's Answer Book, 1978; How To Make Money in Your Spare Time by Writing, 1971; Law and the Writer, 1978. Home: 5450 Beechmont Ave Cincinnati OH 45230 Office: 9933 Alliance Rd Cincinnati OH 45242

POLLACK, JOSEPH, journalist; b. Bklyn., Feb. 3, 1931; s. Samuel H. and Hannah (Weisman) P.; B.A. in Journalism, U. Mo., 1952, postgrad., 1954-55; m. Carol Bryan Atchison, Dec. 1, 1964; children (by previous marriage)—Wendy Leah, Dara Rebecca, Sharon Merrill. Asst. sports editor Jackson (Miss.) Daily News, 1952; sports writer St. Louis Globe-Democrat, 1955-61; pub. relations dir. St. Louis Football Cardinals, 1961-72; film and drama critic, feature writer St. Louis Post-Dispatch, 1972—; freelance writer and critic, 1961—. Served with AUS, 1952-54. Mem. Am. Theatre Critics Assn., Profl. Football Writers Am., U.S. Football Writers' Assn., Mill Creek Valley Athletic Union, Nat. Acad. TV Arts and Sci., Sigma Delta Chi, Kappa Tau Alpha. Club: St. Louis Press. Home: 7417 Oxford Dr St Louis MO 63105 Office: 900 N 12th St St Louis MO 63101

POLLAK, FELIX, librarian; b. Vienna, Austria, Nov. 11, 1909; s. Geza and Helene (Schneider) P.; came to U.S., 1938, naturalized, 1943; student U. Vienna, 1929-36, J.D., 1953; B.L.S., U. Buffalo, 1941; M.L.S., U. Mich., 1949; m. Sara Allen, June 23, 1950. Readers' adviser Buffalo Pub. Library, 1942-43, adminstrv. asst., 1945-47; curator spl. collections Northwestern U. Library, Evanston, Ill., 1949-59; curator rare books U. Wis. Library, Madison, 1959-74, lectr., 1971-72, prof. emeritus, 1974—. Served with AUS, 1943-45. Mem. Beta Phi Mu. Poetry editor: Arts in Society, 1972-76; author: The Castle and the Flaw, 1963; Say When, 1969; (with James Hearst and John Woods) Voyages to the Inland Sea, Vol. II, 1972; Ginkgo, 1973 (1st prize in poetry Council Wis. Writers 1974); Subject to Change, 1978. Home: 3907 Winnemac Ave Madison WI 53711

POLLAK, JAY MITCHELL, lawyer; b. Chgo., Apr. 5, 1937; s. Bertram L. and Florence (Molner) P.; B.S., Miami U., 1959; J.D., Northwestern U., 1962; m. Patricia C. Trexler, May 11, 1963; children—Mitchell E., John A. Admitted to Ill. bar, 1963, also Fed. bar; practiced in Chgo., 1963—; partner firm Pollak & Welsh, Chgo., 1963—; Northbrook village prosecutor, 1964-69. Served with AUS, 1962-63. Mem. Ill., Chgo. bar assns., Zeta Beta Tau, Phi Delta Phi. Home: 846 Dundee Rd Northbrook IL 60062 Office: 150 N Wacker Dr Chicago IL 60606

POLLAK, MICHAEL EDWARD, lawyer; b. Northbrook, Ill., July 6, 1941; s. Bertram L. and Florence (Molner) P.; B.S., Miami U., 1963; J.D., Loyola U., 1966; children—Scott David, Jana Karen. Admitted to Ill. bar, 1966; practiced in Chgo., 1966—; staff atty. Ill. Legis. Reference Bur., Springfield, 1966-67; asso. firm Pollak & Welsh, Chgo., 1967-70; adminstrv. asst. Lt. Gov. State Ill., 1970-72; parliamentarian Ill. Senate, Springfield, 1977, spl. counsel to pres., 1977—; partner firm Pollak & Welsh, Chgo., 1973—. Dir. scheduling and advance for candidate for Democratic gubernatorial nominee for Gov. State Ill., Paul Simon, 1972; bd. dirs., sec. Neighborhood Legal Assistance Center, 1967-70. Mem. Ill. State, Am., Chgo. bar assns., Winnetka-Northfield Jr. C. of C. (dir. 1969-71). Office: 150 N Wacker Dr Chicago IL 60606

POLLARD, HERMAN MARVIN, physician; b. Lamar, Colo., 1906; M.D., U. Mich., 1931, M.S., 1938. Intern, U. Mich. Hosp., Ann Arbor, 1931-33, instr. internal medicine, 1933-38, asst. prof., 1938-45, asso. prof., 1945-51, prof., 1951—; cons. in gastroenterology VA Hosp., Ann Arbor, 1953. Pres., Am. Cancer Soc., 1970-71. Diplomate Am. Bd. Internal Medicine. Master A.C.P. (pres.); mem. A.M.A., Central Soc. Clin. Research, Am. Fedn. Clin. Research, Am. Gastroenterology Soc., Am. Gastroent. Assn. (pres.). Address: Dept Internal Medicine University Mich Med Center Ann Arbor MI 48104

POLLARD, JOHN WILLIAM, cardiologist, internist; b. Mpls., Mar. 13, 1932; s. Donald William and Marian Victoria (Julian) P.; student Harvard U., 1950-51; B.A., U. Minn., 1954, B.S., 1955, M.D., 1957; M.B.A., U. Ill., 1977; m. Gwen Ellen Clanin, Sept. 3, 1955; children—Scott, Anne, Mark, Melissa. Intern, Valley Forge Army Hosp., Phoenixville, Pa., 1957-58; resident Mayo Clinic, Rochester, Minn., 1959-62; practice medicine, specializing in cardiology and internal medicine Carle Clinic, Urbana, Ill., 1963—, med. dir., exec. dir., 1969—; mem. staff Carle Found. Hosp., 1963—; bd. dirs. Regional Health Resource Center, Champaign County, Ill., Found. for Health Care, Champaign County, Ill. Served with AUS, 1956-58. Fellow A.C.P., Am. Coll. Cardiology; mem. Am., Ill. (pres. 1971-72), Champaign County heart assns., Phi Beta Kappa. Home: 1012 Hadley St Champaign IL 61820 Office: 602 W University St Urbana IL 61801

POLLEY, EDWARD HERMAN, educator; b. Chgo., Sept. 20, 1923; s. Sam and Anna (Revzin) P.; B.A., DePauw U., 1947; M.S., St. Louis U., 1949, Ph.D., 1951; m. Jo Ann Welsh, Aug. 11, 1953; children—Lisa, Eric. Instr. anatomy Hahnemann Med. Coll., Phila., 1953-55, asst. prof., 1953-59; asst. prof. anatomy U. Md. Sch. Medicine, Balt., 1964-68, asso. prof., 1968-70; research biologist Edgewood Arsenal, Md., 1959-62, chief neurophysiol. br., 1962-70; prof. anatomy, prof. ophthalmology and neurosurgery U. Ill. Sch. Medicine, Chgo., 1970—. Mem. hearing and vision coms. Nat. Acad. Sci-NRC. Served to lt. (j.g.) USNR, 1942-46. Mem. Am. Assn. Anatomists, AAAS, Am. Soc. for Neurosci., Midwest Soc. Electron Microscopists, Sigma Xi. Clubs: Cajal, Chgo. Lit. Office: U Ill Sch Medicine Dept Anatomy 1853 W Polk St PO Box 6998 Chicago IL 60680

POLLEY, HOWARD FREEMAN, physician; b. Columbus, Ohio, Nov. 12, 1913; B.A., Ohio Wesleyan U., Delaware, 1934, D.Sc. (hon.), 1965; M.D., Ohio State U., 1938; M.S., U. Minn., 1945; m. Georgiana Redrup, June 5, 1938; children—Alice, Mary Ann, William. Intern, St. Luke's Hosp., Chgo., 1938-39, resident, 1939-40; fellow Mayo Grad. Sch., U. Minn., 1940-43; first asst. in rheumatology Mayo Clinic, Rochester, Minn., 1942-43, cons. in medicine and rheumatic diseases, 1943-46, 48—, cons. in phys. medicine, 1946-48, head sect. of medicine, 1962-66, chmn. div. rheumatology, dept. medicine, 1966-76, sr. cons. rheumatology, 1976—; mem. adv. council Nat. Inst. Arthritis, Metabolism and Digestive Diseases, NIH, Bethesda, Md., 1972-76; instr. phys. medicine Mayo Grad. Sch., U. Minn., 1947-48, instr. medicine, 1948-50, asst. prof., 1950-54, asso. prof., 1954-60, prof., 1960-72, prof. medicine Mayo Med. Sch., 1972—. Vice pres. Arthritis Found., 1966-68, mem. exec. bd., bd. dirs., 1964-68; trustee Ohio Wesleyan U., 1967—, mem. exec. com., 1970-72, chmn. student affairs com. of bd., 1970-72. Recipient Alumni Achievement award Ohio State U., 1958. Diplomate Am. Bd. Phys. Medicine. Fellow, A.C.P.; mem. Central Soc. for Clin. Research, AMA, Zumbro Valley Med. Soc., Am. (Spl. citation 1951, pres. 1964-65), Indian (hon.), Japan (hon.), USSR (hon.) rheumatism assns., Nat. Soc. Clin. Rheumatologists (founder, 1st pres.), Sociedad Uruguaya de Rheumatologia (hon.), Sigma Xi, Alpha Omega Alpha. Author: (with others) Physical Examination of the Joints, 1965; asso. editor Arthritis and Rheumatism, 1960-64. Office: Dept Internal Medicine Div Rheumatology Mayo Clinic Rochester MN 55901

POLLEY, ROBERT LUTZ, editor; b. Marion, Ind., Apr. 18, 1933; s. Phillip William and Kathryn (Lutz) P.; m. Constance Fay Safford, July 12, 1958. Reporter, feature writer, book and drama reviewer Middletown (Conn.) Press, 1958; editorial asst. Sat. Eve. Post, Phila., 1959-61; mng. editor Country Beautiful Found., Inc., Waukesha, Wis., 1961-62, exec. editor, 1962-76; editor, v.p. mktg. and prodn. Country Beautiful Corp., 1977—; guest lectr. U. Wis.-Waukesha Center. Served to 1st lt. USAF, 1955-57. Mem. Assn. for Edn. in Journalism. Editor: Lincoln: His Words and His World, 1965; The Beauty of America in Great American Painting, 1965; America the Beautiful in the Words of Henry David Thoreau, 1966; America's Historic

Houses: The Living Past, 1967; America's Folk Art, 1968; America the Beautiful in the Words of Walt Whitman, 1970; The Truman Years, 1976; The Mystery of Beauty: Poems by Emily Dickinson, 1976. Home: 530 S Elm Grove Rd Brookfield WI 53005 Office: 24198 W Bluemound Rd Waukesha WI 53186

POLLINO, PATRICK ANTHONY, pub. relations exec.; b. Johnstown, Pa., Nov. 10, 1942; c. Cozy Anthony and Helene Adeline (Venetico) P.; B.A., U. Pitts., 1964; m. Patricia Lynne Sullivan, Feb. 12, 1972; children—Anthony Vincent, Kathryn Lynne. Pub. relations asso. Western Electric Co., Inc., N.Y.C., 1965-70, regional dir. pub. relations, St. Louis, 1970-75, product cons. staff, St. Louis, 1975-77; pub. relations Supr. Southwestern Bell, St. Louis, 1977—. Corporate adviser Jr. Achievement, St. Louis, 1971-75. Served with AUS Res., 1965-71. Mem. Pub. Relations Soc. Am., Omicron Delta Kappa. Office: 100 N 12th St St Louis MO 63101

POLLITT, DAMON EDWARD, transp. cons.; b. Chgo., Nov. 18, 1930; s. James D. and Geraldine Francis (Tyrrell) P.; B.S. in Economics, Bradley U., 1953, postgrad., 1957; m. Bernita Arlene Giltner, June 1, 1957; children—Michael Edward, Karen Anne, Robert James, Kathryn Susan. Internat. rate analyst Caterpillar Tractor Co., Peoria, Ill., 1956-57; terminal mgr. Milburn, Inc., Chgo., 1957-59; terminal mgr. Brady Motorfreight, Chgo., 1959-66; asst. distbn. mgr. Donahue Sales Corp., Park Forest, Ill., 1965-67; asst. mgr. warehouses, ESB, Inc., Cleve., 1967-69; sr. asso. William Kordsiemon & Associates, Chgo., 1969-70; pres. PC Services, Inc., Oak Brook, Ill., 1970—; speaker Nat. Council of Phys. Distribution, 1975. Served to capt. USAF, 1954-57; Korea. Mem. Am. Soc. Mgmt. Consultants, Nat. Small Bus. Assn., Alpha Kappa Psi. Roman Catholic. Author: Private Carriage Records Manual, 1972. Home: 139 E Sunset St Lombard IL Office: 1301 W 22nd St Oak Brook IL 60521

POLLITT, GERTRUDE STEIN, social worker; b. Vienna, Austria, Sept. 12, 1919; d. Julius and Sidoni (Brauch) Stein; came to U.S., 1949, naturalized, 1951; B.A., Roosevelt U., 1954; M.A., U. Chgo., 1956; certificate Chgo. Inst. Psychoanalysis, 1963; m. Erwin P. Pollitt, Jan. 13, 1951. Resident social worker Anna Freud, Essex, Eng., 1944-45; dep. dir. UN, U.S. Zone, Germany, 1945-48; psychiat. social worker Jewish Children's Bur., Chgo., 1955-63; pvt. practice as psychiat. social worker, Glencoe, Ill., 1961—. Cons., Winnetka Community Nursery Sch., 1962-63, North Shore Congregation Israel Nursery Sch., 1966-69. Registered Nat. Registry Health Care Providers in Clin. Social Work. Fellow Am. Orthopsychiat. Assn., Ill. Clin. Social Workers Assn.; mem. Acad. Certified Social Workers, Nat. Assn. Social Workers (chmn. pvt. practice com. 1967-70), Nat. Assn. Clin. Social Workers, Menninger Found. Author articles in field. Home: 481 Oakdale Ave Glencoe IL 60022 Office: 695 Venron Ave Glencoe IL 60022

POLLNOW, GEORGE GUSTAV, farmer; b. Marengo, Ill., June 28, 1906; s. Gustav A. and Winnie (Oberg) P.; student pub. schs.; m. Clara Lucille Dawson, June 11, 1930; children—Ann Lucille (Mrs. Charles Oswald), Lois (Mrs. Bernard Roberts), Wesley. Farmer, Belvidere, Ill., 1930—; agt. Rockford Dist. Mut. Tornado Ins. Co., 1959—; pres. Belvidere Farmers Mut. Fire & Lightning Ins. Co., 1961—. Mem. Livestock Marketing Bd., 1958-61; active Fed. Farm programs, 1945-73; dir. Co-op. Elevator Co., agt. Grinnell Mut. Reins. Co. Mem. North Boone High Sch. Bd., 1950-63, sch. trustee, 1954-57; mem. Federated Church Bd., 1928-58; mem. No. Ill. Jr. Coll. Steering Com., 1963-65, No. Boone Citizens Com., 1965-66, Doane Countrywide Farm Panels, 1964-73, Boone County Soil and Water Conservation Edn. Com., 1964-65, Boone County Regional Planning Commn., 1964—. Mem. Coop. Milk Marketing Assn., Farm Bur. (dir.). Lion (dir., pres. Poplar Grove). Mem. Goodwill Tour to Russia, 1957. Home: 12950 Poplar Grove Rd Poplar Grove IL 61065

POLLOCK, BRUCE GILLESPIE, realtor; b. Flint, Mich., Oct. 7, 1922; s. Milton and Elizabeth Mary (Gillespie) P.; student Northwestern U., 1940-41, U. Mich., 1942; m. Virginia Mary Cooper, Dec. 23, 1942; children—Linda (Mrs. Arthur Lyle Beckwith), Lauriel (Mrs. Larry Luciani). With A.C. Spark Plug div. Gen. Motors Corp., Flint, 1946-48; with Hachtel-Pollock Bldg. Co., Flint, 1948-53; v.p., treas. Hachtel-Pollock, realtors, Flint, 1953-71; owner Bruce G. Pollock & Assos., realtors, Grand Blanc, Mich., 1971—; dir. First Security Bank Grand Blanc. Pres., Grand Blanc Community Hosp. Assn., 1969—. Trustee, Grand Blanc Twp. Bd., 1964-72, mem. pub. works com., 1964-74. Served with USAAF, 1942-46. Named Realtor of Year, Flint Bd. Realtors, 1964. Mem. Inst. Real Estate Mgmt., Nat., Mich. (bd. dirs. 1964-66) real estate assns., Flint Bd. Realtors (pres. 1964), Flint Assn. Home Builders (pres. 1953), Flint Area C. of C. (dir. 1973—). Club: Warwick Hills Golf and Country (Grand Blanc). Home: 5279 Territorial Dr Grand Blanc MI 48439 Office: 8455 S Saginaw Rd Grand Blanc MI 48439

POLLOCK, JAMES WILSON, librarian; b. Assiut, Egypt., Mar. 21, 1922; s. James Alexander and Ethel Jeanette (Craig) P.; B.A., Monmouth Coll., 1945; M.Div., Pitts. Xenia Theol. Sem., 1945; M.S.T., Andover Newton Theol. Sch., 1952; M.A. in Arabic and Islamics, Hartford Sem. Found., 1961; M.A. in L.S., Ind. U., 1964; m. Rachel Lois Buchanan, Sept. 7, 1945; children—Howard, Juanita, Aida, Lois. Missionary, United Presbyn. Bd. Fgn. Missions, Egypt., 1945-56; minister United Presbyn. Ch., Eskridge, Kans., 1956-57; mem. library staff Hartford Sem. Found., Hartford, Conn., 1957-60; cataloger Near East materials, Ind. U. Library, Bloomington, 1961-65, specialist for Near East studies, 1966—, specialist religious studies, 1975—. Mem. Middle East Studies Assn., Am. Oriental Soc., Middle East Librarians Assn. Author: Periodical 25 year Index to Muslim World, 1936-60. Editor publs. Middle East Librarians Assn., 1973-78. Home: 221 E Chester Dr Ellettsville IN 47429 Office: Indiana University Library Bloomington IN 47401

POLLOCK, JOHN DALE, insulation and related products mfg. co. exec.; b. Van Wert, Ohio, Dec. 31, 1920; s. John Lawrence and Jane (Hughs) P.; student York High Sch., 1954-56; m. Pearl L. Winans, Feb. 4, 1940; children—Gary, John, Robert, Don, Debra. Contractor, 1939-56; maintenance foreman Ohio Decorative Products, Spencerville, 1949-71, plant engr., 1964; constrn. supt. Edgerton Metal Products (Ohio), 1964; plant engr. Hagan Mfg. Co., Delphos, O., 1964-65, v.p. mfg., 1966-71; pres., gen. mgr. Diversified Insulation, Inc., Hamel, Minn., 1972—. Mem. Spencerville Schs. Bd. Edn., 1950-54. Mem. Nat. Cellulose Insulation Mfg. Assn. (pres. 1975-76), Greater Mpls. C. of C. Presbyterian. Club: Mpls. Athletic. Home: 6566 France Ave S Edina MN 55435

POLLOCK, LESLIE STUART, urban and regional planning cons.; b. Chgo., Mar. 25, 1942; s. Reuben and Nettie (Brickman) P.; B.Arch., U. Ill., 1966, M.Urban Planning, 1968; m. Sharon Iris Levine, Jan. 30, 1965; children—Elizabeth Lynne, Barbra Alexandria. Instr. urban planning U. Ill., Urbana, 1967-68; sr. asso. Barton-Aschman Assos., Inc., Planning and Engrng. Cons., Evanston, Ill., 1968-76; prin. Camiros Ltd. Planning Cons., 1976—; lectr. grad. dept. urban studies Loyola U., Chgo., 1973—. Chmn., Wilmette (Ill.) Planning Commn., 1974—; mem. Wilmette Bd. Local Improvements, 1975—, Wilmette Council for Comml. Renewal, 1973—. Mem. Am. Inst. Planners (chmn. edn. and tng. of transp. dept.; Student award 1968), Am. Soc. Planning Ofcls., Urban Land Inst. Contbr. articles to profl. jours. Home: 104 9th St Wilmette IL 60091 Office: 173 W Madison Chicago IL 60602

POLLOCK, ROBERT BAKER, automobile co. exec.; b. Seneca, Mo., Nov. 12, 1928; s. Earl F. and Katie N. (Baker) P.; B.J., U. Mo., 1950; m. Pauline M. Pasley, June 17, 1951; children—Robert D., Melinda K. Mng. editor Inter-City Press, Inc., Kansas City, Mo., 1950-53; editor Kansas City aircraft plant Ford Motor Co., 1953-56, editor employee info., tracter and implement div., Birmingham, Mich., 1956-58, co. employee info. specialist, Dearborn, Mich., 1958-64, supr. employe newspapers, 1964-69, mgr. employe communication dept., 1969—. Mem. Internat. Assn. Bus. Communicators, Pub. Relations Soc. Am. Methodist. Club: Chemung Hills Country, Elks. Home: 5374 Washakie Trail Rural Route 1 Brighton MI 48116 Office: Room 405 Ford World Hdqrs Dearborn MI 48121

POLLOCK, ROBERT JOHN, JR., periodontist, educator; b. Oak Park, Ill., Apr. 15, 1933; s. Robert John and Irma (Runion) P.; student Northwestern U., 1951-52, D.D.S., 1956; certificate splty. periodontics Loyola U., Chgo., 1961, M.S., 1962, Ph.D., 1968; m. Patricia Mary Ann James, Mar. 17, 1956; children—Susan Lynn, Elizabeth Ann. Instr., Northwestern U. Dental Sch., Chgo., 1956, 58-59; teaching fellow Loyola U. Sch. Dentistry, Chgo., 1960-64, research asso., 1964-68, asso. prof., chmn. dept. histology, 1968-76, prof., 1976—, chmn. dept. histology, 1976—; pvt. practice dentistry specializing in periodontics, Oak Park, Ill., 1961—. Served as capt. Dental Corps, USAF, 1956-58. NIH fellow 1960-64. Mem. Am. Dental Assn., Ill., Chgo. dental socs., Odontographic Soc., Am. Soc. Mammalogists, AAAS, Internat. Assn. Dental Research, Am. Acad. Periodontology, Midwest Soc. Periodontology, N.Y. Acad. Scis., Omicron Kappa Upsilon Contbr. articles to profl. jours. Home: 274 South St Elmhurst IL 60126 Office: 937 S Mannheim Rd Westchester IL 60153 also 2160 S 1st Ave Maywood IL 60153

POLOM, FRANK EDWARD, bd. trade exec.; b. Nanty-Glo, Pa., Mar. 30, 1924; s. John Andrew and Anna (Lorinc) P.; student U. Denver, 1950-51; m. Helen Grysiak, Nov. 12, 1949; children—Edward F., Marianne T. Admitted to practice before ICC, 1953; various traffic positions with major Midwest R.R. and Fed. Govt., 1946-54; traffic mgr. Beardstown (Ill.) Mills Co., 1954-59, rate analyst, 1959-63, asst. mgr. trans., 1963-68; exec. dir. transp., commodities exchange trading in agrl. and nonagrl. contracts, Chgo. Bd. Trade, 1968—; lectr. on transp.; transp. cons. grain and grain products. Mem. Harbors and Waterways Com. of Chgo. Assn. Commerce and Industry, 1973-75. Served with USNR, 1943-46. Mem. Assn. Interstate Commerce Commn. Practitioners (chmn. Chgo. regional chpt. 1977-78), Traffic Club Chgo. (mem. ednl. com. 1974-79, dir. 1977-79), Transp. Club Chgo., Calumet Transp. Assn., Midwest Adv. Bd., Nat. Indsl. Traffic League, Ill. Terr. Mfrs. Traffic League, Royal Order Night Riders. Club: Moose. Home: 820 Strieff Ln Glenwood IL 60425 Office: 141 W Jackson Blvd B Level Chicago IL 60604

POLSKY, DONALD PERRY, architect; b. Milw., Sept. 30, 1928; s. Lew and Dorothy (Geisenfeld) P.; B.Arch., U. Nebr., 1951; postgrad. U. Calif. at Los Angeles, 1957, U. So. Calif., 1956, U. Ill., 1965, U. Omaha, 1964; m. Corinne Shirley Neer, Aug. 25, 1957; children—Jeffrey David, Debra Lynn. Job capt. Richard J. Neutra, architect, Los Angeles, 1953-56; prin. Donald P. Polsky & Asso., 1956-62; staff architect MCA, Inc., Universal City, 1962-64; prin. Donald P. Polsky, AIA & Assos., Omaha, 1964—. Chmn. design control Interstate 480 Study, 1969, Mayor's Riverfront Devel., Omaha, 1971; mem. Mayor's adv. panel for selection procedures of design profl. services, 1974; vice chmn. Omaha Zoning Bd. Appeals, 1975-77. Served to 1st lt. USAF, 1951-53. Recipient honor award Canyon Crier newspaper, Los Angeles, 1960. Mem. AIA (sect. pres. 1968, chpt. bd. dirs. 1971—, v.p. Nebr. Soc. Architects 1975, pres. 1976-77; awards 1962, 64, 68), Zeta Beta Tau. Club: Highland Country (Omaha). Home: 106 S 89th St Omaha NE 68114 Office: 7337 Farnam St Omaha NE 68114

POLYDORIS, NICHOLAS GEORGE, bus. exec.; b. Chgo., July 7, 1930; s. George Nicholas and Annetta (Karagianis) P.; B.E.E., Northwestern U., 1954; m. Gloria Lucas, Dec. 28, 1952; children—Steven, Janet, Lynn, Susan, Nancy. Trainee, Fairbanks Morris, Chgo., 1954-55; regional mgr. Fasco Industries, N.Y.C., 1955-57; founder, pres. ENM Co., Chgo., 1957—; dir. Gladstone-Norwood Trust & Savs. Bank. Bd. dirs. North Shore Mental Health Found. Mem. Nat., Ill. socs. profl. engrs., Tau Beta Pi. Clubs: Kenilworth, Michigan Shores. Home: 327 Leicester Rd Kenilworth IL 60043 Office: 20 N Wacker Dr Chicago IL 60606

POMERANTZ, SHERWIN BERNARD, data processing exec.; b. N.Y.C., Nov. 18, 1939; s. Sidney and Anna (Simons) P.; B.Indsl. Engring., N.Y. U., 1960; M.S., U. Ill., 1962; m. Barbara Sue Rashbaum, Jan. 27, 1962; children—Shari, Deborah. Instr. mech. engring. U. Ill., 1960-62; instr. engring. drawing Cuyahoga Community Coll., Cleve., 1962-64; controller Masten Corp., Chgo., 1964-66; pres. Controls for Industry, Inc., Chgo., 1966—. Pres. Me. Twp. Jewish Congregation, Des Plaines, Ill., 1976—, named Israel Bond man of year, 1973; pres. Allied Jewish Sch. Bd. Met. Chgo., 1975—; v.p. Bd. Jewish Edn. Met. Chgo.; v.p. Midwest region United Synagogue of Am., chmn. Commn. Jewish Edn., 1976—. Served to capt. Signal Corps, AUS, 1962-64. Mem. ASME, N.Y. U. Alumni Assn., U. Ill. Alumni Assn. (life), Alpha Epsilon Pi (nat. v.p. 1969-75, Nehemiah Gittelson medallion 1976). Columnist: Chgo. Jewish Post and Opinion, 1975—. Home: 8812 Church St Des Plaines IL 60016

POMERANZ, JEROME RAPHAEL, dermatologist; b. Newark, Dec. 29, 1930; s. Raphael and Zina (Rubinow) P.; B.A., George Washington U., 1952; M.D., Boston U., 1956; children—Russell Carl, William Eric, Emily Suzanne. Rotating intern Kings County Hosp., 1956-57; intern in pathology Johns Hopkins Hosp., Balt., 1957-58, asst. physician out patient dept. allergy clinic, 1963-65; fellow in medicine (dermatology) Johns Hopkins U. Sch. Medicine, 1960-63, fellow in medicine (allergy and infectious disease), 1963-65; dir. dermatology Cleve. Met. Gen. Hosp., 1965—, pathologist in charge skin pathology, 1967—; asso. prof. dermatology Case Western Res. U. Sch. Medicine, 1971—, asst. prof. pathology, 1967—; mem. com. to rev. use of ionizing radiation for treatment of benign diseases Nat. Acad. Scis., 1975—. Served with M.C., U.S. Army, 1958-60. Diplomate Am. Bd. Dermatology. Fellow A.C.P., Am. Acad. Dermatology; mem. Am. Dermatol. Assn., Am. Soc. Dermatopathology, Soc. Investigative Dermatology, Assn. Profs. Dermatology, Am. Fedn. Clin. Research, AAAS, Cleve. Dermatol. Soc. (pres. 1973-75), N.Y. Acad. Scis., Cleve. Soc. Pathologists (asso.), Cleve. Acad. Medicine. Club: Ripon. Home: 490 Merrimak Dr Berea OH 44017 Office: 3395 Scranton Rd Cleveland OH 44109

POMEROY, ELWAINE F(RANKLIN), lawyer; b. Topeka, June 4, 1933; s. Charles Franklin and Ada Frances (Owen) P.; A.B., Washburn U., 1955, J.D., 1957; m. Joanne Carolyn Bunge, Sept. 30, 1950; children—Janella Ruth, Duane Franklin, Carl Fredrick. Admitted to Kans. bar, 1957, since practiced in Topeka; sr. partner Pomeroy and Pomeroy, 1964—; pres. Topeka Escrow Service, Inc. Mem. Kans. State Senate, 1969—; Republican precinct committeeman, 1961—. Mem. Am., Kans., Topeka bar assns. Mason, Moose, Eagle. Author: (with others) Principles of Accounting, 1957. Home: 1619 Jewell St Topeka KS 66604 Office: 1415 Topeka Ave Topeka KS 66612

POMEROY, MAHLON WALTER, nursing home adminstr., clergyman; b. Franklin, N.Y., Oct. 12, 1904; s. Walter Jay and Barbara Helen (Teed) P.; B.A., U. Rochester (N.Y.), 1930; B.D., Colgate Rochester Div. Sch., 1934, M.Div., 1973; M.A., Syracuse (N.Y.) U., 1947, Ph.D., 1958; m. Antoinette M. Agnello, Nov. 29, 1934; children—Carol (Mrs. Maurice Lemelin), Renee Joan. Ordained to ministry Am. Baptist Ch., 1933; pastor First Bapt. Ch., Deposit, N.Y., 1934-39; pastor First Bapt. Ch., Carthage, N.Y., 1939-44; pastor North Bapt. Ch., Post Chester, N.Y., 1944-50; pastor Park Bapt. Ch., St. Paul, 1950-57; pastor Federated Ch., Wauconda, Ill., 1957-70; founder, adminstr. Town Hall Estates Nursing Home, Wauconda, 1970—. Co-originator, permanent panel mem. Town Hall TV show, 1952—; dir. Am. Religious Town Hall Meeting Inc., Dallas, 1952—; organizer Park Counseling Service, St. Paul, 1954-57; producer TV show It's A Family Affair, St. Paul, 1955; mem. White House Conf. Aging, 1971. Mem. Sigma Xi, Psi Chi. Clubs: Masons, Rotary, Lions. Contbg. author: America Prays, 1946; 450 Stories From Life, 1947. Contbr. numerous articles to religious jours. Home: 504 Brown St Wauconda IL 60084 Office: 176 Thomas Ct Wauconda IL 60084

POMINVILLE, HENRY ARTHUR, lawyer; b. Grosse Pointe Farms, Mich., Mar. 11, 1933; s. Arthur Henry and Esther Elizabeth (Stephens) P.; B.J., U. Mo., 1957; LL.B., Wayne State U., 1964; m. Mary Valerie Stackpoole, June 6, 1959; children—Stephen Eric, Lauretta Ann, Garrett Arthur, Kyle Edwin, Kathleen Ann. Newsman, UP Internat., 1957-58; with IRS, 1959-64; admitted to Mich. bar, 1964; staff atty. The Dow Chem. Co., Midland, Mich., 1964-65; asst. U.S. atty. U.S. Dept. Justice, Bay City, Mich., 1965-66; asst. pros. atty. Bay County (Mich.), 1966; practice law, Bay City, 1966—; dir. Internat. Terminals, Inc., Bay City. Mayor, City of Bay City, 1969-72; mem. Bay County Democratic Exec. Com., 1969-71. Served with AUS, 1953-55. Mem. Am., Bay County (treas. 1966-68), Lawyer-Pilots bar assns., State Bar Mich., Am., Mich. trial lawyers assns., Maritime Law Assn. U.S., U.S. Navy League (chpt. v.p. 1970), Kappa Tau Alpha, Delta Theta Phi. Clubs: K.C., Elks, Bay City Country. Office: 304 Davidson Bldg 916 Washington Ave Bay City MI 48706

POMMREHN, RICHARD JUNIOR, publishing co. exec.; b. Iowa City, Apr. 17, 1924; s. Arthur R. and Leone K. (Dick) P.; student U. Louisville, 1944, Westminister Coll., 1944-45; B.B.A., Tulane U., 1947; M.A., Drake U., 1953; m. Patricia A. Bahr, June 6, 1952; 1 son, Mark R. Accountant, Standard Oil Co., Des Moines, 1947-51; dir. research Wallaces Farmer, mag., Des Moines, 1951, Wis. Agriculturist Mag., Racine, 1951—; dir. research Prairie Farmer mag., Chgo., 1957—; asst. gen. mgr. Wallace Homestead Co., Des Moines, 1973, gen. mgr., 1974—, v.p., 1977—; v.p., mgr. Agrl. Insight, 1967—; dir. research Midwest Unit Farm Publs., 1969—; mem. census adv. com. on agrl. statistics, 1962—. Served with USNR, 1944-47. Methodist (state bd. mission 1969-73). Home: 1225 18th St West Des Moines IA 50265 Office: 1912 Grand Ave Des Moines IA 50305

POMROY, CAROL E., guidance counselor; b. Hibbing, Minn., Nov. 7, 1926; d. O. Edwin and Tillie F. (Lycander) Eyberg; A.A., Hibbing Jr. Coll., 1946; B.S.E., U. Minn., 1957, B.S. magna cum laude in Psychology, Library Sci., 1948, M.A. in Ednl. Psychology, 1963; m. James L. Pomroy, Aug. 4, 1950 (dec.); children—Susan J., James E., Robert L., Katherine Ann. Librarian U. Minn., Duluth, 1948-51, Mpls. Pub. Library, 1952-56, Mpls. Pub. Schs., 1957-62; counselor Mpls. Pub. Schs., 1963—. Pres. Mpls. Counselors Forum, 1977. Presenter Commrs. Nat. Conf. Career Edn., Houston, 1976. NDEA fellow; mem. Minn. Assn. Secondary Sch. Counselors and Coll. Admissions Officers (past pres.), Am., Minn. personnel and guidance assns., Minn., Am. sch. counselors assns., Nat. Vocat. Guidance Assn., Minn. Vocat. Guidance Assn., Nat. Assn. Coll. Admissions Counselors, Mpls. Fedn. Tchrs., Pi Lambda Theta Epsilon. Methodist. Home: 3307 Lawrence Rd Minneapolis MN 55429 Office: 700 22d Ave NE Minneapolis MN 55418

PONDROM, LEE GIRARD, physicist, educator; b. Dallas, Dec. 26, 1933; s. Levi Girard and Guinevere (Miller) P.; B.S., So. Meth. U., 1953; S.M., U. Chgo., 1956, Ph.D., 1958; m. Cyrena Jo Norman, Aug. 25, 1961. Instr. physics Columbia U., 1960-63; asso. prof. physics U. Wis., Madison, 1963-69, prof., 1969—; mem. high energy adv. com. Brookhaven Nat. Lab., 1973-75. Trustee Univs. Research Assn., 1973-76. Served as 1st lt. USAF, 1958-60. J.S. Guggenheim Meml. fellow, 1971-72. Fellow Am. Phys. Soc. (sec.-treas. div. particles and fields 1977—). Exptl. researcher elementary particle physics. Home: 2826 Mason St Madison WI 53705

PONITZ, DAVID HENRY, coll. pres.; b. Royal Oak, Mich., Jan. 21, 1931; s. Henry John and Jeanette (Bouwman) P.; A.B., U. Mich., 1952, M.A., 1954; Ed.D., Harvard U., 1964; m. Doris Humes, Aug. 5, 1956; children—Catherine Anne, David Robinson. Supr., Waldron (Mich.) Area Schs., 1958-60; research asso. Harvard U., 1960-62; supt. Freeport (Ill.) Pub. Schs., 1962-65; pres. Washtenaw Community Coll., Ann Arbor, Mich., 1965-75, Sinclair Community Coll., Dayton, Ohio, 1975—; mem. nat. adv. bd. Am. Coll. Testing Program, 1967-73. Pres. Portage Trails council Boy Scouts Am., 1970-71; campaign chmn. Washtenaw United Way, 1974; mem. exec. com. Region VII Boy Scouts Am., 1970—. Served with AUS, 1954-56. Recipient Silver Beaver award Boy Scouts Am., 1974. Mem. Am. Assn. Sch. Adminstrs., Am. Assn. Jr. and Community Colls., Mich. Community Coll. Assn. (pres. 1969-70), Mich. Council Community Coll. Adminstrs. (pres. 1968-69). Editorial bd. Community Coll. Rev., 1971—, Nation's Schs., Community Coll. Jour. Home: 5556 Viewpoint Dr Dayton OH 45459 Office: 444 W 3d St Dayton OH 45402

PONKA, JOSEPH LUKE, surgeon; b. Gary, W.Va., May 18, 1913; s. John and Barbara (Visoglant) P.; A.B., B.S., W. Va. U., 1940; M.D., Wash. U., 1942; M.S.C., U. Mich., 1953; m. Clare Margaret Straub, June 8, 1938; children—Joseph L., Jr., George J., Clare Suzette, Carol Jo. Intern, Henry Ford Hosp., Detroit, 1942-43, resident, 1946-50, dir. surg. edn. program, 1975—; practice medicine specializing in surgery, Detroit, 1951—; asso. clin. prof. U. Mich., Ann Arbor, 1970-77, clin. prof., 1977—. Bd. dirs. Children's Orthogenic Sch., 1960-64. Served with AUS, 1943-46. Recipient Sci. award A.C.S., 1966. Mem. A.C.S., AMA, Am. Proctologic Soc., Am. Surg. Assn., Detroit Surg. Soc. (pres. 1968-69), Detroit Acad. Surgery (pres. 1967-68), Am. Soc. Colon and Rectal Surgeons, Am. Med. Writers Assn., Am. Geriatric Soc., Am. Assn. Med. Clinics, Collegium Internat. Chirurgiae Digestivae, Detroit Gastroenterological Soc., Detroit Physiol. Soc., Detroit Acad. Medicine, Mich. State (mem. jud. com. 1974-75), Wayne County (mem. com. govt. in medicine 1974-75) med. socs., Soc. de Chirurgie Internat., Soc. Surgery Alimentary Tract, Pan Pacific, Western, Central surgical assns. Editor: Detroit Med. News, 1975-76. Contbr. articles in field to med. jours. Home: 1520 W Boston Blvd Detroit MI 48206 Office: Henry Ford Hosp 2799 W Grand Boulevard Detroit MI 48202

PONSETI, IGNACIO VIVES, physician, educator; b. Spain, June 3, 1914; s. Miguel B. and Margaret F. (Vives) P.; B.S., U. Barcelona, 1930, M.D., 1936; m. Helena Pereas, 1961; 1 son, William. Intern, Hosp. Clinico, Barcelona, Spain, 1936-37; resident in orthopedic surgery U. Iowa Hosps., Iowa City, 1941-44; instr. orthopedic surgery U. Iowa, Iowa City, 1944-56, prof., 1956—; cons. orthopedic tng. com. HEW, 1960-66. Recipient Outstanding Orthopedic Research award Kappa Delta, 1956; Shands lectr. in orthopedic surgery, 1975. Mem. A.C.S., Am. Acad. Orthopedic Surgery, Am. Orthopedic Assn., Internat. Soc. Orthopedic Surgery, Sigma Xi. Contbr. numerous articles on bone growth and skeletal anomalies to med. jours. Home: 110 Oak Ridge St Iowa City IA 52240 Office: U Iowa Med Sch Iowa City IA 52240

PONT, JOHN, educator, football coach; b. Canton, Ohio, Nov. 13, 1927; s. Bautista and Susie (Sikurinec) P.; B.S., Miami U., Oxford, Ohio, 1952, M.S., 1956; m. H. Sandra Stoutt, June 23, 1956; children—John W., Jennifer Ann, Jeffrey David. Profl. football player, Can., 1952-53; instr., freshman football-basketball coach Miami U., 1953-55, head football coach, asst. prof., 1955-62; head football coach Yale, 1963-65; head football coach, prof. Ind. U., Bloomington, 1965-73; prof., head football coach Northwestern U., Evanston, Ill., 1973-77, athletic dir., 1973—. Athletic dir. Jewish Community Center, Canton, 1953; mem. Pres.'s Council on Phys. Fitness; mem. legis. spl. com. on recruiting Nat. Collegiate Athletic Assn. Chmn. Ind. Easter Seal, 1968-69; chmn. Ind. div. Cancer Crusade, 1969. Mem. bd. Multiple Sclerosis; bd. dirs. Chgo. council Boy Scouts Am. Served with USNR, 1945-47. Named Football Coach of Year, Coaches Assn., 1967, Football Writers' Coach of Year, 1967; recipient Significant Sig award, 1968. Mem. Am. Football Coaches Assn. (chmn. ethics com.), Blue Key, Sigma Chi (sec. 1951), Phi Epsilon Kappa (pres. 1951), Omicron Delta Kappa. Republican. Home: 2520 Sheridan Rd Evanston IL 60201

PONTIUS, HAROLD JACKSON, trade assn. exec.; b. Ames, Iowa, July 25, 1916; s. Pierce Benjamin and Lenore (Leek) P.; student Iowa State Coll., 1937-39; m. Barbara Straight, July 12, 1942; children—Leann Straight Peach. Supr. adminstrv. services Douglas Aircraft Corp., Long Beach, Calif., 1939-44; exec. sec. Pasadena (Calif.) Bd. Realtors, 1944-48; edn. dir., exec. v.p. Calif. Real Estate Assn., Los Angeles, 1948-70; exec. v.p. Nat. Assn. Realtors, Chgo., 1970—; Internat. Real Estate Fedn. rep. NGO sect. UN 1975—; mem. real estate adv. com. U. Calif., 1957-70; mem. state of Calif. Real Estate Commn., 1959-70; U.S. del. UN Conf. on Human Settlements, 1976. Exec. dir. Pasadena Improvement Assn., 1945-48; mem. Adv. Council on Research in Energy Conservation, 1975-77. Recipient World medal Internat. Real Estate Fedn., 1972. Mem. Am. Soc. Assn. Execs., U.S. C. of C., SAR, Sons of Spanish Am. War Vets., Lambda Alpha (internat. pres. 1974-75, treas. 1976-77). Republican. Editor Calif. Real Estate Mag., 1948-70, REALTOR Headlines, 1970-76, REALTORS Rev., 1977—. Home: 175 E Delaware Pl Apt 8909 Chicago IL 60611 Office: Nat Assn Realtors 430 N Michigan Ave Chicago IL 60601

POOL, ERNEST HOWARD, JR., lawyer; b. Ottawa, Ill., July 22, 1922; s. Ernest Howard and Mildred Helene (Keeler) P.; A.B., U. Ill., 1947, J.D., 1949; m. Sylvia Jean Arnold, Aug. 16, 1947; children—Catherine Anne, Leslie Jean. Admitted to Ill. bar, 1949; since practiced in Ottawa; asso. firm Hibbs, Pool & Langer, 1949-51; partner Pool & Langer, 1951-70, Pool & Pool, 1970—. Master in chancery Circuit Ct. La Salle County (Ill.), 1957-58. Served with AUS, 1944-45; ETO. Decorated Purple Heart with oak leaf cluster. Fellow Am. Coll. Trial Lawyers; mem. Am., Ill. State, LaSalle County (pres. 1968-69) bar assns. Clubs: Masons, Elks, Rotary. Home: Rural Route 1 Ottawa IL 61350 Office: 611 1/2 LaSalle St Ottawa IL 61350

POOL, JOHN DAVID, endocrinologist; b. Zeeland, Mich., Aug. 23, 1923; s. Robert and Wilhelmina Cornelia (Bolier) P.; A.B., Calvin Coll., 1947; M.D., Wayne State U., 1951; m. Miriam Ruth Oom, June 22, 1945; children—Jayne E., Deborah L., Ruth M., Joan R. Intern, Butterworth Hosp., Grand Rapids, Mich., 1951-52; resident Wayne Univ. Hosps., Detroit, 1954-57; fellow in medicine Mass. Gen. Hosp., Boston, 1970-72; gen. practice medicine, Grand Rapids, 1952-54; practice medicine specializing in internal medicine, Kalamazoo, 1957-70; chmn. dept. medicine Broson Hosp., Kalamazoo, 1967-69; dir. endocrine service St. Mary's Hosp., 1972—, dir. edn., med. service, 1972—, chmn. dept. medicine, 1976—; instr. internal medicine Wayne U. Sch. Medicine, 1957; chmn. instnl. rev. com. St. Mary's Hosp., 1974—; asso. prof. medicine Mich. State U. Coll. Human Medicine, 1975—; cons. endocrinology Butterworth, Blodgett, Ferguson hosps. Served with AUS, 1943-45. Diplomate Am. Bd. Internal Medicine. Decorated Purple Heart; Dorothy S. Hutton Traveling scholar, 1970. Mem. AAAS, A.C.P., Mich. State, Kent County med. socs. Mem. Christian Reformed Ch. Home: 50 College NE Grand Rapids MI 49503 Office: 200 Jefferson SE Grand Rapids MI 49503

POOLE, CHARLES PINCKNEY, psychologist; b. Lynn, Ala., Jan. 20, 1893; s. Ephraim Bailey and Mary Caroline (Reynolds) P.; Litt.B., David Lipscomb Coll., 1918; A.B. (fellow in psychology), Clark U., 1920; M.A., Harvard U., 1925; Ph.D., U. Wash., 1948; postgrad. Tex. Christian U., 1919, Vanderbilt U., 1926; m. LaVerne Gossum, Feb. 22, 1936 (dec. May 1976); children—Morgan, Stanley, Charles. Head dept. polit. sci. Abilene (Tex.) Christian Coll., 1920-21; jr. master Boston Latin Sch., Melrose High Sch., Boston, 1922-25; prof. physics, chemistry David Lipscomb Coll., Nashville, 1925-28; prof. psychology Murray (Ky.) State U., 1928-36; head dept. psychology, philosophy Whitworth Coll., Spokane, Wash., 1939-42; bursar, prof. psychology Boise (Idaho) Coll., 1942-43; head dept. psychology U. Alaska, Coll., 1943-46; prof. psychology Central Mich. U., Mt. Pleasant, 1947-65, psychologist U. Clinic, 1948-57; lectr. U. Mich. Grad. Sch., Ann Arbor, 1948-58; cons. psychologist, Mount Pleasant, 1963—. Chmn., Mount Pleasant Housing Commn., 1966; mem. WHO. Fellow Am. Assn. Mental Deficiency; mem. Am., Mich., Midwestern psychol. assns., So. Soc. Philosophy and Psychology, Mich. Soc. Cons. Psychologists, Am. Assn. Marriage and Family Counselors (clin. mem.). Rotarian. Home: 901 Watson Rd Mt Pleasant MI 48858 Office: 901 Watson Rd Mt Pleasant MI 48858

POOLE, JAMES IRA, lawyer; b. Muskogee, Okla., Nov. 3, 1915; s. James Ira and Ethel (Lomax) P.; A.B., U. Kans., 1935, LL.B., 1937; m. Eunice (Betty) Creager, Oct. 16, 1937; children—Judith (Mrs. Achim von der Nuell), Mary (Mrs. Kenneth A. Beattie). Admitted to Mich. bar, 1938, Okla. bar, 1943, Wis. bar, 1944; atty. Phillips Petroleum Co., Mich. and Okla., 1937-42; mem. firm Foley & Lardner, Milw., 1943—; dir., mem. exec. com. Globe-Union Inc., 1964—, Square D Co., 1975—; dir. Compania Gen. De Electronica, S.A., (Mexico), Centralab-Taiwan, Ltd., A.F. Gallun & Sons Corp., officer, dir. Fairfield Greenhouse, Inc., 1965—; officer, dir., mem. exec. com. E.R. Wagner Mfg. Co., 1959—. Mem. exec. com. Goodwill Industries Milw. Area, Inc., 1951—. Officer, bd. dirs. Edel Charitable Found.; bd. dirs. Square D Found., 1975—. Mem. Am., Wis. bar assns., Delta Tau Delta. Republican. Conglist. Clubs: Milwaukee (past pres.), Milwaukee Country, Town (Milw.). Home: 3069 E Newport Ct Milwaukee WI 53211 Office: 777 E Wisconsin Av Milwaukee WI 53202

POOLE, JOHN BAYARD, lawyer; b. Chgo., May 17, 1912; s. John E. and Edna (Carpenter) P.; B.A., U. Chgo., 1932; LL.B., Detroit Coll. Law, 1936; J.D., 1968; m. Leah B. Baldwin, Feb. 25, 1941 (dec.); children—Michael B., Leah Kathleen. Admitted to Mich. bar, 1936, since practiced in Detroit; sr. partner Poole, Littell & Sutherland, 1936-76, Butzel, Long, Gust, Klein & Van Zile, 1976—; sec., v.p., dir. Storer Broadcasting Co., Detroit, 1945-55; chmn. exec. com. Capital Cities Communications Co., N.Y.C., 1960-64; pres., chmn. bd. Poole Broadcasting Co. (WJRT-TV Flint, Mich., WPRI-TV, Providence, WTEN-TV, Albany), 1964—; dir. Mich. Nat. Bank Detroit, Mich Nat. Bank, Lansing, Mich. Nat. Corp., White Motor Corp., Cleve. Bd. dirs. Greater Detroit Area Hosp. Council, 1967—; trustee, pres., chmn. exec. com. William Beaumont Hosp., Royal Oak, Mich., 1963-70; trustee U. Chgo., 1974—, Cranbrook Ednl. Community, 1976. Fellow Am. Bar Found.; mem. Am., Mich., Detroit bar assns., Am. Judicature Soc. Episcopalian. Clubs: Detroit Athletic, Detroit; Bloomfield Hills Country (pres. 1964); Marco Polo (N.Y.C.); Sleepy Hollow Country (Scarborough, N.Y.); Key Largo (Fla.) Anglers; Indian Creek Country (Miami Beach, Fla.); Cat Cay (Bahamas). Home: 229 Barden Rd Bloomfield Hills MI 48013 Office: 1700 N Woodward Ave Bloomfield Hills MI 48013

POOTS, C. ALLAN, real estate broker, developer, contractor, appraiser, certified property mgr.; b. Newton, Iowa, Jan. 29, 1934; s. Clifford Lyman and Helen May (Cool) P.; student Simpson Coll., 1953, Iowa State U., 1953, U. Iowa, 1956-59; m. Kathleen M. LaBudde, Aug. 17, 1957; children—Michael Allan, Patricia Ann. Real estate broker, developer, Coralville, Iowa, 1960—; officer, dir. various corps., 1963—; asst. instr. mech. engring. State U. Iowa, 1957-59. Hon. trustee Cedars Home Children, 1972. Served with AUS, 1954-55. Recipient archtl. design awards Iowa State U., Iowa Homebuilders Assn., 1965-67. Home: 10 Olde Hickory Ridge Lakewood Hills Coralville Iowa City IA 52241 Office: PO Box 5095 Coralville Br Iowa City IA 52241

POPE, DONNA KOLNIK, state legislator; b. Cleve., Oct. 15, 1931; d. John Emil and Marie Josephine (Thiel) Kolnik; ed. pub. schs., adult evening classes; m. Raymond Pope, Oct. 21, 1950; children—Candace (Mrs. George Evans), Cheryl Ann. Supr. Cuyahoga County Bd. Elections, also Parma ward leader, 1966-72; precinct committeeman, 1966—; mem. Rep. State Central Com., 1966-72; rep. Ohio Gen. Assembly, 1972—; mem. Cuyahoga County Rep. Exec. Com., House ways and means, state govt. coms., Nat. Legis. Com. on Sci. and Tech., Gov.'s Task Force on Health Care, spl. study com. health care costs Legislative Service Commn., Parma Women's Rep. Club. Active P.T.A., Greater Cleve. Citizens League. Named an outstanding woman legislator in nation, Eagleton Inst. Politics of Rutgers U., 1972. Mem. Nat. Soc. State Legislators, Nat. Orgn. Women Legislators, Internat. Platform Assn., Am. Bus. Women's Assn., Nat. Travel Club. Roman Catholic. Home: 3915 Longwood Ave Parma OH 44134 Office: State House Columbus OH 43215

POPE, JEAN GROVE, psychologist, educator; b. Cin., June 12, 1927; d. Fred E. and Gertrude (Welch) Grove; B.S., Purdue U., 1966; M.Ed., U. Cin., 1969, Ed.D., 1977; m. Jack H. Pope, Aug. 24, 1946; children—Michael, Nancy, Holly. Tchr., Eastern Hills Elementary Sch., Cin., 1966-67; sch. psychologist Clermont County (Ohio) Pub. Schs., Batavia, 1969-74, Hamilton County (Ohio) Pub. Schs., Cin., 1974-75, instr. Clermont Coll., Batavia, 1975—. Mem. Nat., Ohio assns. sch. psychologists, Am., Cin. psychol. assns., Ohio Orgn. Human Service/Mental Health Educators, Kappa Delta Pi. Home: 6944 Miami Bluff Dr Cincinnati OH 45227 Office: Kenwood Psychological Services Cincinnati OH 45236

POPE, JOHN DAWSON, III, lawyer; b. Butte, Mont., May 29, 1913; s. John Dawson and Abbie Esther (Shaw) P.; student Mont. State Sch. Mines, 1929-30; B.S., Mont. State U., 1933; J.D., Harvard U., 1936; postgrad. Mass. Inst. Tech., 1936; m. Rebecca Elizabeth Callis, May 31, 1952; children—John Daniel (dec.), Judith Anne, Elizabeth Pope Ford. Admitted to Mo. bar, 1937; since practiced in St. Louis; asst. patent atty. Monsanto Chem. Co., St. Louis, 1936-39; asso. firm Haynes & Koenig, St. Louis, 1939-50; partner firm Koenig & Pope and successor, St. Louis, 1950-63; mem. firm John D. Pope III, 1964-76; partner firm Pope & Fishel, 1977—; lectr. Washington U., St. Louis, 1964; mem. bd. admissions U.S. Dist. Ct., Eastern Dist. Mo., 1964-70, chmn., 1969-70. Mem. Am. Chem. Soc., AAAS, U.S. Trademark Assn. (lawyers adv. com. 1952-54, 57-59, 63-66, 74-77), Am. Patent Law Assn., Am., Fed. bar assns., Mo. Bar, Bar Assn. Met. St. Louis (chmn. patent sect. 1958-59), Phi Kappa Phi. Clubs: Mo. Athletic, Media (St. Louis). Editor Am. Philatelic Congress Book, 1954. Home: 55 South Gore Ave Webster Groves MO 63119 Office: 818 Olive St Saint Louis MO 63101

POPE, SARAH GEORGINA, physician; b. N.S., Can., Oct. 29, 1940; d. George Donovan and Hughena (Mac Innis) Donovan; came to U.S., 1969; B.Sc. in Chemistry, Mt. St. Vincent Coll., 1960; M.D., Ottawa U., 1964; m. Dec. 14, 1968; children—Sarah, Patrick. Intern, Ottawa (Can.) Gen. Hosp., 1964-65; resident Royal Victoria Hosp., 1966-68; resident Henry Ford Hosp., Detroit, 1969, asso. radiologist, 1970-73; asso. radiologist Sinai Hosp. of Detroit, 1973—, dir. residency tng. program, 1973—. Mem. AMA, Wayne County Med. Soc., Am. Coll. Radiology, Mich. Radiol. Soc., Am. Soc. Nuclear Medicine. Home: 1884 Balmoral Dr Detroit MI 48203 Office: 6767 W Outer Dr Detroit MI 48235

POPE, SHARON KAY, ednl. adminstr.; b. Kansas City, Mo., Dec. 27, 1944; d. Allen David and Mildred Maybel (Wilcox) P.; B.S. cum laude, U. Mo., 1966, M.Ed., 1967, Ph.D., 1971; m. Bob Callis, Sept. 4, 1971. Adminstrv. asst. U. Mo., Columbia, 1967-68, asst. dir. women student affairs, 1968-69, grad. asst. Inst. Personnel Work, 1969-70, asst. dir. Center for Student Life, 1974—; instr. edn. U. Mo., Kansas City, 1970-71, asst. prof. edn., counseling psychologist, 1971-72, asst. dir. testing and counseling center, asst. prof. edn., 1972-73; mem. adv. bd. Women's Resource Service, U. Mo., Kansas City, 1970-72. Mem. Am. (pres. 1977), Mo. (planning com. 1973) coll. personnel assns., Am., Mo. (chmn. research on changing women's roles 1973) personnel and guidance assns., Nat. Vocat. Guidance Assn., Assn. Counselor Educators and Suprs., Mo. Psychol. Assn., Mo. Guidance Assn., U. Mo. Columbia Edn. Alumni Assn. (dir. 1969-72), Pi Lambda Theta, Phi Delta Kappa, Delta Gamma. Club: Columbia Dance. Home: Route 4 Box 205 Columbia MO 65201 Office: 106 Read Hall U Mo Columbia MO 65201

POPKE, CHESTER A., supt. schs.; b. Birnamwood, Wis., July 9, 1926; s. Walter E. and Orma Marie (St. Thomas) P.; B.S., U. Wis. at Oshkosh; M.A., U. No. Colo., postgrad., 1968; m. Sept. 29, 1954; 1 dau., Suzanne. Tchr., prin. Kiel, Mineral Point, Wis., 1954-61; supt. schs. Lomira, Wis., 1961-67; supt. schs. DeSoto, Wis., 1971—. Insp., Utility Commn., Stoddard, Wis.; cons. ednl. TV. Served with USNR, AUS, USAF. Decorated Purple Heart. Mem. NEA (life), Wis., Am. assns. sch. dist. adminstrs., Nat. Assn. Secondary Sch. Prins., Nat. Assn. U. Profs., Nat. Assn. Lab. Sch. Adminstrs., Phi Delta Kappa. Clubs: Lions, Eagles. Home: Rural Route 2 Box 167B Wausaukee WI 54177 Office: Wausaukee WI 54177

POPOVICH, PETER STEPHEN, lawyer; b. Crosby, Minn., Nov. 27, 1920; s. Peter and Rose Mary (Mihelich) P.; A.A., Hibbing Jr. Coll., 1940; B.A., U. Minn., 1942; J.D. (Minn. Bar Assn. scholar 1946), St. Paul Coll. Law, 1946; children—Victoria Ann, Dorothy Rose, Stephen Peter, Susan Jane. Admitted to Minn. bar, 1947, Fed. bar, 1947, U.S. Supreme Ct. bar, 1956; practiced in St. Paul, 1947—; mem. firm Peterson, Popovich, Knutson & Flynn, St. Paul, 1947—. Counsel, Minn. Sch. Bds. Assn., 1961, Minn. Broadcasters Assn., 1970, various sch. dists., 1947—; chmn. planning com., St. Mary's Point, 1970-77; mem. Minn. Bd. Continuing Legal Edn., 1975—. Mem. State Coll. Bd., 1965-69; mem. Higher Edn. Coordination Com., 1968-69. Mem. Minn. Ho. of Reps., 1953-63. Mem. Am., Minn., Ramsey County, Washington County bar assns., Minn. Hist. Soc. (exec. council 1958—), Nat. Orgn. Legal Problems in Edn. (dir. 1976—), Gamma Eta Gamma. Home: 1400 River Rd St Marys Point Route 1 Lakeland MN 55043 Office: 314 Minnesota Bldg St Paul MN 55101

POPOVSKY, JULIO, physician; b. Buenos Aires, Argentina, Sept. 20, 1936; s. Abraham and Clara (Dimand) P.; Bachiller, Colegio Nacional San Martin, Buenos Aires, 1954; M.D., U. Buenos Aires, 1960; came to U.S., 1960, naturalized, 1975. m. Eliza Jane Goodbar, May 13, 1961; children—Ricardo Jack, Deborah Ann. Intern, Chesapeake and Ohio Hosp., Clifton Forge, Va., 1960-61; resident in surgery Mt. Sinai Hosp., Cleve., 1961-65; resident cancer surgery Meml. Cancer Hosp., N.Y.C., 1965-66; practice medicine specializing in gen. surgery, Bahia Blanca, Argentina, 1966-69; mem. staff Italiano Regional Hosp.; fellow trauma unit U. Md., Balt., 1969; resident in thoracic-cardiological vascular surgery St. Vincent Charity Hosp., Cleve., 1969-71; practice medicine specializing in thoracic cardiovascular surgery, Cleve., 1971—; mem. staff Mt. Sinai Hosp., Suburban Hosp., St. Vincent Hosp. Sr. clin. instr. Case Western Res. U., Cleve., 1975—. Fellow A.C.S., Am. Coll. Angiology Am. Coll. Cardiology. Home: 21449 Shaker Blvd Cleveland OH 44122 Office: 11811 Shaker Blvd Cleveland OH 44120

POPPE, WASSILY, chemist; b. Riga, Latvia, Nov. 10, 1918; s. Wilhelm and Barbara (Gogotoff) P.; student Kaiser Friedrich Wilhelm U., Berlin, 1936-39; cand. chem., U. Tubingen (Germany), 1947; dipl. chem. Inst. Tech. Stuttgart (Germany), 1949; Ph.D., U. Pitts., 1966; m. Larissa Heffner, Oct. 16, 1942; 1 dau., Katherine Poppe Zawadzkas. Came to U.S., 1959, naturalized, 1965. Chemist, Dr. Hans Kittel Chem. Lab., Germany, 1949-50; devel. chemist Karl Worwag Lack & Farbenfabrik, Germany, 1950-51, prodn. mgr. paint Pinturas Iris, Venezuela, 1951-53; lab. supr. Pinturas Tucan, Venezuela, 1953-54, tech. dir., 1954-57, plant mgr. paint prodn. 1957-59; chemist PPG Industries Springfield, Pa., 1959-64; research asst. phys. chemistry U. Pitts., 1964-66; group leader surface chemistry Avisun Corp., Marcus-Hook, Pa., 1966-68; research supr. Amoco Chems., Naperville, Ill., 1968—. Fellow Am. Inst. Chemists; mem. Am. Chem. Soc., Sigma Xi. Home: 105 Main St Lombard IL 60148 Office: PO Box 400 Naperville IL 60540

POPPELBAUM, WOLFGANG JOHANN, physicist; b. Frankfurt, Germany, Aug. 28, 1924; s. Hermann and Edith (Baumann) P.; M.S., Lausanne U., 1948, Ph.D., 1953. Came to U.S., 1957. Prin. investigator charge circuit research group Digital Computer Lab. U. Ill., 1954—, dir. Info. Engring. Lab., 1973—. Fellow IEEE; mem. Swiss, Am. phys. socs., Sigma Xi. Author: Computer Hardware Theory; also articles to profl. jours. Home: 2007 S Anderson Urbana IL 61801 Office: Digital Computer Lab U Ill Urbana IL 61801

POPPEN, BRUCE JENNINGS, real estate appraiser; b. Holland, Mich., May 31, 1932; s. Henry Jennings and Anna (Goorman) P.; student Western Mich. U., 1951-52; grad. real estate program U. Mich., 1964; m. Lois Ruth Bolt, June 19, 1959; children—Jeffrey, SueAnne, MaryLynn. Appraiser Mich. Nat. Bank, Grand Rapids, 1961-67; practice real estate appraising, cons. Grand Rapids, 1967—. Lectr. assessor's Kent County certification program; adj. faculty Aquinas Coll., Grand Rapids, 1971-75. Mem. bd. of rev., Grand Rapids, 1968. Bd. dirs. Calvin Alumni Players, Grand Rapids, 1962-64. Mem. Am. Inst. Real Estate Appraisers (dir. Mich. chpt. 1977—), Appraisal Inst., Soc. Real Estate Appraisers (pres. chpt. 1972-73), Nat. Assn. Realtors, Mich. Real Estate Assn., Grand Rapids Real Estate Bd., Opera Assn. Western Mich. (v.p. 1969-71). Club: Cascade Country. Home: 1203 E Paris Rd Grand Rapids MI 49506 Office: 510 Peoples Bldg 60 Monroe NW Grand Rapids MI 49503

POPRICK, MARY ANN, psychologist, educator; b. Chgo., June 25, 1939; d. Michael and Mary (Mihalcik) P.; B.A., De Paul U., 1960, M.A., 1964; Ph.D., Loyola U., Chgo., 1968. Intern psychology Elgin (Ill.) State Hosp., 1961-62; staff psychologist, 1962; staff psychologist Ill. State Tng. Sch. for Girls, Geneva, Ill., 1962-63. Mt. Sinai Hosp., Chgo., 1963-64; lectr. psychology Loyola U. at Chgo,, 1964-67; asst. prof. Lewis U., Lockport, Ill., 1967-70, asso. prof., 1970-75, chmn. dept. psychology, 1968-72; adj. asso. prof. South Chgo. Community Hosp. Sch. Nursing, Lewis U., 1975; postdoctoral intern clin. psychology Ill. State Psychiat. Inst., Chgo., 1972-73; pvt. clin. practice, asso. with Paul P. David, M.D., Riverdale, Ill., 1973—; mem. asso. sci. staff Riveredge Hosp., Forest Park, Ill., 1975, 76. Co-chmn. commn. on personal growth and devel. Congregation 3d Order St. Francis of Mary Immaculate, Joliet, Ill., 1970-71. Mem. Am., Midwestern, Ill. (sec.-treas. acad. sect. 1975-77, chairperson acad. sect. 1978—, mem. program com. 1977—) psychol. assns., Psychologists Interested in Religious Issues, AAUP, AAAS, Council for Advancement Psychol. Professions and Scis., Kappa Gamma Pi, Psi Chi (sec. 1964-65, pres. 1965-66). Home: 547 Marquette Ave Calumet City IL 60409 Office: 159 E 144th St Riverdale IL 60627

PORCHEDDU, JOSEPH WARREN, display fireworks mfg. co. exec.; b. Danville, Ill., Apr. 29, 1926; s. Joseph P. and Helen (Gray) P.; student Mo. Mil. Acad., 1942-44, McCormick Sch. Commerce, 1946-47; m. Betty Sliva, Aug. 23, 1957; children—Gail, Susan, Stacey, Shelley. With Ill. Fireworks Co., Inc., Danville, 1944—, pres., 1955—. Served with AUS, 1944-46. Mem. Am. Legion (past asst. dep. sgt. at arms 1971-73). Clubs: Elks, Danville Boat, Danville Country. Home: 10 Carriage Ln Danville IL 61832 Office: PO Box 792 Danville IL 61832

POROD, ROBERT FRANCIS, devel. engr.; b. Chgo., Oct. 10, 1946; s. Rudolph F. and Lorraine J. (Budzynski) P.; A.A., Morton Jr. Coll., 1966; B.S. in Mech. Analysis and Design Engring., U. Ill., Chgo., 1968; m. Janet M. Przybyl, Aug. 24, 1968; children—Robert Francis, Karyn M., Eric J. Devel. and product engr. Hawthorne sta. Western Electric Co., Chgo., 1968—. Pres. Med. Engring. Devel. Group, 1977—; publicity chmn. Lincoln PTA, 1976-77. Mem. ASME (asso.), Western Soc. Engrs. (asso.; Charles Ellet award 1976), U. Ill. Alumni Assn. (life), Polish Nat. Alliance. Roman Catholic. Club: Hunting and Fishing. Home: 3235 S 60th Ct Cicero IL 60650 Office: Hawthorne Sta Dept 8212 Chicago IL 60623

PORT, CURTIS DEWITT, veterinarian; b. Cheyenne, Wyo., Aug. 25, 1930; s. Harold DeWitt and Myrtle Elizabeth (Miller) P.; B.S., U. Calif., 1954, D.V.M., 1956; M.S., Northwestern U., 1963; Ph.D., U. Chgo., 1972; m. Janice Michaels, Aug. 10, 1957; children—John, Audrey. Practice veterinary medicine, San Bruno, Calif. and Morton

Grove, Ill., 1958-66; research investigator lab. animal medicine Hines (Ill.) VA Hosp., 1966-68; sr. veterinary pathologist Research Inst., Ill. Inst. Tech.; Chgo., 1970-74, sci. adviser, head exptl. pathology and animal resources, 1974-76; head pathology, pharmacology div. Baxter Labs., 1976; asso. prof. pathology Northwestern U. Med. Sch., Chgo., 1976—. Served with Veterinary Corps, U.S. Army, 1956-58. Diplomate Am. Coll. Lab. Animal Medicine. Mem. AVMA, Am. Assn. Lab. Animal Sci., Am. Soc. Lab. Animal Practitioners, AAAS. Contbr. articles to profl. pubs. Home: 1448 Lois St Park Ridge IL 60068 Office: Northwestern U Med Sch Chicago IL 60611

PORT, RICH BLESER, realtor; b. Chgo., Sept. 17, 1917; s. Fredrick James and Gretchen (Bleser) P.; B.S., U. Ill., 1939; student St. Norbert Coll., 1942; m. Mary Elizabeth Burns, Sept. 5, 1940; 1 dau., Elizabeth Anne Port Hallahan. Pres., Rich Port, Realtor, LaGrange, Ill., 1952-73, chmn. bd., 1973—; v.p. Dewry Ins. Agy., Inc., LaGrange, 1963—; pres. Rich Port Devel. Corp., LaGrange, 1955—, Residential Appraisal Co., Cebert-Rori, Inc.; dir. 1st Nat. Bank of Western Springs (Ill.). Dean, Ill. Realtors Inst.; chmn. bd. Nationwide Find-A-Home Service Inc.; past pres. Realtors Computer Service Inc. Mem. nat. adv. bd. Am. Security Council; army aide to Gov. Ill., 1969-73; past chmn. bd. West Suburban YMCA; trustee Lincoln Acad. Ill. Served to lt. col. AUS, 1939-46. Recipient awards including Ill. Realtor of Year, 1964; Oscar of Salesmanship award Am. Salesmasters; awards West Suburban YMCA, 1961, 65. Mem. LaGrange Real Estate Bd. (past pres.), Ill. (past pres.), Nat. (dir. 1964—, pres. 1970) assns. realtors, Realtors Nat. Mktg. Inst. (life gov.), West Suburban C. of C. (past pres.), Am. Mgmt. Assn., Chgo. Assn. Commerce and Industry, Exec. Club Chgo., U. Ill. Alumni Assn. (life), Nat. Guard Assn. U.S. (life), Assn. U.S. Army, Ill. Police Assn., Ill. C. of C., Am. Legion (past post comdr.; life), Mil. Order World Wars, Res. Officers Assn. U.S. (life), VFW, 40 and 8, Zeta Psi Alumni Assn., Lambda Alpha, Omega Tau Rho. Republican. Home: 801 N Spring Ave LaGrange Park IL 60525 Office: 547 S LaGrange Rd LaGrange IL 60525

PORTENIER, LILLIAN GERTRUDE, emeritus prof., author; b. Guide Rock, Nebr., Aug. 23, 1890; d. Jacob and Susanna (Suess) P.; High Sch. Tchrs. certificate Peru State Coll., 1917; grad. U. Nebr., 1922; A.S., U. Wyo., 1972, LL.D. (hon.), 1974; postdoctoral student U. London, 1939, U. Chgo., 1948. Tchr. pub. schs. Nebr., 1907-22, 1924; asst. prof. Columbia U., 1929-33; asso. prof. ednl. psychology U. Wyo., 1925-65, spl. prof., 1965-70; lectr. in field, 1970—. Mem. Internat. Psychologists, Phi Beta Kappa, Psi Chi. Home: 320 North Seward Red Cross NE 68970

PORTER, ALBERT S., civil engr.; b. Portsmouth, Va., Nov. 29, 1904; s. Albert S. and Lena (Edmonds) P.; B.C.E., Ohio State U., 1928; m. Genevieve J. Shaveyco, Dec. 29, 1949. Draftsman, asst. engr. City Plan Commn. and City Engrs. Office, Columbus, Ohio, 1925-29; engr., cons. Cleve. Hwy. Research Bur., 1929-32; chief dep. county engr. Cuyahoga County, Cleve., 1933-41, 46-47; Cuyahoga County engr., Cleve., 1947-76; mem. Freeway Bd., 1951—. Mem. Mental Health Commn.; exec. com. Metro; chmn. Cuyahoga County Charter Commn., 1959; mem. traffic adv. com. Cleve. Safety Council, 1959, v.p. pub. employees, 1960; chmn. County Airport Bldg. Commn., 1958; exec. bd. Cleve. Open Golf Tournament, 1964—; chmn. policy com. Democratic Exec. Com.; del. Dem. Nat. Conv., 1952, 56, 60, 64, 68, 72; nat. committeeman, 1964-72; Dem. candidate for Mayor Cleve., 1953; chmn. Dem. State Conv., 1958; candidate for gov., 1958; Ohio favorite son candidate for pres., 1960, 64; chmn. Dem. Exec. Com., 1963-69; chmn. Dem. Central Com., Cuyahoga County, 1964-69. Served to comdr. Civil Engr. Corps, USNR, 1941-46; comdr. Res. Named Engr. of Year, Cleve. Soc. Profl. Engr. and Cleve. Engring. Soc., K. C. Civic award, 1964; registered profl. engr., Ohio. Mem. Western Res. Hist. Soc., Phillis Wheatley Assn., Nat. Soc. Profl. Engrs., County Engrs. Assn. Ohio (past pres.), ASCE, Am. Roadbuilders Assn., Aircraft Owners and Pilots Assn., Smaller Bus. Assn., Nat. Assn. County Ofcls. (past mem. hwy. com.). Nat. Assn. County Engrs., Nat. Sojourners, Heroes of 76, SAR, Res. Officers Assn., Res. Officers Naval Services, Am. Legion, VFW, Mil. Order World Wars. Episcopalian. Clubs: Masons, Shriners, Eagles; Koran; Shrine Luncheon: Acacia Country (past dir.); Cleve. Auto, Cleve. Aviation (dir.); Bal Harbour. Home: 31179 S Woodland Rd Cleveland OH 44124

PORTER, DALE LINCOLN, lawyer; b. Des Moines, Jan. 16, 1925; s. Fred Cromer and Anita Louise (Conlee) P.; student St. Ambrose Coll., 1943-44; B.A., Drake U., 1949, J.D., 1949; m. Betty R. Dikeman, Dec. 31, 1945 (div. Feb. 1975); children—Dale Ross, Craig Raymond, Marcia Louise, Candace Anita, Jeffrey Douglas; m. 2d, A. Leta Dice, June 27, 1975. Admitted to Iowa bar, 1949; practiced in Des Moines, 1949—; mem. firms Lehmann, Hurlburt, Blanchard, Cless & Porter, 1949-61, Hurlburt, Blanchard, Cless & Porter, 1962-75; dir. Pioneer Hi-Bred Internat., Inc., Des Moines, Pioneer Hi-Bred Corn Co. of Ill., Princeton, Pioneer Hi-Bred, Inc., Tipton, Ind., Pioneer Hi-Bred Corn Co. of Canada, Ltd., 1960—. Mem. Plant Variety Protection Bd., U.S. Dept. Agr., 1971. Served with USNR, 1943-46. Mem. Nat. Council Comml. Plant Breeders (pres. 1973-74), Am. Seed Trade Assn. (com. chmn. 1955-73), Am., Iowa, Polk County bar assns., Helmet and Spurs, Order of the Coif, Chi Delta, Phi Alpha Delta. Club: Des Moines Golf and Country. Home: 3400 Skyline Dr West Des Moines IA 50310 Office: 1206 Mulberry St Des Moines IA 50308

PORTER, DAVID LINDSEY, historian; b. Holyoke, Mass., Feb. 18, 1941; s. Willis Hubert and Lora Frances (Bowen) P.; B.A., Franklin Coll. Ind., 1963; M.A., Ohio U., 1965; Ph.D., Pa. State U., 1970; m. Marilyn Esther Platt, Nov. 28, 1970; 1 son, Kevin Robert. Asst. prof. history Rensselaer Polytech. Inst., Troy, N.Y., 1970-75, co-dir. Am. studies program, 1972-74; adminstrv. asst. Municipal Civil Service Dept., Troy, 1975-77; prof. history, polit. sci. William Penn Coll., Oskaloosa, Ia., 1977—; participant seminar Inter-U. Consortium for Polit. Research, U. Mich., 1967; organizer lecture series Am.'s Religious Heritage, 1976; lectr. continuing edn. State U. N.Y., Albany, 1976. Chmn. bd. Christian edn. 1st Baptist Ch., Troy, 1971-76; chmn. Troy Area Bicentennial Com., 1975-76; mem. Oskaloosa Community Choir, 1977; bd. dirs. Troy Area Council Chs., 1974-76. Pres.'s scholar, 1959-63; Franklin scholar, 1959-63; Wilson fellow, 1963-65; NSF grantee, 1967; Faculty Travel grantee, 1974. Mem. Am. Hist. Assn., Orgn. Am. Historians, Ia., Mahaska County hist. socs., N. Am. Soc. Sport History, Soc. Am. Baseball Research, Soc. History of Am. Fgn. Relations, Am. Assn. U. Profs., Great Plains, Capital Dist. sports assns., Alpha Kappa Delta Pi, Phi Alpha Theta, Lancers, Blue Key. Author: Your New Career, 1976; also numerous hist. articles. Home: 616 4th Ave E Oskaloosa IA 52577 Office: William Penn Coll Oskaloosa IA 52577

PORTER, DONALD GAMALIEL, floor covering co. exec.; b. Marion, Ohio, Nov. 10, 1920; s. Talmage Newton and Mabel (Wottring) P.; B.Arch., Ohio State U., 1943; m. Jean Alice McCoskey, Nov. 27, 1943; children—Talmage Newton, Stephen Donald. Purchasing agt. Wallace F. Ackley Co., Columbus, Ohio, 1946-48; salesman Wilson Floors Co., Columbus, 1948-70, v.p. sales and mktg., 1970-77; pres. Porter Interior Surfaces Inc., Columbus, 1977—; instr. Builders Exchange Sch., Columbus, 1972—. Mem. Brookside Civic Assn., Worthington, Ohio, 1956—. Served with AUS, 1943-46. Mem. Constrn. Specifications Inst. (tech. com. awards 1968—), Builders Exchange Columbus (dir. 1970), Alpha Rho Chi. Methodist (trustee 1952-58). Clubs: Masons, Shriners, Univ. (Columbus); Ohio State U. Faculty. Home: 6541 Winston Ct Worthington OH 43085 Office: 4243 Diplomacy Dr Columbus OH 43228

PORTER, EARL DOSSETT, JR., garden sales exec.; b. Poplar Bluff, Mo., June 17, 1917; s. Earl Dossett and Pearl Ermine (Mace) P.; student pub. schs. Mattoon, Ill.; m. Helen Ruth, Jan. 1, 1940; children—Patricia Louise, Mary Lynn, Virginia Josephine, Earl D. III, Jeanne Anne, Helen Ruth, William Henry II, Laurie Suzanne, Michael Joseph, James Andrew. Ops. mgr. Hayes Freight Lines, 1934-40, Fed. Express, Inc., Indpls., 1940-46; pres. Porter-Daugherty Agy., Inc., Indpls., 1946-54, Stonybrook Garden Shoppe & Landscaping Corp., 1954-64, Garden Sales Assos., Inc., Indpls., 1964—; partner MW Peat Co.; chmn. MW Garden Supply, Inc.; dir. Patrol Products, Inc., MW Garden Sales, Inc. Mem. Am., Ill., Ind. assns. of nurserymen, So. Nurserymen's Assn. Democrat. Roman Catholic. Clubs: Moose, K.C. Home: 929 S Guilford Rd Carmel IN 46032 Office: PO Box 40265 Indianapolis IN 46240

PORTER, FREDERICK ANDREW, accountant; b. North Henderson, Ill., Nov. 20, 1917; s. George Allingham and Emma Belle (Mann) P.; student Moline Bus. Coll., 1935-37, Drake U. Community Coll., 1959, 65-67; m. June Z. Hanlon, June 6, 1942; children—Gail, Pamela (Mrs. James A. Schoenberger), John, S. Belle. Accountant, Swift & Co., Rock Island, Ill., 1937-41, Sheboygan, Wis., 1941-42, Durham, N.C., 1942-52, Des Moines, 1952-61; accountant Pillsbury Co., Des Moines, 1961-64; with Iowa Employment Security Commn., Des Moines, 1964—, tax functions adminstr. Cons. income tax. Mem. Accountants Assn. Iowa, Nat. Soc. Pub. Accountants. Home: 2615 45th St Des Moines IA 50310 Office: 1000 E Grand Ave Des Moines IA 50319

PORTER, GEORGE DARWIN, computer mfg. co. exec.; b. Dayton, Pa., July 25, 1937; s. Melvin Clair and Mary Gladys (Thomas) P.; diploma Robert Morris Sch., Pitts., 1957; m. Charlotte Louise Ferkan, June 8, 1963; children—George Darwin, II, Faye Ellen, Joseph Clair, David Eugene. Mgr. data processing Magnetics, Inc., Butler, Pa., 1961-62, 63-67; computer operator Mellon Bank, Pitts., 1962-63; systems and procedures mgr. Dresser Industries Co., Bradford, Pa., 1967-68; info. systems mgr. Standard Transformer Co., Warren, Ohio, 1968-69; mgr. br. sales Pryor Corp., Warren, 1969—; instr. data processing Pa. State U. Extension, Butler, 1966. Pres. North Rd. Elementary Sch. PTA, Warren, Ohio, 1974-75; lay pres. congregation St. Paul's Luth. Ch., Warren. Served with U.S. Army, 1958-61; ETO. Recipient numerous sales awards Pryor Corp., 1971-76. Mem. Data Processing Mgmt. Assn., Assn. Systems Mgmt. Republican. Clubs: Avalon Swim and Tennis, Masons. Home: 4272 Aleesa Dr SE Warren OH 44484 Office: PO Box 830 280 N Park Ave Warren OH 44482

PORTER, GEORGE LEROY, ophthalmologist; b. Geneva, Nebr., July 20, 1906; s. George Wray and Kathryn M. (Hafer) P.; B.S., U. Nebr., 1929, M.D., 1931; fellow Mayo Grad. Sch. Medicine, U. Minn., 1932-35; m. Janice O'Brien, June 13, 1931; children—John P., Kathryn A. (Mrs. Frank Keck), Janice L. (Mrs. E.B. Phillippson). Intern, Univ. Hosp., Omaha, 1931-32; resident Mayo Found., Rochester, Minn., 1932-35; practice medicine, specializing in ophthalmology, Urbana, Ill., 1932—; founding mem. Carle Clinic Assn., Urbana, 1935, head dept. ophthalmology, 1935—, chmn. bd. govs., 1958—; clin. asso. U. Ill. Sch. Basic Med. Scis., 1972—. Dir., chmn. bd. Champaign County Bank and Trust Co., Urbana, 1973—; dir. Porter Equipment Co., Schiller Park, Ill. Mem. Arrowhead council Boy Scouts Am., 1958-60. Founding mem., trustee Carle Found., 1947-71, pres., 1962; trustee Carle Meml. Hosp., 1940—, pres. med. staff, 1957—; cons. U.S. Air Force Hosp., Chanute Field, Ill., 1952—. Served to maj. USAF, 1942-45. Diplomate Am. Bd. Ophthalmology; mem. A.M.A., Ill. Med. Soc., Chgo. Ophthalmology Soc., Champaign County Med. Soc. (pres. 1956), Ill. Soc. Ophthalmology (v.p. 1971), Central Ill. Soc. Ophthalmology and Otolaryngology (pres. 1962), Am. Acad. Ophthalmology and Otorhinolaryngology, Soc. Eye Surgeons, Sigma Nu, Nu Sigma Nu, Alpha Omega Alpha. Contbr. to profl. publs. in field. Home: 107 The Meadows Urbana IL 61801 Office: 602 W University Ave Urbana IL 61801

PORTER, HARRY BENTON, JR., optometrist; b. Holton, Kans., Aug. 15, 1925; s. Harry Benton and Matilda A. (Faber) P.; student Washburn U., Topeka, 1943-44, Kansas City U., 1946-47; B.S., No. Ill. Coll. Optometry, 1947, O.D., 1950; m. Cynthia Ann Bransfield, Mar. 11, 1963. Asso. with Dr. Cochran, Topeka, 1952-53, Dr. C.S. Nelson, Leavenworth, Kan., 1953-63; pvt. practice optometry, Leavenworth, 1963—. Served with USNR, 1943-46. Mem. Am., Kans. optometric assns., Am., Kans. optometric founds., Pub. Service Vision League, Heart of Am. Contact Lens Soc. (dir.). Clubs: Masons, Elks, Eagles, Lions, Tower (Leavenworth). Home: Rural Route 1 Box 29A Leavenworth KS 66048 Office 508 Cherokee St Leavenworth KS 66048

PORTER, HARRY LERICHMOND, lawyer; b. Milan, Mo., Aug. 26, 1912; s. N. Harry and Dorothy Ellen (Booth) P.; A.B., Park Coll., 1935; LL.B., U. Kansas City, 1941; J.D., U. Mo., 1943; postgrad. Mass. Inst. Tech., 1944, Washington and Jefferson Coll., 1944; m. Wava Vernelle Field, Dec. 22, 1935; children—Alison Porter Thomas, Stephen Douglas. Admitted to Mo. bar, 1941, Kans. bar, 1942; practiced in Columbus, Kans., 1941-43, Marceline, Mo., 1946—; pros. atty. Cherokee County (Kans.), 1942-43; city atty. Marceline (Mo.), 1946—; pros. atty. Linn County (Mo.), 1965-69. Mem. steering com. Mo. Assn. Social Welfare, 1960-64; mem. Mo. Gov.'s Commn. Commerce and Industry, 1962-64; chmn. Linn County Democratic Com., 1952-56, vice-chmn., 1974-76; chmn. 12th Legis. Dist. Dem. Com., 1973—; pres. Marceline Reorganized Sch. Dist., Sch. Bd., 1962-63. Served with AUS, 1943-46. Mem. Mo., 9th Jud. Circuit (pres. 1962-63, 72-73) bar assns., Am. Legion, Sigma Phi Sigma, Pi Kappa Delta. Presbyterian. Clubs: Lion, Rotary (pres. 1961). Home: 701 N Missouri Ave Marceline MO 64658 Office: 104 S Kansas Ave Marceline MO 64658

PORTER, JOHN EDWARD, lawyer, state legislator; b. Evanston, Ill., June 1, 1935; s. Harry H. and Florence B. (Vahle) P.; student Mass. Inst. Tech., 1953-54; B.S. in Bus. Adminstrn., Northwestern U., 1957; J.D. with distinction, U. Mich., 1961; m. Kathryn Cameron Porter; children—John Clark, David Britton, Ann Lindsay. Admitted to Ill. bar, 1961, Supreme Ct. bar; atty. civil div., appellate sect. Dept. Justice, Washington, 1961-62; practice law, Evanston, 1962-74; partner firm Porter & Hoffman, 1975—; mem. Ill. Ho. of Reps. from 1st Dist., 1973—. Chmn. lawyers sect. United Community Services of Evanston, 1965, 67; bus. and industry chmn. Evanston March of Dimes, 1968-69; mem. East Evanston Community Conf., 1969—. Co-counsel Evanston Republican Club, 1967-70; precinct capt., mem. exec. bd., area chmn. Evanston Regular Rep. Orgn., 1968—; pres. Evanston Young Rep. Club, 1968-69; gen. counsel Cook County Young Rep. Orgn., 1965; v.p. polit. affairs Niles Twp. Young Rep. Orgn., 1966; hdqrs. chmn. Evanston Citizens for Ogilvie, 1966; charter mem. Evanston Rep. Workshops, 1967; bd. dirs. Legal Assistance Found. Cook County, 1967-72, North Cook County Legal Adv. Bd., 1967-72; bd. dirs. YMCA, 1970-75, adv. bd., 1975—; treas. S.E. Evanston Assn., 1967-68, bd. dirs., 1967-69; trustee Evanston Hist. Soc., 1970-73, Cove Sch. for Perceptually Handicapped Children, 1974-76. Served with U.S. Army Res., 1958-64. Named Outstanding Legislator, Independent Voters Ill., 1974, League Conservation Voters, 1974, Chgo. Crime Commn., 1976. Mem. Am., Ill., Chgo., N.W. Suburban bar assns., Evanston C. of C. (past com. chmn.). Presbyn. Clubs: Execs. (Chgo.); Univ. (past v.p., dir.) (Evanston). Asst. editor: Mich. Law Rev., 1960-61. Home: 1124 Sheridan Rd Evanston IL 60202 Office: 2090 State Nat Bank Plaza Evanston IL 60201

PORTER, JOHN WILSON, supt. schs.; b. Fort Wayne, Ind., Aug. 13, 1931; s. James Richard and Ola (Phillips) P.; A.B., Albion Coll., 1953; M.A., Mich. State U., 1957, Ph.D., 1962; D.H.L., Adrian Coll., 1970; LL.D., Western Mich. U., 1971, Eastern Mich. U., 1975; Dr. Pub. Adminstrn., Albion Coll., 1973; H.H.D., Kalamazoo Coll., 1973. m. Lois Helen French, May 27, 1961; children—Stephen James, Donna Agnes. Counselor, Lansing Pub. Schs., 1953-58; cons. Mich. Dept. Pub. Instrn., 1958-61; dir. Mich. Higher Edn. Assistance Authority, 1961-66; asso. supt. for higher edn. Mich. Dept. Edn., 1966-69, state supt. schs., 1969—; pres. Council Chief State Sch. Officer, 1977. Mem. Nat. Commn. Reform of Secondary Edn., 1972—, Nat. Commn. Financing Post-Secondary Edn., 1972—, Nat. Commn. on Manpower Policy, 1974—. Mem. Local Draft Bd. 264, 1967—; mem. Pres.'s Commn. Mental Health Task Panel Mental Health and Family, 1977; advisory bd. Women's Ednl. Equity Communications Network, 1977; bd. dirs. Mich. Internat. Council; trustee Mich. Joint Council Econ. Edn., 1977. Trustee Nat. Urban League. Recipient Phi Beta Sigma Delta Kappa certificate, 1970; recognition Mich. Legislature, 1970; Distinguished Service award Mich. Assn. Secondary Sch. Prins., 1974; Distinguished Alumni award Mich. State U., 1974; Pres.'s award Nat. Alliance Black Sch. Educators, 1977. Home: 622 Camelot Dr East Lansing MI 48823 Office: Michigan National Tower Lansing MI 48933

PORTER, REX VERNON, village ofcl.; b. Hayesville, Iowa, Apr. 8, 1905; s. Frank Edison and Ethel (Shively) P.; student Coe Coll., 1924-26, Iowa State U., 1927-28; student bus. adminstrn. Northwestern U., 1942-45; m. Ella Williams, Apr. 2, 1928; 1 dau., Barbara Ann Porter Pray. Ry. signal engr. Atchison, Topeka and Santa Fe Ry., Gallup, N.Mex., 1928, accountant, estimator div. costs, Winslow, Ariz., 1928-32; Iowa examiner local govt. accounts, Des Moines, 1934-39; accounting supr. fin. statements Gen. Motors Corp., La Grange, Ill., 1940-68; fin. dir., treas. Downers Grove (Ill.), 1969-76. Mem. Ill. Budget Task Force, 1962; treas. Downers Grove Community Fund, 1951-54; rep. to west suburban area Chgo. Crusade of Mercy, 1959; councilman, Downers Grove, 1954-63; bd. dirs. Downers Grove YMCA, 1961-62. Mem. Ill. Municipal Fin. Officers Assn., Am. Accounting Assn., Downers Grove Artist Guild (treas. 1949), Downers Grove Fall Festival (pres. 1951). Congregationalist (deacon 1958). Clubs: Masons, Kiwanis. Home: 4817 Bryan Pl Downers Grove IL 60515

PORTER, ROBERT EUGENE, architect; b. Chgo., July 11, 1933; s. Gene and Virginia P.; student St. Joseph's Coll., 1951-52; B. Archtl. Engring., Chgo. Tech. Coll., 1957; m. Mary Jane Taulman, June 23, 1957; children—Laura Lynn, Robert Scott, Sandra Kay. Staff archtl. engr. Wonder Bldg. Corp., Chgo., 1957-60; staff architect Kruegel-Healy-Moore, Joliet, Ill., 1960-65, Turner & Witt, Kankakee, Ill., 1965-66; architect, partner Porter, Turner, Witt, Moline, Crawfordsville, Ind., 1966-68; architect, owner Robert E. Porter & Assoc., 1968—. Mem. nominating com. Sch. Bd., Crawfordsville, 1970; mem. Crawfordsville Community Redevel. Com., 1967—; Mayor's Commn. on Environment, 1972—. Served with AUS, 1953-55. Mem. Nat. Council Archtl. Registration Bds., AIA, Central-So. Ind. chpt. AIA (bd. dirs. 1975—, pres. 1976—), Sigma Phi Delta. Baptist. (deacon 1971-74, bldg. com. 1971—, trustee 1975—). Prin. archtl. works include White County Jail (design), Monticello, Ind., 1967, First Christian Ch., Crawfordsville, 1968, Culver Union Hosp., Crawfordsville, 1969, Crawfordsville Downtown Redevel. Program, 1966-67, High-rise Apts. for elderly, Sullivan, Ind., 1972-73, Northridge housing and office devel., Crawfordsville, 1976—. Home: 700 North Dr Crawfordsville IN 47933 Office: 221 E Main St Crawfordsville IN 47933

PORTER, SCOTT ELLIS, dentist; b. Humboldt, Tenn., Nov. 15, 1924; s. Deeoder James and Moteller W. (Mootry) P.; B.S., U. Toledo, 1949; B.Sc. in Edn., Ohio State U., 1952, D.D.S., 1957. Pvt. practice dentistry, Toledo, 1958—; asst. to dir. dental services Toledo Health Dept., 1960-66. Bd. mgrs. YMCA, Toledo. Mem. NAACP (life) Am., Ohio dental assns., Toledo Dental Soc., Ohio State U. Alumnae Assn., U. Toledo Alumnae Assn., Kappa Alpha Psi. Republican. Clubs: Masons (32 deg.), Shriners. Club: Worldwide Sportsmen's. Address: 1023 Lincoln Ave Toledo OH 43607

PORTER, STUART WILLIAMS, investment co. exec.; b. Detroit, Jan. 11, 1937; s. Stuart Perlee and Alma Bernice (Williams) P.; B.S., U. Mich., 1960; M.B.A., U. Chgo. (Am. Accounting Assn. fellow), 1967, postgrad., 1967-68; m. Myrna Marlene Denham, June 27, 1964; children—Stuart, Randall. Exec. v.p. Weiss Peck & Greer Investments, Inc., Chgo., 1969—. Chmn. Crusade of Mercy, 1973. Served with USAF, 1961-62. Recipient award for excellence in bus. and accounting Fin. Exec. Inst., 1966. Mem. Inst. for Quantitative Research and Fin. (dir.), Investment Analysts Soc. Chgo., Fin. Analysts Fedn., Beta Gamma Sigma. Presbyterian. (trustee). Clubs: Forest Grove Tennis (Arlington, Ill.); Turnberry Country (Crystal Lake, Ill.); Chgo. Athletic. Home: 130 Wyngate Dr Barrington IL 60010 Office: 30 N LaSalle St Chicago IL 60602

PORTER, TERENCE CLIFTON, lawyer; b. St. Joseph, Mo., Dec. 13, 1934; s. Ernest Clifton and Helen Francis (Denny) P.; B.S. in Agr., J.D., U. Mo., 1958; m. Joyce Newman, June 2, 1956; children—Katherine, Michael, David, Susan. Admitted to Mo. bar, 1958; with firm Clark & Becker, Columbia, Mo., 1958-60, Becker & Porter, 1960-61, Welliver, Porter & Cleveland, 1962-70, Porter, Sprick & Powell, 1970—; partner Porter & Porter Investment & Rental Co., 1963—; sec., dir. Boone County Devel. Co., Hilton Inn of Columbia. Served to lt. U.S. Army, 1958. Mem. Am., Mo. bar assns., Def. Research Inst., Democrat. Presbyterian. Club: Kansas City. Home: 1129 Danforth Circle Columbia MO 65201 Office: 121 S 8th St Columbia MO 65201

PORTER, T(HOMAS) WAYNE, educator; b. Bowling Green, Ohio, Aug. 8, 1911; s. Archie Henry and Ollie (Stocker) P.; A.B., Bowling Green State U., 1935, B.S., 1936; M.A., U. Mich., 1940; Ph.D., U. Kans., 1950; m. Kathryn Lucile Fox, Aug. 4, 1935; children—Thomas Wayne II, James Edwin. Tchr., Salem Oak Harbor High Sch., Oak Harbor, Ohio, 1936-42; tchr. Mt. Pleasant (Mich.) High Sch., 1942-44; mem. faculty Iowa State U., Ames, 1948-50; mem. faculty Mich. State U., East Lansing, 1950—, prof. zoology, 1954—; asst. dir. W.K. Kellogg Gull Lake Biol. Sta., Hickory Corners, Mich., 1954—. Mem. evaluation coms. NSF, 1964-72, dir. summer insts., 1958-72. Served to lt. comdr. USNR, 1944-46. Mem. Am. Inst. Biol. Scis. (mem. governing bd. 1960-69, 75-77), Mich. Entomol. Soc. (pres. 1967-68), Am. Micros. Soc. (treas. 1954-75, pres. 1976), Entomological Soc. Am., Midwest Benthological Soc., Wilson

Ornithol. Soc., Audubon Soc. Research on Hebridae of the world. Home: 272 Kenberry Dr East Lansing MI 48823

PORTER, WILLIAM JOSEPH, JR., real estate exec.; b. Kalamazoo, Sept. 9, 1909; s. William Joseph and Stella Mae (Story) P.; B.E.E., Mich. State U., 1932; m. Lucile L. Hummel, Aug. 25, 1934; children—William Joseph, James A., Richard T. Rental salesman, credit mgr., property mgr., sales mgr., v.p. and gen. mgr. Advance Realty Co., Lansing, Mich., 1932-46; founder, pres. Porter Realty Co., Lansing, 1946—; pres. Lansing Bd. Realtors, 1952, 64; dir. Am. Bankcorp., Lansing, Am. Bank & Trust Co., Lansing. Campaign mgr. Lansing United Way, 1949, bd. pres., 1953; trustee Greater Lansing Found., 1950-73. Named Lansing Realtor of Year, 1965. Mem. Mich. Assn. Realtors (sec. 1957), Certified Property Mgrs. Assn. (pres. Mich. chpt. 1950), Inst. Real Estate Mgmt. (regional v.p. 1945-46), Soc. Real Estate Appraisers (pres. Lansing chpt. 1960, sr. real estate analyst, 1963—) Am. Soc. Appraisers (sr.) (pres. Lansing chpt. 1972), Am. Inst. Real Estate Appraisers, Lansing Regional C. of C. (pres. 1954-55), Soc. Indsl. Realtors, City Club Lansing (pres. 1956). Lutheran (pres. ch.). Club: Country of Lansing (sec. 1965-68). Home: 3035 Westchester Rd Lansing MI 48910 Office: 109 W Michigan Ave Suite 800 Lansing MI 48933

PORTER, WINSTON SEYMOUR, realty co. exec.; b. Port Maitland, N.S., Can., Sept. 17, 1909; s. Lyndon E. and Lillian D. (Sanders) P.; came to U.S., 1926, naturalized, 1935; student Northwestern U., 1936-38; m. Ruth Lyon, Sept. 29, 1934; children—Robert G., Lynne S. With Estate of Marshall Field, 1934-43, asst. regional rent dir. OPA, Chgo., 1944-46; v.p. Oliver S. Turner & Co. (now Turner, Bailey & Zoll, Inc.), Chgo., 1946-67; v.p. Arthur Rubloff & Co., 1967—. Trustee Deerfield, Ill., 1959-63; chmn. finance com. Deerfield, 1959-63, chmn. Deerfield Plan Commn., 1954-59, N.W. Suburban Planning Commn., 1958; active Boy Scouts Am. Mem. Field Mus. Natural History (asso. life), Art Inst. Chgo., Nat. Assn. Bldg. Mgrs., Chgo. Real Estate Bd., Ill. C. of C., Order of Arrow, Smithsonian Assos., Lambda Alpha (chpt. pres. 1940). Presbyterian. Clubs: Builders, Canadian (Chgo.); Northbrook (Ill.) Gun. Home: 944 Clay Ct Deerfield IL 60015 Office: 30 N Michigan Ave Chicago IL 60602

PORTERFIELD, HENRY ANDREW, real estate co. exec.; b. New Philadelphia, Ohio, Sept. 10, 1925; s. Henry A. and Helen J. (Jones) P.; B.S., Ohio State U., 1947; m. Ellen C. Cole, Jan. 1, 1943; children—Michael E., Steven J., C. Anthony, Christopher C. Sales mgr. Ohio Injector, 1947-59; sales mgr. Henry Pratt Co., Chgo., 1960-65; v.p. W.C. Norris Co., Tulsa, 1965-66; gen. mgr. Steinen Co., Parsippany, N.J., 1966-69; pres. Auto Laundry Cons., N.J., 1969-70; pres. Trans-Clean, Glenview, Ill., 1970-72; pres. Porterfield & Co., Hinsdale, Ill., 1972-74; pres. Realty World Midwest, Oakbrook, Ill., 1974—; dir. DuPage Bd. Realtors, Nat. Carwash Council. Served to 1st lt. USAAF, 1943-45. Clubs: Mt. Lakes (N.J.) (dir.); Oak Brook (Ill.) Polo. Home: 611 Woods Ave Oak Brook IL 60521

PORTERFIELD, NEIL HARRY, landscape architect; b. Murrysville, Pa., Aug. 15, 1936; s. Phil Frank and Alvira Clare (Rea) P.; B.S. in Landscape Architecture, Pa. State U., 1958; M. Landscape Architecture, U. Pa., 1964; m. Sandra Jean Beswarick, Aug. 9, 1958; children—Eric Jon, Jennifer Jane, Garrett Andrew. Landscape architect Pitts. Dept. Parks Recreation, 1958-59; land planner Neil H. Porterfield & Assos., Murrysville, 1961-64; dir. landscape architecture and planning Hellmuth, Obata & Kassabaum, Inc., St. Louis, 1964-70, exec. v.p., 1970-72; pres. HOK Assos., 1972—; vis. lectr. landscape architecture Iowa State U. at Ames, 1969-70, U. Ill. at Champaign, 1970-71; vis. lectr. urban design Washington U., St. Louis, 1968-74; mem. adv. council sch. forestry U. Mo. at Columbia, 1973-76. Recipient Honor award for Married Student Housing U. Mich. at Ann Arbor, Am. Soc. Landscape Architects, 1969; Merit award Parkside Campus Study U. Wis. at Kenosha Am. Soc. Landscape Architects, 1969, Merit award Operation Breakthrough Housing Project St. Louis, 1974, Honor award Laclede's Landing Urban Design, St. Louis, Merit award comprehensive plan Village of Lake Placid, N.Y. Mem. Am. Soc. Landscape Architects (chmn. Mo. Valley chpt. St. Louis sect. 1970-72), Mo. Assn. Landscape Architects (v.p. 1967-75). Presbyterian. Contbr. papers to profl. assns. and anthologies. Designer landscape archtl. plans. Home: 920 Singlepath Ln St Louis MO 63122 Office: 100 N Broadway St Louis MO 63102

PORTES, CAESAR, physician, educator; b. Russia, Apr. 14, 1897; s. Solomon and Miriam Debora (Sax) P.; student U. Chgo., 1917-18; M.D., Chgo. Med. Sch., 1928; Ph.D., Triton Coll., Melrose Park, Ill., 1975; m. Rose Rubenstein, Nov. 25, 1929; 1 dau., Miriam Portes Scholnick. Intern, Washington Park Hosp., 1928-29; resident Sloan Clinic, Bloomington, Ill.; practice medicine specializing in proctology, Chgo., 1930—; mem. staffs med. dir. Gottlieb Meml. Hosp., Melrose Park, 1960—; prof. surgery Chgo. Med. Sch., 1960—; med. dir. emeritus Cancer Prevention Center, Chgo. Pres. Chgo. Bd. unit Am. Cancer Soc. Recipient Masada award Govt. of Israel, 1975. Mem. AMA, Ill. State (pres. 1967), Chgo. med. socs. Jewish. Club: Masons, Moose, Standard, Exec., Medinah (Chgo.). Contbr. articles on proctology and cancer control to profl. jours. Home: 1550 N Lake Shore Dr Chicago IL 60610 Office: 25 E Washington St Chicago IL 60620

PORTHAN, EDWARD RICHARD, phys. edn. dir.; b. Ely, Minn., Oct. 6, 1939; s. Edward Emil and Mary Ann (Seme) P.; B.A. in English, Hamline U., 1962, M.A. in Secondary Sch. Adminstrn., 1967, B.A. in Health, Phys. Edn., 1962; m. Kathleen Ann Luhman, Apr. 28, 1962; children—Teresa, Tammy, Todd. Tchr., coach high sch., St. Paul, 1962-67; tchr. coach Irondale High Sch., New Brighton, Minn., 1967—, dist. chmn. health phys. edn. pub. schs., New Brighton, 1971—, prin. summer sch., 1972-73, founder outdoor edn. program, 1973; mem. adv. council health edn. Minn. Dept. Edn., St. Paul, 1972-75; mem. adv. bd. community edn. New Brighton, 1973-75; cons. outdoor edn. Minn., 1974-75. Named Coach of Year Minn. Swimming Coaches Assn., 1973; Honored Citizen, St. Anthony Park, St. Paul, 1966. Mem. Minn. Assn. Health Phys. Edn. Recreation, Nat. Alliance Health Phys. Edn. Recreation, NEA, Mounds View Edn. Assn., Minn. Swim Coaches Assn. (pres. 1975-76). Chmn. Issues in Life, 1970-75. Home: 1588 21st Ave NW New Brighton MN 55112 Office: 2425 Long Lake Rd New Brighton MN 55112

PORTTEUS, ELNORA MARIE MANTHEL (MRS. PAUL PORTTEUS), ednl. adminstr.; b. Rosendale, Wis.; d. H.R. and Anna M. (Kentop) Manthel; student Oshkosh State Coll., 1937-39; B.S., U. Wis., 1941; M.A., Kent State U., 1954; m. Paul Portteus, Oct. 19, 1942; children—Carrie Jo Portteus Thomas, Lane Paul, Andre Eugene. Librarian, tchr. Racine, Kenosha Normal Sch., 1942; library asst. Fed. Res. Bank Cleve., 1943; asst. librarian Indsl. Relations Counselors N.Y., 1947-48; librarian Findlay (Ohio) City Schs., 1948-58; asst. prof. dept. library sci. Kent State U., 1958-65, adj. asso. prof., 1976—; dir. ednl. media Cleve. Bd. Edn., 1965—; dir. NDEA Inst., 1965. Chmn., Findlay Council Youth Serving Agys., 1954-56; adv. bd. Cuyahoga Community Coll. Recipient Distinguished Alumna award Kent State U., 1967. Mem. AAUW, Am. (chmn. adv. com. Midwest Program on Airborn TV Instrn. 1964-67, Ency. Brit. Sch. Library award 1st place 1967, pres. 1972-73), Ohio (pres. 1957-58, Distinguished Service award 1972) assns. sch. librarians, Ohio Library Assn. (chmn. service to schs. 1959-60, book exam. center com. 1964-65, chmn. scholarship com. 1965-69, Librarian of Year 1972), Ohio Edn. Assn., ALA (John Cotton Dana Publicity awards 1967, 69), Women's Nat. Book Assn., Soc. Studies World Affairs (chmn. 1974—), Beta Phi Mu. Mem. Order Eastern Star. Author ednl. handbooks, contbr. articles to profl. jours.; reviewer Sch. Library Jour. and Previews. Home: 7357 West Lake Blvd Kent OH 44240 Office: Woodhill-Quincy Center 10600 Quincy Av Cleveland OH 44106

POSCH, JOSEPH LOUIS, surgeon; b. St. Paul, Dec. 26, 1915; s. Louis Gustav and Frances Martha (Kurz) P.; B.S. cum laude, St. Thomas Coll., 1938; M.D., U. Minn., 1942; m. Martha Jane Stark, May 2, 1942; children—Mary Katherine Posch Gebeck, Joseph Louis. Intern, City of Detroit Receiving Hosp., 1942-43, fellow in surgery, 1943-44, resident in surgery, 1946-49, chief of staff, 1965; practice medicine specializing in surgery, Detroit; dir. hand surgery Hand Center, Harper-Grace Hosp., Detroit Med. Center, Wayne State U.; mem. staff Hutzel Hosp., Detroit Gen. Hosp., St. Joseph Mercy Hosp., Mt. Carmel Mercy Hosp., Children's Hosp. of Mich., St. John's Hosp., Sinai Hosp., Bon Secours Hosp., VA Hosp., USPHS Hosp.; clin. prof. surgery Coll. Medicine, Wayne State U., 1973, Rehab. Services Adminstrn.; HEW trainee in rehab. medicine (hand surgery), micro-surgery research lab. Wayne State U. Served with M.C., U.S. Army, 1944-46; ETO. Diplomate Am. Bd. Surgery. Mem. Am. Soc. for Surgery of the Hand, Am. Assn. for Surgery of Trauma, AMA, A.C.S., Indsl. Med. Assn., Detroit, Central, Western, Midwest surg. assns., Acad. Surgery of Detroit, Detroit Surg. Soc., Mich., Wayne County med. socs., Am. Soc. for Plastic and Reconstructive Surgery (asso.), Mich., Detroit, hist. socs., Detroit Inst. Arts Founders Soc., Anthony Wayne Soc., Grosse Pointe Power Squadron, Phi Chi. Roman Catholic. Clubs: Detroit Athletic, Grosse Pointe Yacht, K.C. Contbr. articles to profl. jours. Home: 73 Webber Pl Grosse Pointe Shores MI 48236 Office: 1408 Kales Bldg 76 W Adams St Detroit MI 48226

POSLUSZNY, GERALD MILTON, electric products mfg. co. exec.; b. Chgo., Dec. 6, 1943; s. Milton Ben and Lottie Ann (Gross) P.; B.S., Quincy Coll., 1966; m. Jacalyn Mary Bonis, Apr. 26, 1969; children—Joy, Jason. Cost accountant Western Electric Co., Inc., mfg. telephone equipment, Chgo., 1966-67, fin. auditor, 1967; cost accountant Aero Research Inst. div. Am. Standard Inc., Franklin Park, Ill., 1967-70, controller, 1970-71; treas., sec. Ari Industries, Inc., mfg. elec. conduction and temperature instrumentation, Franklin Park, 1971—. Mem. Nat. Assn. Accountants (dir.), Am. Accounting Assn. Club: K.C. (warden 1962-63). Home: 1541 Allen Ln St Charles IL 60174 Office: 9000 King St Franklin Park IL 60131

POSNER, JUDITH LOIS, fine arts corp. dir.; b. Milw., Sept. 22, 1941; d. Sol. J. and Miriam F. (Posner) Kahn; B.S. in Fine Art, U. Wis., 1963; m. Jeffry A. Posner, Aug. 17, 1963; children—Wendy Lee, David Adam. Asst. dir. Gallery 12, Daytons, Mpls., 1963-64; partner, dir. fine arts Jeffry A. Posner Corp., Judith L. Posner & Assos., Inc., Milw., 1973—. Mem. corporate bd. Mt. Sinai Med. Center, recipient Hands That Serve award, 1976, chairwoman art purchases com., mem. aux.; mem. womens welfare bd. Mental Health Assn. Mem. Milw. Art Center, Milw. Symphony League and Ballet League. Home: 7945 N Fairchild Rd Milwaukee WI 53217 Office: 152 W Wisconsin Ave Milwaukee WI 53203

POSNICK, IRVING HARVEY, dentist; b. Mpls., Sept. 13, 1923; s. David Michael and Ethel (Kaplan) P.; student U. Minn., 1941-43, D.D.S., 1946; m. Nan Fine, Oct. 31, 1945; children—William, Steven, Jeffrey, Richard. Gen. practice dentistry, St. Louis Park, Minn., 1949—; cons. in hosp. dentistry U. Minn., Mpls.; mem. staffs Mt. Sinai, Methodist hosps., Children's Med. Center; mem. med.-dental staff Golden Valley Health Center, Mpls.; past sec.-treas., pres. Aqualand Pool Co., Inc., Park Enterprises, Inc. Served with AUS, 1943-45, to lt. comdr. Dental Corps, USNR, 1946-48, ret. Res., 1965. Fellow Royal Soc. Health, Am. Acad. Denistry for the Handicapped, Am. Coll. Dentists; mem. Am. Soc. Dentistry for Children (pres. 1971-72), Mpls. Dental Soc. (pres. 1973-74), U. Minn. Alumni Assn., U. Minn. Dental Sch. Century Club (v.p., dir.), Beth El Synagogue Men's Club. Jewish. Club: B'nai B'rith. Co-author: Jimmy's First Visit to the Dentist; Fifteen Years of Hospital Dentistry. Home: 4740 W 27th St Saint Louis Park MN 55416 Office: 3400 Dakota Ave Saint Louis Park MN 55416

POSPISHIL, FRANK FRANCIS, lawyer; b. Omaha, Aug. 9, 1942; s. Frank and Hannah (Hassett) P.; B.A. magna cum laude, U. Nebr., 1964, J.D., Creighton U., 1967; m. Mary Ellen Flaherty, Aug. 20, 1966; children—Bradley, Cynthia, Matthew, Douglas. Admitted to Nebr. bar, 1967; asso. firm Abrahams, Kaslow & Cassman, Omaha, 1967-70, partner, 1971—. Mem. Am., Nebr., Omaha bar assns., Omaha Barristers Assn. Home: 10119 Grover St Omaha NE 68124 Office: 1175 Woodman Tower Omaha NE 68102

POSPISHIL, LLOYD LABAR, lawyer; b. West Point, Nebr., May 19, 1911; s. Paul and Matilda Alice (Yunek) P.; B.A., U. Nebr., 1932, LL.B., 1933; J.D., 1968; m. Margaret E. Reuter, July 14, 1937. Admitted to Nebr. bar, 1933; practiced in Schuyler, 1933—; county atty. Colfax County, 1935-39, 43-51, now dep. county atty.; city atty. Schuyler, 1942-43, 58-60, 62-64; staff legal officer Naval Air Intermediate Tng. Command, 1943-45; judge Ct. Indsl. Relations, 1960-66; dir. First Nat. Bank, Schuyler, FNS, Inc., Schuyler, Clarkson Bank (Nebr.); counsel U.P. R.R.; mem. Nebr. Supreme Ct. Nominating Commn. U. Nebr. rep. Internat. Intercollegiate Debate with U. Oxford, Eng., 1930; mayor Schuyler, 1940-42; bd. dirs. Meml. Hosp., Schuyler, 1953-57, 71—; mem. governance commn. U. Nebr. Served to lt. comdr. USNR, 1943-45. Mem. Schuyler C. of C. (pres.), Nat. Forensic Soc., Nebr. Assn. Trial Lawyers (pres.), Am. (mem. coms.), Nebr. (adv. com. 1951-75), 6th Jud. Dist., Colfax County (pres.) bar assns., Nebr. Bar Found. (dir.), Am. Coll. Probate Counsel, Am. Legion (Distinguished Citizen award 1957, 74, dist. comdr., Nebr. vice comdr., nat. vice chmn. Americanism commn., dept. judge adv.), 40 and 8, Delta Sigma Rho. Club: Rotary (pres.). Contbr. articles to profl. jours. Home: 425 B St Schuyler NE 68661 Office: 324 E 11th St Schuyler NE 68661

POST, DONALD GEORGE, mktg. exec.; b. Milw., Aug. 12, 1946; s. Charles Gilbert and Grace (Strohman) P.; B.S. in Elec. Engring., Purdue U., 1968; postgrad. U. Chgo., 1969; M.B.A., Bradley U., 1973; m. Jessalyn Sue Nicklas, Sept. 7, 1968; children—Gregory George, Geoffrey Michael. Sales engr., indsl. field sales Westinghouse Electric Corp., Peoria and Chgo., Ill., 1968-73, application engr., small motor div., Lima, Ohio, 1973-76, supr. planning and communications, 1976-77, mktg. services mgr., 1977—; instr. bus. techs. Lima Tech. Coll., 1976—. Pres., Profl. Investors of Lima, 1973-77; team capt. YMCA membership drives, 1974-75; chmn. Allen County (Ohio) Vote No on Issue 4-7 Com., 1976; active Indian Guides, 1976—, Conservative Caucus, 1976—; Republican precinct committeeman, 1975—; v.p. Allen County Young Republicans, 1975; councilman, Village of Ft. Shawnee, Ohio, 1976—; mem. adv. com. Allen County Comprehensive Employment Tng. Act, 1976—. Recipient Westinghouse Community Service award, 1975. Mem. Nat. Mgmt. Assn. (chmn. mgmt. devel. com. Lima chpt. 1976—), Lima Area Jaycees (v.p. 1975-76, Distinguished Service award 1976), Lima Area C. of C. (chmn. mgmt. devel. seminars 1976—), IEEE, Pi Kappa Alpha, Tau Beta Pi, Eta Kappa Nu, Omicron Delta Kappa, Phi Eta Sigma. Methodist. Home: 3781 S Amblewood Circle Lima OH 45806 Office: 2025 E 4th St PO Box 566 Lima OH 45802

POST, MARGARET MOORE, journalist; b. Plainfield, Ind., Aug. 16, 1909; d. Robert Wans and Virginia (Rupe) Stephenson; student U. Mich., 1926-27, Butler U., summer 1929; A.B., La. State U., 1930; L.H.D., Franklin Coll., 1973; m. Everett Laurence Moore, Dec. 4, 1932 (dec. Mar. 1952); children—Jo Ann (Mrs. David E. Long), Sue Ellen (Mrs. Philip M. Walker); m. 2d, H. John Post, 1970 (div.). Editor, The Reveille, La. State U. newspaper, 1929-30; reporter Logansport (Ind.) Press, 1930-32; editor Mooresville (Ind.) Times, 1933-38; columnist Indpls. Star, 1932-42; head journalism dept. Franklin Coll., 1942-51; copy editor Indpls. News, 1952-53; pub. relations Indpls. Star and Indpls. News, 1952-68; polit. writer Indpls. News, 1968—. Tchr. journalism Ind. U. at Indpls., 1954-55; tchr. creative writing N. Central High Sch., Indpls., 1962-63. Mem. Mayor's Manpower Commn., 1964—, Indpls. Community Service Council, 1960—, Indpls. Parent-Tchr. Council 1965—, Soc. for Intensified Edn., 1965—, Gov.'s Criminal Justice Planning Agy., 1969—; mem. Nat. Adv. Commn. Criminal Standards and Goals; Ind. chmn. Juvenile Standards and Goals, 1975—; coordinator Indpls. Anti-Crime Crusade; speaker on How To Fight Crime at White House, 1968; founder Indpls. Women United Against Rape, 1973—; chmn. Gov.'s Conf. on Child Abuse, 1977; mem. bd. Midwest Resource Council, Child Abuse, 1977—; mem. Ind. commn. Internat. Women's Year, 1977. Bd. dirs. News Camp for Children, Indpls., 1954-60, Settlements Camping, Inc., 1959—, Concord Center Settlement House, 1959—, Nat. Soc. for Prevention of Blindness, 1954—, United Cerebral Palsy Ind., 1960—. Named Ind. Mother of Year, 1956-66; Sagamore of Wabash, 1976; recipient Soroptimist Internat. award Women Helping Women, 1976. Mem. Woman's Press Club (pres. 1942-44), U.S. C. of C. (crime control panel 1959—), Nat. Council Women (woman of conscience award 1968), Indpls. C. of C., Gen. Fedn. Women's Clubs (law enforcement chmn. 1968—), Bus. and Profl. Women's Club, Ind. Acad., Theta Sigma Phi (nat. sec. 1947-53, nat. headliner 1968), Ind. Forum, Women in Communications (Clarion award 1974, 75), Delta Kappa Gamma. Republican. Quaker. Clubs: Altrusa; Delta Gamma Social Sorority Mothers (pres. 1955-56). Author: (with M. Stanton Evans) The Law Breakers (Book of Month Club Selection), 1968; How to Combat Rape: In Your Home, On Your Street, In Your City, 1975; A Child is Crying, 1976; Bicentennially Hers, 1976. Home: 5010 A Allisonville Rd Indianapolis IN 46205 Office: 307 N Pennsylvania St Indianapolis IN 46206

POSTHUMA, ALBERT ELWOOD, surgeon; b. Grand Rapids, Mich., Apr. 25, 1919; s. Gerrit Pylman and Alice (Mandemaker) P.; A.B., Calvin Coll., 1940; M.D., U. Mich., 1943, M.S., 1949; m. Jean L. Swann, Aug. 17, 1974; children by previous marriage—Beth Alicia Posthuma Jenkins, Ann Maureen Posthuma Lustig, Jane Marie, Sue Swann Frankforter. Intern, St. Mary's Hosp., Grand Rapids, 1943-44, resident, 1944-46, 48-50; practice medicine specializing in surgery, 1950—; cons. surgeon, chief staff St. Mary's Hosp., 1972—; cons. surgeon Ferguson-Drost-Ferguson hosps. Mem. asso. council, trustee Kent County Med. Found. Served from 1st lt. to capt. AUS, 1946-48. Recipient citation U. Mich., 1949. Diplomate Am. Bd. Surgery. Fellow A.C.S.; mem. Pan-Pacific Surg. Assn., Kent County Med. Soc. (pres. 1978-79). Club: Blythefield Country. Home: 2117 Osceola Dr Grand Rapids MI 49507 Office: 153 Lafayette SE Grand Rapids MI 49502

POSTON, FRANKLIN DARRELL, mktg. exec.; b. Canaan Twp., Ohio, Mar. 18, 1938; s. Elmer Frederick and Mearl (Hawk) P.; B.J., Ohio U., 1963; m. Darla Lou Gabriel, Nov. 22, 1957; children—Teressa Ann, Bradley Darrell, Amy Elizabeth. Copywriter, Lazarus Dept. Store, Columbus, Ohio, 1963-65; coordinator product communications Ross Labs., Columbus, 1965-69; mgr. market devel. Worthington Foods (Ohio), 1969—. Vice pres. Northland Community Council, Columbus, 1972-73. Mem. Ohio U. Advt. Mktg. Club (pres. 1962-63), Columbus Advt. Fedn., Northland Jaycees (pres. 1971-72), Sigma Delta Chi. Methodist. Home: 1908 Greenglen Ct Columbus OH 43229 Office: 900 Proprietors Rd Worthington OH 43085

POSZ, ALBERT CONRAD, educator; b. Plainview, Minn., Sept. 11, 1920; s. Albert Daniel and Mary Etta (Gaylord) P.; B.S., Winona State Coll., 1944; M.A., State U. Iowa, 1946; Ed.D., Mich. State U., 1952; m. Marie Genevieve Fjelstad, Aug. 26, 1944; children—Carl Conrad, Sylvia Marie. Radio announcer, engr. Sta. KWNO, Winona, Minn., 1943-44; grad. teaching asst. State U. Iowa, 1944-46; instr., asst. prof. Mich. State U., 1946-59; dir. edn. Palmer Writers Sch. and Art Instrn. Schs., Mpls., 1961—, v.p.; part-time prof. Sch. Bus., U. Minn., 1966—; profl. pub. speaker. Adv. commn. Minn. Pvt. Bus., Trade and Corr. Sch. Mem. Adult Edn. Assn. U.S., Minn. Counselors Assn., Nat. Home Study Council (research and ednl. standards com., recipient Distinguished Service award 1974), Minn. Assn. Pvt. Vocat. Schs., Phi Kappa Psi. Lutheran. Mason. Contbr. articles to profl. jours. Home: 9307 W 23d St Minneapolis MN 55426 Office: 500 S 4th St Minneapolis MN 55415

POSZE, ALEX RICHARD, JR., architect; b. Lorain, Ohio, Dec. 26, 1933; s. Alex Richard and Yolanda Ann (Petrovich) P.; student Kans. State U., 1958-59; B.Arch., Miami U., Oxford, Ohio, 1963; M.Arch., Washington U., St. Louis, 1964; m. Mary Ellen Gens, Aug. 22, 1953; children—Jennifer Lynn, Vanessa Elizabeth. With Architects Dept., London County Council, London, Eng., 1964-65; dir. community devel. City of Berea (Ohio), 1965-67; dir. city plan and zoning commn. City of Middletown (Conn.), 1967-69; dir. planning Heine Crider & Williamson, Inc., Architects and Planners, Berea, 1969-77, Alex Posze & Assos., Berea, 1977—. Served with AUS, 1956-58. Mem. AIA, Am. Inst. Planners, Nat. Council Archtl. Registration Bds. Club: Kiwanis. Home and Office: 176 Manning Dr Berea OH 44017

POTKIN, NATHAN NORMAN, dentist; b. Chgo., Nov. 5, 1914; s. Max and Bessie (Gross) P.; B.S., U. Ill. Sch. Pharmacy, 1933; D.D.S., U. Ill., 1944, M. Bacteriology, 1935; m. Evelyn Goldman, June 3, 1940; children—Steven, Ralph, Jeffrey, Benji. Faculty, researcher U. Ill. Coll. Dentistry, 1944-53; practice dentistry, Chgo., 1944-53, 55—; chief dental staff Northeast Hosp., Chgo.; chief staff Forkosh Hosp. Active Cub Scouts Am., 1955-57. Served with AUS, 1953-55. Mem. Endodontic Soc., Internat. Dental Research Assn., Ill., Chgo. dental socs. Mason (Shriner). Contbr. to profl. publs. in field. Home: 6950 N Kenneth Ave Lincolnwood IL 60646 Office: 7001 N Clark St Chicago IL 60626

POTOCKI, WLADYSLAW JAN, test pilot, aero. engr.; b. Krakow, Poland, June 9, 1919; s. Teofil and Antonina (Filipowicz) P.; student Polish Air Force Coll., 1938-40, Empire Test Pilots Sch. Farnborough, Eng., 1951; m. Marjorie Bennet, Oct. 1, 1953. Commd. 2d lt. 1941, Polish Air Force (RAF), advanded through grades to squadron leader, 1945; comdg. officer 315th Fighter Squadron; test pilot, Farnborough, Eng., 1951-55; ret., 1956; exptl. test pilot, chief test pilot Avro Aircraft Canada, 1956-62; sr. tech. staff N.Am. Aviation/Rockwell Internat. Aircraft and missile divs., Columbus, Ohio, 1962—.

Decorated Order Virtuti Militari, Cross of Valor (3), Air Force Cross (Poland); D.F.C. (England). Asso. fellow Canadian Aeros. and Space Inst.; mem. Am. Inst. Aeros. and Astronautics, Am. Def. Preparedness Assn., Air Force Assn., Nat. Assn. Remotely Piloted Vehicles, Nat. Mgmt. Assn., Polish Air Force Club (England). Roman Catholic. Pioneer in transonic and supersonic flights. Club: DCSC Officers, Columbus. Home: Shamrock Motel Box 87 Rt 40 Etna OH 43018 Office: 4300 5th Ave E Missile Systems Div Columbus OH 43216

POTTER, DENNIS ALVIN, heavy equipment mfg. co. exec.; b. Rockford, Ill., July 13, 1938; s. Hudson M. and Pauline E. (Osborn) P.; B.S., So. Ill. U., 1963; m. Coleen E. Frandsen, June 10, 1961; children—Dianne Lynn, Robert Steven. With Rockford (Ill.) Clutch Co., 1963-64, Prudential Ins. Co., 1964-66; controller Hydro-Line Mfg. Co., 1966-73, Remco Hydraulics div. Stanray Corp., Indpls., 1973-74; controller Rockford Safety Equipment Co., 1974-76, gen. mgr. ops., 1976—. Mem. budget com. Rockford United Fund, 1969-73. Mem. Nat. Assn. Accountants. Mason. Club: Rockford Personnel. Home: 1237 Harlem Blvd Rockford IL 61103 Office: 4620 Hydraulic Rd Rockford IL 61109

POTTER, GEORGE ERNEST, lawyer; b. Flint, Mich., Mar. 1, 1937; s. Ernest Davison and Bonnie Jean (Bayley) P.; student Jackson (Mich.) Jr. Coll., 1954-56; B.A., Albion Coll., 1958; J.D., U. Mich., 1960; m. Donna Elizabeth St. John, June 23, 1956; children—Kevin Ernest, Eric Davison, Melissa Elizabeth. Admitted to Mich. bar, 1960; mem. firm Anderson, Patch, Rosenfeld, Potter & Grover, Jackson, 1961—, partner, 1965—; pres. Jackson Hillsdale Title Co., 1970-75. Mem. Mich. Council Postsecondary Edn., 1971-74, Gov.'s Commn. Higher Edn., 1972-73, Commn. Govtl. Affairs, 1971-75, Edn. Council Mich., 1974—. Trustee Jackson Community Coll., 1962—, chmn. bd., 1969—. Recipient Outstanding Jaycee award Jackson Jaycees, 1966, Outstanding Young Man award, 1967; Nation's Outstanding Community Coll. Trustee award, 1974. Mem. Am., Jackson County (sec. 1961-62) bar assns., State Bar Mich., Am. Trial Lawyers Assn., Am. Judicature Soc., Def. Research Inst., Mich. Community Coll. Assn. (pres. 1970-71, dir. 1969—), Assn. Community Coll. Trustees (dir. 1972—, pres. 1976-77), Am. Assn. Community and Jr. Colls., Jackson C. of C. (dir. 1967-68), Jaycees (local pres. 1966-67, state v.p. 1967-68, nat. dir. 1969-70). Rotarian (dir. 1972-75). Clubs: Jackson Town Jackson Country. Home: 3415 Lookout Circle Jackson MI 49201 Office: 404 S Jackson St PO Box 785 Jackson MI 49204

POTTER, JOHN WESLEY, ret. orthodontist; b. Kinross, Iowa, May 26, 1908; s. William Wolcott and Clara Louise (Mason) P.; student Ia. Wesleyan Coll., 1926-28; D.D.S., U. Iowa, 1932, M.S., 1948; m. Dorothy Lucile Reich, Aug. 15, 1933; children—John Wesley, William R., Jane (Mrs. H.W. Ogilvie, Jr.). Practice dentistry specializing in orthodontics, Muscatine, Iowa, 1933-77. Bd. dirs. YMCA, Muscatine, United Way. Served with AUS, 1941-45. Mem. Am., Iowa, Davenport Dist. dental assns., Fedn. Dentaire Internat., Ret. Officer's Assn., Am. Legion, Farm Bur., Muscatine C. of C. (bd. dirs. 1959-62), Sigma Phi Epsilon, Xi Psi Phi. Republican. Methodist. Mason (Shriner), Elk, Rotarian. Home: Route 2 Box 144 West Liberty IA 52776

POTTER, JUAN WYATT, rancher; b. Carthage, Mo., May 8, 1907; s. Ernest and Leona Gertrude (Starett) P.; student Draughn's Bus. Sch., Springfield, Mo., 1926; m. Ruth Flowers, Apr. 21, 1935; children—Ronald, Ronda (Mrs. Jack Mote), Larry. Draftsman Carthage Marble Corp., 1927-43; rancher, farmer, Jasper County, Mo., 1943—. Dir. Farmers Exchange Carthage, 1956-75, M.F.A. Springfield Milling Co.; mem. bd. Producer Creamery Co., Springfield, Producers Produce Co., Springfield. Mem. extension council, Jasper County, 1965-69. Mem. Mo. Farmers (dir.), Midcontinent Farmers Assn. Columbia (dir. 1969—), Ark. Farmer Assn. (dir.). Methodist. Address: Route 3 Carthage MO 64836

POTTER, MARILYN MEYER, educator; b. Lincoln, Nebr., Aug. 20, 1927; d. Clifford Carrigan and Maude Fae (Myers) Meyer; B.S., U. Wis., 1949; M.A., Syracuse U., 1956; Ed.D., Mich. State U., 1969; m. Ralph McDonald Potter, Aug. 10, 1973. Tchr., John Burroughs Sch., Clayton, Mo., 1949-51; tchr. Evanston Twp. High Sch., Evanston, Ill., 1951-55, counselor, dir. student activities, 1956-64; instr. Mich. State U., East Lansing, 1964-68; faculty U. Wis., Oshkosh, 1968—, prof. counseling psychology since 1976. Mem. Am., Wis. personnel and guidance assns., Nat. Vocat. Guidance Assn., Am. Psychol. Assn., Wis. Psychol. Assn., Assn. Counselor Edn. and Supervision, Am. Coll. Personnel Assn., Wis. Coll. Personnel Assn., AAUW, P.E.O. Home: 1000 Canterbury Dr Oshkosh WI 54901 Office: Univ Wisconsin Counseling Center Oshkosh WI 54901

POTTER, NORMAN RODNEY, psychologist; b. New London, Conn., Oct. 27, 1927; s. Kirby Safford and Lucy Ann (Carter) P.; B.A., U. Conn., 1952; M.S., Trinity U., 1959; Ph.D., Okla. State U., 1966; m. Mary Elizabeth Wallace, Nov. 23, 1950; children—Steven Douglas, Janice Linn, Jeffrey Curtis. Research psychologist various Air Force Labs., 1953-60; engring. psychologist Human Engring. Lab., Griffiss AFB, N.Y., 1960-63; chief Personnel Subsystems Br., Wright-Patterson AFB, Ohio, 1966-69; chief Systems Support Office Human Resources Lab., Brooks AFB, Tex., 1969-70; asst. prof. biometry La. State U. Med. Center, New Orleans, 1970-73; sr. scientist Systems Research Lab., Dayton, Ohio, 1973—; human factors cons. Army-Navy-Air Force Aircrew Standardization Panel, 1966-69, Joint Services Task Force Two, 1966-67; mem. Human Factors Group Joint Services Task Force Eight, 1968. Mem. adv. group for internal reorgan. La. Heart Assn., 1972. Served with USAF, 1952-70. Decorated Air Force Commendation medal with two oak leaf clusters; licensed psychologist, Ohio, Tex. Mem. Am., Southeastern psychol. assns., Soc. Engring. Psychologists, Sigma Xi, Psi Chi. Contbr. articles in field to profl. jours. Home: 2988 Southfield Dr Xenia OH 45385 Office: 2800 Indian Ripple Rd Dayton OH 45440

POTTS, DONALD ALBERT, physician; b. N.Y.C., Mar. 25, 1930; s. Albert C. and Anna B. (Truman) P.; A.A., Graceland Coll., Lamoni, Iowa, 1950; student William Jewel Coll., Liberty, Mo., 1951-52; A.B., U. Kans., 1957, M.D., 1962; m. Barbara Joyce Elledge, Dec. 27, 1953; children—Tedd Albert, Dwight Alan, Douglas Brian, Laura Jean. Intern, Kansas City Gen. Hosp. and Med. Center, 1962-63; practice family medicine, Independence, Mo., 1963—; med. dir. Harry S. Truman Children's Neurol. Center, Kansas City, Mo., 1973—; chmn. dept. medicine Independence Sanitarium and Hosp., 1967, 77-78; sec. staff Med. Center of Independence, 1970-72; asst. clin. prof. medicine U. Mo. at Kansas City, 1973—; preceptor in medicine U. Mo. at Columbia; pres. Family Medicine, Inc. Vice pres. Campo Fiesta; chmn. bd. ethics City of Independence. Served as spl. agt. CIC, AUS, 1953-55. Diplomate Am. Bd. Family Practice. Fellow Am. Acad. Family Practice (charter); mem. Audio Engring. Soc., AMA, Mo. Med. Assn., Jackson County Med. Soc., Mo., Kansas City (pres. 1976). acads. family practice, Christian Med. Soc., Independence C. of C., Reorganized Ch. Latter Day Saints Med.-Dental Assn. (sec.-treas. 1970-74), Phi Beta Pi, Alpha Phi Omega. Mem. Reorganized Ch. of Jesus Christ of Latter-day Saints (elder). Home: 18508 E 30th Terr Independence MO 64057 Office: 1515 W Truman Rd Independence MO 64050

POTTS, FRANK ALEX, restaurant exec.; b. Boone County, Mo., Nov. 6, 1933; s. Millard N. and Beulah C. (Marshall) P.; B.S. in Bus., U. Mo., Columbia, 1955; m. Bette S. Card, May 5, 1962; children—Charles E., Stephen F. Accountant, Ernst & Ernst, 1957-63; controller Sterling div. Fed.-Mogul Corp., 1963-68; with Nantucket, Inc., St. Louis, 1968—, pres., 1970—. Served to 1st lt. U.S. Army, 1955-57. C.P.A. Mem. Christian Ch. Club: Norwood Hills Country. Home: 12777 Mason Manor Saint Louis MO 63141 Office: 40 N Kingshighway Saint Louis MO 63108

POTTS, LESLIE CARROLL, physician; b. Indainola, Nebr., Aug. 15, 1925; s. Lester Cromwell and Ruby Elizabeth (Rozell) P.; student U. Nebr., 1946-49; M.D., Univ. Coll. Medicine, 1954; m. Royce Elaine Walters, Sept. 10, 1949; children—Leslie Carroll, John Rozell, Genie Rae, Debra Lyn. Intern, Immanuel Deaconess Hosp., Omaha, 1954-55; gen. practice medicine, Grant, Nebr., 1955—. Pres. Walking Seven Mfg. Co., Inc.; owner, operator Flying 6 Ranch. Served with AUS, 1943-46. Mem. AMA, Nebr. Med. Assn., Garden, Keith and Perkins County Med. Soc. (past pres.), Assn. Physicians and Surgeons. Republican. Congregationalist. Club: Elks. Home: Box 69 Grant NE 69140 Office: 115 W 3d Grant NE 69140

POULIK, MIROSLAV DAVE, immunologist, protein chemist, clin. pathologist; b. Brno, Czechoslovakia, June 6, 1923; s. John and Maria (Vozdecka) P.; B.A., Real Gymnasium, 1942; postgrad. Masaryk U., 1948, English Inst. br. Victoria Coll., London, Eng., 1942-43; M.D., U. Toronto, Ont., Can., 1960; m. Emily Zalkauskaite, Dec. 21, 1950; children—Michelle, Dinah, Jeanette, Maria. Guest investigator Rockefeller U., N.Y.C., 1960-61; asst. dir. research ARC, Washington, 1961-62; sr. research asst. Child Research Center, Detroit, 1962-71; prof. pediatrics Wayne State U. Sch. Medicine, 1962-73, prof. immunology and microbiology, 1973—; chief immunology William Beaumont Hosp., Royal Oak, Mich., 1971—. Expert panel immunology WHO, Geneva, Switzerland, 1968—. NIH grantee, 1962—. Roman Catholic. Research structure immunoglobin molecule, structure B2 microglobulin. Home: 776 Hampton Rd Grosse Pointe Woods MI 48236 Office: William Beaumont Hosp Royal Oak MI 48072

POULIMAS, CONSTANTINE NICHOLAS, music educator; b. Corfu, Greece, June 6, 1929; s. Nicholas and Sophia (Louissios) P.; B.S., Ithaca Coll., 1951; M.M., Butler U., 1956; Ed.D., U. Ind., 1975; m. Ann Dadoukis, Aug. 31, 1952; children—Michael James, Theodore Nicholas, James Constantine. Dir. orch. Howe High Sch., Indpls., 1955-64; asso. prof. music edn. strings Jordan Coll. Music Butler U., Indpls., 1964—; musician orch. concert tours Andy Williams, U.S., Can., 1967-70, Glenn Campbell, 1971-75, Henry Mancini, U.S., Can., 1963-75; dir. Anthenaeum Turners Orch., Indpls., 1971-74. Chmn. local arrangements com. Ind. Music Educators Nat. Conf., Indpls., 1963; guest clinician N.Am., Ball State U., Muncie, Ind., 1960-63, Ind. State U., Terre Haute, 1959-62. Served with USAF, 1951-54. Mem. Am. Hellenic Ednl. Prog. Assn. (pres. Ind. chpt. 1958-59), Am. String Tchrs. Assn. (pres. Ind. 1975—, chmn. Ind. dist. gold honors com. 1962-75, regional chmn. N. Central div. 1977—), Phi Mu Alpha Sinfonia, Phi Delta Kappa, Pi Kappa Lambda. Greek Orthodox. Author: Fundamental Concepts of Music Elements, 1971. Home: 12529 Windsor Dr Carmel IN 46032 Office: Jordan Coll Music Butler U 4600 Sunset Ln Indianapolis IN 46208

POULIN, MAUREEN JOAN, educator; b. Haverhill, Mass., Nov. 14, 1949; d. Alfred Dominic and Rosemarie Augustine (Dolfe) Poulin; B.S., U. Kans., 1972; M.A., U. Mo., Kansas City, 1975; 1 son, Michael Jeremy. Primary tchr. Our Lady of Lourdes Sch., Raytown, Mo., 1972-74; psychometrist North Kansas City Pub. Schs., Kansas City, Mo., 1975-76, learning specialist, 1976-77, cons. gifted and talented program, 1976-77, psychometrist, 1977—. Mem. Am. Personnel and Guidance Assn., Kappa Delta Pi. Roman Catholic. Home: 10404 E 82d Terrace Raytown MO 64138 Office: 2000 NE 46th St Kansas City MO 64116

POULSEN, LANCE KULD, metals mfg. co. exec.; b. Chgo., June 25, 1943; s. Carl B. and Margrette (Neilsen) P.; B.S., Roosevelt U., 1966; M.A., U. Iowa, 1968; m. Michelle E. Knapp, Dec. 6, 1975; children—Jason, Suzanne. Mgr., Firestone Tire and Rubber Co., Chgo., 1966-67, cons., 1968-70; brand mgr., advt. dir., dir. new products, asst. to pres. Heublein Corp., Hartford, Conn., 1968-72; v.p. marketing Atlantic-India Rubber Co., Chgo., 1972-75; pres. Rajo Motor & Mfg. Co., Racine, Wis., 1975—; dir. Sea Tiger Yachts Inc.; cons. in field. Bd. dirs. Jr. Achievement Wis. Mem. U.S. C. of C., Wis., Nat. mfrs. assns., Am. Marketing Assn. Clubs: Rotary, Racine Yacht. Patentee in field. Office: 1600 Junction St Racine WI 53403

POVLSEN, PAUL KRISTIAN, JR., dentist; b. Bklyn., Jan. 14, 1926; s. Paul Kristian and Helen Letcher (Logan) P.; student Columbia U., 1946-47; D.D.S., Loyola U., 1953; postgrad. No. Ill. U. Grad. Sch. Guidance and Counseling, 1968-72; m. Roberta Beth Rushing, Mar. 28, 1946; children—Paul K. III, Leslie, Holly, Kathryn (Mrs. Charles Hebert). Practice dentistry, Sycamore, Ill., 1953—. Missionary dentist, Honduras, summer 1972; dentist Bus. and Profl. Counselors Assn., 1971-73. Active Boy Scouts Am., 1946-55; pres. Stagecoach Community Theatre; mem. Sycamore Sch. Bd., 1963-72, pres., 1971-72, sec., 1969-70. Bd. dirs. Walden 4 Ecol. Land Devel. Recipient citation award Boy Scouts Am., 1955, statuette, 1955, citation High Sch. Cooperative Edn., 1966, 71. Mem. Am. Dental Assn., Ill., Fox Valley (ethics com. 1960) dental socs., Am. Legion. Methodist. Clubs: Elks, Lions, Sportsman, Kishwaukee Country. Home: 212 E State St Sycamore IL 60178 Office: 220 E State St Sycamore IL 60178

POVONDRA, DENNIS LEE, educator; b. Yankton, S.D., Oct. 12, 1948; s. Stephen Frank and Gladys Mary (Slavik) P.; B.S.E., So. State Coll., 1970; postgrad. U. S.D. at Vermillion, 1974-75; m. Sherlyn Sue Beran, June 5, 1971. Tchr. bus. edn. pub. schs. Gregory, S.D., 1970-75; bus. mgr. Bon Homme Sch. Dist. 4-2, Tyndall, S.D., 1975—. Play dir., Fall Drama Prodn., 1970-75, One-Act Contest Play, 1970-75, Children's Theater, 1970-75, Spring Musical, 1975. Trustee Tabor Town Bd., 1975-77; bd. dirs. Czech Heritage Preservation Soc.; instr. Conf. Christian Doctrine St. Wenceslaus Ch., 1975-77; supporting mem. Nat. Right to Work Com., 1977—. Named Jaycee Outstanding Young Educator Gregory, 1974. Mem. S.D. Assn. Sch. Bus. Ofcls., Assn. Sch. Bus. Ofcls. U.S. and Can., Sch. Adminstrs. S.D., Tabor Area C. of C. (sec.-treas. 1975—), Catholic Workmen. Democrat. Roman Catholic. Compiler The Povondra Family History, Plavec and Merkwan Family History. Home: PO Box 64 Tabor SD 57063 Office: PO Box 28 Tyndall SD 57066

POWDRILL, GARY LEO, plant engring. adminstr.; b. Butte, Mont., Nov. 26, 1945; s. Harold Holmes and Genevieve Marie (Tansey) P.; B.S., Gonzaga U., 1969; M.B.A., U. Detroit, 1973. Plant design engr. Ford Motor Co., Sterling Heights, Mich., 1969-73, div. plant engr. Chassis div., 1973-74, supr. plant engring. sect., Indpls. plant, 1974—. Mem. Indpls. Mayor's Tech. Adv. Com., 1975—. Licensed profl. engr., Ind. Mem. Ind. Soc. Profl. Engrs. Roman Catholic. Elk. Home: 5864-B San Clemente Ln Indianapolis IN 46226 Office: 6900 English Ave Indianapolis IN 46206

POWELL, ERNESTINE BREISCH (MRS. ROGER K. POWELL), lawyer; b. Moundsville, W.Va., Feb. 16, 1906; d. Ernest Elmer and Belle (Wallace) Breisch; student Dayton YMCA Law Sch., 1929; m. Roger K. Powell, Nov. 15, 1935; children—R. Keith (dec.), Diane L. D., Bruce W. Admitted to Ohio bar, 1929; tax analyst tax dept. Wall, Cassell & Groneweg, Dayton, Ohio, 1929-31; pvt. practive law, 1931-40; gen. counsel for Dayton Jobbers and Mfrs. Assn., 1931-41; mem. Powell & Powell, Columbus, Ohio, 1944—. Ohio chmn. Nat. Woman's Party, Washington, 1950-51, nat. chmn. 1953-54, lifetime hon. nat. chmn., 1954—, life mem. Pres. vol. activities com. Columbus State Sch., 1960-61, trustee, 1957-59. Mem. Nat. Assn. Women Lawyers, Am., Ohio, Columbus bar assns., Nat. Assn. Arts and Letters (pres. Columbus chpt.). Clubs: National Lawyers Club (charter mem.) (Washington, D.C.). Co-author: Tax Ideas, 1955; Estate Tax Techniques, 1951—. Editor-in-chief; Women Lawyers Jour., 1943-45. Office: 17 S High St Columbus OH 43215

POWELL, IRA CHESLEY, choral music conductor; b. Luling, Tex., Apr. 20, 1930; s. Ira Milton and Margaret Elizabeth (Anderson) P.; student Baylor U., 1946-47; B.S., Wayland Coll., 1950; M. Sacred Music, Southwestern Baptist Theol. Sem., 1956; D. Music Edn., U. Okla., 1969; m. Elinor Cora Van Dyke, Dec. 31, 1974. Minister of music First Baptist Ch., Norman, Okla., 1961-67; mem. music faculty U. Mo., Columbia, 1967—; choral and vocal clinician and adjudicator; bass oratorio soloist; cons. ch. music; musical dir. Community United Methodist Ch., Columbia, Mo.; co-founder, pres. Galaxy Games, Inc. Named Hon. Citizen of Norman (Okla.), 1967. Mem. Nat. Assn. of Tchrs. of Singing (Mo. gov. 1973-77), Am., Mo. choral dirs. assns., Pi Kappa Lambda, Phi Mu Alpha Sinfonia. Republican. Methodist. Home: 1200 S Glenwood St Columbia MO 65201 Office: Music Dept Univ Missouri Columbia MO 65201

POWELL, JEROME EVAN, ins. agency exec.; b. Dallas, Mar. 30, 1935; s. Harry E. and Myrtle H. (McAlear) P.; B.S., U. Dayton, 1957; m. Constance J. Griffiths, May 10, 1958; children—Lisa M., Judith L., Amy E. Retail store mgr. Gen. Tire Co., Pitts., 1957-60; brokerage cons., asst. mgr. Conn. Gen. Life Ins. Co., Chgo., 1960-65; v.p., sec.-treas. Assurance Agy., Arlington Heights, Ill., 1965—; dir. Community Bank of Hanover Park, Valley Bank of South Elgin. Bd. dirs. Inverness Village Assn. Mem. Nat. Assn. Life Underwriters, Million Dollar Round Table. Republican. Roman Catholic. Club: Inverness Golf. Home: 1600 Pheasant Trail Inverness Palatine IL 60067 Office: 1650 N Arlington Heights Rd Arlington Heights IL 60004

POWELL, RICHARD CINCLAIR, physician, educator; b. South Bend, Ind., July 28, 1929; s. George M. and Frances M. (Smith) P.; A.B., DePauw U., 1951; M.D., Northwestern U., 1955; m. VerNalda Fay Strong, Dec. 21, 1954; children—Ronald S., Steven M. Intern, Ind. U. Med. Center, Indpls., 1955-56, resident in internal medicine, 1956-59; mem. faculty Ind. U. Sch. Medicine, Indpls., 1961—, prof. medicine dept. medicine, 1972—. Active Boy Scouts Am., Am. Heart Assn., Am. Diabetes Assn. Served as capt. U.S. Army, 1959-61. Diplomate Am. Bd. Internal Medicine. Fellow Am. Coll. Physicians; mem. AMA, Am. Soc. Internal Medicine, The Endocrine Soc., Central Soc. Clin. Research. Episcopalian. Club: Masons. Contbr. articles to med. jours. Home: 5359 Hedgerow Dr Indianapolis IN 46226 Office: Dept Medicine Ind Univ Sch Medicine 1100 W Michigan St Indianapolis IN 46202

POWELSON, JAMES SHERMAN, lumber co. exec.; b. Sterling, Ill., May 25, 1931; s. Abram James and Esther Grattan (Mayes) P.; B.A., Knox Coll., 1953; m. Alice Louise Hunter, Dec. 27, 1953; children—James Hunter, David Sherman. With Simpson-Powelson Lumber Co., Galesburg, Ill., 1955—, v.p., dir., 1959-63, exec. v.p., 1963-69, pres., 1969—; also dir.; dir. Res. Supply Corp., Franklin Park, Ill., Farmers & Mechanics Bank, Galesburg, 1965—. Mem. exec. bd. Prairie council Boy Scouts Am., 1966-69. Trustee Galesburg Cottage Hosp. Served with AUS, 1953-55; Korea. Mem. Galesburg C. of C. (dir. 1963-69), Beta Theta Pi. Republican. Methodist. Home: 2060 N Broad St Galesburg IL 61401 Office: 159 S Prairie St Galesburg IL 61401

POWER, JOSEPH ALOYSIUS, lawyer; b. Chgo., June 26, 1916; s. William J. and Edna (Colwell) P.; LL.B., Loyola U., Chgo., 1938; B.S.C., 1942; m. Mary Cavanaugh, Nov. 14, 1942; children—Margaret, Mary Ellen, Catherine, Jean, Joseph, William, Maureen, Thomas, Carole. Admitted to Ill. bar, 1938; real estate agt. County of Cook, 1947-54; asso. judge Municipal Ct. Chgo., 1954-64; asso. judge Circuit Ct., Chgo., 1964, judge, 1964-76; gen. atty. Chgo. Park Dist., 1976—. Bd. dirs. Boy Scouts, Little City, Inc. Served to lt. USNR, 1942-45. Mem. Am. Legion, Ill., Fed., Chgo. bar assns., Cath. Lawyers Guild (dir.), Moose, K.C. Home: 4228 S Wallace St Chicago IL 60609 Office: Chgo Park Dist Adminstrn Bldg 425 McFetridge Dr Chicago IL 60605

POWER, PHILIP HARWICK, publisher; b. Ann Arbor, Mich., June 3, 1938; s. Eugene Barnum and Sayde (Harwick) P.; B.A. summa cum laude, U. Mich., 1960; M.A. (Marshall scholar), Univ. Coll., Oxford, Eng., 1964; m. Sarah Hutchins Goddard, July 5, 1971. Acting city editor Fairbanks (Alaska) Daily News-Miner, 1961-62; fgn. corr. Chgo. Daily News, 1962-64; mem. gubernatorial campaign staff U.S. rep. 1964; adminstrv. asst. to U.S. rep., 1965-66; founder, pub. Observer Newspapers, Inc., Livonia, Mich., 1966-74; co-founder, chmn. Suburban Communications Corp., Livonia, 1974—; co-pub. Observer-Eccentric Newspapers, Livonia, 1974—; chmn. Queen City Suburban Press, Cin., 1974—, Towne Courier Publs., East Lansing, Mich., 1974—, Instructional Fair, Grand Rapids, Mich., 1974—; dir. Suburban Newspapers Am., Eskimo Art, Inc. Ann Arbor, Park Place Motor Inns, Inc. Bd. dirs. Power Found.; chmn. Mich. Found. for Arts. Mem. Council on Fgn. Relations. Club: American (London). Office: care Suburban Communications Corp 36251 Schoolcraft Rd Livonia MI 48150

POWER, SARAH GODDARD (MRS. PHILIP H. POWER), govt. ofcl.; b. Detroit, June 19, 1935; d. Wendell Converse and Katherine (Russel) Goddard; B.A., Vassar Coll., 1957; M.A., N.Y. U., 1965; m. Philip H. Power. Asst. to exec. dir. Asso. Alumnae Vassar Coll., 1957-58; personal asst. to Gov. Nelson A. Rockefeller, 1958-63; exec. dir. N.Y.C. Commn. for the UN and for The Consular Corps, 1966-69; exec. dir. U.S. UN-N.Y.C.; mem. U.S. Nat. Commn. for UNESCO; chairperson Task Force for Internat. Women's Yr. Host Country Adv. Com., N.Y.C., 1969-72. Chmn. U.S. Nat. Commn. for UNESCO, 1976—; del. 19th Gen. Conf. UNESCO, Nairobi, 1976; trustee Elizabeth N. Arnstein Fund, Power Found.; regent U. Mich., 1975—. Democrat. Home: 12 Ridgeway W Ann Arbor MI 48104

POWERS, EARL HERSHEL, realtor; b. Tell City, Ind., May 5, 1934; s. Archie E. and Mabel (Hobbs) P.; B.S., Western Ky. U., 1961; m. Sharon A. Grimes, Jan. 15, 1972; children from previous marriage—Allen, Patricia, Kimberly, Lisa Fentress, Jeff Fentress. Account exec., Wolverine World Wide, Rockford, Mich., 1961-67; owner Powers Cos., Inc. bldg. and devel. real estate, Evansville, Inc., 1967—, Newburgh, Ind., 1969—; dir. Powers Co. Fla. Adviser Council Govts., 1973-75. Served with USNR, 1954-58. Recipient Silver Key award for condominium design U.S. Steel, 1973. Mem. C. of C., Nat. Home Builders Assn. (nat. outstanding achievement award, 1974) Nat. Inst. Real Estate Brokers, Evansville Bd. Realtors, Multiple Listing Service, LaSalle Law Alumni Club, Phi Delta Kappa. Mason (Shriner), Elk. Clubs: Tri State Racquet, Oak Meadow. Office: PO Box 177 11 W Jennings Newburgh IN 47630

POWERS, EARL LOUIS, real estate exec.; b. Bay City, Mich., Apr. 16, 1923; s. Stanley and Nora K. (Englehardt) P.; student various real estate courses U. Mich., Delta Coll.; m. Norma Beatrice Ashcraft, Aug. 31, 1945; children—Earl Louis, Suzanne (Mrs. Dale Meylan), David L., Jennifer Sue. Owner, Powers Grocery, 1948-61; founder, owner Powers Realty Co., Bay City, 1961—, Colonial Apts., 1965—, Powers Apts., 1948—, Powers Investment Co., 1961—, Powers-Kirkbride Bldg. Co., 1968—; co-owner Profl. Center, 1972—. Served with USAAF, 1942-46. Mem. Multiple Listing Service, Bay County Bd. Realtors (pres. 1966, bd. dirs. 1965-68), Nat. Assn. Realtors, Nat. Assn. Real Estate Appraisers. Club: Bay City Country. Home: 4659 Niccolet Pl Bay City MI 48706 Office: 406 7th St Bay City MI 48706

POWERS, JAMES WALTER, compensation and benefits adminstr.; b. Greensboro, N.C., Aug. 19, 1943; s. Frank and Ellen (Harman) P.; B.S.B.A., U. Richmond, 1965; postgrad. U. Md., 1965-68; m. Mary M. Wells, Nov. 26, 1966; children—John, Wendy. Indsl. relations analyst Ford Motor Co., Livonia, Mich., 1968-70; adminstrv. mgr. AMF/Paragon Electric Co., Summerville, S.C., 1970-74, mgr. personnel and indsl. relations, Two Rivers, Wis., 1974-76; mgr. compensation and benefits AMF/Harley-Davidson Co., Milw., 1976—. Bd. dirs. Jr. Achievement, Summerville C. of C.; mem. advisory bd. Lakeshore Tech. Inst., Cleve. Mem. Personnel and Indsl. Relations Assn., Am. Soc. of Personnel Adminstrn., N.E. Wis. Indsl. Assn., Alpha Kappa Psi, Sigma Alpha Epsilon. Episcopalian. Club: Elks. Home: 9317 W Stickney Ave Wauwatosa WI 53226 Office: 3700 W Juneau Ave PO Box 565 Milwaukee WI 53201

POWERS, JOHN JAMES, chem. products co. exec.; b. East Grand Forks, Minn., Nov. 11, 1917; s. Thomas and Mary Ann (O'Leary) P.; student parochial schs., East Grand Forks; m. Margaret Ann Olson, Aug. 12, 1941; children—Patricia, Michael, Timothy, Greg, Steve. With Lystads Inc., Grand Forks, N.D., 1935—, sales mgr., 1956-77, v.p. chem. sales, 1956—; v.p. Miracle Chems. Co.; chmn. bd. Am. Fed. Savs. & Loan Co. Pres. Sch. Bd., East Grand Forks, 1957-59; bd. dirs. March of Dimes, Grand Forks. Served with U.S. Army, 1943-46; ETO. Decorated Silver Star; recipient award United Fund, 1974-76, U. N.D., 1975, St. Michael's Hosp. Fund Dr., 1958. Mem. Internat. Sanitary Supply Assn., Chem. Spltys. Mfrs. Assn., DAV, Am. Legion, VFW. Roman Catholic. Clubs: Eagles, Grand Forks Country. Home: 3400 Cherry St Grand Forks ND 58201 Office: 901 University Ave Grand Forks ND 58201

POWERS, JOHN RICHARD, III, computer services co. exec.; b. Rochester, N.Y., Dec. 11, 1940; s. John Richard and Virginia Estelle (Kindgen) P.; B.A., Hendrix Coll., 1964; M.S., Purdue U., 1969; m. Janey Hershey, June 12, 1965; children—Robert, Matthew, Jason. With Batelle Labs., Columbus, Ohio, 1966-76, mgr. ednl. technology sect., 1975-76, sr. research scientist, computer, info. systems and edn. dept., 1976-77; co-founder, pres. Authorship Resource Inc., Columbus, 1977—. Mem. Assn. Devel. Computer-Based Instructional Systems, Assn. Ednl. Data Systems. Office: 6660 Doubletree Ave Suite 16 Columbus OH 43229

POWERS, RAYMOND EDWIN, JR., distillery exec.; b. Aurora, Ill., Sept. 17, 1937; s. Raymond Edwin and Alma Malinda (Knapp) P.; B.S., No. Ill. U., 1959; M.B.A., U. Chgo., 1968; m. Nancy Jo Kein, Aug. 28, 1936; children—Dawn, Stacy, Raymond Edwin III. Sr. accountant U.S. Gypsum Co., Chgo., 1959-62; accounting mgr. The Paper Mate Co., 1962-66; controller Leaf Brands div. W.R. Grace Co., 1966-70; controller Barton Brands Ltd., 1970—; dir. Manning Savs. & Loan. C.P.A., Ill. Mem. Am. Inst. C.P.A.'s, Ill. Soc. C.P.A.'s, Western Springs Service Club (treas.). Home: 4208 Hampton St Western Springs IL 60558 Office: 200 S Michigan Ave Chicago IL 60604

POYNTON, JOSEPH PATRICK, aerospace engr.; b. Chgo., Aug. 28, 1934; s. Joseph P. and Marvel E. (Gaffney) P.; B.S. Aero. Engring., U. Notre Dame, 1956, M.S. Aero. Engring., 1958; m. Betty Jeanne Gorman, Oct. 1, 1971; 1 dau., Jeanne Louise. Teaching fellow U. Notre Dame, 1956, research asst., 1957; aerodynamics engr. Douglas Missiles Co., Santa Monica, Calif., 1958-59; sr. aerodynamic engr. Honeywell Inc., Mpls., 1959-64, sr. design engr. Fgn. Technology div., Dayton, Ohio, 1964; sr. aerospace engr. Lockheed Space & Missiles Co., Sunnyvale, Calif., 1965-66; supervisory aerospace engr. U.S. Army-Dept. Def. Army Aviation Research and Devel. Command, St. Louis, 1966—. Mem. Am. Inst. Aeros. and Astronautics, Am. Helicopter Soc., Sigma Xi. Roman Catholic. Home: 9624 Yorkshire Estates Crestwood MO 63126 Office: PO Box 209 Saint Louis MO 63166

POYSER, JOHN REED, mgmt. cons.; b. Canton, Ohio, Oct. 16, 1917; s. John Reed and Alice Keith (Orton) P.; B.S. cum laude in Mech. Engring., U. Ill., 1939, M.S. in Theoretical and Applied Mechanics, 1940; m. Paula Jean McNamara, Apr. 19, 1941; children—Paula McNamara (Mrs. Charles Sumner Merrill), James Hicks, Mary Margaret (Mrs. James MacCallum), Joan R. (Mrs. Terrence Kiernan), John Reed; m. 2d, Beate Rost, Oct. 5, 1972. Chief process and standards engr. Chain Belt Co., Milw., 1940-46; chief methods engr. S.C. Johnson & Son, Inc., Racine, Wis., 1946-50; chief indsl. engr. Modine Mfg. Co., Racine, 1950-52; staff mgmt. cons. A.T. Kearney, Inc., Chgo., 1952-57, prin., engagement mgr., 1959—; works mgr. Leece Neville Co., Cleve., 1957-59; instr. U. Wis., Milw., Racine, 1943-50, guest speaker Mgmt. Inst., Madison, 1944—; seminar leader Am. Mgmt. Assn., 1965—. Alderman, Racine City Council, 1950-52, mem. finance com., 1950-52, mem. parks com., 1950-52; mem. Racine City Plan Commn., 1950-52. Registered profl. engr., Wis. Mem. Inst. Mgmt. Consultants (founding), S.A.R., Tau Beta Pi, Pi Tau Sigma, Chi Psi. Contbr. articles to tech. mags. Home: 863 W Lill St Chicago IL 60614 Office: 100 S Wacker Dr Chicago IL 60606

PRAGER, DAVID, justice; b. Fort Scott, Kans., Oct. 30, 1918; s. Walter and Helen (Kishler) P.; A.B., U. Kans., 1939, LL.B., 1942; m. Dorothy Schroeter, Sept. 8, 1945; children—Diane, David III. Admitted to Kans. bar, 1942; practiced in Topeka, 1946-59; dist. judge, Topeka, 1959-71; asso. justice Supreme Ct. Kans., 1971—; lectr. law Washburn Law Sch., 1948-68. Served to lt. USNR, 1943-46. Mem. Am., Kans., Topeka bar assns., Order of Coif, Phi Beta Kappa, Phi Delta Theta, Phi Delta Phi. Home: 5130 SW 53d St Topeka KS 66610 Office: State House Topeka KS 66612

PRALL, ELMER CLARENCE, dentist; b. Lamoni, Iowa, Mar. 9, 1902; s. Oscar Edward and Eleanor Margaret (Gibbons) P.; A.A., Graceland Coll., 1923, U. Iowa, summers, 1920-22, 24, 26; D.D.S., U. Iowa, 1930; m. Irma Caroline Reihman, June 25, 1927; 1 dau., Paula (Mrs. White). Tchr., athletic coach Iowa High Schs., 1920-22, 23-24, 26-27; gen. practice dentistry, Mount Vernon, Iowa, 1930—. Pres., Mount Vernon chpt. ARC, 1947, v.p., water safety chmn., 1948-76. Mem. Mount Vernon City Council, 1934-76; mem. tax com. Iowa League Municipalities, 1936. Fellow Am. Coll. Dentists; mem. Am. Soc. Dentistry for Children (unit pres. 1955), Am. (life), Iowa (supt. clinics. 1950, chmn. ins. council 1956-64) dental assns., University Dist. (pres. 1950, sec. 1945-50, 68—), Cedar Rapids (pres. 1944-45) dental socs., Pierre Fauchard Acad., Alumni Assn. Dental Coll. U. Iowa (pres. 1957, treas. 1958-65), Mount Vernon C. of C. (pres. 1933). Methodist (trustee 1971-74). Lion (pres. 1937). Home: 419 S 2d St Mount Vernon IA 52314 Office: 125 1st St W Mount Vernon IA 52314

PRAML, LAWRENCE ANTHONY, electronic products co. technician; b. St. Paul, Feb. 27, 1939; s. Joseph Patrick and Mildred (Pierce) P.; student Dunwoody Indsl. Inst., 1964-66, student U. Minn., 1961-62, 67—; m. Mary Ellen Johnson, Oct. 5, 1963; children—Patricia, Lawrence Anthony, James. With Xerox Corp., Mpls., 1966—, technician II, 1966-68, technician III, 1968-72, technician IV, 1972—. Chmn. Cottage Grove (Minn.) Econ. Devel. Commn., 1972; dist. chmn. Democratic-Farmer-Labor party, 1971-72, del. county conv., 1972—. Served with Signal Corps, AUS, 1957-61. Named Outstanding Young Man Cottage Grove, 1972; recipient 12 state awards and 5 nat. awards Jaycees. Mem. Cottage Grove Jaycees (pres. 1969-70, dir. 1968-69), Minn. Jaycees (v.p. 1970-71, dir. 1973), Cottage Grove Athletic Assn. K.C. Home: 8976 Inwood Ave S Cottage Grove MN 55016

PRANGE, JAMES ROBERT, realtor; b. Hammond, Ind., Apr. 27, 1936; s. William Edward and Mildred Lorraine (Hutchinson) P.; grad. high sch., Grad. Realtors Inst., 1974; m. Marilyn Joyce Lavery, June 29, 1970; children—James Allen, Thomas Michael, Cynthia Sue. Electrician, No. Ind. Pub. Service Co., Crown Point, Ind., 1957-61; salesman Burkhardt Schmal Realty Inc., Crown Point, 1961-63; broker, co-owner Lake County Realty, Inc., and Prange Devel. Co., 1963—. Owner Jamar Properties mgmt., 1970—; pres. Triangle Constrn. Co., 1976—, Burgundy Builders, 1977—, Wide World of Travel, 1977—. Served with AUS, 1955-57. Mem. Home Builders Assn. (dir., 1973-74), South Lake County Bd. Realtors, Merrillville C. of C., Nat. Assn. Realtors, Nat. Inst. Real Estate Brokers, Ind. Realtors Inst., Nat. Assn. Ind. Fee Appraisers (v.p., 1969-71), Crown Point C. of C. Methodist. Home: 421 Martin Dr Crown Point IN 46307 Office: 8695 Broadway St Merrillville IN 46410

PRANGE, JAMES WILLIAM, educator; b. New Douglas, Ill., Apr. 17, 1924; s. August William and Eugenia (Livingston) P.; B.S., Ill. State U., 1945; M.S., Ind. U., 1949; specialist degree N.Y. U., 1954; postgrad. Mich. State U., 1964-66; m. Cathmar Jeanne Shaw, Aug. 14, 1956; children—Rebecca Jeanne, Margaret Ann, Amy Sue, Robert Bruce. Tchr., Lawrenceville (Ill.) High Sch., 1945-46; instr. Winona (Minn.) State Tchrs. Coll., 1949-51; dir. audio visual York Community High Sch., Elmhurst, Ill., 1952-57; asso. dir. instructional tech., asso. prof. Western Ill. U., 1957—. Served with U.S. Army, 1946-47. Mem. NEA, Nat. Assn. Ednl. Broadcasters, Assn. Ednl. Communication and Tech., W. Central Ill. Ednl. TV Assn. (sec. treas.), Phi Delta Kappa, Alpha Phi Omega, Gamma Theta Upsilon, Pi Gamma Mu. Lutheran. Office: Office Instructional Technology Western Illinois University Macomb IL 61455

PRANGE, WILLIAM HAROLD, realtor; b. Hammond, Ind., Sept. 20, 1934; s. William Edwin and Mildred Lorene (Hutchinson) P.; student Ill. Inst. Tech., 1952-54; B.S., Ind. U., 1957, postgrad., 1960-64; m. Nancy Jane Reiger, June 7, 1956; children—Lisa Denise, Cassandra Lyn, William Robert, Amanda Melinda. Art supr. Celina (Ohio) Pub. Schs., 1957-60; draftsman Avco Co., 1957-58; instr. Sch. Edn., Ind. U., Bloomington, 1960-64; designer, asst. mgr. Furniture Center, Bloomington, 1964-66; designer, buyer, salesman Kennedy & Lewis Furniture, Crown Point, Ind., 1966-68; asst. closing broker Lake County Realty, Inc., Merrillville, Ind., 1968-69, sales tng. mgr., 1970-74, advt. mgr., 1971-74, salesman, 1968-71, asst. office mgr., 1972-73, designer new homes, 1968-74, gen. sales mgr., 1973-74; asst. sec. Alta Corp.-Embassy Homes, 1974-76; exec. v.p. Village View Realty Inc., Highland, Ind., 1974-76; sec.-treas. Burgundy Builders, 1976—. Served with USNR, 1952-53. Named Salesman of the Year, Lake County Realty, Inc., 1972. Mem. Nat. Assn. Real Estate Bds., Ind. Real Estate Assn., So. Lake County and Calumet Bd. Realtors (chmn. edn. com. 1975), Ind. U. Alumni Assn., Gary Artists League. Methodist. Editor Homes for Living, 1973-74. Home: 12307 Hermits Ln Crown Point IN 46307 Office: 8695 Broadway Merrillville IN 46410

PRASAD, ANANDA SHIVA, physician; b. India, Jan. 1, 1928; s. R. K. Lal and M. (Kaur) P.; B.Sc., Patna Sci. Coll., 1946; M.B., B.S., Patna Med. Coll., 1951; Ph.D. in Medicine, U. Minn., 1957; m. Aryabala, Jan. 6, 1952; children—Rita, Sheila, Ashok, Audrey. House physician Patna Med. Coll. Hosp., 1951-52; resident pathology St. Paul's Hosp., Dallas, 1952-53; resident in-patient service U. Minn., 1953-54, resident out-patient service, 1954-55, resident neurology, 1955, resident hematology, 1956; sr. resident metabolism VA Hosp., Mpls., 1956; instr. Dept. Medicine U. Minn. Hosp., 1957-58; vis. asso. prof. medicine Shiraz Med. Faculty and asso. medicine Nemazee Hosp., Shiraz, Iran, 1958-60, chmn. dept. medicine, 1960; asst. prof. nutrition Vanderbilt U., Nashville, also head nutrition project U.S. Naval Med. Research Unit, Cairo, U.A.R., 1961-63; asst. prof. medicine Wayne State U., 1963-64, chief hematology, 1963—, asso. prof., 1964-68, prof., 1968—; mem. staff VA Hosp., Allen Park, Mich., 1964—; sr. attending physician Detroit Gen. Hosp., 1968—. Recipient Caldwell Meml. prize, 1944; Pfizer resident scholarship, 1955-56; Research Recognition award Wayne State U., 1964; Goldberger award AMA, 1975; Am. Coll. Nutrition award, 1976. Diplomate Am. Bd. Nutrition. Fellow A.C.P.; mem. Am. Fedn. Clin. Research, U. Minn. Alumni Assn., Internat. Soc. Internal Medicine, Internat. Soc. Hematology, Am. Soc. Hematology, Central Soc. Clin. Research, Soc. Exptl. Biology and Medicine, Am. Soc. Clin. Investigation, Assn. Am. Physicians, Sigma Xi. Club: Cosmos (Washington). Editor: Zinc Metabolism, 1966, 69; Trace Elements in Human Health and Disease, 2 vols., 1976; co-editor: Zinc Metabolism: Current Aspects in Health and Disease, 1977. Contbr. articles profl. jours. Home: 4710 Cove Rd Orchard Lake MI 48033 Office: Wayne State U Sch Medicine 540 E Canfield Ave Detroit MI 48201

PRASAD, ARYABALA RAY, physician; b. Cuttack, India; d. Birkishore and Saraswati (Pattanayak) Ray; M.B., B.S., Patna (India) U., 1951; M.S., U. Minn., 1958; m. Ananda S. Prasad, Jan. 6, 1952; children—Rita Rochelle, Sheila, Ashok, Nivedita Audrey. Came to U.S., 1952, naturalized, 1968. Resident obstetrics and gynecology St. Paul's Hosp., Dallas, 1952-53, St. Barnabas Hosp., Mpls., 1953-55; resident surgery Mt. Sinai Hosp., Mpls., 1955-56; resident pathology St. Joseph Hosp., St. Paul, 1956-57; teaching asst. physiology U. Minn., 1957-58; vis. staff physician Nemazee Hosp., Pahlevi U., Shiraz, Iran, 1958-61, in charge obstetrics service, 1959-61; physician Planned Parenthood Clinic, Detroit, 1965-71; mem. staff St. Joseph Hosp., Pontiac. Mem. Detroit Founders Soc., Detroit Inst. Arts, Detroit Internat. Inst. Home: 4710 Cove Rd Orchard Lake MI 48033 Office: 435 Hickory St Milford MI 48042

PRASSE, PAUL HENRY, banker; b. South Euclid, Ohio, Oct. 16, 1934; s. Paul Henry and Ann Hill-Adamson (Brown) P.; B.S., John Carroll U., 1956; postgrad. Northwestern U., 1964-66; m. Marilyn Merts, June 23, 1962. With Society Nat. Bank, Cleve., 1958—, asst. dir. pub. relations and advt., 1959-63, head bus. devel. dept., 1963-69, asst. cashier, 1964-67, asst. v.p., 1967-68, mgr. Quick-Credit, 1968-71, head Master Charge/Quick Credit dept., 1971-75, v.p., mgr. mktg. dept., 1975—; v.p. TransOhio Fin. Corp., 1975—; pres. Prasse and Assos., 1977—. Chmn. Sr. Citizens Center, 1969-70; exec. com. Cleve. Garden Center, 1965-73; asst. sec.-treas. Pub. Sq. Assn., 1961-66. Bd. dirs. community services div. Cleve. Welfare Fedn., 1964-73. Served as lt. Transp. Corps, U.S. Army, 1956-58. Mem. Savs. Inst. Mktg. Soc. Am., Am., Bank mktg. assns., Am. Mgmt. Assn., Am. Inst. Banking (bd. govs. 1968-71), Early Settlers Assn. Western Res., Ohio City Community Devel. Assn., Musical Arts Assn., English Speaking Union, Cleve. Growth Assn., John Carroll U. Alumni Assn. Republican. Presbyterian. Clubs: Cleve. Athletic, Playhouse, City, Mid-Day, Cleve. Advt. (treas. 1970-73, v.p. 1973-75). Contbr. articles to profl. jours. Publicity editor Bank Mktg. mag., 1967-68. Home: 1324 Inglewood Dr Cleveland Heights OH 44121 Office: 127 Public Sq Cleveland OH 44114

PRASUHN, LLOYD WAYNE, veterinarian; b. Beansville, Ohio, June 28, 1930; s. Carl Henry and Ellen Victoria (Neal) P.; D.V.M., Ohio State U., 1954; m. Mary Zinn Squibb, Nov. 7, 1963. Practice of vet. medicine, New Palestine, Ind., 1956-57; veterinarian Lake Shore Animal Hosp., Chgo., 1957—, pres., dir., 1963—; cons. Wilson Labs., Beatrice Foods, Kimberly-Clark Corp., Parke-Davis, Ralston Purina, Affiliated Labs.; editor D.V.M. News mag., 1969-72; editor-in-chief Veterinary Digest, 1976—. Mem. adv. bd. manpower devel. and tng. act Ill. Dept. Labor, 1971—. Pres. Lake Shore Found. for Animals, 1966—. Served as capt. USAF, 1954-56. Mem. AMVA, Ohio, Ill. State, Chgo. vet. med. assns., Am. Animal Hosp. Assn., Am. Vet. Radiology Soc., Am. Acad. Vet. Cardiology, Am. Vet. Neurology Assn., Nat. Wildlife Fedn., Lincoln Park Zool. Soc., Humane Soc. U.S., Am. Humane Assn., Internat. Veterinary Acupuncture Soc. (treas. 1976—). Phi Eta Sigma, Phi Zeta. Lutheran. Clubs: International, Whitehall. Contbr. articles to publs. Home: 225 W Division St Chicago IL 60610

PRATER, HORACE MILTON, ret. trucking co. exec.; b. Waxahachie, Tex., Mar. 19, 1909; s. John Wesley and Bessie Irene (Simmons) P.; LL.B., South Tex. Coll. Law, 1937-39, LaSalle U., 1931-34, Alexander Hamilton Inst., 1944-48; m. Dorothy Genevieve Oliver, Dec. 9, 1932; 1 son, John Oliver. Co-founder Missouri Pacific Truck System, St. Louis, 1938—, v.p., gen. mgr., 1944-56, v.p. traffic, 1958-60, v.p. sales, 1960-67, v.p. legis., 1967-74; co-founder, v.p. MP Airfreight, Inc., 1967-74; co-founder, v.p. MP Intermodal Transports, Inc., 1968-74; founder, v.p. MPTL's System Sales Group, 1958-67; v.p. MP Truck Lines, 1960-74, Tex.-Pacific Motor Transport Co., 1960-74; founder MPRR-MPTL Truck Rail Sales Force, 1960-67; mgr. merchandise sales, gen. merchandise agt. Mo. Pacific R.R., 1944-56. Loaned exec. bd. St. Louis United Fund., 1972-73, officer corporate gifts, 1973—. Recipient numerous nat. safety awards Am. Trucking Assn. and Tex. Safety Assn. Mem. Western R.R. Truck Line Assn. (founder 1950, sec.-treas. 1957), Houston Freight Carriers Assn. (co-founder, v.p. 1944), Southwest Shippers (adv. bd. 1947-62), Assn. Am. Railroads (chmn. operating rights com. 1970-74). Republican. Presbyterian. (trustee 1962-63, elder) Mason (32 deg., Shriner). Club: St. Louis Traffic, Houston Traffic. Home: 417 Hill Dr St Louis MO 63122 Office: 210 N 13th St St Louis MO 63103

PRATHER, JAMES KEITH, veterinarian; b. Moberly, Mo., Mar. 4, 1928; s. James Logan and Dorothy Christine (Chapman) P.; B.S., U. Mo., 1955, D.V.M., 1955; m. Edith K. Rechkemmer, Aug. 3, 1973; 1 dau., Valerie; stepchildren—Susan, Karen. Veterinarian, Prather Vet. Clinic, Humston, Iowa, 1955-61; researcher Nat. Research Lab., Ames, Iowa, 1962; veterinarian Flint-Prather Vet. Clinic, Fairbury, Ill., 1963-71; veterinarian Aberdeen (S.D.) Vet. Hosp. P.C., 1972—, pres., 1977—. Served with U.S. Army, 1946-49. Recipient Outstanding Achievement award S.D. chpt. Wildlife Fedn., 1977. Mem. Am., S.D. vet. med. assns. Clubs: Whitetail Bowmen, Elks, Masons. Home: Box 591 Aberdeen SD 57401 Office: Box 1216 Aberdeen SD 57401

PRATT, DAN EDWIN, educator; b. High Point, N.C., Feb. 7, 1924; s. C. Daniel and Carol Druscilla (Wyatt) P.; student U. Tampa, 1946-47; B.S., U. Ga., 1950, M.S., 1952; postgrad. Va. Poly. Inst., 1954, Emory U. Law Sch., 1955-56; U. Mass., 1954-55; Ph.D. (fellow) Fla. State U., 1962; m. Mana Clariece Peacock, Aug. 29, 1959; 1 dau., Mana Lisa. Asst. prof. chemistry U. Ga., Athens, 1955-61; asso. prof., research scientist dept. food sci. and nutrition U. Wis., Madison, 1964-69; research scientist, asso. prof. Purdue U., West Lafayette, Ind., 1969-76, prof., 1976—. Served with USMCR, 1942-45. Fellow Am. Inst. Chemists; mem. Nat. Inst. Food Scientists (sec. Inst.), Inst. Food Technologists, Ga. Acad. Sci., N.Y. Acad. Sci., Sigma Xi, Phi Kappa Phi, Pi Mu Epsilon, Phi Tau Sigma (exec. sec. 1969). Club: Optivestment. Toastmasters (pres.). Contbr. articles to profl. jours. Home: 1600 Northwestern Ave West Lafayette IN 47906 Office: Dept Foods and Nutrition Purdue Univ West Lafayette IN 47906

PRATT, GEORGE EDWARD, assn. exec.; b. River Falls, Wis., Mar. 27, 1925; s. George Edward and Elizabeth Bridgett (O'Connor) P.; student Wis. State U., 1946-48; B.S., U. Wis., 1950, M.S., 1951; postgrad. Washington U., St. Louis, 1955-56, U. Iowa, 1975, U. S.D., 1976-77; m. Mary Jean Bushey, Apr. 18, 1952; 1 son, John Michael. Social worker Wis. State Dept. Pub. Welfare, 1951-54; asst. to dir. Lad Lake Home for Boys, Dousman, Wis., 1954-56; dept. head Health and Welfare Council, St. Louis, 1956-58; exec. asst. United Fund of St. Louis, 1958-64; exec. dir. Siouxland United Way, Sioux City, Iowa, 1964—. Instr. bus. adminstrn. Western Iowa Tech. U., 1969-72; instr. bus., U. Iowa Inst. Pub. Affairs, 1969-72, instr. Grad. Sch. Social Work, 1976. Mem. exec. com. Woodbury County Crime Prevention Com., Sioux City, 1969-73; alt. del. Northwest Iowa Crime Prevention Com., 1972-73; mem. manpower tng. adv. com. State Employment Service; sec. Community Appeals Rev. Bd., 1964-73. Served with USNR, 1943-46. Mem. Am. Statis. Assn. (chpt. treas. 1958-64), Nat. Assn. Social Workers (chpt. sec. and treas. 1975), Acad. Certified Social Workers, Alpha Kappa Delta, Silver R. Honor Soc. Clubs: Rotary, Sioux City Boat. Contbr. articles to various publs. Home: 3606 Court St Sioux City IA 51104 Office: PO Box 204 Sioux City IA 51102

PRATT, LEROY GEORGE, state ofcl.; b. Burlington, Iowa, Mar. 26, 1910; s. Clyde Allen and Louise Christine (Bruhl) P.; student Washington Jr. Coll. (Iowa), 1928-30; B.S., State U. Iowa, 1932, M.A., 1933; postgrad. Drake U., 1948-56; m. Ruth Louise McFadden, Dec. 31, 1938; children—LeRoy George II, Patricia Louanne Mathern. Dist. mgr. Investors Diversified Services, Washington, Iowa, 1934-42; cost accountant Iowa Ordnance Plant, Burlington, 1942-43; vocat. adviser VA, Des Moines, 1945-49, adminstrv. asst., 1949-52, chief, allotment unit 1952-53; supply officer Dept. of Army, Iowa Mil. Dist., Des Moines, 1953-59; supr. statistics Iowa Dept. Pub. Instrn., Des Moines, 1959-67, publs. cons., 1967-70, publs. editor, 1970-75. Mem. Iowa Hist. Bd., 1974—. Served with USNR, 1943-45. Mem. Polk County Hist. Soc. (pres. 1962-64), Iowa Soc. for Preservation Hist. Landmarks (pres. 1964-74), Nature Conservancy (chpt. vice chmn. 1967-73, chmn. 1973-74), Iowa Archeol. Soc. (dir. 1968-71), Living History Farms (dir. 1971—), Des Moines Audubon Soc. (pres. 1970-72), Des Moines Color Film Club (pres. 1956-57, 70-71), Beta Theta Pi, Beta Gamma Sigma, Order of Artus. Author: Summer School Programs in Iowa Public Schools, 1960, 62, 63, 65; From

Cabin to Capital, 1966, rev. edit., 1971, 74; Teaching Iowa History, 1968; A Guide to Historic Iowa, 1968; Discovering Historic Iowa, 1972, rev. edit., 1975; Polk County Coal Mines, 1974; The Counties and Courthouses of Iowa, 1977; co-author Iowa History: A Guide to Resource Material, 1972; Historical Highlights of Polk County, Iowa, 1973; also articles, newsletters, book revs. Editor: Data on Iowa Schools, 1970-75, Iowa Ednl. Directory; asso. editor Ednl. Bull, Iowa Dept. Pub. Instrn., 1959-71. Home: 317 SW 42d St Des Moines IA 50312 Office: State Historical Bldg Des Moines IA 50319

PRATT, WILLIAM CROUCH, JR., educator; b. Shawnee, Okla., Oct. 5, 1927; s. William Crouch and Irene (Johnston) P.; B.A., U. Okla., 1949; M.A., Vanderbilt U., 1951, Ph.D., 1957; m. Anne Cullen Rich, Oct. 2, 1954; children—Catherine Cullen, William Stuart, Randall Johnston. Rotary Internat. fellow U. Glasgow (Scotland), 1951-52; instr. English, Vanderbilt U., 1955-57; instr. Miami U., Oxford, Ohio, 1957-59, asst. prof. English, 1959-64, asso. prof., dir. freshman English, 1964-68, prof., 1968—; adviser Ohio Poetry Circuit, 1964—; Fulbright-Hays lectr. in Am. lit., prof. Am. lit. Univ. Coll., Dublin, Ireland, 1975-76; resident scholar Miami U. European Center, Luxembourg, fall 1976. Served to lt. USNR, 1953-55. Mem. Modern Lang. Assn., Nat. Council Tchrs. English (Ohio awards chmn. 1967-69), Coll. Conf. on Composition, Communication, Internat. Contemporary Lit. and Theatre Soc., Soc. Study So. Lit., Phi Beta Kappa, Sigma Alpha Epsilon. Republican. Episcopalian. Club: Butler County (Ohio) Torch. Author: The Imagist Poem, 1963; The Fugitive Poets, 1965; The College Writer, 1969; contbr. essays, translations, poems, revs. to lit. jours., books. Home: 212 Oakhill Dr Oxford OH 45056 Office: Dept of English Miami U Oxford OH 45056

PRAUSNITZ, WALTHER GUNTHER, educator; b. Cologne, Germany, Oct. 2, 1924; s. Fred F. and Maria E. (Moritz) P.; came to U.S., 1937, naturalized, 1947; A.B., U. Chgo., 1949, M.A., 1950, Ph.D., 1956. Instr., Wright Jr. Coll., Chgo., 1951-52; asst. prof. Concordia Coll., Moorhead, Minn., 1952-54, asso. prof., 1954-56, prof., head English dept., 1956-68, dir. Liberal Arts Studies, 1968—. Mem. exec. com. Conf. on Coll. Composition and Communication, 1956-59; mem. governing bd. Minn. State Arts Council, 1973-76, chmn. bd., 1975-76, dir. long-range planning study, 1973-75; mem. festival panel Minn. Bicentennial Commn., 1973-75. Bd. dirs. Fargo-Moorhead Open Forum, 1954-58; gen. mgr. Fargo-Moorhead Symphony Orch. Assn., 1960-68; producer television course, 1965. Mem. North Central Ednl. TV Assn. (trustee, v.p. devel. 1965-68), Modern Lang. Assn., Nat. Council Tchrs. English, Am. Assn. Higher Edn., Conf. Coll. Composition and Communication, AAUP, Phi Beta Kappa. Author: Introduction to Research; Curriculum Reform; also students manual. Editor: Discourse: A Review of the Liberal Arts, 1957-67; Capsules: A Review of Higher Edn. News and Research, 1970—. Office: Concordia Coll Moorhead MN 56560

PRAY, BRUCE S., clergyman, psychologist; b. Haverhill, Mass., June 5, 1926; s. Roland Call and Elsie (Stevens) P.; B.S., Houghton Coll., 1962; M.Div. Colgate-Rochester Div. Sch., 1966; M.S., Alfred U., 1968; m. Rose Mary Barios, Oct. 30, 1948; children—Steven, Ronald, Karen, Bruce, Douglas, Shirley, Elsie, John, Gerry. Clin. tng. Willard State Hosp., 1962, Gowanda State Hosp., 1963; intern VA Hosp., Sioux Falls, S.D., 1971. Ordained to ministery, Presbyn. Ch., 1956; patrolman Gen. Electric Co., Schenectady, 1946-48; pastor Howard Union Ch., Howard, N.Y., 1960-66; chaplain Bath (N.Y.) VA Hosp., 1966-68; guidance counselor, Kimball, S.D., 1968-69; sch. psychologist Flandreau (S.D.) Ind. Sch., 1969-76; pvt. practice sch. psychology, Pipestone, Minn., 1976—; del. to profl. meetings. Contbr. articles to profl. jours. Home: 114 W 1st Ave Flandreau SD 57028

PRAY, RALPH RUSTIN, physician; b. Fargo, N.D., Feb. 2, 1943; s. Laurence Gesner and Helen Louella (Van Atta) P.; B.A., Grinnell Coll., 1965; M.D., U. Iowa, 1969; m. D. Jean Reay, Apr. 5, 1969; children—Sarah Elaine, Gregory David. Intern, Harborview Med. Center, Seattle, 1969-70; resident in internal medicine U. Iowa Hosps. and Clinics, Iowa City, 1970-73; practice specializing in internal medicine, Des Moines, 1973—; mem. staff Iowa Methodist Med. Center, Broadlawns Polk County Hosp., Iowa Lutheran Hosp.; instr. internal medicine Iowa Meth. Med. Center. Diplomate Am. Bd. Internal Medicine. Mem. AMA, Iowa, Polk County med. socs., Am. Coll. Physicians, Am. Soc. Internal Medicine, Med. Library Club, Alpha Omega Alpha. Republican. Presbyterian. Club: Masons. Home: 4616 Western Hills Dr West Des Moines IA 50265 Office: 1221 Center St Suite 15 Des Moines IA 50309

PRCELA, JOHN IVAN, educator, editor; b. Kosute-Trilj, Croatia, Mar. 9, 1922; s. Petar and Iva (Cabo) P.; came to U.S., 1949, naturalized, 1955; student Internat. Coll. St. Anthony, Rome, 1945-47, Cleve. Coll., 1951-53; B.A., John Carroll U., 1954; M.A., Western Res. U., 1957; postgrad. Institute Catholique, Paris, summer 1958, Am. Acad. in Rome, summer 1960, John Carroll U., summers 1974, 75; m. Amelia Consuelo Mir, Dec. 26, 1963; children—Maria-Consuelo, Joseph-Aloysius, Ana Clara, Therese-Michele Tchr. fgn. lang. dept. St. Edward High Sch., Lakewood, Ohio, 1954-58, Charles F. Brush High Sch., Lyndhurst, Ohio, 1958—. Tchr. Italian and English. Cleve. Bd. Edn. Evening Sch., 1955-59; tchr. Latin and Spanish, Saturday program Cleve. Cath. Diocese, 1964-70; tchr. French, Cuyahoga Community Coll.-Eastern Campus, Cleve., 1974—. Served with Yugoslav Army, 1945. Mem. Nat., Ohio, Northeastern Ohio, South Euclid-Lyndhurst tchrs. assns., United Am. Croatians Cleve. (pres. 1962-65), Croatian Nat. Resistance Movement (sec. for English 1965—), Croatian Cath. Union, Phi Alpha Theta. Editor-in-chief: Operation Slaughterhouse, 1970. Editor, translator: In Tito's Death Marches, 1961; In Tito's Death Marches and Extermination Camps, 1962. Home: 4037 Monticello Blvd Cleveland OH 44121 Office: Charles F Brush High School Lyndhurst OH 44124

PREBE, WILLIAM FRANCIS, automotive and truck parts co. exec.; b. Toledo, O., Aug. 27, 1922; s. Kaiser and Gertrude Mary (Hurley) P.; B.B.A., U. Toledo, 1949; m. Jeanette Marie Burtscher, July 2, 1949; children—Ronald William, Susan Lynette. With Dana Corp., automotive and truck parts mfr., Toledo, 1952—, market research mgr., 1966-68, corp. economist, 1969—, v.p., economist, 1976—; adj. prof. U. Toledo; lectr. Cleve. State U., 1976—. Served to lt. (j.g.) USNR, 1942-46, 50-52. Mem. Am. Statis. Assn., Nat. Assn. Bus. Economists, Automotive Market Research Council, Fourth Dist. Economists Round Table, American Turners, U. Toledo Bus. Alumni Assn. (sec. 1972-73). K.C. Contbr. articles to profl. publs. Home: 4202 Stannard Dr Toledo OH 43613 Office: PO Box 1000 Toledo OH 43697

PREBLE, ROBERT CURTIS, JR., life ins. exec.; b. Oak Park, Ill., Dec. 19, 1922; s. Robert Curtis and Dorothy (Seidel) P.; B.A. (Meml. fellow), Amherst Coll., 1947; M.B.A., Harvard U., 1949, grad. 61st Advanced Mgmt. Program; m. Lidia Blazik, May 29, 1963. Asst. to gen. supt., asst. buyer Carson Pirie Scott & Co., Chgo., 1949-52; sales dept. Northwestern Mut. Life Ins. Co., Chgo., 1952-53, Nat. Life Ins. Co., Chgo., 1953-59; prin. Preble Assos., Chgo., 1959—; pres.-treas. Variable Annuity Life Ins. Agys., Inc.; cons. Iowa Savs. & Loan League; dir. Scandia Savs. & Loan Assn. (Iowa), World Book Life Ins. Co. Consul of Bolivia, 1968-71. Adv. bd. Ill. Dept. Ins., 1965-70. Dep. regional chmn. Democratic Nat. Fin. Com., 1952; bd. dirs. McCormick Theol. Sem. Served to 1st lt. AUS, 1943-46; PTO. Recipient service award Chgo. council Boy Scouts Am., 1962, C.L.U. Mem. Newcomen Soc., Soc. Colonial Wars, Assn. for Advanced Life Underwriting (founding pres. 1957-58), Am. Soc. C.L.U.'s (pres. Chgo. chpt. 1963-64), Nat. Assn. Life Underwriters (life mem. Million Dollar Round Table 1956—), Mil. Order World Wars, Chgo. Council Fgn. Relations (dir. 1971-77), Harvard Bus. Sch. Assn. (exec. council), Inst. Internat. Edn. (Midwest advisory bd.), Chi Psi. Democrat. Presbyterian. Clubs: University, Chicago, Economic, Harvard Bus. Sch. (past pres.), Amherst (past pres.), Harvard (Chgo.). Home: 300 N State St Chicago IL 60610 Office: One IBM Plaza Chicago IL 60611

PREDOLIN, HENRY, transp. co. exec.; b. Zadar, Yugoslavia, Oct. 26, 1924; s. Henry and Bertha (Gregich) P.; came to U.S., 1951, naturalized, 1959; student U. Padua (Italy), 1941-42; m. Helga Hubner, Aug. 14, 1965; 1 dau., Kirsten. With Pirkle Refrigerated Freight Lines, Inc., Madison, Wis., 1954—, pres., owner, 1968—; pres. Henry Predolin Trucking Inc., also chmn.; dir. Pirkle Refrigeratied Freight Lines, Inc., Henry Predolin Trucking, Inc., HPT, Inc., United Banks of Wis., Inc. Served with Tito's Liberation Movement, Yugoslavia, 1943-45. Mem. Am. Trucking Assn. (dir.), Am. Mgmt. Assns., Wis. Motor Carriers Assn. Clubs: Rotary, Maple Bluff Country, Shriners. Home: 639 Farwell Dr Madison WI 53704 Office: PO Box 3358 Madison WI 53704

PREECE, RODNEY JOHN, educator; b. Littleborough, Eng., Aug. 15, 1939; came to Can., 1969, naturalized, 1975; s. Albert Edward and Ivy (Mills) P.; B.A., U. Leicester (Eng.), Ph.D., 1970; m. Nan Morrison Keery, Aug. 12, 1972. Asso. lectr. linguistic, regional studies U. Surrey (Eng.), 1964-66; lectr. polits. U. Leicester, 1966-69; asst. prof. polit. sci., U. Waterloo, Can., 1969-70, asso. prof. 1970-73; asso. prof. Wilfrid Laurier U., Waterloo, Ont., Can., 1973—, mem. bd. dirs. Univ. press, 1974—, mem. grad. faculty exec., 1974—. Author: Land Elections German Federal Republic, 1968; (with R.B. Tilford) Federal Germany, Political Social Order, 1969; The Political Animal, But——, 1975. Home: 124 Manchester Rd Kitchener ON N2B 1A2 Canada

PREFONTAINE, HARRIS LEONARD, optometrist; b. Ludington, Mich., May 28, 1906; s. Ame Louis and Gertrude (Malliat) P.; D. Optometry, Ill. Coll. Optometry, 1931, D. Ocular Sci., 1959; m. Mary Louise Beckman, May 30, 1933; children—Ronald, Linda (Mrs. Donald Lahay), Richard. Pvt. practice optometry, Grand Rapids, Mich., 1944—. Fellow Am. Acad. Optometry, Coll. Optometrists in Vision Devel.; mem. Am., Mich. optometric assns., Optometric Extension Program. Home: 2811 Five Mile Rd NE Grand Rapids MI 49505 Office: 545 Cheshire Dr NE Grand Rapids MI 49505

PREGON, GERALD MICHAEL, dentist; b. St. Louis, Sept. 16, 1935; s. Michael and Alberta Corrine (Barron) P.; student Washington U., 1955-56; D.D.S., St. Louis U., 1963; m. Carole Lee Roberts, Sept. 7, 1957; children—Michael, David, Gregory, Timothy. Profl. baseball player, Boston Red Sox, 1954-56; elec. draftsman Monsanto Chem. Co., St. Louis, 1956-57; with Williamson & Assos., cons. engrs., St. Louis, 1957-63; practice dentistry, St. Louis, 1963—. Alderman, City of Crestwood (Mo.), 1975—. Bd. dirs. St. Louis Football Jr. League, 1970—, v.p., 1971-75. Mem. Profl. Ballplayers Am., Am. Dental Assn., Zi Psi Phi. Contbr. to profl. photog. publs. Home: 9125 Desmond St Crestwood MO 63126 Office: 3717 Bayless St Lemay MO 63125

PRENDERGAST, MARY KATHRYN, mathematician; b. Evergreen Park, Ill., Nov, 16, 1942; d. Francis Justine and Ann (Lanigan) Foley; B.S., Mundelein Coll., 1963; M.A., Loyola U., 1965; m. William Patrick Prendergast, Nov. 21, 1964; children—William Francis, Patrick Joseph. Asso. prof. mathematics Richard J. Daley Coll., Chgo., 1966—, sec. mathematics dept., 1968—, faculty advisor, 1974—. Mem. Math. Assn. Am., Am. Math. Assn. of Two-Yr. Colls. Home: 10108 S Komensky Ave Oak Lawn IL 60453 Office: 7500 S Pulaski Rd Chicago IL 60652

PRENZLOW, ELMER JOHN CHARLES, JR., clergyman, educator; b. Norfolk, Neb., Apr. 4, 1929; s. Elmer Edward and Alvina Carolina (Henning) P.; B.A., Northwestern Coll., 1950; B.D., Evang. Luth. Theol. Sem., 1953; postgrad. U. Minn., 1957-61; M.S. in Ednl. Psychology, U. Wis., 1969; m. Marilyn Ruth Wolff, July 10, 1953; 1 son, Elmer Carl III. Ordained to Luth. Ch., Mo. Synod, 1953; parish pastor St. Paul Luth. Ch., Bloomer, Wis., 1953-62; chaplain Univ. Luth. Chapel, U. Wis., Milw., 1962—; prof. Spencerian Bus. Coll., Milw., 1963—, chmn. humanities dept., 1969-72. Mem. Wis. State Legis. com. for Kerner Report, Madison, 1968-70, U.S. Justice Dept. Commn. Law Enforcement Goals and Standards, 1970-73; mem. ad hoc adv. panel Nat. Inst. Corrections, U.S. Dept. Justice and U.S. Bur. Prisons, 1972—. Bd. dirs. Patricia Stevens Career Coll., Milw., Wis. Inst. Social Research and Devel. Mem. Am., Wis. psychol. assns. Republican. Optimist. Contbr. articles to denominational jours. Home: Juneau Village 1129 N Jackson St Suite 1413-C Milwaukee WI 53202 Office: 2223 E Kenwood Blvd Box 11761 Milwaukee WI 53211

PREROST, FRANK JOSEPH, psychologist, educator; b. Chgo., Jan. 20, 1948; s. Joseph John and Emily Lynn (Dubina) P.; B.S., U. Ill., 1970; M.A., DePaul U., 1973, Ph.D., 1975. Intern psychologist, Childrens Meml. Hosp. Chgo., 1972-73; asst. professorial lectr. St. Xavier Coll., 1974-75; asst. prof., coordinator community psychology Lewis U., Lockport, Ill., 1975—; pvt. practice psychotherapy, 1975—. Mem. Am., Ill., Midwestern psychol. assns., Soc. Pediatric Psychology, AAAS, U. Ill. Alumni Assn. Roman Catholic. Contbr. articles to profl. jours. Home: 8245 S California Ave Chicago IL 60652 Office: Dept Psychology Lewis Univ Lockport IL 60441

PRESCOTT, GERALD JAMES, JR., wholesale distbn. co. exec.; b. Flint, Mich., May 26, 1934; s. Gerald James and Beatrice Louise (Smith) P.; B.B.A., U. Mich., 1956, L.L.D., 1959; m. Lorna Fallis Ball, June 22, 1957; children—Sydney Smith, Thomas Ball, Kristin Wheeler, Dorothy Gordon. Pres. Distbrs. Concepts, Ann Arbor, 1970-75, E.W. Schmidt/Haight Co., Ann Arbor, 1966-75; pres. King/Mich. Sundries, Flint, 1972-76, pres. King Group Inc., Ann Arbor, 1976—; chmn. bd. Internat. Tobacco Wholesalers Alliance Ltd., Dearborn, Mich., 1976—; chmn. bd. Mich. Tobacco, Candy, Vendor and Music Operators Mich., Ann Arbor, 1977—, pres. 1972-76; pub. DEBS Confectionery Marketing Reports, 1973—. Mem. Nat. Assn. Tobacco Distbrs., Nat. Candy Wholesalers Assn., Nat. Assn. Wholesalers, Progressive Buying Assos., Mich. Assn. Tobacco and Candy Wholesalers. Home: 2735 Bedford Rd Ann Arbor MI 48104 Office: 2460 S Indsl Hwy Ann Arbor MI 48106

PRESSEY, ALEXANDER WILLIAM, educator; b. Ethelbert, Man., Can., Feb. 8, 1939; s. William and Anne (Kunka) Prysiazniuk; B.A., U. Man., 1959, M.A., 1961; Ph.D., U. Alta., 1965; m. Joyce Evelyn Hedison, May 16, 1959; children—Cindy Dawn, Heather Lynn, Christopher Alexander. Research psychologist Sask. Training Sch., Moose Jaw, 1961-63; asst. prof. psychology U. Man., Winnipeg, 1965-68, asso. prof., 1968-73, prof. psychology, 1973—. Grain farmer, Winnipeg, Man., 1974—. Nat. Research Council Can. grantee, 1965-77. Fellow Canadian Psychol. Assn.; mem. Man. Psychol. Soc. (pres. 1970), Psychonomic Soc., Sigma Xi. Club: Pembina Curling. Contbr. articles to profl. jours. Author: Readings in General Psychology: Canadian Contributions, 1970. Home: 952 Oakenwald Winnipeg MB Canada

PRESSLER, LARRY, congressman; b. Humboldt, S.D., Mar. 29, 1942; s. Antone Lewis and Lorretta (Claussen) P.; B.A., U. S.D., 1964; diploma in Econs. (Rhodes scholar), Oxford U., Eng., 1966; M.A., Harvard U., 1971, J.D., 1971. Student aide to Sen. Francis Case of S.D., 1960-62; aide S.D. Republican Central Com., 1962; summer legal aide firm Dana, Moore, Golden & Rasmussen, Sioux Falls, S.D., 1970; legal adviser State Dept., 1971-74; mem. 94th-95th Congresses from 1st Dist. S.D., 1974—. All-Am. del. 4-H Agrl. Fair, Cairo, Egypt, 1961. Served to 1st lt. AUS, 1966-68, Vietnam. Recipient Nat. 4-H Citizenship award, 1962, Report to Pres. 4-H award, 1962; selected as one of four All-Am. 4-H dels. to agrl. fair in Cairo, Egypt, 1961. Mem. Am. Assn. Rhodes Scholars, Jaycees, VFW, DAV, Am., D.C. bar assns., Am. Legion, S.D. Hist. Soc., Phi Beta Kappa. Club: Lions. Home: 3822 Van Ness St NW Washington DC 20016 Office: 1132 Longworth House Office Bldg Washington DC 20515

PRESTON, DAVID MICHAEL, lawyer; b. Detroit, Apr. 15, 1930; s. David Harold and Ruth (MacDonald) P.; B.A., U. Mich., 1952, LL.B., 1955; m. Judith Ann Hillner, Aug. 19, 1961; children—Matthew MacDonald, Sarah Elizabeth, Melissa Ann. Admitted to Mich. bar, 1955; partner Long, Preston & Kinnaird, Detroit, and Birmingham, Mich., 1965—. Pres., Tim-Ro-Nan-Go Center for Emotionally Disturbed Children, Birmingham, 1972—. Trustee, Oakland Community Coll., 1969-70. Mem. Am., Mich., Oakland County bar assns., Beta Theta Pi, Phi Delta Phi. Club: Birmingham Athletic (bd. dirs.). Home: 577 Westwood Dr Birmingham MI 48009 Office: 280 N Woodward Ave Birmingham MI 48011

PRESTON, ELIZA HOYT, editor; b. Columbia, Mo., Dec. 12, 1936; d. Charles Edwin and Frances Gertrude (Reynolds) Barkshire; A.B., U. Mo., 1955, B.J., 1956, M.A. Reporter, feature writer Daily Republican Times, Ottawa, Ill., 1956-61; asso. editor Irving Cloud Pub. Co., Lincolnwood, Ill., 1961-63; asst. editor Sci. Research Assos., Chgo., 1963-64; instr., pub. editor, extension div. Coll. Agr., U. Mo., Columbia, 1965-73; editor consumer info. services Sears, Roebuck & Co., Chgo., 1973—. Chmn. pub. relations com. Boone County (Mo.) Assn. Mental Health, 1970-73. Mem. Am. Assn. Agrl. Coll. Editors, AAUW, Newberry Library Assos., Chgo. Council Fgn. Relations, Kappa Epsilon Alpha, Sigma Delta Chi, Theta Sigma Phi, Delta Delta Delta, P.E.O. Contbg. editor Mo. Today. Home: 145 Callan Ave Evanston IL 60202

PRESTON, IVAN L., educator; b. Bryn Mawr, Pa., Dec. 18, 1931; s. Albert W. and Kathryn P.; B.A., Coll. Wooster, 1953; M.A., Mich. State U., 1961, Ph.D., 1964; m. Roberta Williamson, Sept. 2, 1961; children—Micaela, Julie, Terry Jane. Photographer, reporter Elyria (Ohio) Chronicle Telegram, 1955; advt. account asst., Ketchum, McLeod & Grove Agy., Pitts., 1955-57; editor, news service, pub. relations dept. Carnegie Inst. Tech., Pitts., 1957-58; pub. relations account exec. Erwin Wasey, Ruthrauff & Ryan Agy., Pitts., 1958-59; asst. prof. journalism Pa. State U., 1963-68; asso. prof. Sch. Journalism U. Wis., Madison, 1968-74, prof., 1974—; cons. div. nat. advt. FTC, 1973—. Bd. dirs. Wis. Consumers League, 1973-77. Served with AUS, 1953-55. NSF summer fellow, 1963; recipient grants Am. Assn. Advt. Agencies, 1969-71, White House Office Consumer Affairs, 1974-75. Mem. Assn. Edn. in Journalism, Am. Acad. Advt., Am. Council Consumer Interests, Assn. Consumer Research, Madison Advt. Club. Author: The Great American Blow-Up: Puffery in Advertising and Selling, 1975; contbr. articles to scholarly jours. Home: 4108 Yuma Dr Madison WI 53711 Office: School Journalism Univ Wis Madison WI 53706

PRESTON, JAMES FAULKNER, JR., lawyer; b. Lowell, Mass., Dec. 6, 1909; s. James Faulkner and Jane (Mc Lellan) P.; B.A., Harvard U., 1932; LL.B., Mich. Law Sch., 1935; m. Margaret H. Hertrich, Aug. 25, 1935; children—Frederick, James, Henry, Jessie. Admitted to Mass. bar, 1936, Ohio bar 1941; asso. firm Herrick, Smith, Donald and Farley, Boston, 1935-41; asso. firm Squire Sanders and Dempsey, Cleve., 1941-43, partner 1946—. Trustee, vice chmn. 1st Union Real Estate Investments, 1973—, Ashland Coll., 1973-75; dir. White Motor Corp., 1972—, Harris Corp., 1971—, Shaker Savs. Assn., 1967—, Highlights for Children Inc., 1967—, Citizens Gas Fuel Co., Adrian, Mich., 1951—. Served with USNR, 1943-45. Recipient Ohio bar medal, 1970. Fellow Am. Bar Assn. Found.; mem. Ohio State Bar Assn. (pres. 1965-66). Clubs: Union, Tavern Cleve. Home: Rt 1 Polk OH 44866 Office: 1800 Union Commerce Bldg Cleveland OH 44115

PRESTON, NORRIS WAYNE, optometrist; b. Armstrong, Mo., Sept. 28, 1932; s. Norris Scott and Nancy Kathryn (Chism) P.; B.S., Northeast Mo. State Tchrs. Coll., 1964; D.Optometry, So. Coll. Optometry, 1964; m. Mary Helen Porter, Oct. 20, 1957; children—James Wayne, Lucinda Faith. Practice optometry, Moberly, Mo., 1964—. Chmn., Huntsville (Mo.) Planning and Zoning Commn., 1971-72; mem. Huntsville City Council, Randolph County Sch. Bd. Served with USAF, 1952-56. Mem. Am., Mo. optometric assns., Mo. Optometric Found., Optometric Extension Program, Am. Legion, Omega Delta. Lion (pres. 1971-72). Home: 313 E Elm St Huntsville MO 65259 Office: 203 N Williams St Moberly MO 65270

PRESTON, RICHARD LEE, air force officer, educator; b. Durand, Mich., June 16, 1945; s. Paul and Barbara Jane (Sandula) P.; B.S. in Chemistry, Mich. State U., 1967; M.A. in Guidance and Counseling, Wayne State U., 1971; Ed.S. in Ednl. Adminstrn. and Supervision, Bowling Green State U., 1977; m. Nancy Ann Wise, Mar. 29, 1972. Commissioned 2nd lt. U.S. Air Force, 1967, advanced through grades to capt., 1970; site space surveillance officer, Charleston AFB, S.C., 1967-68, Sheyma AB, Alaska, 1968-69, space object identification analyst, 1969; site space surveillance officer Aviane AB, Italy, 1969-73; space system staff officer, project dir. classified system, Aviane AB, Italy, 1973-74; asst. prof. aerospace studies, commandant of cadets, AF Rotc, Bowling Green State U., Bowling Green, Ohio, 1974-77, asst. prof., exec. officer, 1977—. Decorated Nat. Defense Medal, 2 AF commendation medals, 3 AF unit awards. Mem. Am. Chem. Soc. (analytical div.), AAAS, Am. Personnel and Guidance Assn., Am. Coll. Personnel Assn., AF Assn., Nat. Geographic Soc., Smithsonian Assocs., Phi Delta Kappa. Republican. Roman Catholic. Clubs: Wright/Patterson AFB Officers', Bowling Green State U. Faculty. Home: 6211 Marscot Dr Lansing MI 48910 Office: AF ROTC Det 620 Bowling Green State U Bowling Green OH 43403

PRESTWICH, LEONARD WILLIS, educator; b. Huntington, Utah, Oct. 14, 1923; s. Armeldo and Lylia Jean (Johnson) P.; student Utah Agrl. Coll., 1941-43; B.S., Brigham Young U., 1948; M.S., N.Y. U., 1949; Ph.D., Ohio State U., 1957; m. Maurine Riding, Sept. 12, 1947; children—Afton (Mrs. Dennis M. Teague), Donna (Mrs. Kenneth T. Holman), Kathryn A., Daniel S. Instr., asst. prof. Ala. Poly. Inst., Auburn, 1949-51; instr. Brigham Young U., Provo, Utah, 1953-56; asso. prof. mktg. Ala. Poly. Inst., 1956-57; asso. prof. George Washington U., Washington, 1957-63; prof., dir. program retail mgmt. U. Nebr., Omaha, 1963—; vis. prof. U. Utah, summer 1959; cons.; expert witness, small bus. com. U.S. Ho. of Reps. Served with AUS,

1943-46; ETO. Assoc. Retailers Omaha fellow, 1966. Mem. Am. Mktg. Assn. (v.p. 1969-70), Am. Collegiate Retailing Assn., Alpha Kappa Psi, Beta Gamma Sigma. Mem. Ch. of Jesus Christ Latter-day Saints (bishop, stake high council 1964—). Contbr. articles to profl. jours. Home: 13229 Polk St Omaha NE 68144

PREUL, HERBERT CHARLES, educator, engring. cons.; b. Berger, Mo., Jan. 11, 1926; s. Fred C. and Hulda F. (Schake) P.; B.S., U. Ia., 1950; M.S., U. Minn., 1955, Ph.D., 1964; m. Audrey A. Van Roekel, May 27, 1950; 1 son, Mark C. Profl. baseball player N.Y. Yankee System, 1948-49; hydraulic engr. U.S. Bur. Reclamation, Denver, also Goleta, Calif., 1950-52; hydraulic engr. U.S. C.E., St. Paul and Omaha, 1952-60, chief san. engr. design, 1955-60; research fellow div. san. engring., dept. civil and environ. engring. U. Minn., Mpls., 1960-64; mem. faculty U. Cin., 1964—, prof. civil and environ. engring., 1964—, dir. div. water resource, 1964—. Cons. engring. edn. India, USAID, summers 1966, 68, 70, WHO at U. Khartoum, Sudan, 1972; WHO water pollution cons. Govt. Singapore, 1973, Govt. Hungary, 1974, Govt. Papua, New Guinea, 1974, Govt. Yemen, 1975, Libya, 1977. Served with AUS, 1944-46. Registered profl. engr., Ohio, Iowa, Minn. Mem. Am. Waterworks Assn., Internat. Water Resources Assn., Internat. Assn. Water Pollution Research, Am. Soc. Engring. Edn., ASCE, Water Pollution Control Fedn., Ohio Water Pollution Conf., Am. Water Resources Assn. (state pres. 1972-73), Engring Soc. Cin. (dir. 1971-74, v.p. 1974-75, pres. 1975-76), Internat. Water Resources Assn. (co-founder; dir. 1971-75), Sigma Xi. Contbr. numerous articles to profl. publs. in field. Home: 760 Ludlow Ave Cincinnati OH 45220

PREUS, JACOB A.O., clergyman; b. St. Paul, Jan. 8, 1920; s. Jacob A.O. and Idella (Haugen) P.P; B.A., Luther Coll., 1941; M.A., U. Minn., 1946, Ph.D., 1951; m. Delpha Mae Holleque, June 12, 1943; children—Patricia (Mrs. Gerhard Bode), Delpha (Mrs. George Miller), Carolin (Mrs. Louis LaPrarie), Sarah (Mrs. Dennis Schwab), Idella (Mrs. Mark Moberg), Mary (Mrs. William Churchill), Jacob, Margaret (Mrs. Timothy Weible). Ordained to ministry Lutheran Ch., 1945; parish minister, South St. Paul, 1945-46, Luverne, Minn., 1950-56; prof. Greek, Latin Bethany Coll., Mankato, Minn., 1947-50, 56-58; prof. Greek, Latin Concordia Theol.Sem., Springfield, Ill., 1958-62, pres., 1962-69; pres. Mo. Synod, Luth. Ch., 1969—. Republican. Translator: De Duabus Naturis (by Martin Chemnitz), Commentary on Romans (by Martin Luther). Contbr. articles to profl jours. Home: 400 Mansion House 1601 St Louis MO 63102 Office: 500 N Broadway St Louis MO 63102

PREUSS, ROGER E(MIL), artist; b. Waterville, Minn., Jan. 29, 1922; s. Emil W. and Edna (Rosenau) P.; student Mankato Comml. Coll., Mpls. Sch. Art; m. MarDee Ann Germundson, Dec. 31, 1954. Painter of nature art; one man shows St. Paul Fine Art Galleries, 1959, Albert Lea Art Center, 1963, Hist. Soc. Mont., Helena, 1964, LeSueur County Hist. Soc. Mus., 1976; exhibitions include Midwest Wildlife Conf. Exhbn., Kerr's, Beverly Hills, Calif., 1947, Joslyn Meml. Mus., Omaha, 1948, Minn. Centennial, 1949, Federated Chaparral Authors, 1951, Nat. Wildlife Art, 1951, 52, N.Am. Wildlife Art, 1952, Ducks Unltd. Waterfowl exhibit, 1953, 54, St. Paul Winter Carnival, 1954, St. Paul Gallery Art Mart, 1954, Stanley Gallery, Nairobi, Kenya, 1973; Galleria Colosseo, Rome, 1974, Holy Land Conservation Fund Exhbn., Tel Aviv, La Galerie Mouffe, Paris; represented in permanent collections Demarest Meml. Mus., Hackensack, N.J., Smithsonian Inst., N.Y. Jour. Commerce, Mont. Hist. Soc., Inland Bird Banding Assn., Minn. Capitol Bldg., U. Mont., Wildlife Am. Collection, LeSueur Hist. Soc., Nat. Wildlife Fedn. Collection, Minn. Ceremonial House, Fine Arts Center of Brigham Young U., U.S. Wildlife Service Fed. Bldg., Ft. Snelling, Minn., Luxton Collection, Banff, Alta., Can., Inst. Comtemporary Arts London, Museo de Arte Contemporaneo, Ibiza, Spain, Nat. Library Scotland, numerous galleries and pvt. collections; designer Fed. Duck Stamp, U.S. Dept. Interior, 1949. Judge ann. Goodyear Nat. Conservation Awards Program. Del. Nat. Wildlife Conf.; bd. dirs. Voyageurs Nat. Park Assn., N. Am. Conservation Hall and Mus., Wetlands for Wildlife U.S.A.; pres. Wildlife Am.; dir. Minn. Conservation Fedn., 1952-54; panelist Sportsman's Roundtable, WTCN-TV, Mpls., 1953—; Seminar instr. Minn. Coll. Art and Design. Served in USNR, World War II. Recipient Minn. Outdoor award, 1956; Patron of Conservation award, 1956; 1st award Am. Indsl. Devel. Council; citation of merit V.F.W.; award of merit Mil. Order Cootie, 1963; Nat. Art Print of Year award, 1973; merit award Minn. Waterfowl Assn., 1976; named Wildlife Conservationist of Year, Sears Found.-Nat. Wildlife Fedn. Program, 1966, Am. Bicentennial Wildlife Artist, 1976; hon. mem. Ont. Chippewa Nation of Can., 1957. Fellow Internat. Inst. Arts (life), Soc. Animal Artists N. Am. Mycol. Assn.; mem. Nat. Audubon Soc., Internat. Sci. Info. Service, Am. Mus. Natural History, Nat. Wildlife Fedn. (nat. wildlife week chmn. Minn.), Minn. Ducks Unltd. (dir.), Minn. Artists Assn. (v.p., dir.), Soc. Artists and Art Dirs., Outdoor Writers Am., Am. Artists Profl. League, Mpls. Soc. Fine Arts, Wildlife Soc., Zool. Soc., Nature Conservancy, Minn. Mycol. Soc. (pres.), Minn. Conservation Fedn. (hon. life), Le Sueur Hist. Soc. (hon.). Clubs: Beaverbrook (hon. life), Minn. Press; Explorers (N.Y.C.). Contbr. to Christmas Echos, 1955, Wing Shooting, Trap & Skeet, 1955; also illustrations and articles in periodicals. Editor: Sports and Recreation mag., Out-of-Doors mag. Compiler and artist; Outdoor Horizons, 1957; Twilight over the Wilderness, 1972; contbr. Educators Guide to Science Materials; paintings and text Minnesota Today. Creator Preuss Wildlife Calendar; inventor Wildlife Am. Calendar. Studio: 2224 Grand Ave Minneapolis MN 55405

PRICE, C. EUGENE, educator; b. Columbus, Ohio, May 3, 1935; s. Curtis Theodore and Margueret Ann (Busick) P.; B.A., Otterbein Coll., 1958; postgrad. United Theol. Sem., 1958-59, Christian Theol. Sem., 1959, Ohio U., 1965; M.S., St. Francis Coll., 1963, postgrad., 1968-70; m. Carolyn Jean Bondurant, Nov. 25, 1958; children—Cindie Jean, Christie Jean. Tchr. English, Pleasant Mills High Sch., Adams County, Ind., 1960-61; tchr. Pleasant Twp. Sch., Ft. Wayne, Ind., 1961-62; tchr. English, speech and debate New Haven (Ind.) High Sch., 1962-65; tchr. English, guidance counsellor Liberty Union-Thurston Schs., Baltimore, Ohio, 1965-68; tchr. spl. edn. East Allen County Schs., New Haven, 1968-71; tchr. lang. arts, social studies Village Woods Jr. High Sch., Ft. Wayne, 1971—. Pres. Liberty Union-Thurston Classroom Tchrs., 1967-68; feature writer Baltimore News, 1967-68, chmn. Adams/Wells/Allen County Tchr. Coordinating Council, 1975-76. Recipient Ruby award Nat. Forensic League Coaches Key, 1964, Young Man of Year award and scholarship Columbus South Elks, 1958. Mem. NEA (del. Rep. Assembly 1974—), Ind. State Tchrs. Assn. (del. 1970—, dir. human rights IV Dist. 1973-75, mem. legis. com. 1976-77), East Allen Educators Assn. (v.p. 1972-73, parliamentarian 1970-72, pres. 1974-76, legis. chmn. 1976-77), Ind. English Tchrs. Assn. United Methodist. Home: 1850 Fox Point Trail Fort Wayne IN 46816 Office: 2700 E Maple Grove Fort Wayne IN 46806

PRICE, CHARLES MELVIN, Congressman; b. East St. Louis, Ill., Jan. 1, 1905; student St. Louis U.; m. Geraldine M. Freelin, July 7, 1952; 1 son, William Melvin. Newspaper corr. East St. Louis Jour., St. Louis Globe-Democrat; sports editor East St. Louis News-Rev.; sec. to Congressman Edwin M. Schaefer, 1933-43; mem. 79th-95th congresses from 23d Ill. Dist. Mem. St. Clair County Bd. Suprs., 1929-31. Mem. Am. Legion, AMVETS, Nat. Press Club. Clubs: Moose, Eagles, Elks, K.C., Order of Hibernians. Office: Room 2340 Rayburn House Office Bldg Washington DC 20515*

PRICE, CHARLES MORGAN, lawyer; b. Chgo., July 17, 1898; s. L. Morgan and Eva (Lapham) P.; A.B., Northwestern, 1920, J.D., 1923; m. Elinor Rew, Oct. 8, 1932; children—Henry Morgan, Rew (Mrs. Donald F. Carne), Charles Morgan. Admitted to Ill. bar, 1923, partner firm Price, Cushman, Keck, Mahin & Cate, and predecessor firms, Chgo., 1923—. Mem. Am., Ill., Chgo. bar assns., Delta Upsilon, Phi Delta Phi. Republican. Episcopalian. Clubs: Chgo.; Glen View. Home: 1500 Lake Shore Dr Chicago IL 60610 Office: 8300 Sears Tower 233 S Wacker Dr Chicago IL 60606

PRICE, EDWARD FRANCIS, civil engr.; b. Los Angeles, Oct. 3, 1934; s. Francis Edward and Carol Evelyn (Cole) P.; B.S. in Civil Engring., Chgo. Tech. Coll., 1967, B.S. in Archtl. Engring., 1970. Tool designer Chgo. Allis Mfg. Corp., 1963-67; with Met. San. Dist., Chgo., 1967—, engr. technician V, 1969—. Served with Air Def. Command, 1956-60. Registered profl. engr., Ill. Mem. Am. Inst. Design and Drafting (pres. Chgo. council), ASCE, Instrument Soc. Am., Ill. Soc. Profl. Engrs. Republican. Episcopalian. Home: 6011 N Winthrop St Chicago IL 60660 Office: 100 E Erie St Chicago IL 60611

PRICE, EVERETT ALFRED, dentist; b. N.Y.C., Dec. 29, 1917; s. Alfred Lawrence and Amanda (Hokanson) P.; A.B., Lake Forest Coll., 1941; M.S., U. Chgo., 1942; B.S., U. Ill., 1944, D.D.S., 1946; m. Zelma Clara Marker, Jan. 19, 1947; children—Pamela Lee, Rebecca Lynn, Debra Kay. Instr. parasitology U. Chgo., 1942; instr. dentistry U. Chgo., 1948-50; dentist Lying-In Hosp., Chgo., 1949-50; Lee County dentist Ill. Dept. Health, 1950-51; gen. practice dentistry, Rockford, Ill., 1952—; asst. prof. oral diagnosis U. Ill. Dental Sch., 1968. Served with USNR, 1942-48. Mem. Am., Ill., Winnebago County dental socs., AAAS, Acad. Gen. Dentistry, Acad. Oral Medicine, Fedn. Dentaire Internat., Royal Soc. Health (Eng.). Democrat. Lutheran. Home: 5548 Springbrook Rd Rockford IL 61111 Office: 3041 Kishwaukee St Rockford IL 61109

PRICE, JACOB MYRON, historian, educator; b. Worcester, Mass., Nov. 8, 1925; s. Abraham Oscar and Alice (Pike) P.; A.B., Harvard U., 1947, A.M., 1948, Ph.D., 1954; postgrad. Oxford (Eng.) U., 1949-50, London Sch. Econs., 1950-51. Instr. history Smith Coll., 1954-56; instr. U. Mich., 1956-58, asst. prof. history, 1958-61, asso. prof., 1961-64, prof., 1964—; mem. council Inst. Early Am. History, 1974-77. Served with USAAF, 1944-46. Recipient Gilbert Chinard prize Soc. French Hist. Studies, 1974; Guggenheim fellow, 1958-59, 65-66; Social Sci. Research Council faculty fellow, 1962-63; Am. Council Learned Socs. fellow, 1972-73; Nat. Endowment for Humanities fellow, 1977-78. Fellow Royal Hist. Soc.; mem. Am. Hist. Assn. (chmn. program com. 1976), Econ. History Assn., Conf. Brit. Studies, Midwest Conf. Brit. Hist. Studies (pres. 1976-78), Soc. Comparative Study of Soc., History (sec. 1974—). Jewish. Club: Cosmos (Washington). Author: The Tobacco Adventure to Russia, 1961; France and the Chesapeake, 1973 (U. Mich. Press Book award 1974); editor: Reading for Life, 1959; The Dimensions of The Past, 1972; editorial bd. Jour. Modern History, 1968-70, Jour. Brit. Studies, 1974—, William and Mary Quar., 1974-77, Comparative Studies in Soc., History, 1974—. Home: 1050 Wall St Ann Arbor MI 48105 Office: Dept History U Mich Ann Arbor MI 48109

PRICE, JOHN MICHAEL, photographer; b. Indpls., Oct. 10, 1936; s. Chester Morris and Sarah Elizabeth (Ferguson) P.; grad. high sch.; m. Madalene Wing, May 8, 1956; children—Teresa Kay, Michael Chester. Farmer; owner, photographer Price Portrait Studio, Lizton, Ind., 1967—. Cons., judge photography 4-H workshops, state and county fairs (Ind.), high schs., 1967—. Supt. agrl. displays 4-H fairs, Ind., 1966—; mem. youth adv. council Hendricks County (Ind.), 1970-71; pres. band boosters New Salem (Ind.) High Sch., 1970; instr. leather craft local orgns. Recipient honors 4-H Club Continued Service, 1971, 73. Mem. profl. photographers Am., Ind. Address: Box 159 Rd 900 N Lizton IN 46149

PRICE, KENNETH STRAWN, cons. engr.; b. Frankfort, Ind., Aug. 4, 1942; s. Richard Curtis and Dorothy Ellen (Strawn) P.; B.S. in Civil Engring., Purdue U., 1964, M.S. (USPHS grant), 1966, Ph.D., 1968; m. Christine Kay Merrill, Aug. 24, 1963; children—Matthew, Michael, Angela. Instr. civil engring. Purdue U., Lafayette, Ind., 1967-68; research engr. Union Carbide Corp., S. Charleston, W. Va., 1970-73; v.p. operations Clark, Dietz and Assos.-Engrs., Inc., Urbana, Ill., 1973—, bd. dirs., 1974—; adj. prof. W. Va. U., 1971-72. Served to capt. U.S. Army, 1968-70. Recipient Rudolph Hering medal, Environ. Engring. div. ASCE, 1974. Mem. Am. Water Works Assn., Water Pollution Control Fedn., ASCE. Methodist. Home: 2206 Wyld St Urbana IL 61801 Office: 311 N Race St Urbana IL 61801

PRICE, LUCILE BRICKNER BROWN, ret. personnel adminstr.; b. Decorah, Iowa, May 31, 1902; d. Sidney Eugene and Cora (Drake) Brickner; B.S., Iowa State U., 1925; M.A., Northwestern U., 1940; m. Maynard Wilson Brown, July 2, 1928 (dec. 1937); m. 2d, Charles Edward Price, Jan. 14, 1961. Asst. dean of women Kans. State U., Manhattan, 1925-28; mem. bd. student personnel adminstrn. Northwestern U., Evanston, Ill., 1937-41; with personnel research dept. Sears, Roebuck & Co., Chgo., 1941-42; overseas club dir. ARC, Eng., 1942-43, Africa, 1943, Italy, 1944-45; dir. Child Edn. Found., N.Y.C., 1946-56; del. Mid-Century White House Conf. Children and Youth, 1950; mem. Iowa State Extension Adv. Com., 1973-75. Bd. dirs. NE Iowa Mental Health Center, pres., 1960-61; trustee Porter House Mus. Recipient Alumni Merit award Iowa State U., 1975. Mem. Am. Coll. Personnel Assn. (life), AAUW (dir. Decorah br. 1965-75), Nat. Assn. Mental Health, Norwegian-Am. Museum (life), Winneshiek County Hist. Soc., Internat. Platform Assn., DAR, Common Cause, Am. Overseas Assn. (life; nat. bd. 1960—), Pi Lambda Theta, Chi Omega. Instrumental in building of house for retirement living; active on Historic Preservation com. of AAUW which secured grants from Nat. Endowment for Humanities, Nat. Endowment for Arts, also listing on Nat. Register Historic Places. Address: 508 W Broadway Decorah IA 52101

PRICE, PAUL MYRON, JR., zoo adminstr.; b. Ironton, Mo., May 28, 1955; s. Paul Myron and Juanita Murel (Lane) P.; student U.S. Mcht. Marine Acad., 1973-74; student S.W. Mo. State U., 1974-76; m. Terry Lee Grimes, July 31, 1976. Breeding programs coordinator Dickerson Park Zoo, Springfield, Mo., 1975-77, sr. animal technician, 1977—. Mem. Am. Assn. Zookeepers, Raptor Research Found., Am. Assn. Zool. Parks, Aquariums, North Am. Falconry Assn., Greater Ozarks Zool. Soc. (dir. 1975—, treas. 1977-78). Research on breeding of bald eagle in captivity. Home: 2950 Apt J N National St Springfield MO 65803 Office: 3043 N Fort St Springfield MO 65803

PRICE, PAXTON (PATE), librarian; b. Batesville, Ark., June 18, 1913; s. John M. and Clara (Pate) P.; grad. N.Mex. Mil. Inst., 1933; B.S., George Peabody Coll., 1937, B.S. in L.S., 1941; postgrad. Columbia U., 1946; m. Ella Ida Tarbell, Aug. 23, 1941; children—John Scott, Peter Tarbell, Clayton Everside, Sumner Seabury. Instr. Roswell (N.Mex.) Sr. High Sch., 1937-40; librarian N.Mex. Mil. Inst., 1940-43, N.W. Mo. State Coll., Maryville, 1947-49; librarian Mo. State Library, 1949-64; dir. library services br. U.S. Office Edn., 1964-65, acting dir. div. library services, 1965-68; librarian St. Louis Public Library, 1969-77; exec. dir. Urban Libraries Council, 1977—; U.S. rep. UNESCO Conf. Nat. Library Planning Latin Am., 1966, Internat. Team to Develop Nat. Library Plan for Colombia, 1970. Served to 1st lt. AUS, World War II; ETO; lt. col. Mo. NG. Mem. Nat. Assn. State Librarians (pres. 1954), ALA (chmn. joint com. with Rural Sociol. Soc. 1953-55, v.p., pres. library adminstrn. div. 1976), Bibliog. Soc. Am. (council), Mo. Library Assn. (pres. 1959), Mo. Adult Edn. Assn. (sec.-treas.), Am., Mo. NG assns. Past editor Library Trends. Contbr. articles profl. jours., ency. Home: 7414 Lyndover Pl St Louis MO 63143

PRICE, ROBERT EUGENE, banker; b. Fayette County, Ind., Oct. 21, 1929; s. James Thomas and Geneva (McClain) P.; grad. Stonier Grad. Sch. Banking, Rutgers U. 1970; m. Nancy Kay Riggs, Mar. 2, 1957; children—Deron James, David Lewis. With Central State Bank, Connersville, Ind., 1947—, asst. cashier, mktg. officer, 1951-58, v.p., 1959-69, exec. v.p., 1969-71, pres., chmn., 1971—; pres., chmn. Central Ins. Agency, Connersville, 1971—, Central State Realty Corp., Connersville, 1971—, Central State Travel Agency, Connersville, 1974—. Pres. Jr. Achievement Connersville, 1972. Served with U.S. Army, 1951-53. Recipient Connersville Distinguished Citizen's award, 1976; Jaycee Distinguished Service award, 1955, 62, Award of Merit, 1974. Mem. Independent Bankers Assn. Ind. (pres. 1976-77), Ind. Bankers Assn. (dir.), Ind. Automated Exchange (dir.), C. of C. (pres. 1962), Downtown Connersville (pres.). Democrat. Episcopalian. Clubs: Country, Elks, Masons, Knights Templar. Home: PO Box 102 Connersville IN 47331 Office: 531 Central Ave Connersville IN 47331

PRICE, RUSS EDWARD, economist; b. Crenshaw, Miss., Feb. 11, 1934; s. Ransom B. and Edna (Denham) P.; B.S., U. Mo., 1955, M.S., 1956; postgrad. Iowa State U., 1956-57; m. Sallie Elizabeth Kingsborough, Dec. 24, 1955; children—Edward Byron, Kathryn Loree, David Ransom, Carol Elizabeth. Market analyst Mo. Farmers Assn., 1954; research asst. U. Mo., 1955-56; research asso. Iowa State U., 1956-57; econ. analyst, sr. economist, dir. planning and research Farmland Industries, Inc., Kansas City, Mo., 1957-66; pres. Research Ability, Inc., Kansas City, 1966—; v.p. Logistics Research, Inc., 1966—; gen. partner Mgmt. Devel. Assos., 1971—; v.p., gen. mgr. Yellow Cab of Kansas City, Inc., 1972-73; bus. and mgmt. specialist U. Mo., 1973—. Cons. Inst. for Community Studies. Mem. Am. Mktg. Assn. (v.p., dir.), Am. Econ. Assn. Home: 7924 N Washington St Kansas City MO 64118 Office: 4049 Pennsylvania Kansas City MO 64111

PRICE, THOMAS EMILE, export sales, investment, fin. co. exec., sports assn. ofcl.; b. Cin., Nov. 4, 1921; s. Edwin Charles and Lillian Elizabeth (Werk) P.; B.B.A., U. Tex., 1943; postgrad. Harvard U., 1944; m. Lois Margaret Gahr Matthews, Dec. 21, 1970; 1 dau. by previous marriage, Dorothy Elizabeth Wood Price; stepchildren—Bruce Albert, Mark Frederic, Scott Herbert, Eric William Matthews. Co-founder Indsl. Waxes, Inc., 1946, sec., 1946-75, treas., 1946-76, pres., 1975-76; co-founder Climax Products Corp., Cin., 1953, sec., 1957-59, treas., 1956-57, v.p., 1953-57; co-founder Price Y Cia, Inc., Cin., 1946—, sec., 1946-75, treas., 1946—, pres., 1975—, also dir.; co-founder Premium Finishes Sales, Inc., Cin., 1963-75, pres., 1975—, also dir.; co-founder Price Paper Products Corp., Cin., 1956, treas., 1956—, pres., 1975—, sec., 1956-75, also dir.; mem. Cin. Regional Export Expanison Com., 1961-63; dir. Central Acceptance Corp., 1954-55; founding mem. and dir. Cin. Royals Basketball Club Co., 1959-73. Referee Tri-State Tennis Championships 1963-68, Western Tennis Championships, 1969-70, Nat. Father-Son Clay Court Championships, 1974—, Tennis Grand Masters Championships, 1975-77; vol. coach Walnut Hills High Sch. Boys Team, Cin., 1970—; chmn. and coach Greater Cin. Jr. Davis Cup, 1968—; co-founder Tennis Patrons of Cin., Inc., 1951, trustee, 1951—, pres., 1958-63, 68. Participant in Fund Raising Drives for Cin. Boys Amateur Baseball Fund, chmn. Greater Cin. YMCA World Service Fund Drive, 1962-64. Served to 1st lt. USAAF, 1943-46; ETO. Elected to Western Hills High Sch. Sport Hall of Honor. Mem. Cin. Fgn. Credit Club, Cin. World Trade Club (pres. 1959), U.S. Trotting Assn., Cin. Hist. Soc., U.S. Lawn Tennis Assn. (trustee 1959-60, 62-64, chmn. Jr. Davis Cup com. 1960-62, mem. jrs. and boys championships com. 1960—, founder of Col. James H. Bishop award 1962), Ohio Valley (trustee 1948—, Gillespie award 1957, Dredge award 1973, pres. 1951-52), Western (trustee 1951—, mem. championships advisory com. 1969—, pres. 1959-60) tennis assns., Cin., Eastern Hills indoor tennis clubs, Phi Gamma Delta. Republican. Presbyterian. Clubs: Cincinnati Country, University, Cincinnati Tennis (pres. 1957-58, advisory com. 1959—). Nationally ranked jr. tennis player, 1939. Home: 504 Williamsburg Rd Cincinnati OH 45215 Office: 924-929 Dixie Terminal Bldg Cincinnati OH 45202

PRICE, VIRGIL EVON, dentist; b. Litchfield, Ill., July 20, 1911; s. Benjamin R. and Rena Jane (McCaslin) P.; student Blackburn Coll., 1931-33; B.S., U. Ill., 1936; D.D.S., Northwestern U., 1940; m. Mary Alice Wait, Apr. 7, 1935; children—John Martin, Joseph Haskell. Practice dentistry, Mason City, Ill., 1940—; dir., v.p. Mason City Nat. Bank. Commr., Mason City Park Dist., 1951-59; mayor, Mason City, 1961—. Served with AUS, 1943-46. Mem. Am. Legion, Am. Dental Assn., Ill. State, Peoria Dist. dental socs. Republican. Prebyn. Clubs: Havana (Ill.) Post Rifle; Gun (Mason CIty). Home: 1300 E Chestnut St Mason City IL 62664 Office: 110 W Elm St Mason City IL 62664

PRICHARD, MERRILL E., exec.; b. Wheaton, Ill., July 13, 1925; s. Harold C. and Ann F. (Bailey) P.; B.S., U. Ill., 1948; postgrad. U. Chgo., Northwestern U.; m. Betty Ann Tibbits, Sept. 2, 1947; children—Ann (Mrs. James A. Wallace), Sue. Sports reporter Wheaton Daily Jour., Chgo. City News Bur., Lombard (Ill.) Spectator, 1940-42; sports editor Glen Ellyn (Ill.) News, summer 1942; asst. editor Mag. of Sigma Chi and Sigma Chi Bull., 1948-49, editor, 1949-55, also exec. dir. Sigma Chi Frat., 1953-55; asst. to pres. C.P. Clare & Co., mfrs., 1956-59, v.p., 1959-66, exec. v.p., 1966-71, also dir., 1961-71; vice chmn. C.P. Clare Internat. N.V., Tongeren, Belgium, 1962-71; group v.p. Gen. Instrument Corp., 1968-71; dir. C.P. Clare Can., Ltd., 1957-71; v.p. ops. Cummins-Allison Corp., 1971-73; group v.p. Powers Regulator Co., Skokie, Ill., 1973-77, pres., 1977—; vice chmn., dir. Powers Regulator Co. Can. Ltd., Toronto, Ont., 1974—; dir. Mark Controls Corp., Evanston, Ill., Belden Corp., Asso. Steel Co. of Houston, Glenview State Bank. Trustee, exec. com. Ravenswood Hosp., Chgo. Served as staff sgt. AUS, 1945-46; editor, pub. relations Camp McCoy, Wis. Mem. Sigma Chi (past pres. house corp.), Kappa Tau Alpha, Sigma Delta Chi. Clubs: Headline (Chgo.); Westmoreland Country (v.p., dir.). Editor 1950, 52, 54 edits. The Norman Shield, also centennial commemorative issue The Mag. of Sigma Chi, 1955. Home: 3139 Walden Ln Wilmette IL 60091 Office: 3400 Oakton St Skokie IL 60076

PRICHARD, NANCY SAWYER GILBERT (MRS. KENNETH D. PRICHARD), assn. exec.; b. Owosso, Mich., Mar. 9, 1924; d. Morgan Rowland and Helen Morrill (Stone) Gilbert; B.A. cum laude, U. Wash., 1952, M.A., 1954; m. Kenneth D. Prichard, Dec. 9, 1954; 1 son (by previous marriage), Thomas Morgan Davis. Teaching fellow U. Wash., 1952-54; tchr. English and speech St. Nicholas Sch. for Girls, Seattle, 1958-64; prof. English, asst. chmn. humanities div., dir. coll. exploratory program Shoreline Community Coll., Seattle, 1964-69; asst. exec. sec. Nat. Council Tchrs. English, Urbana, Ill.,

1969-73, asso. exec. sec., 1973-77; exec. dir. Unitarian Universalist Women's Fedn., Boston, 1977—. Speaker, cons. at nat. and regional confs. on teaching English. Field reader U.S. Office Edn., 1972-77. Served with WAVES, 1944-45. Recipient Oral Interpretation award U. Wash., 1952. Mem. Nat. Council Tchrs. English, Phi Beta Kappa. Editor: (with J. Strugar, D. Wright, A. Maxwell) Voices, 1970. Contbr. articles on tchr. edn., lit. of Third World. Home: 36 St Germain St Boston MA 02115 Office: 25 Beacon St Boston MA 02108

PRIDDY, ROBERT RAY, educator; b. Muncie, Ind., Jan. 17, 1929; s. Harold Eugene and Dorothy May (Yost) P.; B.S., Huntginton (Ind.) Coll., 1964; M.S., St. Francis Coll., Ft. Wayne, 1967; Ed.D. (Univ. fellow) Ball State U., 1976; m. Helen Rosalie Wright, July 2, 1948; children—Evelyn Jo, Jacqueline Lee, David Alan. Machinist, Dana Corp., Ft. Wayne, Ind., 1947-52, insp., 1952-53, quality control investigator, 1953-63; tchr. math, biology Bluffton-Harrison (Ind.) Met. Sch. Dist., 1964-67; tchr. biology Huntington North High Sch., 1967-71; wildlife biologist, asst. prof. botany, dir. natural resources Huntington Coll., 1971—, dir. Upper Wabash Basin-Regional Resource Center, 1975—. Ind. Dept. Natural Resources Wildlife Research grantee, 1971; Lilly Endowment Inc. Resource Center grantee, 1975; YCC grantee, 1977. Mem. Wildlife Soc., Wildlife Fedn., Ind. Acad. Sci., Conservation-Outdoor Edn. Assn. Ind., Kappa Delta Pi. Mem. Ch. of Nazarene. Home: 1147 College Ave Huntington IN 46750

PRIEDEMAN, WILLIAM ROBBINS, mktg. services co. exec.; b. St. Paul, Dec. 2, 1925; s. George Walter and Cecil (Robbins) P.; B.S., Yale U., 1949; M.B.A., Harvard U., 1951; m. Nancy Katharin Gaver, Apr. 25, 1953; children—Katharin Robbins, William Robbins. Pres. Mpls. Ornamental Iron Co., 1957-63; pres. Consol. Engring. Inc., Mpls., 1963-65; corporate services Piper Jaffray & Hepwood, Mpls., 1965-67; v.p. Waters Instruments, Rochester, Minn., 1967-71, cons., 1971-73; pres. Sci. Med. Inc., Mpls., 1973-75; pres. W.R. Priedeman Asso., Wayzata, Minn., 1975—; community faculty Metro State U.; dir. Regal Industries. Served with AC U.S. Army, 1943-46. Clubs: Lafayette, 555. Home: 19400 Cedarhurst St Wayzata MN 55391 Office: 1421 E Wayzata Blvd 251D Wayzata MN 55391

PRIEHS, GEORGE WILLIAM, corp. exec.; b. Mt. Clemens, Mich., May 24, 1907; s. Edward Carl and Mathilda Amelia (Burdenam) P.; B.A., U. Mich., 1930; postgrad. U. Wis., U. London; m. Hermine Soukup, Oct. 25, 1933; children—Marilyn Louise, Sandra Suzanne. Nat. publicity dir. Nat. Thrift Com., N.Y.C., 1931-32; with toy dept. R.H. Macy Co., N.Y.C., 1931-32; pres. Priehs Dept. Store, Priehs Realty Co. and J. Priehs Merc. Co., Inc., Mt. Clemens, 1933—; sr. partner Medea Corp., Mt. Clemens, 1956-72, Clemens Center Co., 1966-70; drama critic Mich. Daily, Wis. Cardinal; writer Fairchild Publs. Mem. Mt. Clemens City Planning Commn., 1956-71, War Prodn. Retail Trade Adv. Com., Washington, World War II. Recipient Wisdom Award of Honor, 1970, Brookfield Clothing Acad. award, 1961; hon. gen. 1st Fighter Wing USAF. Mem. Nat. Retail Mchts. Assn. (pres. smaller stores div.), Mich. Retailers Assn., AIM, Am. Ordnance Assn., Am. Judicature Soc., AF Assn., U.S., Mich. hist. socs., Alpha Tau Omega. Clubs: Selfridge Air Force Officers (hon.), U. Mich. Alumni, Elks, Macomb County Old Crowd, St. Joseph Hosp. Century, Detroit Econ. Home: 24805 Crocker Blvd Mount Clemens MI 48043 Office: 60 66 Macomb St Mount Clemens MI 48043

PRIEHS, HERMINE SOUKUP, retail co. exec.; b. N.Y.C., Aug. 30, 1909; d. Albert and Maria (Pischel) Soukup; B.A., U. Mich., 1931; m. George William Priehs, Oct. 27, 1932; Marolyn L. Priehs Pagels, Susan S. Priehs Butterwick. Asst. to residence stypist J.L. Hudson Co., Detroit, 1931-32; buyer Priehs Dept. Store, Mt. Clemens, Mich., 1933-65; treas., dir. J. Priehs Merc. Co., Inc., Mt. Clemens, 1947—; sec., dir. Priehs Realty Co., Inc., 1949—. Asst. sec. U. Mich. Alumni Class of 1931, 1931—. Club: Officers Wives (Selfridge Air N.G. Field, Mt. Clemens). Home: 24805 Crocker Ave Mount Clemens MI 48043 Office: 60-66 Macomb St Mount Clemens MI 48043

PRIEST, CHARLES JOSEPH, mfg. co. exec.; b. River Rouge, Mich., May 18, 1924; s. William K. and Ada Regina (Plunkett) P.; B.A. in Chemistry, Trinity U., 1954; m. Annie Louise Tullos, Jan. 5, 1945; children—Sydney Lee, Jo Ann, Mary Katheryn. Coating supr. E. Tex. Pulp & Paper Co., Evadale, Tex., 1954-58; tech. supt. C.A. Venezolana de Pulpa Y Papel Co., Venezuela, 1958-60; supr. tech. services Continental Can Co., Augusta, Ga., 1960-67; br. mgr. Cesco Inc., Charleston, S.C., 1967-70; tech. Augusta Pub. Schs., 1970-74; process chemist Inland Container Corp., Newport, Ind., 1974—, tech. supt., 1975—; cons. of wastewater treating, 1975—. Served with USNR, 1943-46. Mem. Vermillion County Improvement Assn., TAPPI, Nat. Council of Paper Industry for Air and Stream Improvement. Mem. Rock Ch. Home: 17 Park St Danville IL 61832 Office: PO Box 428 Newport IN 47966

PRIEST, WILLIAM ROY, orthodontist; b. Detroit, Oct. 8, 1935; s. William R. and Ora M. (Thompson) P.; D.D.S., U. Mich., 1959, M.S., 1963; m. Judith Ellen Gruitch, Jan. 14, 1961; children—Barbara Ann, Catherine Ann. Pvt. practice orthodontics, Saginaw, Mich., 1963—. Chmn. flouridation campaign Saginaw Twp., 1967, Saginaw, 1973. Served with USNR, 1959-61. Fellow Internat., Am. Colls. dentists; mem. Saginaw Valley Dist. Dental Soc. (pres. 1971-72), U. Mich. Dental Sch. Alumni Soc. (dir. 1972). Rotarian. Club: Trout Unlimited (nat. dir. 1971). Home: 39 E Hannum Blvd Saginaw MI 48602 Office: 100 Harrow Ln Saginaw MI 48603

PRIMACK, VERNE MORAN, dentist; b. Detroit, Mar. 2, 1933; s. Abraham Myer and Florence (Zeman) P.; student Highland Park Jr. Coll., 1950-52, Wayne State U., 1952; D.D.S., U. Mich., 1956; m. Naomi Moore, June 24, 1956; children—Brian, Scott, Glenn. Gen. practice dentistry, Saginaw, Mich., 1959—; pres. Can-Am-Petroleum Corp., Saginaw, 1972—. Cons. VA, OEO, HEW, 1971-72; cons. Saginaw Twp. Sch. Bd., 1964-65; founder Robert E. Moyers Symposium on Cranial Facial Growth, U. Mich. Vice pres. Saginaw Twp. Community Schs. Bd., 1963-66; bd. dirs. Project Area Health Edn. Com., 1971-72. Served to capt. AUS, 1957-59. Recipient State Mich. Bd. Regents Scholarship, U. Mich., 1951. Mem. Internat. Assn. Orthodontics, Am. Acad. Gen. Dentistry, Mich. Dental Assn. (mem. com. on pub. relations 1964), Saginaw County Dental Soc. (pres. 1970-71), Alpha Omega. Club: Saginaw Country. Inventor unilateral bur ejection tool, 1964. Home: 1450 W Delta Dr Saginaw MI 48603 Office: 3456 Shattuck Rd Saginaw MI 48603

PRIMIANO, NICHOLAS PETER, obstetrician, gynecologist; b. N.Y.C., Aug. 13, 1922; s. Michael Anthony and Julia (Franko) P.; B.S., Fordham U., 1942; M.D., Loyola U., 1946; m. Margaret Mary Johnston, May 6, 1950; children—Patrice Marie, Margaret Anne, Elizabeth Anne, Michael Thomas, Nicholas Peter, Robert Mark, John Gerard, Mary Frances, Julie Clare, Thomas Patrick. Intern Cook County Hosp., 1946-47, resident obstetrics and gynecology, 1950-53; practice medicine, specializing in obstetrics and gynecology, Joliet, Ill., 1953—; cancer research fellow Solomon Found. Heokton Inst., Chgo., 1951-53; chief dept. obstetrics and gynecology St. Joseph's Hosp., Silver Cross Hosp., Joliet. Pres., organizer Joliet Catholic Physicians Guild, del. Nat. Fedn. Mem. pres.'s council Coll. St. Frances, Joliet. Served to capt., M.C., USAF, 1947-49. Diplomate Am. Bd. Obstetrics and Gynecology, Am. Bd. Med. Examiners. Fellow Am. Coll. Obstetrics and Gynecology, A.C.S.; mem. A.M.A., Ill. (com. on nursing, com. on medicine and religion), Will-Grundy Counties (president 1966-67) med. socs., Central Assn. Obstetricians and Gynecologists, Joliet Loyola U. Alumni Assn. K.C. (4 deg.), Elk, Rotarian. Clubs: Joliet University, Joliet Country. Home: 700 Western Ave Joliet IL 60435 Office: 201 N Joliet St Joliet IL 60431

PRIMICH, THEODORE, sheet metal and machinery mfg. co. exec.; b. Manassas, Va., May 28, 1915; s. John and Mary (Zudock) P.; student Gary (Ind.) pub. schs.; m. Katherine Pollak, Jan. 30, 1938; children—Geraldine Mary, Katherine Jean. Vice pres. G.W. Berkheimer Co., Gary, 1936-46; pres. Gary Steel Products Corp., Gary, 1945—; v.p. Primich Warehouse Co., Gary, 1955-77; pres. Primich Engineered Products. Mem. Air Distribution Inst., Ind. Mfrs. Assn., Ind. State, Gary C. of C.'s, Nat. Assn. Mfrs., Nat. C. of C., Midwest Indsl. Mgmt. Assn., N.Am. Heating and Air Conditioning Assn. Club: Lions, Gary Country. Patentee numerous items. Home: 1937 W 61st Pl Merrillville IN 46410 Office: 4400 W 9th Ave Gary IN 46406

PRIMMER, GLENN ESTUS, supt. schs.; b. Smith Center, Kans., Oct. 14, 1927; s. Glenn Estus and Mabel Ida (Abernathy) P.; B.A., U. No. Iowa, 1949; M.Ed., Iowa State U., 1960, Ph.D., 1974; postgrad. Drake U., 1962-63; m. June Christ, July 13, 1947; children—Glenda (Mrs. Ray Endicott), Kenneth, Jeffrey. Tchr., McGregor, Iowa, 1949-52; salesman Bender Music Co., Clinton, Iowa, 1952-58; tchr., voice, band, Maxwell, Iowa, 1955-57, Ellsworth, Iowa, 1957-60; instr. band, Waukee, Iowa, 1960-64; prin. jr. high sch. Carlisle, Iowa, 1964-67; supt. schs. Menlo, Iowa, 1967-69, Bondurant, Iowa, 1969-73, Central City, Iowa, 1973—. Mem. Iowa, Am. assns. sch. adminstrs., Phi Delta Kappa. Methodist. Clubs: Lions, Kiwanis (pres. 1977-78), Masons, Shriners. Home: 366 Terrace Dr Central City IA 52214 Office: Box 340 Central City IA 52214

PRINCE, AARON ERASTUS, ret. clergyman, educator; b. Fairfield, Ill., Jan. 1, 1887; s. Rev. Peter and Emma Jane (Young) P.; A.B., Howard Payne U.; S.T.B., LL.D., La Grange Coll.; D.D., Ewing Coll.; m. Pearl Bonner, Aug. 24, 1909 (dec. Oct. 1946); children—Esther E. (Mrs. Howard L. Jackson), Ruth A. (Mrs. R. Allen Hunt), Mary L. (Mrs. Edwin F. Moore), Grace L. (Mrs. Glen Lee Greene), Dorothy E., Aaron, Jr.; m. 2d, Virginia Faye Dixon, June 9, 1949. Ordained to ministry Baptist Ch., 1904; held student pastorates Ill., 1904-10; pastor, Casey, Ill., 1910-12, Ewing, Ill., 1912-14, Charleston, Ill., 1914-16; LaGrange, Mo., 1916-19; Eldorado, Ill., 1919-21, Marion, Ill., 1921-27, Brownwood, Tex., 1927-34, Pineville, La., 1934-39, West Monroe, La., 1939-41, Fifth Street Ch., Hannibal, Mo., 1941-44; pastor emeritus, 1944—; pres. Hannibal LaGrange Coll., 1941-50; pastor First Bapt. Ch. Effingham, Ill., 1950-51; interim pastor Bapt. Tabernacle, Auckland, New Zealand, 1951-52; prin. Hawaiian Bapt. Acad., 1952-53; founder, pres. Honolulu Christian Coll., 1953-55; pastor First Bapt. Ch., Lafayette, La., 1957-58, Emmanuel Chapel, Scott Field Air Base, 1958-59; pastor Maplewood Park Bapt. Ch., Cahokia, Ill., 1960-66, pastor emeritus, 1977—; pastor Water Tower Bapt. Ch., St. Louis, 1966-68, 70-74, pastor emeritus, 1974—. Chaplain, Temple Retirement Home, Bridgeton, Mo. 1965-66. Dir. Four Minute Speakers, Publicity Dept., U.S. Govt. for Northeast Mo., World War, 1917-19. Chaplain U.S. Vet. Hosp., Alexandria, La., 1937-39, Central La. State Hosp., 1935-39, La. State Indsl. Sch. for Girls, 1937-39. Mem. Edn. Bd. So. Bapt. Conv., 1919-21, Bd. Fgn. Missions, 1921-27, Relief Annuity Bd., 1937-40. Rec. sec. exec. bd. Ill. Bapt. State Assn., 1919-27; trustee Ewing Coll., 1919-25, pres. Ewing Coll., 1924-25; trustee Howard Payne Coll., 1927-34; mem. exec. bd. Bapt. Gen. Conv., Tex., 1927-34; moderator Brown Co. (Tex.) Bapt. Assn., 1929-34; mem. La. Bapt. Hosp. Bd., 1935-41; pres. exec. bd. La. Bapt. Conv., 1937-41. Mem. Ewing Coll. Alumni Assn. (pres. 1958—). Mason (32 deg., Shriner). Odd Fellow. Rotarian. Editor: Life's Best, 1940; Meeting Life's Reverses, 1941. Author: Christ Is All, 1940 (English edit.); Cristo E Tudo, 1941 (Portuguese edit.); Back to Bethel, 1942; To My Friends, 1943; History of Fifth Street Baptist Church, 1944; History of Ewing College, 1961; History of Maplewood Park Baptist Church, 1974. Home: PO Box 4015 St Louis MO 63136

PRINCE, FRANCES ANNE KIELY (MRS. RICHARD EDWARD PRINCE, JR.), civic worker; b. Toledo, Dec. 20, 1923; d. John Thomas and Frances (Pusteoska) Kiely; student U. Louisville, 1947-49; A.B., Berea Coll., 1951; postgrad. Kent Sch. Social Work, 1951, Creighton U., 1969, U. Nebr. at Omaha, 1974—; m. Richard Edward Prince, Jr., Aug. 17, 1951; children—Anne, Richard III. Instr. flower arranging Western Wyo. Jr. Coll., 1965, 66. Chmn., Lone Troop council Girl Scouts U.S.A., 1954-57, trainer leaders, 1954-68, mem. state camping com., 1959-61, bd. mem. Wyo. state council, mem. state program com., 1966-69; chmn. Community Improvement, Green River, Wyo., 1959, 63-65, Wyo. Fedn. Women's Clubs State Library Services, 1966-69; mem. Wyo. State Adv. Bd. on Library Inter-Co-op., 1965-69; bd. mem. Sweetwater County Library System, 1962—, pres. bd., 1967-68; mem. adv. council Sch. Dist. 66, 1970—. Mem. Morning Musicale Bd., 1970—; bd. dirs. Opera Angels, 1971—, v.p., 1974—, chmn. fund raising com., 1971-72; mem. bazaar com. Children's Hosp., 1970-74; mem. Nebr. Forest Adv. Bd., 1976—; Nebr. chmn. Am. Land Trust, 1976—. Recipient Library Service award Sweetwater County Library, 1968. Accredited Flower Show judge, Landscape Design critic. Mem. AAUW, New Neighbors League (dir. 1970-72), Docent Joslyn Art Mus., Symphony Guild, Ikebana Internat., Omaha Playhouse Guild, Am., Nebr. library assns., Nebr. Flower Show Judges Council, Internat. Platform Assn., Countryside Garden Club (dir. 1970-72, pres. 1973-74), Omaha Council Garden Clubs (1st v.p. 1973, pres. 1973-75), Nebr. Federated Garden Clubs (1st v.p. 1976). Mem. United Ch. of Christ (intermountain tri-state bd. dirs. 1965-68). Home: 8909 Broadmoor Dr Omaha NE 68114

PRINCE, VIRGINIA FAYE DIXON (MRS. A.E. PRINCE), educator; b. Big Springs, Mo., July 23, 1919; d. William Marcellus and Cassie Mae (Walker) Dixon; A.A., Hannibal-LaGrange Coll., 1946; B.A., N.E. La. State U., 1956; M.Ed., Southwestern La. U., 1959; postgrad. U. Mo., 1948, U. Hawaii, 1952, 53; Specialist Certificate in Edn., So. Ill. U., 1969; m. A.E. Prince, June 9, 1949. Sec. to pres. Hannibal-LaGrange Coll., 1946-48; tchr. pub. schs., Center, Mo., 1947-48, Honolulu, 1952-54, Monroe, La., 1954-56, Jennings, Mo. 1958—; dir. Instructional Materials Center, Jennings, Mo.; dietitian Hannibal-LaGrange Coll., 1948-50; sec. to pastor Auckland (New Zealand) Baptist Tabernacle, 1951-52. Mem. Internat. Reading Assn., Assn. Childhood Edn. (life), NEA (life), Mo. (life), St. Louis Suburban tchrs. assn., Am. Bell Assn., Alpha Delta Kappa, Kappa Delta Pi. Republican. Baptist. Mem. Order Eastern Star. Home: PO Box 4015 St Louis MO 63136

PRINDAVILLE, LAWRENCE ALLEN, psychologist; b. Dixon, Ill., Dec. 28, 1947; s. Raphael Edward and Florence Margarite (Reis) P.; B.S., Loyola U., Chgo., 1970; M.S., Western Ill. U., 1974; 1 dau., Sara Meghan. Psychologist, Sinnissippi Mental Health Center, Dixon, Ill., 1972—, coordinator sustaining care program, 1976—. Mem. Am. (asso.), Ill. psychol. assns., Am. Orthopsychiat. Assn., Acad. Psychologists Marital Family Therapy, Am. Mental Health Counselors Assn. Home: 607 Good St Dixon IL 61021 Office: Sinnissippi Mental Health Center Dixon Sterling Freeway Dixon IL 61021

PRINZ, ANDREW KARL, educator; b. Chgo., July 18, 1935; s. Andrew and Margaret (Keller) P.; B.A. magna cum laude, Augustana Coll., 1957; M.A., Northwestern U., 1958, Ph.D., 1963; m. Carol Elizabeth Knudsen, Aug. 10, 1957; children—Kurt Keller, Linda Elizabeth, Diane Margaret, Mark Edward. Asso. prof. social sci. Faculty, Concordia Tchrs. Coll., 1960-69; prof. social sci. Elmhurst (Ill.) Coll., 1969—, also dir. urban studies. Plan commr. City of Oak Park, 1969-73; v.p., program chmn. Oak Park Community Lecture Series, 1967-73; mem. Ill. Edn. Council, 1974-76. Democratic twp. committeeman, Oak Park, 1974—. William R. Hearst fellow, 1957-58; Nat. Center for Edn. in Politics Faculty fellow, 1964-65; Fed. Exec. Inst. fellow, 1971. Mem. Am. Hist. Assn., Assn. Lutheran Coll. Faculties (v.p. 1967-68, pres. 1968-69), Soc. Am. Archivists, Orgn. Am. Historians, Am. Polit. Sci. Assn., UN Assn. (dir. Ill. and Greater Chgo. dirs. 1973—), Council Univ. Insts. for Urban Affairs, Am. Soc. Planning Ofcls., Phi Beta Kappa, Phi Alpha Theta. Lutheran. Contbr. articles to profl. jours. Home: 800 N Elmwood Ave Oak Park IL 60302 Office: 190 Prospect St Elmhurst IL 60126

PRINZ, LEON MARVIN, urologist; b. Chgo., Nov. 14, 1930; s. George and Helen P.; B.S. in Medicine, U. Ill., 1952, M.D., 1954; m. Dora Pinsky, July 3, 1955; children—Michael, Steven, Paul, Carolyn, Linda. Practice medicine specializing in urology, Chgo., 1961—; clin. asst. Chgo. Med. Sch.; attending physician Michael Reese Hosp.; cons. McHenry Hosp., Jackson Park Hosp. Fellow Am. Coll. Surgeons, Internat. Coll. Surgeons; mem. Michael Reese Alumni Assn. (pres.). Office: 104 S Michigan Ave Chicago IL 60603

PRITCHARD, LEONARD STILTS, physician; b. Pitts., Dec. 27, 1924; s. Leonard C. and Hazel M. (Stilts) P.; B.S., U. Pitts., 1951, M.D., 1952; m. Joanne Sprott, Oct. 15, 1974; children—Virginia, Carl. Intern Shadyside Hosp., Pitts., 1952-53; practice medicine specializing in family practice, Columbiana, Ohio, 1954—; chief dept. medicine Salem (Ohio) City Hosp., 1966-67, 76-77, pres. staff, 1968-70; pres. staff No. Columbiana County Community Hosp., 1970-71, chief staff, 1971-73, mem. exec. com., 1966-77, trustee, 1968-73. Mem. bd. health Columbiana County, 1960-67; dep. coroner Columbiana County, 1965-75. Mem. Park Bd. Columbiana, 1970-73. Served with USAF, 1943-46. Recipient First prize sculpture Kiwanis Art Show, 1971, 72, 73-76, Canfield Fair, 1977. Fellow Am. Acad. Family Practice; mem. Columbiana County Med. Soc. (pres. 1961), Ohio State Med. Assn. (mem. rural health scholarship com. 1965-76), Ohio Acad. Family Practice, Am. Guild Organists, Am. Theater Organ Soc., Sigma Chi, Phi Rho Sigma. Presbyterian (trustee). Kiwanian (pres. 1970). Home: 315 Parkview Dr Columbiana OH 44408 Office: 153 S Main St Columbiana OH 44408

PRITCHARD, MARY HANSON (MRS. C.G. PRITCHARD), parasitologist; b. Lincoln, Nebr., July 16, 1924; d. Paul Gerhard and Ruth (Long) Hanson; B.Sc. in Bus. Adminstrn., U. Nebr., 1946, M.A., 1949; m. Claremont G. Pritchard, Aug. 24, 1956. Asst. curator zoology U. Nebr. State Mus., 1948-57; research asso. dept. zoology and physiology U. Nebr., Lincoln, 1959-68, asst. prof. zoology, 1968-74, asso. prof. zoology, 1974—, asso. curator parasitology U. Nebr. State Mus., 1968-72, curator parasitology, 1972—. Mem. ecology adv. com. U.S. EPA, 1974—. Dept. election commrs. office, Lincoln, 1958. Fellow AAAS; mem. Am. Soc. Parasitologists, Am. Micros. Soc., Helminthological Soc. Washington, Soc. Systematic Zoology, Assn. Systematic Collections (council on standards 1973—, membership com. 1976—), Nebr. Acad. Sci., Nebr. Ornithol. Union, Marquis Biog. Library Soc., Sigma Xi, Phi Beta Kappa, Sigma Delta Epsilon (editor News 1958-66). Asst. editor Jour. Parasitology, 1965-68. Research articles concerning trematodes of marine fishes, principally of Hawaii and S. Africa, and eastern Pacific. Home: 6501 Sumner Lincoln NE 68506

PRITIKIN, JEANNE DUPRE MOORE (MRS. ROLAND I. PRITIKIN), hosp. adminstr.; b. Rockford, Ill., Apr. 13, 1913; d. Homer Frank and Ann (DuPre) Moore; student U. Wis., 1931, Rockford Coll., 1930-34; m. Roland I. Pritikin, May 25, 1940; children—Gloria, Karin (Mrs. Craig Howard Heiser). Cellist Rockford Symphony Orch., 1930-36; Rockford Agt. Am. Mut. Ins. Co., Boston, 1932-40; real estate broker Hawkinson Realty, Rockford, Ill., 1950-60; asst. sec. Henry Holland Mission Hosps., Rockford, 1957—, W. Pakistan, 1957-60, 63, 66, 71, Ethiopia, 1972; sci. proof reader J.B. Lippincott Co., Phila. 1946-50, Moore Pub. Co., Durham, N.C., 1969—; sci. translator, also manuscript supr. Internat. Soc. History of Sci., 1956, Internat. Soc. History of Medicine, 1966, Internat. Coll. Surgeons, 1946—, Ill. State Med. Soc., 1941—, Middle East Med. Assembly, 1956, Internat. Soc. Geog. Ophthalmology, 1971; proofreader, assistant for sci. manuscripts and movies Internat. Congress of Ophthalmology, London, 1950, Montreal and N.Y.C., 1954, Brussels, 1958, New Delhi, 1962, Munich, 1966, Mexico City, 1970, Paris, 1974; asst. to surgeon 33rd div. War Veterans Assn., 1975—. Mem. A.M.A. Womens Aux., Ill. State Med. Soc. Womens Aux., Winnebago County Med. Soc. Womens Aux., Med. Soc. Loyola U., Chgo., D.A.R. (chpt. treas. 1950-60), Daus. of Founders and Patriots Am. Republican. Conglist. Clubs: Officers' Wives, Retired Officers of U.S. Home and Office: 1211 Talcott Bldg Rockford IL 61101

PRITIKIN, ROLAND I., ophthalmologist; b. Chgo., Jan. 9, 1906; s. Edward and Bluma (Saval) P.; B.S., Loyola U., 1928, M.D., 1930; m. Jeanne DuPre Moore, May 25, 1940; children—Gloria Anne, Karen (Mrs. Craig Heiser). With eye dept. Loyola U. Sch. Medicine, 1933-35; resident Ill. Eye and Ear Infirmary, 1936-38; visited eye clinics, Vienna, Zurich, Paris, 1934; vis. eye surgeon, Shikarpur, Sind, Pakistan, 1939, 57, 60, 63, 65, 66, 71; former mem. faculty eye dept. Loyola U., staff Ill. Eye and Ear Infirmary, U. Ill.; mem. eye staff Rockford Meml. Hosp., St. Anthony Hosp., Swedish-Am. Hosp. Rockford; faculty dept. ophthalmology Rockford Sch. Medicine of U. Ill., 1970—; lecture-research tour Western Europe, Near and Middle East, 1951; del. to various med. confs., including Internat. Congress Ophthalmology, 1950, 54, 58, 62, 65, 66, 70, 71, 74. Chief, eye, ear, nose and throat service Stark Gen. Hosp., 1941-45; col. Med. Corps, 1946; col. Med. Corps, research and devel. sect. U.S. Army Res.; cons. ophthalmology 5th U.S. Army, 1969—. Ofcl. del. Assn. Mil. Surgeons U.S. and Am. Assn. Indsl. Phys. and Surgs. to 16th Internat. Congress Ophthalmology, London, 1950. Winner 1st place med. slide contest U.S. Com. World Med. Assn., 1965; Quetta Mission Hosp. medal, 1965; Army Commendation medal, 1966; decorated Order St. John of Jerusalem. Life fellow Weizamann Inst. Sci. Diplomate Am. Bd. Ophthalmology. Fellow Am. Coll. Nuclear Medicine (founding, charter), Indsl. Med. Assn., Am. Med. Writers Assn., Soc. Mil. Ophthalmologists (life), Royal Soc. Health (life), A.C.S., I.C.S., A.A.A.S., Instituto Barraquer (Barcelona); mem. A.M.A., Assn. Research Ophthalmology, N.Y. Acad. Scis., Ill. Soc. Prevention Blindness, Soc. Nuclear Medicine, Internat. Corr. Soc. Ophthalmology and Otolaryngology, Am. Assn. Ophthalmology, Am. Nuclear Soc., Ophthalmol. Soc. U.K., Soc. Mil. Ophthalmologists, Royal Soc. Medicine, Soc. Med. Consultants Armed Forces, Ophthal. Soc. U.K., Ill. State, Winnebago County (treas.) med. socs., Am. Acad. Ophthal. and Otolaryn., Chgo. Ophthal. Soc., Assn. Mil. Surgeons U.S. (life), World Pan-Am. Assn.

Ophthalmology, Internat. Soc. History of Medicine, Am. Assn. History of Medicine, Assn. Am. Physicians and Surgeons, Internat. Agy. for Prevention of Blindness, Internat. Assn. Secs. Opthal. and Otolaryn. Socs. (bd. dirs, editor for ophthalmology), Nat. Soc. Prevention Blindness, Am. Geriatrics Soc., Royal Soc. Promotion Health, Am. Med. Authors, Nat. Guard Assn. U.S. (life), Soc. Ophthalmic Microsurgery (charter mem.), Ophthal. Soc. Canary Islands (hon.), Ophthalmol. Soc. Pakistan, Internat. Assn. Against Trachoma, Contact Lens Assn. Ophthalmologists, Pan-Am. Med. Assn., Ill. Soc. Professions, Internat. Agy. Prevention Blindness, C. of C., N.G. Assn., 33d Div. War Vets. Assn., Am. Legion, Res. Officers Assn. (life), Ret. Officers Assn. (life, pres. No. Ill. 1969), U. Ill. Alumni Assn. (life). Club: University. Author: Essentials of Ophthalmology, 1950, 3d edit., 1976; World War Three Is Inevitable!, 1976; author of sect. in ophthal. Ency. Americana, and Americana Ann., 1946—; also articles in profl. jours. Home: 3505 Highcrest Rd Rockford IL 61107 Office: 1211 Talcott Bldg Rockford IL 61101

PRITSKER, A. ALAN B., systems analyst; b. Phila., Feb. 5, 1933; s. Robert and Gertrude (Leibowitz) P.; B.S. in Elec. Engring., Columbia U., 1955, M.S. in Indsl. Engring., 1956; Ph.D., Ohio State U., 1961; m. Anne Gruner, Sept. 22, 1956; children—Caryl, Pamela, Kenneth, Jeffrey. Researcher Battelle Meml. Inst., Columbus, Ohio, 1956-62; prof., systems analyst Ariz. State U. at Tempe, 1962-69, Va. Poly. Inst., Blacksburg, 1969-70, Purdue U., Lafayette, Ind., 1970—. Cons. Rand Corp., DVR Corp., Unido, U.S. Army. Recipient Distinguished Research award Am. Inst. Indsl. Engrs., 1966; Faculty Achievement award Ariz. State U., 1967. Mem. Am. Inst. Indsl. Engrs. (mem. editorial bd. 1961-70, div. dir. 1970-72), Am. Soc. Engring. Edn., Operation Research Soc. Am., Inst. Mgmt. Sci., AAAS, Sigma Xi, Alpha Pi Mu, Tau Beta Pi. Home: 1201 Wiley Dr West Lafayette IN 47906 Office: Sch Indsl Engring Purdue U Lafayette IN 47907

PRITZKER, A. N., lawyer; b. Chgo., Jan. 6, 1896; s. Nicholas J. and Annie (Cohn) P.; student Northwestern, 1913-14; Ph.B., U. Chgo., 1916; LL.B., Harvard U., 1920; m. Lorraine Colontonio, Jan. 13, 1972; children—Jay, Robert, Donald. Admitted to Ill. bar, 1920, since practiced in Chgo.; mem. firm Pritzker & Pritzker; pres. Hotel Equities Corp.; hon. dir. Hyatt Corp. Chmn. council Pritzker Sch. Medicine. Served as chief petty officer, USNRF, World War I. Home: 1040 N Lake Shore Dr Chicago IL 60611 Office: 20 S Clark St Chicago IL

PRITZKER, LEON, food co. exec.; b. N.Y.C., June 26, 1922; s. Harry and Sophia (Greene) P.; B.S. summa cum laude, Coll. City N.Y., 1942; M.A., U. Pa., 1947; m. Mary Anne E. Watts, Dec. 12, 1970; children—William, David, Paul, Carol, Phillip. With Bur. Census, Washington, 1942-67, chief response research br., 1961-67; dir. mktg. info. services Anheuser-Busch, Inc., St. Louis, 1967-73, dir. mgmt. systems, 1973—; vis. prof. Case Inst. Tech., Cleve., 1954-55; cons. govt. Israel, 1961, Turkey, 1967. Served with AUS, 1943-46. Recipient Meritorious Service award Dept. Commerce, 1954. Fellow Am. Statis. Assn.; mem. Ops. Research Soc. Am., Sigma Xi, Phi Beta Kappa. Club: Missouri Athletic. Contbr. articles to profl. jours. Home: 2108 N Geyer Rd Frontenac MO 63131 Office: Anheuser Busch St Louis MO 63118

PRITZKER, ROBERT ALAN, mfg. co. exec.; b. Chgo., June 30, 1926; s. Abram Nicholas and Fanny (Doppelt) P.; B.S. in Indsl. Engring., Ill. Inst. Tech., 1946; grad. student bus. adminstrn., U. Ill.; m. Audrey Gilbert, Dec. 19, 1948; children—James Nicholas, Linda, Karen. Engaged in mfg., 1946—; pres., dir. The Marmon Group, GL Corp., Marmon Group Inc. (formerly Cerro Marmon Corp.); partner Colson Co., Chgo.; dir. Peoples Gas Co., Chgo., Hyatt Corp., Burlingame, Cal., Prado Hermanos y Cia., Bilbao, Spain. Vice pres., bd. dirs. Pritzker Found., Chgo.; trustee vice chmn., Ill. Inst. Tech. Office: 39 S LaSalle St Chicago IL 60603

PROBASCO, GENE ARLEN, lawyer; b. Creston, Iowa, May 17, 1931; s. Fred T. and LaVada Vesta (Hoffman) P.; student Creston Jr. Coll., 1949-50; B.S. in Accounting, State U. Iowa, 1956, J.D., 1957; m. Patricia Ann Shoemaker, Mar. 8, 1952; children—Sheryl, Debra, Cynthia, Craig. Admitted to Iowa bar, 1957; partner firm Goldberg, Mayne, Probasco & Berenstein, Sioux City, Iowa, 1957—. Lectr. Iowa State Bar Assn. Tax Sch. Mem. Sioux City Bd. Adjustment, 1968-69. Trustee Iowa Law Sch. Fund, 1961-63. Served with USAF, 1951-53. Decorated Air medal with 3 oak leaf clusters. Mem. Am., Iowa (exec. council young lawyers sect. 1960-61), Woodbury County (pres. 1969-70), 4th Jud. Dist. (pres. 1969-70), Sioux City bar assns., Iowa State U. Parents Assn. (dir. 1973-76), Sioux City Zool. Soc. (dir. 1967-73, treas. 1970), Sioux City Bldg. Owners and Mgrs. Assn. (pres. 1967-68), Better Bus. Bur, C. of C., Phi Delta Phi. Republican. Methodist. Clubs: Sioux City Lawyers (pres. 1961-62), Sertoma (pres. 1969-70), Sioux City Boat (v.p. 1968-69, dir. 1966-69), Sioux City Country (dir. 1973-76, v.p. 1976-78). Home: 4432 Perry Way Sioux City IA 51104 Office: 300 Commerce Bldg Sioux City IA 51101

PROBST, WILDENA GEORGIA, speech pathologist; b. Kremlin, Okla., July 13, 1939; d. George Coverdale and Wilma Elizabeth (French) Probst; B.A., U. Okla., 1962. Speech pathologist Wichita (Kans.) Pub. Schs., 1962-63, Larned (Kans.) City Schs., 1964-66, Coldwater (Kans.) Unified Dist. #300, 1967; pvt. practice speech pathology, Protection, Kans., 1965—. Mem. Am. Speech and Hearing Assn. Democrat. Address: Lexington Route Ashland KS 67831

PROCHAZKA, OTTO FRANCIS, radiologist; b. Atwood, Kans., Feb. 24, 1912; s. Frank Francis and Anna Marie (Heble) P.; B.A., U. Kans., 1935, M.D., 1938; m. Susan Furlong, Dec. 31, 1940; children—Ronald D., Carole S., Phillip P., Thomas O., Anne N., Sarah S. Intern, St. Francis Hosp., Wichita, Kans., 1938-39; resident Sedgwick County Hosp., Wichita, 1939-40, supt., 1940-41; asso. chief dept. Wichita Hosp. and St. Josephs Hosp., Wichita, 1946; practice medicine specializing in radiology, Liberal, Kans., 1946-59, 60—; chief radiology Epworth Hosp., Liberal, 1946-59, 60-64; chief resident VA Hosp., Denver, Colo., 1959-60; chief radiology S.W. Med. Center, Liberal and Meade (Kans.) Dist. Hosp., 1960—, chief of staff Epworth Hosp. and S.W. Med. Center, 1957-61; cons. in radiology various hosps. in area; med. cons. Am. Cancer Soc., 1947—. Founder Nat. Fin. Life Underwriters Inc. (now Farm and Ranch Inc.). Served with M.C., U.S. Army, 1941-46. Diplomate Am. Bd. Radiology. Recipient 20 Year award Am. Cancer Soc., 1973. Distinguished fellow Am. Coll. Nuclear Medicine; mem. Kans. (cancer control com.), Seward County (pres. 1956-62) med. socs., AMA, Radiol. Soc. N.Am., Am. Nuclear Soc., Am. Coll. Radiology, Am. Coll. Nuclear Physicians, Soc. Photo-Optical Instrumentation Engrs., Kans. Radiol. Soc., Assn. Am. Physicians Surgeons, Am. Inst. Ultrasound in Medicine, Rocky Mountain Radiol. Soc., Interamerican Coll. Radiology, Kans. Thoracic Soc., AAAS, DAV, Nat. Geog. Soc., Smithsonian Instn. Assos. Republican. Roman Catholic. Clubs: High Plains Petroleum, Por Nada (pres., founder), Elks, K.C. Home: 1105 Elm Blvd Liberal KS 67901 Office: W 15th St Box 1034 Liberal KS 67901

PROCHNOW, HERBERT VICTOR, banker; b. Wilton, Wis., May 19, 1897; s. Adolph and Alvina (Liefke) P.; grad. Wis. U., 1917; B.A. U. Wis., 1921, M.A., 1922, LL.D. (hon.), 1956; Ph.D., Northwestern U., 1947; Litt.D. (hon.), Millikin U., 1952; LL.D. (hon.), Ripon Coll., 1950, Northwestern U., 1963, Lake Forest Coll., 1964; D.H.L. (hon.), Thiel Coll., 1965, Monmouth Coll., 1965, U. N.D., 1966; m. Laura Virginia Stinson, June 12, 1928; 1 son, Herbert Victor. Prin., Kendall (Wis.) High Sch., 1917-18; asst. prof. bus. adminstrn. Ind. U., 1922-23; advt. mgr. Union Trust Co., Chgo., 1923-29; asst. cashier First Nat. Bank of Chgo., 1933-36, asst. v.p., 1936, v.p., 1947-55, gen. v.p. 1956-59, exec. v.p., dir., 1960-62, pres., dir., 1962-68, hon. dir., 1968-73; dir. Banco di Roma, FRS Assos.; sec. Fed. Res. Adv. Council, 1945—; spl. cons. sec. state, 1955, 57; dep. under sec. state econ. affairs, 1955-56; alt. gov. Internat. Bank and IMF, 1955-56. Chmn., U.S. del. GATT, Geneva, 1956; mem. U.S. del. Colombo Conf., Singapore, 1955, OECD, Paris, 1956; pres. Internat. Monetary Conf., 1968, now cons., hon. mem.; Sch. Banking of South, La. State U., Stonier Grad. Sch. Banking, Rutgers U., Sch. for Internat. Banking, U. Colo.; lectr. Loyola U., Ind. U., Northwestern U., dir. summer Grad. Sch. Banking, U. Wis., 1945—; fin. columnist Chgo. Tribune, 1968-70. Treas. Nat. 4-H Clubs, 1962-69. Trustee McCormick Theol. Sem.; former trustee Evanston Hosp. Served with AEF. Decorated comdr. Order of Vasa (Sweden); comdr.'s cross Order of Merit (W.Ger.); recipient award Harvard Bus. Sch. Assn., 1965, Ayres Leadership award Stonier Grad. Sch. Banking, Rutgers U., 1966, Silver Plaque award NCCJ, 1967. Mem. Soc. Midland Authors, Am. Econ. Assn., Chgo. Assn. Commerce and Industry (pres. 1964-65), Chgo. Council Fgn. Relations (pres. 1966-67), Nat. Assn. Bus. Economists, Fgn. Policy Officers Assn., Am. Finance Assn., Beta Gamma Sigma (nat. honoree). Clubs: Chicago Sunday Evening (trustee), University, Chicago, Commercial, Mid-Day, Rotary, Union League (Chgo.); Bankers, Executives, Glen View. Author: Great Stories from Great Lives (an anthology), 1944; Meditations on the Ten Commandments, 1946; The Toastmaster's Handbook, 1949; Term Loans and Theories of Bank Liquidity, 1949; Successful Speakers Handbook, 1951; 1001 Ways to Improve Your Conversations and Speeches, 1952; Meditations on the Beatitudes, 1952; The Speaker's Treasury of Stories for All Occasions, 1953; The Toastmaster's and Speaker's Handbook, 1955; The Speaker's Handbook of Epigrams and Witticisms, 1955; Speaker's Treasury for Sunday School Teachers, 1955; The New Guide for Toastmasters, 1956; A Treasury of Stories, Illustrations, Epigrams and Quotations for Ministers and Teachers, 1957; The New Speaker's Treasury of Wit and Wisdom, 1958; A Family Treasury of Inspiration and Faith, 1958; Meditations on the Lord's Prayer, 1957; The Complete Toastmaster, 1960; Speaker's Book of Illustrations, 1960; Effective Public Speaking, 1960; 1000 Tips and Quips for Speakers and Toastmasters, 1962; 1400 Ideas for Speakers and Toastmasters, 1964; Tree of Life, 1972; Speaker's Source Book, 1969; A Speaker's Treasury for Educators, Convocation Speakers, 1973; the Speaker's and Toastmaster's Handbook, 1973; co-author The Next Century is America's, 1938; Practical Bank Credit, 1939, rev. edit., 1963; The Public Speaker's Treasure Chest, 1942, rev. edit., 1964, 77; A Dictionary of Wit, Wisdom and Satire, 1962; The Successful Toastmaster, 1966; A Treasury of Humorous Quotations, 1969; The Changing World of Banking, 1974; co-author: Quotation Finder, 1971. Editor: American Financial Institutions, 1951; Determining the Business Outlook, 1954; Federal Reserve System, 1960; World Economic Policies and Problems, 1965; The Five-Year Outlook for Interest Rates, 1968; The One-Bank Holding Company, 1969; The Eurodollar, 1970; The Five-Year Outlook for Interest Rates in the United States and Abroad, 1972. Home: 2950 Harrison St Evanston IL 60201 Office: 1 First Nat Plaza Chicago IL 60670

PROCHNOW, HERBERT VICTOR, JR., banker, lawyer; b. Evanston, Ill., May 26, 1931; s. Herbert V. and Laura (Stinson) P.; A.B., Harvard U., 1953, J.D., 1956; A.M., U. Chgo., 1958; m. Lucia Boyden, Aug. 6, 1966; children—Thomas Herbert, Laura. Admitted to Ill. bar, 1957; with 1st Nat. Bank Chgo., 1958—, atty., 1961-70, sr. atty., 1971-73, counsel, 1973—; sec. 1st Chgo. Internat. Banking Corp., N.Y.C., 1st Chgo. Internat., Los Angeles and San Francisco. Mem. Am., Ill. (chmn. sect. internat. law 1967-68), Chgo. (chmn. com. internat. law 1970-71) bar assns., Am. Soc. Internat. Law, Phi Beta Kappa. Clubs: Chicago; Harvard (N.Y.C.); Legal, Law, Onwentsia, Economic, Executives, University (Chgo.). Author: (with Herbert V. Prochnow) A Dictionary of Wit, Wisdom, and Satire, 1962; The Public Speaker's Treasure Chest, 1977; The Successful Toastmaster, 1966; A Treasury of Humorous Quotations, 1969; The Changing World of Banking, 1973; also articles in legal publs. Home: 226 Ravine Forest Dr Lake Bluff IL 60044 Office: 1 First Nat Plaza Chicago IL 60670

PROCHNOW, LAURA S. (MRS. HERBERT V. PROCHNOW), civic worker; b. Camden, Ark., May 15, 1900; d. John McCollum and Alice (Loving) Stinson; student Randolph-Macon Woman's Coll., 1917-19; A.B., U. Mo., 1922; M.A., Northwestern U., 1942; m. Herbert V. Prochnow, June 12, 1928; 1 son, Herbert V. Mem. sr. bd. Infant Welfare Soc., Evanston, 1960. Fin. chmn. Evanston Woman's Club, Evanston, 1947-49. Treas. Woman's Assn. First Presbyn. Ch., Evanston, 1958-60. Presbyterian. Clubs: Fortnightly (Chgo.); Woman's (Evanston); Univ. Guild. Home: 2950 Harrison Evanston IL 60201

PROCTOR, CONRAD ARNOLD, physician; b. Ann Arbor, Mich., July 14, 1934; s. Bruce and Luena Marie (Crawford) P.; M.D., U. Mich., 1959, M.S., 1964; m. Phyllis Darlene Anderson, June 23, 1956; children—Sharon Darlene, Barbara Jan, David Conrad, Todd Bruce. Intern, St. Joseph Mercy Hosp., Ann Arbor, 1959-60; resident Univ. Hosp., Ann Arbor, 1960-65; jr. clin. instr. otorhinolaryngology U. Mich., 1961-63, sr. clin. instr., 1963-65; chief dept. otolaryngology Munson Army Hosp., Ft. Leavenworth, Kans., 1965-67; practice medicine specializing in ear, nose and throat, Royal Oak, Mich., 1967—; v.p. Drs. B. Proctor and C. Proctor, P.C., 1968—; mem. staff Beaumont Hosp., Royal Oak, Detroit Meml., South Macomb hosps., Detroit; mem. Centurion Club for Deafness Research U.S., 1968—. Served with AUS, 1965-67. Fellow A.C.S., Am. Acad. Ophthalmology and Otolaryngology; mem. AMA, Mich., Oakland County, Christian med. socs., Triological Soc., Pan Am. Med. Assn., Mich. Otolaryngol. Soc., Phi Beta Kappa. Republican. Baptist (dir. Christian edn. 1969-72). Clubs: Michigan Deep Sea Fishing (Fenton). Contbr. articles to profl. publs. Home: 1645 Wabeek Way Bloomfield Hills MI 48013 Office: 3535 W 13 Mile Rd Royal Oak MI 48072

PROCTOR, HAZEL PEABODY, savs. and loan exec.; b. Austin, Tex., July 13, 1924; d. Ernest M. and Alva (Simpson) P.; B.A., Los Angeles State Coll., 1945; postgrad. Otis Art Inst., 1947; certificate in fin. mktg. U. Mo., 1975; m. Donald John Proctor, Mar. 29, 1947; children—Donald Peabody, John Ernest, Christopher Alan. Staff artist and writer Pasadena (Calif.) Star News, 1947-49; tchr. Nicholson Remedial Clinic, Los Angeles, 1955-60; market researcher Gold-Thompson, Inc., Pasadena, Calif., 1960-65; account exec. Sam Fine Assos., Ann Arbor, Mich., 1965-58; v.p. mktg. Gt. Lakes Fed. Savs. & Loan Assn., 1968—; cons. in fin. mktg., 1973—; guest lectr. mktg., 1973—. Chmn. St. Joseph's Hosp. Fund Drive, Ann Arbor, 1978; chairperson Community Service Com., Ann Arbor, 1976—; chairperson Washtenaw County Hist. Mus., 1976—; bd. dirs. Ann Arbor Symphony Orch., 1976—. Recipient Nat. Mktg. award, 1970, 72, 73. Mem. Am. Mgmt. Assn., Mich. Savs. and Loan League, Savs. Instns. Mktg. Soc. Am. (dir. 1975—), Mich. State Hist. Soc. Lutheran (ch. council). Club: Zonta Internat. Author of seven pictorial history books on State of Michigan, 1971-75; contbr. articles on mktg. to profl. jours. Home: 1832 Midvale Ave Ypsilanti MI 48197 Office: 407 E Liberty St Ann Arbor MI 48108

PROCTOR, JERRY FRANKLIN, nutrition research adminstr.; b. Westminster, Tex., Jan. 4, 1932; s. Irl Sheridan and Mary Bell (West) P.; Asso. in Sci., Arlington State Coll., 1951; B.S., Tex. A. and M. U., 1955; M.S. in Nutrition, Cornell U., 1958, Ph.D. in Nutrition, 1960; m. Linda Geary Sutter, Dec. 18, 1971; children—Philip Reed, Brian Franklin, Katherine Ann, Richard Sutter. Sr. nutritionist Fundamental Research Lab., Kraftco Corp., Glenview, Ill., 1960-61, group leader Fundamental Research Lab., 1961-65, group leader Indsl. Food Products Lab., 1965-68, mgr. Nutrition Research Lab., 1968—. Village trustee Vernon Hills (Ill.), 1962-64, mayor, 1964-66. Served with OSS, USAFR, 1951-64. Mem. Assn. Vitamin Chemists (sec. 1967—), Nutrition Research Council, Am. Feed Mfrs. Assn., Inst. Food Technologists, Am. Soc. Animal Sci., Am. Oil Chemists Soc., AAAS, Nutrition Soc. Gt. Britain, Chgo. Nutrition Assn., Inst. Edible Oils and Shortening (nutrition com.), Grocery Mfrs. Assn. (nutrition adv. com.), Nat. Assn. Margarine Mfrs. (research com. 1961-64), Equine Nutrition and Physiology Soc. (dir. 1969—), Phi Kappa Phi, Alpha Zeta. Contbr. articles on nutrition to profl. jours. Home: 408 Red Rock Dr Lindenhurst IL 60046 Office: Kraftco Corp Research and Devel 801 Waukegan Rd Glenview IL 60025

PROCTOR, VALERIE FLOYD, ednl. counselor; b. Detroit, Dec. 27, 1932; d. Wallace Walker and Dorcelle (Wingfield) Floyd; B.S. in Edn., Wayne State U., 1956, M.S., 1963; m. Louis Anderson Proctor, Nov. 7, 1953; children—Diane Pearcelle, Rosemarie Doris. Tchr., librarian pub. schs., Highland Park, Mich., 1957-58; tchr., librarian Detroit Bd. Edn., 1959-64, jr. high sch. counselor, 1964-68, counselor sr. high sch., 1968—, also tchr. English and social studies adult edn., 1972—. Second v.p. Raise Aspirations of Youth and Adults, 1972—; fin. sec., recipient Group Leader of Year plaque Detroit chpt. Jack and Jill Inc., 1976. Mem. Am., Mich. personnel and guidance assns., Guidance Assn. Met. Detroit, Assn. Non White Concerns, Nat. Catholic Guidance Assn., Assn. Sch. Counselors, ALA, Mich. Assn. Women Deans, Counselors, and Adminstrs., Am., Mich., Detroit fedns. tchrs., U. Detroit Tchrs. Guild, Wayne State U. Alumni Assn., Delta Sigma Theta. Mem. Detroit Unity Temple. Office: 17525 Wyoming Ave Detroit MI 48221

PROKOPOFF, STEPHEN S., museum exec.; b. Chgo., 1929; B.A., U. Calif. at Berkeley, 1951, M.A., 1952; Ph.D., N.Y.U., 1962; m. Paula Prokopoff; 2 children. Formerly prof. art Skidmore Coll., U. Wash.; dir. Inst. Contemporary Art, Phila., 1967-71; dir. Museum of Contemporary Art, Chgo., 1971—. Author: The Nineteenth Century Architecture of Saratoga Springs, N.Y., 1970. Contbr. articles to profl. jours., exhbn. catalogues. Address: 237 E Ontario St Chicago IL 60611

PROMERSBERGER, WILLIAM JOSEPH, educator; b. Littlefork, Minn., May 28, 1912; s. John and Elizabeth (Hauner) P.; B.S., U. Minn., 1935; M.S., Kans. State U., 1941; m. Ann Katherine Wick, June 9, 1938; children—Kenneth Carol Ann (dec.), Nancy Jane. Instr. U. Minn., Crookston, 1935-38; asst. prof. agrl. engring. N.D. State U., Fargo, 1938-40; chmn. dept., 1941—, prof., 1945—; vis. prof. Univ. Coll., Dublin, Ireland, 1965-66. Mem. Am. Soc. Agrl. Engrs., Am. Soc. Engring. Edn., N.D. Acad. Sci., Phi Kappa Phi, Alpha Epsilon, Sigma Phi Delta, Fargo Moorhead Execs. Club. Elk. Author: (with others) Modern Farm Power, 1962, 2d edit., 71. Contbr. to profl. jours. Home: 55 18th Ave N Fargo ND 58102 Office: State Univ Station ND State U Fargo ND 58102

PROOST, ROBERT LEE, lawyer; b. St. Louis, July 30, 1937; s. Virgil Raymond and Anna Marie (Gaeng) P.; B.S. magna cum laude, St. Louis U., 1959; J.D., Washington U., St. Louis, 1962; m. Mary Jo McDonald, July 1, 1961; children—Timothy Robert, Mary Elizabeth, Thomas Edward, Daniel Joseph. Admitted to Mo. bar, 1962, Ill. bar, 1962; mem. firm Peper, Martin, Jensen, Maichel & Hetlage and predecessor firm, St. Louis, 1962—, partner, 1968—; pres., dir. Silmasco, Inc., St. Louis, 1971—; pres., dir. Executype, Inc., St. Louis, 1971—; lectr. McKendree Coll., 1963, 65; lectr. law Washington U. Sch. Law, 1963-73. Served with USAF, 1962-65. Mem. Am., Mo., Ill. bar assns., Bar Assn. Met. St. Louis (v.p. 1973, sec. 1974, pres. 1978), Washington U. Law Alumni Assn. (pres. 1972-73, mem. alumni council 1972—), St. Louis U. Arts and Scis. Alumni Assn. (v.p. 1971), Order of Coif, Alpha Sigma Nu, Phi Delta Phi. Roman Catholic. Clubs: Media, Washington University Faculty. Home: 319 Claymont Dr Ballwin MO 63011 Office: 720 Olive St 24th Floor St Louis MO 63101

PROPATI, JOSEPH ALEXANDER, dentist; b. Chgo., June 6, 1920; s. Anthony Joseph and Josephine (Lofrano) P.; student Wilson Jr. Coll., 1938-39; D.D.S., Loyola U. at Chgo., 1943; m. Flora Mary Saturno, Feb. 7, 1948; children—Anthony, Jo Ann, Rosanne, John. Gen. practice dentistry, Evergreen Park, Ill., 1946—. Served with AUS, 1943-46. Mem. Am. Dental Assn., Chgo. Dental Soc., Order Sons Italy in Am., Blue Key, Delta Sigma Delta, Omicron Kappa Upsilon. Roman Catholic. Club: Gano Athletic (trustee 1970-73).

PROPHETE, BEAUMANOIR, physician; b. Cap-Haitien, Haiti, Sept. 6, 1920; s. Leonce Anselme and Neolie (Edouard) P.; arrived U.S. 1948; naturalized 1955; grad. Faculte de Medecine d'Haiti, 1947; m. Anne Marie Charles, July 28, 1948; children—Yve Robert, Kathleen, JoAnne, Myrtho, John Pierre. Fellow in urology, Freedman Hosp., Howard U., Washington D.C. 1948-49; resident Homer G. Phillips Hosp., Wash. U., St. Louis, 1951-54; clin. instr. dept. urology St. Louis U. Med. Sch. 1965—; supr. urology Homer G. Phillips Hosp., 1956—; individual practice medicine specializing in urology, St. Louis 1956—; med. dir. N. St. Louis Gen. Hosp., 1977—. Treas. W.End Community Conference, St. Louis 1970-71; pres. Mound City Med. Forum, St. Louis, 1970-72; chmn. bd. edn. St. Rose of Lima Sch., St. Louis, 1973-75. Hon. consul of Haiti in St. Louis, 1960-70. Recipient Fulbright fellowship in urology Howard U., Washington D.C. 1948-49; diplomate Am. Bd. Urology. Mem. St. Louis Med. Sco., Mo. State Med. Assn., Mound City Med. Forum, Am. Urological Assn., AMA, Mo. Pan-Med. Assn., Chi Delta Mu, H.G. Phillips Hosp. Intern Alumni (exec. sec. 1973—). Democrat. Roman Catholic. Clubs: Haitian of St. Louis, Haitian Physicians in Foreign Lands. Contbr. articles in field to profl. jours. Home: 19 Windermere Pl St Louis MO 63112 Office: 3737 N Kings Hwy Suite 109 St Louis MO 63115

PROPSON, THOMAS PETER, civil engr.; b. Detroit, May 16, 1932; s. Edmund Augustine and Irene (Thomas) P.; B.S. in Civil Engring., U. Mich., 1955, M.S., 1959, Ph.D., 1970; m. Janet Mary Ewers, Sept. 22, 1962; children—Thomas Edmund, Brian Louis. Planning engr. Fargo Engring. Co., Jackson, Mich., 1959-62; lectr. civil engring., then research asst. U. Mich., 1962-68; asso. prof. civil engring. S.D. Sch. Mines and Tech., Rapid City, 1968—; cons. in field. Served with AUS, 1956-58. Ford Found. fellow, 1965-67; recipient Standard Oil Good Teaching award, 1973; Danforth asso., 1977. Mem. ASCE, Am. Water Resources Assn., Am. Soc. Engring. Edn., S.D. Engring. Soc., Sigma Xi, Tau Beta Pi, Phi Kappa Phi. Home: 8 Oakland St Rapid City SD 57701 Office: 500 E St Joseph St Rapid City SD 57701

PROST, JOHN CHARLES, ins. co. exec.; b. Detroit, Oct. 16, 1936; s. John L. and Kathryn E. Prost; B.A., Mich. State U., 1959; m. Lucinda Hendricks, July 25, 1959; children—Kathryn E., Elizabeth J.

Asst. purchasing agt. Hupp Corp., 1958-59; spl. agt. Northwestern Mut. Life Ins. Co., 1959-61; brokerage mgr. Occidental Life Ins. Co., Detroit, 1961-63; brokerage mgr. Colonial Life Ins. Co., Detroit, 1963-65; br. mgr. Dominion Life Ins. Co., Detroit, 1965—. Mem. campaign staff Cavanagh for Mayor Detroit, 1962, 65, Romney for Gov. Mich., 1964; mem. Citizens Com. for Better Transp., Detroit, 1964; mem. exec. com. Republican Citizens Mich. 14th Congressional Dist., 1966; chmn. Grosse Pointe Park Rep. Club, 1971, 72; pres. Grosse Pointe PTA/Parent Tchr. Orgn. Council, 1975-76. Recipient Presdl. award of honor Detroit Jaycees, 1964-67; Distinguished Service award Grosse Pointe Jaycees, 1968; citation for civic accomplishments Mich. Senate, 1977. Mem. Mich. State (pres. 1976-77), Detroit (pres. 1970-71) assns. life underwriters, Detroit Gen. Agts. and Mgrs. Assn. (pres. 1977), Fin. and Estate Planning Council Detroit, Greater Detroit C. of C., Am. Coll. Life Underwriters (Gold Key Soc.), Grosse Pointe Park Civic Assn. (pres. 1977), Grosse Pointe Jaycees (founder), Kappa Alpha Mu, Sigma Alpha Epsilon. Roman Catholic. Clubs: Detroit Athletic, Econ. of Detroit; Grosse Pointe Power Squadron. Home: 652 Pemberton Rd Grosse Pointe Park MI 48230 Office: 17220-A W Eight Mile Rd Southfield MI 48075

PROTEAU, ROSEANNE VITULLO, pediatrician; b. Chgo., Sept. 26, 1936; d. Ralph N. and Elvira (Liambo) Vitullo; B.A., Clarke Coll., 1958; M.D., Loyola U., Chgo., 1962; m. Paul Joseph Proteau, Sept. 2, 1967; children—Paul Michael, Susan Marie. Intern, Resurrection Hosp., Chgo., 1962-63; resident in pediatrics Presbyn-St. Luke's Hosp., Chgo., 1963-65, chief resident, 1965-66, dir. Birth Defects Spl. Treatment Center, 1972—; attending pediatrician Mile Sq. Health Center, Chgo., 1966-73; med. dir. Misericordia Homes for Retarded Children, Chgo., 1972—; asst. prof. pediatrics Rush Med. Sch., 1972—; cons. Madden Zone Center; mem. Ill. Gov.'s Adv. Council on Developmental Disabilities, 1973—. Mem. St. Mary's Sch. Bd., Riverside, Ill., 1974-77, sec., 1974-75, vice chmn., 1976-77. NIH fellow, 1974. Diplomate Am. Bd. Pediatrics. Fellow Am. Acad. Pediatrics; mem. Chgo. Pediatric Soc., Ill., Chgo. med. socs., AMA. Roman Catholic. Home: 278 Longcommon Rd Riverside IL 60546 Office: 2916 W 47th St Chicago IL 60632 also 1753 W Congress Pkwy Chicago IL 60612

PROTHERO, EDWARD GEORGE, coal co. exec.; b. Monroe County, Iowa, Oct. 14, 1913; s. George Edward and Signa Elnora (Isaacson) P.; student pub. schs., Albia, Iowa; m. Wilda Geneva Richardson, Apr. 26, 1945; 1 dau., Joy Eddette. Truck driver Perry Chilcote Co., Oskaloosa, Iowa, 1934-39; owner, ops. Prothero Sand & Gravel Co., Oskaloosa, 1940-42; supr. constr. Alcan Hwy., Alaska, 1942-44; farmer, Union Mills, Iowa, 1944-45; owner, operator Kirkpatrick & Prothero Constrn. Co., Oskaloosa, 1945-49; owner Prothero Constrn. Co., Oskaloosa, 1949-58; pres., owner Prothero Coal Co. Inc., Oskaloosa, 1958—. Mem. Mahaska County Bd. Suprs., 1972—. Mem. Iowa Assn. County Bds., Iowa State Realtors Assn., C. of C. Republican. Presbyn. Clubs: Elks, Eagles, Moose, Masons. Address: Rural Route 3 Oskaloosa IA 52577

PROUGH, GEORGE HARRISON, educator; b. nr. Bluffton, Ind., Dec. 27, 1911; s. John Arthur and Ethel P. (Davis) P.; B.S., Ball State Tchrs. Coll., 1933; M.S., Ind. U., 1941; m. Elinor Ruth Landon, June 20, 1936; children—Janice Anne (Mrs. Thomas Farkas), Mary Lynn (Mrs. Duncan MacMillan, Jr.). Tchr., coach, prin. Lancaster Central Sch., Wells County, Ind., 1935-43; tchr., coach Mishawaka (Ind.) Pub. Schs., 1943—. Exec. sec. St. Joseph County 4-H Fair, South Bend, Ind., 1957-68. Dir. Ind. Assn. County and Dist. Fairs, 1962-66, vice pres., 1967, pres., 1968, award of distinction, 1968; spl. dep. sheriff St. Joseph County. Trustee Presbyn. Ch., Mishawaka, 1977-80. Recipient Aux. Mil. Police award, 1943, Civic award, 1961, award Mishawaka Edn. Assn., 1967. Mem. City Council, Bluffton, 1938-42. Mem. Am. Fedn. Tchrs. (charter), Ind. State Tchrs. Assn., Mishawaka Edn. Assn. (pres. 1964-67), NEA, Am. Assn. Ret. Persons, Ind. Ret. Tchrs. Assn., Fraternal Order Police, Phi Sigma Epsilon. Democrat. Rotarian (pres. Mishawaka 1964, dir. 1970—). Clubs: Ball State Varsity, Ball State Alumni. Home: 2327 Homewood Ave Mishawaka IN 46544 Office: 1601 Lincolnway E Mishawaka IN 46544

PROUTY, GARRY FRANKLYN, psychologist; b. Syracuse, N.Y., Aug. 21, 1936; s. Cyrus and Rita (McFall) P.; student Buffalo State Tchrs. Coll., 1954-57; B.A., U. Buffalo, 1959; postgrad. (LaVerne Noyes scholar) U. Chgo., 1966; 1 dau., Gwen Allison. Teaching fellow dept. sociology U. Buffalo, 1961-62; chief psychologist Kennedy Job Tng. Center, Palos Park, Ill., 1966-70; dir. mental health program Prairie State Coll., Chicago Heights, Ill., 1970-74; pvt. practice as psychologist, Park Forest, Ill., 1968-72; psychologist Southwell Inst., Olympia Fields, Ill., 1972—; adj. prof. Union Grad. Sch., Yellow Springs, Ohio, 1972-74. Fellow Chgo. Psychotherapy Center, 1975-77. Mem. Am. Psychol. Assn. (asso.), Am. Sociol. Assn., Internat. Soc. for Study of Symbols. Editorial bd. Psychotherapy Theory, Research and Practice, 1970—, Jour. Mental Imagery, 1977—. Home: 1232 Birch Rd Homewood IL 60430 Office: Southwell Institute 2601 Lincoln Olympia Fields IL 60461

PROVENCHER, RONALD, educator; b. Springerville, Ariz., Oct. 7, 1934; s. George C. and Ada L. (Mann) P.; B.A. with distinction, U. Mo., 1959; Ph.D., U. Calif. at Berkeley, 1968; m. Barbara L. Carlson, June 22, 1935; children—Melodie Anne, Lori Michelle, Sherry Lynne. Asst. prof. anthropology San Diego State U., 1966-69; asst. prof. anthropology Rice U., Houston, 1969-74; asso. prof., chmn. anthropology No. Ill. U., DeKalb, 1974—; vis. scholar Nat. U. Malaysia, 1971-72; asso. dir. NSF Field Sch. in Urban Anthropology, 1969. Served with U.S. Army, 1954-57. Woodrow Wilson Found. fellow, 1959-60, U. Calif. fellow, 1961-62, Fgn. Area Fellowship Found. fellow, 1964-66, George Williams Hooper Found. postdoctoral fellow, 1971-72. Fellow Am. Anthropol. Assn.; mem. AAAS, Assn. Applied Anthropology, Assn. Med. Anthropology, Phi Beta Kappa. Democrat. Episcopalian. Author: (with Douglas Uzzell) Urban Anthropology, 1976; Mainland Southeast Asia; An Anthropological Perspective, 1975; Two Malay Worlds, 1971. Home: 714 Normal Rd DeKalb IL 60115 Office: Dept Anthropology No Ill U DeKalb IL 60115

PROVITT, EVELYN, state ofcl.; b. Massillon, Ohio, Apr. 27, 1930; d. Alfonzo and Lucresie (Anderson) Provitt; diploma in nursing Good Samaritan Hosp. Sch. Nursing, Zanesville, Ohio, 1953; B.S., Wayne State U., 1960, M.S., 1965. Dir. inservice edn. Northville (Mich.) State Hosp., 1960-62, asso. dir. nursing services, 1962-66; psychiat.-mental health nurse cons. Mich. Dept. Mental Health, Lansing, 1966-67, asst. program devel. and planning, mental retardation services, 1967-68, dept. asst. dir., div. dir. mental retardation services, 1966-70, state coordinator, dir. planning for mental retardation services, 1970—. Mem. adv. council Inst. for Study of Mental Retardation and Related Disabilities, U. Mich., 1968—; mem. state adv. com. for vocat. rehab. services Mich. Dept. Edn., 1972-76; mem. State of Mich. Council for Developmental Disabilities Services and Facilities Constrn., 1971—; mem. nat. adv. council on services and facilities for developmentally disabled, HEW, 1973-76, nat. task force on definition of developmental disabilities, 1977. Mem. Am. Assn. Mental Deficiency (mem. social and legislative issues com. 1972-76), Nat. Assn. Coordinators State Programs for Mentally Retarded. Home: 501 Rampart Way East Lansing MI 48823 Office: Mich Dept Mental Health 320 Walnut St Lansing MI 48926

PROVOST, WALLACE BURDETT, journalist; b. Lincoln, Nebr., May 20, 1922; s. Orison C. and Irma (Arbogast) P.; student U. Nebr., 1940-43, Milw. State Tchrs. Coll., 1943; m. Margaret Irene Peckham, May 19, 1947. Rewrite man United Press, Lincoln, 1942; asst. sports editor Nebr. State Jour., Lincoln, 1942-43, Lincoln Evening Jour. 1946-51; courthouse reporter, sports editor, sports columnist Omaha World-Herald, 1951—. Vice-pres. Nat. Golden Gloves Assn., 1961-63; mem. nat. boxing com. Amateur Athletic Union, 1958-60. Pres. World-Herald Good Fellows Charities, Inc., 1964-70. Trustee Fontenelle Forest Assn., 1965-68. Served with USAAF, 1943-46; CBI. Mem. Football Writers Assn., Nat. Assn. Sportscasters and Sportswriters, Omaha Sportscasters Assn. Club: Omaha Press. Home: 5135 Parker St Omaha NE 68104 Office: 14th and Dodge Sts Omaha NE 68102

PROXMIRE, WILLIAM, U.S. senator; b. Lake Forest, Ill., Nov. 11, 1915; s. Theodore Stanley and Adele (Flanigan) P.; grad. The Hill Sch., 1934; A.B., Yale U., 1938; M.B.A., Harvard U., 1940, M.A. in Pub. Adminstrn., 1948; m. Ellen Hodges; children—Theodore Stanley, Elsie Stillman, Douglas Clark. Pres. Artcraft Press, Waterloo, Wis., 1953-57; U.S. senator from Wis., 1957—. Nominee for gov. Wis., 1952, 54, 56; assemblyman Wis. legislature, 1951. Democrat. Home: 4613 E Buckeye Rd Madison WI 53716 Office: Senate Office Bldg Washington DC 20510

PRUIS, JOHN J., univ. pres.; b. Borculo, Mich., Dec. 13, 1923; s. Ties J. and Trientje (Koop) P.; B.S., Western Mich. U., 1947; M.A., Northwestern U., 1949, Ph.D., 1951; Litt.D., Yeungnam U., Taegu, Korea, Ind. State U.; m. Angeline Rosemary Zull, Sept. 14, 1944; children—David Lofton, Daniel J., Dirk Thomas. Tchr. pub. schs., Mich., 1942-43; supervising tchr. Campus Sch., Western Mich. U., 1947-48; instr. speech U. No. Iowa, 1951-52; from asst. prof. to asso. prof. speech So. Ill. U., 1952-55; mem. faculty Western Mich. U., 1955-68, sec. bd. trustees, 1964-68, v.p., 1966-68; pres. Ball State U., Muncie, Ind., 1968—. Cons., evaluator, exec. bd. N. Central Assn., 1959—, bd. dirs., 1972—, v.p., 1976-77, pres., 1977-78. County drive chmn. Kalamazoo Community Chest, 1964. Bd. dirs. Kalamazoo chpt. Am. Cancer Soc., 1963-68, Ball Meml. Hosp., United Fund Delaware County, Muncie Symphony Orch., Muncie Big Bros./Big Sisters. Served with USNR, 1943-46; capt. Res. Mem. Am. Assn. Higher Edn., Muncie C. of C., Speech Communication Assn., Phi Delta Kappa. Mem. U.P. Ch. Am. Rotarian. Home: 1009 N Meadow Ln Muncie IN 47304

PRUITT, RUSSELL CLYDE, elec. co. fin. exec.; b. Damascus, Va., Aug. 31, 1927; s. R. Martin and Pearl K. (Osborne) P.; B.A., Fenn Coll., 1954; postgrad. Western Res. U., 1957-62; m. Clarice Furchess, Apr. 5, 1947; children—Phyllis (Mrs. Dwain Parks), Russell C., Mark, Daniel. Auditor, Standard Oil Co., Cleve., 1948-53; controller Nelson Worldwide div. TRW, Lorain, Ohio, 1953—. Notary pub., Lorain County, 1958—; cons. income tax and investment. Mem. Sheffield Lake (Ohio) Charter Commn., 1960-62; chmn. finance com. Sheffield Lake City Council, 1964-66; pres. bd. edn. Black River, Medina County, Ohio, 1973—. Bd. dirs., treas. Lorain YMCA. Served with USNR, 1944-46, 50-51; PTO, Korea. Mem. U.S. Judo Fedn., Smithsonian Inst., Ohio Sch. Bds. Assn., Nat. Assn. Accountants, Am. Inst. Corp. Controllers, Am. Accounting Assn., Am. Quarter Horse Assn., Appaloosa Horse Club. Eagle. Home: 25600 State Route 58 Wellington OH 44090 Office: E 28th St and Toledo Ave Lorain OH 44055

PRUNER, MARY CAROLYN, pub. utility exec.; b. Hancock, Mich., May 17, 1947; d. Norman Douglas and Eleanor Pearl Pruner; student No. Mich. U., 1965-66, Suomi Coll., 1966-67. Sec., Mich. Life Ins. Co., Royal Oak, Mich., 1967-68; sec. Upper Peninsula Power Co., Houghton, Mich., 1968-70, computer programmer, 1970-72, supr. data processing, 1972-77, mgr. data processing, 1977—. Episcopalian. Office: 616 Shelden Ave Houghton MI 49931

PRUSINSKI, RICHARD CASIMER, archtl. research co. exec.; b. Detroit, Dec. 25, 1923; s. Kazimir and Wladislawa (Wasikiewicz) P.; student St. Mary's Coll., 1943, Oxford U., 1945; B.S., U. Detroit, 1950; postgrad. Mass. Inst. Tech., 1965—, Wayne State U., 1950-51; m. Virginia A. Komorski, Aug. 25, 1947; 1 son, Jan. Author, narrator Pioneers of Am. radio broadcast WJLB, Detroit, 1949-50; U.S. dep. dir. Internat. Trade Fair, Poznan, Poland, 1958; v.p. Everglaze Wall Surfacing Corp., 1958-65; pres., chmn. bd. Archtl. Research Corp., Detroit, 1961—; partner Archtl. Investment Group, 1965-76. Pres. Dearborn (Mich.) Traffic Safety Council, 1956. Served with M.C., AUS, 1944-46; ETO. Named Outstanding Young Man Dearborn Jr. C. of C., 1957. Mem. Constrn. Specifications Inst., Dearborn Jr. C. of C. (pres. 1956), Am. Concrete Inst., Soc. Plastics Engrs. (chmn. plastics in constrn. div.), Lutnia Singing Soc. (dir. 1952-54). Roman Catholic. Clubs: Goodfellows (pres.), St. Alphonsus Ushers, Dearborn, U. Detroit Polish (co-founder). Co-inventor precast polymer concrete panel industry, 1957. Home: 7533 Hartwell St Dearborn MI 48126 Office: 13030 Wayne Rd Livonia MI 48150

PRYOR, CHESTER CORNELIUS, II, ophthalmologist; b. Cin., Jan. 2, 1930; s. Percy G. and Frances Marie (Thompson) P.; B.S. cum laude in Chemistry, Central State Coll., 1951; M.D., Howard U., 1955; postgrad. in ophthalmology, U. Ill., Chgo., 1956; m. Audrey Jean Keals, June 6, 1953; 1 son, Marcus H. Resident, Boston City Hosp., 1957-58; Heed fellow ophthalmic pathology Mass. Eye and Ear Infirmary, 1959; practice medicine specializing in ophthalmology, Cin., 1961—; asso. clin. prof. dept. ophthalmology U. Cin., 1961—; mem. active staff Jewish, Bethesda, Children's hosps.; asso. attending staff Christ, Deaconess hosps. Dir. Unity State Bank, 1970-76. Mem. council aging Community Chest, 1962-68. Bd. dirs. Negro Sightless Soc., 1963-64, Cin. Assn. Blind, 1968—. Served to capt. M.C., AUS, 1959-61. Diplomate Am. Bd. Ophthalmology. Fellow Am. Acad. Ophthalmology and Otolaryngology, A.C.S.; mem. Am. Assn. Ophthalmology, AMA, Nat. Med. Assn. (life), Cin. Ophthal. Soc. (pres. 1976), Alpha Phi Alpha (life mem., chpt. treas. chpt. 1963-77). Methodist (sr. stewart 1965—). Club: Argus (Con.), Masons, Shriners. Home: 3980 Winding Way Cincinnati OH 45229 Office: 2828 Highland Ave Cincinnati OH 45219

PSALMONDS, MAJORIE (MRS. W. GORDON PSALMONDS), educator; b. Taylor, Miss.; d. Fred Winford and June (Wolfe) Varner; B.A., William Jewell Coll., 1943; M.R.E., B.S.M., Southwestern Sem., 1947; M.A., Ariz. State U., 1958; postgrad. Ariz. State U., Columbia U., Washington U.; m. W. Gordon Psalmonds, Mar. 23, 1940; 1 son, Jonathan Lowrie. Organist, music dir. 1st Bapt. Chs., Bartlesville, Okla., 1947-50, McAlester, Okla., 1950-51; organist 1st Bapt. Ch., Duncan, Okla., 1951-54; supr. pub. sch. music Murphy Sch., Phoenix, 1954-60; asso. prof. organ Grand Canyon Coll., Phoenix, 1956-67, asso. prof. music, 1960-70; asso. prof. music Mo. Bapt. Coll., 1970—, also dir. concert choir. Mem. Am. Guild Organists (past dean Central Ariz. chpt.), Music Educator's Nat. Conf., Sigma Alpha Iota, Delta Kappa Gamma. Baptist. Home: 12340 Oak Hollow Dr St Louis MO 63141 Office: Mo Bapt Coll Conway Rd St Louis MO 63141

PSALMONDS, (WALTER) GORDON, educator, clergyman; b. Cotton Plant, Ark., Sept. 24, 1916; s. Walter Lowrie and Ionia (Anderson) P.; A.A., S.W. Bapt. Coll., 1941; B.A., William Jewell Coll., 1943; M.R.E., Southwestern Bapt. Sem., 1947, D.R.E., 1958; m. Marjorie Varner, Mar. 23, 1940; 1 son, Jonathan Lowrie. Ordained to ministry Bapt. Ch., 1940; minister edn. 1st Bapt. Ch., Bartlesville, Okla., 1947-49, Park Cities Bapt. Ch., Dallas, 1950, 1st Bapt. Ch., McAlester, Okla., 1951, Duncan, Okla., 1952-54; prof. religion Grand Canyon Coll., Phoenix, 1954-71, editor coll. catalog, 1965-71; prof. religion Mo. Bapt. Coll., St. Louis, 1971—, also chmn. div. humanities, dir. instl. research. Mem. Mayor's Planning Com., Bartlesville, 1948; mem. exec. com. PTA, Phoenix, 1956-58. Trustee Southeastern Bapt. Sem., Wake Forest, N.C., 1961-71. Mem. Am. Acad. Religion, Ariz. Coll. Assn. (pres. 1971), Ariz. Higher Edn. Coordinating Council, So. Southwestern (v.p.) Bapt. religious edn. assns., So. Bapt. Hist. Soc. Republican. Contbr. to ch. periodicals and study materials. Home: 12340 Oak Hollow Dr St Louis MO 63141 Office: 12542 Conway Rd St Louis MO 63141

PSIHOGIOS, GEORGE THOMAS, machine mfg. co. exec.; b. Sault Ste. Marie, Ont., Can., Sept. 1, 1934; s. Thomas George and Emma Clare (Maxwell) P.; came to U.S., 1954, naturalized, 1955; student N. Park Coll., U. Ill.; m. Olympia B. Carvell, Apr. 23, 1972; children—Thomas G., Athena G., Evan G. Ops. supr. A.C. Nielson Co., Chgo., 1956-62; asst. data processing mgr. J.C. Penney Co., Chgo., 1962-64; data processing mgr. Kay Mus. Instruments Co., Elk Grove Village, Ill., 1964-68; mgr. systems, office services Grotnes Machine Works, Chgo., 1968—. Commr., Boy Scouts Am., 1968-75. Served with AUS, 1954-56. Mem. Data Processing Mgmt. Assn., Assn. for Systems Mgmt., Am. Hellenic Ednl. Progressive Assn. Home: 2019 Seminole Ln Mount Prospect IL 60056 Office: 5454 N Wolcott Ave Chicago IL 60640

PTAK, LOUIS RICHARD, chem. engr.; b. Chgo., May 13, 1916; s. Joseph and Antoinette (Stopka) P.; B.S., U. Lwow (Poland), 1938; m. Helen R. Komperda, July 1, 1944; children—Patricia, Richard, Louis Richard, John, Joseph. With Tech. Center, Continental Can Co., Chgo., 1943—, mgr. product and engrng. standards, 1977—. Served as 2d lt. U.S. Army, 1938-41. Decorated Purple Heart; Croix de Guerre (France). Mem. Am. Chem. Soc., Packaging Inst., Inst. Food Technologists. Home: 5317 Johnson Ave Western Springs IL 60558

PU, PIN HSIU, pathologist, lab. dir.; b. Shanghai, China, Feb. 11, 1924; s. Yien Bei and Hsiu Ching (Chang) P.; came to U.S., 1949, naturalized, 1962; B.S., St. Johns U., Shanghai, China, 1944, M.D., 1947; m. Elise Yao, May 25, 1948; children—Lillian, Steve, Sheila, Debbie. Pathologist, St. Anthony Hosp., Terre Haute, Ind., 1960-67, Mary Sherman Hosp., Sullivan, Ind., 1963-67, Valley Med. Lab., Terre Haute, Ind., 1963-67; pathologist, dir. labs. Dunklin County Meml. Hosp., Kennett, Mo., 1968—; cons. pathologist Dexter Meml. Hosp. (Mo.), 1970—, Pemiscot County Meml. Hosp., Hayti, Mo., 1971—, Presnell Hosp., Kennett, Mo., 1968—; dir. SE Mo. Found. Med. Care; dir. SE Mo. Profl. Standard Rev. Orgn.; chmn. rev. com. Bootheel Comprehensive Health Planning Council, 1972-76. Diplomate Am. Bd. Pathology. Methodist. Office: 611 Teaco Rd Kennett MO 63857

PUCCIO, JAMES SALVATORE, dentist; b. N.Y.C., May 23, 1933; s. James Vincent and Phyllis (Ranni) P.; D.D.S., Ind. U., 1958; m. Nancy Ruth Richards, Sept. 6, 1952; children—Shelley Lynn, James Curtis. Practice dentistry, Middletown, Ohio, 1960—. Pres. Realestate Holding Corp., Middletown, 1966—, Denopt Corp., 1967—, Middletown Dental Group, Inc., 1973—. Served with USAF, 1958-60. Home: 2108 Tullis Dr Middletown OH 45042 Office: 2226 Central Ave Middletown OH 45042

PUCKETT, ROBERT HUGH, polit. scientist, educator; b. Kansas City, Mo., July 16, 1935; s. John William and Marjorie (Shirlaw) P.; B.A., De Pauw U., 1957; M.A., U. Chgo., 1958, Ph.D., 1961; m. Barbara Ann Chandley, Dec. 23, 1964; 1 dau., Sarah Anne. Asst. prof. polit. sci. Mary Washington Coll., Fredericksburg, Va., 1961-63; vis. scholar, postdoctoral fellow social sci. research council Mass. Inst. Tech., Cambridge, 1963-64; asst. prof. govt. and fgn. affairs U. Va. at Charlottesville, 1964-66; asst. prof. social sci. Mich. State U., E. Lansing, 1966-68; prof. polit. sci. Ind. State U., Terre Haute, 1968—. Cons. The Rand Corp., Santa Monica, Calif., 1962-63. Mem. DePauw U. Alumni Assn. (pres. chpt. 1973-74), Am. Polit. Sci. Assn., Indpls. Com. Fgn. Relations, Midwest Polit. Sci. Assn., Internat. Studies Assn., So. Polit. Sci. Assn., Ind. Acad. Social Scis., Phi Beta Kappa, Phi Eta Sigma. Kiwanian (dir.). Author: America Faces the World: Isolationist Ideology in American Foreign Policy, 1972; (with Oscar H. Rechtschaffer), Reflections on Space, 1964. Contbr. articles in field to polit. sci. jours. Home: 122 Marigold Dr Terre Haute IN 47803

PUCKORIUS, PAUL RONALD, water treatment, cooling water and pollution control cons.; b. Chgo., Apr. 7, 1930; s. Paul Joseph and Lucy (Adulis) P.; B.A., North Central Coll., Naperville, Ill., 1953; postgrad Northwestern U., 1953-54; m. Joyce Elaine Heinzman, Feb. 14, 1953; children—Susan, David, Cynthia. With Nalco Chem. Co., Chgo., 1948-69, product mgr. cooling water, 1963-65, mgr. cooling water chems. dept., 1965-69; v.p., exec. v.p. Zimmite Corp., Cleve., 1969-76; owner, pres. P.R. Puckorius & Assos. Inc., Cleve., 1976—; dir. Cooling Tower Inst.; mem. adv. bd. Internat. Water Conf. Leader, Explorer Scouts, 1964, active Boy Scouts Am., 1964-72; hon. bd. dirs. Clague Playhouse Theatre; mem. vestry Episcopal Ch., 1964-69, 70-72. Served with Ill. N.G., 1949-58. Mem. Nat. Assn. Corrosion Engrs. (chmn. coms.), Korean Inst. Chem. Engrs. (hon.), Engrs. Soc. Western Pa., Am. Chem. Soc., Am. Water Works Assn., Am. Petroleum Inst., Am. Inst. Chem. Engrs., ASTM, Am. Electroplaters Soc. Author: (with others) Cooling Water Primer, 1971; also articles in profl. jours., papers presented at profl. confs. Patentee in water treatment chemicals. Home: 20800 Valley Forge Dr Cleveland OH 44126 Office: Box 4846 Cleveland OH 44126

PUDLO, EDMUND MARION, chemist; b. Chgo., June 20, 1927; s. Louis John and Apolonia Mary (Krol) P.; B.S., De Paul U., 1950; m. Regina Suzanne Samborski, Apr., 1953; children—Robert, Richard, Raymond. Chemist indsl. coatings Armstrong Paints Co., Chgo., 1950-57; mgr. chem. coatings lab. Mobil Chem. Co., Kankakee, Ill., 1957—; cons. Underwriter's Labs. Served with USAAF, 1945-46. Mem. Fedn. Socs. Coatings Tech. Club: Elks. Home: 27 Guildford Dr Bourbonnais IL 60914 Office: 901 N Greenwood St Kankakee IL 60901

PUEPPKE, GLENN HOWARD, furniture co. exec., farmer; b. Amenia, N.D., Apr. 12, 1927; s. Howard Monroe and Malinda Wilhelmina (Judisch) P.; student Concordia Coll., 1945-46; m. Letha Pauline Mitchell, Sept. 4, 1948 (dec.); children—Steven, David, Eric, Howard, Clinton; m. 2d, Ruth Bernice Kleinsasser, Sept. 19, 1965. With Macklanborg Supply Co., Oklahoma City, 1947, Collins, Dietz, Morris Co., Oklahoma City, 1948-50; farmer nr. Erie, N.D., 1950—; pres. G & G Transport Co., Erie, 1960-66; with Arkota Industries, furniture mfg. co., Valley City, N.D., 1971—, vice chmn., 1970—; mem. N.D. Trade Mission to Middle East, 1976. Pres. Erie (N.D.) Sch. Bd., 1965-67, Dakota Sch. Bd., 1973-77; chmn. Cass County 4C's, 1966. Bd. dirs. St. Lukes Hosp., 1958-60. Mem. Nat. Sunflower Growers Assn., Red River Valley Bean Growers Assn., N.D. Farm

Bur., Profl. Farmers Am., Alpha Epsilon Sigma. Mem. Ch. of God (vice chmn. N.D. mission 1971-73). Republican. Home: Erie ND 58029

PUETZ, WAYNE EDWARD, polit. scientist, educator; b. Joliet, Ill., Feb. 20, 1946; s. Arthur A. and Anne C. (Scheri) P.; B.A. with high honors, Lewis U., 1968; M.A., Georgetown U., 1970; Ph.D., U. Ind., 1978; m. Dale Duda, July 9, 1977. Asst. dept. mgr. Hardlines Corp., retail outlets, Joliet, Ill., 1963-68; vis. prof. polit. sci. dept. Hanover (Ind.) Coll., 1975—; prof. law and govt. Coll. St. Francis, Joliet, 1975—; faculty Bolingbrook High Sch., Romeoville, Ill., 1975-76; dir. gifted program Jane Addams Sch., Bolingbrook, Ill., 1977—; researcher role technosci. progress and internat. law. Mem. Am. Polit. Sci. Assn., Am. Soc. Internat. Law, Delta Epsilon Sigma, Pi Sigma Alpha. Home: 1321 N William St Joliet IL 60435

PUGH, DANIEL WILBERT, costume designer, educator; b. Bluffton, Ind., Sept. 6, 1945; s. Ralph Moody and Doris L. (Baker) P.; B.A. in Drama, Butler U., 1968; M.F.A. in Costume Design, Goodman Sch. of Drama, Chgo., 1974. Faculty asst. in charge of costume design dept. of speech and performing arts Northeastern Ill. State Coll., Chgo., 1968-71; costume designer, shop supr. U. Chgo. Court Theatre, summers 1971, 73, 74, 75, 76, 77; asst. prof. costume history and design, stage makeup and acting Butler U., Indpls., 1971—, also costume designer, dir. maj. prodns., 1971—. Writer, researcher Nat. Sch. of Dress Design div. Americana Interstate Corp., Mundelein, Ill., 1969-72. Mem. Blackford County (Ind.) Hist. Soc., Montpelier Hist. Soc. Home: 3055 N Meridian St #18B Indianapolis IN 46208 Office: Butler U 46th St and Sunset Indianapolis IN 46208

PUGLIESE, JOSEPH MARGIOTTI, geophysicist; b. Pitts., Aug. 19, 1936; s. Sebastian Charles and Grace (Margiotti) P.; B.S. in Geophysics and Geochemistry, Pa. State U., 1958; m. Ann Marie Johnson, Apr. 12, 1969; 1 dau., Marie Christina. Geophysicist, Bur. Mines U.S. Dept. Interior, College Park, Md., 1958-65, geophysicist project engr., Mpls., 1965-68, head thermal and elec. fragmentation lab., Mpls., 1968-70, geophysicist, environ. specialist, sr. research investigator adviser team leader, Mpls., 1970—. Adviser, tchr. seminars in field including Canadian Mines dept., Ottawa, U.S. C.E., others; tech. adviser met. clean air com. Mpls., 1974—. Vol. Little Bros. Poor, Mpls., St. Paul, 1972—. Served with USNR, 1959. Mem. Twin Cities Geologists, Soc. Exptl. Stress Analysis, Internat. Soc. Rock Mechanics, Sigma Gamma Epsilon. Roman Catholic (lector-in-charge). Author tech. papers research rock disintegration. Home: 5016 18th Ave S Minneapolis MN 55417 Office: PO Box 1660 Twin Cities MN 55111

PUKITE, JANIS, elec. engr.; b. Valka, Latvia, Sept. 13, 1928; s. Reinholds Gustavs and Anna Elizabete (Traubergs) P.; came to U.S., 1949, naturalized, 1959; B.S. with honors, U. Wis., 1957, postgrad., 1957-60; postgrad. U. Calif., U. Ariz.; m. Astrida Liliana Bititis, May 18, 1958; children—Sandra Jane, Paul Raymond, John Allan. Engring. analyst Allis Chalmers Mfg. Co., Milw., 1957-60; project engr. AC Electronics, Milw., 1960-62; sr. engr. CDI, cons., Mpls., 1962-64; sr. prin. engr. Honeywell, Inc., 1964-74, supr. data processing, 1974—. Instr. evening tech. courses. Served with AUS, 1951-53. Recipient H.W. Sweatt award Honeywell, Inc., 1966. Mem. Assn. Computing Machinery, Pattern Recognition Soc. Home: 4960 Fillmore St NE Minneapolis MN 55421 Office: 12001 State Hwy 55 Minneapolis MN 55441

PULITZER, EMILY RAUH (MRS. JOSEPH PULITZER, JR.), museum curator; b. Cin., July 23, 1933; d. Frederick and Harriet (Frank) Rauh; A.B., Bryn Mawr Coll., 1955; student Ecole du Louvre, Paris, France 1955-56; M.A., Harvard U., 1963; m. Joseph Pulitzer, Jr. Mem. staff Cin. Art Mus., 1956-57; asst. curator drawings Fogg Art Mus., Harvard, 1957-64, asst. to dir., 1962-63; curator City Art Mus., St. Louis, 1964-73. Mem., chmn. visual arts com. Mo. State Council Arts, 1976—. Vice pres. bd. dirs. Rothko Found. Home: 4903 Pershing Pl St Louis MO 63108

PULITZER, JOSEPH, JR., newspaper publisher; b. St. Louis, May 13, 1913; s. Joseph and Elinor (Wickham) P.; student St. Mark's Sch., Southborough, Mass.; A.B., Harvard, 1936; m. Louise Vauclain, June 2, 1939; 1 son, Joseph IV. Reporter, San Francisco News, 1935; mem. staff, St. Louis Post-Dispatch, 1936-48, asso. editor, 1948-55, editor, pub., pres., 1955—. Served from ensign to lt. USNR, 1942-45. Home: 4903 Pershing Pl St Louis MO 63108 Office: Post-Dispatch St Louis MO 63101

PULLEN, JAMES RALPH, educator; b. Oklahoma City, Feb. 16, 1936; s. Ralph and Anna Margaret (Kiely) P.; m. Janice Louise Robinson, Dec. 9, 1965; 1 son, James Arthur; B.S., U. Mo., 1958, M.Ed., 1963; Ed.D., U. S.D., 1971. With Dept. Def., Germany and P.R., 1963-65; high sch. counselor, Casper, Wyo., 1965-67; counselor, dir. adult edn., Keokuk, Iowa, 1967-69; asso. prof. Central Mo. State U., Warrensburg, 1971—; cons. human relations USAF. Vice pres. Johnson County Mental Health Assn., 1974; bd. dirs. Warrensburg Planned Parenthood Assn. Served with USNR, 1958-60. HEW grantee, 1973-75. Mem. Am. Personnel and Guidance Assn., Am. Psychol. Assn., Phi Delta Kappa. Clubs: Masons, Rotary. Contbr. articles to profl. jours. Home: Route 2 Northfield Warrensburg MO 64093

PULLIAM, JACK CARL, ret. state ofcl.; b. Cheney, Kans., Aug. 18, 1911; s. Henry Bascum and Elfa Alice (Grice) P.; student Coll. Emporia, Kans., 1929-30; student Kans. State Tchrs. Coll., Emporia, 1930-33, B. Gen. Studies, 1976; m. Dorothy Edythe Kendall, June 15, 1935; children—Jacquelyn (Mrs. Jerome Statman), James, Judith (Mrs. Paul Joines). News editor Kingman (Kans.) Leader-Courier, 1933-39; news editor Monett (Mo.) Daily Times, 1939-41; writers project Mo. WPA, 1941; asst. field dir. Midwest area ARC, 1941-44; contact rep. VA, 1946-49; chief adminstrv. div. VA Hosp., Topeka, 1949-51; asst. supr. Kans. Instns., 1951-53; biometrics supr. Kans. Div. Insts., Topeka, 1953-55, coordinator childrens services, 1969-76; supt. Boys Indsl. Sch., Topeka, 1955-69; adj. instr. criminal justice Washburn U., Topeka, 1977—. Pres., Kans. Council for Children and Youth, 1961; mem. adv. bd. Kans. Council on Crime and Delinquency, 1971—. Served with AUS, 1944-45. Recipient Distinguished Citizens award Mayor of Topeka, 1967, Presdl. award Kans. Correctional Assn., 1977, others. Life mem. Kans. Kiwanis Found. Mem. Nat. Assn. Tng. Schs. of Juvenile Agys. (pres. 1963-65, editor procs. 1967-76), Nat. Council on Crime and Delinquency, Kans. Conf. Social Welfare, Kans. Congress Parents and Tchrs. (dir.; treas. 1973-75), Am. Assn. Ret. Persons, Am. Legion, Menninger Sch. Psychiatry Alumni Assn. (hon.). Mem. Christian Ch. Clubs: Masons, Kiwanis (Kans. dist. gov. 1967). Home: 615 W 5th St Topeka KS 66603

PULLUKAT, THOMAS JOSEPH, chemist; b. Kerala, India, Apr. 28, 1941; s. Joseph Thomas and Annamma (Thomas) P.; came to U.S., 1962, naturalized, 1975; Ph.D., Purdue U., 1967; m. Laila Thomas, Feb. 23, 1970; children—Tara Ann, Jeena Elizabeth. Research scientist Chemplex Co., Rolling Meadows, Ill., 1967-71, group leader, 1971-72, sr. research scientist, group leader, 1972—. Mem. Am. Chem. Soc., ASTM. Roman Catholic. Patentee polyethylene catalysis; inventor numerous polyethylene grades. Home: 112 E Charleston Ln Hoffman Estates IL 60195 Office: 3100 Golf Rd Rolling Meadows IL 60008

PULSIPHER, DEE WAYNE, dentist; b. Brigham City, Utah, July 23, 1937; s. Orson Wayne and Leah Mae (Carlson) P.; student Idaho State Coll., 1958-62; D.D.S., Washington U., 1966; m. Grace Neolia Anderson, Aug. 5, 1960; children—Brit Dee, Temia Lyn., Dyan Neolia. Pvt. practice dentistry, Warson Woods, Mo., 1966—; asst. prof. clin. pedodontics Washington U., St. Louis, 1966—; head dental dept. Shriners Hosp., St. Louis, 1970-74; pedontic cons. for dental interns VA Hosp., St. Louis, 1971—. Vice pres. local PTA, 1975-76; active Boy Scouts Am. Served with AUS, 1955-58. Recipient Recognition award Am. Soc. Dentistry for Children, 1971. Mem. Am. Soc. Preventive Dentistry, Am. Soc. Dentistry Children, Am. Assn. Dental Schs., Nat. Analgesia Soc., Am., Mo. dental assns., Acad. Sci., Am. Analgesia Soc., West Dist. Dental Soc. (pres. 1974-76), Greater St. Louis Dental Soc. (chmn. council profl. affairs 1973-75, dir. 1974-77), Nat. Rifle Assn., Am. Numis. Assn., Postal Commemorative Soc., Boat Owners Assn., Mo. Bot. Garden, St. Louis Zoo Assn., Xi Psi Phi. Mason (Shriner). Club: Lake St. Louis Sailing. Home: 843 Briarfarm Ln Kirkwood MO 63122 Office: 9929 Manchester Rd Warson Woods MO 63122

PULVE, FREDERICK MASON, realtor; b. Detroit, June 28, 1940; s. James Constantino and Mildred Agatha (Rossman) P.; student Eastern N.Mex. U., 1959-62, Wayne State U., 1963-68, Highland Park Jr. Coll., 1958-59; m. Michelle Florence Lomske, Dec. 11, 1965; children—Rochelle Renee, Matthew Frederick. Salesman, Schweitzer Real Estate Inc., Detroit, 1969-71, asst. mgr., 1970-71, mgr., 1971-72, dist. mgr., 1972-73, regional mgr., 1973-74, v.p., gen. mgr. sales, 1974—. Realtor cons. Oakland U., 1975-76; cons. Wayne State U., U. Mich. Served with USAF, 1959-63. Mem. S. Oakland Bd. Realtors (sec. 1977, treas. 1978), Macomb County Bd. Realtors, Eastern Detroit Realty Assn., Delta Chi. Lutheran. Home: 1426 Glenwood Dr Leonard MI 48038 Office: 3555 Fourteen Mile Rd Sterling Heights MI 48077

PUNDT, RICHARD ARTHUR, lawyer; b. Iowa City, Iowa, Apr. 18, 1944; s. Arthur Herman and Johanna Celeste (Pasterik) P.; B.A., State U. Iowa, 1966; J.D., Drake U., 1969; m. Joyce Kay Schoenfelder, Dec. 1, 1968; children—Vincent Arthur, Jennifer Johanna, Heather Ann. Temporary claims dep. Iowa Employment Security Commn., 1968-69; admitted to Iowa bar, 1969; staff atty. Polk County Legal Aid, Office Econ. Opportunity, 1969; spl. agt. FBI, 1969-71; law asso. Keys & Crawford, Cedar Rapids, 1971-72, Faches, Klinger & Gloe, Cedar Rapids, 1972-75, Silliman, Gray & Stapleton, Cedar Rapids, 1975—; dir. Cedar Rapids Profl. Football Corp., 1972-73, pres., 1972-73. Exec. dir. Iowans for Rockerfeller, 1968; exec. dir. Polk County Republican Com. 1968-69; mem. Linn County Rep. Central Com., 1972—; chmn. Linn County Rep. party, 1977—; asst. atty. Linn County, 1972-76. Mem. Am., Iowa, Linn County bar assns., Metro Athletic Assn. (dir. 1976—). Roman Catholic. Club: Sertoma. Home: 4118 Hickory Hill Ln SE Cedar Rapids IA 52403 Office: 807 American Bldg Cedar Rapids IA 52401

PUNNETT, AUDREY FRANCES, ednl. psychologist; b. Bremerton, Wash., Oct. 25, 1947; d. Louis and Marjorie Velma (Gibson) P.; A.A., Victor Valley Coll., 1967; B.S., U. Utah, 1971, M.S., 1975. Psychologist, Utah State Dept. Health, Salt Lake City, 1970-71, 73-74; proctor, supr. testing div., counseling and psychol. services U. Utah, Salt Lake City, 1974; psychometrist Washington U. Med. Sch. Psychology Lab., St. Louis Children's Hosp., 1974-75; psychol. examiner, spl. sch. dist. St. Louis County, St. Louis, 1976—; asst. clin. psychologist to Libby Bass, 1977—. Mem. altar guild Episcopal Ch. St. Michael and St. George, Clayton, Mo. Mem. Am. (asso.), Mo. (asso.) psychol. assns., Assn. Advancement of Psychology. Club: Jr. League St. Louis (placement com. 1975-77). Home: 813 Westwood Dr Clayton MO 63105 Office: 12110 Clayton Rd Town and Country MO 63131

PURCELL, JAMES FRANCIS, pub. utilities co. exec.; b. Miles City, Mont., May 13, 1920; s. Robert E. and Mary (Hickey) P.; A.B. magna cum laude, U. Notre Dame, 1942; A.I., Harvard Grad. Sch. Bus. Adminstrn., 1943; m. Dorothy Abel, Nov. 4, 1944; children—Angela, Ann, Alicia, Anita, Alanna, James, Andrea, Adria, Michael, Gregory, Amara. Writer McGraw Hill Pub. Co., N.Y.C., 1946-48; dir. pub. relations Am. Maize Products Co., N.Y.C., 1948-51; pub. relations cons. Selvage & Lee, Chgo., 1951-53; mgr. pub. relations No. Ind. Pub. Service Co., Hammond, 1953—, v.p. pub. relations, 1961-75, sr. v.p., 1975—, also dir.; dir. Bank of Ind., Money Mgmt. Corp. Past pres. adv. bd. Our Lady Mercy; bd. dirs. Diocese Gary Catholic Charities. Served to lt. USNR, 1943-46. Recipient Man of Year award Calumet Notre Dame Alumni, 1967. Mem. U.S. C. of C. (bus. relations com. 1959-61), Am. Gas Assn. (chmn. pub. relations com.), Pub. Relations Soc. Am. (pres. Hoosier chpt.), Newcomen Soc. N.Am. Rotarian. Clubs: Woodmar Country, Notre Dame, Harvard Bus. Sch. Club Chgo. Home: 8350 Parkview Ave Munster IN 46321 Office: 5265 Hohman Ave Hammond IN 46325

PURDUM, JACK JAY, educator, economist; b. Kansas City, Mo., May 3, 1943; s. John Wesley and Janette B. (Black); B.A., Muskingum Coll., 1965; M.A., Ohio State U., 1967, Ph.D. (NSF fellow), 1972; m. Karol Ruth Pfeiffer, Aug. 26, 1967; children—Katie Janette, John Paul. Teaching asso. econs. Ohio State U., Columbus, 1965-70; asst. prof. econs. Creighton U., Omaha, 1970-74, chmn. dept., 1972-73; asso. prof. econs. Butler U., Indpls., 1974—; regional cons. State Farm Ins. Cos., 1975—. Legal cons. tort litigation. Econ. adviser to mayor Indpls., in Republican campaign for U.S. Senate, 1974. Mem. Am. Econs. Assn., Econ. History Assn., Econ. History Soc., Agrl. History Soc. Home: 525 Buckingham Dr Indianapolis IN 46208 Office: Dept Economics Butler U Indianapolis IN 46208

PURDY, CHARLES WILLIAM, III, vet. biol. researcher; b. St. Joseph, Mo., Oct. 25, 1934; s. Charles William and Ethel Rose (Davis) P., Jr.; B.S. in Agr. cum laude, U. Mo., 1963, D.V.M., 1963, M.S., 1967, Ph.D., 1969; m. Carol Ann Wright, Oct. 23, 1955; children—Jeffrey Charles, Michael William, Lisa Ann. Asso. veterinarian County Animal Hosp., St. Louis, 1963-65; research asso. dept. vet. microbiology U. Mo., Columbia, 1965-69; dir. immunological research Philips Roxane, Inc., St. Joseph, 1969—. Dep. veterinarian State of Mo., 1963—. Served with USN, 1953-57. USPHS postdoctoral fellow, 1966, NIH grantee, 1967. Mem. Am., Mo. vet. med. assns., Am. Assn. Equine Practitioners, Gamma Sigma Delta, Phi Zeta. Methodist. Mason (32 deg., Shriner). Home: 71 Leopard Circle St St Joseph MO 64506 Office: 2621 N Belt Hwy St Joseph MO 64502

PURDY, RALPH DAVID, educator; b. Mt. Vernon, Ohio, Sept. 1, 1906; s. Chauncey V. and Emma (Kerr) P.; A.B., Asbury Coll., 1929; postgrad. George Peabody Coll. Tchrs., summer 1931; M.A., U. Ky., 1933; Ph.D., Ohio State U., 1949; m. Chrystabelle D. Yust, Aug. 20, 1930; children—Gary D., Rosemary L. Rauch, Kathleen (Mrs. Bruce Boyd.). Instr., Asbury Coll., 1929-34; tchr., coach Gambier (Ohio) High Sch., 1934-36; exec. head Rushville (Ohio) Union Sch., 1936-40; supt. Wellington (Ohio) Exempted Village Schs., 1940-44; supt. Conneaut (Ohio) City Schs., 1944-50; prof. Marshall U., 1950-56; mem. SSCPEA research staff George Peabody Coll., 1951-52; dir. Bur. Ednl. Field Services, Miami U., Oxford, Ohio, 1956-66, chmn. dept. ednl. adminstrn., 1961-66, project dir. Master Plan for Sch. Dist. Orgn., Ohio Dept. Edn., 1965-66; dir. Great Plains Sch. Dist. Orgn. Project, Nebr. State Dept. Edn., 1967-68; prof. ednl. adminstrn. Miami U., 1956-73, Distinguished prof., prof. emeritus, 1973—. Cons. ednl. evaluation ICA, Afghanistan, 1959, AID, Ethiopia, 1969, AID, Vietnam, 1971. Recipient Distinguished Service award Miami U., 1972, recognition and commendation Ohio Gen. Assembly, 1973. Mem. Am. Ednl. Research Assn., Am. Assn. Sch. Adminstrs., Nat. Orgn. Legal Problems in Edn. Mason (Shriner); mem. Order Eastern Star, Kiwanian. Author: A Master Plan for School District Organization in Ohio; Evaluation and Planning for Secondary Education in South Vietnam, 2 vols.; author, editor numerous publs. in field. Home: Route 3 Hopewell Rd Mt Vernon OH 43050

PURIFOY, CECIL ERNEST, JR., educator; b. Houston, Sept. 22, 1927; s. Cecil E. and Ruth Agnes (Dupre) P.; B.S., U. Tex., 1949; M.A., Mich. State U., 1952, Ph.D., 1970. Tchr. pub. schs., Prince George's County, Md., 1954-55, Houston, 1955-64; mem. faculty Mich. State U., 1964-66, U. Tenn., 1966-71; mem. faculty Ball State U., Muncie, Ind., 1971—, asst. prof. English. Mich. State U. fellow, 1950-54, 64-66. Mem. ALA, Nat. Council Tchrs. English, Internat. Reading Assn., Children's Lit. Assn., Midwest Modern Lang. Assn., Phi Delta Kappa. Contbr. articles to profl. pubs. Home: 4501 Wheeling St Muncie IN 47304 Office: 207 D English Bldg Ball State U Muncie IN 47306

PURPLE, EDWARD BENNETT, automotive parts co. exec.; b. Chgo., Jan. 27, 1938; s. George Sutor and Louise (Bennett) P.; B.S., U. Ill., 1966; m. Lynn Kingsbury, Sept. 10, 1966; children—Christopher R., Eric S. With Caterpillar Tractor Co., Peoria, Ill., 1966-68; exec. v.p. Nash Bros. Co., truck stampings, Joliet, Ill., 1968—, also dir.; dir. First Savs. and Loan Assn., Wilmington, Ill., Flexible Steel Lacing Co., Downers Grove, Ill.; dir. Bolingbrook Travel Center (Ill.), Quin-T Corp., Tilton, N.H. Engring. cons. Served with AUS, 1961-63. Registered profl. engr., Ill. Mem. Delta Upsilon, Sigma Tau. Home: 147th St Forest Hills Lockport IL 60441 Office: PO Box 458 Joliet IL 60434

PURSELL, CARL D., Congressman; b. Plymouth, Mich., Dec. 19, 1932; B.A., Eastern Mich. U., 1957, M.A., 1962; LL.D. (hon.), Madonna Coll.; m. Peggy Jean Brown, 1956; children—Philip, Mark, Kathleen. Educator, small bus. owner; mem. Mich. Senate, 1971-76, mem. appropriations com.; mem. 95th Congress from 2d Mich. Dist., mem. Edn. and Labor Com., Sci. and Tech. Com.; past mem. Mich. Crime Commn. Mem. Wayne County Bd. Commrs., 1960-70. Named Outstanding Young Man of Year Jr. C. of C., 1965; recipient Outstanding Environ. Legislator in Mich. award Fed. Environ. Protection Agy., 1976. Served as officer, inf., U.S. Army, 1957-59. Republican. Office: Room 1709 Longworth House Office Bldg Washington DC 20515*

PURSELL, WARREN BENJAMIN, trade assn. exec., pub. relations counsel; b. Chgo., Sept. 19, 1920; s. William Benjamin and Virginia (Goodrich) P.; student Wright Jr. Coll., Chgo., 1939-40; A.B. in Polit. Sci. U. Chgo., 1942; m. Josephine Venecia Brown, Oct. 10, 1945 (dec. Apr. 1975); children—Wayne Bruce, Marcia Denise Bleck; m. 2d, Arlowyne D. Maddox, Feb. 29, 1976. Mem. editorial dept. Chgo. Tribune, 1936-43; partner Pursell, O'Connell & Pierson, 1946; pres. Pursell Public Relations, Chgo., 1947—; exec. dir. Cook County Council of Insured Savs. Assns. 1959-73; sec.-treas. Savs. Assn. Council, 1969-73; exec. v.p. Ill. Savs. and Loan League, 1973—; lectr. pub. relations. Council committeeman Boy Scouts Am., asst. scout master, 1955-63. Served with USNR, 1943-45, aboard U.S.S. Austin, U.S.S. Willis; now comdr. ret. Res. Decorated Presdl. Unit Citation with bronze star, Am., ETO, Asian theatre medals, Naval Res. Medal, Victory medal; recipient pub. service citation Sec. Navy. Mem. Pub. Relations Soc. of Savs. Assn. (pres. 1955), Pub. Relations Soc. Am. (accredited), Navy League (v.p. 1961, dir. 1960, pres. Chgo. council 1966-67, state pres. 1969-72, nat. dir. 1969—, nat. exec. com. 1972-75, 76—, regional pres. 1972-75, nat. v.p. 1976—), Am. Soc. Assn. Execs., Naval Order U.S. (nat. dep. recorder 1977), Am. Legion, Naval Res. Assn. Inc., U. Chgo. Alumni Assn., Amateur Fencers League Am., Chgo. (dir. 1970-73), Ill. socs. assn. exec., U-505 Pub. Relations Com., Am. Acad. Polit. and Social Sci., Assn. Execs. Club Chgo. (dir. pres. 1966), Savs. Instns. Mktg. Soc. Am., Publicity Club (past Chgo. dir.), Kappa Sigma (past pres., dir. Chgo. alumni chpt.). Presbyterian (deacon). Clubs: University, Executives (Chgo.); Illini, Sangamo (Springfield). Home: 2308 Wiggins St Springfield IL 62704 Office: 220 E Adams St Springfield IL 62701

PURVES, ALAN CARROLL, educator; b. Phila., Dec. 14, 1931; s. Edmund Randolph and Mary Carroll (Spencer) P.; A.B., Harvard U., 1953; M.A., Columbia U., 1956, Ph.D., 1960; m. Anita Woodruff Parker, June 18, 1960 (dec. Mar. 1975); children—William Carroll, Theodore Rehn; m. 2d, Anne H. Nesbitt, July 14, 1976. Lectr. Hofstra Coll., 1956-58; instr. Columbia, 1958-61; asst. prof. English, Barnard Coll., N.Y.C., 1961-65; examiner in humanities Ednl. Testing Service, 1965-68, asso. prof. English, U. Ill., Urbana, 1968-70, prof., 1970-73, prof. English edn., 1973—, dir. curriculum lab., 1976—; staff asso. Central Midwest Regional Ednl. Lab., St. Ann, Mo., 1968-72. Pres. Wonalancet (N.H.) Corp., 1967-70. Served with AUS, 1953-55. Recipient Internat. Assn. Evaluation Edn. Achievement Internat. Fellowship, 1971; Fulbright-Hayes Research award, 1977. Mem. Nat. Council Tchrs. English (trustee research found. 1969-72, mem. com. research 1968—, dir. 1973—, v.p. 1977-78), Newcomen Soc. (hon.), Ill. Assn. Tchrs. English, Nat. Council Research English, Ill. Council English Edn., Am. Edn. Research Assn. Episcopalian (mem. vestry 1970-73). Clubs: Wonalancet Outdoor (pres. 1965-69), Appalachian Mountain. Author: The Essays of Theodore Spencer; The Elements of Writing about a Literary Work, 1968; Testing in Literature, 1971; How Porcupines Make Love, 1972; Literature and the Reader, 1972; Responding, 1973; Literature Education in Ten Counties, 1973; Educational Policy and International Assessment, 1975; Evaluation in English, 1977. Editor: Research in the Teaching of English, 1973—. Home: Main St Fithian IL 61844 Office: U Ill Coll Edn Urbana IL 61801

PUSATERI, LAWRENCE XAVIER, judge; b. Oak Park, Ill., May 25, 1931; s. Lorenzo and Josephine (Romano) P.; LL.B. summa cum laude, DePaul U., 1953; m. Eve Graf, July 9, 1956; children—Joanne, Lawrence, Paul Leo, Mary Anne, Eva Marie. Admitted to Ill. bar, 1953; asst. states atty. Cook County, Chief Cook County Narcotics Bur., 1957-59; spl. asst. atty. gen. State of Ill., 1959; mem. firm Newton, Wilhelm & Kenny, Chgo., 1960-63; partner firm Newton, Wilhelm, Kenny & Pusateri, Chgo., from 1963; justice Ill. Appellate Ct., 1977—; mem. Ill. Ho. of Reps., 1964-68; chmn. Ill. Parole and Pardon Bd., 1968-69; chief legal services Ill. Dept. Corrections, 1972-75; mem. Ill. Liquor Control Commn., 1970-73. Lectr. various ednl. instns. Chmn. Village Cancer Dr., 1963-64; mem. West Suburban Cancer Bd., 1965-66; mem. Melrose Park Library Bd., 1959-63. Chmn. Cook County Young Republicans, 1959; mem. Young Rep. Jr. Nat. Com., 1961; mem. Young Rep. Nat. Exec. Bd., 1961-62; chmn. Ill. Crime Investigating Commn., 1966-69. Served to capt. AUS, 1953-57. Recipient Abraham Lincoln award Ill. Bar Assn., 1964; named one of ten outstanding young men in Chgo., 1959, 65. Mem. Am. (mem. com. on regulation consumer credit), Ill. (pres.

1975-76, gov. 1969—), Chgo. (bd. mgrs. 1965-67) bar assns., Ill. Consumer Finance Assn. (pres. 1971, chmn. bd. 1973—), Justinian Soc. Lawyers (past pres.). Home: 525 Auvergne Pl River Forest IL 60305 Office: 105 W Madison St Chicago IL 60602

PUSTELL, JOHN FRANCIS, tool co. exec.; b. Detroit, July 23, 1913; s. Stanley Anthony and Julia P.; grad. Henry Ford Trade Sch., 1931, Henry Ford Apprentice Sch., 1934; m. Matilda Rose, June 19, 1937; children—J. Thomas, Linda (Mrs. Edgar Capp, Jr.). With Ford Motor Co., 1931-45, asst. quality control mgr., 1940-45; partner PM Tool Co., 1940-46; partner PM Tool & Mfg. Co., Dearborn, Mich., 1946-54, pres., gen. adminstrv. officer, 1954—. Pres., Woodworth Heights Civic Assn., 1955-56. Trustee Dearborn Retarded Children Assn., Detroit Archdiocese Appraisal Center Funds, Inc. K.C., Order of Alhambra (past grand comdr.), Elk, Moose. Home: 233 Brentwood St Dearborn MI 48124 Office: 13121 Prospect St Dearborn MI 48126

PUSTMUELLER, DEBRA RUTH TYBERENDT, counselor; b. St. Louis, Feb. 10, 1953; d. Martin E. and Irma R. (Rixmann) Tyberendt; A.A., Kaskaskia Jr. Coll., 1973; B.A. in Psychology, Eastern Ill. U., 1975, M.S. in Edn., 1977; m. Stephen C. Pustmueller, Oct. 29, 1977. Student worker Warren G. Murray Devel. Center, Centralia, Ill., 1974-76; youth counselor Embarras River Basin Agy., Greenup, Ill., 1977—. Certified guidance counselor. Mem. Am. Personnel and Guidance Assn. Lutheran. Home: 1537 1st St Charleston IL 61920

PUTH, JOHN WELLS, mfg. co. exec.; b. Orange, N.J., Mar. 14, 1929; s. Lenard G. and Elizabeth (Wells) P.; B.S. cum laude, Lehigh U., 1952; m. Betsey Leeds Tait, Mar. 1, 1952; children—David Wells, Jonathan Craig, Alison Leeds. With United Advt. Corp., Newark, 1952-55, Purolator Products, Rahway, N.J., 1955-62; pres., dir. Bridgeport Hardware Mfg. Corp. (Conn.), 1962-65; v.p., div. gen. mgr. H.K. Porter Co., Inc., Pitts., 1965-72; pres., chief exec. officer Disston Inc., Pitts., 1972-75; pres., chief exec. officer, dir. Vapor Corp., Chgo., 1975—; dir. Red Devil Inc., Union, N.J., L.B. Foster Co., Pitts., Nihon Regulator, Japan. Home: 180 De Windt Rd Winnetka IL 60093 Office: 5420 W Howard St Niles IL

PUTKA, ANDREW CHARLES, city and county govt. ofcl.; b. Cleve., Nov. 14, 1926; s. Andrew George and Lillian M. (Koryta) P.; grad. John Carroll U., 1944, U.S. Naval Acad. 1945-46; A.B., Adelbert Coll., Western Res. U., 1949, LL.B., J.D., 1952. Admitted to Ohio bar, 1952, since practiced in Cleve.; instr. govt. Notre Dame Coll. for Women, South Euclid, Ohio, lectr. state and local govt., 1954-58; supt. div. bldg. and loan assns. Ohio Dept. Commerce, 1959-63; pres., chmn. bd., chief exec. officer Am. Nat. Bank, Parma, Ohio, Cleve., 1963-69; dir. finance City of Cleve., 1971-74, dir. port control, 1974—. Mem. Ohio Ho. of Reps. from Cuyahoga County, Cleve., 1953-56; mem. Ohio Sen., 1957-58; dep. auditor, acting sec. Bd. Revision. Cuyahoga County, 1970-71; mem. exec. com. Cuyahoga County Dem. Com., 1963—. Bd. govs. Sch. Law, Western Res. U. Mem. exec. com. World Student Service Fund, 1950-52; U.S. rep. Internat. Pax Romana Congress, Amsterdam, Holland, 1950, Toronto, Can., 1952; mem. lay adv. bd. Notre Dame Coll., trustee Case-Western Res. U. Voted an outstanding legislator by Ohio Press Corrs., 1953; named to All-Star legislative team by Ohio newspaper corrs., 1955, named one of Fabulous Clevelanders. Mem. Am., Ohio, Cuyahoga County, Cleve. bar assns., Nat. Assn. State Savs. and Loan Suprs. (nat. pres. 1962-63), U.S. Savs. and Loan League (legislative com. 1960-63), Am. Legion, Ohio Municipal League (trustee 1973), Parma C. of C. (dir., treas. 1965-67), Newman Fedn. (nat. pres. 1951-53), Nat. Assn. Christians and Jews, Catholic Lawyers Guild (treas.), Am., Ohio bankers assns., Am. Inst. Banking, Adelbert Alumni Assn. (exec. com.), Internat. Order of Alhambra (internat. parliamentarian 1971—, past grand comdr., Supreme Advocate 1973—), Pi Kappa Alpha, Delta Theta Phi (parliamentarian, pres. Cleve. alumni senate 1960-61, Master Inspector 1975—). K.C. (4 deg.). Home: 17013 Scottsdale Blvd Shaker Heights OH 44120 Office: Cleveland Hopkins Internat Airport Cleveland OH 44135

PUTNAM, CLYDE CHARLES, JR., lawyer; b. Iowa City, June 30, 1911; s. Clyde C. and Clara F. (Rittenmeyer) P.; student U. Iowa, 1931; LL.B., Drake U., 1934; m. Dorothy Rolofson, May 5, 1946; children—Tom, Kim. Admitted to Iowa bar, 1934; partner Putnam, Putnam & Putnam, Des Moines, 1934—. Mem. Mayor's Com. Civil Def., Des Moines, 1958. Served with AUS, 1942-46. Mem. Internat. Assn. Ins. Counsel, Iowa Acad. Trial Lawyers, Iowa Def. Lawyers Assn., Iowa (bd. govs. 1972—, jud. nominating commn. 1968—), Polk County (pres. 1970-71) bar assns., Iowa Res. Officers Assn. (pres. 1949). Mason (Shriner). Home: 1919 56th St Des Moines IA 50310 Office: 940 Des Moines Bldg Des Moines IA 50309

PUTNAM, DAVID ARMS, computer co. exec.; b. Mpls., Mar. 31, 1937; s. Norcross and Ruth Ann (Vigoren) P.; B.S., Beloit Coll., 1959; M.S., U. Iowa, 1962; m. Karen Maria Nielsen, June 18, 1960; children—Steven, Jeffrey, Kenneth. Tchr. schs., Chgo. and Iowa City, Iowa, 1959-64; systems analyst Univac, 1964-65; mgr. design data processing Lear Siegler, Inc., Grand Rapids, Mich., 1965-68; v.p. L. and H. Computer Co., Chgo., 1968-70; dir. computer info. services U.S. League of Savs. Assns., Chgo., 1970-76; dir. data shops Systems Mgmt. Inc., Chgo., 1976—; tchr. computer sci. Roosevelt U., 1973; mem. nat. review bd. Nat. Home Study Council, 1973-74. Mem. Data Processing Mgmt. Assn., Soc. Certified Data Processers, SAR. Author home study course Computer Programming Concepts, 1968. Creator BIO-CURVE R method of computerized biorhythmic analysis, 1971. Home: 6525 Taylor Dr Woodridge IL 60515 Office: SMI Data Shop 111 E Wacker Dr Chicago IL 60601

PUTNAM, THEODORE DELANO, educator; b. Waynesville, N.C., Mar. 1, 1944; s. Robert Edward Lee and Esther (Buchanan) P.; B.S., Maryville Coll., 1966; M.S., Auburn U., 1968; m. Phyllis Mae Sauerbrey, Aug. 27, 1966; children—Theodore Delano, Jelena Mae. Instr. chemistry Ohio No. U., Ada, 1968-71, asst. prof. chemistry, dir. chemistry labs., 1971—. Dir. High Sch. Chemistry Bowl N.W. Ohio, Ada, 1974. Mem. Am. Chem. Soc. (sec.-treas. N.W. Central Ohio sect. 1975, chmn. 1977), Am. Inst. Chemists. Methodist. Club: Rotary (v.p. 1976-77, sec.-treas. dist. 1977). Home: PO Box 45 Ada OH 45810

PUTNEY, RICHARD WALLINGTON, realtor; b. Lincoln, Nebr., June 7, 1921; s. Fred Wallington and Cornelia (Frazier) P.; B.A., U. Nebr., 1944; m. Rae-Hope Quimby, May 31, 1943; children—Ray, Ronald, Polly. Vice pres. Hwy. Equipment & Supply Co., Lincoln, 1958-60, pres., 1960-63; broker, appraiser Harrington Assos., Inc., Lincoln, 1964—. Served with USAF, 1943-46. Mem. Lincoln Bd. Realtors. Mem. Nebr. Realtors Assn., Nat. Assn. Realtors. Mem. Ch. Disciples of Christ (deacon). Home: 4410 Stockwell St Lincoln NE 68506 Office: 107 Wedgewood Dr Lincoln NE 68510

PUTTERMAN, ALLEN MICHAEL, ophthalmologist, oculoplastic surgeon; b. Beloit, Wis., May 19, 1938; s. Mayer Leon and Mollie Tankel P.; B.S., U. Wis., 1960, M.D., 1963; m. Jacqueline Orner, Dec. 23, 1962; 1 dau., Jill Tracy. Intern, Cook County Hosp., Chgo., 1963-64; resident ophthalmology Michael Reese Hosp., Chgo., 1966-69; oculoplastic surgery fellow Manhattan Eye and Ear and Throat Hosp., N.Y.C., 1969; asso. prof., chief oculoplastic surgery service U. Ill. Eye and Ear Infirmary, Chgo., 1970—; pvt. practice ophthalmology and oculoplastic surgery Chgo., 1970—; cons. in field. Served to capt. USAF, 1964-66. Fellow A.C.S., Am. Soc. Ophthalmic Plastic and Reconstructive Surgery, Am. Acad. Ophthalmology and Otolaryngology, Am. Assn. Cosmetic Surgery, Am. Soc. Ocularists; mem. AMA, Ill., Chgo. med. socs., Chgo. Ophthalmol. Soc. Contbr. articles to profl. publs. Home: 1555 N Sandburg Terr Chicago IL 60610 Office: 111 N Wabash Ave Chicago IL 60602

PUTZ, LOUIS J., pub. co. exec., diocesan adminstr., clergyman; b. Simbach, Germany, June 1, 1909; s. Ludwig and Anna (Leidmann) P.; A.B., U. Notre Dame, 1932; S.T.B., Institut Catholique, Paris, France, 1936; LL.D., U. Portland, 1959; H.H.D., St. Mary's Coll., Notre Dame, Ind., 1970. Came to the U.S., 1923. Joined Congregation Holy Cross Fathers; ordained priest Roman Catholic Ch.; asso. prof. theology U. Notre Dame, Notre Dame, Ind., 1940-66; rector Moreau Sem., 1966-72; dir. Family Life Services Diocese Fort Wayne-South Bend, Ind., 1972—; pres., chmn. bd. Fides Pub. Co., Notre Dame. Nat. co-chmn. Christian Family Movement; active Young Christian Students, Young Christian Women, Modern Apostles. Home: 309 S Taylor St South Bend IN 46625 Office: 120 S Taylor St South Bend IN 46601

PYLE, BEATRICE ALZIRA, educator; b. West Chester, Pa., May 21, 1922; d. Norman James and Audrey (Dilks) Pyle; B.S., Gettysburg Coll., 1944; M.S. in Hygiene and Phys. Edn., Wellesley Coll., 1946; certificate U. Oslo, (Norway), 1960. Instr. Gettysburg Coll., 1943-44, Vassar Coll., 1946-52; tchr. pub. schs., Winnetka, Ill., 1952-57; asso. prof. phys. and health edn. Miami U., 1957—. Mem. Am. Pub. Health Assn., Royal Soc. Health Assn., Royal Soc. Health Can. and Eng., Nat., Ohio edn. assns., AAHPER (chairperson aquatic council), Ohio Coll. Assn. Am. Camping Assn., AAUW. author textbooks. Home: 119 N Campus Ave Oxford OH 45056

PYLE, H(ERBERT) WAYNE, educator, musician; b. Ottawa, Ill., Oct. 24, 1921; s. Herbert W. and Violet Evelyn (Stephens) P.; Mus.B., Ill. Wesleyan U., 1943; Mus.M., Northwestern U., 1956; m. Riva Betty Hoff, July 10, 1943; children—Gary, Terry, Wendy. Dir. instrumental and vocal music Mazon (Ill.) Elementary and Twp. High Schs., 1946-49; dir. instrumental music and orchs. Quincy (Ill.) Pub. Schs., 1949—. Violinist, violist Quincy Symphony Orch. and Ensemble, 1949—; instr. string instrument methods and violin repertory and performance Quincy Coll., 1956-61; instr. condr. Summer Youth Music, U. Ill., 1959-66, 72, Ill. Wesleyan U., 1960, 61, Western Ill. U., 1966, So. Ill. U., Carbondale, 1966, 67, 71; coop. instr. student tchrs. various univs.; orch. rep. Nat. Interscholastic Activities Commn., also Ill. High Sch. Assn., 1957-61. Served with USAAF, 1943-46. Mem. Internat. Soc. Music Edn., NEA, Ill. Edn. Assn., Nat. Sch. Orch. Assn. (pres. 1967-69), Am. Chamber Music Players, Am. String Tchrs. Assn. (dist. pres. 1960-63), Ill. Music Educators Assn. (exec. bd. 1957-61, 1st state orch. chmn. 1964-67), Adams County Music Educators Assn. (pres. 1958-60), Pi Kappa Lambda, Phi Mu Alpha. Baptist (deacon, dir. choir and orch. 1949—). Home: 47 Granview Dr Quincy IL 62301 Office: 3322 Me St Quincy IL 62301

PYNE, ALVAN WESLEY, food co. exec.; b. Everett, Mass., Sept. 18, 1931; s. Herbert H. and Alma May (Butt) P.; A.B., Eastern Nazarene Coll., 1953; Ph.D. (Campbell fellow), Mass. Inst. Tech., 1962; m. Marie Evelyn Copeland, Sept. 3, 1954; children—Jeffrey Mark, Wesley Glenn, John David. Research chemist Kimberly-Clark Corp., Neenah, Wis., 1962-64; sr. research chemist Gen. Mills. Inc., Mpls., 1964-68, head research isolated protein program, 1968-69, mgr. research and devel. protein ops., 1969, mgr. research and devel. protein products, protein div., 1969-70, mgr. research and devel., protein products food service and protein products div., 1970; dir. corp. research and devel. Internat. Multifoods, Mpls., 1970, v.p. tech., 1971—. Mem. vis. com. Mass. Inst. Tech., 1972-75. Recipient Kirkpatrick Engring. award, 1969, Mem. Inst. Food Technologists, Am. Chem. Soc., Sigma Xi. Clubs: Wayzata Country, Mpls. Athletic. Patentee puffed fibrous food product. Home: 144 Edgewood Av Wayzata MN 55391 Office: Internat Multifoods 1200 Multifoods Bldg 8th and Marquette Minneapolis MN 55402

PYSH, JOSEPH JOHN, life scientist, educator; b. Olyphant, Pa., Nov. 14, 1935; s. John Andrew and Anna Mary (Marusin) P.; D.O., Chgo. Coll. Osteopathic Medicine, 1962; B.A., Wayne State U., 1963; Ph.D., Northwestern U., 1967; m. Margaret Ann Van Dusen, Aug. 1, 1969. Mem. faculty Northwestern U., Chgo., 1966—, asst. prof. anatomy, 1968-72, asso. prof. Med. Center, 1972—; NSF grant referee, 1974—; mem. neurol. research study sect. NIH, 1976-77. Named Basic Sci. Tchr. of Year, Northwestern U. Med. Sch., 1974; USPHS postdoctoral fellow, 1964-66; NIH grantee, 1969-72, 74—. Mem. AAAS (life), Am. Assn. Anatomists, Am. Soc. Cell Biology, Electron Microscopy Soc. Am., Soc. Neuroscience, Sigma Xi. Contbr. to profl. jours. Home: 535 Hinman St Evanston IL 60202

PYUN, SEONG KYUN, obstetrician, gynecologist; b. Seoul, Korea, Sept. 23, 1938; s. Woo Chang and Chung (Sook) P.; came to U.S., 1964, naturalized, 1976; M.D., Yonsei U. Coll. Medicine, 1964; m. Boo Whan Oh, Oct. 30, 1964; 2 daus., Jean, Sandra. Intern, Euclid (Ohio) Gen. Hosp., 1965; resident in obstetrics and gynecology, Wayne State U., Detroit, 1966-70; fellow dept. pathology, Hutzel Hosp., Detroit, 1971; program dir. St. Joseph Mercy Hosp., Detroit, 1971-73; practice medicine specializing in obstetrics and gynecology, St. Clair, Mich., 1973—; pres. profl. corp. Diplomate Am. Bd. Obstetricians and Gynecologists. Fellow Am. Coll. Obstetricians and Gynecologists; mem. AMA, St. Clair County, Mich. State Med. Socs., Mich. Soc. Obstetricians and Gynecologists. Club: Rotary (St. Clair). Home: 200 Hawthorne St Saint Clair MI 48079 Office: 132 Trumbull Saint Clair MI 48079

QADRI, SHANE HAIDER, elec. engr.; b. Abbottabad, Pakistan, Feb. 2, 1948; s. Motaqid Haider and Sardar (Begum) Q.; came to U.S., 1973; B.S. in Elec. Engring., Ind. Inst. Tech., 1975. Project engr. Nat. Oils Ltd., Karachi, Pakistan, 1966-72; tech. rep. A.B. Dick Co., Ft. Wayne, Ind., 1976-77; elec. design engr. B.F. Goodrich Co., Ft. Wayne, 1977—; instr. Ind. Vocat. Tech. Coll., 1977. Mem. IEEE, Soc. Automotive Engrs. (asso.). Home: 3910 Newport St Apt 10 Fort Wayne IN 46805 Office: B F Goodrich Co Woodburn IN 46797

QUAAL, WARD LOUIS, broadcasting exec.; b. Ishpeming, Mich., Apr. 7, 1919; s. Sigfred Emil and Alma Charlotte (Larson) Q.; A.B., U. Mich., 1941; LL.D., Mundelein Coll., 1962, No. Mich. U., 1967, DePaul U., 1974; D. Pub. Service (hon.), Elmhurst Coll., 1967; L.H.D., Lincoln Coll., 1968; m. Dorothy Graham, Mar. 9, 1944; children—Graham Ward, Jennifer Anne. Announcer, writer radio station WDMJ, Marquette, Mich., 1936-37; announcer, writer, producer WJR, Detroit, 1937-41; spl. events announcer-producer WGN, Chgo., 1941-42, asst. to gen. mgr., 1945-49; dir. Clear Channel Broadcasting Service, Washington, 1949-52; chief exec. officer, asst. gen. mgr. Crosley Broadcasting Corp., Cin., 1952, v.p., asst. gen. mgr., 1953-56; v.p., gen. mgr. WGN, Inc., Chgo., 1956-61, exec. v.p., pres., 1961-74; chmn. bd. United Telecom Corp., 1974—; pres. Ward L. Quaal Co., 1974—; dir. Christine Valmy, Inc., Universal Resources Corp.; dir. WLW Radio, Inc., also chmn. exec. com.; pres., chief exec. officer Clear Channel Broadcasting Service, 1964-74; bd. dirs. Assn. Maximum Service Telecasters, Inc., 1954-73. Chmn. exec. com. Council for TV Devel., 1969-70; bd. dirs. Broadcasters Found.; bd. dirs. Chgo. Better Bus. Bur., chmn., 1964-65; pres., dir. Broadcast Pioneers, 1962-63; bd. dirs. Farm Found.; chmn. exec. com., dir., vice chmn. Research and Edn. Found., also nat. gov., immediate past chmn. Assn. Better Bus. Burs.; bd. dirs. Sears, Roebuck Found., 1970-73, Internat. Radio and Television Found.; mem. Ethics com. Am. Advt. Fedn.; mem. bd. control collegiate athletics U. Mich. Served as lt. USNR, 1942-45. Recipient Distinguished Alumnus award U. Mich., 1967; Washington honor medal Freedoms Found., 1969; named Broadcast Man of Year, 1968; Chgo. Advt. Club Man of Year, 1969; Ill. Broadcaster of Yr., Ill. Broadcasters Assn., 1973; recipient Distinguished Service award Nat. Assn. Broadcasters, 1973; Outstanding Achievement in Field of Communications award Brandeis U., 1973; Advt. Man of Yr. Golden medallion Chgo. Advt. Club, 1969; named Communicator of Yr., Jewish United Fund; recipient Key to Loyola, Loyola U., Chgo., 1971; named to Better Bus. Bur. Hall of Fame, 1975. Mem. Delta Tau Delta. Clubs: Mid-Am., Chicago; Lakeside Country (Hollywood, Calif.); Kenwood Golf and Country (Washington); Exmoor Country. Author: (with Leo A. Martin) Broadcast Management, 1968, (with James A. Brown) 2d edit., 1976. Home: 1706-D Northfield Sq Northfield IL 60093 Office: Suite 370 O'Hare Plaza 5725 E River Rd Chicago IL 60631

QUACKENBUSH, GERALD GLENN, dairy assn. exec.; b. Melrose, Wis., July 11, 1916; s. Ward Wesley and Bessie Valentine (Radcliffe) Q.; B.S., U. Wis., 1941; M.S., Purdue U., 1942, Ph.D., 1947; m. Margaret Lee McLean, Oct. 31, 1945; children—Joann, Robert, Kelly. Asst. prof. Mich. State U., East Lansing, 1947-51, asso. prof., 1951-57, prof. 1957-60; dir. market research and econs. Am. Dairy Assn., Chgo., 1960-71; dir. mktg. and econs. research United Dairy Industry Assn., Rosemont, Ill., 1972—. Served with USAAF, 1943-45. Mem. Am. Agrl. Econs. Assn., Am. Mktg. Assn., Phi Eta Sigma, Alpha Zeta, Sigma Xi. Author: (with Warren Vincent) Economics and Management in Agriculture, 1962. Home: 229 Fairfield Ave Elmhurst IL 60126 Office: United Dairy Industry Assn 6300 N River Rd Rosemont IL 60018

QUADRACCI, HARRY R., printing co. exec.; b. Racine, Wis., Nov. 17, 1913; s. Virgil and Pietta (Rompietti) Q.; m. Angeline Wierbe, Oct. 27, 1934; children—Harry V., Leonard, Thomas. Co-founder W.A. Krueger Co., Brookfield, Wis., 1934, exec v.p., 1944-71, pres. Brock & Rankin subs., 1965-71; chmn. bd. Quad/Graphics, Pewaukee, Wis., 1971—. Mem. Milw. Lithographers Club (past pres.), Milw. Racine Craftsmen Club, Lithographers Clinic. Club: Westmoor Country. Home: 7400 Maple Terrace Wauwatosa WI 53213 Office: W 224 N 3322 DuPlainville Rd Pewaukee WI 53072

QUALE, GLADYS ROBINA, historian, educator; b. Manistee, Mich., Jan. 10, 1931; d. Leslie Alexander and Gladys Robina (Dyer) Quale; B.A., U. Mich., 1952, M.A., 1953, Ph.D., 1957; postgrad. Columbia U., 1955-56. Instr. history Albion (Mich.) Coll., 1957-61, asst. prof., 1961-65, asso. prof., 1965-70, prof. history, 1970—. Mem. Albion W. Central Urban Renewal Adv. com., 1966-68; mem. Albion City Planning commn., 1971-73. AAUW fellow, 1955-56; Carnegie Found. fellow, 1961-62; Ford Found. fellow, 1966-67; Fulbright-Hays travel grantee, 1964; Albion Coll. Outstanding Faculty scholar, 1976; recipient Mich. Acad. Sci. Arts and Letters citation, 1968. Mem. Mich. Acad. Sci., Arts and Letters (chmn. Asian Studies sect. 1964-65), Great Lakes Colls. Assn. (bd. dirs. 1976—), Am. Hist. Assn., Assn. for Asian Studies, Middle E. Studies Assn., Am. Acad. Polit. and Social Scis., AAUP, AAUW, Phi Beta Kappa, Pi Lambda Theta, Phi Alpha Theta, Pi Beta Phi. Republican. Episcopalian. Author: Eastern Civilizations, 1966, 2d edit., 1975. Home: 404 E Erie St Albion MI 49224 Office: Albion Coll Albion MI 49224

QUALEY, CARLTON CHESTER, historian, educator; b. Spring Grove, Minn., Dec. 17, 1904; s. Ole O. and Clara (Knatterud) Q.; B.A., St. Olaf Coll., 1929; M.A., U. Minn., 1930; Ph.D., Columbia U., 1938; m. Elizabeth Frances Cummings, Apr. 29, 1933; children—John, Mary. From lectr. to asso. prof. history Bard Coll. of Columbia U., 1936-44, asso. prof. at univ., 1945-46, vis. summer prof., 1938-46; asso. prof. Swarthmore Coll., 1944-45; prof. Am. history Carleton Coll., 1946-67, Laird Bell prof. history, 1967-70, chmn. dept., 1960-67; research fellow Minn. Hist. Soc., St. Paul, 1970—; dir. Minn. Ethnic History Project, 1973-78; vis. prof. Northwestern U., summer 1951; vis. Coe prof. Am. history Stanford U., summer 1966; vis. prof. Cleve. State U., 1971-72, Carleton Coll., 1972, Augsburg Coll., 1976; part-time dir. Minn. Hist. Soc., 1947-48. Participant Minn. Russian Seminar, USSR, 1958, Internat. Congress Hist. Scis., Stockholm, 1960, San Francisco, 1975. Teaching fellow U. Minn., 1929-31, Shevlin fellow, 1931-32; Univ. fellow Columbia U., 1932-33; research grantee Hill Found., St. Paul, 1954-55; travel grantee Social Sci. Research Council, 1960; research grantee Am. Council Learned Socs., 1962-63; research grantee Huntington Library Jan.-Mar. 1968, Bush Found., 1973-75, Nat. Endowment Humanities, 1975-77. Mem. Immigration History Soc. (editor newsletter 1973—), Orgn. Am. Historians (mem. of nominating com. 1966-68), Am., Norwegian-Am. (bd. editors), Western hist. assns., Minn. Hist. Soc., AAUP. Unitarian. Author: Norwegian Settlement in the United States, 1938; Thorstein Veblen, 1968; On Being An Ethnic Historian, 1972; also articles on immigration, book revs. Home: 2110 Carter Ave St Paul MN 55108 Office: Minn Hist Soc St Paul MN 55101

QUANDT, DAVID MYLO, mech. engr.; b. Mpls., Aug. 9, 1946; s. Werner Frank and Grace H. (Hjelmstad) Q.; grad. St. Luke's Sch. Radiol. Tech., Fargo, N.D., 1968; B.S. in M.E., N.D. State U., 1971; m. Kristine Knutson, June 30, 1973; children—Brett David, Erik Todd. Sales engr. Schilling Trane, Indpls., 1972-73; project engr. Meridian Trane, Indpls., 1973-74, Paul R. Hosler, Inc., Indpls., 1974-75; project mgr. Stanley Consultants, Inc., Inopls., 1976—. Councilman Messiah Lutheran Ch., 1976—. Served with USAR, 1970-76. Registered profl. engr., Ino., Ky.; registered technician Am. Registry Radiol. Technologists. Mem. ASME, Nat., Ind. socs. profl. engrs., Profl. Engrs. in Constrn. (sec.), Indpls. Sci. and Engring. Found., Ind. Water Pollution Control Fedn. Home: 197 Sheffield Ct Danville IN 46122 Office: 5610 Crawfordsville Rd Indianapolis IN 46224

QUAST, GARY LYNN, oral surgeon; b. Hastings, Nebr., Nov. 8, 1939; s. Arthur John and Myrtle (Brown) Q.; student Augustana Coll., 1958-59; B.A., State U. Iowa, 1963, D.D.S., 1964, M.S., 1967; m. Susan Jane Hansow, Aug. 31, 1963; children—Wendy Sue, Kevin Jon. Intern, U. Iowa Med. Center, Iowa City, 1964-65; resident, 1966-68; practice dentistry specializing in oral and maxillofacial surgery, Omaha, 1967—; asst. prof. surgery U. Nebr. Coll. Medicine at Omaha, 1967—, asst. prof. oral surgery Coll. of Dentistry at Lincoln, 1970-71; pres. staff Children's Meml. Hosp., Omaha, 1971-72; mem. staffs Nebr. Meth. Hosp., Bishop Bergen Mercy Hosp., Immanuel Luth. Hosp., Clarkson Hosp., Veterans' Hosp., Univ. Hosp., Douglas County Hosp., Children's Hosp., Omaha, Mercy Hosp., Council Bluffs, Iowa, Jennie Edmundson Hosp., Council Bluffs. Recipient Fenton Meml. award Iowa Soc. Oral Surgeons, 1964. Diplomate Am. Bd. Oral Surgery. Mem. Am., Midwest, Nebr. (pres. 1970), Iowa socs. oral surgeons, Am. Soc. Dental Anesthesiology, Am. Acad. Oral Pathologists, AMA, Am., Nebr., Douglas County dental assns. Mason (32 deg.). Clubs: Porsche of America (Gt. Plains regional v.p. 1972—); Sports Car of America (Neb. region). Home: 3120 S 99th Ave Omaha NE 68124 Office: 220 N 89th St Omaha NE 68114

QUAY, QUENTIN Q., dentist, educator; b. Lincoln, Nebr., Feb. 3, 1914; s. Thomas Robert and Josephine L. (Wagner) Q.; D.D.S., U. Neb., 1941; m. Dorothy May Dworak, Oct. 19, 1956 (dec. Nov. 1976); children—Margaret Jo (Mrs. Harry Howard), Thomas Ray Keith, Kathy Lou (Mrs. Richard Ricker), Patti Sue (Mrs. Kevin Brummell). Gen. practice dentistry, Lincoln, 1945—; instr. restorative dentistry U. Nebr. Coll. Dentistry, 1965—. Served to lt. col. Dental Corps AUS, 1942-45. Mem. Am., Neb. dental assns., Am. Acad. Gold Foil Operators, Woodbury Study Club (nat. sec. 1971—), Delta Sigma Delta. Congregationalist. Home: 2919 S 25th St Lincoln NE 68502 Office: 400 N 27th St Lincoln NE 68503

QUAYLE, JAMES DANFORTH, Congressman; b. Indpls., Feb. 4, 1947; s. James C. and Corinne (Pulliam) Q.; B.A. in Polit. Sci., DePauw U., Greencastle, Ind., 1969; postgrad. Ind. U. Law Sch., 1970-74. m. Marilyn Tucker, Nov. 18, 1972; children—Tucker Danforth, Benjamin Eugene; Admitted to Ind. bar, 1974. Ct. reporter, pressman Huntington (Ind.) Herald-Press, 1965-69, asso. pub., gen. mgr., 19/4-/6; mem. Consumer Protection div. Atty. Gen.'s Office, 1970-71; adminstrv. asst. to Gov. Edgar Whitcomb, 1971-73; dir. Ind. Inheritance Tax Div., 1973-74; mem. 95th Congress from 4th Ind. Dist. Tchr. bus. law Huntington Coll., 1975. Mem. Ind., Huntington bar assns., Ft. Wayne Press Club, Hoosier State Press Assn., Huntington C. of C., Elks Club, Rotary Club. Home: 7 N Jefferson St Huntington IN 46750 Office: 1407 Longworth House Office Bldg Washington DC 20515

QUEEN, DANIEL, cons. elec. engr.; b. Boston, Feb. 15, 1934; s. Simon and Ida (Droker) Q.; student U. Chgo., 1951-54; m. Helen Pantazopoulos, Mar. 23, 1957; 1 son, Aaron Jacob. Quality control mgr. Magnacord, Inc., Chgo., 1955-57; project engr. Revere Camera Co., Chgo., 1957-62; dir. engring. for Amplivox products Perma Power Co., Chgo., 1962-70; prin. engr. Daniel Queen Assos., Chgo., 1970—; chmn. Am. Nat. Standards Subcom. PH 7-6; mem. standards com. P8-5 Electronic Industries Assn. Bus. mgr. 5300-5500 Gladys Block Club, Chgo., 1970—. Fellow Audio Engring. Soc.; mem. IEEE (sr.), Am. Nat. Standards Inst. (S-4 and PH-7 com.), Audio Engring. Soc., Acoustical Soc. Am. (vice chmn. Chgo. regional chpt. 1975-77, mem. engring. acoustics com.) Midwest Acoustics Conf. (pres. 1971-72), Chgo. Acoustical and Audio Group (pres. 1969-70), Assn. Ednl. Communications and Tech., Soc. Motion Picture and TV Engrs. (mem. audio rec. and reprodn. com.). AAAS, Catgut Acoustic Soc. Contbr. editor Sound and Communications, 1973—. Patentee in field. Contbr. papers to profl. jours., also articles to trade and popular mags. Address: 5524 W Gladys Ave Chicago IL 60644

QUERY, JOY MARVES NEALE (MRS. WILLIAM T. QUERY), educator; b. Worcestershire, Eng., June 18, 1926; d. Samuel and Dorree (Oakley) Neale; came to U.S., 1952; A.B., Drake U., 1954, M.A., 1955; Ph.D., U. Ky., 1960; postgrad. U. Syracuse, 1955-56; m. William T. Query, June 1, 1956; children—Jonathan, Evan, Margaret. Tchr. secondary schs., Staffordshire, 1946-52; dep. prin. Smethwich Hall Girls' Sch., Staffordshire, 1948-52; instr. U. Ky., 1956-57, asst. prof., 1960; asso. prof. sociology and psychology Transylvania Coll., Lexington, Ky., 1961-66; asso. prof. N.D. State U., Fargo, 1966-68, prof. sociology and psychology, 1968—, chmn. dept. sociology and anthropology, 1968-73, acting chmn. dept. psychology, 1969-70; prof. behavioral scis. in medicine Med. Sch., U. N.D., Grand Forks, 1975—. Field dir. Girl Scouts U.S.A., 1953-55; bd. dirs. Fargo-Moorhead Family Service Agy. Fellow Inst. Social and Policy Studies, Yale, 1975. Fellow Internat. Assn. Social Psychiatry, Am. Sociol. Assn.; mem. Am., N.D. psychol. assns., AAUP, Midwestern Sociol. Soc. (bd. dirs. 1971-73, 75—), Marquis Biog. Library Soc., Alpha Kappa Delta. Unitarian (mem. ch. bd.). Contbr. articles to profl. jours. Home: 1202 Oak St N Fargo ND 58102

QUESNELL, JOHN GEORGE, social worker; b. Thief River Falls, Minn., Sept. 19, 1936; s. Lloyd W. and Fern (Collins) Q.; B.A., St. John's U., 1959; M.Social Work, U. Minn., 1961; m. Alice V. Lehar, June 6, 1959; children—Catherine, Michael, Timothy. With Hennepin County Dept. Ct. Services, Mpls., 1959-61; probation officer Mpls. Cath. Welfare Services, 1965—. Lectr. St. Paul (Minn.) Sem., 1968—. Served with USAF, 1961-64. Recipient Monsignor John O'Grady award Nat. Conf. Cath. Charities, 1967, 69. Mem. Nat. Assn. Social Workers. Nat. Council Family Relations. Am. Assn. Marriage and Family Counselors. Home: 3429 Stinson Blvd Minneapolis MN 55418 Office: 1653 Med Arts Bldg Minneapolis MN 55402

QUICK, GERALD NORMAN, electric and gas utility exec.; b. Centralia, Ill., July 24, 1927; s. Norvell Edgar and Josephine (Lottie) Q.; student Knox Coll., 1946-47; B.S. in Elec. Engring., U. Ill., 1950; m. Mary Lou Parrish, July 27, 1947; children—Charles Preston, Rebecca Kay, David Paul. Test engr. Wis. Steel Works, Chgo., 1950-51; with Ill. Power Co., Decatur, 1951—, service area engr., 1955-60, mgr. indsl. and comml. sales, 1960-70, service area mgr., Bloomington, 1970—. Dist. chmn. Boy Scouts Am. Bd. dirs. Jr. Achievement Central Ill., Bloomington Unltd., St. Joseph Hosp.; mem. Mennonite Hosp. Adv. Bd. Served with USNR, 1945-46. Mem. Petroleum Electric Power Assn. (dir. 1964-66, 68-70), McLean County Assn. Commerce and Industry (dir. 1971—). Clubs: Great Lakes Power (pres. 1965-66), Rotary (dir. 1977—). Home: Rural Route #2 Bloomington IL 61701 Office: 319 N Main St Bloomington IL 61701

QUICK, GUY HAYDEN, ins. co. exec.; b. Crawfordsville, Ind., May 4, 1920; s. Guy Hayden and Helen Naomi (Eltzroth) Q.; student Ill. State U., 1938-41; m. Martha Malinda March, Nov. 6, 1942; children—Guy Hayden, III, Jeffry March, Jean Marie. Joined Chem. Corps, U.S. Army, 1942, commd. 2d lt., 1943, advanced through grades to lt. col., 1962; faculty Army Bomb Disposal Sch., 1943-46; bomb disposal officer JTF-1, Bikini atomic bomb tests, 1946; asso. prof. mil. sci. Hofstra Coll., Hempstead, N.Y., 1951-55; sr. ammunition advisor Republic of Korea Army, 1955-57; ops. officer, insp. gen.'s office Def. Atomic Support Agy., Sandia Base, N.Mex., 1957-59; chief tech. inspection div., insp. gen.'s office Hdqrs. U.S. Army Pacific, Ft. Shafter, Hawaii, 1959-63, ret., 1963; with Fireman's Fund Ins. Cos., St. Louis, 1964-70, Davenport, Iowa, 1970-73, Detroit, 1973—, mgr. loss control depts., 1970—; mem. Mayor's Explosive Safety Commn., Florissant, Mo., 1968-70; pres. Scott County (Iowa) Safety Council, 1972-73. Certified safety profl.; registered profl. engr., Calif. Mem. Am. Soc. Safety Engrs. (profl. mem.), Vets. of Safety, Nat. Safety Mgmt. Soc., Nat. Fire Protection Assn., Nat. Safety Council, Ret. Officers Assn., Am. Def. Preparedness Assn., Nat. Assn. Watch and Clock Collectors. Home: 31207 Kendall St Livonia MI 48154 Office: 23777 Greenfield Rd Southfield MI 48075

QUICK, JOHN LOWELL, pharm. exec.; b. San Diego, Calif., Aug. 9, 1944; s. John Biery and Adele (Lowell) Q.; B.A. in Chemistry, Ind. U., 1966; M.B.A., Northwestern U., 1972; m. Carol Sue Burke, Nov. 16, 1968; children—John Patrick, James Michael. Staff asst. Baxter Co., Morton Grove, Ill., 1969-73, mgr. biomed. engring., 1973-74; mgr. biomed. engring. Travenol Co., Round Lake, Ill., 1974-76, group mgr. biomed. engring., 1976—; speaker high sch. careers. Commr. Buffalo Grove Zoning Bd. Appeals, 1972—. Recipient citation, Outstanding Performance award, Early Bird award, Crusade Mercy, 1973. Methodist. Patentee in field. Home: 491 Castle Wood Ln Buffalo Grove IL 60090 Office: Rt 120 and Wilson Rd Round Lake IL 60073

QUIE, ALBERT HAROLD, congressman; b. nr. Dennison, Minn., Sept. 18, 1923; s. Albert K. and Nettie (Jacobson) Q.; B.A. in Polit. Sci., St. Olaf Coll., 1950; hon. degrees St. Olaf Coll., Greenville Coll., Gettysburg Coll., Buena Vista Coll., Capital U., Gallaudet Coll.; m. Gretchen Hansen, June 6, 1948; children—Fredric, Jennifer, Daniel, Joel, Benjamin. Dairy Farmer; mem. Minn. Senate, 1955, 57; mem. 85th-95th Congresses from 1st Minn. dist.; mem. com. edn. and labor, standards of ofcl. conduct com. Past soil conservation dist. dir. Named Young Man of Yr., Minn. Jr. C. of C., 1957; recipient Distinguished Alumni award, St. Olaf Coll., 1963, Legislative Statesmanship award Council For Exceptional Children, 1968, Ann. award Nat. Council Local Adminstrs., 1971, citation Am. Vocat. Assn., 1972, Distinguished Govt. award Minn. Speech and Hearing Assn., others; named Distinguished Citizen of Agr., Nat. Milk Producers Fedn., 1974. Republican. Home: Dennison MN 55018 Office: Rayburn House Office Bldg Washington DC 20515

QUILTY, FLORENCE ELIZABETH MACINNIS (MRS. FRANCIS C. QUILTY), physician; b. Bowdle, S.D.; d. Austin Edward and Ella (Juntilla) MacInnis; student St. Mary's Coll., Notre Dame U., 1920-22; B.S. in Medicine, Marquette U., 1927, M.D., 1928; m. Francis C. Quilty, Sept. 8, 1951. Intern, St. Anthony's Hosp., Terre Haute, Ind.; resident Wis. Anti-Tb Assn., 1928-41; dir. Tb, Milw. Health Dept., 1941-44; practice medicine specializing in pulmonary diseases, Kansas City, Mo., 1944—, dir. pub. health Tb div. Tb Out-Patient Dept., Kansas City Gen. Hosp.; mem. staff St. Mary's Hosp., Research Hosp., Bapt. Hosp.; asso. clin. prof. medicine Mo. U., 1964—. Med. dir. Heart of Am. Tb Assn. Bd. dirs. Heart Assn., Social Health Soc. Recipient Dearholt medal Miss. Valley Tb Conf., 1965. Mem. Women's C. of C. Clubs: Soroptimist, Woman's City. Home: 609 Romany Rd Kansas City MO 64113 Office: 4620 JC Nichols Pkwy Kansas City MO 64112

QUINLAN, JOHN WILBERT, chiropractor; b. Dubuque, Iowa, Mar. 20, 1944; s. Raphael William and Genevieve Caroline (Timmerman) Q.; student Loras Coll., 1962-63, postgrad., 1971-72; D.C., Nat. Coll. Chiropractic, 1967, postgrad. in Roentgenology, 1972-75; student Northwestern Coll., La., 1969-70; m. Mary Susan Vogt, Aug. 5, 1967; children—John Patrick, Matthew John. Practice chiropractic, Dubuque, 1971—. Mem. exec. bd. Dubuque Children's Zoo, 1972—. Served with AUS, 1968-71; Vietnam. Decorated Bronze Star with three oak leaf clusters (U.S.); Cross of Gallantry (Vietnam); Ky. col. Mem. Iowa Chiropractic Soc. (sec. council on roentgenology 1975, pres. elect 1977-78), Am. Legion, Am. Fedn. Musicians. Democrat. Roman Catholic (extraordinary minister 1974—). Optimist (Outstanding Service award 1972-73). Home: 3258 St Anne Dr Dubuque IA 52001 Office: 630 Dubuque Bldg Dubuque IA 52001

QUINN, CHARLES LEWIS, judge; b. Garrett, Ind., Dec. 23, 1941; s. Franklin Charles and Goldie Ellen (Lewis) Q.; A.B., Manchester Coll., 1964; J.D., Ind. U., 1967. Admitted to Ind. bar, 1967, U.S. Supreme Ct. bar, 1973; mem. legal dept. Midwestern United Life Ins. Co., Fort Wayne, 1967-69; law clk. Allen Superior Ct., Fort Wayne, 1969; mem. firm Smith & Quinn, Auburn, Ind., 1969-75; judge Garrett (Ind.) City Ct., 1974-75, DeKalb County Ct., Auburn, Ind., 1976-77, DeKalb Superior Ct., Auburn, 1977—. State chmn. Ind. Young Republicans, 1973-75; chmn. adminstrv. bd. Garrett United Meth. Ch., 1977—; trustee Garrett Library, 1977—, Auburn Community Thetre; mem. exec. com. No. Ind. Health Systems Agy., Inc. Recipient Bronze and Silver medallions Northeast Ind. Heart Fund Drive. Mem. Ind. Judges Assn. DeKalb County (past pres.), Ind., Am. bar assns., Nat. Trust Historic Preservation, Manchester Coll. and Ind. U. Alumni assns. Bd. dirs. Big Brothers and Sisters NE Ind., 1974-75. Republican. Methodist. Home: 115 Clark St Garrett IN 46738 Office: Court House Auburn IN 46706

QUINN, JAMES LELAND, III, physician; b. Pitts., July 12, 1933; s. James Leland, Jr. and Mary (Dunn) Q.; B.S., Belmont Abbey Coll., 1955, LL.D., 1973; M.D., Bowman Gray Sch. Medicine, 1959; m. Mary Jacqueline Leonard, Jan. 9, 1960; children—Megan Ann, Michelle Diane, James Leland IV, Michael Dennis; m. 2d, Marie Magdalene Boschman, Aug. 26, 1973. Intern, Pa. Hosp., Phila., 1959-60; resident radiology N.C. Baptist Hosp., Winston-Salem, 1960-63, dir. nuclear medicine, 1963-64; instr. radiology Bowman Gray Sch. Medicine, 1963-64; practice medicine, specializing in radiology, Chgo., 1964—; dir. nuclear medicine Northwestern Meml. Hosp., 1964—; asst. prof. radiology Northwestern U., 1964-66, asso. prof., 1966-68, prof., 1968—, asso. chmn., 1974—; expert Panel on Radiation Medicine, WHO, 1975—. Named Outstanding Young Man of Am., 1966. Hon. fellow Royal Coll. Surgery (Ireland); fellow Am. Coll. Radiology; mem. A.M.A., Assn. U. Radiologists, Soc. Nuclear Medicine (trustee, v.p. Central chpt., nat. pres. 1971-72), Radiol. Soc. N. Am., Am. Roentgen Ray Soc., Soc. Clin. Research, Alpha Omega Alpha. Democrat. Roman Catholic. Editor: Scintillation Scanning in Clinical Diagnosis, 1964; Yearbook of Nuclear Medicine, 1964—. Contbr. articles to profl. jours. Home: 1448 N Lake Shore Dr Chicago IL 60610 Office: 250 E Superior St Chicago IL 60611

QUINN, ROBERT HENRY, surgeon; b. Omaha, July 3, 1919; s. Henry T. and Esther (Hecklin) Q.; B.S., Creighton U., 1941, M.D., 1943; m. Ruth Elizabeth Binder, Aug. 1, 1942; children—Karen Quinn Tufty, Terence Robert, Thomas Henry, Lisa Ann. Intern, St. Josephs Hosp., Denver, 1943-44; gen. practice medicine, Sioux Falls, S.D., 1946-54, specializing in surgery, 1958—; fellow surgery Ochsner Found., New Orleans, 1954-58; clin. prof. surgery U. S.D. Med. Sch., 1958—, now asso. dean; med. dir. Atlas Life Ins. Co., 1960-63; chmn. adv. com. Regional Med. Planning Nebr., S.D., 1969—. Pres., Sioux Falls chpt. Am. Cancer Soc.; bd. dirs. Sioux council Boy Scouts Am. Served to lt. M.C., USNR, 1944-46. Fellow A.C.S. (past chpt. pres.); mem. AMA (del.), S.D. (pres.), N. Central (pres.) med. assns., Ochsner Surg. Soc., Sioux Falls C. of C., Alpha Omega Alpha, Alpha Sigma Nu, Phi Chi. Republican. Roman Catholic. Clubs: Rotary, K.C. Home: 233 E 30th St Sioux Falls SD 57105 Office: 250 W 22d St Sioux Falls SD 57101

QUINN, ROBERT J., city ofcl.; b. Chgo., May 12, 1905; s. Patrick James and Nellie (O'Boyle) Q.; student evening coll. Entire career with Chgo. Fire Dept., commr., 1957-78. Mem. Chgo. Mayor's Cabinet, 1957—. Bd. dirs. Hemophilia Found. Served with U.S. Navy, 1923; from lt. to comdr. USNR, 1940-45. Decorated Army and Navy medal. Roman Catholic. Home: 300 N State St Chicago IL Office: City Hall Chicago IL 60602

QUINN, ROBERT LITTEN, lawyer; b. Mingo Junction, Ohio, June 9, 1906; s. Robert S. and Mary Virginia (Litten) Q.; A.B., Ohio Wesleyan U., 1928; J.D., U. Mich., 1931; m. Margaret C. Collins, Dec. 9, 1933; children—Mary (Mrs. James Schafer), Robert C. Admitted Ohio bar, 1931; practiced in Steubenville, 1931—; mem. firms Huston, Quinn & Weinman, 1931-43, Kinsey & Allebrugh, 1943-65, Weinman, Downer, Quinn, Adulewicz & Kerr, Steubenville, 1965—; dir., gen. counsel Ohio Valley Savs. and Loan Assn., Steubenville. U.S. Commr., 1932-36; mem. Ohio Ho. Reps., 1943-44; mem. Ohio Senate, 1947-48. Bd. dirs. Ohio Valley Hosp. Fellow Am., Ohio (mem. exec. com. 1961-64) bar assns.; mem. Jefferson County Bar Assn. (pres. 1941). Mason, Elk. Clubs: University (Pitts.); Williams Country (Weirton, W. Va.); Steubenville Country. Author: (with R.L. Smith) Arells Conversions, 1951. Home: 140 Sharmont Dr Steubenville OH 43952 Office: 600 Ohio Valley Towers Steubenville OH 43952

QUINTANILLA, ANTONIO PAULET, physician, educator; b. Peru, Feb. 8, 1927; s. Leandro Marino and Edel Paulet Q.; came to U.S., 1963, naturalized, 1974; Ph.D., San Marcos U., 1948, M.D., 1957; m. Mary Parker Rodriguez, May 2, 1958; children—Antonio Paulet, Angela, Francis, Cecilia, John. Asso. prof. physiology Univ. Arequipa, Peru, 1960-63; asso. in physiology Cornell Univ., N.Y., 1963-64; prof. physiology Univ. Arequipa, 1964-68; asso. prof. medicine Northwestern Univ., 1969—; chief renal sect. VA Lakeside Hosp., 1976—; mem. advisory bd. Kidney Found. Ill., Am. Fedn. Clin. Research. Fellow Am. Coll. Physicians; mem. Chgo. Heart Assn. (hypertension council), Central Soc. for Clin. Research, Am. Soc. Clin. Pharmacology and Therapeutics, Am., Internat. Soc. Nephrology, Chgo. Soc. Internal Medicine. Contbr. articles on renal disease to med. jours. Home: 500 Ridge Ave Evanston IL 60202 Office: 333 E Huron St Chicago IL 60611

QUINTERO, CESAR, computer services co. exec.; b. Cali, Columbia, Aug. 12, 1942; s. Jose Ramon and Carolina (Cifuentes) Q.; came to U.S., 1964; student Colegio Villegas, Cali, 1960, N.Y. U., 1965, U. Md. Extension, 1966-67, Chgo. City Coll., 1969-70, DuPage U., 1974-75. With IBM of Colombia, 1961-62, Empresas Municipales de Cali, 1962-64; asso. rep. programming staff Burroughs Corp., Chgo., 1969-71; co-founder, co-owner, pres. L-Data Corp., Clarendon Hills, Ill., 1971—. Mem. Latin Am. C. of C. (charter mem. Chgo.). Roman Catholic. Home: 4522 Lee St Downers Grove IL 60515 Office: 6347 Clarendon Hills Rd Clarendon Hills IL 60514

QUIRK, JANE HELEN WAGNER, employment counselor; b. Eagle River, Wis., Jan. 18, 1915; d. William Walter and Sarah Ann (Carter) Wagner; student Oshkosh State Tchrs. Coll., 1934-35, Am. U., 1944, Chgo. U. Extension, 1948, Purdue U. Extension, 1965, 68; m. Neil A. Hall, Sept. 17, 1934 (div. May 1939); 1 son, Carter Lee (dec.); m. 2d, John J. Quirk, Jan. 25, 1949 (div. Oct. 1955); 1 dau., Sarah Jane. Jr. welfare worker, employee relations counselor Selective Service System, Washington, 1942-46; personnel counselor Western Electric Co., Chgo., 1946-49; exec. sec. speakers bur. Indpls. chpt. ARC, 1950-51; editor, personnel dir. Monument Engring. Co., Indpls., 1952-55; employee publs. mgr. Internat. Tel. & Tel. Kellogg, Chgo., 1960-61; editor Buehler Corp., Indpls., 1955-60, pub. relations mgr. 1961-71; dir. advt. Review Pub., 1971-73; placement interviewer Ind. Employment Security Div., Indpls., 1973—. Mem. Community Service Council, Indpls., 1968—; mem. women's council Indian Lake Devel. Assn., 1970. Recipient Hon. awards Nat. Found. March of Dimes, 1964-68, certificate of merit United Fund, 1968, 69. Mem. Ind. Indsl. Editors Assn. (Best Newspaper award 1969, pres. 1965), Internat. Council Indsl. Editors (exec. bd. 1964-65), Ind. Mfrs. Assn. (mem. pub. relations com. 1968-70), Indpls. C. of C. Home: 7023 Indian Lake N Dr Indianapolis IN 46236 Office: 6350 E 82d St Indianapolis IN 46250

QUO, PHILLIP C., engring. co. exec., educator; b. Fukien, China, Oct. 4, 1930; came to U.S., 1956, naturalized, 1974; m. Consuelo Perez, Aug. 5, 1932; children—Marcia Ann, Stacey Dagmar, Geoffrey Quintin, Brian Christopher. LL.B., J.D., Nat. Amoy (China) U., 1949; B.S. in Mech. Engring., U. Kans., 1960, M.S. in Mech. Engring., 1965. Mech. designer, power plant div. Black and Beatch Cons. Engrs., Kansas City, Mo., 1960-64, project engr., 1964-66; lectr. Finley Engring. Coll., Kansas City, Mo., 1964-66; with A.M. Kinney, Inc., Cin., 1966—, dir. computing engring., 1966-75, acting dir. power and nuclear engring., 1968-70, v.p., 1975—; adj. lectr. U. Cin., 1968-71, adj. asso. prof., 1971-74, adj. prof. civil engring., 1974—. Mem. AAUP, Am. Nuclear Soc. (papers review and publs. com., power div., 1974—, Engring. Soc. Cin. (chmn. energy com., 1974-76, chmn. environ. profl. interest com. 1976—), ASME (dir. Cin. Sect., 1969-71, vice chmn., 1972-73, chmn., 1973-74, v.p. Ohio Council, 1974—, chmn. honors and awards com. Gt. Lake Region V, sr. del. nat. agenda conf., 1973-75, nat. policy bd. gen. engring. dept., 1974-76, policy bd. edn. dept., 1975—, nat. metric study com., 1975—, editor Metric News, 1975—, certificate of awards Nat. Council, 1974), Pi Tau Sigma, Sigma Tau, Alpha Sigma Lambda (hon.). Recipient citation Kansas City Internat. Club, 1959; citation Kansas City Jr. Achievement Assn., 1966, Profl. Accomplishment in Industry of Year award, Tech. and Sci. Socs. Council of Cin., 1976. Author: Introduction to Fortran Programming for Engineers, 1967; CPM and Network Diagramming, 1970; contbr. papers to profl. publs. Home: 12067 Deerhorn Dr Cincinnati OH 45240 Office: 2900 Vernon Place Cincinnati OH 45219 also Univ Cincinnati Cincinnati OH 45221

QUTUB, MUSA YACUB, scientist, educator; b. June 2, 1940; s. Yacub and Sarah (Ansari) Q.; came to U.S., 1960, naturalized, 1975; B.A., Simpson Coll., 1964; M.S., Colo. State U., 1966; Ph.D., Ia. State U., 1969; m. Abeer Hashem, Aug. 21, 1970; 1 dau., Hania. Instr. earth sci. Ia. State U., Ames, 1966-69; asst. prof. earth sci. Northeastern Ill. U., Chgo., 1970-72, asso. prof., 1972-77, prof., 1977—, chmn. dept. 1973-74. Cons. NSF, 1970—. Bd. dirs. Earth Sci. Consortium Project, 1971—, Earth Sci. Inst., 1969—, Environ. Sci. Research Center, 1973—, Earth Sci. Learning Project, 1971—; gen. chmn., organizer World Congress Resource Depletion, Energy Alternatives and the Quality of Life in the Year 2000, 1978. NSF grantee, 1970-75. Mem. Internat. Assn. for Advancement of Earth and Environmental Scis. (pres. 1972-75), Nat. Assn. Geology Tchrs., Nat. Sci. Tchrs. Assn., Ill. Earth Sci. Assn. (pres. 1972-74), AAAS, Environ. Sci. Inst., Phi Delta Kappa. Editor: Environmental Resource Mag., 1974-75. Home: 780 Kenilworth Court Des Plaines IL 60016 Office: Northeastern Illinois University 5500 N St Louis Chicago IL 60625

RAACH, FRANCIS ANTHONY, mfg. co. exec., chemist, art gallery exec.; b. Kansas City, Mo., Oct. 4, 1926; s. Francis Anthony and Ethel Cecilia (Stephan) R.; B.S., Rockhurst Coll., 1947; postgrad. U. Calif. at Berkeley, 1947-49, U. Wash., 1951. Vice pres. RO Mfg. Co., Kansas City, Mo., 1950-55, pres., 1955—; chemist Remington Arms Co. Inc., Independence, Mo., 1951—; dir., owner Raach's Plaza Gallery and Raach's Ringstrassa Gallery, Kansas City, 1963—, Raach's Minn. Gallery, 1963—; buyer European art, exporter Kansas City art, 1953—; partner Raach's Galleries Inc., Kansas City, 1957-63; art appraiser, critic, judge; cons. probate, travel, chems.; lectr. U.S. and Europe. Mem. Am. Soc. Metals, Am. Chem. Soc., Am. Indsl. Hygiene Assn., ASTM, Kansas City Friends of Art, Jackson County (Mo.) Hist. Soc. Set up exhbns. of Midwest artists in Europe; promotes local artists in Midwest. Home: 630 W 50th St Kansas City MO 64112 Office: 303 W 47th St Kansas City MO 64112

RAATIKKA, THEODORE RICHARD, educator; b. Bruce Crossing, Mich., Aug. 19, 1923; s. Olli Alexander and Hilma Gustava (Olson) R.; B.S., Mich. State U., 1956, M.A. (Fellow), 1957; m. Anna Mae McIntyre, Mar. 15, 1947; 1 dau., Catherine Ann. Machine operator Cadillac Motor Co., Detroit, 1942-43; rehab. counselor State of Mich., Jackson, 1957-60, disability examiner, Lansing, 1960-64; tchr. Everett High Sch., Lansing, 1964-65; spl. edn. tchr. Durand (Mich.) Area High Sch., 1965—. Served with U.S. Army, 1943-46; PTO. Mem. Am. Personnel and Guidance Assn., Nat. Rehab. Assn., NEA,

Mich., Durand edn. assns. Home: 404 N Oak St Durand MI 48429 Office: 9575 Monroe Rd Durand MI 48429

RABB, GEORGE B., zoologist; b. Charleston, S.C., Jan. 2, 1930; s. Joseph A. and Teresa C. (Redmond) R.; B.S., Coll. Charleston, 1951; M.A., U. Mich., 1952, Ph.D., 1957; m. Mary Sughrue, June 10, 1953. Teaching fellow zoology U. Mich., 1954-56; curator, coordinator research Chgo. Zool. Park, Brookfield, Ill., 1956-64, asso. dir. research and edn., 1964-75, dep. dir., 1969-75, dir., 1976—; research asso. dept. psychology U. Chgo., 1960—; research asso. Field Mus. Natural History, 1965—; lectr. dept. zoology U. Chgo., 1965—, mem. Com. on Evolution Biology, 1969—. Fellow A.A.A.S.; mem. Am. Soc. Ichthyologists and Herpetologists (pres. 1978), Herpetologists League, Soc. Systematic Zoology, Soc. Mammalogists. Soc. Study Evolution, Ecol. Soc. Am., Chgo. Zool. Soc. (pres. 1976—), Am. Soc. Zoologists, Soc. Study Animal Behavior, Am. Assn. Museums, Am. Soc. Naturalists, Am. Assn. Zool. Parks and Aquariums, Internat. Union Dirs. Zool. Gardens, Sigma Xi. Office: Chgo Zool Park Brookfield IL 60513

RABBERS, NORMAN LLOYD, cons. engring. co. exec.; b. Kalamazoo, Dec. 31, 1925; s. Oscar Archibald and Nellie Heartha (Jones) R.; student Oberlin Coll., 1943-44; B.S. in Civil Engring., U. Mich., 1946; postgrad. Western Mich. U., 1946, Northwestern U., 1972—; m. Violet Marie Hornoff, Dec. 14, 1972; children by previous marriage—David, Kenneth, Thomas, Vicki. Hwy. engr. Mich. Hwy. Dept., Kalamazoo, 1946-47; civil engr. L.C. Kingscott & Assos., Kalamazoo, 1947-48; structural designer Sargent & Lundy, Chgo., 1948-50, structural engr., 1953-63; structural engr. F.G. Browne & Assos., Marion, Ohio, 1952-53; cons. engr., Chgo., 1963-64, 70-71; structural engr. Pioneer Service Engring. Co., Chgo., 1964-67; project mgr., dir. bus. devel. DeLeuw, Cather & Co., Chgo., 1967-70; project mgr. Mark Lovejoy & Assos., Burr Ridge, Ill., 1971-72; mgr. bus. devel., mgr. civil div. The Engrs. Collaborative, Chgo., 1972-73; project engr. Sargent & Lundy, Chgo., 1974—. Mem. exec. council Lake Mich. Fedn., 1972-73. Chmn. east central region exec. com. Y-Indian Guides, 1967; mem. Nat. Exec. Com. Y-Indian Guides, 1963-67; vice chmn. DuPage County (Ill.) Planning Council, 1967-68. Bd. dirs. B.R. Ryall YMCA, Glen Ellyn, Ill., 1963-71, chmn., 1969. Served with USMCR, 1943-46, 1950-52. Registered profl. engr., Ill., Ohio. Fellow ASCE (chmn. urban planning div. Ill. sect. 1969). Kiwanian. Home: 7921 Farmingdale Dr Darien IL 60559 Office: 55 Monroe St Chicago IL 60603

RABE, CHARLES CASTENS, coll. pres.; b. Steeleville, Ill., July 14, 1916; s. Charles H. and Emma (Castens) R.; student Valparaiso U., 1935-37; B.S. in Pharmacy, St. Louis Coll. Pharmacy, 1939; M.S., Mass. Coll. Pharmacy, 1950, D.Sc. (hon.), 1966; m. Martha Zority, June 12, 1948; children—Constance Anne, Pamela Martha. Sales rep. Merck, Sharp & Dohme, St. Louis, 1939-41, Warner-Lambert Co., Mo., Ill., Iowa, 1941-42; instr., asst. prof. St. Louis Coll. Pharmacy, 1942-48, asso. prof., 1950-54, pres., 1961—; teaching fellow Mass. Coll. Pharmacy, 1948-50; asst. to sec. Am. Pharm. Assn., Washington, 1954-57; mgr. profl. relations J.B. Roerig & Co., N.Y.C., 1957-61. Trustee O.J. Cloughly Ednl. Found., Pharmacists Ins. Trust. Recipient Distinguished Alumnus award Alumni Assn. St. Louis Coll. Pharmacy, 1963. Mem. Am. Pharm. Assn., Nat. Assn. Retail Druggists, Am. Coll. Apothecaries, A.A.A.S., Mo. Pharm. Assn., Internat. Pharm. Fedn., Kappa Psi, Rho Chi, Delta Sigma Theta. Republican. Presbyn. Clubs: University, Greenbriar Hills Country. Home: 530 Flanders Dr Warson Woods MO 63122 Office: 4588 Parkview Pl St Louis MO 63110

RABE, RICHARD FRANK, dentist, lawyer; b. Crystal Lake, Iowa, May 19, 1919; s. Otto Henry and Agnes Marie (Juhl) R.; A.A., Waldorf Luth. Coll., 1938; D.D.S., U. Iowa, 1942; J.D., Drake U., 1952; m. Barbara Jean McNeal, Mar. 15, 1946; children—Richard Frank, Mary Elizabeth, Kathleen Ann. Practice dentistry, Des Moines, 1946—; limited practice law, Des Moines, 1952—; cons. M.F. Patterson Dental Supply Co. div. Ritter Pfaudler Co., 1956-61; cons. Nat. Bd. Dental Examiners, 1955-60; chmn. bd. Iowa Dental Examiners, 1962; mem. Iowa Bd. Nursing Home Adminstrs., 1975—. Served to capt. Dental Corps, AUS, 1942-46. Fellow Am. Coll. Dentists; mem. Iowa (pres. 1973, trustee), Am. (council on legis. dental assns., Des Moines Dist. Dental Soc. (pres. 1955), Am. Bar Assn., Iowa Dental Study Club (past pres.), Am. Acad. Practice Adminstrn., Milw. Dental Research Group, Psi Omega, Delta Theta Phi. Episcopalian. Clubs: Masons Shriners, Kiwanis; Des Moines Golf and Country. Contbr. articles to profl. jours. Home: 5709 N Waterbury Rd Des Moines IA 50312 Office: 5731 Urbandale Ave Des Moines IA 50310

RABIN, JOSEPH HARRY, mktg. research co. exec.; b. Chgo., Dec. 12, 1927; s. Morris and Libby (Broder) Rabinovitz; B.C.S., Roosevelt U., 1950; M.B.A., DePaul U., 1951; m. Barbara E. Leader, Oct. 31, 1954; children—Marc Jay, Michelle Ann, Deborah Susan. Account exec. Gould, Gleiss & Benn, 1951-56; asst. dir. market research Paper Mate Co., Chgo., 1956-63; pres. Rabin Research Co., Chgo., 1963—. Pres. Mather High Sch. Council, 1972-74; bd. dirs. Market Research Inst., 1973, 74, Ner Tamid Synagogue, 1976—, Jewish Vocat. Service, 1977—. Served with AUS, 1946-47. Mem. Am. Mktg. Assn. (chpt. pres. 1961-62, nat. dir. 1973-75), Assn. Consumer Research, Am. Statis. Assn. (chpt. pres. 1962-63), Am. Assn. Pub. Opinion Research. Home: Apt 308 7061 N Kedzie Chicago IL 60645 Office: 520 N Michigan Ave Chicago IL 60611

RABINOVITZ, ADOLPH J., physician, pathologist; b. Chgo., July 3, 1927; s. Samuel and Esther Hannah (Callner) R.; A.A., Herzl Jr. Coll., 1946; B.S. in Chemistry, Roosevelt U., 1948; M.D., U. Ill., 1952; m. Miriam Pogrund, June 19, 1951; children—Esther Ann, Isaac Aaron, Rena Ruth, Don Joseph. Intern, Cook County Hosp., Chgo., 1952-53; resident in pathology, U. Ill. Research and Edn. Hosp., Chgo., 1953-54, 56-57, Augustana Hosp., Chgo., 1957-59; pathologist Lutheran Gen. Hosp., Park Ridge, Ill., 1959-60; research asso. dept. pathology Michael Reese Hosp., Chgo., 1961-63; asso. pathologist St. Anne's Hosp., Chgo., 1960-72, dir. labs., 1972-75; dir. labs. St. Elizabeth Hosp., Chgo., 1972-75; dir. clin. labs., dir. dept. nuclear medicine Augustana Hosp., Chgo., 1975—; clin. asst. prof. pathology U. Ill. Coll. Medicine, Chgo., 1964—. Served with AUS, 1946-47, USAF, 1954-56. Diplomate Am. Bd. Pathology, Am. Bd. Nuclear Medicine. Mem. AMA, Ill. State, Chgo. med. socs., Am. Soc. Clin. Pathologists, Coll. Am. Pathologists, Chgo. Pathol. Soc. Jewish. Book rev. staff Jour. AMA, 1977—. Home: 2844 West Touhy Ave Chicago IL 60645 Office: Augustana Hosp 441 W Dickens St Chicago IL 60614

RABKIN, ERIC S., humanist; b. Queens, N.Y., Mar. 8, 1946; s. Joseph and Annette (Schwartz) R.; A.B., Cornell U., 1967; Ph.D., U. Iowa, 1970; m. Elizabeth Jane Backer, July 1, 1967; children—David Ivan, Rachel Ann. Asst. prof. English, U. Mich., Ann Arbor, 1970-74, asso. prof., 1974-77, prof., 1977—; cons. in field. Am. Council Learned Socs. fellow, 1973; Horace H. Rackham faculty research grantee, 1973. Mem. Modern Lang. Assn., Popular Culture Assn. Author: Narrative Suspense, 1973; (with David Hayman) Form in Fiction, 1974; The Fantastic in Literature, 1976; (with Robert Scholes) Science Fiction: History, Science, Vision, 1977. Home: 1530 Hanover Ct Ann Arbor MI 48103

RACH, ROY DEAN, engr.; b. Edwardsburg, Mich., Apr. 24, 1930; s. Edward Carl and Edna Elberta (Dargin) R.; B.S. in Physics, Ind. U., 1971; m. Delores Ann Irvin, Nov. 24, 1951; children—Kathryn Ann, Thomas Dean, Karen Lynn. Product service mgr. Lab. Equipment Corp., St. Joseph, Mich., 1965-72; instrumentation engr. J.A. Jones Constrn. Co., Donald C. Cook Nuclear Plant, Bridgman, Mich., 1972-73; plant engr. Modern Plastics Corp., Benton Harbor, Mich., 1973-75; engring. and maintenance mgr. Dynac Corp., St. Joseph, 1975—; instr. Lake Mich. Coll., Benton Harbor; cons. Wightman Assos., St. Joseph. Served with USN, 1951-55. Registered profl. engr., Mich.; certified flight instr. Mem. Nat., Blossomland profl. engr. socs., Instrument Soc. Am., Am. Phys. Soc., Nat. Flight Instr. Assn. Baptist. Home: 1920 Brown School Rd Saint Joseph MI 49085 Office: 229 Kerth St Saint Joseph MI 49085

RACHELS, CHARLES THOMAS, lawyer; b. Griffin, Ind., Oct. 15, 1922; s. John Calvin and Stella (Hyatt) R.; A.B., Evansville (Ind.) Coll., 1952; LL.B., Ind. U., 1954; m. Jacqueline M. Faler, Mar. 22, 1942 (dec. 1976). Admitted to Ind. bar, 1954, U.S. Supreme Ct. bar, 1973; practiced in Mt. Vernon, 1954-77; pros. atty. 11th Jud. Circuit, Ind., 1968-77; mem. Ind. Gen. Assembly, 1955-56. Served with AUS, 1942-46. Mem. Ind. Pros. Attys. Council (dir. 1974-77), Mt. Vernon C. of C. (dir. 1956-58), Posey County Bar Assn. (pres. 1975-76), Am. Legion, Blind Vets. Am. Clubs: Masons, Lions, Elks. Home: 311 Mulberry St Mount Vernon IN 47620 Died Aug. 12, 1977.

RACHESKY, STANLEY ROBERT, entomologist; b. Red Bank, N.J., Feb. 28, 1939; s. Alex and Rose (Albert) R.; B.S. in Zoology, Kans. State U., 1963, M.S. in Entomology, 1966; m. Carole Prochazka, June 5, 1965; children—Peter, Stacey. Urban entomologist U. Ill. Co-op. Extension Service, Chgo., 1966—, pesticide adviser, 1966—, mass media coordinator, 1973—; cons. pesticides S. Rachesky & Assos., Bloomingdale, Ill., 1971—; instr. Coll. DuPage, Glen Ellyn, Ill., 1971, William Rainey Harper Jr. Coll., Palatine, Ill., 1972, Triton Jr. Coll., River Grove, Ill., 1973; lectr. entomology to various colls., clubs, 1966—; TV appearances Chgo. stas. WBBM, WGN, WLS and WMAQ, 1966—; mem. Ill. Turfgrass Found., 1966—. Mem. Sch. Bd. Dist. 13, Bloomingdale, 1973—. Served with M.C., AUS, 1958-60. Mem. Entomol. Soc. Am., Nat. Environ. Health Assn., Environ. Mgmt. Assn., Garden Writers Assn. Am., Ill. (cons. 1974—), Nat. pest control assns., Am. Forestry Assn., Ill. Mosquito Control Assn., Nat. Assn. County Agts. Am. (Feature Story award 1975), Ill. Landscape Contractors Assn. (exec. sec. 19—), Kans. Entomol. Soc., Pi Chi, Gamma Sigma Delta. Contbr. articles on research in pesticides to profl. jours.; columnist Chgo. Tribune, 1967—. Author: Getting Pests to Bug Off, 1978. Home: PO Box 484 Bloomingdale IL 60108 Office: 36 S Wabash Room 1402 Chicago IL 60603

RACHFORD, EDWARD JOHN, ednl. adminstr.; b. Chgo., Feb. 23, 1937; s. Edward Nicholas and Gladys Loretta (Faber) R.; B.A., Beloit Coll., 1959; M.Ed., Loyola U., 1963; Certificate Advanced Study, U. Ill., 1973; m. Helen C. Anderson, June 17, 1961; children—Susan L., Gary E. Tchr. high sch., Oak Lawn, Ill., 1959-62; tchr. Morgan Park High Sch., Chgo., 1962-63; tchr., counselor, chmn. dept., adminstrv. asst. Homewood-Flossmoor (Ill.) High Sch., 1963-70, asst. supt., 1971, supt., 1972—; asst. supt. ednl. service, region Cook County, Ill., 1970-71; cons. ethnicity, Chgo. Recipient certificate of appreciation March of Dimes, 1968-69, 69-70. Mem. Am. Personnel and Guidance Assn. (asst. coordinator nat. conv. 1971), Supt's. Round Table No. Ill., South Interconf. Assn. (treas., v.p.), Am., Ill. (dir.) assn. sch. adminstrs., Ill. Guidance Personnel Assn. (sec. 1969-70), South Cook County Sch. Adminstrs. Assn. (sec.-treas.), Phi Delta Kappa (del. nat. council 1969). Clubs: Masons, Shriners, Rotary. Home: 19037 Center Ave Homewood IL 60430 Office: 999 Kedzie Ave Flossmoor IL 60422

RACHIE, GEORGE LOUIS, dentist; b. Mpls., Apr. 20, 1919; s. Elias and Amanda Marie (Lein) R.; B.A., U. Minn., 1945, D.D.S., 1945; m. Lucille Margaret Schumann, July 19, 1946; children—Susan (Mrs. Robert William Groth), Jeanne (Mrs. Todd Andrew Teske), Thomas George. Practice dentistry, Mpls., 1946-65, Edina, Minn., 1965—. Chmn. troop Boy Scouts Am., 1971-73. Served to 1st lt. Dental Corps USNR, 1945-47. Mem. Am. Acad. Prosthetics, Am., Minn. prosthetic socs., Children Dental Soc., Acad. Gen. Practice, Am., Mpls. dental assns., International Dentaire, Sons of Norway, Silver Spur, Grey Friars, Psi Omega. Lutheran. Optimist. Club: Ys Mens (Mpls.). Home: 5603 Interlachen Circle Edina MN 55436 Office: 535 Southdale Med Bldg Edina MN 55435

RADCHUK, SERGE, lawyer; b. Volyn, West Ukraine, Oct. 25, 1926; s. Chariton and Vera (Novosad) R.; came to Can., 1947, naturalized, 1953; LL.B., Man. Law Sch., 1954; LL.M., U. Man., 1957; D.Jur., Ukrainian Free U., Munich, W.Ger., 1975; m. Leona Kosjar, Oct. 26, 1957; children—Julie, Natalie. Called to Man. bar, 1955; practiced in Winnepeg, 1955—; asso. firm Solomon & Baryluk, 1955-60; mem. firm Karasevich & Radchuk, 1960-67, Radchuk & Peters, 1973—. Liberal candidate for constituency of Winnipeg North in fed. election, 1972; pres. Liberal Assn. Winnipeg North Fed. Constituency, 1963-64; pres. Research Inst. Volyn, 1967—, Ukrainian Can. Congress, 1974—; adv. bd. Internat. Center and Citizenship Council Man., Winnipeg, 1970—. Recipient Queen Elizabeth Royal Silver Jubilee medal, 1977. Mem. Canadian Bar Assn., Ukrainian Fraternal Soc. Can. (pres. 1974—), Carpathia Credit Union Ltd. (pres. 1961-76), Ukrainian Profl. Businessmen's Club. Ukrainian Greek Orthodox (presidium consistory Can. 1974-75). Clubs: Masons, Shriners. Contbr. articles on legal matters to ethnic newspapers. Home: 10 Salvia Bay Winnipeg MB R2V 2L8 Canada Office: 330 Portage Ave Winnipeg MB R3C 0C4 Canada

RADCLIFF, WILLIAM FRANKLIN, lawyer; b. Fredericksburg, Ind., May 21, 1922; s. Samuel Pearl and Hester Susan (Sherwood) R.; B.A., Yale U., 1948; J.D., Ind. U., 1951; m. Margery Anne Glass, Aug. 18, 1962; children—Forrest Lee, Stephanie Anne; foster children—Cheryl Lynn, Sandra Lee, Richard Alan, Lezlie Laverne. Admitted to Ind. bar, 1951; with firm DeFur, Voran, Hanley, Radcliff & Reed, and predecessors, Muncie, Ind., 1951—, partner, 1954—; dir., mem. exec. com. Am. Nat. Bank and Trust Co. of Muncie; dir. Marhoefer Packing Co., Inc., Muncie, Ben Zeigler Co., Inc., Muncie. Pres., Delaware County Mental Health Assn., 1962-63; a founder Ind. Mental Health Meml. Found., 1962, sec., 1962—. Served with AUS, 1940-46; PTO; lt. col. Res., ret. Mem. Am., Ind., Muncie bar assns., Muncie-Delaware County C. of C. (pres. 1972-73). Clubs: Masons, Exchange (pres. 1962); Delaware Country (pres. 1974), Muncie Tennis and Country (dir., sec.), Muncie (Muncie). Home: 1809 N Winthrop Rd Muncie IN 47304 Office: 320 S High St Muncie IN 47305

RADCLIFFE, BYRON MASON, engr., educator; b. Weehawken, N.J., Oct. 17, 1919; s. Harry Southwell and Sarah Ester (Randall) R.; B.M.E., Purdue U., 1948, M.S., 1951; m. Marguerite Evelyn Harpster, Jan. 26, 1943; children—Ray Stephen, Gregory S. Instr. in engring. Purdue U., Lafayette, Ind., 1948-51, asso. prof., dir. Wood Research Lab., 1951-56; dir. research Place Constrn. Co., South Bend, Ind., 1956-58; asso. prof. bldg. constrn. Mich. State U., East Lansing, 1958-66; prof. constrn. sci. Coll. Engring. U. Nebr., Lincoln, 1966—, chmn. dept., 1966—; cons. in field. Served to maj. USMCR, 1941-46. Decorated D.F.C.; registered profl. engr., Mass., La., Miss., Ala. Mem. Am. Soc. Engring. Edn., Nat. Soc. Profl. Engrs., Am. Inst. Constructors, ASCE, Assn. Schs. Constrn. (past pres.), Sigma Xi, Sigma Tau, Pi Tau Sigma, Xi Sigma Pi, Sigma Lambda Chi, Tau Beta Pi. Author: Critical Path Method, 1966; contbr. articles to profl. jours., chpts. to engring. handbooks. Home: 3300 E Pershing St Lincoln NE 68502

RADCLIFFE, DONALD VANE, author, editor; b. Belle Plaine, Iowa, Mar. 23, 1920; s. Glen George and Elizabeth (Vane) R.; B.S. in Chemistry, Iowa State A. and M. Coll. (now Iowa State U.), 1943; m. Shirley Sawyer, Oct. 18, 1953. Agt.-telegrapher Chgo. & Northwestern R.R., Chgo., 1946-60; reporter Chgo. City News Bur., 1961-63; quotations reporter Chgo. Bd. Trade, 1964-66; owner, mgr. Sidebar/Chgo. News Service, 1966—; lectr. communications Chgo. Community Coll., 1974-75, Iota Sigma Epsilon, Chgo., 1972; instr. sci. communications Chgo. Med. Sch., 1975—; staff cons. Am. Soc. Contemporary Medicine and Surgery, 1973-75, MediPhone Consultation Service, Chgo., 1974-75. Served with USNR, 1943-46. Mem. Am. Med. Writers Assn. (pres. 1977-78, chpt. Distinguished Achievement award 1975), Publicity Club Chgo., Assn. Bus. Writers Am., Nat. Assn. Sci. Writers, Am. Soc. Bus. Press Editors, Alpha Sigma Chi. Author: Motivation and the Disadvantaged Trainee, 1972; Instructing Older Workers, 1973; To See or Not, 1974; contbg. author: Best American Shorts Stories, 1967; Above and Beyond, Ency. of Aviation and Space Science, 1974; Life Cycle Library, 1974; author plays: Remember Me in the Morgue, Man, 1966, How Kind the Keeper, 1968. Editor Hearing Aid Jour., 1974-75; cons. editor Comprehensive Therapy Med. Jour., 1975. Address: 5615 N Wayne Ave Chicago IL 60660

RADCLIFFE, ROBERT PUTNAM, retail clothing co. exec.; b. Wichita, Kans., June 22, 1939; s. Charles Ober and Maxine (Fisher) R.; B.S., U. Kans., 1963; m. Jane Fothergill, Apr. 23, 1971; 1 son, William Ober. Pres., Gen. Jeans (Ober's Inc.), Lawrence, Kans., 1971—. Vice chmn. Lawrence chpt. ARC, 1977—; membership chmn. Friends of Art, Helen Foresman Spencer Mus. Art, U. Kans., 1977—. Mem. Menswear Retailers Am. (regional v.p. 1970-72), Nat. Retail Mchts. Assn., Lawrence C. of C. (chmn. central bus. dist. com. since 1976—), Phi Delta Gamma (chpt. adviser Kans., Kans. State univs. 1963—, sec. nat. chpt. 1972-75). Republican. Episcopalian. Club: Rotary. Home: 515 Lindley St Lawrence KS 66044 Office: PO Box 724 1000 Massachuttes St Lawrence KS 66044

RADDE, BERNARD CARL, dentist; b. St. Joseph, Mich., Apr. 2, 1908; s. William Otto and Willhemina (Raschke) R.; student Crane Jr. Coll., 1927-28, Mich. State U., 1928-29, Kalamazoo Coll., 1929-31; A.B., Valparaiso U., 1932; B.Sc.D., U. Nebr., 1938; postgrad. U. Ill., 1938-39; m. Sally Bicknell, Sept. 27, 1932; children—Sallyanne Radde Pagel, Bernard Carl. Staff mem. U. Ill., Chgo., 1938-39; pvt. practice dentistry, Benton Harbor, Mich., 1940—; mem. dental staff Mercy Hosp., Benton Harbor, chmn., 1964; dental staff Meml. Hosp., St. Joseph, chmn., 1965; pres. Sport-O-Rama, St. Joseph, 1965—. Trustee Lake Mich. Coll., 1963-79, now chmn.; v.p. Lake Mich. Coll. Bd., 1971-75. Mem. Mich. Acad. Sci., Arts and Letters, Berrien County Retarded Assn. (dir.), Mil. Surgeons (life), Lutheran Edn. Assn. (life), U. Nebr. Alumnus Assn. (life), Am. (life), Mich. (life), Lakeland Valley (life), Chgo. dental assns., Mich. Assn. Professions, Century Club of Concordia Tchrs. Coll., Century Club of U. Nebr. Dental Coll., Mich. Conservation Club. Lutheran (chmn. Christian bd. edn. 1957-63). Club: Berrien County Sportsmans. Home: 3621 Lake Shore Dr Saint Joseph MI 49085 Office: 777 Riverview St Benton Harbor MI 49022

RADEN, LOUIS, tape and label corp. exec.; b. Detroit, June 17, 1929; s. Harry M. and Joan (Morris) R.; B.A., Trinity Coll., 1951; postgrad. N.Y. U., 1952; m. Mary K. Knowlton, June 18, 1949; children—Louis, Pamela, Jacqueline. With Time, Inc., 1951-52; with Quaker Chem. Corp., 1952-63, sales mgr., 1957-63; exec. v.p. Gen. Tape & Supply, Inc., Detroit, 1963-68, pres., bd. chmn., 1969—. Pres. Michigan Gun Clubs, Inc., Orchard Lake, 1973—. Mem. Nat. Rifle Assn. (life), Nat. Skeet Shooting Assn. (life, nat. dir. 1977—), U.S., Mich., Greater Detroit chambers commerce, Theta Xi (life, Distinguished Service award 1957). Republican. Episcopalian. Clubs: Univ., Pine Lake Country; Fairlane; Detroit Gun, Detroit Golf. Home: 2900 Pine Lake Rd Orchard Lake MI 48033 Office: 7451 W Eight Mile Rd Detroit MI 48221

RADFORD, EDWARD EARL, mgmt. cons. co. exec.; b. Cin., July 6, 1943; s. Earl E. and Thelma (Judd) R.; B.B.A., U. Cin., 1967. Merchandising mgr. Swallen's Co., Cin., 1968-70, Cook United Co., Cleve., 1970-71; founder, pres. Audio Warehouse Companies of Ohio, 1972—; pres. Radford Enterprises, Inc., 1975—; propr. Performance Sales Co., 1977—. Spl. dep. sheriff of Summit County, Ohio, 1977-81; mem. Akron (Ohio) Crime Clinic, 1976—. Served with U.S. Army, 1968-74. Mem. Small Bus. Assn., Fraternal Order of Police, Akron C. of C. Home: 1266 N Howard St Akron OH 44310 Office: 855 E Market St Akron OH 44305

RADKE, DONALD GILBERT, indsl. engr.; b. Milw., July 19, 1940; s. Frank K. and Ottilie (Tucholke) R.; B.S., U. Wis., 1972; m. Ruth Ann Dusterhoft, Aug. 13, 1960; children—Patricia, Suzanne, Christopher. Jr. indsl. engr., Ladish Co., Milw., 1964-66; indsl. engr. Milw. Gear Co., 1966-68; indsl. engr. E.R. Wagner Mfg. Co., Hustisford, Wis., 1968-72, sr. indsl. engr., 1972-75, mgr. indsl. engring., Milw., 1975—. Mem. Am. Inst. Indsl. Engrs., Nat. Mgmt. Assn., Methods Time Measurement Assn., Nat. Bd. Realtors. Author: Cheese Making at Home, 1974. Home: 4753 N 70th St Milwaukee WI 53218 Office: 4611 N 32d St Milwaukee WI 53209

RADKINS, ANDREW PETER, mfg. co. exec.; b. Chgo., Aug. 22, 1926; s. Laurent Vincent and Helen (Petrulis) R.; B.S., Iowa State U., 1947; M.S., Purdue U., 1950; Ph.D., 1958; m. Joanne Lyon, Sept. 18, 1948; children—Susan, James, John, Nancy. Research engr. Standard Oil Ind., Chgo., 1947-49; engr. Kimberly Clark Corp., Neenah, Wis. and Niagara Falls, N.Y., 1950-54; instr. Purdue U., 1954-58; v.p. M&M/Mars Candies, Hackettstown, N.J. and Chgo., 1958-72; asso. prof. bus. adminstrn. Central Mich. U., Mount Pleasant, 1972-73; gen. partner Hindu Incense, Chgo., 1973—; dir. Bartlett State Bank (Ill.). Bd. dirs. Fathers Assn. Choate Sch., Wallingford, Conn., 1971-73. Served with USNR, 1943-46. Fellow Am. Psychol. Assn.; mem. Am. Mktg. Assn., Sigma Xi, Tau Beta Pi, Pi Tau Sigma. Patentee in method for mfr. wax objects. Home: 111 Jervey Ln Bartlett IL 60103 Office: 200 N Laflin St Chicago IL 60607

RADMACHER, CAMILLE J., librarian; b. Monmouth, Ill., Apr. 14, 1917; d. Harry M. and Esther (Greenleaf) R.; student Monmouth Coll., 1935-37. With adult dept. Warren County Library, Monmouth, 1937-48, head county librarian, 1948—, exec. dir. Western Ill. Library System, 1965—; exec. dir. Nat. Library Week in State of Ill., 1959. Mem. Monmouth Coll. Community Concert Lecture Bd., 1967-72; mem. adv. com. Ill. State Library, 1962-72. Mem. Ill. Library Assn. (Ill. Librarian Citation award 1967), Womens Nat. Book Assn., DAR. Methodist. Clubs: Order Eastern Star, Altrusa (treas. 1968-69). Home: 500 N 1st St Monmouth IL 61462 Office: 60-62 Public Sq Monmouth IL 61462

RADOCHONSKI, STEPHEN PETER, dentist; b. Chgo., Apr. 22, 1919; s. Peter Simon and Stephanie Charolette (Noga) R.; student DePaul U., 1937-40; D.D.S., Loyola U., Chgo., 1944; m. Jeanette Marie Kolodziejczyk, Sept. 9, 1944; children—Bernard S., Paul B., Donna M. Practice dentistry, Chgo., 1945—. Mem. elementary sch. bd. dist. 124, Evergreen Park, Ill., 1970-76; sec. Fire and Police Commn. Evergreen Park, 1971—. Served as lt. USNR, 1942-45. Named hon. alumnus St. Cyril and Methodius Sem., Orchard Lake, Mich., 1960. Mem. Acad. Gen. Dentistry, Dental Arts Soc. Chgo. (pres. 1950-51), Internat. Prosthodontic Conf. Soc., ADA, Ill., Chgo. (chmn. table clinics) dental socs., Am. Legion, 40 and 8, Holy Name Soc. (pres. St. Camilius 1949), Delta Sigma Delta. Clubs: Polish Nat. Alliance Lodge; Elks; Beverly Country, Holy Cross Hosp. Physicians and Dentists, New City Lions (pres. 1952-53) (Chgo.). Home: 9641 S Ridgeway Ave Evergreen Park IL 60642 Office: 1725 W 47th St Chicago IL 60609

RADOVANOV, RADMILA, physician; b. Belgrad, Yugoslavia, Nov. 17, 1934; d. Cvetko and Jelena (Kandic) Lazarevic; M.D., Med. U. Belgrad, 1960; m. Milan Radovanov, Nov. 8, 1959; children—Jelena, Nicol; came to U.S., 1967, naturalized, 1972. Intern, St. Francis Hosp., Wichita, Kans., 1968-69, resident, 1969-72; practice medicine specializing in radiology Newton (Kans.) Radiologists Assn., 1972—; mem. staff Bethel Deaconess Hosp., Newton. Diplomate Am. Bd. Radiology. Mem. AMA, Kans. Med. Soc., Am. Coll. Radiology, Women Med. Assn. Club: Racquet. Home: 8705 Stoneridge Wichita KS 67206 Office: 500 Main St Newton KS 67114

RADTKE, LORRAINE M., pub. relations dir.; b. Milw., Nov. 21, 1922; d. Fred G. and Ella L. (Patzke) R.; Ph.B., Marquette U., 1944; A.M., U. Minn., 1946. State editor Milw. Sentinel, 1944-45; part-time lectr. Marquette U., 1944-45, instr., 1946-48; administrv. fellow in radio U. Minn., Radio Sta. KUOM, 1946; instr. Ohio Wesleyan U., 1948-49, asst. prof., 1949-50; advt. specialist Wis. Gas Co., 1950-56; editor Badger Lutheran, 1956-68; owner Radtke Reports, Milw., 1957-68; pub. relations dir. Wis. Heart Assn., Milw., 1968-70, Home for Aged Lutherans, 1970—. Publicity dir. Music Under the Stars, Milw. County Park Commn., 1946-48; bd. dirs. Milw. Sch. Bd., 1955—, pres., 1963-65. Mem. Assn. Edn. in Journalism, Luth. Collegiate Assn., Minn. Alumni Assn., Mo. Synod Luth., Milw. County Hist. Soc., Zool. Soc. Milw. County, Milw. Symphony, Women's League, Marquette U. Alumni Assn., AAUW, Pub. Relations Soc. Am., Women in Communications, Phi Alpha Theta, Delta Zeta. Clubs: Coll., Milw. Advt., Milw. Press. Author: The Story of the Wilhelm Friedrich Radtke Family. Home: 2654 N 57th St Milwaukee WI 53210 Office: 7500 W North Ave Wauwatosa WI 53213

RADWAY, JERROLD EVERETT, chem. research and devel. co. exec.; b. Chgo., July 3, 1930; s. Samuel and Sarah (Myers) R.; B.S. in Chem. Engring., U. Ill., 1952; M.B.A., U. Tenn., 1963; m. Evelyn Jean Levis, June 21, 1952; children—Scott, Shelley, Larry. Devel. engr. Abbott Labs., North Chicago, Ill., 1952-54, Pitman Moore & Co., Zionsville, Ind., 1954-57, Union Carbide Nuclear Co., Oak Ridge, 1957-62; with Basic Chems. Co., Cleve., 1962—, tech. dir., 1965-67, asst. v.p. tech., 1972—. Mem. Cleve. Assn. Research Dirs. (v.p.), Air Pollution Control Assn., Am. Inst. Chem. Engrs., Am. Chem. Soc., ASME (research com. corrosion and deposits from 1975; Vocat. Info. program inner city youth). Author: Business Ethics and the Polygraph, 1963; editor Electric Utility Briefs, 1974; patentee in field. Office: Basic Chems 2532 Saint Clair Ave Cleveland OH 44114

RADY, JOHN MORTIMER, pipeline co. exec.; b. Chgo., Feb 16, 1921; s. Mortimer D. and Clara J. (Wiegers) R.; Ph.B., U. Detroit, 1947, LL.B., 1949; m. Shirley M. Moore, Nov. 4, 1950; children—John Mortimer, Paul Moore, Jane Kathryn, Thomas More. Admitted to Mich. bar, 1949; war materiel expediter Rolls-Royce, Inc., Detroit, 1941-42; asso. counsel legal dept. Mich. Wis. Pipe Line Co., 1949-67; sec. Great Lakes Gas Transmission Co., Detroit, 1967—, gen. atty., 1969-73, v.p., 1972—, gen. counsel, 1973—. Active United Fund. Served with USNR, 1942-45. Mem. Am. Gas Assn., Am., Fed. Power, Detroit bar assns., State Bar Mich., Greater Detroit C. of C., Interstate Natural Gas Assn. Am., Midwest Gas Assn., Econ. Club Detroit, Gamma Eta Gamma. Republican. Roman Catholic. Clubs: Detroit Athletic; Birmingham (Mich.) Athletic. Home: 367 Suffield St Birmingham MI 48009 Office: 2100 Buhl Bldg Detroit MI 48226

RADZIUS, JOSEPH RAYMOND, lawyer; b. Athol, Mass., Jan. 8, 1936; s. Joseph and Rozilda (Champagne) R.; B.A., U. Vt., 1960; LL.B., Wake Forest U., 1965; m. Irene Georgiana Cheney, Nov. 7, 1955; children—Timothy Jay, Christopher Joseph, Matthew Paul. Asst. to dir. research Athol Mfg. Co., Butner, N.C., 1960-62; admitted to Mich. bar, 1965; with Dow Corning Corp., Midland, Mich., 1965-77, atty., food and drug counsel, 1967-77; partner firm Burditt & Calkins, Chgo., 1977—. Mem. Food and Drug Law Inst., Washington, 1968—, Health Industries Assn., Chgo., 1971-72; asso. mem. food protection com. Nat. Acad. Scis./NRC, Washington, 1968—. Mem. Recreation and Parks Com., Williams Twp., Midland, 1969-72. Bd. dirs. Family Service of Midland, 1967-71. Served with AUS, 1954-56. Mem. Am. Coll. Legal Medicine (asso.-in-law), Am. (chmn. med. devices subcom. 1972—), Midland County bar assns., State Bar Mich., Chem. Specialties Mfrs. Assn. (mem. task force on child resistant packaging 1973), Pharm. Mfrs. Assn. (mem. inter-assn. task force on med. device legislation 1973—), Assn. for the Advancement of Med. Instrumentation (dir. 1972—), Elk. Home: 25245 Mayfield St Glen Ellyn IL 60137 Office: 135 S LaSalle St Chicago IL 60603

RAETZMAN, RONALD MURA, educator; b. Chgo., June 24, 1935; s. Merwyn Ewald and Margaret (Mura) R.; student Chgo. Jr. Coll., 1953-55, U. Chgo., 1955-59; B.F.A., Sch. Art Inst. Chgo., 1959, M.F.A., 1966; m. Barbara Lee Johnson, Apr. 7, 1962; children—Amanda Lee, Jon. Pvt. design cons. practice, Ill., Mich., Colo., 1958-69; spl. design cons. Castle-West, Inc., Denver, 1967; asst. prof., area chmn. interior design concentration dept. art Colo. State U., Fort Collins, 1965-69; head interior design, instr. indsl. design Layton Sch. Art, Milw., 1962-65; dir. interior design Kendall Sch. Design, Grand Rapids, Mich., 1959-62; project dir. Westburg-Klaus Assos., Mpls., 1969-70; corporate facilities planner, operational planning and facilities div. Graco, Inc., Mpls., 1970-71; adminstrv. services mgr., operational planning and facilities div., 1971-72; asst. prof. environ. design and housing U. Ill., Urbana, 1972—, adj. prof. dept. architecture, 1976—; asst. prof. environ. design and housing Small Homes Council-Bldg. Research Council, 1974; design cons. Synectics Groups, Inc., Chgo., 1972—; pvt. design cons. practice Champaign-Urbana, Ill., 1972—; asso. dir. research and devel. Interior Design Services, Inc., Champaign. Mem. Colo. Arts and Humanities Council, 1966-69, mem. visual arts com., 1966-69. Bd. dirs. Fort Collins (Colo.) Arts and Humanities Council, 1967-69, chmn. environ. design com., 1967-69. Served with USNG, 1957-63. Daniel D. Van Degrift scholar Sch. Art Inst. Chgo., 1958, U. Ill. grantee, 1974, Am. Friends of Attingham scholar British Nat. Trust Summer Sch., 1967. Mem. Constrn. Specifications Inst. (mem. edn. com. Central Ill. 1973—), Interior Design Educators Council (chmn. Rocky Mountain region, nat. mem. exec. com. 1968-69, nat. chmn. traveling exhbn. com.), Illuminating Engring. Soc. (co-chmn. edn. com. Ill. chpt.), Nat. Trust Historic Preservation, AIA (mem. edn. com. Central Ill. chpt. 1974, vice chmn. com. on regional devel. Ill. council), Am. Soc. Interior Designers (mem. nat. com. on profl. competitions and standards 1975, mem. nat. environ. design com., co-chmn. com. legislation Ill. chpt.). Home: 2201 Duncan Rd Champaign IL 61820

RAFAILL, THOMAS DENNIS, orthodontist; b. Detroit, Feb. 27, 1935; s. Dennis and Helen (Zampas) R.; B.S., U. Detroit, 1957, D.D.S., 1961; M.S., State U. N.Y., 1965; m. Katie Athans, July 24, 1960; children—Dennis, Nicholas, Cynthia. Pvt. practice dentistry specializing in orthodontics, Roseville, Mich., 1965—. Served with USAF, 1961-63. Mem. Am., Mich. dental assns., Macomb Dental Soc., Am., Great Lakes, Mich. orthodontic socs. Home: 71 Stillmeadow Ln Grosse Pointe Shores MI 48236 Office: 31513 Gratiot St Roseville MI 48066

RAGAN, WILLIAM DARBY, physician; b. Logansport, Ind., Oct. 2, 1927; s. Virgil D. and C. Eve (Fouts) R.; B.S., Butler U., Indpls., 1949; M.D., Ind. U., 1954; m. Patricia L. Wilson, June 29, 1957; children—Christopher, Darby, Melissa. Intern, then resident in obstetrics and gynecology Ind. U. Med. Center, 1954-59; practice medicine specializing in obstetrics and gynecology, Indpls., 1959-72; asso. prof. Ind. U. Med. Sch., 1972—; dir. Obstetrics-Gynecology Ultrasound Lab.; chmn. Ind. Maternal Mortality Comm. Served with AUS, 1946-47. Diplomate Am. Bd. Obstetrics and Gynecology. Fellow Am. Coll. Obstetricians and Gynecologists; mem. Central Assn. Obstetricians and Gynecologists, AMA, Ind. Med. Soc. Contbr. med. jours. Home: 11416 Lakeshire Dr E Carmel IN 46032 Office: 1100 W Michigan St Indianapolis IN 46202

RAGAS, LEONIDAS JOSEPH, dentist; b. Kaunas, Lithuania, July 2, 1934; s. Anthony and Sophie (Stanevicius) Ragauskas; came to U.S., 1949, naturalized 1954; student U. Ill., 1953-54; D.D.S., Loyola U., Chgo., 1960; m. Rima Krasauskas, Sept. 1, 1957; children—Paul, Laura. Practice dentistry, South Elgin, Ill., 1962-63, Itasca, Ill., 1963—. Bd. dirs. DuPage County (Ill.) Tb Assn. Served from 1st lt. to capt. AUS, 1960-62. Mem. Am., Chgo., West Suburban dental assns., Far West Dental Study Club, Xsi Psi Phi. Roman Catholic. Lion. Home: 163 W Schick Rd Bloomingdale IL 60108 Office: 421 W Irving Park Rd Itasca IL 60143

RAGG, THEODORE D. B., Anglican bishop of Huron (London, Ont., Can.). Office: Box 308 London ON N6A 4W3 Canada*

RAGHIB, GUNAY MUSTAFA, physician; b. Cyprus, June 20, 1931; s. Mustafa M. and Zekiye (Suleyman) R.; came to U.S., 1957, naturalized, 1974; M.D., U. Istanbul (Turkey), 1957; m. Diane Eggl, Nov. 7, 1966; children—Sevda, Metin, Ender, Aysum, Timur. Intern, U. Minn. Hosps., Mpls., 1959-60, resident, 1960-65; resident St. Boniface Hosp., Winnipeg, Man., Can., 1965-67; practice medicine specializing in pediatrics, Minot, N.D., 1965—. Mem. AMA. Home: 1808 11th St SW Minot ND 58701 Office: Medical Arts Bldg Minot ND 58701

RAGLAND, ALBERT M., orgn. exec.; b. Louisville, Mar. 16, 1929; s. John and Elizabeth R.; B.A., Roosevelt U.; postgrad Sch. Social Adminstrn., U. Chgo.; L.H.D., Daniel Payne Coll., Birmingham, Ala., 1974. Past dir. Woodlawn Urban Progress Center; various positions Cook County (Ill.) Dept. Pub. Aid.; asso. dir. Ch. Fedn. Greater Chgo.; now exec. dir. Chgo. Conf. Religion and Race, 1971—; exec. dir. Chgo. Coordinating Com. Black Churchmen; cons. Lutheran Child and Family Services, Beacon House, United Community Christian Service, Chgo. Mem. Mayor's Com. Manpower City Chgo. Bd. dirs. Anne Tyskling Consortium for Midwest, Opportunities Industrialization Center, Chgo., Black and Brown, Chgo., Delta Ministry Nat. Council Chs. Christ, Greenville, Miss. Served with AUS. Address: Chgo Conf Religion and Race 1020 S Wabash Ave Chicago IL 60605

RAGLAND, SAM BENTON, JR., cons.; b. Fort Benton, Mont., Oct. 8, 1936; s. Sam Benton and Madeline Elizabeth (Fultz) R.; B.B.A., U. Mont., 1959; m. Sandra J. Taylor, Dec. 25, 1963; children—Laura Joan, Deborah Sue, Daniel Coy. Asst. v.p. sales planning and promotion Union Bank, Los Angeles, 1963-70; asst. v.p., dir. bus. devel. First City Nat. Bank, Houston, 1970-73; v.p., dir. mktg. Ohio Nat. Bank, Columbus, 1973-77; exec. v.p. Fin. Tng. Resources, Columbus, 1978—. instr. Am. Inst. Banking. Trustee Leukemia Soc. Am., recipient Achievement certificate; chmn. media com. Franklin County United Way; Deacon, mem. fin. com. Northwest Christian Ch. Served with U.S. Army, 1960-63. Mem. Am. Mgmt. Assn., Am. Mktg. Assn., Bank Mktg. Assn., Sales and Mktg. Execs. Assn. (dir. Columbus chpt.). Republican. Club: Athletic (Columbus). Home and office: 1838 Victorian Ct Columbus OH 43220

RAGSDALE, EDWARD FLOYD, radiologist; b. Little Rock, Mar. 24, 1939; s. Floyd Thomas and Elizabeth (Murphy) R.; B.A. (sr. scholar), U. Ark., 1960; M.D., Washington U., St. Louis, 1964; m. Meredith Lynn Smith, Nov. 20, 1968; children—Lynda Elizabeth, Edward Alan. Intern, Phila. Gen. Hosp., 1964-65; resident in radiology Barnes Hosp-Washington U. Med. Sch., 1965-68; practice medicine specializing in radiology, Alton, Ill., 1970—; v.p., sec., mem. staff Drs. Hooker, Ragsdale & Assos., Radiologists, 1971—; mem. staff Alton Meml. Hosp., Jersey (Ill.) Community Hosp., Boyd Meml. Hosp., Carrollton, Ill., Community Meml. Hosp., Staunton, Ill.; vis. fellow in radiology So. Ill. U., 1977. Vice pres. Madison County (Ill.) unit Am. Cancer Soc., 1975-76, pres., 1976-77; v.p. St. Louis County Young Republicans, 1966, pres., 1967; chmn. Madison County Rep. Com., 1977. Served with USAF, 1968-70. Recipient Ostrum Radiology award Phila. Gen. Hosp., 1965. Diplomate Am. Bd. Radiology. Mem. Madison County (alt. del.), Ill. (dir.) med. socs., Ill. Med. Polit. Action Com., AMA, Greater St. Louis Soc. Radiologists, Phi Beta Kappa, Omicron Delta Kappa, Pi Sigma Pi. Roman Catholic. Editor: Madison County Rep. Newsletter, 1976—. Home: 5316 Shannon St Godfrey IL 62035 Office: Alton Meml Hosp Alton IL 62002

RAGSDALE, RICHARD MICHAEL, obstetrician and gynecologist; b. Madison, Wis., Sept. 1, 1935; s. Clarence E. and Marie (Zettler) R.; B.S., U. Wis., Madison, 1956, M.D., 1959; m. Susan Collins, June 21, 1958; children—David, Christina, Robert, Jennifer, Thomas. Intern, Virginia Mason Hosp., Seattle, 1959-60; resident in obstetrics and gynecology U. Wis., 1962-66; practice medicine specializing in obstetrics and gynecology, Rockford, Ill., 1971—; founder, pres. No. Ill. Women's Center, 1973—; clin. asst. prof. obstetrics and gynecology U. Tex., San Antonio, 1969-71, U. Ill., Rockford, 1973—. Bd. dirs. Ill. Children's Home and Aid Soc., N.W. Region, 1972—, pres., 1974. Served to lt. col. M.C., USAF, 1960-71. Decorated USAF Commendation Medal. AMA, Ill. Med. Soc. Republican. Unitarian. Clubs: Rockford Country, University (Rockford). Home: 9206 Shore Ave Rockford IL 61107 Office: 2500 N Rockton Ave Rockford IL 61103

RAHA, CHITTA RANJAN, biochemist, educator; b. Faridpur, Bangladesh, Apr. 1, 1926; s. Jogendra Nath and Chapala Bala (Mitra) R.; came to U.S., 1965; B.Sc., U. Calcutta (India), 1945, M.Sc., 1947, D.Phil., 1954; m. Dipa Basu, Jan. 24, 1954; children—Abhiji, Mono, Josho. Asst. prof. oncology Chgo. Med. Sch., 1965-68; asso. prof. biochemistry coll. medicine U. Nebr., Omaha, 1968—, asso. prof. Eppley Cancer Inst., 1973—; mem. spl. studies sect. exptl. therapeutics NIH. Internat. Agy. Cancer Research travel fellow Wennergren Inst. U. Stockholm, 1970. Fellow Royal Inst. Chemistry (London), Am. Inst. Chemists; mem. Am. Assn. Cancer Research, Am. Chem. Soc., Biochem. Soc. London, Biochem. Soc. France, Soc. Applied Spectroscopy, AAAS. Contbr. articles to profl. jours. Home: 7432 Spring St Omaha NE 68124

RAHMANN, JOHN CHARLES, television sta. exec.; b. Tarentum, Pa., Aug. 11, 1927; s. Carl Antone and Dorothy Lucille (Klein) R.; B.S., U. Md., 1960; M.B.A., Syracuse U., 1962; grad. Army Lang. Sch., Command and Gen. Staff Coll., 1961; postgrad. George Washington U., 1968—; m. Margaret Lane Shattuck, July 27, 1954; children—John Charles, Pamela Lane, Susan Marion. Commd. 2d lt. U.S. Army, 1947, advanced through grades to lt. col., 1964; ret., 1967; teaching fellow George Washington U., 1968; dir. adminstrn., dep. gen. mgr. WETA-TV, Washington, 1969-71; sta. mgr. WTTW-TV, Chgo., 1972—. Decorated Joint Services Commendation medal, Army Commendation medal, Bronze Star, Purple Heart, Combat Inf. badge; recipient Nat. Pub. TV Devel. award, 1973. Mem. Ret. Officers Assn., Chgo. Assn. Commerce and Industry. Home: 599 Greenleaf Ave Glencoe IL 60022 Office: 5400 N Saint Louis St Chicago IL 60625

RAHTJEN, BRUCE DONALD, clergyman, educator; b. Rochester, N.Y., May 14, 1933; s. Donald F. and Anne Elizabeth (Miller) R.; B.A., U. Rochester, 1955; B.D., Colgate Rochester Div. Sch., 1958; Ph.D., Drew U., 1964; m. Irma Lea McCormac, July 21, 1973; children by previous marriage—Donald, Nancy, James. Ordained to ministry United Meth. Ch., 1958; pastor, Holley, N.Y., 1955-58, Browne Meml. Meth. Ch., Jersey City, 1958-60; instr. bibl. langs. Colgate Rochester Div. Sch., 1960-62; prof. bibl. theology St. Paul Sch. Theology, Kansas City, Mo., 1962—; cons., trainer Group Dynamics, Cons. Trainers S.W. Lecturing fellow Interpreter's House, Lake Junaluska, N.C. Mem. Greater Kansas City Meml. Soc. (dir.), Soc. Bibl. Lit., Am. Acad. Religion, Assn. Creative Change, Phi Beta Kappa. Democrat. Author: Scripture and Social Action, 1966; Biblical Truth and Modern Man, 1968; translator Am. Bible Soc., 1968-70. Home: 1019 W 70th St Kansas City MO 64113

RAHTJEN, IRMA LEA, employment counselor; b. Kansas City, Mo., Oct. 5, 1929; d. George Levi and Leona Eleanor (Perkins) McCormac; B.A., U. Mo., Columbia, 1950; M.A., U. Mo., Kansas City, 1975; m. John L. Evans, Feb. 3, 1951 (div. 1973); children—Carol Jeanne, Ruth Ann, Laurie Susan; m. 2d, Bruce D. Rahtjen, July 21, 1973. Program asst. Kansas City (Mo.) Regional Council for High Edn., 1972-74; exec. sec. to dir. Mid-Am. Arts Alliance, Kansas City, 1974; adminstrv. asst. to exec. dir. Project Equality, Kansas City, 1974-76; placement interviewer Career Info. and Placement Center U. Mo., Kansas City, 1976-77, placement supr., 1977—; led groups on divorce/remarriage, marriage enrichment, assertiveness training, communication skills, personal growth, job-seeking/employment. Active Kansas City Philharmonic Assn.; mem. Women's Political Caucus; active Kansas City Civic Orchestra. Recipient Achievement Award U. Mo.-Kansas City Sch. Edn., 1976. Mem. Am. Personnel and Guidance Assn., Phi Beta Kappa, Psi Chi, Mu Phi Epsilon, Alpha Delta Pi. Republican. Episcopalian. Clubs: Kansas City Musical (sponsor Young Artists' Div.). Home: 1019 W 70th St Kansas City MO 64113 Office: 5100 Rockhill Rd Kansas City MO 64110

RAIKE, SYDNEY RALPH, printing and converting co. exec.; b. Chgo., June 22, 1909; s. Louis and Fannie (Chacofski) R.; B.A., U. Mich.; m. Virginia Trowe, June 22, 1937; children—William Michael, Robin Raike Mitchell. Vice pres. Schenker Co., 1937-39, pres., 1939-70; chmn. bd. Rollprint Packaging Products Co., Inc., Chgo., 1970—. Served with USNR, 1943-45. Club: Mission Hills Country (Northbrook, Ill.). Home: 580 Hawthorne Pl Chicago IL 60657 Office: 2301 Wabansia Ave Chicago IL 60647

RAIKE, VIRGINIA CHARLOTTE, civic worker; b. Chgo., Jan. 7, 1914; d. William H. and Jane (Silverman) Trowe; student Northwestern U., 1931-34; m. Sydney Ralph Raike, June 22, 1937; children—William, Robin Raike Mitchell. Pres. P.T.A., Nettelhorst, 1955-57, Ill. P.T.A., 1970-72, v.p. region 4, 1973-75; mem. Citizens Schs. Com., Chgo.; mem. Gov.'s Commn. on Status Women, 1970-71; chmn. Ill. Joint Com. P.T.A.-Ill. Assn. Sch. Adminstrs.-Ill. Assn. Sch. Bds.-Ill. Edn. Assn., 1970-71; pres. Inst. Sex Edn., 1975. Hon. life mem. Nat., Ill. P.T.A.'s; mem. Chgo. Woman's Aid, Am. Inst. Parliamentarians, Friends Am. Writers, Alpha Epsilon Phi. Contbr. to Ill. Parent-Tchr. Bull., monthly. Home: 580 Hawthorne Pl Chicago IL 60657

RAIKES, JAMES ALFRED, physician; b. Woodbury, N.J., Oct. 20, 1927; s. Edward Alfred and Gertrude Julia (English) R.; B.S., Wayne State U., 1952; M.D., Howard U., 1957; m. Novella Adelaide Harrison, Feb. 14, 1953; children—Keith A., Linda A., Susan A. Intern, Detroit Gen. Hosp., 1957-58; resident in phys. medicine VA Research Hosp., Chgo., 1960-63; practice phys. medicine and rehab., Detroit. Served with USN, 1958-60. Mem. AMA, Nat. Med. Assn., Mich., Wayne County med. socs., Am. Acad. Phys. Medicine Rehab. Episcopalian. Home: 19529 Northlawn St Detroit MI 48221 Office: Sinai Hosp Detroit Detroit MI 48235

RAILSBACK, TOM, congressman; b. Moline, Ill., Jan. 22, 1932; s. Fred Harold and Elizabeth (Johnston) R.; B.A., Grinnell Coll., 1954, LL.D.; J.D., Northwestern U., 1957; LL.D., Monmouth Coll.; m. Patricia Sloan, Aug. 27, 1955; children—Kathryn, Julia. Margaret, Lisa. Admitted to Ill. bar, 1957; practice law, Moline; became mem. Ill. Ho. Reps., 1963; mem. 90th-95th Congresses from 19th Ill. dist., mem. House Judiciary Com., House Select Com. Narcotics Abuse and Control; rep. U.S. Franch Parliamentary Exchange Program, U.S.-Japan Parliamentary Exchange Program, Rep. Task Force Internat. Econ. Devel.; chmn. Ill. Republican del. to Congress. Bd. dirs. Blackhawk chpt. ARC; pres. alumni bd. dirs. Grinnell Coll., 1964—. Served with AUS, 1957-59. Recipient Alumni award Grinnell Coll., 1973, Flandrau award Nat. Council on Crime and Delinquency, 1974, others. Mem. Am., Ill. (pres. Younger Mems. Conf.), Rock Island County bar assns., Jr. C. of C., Phi Delta Phi, Phi Gamma Delta, Blue Key. Conglist. Home: 2800 12th St Moline IL 61265 Office: House Office Bldg Washington DC 20515 also Fed Bldg Rock Island IL 61201

RAIM, ROLAND LEO, musician, band dir.; b. Cedar Rapids, Iowa, Mar. 12, 1936; s. Leo Anton and Libbie Marie (Vessely) R.; Mus.B., U. Iowa, 1958, M.A., 1965; m. Nancy Ann Springer, Aug. 7, 1966; children—Jay Roland, Janelle Joy. Band dir., Milledgeville, Ill., 1958-59, Lone Tree, Iowa, 1959-63; dir. instrumental music Cedar Rapids (Iowa) Community Schs., 1965—; musician, guest condr., soloist Cedar Rapids Municipal Band. Sec. Cedar Rapids Community Concerts Assn., 1968-77; dir. programs Cedar-Rapids-Marion Fine Arts Council, 1970-75; pres. Czech Heritage Found., 1977, Czech Fine Arts Found., 1976. Mem. NEA, Music Educators Nat. Conf., Iowa Band Masters Assn., Assn. Coll. Univ. and Community Arts Adminstrs. Home: 1455 Parkview Dr Marion IA 52302

RAIMUNDO, HUGO SA, anesthesiologist; b. Pangim, Goa, India, Feb. 13, 1937; s. Antonio Macario DeSousa and Teresa Maria Aspulqueta (De Barros) R.; came to U.S., 1965, naturalized, 1972; M.D., Med. Sch. Oporto, Portugal, 1961; m. Joan Porter, Nov. 13, 1967; children—Brian Charles, Lisa Dian. Intern, Robert Packer Hosp., Guthrie Clinic, Sayre, Pa., 1966; resident, fellow Mayo Grad. Sch. Medicine, Mayo Clinic, Rochester, Minn., 1967-72; practice medicine specializing in anesthesiology, Rochester, mem. staff Mayo Clinic, 1972—; asst. prof. anesthesiology Mayo Med. Sch., Rochester, 1972—; cons. anesthesiology Mayo Clinic, 1972. Recipient Physician Recognition award AMA, 1969, 75. Diplomate Am. Bd. Anesthesiology, Ednl. Council Fgn. Med. Grads., Min. State Bd. Med. Examiners. Fellow Am. Coll. Anesthesiologists; mem. AMA, Am. Soc. Anesthesiologists, Internat. Anesthesia Research Soc., Soc. Obstetrical Anesthesia and Perinatology, Minn. State Med. Assn., Minn. Soc. Anesthesiologists, Nat. Wildlife Fedn., Nat. Assn. Residents and Interns, Nat. Geog. Soc., Rochester Area C. of C. Author: Escola de Medicina do Porto e Escola de Medicina de Goa, 1961. Home: 2505 Crest Ln SW Rochester MN 55901 Office: 200 1st St SW Rochester MN 55901

RAINBOW, KATHRYN ADELINE (MRS. WILLIAM EARHART), physician; b. Wheeling, W.Va., Mar. 21, 1921; d. John Henry and Addaline (Holly) Rainbow; B.S., Fort Valley State Coll., 1942; M.D., Meharry Med. Coll., 1948; m. William Earhart, July 29, 1966; children—(by previous marriage) Frederic B., Holly R. Bryant. Intern, Harlem Hosp., N.Y.C., 1948-49; pediatric resident Mercy-Douglas, Children's hosps., Phila., 1949-50, Freedman's Hosp., Washington, Nat. Found. for Infantile Paralysis fellow, 1950-52; NIMH psychiat. residency fellow Menninger Sch. Psychiatry, Topeka, 1962-65, grad. 1965; pvt. pediatric practice, Rocky Mount, N.C., 1952-54; staff physician Lakin State Hosp., W.Va., 1954-60, supt. 1960-62; staff psychiatrist Topeka State Hosp., 1965—, adviser to Psychiat. Aide Orgn., 1969-71. Bd. dirs. The Villages, Topeka, Topeka Assn. Retarded Children. Recipient 5-years Service to Humanity pin Lakin State Hosp., 1961, 25 years service to humanity plaque Meharry Med. Coll., 1973. Mem. Am., Nat., Kans. med. assns., W.Va. (pres. 1961-62), Shawnee County med. socs., Am. Med. Women's Assn., Am. Psychiat. Assn., Menninger Sch. Psychiatry Alumni Assn., Mental Health Assn. Shawnee County, NAACP, Quota Internat., (pres. chpt. 1976-77), Links, (pres. chpt. 1976-78), Alpha Kappa Alpha. Mem. St. John A.M.E. Ch. Home: 2916 Kentucky Ave Topeka KS 66605 Office: 2700 W 6th St Topeka KS 66606

RAINVILLE, HAROLD E., pub. relations counsel; b. Chgo., Jan. 30, 1907; s. William Van Buren and Agnes Marie (Ward) R.; B.S. in Journalism, Northwestern U., 1929; m. Mariann Rita Pack, Aug. 6, 1932; children—Nancy, Roger Harold. Worked on Chgo. papers and for U.P.I., Chgo.; midwestern fin. editor U.P.; entered publicity field, 1933, established own office, 1937; exec. dir. Nat. Rep. Senatorial Com., Washington, 1952, asst. to the chmn., 1953-54; adminstrv. asst. to Senator Everett Dirksen, 1953, mgr. campaign, 1950, 56, 62, 68, spl. asst. Sen. Dirksen, 1953-69; pres., dir. Sage Ventures, Inc.; chmn. bd. Sage Devel. & Expln. Co.; chmn. bd. Roger Rainville & Assos. Ltd., pres. Genesis Co. Past pres. 8th ward Civic Improvement Assn., Evanston; gen. chmn. Evanston Red Cross fund campaign, 1949. Trustee Everett McKinley Dirksen Meml. Library; bd. dirs. North-lake Community Hosp.; pres., bd. dirs. Health Resources Found. Mem. Ill. Press Assn., Chgo. Press Vets. Assn., The Headline, Pi Kappa Alpha, Hammer and Coffin, Sigma Delta Chi, Mu Alpha. Congregationalist. Clubs: Boswell, Press (Chgo.). Home: 222 E Pearson St Chicago IL 60611 Office: 8 S Michigan Ave Chicago IL 60603

RAINVILLE, ROGER HAROLD, pub. affairs and pub. relations cons.; b. Chgo., Nov. 18, 1940; s. Harold and Mariann (Pack) R.; A.B., Dartmouth Coll., 1962; M.A., U. Pa., 1966; m. Jane Young, 1967; children—Lynn, Keith. Founder, owner Roger Rainville & Assos., Ltd., Chgo., 1966—; White House advanceman, 1972-76; officer, dir. Power Ski Corp., Chgo., 1971-73; cons. to real estate and urban planning firms, 1968—. Campaign mgr. Sen. Dirksen for Re-election, 1968; dir. E.M. Dirksen Congressional Leadership Research Center, 1969-72; active Republican politics; lectr. Urban interstate hwy. projects 1969—; bd. dirs. Near North Family Guidance Center, 1970—, treas., 1974-76; precinct coordinator Evanston mayoral election, 1977. Served to 1st lt. USAF, 1962-65. Mem. Am. Polit. Sci. Assn., Chgo. Council Fgn. Relations, Hwy. Action Coalition, Internat. Wildlife Fedn., Internat. Visitors Center. Clubs: Dartmouth, Press, City (Chgo.); Elephant (exec. dir. 1976—) (Evanston, Ill.). Home: 1626 Lincoln St Evanston IL 60201 Office: 8 S Michigan Ave Chicago IL 60603

RAIT, GEORGE, state senator; b. Noonan, N.D., Dec. 5, 1907; s. Robert and Williamina (Morrison) R.; student pub. schs., Noonan; m. Olga Hanson, June 17, 1947. Dir., Farmers Union Oil Co., 1940-66, pres. bd., 1943-56; dir. Burke Divide Electric Co-op, 1953—, v.p., 1956-64, pres. bd., 1964-71; v.p. Upper Mo. Generation & Transmission Coop., from 1964, pres., 1971—; mem. N.D. Senate, 1965—, asst. minority leader, 1969—, mem. state and fed. govt., also Social welfare coms., 1975—. Twp. supr., 1940-43; county pres. Farmers Union, 1947-55; pres. Soil Conservation Dist., 1946-52; committeeman AAA farm program, 1940-46, Farm Security Adminstrn., 1940-45; mem. N.D. Legis. Research Com., 1967—, chmn. natural resources subcom., 1967—; mem. Gov.'s Policy Bd. for Vocat. Rehab. Service, 1967; mem. N.D. Legis. Council, 1967, 69-71, chmn. polit. subdivs. subcom., 1971, v.p. subcom. state of fed. govt., 1973, mem. subcom. natural resources, 1973; mem. social welfare com. Council State Govts., 1969-73. Mem. governing bd. St. Luke's Hosp., Crosby, N.D., 1968-71; adv. bd. Good Samaritan Soc. Home, Noonan. Recipient numerous soil conservation awards, 1948-53; N.D. Dir. of Year award N.D. Assn. Rural Electric Coops., 1970, 71. Mem. Farmer's Union. Democrat. Address: Noonan ND 58765

RAITT, JOHN WELLESLEY, musician; b. Chgo., Oct. 17, 1923; s. Charles Henry and Vie Clinton (Hanna) R.; student Chgo. Mus. Coll., 1946-48; m. Marjorie Ann McLain, May 13, 1950; children—Michael John, Leslie, Barbara, Robin. With Chgo. Civic Orch., 1942, 46, Ark. State Symphony, Little Rock, 1947-48; asst. prin. bassoonist Chgo. Symphony Orch., 1949—; faculty Sherwood Mus. Coll., Chgo., 1951-61, Roosevelt U., Chgo., 1951-57; prin. bassoon Ravinia Festival, Highland Park, Ill., 1962. Served with USAAF, 1943-46. Home: 1510 E Fremont St Arlington Heights IL 60004 Office: 220 S Michigan Ave Chicago IL 60604

RAJENDRA, KUNWAR, engineer; b. Lahore, India (now Pakistan), Sept. 10, 1938; s. Ram Murti and Raj Rani Pawsey; came to U.S., 1970; B.S. in Civil Engring., Roorkee U., India, 1960; Postgrad. Mich. State U., 1970—; m. Shanno Tandon, Dec. 6, 1963; children—Archana, Rachana, Anuja. Engineer, State of India, 1961-70; project engr., coordinator high energy physics, Mich. State U., East Lansing, 1971-74; transp. coordinator City of Lansing, Mich., 1974—; mem. ad-hoc com. transp. of mobility handicapped Mich. Transp. Research Program; speaker profl. confs. Lectr. yoga Mich. State U., 1971—. Mem. Nat. Council Transportation Disadvantaged (Founder), Transp. Research Bd., Am. Soc. Civil Engrs., Indian Roads Congress. Contbr. articles to profl. jours. Home: 5244 Bluehaven Dr East Lansing MI 48823 Office: 2d Floor Washington Sq Annex City Hall Lansing MI 48933

RAJPUT, AQIL KHAN, city ofcl.; b. Mundawar, India, July 1, 1944; s. Rafi Khan and Mijazan A. (Rao) R.; came to U.S., 1975, naturalized, 1975; M.S., U. Sind, 1967; m. Jane Mary Thompson, Oct. 29, 1974; 1 dau., Sabina Saerah. Research asst. Harrods Ltd., London, 1971-74; officer Brit. Railways, London, 1974-75; sr. programmer Harley-Davidson Motor Co., Milw., 1975; project statistician City of Milw., 1975—. Fellow Royal Statis. Soc.; mem. Data Processing Mgmt. Assn., Am. (sec.-treas. Milw. chpt. 1977—), Sind U. statis. assns., Ops. Research Soc., Am. (1st vice chmn. Milw. chpt. 1977—), Inst. Mgmt. Scis., Canadian Ops. Research Soc., Internat. Assn. Survey Statisticians, Inst. Mgmt. Scis. (chmn. elect Milw. chpt. 1977—), Statis. Sci. Assn. Can. Asso. editor: Al-Manar. Home: 10331 W Greenwood Terr Milwaukee WI 53224 Office: Central Electronic Data Services Milw City Hall Room B-8 Milwaukee WI 53202

RAKUSAN, JEROME JOHN, mag. editor; b. Chgo., Sept. 7, 1923; O.D., Chgo. Coll. Optometry, 1948; m. Virginia Blanche Broz, June 15, 1956. Editor ann. book Digest Books, Chgo., 1959-63; editor monthly consumer and trade mag. Guns, The Shooting Industry, The Am. Handgunner, Guns Annuals, Skokie, Ill., 1963—; bd. dirs. Outstanding Am. Handgunner Found., 1976-77; firearms adviser U.S. Bicentennial Soc., 1976, U.S. Hist. Soc., 1976—. Served with AUS, 1943-46. Home: 10483 Greenford Dr San Diego CA 92126 Office: 8150 N Central Park Skokie IL 60076

RALL, KENNETH LOEM, radiologist; b. Independence, Mo., Feb. 11, 1935; s. Albert A. and Roberta F. R.; B.S., Central Mo. State U., 1956; M.D., U. Mo., 1960; m. Sara B. Thoma, May 27, 1956; children—Kenneth, Susan, Kurt. Intern, Pontiac (Mich.) Gen. Hosp., 1960-61; resident U. Mo., Columbia, 1961-64; practice medicine specializing in radiology, 1966—; mem. staffs Boone County Hosp., Cooper County Hosp., Woodland Hosp.; clin. asso. prof. radiology U. Mo., 1966—; mem. staff Radiology, Inc., Columbia, 1966—. Active Boy Scouts Am., 1967—. Served with U.S. Army, 1964-66. NIH fellow, 1965-66; Am. Cancer Soc. fellow 1963-64. Diplomate Am. Coll. Radiology. Mem. AMA, Mo. State, So. Med. assns., Radiol. Soc. N. Am. Presbyterian. Clubs: Cosmopolitan Internat., Masons, Shriners. Home: 1121 Danforth St Columbia MO 65201 Office: 1502 E Broadway Columbia MO 65201

RALSTON, MARY AGNES, lectr., writer; b. Caledonia, Ill., d. William D. and Agnes (Kelly) Ralston; student Rockford Coll., U. Wis. Extension; B.S., Northwestern U. Lectr., free lance writer. Mem. Nat. Assn. Bank Women, Council for Wis. Writers, Am. Assn. U. Women Indsl. and Ednl. Counselors Assn., Asso. Bus. Writers Am., Wis. Regional Writers Assn., Internat. Platform Assn., Wis. Press Women, Nat. Fedn. Press Women, Women in Communications, Author's Guild, Authors' League Am., Am. Profl. Inst., Milw. Press Club, Kappa Alpha Theta. Club: Zonta. Author: How to Return to Work in an Office, 1973. Contbr. numerous articles to profl., trade jours. Home: 1006 E State St Milwaukee WI 53202

RAMACCIOTTI, WILLIAM STEPHEN, bus. exec.; b. Nebraska City, Nebr., Oct. 26, 1934; s. William S. and Ella K. (Havisen) R.; B.S. in Econs., Creighton U.; B.S. in Agrl. Econs., U. Nebr., Lincoln; m. Felicia Mariam McCargill; children—William F., Ann K., Kathleen E., Robert L., William S., Margaret A. Owner, mgr. Ramacciotti Equipment Co., Inc.; mktg. dir. Blatz Brewing Co., LaCrosse, Wis.; spl. products sales mgr., gen. mgr. Grain Belt-Storr Brewing Co.; owner, pres. Ram Distbg. Co.; former dir. Dugdale Construction Co. Mem. St. Margaret Mary's Parish athletic com. also soccer chmn. Served with USNR. Mem. Am. Production and Inventory Control Soc., Nat. Beer Wholesaler's Assn. (dir.), Midwest Farm Equipment Assn., Nebr. Equipment Dealers Assn. (pres.), Assn. Equipment Distbrs. Roman Catholic lectr. infield. Home: 107 N Happy Hollow Omaha NE 68132 Office: 13603 O St Omaha NE 68137

RAMADANOFF, DIMITER, engring. and research cons.; b. Kustendil, Bulgaria, Oct. 8, 1900; s. Christo Ivan and Elena (Stoyanova) R.; came to U.S., 1920, naturalized, 1938; B.S. in Elec. Engring., U. Ill., 1924; Ph.D. in Physics, Cornell U., 1932; m. Thelma A. Briggs, Sept. 12, 1926; 1 son, David Dimitri; McMullen research scholar, instr. elec. engring. Cornell U., 1926-37; research elec. engr., physicist Nat. Carbon Co. div. Union Carbide Corp., Cleve., 1937-58, gen. cons. Carbon Products div., 1958-65; engring. and research cons., Berea, Ohio, 1965—. Fellow IEEE; mem. Inst. Aeros. and Astronautics, Soc. Lubrication Engrs., Soc. Automotive Engrs., Sigma Xi, Phi Kappa Phi. Patentee aircraft and automotive elec. equipment. Address: 661 Grayton Rd Berea OH 44017

RAMAH, SIMON JOSEPH, pathologist; b. Springfield, Mass., Mar. 10, 1919; s. Peter and Bedar (Saloomey) R.; B.S., Springfield, Coll., 1940; M.D., Chgo. Med. Sch., 1943; m. Geraldine Brown, Feb. 7, 1951; children—Greg, Gary. Intern, Loretto Hosp., Chgo., 1944, mem. attending staff, 1944-51, dir. labs., 1962-71; resident West Side VA Hosp., Chgo., 1958-62; mem. attending staff Mercy Hosp., Springfield, Mass., 1951-58; dir. labs. Edgewater Hosp., Chgo., 1971-72, St. Bernard Hosp., Chgo., 1972-75; dir. labs. Suburban Hosp., Hinsdale, Ill., 1975—; med. dir. Hinsdale Clin. Lab., 1975—; clin. asst. prof. Chgo. Med. Sch., 1965—. Served with USPHS, 1945-46, U.S. Army, 1952. Diplomate Am. Bd. Pathology. Fellow Coll. Am. Pathologists, Am. Soc. Clin. Pathologists, Am. Soc. Cytology; mem. AMA, Chgo., Ill. med. socs. Roman Catholic. Clubs: Edgewood Valley Country, Indian Head Racquet. Contbr. articles to profl. jours. Home: 6301 County Line Rd Hinsdale IL 60521 Office: 55th and County Line Rd Hinsdale IL 60521

RAMAKRISHNAN, VENKATASWAMY, educator; b. Coimbatore, India, Feb. 27, 1929; s. Venkataswamy and Kondammal (Krishnaswamy) R.; came to U.S., 1969; B.E., U. Madras (India), 1952, D.S.S., 1953; D.I.C. in Hydropower and Concrete Tech., Imperial Coll. (Eng.), 1957; Ph.D., Univ. Coll., U. London (Eng.), 1960; m. Vijayalakshmi Unnava, Nov. 7, 1962; children—Aravind, Anand. Lectr., P.S.G. Coll. Tech., U. Madras (India), 1952-55, asst. prof., 1960-61, prof., head dept. civil engring., 1961-69; vis. prof. S.D. Sch. Mines and Tech., Rapid City, 1969-70, prof. civil engring., 1970—, dir. concrete tech. research, 1970-71, head grad. div. structural mechs. and concrete tech., dept. civil engring., 1971—; cons. architecture and structural engring., India. Founding mem. PSGR Children's Sch., 1961—; founding dir. World Open U. Columbo Plan fellow, 1955-60 named Outstanding Educator Am., 1975. Mem. Internat. Assn. Bridge and Structural Engring., ASCE (vice chmn. constrn. div. publs. com.), Am. Concrete Inst. (chmn. subcom. gen. considerations for founds.), Instn. Hwy. Engrs. (London), Transp. Research Bd. (mech. properties of concrete com., curing of Concrete com.), Sigma Xi (chpt. treas.). Author: Ultimate Strength Design for Structural Concrete, 1969; contbr. articles to profl. jours. and procs. Home: 1809 Sheridan Lake Rd Rapid City SD 57701

RAMBERT, GORDON ARTHUR, corp. exec.; b. Rochester, N.Y., Mar. 6, 1922; s. Arthur Frederick and Mildred (Baker) R.; grad. Lehigh U., 1949; m. Jeanne Audrey Bucher, Dec. 27, 1947; children—Paul A., Cynthia L., Gregory N., Michele M. Personnel mgr. Jamestown Malleable Iron Corp. (N.Y.) 1955-58; mgr. compensation Burroughs Corp. Todd div., Rochester, N.Y., 1958-64; asst. sec., dir. personnel Consol-Vacuum Corp., Rochester, 1964-66; v.p. indsl. relations Josyln Mfg. & Supply Co., Chgo., 1966-70; pres. Rambert & Co., Inc., Lake Bluff, Ill., 1970—. Bd. dirs. The Lambs, Inc. Served with Signal Corps, AUS, 1942-46. Mem. Am. Soc. Personnel Adminstrn. (dir. 1968—, treas. 1970, 71), Indsl. Relations Assn., Indsl. Relations Research Assn., NAM (indsl. relations com.). Home: 415 Park Ln Lake Bluff IL 60044 Office: 21 N Skokie Hwy Lake Bluff IL 60044

RAMLER, WARREN JOSEPH, radiation equipment co. exec.; b. Joliet, Ill., Jan. 1, 1921; s. John George and Anna Louise (Kohlmeyer) R.; B.S. in Elec. Engring., Ill. Inst. Tech., 1943, M.S. in Elec. Engring., 1953; postgrad. Carnegie-Mellon U., 1943-46, U. Pitts., 1943-46; m. Ruth E. Wilder, Sept. 4, 1943; children—John W., Richard W., Barbara Anne. Instr. elec. engring. and physics Carnegie Inst. Tech., 1943, 44, 46; elec. engr. Tenn. Eastman Corp., Oak Ridge, 1944-46; sr. scientist, project dir. low energy accelerators Argonne (Ill.) Nat. Lab., 1946-73, cons., 1973—; gen. mgr. Radiation Polymer Co. div. PPG Industries, Plainfield, Ill., 1973—; cons. to univs. and industry. Asso. chmn. Boy Scouts Am., Elmhurst, Ill., 1956-60; mem. sci. adv. com. York High Sch., 1962. Mem. IEEE, Am. Phys. Soc., Am. Mgmt. Assn., AAAS, N.Y. Acad. Scis., U.S. Power Squadron, Eta Kappa Nu, Tau Beta Pi, Rho Epsilon. Home: 15 Buckingham Dr Prestbury Aurora IL 60504

RAMNATH, RAMCHANDRA, plastic surgeon; b. Bombay, India, Aug. 8, 1929; s. K.S. Ramchandra and Chelli (Ammal) Iyer; came to U.S., 1962, naturalized, 1976; B.S., M.B., U. Bombay, 1954; m. Irmgard Pfitzer, June 20, 1963; children—Urmila, Albert, Erik, Michelle. Intern, Elizabeth (N.J.) Gen. Hosp., 1962-63; resident in surgery Provident and St. Agnes Hosps., Balt., 1962-66; resident in plastic surgery Christ Hosp., Cin., 1966-69; practice medicine specializing in plastic surgery, Dayton, Ohio, 1970—; mem. staff St. Elizabeth Med. Center, Miami Valley Hosp., Good Samaritan Hosp., Kettering Med. Center, Childrens Med. Center; asst. clin. prof. surgery Wright State U. Sch. Medicine; cons. in plastic surgery Dayton VA Center. Diplomate Am. Bd. Plastic Surgery. Mem. AMA, Ohio State, Pan Am. med. assns., Montgomery County Med. Soc., Dayton Surg. Soc., Internat. Cosmetic Surgery Assn., Assn. Surgeons of India, Am. Soc. Plastic Reconstructive Surgery, Ohio Valley Plastic and Reconstructive Soc. Clubs: Racquet (Dayton); Lions; Ghatkoper (India). Home: 430 E Schantz Ave Dayton OH 45409 Office: 3080 Ackerman Blvd Dayton OH 45429

RAMP, ALVON DENEAL, coll. data processor; b. Dixon, Ill. Sept. 10, 1947; s. Jacob Levi and Bertha Mae (Rucker) R.; B.S. in Math., No. Ill. U., 1969; M.B.A., Loyola U., Chgo., 1977; m. Jeryl Ann McGreevy, Aug. 25, 1968; children—Alette Christine, Patrick Christian, Megan Ann. Systems programmer No. Ill. U., DeKalb, 1968-70; adminstrv. systems analyst Coll. of DuPage, Glen Ellyn, Ill., 1970-72, asso. dir. data processing and programming, 1972-74, dir. data processing, 1974—; instructional specialist for data processing Boulder (Colo.) Valley Schs., 1972; instr. Coll. of DuPage, 1971-72, Waubonsee Community Coll., Sugar Grove, Ill., 1970-72; EDP cons., 1971—. Mem. Data Processing Mgmt. Assn., Ill. Assn. Ednl. Data Systems (dir.), Lincoln Sch. PTA, Loyola U. of Chgo. Grad. Sch. Bus., No. Ill. U. alumni assns., Internat., Wheaton Jaycees, S.E. Wheaton Homeowners Assn. Roman Catholic. Home: 1522 Gainesboro Dr Wheaton IL 60187 Office: 22d and Lambert Rd Glen Ellyn IL 60137

RAMP, WILBER FRANKLIN, JR., bus. exec.; b. Anthony, Kans., July 21, 1924; s. Wilber Franklin and Edna (Childers) R.; student U. Houston, 1942, U. Wichita, 1942, Northwestern Coll. Law, 1962; m. Gerd Vendela Johnson, Nov. 29, 1946; children—Karen V., Deborah Ann. Co-owner, sales mgr. Alemite Co. of N.W., Portland, Oreg., 1945-66, automotive sales mgr. Alemite div. Stewart-Warner Corp., Chgo., 1967-69, dir. mktg., 1969-74; pres. Heavy Duty Parts Inc. div. Bandag Inc., Muscatine, Iowa, 1974-75; group v.p. mktg. Applied Power Inc., Milw., 1975-77; nat. sales mgr. Robert Bosch Corp., Broadview, Ill., 1977—; lectr. Am. Mgmt. Assn. Served with USAAF, 1942-45; USAF, 1951-52. Decorated Air medal with five clusters, Bronze Star; named Internat. Booster of Year Automotive Booster Clubs Internat., 1962. Mem. Equipment and Tool Inst. (pres.), Automotive Booster Clubs Internat. (past pres.), Aircraft Owners and Pilots Assn., Nat. Aero. Assn., Nat. Pilots Assn., Automotive Service Industry Assn. Republican. Presbyterian. Club: Oswego Lake Country (past pres.), (Portland, Oreg.); Knollwood (Lake Forest, Ill.). Office: Robert Bosch Corp Broadview IL 60153

RAMSEY, WILLIAM EUGENE, sch. adminstr.; b. Council Bluffs, Iowa, Dec. 14, 1929; s. George Franklin and Rose Beatrice (Roarty) R.; B.S., Creighton U., 1956; JRN (hon.), Duchesne Coll., 1964; m. Patricia Ann Cleary, July 23, 1931; children—Jeanne, Mark, Ellen, James, Margaret Mary. Reporter, photographer WOW-TV, Omaha, 1956-60; dir. pub. relations Duchesne Coll. and Acad., Omaha, 1960-65; dir. pub. relations Creighton U., Omaha, 1965-68; account exec. Holland Dreves Reilly Advt., Omaha, 1968-72; account exec. Bozell & Jacobs, Inc., advt., Omaha, 1972-74; dep. dir. devel. and pub. relations Boys' Town (Nebr.), 1974—. Chmn. Omaha Transit Authority, 1972-77; mem. Interracial Com.; bd. regents Conception Sem. Coll. Served with USMCR, 1948-49, 50-52. Decorated Purple Heart; recipient Nat. Edn. award Am. Advt. Fedn., 1970, Outstanding Citizen award Woodmen of the World Ins. Soc., 1971, Nat. award Coll. Pub. Relations Assn., 1964, Service award Arthritis Found., 1972, Man of Year award Navy Marine Corps Council, 1971. Mem. 1st Marine Div. Assn. (past pres.), Pub. Relations Soc. Am. (pres. Nebr. chpt. 1976), Omaha Press Club (pres. 1974-75), Alpha Sigma Nu. Club: Rotary (v.p.). Home: 307 S 51st Ave Omaha NE 68132 Office: Boys Town Boys Town NE 68010

RAMSLAND, MAXWELL O., real estate appraiser and cons.; b. Duluth, Minn., Aug. 13, 1939; s. Maxwell O. and Virginia (Mendenhall) R.; B.A., U. Minn., 1963; m. Betty S. Golden, Sept. 23, 1967; 1 son, Austin W. Staff appraiser Equitable Life Assurance Soc. U.S., Washington, 1964-68; asso. Wilbur S. Ratcliffe & Assos., Washington, 1968-70, C. Robert Boucher & Assos., Washington, 1970-71; cons. and appraiser real estate, Duluth, 1971-77; pres. Ramsland, Johnson & Vigen Inc., Duluth, 1977—. Mem. Am. Soc. Appraisers (dir. ednl. found. 1972—), Am. Inst. Real Estate Appraisers (dir. Minn. chpt. 1978—), Soc. Real Estate Appraisers, Am. Arbitration Assn. Club: Kitchi Gammi. Contbr. articles to profl. publs. Home: 2401 E 1st St Duluth MN 55812 Office: Torrey Bldg Duluth MN 55802

RANA, MOHAMMED WAHEED-UZ-ZAMAN, educator; b. Lahore, Pakistan, May 28, 1934; s. Nizam-ud-Din and Zainib (Begum) R.; came to U.S., 1962, naturalized, 1969; A.B., Olivet Coll., 1964; M.S., Wayne State U., 1966, Ph.D., 1968; m. Janice Adrian Wolford, Aug. 21, 1965; children—Jamil Zaman, Anissa Jan. Instr., Med. Sch. St. Louis U., 1968-70, asst. prof., 1970—. Chmn. religious affairs Moslem Student Assn. Greater St. Louis, 1970—; bd. dirs. Internat. Inst. St. Louis, 1975—; bd. dirs., chmn. Islamic Center Greater St. Louis, 1974—. Served with Pakistan Navy, 1953-59. Mem. Am. Assn. Anatomists, So. Soc. Anatomists, Islamic Med. Assn., Soc. Exptl. Biology and Medicine, N.Y. Acad. Sci., Sigma Xi.

Contbr. articles to sci. publs. Home: 5610 Valleyside St Saint Louis MO 63128

RAND, SIDNEY ANDERS, coll. pres., clergyman; b. Eldred, Minn., May 9, 1916; s. Charles William and Ida Alice (Pedersen) R.; B.A., Concordia Coll., Moorhead, Minn., 1938, D.D. (hon.), 1956; C.T., Luther Theol. Sem., St. Paul, 1943; student U. Chgo., 1947-48, 49, 50; LL.D. (hon.), Colo. Coll., 1976; m. Dorothy Alice Holm, Sept. 1, 1942 (dec. Jan. 1974); children—Peter Anders, Mary Alice; m. 2d, Lois M. Ekeren, Nov. 23, 1974. Ordained to ministry Lutheran Ch., 1943; pastor in Nashwauk, Minn., 1943-45; asst., then asso. prof. religion Corcordia Coll., 1945-51; pres. Waldorf Coll., Forest City, Iowa, 1951-56; exec. dir. bd. Christian edn. Evang. Luth. Ch., 1956-61; exec. dir. bd. coll. edn. Am. Luth. Ch., 1961-63; pres. St. Olaf Coll., Northfield, Minn., 1963—; dir. N.Am. Life and Casualty Co., Northfield Nat. Bank Minn. Bd. for Continuing Legal Edn. Tutor Ecumenical Inst., World Council Chs., 1962-63; trustee Fairview Hosp., Mpls. Decorated knight 1st class Order of St. Olaf (Norway), 1974. Mem. Norwegian Am. Hist. Assn., Assn. Am. Colls. (dir.), Phi Beta Kappa. Club: Rotary. Co-author: Christian Faith and the Liberal Arts, 1960. Home: 1215 Saint Olaf Ave Northfield MN 55057

RAND, THEODORE ARNOLD, accountant; b. Presque Isle, Me., Aug. 31, 1936; s. Glen C. and Irene (Collier) R.; B.S., Aurora Coll., 1958; postgrad. No. Ill. U., 1961, Northwestern U., 1965, DePaul U., 1966; m. Pauline A. Davenport, Sept. 2, 1955; children—Barbara Anne, Terri Lynn. Salesman, Swalley Realty, Aurora, Ill., 1958-59, Sears Roebuck & Co., Chgo., 1959-63; sr. accountant Peat, Marwick, Mitchell & Co., Chgo., 1963-67; treas., controller Queen's-Way to Fashion, Inc., Niles, 1967-71, v.p.-fin., 1971-75, mktg. dir., 1975—, also dir.; group v.p. Aparacor, Inc., 1976—. C.P.A., Ill. Mem. Ill. Soc. C.P.A.'s, (charter mem. Fox Valley chpt.), Am. Inst. C.P.A.'s, Nat. Assn. Accountants. Home: 1003 Brookwood Dr E Arlington Heights IL 60004 Office: 7300 N Melvina Ave Niles IL 60648

RANDALL, DUDLEY FELKER, librarian; b. Washington, Jan. 14, 1914; s. Arthur George Clyde and Ada Viola (Bradley) R.; B.A., Wayne U., 1949; M.L.S., U. Mich., 1951; m. Ruby Hudson Hands, June 28, 1935 (div. 1942); 1 dau., Phyllis Randall Sherron III; m. 3d, Vivian Barnett Spencer, May 4, 1957. Librarian, Lincoln U., Jefferson City, Mo., 1951-54, instr. library sci., 1952-54; librarian Morgan State Coll., Balt., 1954-56, Wayne County (Mich.) Federated Library System, 1956-69; librarian U. Detroit, 1969—, instr. English, 1969, poet-in-residence, 1969-74; instr. English, U. Mich., 1969; founder, editor Broadside Press, 1965—; chmn. poetry com. Detroit Soc. Advancement of Culture and Edn., 1966-76; mem. arts com. New Detroit, Inc., 1971-76; mem. lit. com. Mich. Council on Arts, 1970-76. Served with AUS, 1942-46. Mem. ALA, Mich. Library Assn. (chmn. hosp. div. 1963), Detroit Council Arts, Kappa Alpha Psi. Congregationalist. Club: Motor City Tennis (Detroit). Author: Poem Counterpoem, 1966; Cities Burning, 1968; Love You, 1970; More to Remember, 1971; After the Killing, 1973; Broadside Memories, 1975; A Capsule Course in Black Poetry Writing, 1975; editor: For Malcolm, 1967; Black Poetry, 1969; The Black Poets, 1971. Home: 12651 Old Mill Pl Detroit MI 48238 Office: 12652 Livernois Ave Detroit MI 48238

RANDALL, JOHN DANIEL, lawyer; b. Lisbon, Iowa, Nov. 30, 1899; s. Mac J. and Katharine R. (Stahl) R.; LL.B., Coe Coll., Cedar Rapids, Iowa, 1923, LL.D., 1959; m. Margaret E. Graham, June 20, 1925; children—Margaret Sue (Mrs. William J. Jameson, Jr.), John D. Admitted to Iowa bar, 1923, since practiced in Cedar Rapids. Fellow Am. Coll. Trial Lawyers; mem. Am. (chmn. ho. of dels., 1954-56, state del. Iowa, 1948-54, unauthorized practice of law com. 1944-54, chmn. rules and calendar com. 1952-54, chmn. 1946-52, co-chmn. joint conf. on profl. responsibility, pres., 1959-60; gov. 1960-61, pres. Am. Bar Found. 1959-60, chmn. sect. gen. practice 1962-63, chmn. profl. grievances com. 1967-68, dir., pres. bar endowment 1967-69, chmn. grants com. 1969-71), Inter-Am. (v.p. 1959-60), Internal., Iowa (unauthorized practice com., 1939-42 chmn. 1946-52), Linn County (pres. 1947-48), Ill., Chgo., Canadian bar assns., Assn. Bar City N.Y., Law Soc. Eng., Am. Law Inst., Am. Judicature Soc., Internat. Assn. Ins. Counsel, Assn. Inst. Attys. (v.p. 1961-62, pres. 1962-63), Fedn. Ins. Counsel, Nat. Conf. Realtors and Lawyers (co-chmn, 1945-46) Nat. Conf. Lawyers and Reps. of Am. Bankers Assn. trust div., 1945-49, Nat. Conf. Lawyers and C.P.A.'s, (co-chmn. 1950-56). Nat. Conf. Lawyers and Life Underwriters, Nat. Conf. Lawyers and Adjusters, Nat. Conf. Lawyers and Liability Insurers (chmn.), Am. Legion, Selden Soc., Nat. Legal Aid and Defender Assn. (v.p. 1959-60), Order of Coif, Sigma Phi Epsilon, Phi Alpha Delta. Republican. Presbyn. Mason (Shriner). Clubs: Pickwick (Cedar Rapids); Union League (Chgo.). Author articles on unauthorized practice of law. Home: 328 Forest Dr SE Cedar Rapids IA 52407 Office: 330 1st St SE Cedar Rapids IA 52407

RANDALL, JOHN DANIEL, JR., lawyer; b. Cedar Rapids, Iowa, July 30, 1935; s. John Daniel and Margaret (Graham) R.; B.A., State U. Iowa, 1958, LL.B., 1959; m. Melissa Lyon, Nov. 10, 1962; 1 son, John Daniel III. Admitted to Iowa bar, 1959; asso. John D. Randall Law Office, Cedar Rapids, 1959—. Vice pres. exec. com. Old Shad's Assn., Shattuck Sch., Minn., 1972-76. Mem. Am. (gen. practice sect. council 1967-73, vice chmn. com. on coms. 1967-68, membership com. 1967-74, lay assts. to lawyers com. 1969-70, utilization lay assts. to lawyers com. 1970-72, budget and fin. com. 1972-76, sub-com. legal assts. 1972-75), Iowa, Linn County bar assns., Cedar Rapids C. of C., Sigma Nu, Phi Alpha Delta. Clubs: University Athletic, Pickwick. Mason (Shriner). Home: PO Box 2131 330 1st St SE Cedar Rapids IA 52406 Office: 330 1st St SE Cedar Rapids IA 52407

RANDALL, PRISCILLA RICHMOND (MRS. RAYMOND V. RANDALL), pub. relations exec.; b. Arlington, Mass., Mar. 19, 1926; d. Harold B. and Florence (Hoefler) Richmond; student Wellesley Coll., 1943-44, Garland Sch., 1944-46, Winona State U. extension, 1967—; m. Raymond V. Randall, Mar. 2, 1946; children—Raymond R., Priscilla, Susan. Publicity and publs. coordinator Rochester (Minn.) Meth. Hosp., 1960-66, pub. relations cons., 1966-69; pub. relations dir. Sheraton-Rochester Hotel, Rochester, 1969-71; owner, sr. cons. Ideas Unltd., Rochester, 1971—; sr. cons. Med. Travel; pres. Randall Travel, Inc., Rochester, 1977, SABU, Inc., 1972-74; travel writer, 1976—; producer TV show Priscilla's World, 1972-75. Mem. Am. Soc. Hosp. Pub. Relations Dirs., Internat. Platform Assn., Acad. Hosp. Pub. Relations, Pub. Relations Soc. Am., Coordinated Health Communications Soc. (sec.-treas. 1970), Rochester Meth. Hosp. Aux. (pres. 1955-57). Editor: Inside Story, Rochester Meth. Hosp. News, 1960-69. Address: 611 Memorial Pkwy Rochester MN 55901

RANDALL, ROBERT WILLIAM, realtor; b. Danville, Ill., May 16, 1938; s. Buell Hubert and Mary Alys (Pittaway) R.; student Danville Jr. Coll., Henry George Sch. Social Sci.; m. Deborah Sue Petro, May 3, 1974; children—Kristi Lynn (dec.), Mark Alan. Frameman Ill. Bell Telephone Co., 1956-59, switchman, 1959-63, central office foreman, 1963-67, assignment foreman, 1967-70; real estate salesman B. W. Cooper Broker & Builder, 1964-69; owner Cooper-Randall Realtors & Builders, 1970-76, Robert W. Randall, Realtor, 1976—; bd. dirs. Danville Area Bd. Realtors, 1973-74, Multiple Listing Service, 1975-77. Mem. Vermillion County (Ill.) Mental Health Bd., 1969-74, chmn., 1973; bd. dirs. Retarded Children Center, 1972, Vermillion County Rehab. Center, 1971-72. Mem. Ill. Assn. Realtors, Nat. Assn. Real Estate Bds., Danville C. of C., Am. Bus. Club. Mem. Christian Ch. Clubs: Danville Country, Elks. Home: 161 Thornhill Dr Danville IL 61832 Office: 807 Oak St Danville IL 61832

RANDALL, ROGERS ELLIS, educator; b. Browntown, La., Feb. 2, 1925; s. Wilson and Calvie (Haughton) R.; B.A., Dillard U., 1950; M.A., U. Mich., 1951; M.A. in Teaching, Miami U., Oxford, Ohio, 1961; Ph.D., Ohio State U., 1974; m. Mildred Hamm, Aug. 25, 1950; children—Rogers Ellis, Della Carol. Instr., So. U., Baton Rouge, 1951-55, asst. prof., 1955-57, acting chmn. physics, math. dept., 1956-57; instr. sci. Roosevelt Sch., Gary, Ind., 1958-74, chmn. sci. dept., 1965-74; instr. chemistry, physics Adult Edn. Program, Gary, 1964-74; asst. prof. chemistry and physics Calumet Coll., Hammond, Ind., 1974—, chmn. div. sci. and math., 1977—. Bd. dirs. Stewart Settlement House, Gary. Served with AUS, 1942-46. Mem. Am. Inst. Chemists, Nat. Sci. Tchrs. Assn., Ind. Acad. Sci. (speakers bur.), Am. Assn. Physics Tchrs., Gary Sci. Council (pres. 1967-69, 72-73), NAACP, N. Central Crediting Assn. Colls. and Secondary Schs., Beta Kappa Chi, Phi Delta Kappa, Alpha Phi Alpha. Methodist (outstand-layman Calumet dist. 1971, asso. lay leader 1971—, lay speaker). Mason. Home: 2395 W 20th Pl Gary IN 46404

RANDOLPH, ALICE HARRINGTON, rehab. counselor; b. East Liverpool, Ohio, Aug. 24, 1948; d. Clarence Edwin and Raffaela Marie (Familia) Harrington; B.S., W.Va. U., 1968, M.S., 1970, Ed.D., 1974; m. Douglas Guy Randolph, Aug. 3, 1968; children—Matthew Harrington, Lance Coffman. Rehab. counselor W.Va. Div. Vocat. Rehab., Fairmont, 1970-72; tng. asst., materials devel. specialist Rehab. Research and Tng. Center, W.Va. U., Morgantown, 1972-75; asso. dir. tng. W.Va. Rehab. Research and Tng. Center, W.Va. Rehab. Center, Institute, 1975—; cons. JWK Internat.; cons. dept. counselor edn. U. Mich.; cons. Rehab. Inst., So. Ill. U., others. Charter mem., 1st sec. Marion County Community Council. Mem. Am. Personnel and Guidance Assn., Nat. Council on Rehab. Edn., Am., Nat. rehab. counseling assns., Assn. Counselor Educators and Suprs., Nat., W.Va. rehab. assns. Home: 1334 Fisher Rd Burton OH 44021 Office: W Va Rehab Research and Tng Center W Va Rehab Center Institute WV 25112

RANDOLPH, FRANKLIN LEE, agrl. engr.; b. Golconda, Ill., July 4, 1932; s. Winfield Scott and Mattie Jane (Julian) R.; student Central Mich. U., 1956-58; B.S., Mich. State U., 1960; m. Phyllis Joyce Nystrom, Nov. 13, 1954; children—Victoria, Marilyn, Jonathan. Design engr. Internat. Harvester Co., farm equipment mfg., Hinsdale, Ill., 1960-66; chief engr. Panduit Corp., design of plastic parts and machines, Tinley Park, 1966-74; owner, pres. Randolph Co., Mattoon, Ill., 1974—. Served with USNR, 1952-56. Registered profl. engr., Ill. Mem. Am. Soc. Agrl. Engrs., Kappa Mu Epsilon. Baptist (chmn. bd. trustees 1962-65). Home: 1220 Wabash Ave Mattoon IL 61938 Office: 1815 Broadway Mattoon IL 61938

RANDOLPH, JACKSON HAROLD, utility co. exec.; b. Cin., Nov. 17, 1930; s. Deward Bradley and Cora Belle (Puckett) R.; B.B.A., U. Cin., 1958, M.B.A., 1968; postgrad. U. Mich., 1969; m. Angelina Losito, June 28, 1958; children—Terri Lynn, Patti Dawn, Todd Jackson, Craig Louis. Accountant, Arthur Andersen & Co., C.P.A.'s, Chgo., 1958-59; accountant, auditor Cin. Gas & Electric Co., 1959—; tax cons., 1963—. Chmn. fin. com. Oak Hills Sch. Bd., Cin., 1970-71; bd. dirs. Gen. Protestant Orphan's Home, Cin. chpt. ARC. Served with USNR, 1951-55. C.P.A., Ohio. Mem. Am. Inst. C.P.A.'s, Ohio Soc. C.P.A.'s (state tax com. 1970-71), Tax Execs. Inst. (chmn. state tax com. 1970-71), Phi Eta Sigma, Beta Alpha Psi, Delta Sigma Pi. Mem. United Ch. Christ (pres. 1970). Home: 7084 Goldengate Dr Cincinnati OH 45244 Office: 4th and Main Sts Cincinnati OH 45202

RANDOLPH, KENNETH HENRY, veterinarian; b. McCausland, Iowa, June 23, 1923; s. Clarence Raymond and Lillian Henrietta (Litscher) R.; B.S., Iowa State U., 1943, M.S., D.V.M., 1950; m. Carmaleta Frances Stephens, Dec. 21, 1946; children—Joylene Ann, Kerry Alden, Jody Lee. Grad. asst. dept. anatomy Iowa State U., 1947-50; pvt. veterinary practice, Lost Nation, Iowa, 1950—. Mem. Lost Nation City Council, 1957-62. Served with AUS, 1944-46. Mem. AVMA, Eastern Iowa, Iowa veterinary med. assns., Soc. Gentle Doctor, Phi Kappa Phi, Alpha Zeta. Republican. Presbyterian (elder 1962-75). Clubs: Masons, Shriners, Order Eastern Star, Lost Nation Booster, Cyclone Century. Home: 304 Esther St Lost Nation IA 52254 Office: 311 Main St Lost Nation IA 52254

RANDOLPH, ROBERT MARSHALL, mgmt. cons., cons. engring. co. exec.; b. Lincoln, Ill., Nov. 21, 1935; s. Harry Marshall and Mildred Maud (Smith) R.; B.S. in Civil Engring., U. Ill., 1958; M.B.A., Bradley U., 1971; m. JoAnn Cudworth, Sept. 5, 1959; children—Gregory Marshall, Bradley Alan, Jeffery Phillip. With Clark, Daily & Dietz, cons. engrs., Urbana-Champaign, Ill., 1958-60, Warren & Van Praag, Inc., Decatur, Ill., 1960-65; chief engr. Wiegand & Storrer, Inc., East Peoria, Ill., 1965-69; v.p., mgr. Daily & Asso., Engrs., Inc., Peoria, Ill., 1969-74; pres., chmn. bd. Randolph & Asso., Inc., Peoria, 1974—; instr. bus. occupations div. Ill. Central Coll., East Peoria, 1972-74. Co-capt., instr. Macon County Underwater Recovery Team, Decatur, Ill., 1961-64; chmn. recreation area com. Peoria (Ill.) Assn. of Commerce, 1970-71; chmn. Peoria Area Continued Tech. Edn. Com., 1973-74; mem. East Peoria Dist. 85 Bd. of Edn., 1974—, pres., 1976—. Registered profl. engr. Ill. Mem. ASCE, Am. Mktg. Assn., Am. Water Works Assn., Am. Pub. Works Assn., Central States Water Pollution Control Fedn., Farm Bur., Nat., Ill. (pres. Peoria chpt. 1972-73) socs. profl. engrs. Mason (K.T., Shriner), Rotarian. Club: Creve Coeur. Home: 405 Timber Ln East Peoria IL 61611 Office: 2000 W Pioneer Pkwy Peoria IL 61614

RANDOLPH, ROSS V., state ofcl.; b. Hazen, Ark., May 9, 1907; s. Roy and Laura (Hunt) R.; grad. Ill. State Normal U.; m. Irene Stroub, May 17, 1941; 1 son, Ronald. Tchr., prin. pub. schs., rural areas, Ill.; dep. sheriff DeWitt County (Ill.); dir. edn. Ill. Penitentiary, Pontiac, warden, Menard; asst. supt. parole supervision State of Ill., Springfield; spl. agt. FBI, Washington; adminstrv. asst. to gov. State of Ill., Springfield, dir. Dept. Pub. Safety; dir. police East St. Louis (Ill.), from 1969; now under-sheriff Cook County (Ill.). Recipient numerous awards including Certificate of Honorable War Service, FBI, Humanitarian award Rabbinical Soc. Greater St. Louis, 1961, Distinguished Service award So. Ill. U., 1962, Outstanding Citizen award Chester C. of C., 1965; named Mr. So. Illinoisan So. Ill. Editorial Assn., 1965. Mem. Am. Correctional Assn. (v.p. 1965-66), Wardens Assn. Am. (pres. 1965-66), W. Central Wardens Assn. (pres.), Ill. Police Assn., Soc. Former Spl. Agts. FBI, Inc., Nat., Ill. sheriffs assns., Nat. Jail Assn., Central States Corrections Assn., Ill. Rifle Assn., Am. Soc. Pub. Adminstrs., Med. Correctional Assn. Am. Home: Lake Point Tower 505 N Lake Shore Dr Chicago IL 60611

RANEY, EUGENE HUBERT, obstetrician-gynecologist; b. Effingham, Ill., Oct. 11, 1927; s. Jeremiah Raymond and Marie Mary (Grauel) R.; B.S., Eastern Ill. State U., 1950; M.D., U. Ill., 1955; m. Joan Marion Scheve, Apr. 21, 1956; children—Keith Eugene, Brian Joseph, Patrick Jeremiah, Jeanne Marie. Intern, Cook County Hosp., Chgo., 1955-56, resident in obstetrics and gynecology, 1956-59; practice medicine, specializing in obstetrics and gynecology Med. Arts Clinic, Appleton, Wis., 1959—; chmn. obstetrics and gynecology dept. Appleton Meml. Hosp., 1963-64, St. Elizabeth Hosp., Appleton, 1967-68, 71-72. Served with USNR, 1945-46. Diplomate Am. Bd. Obstetrics and Gynecology. Mem. Am. Coll. Obstetrics and Gynecology, Central Assn. Obstetrics and Gynecology, Outagamie Med. Soc. (pres. 1975-76), Wis. Assn. Perinatal Care (pres. 1973-76). Home: 40 River Dr Appleton WI 54911 Office: 401 N Oneida St Appleton WI 54911

RANIERI, DOMINIC GILBERT, pub. accountant; b. DuBois, Pa., May 11, 1921; s. Julio and Angelina (Ronda) R.; student Du Bois Bus. Coll., 1944-45; m. Rita Clara Schock, Oct. 21, 1950; children—Jane F., Paul W., Christopher J., Gerard J., Maria V., Anthony M. Assembly worker Piper Air Craft, Lock Haven, Pa., 1943-44; bookkeeper Auto Aligning Co., DuBois, 1945-46; inventory clk., Vulcan Soot Corp., DuBois, 1946-47; accountant WDAD Radio Sta., Indiana, Pa., 1947-49; accountant-treas. Tiffin (Ohio) Dairy, Inc., 1950-51; accounting dept. staff mem. NOBA Inc., Tiffin, 1951-63; dep. personal property dept. Seneca County Auditor's Office, Tiffin, 1963-68; individual practice accounting, Tiffin, 1968—; dir. Fry Foods Inc., Seneca Leasing Inc. Mem. Nat. Soc. Pub. Accountants. Home: 143 Melmore St Tiffin OH 44883 Office: 360 S Washington St Tiffin OH 44883

RANIVILLE, FRANCIS OLIVER, indsl. belting co. exec., poet; b. Grand Rapids, Mich., Oct. 19, 1920; s. Francis Felix and Charlotte Marie (Blickle) R.; D.Divine Lit. (hon.), Free U. Asia, 1976; D.Liberal Arts, Republic of China. With Raniville Co., Grand Rapids, 1940—, asst. sec., 1970—. Vol. worker Kent Community Hosp. Recipient gold medal Internat. Poet's Shrine, Hollywood, Calif., 1971, Centro Studi e Scambi Internazionali, 1975; silver laurel United Poets Laureate Internat., 1976; World Belletrist award Internat. Poetry Centre. Mem. World Poetry Soc. Intercontinental (magna cum laude award 1970), Hymn Soc. Am. (life), World Poets Resource Center (life), N.Y. Poetry Forum. Author: Bardic Echoes, 1971; Poet, 1971; Twentieth Century Hymns; Yearbook of Modern Poetry, 1971; Lyrics of Love, 1972; Melody of the Muse, 1973. Home: PO Box 1524 Grand Rapids MI 49501 Office: Raniville Co 247 Pearl St Grand Rapids MI 49502

RANKIN, MICHAEL RAE, mortgage banker; b. Coffeyville, Kans., July 16, 1945; s. Sam Harrison and Irene (Kochwelp) R.; B.S., Central Mo. State U., 1967; M.B.A., S.W. Mo. State U., 1976; m. Deborah K. Harmon, Aug. 31, 1968; children—Heather Rae, Ashley Mae. With Central Mortgage Bancshares, Inc., Springfield, Mo., 1970—, v.p., dir., chief exec. officer mortgage banking div., 1972—. Mem. Springfield Airport Commn.; bd. dirs. Ozarks council Boy Scouts Am. Served as 1st lt. U.S. Army, 1967-70; Vietnam. Decorated Bronze Star with oak leaf cluster. Mem. Am., Mo. (dir.), Kansas City mortgage bankers assns., S.W. Mo. Better Bus. Bur. (dir.). Lutheran. Clubs: Rotary (dir.), Twin Oaks Country. Home: 1934 E Lark St Springfield MO 65804 Office: MPO Box 631 Springfield MO 65801

RANNEY, G. DURBIN, ret. judge, cons.; b. Monmouth, Ill., Aug. 24, 1911; s. J. and Iva D. R.; B.S., Monmouth Coll., 1933; J.D., U. Mich., 1939; m. Betty Jane Marshall, June 4, 1940; children—Stephen M., Sue Ann. Admitted to Ill. bar, 1939; individual practice law, Monmouth, Ill. and Los Angeles, 1939-65; state's atty. Warren County (Ill.), 1940-43; judge 9th Ill. Jud. Circuit, Monmouth, 1950-53, 65-75; cons. law, Monmouth, 1976—; lectr. in field. Served with USNR, 1943-44. Mem. Am., Internat. bar assns. Home: 220 S 3d St Monmouth IL 61462 Office: PO Box 306 Monmouth IL 61462

RANOUS, CHARLES ALBERT, educator; b. Ann Arbor, Mich., July 18, 1912; s. Adelbert and Cora (Sink) R.; A.B., U. Mich., 1936, M.A., 1938; postgrad. Columbia U., 1949-53; m. Dorothy Diefendorf, June 7, 1940; 1 son, Karl E. Instr. English and speech U. Tenn., 1938-42, Drake U., 1944-47; instr. Air Force and Army programs Memphis State Coll. and U. Oreg., 1942-44 asst. prof., head freshman English, Fairleigh Dickinson U., 1949-53; tech. writer IT&T Labs., Nutley, N.J., 1953-57; tech. editor, engr. mgmt. staff Burroughs MECD, Detroit, 1957-60; asso. prof. tech. writing U. Wis., Madison, 1960-77, prof., 1977—; editorial cons. Mem. IEEE (sr.), Profl. Group on Edn., Am. Bus. Communication Assn., Republican. Club: Madison Technical. Author: (with Dunn and Allen) Learning Our Language, 1950; Communication for Engineers, 1964; (with D. Ranous) The Inner Zone, 1968; The Engineer's Interfaces, 1974; contbr. articles to profl. jours. in English, edn., engring. Home: 1321 Rosedale Madison WI 53714

RANSDELL, EDGAR CURTIS, III, obstetrician, gynecologist; b. Nebraska City, Nebr., Mar. 17, 1941; s. Edgar C. and Marjorie A. (Rivett) R.; M.D., U. Nebr., 1966; m. Jane E. Lowrey, Sept. 1, 1963; children—Travis Scott, Clay Edward. Intern, Wesley Med. Center, Wichita, Kans., 1966-67; resident U. Nebr. Hosp., Omaha, 1967-70; practice medicine specializing in obstetrics and gynecology, Drs. Tappen, Gleason, Ransdell, Topeka, 1970—; chief of obstetrics Stormont-Vail, St. Francis Hosps., Topeka; sec., treas. Tappen, Gleason, Ransdell. Served to maj. USAR, 1969-75. Fellow Am. Coll. Obstetricians; mem. AMA, Kans. Med. Assn., Topeka C. of C. Republican. So. Baptist. Clubs: Topeka, Topeka Town. Home: 141 Meadow Ln Topeka KS 66606 Office: 800 Lincoln St Topeka KS 66603

RANSOM, HENRY KING, surgeon, educator; b. Jan. 21, 1898; s. Fred C. and Gayle (King) R.; A.B., U. Mich., 1920, M.D., 1923, M.S. in Anatomy, 1934. Intern U. Mich. Hosp., 1923-24, asst. resident, 1924-25, instr. in surgery, 1925-26, sr. instr. in surgery, 1926-29, asst. prof., 1929-33, asso. prof., 1933-50, prof., 1950-68, acting chmn. dept. surgery, 1957-59, prof. emeritus, 1968—; surgeon U. Hosp., 1930-67, surgeon emeritus St. Joseph Mercy Hosp., 1942-60, cons. Ann Arbor VA Hosp., 1950-70. Diplomate Am. Bd. Surgery. Mem. Washtenaw County, Mich. State med. socs., AMA (vice chmn. sect. surgery and gen. abdominal 1956-57), A.C.S., Am., Western, Central (founder, pres. 1952-55), Frederick A. Coller (pres. 1952-55), St. Paul (Minn.), Internat. surg. socs., Soc. Surgery Alimentary Tract, Am. Gastroenterological Assn., Surgeons Club, Acad. Surgery Detroit, Flint Acad. Surgery, Galens Hon. Med. Soc., Alpha Omega Alpha (pres. 1922-23), Phi Kappa Phi, Phi Sigma, Phi Chi. Mem. editorial bd. Archives Surgery, 1956-63. Contbr. numerous articles to med. jours. Office: U Mich Med Sch Ann Arbor MI 48109

RANSOM, JAMES HARLEY, allergist, clin. adminstr.; b. Des Moines, Mar. 9, 1936; s. H.C. and Annabelle (Rutledge) R.; student Stanford, 1954-56; B.A., U. Iowa, 1958, M.D., 1962; m. Marcia Frances Mohler, May 20, 1972. Practice medicine specializing in allergy and immunology, Topeka, 1967—; mem. staff Topeka Allergy Clinic P.A., 1967—, pres., 1975—; pres. med. staff Stormont-Vail Hosp., Topeka. Diplomate Am. Bd. Allergy and Immunology. Fellow Am. Coll. Allergists, Am. Assn. Clin. Immunology; mem. Kans. Allergy Soc. (pres.). Episcopalian. Editor: Stormont-Vail Hosp. Profl. Bull., 1975—. Office: Topeka Allergy Clinic Medical Plaza 10th and Garfield Sts Topeka KS 66604

RAO, DESIRAJU BHAVANARAYANA, educator, meteorologist and oceanographer; b. Visakhapatnam, India, Dec. 8, 1936; s. Desiraju Sreeramulu and Desiraju Hanumayamma Adavikolanu; B.Sc., Andhra U., Waltair, India, 1956, M.Sc., 1959; M.S., U. Chgo., 1962, Ph.D., 1965; m. Vundavalli Uma Devi, Oct. 3, 1965; children—Desiraju

Pramila, Desiraju Kavitha. Came to U.S., 1960, naturalized, 1974. Research scholar Indian Naval Phys. Labs., Cochin, India, 1959-60; post-doctoral fellow Nat. Center Atmospheric Research, Boulder, Colo., 1965-67; research scientist marine scis. br. Canadian Dept. Energy, Mines and Resources, Ottawa, Ont., 1967-68; asst. prof. dept. atmospheric sci. Colo. State U., Fort Collins, 1968-71; asso. prof. dept. energetics, also Center for Gt. Lakes Studies, U. Wis.-Milw., 1971-74, prof., 1974-76; head phys. limnology and meteorology group Gt. Lakes Environ. Research Lab., NOAA, Ann Arbor, Mich., 1975—; adj. prof. limnology and meteorology U. Mich., 1977—; cons. Can. Center Inland Waters, Burlington, Ont., summer 1971; cons. to Canadian govt. on Bay of Fundy tidal power, 1972, Marine Environ. Data Services, Dept. Environment, Ottawa, Can., summer 1974. Mem. Am. Meteorol. Soc. (v.p. Denver chpt. 1969-70), Am. Soc. Limnology and Oceanography, AAAS, Meteorol. Soc. Japan, Internat. Water Resources Assn. (charter), Sigma Xi. Contbr. articles on atmospheric, oceanic and lake dynamics to sci. jours. Office: Great Lakes Environmental Research Lab 2300 Washtenaw Ave Ann Arbor MI 48104

RAOUL, JOSEPH, JR., hydraulic engr.; b. Haiti, Oct. 3, 1937; s. Joseph and Livie (Pierre) R.; M.S., U. Calif., 1962; diploma in hydraulic eng. U. Delft (Netherlands), 1965; M.S., U. Ill., 1977; m. Marie-Rose Hypolite, Oct. 15, 1966; children—Joseph, Mireille, Pascale. Head hydrology Consoes Townsend & Assos., Chgo., 1965-67; chief Great Lakes regulation C.E., U.S. Army, 1973-75; chief hydrologic and hydraulic engring. sect., Chgo., 1975—. Coach soccer Naperville (Ill.) Park Dist. Mem. ASCE, Am. Geophysical Union, Internat. Assn. Sci. Hydrology, Internat. Assn. Great Lakes Research, Internat. Assn. Hydraulic Research. Nat. Soc. Profl. Engrs. Home: 563 Dorset Ct Naperville IL 60540 Office: 536 S Clark Chicago IL 60605

RAPHAEL, RICK, govt. relations rep.; b. N.Y.C., Feb. 20, 1919; s. Louis Nevin and Viola (Felix) R.; B.A., U. N.Mex., 1952; postgrad. U. Philippines, 1938, Boise State Coll., 1961; m. Donna Edith Swenson, May 19, 1972; children—Christopher, Patricia, Melanie Raphael Swensen, Karen Raphael Pleak, Teresa, Stephanie Raphael Martinez. Editor, reporter Albuquerque Jour., 1946-50, Denver Post, 1950-51, Ariz. Republic, Phoenix, 1951-53, San Bernardino (Calif.) Sun, 1953-56, Middleton (N.Y.) Record, 1956-58, Idaho Daily Statesman, Boise, 1958-59; news dir., polit. editor Sta. KBOI-TV, Boise, 1959-63; press sec., exec. asst. U.S. Senator Frank Church, Washington, 1963-69; legis. rep. J.C. Penny Co., Mpls., 1969-74, sr. govt. relations rep., 1974—; lectr. polit. sci. Coll. Idaho, 1960-61, George Washington U., Am. U., Washington, 1964-66. Bd. dirs. State Govtl. Affairs Council. Served to capt. AUS, 1936-45. Decorated Bronze Star with oak leaf and valor clusters, Purple Heart with oak leaf cluster; named Outstanding Nat. Producer-Dir. TV Documentary News, Nat. Radio and TV News Dirs. Assn., 1962. Mem. Nuclear Energy Writers Assn., Sci. Fiction Writers Assn., Guthrie Found., U.S. Ski Assn., Nat. Geog. Soc., Minn. Press Club, Jefferson Forum, Sigma Delta Chi. Episcopalian. Club: Tower. Author: The Thirst Quenchers, 1965; Code Three, 1966; contbr. articles, short stories, novellas to mags. Home: 3320 Niagara Ln Minneapolis MN 55441 Office: 730 2d Ave S Minneapolis MN 55402

RAPP, RALPH L., ins. co. exec.; b. Boonville, Mo., Sept. 27, 1934; s. Walter and Wilma L. (Richerson) R.; grad. high sch.; m. Mildred C. Schuster, Jan. 17, 1953; children—Ronald, Donald, William, Edward, Barbara, Wanda, Patricia. Asst. Modern Am. Life, Springfield, Mo., 1965-66, mgr., 1966-67, v.p., 1967-70; pres. Modern Income Life Ins. Co., Decatur, Ill., 1970—; chmn. bd. dirs. United Empire Life Ins. Co., Indpls. Mem. Ill. Assn. Life Ins. Cos. 1st v.p. 1976—), Decatur C. of C. Rotarian. Home: 4431 Country Manor Ct Decatur IL 62521 Office: 788 N Sunnyside Rd Decatur IL 62521

RAPPANA, DUANE ARCHIE, laundry exec.; b. Mpls., Jan. 21, 1924; s. Archie W. and Hilda (Mattila) R.; B.A., U. Minn., 1948; m. Jean L. Modahl, July 2, 1948; children—Diane, Richard. With Duluth Laundry, Inc. (Minn.), 1948—, v.p., 1954—; dir. Duluth Nat. Bank; mem. Minn. Ho. of Reps., 1964-71. City councilman, Duluth, 1959-63. Served with USNR, 1942-46, 52-54; Korea; comdr. Res. (ret.). Mem. Minn. Fabricare Inst. (pres. 1977), Am. Legion, C. of C., West End Bus. Club (pres. 1957-58). Clubs: Masons (32 deg.), Shriners, Kiwanis. Home: 62 Pike Lake Duluth MN 55811 Office: 17 N 20th Ave W Duluth MN 55806

RAPPOPORT, ARTHUR EVERETT, physician; b. Bklyn, Dec. 23, 1911; s. Samuel and Mary (Babes) R.; student N.Y. U., 1929-32 M.D., Hamburg, U. (Germany), 1936; m. Eleanor J. Moses, Oct. 2, 1938; children—Ronald, William, Mark, Bruce, Catherine; m. 2d. Dolores L. Williams, July 3, 1964; children—Kevin, Scott, Marlyse Joy. Intern, Rochester Gen. Hosp., 1937-38; resident Barmbeck Gen. Hosp., Hamburg, 1933-36; practice medicine specializing in pathology, Youngstown, Ohio, 1946—; pres. A.E. Rappoport, Inc., Research Tech., Inc.; cons. lab. medicine IBM; also pathologist, dir. labs. Youngstown Hosp. Assn.; physician in residence VA, Washington; faculty Grad. Sch., Youngstown State U.; prof. pathology N.E. Ohio Univs. Coll. Medicine; cons. health facilities planning and constrn. H.S.M.H.A., HEW. Dir. Sci. Seminar for Gifted Students, Boardman High Sch. Mem. gov.'s adv. bd., bur. labs. Ohio Lab. Improvement Program; bd. dirs. Youngstown Symphony Soc. Served from lt. to lt. col., AUS, M.C., 1940-46. Recipient research grants USPHS, Hartford Found., AMA. Fellow Am. Soc. Clin. Pathologists, Coll. Am. Pathologists (gov.), Internat. Acad. of Pathology, Royal Coll. Pathology (founder fellow; Gt. Britain), Am. Soc. Cytology, Am. Assn. Pathology, Am. Soc. Nuclear Medicine, Am. Assn. Blood Banks, Soc. Advanced Med. Systems; mem. Academic Clin. Lab. Physicians and Scientists, Ohio Soc. Pathology (pres.), Am. Soc. Cytology, Am. Assn. Clin. Scientists, N.Y. Acad. Sci., Assn. for Advancement Med. Instrumentation, World Assn. Socs. Pathology (chmn. commn. on automation and documentation, chmn. subcom. on quality control), Soc. Computer Medicine, Am. Assn. Hosp. Consultants (affiliate), Inst. for Standardizierung und Dokumentation in Medizinische Laboratorium (corr. mem.), Deutsche Gesellschaft fur Klinische Chemie, Deutsche Gesellschaft fur Laboratoriums-Medizin, Deutsche Gesellschaft fur Angewandte Datenverarbeitung d. Medizin, Societe Francaise de Biologie Medicale. Author: Manual on Laboratory Planning and Design; Computer Assisted Pathology; also chpts. in books, articles in sci. jours. Editorial bd. Nat./Internat. Lab World, Biometrica, Lab, Revue d' Informatique Medicale; editor Quality Control in Clinical Chemistry, 1971. Home: 19024 Bob-o-Link Dr Country Club of Miami Hialeah FL 33015 Office: Youngstown Hosp Assn Youngstown OH 44501

RASH, JACK DEAN, med. found. adminstr.; b. Corsicana, Tex., Oct. 22, 1948; s. Charles Grant and Billie Maxine (Long) R.; A.A., Navarro Coll., 1969; student U. Tex., 1969-71; B.A., Baker U., 1975; M.A., Webster Coll., 1977. Adminstr. Brandon Psychiat. Group, Kansas City, Mo., 1973-76; mng. editor Corrective and Social Psychiatry, Olathe, Kans., 1973-76; chief exec. officer Martin Psychiat. Research Found., Olathe, 1976—. Mem. Assn. Mental Health Adminstrs., Kans. Hosp. Assn., Nat. Assn. Pvt. Psychiat. Hosps., Kans. Hosp. Personnel Mgmt. Assn., Kansas City Area Hosp. Assn. Home: 1617 Central Kansas City KS 66102 Office: 122 N Cooper Olathe KS 66061

RASMUSSEN, OSCAR GUSTAV, pharm. co. exec.; b. Chgo., Jan. 24, 1932; s. Knud Boyer and Anna Catherine (Waldau) R.; B.S., U. Ill., 1954, M.S., 1958, Ph.D., 1965; m. JoAnn F. Simpson, June 21, 1952; children—Shelly, Jeff, Mark. Sr. lab. technician U. Ill., Urbana, 1954, grad. asst., 1957-58; biochemist Am. Meat Inst. Found., Chgo., 1958-64; with nutrition dept. Armour Co., Oak Brook, Ill., 1964-66; research and lab dir. Triple F Feeds, Des Moines, 1966-71; with Miller Pharmacal Co., West Chicago, Ill., 1971-76, exec. v.p.; now pres. M2 Ethicals, Inc. Served with AUS, 1955-56. Mem. Animal Nutrition Research Council, Chgo. Nutrition Assn., Poultry Sci. Assn., Am. Soc. Animal Sci., Assn. Vitamin Chemists (pres. 1973-74), Inst. Food Technologists, Internat. Acad. Preventive Medicine, Internat. Coll. Applied Nutrition, Sigma Xi, Chi Gamma Iota. Home: 64 Waxwing St Naperville IL 60540 Office: PO Box 922 Naperville IL 60540

RASTAS, VYTAS PRANAS, veterinarian; b. Lithuania, May 10, 1922; s. Pranas and Josephine R. came to U.S., 1951, naturalized, 1957; student Baltic U., 1946-48, Hannover (Germany) Veterinary Coll., 1948-51; V.M.D., U. Pa., 1954; m. A. Jane Rosell, June 2, 1956; children—Carolyn, John, Paul, Christine. Meat insp. Fed. Meat Insp., South St. Paul, 1954-55; pvt. veterinary practice, Morris, Minn., 1955-58; with Wis. Dept. Agr., Madison, 1958—, veterinary diagnostician, animal health lab., 1962—. Mem. Wis., Lithuanian veterinary med. assns. Roman Catholic. Home: 2406 Jonquil Rd Madison WI 53711 Office: 6101 Mineral Point Rd Madison WI 53705

RATCHFORD, CHARLES BRICE, educator; b. Gastonia, N.C., July 30, 1920; s. Earl B. and Mary (Woods) R.; B.S., N.C. Coll., 1942, M.S., 1947; Ph.D., Duke U., 1951; m. Betty Brown, June 13, 1942; children—Charles Brice, Mary Eloise. Mem. faculty N.C. State Coll., Raleigh, 1942, 46-54, project leader extension farm mgmt. and mktg., 1948-54, asst. dir. N.C. Agr. Extension Service, 1954-59; mem. faculty U. Mo., Columbia, 1959—, dean extension div., 1960-65, v.p., 1965-70, interim pres., 1970, pres., 1971— prof. agrl. econs., 1977—; cons. U.S. Dept. Commerce, Washington, 1963—, Office Econ. Opportunity, 1964—, U.S. Dept. Agr., 1965—, AID, 1966—. Chmn. bd. trustees Ozarks Unlimited, Am. Inst. Cooperation, 1965—; trustee Mo. Sch. Religion. Served from pvt. to capt. AUS, 1942-46. Mem. Am. Farm Econ. Assn., Mo. Acad. Scis., Acad. Polit. Sci., Phi Beta Kappa, Phi Kappa Phi, Gamma Sigma Delta, Epsilon Sigma Phi, Omicron Delta Kappa. Home: 1900 S Providence Rd Columbia MO 65201

RATCLIFFE, MYRON FENWICK, investment mgmt. exec., banker; b. Evanston, Ill.; s. James Lewis and Jean (Gardner) R.; B.S., U. Ill., 1925; m. Margaret Archibald; 1 dau., Elizabeth Ratcliffe Heinze. With Goldman, Sachs & Co., N.Y.C., 1925-33; adminstr. fin. codes NRA, 1934-35; syndicate mgr. Lehman Bros., N.Y.C., 1936-49; partner Bache & Co., Chgo., 1949-56; pres., dir. Miami Corp., Chgo., 1956—, Cutler Oil & Gas Corp., 1956—; chmn. bd., dir. Nat. Blvd. Bank of Chgo., 1956—; dir. Nat.-Standard Co., Niles, Mich. Bd. govs. Midwest Stock Exchange, 1949-56; trustee Ill. Children's Home and Aid Soc. Served as lt. col. AUS, 1942-46. Decorated Legion of Merit. Clubs: Masons, Bond, Chicago, Casino, Mid-Am. (Chgo.); Indian Hill Country (Winnetka); Old Elm (Ft. Sheridan, Ill.); Birnam Wood Golf (Santa Barbara, Calif.). Home: 82 Indian Hill Rd Winnetka IL 60093 Office: 410 N Michigan Ave Chicago IL 60611

RATH, PATRICIA MINK (MRS. MELVIN EUGENE RATH), educator, author; b. Chgo.; d. Dwight L. and Margaret (Strom) Mink; A.B., Oberlin Coll.; M.S. in Merchandising, Simmons Coll.; postgrad. U. Ill., Northwestern U.; m. Melvin Eugene Rath; 1 son, Eric Clemence. Cons. mktg. and distbv. edn. Bd. dirs. Ill. Found. for Distbv. Edn., Inc. Mem. Am. Mktg. Assn., LWV, Am. Vocat. Assn. Congregationalist. Author: (with Gerald R. Tapp, Ralph E. Mason) Case Studies in Marketing and Distribution, 1965; (with Ralph E. Mason, Lloyd J. Phipps) Applying for a Job, 1967; (with Ralph E. Mason) Distributive Education Notebook for Occupational Growth, 1963; Marketing and Distribution, 1968, 2d edit., 1974; (with Ralph E. Mason and Lloyd J. Phipps) Succeeding on the Job, 1970, Supervising on the Job, 1971; Career Education Kit, 1977. Address: 1037 Cherry St Winnetka IL 60093

RATH, VIRGIL KENNETH, optometrist; b. Bismarck, N.D., Oct. 11, 1928; s. John A. and Emma Lydia (Kempf) R.; student U. N.D., 1946-49; B.S., Chgo. Coll. Optometry, 1953. Dr. Optometry, 1953; m. Mary Jean Larson, Dec. 28, 1951; children—Sandra Lee, Timothy Scott. Practice optometry, Bowman, N.D., 1956—. Pres. local PTA, 1962; comdr. squadron CAP, 1972—, state dir. communications, 1977—. Mem. Am. Optometric Assn., Optometric Extension Program, Bowman C. of C., Phi Theta Upsilon, Lambda Chi Alpha. Republican. Methodist. Mason, Moose, Lion (past pres.). Home: 105 8th Ave NW Bowman ND 58623 Office: Professional Bldg Bowman ND 58623

RATHERMEL, EUGENE MELVIN, mgmt. cons.; b. Fort Dodge, Iowa, Nov. 18, 1930; s. Ernest Fred and Lillian (Walters) R.; student Fort Dodge Jr. Coll., 1950-51; m. Elaine F. Will, Mar. 28, 1953; children—Mick Gene, Kenton Jay, Timothy Brad. Owner Rathermel Marketing Agy., Fort Dodge, 1952-65; pub. Socialite of Fort Dodge, 1962-65; pres. Creative Press, Inc.; now mgmt. cons., cons. to advt. agys.; author, lectr. advt. agy. mgmt. Pres., Community Nursing; pub. relations United Fund, 1959-65; dist. chmn. Boy Scouts Am., 1962-63; mem. publicity chmn. Republican Central Com., 1962; bd. dirs. Art Fedn. Recipient Advt. award Stanley Pub. Co., 1967. Mem. Direct Mail Advt. Assn., Am. Soc. Mgmt. Cons. (charter), Internat. Platform Assn., Jr. C. of C. (pres. 1962-63), C. of C., Blanden Gallery Fedn. Arts (pres.). Methodist. Clubs: Sertoma (sec. 1960-64), Fort Dodge Booster (chmn. conv. and tourist bur.). Editor-pub.: Management Digest. Home: 1417 2d Ave N Box 851 Fort Dodge IA 50501

RATHI, MANOHAR, physician; b. Beawar, India, Dec. 25, 1933; s. Bagtawarmal and Sitadevi (Laddha-Palod) R.; M.B., B.S., Rajasthan (India) U., 1961; D.C.H., Royal Coll. Surgeons and Physicians, London, 1964; came to U.S., 1969; m. Kamla Jajoo, Feb. 21, 1960; children—Sanjeev, Rejeev. Resident house physician in pediatrics and internal medicine hosps. in India and Eng., 1961, 63-64; casualty med. officer Bombay Hosp., 1961-62; resident sr. house physician pediatrics Gen. Hosp., Oldham, Eng., 1964-65; registrar physiciansin pediatrics hosp. in Newcastle-on-Tyne and Ashington, Eng., 1965-68; fellow neonatology Methodist Hosp., Bklyn., 1969-70, chief resident, 1969-70, chief div. neonatology, asst. attending pediatrics, 1971-73; clin. instr. pediatrics Downstate Med. Center, Bklyn., 1971-72; dir. newborn medicine, coordinator pediatric edn., asst. dir., sr. attending div. pediatrics Little Company of Mary Hosp., Evergreen Park, Ill., 1972-74, cons. neonatologist, 1974—; dir. perinatal medicine Christ Hosp., Oak Lawn, Ill., 1974—; asst. prof. pediatrics Rush Med. Coll., Chgo., 1974—. Grantee Hummel Found., 1976-77. Diplomate Am. Bd. Pediatrics with subsplty. neonatal peinatal medicine, 1970, 76. Fellow Am. Acad. Pediatrics; mem. AMA (Physicians Recognition award 1971, 74), N.Y. State, Kings County, N.Y., Chgo. med. socs., Chgo. Pediatric Soc. Contbr. to med. jours. Home: 9221 S Tripp Ave Oak Lawn IL 60453 Office: 4440 W 95th St Oak Lawn IL 60453

RATHS, OTTO NICHOLAS, JR., psychiatrist; b. St. Paul, Minn., Oct. 9, 1915; s. Otto N. and Ellen (Menalis) R.; B.S., St. Thomas Coll., 1940; M.D., St. Louis U., 1942; m. Lois V. DeVall, Sept. 4, 1943; children—Ana Katherine, Karen Elizabeth, Otto Nicholas. Intern, St. Mary's Hosp., Mpls., 1942-43; resident; U. Minn., Mpls., 1946-48; practice medicine specializing in psychiatry, St. Paul, 1959—; inst. psychiatry, Wayne State U., Detroit, 1951-55; clinical prof. psychiatry, U. Minn., Mpls., 1955—. Served with N.G. and USAR, 1936-73; recipient purple heart. Diplomate Am. Bd. Psychiatry. Fellow Am. Psychiat. Assn.; mem. Acad. Psychoanalysis, AMA, Minn., St. Paul psychiat. socs., Minn. Soc. Neurol. Sci., Soc. Adolescent Psychiat. Democrat. Roman Catholic. Club: K.C. Home: 1792 Hillcrest Ave St Paul MN 55116 Office: 1562 University Ave St Paul MN 55104

RATIGAN, WILLIAM O., author, historian; b. Detroit; s. Bernard Joseph and Bertie (Laing) R.; student U. Detroit, 1931; A.B., U. Tenn. at Chattanooga, 1935; M.A., Mich. State U., 1961, Ph.D., 1963; m. Eleanor Dee Eldridge, Sept. 12, 1935; children—Patsy Ratigan Ranger, Anne Ratigan Pelton, Bobbie Laing (dec.), Shannon Leitrim. Continuity dir., producer NBC, Denver, 1937-40, supervisor NBC, Far Eastern Listening Post, 1940-42, mng. news editor Western Div., supr. commentators and war corrs. PTO, 1942-45, news editor, scriptwriter UN Conf., 1945; short story and serial writer Curtis Pub. Co. and other magazine chains, 1946—; founder Dockside Press, Charlevoix, Mich., 1954—; founder counseling center pub. schs., Charlevoix, 1959—; sr. extension lectr. Mich. State U., 1962—; staff mem. NDEA Counseling Inst., 1962; vis. lectr. Fla. State U., 1965, U. Wis. at Milw., 1966, 68, U. Miami, 1967; mem. at large U.S. Adv. Council Naval Affairs, 1957—; cons. Smithsonian Instn. on tech. devel. of Great Lakes craft, 1959—. Adopted chief Ottawa Indian Tribe, 1957; named Knight of Mark Twain, 1970. Mem. Am. Psychol. Assn., Am. Personnel and Guidance Assn., Mich. Acad. Profl. Educators (charter), Blue Key, Phi Kappa Phi. Author: Soo Canal! (foreword by Gen. Douglas McArthur), 1954, 2d edit., 1968; Young Mr. Big, 1955; Hiawatha and America's Mightiest Mile, 1955; The Adventures of Captain McCargo, 1956; Straits of Mackinac, 1957; The Blue Snow, 1958; Tiny Tim Pine, 1958; Adventures of Paul Bunyan and Babe, 1958; The Long Crossing, 1959; Highways Over Broad Waters, 1959; Great Lakes Shipwrecks and Survivals, 1960, 69, 77; Conflicts Within Counseling, 1964; (with others) Theories of Counseling, 1965, 2d edit., 1972, A View from Within, 1967. Editor centennial facsimile edit. The Song of Hiawatha, 1955. Contbr. to The Great Lakes Reader, 1966, Ency. Americana, 1968—. Home: 223 Park Ave Charlevoix MI 49720 Office: The Dockside Press 1 Shipyard Row Box 1 Charlevoix MI 49720

RATKOVICH, JOHN MARK, lawyer, inventor; b. Chgo., Sept. 28, 1936; s. John Mark and Marie (Schackle) R.; B.B.A. (Evans scholar), Wis. U., 1958; J.D., Loyola U., 1966; m. Evely Joan Architect, Oct. 24, 1959; children—Diana, John Mark, David, Kristina, Marlaina, Aaron. Admitted to Ill. bar, 1965; individual practice law, Elmhurst, Ill., 1974—. Mem. Chgo. Bar Assn., Inventors Soc. Am. (pres.). Inventor hunting arrow with electronic transmitter, elbow-rest for use in holding binoculars. Office: 188 Industrial Dr Suite 16 Elmhurst IL 60126

RATLIFF, TEDDY LAVERN, computer co. exec.; b. St. Louis, Sept. 17, 1928; s. Theodore Newton and Pearl (Wells) R.; B.S. in Bus. Adminstrn., Washington U., 1949; M.B.A., U. Detroit, 1975; m. Evelyn Marie Trubey, May 27, 1953; children—Gail Denise, Charles Stewart, Pamela Ann. Travel cons. Am. Express, St. Louis, 1953-55, Buffalo, 1955-58, mgr., Milw., 1958-60, asst. mgr., Chgo., 1960-61, mgr., Memphis, 1961-64, dist. travel mgr., Detroit, 1965-75; dist. sales mgr. Universal Chem. Co., Detroit, 1975-76; mgr. Ednl. Recovery Service, Southfield, Mich., 1976; exec. v.p., gen. mgr. CoSe Co. Inc., Southfield, Mich., 1977—; mem. adj. faculty Mich. Christian Coll., Rochester. Mem. Greater Detroit C. of C. (chmn. aviation com. 1973-75), Internat. Assn. Des Skal Clubs (pres. Detroit 1974), Kappa Sigma, Pi Sigma Epsilon. Clubs: Rotary, Circumnavigators, Masons, Shriners. Contbr. religious publs. Home: 31319 Rayburn St Livonia MI 48154 Office: 29200 Southfield Rd Suite 209A Southfield MI 48076

RATNER, MARK ALAN, educator; b. Cleve., Dec. 8, 1942; s. Max and Betty (Wohlvert) R.; B.A., Harvard U., 1964; Ph.D., Northwestern U., Evanston, Ill., 1969; m. Nancy Ball, June 16, 1969; children—Stacy, Daniel. Amanuensis, Aarhus U., Denmark, 1969-70; asst. prof. chemistry N.Y.U., 1970-74, asso. prof., 1974-75; asso. prof. Northwestern U., 1975—. Sloan fellow, 1974-76. Mem. AAAS, Am. Chem. Soc., Am. Phys. Soc., Chem. Soc., Sigma Xi. Jewish. Contbr. articles to profl. jours. Home: 25 Locust Rd Winnetka IL 60093 Office: Dept Chemistry Northwestern Univ Evanston IL 60201

RATTEREE, WILLIAM ADOLPH, investment co. exec.; b. St. Louis, Jan. 28, 1932; s. Olivie Frank and Annie Laurie (Remley) R.; student Harris Coll., 1949-51; children—Stephen Michael, Matthew Jeffrey, Mark Alan. With Henges Co., St. Louis, 1956-57; salesman, archtl. cons. Home Erection Service Corp., St. Louis, 1958-60; with Adolph Investment Corp., St. Louis, 1960—, pres., chmn. bd., 1960—; dir. Pulaski Savs. & Loan. Fin. advisor Jefferson Nat. Trust Co. Mem. Homebuilders Assn. (dir. 1966-70), Antique Auto Collectors Am. Clubs: Norwood Country, St. Louis Ambassadors. Home: 1630 Rosado Dr St Louis MO 63138 Office: 8444 Florissant Rd St Louis MO 63121

RAU, JEROLD MATTHEW, dermatologist; b. Wichita, Kans., July 3, 1939; s. Peter Joseph and Clara Theresa (Scheer) R.; B.A., U. Wichita, 1961; M.D., U. Kans., 1965; m. Jacqueline Anne Nickerson, Aug. 8, 1970. Intern, Fitzsimons Army Gen. Hosp., Denver, 1965-66, resident Walter Reed Army Hosp., D.C., 1966-69; commd. capt. M.C. U.S. Army, 1964, advanced through grades to lt. col., 1969-73; asst. chief dermatology Walter Reed Hosp., 1969-70; mem. faculty George Washington U., Georgetown U. Med. Schs., D.C., 1969-70; chief dermatology 225th Station Hosp., Munich, W.Ger., 1970-71; chief 130th Station Hosp., Heidelberg, W.Ger., 1971-73; chief cons. U.S. Army, Europe, 1971-73; chief dermatology Kansas City VA Hosp., Kans., 1973—; asst. prof. medicine U. Kans., 1973-77, asso. prof., 1977—; asso. clin. prof. U. Mo., Kansas City, 1977—; spl. cons. U.S. Army, 1974—. Pres. Kans. City, Mo. Community Neighborhood Assn., 1976—. Diplomate Am. Bd. Dermatology, Am. Bd. Pathology. Mem. AMA, Mo., Jackson County med. socs., Kans. City, Mo. dermatol. socs., Am. Acad. Dermatology, Soc. Internat. Dermatology and Tropical Medicine. Contbr. articles to profl. jours. Home: 6024 Morningside Dr Kansas City MO 64113 Office: 315 Nichols Rd Suite 235 Kansas City MO 64112

RAUCH, IRMENGARD, linguist, educator; b. Dayton, Ohio, Apr. 17, 1933; d. Konrad and Elsa (Knott) Rauch; student Nat. U. Mexico, summer 1954; B.S. with honors, U. Dayton, 1955; M.A., Ohio State U., 1957; postgrad. (Fulbright fellow) U. Munich (W.Ger.), 1957-58; Ph.D. (dissertation grantee summer 1962), U. Mich., 1962; m. Gerald F. Carr, June 12, 1965; children—Christopher, Gregory. Instr. German and linguistics U. Wis., Madison, 1962-63, asst. prof., 1963-66; asso. prof. German, U. Pitts., 1966-68; asso. prof. German and linguistics U. Ill., 1968-72, prof., 1972—. Named Outstanding Woman on Campus, U. Ill. Radio Sta. WILL, 1975; research grantee

U. Wis., summer 1966, U. Ill., 1975, 76, 77; NSF and Linguistics Soc. Am. travel grantee, 1972. Mem. Linguistics Soc. Am., Modern Lang. Assn., Am. Assn. Tchrs. German, Societas Linguistica Europaea, Internat. Linguistic Assn., AAAS, AAUP, Phonetics Assn., Semiotic Soc. Am., Alpha Sigma Tau, Delta Phi Alpha. Author: The Old High German Diphthongization: A Description of a Phonemic Change, 1967; co-editor: Approaches in Linguistic Methodology, 1967, Spanish edit., 1974; Der Heliand, 1974; Linguistic Method: The Herbert Penzl Festschrift, 1977; contbr. articles to profl. jours. Home: 200 Cherry Ln Villa Grove IL 61956 Office: Dept Germanic Languages and Literatures U Illinois Urbana IL 61801

RAUFEISEN, RAYMOND ROBERT, advt. exec.; b. Rochester, N.Y., Nov. 21, 1930; s. Raymond W. and Eleanor R. (Froelicher) R.; B.A., U. Ill., 1955; postgrad. Northwestern U., 1957-58; m. Phyllis Arlene Luebbers, Feb. 5, 1955; children—David Craig, Julie Christine, Lisa Marie. Vice pres. Edelstein-Nelson Advt. Agy., Chgo., 1957-61; advt. mgr. Illinois Tool Works Inc., Elgin, 1961-62, Sloan Valve Co., Franklin Park, Ill., 1962—. Served with U.S. Army, 1955-57. Mem. Bus./Profl. Advt. Assn. (chmn. com. 1977-78). Republican. Episcopalian. Club: Tropicana Swim and Tennis (trustee 1974—). Home: 129 Elmwood Ln Hoffman Estates IL 60195 Office: 10500 Seymour Ave Franklin Park IL 60131

RAUSCH, FRANCIS DAVID, veterinarian; b. Logansport, Ind., Oct. 20, 1945; s. Francis Charles and Gertrude Mary (Meyer) R.; student Ind. U., 1963-65; D.V.M., Purdue U., 1970; m. Linda Faye Lancaster, June 6, 1968. Asso. Plaza Vet. Hosp., Farmington, Mich., 1970-71; partner Animal Clinic Plainfield (Ind.), 1971—. Adviser, Explorer Scouts, 1974-76; asst. coach football Little League, 1972. Recipient award Indpls. Humane Soc., 1972. Mem. Ind. Acad. Vet. Continuing Edn., Ind., Central Ind. vet. med. assns., Ark. Humane Soc. AVMA, Am. Animal Hosp. Assn. (affiliate), Phi Zeta. Republican. Developer surg. technique for long term jugular catheterization in swine. Office: Box 336 Plainfield IN 46168

RAUSCHERT, KARL ALFRED, metal fabricating co. exec., architect; b. Sheboygan Falls, Wis., July 30, 1929; s. Arthur E. and Anna J. (Prange) R.; B.A., Princeton U., 1951; B.Arch., U. Ill., 1955; m. Eileen Elenor Norcross, June 19, 1955; children—Philip, Laura Ann, Mark. Asso., Charles F. McKirahan, Architect, Ft. Lauderdale, Fla., 1955-57; pvt. practice architecture, Ft. Lauderdale, 1957-59, Bushnell, Ill., 1959—; v.p. C.S. Norcross & Son Co., Bushnell, 1959-66; pres. Midwest Control Products Corp., Bushnell, 1967—. Pres., Civic Improvement Assn., 1958, City Housing Commn., 1968—, Macomb Community Chorus, 1970; mem. County Nursing Commn., 1966; trustee Wayland Acad., Beaver Dam, Wis. Served with USNR, 1951-53. Mem. AIA. Republican. Presbyterian (ch. elder). Prin. archtl. works located Broward County, Fla., McDonough and Knox counties, Ill. Home: 24 Hillcrest Dr Bushnell IL 61422 Office: 590 E Main St Bushnell IL 61422

RAVEN, EDWIN DEAN, county ofcl.; b. Cadillac, Mich., July 9, 1925; s. Christian and Gladys Lucille (Dunbar) R.; B.S., Mich. State U., 1950, M.S., 1957; postgrad. Colo. State U., summer 1968; m. Marilyn Louise Peterson, Oct. 6, 1951; children—Mark, Marcia, Chris, Lori. 4-H agt. Mason, Manistee and Lake Counties, Mich., 1950-54; asst. agrl. agt. Mich. State U. Extension Service, Mason County, Scottville, Mich., 1954-59, county extension dir., 1960—. Chmn. Scottville City Planning Commn., 1961; bd. dirs. Western Mich. Fair, 1960-74; chmn. bd. trustees West Shore Community Coll., Scottville, 1973—. Served with USNR, 1944-46. Mem. Scottville C. of C. (sec. 1960-65), Mich. Assn. County Agrl. Agts. (Distinguished Service award 1975), Mich. Acad. Sci., Arts and Letters. Methodist. Clubs: Elks, Optimist (Scottville); Lincoln Hills Golf. Home: 211 N Reinberg St Scottville MI 49454 Office: Computer Bldg Scottville MI 49454

RAVER, PAUL JOSEPH, county ofcl.; b. Batesville, Ind., Nov. 25, 1926; s. Clem Joseph and Anna Elizabeth (Berkemeier) R.; B.S., Purdue U., 1952, M.S., 1961; m. Shirley F. Schultz, Oct. 25, 1947; children—Barbara Raver Peterson, Paul T., Rita Raver Sale, Mark, Beth. Asst. county agrl. agt. U.S. Dept. Agr. Extension Service, Shelby County, Ind., 1952-54, Fayette County, Ind., 1954-55, county agrl. agt. Hendricks County, Ind., 1956-63, Howard County, Kokomo, Ind., 1963—. Mem. Howard County Plan Commn., 1963—, pres., 1965-68; mem. Park Bd., 1967—, pres., 1976-77. AUS, 1945-47. Recipient Distinguished Service award, Nat. County Agts. Assn., 1973. Mem. Ind. Extension Agts. Assn. (pres. 1970), Nat. County Agts. Assn., Kokomo C. of C., Ind. Planning Assn., Purdue Agrl. Alumni Assn., Epsilon Sigma Phi. Roman Catholic. Club: Rotary (pres. 1972-73). Home: 2100 Mohr Dr Kokomo IN 46901 Office: Courthouse Kokomo IN 46901

RAVES, PETER HARLEY, product engr.; b. London, Eng., Mar. 12, 1930; s. Henry Alfred and Josephine Esther (Smart) R.; came to U.S., 1969; higher nat. certificate in mech. engring., S.E. Essex Tech. Coll., Eng., 1963; m. Ena Joyce Williamson, Aug. 17, 1957; children—Amanda Jane, Mark Andrew, Melanie Ann. Phys. test lab. supr. Ford Motor Co., Eng., 1956-64, sr. devel. engr., 1964-67, sr. test engr., 1967-70; sr. product engr. Kelsey Hayes Co., Romulus, Mich., 1970—. Served with Brit. Army, 1951-53. Mem. Soc. Automotive Engrs. Home: 317 Surrey Heights Dr Westland MI 48185 Office: 38481 Huron River Dr Romulus MI 48174

RAVINDRANATHAN, P. G., surgeon; b. Kerala, India, May 1, 1938; s. Govindan Pukattu Raman and Kamalakshi Govindan; came to U.S., 1966; B.S., Kerala U., 1958, M.B., B.S., 1963; m. Ambika, Mar. 11, 1970; children—Hari, Meera. Intern, McNeil Meml. Hosp., Berwyn, Ill., 1966; resident Mo. Pacific Hosp. Assn., St. Louis, 1967-71; staff surgeon VA Hosp., Marion, Ill., 1972-73, cons. surgeon, 1973—; attending surgeon Marion Meml. Hosp., 1973—; clin. asso. dept. surgery So. Ill. U. Med. Sch., Springfield, 1975—. Diplomate Am. Bd. Surgery. Mem. Internat. Coll. Surgeons, AMA. Hindu. Home: 305 Sunset Terr Marion IL 62959 Office: 617 E Broadway Johnston City IL 62950

RAWITCH, ALLEN BARRY, biochemist; b. Chgo., Dec. 29, 1940; s. Samuel and Jean (Riefman) R.; student Pierce Coll., 1958-60; A.A., U. Calif. at Los Angeles, 1961, B.S., 1963, Ph.D., 1967; m. Patricia Nan Karlan, July 21, 1962; children—Bruce Howard, David Andrew. Research fellow U. Ill., 1967-69; asst. prof. chemistry Kent State U., 1969-73, asso. prof., 1973-75; asso. prof. dept. biochemistry U. Kans. Med. Center, Kansas City, 1975—; cons. chiefs of police pub. service communications, Portage County, Ohio, 1974-75; research scientist Mid Am. Cancer Center Program. Recipient NIH Research Career Devel. award, 1973; NIH grantee, 1971—; NSF grantee, 1970-72; Nat. Heart Assn. grantee, 1976-77. Mem. Am. Chem. Soc., Am. Soc. Biol. Chemists, AAAS, Sigma Xi. Home: 10112 Oakridge Dr Overland Park KS 66212 Office: Dept Biochemistry U Kans Med Center Kansas City KS 66103

RAWLINGS, GARY DON, environ. engr.; b. Houston, Tex., Feb. 6, 1948; s. William Lee and Sarah Jeanette (Lanham) R.; B.S., S.W. Tex. State U., 1970, M.S., 1971; Ph.D. (Tex. Expt. Sta. grantee), Tex. A. and M. U., 1974; m. Janna Sue Kelley, Mar. 15, 1969. Sr. research engr. environ. engring. research and devel. sect. Monsanto Research Corp., Dayton, Ohio from 1974, now project. mgr. EPA Project, Dayton. Mem. Air Pollution Control Assn., ASCE, Am. Soc. Chem. Engrs., Sigma Xi, Alpha Chi. Author: (with H.B.H. Cooper, Jr.) Sampling and Analysis of Trace Metals in Urban Atmospheres, 1976; contbr. articles in field to EPA Publs. and symposiums. Home: 402 East Dr Dayton OH 45419 Office: 1515 Nicholas Rd Dayton OH 45407

RAWLINGS, MAURICE EDWARD, judge; b. Omawa, Iowa, Aug. 17, 1906; s. Ed Eugene and Effie (Miller) R.; student Iowa U., 1925-27; LL.B., S.D. Coll. Law, 1930; m. Helen Chausee Fowler, Feb. 9, 1928; children—Richard R. (dec.), Maurice F., William J., Janet (Mrs. Robert Pulscher), Mary (Mrs. James Gaukel), Robert C. Admitted to Iowa bar, 1931; practice law, Sioux City; county atty., Woodbury County, Iowa, 1935-43; dir. Sioux City dist. OPA, 1943-45; city corp. counsel, Sioux City, 1948-51; judge Dist. Ct., 4th Jud. Dist. Iowa, Sioux City, 1958-65; asso. justice Iowa Supreme Ct., Sioux City, 1965—. Trustee Goodwill Industries, Sioux City. Served to capt. JAG, AUS, 1937-42. Mem. Am., Iowa, Woodbury County bar assns., Phi Gamma Delta. Democrat. Episcopalian. Mason. Home: 3433 Court St Sioux City IA 51104 Office: Court House Sioux City IA 51101

RAY, ARUN BIKAS, psychologist; b. Bangladesh, May 28, 1936; s. Woo Mesh Chandra and Amiya Prava (Raychoudhury) R.; came to U.S., 1969; B.Sc., U. Calcutta, 1955, M.Sc., 1958, Ph.D., 1967; m. Sipra Guha, June 20, 1973; 1 dau., Anita. Chief psychologist Moose Jaw (Sask., Can.) Union Hosp., 1967-69; sr. psychologist Alta. Guidance Clinic, Calgary, 1970; psychologist, tng. dir. Mental Hygiene Clinic, Toledo, 1971—. Postdoctoral fellow U. N.C., Chapel Hill, 1969-70. Mem. Am., Canadian psychol. assns., Am. Soc. Clin. Hypnosis, Am. Group Psychotherapy Assn., Indian Psychoanalytical Soc. Contbr. articles to profl. jours. Home: 4002 Sylvania Ave Toledo OH 43623 Office: 3450 W Central Ave Toledo OH 43606

RAY, CHARLES DEAN, neurosurgeon; b. Americus, Ga., Aug. 1, 1927; s. Oliver Tinsley and Katherine (Broadfield) R.; A.B., Emory U., 1950; M.S., U. Miami (Fla.), 1952; M.D., Med. Coll. Ga., 1956; children—Bruce, Kathy, C. Marlene, Thomas. Intern, Baptist Meml. Hosp., Memphis, 1956-57; resident, research asso. in neurosurgery U. Tenn. Hosp., Memphis, 1957-62; fellow, research asst. Mayo Clinic and Found., Rochester, Minn., 1962-64; asst. prof. neurosurgery, lectr. bioengring. Johns Hopkins Med. Sch., 1964-68; chief dept. med. engring. F. Hoffmann-LaRoche, Basel, Switzerland, also lectr. U. Basel, 1968-73; practice medicine specializing in neurosurgery, Mpls., 1973—; mem. staff Sister Kenney Inst., Children's, Abbott-Northwestern hosps.; clin. asso. prof. U. Minn. Med. Sch.; v.p. research Medtronic, Inc.; adviser med. devices FDA; chmn. com. materials and devices World Fedn. Neurosurg. Socs. Mem. vestry St. Martin's Episcopal Ch., Wayzata, Minn. Served with USNR, 1945-49. Diplomate Am. Bd. Neurol. Surgery. Fellow A.C.S., Royal Soc. Health; mem. Am., Pan-Am. med. assns., Am. Assn. Neurol. Surgeons, Congress Neurol. Surgeons, W. Ger. Armed Forces Med. Soc., IEEE, Internat. Fedn. Med. Biol. Engring., Internat. Soc. Stereotaxic and Functional Neurosurgery, ASTM, Internat. Orgn. Standardization, Assn. Advancement Med. Instrumentation, AAAS, Bioengring. Soc., Minn., Hennepin County med. socs., Minn. Neurosurg. Soc., Sigma Xi, Alpha Omega Alpha, Psi Chi. Clubs: Cosmos, Lafayette. Author: Principles of Engineering Applied to Medicine, 1964; Medical Engineering, 1974; also monographs, numerous articles. Home: 2020 Willow Dr Long Lake MN 55356 Office: Medtronic Inc Box 1453 Minneapolis MN 55440 also Sister Kenny Inst 2545 Chicago Ave Minneapolis MN 55404

RAY, HOPE WALKER (MRS. KENNETH C. RAY), club woman; b. McConnelsville, Ohio, Oct. 11, 1906; d. S. Carlton and Grace (Wells) Walker; student Malta Normal Sch., 1924-25, Ohio U., 1940-41; B.A. in Edn., George Washington U., 1958; m. Kenneth C. Ray, June 24, 1931; children—John Walker, Beverly Ann. Tchr., Morgan County (Ohio) Schs., 1925-31. Mem. DAR (past regent), Daus. Colonial Wars, AAUW, Pi Lambda Theta. Republican. Methodist. Club: Order Eastern Star. Author: (elementary grade workbooks) Number Trails, 1938. Home: 263 E Main St McConnelsville OH 43756

RAY, JOHN WALKER, physician; b. Columbus, Ohio, Jan. 12, 1936; s. Kenneth Clark and Hope (Walker) Ray; A.B. magna cum laude, Marietta Coll., 1956; M.D. cum laude, Ohio State U., 1960; postgrad. Temple U., 1964, Mt. Sinai Hosp. and Columbia U., 1964, 66, Northwestern U., 1967, 71, U. Ill., 1968, U. Ind., 1969, Tulane U., 1969; m. Susanne Gettings, July 15, 1961; children—Nancy Ann, Susan Christy. Intern, Ohio State U. Hosps., Columbus, 1960-61, clin. research trainee NIH, 1963-65, resident dept. otolaryngology, 1963-65, 1966-67, instr. dept. otolaryngology, 1966-67, 70-75, clin. asst. prof., 1975—, resident dept. surgery 1965-66; active staffs Bethesda, Good Samaritan hosps., Zanesville, Ohio, 1967—; courtesy staff Ohio State U. Hosps., Columbus, 1970—; Past pres. Muskingum chpt. Am. Cancer Soc. Served to capt. USAF, 1961-63. Recipient Barraquer Meml. award, 1965; named Ky. col., 1966. Diplomate Am. Bd. Otolaryngology. Fellow A.C.S., Am. Soc. Ophthalmol. and Otolaryn. Allergy, Am. Acad. Ophthalmology and Otolaryngology, Am. Acad. Facial Plastic and Reconstructive Surgery; mem. Muskingum County Acad. Medicine, Am., Ohio med. assns., Columbus Ophthalmol. and Otolaryngol. Soc., Ohio Soc. Otolaryngology (pres.), Pan-Am. Assn. Otolaryngology and Bronchoesophagology, Phi Beta Kappa, Alpha Tau Omega, Alpha Kappa Kappa, Alpha Omega Alpha, Beta Beta Beta. Republican. Presbyterian. Contbr. articles to sci., med. jours. Collaborator, surg. motion picture Laryngectomy and Neck Dissection, 1964. Office: 2927 Bell St Zanesville OH 43701

RAY, KENNETH C., ret. educator; b. McConnelsville, Ohio, Nov. 17, 1901; s. Thomas Vincent and Mary (Harmon) R.; student Malta Normal Sch., 1920-21; B.S. in Edn., Muskingum Coll., New Concord, Ohio, 1925; M.A., Ohio U., 1931; Ph.D., Ohio State U., 1943; L.H.D., Central State U., 1973; m. Hope Walker, June 24, 1931; children—John Walker, Beverly Ann. Prin., Meigsville (Ohio) High Sch., 1921-23, Chesterhill (Ohio) High Sch., 1924-27; tchr. math. McKeesport (Pa.) High Sch., 1927-28; prin. Coolville High Sch., 1929-32; county supt. schs. Athens County (Ohio), 1932-38; city supt. schs. Zanesville (Ohio), 1938-41; dir. edn. State of Ohio, 1941-45; dir. edn. Grolier Soc., Inc., N.Y.C., 1945-54; chief edn. div. Internat. Coop. Adminstrn., Washington, 1954-59; vis. lectr. edn. Ohio U., Athens, 1959-70, ret., 1970. Mem. Ohio Ho. of Reps., 1928-32. Mem. NEA, Ohio Edn. Assn., Am. Assn. Sch. Administrs., SAR, Kappa Delta Pi, Phi Delta Kappa. Clubs: Masons (32 deg.), Shriners. Home: 263 E Main St McConnelsville OH 43756

RAY, MRS. ROBERT D., wife of Iowa gov.; b. Colombus Junction, Iowa, May 16, 1928; d. Herbert F. and Eva (Hickman) Hornberger; B.S. in Edn. cum laude, Drake U., 1950; m. Robert D. Ray, Dec. 22, 1951; children—Randi Sue, Lu Ann, Vicki Jo. Tchr. elementary sch., 1950-55. Active United Campaign, Heart Fund, March of Dimes, Easter Seals, Mental Health drives, Polk County (Iowa) Cancer Soc., Campfire Girls, ARC, Fedn. Republican Women; state chmn. Iowa Friendship Force. Mem. Polk County Atty. Wives, Drake Nat. Alumni Assn. (dir. 1970—), Mid-Am. Arts Alliance, P.E.O., Beta Sigma Phi, Delta Kappa Gamma, Chi Omega. Address: 2300 Grand St Des Moines IA 50312

RAY, ROBERT D., gov. Iowa; b. Des Moines, Sept. 26, 1928; s. Clark A. and Mildred (Dolph) R.; B.A. in Bus. Adminstrn., Drake U., 1952, J.D., 1954; hon. degrees Central Coll., Iowa Wesleyan Coll., Grinnell Coll., Still Osteo. Coll., Cornell Coll., St. Ambrose Coll., Upper Iowa Coll., Westmar Coll., Luther Coll.; m. Billie Lee Hornberger, Dec. 21, 1951; children—Randi Sue, Lu Ann, Vicki Jo. Admitted to Iowa bar, 1954; mem. firm Lawyer, Lawyer & Ray, Des Moines, 1954-69; owner Emmet Broadcasting Co.; gov. State of Iowa, 1969—; mem. exec. com. Nat. Gov.'s Conf., 1970—, also com. on rural and urban devel., com. on natural resources and environ. mgmt., 1974-75; mem. exec. com. Republican Govs. Assn., 1970—, chmn. policy council, 1975-76; chmn. Midwest Gov.'s Conf., 1972, Nat. Gov.'s Conf., 1975-76, Iowa Exec. Council; v.p. exec. com. Council State Govts.; mem. Adv. Commn. Intergovtl. Relations; chmn. del. govs. to Japan, People's Republic of China, 1972-74, USSR, 1975; spl. adviser to Adv. Com. Intergovtl. Affairs vice chmn. Rep. Gov.'s Assn., 1976-77; mem. subcoms. clean air mgmt., fgn. trade, tourism task force Nat. Gov.'s Assn.; hon. vice chmn. nat. distinguished guests com. Am. Legion, 1977-78. State chmn. March of Dimes, 1960-62; hon. adviser nat. council Boy Scouts Am.; chmn. Iowa Republican party, 1963-68, Midwest Assn. Rep. State Chmn., 1965-68; chmn. Nat. Rep. State Chmns. Assn., 1967-68; chmn. platform com. Rep. Nat. Conv., 1976; bd. dirs. Family Service Des Moines; hon. chmn. Everett McKinley Dirksen Library; hon. trustee Am. Acad. Achievement; chmn. Geol. Bd. Iowa; hon. bd. dirs. Make Today Count, Burlington, Iowa, Practicing Law Inst. Served with AUS, 1946-48. Recipient Nat. Distinguished Service award Future Farmers Am., 1970; Distinguished Alumni award Drake U.; named One of Am.'s 200 Rising Young Leaders, Time Mag., 1974. Mem. Iowa Acad. Trial Lawyers, Am. Trial Lawyers Assn., Iowa State, Polk County, Am. bar assns., Nat. Reading Council, Order of Coif, Alpha Zeta, Delta Theta Phi, Alpha Kappa Psi, Omicron Delta Kappa, Sigma Alpha Epsilon. Mem. Disciples of Christ Ch. Home: 2300 Grand Ave Des Moines IA 50312 Office: State Capitol House Des Moines IA 50319

RAY, RUTH, violinist; b. Alvin, Ill., July 19, 1899; d. Frank H. and Anna L. (Moyer) R.; student U. Chgo., Am. Conservatory of Music, Chgo.; Mus. M., Eastman Sch. Music, U. Rochester (N.Y.), 1941; violin pupil Leopold Auer in Europe and Am. for 6 yrs. Début Carnegie Hall, N.Y.C., Nov. 4, 1919; appeared as soloist with N.Y. Philharmonic Orch., N.Y. Nat. Symphony, Chgo. Symphony, Balt. Symphony and Mpls. Symphony orchs., Woman's Symphony Orch. Chgo., and U. Chgo. Orch., and in individual recitals throughout U.S. and Can.; recitals in Germany and France, summer 1952, 54, 65, Holland, Germany, Switzerland, summer 1968; adv. bd. and head of ensemble dept. Columbia Sch. Music, Chgo., 1924-33; pvt. studio, Chgo. 1933—; head violin dept., also classes and lectures in musical history and appreciation Bradley Coll. Music, Peoria, Ill., 1929-45, Cornell Coll., Mt. Vernon, Iowa, 1945-57; string coach U. Chgo. Orch., 1933-38; concertmaster Woman's Symphony Orch. 1927-30. Mem. AAUP, Soc. Am. Musicians (dir.), Pi Kappa Lambda, Mu Phi Epsilon. Composer short pieces for violin and piano, Midland Tune and My Lord, What a Mournin'. Home: 815 Judson Ave Evanston IL 60202

RAYLE, EDWIN BEARD, ednl. adminstr.; b. Lebanon, Ind., Sept. 2, 1922; s. Pervey Thesel and Sarah Ellen Rayle; student Asbury Coll., Wilmore, Ky., 1945-47; B.S. in Elementary Edn., U. Ky., Lexington, 1949; M.A., Butler U., Indpls., 1958; m. Bette Ruth Greene, Sept. 1, 1949; 1 son, Edwin Kent. Teaching prin., Catlettsburg, Ky., 1949-51; farmer, Westfield, Ind., 1951-53; tchr. Durbin (Ind.) Elementary Sch., 1953-55, Westfield, 1955-57; tchr., asst. prin. Crooked Creek Elementary Sch., Indpls., 1957-61; prin. Harcourt Sch., Indpls., 1961-68, Greenbriar Sch., Indpls., 1968—. Served with AUS, 1942-45. Decorated Purple Heart, Bronze Star. Named Ky. col. Mem. Nat. Assn. Elementary Sch. Prins., Phi Delta Kappa. Home: Rural Route 1 Box 307 Westfield IN 46074 Office: 8201 North Ditch Indianapolis IN 46260

RAYMER, DONALD GEORGE, utility co. exec.; b. Jackson, Mich., July 16, 1924; s. Donald Rector and Vivian Alverda (Wolfinger) R.; B.E.E., U. Mich., 1948; M.S. (Sloan fellow), Mass. Inst. Tech., 1960; m. Joan Elizabeth Steck, Oct. 16, 1948; children—Mary Margaret, Dorothy Elizabeth, Charles George. Relay engr. Central Ill. Pub. Service Co., Springfield, 1948-56, mgr. system ops., 1956-65, div. mgr., Mattoon, Ill., 1965-68, v.p., Springfield, 1968-78, exec. v.p., 1978—, also dir.; dir. Electric Energy, Inc., Springfield Marine Bank. Vice-chmn. Springfield United Fund Campaign, 1964, asso. chmn., 1974; vice-chmn. Mattoon United Welfare Fund, 1967. Served to lt. (j.g.) USNR, 1943-46. Mem. IEEE, Am. Mgmt. Assn., Greater Springfield C. of C. (dir. 1968-71), Chi Phi. Republican. Episcopalian. Clubs: Illini Country, Sangamo (Springfield, Ill.); Union League (Chgo.). Home: 2328 Bates Ave Springfield IL 62704 Office: 607 E Adams St Springfield IL 62701

RAYMOND, LOREN ANDREW, dentist; b. Barberton, Ohio, Sept. 21, 1940; s. Loraine William and Nelle Josephine (Marshall) R.; B.A., U. Rochester, 1961; D.M.D., Tufts U., 1965; m. Gretchen Elizabeth Mueller, Aug. 11, 1962; children—Katherine Ingrid, Kelly Jo. Pvt. practice dentistry, South Lynnfield, Mass., 1967-68, Barberton, 1968—. Mem. Norton (Ohio) Bd. Edn., 1972—, v.p., 1975, 77, pres., 1978. Served to capt. USAF, 1965-67. Recipient award for outstanding achievement Internat. Coll. Dentists, 1965. Mem. Am., Ohio, Akron Area dental assns., Barberton Area C. of C., Omicron Kappa Upsilon. Club: Elks. Home: 4373 Suttle Dr Norton OH 44203 Office: 544 1/2 W Tuscarwas Ave Barberton OH 44203

RAYMOND, WALTER, dentist; b. Quakenbrueck, Germany, Sept. 21, 1915; s. Max and Bertha (Drucker) Reinsberg; came to U.S. 1935, naturalized 1941; B.S., U. Ill., 1947, D.D.S., 1949; m. Marjorie Isabelle Melum, Oct. 2, 1955; 1 dau., Inger Berte. Practice dentistry, Wilmette, Ill., 1949-53, 55-74, Sturgis, S.D., 1974—. Served to capt. USAF, 1953-55. Fellow Acad. Gen. Practice Dentistry; mem. Am., S.D. dental assns. Lutheran. Contbr. articles to profl. jours. Home: 1440 Davenport St Sturgis SD 57785 Office: 1240 Junction Ave Sturgis SD 57785

RAYNOLDS, RANDALL CRANE, realtor; b. Champaign-Urbana, Ill., Oct. 15, 1948; s. John Lloyd and Mary Margaret (Crane) R.; B.A., Ill. Coll., 1970; grad. Realtors Inst., 1974; m. Lynn Ellen Paisley, Nov. 27, 1970; 1 dau., Julie Crane. Partner, Raynolds Realty, Springfield, Ill., 1972—, Raynolds and Albert, Springfield, 1974—; co-chmn. ednl. com. Springfield Bd. Realtors, 1975-76, dir.; dir. Warren Boynton State Bank. Mem. Citizens Adv. Com., Springfield, 1974, mem. spl. adv. com. Community Devel. Project, Springfield, 1975; mem. Springfield Fair Housing Bd., 1975—; active YMCA. Served with AUS, 1970-72. Mem. Am. Bus. Club, Nat. Assn. Realtors, Nat. Inst. Real Estate Bds., Sigma Pi (pres. 1969). Home: 208 S Douglas St Springfield IL 62704 Office: 1430 S 7th Springfield IL 62703

RAYNOR, JOHN P., univ. pres.; b. Omaha, Oct. 1, 1923; s. Walter V. and Mary Clare (May) R.; A.B., St. Louis U., 1947, M.A., 1948 L.Ph., 1949, S.T.L., 1956; Ph.D., U. Chgo., 1959; LL.D., Cardinal Stritch Coll. Joined S.J., 1941, ordained priest Roman Cath. Ch.,

1954; tchr. St. Louis U. High Sch., 1948-51, asst. prin., 1951; instr. dept. edn., asst. to dean Coll. Liberal Arts, Marquette U., Milw., 1960, asst. to v.p. academic affairs, 1960-62, v.p. academic affairs, 1962-65, pres. Marquette U., 1965—; dir. Kimberly-Clark Corp.; mem. Wis. gov.'s adv. com. Higher Edn. Act of 1965; mem. N. Central Assn. Colls. and Secondary Schs., also cons., examiner; corporate mem. Wis. Regional Med. Program, Inc.; sponsor United Negro Coll. Fund; mem. Wis. Higher Ednl. Aids Bd. Corp. mem. United Community Services of Greater Milw.; hon. bd. dirs. Goethe House, Milw. Recipient Distinguished Service award Edn. Commn. of the States, 1977. Mem. Met. Milw. Assn. Commerce, Citizens Govtl. Research Bureau Greater Milw. Com., Newcomen Soc. N.Am., Internat. Fedn. Cath. Colls. and Univs., Nat. Cath. Edn. Assn., U.S. Cath. Conf. (higher edn. com.), Am. Council Edn. (dir.), Wis. Assn. Ind. Colls. and Univs. (exec. com., past pres.), Assn. Jesuit Colls. and Univs. (chmn. bd. dirs.), NCCJ (past Wis. chmn.), Wis. Found. Ind. Colls. (past pres.), Phi Beta Kappa, Phi Delta Kappa, Alpha Sigma Nu. Home: 615 N 11th St Milwaukee WI 52233

RAYSON, LELAND HOMER, lawyer, state legislator; b. Oak Park, Ill., Aug. 23, 1921; s. Ennes Charles and Beatrice (Rowland) R.; B.A., U. Rochester, 1946; J.D., Northwestern Law Sch., 1949; m. Barbara Chandler, May 30, 1944; children—Ann, John, William, Anthony, Leland, Thomas, James. Admitted to Ill. bar, 1949; practiced in Tinley Park, Ill., 1949—; mem. firm Rayson Williams, Pisanian and Rayson, community prof. Govs. State U.; pub. Palos-Worth Reporter, 1960—; mem. Ill. Ho. of Reps., 1965—. Dir. Palos-Worth Press, Inc., Worth, Ill. Mem. Tinley Park Sch. Bd., 1950-54; town assessor, Bremen Twp. 1953-61, magistrate, 1961-65. Bd. dirs. Ams. for Democratic Action; pres. Bremen Twp. Regular Dem. Orgn., 1954-73. Served with USNR, World War II. Mem. Ill., Chgo. bar assns., Chgo. Council on Fgn. Relations, UN Assn. Greater Chgo. (dir.), Nat. Soc. State Legislators, Alpha Delta Phi, Phi Alpha Delta. Methodist (mem. world service and finance commn.) Club: Chicago City. Home: 6500 W 166th St Tinley Park IL 60477 Office: 16740 S Oak Park Ave Tinley Park IL 60477

RAZIM, EDWARD ANTON, physician; b. Chgo., Aug. 4, 1928; s. Edward Anton and Ann Antoinette (Padur) R.; B.S., Northwestern U., 1948, M.D., 1952; m. Mary Templar Nesbit, June 14, 1958; children—Mary, Sarah, Nancy, Edward. Intern, Cook County Hosp., Chgo., 1952-53; resident U. Ill., 1953-54, now mem. staff; practice medicine specializing in otolaryngolgy, Riverside, Ill., 1958—; mem. staff St. Luke's Hosp., Chgo., McNeal Hosp., Berwyn, Ill., Hinsdale (Ill.) San., Community Meml. Hosp., LaGrange, Ill.; asst. prof. otolaryngology U. Ill. Med Center, Chgo., 1966—, Rush Med. Coll., Chgo., 1971—. Served with USAF, 1954-56. Mem. AMA, A.C.S., Am. Acad. Ophthalmology and Otolaryngology, Chgo. Laryngol. and Otol. Soc., Inst. Medicine Chgo. Address: 348 Evelyn Rd Riverside IL 60546

REA, ROBERT EUGENE, educator; b. Benton, Ill., Aug. 31, 1936; s. Guy D. and Ruth L. (Tisdale) R.; B.S., So. Ill. U., 1961, Ph.D., 1966; M.A., U. No. Colo., 1964; postgrad. NSF Insts., U. Colo., Boulder, 1961-62, U. Ill., summer 1970; m. Barbara Andrea Broman, Dec. 20, 1959; children—Valerie, Kimberly, Melanie, Robert. Tchr. pub. schs., Jefferson County, Colo., 1961-63; lectr. instr. So. Ill. U., 1962-66; workshop dir. new math. Dept. Pub. Instrn. State Ill., 1965; asst. prof. math. edn. U. Mo., St. Louis, 1966-70, asso. prof., 1970—, mem. grad. faculty, 1967—, doctoral faculty, 1975-80, chmn. Sch. Edn. Assembly, 1974-75, chmn. dept. childhood edn., 1976—; math. coordinator Parkway Schs., Chesterfield, Mo., 1973-74; cons. various schs., colls., profl. groups, Mo., Ill., Mich., Tex., Fla., Ind., Calif. Mem. citizens adv. council Pkwy. Schs., 1973-75. Served with USAF, 1954-58. NDEA fellow, 1963-66; named Outstanding Young Educator St. Louis Met. Jr. C. of C., 1971. Mem. Math. Club. St. Louis (pres. 1976-77), Nat. Council Tchrs. Math., Assn. Supervision and Curriculum Devel., Sch. Sci. and Math. Assn. Mem. Christian Ch. (exec. bd. 1973-75). Contbr. to profl. publs. in field. Home: 1478 Glenpeak Dr Maryland Heights MO 63043 Office: 8001 Natural Bridge Rd U Mo Saint Louis MO 63121

READ, GEORGE SULLIVAN, banker; b. Madison, Wis., May 20, 1916; s. James Burton and Elvira (Boehner) R.; B.A., U. Wis., 1937; M.A., Columbia U., 1943; m. Julia Elizabeth Schairer, July 10, 1946; 1 son, George Sullivan. Br. officer First Nat. City Bank, Shanghai, China, 1940-42, 45-47, Manila, 1947-49, Hong Kong, 1950-51, Singapore, 1951-53, asst. mgr. internat. banking dept. No. Trust Co., Chgo., 1953-55, 2d v.p., 1955-59, v.p., 1959-65; v.p. internat. City Nat. Bank Detroit, 1966-76, cons., 1976—. Served to lt. USNR, 1942-45. Clubs: Hong Kong (life), Am. (life) (Hong Kong); Tanglin (Singapore), (life), Singapore (life); Detroit. Home: 405 Rivard Blvd Grosse Point MI 48230 Office: City Nat Bank Bldg Detroit MI 48226

READ, ROBERT BENJAMIN, city ofcl.; b. Detroit, Apr. 30, 1918; s. Benjamin K. and Adah M. (Lloyd) R.; B.S., U. Wis., 1943; m. Lydia Emma Porte, July 11, 1953; Field engr. Consoer, Townsend & Assos., Chgo., 1946; constrn. engr. Dept. Pub. Works Madison (Wis.), 1947-69, pub. works planning engr., 1969—. Mem. adv. bd. Madison Area Tech. Coll., 1971-77. Served with USNR, 1943-46. Registered profl. engr., Wis. Mem. Wis. (dir. 1963-65, v.p. 1967-71, Profl. Engr. in Govt., 1975, Engr. of Year in Govt. award 1974, Pres.'s Achievement award 1974, Resolution of Distinguished Service 1974), Nat. (dir. 1971-74) socs. profl. engrs., ASCE, Am. Pub. Works Assn. Presbyterian (deacon 1973-76). Clubs: Masons, Shriners. Home: 645 Charles Ln Madison WI 53711 Office: 210 Monona Ave Madison WI 53709

REALS, WILLIAM JOSEPH, physician; b. Hot Springs, S.D., June 22, 1920; s. Reuben J. and Gertrude C. (Harrigan) R.; B.S., Creighton U., 1944, M.D., 1945, M.S., 1949; m. Norma Rosalie Monahan, May 6, 1944; children—William Joseph, John Francis, Elaine Ann, Thomas Christian, Mary Catherine. Intern, Creighton Meml.-St. Joseph Hosp., Omaha, 1945-46, resident, 1946-49; practice medicine, specializing in pathology, Omaha, 1949-50, Wichita, Kans., 1950—; instr. pathology Creighton U., Omaha, 1949-50; asst. pathologist St. Joseph Hosp., Omaha, 1949-50; attending pathologist, dir. labs. St. Joseph Hosp., Wichita, 1950—; prof. pathology U. Kans. Sch. Medicine, Wichita; adv. lab. commn. Kans. Bd. Health, 1958-72; cons. pathologist to surgeon gen. USAF, VA Central Office, Washington. Served with AUS, 1943-45, USAF, 1951-53; brig. gen. Res. Diplomate Am. Bd. Pathology (trustee). Fellow Am. Soc. Clin. Pathologists, Coll. Am. Pathologists (past sec.-treas., past pres.); mem. AMA, Kans. (pres. 1971-72), Sedgwick County (pres. 1961) med. socs., SAR. Roman Catholic. Author: Medical Investigation of Aviation Accidents, 1968. Home: 706 Stratford Rd Wichita KS 67206 Office: 3600 E Harry St Wichita KS 67218

REAMS, BERNARD DINSMORE, JR., lawyer, educator; b. Lynchburg, Va., Aug. 17, 1943; s. Bernard Dinsmore and Martha Eloise (Hickman) R.; B.A., Lynchburg Coll., 1965; M.S., Drexel U., 1966; J.D., U. Kans., 1972; m. Rosemarie Bridget Boyle, Oct. 26, 1968; 1 son, Andrew Dennet. Instr., asst. librarian Rutgers U., Camden, N.J., 1966-69; admitted to Kans. bar, 1973; asst. prof. law and librarian U. Kans., Lawrence, 1969-74; asst. prof. law and librarian Washington U., St. Louis, 1974-76, asso. prof., 1976, prof., 1976—. Mem. Am., Spl. library assns., Am. Assn. Law Libraries, Am. Bar Assn., Beta Phi Mu, Phi Delta Phi, Order of Coif. Author: Law for the Businessman, 1974; (with Wilson) Segregation and the Fourteenth Amendment in the States, 1975; (with Kettler) Historic Preservation Law: An Annotated Bibliography, 1976; Reader in Law Librarianship, 1976. Office: Washington U Sch Law Box 1120 Saint Louis MO 63130

REARDON, PATRICK JOSEPH, lawyer; b. Leavenworth, Kans., Dec. 8, 1934; s. William Joseph and Esther Marie (Collins) R.; A.B. cum laude, Rockhurst Coll., 1957; LL.B. (scholar), Georgetown U., 1961; m. Dolores Ellis, Feb. 23, 1968. Law clk. Circuit Judge Walter M. Bastian, U.S. Ct. Appeals, Washington, 1961-62; admitted to Kans. bar, 1961; practiced in Leavenworth, 1962—; Leavenworth County atty. chief pros. atty., 1971—. Head legal aid program Georgetown U. Law Center, 1959. Leavenworth County chmn. for election Kans. Gov. Robert Docking, 1970, 72. Mem. Alpha Sigma Nu. Democrat. Roman Catholic. Elk, Eagle, K.C. Home: 118 Spruce St Leavenworth KS 66048 Office: 520 S 4th St Leavenworth KS 66048

REARICK, GARY ROGER, painter; b. Milroy, Pa., Mar. 14, 1948; s. Harold William and Lucille Frieda (Smith) R.; A.B., Ringling Sch. Art, Sarasota, Fla., 1971; Postgrad. Miami (Ohio) U., 1977—. Painter portraits of presidents Miami (Ohio) U., portraits Gulf Western Corp., Fla.; one-man shows: Studio II, Hamilton, Ohio, 1977, Canton (Ohio) Art Inst., 1978; represented in pvt. collections. Served with U.S. Army, 1965. Winner first place All Hamilton, Butler Inst., 1976, 77, Cin. Fin. Center, 1977, first in painting Carnegie Arts Center, 1977, second place Cin. Art Club, 1976; Am. Artist in Paris, Ligoa Duncan Salon of the States (Prix de Paris), 1976. Home: 16 Mavern Ave Hamilton OH 45013 Office: Room 83 Peabody Hall Miami U Oxford OH 45056

REASER, DONALD CLAIRE, pub. co. exec.; b. Battle Creek, Mich., Apr. 20, 1925; s. Daniel Tulle and Josephine (Farrell) R.; student La. State U., 1943-44; A.B., U. Mich., 1950; certificate French studies Sorbonne U., Paris, 1954; m. Barbara Fletcher, Dec. 22, 1948. Indsl. editor Kellogg Co., Battle Creek, 1950-53; editor, sales promoter Nat. Research Bur., Chgo., 1954-59; v.p. Nat. Communications Corp., Chgo., 1960-64, Nightingale-Conant Corp., Chgo., 1965—. Served with AUS, 1943-46. Decorated Bronze Star, Purple Heart. Recipient Avery and Jule Hopwood Maj. Lit. award U. Mich., 1950. Mem. Mail Advt. Club Chgo. (v.p. 1959), U. Mich. Alumni Assn. (life). Author: The Toy Soldier, 1951. Home: 6101 N Sheridan Rd E Apt 10-C Chicago IL 60660 Office: 3730 W Devon Ave Chicago IL 60659

REASOR, GERALD LESTER, chiropractor; b. Eckerty, Ind., Dec. 14, 1914; s. Edgar Webster and Lillie Bell (Lytle) R.; D. Chiropractics, Palmer Coll. Chiropractics, 1958; diploma Parker Research Found., 1973; m. Alma Ruth Hanaver, Jan. 20, 1943; children—Nancy (Mrs. Charles W. Walters), Darrell Ray, Rowlen Lee, Irris (Mrs. David Biro), Winnona Sue (Mrs. Donnie Main), Reneta Kay (Mrs. Mike Toliver), Lenita Jan, Lolita Ann. Practice chiropractics, Paoli, Ind., 1959—. Served with USAAF, 1942-45. Mem. Am. Legion, Internat., Ind. chiropractic assns., Sherman Coll. Chiropractics Alumni Assn. (hon.). Home: 210 College St French Lick IN 47432 Office: Hwy 150 W Paoli IN 47454

REBEIZ, CONSTANTIN ANIS, educator; b. Beirut, July 11, 1936; s. Anis C. and Valentine A. (Choueyri) R.; came to U.S., 1969, naturalized, 1975; B.S., Am. U. Beirut, 1959; M.S., U. Calif. at Davis, 1960, Ph.D., 1965; m. Carole Louise Conness, Aug. 18, 1962; children—Paul A., Natalie, Mark J. Dir. dept. biol. scis. Agrl. Research Inst., Beirut, 1965-69; research asso. U. Calif. at Davis, 1969-71; asso. prof. plant physiology U. Ill., Urbana-Champaign, 1972-76, prof., 1976—. Mem. Am. Soc. Plant Physiologists, Comité Internat. de Photobiologie, AAAS, Lebanese Assn. Advancement Scis. (exec. com. 1967-69), Sigma Xi. Mem. Greek Orthodox Ch. Research and publ. in plant physiology. Home: 301 W Pennsylvania Ave Urbana IL 61801 Office: Vegetable Crops Bldg U Ill Urbana-Champaign IL 61801

REBER, DONALD DAVID, supt. schs.; b. Allentown, Pa., Sept. 16, 1915; s. Charles A. and Hattie (Smith) R.; B.S., Franklin-Marshall Coll., 1937; M.A., Lehigh U., 1948; post-grad. Harvard U., 1942, Stanford U., 1948-52; Ed.D., U. So. Calif., 1958; m. Alma A. Yons, Aug. 23, 1941; children—Donna G. Reber Ebell, Jane M. Reber Grady, Becke A. Reber McKnight. Sch. tchr. prin., Coopersburg, Pa., 1937-42; prin., Allentown, Pa., 1945-48, Punahou Sch., Honolulu, 1948-50; prin., supt. schs., Lynwood, Calif., 1950-59; supt. schs., Claremont, Calif., 1959-63, Lyons Twp. High Sch. and Jr. Coll., LaGrange, Ill., 1963—; asso. prof. Claremont Grad. Sch., 1959-62, U. So. Calif., 1959-63. Bd. govs. LaGrange Community Meml. Hosp.; bd. dirs. United Fund, W. Suburban YMCA, W. Suburban Heart Assn. Served with USNR, 1941-45. Named Lynwood Man of Year, 1959; recipient Honor medal Freedoms Found., 1959; named Ednl. Adminstr. of Year, IAES, 1976; Eisenhower exchange fellow, Europe, 1958-59. Mem. Am., Ill. assns. sch. adminstrn., N. Central Assn. (dist. dir. Ill.), No. Ill. Supts. Round Table, Ill., Nat. (hon. life), Calif. (hon. life) parent-tchs. assns., Phi Delta Kappa. Congregationalist. Club: Kiwanis. Contbr. articles to ednl. jours. Home: 421 Blackstone St LaGrange IL 60525 Office: 100 S Brainard St LaGrange IL 60525

REBERTUS, ROBERT LEE, chemist; b. Pella, Iowa, Aug. 6, 1929; s. John and Ida (Hurwitz) R.; student Mexico City Coll., Mexico, summer 1950; B.S. summa cum laude, Central Coll. Iowa, 1951; M.S., U. Ill., 1952, Ph.D., 1954; m. Delores Vivian Momberger, Jan. 4, 1973; children—Diane, Robert, Alan, Ronald, Chrisanne. Research chemist, Shell Devel. Co., Emeryville, Calif., 1954-57; chemist Shell Oil Co., Wood River, Ill., 1957-59; sr. chemist 3M Co., St. Paul, 1959-63, research specialist, 1963-65, research asso. 1965-68, research lab. mgr., 1968-69, graphic arts lab. mgr., 1969-70, mgr. product devel., 1970-71, tech. dir., 1971—. Served with USN, 1946-48. Mem. AAAS, Am. Chem. Soc., Soc. Photog. Scientists and Engrs., Sigma Xi, Phi Lambda Upsilon. Author: (with others) Chemistry of Coordination Compounds, 1952, Analytical Chemistry of Nitrogen and Its Compounds, 1970. Contbr. articles to profl. jours. Patentee in field. Home: 2069 Timmy St St Paul MN 55120 Office: 3M Center St Paul MN 55101

REBSTOCK, THEODORE LYNN, educator; b. Elkhart, Ind., June 24, 1925; s. Adolph and Redna (Dunkelberger) R.; B.A., N. Central Coll., Ill., 1949; M.S., Mich. State U., 1951, Ph.D., 1956; m. Barbara Jean Lee, Nov. 30, 1957; children—David Lynn, Donald Lee. Instr., Mich. State U., 1951-56, asst. prof. agrl. chemistry, 1956-59, vis. prof. biochemistry, summer 1965; asso. prof. chemistry Westmar Coll., Le Mars, Iowa, 1959-66, prof., 1966—, chmn. dept., 1963—, dir. div. natural sci., 1970. Fellow AAAS, Am. Inst. Chemists, Sigma Xi; mem. Am. Chem. Soc. Methodist (lay leader 1969-70, trustee). Contbr. articles to profl. jours. Home: 1026 6th Ave SE Le Mars IA 51031

RECK, W(ALDO) EMERSON, ednl. pub. relations specialist, writer; b. Gettysburg, Ohio, Dec. 28, 1903; s. Samuel Harvey and Effie D. (Arnett) R.; A.B., Wittenberg U., 1926; A.M., U. Iowa, 1946; LL.D., Midland Coll., 1949; m. Hazel Winifred January, Sept. 7, 1926; children—Phyllis Reck Welch, Jr., Elizabeth Ann Reck Lada. Reporter, Springfield (Ohio) News, 1922-26; publicity dir. Midland Coll., Fremont, Nebr., 1926-28, dir. pub. relations, prof. journalism, 1928-40; dir. pub. relations Colgate U., 1940-48; v.p. Wittenberg U., Springfield, Ohio, 1948-70, v.p. emeritus, 1970—; pub. relations specialist Cumerford Corp., Ft. Lauderdale, Fla., 1970—; columnist Springfield (Ohio) Sun, 1973—; corr. AP, 1928-38; mng. editor Fremont Morning Guide, 1939; vis. lectr. pub. relations State U. Iowa, summers 1941, 42, U. Wyo., summer 1948; co-dir. Seminar on Pub. Relations for High Edn., Syracuse U., summers 1944, 45, 46. Recipient award Am. Coll. Pub. Relations Assn. for Distinguished Service, 1942, for Outstanding Achievement in Interpretation of Higher Edn., 1944, 47; award Council for Advancement and Support of Edn., 1977. Mem. Am. Coll. Pub. Relations Assn. (v.p. in charge research 1936-38, editor assn. mag. 1938-40, pres. 1940-41, chmn. plans and policies com. 1944-50, dir. 1956, historian 1967-76), Luth. Coll. Pub. Relations Assn. (pres. 1951-53), Pub. Relations Soc. Am. (nat. jud. council 1952), Sch. Pub. Relations Assn., Assn. Am. Colls. (com. on pub. relations 1945-48), AAUP, Springfield C. of C. (dir. 1958-60), Council Advancement and Support Edn., Nat. Luth. Ednl. Conf. (chmn. com. pub. relations 1949-50), Ohio Coll. Pub. Relations Officers (pres. 1954-55), Nat. Hist. Soc., Smithsonian Assos., Nat. Trust Historic Preservation, Omicron Delta Kappa, Sigma Delta Chi, Pi Delta Epsilon, Delta Sigma Phi, Blue Key, Elbeetian Legion. Author: Public Relations: a Program for Colleges and Universities, 1946; (with others) The American College, 1949; Public Relations Handbook (with others), 1950, 60, 67; The Changing World of College Relations, 1976; editor: Publicity Problems, 1939; College Publicity Manual, 1948; contbr. to ednl., profl. mags., also hist. publs. Mem. commn. on ch. papers, 1951-62, cons. com. dept. of press, radio and TV United Luth. Ch., 1955-60; vice chmn. commn. on ch. papers Luth. Ch. in Am., 1962-64, mem. exec. com., also chmn. com. periodicals of bd. publ., 1962-72, mem. mgmt. com. Office of Communications, 1972-76; chmn. pub. relations com. Council Protestant Colls. and Univs., 1961-65; mem. adminstrv. com. Wittenberg U., 1968-69. Home: 61 Hedgely Rd Springfield OH 45506

RECKER, EDWARD ANTHONY, floor co. exec.; b. Covington, Ky., July 10, 1920; s. Frank William and Corrine (Sprague) R.; student U. Cin., 1946-48; m. Virginia Lee Cromwell, Dec. 14, 1940; children—Donna L. Recker Becker, Judith A. Recker Auge, Leslie J. Recker Ayres. Salesman Cin. Floor Co., Inc., 1940-75, sr. v.p. sales, 1974—, bd. dirs. 1964—; dir. Allied Constrn. Industries, Cin., 1967-75, ednl. com. 1971-75. Treas. constrn. advancement program, Cin., 1969-75. Served with USMCR, 1943-45. Mem. Constrn. Specification Inst., Bldg. Mgrs. Assn., Ceilings and Interior Systems Contractors Assn., Cin. Acoustical Assn., Greater Cin. Subcontractors Assn. Home: 3816 Hope Ln Erlanger KY 41018 Office: 4785 Eastern Ave Cincinnati OH 45226

RECKERT, ROBERT DEAN, civil engr., land surveyor; b. Norfolk, Nebr., Nov. 11, 1925; s. William Frederick and Zella (Kissinger) R.; B.S. in Civil Engring., Iowa State U., 1948; m. Ann Ruth Rozeboom, July 17, 1948; children—William Bernard, Roberta Ann, Meredith Sue. Asst. dept. head firm Leo A. Daly Co., Omaha, 1952-54; with DeWild Grant Reckert & Assos. Co., Rock Rapids, Iowa, 1954—, v.p., 1965-72, sr. v.p., 1972-75, exec. v.p., 1975—; pres. Environs Inc., Rock Rapids, 1968—; dir Woodbury Devel. Corp., Sioux City, Iowa, Sec., Lyon County Planning and Zoning Commn., 1960-70; chmn. N.W. Iowa Regional Planning Commn., 1969; mem. Gov's Com. Rural Water and Waste Disposal, 1970-71. Served with USNR, 1943-44. Recipient John S. Dodds award, 1977; registered profl. engr., Iowa, Alaska, Minn., S.D., Nebr. Fellow ASCE; mem. Iowa Bd. Engring. Examiners (chmn. 1967-75), Nat. Council Engring. Examiners (chmn. land surveying com. 1972), Am. Congress Surveying and Mapping (past pres.), Cons. Engrs. Council Iowa (treas. 1969), Ia. Engring. Soc. (dir. 1966), Soc. Land Surveyors Iowa, Nat. Soc. Profl. Engrs., Water Pollution Control Fedn., Am. Water Works Assn., Nat. Water Well Assn., Royal Soc. Health (London, Eng.), Alpha Tau Omega. Developer uniform nat. exam. land surveying, 1972. Home: 204 Briar Ln Rock Rapids IA 51246 Office: 315 1st Ave Rock Rapids IA 51246

RECTENWALD, GARY MICHAEL, data processing adminstr.; b. Toledo, Ohio, Dec. 31, 1949; s. Edgar E. and Dorothy C. (Antieau) R.; B.S. (cum laude), Ohio State U., 1971, M.S. in Computer Sci., 1972, M.B.A., 1978. Programmer trainee Ohio State U., 1970-71, grad. research asso., 1971-72; application systems programmer, 1 (1972), 2 (1973-75), 3 (1976-77); mgr. application systems programming, 1977—. Mem. Instruction and Research Computer Center, Ohio State U., Ohio State U. Marching Band, 1967-75, (most inspirational bandsman, 1973), Phi Beta Kappa, Pi Mu Epsilon, Kappa Kappa Psi. Roman Catholic. Home: 4183 Kenridge Dr Columbus OH 43220 Office: Instruction and Research Computer Center Ohio State U 1971 Neil Ave Columbus OH 43210

REDDING, FOSTER KINYON, neurologist, educator; b. Owatonna, Minn., July 22, 1929; s. James Alfred and Dorothy Elizabeth (Kinyon) R.; M.D., U. Pa., 1954; Ph.D., McGill U., 1964; m. Beverly Carol Hanson, Jan 9, 1960; children—Susan, Stephen, Karen, Jane. Intern, U. Minn. Hosps., Mpls., 1954-55; resident U. Pa. Hosp., Phila., 1958-60, Montreal Neurol. Inst., 1960-64; practice medicine specializing in neurology, Chgo., 1964-67, Detroit, 1967—; physician surgeon Palen Clinic, Mpls., 1955-56; asst. prof. neurology U. Ill., Presbyn.-St. Lukes Hosp., Chgo., dir. encephalography, 1964-67; neurologist, neurophysiologist Henry Ford Hosp., Detroit, 1967-73, chief neurology, 1972-73; prof. neurology Wayne State U. Sch. Medicine, 1973—. Served with M.C., USAF, 1956-58. Inst. Neurol. Diseases and Blindness spl. fellow, 1960-64; USPHS research grantee, 1966-69. Fellow Am. Acad. Neurology; mem. Am. Electroencephalographic Soc., Am. Epilepsy Soc., Mich. Neurol. Assn., Soc. Neurosci. Home: 15800 Lakeview Ct Grosse Pointe Park MI 48230 Office: 3990 John R St Detroit MI 48201

REDER, WILLIAM ROGER, advt. exec.; b. Chgo., Aug. 23, 1935; s. Philip A. and Rosalie (Bunois) R.; B.A., U. Ill., 1956; children—Elizabeth R., Jonathan, Philip. Mgr. advt. Dutch Brand div. Johns Manville, Chgo., 1958-60, Ekco Alcoa Containers, Wheeling, Ill., 1956-58; v.p. mktg. Radiant Mfg. Corp., Morton Grove, Ill., 1960-63; exec. v.p. Edro Advt. Inc., Chgo., 1963-67, Garfield Linn Advt., Chgo., 1968—; dir. Simplex/Scribe Internat., J.B. Roger Inc. Adviser, Jr. Achievement of Chgo., 1956-60, Boy Scouts Am., 1966-70. Mem. Am. Archery Council (exec. sec. 1966-68), Archery Mfrs. Orgn. (founding chmn. 1966-69), Chgo. Advt. Club, Nat. Restaurant Assn. (personnel devel. com.), Travelers Aid Soc. (counselor Looking Glass div. 1970-72), Sigma Delta Chi, Alpha Delta Sigma, Tau Delta Phi. Clubs: Wembley Spinner, Northbrook Sports. Contbg. editor Advt. Age, 1968-71, Broadcasting, 1975, 76, Avenue M, 1975, 76, 77. Home: 1000 Lake Shore Dr Chicago IL 60611 Office: 875 N Michigan Ave Chicago IL 60611

REDFIELD, NICHOLAS PRIDMORE, physician; b. Detroit, Apr. 17, 1935; s. Harold and Alma Lillian Gertrude (Bramley) R.; B.S., U. Mich., 1958; M.D., Wayne State U., 1962; m. Ellen Elizabeth Pearson, Aug. 27, 1958; children—Nicholas Pridmore, Duncan, Douglas. Intern, Harper Hosp., Detroit, 1962-63; resident in otolaryngology Mayo Clinic, Rochester, Minn., 1963-66, 68-69; practice medicine specializing in otology, Saginaw, Mich., 1969—; mem. active staff St. Mary's Hosp., Saginaw; sr. staff St. Luke's Hosp., Saginaw; asso. staff Saginaw Gen. Hosp.; cons. staff Central Mich. Community Hosp., Mt. Pleasant, Midland (Mich.) Community Hosp.;

adj. prof. otolaryngology Central Mich. U., Mt. Pleasant, 1970—; asst. clin. prof. otolaryngology Mich. State U. Coll. Human Medicine, 1973—; vis. scientist U. Ill., Chgo., 1971. Served with AUS, 1966-68. Diplomate Am. Bd. Otolaryngology. Mem. Mich. State, Saginaw County med. socs., AMA, Saginaw Valley Acad. Ophthalmology and Otolaryngology (pres. 1972-73), Phi Rho Sigma. Club: Bay City Yacht. Contbr. articles to med. bulls. Home: 1787 E Packard St Saginaw MI 48603 Office: 1811 N Michigan Ave Saginaw MI 48602

REDGRAVE, JOHN ROBERT, heavy machinery mfg. co. exec.; b. Phila., Nov. 9, 1925; s. DeWitt Clinton and Hope (Pillsbury) R.; M.E., Rittenhouse Coll., 1948; m. Nancy Jean Rosendale, Aug. 17, 1951; children—Martyn Robert, Timothy Douglas, John Robert, Barbara Jean. Regional sales mgr. Beloit Corp., Portland, Oreg., 1963-67, gen. mgr. control systems div., Beloit, Wis., 1967-70, v.p. sales, 1974-77; pres. Beloit Sorel Walmsley, Ltd., Sorel, Que., Can., 1970-74, also dir.; chmn., pres. Dolphin Machining Inc., South Beloit, Ill., 1977—. Vice chmn. Citizen's Adv. Com., Beloit, 1968-70; bd. dirs. Meml. Hosp. Served with USNR, 1943-46. Mem. Nat. Assn. Parliamentarians, Robert's Rules Assn. (chmn. 1965), Am. Mgmt. Assn., Am. Inst. Parliamentarians, Instrument Soc. Am., TAPPI, Paper Industry Mgmt. Assn. Clubs: Rotary, Beloit Country (dir.). Home: 3709 Oak Lane Dr Beloit WI 53511 Office: 1st Lawrence St Beloit WI 53511

REDLEAF, PAUL DAVID, physician, educator; b. N.Y.C., Apr. 24, 1931; s. Harry and Myrtle (Goodfriend) R.; A.B. with distinction in Zoology and Gen. Studies, Cornell U., 1951; M.D., Columbia, 1955; m. Rhoda Eileen Rosen, May 29, 1953; children—Diane, Andrew, Karen, Eric. Nat. Heart Inst. postgrad. fellow internal medicine U. Minn., Mpls., 1955-57, 59-61, clin. prof. medicine, 1975—; practice medicine specializing in internal medicine, St. Paul, 1961—; attending physician St. Paul Ramsey Hosp., Diplomate Am. Bd. Internal Medicine. Fellow A.C.P.; mem. Phi Beta Kappa, Alpha Omega Alpha, Phi Kappa Phi. Contbr. articles to med. jours. Home: 2090 Upper St Dennis St St Paul MN 55116

REDMOND, GEORGE FOOTE, lawyer; b. Racine, Wis., Oct. 23, 1911; s. Leo Ira and Elizabeth (Foote) R.; B.A., U. Wis., 1933, J.D., 1935; m. Doris R. Roethke, Oct. 26, 1942; children—Margaret, Kathleen, Gail. Admitted to Wis. bar, 1935; atty. U.S. Dept. Agr., Washington, Milw., 1935-42; pvt. practice law, Milw., 1943—, partner Von Briesen, Redmond, Schilling and Kreunen, 1948—; municipal justice Village of River Hills, 1953—. Served as 1st lt. USAAF, 1942-43. Mem Wis. Bar Assn. (past gov., sec. bus. and corp. law sect. 1953-76). Home: 8150 N Green Bay Rd Milwaukee WI 53209 Office: 757 N Broadway Milwaukee WI 53202

REDONDO, DIEGO, pediatrician; b. Barranquilla, Colombia, Apr. 22, 1936; s. Diego and Regina (Villarreal) R.; came to U.S., 1953, naturalized, 1973; A.A., Christian Bros. Coll., 1955; M.D., Tulane U., 1961; m. Susan Biebel, Feb. 16, 1963; children—Diego, Dorothy, Peter, Ramon. Intern, Charity Hosp., New Orleans, 1961-62; resident in pediatrics Children's Meml. Hosp., Chgo., 1962-64, chief resident in pediatrics, 1964-65, fellow in hematology, 1965-66; practice medicine specializing in pediatrics, Deerfield, Ill., 1966—; asst. prof. clin. pediatrics Northwestern U. Med. Sch.; bd. dirs. Children's Meml. Hosp., 1976—. Mem. Gov's. Transition Task Force, Ill., 1972-73, Ill. Bd. Higher Edn., 1974—; chmn. Ill. Ednl. TV Commn., 1976—. Fellow Am. Acad. Pediatrics; mem. Ill. State, Lake County med. socs., AMA. Roman Catholic. Author: (with Edith Freund) Growing Up Healthy, 1976. Home: 1345 Montgomery Dr Deerfield IL 60015 Office: 956 Deerfield Rd Deerfield IL 60015

REDSHAW, WARD FULLER, audio-visual co. owner; b. Great Falls, Mont., Mar. 31, 1923; s. Thomas Alfred and Elvina Anne (Fuller) R.; student U. Md., 1958-59, Army Command and Gen. Staff Coll., 1960; m. Margaret MacPherson, Feb. 9, 1946; children—Neil, Barbara, Janet Redshaw Prochnow, Mark. Commd. 2d lt., U.S. Army, 1950, advanced through grades to maj., 1962, ret. as chief pictorial officer, 1963; with Keuffel & Esser Co., engring. and audio-visual, Dallas, 1963-65, Chgo., 1965-66; mfrs. rep. Vern Schultz & Assos., Crystal Lake, Ill., 1966-69; propr. Redshaw Audio-Visual Co., mfrs. rep., also bus. cons., Libertyville, Ill., 1969—; instr., also bd. dirs. Nat. Audio-Visual Assn., 1972-75. Decorated Combat Infantryman's badge, Army Commendation medal with 2 oak leaf clusters. Presbyterian. Club: Masons. Home: 1349 Redwood Ln Libertyville IL 60048 Office: 110 Lake St Libertyville IL 60048

REECE, WILBUR TAYLOR, dentist; b. Normal, Ill., Aug. 23, 1910; s. John Stewart and Estella Jennie (Schaeffer) R.; B.E., Ill. State U., 1932; M.A., U. Chgo., 1937; D.D.S., Northwestern U., 1949; m. Lois Conover, Mar. 15, 1935 (dec. Oct. 1968); children—John C., Sharon Reece Clark; m. 2d, Mildred Welch, Nov. 28, 1969. Sci. tchr., prin. high sch., Petersburg, Ill., 1932-36; sci. tchr. Elmhurst (Ill.) Jr. High Sch., 1936-40; research asst. Ill. Edn. Assn., Springfield, 1941-43, 1946; gen. practice dentistry, Springfield, Ill., 1949—; trustee Trustee, Ill. Dental Service, non profit dental service corp., 1969—. Served with USNR, 1943-46; lt. Res. ret. Fellow Am. Coll. Dentists; mem. Ill. Dental Soc. (chmn. com. legis. 1960-68), G.V. Black Dist. Dental Soc. (pres. 1962-63), Kappa Delta Pi, Phi Delta Kappa, Delta Sigma Delta., Am. Legion, ADA, Am. Acad. Gen. Dentistry, Fedn. Dentaire Internat., Chgo. Dental Soc., Ill. Assn. Profs. Congregationalist (moderator 1970-71). Contbr. to profl. publs. in field. Home: 41 Andover Dr Springfield IL 62704 Office: 425 W Ash St Springfield IL 52704

REED, ARTHUR LACHLAN, business exec.; b. Izmir (Smyrna) Turkey, Mar. 22, 1917 (parents American citizens); s. Cass Arthur and Rosalind Blackler (Maclachlan) R.; grad. Phillips Acad., 1935; A.B., Yale, 1939, A.M., 1941; Ph.D., U. Minn., 1953; m. Martha Sweatt, Sept. 3, 1942; children—William, Lachlan, Mark, Mary, Harold, John. Asst. mgr. advt. Honeywell, Mpls., 1945-47, various exec. positions, 1956-66; tchr. Silver Lake (Minn.) High Sch., 1947-48; instr. Phillips Acad., Andover, Mass., 1948-51; headmaster Northrop Collegiate Sch., Mpls., 1951-53; spl. asst. U.S. commr. edn. HEW, 1954-56; venture capitalist, Mpls., from 1966; founder, partner Gulf Machinery Co., Abu Dhabi, 1975, Lachlan Castle Co., Dubai, 1976, Saha Co., Geneva, 1976; founder, chmn. Internat. Timesharing, Mpls., Lachlan Internat., London and Mpls.; founder, dir. Interpoint Corp., Chgo., 1966-75, Roart Plastics, Mpls.; bd. mgrs. Investors Diversified Services Life Ins. Co., Mpls.; dir. Abercrombie & Fitch, 1966-75. Mem. Minn. Gov.'s Com. on Human Rights, 1958-63; mem. adv. com. Minn. Jr. Coll. Bd., 1960-65; gen. chmn. Yale Regional Conf., 1960; pres. Choate Sch. Fathers' Assn., 1962-63; dir. exec. bd. Viking council Boy Scouts Am., 1960-66. Trustee, Fisk U., 1957-74, chmn. centennial fund dr., 1965; trustee Internat. Coll., Beirut, Am. U. in Cairo (Egypt), Northstar Research Inst., Mpls., 1968-74; founder, trustee Minn. Outward Bound Sch., 1962-72; chmn. bd. trustees, 1971; founder, dir. Dynamy Program Mass., 1968-76, founder, chmn. Dynamy Minn., 1972-76; bd. dirs. Que.-Labrador Fedn., Middle East Inst.; vis. com. Center for Middle East Studies, Harvard U., 1974—. Served from ensign to lt. comdr., USNR, 1941-45. Clubs: Minneapolis; Woodhill Country (Wayzata); Yale (NYC); Bath and Tennis (Palm Beach); Hurlingham (London). Home: 1500 Brackett's Point Rd Wayzata MN 55391 Office: 1560 Dain Tower Minneapolis MN 55402

REED, DONALD IRVING, assn. exec.; b. Oak Park, Ill., June 25, 1929; s. Samuel Irving and Pearl Hart (Kniffen) R.; B.A., Ripon Coll., 1951; m. Beverly Burner Cram, July 17, 1954; children—Diana, David. Design engr. Internat. Harvester Co., Melrose Park, Ill., 1956-59; with Boating Industry Assn., Chgo., 1959—, dir. engring., 1971—, also exec. sec. Trailer Mfrs.' Assn. (an affiliate). Served with U.S. Army, 1951-56; served to maj. CAP, 1960—. Mem. Soc. Automotive Engrs. (chmn. specialized vehicle and equipment council), Am. Boat and Yacht Council (div. dir. standards div.), Soc. Naval Architects and Marine Engrs., Am. Def. Preparedness Assn., Aircraft Owners and Pilots Assn., Nat. Rifle Assn., Internat. Orgn. for Standardization (U.S. del. leader to internat. meetings), ASTM (panel chmn.). Home: 1216 3d Ave Des Plaines IL 60018 Office: 401 N Michigan Ave Chicago IL 60611

REED, E. SMITH, JR., mech. engr.; b. Washington, Dec. 8, 1945; s. E. Smith and Josephine (Lewis) R.; B.S. in Mech. Engring., U. Ark., 1968; m. Virginia Ann Burch, June 13, 1970; children—Robyn Cathleen, Karen Lindsay. Production engr. ordnance div. Honeywell Inc., Mpls., 1968-70; chief product engr. Toro Co., Mpls., 1970—. Elder, Faith Presbyn. Ch., 1974—. Recipient James F. Lincoln Found. award, 1976; registered profl. engr., Minn. Mem. Soc. of Automotive Engrs., Phi Delta Theta. Inventor of golf course greens spikers. Home: 20225 Cottagewood Ave Deephaven MN 55331 Office: 8111 Lyndale Ave S Minneapolis MN 55420

REED, EDSEL SHERWOOD, radiologist; b. Bowen, Ky., Aug. 19, 1923; s. George W. and Mattie Elizabeth (Palmer) R.; B.S., Morehead State U., 1943; M.D., U. Louisville, 1946; m. Allie Carey, Dec. 23, 1947; children—Patricia Jayne Reed Tate, Cynthia Lynn, Edsel Sherwood. Intern, Good Samaritan Hosp., Lexington, Ky., 1947, U. Pa., 1950-51; resident in radiology U. Louisville, 1948-51, asst. in radiology 1948-50, instr., 1951, 58-68, asst. clin. prof., 1969—; staff med. isotopes U. Tex. at Houston, 1957; pvt. practice radiology, St. Joseph, Mo., 1953-56; assoc. radiologist, asst. dir. dept. radiology Miners Meml. Hosp. Assn., Harlan, Ky., 1956-58; dir. radiology Clark County Meml. Hosp., Jeffersonville, Ind., 1958—; chief med. staff, 1973; pres. Radiology Assos. Inc., 1969-71. Deacon, 1st Bapt. Ch., Jeffersonville, 1969—. Served with AUS, 1943-46, to capt. USAR, 1951-53. Diplomate Am. Bd. Radiology. Mem. Clark County Med. Soc. (pres. 1962), Greater Louisville Radiology Soc. (pres. 1970), Ind. Med. Assn., AMA, Ind. Roentgen Soc., Am. Coll. Radiology, Radiol. Soc. N.Am., Ky., Ind. hist. socs. Clubs: Mason, Elks, Shriners. Contbr. articles to profl. jours. Home: 111 Pawnee Dr Jeffersonville IN 47130 Office: 1220 Missouri Ave Jeffersonville IN 47130

REED, ELMETHRA LUSTER, educator; b. Dundee, Miss., Mar. 31, 1918; d. Donnell and Willie Mae (Rhodes) Luster; B.S. in Edn., Chgo. State U., 1969; M.Ed. in Guidance and Counseling, DePaul U., Chgo., 1977; m. Alonzo L. Reed, Nov. 24, 1937; children—Wilimethra Davenport, James, Leonard, Byron, Carl, Crystal, Darryl. Cosmetic demonstrator, saleslady Noblesse Cosmetic Co., 1936; civilian naval insp., 1942-44; fiscal clk. VA, 1944-51; tchr. Chgo. pub. schs., 1969—; tchr. arts and crafts Lawndale Youth Program, Chgo., 1968-77. Chmn. Lawndale Youth Cultural Program, 24th Ward, 1965-68; pres. Altar and Rosary Soc., St. Agatha Roman Catholic Ch., 1965-69. Recipient various civic service awards. Mem. Am. Personnel and Guidance Assn. Home: 1517 S Spaulding Ave Chicago IL 60623 Office: 2740 W Roosevelt Rd Chicago IL 60608

REED, EMELYNE ELY, civic worker; b. Oak Hill, Ohio, Jan. 15, 1912; d. George Leonard and Jessie (Climer) Ely; grad. Office Tng. Sch., 1931; m. Richard A. Reed, May 2, 1943 (div. Mar. 1948); 1 dau., Alice Jane. Steno-sec. Ohio Nat. Bank, Columbus, 1931-34, Brunson Bank & Trust Co., Columbus, 1934-37, Standard Savs. & Loan Co., Columbus, 1937-43; underwriter Trafford Tallmadge Agy., Columbus, 1943-47; statis. sec. Mead Corp., Chillicothe, Ohio, 1947-65, tech. sec. Central Research Labs., 1965-77; pvt. practice sci. editing, lit. services, Londonderry, Ohio, 1977—. Publicity chmn. bd. mgrs. Ohio PTA, 1963-66, dir. Dist. 11, 1966-70, 71-75, communications chmn. 1970-71; mem. State Library of Ohio Adv. Council for Fed. LSCA Programs, 1971—. Pres. OVAL Council, 1971-73, pres. OVAL trustees, 1973—; trustee Ross County Dist. Library, 1959-69, pres., 1963-69; trustee Ross County Community Action Commn., 1963-71; trustee Chillicothe and Ross County Pub. Library, 1970—, v.p., 1976—; trustee Ross County chpt. Am. Heart Assn. Mem. Am., Ohio (exec. com. 1972-73, sec. 1973—; Trustee of Year award 1974). library trustees assns., PTA (life). Home: Box 165 Londonderry OH 45647

REED, FRANK FREMONT, II, lawyer; b. Chgo., June 15, 1928; s. Allen Martin and Frances (Faurot) R.; student Chgo. Latin Sch.; grad. St. Paul's Sch., 1946; A.B., U. Mich., 1952, J.D., 1957; m. Jaquelin Silverthorne Cox, April 27, 1963; children—Elizabeth Matthiessen, Laurie Matthiessen, Mark Matthiessen, Jeffrey, Nancy, Sarah. Admitted to Ill. bar, 1958; asso. Byron, Hume, Groen & Clement, 1958-61, Marks & Clerk, 1961-63; individual practice, Chgo., 1963—; dir. Western Acadia (Western Felt Works), 1960-75, chmn. exec. com., 1969-71. Cubmaster, Cub Scout Pack 3014, Chgo. Area council Boy Scouts Am., 1964-70; Republican precinct capt. 1972—; candidate for 43d ward alderman, 1975; bd. dirs., sec. Chgo. Found. Theater Arts, 1959-64; vestryman St. Chrysostom's Ch., 1975—, chmn. ushers guild, 1976-78; bd. dirs. North State, Astor, Lake Shore Dr. Assn., 1965—, pres. 1977—. Served from pvt. to cpl. AUS, 1952-54. Mem. Am., Ill., Chgo. bar assns., Chgo. Patent Law Assn. (chmn. by-laws com. 1962), Am. Judicature Soc., Phi Alpha Delta. Republican. Episcopalian. Clubs: Racquet, Wausaukee (sec., dir. 1968-71, chmn. sailing com. 1962-70, 72—), Univ. (Chgo.). Home: 1500 Lake Shore Dr Chicago IL 60610 Office: 135 S LaSalle St Suite 3810 Chicago IL 60603

REED, GARETH LAVERNE, elec. co. exec.; b. Cedar Rapids, Iowa, Dec. 22, 1932; s. John Ivan and Florence Lorene (Larson) R.; B.S., Iowa State U., 1954; M.S., U. N.Mex., 1958; Ph.D., U. Md., 1966; M.B.A., U. Mich., 1974; m. LaVonne Doris Bartels, June 13, 1954; children—Richard K., Robin R., Kathryn S. Sr. engr. N.Am. Aviation, Canoga Park, Calif., 1958-62; project engr. Martin-Marietta, Balt., 1962-67; dir. product devel. Allis Chalmers, Milw., 1967-70; dir. corporate planning Masco Corp., Detroit, 1970-72, div. gen. mgr., 1972—. Served to capt. USAF, 1955-58. Mem. Am. Inst. Chem. Engrs., Soc. Mfg. Engrs., Am. Mgmt. Assn., Tau Beta Pi, Pi Tau Sigma, Sigma Xi. Lutheran. Contbr. articles to profl. jours. Inventor in field. Home: 3670 Chatham Way Ann Arbor MI 48105 Office: 12085 Dixie St Detroit MI 48239

REED, MARGARET FOX, educator; b. Chgo., Mar. 13, 1916; d. Paul Christopher and Sarah (Pruner) Fox; B.A., U. Chgo., 1938, M.A., 1941, Ph.D., 1951; m. Richard Yates Reed, May 17, 1952; children—Christopher Yates, Sarah Margaret Yates. Employment mgr. U. Chgo., 1947-49, vocat. counselor, 1943-47; counselor for socially maladjusted Bloom Twp. High Sch., Chicago Heights, 1951-52; asst. editor Scott, Foresman & Co., Chgo., 1952-53; pvt. practice as marriage and family counselor, Miami, Fla., 1953-64; mem. faculty Moorhead (Minn.) State U., 1964—, prof., 1967—, chmn. dept. social work, 1971—. Mem. Am. Psychol. Assn., Nat. Assn. Social Workers, Council Social Work Edn., P.E.O. Mem. United Ch. of Christ. Home: 1309 13th St S Moorhead MN 56560 Office: Dept Social Work Moorhead State Univ Moorhead MN 56560

REED, PHILIP G., book illustrator, designer; b. Park Ridge, Ill., Jan. 17, 1908; s. John Wesley and Grace C. (Hibbard) R.; grad. Art Inst. Chgo., 1930; m. Nancy L. Price, April 30, 1954; children—Keith O., Scott H., Ian Campbell. Founded Broadside Press, Barrington, Ill., 1930-33, Katonah, N.Y., 1933-36, Park Ridge, Ill., 1936-39; founder Philip Reed, Printer, Ltd., 1977; dir. The Monastery Hill Press, Chgo., 1939-43; founded Printing Office of Philip Reed, 1946, pres., 1948—; asso. A. & R. Roe Printers, St. Joseph, Mich., 1956-73; work exhibited in Moscow Am. Nat. Exhbn. Served with C.E., AUS, 1943-45. Recipient awards for printing design Chgo. Soc. Typographic, Arts, 1937, 40, 47, 51-53, book design, 1951; nominee Caldecott medal, 1963. Mem. Am. Inst. Graphic Arts (50 books of year 1939, 40, 47, 51-53, 63, printing for commerce 1937, 49, 50-56). Republican. Episcopalian. Club: Cliff Dwellers. Specialist in book design and illustration. Home: 2901 Cleveland Ave Saint Joseph MI 49085 Office: 191 Michigan Ave Benton Harbor MI 49022

REED, ROBERT HOLBROOKE, educator; b. Anadarko, Okla., Sept. 29, 1922; s. Otie Watson and Mattie Elizabeth (Ratliffe) R.; B.S., U. Calif. at Berkeley, 1949, M.S., 1953, Ph.D., 1961; m. Luise Antonina Rosalewski, June 11, 1950; children—Elisabeth Luise, Susan Holly. Agrl. economist U. Honolulu, 1952-53; mgmt. trainee Del Monte Foods, San Francisco, 1953-54, plant foreman, Emeryville, Calif., 1954-55; agrl. economist, asso. exptl. sta., econ. research service U.S. Dept. Agr. and U. Calif. at Berkeley, 1955-60; research economist United Fruit Co., LaLima, Honduras, 1960-61; agrl. economist Econ. Research Service, Berkeley, 1962-65; prof. agrl. econs. U. Wis., Madison, 1965—; cons. World Bank, Colombia, 1966, Stanford Research Inst., 1959; prof. U. Wis./AID, Universidade Federal do Rio Grande do Sul, Porto Alegre, Brazil, 1968-72; cons. Asian Devel. Bank, Manila, Philippines, 1972-75, Multinat. Agri Bus. Assos., Washington, 1974—, OAS, Ecuador, 1976; vis. scholar U. Cal. at Berkeley, 1974. Served with AUS, 1940-45; ETO. U. Calif. and Econ. Research Service grantee, 1974—. Mem. Agrl. Econs. Assn., Am. Econ. Assn. Clubs: British (Porto Alegre). Author: Economia de Comercializacao, 1971. Home: 904 Arden Ln Madison WI 53711

REEDER, EILEEN BERENDT, bus. cons.; d. Edward and Hilda Christina (Buchholz) Berendt; M.Ed., U. Mo. at Kansas City; M.B.A., So. Ill. U., Edwardsville, 1973; m. John Charles Reeder; children—John Robert, Valerie Ann, Deborah Eileen. Writer, advt. staff Crown Drug Co., Kansas City, Mo.; tchr. pub. schs., Kansas City, St. Charles, Mo., Ferguson-Florissant Pub. Schs.; mem. pub. relations staff Land of the Fifth Season, St. Louis; real estate agt. Kelly Real Estate, Florissant; bus. cons. extension bus. and industry program U. Mo., St. Louis, 1974—. Mem. Am. Mktg. Assn., Am. Statis. Assn., AAUW. Methodist. Office: 724 Union St N St Louis MO 63108

REEDER, STANLEY WAYLETT, indsl. engr.; b. Gering, Nebr., Oct. 15, 1922; s. Harry Hobart and Albertine Emily (Waylett) R.; student U. Nebr., 1940, 50, 59, 62, DePaul U., 1943, Northeastern U., 1944; m. Elizabeth Nelson Barker, June 7, 1941; children—Enid Loretta Reeder Burrows, Jody Deven Reeder Brown. Rate clk. Consol. Aircraft Corp., San Diego, 1941-42; time study engr., Bell & Howell, Chgo., 1942-44; chief time study engr. Food Machinery Corp., Hoopeston, Ill., 1944-46; with Cushman Motors, (now Outboard Marine Corp.), Lincoln, Nebr., 1946—, foreman engine assembly, 1948-56, time study engr., 1965-72, chief methods, engr., 1972—. Mem. San. and Improvement Dist. #2 Bd., 1965-73, chmn., 1966-73. Served with AUS, 1940-41. Mem. Am. Inst. Indsl. Engrs., Am. Inst. Plant Engrs., Indsl. Club. Republican. Clubs: Lions (dep. dist. gov.), Elks, Masons, Order Eastern Star. Lincoln Chess. Home: 6345 East Shore Dr Lincoln NE 68516 Office: 920 N 21st St Lincoln NE 68501

REES, WARREN JAMES, judge; b. Anamosa, Iowa, Aug. 2, 1908; s. Barlow G. and Anna (Lowe) R.; student Grinnell Coll., 1926-27; m. Alma Davis, Aug. 20, 1938; children—Mary Ann (Mrs. R. Ashley Lyman), William (dec.). Clk. Dist. Ct., Jones County, Iowa, 1929-32; admitted to Iowa bar, 1934; pvt. practice law, Anamosa, 1934-63; county atty., Jones County, 1939-45; judge 18th and 8th Jud. Dists. Iowa, 1963-69; justice Iowa Supreme Ct., 1969—. Chmn., Jones County Republican Central Com., 1938-50; mem. Rep. State Central Com., 1950-54; trustee Cornell Coll., Mt. Vernon, Iowa. Mem. Am., Iowa, Jones County bar assns., Am. Judicature Soc., Order of Coif. Methodist. Mason (Shriner), Lion. Home: 307 E 2d St Anamosa IA 52205 Office: Jones County Courthouse Anamosa IA 52205

REESE, DONALD JOSEPH, bus. exec.; b. Blairsville, Pa., Oct. 5, 1923; s. Elmer James and Mary Ellen (Litzinger) R.; B.S. in Bus. Adminstrn., Ohio State U., 1948; m. Evelyn Van Huffel, Sept. 14, 1946; children—Kareen, Donald, Stephen, Monica. Sales trainee Republic Steel Corp., Warren, Ohio, 1948-49; pres., treas. Reese Tool & Supply Co. Warren, 1950—, Reewood Inc., Warren, 1960—, Metal Services Co., Warren, 1970—; dir. Union Savs. & Trust Co., I.J. Investment Co. Trustee Trumbull Meml. Hosp., Trumbull County chpt. ARC, Blessed Sacrament Ch.; chmn. United Negro Coll. Fund Dr. Served with U.S. Army, 1942-46. Mem. Warren-Youngstown Indsl. Supply Assn. (pres. 1965). Republican. Roman Catholic. Clubs: Trumbull Country (pres. 1976-77), Univ. Pitts., Sales Execs. Steubenville. Office: 30 N River Dr PO Box 1070 Warren OH 44481

REESE, RAYMOND CASTLE, structural engring. cons.; b. Pittsfield, Mass., Dec. 22, 1893; s. John Miles and Minnie Victoria (Castle) R.; B.S., Mass. Inst. Tech., 1920; postgrad. Harvard; D.Sc. (hon.), U. Toledo, 1977; m. Florence Miller, Dec. 30, 1920; children—Carolyn M. Reese Clark, Allen M., Virginia F. Reese White. Draftsman Bldg. Dept., Gen. Electric Co., Pittsfield, Mass., 1907-14, designer, 1914-16, chief draftsman, 1916-20; pvt. practice indsl. engring., Pittsfield, Mass., 1920-22; chief engr. Bldg. Products Co., Toledo, 1922-64; pvt. practice cons. structural engr., Toledo, 1922—; partner, cons. Raymond C. Reese, Asso., Toledo, 1960-73; lectr. U. Toledo, 1924-52. Mem. editorial com. on codes for developing countries UNESCO, 1963-64; dir. Toledo Concrete Improvement Bd., 1965-66; v.p. Arthritis Found., 1971-75. Recipient 25 Year award ASTM, 1969; Founders award Toledo area Concrete Improvement Bd., 1969; Lindau award Am. Concrete Inst., 1957, Kennedy award, 1964, Henry C. Turner award, 1977, Arthur R. Moy award Mich. chpt., 1977; named Engrings. News Record Man of the Year, 1966; Engr. of the Year, Toledo Soc. Profl. Engrs., 1962. Fellow Am. Inst. Cons. Engrs.; mem. Mass. Inst. Tech. Alumni Assn., Am. Nat. Standards Inst., Concrete Reinforcing Steel Inst., ASTM, Cons. Engrs. Ohio, Comite Europeen du Beton, Internat. Soc. Bridge and Structural Engrs., Nat., Ohio, Toledo socs. profl. engrs., Réunion Internationale Des Laboratoires D'Essais et De Recherches Sur Les Materiaux et Les Constructions, Brit. Instn. Civil Engrs., Internat. Assn. Shell Structures, Prestressed Concrete Inst., Am. Soc. Engring. Edn., Nat. Bd. Accreditation in Concrete Constrn. (chmn. bd. 1973—), ASCE, Am. Concrete Inst. Rotarian. Club: Toledo. Author: Reinforced Concrete Design, 1943, CRSI Design Handbook, 1952, others. Contbr. articles to profl. jours. Address: 3821 Sulphur Spring Rd Toledo OH 43606

REESE, RICHARD SCOTT, pottery co. exec.; b. New Cumberland, W.Va., Mar. 2, 1933; s. Scott Charles and Gertrude Pearl (Starr) R.; student Wooster Coll., 1950-52; B.S., Ashland Coll., 1955; m. Carol Jane Garver, May 1, 1955; children—Steven Reese, Douglas, Christopher. With Scio Pottery Co. (Ohio), 1954—, v.p., chmn. bd., 1966—; pres. Scio Bank Co. 1965—. Chmn. Am. Dinnerware Emergency Com., Washington, 1970—. Bd. dirs. Twin City Hosp., 1964. Served with AUS, 1956-57. Recipient Citizens award City of Scio, 1970, Award letter Ohio Ho. of Reps., 1970. Mason. Patentee in field. Home: RD 1 Scio OH 43988 Office: Box 565 Scio OH 43988

REESE, THOMAS LELAND, steel co. exec.; b. Louisville, Feb. 3, 1936; s. Harry Leland and Rose Vivien (Peitzman) R.; B.S., Rose Hulman Inst. Tech., 1958; M.B.A., Ind. U., 1958-59; m. Sharon Krieger, Dec. 12, 1976; children—Susan, Richard, David, Jonathan. With Universal Tank & Iron Works, Inc., Indpls., 1960—, pres., chief exec. officer, 1975—; dir. Marsh Foods, Inc. Nat. alumni fund chmn., bd. mgrs. Rose Hulman Inst. Tech., 1970-71, Named Outstanding Young Man Am., 1968; recipient Distinguished Achievement award Rose Hulman Inst. Tech., 1975; registered profl. engr., Ind., Tex., Iowa, La. Mem. Young Pres.'s Orgn., ASCE, Steel Plate Fabricators Assn. (dir. 1973-76), Sigma Iota Epsilon. Club: N.E. Tennis, Woodstock Country. Home: 7474 Noel Rd Indianapolis IN 46278 Office: 11221 Rockville Rd Indianapolis IN 46231

REESE, WENDELL BLAINE, city ofcl.; b. Empire, Ohio, July 5, 1929; s. Harry Andrew and Dorothy Rebecca (Keenan) R.; grad. high sch.; m. Susan Jane Elliott, June 10, 1955; children—Byron Elliott, Wendell Andrew. With Ohio Edison Co., Toronto, 1947-69; owner Reese Trailer Sales, Empire, 1950-67, Reese Mobile Homes, Inc., Empire, 1967—; pres. Reese Devel., Inc., 1970—. Mem. Village Council Empire, 1959-61, mayor, 1961—; mem. Jefferson County Democratic Exec. Com., 1966-67. Served with AUS, 1951-53. Home and Office: PO Box 118 Empire OH 43926

REEVES, DUANE LEE, newspaper editor; b. Greenville, Ill., June 10, 1932; s. Leo Forrest and Viola Electa (McCullah) R.; student Greenville Coll., 1950-52; m. Marilyn Marie Zeller, July 17, 1955; children—Jane Ann, Richard Duane. Mem. staff Greenville Advocate, 1951—, a pub., 1964—, editor, 1966—; co-owner Greenville Lumber Co., 1976—. Mem. Bond County Community unit 2 Citizen Adv. Council. Served in USAF, 1952-56. Recipient Presdl. award Greenville Coll., 1976. Mem. Nat. Newspaper Assn., Ill. Press Assn., So. Ill. Editorial Assn. Baptist. Home: 12 Springhill St Greenville IL 62246 Office: 305 S 2d St Greenville IL 62246

REEVES, ELTON TRAVER, educator; b. Rigby, Idaho, Sept. 23, 1912; s. James Marshall and Bertha Beatrice (Traver) R.; B.S., U. Idaho, 1932; M.A., U. Wash., 1938; postgrad. La. State U., 1959-61; m. Elsie May Wolfinger, children—Delores Reeves Blackman, Rosemary Reeves Sonnikson. High sch. tchr. and prin., Idaho, 1936-45; rubber supr. U.S. Rubber Co., Detroit, 1945-48; med. rep. Lederle Labs., Spokane, 1948-54; with Kaiser Aluminum & Chem. Corp., 1954-63; indsl. relations Warwick Electronics, Inc., Niles, Ill., 1963-64; dir. tng. The Boeing Co., Seattle, 1964-69; prof. bus. and mgmt. U. Wis. Extension, Madison, 1969—; cons. Allen-Bradley, Sherwin-Williams, Hannah Mining, U.S. CSC, Cuna Sch., Harper Coll. Served with USNR, 1945. Mem. Am. Soc. Personnel Adminstrn., Internat. Platform Assn., Smithsonian Assos. Club: Internat. (Chgo.). Author: Management Development for the Line Manager, 1969; The Dynamics of Group Behavior, 1970; So You Want to Be A Supervisor, 1971; So You Want to Be a Manager, 1971; So You Want to Be an Executive, 1971; How to Get Along with Almost Everybody, 1973; Practicing Effective Management, 1975. Home: 4859 Sheboygan Ave Madison WI 53705 Office: 432 N Lake St Madison WI 53706

REEVES, WALTER HAROLD, psychologist; b. Chgo., May 18, 1931; s. Harold Elmer and Betty (Cihla) R.; B.A., Roosevelt U., 1953, M.A., 1960; M.Ed., Loyola U., Chgo., 1968; Ph.D. (Univ. fellow), Northwestern U., 1972; m. June Hubert, June 25, 1960; children—Pamela, Brenda. Intern, staff psychologist Ill. Dept. Mental Health, Kankakee State Hosp., 1957-60; staff psychologist Ill. Dept. Correction, St. Charles, 1960-62; staff psychologist Sch. Assn. for Spl. Edn., Naperville, Ill., 1962-63, chief psychologist, 1963—; pvt. practice psychology, 1973—; instr. Elgin (Ill.) Community Coll., 1961-63, Nat. Coll. Edn., 1967, Ill. Benedictine Coll., 1975. Served with AUS, 1953-55. Mem. Am., Midwestern, Ill. psychol. assns. Home: 4903 Valerie Dr Crystal Lake IL 60014 Office: 6S331 Cornwall Rd Naperville IL 60540

REGAGNON, PAUL, bioanalyst; b. Mexico, D.F., Mex., Nov. 5, 1916; s. Antoine and Ana M. (Rangel) R.; came to U.S., 1944, naturalized, 1945; B.B.Sc., Colegio Frances De La Salle, 1936; B.B.S.C., Universidad Nationale Mexico, 1936, 38-43; m. Opal Faye McHenry, July 28, 1949; children—Donnie May, Tom H., Peggy D., Paulette, Diana, Daniel P. With Sid Richardson Refining Co., 1948-49, Eddy Clinic, Hays, Kans., 1953-70; with Laughlin Hosp. & Clinic, Inc., Kirksville, Mo., 1970—, dir. of labs., 1953—. Chmn. blood com. Adair County chpt. ARC, 1970—. Served with U.S. Army, 1944-47, 49-53. Diplomate Am. Bd. Bioanalysis. Mem. AAAS, Am. Assn. Bioanalysts, Med. Electronics and Data Assn., Am. Chem. Soc., Heart of Am. Assn. of Blood Banks, Am. Legion. Mormon. Home: 406 E Jefferson St Kirksville MO 63501 Office: 711 W Jefferson St Kirksville MO 63501

REGGIO, VITO ANTHONY, mgmt. cons.; b. Rochester, N.Y., Dec. 17, 1929; s. Salvatore and Carrie Angelina (LoRe) R.; student Middlebury Coll. Grad. Sch. Modern Langs., 1948; B.S., Purdue U., 1952; postgrad. (Inter-Univ. Exchange fellow) grad. schs. Univs. Ala., Tenn., Ky., 1952-53; m. Mary Ann Dolores Pippie, Sept. 28, 1957; children—Salvatore, Angela. Position classifier Navy Dept. Office Indsl. Relations, Indpls., 1955-56; asso. prin. Bus. Research Corp., mgmt. cons., Chgo., 1956-60; dir. personnel mgmt. cons. services Ebasco Services, Inc., Chgo., 1960-77; pres. Reggio and Assos., Human Resources Consultants, Chgo., 1977—. Served with Adj. Gen. Corps, AUS, 1953-55. Mem. Am. Mgmt. Assn., Am. Compensation Assn., Am. Soc. Personnel Adminstrn., Indsl. Relations Assn. Chgo., Western Soc. Engrs. Home: 441 S 6th Ave La Grange IL 60525 Office: 125 S Wacker Dr Chicago IL 60606

REGULA, RALPH STRAUS, lawyer, congressman; b. Beach City, Ohio, Dec. 3, 1924; s. O.F. and Orpha (Walter) R.; B.A., Mt. Union Coll., 1948; LL.B., William McKinley Sch. Law, 1952; m. Mary Rogusky, Aug. 5, 1950; children—Martha, David, Richard. Sch. adminstr. Stark County Bd. Edn., 1948-55; admitted to Ohio bar, 1952; practiced law, Navarre; mem. Ohio Ho. of Reps., 1964-65, Ohio Senate, 1965-72; mem. 93d-95th congresses, 16th Dist. Ohio. Partner Regula Bros. Mem. Pres.'s Commn. on Financial Structures and Regulation, 1970-71; mem. Ohio Bd. Edn., 1960-65; mem. adv. bd. Walsh Coll., Canton, Ohio. Trustee Mt. Union Coll., Alliance, Ohio, Stark County Hist. Soc.; Stark County Wilderness Soc. Served with USNR, 1944-46. Recipient Community Service award Navarre Kiwanis Club, 1963; Meritorious Service in Conservation award Canton Audubon Soc., 1965; Ohio Conservation award Gov. James Rhodes, 1969; named Outstanding Young Man of Year, Canton Jr. C. of C., 1957. Legislative Conservationist of Year, Ohio League Sportsman, 1969. Mem. Am., Ohio, Stark County bar assns. Republican. Episcopalian. Home: 8787 Erie Ave SW Navarra OH 44662

REH, THOMAS EDWARD, physician; b. St. Louis, Sept. 12, 1943; s. Edward Paul and Ceil Anne (Golden) R.; B.A., St. Louis U., 1965, M.D., 1969; m. Benedette Texada Gieselman, June 22, 1968; children—Matthew J., Benedette T. Intern, St. John's Mercy Med. Center, St. Louis, 1969-70; resident in radiology St. Louis U., 1970-73; clin. fellow in vascular radiology Beth Israel Hosp., Harvard Med. Sch., Boston, 1973-74; radiologist St. Louis U. Hosp., St. Mary's Health Center, St. Louis, 1974—; clin. asst. prof. radiology St. Louis U. Med. Sch., 1975—. Mem. AMA, Mo. Med. Assn., St. Louis Med. Soc., Am. Coll. Radiology, Radiol. Soc. N.Am., Mo. Radiol. Soc., Alpha Omega Alpha. Roman Catholic. Home: 1425 Frontenay Ct St Louis MO 63122 Office: 6420 Clayton Rd St Louis MO 63122

REHAK, JAMES RICHARD, orthodontist; b. Chgo., Jan. 2, 1938; s. James Joseph and Lydia Ann (Thomas) R.; B.S., U. Ill., 1960, D.D.S. cum laude, 1962, M.S., 1967, certificate in orthodontics, 1965; m. Joann Marie Tabbert, Oct. 15, 1969; children—James Collins, Timothy Joseph, Laura Jean, Suzanne Therese. Practice dentistry, Chgo., 1962-63, practice orthodontics, Chgo. and Arlington Heights, Ill., 1965—; asst. prof. U. Ill. Coll. Dentistry, 1966-68. Kellogg Found. fellow, 1958. Fellow Royal Soc. Health; mem. ADA, Ill. Dental Assn., Chgo. Dental Soc., Am., Ill., Midwest socs. orthodontists, Internat. Platform Assn., Psi Omega, Omicron Kappa Upsilon. Home: 307 Ottawa Ln Oak Brook IL 60521 Office: 6441 S Pulaski Rd Chicago IL 60629

REHE, ROLF FRIEDRICH, typographer; b. Zwickau, Germany, May 28, 1935; s. Fritz and Melanie (Mueller) R.; came to U.S., 1960, naturalized, 1966; B.A., Ind. U., 1970, M.A., 1972. Apprentice, E. Schwendt, Schw. Hall (Germany), 1949-52, journeyman typesetter, 1952-60; dir. typographic design Roger Typesetting Co., Indpls., 1963-67; instr. Herron Sch. Art, Ind./Purdue U., Indpls., 1972-75, asst. prof., 1975-78, asso. prof., 1978—; dir. Design Research Internat., Carmel, Ind. Mem. pub. relations bd. Indpls. chpt. ARC, 1974—; adv. bd. Advt. Prodn. Art Inst., Ltd., St. Louis, 1976—. Recipient Best of Show award Ind. Art Dirs. Club Ann. Contest, 1974, Outstanding Vol. award Indpls. chpt. ARC, 1977. Mem. Assn. Typographique Internationale, Soc. for Typographic Arts, AAUP, Sigma Delta Chi. Roman Catholic. Clubs: Carmel Toastmasters (pres. 1976-77); Athenaeum Turners (Indpls.). Author: Typography: How to Make It Most Legible, 1972, rev. edit., 1976. Contbr. articles to trade publs. Home: 520 Lark Dr Carmel IN 46032 Office: 1701 N Pennsylvania St Indianapolis IN 46202

REHKOPF, CHARLES FREDERICK, ch. exec.; b. Topeka, Dec. 24, 1908; s. Frederick A. and Mary G. (Jennings) R.; B.S., Washburn Coll., 1932; certificate Episcopal Theol. Sch., 1935; m. Dorothy A. Getchell, July 30, 1936; children—Frederick, Jeanne, Susan. Civil engr. Kans. Engring. Co., Topeka, 1927-30; rector Trinity Episc. Ch., El Dorado, Kans., 1935-44, St. John's Eipsc. Ch., St. Louis, 1944-52; archdeacon and exec. sec. Diocese Mo., Protestant Episc. Ch., St. Louis, 1953-76; chmn. dept. research and planning Met. Ch. Fedn. Greater St. Louis, 1954-64; chmn. div. adminstrn. Mo. Council Chs., 1965-68, chmn. div. communications, 1970-72, chmn. div. Christian unity, 1972-73; registrar Diocese of Mo., 1949—; staff Episc. Ch., Webster Groves, Mo., 1976—. Trustee Episcopal Presbyn. Found. for Aging, Inc., mem. Religious Pub. Relations Council. Mem. Soc. Am. Archivists, Hist. Soc. Protestant Episc. Ch. (dir.). Editor The Historiographer's News Letter; author articles pub. profl. jours. Home: 642 Clark Ave Webster Groves MO 63119 Office: 1210 Locust St Saint Louis MO 63103

REHNER, HERBERT ADRIAN, writer, educator; b. Vincennes, Ind., Dec. 14, 1926; s. Herbert O. and Anna-Blanche (Chapman) R.; A.B., Ind. State U., M.A., 1948; LUD, Royal Acad. Dramatic Art, U. London, 1949, student Acad. Arts and Design in Mex., Litt.D., 1960; Litt.D., Brantridge Forest Sch., Eng., 1967. Tchr., Ind. State U., 1947-48; lectr. Royal Acad. Dramatic Art, 1949-50; head theatre dept. Wilson Br., Chgo. City Coll., 1950-68, head speech dept., 1959-68, chmn. and prof. speech and drama, 1968—; producer, dir. Shawnee Summer Theatre, Greene County, 1960; pres. Ind. Acad. Dramatic Art, 1953-56; producer, dir. profl. tour of You Can't Take It with You for Def. Dept., Europe, 1959; programs over radio sta. WBOW and WIHI, 1946-48; summer producer White Barn Profl. Theater, Terre Haute, Ind.; cultural rep. Internat. Theater Inst., Chgo., 1955; dir. All City Chicago Drama Festival, 1957; dir. Shakespeare on TV, 1961, 69; producer Guys and Dolls, Chgo., 1960, Westward the River hist. drama, 1967; mgr. theatre tour to S. Pacific, Dept. Def., 1971; dir. TV variety hour, Seoul, Korea, 1971; prod. Profl. Performing Equity Co., Drama Guild, Chgo., 1972-75; mng. producer Sta. WKKC, Chgo., 1978. Contracted to develop 5 curricula, also design performing arts center for new university, Iran, 1973. Fulbright grant to study in Eng. and Europe; James Yard award for human relation NCCJ, 1960; named Chgo. Tchr. of Year, 1965; recipient Kate Moremont travel grant, 1965. Mem. Speech Assn. Am., Sadlers Wells-Old Vic Assn., Soc. Midland Authors, ANTA (Chgo. bd. 1960-61), Theta Chi, Theta Alpha Phi (nat. v.p. 1968, 72-74, nat. pres. 1974-76, nat. council 1977—), Blue Key. Club: Players (N.Y.C., hon.). Author: Sons of the Prairie, 1950; Pastime of Eternity, 1948; The Dramatic use of Oral Interpretation and Choral Speaking, 1951; The Constant Heritage, 1952; Out of this Land, 1954; Practical Public Speaking, 1957; Communication Through Speaking, 1959, rev., 61, 62, 65, 68, 77, 78; Speaking in Public, 1961; Activities In Living and Speaking, 1965, rev., 1967, 73; nat. editor Cue mag., 1962-64. Home: Valhalla Star Route 1 Owensburg IN 47453 Office: 6904 S Harvard Ave Chicago IL 60621

REICH, DAVID LEE, librarian; b. Orlando, Fla., Nov. 25, 1930; s. P.F. and Opal Katherine (Wood) Reichelderfer (now Reich); Ph.B. magna cum laude, U. Detroit, 1961; A.M. in L.S. (Carnegie Library Sci. Endowment scholar), U. Mich., 1963; m. Kathleen Johanna Weichel, Aug. 2, 1954 (div. Sept. 1964); 1 son, Robert Weichel. Tchr. English, Jefferson Davis Jr. Sch., San Antonio, 1961-62; dir. engring. library Radiation Inc., Melbourne, Fla., 1963-64; asst. to dir. libraries Miami-Dade Jr. Coll., Miami, Fla., 1964-65; dir. learning resources Monroe County Community Coll., Monroe, Mich., 1965-68; dep. dir. Dallas Pub. Library, 1968-73; dep. chief librarian Chgo. Pub. Library, 1973-74, commr., 1975—; library cons. Macomb County Community Coll., Warren, Mich., 1967; mem. adv. council, dept. library sci. No. Ill. U.; chmn. adv. com. to library tech. asst. program El Centro Coll., Dallas, 1969-71. Mem. Inter-Task Working Group, Goals for Dallas, 1968-70; mem. Dallas Area Library Planning Council, Goals for Dallas, 1970-73; bd. dirs. Harris Sch., Chgo., 1975-76. Served as sgt. AUS, 1952-55. William B. Calkins Found. scholar, Orlando, 1963. Mem. Am. Assn. Community and Jr. Colls., ALA (council mem.-at-large 1968-72, 75—), South, S.W., Fla. (sec.-treas. coll and spl. libraries div. 1965), Ill. library assns., Assn. Coll. and Research Libraries, Alumni Assn. U. Mich. (pres. L.S. alumni 1973), German Club Chgo. (v.p. 1975—). Clubs: Execs., Caxton, Arts (Chgo.). Author: (with Jean Brooks) The Public Library in Non-Traditional Education, 1974; contbr. articles to library jours. Home: 2650 N Lakeview Ave Chicago IL 60614 Office: Chgo Pub Library 78 E Washington St Chicago IL 60602

REICHERT, NORMAN VERNON, transp. co. exec.; b. Berwyn, Ill., Apr. 17, 1921; s. John G. and Valeria (Hoffman) R.; B.S. in Bus. Adminstrn., Northwestern U., 1943; postgrad. Harvard U., 1943-44; m. Wilma Eleanor Catey, Feb. 5, 1944; children—Susan, Norman V. Accountant, Arthur Young & Co., Chgo., 1946-50; central fin. staff, controller styling div. Ford Motor Co., Dearborn, Mich., 1950-61; asst. treas. Philco Ford Corp., Phila., 1961-69; asst. treas. United Air Lines, Inc., 1969-72; v.p. finance, treas. Trailer Train Co., Chgo., 1972—, Am. Rail Box Car Co., Chgo., 1972—; dir. Hamburg Industries, Inc., Augusta, Ga., Calpro, Inc., Riverside, Calif. Served to lt. USNR, 1943-46. C.P.A., Ill. Mem. Am. Inst. C.P.A.'s, Fin. Execs. Inst., Beta Alpha Psi, Sigma Alpha Epsilon. Clubs: Union League, Knollwood, Execs. Home: 921 Grandview Ln Lake Forest IL 60045 Office: 300 S Wacker Dr Chicago IL 60606

REICHL, MARY THOMAS, sch. ofcl.; b. Wis., Nov. 29, 1928; d. George Joseph and Susan (Rauen) Reichl; B.A., Cardinal Stritch Coll., 1960; M.A., Marquette, U., 1965. Joined Sisters of Mary of Holy Cross, Roman Catholic Ch., 1946; tchr. Holy Cross High Sch., Merrill, Wis., 1955-65, counselor, dir. guidance, adminstrv. asst., 1965-72, provincial supr., 1972—. Mem. Lincoln County Mental Health Assn. (v.p. 1969-72), Am. Personnel and Guidance Assn., Wis. Hist. Soc., Der Deutsche Klub, Nat. Cath. Guidance Conf., Leadership Conf. Women Religious, Nat. Cath. Edn. Assn., Nat. Assn. Religious Women. Home and office: Holy Cross Convent Merrill WI 54452

REICHLIN, WILLIAM JOSEPH, mgmt. cons.; b. Hartford, Conn., Dec. 31, 1940; s. Meyer Aaron and Sophia Ann (Skuhul) R.; A.B., Mitchell Coll., 1961; B.B.A., U. Miami, Coral Gables, Fla., 1963, M.B.A., 1971, Ph.D., 1973; m. Joyce Lee Williams, Aug. 16, 1975; children—Amy Elizabeth, Michael Shane. Asso. prof. U. Miami, 1972; asso. firm Donahue, Groover & Assos., Coral Gables, 1972—; pres. Sterling Wood Assos. Ltd., St. Louis, 1975—. Served with USN, 1963-70. U. Miami dept. bus. decision scis. fellow, 1970-71. Mem. Am. Mgmt. Assn., Am. Mktg. Assn., Soc. Profl. Sales Personnel, Sigma Chi. Republican. Methodist. Clubs: Elks, Optimists. Office: 232 S Meramec Dr Clayton MO 63105

REICHNER, ROBERT JAMES, accounting co. exec.; b. Warren, Ohio, Nov. 21, 1944; s. Stephen and Lillian (Simon) R.; B.S., Duquesne U., 1966; M.B.A., Northwestern U., 1967; m. Lucille Patrick Hoyle, Jan. 20, 1973; children—Robert James II, Danielle Marie. Sr. accountant Arthur Andersen & Co., Chgo., 1967, 69-71; pres. Robert J. Reichner & Assos. Inc., Wilmette, Ill., 1971—; partner Reichner & Nykiel, Wilmette, 1974-75; lectr. in field; dir. House of Salads Inc. Founding com. Chgo. Community Ventures Inc., 1971—. Served with U.S. Army, 1967-69. Decorated Bronze Star. Home and office: 807 Chestnut St Wilmette IL 60091

REID, BILL, psychotherapist; b. Joplin, Mo., Mar. 8, 1936; s. James L. and Josephine (Kelley) R.; Ph.D., Brantridge Forest Sch., 1972; Litt.D. (hon.), U. Ryukyus, 1962; children—Cathy, James, Naida, Johanna, Jean. Pvt. practice psychotherapy, Louisville and Jeffersonville, Ind., 1974—; tchr. Spencerian Coll., Louisville, 1969-77; editor, pub. Internat. Violin and Guitar Makers Jour., 1967—; v.p. Spectro-Chem., Inc., 1970-77. Diplomate Am. Bd. Examiners Psychotherapy. Mem. Internat. Transactional Assn., Interam. Soc. Psychology, AAUP, Nat. Assn. Sch. Psychologists, Internat. Rorshach Soc., Data Processing Mgmt. Assn. Buddhist. Author: Just A Girl and A Night, 1969; Calling All Really Obscure Lovers, 1976; Do What Works, 1977. Originator Causative Agency method of psychotherapy. Home: 403 W Maple St Jeffersonville IN 47130 Office: 834 E Broadway Suite 218 Louisville KY 40204

REID, CLYDE MYER, microbiologist, educator; b. Birmingham, Ala., Jan. 15, 1930; s. Fred Reid and Alma Arlene Reid McDonald; B.A., Rust Coll., 1954; Med. Technologist, Homer G. Phillips Sch. Med. Tech., 1955; postgrad. St. Louis U., 1957-58, 66-68; m. Elsa Maxine Sydner, July 30, 1955; children—Sandra, Kim, Clyde, Jannette. Lab. supr. De Paul Hosp. Lab., St. Louis, 1955—; instr. microbiology St. Louis U. Sch. Medicine, 1958—; lab. dir., pres. Reid Lab. Inc., St. Louis, 1960—. Active Boy Scouts Am.; exec. bd. McKnight Sch. Parent Tchr. Orgn., 1972-73, treas., 1974-75. Served with AUS, 1950-52. Diplomate Am. Soc. Clin. Pathologists. Mem. Am. Soc. Microbiology, Am. Soc. Clin. Pathology Tech., Mo., Am., St. Louis socs. med. tech. Home: 847 Saxony Ct University City MO 63130 Office: 1402 S Grand St Saint Louis MO 63104

REID, DOUGLAS GORDON, counselor; b. Detroit, Nov. 3, 1936; s. John Arthur and Margaret Marie (Engwall) R.; B.S., Central Mich. U., 1958; M.Ed., U. Mich., 1962. Tchr., L'Anse Creuse Pub. Schs., Mt. Clemens, Mich., 1958-63; counselor Lakeview Pub. Schs., St. Clair Shores, Mich., 1963—, guidance chmn., 1966—. Bd. dirs. Macomb County Youthscope, 1971-74; mem. Mich. Task Force for Entry Level Counselor Competencies, 1972; active ch. bds. Presbyn. Ch. Served in U.S. Army, 1959. Certified sch. counselor, Mich. Mem. NEA, Mich. Edn. Assn., Mich. Guidance Dirs. Assn. (dir. 1972—, v.p. 1976, pres. 1977), MaComb County Personnel and Guidance Assn. (past v.p., past sec.-treas.), Am. Coll. Testing Secondary Sch. Council, Mich. Assn. Counselor Edn. and Supervision (dir. 1975—, program chmn. 1977). Home: 20851 Maple St Saint Clair Shores MI 48081 Office: 21100 Eleven Mile Rd Saint Clair Shores MI 48081

REID, ELLIS EDMUND, lawyer; b. Chgo., May 19, 1934; s. Ellis Edmund and Carrie B. (Graham) R.; B.A. in Polit. Sci., U. Ill., 1956; J.D., U. Chgo., 1959; m. Barbara A. Kline, May 25, 1957; children—Ellis Edmund, David E. Admitted to Ill. bar, 1959; with firm McCoy, Ming & Black, Chgo., and predecessor, 1959—, partner, 1964—; dir. Highland Community Bank; cons. legal services program Office Econ. Opportunity; real estate broker; spl. asst. states atty. Cook County (Ill.), 1970-73; hearing examiner Fair Employment Practices Commn., 1968-76; exec. dir. Cook County Bar Found. Vice pres. Chatham Avalon Park Community Council, 1963-65, 67, Better Boys Found. Served to capt. AUS, 1957. Mem. Nat., Ill., Chgo., Cook County (pres.) bar assns., Bar Assn. 7th Fed. Circuit, Am. Arbitration Assn. (nat. panel), Kappa Alpha Psi, Phi Delta Phi. Home: 505 N Lake Shore Dr Chicago IL 60611 Office: 39 S LaSalle St Chicago IL 60613

REID, JAMES CALVIN, physician; b. Urbana, Ill., May 29, 1937; s. George Calvin and Gertrude Louise (Ross) R.; student Blackburn Coll., 1956-57; B.S., U. Ill., 1960, M.D., 1963; m. Doris Jean Rosentreter, Sept. 16, 1961; children—Julia Ann, Joan Marie, Laura Jane, Monica Suzanne, Christine Lucille. Intern, Decatur-Macon County Hosp., Decatur, Ill., 1963-64; practice medicine specializing in family practice, Greenfield, Ill., 1964—; mem. staffs Boyd Meml. Hosp., Carrollton, Ill., Passavant Meml. Area Hosp., Jacksonville, Ill. Diplomate Nat. Bd. Med. Examiners, Am. Bd. Family Practice. Mem. AMA, Am. Acad. Family Practice, Ill. (del. state conv. 1969-76), Greene County (pres. 1968-69, sec., treas. 1969—) med. socs. Roman Catholic. Home: Rural Route 1 Greenfield IL 62044 Office: 712 S College St Greenfield IL 62044

REID, ROBERT ALTON, environ. engr.; b. Hampton, Va., Sept. 26, 1940; Asso. Applied Sci. with honors, Old Dominion Tech. Inst., 1962; B.S. in Mech. Engring., N.C. State U., 1967; M.S., U. Minn., 1971. Spl. problems engr. Newport News Shipbldg. and Dry Dock Co.

(Va.), 1962-67; life support engr. Northrop Corp. /NASA LangleyResearch Center, Hampton, Va., 1967-68; sr. environ. engr.U. Minn. Dept. Physical Plant, Mpls., 1971-76, principal plan.engr., 1976—; participant numerous coms., task forces on environ. protection, 1971—. NASA traineeship environ. health U. Minn., 1969; water quality research traineeship Dept. Interior U. Minn., 1970, 71; USPHS grantee environ. health, hosp. engring., 1970; named Ecologist of the Week Metro Clean Air Com., 1971; certified Bd. Safety Profls. Home: 821 Weeks Ave SE Minneapolis MN 55414 Office: 319 15th Ave SE Minneapolis MN 55455

REID, WILLIAM TURNBULL, JR., utility co. exec.; b. Chgo., Oct. 5, 1922; s. William Turnbull and Dorothy Lucille (Mook) R.; B.S. in Engring., Bradley U., 1944; student U. Ill., 1943, U.S. Naval Acad., 1944; m. Jane Miles Meldrum, July 8, 1947; children—William Turnbull, Margaret Lucille. Instr. mech. engring. Bradley U., Peoria, Ill., 1946-49; engring. and operation positions Central Ill. Light Co., Peoria, 1949—, mgr. power supply, 1968-70, v.p. ops., 1970—; mem. U. Ill. Alumni Com. for Power Industry, 1969—. Mem. grade sch. and high sch. bds., Peoria, 1965-68; swimming ofcl. Ill. High Sch. Assn., 1965—; mem. curriculum adv. bd. Ill. Central Coll., 1968—; active Am. Field Service; bd. dirs. Central Ill. sect. ARC, chmn. water safety com. Served with USNR, World War II, Korea; comdr. Res., ret. Mem. NAM (environ. policy com.), ASME (utility ops. com. power div.), ASTM (co. rep.), U.S. Power Squadron (safety officer Ill. Valley sect.), Peoria Assn. Commerce (water resources com.), Tau Sigma, Theta Alpha Phi. Club: Ill. Valley Yacht (chmn. aquatic and water safety coms.). Home: 4533 Bournedale St Peoria IL 61614 Office: Central Illinois Light Co 300 Liberty St Peoria IL 61602

REIDDA, PHIL, psychologist; b. Hackensack, N.J.; s. Benedict and Vera (Sandino) R.; B.A., U. Hartford, 1961; M.S., Coll. City N.Y., 1963; Ph.D., Ill. Inst. Tech., 1971; m. Ellen Kapsis, Dec. 27, 1958; children—Barry, Sloane. Psychometrist, N.Y. U. Testing Center, N.Y.C., 1963; psychology intern Chgo. State Hosp., 1963-64, psychologist, 1964-65; psychologist Lakeview-Uptown Community Mental Health Center, Chgo., 1966-67, Harbor Light Out-Patient Clinic, 1965-66; dir. Garfield Park Community Mental Health Center, Chgo., 1966-70; coordinator of research and evaluation Chgo. Bd. Health, 1970-71; clin. cons. psychologist Affiliated Psychologists, Ltd., Elk Grove Village, Ill., 1971—; instr. psychology Elmhurst (Ill.) Coll., 1967. Served with USNR, 1948-50. Mem. Am., Ill. (standards and tng. com. 19—) psychol. assns., Ill. Group Psychotherapy Soc. Contbr. articles to profl. jours. Office: 500 E Higgins Rd Elk Grove Village IL 60007

REIDENBERG, LOUIS MORTON, lawyer; b. Phila., Dec. 1, 1939; s. Bernard M. and Beatrice (Rauer) R.; B.B.A., U. Miami, Coral Gables, Fla., 1961; J.D., U. Minn., 1965; children—Daniel Jay, Jeffrey Brian. Admitted to Minn. bar, 1965; pvt. practice law, Mpls., 1966—; Law clk. Minn. Supreme Court, 1965-66; lectr. continuing legal edn., 1971—. Sec., Hennepin County Family Law Com., 1972-73. Mem. Minn., Hennepin County bar assns., Minn. Bar Assn. Family Law Com., Am. Trial Lawyers Assn., Am. Acad. Matrimonial Lawyers. Contbr. articles to profl. publs. Home: 9605 Cimarron Trail Minnetonka MN 55343 Office: 2112 IDS Center 80 S 8th St Minneapolis MN 55402

REIDER, JAMES EUGENE, internat. trade mgmt. co. exec.; b. Marion, Ohio, Jan. 18, 1928; s. Robert J. and Mary Belle (Willey) R.; B.S., Ohio State U., 1951, M.S., 1951; m. Jeannie Johnson, July 5, 1952; children—Brent Carleton, Carson Robert. Applications engr. Indsl. Nucleonics Corp., Columbus, Ohio, 1953-54, sales engr., 1954-55, metals industry mgr., 1955-59, sales mgr. Columbus area, 1959-61, sales ops. mgr., 1961-62, mktg. and product mgr., 1962-64, mgr. adminstrn., 1964-66, mgr. mktg., 1966-67, gen. mgr. market devel. group, 1967-68, gen mgr., 1968-69, v.p., gen. mgr., 1969-72, group v.p., 1972-74; pres. Internat. Trade Group Ohio, Inc., Columbus, 1975—. Pres., Upper Arlington Civic Assn., 1973; bd. dirs. Silver Bay Assn., Glens Falls, N.Y. Served with USNR, 1945-46, USMCR, 1951-53. Recipient Distinguished Alumnus award Coll. Engring., Ohio State U., 1972. Club: Rotary. Patentee in field. Home: 2920 North Star Rd Columbus OH 43221 Office: 100 E Broad St Columbus OH 43215

REIFF, GUY GENE, educator; b. Los Angeles, May 8, 1926; s. Emil and Marcelle (Erhart) R.; B.S., U. So. Calif., 1952; M.A., Colo. State Coll., 1955; Ph.D., U. Mich., 1964; m. Geraldine Bruce, June 12, 1955; children—Sheri, Teri, Craig. Athletic coach Calif. Mil. Acad., Los Angeles, 1948-50, St. John's Acad., Los Angeles, 1950-52; grad. fellow recreation Colo. State Coll., Greeley, 1952-53; athletic coach, dir. phys. edn. program Coll. High Sch., Greeley, 1953-55; asst. prof. phys. edn. Colo. State Coll., Greeley, 1955-60; instr. phys. edn. U. Mich., Ann Arbor, 1960-64, asst. prof., 1964-67, asso. prof., 1967-71, prof. phys. edn., 1971—; cons. HEW, Ednl. Testing Service, U.S. Golf Found., Pres.'s Council on Phys. Fitness and Sports. Served with USN, 1943-46. Fellow AAHPER, Am. Coll. Sports Medicine; mem. AAUP. Contbr. articles to profl. jours.; asso. editor Research Quarterly, 1970—. Home: 1906 Crestland Dr Ann Arbor MI 48104

REIGEL, DON, corp. exec.; b. Deer River, Minn., Sept. 4, 1914; s. Jake and Marion (Shabel) R.; B.A., cum laude, Carleton Coll., 1936; postgrad. Minn. Sch. Bus., 1942; grad. Command and General Staff Coll., Fort Leavenworth, Kans., 1963; postgrad. in polit. sci. Mankato (Minn.) State Coll.; m. Mary Jane Scott, Oct. 24, 1942; children—Marc, Kent. Auditor, Stearns Lumber Co., Hutchinson, Minn., 1936-42; advt. mgr. U.S. Check Book Co., Omaha, 1946-50, Journ.-Chronicle Co., Owatonna, Minn., 1950-56; pub., owner Photo News, Owatonna, 1956-73; pres. Reigel Corp., 1973—; info. officer Minn. Vocat. Rehab., 1974—. Tchr. U. Omaha and Van Sant Sch. of Bus., Omaha, 1946-50, Mankato State Coll., 1972-73. Pres. Owatonna Community Chest, 1954; dist. chmn. Wasioja dist. Boy Scouts of Am., 1955-56. Mem. Minn. Ho. of Reps. from Steele County, 1968-70. Bd. dirs. Paul Watkins Home, Winona, 1966-72. Served to capt. AUS, 1942-46; to lt. col. Res. Mem. Minn. Newspaper Assn. (chmn. advt. com. 1962-63), Nat. Editorial Assn. Methodist. Mason. Clubs: Rotary (sec. 1955—), Minneapolis Athletic, Elks. Home: 558 E South St Owatonna MN 55060 Office: PO Box 292 Owatonna MN 55060

REILLY, FRANK KELLY, educator; b. Chgo., Dec. 30, 1935; s. Clarence Raymond and Mary Josephine (Ruckrigel) R.; B.B.A., U. Notre Dame, 1957; M.B.A., Northwestern U., 1961, U. Chgo., 1964; Ph.D., U. Chgo., 1968; m. Therese Adele Bourke, Aug. 2, 1958; children—Frank Kelly, Clarence Raymond, Therese B., Edgar B. Trader, Goldman Sachs & Co. stocks, Chgo., 1958-59; security analyst Technology Fund, Chgo., 1959-62; asst. prof. U. Kans., Lawrence, 1965-68, asso. prof., 1968-72; prof. bus., asso. dir. div. bus. and econ. research U. Wyo., Laramie, 1972-75; prof. fin. U. Ill., Urbana, 1975—. Bd. dirs. Heart of Am. Growth Fund, Kansas City, Mo., 1971—. Arthur J. Schmidt Found. fellow, 1962-65; U. Chgo. fellow, 1963-65; chartered fin. analyst. Mem. Midwest Bus. Adminstrn. Assn. (pres. 1974-75), Southwestern, Western (exec. com. 1973-75), Am. fin. assns., Fin. Analysts Fedn., Fin. Mgmt. Assn. (v.p. 1977-78), Nat. Bur. Econ. Research, Beta Gamma Sigma. Roman Catholic. Editor: Readings and Issues in Investments, 1975. Asso. editor Fin. Mgmt., 1977—. Home: 54 Chestnut Ct Champaign IL 61820 Office: Coll Commerce U Ill Urbana IL 61801

REIMER, DONALD ROSS, physician; b. Colorado Springs, Colo., July 12, 1934; s. Chester John and Hazel Mildred (Stuart) R.; B.A., U. Colo., 1958, M.D., 1962; m. Darlene Carole Erickson, June 25, 1955 (dec. May 1965); children—Suzanne Jeanne, Robert Ross; m. Jeaniece D. Fiedler, Apr. 1, 1972. Commd. ensign U.S. Navy, 1961, advanced through ranks to lt. comdr. 1967, resigned, 1969; intern U.S. Naval Hosp., Jacksonville, Fla., 1962-63; resident anesthesiology U.S. Naval Hosp., Chelsea, Mass., 1963-65, Boston Children's Hosp. Med. Center, 1964, Boston Lying-In Hosp., 1965; instr. anesthesiology Boston U. Sch. Medicine, 1966-67; chief anesthesiologist U.S. Naval Hosp., Key West, Fla., 1968-69; fellow psychiatry Menninger Found., Topeka, Kans., 1971-74; practice medicine, specializing in anesthesiology, Cape Girardeau, Mo., 1969-71, anesthesiology and psychiatry, Topeka, 1971—; active staff St. Francis Hosp., Topeka. Diplomate Am. Bd. Anesthesiology. Fellow Am. Coll. Anesthesiologists, Am. Acad. Psychosomatic Medicine; mem. A.M.A., Internat. Anesthesia Research Soc., Am., Mo., Kans. socs. anesthesiologists, Am. Psychiat. Assn. Home: 234 Greenwood Ave Topeka KS 66606 Office: St Francis Hosp Topeka KS 66606

REIMER, ROBERT CHARLES, lawyer; b. Schleswig, Iowa, May 28, 1927; s. William Christian and Emma Marie (Hansen) R.; B.A. with highest distinction, U. Iowa, 1948, J.D. with highest distinction, 1950; m. Mary Ann Gray, Nov. 23, 1955; children—Amy Jo, Robert Hugh. Admitted to Iowa bar, 1950, Neb. bar, 1951; practiced in Denison, 1954—; mem. firms L.W. Powers, 1954, Powers & Reimer, 1955-66; sr. partner Reimer, Boddicker & Vipond, 1967, Reimer & Vipond, 1968-72, Reimer, Vipond & Nixt, 1973-74, Reimer & Vipond, 1975—; dir. Farmers' State Bank, Schleswig, Feeders Supply Service Inc., Schleswig. Co-chmn. Iowa Joint Editorial Bd. for Uniform Probate Code, 1973—; lectr. on probate and tax law Ia. Bar Assn., 1964, 67-71, 74. Trustee Crawford County (Iowa) Meml. Hosp., Denison, 1960-72. Served to 1st lt. AUS, 1950-53. Decorated Bronze Star. Fellow Am. Coll. Probate Counsel (Iowa chmn. 1966-73, 75-77); mem. Am., Iowa (chmn. spl. com. probate property and trust law 1973-75), 3d Jud. Dist. (bd. govs. 1975-77), Nebr. (v.p. 1977-78), Crawford County (pres. 1968-69) bar assns., Order of Coif, Phi Beta Kappa, Eta Sigma Phi, Gamma Eta Gamma. Democrat. Methodist. Co-author: Iowa Estates-Taxation and Administration, 1975. Home: Plum Thicket Rural Route 1 Denison IA 51442 Office: Box 25 S Main St Denison IA 51442

REIMERS, RICHARD H., ins. co. exec.; b. Des Moines, Nov. 20, 1937; s. Wilfred A. and Signa P. (Hendersen) R.; student Iowa State U., 1956-57; B.B.A., U. S.D., 1960; m. Jeanne R. Iverson, Dec. 21, 1958; children—Cheri, Laura, Mark, John. Sales surp. The Travelers Ins. Co., San Francisco, 1962-65; pres. Peters & Reimers Insurors, Inc., Spencer, Iowa, 1965—. Served to lt. U.S. Army, 1960-62. Mem. Nat. Assn. Ind. Agts. Clubs: Spencer Golf and Country, Embassy (Des Moines). Home: Rural Route Box 5374 Spirit Lake IA 51360 Office: 800 Grand Ave Spencer IA 51301

REIMNITZ, RAYMOND FREDERICK, financial exec.; b. Mt. Vernon, S.D., May 21, 1931; s. William F. and Amelia (Meoge) R.; student Dakota Wesleyan U., 1948-49; B.S., Drake U., 1959; M.B.A., U. Chgo., 1969; m. Bessie M. Batalis, Oct. 25, 1964; children—George, William. Auditor, Bendix Corp., South Bend, Ind., 1959-65; mem. controller's staff Whirlpool Corp., Benton Harbor, Mich., 1965-66; plant controller Colt Industries, Moline, Ill., 1966-67; treas., Jarke Corp., Niles, Ill., 1967-71; controller, Wen Products, Chgo., 1971—. Served with USAF, 1951-55. Mem. Niles C. of C. (dir. 1970-71). Club: Executive Program (Chgo.). Home: 657 S Mallard St Palatine IL 60067 Office: 5810 NW Hwy Chicago IL 60631

REINBOLD, JAMES WILLIAM, elec. co. exec.; b. Brownstown, Ind., May 27, 1932; s. Thomas Lorin and Ruth Jane (Spurgeon) R.; student Rose Poly. Inst., 1950-52; B.S., U. Louisville, 1956; m. Mary-jo Ann Warren, June 10, 1956; children—Jodi Lynne, Jon William, James Warren. Mgr. product safety design Gen. Electric Co., Louisville, 1956-57, evaluation engr., 1957-60, evaluation supr., 1961-62, prodn. engr., 1962-69. mgr. prodn. engring., 1969-70, program group leader, 1970-71, sr. project engr., 1971-75, mgr. safety engring., 1972—. Served with AUS, 1957. Registered profl. engr., Ky. Mem. ASME, Appliance Engrs. Soc., Lambda Chi Alpha. Democrat. Methodist (chmn. adminstrv. bd. 1969-77). Home: 825 Beechwood Dr Sellersburg IN 47172 Office: Appliance Park Louisville KY 40225

REINERTSON, JAMES WAYNE, pediatrician; b. Des Moines, Jan. 25, 1927; s. Adolph Jennings and Bonnie Viola (Wald) R.; B.A., Luther Coll., 1948; M.S.P.H., U. N.C., 1949; postgrad. Wayne U., 1952-54; M.D., U. Ia., 1959; m. Beverly Elaine Sampson, June 6, 1948; children—Mark Wayne, Marilee. Asso. research parasitologist Parke, Davis & Co., 1949-54; intern Mercy Hosp., Cedar Rapids, Iowa, 1959-60; resident in pediatrics, Wyeth pediatric fellow Blank Meml. Hosp., Des Moines, 1960-62; practice medicine specializing in pediatrics, Cedar Rapids, Iowa, 1962—; mem. staff St. Lukes Meth. Hosp., 1962—, v.p. elect, 1978—; staff Mercy Hosp.; instr. Cedar Rapids Med. Edn. Program. Mem. ch. council First Lutheran Ch., 1965-71; bd. dirs. Linn County Assn. Retarded Citizens, 1972—. Diplomate Am. Bd. Pediatrics. Fellow Am. Acad. Pediatrics; mem. AMA, Iowa, Linn County med. assns., Am. Acad. Pediatrics. Lutheran. Developer exptl. drug amebiasis. Home: 1130 27th St Cedar Rapids IA 52402 Office: 1300 2d Ave Cedar Rapids IA 52403

REINHART, MELVIN JOSEPH, psychiatrist; b. Detroit, Dec. 2, 1929; s. William Aron and Augusta (Shapiro) R.; A.B., U. Mich., 1951, M.D., 1955; m. Malverne Gleiber, Aug. 12, 1954; children—Janet Lee, Robert David. Intern, U. Mich. Med. Center, Ann Arbor, 1955-56, resident, 1956-58, 60-61, now staff; practice medicine specializing in psychiatry, Ann Arbor, 1962—; staff St. Joseph Mercy Hosp., Ann Arbor, 1975—; instr. U. Mich. Med. Sch., Ann Arbor, 1961-65, asst. prof., 1965-69, asso. prof. psychiatry, 1969—; cons. Battle Creek (Mich.) Child Guidance Clinic, 1961-65, Washington County Commn. on Alcoholism, 1962-65. Served as lt., USNR, 1958-60. Diplomate Am. Bd. Psychiatry and Neurology. Fellow Am. Psychiat. Assn.; mem. AMA, N.Y. Acad. Scis., AAAS, Mich. Assn. of the Professions, Mich., Washtenaw County med. socs., Mich. Psychiat. Soc., Common Cause. Jewish (v.p. 1966-69). Contbr. articles to profl. jours. Home: 1921 Hampton Ct Ann Arbor MI 48103 Office: U Mich Med Center Ann Arbor MI 48104 also 517 1st Nat Bldg Ann Arbor MI 48108

REINIS, STANISLAV, educator; b. Nitra, Czechoslovakia, Dec. 22, 1931; s. Stanislav and Jaroslava (Vojtova) R.; M.D., Charles U., Prague, Czechoslovakia, 1957; Ph.D., 1962; m. Milada Chytrova, Apr. 25, 1966; children—Renata, Stanislav, Teresa. Scientist, Charles U., Prague, 1961-66; sr. lectr., asso. prof., head dept. Ghana Med. Sch., Accra, 1966-70; postdoctoral fellow, asso. prof. York U., Toronto, 1970-73; prof. psychology U. Waterloo (Ont. Can.), 1973—; research asso. Hosp. for Sick Children, Toronto, 1973-76, U. Toronto Inst. Aerospace Studies, 1973—. Mem. Can. Physiol. Soc., Soc. Neurosci., Am. Soc. Neurochemistry. Author: The Chemistry of The Brain, 1978. Contbr. articles to profl. jours. Home: 348 Ascot Pl Waterloo ON N2J 3V8 Canada Office: Dept Psychology U Waterloo Waterloo ON N2L 3G1 Canada

REINKE, JOHN HENRY, priest, univ. chancellor; b. Covington, Ky., Sept. 14, 1915; B.A. in Greek, Loyola U., Chgo., 1937, M.A., 1942, postgrad., 1947-54; resident intern clin. psychology Patton (Calif.) State Hosp., 1951-52. Ordained priest Roman Cath. Ch., 1945; instr. Loyola Acad., Chgo., 1939-42, dir. guidance, 1959-60, headmaster, 1960-65, rector Jesuit community 1965-70; pres. Loyola Acad., Wilmette, Ill., 1965-75; teaching fellow gen. and clin. psychology Loyola U., Chgo., 1947-54, trustee, 1973-75, vice chancellor, 1975-76, chancellor, 1976—; asst. prof. psychology Xavier U., Cin., 1954-59; instr. psychology and music therapy Ind. U., summers 1958-60. Appeared with Loyola Community Theater Forum, 1952-54; producer weekly TV variety and discussion show Xavier Presents, WCPO-TV, Cin., 1954-59; piano soloist Cin. Symphony Orch., 1956, 57, 60; trustee Xavier U., Regis Coll., Denver, Hadly Sch. for Blind, Winnekta. Office: Lewis Towers 820 N Michigan Ave Chicago IL 60611

REINSDORF, JERRY MICHAEL, bus. exec., lawyer; b. Bklyn., Feb. 25, 1936; s. Max and Marion (Smith) R.; B.A., The George Washington U., 1957; J.D., Northwestern U., 1960; m. Martyl F. Rifkin, Dec. 29, 1956; children—David Jason, Susan Janeen, Michael Andrew, Jonathon Milton. Admitted to D.C., Ill. bars, 1960; atty. staff regional counsel IRS, Chgo., 1960-64; asso. law firm Chapman & Cutler, 1964-68; partner law firm Altman, Kurlander & Weiss, 1968-73; of counsel firm Katten, Muchin, Gitles, Zavis, Pearl & Galler, 1973—; gen. partner Carlyle Real Estate Ltd. Partnerships, 1971-72; former pres. The Balcor Co., Skokie, Ill., chmn. bd., 1974—; mng. partner TBC Films, 1975—; lectr. John Marshall Law Sch., 1966-68; dir. Real Estate Securities and Syndication Inst. Co-chmn., Ill. Profls. for Sen. Ralph Smith, 1972-76. C.P.A., Ill. Mem. Am., Ill., Chgo., Fed. bar assns., Order of Coif, Omega Tau Rho. Author: (with L. Herbert Schneider) Uses of Life Insurance in Qualified Employee Benefit Plans, 1970. Office: 4711 Golf Rd Skokie IL 60076

REISCHAUER, ROBERT EUGENE, mktg. exec.; b. St. Louis, Jan. 22, 1931; s. Robert Eric and Dora Mae (Sauerbrunn) R.; B.S., Ill. Inst. Tech., 1952; postgrad. U. So. Calif., 1964; m. Audrey Helen Ruess, June 9, 1951; children—Robert Steven, Cynthia Jane, Kenneth John. Commd. ensign, U.S. Navy, 1952, advanced through grades to lt. comdr., 1962, ret., 1963; applications analysis Sperry Univac, San Diego, 1963, supervising system design engr., 1965, supervising engr., St. Paul, 1969-70, prin. system design engr., 1970-71, tech. staff, 1971-73, prin. advance system engr. Navy/Marine Corps Advanced Systems, 1973, prin. system engr. for preparation Iranian DD993 Combat System, 1974, mgr. program devel., naval applications, 1974-76, mgr. navy mktg., combat systems and new bus. devel., 1976—. Active PTA, San Diego and Minnetonka, Minn., 1963-75; chmn. cub scout pack Boy Scouts Am., San Diego, 1962. Recipient Tiger awards (2) Sperry Univac, 1976. Mem. Am. Def. Preparedness Assn., Nat. Security Indsl. Assn., Am. Soc. Naval Engrs., V.F.W., Sigma Phi Epsilon. Republican. Lutheran. Club: Masons. Home: 3000 Keating Ct Burnsville MN 55337 Office: MS U2L14 PO Box 3525 Saint Paul MN 55156

REISMAN, ARNOLD, educator; b. Lodz, Poland, Aug. 2, 1934; s. Isadore and Rose (Joskowitz) R.; came to U.S., 1946, naturalized, 1955; B.S., U. Calif. at Los Angeles, 1955, M.S., 1957, Ph.D., 1963; m. Judith Ann Gelernter, Mar. 12, 1955; children—Miriam Jennie, Ada Jo, Deborah Fawn, Nina Michelle. Design engr. Los Angeles Dept. Water and Power, 1955-57; asso. prof. Calif. State U., Los Angeles, 1957-66; prof. U. Wis., Milw., 1966-68; prof. ops. research Case Western Res. U., Cleve., 1968—; vis. prof. Hebrew U., Jerusalem, 1975, Japan-Am. Inst. Mgmt. Sci., Honolulu, 1975, Bus. Econ. and Quantitative Methods, U. Hawaii, Honolulu, 1971; asso. research engr. Western Mgmt. Sci. Inst., U. Calif. at Los Angeles, 1964-65; coordinator programs between Inst. Mgmt. Scis. and AAAS, 1971—; examiner North Central Assn. Colls., Univs. and Secondary Schs., 1971; v.p. Univ. Assos., Inc., Cleve., 1968—; expert witness Solicitor Gen., Dept. Labor, 1969-70, U.S. Equal Opportunities Commn., 1976-77; cons. to asst. sec. HEW, 1971-72, Office Program Planning and Evaluation, U.S. Office Edn., 1972-73; cons. in gen. field systems analysis numerous corps. and instns. U.S. del. to Internat. Fedn. Ops. Research Socs., Conv., Dublin, Ireland, 1972. Review bd. mem. Lake Erie Regional Transp. Authority, 1974-75; mem. del. assembly Jewish Community Fedn. Cleve., 1974—; mem. Shaker Heights (Ohio) Citizens adv. com., 1972—. Trustee Hillel Found. Named Cleve. Engr. of the Year, 1973. Registered profl. engr., Calif., Wis., Ohio. NSF fellow, 1963. Fellow AAAS (council); mem. Ops. Research Soc. Am., Inst. Mgmt. Scis., ASME, Am. Soc. Engring. Edn., AAUP, Am. Inst. Indsl. Engrs., N.Y. Acad. Sci., Phi Delta Kappa, Sigma Xi. Contbr. numerous articles to profl. jours. Author: Managerial and Engring. Economics, 1971; Systems Approach and The City, 1972; Industrial Inventory Control, 1972; Health Care Delivery Planning, 1973, others. Series editor: Operations Management. Asso. editor: Socio Economic Planning Sciences. Home: 18428 Parkland Dr Shaker Heights OH 44122 Office: Case Western Reserve U Dept Operations Research Sears Bldg Cleveland OH 44106

REISMAN, BETTY LOU, coll. adminstr.; b. Youngstown, Ohio, Nov. 9, 1941; d. Bernard and Florence Esther (Liebermann) Reisman; B.A., Case Western Res. U., 1963; M.A., Kent State U., 1965, Ph.D., 1977. Asst. dean students State U. Coll. at Buffalo, 1965-68; asst. dean student affairs Clarion (Pa.) State Coll., 1968-69; asst. dir. housing, adj. instr. sch. psychology and counseling State U. N.Y. Coll. at Oswego, 1969-75; organizational Specialist Kent State U., 1976-77, mem. grad. faculty, 1977—; counselor U. Md., Balt. County, 1977—; adviser Hillel Group, 1973. Mem. Am. Coll. Personnel Assn., Am. Coll. and U. Housing Officers, Nat. Assn. Women Deans, Adminstrs. and Counselors (exec. bd. 1977-78), N.Y. Assn. Women Deans, Adminstrs. and Counselors (mem. adv. bd. 1973-75), Sigma Psi. Author monographs; contbr. articles to profl. jours. Home: 3475 5th Ave Youngstown OH 44505

REISS, JEROME LEE, real estate broker; b. Detroit, Apr. 23, 1928; s. Joseph A. and Rita V. (Levinson) R.; B.S., U. Mich., 1950; m. Lillian J. Rome, Nov. 25, 1954; children—Robin Lynn, Wendy Ann. Vice-pres. leasing Byron W. Trerice Co., Detroit, 1959-67; sec.-treas. Burland, Reiss, Murphy & Mosher Inc., Southfield, Mich., 1967—. Pres. Detroit Bd. Realtors, 1974. Served with AUS, 1950-52. Mem. Realtors Nat. Mktg. Inst. (council), Met. Detroit C. of C., Mich. Assn. Realtors (dir. 1972—), Sale Mktg. Execs. Detroit (dir. 1970—), Nat. Assn. Realtors. Office: Burland Reiss Murphy & Mosher Inc Suite 815 17117 W Nine Mile Rd Southfield MI 48075

REISTER, RAYMOND ALEX, lawyer; b. Sioux City, Iowa, Dec. 22, 1929; s. Harold William and Anna (Eberhardt) R.; A.B., Harvard, 1952, LL.B., 1955; m. Ruth Elizabeth Alkema, Oct. 7, 1967. Admitted to N.Y. bar, 1956, Minn. bar, 1960; asso. firm Paul, Weiss, Rifkind, Wharton & Garrison, N.Y.C., 1955-56; asso. firm Dorsey, Windhorst, Hannaford, Whitney & Halladay, Mpls., 1959-63, partner, 1964—; instr. law U. Minn. Extension Div., 1964-66. Served to 1st lt. AUS, 1956-59. Mem. Am. Coll. Probate Counsel, Am., Minn., Hennepin County bar assns. Clubs: Minneapolis, Harvard of Minn. (pres. 1969-70). Editor (with Larry W. Johnson) Minnesota Probate Administration, 1968. Home: 93 Groveland Terr Minneapolis MN 55403 Office: 2300 1st Nat Bank Bldg Minneapolis MN 55402

REISTROFFER, DIANNE, educator; b. Davenport, Iowa, Oct. 20, 1949; d. Eugene Francis and Geraldine Claire (Leach) Reistroffer; B.A. summa cum laude, History and Theology, Coll. of St. Teresa, 1972; M.A. in History, Villanova U., 1975; postgrad. U. Minn., 1975-77. Instr. in religion Winona (Minn.) Cotter High Sch., 1972-73, girls intramural basketball coach, 1972-73; teaching asst. dept. history Villanova (Pa.) U., 1973-75; teaching asst. dept. history U. Minn., Mpls., 1975; researcher and legis. aide Minn. Ho. of Reps., 1975-77; instr. religion Austin Pacelli High Sch., Austin, Minn., 1977—, newspaper moderator, 1977—, girls basketball coach, 1977—. Mem. Am. Hist. Assn., Am. Acad. of Polit. and Social Scis., Minn. Hist. Soc., Met. Museum of Art Assn., Villanova U. Alumni Assn., Coll. of St. Teresa Alumnae Assn. Democrat. Roman Catholic. Club: Villanova Varsity. Home: 507B NW 6th Ave Austin MN 55912 Office: 311 NW 4th St Austin MN 55912

REJAI, MOSTAFA, educator; b. Tehran, Iran, Mar. 11, 1931; s. Taghi and Forough (Lashgari) R.; came to U.S., 1954; A.A., Pasadena City Coll., 1957; B.A., Calif. State U. at Los Angeles, 1959, M.S., 1961; Ph.D., U. Calif. at Los Angeles, 1964. Asst. prof. polit. sci. Miami U., Oxford, Ohio, 1964-67, asso. prof., 1967-70, prof., 1970—; vis. prof. Western Coll., Oxford, 1971, 72; vis. scholar Center for Internat. Affairs, Harvard, 1972, Hoover Instn., Stanford, 1973, Inst. Internat. Studies, Iran, 1974-75. Adminstrv. and research asst. to mgr. City of Temple, Calif., 1959-61. Summer research fellow Miami U., 1967, 70, 76. Recipient Outstanding Teaching award Miami U., 1970. Mem. Am. Polit. Sci. Assn., Conf. for Study of Polit. Thought, Internat. Studies Assn., Pi Sigma Alpha, Pi Gamma Mu. Author: The Strategy of Political Revolution, 1973; Ideologies and Modern Politics, 1971, 2d edit., 1975; Decline of Ideology, 1971; Mao Tse-Tung on Revolution and War, 1969, 2d edit., 1970; Democracy: The Contemporary Theories, 1967; The Comparative Study of Revolutionary Strategy, 1977; Leaders of Revolution, 1978. Asso. editor Jour. Polit. and Mil. Sociology. Contbr. articles to profl. jours. Home: 208 Oakhill Dr Oxford OH 45056 Office: Dept Polit Sci Miami U Oxford OH 45056

RELFORD, REGINA FRANCES, rehab. counselor; b. St. Louis, Mar. 16, 1952; d. Arthur D. and Clote V. Relford; B.S. in Adminstrn. of Justice, So. Ill. U., Carbondale, 1973; M.Ed., Loyola U., Chgo., 1977. Intern, St. Clair County (Ill.) Criminal Justice System, 1973; rehab. counselor Ill. Div. Vocat. Rehab., Chgo., 1974—, mem. dir.'s counselors' adv. com., 1975—. Mem. Nat. Rehab. Assn., Am. Personnel and Guidance Assn. Roman Catholic. Home: PO Box 3531 Merchandise Mart Bldg Chicago IL 60654 Office: 1020 160 N LaSalle St Chicago IL 60601

RELIC, MILAN RAYMOND, photography co. exec.; b. Cleve., Mar. 8, 1922; s. John and Mary (Boich) R.; certificate bus. adminstrn., Fenn Coll., 1948; m. Helen Irene Ponikvar, Sept. 20, 1947. Partner, Euclid Studio, Cleve., 1950-54; pres. Euclid Studio, Inc., Cleve., 1954—, Edcom Prodns., Inc.; Cleve., 1973—; v.p. Tungsten Corp., Cleve., 1964—; mgmt. dir. Tungsten Music Pub. Co., Cleve., 1971—. Vice pres., trustee, dir. State Troopers of Ohio, 1970-75. Served with AUS, 1942-46. Decorated Purple Heart. Mem. Soc. No. Ohio Profl. Photographers (pres. 1960-61), VFW (comdr. 1947), Assn. Indsl. Advertisers. Home: 273 E 280th St Euclid OH 44132 Office: 26991 Tungsten Rd Cleveland OH 44132

REMBUSCH, JOSEPH JOHN, coll. adminstr.; b. Joliet, Ill., June 29, 1939; s. Joseph Earl and Agnes Cecilia (Heinen) R.; diploma Joliet Jr. Coll., 1959; B.S., U. Ill., 1962; postgrad. No. Ill. U., 1961-62, 63-72; M.A.T., Rockford Coll., 1970; Ph.D., Western Colo. U., 1977. Psychologist intern Ill. Div. Criminologist, Ill. State Prison, Joliet, 1962; instr. sci. Crete (Ill.) Monee High Sch., 1963-64; clin. counselor Ill. Tng. Sch. for Boys, St. Charles, 1964-65; dir. guidance Hiawatha unit Sch. Dist. 426, Kirkland, Ill., 1966-69; registrar Kishwaukee Community Coll., Malta, Ill., 1969—, also prof. social scis. Evening Sch., 1969—. Pvt. practice as psychologist, DeKalb, 1971—; psychol. cons. Ill. Div. Vocat. Rehab., DeKalb, 1971—. Pres., Hiawatha unit Sch. Dist. PTA, 1968-69; mem. guidance dept. adv. bd. DeKalb Sr. High Sch., 1974—. Mem. Ill. Acad. Criminology, No. Ill. U. Assn. Guidance Personnel (life), U. Ill. Alumni Assn. (life), Delta Upsilon, Phi Delta Kappa. Republican. Roman Catholic. Home: 104 Laurel Ln DeKalb IL 60115 Office: Kishwaukee Coll Malta IL 60150

REMER, RICHARD CHARLES, banker; b. Des Moines, July 6, 1944; s. Vernon Ralph and Jane Viola (Bush) R.; B.A. in Econs., U. Iowa, 1966, M.A., 1970; m. Deanne Marie Anderson, Oct. 23, 1973; 1 son, Michael Edward. With N.W. Brenton Nat. Bank, Des Moines, 1970—, v.p., mgr. Johnston office, 1975—. Mem. Johnston Bd. Adjustment, 1977—, sec., 1977-78. Served with U.S. Army, 1967-69. Mem. Am. Bankers Assn., Am. Inst. Banking. Republican. Congregationalist. Clubs: Johnston Lions, N.W. Des Moines Optimist. Home: 5204 N W 64th Pl Des Moines IA 50323 Office: 5965 Merle Hay Rd Des Moines IA 50323

REMINGER, RICHARD THOMAS, lawyer; b. Cleve., Apr. 3, 1931; s. Edwin Carl and Theresa Henrietta (Bookmyer) R.; A.B., Case-Western Res. U., 1953; J.D., Cleve.-Marshall Law Sch., 1957; m. Billie Carmen Greer, June 26, 1954; children—Susan Greer, Patricia Allison, Richard Thomas. Admitted to Ohio bar, 1957, U.S. Supreme Ct. bar, 1961; personnel and safety dir. Moton Express, Inc., Cleve., 1954-58; mng. partner firm Reminger & Reminger Co., Cleve., 1958—; lectr. transp. law Fenn Coll., 1960-62, bus. law Case-Western Res. U., 1962-64. Mem. joint com. Cleve. Acad. Medicine and Greater Cleve. Bar Assn. Trustee Cleve. Zool. Soc., Huron Road Hosp., Cleve. Served with AC, USNR, 1950-58. Mem. Fedn. Ins. Counsel, Trial Attys. Am. (mem. sect. litigation, also ins., compensation and negligence), Fed., Am. (com. on law and medicine, profl. responsibility com. 1977—), Internat., Ohio, Cleve. (med. legal com. 1977—, profl. liability com. 1977—), bar assns., Motor Carrier Lawyers Assn., Cleve. Def. Attys. Assn., Am. Soc. Hosp. Attys., Ohio Def. Assn., Am. Judicature Soc., Def. Research Inst. (law inst. com. 1977—), Maritime Law Assn. U.S. Clubs: Mayfield Country (dir. 1977—), Cleveland Playhouse, Hermit (pres. 1973-75) (Cleveland); Lost Tree (Fla.). Home: 32450 Meadowlark Way Pepper Pike OH 44124 Office: Leader Bldg Cleveland OH 44114

REMPERT, LAWRENCE ARNOLD, engr.; b. Oak Park, Ill., Oct. 14, 1942; s. Arnold William and Eleanor Emma (Melchin) R.; B.S. in E.E., Purdue U., 1964, M.S. in E.E., 1966; m. Susan Hopkins Wrenn, June 24, 1967; children—Laura Louise, Carl Halder. Mem. tech. staff RCA Labs., Princeton, N.J., 1966-70; tech. advisor to patent dept. RCA Corporate staff, Princeton, 1970-72; sr. project engr. Esterline Angus Instrument Co., Indpls., 1972-77, chief digital engr., 1977—. Recipient outstanding achievement award RCA Labs., 1969. Mem. Instrument Soc. Am., Tau Beta Pi, Eta Kappa Nu. Episcopalian. Club: Danville (Ind.) Optimist. Patentee in field. Home: 540 N Washington St Danville IN 46122 Office: 1200 Main St Speedway IN 46224

RENCH, RICHARD EUGENE, real estate broker; b. Findlay, Ohio, May 3, 1941; s. Harold E. and Geraldine (Dysinger) R.; student Ohio State U., 1959-60, Ohio State Hwy. Patrol Acad., 1963, Ohio Sch. Real Estate, 1971; m. Cheryl Rose Tom, Sept. 5, 1964; children—Thomas E., Steven R. Salesman West Bend Co., Findlay, 1960-62; patrolman Ohio State Hwy. Patrol, Van Wert, 1962-68; pres. Rench Diversified Builders, Norwalk, O., 1968—; v.p. Airwalk Inc., Norwalk, 1972—; broker, pres. Rench Diversified Real Estate Co., Norwalk, 1971—. Dep. Erie County (O.) Sheriff's Dept., 1968-76; Erie County appraiser, VA, 1973—; pres. Multi-Media of Norwalk, 1974; cubmaster Boy Scouts Am., Norwalk, 1976—; pres. Huron County (Ohio) Airport Authority, 1974-75; finance dir. Huron County Rep. Party, 1974—. Mem. Erie County Bd. Realtors, Milan Jaycees (Outstanding Young Man 1974), Nat. Rifle Assn., Ohio Gun Collectors Assn., Norwalk C. of C., Nat. Muzzle-loading Rifle Assn. Methodist (dir. ch. 1973-74). Club: Kiwanis. Home: 5 Milan Manor Dr Milan OH 44846 Office: Suite 201 Citizens Nat Bank Norwalk OH 44857

RENCHER, MARK JULIUS, machining co. exec.; b. Huntington, N.Y., Apr. 19, 1947; s. Julius Kilian and Wanda Anne (Kurpita) R.; B.Mech. Engring., U. Detroit, 1969, M.Engring. in Mfg., 1977; M.A., Ball State U., 1974; m. Charlene Starman, May 20, 1972. Jr. engr. LTV Aerospace Corp., Warren, Mich., 1966-68; asso. engr. Burroughs Corp., Plymouth, Mich., 1973-76; tech. asst. to pres. Cleary Devel. Inc., Madison Heights, Mich., 1976—. Served with USAF, 1969-73; mem. Ohio Air NG. Certified mfg. technologist. Mem. ASME, Soc. Die Casting Engrs., Soc. Mfg. Engrs., Mfg. Engring. Inst. U. Detroit, Soc. Plastic Engrs., Am. Powdered Metallurgy Inst. Roman Catholic. Home: 2147 Park Place Walled Lake MI 48088 Office: 32033 Edward St Madison Heights MI 48071

RENDLEMAN, GEORGE FRANKLIN, JR., physician; b. St. Louis, Aug. 31, 1929; s. George Franklin and Lorraine (Meyer) R.; B.S., Northwestern U., 1951; M.D., U. Mo., 1958; postgrad. St. Louis U., 1952-54; m. Nancy Lou Smith, Aug. 2, 1963; children—George Franklin III, Carl Christian. Intern, resident St. Louis City Hosp., Ohio State U. Group, 1958-63; practice medicine specializing in surgery, St. Louis, 1963—; mem. staff Deaconess, Mo. Bapt., St. Anthony's, Incarnate Word, Lutheran hosps. Diplomate Am. Bd. Surgery. Fellow A.C.S.; mem. AMA, Mo. State, St. Louis med. assns., Sigma Nu, Phi Beta Pi. Presbyterian. Mason (32 deg., Shriner). Home: 2 Vista Brook Ln St Louis MO 63124 Office: 812 Olive St St Louis MO 63101

RENDON, LEANDRO, chem. co. exec.; b. Port Lavaca, Tex., July 27, 1918; s. Alfredo and Fannie (Mena) R.; student St. Edward's U., 1936-39; A.B., U. Tex., 1941; M.S., St. Louis U., 1949; m. Margaret Mary Martin, Sept. 4, 1948; 1 son, Martin Stephen. Instr. chemistry and microbiology Coll. Mortuary Sci., St. Louis, 1949-50; asst. dir. chem. research The Champion Co., Springfield, Ohio, 1950-51, dir. chem. research, 1951-54, asst. dir. service and research, 1954-58, dir. service and research, 1958-72, dir. research and ednl. programs, 1972—. Bd. dirs. Parish News Assos., Springfield, 1965—, pres., 1973—. Served with USAAF, 1942-46. Decorated Air Force Commendation Medal. Mem. AAAS, Am. Chem. Soc., Am. Leather Chem. Assn., Am. Pub. Health Assn., N.Y. Acad. Scis., Ohio Acad. Scis., Res. Officers Assn., Springfield Sci. Seminar Program (chmn. 1959-60). K.C. (4 deg.). Contbg. editor: Ency. Indsl. Chem. Analysis, 1971. Patentee in field. Home: 100 N Broadmoor Blvd Springfield OH 45504 Office: 400 Harrison St Springfield OH 45501

RENEKER, BETTY CONGDON (MRS. ROBERT W. RENEKER), civic worker; b. Coffeyville, Kans., Feb. 2, 1913; d. Carl Otto and Eva (Budge) Congdon; student Purdue U., 1930-33; m. Robert W. Reneker, Mar. 2, 1935; children—William Carl, David Lee. State pres. Congl. Christian Womens Fellowship, 1956-59, nat. pres., 1959-62; pres. womens bd., mem. nat. coms. Boy Scouts Am., Chgo., 1966-68; pres. womens bd. Ridge Service Guild, 1967-69; pres. Fortnightly Club, Chgo., 1973-75; chmn. John Crerar Library Assos., 1969-77; acting pres. Chgo. Theol. Sem., summer, 1971. Chmn. bd. dirs. Chgo. Theol. Sem.; bd. dirs., mem. exec. com., Adler Planetarium; bd. dirs. Ill. Children Home and Aid Soc., John Crerar Library; women's bd. Chgo. Heart Assn., U. Chgo.; mem. exec. com. Chgo. area council Boy Scouts Am. Mem. Heart Assn. Mem. United Ch. of Christ. Home: 1300 Lake Shore Dr Chicago IL 60610

RENEKER, ROBERT W(ILLIAM), bus. exec.; b. Chgo., Aug. 4, 1912; s. William Turner and Mary Ethel (Gilmour) R.; Ph.B., U. Chgo., 1933; spl. course Harvard U., 1954; m. Eva Elizabeth Congdon, Mar. 2, 1935; children—William Carl, David Lee. With purchasing dept. Swift & Co., Chgo., 1934-44, asst. office of v.p. charge purchasing, 1944-46, tech. product sales, 1946-50, asst. in office of pres., 1950-55, v.p., 1955-64, pres., 1964—, chief exec. officer, 1967—, also dir.; chmn., chief exec. officer Esmark, Inc., 1973—; dir. Continental Bank, Jewel Co., Trans Union Co., U.S. Gypsum, Gen. Dynamics Co., Chgo. Community Trust. Vice pres. Chgo. Community Fund. Mem. nat. exec. bd. Boy Scouts Am.; bd. dirs. Mus. Sci. and Industry; chmn. bd. trustees U. Chgo.; trustee Nat. Merit Scholarship Found. Clubs: Mid-Am., Economic, Chgo., Comml., Chgo. Sunday Evening (trustee). Home: 1300 Lake Shore Dr Chicago IL 60610 Office: 55 E Monroe St Chicago IL 60603

RENFREW, JAMES, lawyer; b. Detroit, Aug. 16, 1924; s. Samuel Murray and Elizabeth (Maxwell) R.; student U. Idaho, 1945-46; B.A. with distinction, Wayne State U., 1948, J.D., 1950, postgrad., 1948; postgrad. Harvard U., 1949; m. Alicia Gonzalez, June 23, 1962. Admitted to Mich. bar, 1953; legal adviser research and devel. Detroit Arsenal, Center Line, Mich., 1951-54; practiced in Detroit, 1954-56, Royal Oak, Mich., 1956—; mem. firms Renfrew, Moir & Burgett, 1956—; instr. adult edn. program U. Mich. Referee Mich. Civil Rights Commn., 1970-72. Judge, City of Huntington Woods, Mich., 1957-61; spl. asst. atty. gen., 1963. Bd. dirs., pres. Oakland County Legal Aid Soc. Served with USNR, 1943-46. Mem. Selden Soc., Am. Soc. Legal History, Am. Judicature Soc., Am., Oakland, South Oakland County bar assns., State Bar Mich. (commr.), Oakland County Judicial Assn. (pres. 1959-61), Mich., Oakland County, Sublette County, Wyo. hist. socs., Delta Theta Phi. Author: Rationale and Method for Circuit Court Supervision of Justice Courts, 1960; Dan Judd's Way West - Its Why and How, 1967; Clio in the Service of Advocacy, 1970. Home: 3050 Stanton Rd Lake Orion MI 48035 Office: 714 W Eleven Mile Rd Royal Oak MI 48067

RENICH, PAUL WILLIAM, educator; b. LaJunta, Colo., May 5, 1919; s. Edward Alexander and Anna (Andres) R.; A.B., Bethel Coll., Newton, Kans., 1942; M.A., U. Kans., 1944, PH.D. (Cady fellow from 1947-48), 1949; m. Roberta Merle Enns, May 15, 1943; children—Rebecca (Mrs. T.J. Lynch), Stephen, Thomas. Prof. chemistry Kans. Wesleyan U., Salina, 1948-74, dean univ., 1951-69, pres., 1969-73; instr. life sci. Haskell Indian Jr. Coll., 1974—. Pres. Saline County Mental Health Assn., 1953-54; sec. Community Welfare Council, 1952-53, v.p., 1956-57; chmn. Salina County Ednl. Survey Com., 1958-59; asso. N. Central Assn., 1959-60, cons., 1960—, commr., 1967-71; chmn. Salina Urban Renewal Agy., 1965-69; del. World Meth. Conf., Denver, 1971; vice chmn. program council Kans. West Conf., United Meth. Ch., 1968-72, del. Gen. Conf., 1972; bd. dirs. Kans. Found. for Pvt. Colls., 1971-73. Served from ensign to lt. (j.g.), USNR, 1944-46. Ford Found Faculty fellow Mass. Inst. Tech., 1954-55; recipient Distinguished Service award Kans. Wesleyan U., 1958. Mem. AAAS, Am. Chem. Soc., Sigma Xi, Phi Lambda Upsilon, Alpha Chi Sigma. Methodist. Mem. study tour Egypt, 1964. Home: 2133 Carolina St Lawrence KS 66044 Office: Haskell Indian Jr Coll Lawrence KS 66044

RENICK, MURRAY CHESTER, JR., pet food mfg. exec.; b. Rolla, Mo., Nov. 28, 1941; s. Murray C. and Virginia L. (Blue) R.; student Westminster Coll., 1960-62; grad. Draughon Bus. Sch., 1964; m. Ruth Ann Ashmore, Aug. 25, 1961; children—Angela Lea, Murray Chester III. Realtor, Ashmore-Renick Properties Co., Carl Junction, Mo., 1963-67; v.p. Bow Wow Pet Foods, Rolla, 1967—, gen. mgr., 1969—. Chmn. Rolla Personnel Bd., 1975-77; mem. Rolla Police Merit Bd., 1972-74; bd. dirs. Rolla Skillsbuilder Sch., 1972-74, Rolla Big Bros. and Big Sisters, 1977—. Mem. Am. Feed Mfrs., U.S., Rolla Area chambers commerce, Rolla Jaycees (pres. 1966). Episcopalian. Home: 18 Country Club Terr Rolla MO 65401 Office: PO Box 938 Rolla MO 65401

RENISON, HERBERT JOHN, educator; b. Quilmes, Argentina, Apr. 7, 1915; s. Sidney and Inez Maria (Clark) R.; student Trinity Coll. Music London extension at Buenos Aires, 1934; student Jorge de Lalewicz, 1935-46; grad. Conservatorio Nacional Buenos Aires, 1937; m. Paula Gerard, Aug. 28, 1965. Came to U.S., 1946, naturalized, 1956. Pvt. tchr. piano, 1935—; tchr. St. George's Coll., Quilmes, 1938-46; tchr. Sherwood Music Sch., Chgo., 1946—; piano recitals, Argentina, Uruguay, U.S.; soloist with Peoria Symphony, 1960; contest dir. Chgo. Tribune, 1965. Bd. dirs. Sherwood Music Sch., 1970—. Mem. Nat. Music Tchrs. Assn., Soc. Am. Musicians (pres. 1970-72). Club: Cliff Dwellers. Home: 2043 N Mohawk St Chicago IL 60614 Office: 1014 S Michigan St Chicago IL 60605

RENO, OTTIE WAYNE, judge; b. Pike County, Ohio, Apr. 7, 1929; s. Eli Enos and Arbannah Belle (Jones) R.; Asso. in Bus. Adminstrn., Franklin U., 1949; LL.B., Franklin Law Sch., 1953; J.D., Capital U., 1966; grad. Coll. Juvenile Justice, U. Nev., 1973; m. Janet Gay McCann, May 22, 1947; children—Ottie Wayne II, Jennifer Lynn, Lorna Victoria. Admitted to Ohio bar, 1953; practiced in Pike County; recorder Pike County, 1957-73; common pleas judge Probate and Juvenile divs. Pike County, 1973—. Mem. adv. bd. Ohio Youth Services, 1972-74. Mem. Democratic Central Com. Camp Creek precinct, 1956-72; sec. Pike County Central Com., 1960-70; chmn. Pike County Democratic Exec. Com., 1971-72; del. Dem. Nat. Conv., 1972; mem. Ohio Dem. Central Com., 1969-70; Dem. candidate 6th Ohio dist. U.S. Ho. of Reps., 1966; pres. Scioto Valley Local Sch. Dist., 1962-66. Recipient Distinguished Service award Ohio Youth Commn., 1974; 13 times Ala. horseshoes pitching champion; mem. internat. sports exchange, U.S. and Republic South Africa, 1972. Mem. Ohio, Pike County (pres. 1964) bar assns., Nat. Council Juvenile Ct. Judges, Am. Legion. Mem. Ch. of Christ. Author: Story of Horseshoes, 1963; Pitching Championship Horseshoes, 1971, 2d rev. edit., 1975. Home: RD 5 Box 305 Lucasville OH 45648 Office: Common Pleas Ct Waverly OH 45690

RENSEL, LLOYD ALOYSIUS, univ. adminstr; b. Cleve., May 26, 1921; s. Lloyd R. and Florence Marie (Mahoney) R.; A.B. in Psychology, U. Dayton, 1943; m. Bette J. Hempelman, Aug. 23, 1943; 1 son, John Edward. Employee counselor White Motor Co., Cleve., 1945—46; dir. testing services, coordinator student employment U. Dayton (Ohio), 1946—; cons. McGraw-Hill Calif. Test Bur., 1970—76. Chmn. St. Brendan Fund Raising Program 1961—64. Served with U.S. Army, 1942—45. Recipient Chpt. award Montgomery County Univ. Dayton Alumni Assn., 1953; Parish, 1965; Sponsor's award U. Dayton Arena, 1967; certificate of appreciation U. Dayton, 1971. Mem. Nat. Vocat. Guidance Assn., Am., Ohio, Miami Valley personnel and guidance assns., Nat. Catholic Counselors Assn., Nat. Travel Club, Optimist Club, U. Dayton Alumni Assn., Univ. Colleagues Assn., K.C. Democrat. Roman Catholic. Home: 5177 Scarsdale Dr Dayton OH 45440 Office: Univ Dayton Dayton OH 45469

RENSNER, DELMAR A., dentist; b. Chgo., Sept. 2, 1923; s. Adolph Gustav and Amalia (Dams) R.; student Lake Forest Coll., 1941-43, Tex. A. and M., 1944; B.S., U. Ill., 1945, D.D.S., 1947; m. Billie Kathleen Crumm, May 10, 1947; children—Gary, Warren, Michael, Donald. Pvt. practice dentistry, Chgo., 1947-51, Wichita (Kans.) Clinic, 1953—, head dept., 1956—; mem. staff St. Francis Hosp., Wesley Med. Center, St. Joseph Hosp.; adj. asso. prof. dental hygiene Wichita State U., 1966—; guest lectr. Kans. Med. Sch. at Wichita State U., also adviser Dental Assts. Sch.-Coll. Health Related Professions. Instrumental in creating Wichita Dental Hygiene Sch., 1966. Served with AUS, 1943-45, to capt. USAF, 1951-53. Mem. Am., Kan. dental assns., Wichita (pres. 1964-65), Sunflower (pres. 1972—), Chgo. dental socs., Acad. Childrens Dentistry, Wichita C. of C., Delta Sigma Delta. Clubs: Knife and Fork; Crestview Country, Masons, Shriners, Kiwanis (pres. 1974). Home: 1902 N Charlotte St Wichita KS 67208 Office: 3244 E Douglas St Wichita KS 67208

RENTSCHLER, WILLIAM HENRY, bus. cons.; b. Hamilton, Ohio, May 11, 1925; s. Peter Earl and Barbara (Schlosser) R.; grad. Berkshire Sch., Sheffield, Mass.; A.B., Princeton, 1949; m. Sylvia Gale Angevin, Dec. 20, 1948; children—Sarah Yorke, Peter Ferris, Mary Angevin, Phoebe Mason; m. 2d, Martha Snowdon, Jan. 21, 1967; 1 dau., Hope Snowdon. Reporter, Cin. Times-Star, 1946; successively reporter, exec. trainee, asst. to exec. editor Mpls. Star & Tribune, 1949-53; mgr. pub. relations The Northern Trust Co., Chgo., 1953, mgr. pub. relations and advt., 1953-54, 2d v.p., 1954-56; pres. Martha Washington Kitchens, Inc., 1957-68, Stevens Candy Kitchens, Inc., 1957-66; investor closely-held cos., 1970-73; bus. cons., ins. counselor, 1973—; dir. Mopeds Midwest USA, Inc., 1977—. Spl. adviser Pres.'s Nat. Program for Vol. Action, 1969; bd. dirs. Better Boys Found. Republican candidate U.S. Senate, 1960, 70. chmn. Ill. Citizens for Nixon, 1968; pres. Young Reps. Ill., 1957-59; exec. com. 1963-69. United Rep. Fund Ill.; former trustee Rockford Coll., Goodwill Industries. Recipient 1st ann. Buddy Hackett award for service to young men, 1968. Clubs: Onwentsia (Lake Forest, Ill.); Executives, Economic, Tavern (Chgo.). Home: 361 Cherokee Rd Lake Forest IL 60045

REPP, DUANE LESLIE, engine and generator distbn. exec.; b. South Bend, Ind., Apr. 26, 1931; s. Earl C. and Marie A. (Zepka) R.; B.S. in Mech. Engring., Purdue U., 1953; m. Shirline L. Bierbaum, Apr. 14, 1956; children—Duane M., Mark A., Thomas S. Sales engr. Cummins Engine Co., Columbus, Ind., 1953, 55-57, indsl. sales supr., 1957-58, regional rep., Chgo., 1958-60, regional mgr., N.Y.C., 1960-62, constrn. and indsl. div. mgr., 1962-66, div. mgr., 1966-70, gen. mgr. N.Am. sales and service, Columbus, 1970-72, chmn. indsl. distbr. council, 1978—, pres. Cummins Wis., Inc., Milw., 1972—; pres. DMT Corp., Milw., 1973—. Chmn., Met. Hwy Users Comf., Milw., 1973—; trustee Univ. Lake Sch., Hartland, Wis., 1975—; chmn. fund dr. St. Clare Ch., North Lake, Wis., 1975-76. Served with USAF, 1953-55. Mem. U.S., Milw. chambers commerce, Wis. Mfrs. Assn., Milw. World Trade Assn., Wis. Motor Carriers, Wis. Equipment Distbrs., Am. Automobile Assn. (dir. Wis. div. 1976—), Hwy. Users Fedn. (dir. 1977—). Republican. Roman Catholic. Clubs: Kiwanis, Athletic (Milw.); Chenequa Country. Office: 1921 S 108th St Milwaukee WI 53227

REPUCCI, LAWRENCE CARL, mgmt. cons.; b. Mansfield, Mass., May 23, 1927; s. Victor Umberto and Josephine (DePrizio) R.; A.B., King's Coll., 1950; M.S. (scholar; fellow), Coll. William and Mary, 1954; Ph.D. (fellow), Wayne State U., 1962; m. Rosalie Mae Johnson, June 10, 1954; children—John, Thomas, Shirine, Richard, William,

Christina, Mark. Instr. U. Detroit, 1955-57, Wayne State U., 1958-59; research dir. psychology Wayne County Gen. Hosp., 1958-59; asst. staff psychologist Dow Chem. Co., Midland, Mich., 1959-65; mgmt. cons., Midland, 1965—. Editor, publisher Creativity Rev., 1965—. Dir. Smith Korona, 1974. Instr. Central Mich. U., part time 1962-65. Pres., Young Republicans, Midland, 1964. Bd. dirs. Saginaw Guidance Clinic, 1960-61, Big Sisters, Midland, 1961-63. Mem. Am., Midwestern, Mich. psychol. assns., AAAS, Sigma Xi, Psi Chi. Contbr. profl. jours. Home: 1115 E Park Dr Midland MI 48640

RESER, BILLY JOE, banker; b. Galena, Mo., Mar. 7, 1933; s. Lloyd William and Audie Lela (Smith) R.; Asso. Sci., Mo. So. Coll., 1953; diploma banking U. Wis.-Madison, 1976; m. Catherine R. Jones, Apr. 9, 1955; 1 son, Ronald William. Br. mgr. Beneficial Fin. Co., Joplin, Mo., 1957-58, Springfield, Mo., 1958-68; v.p. 1st. City Bank, Springfield, 1968-71; v.p. mktg. Merc. Bank, Springfield, 1971-76; v.p. mktg. and personnel Empire Bank, Springfield, 1976—; dir. Ind. Mut. Ins. Co., St. Louis. Adv. bd. St. John's Hosp.; v.p. Springfield Greene County United Way, 1976—, Springfield Area Council Chs., 1976—. Mem. Springfield C. of C., Mo. Bankers Assn. (dir. 1975—). Methodist. Club: Masons (Shriner). Home: 3144 E Wayland Dr Springfield MO 65804 Office: 1800 S Glenstone St Springfield MO 65804

RESLER, PAUL EDWARD, optometrist; b. Pittsburg, Kans., Aug. 21, 1922; s. L.M. and Margaret (Kelly) R.; A.B., Kans. U., 1948; B.S., Ill. Coll. Optometry, 1952, O.D., 1953; m. Marion M. Twardokus, Oct. 8, 1953; children—John L., Tammy J. Pvt. practice optometry, Kans., 1953-58; mem. edn. dept. Plastic Contact Lens Co., Chgo., 1959-60; dir. St. Louis Wesley-Jessen, 1960-64, regional mgr. Midwest, St. Louis, 1965-67; pvt. practice, Florissant, Mo., 1967—, Chesterfield, Mo., 1975—; pres. Resler Optometry Inc., 1974—; co chmn. membership com. Nat. Eye Research Found. Served with USN, 1942-46. Fellow Nat. Eye Research Found. (Distinguished Service award 1974), Internat. Orthokeratology Soc.; mem. Am., Mo., St. Louis optometric assns., Am. (life), Mo. optometric founds., Am. Pub. Health Assn., Florissant Fine Arts Council (charter), St. Louis Art Mus. (life), St. Louis Symphony Soc. (sustaining), Heart of Am. Contact Lens Soc., Better Vision Inst. Clubs: Elks, Rotary. Internat. lectr. contact lenses. Home: 1660 Featherstone Dr St Louis MO 63131 Office: 875 St Francis St Florissant MO 63031 also 177 The Village Chesterfield MO 63017

RESLOCK, PAUL VERNON, optometrist; b. Devils Lake, N.D., Apr. 22, 1925; s. Paul and Gertie (Kjelbertson) R.; student Valley City State Coll., 1944; D.Optometry, No. Ill. Coll. Optometry, 1949; m. Caryl Ann Kelly, Feb. 22, 1946; children—Chris, Jane (Mrs. Terry Willson), David, William. Pvt. practice optometry, Valley City, N.D., 1949—; sec., dir. Farmers & Mchts. State Bank, 1970—, Farmers & Mchts. Ins. Agy., 1970—. Mem. Valley City Drum and Bugle Corps, 1949-59. Served with USNR, 1943-46. Mem. N.D. State Bd. Examiners Optometry, N.D. Optometric Assn. (pres. 1954-55), Am. Legion (post comdr. 1960). Lutheran. Elk, K.P., Rotarian (pres. 1955). Club: Valley City Country (pres. 1954, 75-75). Home: 1319 Chautaugua Blvd Valley City ND 58072 Office: 117 NW 3d St Valley City ND 58072

RESNECK, ELLIOTT JACK, mgmt. cons., ins. agt.; b. Lepanto, Ark., July 14, 1920; s. William V. and Bess (Adams) R.; B.A., U. Wis., 1941; postgrad. Harvard U., 1941-42; m. Dora Block, Apr. 12, 1942; children—Susan Dale, Linda Ian, Brenda Jane. Vice pres. Elliott's Fashion Apparel Group Wis., 1945-54, pres., 1954-60, chmn., 1960-71; mgmt. cons. to retail trades, 1971—; cons. on pension plans, life ins. and securities sales, 1972—; dir. Mchts. and Savs. Bank, Janesville. Dir. Janesville Indsl. Devel. Corp., 1952-53; dir. Greater Janesville Corp., 1970—, pres., 1972; bus. chmn. Janesville United Givers Fund, 1965. Served with USAAF, 1942-44. C.L.U. Mem. Janesville C. of C. (pres. 1952), Aircraft Owners and Pilots Assn., Wis. Alumni Assn., Million Dollar Roundtable, Nat. Assn. Life Underwriters (Nat. Quality award, Sales Achievement award), Artus, Phi Beta Kappa, Phi Kappa Phi, Phi Eta Sigma. Rotarian (mem. Speakers Bur. 1960—). Club: Janesville Country (dir. 1976—). Contbr. articles to retail trade publs. and ins. mags. Home: 714 N Marion Ave Janesville WI 53545 Office: 1425 W Memorial Dr Janesville WI 55345

RESNICK, LOUIS, corp. architect; b. N.Y.C., July 14, 1916; s. Charles and Pauline (Schmaltz) R.; student Coll. City N.Y., 1934-35, N.Y. U. Sch. Architecture, 1937-41, Columbia Sch. Architecture, 1947-52; m. Gertrude Berlin, Dec. 24, 1936; 1 son, Curt Alan. Corp. architect Stein's Stores Inc., N.Y.C., 1955-59, Richman Bros. Co., Cleve., 1959-68, Jacobs, Visconsi & Jacobs Co., Cleve., 1968-77; pvt. practice architecture, 1977—; lectr. architecture Kent (Ohio) State U., 1971. Bd. trustees Inst. Store Planners. Served with USNR, World War II; PTO. Registered architect; certified Nat. Council Archtl. Registration Bds. Mem. AIA, Archtl. Soc. Ohio. Home: 3809 Faversham Rd University Heights OH 44118

RESNIK, MARVIN, optometrist; b. Kiev, Russia, Jan. 24, 1921; s. Jacob and Anna (Cohen) R.; came to U.S., 1929, naturalized, 1943; student Case Inst. Tech., 1937-38; B.Sc., Ohio State U., 1939, O.D., 1946; student U. Wyo., 1943, State U. Iowa, 1943; m. Elizabeth Stalnaker, Nov. 28, 1942; children—Judy (Mrs. Michael Oldak), Charles. Practice optometry, East Akron, Ohio, 1946—. Trustee Ohio Lions Eye Research Found. (charter). Served with AUS, 1942-46. Decorated Bronze Star. Mem. Am., Ohio optometric assns. Jewish (soloist congregation choir 1947-73). Mason (Shriner), Lion (pres. 1965-66); mem. B'nai B'rith. Home: 202 Durward Rd Akron OH 44313 Office: 863 E Market St Akron OH 44305

RESSEGUIE, JAMES LYNN, clergyman; b. Buffalo, Jan. 1, 1945; s. Leon Arthur and Mable (Vary) R.; A.B., U. Calif., Berkeley, 1967; M.Div., Princeton Theol. Sem., 1972; postgrad. Fuller Theol. Sem., 1972—; m. Dianne Laverne Paulson, Oct. 24, 1970; children—Timothy, Carin. Ordained to ministry United Presbyterian Ch. U.S.A., 1976; teaching fellow Fuller Theol. Sem., Pasadena, Calif., 1973-76; asst. prof. N.T., Winebrenner Theol. Sem., Findlay, Ohio, 1976—. Peace Corps vol., Cameroon, 1967-69, presdl. certificate of appreciation, 1969. Mem. Soc. Bibl. Lit. Contbr. articles to Studia Biblca et Theologica. Home: 2105 Jennifer Ln Findlay OH 45840 Office: 701 E Melrose Ave Findlay OH 45840

RESTIVO, RAYMOND M., health assn. exec., pub. health cons.; b. Chgo., Aug. 19, 1934; s. Frank M. and Angeline (Franzone) R.; B.S.A., Loyola U., Chgo., 1956; certificate pub. health adminstrn. U. Ill., 1968; children—Laura, Maria, Mark, Susan, Steven, John. Adminstrv. asst. to pres. of S.K. Culver Co., Chgo., 1954-59; projects coordinator Chgo. Heart Assn., 1959-66, exec. dir., 1973—; pub. health adminstr. Chgo. Bd. Health, 1966-73, mem. advisory com., 1967-73, mem. editorial rev. com. for newsletter, 1968-73; cons. community health to various pub., vol. and ofcl. health agys., 1962—; del. to Pub. Service Inst. of City of Chgo., 1973; notary pub., Cook County (Ill.), 1971—; mem. oral bd. examiners for cardiovascular technologist, City of Chgo. Civil Service Commn., 1971-73. Sec., Morris Fishbein, Jr. Meml. Fund, 1973—; mem. Zoning Bd. Appeals, Forest Park, Ill., 1964-68; mem. Health Services Task Force, Oak Park, Ill., 1974-75; bd. dirs. Chgo. Health Research Found., 1976—; mem. Planning Com. 4th Nat. Congress Quality of Life AMA, 1977-78. Recipient Meritorious Service award Village of Oak Park, 1975. Mem. Ill. Pub. Health Assn. (mem. policy com. 1971-73, mem. health issues com. 1972-73), Am. Pub. Health Assn., Am. Heart Assn. Profl. Staff Soc., Am. Soc. of Assn. Execs., Am. Mgmt. Assn., Nat. Assn. of Emergency Care Technicians, Epidemiology Club of Chgo., City of Chgo. Exec. Devel., Loyola U. alumni assns. Clubs: Tower, University. Contbr. articles on heart disease to profl. publs. Office: 20 N Wacker Dr Chicago IL 60606

RESTORICK, WILLIAM HOWARD, utility co. engr.; b. Newark, O., Feb. 20, 1945; s. Earl C. and Leona F. (Prysi) R.; B.S. in Elec. Engring., U. Toledo, 1972, M.S. in Indsl. Engring., 1976; m. Aline Edith Clark, June 14, 1968; children—William Howard, Christopher Aaron, Bryan Matthew. Design draftsman City of Toledo, 1967-72; asst. engr. Toledo Edison Co., 1972-74, power engr., 1974, load mgr. engr., 1974-75, custom substa. engr., 1975-77, substa. sect. head, 1977—; instr. Electric Heating Equipment Sizing Sch., Toledo, 1972-74; instr. U. Toledo Community and Tech. Coll., 1976—. Registered profl. engr., Ohio. Mem. Constrn. Specification Inst. (sec. Toledo chpt. 1975, editor newsletter 1973-75), IEEE, Phi Kappa Psi. Author: Electric Heating Reference Manual, 1973. Home: 800 Ransom Rd Maumee OH 43537 Office: Toledo Edison Co 300 Madison St Toledo OH 43652

RESZKA, ALFONS, computer systems architect; b. Imielin, Poland, Dec. 17, 1924; s. Alfons and Maria (Galazka) R.; B.Sc., U. London, 1954; M.S. in E.E., Northwestern U., 1960; Ph.D., Northwestern U., 1976; children—Ann, Elizabeth, Alfred, Cathrine. Engr., British Jeffrey Diamond, Wakefield, Eng., 1954-55; lectr. Bradford (Eng.) Tech. Coll., 1955-56; engr. A.C. Nielson, Chgo., 1956-59; with Teletype Corp., Skokie, Ill., 1959—, project dir., 1969-75, sr. staff engr., 1975—. Mem. IEEE, Computer Soc., Tech. Com. of Computer Architecture. Patentee in electronics. Home: PO Box 373 Northbrook IL 60062 Office: 5555 Touhy Ave Skokie IL 60076

RETSKY, MICHAEL WALTER, physicist; b. Chgo., June 26, 1939; s. Meyer and Helen (Block) R.; B.S., Ill. Inst. Tech., 1961; S.M., U. Chgo., 1969, Ph.D., 1974; m. Myrna Marks, Oct. 22, 1961; children—Paula, Karen. Research engr. Magnaflux Corp., Chgo., 1961-64; scientist Zenith Radio Corp., Chgo., 1964-73, mgr. electron physics, 1974-75, mgr. gun design and finishing engring., 1975—. Recipient 1st prize for sci. importance in micrographic competition, Royal Microscopical Soc., 1974. Contbr. articles in field to profl. jours. including Optik, Am. Jour. Physics, and others. Home: 2942 W Jarlath Ave Chicago IL 60645 Office: 2407 W North Ave Melrose Park IL 60160

RETTMER, FORREST RUDOLPH, chem. co. exec.; b. Tracy, Minn., Nov. 27, 1931; s. Ralph John and Louise Georgia (Anderson) R.; B.A., Mankato (Minn.) State Coll., 1954; m. Georgia Mae Stoll, Dec. 29, 1954; children—Rebecca Louise, Kimberly Ruth, Peter Stoll, John Thomas. Self-employed as interior decorator, Mankato, 1959-62; with Standard Oil Co. (Ind.), Mankato, Mpls. and Rochester, Minn., 1955-59; salesman Nat. Poly Products, Inc. (merged into No. Petrochem. 1967), Mankato, 1962-64, sales mgr., 1964-66, v.p. marketing, 1966-68, pres., 1968—; gen. mgr. expanded operation No. Petrochem., Mankato, 1969—. Served with M.C. AUS, 1950-52. Home: 157 W Glencrest St Mankato MN 56001 Office: PO Box 1180 21113d Ave Mankato MN 56001

RETZER, KENNETH ALBERT, educator; b. Jacksonville, Ill., Nov. 6, 1933; s. Samuel Starks and Cora Edith (Martin) R.; A.B., Ill. Coll., 1954; M.Ed., U. Ill., 1957; postgrad. U. Wyo., summer 1957, La. State U., summer 1958; Ph.D., U. Ill., 1967; m. Dorcas Anne Schroeder, Apr. 18, 1953; children—Martin Wayne, Kent Arnold, Sheryl Kaye. Math and sci. tchr. Saunemin (Ill.) Twp. High Sch., 1954-58; asst. supt. schs. Saunemin, Ill., 1955-58; asst. prof. Ill. State U., Normal, 1959-67, asso. prof., 1967-72, prof. math., 1972—, asst. chmn. math. dept., 1969-71; guest lectr., vis. prof. Taylor U., 1973-74, Abilene Christian Coll., 1973-74, U. Ga., 1972-74. Advancement chmn. Boy Scouts Am., Normal, Ill., 1964-69; sec. Ill. State U. Householder Assn., 1967-68. HEW grantee, 1968-69; NSF grantee, 1968-75, 77—; Ill. State U.-Instrnl. Devel. Program grantee, 1961-63, 71-75; State Ill. fellow, 1964-65; State Fla., U.S. Office Edn. traineeship, 1973-74; NSF fellow, 1958-59, summer 1958, 57; Laverne Noyes scholar, 1951-54. Mem. Ill. Council Tchrs. Math (bd. dirs. 1972-75), Am. Sci. Affiliation, Nat. Council Tchrs. Math., Math. Assn. Am., NEA, AAUP, Nat. Soc. Profs., AAAS, Nat. Council Suprs. Math., Am. Soc. Profs., Am. Edn. Research Assn., Ill. Assn. Higher Edn. (v.p. 1973-74), Kappa Delta Pi, Pi Mu Epsilon, Phi Delta Kappa. Ch. of Christ (deacon 1969-72, elder 1972—). Contbr. articles to profl. jours. Home: 316 S Grove St Normal IL 61761

RETZER, MARY ELIZABETH HELM (MRS. WILLIAM RAYMOND RETZER), librarian; b. Balt.; d. Francis Leslie C. and Edna (Smith) Helm; B.A., Western Md. Coll., 1940; M.A., Columbia U., 1946; postgrad. George Washington U., Ind. U., U. Ill., Ill. State U., Bradley U.; Ph.D., Western Colo. U., 1972; m. William Raymond Retzer, June 28, 1945; children—Lesley Elizabeth, April Christine. Mem. faculty Rockville (Md.) Bd. Edn., 1940-47, elementary supr., 1945-47; cons. librarian Bergan High Sch., 1964-67; condr. library sci. course in reference Bradley U., 1966—; librarian Hines Elementary Sch., 1963-66, Roosevelt Jr. High Sch., 1966-69; head librarian Manual High Sch., Peoria, Ill., 1969—. Instr. water safety courses ARC, summers 1940—; pres. women's bd. Salvation Army, 1952-54; mem. Crippled Children's Adv. Com., Peoria, 1957-60; mem. women's adv. bd. Peoria Journal Star, 1970-73; active various community drives. Mem. ALA, Ill., Ill. Valley (pres. 1971-72) library assns., NEA, Ill. (audio visual com. 1972-74), Peoria edn. assns., AAUW, Internat. Platform Assn., Ill. Assn. Sch. Librarians (certification com. 1973-75). Republican. Presbyn. Mem. Order Eastern Star. Clubs: Ill. State University Administrators, Willowknolls Country. Home: 1317 W Moss Ave Peoria IL 61606

RETZER, WILLIAM RAYMOND, ret. indsl. hygiene engr.; b. Bklyn.; s. William Michael and Mildred Adalaide (Engles) R.; B.S. in Chem. Engring., Lehigh U., 1934; m. Elizabeth Helm, June 28, 1945; children—Lesley Elizabeth Retzer Cowley, April Christine Meacham. Control chemist Dupont Co., Nat. Lead Co., 1934-36; indsl. hygiene and safety engr. Pulmosan Co., 1936-34, Ky. Health Dept., 1940-42, Md. Health Dept., 1946-47; indsl. hygiene and safety engr. East Peoria plant Catepillar Tractor Co., 1947-68, worldwide plants, 1968-77. Mem. Peoria mayor's coms. noise and smoke abatement; mem. Ill. Com. Indsl. Hygiene. Served with U.S. Army, 1942-46. Diplomate Am. Bd. Indsl. Hygiene. Mem. Am. Indsl. Hygiene Assn., Am. Acad. Indsl. Hygiene, Am. Pub. Health Assn. Club: Masons (Scottish Rite). Home: 1317 W Moss Ave Peoria IL 61606

RETZLAFF, HORST FRANZ ALBERT, non-commd. air force officer; b. Stettin, Germany, Oct. 14, 1932; s. Franz Hermann Conrad and Elfriede Ilse (Kuhnrich) R.; came to U.S., 1956, naturalized, 1962; diploma Devry Inst., 1971, Non-Commd. Officers Acad., 1961; m. Thelma Louise Kennedy, Feb. 10, 1962; 1 dau., Crystal Ann. Enlisted U.S. Air Force, 1957, advanced through grades to tech. sgt., 1974; airborne radio team chief McConnell AFB, 1959-62; crew chief, radio repairman various locations; work center supr. 665th Radar Squadron, Calumet Air Force Sta., Mich., 1976—; adviser Electronics mag., 1977-78. Recipient Airman Achievement award, 1960. Mem. Smithsonian Inst., Nat. History Mus. of N.Y. Lutheran. Home: 307 W Wisconsin Ave Greensburg KS 67054 Office: 665 RADS Calumet AFS MI 49913

RETZLOFF, DAVID GEORGE, educator; b. Pitts., Feb. 19, 1939; s. John Joseph and Georgia Ruth (Hook) R.; B.S., U. Pitts., 1963, M.S., 1965, Ph.D., 1967; postgrad. Kans. State U., 1970-73, U. Houston, 1974-75; m. Debra Rae Renz, July 31, 1971. Wetenschaplijk medewerker U. Delft (The Netherlands), 1967-68; research asso. U. Colo., Boulder, 1968-69; asst. prof. Kans. State U., Manhattan, 1969-73; research engr. Exxon Research and Engring. Co., Baytown, Tex., 1973-75; asst. prof. chem. engring. U. Mo., Columbia, 1975—. Served with USAF, 1956-60. Mem. AAAS, Am. Inst. Physics, Am. Chem. Soc., Am. Inst. Chem. Engring., Sigma Xi. Republican. Roman Catholic. Home: 1461 S Mesa Dr Columbia MO 65201 Office: U Mo Dept Chem Engring Columbia MO 65201

RETZLOFF, JAMES GAIL, fire protection engr.; b. Lansing, Mich., May 31, 1939; s. Gail Frederick and Winifred Leonora Else (Hay) R.; B.M.E., Gen. Motors Inst., 1962; m. Julia Francis White, Aug. 8, 1959; children—Peggy Lynn, Bonnie Lynn, Wendy Lynn. Fire protection engr. Oldsmobile div. Gen. Motors Corp., Lansing, Mich., 1963-73, Viking Fire Protection Assos., Hastings, Mich., 1973-74; v.p., Viking Fire Protection Assos., 1974—; chief engr. Viking Corp., Hastings, 1976—. Registered profl. engr., Mich.; certified safety profl., Ill. Mem. Mich. Soc. Profl. Engrs., Mich. Assn. Profls., Soc. Fire Protection Engrs., Nat. Fire Protection Assn., Mich. Fire Insps. Soc. Lutheran. Home: 4773 Grand Woods Dr Lansing MI 48917 Office: 210 N Industrial Park Rd Hastings MI 49058

REUBEN, DAVID J., computer scientist; b. Akron, Ohio, Sept. 22, 1944; s. Albert G. and Sara I. (Rifkin) R.; B.A., Yale U., 1966; M.S., Johns Hopkins U., 1970. Sr. planner Indpls. Dept. Met. Devel., 1971; asst. project mgr. Census Use Study, U.S. Census Bur., Indpls., 1972-76; systems cons. Melvin Simon & Assos., Indpls., 1976—; mem. asso. faculty Ind. U., 1972-73. IBM fellow, 1968-70. Mem. Phi Beta Kappa. Club: Yale. Office: Melvin Simon and Assos 1712 N Meridian St Indianapolis IN 46202

REUBEN, DON H., lawyer; b. Chgo., Sept. 1, 1928; s. Michael B. and Sally (Chapman) R.; B.S., Northwestern U., 1949, J.D., 1952; m. Evelyn Long, Aug. 27, 1948 (div.); children—Michael Barrett, Timothy Don, Jeffrey Long, Howard Ellis; m. 2d, Jeannette Hurley Haywood, Dec. 13, 1971; stepchildren—Harris, Jeannette, Edward. Admitted to Ill. bar, 1952; practiced with firm Kirkland & Ellis, Chgo., 1952—, now sr. partner; gen. counsel for Tribune Co. and subsidiaries, Ill. C. of C., 1961—, Chgo. Bears Football Club, Inc., Regensteiner Pub. Enterprises, Inc.; spl. asst. atty. gen. State of Ill., 1963-64, 69—; counsel spl. session Ill. Ho. of Reps., 1964, for Ill. treas. for congl., state legis. and jud. reapportionment, 1963—; spl. fed. ct. master, 1968-70. Dir. Lake Shore Nat. Bank. Mem. citizens adv. bd. to Sheriff Cook County, 1962-66; mem. jury instrns. com., 1963-68, com. rules Ill. Supreme Ct., 1963-73; mem. pub. relations com. Nat. Conf. State Trial Judges; mem. Chgo. Better Schs. Com., 1968—, Chgo. Crime Commn., 1970—; mem. supervisory panel Fed. Defender Program. Mem. nat. legacy com. Multiple Sclerosis Soc., also vice chmn. Central region; pres. Weymouth Kirkland Found.; bd. dirs. Lincoln Park Zool. Soc., Rehab. Inst. Chgo., United Cerebral Palsy Assn. Chgo.; mem. citizens bd. Loyola U. of Chgo. Mem. Ill., Chgo. (chmn. subcom. on propriety and regulation of contingent fees com. devel. law 1966-69) Am. (standing com. on fed. judiciary) bar assns., Am. Law Inst., Am. Judicature Soc., Fellows Am. Bar Found., Bar Assn. 7th Fed. Circuit, Am. Coll. Trial Lawyers, rule 23 and multi-dist. litigation com., adj. state com.), Internat. Acad. Trial Lawyers, Ill. Trial Lawyers Assn., Assn. Trial Lawyers Am., Am. Arbitration Assn. (nat. panel arbitrators) Phi Eta Sigma, Beta Alpha Psi, Beta Gamma Sigma, Order of Coif. Clubs: University, Chicago, Tavern, Mid-Am., Chgo. Yacht (Chgo.); Butterfield Country; Oak Brook (Ill.) Polo; Comml.; Dunham Woods Riding. Lectr. on libel, slander, privacy and freedom of press. Home: 2430 Lake View Ave Chicago IL 60614 Office: 200 E Randolph Dr Chicago IL 60601

REUSS, CARL FREDERICK, sociologist, ch. orgn. exec.; b. Phila., June 7, 1915; s. Charles F. and Marie (Kick) R.; B.S., U. Va., 1934, M.S., 1935, Ph.D., 1937; m. Thelma Lucille Steinmann, June 24, 1938; children—Paula Lucille (Mrs. Robert Schanz), Ellen Marie (Mrs. Thomas Jeppesen), Betty Jeanne (Mrs. Wayne Shovelin). Asst. rural sociologist State Coll. Wash., 1937-44; social sci. analyst U.S. Dept. Agr., Berkeley, Calif., 1944; prof. sociology Capital U., 1944-48; dean of faculty Wartburg Coll., 1948-51; exec. sec. bd. for Christian Social Action. Am. Luth. Ch., Columbus, Ohio, 1951-60; dir. research and analysis Am. Luth. Ch., Mpls., 1960—. Sec. Commn on Inner Missions, Luth. World Fedn., 1952-63; mem. com. on church and soc. World Council Chs., 1954-61; del. 1968 assembly World Council Chs.; del. assemblies Luth. World Fedn., 1957, 63, 70; mem. various coms. Lutheran Council U.S.A. Bd. dirs., v.p. conf. religious leaders Nat. Safety Council, 1973—. Mem. Am. Sociol. Assn., Rural Sociol. Soc., Nat. Council Family Relations, Phi Kappa Phi, Alpha Kappa Delta. Editor: The Christian in His Social Living, 1960, Conscience and Action, 1971. Home: 5311 Vincent Ave S Minneapolis MN 55410 Office: 422 S 5th St Minneapolis MN 55415

REUSS, HENRY S(CHOELLKOPF), congressman; b. Milw., Feb. 22, 1912; s. Gustav A. and Paula (Schoellkopf) R.; A.B., Cornell U., 1933; LL.B., Harvard, 1936; m. Margaret Magrath, Oct. 24, 1942; children—Christopher, Michael, Jacqueline, Anne. Admitted to Wis. bar, 1936, practiced in Milw., 1936-55; lectr. Wis. State Coll., Milw., 1950-51; asst. corp. counsel Milwaukee County, 1939-40; asst. gen. counsel OPA. Washington, 1941-42; dep. gen. counsel Marshall Plan, Paris, France, 1949; spl. prosecutor Milw. Co. Grand Jury, 1950; personal counsel to Sec. State in reapportionment case Wis. Supreme Court, 1953; mem. 84th to 95th congresses from 5th Dist. Wis. Mem. legal adv. com. Nat. Resources Bd., Washington, 1948-52; chmn. House Banking, Fin. and Urban Affairs Com., mem. Joint Economic Com. Mem. Milw. Sch. Bd., 1953-54; chmn. clubs and orgns. com. Milw. March of Dimes, 1953; nat. adv. bd. Am. Youth Hostels. Bd. visitors Cornell U. Coll. Arts and Scis. Served from 2d lt. to capt. 63d, 75th Inf. Divs., AUS, 1943-45; chief price control br. Office Mil. Govt. Germany, 1945. Decorated Bronze Star. Mem. Children's Service Soc. (dir.), Jr. Bar Assn. of Milw. (vice chmn.), Milwaukee County (chmn. constn. and citizenship com.), Milw. bar assns., Chi Psi Alumni Assn. (v.p.). Club: Milwaukee City, Alumni Trustee Harvard Law Rev., 1956-60. Author: The Critical Decade, 1964; Revenue Sharing, Crutch or Catalyst, 1970; On the Trail of the Ice Age, 1976; To Save Our Cities, 1977. Home: 1028 E Juneau St Milwaukee WI 53202 Office: 2413 Rayburn House Office Bldg Washington DC 20515 also 517 E Wisconsin Ave Milwaukee WI 53203

REUTER, GEORGE SYLVESTER, JR., educator, writer; b. Holden, Mo., Feb. 9, 1920; s. George Sylvester and Laura Ethelyn (Angle) R.; B.S., Central Mo. State U., 1941, M.S., 1949; Ed.D., U. Mo., 1952, post-doctoral student Harvard, 1964-65; m. Helen Frances Hyde, Aug. 18, 1956; children—Don, Allan, Kim. Tchr. high sch., Lone Jack, Mo., 1941-42; asst. credit mgr. A.C. Becken & Co., 1946-48;

grad. asst. Central Mo. State Coll., 1948-49; supt. schs. R-VIII, Henry County, Mo., 1949-50; prof., chmn. dept. edn., dir. research Ark. A. and M. Coll., 1952-57; dean of coll., dir. summer session Minot State Coll., 1957-60; research dir. Am. Fedn. for Tchrs., 1958-65; prof. edn., So. Ill. U., Edwardsville, 1965-66; pres. Sioux Empire Coll., Hawarden, Ia., 1966-70; supt. schs. New Madrid County R-I Enlarged, 1970—. Spl. cons. Ill. Dept. Pub. Instrn., 1969-70. Nat. Com. for Support of Pub. Schs. Producer weekly radio program Know Your College, 1955-57, co-producer daily radio program From the Music Room, 1955-57. State dir. Senior Citizens of America, 1956—. Served from apprentice seaman to lt. (j.g.) USNR, 1942-46. Mem. Am. Assn. Sch. Adminstrs., N.E.A., UN Assn. U.S.A., Internat. Platform Assn., Phi Delta Kappa, Kappa Delta Pi, Phi Sigma Pi, Zeta Kappa Epsilon. Baptist (deacon 1951). Rotarian. Club: Harvard (Chgo.). Author: (with August M. Hintz and Helen H. Reuter) One Blood; (with Helen H. Reuter) Democracy and Quality Education, 1965. Editor: (film strip) A Proud Heritage, 1957; Achieving Quality Education, 1971; Emergency School Assistance Program Seminars, 1972; editor: Occupational Educational Leadership, a Performance Based Approach. Condr. study Asociacion Escuelas Lincoln of Buenos Aires. Home: 1111 E Alder Ln Mt Prospect IL 60056 Office: PO Box 56 New Madrid MO 63869

REUTER, HELEN HYDE, psychologist; b. McGehee, Ark., July 26, 1917; d. John Lloyd and Sallie Elizabeth (Holcomb) Hyde; B.A., Westmar Coll., 1965; A.M., U. S.D., 1969; L.H.D., Sioux Empire Coll., 1970; m. George S. Reuter, Jr., Aug. 18, 1956; children—Don N., M. Allan, K.L. Postmaster, Coll. Heights, Ark., 1952-65; counselor various pub. schs., 1965-70; sch. psychologist New Madrid County (Mo.) Pub. Schs., 1970-75, Oak Park and River Forest (Ill.) High Schs., 1975—; cons. in field. Named Mother of Yr., Monticello, Ark., 1960. Mem. Ill. Psychol. Assn., Nat. Assn. Sch. Psychologists, AAUW, P.E.O., Council Exceptional Children, Assn. Learning Disabilities, Profl. Counsellors Assn., Psi Chi, Alpha Chi, Phi Delta Kappa, Delta Kappa Gamma. Democrat. Baptist. Author: (with G.S. Reuter, Jr., A.M. Mintz) One Blood, 1964; (with G.S. Reuter) Democracy and Quality Education, 1965; contbr. articles to profl. jours. Home: 1111 E Alder Ln Mount Prospect IL 60056 Office: 201 N Scoville Ave Oak Park IL 60302

REUTHE, JOHN JULIUS, orthodontist; b. Lima, Ohio, Dec. 18, 1913; s. Alfred E. and Agnes Mary (Welch) R.; D.D.S., Ind. U., 1937; postgrad. Northwestern U., 1956, Columbia U., 1957, Temple U., 1957, Ind. U., 1951; m. Marjorie Mathes Snyder, July 29, 1939; children—John Edward, Susan Kay. Intern, Forsyth Dental Infirmary for Children, Boston, 1937-38; med. missionary Internat. Grenfell Assn., Newfoundland and Labrador, 1938-39; practice dentistry, South Bend, 1939-53; practice orthodontics, South Bend, Ind., 1960—; chief dental staff No. Ind. Children's Hosp., South Bend, 1948—; mem. staff Meml. Hosp. In-service instr. dental aux. tng. program Ind. U. at South Bend, 1969—; mem. Ind. Health Planning Bd., 1967—. Vice pres. No. Ind. council Boy Scouts Am., 1966—. Served from maj. to lt. col. AUS, 1953-55; Recipient Silver Beaver award Boy Scouts Am., 1966. Fellow Internat. Coll. Dentists; mem. Am., Ind. dental assns., St. Joseph County (pres. 1942-43), N. Central (Ind.) dental socs., Tweed Found. for Orthodontic Research, Ind. Alumni Assn. (bd. dirs. 1968—), South Bend Power Squadron, Delta Chi, Xi Psi Phi. Republican. Presbyn. (deacon 1945—, elder 1952—, trustee 1948—). Mason (32 deg., K.T., Shriner). Clubs: Exchange (pres. 1950-51) (South Bend); Corey Yacht (Three River, Mich.). Home: 51880 Lilac Rd South Bend IN 46628 Office: 926 E Jefferson Blvd South Bend IN 46617

REUTTER, CLIFFORD JOHN, historian; b. St. Louis, Aug. 6, 1921; s. Henry John and Marie (Goodpasture) R.; student William T. Harris Tchrs. Coll., St. Louis, 1939-43, U. Wis., 1943-44; M.A., St. Louis U., 1948, Ph.D., 1950; m. Joan Miriam Gutting, Feb. 2, 1952; children—John, Jeanne, Cathy, Ruth, Tom, Mary Joan, Claire, Cliff, Jim, Meg, Beth, Joseph, Michele. Instr. history St. Louis U., 1948-50, U. Detroit, 1950-52, asst. prof., 1952-57, asso. prof., 1957-68, prof., 1968—. Participant, U.S. Bishop's Conf., 1976; del. Mich. Democratic Conv., 1976. Served with U.S. Army, 1943-46. Mem. Soc. Historians Am. Fgn. Relations (charter), Immigration History Soc., Am. Folklore Soc., Am. Hist. Assn., Orgn. Am. Historians, Mich. Acad. Sci., Art and Letters. Roman Catholic. Contbr. articles on ethnicity, nationalism and diplomacy to hist. jours. Home: 15442 Ashton Rd Detroit MI 48223 Office: Dept History U Detroit 4001 W McNichols St Detroit MI 48221

REWOLDT, STEWART HENRY, educator; b. Dundee, Ill., Jan. 26, 1922; s. Frank Frederick and Elsa Caroline (Schultz) R.; B.B.A., U. Mich., 1946, M.B.A., 1947, Ph.D., 1952; m. May Allison Hilliard, Dec. 28, 1946; children—Gregory, Jeffrey, Thomas. Instr., U. Mich., Ann Arbor, 1947-52, asst. prof., 1952-53, prof. mktg., 1960—; asst. prof. Ind. U., Bloomington, 1953-55, asso. prof., 1955-56. Adviser Inst. Research in Productivity Waseda U., Tokyo, Japan, 1959-60. Mem. Am. Mktg. Assn. (dir. Ind. chpt. 1954-56), Sales/Mktg. Execs. (ednl. adv. bd. 1960-75), Beta Gamma Sigma, Phi Kappa Phi. Club: University (Ann Arbor). Author: Economic Effects of Marketing Research, 1953; Introduction to Marketing Management: Text and Cases, 1969; (with J.D. Scott and M.R. Warshaw) Teachers Manual to Accompany Introduction to Marketing Management, 1969, Introduction to Marketing Management: Text and Cases, 1973, Teacher's Manual to Accompany Introduction to Marketing Management, 1973; Introduction to Marketing Management: Text and Cases, 1977, also tchrs. manual. Editor: Frontiers in Marketing Thought, 1955; Conference on Sales Management, 1957, others. Home: 1213 Manhattan Dr Ann Arbor MI 48103

REYES, MILAGROS PAGADUAN, physician, educator; b. Quezon, Nuevaecija, Philippines, June 9, 1942; d. Olegario F. and Estela R. (Pagaduan) Reyes; student U. Philippines, 1958-61, M.D., 1966. Came to U.S., 1969. Intern Philippine Gen. Hosp., Manila, 1965-66, resident, 1966-69; trainee in infectious diseases, research fellow in medicine Wayne State U., Detroit, 1969-72, asst. prof. medicine, 1972-77, asso. prof., 1977—; cons. medicine, infectious diseases Harper Hosp., Detroit Gen. Hosp., Detroit Meml. Hosp.; cons. Hutzel Hosp., Detroit, 1972—, hosp. epidemiologist, 1975—. Recipient Samia award Philippine Med. Assn., 1968. Mem. Philippine Med. Assn. in Mich. (sec. 1970-73), Am. Soc. Microbiology. Contbg. author: Antimicrobial Therapy, 1974. Contbr. articles to profl. jours. Home: 1937 Severn Ave Grosse Pointe Woods MI 48236 Office: 432 E Hancock St Detroit MI 48201

REYMOND, RALPH DANIEL, radiologist; b. Geneva, Switzerland, Mar. 31, 1937; s. Ernest and Dolores (Francini) R.; came to U.S., 1950, naturalized, 1955; A.B. in Physics and Egyptology, Johns Hopkins U., 1959, M.A. in Physics, 1963; M.D., 1967; m. Patricia Ann Bulger, Feb. 4, 1961; 1 son, Eric Daniel. Intern Md. Gen. Hosp., Balt., 1967-68; resident in radiology Johns Hopkins Hosp., Balt., 1968-72; radiologist in radiology and nuclear medicine, Topeka, Kans., 1972—; physicist Harry Diamond Labs., Dept. Army, Washington, D.C., summers 1957-66; jr. instr. physics Johns Hopkins U., 1960-62. Bd. dirs. Topeka Zoo, 1972-75. Diplomate Am. Bd. Radiology, Nat. Bd. Med. Examiners. Mem. Am., So. med. assns., Am. Radium Soc., Royal Soc. Medicine (London), Radiol. Soc. N. Am., Am. Coll. Radiology, Am. Med. Soc. of Vienna, Am. Phys. Soc., Am. Assn. Physicists in Medicine, Am. Coll. Nuclear Physicians, Kans. Med. Soc., Kans. Radiol. Soc., AAAS, Med. and Chirurgical Faculty Md., Nat. Assn. Residents and Interns, Am. Coll. Nuclear Medicine, Am. Research Center Egypt. Republican. Clubs: Rolls-Royce Owners, Saturday Night Literary. Patentee in field. Home: 2816 MacVicar Ave Topeka KS 66611 Office: 310 Med Arts Bldg 10th and Horner Sts Topeka KS 66604

REYNOLDS, DALE RICHARD, furniture co. exec.; b. Wakarusa, Ind., July 11, 1924; s. H. Otis and Mary Victoria (Kehr) R.; student Dale Carnegie Inst., 1965; m. Marjorie L. Holdeman, Apr. 2, 1946; children—Judith Ann, Dennis, Thomas, Clifton, Donald. Foreman, Comfo Sleep, Inc., 1949-52; plant mgr. Fred V. Gentsch, Inc., 1952-56; v.p., gen. mgr. Kinder Mfg. Co., Inc., Elkhart, Ind., 1956-71; pres. Wakarusa Devel. Corp., 1969-71; pres. Mastercraft, Inc., Shipshewana, Ind., 1971—, Mem. Elkhart County Planning Commn., 1970-71. Del. Republican Ind. State Conv., 1970. Served with AUS, 1943-47. Mem. United Comml. Travelers, Am. Legion. Methodist (mem. finance com. 1968-71, pres. exec. bd. 1969-71). Mason (32 deg., Shriner), Lion. Home: 401 S Washington St Wakarusa IN 46573 Office: Mastercraft Inc PO Box 326 Hwy 5 So Shipshewana IN 46565

REYNOLDS, FREDERICK CHARLES, savs. and loan exec.; b. Clio, Mich., July 4, 1918; s. Leo Burnham and Esther Leah (Geiger) R.; certificate Baker Bus. U., 1936; m. Velma Eileen Nash, Oct. 11, 1941; children—Gary Nash, Susan Lynn (Mrs. Wayne Fisher), Lee Ann (Mrs. Darwyn Sanborn). Billing clk. Veit & Davison Lumber Co., Flint, Mich., 1936; teller Detroit and No. Savs. & Loan Assn., Flint, 1937-40; auditor Mutual Savs. & Loan Assn., Bay City, Mich., 1940-43; examiner Fed. Deposit Ins. Corp., Washington, 1943-45, Fed. Home Loan Bank Bd., Washington, 1946; exec. officer, dir. Kalamazoo Savs. & Loan Assn., 1947—, sec.-treas., 1947-55, exec. v.p., 1955-57, pres., 1957—, chmn. bd., 1973—; dir. Kalamazoo Home Builders Assn., Builders Supply div. Credit Bur. Kalamazoo; dir. Fed. Home Loan Bank of Indpls., 1966-69, vice chmn. bd., chmn. exec. com., 1969. Pres. Constance Brown Soc. for Better Hearing, 1959-60; past pres. Washington Elementary PTA, Past v.p. Kalamazoo Area PTA Council, mem. Downtown Kalamazoo Planning Com., 1961—; pres. Kalamazoo YMCA, 1961-62; mem. Kalamazoo County Planning Bd. 1969; sec. Kalamazoo City Planning Commn., 1966-69, Kalamazoo City Zoning Bd. Appeals, 1954-65; past mem. Kalamazoo City Plumbing Bd. Bd. dirs., gen. crusade chmn. Kalamazoo County unit Am. Cancer Soc., bd. dirs., mem. standing crusade chmn. Mich. div.; bd. dirs. Kalamazoo Safety Council. Mem. U.S. (dir. 1961-63, mem. legis. com. 1959—), Mich. (pres. 1959-60) savs. and loan leagues, Soc. Residential Appraisers (pres. Kalamazoo chpt. 1952-53), Kalamazoo County C. of C. (dir. 1961-64), Kalamazoo Mgmt. Assn. (dir. 1965-68). Methodist (mem. ofcl. bd.). Elk. Kiwanian. Home: 6280 Saybrook Dr Kalamazoo MI 49009 Office: 215 E Michigan Ave Kalamazoo MI 49006

REYNOLDS, JAY DON, lawyer; b. Avard, Okla., Oct. 3, 1940; s. Henry Homer and Cordelia Olive (Prigmore) R.; B.A., Northwestern State Tchrs. Coll., 1962; J.D., Washburn U., 1966; m. Marian K. Schartz, July 28, 1973; 1 son, Mark; children by previous marriage—Christopher, Chad. Admitted to Kans. bar, 1966; gen. practice law, Cimarron, Kans., 1969—; co. atty. Gray Co., Kans., 1971—; city atty., Montezuma, Kans., 1971-74; municipal judge, Scott City, Kans., 1972—; asso. dist. judge, 10th Jud. Dist., Kans., 1977—. Served to capt. USMCR, 1966-69; Viet Nam. Recipient Law Week award Washburn Law Sch., 1966. Mem. Kans. Bar Assn. (ins. com.), Kansas County Atty. Assn. (pres. 1973). Rotarian (v.p., 1972-73). Club: Cimarron Crossing Saddle and Roping (chmn. bd. 1970). Home: West Park Dodge City KS 67801 Office: Courthouse Dodge City KS 67801

REYNOLDS, JOHN W., dist. judge; Green Bay, Wis., Apr. 4, 1921; s. John W. and Madge (Flatley) R.; B.S., U. Wis., 1946, LL.B., 1949; m. Patricia Ann Brody, May 26, 1947 (dec. Dec. 1967); children—Kate M., Molly, Jimmy; m. 2d, Jane Conway, July 31, 1971; children—Tom, Jake, Frances. Admitted to Wis. bar, 1949, since practiced in Green Bay; atty. gen., Wis., 1959-63; gov. State of Wis., 1963-65; U.S. dist. judge Eastern Dist. Wis., 1965—, now chief judge. Mem. Am., Wis. State, Brown County bar assns. Democrat. Home: 4654 N Woodburn Milwaukee WI 53211 Office: Federal Bldg Milwaukee WI 53202

REYNOLDS, KELLY PETER PATRICK, fire protection engr.; b. Los Angeles, June 2, 1944; s. Reta Ellen (Petty) R.; student Okla. State U.; m. Patricia Anne Boyd, July 27, 1970. Sr. fire insp. Scottsdale (Ariz.) Municipal Fire Dept., 1970-74; chief fire marshal, Albemarle County, Va., 1974-77; chief fire protection engr. Bldg. Ofcls. and Code Adminstrs., Chgo., 1977—; nat. chmn. BOCA Basic Fire Prevention Code, 1975-77. Served with USMC. Decorated Bronze Star medal; recipient Outstanding Young Man of Year award Va. Fire Prevention Assn., 1977. Mem. Soc. Fire Protection Engrs., Nat. Fire Protection Assn., Nat. Acad. Code Adminstrs., Fire Marshals Assn. N.Am., Smoke Control Assn., Internat. Assn. Fire Chiefs, Am. Legion. Roman Catholic. Contbr. Nat. Policy on Fire Research and Devel. Office: 1313 E 60th St Chicago IL 60637

REYNOLDS, RICHARD WILLIAM, mag. exec.; b. Milw., Aug. 22, 1923; s. James Francis and Mary Mabel (Driscoll) R.; B.S., U. Wis., 1949; m. Joan Carolyn Borgerding, July 21, 1951; children—Jane Frances, Barbara Joan, Anne Elizabeth. With Time Inc., N.Y.C., 1950-64; mem. mktg. sales staff Curtis Publ. Co., Phila., 1964-68, Forbes mag., N.Y.C., 1968—. Served with inf. AUS, 1942-45; PTO. Decorated Bronze Star, Purple Heart. Mem. Bus. Profl. Advt. Assn., Ins. Advt. Conf., Milw. Advt. Club, Agate Club Chgo. Clubs: Mid-Am., Chgo. Athletic Assn.; Milw. Athletic, Club International. Home: 1173 Scott St Winnetka IL 60093 Office: 435 N Michigan Ave Chicago IL 60611

REYNOLDS, WILLIAM PRESTON, r.r. exec.; b. Janesville, Wis., Aug. 24, 1940; s. James William and Helen Sophia (Pitzen) R.; student U. Wis., 1959-60; B.A., Milton Coll., 1964. Claims examiner U.S. R.R. Retirement Bd., Chgo., 1965-68; sta. clk., receiver, transit technician Chgo. Transit Authority, 1969—; secondary sch. tchr., Stephenson Town (Wis.) High Sch., 1964-65. Mem. Lake View Citizens Council, Landmarks Preservation Council; mem. Chgo. Sch. Architecture Found. Named Chgo. Transit Authority Employee of Year, 1970. Mem. Omnibus Soc. Am. (dir. 1974-76), Central Electric Rail Fans Assn. (activities dir. 1969-70), R.R. Club Chgo., Ill. Psychic Research Soc., Wis. Electric Ry. Hist. Soc., Spiritual Frontiers Fellowship. Republican. Roman Catholic. K.C. (4 deg.). Home: 722 W Grace St Chicago IL 60613 Office: Room 7140 Merchandise Mart 222 N Bank Dr Chicago IL 60654

REZNER, CHARLES THOMAS, law enforcement coordinator, educator; b. Chgo., Oct. 14, 1942; s. Charles Louis and Lois Gladys (Baskin) R.; B.A., Monmouth (Ill.) Coll., 1964; M.A., U. Ill., 1965; postgrad. Roosevelt U., 1967, Western Ill. U., 1968-71, Middle Tenn. State U., 1971, Nova U., 1976-78; m. Karen Jean Carman, Aug. 25, 1968; children—Anne Elizabeth, Charles Louis. Instr. social sci., coach jr. high sch., Mt. Prospect, Ill., 1965-66, Northwestern Mil. Naval Acad., Lake Geneva, Wis., 1966-67; head swim coach Monmouth (Ill.) Coll., 1971-75; instr. social sci. Carl Sandburg Coll., Galesburg, Ill., 1967-76, coordinator law enforcement, 1976—. Registrar, Episcopal Diocese Quincy (Ill.), 1971—, lic. lay reader, 1962—. Contbr. book revs. to Community Coll. Social Sci., Quar., 1970-73, Jour. Am. History, 1977; articles to Swimming World Mag., 1974, 75. Home: 1920 Patterson Dr Galesburg IL 61401 Office: Carl Sandburg Coll Galesburg IL 61401

RHEMBRANDT, CARLTON KAYO, city ofcl.; b. Amarillo, Tex., Dec. 16, 1926; s. Chester H. and Lois Olita (Nash) McDermett; student U. N.M., 1946-48; m. Sylva Sieberta Stalker, Mar. 23, 1954; children—David Kayo, Dan Dee, Coy Duane. Geologist, Lone Star Mining Co., Albuquerque, 1956-59, Consolidated Metals, Roswell, N.Mex., 1959-61; supt., Garnier Pipeline Constrn. Co., Albuquerque, 1961-64; st. supt., City of Alamosa, Colo., 1964-67; dir. pub. works City of Belleville, Kans., 1967-68, city mgr., 1968-70; city mgr. City of Chadron, Nebr., 1970—. Served with USNR, 1944-46; PTO. Recipient Leadership award Nebr. Community Improvement Program, 1971, 74, 75. Mem. Internat., Nebr. (sec.-treas. 1972-73, v.p. 1973-74, pres. 1974-75) city mgmt. assns., Municipal Treas. Assn. U.S., VFW, Am. Legion. Elk, Lion. Editor: Nebr. City Mgmt. Newsletter, 1971—. Home: 330 Pine St Chadron NE 69337 Office: Box 390 Chadron NE 69337

RHIEW, HYOMYEONG BENJAMIN, psychiatrist; b. Seoul, Korea, May 14, 1939; s. Choon-San and Sun-Ae (Chang) R.; student Seoul Nat. U., Korea, 1958-60; M.D., Seoul Nat. U., 1964; came to U.S., 1967; m. Dongsun Shin, June 7, 1967; children—Albert, Catherine, Margaret. Intern, Detroit-Macomb Hosps. Assn., Detroit, 1967-68; resident Phila. Gen. Hosp., 1968-70, Detroit Psychiat. Inst., 1970-71; staff psychiatrist, sect. dir. Northville (Mich.) State Hosp., 1971-75; pvt. practice psychiatry, Detroit and Livonia, Mich., 1972—; staff psychiatrist Adult Psychiat. Clinic, Detroit, part time 1971-72, Detroit Meml. Hosp., 1977—, Ardmore Acres Hosp.; cons. psychiatrist Evang. Deaconess Hosp., Alexander Blain Hosp., S.W. Detroit Hosp., Dearborn Med. Center; clin. Ward dir. Detroit Psychiat. Inst., 1975—; clin. asst. prof. Wayne State U., 1976—. Served with Korean Army, 1964-67. Diplomate Am. Bd. Psychiatry and Neurology. Mem. AMA, Mich. Psychiat. Soc., Am. Psychiat. Assn., Mich. State, Wayne County med. socs. Home: 25451 Liberty Ln Farmington Hills MI 48018 Office: 841 David Whitney Bldg Detroit MI 48226

RHOAD, FLOYD GERALD, agrl. co. exec.; b. Latty, Ohio, Nov. 23, 1916; s. John Archer and Gertrude Sylvia (Gantt) R.; grad. high sch.; m. Denelda Halter, May 14, 1942; 1 son, Darrel Floyd. With Paulding (O.) Consumers, 1939-40; with Paulding County Farm Bur., 1940—, petroleum mgr., 1965—. Mem. Blue Creek Local Sch. Bd., Haviland, O., 1960-71. Councilman, Scott Village, Ohio, 1950-51, 72-73, treas., 1952-59, mayor, 1973—. Mem. Pentecostal Ch. of God (mem. bd. trustees 1940—). Home: PO Box 5 Scott OH 45886 Office: Wall and Walnut Sts Paulding OH 45879

RHOADES, THOMAS PERRY, III, automotive co. exec.; b. Indpls., Jan. 16, 1941; s. Thomas Perry and Frances Elizabeth (Kirkpatrick) R.; student U. Va., 1959-62; B.A., Northland Coll., Ashland, Wis., 1964; m. Myra Gertrude Aichholz, Jan. 24, 1970; children—Melinda Ann, Thomas Perry. Reporter Daily Item, Port Chester, N.Y., 1964-65; reporter Kansas City Star, 1965-66, copy editor, 1967-69; pub. relations specialist Ford Motor Co., N.Y.C., 1969-70, Ford div., Dearborn, Mich., 1970-74, Lincoln-Mercury div., Dearborn, 1974-76, asst. pub. relations mgr. Ford Parts and Service div., Livonia, Mich., 1976—. Served with U.S. Army, 1965-67. Mem. Pub. Relations Soc. Am., Internat. Motor Press Assn., Northland Coll. Alumni Assn. (past bd. dirs.). Episcopalian. Club: Detroit Press. Home: 588 Lincoln Rd Grosse Pointe MI 48230 Office: 29500 Plymouth Rd Livonia MI 48151

RHODES, ARTHUR EDWARD, utility exec.; b. Seymour, Mo., Sept. 19, 1925; s. Washington Hope and Lillie Mae (Cawthra) R.; student pub. schs.; m. Nadine Ruth Fauscett, Dec. 23, 1966. Pressman, Mountain Grove (Mo.) Jour., 1946-50; shop foreman Mansfield (Mo.) Mirror newspaper, 1950-56; editor Sho-Me Live Wire, Marshfield, Mo., 1956-60; with G & T Sho-Me Power Corp., Marshfield, 1960—, dir. pub. relations, 1966-73, dir. personnel and pub. relations, 1974-75, mgr. dept. personnel and pub. relations, 1975—. Chmn., Mo. Ozarks Mem. Services Group, 1974—. Pres., Webster County Fair Bd., 1968-69; chmn. publicity Webster County Red Cross, 1963-65; v.p. Ozark Area Community Action Corp., 1968-72. Chmn. Webster County Republican Com., 1972-73. Chmn. bd. dirs. Webster County OEO, 1966-72. Served with C.E., AUS, 1943-46: ETO. Recipient 1st place award photography Nat. Rural Electrification Coop. Assn., 1964. Mem. Springfield Personnel Assn., Am. Legion. Mem. Christian Ch. (elder). Rotarian. Club: Marshfield. Home: 706 NW Hubble Dr Marshfield MO 65706 Office: 301 W Jackson St Marshfield MO 65706

RHODES, DONALD ELLSWORTH, lawyer, ins. co. exec.; b. New Castle, Pa., Oct. 21, 1915; s. Oscar E. and Alice R. (Heasley) R.; A.B., Grove City Coll., 1937; LL.B., U. Mich., 1948; postgrad. in ins. mgmt. U. Wis.-Madison, 1965-66; m. Emily Swanson, June 15, 1940; children—Susan (Mrs. James Stefanski), Jeffrey E. Draftsman Bell Telephone Co. of Pa., New Castle, 1937-38; draftsman Pa. Dept. Hwys., New Castle, 1938-39; mgr. Retail Credit Co., Johnstown and Beaver, Pa., 1939-41; supr. drafting Curtiss-Wright Corp., Beaver, also Caldwell, N.J., 1941-46; admitted to Mich. bar, 1948; v.p., gen. counsel, sec. Citizens Mut. Ins. Co. (name later changed to Citizens Ins. Co. of Am.), Howell, Mich., 1948—; v.p., gen. counsel, sec. Beacon Mut. Indemnity Co., Columbus, Ohio, Am. Select Risk Ins. Co., Columbus. Chmn. Mich. Auto No Fault Legal Com., 1972-73. Chmn. Howell Citizens Adv. Com. on Schs., 1956-58; co-chmn. Howell Area United Fund, 1969. Bd. dirs. Lansing (Mich.) Mental Health Clinic, 1956-61, pres., 1959-60; trustee Child and Family Services of Mich. Inc. Mem. State Bar of Mich. (chmn. com. ins. law 1958-59), Am. Bar Assn., Fedn. Ins. Counsel (v.p. 1961), Ins. Fedn. Ohio (mem. legis. com., exec. com.), Mich. Ins. Lawyers Council (pres. 1960), Mich. Ins. Info. Service (gov. 1967-71), Mich. Assn. Mut. Ins. Cos. (pres. 1969-70), Mich. Assn. Ins. Cos. (chmn. legis. com., 1971—), Howell Area C. of C. (pres. 1964), Highlander Athletic Boosters (pres. 1969-70), Pi Gamma Mu, Nu Lambda Phi. Presbyterian (elder 1969). Mason (Shriner, K.T.), Elk; mem. Order of Eastern Star. Home: 1444 Crest Rd Howell MI 48843 Office: 645 W Grand River Ave Howell MI 48843

RHODES, IRWIN SEYMOUR, lawyer; b. Cin., Nov. 21, 1901; s. Solomon and Lina (Silberberg) R.; B.A., U. Cin., 1921; LL.B., Harvard, 1924; M.A., Xavier U., 1962; m. Mary Elizabeth Frechtling, Dec. 12, 1941; children—Elana Susan, Irwin Lawrence. Admitted to Ill. bar, 1924, Ohio bar, 1925; pvt. practice Chgo., 1924-29, Cin., 1929—; editor Pub. Utilities and Carrier Service, 1926-29; contbg. editor Ohio Jurisprudence, 1933-35; chmn. com. for Preservation John Marshall Papers, 1953, mem. editorial bd., 1953-59, chmn. spl. com., 1957-59; co-dir. Irwin S. and Elizabeth F. Rhodes Legal History Collection, U. Okla.; past chmn. John Marshall Papers Project, Am. Bar Found. Mem. Cin. (chmn. com. for preservation legal hist. documents 1961), Fed. (com. law compliance) bar assns. Acad. Univ. Fellows U. Okla., Phi Beta Kappa (hon.) Clubs: Harvard, Harvard Business School, Cincinnati, Bankers; Cosmos (Washington). Author articles in field. Author-editor: The Papers of John Marshall, a Descriptive Ave The Papers of Roger Brooke Taney. Home: 3815 Erie Ave Cincinnati OH 45208 also 2122 Massachusetts Ave NW Washington DC 20008

RHODES, LESTER LEGERE, soybean assn. ofcl.; b. Spencer, Iowa, Feb. 19, 1919; s. William H. and Ethel M. (Legere) R.; B.S. in Dairy Industry and Econs., Iowa State U., 1942; m. Luetta Christine Norland, Dec. 9, 1949; children—Christine (Mrs. G.D. Knoll), Leslee (Mrs. John Madison), Rebecca. Quality fieldman Palo Alto Dairy Products Improvement Assn., Emmetsburg, Iowa, 1946-48; fieldman Farm Bur., Palo Alto County, 1948-51, farm bur. Marion and Kossuth counties, Iowa, 1953-54; farmer Clay County, Iowa, 1951-53; regional supr. Iowa Farm Bur. Fedn., northeast Iowa counties, 1954-58; asst. dir. of field service Iowa Farm Bur., Des Moines, 1958-63; dir. pub. relations Am. Dairy Assn. of Iowa, Des Moines, 1963-71, dir. field service, 1971-73; mgr. Iowa State Dairy Assn., Des Moines, 1972-75; mgr. no. markets Midland United Dairy Industry Assn. Ankeny, Ia., 1972-75; mgr. Iowa Dairy Industries Commn., 1972-75; field service rep. Am. Soybean Assn., Hudson, Iowa, 1975—; also exec. dir. Iowa Soybean Promotion Bd., 1975—, owner, mgr. Laminating Co. Iowa, Grimes. Mem. rev. bd. Farm Home Adminstrn., Onkeny, Iowa, 1973-76. Served with USNR, 1942-59; aviator Iowa NG, 1959—. PTO. Decorated D.F.C., Air medal with three gold stars. Mem. Am., Iowa socs. of assn. execs., Central Iowa Dairy Tech. Soc. (pres. 1968-69), Des Moines, Ankeny (chmn. airport com. 1972-75) chambers commerce, Am. Legion. Lutheran (mem. resolutions com. 1973, youth com. 1961-63, fellowship com. 1967-70). Lion (dir. 1971-75, pres. 1977). Home: 7832 NW 114th St Grimes IA 50111 Office: 1200 35th St West Des Moines IA 50265

RHODES, MARY ELIZABETH FRECHTLING, writer, editor; b. Madison, Ind., May 3, 1911; d. George William and Laura (Lory) Frechtling; student, Butler U., 1928-30; student Herron Art Sch., 1925-30; m. Irwin S. Rhodes, Dec. 12, 1941; children—Elana Susan, Irwin Lawrence. With Marx-Flarsheim Advt. Co., Cin., 1930-32; exec. sec. Perfect Mfg. Co., Cin., 1932-36; sales promotion, real estate mgmt. Am. Service Assos., Cin., 1936-40. Chmn. Cin. Fine Arts Dr., 1947-59, Cin. Summer Opera Womens Com., 1966-67; mem. adv. bd. Air Pollution Control League, 1958-62; adv. com. Cin. Juvenile Ct., 1960—; mem. exec. com. Am. Cancer Soc. Balls, 1966—; chmn., v.p. Women's Com. Cin. Symphony Orch., 1959-64; sponsor Irwin S. and Elizabeth F. Rhodes Legal History Collection, U. Okla. Mem. Soc. Ind. Pioneers, Cin., Ky., Lancaster County (Pa.) hist. socs., Md. Hist. Soc., Hon. Order Ky. Cols., Ky. Soc. Washington, Smithsonian Instn., D.A.R. (editor nat. mag. Children Am. Revolution 1966-67). Clubs: Woman's Nat. Dem., Nat. Press (Washington). Asst. editor The Papers of John Marshall, 1969, The Papers of Roger Brooke Taney. Home: 3815 Erie Ave Cincinnati OH 45208 also 2122 Massachusetts Ave Washington DC 20008

RHODES, PAUL EARL, plastics co. ofcl.; b. Akron, Ohio, Mar. 15, 1947; s. Louis Earl and Evelyn Margaret (Meyers) R.; B.S. in Chem. Engring., Purdue U., 1969; m. Phyllis Ann Jeffrey, June 8, 1969; children—Jeffrey Paul, Scott Louis. Chief process engr. Rostone Corp., Lafayette, Ind., 1967-71; mgr. engring. Haysite Div. Synthane Taylor Corp., Erie, Pa., 1971-75; mktg. mgr., Premix Inc., N. Kingsville, Ohio, 1975—. Mem. Soc. Plastic Engrs., Am. Chem. Soc., Am. Inst. Chem. Engrs. Methodist. Home: 4641 Dorchester Dr Erie PA 16509 Office: Box 281 Route 20 and Harmon Rd North Kingsville OH 44068

RHOTEN, OGLE ELDRIC, civil engr.; b. Bluejacket, Okla., May 6, 1919; s. Daniel Franklin and Nellie Elzina (Essary) R.; Certificate in Engring., Coffeyville Jr. Coll., 1941; student Wichita State U., 1945-46; m. Lucille Huffman, Dec. 18, 1944; children—Rodney Ogle, Deborah Ann (Mrs. Kirk Hamersky), Rickey Franklin. Instr., Engr. Sch., U.S. Army C.E., Ft. Belvoir, Va., 1944-45; instrument man, party chief Sedgwick County (Kans.) Engrs. Office, Wichita, 1946; engring. aide Kan. Hwy. Commn. (name changed to Kans. Dept. Transp. 1975), Wichita, 1947-53, civil engr. I, 1953-57, civil engr. II, resident engr., 1958—. Instr. Wichita Bus. Coll., 1971. Plotting officer Control Center Civil Def., Wichita, 1953—; committeeman, asst. adviser to Explorers, Boy Scouts Am., Wichita, 1953-54, asst. cub master Cub Scouts, 1955-56, chmn. pack com., 1956-58; v.p. North Pleasant Valley PTA, Wichita, 1964-65, pres., 1965-66. Served with C.E., AUS, 1941-45; Aleutian Islands. Registered profl. engr., Kans. Mem. Nat. Soc. Profl. Engrs., Kans. Engring. Soc. (speakers' bur. 1962—, chmn. membership 1964-66), Wichita Profl. Engring. Soc. (pres. 1972-73). Methodist. Mason (Shriner, 32 deg.). Home: 4018 N Charles St Wichita KS 67204 Office: 4448 W Kellogg St Wichita KS 67209

RHYKERD, CHARLES LOREN, educator; b. Cameron, Ill., Apr. 7, 1929; s. James Augustus and Blanche Adela (Olson) R.; B.S., U. Ill., 1951, M.S., 1952; postgrad. Ohio State U., 1954-55; Ph.D., Purdue U., 1957; m. Jessie Eileen McIlrath, June 19, 1954; children—Charles Loren, Robert Lee, Linda Marie. Technician, DeKalb Agrl. Assn., Tuscola, Ill., 1952; technician, asst. plant breeder Producers Seed Co., Piper City, Ill., 1953-54; instr. Ohio State U., 1954-55; instr. Purdue U., West Lafayette, Ind., 1955-57, prof. agronomy, 1960—; soil scientist U.S. Dept. Agr. Regional Pasture Lab., State College, Pa., 1957-60. Cons., IRI Research Inst., Brazil, 1965; vis. prof. U. Calif., Davis, 1967-68; co-dir. nat. corn and sorghum project in Brazil, AID contract with Brazilian Ministry Agr. and Purdue U., 1973-75. Fellow Am. Soc. Agronomy; mem. Crop Sci. Soc. Am., Internat. Soil Sci. Soc., Am. Forage and Grassland Council, Ind. Acad. Sci., Farmhouse, Sigma Xi, Gamma Sigma Delta, Alpha Zeta. Lion. Author: Forage Technology, 1970; asso. editor Forage Fertilization, 1974. Home: 164 Blueberry Ln West Lafayette IN 47906

RIBORDY, DENIS EUGENE, drug co. exec.; b. East Chicago, Ind., July 20, 1929; s. Myrel I. and Lela (Hunsley) R.; B.S. in Pharmacy, Butler U., 1952; m. Carolyn Ann McClurg, June 20, 1954; children—Cheryl, Scott, Nancy, Mark. Partner Hill Drug Co., Augusta, Ga., 1954; pres. Ribordy's Pharmacy, Gary, Ind., 1955; founder, pres. Ribordy Drugs Inc., retail chain, Highland, Ind., 1955—; dir. Gary Nat. Bank, Affiliated Drug Stores, N.Y.C. Pres. Gary Downtown Council, 1962, Ogden Dunes (Ind.) Home Owners Assn., 1972. Pres. Town Bd. trustees Town of Ogden Dunes, 1974—. Bd. dirs. N.W. Ind. Better Bus. Bur., 1959—, v.p., 1969—; adv. bd. Butler U. Coll. Pharmacy, 1964—; pres. bd. trustees Methodist Hosp., Gary, 1974—; chmn. Highland ARC, 1975-76. Served with AUS, 1952-54. Mem. Lake County (pres. 1957-58), Ind., Am. pharm. assns., Nat. Assn. Retail Druggists, Nat. Assn. Chain Drug Stores, Gary U. Club (pres. 1972), Ind. Soc. Chgo. Methodist (pres. bd. trustees). Mason (Jester, Shriner). Club: Gary Country. Home: 530 40 Diana Rd Ogden Dunes IN 46368 Office: Ribordy Drugs Inc 9626 Cline Ave Highland IN 46322

RICCARDO, EDWARD PETER, educator; b. St. Louis, Dec. 15, 1943; s. Nicholas John and Eileen (Fenlen) R.; B.A., Old Dominion U., 1966; M.A., Northwestern U., 1967, postgrad., 1967-70; m. Margaret Mulroy, Dec. 28, 1968 (div.); children—Patricia Eileen, Catherine Ann. Instr. philosophy Triton Coll., River Grove, Ill., 1969—; exec. dir. Am. Humanistic Philosophy Assn.; dir. Hegire Corp. Bd. dirs. Ill. Center Psychol. Research. Woodrow Wilson fellow, 1966-67; Northwestern U. fellow, 1967-68. Mem. Am., Ill. philos. assns., Humanistic Psychology Assn., Ill. Inst. Diving, Chgo. Mountaineering Club, NOW, Delta Phi Omega, Phi Alpha Theta, Sigma Beta Tau. Contbr. to Poetry, Nat. Poetry Press, 1965, Intercollegiate Poetry Congress, 1965; editor: Introduction to Humanistic Philosophy, 1975. Home: 5451 N East River Rd Chicago IL 60656 Office: Triton College 2000 5th Ave River Grove IL 60171

RICCARDO, JOHN JOSEPH, automotive co. exec.; b. Little Falls, N.Y., July 2, 1924; s. Peter and Mary (Cirillo) R.; student N.Y. Coll. for Tchrs., 1942; B.A., U. Mich., 1949, M.A., 1950; LL.B. (hon.), No. Mich. U., 1971; Sc.D., Lawrence Inst. Tech., 1972; m. Thelma L. Fife, Aug. 5, 1950; children—Mary Catherine, Teresa Anna, Margaret Lynn, Peter Douglas, John Christopher. Mgr., Touche, Ross, Bailey & Smart, Detroit, 1950-59; financial staff exec. internat. ops. Chrysler Corp., Highland Park, Mich., 1959-60, gen. mgr. Export-Import div., 1960-61, v.p., ops. mgr. Chrysler Can., 1961-62, exec. v.p. Chrysler Can., 1962-63, gen. sales mgr. Dodge div., 1963-64, asst. gen. mgr. Dodge div., 1964-65, asst. gen. mgr. Chrysler-Plymouth div., 1965-66, v.p. mktg., 1966, group v.p. domestic automotive, 1967, group v.p. U.S. and Can. automotive, 1967-70, pres., 1970—, dir., 1967—, chmn., chief exec. officer, 1975—. Mem. Nat. Bus. Council for Consumer Affairs; mem. automotive sub-council Nat. Indsl. Pollution Control Council. Lay chmn. Archdiocesan Devel. Fund, Detroit, 1968; gen. chmn. Meadowbrook Music Festival and Theater, Rochester, Mich., 1971; v.p., mem. exec. com. United Found., Detroit. Bd. dirs., mem. devel. council U. Mich. Served with AUS, 1943-45; CBI. C.P.A., Mich. Mem. Am. Inst. C.P.A.'s, Mich. Assn. C.P.A.'s, Motor Vehicle Mfrs. Assn. (vice chmn.), Sales and Mktg. execs., Hwy. Users Fedn. (dir.), Phi Beta Kappa. Clubs: Bloomfield Hills Country; Detroit Athletic (pres. 1975), Detroit. Home: 2243 Tottenham St Birmingham MI 48009 Office: Chrysler Corp 12000 Lynn Townsend Dr Highland Park MI 48231

RICE, ARTHUR RAYMOND, computer service mgr.; b. Lexington, Va., Oct. 27, 1940; s. Raymond Guy and Frances Allene (Spangler) R.; student Ind. U. NW; m. Diana Charmaine Sage, June 5, 1971; children—Alicia Rene, Anthony Rea, Dianna Michele; adopted stepchildren—Lisa Marie, Mark Timothy. With industry control dept. Gen. Electric Co., Salem, Va., 1964-66, with process computer dept. Phoenix, Ariz., 1966-68, with installation and service engring., div. Chgo., 1968—, service supr. digital processors, 1975-77, mgr. machine tool/computers St. Louis/Mpls. unit, 1978—. Served with USAF, 1959-64. Republican. Baptist. Home: 3320 W 73d Pl Merrillville IN 46401 Office: 2015 Spring Rd Oak Brook IL 60521

RICE, CHARLES WAYNE, assn. exec.; b. Oklahoma City, Nov. 9, 1941; s. Charles Wesly and Cecil Loraine (Plymate) R.; student U. Tulsa, 1961; B.S., Bethany Nazarene Coll., 1964; M.Hosp. Adminstrn., U. Minn., 1966; m. Gwynneth Kay Taylor, Aug. 28, 1964; children—Julie Ann-Marie, Lauri Lynn. Adminstrv. resident Eitel Hosp., Mpls., 1965-66; asst. exec. dir. Greater Cleve. Hosp. Assn., 1966, exec. dir., 1967-72, pres., 1973—. Mem. hosp. lay adv. panel to Am. Hosp. Assn. Bd. Trustees, 1975-76; mem. nat. adv. panel State and Met. Hosp. Assn., 1974-77; treas. Am. Hosp. Assn. Metro. Execs. Conf.; cons. Wis. Regional Med. Program, 1974; mem. health adv. com. Ohio State Dir. Health, 1972-74; sec. hosp. adv. com. Blue Cross N.E. Ohio, 1966—. Mem. lay adv. bd. to pres. Mt. Vernon Nazarene Coll., 1974. Bd. dirs. Greater Cleve. Growth Assn., Regional Council on Alcoholism. Named One of Year's Outstanding Alumni, Bethany Nazarene Coll., 1969, 75. Mem. Am. Hosp. Assn. (com. on health care for disadvantaged 1974—, chmn. subcom. edn. 1976-77), Am. Coll. Hosp. Adminstrs., Am. Soc. Adminstrv. Execs., Ohio Hosp. Assn. Rotarian. Clubs: Cleveland Athletic, Citizens League, City, Mid-Day (Cleve.). Home: 11700 Parkview Rd Brecksville OH 44141 Office: 1021 Euclid Ave Cleveland OH 44115

RICE, DAVID LEE, univ. pres.; b. New Mrket, Ind., Apr. 1, 1929; s. Elmer J. and Katie (Tate) R.; B.S., Purdue U., 1951, M.S., 1956, Ph.D., 1958; m. Betty Jane Fordice, Sept. 10, 1950; children—Patricia Denise Rice Dawson, Michael Alan. Dir. research, educator Ball State U., Muncie, Ind., 1961-66; v.p. Coop. Ednl. Research Lab., Inc., Indpls., 1965-67, also research coordinator, bur. research HEW, Washington; dean campus Ind. State U., Evansville, 1967-71, pres. campus, 1971—; adminstrv. asst. Gov.'s Com. on Post High Sch. Orgn. Mem. State Citizens Adv. Bd. Title XX Social Security Act; bd. dirs. Ind. Forum; bd. commrs. Evansville Housing Authority; mem. South Ind. Conf. Div. Church Relted Colls.; chmn. Mayors Riverboat Com.; treas. Leadership Evansville, 1976-77; v.p. S.W. Ind. Pub. TV, 1972—; mem. Buffalo Trace council Boy Scouts Am., 1968—. Served with inf. AUS, 1951-53. Decorated Combat Infantryman's Badge; recipient Service to Others award Salvation Army, 1972, Citizen of Year award Westside Civitan Club, 1972, Boss of Year award Am. Bus. Womens Assn., 1976. Mem. Am. Assn. Higher Edn., Am. Ednl. Research Assn., Nat. Soc. Study Edn., Alpha Kappa Psi, Alpha Zeta, Phi Delta Kappa. Methodist. Clubs: Petroleum, Rotary. Contbr. articles to profl. jours. Home: 611 Mels Dr Evansville IN 47712 Office: 8600 University Blvd Evansville IN 47712

RICE, DONALD LEE, wholesale grocery exec.; b. Danville, Ill., Sept. 12, 1926; s. James Thomas and Margaret Louise (Paxton) R.; B.A. with honors, Wabash Coll., 1950; student Hampshire U., 1948, DePaul U., 1947; m. Nancy June Hamblin, Dec. 2, 1951; children—Nanette Lee, James Michael. Clk., asst. mgr., mgr. Grab It Here Stores, 1950-55; office accounting, advt. ins. The Paxton Wholesale Grocery Co., Danville, Ill., 1958-68, dir. adminstrn., 1969-71, advt. mgr., retail buyer, 1970—, dir., 1950—; dir. Mann's Service Bur., Danville, Ill. Mem. disaster com. ARC, Danville, Ill., 1951—. Served with AUS, 1943-45. Decorated Bronze Star medal with oak cluster; presdl. citation. Mem. Men's Golf Assn. (pres. 1962-63, sec. 1960-62), Lambda Chi Alpha (sec., social chmn. 1946-47). Mason (33 deg.), Elk. Clubs: Danville Country (pres. 1964-66), Boat. Home: 1115 Lake Ridge Rd Danville IL 61832 Office: 815 N Oak St Danville IL 61832

RICE, PAUL FREDERICK, structural engr.; b. Mandan, N.D., Dec. 8, 1921; s. Paul Frederick and Claire Olive (Des Jardins) R.; B.S., N.D. State Coll., 1941; postgrad. Ill. Inst. Tech., 1942; M.S., Mass. Inst. Tech., 1947; postgrad. U. Mich., 1953-57; m. Joan Carol Cannon, June 22, 1946; children—Paul Frederick, Clair Patrick, John Cassius, Richard Clay. Structural design engr. Cunningham-Limp Co., Detroit, 1947-49; structural field engr. Mich., Portland Cement Assn., Chgo., 1949-54; tech. dir. Am. Concrete Inst., Detroit, 1954-58; v.p. engring. Concrete Reinforcing Steel Inst., Chgo., 1958—. Chmn., Concrete Improvement Bd., Detroit, 1955-56; vice chmn. Reinforced Concrete Research Council, ASCE, 1974-76. Served with C.E., AUS, 1942-46; ETO. Registered profl. engr., Mich.; registered structural engr., Ill. Mem. ASCE, Am. Concrete Inst., Am. Welding Soc., ASTM, Structural Engs. Assn. Ill., Reinforced Concrete Research Council Clubs: Engrings. Soc. Detroit, Chgo. Engrs., N.Y. Engrs., Rotary, Masons. Editor, author: Concrete Reinforcing Steel Institute (CRSI) Handbook, 1968, 71, 75; Co-author: Structural Design Guide to ACI Building Code, Structural Design Guide to AISI Specifications. Home: 2033 Sherman Ave Evanston IL 60201 Office: 180 N LaSalle St Chicago IL 60601

RICE, PONY RALPH, chem. engr.; b. Louisville, May 24, 1944; s. Pony Ralph and Mary Agnes (Robertaccio) R.; B.S. in Chem. Engring., U. Louisville, 1967, M.S. in Chem. Engring., 1975; m. Sandra Lee Willis, Dec. 17, 1966; 1 dau., Kristin Lauren. Mem. staff tech. and prodn. supervision Am. Can Co., Carrollton, Ky., 1972-76, mgr. chem. plant, Rothschild, Wis., 1976—. Served to capt. USAF, 1968-72. Decorated Commendation medal. Mem. Am. Inst. Chem. Engrs. Roman Catholic. Home: 2354 Rainbow Dr Mosinee WI 54455 Office: Am Can Co US Business 51 Rothschild WI 54474

RICE, WILFRED FRANCIS, JR., lawyer; b. Dayton, Ohio, May 25, 1932; s. Wilfred Francis and Elisabeth (Flanagan) R.; B.S. magna cum laude, U. Notre Dame; J.D., Georgetown U., 1958; m. Rita Jean Cerenzia, Apr. 28, 1956; children—Paula Jean, Mary Catherine. Admitted to Ill. bar, 1959; with firm Seyfarth, Shaw, Fairweather & Geraldson, 1958—, partner, 1965—, Chgo. Served with USAF, 1954-56. Mem. Am., Ill., Chgo. bar assns., Delta Theta Phi. Clubs: Chicago, Saddle and Cycle, Chicago Athletic, Long Beach Country. Home: 2142 Farwell Ave Chicago IL 60645 also Grand Beach MI Office: 55 E Monroe St Suite 4200 Chicago IL 60603

RICH, DONALD JOSEPH, sales, mktg. exec.; b. Apr. 2, 1933; s. Edwin Peter and Lucy Mary (Casey) R.; student pub. schs., Washington; m. Marjorie Belle Statler, June 17, 1952; children—Gwen, Jolisa, Scott, Sonja, Donja. Salesman, Yoder, Inc., Kalona, Iowa, 1957-62, dist. sales mgr., 1963-69, sales mgr., 1969-73, v.p. sales and mktg., 1973—. Leader Boy Scouts Am.; mem. parish council; mem. sch. bd. Mem. Am. Feed Mfrs. Assn., Am. Mgmt. Assn. (exec. com. mktg. council 1971-73), Iowa Feed & Grain, United Egg Producers, Iowa Turkey Fedn., Washington County Pork Producers. Democrat. Roman Catholic. Clubs: Eagles (pres.), K.C., Elks. Home: Rural Route 1 Washington IA 52353 Office: Rural Route 2 Kalona IA 52237

RICH, MARVIN LEWIS, lawyer; b. Kansas City, Mo., Nov. 21, 1933; s. Isadore and Ethel (Levy) R.; B.S., U. Mo., 1956; LL.B., Harvard, 1959; m. Patricia C. Uhlmann, Aug. 31, 1963; children—Alison, Meridith. Admitted to Mo. bar, 1959, Fed. bar, 1960; mem. firm Rich, Granoff & Levy, and predecessor firms, Kansas City, Mo., 1959—, partner, 1962—; dir. H & R Block, Inc. Mem. Mo., Kansas City, Am. bar assns. Jewish. Home: 6320 Verona Rd Mission Hills KS 66208 Office: 900 Walnut St Kansas City MO 64106

RICHARD, JACK, artist; b. Akron, Mar. 7, 1922; s. John Peter and Maude Anna (Williams) R.; student Chgo. Profl. Sch. Art, 1940-42, Kent State U., 1953-54, Akron U., 1947-48, U. Ohio, 1958-58. One-man shows: Canton (Ohio) Art Inst., Ambassador Coll. Gallery, Pasadena, Calif., 1969, Cuyahoga Valley Art Sch., French Colony Gallery, Gallopolis, Ohio, 1975; exhibited in group shows; represented in permanent collection: Canton Art Inst., Taylor Meml., Albany, Ohio; executed portraits Pres. and Mamie Eisenhower, also murals; dir. Cuyahoga Valley Art Center, 1952-62, Almond Tea Galleries, Cuyahoga Falls, 1962—; conservator, lectr. Served with AUS, 1942-45. Huntington Hartford Internat. fellow. Mem. Fifty Am. Artists, Internat. Platform Assn. Home and studio: 2250 Front St Cuyahoga Falls OH 44221

RICHARDS, EARL FREDERICK, elec. engr.; b. Detroit, Mar. 11, 1923; s. Earl F. and Esther Stancer (Branning) R.; B.S. in E.E., Wayne U., 1951; M.S. in E.E., Mo. Sch. Mines and Metallurgy, 1961; Ph.D. in E.E., U. Mo., 1971; m. Marjorie P. Holt, Jan. 12, 1946; children—Dennis Lee, Laura Lee. Project engr. Pa. Salt Mfg. Co., Wyandotte, Mich., 1952-53; elec. engr. Revere Copper & Brass, Inc., Detroit, 1954-58; plant engr., elec. engring. U. Mo., Rolla, 1958—; tchr. U. Detroit, 1956-58; research asso. Argonne (Ill.) Nat. Lab., 1963; cons. Firestone Rubber Corp., 1954-56, Electronic Control Corp., Detroit, 1950-51. Served with OSS, 1942-46. Registered profl. engr. Mo., Mich. Mem. Sigma Xi, Tau Beta Pi, Eta Kappa Nu, Theta Xi. Roman Catholic. Club: Lions. Home: 8 Hyer Ct Rolla MO 65401 Office: U Mo Rolla MO 65401

RICHARDS, FRANCIS LEE, physician; b. Ashland, Nebr., Feb. 19, 1908; s. Earl Webster and Ida Belle (Wortman) R.; A.B., Doane Coll., 1932; M.D., U. Nebr., 1938; m. Dorothy Waters Hamilton, Jan. 29, 1938; 1 son, Donald Lee. Intern, University Hosp., Omaha, 1938-39; practice medicine specializing in eye, ear, nose and throat, Kearney, Nebr., 1946—; mem. staff Good Samaritan Hosp., Kearney, chief of staff, 1953-54; pres. Valley Plaze Corp., 1967—; charter dir. Kearney State Bank. Mem. Kearney City Council, 1961-63; mayor, Kearney, 1963—; mem. So. Route Commn., 1976—. Served with AUS, 1941-46. Recipient distinguished service award Cosmopolitan Internat., 1967. Mem. AMA, Nebr. Acad. Ear, Nose Throat, Kearney C. of C. (dir. 1956-57). Republican. Presbyn. (deacon 1953-54, trustee 1949-50). Mason, Elk. Club: Cosmopolitan (pres. 1955). Home: 3206 1st Av Kearney NE 68847 Office: 214 W 25th St Kearney NE 68847

RICHARDS, GRAYDON EDWARD, agronomist; b. Lockney, W.Va., July 2, 1933; s. Graydon Mack and Thelma Leah (Yoak) R.; A.A., Potomac State Coll., 1953; B.S., W.Va. U., 1955; M.Sc., Ohio State U., 1959, Ph.D., 1961; m. Patricia Ann Royster, July 28, 1956; children—Kent Stuart, Craig Steven. Tchr. vocat. agr. high sch., Troy, W.Va., 1955-57; research agronomist Internat. Mineral & Chem. Corp., Skokie and Libertyville, Ill., 1961-67; sr. research scientist, project leader Continental Oil Co., Ponca City, Okla., 1967-70; regional agronomist Olin Corp., Oak Brook, Ill., 1970-73, St. Louis, 1973—. Coach, Little League and Khoury League Baseball, 1972—. Mem. Am. Chem. Soc., AAAS, Am. Soc. Agronomy (Journalism award 1976), Soil Sci. Soc. Am. (chmn. fertilizer tech. and usage div. 1977, com. tng. soil scientists 1977-78, bd. dirs. 1978), Ponca City C. of C., Sigma Xi, Phi Lambda Upsilon, Gamma Sigma Delta, Alpha Zeta, Alpha Tau Alpha. Republican. Methodist. Home: 5 Newfield Ct Ballwin MO 63011 Office: 1177 N Warson Rd Saint Louis MO 63132

RICHARDS, JANE GRILLS, ednl. adminstr.; b. Flint, Mich., Oct. 7, 1919; d. James William and Edna Allen (Beebe) Grills; B.A., U. Mich., 1941, M.A., 1943; Ph.D., Mich. State U., 1959; postgrad. Northwestern U., 1949-50; m. Bertrand F. Richards, July 20, 1966. Instr., Sullins Coll., Bristol, Va., 1943-44; asst. prof. Alma (Mich.) Coll., 1944-45; asso. prof. radio, TV and film U. N.C., Chapel Hill, 1945-49; womens programming and edn. officer, civil info. and edn., radio br., Supreme Comdr. Allied Power, Tokyo, 1950-51; tchr. high sch., Saginaw, Mich., 1953-55; publicity and pub. relations asst. Peet Packing Co., Grand Rapids, Mich., 1955-59; area coordinator Midwest program on airborne TV instrn., prof. speech Ind. State U., Terre Haute, 1962-72; exec. dir. Ind. Higher Edn. Telecommunication System, Indpls., 1972—. Mem. Nat. Assn. Ednl. Broadcasters, NEA, Speech Communication Assn., Central States Speech Assn., Assn. Profl. Broadcast Edn., Assn. Ednl. Communications Technology, Internat. Inst. Communications, Joint Council Ednl. Telecommunications (dir.), Pub. Service Satellite Consortium (vice chmn., dir.), Indpls. Press Club, Sigma Delta Chi. Presbyn. Club: Country of Terre Haute. Contbr. articles to ednl. periodicals. Home: 25 E 40th St Apt 6U Indianapolis IN 46205 Office: 1100 Michigan St W Indianapolis IN 46202

RICHARDS, JONATHAN BARLOW, lawyer; b. Red Oak, Iowa, Feb. 14, 1913; s. Paul William and Stella Erie (Powell) R.; A.B. magna cum laude, Harvard U., 1934, J.D., 1937; m. Elizabeth Miller, Oct. 1, 1935; children—Jonathan Barlow, Kathleen, Victoria Kimball (dec.), Charles Emery. Admitted to Iowa bar, 1937; staff atty. Home Owners Loan Corp., Washington, 1937-40; asso. gen. counsel OPA, Atlanta, 1942-44, Washington, 1944-46; practiced in Red Oak, 1946—. Mem. Iowa Bd. Law Examiners, 1962-64; mem. Iowa Bd. Regents, 1964-69. Mem. Phi Beta Kappa. Democrat. Clubs: Classic Car Am.; Nat. Horseless Carriage; Antique Car, Classic Jaguar, New Eng. MG Register, Elks. Home: 1112 Boundary St Red Oak IA 51566 Office: 204 Reed St Red Oak IA 51566

RICHARDS, LACLAIRE LISSETTA JONES (MRS. GEORGE A. RICHARDS), social worker; b. Pine Bluff, Ark.; d. Artie William and Geraldine (Adams) Jones; B.A., Nat. Coll. Christian Workers, 1953; M.S.W., U. Kans., 1956; postgrad. Columbia U., 1960; m. George Alvarez Richards, July 26, 1958; children—Leslie Rosario, Lia Mercedes. Psychiat. supervisory, teaching, adminstrv. and consultative duties Hastings State Hosp., Ingleside, Nebr., 1956-60; supervisory, consultative and adminstrv. responsibilities for psychiat. and geriatric patients VA Hosp., Knoxville, Iowa, 1960-70, 71-74, Fed. women's program coordinator, 1973-74, equal employment counselor, 1971-74; chief social worker, adult female service Mental Health Inst., Cherokee, Iowa, 1974-77; outpatient social worker VA Center, Sioux Falls, S.D., 1978—; field instr. for grad. students from U. Mo., 1966-67, also equal employment opportunity counselor, 1969-70, 71-74, com. chmn., 1969-70; field instr. Drake U., 1969-70, 73, also U. Iowa, U. No. Iowa, Morningside Coll., Buena Vista Coll., Westmar Coll.; mem. civil rights com. Mental Health Inst. Mem. Knoxville Juvenile Adv. Com., 1963-65, 68-70, sec., 1965-66, chmn., 1966-68; sec. Urban Renewal Citizens' Adv. Com., Knoxville, 1966-68; canvasser community fund drives, Knoxville; mem. Conf. Bd. Edn. United Meth. Ch., also worship commn., music com. St. Paul's United Meth. Ch. Fellow Royal Soc. Health; mem. Nat. Assn. Social Workers (co-chmn. Neb. chpt. profl. standards com. 1958-59), Acad. Certified Social Workers, Neb. Assn. Social Workers (chmn. 1958-59), AAUW (sec. Hastings chpt. 1958-60). United Methodist (past Sunday sch. tchr. adult div.; mem. commn. on edn. and missions 1968-74, chmn. health and welfare commn. 1973-74, mem. task force experimental styles ministry and leadership). Methodist (mem. worship com.). Home: 1701 Ponderosa Dr Sioux Falls SD 57103

RICHARDS, MAURICE LYMAN, JR., assn. exec.; b. Ferndale, Mich., Jan. 14, 1928; s. Maurice Lyman and Tressa Olive (Fox) R.; student U. Mich., 1946-48; B.B.A., U. Tulsa, 1952. Owner, Stewart Howe Alumni Service, Inc., alumni and pub. relations, Ann Arbor, Mich., 1958-68; v.p. Huron Valley Nat. Bank, Ann Arbor, 1968-70; exec. v.p. South Oakland County Bd. Realtors, Royal Oak, Mich., 1970—; dir. SOCBOR Credit Union, Royal Oak, 1971-74. Served with AUS, 1952-54. Decorated Army Commendation medal with metal pendant; named Soldier of Year Ft. Bliss, Tex., 1952, 30th A.A.A., 1954. Mem. Met. Detroit Council Real Estate Bds., Nat. Assn. Realtors, Mich. Exec. Officer's Council (pres. 1971-74), Assn. Execs. Met. Detroit, Am. Soc. Assn. Execs., Am. Mgmt. Assn., Am. Inst. Parliamentarians. Rotarian. Home: 18903 Fairfield St Detroit MI 48221 Office: 3318 N Main St Royal Oak MI 48073

RICHARDS, MICHAEL STEVEN, retail foods exec.; b. Ft. Wayne, Ind., Nov. 17, 1947; s. Roland Ray and Sharon Ann (Shive) R.; B.S., Purdue U., 1971; m. Cheryl June Siebert, June 1, 1967; children—Michelle Joanne, Carl David. Unit mgr. Burger King, Gary, Ind., 1971-73, Justrite Systems Co., Indpls., 1973-74; exec. v.p. Jack's 33 Flavors of Ind., Hammond, 1974—. Mem. Mensa. Home: 640 E 91st St Indianapolis IN 46240 Office: 6508 Indianapolis Blvd Suite 204 Hammond IN 46320

RICHARDS, PAUL FREDERICK, ophthalmologist; b. Pitts., June 23, 1939; s. S. Herbert and Anne (Busse) R.; A.B., Ohio Wesleyan U., 1961; M.D., Case Western Res. U., 1965; Heed postgrad. fellow Wilmer Inst.-Johns Hopkins, 1969, Mass. Eye and Ear Infirmary, 1969; m. Margaret Jane Mitchell, June 23, 1962; children—Jennifer Ellen, Julia Elizabeth, John Herbert Secrest. Intern, Riverside Meth. Hosp., Columbus, Ohio, 1965-66; resident in ophthalmology Ohio State U., Columbus, 1966-69; practice medicine specializing in ophthalmology, Columbus, 1970—; clin. instr. dept. ophthalmology Ohio State U., 1971—; mem. staffs Grant Hosp., Univ. Hosp., Riverside Meth. Hosp. Ophthalmologist Ohio State Sch. for Blind, 1971—; regional cons. Bus. Services for Blind, Ohio Rehab. Services Commn., 1971—; program chmn. Ohio Soc. for Prevention Blindness, 1977, med. adv. vice chmn., 1972-73. Served to capt. USAF. Diplomate Am. Bd. Ophthalmology. Mem. Columbus Eye, Ear, Nose and Throat Soc., Ohio State Med. Assn., AMA, Phi Rho Sigma, Phi Delta Theta. Episcopalian. Home: 4083 Clairmont Rd Columbus OH 43220 Office: 300 E Town St Columbus OH 43215

RICHARDSON, ARTHUR HAMILTON, bus. exec.; b. Lead, S.D., May 7, 1937; s. Olney Arthur and Orva Louise (Hilgenbocker) R.; student Black Hills State Coll., 1955-57; B.S., Oreg. State U., 1960; m. Karen Kay Wright, June 30, 1962; children—Troy Arthur, Timm Kent. Dist. game mgr. S.D. Dept. Game, Fish and Parks, Custer, 1961-70; asst. regional supr., Sioux Falls, 1970-72, regional supr., Rapid City, 1972-76; with A & K Market, Custer, 1976—. Mem. S.D. Wild Turkey Fedn. (pres. 1977), Wildlife Soc. (state rep. Central Mountains and Plains sect. 1974-75, Profl. award 1971). Lion (Lion of Year 1968, 70). Home: West of City Custer SD 57730 Office: 214 Mt Rushmore Rd Custer SD 57730

RICHARDSON, CHARLES EVERETT, univ. ofcl.; b. Aledo, Ill., Dec. 23, 1928; s. Riley E. and Velma P. (Neal) R.; A.B., So. Ill. U., 1950, M.S., 1951; M.P.H. (Horace B. Rackham fellow), U. Mich., 1952; Ed.D., U. Calif., Los Angeles, 1959; m. Mary A. Newton, Dec. 23, 1947; children—Leigh Richardson Stockton, Charles. Lectr. and coordinator health sci. curriculum So. Ill. U., Carbondale, 1954-56, asst. prof. dept. health edn., 1957-62, asso. prof., 1962-68, prof., 1969-72, spl. asst. to provost, 1972-73, prof. Sch. Medicine, 1973—, asst. dean for faculty, 1973-74, asso. dean, 1974—; vis. prof. Sch. Pub. Health, U. Calif., Los Angeles, summer, 1965, Sch. Pub. Health, U. Hawaii, summer, 1968; expert cons. to Pres.'s Council on Youth Fitness, Washington, 1961. Mem. Carbondale Elementary Sch. Bd., 1970-73. Served with U.S. Army, 1953-54. Mem. Ill. Pub. Health Assn., Ill. Soc. Pub. Health Educators (pres. 1960-61), Jackson County Heart Assn. (pres. 1970-71), Jackson County Mental Health Assn., Eta Sigma Gamma. Club: Elks. Author: Living: Health, Behavior and Environment, 1975. Home: 1501 Taylor Dr Carbondale IL 62901 Office: Life Science I School of Medicine Southern Illinois Univ Carbondale IL 62901

RICHARDSON, EMANUEL ROSS, govt. ofcl.; b. Richmond, Va., Dec. 23, 1924; s. George C. and Lilia Ann (Gibbs) R.; B.S., Hampton Inst., 1950; M.A., Central Mich. U., 1973; Cornell U. Law Sch., 1950-53; m. Irene Hortense Burnette, Dec. 1, 1963; children—Angela Dawn, Eric Bernard. Substitute tchr. secondary schs., Richmond, 1953-54; recreation dir. City of Richmond, 1953-54; group leader and supply commodity mgr. officer U.S. Naval Aviation Supply Office; exec. agt. for retail agreements U.S. Air Force Logistics Command, Wright-Patterson AFB, Ohio, 1963-70, systems analyst, 1970—; propr. A to Z Rental Center, Xenia, Ohio, 1969-71. Pres. Wilberforce Community Property Owners and Voters Assn., 1966-68; chmn. Xenia Area Human Relations Council, 1969-72; sec. treas. Greene County chpt. Greene-Montgomery Health and Welfare Planning Council, 1972-76; mem. affirmative action com. Xenia Pub. Schs., 1977; treas. Greene County Farm City Tour Com., 1976-77; mem. pres.'s club Nat. Democratic Party Com., Washington, 1977-78. Served with U.S. Army, 1943-46, 55-58. Decorated Bronze Star (3). Mem. Air Force Assn., Am. Def. Preparedness Assn., Assn. for the Study of Afro-Am. Life and History, Xenia C. of C., NAACP (negotiating com. 1976—), Am. Legion, Greene County Hist. Soc. Democrat. Episcopalian. Clubs: Kiwanis, Optimist; Town and Country. Home: PO Box 512 Wilberforce OH 45384 Office: US Air Force Logistics Command Wright Patterson AFB OH 45433

RICHARDSON, EUGENE STANLEY, JR., paleontologist; b. Phila., Oct. 17, 1916; s. E. Stanley and Jessica (Ripple) R.; A.B., Williams Coll., 1938; postgrad. Wash. State Coll., 1939-41; M.S., Pa. State Coll., 1942; Ph.D., Princeton, 1954; m. Priscilla Lewis Cox, May 31, 1958; children—Edwards N., Helen Maude Southwell (Mrs. James Wahlman), Peter Nichols, Victoria Cox Southwell (Mrs. Victoria C.S. Sharvy), Priscilla Lewis Southwell. Instr., Bryn Mawr Coll., 1943-45; geologist Ohio Oil Co., 1944-45; curator fossil invertebrates Field Mus., Chgo., 1946—. Propr., Vanishing Press, Gurnee, Ill., 1933—. Mem. Paleontol. Soc., A.A.A.S., Pa., Ill. acads. sci., Yorkshire Geol. Soc., Soc. Vertebrate Paleontology. Home: 1765 S River Rd Gurnee IL 60031 Office: Field Mus Natural History Chicago IL 60605

RICHARDSON, GEORGE BOWN, sales exec.; b. Akron, Ohio, Nov. 3, 1926; s. William Samuel and Margaret (Bown) R.; B.S. in Commerce, U. Va., 1950; m. Helen Miller, Dec. 1, 1956; 1 dau., Denise. Nat. mgr. indsl. maintenance and transp. sales Glidden Co., 1950-59; pres., chmn. bd. R/C Assos., Inc., R/C-NSO, Inc., Beachwood, Ohio, 1949—. Served with USMCR, 1944-46; PTO. Mem. Elec. League Cleve., Nat. Elec. Mfrs. Reps. Assn. (bd. govs.). Republican. Episcopalian. Club: Country of Cleve. Home: 2840 Lander Rd Pepper Pike OH 44124 Office: 24100 Chagrin Blvd Beachwood OH 44122

RICHARDSON, JAMES LEWIS, artist; b. Monett, Mo., Oct. 8, 1927; s. Kenley H. and Kate (Lewis) R.; B.S., S.W. Mo. State U., Springfield, 1952; M.A., U. Ark., 1961; M.F.A., Wichita State U., 1970. Tchr., pub. schs., Monett, 1952-61; prof. S.W. Mo. State U., 1961-74, head art dept., 1974—; regional and nat. print exhbns., 1952—. Served with AUS, 1946-48. Mem. NEA, AAUP. Home: Route 10 Box 448 Springfield MO 65803 Office: Dept Art Southwest Mo State Univ Springfield MO 65803

RICHARDSON, JOHN ADKINS, art scholar, educator; b. Gillette, Wyo., Oct. 24, 1929; s. John Wesley and Joyce L. (Adkins) R.; B.A., Eastern Wash. State U., 1951; M.A., Columbia U., 1952, Ed.D., 1958; m. Betty Joyce Ritchie, Oct. 8, 1971; children by previous marriage—Christopher, Robin. Prof. art and design State U. N.Y., Geneseo, 1957-58, Fresno (Calif.) State Coll., 1958-59, So. Ill. U., Edwardsville, 1959—. Author: Modern Art and Scientific Thought, 1971; Art: The Way It Is, 1974; The Complete Book of Cartooning, 1976. Home: 802 W High St Edwardsville IL 62025 Office: Box 64 Southern Illinois Univ Edwardsville IL 62025

RICHARDSON, JOSEPH HILL, physician; b. Rensselaer, Ind., June 16, 1928; s. William Clark and Vera (Hill) R.; M.S. in Medicine, Northwestern U., 1950, M.D., 1953; m. Joan Grace Meininger, July 8, 1950; children—Lois N., Ellen M., James K. Intern, U.S. Naval Hosp., Great Lakes, Ill., 1953-54; fellow in medicine Cleve. Clinic, 1956-59; individual practice medicine specializing in internal medicine and hematology, Marion, Ind., 1959-67, Ft. Wayne, Ind., 1967—; instr. medicine Ind. U. Sch. Medicine. Served to lt. MC USNR, 1954-56. Diplomate Am. Bd. Internal Medicine. Fellow A.C.P., AAAS; mem. Am. Fedn. for Clin. Research, Am. Med. Writers Assn., AMA. Mason. Contbr. articles to med. jours. Home: 8726 Fortuna Way Ft Wayne IN 46805 Office: 3010 E State Blvd Fort Wayne IN 46805

RICHARDSON, LONNIE ALLEN, clergyman; b. Indpls., Mar. 3, 1953; s. Truman Rudolph and Bertha Irene (Caulk) R.; B.A., Greenville Coll., 1975; m. Maria Mercedes Sanchez. Program dir. WGRN-FM, Greenville, Ill., 1972-73, sta. mgr., 1972-75; ordained minister Free Meth. Ch., 1974; pastor Cumberland Presbyn. Ch., Dudleyville, Ill., 1972-74; asst. minister Centenary United Meth. Ch., St. Louis, 1974-76; clergyman United Meth. Ch., 1976; minister Centenary United Meth. Ch., 1976-77, Faith United Meth. Ch., 1978—; producer religious shorts and commls. for TV. Recipient Outstanding Aid to Law Enforcement Award City of St. Louis Police. Mem. Pi Kappa Delta. Address: 6941 Bonanza House Springs MO 63051

RICHARDSON, MYRTLE, abstracter, judge; b. Jefferson County, Ohio, July 2, 1907; d. Thomas and Blanche (Whitecotton) Heinselman; student Kansas State Tchrs. Coll., 1926; m. Harold Richardson, Mar. 4, 1929 (div.); 1 dau., Nancy Lee (Mrs. Donald W. Ridgway). Tchr. pub. schs. Edwards County, Kans., 1924-28; reporter, advertiser Kinsley Graphic, Kinsely, Kans., 1928-35; editor, advt. mgr. S. Standard, McMinnville, Tenn., 1935-36; mgr. Kinsley Graphic, 1937-41; abstracter H.F. Thompson, Kinsley, 1943-54; editor Kinsley Mercury, 1954-57; abstracter, Kinsley, 1957—; owner, mgr. Richardson Abstract Co.; probate judge, Kinsley, 1958-68; police judge, City of Kinsley, 1958-68. Bd. dirs. United Drive, 1947-57; mem. bd. Edwards County chpt. ARC, 1940-50; community and project leader 4-H Club, 1943-52; community and project leader Edwards County 4-H Who's Who Club, 1943-52; pres. PTA, 1940-44; vice chmn. Edwards County Dem. Party, 1956—; charter mem. Edwards County Dem. Women's Federated Club, pres., 1970—. Mem. C. of C. (Sec.-mgr. 1947-54), Edwards County Hist. Soc. (historian 1950). Nat. Council Juvenile Ct. Judges, Internat. Platform Assn., S. Central Kan. Probate Judges Assn. (pres. 1966). Author: Oft' Told Tales, a history of Edwards County, Kansas, to 1900, 1976. Home: 120 N 2d St Kinsley KS 67547 Office: 218 W 8th St Kinsley KS 67547

RICHARDSON, ROBERT A, lawyer; b. Cleve., Feb. 15, 1939; s. Allen B. and Margaret C. (Thomas) R.; B.A., Ohio Wesleyan U., 1961; LL.B., Harvard, 1964; m. Carolyn Eck. Admitted to Ohio bar, 1964; asso. firm Calfee, Halter & Griswold, 1969-72, partner, 1972—. Mem. Nat. Panel Arbitrators, Am. Arbitration Assn., 1966—; lectr. securities law, corp. law Cleve. State U., 1972-76. Trustee Big Bros. Greater Cleve., 1974—, v.p., 1975-76, exec. v.p., 1976-77, pres., 1977—. Mem. Am. Ohio St., Cleve. (social chmn. young lawyers sect. 1967, law day chmn. 1968) bar assns., Cleveland Council on World Affairs (chmn. world affairs forum, trustee, mem. exec. com. 1973—), English Speaking Union (treas., dir. 1973-75), Cleve. Philos. Club, Omicron Delta Kappa, Delta Sigma Rho. Clubs: Cleve. Skating, Hillbrook, Cleve. Athletic, Downtown Cleve. Rotary. Home: 2870 Plymouth Pepper Pike OH 44124 Office: Central Nat Bank Bldg Cleveland OH

RICHARDSON, RUTH ANN, librarian; b. Vinton, Iowa, Dec. 30, 1923; d. Ashley Ryther and Elsie Elizabeth (Schmidt) Richardson; B.A., U. No. Iowa, 1946; M.A., U. Wis., 1955. Tchr. Benton County (Iowa) Pub. Schs., 1942-43, Decorah (Iowa) High Sch., 1946-52, Harlandale High Sch., San Antonio, 1952-54; classifier Iowa State U. Library, 1955-56; head reference Cedar Rapids (Iowa) Pub. Library, 1956-60, head adult services, 1960-76, asst. dir., 1976—; vis. asst. prof. Fla. State U., 1959-60. Mem. ALA, Iowa Library Assn. (pres. adult services sect. 1961), Iowa Adult Edn. Assn., Conn. Hist. Soc., New Eng. Hist. Geneal. Soc., Beta Phi Mu, Kappa Delta Pi. Presbyterian. Home: 1400 2d Ave SE Cedar Rapids IA 52403 Office: 428 3d Ave SE Cedar Rapids IA 52401

RICHCREEK, JAMES MARION, coll. adminstr.; b. Warsaw, Ind., June 18, 1918; s. Rex. R. and Hazel E. (Banghart) R.; B.S., Ashland Coll., 1941; M.A., Ohio State U., 1948; Ed.D. (Univ. fellow), U. Nebr., 1958; m. Marilyn Carpenter, Sept. 6, 1942. Prof. phys. edn. Ashland (Ohio) Coll., 1946-52, prof. psychology, 1961-65, dir. div. social sci., 1966—; prof. phys. edn. U. S.D., Vermillion, 1953-57; dir. div. phys. edn. Henderson State Coll., Arkadelphia, Ark., 1957-58; prof. phys. edn. Central Mich. U., Mt. Pleasant, 1958-61; dir. div. phys. edn. Edinboro (Pa.) State Coll., 1965. Served to maj. AUS, 1941-46. Mem. Internat. Platform Assn. Home: 727 Buena Vista Ave Ashland OH 44805

RICHELIEU, CLYDE CARL, banjo mfg. co. exec.; b. Greengrove Twp., Owen, Wis., Aug. 9, 1909; s. Chris and Gena (Severson) R.; B.S., Dodge Radio Coll., Valparaiso, Ind., 1928; m. Lucy E. Baker, Aug. 29, 1929; children—Judith Lou, Rochelle Lou. Communications engr. radio stas. WBL, WGO, WRL, RCA, 1928-31; radio operator U.S.S. Sumac, U.S. Lighthouse Service, 1932-36; radio engr., maintenance electrician CAA, Milw., Burlington, Iowa, North Platte, Nebr. and Washington, 1937-45; dist. mgr. Simplex Time Recorder, Milw., gen. sales mgr., Gardner, Mass., 1945-53; gen. sales mgr. Cin. Time Recorder, 1953-58; regional sales mgr. Stromberg Time Recorder, Chgo., 1959-64; owner, operator Banjos by Richelieu, Oregon, Wis., 1964—; profl. banjoist; dir. Central div. Am. Radio Relay League, 1947-48; owner, operator stas. W9ARE and W9JS. Mem. Quarter Century Wireless Assn., Soc. Wireless Pioneers. Club: Masons (Shriners). Composer: Oh, How I Love the Banjo, 1970. Contbr. articles to profl. jours. Home: 215 S Washington St Wheaton IL 60187 Office: 786 N Main St Oregon WI 53575

RICHIE, ERNEST CARL, mfg. exec.; b. Mannheim, Germany, Aug. 25, 1912; s. Carl and Maria (Aberle) R.; M.S. in Electronics, Tech. U. Berlin, 1936; m. Gertrude E Heyartz, Apr. 16, 1948; children—Peter Carl, Patricia Monica, Raymond Ronald. Came to U.S., 1954, naturalized, 1959. Mgr. electronics factory Gen. Electric Co., Buenos Aires, 1938-54, dir., 1952-54; works mgr. tuner div. Sarkes Tarzian, Inc., Bloomington, Ind., 1954-77; pres. Tuner Service Corp., 1954—, Cable Converter Service Corp., 1977—; exec. v.p. Eastern Electronics Co.; gen. mgr. Sarkes Tarzian Mexicana, Tarmex. Cons. Tonfunk, Karlsruhe, Germany, 1961, Dean Bros., Indpls., 1961-65. Mem. Bloomington C. of C. Author: Appliances, 1945; Radio Equipment for FM, 1945, also articles in field. Home: 316 Lakewood Dr Bloomington IN 47401 Office: Tuner Service Corp 537 S Walnut Bloomington IN 47401

RICHMAN, MARVIN JORDAN, developer; b. N.Y.C., July 13, 1939; s. Morris and Minnie (Graubart) R.; B.Arch., Mass. Inst. Tech., 1962; M.Urban Planning, N.Y.U., 1966; M.B.A., U. Chgo., 1977; m. Amy Paula Rubin, July 31, 1966; children—Mark Jason, Keith Hayden, Suzanne Elizabeth. Architect, planner Skidmore, Owings & Merrill, N.Y.C., 1964, Conklin & Rossant, N.Y.C., 1965-67, Jonas Vizbaras & Assos., N.Y.C., 1968-69; v.p. Urban Investment & Devel. Co., Chgo., 1969—; lectr. N.Y.U., 1967-69. Served with USAF, 1963-64. Registered profl. architect, N.Y.; licensed real estate broker, Ill. Mem. AIA, Am. Inst. Planners, Am. Arbitration Assn., Internat. Council Shopping Centers, Chgo. Real Estate Bd. Home: 3250 University Ave Highland Park IL 60035 Office: 845 N Michigan Ave Chicago IL 60611

RICHMOND, HAROLD WAYNE, physician; b. Oakdale, La., July 11, 1925; s. Harold Easborn and Essie (Seals) R.; B.S., U. Southwestern La., 1946; M.D., La. State U., 1948; m. Frances Alexa Womack, Sept. 30, 1950; children—Mark Kimbrough. Intern, Confederate Meml. Med. Center, Shreveport, La., 1948-49, resident surgery and orthopedics, 1949-50; pvt. practice gen. medicine and surgery, Oakdale, 1953-60; med. dir. Cummins Engine Co., Inc., Columbus, Ind., 1960-74, corporate med. dir., 1974—. Co-founder, med. dir. Columbus Occupational Health Center, 1970—. Served to lt. (j.g.), M.C., USNR, 1951-53. Diplomate Am. Bd. Preventive Medicine, Am. Bd. Family Practice. Fellow Am. Coll. Preventive Medicine, Am. Acad. Family Practice, Am. Acad. Occupational Medicine. Clubs: Harrison Lake Country; Columbia (Indpls.). Home: 3960 Waycross Dr Columbus IN 47201 Office: 605 Cottage Av Columbus IN 47201

RICHMOND, QUINTON BLAINE, accountant; b. New, W.Va., Mar. 7, 1924; s. Calvin H. and Nora Ellen (Garten) R.; student Southeastern Bible Coll., 1950-51; B.A., Southwestern Bible Inst., 1952, Th.B., 1952; m. Patricia Lee Haley, Oct. 4, 1944; children—Carolyn Sue Richmond Terry, Larry Dean, Ronald David. Ordained to ministry Gen. Council of Assemblies of God, 1955; pastor chs., Kaufman, Tex., 1952-54, Dallas, 1954-56, New Carlisle, Ohio, 1963-66; accountant, auditor States Seed Co., Inc., Garland, Tex., 1952-53; with Indsl. Towel Co., Dallas, 1953-54; contract statistician Chance Voight Aircraft Corp., Dallas, 1954-55; auditor Tex. Automatic Sprinkler Corp., Dallas, 1955; accountant Wright-Patterson Air Force Base, Ohio, 1955-56; supr. cost accountant Dayton Air Force Depot, Dayton, Ohio, 1956-60; supervisory accounting tech. Detroit Air Force Contract Mgmt. Dist., 1960-61, contract specialist, 1961-63; contract price analyst/negotiator Wright Patterson AFB, Ohio, 1963-74; accountant, corporate officer, pres., chmn. bd. dirs. South Ohio Profl. Service & Sales Co., Inc., Dayton, 1973—; owner Beauty World Salon, Dayton, O., 1975—. Served with USNR, 1942-44. C.P.A., Ohio. Mem. Nat. Soc. Pub. Accountants. Composer songs. Home: 2860 Nacoma Pl Kettering OH 45420 Office: 3108 Wilmington Pike Dayton OH 45429

RICHMOND, RICHARD (DICK) THOMAS, journalist; b. Parma, Ohio, May 16, 1933; s. Arthur James and Frances Marie (Visosky) R.; A.B., Washington, U., St. Louis, 1961; m. Charlotte Jean Schwoebel, Dec. 18, 1954; children—Kris Elaine, Leigh Alison, Paul Evan. Bur. mgr. UPI Newspictures, St. Louis, 1961-62; asst. picture editor St. Louis Post-Dispatch, 1962-64, editor of color sect., 1964—, columnist, 1971—; v.p. Golden Royal Enterprises, St. Louis, 1976—; pres. OroQuest Press, Inc., St. Louis, 1977; dir. U.S. Mortgage & Investment Corp., 1977—; treas. Magalar Diversified Industries, 1977—. Served with USAF, 1953-57. Author: (with Roy Volker) Treasure Under Your Feet, 1974; In the Wake of the Golden Galleons, 1976. Home: 307 Lebanon Ave Belleville IL 62221 Office: Post-Dispatch 900 N 12th Blvd St Louis MO 63101

RICHMOND, TULLIE TAYLOR, pub. accountant; b. Columbus, Ohio, Oct. 31, 1923; s. Loren M. and Ruth (Shannon) R.; B.S., Ohio State U., 1950; m. Mary Jane Gabriel, July 24, 1943; children—Shera Lynn (Mrs. J. Hunter Skaggs). Dana Gabriel, Mark Loren, Michael Kent. Sr. accountant Lybrand, Ross Bros. & Montgomery, C.P.A.'s, Columbus, 1950-62; pres. Comp-Tool, Inc., Ashtabula, Ohio, 1963-66; partner Adams & Richmond, C.P.A.'s, Ashtabula, 1962-65; partner Adams, Richmond & Moore, C.P.A.'s, Ashtabula, 1965-66; treas. H. W. Satchell & Co., Columbus, 1962-68; treas., v.p., dir. Turner & Shepard, Inc., Columbus; owner Tullie T. Richmond, C.P.A., Columbus, 1966—. Mem. Ashtabula Area Devel. Assn., 1965-66, Copyright-Table to Find Transp.; patron Ashtabula Fine Arts Center; advisor to bd. dirs. Bethel Goodwill Industries, Ashtabula, O. Served with AUS, 1943-46. Mem. Am. Inst. C.P.A.'s, Ohio Soc. C.P.A.'s, Nat. Assn. Accountants, Am. Accounting Assn., Ohio State U. Assn. (life), Assn. for Systems Mgmt. Methodist. Mason (32 deg.), Lion. Home: 5955 Litchfield Rd Worthington OH 43085 Office: 17 S High St Columbus OH 43215

RICHMOND, WILLIAM LLOYDE, JR., cons. civil engr.; b. Grand Forks, N.D., July 21, 1937; s. William Lloyde and Wilhelmina Alice (Ogden) R.; B.S. in Civil Engring., U. N.D., 1959, M.S., 1960, fallout shelter analyst, 1967; m. Blanca Aniceta Humerez, Feb. 16, 1963; children—William Lloyde III, Blanca Elizabeth, Alice Julliette, James Bernard, Aileen Millicent. Engr. trainee L. Richmond, cons. engr., Grand Forks, 1958-61; asst. to chief structural engr. Stanley Engring., Inc., Muscatine, Iowa, 1961-64; chief design engr. Richmond Engring., Inc., Grand Forks, 1964—, corporate sec., 1968—. Registered profl. engr., N.D., S.D., Iowa, Minn., Mont. Mem. ASCE, ASTM (dir. No. Plains dist. 1967—), Nat., N.D. socs. profl. engrs., Nat. Assn. County Engrs., U. N.D. Varsity Alumni Lettermen Club (pres. 1971, 72), Grand Forks County His. Soc. (charter), Phi Delta Theta. K.C., Elk. Author: (with Dimitri Nesterenko) Coefficients for Four Span Beams, 1963. Contbr. articles to tech. jours. Bridge tchr., life master. Home: 1800 Riverside Dr Grand Forks ND 58201 Office: Box 577 Grand Forks ND 58201

RICHTER, HAROLD, lawyer; b. N.Y.C., Nov. 30, 1924; s. Joseph and Mary (Slutzker) R.; student U. Okla., 1943-44; B.S.E., U. Mich., 1948; J.D., Harvard, 1952; m. Renee Katz, Aug. 31, 1952; children—Neal, Carol. Admitted to Ill. bar, 1952, Ind. bar, 1953; since practiced in Chgo., city prosecutor Calumet City, Ill., 1962-65; village prosecutor Burnham, Ill., 1964-67; village atty. Calumet Park, Ill., 1970—; dir. ITA Leasing Co., Hammond, Ind. Served with USNR, 1943-46. Mem. Am., Chgo., South Chgo. (pres. 1967-68) bar assns., Am. Acad. Matrimonial Lawyers. Kiwanian. (pres. 1965-66). Home: 8327 Oakwood St Munster IN 46321 Office: 69 W Washington St Chicago IL 60602

RICHTER, ROBERTA BRANDENBURG (MRS. J. PAUL RICHTER), educator; b. Osborn, Ohio, Dec. 29; d. Warren F. and Mary M. (Davis) Brandenburg; student Miami-Jacobs Coll., 1930, Wittenberg U., 1930-31, Coll. Music, U. Cin., U. Dayton, 1954, 64; B.S., Miami U., Oxford, Ohio, 1958, M.Ed., 1959; postgrad. Wright State U., 1966-70, Ohio State U., 1969—; m. Jean Paul Richter, Oct. 6, 1934; 1 son, James Paul. Bus. mgr. T.D. Peffley, Inc., 1929-32; sec., prodn. mgr. Delco Products div. Gen. Motors, 1932-34; exec. sec. League Women Voters, 1935-38, Elder & Johnston Dept. Store, 1938-40; cts. and conv. reporter Montgomery County, 1940-46; adminstrv. asst. Ch. Fedn. Greater Dayton, Ohio, 1946-50; audio-visual cons. schs., chs. Twyman Films, 1950-53; legal asst. Nadlin Law Offices, 1953-58; instr. stenotype, office practice Miami-Jacobs Coll., Dayton, 1952-59; tchr. stenotype, guidance counselor Stebbins High Sch., Dayton, 1958-74; vocat. guidance coordinator Mad River Planning Dist., Montgomery County, Ohio, 1968-74; adviser Nat. Honor Soc.; lectr. in field; profl. cellist. Instr. workshop in stenotype and ct. reporting Wright State U., Dayton, 1970—; owner Dayton Stenographic Studio. Supt., tchr., adviser youth div. Grace United Meth. Ch., Dayton, 1942-72, sec. adminstrv. bd., 1940—, past pres. Ex-cel Club, mem. council on ministries, 1970-73, work area, Christian social concerns, Christian missions Women's Soc. Christian Service; counselor Camp Miniwanca, Am. Youth Found., 1953-68; circle leader United Meth. Women, 1976—. Mem. Am., Ohio, Miami Valley personnel and guidance assns., Ohio Bus. Tchrs. Assn., Am., Ohio sch. counselor assns., Nat., Ohio edn. assns., Nat. Vocat. Guidance Assn., Ohio Assn. Counselors, Deans and Adminstrs., Dayton Bus. Soc. (v.p. 1969—), Pub. Speaker Bur., Council World Affairs, Delphian (past pres.), League Women Voters (past pres., dir., treas.), Greater Dayton C. of C., Bus. and Profl. Women, Pi Omega Pi. Mem. Order Eastern Star. Clubs: Progressive Mothers (chmn. program Dayton 1969-70), World Trade. Author numerous ednl. handbooks, pamphlets. Contbr. articles to profl. jours. Home: 3865 Seiber Ave Dayton OH 45405

RICHTER, WILLIAM ARTHUR, lawyer; b. St. Louis, Feb. 10, 1932; s. Arthur William and Fredda Marie (Memhardt) R.; student Grinnell Coll., 1950-51; A.B., Washington U., St. Louis, 1955, LL.B., 1955; m. Patricia Eileen Scoles, July 18, 1959; children—Eric Scoles, Dana Marie, Kurt William. Admitted to Mo. bar, 1955; practiced in St. Louis, 1955, 57—; mem. firm Coburn & Croft, St. Louis, 1955, Stamm, Millar, Neuhoff & Campbell, St. Louis, 1955-59, Peper, Martin, Jensen, Maichel & Hetlage, 1959—. Lectr. law Washington U. Law Sch., 1961-63, 66-67. Served to 1st lt. AUS, 1955-57; col. Res. Mem. Am., Mo., St. Louis bar assns., Newcomen Soc., Order of Coif, Phi Beta Kappa, Phi Delta Phi. Lutheran. Club: Mo. Athletic (St. Louis). Home: 1887 Candlewick St Des Peres MO 63131 Office: 720 Olive St St Louis MO 63101

RICKBEIL, CLARA EVELYN SHELLMAN (MRS. RAYMOND E. RICKBEIL), club woman; b. Gibson City, Ill.; d. Kilian and Anna Marie (Johnson) Shellman; grad. Brown's Bus. Coll., Champaign, Ill., 1922; student U. Ill., 1927-28; m. Raymond Earl Rickbeil, May 8, 1930. Office sec. Ford County Farm Bur., Gibson City, Ill., 1922-26; secretarial position Raymond E. Rickbeil, C.P.A., Springfield, Ill., 1928-61, Ernst & Ernst, Springfield, 1961-65. Program chmn. 21st dist. Ill. Fedn. Women's Clubs, 1968-69, corr. sec., 1969-71, dir., 1971-73; mem. Republican Women's Club Sangamon County, Nat. Fedn. Rep. Women Mem. Sangamon County Farm Bur., Child and Family Service Sangamon County; bd. dirs. Carrie Post King's Daus. Home for Women, 1967-69, also mem. Willing Circle. Recipient award for work pub. accounting legislation Ill. Soc. C.P.A.'s, 1956. Mem. U. Ill. Alumni Assn., Am. Legion Aux., YWCA, Sangamon County Hist. Soc., Meml. Hosp. Aux., Abraham Lincoln Assn., Am. Assn. Ret. Persons. Republican. Presbyterian. Mem. Order Eastern Star. Clubs: Springfield Woman's (reception com. 1962-63, social com. 1963-64, corr. sec. 1972-74), Mariama (chpt. chmn., mem. bd. 1969-71), Amateur Musical, Zonta (treas. 1954-57, finance chmn. 1957, 63, 66, service chmn. and mem. service com. 1953-62), Sangamo, U. Ill. Presidents. Home: 937 Feldkamp Ave Springfield IL 62704

RICKER, OTTO LEE, oral surgeon; b. Cadillac, Mich., Mar. 20, 1910; s. Otto Lee and Nelle B. (Shupe) R.; B.S., Mich. State U., 1931; D.D.S., U. Mich., 1934, M.S., 1948; m. Genevieve Louis Ricker, Jan. 1, 1939. Pvt. practice dentistry, East Lansing, Mich., 1935-42; resident U. Mich. Hosp., 1945-48; pvt. practice oral surgery, Grand Rapids, Mich., 1948—. Cons. Council on Dental Edn., 1960-75. Pres., Symphony Orch. Bd., active Am. Cancer Soc. Served to maj., AUS, 1942-46; ETO. Mem. Am. Bd. Oral Surgery (pres. 1969), Mich. Dental Assn. (pres. 1968). Club: Kent. (Grand Rapids, Mich.). Home: 2853 Woodclift Circle Grand Rapids MI 49506 Office: 153 Lafayette St SE Grand Rapids MI 49503

RICKERT, RICHARD MICHAEL, engr. b. Bklyn., Aug. 17, 1936; s. Richard and Louisa (Hofbauer) R.; A.B., Columbia U., 1958, B.S. in Elec. Engring., 1959, M.S. in Elec. Engring., 1960; m. Carla Schmidt, Jan. 16, 1961; children—Richard, Louisa, Adam. Mem. tech. staff Bell Telephone Labs., Indpls., supr. telephone circuit design, 1964—. Mem. IEEE (editor newsletter Central Ind. sect. 1969-71), K. of C., Phi Beta Kappa Kappa, Eta Kappa Nu, Tau Beta Pi, Indpls. Art Mus., Children's Mus., Smithsonian Asso. Contbr. articles in field to profl. jours. Patentee in field. Office: 2525 Shadeland Ave Indianapolis IN 46219

RICKETTS, JOHN WILLIAM, corp. exec.; b. Boonville, Mo., Aug. 26, 1939; s. William Arthur and Olive Estelle (Bess) R.; B.S., Mo. Sch. Mines, 1961; M.B.A., Drury Coll., 1971; m. Camille Curtis, July 1, 1961; children—Laurel Marie, Elizabeth Marie. With Southwestern Bell Telephone Co., 1961-66, test center foreman, Joplin, Mo., 1965, supervising wire chief, Sikeston, Mo., 1966; with Tamko Asphalt Products, Joplin, 1966—, plant mgr., 1967-69, v.p. mfg., 1969—; with Royal Brand Roofing Co., 1969—, exec. v.p., 1972—, dir., 1969—; v.p. mfg. Am. Eagles Homes, Inc. Regiment leader United Fund, Joplin, Mo., 1969-70. Bd. dirs. Joplin Civic Theater, 1967-70, Salvation Army, 1977—; trustee Tamko Employees Profit Sharing Trust Fund. Served with AUS, 1962-64. Recipient Outstanding Young Engineer of the Year award Southwest chpt. Mo. Soc. Profl. Engrs., 1968. Registered profl. engr., Mo., Kans., Ala., Tenn. Mem. Mo. Soc. Profl. Engrs., Nat. Soc. Profl. Engrs. Methodist (mem. ofcl. bd. 1967-73, layleader, lay speaker 1974—, trustee W. Mo. Conf). Kiwanian. Home: 802 N Moffet St Joplin MO 64801 Office: 601 N High St Joplin MO 64801

RICKETTS, RALPH LYNN, cons. agrl. engr., former educator; b. Springfield, Mo., July 12, 1910; s. Gilbert L. and Sarah B. (Smith) R.; B.S. in Agrl. Engring., U. Mo., 1937, M.S., 1960; m. Lillian Adeline Goodwin, Apr. 24, 1937; children—David L., Sharon Sue (Mrs. Donald Goff). Drainage engr. U.S. Dept. Agr., S.E. Mo. delta, 1937-42; asst. prof. U. Mo., Columbia, 1942-47, asso prof., 1947-51, prof. agrl. engring., 1951-71; cons. engr., Hallsville, Mo., 1971—. Engr. water dist. 4 Boone County, chmn., 1968-71. Recipient Meritorious Service award U. Mo., 1971. Fellow Am. Soc. Agrl. Engrs.; mem. Gamma Sigma Delta (award of merit 1964), Epsilon Sigma Phi (certificate of recognition 1964). Contbr. articles to profl. jours.; author U. Mo. bulls. Home: Route 1 Hallsville MO 65255

RICKS, BERNARD E., auto mfg. co. exec.; b. Boscobel, Wis., Jan. 25, 1914; s. Clarence G. and Idllie Bell (Hubanks) R.; B.S.M.E., Detroit Inst. Tech., 1943; m. Ruth M. Guenther, Sept. 29, 1946; children—William (adopted), Jeff, Jon, Michal. With TRW, various locations, 1940—, dir. quality control and reliability, Warren, Mich, 1962—71, dir., coordinator quality control and relations, automotive world wide, Warren, 1971—. Mem. Soc. Auto. Engrs., Am. Soc. Quality Control, Am. Mgmt. Assn. Presbyterian. Clubs: Birmingham Country, Spring Lake Country, Recess, Masons. Patentee in field. Home: 31702 Auburn Dr Birmingham MI 48009 Office: 34201 Van Dyke St Warren MI 48092

RIDDLE, MAXWELL, newspaper columnist; b. Ravenna, Ohio, July 29, 1907; s. Henry Warner and Mary E. (Fitz-Gerald) R.; B.A., U. Ariz., 1929; m. Martha A. Hurd, Mar. 31, 1933; children—Betsy (Mrs. Richard H. Whitmore), Henry W. III. Turf editor, columnist NEA Service, 1930, 39; kennel editor, columnist, pets columnist Cleve. Press, 1938-69; columnist Columbia Features, Inc., 1959-66; columnist Ledger Syndicate, 1966-73, Scott Editor Service, 1973—, Allied Feature Syndicate, 1975—; all breed dog judge, fgn. countries, 1955. U.S., 1960—. Recipient Cruikshank medal, 1941; Dog Writer of Year, 1949, 61; Dogdom's Man of the Year, 1968, Dog. Journalist of Year, 1970, 72. Mem. Ohio Dog Owners Assn., Dog Writers Assn. (past pres.), Sigma Delta Chi. Clubs: Western Reserve Kennel, Ravenna Kennel. Author: The Springer Spaniel, 1939; The Lovable Mongrel, 1954; This Is The Chihuahua, 1959; The Complete Book of Puppy Training and Care, 1962; Dog People are Crazy, 1966; Your Show Dog, 1968; A Quick Guide to the Standards of Show Dogs, 1972; (with Mrs. M.B. Seeley) The Complete Alaskan Malamute, 1976. The Complete Brittany Spaniel, 1974; The New Shetland Sheepdog, 1974; also articles in field. Contbr. New Dog Ency., 1967, Internat. Dog Ency., 1972, World Book Ency. Asso. editor Dog World Mag., 1961—. Home: PO Box 286 Ravenna OH 44266

RIDDLEBARGER, LARRY DEVON, accountant; b. Lucasville, Ohio, Mar. 19, 1941; s. Melford William and Florence (Fraley) R.; B.B.A., U. Cin., 1964; postgrad. Wright State U., 1969-70; m. Rosalie Rase, Apr. 19, 1967; children—Kimberly, Keri Rose. Internal auditor Mead Corp., Dayton, Ohio, 1965-66, plant accountant Mead Packaging div., Chgo., 1966-68; budget and financial analyst Chrysler Corp. Airtemp div., Dayton, 1968-70; controller Jabsco-par div ITT, Springfield, Ohio, 1970; prin., owner Larry Riddlebarger & Co., computerized accounting systems, Portsmouth, Ohio, 1971—; auditor Citizens Savs. & Loan Assn. Mem. Accreditation Council for Accountancy. Mem. Accountancy Bd. Ohio, Nat. Assn. Accountants, Nat. Soc. Pub. Accountants, Fin. Mgrs. Soc. Savs. Instns., YMCA. Republican. Baptist. Home: 5340 Wilson Ave Sciotoville OH 45662 Office: 627 Nat Bank Bldg Portsmouth OH 45662

RIDEN, JOSEPH ROBERT, chemist; b. Gettysburg, Pa., Dec. 13, 1922; s. Joseph Robert and Anna Mary (Stevenson) R.; B.S., Pa. State U., 1944, M.S., 1949, Ph.D., 1951; m. Sarah Jane Schmidt, Nov. 30, 1946; children—Ellen (Mrs. David L. Perry), Susan, Martha, Daniel, Rebecca Jo. Research asso. Johns Hopkins, Balt., 1951-55; biochemist Chemagro Corp. Pitts., 1955-57; research scientist Spencer Chem. Co., Gulf Oil Corp., Merriam, Kans., 1957-74; chem. research mgr. Gulf Oil Chem. Co., 1974—. Served with USNR, 1944-46. Mem. Am. Chem. Soc., Alpha Chi Sigma, Phi Lambda Upsilon, Gamma Sigma Delta, Pi Kappa Phi. Home: 8447 Lamar St Overland Park KS 66207 Office: 9009 W 67th St Merriam KS 66202

RIDGE, WILLIAM CLAYTON, educator; b. Detroit, Feb. 28, 1937; s. Thurman Garrison and Helen Marpe (Vanderburgh) R.; B.A., Ind. U., 1959, M.A., 1963, Ph.D. (research fellow), 1969; m. Arob Watanavicharn, Apr. 6, 1967; 1 son, Robert Hunt. Instr. Faculty Med. Sci., Bangkok, Thailand, 1964-65; asst. prof. math. Suffolk U., Boston, 1969-70; asst. prof. Ind. U.-Purdue U. at Indpls., 1970—. Founding mem. Internat. Center Indpls., 1974—; mem. Ind. Consortium for Internat. Activities, 1974—. Served with AUS, 1959-61. Recipient Merle Sidener award in journalism, 1955. Mem. Phi Beta Kappa. Author: Differential Equations, 1976. Home: 5619 Beechwood Ave Indianapolis IN 46219 Office: 1135 E 38th St Indianapolis IN 46205

RIDGWAY, GEORGE MARTIN, computer cons. co. exec.; b. Rockford, Ill., Aug. 15, 1936; s. William Franklin and Marjorie Ann (Bolin) R.; Ph.B., Northwestern U., 1966; postgrad. U. Colo., 1966-67; m. Nanette Marie Populorum, Dec. 23, 1961; children—Philip Esta, Paul Franklin, Elizabeth Ann. Program analyst Abbott Labs., Chgo., 1960-66; systems mgr. Colo. Interstate Computer Services, Colorado Springs, 1966-67; mgr. computer services Greyhound, Chgo., 1967-68, asst. to pres., 1968-69; founder Systems Mgmt., Des Plaines, Ill., 1969—, also pres.; cons. Joint Commn. on Accreditation Hosps., 1974-75, HEW, 1974-75. Treas., Republican County Com., 1967-73, precinct committeeman, 1965-67. Served with AUS, 1957-59. Mem. Assn. Computing Machinery, Data Processing Mgmt. Assn., Am. Contract Bridge League. Presbyterian. Home: 681 Monticello Circle Lake Forest IL 60045 Office: 10400 W Higgins Rd Des Plaines IL 60018

RIDINGS, CRAIG ASHER, lawyer; b. Bradford, Ill., Dec. 13, 1920; s. Charles Hendricks and Katherine (Kirchhubel) R.; J.D., U. Louisville, 1943; postgrad. John B. Stetson U., 1946-47; m. Marry Margaret Helm, June 9, 1942; children—Carey, Kevin, G. Franklin. Admitted to Ky. bar, 1947, Ill. bar, 1956; title examiner Louisville Title Ins. Co., 1939-42, 44-46; claims adjuster Am. Mut. Liability Ins. Co. of Boston, 1947-51, claims mgr., 1951-56; asso. Yalden & Ridings, Rockford, Ill., 1956—. Del., Democratic Nat. Conv., 1976; bd. dirs. Rockford chpt. Big Bros. Am., 1960-68, sec., 1965-68; trustee Midwestern Baptist Theol. Sem., Kansas City, Mo., 1971—, Judson Coll., Elgin, Ill., 1972—. Served with AUS, 1942-44. Mem. Ill. (unauthorized practice of law com. 1967—, chmn. 1975-76), Winnebago County, Ky., Am. bar assns., Am. Trial Lawyers Assn., Am. Judicature Soc. Democrat. Baptist (bd. dirs. Ill. Bapt. Assn. 1970-76, preaching mission Philippines 1970, fgn. mission crusade, Sao Paulo, Brazil 1974). Mason. Home: PO Box 5084 Rockford IL 61125 Office: 408 Camelot Tower 1415 E State St Rockford IL 61108

RIDLEN, JAMES HERMAN, dentist, educator; b. Chicago Heights, Ill., Apr. 5, 1926; s. Herman and Ruth Avis (Duffy) R.; student N. Central Coll., Naperville, Ill., 1946-48; D.D.S., Chgo. Coll. Dental Surgery, Loyola U., 1952; m. Dolores Mary Israels, Nov. 24, 1948; children—Cheryl Lynn, Cynthia Lee, James Robert. Practice dentistry, Western Springs, Ill., 1952—; instr. Loyola U. Sch. Dentistry, Chgo., 1952-59; asso. prof. U. Ill. Sch. Dentistry, Chgo., 1963—. Health commr., also trustee Village of Willowbrook, Ill., 1970-75. Served with USMCR, 1944-46. Mem. Internat. (exec. council, dir. U.S. sect.), Am. (pres. Ill. sect. 1972) colls. dentists, Ill. (councilman 1966-69), W. Suburban (pres. 1965), Chgo. (treas.) dental socs., Western Springs C. of C. (dir. 1954-60), P.T.A. Mason, Rotarian. Home: 800 Ridgemoor W Hinsdale IL 60521 Office: 1052 Hillgrove St Western Springs IL 60558

RIDLEY, ELTON TAFT, hosp. adminstr., med. center planning cons.; b. Syracuse, N.Y., July 26, 1926; s. Clarence Eugene and Edna Esther (Taft) R.; B.S. in Commerce, U. Ill., 1950; M.B.A. in Hosp. Adminstrn., U. Chgo., 1952; m. Mary Elizabeth Ross, Oct. 3, 1953. Adminstrv. resident Ind. U. Med. Center, Indpls., 1951-52, adminstrv. asst., 1952-53, asst. to adminstr., 1953-54, acting personnel dir., 1954-55, asst. adminstr., 1954-64, acting adminstr., 1964-66; dir. Ind. U. Hosps., Indpls., 1966-72, spl. cons. to chancellor dir. for med. center planning, 1973—; interim dir. div. allied health scis., asso. prof. hosp. adminstrn. Ind. U. Sch. Medicine. Cons. communicative disorders program project rev. com. Nat. Inst. Neurol. Diseases and Stroke; pres. Indpls. Dist. Hosp. Council, 1962-63, 72-73. Bd. dirs. Blue Cross Hosp. Service, 1972-73; bd. dirs., chmn. Ind. Health Careers; bd. dirs. United Hosp. Services, 1965-73, Ind. Hosp. Services, 1967-72, Central Ind. Comprehensive Health Planning Council, Ind. Adv. Hosp. and Health Facilities planning Council; bd. dirs. Marion County Comprehensive Health Planning Council, pres., 1972-74; pres. In Health Council; mem. exec. council Univ. Hosps., 1952-72, Childrens Hosps.; bd. dirs. Tri-State Hosp. Assembly, Scientech Club of Indpls. adv. com. Indpls. Alcohol Safety Action Project. Served with AUS, 1945-46. Fellow Am. Coll. Hosp. Adminstrs.; mem. Am. (del.), Ind. (pres. 1970-71, dir.) hosp. assns., Assn. Am. Med. Colls. (council on teaching hosps. 1966-72), U. Chgo., U. Ill. alumni assns., James W. Riley Meml. Assn., Psi Upsilon. Methodist. Home: 2815 N High Sch Rd Indianapolis IN 46224 Office: 1100 W Michigan St Indianapolis IN 46202

RIDZON, JAMES RONALD, orthodontist; b. Canton, Ohio, Mar. 25, 1941; s. Joseph John and Marcella Norma (McMahan) R.; student John Carroll U., 1959-61; B.S., Western Res. U., 1963, D.D.S., 1965, M.S., 1971; m. Marilyn Lee McQuern, July 3, 1965; children—Richard, Susan. Asso. in practice of gen. dentistry, Canton, 1968-70; asso. in practice of orthodontics, Wooster, Ohio, 1970-72; pvt. practice orthodontics, Massillon, Ohio, 1972—. Served as lt. U.S. Navy, 1965-68. Recipient award of achievement Am. Coll. Dentists. Mem. Royal Soc. Health, ADA, Am. Assn. Orthodontists, Gt. Lakes Orthodontic Assn., Ohio Dental Assn., Omicron Kappa Upsilon. Roman Catholic. Home: 5772 West Blvd NW Canton OH 44718 Office: 3140 Lincoln Way E Massillon OH 44646

RIECKER, JOHN E(RNEST), lawyer, bank exec.; b. Ann Arbor, Mich., Nov. 25, 1930; s. Herman H. and Elizabeth (Wertz) R.; A.B. with distinction, University Michigan, 1952, J.D. with distinction, 1954; m. Margaret Ann Towsley, July 30, 1955; children—John Towsley, Margaret Elizabeth. Admitted to Mich. bar, 1954, Cal. bar, 1955, bar U.S. Tax Ct., U.S. Supreme Ct. Bar, U.S. Treasury Bar; asso. law firm Bonisteel & Bonisteel, Ann Arbor, 1954-55; partner firm Francis, Wetmore & Riecker. Midland, Mich., 1958-65; partner firm Gillespie Riecker & George, Midland, 1966—; chmn. bd. dirs. First Nat. Bank & Trust Co. Midland; sec. numerous Mich. corps. Mem. N.A.M. trade mission to EEC, 1964. Trustee, treas. Delta Coll., 1965-68; mem. bd. mgrs. United Fund Midland 1960-64; sec. Midland City Charter Rev. Com., 1964, mem. Spl. Charter Commn., 1972; mem. Midland Community Found., 1974; mem. Bd. Ethics State of Mich., 1976—; asst. sec. Mich. Found. for Advanced Research, Dow Found., Towsley Found. Ann Arbor; mem. exec. com. Mich. United Fund, 1970-71; bd. govs. Northwood Inst., 1969-71; bd. dirs. U. Mich. Devel. Council. Served as 1st lt., Judge Adv. Gens. Corps, AUS, 1955-58; now capt. Res. Mem. Midland County (pres. 1962-63), Am., Calif., Mich. (tax council) bar assns., Midland C. of C. (pres. 1971), Phi Beta Kappa, Phi Kappa Phi, Phi Eta Sigma, Sigma Iota Epsilon, Alpha Delta Phi, Phi Delta Phi. Republican. Episcopalian. Clubs: Benmark, Midland Country, Saginaw, Saginaw Valley Torch, President's (U. Mich). Mem. bd. editors Mich. Law Rev., 1953-54. Contbr. articles to profl. jours. Benefactor U. Mich. Home: 3211 Valley Dr Midland MI 48640 Office: 414 Townsend St Midland MI 48640

RIECKER, MARGARET ANN TOWSLEY (MRS. JOHN E. RIECKER), polit. worker, found. exec.; b. Ann Arbor, Mich., Nov. 9, 1933; d. Harry A. and Margaret (Dow) Towsley; B.A., Carleton Coll., 1954; postgrad. Mt. Holyoke Coll., 1955; m. John E. Riecker, July 30, 1955; children—John Towsley, Margaret Elizabeth. Vice chmn. Midland County Republican Com., Midland, Mich., 1962—; vice-chmn. 10th Congl. Dist. (Mich.) Com., 1964—; spl. asst. for women's affairs Rep. state chmn. Mich., 1966—; 1st vice chmn. Mich. Rep. party, 1968—; mem. Rep. Nat. Com. from Mich., 1970—, mem. exec. com., 1973—. Trustee Herbert H. & Grace A. Dow Found., 1962—, Harry A. and Margaret D. Towsley Found., 1961—; trustee Central Mich. U., 1974—, chmn. bd., 1976—. Mem. Midland Little Theatre Guild, 1958—; women's bd. trustees Northwood Inst., Midland, 1965—; mem. Midland Center for Arts, Midland Community Concerts. Mem. Midland Symphony Guild, Carleton

Coll. Alumni Assn., Midland Art Assn. Clubs: Women's Study, Midland Country, Zonta, Northwood Town and Campus (sec. 1967—), University of Michigan President's. Benefactor U. Mich. Address: 3211 Valley Dr Midland MI 48640

RIECKUS, ALOYSIUS MICHAEL, ret. clergyman, librarian; b. St. Louis, Aug. 6, 1905; s. Aloys and Anna Elizabeth (Wohlschlaeger) R.; A.B., St. Louis U., 1928, A.M., 1930; S.T.L., St. Mary's Coll., 1938. Joined Soc. of Jesus, 1924, ordained priest Roman Catholic Ch., 1937; instr. classical langs. Creighton U., Omaha, 1932-34; tchr. classical langs. Rockhurst High Sch., Kansas City, Mo., 1941-44, St. Stanislaus Sem., Florissant, Mo., 1944-46, Regis High Sch., Denver, 1946-51; supt. grounds and bldgs. Regis Coll., Denver, 1951-54; instr., asst. prof. classical langs. Rockhurst Coll., Kansas City, Mo., 1954-63, also dir. residence hall, 1954-63, student chaplain, 1963-67; librarian St. Stanislaus Sem., 1967, Fusz Meml. Library, St. Louis U., 1968-76; archivist Mo. Province Ednl. Inst., St. Louis, 1976—. Home: 4511 W Pine Blvd St Louis MO 63108

RIEDEL, PAUL SCHREITER, mobile homes co. ofcl.; b. Minden City, Mich., Oct. 8, 1911; s. Louis Herman and Anna (Schreiter) R.; student Mich. State U., 1928-31, Detroit Bus. U., 1932; m. Dorothy Artha Slack, Oct. 17, 1932; children—Daniel P., Andrea Lynn. Propr., L.H. Riedel Lumber Co., 1941-46, pres. L.H. Riedel Lumber Co., Inc., 1946-53; hon chmn.; Vindale Corp., mobile homes, Brookville, Ohio; dir. First Nat. Bank of Dayton. Presbyterian. Clubs: Racquet, Dayton Country, Bicycle (Dayton); Capitol Hill (Washington). Home: 2230 S Patterson Blvd Kettering OH 45409 Office: 1222 First Nat Bank Bldg Dayton OH 45402

RIEDELL, JOHN ALOYSIUS, cartoonist; b. Sac County, Iowa, May 20, 1932; s. Joseph Alois and Flotilla Elizabeth (Frisbie) R.; student The Creighton U., 1953-54; B.A., St. Benedict's Coll., 1958; student Am. Inst. of Air, 1952; m. Serafina Maria Gonzalez, June 4, 1961; children—Shaun, Shane Eduardo, Aaron Matthew. News editor Radio sta. KCIM, Carroll, Iowa, 1952-53; counselor Father Flanagan's Boys Home, Boy's Town, Nebr., 1953-54; editorial dept. employee Hallmark Cards, Kansas City, Mo., 1958; tchr. Atchison, Kans., 1958-59, Immaculate Conception Grade Sch., Leavenworth, Kans., 1959-60; faculty Muffle's Coll., Orange Walk, British Honduras, 1960-61; tchr. Odebolt (Iowa)-Arthur Community Sch., 1961-65, Wall Lake (Iowa) Community Sch., 1965-67; cartoonist Peoria (Ill.) Jour. Star, 1967—. Served with USN, 1949-51. Recipient Freedoms Found. awards, 1967, 68, 69, 70, 71, 72, 73, 74, 75, 76; Nat. Found. for Hwy. Safety awards, 1968, 73. Mem. Assn. Am. Editorial Cartoonists. Roman Catholic. Cartoonist, illustrator Hawkeye Adventure, 1966. Cartoons reprinted in books and newspapers including Chgo. Tribune, San Diego Union. Cartoon exhibition Little Art Gallery, KVFD Radio Studios, Ft. Dodge, Iowa 1967. Home: Route 4 Metamora IL 61548 Office: Journal Star War Meml Dr Peoria IL 61601

RIEDL, FRANK WILLIAM, physician; b. Chatham, Ont., Can., Apr. 22, 1940; s. Frank and Helen (Bernath) R.; M.D., U. Western Ont., 1965; m. Mary Lynne Lampitt, Apr. 27, 1968; children—Becky Elizabeth, Craig Allan Lampitt, Jennifer Lynne, Frank Douglas. Intern, St. Joseph's Hosp., London, Ont., 1965-66; resident, U. Alta. Hosp., Edmonton, 1966-67; family practice medicine, Petrolia, Ont., 1967—; home physician Lambton Twight Haven, Petrolia, 1970-71; dir. Lambton Pharmacie Ltd., 1969—; chief staff Charlotte Elleanor Englehart Hosp., Petrolia, 1970-71, also trustee, 1970-71. Mem. adv. bd. Ont. Addiction Research Found., Lambton, 1971-74. Served with RCAF, 1961-64. Fellow Ont. Geriatrics Research Soc.; mem. Canadian, Ont. med. assns., Canadian, Ont. colls. family physicians, Coll. Physicians and Surgeons Ont., Southwestern Ont. Anaesthetists Soc., Lambton County Med. Soc. (pres. 1977—). Roman Catholic. Club: Rotary. Home: 513 Queen St Petrolia ON N0N 1R0 Canada Office: 4141 Lorne Ave Petrolia ON N0N 1R0 Canada

RIEDMANN, WILLIAM JOSEPH, lawyer; b. Omaha, Dec. 19, 1941; s. William J. and Elizabeth (Welch) R.; J.D., Creighton U., 1965; m. Agnes A. Czerwinski, Aug. 17, 1963; children—Elizabeth, William. Admitted to Neb. bar, 1965; asso. law firm Kennedy, Holland, DeLacy & Svoboda, Omaha, 1965-68, partner, 1968-72; sr. partner law firm Riedmann & Welsh, Omaha, 1972—; dir. Sawyer's Safety Service Inc.; lectr. nursing and law Creighton Meml. Hosp., St. Joseph Hosp., St. Mary's Coll. Mem. Omaha Symphony Council, 1971—; mem. Omaha Citizens Crime Commn., 1967; spl. asst. to Mayor for Implementation of Crime Commn. Recommendations, 1968; chmn. Lawyers Com. Heart Fund Drive, 1969; mem. Mayor's Crime Study Com., 1969; mem. com. Omaha Hearing Sch. Fund Drive, 1968; mem. com. United Community Services Fund Drive, 1969; chmn. probation com. United Community Services Cts. Correction and Legal Services Task Force, 1970; bd. dirs. Crime Crisis Council. Mem. Omaha, Nebr., Am. bar assns., Nebr. Assn. Trial Attys. (v.p. 1976—), Omaha Barristers Club (pres. 1967), Def. Counsel Assn. Neb. (pres. 1972), Phi Alpha Delta. Republican. Roman Catholic. Clubs: Omaha Ski (dir. 1970-72). Home: 2322 S 91st St Omaha NE 68124 Office: 2040 First Nat Center Omaha NE 68102

RIEG, GEORGE STANLEY, JR., lawyer, accountant; b. Chicago., Nov. 28, 1926; s. George Stanley and Helene (Hermanns) R.; Ph.B., U. Chgo., 1945, M.B.A., 1949, J.D., 1953; m. Helga Mattern, Aug. 3, 1962; children—George S. VI, Monica. C.P.A., Arthur Andersen & Company, 1949-51, George Rieg, Sr., 1953-54, George S. Rieg, Jr., 1954—; admitted to the Ill. bar, 1954, since in pvt. practice; professorial lectr. in fed. taxation and accounting U. Chgo. Sch. Bus. 1954—, also prof.; mgr. ins. dept. Chgo. Bridge & Iron Co., 1956-57. Served from pvt. to pfc. Mil. Police, AUS, 1946-47; now col. Res. d'Lustige Holzhacker Baum, Schlaraffia Chicagoana, City Club Chgo. C.P.A., Ill. Mem. Am., Ill., Chgo. bar assns., U. Chgo. Alumni Assn., Mil. Order World Wars, Res. Officers Assn., Ill. Soc. C.P.A.'s, Am. Youth Hostels, Chgo. Council Fgn. Relations, Sigma Chi. Elk, K.C. Clubs: Germania, Riviera Country, Catholic University, City, German (Chgo.); Turnverein Eiche. Home: 10449 S Hamilton Ave Chicago IL 60643 Office: 19 S LaSalle St Chicago IL 60603

RIEGEL, FARALD LLOYD, accountant; b. Dayton, Ohio, Sept. 26, 1940; s. James Lloyd and Olive Anne (Heiden) R.; student Ohio State U., 1960-62; B.S., Wright State U., 1969, M.B.A., 1972; m. Mary Carolyn Paige, Sept. 25, 1969; children—James Lloyd, Paige Renee Anne. Supr., Bertram Plotnick Co., C.P.A.'s, Dayton, Ohio, 1972-73; pvt. practice accounting, Dayton, Ohio, 1973—. Served with U.S. Army, 1958-60. Mem. Am. Inst. C.P.A.'s, Ohio Soc. C.P.A.'s, Nat. Soc. Pub. Accountants, Pub. Accountants Soc. Ohio, Nat. Assn. Accountants, Dayton Tax Club. Club: Trailsend. Home: 3204 Allendale Dr Kettering OH 45409 Office: 4140 Linden Ave Dayton OH 45432

RIEGER, HELEN BREEDEN HEDRICK (MRS. WRAY MONTGOMERY RIEGER), mus. curator; b. Columbia, Mo., Oct. 13, 1903; d. Earle Raymond and Helen Breeden (Seidensticker) Hedrick; B.S., U. Mo., 1925; postgrad. Pomona Coll., 1926-27; m. Wray Montgomery Rieger, Sept. 15, 1927; children—Helen B. (Mrs. John Robert Anderson), Wray Montgomery. Substitute tchr., Chgo., 1927-28, Kirksville, Mo.; 1941-57; curator E.M. Violette Mus., Kirksville, 1958—; archivist N.E. Mo. State U., Kirksville, 1966—. Bd. dirs. Sojourners Pub. Library, 1946-70. Mem. Alpha Gamma Delta. Baptist. Clubs: Sojourners, University Dames (pres. 1937) (Kirksville). Home: 516 Halliburton Ave Kirksville MO 63501

RIEGER, MITCHELL SHERIDAN, lawyer; b. Chgo., Sept. 5, 1922; s. Louis and Evelyn (Sampson) R.; A.B., Northwestern U., 1944; J.D., Harvard, 1949; m. Nancy Horner, May 30, 1961 (div. Mar. 1972); 1 dau. by previous marriage, Karen Rieger Gross (Mrs. Walter Abelmann); step-children—Jill, Susan and James Geoffrey Felsenthal, Linda Hanan; m. Pearl Handelsman, June 10, 1973; stepchildren—Steven Newman, Mary Ann Crowe, Nancy Newman. Admitted to Ill. bar, 1950; asso. Rieger & Rieger, Chgo., 1950-54; asst. U.S. Atty., No. Dist. of Ill., 1954-60, chief tax div., 1954-55, chief criminal div., 1955-58, first asst. 1958-60; asso. gen. counsel Securities and Exchange Commn., Washington, 1960-61; partner Schiff Hardin & Waite and predecessor firm, Chgo., 1961—; instr. law John Marshall Law Sch., Chgo., 1952-54. Past pres., dir. Park View Home. Mem. Chicago Crime Commn. Served from lt. (j.g.) to comdr. USNR, 1943-46, ret. 1967. Mem. Am., 7th Circuit, Ill., Chgo., Fed. (pres. Chgo. chpt. 1959-60, nat. v.p. 7th dist. 1960-61) bar assns., Am. Judicature Soc., Phi Beta Kappa. Clubs: The Standard (Chgo.), Lake Shore Country (Glencoe); Metropolitan. Contbr. articles in field to profl. jours. Home: 5333 S Hyde Park Blvd Chicago IL 60615 Office: 7200 Sears Tower 233 S Wacker Dr Chicago IL 60606

RIEGER, PEARL HANDELSMAN, psychologist; b. Chgo., Feb. 8, 1928; d. Meyer and Anne (Goldkin) Handelsman; B.A., U. Mich., 1948; M.A., U. Chgo., 1974; m. Mitchell Sheridan Rieger, June 10, 1973; children from previous marriage—Steven B. Newman, Mary Ann Crowe, Nancy L. Newman. Speech therapist Michael Reese Hosp. and Med. Center, Chgo., 1948-51; ednl. diagnostician Ancona Montessori Sch., Chgo., 1974-77; cons. ednl. diagnostician U. Chgo. Lab. Schs., Near North Montessori Sch., Harris Sch., 1974—, Ancona Montessori Sch., 1977—; pvt. practice ednl. diagnostician, Chgo., 1974—. Trustee, Chgo. Inst. Psychoanalysis; chmn. bd. com. Barr Harris Center Study of Separation and Loss During Childhood, 1976—; v.p. bd. govs. U. Chgo. Lab. Schs., 1966-69, 74-75; women's bd. Jewish Fedn. Met. Chgo., 1952-60, Michael Reese Hosp., 1955-69, Jewish Community Centers, 1956-61. Registered psychologist, Ill. Mem. Council Exceptional Children, Assn. Children with Learning Disabilities, Am. Speech and Hearing Assn., Zeta Phi Eta, Pi Lambda Theta. Jewish. Club: Quandrangle. Home and Office: 5333 S Hyde Park Blvd Chicago IL 60615

RIEGLE, DONALD WAYNE, JR., Senator; b. Flint, Mich., Feb. 4, 1938; s. Donald Wayne and Dorothy (Fitchett) R.; B.A. in Bus. Adminstrn. and Econs., U. Mich.; M.B.A., Mich. State U., 1961; postgrad. Harvard Bus. Sch., 1964-66; children—Catherine Anne, Laurie Elizabeth, Donald Wayne III. Faculty Mich. State U., 1960-61; sr. pricing analyst IBM, 1961-64; cons. Harvard-Mass. Inst. Tech. Joint Center on Urban Studies; mem. 90th-94th congresses Mich. 7th Dist.; Senator from Mich., 1976—, mem. Com. on Banking, Com. on Housing and Urban Affairs, Com. on Human Resources, Com. on Commerce, Sci. and Transp.; fellow-in-residence John Kennedy Inst. for Politics, Harvard, 1971. Recipient Distinguished Alumni award U. Mich. Bus. Adminstrn. Soc., 1967; named one of 10 Outstanding Young Men in Am., U.S. Jaycees, 1967; one of 200 Nat. Leaders Under Age 45, Time mag., 1974. Mem. Beta Gamma Sigma. Democrat. Author: O Congress, 1972. Office: Dirksen Senate Office Bldg Washington DC 20510

RIEMAN, DWIGHT WALKER, educator; b. Berlin, Pa., Mar. 30, 1918; s. George S. and Emma (Walker) R.; A.B., Juniata Coll., 1940; M.S., Case Western Res. U., 1949; m. Emily Hutton Griest, Jan. 11, 1947; children—Eliot, Janice, Michael, Elizabeth. Psychiat. social worker Fed. Employee Mental Health Clinic, USPHS, Washington, 1946-50; cons. psychiat. social worker Tex. Dept. Health, 1950-60, chief psychiat. social worker, 1960-65; adminstrv. cons. community services Tex. Dept. Mental Health, Austin, 1965-68; asso. prof. Social Work Extension Program, U. Mo., Sch. Social and Community Services, Columbia, 1968—; program dir. NIMH continuing edn. projects, 1970-73, 75—; cons. on prodn. film "Community Mental Health", Mental Health Film Bd., N.Y.C., Hollywood, Calif., 1959; cons. Mid-Continent Inst., Nat. Assn. Social Workers, 1965, Confs. Chief Psychiat. Social Workers in State Mental Health Programs, USPHS, Region IV, 1965, Ga. Dept. Pub. Health, Community Mental Health Services, 1966, Greater Kansas City Mental Health Found., Inst. for Pupil Study, 1967. Served with M.C., AUS, 1944-45. Mem. Nat. Assn. Social Workers (del. Mo. council, Region VI cons. continuing edn. 1972-73), Nat. Conf. on Social Welfare, Acad. Certified Social Workers, Council on Social Work Edn., Mo., Tex. (past v.p., treas.) social welfare assns. Contbr. to Consultation in Social Work Practice, 1963; Mental Health and the Community-Problems, Programs and Strategies, 1969; Consultation in Community Mental Health Services, 1973. Home: 405 S Garth St Columbia MO 65201 Office: 826 Clark Hall U Mo Columbia MO 65201

RIES, EDWARD OTTO, vending service co. exec.; b. Sandusky, Ohio, Sept. 13, 1937; s. Edward L. and Dorothy V. (Rudolph) R.; m. Betty J. Brady, Aug. 7, 1954; children—Thomas E., Katherine Ries Krauzer, Dotti M. Pres., Ries Vending Service Inc., Sandusky, Ohio, 1967—; sec., treas. Lum's Vending & Food Service Inc., Cleve.; v.p. Steele's of Sandusky. Mem. Nat., Ohio (pres. 1972-73, dir. 1977—) automatic merchandising assns., Sandusky C. of C. Republican. Roman Catholic. Clubs: Sandusky Yacht (dir. 1976—), Plum Brook Country. Home: 3921 Hilltop Dr Huron OH 44839 Office: 608 Feick Bldg Sandusky OH 44870

RIESTER, GEORGE P., orthodontist; b. Salem, Ind., Feb. 4, 1915; s. John Otto and Glenn (Hayes) R.; D.D.S., Ind. U., 1938; m. Mary Ellen Baugh, Nov. 21, 1965; children—Joan (Mrs. James E. Engeler, Jr.), Kathleen (Mrs. Daniel Earl Sparks), John Leslie. Instr., Ind. U. Sch. Dentistry, 1938-39; practice gen. dentistry, Paoli, Ind., 1940-54; practice orthodontics, Bloomington, Ind., 1954—. Mem. Am. Assn. Orthodontists, Am. Dental Assn., Omicron Kappa Upsilon, Phi Kappa Psi. Presbyterian (elder 1950—). Clubs: Bloomington Country (pres. 1960-62), Indiana University Varsity (pres. 1964) (Bloomington). Home: 1017 Commons Dr Sherwood Green Bloomington IN 47401 Office: 857 Auto Mall Rd Bloomington IN 47401

RIETZ, EDWARD GUSTAVE, educator; b. Chgo., Feb. 24, 1911; s. Edward Jacob and Emily Olive (Olsen) R.; B.S., U. Chgo., 1933, M.S., 1935, Ph.D., 1938. Chemist, U.S. FDA, Chgo., 1939-42; research chemist U.S. Dept. Agr., Albany, Calif., 1942-46; asso. prof. U. Fla., Gainesville, 1946-52; prof., chmn. dept. Chgo. City Colls., 1952—; staff U. Ill., Chgo., 1956—; vis. asso. prof. chemistry St. Louis U., 1955. Active Rec. for the Blind; bd. dirs. Family Counseling Service Evanston and Skokie Valley, 1975—. Served with USNR, 1943-46; PTO; capt. USNR ret. Mem. Am. Chem. Soc. (councilor 1973—, chmn. Chgo. sect. 1973), Ret. Officers Assn., Episcopalian. Club: Cliff Dwellers (Chgo.). Author: (with others) Chemical and Biological Warfare Defense, 1952; (with Pollard) Problems in Organic Chemistry, 1952. Contbr. articles to profl. jours. Home: 2948 N Laramie Ave Chicago IL 60641

RIGG, ROBINSON PETER, ins. co. exec.; b. Blackpool, Eng., Jan. 13, 1918; s. Robinson Patrick and Lilian Mary (Clough) R.; came to U.S., 1969; A.B., U. of Liverpool (Eng.), 1939; m. Jane Lane Chadwick, Apr. 3, 1952. Vice chmn. Foreign Office Whitley Council, (German Sect.), 1947-52; pub. editor Indsl. Screen, London, 1957-62; indsl. firm corr. Financial Times, London, 1958-63; communications cons., 1963-69; chmn. indsl. film corrs. group, 1966-69; pub. relations asso. Combined Ins. Co., Chgo., 1969-72, dir. pub. relations advt., 1972, v.p., 1972—. Mng. dir. Robin Publs. Limited, London, 1957—; trustee Ill. Council Economic Edn., 1977—. Served with British Army, 1939-46. Fellow Royal Photographic Soc.; mem. Pub. Relations Soc. of Am., Inst. of Pub. Relations (Eng.), Inst. of Journalists (Eng.), Soc. of Authors, Health Ins. Assn. of Am. (chmn. consumer relations com.). Clubs: Inst of Dirs., Sportsmans (London), Press Club (Chgo.), Michigan Shores (Wilmette). Author Audiovisual Aids & Techniques, 1969; contbr. to Indsl. Advt. Mgrs. Handbook, 1968, Dirs. Handbook, 1970, The Times, Financial Times, The Dir., Investors Chronicle. Home: 1234 Isabella St Evanston IL 60201 Office: 5050 Broadway St Chicago IL 60640

RIGGS, BYRON LAWRENCE, JR., physician; b. Hot Springs, Ark., Mar. 24, 1931; s. Byron Lawrence and Elizabeth Ann (Patching) R.; student U. Ark., 1948-51, B.S., 1953, B.S. in Medicine, 1953, M.S., 1955; M.S. in Medicine, U. Minn., 1962; m. Janet Templeton Brewer, June 24, 1955; children—Byron Kent, Ann Templeton. Intern, Lettermen Army Hosp., San Francisco, 1958-59; resident internal medicine Mayo Grad. Sch. Medicine, 1958-61; asst. to staff Mayo Clinic, Rochester, Minn., 1961, mem. staff internal medicine and metabolism Mayo Clinic and Found., 1962—; instr. medicine U. Minn., 1962—; asst. prof. U. Minn., 1967-70, asso. prof., 1970—; prof. medicine Mayo Med. Sch., 1974—; chmn. div. endocrinology Mayo Clinic and Med. Sch., 1974—. Served with M.C., AUS, 1956-58. Recipient Mayo Found. Postgrad. Travel award, 1961; Kappa Delta award Am. Acad. Orthopedic Surgery, 1972. Royal Soc. Medicine Found. traveling fellow, 1973. Diplomate Am. Bd. Internal Medicine. Fellow A.C.P., mem. Am. Diabetes Assn., AMA, Minn., Zumbro County med. socs., Am. Soc. Clin. Investigation, Endocrine Soc., Am. Fedn. Clin. Research (councillor Midwest sect.), Central Soc. Clin. Research, Central Clin. Research Club, AAAS, N.Y. Acad. Scis. Contbr. articles to profl. jours. Research in metabolism. Home: 432 SW 10th Ave Rochester MN 55901 Office: 200 SW 1st St Rochester MN 55902

RIGGS, RODERICK DOUGLAS, educator; b. Racine, Wis., Apr. 15, 1931; s. Ardath and Elizabeth (Davies) R.; B.S. magna cum laude, U. Dubuque, 1955; M.S., Iowa State U., 1957; Ph.D., Mich. State U., 1971; m. Patricia Alice Pav, June 4, 1955; children—Elizabeth Anne, Kathryn Irene, David William. Physics instr. Jackson (Mich.) Jr. Coll., 1958-61, dean men, 1961-62, dean students, 1962-65, prof., chmn. physics dept., 1965—; owner Sci. Assos., Ednl. and Mgmt. Cons. firm, Jackson, Mich., 1965—. Regional cons. State Farm Mut. Ins. Co. of Mich., 1967—; lectr. physics Spring Arbor Coll. Co-chmn. Jackson Met. Information Com.; mem. Gov.'s Com. to Mich. Higher Edn. Assistance Authority; budget chmn. Jackson United Fund. Served with USN, 1949-53. Mem. Am. Assn. Physics Tchrs. (pres. Mich. sect. 1965-66), Jackson Area Guidance and Personnel Assn. (pres. 1961-62), NAACP. Presbyterian (ruling elder 1962-66). Rotarian. Contbr. articles to profl. jours. Home: 2605 S St Anthony St Jackson MI 49203 Office: Jackson Community Coll Jackson MI 49201

RIGGS, WILLIAM NORMAN, agrl. engr.; b. Wentzville, Mo., May 7, 1936; s. Paul Flood and Ella Lucille (Ridgway) R.; B.S. in Agrl. Engring., U. Mo., 1958; m. Ruby Arlene Booth, Dec. 27, 1964; 1 son, Russell Paul. Engr., U.S. Soil Conservation Service, Dept. Agr., Elsberry, Mo., 1958, Bethany, Mo., 1961-62, Maryville, Mo., 1962-66, area engr., Bethany, 1966—. Bd. dirs. United Fund, 1971-76, v.p., 1973, pres., 1974. Served with AUS, 1958-60. Recipient Spl. Achievement award Soil Conservation Service, 1974. Registered profl. engr., Mo. Mem. Orgn. Profl. Employees U.S. Dept. Agr., U. Mo. Alumni Assn., Jaycees (Distinguished Service award 1973), Am. Soc. Agrl. Engrs. (Young Engr. award Mo. sect. 1975), Soil Conservation Soc. Am. Methodist (ch. adminstrv. bd. 1973, chmn. council on ministries 1974-76, trustee 1977). Mason. Club: Bethany Kiwanis (v.p. 1968-69, pres. 1969-70). Home: 1103 Maple Terrace Bethany MO 64424 Office: PO Box 232 Bethany MO 64424

RIGHTER, WALTER CAMERON, clergyman; b. Phila., Oct. 23, 1923; s. Richard and Dorothy Mae (Bottomley) R.; B.A., U. Pitts., 1948; M.Div., Berkeley Div. Sch., 1951, D.D., 1972; m. Marguerite Jeanne Burroughs, Jan. 26, 1946; children—Richard Stanton, Rebecca Jean. Ordained to ministry Episcopal Ch., 1951; vicar All Saints Ch., Aliquippa, Pa., 1951-54; rector Ch. of Good Shepherd, Nashua, N.H., 1954-71; consecrated bishop, 1972; bishop diocese of Ia., Des Moines, 1972—. Bd. dirs. Orchard Place Home for Children, Des Iowa, 1975—, Door of Faith Mission, Des Moines; past bd. dirs. Protestant Home for Children, Nashua, 1954-70; trustee Nashua Pub. Library, 1968-71. Served with AUS, 1943-45; ETO. Fellow Coll. Preachers Washington Cathedral; mem. Newcomen Soc. Mason, Rotarian (dir.). Contbr. articles to religious publs. Address: 225 37th St Des Moines IA 50312

RIGHTER, WILLIAM HOWARD, JR., fin. mgmt. co. exec.; b. Salem, N.J., Apr. 27, 1936; s. William Howard and Lillian (Cole) R.; B.S., U. S.C., 1958, M.B.A., 1960. Product mgr. duPont Co., Del., 1960-67; v.p. new product devel. Morton-Norwich, Chgo., 1967-75; pres. Nat. Retirement Services, Inc., Chgo., 1975—; owner Righter Assos. Personnel Agy., 1972—; dir. Farmers Nat. Ins. Served with C.E., AUS, 1953-55. Democrat. Episcopalian. Developer thixotropic paint, Nature's Seasons, Handi-Melt, Salt Substitute; developer, patentee Lite Salt. Home: 1415 N Astor St Chicago IL 60610 Office: 1200 N State St Chicago IL 60610

RIGONI, RAYMOND JOHN, JR., supt. schs.; b. Ramsay, Mich., July 3, 1937; s. Raymond John and Marie T. (Reinikka) R.; A.A., Gogebic Community Coll., 1957; B.S., No. Mich. U., 1959, M.A., 1964, postgrad., 1966—; m. Bette Lou Toomey, Oct. 6, 1962; children—Rae Marie, Rhonda, Renee, Regan. Indsl. arts tchr., Bergland (Mich.) Community Schs., 1959-66, prin., 1964-66; supt. schs. Ewen (Mich.) Pub. Schs., 1966-67, Ewen-Trout Creek Consol. Schs., Ewen, 1967—. Mem. Vol. Fire Dept., 1973—. Mem. Am., Mich. (mem. state council 1972-74) assns. sch. adminstrs., Mich. Assn. Sch. Bds. and Adminstrs. Assn., Ewen Businessmen's Assn. (pres. 1971). Roman Catholic (mem. parish council 1972—). Home: Elm St Ewen MI 49925 Office: Box 218 Ewen MI 49925

RIKER, CHARLES MARR, III, banker; b. Chgo., Apr. 27, 1938; s. Charles Marr II and Mary Jeanne (Handy) R.; student Ill. State Normal U., 1964; grad. So. Ill. U. Sch. Banking, 1971; m. Barbara Jean Schierer, Sept. 5, 1964; children—Kimberly Marie, Deborah Sue, Charles Marr IV. Asst. mgr., sec. Pontiac Savs. & Loan Assn. (Ill.), 1964-69; v.p., cashier Manteno State Bank (Ill.), 1969-74; pres., chief exec. officer State Bank of Herscher (Ill.), 1974—, also dir. Alderman, Pontiac, 1966-69, named outstanding alderman City of Pontiac, 1968; pres. Livingston County Young Republican Club, 1965-66. Served with USNR, 1956-60. Mem. Am., Ill. bankers assns. Roman Catholic.

Clubs: Lions, Moose, Kiwanis (treas. 1967). Home: 524 4th St Herscher IL 60941 Office: 104 S Main St Herscher IL 60941

RIKIMARU, YUKI, archtl. designer, planner; b. Sacramento, Oct. 7, 1927; s. Joseph Iwasuke and Kiyono (Aramaki) R.; A.B. in Architecture, San Mateo City Coll., 1949; B.A. in Architecture Washington U., St. Louis, 1953; m. Kaoru Goto, Nov. 8, 1958; children—Raymond Kenji, Loryn Tamiko. Archtl. draftsman William B. Ittner, St. Louis, 1953-55; archtl. designer Russell, Mulgardt Schwarz, Van Hoeflin, St. Louis, 1956—; archtl. partner W.B. Kromm Asso., St. Louis, 1957—; prin. Kromm Rikimaru & Johansen Inc., architects, St. Louis, 1960—; v.p. Kromm, Rikimaru, Johansen & Aach Inc., architects, engrs. and planners, St. Louis, 1972, Archtl. Mgmt. Group Inc. Served with AUS, 1946-47. Mem. AIA, Nat. Council Archtl. Registration Bds., Mo. Council Architects. Prin. archtl. works include: Maplewood Municipal Bldg., St. Louis, 1961; Mineral Area Coll., Flat River, Mo., 1966; Fulton (Mo.) Juvenile Center, 1967; Delmar Gardens Nursing Home, St. Louis, 1968; Columbia (Mo.) Regional Hosp., 1972. Office: 112 S Hanley Rd St Louis MO 63105

RIKKER, LESLIE DENES, engring. co. exec.; b. Hungary, Mar. 12, 1937; s. Josef and Ilona (Egri) R.; came to U.S., 1957, naturalized, 1962; diploma in power engring., Budapest (Hungary) Inst. Tech., 1950-55; m. Cecilia Eva Mucska, Feb. 15, 1957; children—George Leslie, Eva Katerina. Plant engr. Budapest Motor Casting, 1955-56; engr. Combustion Engring. East Chgo. Div., 1957-60, Raymond Div., Chgo., 1960-64, asst. squad leader, 1962-64; designer Nat. Engring. Co., Chgo., 1964, sr. mech. engr., 1965-67, asst. chief mech. engr., 1969-71, v.p. 1973-76, exec. v.p., 1976—, also dir.; v.p. Neco of Can., Toronto, Ont., 1971-76, exec. v.p., 1976—. Recipient of certificate of appreciation Dept. Commerce, 1971, 72. Mem. Am. Foundrymen Soc. Roman Catholic. Patentee in field. Home: 15441 Betty Ann Ln Oak Forest IL 60452 Office: 20 N Wacker Dr Chicago IL 60606

RILEY, DONALD ALAN, mfg. co. info. systems exec.; b. Youngstown, Ohio, July 11, 1937; s. Perry W. and Dorothy E. (Battin) R.; B.S. in Bus. Adminstrn., Youngstown U., 1960; diploma U.S. Army Command Gen. Staff Coll., 1974, Indsl. Coll. Armed Forces, 1976; postgrad. bus. adminstrn. Ohio State U., 1964-65; m. Barbara Kiskaddon, Jan. 29, 1960; children—Robert Alan, Kathleen Joyce. Commd. 2nd lt. U.S. Army, 1960, advanced through grades to maj., 1967; asst. prof. mil. sci. Ohio State U., 1964; comdg. officer signal co., Vietnam, 1966-67; chief EDP facility, Ft. Leavenworth, Kans., 1967-70; mgr. data processing Kansas City (Mo.) div. Bendix Corp., 1970—. Active Boy Scouts Am., YWCA, PTA. Served as lt. col. USAR, 1970—. Decorated Bronze Star medal, Air medal. Mem. Bendix Mgmt. Club, U.S. Army Res. Assn., Theta Chi. Home: 11128 E 85th St Raytown MO 64138 Office: PO Box 1159 Kansas City MO 64141

RILEY, FENWICK CHARLES, JR., ophthalmologist; b. Bellingham, Wash., Mar. 31, 1934; s. Fenwick Charles and Helen Elizabeth (Grace) R.; A.B., Dartmouth Coll., 1956; M.D., Harvard Med. Sch., 1961; m. Jenifer O. M. Jowsey, Sept. 9, 1967; children—John Benjamin Jowsey, Pamela Grace. Intern, U. Oreg. Med. Sch. Hosp., 1961-62; resident Mayo Grad. Sch., Rochester, Minn., 1964-67; asso. cons. ophthalmology Mayo Clinic, Rochester, 1967-68; cons., 1968-74; practice medicine specializing in ophthalmology, Austin, Minn., 1974—; instr. ophthalmology Mayo Grad. Sch., Rochester, Minn., 1969-71; asst. prof. ophthalmology Mayo Med. Sch., 1971-74. Served with M.C., USN, 1962-64. Heed Found. fellow, 1968; Sicot fellow, 1972; recipient ophthalmology award Mayo Found., 1968. Diplomate Am. Bd. Ophthalmology. Mem. Mower County (pres. 1976), Minn. med. socs., Am., Minn. assns. ophthalmology, Am. Acad. Ophthalmology and Otolaryngology, Am. Intraocular Implant Soc. Author various research publs. Home: Nether Wallop Farm Rock Dell Route 2 Byron MN 55920 Office: 100 Bldg 109 N Main Austin MN 55912

RILEY, JOHN EDWARD, psychologist; b. Dayton, Ohio, Nov. 5, 1930; s. John William and Marie Eileen (Healey) R.; B.A., U. Dayton, 1952; M.A., Miami U., Oxford, Ohio, 1959; children—Kevin, Thomas, Ann, Robert. Staff psychologist U. Dayton Psychol. Services Center, 1957-65, dir. vets. guidance, 1965-74, dir. center, 1974—; asst. prof. U. Dayton, 1960-73; pvt. practice, 1970—. Vice pres. Gaslight Acad., Dayton. Served with U.S. Army, 1952-54. Mem. Am., Ohio psychol. assns. Home: 5530 Bigger Rd Kettering OH 45440 Office: 300 College Park Ave Dayton OH 45469

RILEY, LYMAN GUYTON, cons. evangelism; b. Little Sioux, Iowa, May 13, 1918; s. Elias Lyman and Anna Marie (Johnson) R.; A.S., Graceland Coll., 1937; B.A., Trinity Coll., Sioux City, 1938; m. Velma Ruth Benson, Feb. 23, 1939; children—Patricia (Mrs. Robert L. Wallis), Linda Maureen (Mrs. Dennis Steele). Prin., St. Joseph High Sch., Salix, Iowa, 1937-38; dist. mgr. Econs. Lab., St. Paul, 1939-43; mgr. Meramec Caverns, Stanton, Mo., 1946-49; owner, mgr. Onondaga Cave, Leasburg, Mo., 1950-67; dir. Woodland Hills Camp Found., 1971—. Vice pres. Meramec Basin Corp., Kirkwood, Mo., 1962-67. Chmn. Mo. Travel Commn., 1958-63. Mem. Republican County Com., 1968-77. Bd. dirs. Nat. Youth Found., St. Louis, 1973-75. Mem. Am. Cave Men (pres. 1946-50, Cave Man of year 1962, 63, 64), US 66 Assn. (dir. 1947-66), Meramec Basin Assn. (pres. 1964-67), Nat. Assn. Travel Ofcls. Mem. Reorganized Ch. Jesus Christ Latter-day Saints (elder). Clubs: Masons, Shrine, Lion, Rotary. Home: Route 1 Leasburg MO 65535

RILEY, ROBERT GREEN, lawyer; b. Des Moines, Aug. 25, 1916; s. William Francis and Catherine Mary (Green) R.; student Holy Cross Coll., 1934-37; LL.B., Drake U., 1941; m. Mary Ann Warren, Oct. 2, 1943; children—Anne (Mrs. John Green), Robert Green, Philip, Timothy, Ben. Admitted to Iowa bar, 1941, since practiced in Des Moines; mem. firm Duncan Jones, Riley and Finley, 1941—. Mem. Community Planning Council, Des Moines, 1967-70, pres., 1969-70; bd. dirs. Iowa Home for Sightless Women, 1946-58, pres., 1955-58; pres. Health Planning Council Central Iowa, 1971-72; bd. dirs. Roadside Settlement House, 1947-59, pres., 1958-59; bd. dirs. Legal Aid Soc. Des Moines, 1962-72, pres., 1964; v.p. Greater Des Moines United Way, 1970. Served with AUS, 1942-46. Mem. Am., Iowa State, Polk County (pres. 1963-64) bar assns., Sigma Alpha Epsilon. Clubs: Pow Wow, Lincoln Inne, Des Moines, Embassy, Wakonda. Home: 2834 Forest Dr Des Moines IA 50312 Office: 404 Equitable Bldg Des Moines IA 50309

RILEY, TOM JOSEPH, lawyer; b. Cedar Rapids, Iowa, Jan. 9, 1929; s. Joseph Wendell and Edna (Kyle) R.; B.A., State U. Iowa, 1950, J.D., 1952; m. Nancy Evans, Jan. 21, 1952; children—Pamela, Peter, Lisa, Martha, Sara, Heather. Admitted to Iowa bar, 1952; practiced in Cedar Rapids, 1954—; asso. Simmons, Perrine, Albright, Ellwood & Neff (now Simmons, Perrine, Albright and Ellwood), 1954-59, partner, 1960—; dir. Iowa Surety Co.; mem. Iowa Ho. of Reps., 1960-64; mem. Iowa Senate, 1964-74; Republican candidate for Congress, 1968, 74, 76. Chmn. Govs. Com. on Aging, 1963-65, mem. Iowa Commn. Aging; del. White House Conf. Aging, 1971. Bd. dirs. Iowa Assn. Mental Health, Linn County Assn. Retarded Children. Served to 1st lt. USAF, 1952-54. Named Outstanding Freshman Legislator, Des Moines Press and Radio Club, 1961; selected by Nat. Young Republicans to attend 1st Ann. Young Rep. Conf., 1962. Mem. Am., Iowa, Linn County bar assns., Am. Legion. Presbyterian. Mason. Author: Response to Crisis. Home: 3610 Clark Rd SE Cedar Rapids IA 52406 Office: Mchts Nat Bank Bldg Cedar Rapids IA 52401

RINELLA, SALVADOR ANTHONY, physician; b. Chgo., June 7, 1941; M.D., Loyola U., 1966. Intern, St. Francis Hosp., Evanston, Ill., 1966-67, resident in radiology, 1969-72; physician, Asso. Radiologists of Joliet (Ill.), 1972—; mem. staff Silver Cross Hosp., Joliet, St. Mary's Hosp., Kankakee, Ill. Served with USN, 1967-69. Diplomate Am. Bd. Nuclear Medicine. Diplomate Am. Bd. Radiology. Mem. AMA, Radiol. Soc. N.Am., Soc. Nuclear Medicine, Am. Coll. Radiology. Office: 120 Scott St Joliet IL 60431

RING, GERALD JOHN, real estate developer; b. Madison, Wis., Oct. 6, 1928; s. John George and Mabel Sarah (Rau) R.; student pub. schs., Madison; m. Armella Marie Dohm, Aug. 20, 1949; children—Michael J., James J., Joseph W. With Sub-Zero Freezer Co., Madison, 1948-70, mfr.'s rep., 1954-70; founder, sec.-treas. Parkwood Hills Corp., Madison, 1965—; founder, sec.-treas. Park Towne Devel. Corp., Madison, 1969—; chmn. bd. dirs. Cumis Ins. Soc.; vice-chmn. CUNA Mutual Ins. Soc., CUNA Mut. Ins. Group; treas. Cunadata Corp. Pres. Wis. Credit Union League, 1965-67; mem. Wis. Credit Union Rev. Bd., 1967—. Served with USMC, 1951-53. Mem. Aircraft Owners and Pilots Assn. Roman Catholic. Club: Rotary. Home: 721 Anthony Ln Madison WI 53711 Office: 6622 Mineral Point Rd Madison WI 53705

RING, LEONARD M., lawyer; b. Tauragena, Lithuania, May 11, 1923; s. Abe and Rose (Kahn) R.; brought to U.S., 1930, naturalized, 1930; student N.Mex. Sch. Mines, 1943-44; LL.B., DePaul U., 1949, J.D., 1971; m. Donna R. Cecrle, June 29, 1959; children—Robert Steven, Susan Ruth. Admitted to Ill. bar, 1949; since practiced in Chgo.; spl. asst. atty. gen. State Ill., 1967-72; spl. atty. Ill. Dept. Ins., 1967-73; spl. trial atty. Met. Sanitation Dist. Greater Chgo., 1967—; lectr. civil trial, appellate practice, tort law Nat. Coll. Advocacy, San Francisco, 1971-72; guest lectr. civil trial practice U. Chgo. Law Sch., 1973; mem. com. jury instrns. Ill. Supreme Ct., 1967-71, 74—; nat. chmn. Attys. Congl. Campaign Trust, Washington, 1975—. Trustee Roscoe Pound-Am. Trial Lawyers Found., Cambridge, Mass., 1974—; chmn. bd. trustees Avery Coonley Sch., Downers Grove, Ill. Served with AUS, 1943-46. Decorated Purple Heart. Fellow Am. Coll. Trial Lawyers, Internat. Acad. Trial Lawyers, Internat. Soc. Barristers; mem. Soc. Trial Lawyers, Appellate Lawyers Assn. (pres. 1974-75), Assn. Trial Lawyers Am. (nat. pres. 1973-74), Ill. Trial Lawyers Assn. (pres. 1966-68), Chgo. Bar Assn. (bd. mgrs. 1971-73), Am., Ill. bar assns., Lex Legio (pres. 1976—). Club: Oak Brook Polo (Ill.); Met. (Chgo.). Author: (with Harold A. Baker) Jury Instructions and Forms of Verdict, 1972; contbr. articles to profl. jours. Home: 6 Royal Vale Dr Oakbrook IL 60521 Office: 111 W Washington St Chicago IL 60602

RINGEL, MARY FRANCES CHEATHAM (MRS. WILLIAM SHELDON RINGEL), banker; b. Peoria, Ill., Nov. 30, 1934; d. Guy Raymond and Mary V. (Hovenden) Cheatham; student Grad. Sch. Banking U. Wis.-Madison; m. William Sheldon Ringel, June 10, 1953; children—Richard Allen, Stephen Paul. With traffic dept. Ill. Bell Telephone Co., Peoria, 1962-64; with Sheridan Bank of Peoria (Ill.), 1964—, asst. cashier, 1969-73, asst. v.p., 1973-75, v.p., 1975-76, exec. v.p., 1976—, also dir. Mem. Am. Inst. Banking, Nat. Assn. Bank Women, Inc., Bank Mktg. Assn., Ill. Bankers Assn., Bankers Adminstrn. Inst., Peoria Area Assn. Banks (v.p.) St. Jude Childrens Hosp. (dir. Central Ill. affiliate) Lutheran. Home: 6325 N Imperial Dr Peoria IL 61614 Office: 4125 N Sheridan Rd Peoria IL 61614

RINGER, ALFRED VICTOR, lawyer; b. Williamsport, Ind., Nov. 10, 1903; s. Victor Howard and Alice (Thomas) R.; A.B. with distinction, Ind. U., 1926, J.D., 1928; m. Dorothy Evelyn Slabaugh, Apr. 19, 1929; children—Thomas L. William A., Joan L. (Mrs. John Larson). Admitted to Ind. bar, 1927, U.S. Dist. Ct., 1928; practiced in Williamsport, 1928—; pros. atty. Warren Circuit Ct., Ind., 1935-40; atty. Town of Williamsport, 1940-72; atty. Warren County, Williamsport, 1953-70. Mem. Am., Ind. (pres. 6th dist. 1952; bd. mgrs. 1964-66), 7th Circuit bar assns., Ind. Bar Found. (dir., pres. 1972-73), Am. Judicature Soc., Ind. Soc. Chgo., Shrine, Phi Beta Kappa, Phi Delta Phi, Sigma Nu. Republican. Presbyn. Mason (Scottish Rite); Elk, Lion, Rotarian (dist. gov. 1951-52). Club: Columbia (Indpls.). Home: 311 Lincoln St Williamsport IN 47993 Office: 110 N Monroe St Williamsport IN 47993

RINGO, BOYD COLBURN, civil engr.; b. Tulsa, Okla., May 16, 1927; s. Boyd Riley and Helen (Colburn) R.; B.S. in Archtl. Engring., Washington U., 1950, M.S. in Civil Engring., 1954; Ph.D. in Civil Engring., U. Mich., 1964; postgrad. Mich. State U., 1956-58; m. Marie Helen Smolicek, Sept. 13, 1948; children—Kim Ellen, Lynn Ann, William Colburn. Archtl. draftsman, Gallmaier Engring. Co., Oklahoma City, 1950-51; asst. project engr. Granco Steel Products Co., Granite City, Ill., 1951-52; structural designer Sverdrup & Parcel Consulting Engrs., St. Louis, 1952-54; instr. dept. civil engring. Mich. State U., East Lansing, 1954-57, asst. prof., 1957-61; asst. prof. dept. of civil engring. U. Cin., 1961-64, asso. prof., 1964-67, prof., 1967—; cons. to various indsl. and mfg. firms, 1955—; reviewer for McGraw Hill Book Co., 1966; judge for Lincoln Arc Welding Found. Competition, 1964, 69; lectr. on tornadoes and structural damage to Civil Defense and the community, 1974—. Committeeman Dan Beard council Cub Scouts Am., 1968-72, asst. scoutmaster 1972—; Sunday sch. tchr. Faith Luth., Cin., 1972-74. Served with USN, 1946-47. Recipient Entry of Merit award Lincoln Arch Welding Found., 1975; registered profl. engr. Mich., Mo., Ohio. Mem. ASCE (faculty adviser 1962-64, reviewer Jour. for structural div. 1968-72), Am. Concrete Inst. (ednl. activities com. 1972-78), Am. Inst. of Steel Constrn. (Spl. Citation award 1972), Am. Soc. for Engring. Edn. (Western Electric Fund award for Teaching Excellence 1976), Tau Beta Pi, Chi Epsilon, Pi Mu Epsilon. Author: (with J.F. McDonough and C.J. Keaney), Use of Computer by the Practicing Civil Engr., 1967; contbr. articles on structural design and engring. edn. to profl. jours.; developed the structural curriculum for undergrad. and grad. courses at U. Cin. Home: 9098 Arrowhead Ct Cincinnati OH 45231 Office: Mail Loc 71 Univ of Cincinnati Cincinnati OH 45221

RINGO, MIRIAM K., cons.; b. N.Y.C.; B.A., Hunter Coll.; M.A., U. Chgo.; 3 children. Economist, War Manpower Commn.; research asst. Inland Steel Co.; staff dir. Gov.'s Com. on Unemployment; asst. to Gov. Otto Kerner, Springfield, Ill.; dir. Dept. Personnel, State of Ill.; staff dir., mem. adv. com. on research U.S. Employment Service; staff dir. Ill. Commn. on Labor Law; formerly dir. personnel Office Ill. Sec. State, Springfield; former dir. ops. Ill. Ho. of Reps., Springfield; now cons., writer. Mem. Am. Econ. Assn., Indsl. Relations Research Assn., Jane Austen Soc. Home: 16 W 220 97th St Hinsdale IL 60521

RINGO, PHILIP JANSEN, transp. mgmt. co. exec.; b. Cin., Feb. 23, 1942; s. David Leer and Ruth Jean (McDonell) R.; B.A. cum laude, Princeton U., 1964; M.B.A., Harvard U., 1966; m. Margaret Randolph Foote, June 12, 1965; children—Ramsay McCall, Ruth Jean, Margaret Randolph. Asso., McKinsey & Co., Washington, 1966-69; exec. v.p. Oceanography Devel. Corp., Rivera Beach, Fla., 1969-71; pres. ATE Mgmt. and Service Co., Cin., 1971—. Served with U.S. Army, 1967-69; Vietnam. Decorated Bronze Star. Mem. Am. Pub. Transit Assn., Transp. Research Bd. Episcopalian. Clubs: Princeton Club So. Ohio (exec. com.); Glendale Lyceum (dir.). Home: 740 Ivy Ave Cincinnati OH 45246 Office: 617 Vine St Suite 800 Cincinnati OH 45002

RINKE, DWIGHT CLARENCE, educator; b. Mt. Clemens, Mich., Aug. 28, 1945; s. Clarence Henry William and Elsie Jane (Eddinger) R.; B.A., Wayne State U., 1968; certificate, 1969, postgrad., 1968—. Tchr., Madison High Sch., Madison Heights, Mich., 1967—; tchr., dir. Cranbrook Theatre Sch., Bloomfield Hills, Mich., 1970—. Prodn. dir. Miss East Detroit Pageant, 1967-69; gen. com. chmn. St. Dunstan's Players Guild, Cranbrook, 1972-74; mem. adv. bd. Wayne State Fund, 1973-75. Mem. Am. Theatre Assn., Nat., Mich. councils tchrs. English, Mich. Edn. Assn., Detroit Met. English Club, Bloomfield Art Assn., Detroit Artists' Market, Wayne State U. Alumni Assn. (dir. 1973-76), Omicron Delta Kappa, Pi Kappa Alpha. Unitarian-Universalist (chmn. religious edn. com. 1975-76, worship com. 1976—). Club: Harmonie (Detroits). Home: 498 E Southlawn St Birmingham MI 48009 Office: 915 E 11 Mile Rd Madison Heights MI 48071

RINSLEY, DONALD BRENDAN, psychiatrist; b. N.Y.C., Jan. 31, 1928; s. Louis and Annamay (Hindle) R.; A.B. with honors, Harvard, 1949, postgrad., 1949-50; M.D., Washington U., St. Louis, 1954; diploma in child psychiatry honoris causa Menninger Found., 1975; m. Jacqueline Ann Louk, May 28, 1955. Intern pediatrics St. Louis Children's Hosp., 1954-55; fellow in psychiatry Menninger Found., Topeka, 1955-56, 58-60; staff psychiatrist Dept. Justice, U.S. Med. Center for Fed. Prisoners, Springfield, Mo., 1956-58; resident psychiatrist Topeka State Hosp., 1955-56, 58-60, asst. chief adolescent unit, children's sect., 1960-68, chief, 1968-70, dir. sect., 1970-75; asso. chief psychiatry edn. Topeka VA Hosp., 1975—; cons. psychiatrist C.F. Menninger Meml. Hosp., 1976—; asst. in pediatrics Washington U. Sch. Medicine, St. Louis, 1954-55; faculty gen. psychiatry, Menninger Sch. Psychiatry, Topeka, 1960—, faculty child psychiatry, 1968—, exec. and tng. faculty in child psychiatry, 1969-75, 77—; asso. clin. prof. psychiatry U. Kans. Sch. Medicine, 1970-77, clin. prof., 1977—. Sr. asst. surgeon to surgeon USPHS, 1956—. Recipient Edward A. Strecker Meml. award Inst. Pa. Hosp., 1968. Spencer Found. fellow in advanced studies Menninger Found., 1976—. Diplomate in psychiatry Am. Bd. Psychiatry and Neurology. Fellow Am. Psychiat. Assn. (br. chmn. com. research, 1964-65), Royal Soc. Health, AAAS, N.Y. Acad. Scis., Am. Orthopsychiat. Assn., Soc., Am. Assn. Children's Residential Centers; mem. Assn. for Research Nervous and Mental Disease, Am. Soc. Adolescent Psychiatry (com. residential treatment adolescents 1968—, com. tng. in adolescent psychiatry 1969—), Am. Acad. Psychoanalysis, Am. Acad. Child Psychiatry, Canadian Psychiat. Assn. (corr.), Am. Assn. Psychiat. Services for Children, Argentine Assn. Child and Adolescent Psychiatry and Psychology (hon.), Sigma Xi (zone cons. to chpt.-at-large 1969-71, mem. com. on membership-at-large 1972-75). Editorial bd. Psychiat. Quar. Adolescent Psychiatry, Argentine Jour. Child and Adolescent Psychiatry and Psychology. Contbr. articles to profl. publs. Home: 3212 Eveningside Dr Topeka KS 66614 Office: 2200 W Gage Blvd Topeka KS 66622

RINSLEY, JACQUELINE ANN (MRS. DONALD BRENDAN RINSLEY), hosp. adminstr.; b. Chgo., Apr. 5, 1933; d. John Lancelot and Margaret Elizabeth (Zeilinger) Louk; student Washington U., St. Louis, 1951-52; diploma in nursing St. Luke's Hosp. Sch. Nursing, 1955; m. Donald Brendan Rinsley, May 28, 1955. Psychiat. nurse Topeka State Hosp., 1955-56, sect. head nurse, 1955-56; gen. and pediatric nurse St. John's Hosp., Springfield, Mo., 1956-57, Burge Hosp., 1957-58; head pediatric nurse Stormont-Vail Hosp., Topeka, 1958-60; psychiat. nurse. Kans. Neurol. Inst., Topeka, 1960-70, adminstr., 1970—. Mem. Am. Nurses Assn., Am. Assn. for Mental Deficiency, Nat. Rehab. Assn., Nat. Audubon Soc., Am. Mus. Nat. History, Smithsonian Assos., Zeta Tau Alpha. Democrat. Lutheran. Home: 3212 Eveningside Dr Topeka KS 66614 Office: Kansas Neurological Institute 3107 W 21st St Topeka KS 66604

RIORDAN, RAY JOSEPH, trade assn. exec.; b. Green Bay, Wis., Jan. 27, 1916; s. Daniel E. and Florence E. (Brooks) R.; student St. Norbert Coll., 1933-35; B.S., Marquette U., 1937; m. Eileen Kelly, June 25, 1941; children—Mary Eileen (Mrs. Richard Harper), Ray Joseph, Patrick D., Robert H. Editor, pub., Tri County News, Pulaski, Wis., 1938-41; salesman Yellow Pages, Mich., Wis. and Ind., 1941-42; telephone engr. Hercules Powder Co., Wilmington, Del., 1942-43; comml. mgr. Gen. Telephone Co., Wausau and Madison, Wis., 1943-46; comml. mgr. 6 state area Central Telephone Co., LaCrosse, Wis., 1946-52; exec. v.p. Wis. State Telephone Assn., Madison, 1952—; pres. Shamrock Affiliates, Madison, 1959—; sec.-treas. Wis. State Telephone Found., Madison, 1965—, N.E. Telephone Co., Pulaski, 1950—. Mem. Council Telephone Execs. (pres. 1962, 70), Ind. Telephone Pioneers (pres. Badger chpt. 1954-55). Clubs: Elks, Madison. Home: Box 234 Dunlap Hollow Rd Mazomanie WI 53560 Office: 30 W Mifflin St Suite 601 Madison WI 53703

RIPLEY, KENNETH LAUREN, elec. engr.; b. Durham, N.C., Apr. 24, 1945; s. Webb Pendleton and Pauline Thelma (Hall) R.; B.A., N.C. State U., 1969; M.S., Washington U., 1976; m. Carole Louise Smith; children—Timothy Michael, Jeffrey Glenn. Research technician research div. N.C. Dept. Mental Health, 1966-70; NIH trainee dept. psychology Washington U., St. Louis, 1970-73, research engr. Biomed. computer lab., 1973—, mgr. dept. computer sci., 1977—. Mem. AAAS, Soc. Neurosci., IEEE, Am. Heart Assn. Office: Washington Univ 700 S Euclid St Louis MO 63110

RIPPY, FRANCES MARGUERITE MAYHEW, educator, editor; b. Ft. Worth, Sept. 16, 1929; d. Henry Grady and Marguerite Christine (O'Neill) Mayhew; B.A., Tex. Christian U., 1949; M.A., Vanderbilt U., 1951, Ph.D. (fellow), 1957; postgrad. Birkbeck Coll. U. London (Eng.), 1952-53; m. N. Merrill Rippy, Aug. 29, 1955; children—Felix O'Neill, Conrad Mayhew, Marguerite Hailey. Teaching fellow Vanderbilt U., Nashville, 1951-52; instr. Tex. Christian U., 1953-55; instr. to asst. prof. Lamar State U., 1955-59; successively asst., asso., prof. dept. English, Ball State U., Muncie, Ind., 1959—; vis. prof. U. Puerto Rico, summers 1959, 60, 61, Sam Houston State U., summer, 1957; cons., evaluator North Central Assn. Colls. and Secondary Schs., 1973—. Treas., Friends of Muncie Pub. Library, 1976—. Named Danforth Asso., 1965—; Danforth summer grantee, 1962; MacClintock research scholar, 1965. Mem. Modern Lang. Assn., Am. Soc. 18th Studies (charter), Johnson Soc. Midwest (sec. 1961-62), Coll. English Assn., Nat. Council Tchr. English, AAUP, Ind. Coll. English Assn., Ind. Council Tchrs. English. Editor Ball State U. Forum. Home: 4709 W Jackson St Muncie IN 47304

RISDALL, JOHN ROBERT, advt. exec.; b. St Paul, May 25, 1945; s. Newell V. and Mary L. (Diebel) R.; B.A. in Speech, U. Minn., 1968; m. Cathy Ann Stark, Sept. 20, 1969; children—Ted, Tim, Jennifer. Account exec. Harold C. Walker Advt., Mpls., 1964-68; account supr. Autographics Corp., Mpls., 1969-70; copywriter Blanchard & Assos., Mpls., 1971-72; partner Dorsch Risdall & Assos., Roseville, Minn., 1972-76; pres. John Risdall & Assocs., New Brighton, Minn., 1977—. Mem. Midwest Mail Mkgt. Assn. Mem. United Ch. of Christ. Club:

Rotary Internat. Author: Winter Fun in Minn., 1976. Contbr. articles to profl. jours. Home: 1561 15th St NW New Brighton MN 55112 Office: 1433 Silver Leaf Rd New Brighton MN 55112

RISELEY, MARTHA SUZANNAH HEATER (MRS. CHARLES RISELEY), psychologist, educator; b. Middletown, Ohio, Apr. 25, 1916; d. Elsor and Mary (Henderson) Heater; B.Ed., U. Toledo, 1943, M.A., 1958; Ph.D., Toledo Bible Coll., 1977; student Columbia U., summers 1943, 57; m. Lester Seiple, Aug. 27, 1944 (div. Feb. 1953); 1 son, L. Rolland, III; m. 2d, Charles Riseley, July 30, 1960. Tchr. kindergarten Maumee Valley Country Day Sch., Maumee, Ohio, 1942-44; dir. recreation Toledo Soc. for Crippled Children, 1950-51; tchr. trainable children Lott Day Sch., Toledo, 1951-57; psychologist, asst. dir. Sheltered Workshop Found., Lucas County, Ohio, 1957-62; psychologist Lucas County Child Welfare Bd., Toledo, 1956-62; tchr. educable retarded, head dept. spl. edn. Maumee City Schs., 1962-69; pvt. practice clin. psychology, 1956—; instr. spl. edn. Bowling Green State U., 1962—; instr. Owens Tech. Coll., 1973; interim dir. rehab. services Toledo Goodwill Industries, summer 1967, clin. psychologist Rehab. Center, 1967—. Dir. camping activities for retarded girls and women Camp Libbey, Defiance, Ohio, summers 1951-62; group worker for retarded women Toledo YWCA, 1957-62; guest lectr. Ohio State U., 1957. Mem. Ohio Assn. Tchrs. Trainable Youth (pres. 1956-57), N.W. Ohio Rehab. Assn. (pres. 1961-62), Toledo Council for Exceptional Children (pres. 1965), Greater Toledo Assn. Mental Health, Nat. Assn. for Retarded Children, Ohio Assn. Tchrs. Slow Learners, Am. Assn. Mental Deficiency, Am. Soc. Psychologists in Marital and Family Counseling, Psychology and Law Soc., Am. (asso.), Ohio, N.W. Ohio (sec.-treas. 1974-77, pres.-elect 1977) psychol. assns., NEA, AAUW, Am. Soc. Psychologists in Pvt. Practice (nat. dir. 1976—), Bus. and Profl. Women's Club, (pres. 1970-72), Ohio Fedn. Bus. and Profl. Womens Clubs (dist. sec. 1970-71, dist. legislative chmn. 1972-74), Toledo Art Mus., Women's Aux. Toledo Bar Assn., Zonta Internat. (local pres. 1973-74, area dir. 1976-78), Maumee Valley Hist. Soc., M.B.L.S. P.E.O. (chpt. pres. 1950-51), Toledo Council on World Affairs, Internat. Platform Assn. Baptist. Home: 322 River Rd Maumee OH 43537 Office: 706 Madison Ave Toledo OH 43624

RISK, GEORGE, electronic mfg. co. exec.; b. Cedar Rapids, Iowa, Dec. 8, 1912; s. Joseph A. and Sadie (Nemer) R.; student pub. schs., Cedar Rapids; m. Eileen M. Johnson, May 25, 1940; children—Dale Joseph, Delores Eileen, Kenneth Ross, Victor (dec.). Pres., dir. Electronic Devel. Corp., Omaha, 1937-49, Dale Electronic Corp., Columbus, Nebr., 1951-62, Hathaway Instruments, Inc., Denver, 1960-61; chmn. exec. com. Lionel Corp., N.Y.C., 1961-62; pres. dir. George Risk Industries, Inc., Kimball, Nebr., 1966—. Bd. dirs. St. Jude Childrens Research Hosp., Memphis. Mem. IEEE (sr.). Republican. Episcopalian. Clubs: Kimball Country, Lincoln University, Masons, Shriners. Inventor numerous electrical components. Home: 716 E 5th St Kimball NE 69145 Office: GRI Plaza Kimball NE 69145

RISTOLA, EUGENE GUSTAF, electronics engr.; b. Withee, Wis., Mar. 18, 1920; s. Nestor and Gunilla (Alline) R.; B.S., U. Wis., 1947; m. Mary Jane Hubbard, July 28, 1950; 1 son, Stephen Eugene. Electronic design engr. Collins Radio Co., Cedar Rapids, Iowa 1947-60, adminstrv. mgr. research div., 1960-64, mem. tech. staff electronics research dept., 1964-69, mem. inertial navigation systems dept., 1969-71; engring. bus. mgr. Norand Corp., Cedar Rapids, 1971-75; mem. avionics div. Collins Radio Group Rockwell Internat., 1976—. Active Boy Scouts Am. Served with AUS, 1943-46. Mem. IEEE, Eta Kappa Nu. Lutheran (mem. finance com.). Home: 4208 Northwood Dr NE Cedar Rapids IA 52402

RITCHIE, ALEXANDER BUCHAN, lawyer; b. Detroit, Apr. 19, 1923; s. Alexander Stevenson and Margaret (May) R.; B.A., Wayne State U., 1947, LL.D., 1949; m. Gladys Bilkow, Aug. 12, 1944; children—Alexander K., Barbara Sharon. Admitted to Mich. bar, 1949; practiced in Detroit, 1949—; asst. gen. counsel Maccabees Mut. Life Ins. Co., Southfield, Mich., 1952-65, v.p., gen. counsel, 1977—; sec., Wayne Nat. Life Ins. Co., 1966-67; mem. firm Fenton, Nederlander, Dodge, & Ritchie and predecessor firm, Detroit, 1967-76. Mem. bd. edn., Detroit, 1970—; mem. Central Bd. Edn., 1973; mem. bd. police commrs. City of Detroit, 1974—, chmn., 1977—. bd. dirs. Doctors Hosp. Served with AUS, 1943-46. Lutheran. Home: 12479 Riad St Detroit MI 48224 Office: 25800 Northwestern Hwy Southfield MI 48037

RITCHIE, JOHN DUNCAN, coll. adminstr.; b. Newtownards, North Ireland, Aug. 22, 1943; s. Harold Dennison and Jessie Marshall (McLean) R.; came to U.S., 1962, naturalized, 1967; student Coll. Great Falls, 1964-66; B.S., U. Nebr., 1969, M.A., 1971, postgrad., 1971—; m. Linda Carol Sarpen, Aug. 24, 1968. Asst. dir. student fin. assistance U. Nebr., Lincoln, 1971-72, dir. student fin. assistance, 1972—. Midwest cons., Coll. Scholarship Service, Evanston, Ill., 1974-75, 75-76, mem. com. guidance and publ. Coll. Scholarship Service, 1975—. Served with USAF, 1963-67. Mem. Big Eight Fin. Aid Officers Assn. (chmn., 1972), Neb. (sec. 1972-73, pres. 1975-76), Nat. assns. student fin. aid adminstrs., Omicron Delta Epsilon, Phi Delta Kappa. Home: 7700 Yankee Hill Rd Lincoln NE 68506 Office: Administration Bldg Univ Nebraska Lincoln NE 68508

RITENOUR, JOHN JOSEPH, JR., air force officer; b. Springfield, Ohio, May 22, 1941; s. John Joseph and Ivis Gwendolyn (Bessey) R.; B.S. in Math., Ohio State U., 1965; M. Computing Scis., Tex. A. and M. U., 1969; m. Carolyn Ann Thompson, Feb. 11, 1967; children—Steven Keith, Deborah Lynn. Commd. 2nd lt. U.S. Air Force, 1965, advanced through grades to maj., 1977; data automation officer, Vietnam, 1969-70; computer systems analyst, design engr. Def. Intelligence Agency, Washington, 1970-73; computer systems design engr., hdqrs. USAF communications service Richards Gebaur AFB, Mo., 1973-75, staff officer, computer systems, 1975-77; student Telecommunications Staff Officer Course, Keesler AFB, Miss., 1977-78; communications staff mgmt. officer Def. Communications Agy., Washington, 1978—. Decorated USAF Commendation medal. Contbr. publs. in field. Home: Drawer 507 Devine TX 78016

RITTENHOUSE, JOSEPH WILSON, elec. products mfg. co. exec.; b. Neosho, Mo., Jan. 22, 1917; s. George Eddy and Nannie Stewart (Morgan) R.; B.S. in Elec. Engring., Purdue U., 1939; M.S. in Elec. Engring., U. Mo., 1949; m. Jane Eileen Peterson, June 3, 1939; children—Joseph Wilson II, John David, Jane Eileen, Judith Anne, James Jay, Jeffrey Lee. Mem. staff radio sta. WBAA, Purdue U., Lafayette, Ind., 1936-39; various engring. positions James R. Kearney Corp., St. Louis, 1939-43; mem. faculty elec. engring. dept. U. Mo. at Rolla, 1947-54, asso. prof. elec. engring., 1952-54; tech. dir. hi-voltage equipment div. Joslyn Mfg. and Supply Co., Cleve., 1954-65, div. gen. mgr., 1965-69, group v.p. elec. products, Chgo., 1969-73, pres. co., chmn. bd., 1973—, dir., 1970—. Guest speaker at meetings of profls. and other socs. Mem. indsl. devel. com. City Council, Aurora, Ohio, 1960-62. Served to maj. AUS, 1943-46. Registered profl. engr., Mo. Fellow IEEE (mem., chmn. numerous coms.); mem. Nat. Soc. Profl. Engrs., Am. Soc. Engring. Edn., Ill. Soc. Profl. Engrs., Conf. Internationale des Grands Reseaux Electriques, Nat. Elec. Mfrs. Assn. (bd. govs. 1970—, vice chmn. 1974—), Cleve C. of C., Sigma Xi, Eta Kappa Nu (nat. adv. bd. 1955-57), Tau Beta Pi, Tau Kappa Alpha, Lambda Chi Alpha. Co-author: Electric Power Transmission, 1953. Contbr. articles to profl. publs. Patentee in field. Home: Rt 1 Box 26 Barrington IL 60010 Office: Joslyn Mfg and Supply Co 2 N Riverside Plaza Chicago IL 60606

RITTER, HARTIEN SHARP, chemist; b. Iola, Kans., Oct. 13, 1918; s. Christopher Sharp and Harriet Ann (Welker) R.; A.B., U. Kans., 1940; M.S., U. Akron, 1954, Ph.D., 1963; m. Charlotte Eloise Burtnett, June 21, 1941; children—Harriet Ann, Christopher Sharp II. Chemist, lab. supr. Olin Industries, East Alton, Ill., 1941-46; asst. research dir. Calcium Carbonate Co., Quincy, Ill., 1946-48; sr. chemist PPG Industries, chem. div., Barberton, Ohio, 1948-59, supr., 1959-65, sr. supr., 1965—. Mem. Am. Chem. Soc., Fedn. Socs. Paint Tech., Ohio Geneal. Soc. (mem. exec. com. Summit County chpt., 1972—, trustee, 1975—, pres. 1975-77), Ohio State Hist. Soc., Western Reserve Hist. Soc., Alpha Chi Sigma. Clubs: Kiwanis, Torch. Patentee in field. Home: 1495 Shanabrook Dr Akron OH 44313 Office: PO Box 31 Barberton OH 44203

RITTER, HUBERT AUGUST, obstetrician, gynecologist; b. St. Louis, Aug. 30, 1924; s. Hubert C. and Louise (Laipple) R.; A.B., Westminster Coll., 1945; M.D., St. Louis U., 1948; m. Harriette Hudson, Feb. 27, 1949; 1 dau., Lisa. Intern, St. Louis U. Hosp., 1948-49, resident, 1950-53; practice medicine specializing in obstetrics and gynecology, St. Louis, 1955—; founder Ritter Obstetrics-Gynecology Assos., Inc., St. Louis, 1969—; acting chmn. obstetrics-gynecology St. Louis U., 1976;. Served with USN, 1949-55. Recipient Key to City, St. Louis, from Mayor J. Peelker for community serivce, 1975. Fellow Am. Coll. Obstetricians and Gynecologists; mem. AMA (trustee 1976—), Missouri State, So. med. assns., St. Louis Med. Soc., St. Louis Gynecol. Soc., Internat., Am. fertility socs. Presbyterian. Clubs: Univ. St. Louis, Old Warson Country, St. Louis Skeet and Trap, Masons Shriners. Contbr. articles in field to med. jours. Office: 1035 Bellevue Ave Suite 208 Saint Louis MO 63117

RITTERBUSCH, ROBERT KARL, dentist; b. Bland, Mo., June 5, 1929; s. Loel Clarence and Mabel Leatha (Rohrer) R.; B.A., Westminster Coll., 1951; D.D.S., U. Mo., 1955; m. Nancy Elizabeth Titus, July 4, 1953; 1 son, Eric Karl. Pvt. practice dentistry, Kansas City, Mo., 1957-58, Smithville, Mo., 1958—. Cons. med. and dental staff Spelman Meml. Hosp., 1970-77. Served to capt. AUS, 1955-57. Mem. Am., Mo. (chmn. advisory com. women's aux.), N.W. Mo. dental assns., Kansas City Dist. Dental Soc., Delta Tau Delta. Mason. Address: Box 271 Smithville MO 64089

RITZ, GORDON H., pres. Minn. North Stars Hockey Team. Office: 7901 Cedar Ave S Bloomington MN 55420*

RIVERA, MARIO PABLO, tribologist, mathematician; b. Sucre, Bolivia, Aug. 17, 1944; s. Roman Paredes and Elia Maria (Espinoza) R.; came to U.S., 1964, naturalized, 1976; B.S. (Inst. Internat. Edn. scholar), Rensselaer Poly. Inst., 1968, M.S., 1971, Ph.D., 1973; m. Michele V. McKee, Jan. 31, 1971; children—Elia Theresa, Jennifer Eir, Chad Mateo. Research fellow, teaching asst., dept. mechanics Rensselaer Poly. Inst., 1968-73; materials scientist U.S. Air Force Materials Lab. Wright-Patterson AFB, Ohio, 1973—, research materials scientist, 1977—. Roman Catholic. Home: 3326 Oakmont Ave Kettering OH 45429 Office: Air Force Materials Lab MBT Wright-Patterson Air Force Base Dayton OH 45433

RIVERS, MOZELLE WILSON (MRS. JOHN J. RIVERS), educator; b. East Chicago, Ind., Sept. 15, 1932; d. Raymond Louis and Annie (Nichols) Wilson; A.B., Ky. State Coll., 1954; M.S., Ind. U., 1956, postgrad. 1957-59, 64, 68-69, 70-71; postgrad. U. So. Calif.; m. Robert Lee Williams, Dec. 22, 1959 (div.); 1 dau., Teresa Ann; m. 2d. John J. Rivers, Jan. 22, 1971; children—Katrina Joi, Marvina Rae. Elementary math., language arts tchr. Columbus Sch., East Chicago, Ind., 1954-59, instr. in adult edn., 1967-68, co-dir. in adult edn. workshop, summer 1969, phys. ednl. instr. for recreational activities, 1961-64; elementary tchr. Eugene Field Sch., East Chicago, 1961-63, ednl. adjustment tchr. in math., reading, 1963-70, instr. in adult edn., 1961-64; remedial reading tchr. Franklin Elementary Sch., East Chicago, from 1970; now dir. East Chicago Head Start Program. Supr. East Chicago Jr. Police, 1970-71; pink lady St. Catherine's Hosp., East Chicago, 1957; co-leader Girl Scouts of the U.S.A. Field Sch., 1969-70; sec., treas. St. Luke's Housing Corp., 1968—. Recipient Nat. Student award for most outstanding student Ky. State Coll., 1954. Mem. Am. Childhood Edn. Internat. (chpt. pres. 1971-72), Am. Fedn. Tchrs. (bldg. rep. Field Sch. 1966-70), Nat. Fedn. of Colored Women's Club (chpt. sec. 1969—), Ky. State Coll. Alumni Assn., Historical Soc., Ind. Classroom Tchrs. Assn., Ind. U. Alumni Assn., Eta Kappa Omega. Home: 2414 W 5th Ave Gary IN 46404 Office: Field Elementary Sch 3551 Block Ave East Chicago IN 46312

RIVES, JAMES HENRY, JR., structural engr.; b. Bessemer, Ala., Mar. 9, 1931; s. James Henry and Bessie Lillian (Hardy) R.; B.S. in Civil Engring., U. Ala., 1954; m. Mary Jo Wiggins, Jan. 14, 1954; children—James Gordon, Thomas Scott. Structural engr. So. Services, Inc., Birmingham, Ala., 1955-62; prin. engr. Barnard & Burk, Inc. cons. engrs., Baton Rouge, La., 1962-72; chief structural engr. Gibbs & Hill, Inc., Omaha, 1972—. Coach Baton Rouge Little League, 1966-69; Am. Legion Baseball, 1970; mem. indsl. cons. group Southeast Community Coll., Milford, Neb., 1975—. Served with AUS, 1953-55. Recipient Am. Def. award U.S. Govt., 1955. Mem. Nat. Soc. Profl. Engrs., Profl. Engrs. Nebr., La. Engring. Soc. (sec., vice chmn. 1971-72), Am. Concrete Inst., Am. Welding Soc., Theta Tau, Theta Chi. Episcopalian. Clubs: Piedmont (sec. bd. govs. 1969-70), Acadian (dir. 1971-72). Home: 2206 S 138th St Omaha NE 68144 Office: 8420 W Dodge Rd Omaha NE 68114

RIVES, STANLEY GENE, educator; b. Decatur, Ill., Sept. 27, 1930; s. James A. and Frances (Bunker) R.; B.S., Ill. State U., 1952, M.S., 1955; Ph.D., Northwestern U., 1963; m. Sandra Lou Belt, Dec. 28, 1957; children—Jacqueline Ann, Joseph Alan. Instr. W.Va. U., 1955-56, Northwestern U., 1956-58; asst. prof. Ill. State U., Normal, 1958-63, asso. prof., 1963-67, prof., 1967—, acting asst. dean Coll. Arts and Scis., 1968-70; chmn. gen. speech area dept. speech, 1968-70, asso. dean faculties, 1970-72, dean undergrad. instrn., 1972—, asso. provost, 1976—; vis. prof. U. Hawaii, 1963-64. Trustee Nat. Debate Tournament. Served with AUS, 1952-54. Mem. Central States, Ill. speech assns., Speech Communication Assn., Internat. Communication Assn. Am., Midwest (pres. 1961-63) forensic assns. Am. Studies Assn., AAUP, Am. Assn. Higher Edn., Theta Alpha Phi, Pi Kappa Delta, Pi Gamma Mu. Author: (with Donald Klopf) Individual Speaking Contests: Preparation for Participation, 1967; (with Gene Budig) Academic Quicksand: Trends and Issues in Higher Education, 1973. Contbr. articles to profl. jours. Home: 402 Marian St Normal IL 61761

RIVKIN, WILLIAM B., physicist; b. Chgo., Jan. 6, 1921; s. Oscar I. and Fannie Mary (Ovchinsky) R.; B.S. in E.E., Ill. Inst. Tech., 1946; m. Dolores Weinstein, July 10, 1955; children—Francine Vicky, Debra Ilene. Field engr. Tracerlab, Inc., Boston, Baird Atomio, Inc., Balarica, Mass.; radiation safety officer Westinghouse Electric Co., Cheswick, Pa., 1955-56; pres. Midwest Nuclear Industries, Inc., Chgo., 1957-61; v.p. Health Physics Assos. Ltd., Northbrook, Ill., 1961—; lab mgr., dir. Isotope Measurements Labs., Inc., Northbrook, 1969—; cons. VA Hosp., Hines, Ill., 1963—. Served with U.S. Army, 1941-42. Mem. Health Physics Soc., Am. Nuclear Soc., Soc. Nuclear Medicine, Am. Assn. Physicists in Medicine, Am. Pub. Health Assn., AAAS. Home: 1170 Ridge Rd Highland Park IL 60035 Office: 3304 Commercial Ave Northbrook IL

RIZIK, MICHAEL BERNARD, accountant; b. Flint, Mich., Jan. 8, 1920; s. Assad M. and Rose H. (Faris) R.; M. Accounting, Flint Jr. Coll., 1940; m. Matilda Bouhasin, Jan. 14, 1951; children—Michael, George, Regina, Matthew, Mark, David, Christopher. Pres., chief accountant Mich. Bookkeeping, Inc., Flint, 1945—, Income Tax Service Co., Fling, 1945—, Bus. Analysts. Co., Flint, 1970—; pres. Johnny Fast Print Co., Flint, 1969—, MABE, Inc., Flint, Mich., 1958—, Larner-Rizik Co., Flint, 1970—. Fin. dir. Our Lady of Lebanon Catholic Church., Flint, 1973—. mem. Catholic Social Services Bd., 1956-57; pres. council Boy Scouts Am., Flint, 1964-65. Served with U.S. Army, 1942-45. Named Michigan's Outstanding Accountant, 1958. Mem. Independent Accountants Assn., Nat. Apostolates of Maron, Serra Club (pres. 1967), Nat. Assn. Income Tax Accountants, Downtown Merchants Assn. Democrat. Roman Catholic. Author: Income Tax Textbook, 1969. Home: G-3266 Martharose Ct Flint MI 48504 Office: 116 E Kearsley St Flint MI 48502

ROACH, JOHN PAGE, agr. bus. exec.; b. Plainfield, Iowa, May 30, 1921; s. Howard Luverne and Frieda Rebecca (Page) R.; student Wartburg Coll., 1938-39, Iowa State U., 1939-41; m. Esther Louise Van Syoc, Mar. 12, 1944; children—Edwin A., Joanne (Mrs. Gary M. Fober). Mgr. soybean processing J. Roach Sons, Inc., Plainfield, 1946-53, mgr. animal feed div., 1953-55; sec. Roach Farms, Inc., 1955-67, pres., 1967—; real estate broker, farmer, farm cons. and appraiser.; dir. Plainfield Mills, Inc., 1969—; v.p. Arrow Supply Co., 1972—. Chmn., Bremer County Planning & Zoning Commn., 1963—; chmn. Veteran Affairs Commn., 1964—; mem. Met. Regional Planning Commn., 1971—. Precinct chmn. Rep. party, 1972—. Served with USNR, 1942-46. Recipient Silver Beaver award Boy Scouts Am., 1960; named Farm and Land Broker of the Year Nat. Inst. Farm & Land Brokers, 1969, Farm and Land Broker Achievement award, 1964, 67. Mem. Nat. Inst. Farm and Land Brokers (chpt. pres. 1964), Am. Legion. Baptist (deacon 1971—, bd. trustees Iowa Baptist Convention 19——). Clubs: Masons, Rotary, Elks. Home: 311 Main St Plainfield IA 50666 Office: 714 Main St Plainfield IA 50666

ROACH, JOHN ROBERT, archbishop; b. Prior Lake, Minn., July 31, 1921; s. Simon J. and Mary V. Roach; B.A., St. Paul Sem.; M.A., U. Minn. Ordained priest Roman Catholic Ch., 1946; named domestic prelate, 1966; instr. St. Thomas Acad., 1946-50, headmaster, 1951-68; rector St. John Vianney Sem., 1968-71; aux. bishop St. Paul and Mpls., 1971; pastor St. Charles Borromeo Ch., Mpls., 1971, St. Cecilia Ch., St. Paul, 1973-75; archbishop of St. Paul and 1975—. Apptd. vicar for parishes, 1971-75; vicar for clergy, 1972-75; mem. Priests Senate, 1968-72; pres. Priests Senate and Presbytery, 1970; Episcopal moderator Nat. Apostolate for Mentally Retarded, 1974. Chmn., Com. on Accreditation Pvt. Schs. in Minn., 1952-57; mem. adv. com. Coll. Entrance Exam. Bd., 1964. Trustee St. Paul Sem., Coll. of St. Thomas, St. Thomas Acad., Coll. of St. Catherine, Visitation Convent and Sch. Mem. Minn. Cath. Edn. Assn. (pres. 1959-61), Assn. Mil. Colls. and Schs. U.S. (pres. 1961-62), N.Central Assn. Colls. and Secondary Schs. (adv. com. 1963-66), Am. Council Edn. (del. 1963-65), Am. Assn. Theol. Schs. (dir.), Nat. Conf. Cath. Bishops. Office: 226 Summit Ave St Paul MN 55102

ROACH, RONALD THOMAS, ins. broker; b. Martinton, Ill., Feb. 6, 1926; s. John and Aldea (Benoit) R.; grad. high sch.; m. Esther Duclos Wehling, June 18, 1966; step-children—David A., Sandra (Mrs. David Webster). Salesman Leatherman Ins. Agy., Woodland, 1960-61; owner Ronald T. Roach Ins. Agy., Martinton 1960—; salesman Eaken Realty, Watseka, 1966-69; real estate broker Ronald T. Roach Ins. & Real Estate, Martinton, 1969—; pres. Miller-Roach Ins. Agy., Donovan, Ill., 1973—. Village trustee, Martinton, 1955, village clk., 1960—; clk. Martinton Twp., 1967—. Served with M.C., AUS, 1951-53. Mem. Iroquois-Ford Counties Bd. Realtors, Twp. Ofcls. Ill. Assn. Am. Legion, V.F.W. Roman Catholic. Home: 201 S 2d St Martinton IL 60951 Office: PO Box 11 Martinton IL 60951

ROACHE, ESTHER WILSON (MRS. FRED W. ROACHE), civic worker; b. Osgood, Ind.; d. Clarence B. and Alice (Garrigues) Wilson; student Franklin Coll., 1915-16, Ind. U., 1919; m. Fred W. Roache, June 12, 1942 (dec. 1960). Asst. cashier Aurora (Ind.) State Bank, 1936-50, cashier, 1950-56; v.p. 1st Nat. Bank, Aurora, Ind., 1956-65, dir., 1956-76, dir. emeritus, 1976—. Sec.-treas. Dearborn County Council Social Action 1962-74; mem. Gov. Commn. of the Arts, 1964-66; exec. sec. Hillforest Hist. Found., 1956—; sec.-treas. Southeastern Ind. Recreational Council, 1963-74, dir., 1964. Bd. dirs. Tri State Air Com., 1970-72, Historic Hoosier Hills Inc., Regional Council on Aging, Area 12. Named 1 of 10 Greater Cin. Women of Year, Cin. Enquirer, 1971. Mem. Nat. Assn. Bank Women, D.A.R. (regent Col. Archibald Lochry chpt. 1969-71), Aurora C. of C., Tri Kappa, Delta Delta Delta, Aurora Research Club. Home: 415 Manchester St Aurora IN 47001

ROAN, FRANK JOSEPH, lawyer; b. Pitts., May 2, 1925; s. Frank Joseph and Margaret Loretta (Gordon) R.; grad. The Hill Sch., 1942; student Amherst Coll., 1942-43; J.D., St. Louis U., 1948; m. Elfleda L. Gillespie, Dec. 23, 1945; children—Catherine (Mrs. Robin A. deTurk), Beverly (Mrs. Wilson J. Seldon, Jr.). Admitted to Ill. bar, 1949, Fla. bar, 1976; practiced in Marion until 1955; asso. firm Rathje, Kulp, Sabel & Sullivan, Chgo., 1955-63; partner Shorey, Floberg & Roan, Chgo., 1963-65, Ross, Hardies, O'Keefe, Babcock, McDugald & Parsons, Chgo., 1965-70; sr. partner Roan & Grossman, Chgo., 1970—. Mem. adv. council Ill. Inst. Continuing Legal Edn., 1961-73, exec. com., 1972-73; counsel Ill. Election Laws Commn., 1962—, co-drafter Election Code 1972. Asst. atty. gen. of Ill., 1949-53. Served with USNR, 1943-46. Fellow Am. Coll. Probate Counsel; mem. Am., Ill. (chmn. jr. bar 1952-54, vice chmn. probate and trust law 1960-61), Chgo., Fla. bar assns., Law Club Chgo., Legal Club Chgo. Clubs: Munroe, University (Chgo.); Glen Oak Country (Glen Ellyn, Ill.). Author: (with others) Administering Illinois Estates, 1969; (with others) Creditors Rights in Illinois, 1968. Home: 21W441 Clifton St Glen Ellyn IL 60137 also 5855 Midnight Pass Rd Sarasota FL 33581 Office: 120 S LaSalle St Chicago IL 60603 also Suite 640 1390 Main St Sarasota FL 33577

ROARK, JEAN CARROLL, metallurgist; b. Anderson, Mo., Apr. 9, 1919; s. Wiley Edward and Bertha (Dunn) R.; student Southwest Mo. State, 1938-41; m. Miriam Virginia Coble, Oct. 18, 1941; children—Bobbie Jean (Mrs. Robert M. Miller), James Nicholas, Terry Lee, Dale Edward. Metal process insp. Beech Aircraft Corp., 1941-44; chemist and metallographer Triplett and Barton Inc., 1944-45; process engr., lab. supr. Swallow Airplane Co., Inc., 1945-49; founder, partner, mgr. Arrow Lab., 1949-61, pres., 1961—; cons. metallurgist. Fellow Am. Inst. Chemists; mem. Assn. Cons. Chemists and Chem. Engrs., Inc., Am. Foundrymen's Soc., Am. Soc. for Metals, ASTM. Methodist. Home: 1756 Burns St Wichita KS 67203 Office: 1333 Main St Wichita KS 67203

ROARK, LAVERNE WALDO, computer cons.; b. Canute, Okla., Jan. 23, 1922; s. Waldo Walton and Luella Gertrude (Cox) R.; student Kans. State Tchrs. Coll., 1941-43; m. Donnetta Molz, Feb. 15, 1947; children—Sandra K. Broadstreet, LaNita Rae (Mrs. Thomas M. Dick). Owner, mgr. W-R Grocery Store, Johnson, Kans., 1945-48; tool attendant Boeing Airplane, Wichita, 1948-52, sr. systems analyst, 1958-70; owner farm, Animas, N.Mex., 1952-55; cons., program mgr. Boeing Computer Service, Inc., Wichita, Kans., 1970—. Served with USAF, 1943-45. Mason. Home: 11204 Valley Hi Ct Wichita KS 67209 Office: 3801 S Oliver St Wichita KS 67210

ROATH, RICHARD STERLING, elec. controls mfg. co. exec.; b. Lake County, Ohio, Apr. 15, 1926; s. Howard Delos and Clara Jane (Willm) R.; grad. high sch.; m. Betty Jean Reeves, June 21, 1952; 1 son, Alan Lee. Asst. plant mgr. EMD Components, Inc., Wickliffe, Ohio, 1957-70; mgr. mfg., purchasing agt. MEM Controls, Inc. Wickliffe, 1970-74; mgr. mfg. Cyberex, Inc., Mentor, Ohio, 1974—. Mem. Am. Theatre Organ Soc., Western Reserve Theatre Organ Soc., Lake County Internat. Mgmt. Club, Soc. Mfg. Engrs. Methodist. Home: 14724 Ford Rd Madison OH 44057 Office: 7171 Indsl Park Mentor OH 44060

ROBA, WILLIAM HENRY, educator; b. Moline, Ill., Mar. 8, 1946; s. Roy Clarence and Elsie Preciosa (Knaack) R.; A.B., Augustana Coll., Rock Island, Ill., 1968; M.A., Cornell U., 1971; m. Sylvia Linea Lee, June 10, 1967; children—Jennifer Sarah, Allison Courtney. Chmn. social sci. dept. Palmer Jr. Coll., Davenport, Iowa, 1971-74; asso. planner criminal justice Bi-State Met. Planning Commn., Rock Island, 1974-76; instr. interdisciplinary studies Black Hawk Jr. Coll., Moline, 1977—; cons. in field. Trustee Davenport Pub. Library, 1968-72; del. Iowa Democratic Nominating Com., 1972. NDEA grantee, 1968-70. Mem. A. Philip Randolph Inst., Am., Iowa library assns., Am. Hist. Assn., Am. Studies Assn., Popular Culture Assn., Soc. Study Midwest Lit., Phi Alpha Theta, Pi Kappa Delta. Unitarian. Contbr. articles to profl. jours. Home: 1137 Kirkwood Blvd Davenport IA 52803 Office: 6600 34th Ave Moline IL 61265

ROBACK, RAYMOND ROGER, banker; b. Chgo., Mar. 22, 1939; s. Frank and Pauline Ann (Malikowski) R.; B.A., DePaul U., 1960; m. Dorothy A. Lomasney, July 22, 1961; children—Sherry Lynn, Mark Francis. Data processing supr. Allstate Ins. Co., Skokie, Ill., 1960-65; mgr. data processing Bankers Data Corp., Chgo., 1965-67; mgr. systems programming Chgo. Tabulating Service, Inc., 1967-70; dir. data processing 1st Nat. Bank Elgin (Ill.), 1970-77; asst. v.p. Glenview (Ill.) State Bank, 1977—; instr. Elgin Community Coll., 1974-77. Roman Catholic. Club: Kiwanis. Home: 833 Canterbury Dr Crystal Lake IL 60014 Office: 800 Waukegan Rd Glenview IL 60025

ROBB, DAVID DOW, cons. engr.; b. Salina, Kans., Feb. 13, 1922; s. Francis and Florence May (Dow) R.; B.S., U. Kans., 1943, M.S., 1948, Ph.D., 1964; m. Mildred Hershey, Dec. 21, 1946; children—Mildred Ellis, Bruce Dow. Instr. elec. engring. U. Kans., 1943-48; asst. prof. elec. engring. Iowa State Coll., 1948-52; elec. engr. Wilson & Co., Salina, Kans., 1952-68; asso. prof. elec. engring. Iowa State U., 1968-71, prof., 1971-76; pres. D.D. Robb & Assos., Profl. Assn., cons. engrs., 1976—. Registered profl. engr., Kans., Iowa, Mo., Okla., Colo., Nebr. Mem. IEEE, Nat. Soc. Profl. Engrs., Eta Kappa Nu, Kappa Eta Kappa, Sigma Xi. Republican. Presbyn. Patentee in field. Home: 206 E Wayne St Salina KS 67401 Office: PO Box 941 Salina KS 67401

ROBB, WILLIAM JOHN, orthopedic surgeon; b. Denver, Oct. 10, 1916; s. William John and Zina M. (McKenzie) R.; B.A., Yale U., 1939; M.D., U. Colo., 1943; m. Cora Georgene Iles, Dec. 13, 1942; children—William, George, Don, Barbara, Anne. Intern, Bellevue Hosp., N.Y.C., 1944; orthopedic resident Colo. Gen. Hosp., Denver, 1946-47, Children's Hosp., Denver, 1947-48, St. Luke's Hosp., Denver, 1948-49; practice medicine specializing in orthopedic surgery, Cedar Rapids, Iowa, 1949—. Instr. surg. anatomy U. Colo., Denver, 1947-48. Served with USNR, 1944-46, 50-51; PTO. Decorated Bronze Star. Diplomate Am. Bd. Orthopedic Surgery. Mem. Am. Acad. Orthopedic Surgeons, Mid-Central States Orthopedic Soc., Clin. Orthopedic Soc. Mason (Shriner). Home: 2330 Linden Dr SE Cedar Rapids IA 52403 Office: 115 8th St NE Cedar Rapids IA 52401

ROBBINS, EDWARD LOUIS, educator; b. Eaton, Ind., Feb. 11, 1933; s. Ora Clayton and Marcella Pearl (Smoot) R.; B.S., Ball State U., 1958, M.A., 1959; postgrad. (grad. fellow) Wayne State U., 1960, (NDEA fellow) No. Colo. U., 1965; Ed.D., Ind. U., 1971; m. Beverly Ann Williams, Jan. 31, 1954; children—Ann, Kay. Elementary sch. tchr. Fort Wayne (Ind.) community schs., 1958-66; dir. Title I Elementary and Secondary Edn. Act, Ind. Dept. Pub. Instrn., Indpls., 1966-69; vis. lectr. Ind. U., Bloomington, 1969-71; asst. prof. edn. Ind. U.-Purdue U. Indpls., 1971-74, asso. prof., 1974—; pres. Edcar Ind., Bloomington, 1975—; dir. Ind. Head Start Supplementary Tng., 1969-76, Comprehensive Tng. Program for Tchrs. of Reading, 1972-73; community resource Model Cities Schs. Town Meeting, Indpls., 1972. Served with AUS, 1953-55. Mem. Nat. Soc. Study Edn., Am. Ednl. Research Assn., Internat. Reading Assn., Assn. Supervision and Curriculum Devel., Ind. Schoolmen's Club, Kappa Delta Pi, Phi Delta Kappa. Methodist. Author: Handbook for Volunteer Tutors, 1971; (with Blanton, Laffey, Smith) POWER Reading Program, 1972; (with Carl Smith) Robbins and Smith Reading Tests, 1972; Testing Program, Macmillan Series R Basal Reading Program, 1975. Editor: Ind. Reading Quar., 1970-71. Home: 7346 Shamrock Dr Indianapolis IN 46217 Office: 902 N Meridian St Indianapolis IN 46204

ROBBINS, FREDERICK CHAPMAN, physician; b. Auburn, Ala., Aug. 25, 1916; s. William J. and Christine (Chapman) R.; A.B., U. Mo., 1936, B.S., 1938; M.D., Harvard, 1940; D.Sc. (hon.), John Carroll U., 1955, U. Mo., 1958; LL.D., U. N.Mex., 1968; m. Alice Havemeyer Northrop, June 19, 1948; children—Alice, Louise. Sr. fellow virus disease NRC, 1948-50; staff research div. infectious diseases Children's Hosp., Boston, 1948-50, asso. physician, asso. dir. isolation service, asso. research div. infectious diseases, 1950-52; instr., asso. in pediatrics Harvard Med. Sch., 1950-52; dir. dept. pediatrics and contagious diseases Cleve. Met. Gen. Hosp., 1952-66; asso. pediatrician U. Hosps., Cleve., 1952—; prof. pediatrics Case-Western Res. U., 1952—, dean Sch. Medicine, 1966—; vis. scientist Donner Lab., U. Calif., 1963-64. Served as maj. AUS, 1942-46; chief virus and rickettsial disease sect. 15th Med. Gen. Lab.; investigations infectious hepatitis, typhus fever and Q fever. Decorated Bronze Star, 1945; received 1st Mead Johnson prize application tissue culture methods to study of viral infections, 1953; co-recipient Nobel prize in physiology and medicine, 1954; Med. Mut. Honor Award for 1969. Diplomate Am. Bd. Pediatrics. Mem. Am. Epidemiol. Soc., Am. Acad. Arts and Scis., Am. Soc. Clin. Investigation (emeritus mem.), Am. Acad. Pediatrics, Soc. Pediatric Research (pres. 1961-62, emeritus mem.), Am. Assn. Immunologists, Soc. Exptl. Biol. and Medicine, Am. Pediatric Soc., Nat. Acad. Scis., Nat. Inst. Medicine, Am. Philos. Soc., Phi Beta Kappa, Sigma Xi, Phi Gamma Delta. Home: 2467 Guilford Rd Cleveland Heights OH 44118 Office: 2119 Abington St Cleveland OH 44106

ROBBINS, GLENN KINGSLAND, lawyer; b. St. Louis, May 9, 1923; s. Leroy Kingsland and Ruth (Southward) R.; B.S. in Chem. Engring., Washington U., 1947; J.D., LL.B. George Washington U., 1950; m. Anna Brozovic, Dec. 1, 1956; children—Joseph K., Edward S., Glenn Kingsland II, Richard S. Admitted to D.C. bar, 1950, Ill. bar, 1951, Mo. bar, 1952, U.S. Supreme Court, 1960; examiner U.S. Patent Office, Washington, 1947-51; patent counsel Nat. Cylinder Gas Co., Chgo., 1951; asso. Kingsland, Rogers, Ezell, 1951-58; partner Rogers, Ezell, Eilers, & Robbins, and predecessor firm, St. Louis, 1958-72, pvt. practice, 1972—. Served with AUS, 1942-46; lt. col. Res. (ret.). Mem. Am., Mo. bar assns., Bar Assn. Met. St. Louis, Am. Patent Law Assn., U.S. Trademark Assn, Am. Chem. Soc., Am. Legion (comdr. 1962), Alpha Chi Sigma. Presbyn. Clubs: Missouri Athletic (St. Louis); Engineers; Franklin County Country; Washington University (St. Louis). Home: Route 2 Union MO 63084 Office: 314 N Broadway St Louis MO 63102

ROBBINS, NORMAN NELSON, lawyer; b. Detroit, Sept. 27, 1919; s. Charles and Eva (Gold) R.; J.D., Wayne State U., 1943; m. Elaine Helen Israel, June 22, 1946; children—Aimee Carol (Mrs. Stephen B. Malkin), Susan Lynn (Mrs. Ira Stuart Jacobs). Admitted to Mich. bar, 1943, practice specializing in family law, Detroit, 1946—; lectr. Inst. Continuing Legal Edn. under auspices of U. Mich., Ann Arbor, and Wayne State U., Detroit, 1971-75; instr. Eastern Mich. U., Ypsilanti, 1973. Pres. Wayne County (Mich.) unit Am. Cancer Soc., 1969-74, recipient achievement award, 1974. Bd. dirs. Mich. State Bd. Marriage Counselors, 1968-77, chmn. bd., 1971-77; bd. dirs. Mich. State Bd. Vets. Trust Fund, 1964—, chmn. bd., 1974—. Served to capt. USMCR, 1943-46. Named Mich. State Judge Adv., Am. Legion, 1966-67; named Boss of the Year, Southfield Bus. and Profl. Women, 1972; recipient Pub. Service commendation Sta. WOMC, 1974; Mich. Minuteman Gov.'s award, Mich. Minuteman citation of honor Jewish War Vets. Mem. Mich. Interprofl. Assn. Marriage, Divorce and the Family (pres. 1967-70); mem. Am., Detroit (chmn. family law com. 1967-74), Oakland bar assns., State Bar of Mich. (chmn. family law com. 1969-71, chmn. family law sect. 1974-75), Am. Judicature Soc., Am. Arbitration Assn., Am. Legion (vice-comdr. Mich. chpt. 1964-65, comdr. Detroit dist. 1963-64). Mason. Author: Domestic Relations Course Book, 1972. Editor: State Bar Mich. Family Law Jour. Contbr. numerous articles on family law to The Family Coordinator and other profl. jours. Home: 23071 Riverside Dr Southfield MI 48075 Office: 30400 Telegraph Rd Suite 452 Birmingham MI 48010

ROBBINS, OREM OLFORD, ins. co. exec.; b. Mpls., Feb. 5, 1915; s. Douglas Ford and Grace (Rorem) R.; B.B.A. with distinction, U. Minn., 1936; B.S.L., William Mitchell Coll., Law, 1946, J.D. cum laude, 1948; m. Margaret Linderberg Thomson, July 4, 1968; children—Ford, Ross, Gail, Cynthia (Mrs. David Rothbard). Admitted to Minn. bar, 1948; with Northwest Bell Tel. Co., Mpls., 1936-47; dep. dir. Savs. Bond div. U.S. Treasury Dept., 1947-49; agt. Conn. Gen. Life Ins. Co., Mpls., 1949-59; founder-chmn. Security Life Ins. Co. of Am., Mpls., 1956—; chmn. bd., pres. Security Am. Fin. Enterprises, Inc.; chmn. bd. Congress Life Ins. Co., Santa Ana, Calif., Home Life Ins. Co., Springfield, Mo.; mem. faculty bus. ins. and estate planning U. Minn. Ext. Div. Bd. dirs. Methodist Hosp., Family and Children's Service. Served as Col. U.S. Army ret. Decorated Legion of Merit. Fellow Life Office Mgmt. Assn.; mem. Am. Soc. Chartered Life Underwriters, Minn. State Bar Assn., Nat. Eagle Scout Assn., Res. Officers Assn., Assn. U.S. Army, Delta Sigma Pi, Beta Gamma Sigma. Clubs: Skylight, Mpls., Interlachen Masons. Home: 4916 Sunnyside Rd Edina MN 55424 Office: 1200 2d Ave S Minneapolis MN 55403

ROBERTO, EDWARD A., hosp. adminstr.; b. Canton, Ohio, Dec. 21, 1924; s. Salvatore Anthony and Angela Marie (DeStefano) R.; B.S., Ohio State U., 1949; m. Doris Mae Leslie, July 1, 1950; children—Leslie Anne Roberto Ring, Mark Salvatore, Christine Grace Roberto Layman. Adminstr., Brown County Gen. Hosp., Georgetown, Ohio, 1960—; dir. 1st Nat. Bank Georgetown, So. Ohio Savs. Assn. Chmn., Ohio Statewide Health Coordinating Council; past chmn. bd. dirs. Ohio Hosp. Mgmt. Service. Served with AUS, 1942-46. Fellow Am. Coll. Hosp. Adminstrs.; mem. Ohio Hosp. Assn. (past chmn. bd. dirs.), Greater Cin. Hosp. Council (exec. com.). Home: 610 S Pleasant St Georgetown OH 45121 Office: Brown County Gen Hosp Georgetown OH 45121

ROBERTON, LOIS RICKERT (MRS. THEODORE S. ROBERTON), banker, nurse, civic worker; b. Reinback, Iowa, Oct. 6, 1916; d. Elmer Carl and Viola (French) Rickert; student pub. schs.; B.A., Winona (Minn.) State U., 1978; m. Theodore S. Roberton, Jan. 23, 1943; children—Theodore S., II, Teryl Lynn. Gen. duty nurse St. Lukes Hosp., Chgo., 1938, Cornell Med. Center, N.Y.C., 1939-40; pvt. duty nurse, Chgo., 1942; indsl. nurse Internat. Harvester Co., 1943; vol. nurse A.R.C., Community Immunization Clinics, 1945—, Tuberculin Testing Team, S.E. region Minn. Tb and Health Assn., 1964—; v.p., dir. Rushford State Bank, 1952—; city treas., Rushford, Minn., 1961—. Finance sec., bd. incorporators Rushford Clinic Corp., 1959—. County treas. Nat. Found. Infantile Paralysis, Fillmore County, Minn., 1947, county pres., 1948; adv. bd. Fillmore County Nursing, 1952, County Mental Health, 1965, S.E. Minn. dist. Project Head Start, 1967—. Vice chairwoman Fillmore County Republican Com., 1952, chairwoman, 1969. Mem. Minn. Respiratory Health Assn. (exec. bd. 1963-71), Miss. Valley Conf. Nat. Tb Assn. (governing council 1964-71), Community Meml. Hosp. Aux. (nursing scholarship com. 1962-64), St. Lukes Alumni Assn. (life), Sweet Adelines, Am. Lutheran. Mem. Order Eastern Star. Club: Rushford Federated Women's (1st pres. 1958). Home: 304 W Stevens Ave Rushford MN 55971 Office: 219 Mill St Rushford MN 55971

ROBERTS, CHARLES CHESTER, JR., mech. engr.; b. New Bedford, Mass., May 6, 1944; s. Charles Chester and Janina (Patykula) R.; B.S. in M.E., Worcester Tech. Inst., 1966, M.S. in M.E., 1967; Ph.D., U. N.Mex., 1972; m. Lydia Justine Laquer, June 15, 1972. Devel. engr. Jamesbury Corp., Worcester, Mass., 1967-68; mech. engr. Yuma (Ariz.) Proving Ground, 1968-70; mem. tech. staff Bell Labs., Naperville, Ill., 1972-76; sr. profl. engr. Packer Engring. Assos., Naperville, 1976—; cons. heat transfer, probabilistic design, computer design techniques, structural analysis. Served with AUS, 1968-70. Registered profl. engr., Ill.; certified Profl. Ski Instrs. Am. Mem. Am. Soc. M.E., Am. Inst. Aeros. and Astronautics, Inst. Environ. Scis., Sigma Tau. Roman Catholic. Clubs: North Shore Yacht, Toast Masters. Contbr. articles on heat pipe design, probabilistic design and temperature measurements to tech. jours. Patentee in field. Office: Box 353 Packer Engineering Co Naperville IL 60540

ROBERTS, CHARLES EUGENE, chem. co. exec.; b. Nashville, Sept. 21, 1915; s. Charles E. and Maude E. (Hutton) R.; B.A., Vanderbilt U., 1941; J.D., Cornell U., 1948; m. Josephine Edwards Smith, Aug. 26, 1944; children—Susan (Mrs. William R. Hines), Louise, Ann (Mrs. Gary B. Johnson), Carol. Spl. agt. FBI, 1941-46; admitted to N.Y. bar, 1950, Ohio bar, 1968; atty. Mackenzie, Smith & Michell, Syracuse, N.Y., 1948-53; atty. dir. labor relations Smith-Corona Marchant Inc., Syracuse, 1953-61; individual law practice, Syracuse, 1961-65; atty., dir. personnel Harshaw Chem. Co. subs. Kewanee Oil Co., Cleve., 1965—. Mem. Am., N.Y., Ohio, Cleve. bar assns., Soc. Former Spl. Agts. FBI Inc., Cleve. Indsl. Relations Assn., Greater Cleve. Growth Assn. Democrat. Episcopalian. Home: 20 Greentree Rd Chagrin Falls OH 44022 Office: 1945 E 97th St Cleveland OH 44106

ROBERTS, EDGAR LEE, heavy equipment mfg. co. exec.; b. Chgo., Aug. 8, 1902; s. Thomas J. and Inestine (Bush) R.; grad. pub. high sch.; m. Gertrude Nancy Martin, May 29, 1930 (dec. May, 1963); children—Nancy (Mrs. C. Rodney Antrim), Janet (Mrs. Terry Johnson); m. 2d, Christie Mae Yates, Mar. 11, 1972. With Link Belt Co., Chgo., Toronto, Phila., 1922-48, adminstrv. asst. to v.p. mfg., 1942-48; asst. gen. mgr. Palmer Bee Co., Detroit, 1948-54; founding pres. Roberts-Formetals, Inc. Grand Rapids, Mich., 1955—. Mem. Library Bd. City Kentwood, Mich., 1965—. Home: 1356 Camille Dr SE Grand Rapids MI 49506 Office: 3032 Stafford Ave SW Grand Rapids MI 49508

ROBERTS, ERSKINE GOODE, mech. engr.; b. Cambridge, Mass., Aug. 23, 1914; s. Erskine Cathlitt and Alice (Goode) R.; B.S., Northeastern U., 1932; B.S., Mass. Inst. Tech., 1932, M.S., 1933; m. Catherine Claughton, Dec. 31, 1955; children—Alice Jozelda Robinson, Erskine N., Lillian D. Registered profl. engr., Ill., Ind., N.C. Lectr., asst. prof., univ. engr. Tuskegee Inst., Howard U., Lincoln U., 1935-42; asso. engr. examiner Fed. Works Agy., 1935-38; devel. and prodn. engr. P.R. Mallory & Co., Inc., Indpls., 1942-45; chief engr. W.C. Grant Co., Inc., Indpls., 1945-47; self employed profl. engr. and cost cons., Indpls., 1947-54; supervisory project engr. Ind. Dept. Pub. Works and Supply, Indpls., 1954-56; ops. engr., mgmt. div. Chgo. Regional Office, HUD, 1956-60; asso. engr., project mgr. devel., facility engr. Bus. Mgr.'s Office, Argonne Nat. Lab., 1960-68; prin. engr. Perkins & Wills Engrs., Inc., 1969-71; v.p. W.V. Rouse Assos., Ltd., Chgo.; dir. engring. Health and Hosps. Governing Commn. Cook County, Chgo.; profl. cons., personnel dept. Met. San. Dist. Greater Chgo.; cons. engr. N.Central Dist., 1970-71. Trustee, Good Shepard Congl. Ch.; ednl. counsellor Mass. Inst. Tech.; active Quarter Century Group. Mem. ASCE, Ill. Soc. Profl. Engrs., Western Soc. Engrs., Chgo. Assn. Commerce and Industry, Masons (32 deg.), Frogs, Twenty fifth Century KAV. Contbr. articles to profl. jours. Home: 5471 Hyde Park Blvd Chicago IL 60615 Office: 1900 W Polk St Chicago IL 60612

ROBERTS, HELEN CATHERINE GOLDEN, counselor; b. Bethlehem, W. Va., Aug. 1, 1924; d. Edward Evans and Charlotte Eleanore (Ball) Golden; A.B., Bethany Coll., 1946; postgrad. U. Pitts., 1947, 63, Coll. St. Francis, Joliet, Ill., 1969-70, Joliet Jr. Coll., 1970, Lewis U., 1970; M.S. in Edn., No. Ill. U., 1971, certificate advanced studies, 1974, Ed.D. in Counselor Edn., 1978; m. Charles Gilbert Roberts, Nov. 4, 1950 (dec. 1969); children—Charlotte Eleanore, Charles Gilbert. Quality control chemist H.J. Heinz Co., Pitts., Salem, N.J., 1945; tech. librarian, research chemist Harbison-Walker Refractories Co., Pitts., 1946-48; chief chemist Centre Foundry & Machine Co., Wheeling, W. Va., 1948-50; abstractor chem. abstracts service Am. Chem. Soc., Ohio State U., Columbus, 1959-74; subs. tchr. Joliet (Ill.) Twp. Grade and High Schs., 1967-71, Rockdale (Ill.) Pub. Schs., 1967-71, Troy Community Consol. Schs., 1967-70; counselor Valley View Community Unit Sch. Dist. 365U, Romeoville, Ill., 1972—; counselor Bolingbrook, Ill., 1972, coordinator elementary social work and counseling services, 1974-76; v.p., corp. dir. Park Place, Inc., Wheeling, 1972—; item writer Scholastic Testing Service, Bensenville, Ill., 1974—; cons. in field. Patron Family Counseling Agy. Recipient Gans Grant Award for Sci. Research, 1945. Mem. Am., Ill. personnel and guidance assns., No. Ill. U. Assn. Guidance Personnel, Inst. Logotherapy, Nat. Character Lab., Am. Chem. Soc., Zeta Tau Alpha. Contbr. articles to profl. jours. Home: 3005 Twin Oaks Dr Joliet IL 60435 Office: West View Middle Sch Romeoville IL 60441

ROBERTS, HUGH EVAN, metals mfg. and engring. co. exec.; b. Marion, Ind., Aug. 29, 1923; s. Arthur Edwin and Georgina (Fankboner) R.; student De Pauw U., 1941-43; B.S. in Mech. Engring., U. Cin., 1950; m. Ellen Langtree Gordon, Sept. 16, 1950; children—Ellen Langtree, Daniel Evan, Robert Gordon. Project engr. Procter & Gamble Co., Cin., 1950-53, master mechanic, 1953-56, dir. field constrn., 1957-60, dir. plant engring., 1960-63; mgr. comml. devel. Monsanto Co., St. Louis, 1963-65, product sales mgr., 1965-68, dir. solid pollution bus. group, 1968-69; pres. Binkley Co., Warrenton, Mo., 1969—. Pres. Bd. Edn. Spl. Sch. Dist., St. Louis County (Mo.), 1973-75. Served to 1st lt. USAAF, 1943-45. Decorated D.F.C., Air medal with oak leaf clusters. Mem. Mo. Quail and Gun Club, Nat. Assn. Watch and Clock Collectors. Patentee in field. Home: 17 Frontenac Estate St Louis MO 63131 Office: Main and Elm Sts Warrenton MO 63383

ROBERTS, JAMES ALFRED, dentist; b. New Rochelle, N.Y., June 29, 1941; s. Lawrence David and Margaret Julia (Vernier) R.; student U.S. Air Force Acad., 1959-60; B.S., Furman U., 1963; D.M.D., U. Pa., 1967; m. Rachel Sherwood, Apr. 1, 1966; children—Anne Margaret, Edward Hammond, Emily Allen. Dentist, Fort Wayne (Ind.) State Hosp. and Tng. Center, 1968; practice dentistry, Auburn, Ind., 1968—; mem. staff DeKalb Meml. Hosp. Asst. coordinator Civil Def. Mem. Am., Ind. dental assns., Isaac Knapp Dist. Dental Soc., Am. Analgesic Soc., Auburn Jaycees, Am. Endodontic Soc., Am. Acad. Orthodontics for Gen. Practioner, Am. Soc. Dentistry for Children, Auburn C. of C. (dir. 1970-72), Pi Kappa Phi, Delta Sigma Delta. Republican. Presbyterian (deacon 1970—). Club: Greenhurst Country. Ham radio operator. Home: 509 Greenbriar Blvd Auburn IN 46706 Office: 102 N Clark St Auburn IN 46706

ROBERTS, JO ANN (WOODEN), speech pathologist; b. Chgo., June 24, 1948; d. William Dean and Annie Mae (Wardlaw) Dean Wooden; B.S., Wayne State U., 1970, M.Ed., 1971; Ph.D., Northwestern U., 1977; m. Edward Allen Roberts, May 27, 1972; 1 son, Edward Allen, Jr. Speech pathologist Holy Cross Hosp., Chgo., 1971, Chgo. Bd. Edn., 1971—; instr. Mayfair City Community Coll., Chgo., 1975-76; project dir. Ednl. Testing Service, Evanston, Ill., 1976; cons. Frank Cassell and Assos., Evanston. Mich. ednl. grantee, 1969-70, ednl. fellow, 1970-71. Mem. Chgo. Assn. Sch. Speech Therapists, Ill. Speech and Hearing Assn., Christian Bus. and Profl. Women's Club (ticket chmn. 1976-77), Phi Delta Kappa. Roman Catholic. Author: Learning to Talk, 1975. Home: 2353 E 70th St Chicago IL 60649 Office: 1750 E 71st St Chicago IL 60649

ROBERTS, LEIGH MILTON, educator; b. Jacksonville, Ill., June 9, 1925; s. Victor Harold and Ruby Harriet (Kelsey) R.; B.S., U. Ill., 1945, M.D., 1947; m. Marilyn Edith Kadow, Sept. 6, 1946; children—David, Carol (Mrs. Thomas Mayer), Paul, Nancy. Intern, St. Francis Hosp., Peoria, Ill., 1947-48; resident U. Wis. Hosps., Madison, 1953-56; gen. practice medicine, Macomb, Ill., 1948-50; staff psychiatrist Mendota (Wis.) State Hosp., 1956-58; prof. psychiatry U. Wis. Med. Sch., Madison, 1959—, acting chmn. dept. psychiatry, 1972-75. Mem. spl. rev. bd. Wis. Parole Bd. for Sex Crimes Law, 1962—; cons. Wis. Div. Mental Hygiene, 1965—, VA, Milw., 1962-75. Mem. Dane County Devel. Disabilities Bd., 1972—; mem. Wis. State Planning Coms., Mental Health, 1963-65, Health, 1969-71, Vocat. Rehab., 1966-68, Mental Health Centers, 1967-71, Mental Health Adv., 1973—; v.p. Wis. Council Chs., 1976—. Bd. dirs. Meth. Hosp., Madison, Madison Campus Ministry, Dane County Rehab.

House, Dane County Assn. Mental Health, St. Benedict Center. Served with USNR, 1943-45, 50-53. Decorated Bronze Star medals, Purple Heart. Diplomate Am. Bd. Neurology and Psychiatry. Fellow Am. Psychiat. Assn. (area rep. 1976—); mem. Wis. Psychiat. Assn. (pres. 1967). Methodist (gen. council ministries 1973—). Editor: Community Psychiatry, 1966; Comprehensive Mental Health, 1968. Contbr. articles to profl. jours. Home: 7924 Deer Run Rd Cross Plains WI 53528 Office: 427 Lorch St Madison WI 53706

ROBERTS, LEO JAMES, eye physician and surgeon; b. Chgo., Sept. 1, 1933; s. Leo Joseph and Marjorie (Palmer) R.; B.S., Loyola U., 1956, M.D., 1958; m. Joyce Ann Woods, May 24, 1969; children—Mary Joyce, Elizabeth Ann, Jennifer Lea, Catherine Nell. Intern, Cook County Hosp., 1958-59; resident West Side VA Hosp., Chgo., 1959-60, Ill. Eye and Ear Infirmary, 1962-65, U. Calif. at Los Angeles Med. Center, 1965-66; practice medicine specializing in ophthalmology, Hinsdale, Ill., 1966—; mem. staffs Hinsdale Sanitarium and Hosp., Community Meml. Hosp., LaGrange, Ill. Instr. ophthalmology U. Ill., 1966-70, Loyola U., 1970—. Served with USAF, 1960-62. Fellow A.C.S., Am. Acad. Ophthalmology and Otolaryngology; mem. Flying Physicians Assn., Chgo., Dupage County med. socs. Club: Hinsdale Golf. Home: 55 Devonshire Dr Oak Brook IL 60521 Office: 40 S Clay St Hinsdale IL 60521

ROBERTS, RICHARD LEE, chemist; b. Mattoon, Ill., Jan. 22, 1949; s. John Paul and Martha Marie (Miller) R.; B.S., U. Tex. at Arlington, 1971; M.S., Tex. Tech. U., 1974; postgrad. Ind. U., Indpls.; m. Sarah Ann Russell, June 5, 1976. Devel. cosmetic chemist, Lilly Research Labs., Eli Lilly & Co., Indpls., 1974-76, research cosmetic chemsit, 1976—. Robert A. Welch Found. fellow, 1973-74; Tex. Tech. U. fellow, 1972. Mem. Delta Tau Delta. Home: 6208 Hoover Rd Indianapolis IN 46260 Office: PO Box 2046 Indianapolis IN 46206

ROBERTS, ROY, marketing exec.; b. Chgo., June 18, 1927; s. Irwin Leon and Berenice Muriel (Lindenthal) R.; B.A., Stanford U., 1950; m. Marian Cecily Fried, Dec. 14, 1952; children—Julia Ann, Charles Harry. Asst. account exec. Ruthrauff & Ryan, Chgo., 1951-52; account exec. Bozell & Jacobs, Chgo., 1952-56; advt. mgr. Duraclean Internat., Deerfield, Ill., 1956-57; v.p. Home Arts Guild Corp., Chgo., 1957-69, pres., 1969—, owner, 1969—. Served with AUS 1945-47. Mem. Am. Marketing Assn., Marketing Research Assn., Alpha Delta Sigma. Office: 35 E Wacker Dr Chicago IL 60601

ROBERTS, THOMAS CHELCIE, constrn. co. exec.; b. Harlan, Ky., Dec. 20, 1935; s. Alfred Adam and Gladys Virginia (Cook) R.; student Lawrence Inst. Tech., 1961-63; m. W. Lee Barker, May 21, 1956; children—Guy T., Alfred A., Wade E. Elec. worker, 1957-70; salesman Roberts Co., 1970-72; v.p. Robco Homes, Inc., Energy, Ill., 1972-73, pres., 1973—, also dir.; pres. Wood-Vale Homes, Inc., Energy; v.p. Pyramid Title Co.; sec.-treas., dir. Cedar Grove Devel., Inc., Marion, Ill. Mem. Nat. (dir.), Ill., So. Ill. (dir.) home builder assns., Herrin C. of C. Club: Kiwanis (pres. Herrin 1973-74, lt. gov. div. 16 Ill.-Iowa dist.). Home: 1712 W Adams St Herrin IL 62948 Office: Hwy 148 S Energy IL 62933

ROBERTS, VALERIE SAWYER, counseling psychologist; b. Tarrytown, N.Y., Apr. 29, 1953; s. Alfred Worcester and Elinore (Mooney) Sawyer; student Wheaton Coll., 1971-73; B.A., Smith Coll., 1975; M.Ed., U. N.C., Chapel Hill, 1977; m. Charles Roberts, July 24, 1977. Tchr. lower sch. Fessenden Sch., West Newton, Mass., 1975-76; counseling intern Carrboro Elementary Sch., (N.C.), 1976-77; counseling psychologist Weber Sch., Creve Coeur, Mo., 1977—. Volunteer, Crisis Intervention Center, Carrboro, 1977. Mem. Am. Personnel and Guidance Assn., AAUP, Mo. Tchrs. Assn., Parkway Ind. Community, Greater St. Louis tchrs. assns., Smith Coll. Club of Wellesley (Mass.). Republican. Episcopalian. Home: 711A Wiggens Ferry Dr Creve Coeur MO 63141 Office: 300 N New Ballas Rd Creve Coeur MO 63141

ROBERTS, WILLIAM KEITH, indsl. psychologist; b. Arcola, Ill., Dec. 19, 1922; s. Dewey N. and Anna E. (Franklin) Roberts; m. Patricia R. Park, June 12, 1948; children—Christopher, Scott, Andrew, Theodore, Rebecca; B.S., Purdue U., 1950, M.S., 1951. Registered psychologist, Ill. Instr. psychology Gen. Motors Inst., Flint, Mich, 1951, personnel evaluation specialist, 1953-54, supr. edn. and training. Gen. Motors Corp., Linden, N.J., 1954-56; adminstr. training and devel. Am. Standard Corp., N.Y., 1956-59; mgr. management devel. Raytheon Co., Lexington, Mass., 1959-64; personnel and organizational cons. Abbott Labs., N. Chgo., 1964-66; mgr. training and devel. services Allis-Chalmers Corp., Milw., 1966—; instr. U. Wis. extension div., 1971—. Pilot USAAF, 1943-45; pilot psychology branch Aeromed. Lab. U.S. Air Force, 1951-53. Mem. Am. Soc. for Training and Devel., Am. Psychol. Assn., Nat. Soc. of Sales Tng. Execs. Contbr. articles in field to profl. jours. Home: 2390 Hannemann Rd Grafton WI 53204 Office: Box 512 Milwaukee WI 53201

ROBERTSON, ABEL ALFRED LAZZARINI, JR., pathologist; b. St. Andrews, Argentina, July 21, 1926; s. Abel Alfred Lazzarini and Margaret Therese (Anderson) R.; came to U.S., 1952, naturalized, 1957; B.S., Coll. D.F. Sarmiento, Buenos Aires, Argentina, 1946; M.D. cum laude, U. Buenos Aires, 1951; Ph.D., Cornell U., 1959; m. Irene Kirmayr Mauch, Dec. 26, 1958; children—Margaret Ann, Abel Martin, Andrew Duncan, Malcolm Alexander. Fellow tissue culture div. Inst. Histology and Embryology, U. Buenos Aires Sch. Medicine, 1947-49; surg. intern Hosp. Ramos Majia, Buenos Aires, 1948-50; fellow in tissue culture research Ministry of Health, Buenos Aires, 1950-51; resident Hosp. Nacional de Clinicas, Buenos Aires, 1950-51; head blood vessel bank and organ transplants Research Center, Ministry of Health, Buenos Aires, 1951-53; fellow dept. surgery and pathology Cornell U. Sch. Medicine, N.Y.C., 1953-55; asst. vis. surgery U. Hosp. N.Y., N.Y.C., 1955-60; asst. prof. research surgery N.Y. U. Postgrad. Med. Sch., N.Y.C., 1955-56; asst. vis. surgeon Bellevue Hosp., N.Y.C., 1955-60; asso. prof. research surgery N.Y. U. Postgrad. Med. Sch., 1956-60, asso. prof. pathology Sch. Medicine and Postgrad. Med. Sch., 1960-63; staff mem. Cleve. Clinic Found. Div. Research, 1963-73, prof. research, 1972-73; asso. clin. prof. pathology Case Western Res. U. Sch. Medicine, Cleve., 1968-72, prof. pathology, 1973—, dir. interdisciplinary cardiovascular research, 1975—. Research fellow N.Y. Soc. Cardiovascular Surgery, 1957-58; mem. research study subcom. of heart com. N.E. Ohio Regional Med. Program, 1969—. Recipient Research Devel. award NIH, 1961-63. Fellow Am. Coll. Cardiology, Am. Coll. Clin. Pharmacology, Am. Heart Assn. (nominating com. council on arteriosclerosis 1972), Royal Microscopical Soc. (Gt. Britain), Royal Soc. Promotion Health (Gt. Britain), Am. Geriatrics Soc., N.Y. Acad. Scis., Cleve. Med. Library Assn.; mem. AAAS, Am. Assn. Pathologists and Bacteriologists, AAUP, Am. Inst. Biol. Scis., Am. Judicature Soc., Am. Soc. Cell Biology, Am. Soc. Exptl. Pathology, Am. Soc. Nephrology, Assn. Am. Physicians and Surgeons, Assn. Computing Machinery, Electron Microscopy Soc. Am., Internat. Acad. Pathology, Internat. Cardiovascular Soc., Internat. Soc. Cardiology (sci. council on arteriosclerosis and ischemic heart disease 1960-64), Internat. Soc. Nephrology, Internat. Soc. Stereology, Pan Am. Med. Assn. (life, councillor in angiology 1966-72), Reticuloendothelial Soc., Soc. Cryobiology, Tissue Culture Assn., Ohio Soc. Pathologists, Electron Microscopy Soc. Northeastern Ohio (pres., trustee 1966-68), Heart Assn. Northeastern Ohio, N.Y. Soc. Cardiovascular Surgery, N.Y. Soc. Electron Microscopists, Cuyahoga County Med. Soc., Cleve. Soc. Pathologists, Sigma Xi. Mem. internat. editorial bd. Atherosclerosis, Jour. Exptl. and Molecular Pathology, 1964—. Contbr. articles to profl. jours. Home: 3596 Beverly Hills Dr Rocky River OH 44116 Office: 2085 Adelbert Rd Cleveland OH 44106

ROBERTSON, BILLY O'NEAL, sch. adminstr.; b. Columbia, S.C., Mar. 27, 1930; s. William Anglo and Ollie Vandora (Freeman) R.; student Furman U., 1955-58; B.A., U. Louisville, 1959; M.A., Ind. U., 1962; postgrad. Mich. State U., 1971-74; m. Helen Noreen Oglesby, May 21; children—Larry, Ronald, Marcia. Tchr.-librarian North Central Sch., Ramsey, Ind., 1959-61; tchr.-librarian Dennis Jr. High Sch., Richmond, Ind., 1961-63; sch. library supr. Greeley (Colo.) Pub. Schs., 1963-65; dir. media. Pub. schs., Lincoln, Nebr., 1965-70; coordinator instructional media Pub. Schs., Midland, Mich., 1970—; asso. prof. library and audio visual U. Nebr. Served with USAF, 1948-50, 50-51. Recipient Media Educator award Nebr. Ednl. Media Assn., 1970. Mem. Mich. Library Assn. (chmn. elect sch. sect.), Nat. Council Accreditation of Tchr. Edn., ALA, Assn. Ednl. Communications and Tech., Mich. Assn. Media in Edn., Assn. Supervision and Curriculum Devel., Am. Ednl. Research Assn. Democrat. Baptist. Club: Lions, Gideons. Home: 4411 Swede Rd Midland MI 48640 Office: 600 Carpenter St E Midland MI 48640

ROBERTSON, CHARLES HARRY, lawyer; b. Bloomington, Ind., Oct. 19, 1902; s. Charles Wesley and Rose E. (Whisenand) R.; student Ind. U., 1921-24; LL.B., Cumberland U., 1925, J.D., 1969; m. Lottie Luetta Coumbe, June 24, 1927; children—Luetta Coumbe (Mrs. Tor D. Kolflat), Malcoumbe Clark. Admitted to Ind. bar, 1923, Fla. bar, 1925; practiced law in Fla., 1925-26, Lafayette, Ind., 1926—; judge Superior Ct., Tippecanoe County, Ind., 1943-45; Tippecanoe County Atty., civil law, 1946-64. Lectr. law domestic relations Purdue U., 1946-47, philos. aspects law, 1963, Zen-Christianity. Lafayette, West Lafayette, Inc., 1963-65; daylily hybridist. Past mem. bd. dirs. YMCA, Salvation Army, Lafayette Art Assn.; past pres. Community Fund Greater Lafayette; pres. bd. dirs. Sunnyside Sch. Bldg. Corp., 1955-72. Pres. bd. Pub. Welfare, Tippecanoe County 1940-42; chmn. Ind. 2d Congl. Dist., Pres. Eisenhower's Am.-Korean Campaign; mem. Ind. Corp. Survey Commn., 1957-69; Tippecanoe County chmn. of First Law Day U.S.A., 1958. Sec. Tippecanoe County Republican Central Com., 1946-52; personal campaign mgr. for Senator Robert E. Taft for Pres., 2d Congl. Dist. Ind., preliminary to Rep. Nat. Conv., 1952; del. Rep. Nat. Conv., 1952; incorporator, bd. dirs. Jerry E. Clegg Meml. Found., 1965-67. Apptd. Sagamore of Wabash by gov. Ind., 1965. Mem. Am., Ind. (presdl. citation for exceptional contbn. to profession law 1966), Tippecanoe County (pres. 1935-36) bar assns., Nat. Rifle Assn., Wildcat Valley Rifle and Pistol Club, Am. Hemerocallis Soc. (life), Tippecanoe County Hist. Soc. (past dir.), Kappa Sigma, Gamma Eta Gamma, Theta Alpha Phi. Mason, Elk (life). Clubs: Lafayette Country (pres. 1940-41); Diana Skeet (co-founder 1969). Composer music for 1923 Union Revue and Jordan River Revue, Ind. U., Song My Valentine. Home: Terrace Gardens 600 Lingle Terr Lafayette IN 47901 Office: Robertson Law Office Lafayette Bank & Trust Bldg Lafayette IN 47901

ROBERTSON, JAMES EDWARD, tire and motor supply co., investment co. exec.; b. St. Joseph, Mo., Nov. 27, 1931; s. James Leo and Laura E. (Rupp) R.; student St. Joseph Jr. Coll., 1949-51; m. Jolene Ann O'Connor, Sept. 3, 1956; children—Mike, Jina, John, Jan. With Leo Robertson Tire & Motor Supply, Inc., St. Joseph, 1952—, pres., dir., 1959—; partner Robertson Bros., St. Joseph, 1964—; chmn. bd. Citizens State Bank, Seneca, Kan.; pres. Seneca Bancshares; sec.-treas., 1st Mo. Bancshare; sec.-treas., dir. Kans. BanCorp., Kansas City, Kan., 1970—, Central Bank Shares, Hutchinson, Kans., 1970-73; dir. Belt Nat. Bank, St. Joseph, 1st Am. Bancshares; adv. dir. Home State Bank, Kansas City, Kans. Chmn., Mayor's Drug Abuse Commn., 1970—. Pres., bd. dirs. J. Leo Robertson Found., 1965—, New Life-Inner City, 1969-74, St. Joseph Sch. System, 1968—; bd. dirs. St. Joseph Hosp. Served with USAF, 1951-52. Mem. Nat. Tire Dealers and Retreaders Assn., Young Tire Dealers (pres. 1960-62), C. of C. Home: 35 Stonecrest St St Joseph MO 64506 Office: 1801 Frederick St St Joseph MO 64501

ROBERTSON, JAMES EDWIN, physician; b. Hillsboro, Tex., Jan. 6, 1915; s. Abram Nangle and Altha (Dilworth) R.; B.S., U. Tex., Austin, 1936; M.D., U. Tex., Galveston, 1940; m. Viola Startzman, Aug. 29, 1954; children—Dean Edwin, James Frederick, David Leon, Martin Scott. Intern, Met. Gen. Hosp., Cleve., 1940-41, asst. resident, 1941-42; practice medicine specializing in internal medicine, Wooster, Ohio, 1946—; fellow Cleve. Clinic, 1954-55. Active Wayne County, E. Central heart assns.; mem. research com. Ohio Heart Assn., 1970—. Served with U.S. Army, 1942-46. Diplomate Am. Bd. Internal Medicine. Fellow ACP; mem. AMA, Ohio State Med. Assn., Wayne County Med. Soc. Presbyterian. Club: Century. Home: 1137 Forest Dr Wooster OH 44691 Office: Wooster Clinic 1740 Cleveland Rd Wooster OH 44691

ROBERTSON, JOSEPH EDMOND, indsl. grain processing co. exec.; b. Brownstown, Ind., Feb. 16, 1918; s. Roscoe Melvin and Edith Penina (Shields) R.; B.S., Kans. State U., 1940, postgrad., 1940; m. Virginia Faye Baxter, Nov. 23, 1941; 1 son, Joseph Edmond. Cereal chemist Ewing Mill Co., 1940-43, flour milling engr., 1946-50, feed nutritionist, 1951-59; v.p., sec. Robertson Corp., Brownstown, Ind., 1960—. Pres. Jackson County (Ind.) Welfare Bd., 1948-52. Served with USAAF, 1943-45. Mem. Hardwood Plywood Mfrs. Assn. (v.p. affiliate div. 1971-73), Am. Assn. Cereal Chemists, Assn. Operative Millers, Am. Legion, Brownstown C. of C. (dir. All Am. city program 1955), Kans. State U. Alumni Assn. (life), Blue Key, Phi Delta Theta, Phi Kappa Phi, Alpha Mu. Presbyn. (elder 1954-69). Elk. Clubs: Country (Seymour, Ind.); Hickory Hills Country (Brownstown, Ind.). Home: Route 2 Lake and Forest Club Brownstown IN 47220 Office: 200 Front St Brownstown IN 47220

ROBERTSON, RODNEY CHARLES, accountant; b. Eaton Rapids, Mich., July 31, 1949; s. Charles Marion and Thena Maxine (Jeffery) R.; B.A., Mich. State U., 1971; m. Doris Ann Gillett, Dec. 19, 1970; one dau., Sara Marie. Sr. accountant Young, Skutt & Breitenwischer, Jackson, Mich., 1971-74; partner Robertson & Zick, Rose City, Mich., 1974—. Mem. Ogemaw Valley Jr. (adminstrv. v.p. 1977), Rose City Area chambers commerce, Mich. Assn. C.P.A.'s. Am. Inst. C.P.A.'s, Beta Alpha Psi. Methodist. Home: 1144 E Rose City Rd Rose City MI 48654 Office: 103 E Main St Rose City MI 48654

ROBERTSON, WILLIAM BRUCE, pub. relations cons.; b. Beverly, Mass., Dec. 2, 1927; s. William Hoare and Janet Irene (Robertson) R.; B.A., Dartmouth Coll., 1951; m. Mary Joan Rowe, Dec. 30, 1953; children—Emily Marie, William Bruce. Copywriter, Marshall Field & Co., Chgo., 1956-58, Batten Barton Durstine & Osborne Co., Chgo., 1959-61; asst. advt. mgr., pub. relations dir. Kemper Ins. Group, Chgo., 1962-69; mgr. pub. relations dept. communications div. Motorola Corp., Chgo., 1970-72; exec. dir. Health Care At Home, Northbrook, Ill., 1973-75; v.p. pub. relations Stevens Kirkland Kreer, Co., Chgo., 1975—. Served with USNR, 1951-55. Mem. Pub. Relations Soc. Am. Club. Mich. Shores (Wilmette, Ill.). Home: 1216 Ashland Ave Wilmette IL 60091 Office: 111 E Wacker Dr Chicago IL 60601

ROBIE, FRED SMITH, coll. pres.; b. Aspinwall, Pa., Mar. 7, 1920; s. George Randolph and Blanche (Hilliard) R.; B.A., U. Pitts., 1941; M.A., U. Mich., 1949; Ph.D., U. Pitts., 1970; m. Mary Louise Kent, May 9, 1943; children—William Randolph, Nancy Ann, Fred Kent. Instr. speech W.Va. U., 1946-47; asst. prof. U. Pitts., 1947-51, alumni dir., 1960-67, asst. dir., dir. admissions, 1967-70; spl. agt. FBI, 1951-60; pres. Jefferson Tech. Coll., Steubenville, Ohio, 1970—. Pres., Steubenville Area United Way, 1977; campaign chmn. Jefferson County Heart Assn., 1974-77; bd. dirs. Fort Steuben council Boy Scouts Am. Served to capt. U.S. Army, 1942-46; PTO. Ford. Found. grantee, 1968-69. Mem. Ohio Assn. Tech. Colls. (pres. 1974), Steubenville Area C. of C. (v.p. 1977-78). Presbyn. Clubs: Rotary, Williams Country, Mason. Home: 1718 Williams Pl Steubenville OH 43952 Office: 4000 Sunset Blvd Steubenville OH 43952

ROBILLARD, JAMES LAWRENCE, independent researcher; b. Milw., Feb. 5, 1926; s. Lionel Ovila and Diana Helen (Rousseau) R.; certificate Laval U., Quebec, Que., 1948; Ph.B., Marquette U., 1950; postgrad., summer 1956; M.A., U. Wis., 1951; postgrad. Leadership Tng. Inst., Washington, 1968-69. Grad. teaching asst. U. Wis., 1950-51; English teaching asst. Lycee Chaptal, Paris, France, 1951-52; tour mgr. Am. Express Travel Service, Chgo., 1953-54, 57-60; jr. officer trainee USIA, Washington, asst. to press attache USIS, Rome, Italy, sub-post duty USIS and Am. Consulate, Florence, Italy, 1955-56; spl. asst. devel. projects, dir. found. relations U. Chgo., 1960-62; exec. dir. Jesuit Ednl. Assn., Washington, 1962-67; ednl. cons. J. Lawrence Robillard, Washington, 1967-68; dir. ednl. programs Stanwick Corp., Arlington, Va., 1968-69; cons., proposal writer for John W. Gardner, then pres. Nat. Urban Coalition, Washington, 1969; independent research scholar dept. English U. Wis.-Milw., 1969—. Served with USNR, 1944-46; ETO, PTO. Named hon. citizen New Orleans, 1976; teaching fellow U. Wis., 1950, Inst. Internat. Edn./French Govt., 1951. Mem. Am. Acad. Polit. and Social Scis., Am. Council on Edn., Am. Assn. Fund-raising Council, Assn. Am. Colls. Author: The Jesuit Order and Higher Education in the United States, 1789-1966, 1966; Program Funding for Educational Activities in the Jesuit Colleges and Universities of the United States: 1962-1967, 1967; Involvement in International Education of American Jesuit Higher Education, 1967.

ROBILLIARD, WALTER HENRY, mfg. co. exec.; b. Faribault, Minn., Aug. 3, 1921; s. Charles Morton and Virginia Harriet (Schutt) R.; student Grinnell Coll., 1939-41, U. Minn., 1941-43; m. Caroline Ann Gilbert, May 30, 1941; children—Walter Henry, Bonnilee. Accountant, Holloway, Knutson & Bowers, Mpls., 1942-45; internal revenue agt. U.S. Treasury Dept., 1945-54; asst. gen. auditor Minn. and Ont. Paper Co., Mpls., 1954-59, asst. treas., 1959-61, sec.-treas., 1962-66; treas. McQuay-Perfex Inc., air-conditioning and other heat transfer products, Mpls., 1966-73, v.p., treas., 1973—; dir. Foto-Mark Inc., metal finishing. Owner Carawal Arabians, horse breeding farm, Buffalo, Minn., 1965—. C.P.A., Minn. Mem. Am. Inst. C.P.A.'s, Minn. Soc. C.P.A.'s, Financial Execs. Inst., Am. Horse Shows Assn., Minn. Arabian Horse Assn. (past pres.), Arabian Horse Registry Am. Mason. Club: Minneapolis Athletic. Home: Route 3 Box 218A Buffalo MN 55313 Office: 5401 Gamble Dr PO Box 9316 Minneapolis MN 55440

ROBINDER, CATHERINE MAE FITZPATRICK, mathematician; b. East Moline, Ill., July 24, 1922; d. Walter H. and Belva M. (Westerfield) Fitzpatrick; A.B. cum laude, Augustana Coll., 1956; M.S., U. Iowa, 1961; m. Wallace R. Robinder, Nov. 5, 1966. Draftsman, Rock Island (Ill.) Arsenal, 1942-45, Swanson & Maiwald, Architects, Moline, Ill., 1946-47; mathematician-engr. Rock Island Arsenal, 1948-77; cons. field stress analysis, 1970—. Recipient Rock Island Arsenal spl. award for published article, 1966, for outstanding analysis work, 1960, 69, 75. Mem. Am. Math. Soc., AAUW, (br. treas. 1962-65) Illowa Gem and Mineral Soc., Sigma Xi. Baptist (chmn. music com. 1963—, fin. sec. 1956-63, youth work com. 1954—). Club: Blackhawk Gem and Mineral (v.p., program chmn. 1967, pres. 1973). Home: 2115 25th Ave Rock Island IL 61201

ROBINS, ELI, psychiatrist, neurochemist; b. Houston, Feb. 22, 1921; s. Abe and Ida (Schaffer) R.; B.A., Rice U., 1940; M.D., Harvard, 1943; m. Lee Nelken, Feb. 22, 1946; children—Paul, James, Thomas, Nicholas. Asst. in psychiatry Harvard, 1944-45; Boston U., 1948; intern Mt. Sinai Hosp., N.Y.C., 1944; resident Mass. Gen. Hosp., Boston, 1944-45, McLean Hosp., Waverly, Mass., 1945-46, Pratt Diagnostic Hosp., Boston, 1948-49; instr. neuropsychiatry Washington U., St. Louis, 1951-52, asst. prof. psychiatry, 1953-56, asso. prof., 1956-58, prof., 1958-66, head dept psychiatry, 1963-75, Wallace Renard prof., 1966—. Served to capt U.S. Army, 1946-48. Recipient career research award USPHS, 1961-63; gold medal Soc. Biol. Psychiatry, 1974; Paul H. Hoch award Am. Psychopath. Assn., 1977. Diplomate Am. Bd. Am. Bd. Psychiatry and Neurology. Fellow Am. Psychiat. Assn., Royal Coll. Psychiatrists; mem. Am. Soc. Clin. Investigation, Am. Soc. Biol. Chemists, Soc. Biol. Psychiatry, Psychiatric Research Soc., Am. Psychopath. Assn. Internat. Soc. Neurochemistry, Assn. for Research in Nervous and Mental Disease (v.p. 1960), Soc. Neurosci. Contbr. articles to med. jours. Home: 1 Forest Ridge St Louis MO 63105 Office: 4940 Audubon St Louis MO 63110

ROBINS, GARY BRUCE, beverage co. exec.; b. Columbus, Ohio, June 6, 1946; s. Louis and Sara (Kahn) R.; student Ohio State U., 1964-66; m. Constance Kiefer, Aug. 11, 1967; children—Dean, Chad, Bret. Salesman, Excello Wine Co., Columbus, 1967-70, v.p., 1971—; pres. Hi-State Beverage Co., Columbus, 1977—, also dir. Active United Jewish Fund, 1970—; bd. dirs. Jewish Family Service, 1975. Mem. Wholesale Beer Assn. Ohio, Nat., Beer Wholesalers Assn., Wine and Spirits Wholesalers Am., Ohio Wholesale Wine Dealers Assn. Club: B'nai B'rith, Winding Hollow Country. Home: 389 S Merkle Rd Columbus OH 43209 Office: 949 King Ave Columbus OH 43212

ROBINSON, CLAUDE GARTH, steel fabricating co. exec.; b. Detroit, July 13, 1925; s. Claude W. and Gladys (Bricker) R.; B.S., Wayne State U., 1949, M.S., 1960, postgrad. bus. adminstrn., 1960—; m. Marion Keith, Aug. 15, 1947. Bridge and expressway engr. Wayne County Rd. Commn., Detroit, 1949-56; design engr. to chief engr. archtl., spl. and transp. products divs. Stran Steel Corp. unit Nat. Steel Corp., Detroit, 1956-59; chief product engr., steel div. Fenestra, Inc., Detroit, 1960; chief engr. Safway Steel Products, Inc., Milw., 1960-63, v.p. engring., 1963-69 (became div. Automatic Sprinkler Corp. Am. 1966); pres. Universal Bleacher Co., Champaign, Ill., 1969—; exec. v.p. Endion, Inc., Chgo., 1972-73; pres. E.H. Sheldon & Co., Muskegon, Mich., 1973—, Archtl. Products Group, Am. Seating Co., 1974—. Served to 2d lt. USAAF, 1943-45. Registered profl. engr., Mich., Wis., N.J. Mem. ASCE, Am. Welding Soc., Am. Mgmt. Assn. Patentee in field. Office: 716 Nims St Muskegon MI 49443

ROBINSON, ELIOT FINLEY, architect; b. Detroit, July 19, 1918; s. Mitchell Barther and Alma (Finley) R.; B.A. in Econs., U. Mich., 1939; M.Arch., Harvard U., 1942; m. Sarah Winston, June 28, 1949; children—Peter, Lydia, Suzanne, Sarah. Project dir. Albert Kahn, Inc., 1946-49; liaison architect Eero Saarinen & Assos., Bloomfield Hills, Mich., 1949-53; pvt. practice architecture, Birmingham, Mich., 1953-58; asso. Frederick Stickel Assos., Birmingham, 1961—; pres.

Beacon Bldg. Products Co., Detroit, 1958-61; asst. prof. Lawrence Inst. Tech., 1956. Chmn., mem. Birmingham Planning Bd., 1957—; pres., trustee Bloomfield Art Assn. Mem. adv. bd. dirs. City and Country Sch. Bloomfield Hills. Served to lt. comdr. USNR, 1942-45. Decorated Bronze Star medal. Registered architect, Mich. Mem. AIA. Club: Bloomfield Open Hunt. Patentee support bracket. Home: 572 Linden Rd Birmingham MI 48009 summer Old Bennington VT 05201 Office: 2900 W Maple Troy MI 48084

ROBINSON, FORREST DEAN, educator, poet, editor; b. Berea, Ohio, Nov. 4, 1931; s. Harry Forest and Mary Ella (Dean) R.; A.B., Miami U., Oxford, Ohio, 1953, M.A., 1957; Ph.D., Ohio U., 1966; m. Margaret Ann McLaughlin, July 9, 1955; children—Benjamin Grant, Kristen Lorene, Rachel Lynn. Instr., English, Ohio U., 1959-66; asst. prof. English, Heidelberg Coll., 1966-68; prof. Western Ill. U., 1968—. Served with U.S. Army, 1953-55. Recipient prize for work-in-progress in field of poetry Ind. U. Writers' Conf., summer 1971. Mem. Coll. English Assn., Modern Lang. Assn., Soc. Study Midwestern Lit. Contbr. poems to lit. jours.; poetry editor Mississippi Valley Rev., 1971-73, editor, 1973—. Office: Dept English Western Ill U Macomb IL 61455

ROBINSON, GEORGE ALBERT, accountant; b. Elgin, Ill., Dec. 2, 1941; s. Joseph and Myrtle Louise (Beyer) R.; student Elgin Community Coll., 1964-65; m. Christine Ann Schneider, Sept. 2, 1961; children—Brian, Karen, Jaclyn. Accountant, Grant Motor Sales, Lake Zurich, Ill., 1959-60, W. Ray Davis & Asso., pub. accountant, Elgin, 1960-69; owner George A. Robinson Tax and Accounting Service, Elgin, 1969—; dir. Rasmussen Steel Co., Inc. Spl. adviser to pres. John Ericsson Republican League Ill., 1974. Mem. Nat. Soc. Pub. Accountants, Independent Accountants Assn. Ill. (chpt. pres. 1971-72), Assn. Enrolled Agts. Moose. Club: Elgin Riverside. Home: 240 S Edison Ave Elgin IL 60120 Office: 305 Ramona Ave PO Box 633 Elgin IL 60120

ROBINSON, GLADYS MABEL CHAMBERS (MRS. CARL TAPLEY ROBINSON), educator; b. New Orleans, Dec. 5, 1909; d. Oscar Louis and Susie Elizabeth (Lang) Chambers; A.B., Northwestern State Coll., 1929; M.S., U. Chgo., 1931, postgrad., 1947, 68; postgrad. Tulane U., 1932, Marine Biol. Lab., Woods Hole, Mass., 1938, U. Ill., 1955-57, Ill. Inst. Tech., 1964-65; m. Carl Tapley Robinson, Dec. 24, 1932. Asst. prof. biology Tougaloo (Miss.) Coll., 1931-41, U. Arkon (Ohio), 1942-48; instr. George William Coll., Downers Grove, Ill., 1948-50, prof. biology, 1959-75, prof. emeritus, 1975—, dir. div. natural scis., 1965-73; instr. Cook County Sch. Nursing, Chgo., 1950-59. Recipient Golden Apple award for excellence in teaching, student body George Williams Coll., 1972, Gladys C. Robinson Marsh named in honor, 1975. Ford Found. scholar, 1953, NSF scholar, 1964-65, 65, 68. Mem. Bot Soc. Am., Am. Inst. Biol. Sci., Assn. Midwest Coll. Biology Tchrs., Ill. Acad. Sci., Nature Conservancy, Phi Sigma, Sigma Delta Epsilon. Democrat. Baptist. Home: 7920 S Lafayette St Chicago IL 60620 Office: 555 31st St Downers Grove IL 60515

ROBINSON, JACK F(AY), clergyman; b. Wilmington, Mass., Mar. 7, 1914; s. Thomas P. and Ethel Lincoln (Fay) R.; A.B., Mont. State U., 1936; D.B., Crozer Theol. Sem., 1939; A.M., U. Chgo., 1949, postgrad., 1950-52; m. Eleanor Jean Smith, Sept. 1, 1937 (dec. 1966); 1 dau., Alice Virginia Dungey; m. 2d, Lois Henze, July 16, 1968. Ordained to ministry Baptist Church, 1939; minister Bethany Ch., American Falls, Idaho, 1939-41, 1st Ch., Council Grove, Kans., 1944-49; ordained (transfer) to ministry Congl. Ch., 1945; minister United Ch., Chebanse, Ill., 1949-52, 1st Ch., Argo, Ill., 1954-58, Congl. Ch., St. Charles, Illinois, 1958-64; asso. minister Plymouth Congregational Ch., Lansing, Mich., 1964-66; tchr. Chgo. Pub. Schs., 1966-68; minister Waveland Ave. Congl. Ch., Chgo., 1967—. Asso. Hyde Park dept. Chgo. YMCA, 1942-44. U. Chgo. Library 1952-54; chmn. com. evangelism Kans. Congl. Christian Conf., 1947-48; city chmn. Layman's Missionary Movement, 1946-51; trustee Congl. and Christian Conf. Ill., v.p., 1963-64; mem. exec. council Chgo. Met. Assn. United Ch. of Christ.; mem. gen. bd. Ch. Fedn. Greater Chgo. Library board Council Grove, 1945-49; city chmn. NCCJ, 1945-49; dean Northside Mission Council United Ch. of Christ, 1975-77. Mem. Am. Soc. Ch. History. Am. Hist. Assn., C. of C. (past dir.), Internat. Platform Assn. Author: The Growth of the Bible, 1969; From A Church to a Mission, 1976. Home: 2614 Lincolnwood Dr Evanston IL 60201 Office: PO Box 4578 Chicago IL 60680

ROBINSON, JOHN EDMUND, dentist; b. Kearny, N.J., Nov. 27, 1924; s. John Edmund and Norma (McDonald) R.; D.D.S., State U. N.Y. at Buffalo, 1952; m. Mary Bolinski, Nov. 23, 1946. Practice dentistry, North Syracuse, N.Y., 1952-56; instr. dental surgery Zoller Dental Clinic, U. Chgo. Hosps. and Clinics, 1957-58, asst. prof., 1958-64, asso. prof., 1964-70, prof. dental surgery, 1970—. Cons. U. Ill. Center for Craniofacial Anomalies. 1968—. Served with USNR, 1943-46; PTO. Fellow Am. Coll. Dentists, Inst. Medicine Chgo., N.Y. Acad. Scis., Midwest Acad. Prosthodontists, Am. Acad. Maxillofacial Prosthetics (pres. 1970-71), Fedn. Prosthodontic Orgns. (pres. 1973-74). Home: 5530 S Shore Dr Apt 5C Chicago IL 60637 Office: 950 E 59th St Chicago IL 60637

ROBINSON, JOHN F., editor; b. New Rochelle, N.Y., Sept. 4, 1937; s. John and Isabelle (Petersen) R.; B.A., U. Scranton, 1963; M.A., Duquesne U., 1965; postgrad. Ohio State U., 1965-66. Reference writer Ency. Britannia, Chgo., 1966-69, sr. editor history, 1969-73; asso. editor U. Chgo. Press, 1974—, Served with U.S. Army, 1956-59. Mem. Am. Hist. Assn. Club: Quadrangle. Home: 1035 Wolfram St W Chicago IL 60657 Office: 5801 Ellis Ave Chicago IL 60637

ROBINSON, LARRY RAPPORT, retail jewelry co. exec.; b. Detroit, Oct. 28, 1928; s. Joseph Barther and Minnie (Rapport) R.; B.A. cum laude, Ohio State U., 1950; M.B.A. with distinction, Harvard U., 1952, D.Bus., 1958; m. Barbara Shultz, May 23, 1953; children—Lisa, John, James. Research asso. in bus. adminstrn. Harvard U., 1952-55; asst. to chief execs. Material Service Corp., Chgo., 1955-59; pres. J.B. Robinson Co. Jewelers, Inc., Cleve., 1960—. Pres. Citizen's League of Cleve., 1977—; mem. Cleve. Mayor's Internat. Trade Commn.; mem. Criminal Justice Coordinating Council, Cleve. Mem. Nat. Jewelry Industry Council (dir.), Cleve. Bar Assn. (lay trustee), Harvard Bus. Sch. Alumni Assn. (nat. sec.-treas.). Club: City (pres. 1972) (Cleve.). Office: 811 Euclid-Ninth Tower Cleveland OH 44115

ROBINSON, PETER CLARK, stone co. exec.; b. Brighton, Mass., Nov. 16, 1938; s. Richard and Mary Elizabeth (Cooper) R.; B.S. in Fgn. Service, Georgetown U., 1961; M.B.A., Babson Inst., 1963; m. Sylvia Phyllis Petschek, Aug. 26, 1961 (div. 1973); children—Marc Louis, Nicholas Daniel, Andrea Suzanne. Asst. supt. prodn. Mass. Broken Stone Co., Weston, 1961-62, night shift supt., 1962-65, v.p. operations, 1968, v.p., dir., 1969-75; gen. supt. Berlin Stone Co., 1965-67, v.p. operations, 1968, v.p., dir., 1969-75; v.p., dir Holden Trap Rock Co., to 1975; pres. J.P. Burroughs & Sons, Inc. aggregate div., subsidiary Blount, Inc., Saginaw, Mich., and Montgomery, Ala., 1975-78, v.p. mktg. Blount, Inc., 1978—. Mem. Am. Mgmt. Assn., Am. Mktg. Assn., Engring. Soc. Detroit, Nat. Crushed Stone Assn. (dir.), Clubs: Economic (Detroit), Saginaw Home: PO Box 1202 Saginaw MI 48606 Office: Po Box 1468 3801 E Holand Ave Saginaw MI 48605

ROBINSON, RAYMOND WAYNE, educator; b. Tonkawa, Okla., Nov. 24, 1923; s. Charles Wesley and Vera Jennie (Reed) R.; student No. Okla. Jr. Coll., 1941-43, U. Okla., 1943-44, Columbia U., 1944; B.S., Okla. State U., 1947, M.S., 1949; postgrad. Auburn U., 1949-52; Ph.D. (Gen. Edn. Bd. fellow), U. Wis., 1957; m. Etha Lois Campbell, Aug. 12, 1945; children—Larry Wayne, T(homas) Kent, P(aul) Scott. Asso. prof., asso. agrl. economist Auburn U., 1948-52; instr. agrl. econs. U. Wis., Madison, 1954; asst. prof., extension specialist in marketing info. Kans. State U. Coop. Extension Service, Manhattan, 1954-57; extension economist U. Idaho, Boise, 1957-67; prof. Univ. Center for Coops. and dept. agrl. econs. and extension specialist in mktg. U. Wis., Madison, 1967—. Cons., Western Nuclear Corp., Idaho Falls, Idaho, 1963-64, Near East Found., N.Y.C., 1966-67, Asian-Am. Free Labor Inst., Washington, 1975; mem., adviser various coops. Mem. Boise Valley World Affairs Assn., 1957-67; mem. troop com. Boy Scouts Am., Boise, 1960-63. Served to lt. (j.g.), USNR, 1943-46; PTO. Recognized for Outstanding Contbn. to edn. Am. Inst. Cooperation and Idaho Coop. Council, 1967. Mem. Am., Western agrl. econs. assns., Am. Acad. Polit. and Social Sci., Internat. Assn. Agrl. Economists. Am. Legion (comdr. 1951-52), Pi Gamma Mu, Epsilon Sigma Phi. Democrat. Congregationalist (chmn. social action com., Boise 1963-64). Contbr. articles to profl. lit. Home: 5330 Coney Weston Pl Madison WI 53711

ROBINSON, RENAULT ALVIN, police assn. exec.; b. Chgo., Sept. 8, 1942; s. Robert S. and Mabel (Stevenson) R.; B.A., Roosevelt U., 1970; M.A., 1971; postgrad. (urban fellow) Northwestern U., 1972-73; m. Annette Richardson, Feb. 23, 1963; children—Renault Alvin, Brian, Kivu, Kobie. With Chgo. Post Office, 1960-62; printer, Union Tank Car Co., Chgo., 1963-64; patrolman, Chgo. Police Dept., 1964—; pres. Afro-Am. Patrolmen's League, Chgo., 1968-70, exec. dir., 1970—. Mem. Com. on Fgn. and Domestic Affairs, Chgo. Forum, 1971—. Bd. dirs. League to Improve the Community, Chgo. Recipient Citizens award Malcolm X Coll., 1972; Cabrini Green Alternative High Sch., 1972; Outstanding Service award NIU Black Arts Festival, 1971; Appreciation award Youth for Christ Choir, 1973; Outstanding Young Man award Chgo. South End Jr. C. of C., 1970; Community Service awards Black Olympics Com., 1973, Nat. Assn. Black Social Workers, 1974; Dr. Martin Luther King Jr. award SCLC, 1975; Image award League Black Women, 1975; I am my Brother's Keeper award Policemen for a Better Gary, 1975; AABS award excellence, 1976; Service to Community award Newspaper Guild, 1976; Humanitarian Service award Centers New Horizons, 1976; Gratitude award Kiwanis Club of Roseland, 1976; Affirmative Action award Breadbasket Comml. Assn., 1976; Affirmative Action, Pub. Service award Cook County Bar Assn., 1976; named Man of Year, Guardians Police Orgn., 1975. Mem. Nat. Black Police Assn. (nat. info. officer). Office: 7126 S Jeffery Blvd Chicago IL 60649

ROBINSON, RUSSELL DEAN, educator; b. Mauston, Wis., Feb. 5, 1927; s. Dean Daniel and Dorothea (Carter) R.; B.S., U. Wis., 1950, M.S., 1961, Ph.D., 1963; m. Edith Norma Drajeske, Aug. 31, 1957 (div.); children—Dean William, Daniel Mark, Lynn Louise; m. 2d, Janet Talkington Clizbe, Oct. 18, 1974. County extension agt., Waukesha, Wis., 1950-60; mem. faculty U. Wis., Milw., 1963—, prof. edn., coordinator grad. program adult edn., 1965—, extension youth devel. specialist, 1963-68, extension program leader, 1968-69. Cons. to schs., orgns. Project dir. Project Understanding, Milw., 1965—; pres. Milw. Council Adult Learning, 1968-69; mem. adv. com. Internat. Coop. Tng. Center, Madison, Wis., 1966-69. Regional v.p. Albert Baker Meml. Scholarship Fund for Higher Edn., San Francisco, 1968—; trustee Student Center Found., Madison, Wis. Served with AUS, 1945-46. Fellow Nat. Extension Center for Advanced Study, 1960-63. Mem. Adult Edn. Assn. U.S.A. (exec. com. 1972-73), Am. Sociol. Assn., Am. Acad. Religion, Nat. Council Family Relations, Adult Edn. Assn. Wis. (pres. 1970-71), Phi Kappa Phi. Christian Scientist. Author: Teaching the Scriptures, 1966. Home: 1111 E Fairy Chasm Rd Milwaukee WI 53217

ROBINSON, SALLY WINSTON, artist; b. Detroit, Nov. 2, 1924; d. Harry Lewis and Lydia (Kahn) Winston; B.A., Bennington Coll., 1947; student Cranbrook Acad. Art, 1949; grad. Sch. Social Work, Wayne State U., 1948, M.Art, 1973, M.F.A., 1974; m. Eliot F. Robinson, June 28, 1949; children—Peter Eliot, Lydia Winston, Suzanne Finley, Sarah Mitchell. Psychol. tester Detroit Bd. Edn., 1944; pyschol. counselor and tester YMCA, N.Y.C., 1946; social caseworker Family Service, Pontiac, Mich., 1947; one-man shows: Arnold Klein Gallery, Mich., Bertha Urdang Gallery, N.Y.C., Williams Coll.; exhibited group shows Bennington Coll., Cranbrook Mus., Detroit Inst. Art, Detroit Artists Market, Soc. Women Painters, Soc. Arts and Crafts; represented in permanent collections, Detroit, N.Y.C.; represented by Asset Gallery, Zella Gallery, London; tchr. children's art Detroit Inst. Art, 1949-50; instr. printmaking Wayne State U., 1974. Bd. dirs. Planned Parenthood, 1951-55, 65—, exec. bd., 1963; bd. dirs. PTA, 1956-60; exec. com. Detroit Adventure; bd. dirs. City and Country Sch., Drawing and Print Orgn. Detroit Inst. Arts. Mem. Detroit Artists Market (mem. bd. dirs. 1956—), Bennington Coll. Alumnae Assn. (regional chmn. 1963, 65), Birmingham Soc. Women Painters (dir.), Bloomfield Art Assn. (program co-chmn. 1956), Founders Soc. Detroit Inst, Drawing and Print Club (dir.). Art, Detroit Soc. Women Painters. Clubs: Village Women's, Democratic (Birmingham, Mich.). Home: 572 Linden Rd Birmingham MI 48009 also 7 Monument Circle Old Bennington VT 05201

ROBINSON, THEODORE CURTIS, lawyer; b. Chgo., Jan. 22, 1916; s. Theodore Curtis and Edna (Willard) R.; A.B., Western Res. U., 1938, LL.B., 1940; m. Marynel Werner, Dec. 28, 1940; children—Theodore Curtis III, Peter Shipley. Admitted to Ohio bar, 1940, Ill. bar, 1956; asso. mem. firm Davis & Young, Cleve., 1940; law clk. U.S. Dist. Ct., No. Dist. Ohio, Cleve., 1940-42; asso. mem. firm Ray, Robinson, Keenen & Hanninen and predecessor firms, Cleve., 1945-52, partner, 1952—, resident partner, Chgo., 1957—. Served with USCGR, 1942-45. Fellow Am. Coll. Trial Lawyers; mem. Am., Chgo., Cleve. bar assns., Maritime Law Assn. U.S., Internat. Assn. Ins. Counsel, Internat. Shipmasters Assn. (sec. treas.), Order of Coif. Presbyterian (trustee). Clubs: Traffic, Propeller (pres.) (Chgo.). Author: Private and Contract Carriage and Towage on the River, 1971. Home: 332 S Brainard Ave LaGrange IL 60525 Office: 135 S LaSalle St Chicago IL 60603

ROBINSON, WALTER STITT, JR., historian; b. Matthews, N.C., Aug. 28, 1917; s. Walter Stitt and Mary Irene (Jamison) R.; B.A. summa cum laude, Davidson Coll., 1939; M.A., U. Va., 1941, Ph.D., 1950; m. Constance Lee Mock, Mar. 18, 1944; children—Ethel Barry, Walter Lee. Asst. prof. history Florence (Ala.) State Coll., 1946-47, asso. prof., 1947-48; asst. prof. U. Kans., Lawrence, 1950-54, asso. prof., 1954-59, prof., 1959—, chmn. dept., 1968-73; mem. Nat. Civil War Centennial Commn., 1961-65; mem. Kans. Com. for Humanities, 1971—. chmn., 1976, 77. Adminstrv. bd. 1st United Methodist Ch., Lawrence; mem. exec. com. bd. dirs. Kans. Sch. Religion. Served to capt. U.S. Army, 1941-45. Decorated Bronze Star; Social Sci. Research Council grantee, 1959-60; Am. Philos. Soc. grantee, 1967; recipient Distinguished Scholarship award U. Kans., 1976. Mem. Am., So. hist. assns., Orgn. Am. Historians (chmn. program com. 1959), Kans. State (dir.), Douglas County (dir., mem. exec. com.) hist. socs., Raven Soc., Phi Beta Kappa. Author: Land Grants in Virginia, 1607-1699, 1957; mem. editorial bd. 18th century bibliography in Philol. Quar., 1975—; contbr. articles in field to Jour. So. History, Miss. Valley Hist. Rev., others. Home: 801 Broadview Dr Lawrence KS 66044 Office: Dept History Univ Kansas Lawrence KS 66045

ROBINSON, WILLIAM NATHANIEL, educator; b. St. Joseph, Mo., May 7, 1919; s. William Eugene and Maude (Cummings) R.; B.S., U. Ariz., 1947; B.S., U. Kans., 1950, M.E., 1953; Ed.D., U. Neb., 1965; m. Analee June McClung, Aug. 25, 1946; children—June Ann Sutley, William Steuert. Dep. county sch. supt., Pima County, Ariz., 1947-49; tchr., prin. Sabetha (Kans.) High Sch., 1950-54; prin. Holyrood (Kans.) High Sch., 1954-58; asst. prof. edn. Tarkio Coll., 1958-64; prof. edn. Fort Hays (Kans.) State Coll., 1964—; cons. North Central Kans. Regional Resource Center; mem. Kans. Title IV Adv. Council. Chmn., March of Dimes, Holyrood, 1956. Bd. dirs. Cedar Bluff North Shore Lake Assn. Served with USAAF, 1940-43. Mem. Nat. Assn. Secondary Sch. Prins., NEA, Kans. Edn. Assn., Kans. Classroom Tchr. Commn., Soc. Profs. Edn., Ellsworth County Tchrs. Assn. (pres. 1956), Phi Delta Kappa. Presbyn. (deacon 1967-70, trustee 1970-73). Lion. Author: American Education: Its Organization and Control, 1968. Contbr. articles to various jours. Home: 2906 Hillcrest St Hays KS 67601 Office: Edn Dept Fort Hays Kan State Coll Hays KS 67601

ROBLING, JOHN STEVENS, publishing co. exec.; b. Clinton, Ia., May 16, 1922; s. Christopher M. and Mary (Stevens) R.; student Dowling Coll., 1939-41; B.J., U. Mo., 1943; m. Charlotte L. Fitz Henry, July 6, 1946; children—Mary Charlotte, Stevens, Christopher, Julia. Editor, A.P., Chgo., 1943-45; pub. relations mgr. Meredith Pub. Co., Des Moines, 1945-51; dir. advt. and pub. relations McCall Corp., N.Y.C., 1951-57; dir. Nat. Library Week, Nat. Book Com., N.Y.C., 1957-61; v.p. advt. and pub. relations Ency. Brit., Inc., Chgo., 1961—. Cons., This Week Mag., 1958-59. Mem. steering com. Nat. Library Week, N.Y., 1964-67; chmn. Ill. State Com. for Library Week, 1966; mem. Citizens Com. for Chgo. Pub. Library, 1969; dir. Nat. Citizens Com. to Save Edn. and Library Funds, 1969. Chmn. pub. relations planning com. Am. Ednl. Publs. Inst., 1968-69. Treas., Des Moines Child Guidance Center, 1950. Pres., Polk County Young Democrats, 1949. Trustee Winnetka Pub. Library Bd., 1968-74, Ill. Library Bd., 1972—; bd. dirs. Chgo. Pub. Library Friends, Civitas Found. Served with AUS, 1942-43. Recipient Spl. Honor citation Am. Assn. Sch. Librarians, 1967. Mem. Pub. Relations Soc. Am. (Silver Anvil award for Better Homes and Gardens, 1948, Ency. Brit. 1967). Clubs: Overseas Press. Grolier (N.Y.C.); Nat. Book League (London); Chgo. Arts, Chgo. Press, Chgo. Racquet, Caxton. Contbr. articles to profl. jours. Home: 50 W Schiller St Chicago IL 60610 Office: 425 N Michigan Ave Chicago IL 60611

ROBSON, EDWIN A., dist. judge; b. Chgo., Apr. 16, 1905; s. Clarence T. and Alice B. (Andres) R.; LL.B., DePaul U., 1928; m. Leah M. Kinne, Sept. 11, 1928; children—Edwin A., Clark K., David K. Admitted to Ill. bar, 1928; practiced with Kinne, Scovel & Robson, 1928-45; judge Superior Ct. Cook Co., 1945-51; dir. organizer in Superior Ct. of the Central Assignment System and Pre-trial Conf. of civil cases, 1949-51, chief justice, 1950-51; judge Ill. Appellate Ct., 1951-58, U.S. dist. judge, 1958—, chief judge No. Dist. Ill., 1970-75, sr. dist. judge, 1975—. Mem. Nat. Panel Multidist. Litigation, 1968. Mem. Am. Judicature Soc., Am., Ill., Chgo. bar assns., Phi Alpha Delta. Methodist. Clubs: Legal, Union League, Standard, Law (Chgo.). Home: 2418 Iroquois Rd Wilmette IL 60091 Office: 219 S Dearborn St Chicago IL 60604

ROBSON, JOHN HENRY, retail fuel co. exec.; b. Evanston, Ill., Apr. 14, 1932; s. William Wallace and Ruth Ridgeway (Wright) R.; B.S. in Agr., Iowa State U., 1955; m. Freida B. Davis, Dec. 11, 1954. Operator dairy farm, Crystal Lake, Ill., 1957-65; tech. dir. Marcook Corp., Evanston, 1965-67; partner, v.p. Marquette Fuels, Evanston, 1967—; partner, pres. Cooksy Oil Co., Northbrook Ill., 1967—; mem. natural gas transmission and distbn. advisory com. Fed. Energy Adminstrn.; mem. natural gas servey advisory com. FPC. chmn. Mundelein (Ill.) Planning Commn. Served to capt. USAF, 1955-57. Recipient numerous Jaycees awards. Mem. Oil Heat Marketers Assn. (pres.), Nat. Oil Jobbers (council fuel oil steering com.). Republican. Club: Rotary. Holder 2 U.S. patents; contbr. articles on energy and natural gas policies to jours. and mags. Home: 1167 Lomond Dr Mundelein IL 60060 Office: 730 Pitner Ave Evanston IL 60204

ROBY, MAX, JR., TV broadcaster; b. Alva, Okla., Aug. 14, 1922; s. Maxwell Frank and Dot (Keller) R.; B.A. in Polit. Sci., U. Utah, 1949; m. Mary Alice Fisher, Mar. 13, 1943; children—Irene, Maxine, Frank. Reporter, Daily Rev.-Courier, Alva, 1941; news announcer Radio Sta. KFBI, Wichita, Kans., 1942; news dir. stas. KSL, KSL-TV, Salt Lake City, 1946-51; news reporter-broadcaster KNX, CBS, Hollywood, Calif., 1951-58; asst. news dir., anchorman on 6 and 10 p.m. news broadcasts KMOX-TV, CBS, St. Louis, 1958-73; commentator-anchorman KSD-TV, 1973—; mem. communications faculty St. Louis Community Coll., 1975-76, adv. bd., 1976—. Bd. dirs. St. Louis Conv. and Visitors Bur., 1976—. Served with Signal Corps, AUS, 1943-46; ETO. Recipient Citizenship award VFW, 1967; DeMolay Hon. Legion Honor. Mem. Radio and Television News Dirs. Assn., Radio and Television Corrs. Assn. Washington, Nat. Broadcast Editorial Assn., St. Louis Press Club (past pres.), Sigma Delta Chi (pres. 1970-71), Kappa Tau Alpha. Methodist. Mason (Shriner, Jester). Home: 1630 View Woods Dr St Louis MO 63122 Office: 1111 Olive St St Louis MO 63101

ROCCO, VINCENT ANTHONY, consulting co. exec.; b. Hoboken, N.J., Mar. 13, 1945; s. Bernard James and Margaret Gloria (Monaco) R.; Mech., Engr. (Gen. Motors scholar), Stevens Inst. of Tech., 1967; M.S., U. Tenn., 1970; m. Mary Elizabeth Bathe, Oct. 11, 1969. Asst. chief environ. planning div. Tenn. Dept. of Transp., Nashville, 1972-73; dir. environ. planning RETA, St. Louis, 1973; supt. environ. planning and policy Wis. Electric Power Co., Milw., 1973-74; v.p. and gen. mgr. Midwestern ops. Environ. Research & Tech. Inc., Lombard, Ill., 1975-77, v.p., dir. corporate programs, 1977—; vis. instr. N.Y. U., 1967; cons. Fed. Hwy. Adminstrn., Nat. Hwy. Inst., 1973-74. Served to capt. USAF, 1968-72. Recipient USAF Systems Command award for Sci. Achievement, 1971, Meritorious Service medal, 1972. Registered profl. engr., Ill., Mo., N.J., Tenn., Tex., Wis. Mem. Nat. Soc. of Profl. Engrs., ASME, Air Pollution Control Assn., Am. Inst. of Planners, Sigma Phi Epsilon. Roman Catholic. Contbr. articles to profl. jours. Home: 3 S 364 Shagbark St Glen Ellyn IL 60137 Office: 131 Eisenhower Ln Lombard IL 60148

ROCH, LEWIS MARSHALL, II, ophthalmic surgeon; b. Mineola, Tex., Aug. 13, 1934; s. Lewis Marshall and Gladys Irene (Hoover) R.; B.A., U. Tex., 1954, M.D., 1959; m. Lois Afton Price; children—Lewis Marshall III, Katrina Ann. Intern USPHS Hosp., Boston, 1959-60; resident ophthalmology USPHS Hosp., New Orleans, 1960-63, dep. chief ophthalmology, 1963-64; chief ophthalmology USPHS Hosp., Seattle, 1964-67; practice medicine specializing in ophthalmology, Muncie, Ind., 1967—; attending ophthalmic surgeon Ball Meml. Hosp., Muncie, chmn. dept. surgery, 1973, chmn. clin. staff, 1975. Served with USPHS, 1959-67.

Diplomate Am. Bd. Ophthalmology. Fellow Am. Acad. Ophthalmology and Otolaryngology, A.C.S.; mem. AMA, So. Med. Assn., Soc. Eye Surgeons Internat. Eye Found., Contact Lens Assn. Ophthalmologists, Am. Assn. Opthalmology, Ind. Acad. Ophthalmology and Otolaryngology, Muncie Acad. Medicine (past pres.), Am. Intra-Ocular Implant Soc. Home: 2006 Robinwood Dr Muncie IN 47304 Office: 308 White River Blvd Muncie IN 47303

ROCHETTO, EVELYN MARIE, educator; b. Chgo.; d. Lucius J. and Clara M. (Jung) Young; Ph.B., Northwestern U., 1952; m. Paul A. Rochetto, June 9, 1937. Profl. musician, 1930-50; membership sec. Internat. Soc. for Gen. Semantics, 1950-55, exec. sec., 1955-68, dir., 1952-68; tchr. Aurora Coll., 1968—; counselor State of Ill., 1970—. Pres., Chgo. Story League. Dir. Pan Am. Bd. Edn. Mem. AAUW (pres. Chgo. br. 1956—, mem. bd. 1953—), Am. Legion Auxiliary (mem. bd.), Alpha Sigma Lambda (dir.). Club: Woman's University (pres. 1966—). Home: 5240 Sheridan Rd Chicago IL 60640

ROCHMAN, MICHAEL DAVID, chem. co. exec.; b. St. Louis, Dec. 23, 1940; s. Nathan George and Virginia Ruth (Paul) R.; B.S., U. Okla., 1963; m. Judith Ann Walraven, Dec. 27, 1966; children—Ruth Ester, Melissa Valia. Store mgr. Zale Jewelers, Dallas, 1963-67; salesman Nat. Chemsearch Corp., Dallas, 1967-69; salesman, mgr. Continental Research Corp., St. Louis, 1969-71; pres. Ruth Industries Inc., St. Louis, 1971—. Mem. St. Louis (v.p. 1976—), Internat. sanitary supply assns., St. Louis C. of C., Am. Mgmt. Assn. Republican. Jewish. Club: Stadium St. Louis. Author: The Ruth Guide to Successful Selling, 1975. Home: 11 Kirken Knoll Town and Country MO 63131 Office: 1170 Adminstrn Dr St Louis MO 63141

ROCK, RONALD STEPHEN, lawyer; b. Chgo., Jan. 19, 1936; s. Stephen Louis and Irene (Krivan) R.; B.A., Ripon Coll., 1958; J.D. (Univ. scholar), U. Chgo., 1961; m. Yolanda Bertha Szabo, June 17, 1961; children—Michelle, Ronald Stephen. Admitted to Ill. bar, 1962; project dir. Am. Bar Found., Chgo., 1961-76. Lectr., U. Chgo., 1968, Chgo. City Coll., 1969, Northwestern U., 1972, various profl. orgns. Mem. Ill. Commn. to Revise Mental Health Code, 1973—; exec. com., chmn. Civil Hospitalization Com., Chgo., 1973-74; cons. to various fed., state, local mental health orgns. NIMH grantee, 1961-68; Law Enforcement Assistance Adminstrn. grantee, 1973-75. Author: Hospitalization and Discharge of the Mentally Ill, 1968; (with J. Brakel) Mentally Disabled and the Law, 1971. Office: 1155 E 60th St Chicago IL 60637

ROCK, WILLIAM RAY, historian; b. Mercersburg, Pa., Apr. 8, 1930; s. David Ray and Mildred Cecelia (Glee) R.; B.A., Gettysburg Coll., 1951; M.A., Duke U., 1953, Ph.D., 1956; m. Suzanne Joyce Beck, June 18, 1955; children—Stephen, Anne, Brian. Instr. history Duke U., Durham, N.C., 1957-58; instr. history Bowling Green (Ohio) State U., 1958-61, asst. prof., 1961-64, asso. prof., 1964-67, prof., 1967—. Served with U.S. Army, 1955-57. Mem. Am. Hist. Assn., Ohio Acad. History. Author: Appeasement on Trial: British Foreign Policy and Its Critics, 1938-1939, 1966; Neville Chamberlain, 1969: British Appeasement in the 1930s, 1977. Home: 14543 Sand Ridge Rd Bowling Green OH 43402

ROCKE, R. THOMAS, orthodontist; b. LaPorte, Ind., Feb. 12, 1940; s. Robert A. and Dorothy J. (Wilhelm) R.; B.S., Ind. U., 1962, D.D.S., 1965; M.S., St. Louis U., 1969; m. Carol Ann Wessel, Dec. 20, 1969; children—Jennifer, Jeffrey. Mem. Kesling-Rocke Orthodontic Group, Westville, Ind., 1969—; instr. orthodontics St. Louis U. Grad. Sch., 1970—. Served to capt. U.S. Army, 1966-67. Mem. ADA, Am. Assn. Orthodontists, Begg Soc. Orthodontists (P. Raymond Begg award 1973), Phi Delta Theta, Delta Sigma Delta, Omicron Kappa Upsilon. Home: 2606 Belle Plaine Trail LB Michigan City IN 46360 Office: Orthodontic Center Westville IN 46391 also 210 Sherland Bldg South Bend IN

ROCKE, ROBERT ALFRED, orthodontist; b. Chgo., Dec. 7, 1911; s. Alfred Ebhardt and Hedwig (Lippold) R.; D.D.S., Loyola U., 1934; m. Dorothy Jane Wilhelm, Jan. 28, 1939; children—R. Thomas, Mary Susan (Mrs. Thomas F. Armstrong), Paul A. Pvt. practice dentistry Laporte, Gary, Highland, Ind., 1934-59; partner Kesling & Rocke Orthodontic Center, Westville, Ind., 1959—. Tchr. Begg Light Wire Orthodontic Technique, 1959—, also continuing edn. courses; cons., asso. T-P Labs., LaPorte, Ind. Bd. dirs. YMCA, LaPorte, 1962—. Served with Dental Corps., AUS, 1953-55. Mem. Northwest (past pres.), Ill. dental socs., Ind. (past pres.), Ill., Great Lakes socs. orthodontists, Am. Begg Soc. Orthodontists (past pres.), Am., Ind. dental assns., Omicron Kappa Upsilon. Presbyn. (past pres. bd. trustees). Lion (past pres.). Club: South Bend (Ind.) Country. Home: 10 Greenacres St La Porte IN 46350 Office: Kesling and Rocke Orthodontic Center Westville IN 46391

RODD, FOREST WILLARD, lawyer; b. Rhinelander, Wis., May 14, 1916; s. Hans and Tillie Caroline (Nelson) R.; Ph.B., U. Wis., 1938, LL.B., 1941; m. Margaret M. Conkey, Mar. 4, 1939; 1 son, William Hans. Admitted to Wis. bar, 1942; claims rep. Hartford Accident and Ins. Co., Rhinelander, 1942-44; practice law, Rhinelander, 1946—; pres. firm Korth, Rodd, Sommer & Mouw, Rhinelander, 1970—. Dir. First Nat. Bank, 1965—. Dist. atty., Oneida County, Wis., 1949-53; pub. adminstr. Oneida County, 1953-73. Served to lt. (j.g.) USNR, 1944-46. Mem. Am., Wis., Oneida County (pres. 1959), Lincoln Oneida Vilas (pres. 1951) bar assns., Rhinelander C. of C. (dir. 1956). Mason (Shriner, K.T.). Home: Route 2 Rhinelander WI 54501 Office: First Nat Bank Bldg Rhinelander WI 54501

RODDIS, WILLIAM HENRY, banker; b. Marshfield, Wis., Nov. 6, 1917; s. Hamilton and Catherine Sara (Prindle) R.; student Mass. Inst. Tech., 1 en—Grace, Thomas. Plant mgr. Roddis Plywood Corp., Marshfield, Wis., 1946-56, corporate sec., 1946-60, dir., 1951-60; profl. specialist Weyerhaeuser Co., Longview, Wash., 1961-62; v.p. Swords Veneer Ill., 1962-64; dir. Citizen's Nat. Bank & Trust Co., Marshfield, 1972—. Mem. Wood County Bd. Suprs., 1943-44. Served with USNR, 1944-46. Mem. Aircraft Owners and Pilots Assn., Forest Products Research Soc., Mayflower Soc., Soc. Colonial Wars, SAR, Huguenot Soc. Republican. Episcopalian. Clubs: Union League Chgo.; Milw. Athletic. Home: 2433 N Wahl Ave Milwaukee WI 53211

RODECK, WILLIAM FRED, JR., mech. engr.; b. Chgo., Nov. 30, 1925; s. William Fred and Martha (Schultz) R.; B.S. in Mech. Engring., U. Ill., 1952; m. Virginia M. Springs, July 12, 1952; 1 Alan. Mech. engr. N.Y. Central R.R., Chgo., 1952-54; mech. engr. Schmidt, Garden & Erikson, Chgo., 1954—; asso. dir. mech. engring. Schmidt, Garden & Erikson, Chgo., 1975—, dir. co-op. engring. edn., 1975—. Served with USAAF, 1943-45. Decorated Air medal with 1 oak leaf cluster. Registered profl. engr., Ill., Mich., Wis., Fla. Roman Catholic. Club: Elks. Home: 15230 Irving Ave Dolton IL 60419 Office: 104 S Michigan Ave Chicago IL 60603

RODERICK, HARRY EDWARD, ret. govt. ofcl.; b. Brodhead, Wis., May 22, 1913; s. Harry and Sophie (Alleman) R.; B.S. in Elec. Engring., U. Wis., 1936; grad Air War Coll., 1957; m. Jacqueline Brouillard, May 14, 1938; children—Douglas, Bruce, Jane. Radio engr. sta. WHA, Madison, Wis., 1932-35, Ken-Rad Tube Corp., Owensboro, Ky., 1936-37, Westinghouse Radio div., Chicopee Falls, Mass. and Balt., 1938-39; pvt. engring, cons., 1947-50; dir. attack warning br. FDCA, Washington, 1951-53, dir. attack warning div., Battle Creek, Mich., 1954-57, dir. warning office OCDM, Exec. Office of Pres., 1958-61; dir. warning office Office of Civil Def., Dept. Def., 1961-64, chief communications ops., 1964-66, chief communications and warning research, 1967-71; dep. dir. support systems research Def. Civil Preparedness Agy., 1972-74, ret., 1974; U.S. rep on Can. warning group, 1952-64, NATO warning group, 1957-61, Central Treaty Orgn. Civil Def. Meeting, 1959. Chmn. Evansville Historic Preservation Commn., 1977. Served from 1st lt. to lt. col., USAAF, 1940-46; col. USAF Res. (ret.). Mem. Air Force Assn., Res. Officers Assn. (pres. Janesville, Wis. and Battle Creek), Wis., Rock County (Tallman House com., trustee 1976-77), hist. socs., Am. Legion (post comdr.), S.A.R. Clubs: Masons (32 deg.), Lions. Contbr. articles to profl. publs. Home: 33 N 1st St Evansville WI 53536

RODGERS, DENNIS BRUCE, lawyer; b. Decatur, Ill., Oct. 16, 1940; s. Richard Wilbur and Eleanor Frances (Cobb) R.; B.S., Trinity Coll., Hartford, Conn., 1962; J.D., Georgetown U., 1966; m. Marilynne Linda Wilson, Nov. 30, 1974; children—John, Andrew. Tchr., Bloomfield (Conn.) pub. schs., 1962-63; admitted to Ill. bar, 1966, since practiced in Decatur; mem. firm Denz, Lowe, Moore, Rodgers & See, 1966-77; legal planner Macon County Regional Plan Commn., 1970-76; part time prof. Richland Community Coll., 1976—; dir. Redwood Devel. Co., Inc. Crusade chmn. Macon County unit Am. Cancer Soc., 1971-72, bd. dirs., 1972—, chmn. bd., 1974-75; mem. Now and Tomorrow Council of Decatur Meml. Hosp., 1971-77; bd. dirs. Council Community Services, 1970—, pres., 1975—; pres. Sangamon Valley Assn., 1972-76; mem. Scholarships for Ill. Residents, 1970—. Pres. Young Republican Orgn. Macon County, 1967-68. Named to Outstanding Young Men of Am., 1969-72. Mem. Ill., Decatur bar assns., Decatur Jaycees (adminstrv. v.p. 1969-70), Alpha Chi Rho, Phi Alpha Delta (certificate distinguished service 1966). Kiwanian (bd. dirs. Decatur 1970-72). Co-author: Oakley Reservoir and Water Development for Central Illinois, 1968. Home and office: 6 Louise Ct Decatur IL 62521

RODGERS, EUGENE MERLE, banker; b. South Bend, Ind., Dec. 14, 1932; s. Joseph Merle and Bertha Ann (Bauwens) R.; student U. Calif., 1954; B.S., Ind. U., 1970; m. Grace Anne Morrow, July 7, 1958; children—Craig Eugene, Kimberly Sue. With U.S. Rubber Co., Mishawaka, Ind., 1951-53, 55-60, data processing supr., 1955-60; asst. v.p., systems dir. Assos. Investment Co., South Bend, 1960-68; v.p., computer center mgr. St. Joseph Bank & Trust Co., 1968-73; mktg. dir. Nat. Computing Corp., South Bend, 1973-74; computer center mgr. Systematics Inc., 1974—. Mem. data processing adv. com. Ind. Vocat. Tech. Coll., 1970-73. Served with AUS, 1953-55. Mem. Assn. Systems Mgmt. (chpt. pres. 1968), Data Processing Mgmt. Assn., Deans Assos. Ind. U., South Bend C. of C. Republican. Methodist. Home: 61500 Druid Ln South Bend IN 46614 also 48 Allendale St Terre Haute IN 47802 Office: 4500 Dixie Bee Rd Terre Haute IN 47802

RODGERS, ORLAN CLEEVE, steel tubing co. exec.; b. Colebrook, Ohio, May 14, 1916; s. Gaylord Fulton and Bertha (Cleeve) R.; grad. high sch.; m. Jennie Stepnik, June 30, 1936; children—Ronald, Dennis, Gregory. Timber jack truck driver Midwest Haulers Alford div. Glenn Cartage Co., 1933-39; punch press operator, set-up man U.S. Gypsum Co., 1939-41; ordnance worker U.S. Arsenal, Ravenna, Ohio, 1941-42; electrician, supt. Brainard Steel Corp., 1943-47; plant mgr. Sharon Steel Corp., 1947-58; mgr. operations Welded Tubes, Inc., Orwell, Ohio, 1958—. Pres. Orwell Village Council, 1955-58. Methodist. Mason (32 deg.). Home: 61 N Park St Orwell OH 44076 Office: 1st Penniman St Orwell OH 44076

RODGERS-SULLIVAN, ROSEMARY FLORENCE, physician; b. Cin., July 10, 1945; d. James Chester and Rosemary Virginia (Koenig) Rodgers; B.S., Northwestern U., 1967, M.D., 1969. Intern, Evanston (Ill.) Hosp., 1969-70; resident internal medicine Northwestern U. Med. Sch., Chgo., 1970-74; fellow thoracic diseases Mayo Clinic, Rochester, Minn., 1974—; now attending physician Mt. Sinai Hosp.; faculty Rush. Med. Sch. Mem. honors med. program Northwestern U., 1963-69. Diplomate Am. Bd. Internal Medicine, Am. Bd. Pulmonary Disease. Fellow Am. Coll. Chest Physicians; mem. AMA, A.C.P., Am. Thoracic Soc., Zeta Tau Alpha. Home: 701 S Arlington Heights Rd Arlington Heights IL 60005 Office: Mt Sinai Hosp 25th and California Ave Chicago IL 60612

RODIN, ERNEST ANTON, neurologist; b. Vienna, Austria, Aug. 30, 1925; s. Mathias and Erna (Diner) R.; came to U.S., 1950, naturalized, 1955; M.D., U. Vienna, 1949; M.S., U. Minn., 1955; m. Martha Joanne Kinscher, Dec. 23, 1951; children—Krista, Peter, Eric. Intern, Staten Island Hosp., N.Y., 1950-51; instr., asst. prof. psychiatry U. Mich., 1955-58; asst. prof. neurology Wayne State U., Detroit, 1958-64, asso. prof., 1964-70, prof., 1970—; chief, neurology and electroencephalogrphy Lafayette Clinic, Detroit, 1958—; med. dir. Epilepsy Center Mich., 1971—; dir. EEG Lab., Childrens Hosp. Mich., 1962—. Served with World War II, 1943-45. Diplomate in neurology Am. Bd. Psychiatry and Neurology. Mem. Central (past pres.), Eastern (past pres.), Am. (sec. 1970-73, pres. 1975-76) EEG socs., Mich. Neurol. Assn., AMA, Am. Acad. Neurology (S. Weir Mitchell award 1957), Assn. for Research in Nervous and Mental Disease, Am. Epilepsy Soc. Club: Grosse Pointe Sail. Author: The Prognosis of Patients with Epilepsy, 1969. Contbr. articles to profl. jours. Home: 773 Balfour St Grosse Pointe Park MI 48230 Office: 951 E Lafayette St Detroit MI 48207

RODIS, THEMISTOCLES CONSTANTINE, historian; b. Bridgeport, Conn., Aug. 20, 1917; s. Constantine Themistocles and Euphrosyne (Panagiotacopoulou) R.; A.B., Miami U., Oxford, Ohio, 1941; A.M., Case Western Res. U., 1949, Ph.D., 1968; postgrad. George Washington U., 1941-42; m. Rose Panoraia Simon, Aug. 19, 1956; children—Constantine, Marian, Peter, Eleni, Estelle. Instr. humanities Case Inst. Tech., 1952-53; instr. history Baldwin Wallace Coll., 1953-54; asst. prof. history and sociology U. Md. Overseas, 1954-55, 56-57; asst. prof. history and polit. sci. Baldwin Wallace Coll., Berea, Ohio, 1955-56, 57-68, chmn. dept. history, 1963-66, asso. prof., 1968-72, prof., 1972—, chmn. div. humanities, 1976—; dean faculty, prof. history Hellenic Coll., Brookline, Mass., 1969-70; asst. to registrar Harvard U., summer 1970; vis. lectr. econ. history Fenn Coll., 1956-57; vis. lectr. French history Case Western Res. U., 1968, 70, vis. scholar, 1972, 73. Mem. Ethnic Heritage and Lang. studies Com. Cleve., 1975—, Cleve. Ethnographic Com., 1976—; mem. program bd. Nat. Council Chs., 1970-75; bd. govs., chmn. edn. com. Annunciation Greek Orthodox Ch., 1971—. Served with M.I., U.S. Army, 1942-46. Recipient grants Danforth Found., 1962-64, Baldwin wallace, 1972-73, HEW, 1975-76. Mem. AAUP, Am. Hist. Assn., Am. Soc. 18th Century Studies, Hellenic U. Club, Ohio Acad. History, Soc. French Hist. Studies, Modern Greek Studies Assn., Western Soc. French Hist. Studies. Contbr. articles to profl. jours. Home: 17622 Indianola Dr Lakewood OH 44107 Office: Dept History Baldwin Wallace Coll Berea OH 44017

RODISCH, ROBERT JOSEPH, clergyman, synod exec.; b. Phila., Sept. 22, 1919; s. Edward and Isabella (Dugan) R.; A.B., Grove City Coll., 1941; B.Th., Princeton Theol. Sem., 1943; postgrad. Union Sem., 1944, Temple U., 1946-48; D.D., Tarkio Coll., 1962; m. Ruth M. Weisner, Aug. 14, 1943; children—Ruth E., Lynda J. Ordained to ministry Presbyn. Ch., 1943; pastor First Ch., Galeton, Pa., 1943-45, Langhorne, Pa., 1945-51; dir. S.E. Okla. Larger Parish, 1951-53; pastor Second Ch., Tulsa, 1953-62; moderator Muskogee Presbytery, 1952-53, Tulsa Presbytery, 1957-58; chmn. nat. missions com. Okla. Synod; synod exec. Mo. Synod, U.P. Ch. U.S.A., 1962-69, Synods Mo. of United Presbyn. Ch. in U.S.A. and Presbyn. Ch. in U.S., 1969-72, exec. Synods of Mid-Am., 1972—. Former pres. Mo. Council Chs.; mem. gen. assembly Mission Council, U.P. Ch. U.S.A. and Presbyn. Ch. in U.S. Trustee Presbyn. Children's Home Mo. Mem. Mo. Assn. Social Welfare, Pi Gamma Mu. Mason, Rotarian. Home: 3002 W 71st Terr Prairie Village KS 66208 Office: 6400 Glenwood Overland Park KS 66202

RODMAN, JAMES PURCELL, astrophysicist, educator; b. Alliance, Ohio, Nov. 11, 1926; s. Clarence James and Hazel (Purcell) R.; B.S. in Physics and Math., Mt. Union Coll., 1949; M.A. in Nuclear Physics, Washington U., St. Louis, 1951; Ph.D. in Astrophysics, Yale, 1963; m. Margaret Jane Kinsey, Aug. 14, 1950; children—William James, Jeffrey Kinsey, David Lawrence, Gretchen. Sec., Alliance Ware, Inc., 1954-55. Alliance Machine Co., 1959-69; v.p., treas. Alliance Tool Co., 1951-54, pres., 1954-59; instr. dept. physics and math. Mt. Union Coll., Alliance, 1951-59, asso. prof. physics, 1962-66, prof., 1966—, head dept. physics, 1963-65, head dept. physics and astronomy, 1965-74, 77—, dir. Clarke Obs., 1953—, dir. Computer Center, 1967-74, 77. Research asso. dept. astronomy Yale, 1963-68; cons. engr. astron. instrumentation, 1962—. Dir. United Nat. Bank & Trust Co. Mem. Alliance Bd. Edn., 1957-59, pres., 1959; exec. com. Buckeye council Boy Scouts Am. 1963-77, mem. nat. scouting com., 1973-77. Dep. sheriff Stark County, 1972—; spl. police officer Alliance Police Dept., 1974—, tech. insp., 1976—. Trustee Western Res. Acad., 1969—. Served with USNR, 1944-45. Fellow A.A.A.S., Royal Astron. Soc.; mem. Am. Phys. Soc., Am. Astron. Soc. Astron. Soc. of Pacific, Am. Assn. Physics Tchrs., Optical Soc. Am., Am. Geophys. Union, Maria Mitchell Assn. (pres. 1974), Sigma Xi. Republican. Mason (32 deg., Shriner). Clubs: Corinthian Yacht, Cape May (N.J.) Beach. Contbr. articles to profl. jours. Home: 1125 Fernwood Blvd Alliance OH 44601 also 1613 Beach Ave Cape May NJ 08204

RODNEY, SAM, city ofcl.; b. Sunflower, Miss., Aug. 25, 1919; s. Sam and Pearl (Brunson) R.; grad. high sch.; m. Jessie L. Leavy, Dec. 21, 1939; children—Frances M. (Mrs. Joseph V. Mason), William S. With City of Chgo., 1954—, supervisor st. cleaning Bur. Sanitation, 1975—. Mem. Selective Service Bd. 18, 1970—, recipient spl. citation, 1971. Mem. NAACP (pres. Chgo.'s Northside 1969-72, 1st. v.p. 1973—). Baptist (deacon 1943—, mem. exec. bd. Sunflower County gen. Bapt. assn. 1945-50). Home: 413 W Blackhawk St Chicago IL 60610

RODRIGUEZ, MANUEL BAELLO, JR., pathologist; b. Manila, Feb. 21, 1923; s. Manuel Juan and Nicandra Trinidad (Baello) R.; M.D. cum laude, U. Santo Tomas, Manila, 1948; m. Ruth Gundrun Eisele, Sept. 3, 1955; children—Manuel, Luz, Mark. Resident in pathology U. Santo Tomas Hosp., Manila, 1948-51; fellow in pathology Mt. Sinai, Hosp., Cleve., 1951-54; asst. pathologist Huron Rd. Hosp., Cleve., 1955-59, asso. pathologist 1966-71, dir. sch. med. tech., 1967-71, clin. labs., 1968-71; asst. pathologist Doctors' Hosp., Cleve., 1954-55, St. Luke's Hosp., Cleve., 1965-66; asso. pathologist Lakewood Hosp., Cleve., 1971-73; pathologist Suburban Hosp., Cleve., 1959-65, Hilcrest Hosp., Cleve.; clin. instr. Case Western Res. U. Certified Am. Bd. Pathology. Mem. Cleve. Acad. Medicine, AMA, Ohio State Med. Soc., Coll. Am. Pathologist, Am. Soc. Clin. Pathologists, Ohio Soc. Pathologists Cleve. Soc. Pathologists. Lutheran. Contbr. aritcles to med. jours. Home: 34605 McAfee Dr Solon OH 44139 Office: 6780 Mayfield Heights OH 44124

RODRIGUEZ, RAYMOND, state ednl. adminstr.; b. N.Y.C., July 5, 1944; s. Ramon and Pura Concepción (Santiago) R.; B.S., U. Wis., Lacrosse, 1967; M.A., Northeastern U., 1971; M.A. in Ednl. Adminstrn., Roosevelt U., 1974; m. Sandra Diann Williams, June 18, 1966; 1 dau., Navarra Valencia. Tchr., English as second lang., pub. schs., Waukegan, Ill., 1967-71, coordinator bilingual edn. program, 1971-75; asst. dir. dept. bilingual edn. Ill. Dept. Edn., Chgo., 1975—. Home: 616 Yeoman Park Waukegan IL 60085 Office: 188 W Randolph St Chicago IL 60601

RODRIGUEZ, ROBERT ALAN, sch. adminstr.; b. St. Louis, Jan. 30, 1946; s. Joseph and Claire Rita (Burke) R.; B.A., Rockhurst Coll., 1968; M.A., U. Mo., 1971, Ed.S., 1975; Ed.D., U. Kans., 1977; m. Patricia Ann Tuttle, May 29, 1977; children—Shawn Steven, Michele Marie. Tchr. pub. schs., Kansas City, Mo., 1968-71; prin. Blessed Sacrament Sch., Kansas City, Kans., 1971-75; prin. Curé of Ars Sch., Leawood, Kans., 1975-78. Mem. Nat., Kans. assns. elementary sch. prins. Home: 4209 W 70th St Prairie Village KS 66208 Office: 9403 Mission Rd Leawood KS 66206

RODRIGUEZ-TORRES, RAMON, pediatric cardiologist, educator; b. Havana, Cuba, Mar. 6, 1926; came to U.S., 1960, naturalized, 1967; s. Narciso and Clara (Torres) R.; M.D., Hava U., 1951; m. Gudelia Garcia, Sept. 11, 1955; children—Raul, Rafael, Raymond. Rotating intern Mercedes Hosp., Cuba, 1951-52; resident in internal medicine Calixto Garcia Hosp., Havana, 1952-55; rotating intern Fajardo (P.R.) Dist. Hosp., 1960-61; fellow in pediatrics Kings County Hosp., Bklyn., N.Y., 1961-63; sr. resident, 1963-64, fellow in pediatrics, 1964-65; adscripto, clin. medicine Havana Sch. Medicine, 1953-55; scholar in cardiology Manchester U., London, Eng., 1957-58; instr. pediatrics State U. N.Y. Downstate Med. Center, Bklyn., 1961-63, asst. prof., 1963-66, acting chmn., 1966, asso. prof., 1966-70, prof., 1970-73, acting chmn., 1972-73; prof., chmn. pediatrics Med. Coll. Ohio, Toledo, 1973—; dir. pediatric service Med. Coll. Ohio Hosp., 1973—. Diplomate Am. Bd. Pediatrics. Fellow Sociedad de Estudios Clinicos de la Habana, Am. Coll. Cardiology, Am. Acad. Pediatrics, Bklyn. Acad. Pediatrics, Royal Soc. Health, Ohio Acad. Sci.; mem. Sociedad Cubana de Cardiology, Am. Heart Assn., Am. Fedn. Clin. Research, Kings County, N.Y. State med. socs., AMA, N.Y. Acad. Sci., Pan Am. Med. Soc., Toledo Pediatric Soc., Assn. Med. Sch. Pediatric Dept. Chmn., Acad. Medicine Toledo and Lucas County, Am. Pediatric Soc., Sigma Xi. Roman Catholic. Contbr. numerous articles, book review, to profl. jours. Home: 2129 Emkay St Toledo OH 43606 Office: Caller Service 10008 Toledo OH 43699

ROE, CLAUDE LEIGHTON, retirement community adminstr.; b. Berne, Ohio, Feb. 26, 1916; s. Claude Haskell and Margaret (Logan) R.; B.S. cum laude, Baldwin-Wallace Coll., 1939; B.D., Oberlin Grad. Sch. Theology, 1946, S.T.M., 1949; D.Ministry, Vanderbilt U. (merger with Oberlin), 1974; m. Gladys Marie McConnaughy, June 14, 1939; children—Richard Lewis, Kay Marie (Mrs. Thomas Stewart). Ordained to ministry Methodist Ch., 1944; pastor chs., Fredericksburg, Ohio, 1942-45, Brewster, Ohio, 1945-47, E. Liverpool, Ohio, 1947-48, Cleve., 1948-55, Montclair, N.J., 1955-58, Whippany, N.J., 1958-62; asst. exec. dir. Presbyn. Homes N.J., Princeton, 1962-72; exec. dir. Copeland Oaks Retirement Community, Sebring, Ohio, 1972—. Mem. faculty extenion div. Rutgers U., 1965-72, also mem. health facilities mgmt. com.; mem. N.J. Adv. Com. on Nursing Edn., 1968-72; licensed nursing home adminstr. preceptor Ohio Dept. Health, 1972—. Chaplain, Montclair (N.J.) chpt. ARC, 1955-58; chaplain Hanover Twp., N.J., 1958-62,

Whippany (N.J.) Fire Dept., 1958-62; mem. Morris County, N.J. Com. Mental Health, 1958-62. Fellow Am. Coll. Nursing Home Adminstrs.; mem. Am. Assn. Homes for Aging (treas., trustee, 1964-71), Nat. Council on Aging, Nat. Geriatrics Soc., Gerontol. Soc., Menninger Found., Mensa. Mason, Lion, Kiwanian, Rotarian. Contbr. articles to profl. jours. Home: 1-730 800 S 15th St Sebring OH 44672 Office: 800 S 15th St Sebring OH 44672

ROEING, RICHARD SVEN, mfg. co. exec.; b. Chgo., Dec. 29, 1926; s. Sven Eric and Grace Lydia (Hanson) R.; B.S. in Elec. Engring., U. Ill., 1948; M.B.A., No. Ill. U., 1972; m. Shirley Marie Walsh, Nov. 13, 1948; children—Richard Alan, Randall Robert, Karen Marie. Asst. chief engr., dir. tech. mktg. C.E. Niehoff & Co., Chicago, 1953-68; plant mgr. Dixon div. Borg-Warner Corp. (Ill.), 1968-74; v.p., co-owner Mallard Mfg. Corp., Sterling, Ill., 1974—. Pres., Rock River Diabetes Assn., 1972—; bd. dirs. Martha Home for Girls, Dixon, 1970; v.p. Dixon C. of C., 1972. Served with USNR, 1944-48. Mem. Soc. Automotive Engrs. (chmn. tech. com. ignition mfg. inst. sect. 1964—), Material Handling Inst. Republican. Clubs: Rotary, Sterling Rock Falls Toastmaster, Rock River Country, Elks. Author: Automobile Engine Tune-up, 1968. Home: 3308 15th Ave Sterling IL 61081 Office: 101 Mallard Rd Sterling IL 61081

ROEPER, GEORGE ALEXANDER, ednl. adminstr.; b. Hamburg, Germany, Sept. 7, 1910; s. George Paul and Anna H. (Meyer) R.; came to U.S., 1938, naturalized, 1946; student U. Munich, 1930-31, U. Berlin, 1931-32; Dipl. Kfm., U. Cologne, 1935; postgrad. U. Greifswald, 1936-38; m. Annemarie M. Bondy, Apr. 20, 1939; children—Tom, Peter, Karen Roeper Carman. Headmaster, Windsor Mt. Sch., Lenox, Mass., 1940-41; headmaster, founder Roeper City and Country Sch., Bloomfield Hills, Mich., 1941—; research asso. prof. spl. edn. Eastern Mich. U., Ypsilanti, 1963-70. Mem. Mich. Soc. Mental Health, Nat. Assn. Elementary Sch. Prins., Nat. Assn. Supervision and Curriculum Devel., Assn. Gifted Children, Council Exceptional Children, NEA, Nat. Assn. Ind. Schs. Author books, contbr. articles profl. publs. Home: 7400 Franklin Rd Franklin MI 48025 Office: Roeper City and Country Sch 2190 N Woodward St Bloomfield Hills MI 48013

ROESE, ALBERT JUNIOR, researcher; b. South Bloomfield, Ohio, Feb. 11, 1924; s. John Nathan and Sadie Francis (Bragg) R.; B.A., Burton Coll., 1965; student Pa. State, 1971; m. Jewell Polley, Feb. 23, 1948; children—John, Frances, Melody, Susan, Patrick. Various positions with Battelle Mem. Inst., Columbus, Ohio, 1951-57, researcher, head particle characterization lab., 1968—. Pres. South Bloomfield Village Council 1973-75, mayor 1975—. Served with USCG, 1942-45. Mem. Fine Particle Soc. Democrat. Roman Catholic. Home: 5016 S Concord St Ashville OH 43103 Office: 505 King Ave Columbus OH 43201

ROESEL, RUDOLPH WALTER, surgeon; b. Muenchen Bernsdorf, Germany, Mar. 3, 1924; s. Walter Hermann and Ida (Praessler) R.; came to U.S., 1952, naturalized, 1958; M.D., U. Zurich, 1952; m. Erica Erna Hirsig, Mar. 1, 1952; children—Thomas, Michael. Intern, Sioux Valley Hosp., Sioux Falls, S.D., 1952-53, resident in surgery Augustana Hosp., Chgo., Creighton U., Omaha, 1954-61; practice medicine specializing in surgery, S.D., 1952-54, Chgo., 1963—; mem. attending staffs Augustana Hosp., Ravenswood Hosp., also mem. tumor bd., chmn. continuing edn. com. and Nelson M. Percy Research Com.; mem. vis. attending staff U. Ill., clin. asst. prof. surgery Abraham Lincoln Sch. Medicine. Diplomate Am. Bd. Surgery. Fellow A.C.S.; mem. Chgo. Med. Soc., AMA. Lutheran. Contbr. articles to profl. jours. Home: 1212 N Lake Shore Dr Chicago IL 60610 Office: 700 N Michigan Ave Chicago IL 60611

ROESER, THOMAS FRANCIS, food co. exec.; b. Evanston, Ill., July 23, 1928; s. Harold Nicholas and Frances Catherine (Cleary) R.; B.A., St. John's U., 1950; postgrad. DePaul U., 1950-52; m. Lillian Kathleen Prescott, Oct. 10, 1959; children—Thomas Francis, Mary Catherine, Michael Joseph, Jeanne Marie. Asst. to gov. Minn., 1961-63; asst. to sec. Commerce for Minority Enterprise, 1969-70; dir. pub. affairs Peace Corps, 1970-71; with Quaker Oats Co., Chgo., 1964—, dir. pub. affairs, 1967—; lectr. Wharton Sch., U. Pa., Northwestern U. Bd. dirs. Pub. Affairs Council, 1971-72, Learning Exchange. Fellow, Inst. of Politics, John F. Kennedy Sch. Govt., Harvard U., 1977-78. Mem. Conf. Bd., Ill. C. of C. Republican. Roman Catholic. Clubs: Federal City, Capitol Hill (Washington); Mchts. and Mfrs., Athletic Assn. (Chgo.). Home: 200 Cherry St Park Ridge IL 60068 Office: 345 Merchandise Mart Chicago IL 60654

ROESNER, PETER LOWELL, mfg. co. exec.; b. Winchester, Ind., July 3, 1937; s. Lowell LeClair and Martha C. (Overmyer) R.; B.A., DePauw U., 1959; LL.B., U. Mich., 1962; M.B.A., Harvard U., 1964; m. Rebecca Anne Roleson, Aug. 25, 1962; children—Peter Lowell II, David Brandon, John Franklin. Pres., dir. Overmyer Corp., supplier to glass industry, Winchester, Ind., 1969—, Overmyer Mould Co. of Pa., Greensburg, 1969—, Overmyer Mould Co. (Calif.) Inc., Downey, 1969—; dir. Mchts. Nat. Bank, Muncie, Ind., N.V. OMCO, S.A., Aalter, Belgium, OMCO (Espana) S.A., Barcelona, Spain; chmn. bd., dir. Aquality, Inc., Chatsworth, Cal. Chmn. Glass Industry Award Com. Mem. Am. Bar Assn., Ind. Mfrs. Assn. (dir., pres.), Delta Theta Phi, Phi Gamma Delta. Rotarian. Clubs: Columbia (Indpls.); Muncie, Delaware Country (Muncie). Home: 2207 Wiltshire Rd Muncie IN 47304 Office: PO Box 489 Winchester IN 47394

ROESSLER, DAVID MARTYN, physicist; b. London, Eng., Apr. 29, 1940; s. Alfred Ernest and Elizabeth Minnie (Cornish) R.; came to U.S., 1966; B.Sc., U. London, 1961, Ph.D., 1966. Mem. tech. staff Bell Telephone Labs., Murray Hill, N.J., 1968-70; asso. Gen. Motors Research Labs., Warren, Mich., 1970-71, sr. research physicist, 1971—. Asso. Kings Coll., 1961. Mem. Inst. Physics U.K. Contbr. articles to profl. jours. Research ultra-violet and visible spectroscopy, optical properties of materials. Home: 31720 Concord Dr Madison Heights MI 48071 Office: Dept Physics Gen Motors Research Labs Warren MI 48090

ROFFMANN, HAROLD, civil engr.; b. Carlyle, Ill., Aug. 10, 1929; s. William and Lura (Orrell) Roffmann; m. Phyllis Zenzen, Dec. 29, 1956; children—Jennifer, Amy, Emily, William Harold, John. B.C.E., U. Ill., 1958; student U. Wis., 1970-77. Registered Profl. Engr., Ill., Ia., Ind., Ohio, Mo., Ky., Fla., N.C.; Licensed Land Surveyor, Ill., Mo.; Registered Structural Engr., Ill. Design engr. Rochester & Godell Engrs., Salem, Ill., 1958-62; owner Harold Roffmann Consulting Engr., Mt. Vernon, Ill., 1962—; city engr., Mt. Vernon, Ill., 1970-75; owner Nature Trail Nursing Home, Mt. Vernon, Ill., 1970—; partner Rockford Manor Nursing Home; partner Rochelle (Ill.) Manor Nursing Home; partner Fairview Nursing Home, Bellevidere, Ill.; v.p., gen. mgr. Regal 8 Inns, Mt. Vernon, Ill., 1976—. Mem., Ill. Constrn. Industry Commn., 1970-71. Mem. Nat., Ill. (v.p. 1976-77) socs. profl. engrs., Am. Hotel-Motel Assn., Mason, Shriners, Elks Club. Home: 20 Wildwood St Mt Vernon IL 62864 Office: 713 Harrison St Mt Vernon IL 62864

ROGERS, CHARLES THOMAS, mech. engr.; b. Grand Rapids, Mich., June 13, 1912; s. Charles Erwin and Helen Pearl (Smedley) R.; M.S., Detroit Inst. Tech., 1944; certificate completion engr. tech. orientation course U.S. Army Engr. Sch., 1960; m. Hilda Belle Busey, Aug. 17, 1944. Indsl. engr., Detroit Ordnance Dist., 1941-46; quality control analyst Cadillac Motor car div. Gen. Motors Corp., Detroit, 1948-54; mech. engr. U.S. Army Tank Auto. Command, Warren, Mich., 1954—. Registered profl. engr., Mich.; recipient fallout shelter analysis certificate Dept. Def., 1970. Mem. Am. Def. Preparedness Assn. (life), Mich. Soc. Profl. Engrs., Nat. Soc. Profl. Engrs., Mich. Assn. Professions. Presbyterian. Clubs: Mason, Order Eastern Star. Home: 10622 Outer Dr W Detroit MI 48223

ROGERS, DAVID ALAN, mgmt. cons.; b. Huntington, Ind., Jan. 4, 1940; s. Eldon J.C. Rogers; B.S., Ind. U., 1963; M.B.A., Butler U., 1970; m. Suzanne Moffitt, Oct. 20, 1960; children—Julie Ann, Lisa Kay. Tchr. biology Indpl. Pub. Schs., 1963-65; sales rep. Med. Protective Co., Indpls., 1965-66; mgr. advt. and customer service Bowes Seal Fast Corp., Indpls., 1966-70; clinic adminstr. Meml. Clinic, Indpls., 1970-75; mgmt. cons., pres. owner Profl. Econs., Inc., Indpls., 1975—; lectr. Butler U. Bd. dirs. Delaware Trail Civic Assn. Served with USMCR, 1957-63. Mem. Adminstrv. Mgmt. Soc. (dir.), Med. Group Mgmt. Assn., Ind. Clinic Mgrs. Assn., Methodist. Clubs: Masons, Shriners. Home: 905 77th South Dr Indianapolis IN 46260 Office: 1633 N Capitol St Indianapolis IN 46202

ROGERS, FELIX MICHAEL, air force officer; b. Somerville, Mass., July 6, 1921; s. Francis F. and Margaret Louise (Barnes) R.; student U. Va., 1947-49; B.S., U. Md., 1952; postgrad. Lacaze Acad., Washington, 1952-53, Nat. War Coll., Washington, 1961; m. Virginia Gordon Baker, June 10, 1949; children—Virginia C., Stephen B., Derek A., Ian A.G. Commd. 2d lt. USAAF, 1943, advanced through grades to gen. USAF, 1975; asst. air attache, Madrid, Spain, 1953-57; chief Current Intelligence br. Office Dep. Chief of Staff, Ops., dir. current intelligence Orgn. Joint Chiefs of Staff, Washington, 1957-60; with Office of Asst. Sec. Def. with duty sta. at Dept. State, 1961-62; sec. Air Force Council, Office Vice Chief of Staff, 1962-63, dir. Secretariat, Air Force Council Designated Systems Mgmt. Group, 1963-66; asst. dep. chief of staff, devel. plans Air Force Systems Command, Andrews AFB, Md., 1966-70; sr. mem. UN Command, Mil. Armistice Commn., Korea, 1970-71; dep. chief of staff for tech. tng. Air Tng. Command Hdqrs., Randolph AFB, Tex., 1971-72, vice comdr., 1972-73; comdr. Air U., Maxwell AFB, Ala., 1973-75; comdr. Air Force Logistics Command, Wright-Patterson AFB, Ohio, 1975—. Co-chmn. United Negro Coll. Fund, Greater Dayton Area, 1975-76; trustee Aviation Hall of Fame; bd. mgrs. Air Force Mus. Found. Mem. Air Force Assn., U.S. Strategic Inst., Soc. Logistic Engrs., Order Daedalians (hon. flight capt.), Am. Fighter Aces Assn., Metropolitan Club Washington, Admirals Club Washington, 100 Club of Dayton, Dayton Racquet Club, Moraine Country Club. Decorated D.S.M. with 2 oak leaf clusters, Silver Star medal, Legion of Merit with oak leaf cluster, D.F.C. with oak leaf cluster, Bronze Star medal, Air medal with 20 oak leaf clusters, Army Commendation medal, Order Aero. Merit (Spain), Order Nat. Security Merit (Republic of Korea). Home: 531 1st St Wright-Patterson Air Force Base OH 45433 Office: Air Force Logistics Command Wright-Patterson Air Force Base OH 45433

ROGERS, GIFFORD EUGENE, civil engr.; b. Grand Island, Nebr., May 22, 1920; s. Frederick Charles and Beaulah (Crabtree) R.; B.S., U. Nebr., 1943; M.S., Purdue U., 1948; Diploma Honor, Cartographic Inst. Guatemala, 1962, Agrarian Reform Inst. Guatemala, 1961; m. Edna Marjorie Mull, Dec. 25, 1942; children—Robert Dennis, Michael Edwin, Barry David, Gifford Eugene Jr. With United Fruit Co., various internat. locations, 1948-60, field engr., soils engr., project engr., Panama, Honduras, Guatemala, 1948-56, chief engr., Costa Rica, Dominican Republic, 1956-60; with Internat. Devel. Services Inc., Guatemala and Dominican Republic, 1960-64, regional planning engr., 1960-61, chief engr., Guatemala City, 1961-62, project. mgr., 1962-64; cons. Agrarian Reform Inst., Santo Domingo, Dominican Republic, 1964-65, Nicaragua, 1967-69; sr. engr. Devel. & Resources Corp., Malaysia and Nicaragua, 1965-67, Robert R. Nathan Assos., El Salvador and Ghana, 1969-70; project mgr. Engring. Cons. Inc., Bangladesh, Turkey and Indonesia, 1970—. Adviser Boy Scouts Guatamala, 1960-62. Bd. dirs. Dominican-Am. Cultural Inst., 1962-64. Served to 1st lt. C.E., AUS, 1943-46; PTO. Registered profl. engr., Nebr. Regents scholar, 1938-42; Standard Oil fellow, 1946-48. Fellow ASCE; mem. Soc. Internat. Devel., Am. Soc. Pub. Adminstrn., Nat. Soc. Profl. Engrs., Sigma Xi. Mem. Union Ch. Mason. Author: Agrarian Reform Defined and Analyzed, 1964. Editor: Engineering Design of Drainage Systems, 1973. Home: 916 A St Apt 6 Lincoln NE 68502 Office: 1901 S Navajo St Denver CO 80223

ROGERS, JAMES FRANKLIN, leisure products mfg. co. exec.; b. Mankato, Minn., Feb. 15, 1939; s. James Franklin and Marilynn Marcella (Fenger) R.; B.S., U. Minn., 1961; m. Mary Pauline Bever, Dec. 10, 1960; children—David, Steven, Richard, Timothy. Reporter, Pioneer Press, St. Paul, 1958-61; staff writer AP, Mpls., 1961-62; pub. relations specialist Minn. Mining and Mfg. Co., St. Paul, 1964-69; mktg. communications specialist N.Am. Rockwell, Pitts., 1969-70; nat. sales mgr. Crestliner div. AMF, Inc., Little Falls, Minn., 1970-73; v.p. sales Riddell, Inc., Chgo., 1973-76, sr. v.p., 1976-77; gen. mgr. Graftek Leisure Products div. Exxon Enterprises, Raleigh, N.C., 1977—. Served with AUS, 1962-64. Mem. Nat. Sporting Goods Assn., Sporting Goods Mfrs. Assn., U. Minn. Alumni Assn., Am. Mgmt. Assn. Club: U. Minn. M. Home: 353 Hillside Dr Roselle IL 60172 Office: 242 St Nicholas Ave South Plainfield NJ 07080

ROGERS, JAMES MAURICE, pub. relations exec.; b. Frankfort, Ind., Jan. 1, 1934; s. Maurice Matthew and Mary Sims (Aughe) R.; B.S. in Radio-TV, Ind. U., 1956; m. Julia Lee Morrow, June 22, 1957; children—Evan Morrow, Alexander Burke. Account exec. LaGrange & Garrison Advt., Indpls., 1959-60; pub. relations dir. Hook Drugs, Inc., Indpls., 1960—, asst. v.p., 1967. Pres., Indpls. Speech & Hearing Center, 1967, Indpls Hist. Preservation Commn., 1974—; dir. Hist. Landmarks Found. of Ind., Inc., v.p., 1975—; dir., Travel, Ind., Inc. Served to 1st lt. U.S. Army, 1957-59. Mem. Pub. Relations Soc. Am., Nat. Assn. Chain Drug Stores (pub. relations com.). Republican. Methodist. Clubs: Athenaeum-Turners, Phi Kappa Psi. Home: 6331 Knyghton Rd Indianapolis IN 46220 Office: 2800 Enterprise St PO Box 26285 Indianapolis IN 46226

ROGERS, JOANN, educator; b. Canfield, Ohio, Jan. 13, 1954; d. Malcolm Hall and Bernadine Marjorie Elene (Peterson) Wilkin; B.S. magna cum laude in Mathematics and Edn. (Luth Ch. women's scholar, Undergrad. fellow), Miami U., Oxford, Ohio, 1976; m. Lawrence Robert Rogers, July 16, 1977. Clk. accounting dept. U.S. Steel Corp., McDonald, Ohio, 1973, 74; lecture asst., dept. math. and statistics Miami U., 1976; tchr. math. high sch., Ottawa, Ohio, 1976-77. Recipient Christofferson award Best Potential Secondary Tchr., Miami U., 1976. Mem. Am. Math. Soc., Math. Assn. Am., Nat. Council Tchrs. Math., Phi Beta Kappa, Pi Mu Epsilon. Lutheran. Home: 126 Hilltop Blvd Canfield OH 44406

ROGERS, JOHN FRANCIS, mfg. co. exec., hist. soc. ofcl.; b. Chgo., Aug. 12, 1922; s. Michael and Anna (Auksas) R.; diploma, Mech. Industries Tech. Inst., 1941; grad. Pullman Aircraft Inst., 1941; m. Marie Catherine Schwartz, Oct. 7, 1945; children—Kathleen Marie Rogers Henry, Anita Doreen Rogers Gomolski. Foreman, Pullman Aircraft Co., Chgo., 1941-43; supr. Dodge Chrysler Aircraft Co., Chgo., 1943-45; machine trainee Athey Mfg. Co., Chgo., 1946-47; v.p. Aarness Corp., Chgo., 1947-56; plant supt. Tanko Screw Products Corp., Chgo., 1965—. Pres., Ruth Burns Lord Found., 1973—. Vice pres. Palos Hist. Soc., Palos Park, Ill., 1965-66, pres., 1966—. Home: 12021 S 93d Ave Palos Park IL 60464 Office: 9244 S Stony Island Ave Chicago IL 60617

ROGERS, JOHN RUSSELL, engr.; b. St. Louis, May 12, 1929; s. John Flint and Faye (Russell) R.; A.B., Washington U., St. Louis, 1951; m. Lorraine Esther Klockenbrink, Sept. 15, 1951; children—John Oliver, Gail Joanne. Plant supt. Daybrite Lighting, Inc., Tupelo, Miss., 1959-64; plant mgr. White Rodgers Ltd., Markham, Ont., Can., 1964-66; ops. mgr. Metal Goods Corp., St. Louis, 1966-71; engr., v.p. Ross & Baruzzini, Inc., Cons. Engrs., St. Louis, 1971—. Dir. indsl. div. St. Louis Safety Council, 1968; leader Boy Scout Am., 1963-71, Girl Scouts U.S.A., 1972; dep. gen. conv. Protestant Episcopal Ch., 1976, del. diocesan conv., 1967-77, pres. diocesan standing com., 1975; dir. Episc. Ednl. Center, St. Louis, 1974; bd. dirs. Episc. Neighborhood Sch., St. Louis, 1974, Care and Counseling, 1975; bd. mgrs. Thompson Retreat House, St. Louis, 1975. Served to capt., inf., USAF, 1951-54. Registered profl. engr., Mo, Ill. Mem. Assn. Profl. Material Hadling Cons.'s, Internat. Materials Mgmt. Soc., Am. Soc. Safety Engrs., Res. Officers Assn., Phi Delta Thea. Home: 10332 Richview Dr Saint Louis MO 63127 Office: 7912 Bonhomme Ave Saint Louis MO 63105

ROGERS, JOY JEANNE, psychologist; b. St. Joseph, Mich., Dec. 9, 1942; d. Harold John and Frieda (Ulmer) Rogers; B.A. in Psychology and English, Western Mich. U., 1964; M.A. in Sch. Psychology, 1966, Ed.S., 1966; Ph.D., U. Mich., 1970. Teaching asst. Western Mich. U., 1964-66, part-time instr., 1965-67; clin. psychologist Kalamazoo State Hosp., 1966-68; research asst. Center Research on Learning and Teaching, U. Mich., 1968-70; asst. prof. psychology Purdue U., 1970-73; asso. prof. psychology Loyola U., Chgo., 1972—; cons. in field. Mem. Park Forest (Ill.) Youth Commn. Recipient Purdue U. award for excellence in undergraduate teaching, 1971. Mem. Am. Psychol. Assn., Am. Ednl. Research Assn., Nat. Soc. for Programmed Instn., AAUP. Contbr. articles to profl. jours. Home: 520 Chase St Park Forest IL 60466 Office: Loyola Univ 820 N Michigan Ave Chicago IL 60611

ROGERS, RAYMOND EARL, pub. relations exec.; b. St. Louis, Sept. 17, 1941; s. Ralph Raymond and Mary Louise (Wright) R.; B.J., U. Mo., 1963, M.A., 1973; m. Carolyn Jeanne Martines, Sept. 7, 1963; children—Mark, Kent. Asst. mgr. pub. info. and bank relations Fed. Res. Bank, St. Louis, 1966; mgr. advt. and pub. relations Credit Systems, Inc., St. Louis, 1968-70; dir. advt. and pub. relations Bank Bldg. Corp., St. Louis, 1970—. Served to capt. U.S. Army, 1964-66. Mem. Bus. Profl. Advt. Assn. (pres. St. Louis 1975), Pub. Relations Soc., Advt. Club. Republican. Methodist. Office: 1130 Hampton St St Louis MO 63139

ROGERS, THOMAS KAY, corporate ednl. adminstr.; b. Lorain, Ohio, May 4, 1933; s. Ralph Clark and Alice (Kay) R.; B.S. in Edn., Ohio U., 1957, M.Ed., 1958; postgrad. John Carroll U., 1962, Wayne State U., 1961; m. Betty Ann Kovacs, Apr. 24, 1954; children—Thomas K., David A., Robert D. Grad. asst. Ohio U., Athens, 1957-58; tchr., coach Warrensville (Ohio) Heights Schs., 1958-64; dist. sales mgr. Brodhead-Garrett Co., Cuyahoga Heights, Ohio, 1965-66, ednl. cons., 1967—; speaker, lectr. in field. Trustee Walsh Jesuit High Sch., 1975—. Served with U.S. Army, 1953-55. Mem. Am. Sch. Bus. Offcls., Am. Vocat. Assn., Am. Indsl. Arts Assn., Edn. Industry Assn. (pres. 1976), Ednl. Exhibitors Assn. (pres. 1977), Epsilion Pi Tau, Phi Delta Kappan, Iota Lamba Sigma. Contbr. articles to profl. jours. Home: 130 Pickwick St Northfield OH 44067 Office: 4560 E 71st St Cleveland OH 44105

ROGERS, VAN RENSSELAER, exhbn. center exec.; b. nr. Lexington, Ky., Jan. 9, 1914; s. Edgar Alfred and Nellie Estella (Burton) R.; grad. Cleve. Inst. Art, 1937; m. Ruth Charlotte Reichelt, Aug. 3, 1941; 1 son, Peter Van. Commd. sculptor Walt Disney Enterprises, Hollywood, Calif., 1937-38; co-founder Rogers Bennett Studios, Cleve., 1938; pres., owner Rogers Display Studios div. NESCO, Inc., Cleve., 1959—. Asst. registrar John Huntington Poly. Inst., Cleve., 1938-41. Chmn. Zoning Commn., Russell Twp., Geauga County, O., 1974. Served to lt. comdr. USNR, 1942-46. Mem. Exhibit Designers and Producers Assn., Nat. Trade Show Exhibitor Assn. (founder, citation as Godfather of orgn. 1977), North and South Skirmish Assn., Nat. Muzzle Loading Rifle Assn., Greater Cleve. Growth Assn., Western Reserve Hist. Soc. Mason (32 deg., K.T.). Club: Advertising (Cleve.). Home: 8230 Fairmount Rd Novelty OH 44072 Office: Rogers Display Studios Inc 1000 Wayside Rd Cleveland OH 44110

ROGERS, WILBUR FRANK, educator; b. Willow Lake, Nebr., July 23, 1916; s. Hubert Melvin and Bertha (Dumke) R.; B.Sc., U. Nebr., 1939, M.Sc., 1941; postgrad U. Ariz., 1966-67, Colo. State U., 1967-68; Ph.D., Pa. State U. 1970; m. Priscilla F. Chain, June 12, 1941; children—John C., William F., Martha (Mrs. James W. Davis). Geologist, Carter Oil Co., Lander, Wyo., 1945-48; dist. geologist W.C. McBride Co., Lander, 1948-49, Sinclair Oil Co., Scottsbluff, Nebr., 1949-50; cons. geologist and civil engr., Scottsbluff, 1950-68; prof. civil engring. U. Nebr., Omaha, 1970—. Pres., Rogers Oil Co., Scottsbluff, 1950-55, W.F. Rogers Drilling Co., Scottsbluff, 1955-67, Plains Supply Co., Scottsbluff, Oil Well Cementing Co., Scottsbluff, 1965-66; vis. prof. U. Padua (Italy), 1969; guest lectr. Imperial Coll. Sci. and Tech., London, 1974; cons. engr., 1945—. Served to lt. comdr. USNR, 1941-45. Registered profl. engr., Nebr., Wyo., S.D. Mem. Am. Assn. Petroleum Geologists, ASCE, Am. Geophys. Union, Nebr. Oil and Gas Assn. (1st pres.), Rocky Mountain Oil and Gas Assn. (past v.p.), Sigma Xi, Alpha Tau Omega, Sigma Gamma Epsilon. Mason (Shriner), Elk, Rotarian (chmn. internat. service com. 1973-74). Patentee and publs. in field. Home: 713 S 84th St Omaha NE 68114 Office: Dept Civil Engineering Box 688 Omaha NE 68101

ROGERS, WILLIAM ARTHUR, photojournalist; b. Chgo., Apr. 12, 1920; s. Edwin Arthur and Astrid (Svendsen) R.; student U. Dubuque, 1938; seminars various univs., 1959—; m. Pauline Elizabeth King, Apr. 6, 1945; 1 dau., Pamela Kay. Reporter, writer, newscaster, news dir. WSAI and WCKY, Cin., 1947-48; sales promotion mgr. Frederic W. Ziv Co., Cin., 1949-52; self-employed publicity and promotion, Chgo., 1953-58; reporter, feature writer Economist Newspapers, Chgo., 1959-60; prin. Bill Arthur Rogers, photojournalist, Oak Park, Ill., 1960—; instr. photography part time, Triton Coll., 1971-76, U. Ill. Med. Center, Chgo., 1972-73, Winona Sch. Photography, 1977; exhibited photographs one-man show, Chgo., 1970, also group shows, Chgo., N.Y., Phila., Los Angeles. Chmn., coordinator Chgo. 74, 1974. Aldermanic candidate, Chgo., 1958-59. Served with USMCR, 1941-45. Mem. Am. Soc. Mag. Photographers (past pres. Chgo. chpt.), Artists Guild Chgo. (v.p.), Indsl. Editors Assn. Chgo. (past treas.), Nat. Press Photographers Assn. Episcopalian (past vestryman). Columnist, Oak Park World, 1975-76. Home and Office: 713 Washington Blvd Oak Park IL 60302

ROGNAN, LLOYD NORMAN, artist, illustrator; b. Chgo., June 14, 1923; s. John and Gertrude Sophia (Hagen) R.; student Am. Acad. Art, 1941, 50, 51; diploma Acad. de la grande Chamiere, 1949; m.

Sylvia Marcella Erickson, July 18, 1953; children—Bruce Byron, Cindy Lou. Cover artist French edit. Ellery Queen, Paris, France, 1947-49; sci. fiction cover artist Greenleaf Publs., Evanston, Ill., 1956-58; with Meyer and Booth Studio, Chgo., 1958-61; biol. artist Golden Books Press, N.Y.C., 1961-63; cartoonist United Card Co., Rolling Meadows, Ill., 1966-71; art dir. Gallant Greetings, Chgo., 1972; calendar artist, hillbilly series Corn Squeezins, Brown and Bigelow, St. Paul, 1976—; with Saga, Inc., ltd. edits. Western prints Albuquerque, 1977—. Art counsellor Boy Scouts Am. Served with U.S. Army, 1944-46; ETO. Decorated Purple Heart. Home and studio: 3620 Linneman St Glenview IL 60025

ROGOLS, SAUL, biochemist; b. Cambridge, Mass., July 27, 1933; s. Barney Barken and Dora (Cohen) R.; B.Sc., Antioch Coll., 1956; M.Sc., Ohio State U., 1958; certificate paper tech. Western Mich. U., 1962; m. Delores Valentine, June 14, 1958; children—Marc, Kevin. With Columbus div. A.E. Staley Mfg. Co., Columbus, Ohio, 1961—, group leader, 1968-69, div. tech. dir., 1969—. Mem. lab. research staff Childrens Hosp., Columbus, 1965-72. Mgr., Little League Baseball, 1967-71. Recipient certificate counting computer tech. Coulter Electronics, 1976. Fellow Am. Inst. Chemists; mem. Am. Chem. Soc., Am. Assn. Cereal Chemistry, N.Y. Acad. Scis., Sigma Xi. Patentee in field. Contbr. articles to profl. jours. Office: 324 Dering Ave Columbus OH 43207

ROHL, DAVID WILLIAM, dentist; b. Hutchinson, Kans., Feb. 2, 1919; s. Forrest Edgar and Sydney Mae (Sheldon) R.; D.D.S., Southwestern Coll., 1936-40; B.A., Washington U., 1946-50; m. Carolyn Jean Hall, Aug. 4, 1949; children—Russell David, Suzanne Beth (Mrs. Kenny Joe Teeple). Pvt. practice dentistry, Independence, Mo., 1952-65, Versailles, 1965—. Served with USAAF, 1941-45, AUS, 1950-52. Mem. Am. Dental Assn., Jefferson City Dental Soc. (pres. 1971), Xi Psi Phi. Methodist. Republican. Lion (pres. 1958-59). Home: 309 N Walnut St Versailles MO 65084 Office: 117 S Monroe St Versailles MO 65084

ROHLING, PAUL VERNON, stainless steel utensils mfg. co. exec.; b. Kenosha, Wis., Mar. 6, 1917; s. Mads Lange and Anna Katrina (Egmose) R.; B.S. in Mech. Engring., U. Wis., 1944; m. Hazel Marie Sorensen, July 1, 1944; children—Paul, Joanne. Methods engr., Vollrath Co., Sheboygan, Wis., 1944-46, chief engr., 1947-51, asst. factory mgr., 1951-59, factory mgr., 1959-60, mfg. v.p., 1960-64, sr. v.p., 1964-65, exec. v.p., 1965-68, pres., 1968—, chmn. bd., chief exec. officer, 1976—. Registered profl. engr., Wis. Mem. Soc. Mfg. Engrs. (pres. 1952-53), Assn. Commerce (dir. 1966-68), Sheboygan Econ. Club. Lutheran (mem. council 1948-54, 56-60, 67-71). Club: Country (Sheboygan). Home: 1244 Riverview Dr Sheboygan WI 53081 Office: 1236 N 18th St Sheboygan WI 53081

ROHLINGER, MERLIN JOSEPH, chemist; b. Saxon, Wis., Jan. 8, 1916; s. Adam Frederick and Margaret (Weidig) R.; B.S., Marquette U., 1936; postgrad. U. Wis., 1936-37; m. Virginia Catherine Flad, Oct. 9, 1937; children—Dennis, Marion, Gordon. Chief quality control chemist U.S. Standard Products Co., 1938-41, dir. labs., 1942-48; chief spectrographer Globe Steel Tubes Co., Milw., 1941-42; chief research chemist Allied Mills Inc., 1948-64; chief chemist Bur. Air Pollution Control, Ill. Dept. Pub. Health, Springfield, 1964-70; chief chemist Air Pollution Control div. Ill. Environ. Protection Agy., 1970-73. Cons., Merlin J. Rohlinger & Assos., Libertyville, Ill., 1965—, Beling Engring. Cons., 1973-74. Mem. Am. Chem. Soc., Am., Ill. pub. health assns., Am. Inst. Chemists. Address: 142 Kenloch Ave Libertyville IL 60048

ROHRBACH, MAX SIDNEY, mfg. co. exec.; b. Heidenheim, Germany, July 10, 1914; s. Sigmund R. and Mathilde (Sachsendorfer) R.; came to U.S., 1936; naturalized, 1941; Abitur degree, Real & Handelschule, Marktbreit am Main, 1930; student Heehere Preussische Textil Fachschule, Munchen-Gladbach-Rhein, Germany, 1931-33; m. Susan Bendheim, Apr. 11, 1954; children—Monica, Stuart. With Cohn-Hall-Marx, N.Y.C., 1938-67, nat. sales mgr.; pres., founder Fabric Distributers, Inc., Cin., 1968—, Fabric Merchants, Inc., Cin., 1968—, Fabric Circle U.S.A., Cin., 1968—; pres. Monique Fabric & Daytex Outlet Stores, Dayton, Ohio, 1976—. Bd. dirs. Jewish Welfare Fund, Cin., 1975-78; bd. dirs. Jewish Nat. Fund; active Bonds for Israel, Cin., 1975-77; founder Center Internat. Security Studies, Am. Security Council Edn. Found. Served as spl. agent counter Intelligence Corps, U.S. Army, 1941-44. Decorated 2 Invasion Arrowheads, Battle Stars, etc. Mem. Internat. Council of Shopping Centers, Nat. Mass Retail Inst., Am. Security Council, Prime Ministers Club of Israel. Clubs: Capitol Hill Club, of Washington, Crest Hills Country, New Hope Congregation. Home: 6673 E Farm Acres Rd Cincinnati OH 45237 Office: 8911 Rossash Rd Cincinnati OH 45236

ROHRMAN, DOUGLASS FREDERICK, lawyer; b. Chgo., Aug. 10, 1941; s. Frederick Alvin and Velma Elizabeth (Birdwell) R.; A.B., Duke U., 1963; J.D., Northwestern U., 1966; m. Alice Anne Bliss, Aug. 23, 1969. Admitted to Ill. bar, 1966; legal coordinator Nat. Communicable Disease Center, Altanta, 1966-68; asso. firm Keck, Cushman, Mahin & Cate, Chgo., 1968-73, partner, 1973—; v.p., dir. Kerogen Oil Co., 1967—; dir. Valley View, Inc. Vice chmn., commr. Ill. Food and Drug Commn., 1970-72. Served as lt. USPHS, 1966-68. Mem. Am., Chgo. (chmn. com. on food and drug law 1972-73), 7th Circuit bar assns., Am. Soc. Law and Medicine, Selden Soc. Democrat. Episcopalian. Club: Union League of Chgo. Contbr. articles on law to various profl. jours. Home: 2666 Prairie Ave Evanston IL 60201 Office: 8300 Sears Tower Chicago IL 60606

ROHRS, KENNETH VERNON, mfg. co. exec.; b. Johnson, Nebr., Mar. 18, 1924; s. Vernon K. and Ellen (Rademacker) R.; B.S., U. Nebr., 1949; m. Elsa Glendora Galloway, July 26, 1945; children—Ronald, Rick, Patricia, Teresa. Sales mgr. Reimers Kaufman Concrete Products, 1949-58; coordinating mgr. all products Abel Investment Co., 1958-59; gen. sales mgr. Plant City Steel Corp., 1959-63; pres. Stormor, Inc., steel fabrication, Fremont, Nebr., 1963—; dir. First Nat. Bank, Fremont, Fuqua Industries. Bd. dirs. YMCA, Fremont. Served with USAAF, 1943-45 (prisoner of war). Decorated 4 Air medals, Purple Heart. Mem. C. of C. (bd. dirs. 1969-71). Presbyn. (deacon 1962-63). Clubs: Raw Hide Ski, Fremont Country, Frelin Soaring. Home: 1801 La Playa Ln Rural Route 1 Fremont NE 68025 Office: 1255 Front St Fremont NE 68025

ROLAND, CARROLL DUDLEY, psychologist; b. Woodland, Calif., Jan. 8, 1944; s. Carroll and Joyce Lee (Lillard) R.; B.A., Adams State Coll., 1966; M.S., U. Nebr., 1968; Ed.S., U. Iowa, 1973; Ph.D., Iowa State U., 1977; m. Nadine Mary Ward, Feb. 12, 1972; children—Michelle Marie, Richard Carroll. Psychologist, Tama—Poweshiek and Benton Joint County Dept. Spl. Edn., Tama, Iowa, 1968-70; psychologist Benton Tama County Dept. Spl. Edn., 1971-72; coordinator psychol. and ednl. strategists services Marshall Poweshiek Joint County Dept. Edn., Marshalltown, Iowa, 1972-75; psychologist Area Edn. Agy. 11, Ankeny, Iowa, 1975-77; cons. psychology, marriage counselor, Marshalltown, 1975—, Marshalltown Counseling Services, 1975—. Tchr. Church Sch., 1st United Meth. Ch. Served with AUS, 1970-71. Mem. Iowa Psychol. Assn., Council Exceptional Children, Blue Key, Phi Kappa Phi. Club: Flying, Skiing. Home: 1515 W Church St Marshalltown IA 50158 Office: 104 S 1st St Marshalltown IA 50158

ROLF, FRANK PAUL, mech. engr.; b. Peekskill, N.Y., July 30, 1928; s. Frank and Paula (Hartman) R.; B.M.E., Clarkson Coll., 1954; m. Eleanor Gaines, Feb. 16, 1951; children—James E., John A., Jeffrey O., Cecilia A., Catharine L., Cristin M. Test engr. Aberdeen Proving Ground, 1954-55; design engr. New Departure div. Gen. Motors Corp., Bristol, Conn., 1955-56, applications engr., 1956-57, project engr., 1957-59, supr. auto testing, 1959-67; maintenance supr. Lane Constrn. Co., Fulton, N.Y., 1967; project engr. Lubrizol Corp., Wickliffe, Ohio, 1967-70, supr. fleet test, 1970—. Served with USN, 1946-48, 51-52. Mem. Soc. Automotive Engrs., Coordinating Research Council, Regular Common Carrier Conf. Republican. Roman Catholic. Club: Elks. Office: 29400 Lakeland Blvd Wickliffe OH 44092

ROLFS, MARVIN EUGENE, mathematician; b. Geneseo, Kans., Feb. 15, 1913; s. Henry Rudolf and Clara Ruth (Schroeder) R.; B.S., Ottawa U., 1934; M.A., U. Kans., 1935; postgrad U. Minn., summer 1939; m. Ardelle Lavinia Baker, July 27, 1938; children—Leland Eugene, Jane Ann, Kay Helen. Instr. Dodge City (Kans.) Jr. Coll., 1936-43, U. Kans., 1943-44; mathematician U. Iowa, Iowa City, 1945; instr. U. Kans., 1945-47; asso. prof. No. Mich. Coll. Edn., Marquette, 1947-51; analyst USAF, Forbes AFB, Topeka, 1951-61; instr. Fort Hays (Kans.) State Coll. (now U.), 1961-63, asst. prof., 1963-72, asso. prof., 1972—. Mem. Nat. Council Tchrs. Math., Math. Assn. Am., Kans. Assn. Tchrs. Math, Fort Hays Kans. State Coll. Faculty Assn., Fort Hays Kans. State Coll. Faculty Men, Nat., Topeka Audubon socs., Kans. Ornithol. Soc., Nat., Internat. wildlife fedns., Sigma Pi Sigma, Pi Mu Epsilon. Republican. Baptist. Home: 211 W 24th St Hays KS 67601 Office: Dept Math Fort Hays State U Hays KS 67601

ROLLAND, PAUL, music educator; b. Budapest, Hungary, Nov. 21, 1911; grad. Franz Liszt Acad. Music, 1937; B.Mus., Simpson Coll., 1943; m. Clara Szekely, Dec. 24, 1940; children—Peter, John. First violist Budapest Symphony Orch., 1935-38; Pro Ideale Quartet, Budapest, 1936-40; violist Westminster Choir Coll., Princeton, N.J., 1938-40; fellow Simpson Coll., Indianola, Iowa, 1940-45; prof. music U. Ill., 1945—; dir. Strings Nat. Acad. Arts, Champaign, Ill., 1974—; dir. U. Ill. HEW String Research Project, 1967-70. Recipient Outstanding Tchr. of Year award U. Ill., 1976; Dept. State Am. Specialist grantee, 1960-61. Mem. Am. String Tchrs. Assn. (founding mem., editor, past pres., chmn. publs.), Music Tchrs. Nat. Assn., Music Educators Nat. Conf., Nat. Sch. Orch. Assn. Author: Basic Principles of Violin Playing, 1960; Prelude to String Playing, Method, 1972; The Teaching of Action in String Playing (series 17 films, books, audio-visual aids), 1973. Home: 404 E Oregon St Urbana IL 61801 Office: Sch Music U Ill Urbana IL 61801

ROLLER, MAC C., physician; b. Ft. Wayne, Ind., Apr. 25, 1935; s. George Franklin and Dortha (Cottrell) R.; student Purdue U., 1953-56; M.D., Ind. U., 1960; m. Velva Ann Roller, Aug. 14, 1959; children—Douglas Alan, Gregory Lee, Brian Christopher. Intern St. Joseph's Hosp., Denver, 1960-61; practice medicine specializing in family practice, Chetek, Wis., 1961-62, Purdue U., 1964-66, Franklin, Ind., 1966—; mem. med. staff Johnson County (Ind.) Meml. Hosp. clin. instr. medicine dept. family practice Ind. U. Med. Center, 1976—. Served with U.S. Army, M.C., 1962-64. Diplomate Am. Bd. Family Practice. Mem. AMA, Ind. Med. Assn., Am. Acad. Family Practice. Contbr. articles to profl. jours. Home: 1260 E Adams St Franklin IN 46131 Office: 1551 N Main St Franklin IN 46131

ROLOFF, LELAND HAROLD, educator; b. San Diego, Aug. 15, 1927; s. Herman H. and Sophie Dietz; children—Peter Jared, Kent Durham. Instr., U. Vt., Grossmont, 1952-57, tchr. pub. schs., Glendale, Calif., 1957-62; asst. prof. Occidental Coll., Los Angeles, 1962-66, So. Methodist U., Dallas, 1966-68; prof. interpretation Northwestern U., Evanston, Ill., 1968—. Pres., bd. dirs. C.G. Jung Inst., Chgo. Served with USN, 1945-46. Author: Perception and Evocation of Literature, 1973. Home: 1745 Orrington St Evanston IL 60201 Office: Northwestern Univ Evanston IL 60201

ROLSTEN, ROBERT FRED, materials mech. engr.; b. Fort Wayne, Ind., Feb. 6, 1925; s. Chalice Lloyd and Nell Jane (Good) R.; B.Sc., Capital U., 1948; Ph.D., Ohio State U., 1955. Research scientist Battelle Meml. Inst., 1950-55, E. I. duPont deNemours & Co., 1955-59; research chemist, head tech. engring. service U.S. Borax Research Corp., 1959; engring. design specialist Gen. Dynamics, 1960-63; asso. prof. sci. dept. Calif. Western U., 1960-64; sect. mgr. Am. Machine & Foundry Co., 1964; sr. staff scientist Tech. Operations Research, Lexington, Mass., 1964-65; pvt. practice as cons., Kettering, O., 1965—; prof. dept. engring. Wright State U., Dayton, O., 1971—, acting chmn., 1974-75, asst. dean Coll. Continuing and Community Edn., 1975-77, asst. dean Coll. Sci. and Engring., 1975—. Served with USAAF, 1943-46. Mem. AAAS, AAUP, Am. Chem. Soc., Am. Geophys. Union, Am. Inst. Aeros. and Astronautics, Am. Ordnance Assn. (life), Chem. Abstracts, Electrochem. Soc., Marine Tech. Soc., Ohio Acad. Scis., Sigma Xi, Phi Lambda Upsilon. Author: Iodide Metals and Metal Iodides, 1961; contbr. articles to profl. jours.; tech. adviser motion picture Overlords; patentee in field. Home: 1436 Adirondack Trial Kettering OH 45409 Office: Coll Sci Engring Wright State U Dayton OH 45431

ROLSTON, RODRICK RIGGS, sociologist; b. Sheldon, Iowa, Aug. 7, 1931; s. William Wendell and Frances Elizabeth (Fitzsimmons) R.; A.B., Manchester Coll., Ind., 1954; M.A., No. Ill. U., 1960; Ph.D., Iowa State U., 1966; m. Wilma Mae Craig, Dec. 30, 1955; children—Raleigh, Ronda. High sch. tchr., Ill., 1958-60; instr. Manchester Coll., 1961-63; asst. prof. sociology Bradley U., Peoria, Ill., 1966-68, U. Wis., Platteville, 1968-73; asso. prof. sociology Ind. U., South Bend, 1973—; program coordinator, bd. dirs. Ind. Council Family Relations; cons. in field. Mem. Am., North Central, Wis. sociol. assns., Midwest Sociol. Soc. (sect. chmn. 1971), Nat. Council Family Relations, Ind. Acad. Social Scis., Common Cause, Alpha Kappa Delta. Mem. Ch. of Brethren. Clubs: Torch, Optimist. Author: The Sociological Vitamin Book, 1975; also articles. Home: 52330 Kenilworth Rd South Bend IN 46637 Office: 1825 Northside Blvd South Bend IN 46615

ROLWING, RAYMOND HUGH, educator; b. Toledo, Mar. 22, 1931; s. E. Merlin and Rose (Marbaugh) R.; B.S., Christian Brothers Coll., Memphis, 1955; M.S., U. Notre Dame, 1958; Ph.D., U. Cin., 1963; m. Nancy J. Pomeroy, Sept. 3, 1956; children—Helen E., Donna J., Marcia Kay, Robert M. Teaching fellow U. Notre Dame, 1955-58; instr. math. Christian Brothers Coll., Memphis, 1958-60, U. Cin., 1960-63, asst. prof. math., 1964-69, asso. prof., 1969—, asst. dean Coll. Arts and Scis.; dir. NSF, In-Service Inst. at U. Cin. for Secondary Tchrs., also Summer and Academic Yr. Insts. NSF Sci. faculty fellow U. Cin., 1963-64. Mem. Am. Math. Soc., Math. Assn. Am. (sec.-treas. Ohio sect. 1973—), Soc. for Indsl. and Applied Math., AAUP, Nat. Council Tchrs. Math., Sigma Xi. Home: 11636 Hollingsworth Way Cincinnati OH 45240

ROLWING, ROBERT EUGENE, constrn. co. exec.; b. Chgo., Nov. 12, 1926; s. Edward Merlin and Rose (Marbaugh) R.; B.S. in Mech. Engring., U. Notre Dame, 1948; m. Judith A. Turk, June 6, 1953; children—Ann, Roberta, Maria, Joan. Project engr. F.H. McGraw & Co., Hartford, Conn., 1951-60; prin. firm D.W. Neville & Assos., Chgo., 1960-62; chief engr., mgr. constrn. Edward Gray Corp., Chgo., 1962—, also v.p. constrn. div., 1971—. Instr. St. Irenaeus Parish Sch. System, Park Forest, Ill., 1969-75. Served with USNR, 1944-45. Mem. Chgo. C. of C., Am. Mgmt. Assn. K.C. Home: 20950 Cambridge Ln Olympia Fields IL 60461 Office: 12233 Ave O Chicago IL 60633

ROMAGER, JIMMIE L., realtor; b. Piper, Ala., Oct. 8, 1939; s. Odis and Ruth (Arnold) R.; student Eastern Ill. U., 1959-61; m. Nancy Galene Cochran, Oct. 2, 1965; children—Stacey Lee, Eric Bayard. Asst. prodn. mgr. A.W. Cash Value Mfg. Co., Decatur, Ill., 1962-65; circulation adviser Decatur Herald & Rev., 1965-69; broker, sales mgr. Tom Brinkoetter & Co., Decatur, 1969—. Mem. Ill. Assn. Realtors, Decatur Bds. Realtors. Elk. Home: 4751 Willowbrook Ln Decatur IL 62521 Office: 1043 E Eldorado St Decatur IL 62521

ROMANO, PAUL EDWARD, ophthalmologist; b. N.Y.C., Oct. 30, 1934; s. Paul Salvatore and Mary Elizabeth (Simms) R.; A.B., Cornell U., 1955, M.D., 1959; M.S. in Ophthalmology, Georgetown U., 1967; m. Judith Ann Robinson, Oct. 18, 1969. Intern, Albany (N.Y.) Med. Center, 1959-60, surg. resident, 1960-61; ophthalmology resident Georgetown U. Hosp., Washington, 1964-67; practice medicine specializing in pediatric ophthalmology, Chgo., 1970—; asst. dir. div. ophthalmology Children's Meml. Hos., 1969-70, dir., 1970—; asst. prof. Northwestern U. Med. Sch., 1969-73, asso. prof., 1973—. Served to capt. AUS, 1961-64. Heed Ophthalmologic fellow, 1968; NIH spl. fellow, 1968-69. Mem. Am. Acad. Ophthalmology and Otolargyngology, Chgo. Ophthal. Soc. (program chmn. 1971-73, Am. Assn. Pediatric Ophthalmology (charter). Contbr. articles to profl. jours. Home: 2116 N Halsted St Chicago IL 60614 Office: 2300 N Children's Pl Chicago IL 60614

ROMBS, VINCENT JOSEPH, accountant, lawyer; b. Newport, Ky., Mar. 8, 1918; s. John Thomas and Mathilda (Fromhold) R.; student Xavier U., 1936-37; B.S. with honor, Southeastern U., 1941; J.D., Loyola U., Chgo., 1952; m. Ruth Burns, Aug. 15, 1942; 1 dau., Ellen (Mrs. James P. Herman). Admitted to Ill. bar, 1952; tax partner with local and nat. pub. accounting firms, Chgo., 1952—; with firm Laventhol & Horwath, Chgo., 1970-75; of counsel Edelman & Rappaport, Chartered, 1975—. Bd. dirs. Miller Found. Served to lt. comdr., USNR, 1941-46. Recipient Scholarship Key award Delta Theta Phi, 1953. C.P.A., Ill. Mem. Am. Inst. C.P.A.'s, Ill. Soc. C.P.A.'s. Home: 1295 Sterling St Palatine IL 60067 Office: 1 N LaSalle St Suite 1714 Chicago IL 60602

ROMERO, JOSEFINO TABERNILLA, artist; b. Tayabas, Quezon, Philippines, Mar. 19, 1939; d. Melanio Romero and Teodorica Talavera (Tabernilla) R.; grad. nurse Quezon Meml. Hosp., 1961; grad. nurse anesthetist Mt. Carmel Hosp., Detroit, 1968. Psychiat. nurse Nat. Mental Hosp., Mandaluyong Rizal, Philippines, 1961-63; operating room nurse St. Vincent Hosp., Worcester, Mass., 1963-64, Michael Reese Hosp., Chgo., 1964-65, Sarnia (Ont., Can.) Gen. Hosp., 1965-66; nurse Quezon Meml. Hosp., Lucena City, Philippines, 1971-72; nurse anesthetist Mt. Carmel Hosp., Detroit, 1972-74; nurse anesthetist Brent Hosp., Detroit, 1974-76; one-man shows include: Ramada Inn, Southfield, Mich., 1975, Romero Art Gallery, 1976; group shows include: Scarab Club Art Show, Troy, Mich., 1975, 77, Keatington Antique Village Art Show, Lake Orion, Mich., 1975. Recipient Merit award Mich. Ann. Art Festival Show, Livonia, 1975; award Cambridge Village Assn., 1976. Mem. Am. Assn. Nurse Anesthetists, Internat. Soc. Artists, Mich. Watercolor Soc., Friends of Paris Am. Acad. Club: Scarab (Detroit). Home and Office: 27360 Lexington Pkwy Southfield MI 48076

ROMESBERG, FLOYD EUGENE, chemist; b. Somerset, Pa., Jan. 31, 1927; s. Ephraim J. and Mayme Susan (Swearman) R.; B.S., Pa. State U., 1949; M.S., Bucknell U., 1950; Ph.D. in Chemistry, U. Cin., 1953; m. Jennied Naomi King, Sept. 19, 1948; children—Beverly Ann, Cynthia Anne, Floyd Eric. With Dow Chem. Co., Midland, Mich. and Granville, Ohio 1953—, tech. dir. films research, 1966-70, films research specialist, 1970—. Active PTA, Boy Scouts Am., Little League. Mem. Toastmasters Internat. Kiwanian. Patentee in field. Home: 18 Wyddfa Ct Route 2 Snowden Estates Granville OH 43023 Office: Dow Chemical Co Granville OH 43023

ROMIG, JAMES LYLE, editor; b. Whittier, Calif., Oct. 19, 1938; s. Lawrence M. and Lois Jane (Morris) R.; A.B., Whittier Coll., 1960; Ed.D., U. So. Calif., 1972; m. Angela Carol LaBella, June 1, 1968; children—Teri Lyn, James Carl, Andrew John, Seth Joseph. Elementary tchr. East Whittier (Calif.) Schs., 1960-61, 64-65; instr. gen. studies Whittier (Calif.) Coll., 1961-64, dir. freshman English, 1967-70, dean of students, 1970-71, asst. prof. edn., 1971-74, asso. prof., 1974-75; editor field rep., asst. to nat. sales mgr. Scott Foresman & Co., Glenview, Ill., 1965-67, exec. editor, 1975—. Mem. Am. Psychol. Assn., Am. Ednl. Research Assn. Office: 1900 E Lake Ave Glenview IL 60025

ROMINE, CHARLES ALVA, govt. ofcl.; b. Ft. Wayne, Ind., July 1, 1927; s. Chalres Everett and Ruby Irene (Griesinger) R.; student Ind. U., 1946-47, DeVrie Inst., 1948; m. Betty Jean Allisbaugh, Sept. 15, 1950; children—Vicky Sue, Gina Marie. Coil winder Phelps Dodge Copper Co., Ft. Wayne, 1945-48; asst. mgr. Standard Lumber & Supply Co., New Haven, Ind., 1949-50; electrician apprentice Internat. Harvester Co., Ft. Wayne, 1949-53; electrician Good Year Atomic Corp., Postsmouth, Ohio, 1953-64; tng. rep. Bur. Apprenticeship and Tng., U.S. Dept. Labor, Battle Creek, Mich., 1964—. Vice pres. Ohio AFL-CIO, 1960-64, pres. local, 1954-60. City councilman Waverly, Ohio, 1958-64; chmn. Pike County Planning Commn., 1960-63; CD dir., Waverly, 1955-57. Served with USNR, 1945-46. Recipient Civil Service Quality award, 1973. Presbyn. (ruling elder 1966-74, commr. gen. assembly Nebr. 1973, presbytery commr. 1974). Home: 534 Sylvan Dr Battle Creek MI 49015 Office: Federal Center Bldg 74 N Washington St Battle Creek MI 49017

ROMINE, ROBERT JOSEPH, JR., educator; b. Independence, Kans., May 9, 1947; s. Robert Joseph and Phyllis Jean (Thomas) R.; A.A., Independence Community Coll., 1967; B.A. cum laude, Emporia (Kans.) State Coll., 1969, M.A. cum laude, 1971, M.S. cum laude, 1975; m. Janet Kay Relph, Jan. 1, 1968. Instr., Pratt (Kans.) Community Coll., 1971—, chmn. div. social scis., 1973—, dir. human services, 1974—. Project dir., program devel. Kans. Com. for Humanities, 1973—, state field humanist, 1975-76; mem. criminal justice adv. commn. Indian Hill Regional Planning Commn., 1972—. Bd. dirs. Community Concert Assn., 1973—, Pratt County Mental Health Inst., 1971—. Mem. Am., Polit. Sci. Assn., Am. Sociol. Assn., Acad. Polit. Sci., Community Coll. Social Sci. Assn., AAUP, Orgn. Am. Historians, Kans. History Tchrs. Assn. (exec. com. 1976—), Pratt Higher Edn. Assn. (pres. 1977—), ACLU, Phi Theta Kappa, Pi Gamma Mu. Home: 902 W 2d St Pratt KS 67124

ROMITO, WALTER RICHARD, furniture mfg. co. exec.; b. Cuyahoga Falls, Ohio, Dec. 5, 1922; s. Leopold S. and Palma M. (Romito) R.; A.B., U. Notre Dame, 1947; m. Dolly May Bell, Oct. 7, 1950; children—Leopold, Stephen, Pamela. With Romito-Donnelly Corp., Ravenna, Ohio, 1947—, pres., 1969—; dir. 1st Nat. Bank

Ravenna, R.D. Seating Co., Inc., Tupelo, Miss.; partner CMR Oil & Gas Co., Spencer, W.Va., 1970—. Served with USNR, 1942-45. Recipient Distinguished Service award Jaycees, 1956. Mem. Italian Am. Soc. (past pres.), VFW. Eagle, K.C. (4 deg.). Home: 416 Woodland St Ravenna OH 44266 Office: 849 Romito St Ravenna OH 44266

ROMMEL, RICHARD EARL, structural engr.; b. Oak Park, Ill., Nov. 15, 1927; s. Carl Martin and Gertrude (Lochmann) R.; B.S. in C.E., Ill. Inst. Tech., 1951; m. Corrine Joyce Will, May 17, 1952; children—Duane, Joyce, Jeffrey. Structural engr. William Schmidt & Assos., structural engrs., Chgo., 1951-66; structural engr. Rittweger & Tokay, Inc., cons. structural engrs., Park Ridge, Ill., 1966—. Served with USN, 1946-48. Mem. ASCE, Am. Concrete Inst., Structural Engrs. Assn. Ill. Lutheran (financial sec. 1965-73). Club: Men's (Park Ridge, Ill.). Home: 625 N Hamlin Park Ridge IL 60068 Office: 1580 N Northwest Hwy Park Ridge IL 60068

ROMNEY, GEORGE, govt. ofcl.; b. Chihuahua, Mexico, July 8, 1907; s. Gaskell and Anna (Pratt) R.; student high sch., jr. coll., U. Utah, 1929, George Washington U., Wash., 1929-30; m. Lenore LaFount, July 2, 1931; children—Lynn (Mrs. Loren G. Keenan), Jane (Mrs. Bruce H. Robinson), Scott, Willard Mitt. Missionary, Scotland and England, 1927-28; tariff specialist for U.S. Senator David I. Walsh, 1929-30; apprentice, Aluminum Co. Am., 1930, salesman, Los Angeles office, 1931, Washington rep. Aluminum Co. Am. and Aluminum Wares Assn., 1932-38; Detroit mgr., Automobile Mfrs. Assn., 1939-41, gen. mgr. assn., 1942-48; v.p. Nash-Kelvinator Corp., 1950-53, exec. v.p., 1953-54, dir., 1953-63; pres., chmn. bd., gen. mgr. Am. Motors Corp., 1954-62; gov. Mich., 1963-69; U.S. sec. HUD, 1969-73; chmn. Nat. Center for Vol. Action, 1974—. U.S. employer del. to Metal Trades Industry Confs., 1946-49; mng. dir. Automotive Council War Prodn., 1942-45; chmn. Citizens for Mich.; mgmt. mem. War Manpower Commn., Labor-Mgmt. Commn., Detroit area, pres. Washington Trade Assn. Execs., 1937-38; pres. Detroit Trade Assn., 1941; dir. Am. Trade Assn. Execs., 1944-47. Mng. dir. Nat. Auto. Golden Jubilee Com., 1946; former dir. NCCJ, United Found., Cranbrook Sch.; past pres. Detroit Stake Ch. Jesus Christ of Latter Day Saints. Clubs: Athletic, Detroit (Detroit); Burning Tree, Bloomfield Hills Country, Nat. Press. Author: The Concerns of A Citizen, 1968. Home: East Valley Rd Bloomfield Hills MI 48013

ROMON, PACIFICO CRUZ, JR., pathologist; b. Manila, Philippines, Feb. 25, 1936; s. Pacifico N. and Adriana G. (Cruz) R.; A.A., Letran Coll., Manila (Philippines), 1953; M.D., U. St. Thomas, Manila, 1958; m. Maria Luisa Buenafe; children—Dilcie Marie, Darryl Anthony. Intern, Jamaica (N.Y.) Hosp., 1959-60, resident in pathology, 1960-64, asso. pathologist, 1964-74; asso. pathologist St. John's Hosp., Queens, N.Y.C., 1966-68; pathologist and dir. labs. Cass County Meml. Hosp., Atlantic, Iowa, 1974—; cons. pathologist Audubon (Iowa) County Meml. Hosp., Manning (Iowa) Gen. Hosp., 1974—; asst. clin. prof. pathology, Sci. Medicine Creighton U., Omaha. Mem. Atlantic C. of C. Diplomate Am. Bd. Pathology. Fellow Coll. Am. Pathologists, Am. Soc. Clin. Pathologists, Internat. Acad. Pathology, Am. Soc. Cytology, Assn. Clin. Scientists. Roman Catholic. Clubs: Rotary. Home: 101 E 21st St Atlantic IA 50022 Office: 1501 E 10th St Atlantic IA 50022

RONEY, PATRICK ATKINS, wine cons.; b. Palo Alto, Calif., Mar. 9, 1956; s. William Patrick and Elizabeth Ann (Atkins) R.; B.S. in Speech, Northwestern U., 1978. Head wine steward Pump Room, Ambassadors Hotels, Chgo., 1976—; cons. Connoisseur Wines, Chgo., 1977—; owner The Wine Cellar, Chgo.; tchr. wine class Northwestern U. Registered head wine steward, London. Mem. Chevalier de la Chaine des Rotisseurs, French, Spanish wine socs. Republican. Roman Catholic. Clubs: Elks. Home: 562 Lincoln St Evanston IL 60201

RONINGEN, JEWEL EDGAR, stockyards exec.; b. Pelican Rapids, Minn., Jan. 15, 1922; s. James Marion and Effie Amanda (Holt) R.; B.S., N.D. State U., 1943; m. Grace Marlyn Carlen, Jan. 16, 1943; 1 son, Bruce Jewel. Instr. vocat. agr., Pelican Rapids, Minn., 1944-45; county extension agt., McIntosh, Minn., 1945-47; dist. supt. U.S. Dept. Agr., Packers & Stockyards Adminstrn., Sioux City, Ia., 1948-58; pres., gen. mgr. Sioux Falls (S.D.) Stockyards Co., 1958-67; pres., gen. mgr. Union Stockyards Co. of Fargo, West Fargo, N.D., 1967—, also dir. Served with USMCR, 1943-44. Recipient Pilot Study Grant, EPA, 1970, Gamma Sigma Delta award, 1966. Mem. Fargo (chmn. N.D. hwy. users conf. 1973—, chmn. N.D. Hwy. Hall of Honor com. 1974—), West Fargo chambers commerce. Lutheran (mem. stewardship com. 1968—). Mason (Shriner), Elk, Rotarian. Home: 213 21st Ave N Fargo ND 58102 Office: Livestock Exchange Bldg West Fargo ND 58078

RONINGEN, ROBERT NOEL, lawyer; b. Duluth, Minn., Aug. 7, 1935; s. Henry Noel and Myrtle Ann (Hendricksen) R.; B.A., U. Minn., 1957, J.D., 1962; m. Margaret Ann Murphy, Dec. 14, 1957; children—Robert Noel, Chris Henry, Jean Linda. Geophysicist, Continental Geophys. Co., Guatemala, 1957-59; admitted to Minn. bar, 1962; asso. firm Martini, Harper and Gustafson, Duluth, 1962-65; individual practice law, Duluth, 1966—; lectr. in field; dir. Lyric Block Devel. Corp. Active Boy Scouts Am. Mem. Minn., St. Louis County bar assns., Nat. Rifle Assn., Minn. Weapons Collectors Assn., Wally Byam Caravan Club Internat., Minn., Nat. Eagle Scout assns., Sons of Norway (v.p., exec. council Lake Superior region 1967—). Republican. Methodist. Home: 155 E Strand Rd Duluth MN 55804 Office: 816 1st Nat Bank Bldg Duluth MN 55802

ROOKS, CHARLES SHELBY, clergyman: b. Beaufort, N.C., Oct. 19, 1924; s. Shelby A. and Maggie (Hawkins) R.; A.B., Va. State Coll., 1949; B.D., Union Theol. Sem., 1953; D.D., Coll. Wooster, 1968; m. Adrienne Martinez, Aug. 7, 1946; children—Laurence Gaylord, Carol Ann. Ordained to ministry United Ch. of Christ, 1953; pastor Shanks Village Ch., Orangeburg, N.Y., 1951-53; pastor Lincoln Meml. Congl. Temple, Washington, 1953-60; asso. dir. Fund for Theol. Edn., Princeton, N.J., 1960-67, exec. dir., 1967—; mem. exec. bd. dept. ministry Nat. Council Chs., 1962—; chmn. bd. Office of Communication, United Ch. of Christ, 1964—, chmn. com. structure Central Atlantic Conf., 1970-72; mem. Union Theol. Sem. Alumni Council, 1968—, Theol. Perspectives Commn. Nat. Com. Black Churchmen; now pres. Chgo. Theol. Sem.; vis. fellow Epis. Theol. Sem. Southwest, Austin, Tex., 1966; lectr. in field. Chmn. planning com. Nat. Consultation Negro in Christian Ministry, 1965. Mem. Princeton Regional Sch. Bd., 1969-70. Bd. dirs., chmn. housing com. Washington Urban League; trustee Bexley Hall Theol. Sem., Colgate Rochester Div. Sch., Lancaster Theol. Sem., Eastern Career Testing Center, Communications Improvement, Inc. Served with U.S. Army, 1943-46; PTO. Recipient Elizabeth Taylor Byrd Fund award for outstanding community service, 1969. Mem. Va. State Coll. Nat. Alumni Assn. (pres. 1966-67), Am. Assn. Theol. Schs. (cons. Black ch. studies 1970-71). Editor: Toward a Better Ministry, 1965. Contbr. articles to religious jours. Address: 5727 University Ave Chicago IL 60637

ROOKS, CHARLES WENDELL, chem. engr.; b. Memphis, Dec. 10, 1945; s. Charles Elkins and Rose Marie (Hargett) R.; B.Ch.E., U. Miss., 1969; M.S., U. Okla., 1971, Ph.D., 1973; m. Dana Jane Collier, Dec. 28, 1971. Research engr. Esso Prodn. Research, Houston. 1968; research engr. Shell Research and Devel. Co., Deer Park, Tex., 1969; cons. engr. Univ. Engrs., Inc., Norman, Okla., 1972-73; sr. research engr. Monsanto Textiles Co., Pensacola, Fla., 1973-74; sr. research engr. Monsanto Polymers and Petrochem. Co., St. Louis, 1975—. NSF grantee, 1969-72. Mem. Am. Inst. Chem. Engrs., S.A.R., Phi Kappa Phi, Tau Beta Pi. Home: 1703 Pensacola Dr St Louis MO 63141 Office: 800 N Lindbergh St St Louis MO 63132

ROONEY, EDWIN ANTHONY, chemist; b. Seneca, Ill., July 12, 1919; s. Michael James and Mary (Kelleher) R.; B.S., DePaul U., 1942; Mus.B., Am. Conservatory Music, 1958. Chemist F.E. Schundler & Co., Joliet, Ill., 1941, 42; with Apco Oil Corp., Chgo., 1945—, lab. dir., 1964—. Mem. Sheffield Neighborhood Assn., Chgo., 1964—; mem. Lincoln Park Conservation Assn., Chgo., 1966—. Served with AUS, 1942-45. Mem. Am. Chem. Soc., ASTM, Am. Indsl. Hygiene Assn., Nat. Paint and Lacquer Assn., Nat. Fedn. Paint Tech., Internat. Soc. Contemporary Music, Holy Name Soc., Phi Beta Epsilon. Roman Catholic. Home: 1248 W Norwood St Chicago IL 60660 Office: 3921 N Ravenswood Ave Chicago IL 60613

ROONEY, GEORGE EUGENE, prosthodontist; b. Joliet, Ill., Sept. 12, 1939; s. George Eugene and Mona Mary (Horn) R.; B.S., Lewis Coll., 1961; D.D.S., Loyola U., 1965; m. Carol Elizabeth Bruns, July 1, 1967. Intern, Hines VA Hosp., 1965-66; resident in prosthodontics Memphis VA Hosp., U. Tenn., 1966-68; staff prosthodontist Hines VA Hosp. (Ill.), 1968, chief dental clinic II, 1968-70, dental internship dir., 1970-73, coordinator dental technician program, 1971-73; asst. chief, dir. dental clinic Wood (Wis.) VA Hosp., 1973-74, chief dental service, 1974—; coordinator dental externship Elmhurst Coll., Triton Coll., 1971-73; mem. staff Milwaukee County Med. Complex; asst. prof. Marquette Dental Sch., Milw., 1973-75, asso. prof., 1975—; coordinator dental programs Milw. Area Tech. Coll., 1975—; instr. U. Tenn. Dental Sch., 1967-68, Loyola Dental Sch., Chgo., 1968-70; asst. prof. Loyola Dental Sch., Chgo., 1970-73; cons. dental tech. bd. Triton Coll., 1970-73. Recipient Certificate of Appreciation, Triton Coll., 1972, performance awards Hines VA Hosp., 1970, Wood VA Hosp., 1974, 77. Fellow Midwest Acad. Prosthodontics (mem. finance com. 1973, chm. local arrangements com. 1977); mem. Am., Wis. (audio visual com. 1977—), Greater Milw. (edn. com. 1977—), Am. Cancer Soc. (profl. com. 1976—), Mil. Surgeons U.S., Am. Prosthetic Soc. (edn. com. 1976), Delta Sigma Delta. Club: Chambord Tennis (Oakbrook, Ill.). Home: 18230 LeChateau Dr Brookfield WI 53005 Office: Wood VA Hosp Wood WI 53193

ROONEY, WILLIAM BOYD, JR., educator, broadcasting exec.; b. Martinsburg, W.Va., June 11, 1934; s. William Boyd and Grace Catherine (Wheeler) R.; A.B., Shepherd Coll., 1955; M.A., U. Nebr., 1957; m. Sandra Jean Reimers, Sept. 1, 1959; children—Catherine, Lisa, Susan. Announcer, Sta. WFTR, Front Royal, Va., 1953, Sta. WEPM-AM-FM, Martinsburg, 1954; grad. asst. U. Nebr., 1955, asst. prof. journalism, 1961-68, asso. prof., 1968-75, prof., 1975—; asst. gen. mgr. ops. Nebr. Ednl. TV Network, Lincoln, 1956—; cons. on TV broadcasting to bus., industry, govt. Served with USAR, 1957. Mem. Nat. Assn. Ednl. Broadcasters. Mem. United Ch. of Christ. Home: 345 Glenhaven Dr Lincoln NE 68505 Office: PO Box 83111 Lincoln NE 68501

ROOS, JAMES PAUL, constrn. co. exec.; b. Dale, Ind., Mar. 30, 1930; s. Raymond Michael ad Magdelene Mary (Gogel) R.; B.S., U. Evansville, 1948-52; M.S., Ind. U., 1960; m. Betty Louise McDaniel, July 8, 1949; children—Michael E., Patricia Lou, Eric Paul, James Scott, Tina Marie. Tchr., coach, Tell City, Ind., 1952-55; tchr., coach, dean boys Washington (Ind.) High Sch., 1955-59; prin. Ireland (Ind.) High Sch., 1959-62; prin., supt. Rockport (Ind.) Schs., 1962-64; gen. mgr. Guy N. Ramsey Co. real estate holding and constrn., Tell City, 1964—; v.p., dir. Ramsey Realty Corp., 1965—; sec., dir. Wesleyan Investment Co., Inc., 1965—. Pres., PTA, 1966-67, ARC, 1966-67. Pres. Tell City Sch. Bd., 1969-70, sec., 1965-70; mem. bd. Tell City Housing Authority, 1973—. Bd. dirs. Ind. Assn. Retarded Children, 1967-70. Mem. C. of C. Democrat. Roman Catholic. Lion, K.C. Home: 502 26th St Tell City IN 47586 Office: PO Box D Tell City IN 47586

ROOT, JOHN O., assn. exec.; b. Flint, Mich., Mar. 10, 1919; s. John C. and Hazel (McEwen) R.; B.S., George Williams Coll., 1946, grad. study group work adminstrn., 1946-48; m. Betty Van Haften, Aug. 3, 1946; children—Jacalyn Mueller, Rebecca Rich, Victoria, John Alan. Phys. dir. Sears YMCA, 1946-48; program dir. Harvey Meml. YMCA, 1948-50, exec. sec., 1950-54; asst. gen. sec. program services YMCA Met. Chgo., 1954-62, asso. gen. sec., 1962, gen. sec., 1963-70, pres., 1970—. Nat. YMCA rep., Exchange Program with USSR, 1962. Chmn. priorities com. Area Manpower Planning Council; adv. bd. Cook County Pub. Aid. Mem. Nat. Bd. YMCA's; exec. com. YMCA Urban Group; trustee, exec. com. George Williams Coll.; mem. advisory bd. City of Chgo. Health Systems. Served to maj. USAAF, 1941-46. Recipient Thomas and Eleanor Wright award Chgo. Commn. Human Relations; award Nat. Com. Prevention Child Abuse; award United Way Am. Clubs: Economic, Metropolitan, Plaza. Home: 155 N Harbor Dr Chicago IL 60601 Office: 19 S LaSalle St Chicago IL 60603

ROOTARE, HILLAR MUIDAR, chemist; b. Tallinn, Estonia, Apr. 26, 1928, came to U.S., 1946, naturalized, 1951; s. Karl Johannes and Karin (Kangas) R.; m. Norene Catherine Kindstrand, June 27, 1959; children—Laura, Paul, Neil, Eva, Lennart, Margrethe. A.A., Jersey City Jr. Coll., 1951; B.S., Wagner Coll., 1952; Ph.D., U. Mich., 1973; grad. Dale Carnegie Course, 1974. Observer, USAF, Japan, 1954-56; chemist, research asso. Bone Char Research Project, Inc., Nat. Bur. Standards, Washington, D.C., 1957-63; dir. Materials Technology Lab., Am. Instrument Co., Silver Spring, Md., 1963-66; NIH trainee, research asst. dept. dental materials Sch. Dentistry, U. Mich., Ann Arbor, 1966-73; dir. tech. research L.D. Caulk Co., Div. Dentsply Internat. Inc., Milford, Del., 1973-75; chmn. research and devel. Micrometrics Instruments Corp., Norcross, Ga.; sr. research asso. dept. dental materials Sch. Dentistry, U. Mich., 1975—; cons. Rootare Assos., Ann Arbor, 1975—. Mem. Internat. Assn. Dental Research, Dental Materials Group, Mineralized Tissue Group, Am. Chem. Soc., Am. Soc. Metals, Fine Particle Soc., Rotalia, Estonian Student Fraternity, Amateur Trapshooting Assn. Author: A Review of Mercury Porosimetry, 1970, Analytical Calorimetry, 1974, 77. Home: 1206 Bydding Rd Ann Arbor MI 48103 Office: Dept Dental Materials Sch Dentistry U Mich Ann Arbor MI 48109

ROOTS, CLIVE GEORGE, zoo exec.; b. Coventry, Eng., Aug. 14, 1935; s. George William and Kathleen Elsie (Waters) R.; came to Can., 1970; certificate in biology Poly. Inst., London, 1958; m. Jean Rosalie Cox, Oct. 1, 1960; children—Helen Lesley, Simon Paul. Free lance animal collector, S.Am., W.I., 1959-60; supt. Emperor Valley Zoo, Trinidad, W.I., 1960-62; gen. curator Dudley (Eng.) Zoo, 1962-66; curator Winged World, Lancashire, Eng., 1966-70; dir. Assiniboine Park Zoo, Winnipeg, Man., Can., 1970—; pres. Design for Zoos Inc., zoo planning cons. Served with Royal Arty., 1954-56. Can. Council grantee, 1973. Mem. Canadian Am. (profl. fellow) assns. Zool. parks and aquariums, Internat. Union Dirs. Zool. Gardens. Anglican. Author books in field, latest being: Exotic Pets, 1972; Animals of the Dark, 1974; Animal Invaders, 1976; research on rare and endangered animals in Can., 1973. Home: 683 Community Row Winnipeg MB R3R 1H8 Canada Office: 2355 Corydon Ave Winnipeg MB R3P 0R5 Canada

ROOZBAZAR, AZIZ, human factors engr.; b. Abadan, Iran, Mar. 23, 1939; s. Saneh and Zainab (Mirtalebi) R.; B.Sc., Abadan Inst. Technology, 1965; M.S., U. So. Calif., 1971; Ph.D., N.C. State U., 1974; m. Nora H. Tehrani, July 28, 1965; children—Tommy, Emily. Sr. engr., Nat. Iranian Oil Co., Abadan, 1965-70; asst. prof. indsl. engring. Wichita State U., 1974—. EPA trainee, 1972; Nat. Inst. Occupational Safety trainee, 1972-74. Mem. Am. Inst. Indsl. Engrs. (sr.), Am. Indsl. Hygiene Assn., Human Factors Soc., Am. Soc. Safety Engrs. Contbr. articles to profl. jours. Home: 1826 Farmstead St Wichita KS 67208 Office: Dept Industrial Engineering Wichita State Univ Wichita KS 67208

ROPER, DAVID JAMES, realtor; b. Globe, Ariz., Jan. 13, 1947; s. Robert George and Loismarie (Brewer) R.; student (scholar) U. Minn., 1965-68; m. Carol Jean Meyer, Mar. 21, 1975; children—Jeffry M., Todd M. Sales staff L.F. Bowman Realty, Duluth, Minn., 1969-71; v.p. Apollo Realty, Inc., Duluth, 1971—; mem. profl. standards com. Duluth Bd. Realtors. Mem. Nat. (Certified Comml. Investment Mem. candidate), Minn., Duluth realtors assns., Sertoma Club of Duluth (v.p.). Home: 417 Aspen Ln Duluth MN 55804 Office: 400 Sellwood Bldg Duluth MN 55802

ROPER, LAROY RAYMOND, JR., oil and auto parts distbg. co. exec.; b. Cape Girardeau, Mo., Jan. 15, 1943; s. LaRoy Raymond and Lucy Leone (Lovell) R.; B.A., Westminster Coll., Fulton, Mo., 1964; m. Susam K. Campbell, Aug. 23, 1964; children—Reagan Sue, Shannon Campbell, Rachel Avis, La Roy Raymond. Vice-pres. United Oil Co., Cape Girardeau, Mo., 1964—; chief exec. officer Horton Sales Co., Cape Girardeau, 1972—; dir. Fleetwood Tire & Rubber Co., Heritage Savs. & Loan Assn. Pres. SE Mo. Dist. Fair, 1976; adviser SBA St. Louis Dist., 1976-77; chmn. spl. gifts div. local Am. Cancer Soc., 1977; fund raising chmn. Otahkd council Girl Scouts U.S., 1977—; bd. dirs. Greater Cape Girardeau Devel. Corp. Named outstanding young man Mo., 1977; recipient distinguished service award Mo. Jaycees, 1977. Mem. Cape Jaycees (v.p. 1964—), Nat. Tire Dealers Assn., Automotive Service Industries Am., Automotive Wholesalers Mo., Nat. Fedn. Ind. Businessmen. Presbyterian. Clubs: Rotary (pres. Cape West 1977-78), Masons, Shriners. Home: 2521 Allendale St Cape Girardeau MO 63701 Office: United Oil Co 101 N Kingshwy Cape Girardeau MO 63701

ROPER, RAYMOND WARREN, JR., assn. exec.; b. Springfield, Mo., Apr. 26, 1940; s. Raymond Warren and Mary (Hacker) R.; B.A. cum laude, Benedictine Coll., 1961; m. Judith Ann Haynes, Jan. 5, 1963; children—Mark Christopher, Sean Gregory, Douglas Warren. Personnel officer Frisco Ry., Springfield, Mo., 1965-69; dept. dir. U.S. Jaycees, Tulsa, 1969-72, exec. v.p., 1972-74; exec. v.p. Mo. Assn. Realtors, Columbia, 1974—. Commr. Springfield (Mo.) Human Rights Commn., 1969; mem. Mo. Task Force on Med. Malpractice Ins., 1975. Trustee, sec.-treas. U.S. Jaycees War Meml. Fund, 1972-74; trustee U.S. Jaycees Found., 1972-74. Served with AUS, 1963. Certified assn. exec. Mem. Am. Soc. Assn. Execs., Mo. Soc. Assn. Execs., Mo. Assn. Realtors, Nat. Assn. Realtors. Clubs: Columbia Country, Rotary. Home: 2216 Ridgefield Rd Columbia MO 65201 Office: PO Box 1327 Columbia MO 65201

ROPER, WILLIAM ZACHARIAS, orthodontist; b. New Orleans, Feb. 2, 1937; s. Irven Moore and Isabella Louise (Vath) R.; student Loyola U. of South, New Orleans, 1955-57, D.D.S., 1961; postgrad. Ind. U., 1966-68; m. Elaine Teresa Fuelling, Aug. 22, 1959; children—William Michael, Loraine Therese, Gerald James, Gregory Paul. Pvt. practice orthodontics, Marion, Ind., 1968—; instr. orthodontics Ind. U., 1968-69. Precinct vice-committeeman Washington Twp., Republican Com., 1968-74, precinct Committeeman, 1974—. Served to lt. comdr., Dental Corps, USNR, 1961-66. Mem. Am. Assn. Orthodontists, ADA, Great Lakes Soc. Orthodontists, Ind. Soc. Orthodontists, Ind. Dental Assn. (long range planning com. 1974—, dental law com. 1975—), Wabash Valley (pres. 1972-73), Grant County (pres. 1969-70) dental socs., Found. Orthodontic Research, C. Victor Vignes Odontological Soc., Psi Omega, Blue Key. Republican. Roman Catholic. Home: 2610 E Bocock Rd Marion IN 46952 Office: 1102 N Wabash Ave Marion IN 46952

ROPPEL, RICHARD MEREDITH, biophysicist; b. Williamsport, Penn., Jan. 15, 1929; s. Albert Carl and Susan Isabelle (Meredith) R.; B.A. in Physics, Lehigh U., 1951; Ph.D. in Biophysics, Yale U., 1959; m. Lola Burkowsky, Oct. 1, 1950; children—Thaddeus, Meredith Roppel Henry. Sr. research scientist Battelle Meml. Inst. Columbus, Ohio, 1960-66; research biophysicist USDA Savannah, Ga., 1966-71; research asso., mem. grad. faculty U. Ga., 1969-71; mem. faculty Mich. State U., 1973—. Served with U.S. Army Air Force, 1945-46. Decorated Purple Heart. Fellow Am. Cancer Soc., mem. Am. Assn. Advanced Sci., Biophysical Soc., N.Y. Acad. Sci., Georgia Acad. Sci., Entomological Soc. Am. Contbr. numerous articles in field to profl. jours. Patentee in field. Home: 2248 Kent St Okemos MI 48864 Office: Biomechanics dept Michigan State Univ East Lansing MI 48824

RORIG, KURT JOACHIM, chemist; b. Bremerhaven, Germany, Dec. 1, 1920; s. Robert Herman and Martha (Grundke) R.; came to U.S., 1924; naturalized, 1929; B.S., U. Chgo., 1942; M.A., Carleton Coll.; Ph.D., U. Wis., 1947; m. Helen Yonan, Mar. 20, 1949; children—James, Elizabeth, Miriam. Lectr. Loyola U. Chgo., 1950-62; chemist to asso. dir. Chem. Research G.D. Searle & Co., Chgo., 1947—. Mem. Sch. Bd., Wilmette, Ill., 1969-71. Mem. Am. Chem. Soc. (dir. Chgo. sect.), N.Y. Acad. Sciences, AAAS, Chgo. Chemists Club (past pres.). Presbyterian. Patentee in field. Home: 337 Hager Ln Glenview IL 60025 Office: G D Searle & Co PO Box 5110 Chicago IL 60680

ROSCOE, WAYNE LYNN, chem. co. exec.; b. St. Louis, Nov. 28, 1924; s. Valjean Whitney and Olivia Wilma (Appel) R.; A.B., Washington U., St. Louis, 1948; m. Elvira Lorraine Herzlik, Oct. 23, 1948; children—Cheryl L. (Mrs. Kenneth Eugene Komor), Terry L. Analytical and research chemist Mallinckrodt Co., St. Louis, 1948-51, order expediter, clerical supr., 1951-55, supr. inventory control, 1956-69; process engr. Lewis-Howe, St. Louis, 1969-70, mgr. phys. distbn. services, 1970—. Loaned exec., solicitor United Fund, 1956—. Served with AUS, 1943-46. Mem. Internat. Material Mgmt. Soc. (v.p. St. Louis chpt. 1974), St. Louis Traffic Club, United Shippers and Asso. Shippers, Archway Shippers Assn. (v.p., dir.), Nat. Small Shipments Traffic Conf. (mem. exec. com., treas.). Methodist. Mason. Home: 11225 Mimosa Ln St Louis MO 63126 Office: 319 S 4th St St Louis MO 63102

ROSDAIL, JAMES RUSSELL, veterinarian; b. Norway, Iowa, Apr. 13, 1917; s. LeRoy and Mabel Olena (Olson) R.; m. Mildred Annetta Cruzen, July 3, 1948; children—Jay, Gail, Jan, Joy, Leanne, Tom, Jon. Pvt. practice vet. medicine specializing in large animals, Pomeroy, Iowa, 1951—. Mem. Iowa State Bd. Med. Examiners, 1969-75, chmn., 1970-71; mem. Nat. Bd. Examiners in Vet. Medicine, 1972—; mem. Ednl. Commn. for Fgn. Vet. Grads., 1971—. Mem. Pomeroy Town Council, 1955-57; mem. Pomeroy Community Sch. Bd. Edn.,

1961-64; mem. Calhoun County Bd. Edn., 1965-71, 74-75. Bd. dirs. Iowa Vet. Med. Assn. Found., 1963-71, pres., 1965-71. Served to capt. AUS, 1942-46. Decorated Bronze Star medal; recipient Stange award for meritorious service Iowa State U., 1971. Mem. Iowa Vet. Med. Assn. (exec. bd. 1957-75, v.p., 1971, pres. elect 1972, pres. 1973; Veterinarian of Year award 1976), Assn. Am. State Bds. Examiners in Vet. Medicine (v.p. 1970, pres. 1971), Am. Vet. Med. Assn. Republican. Lutheran (congregation pres. 1969-73). Club: Met. Dinner of Greater Fort Dodge (gov. 1975—, pres. 1976). Address: Pomeroy IA 50575

ROSE, ALLAN, owner greeting card co.; b. Chgo., Aug. 12, 1934; s. Nathan and Rose (Zfaney) R.; B.S., Northwestern U., 1955. Exec. supr. George S. May Internat., bus. cons., Chgo., 1960-62; owner, mgr. Custom Card Co., Chgo., 1962—; owner, mgr. Buss Bros., greeting cards, Chgo., 1967—, Am. Greeting Card Co., 1967—, Custom Craft Greetings, 1970—. Cook County regional dir. Ill. Young Democrats, 1959-61. Mem. Chgo. Council Fgn. Relations, Am. Mktg. Assn., Chgo. Assn. Commerce and Industry, Jewish Fedn. Chgo., Northwestern U. Alumni. Home: 6236 N Richmond St Chicago IL 60659 Office: 2054 W Irving Park Rd Chicago IL 60618

ROSE, BETTY ANN, environ. engring. corp. exec.; b. Kenosha, Wis., May 17, 1934; d. Albert and Emily Albertine (Johnson) Rose; B.S. (Kemper K. Knapp scholar), U. Wis., 1955; postgrad. Northwestern U., 1959, Ind. U., 1961. Tchr., Luxemburg (Wis.) High Sch., 1955-57; tchr., pub. relations dir. Ela-Vernon High Sch., Lake Zurich, Ill., 1957-63; Mid-west advt. mgr. Harcourt, Brace & World, Inc., Chgo., 1963-64; asst. editor Reuben H. Donnelley Corp., Chgo., 1964-68; presentation editor Scranton Pub. Co., Inc., Chgo., 1968-70; asst. to pres. Curnham & Assos., Inc., Chgo., 1970—, asst. sec.-treas., 1972—; asst. sec. Peter F. Loftus Corp. (Ill.), 1975—. Mem. Central States Water Pollution Control Assn. (Select Soc. Sludge Shovelers), Chgo. Indsl. Water, Waste and Sewage Group (chmn. 1974-76), Am. Inst. Chem. Engrs., Soc. Women Engrs., Water Pollution Control Fedn., Constrn. Writers Assn. (dir.), Sigma Epsilon Sigma, Phi Kappa Phi. Co-author chpt. in handbook, 1976. Contbr. articles on pollution control to profl. jours. Office: 223 W Jackson St Chicago IL 60606

ROSE, BEVERLY JEAN, wildlife biologist; b. Sedalia, Mo., Mar. 21, 1929; s. John Adam and Irma Leota (Love) R.; B.S., U. Mo., Columbia, 1952; M.S., Mont. State U., 1956; m. Sharon Kay Blair, Dec. 19, 1977; children by previous marriage—Alan Duane, Douglas Lloyd, Roger Adam. Dist. game biologist Mont. Fish and Game Dept., Miles City, 1956-58, dist. info. and edn. specialist, Missoula, 1959-61; dist. game mgr. S.D. Dept. Game, Fish, and Parks, Aberdeen, 1958-59, dist. game mgr., 1966, asst. chief game mgmt., Rapid City, 1967-70, staff game specialist, Pierre, 1970-75; regional dir. Ducks Unltd., Inc., 1975—; waterfowl biologist Nat. Wildlife Fedn., Bismarck, N.D., 1961-66. Served to 1st lt., AUS, 1952-54. Decorated Silver Star. Mem. S.D. Ornithologists Union (dir.), Bismarck (pres. 1963-65), Black Hills (pres. 1968-70) Audubon socs., Wildlife Soc. (dir. S.D. chpt. 1971-73), Am. Birding Assn. (life), VFW (life), Am. Legion, Phi Sigma. Methodist. Contbr. photographs and articles to profl. publs. Address: Box 127 Boys Town NE 68010

ROSE, CHARLES WILLIAM, educator; b. Columbus, Ohio, May 20, 1940; s. Gordon Snyder and Wilma Louise (Cutshall) R.; B.S. in Elec. Engring. magna cum laude, Duke U., 1962, M.S. (James B. Duke fellow), 1963; Ph.D., Case Western Res. U., 1970; m. Mary Sue Skaggs, June 22, 1963; children—Mary Elizabeth, David Douglas. Sr. engr. Tex. Instruments, Inc., Dallas, 1963-70; asst. prof. info. scis. and engring. Case Western Res. U., Cleve., 1970-73, asso. prof., 1973—. Mem. faculty Nat. Engring. Consortium, 1973—; cons. to U.S. Govt. and industry. Mem. Assn. Computer Machinery (chmn. group on design automation 1975-77), IEEE, Phi Beta Kappa, Omicron Delta Kappa, Tau Beta Pi, Sigma Pi Sigma, Eta Kappa Nu, Pi Mu Epsilon, Sigma Nu. Presbyn. Contbr. articles to profl. lit. Home: 3796 Montevista Rd Cleveland Heights OH 44121

ROSE, ERNST, dentist; b. Oldenburg, Germany, July 22, 1932; s. William and Elsie (Lowenbach) R.; came to U.S., 1940, naturalized, 1946; B.S., Georgetown U., 1955; D.D.S., Western Res. U., 1963; m. Shirley Mae Glassman, Dec. 24, 1960; children—Ruth Ellen, Michele Ann, Daniel Scott, Seth Joseph. Intern, Waterbury (Conn.) Hosp., 1964; pvt. practice dentistry, Hubbard, Ohio, 1964—; pres., treas. Dr. Ernst Rose, Inc. Lab. instr. Ohio State U., Columbus, 1956-57; dental adviser Asso. Neighborhood Center. Mem. Liberty Twp. Zoning Commn., 1967-74; chmn., 1970-74; chmn. Hubbard (Ohio) Urban Renewal Com., 1968-74. Served with AUS, 1957-59. Fellow Royal Soc. Health; mem. Chgo. Dental Soc., Am., Ohio dental assns., Corydon Palmer Dental Soc., Warren Dental Soc., Hubbard C. of C. (dir. 1973—), Jewish Chatauqua Soc. (life), Alpha Omega (council mem. 1968—, sec. 1970-71, v.p. 1971-72, pres. 1972-73). Jewish (mem. brotherhood bd. 1967—, treas. 1971-73, pres. 1975-77, temple bd. dirs. 1975—). Mem. B'nai B'rith (pres. 1970-71, trustee 1971—), Rotarian. Home: 418 Arbor Circle Youngstown OH 44505 Office: 30 N Main St Hubbard OH 44425

ROSE, FREDERICK ALBERT, physician; b. Erie, Pa., Aug. 6, 1912; s. Albert Eugene and Henrietta Sophia (Hornaman) R.; A.B., Western Res. U., 1933, M.D., 1936; m. Mary Elizabeth Sutherland, June 16, 1941; children—Elizabeth Ann, Douglas Frederick, Chester Malcolm. Intern, Hosp. U. Pa., 1936-38; resident in internal medicine Univ. Hosps., Cleve., 1938-41, radiology, 1947-50; asso. radiologist Univ. Hosps., Cleve. 1950—, dir. diagnostic radiology, 1957—; prof. radiology Case Western Res. U., 1976—. Served to maj. AUS, 1941-46. Fellow Am. Coll. Radiology; mem. Am. Roentgen Ray Soc., Radiol. Soc. N.Am., AAAS. Republican. Home: 16233 Cleviden Rd E Cleveland OH 44112 Office: 2065 Adelbert Rd Cleveland OH 44106

ROSE, HUGH LEE, clearing house exec.; b. Wurtland, Ky., June 7, 1944; s. Clarence Edwin and Edna Mae (Savage) R.; B.S., DePaul U., 1971, M.B.A., 1976; m. Sandra June Maniatis, Oct. 24, 1970; children—Nicole Elizabeth, James Edwin. Plant controller Allied Chem. Corp., Chgo., 1966-70; sr. staff accountant Chemplex Co., Rolling Meadows, Ill., 1970-72; tax accountant Interlake, Inc., Chgo., 1972-73; controller Real Estate Devel. & Constrn. Co., Joliet, Ill., 1973-74; v.p., treas. Options Clearing Corp., Chgo., 1974—. Mem. Financial Execs. Inst., Am. Mgmt. Assn., Assn. M.B.A. Execs., Sigma Alpha Epsilon. Home: 10151 S 84th Ave Palos Hills IL 60465 Office: 233 S Wacker Dr Chicago IL 60606

ROSE, KENNETH DWIGHT, physician; b. Hastings, Nebr., Sept. 8, 1912; s. Ralph A. and Iva (Snyder) R.; B.A., U. Nebr., 1941, M.A., 1943, M.D., 1947; m. Margaret Ellen McMaster, June 13, 1943; children—Beth Marie (Mrs. Robert Dwyer), Susan Kay (Mrs. Victor Kuklin), Douglas Kenneth, Priscilla Margaret (Mrs. Barry Cross), James Allen, John Steven, Mary Elizabeth. Instr. bacteriology U. Nebr., Lincoln, 1943, research asst. Coll. Medicine, 1943-47, clinician, dir. div. med. research Health Service, 1959-73, dir. Phys. Fitness Research Lab., 1970-73, cons. physician, 1973—; intern Cin. Gen. Hosp., 1947-48; gen. practice medicine, Lincoln, 1948-59; mem. attending staff Bryan Meml. Hosp., staff physician emergency medicine, 1973—; mem. courtesy staff Lincoln Gen. Hosp. Served with M.C., AUS, 1943-46; to capt., M.C., AUS, 1954-56. Recipient Service citation USMC, Quantico, Va., 1969, Phys. Fitness Leadership award Nat. Jr. C. of C., 1971. Fellow Am. Coll. Sports Medicine (recipient Distinguished Service citation 1967, trustee 1969-73); mem. AMA (chmn. com. exercise and phys. fitness 1965-72), Am. Coll. Health Assn. (chmn. research adv. com.), Am. Acad. Family Practice, Nebr., Lancaster County med. socs., Nebr. Heart Assn., Nat. Athletic Trainers Assn. (hon.), Am. Orthopedic Soc. for Sports Medicine (hon.), Phi Beta Kappa, Sigma Xi, Phi Lambda Upsilon, Alpha Omega Alpha. Author: (with Jack Dies Martin) The Lazy Man's Guide to Physical Fitness, 1974. Editorial bd. The Physician and Sports Medicine. Contbr. articles to med. jours. Home: RFD 8 Lincoln NE 68506 Office: Bryan Meml Hosp Lincoln NE 68510

ROSE, KURT RAINER, gas co. exec.; b. Vienna, Austria, July 26, 1931; s. Otto and Caroline (Deininger) R.; B.S., Case Western Reserve U., 1953; m. Carol Thut, July 19, 1952; children—Susan A., Thomas A., Frederick S. Came to U.S., 1939, naturalized, 1944. Welding engr. Lincoln Electric Co., Cleve., 1953-58; supt., Ryan Industries, 1958-62; plant mgr. Struthers Wells Corp., Titusville, Pa., 1962-63; asst. to pres. Patterson Industries, Cleve., 1963-65; v.p. operations Burdett Oxygen Co., Cleve., 1965—. Mem. Case Alumni Council. Office: 3300 Lakeside Ave Cleveland OH 44114

ROSE, LEONARD GEORGE, credit agy. exec.; b. Highland Park, Mich., Mar. 6, 1927; s. Frank S. and Gladys (Piper) R.; B.A., Wayne State U., 1949; m. Rosemary M. Macaulay, Aug. 23, 1952; children—Martha L., Sheila E., Suzanne E. Exec. v.p. Creditors Service, Inc., Detroit, 1955-68; pres., chief exec. officer Nat. Account Systems, Inc. subsidiary Diners Club, Chgo., 1968—. Accredited instr. Am. Collectors Assn. Pres. Green Lake Village, Mich., 1964-68; mem. planning commn., W. Bloomfield Twp., Mich., 1966-67. Served with USNR, 1944-46, 50-52. Named Pres. of Year Am. Collectors Assn., 1961-62; recipient Outstanding Achievement award Mich. Assn. Credit Agys., 1968. Mem. Am. Collectors Assn. (pres.), Am. Inst. Mgmt. (pres.'s council 1969-70). Roman Catholic. Clubs: Lake Forest (Ill.); Executives, Metropolitan (Chgo.); Racquet (Libertyville, Ill.). Contbr. articles to newspapers, trade jours.; numerous radio and tv. appearances on use of credit. Home: 150 W Onwentsia Lake Forest IL 60045 Office: 53 W Jackson St Chicago IL 60604

ROSE, MERRITT DEVON, publisher, author; b. Lebanon, Ind., May 19, 1923; s. Don Carl and Minnie Myrtle (Airhardt) R.; B.A., Canterbury Coll., Danville, Ind., 1951; postgrad. U. Montreal (Can.), 1951. Author, contbr. to poetry mags., to 1959; advt. mgr. Monroe County Appeal, Paris, Mo., 1959-63; mem. staff Pampa (Tex.) Daily News, 1963-64; nat. advt. mgr. Nat. Jewish Post Opinion, 1965-66; advt. mgr. Community Press, Inc., Carmel, Ind., 1965-66, treas., owner, 1966-69; owner, pub. Hoosier Graphic, Thorntown, Ind., 1969—. Democrat. Home and office: Route 2 Box 163 Jamestown IN 46147

ROSE, ROBERT EMBREE, physician; b. Cleve., Sept. 10, 1925; s. Embree Rector and Effie Mae (Gordon) R.; A.B., Ind. U., 1949, M.D., 1952; m. Renee Andree Arnoux, Oct. 31, 1969; children—Robert Embree, Dennis John. Intern, St. Joseph's Hosp., Reading, Pa., 1952-53; resident Sacred Heart Hosp., Norristown, Pa., 1953-54; practice medicine specializing in gen. medicine, Norristown, 1954-68, Spencer, Ind., 1970—; physician Variety Club, Phila., 1955-67; physician in charge St. Gabriel's Hosp., Phoenixville, Pa., 1955-58; med. dir. Breckinridge Job Corp Center, Morganfield, Ky., 1968; student health physician Ind. U., Bloomington, 1968-69; mem. staffs Bloomington Hosp., Ind.; health officer Owen County, 1976—. Served with AUS, 1943-46. Mem. Aerospace Med. Assn., Civil Aviation Med. Assn., Flying Physicians Assn., Owen-Monroe County Med. Soc. Home: Rural Route 3 Spencer IN 47460 Office: 792 E Morgan St Spencer IN 47460

ROSE, STANLEY JAY, newspaper exec.; b. Kansas City, Mo., June 3, 1918; s. Joseph and Mae (Lund) R.; A.A., Los Angeles City Coll., 1939; B.J., U. Mo., 1941; m. Shirley Mallin, Oct. 7, 1942; children—Roberta Susan (Mrs. Stephen Q. Small), Stephen F. Chmn. bd., pub. Sun Publs., Inc., Overland Park, Kans., 1950—; pub. Kansas City (Mo.) Jewish Chronicle, Inc., 1964—. Bd. dirs. Kaw Valley Heart Assn., Kans. Assn. Commerce and Industry, Heart of Am. council Boy Scouts Am. Served to lt. (j.g.) USNR, World War II; PTO. Recipient Sweepstakes, 1st Pl. awards Kans. Better Newspaper Contest, 1968, 69, 70, 72, 73, William Allen White News Enterprise award, 1975; named hon. col. Ky. cav. Mem. Overland Park C. of C. (dir.), Sigma Delta Chi. Mason (Shriner), Rotarian. Clubs: Kansas City (Mo.) Press; Optimist (Prairie Village, Kans.). Home: 7 Navajo Ln W Lake Quivira KS 66106 Office: Sun Publs Bldg Overland Park KS 66212

ROSE, WILLIAM, bus. service co. exec.; b. Waukegan, Ill., Nov. 7, 1919; s. Louis and Bertha (Rose) R.; student pub. schs.; m. Vivian May Gulledge, July 15, 1951; children—Whyland, Calvin, Marcia. Pres., Jobs, Inc., Waukegan, 1951—, dir., 1951—. Mem. adv. com. Bus. Edn. Dept. N. Chicago Community High Sch., 1963-64, Graphic Arts Dept. Waukegan High Sch., 1963-71, Career Program Devel. Coll. Lake County, 1968-75; mem. Lake County Mental Health Adv. Com., 1971—. Justice of peace, Lake County, Ill., 1957-61, police magistrate, 1959-61; mem. Shields Twp. Bd. Auditors, 1957-61. Fin. chmn. Boy Scouts Am., 1959-60, bd. dirs., 1966-71; bd. dirs. Lake County Mental Health Clinic, 1957-68, United Community Services, 1964-71, Lake County Crime Commn., 1969-75; bd. dirs., v.p. Lake County Welfare Council, 1963. Served with Signal Corps, AUS, 1944-46. Mem. Ind. Office Services Inst. (pres. 1971-73), Nat. Assn. Temporary Services (dir. 1975—), Am. Legion (comdr. 1951) Lake County Mental Health Soc. (pres. 1961), Waukegan-North Chicago C. of C. (dir. 1968-74, pres. 1973. Jewish (treas. congregation 1968-74, pres. 1976). Mem. B'nai B'rith. Clubs: Waukegan Exchange (pres. 1963-64), North Shore Craftsman (pres. 1965). Home: 2439 Dunlay Ct Waukegan IL 60085 Office: 1534 Washington St Waukegan IL 60085

ROSEMOND, JOHN HENRY, physician; b. Jacksonville, Fla., Oct. 17, 1917; s. John Henry and Ida Bell (Taylor) R.; B.S., Fla. A. and M. U., 1941; M.D., Howard U., 1951; m. Rosalie Edge, Mar. 15, 1943; children—John Henry, Janith Sheryl, Ronald Elliot. Tchr. math. and sci. pub. schs., Winterhaven, Fla., 1941-42; chemist U.S. Govt., Chattanooga, 1942-43; intern D.C. Gen Hosp., 1951-52; civilian physician U.S. Army, Fort Belvoir, Va., 1952-53; practice medicine specializing in family practice, Columbus, Ohio, 1953—; mem. staffs Grant Hosp., Mt. Carmel Hosp., Ohio State U. Hosp., St. Anthony Hosp., Children's Hosp., all Columbus. Councilman, City of Columbus, 1970—; nominee for mayor City of Columbus, 1975. Trustee, Columbus Tech. Inst., chmn. 1969-71. Served to 1st lt. USAAF, 1943-46. Named Practitioner of Year, Nat. Med. Assn., 1970, Omega Man of Year Omega Psi Phi, 1970. Mem. Am., Ohio, Columbus med. assns., Am., Ohio (Family Physician of Year 1974), Central Ohio acads. family practice, Council Community Coll. Bds. (steering com. 1970), Nat. Sch. Bds. Assn., Columbus C. of C. (development com. 1960), Sigma Pi Phi. Democrat. Presbyterian (elder 1964—). Home: 3300 E Livingston Ave Columbus OH 43227 Office: 1314 Mount Vernon Ave Columbus OH 43203

ROSEN, CARL LEONARD, psychotherapist, Reiki healer; b. Mpls., June 9, 1930; s. Leonard Carl and Esther Matilda (Anderson) R.; B.A., St. John's U., 1954; postgrad. St. John's Sem., 1954-58; M.S., St. Cloud State U., 1972; postgrad. Moorhead State U., 1969-70, U. San Francisco, 1968, U. Minn., 1969, U. New Mex., 1971; m. Natalie Ann Fish; children—Michael, Patrick, Edward, Joy. Mem. St. John's Abbey, Gollegeville, Minn., 1951-70; ordained priest, Roman Catholic Ch., 1958; asst. pastor St. Boniface Ch., Mpls., 1958-61; St. Bernard's Ch., St. Paul, 1961-63; Sts. Peter & Paul Ch., Richmond, Minn., 1963-65; dir. religious edn. St. Boniface High Sch., Cold Spring, Minn., 1965-68; dir. Newman Center Moorhead State U., 1968-70; asst. dir. fin. aids St. Cloud State U., 1972-73; adminstr. fin. aids Minn. Higher Edn. Coordinating Bd., St. Paul, 1973-76; dir. Carl's House, St. Paul, 1974—; instr. continuing edn. Coll. St. Francis, St. Paul, 1976—; cons. St. Cloud Sch. Nursing, 1972. Mem. Am., Minn. personnel and guidance assns., Am. Rehab. Assn. Democratic Farm Labor. Author: Since I Think, I Exist, 1975; Persons, 1976. Home: 1949 Ebertz Ct St Paul MN 55119

ROSEN, GEORGE, economist, educator; b. Leningrad, USSR, Feb. 7, 1920; s. Leon and Rebecca (Rosenoer) R.; B.A., Bklyn. Coll., 1940; M.A., Princeton U., 1942, PH.D., 1950; m. Kusum Parekh, Aug. 11, 1956; 1 son, Mark. Prof. econs. Bard Coll., Annadale-on-Hudson, N.Y., 1946-50; economist Dept. State, Washington, 1951-54, Council Econ. Indsl. Research, Washington, 1954-55, Mass. Inst. Tech., Cambridge, 1955-59, UN, N.Y.C., 1959-60, Ford Found., N.Y.C., India, 1960-62, Rand Corp., Santa Monica, Calif., 1962-67; chief economist Asian Devel. Bank, Manila, Philippines, 1967-71; prof. econs. U. Ill., Chgo., 1972—, head dept., 1972-77. Ford Found. fellow N.Y. U., 1971-72. Author: Industrial Change in India, 1958; Some Aspects of Industrial Finance in India, 1962; Democracy and Economic Change in India, 1966, 67; Peasant Society in a Changing Economy, 1975. Home: 1400 Chicago Ave Evanston IL 60201 Office: Univ Illinois PO Box 4348 Chicago IL 60680

ROSEN, RONALD HAIAM, educator; b. Cleve., June 13, 1933; s. Nathan Abraham and Celia Shana (Narotsky) R.; student Cleve. Music Sch. Settlement, 1951, B.A., Western Res. U., 1955; M.A., U. Wis., 1957, Ph.D., 1959. Instr., U. Mich., Ann Arbor, 1959-61, asst. prof., 1961-66, asso. prof. math., 1966—. Office Naval Research asso. Columbia, 1962-63; NSF fellow, mem. Inst. for Advanced Study, 1963-64. Mem. Am. Math. Soc., U.S. Chess Fedn., Nat. Wildlife Fedn., Phi Beta Kappa. Cons., reviewer Math. Revs., Ann Arbor, also ZentralBlatt fur Mathematik, W.Berlin, 1963—; contbr. articles to profl. jours.; chess journalist, 1950-74. Home: 1050 Wall St Ann Arbor MI 48105

ROSEN, SAMUEL MORRIS, chem. co. exec.; b. N.Y.C., July 24, 1919; s. Abraham and Sadie (Sominsky) R.; student arts, scis., and sch. law St. Johns U., Bklyn., 1936-42; m. Maxine Schwartz, Jan. 25, 1962; children (from previous marriage)—Myrna, Neill, Jay; stepchildren—Laura Belcove, Wendy Belcove. Salesman, Bell Sewing Machine Co., 1946-47; sales mgr. Belle Electronic Corp., 1947-51; sales mgr. eastern region S & W. Fine Foods, 1951-56; salesman Eastern Paint Concern, 1956-58; pres., chmn. bd. Nucleonics Internat., Inc., Astratek Internat. Ltd. and following divs. Alco-Flex, Astrachem Polymer, Hydralum Industries, Process Chems., Protective Coatings Unltd., Silmica, Spramor, Terrastan Seamless Surfaces, Uniques, Chgo., 1958—; chmn. bd., pres. Moly Protech. Corp. Active City of Hope, Chgo. Boys Club, United Jewish Appeal. Served with AUS, 1942-45. Named One of 10 Best Dressed Men in World, 1968. Mem. Better Bus. Burs., U.S. C. of C., Chgo. Assn. Commerce and Industry, Ill. Mfrs. Assn., Am. Legion, V.F.W. K.P. Patentee in field. Home: 403 Desert Willow Circle Palm Springs CA 92262 Office: 550 Frontage Rd Suite 2012 Northfield IL 60093 Died Mar. 10, 1977.

ROSENBAUM, EARL LEWIS, nursing home adminstr.; b. Chgo., May 11, 1942; s. Edward and Martha (Wax) R.; A.A., Wright Jr. Coll., Chgo., 1963; B.S., B.A., Roosevelt U., 1969; m. Pearl Berman, Jan. 26, 1964; children—Alan, Ivy. Social worker with mentally retarded youngsters Deborah Boys Club, Chgo., 1963-69; sales mgr. DuBois Chem. Co., Chgo., 1970; adminstr. All Seasons Nursing Center, Waukegan, Ill., 1970—. Mem. Skokie (Ill.) Recreation Commn., 1973-75; financial sec. Michael Earl Found. for Retarded, 1973-74, pres., 1974-75, also bd. dirs.; group leader Contact Teleministry Crisis Intervention, Waukegan, 1974-75, group leader tng. program, 1974—, treas., 1977—. Mem. Am. Coll. Nursing Home Adminstrs., Ill. Health Care Facilities, Nat. Geriatric Soc. Office: 919 Washington St Waukegan IL 60085

ROSENBERG, DALE HENRY, plastic and reconstructive surgeon; b. Belleville, Ill., Sept. 13, 1927; s. Henry and Evelyn (Miller) R.; student Springfield Jr. Coll., 1946-48; B.S., U. So. Calif., 1949; M.D., U. Ill., 1953; m. Nancy E. Biggs, July 1, 1950; children—Dirk, Jenny, Candra, Charles. Intern, Sacramento County Hosp., 1953-54; resident in plastic surgery Orange Meml. Hosp., Orlando, Fla., 1963-65; asso. Plastic Surgery Consultants, Ltd., Belleville, Ill., 1966—; pres. med. staff Belleville Meml. Hosp., 1974-75; exec. sec.-treas. So. Ill. Med. Assn. Served with USNR, 1944-46. Mem. AMA, Ill., St. Clair County med. socs., Midwestern Assn. Plastic Surgeons, Am. Assn. Plastic and Reconstructive Surgeons. Home: 303 Paddock Rd Belleville IL 62223 Office: Suite 3E 6401 W Main St Belleville IL 62223

ROSENBERG, EDWARD DANIEL, lawyer; b. Orange, N.J., Dec. 17, 1929; s. Soloman and Fannie Mary (Seidlin) R.; student De Paul U., Chgo., 1950, Roosevelt U., 1950, Union Coll., 1947-49; J.D., John Marshall Law Sch., 1954; children—Nina Diane, Beth Adrienne. Admitted to Ill. bar, 1954; since practiced in Chgo.; mem. firm Rosenberg & Kosin, 1954—. Adj. prof. law John Marshall Law Sch., 1972-74; vis. lectr. U. Chgo., 1962-67, Northwestern U., 1962-67; cons. Commrs. Uniform State Divorce Laws, 1970—. Mem. Ill. Family Study Commn. Marriage-Divorce and Parental Responsibility, 1967. Served with AUS, World War II. Fellow Am. Acad. Matrimonial Lawyers (nat. v.p. 1968-73, gov. 1962—); mem. Chgo. Bar Assn. (recipient certificate appreciation 1969, mem. com. profl. fees 1974—), Ill. Inst. Continuing Legal Edn. (recipient certificate appreciation 1968), Am. Bar Assn. (vice chmn. com. divorce laws and procedures 1974-75, vice chmn. com. liaison commrs. uniform state laws 1974-75, chmn. com. uniform recognition fgn. divorce act 1975—), Ill. Bar Assn. (chmn. family law sect. 1970). Contbr. articles to profl. jours. and family law handbooks. Office: 134 N LaSalle St Chicago IL 60602

ROSENBERG, GUY LOURIE, psychologist; b. Moline, Ill., Apr. 3, 1935; s. Guy Fay and Mabel Hilda (Anderson) R.; A.A., Blackhawk Coll., Moline, 1955; B.S. in Edn., Western Ill. U., 1957, M.S. in Edn., 1960; Ph.D., U. Iowa, 1969; m. Sharon Kay Miller, Aug. 24, 1958; children—Guy John, Gary Lundell. Tchr., Sterling (Ill.) Sch. Dist. 134, 1957-58; instr. guidance and counseling Western Ill U., 1960-62, also head resident advisor; counselor Park Forest (Ill.) Sch. Dist. 163, 1959-60; bus. and indsl. placement counselor U. Iowa, 1965-66; asso. prof. psychology Peru (Nebr.) State Coll., 1966-71, also dean of students, v.p. student affairs, 1971-73, dir. student life, 1973-76, dir. career counseling and placement, 1976-77; sr. test editor mental abilities tests Houghton Mifflin Co., Iowa City, Iowa, 1978—. Mem. Am. Personnel and Guidance Assn., Am. Coll. Personnel Assn., Nat.

Vocat. Guidance Assn., Rocky Mountain Placement Assn., Peru C. of C. (v.p. 1970-71), Phi Delta Kappa. Clubs: Masons, Elks. Home: 17 Lakeview Knoll River Heights Iowa City IA 52240 Office: Houghton Mifflin Co Test Dept Box 1970 Iowa City IA 52240

ROSENBERG, KENYON CHARLES, library adminstr.; b. Chgo., Sept. 9, 1933; s. Dave and Esther Mildred (Friedman) R.; A.A., Los Angeles City Coll., 1957; A.B., U. Calif., Los Angeles, 1959; M.S., U. So. Calif., 1961; m. Judith Karen Campbell, Apr. 30, 1971; children—Lorna Serene, Victoria Lynn, Dana Rebecca, Katherine Eleanor. Reference librarian Los Angeles County Law Library, 1955-60; librarian Los Angeles office Calif. Dept. Justice, 1960-62; cons. Alaska Ct. System, 1962; head tech. library services Hughes Aircraft Co., 1962-66; dir. tech. info. services Ampex Corp., 1966-69; asso. prof. library sci. Kent (Ohio) State U., 1968-76, asst. dir. libraries, 1976—. Served with AUS, 1953-55. Mem. ALA, Am. Soc. Info. Sci. (pres. San Francisco chpt. 1967-68), IEEE, Chi Delta Pi, Alpha Mu Gamma. Jewish. Author: Young People's Literature in Series, Vol. 1, 1972, Vol. 2, 1973; Watergate, 1975; Media Equipment, 1976; editor Previews Mag., 1973-75. Home: 2154 White Oak Dr Stow OH 44224 Office: Kent State U Libraries Kent OH 44242

ROSENBERG, NORMAN JACK, agrl. meteorologist; b. Bklyn., Feb. 22, 1930; s. Jacob and Rae (Dombrowitz) R.; B.S., Mich. State U., 1951; M.S., Okla. State U., 1958; Ph.D., Rutgers U., 1961; m. Sarah Zacher, Dec. 30, 1950; children—Daniel Jonathon, Alyssa Yael. Soil scientist Israel Soil Conservation Service, Haifa, 1953-55, Israel Water Authority, Haifa, 1955-57; research asst. Okla. State U., 1957-58; research fellow Rutgers U., 1958-61; asst. prof. agrl. meteorology U. Nebr., 1961-64, asso. prof., 1964-67, prof., 1968—, leader sect. agrl. meteorology, 1974, prof. agrl. engring., 1975—, prof. agronomy, 1976—; cons. AID, Dept. Commerce; mem. numerous ad hoc coms., mem. standing com. on atmospheric sci. Nat. Acad. Scis./NRC; vis. prof. agrl. meteorology Israel Inst. Tech., Haifa, 1968; Lady Davis fellow Hebrew U., Jerusalem, 1977. Recipient Centennial medal lNat. Weather Service, 1970; NATO sr. fellow in sci., 1968. Fellow AAAS; mem. Am. Soc. Agronomy, Am. Meteorol. Soc., Malib Poker Soc. Lincoln, Sigma Xi, Alpha Zeta, Gamma Sigma Delta. Jewish. Author: Microclimate: The Biological Environment, 1974. Tech. editor Agronomy Jour., 1974—. Contbr. numerous articles to profl. jours. Home: 3950 Pace Blvd Lincoln NE 68502 Office: 211 Agrl Engring Bldg U Nebr Lincoln NE 68583

ROSENBERGER, HELEN MARIE, chemist; b. Toledo, Dec. 6, 1923; d. Ferdinand Anthony and Helen Barbara (Schmider) Rosenberger; B.S., Mary Manse Coll., 1945; postgrad Northwestern U., 1949-50. Chemist, Monsanto Chem. Co., Dayton, 1945-47; with A.B. Dick Co., Chgo., 1947—, research asso., 1969-72, mgr. analytical services, materials research, 1972—, tech. adviser Creative Products, 1970—. Mem. Am. Chem. Soc., Am. Inst. Chemists (chmn. Ill. accreditation program), Photog. Soc. Am. Roman Catholic. Patentee reprographic processes and supplies. Contbr. articles to profl. jours. Home: 7643 Park Ave Skokie IL 60076 Office: 5700 Touhy Ave Niles IL 60648

ROSENBLATE, HOWARD JEROME, hepatologist; b. Chgo., July 1, 1936; s. Adolph Jon and Elizabeth (Bernstein) R.; B.A., Northwestern U., 1958; M.D., U. Ill., 1962; m. Karen Kohn, June 11, 1961; children—Elizabeth Ann, Robin Lynn, Adam Hunter. Intern, Presbyn. St. Lukes Hosp., Chgo., 1962-63, resident in internal medicine, 1965-67, attending physician, mem. sect. hepatology, 1969-73; chief sect. hepatology Luth. Gen. Hosp., Park Ridge, Ill., 1972-77; asst. prof. medicine Rush Med. Coll., also instr. U. Ill., 1972—. Served with M.C., AUS, 1963-65. Decorated Army Commendation Medal. USPHS fellow, 1967-69. Fellow A.C.P.; mem. Am. Assn. Study of Liver Disease, Internat. Acad. Pathology, Chgo. Soc. Gastroenterology, Am. Fedn. Clin. Research. Jewish. Research on the liver in sickle cell anemia, liver injury in heroin addiction, alcoholic liver disease. Home: 954 Golfview Rd Glenview IL 60025 Office: 950 Northwest Hwy Park Ridge IL 60068

ROSENBLATT, SUZANNE MARIS, artist; b. Hackensack, N.J., July 2, 1937; d. David and Rose Mary (Richman) Freedman; B.A., Oberlin Coll., 1959; student Central Sch. Arts and Crafts (Eng.), 1957-58, Cooper Union, 1960, Art Students League, 1961-63; m. Adolph Rosenblatt, Mar. 26, 1961; children—Sarah, Eli, Joshua. One man shows include: Bradley Gallery, Milw., 1971, Wustum Mus., Racine, Wis., 1972, Oshkosh (Wis.) Pub. Mus., 1972, N.Y. City Center, 1976, Ft. Wayne (Ind.) Mus. Art, 1976, Performing Arts Center, Milw., 1976, 77, 78; group shows include: Milw. Art Center, 1971, 76-78, Roko Gallery, N.Y.C., 1972, Tenn. Fine Arts Center, Nashville, 1974, Phila. Art Alliance, 1976, Weyne Gallery, N.Y.C., 1976, Lohman Gallery, N.Y.C., 1977; represented in permanent collections N.Y. Library, Mus. Performing Arts, N.Y.C., N.Y. City Center; artist of courtroom drawing for TV for Milw.'s CBS and NET affiliates. Recipient 1st prize creative expression Shasta Film Festival, Redding, Calif., 1976. Mem. Nat. Artworkers Coalition, Wis. Women in Arts, Phi Beta Kappa. Writer, illustrator: Everyone is Going Somewhere, 1976; illustrator (book of drawings) Dancers, 1977; Desk Diary, 1978. Address: 4211 N Maryland St Milwaukee WI 53211

ROSENCRANZ, ROBERT, elec. engr.; b. Chgo., July 2, 1926; s. Bernard and Lillian (Greenstein) R.; B.S. in Elec. Engring., U. Ill., 1948; B.S. in Indsl. Engring., Ill. Inst. Tech., 1955, B.S. in Mech. and Aerospace Engring., 1969; M.B.A., Roosevelt U., 1977; m. Judith Diane Levey, June 29, 1952; children—Leslie Joyce, Holly Ann. Chief engr. Standard Stamping & Perforating Co., Chgo., 1948-58, also cons. engr.; research engr. Clearing Machine Corp. div. U.S. Industries, Chgo., 1958-60; sr. elec. engr. U.S. Industries Tech. Center, Pompano Beach, Fla., 1960-61; chief engr. Lumen Electronics div. Esterline Angus Instrument Co., Joliet, Ill., 1961-65, Zenith Electric Co., Chgo., 1965-66; mgr. electronic and optical engring. Sargent-Welch Sci. Co., 1966-73; sr. engr. Abbott Labs., North Chicago, 1973—; Served with USNR, 1944-46. Mem. IEEE, Soc. Photog. Scientists and Engrs. (pres. 1970-71; service award 1972), Instrument Soc. Am. (sr.), Beta Gamma Sigma. Clubs: Masons, Shriners. Contbr. articles to profl. jours. Patentee in field. Home: 1762 McCraren Rd Highland Park IL 60035

ROSENFELD, ROBERT SANFORD, lawyer; b. Highland Park, Mich., Feb. 28, 1933; s. Michael and Fay (Dubin) R.; B.S.E. in Indsl. Mgmt., U. Mich., 1954, LL.B., 1957; LL.M., Georgetown U., 1960; m. Ruth Ellen Donner, Feb. 4, 1956; children—Lori Jane, Debra Lynn, Amy Beth. Admitted to Mich. bar, 1957, N.Y. bar, 1960; legal cons. social security dept. Internat. Union, U.A.W., 1960-62, asst. gen. counsel, 1962-64; partner law firm Keywell and Rosenfeld, Birmingham, Mich., 1964—; labor arbitrator in pub. employment, chem., automotive, paper and other industries. Served to lt. (s.g.), USNR, 1957-60. Mem. Detroit (chmn. young lawyers sect. 1966-67), Mich. (council man of young lawyers sect., 1965-66), bar assns. Jewish (pres. congregation 1975). Home: 110 Lone Pine Rd Bloomfield Hills MI 48013 Office: 30100 Telegraph Rd Birmingham MI 48010

ROSENFELD, STEVEN ALAN, computer systems co. exec.; b. Queens, N.Y., Aug. 25, 1950; s. Morton and Carol Lois (Leibowitz) R.; B.A., Brandeis U., 1971; postgrad Boston U., 1973-75, in data processing master's program, 1977—, m. Gwendolyn Jane Kerstetter, June 22, 1974. Asso. programmer Nixdorf Computer Inc., Wellesley, Mass., 1973, programmer, 1973-74, programmer, analyst, 1974, systems rep., 1974-75, systems mgr., 1975—. Jewish. Home: 3463 Norberg Dr Florissant MO 63031 Office: 100 Progress Parkway Maryland Heights MO 63043

ROSENGARD, ABE BENJAMIN, wholesale furniture co. exec.; b. Chgo., Sept. 30, 1914; s. Charles L. and Anna (Braude) R.; grad. Morton Coll., 1936; m. Maeta Kaplan, June 23, 1946; children—Frances, Charles, Allen, Shelley, Sue. Sales mgr. Louisville Chair Co., Chgo., 1960—; pres. Abe Rosengard and Assos., Inc., Chgo., 1962—. Pres., Morton Parents' Swim Team Club, 1966—; precinct capt. Combined Jewish Appeals, 1965—. Bd. dirs. Dialogue Mag. for Blind. Served with inf., AUS, 1941-45. Mem. Mfrs. Agts. Club (pres., chmn. bd.), Furniture Club Am. (head com.), Nat. Wholesale Furniture Assn., Am. Legion (comdr. furniture mart post). Jewish religion (pres. temple). Mason (Shriner). Clubs: Village Field (dir.) (La Grange Park, Ill.); La Grange YMCA Bus. Men's. Home: 6858 Riverside Dr Berwyn IL 60402 Office: 666 Lake Shore Dr Chicago IL 60611

ROSENGREN, CHESTER GORDON, dist. judge; b. Brandon, Minn., Nov. 12, 1908; s. Charles Geodfrey and Emily (Olson) R.; student St. Olaf Coll., 1925-27; B.B.A., U. Minn., 1929; J.D., U. Mich., 1932; m. Frances L. Anderson, Dec. 25, 1932 (dec. Oct. 1973); children—Janet (Mrs. R.R. Dils), C. Jon; m. 2d, Evelyn Johnson Cole, June 27, 1974. Admitted to Minn. bar, 1932; practiced in Fergus Falls, Minn., 1932-64; city atty. Fergus Falls, 1935-42; mem. firm Dell & Rosengren, 1932-53, Rosengren, Rufer, Blatti, Hefte & Pemberton, 1953-64; judge Minn. Dist. Ct., Fergus Falls, 1964—; temporary guest mem. Minn. Supreme Ct., 1974, 75. Mem. Ind. Sch. Dist. Sch. Bd., 1954-62, Fergus Falls Park Bd., 1940-46. Trustee 1st Luth. Found., Lake Region Hosp. Mem. Am. Coll. Trial Lawyers, Am. (trustee), Minn. (bd. govs. 1959—) bar assns., Am. Judicature Soc., Minn. Bd. Law Examiners, Alpha Delta Phi, Phi Delta Phi. Lutheran (trustee). Elk (trustee home lodge). Home: 909 Mt Faith Ave Fergus Falls MN 56537 Office: Courthouse Fergus Falls MN 56537

ROSENKOETTER, GERALD EDWIN, engring. exec.; b. St. Louis, Mar. 16, 1927; s. Herbert Charles and Edna Mary (Englege) R.; B.C.E. (St. Louis Engrs. Club scholar), Washington U., St. Louis, 1951; M.C.E., Sever Inst., 1957; m. Ruth June Beekman, Sept. 10, 1949; children—Claudia Ruth, Carole Lee. Engr. and group leader Sverdrup & Parcel, Engrs. and Architects, St. Louis, 1951-58, project engr., 1959-63, project mgr., 1964-69, asst. chief engr., 1970-72, asst. v.p., chief engr. indsl. div., 1972-74, v.p., mgr. indsl. div., 1975-76, corporate v.p., corporate indsl. prin., 1977—, also dir.; lectr., cons. in field. Councilman, City of Berkeley (Mo.), 1957-59, councilman-at-large, 1959-60, mem. Zoning Bd. and Bd. Adjustment, 1957-64. Served with U.S. Army, 1945-46. Registered profl. engr., Mo., Colo., Ind., N.J., Tex., Wis., Pa., Del., Idaho, N.C. Mem. ASCE (Outstanding Sr. award 1951), Air Force Assn. Club: St. Louis Media. Home: 42 Ballas Ct Town and Country MO 63134 Office: 800 N 12th Blvd Saint Louis MO 63101

ROSENOW, OSCAR FERDINAND, physician; b. Alma, Wis., Dec. 27, 1906; s. Ferdinand G. and Clara (Keller) R.; A.B., M.D., U. Wis., 1924-31; m. Mildred Irene Eichelberger, July 7, 1933; children—Edward Carl III, Kathleen Ann (Mrs. Gerald Fugazzi). Intern, White Cross Hosp., 1931-32, resident medicine, 1932-33, former dir. medicine; asst. clin. prof. medicine Ohio State U.; pvt. practice internal medicine, 1933-76; cons. medicine Mt. Carmel Hosp., sr. attending Riverside Meth. Hosp. Medicine. Served as maj. AUS, 1942-46. Diplomate Am. Bd. of Internal Medicine, Pan Am. Med. Assn. Fellow Am. Coll. Gastroenterology, AMA, A.C.P., Am. Coll. Cardiology, Royal Soc. Health; mem. Ohio State Med. Assn., Am. Heart Assn., Am. Soc. Clin. Hypnosis (charter), Columbus Acad. Medicine, Am. Legion. Mem. First Community Ch. Mason (Shriner). Club: Scioto Country. Home: 3140 Carlsbrook Rd Columbus OH 43221

ROSENSTROCK, PHILIP, accountant, lawyer; b. Chgo., June 3, 1915; s. Benjamin and Mollie (Borenstein) R.; grad. Crane Jr. Coll., 1933; B.C.S., Northwestern U., 1954; J.D., John Marshall Law Sch., 1957; m. Mildred Hoffman, Dec. 24, 1935; children—Edith Ann, Paul Myron, Bruce Benjamin. Partner, Philip Rosenstrock & Co., Chgo., 1942—; admitted to Ill. bar, 1957, since practiced in Chgo. Legal adviser Chgo. Businessmen's Orch., 1933—, Evans Symphony Orch., 1965—. Mem. Am., Ill., Chgo. bar assns., Am. Inst. C.P.A.'s, Ill. Soc. C.P.A.'s, Am. Assn. Atty.-C.P.A.'s. Mason (Shriner). Club: Covenant (Chgo.). Home: 75 Brentwood Dr Glencoe IL 60022 Office: 105 W Adams St 34th Floor Chicago IL 60603

ROSENTHAL, HERBERT M., real estate exec.; b. Chgo., Oct. 1922; s. Nathan and Bess (Jacobson) R.; B.S. in Econs., U. Ill., 1947; m. Kaye L. Kimbro, June 27, 1950; children—Robert N., Richard M., Steven E., James D. Pres. Hyland Builders, 1949-55; pres. Dunbar Corp., Chgo., 1955—, chmn. bd., 1973—. Served in USAAF, 1943-47; ETO. Recipient Builder of Yr. award Home Builders Assn. Chgo., 1966; Recognition award Commonwealth Edison, 1971. Mem. Nat. Assn. Home Builders, Sigma Alpha Mu. Clubs: Mid-Am., Carlton, Plaza. Introduced condominium type dwelling to U.S., 1962. Home: 1353 Westmoor Trail Winnetka IL 60093 Office: 3201 W Devon Ave Chicago IL 60693

ROSENTHAL, JOYCE ELAINE, lawyer; b. Detroit, Mar. 30, 1944; d. Marvin James and Madolyn (Lefkovits) Rosenthal; B.A., U. Mich., 1965; J.D., Wayne State U., 1969. Research law clk. Greyhound Food Mgmt., Inc., Detroit, summers 1968-69, corporate atty., 1974-76; asst. gen. counsel Oxx Metal Industries Corp., Madison Heights, Mich., 1976—; admitted to Mich. bar, 1969; staff atty. Kelly Services, Inc., Southfield, Mich., 1969-74. Campaign mgr. Oakland County Young Republicans, 1973; treas. Mich. Fedn. Young Reps., 1973; treas. state legislator campaign, 1974; mem. Oakland County Rep. Comm., 1973. Recipient Am. Jurisprudence award for labor law, 1969, Sales award Jr. Achievement, Curved bar Girl Scouts Am. Mem. Am., Mich., Detroit bar assns., U. Mich. Alumni Assn. Law Study Soc., Phi Alpha Delta. Home: 2329 Golfview Dr Troy MI 48084 Office: 32100 Stephenson Hwy Madison Heights MI 48071

ROSENTHAL, JULIAN SANFORD, dentist; b. Detroit, Mar. 2, 1928; s. Manuel Mandel and Shirley K. (Kukes) R.; B.S., Wayne U., 1950; D.D.S., U. Detroit, 1957; m. June 20, 1967; children—Carisa, Gregory. Pvt. practice dentistry, Inkster, Mich., 1957, Royal Oak, Mich., 1958—. Served with AUS, 1950-52. Mem. Am. Soc. Dentistry for Children, Am. Dental Assn., Mich. State, Oakland County dental socs., Mich. Soc. Psychosomatic Dentistry, Detroit Dist. Dental Soc., Founders Soc. Detroit Inst. Arts, Alpha Omega. Jewish. Office: 2530 Crooks Rd Royal Oak MI 48073

ROSENTHAL, MARK ALAN, zoo curator; b. Chgo., Jan. 3, 1946; s. Harry and Betty (Meltzer) R.; B.A., So. Ill. U., 1968; M.A., Northeastern Ill. U., 1976. Mem. staff Lincoln Park Zoo, Chgo., 1967—, zoologist, 1969-71, asso. curator mammals, 1971-76, curator, 1976—; lectr. in field. Mem. Am. Assn. Zool. Parks and Aquariums, Internat. Brotherhood Magicians. Jewish. Home: 347 W Menomonee St Chicago IL 60614 Office: 2200 N Cannon Dr Chicago IL 60614

ROSENTHAL, SAMUEL ROBERT, lawyer; b. Manistique, Mich., June 6, 1899; s. Lazarus and Rachel (Blumrosen) R.; A.B. summa cum laude, U. Mich., 1921; J.D., Harvard, 1924; m. Marie-Louise Dreyfus, July 30, 1932; children—Martin Raymond (dec.), Louise R. (Mrs. James J. Glasser). Admitted to Ill. bar, 1925, since practiced in Chgo.; asso. firm Foreman, Bluford, Steele & Schultz, 1924-26; asso. firm Sonnenschein, Carlin, Nath & Rosenthal, 1926-36, partner, 1937—; pres. D and R Fund, Chgo. Pres. bd. edn. Highland Park High Sch., 1955-59; pres. Highland Park Community Chest, 1947-48. Bd. mgrs. Highland Park Hosp. Found., 1942-53, life trustee; trustee Grinnell Coll., 1962-77, Ravinia Festival Assn. (life), Newberry Library, Michael Reese Hosp. and Med. Center, Chgo. (life), Highland Park Pub. Library, 1962-72; fellow Brandeis U. Served as lt. U.S. Army World War I. Mem. Am., Ill., Chgo. bar assns., Am. Bar Found., Am. Coll. Probate Counsel, Am. Antiquarian Soc., Phi Beta Kappa. Clubs: Mid-Day, Metropolitan, Standard, Caxton (pres. 1974-76), Mid-America (Chgo.); Lake Shore Country (Glencoe, Ill.); Grolier (N.Y.). Home: 910 Baldwin Rd Highland Park IL 60035 Office: 8000 Sears Tower Chicago IL 60606

ROSENTRETER, MYRON ADOLPH, lawyer; b. Oak Harbor, Ohio, Dec. 3, 1904; s. Charles R. and Bertha (Brodersen) R.; student U. Toledo, 1930-31; J.D., Ohio State U., 1935; m. Margaret M. Tucker, Nov. 23, 1943; 1 dau., Marcia (Mrs. Daniel W. Almendinger). In craft leather bus., shoe and harness repair with father, Oak Harbor, 1924-30; admitted to Ohio bar, 1935; practice in Oak Harbor, 1935—; mem. firm Rosentreter & Zeitzheim, 1972—; dir. Nat. Bank of Oak Harbor, 1949—, 1st v.p., 1965—. Mem. Village Council, Oak Harbor, 1930-31; mem., pres. Bd. Pub. Affairs, Oak Harbor, 1936-43; pros. atty. Ottawa County, Ohio, 1949-56. Served to capt. AUS, 1942-46, Mem. Am., Ohio, Ottawa County bar assns. Democrat. Mem. United Ch. of Christ (pres. 1965-68). Mason (dist. dep. grand master 1949-51), Moose, Elk, K.P., Rotarian (pres. 1946-47, charter mem.). Home: 604 E Water St Oak Harbor OH 43449 Office: 119 W Water St Oak Harbor OH 43449

ROSENZWEIG, DAPHNE LANGE, Orientalist; b. Evanston, Ill., July 7, 1941; d. William Ward and Elizabeth Terence (Neidlinger) Lange; A.B., Mt. Holyoke Coll., 1963; M.A., Columbia U., 1967, Ph.D., 1973; m. Abraham Rosenzweig, May 31, 1969; 1 dau., Victoria Lange. Lectr., Adelphi U., Garden City, N.Y., summer 1967; translator, lectr. Nat. Palace Museum, Taipei, Taiwan, 1967-69; lectr. U. N.Mex., 1969-73; asst. prof. Oriental and Islamic art history Oberlin (Ohio) Coll., 1973—; cons. in field. White House fellow, 1963; Nat. Def. Fgn. Lang. fellow, 1964-67; Fulbright fellow, 1967-69; grantee Columbia U., Gt. Lakes Colls. Assn., Oberlin Coll. Mem. Asia Soc., Japan Soc., Assn. Asian Studies, Fulbright Alumni Assn., Midwest Art Historians Assn., Coll. Arts Assn., Internat. House Japan. Democrat. Episcopalian. Author articles. Home: 143 E College St Oberlin OH 44074 Office: Dept Art Oberlin Coll Oberlin OH 44074

ROSEVEAR, ROBERT ALLEN, orthodontist; b. Aberdeen, Wash., Mar. 11, 1943; s. Richard Clarence and Elizabeth Julia (Northgren) R.; B.S., U. Puget Sound, 1965; D.D.S., U. Mo., 1968; M.S., W.Va. U., 1971. Individual practice dentistry, Portland, Oreg., 1968-69; practice as orthodontist, Eugene, Ore., 1971-72, Frankfurt, Germany, 1972, Overland Park, Kans., 1973—; former chmn. dept. occlusion U. Mo., Kansas City; mem. staff Washington County Indigent Children's Clinic, 1969. Cons. Jackson County Hosp., 1972. Mem. Am. Assn. Orthodontists, Am., Mo. dental assns., Greater Kansas City Orthodontic Soc., Kansas City Dental Soc., Phi Delta Theta. Home: 4443 Jefferson St Kansas City MO 64111 Office: 11055 Cedar Pkwy Overland Park KS 66211

ROSHEL, JOHN ALBERT, JR., orthodontist; b. Terre Haute, Ind., Apr. 7, 1941; s. John Albert and Mary M. (Griglione) R.; B.S., Ind. State U., 1963; D.D.S., Ind. U., 1966; M.S., U. Mich., 1968; children from previous marriage—John Albert III, James Livingston, Angela Kay. Individual practice dentistry, specializing in orthodontics Terre Haute, 1968—. Mem. Am. Dental Assn., Am. Assn. Orthodontists, Terre Haute C. of C., Lambda Chi Alpha, Delta Sigma Delta, Omicron Kappa Upsilon. Clubs: Terre Haute Country, Lions, Elks, K.C. Roman Catholic. Home: 1829 43d Dr Terre Haute IN 47802 Office: 4241 S 7th St Terre Haute IN 47802

ROSINGER, GEORGE, research psychologist; b. Prague, Czechoslovakia, Jan. 27, 1935; s. Julius and Anna (Lichtig) R.; m. Joyce Marlene Burger, Aug. 23, 1958; children—David Steven, Alan Scott, Julie Lynn; came to U.S., 1946, naturalized, 1951; student Hunter Coll., 1953-54; B.B.A., City Coll. N.Y., 1957; M.A. (scholar), Lehigh U., 1959. Licensed psychologist, Ohio. Research psychologist Army Natick (Mass.) Labs., 1958-60; human factors specialist Martin Marietta Corp., Balt., 1961-65; project leader, sr. human factors engr. Rockwell Internat., Columbus, Ohio, 1965-67; asso. mgr. Center for Improved Edn., Battelle-Columbus Labs., 1967—; participant, rev. panel NSF, 1977. Mem. Am. Psychol. Assn., Soc. Applied Learning Tech., Am. Soc. for Tng. and Devel., Columbus C. of C. (sch. issues com. 1974-76, subcom. chmn. 1975), Psi Chi. Contbr. articles to profl. jours. Home: 2840 Berwick Blvd Columbus OH 43209 Office: Battelle-Columbus Labs 505 King Ave Columbus OH 43201

ROSKENS, RONALD WILLIAM, univ. system pres.; b. Spencer, Iowa, Dec. 11, 1932; s. William E. and Delores A.L. (Beving) R.; m. Lois Grace Lister, Aug. 22, 1954; children—Elizabeth, Barbara, Brenda, William; B.A., U. No. Iowa, 1953, M.A., 1955; Ph.D., State U. Iowa, 1958. Tchr., Minburn (Iowa) High Sch., 1954, Woodward (Iowa) State Hosp., summer 1954; asst. counselor to men State U. Iowa, 1956-59; dean man, asst. prof. spl. edn. Kent (Ohio) State U., 1959-63, asso. prof. spl. edn., 1963-68, prof., 1968-72, asst. to pres., 1963-66, dean for adminstrn., 1965, v.p. univ. relations and devel., 1966-68, v.p. for adminstrn., 1968-71, exec. v.p., prof. ednl. adminstrn., 1971-72; chancellor, prof. ednl. adminstrn. U. Nebr. at Omaha, 1972-77, pres. U. Nebr. system, 1977—; dir., Omaha Nat. Bank; mem. Nat. Exec. Res. Corps. Mem. Kent City Planning Commn.; bd. dirs. Found. Study Presdl. and Congl. Terms, Met. YMCA, Boy Scouts Am., United Community Services, NCCJ; trustee Huston Tillotson Coll., Austin, Tex., chmn., 1976—; trustee Brownell-Talbott Sch., Harry S Truman Inst. Named Nat. 4-H Alumnus, 1968, Outstanding Alumnus, U. No. Iowa, 1974; recipient NCCJ Brotherhood award, 1977. Mem. AAAS, Am. Personnel and Guidance Assn., Am., Ohio coll. personnel assns., Assn. Urban Univs. (pres. 1976-77), AAUP, Am. Ednl. Research Assn., Am. Psychol. Assn., Kent Area C. of C. (pres. 1966), Young Pres.'s Orgn., Com. on Fgn. Relations, Phi Delta Kappa, Phi Eta Sigma, Sigma Tau Gamma (pres. grand council 1968-70), Omicron Delta Kappa, Mason (32 deg.). Co-editor: Paradox, Process and Progress, 1968; Contbr. articles to profl. jours. Home: 5930 Norman Rd Lincoln NE 68512

ROSLYCKY, EUGENE BOHDAN, microbiologist; b. Tluste, Ukraine, May 8, 1927; s. Mykola and Felicia (Stoyanovych) R.; B.Sc., U. Man., 1953, M.Sc., 1955; Ph.D., U. Wis., 1960; came to Can., 1948, naturalized, 1954; m. Halina Czerepacha, Oct. 9, 1971; children—Oleh, Lada. Research scientist Research Inst. Agr. Can., U.

Western Ont., London, 1959—. Chmn. Com. for Defece of Human Rights, London, 1971-75. Mem. Shevchenko Sci. Soc. Can., Ukrainian Free Acad. Sci. Can., Am. Soc. Microbiology, Canadian, Brit. socs. microbiology, Internat. Com. Systematic Bacteriology (chmn. subcom. Agrobacterium and Rhizobium, 1974—). Discoverer of rhizobiocins, 1966; introduced new procedure for silica gel media, 1972. Home: 195 Tarbart Terr London ON N6H 3B3 Canada Office: Research Inst Agriculture Canada Univ Sub PO London ON N6A 5B7 Canada

ROSS, ALBERT MERRITT, lawyer; b. Kansas City, Kans., Nov. 20, 1923; s. Albert Mettie and Marion Birch (Damrell) R.; B.A., Washburn U., 1947, LL.B., 1949, J.D., 1970; m. Ora M. Nuttle, Dec. 18, 1948; children—Harriett, Gretchen, Nava, Albert. Admitted to Kans. bar, 1949; practiced in Kansas City, 1949-69, Overland Park, 1969—; mem. firm Ross & Hoagland, 1975—; Workmen's Compensation examiner, 1953-55, mem. commn., 1955-56. Asst. scoutmaster Boy Scouts Am., 1969-75, Bd. dirs. Sunflower Campfire Girls, 1958-75, Johnson County Mental Retardation Com., 1969-75. Served with USNR, 1942-46. Mem. Kan. Trial Lawyers Assn. (pres.), Delta Theta Phi, Phi Delta Theta. Presbyterian (trustee United Presbyn. Found. Kan.). Mason (Shriner). Home: 6740 Fonticello Prairie Village KS 66208 Office: 5454 W 110th St Overland Park KS 66211

ROSS, CHARLES HOWARD, physician, author; b. Troy, Ohio, July 6, 1890; s. Charles Clemdenning and Eusebia Lydia (Wagner) R.; A.B. with high distinction, U. Mich., 1916; M.D. with distinction, 1931; m. S. Cecelia Graham, June 29, 1920 (dec. July 31, 1960); 1 son, Howard Graham; m. 2d, Jeannette Marguerite Albert, July 21, 1962. Village sch. master, 1909-11; instr. botany U. Mich., 1913-16; high sch. tchr., Moline, Ill., Sioux City, Ia., 1916-17; gen. mgr. Union Malleable Iron Co., E. Moline, Ill., 1924-27; instr. internal medicine U. Mich. Med. Sch., 1932-36; practice medicine specializing in geriatrics, 1932-69; author, 1908—. Lectr. medicine, history, herbal lore, lectr. med. ethics and econs. U. Mich., 1955-66, 70; adv. councilor Am. Med. Edn. Found.; mem. Gov.'s adv. com. White House Conf. on Aging, 1971. Served to 1st lt. AUS, 1917-19. Recipient Swanberg Distinguished Service award Am. Med. Writers Assn., 1967. Fellow Am. Med. Writers Assn. (nat. bd. dirs. 1966-68, 70-72); mem. Mich. Acad. Gen. Practice (pres. 1959-60), North Tri State Med. Assn. (pres. 1955-56), Am. Geriatrics Soc. (bd. dirs. 1962-69), Mich. State Med. Soc. (active on numerous coms.), Ann Arbor Hist. Found., Washtenaw Hist. Soc., Theta Kappa Psi, Phi Kappa Phi, Alpha Omega Alpha. Clubs: Emeritus, Exchange, Thursday Study Luncheon, U. Mich. Author of numerous books including: Ethics in Medical Writing, 1961; Nutrition in Geriatrics, 1963; Granny's Herbs and the Witch Doctor, 1966; The Evangelism of Communication, 1967. Guest editor The New Physician, 1961. Contbr. numerous articles to profl. pubs. Home: 1725 Glastonbury Rd Ann Arbor MI 48103

ROSS, DAVID EUGENE, JR., physician; b. Lorain, Ohio, June 15, 1930; s. David Eugene and Linnie S. (Feazell) R.; A.B., Tougaloo Coll., Miss., 1950; M.D., Meharry Med. Coll., 1955; m. Ruthie Ellison, March 26, 1968; children—David, Karen, Anthony, Michael, Mildred, Nathaniel, Ruth, Rachael, Rebeccah. Intern, Madigan Army Hosp., Tacoma, 1955-56; practice medicine specializing in family practice, Gary, Ind., 1960—; dir. emergency dept. Meth. Hosp., Gary, 1970-76, dir. family residency program, 1975, med. dir. paramedic program, 1974-76; asso. prof. Ind. U.; pres. med. staff Meth. Hosp., 1974-75. Police civil service commr., Gary, 1972-74. Diplomate Am. Bd. Family Practice. Mem. Lake County Med. Soc. (v.p. 1975-76), Am. Acad. Family Physicians, Am. Acad. Emergency Physicians, AMA. Lutheran. Home: 433 Arthur St Gary IN 46404 Office: 2318 W 5th Ave Gary IN 46404

ROSS, DAVID KINSEY, natural gas co. exec.; b. Columbus, O., Apr. 4, 1934; s. Herbert H. and Ruth Elizabeth (Purcell) R.; B.S., U. Tulsa, 1961; m. Jimmie Kay Mitchell, Dec. 27, 1956; children—James David, Mark Edwin, Phillip Scott. Sales rep. Continental Oil Co., Oklahoma City, 1961-63, dist. sales rep., 1963-65, acting div. sales mgr., 1965; v.p. operating dept. Ind. Natural Gas Corp., Paoli, 1965-67, v.p., 1967-70, pres., 1970—. Pres., Springs Valley Community Park Bd., 1967, 68, 71. Pres. Springs Valley Community Schs. Bd., 1973-74. Bd. dirs. West Washington Bldg. Trades Sch. Served with AUS, 1956-58. Mem. Ind. Natural Gas Corp. (dir. 1968—), Ind. Gas Assn. (dir. 1970—), Ind. Mfrs. Assn. Methodist (chmn. stewardship and fin. 1969-74). Home: Rural Route 1 West Baden IN 47469 Office: Hospital Rd Paoli IN 47454

ROSS, EARL E., juvenile worker; b. St. Louis, July 3, 1942; s. Edward Earl and Ruth Randles (Loewen) R.; B.A. in Psychology, Central Mo. State U., 1965; M.A. in Corrections, Webster Coll., Webster Groves, Mo., 1976; m. Mary Donna Moore, May 31, 1964; 1 son, Damon Moore. Reporter, Warrensburg (Mo.) Daily Star-Jour., 1965; social worker St. Louis County Welfare Div., Maplewood, Mo., 1966-68; asso. dist. scout exec. Boy Scouts Am., St. Louis, 1968; dep. juvenile officer St. Louis County Juvenile Ct., Clayton, Mo., 1969-72; program dir. St. Louis County Detention Center, Clayton, 1972—; asst. supt. St. Louis County Detention Center, Clayton, 1978—; instr. tng. sessions. Mem. Am. Personnel and Guidance Assn., Pub. Offender Counselors Assn., Mo. Corrections Assn., Mo. Juvenile Officers Assn., Greater St. Louis Probation and Parole Assn. Home: 15333 Appalachian Trail Chesterfield MO 63017 Office: 501 S Brentwood Blvd Clayton MO 63105

ROSS, EUGENE IRWIN, real estate co. exec.; b. Lewis D. and Dorothy (Levy) R.; B.S., U. Colo., 1956; postgrad. Ill. Inst. Tech., 1959-60; m. Patti Ann Packman, Dec. 18, 1956; children—Kenneth, Douglas, Terri. Salesman, Ryerson Steel Co., 1959-61; sales mgr. Circle Security Agy., 1961-62; v.p. Arthur Rubloff and Co., Chgo., 1962-70; pres. Seay & Thomas, Inc., 1971-75, Ross, Kotin & Co., Chgo., 1975—; dir. Phillipsborn Equities Corp., Treasure Lakes Corp.; treas. IC Leasing Corp. Real estate cons., lectr. nat. convs. Active Met. Crusade Mercy; mem. Deerfield (Ill.) Interurban Council, 1964-65. Bd. dirs. Charles G. Kramer Found., Young Men's Jewish Council, Apt. Council Met. Chgo., Greater Chgo. Com., Invarrary Assn., Greater North Mich. Ave. Assn., real estate div. United Settlement Appeal. Served to capt. USAF, 1956-59. Recipient Certified Property Mgr. awards Crusade Mercy, 1966; United Jewish Appeal, 1962. Mem. Inst. Real Estate Mgmt., Urban Land Inst., Nat. Assn. Real Estate Bds., Bldg. Owners and Mgrs. Assn. (dir.), Apartment Owners and Mgrs. Assn. (dir.), Internat. Council Shipping Centers, Res. Officers Assn., Young Pres.'s Orgn., Alpha Kappa Psi, Zeta Beta Tau, Lambda Alpha. Clubs: Standard, International, Briarwood. Home: 875 Fairview St Highland Park IL 60035 Office: 179 W Washington St Chicago IL 60602

ROSS, GEORGE EDWIN, social scientist; b. St. Louis, June 12, 1927; s. Isaac Felix and Emma Antoinette (Basola) R.; B.S., U. Ill., 1951, M.Ed., 1953, D.Ed., 1960. Tchr. pub. schs., Sandoval, Ill., 1949-50; prin., Centralia (Ill.) City Schs., 1950-56; prof. edn. Western Ill. U., Macomb, 1960-67; asst. dir. Ill. Office Edn., 1967-69; staff devel. coordinator Ill. Dept. Children and Family Services, E. St. Louis, Ill., 1969-74, child welfare adminstr. Salem area, 1974—. Chmn. Human Relations Com. City of Macomb, 1964-67, REgional Manpower Com., 1976—; mem. Gov.'s Com. on Spl. Edn., 1964-67. Mem. Western Ill. Higher Edn. Assn. (pres. 1966), Ill. Welfare Assn. (dir.), Child Care Assn. Ill., NEA, Ill. Edn. Assn. Republican. Mem. Ch. Disciples of Christ. Clubs: Elks (past state chmn), Odd Fellows (past dist. pres.), Moose. Contbr. articles to profl. jours. Home: 19 Orchard Dr Sandoval IL 62882 Office: 205 E Locust St Salem IL 62881

ROSS, HAROLD ANTHONY, lawyer; b. Kent, Ohio, June 2, 1931; s. Jules and Helen Assumpta (Ferrara) R.; B.A. magna cum laude, Western Res. U., 1953; J.D., Harvard U., 1956; m. Elaine Louise Hunt, July 1, 1961; children—Leslie Ann, Gregory Edward, Jonathan Harold. Admitted to Ohio bar, 1956; with firm Hornbeck, Ritter & Victory, Cleve., 1958-59; regional atty. NLRB, Cleve., 1959-61; with firm Marshman, Hornbeck, Hollington, Steadman & McLaughlin, Cleve., 1961-64; partner firm Ross & Kraushaar, and predecessor, 1964—; gen. counsel Brotherhood Locomotive Engrs., 1966—. Mem. Charter Rev. Com., N. Olmsted, Ohio, 1970-75; Democratic primary candidate for Ohio Ho. Reps., 1964; Dem. party nominee, law dir., N. Olmsted, 1967; trustee Citizens League Greater Cleve., 1969—. Served with AUS, 1956-58. Mem. Am., Ohio, Cleve. bar assns., Phi Beta Kappa, Delta Sigma Rho, Omicron Delta Kappa, Pi Kappa Alpha. Roman Catholic. Home: 23195 Stoneybrook Dr North Olmsted OH 44070 Office: 1548 Standard Bldg Cleveland OH 44113

ROSS, JAY BERNARD, lawyer; b. N.Y.C., Feb. 12, 1942; s. Leon and Leah (Kramer) R.; B.S., U. Wis., 1964; J.D., U. Ill., 1967. Admitted to Ill. bar, 1968, U.S. Supreme Ct. bar, 1972; individual practice law, Chgo., 1968—; adj. prof. U. Ill. Extension; staff writer Ill. Inst. Continuing Edn., Chgo. Law Bull. Vice-pres. Variety Club; pres. Variety Club Children's Charities for La Rabida Hosp., 1978; active City of Hope, Chgo. One Hundred, Red Cloud Athletic Found. Recipient Jaycees Citizenship award, 1960, Gold Medal award, Found. Faith of the Millennium, 1977. Mem. Am., Chgo., Fed., Ill. bar assns., Nat. Assn. Recording Arts Scis., Nat. Assn. TV Arts and Scis. Clubs: Chgo. Unlimited, Chgo. Advt. Office: 11 S LaSalle St Chicago IL 60603

ROSS, MONTE, elec. engr.; b. Chgo., May 26, 1932; s. Jacob Henry and Mildred Amelia (Feller) R.; B.S. in Elec. Engring., U. Ill., 1953; M.S., Northwestern U., 1962; m. Harriet Jean Katz, Feb. 10, 1957; children—Karyn, Dianne, Ethan. Devel. engr. Chance Vought, Dallas, 1953-54; sr. electronics engr. Motorola, Chgo., 1955-56, project engr., 1957-59, asso. dir. research, 1960-63; dir. research Hallicrafters Co., Chgo., 1964-65; mgr. laser tech. McDonnell Douglas Astronautics Co., St. Louis, 1966—; program mgr. Laser Space Communications, 1971—. Guest lectr. various univs.; cons. NSF. Fellow IEEE; mem. Sigma Xi. Author: Laser Receivers, 1966. Tech. editor Laser Application Series, vol. 1, 1971, vol. 2, 1974. Patentee in field. Home: 226 Wenneker St St Louis MO 63124 Office: PO Box 516 McDonnell Douglas St Louis MO 63166

ROSS, MYLAN EVERETT, bus. exec.; b. Rosalie, Nebr., Mar. 6, 1920; s. Ura S. and Eva Mae (Copple) R.; B.S., U. Nebr., 1941; M.B.A., U. Chgo., 1947, postgrad., 1948-50; m. Helen Maxine Travis, June 16, 1946; children—Melanie Jo, Michael Allen. Spl. lectr. Drake U., summer 1947; asst. prof. Sch. Econ. and Bus. Wash. State Coll., 1947-51; dir. mktg. research, advt. mgr. Western Cottonoil Co., Abilene, Tex., 1951-52; sr. analyst market research Armour & Co., Chgo., 1952-54; dir. market research Feed div. Pillsbury Co., Clinton, Iowa, 1954-59; v.p., gen. mgr. Nat. Food Co., Fond du Lac, Wis., 1959-61; dir. research Nat. Livestock Producers Assn., Chgo., 1961-63, sec., gen. mgr., 1963-66, exec. v.p., gen. mgr., 1966-72; exec. v.p., gen. mgr. Nat. Feeder & Fin. Corp., 1966-72; exec. v.p. Nat. Livestock Pub. Assn., 1966-72; sec., gen. mgr. Nat. Producers Service Co., 1968-72; mktg. dir. Tekseed Hybrid Co., Tekemah, Nebr., 1972-74, exec. v.p., gen. mgr., 1974—. Served to lt. col. USAAF, 1941-46. Decorated Bronze Star. Mem. U.S. Feed Grains Council (dir.), Nebr. Seedsmens Assn. (dir.), Farm House, Alpha Kappa Psi. Presbyn. (elder). Mason (shriner), Lion. Home: 720 K St Tekamah NE 68061 Office: Rural Route 2 Tekamah NE 68061

ROSS, MYRON DONALD, office adminstrn. cons.; b. Chgo., Sept. 30, 1909; s. Michael J. and Bertha (Krutch) R.; B.S., Northwestern U., 1934; m. Marie V. Manning, June 13, 1935; children—Donald R., Darlene M. With Jewel Tea Co., Inc. (name changed to Jewel Cos., Inc.), Melrose Park, Ill., 1932-70, mgr. inventory control, cost accounting depts., mgr. cash, payroll dept., store personnel mgr., office mgr., 1932-45, mgr. cash operating div., 1945-54, mgr. systems div., 1954-63, mgr. electronic data processing div., 1963-66, asst. controller Chicagoland Stores, 1966-67, asst. to exec. v.p., 1967-70; cons. office adminstrn., 1970—. Recipient Merit Award key Office Mgmt. Assn. Chgo., 1950, Leadership plaque Nat. Office Mgmt. Assn., 1951. Mem. Nat., Chgo. (pres. 1949-50) office mgmt. assns., Bus. Electronics Round Table Assn. (pres. 1949-50), Exec. Club Chgo. Home and Office: 10543 Dorchester Rd Westchester IL 60153

ROSS, RICHARD, cons. engr.; b. Halstead, Kans., Jan. 14, 1933; s. Fay Preston and Bertha Clara (F0yar) R.; B.S. in Aero. Engring., U. Wichita, 1956; M.S., U. So. Calif., 1958; doctoral candidate in fluid mechanics Stanford U.; m. Leah May Vaughan, Aug. 1, 1954; children—Charles, Lynn, George. Aerodynamicist, Lockheed-Calif. Co., 1956-58, sr. aerodynamics engr., 1960-65; summer faculty fellow NASA Ames Research Center, 1967; asst. prof. aero. engring. Wichita (Kans.) State U., 1965-68; sr. tech. engr. Lear Jet Co., summer 1968; chief aerodynamics and propulsion Gates Learjet Corp., 1971-77; vis. asso. prof. U. Kans., 1976-77; dir. Ross Aviation Assos., Sedgwick, Kans., 1977—; cons. Canadair Ltd., Aeronca, Inc., Flight Safety, Inc., ROS, Inc, Cerebral Palsy Research Found. Kans. Mem. Bd. Edn., 1975—; scoutmaster, Sedgwick, 1971—. Served in USAF, 1958-60. Named Outstanding Sr. Engr., U. Wichita, 1956; NSF trainee, 1968-70, sci. faculty fellow, 1970-71; Am. Soc. Engring. Edn.-NASA summer faculty fellow, 1967; Walter H. Beech scholar, 1951-55. Asso. fellow Am. Inst. Aeros. and Astronautics (faculty adviser 1966-68; program chmn. Wichita sect. 1973-74, treas. 1974-75, vice-chmn. 1975-76, chmn. 1976-77; gen. aviation systems tech. com. 1976—, turbojet engine testing working group 1972—); mem. Soc. Automotive Engrs. (chmn. session on aerodynamics for 1976 nat. meeting), Nat., Kans. (sec.-treas. engrs. in edn. sect. 1968-69; Outstanding Young Engr. 1968), Wichita (chmn. young engrs. com. 1968-69; Outstanding Young Engr. 1968) profl. engrs. socs. Methodist. Contbr. aLticles to profl. jours. Home and Office: RFD 1 Sedgwick KS 67135

ROSS, RICHARD HALL, pub. co. exec.; b. St. Louis, June 27, 1935; s. Glen Alexander and Dorthy Maria (Hall) R.; B.B.A., Western Mich. U., 1957; m. Alma Jean Powers, May 4, 1963; children—Gregory A., Richard D. Advt. coordinator Clark Equipment Co., Battle Creek, Mich., 1960-62; with Campbell-Ewald Co., Detroit, 1962-69, supr. dir. mail dept., 1967-68, account exec., 1968-69; v.p., gen. mgr. Ceco Publ. Co., Warren, Mich., 1969-77, pres., 1977—, also dir. Trustee New Horizons Oakland County, Inc., 1972—. Mem. Direct Mail Advt. Assn., Mktg. Communications Execs. Internat., Direct Mail Club Detroit (pres. 1967), Sigma Phi Epsilon. Home: 3675 Bradford St Birmingham MI 48010 Office: 30400 Van Dyke St Warren MI 48093

ROSSEELS, GUSTAVE ALOIS, educator; b. Malines, Belgium, Jan. 19, 1911; s. Karel Hubert and Elisabeth (Rooms) R.; came to U.S., 1946, naturalized, 1952; grad. with great distinction Royal Conservatory (Belgium), 1929; m. Jacqueline Crepin, Sept. 5, 1944; children—Marc, Elisabeth Rosseels Reed, Susanne. Asst. prof. violin, chamber music Royal Conservatory, Brussels, Belgium, 1938-45; concert artist Paganini Quartet touring U.S.A., S.Am., Can., Europe, 1946-57; prof. music U. Mich., Ann Arbor, 1957—. Mem. A.A.U.P., Mich. Acad. Arts and Scis., Am. String Tchrs. Assn., Pi Kappa Lambda. Home: 1233 Bending Rd Ann Arbor MI 48103

ROSSI, DONALD, psychologist; b. Chgo., Oct. 3, 1940; s. Raymond R. and Dora R. (Rante) R.; B.S., No. Ariz. U., 1964; M.S., N.M. Highlands U., 1966; Ph.D., U. Sheffield (Eng.), 1969; m. J. Antoinette Chapados, Aug. 27, 1966; 1 dau., Tamara Dawn. Clin. intern N.M. State Hosp., Las Vegas, 1965; asst. lectr. dept psychology U. Sheffield, 1967-68; clin. intern Springfield State Hosp., Sykesville, Md., also Sinai Hosp. of Balt., 1968-69; postdoctorate tng. Mich. Psychoanalytic Inst., 1970-75; staff psychologist York Woods Center, Ypsilanti, Mich., 1969-70, dir. day treatment program, 1974-75, chief psychologist, instr. child psychiatry, cons. child devel., 1974-76; sr. research asso., child psychoanalytic study program U. Mich. Med. Sch., Ann Arbor, 1970-74; lectr. dept. psychology Eastern Mich. U., Ypsilanti, 1974-75; asso. prof. psychology Hillsdale (Mich.) Coll., 1976—; pvt. practice child and adult psychotherapy, Ann Arbor, 1971—; cons. Friends of Psychiat. Research, Balt., 1968-69, House of Good Shepherd, Balt., 1969, Center for Forensic Psychiatry, Ann Arbor, 1969-70, Mich. State Police, Lansing, 1974—, Meth. Children's Home Soc., Detroit, 1975-76, Hillsdale County Juvenile Ct., 1976—, Internat. Assn. Chiefs of Police, Gaithersburg, Md., 1977—. Mem. Am., Mich. psychol. assns., Mich. Soc. Cons. Psychologists, Midwest Psychoanalytic Soc., Council for Exceptional Children, Psi Chi. Home: 220 Osseo Rd Osseo MI 49266 Office: Mercy Med Plaza Suite 10 4116 Jackson Rd Ann Arbor MI 48103

ROSSI, JEAN JOSEPH, clin. and social psychologist; b. Plainfield, N.J., Mar. 30, 1926; s. Jean and Margaret (Marra) R.; B.Sc., Seton Hall U., 1949; M.A., Cath. U. Am., 1954; Ph.D., U. Ottawa, 1957; m. Ilene Georgene Lindsoe, Dec. 31, 1956; children—Mary Beth, Anna Christine, Paula Jeanne, John Paul. Psychologist, Cath. U. Counseling Center, 1949-51, Nat. Tng. Sch. for Boys, 1950-51, Willmar State Hosp., 1951-61; clin. psychologist West Central Minn. Mental Health Center, 1958-61; pvt. practice, chief psychologist Luth. Gen. Hosp., Des Plaines, Ill., 1961-69, program dir. alcohol treatment center, 1968-74, dir. research and evaluation psychiatry, 1974, dir. personality lab., 1967—; pres. Behavioral Consultants, Inc., 1972—; mental health cons. Govt. of Can. Health and Welfare, Provinces of Alta. and Man., States of Ill., Ky., Iowa; invited faculty U. Alaska, Alaska Meth. U., U. Iowa, Northwestern U., U. Ala. Served with USNR, 1943-46; PTO. Recipient grants Hill Found., 1956-60, Am. Luth. Ch., 1976-77. Mem. Am., Ill. psychol. assns., AAAS, Assn. Advanced Behavior Therapy, Ill. Group Psychotherapy Soc., Internat. Council Alcoholism and Addictions, Alcohol and Drug Problems Assn. N.Am. Democrat. Roman Catholic. Author: Treatment Issues in Alcoholism, 1977. Editor: (with others) Therapeutic Community, 1975; Alcohol and Alcohol Problems, New Thinking and New Directions, 1976; Core Knowledge Package-Alcoholism Treatment, 1977; contbr. articles profl. jours. Office: 2474 Dempster St Suite 117 Des Plaines IL 60016

ROSSING, WILLIAM OSMUND, physician; b. Bagley, Minn., June 6, 1934; s. Erling W. and Irene Clara (Norby) R.; B.A., Augustana Coll., Sioux Falls, S.D.; M.D., Northwestern U.; m. Ihlene Aubry Beade, Dec. 29, 1958; children—Karen Ihlene, Rebecca Marie, William Robert, Signe Ann. Intern, Brooke Gen. Hosp., Ft. Sam Houston, Tex., 1959-60, resident in internal medicine, 1960-63; practice medicine specializing in internal medicine, Sioux Falls, 1966—; chief staff Sioux Valley Hosp., 1976—. Bd. dirs. Vis. Nurses Assn., Civic Symphony, Sioux Falls. Served with M.C., U.S. Army, 1959-66. Fellow A.C.P.; mem. Am., S.D. med. assns., 7th Dist. Med. Soc. (pres. 1975-76), Am., S.D. (pres. 1971-73) socs. internal medicine, Augustana Coll. Alumni Assn. (pres. 1972-73), Am. Heart Assn. Republican. Lutheran. Club: Kiwanis. Home: 2604 S Lyndale St Sioux Falls SD 57105 Office: 1200 S Euclid St Sioux Falls SD 57105

ROSSMAN, MARGARET MARY DRYZ, search and cons. co. exec.; b. Chgo., July 6, 1939; d. Gregory T. and Margaret M. Dryz; B.A., Rosary Coll., River Forest, Ill., 1971; m. Donald L. Rossman, June 27, 1959; 1 dau., Theresa Lynn. Copywriter, Butler Bros. Co., Chgo., 1958-60; tchr. elementary schs., Chgo., 1960-68; with advt. sales dept. Paddock Crescent Newspapers, Downers Grove, Ill., 1971-73; co-founder, pres. Women's Inc., Hinsdale, Ill., 1973—, also dir.; instr. career oevel. Harper Coll., Palatine, Ill. Mem. Woodridge (Ill.) Bd. Library Dirs., 1969-75; mem. Woodridge Youth Commn., 1970-71. Mem. Bus. and Profl. Women. Office: 15 Spinning Wheel Rd Suite 14 Hinsdale IL 60521

ROSSWAY, MELVIN WEAVER, r.r. exec.; b. Belle Plaine, Iowa, Sept. 7, 1918; s. Samuel W. and Edna (Weaver) R.; diploma in certified pub. accounting, Internat. Corr. Schs., 1953; m. Marian Ruth Morehead, Oct. 31, 1946; children—Ronald Alan, Rhonda Kay, Rita Jean. Agt. helper C. & N. W. Ry., 1937-38, telegraph, sta. agt., 1938-53, travelling accountant, Chgo., 1953-56; asst. controller, auditor Lake Superior & Ishpeming R.R. Co., Marquette, Mich., 1956-58, treas., controller, 1958-61, v.p., treas., controller, 1961-73, sr. v.p., 1973—; dir. Lasco Devel. Corp.; dir. 1st Nat. Bank & Trust Co., Mich. Fin. Corp. Treas. Marquette Hosp. Bond Authority. Served with AUS, 1944-46; dist. staff officer USCG Aux. Mem. Tax Execs. (Wis. chpt.), Am. Legion, Marquette Range Engrs., Marquette C. of C. Republican. Lutheran. Clubs: Masons, Lions, Elks. Home: 800 W Magnetic St Marquette MI 49855 Office: 105 E Washington St Marquette MI 49855

ROST, J. WALDO, accountant; b. Axtell, Nebr., June 21, 1927; s. John A. and Martha (Lonnquist) R.; A.A., Luther Coll., 1948; certificate in Accounting, LaSalle Extension U., 1955; m. Marcia V. Stohl, July 23, 1950; children—Genon Verlene, Monica Raye, Clendon Waldo. Office mgr. Grainger Bros. Wholesale 1949-50; pvt. practice pub. accounting J. Waldo Rost, Holdrege, Nebr., 1954—. Chmn. Phelps County chpt. ARC, 1960-61; mem. Bd. Edn. Holdrege Pub. Schs., 1968-72, v.p., 1968-72; trustee Found. of Nebr. Soc. C.P.A.'s. Served with AUS, 1951-53. Mem. Nebr. Soc. C.P.A.'s (dir. 1976—), Am. Inst. C.P.A.'s, Am. Legion, Holdrege C. of C., Ak-Sar-Ben. Lutheran (mem. council). Elk, Rotarian (sec. Holdrege 1961-62, dir. 1962—, pres.). Club: Country (sec. Holdrege, 1955-57). Contbg. author: Portfolio of Accounting Systems for Small and Medium-Sized Businesses. Home: 1130 Sheridan St Holdrege NE 68949 Office: 709 4th Ave Holdrege NE 68949

ROST, WILLIAM JOSEPH, educator; b. Fargo, N.D., Dec. 8, 1926; s. William Melvin and Christine Ruth (Hamerlik) Rost; m. Rita Cincoski, Sept. 15, 1951; children—Kathryn, Patricia, Carol. B.S., U. Minn., 1948, Ph.D., 1952. Registered Pharmacist, Minn. Asst. prof. pharmaceut. chemistry Sch. Pharmacy, U. Kansas City, 1952-56, asso. prof., 1956-61, prof., 1961-63; prof. pharmaceut. chemistry Sch. Pharmacy, U. Mo. at Kansas City, 1963—. Mem. Am. Pharmaceut.

Assn., Am. Chem. Soc., Kappa Psi, Rho Chi, Phi Lambda Upsilon, Sigma Xi. Recipient Wulling Club Key, U. Minn., 1948. Co-author (with William O. Foye et al): Principles of Medicinal Chemistry, 1974. Contbr. articles to profl. jours. Home: 10910 Washington St Kansas City MO 64114 Office: Sch Pharmacy U Mo Kansas City MO 64110

ROSTENKOWSKI, DAN, congressman; b. Chgo., Jan. 2, 1928; s. Joseph P. and Priscilla (Dombroski) R.; student St. John's Mil. Acad., 1942-46, Loyola U., 1948-51; m. LaVerne Pirkins, May 12, 1951; children—Dawn P., Kristie M., Gayle A., Stacy L. Mem. Ill. Gen. Assembly, 1952, Senate, 1954, 56; mem. 86th-95th congresses, 8th Dist. Ill., mem. ways and means com., chmn. subcom. on health; mem. joint com. on taxation; chmn. Democratic Caucus 90th, 91st Congresses; now chief dep. majority whip. Exec. dir. Automobile Assn., 1956-58. Chmn. Northwest Town Joint Appeal Fund, 1958; mem. mayor's youth adv. commn., Chgo.; mem. N.W. area redevel. commn., Chgo., 1952—. Served as cpl. 7th Inf. Div., AUS, 1946-48. Mem. YMCA, V.F.W. Democrat. K.C., Kiwanian. Home: 1372 W Evergreen St Chicago IL 60622 Office: House Office Bldg Washington DC 20515

ROTELLI, LEO ANTHONY, advt. and design agy. exec.; b. Waterman, Pa., Jan. 8, 1924; s. Placido and Jenny (Sia) R.; student Art Inst. Pitts., 1946-50, Art Inst. Chgo., 1951-52; m. Martha Yancic, May 4, 1953; children—Mason, Eric, Jennifer. Advt. dir. Edelstein Nelson, Chgo., 1952-53; partner Bendelow & Assos. Art Studio, 1953-65; owner Leo Rotelli Assos., Chgo., design studio, 1965—. Served with AUS, 1943-46. Recipient Design award Am. Paper Mfg. Assn., 1968; Design award Publicity Club Chgo., 1970-72. Mem. Nat. Indsl. Recreation Assn. (art dir., asso. dir. 1966-70), Artist Guild Chgo. (dir. 1969-70). Club: Chicago Press. Home: 513 S Wille St Mount Prospect IL 60056 Office: 535 N Michigan Ave Chicago IL 60611

ROTH, CARL FREDERICK, exec.; b. Bklyn., Apr. 29, 1932; s. John Julius and Charlotte (Vogel) R.; B.S. in Civil Engring., U. Miami (Fla.), 1958; M.B.A., DePaul U., 1968; m. Cecilia Carmella De Marco, Aug. 17, 1957; children—Janet Victoria, Victoria Christine, Carl Louis. Civil engr. Chgo. Bur. Engring., 1958-60; exec. dir. region 5 Structural Clay Products Inst., 1960-63; dir. mktg. Portland Cement Assn., Skokie, Ill., 1963-73; dir. marketing Precast Systems, Inc., 1973-76; pres. Modern Project Mgmt., Inc., 1976—; instr. civil engring. Midwest Coll. Engring., 1976—; lectr. bldg. constrn. Mem. bd. local improvements Village of Villa Park, Ill., 1971-77, trustee, 1971-75, pres. village, 1975—. Mem. St. Pius X Sch. Bd., 1970-71. Adminstr. bd. Sugar Creek Golf Course, 1974-75. Served with AUS, 1952-54. Recipient certificate appreciation Nat. Assn. Home Builders, 1971; Freedom Guard award Villa Park Jaycees, 1971. Registered profl. engr., Ill. Mem. Ill. Soc. Profl. Engrs., Prestressed Concrete Inst., Am. Marketing Assn., V.F.W., Beta Gamma Sigma, Delta Mu Delta. Clubs: Villa Park Kiwanis, K.C. (4 deg.). Home: 1100 Rand Rd Villa Park IL 60181

ROTH, CLAUDE A., lawyer; b. Galena, Ill.; LL.B., U. Chgo., 1923; m. Maryrose Racicot, July 12, 1927; 1 dau., Mrs. Claudette Kotrich. Admitted to Ill. bar, 1923; gen. practice of law, Chgo.; trustee C & N-W Ry., 1944-45. Served in USAAC, World War I. Mem. Am., Ill., Chgo. bar assns., Phi Delta Phi. Clubs: Mid-day (Chicago); Skokie Country. Home: 175 E Delaware Pl Chicago IL 60611 Office: 120 S LaSalle St Chicago IL 60603

ROTH, DAVID FRANCISCO, polit. scientist; b. Mar. 22, 1939; B.A., Claremont Men's Coll., 1960; M.A., San Francisco State Coll., 1964; Ph.D., Claremont Grad. Sch., 1968; postgrad. U. Calif., Berkeley, 1968. Condr. seminars for Good Neighbors Abroad in Latin Am., Asia, Western and Eastern Europe and Africa, summers 1960-66; vis. prof. U. Philippines, 1967; asst. prof. polit. sci. U. Wis., Oshkosh, 1968-69; research asso. Politicometrics Research Program, Ohio State U., 1969-70; asst. prof. polit. sci. Purdue U., West Lafayette, Ind., 1970—, adviser Black Opportunity Program, 1972-74, Iranian Student Assn., 1975-76, faculty fellow, 1973—; mem. MUCIA, Rural Devel. Task Force (Trinidad Project), 1974-76; cons. exec. sec. Philippine Cabinet, 1967-68, minister Health, Malaysia, summers 1972-75, minister Rural Devel. and Sci. and Tech., Malaysia, summers 1973-74, minister Agr., Sarawak, Malaysia, 1974-75, UNECAFE, 1974-75, exec. sec. to pres. Philippines, 1975, Foster Parents, Haiti, 1976, Ministry of Devel., Columbia, 1976. Recipient Internat. Devel. Research Center award, UN Asian Center for Devel. Adminstrn. award, 1975; Good Neighbors Abroad grantee, 1965, Purdue Research Found. summer travel grantee, 1971, World Order Project grantee, 1971, Malaysian Govt. research grantee, 1972; Author: (with Lee Wilson) The Comparative Study of Politics: China, Soviet Union, Britain, France, Mexico and Nigeria, 1976; Political Change in a Technocratic Society: The United States, 1977; contbr. articles on politics to profl. jours. Home: 2233 Miami Trails West Lafayette IN 47906

ROTH, DAVID MAURICE, realtor; b. Fort Wayne, Ind., Sept. 21, 1922; s. Rufus and Flossie Mildred (Deatrick) R.; B.S., Ind. U., 1948; m. Margaret Lourena Harrod, Aug. 24, 1946; children—John, Sharon (Mrs. Robert S. Wartenbe), Gregory, Kathryn. Partner, Mallough Roth Assos., Ft. Wayne, 1956-64; v.p. Banks Mallough Roth, Inc., 1964-71; pres. Roth Wehrly Heiny, Inc., 1971—. Co-capt. Fine Arts Drive, 1969-70. Bd. dirs. TB Assn., 1972-73, Better Bus. Bur., 1977; chmn. fund dr. Am. Cancer Soc., 1977, bd. dirs., 1977—. Served as lt. (j.g.) USNR, World War II; PTO. Mem. Realtors Nat. Mktg. Inst., Realtors Assn. (dir. 1971-72), Nat. Assn. Realtors, Multiple Listing Assn. (dir. 1970-73), C. of C., Exec. Club, Soc. Real Estate Appraisers, Home Builders Assn., Ind. U. Alumni Club. Mem. United Ch. Christ. Kiwanian. Home: 3427 Maxim Dr Fort Wayne IN 46805 Office: 230 E Berry St Fort Wayne IN 46802

ROTH, JOHN REECE, engring. physicist; b. Washington, Pa., Sept. 19, 1937; s. John Meyer and Ruth E. (Iams) R.; B.S., Mass. Inst. Tech., 1959; Ph.D., Cornell U., 1963; m. Helen Marie DeCrane, Jan. 14, 1972; 1 dau., Nancy Ann. Engring. aide Aerojet-Gen. Corp., Azusa, Calif., summers 1957, 58; research engr. N. Am. Aviation, Canoga Park, Calif., summer 1959; aerospace research scientist NASA-Lewis Research Center, Cleve., 1963—. Mem. IEEE (sr.), Am. Phys. Soc., AAAS, Am. Nuclear Soc., Archaeol. Inst. Am., Am. Inst. Aero. and Astronautics, Nuclear and Plasma Scis. Soc., Sigma Xi. Contbr. numerous articles in field to profl. jours. Research in high temperature plasma physics. Home: 21125 S Park Dr Fairview Park OH 44126 Office: 21000 Brookpark Dr Cleveland OH 44135

ROTH, NORMAN GILBERT, microbiologist; b. Chgo., Dec. 11, 1924; s. Joseph and Clara (Schein) R.; B.S., U. Chgo., 1947; M.S., U. Ill., 1949, Ph.D., 1951; m. Rose Marie Klein, Feb. 5, 1950; children—Susan, William, Joseph, Virginia, Sandra, David. Research microbiologist U.S. Army Chem. Corps, Frederick, Md., 1951-57; with Whirlpool Corp., Benton Harbor, Mich., 1957—, dir. life support, space programs, 1960-72, dir. waste mgmt. systems, 1972-77, dir. research and edn. spl. project, 1977—. Mem. finance com. Twin City Players, St. Joseph/Benton Harbor Community Theater, 1970—; active Boy Scouts, Girl Scouts, United Fund, YMCA. Mem. Library Bd. St. Joseph Twp., 1972—. Recipient NASA awards for achievements in manned space programs. Mem. AAAS, Water Pollution Control Fedn., Am. Soc. Microbiologists, Aerospace Med. Assn., Sigma Xi. Contbr. articles to profl. jours. Home: 1801 Briarcliff Dr St Joseph MI 49085 Office: Whirlpool Corp Research and Engineering Center Monte Rd Benton Harbor MI 49022

ROTH, SYDNEY MARTIN, advt. and mass market planning specialist; b. Jersey City, June 3, 1903; s. Edward M. and Bessie (Kauffman) R.; ed. Ill. Inst. Tech., U. Chgo.; m. Adele Cashwan, Nov. 24, 1944 (div.). Vice pres. Morris Schenker Roth, advt. agy., Chgo., 1935-39; pres. Roth, Schenker & Bernhard, advt. agy. and mass market devel., Chgo., 1939-43; pres. Roth Bros. & Co. (successors to Roth, Schenker & Bernhard, Inc.), 1943—; exec. dir. Roth Market Devel. Co., 1967—; founding dir. Growth Industries Shares, Inc., mut. fund. Wartime cons. U.S. Dept. Agr., Food Distbn. Adminstrn. Served on business adv. com. Presidents Council Econ. Advisers. Founding pres. Community Child Guidance Centers of Chgo.; past pres. Individual Psychology Assn. Hon. fellow Harry S. Truman Library. Mem. Am. Soc. Adlerian Psychology, Fgn. Policy Assn., Chgo. Assn. Commerce and Industry, Chgo. Council on Fgn. Relations, Advt. Fedn. Am., Chemurgic Council, Internat. Platform Assn., Ill. Soc. Mental Hygiene, Am. Mgmt. Assn., Am. Marketing Assn., Nat. Planning Assn., Ore. Soc. Individual Psychology (hon. life), Am. Inst. Graphic Arts. Club: City. Founder and pub. Am. edit. Internat. Jour. Individual Psychology. Home: 880 N Lake Shore Dr Chicago IL 60611 Office: 1 E Wacker Dr Chicago IL 60601

ROTHENBERG, HAROLD JAY, II, pathologist; b. Chgo., Sept. 30, 1941; s. Harold J. and Florence (Light) R.; M.D., U. Ill., 1966. Rotating intern Cook County (Ill.) Hosp., 1966-67; resident pathology Passavant Meml. Hosp., Chgo., 1967-68, Presbyn. St. Luke's Hosp., 1970-72; clin. pathology fellow U. Ill. Hosp., Chgo., 1972-73, dir. blood bank, 1973-77; asst. dir. dept. pathology Abraham Lincoln Sch. Medicine, U. Ill., Chgo., 1976—; dir. Phys. and Surg. Labs., Waukegan, Ill., 1976—. Served with USNR, 1968-70; comdg. officer environ. and preventive medicine, 1975—. Mem. AMA, Am. Soc. Clin. Pathologists, Coll. Am. Pathologists, Ill., Chgo. med. scos., Chgo. Pathol. Soc. Jewish. Address: Dept Pathology 1853 W Polk St Chicago IL 60612

ROTHERMEL, BRADLEY LEGEORGE, coll. adminstr.; b. Monroe Center, Ill., Dec. 4, 1937; s. Milford Olen and Ruth Leona (Fager) R.; B.S., No. Ill. U., 1960; M.S., U. Ill., 1961, Ph.D., 1965; m. Suzanne Kay Menz, June 8, 1963; children—Beth Kristin, Christine Anne. Asst. and asso. prof. U. Ill., Champaign-Urbana, 1965-71, dir. phys. fitness lab., 1965-66, supr. research devel. and counseling in athletics, 1966-68; prof. health and phys. edn. George Williams Coll., Downers Grove, Ill., 1971-74, dir. div. health and phys. edn., 1971-74; asst. dir. and bus. mgr. dept. intercoll. athletics Kans. State U., Manhattan, 1974—. Research cons. Chgo. Cubs, 1963-65, univs., coll., high sch. athletics health and phys. edn. programs. Capt., United Fund drive, Urbana, Elmhurst, Ill., Manhattan, Kans.; mem. research devel. com., nat. bd. dirs. YMCA, 1971-74. Recipient med. sch. research grant U. Ill., 1970-71. Mem. Coll. Athletic Bus. Mgrs. Assn., Internat. Fedn. Phys. Edn., Nat. Coll. Athletic Assn., Nat. Amateur Athletic Union, Nat. Coll. Phys. Edn. Assn., AAHPER, Ill. Assn. Health, Phys. Edn. and Recreation (state pres. 1972-74), Ill. Assn. Profl. Preparation in Health, Phys. Edn. and Recreation (state pres. 1973-74), Phi Epsilon Kappa. Author: Selected Physical Fitness Characteristics of Professional Baseball Players, 1970. Contbr. articles to profl. jours. Home: 1853 Fairchild St Manhattan KS 66502 Office: Ahearn Gymnasium Kans State U Manhattan KS 66506

ROTHFUS, JOHN ARDEN, chemist; b. Des Moines, Dec. 25, 1932; s. Truman Clinton and Beatrice (Keeney) R.; B.A., Drake U., 1955; Ph.D., U. Ill., 1960; m. Paula Kay Harris, Sept. 26, 1959; children—Lee Ellen, David Merrill. Asst. biochemistry U. Ill. at Urbana, 1955-59; instr. U. Utah Coll. Medicine, Salt Lake City, 1961-63; asst. prof. U. Calif. Med. Sch., Los Angeles, 1963-65; prin. research chemist U.S. Dept. Agr., Peoria, Ill., 1965-70, investigations head, 1970-74, research leader, 1974—. Proctor & Gamble Co. fellow, 1957-58; USPHS postdoctoral fellow, 1959-61. Mem. Am. Chem. Soc., AAAS, Am. Assn. Cereal Chemists, N.Y. Acad. Scis., Phi Beta Kappa, Sigma Xi, Phi Lambda Upsilon, Omicron Delta Kappa, Alpha Chi Sigma. Home: 5615 N Sherwood Ave Peoria IL 61614 Office: 1815 N University St Peoria IL 61604

ROTHFUSS, FRED DOTY, metal furniture mfg. co. exec.; b. Sylvania, Ohio, Nov. 15, 1918; s. Herman William and Helen (Doty) R.; student Toledo U., 1939-43, Toledo Mus. Art, 1942-43; m. Stella Schmabel, Apr. 14, 1946; children—Michael, Nancy. Pres., Rothfuss Industries, Inc., Ottawa Lake, Mich., 1947—. Served with USNR, 1943-46. Mem. Quiet Birdmen (Keyman 1975-76), Alpha Sigma Phi. Conglist. Home: 12951 Yankee Rd Ottawa Lake MI 49267 Office: 12953 Yankee Rd Ottawa Lake MI 49267

ROTHHAAR, RAYMOND EUGENE, pedodontist; b. Muncie, Ind., Mar. 18, 1925; s. Raymond Charles and Estella Iva (Leininger) R.; student Ball State U., Muncie, 1946-48; D.D.S., Ind. U., 1952; postgrad. U. Pa., 1958; m. Frances Wynne Kimbrough, Aug. 12, 1949 (dec. 1966); children—Gayle, Karen, Gretchen, Karl, Kendra; m. 2d, Arlene Helen Campbell, Dec. 1, 1966; children—Eric Ray, Kirk Tyler. Practice dentistry, Muncie, 1952—; mem. pedodontics faculty Ind. U. Dental Sch., 1957-58; sr. class guest lectr. preventive dentistry, 1961—. Mem. Ind. Bd. Dental Examiners, 1971—; dental examiner Nat. Testing Service Bd., 1974—. Mem. Muncie Community Bd. Sch. Trustee, 1964-72. Bd. dirs. local Am. Cancer Soc., Soc. Crippled Children and Adults, Boy Scouts Am.; mem. Ind. State Controlled Substance Adv. Bd., 1973—. Served with USNR, 1943-46. Recipient Distinguished Service award Muncie Jaycees, 1958. Fellow Am. Acad. Pedodontics, Acad. Internat. Dentistry, Acad. Canadienne des Scis. Dentaires; mem. Ind. Soc. Dentistry Children (pres. 1963-64), E. Central (pres. 1957-58), Del. County (pres. 1953-54) dental socs. Methodist (trustee). Mason. Club: Delaware Country (Muncie, Ind.). Home: 2605 Wood-Bridge St Muncie IN 47304 Office: 510 S Tillotson St Muncie IN 47304

ROTHMAN, DAVID, physician; b. St. Louis, Apr. 30, 1911; s. Ben and Ida (Gidansky) R.; B.S., M.D., Washington U., 1935; m. Frances Strauss, June 14, 1934; children—Helen Jean (Mrs. Normal Flegel), Elaine Pearl, Sally Ann. Intern, Jewish Hosp., St. Louis, 1935-36; resident St. Louis Maternity Hosp., 1936-37, Jewish Hosp., St. Louis, 1937-38; practice medicine specializing in obstetrics and gynecology, St. Louis, 1938—; staff mem. Jewish Hosp., Barnes, St. Louis Maternity, all St. Louis, 1938—; dir. dept. obstetrics and gynecology Jewish Hosp., St. Louis, 1956-72; pres. med. staff, 1959-61; asso. clin. prof. obstetrics and gynecology Washington U. Med. Sch., St. Louis, lectr. obstetrics Warren Brown Sch. Social Service, 1954—. Bd. dirs. Jewish Med. Social Service Bur., 1951-54, Jewish Childrens Home, 1956-57, St. Louis Psychoanalytic Found.; med. adv. bd. Salvation Army. Served to capt. M.C., USAF, 1942-45. Diplomate Am. Bd. Obstetrics and Gynecology. Mem. AMA, Am. Coll. Obstetrics and Gynecology, Central Assn. Obstetrics ano Gynecology, St. Louis Gynecol. Soc., Acad. Psychosomatic Medicine, Am. Fertility Soc. Home: 8033 Davis Dr Clayton MO 63105 Office: 2821 N Ballas Rd St Louis MO 63131

ROTHMANN, BRUCE FRANKLIN, pediatric surgeon; b. Akron, Ohio, July 11, 1924; s. Edwin Franklin and Mary Madelene (Policy) R.; student Western Res. U., 1942-43, Wesleyan U., 1943-44; M.D., N.Y.U., 1948; postgrad. surgery U. Pa., 1952-53; m. Lola Secor, June 14, 1947; children—Susan Ann Rothmann Hamburger, Pamela Jane Rothmann Perkins, Elizabeth May. Intern, Akron City Hosp., 1948-49, resident in surgery, 1949-50, gen. surg. resident, 1953, chief surg. resident, 1954-55; resident in pediatric surgery Children's Hosp., Akron, 1953-54, mem. staff, 1955—, chief of surgery, 1969-74, chief of staff, 1973-74; practice medicine specializing in surgery, Akron, 1955-68, practice limited to pediatric surgery, 1968—; asst. surgeon Univ. Hosps., Cleve., 1962—; clin. instr. pediatric surgery Case-Western Res. U., Cleve., 1962-64, sr. instr., 1964-67, asst. clin. prof., 1967—. Mem. advisory com. Coll. Fine and Applied Arts, U. Akron, 1972—, Blossom Music Center, 1973—, Children's Concert Soc. Akron, 1972—; bd. mgrs. Cuyahoga Falls Community YMCA, 1957-63; bd. trustees 1st Congl. Ch., Akron, 1960-64, Performing Arts Hall Assn., 1974—, Akron Symphony Orch., 1958—. Served with USN, 1943-45, 50-52. Diplomate Nat. Bd. Med. Examiners, Am. Bd. Surgery. Fellow Am. Acad. Pediatrics, A.C.S.; mem. Am. Pediatric Surg. Assn., Am. Burn Assn., British Assn. Pediatric Surgeons, AMA, Cleve. Surg. Soc., Summit County Med. Soc. Contbr. articles to med. jours. Clubs: Akron City, Silver Lake Country. Home: 3020 Kent Rd Silver Lake Cuyahoga Falls OH 44224 Office: 300 Locust St Akron OH 44302

ROTHNEM, MORRIS STANLEY, obstetrician, gynecologist; b. Fargo, N.D., Dec. 3, 1919; s. Thomas Peter and Ovidia (Rosten) R.; student St. Olaf Coll., 1937-40; B.S., U. Minn., 1942; M.S., 1944, M.D., 1944; m. Lorraine Elizabeth Englert, Oct. 5, 1948; children—Bradford Thomas, Susan Lorraine, Gregory Lambert. Intern, resident in obstetrics and gynecology St. Barnabas Hosp., Mpls., 1946-48; practice medicine specializing in obstetrics and gynecology Paul Larson Obstetrics and Gynecology Clinic, Mpls., 1950—; pres. Northwestern Hosp. Med. staff, Mpls., 1966, mem. hosp. bd. and corp., instr. in intern and residency tng. program in obstetrics and gynecological surgery; mem. med. staff Abbott-Northwestern Hosp., 1950—, Fairview Community Hosps., 1962—; med. dir. Planned Parenthood, Mpls., 1954-55; mem. com. for orgn. pub. health services Hennepin County (Minn.), 1973, 74; mem. Morse Twp. Planning and Zoning Commn., 1974—; active Physicians Met. Health Force, 1975—; mem. Hosp. and Physician Health Resource Advisory Com. to Met. Health Bd., 1975—. Served to capt. M.C., U.S. Army, 1944-46. Diplomate Am. Bd. Obstetrics and Gynecology. Mem. Am. Coll. Obstetrics and Gyncology, Mpls. Acad. Medicine, Mpls. Council Obstetrics and Gynecology, AMA, Minn. State, Hennepin County med. socs., Minn. State Obstetrics and Gynecology Soc. Lutheran. Club: Decathalon Athletic (Mpls.). Contbr. articles in field to med. jours. Home: 4605 Townes Circle Minneapolis MN 55424 Office: 6517 Drew Ave S Edina MN 55436

ROTHNER, ARNOLD DAVID, pediatric neurologist; b. Chgo., Nov. 19, 1940; s. Nathan Michael and Shirley R.; A.B., Yeshiva Coll., 1961; M.D., U. Ill., Chgo., 1965; m. Sarah Hurwitz, Aug. 25, 1963; children—Yehuda, Malka. Intern, Presbyn.-St. Luke's Hosp., Chgo., 1965-66; resident in pediatrics Presbyn.-St. Luke's Hosp., Chgo., 1966-67; Babies Hosp., Columbia-Presbyn. Med. Center, N.Y.C., 1967-68; NIH fellow in pediatric neurology Neurol. Inst., Columbia U., 1970-73; chief sect. child neurology, dept. pediatrics The Cleve. Clinic Found., 1973—. Pres. Cleve. chpt. Epilepsy Found. Served as major U.S. Army, 1968-70. Diplomate Nat. Bd. Med. Examiners, Am. Bd. Pediatrics, Am. Bd. Psychiatry and Neurology. Mem. Child Neurology Soc., Epilepsy Assn. Ohio, Contbr. numerous articles in field to med. jours. Home: 3495 Severn Rd Cleveland Heights OH 44118 Office: 9500 Euclid Ave Cleveland OH 44106

ROTHSCHILD, ROBERT LEHWALD, pub. co. exec.; b. N.Y.C., Aug. 22, 1911; s. Moses J. and Mabel (Pike) Lehwald;; A.B., U. Wis., 1932. Vice pres., prodn. mgr. Spencer Press Inc., 1945-61; pres. Am. Peples Press Inc., 1961-65; pres. Lexicon Publs. Inc., Chgo., 1965—. Past pres., bd. dirs. Chgo. Book Clinic; trustee U. Wis. Scholarship Trust, Columbia Coll., Chgo. Served with USAAF, 1942-45. Club: U. Wis. of Chgo. (past pres.). Home: 505 Lake Shore Dr Chicago IL 60611 Office: 201 N Wells St Chicago IL 60606

ROTHSTEIN, DAVID ANTHONY, psychiatrist; b. Chgo., Jan. 14, 1935; s. Alexander and Lillian Alice (Spitler) R.; B.S., U. Ill., 1957, M.S., 1959, M.D. cum laude, 1959; m. Laila Usprich Cohen, June 30, 1957; children—Lisa Anne, Peter David. Intern. St. Francis Hosp., Evanston, Ill., 1959-60; resident Michael Reese Hosp., Chgo., 1960-63; pvt. practice psychiatry, Chgo., 1965—; attending physician Michael Reese Hosp. Psychosomatic and Psychiat. Inst., 1965—; attending psychiatrist Chgo. Lakeshore Hosp., 1972—; asst. prof. psychiatry U. Chgo. Med. Sch., 1974—; sr. cons. Ill. State Psychiat. Inst., 1973-75; cons. Ill. Dept. Mental Health Inst. for Juvenile Research, 1964-66, community mental health program, 1972; cons. Warren Commn., 1964, Nat. Commn. on Causes and Prevention of Violence, 1968; del. Inst. Govt. Ops., 1976. Pres., Dist. 2 Edn. Council, Chgo. Bd. Edn., 1974-76; pres. Jamieson Sch. Community Council, 1972-73; mem. city-wide adv. com. to desegregate Chgo. Pub. Schs., 1977—; bd. mgrs. Montefiore-Motley Spl. Schs. PTA. Served to lt. comdr. USPHS, 1963-65. Diplomate Am. Bd. Psychiatry and Neurology. Fellow Am. Orthopsychiat. Assn., Am. Psychiat. Assn. (com. financing mental health care); mem. AMA (recipient Physicians Recognition award 1970, 73, 76, Roche award 1957), Ill. Psychiat. Soc. (editor Psychiat. Examiner, legis. liaison com., chmn. malpractice subcom., residents research award 1963), Am., Chgo. (chmn. ad hoc com. desegregation, co-chmn. com. on revised mental health code) socs. adolescent psychiatry, Ill. Group Psychotherapy Soc. (councillor), Ill. Med. Soc. (ho. dels., task force on profl. liability, council affiliated socs.), AAAS, ACLU, Center Study Dem. Instns., SANE, Ams. for Democratic Action, Ind. Voters Ill., Alpha Omega Alpha. Research on presdl. assassination and study of leaders, info. theory applications to psychiatry, study of diagnosis and treatment of deaf patients, econs. of health care, group process in community and profl. groups. Contbr. articles to profl. jours. Office: 55 E Washington St Chicago IL 60602

ROTHSTEIN, STANLEY HAROLD, mental health center exec.; b. Louisville, Mar. 10, 1926; s. Jack and Sara (Fine) R.; B.A., U. Louisville, 1948; M.A., U. Chgo., 1951, Ph.D., 1967; m. Linda Rae Smith, Feb. 13, 1960; children—Jan Stephen, Jason Joel. Dir. social service Loretto Hosp., Chgo., 1960-64; dir. South East Community Mental Health Center, Chgo., 1967—; exec. dir. South East Community Health Orgn. Alcoholism Treatment Program, 1976—; mem. faculty Stritch Sch. Medicine Loyola U., 1955-70, Chgo. City Coll., 1955-70; cons. in field. Mem. adv. council Olive-Harvey br. Chgo. City Coll. Served with AUS, 1943-45; ETO. Decorated Purple Heart. USPHS fellow gerontology, 1964-67. Mem. Am. Orthopsychiat. Assn., Nat. Assn. Social Workers. Home: 4748 S Kenwood Ave Chicago IL 60615 Office: 30 N Michigan Ave Chicago IL 60602 also 80 River Oaks Center Calumet City IL 60409

ROUDANÉ, CHARLES, metal products co. exec.; b. Los Angeles, July 16, 1927; s. Rudolph and Irene (Warner) R.; B.S., Tulane U., 1950; m. Orient Fox, Aug. 20, 1948; children—Mark, Matthew. Gen. mgr. Master div. Koehring Co., Chgo., 1955-67; gen. sales mgr.

Wilton Corp., Schiller Park, Ill., 1967-70; dir. mktg. Flexonics div. UOP Inc., Bartlett, Ill., 1970-73, v.p., gen. mgr. Flexonics div., 1973—. Served with U.S. Army, 1945-46. Mem. Am. Mgmt. Assn. (mem. marketing council), ASME (exec. affiliate). Republican. Presbyterian. Office: 300 E Devon Ave Bartlett IL 60103

ROUNDY, LLOYD RUSSELL, owner supermarkets; b. Panama, Iowa, Apr. 18, 1913; s. Albert Ross and Ida Pearl (Razee) R.; grad. high sch.; m. Bonnie Glee Musgrave, Dec. 15, 1947; 1 dau., Dina Glee. Owner, operator Foodland Super Markets, Woodbine, Iowa, and Missouri Valley, Iowa, 1947—. Served with AUS, 1942-45. Mem. V.F.W., Am. Legion. Methodist. Odd fellows. Home: 45 5th St Woodbine IA 51579 Office: Foodland Super Market 5th and Lincoln Way Woodbine IA 51579

ROUSE, GENE GORDON, community services worker; b. Mt. Vernon, Ohio, Apr. 23, 1923; s. Horace Kenneth and Louise (Carrington) R.; B.S., Central State U., 1951; postgrad. Chgo. Tchrs. Coll., 1960-61; m. Estelle Lewis, June 4, 1949; children—Gene Gordon, Eric Von. Clk., U.S. Post Office, Chgo., 1951-66; neighborhood worker Chgo. Dept. Human Services City of Chgo., 1966-68, unit dir. Englewood Unit Community Services, 1968—. Tchr., 7th grade, Chgo., 1960-65. Hon. mem. P.R. Congress, 1972—; chmn. blood drives Engelwood Hosp., 1974; mem. Mendel Parents Club, 1968—; pres. Mendel Boosters, 1974-75; mem. Ill. selection com. Navy ROTC, 1971. Served with AUS, 1943-45; ETO. Recipient Appreciation award Puerto Rican Congress, 1971; Service award Central State U. Alumni Assn., 1971; Austin Town Hall Assembly, 1971, Great Guy award Sta. WGRT, 1971. Mem. Nat. Assn. Community Devel., Kappa Alpha Psi. Roman Catholic. Named Midwest Football All-Am., 1950, Little Ohio Football All-Am., 1950. Home: 1054 W 109th Pl Chicago IL 60643 Office: 6005 S Halsted St Chicago IL 60620

ROUSE, JOHN RATCLIFFE, art museum dir., curator; b. Cunningham, Kans., Aug. 27, 1917; s. John R. and Edith Belle (Cole) R.; B.A., Bethel Coll., Newton, Kans., 1939. With 4th Nat. Bank & Trust Co., Wichita, 1940-46; mgr. Commodore Hotel, Wichita, 1946-56; pvt. cons. antiques, 1955—; curator, dir. Wichita Art Assn. Galleries, Inc., 1973—. Mem. Wichita Hist. Mus. Assn. (trustee 1972—), Wichita Art Assn. (trustee 1973—, pres., 1973-75), Wichita Art Mus. Mems. Found., Fine Arts Council Wichita, Am. Assn. Museums, Mountain Plains Mus. Conf., Kans. Mus. Assn., Am. Crafts Council. Republican. Christian Scientist. Home: 1400 N Woodlawn Ave Wichita KS 67208 Office: 9112 E Central St Wichita KS 67206

ROUSH, ALLAN NELSON, chemist; b. DeKalb, Ill., Mar. 21, 1939; s. Glenn William and Maryon Eleanor (Nelson) R., B.S., No. Ill. U., 1962, M.S., 1966; m. Patricia Rose Latham, Feb. 4, 1961; children—Allan Richard, Stephanie Lyn. Project leader Synthetic Aircraft Lubricant R & D Sinclair Research, Inc., Harvey, Ill., 1967-69; project mgr. Lubricants R & D Atlantic Richfield Co., Harvey, 1969-72, sr. product compliance specialist fuels, 1972-74; mgr. product research D-A Lubricant Co., Indpls., 1974-77, asst. v.p. research, 1977—. Dir. Home Owners Assn., Park Forest South, Ill., 1968; cub scout leader, Boy Scouts Am., 1972. Mem. Soc. Automotive Engrs., Am. Soc. Testing and Materials. Patentee stable synthetic ester lubricant composition. Home: 3406 Beech Dr Carmel IN 46032 Office: 1331 W 29th St Indianapolis IN 46208

ROUSOS, MICHAEL GEORGE, structural engr.; b. Delphos, O., Feb. 16, 1929; s. George and Theodora (Frangake) R.; B.S. in Archtl. Engring., with honors, Ohio U., 1951; m. Alfreda W. Mannossos, May 8, 1955; children—George Michael, Theodore Michael, William Michael, James Michael. With the Hausman Steel Co., Toledo, 1953-54; with Samborn, Steketee, Otis and Evns, architects and engrs., Toledo, 1954-59; asso., asst. chief structural engr., Richards, Bauer & Moorhead, architects and engrs., Toledo, 1959-70; partner Leruth & Rousos, cons. structural engrs., Toledo, 1970-72; prin. and structural engr. The Collaborative, Inc., architects, engrs. and landscape architects, Toledo, 1973—. Served to lt., USAF, 1951-53. Registered profl. engr., Ohio, Fla., Colo., Mich., N.J., Ind., Pa., Tenn.; registered profl. structural engr., Ill., Ky. Mem. Nat., Ohio, Toledo socs. profl. engrs., ASCE, Am. Concrete Inst., Prestressed Concrete Inst., Post-Tensioning Inst. Mem. Greek Orthodox Ch. (treas.. sec.). Home: 1459 Sabra Rd Toledo OH 43612 Office: 1647 S Cove Blvd Toledo OH 43606

ROUTMAN, BURTON NORMAN, osteo. physician, educator; b. Youngstown, Ohio, Apr. 21, 1941; s. Samuel Leonard and Beatrice Roberta (Epstein) R.; B.A., Johns Hopkins, 1963; D.O., Coll. Osteo. Medicine and Surgery, Des Moines, 1968; m. Teri Lisa Laybourn, June 12, 1964; children—Stephanie Lynn, Leslie Gail. Intern, Green Cross Gen. Hosp., Cuyahoga Falls, Ohio, 1968-69; practice osteo. medicine, Des Moines, 1972—; mem. staffs Des Moines Gen. Hosp., Broadlawns Polk County Hosp.; asst. dean student affairs, prof. Coll. Osteo. Medicine and Surgery, 1972—, pvt. practice family medicine, 1976—. Mem. Gov. Iowa Adv. Council to Iowa Drug Abuse Authority, 1974—; bd. dirs. Inner Urban Community Health Center, Central Iowa Health Services Inc., Greater Opportunities Inc., Bur. Jewish Edn. Served to capt., Med. Service Corps., USAF, 1969-72. Mem. Am. Osteo. Assn., Polk County, Iowa socs. osteo. physicians, Aerospace Med. Assn., Sigma Sigma Phi (dir.), Lambda Omicron Gamma, Alpha Epsilon Pi. Jewish (Men's Club). Home: 404 33d St West Des Moines IA 50265 Office: 812 Ashworth Rd West Des Moines IA 50265

ROUWENHORST, DONALD LEE, chem. co. exec.; b. Oskaloosa, Iowa, July 18, 1938; s. John Lester and Florence A. (Grandia) R.; B.S., Iowa State U., 1960; M.S., So. Ill. U., 1970; m. Janet A. Berglund, Aug. 3, 1963; children—John Lee, Beth Ann, Lisa Kay. With Rudy Patrick Co., Princeton, Ill., 1961-74, asst. prodn. mgr., 1961-69, prodn. mgr., 1970-74; area research and devel. rep. Uniroyal Chem., Oskaloosa, 1974—. Recipient Presdl. citation Rudy Patrick Co., 1973. Mem. Am. Soc. Agronomy, Phi Kappa Phi. Mem. Ref. Ch. Am. Club: Optimist (internal v.p. 1973). Home: 1032 1st Ave E Oskaloosa IA 52577

ROVELSTAD, TRYGVE A., sculptor; b. Elgin, Ill., Sept. 27, 1903; s. Theador and Anna (Evensen) R.; student of Lorado Taft, 1922, Frederick Hibbard, Chgo., 1923, U. Wash., 1927; m. Gloria G. Michel, July 8, 1950; 1 dau., Gloria-Ann. Exhibited at Acad. Galleries, Elgin, Gallery of Pallette and Chisel Club, Chgo., 1938-39, Peabody Inst., Balt., 1959-60, Pub. Library, Washington, 1964, North Mississippi Valley Artists Exhbn., Ill. State Mus., 1964, Elgin Coin Club, 1966, Hudson Valley Art Assn., Inc., 1970; in permanent collections Smithsonian Instn. Numis. Hall, Washington, Am. Meml. Chapel St. Paul's Cathedral, London, Eng., Crane Tech. High Sch., Chgo., Ill. State Capitol, Ill. State Office Bldg.; instr. sculpting U.S. Army U., Shrivenham, Eng., 1945-46; designed, executed Elgin Commemorative Half Dollar U.S. Mint, Phila., 1936; designer, editor Am. Roll Honor St. Paul's Cathedral, London, 1951; designer U.S. Army Occupation Germany medal, Roland Victor Libonati I Will medal-award, 1964; designer-sculptor Logan Hay Lincoln medal award of Abraham Lincoln 1967; Mark Twain medal Chase Commemorative Soc., 1967; Ill. Sesquicentennial medals, 1968; Chgo. Coin Club 50th Anniversary medal, 1969; Lincoln Heritage Trail medal, 1969; 101st Airborne Div. medal, 1969; Eisenhower Proclamation medal, 1969; Chgo. Fire Centennial medal, 1971; Rovelstad Pioneer-I Will medal, 1971; heroic sculptures, 1971—; pres., bd. dirs. Pioneer Meml. Found. Ill.; pres., bd. govs. Asso. I Will Sculptors Chgo., 1964-75; pres., dir. Tryg's Sculpture Sch., 1963-72; pres., dir. Pathfinder Inc., 1973-75. Recipient silver Ill. Sesquicentennial medal Ill. Sesquicentennial Commn., 1968; ofcl. commemorative medal Lincoln Heritage Trail Found., 1969; silver CCC Golden Anniversary medal Chgo. Coin Club, 1969; Captive Nations Eisenhower Proclamation medals and certificate Captive Nations Friends Com., 1969; Charlotte Dunwiddie prize for heroic Pioneer Father bronze head Am. Artists Profl. League, 1971, Anna Hyatt Huntington Meml. award for heroic Pioneer Scout aluminum sculpture head, 1974; hon. mention for Pioneer Mother heroic aluminum head Hudson Valley Art Assn., 1972; Ill. Bicentennial Medal design prize Franklin Mint, 1972. Mem. Elgin Area Hist. Soc. (dir. 1966-67), Am. Artists Profl. League, Elgin Coin Club (hon.). Address: 535 Ryerson Ave Elgin IL 60120

ROWAN, RICHARD JOHN, automotive equipment mfg. co. exec.; b. Cleve., Aug. 20, 1931; s. Rudolph George and Mary (Magdalene) R.; B.S. in Mech. Engring. (Am. Steel & Wire scholar), Case Inst. Tech., 1953; M.B.A. (univ. scholar), Syracuse U., 1967; m. Julia Park, Dec. 28, 1957; children—Carol, Kathleen, Richard, Robert. With Am. Steel & Wire div. U.S. Steel Corp., Cleve., 1953-62, indsl. engr., 1957-59, foreman, combustion control, maintenance engr., 1959-62; sr. system analyst Corning Glass Works, (N.Y.), 1962-63, supr. equipment engring., 1963-67; asst. plant mgr. Continental Can Co., N.Y.C., 1967-69; mgr. mfg. Rockwell Standard div. Rockwell Internat., Newark, Ohio, 1969-71, plant mgr., Tilbury, Ont., Can., 1971-72, New Castle, Pa., 1972-75; gen. mgr. O.E.M. div. Heavy Vehicle System Group, Bendix Corp., Elyria, Ohio, 1975—. Councilman-at-large, Heath, Ohio, 1970-71; mem. Greater New Castle Assn., 1972—; mem. Parents Tchrs. Orgn., New Castle; coach Poland (Ohio) Little League Football. Bd. dirs. Lawrence County (Pa.) United Fund. Served with USNR, 1953-57. Recipient outstanding adviser jr. achievement area award Am. Soc. Tng. Dirs., 1961. Mem. ASME, Am. Inst. Indsl. Engrs., Am. Mktg. Assn., Greater New Castle Assn., Canadian Mfg. Assn., Automotive Parts Mfg. Assn., Syracuse Alumni Assn., Rockwell Axle Club, Horse Heads Transp. Com. Author: Market Planning and Behavioral Concepts, 1963. Home: 2475 Timothy Knoll Dr Poland OH 44514 Office: 901 Cleveland St Elyria OH 44035

ROWE, CLARENCE JOHN, psychiatrist; b. St. Paul, May 24, 1916; s. Clarence John and Sayde E. (Mabin) R.; B.A., Coll. St. Thomas, 1938; M.B., U. Minn., 1942, M.D., 1943, fellow in psychiatry, 1946-49; m. Patricia A. McNulty, Jan. 15, 1945; children—Padraic, Rory, Kelly Michael. Intern St. Joseph's Hosp., St. Paul, 1942-43; resident VA Hosp., Mpls., U. Minn. hosps., Mpls., 1946-49; instr., asst. prof. U. Minn., 1949-54; dir. Hamm Meml. Psychiat. Clinic, St. Paul, 1954-57; pvt. practice St. Paul, 1957—; cons. 3M Co., 1957-72, Ramsey County Mcpl. Ct., 1958—, Constance Bultman Wilson Center, Faribault, Minn., 1973—; clin. prof. psychiatry U. Minn. Med. Med. Sch., 1964—; adj. faculty mem. Antioch Coll., 1974—; cons. St. Thomas Acad., 1970—; chmn. Minn. Mental Health Planning Council, 1963—; mem. Mayors Com. on Drug Use and Abuse, 1969-71, Govs. Council on Employment of Handicapped, 1965—; mem. adv. bur. hearing and appeals Social Security Adminstrn., 1965—. Trustee St. Thomas Acad., 1970-76; bd. dirs. St. Johns U. Inst. Mental Health, Collegeville, Minn., 1954—. Served with M.C., AUS, 1943-46. Fellow Am. Psychiat. Assn. (chmn. mental health in industry com., 1959-64); mem. AMA, Group for Advancement Psychiatry, Minn. Psychiat. Soc. (pres., 1973—), Minn. Soc. Adolescent Psychiatry (pres. elect), St. Paul Soc. Psychiatry and Neurology (pres., 1971-72). Roman Catholic. Clubs: St. Paul Athletic, Town and Country, Informal. Author: An Outline of Psychiatry, 6th ed., 1975; The Mentally Ill Employee, 1965; (with Allan McLean) The Clergy and Pastoral Counselling, 1969. Home: 1770 Colvin St St Paul MN 55116 Office: 551 S Snelling St St Paul MN 55116

ROWE, FRED HERBERT, urologist; b. Chgo., Feb. 13, 1933; s. Charles J. and Rose (Lessick) R.; B.S., U. Ill., 1952, M.D., 1956; m. Joyce G. Singer, Feb. 26, 1961; children—Steven, Mark, Robert. Intern, Cook County Hosp., Chgo., 1956-57, resident in urology, 1957-61; practice medicine specializing in urology, Chgo., 1963—. Served to capt. USAF, 1961-63. Mem. AMA, A.C.S., Ill., Chgo. med. socs., Am., Chgo. urol. assns. Home: 1701 S Millburne Rd Lake Forest IL 60045 Office: 3333 W Peterson St Chicago IL 60659

ROWE, FRED WERNER, mfg. co. exec.; b. Heilbronn, West Germany, Sept. 14, 1921; s. William A. and Irma (Rothschild) R.; came to U.S., 1939, naturalized, 1944; B.E.E. (Rackham Found. scholar), U. Detroit, 1944; m. Betty S. Shaffer, Aug. 16, 1947; children—Linda Ann, Steven Shelby. Elec. engr. Bulldog Electric Products Co., Detroit, 1941-44; research engr., fgn. tech. coordinator Bundy Tubing Co., Detroit, 1946-66; with Mich. Seamless Tube Co. (now Quanex Corp.), South Lyon, Mich., 1966—, corporate dir. research and devel., 1966—. Served with USNR, 1944-46. Mem. Am. Soc. Metals, Am. Soc. Nondestructive Testing (dir. 1976-78), IEEE, Engring. Soc. Detroit. Jewish. Club: Optimist (dir. 1970-74). Home: 7178 Heatherheath Ln West Bloomfield MI 48033 Office: Quanex Corp 400 McMunn St South Lyon MI 48178

ROWE, NATHANIEL HAWTHORNE, dentist; b. Hibbing, Minn., May 26, 1931; s. Nathaniel Hawthorne and Edna (Bockler) R.; D.D.S., B.S., U. Minn., 1955, M.S.D., 1958; m. Norma Estelle Quinlan, June 24, 1954; children—Bradford Scott, Nathaniel Edwin, Lorna Michelle, Jonathan Alan. Teaching asst. dept. oral pathology Sch. Dentistry, U. Minn., 1955-56, research fellow, 1956-58, clin. instr., 1958-59; asst. prof. pathology Washington U. Sch. Dentistry, St. Louis, 1959-65, asso. prof., 1965-69, prof. Grad. Sch. Arts and Scis., 1966-69, vis. prof. pathology Sch. Dentistry, 1969-71, chmn. dept. gen. and oral pathology, 1959-68, coordinator oral cancer teaching, 1959-68; asso. research scientist Cancer Research Center, Columbia, Mo., 1967-71; asso. prof. pathology Sch. Medicine, U. Mich., Ann Arbor, 1969-76, prof. pathology, 1976—, prof. dentistry Sch. Dentistry, 1968—, asso. dir. Dental Research Inst., 1970—, sr. research scientist Virus Research Group, 1977; cons. staff Jewish Hosp., St. Louis, 1960-68; cons. Ellis Fischel State Cancer Hosp., Columbia, 1967—, sci. adv. bd. Cancer Research Center, 1975—; cons. oral pathology U.S. VA Hosps., St. Louis, 1965-68, Ann Arbor, 1973—, Mo. Dental Assn., St. Louis, 1967-69; civilian profl. cons. Office of Surgeon, 5th U.S. Army, 1967—; cons. Bur. Medicine Adv. Panel System, HEW, dental agts. adv. com. FDA, 1968-70; mem. profl. adv. council on cancer Mich. Assn. Regional Med. Programs, 1969-73; mem. policy council Met. Detroit Cancer Control Program, 1976—; Recipient D.E. Listiac award, faculty U. Minn. Sch. Dentistry, 1955; named Hon. Alumnus Washington U. Sch. Dentistry, 1966. Diplomate Am. Bd. Oral Pathology. Fellow Am. Acad. Oral Pathology (councillor 1971-74, pres. 1977-78), Am. Coll. Dentists; mem. AAAS, N.Y. Acad. Scis., Am. Assn. Cancer Research, ADA (cons. Council on Dental Edn. 1971-72, 75—, mem. commn. on accreditation 1976—), Mich. (cons. com. on cancer control 1971—), Dist. dental assns., Mich. Soc. Pathologists, Am. Acad. Periodontology, Internat. Assn. Dental Research, Royal Soc. Health (Eng.), Fedn. Dentaire Internationale, Internat. Acad. Pathology, Am. Cancer Soc. (dir. St. Louis City and County unit 1964-68, chmn. profl. edn. com. 1967-68, v.p., 1967-68, dir. Mo. div. 1965-68, dir., mem. exec. com. Mich. div. 1970—, chmn. profl. edn. com. 1973-76, v.p. unit 1975-76, pres. 1976-77), Sigma Xi, Xi Psi Phi, Omicron Kappa Upsilon. Editor Proc. of Symposium: Salivary Glands and Their Secretion, 1973; Proc. of Symposium: Dental Plaque: Interfaces, 1974; Proc. of Symposium: Oral and Perioral Ulcerations: Cause and Control, Emphasis on Herpes Simplex Virus, 1975; Proceedings of Symposium: Research in Form and Function, 1976. Mem. editorial bd. Jour. Mo. Dental Soc., 1963-69, Bull. Greater St. Louis Dental Soc., 1964-68, Cancer, 1967—, Oral Research Abstracts, 1967—, Jour. Dental Research, 1971-73; contbr. articles to profl. jours.; also chpts. to books. Home: 2107 Devonshire Rd Ann Arbor MI 48104

ROWE, ROBERT B., supt. schs.; b. Bloomington, Ind., Aug. 23, 1929; s. Basil W. and Mae E. (Farley) R.; B.A., Franklin Coll., 1952; M.S., Ind. U., 1959; m. Betty G. Adkins, Nov. 15, 1953; children—Mary Beth, Robert Eugene, Michael Kevin. Tchr., coach high sch., Oolitic, Ind., 1954-59; prin. high sch., Hardinsburg, Ind., 1959-62; prin. Hope, Ind., 1962-65, supt. schs., Hope, Ind., 1965—. Bd. dirs. United Fund, Bartholomew County, Ind., 1967-68, Tb. Assn., 1971-72. Served with AUS, 1952-54. Mem. Am. Assn. Sch. Adminstrs., Ind. Assn. Pub. Sch. Supts. Club: Lions (pres. 1968-69). Home: Rural Route 1 Hope IN 47246 Office: Box 34 Hope IN 47246

ROWE, ROBERT BRADFORD, urologist; b. Binghamton, N.Y., Aug. 15, 1918; s. Charles Eckert and Ethel Alice (Quick) R.; A.B., Williams Coll., 1940; M.D., Syracuse U., 1943; m. Elizabeth Reed Spencer, Mar. 22, 1943; children—Linda H., Barbara S., Susan S., Robert B., Sarah H., Constance K. Intern, St. Joseph Hosp., Syracuse, N.Y., 1943-44; resident in gen. surgery Syracuse Med. Center, 1944-45; commd. 1st lt. U.S. Army, 1945, advanced through grades to lt. col., 1951; resident in urology Walter Reed Gen. Hosp., Washington, 1947-50; chief urology Valley Forge Gen. Hosp., Phoenixville, Pa., 1950-54; urologist Carle Clinic Assn., Urbana, Ill., 1954—, bd. govs., 1968-74, sec.-treas., 1968-69, chmn., 1971-73; mem. staff Carle Hosp., 1954—, chief of staff, 1966; trustee Carle Found., 1974—; cons. Chanute Air Force Hosp., div. vocat. rehab. U. Ill. Chmn. Urbana Civic Center Com., 1966-72. Diplomate Am. Bd. Urology. Fellow A.C.S.; mem. Am. Group Practice Assn. (credentials chmn. 1964-70, sec.-treas. 1970-74, v.p. 1974-76, pres. 1976—), AMA, Royal Soc. Health, Midwest Surg. Soc. (founding mem.), Ill. State, Champaign County med. socs., Am. Assn. Med. Clinics (N. Central sect.), Pan Am. Med. Assn., Am. Urol. Assn., Urbana Assn. Commerce (dir. 1961-64). Republican. Presbyterian. Clubs: Lions (pres. 1960-61); Levis Faculty Center (U. Ill.). Contbr. articles to med. jours. Home: 1501 N Coler Ave Urbana IL 61801 Office: Carle Clinic Urbana IL 61801

ROWEN, KENNETH ALEXANDER, agrl. engr.; b. Wessington, S.D., May 13, 1927; s. Alexander Michael and Francis Wilheimina (Lichty) R.; B.S., S.D. State U., 1951, M.S., 1960; m. Mary Margaret Robinson, June 30, 1957; children—Rodney Alan, Donald Wayne. Irrigation engr. Bur. Reclamation, Huron, S.D., 1951; farmer, Wessington, S.D., 1951-55; with U.S. Army C.E., 1955—, office engr. Tuttle Creek Lake Project, Manhattan, Kan., 1958-62, Milford Lake Project, Junction City, Kans., 1962-67; resident engr. Melvern Lake Project, 1967-72, Clinton Lake Project, Lawrence, Kans., 1972—. Coach Little League Baseball, 1969-75. Served with AUS, 1945-47. Registered profl. engr., Kans. Mem. Am. Soc. Agrl. Engrs., Kans. Profl. Engring. Soc., Nat. Profl. Engring. Soc. Republican. Methodist (chmn. adminstrv. bd. 1968-72, chmn. bldg. com. 1970-73, trustee 1974-75 77, chmn. 1977), Lion, (dir. 1974-75, pres. 1975-76, zone chmn. 1976-77), Elk. Home: Route 5 Box 63 Lawrence KS 66044 Office: Route 1 Box 120G Lawrence KS 66044

ROWLAND, DONALD CHARLES, librarian; b. Kansas City, Mo., Oct. 5, 1939; s. Leonard Clarence and Clastine Elizabeth (Mason) R.; B.A., Mankato State Coll., 1954; M.S. in L.S., U. Denver, 1966; Ph.D. (hon.), Eastern Neb. Christian Coll., 1970; m. Shirley Jean Harding, June 1, 1969. Tchr. English Sentral Community Sch., Fenton, Iowa, 1964-66; county librarian Pitkin County, Aspen, Colo., 1966-67; dir. learning resources Colo. Mountain Coll., Glenwood Springs, 1967-68; dir. Learning Resources Center, Black Hawk Coll., Moline, Ill., 1968—; v.p. research and devel. Internat. Computer Services, Denver, 1970—; cons. in field. Active local Boy Scouts Am. Served with USMC, 1958-61. Library grantee State Colo., 1965; recipient 1st place world-wide USMC photography contest, 1961. Mem. Am., Ill. library assns., Ill. Audio Visual Assn., Assn. Ednl. Communications and Tech., DAV, Am. Radio Relay League, U.S. Power Squadron, USCG Aux. Home: 3411-6D 60th St Moline IL 61265 Office: 6600 34th Ave Moline IL 61265

ROWLAND, HENRY SANDERS, III, constrn. co. exec.; b. Hartford, Conn., May 18, 1934; s. Henry Sanders and Helen Louisa (Kenyon) R; B. Indsl. Engring., Ga. Inst. Tech., 1957; M.B.A., Harvard U., 1959; postgrad. Technische Hochschule, Stutgart, Germany, 1954-55; m. Susan Frances DeSantis, Jan. 28, 1959; children—Frank, Fred, Andrew, Bruce, Sarah, Eve. Asst. to exec. v.p. Cinerama, Inc., N.Y.C., 1959; project dir., dir. devel., Phillippines, Pan. Am. Airways, N.Y.C., 1959-63; dir. planning group, dir. marketing services Rust Engineering Co., Birmingham, Ala., 1963-72, Brussels, Belguim, 1968-70, Pitts., 1970-72; mgr. quality assurance Azco, Inc., Appleton, Wis., 1972—. Mem. Am. Soc. for Non-destructive Testing (chmn. NE Wis. sect. 1977-78), Neenah-Menasha (Wis.) Amateur Radio Club (past pres.), A.S.M.E., Am. Welding Soc., Am. Soc. for Quality Control. Republican. Presbyterian. Home: 320 9th St Neenah WI 54956 Office: PO Box 567 Appleton WI 54911

ROWLANDS, DAVID JAMES, educator; b. Watertown, Wis., Jan. 11, 1937; s. John Wilson and Alyce Lenora (Freitag) R.; B.S. (Lawrence Clinard scholar), U. Wis. at Madison, 1958, M.S., 1962; Ph.D., U. Utah, 1974; m. Lou Ella Stoltenburg, June 21, 1958; children—Mark, Robert. Dir. athletics, chmn. phys. edn. Truman Coll., 1962—, golf coach, 1967—. Mem. golf course staff Glenview (Ill.) Park Dist., 1963—. Pres. phys. edn. council City Colls. Chgo., 1970-71; mem. gymnastics com. U.S. Olympics, 1972—; ednl. cons. Nat. Golf Found., 1975—. Mem. Nat. Jr. Coll. Athletic Assn. (dir. 1972—), AAHPER, Ill. Assn. Health, Phys. Edn. and Recreation, Phi Delta Kappa, Phi Kappa Phi, Phi Epsilon Kappa, National W Club. Home: 2501 Robin Crest Lane Glenview IL 60025 Office: 1145 W Wilson Ave Chicago IL 60640

ROYALTY, DENNIS MARION, material handling equipment co. exec.; b. Bloomington, Ind., Nov. 17, 1923; s. Henry Dennis and Lois Vivian (Malicote) R.; student King Coll., 1943; B.S., Ind. U., 1946-49; postgrad. Butler U., 1955, Youngstown U., 1957-58; m. Kathleen Hollis Barnhart, Aug. 26, 1946; children—Dennis Michael, David Alan. With RCA, 1949-54; personnel mgr. Mallory-Sharon Metals, Niles, O., 1955-58; chief plans and controls Martin-Marietta, Denver, 1958-64; personnel mgr. Fed.-Mogul Corp., Frankfort, Ind., 1964-70; dir. personnel Mallory Timers Co., Indpls., 1970-71; plant mgr. Delphi Body Works (Ind.), 1972-73; mgr. employee and community relations Stephens-Adamson Inc. sub. Allis Chalmers, Aurora, Ill., 1974—. Bd. dirs. Jr. Achievement Aurora, 1976-78. Served with USAF, 1943-46. Recipient Award of Merit, U.S. Treasury Dept.,

1964-70, Nat. Safety Council, 1953, 57. Mem. Valley Personnel Assn. (pres. 1977), Greater Aurora C. of C. (chmn. congl. action com. 1977-78), Ind. U. Club of Clinton County (dir. 1966-69, pres. 1970). Elk. Home: 378 Michigan Ave Aurora IL 60506 Office: Stephens-Adamson Ridgeway Ave at Woodlawn Aurora IL 60507

ROYHL, JOHN CHARLES, ins. agt.; b. Chgo., June 26, 1943; s. John Henry and Florence Adelaide (Miller) R.; B.A., Valparaiso U., 1966; M. Ed., Loyola U., Chgo., 1973; m. Marcia Ann Kniph, Feb. 1, 1969; children—Heather Renee, Annette Michele. Sales, customer service Pyramid Moulding Inc., Chgo., 1969-73; guidance counselor, tchr. Lisle (Ill.) Community Sch. Dist., 1973-77; spl. agt. Northwestern Mut. Life Ins. Co., Chgo., 1977—; systems cons. Norelco WPS, Philips Bus. Systems. Sponsor, Future Bus. Leaders Am., Lisle Sr. High Sch., 1973-75; sponsor Kiwanis Builders CLub, Lisle Jr. High Sch., 1977. Mem. Ill., Am. personnel and guidance assns. Lutheran. Club: YMCA Y's Men's (sec. 1969-70) (Elmhurst, Ill.). Home: 44 W Sunset St Lombard IL 60148 Office: 150 S Wacker Dr Chicago IL 60606

ROYKO, MIKE, newspaper columnist; b. Chgo., Sept. 19, 1932; s. Michael and Helen (Zak) R.; student Wright Jr. Coll., 1951-52; m. Carol Joyce Duckman, Nov. 7, 1954; children—M. David, Robert F. Reporter, Chgo. North Side Newspapers, 1956; reporter, asst. city editor Chgo. City News Bur., 1956-59; reporter, columnist Chgo. Daily News, 1959-78, Chgo. Sun Times, 1978—. Served with USAF, 1952-56. Recipient Heywood Brown award, 1968, Pulitzer prize for commentary, 1972. Mem. Chgo. Newspaper Reporters Assn. Club: LaSalle St. Rod and Gun. Author: Up Against It, 1967; I May Be Wrong but I Doubt It, 1968; Boss—Richard J. Daley of Chicago, 1971; Slats Grobnik and Some Other Friends, 1973. Home: 6657 N Sioux Ave Chicago IL 60646 Office: Chgo Sun Times 401 N Wabash Ave Chicago IL 60611

ROZAN, DOROTHY NATALEE CAMIN (MRS. JOSEF S. ROZAN), social worker; b. Detroit, Oct. 9, 1911; d. David Samuel and Minnie (Oppenhiem) Camin; student Lasell Jr. Coll., 1928-30; B.A., Mich. State U., 1938, M.S.W., 1958; m. Josef S. Rozan, Oct. 6, 1931 (dec. Dec. 1965); children—Dale (Mrs. Melvin Applebaum), Gerry Michael. Caseworker, ARC, 1944-45; caseworker Lansing (Mich.) Family Service Agy., 1958-63, supr. Grad. Sch. Social Work Students, 1963-67, exec. dir., 1967-68; psychiat. social worker Community Mental Health Center, St. Lawrence Hosp., Lansing, 1969—; med. social work cons. Vis. Nurses Assn., Lansing, 1963-68. Pres. Ingham County Med. Aux., 1951; mem. Gov's. Conf. on Children and Youth, 1950-51; chmn. family and children's services Community Service Council, 1948-52; bd. dirs. Jean Granger March of Dimes Prenatal Clinic 1974—. Recipient award Radar Air Warning Service, 1942, awards ARC, 1940-43, award Mich. Hosp. Assn.-Blue Cross, 1973. Mem. Nat. Assn. Social Workers, Acad. Certified Social Workers, Coll. Women's Vol. Service (pres. 1950), Planned Parenthood Assn., Mich. Assn. Emotionally Disturbed Children. Republican. Author: (with Anne K. DeRose) Volunteers in a CMHC-A Blueprint, 1973. Contbr. articles, short stories to nat. publs. Home: 1271 Mulberry Ln East Lansing MI 48823 Office: St Lawrence Hosp Community Mental Health Center Oakland Ave Lansing MI 48914

ROZMAN, JOSEPH JOHN, JR., artist, educator; b. Milw., Dec. 26, 1944; s. Joseph J. and Julia Mary (Vicic) R.; B.F.A. with honors, U. Wis., 1967, M.F.A., 1969; m. Nicolee Teegarden, Dec. 26, 1973; children—Terri Nicole, Eric Todd. Instr. in art U. Wis., Milw., 1967-69, vis. lectr. in art, 1972-73, also vis. lectr. U. Wis. at Parkside, 1970-71; instr. in printmaking Milw. Art Center, 1968-76; instr. in art Carthage Coll., Kenosha, Wis., 1969-72; instr. design and printmaking Layton Sch. of Art and Design, Milw., 1973-74; asst. prof. art Mount Mary Coll., Milw., 1975—; juror for various art exhbns., 1969—; one man shows of Prints/paintings include: Southwest Tex. State Coll., San Marcos, 1969, U. Wis., Milw., 1969, Northern State Coll., Aberdeen, S.D., 1971, Carroll Coll., Waukesha, Wis., 1972, Milw. Art Center, 1973, Fanny Garver Gallery, Madison, Wis., 1973, Wustum Mus., Racine, Wis., 1975, others; group shows include: Chgo. and Vicinity Exhbn., Chgo. Art Inst., 1966, 68, 73, 77, Nat. Boston Printmakers Exhbn., Boston Mus. Fine Arts, 1967-69, Pratt Internat. Miniature Print Exhbn., N.Y.C., 1968, 71, 75, Tex. Tech. U., 1969-71, State Univ. N.Y., Oneonta, 1972, So. Ill. U., 1972, Okla. Art Center; represented in permanent collections: Milw. Art Center, Decordova Mus., Lincoln, Mass., U. Wis., Milw., SW Tex State Coll., San Marcos, Carthage Coll., Kenosha, 1st Wis. Center, Milw., Wis. State U., Stevens Point, Sears Tower, Chgo., others. Recipient numerous awards including: Wis. Salon of Art award, 1966; Logan award and prize Chgo. Art Inst., 1966; Carthage Coll. Faculty Research grantee, 1970; Lakefront Festival of Arts award, 1977; Main award Watercolor Wis., 1977. Mem. Boston Printmakers, Art Inst. Chgo., Milw. Art Center. Christian Scientist. Home: 4419 Lindermann Ave Racine WI 53405 Office: 2900 N Menomonee River Parkway Milwaukee WI 53222

RUBENS, SIDNEY MICHEL, physicist, cons.; b. Spokane, Wash., Mar. 21, 1910; s. Max Zvoln and Jennie Golda (Rubinovich) R.; B.S., U. Wash., 1934, Ph.D., 1939; m. Julienne Rose Fridner, May 11, 1944; 1 dau., Deborah Janet. Instr. U. So. Calif., 1939-40; research asso. U. Calif. at Los Angeles, 1940-41; physicist Naval Ordnance Lab., Washington, 1941-46; physicist Engring. Research Assos., St. Paul, 1946-52; mgr. physics Univac div. Sperry Rand, St. Paul, 1958-61, dir. research, 1961-66, staff scientist, 1969-71, dir. spl. projects, 1971-75; cons., 1975—. Lectr., U. Pa., 1960-61; mem. adv. subcom. on instrumentation and data processing NASA, 1967-69, panel on computer tech. Nat. Acad. Sci.. 1969. Hon. fellow U. Minn., 1977—. Fellow IEEE; mem. Am. Phys. Soc., Am. Geophys. Union, AAAS, Acad. Applied Sci., Minn. Acad. Sci., Am. Optical Soc., Phi Beta Kappa, Sigma Xi, Pi Mu Epsilon. Patentee in magnetic material and devices. Author: Amplifier and Memory Devices, 1965. Contbr. articles to profl. jours. Home: 1077 Sibley Hwy Apt 506 St Paul MN 55118

RUBIN, STANLEY J., realtor; b. Chgo., July 26, 1913; s. David M. and Anna (Rosengarden) R.; Ph.B., U. Chgo., 1934; m. Doris Patinkin, Apr. 21, 1974; children by previous marriage—Neal, Alan, Robert, Joanne. Pres., owner, Stanley Realty Co., Chgo., 1934-69; v.p. Arthur Rubloff & Co., Evergreen Park, Ill., 1969—. Bd. dirs. Hyde Park Jewish Community Center. Served with AUS, 1944-45; ETO. Mem. pres.'s council St. Xavier Coll., 1974. Jewish. Home: 5471 Hyde Park Blvd Chicago IL 60615 Office: 9730 S Western Ave Evergreen Park IL 60642

RUBIN, STEPHEN DAVID, wholesale distributor; b. Milw., May 30, 1939; s. Ephraim I. and Ruth (Grodin) R.; B.B.A., U. Wis., 1961; LL.D., 1965; m. Marcia Rubin; children—Wendy Lynn, Michael Allen. Vice pres. Liberman & Gittlen Metal Co., Grand Rapids, Mich., 1965-74; pres. Graver-Dearborn Corp., Chgo., 1966—, Mercil Plating Co., Chgo., 1968-74, Master Plating Co., Chgo., 1968-74; v.p. P.J. Gould Co., 1973-74, Odd 02 Amusements; pres. Donnell Co., Fla., Tex., Ga., 1975—; pres. Baker Rite Baking Co., Stevens Point, Wis., 1976—. Pres. Swiss Internat. Marketing Group. Mem. Young Men's Jewish Council (dir.). Zeta Beta Tau. Home: 7314 N Lowell Ave Lincolnwood IL 60646 Office: 224 N Ada St Chicago IL 60607

RUBINOW, STEVEN CHARLES, biochemist; b. Chgo., Dec. 6, 1952; s. Solomon and Etty (Kain) Rubinow; m. Marlene Suzette Karbin, Aug. 4, 1974. B.S., U. Ill., 1973, M.S., 1974. Teaching asst., research asst., U. Ill. Chgo.-Circle, 1973—; cons. patents and licensing dept. Standard Oil Co. of Ind., Chgo., 1976. Volunteer research asst. U. Ill. Med. Center, Chgo., 1972; volunteer histopathologist VA Research Hosp., Chgo., 1973; judge dist. 21 Science Fair, Bd. Edn., Chgo., 1976—. Mem. Am. Chem. Soc., AAAS, Ill. State Acad. Sci., Am. Mktg. Assn., Assn. M.B.A. Execs., Internat. Oceanographic Found., U.S. Racquetball Assn. Home: 6210 N Fairfield St Chicago IL 60659 Office: Box 4348 Chicago IL 60680

RUBINS, IRA MARC, ednl. adminstr.; b. Cleve., Nov. 4, 1947; s. Alex and Betty (Buller) R.; B.A., Miami U., Ohio, 1969, M.A., 1971; m. Sherry Ruth Weintraub, Aug. 24, 1969; 1 dau., Jennifer Sarah. Producer of Radio Talk Music Show, sta. WIXY, Cleve., 1970-71; chmn. broadcast mgmt. dept. Jones Coll., Jacksonville, Fla., 1971-72; announcer Sta. WKTZ, Jacksonville, Fla., 1971-72; faculty coordinator WIXY Sch. Broadcast Technique, Cleve., 1973-75; dir. edn. Ohio Sch. Broadcast Technique, Cleve., 1975—; v.p. Ednl. Broadcast Services, Inc., Cleve., 1975—. Dir. auctions Renaissance Fine Arts Gallery, Cleve., 1974—. Mem. Nat. Assn. of Trade and Tech. Schs. (pub. relations com. 1976-77), Nat. Assn. Ednl. Broadcasters (mem. broadcast edn. com. 1975-77), Radio TV Council Greater Cleve., Northeastern Ohio chpt. Proprietary Schs. (sec.), Ohio Council Pvt. Colls. and Schs. (sec.). Jewish. Home: 16004 Fernway Rd Shaker Heights OH 44120 Office: 3940 Euclid Ave Cleveland OH 44115

RUBINSTEIN, JACK HERBERT, physician; b. N.Y.C., Aug. 4, 1925; s. Saul David and Anna (Gordon) R.; A.B., Columbia U., 1947; M.D., Harvard U., 1952; m. Thelma Regent, Nov. 22, 1952. Intern, Beth Israel Hosp., Boston, 1952-53; pediatric intern and resident Mass. Gen. Hosp., Boston, 1953-55; pediatric resident and fellow Children's Hosp., Cin., 1955-57; dir. Hamilton County Diagnostic Clinic, Cin., 1957—, dir. Children's Neuromuscular Clinic, Cin., 1962—, dir. Univ. Affiliated Clin. Program for Mentally Retarded Diagnostic Clinics., Cin., 1967—, now dir. amalgamated programs Univ. Affiliated Cin. Center Developmental Disorders; prof. pediatrics U. Cin., 1970. Served with AUS, 1944-46. Mem. Acad. Pediatrics, Am. Pediatric Soc., Am. Assn. Mental Deficiency, Am. Acad. Cerebral Palsy, Cin. Pediatric Soc., Teratology Soc., Boylston Med. Soc., Phi Beta Kappa, Alpha Omega Alpha. Home: 3408 Manor Hill Dr Cincinnati OH 45220 Office: Pavilion Bldg Elland and Bethesda Aves Cincinnati OH 45229

RUBLE, RONALD ALVIN, educator; b. Los Angeles, Sept. 14, 1929; s. Ronald A. and Maria Alvina (Abeyta) R.; B.A., U. N.Mex., 1952, M.A., 1959, Ed.D., 1964; m. Angelina Garcia, June 28, 1952; 1 dau., Regina Christine. Tchr., Otero County (N.Mex.) Schs., 1952-53; tchr. mcpl. schs. Taos, N.Mex., 1954-56, counselor, 1956-57; counselor, asst. dir., dir. Lincoln Guidance Research Project, Albuquerque Pub. Schs., 1957-65; prof., counselor edn., chmn. div. counselor edn. St. Louis U., 1965—. Mem. Am. Personnel and Guidance Assn., Assn. Specialists in Group Work, Assn. Counselor Edn. and Supervision, Am. Psychol. Assn., Profl. Counselors' Assn. Home: 7605 Arlington Ave St Louis MO 63119 Office: 221 N Grand Blvd St Louis MO 63103

RUBLOFF, BURTON, real estate broker; b. Chisholm, Minn., June 1, 1912; s. Solomon W. and Mary R.; grad. Northwestern U., 1940; m. Patricia F. Williams, July 17, 1943; 1 dau., Jenifer. Entire business career with Arthur Rubloff & Co., Chgo., 1930—, v.p., 1947-76, sr. v.p., 1976—. Bd. dirs. Citizens of Greater Chgo., Municipal Art League of Chicago, West Central Assn. Chgo. Served as sgt. AUS, 36th Div., ETO, 1943-46. Mem. Am. Inst. Real Estate Appraisers, Nat., Ill., Chgo. assns. real estate bds., Bldg. Mgrs. Assn. Chgo., Wacker Dr. Assn. (dir.), Lambda Alpha. Club: John Evans (Northwestern U.). Home: 633 N Waukegan Rd Lake Forest IL 60045 Office: 69 W Washington St Chicago IL 60602

RUCH, RICHARD HURLEY, furniture and fixtures co. exec.; b. Plymouth, Ind., Apr. 15, 1930; s. Dallas Claude and Mable Elizabeth (Hurley) R.; A.B. with high honors, Mich. State U., 1952; m. Patricia Lou Overbeek, July 23, 1948; children—Richard, Christine, Michael, Douglas. Accountant, Automobile div. Gen. Motors Corp., Lansing, Mich., 1952-54; accounting supr. Kroger Co., Grand Rapids, 1954-55; chief accountant Herman Miller, Inc., Zeeland, 1955-58, controller, 1958-63, dir. mfg., 1963-69, v.p. mfg., 1969—; pres. Scanlon Plan Assos., 1969-70, 75—, also dir.; dir. Herman Miller of Can., H.L. Hubbell Inc., Star Industries, Inc. Mem. New Groningen Sch. Bd., Zeeland, Mich., 1962-68. Mem. Reformed Ch. (elder 1967-70, 73-76, chmn. ch. edn. com. 1967-70). Home: 30 Lee St Zeeland MI 49464 Office: 140 McKinley St Zeeland MI 49464

RUCK, CHARLES MITCHELL, veterinarian; b. Jeffersonville, Ind., Oct. 12, 1924; s. Charles Jacob and Nina Maude (Mitchell) R.; student Franklin Coll. Ind., 1941-42; D.V.M., Mich. State U., 1946; m. Annette Joyce Wolfe, Sept. 4, 1946; children—Carol Ann Ruck Cook, Patricia Jean Ruck Whitworth, Charlene Diane. Practice veterinary sci., Normal, Ill., 1947-50; veterinarian Ruck Animal Hosp., East St. Louis, Ill., 1950-65; owner, dir. Bel East Animal Hosp., Belleville, i Ill., 1965—; cons. veterinarian East Side Health Dept., East St. Louis, 1950-65. Pres. Belleville Humane Soc., 1970-75, bd. dirs., 1970-77. Served with U.S. Army, 1943-44. Mem. Greater St. Louis (past pres.), So. Ill. (past pres.), Ill. veterinary med. assns., AVMA. Republican. Mem. Christian Ch. (elder). Clubs: Masons, Shriners, Rotary. Home: 116 Powder Mill Rd Belleville IL 62223 Office: Rt 161 & Carson Rd Belleville IL 62223

RUDD, RALPH CORLIES, lawyer; b. Suifu (now Ipin), Szechuan, China, May 22, 1915 (parents Am. citizens); s. Herbert Finley and Anna (Corlies) R.; B.A., U. N.H., 1936; LL.B., Yale, 1942; postgrad. Columbia 1942-43; m. Mary Carolyn Clausen, June 17, 1941; children—Darnell (Mrs. David Mandelblatt), Herbert Finley II, Corlies Anna (Mrs. Gregory Delf), Rachel Clausen (Mrs. Eric Christensen). Admitted to Ohio bar, 1946, since practiced in Cleve., asso. firm Schaefer & Schaefer, 1946, Harrison, Thomas, Spangenberg & Hull, 1946-49; asso. firm Harrison, Spangenberg & Hull, 1949-54, partner, 1954-59; partner firm Rudd, Ober, Finley & Miller, 1959-61, Rudd, Ober & Miller, 1961-68, Rudd, Miller, Sheerer & Lybarger, 1968-71, Rudd, Karl, Sheerer & Lybarger, 1971-72; pres. Rudd, Karl, Sheerer, Lybarger & Campbell Co., L.P.A. and predecessor firm, 1972-76; adj. prof. law Cleve.-Marshall Coll. Law, Cleve. State U., 1975-76; atty. Legal Aid Soc. Cuyahoga County, 1977—. Adviser, Draft Counselling Assn., Cleve., 1968-73; hearing examiner Ohio Civil Rights Commn., 1972; mem. policy com. Friends Com. Nat. Legislation, 1968-76, mem. exec. com., 1974—, chmn. gen. com., 1975—. Mem. Ohio Ho. of Reps., 1959-62; mem. Lake County Democratic Exec. Com., 1966—; trustee West Lake County Dem. Club; chmn. ACLU, Cleve., 1952-55, 74-76, chmn., Ohio, 1954-56, treas., Ohio, 1975-76; chmn. bd. dirs. Elizabeth S. Magee Edn. and Research Found., Cleve.; trustee Ohio Consumers' League. Mem. Lake County, Cuyahoga County, Cleve., Ohio, Am. bar assns., Am. Trial Lawyers Assn. Mem. Soc. Friends. Kiwanian. Author: Syllabus on Selective Service Procedure, 1968; Syllabus on Law of Conscientious Objection, 1968; Suggestions for Answering CO Questionnaire, 1970. Home: 4777 Wood St Willoughby OH 44094 Office: 1223 W 6th St Cleveland OH 44113

RUDDLE, JAMES FARRIS, TV newscaster; b. Oakhurst, Okla., May 20, 1932; s. George Lawrence and Evelyn Lucille (Baxter) R.; B.A., U. Tulsa, 1956, M.A., 1957; postgrad. (Univ. fellow), U. N.Mex., 1963; m. Patricia Anne Abbett, May 25, 1956; children—Kathryn, Blake, Valerie, Kristin. Newscaster, KOTV, Tulsa, 1955-58, XEAK, Tijuana, Mexico, 1958-59, WTVT, Tampa, Fla., 1963-65, WGN, Chgo., 1965-67, WMAQ, Chgo., 1967-75, sr. editor, corr. WTTW, Chgo., 1975—; Instr. U. N.Mex., 1959-62, U. South Fla., Tampa, 1963-65. Chmn. grand council Am. Indian Center, Chgo., 1976—. Served with USCGR, 1951-54. Recipient Silver Gavel award Am. Bar Assn., 1968. Mem. Am. Studies Assn., Chgo. Council Fgn. Relations, Civil War Roundtable, Nat. Acad. TV Arts and Scis. (pres. 1973, nat. trustee 1974—). Home: 1621 Barry Ln Glenview IL 60025 Office: Public News Center 233 N Michigan Ave Chicago IL 60601

RUDEN, VIOLET HOWARD (MRS. CHARLES VAN KIRK RUDEN), Christian Sci. tchr., practitioner; b. Dallas; d. Millard Fillmore and Henrietta Frederika (Kurth) Howard; B.J., U. Tex., 1931; C.S.B., Mass. Metaphys. Coll., 1946; m. Charles Van Kirk Ruden, Nov. 24, 1932. Radio continuity writer Home Mgmt. Club broadcast Sta. WHO, Des Moines, 1934; joined First Ch. of Christ Scientist, Boston, 1929; C.S. practitioner, Des Moines, 1934—; C.S. minister WAC, Ft. Des Moines, 1942-45; 1st reader 2d Ch. of Christ Scientist, Des Moines, 1952, Sunday sch. tchr., 1934—; instr. primary class in Christian Sci., 1947—. Trustee Asher Student Found. Drake U., Des Moines, 1973. Mem. Women in Communications, Mortar Bd., Orchesis, Cap and Gown. Republican. Club: Des Moines Women's. Home: 5808 Walnut Hill Dr Des Moines IA 50312 Office: 206 Kresge Bldg Des Moines IA 50309

RUDICK, MILTON MARTIN, civil engr., contractor; b. Youngstown, Ohio, July 11, 1920; s. Ben and Dina (Greenblatt) R.; B.S., Carnegie Mellon U., 1946; m. Marie Taussig, June 28, 1945; children—Jerald David, Leonard Taussig, Lois. Engr., Truscon Steel Co., Youngstown, 1946-48; asst. chief engr. Ring Constrn. Co., Albany, N.Y., 1948-49; exec. v.p. Ben Rudick & Son, Inc., Youngstown, 1949-74, pres., 1974—; pres. Nat. Fire Repair, Inc., 1976—; bldg. damage cons., 1965—. Trustee Labor Pension Fund, 1965, 66; bd. mem. Rodef Shalom Temple. Served to 2d lt. C.E., AUS, 1943-45. Mem. ASCE, Nat. Soc. Profl. Engrs., Builders Assn. Eastern Ohio and Western Pa., Jewish War Vets. Clubs: Rotary, B'nai B'rith, Squaw Creek Country. Home: 532 Madera Ave Youngstown OH 44504 Office: 855 Tod Ave Youngstown OH 44502

RUDISILL, ROBERT MACK, anesthesiologist; b. Lincolnton, N.C., Mar. 4, 1923; s. Joseph Luther and Espie Iowa (Sharp) R.; B.S., U. S.C., 1943; M.D., La. State U., 1951; m. Peggy Lucille Lawhead, Feb. 5, 1971; children by a previous marriage—Robert M., Tim Hall; adopted children—Wendy Ellen, Stephanie Lynn. Intern, St. Joseph's Hosp., South Bend, Ind., 1951-52; gen. practice medicine, S. Bend, Ind., 1952-54; anesthesiology preceptorship Reno, Nev. and U. Calif. at Los Angeles Med. Center, 1954-58; practice medicine specializing in anesthesiology, Reno, Nev., 1954-66; dir. dept. anesthesia and respiratory care Mercy Hosp., Urbana, Ill., 1966-72; clin. asso. U. Ill. Sch. Basic Med. Scis., 1969-72; staff mem. and vice-chmn. div. anesthesiology Cleve. Clinic, 1972—; instr. various anesthesiology programs. Served with USN, 1942-46. Diplomate Am. Bd. Anesthesiology. Fellow Am. Coll. Anesthesiology; mem. AMA, Ohio State Med. Assn., Cleve. Acad. of Medicine, Am., Ohio, Cleve. soc. of anesthesiologists, Regional Anesthesia Soc., Ohio Thoracic Soc., No. Ohio Lung Assn. Methodist. Editorial bd. Anesthesiology Staff News, 1974—. Home: 5305 Northfield Rd Apt 317 Bedford Heights OH 44146 Office: Cleveland Clinic 9500 Euclid Ave Cleveland OH 44106

RUDMAN, DANIEL STEPHEN, cons. firm exec.; b. Galesburg, Ill., Nov. 15, 1945; s. Mitchell and Rose (Levy) R.; B.S., U. Ill., 1969; m. Susan B. Meyer, June 22, 1969; children—Deborah, Julie. Controller, Brown Splty. Co., Galesburg, Ill., 1969-75; pres. Rudman & Asso., cons., Galesburg, 1975—; cons., lectr. in field. Chmn. mayor's com. on swimming pool constrn., 1977-78. Mem. Am. Bus. Clubs U.S., Ill. Soc. C.P.A.'s, Am. Soc. Tng. and Devel., Galesburg C. of C., Beta Alpha Psi (regional Howard), Beta Gamma Sigma (award), Ill. Jaycees (named outstanding local pres. 1975), Alpha Kappa Psi. Republican. Jewish. Clubs: Masons, B'Nai B'Rith (past pres.). Office: PO Box 447 1320 N Henderson St Galesburg IL 61401

RUDMAN, HERBERT CHARLES, educator; b. N.Y.C., July 29, 1923; s. Abraham and Celia (Factor) R.; B.S., Bradley U., 1947; M.S., U. Ill., 1950, Ed.D., 1954; m. Florence Bromberg, Dec. 22, 1923; 1 dau., Jane Ann. Tchr., asst. to prin. Peoria (Ill.) Bd. Edn., 1946-51; instr. U. Ill., 1951-53; chmn. dept. elementary edn., U. S.C., 1954-56; prof. adminstrn. and higher edn. Mich. State U., East Lansing, 1956—. Served with USAAF, 1942-46. Ford Found. fellow, USSR, 1958; head U.S. del. to USSR for U.S. State Dept., 1963-64. Author: (with Truman Kelly, Richard Madden, Eric Gardner) Stanford Achievement Tests, 1964; (with Richard Featherstone) Urban Schooling, 1968; (with Donald J. Leu) Preparation Programs for School Adminstrators 1963; (with Frederick King, Herbert Epperly) Concepts in Social Science, 1970; School and State in the USSR, 1967; (with others) Stanford Achievement Tests, 1973; (with Frederick King) Understanding People, 1977, Understanding Communities, 1977, Understanding Regions, 1978; At Your Best, 1977; Toward Your Future, 1977; Balance In Your Life, 1977. Home: 4401 Greenwood Dr Okemos MI 48864 Office: Coll Edn Mich State U East Lansing MI 48823

RUDOLPH, JACK WALLACE, freelance writer; b. Ellsworth, Wis., Oct. 22, 1908; s. Solomon Francis and Mary (Casey) R.; student Lawrence Coll., 1926-29; B.S., U.S. Mil. Acad., 1933; m. Leora O. Calkins Quinn, Apr. 12, 1958; 1 step dau., Leora Jane (Mrs. Thomas Marshall). Commd. 2d lt. U.S. Army, 1933, advanced through grades to col., 1945-53, ret., 1953; served in War Dept. Mil. Intelligence div. during World War II, comdg. officer 38th Inf. Regt., 1949—; music-drama critic, feature writer Green Bay (Wis.) Press-Gazette, 1954-71; news editor, music-drama critic Green Bay (Wis.) The Spirit, 1971-73; free lance writer, 1974—. Mem. Brown County Hist. Soc. (pres. 1961), Music Critics Assn., Assn. U.S. Army, Ret. Officers Assn. Republican. Roman Catholic. Club: Army and Navy (Washington). Home: 703 Glenwood Ave De Pere WI 54115

RUDRAUFF, ANN AUDGERIE, ednl. TV coordinator; b. Seattle, Feb. 6, 1946; d. Jerome William and Audgerie Phyllis (Anderson) Rudrauff; B.S., Wash. State U., 1967; M.A., Ohio State U., 1970. Tchr., Kirkland (Wash.) Jr. High Sch., 1967-69; grad. asst. health edn. Ohio State U., Columbus, 1969-70; instr. health edn. U. Toledo, 1970-71, 72-75; tchr. Calgary (Alta., Can.) Pub. Schs., 1971; educative services specialist Sta. WGTE-TV, Toledo, 1975-77, coordinator instructional TV, 1977—; co-producer TV program Thirty-Bird Calls, 1976-77, producer, 1975-76; cons., Bowling Green State U., Ohio Dept. Edn., Ohio Planning Com. Health Edn. Trustee Mental Health Assn. Greater Toledo, 1975—. Recipient Instructional TV

Promotions award Sta. WGTE-TV, 1976. Author articles in field. Office: 415 N St Clair St Toledo OH 43604

RUDY, DAVID ROBERT, physician; b. Columbus, Ohio, Oct. 19, 1934; s. Robert Sale and Lois May (Arthur) R.; B.Sc., Ohio State U.,1956, M.D., 1960; m. Hester A. Armstrong, Dec. 30, 1971; children by previous marriage—Douglas D., Steven W., Katharine L. Intern, Northwestern Meml. Hosp., Chgo., 1960-61; resident in internal medicine, Ohio State U. Hosp., 1963-64, in pediatrics Children's Hosp., Columbus, Ohio, 1964; practice medicine specializing in family practice, Columbus, 1964-75; dir. Family Practice Center and residency program Riverside Meth. Hosp., Columbus, 1975—; clin. asst. prof. Ohio State U. Served as capt., Flight surgeon, M.C., USAF, 1961-63. Diplomate Am. Bd. Family Practice. Fellow Am. Acad. Family Physicians; mem. AMA, Ohio Med. Assn., Central Ohio Acad. Family Practice (pres. elect 1978), Am. Mensa Soc., Columbus Maennerchor, Columbus Med. Symposium. Republican. Contbr. articles to profl. jours. Home: 1206 Kenbrook Hills Dr Columbus OH 43220 Office: 797 Thomas Ln Columbus OH 43214

RUDY, ELMER CLYDE, lawyer; b. Elgin, Ill., Apr. 10, 1931; S. Elmer Carl and Bernice (Tobin) R.; B.A., Beloit (Wis.) Coll., 1953; LL.B., U. Mich., 1958; m. Margaret L. Meyer, July 5, 1953; children—Lynne, Elizabeth, Paul, Charles, Leslie. Admitted to Ill. bar, 1958, since practiced in Rockford; partner firm Williams, McCarthy, Kinley, Rudy & Picha, 1965—. Bd. dirs. Rosecrance Meml. Homes, Rockford, Ill., 1973—, chmn., 1974; bd. dirs. Rockford Jaycees, 1962-68, Booker Washington Center, 1962-66, Rockford Mus. Assn., 1973—. Served with AUS, 1953-55. Mem. Am., Ill., Winnebago County bar assns., Am. Judicature Soc., Rockford C. of C. (bd. dirs.), Phi Beta Kappa. Home: 5024 Braewild Rd Rockford IL 61107 Office: 400 Talcott Bldg Rockford IL 61101

RUDY, JOEL SANFORD, coll. adminstr.; b. Bklyn., Jan. 20, 1941; s. Sidney T. and Selma (Rayvis) R.; B.S., Bethany Coll., 1962; M.A., Kent State U., 1964; m. Marlene Yourga, Nov. 24, 1965; children—Lisa Michele, Brian Scott. Dir. student activities, asst. dean, instr. Hunter Coll. in Bronx, 1964-67; asso. dir. housing, dir. resident student devel. U. Miami, Coral Gables, Fla., 1967-71; dean student residence life Kent (Ohio) State U., 1971-75, asst. v.p. for edn. and student services, 1975-76; dir. residence life Ohio U., Athens, 1976—. Chmn. bd. dirs. Tallmadge Coop PreSchool, 1973-75; v.p. Athens City Elementary Sch. PTA, 1977-78. Mem. Am. Personnel and Guidance Assn., Ohio Coll. Personnel Assn., Nat. Assn. Student Personnel Adminstrs., Ohio Assn. Student Personnel Adminstrs., Assn. Coll. and Univ. Housing Officers, Internat. Narcotic Enforcement Officers Assn., Phi Delta Kappa, Beta Beta Beta, Alpha Phi Omega, Phi Kappa Tau. Pi Gamma Mu. Home: 19 Roxbury Dr Athens OH 45701 Office: 50 Chubb Hall Ohio Univ Athens OH 45701

RUDY, ROBERT SALE, ret. restaurant exec.; b. Champaign, Ill., Aug. 20, 1907; s. Franklin Tipton and Minnie Mable (Sale) R.; B.S., Ohio State U., 1928; m. Lois May Arthur, Feb. 8, 1930; children—John, James, David, Theodore, Carolyn (Mrs. Daniel Jensen). Auditor, Ohio Farm Bureau Corp., Columbus, Ohio, 1928-30; clerk receivables Columbus Coated Fabrics Corp., 1930-35; treas. Summer & Co., Columbus, 1935-54; controller White Castle System Inc., 1954-73. Tchr. Franklin U., Ohio Wesleyan U., Ohio State U. Treas. Hosp. Certification Service. Trustee-at-large Palatines to Am., 1975—, pres., 1977. C.P.A. Mem. Ohio Soc. C.P.A. (pres. chpt. 1940). Nat. Assn. Accountants (pres. chpt. 1948), Financial Execs. Inst. (pres. chpt. 1962), Inst. Scrap Iron and Steel (sec. chpt. 1948), Ohio, Pa. hist. socs., Ohio C. of C., Newcomen Soc., Phi Sigma Kappa, Phi Delta Gamma. Republican. Kiwanian (pres. N.W. Columbus 1960). Home: 1492 Guilford Rd Columbus OH 43221

RUEBKE, HENRY JACOB, state ofcl.; b. Ada, Minn., Sept. 12, 1920; s. Albert G. and Irma Sophie (Schwartz) R.; D.V.M., Iowa State U., 1943, M.S., 1950; m. Marybelle Janet Mohler, June 15, 1946; children—Linda Lou, Dan Albert. Practice vet. medicine, Wadena, Minn., 1944-47; mem. faculty Iowa State U., 1947-50, Tex. A. and M. U., 1950; practice vet. medicine, Ada, 1951-62; dist. supr. Minn. Livestock San. Bd., Ada, 1962—. Mem. Ada Sch. Bd., 1956-62, pres. bd., 1960-61. Served with AUS, 1941-43. Mem. AVMA, Minn. Veterinary Med. Assn., Red River Valley Angus Assn. (pres. 1968-69), Lake Region Vet. Assn. (pres. 1955-56), Am. Legion, Phi Mu Alpha, Phi Zeta. Home: Route 2 Ada MN 56510 Office: Ada MN 56510

RUEGER, HOMER EDWIN, mgmt. accountant; b. Highland Park, Mich., May 20, 1919; s. Charles J. and Charlotte D. (Jominy) R.; B.A., U. Mich., 1940, M.B.A., 1941. Supr., Ford Motor Co., Dearborn, Mich., 1941-49; controller Dixie Shops, Inc., Ypsilanti, Mich., 1949-57; dir., controller, treas. Univ. Microfilms, Inc., Ann Arbor, Mich., 1957-70; mgr. Arbor Accounting Service, mgmt. accounting cons., Ann Arbor, 1970—; pres., dir. G C O, Inc., Fountain Valley, Calif.; dir. Rectron, Inc., Chelsea, Mich. Mem. Nat. Assn. Accountants (past chpt. pres.). Republican. Lutheran. Clubs: Detroit Athletic, Ann Arbor Golf and Outing, Ann Arbor Town, Kiwanis. HOme: 3399 Dale View Dr Ann Arbor MI 48103 Office: 1830 Washtenaw Ave Ann Arbor MI 48104

RUEGSEGGER, DONALD RAY, JR., radiol. physicist; b. Detroit, May 29, 1942; s. Donald Ray and Margaret Arlene (Elliot) R.; B.S., Wheaton Coll., 1964; M.S., Ariz. State U., 1966, Ph.D. (NDEA fellow), 1969; m. Judith Ann Merrill, Aug. 20, 1965; children—Steven, Susan, Mark, Ann. Radiol. physicist Miami Valley Hosp., Dayton, Ohio, 1969—; physics cons. X-ray dept. VA Hosp., Dayton, 1970—; adj. asst. prof. physics Wright State U., Fairborn, Ohio, 1973—, clin. asst. prof. radiology, 1976—. Diplomate Am. Bd. Radiology. Mem. Am. Assn. Physicist in Medicine, Am. Coll. Radiology, Am. Phys. Soc., AAAS, Ohio Radiol. Soc., Health Physics Soc. Baptist. Home: 2018 Washington Creek Ln Centerville OH 45459 Office: Radiation Therapy Miami Valley Hospital 1 Wyoming St Dayton OH 45409

RUEGSEGGER, LOYAL, JR., elec. co. exec.; b. Canton, Ohio, June 19, 1920; s. Loyal and Dora (Leyman) R.; student Purdue U., 1945-46; B.S. in Elec. Engring., Ohio No. U., 1950; m. L. June Smith, May 20, 1944; children—Carol June, Loyal III. Test engr. Eureka Williams Corp., Bloomington, Ill., 1950-51; system relay engr. Ohio Power Co., Canton, 1951-54; coordinator field engrs. Ohio Valley Electric Corp., Gallipolis, Ohio, 1954-56, system meter engr. supr., Piketon, Ohio, 1956—. Corr. Edison Electric Inst. Judge Jr. Sci. Fair, Ohio U., Athens. Served from pvt. to tech. sgt. USAAF, 1941-45. Decorated D.F.C., Air medal with 10 oak leaf clusters (Army). Mem. Mid-South Metermens Assn. (2d v.p. 1957-58), IEEE (sr.), Power Engring. Soc. (sr.), Nat., Ky. Socs. profl. engrs., Instrument Soc. Am. (sr.), VFW, Am. Legion. Mason (Shriner); member Order Eastern Star. Contbr. articles to profl. jours. Home: Box 220 Route 2 Waverly OH 45690 Office: PO Box 468 Piketon OH 45661

RUEHL, PHILLIP CHRISTIAN, IV, mech. engr.; b. Milw., July 16, 1946; s. Milton Phillip and Barbara Dorris (Bachelder) R.; B.S. in Mech. Engring., Marquette U., Milw., 1969, M.S., 1974; m. Virginia Ann Grigg, Jan. 7, 1978. With A.O. Smith Corp., Milw., 1969—, prodn. supr., 1974-75, supr. quality control engring., 1975—; judge freshman engring. competition Marquette U., 1977. Class agt. Greater Marquette Fund, 1972-77; fund solicitor Milw. YMCA, 1976-77; account chmn. United Way of Greater Milw., 1977. Mem. Am. Soc. Metals, Soc. Automotive Engrs. (gov. bd. Milw. sec. 1974-77, asst. chmn. tech. session passenger car meeting 1977), Triangle. Republican. Lutheran. Office: PO Box 584 Milwaukee WI 53201

RUF, JACOB FREDERICK, info. systems devel. exec.; b. Kansas City, Mo., Dec. 30, 1936; s. Paul William and Amalia (Maier) R.; Asso. Sci. in Engring., Met. Jr. Coll. Kansas City; B.S. in Chem. Engring., Kans. U., 1959, M.S., 1967; m. Sondra Sue Ramsey, Aug. 30, 1957; children—Kurtis M., Brian A., Eric J., Jacob Frederick II. Research engr. Panhandle Eastern Pipe Line, 1959-61; supr. sci. systems Great Lakes Pipe Line, 1961-63; mgr. systems devel. Black & Sivals & Bryson, Kansas City, Mo., 1963-66; dir. data systems Met. Planning Commn., Kansas City region 1966-69; pres. Mid-Continent Computing Inc., Kansas City, Mo., 1967-69; exec. v.p. Info. Systems Devel. Inc., Kansas City, 1969-77; v.p. NLT Computer Services Corp., 1976-77; pres. Ruf Corp., Olathe, Kans., 1976—. Mem. accrediting study team Nat. Assn. for Trade and Tech. Schs.; math. judge Nat. Sci. Fair, 1973, Kansas City Sci. Fair; mem. adv. bd. Mid-Am. regional council Emergency Med. Systems; mem. Gov. Kans.'s Adv. Council Info. and Communication Systems, 1968-74, Gov. Mo.'s Adv. Council Comprehensive Health Planning, 1972-73, Gov. Mo.'s Adv. Council State Center Health Statistics; mem. Jo. County (Kans.) Mayors Adv. Bd. Transp. Planning, 1971-72; mem. mid-Am. regional council Population Projection Adv. Bd. and econ. devel. adv. com.; mem. Merriam (Kans.) Zoning Bd. Appeals, Jo. County Water Bd., 1970-72; tech. adv. com. Kansas City Heart Assn., 1975—. Served with USNR, 1954-59. Mem. Assn. for Computing Machinery (chmn. Kansas City chpt. 1967), Am. Inst. Chem. Engrs. Contbr. articles on chem. engring., urban planning, Info. systems to tech. jours. Home: 13700 Pflumm Rd Olathe KS 66061 Office: Rural Route 2 Olathe KS 66061

RUF, PATRICIA KAYE, metallurgist; b. McCook, Nebr., May 6, 1949; d. Manuel LeRoy and Margalee Alice (Lyons) Ruf; B.S., U. Nebr., 1971; M.S., Mich. Tech. U., 1973; postgrad. U. Calif., 1973-74. Metall. scientist U. Calif., Berkeley and Livermore, 1973-74; metallurgist Bechtel Corp., San Francisco, 1974-75, welding engr. on Alaska Pipeline, Fairbanks, 1975-78; chmn., speaker workshops. Sci. fellow Alpha Sigma Mu. 1972; grantee AEC, 1970, 73. Registered profl. engr., Calif. Mem. Am. Soc. Metals, Am. Soc. Quality Control, Am. Welding Soc., Soc. Women Engrs., League Acad. Women. Contbr. profl. jours. Home and office: 120 Warner St Marietta OH 45750

RUGG, JOHN DAILY, genealogist; b. Newark, Ohio, Feb. 27, 1921; s. Paul Prior and Ruth Naomi (Daily) R.; student Ohio Wesleyan U., 1938-42; B.A., U. Tex., Austin, 1948, M.A., 1949; M.L.S., Brigham Young U., 1974; m. Mildred Catherine McDonald, June 17, 1945; 1 son, Paul McDonald. Writer, editor U. Tex. Bur. Bus. Research, 1949; asst. pub. info. officer USAF, Washington, 1949-51, dep. chief info. services Air Weather Service, 1951-58, founding editor AWS Observer, 1954-58, exec. editor, 1958-72, dir. info., 1958-72; dir. research Ohio Roots, Granville, 1974—. Mem. Mayors Com. on Sewers, Collinsville, Ill., 1969-70; Mem. adv. bd. Licking County Bicentennial Commn. Bd. dirs. Madison County (Ill.) Mental Health Center, 1967-72, v.p., 1970-72. Served with AUS, 1942-43. Mem. ALA, Nat., Ohio geneal. socs., Ohio Hist. Soc., Am. Meteorol. Soc., S.A.R., So. Ill. Editorial Assn., Air Force Assn., Ohio Geneal. Soc. (trustee), Phi Kappa Phi, Beta Phi Mu, Sigma Chi. Methodist. Home: 112 Thresher St Granville OH 43023 Office: PO Box 332 Granville OH 43023

RUGGLES, ROBERT BLAIR, advt. agy. exec.; b. Cleve., June 3, 1934; s. Ralph Austin and Winifred Regina (Cunningham) R.; B.S., Grove City Coll., 1957; m. Jo Ann Marie Burg, Sept. 7, 1957; children—Rand C., Dale Royce. Advt. mgr. James C. Heintz Co., tire equipment mfr., Cleve., 1959-66; dir. mktg. Wattenmaker Advt., 1966-72; partner The Second Floor, advt. agy., Cleve., 1972-73; pres. Show & Tell, Inc., advt., 1974—. Packmaster, Cub Scouts Am., Berea, Ohio, 1968-71. Served with AUS, 1957-59. Mem. Am. Mktg. Assn., Cleve. Soc. Communications Arts, Cleve. Advt. Club. Clubs: Sales Mktg. Execs., Cleve. Athletic. Home: 10501 Lake Shore Blvd Apt 4 Bratenahl OH 44108 Office: Suite 236 The Arcade Cleveland OH 44114

RUGH, WILLIAM BATMAN, mech. engr.; b. Alton, Ill., Nov. 6, 1947; s. Robert Handlin and Elizabeth Lenore (Batman) R.; B.S. in Mech. Engring., Duke U., 1969; M.B.A., U. N.C., 1972. Mem. indsl. engring. staff Owens-Ill., Inc., North Bergen, N.J., 1972-74, engr. glass container div. engring. group, Toledo, 1974—. Dist. committeeman Boy Scouts Am., 1974—. Recipient Eagle Scout award Boy Scouts Am., 1962. Mem. ASME, Nat. Soc. Profl. Engrs., Internat. Brotherhood Magicians, Nat. Flag Found., Alpha Phi Omega (nat. bd.), Beta Gamma Sigma. Club: Onized Singles (pres.). Home: 2401 Cheyenne Blvd Apt 146 Toledo OH 43614 Office: Box 1035 N T C Toledo OH 43666

RUGOLO, LAWRENCE, artist; b. Milw., Oct. 2, 1931; s. Joseph and Antonia (Draga) R.; B.S., U. Wis., Milw., 1954; M.F.A., U. Iowa, Iowa City, 1959; m. Carol Mary Thorndyke, Aug. 9, 1958; children—Gregg Noland, Elise Ann. Instr. art U. Iowa, 1959-60; instr. art U. Mo., Columbia, 1960-64, asst. prof., 1964-68, asso. prof., 1968-74, prof., 1974—, chmn. dept. art, 1973-76; design cons. McGraw-Edison Mfg. Co., Boonville, Mo., 1962-64; art editor Mo. Alumnus Mag., 1967-69; artist, works exhibited 8 one-man shows, 4 two-man shows, 44 juried and competitive exhbns., other invitational exhbns. Bd. dirs. U. Mo. YMCA, 1977—. Served with AUS, 1955-57. Recipient 15 awards for art work from juried competitions. Mem. Nat., Midwest coll. art assns., NEA, Columbia Art League (dir.), Kappa Delta Pi. Home: 415 Parkade Blvd Columbia MO 65201 Office: A126 Fine Arts University of Missouri Columbia MO 65201

RUHALA, RICHARD JOHN, lawyer; b. Flint, Mich., Mar. 28, 1936; s. John and Anna Elizabeth (Mucha) R.; B.A., U. Mich., 1958; postgrad. U. Rochester, 1958-59; J.D., Wayne State U., 1962; m. Hildreth Arlene DeCook, Aug. 9, 1958; children—Karen Lynn, John Charles, Richard James, Philip Neil. Admitted to Mich. bar, 1962, U.S. Supreme Ct. bar, 1976; practice law Genesee County, Mich., 1962—; mem. firm Draper, Mansour, Daniel, Sordyl & Ruhala, 1962-64; Genesee Co. asst. prosecutor, 1964-65; mem. firm Thomas & Delaney, 1965-67, Draper, Daniel & Ruhala, 1967-72, Draper, Daniel, Ruhala & Seymour, P.C., 1973—. City atty. Davison, Mich., 1967—; asst. city atty. Flint, Mich., 1966—; dir. Grand Eta Corp., 1967-71; legal adv. Genesee County Parents Without Partners Assn., 1964—. Mem. Flint YMCA Camp Com., 1965-72; mem. Genesee County Red Feather Fund Raising Com., 1964-67; chmn. council ministries Central United Methodist Ch., 1973-76; chmn. com. on ethics Nat. Sch. Bds. Assn., 1974-76; pack master Cub Scouts, Flint, 1974-76. Democratic candidate U.S. Congress, 1970; mem. Flint Bd. Edn., 1967—, pres., 1972-73; mem. Flint Charter Commn., 1964-66; chmn. Com. for Flint's New City Charter, 1974. Bd. dirs. Genesee Co. Cystic Fibrosis Found., Genesee Co. Planned Parenthood Assn., 1964-66. Named Outstanding Young Man of Year Flint, 1967; Outstanding Young Man of Year Mich., 1968; recipient Key to City Flint, 1967. Mem. Mich. Assn. Sch. Bds. (pres. 1971-72, dir. 1968-74), Nat. Sch. Bds. Assn. (dir. 1973—), U. Mich. Flint Alumni Club (dir.), Flint Jr. C. of C. (dir. 1963-67), Wayne State U. Alumni Club, Am., Mich., Genesee County bar assns., Am. Judicature Soc., Mich., Am. trial lawyers assns., Greater Flint C. of C., Genesee Co. Young Lawyers Assn. (pres. 1966), Phi Kappa Sigma. Clubs: University (Flint, Mich.), Elks. Contbr. articles to profl. jours. Home: 6289 Tanbark Ct Flint MI 48504 Office: 717 S Grand Traverse St Flint MI 48502

RUKSENAS, ALGIS PIUS, city ofcl.; b. Kaunas, Lithuania, May 7, 1942; s. Anthony and Elena (Maciokas) R.; came to U.S., 1949, naturalized, 1955; B.A., Western Res. U., 1965; M.A., Ill. State U., 1971. Reporter, The Telegraph, Painesvile, Ohio, 1968; writer Ednl. Research Council Am., Cleve., 1968; tchr., Willoughby-Eastlake (Ohio) Sch. System, 1967-68; reporter UPI, Cleve., 1968-71; sec. to dir. dept. pub. utilities City of Cleve., 1973—; instr. tech. writing Lakeland Community Coll., 1976. Pres., Lithuanian Am. Council, Cleve., 1973—; sec. Lithuanian Civic Club, 1975—. Recipient Best Non-fiction award Ohioana Library Assn., 1975, Most Outstanding Individual of Year award Vydunas Fund, 1973, Ann. prize for outstanding civic contbn. Lithuanian Med. Assn. Ohio, 1973. Mem. Soc. Lithuanian Journalists. Roman Catholic. Author: Day of Shame, 1973. Contbr. articles to mags., newspapers. Home: 5682 French Blvd Mentor OH 44060 Office: 1201 Lakeside Ave Cleveland OH 44114

RULAU, RUSSELL, editor; b. Chgo., Sept. 21, 1926; s. Alphonse and Ruth (Thorsen) R.; student U. Wis., 1946-48; m. Hazel Darlene Grizzell, Feb. 1, 1968; children—(by former marriage) Lance Eric, Russell A.W., Marcia June, Scott Quentin, Roberta Ann, Kyle Christopher; 1 step-dau., Sharon Maria Modia. Entered U.S. Army, 1944-1950, served to master sgt. USAF, 1950-62; resigned active duty, 1962; asst. editor Coin World newspaper, Sidney, Ohio, 1962-74, editor World Coins mag., 1964-74, Numis. Scrapbook mag., 1968-74; editorial coordinator How to Order Fgn. Coins guidebook, 1966-74; mng. editor World Coin News newspaper, 1974—; fgn. editor Numis. News newspaper, 1974—; editor-in-chief Standard Catalog of World Paper Money, 1975—; contbg. editor Standard Catalog of World Coins, 1974—. Mem. U.S. Assay Commn., 1973. Sec., Numismatic Terms Standardization Com., 1966-74. Vice-chmn. Waupaca County Republican party, 1977—. Fellow Royal Numis. Soc., Am. Numis. Soc. (asso.); mem. Token and Medal Soc. (editor 1962-63), Am. Numis. Assn., Canadian, S. African numis. assns., Mont. Hist. Soc., Am. Vecturist Assn., Numis. Lit. Guild (dir. 1974—). Lutheran. Author: (with George Fuld) Spiel Marken, 1962-65, American Game Counters, 1972: World Mint Marks, 1966; Modern World Mint Marks, 1970; (with J. U. Rixen and Frovin Sieg) Seddelkatalog Slesvig Plebiscit Zone I og II, 1970; Numismatics of Old Alabama, 1971-73; (with Chester L. Krause) Hard Times Tokens, 1977. Contbr. numis. articles to profl. jours. Home: Rt 2 Box 15-BA Iola WI 54945 Office: Krause Publications Iola WI 54945

RULIS, ROBERT ALEXANDER, corp. exec.; b. Vandergrift, Pa., Feb. 8, 1928; s. Charles and Alexandria R.; B.S., U. Md., 1956; m. Diane Kay Brower, Aug. 26, 1972; children by previous marriage—Ines Denise, Suzanne A. Commd. ensign U.S. Navy, 1950, advanced through grades to comdr., 1966; ret., 1969; v.p. fin. planning Platte Valley Oil Co., Inc., Ralston, Nebr., 1969-70; pres. Standard Capital Corp., Omaha, 1970—; guest lectr. fin. planning U. Calif. (Berkeley). Bd. dirs. Park East, Inc. Mem. Ret. Officers Assn. (past pres. Offutt chpt.). Actively involved in rehab. of inner city. Home: 12815 Dewey St Omaha NE 68154 Office: 2626 Dewey Ave Omaha NE 68105

RUMELY, EMMET SCOTT, automobile co. exec., banker; b. N.Y.C., Feb. 15, 1918; s. Edward A. and Fanny (Scott) R.; grad. Phillips Exeter Acad., 1935; B.S., Yale, 1939; postgrad. U. Mich., 1940-41; m. Elizabeth Hodges, July 5, 1947; children—Virginia H., Elizabeth Rumely Visser, Scott Hodges. Mgr., Marenisco Farms, La Porte County, Ind., 1939-73; dir. La Porte Hotel Co., Inc., 1938-70, pres., 1965-70; pres., dir. Rumely Corp., 1970—; product planning mgr. tractor ops. Ford Motor Co., Birmingham, Mich., 1961-70, asst. to v.p., gen. mgr., 1970-75; dir. 1st Nat. Bank & Trust Co., La Porte. Mem. Detroit Fine Arts Founders Soc., Am. Soc. Agrl. Engrs., Soc. Orchard Lake (Mich.) Country; Huron Mountain (Big Bay, Mich.); Otsego Ski (Gaylord, Mich.); Yale (Detroit). Home: 207 Abbey Rd Birmingham MI 48008 Office: 800 Michigan Ave La Porte IN 46350

RUNGE, ROBERT HENRY, realtor; b. Fort Wayne, Ind., Feb. 1, 1929; s. Herman Albert and Helen Marie (Fortmeyer) R.; B.S.C., Internat. Coll., 1950; m. Helen Ann Hartsough, Dec. 26, 1953; children—SuzAnne Diane, Kathryn RoxAnne. Mem. indsl. mgmt. staff Cleve. Graphite Bronze, Fort Wayne, 1950-58, Essex Internat., 1958-66; broker Runge Realtor, Fort Wayne, 1966-71; owner operator Robert Runge Realtor, Fort Wayne, 1972—. Served with AUS, 1950-52: Korea. Mem. Ind., Internat. real estate assns., Fort Wayne Bd. Realtors, Fort Wayne C. of C., Am. Legion, Young Men's Indsl. Mgmt. Club, Transp. Club, 75 Club, Delta Nu Omega. Clubs: Olimpia, Kiwanis. Home and office: 7223 Illinois Rd Fort Wayne IN 46804

RUNICE, ROBERT E., telephone co. exec.; b. Fargo, N.D., Aug. 20, 1929; s. Elmer M. and Ruth F. (Soule) R.; B.S., N.D. State U., 1951; m. Geraldine Kharas, June 26, 1954; children—Michael, Christopher, Paul, Karen. With N.W. Bell Telephone Co., 1951—, v.p. Neb., 1966-69, v.p. pub. relations, pub. affairs, Omaha, 1969-73, v.p. mktg., 1973—; dir. Neb. Savs. & Loan. Chmn. United Appeal Campaign, 1969. Bd. dirs. Coll. St. Mary, Nebr. Meth. Hosp.; trustee Omaha-Indsl. Found. Mem. Omaha C. of C. (pres. 1972), Soc. of Mayflower, Air Force Assn. (pres.). Episcopalian. Rotarian. Clubs: Omaha; Plaza, Country (Omaha). Home: 9512 Valley St Omaha NE 68124 Office: 100 S 19th St Omaha NE 68102

RUNNEBOHM, NICHOLAS JOSEPH, constrn. co. owner; b. Shelby County, Ind., July 31, 1939; s. John Louis and Rose Marie (Cord) R.; grad. high sch.; m. Julia Carolyn Jenkins, Sept. 30, 1967; children—Michael, Kathleen, Cynthia, Susan. Vice pres. Runnebohm Shaeffer Inc., Shelbyville, Ind., 1965-67; pres. Nick Runnebohm Constrn. Co., Inc., Shelbyville, 1968—. Pres., Try Enterprises, Shelbyville, 1966—; owner, operator Justermere Farm, 1967—. Served with USMC, 1957-60. Mem. Ind. Metal Bldg. Dealers Assn. (sec. 1974-75, pres. 1976-77), Nat. Rifle Assn., Shelbyville Rifle and Pistol Club (dir. 1964-67), Roman Catholic. Lion, K.C. Home: RD 6 Box 317 Shelbyville IN 46176 Office: Box 30A Route 6 Shelbyville IN 46176

RUNSER, CHARLES ALLAN, lawyer; b. Van Wert, Ohio, June 28, 1942; s. Charles H. and Bina F. (Restar) R.; B.S. in Bus. Adminstrn., Northwestern U., 1964; J.D., Ohio No. Coll. of Law, 1967; m. Rebecca Ellen Roggenkemper, Sept. 9, 1967; children—Charles Allan, Jr., Jennifer Anne. Admitted to Ohio bar, 1967; partner firm Beard, Childs & Runser, Van Wert, 1967-72; mem. firm Childs & Runser, Van Wert, 1973-75; individual practice law, Van Wert, 1976—; prosecuting atty. Van Wert County, 1973-76; dir. First Fed. Savs. & Loan Assn., Van Wert; dir., officer Bob Dunn Ford, Inc., Bob

Dunn Leasing, Inc., Blue Rock Estates, Inc. Pres. United Fund, 1972-74; mem. Civil Service Commn., 1968-77. Served with U.S. Army, 1967-68. Mem. Am., Ohio, Northwestern Ohio bar assn., Am. Judicature Soc., Nat. Dist. Attys. Assn., Ohio Info. Com., W. Central Ohio Health Assn., Am. Fedn. Police, Nat. Council on Crime and Delinquency, C. of C. (chmn. congressional action com. 1972, recipient Ray Miller Award for Outstanding Com. Chmn. 1972). Republican. Presbyterian. Clubs: Willow Bend Golf (Van Wert), Van Wert Rotary, Elks. Home: 1056 Indian Hill Dr Van Wert OH 45891 Office: Suite 105 First Fed Savs Bldg Van Wert OH 45891

RUPE, BILLY DEAN, pharmacologist; b. Lynn, Ind., Nov. 7, 1931; s. Dow Elsworth and Garnet Irene (Betts) R.; B.S., Purdue U., 1960, M.S., 1961, Ph.D., 1963; m. Wanda Mae Harris, July 29, 1950; children—Towanna Lynn, Jon Eric, Matthew Karl. Sect. head Strasenburg Labs., Rochester, N.Y., 1963-68; mgr. pharm. research Cutter-Haver-Lockhart, Shawnee, Kan., 1968-73; mgr. spl. sci. projects Marion Labs., Kansas City, Mo., 1973-75; dir. pharm. research and devel. Jensen-Salsbery Labs. div. Richardson-Merrell Inc., Kansas City, Mo., 1975—. Served with AUS, 1952-54. Mem. Am. Pharm. Assn., N.Y. Acad. Scis., AAAS, Sigma Xi, Phi Eta Sigma, Rho Chi, Phi Lambda Upsilon. Home: 10516 Pawnee Ln Leawood KS 66206 Office: 520 W 21st St Kansas City MO 64141

RUPP, DOUGLAS ALAN, constrn. co. exec.; b. Slayton, Minn., July 1, 1944; s. Calvin A. and Norma A. (Koopman) R.; B.S. in Constrn., Ariz. State U., 1966; postgrad. in bus. U. S.D., 1966-67; m. Joan D. Phillips, Dec. 10, 1971, children—Lincoln Douglas, Tyson David, Rylan Mitchell. Vice pres. Rupp Constrn. Co. Inc., Slayton, 1970-71, pres., 1971—; pres. D.A. Rupp Asphalt Co. Inc., 1972—, Rupp Contracting Corp., 1976—, Pipestone Bituminous Corp., 1976—; dir. Peoples State Bank of Slayton, Slayton Service Corp. Served with USNR, 1967-69. Mem. Am. Inst. Constructors, Associated Builders and Contractors, Minn. Asphalt Pavement Assn. Home: 3035 Queen Ave Slayton MN 56172 Office: Box 1 Slayton MN 56172

RUPP, ROBERT GEORGE, mag. editor; b. Aurora, Nebr., Oct. 28, 1918; s. Laurin Everett and Cassie Ellen (Dean) R.; B.Sc., U. Nebr., 1941; postgrad. U. Minn., 1945-46; m. M. Dee Schill, 1942 (dec. 1961); children—Victoria Ann, Robert George II, Lorna Lee; m. 2d, Matilda Alice Towne, May 26, 1962. News editor Agr. Extension Service, Iowa State U., Ames, 1946-48; extension news editor Agrl. Extension Service, U. Minn., St. Paul, 1948-50; asso. editor The Farmer mag., St. Paul, 1950-59, mng. editor, 1959-69, editor, 1969—. Dir. farms Nat. Safety Council, 1970—; mem. adv. council U. Minn. at Crookston, Waseca, Minn. Dept. Edn. vocat. agrl. div.; vice-chmn. Minn. Humanities Commn., 1976—. Named hon. state farmer Minn. Future Farmers Am.; recipient Meritorious Service award 4H Fedn., 1961; Nat. Soil Builders award Nat. Plant Food Council, 1957. Mem. Internat. Fedn. Agrl. Journalists (U.S. dir. 1971—), Minn. Assn. Commerce and Industry (v.p. agr. 1972-75), Minn. Agri-Growth Council (dir. 1973—), Minn. Safety Council (chmn. agr. div. 1964—, Meritorious Service award, 1966), Am. Agrl. Editors Assn. (pres. 1966-67). Rotarian. Home: 14906 50th St S Afton MN 55001 Office: 1999 Shepard Rd St Paul MN 55116

RUPPEL, HOWARD JAMES, JR., sociologist; b. Orange, N.J., July 22, 1941; s. Howard J. and Lillian M. (Wordley) R.; B.A., St. Joseph's Coll., Ind., 1963; M.A., No. Ill. U., 1968; postgrad. U. Iowa, 1968—; m. Barbara Margaret Wiedemann, June 3, 1967. Instr. social sci. St. Francis High Sch., Wheaton, Ill., 1963-65, debate coach, 1963-65; instr. sociology St. Dominic Coll., St. Charles, Ill., 1966-67; instr. sociology Cornell Coll., Mt. Vernon, Iowa, 1969-70, asst. prof., 1970-72, lectr., 1972-73; research dir. Social Sci. Research Assos., Cedar Rapids, Iowa, 1973—; instr. div. continuing edn. U. Iowa, 1976—; instr. continuing edn. program Mt. Mercy Coll., Cedar Rapids, 1976—; cons. Iowa Dept. Social Services, Mankato (Minn.) State Coll., Ohio State Chiropractors Assn., Cath. U., Nijmegen, Holland, Sch. Social Work, U. Iowa, Kirkwood Community Coll., Cedar Rapids, Families Inc., West Branch. Bd. dirs. Hawkeye Area Community Action Program, Cedar Rapids, Ia., 1970-71. NSF fellow, 1968. Mem. Am. Sociol. Assn., Midwest Sociol. Soc., Nat., Iowa (dir. 1976-77) councils family relations, Assn. for Sociology of Religion, Soc. Sci. Study Religion, Soc. for Study of Social Problems, Fedn. Am. Scientists, Soc. for Sci. Study Sex, Am. Assn. Sex Educators, Counselors and Therapists, Nat. Forensic League, No. Ill. U. Alumni Assn., Alpha Kappa Delta. Democrat. Contbr. articles on complex orgns., marriage and the family, methodology and child care theory to profl. publs. Home: 608 5th Ave N Mount Vernon IA 52314 Office: Box 1564 Cedar Rapids IA 52406

RUSCH, HERMAN AUGUST, museum garden owner; b. nr. Arcadia, Wis., Oct. 7, 1885; s. Fredrick and Pauline (Finner) R.; ed. pub. schs.; m. Sophia Berg, Sept. 3, 1914; children—Evlyn (Mrs. DeGraw), Lewis (Mrs. Ed Kaiser). Farmer, Arcadia, 1912-52, ret. part-time farming 1952-67; museum founder, owner, Prairie Moon Museum, nr. Cochrane, Wis., 1967—. Mem. Cochrane Sch. Bd. Address: Route 1 Cochrane WI 54622

RUSH, DAVID HARRY, lumber co. exec.; b. Cleve., Mar. 31, 1927; s. Harry John and Minnie (Schwarzer) R.; B.S. in M.E., Case Inst. Tech., 1951; m. Marjorie Lillian Couch, Mar. 31, 1951; children—Cynthia Lynn, Janet Lee. Application engr. Relianc Electric Corp., 1951-53, dist. mgr., Rochester, N.Y., 1954-55; v.p. Hilton & Rush Co., Cleve., 1956-59; pres., 1960—. Served with USN, 1945-46. Mem. N. Am. Wholesale Lumber Assn. (pres. 1973-74), Nat. Assn. Wholesalers (dir. 1973-75), Econ. Council Forest Products Industries, Case Alumni Assn. (pres. 1976-77), Phi Delta Theta, Tau Beta Pi, Theta Tau, Pi Delta Epislon. Home: 134 Lakeview Ln Chagrin Falls OH 44022 Office: PO Box 16430 Cleveland OH 44116

RUSH, JOSEPH THORNTON, photographer; b. Milburn, Ill., Apr. 9, 1933; s. Thala W. and Helen G. (Thomas) R.; B.Music, DePauw U., 1956; M.Music, Vandercook Coll. Music, 1961; student Sch. Modern Photography, 1968-69, Winona Sch. Profl. Photography, 1971, 73; m. Barbara Jean Anderson, June 13, 1953; children—Gary Robert, David Howard, Lori Jo. Pub. sch. music instr., Wawaka, Ind., 1956-58; dir. fine arts Antioch (Ill.) Community High Sch., 1958-71; owner, pub. Antioch News, 1971-74; owner B-J Rush Studio, 1971—, Langdon's of Barrington Portrait Studio, 1975—. Mem. Leblanc Music Educators Nat. Adv. Bd., 1967-70; North Central Evaluating Com., 1970. Mem. No. Ill. Profl. Photographers Assn. (bd. dirs., program chmn. 1974-75, 1st v.p. 1978), Asso. Profl. Photographers Ill., Profl. Photographers Am., Barrington C. of C., Antioch Chamber Commerce and Industry. Club: Rotary. Address: 141 Cheri Lane Antioch IL 60002

RUSHTON, WILLIAM EDWIN, chem. engr.; b. Blue Island, Ill., Dec. 11, 1926; s. William E. and Eva M. (Hawkins) R.; B.S., U. Mo., 1951; m. Suzanne Scoville, May 19, 1951; children—Cynthia Anne, Robert W. Application engr. pulp and paper dept. Swenson div. Whiting Corp., Harvey, Ill., 1956-57, chem. equipment dept., 1957-60, asst. mgr., 1960-66, mgr. phosphate dept., 1966-71, mgr. environ. control dept., 1971-77, asst. div. mgr., 1977—; lectr. on use of evaporation equipment local colls. Served with AUS, 1945-47. Mem. Am. Inst. Chem. Engrs., Alpha Chi Sigma. Patentee in field. Home: 16539 Claire Ln South Holland IL 60473 Office: 15700 Lathrop Ave Harvey IL 60426

RUSKAUP, CALVIN FREDERICK, historian, writer; b. St. Louis, Feb. 5, 1939; s. Henry Clarence and Viola Alvina (Vogt) R.; B.S., U. Mo., 1967; M.A., Ohio State U., 1975, postgrad. 1975-77. Writer, Sta. KDHL, Faribault, Owatonna, Mpls., Minn., 1960-61, Bahamian Rev., Nassau, 1971-72; asso. editor Knapsack, St. Louis, 1962-65; instr. history, English, Normandy (Mo.) Schs., 1966, St. Louis City Schs., 1967-68, Fresno (Calif.) Schs., 1968-69; community organizer City of Isla Vista (Calif.), 1969-70; dir. student publs. Aquinas Coll., Nassau, 1971-72; co-founder, program dir. Community radio Sta. WFAC, Columbus, Ohio, 1974-76; chief writer Radish Guild Comedy Hour, CCE Broadcasting Corp., Columbus, Ohio, 1975-76; broadcast historian Ohio State U., Columbus, 1975—; co-founder Environmental Action, Santa Barbara, Calif., 1970; columnist Spectra, 1963-64; author (play): 40 Miles Away, 1962. Mem. Am. Hist. Assn. Home: 101 Curl Dr Columbus OH 43210 Office: 230 W 17th Ave Columbus OH 43210

RUSSELL, DAVID GARTH, counselor; b. Manhattan, Kans., Dec. 31, 1951; s. Garth Samuel and Ruth Christina (Erwin) R.; B.S.Ed., U. Mo., Columbia, 1973, M.Ed., 1977; 1 dau. by previous marriage—Sean Ashleigh. Tchr., New South Wales (Australia) Dept. Edn., 1973-76; counselor elementary sch., psychol. examiner High Ridge (Mo.) Bd. Edn., 1977—. Mem. Am. Personnel and Guidance Assn., Am. Sch. Counselors Assn., Assn. Humanistic Edn. and Devel., Phi Kappa Psi., Kappa Delta Pi. Home: 12172-C Vivacite Walk St Louis MO 63141 Office: R-1 Sch Dist PO Box 500 High Ridge MO 63049

RUSSELL, DAVID LAWSON, psychologist; b. N.Y.C., Apr. 1, 1921; s. Charles and Kathleen (Lawson) R.; B.A. with Honors, with Distinction in Psychology, Wesleyan U., 1942; Ph.D., U. Minn., 1953; m. Jean Williams, Mar. 18, 1943; children—David Williams, Nancy Kathleen. Instr. Bowdoin Coll., 1950-54, dir. student counseling, 1950-59, asst. prof. psychology, 1954-59; asso. prof. Ohio U., 1959-67, prof. psychology, 1967—, also chmn. dept., 1968-72; vis. prof. psychology U. N.H., summer, 1958; sec., treas. Maine Bd. of Examiners of Psychologists, 1957-59, chmn., 1959; mem. Maine Com. on Mental Health, 1957-59. Mem. superintending sch. com., Topsham, Maine, 1953-59, chmn., 1953-54, 56-57, sch. bldg. com. chmn., 1953-55, mem. zoning com., 1946-47; pres. Maine Psychol. Assn., 1956-57. Served from ensign to lt. USCGR, 1942-46. Licensed psychologist, Ohio. Fellow Ohio Psychol. Assn.; mem. Am., Midwestern psychol. assns., Am. Personnel and Guidance Assn., Nat. Vocat. Guidance Assn., Am. Edml. Research Assn., AAUP, Sigma Xi, Psi Chi. Co-author: Applied Psychology, 1966; also articles and research papers in field. Home: 41 Elmwood Pl Athens OH 45701

RUSSELL, DAVID WILLIAMS, lawyer; b. Lockport, N.Y., Apr. 5, 1945; s. David Lawson and Jean Graves (Williams) R.; A.B. (Army ROTC scholar, Daniel Webster scholar), Dartmouth Coll., 1967, M.B.A., 1969; J.D. cum laude, Northwestern U., 1976; m. Frances Yung Chung Chen, May 23, 1970. English tchr. Talledega (Ala.) Coll., summer 1967; math. tchr. Lyndon Inst., Lyndonville, Vt., 1967-68; instr. econs. Royalton Coll., South Royalton, Vt., part-time 1968-69; asst. to pres. for planning Tougaloo (Miss.) Coll., 1969-71, bus. mgr., 1971-73; mgr. will and trust rev. project Continental Ill. Nat. Bank & Trust Co. Chgo., summer 1974; law clk. Montgomery, McCracken, Walker & Rhoads, Phila., summer 1975; admitted to Ill. bar, 1976; asso. firm Winston & Strawn, Chgo., 1976—; cons. Alfred P. Sloan Found., 1972-73. Mem. nat. selection com. Woodrow Wilson Found. Adminstrv. Internship Program, 1973-76; vol. Lawyers for Creative Arts, Chgo., 1977. Woodrow Wilson Found. adminstrv. intern, 1969-72. Mem. Am., Ill., Chgo. bar assns., Chgo. Council Lawyers, ACLU, Chinese Music Soc., Zeta Psi. Presbyterian. Home: Apt 3A 1622 W Farwell St Chicago IL 60626 Office: Suite 5000 1 1st Nat Plaza Chicago IL 60603

RUSSELL, EDWARD HENRY, advt. exec.; b. Manila, Philippines, Dec. 6, 1922; s. John Joseph and Socorro Moreno (Lacalle) R.; student U. Philippines, 1940; B.S., U. Ill., 1947; m. Sophia Zombolas, July 12, 1969; children—Teresa Pamela, Jonathan Edward. Telegraph editor Champaign-Urbana (Ill.) News Gazette, 1947-48; promotion dir. Asso. Tech. Writers, N.Y.C., 1949; with The Biddle Co., 1950-63, sucessively prodn. mgr., asst. to pres. and plans mgr., asst. to pres., account exec., account supr., 1950-54, v.p., 1955-58, sr. v.p., 1958-63, plans bd., mgr., 1956, steering com. chmn. 1957, dir., 1958-63; pres. E.H. Russell & Co., Chgo., 1963-66; sr. v.p. Arthur Meyerhoff Assos., Chgo., 1966-68; pres. Vivox, Inc., St. Joseph, Mich., 1969—. Served to lt. (j.g.) USNR, 1943-46. Mem. Alpha Sigma Phi. Clubs: Bloomington Country, Am. Business (dir.) (Bloomington Ill.); Lake Shore, Rotunda, Bob-o-Link Golf, Press (Chgo.); Berrien Hill Country, Southshore Racquet (St Joseph). Home: 2727 Lake Shore Dr St Joseph MI 49085 Office: Box 379 St Joseph MI 49085

RUSSELL, ERWIN DEE, psychologist; b. Salt Lake City, May 26, 1924; s. Harry James and Agnes Nancy (Gardner) R.; B.A., Miami U., Oxford, Ohio, 1946; M.S., Purdue U., 1949, Ph.D., 1952; m. Joan Patricia Ramsay, Sept. 29, 1973; children—Scott, Michael, Kent. Asst. prof. Wabash Coll., 1951-52; with Rohrer, Hibler & Replogle Inc., Milw., 1952—, partner, 1957—, mgr., 1971—. Bd. dirs. YMCA, 1957-74; pres. Cambridge House, 1967; bd. dirs. Lad Lake Inc., 1975—. Licensed psychologist, Wis. Mem. Am., Midwestern, Wis., Milwaukee County psychol. assns., Am. Assn. Advancement Psychology, Wis. Acad. Arts, Scis. and Letters, Sigma Xi. Clubs: Milw. Athletic, Lake Shore, North Shore Racquet. Home: 5253 Mohawk Ave N Milwaukee WI 53217 Office: 660 Mason St E #402 Milwaukee WI 53202

RUSSELL, GARTH SAMUEL, orthopaedic surgeon; b. Kingsland, Ark., Aug. 4, 1929; s. Lindsay W. and Nancy (Bussey) R.; student U. Ark., 1946; B.S., Kan. State U., 1953; M.D., U. Kans., 1959; m. Ruth Cristine Erwin, Dec. 19, 1948; children—David Garth, Kyle Erwin. Dir. health dept., Gt. Bend, Kans., 1953-55; intern Wesley Hosp., Wichita, Kans., 1959; resident in orthopaedic surgery U. Mo., 1960-65; practice medicine specializing in orthopaedic surgery, Columbia, Mo., 1965—; mem. staff Columbia Regional Hosp., Boone County (Mo.) Hosp.; asst. prof. orthopaedic surgery U. Mo. Sch. Medicine; dir. Med. Dental Co. of Am., trustee Columbia Regional Hosp., 1975—; vis. prof. orthopaedic surgery U. Mancipal, India, 1977. Served with AUS, 1946-49. Diplomate Am. Bd. Orthopaedic Surgery. Mem. Am. Acad. Orthopaedic Surgery, Mo. Orthopaedic Assn. (pres. 1976). Editorial cons. Jour. Continuing Edn., 1973—. Contbr. articles in field to profl. jours. Address: 3205 Lansing Ave Columbia MO 65201

RUSSELL, JOHN ROBERT, physician; b. Bloomington, Ind., Mar. 17, 1922; s. John Dale and Elsie Violet (Hattery) R.; B.S., U. Chgo., 1941, M.S., 1941, M.D., 1945; m. Jane Elizabeth Bureau, Aug. 21, 1943; children—Thomas William, John Bureau, Ann Elizabeth, Amy Catherine. Intern, Chgo. Meml. Hosp., 1945-46, resident in neurol. surgery, 1948-50; resident in neurol. surgery Baptist Meml. Hosp., Memphis, 1950-51; practice medicine specializing in neurol. surgery, Indpls., 1951—; faculty Sch. Medicine, Ind. U., 1951-59, asso. prof., 1959; asso. clin. prof. surgery, part-time 1959—; teaching staff Meth. Hosp. Grad. Med. Center, 1959—. Served from 1st lt. to capt. M.C., AUS, 1946-48. Fellow A.C.S.; mem. AMA, Congress Neurol. Surgeons (pres. 1966-67), Am. Assn. Neurol. Surgeons (dir. 1967-70), Phi Beta Kappa, Sigma Xi. Episcopalian. Home: 4020 Washington Blvd Indianapolis IN 46205 Office: 1633 N Capitol Ave Indianapolis IN 46202

RUSSELL, JUDITH GRAY, counselor; b. Washington, Aug. 16, 1939; d. William Ralph and Jean Grace (Hamilton) Gray; B.S., U. Md., 1961; M.A. in Counseling and Guidance, No. Mich. U., 1973; m. John Mills Russell, June 9, 1962; children—Heather Jean, Dan William. Editorial asst. Nat. Geog. Soc., Washington, 1961-65; counselor Women's Center for Continuing Edn., No. Mich. U., Marquette, 1973—; cons. chs., hosps., profl. agys.; instr. adult enrichment, community schs.; speaker local orgns. Mem. Am. Personnel and Guidance Assn., Phi Kappa Phi. Democrat. Presbyterian. Contbr. paper to workshop, 1975. Home: 301 E Hewitt Ave Marquette MI 49855 Office: 403 Cohodas Bldg No Mich U Marquette MI 49855

RUSSELL, MAX RAY, veterinarian; b. Courtland, Kans., Dec. 15, 1938; s. Carl Hoffman and Dorothy Adelaide (Anderson) R.; D.V.M., Kans. State U., 1970; m. Kay L. Nagely, Dec. 22, 1968; children—Sean Michael, Elizabeth Louise, Patrick Joseph. Gen. practice Patton Rd. Veterinary Clinic, Great Bend, Kans., 1970-71, Northside Animal Hosp., Wamego, Kans., 1971—. Active Wamego C. of C., 1971-77. Served with U.S. Army, 1961-64. Mem. Am., Kans., Blue Valley veterinary med. assns. Presbyterian. Home and Office: Rural Route 1 Wamego KS 66547

RUSSICK, BERTRAM WARREN, mktg. research co. exec.; b. Des Moines, Oct. 29, 1921; s. David Frank and Blanche (Weiser) R.; student Drake U., 1939-42; B.S., U. So. Calif. 1946; M.A., U. Minn., 1960; m. Harriet Helen Halperin, Oct. 5, 1950; children—Betsy Louise, Constance Eve, Bertram Warren. Market analyst Gen. Mills Inc., Mpls., 1946-47, Minn. & Ont. Paper Co., Mpls., 1947-50; pres. Mid Continent Surveys Inc., Mpls., 1953—; lectr. mktg. research U. Minn., 1970—. Served with USAAF 1943-45. Decorated Air medal with oakleaf clusters. Certified cons. psychologist, Minn. Mem. Am. Mktg. Assn. (past pres.), Am. Psychol. Assn., Am. Assn. Pub. Opinion Research. Jewish. Clubs: Mpls., Oakridge County, Minn. Alumni. Author: Choice or Change, 1976. Home: 99 Forest Dale Minneapolis MN 55410 Office: 802 Midwest Plaza Minneapolis MN 55402

RUSSO, JOSEPH ROBERT, educator; b. Wilmington, Del., Feb. 16, 1934; s. Joseph R. and Edith M. (Williamson) R.; m. Lee Kroeger, Jan. 1970; children—Mark, Andrew, Richard, Sean, Joseph, Timothy. B.S., Pa. State U., 1955; student U. Fla., 1956-57, U. Rochester, 1957; M.S., Pa. State U., 1959, D.Ed., 1963. Dir., McKim Community Assn., Balt., 1955-57; tchr. Kissimmee (Fla.) Pub. Schs., 1957-58, dir. guidance, 1959-62; research dir. delinquency study porject So. Ill. U., Edwardsville, 1963-68, coordinator research, 1968-72, asso. dean Grad. Sch., 1972—, prof. psychology, 1975—. Mem. Ill. Gov.'s Adv. Bd. Youth Corrections, Council Diagnosis and Evaluation Criminal Defendants, 1972. Mem. Am. Psychol. Assn., Phi Delta Kappa. Named Fla. Tchr. Year, 1962; Social and Rehab. Service and Office Edn. grantee, 1972-74. Contbr. articles to profl. jours. Author: Amphetamine Abuse, 1972, The Job of Help-Giving. Home: 447 Shady Ln Edwardsville IL 62025 Office: Box 46 Southern Ill U Edwardsville IL 62026

RUSSO, MARTIN A., congressman; b. Chgo., Jan. 23, 1944; s. Anthony and Lucille Russo; B.A., DePaul U., 1965, J.D., 1967; m. Karen Jorgensen, Dec. 19, 1965; 1 son, Tony. Admitted to Ill. bar, 1967; law clk. Ill. Appellate Ct., 1967-68; practiced in Chgo., 1968-71; asst. states atty. Cook County (Ill.), 1971-73; mem. 95th Congress from 3d Ill. Dist. Named One of Roseland's Ten Outstanding Young Men, Gateway br. Chgo. Assn. Commerce and Industry, 1968; Man of Year, Chgo. West Suburban chpt. United Neighbors of Italian Community Orgns., 1975, Man of Year Justinian Soc., 1976, Outstanding Legislative Leader Soc. of Little Flower, 1975. Mem. Am., Ill., South Suburban bar assns., Order Sons of Italy, Blue Key, Joint Civil Com. Italian-Ams., Delta Theta Phi, Alpha Phi Delta. Club: Elks. Home: 1116 E 160th Pl South Holland IL 60473 Office: 126 Cannon House Office Bldg Washington DC 20515

RUSSO, MICHAEL EUGENE, pharm. corp. ofcl.; b. St. Louis, Aug. 5, 1939; s. Michael W. and Lyda Mae (Wootten) R.; A.B., Washington U., 1961, Ph.D. in Phys. Chemistry, 1970. With Mallinckrodt, Inc., St. Louis, 1967—, research investigator, 1967-72, research asso., 1972-74, group leader, 1974-75, research mgr. drug and cosmetic chem. div., 1975—; v.p., dir. Parkside Devel. Corp., St. Louis. NSF fellow, 1963, Shell fellow, 1964-65, NASA trainee, 1965-67. Mem. Am. Chem. Soc., Soc. Cosmetic Chemists, AAAS, Sigma Xi, Sigma Chi. Club: Washington U. (St. Louis). Home: 10 Kingsbury Pl Saint Louis MO 63112 Office: 3700 N Broadway St Saint Louis MO 63147

RUSTEN, ELMER MATHEW, dermatologist; b. Pigeon Falls, Wis., Oct. 5, 1902; s. Ener E. and Clara L. (Benrud) R.; B.A., St. Olaf Coll., 1925; B.S., U. Minn., 1928, B.M., 1928, M.D., 1929, postgrad., 1929-31, U. Vienna, 1932; m. Helen Marthine Steidl, July 19, 1930; 1 son, Elmer Michael. Intern, Mpls. Gen. Hosp., 1929, resident, 1929-31; practice medicine specializing in dermatology, Mpls., 1933—; instr. dermatology U. Minn., Mpls., 1934-38, clin. instr., 1938-42, clin. asst. prof., 1942-71; mem. cons. staff Mpls. Gen. Hosp., 1933-40, 51-60, Glen Lake Sanatorium, Oak Terrace, Minn., 1936-60; mem. attending staff Methodist Hosp., St. Louis Park, Minn., 1959-77, Abbott Hosp., Mpls., Minn., 1935—, Asbury Hosp., Mpls., 1934-50. Del. to 14th Internat. Tb Conf., New Delhi, India, 1957. Mem. Minn. Citizens Council, 1963-66; judge Big Game Competition, 1959, chmn., 1961, 64, v.p., 1965-74. Bd. dirs. Correctional Service of Minn., pres., 1963-67; bd. dirs. Minn. Dermatol. Found., 1950-54. Diplomate Am. Bd. Dermatology. Mem. Am., Minn. med. assns., Am. Acad. Dermatology, Soc. for Investigative Dermatology, Minn., Chgo. dermatol. socs., Internat. Soc. Tropical Dermatology, Am. Acad. Allergy, Internat. Corrs. Soc. of Allergists, Hennepin County Med. Soc., Alaska Territorial Assn. (hon.). Republican. Lutheran. Rotarian (pres. 1961). Clubs: Boone and Crockett (hon., life), Six O'Clock Club, Minneapolis Club. Author: Wheat, Egg and Milk-Free Diets, 1932. Home: 18420 D 8th Ave N Wayzata MN 55391 Office: 1645 Medical Arts Bldg Minneapolis MN 55402

RUTH, THOMAS EDWIN, chem. co. exec.; b. Binghamton, N.Y., Dec. 4, 1945; s. Harold Edwin and Eleanor Margaret (Thomas) R.; B.S. in Chemistry, Syracuse U., 1967; M.B.A., Central Mich. U., 1973; m. Judith Anne Bennett, June 24, 1967; children—Erika, Scott. Chemist, Dow Corning Corp., Midland, Mich., 1967-70, tech. service and devel. chemist, 1970-73, bus. research coordinator, 1973-76, bus. research supr., 1976—; guest lectr. Central Mich. U. Chmn. fund raising com. Siebert Elementary Sch. Parent Tchrs. Orgn., Midland, 1975-76, pres., 1976-77. Mem. Am. Mktg. Assn. Home: 3843 Ken Ln Midland MI 48640 Office: Mail 153 Midland MI 48640

RUTHEMEYER, THOMAS JAMES, hosp. adminstr.; b. Cin., May 10, 1947; s. Charles Joseph and Barbara Marie (Stoffel) R.; B.B.A. in Accounting, U. Cin., 1971; m. Patricia J. Muszynski, Sept. 6, 1975.

Accountant William H. Mers & Co., Cin., 1970-73; controller Clermont County Hosp., Batavia, O., 1973—, trustee, 1972—, mem. lay adv. bd., 1973—, mem. planning com., 1975—. Bd. dirs. Clermont County Human Services, 1974-75. Mem. Our Lady of Mercy Hosp. Planning Council, Cin. Hosp. Council. C.P.A., Ohio. Mem. Am. Inst. C.P.A.'s, Ohio Soc. C.P.A.'s, Nat. Assn. Accountants, Am. Accounting Assn., Am., Ohio hosp. assns., Am. Pub. Health Assn., Hosp. Financial Mgmt. Assn., Clermont County C. of C. (dir. 1975-78), Beta Alpha Psi, Delta Sigma Pi. Clubs: Kiwanis, Rotary. Home: 6405 Clough Pike Cincinnati OH 45244 Office: 3000 Hospital Dr Batavia OH 45103

RUTHERFORD, JOHN SHERMAN, III, profl. race car driver; b. Coffeyville, Kans., Mar. 12, 1938; s. John Sherman and Mary Henrietta (Brooks) R.; student Tex. Christian U., 1956; m. Betty Rose Hoyer, July 7, 1963; children—John Sherman, Angela Ann. Profl. race car driver, 1959—; driver super-modified race cars, sprint cars, stock cars, midgets, sports cars, and formula 5000; winner fifteen championship car races in U.S. Auto Club: winner Indpls. 500, 1974, 76, second place, 1975; set new world's record for stock cars, Daytona Beach, Fla., 1963; U.S. Auto Club Nat. Sprint Car Champion, 1965; host TV show The Recers; rep. for Car Quest Auto Parts, Central Ind. Oldsmobile Dealers; appeared in numerous TV commls.; lectr. in field. Hon. state chmn. Am. Cancer Soc., Tex.; appeared in TV and radio pub. services messages for Nat. Safety Council, Calif. Hwy. Patrol, Muscular Dystrophy Assn. Named Fort Worth Newsmaker of Yr., 1974; Driver of Yr., Sport Mag., 1976; Driver of Yr., Am. Sports Writers and Broadcasters, 1974; recipient Jim Clark award, 1969, Jim Malloy award, 1974, Eddie Sachs award, 1975, Extra Mile award, 1973; chosen for Internat. Race of Champions, 1974, 76, 77. Mem. U.S. Auto Club. Fedn. Internat. Automobile, Exptl. Aircraft Assn., Warbirds of Am. Baptist. Clubs: Lions, Diamond Oaks Country, Shady Oaks Country. Home: 4919 Black Oak Ln Fort Worth TX 76114 also Rural Route 18 Box 340 B Indianapolis IN 46234

RUTHERFORD, WILLIAM KENNETH, former sch. prin.; b. Cairo, Mo., Sept. 24, 1907; s. William N. and Myrtle (Halliburton) R.; B.S., N.E. Mo. State Tchrs. Coll., 1935; M.Ed., U. Mo., 1948, postgrad., 1949-55; m. Anna Clay Zimmerman, Nov. 20, 1940; children—Anna Christene, Shirley Kay, William Clay. Tchr., sch. adminstr., Northeast, Mo., 1929-42; tchr., elementary prin., Moberly, Mo., 1945-50; elementary supr., Fulton, Mo., 1950-51; supervising prin., dir. guidance, Lexington, Mo., 1951-57, prin., 1957-73, ret. Served with U.S. Army, 1942-45. Mem. State Hist. Soc. Mo., New Eng. Gen. Hist. Soc., Peyton Soc. Va., Soc. Genealogists (London), Alden Kindred Am., Nat. Geneal. Soc., N.Y. Geneal. and Brog. Soc., Gen. Soc. Mayflower Descs., S.A.R., Phi Delta Kappa. Mem. Christian Ch. (elder, chmn. ch. bd. 1964-66). Mem. Magna Charta Barons; Rotarian. Author: Genealogical History of the Halliburton Family, 1959, rev. edit., 1972; John Rutherford, Pioneer of Lincoln County, Ky. and His Descendants, 1963; Genealogical History of the Rutherford Family, 1969; Genealogical History of Our Ancestors, 1970, rev. edit., 1977. Home: 2101 Forest Ave Lexington MO 64067

RUTKOWSKI, KAREN ANN, sch. counselor; b. Detroit, Jan. 23, 1945; d. Anthony and Sylvia Jane (De Zutter) Rutkoski; B.S., Wayne State U., 1967, M.Ed., 1970, Ed.S., 1974, also postgrad. Tchr., counselor, adminstrv. intern Lake Shore Sch., St. Clair Shores, Mich., 1967-73; coordinator, leader-counselor edn. Wayne State U., Detroit, 1974-76; counselor Chippewa Valley (Mich.) Schs., 1973; mem. coms. Supts. Vocatl. Edn., Career Edn., Health Curriculum. Mem. Am., Mich., Macomb County (pres. 1976-77) personnel and guidance assns., Am., Mich. counselors assns., N.E.A., Mich. Edn. Assn. Researcher in field. Home: 850 Notre Dame St Grosse Pointe MI 48230 Office: 42755 Romeo Plank Mt Clemens MI 48043

RUTLEDGE, HENRY TRENAMAN, ret. banker; b. Glencoe, Minn., May 27, 1912; s. Henry B. and Eva (Trenaman) R.; grad. Stonier Grad. Sch. Banking; m. Helen Raichert, Oct. 29, 1938; children—Lynn (Mrs. John Swon), Anne. With Northwestern Nat. Bank of Mpls., 1929-65, exec. v.p., 1957-65, also dir.; pres. Northwest Bancorp., Mpls., 1965-71, chmn. bd., chief exec. officer, 1971-77, also dir.; dir. McQuay-Perfex, Inc., No. States Power Co. Clubs: Minneapolis, Minikahda (Mpls.). Home: 5 Orchard Ln Minneapolis MN 55436 Office: 1150 Northwestern Bank Bldg Minneapolis MN 55402

RUTLEDGE, VIRGINIA ALICE, bus. services co. exec.; b. Grant Tower, Ill., Dec. 15, 1919; d. Emora F. and Dora A. (Davis) Howe; children by former marriage—Walter, Patricia. Corporate pres. Gateway Account Service Inc., St. Louis, 1968—; lectr. in field. Recipient exec. achievement award Asso. Credit Burs. Inc., 1976. Mem. Mo. (pres. 1974-75, credit exec. of yr. award 1973), Internat. (distinguished service award 1975) consumer credit assns., Mo. Collector Assn. (pres. 1973-74), Soc. Consumer Credit Execs., Asso. Credit Burs. Inc., Credit Women Internat. Nat. leader in consumer credit. Office: 8460 Watson Rd St Louis MO 63126

RUZICKA, FRANCIS FREDERICK, JR., radiologist, educator; b. Balt., June 30, 1917; s. Francis Frederick and Anne (Kaspar) R.; A.B. cum laude, Holy Cross Coll., Worcester, Mass., 1939; M.D., Johns Hopkins, Balt., 1943; m. Margaret M. Kernan, May 31, 1941; children—Margaret M., Mary Frances, John F., Francis Frederick III, M. Therese, Joseph T. Intern, Univ. Hosp., Balt., 1943, resident in radiology, 1944-45; fellow Univ. Hosp., Mpls., 1948-49, instr. in radiology, 1949-50; dir. radiology St. Vincent's Hosp. and Med. Center, N.Y.C., 1950-73; prof. radiology U. Wis., Madison, 1973-76; prof., chmn. dept. radiology U. Wis. Health Center, 1976—; asso. clin. prof. to clin. prof. N.Y.U., 1950-73; acting chmn., clin. prof. radiology N.J. Coll., Jersey City, 1964-67; cons. Nat. Acad. Scis., 1975-76. Served with M.C., AUS, 1945-47. Diplomate Am. Bd. Radiology. Fellow Am. Coll. Radiology; mem. Am. Roentgen Ray Soc., Radiol. Soc. N.Am., AMA, Wis. Med. Soc., N.Y. Acad. Scis., Soc. Gatrointestinal Radiology, Soc. Cardiovascular Radiology, Cath. Physicians Guild, N.Y. Roentgen Soc. (past pres.). Editor: (with others) Vascular Roentgenology, 1964. Contbr. articles to profl. jours. Home: 5705 Cove Circle Monona WI 53716 Office: 1300 University Ave Madison WI 53706

RYAN, ALLAN CHARLES, III, metal decorating co. exec.; b. Balt., Feb. 14, 1938; s. Allan Charles and Jean (Hawley) R.; B.S. in Elec. Engring., Purdue U., 1960; M.B.A., U. Chgo., 1972; m. Catherine Crowley, Feb. 10, 1968; children—Allan IV, Brian. Sales rep. Square D Co., Chgo., 1963-69, S & C Electric Co., Chgo., 1969-72; exec. v.p. Am. Metal Decorating Co., Alsip, Ill., 1972—. Served with USNR, 1961-63. Registered profl. engr., Ill. Mem. Nat. Soc. Profl. Engrs. Democrat. Roman Catholic. Home: 5555 Sheridan Rd Chicago IL 60640 Office: 12701 S Ridgeway Ave Alsip IL 60658

RYAN, CLARENCE EDWARD, JR., indsl. cons.; b. Moline, Ill., Jan. 27, 1919; s. Clarence Edward and Dorothy A. (Olson) R.; B.S., St. Ambrose Coll., 1943; LL.B., Blackstone Sch. Law, 1956; postgrad., Augustana Coll., U. Ill., U. Ala., Mich. State U., John Marshall Law Sch., U. Notre Dame, 1943-56; m. Josephine Ann Frankville, Sept. 22, 1941; 1 dau., Dorothy A. Lab. technician Ill. Dept. Pub. Welfare, East Moline, 1938-39; instr. U. Ill. Extension Div., 1946-47; chemist Aluminum Co. Am., Davenport, Iowa and Richmond, Ind., 1948-50; tech. dir., chief chemist Casper Tinplate Co. (now Ball Metal Decorating and Services Div.), Chgo., 1950-74; cons. various coal, petroleum, organic coating cos., 1974—; pres. C R Land Corp.; v.p., dir. Transcontinental Internat., Inc. Served with USNR, 1941-67; PTO. Fellow Am. Inst. Chemists; mem. Am. Chem. Soc., Am. Def. Preparedness Assn., Internat. Platform Assn., VFW, Ret. Officers Assn. Democrat. Roman Catholic. Contbr. articles in chem. field to profl. jours. Home: Rural Route 1 Box 32 Matteson IL 60443 Office: C R Land Corp PO Box 23 Oak Forest IL 60452

RYAN, DAVID MATHER, corp. exec.; b. Toledo, Jan. 19, 1933; s. Burt T. and Nathalie (Mather) R.; A.B., Colgate U., 1956; m. Ellen Moran, Aug. 24, 1963; children—David M., Ellen Marie, Richard P. Salesman, H.H. Donnelly, Toledo, Ohio, 1958—, 1958-75, pres., 1975—. Served with U.S. Army, 1956-58. Mem. Material Handling Equipment Soc., Soc. Packaging and Handling Engrs. Republican. Roman Catholic. Clubs: Toledo, Sylvania Country, Toledo Racquet. Home: 5342 Northbrook Ct Sylvania OH 43560 Office: 853 S Reynolds Rd Toledo OH 43615

RYAN, DONALD PATRICK, contractor; b. Janesville, Wis., July 13, 1930; s. William H. and Myrtle (Westrick) R.; B.S. in Civil Engring., U. Wis., 1953, B.S. in Naval Sci., 1953; m. Diana Houser, July 17, 1954; children—Patrick, Susannah, Nancy, David, Josephine, Rebecca, Polly, Adam. Partner, Ryan Bros. Co., Janesville, Wis., 1949—; sec., treas., dir. Ryan, Inc., Janesville, 1957—; pres. Engring. Service Corp., Janesville, 1959—, P.W. Ryan Sons, Janesville; dir. Mchts. and Savs. Bank, Janesville. Mem. U. Wis. Meml. Union Bldg. Assn. Served with USNR, 1953-55. Registered profl. engr., Wis., Ill. Mem. Nat. Soc. Profl. Engrs., U. Wis. Alumni Assn., Chi Epsilon, Phi Delta Theta. Home: 703 St Lawrence St Janesville WI 53545 Office: PO Box 206 Janesville WI 53545

RYAN, EDWARD JOSEPH, physician; b. Council Bluffs, Iowa, Nov. 14, 1912; s. Edward Joseph and Ann E. (O'Hara) R.; A.A., Jr. Coll. Kansas City (Mo.), 1932; M.D., U. Kans., 1936; m. Helen Louise Harvey, Dec. 29, 1937; children—Michael, Terence, Scott, Christopher, Philip. Intern U. Kans. Med. Center, 1936-37; fellow in internal medicine Cleve. Clinic, 1937-40, spl. fellow in endocrinology, 1940-41, mem. staff, 1941-46; practice medicine specializing in internal medicine, Emporia, Kans., 1947—; mem. staff St. Mary's Hosp., Newman Meml. Hosp.; lectr. U. Kans. Med. Sch., 1948-53; pres. Kans. Blue Shield, 1958-60, pres. Gen. Devel. Corp., Emporia, 1976-77. Served to lt. comdr., USNR, 1942-46. Diplomate Am. Bd. Internal Medicine. Fellow A.C.P.; mem. Am. Diabetes Assn., Endocrine Soc., Central Soc. Clin. Research, Am. Fedn. Clin. Research, AMA, Kans., Flint Hill med. socs., Audubon Soc., Nature Conservancy, Sierra Club. Republican. Roman Cath. Club: Emporia Rotary. Contbr. profl. jours. Home: 1820 Canterbury Rd Emporia KS 66801 Office: 919 W 12th Ave Emporia KS 66801

RYAN, ELEANOR ABELL, educator; b. Mendota, Ill., Sept. 14, 1932; d. Otto Henry and Lelia Dorothy (Cradduck) Abell; B.A. in Spanish, No. Ill. U., 1967; M.A., Ill. State U., 1972; m. Glen Ryan, Jr., Sept. 14, 1950; children—Eileen Lorraine Ryan Martin, Colleen Lavonne Ryan Grafton. Tchr. Spanish, LaSalle (Ill.)-Peru Twp. High Sch., 1967—; legis. co-ordinator 45th dist. Ill. Fedn. Tchrs., 1977—; pres. No. LaSalle Bur. and Putnam Counties council AFL-CIO, 1976—; chmn. 15th congl. dist. com. on polit. edn. AFL-CIO, 1976—. Sec. overall econ. devel. com. LaSalle County Regional Planning Commn., 1976—; mem. jobs div. Ill. Valley C. of C., 1976-77, mem. indsl. devel. com., 1977—; mem. budget com. Ill. Valley United Fund, 1976. Mem. Am. Assn. Tchrs. Spanish and Portuguese (pres. chpt. 1974), Am. Fedn. Tchrs. v.p. local 1973), Phi Alpha Theta, Sigma Delta Pi. Democrat. Methodist. Home: 2517 Rock St Peru IL 61354 Office: 541 Chartes St LaSalle IL 61301

RYAN, JAMES HERBERT, physician; b. Centralia, Ill., Apr. 12, 1928; s. Charles William and Marie (Waggoner) R.; B.S., St. Louis U., 1948, M.D., 1952; m. Anita Joyce Gazin, July 11, 1948; children—Kathryn J., Thomas P., Colleen M. Intern, St. Vincent's Hosp., Toledo, 1952-53; resident in pediatrics Brooke Army Med. Center, San Antonio, 1953-56; practice medicine specializing in pediatrics, Kankakee, Ill., 1958—; coroner Kankakee County (Ill.), 1964-76; chief pediatrics St. Mary's Hosp., 1962-63, 70-71, pres. elect med. staff, 1973; chief pediatrics Riverside Hosp., 1963-66 (both Kankakee); cons. pediatrics Kankakee State Hosp., 1962—, Manteno State Hosp., 1964—, Kankakee County Juvenile Ct., 1962—; pres. Pediatrics, Ltd., Kankakee, Ill., 1965—. Cons. Family Life Achievement Center, Chgo., 1973—. Mem. Gov's Commn. to investigate hospitalization for paraplegics, 1959-60; chmn. oral polio campaign Kankakee County, 1963; mem. adv. bd. necropsy service Coroner's Office, Ill. Dept. Pub. Health; bd. dirs. St. Mary's Hosp., 1976—. Served with AUS, 1953-58. Fellow Am. Acad. Pediatrics; mem. A.M.A., Ill. (legis. com., govtl. affairs com., forensic medicine com.), Kankakee County (pres. 1968) med. socs., Ill. Pediatric Soc., Am. Bd. Pediatrics, Authors Guild, Authors League Am., Phi Beta Pi. Republican. Roman Catholic. Clubs: Union League (Chgo.); Kankakee (Ill.) Country. Author: Suffer the Little Ones, 1972; Pablum, Parents and Pandemonium, 1975. Home: Rt 2 Box 41 Kankakee IL 60901 Office: 401 N Wall St Kankakee IL 60901

RYAN, JAMES JAY, dentist; b. Peoria, Ill., July 5, 1935; s. Earle Vincent and Gladys Elizabeth (Vonachen) R.; student Spalding Inst., 1949-53; D.D.S., Marquette U., 1959; m. Margaret Caroline Campbell, Nov. 25, 1961; children—Jennifer, James, Beth. Pvt. practice dentistry, Peoria, Ill., 1962—. Bd. dirs. Legis. Interest Com. Ill. Dentists, 1971-74. Served with USNR, 1959-62. Mem. Am., Ill., Peoria Dist. (dir. 1970-73), Bahamian dental socs., Am. Soc. Preventive Dentistry, Pierre Fauchard Acad., Internat. Platform Assn., Royal Soc. Health (Eng.). Rotarian. Patentee dental unit, 1967. Home: 1900 Lakeview St E Peoria IL 61611 Office: 6320 N Sheridan Rd Peoria IL 61614

RYAN, JAMES RAYMOND, physician; b. Benton Harbor, Mich., Apr. 25, 1936; s. Leonard Joseph and Beulah May (Southworth) R.; student Western Mich. U., 1954-57; M.D., Wayne State U., 1961; Intern Grace Hosp., Detroit, 1961-62; resident orthopedic surgery U. Ark., 1962-67; asst. prof. orthopedic surgery U. Ark., Little Rock, 1967; dep. chief orthopedics USPHS, San Francisco, 1967-69; asst. prof. orthopedics Wayne State U., Detroit, 1969-77, asso. prof., 1977—; Fellow ACS; mem. Clin. Orthopedic Soc., Aesculapian Soc., Am. Acad. Orthopedic Surgery, Midwest Surg. Soc., Detroit Orthopedic Soc., Am., Mich. med. assns., Wayne County Med. Soc. Contbr. articles to research publs. Home: 3381 Squirrel St Bloomfield Hills MI 48013

RYAN, JAY JAMES, food co. exec.; b. N.Y.C., Oct. 24, 1936; s. Raymond Thomas and Kathryn (Parsons) R.; B.A., Notre Dame U., 1958; M.B.A., U. Pa., 1960; m. Nancy McIntyre, May 14, 1966; children—Jay, Timothy, Michael, Katherine. Salesman, Procter & Gamble, Phila., 1960-62; purchasing agt. Container Corp. Am., Phila., 1962-64; mem. product mgmt. staff Nestle Co., White Plains, N.Y., 1964-66, Colgate Co., N.Y.C., 1966-74; with Ralston Purina Co., St. Louis, now dir. pet products spl. markets. Served with U.S. Army, 1960. Republican. Roman Catholic. Club: Rotary. Home: 630 N Taylor St Kirkwood MO 63122 Office: Checkerboard Square Saint Louis MO 63188

RYAN, JOHN WILLIAM, univ. adminstr.; b. Chgo., Aug. 12, 1929; s. Leonard John and Maxine (Mitchell) R.; A.B., U. Utah, 1951; M.A., Ind. U., 1954, Ph.D., 1958; m. D. Patricia Goodday, Mar. 20, 1949; children—Kathleen Elynne, Kevin Dennis, Kerrick Charles Casey. Research analyst Ky. Dept. Revenue, 1954-55; vis. research prof. U. Thammasat, Bangkok, Thailand, 1955-57; asst. dir. Inst. Tng. for Pub. Service, Ind. U., 1957-58; successively asst. prof., asso. prof. polit. sci., also asso. dir. Bur. Govt., U. Wis., 1958-62; exec. asst. to pres., sec. of univ. U. Mass., 1962-63, chancellor, 1965-68; v.p. acad. affairs Ariz. State U., 1963-65; v.p., chancellor regional compuses Ind. U., 1968-71, pres. Ind. U., 1971—. Chmn. tech. rev. com. Mass. Commn. Aging, 1965-68; mem. Mayor Madison (Wis.) Com. Minority Housing, 1961-62; pres. Ind. Newman Found., 1969—; mem. regional exec. com. State Tech. Services Act New Eng., 1966-68. Mem. Am. Soc. Pub. Adminstrn. (pres. Ind. chpt. 1969—, pres. nat. chpt. 1972-73), Indiana Soc. Chgo., Am. Polit. Sci. Assn., Assn. Asian Studies, Adelphia (hon.), Phi Kappa Phi, Phi Alpha Theta, Pi Sigma Alpha, Kappa Sigma. Roman Catholic. K.C. Author papers and reports in field. Home: Presidents House Indiana U Bloomington IN 47401

RYAN, RICHARD JOHN, sanitary dist. ofcl.; b. Hector, Minn., Apr. 21, 1948; s. Douglas Edward and Julia Grace (Novotny) R.; B.C.E. with distinction, U. Minn., 1970; postgrad. Ill. Inst. Tech., 1971-72, Bradley U., 1973-74; m. Ruth Annabel Whetstine, Aug. 19, 1972; children—Valerie Lea, Rebecca Ann. Field asst. hydraulic div. U.S. Geol. Survey, St. Paul, part-time 1970; with Met. Sanitation Dist. Greater Chgo., 1971—, resident engr. constrn. Fulton County Project, Canton, Ill., 1972—. Registered profl. engr., Ill. Mem. ASCE (Outstanding Civil Engring. award 1974), Ill. Soc. Profl. Engrs. Roman Catholic. Home: 14 Mar Lee Dr Canton IL 61520 Office: Met Sanitation Dist Greater Chgo PO Box 236 Canton IL 61520

RYAN, ROBERT BRENNAN, food co. exec.; b. O'Neill, Nebr., May 25, 1920; s. James B. and Sarah (Brennan) R.; student Loyola U. Chgo., 1939-41; J.D., DePaul U., 1947; m. Josephine Wall, Oct. 1, 1949; children—Michael B., Mary Jo. Internal revenue agt. U.S. Govt., Chgo., 1948-56; spl. agt. Northwestern Mut. Life Ins. Co., Evanston, Ill., 1956-63; asst. sec., asst. treas. McDonald's Corp., Chgo., 1963-67, v.p., 1967—, treas., 1973—. Served to 1st lt. USAAF, 1941-45. Mem. Fed. Bar Assn., Delta Theta Phi. Roman Catholic. Home: 1531 Basswood Circle Glenview IL 60025 Office: McDonald's Plaza Oak Brook IL 60521

RYAN, ROBERT DALE, educator; b. Newman Grove, Nebr., Apr. 9, 1931; s. Wallace Lee and Hulda Lillian (Nelson) Ryan; m. Barbara Anderson, June 2, 1956; children—Cynthia, Sara. B.A., Wayne State Coll., 1955; M.A., U. No. Colo., 1957, Ed.D., 1964. Instr., Scottsbluff (Nebr.) Pub. High Sch., 1955-57; instr. U. Minn., Duluth, 1957-59; dir. tech. tng. Alpena (Mich.) Community Coll., 1959-62; chmn. dept. tech. St. Cloud State U., 1962—; lectr. U. No. Iowa, Cedar Falls, 1968, San Jose State U., 1972. Mem. council Salem Lutheran Ch., 1965-67, 69-72, 75—. Mem. World Future Soc. (v.p. 1974—), ASME (v.p. Central Minn. chpt. 1974—), Am. Soc. Engring. Educators, Nat. Assn. Indsl. Tech., Smithsonian Assos. Author: Primer of Blue Print Reading, 1967; Drafting Aids Transparencies, 1967; Advancing Technology: It's Impact on Society, 1971; Future Alternatives for Industrial Arts, 1976. Home: 912 24th Ave N St Cloud MN 56301 Office: St Cloud State U St Cloud MN 56301

RYAN, ROBERT EMMETT, otolaryngologist; b. St. Louis, July 1, 1917; s. Linus M. and Corinne C. (Fuchs) R.; B.S., St. Louis U., 1938, M.D., 1943; M.S. in Otolargynology, U. Minn., 1947; m. Eunice M. Burtt, Dec. 4, 1943; children—Robert Emmett, Ronald Emmett. Intern St. John's Hosp., St. Louis, 1943-44, Mayo Clinic, 1944-47; practice medicine specializing in otolaryngology, St. Louis, 1948—; chief dept. otolaryngolgoy St. John's Mercy Med. Center, 1968—; asso. otolaryngology St. Louis U. Hosp., 1948—; prof. St. Louis U. Med. Sch., 1968—. Bd. dirs. St. Louis U. High Sch., 1949—, Khoury League, 1953—; mem. lay adv. bd. Fontbonne Coll., 1959-64. Recipient Pres.'s award St. Louis U. High Sch. Sch., 1971; certificate of award St. Louis U., 1972, Man of Year award Khoury League, 1977. Diplomate Am. Bd. Otolaryngology. Fellow A.C.S.; mem. Am., Mo., So., Pan Am. med. assns., Am. Acad. Ophthalmology and Otolaryngology (certificate 1952, Honor award 1966), St. Louis Med. Soc., Mayo Clinic Alumni Assn., Am. Assn. Study Headache (pres. 1966-68; certificate appreciation 1970), Am. Triological Soc., Am. Council Otolargynology, Royal Soc. Medicine, Sigma Xi. Clubs: Missouri Athletic (St. Louis); Stadium, Centurion. Author: The Nose in Health and Disease, 1968; Headache-Diagnosis and Treatment, 1954; Headache, 1957; Synopsis of Ear, Nose and Throat Diseases, 3d edit., 1970; Tratao and International de Alergia, 1957, Tratado De Prognostico y Therapeutica, 1972; Headache, 1978, also papers. Home: 1 West Point Lane St Louis MO 63131 Office: 621 S New Ballas Rd St Louis MO 63141

RYAN, THOMAS GRADY, lawyer; b. Evanston, Ill., Oct. 12, 1949; s. Jack T. and Elizabeth Jane (Pokorney) R.; A.B. cum laude, Amherst Coll., 1972; J.D., U. Calif., Los Angeles, 1975; m. Caroline Grage Gregory, Nov. 5, 1977. Admitted to Ill. bar, 1975; asso. firm Isham, Lincoln and Beale, Chgo., 1975—. Mem. Art Inst. of Chgo. Winner Edward Serues Meml. Tennis Trophy, 1972. Mem. Ill. State, Chgo., Am. bar assns., Am. Acad. Polit. Sci. and Social Studies. Roman Catholic. Clubs: Univ. of Chgo., Sierra, Amherst of Chgo. (sec.). Office: One First National Plaza Suite 4200 Chicago IL 60603

RYAN, WILLIAM EDWARD, trade assn. exec.; b. Chgo., Apr. 11, 1922; s. John Michael and Lucy Kathleen (Burke) R.; m. Jean M. Schaid, Sept. 18, 1948; children—William Edward, Timothy J., Daniel T., Kevin D., Robert M.; B.A. in Philosophy, St. Mary's on the Lake Coll., Chgo., 1944. Rep., br. mgr., mgr. group promotion dept. Blue Cross/Blue Shield Plan, Chgo., 1946-60; v.p. enrollment, sr. v.p. mktg. Blue Shield Assn., Chgo., 1960-76, pres., 1976-77; sr. exec. v.p. Blue Cross Assn. and Blue Shield Assn., 1978—. sec. Med. Indemnity of Am., Inc.; council mem. Internat. Fedn. Vol. Health Service Funds; mem. AMA Commn. on Cost of Med. Care. Mem. Internat. Found. Employee Benefit Plans, Am. Soc. Assn. Execs., Am. Mgmt. Assn., Am. Pub. Health Assn. Clubs: Chgo. Athletic, International (Washington). Office: 211 E Chicago Ave Chicago IL 60611

RYCHLEWSKI, JUDITH ANNE, coll. adminstr.; b. Memphis, Apr. 10, 1948; d. Thomas Whitten and Beatrice Lillian (Klingenberg) Denham; B.A., U. Mo., 1970, M.S., 1972; m. Walter Joseph Rychlewski, Aug. 15, 1970. Counselor, instr. psychology Stephens Coll., Columbia, Mo., 1972-76, dir. career devel. center, 1974-76; dir. career devel. and placement, dir. student activities William Jewell Coll., Liberty, Mo., 1976—. Pres., Ruth Circle, 1975—. Mem. Am. Personnel and Guidance Assn., Assn. Coll. Personnel Adminstrs., Nat. Vocat. Guidance Assn., Midwest, Rocky Mountain coll. placement assns., Coll. Placement Council, Personnel Mgmt. Assn., Am. Soc. for Personnel Adminstrn., Assn. Coll. Unions Internat. Republican. Methodist. Club: Dudes and Dames. Home: 603 Spruce St Liberty MO 64068 Office: William Jewell Coll Liberty MO 64068

RYCKMAN, DEVERE WELLINGTON, cons. environ. engr.; b. South Boardman, Mich., May 27, 1924; s. Seymour Willard and Laverne Eliza (Jenkins) R.; student U. Maine, 1941-43; B.S., Rensselaer Poly. Inst., 1944; M.S., Mich. State U., 1949; Sc.D., Mass. Inst. Tech., 1956; m. Betty Jane Rendall, May 28, 1949; children—Mark, Jill, Stewart, Cons. san. engr. Frank R. Theroux & Assos., East Lansing, Mich., 1946-53; asst. prof. Mich. State U., East Lansing, 1946-53; environ. engr., research asst. Mass. Inst. Tech., Cambridge, 1953-56; A. P. Greensfelder prof. environ. engring. Washington U., St. Louis, 1956-69; founder, pres. Ryckman, Edgerley, Tomlinson & Assos., Inc., St. Louis, 1956-75; founder, pres. D.W. Ryckman & Assos., Inc., also Ryckman's Emergency Action Cons. Team, St. Louis, 1975—; dir. Environ. Triple S. Co., St. Louis. Vis. prof. U. Hawaii, Honolulu, 1962-63; dir. Center for Biology, Washington U., St. Louis, 1964-70. Dir., mem. Mo. Gov's. Sci. Adv. Bd., 1959-66; mem. Washington Architect and Engrs. Pub. Affairs Conf., 1969-75; mem. Arts and Ednl. Fund, St. Louis, 1970-75. Bd. dirs. Mass. Inst. Tech. Alumni Leadership Fund., St. Louis, 1970-74. Served with C.E.C., USNR, 1944-46. Recipient Man of Year award Am. Water Works Assn., 1965, Award of Merit, Engrs. Club St. Louis, 1970, Grand Conceptor award Cons. Engring. Council, 1969. Registered profl. engr., Mich., Mo., Ill., Wyo., Cal., Mont., Nev., Tex., Colo. Fellow ASCE; mem. Nat. Soc. Profl. Engrs., Air Pollution Control Assn., Am. Water Works Assn., Water Pollution Control Fedn., Am. Cons. Engrs. Council U.S.A. (dir. 1974-75), Cons. Engrs. Council Mo. (dir. 1971-75, pres. 1973-75), Sigma Xi, Tau Beta Pi, Chi Epsilon, Lambda Chi Alpha. Republican. Conglist. (chmn. exec. com., deacon 1960-72). Mason (Shriner), Rotarian. Club: Washington U. Century. Inventor process for removal phosphates by biochem. techniques. Address: 1000 Joanna St St Louis MO 63122

RYCKMAN, GEORGE FRANKLIN, mfg. co. exec.; b. London, Ont., Can., Nov. 16, 1925; (parents U.S. citizens); s. Clarence and Ellen May (Murphy) R.; B.S. in Naval Sci., U. Va., 1946; B.S. in Elec. Engring., U. Mich., 1949; m. Mary Elizabeth Kerr, July 1, 1955; children—Mary Louise, Judith Ann, Thomas Edward. Engr., Mich. Bell Telephone Co., 1949-51; mem. tech. staff Bell Telephone Labs., 1951-52; asst. head computer sci. dept. Gen. Motors Research Lab., Warren, Mich., 1952—. Served with USNR, 1943-47. Mem. SHARE (pres. 1962-63), Sigma Chi. Republican. Presbyn. (mem. session 1965—). Home: 487 Rivard Blvd Grosse Pointe City MI 48230 Office: General Motor Research Labs 12 Mile and Mound Rds Warren MI 48090

RYCKMAN, MARK DEVERE, environ. systems engr.; b. Lansing, Mich., July 8, 1951; s. DeVere Wellington and Betty Jane (Rendall) R.; B.A. in Math., DePauw U., 1974; B.S. in Civil Engring. with honors, Clemson U., 1974, M.S. in Environ. Systems Engring., 1975; m. Jean Diane Lorch, Aug. 3, 1974. Environ. technician St. Louis County Health Dept., summers 1970-71; engr. asst. Ryckman, Edgerley, Tomlinson & Assos., St. Louis, summer 1971; environ. cons. Town Hall, LaPlata, Md., 1971-72; asst. dir. Rome (Italy) operation Ryckman, Edgerley, Tomlinson & Assos., St. Louis, summer 1972; environ. engr. Ryckman, Edgerley, Tomlinson & Assos., St. Louis, summer 1973; research asst. dept. environ. systems engring. Clemson (S.C.) U., 1972-75; environ. engr. Environ. Triple S Co., St. Louis, 1974; mgr. environ. systems engring. D.W. Ryckman & Assos., Inc., St. Louis, 1975—, v.p. and founder Ryckman's Emergency Action Cons. Team, 1976—. Jr. high youth sponsor Kirk of the Hills Presbyn. Ch., 1976-77; campaign solicitor United Way, 1976-77. Recipient Service award Rough Rock Demonstration Sch., Ariz., 1968; engr.-in-training, S.C. Mem. ASCE, Water Pollution Control Fedn., Air Pollution Control Assn., Am. Water Works Assn., Tau Beta Pi, Theta Chi Epsilon. Clubs: St. Louis DePauw Alumni, St. Louis Engrs. Author: Design Manual for Thickening of Biological Sludges in Seconday Settling Tanks, 1975; contbr. papers to confs. and jours. Home: 283 Oak Pass Ct Ballwin MO 63011 Office: 689 Craig Rd PO Box 27310 St Louis MO 63141

RYDSTROM, ROGER THEODORE, dentist; b. Chgo., Sept. 26, 1934; s. John and Elsie (Nelson) R.; D.D.S., Northwestern U., 1959; m. Barbara Ann Reinlie, Aug. 10, 1957; children—Gary Roger, Beth Ann. Practice dentistry, Elmhurst, Ill., 1961—. Exec. dir., founder Home Care Dental Service DuPage County (Ill.) Inc., 1965-74; guest lectr. community dentistry, Loyola U. Dental Sch., 1971-73, Harper Jr. Coll. Sch. Hygiene, West Suburban Dental Hygienist Soc. Mem. DuPage County Bd. Health, 1964—, v.p. 1968-75, pres., 1975—; mem. com. of 300, Sch. Dist. 88, 1963. Served to lt. Dental Corps, USNR, 1959-61. Mem. ADA, Ill., Chgo. (pres. West Suburban br. 1976-77, chmn. pub. relations com.) dental socs., Ill. Pub. Health Assn., Odontographic Soc. Chgo., Am. Soc. Clin. Hypnosis, Acad. Gen. Dentistry, Far West Study Club (pres. 1969), Am. Soc. Geriatric Dentistry. Methodist. Home: 217 Elmhurst St Elmhurst IL 60126 Office: 333 1st St Elmhurst IL 60126

RYHAL, JAMES LAWRENCE, JR., lawyer; b. Cleve., Dec. 24, 1924; s. James Lawrence and Eleta (Hoffman) R.; A.B. magna cum laude, Western Res. U., 1949, J.D., 1952. Admitted to Ohio bar, 1952, since practiced in Cleve.; partner firm Gallagher, Sharp, Fulton, Norman & Mollison, 1970—; lectr. law Cleve. Marshall Coll. Law; sec., dir. Stevenson Oil & Chem. Corp. Bd. dirs. Cleve. Ballet Guild. Served with AUS, 1944-46. Mem. Am., Ohio, Cuyahoga County, Cleve. (chmn. speakers bur. 1960-65) bar assns., Cleve. Coll. Alumni Assn. (pres. 1952-56), Omicron Delta Kappa, Tau Delta Alpha, Phi Soc., Delta Theta Phi. Democrat. Episcopalian. Composer: Prelude in A Flat Minor, 1942. Home: 14724 Clifton Blvd Lakewood OH 44107 Office: 630 Bulkley Bldg 1501 Euclid Ave Cleveland OH 44115

RYMAR, JULIAN W., mfg. co. exec.; b. Grand Rapids, Mich., June 29, 1919; student Grand Rapids Jr. Coll., 1938-40, U. Mich., 1940-42, Wayne U., 1948-52, Rockhurst Coll., 1952-53; m. Margaret Macon Van Brunt, Dec. 11, 1954; children—Margaret Gibson, Gracen Macon, Ann Mackall. Entered USN as aviation cadet, 1942, advanced through grades to capt., 1964; chmn. bd., pres., dir. Grace Co., Belton, Mo., 1955—; chmn. bd. dirs. Shock & Vibration Research, Inc., 1956—; comdg. officer Naval Air Res. Squadron, 1957-60, asst. staff comdr., 1960-64. Bd. dirs. Bros. of Mercy; trustee Missouri Valley Coll., 1969-74. Mem. Mil. Order World Wars, Navy League U.S. (pres. 1959-60, dir. 1960—), Rockhill Homes Assn. (v.p.) Friends of Art (pres., chmn. bd. govs. 1969-70, exec. bd. 1971—), Soc. of Fellows of Nelson Gallery Found. (exec. bd. 1972—), Sigma Delta Chi. Episcopalian (dir., lay reader, lay chalice, vestryman, sr. warden). Clubs: Press, University of Mich. (Kansas City); Arts (Washington). Home: 1228 W 56th St Kansas City MO 64113 Office: Mill St Belton MO 64012

RYU, JAI HYUN, research scientist; b. Ham-nam, Korea, Oct. 27, 1940; s. Chang Yul and Byung Sun (Park) R.; came to U.S., 1960, naturalized, 1973; B.S.E. in Aerospace Engring., U. Mich., 1966, M.S.E. in Bio-Mech. Engring., 1972, postgrad. in Bio-Systems Engring., 1972—; m. Jacqueline Ellen Brisbin, June 16, 1973; 1 dau., Juliette Jaie. Research asst. dept. otorhinolaryngology U. Mich., 1961-66; asso. research scientist dept. otolaryngology U. Iowa, 1966-74, research scientist, 1974—, dir. vestibular research labs., 1974—. Mem. Barany Soc., Am. Inst. Aeros. and Astronautics, Aerospace Med. Assn., Soc. Neurosci., Biomed. Soc., Sigma Xi. Author: The Vestibular System, 1975; contbr. articles to profl. jours. Home: 1111 East Ct Iowa City IA 52240 Office: Med Research Center U Iowa Iowa City IA 52242

RZEMINSKI, PETER JOSEPH, personnel adminstr.; b. Chgo., Apr. 19, 1947; s. Casmir Stanley and Bertha Emma (Rudisill) R.; B.S., U. Ill., 1973; M.B.A., De Paul U., 1976; m. Dorothy Morowczynski, Jan. 10, 1970; children—Peter Joseph, Stacey Bobbe. Asst. dir. personnel St. Francis Hosp., Blue Island, Ill., 1974—. Mem. advisory com. Sauk Area Career Advisory Com., 1974-77. Served with U.S. Army, 1967-72, USAR, 1972—. Decorated D.F.C., Bronze Star, Air medals (22), Purple Heart, Army Commendation medal; Vietnam Cross of Gallantry with Palm. Mem. Southwest Area Hosp. Personnel Dirs. Assn. (sec.), Ill. Soc. Human Resource Adminstrn. in Health Care, Chgo. Hosp. Personnel Mgmt. Assn. (sec.), Am. Soc. for Personnel Adminstrn. (accredited; mem. program com.), Young Adminstrs. Chgo., Res. Officer Assn., Am. Soc. Hosp. Personnel Adminstrs. Roman Catholic. Home: 13417 S Medina Dr Orland Park IL 60462 Office: 12935 S Gregory St Blue Island IL 60406

SABA, KHAMIS ALEXANDER, surgeon; b. Jaffa, Palestine, Feb. 16, 1927; s. Alexander Suleiman and Marie (Kiriazi) S.; came to U.S., 1956, naturalized, 1964; B.A., Am. U., Beirut, 1949, M.D., 1953; m. Judith Clare Diehl, Sept. 3, 1960; children—Maria, Alexander, Clare, Peter, Monica, Paul. Rotating intern Am. U. Hosp., Beirut, 1952-53; med. officer Trans-Arabian Pipeline Co. Hosp., Beirut, 1953-56; surg. intern Good Samaritan Hosp., Cin., 1956-57, resident in surgery, 1957-60, chief surg. resident, 1960-61; practice medicine specializing in surgery, Cin., 1961—; attending surgeon Good Samaritan, Providence, Deaconess, St. George hosps.; courtesy staff Christ, Our Lady of Mercy, Bethesda hosps. Diplomate Am. Bd. Surgery. Fellow A.C.S., Am. Soc. Abdominal Surgeons; mem. Cin. Acad. Medicine, Cin. Surg. Soc., Ohio Med. Assn. Roman Catholic. Club: Medi. Home: 2112 Raeburn Dr Cincinnati OH 45223 Office: 328 Probasco St Cincinnati OH 45220

SABATES, FELIX NABOR, ophthalmologist; b. Camaguey, Cuba, July 12, 1930; s. Jose and Maria (Sabates) S.; M.D., Havana U., 1948; postgrad. Harvard Med. Sch., 1956, State U. N.Y., 1959; m. Carmen Corripio, June 2, 1957; children—Carmen Maria, Felix N., Nelson R. Resident Downstate Med. Center U. N.Y.; practice medicine specializing in ophthalmology, Boston; mem. staff Mass. Eye and Ear Infirmary; asso. prof., chief ophthalmology, U. Mo., 1964-66; clin. prof., chief ophthalmology, U. Mo.-Kansas City Sch. Med., 1966—; chmn. dept. ophthalmology Kansas City Gen. Hosp. and Med. Center, 1966—. Fellow Retina Found., Mass. Eye and Ear Infirmary, A.C.S., Am. Acad. Ophthalmology; mem. A.M.A., Mo. state med. assn., Retina Soc., Mo. Ophthalmological Soc. (pres. 1973-74). Home: 2503 W 70th Terrace Shawnee Mission KS 66208 Office: 6700 Troost Ave S-110 Kansas City MO 64131

SABATINO, ANTHONY CARMEN, ins. co. exec.; b. Chgo., June 22, 1930; s. Russell Anthony and Isabel Fradinardo S.; B.S. in Accounting, Walton Sch. Commerce, 1968; m. Dolores M. Rito, May 5, 1951; children—Paul, Susan, Pamela. Office mgr. accountant Elgin Gravure Service (Ill.), 1956-57; sr. accountant Edward J. Hutchens, C.P.A., Chgo., 1957-69; treas. Casualty Ins. Co., Chgo., 1969—; treas. CIC Financial Corp., Chgo., 1971—; dir. treas. CIC Acceptance Corp., Walro Shoes Inc. Served with U.S. Army, 1951-53; ETO. Mem. Am. Accounting Assn., Ins. Accounting and Statis. Assn., Adminstrv. Mgmt. Soc., Am. Mgmt. Assn. Moose. Clubs: North Riverside (Ill.) Sportsman's (pres. 1970-71), Columbian (sec.). Home: 2225 S Burr Oak Ave North Riverside IL 60546 Office: 222 N Michigan Ave Chicago IL 60601

SABIN, HAROLD PORTER, sch. adminstr.; b. Hale, Mich., Aug. 20, 1927; s. James Kellog and Grace May (Gillette) S.; B.A., Central Mich. U., 1949; M.A., U. Mich., 1956; postgrad. Mich. State U., 1970-75; m. Alberta May Arquilla, June 10, 1950; children—William, Samuel, David, Patricia, Jeanne. Tchr., Springport (Mich.) Pub. Schs., 1949-52; prin. Sandusky (Mich.) Community High Sch., 1954-65, Glennie-County Line Elementary Sch., Oscoda, Mich., 1966-73, River Rd. Elementary Sch., Oscoda, 1973—. Counselor for youth for understanding Exchange Student Program, Germany, 1965; dir. Operation Head Start, Oscoda, 1966-70. Dir. publicity McKenzie Meml. Hosp., Sandusky, 1963-65; sec. Oscoda Schs. Employee's Credit Union, 1974—; mem. Blue Snow Arts Council, Oscoda, 1974—; mem. Domestic Action Council, 1970—; mem. adv. council Oscoda Bd. Edn., 1974—. Served with CIC, U.S. Army, 1952-54. Mem. Nat. (region dir. 1962-64), Mich. (pres. region XI, 1960-61) edn. assns., Nat., Mich. assns. elementary prins., Phi Delta Kappa. Democrat. Methodist (lay speaker). Clubs: Masons, Lions (sec. 1976—). Home: 6060 Stage Coach Trail Oscoda MI 48750 Office: 3510 River Rd Oscoda MI 48750

SABIN, NORBERT MICHAEL, dentist; b. Ladysmith, Wis., June 12, 1925; s. Floyd Burt and Mary Florence (Fisher) S.; student Lawrence U., 1946-47, Eau Claire State U., 1947-48; D.D.S., Marquette U., 1952; m. Carol Anne Miessler, June 18, 1949; children—Mark, Elizabeth, Paul. Pvt. practice dentistry, Elkhorn, Wis., 1952—. Clin. instr. Marquette U., 1952-53. Mem. exec. bd. Sinissippi council Boy Scouts Am., 1960-73; pres. Walworth Central Council, 1954. Served with USNR, 1943-45. Recipient Silver Beaver Boy Scouts Am., 1963. Fellow Internat. Coll. Dentists; mem. Acad. Gen. Dentistry (pres. Wis. chpt. 1962-69), Soc. Dentistry for Children, Am. Analgesic Soc., Orthodontic Acad., Wis. Dental Assn. (pres. 1976-77), Burlington Dental Soc. (pres. 1961). Sigma Phi, Epsilon. Republican. Lutheran (pres. ch. council 1971-72). Kiwanian. Club: Wisconsin (Milw.). Office: 104 S Wisconsin St Elkhorn WI 53121

SABLE, LOUIS ANTHONY, assn. exec.; b. Wamego, Kans., June 16, 1934; s. Henry Francis and Alice Viola (Weltsch) S.; B.S. in Tech. Journalism, Kans. State U., 1957; certificate Career Sch. Real Estate, 1970, Real Estate Inst. of Kansas City Realtors, 1961; m. Mary Therese Wieland, Aug. 17, 1957; children—Jeffrey Joseph, Angela Marie. Reporter, photographer Pratt (Kans.) Daily News, 1957-58; advt. mgr. Richmond (Mo.) News, 1958-59, Liberty (Mo.) Tribune, 1959-60; asst. exec. v.p. Kansas City (Mo.) Real Estate Bd., 1960-66; exec. v.p. Springfield (Mo.) Bd. Realtors, 1966—; instr. Realtors Sch. Real Estate; former instr. Career Sch. Real Estate, Springfield. Past bd. dirs. Greene County Heart Assn., St. Louis Blue Shield, Served with AUS, 1957-63. Mem. Springfield C. of C., Am. Soc. Assn. Execs., Nat. Assn. Realtors (mem. exec. officers com., bd. govs. real estate bd.), Sigma Delta Chi. K.C. Home: 6216 Emblem St Route 4 Box 472 Rogersville MO 65742 Office: 1501 E Sunshine St Springfield MO 65804

SABLE, MARTIN HOWARD, educator; b. Haverhill, Mass., Sept. 24, 1924; s. Benjamin and Ida (Saberlinsky) S.; student Northeastern U., 1942-43; A.B., Boston U., 1946, M.A., 1952; Dr. en Letras, Nat. U. Mexico, 1952; M.S., Simmons Coll. Sch. Library Sci., 1959; m. Minna Gibbs, Feb. 5, 1950; children—James S., Charles D. Bibliographer, reference librarian Northeastern U., Boston, 1959-63; research librarian Harvard U., part-time 1962-63; lang. librarian Calif. State Coll., Los Angeles, 1963-64; asst. research prof. Latin Am. Center, U. Calif. at Los Angeles, 1965-68; asso. prof. Sch. Library and Information Sci., U. Wis. at Milw., 1968-72, prof., 1972—. Mem. ALA, Latin Am. Studies Assn., AAUP, Wis. Council Latinamericanists, Pacific Coast Council Latin Am. Studies (newsletter editor 1965-68). Author books including A Guide to Latin American Studies I-II, 1967; A Bio-Bibliography of the Kennedy Family, 1969; Latin American Urbanization, 1971; Guerrilla Movement in Latin America, 1977. Adv. editor for Latin Am., Ency. Americana, 1967—. Home: 4518 N Larkin St Milwaukee WI 53211 Office: U Wis Milwaukee WI 53201

SABO, RICHARD STEVEN, found. exec.; b. Walkertown, Pa., Jan. 1, 1934; s. Alex S. and Elizabeth (Haluska) S.; B.S. in Edn., Cal. State Coll., 1955; M.S. in Edn., Edinboro State Coll., 1965; m. Gail Digon, Feb. 15, 1954; children—Gailyn, Richard, Kerry, Dale. Instr. Cleve. State U., 1972—; tchr., coach Northwestern Schs., Albion, Pa., 1955-65; mgr. publicity and ednl. services Lincoln Electric Co., Cleve., 1966—; sec. James F. Lincoln Arc Welding Found., Cleve., 1970—; pres. Grand Valley Organics, bd. dirs. Grand Valley Enterprises. Chmn. Geauga County Health Fund, 1970-72; chmn. welding U.S. Skill Olympics, 1972-75. Recipient Outstanding Service award Vocational Indsl. Clubs Am., 1970. Mem. Am. Welding Soc., Am. Soc. Engring. Edn., W.Va. Wildlife Fedn., Northwestern Pa. State Ednl. Assn. (pres. 1957-59), West Geauga Baseball Fedn. (sec. 1972—). Presbyn. (ruling elder 1968-72). Clubs: Albion Sportsman, Mason (Pa.). Author: Modern Welded Structures, Vol. 3, 1971; Design Ideas for Weldments, Vol. 2, 1972. Contbr. articles to profl. jours. Home: 11951 East Hill Dr Chesterland OH 44026 Office: 22801 St Clair Ave Cleveland OH 44117

SACHO, EMORY ROY, village ofcl.; b. Edgar, Wis., July 3, 1923; s. Frank Stanley and Dale Elizabeth (Meyer) S.; student U. Wis., 1941-42, U. Denver, 1944-45, 47-48; B.B.A., U. Marquette, 1952; m. Marie Magdalen Schaeffer, Aug. 21, 1948; children—Daniel T., Joel M., Lori B. Prodn. and material control mgr. Sprague Electric Co., Grafton, Wis., 1948-67, also mgr. sales office, purchasing agt., 1948-67; mgr. materials, indsl. engr. Astronautics Corp., Milw., 1967-69; mgr. plant and co. service Sprague Electric Co., Grafton, 1969-71; v.p., regional dir. Nat. Exec. Search, Inc., Milw., 1971; village clk. Village of Grafton, 1956—, village treas., 1957—, village assessor, 1960-75, village adminstr., 1971—; mem. Tax Bd of Rev., 1956—. Mem. Ozaukee County Health Planning Com. Bd. dirs. A.R.C., 1965-68, Manpower Planning Council Waukesha, Ozaukee and Washington Counties, 1974-76. Served with U.S. Army, 1945-46. Mem. Internat. City Mgmt. Assn., Wis. City Mgrs. Assn. (pres. 1976-77), League Wis. Municipalities, League Suburban Municipalities, Mid-Morraine Municipal Assn., Ozaukee Traffic Club (treas. 1965-66), Am. Legion, Holy Name Soc. (sec. 1958, 59, 62). Lion. Home: 1104 Sunset Ct Grafton WI 53024 Office: 1102 Bridge St Grafton WI 53024

SACHS, HARLEY LUTHER, educator; b. Chgo., Jan. 1, 1931; s. Jack S. and Miriam S.; A.B., Ind. U., 1953; M.A.T., 1956; Ph.D., Ind. Christian U., 1971; m. Ulla Deborah Hintz, 1960; children—Anna-Lena, Belinda, Cynthia. Asso. prof. humanities Mich. Technol. U., Houghton, 1965—; pres. Idea Devel. Co., Houghton, 1973—; cons. Volvo A/B, Gothenberg, Sweden. Mem. Houghton County Commn., 1968-69, Houghton County Housing Commn., 1969-70, Parks and Recreation Commn., 1968-69. Served with AUS, 1953-55. Recipient Article of Year award Soc. Tech. Communication, 1975, Distinguished Tech. Communication award, 1976, Merit award, 1976. Mem. Upper Peninsula Mich. Writers Assn. (past pres.), AAUP, Nat. Assn. Simulation and Gaming, Nat. Council Tchrs. English, Soc. Tech. Communication. Inventor game Police State, 1969; contbr. over 165 articles to profl. jours. Home: 113 Houghton St W Houghton MI 49931 Office: Dept Humanities Mich Technol U Houghton MI 49931

SACHS, HERBERT L., educator, counselor, psychologist; b. Chgo., May 1, 1929; s. Morris and Esther (Ross) S.; B.Sc., Roosevelt U., Chgo., 1949; M.A. in Psychology, Loyola U., Chgo., 1951, M.Ed., 1953; postgrad. DePaul U., Northeastern Ill. U., Gov.'s State U.; m. Renee Goldfarb, Aug. 14, 1949; children—Michael, Kerry, Richard. Asst. prin., prin. Chgo. pub. schs., 1955-66; prof. psychology and counseling Truman Coll. City Colls. Chgo., 1965—, chmn. dept. Counseling and Social Sci., 1970—; psychol. cons., pvt. clinician, lectr. Mem. Am., Midwestern, Ill. psychol. assns., Am. Assn. U. Profs., Am., Ill. personnel and guidance assns. Jewish. Mem. B'nai B'rith. Clubs: George Howland Principal's, Chgo. Principals. Author: Student Projects in Child Psychology, 1967; Dynamic General Psychology: An Introduction, 1971; Student Workbook to Accompany Dynamic General Psychology: An Introduction, 1971; Dynamic Personal Adjustment, 1974; Every Parent Is a Tutor, 1977. Contbr. articles to profl. jours. Home: 6251 N Harding Ave Chicago IL 60659

SACHS, HOWARD F(REDERIC), lawyer; b. Kansas City, Mo., Sept. 13, 1925; s. Alex F. and Rose (Lyon) S.; B.A. summa cum laude, Williams Coll., 1947; J.D., Harvard, 1950; m. Susanne Wilson, 1960;children—Alex Wilson, Adam Phinney. Admitted to Mo. bar, 1950; law clk. U.S. Dist. Ct., Kansas City, Mo., 1950-51; practiced in Kansas City, 1951—; mem. firm Spencer, Fane, Britt & Browne. Mem. Kansas City Commn. on Human Relations, 1967-73; chmn. Jewish Community Relations Bur., 1968-71; mem. exec. com. Nat. Jewish Community Relations Adv. Council, 1968-71; pres. Urban League of Kansas City, 1957-58; co-chmn. Nat. Conf. Christians and Jews, Kansas City, 1958-60; chmn. Kansas City chpt. Am. Jewish Com., 1963-65; pres. Kansas City (Mo.) chpt. Am. Jewish Congress, 1974-77; mem. Sch. Desegregation Task Force, Kansas City Sch. Dist., 1976—. Pres., Jackson County Young Democrats, 1959-60; treas. Kennedy-Johnson Club Jackson County, 1960. Served with USNR, 1944-46. Mem. Am., Kansas City bar assns., Mo. Bar, Phi Beta Kappa. Democrat. Jewish. Club: Kansas City. Contbr. articles on labor law, Mo. legal history, history of Jewish community of Kansas City to various publs. Home: 816 W 68th Terrace Kansas City MO 64113 Office: 106 W 14th St Kansas City MO 64105

SACHS, ROBERT GREEN, physicist, educator, lab. adminstr.; b. Hagerstown, Md., May 4, 1916; s. Harry Maurice and Anna (Green) S.; Ph.D., Johns Hopkins, 1939; D.Sc. (hon.), Purdue U., 1967; D.Sc. (hon.), U. Ill., 1977; m. Selma Solomon, Aug. 28, 1941; m. 2d, Jean K. Woolf, Dec. 17, 1950; children—Rebecca, Jennifer, Jeffrey, Judith, Joel; m. 3d, Carolyn L. Wolf, Aug. 21, 1968; stepchildren—Thomas Wolf, Jacqueline Wolf, Katherine Wolf. Served as research fellow George Washington U., 1939-41; instr. physics Purdue U., 1941-43; on leave as lectr., research fellow U. Calif. at Berkeley, 1941; sect. chief Ballistic Research Lab., Aberdeen (Md.) Proving Ground, 1943-45; dir. theoretical physics div. Argonne Nat. Lab., 1945-47; asso. prof. physics U. Wis., 1947-48, prof., 1948-64; asso. dir. Argonne Nat. Lab., 1964-68; prof. physics U. Chgo., 1964—, dir. Enrico Fermi Inst. of U. Chgo., 1968-73; dir. Argonne Nat. Lab., 1973—; Higgins vis. prof. Princeton, 1955-56; vis. prof. U. Paris (France), 1959-60; cons. Ballistic Research Labs., 1945-59; cons. to Argonne Nat. Lab., 1947-50, 60-64; cons. radiation lab. U. Calif. at Berkeley, 1955-59; adv. panel physics NSF, 1958-61; chmn. elementary particle physics panel Nat. Acad. Scis., 1969—; high energy physics adv. panel div. research AEC, 1966-69. Research in theoretical nuclear and atomic physics, terminal ballistics, nuclear power reactors, theoretical particle physics. Guggenheim fellow, 1959-60. Fellow Am. Acad. Arts and Scis.; mem. Nat. Acad. Scis. (chmn. physics sect. 1977—), Am. Phys. Soc. (council 1968-71), regional sec. Central States 1964-69), A.A.A.S., (v.p., chmn. physics sect. 1970-71), Am. Inst. Physics (mem. governing bd. 1969-71), Phi Beta Kappa, Sigma Xi. Author: Nuclear Theory, 1953. Chief editor: High Energy Nuclear Physics, 1957. Home: 5490 South Shore Dr Chicago IL 60615 Office: Argonne Nat Lab Argonne IL 60439

SACHS, SAMUEL, mech. and elec. engr.; b. Chgo., Aug. 14, 1917; s. Benjamin and Gertrude (Soloducho) S.; student Wright Jr. Coll., 1934-36; B.S., U. Ill., 1939, M.S., 1942; m. Rita Chilow, Feb. 8, 1942; children—Barbara (Mrs. Charles Allen Linn), Laurie Ellen. With Skidmore, Owings & Merrill, Chgo., 1947—, asso. partner, 1955—, dir. of design, 1972—; trustee dept. mech. and indsl. engring. U. Ill.; vice pres. Automated Procedures for Engring. Mem. Winnetka Caucus Com., 1964-65; mem. exec. bd. Anti-Defamation League, Chgo., 1969-77. Served with AUS, 1943-45. Named Distinguished Alumnus, Dept. Mech. and Indsl. Engring., U. Ill., 1972. Fellow Am. Soc. Heating, Refrigerating and Air Conditioning Engrs.; mem. Nat. Soc. Fire Prevention Engrs., Nat. Soc. Profl. Engrs., Solar Energy Industries Assn., Art Inst. Chgo., Brain Research Found. Club: Standard. Engring. design projects include USAF, Colorado Springs, 1958, U. Ill. Chgo., 1965, 60" Solar Telescope, Kitt Peak Ariz., 1961, 150" Stellar Telescopes, Kitt Peak A and Cerro Tololo, Chile, 1972, Chgo. Civic Center, 1968. Home: 860 Burr Ave Winnetka IL 60093 Office: 30 W Monroe St Chicago IL 60603

SACHS, SAMUEL, II, mus. dir.; b. N.Y.C., Nov. 30, 1935; s. James Henry and Margery (Fay) S.; B.A. cum laude, Harvard U., 1957; M.A., N.Y. U., 1962; m. Susan McAllen, 1957 (div. 1968); children—Katherine, Eleanor; m. 2d, Jerre S. Hollander, 1969; 1 son, Alexander. Asst. in charge prints and drawings Mpls. Inst. Arts, 1958-60; asst. dir. U. Mich. Mus. of Art, Ann Arbor, 1963-64; chief curator Mpls. Inst. of Arts, 1964-73, dir., 1973—. Bd. dirs. Harvard U. Alumni Assn.; trustee Middlesex Sch. Decorated Knight 1st class Order North Star (Sweden). Mem. Am. Fedn. Arts, (exhbn. com.), Coll. Art Assn., Am. Assn. Museums. Clubs: Skylight; 555; Century; Harvard (pres. 1966). Home: 1786 James Ave S Minneapolis MN 55403 Office: 2400 3d Ave S Minneapolis MN 55404

SACHS, WILLIAM LEWIS, clergyman; b. Richmond, Va., Aug. 22, 1947; s. Lewis S. and Dorothy M. (Creasy) S.; B.A., Baylor U., 1969; M.Div. (Stevenson fellow), Vanderbilt U., 1972; S.T.M., Yale U., 1973; postgrad. (Episcopal Ch. Found. fellow), U. Chgo., 1975—; m. Suzanne Kay Parker, July 11, 1976. Ordained to ministry Episcopal Ch., 1973; curate Emmanuel Episcopal Ch., Richmond, Va., 1973-75; asst. rector St. Chrysostom's Ch., Chgo., 1975—; mem. bd. Episcopal Book Store, Richmond, In-Home Health Care, Inc.; program chmn. Richmond Episcopal Clergy; chaplain Boston State Hosp., 1972. Mem. Arts Club Chgo. Contbr. articles to theol. jours.; researcher Huntington Library. Home and office: 1424 N Dearborn Pkwy Chicago IL 60610

SACKETT, ROBERT WILSON, lawyer; b. Spencer, Iowa, Nov. 20, 1933; s. Wilber Wilson and Edith Rose (Murphy) S.; B.S., Iowa State U., 1957; LL.B., Drake U., 1960; m. Rosemary Shaw, June 20, 1964; children—Murphy, Morgan, Barry, Frank, Mary. Livestock and grain farmer, Clay and Dickinson counties, Ia., 1952-57; with casualty claims depts. State Auto Ins. Co., then Employers Mut. Casualty Ins. Co., 1957-60; admitted to Iowa bar, 1960, U.S. Dist. Cts., 1962, 67; mem. firm Sackett, Sackett & Hemphill and predecessors, Spencer, 1960—; dir. Farmers Savings Bank, Fostoria. Chmn. adv. bd. Northwest Iowa Alcoholism and Drug Treatment Unit, 1971-75; mem. Northwest Iowa Mental Health Bd., 1973-75. Precinct committeeman Republican Party, 1964-68; Clay County atty., 1965-71; city atty. numerous cities, Iowa. Mem. Am., Iowa, Clay County (pres. 1964-66) bar assns., Clay County Iowa State Alumni Assn. (pres. 1967-69), Phi Kappa Psi, Delta Theta Phi. Roman Catholic. Elk, Moose, Kiwanian (pres. 1973), K.C. (4 deg., pres. 1976). Club: Okoboji Yacht (dir. 1975—). Home: Rural Route Box 6136 Haywards Bay Okoboji IA 51355 Office: 1823 Highway Blvd Spencer IA 51301

SADD, JOHN ROSWELL, plastic surgeon; b. Chgo., Apr. 18, 1933; s. Sumner Harry and Louise Elizabeth (Beardsley) S.; B.S., Purdue U., 1955; M.D., U. Rochester, 1959; m. Valerie Crim Lavery, June 23, 1956; children—Elizabeth, Katherine, Virginia, Dorothy. Intern, U. Wis., Madison, 1959-60, resident in plastic surgery, 1960-62, 64-67; practice medicine specializing in plastic surgery, Toledo, 1967—; chmn. dept. surgery Toledo (Ohio) Hosp., 1973—; asst. clin. prof. surgery Med. Coll. Ohio. Diplomate Am. Bd. Plastic Surgery. Mem. Toledo Surg. Soc. (pres. 1975). Republican. Contbr. articles to med. jours. Office: 3939 Monroe St Toledo OH 43606

SADEK, SALAH EDLINE, pathologist; b. Cairo, Egypt, June 9, 1920; s. Ahmad A. and Zienab (Zahran) S.; D.V.M., U. Cario, 1945; M.R.C.V.S., U. Edinburgh, 1948; M.S., Mich. State U., 1950; Ph.D., U. Ill., 1956; m. Helen Ann Phoenix, Apr. 12, 1952; children—Craig, Ramsay, Mark. Asst. prof. U. Cairo, Egypt, 1945-48; asst. U. Ill., Urbana, 1953-55; pathologist Dow Chem. Co., Midland, Mich., 1956-67; head of pathology Hoffmann La Roche, Nutley, N.J., 1967—; clin. prof. pathology N.J. Coll. Medicine and Dentistry, Newark. Pres., Midland County Humane Soc., 1965-67. Diplomate Am. Bd. Indsl. Hygiene. Mem. Am. Vet. Med. Assn., N.Y. Acad. Sci., British Vet. Assn., Royal Coll. Veterinary Surgeons, Mich. Soc. Pathologists, N.Y. Pathol. Soc., Soc. Toxicology, Soc. Pharmacological and Environ. Pathologists, Am. Acad. Indsl. Hygiene. Research in exptl. pathology and toxicology. Club: Midland Country. Home: 3910 Valley Dr Midland MI 48640 Office: Hoffmann La Roche Nutley NJ 07110

SADLER, CARL LEON, civil engr.; b. Cameron, Mo., July 25, 1878; s. Rufus B. and Nannie J. (McComb) S.; U. Ark., 1901; m. Lucy McRae, Apr. 26, 1905; 1 son, Carl Leon. Asst. topographic engr. U.S. Geol. Survey, 1902-17, Topographic engr. sect. chief, 1919-40, div. engr. charge central div. topographic div., 1940-48. Campaign chmn. Phelps County chpt. A.R.C., 1957; committeeman Nat. U.S.O., 1969-71; hon. mem. Rolla (Mo.) Bicentennial Com. Served to capt. U.S. Army, 1917-19. Recipient Community Service awards Kiwanians, Jr. C. of C., C. of C., Lions Club, Mo. Sch. Mines, Mo. Geol. Survey, 1948; Distinguished Service award Dept. Interior, 1949, certificate of award Armed Services div. Salvation Army, Service award A.R.C., 1957. Mem. Am. Soc. C.E. (life), Nat. Geog. Soc., Kappa Alpha. Republican. Presbyn. (elder 1945-63). Rotarian (Man of Year award City of Rolla 1957, Paul Harris fellow 1977). Home: Apt 3B Homelife Plaza Rolla MO 65401

SADLER, JOHN REUEL, data processing services co. exec.; b. Mpls., June 15, 1934; s. Reuel Raymond and Veronica (Schweiss) S.; B.A., Coll. of St. Thomas, 1961; m. Patricia Lee Henry, Sept. 28, 1963; 1 dau., Susan Marie. Salesman 3M Co., St. Paul, 1961-62; prodedure analyst Fed. Res. Bank, Mpls., 1962-65; lead programmer N.Am. Life and Casualty Co., Mpls., 1965-68; v.p., data processing mgr. Ministers Life Info. Services Corp., Mpls., 1968—. Served with U.S. Army, 1957-59. Mem. Assn. for Systems Mgmt. Home: 8751 Bentwood Dr Eden Prairie MN 55344 Office: 3100 W Lake St Minneapolis MN 55416

SAETHER, KOLBJORN, structural engr.; b. Trondheim, Norway, July 16, 1925; s. Arne and Beatrice (Thommesen) S.; M.S., E.T.H. (Inst. Tech.) (Zurich, Switzerland), 1949; children—Eva, Erik, Linda. Pres., Kolbjorn Saether & Assos. Inc., Chgo., 1956—, also Saether Industries, Inc. Served with C.E., Norwegian Air Force, 1949-50. Registered structural engr., Ill.; registered profl. engr., Ill., Cal., Wis., Minn., Ind., Mich., Pa., Mo. Mem. Am. Soc. C.E., Norwegian Soc. Civil Engrs., Structural Engrs. Assn. Ill. (dir.), Prestressed Concrete Inst., Am. Concrete Inst. Patentee in field. Home: 934 Linden Ave Wilmette IL 60091 Office: 221 N La Salle St Chicago IL 60601

SAFFELL, HAL DUANE, research co. exec.; b. New Lexington, O., Nov. 5, 1934; s. Kenneth Eugene and Mildred Lois (Paxton) S.; B.A., Ohio State U., 1956; m. Kay Frances Stoneburner, May 5, 1957; children—Ann, David, Susan. Supr. personnel relations Battelle Inst., Columbus, O., 1958-65; mgr. personnel and pub. relations Spindletop Research, Lexington, Ky., 1965-67; dir. personnel Ross Labs. div. Abbott Labs., Columbus, 1967-69; co-founder, pres. Columbia Marketing Research, Columbus, 1969—, Columbia Personnel; partner Columbus Marine Distbrs. Mem. bd. mgmt. YMCA, Columbus, 1974—; mem. adv. bd. Nationwide Network Co. Served with U.S. Army, 1957. Named Outstanding Indian Guide, North Columbus br. YMCA, 1971; Ky. adm., Ky. col. Mem. Columbus Area C. of C., Am. Marketing Assn. Methodist. Contbr. articles to profl. jours. Home: 580 Timberlake Dr Westerville OH 43081 Office: 50 W Broad St Columbus OH 43215

SAFFELL, JOHN EDGAR, educator; b. North Georgetown, O., July 22, 1916; s. Byron Edgar and Isabella (Anderson) S.; A.B., Mt. Union Coll., 1937; A.M., Western Res. U., 1938, Ph.D., 1965; m. Helen Virginia Weaver, Oct. 8, 1955. Tchr. pub. schs. Stark County (O.) 1939-41, Paineville, O., 1941-43; polit. analyst Gen. Hdqrs., Far East Command, U.S. War Dept., 1946-47; asst. prof. history Mt. Union Coll., Alliance, O., 1948-56, asso. prof., 1956-65, prof., 1965—. Owner cattle farm; cons. CHOICE. Served with U.S. Army, 1943-46. Recipient Gt. Tchr. award Mt. Union Coll., 1965. Mem. Ohio Acad. History, Am. Hist. Assn., Orgn. Am. Historians, Assn. for Asian Studies. Home: Homeworth OH 44634 Office: Mt Union Coll Alliance OH 44601

SAFFIR, MILTON A(BRAHAM), psychologist; b. Peoria, Ill., Feb. 22, 1910; s. Max and Bloome (Matthew) S.; Ph.B., U. Chgo., 1930, Ph.D., 1935; clin. tng. Ill. Inst. Juvenile Research, 1935-36; m. Ruth Edith Levine, Aug. 21, 1938; children—Sarah Leah (Mrs. Matisyohu Weisenberg), Kaye Betsy (Mrs. Mark Ira Flanzer), Max Isser. Psychologist, Bur. Child Study, Chgo., 1936-50; instr. Wright Jr. Coll., Chgo., 1950-53; prin. Chgo. pub. schs., 1953-72; dir. Chgo. Psychol. Guidance Center, 1943—; part-time psychologist, instr. Cook County (Ill.) Hosp., Elgin (Ill.) State Hosp., Pestalozzi-Froebel Tchrs. Coll., Nat. Coll. Edn., Evanston, Ill. Chmn. awards com. Youth of Year Scholarship, 1960-77; mem. House of Correction Spl. Selective Service Bd., World War II; mem. com. on approval qualified psychol. examiners Ill. Supt. Pub. Instrn., 1954-60; mem., vice chmn. bd. edn. Arie Crown Hebrew Day Sch., Chgo. Diplomate Am. Bd. Profl. Psychology. Fellow Am. Psychol. Assn. (council reps. 1949-52), Div. Sch. Psychologists (pres. 1953-54), Div. Clin. Psychology, Div. Cons. Psychology. Mem. B'nai B'rith (lodge pres. 1974-76). Author: (with L.L. Thurstone, Leone Cheshire), Computing Diagrams for the Tetrachoric Correlation Coefficient, 1933. Contbr. articles to profl. jours. Home: 5257 N St Louis Chicago IL 60625 Office: Chgo Psychol Guidance Center 55 E Washington St Chicago IL 60602

SAFFORD, WILLIAM CULLEN, ins. exec.; b. Columbus, Ohio, Dec. 2, 1898; s. William C. and Martha (Reese) S.; student Aquinas Coll., 1916-17, Columbus Law Coll., 1926-27; m. Frances Fobiano, July 21, 1956; children—Melissa Jane Compton, Susan. Dep. supt. ins. of O., 1925-26, supt., 1927-28; v.p. The Western and So. Life Ins. Co., Cin., 1928-57, pres., 1957-73, chmn. bd., 1973—. Mem. adv. council Ohio Bur. Employment Services, 1937-72; mem. Ohio Devel. Commn., 1965-71. Trustee Ohio State U., 1967-75, bd. regents, 1975—; bd. visitors U.S. Mil. Acad., 1950-52 (chmn. 1952). Democrat. Clubs: Queen City, Hyde Park Country, Columbus; N.Y. Athletic, N.Y. Economic, Commercial. Home: 550 E 4th St Cincinnati OH 45202 Office: 400 Broadway Cincinnati OH 45202

SAGARTZ, JOHN WILLIAM, veterinary pathologist; b. Chgo., Aug. 29, 1940; s. John Peter and Anna Marie (Fasekas) S.; B.S., U. Ill., 1962, D.V.M., 1964, M.S., 1969; m. Barbara Elizabeth Crane, July 7, 1962; children—Michael J., William M., John E., Andrew P., Liesl M., Barbara L. Sr. research investigator G.D. Searle & Co., Chgo., 1967-69; gen. practice veterinary medicine, W. Point, Iowa, 1975—; cons. Ill. Inst. Tech., Pitman-Moore Inc., Schering Corp., Chemagro Corp., Biometric Labs., Inc. Served with U.S. Army, 1969-75. Mem. Am., Iowa veterinary med. assns., Am. Coll. VeterinaryPath Assn. Swine Practitioners, Am. Assn. Bovine Practitioners, Soc. Theriogenology, Eastern Iowa Veterinary Assn. Republican. Roman Catholic. Club: K. of C. Contbr. articles in field to profl. jours. Home: Rural Route 1 Donnellson IA 52525 Office: Box 276 West Point IA 52656

SAGE, MYRON ALVIN, heavy constrn. co. exec.; b. Cardington, O., July 8, 1920; s. Walter J. and Inez (Caris) S.; student Marion Bus. Coll., 1939; m. Vivian Gaynell; children—Judith Ann Addis, Michael Allen, Cynthia Lynn (Mrs. Edwin McCleese), James. With Gledhill Road Machinery Co., Galion, O., 1939-59, v.p., 1955-59; founder, pres. Iberia (O.) Earthmoving Service, Inc., 1950—; founder, sec.-treas. Cliffshire Estates, Inc., Galion, O., 1960—, Iberia Mining Corp., 1965—, Mylan Co., Iberia, 1965—, Sagler Realty Co., Iberia, 1966—, Golf Courses by Iberia, Inc., Galion, 1970—; Peoples Bank, Mt. Gilead, O., Gledhill Road Machinery Co.; pres. Roofing Cons., Inc., Iberia, Ohio; founder sec.-treas. Saber Equipment Corp. Pres. U.S. SSS Draft Bd., Mt. Gilead, 1952-70, bd. dirs. Harding Area Council Boy Scouts Am., Galion Community Hosp.; adv. council Ohio State U., Marion. Served as staff sgt. AUS, World War II; ETO. Decorated Bronze Star. Named Ohio commodore. Mem. Ohio Contractors Assn. (dir.), Internat. Brotherhood of Magicians, Mason, (32 deg.). Home: Iberia OH 43325 Office: Iberia OH 43325

SAGE, RICHARD BRUCE, bindery exec.; b. Detroit, Jan. 6, 1927; s. William Frederick and Bessie (Sheeks) S.; B.A., Mich. State U., 1952; m. Patricia Ann Traffalis, June 30, 1962; children—Jeffrey Alan, Kimberley Anne. Gen. mgr. Papeles Adhesivos de Mexico, S.A., Mexico City, 1963-65; sales mgr. Comml. Bindery Inc., Dearborn, Mich., 1954-63, pres., 1965—. Served to 1st lt. AUS, 1952-54; Korea. Mem. Graphic Arts Assn. Mich., V.F.W., Beta Theta Pi. Presbyterian. Mason. Clubs: Adcraft (Detroit); Oakland County Sportsmen's (Waterford, Mich.). Home: 30370 Red Maple Ln Southfield MI 48076 Office: 6620 Lonyo St Dearborn MI 48126

SAGEEV, SHMUEL GERSHON, educator; b. N.Y.C., July 5, 1937; s. Paul and Sheva (Tussman) Weiselberg; B.Sc., Hebrew U. Jerusalem, 1963, M.Sc., 1967, Ph.D., 1973; m. Pneena Pearl Soudack, Mar. 25, 1962; children—David, Abraham, Gideon, Hannah, Michah, Yair. Teaching asst., instr. Hebrew U. Jerusalem, 1967-72; E. R. Hedrick asst. prof. U. Calif. at Los Angeles, 1973-75; lectr. Mass. Inst. Tech., Cambridge, 1975-76; asst. prof. math. Ohio State U., Columbus, 1976—. Recipient Glora Yoel Yeshinski Prize, Weizman Inst. and Hebrew U. Jerusalem, 1973; NSF grantee, 1973-76. Mem. Am. Math. Soc., Assn. Symbolic Logic, Smithsonian asso. Home: 2431 Bexley Park Rd Bexley OH 43209 Office: 231 W 18th Ave Columbus OH 43210

SAGER, DONALD JACK, library exec.; b. Milw., Mar. 3, 19 38; s. Alfred Herman and Sophia (Sagan) S.; B.S., U. Wis., Milw., 1963; M.S. L.S., U. Wis., Madison, 1964; m. Irene Lynn Sleeth, June 28, 1969. Sr. documentalist AC Electronics div. Gen. Motors Corp., Milw., 1958-63; teaching asst. U. Wis., 1963-64; dir. Kingston (N.Y.) Pub. Library, 1964-66, Elyria (Ohio) Pub. Library, 1966-71, Mobile (Ala.) Pub. Library, 1971-75, Pub. Library of Columbus and Franklin County (Ohio), 1975—; instr. U. Ala. Grad. Library Sch., summer 1974; bd. dirs. Ohio Coll. Library Center. Chmn., Columbus Area CATV Commn., 1976—; bd. dirs. Options, Adult Edn. of Met. Columbus; active Columbus Symphony Orch. Assn., Gallery Fine Arts Assn., N.W. Civic Assn. Mem. Am., Ohio (dir.), Pub. (dir.) library assns., Info. Sci. and Automation Assn., Rotary. Author: Reference: A Programmed Instruction, 1970; Binders, Books and Budgets, 1971; contbr. articles to profl. jours. Home: 5485 Millington Rd Columbus OH 43220 Office: 96 S Grant Ave Columbus OH 43215

SAHU, SAHEB, pediatrician; b. Mulbar, India, Mar. 5, 1944; s. Bidyadhar and Sakuntala S.; came to U.S., 1970, naturalized, 1972; M.D., All India Inst. Med. Scis., New Delhi, 1969; m. Krushnapriya Pradhan, June 8, 1970. Intern, resident Raymond Blank Meml. Hosp. Children, Des Moines, 1970-72; fellow in perinatomy Milw. (Wis.) County Hosp., 1972-73; practice medicine specializing in pediatrics and neonatology, Des Moines, 1973—; mem. staff Mercy Hosp., dir. neonatal intensive care unit, 1973—; mem. staff Mercy Hosp., Iowa Meth. Hosp., Iowa Luth. Hosp.; asst. prof. pediatrics Coll. Osteo. Medicine Surgery, Des Moines, 1973-76, asso. prof., 1976—. Diplomate Am. Bd. Pediatrics. Fellow Am. Acad. Pediatrics, Internat. Coll. Pediatricians; mem. Iowa, Polk County med. socs., Indo-Am. Assn. Des Moines (founding pres. 1974). Hindu. Clubs: Rotary, Study Forum. Contbr. articles to med. jours. Home: West Des Moines IA 50265

SAINT DENIS, BARBARA LOUISE DION, artist; b. Muskegon, Mich., Sept. 8, 1928; d. Halley Joseph and Helen Sophia (Johnson) Dion; grad. high sch.; m. Richard Breen Saint Denis, Sept. 20, 1947 (div. 1969); children—Peggy (Mrs. David Scouten), Michele (Mrs. Joseph Hecksel), Richard L. Advt. mgr. Muskegon Grocery Wholesale Co. Co-op. (Mich.), 1953-56; dir. Grand Haven (Mich.) Art Center, 1957-60; founder, pres. Custom Service Printers, 1959-60; account exec. Indsl. Advt. Agy., Muskegon, 1960-63; owner Saint Denis Fine Arts Studios, Muskegon, 1963—, Traverse City, Mich., 1975—; exhibited one-woman shows Grand Haven Art Center, 1960, Battle Creek (Mich.) Civic Art Center, 1969, Chgo. Uptown Savs. & Loan, 1967, Grand Haven Civic Center, 1968, Americana Hotel, N.Y.C., 1967, Jenny Wren Art Gallery, Pentwater, Mich., 1971; groups shows Hackley Art Gallery, Muskegon, 1962-66, Grand Rapids Art Museum, 1965, 67-69; represented in permanent collections Mus. Contemporary Crafts, N.Y.C., 1963, W.K. Kellogg Found., Battle Creek, Mich., 1970. Chmn. Seaway Art Festival, 1961-62, Am. Art Week, 1965, Muskegon Cultural Series, 1964-66; mem. bldg. com. St. Francis de Sales Ch., Muskegon, Mich., 1965-67; mem. Liturgical Art Commn., Diocese Grand Rapids, Mich., 1969; mem. Muskegon Mayor's Art Commn., 1976. Recipient Major Art award Hackley Art Gallery, 1965. Mem. Mich. Acad. Arts. Sci. and Letters, NAACP. Roman Catholic. Home: 2108 LeTart Ave Muskegon MI 49441 Office: 2005 Lakeshore Dr Muskegon MI 49441 also 618 E Front St Traverse City MI 49684

ST. IVES, RAYMOND, investment analyst; b. Alaska, Dec. 25, 1945; s. Charles Luciano II and Susan L. (Luciano) St. I.; Ph.D., Clinton U., 1968; m. Cassandra Patch, June 15, 1970. Investment analyst, researcher St. Ives, Inc., Chgo., 1974—; dir. St. Ives Juke Box Corp., Pirania Ltd.; bodyguard to Calif. Gov. Ronald Regan, 1974-75. Served with CIA, 1969-72; Vietnam. Office: 2146 N Dayton St Suite 103 Chicago IL 60614

ST. JEAN, CHARLES ALBERT, veterinarian; b. Pawtucket, R.I., Apr. 15, 1945; s. Albert Henri and Emerica (Palagi) S. J.; B.S., Ohio State U., 1966, D.V.M., 1971; m. Kathryn Sue Starrett, July 5, 1975. Partner, Chittenden Veterinary Clinic, Columbus, Ohio, 1971—; tchr. Columbus Tech. Inst., 1971—, chmn. dept. animal health technology, 1972-74; owner, mgr. Yorkshire Pacers Standardbred Farm; mem. Columbus Veterinary Emergency Service. Mem. AMVA, Ohio Veterinary, Med. Assn., Columbus Acad. Veterinary Medicine, Am. Assn. Equine Practitioners, U.S. Trotting Assn., Ohio Horsemen Assn., 5th Dist. Equine Practitioners Assn., Internat. Veterinary Acupuncture Soc. Democrat. Roman Catholic. Home: 1739 State Rt 61 Sunbury OH 43074 Office: 239 Chittenden Ave Columbus OH 43201

ST. JOHN, CHARLES RAYMOND, metal processing co. exec.; b. Jackson, Mich., Apr. 1, 1917; s. J.F. and Mary (Ezoa) St. J.; student Jackson Jr. Coll., 1936-37; B.S. in Metall. Engring., U. Mich., 1938-39; m. Dorothy Marie West, Dec. 21, 1939; children—Kenneth. Lab. technician Frost Gear & Forge Co., 1939-41; metallurgist Jackson Comml. Heat Treat Co., 1941-42; owner Indsl. Steel Treating Co., Jackson, 1942—, pres., 1950-70, chmn. bd., 1970—; owner St. John Mfg. Co., Jackson, 1949-77; v.p. White Star Moving & Storage Co.; pres. Cascade Ice Co., Jackson Sports Arena; v.p. Jada Mfg. Co., Rives Junction, B. & S. Machine & Tool Co., Stanton Co., Jackson; partner, dir. St. John Enterprises. Mem. Jackson Mfg. Assn. (past pres.), Am. Soc. Metals (past chmn.), Am. Soc. Tool and Mfg. Engrs. (past chmn.), Jackson Jr. (nat. dir. 1950, chmn. regional planning commn. 1971-77), Jackson (dir.) chambers commerce. Lion Club: Jackson Country. Home: 3776 Maidstone Rd Jackson MI 49203 Office: 613 Carroll St Jackson MI 49202

SAINT JOHN, CHARLES VIRGIL, pharm. co. exec.; b. Bryan, Ohio, Dec. 18, 1922; s. Clyde W. and Elsie V. (Kintner) St. J.; A.B., Manchester Coll., 1943; M.S., Purdue U., 1946; m. Ruth Ilene Wilson, Oct. 27, 1946; children—Janet St. John Amy, Debra Ann. Research chemist Manhattan Dist. atomic energy project, West Lafayette, Ind., 1944—46; chemist Eli Lilly & Co., Lafayette, Ind., 1946—; asst. gen. mgr., dir. ops. Clinton (Ind.) 1971—74; gen. mgr. Tippecanoe and Clinton Labs., Lafayette and Clinton, 1974—. Bd. dirs. Purdue Nat. Bank, Lafayette, Capital Funds Found. Greater Lafayette; vice chmn. lay advisory bd. St. Elizabeth Hosp., Lafayette. Mem. adminstrv. bd., fin. com. 1st United Meth. Ch., Lafayette. Mem. Am. Chem. Soc., Lafayette C. of C. Club: Lafayette Country. Contbr numerous articles in field to profl. jours. Home: 320 Overlook Dr W Lafayette IN 47906 Office: POB 685 Lafayette IN 47902

ST. ROSE, JOHN ELLISTON MACDONALD, biologist; b. St. Lucia, West Indies, Mar. 27, 1934; s. Maximillien Philip Victor and Blanche Felicia (French) St.R.; B.A., U. Toronto (Can.), 1958, M.A., 1960, Ph.D., 1967; m. Irene Sawchuk, Aug. 27, 1958; children—Abigail Irene, Marc Andrew, Laura Blanche, Jonathan Bede. Jr. master St. Mary's Coll. Secondary Sch., St. Lucia, West Indies, 1952-54; research asst., div. biol. research Ont. Cancer Inst., Toronto, Can., 1960-66; teaching fellow dept. path. chemistry U. Toronto (Ont.), 1964-65; sci. officer Def. Research Med. Labs.,

Downsview, Ont., 1966-69; tech. sec. panel on Arctic medicine and climatic physiology Def. Research Bd., Dept. Nat. Def., Can., 1968-71, head metabolism group, 1960-71; research asso., faculty medicine, dept. clin. biochemistry U. Toronto, 1970—. Head environ. biology Def. and Civil Inst. Environ. Medicine, Downsview, 1971—, acting dir. bioscis. div., 1971-72; with Service d'Immunologie Cellulaire, Pasteur Inst., Paris, France, 1973-74. Mem. Chem. Inst. Can., Ont. Antibody Club, N.Y. Acad. Sci., Canadian Soc. Immunology, A.A.A.S., Profl. Inst. Pub. Services Can., Clin. Research Soc. Toronto. Home: 68 Bobmar Rd West Hill ON M1C 1C9 Canada Office: 1133 Sheppard Ave W Downsview ON M3M 3B9 Canada

SAKONYI, JOHN JOSEPH, elec. engr.; b. Orient, Ill., Oct. 18, 1926; s. Charles and Anna (Vrtel) S.; B.S., Mo. Sch. Mines and Metallurgy, 1950. Elec. engr., estimating, design, J. Livingston & Co., Chgo., 1950-67; supt. elec. constrn. Gust K. Newberg Constrn. Co., Chgo., 1967—. Served with USNR, 1944-46; PTO. Mem. Chgo. Elec. Estimators Assn. Roman Catholic. Home: 644 Exchange Ave Calumet City IL 60409 Office: 2040 N Ashland Ave Chicago IL 60614

SALACH, ROBERT LEE, JR., counselor; b. East Chicago, Ind., Dec. 10, 1946; s. Robert Lee and Pearl (Paul) S.; student Purdue U., 1964-66; B. Gen. Studies, U. Nebr. at Omaha, 1972, M.S., 1976; m. June 20, 1970 (div.); 1 son, Steven Robert. Program supr. Bellevue Indsl. Tng. Center, Eastern Nebr. Community Office Retardation, Omaha, 1971-72, workshop supr., 1972-73; dir. Bellevue 1974—; pvt. cons. with Awareness Center, 1977—. Mem. organizing com. Sarpy County Assn. Retarded Citizens. Served with USAF, 1967-71. Mem. Bellevue Businessmens Assn., Am. Personnel and Guidance Assn., Am. Rehab. Counseling Assn., Nat. Greater Omaha assns. retarded citizens. Democrat. Roman Catholic. Home: 7110 Chandler Acres Dr Omaha NE 68147 Office: 114 W Mission St Bellevue NE 68005

SALAMONE, ANTHONY AUGUSTUS, nursing home adminstr.; b. Montedoro, Sicily, Italy, Oct. 21, 1904; s. Frank and Josephine (Spirazza) S.; came to U.S., 1906, naturalized, 1917; student Mechanics Inst. (name later changed to Rochester (N.Y.) Inst. Tech.), 1919-23; student Art Students League, N.Y.C., 1924; m. Lee Rose Fortunato, Oct. 1, 1927; 1 son, Robert. Freelance advt. artist, Rochester, 1924-28; artist letterhead and checks Todd Co., checks and bus. stationery, Rochester, 1928-31; art dir. Hav Nash Advt. Co., Rochester, 1931-39; artist-tchr. N.Y. Dept. Edn., Rochester, 1940-50; first dir. adult edn. St. Louis U., 1950-63; dir. pub. relations, exec. dir. Fountain Blue, Bridgeton, Mo., 1963-69; exec. dir. Barat Hall, pvt. sch. for boys, St. Louis County, Mo., 1969-72; founder, exec. dir. Villa Capri Manor Nursing Home, Maryland Heights, Mo., 1972—. Advt. dir. Paramount Theatres, Rochester, 1940-50, Schine Theatres, Rochester, 1940-50; chmn. com. long term care project rev. Alliance for Regional Community Health, 1972—, Mem. health services planning task force, 1973—; chmn. Greater St. Louis Com. on Aging, 1955-65; pres. Greater St. Louis Centers for Sr. Citizens, 1953-65; chmn. adv. council Nat. Golden Age and Sr. Citizens Clubs of U.S.A., 1956-65; mem. St. Louis Council on Human Relations, 1957-60; mem. Mo. com. White House Conf. on Aging, 1958-62; speaker on gerontology, adult edn.; organizer preparation for retirement programs, adult edn. programs. Named Ofcl. Cavalier Italian Govt., 1957, Hon. Col. Mo., 1961; recipient Unico dr. Vastola. Fellow Gerontol. Soc., Harry S. Truman Library Inst. (hon.); mem. Mo. Nursing Home Assn. (chmn. edn. 19—), Am. Health Care Assn., Mo. Adult Edn. Assn., Adult Edn. Assn. of U.S.A., Unico (nat. exec. sec. 1958-65, pres. chpt. 1960-62), Am. Coll. Nursing Home Adminstrs. (Educator of Year award 1976). Disable Persons Assn. Am. (hon. life). Author: Retiring Into A Fuller Life, 1956. Contbr. articles to profl. jours. Founder first St. Louis center for sr. citizens, 1953. Home: 885 Club House Dr Ballwin MO 63011 Office: 2920 Fee Fee Rd Maryland Heights MO 63043

SALANCIK, GERALD ROBERT, social psychologist; b. Chgo., Jan. 29, 1943; s. Andrew and Anne (Hanson) S.; B.S. in Journalism, Northwestern U., 1965, M.S., 1966; Ph.D., Yale U., 1970; m. Charytyna Helen Krupka, Dec. 27, 1969; 1 dau., Sofia Katerina. Research asso. Mktg. Control, Inc., N.Y.C., 1968-70, Inst. for Future, Middletown, Conn., 1970-71; mem. faculty U. Ill., Urbana, 1971—, prof. organizational behavior, dir. grad. studies, 1977—; mem. rev. panels Nat. Inst. Edn., Adminstr. Sci. Quar.; cons. to govt. and industry. Fellow Chgo. Advt. Club, 1965, Yale U., 1966-68, Stanford U., NIMH, 1975; grantee NATO Advanced Study Inst., 1972; hon. fellow U. Bradford (Eng.), 1976. Mem. Am. Psychol. Assn., Acad. Mgmt., Human Systems Mgmt. Circle, Phi Theta Kappa. Mem. Ukrainian Cath. Ch. Club: Yale (Chgo.). Author: The Interview, 1966; New Directions in Organizational Behavior, 1977; The External Control of Organizations, 1977; also articles. Home: 704 Park Lane Dr Champaign IL 61820 Office: 350 Commerce West Univ Ill Urbana IL 61801

SALANTRIE, FRANK, artist; b. Newburgh, N.Y., Jan. 25, 1926; s. Edward Ferdinand and Mary (Caltabiano) S.; student Art Students League, N.Y.C., 1950-51; m. June Pines Katz, Nov. 25, 1970; children—Mary Frances, Frank; stepchildren—Judith (Mrs. Roger Broz), Eugene Katz. Artist, Chgo., 1951—; editor Cuneo Press, Chgo., 1964-71; mng. editor Publishers Devel. Corp., Skokie, Ill., 1971-73; art tchr. Loop Center YWCA, Chgo., 1963-64; founder, 1967, since pub., editor The Original Art Report, 1967—; co-founder, 1st pres. Mid Am. Art Assn., 1968; exhbns. in nat. open competitions, 1963-70. Served with USAF, 1944-46. Fellow Huntington Hartford Found., 1961. Mem. Artists Equity Assn. (pres. Chgo. chpt. 1971-72). Pen and ink drawings reproduced in mags. Address: PO Box 1641 Chicago IL 60690

SALAZAR, JOSE LUIS, neurosurgeon; b. Durango, Mex., Nov. 25, 1940; s. Juan F. and Josefa G. (Guereca) S.; came to U.S., 1966; M.D., Nat. U. Mex., 1964; m. Cynthia Sue Bieber, May 6, 1972; children—Alicia Marie, Michael Joseph, Elisabeth Anne. Intern, North York Branson Hosp., Toronto, Can., 1964-65; rotating intern Fairview Park Hosp., Cleve., 1966-67; resident in gen. surgery Michael Reese Hosp., Chgo., 1967-68; resident in neurosurgery U. Ill. Med. Center, 1968-71; practice medicine specializing in neurosurgery, Chgo., since 1971; attending Ill. Masonic Med. Center; surg. dir. microneurosurgery lab. U. Ill. Hosp.; asst. prof. Abraham Lincoln Med. Sch., U. Ill. Diplomate Am. Bd. Neurol. Surgery. Fellow A.C.S.; mem. Am. Assn. Neurol. Surgeons, AMA, Ill., Chgo. med. socs., Central, Ill. neurosurg. socs., Am. Coll. Internat. Physicians. Roman Catholic. Contbr. articles to med. jours. Home: 2527 Laurel Ln Wilmette IL 60091 Office: 912 S Wood St Chicago IL 60612

SALIBI, BAHIJ SULAYMAN, neurosurgeon; b. Omdurman, Sudan, May 16, 1922; s. Sleiman Khalil and Salva Ibrahim (Salibi) S.; came to U.S., 1946, naturalized, 1961; B.A., Am. U. Beirut (Lebanon), 1941, M.A., 1944; postgrad. U. Mich., 1946; M.D., Harvard, 1950; m. Margaret Elizabeth Beverley, May 16, 1954; children—Lillian Salwa, Charles Khalil, Ernest Kamal. Intern in pathology and clin. pathology Children's Hosp., Boston, 1950-51, research fellow in neurosurgery, 1956; intern in surgery Barnes Hosp., St. Louis, 1951-52, asst. resident in surgery, 1952-53; resident in neurosurgery St. Lukes Hosp., Chgo., 1953-54; resident in neurosurgery U. Ill. Neuropsychiat. Inst., Chgo., 1954-56, chief resident in neurosurgery, 1955-56; asst. in surgery (neurosurgery) Harvard Med. Sch., Boston, 1956; neurosurgeon Marshfield Clinic, Marshfield, Wis., 1958—; mem. staff St. Joseph's Hosp.; asst. clin. prof. neurol. surgery U. Wis. Med. Sch., Madison. Served as capt. MC, U.S. Army, 1956-58. Diplomate Am. Bd. Neurol. Surgery. Fellow A.C.S.; mem. AMA, Wis. State Med. Soc., Wood County Med. Soc., Chgo. Neurol. Soc., Congress Neurol. Surgeons, Central Neurosurg. Soc. (pres. 1968-69), Am. Assn. Neurol. Surgeons, Internat. Med. Soc. Paraplegia. Democrat. Episcopalian. Contbr. articles in field to profl. jours. Inventor artery clamp. Home: 1006 W 8th St Marshfield WI 54449 Office: Marshfield Clinic Marshfield WI 54449

SALISBURY, ALVIN BURTON, JR., physician; b. Rockford, Ill., Mar. 11, 1922; s. Alvin Burton and Mildred Elizabeth (Scott) S.; student Beloit Coll., 1941-43, Vanderbilt U., 1943-44; M.D., Ohio State U., 1949; m. Cecelia Mitchell, Aug. 26, 1944; m. 2d, Jane Jefford, Aug. 26, 1976. Intern, White Cross Hosp., Columbus, Ohio, 1949-50; practice medicine, Fairborn, Ohio, 1952—; mem. staff Greene Meml. Hosp., Xenia, Ohio; courtesy staff Miami Valley, St. Elizabeth's hosps., both Dayton, Ohio; founder, pres. Ankh Labs., Inc., Fairborn, 1955-69. Founder, Mus. of Old Northwest Frontier, Lockington, 1970. Served to capt. M.C., AUS, 1943-46, 51-52. Mem. Ohio State Med. Assn., Greene County Med. Soc. (pres. 1962, 74), Am. Assn. State and Local History. Patentee med. instruments. Editor, pub. Adventures of Col. Daniel Boone (John Filson), 1968. Address: 415 W Ash St Piqua OH 45356

SALISBURY, ARNOLD WIRT, educator; b. Bristol, Ill., Dec. 6, 1913; s. Glen M. and Elsie (Arnold) S.; B.A., Wesleyan Coll., Ia., 1935, LL.D., 1962; M.A., State U. Iowa, 1941, Ph.D., 1963; student Columbia, 1956; student Nat. Coll. Edn., 1953; L.H.D. (hon.), Lower Columbia Coll., 1969; m. Mildred A. Reusch, Aug. 17, 1935; children—Sue Ann, Mary Frances. Tchr., Fremont, Iowa, 1935-39; prin. Strawberry Point, Iowa, 1939-42, Marion, Iowa, 1942-45, Spencer, Iowa, 1945-50, Fairfield, Iowa, 1950-53; prin. sr. high sch., Galesburg, Ill., 1953-54; supt. schs. Galesburg, Ill., 1954-58; supt. schs. Cedar Rapids, Iowa, 1958-68; chmn. dept. ednl. adminstrn. Western Ill. U., Macomb, 1968—. Vis. lectr. State U. Iowa, summers 1952, 64, 65, 66. Exec. sec. Nat Sch. Facilities Council, 1970-76. Mem. Am. Assn. Sch. Adminstrs. (pres. 1969-70), exec. com.), Ill. Assn. Sch. Adminstrs., Am. Assn. U. Profs., Assn. Sch. Bus. Ofcls., Horace Mann League (dir.), Phi Delta Kappa, Sigma Phi Epsilon. Methodist. Mason; Rotarian. Author: How Ivan Learns. Home: 807 Jamie Lane Macomb IL 61455

SALKIN, HARVEY MARSHALL, educator; b. N.Y.C., June 22, 1945; s. Sol and Rose (Moritz) S.; B.S., Bklyn. Poly. Inst., 1967; M.S., Cornell U., 1968; Ph.D., Rensselaer Poly. Inst., 1969; m. Laura May Wolfsohn, Oct. 22, 1966; children—Jonathan Otto, Randy Sean. Teaching fellow Cornell U., 1967-68; asst. prof. Case Western Res. U., 1969—, asso. prof. ops. research, 1972—; cons. in field. Grantee Office Naval Research, 1973, NSF grantee, 1974-76. Mem. Ops. Research Soc. Am., Inst. Mgmt. Sci., Math. Program Soc. (charter), Tau Beta Pi, Sigma Chi. Author: Integer Programming, 1975; also articles. Co-editor: Studies in Linear Programming, 1975. Home: 23401 S Woodland Rd Shaker Heights OH 44122 Office: Univ Circle Cleveland OH 44106

SALLEE, FRANK, banker; b. Manhattan, Mont., Mar. 29, 1930; s. Frank and Mildred (Easton) S.; B.S., U. Mo., 1951; m. Nancy Ann Foster, Jan. 27, 1952; children—Deborah Ann and Linda Gail (twins), Frank Foster, David Reid. Asso. county agt. U. Mo. Extension Service, 1951-55; dist. mgr. Penn. Mut. Life Ins. Co., 1955-56; zone dist. mgr. Investors Diversified Services, 1956-62; pres. Camden County Bank, Camdenton, Mo., 1962—; now chmn. bd. Financial Computing Corp., Lebanon, Mo. Mem. at large Great Rivers council Boy Scouts Am.; bd. dirs. Lake of Ozarks Assn. Served with AUS, 1951-55. Mem. Mo. Bankers Assn. (dir.), Am. Legion, Mo. Trapshooters Assn., Inc. (sec.-treas.). Democrat. Mem. Christian Ch. Clubs: Media (St. Louis); Country Mo. (Columbia); Lake Valley Golf and Country (dir.). Home: RFD 1 Box 146N Camdenton MO 65020 Office: Camden County Bank Camdenton MO 65020

SALMON, JAMES HENRY, neurosurgeon; b. Centerville, Pa., Feb. 25, 1932; s. Ray J. and Ruth (Humes) S.; B.S., Pa. State U., 1953; M.D., Hahnemann Med. Coll., 1957; m. Louisa Potts, Oct. 14, 1967; children—Rebecca, James Thomas. Intern, Charity Hosp. La., New Orleans, 1957-58; resident gen. surgery Hahneman Hosp., Phila., 1960-61; resident neurol. surgery Yale-New Haven and Hartford Hosp., 1961-65; Knight fellow neuropathology Yale, 1962-63, instr. neurol. surgery Sch. Medicine, 1964-65; postgrad. fellow Inst. Neurology, Queen Sq., London, 1965; practice medicine specializing in neurosurgery, Cin., 1966-72, Springfield, Ill., 1972—; instr. neurosurgery U. Cin. sch. Medicine, 1966-67, asst. prof. 1967-69; asso. prof. 1969-72; prof., chmn. div. neurosurgery So. Ill. U. Sch. Medicine, 1972-77; clin. asst. prof. U. Pitts., 1977—; chief neurosurgery VA Hosp., Cin., 1966-72; asst. dir. neurosurgery Children's Hosp., 1967-72; attending surgeon St. Vincents Hosp., Hamot Hosp., both Erie, Pa. cons. Pitts. Childrens Hosp. Served with USNR, 1958-60. NIH travel grantee award for outstanding jr. investigators, 1965. Mem. Congress Neurol. Surgeons, Assn. for Acad. Surgery, A.C.S., Am. Assn. Neurol. Surgeons, Internat. Soc. Pediatric Neurosurgery (charter), Soc. for Neurosci. Contbr. articles to profl. jours. Home: 220 Anderson Dr Erie PA 16502 Office: 225 W 25th St Erie PA 16502

SALOIS, JEAN PAUL, broadcasting exec.; b. Willimantic, Conn., Aug. 15, 1932; s. Donat Pierre and Anita Eva (Gauthier) S.; grad. high sch.; m. Betty Alice Ronan, Nov. 27, 1952; children—Michelle, Joseph, Patricia, Mary, Margaret. With McDonnell Aircraft, St. Louis, 1955-56; Ozark Air Lines, St. Louis, 1956-57, KWK radio and TV, St. Louis, 1957-66; founder, pres., gen. mgr., KPCR radio, Bowling Green, Mo., 1966—. Mem. steering com. Pike County Health Dept., 1971—; bd. dirs. Cuivre Twp. United Fund, 1968—. Served with USAF, 1951-55. Mem. Nat. Assn. Broadcasters, Bowling Green C. of C. (pres. 1972-74), Soc. Broadcast Engrs. (sr.). Roman Catholic. K.C., Rotarian. Inventor parlor game 'Campaign', electric clavichord. Home: RFD 1 Bowling Green MO 63334 Office: PO Box 1 Bowling Green MO 63334

SALOMON, SID, III, hockey club exec.; b. St. Louis, Nov. 9, 1937; s. Sidney and Jean (Korach) S.; ed. U. Miami (Fla.), Washington U., St. Louis; children—Sid IV, Tim, Patti. Vice pres. Sidney Saloman, Jr. & Assos. Inc., life ins. underwriters and cons.; pres., mng. dir. St. Louis Blues Hockey Club. Mem. Mo. Athletic Commn. Bd. dirs. St. Louis Country Day Sch., DeSmet Prep. Sch. Recipient Knute Rochne award; Hockey News Exec. of Year award; Dr. Robert F. Hyland award for service to sports. Mem. Nat. Hockey League (gov.), Million Dollar Round Table (life). Mo. Amateur Hockey Assn. (dir.), Mo. State Golf Assn. (past pres.), Young Pres.'s Orgn., Zeta Beta Tau. Clubs: University, Westwood Country, Mo. Athletic (St. Louis); Country of Mo. (Columbia); Voca Rio Country (Boca Raton); Pinetree Country (Delray Beach, Fla.). Home: Rural Route 2 Villa Ridge MO 63089 Office: 5700 Oakland Ave St Louis MO 63110

SALOMON, SIDNEY, JR., ins. exec., former govt. ofcl.; b. N.Y.C., Apr. 20, 1910; s. Sidney and Mollie (Jesselson); grad. Culver Mil. Acad., 1929; m. Jean Korach, Nov. 19, 1936; children—Sid, Susan. Asso. agy. mgr. Equitable Life Assurance Soc. of U.S., St. Louis, 1929-42; exec. asst. to Postmaster Gen., Washington, 1945-46; pres. Sidney Salomon, Jr. and Assos., Inc., St. Louis, 1946—; former chmn. bd. Bank of Ladue (Mo.). Mem. Am. Battle Monuments Commn., 1961; former exec. v.p. and mem. bd. St. Louis Brown Am. League Baseball; chmn. bd. St. Louis Blues Hockey Club, Inc. Mem. Appellate Jud. Commn., 1959-64, 70—; mem. Mo. Cancer Bd. Treas. Democratic Nat. Com., 1950-51, fin. dir. senatorial campaign com., 1954, hon. fin. dir., 1956; chmn. city campaign fin. com., 1959; nat. fin. chmn. Kennedy-Johnson Campaign, 1960; mem. adv. com. 750 Club of Dem. Nat. Com.; del. at large Dem. Nat. Conv., Chgo., 1956, Los Angeles, 1960, Atlanta, 1964, Chgo., 1968; Dem. nat. committeeman Mo., 1968-70; mem. Mo. Dem. Com. Mem. bd. Devel. Council St. Louis U.; bd. dirs. St. Louis, St. Louis County chpts. Nat. Found. Infantile Paralysis; nat. trustee Am. Med. Center, Denver; trustee Harry S. Truman Library; bd. dirs. Nat. Jewish Hosp. and Research Center, St. Anthony Hosp., St. Louis Civic Alliance for Housing, St. Louis Art and Edn. Council, Lovelace Clinic, Albuquerque, Am. Med. Center, Denver. Recipient Michael Angelo award for service to children Boys' Town of Italy, 1959; Bruce Campbell award, 1968; Robert F. Hyland award Baseball Writers; Unico award, 1971. Mem. Life Underwriters Assn. St. Louis, St. Louis C. of C., Eastern Mo. Profl. Golfers Assn., Profl. Golfers Assn. Am., Jewish War Vets., Navy League (life), Mil. Order World Wars, Culver Legion (life). Mem. B'nai B'rith. Clubs: Westwood Country, Meadowbrook Country, Univ. (St. Louis); Standard (Chgo.); Boca Rio Country (Boca Raton, Fla.). Home: Rural Route 2 Box 108 Villa Ridge MO 63089 also 21136 Juego Circle Boca Raton FL 33433 Office: 5700 Oakland Ave St Louis MO 63110

SALOWICH, LEROY GEORGE, educator; b. Detroit, Mar. 20, 1940; s. George and Susan S.; B.S. in Biology, Chemistry, Wayne State U., Detroit, 1963, M.S. in Microbiology, 1965, Ph.D., 1971; postgrad. in Epidemiological Scis. U. Mich., 1966-68; m., May 1, 1966. Instr., Coll. Mortuary Sci. Wayne State U., 1961-63. Charter faculty mem., prof. Oakland Community Coll., Union Lake, Mich., 1965-75, prof. allied health, dir.-coordinatory med. technician program, 1975—. Cons. in microbiology, epidemiology for med. labs.; mem. Med. Lab. Adv. Com. for Oakland County (Mich.), 1968-75. Active Univ. Dist. Community Assn., action group for maintenance, improvement of Detroit neighborhoods. Served with AUS, 1958-59. Basic Allied Health Improvement grantee, 1970, 71; recipient Outstanding Educators award, 1972. Mem. Speakers Bur., Just Right Club, Sigma Xi, Phi Sigma. Lutheran (ch. council 1974-75). Author: Reversion of Staphylococcal L Forms, 1965; Bacterial Morphology Programmed Text, 1967; Biochemistry of Memory and Cognitive Style, 1971. Office: 7350 Cooley Lake Union Lake MI 48085

SALTER, MAUD (MRS. LESLIE E. SALTER), music educator, composer; b. Galena, Kans., Oct. 13, 1899; d. Gideon Pitt and Ethel (Goodner) Carroll; A.A., Stephens Coll., 1917, B.M., 1918; Mus.B., U. Okla., 1922; postgrad. Am. Conservatory of Music, 1951-53; m. Leslie Earnest Salter, March 7, 1925 (dec. Feb. 1964); children—Edwin Carroll, Robert Earnest. Composed series of piano pieces for beginners known as Story Solos including Little Horny Horn, Seven Stars, Mistress Mouse, Tall Grass Green, Fishing Is My Dream, Susy Waves, Galoshes, and Tecolote, 1951-52. Mem. D.A.R., Am. Coll. Musicians, Nat., State mus. tchrs. assns., Fedn. Music Clubs, Guild Piano Tchrs., Ill. Fedn. Music Clubs (dist. chmn. jr. and sr. composers 1956—), Mu Phi Epsilon. Mem. Order Eastern Star. Author: The Piano Party, 1962; Seven Star Harmony, 1963; Nocturne, 1964; Summer Garden, 1964. Home: 716 Park Dr Flossmoor IL 60422

SALTER, RICHARD MACKINTIRE, artist, photographer; b. Iowa City, May 7, 1940; s. John Randall and Josephine Senn (Heath) S.; B.A., No. Ariz. U., 1964; M.F.A., Instituto Allende, San Miguel Allende, Mex., 1968; m. Sonette E. Chanson, Dec. 22, 1968; children—Richard Mackintire, Michele, Robert, Mary. One-man shows U. Wis., Green Bay, 1977, Rockford (Ill.) Coll., 1974, Concordia Coll., Milw., 1977, Rock Valley Coll., Rockford, 1976, Ozaukee County Art Center, Cedarburg, Wis., 1977; exhibited in group shows Gallery A., Taos, N.Mex., 1977, Elaine Horwitch Gallery, Scottsdale, Ariz., 1976, Wis. Gallery, Milw. Art Center, 1977, Turtle Mountain Gallery, Phila., 1977; represented in permanent collections U.S. Dept. Interior, Bur. Indian Affairs, Phoenix Indian Sch., Will Harnsen Western Collection, Denver, No. Ariz. U., Arthur Adams Western Collection, Beloit, Wis., Pioneer Savs. & Loan, Walworth, Racine, Wis., Walworth State Bank, Lake Geneva Pub. Library, Red Cloud Indian Sch., Pine Ridge, S.D.; tchr. art Colinga Jr. Coll., 1967-68, Albuquerque Pub. Schs., 1967-68, Rockford Art Assn., 1968-69, U. Wis., Green Bay, 1973, Big Foot High Sch., Walworth, 1969-77. Recipient 1st prize Red Cloud Indian Art Show, 1976, 2d prize, 1977; award Heard Mus. Indian Arts and Crafts Show, Phoenix, 1976. Mem. Coll. Art Assn. Am., Wis. Painters and Sculptors Assn. Home: Route 1 Box 524AA Lake Geneva WI 53147

SALTER, ROBERT LAWRENCE, hosp. adminstr.; b. St. Louis, June 1, 1948; s. Edward Burghart and Lucille (Croom) S.: B.S. in Pharmacology, Pharm. Sci., St. Louis Coll. Pharmacy, 1970; M.S. in Hosp. and Health Care Adminstrn., St. Louis U., 1973. Adminstr. St. Louis Christian Med. Center, 1974—, exec. v.p., 1976—; exec. v.p. CMC Hosp. Corp., Central Med. Center, 1976—; v.p. Lawrence & Lawrence Assos., advt. and pub. relations, St. Louis, 1974—; asst. program dir. radio sta. KKss-FM, St. Louis, 1975—; adminstrv. preceptor Meharry Med. Coll./Fisk U., Nashville; mem. adv. bd. Human Devel. Corp. Head Start Program; mem. gen. assembly Greater St. Louis Health Systems Agy.; treas. Mo. chpt. Nat. Assn. Health Service Execs. Finance chmn. 6th ward aldermanic campaign Atty. Bernard Edwards, 1975. Mem. adv. council St. Louis Comprehensive Health Center, 1975—. Mem. St. Louis Media Club. Home: 4501 Lindell St Apt 10C St Louis MO 63108 Office: 4411 N Newstead St St Louis MO 63115

SALTZSTEIN, HARRY C., ret. surgeon and educator; b. Washington, Nov. 11, 1890; s. Abraham Louis and Fannie (Cohen) S.; B.S., Yale, 1910; M.D., Johns Hopkins U., 1914; Resident in surgery Mt. Sinai Hosp., N.Y.C., 1914-17; practice medicine specializing in surgery, Detroit, 1922-59; mem. active staff Harper Hosp., Detroit, 1921-56, mem. cons. staff, 1956-69, mem. emeritus, 1969-77, dir. med. edn., 1957-60; clin. asso. prof. Wayne State U. Sch. Medicine, Detroit, 1955-63, clin. prof. emeritus, 1963-77. Served from 1st lt. to capt. M.C. U.S. Army, World War I. Diplomate Am. Bd. Surgery. Fellow Am. Coll. Surgeons. Editor, Bull. Hosp., 1968-77; contbr. numerous articles to med. jours. Home: 16500 N Park Dr Southfield MI 48075

SALVA, VLADIMER MICHAEL, JR., accountant; b. Cleve., Nov. 21, 1948; s. Valdimer Michael and Concetta (Corrado) S.; student U. Dayton, 1967-68, Cuyahoga Community Coll., 1969, San Angelo State Coll., 1970, U. Md., 1971-72, U. Balt., 1972-73; B.B.A., Kent State U., 1976, postgrad. 1977—; m. Karen Ann Matyaszek, Nov. 19, 1969; children—Bradley Scott, Bryan Spencer. Pvt. practice accounting, Balt., 1973-74, Cleve., 1974-77; tax accountant, supr. Revco D.S. Inc., Cleve., 1974-76; pvt. practice, S. Euclid, Ohio, 1975—; tax accountant Cook United Inc., Maple Heights, Ohio, 1977—. Served with USAF, 1969-73. Mem. Nat. Accounting Assn., Kent Accounting Assn., Nat. Hist. Soc., Musical Arts Assn., Smithsonian Assn., South Euclid Lyndhurst Jr. C. of C. (sec. 1976-77), Cleve. Orch. Assn., Sigma Pi, Sigma Phi Epsilon. Roman Catholic. Home: 1073 Avondale St South Euclid OH 44121 Office: 16501 Rockside Rd Maple Heights OH 44137

SALVATORE, JAMES DANIEL, data processing exec.; b. Columbus, Ohio, Sept. 20, 1947; s. Dante and Lulu Louise (Kinzelman) S.; B.S. in Bus. Adminstrn., Ohio State U., 1970; certificate Mata Coll., 1970; M.B.A., Xavier U., 1975. Data processing mgr. Robertshaw Controls Co., Grove City, Ohio, 1971-75; dir. data processing W.A. Butler Co., Columbus, 1975—; cons. Mem. Assn. M.B.A. Execs., Data Processing Mgmt. Assn. Republican. Roman Catholic. Clubs: Pres.'s of Ohio State U., Guild Athletic. Home: 777 Clubview Blvd Worthington OH 43085 Office: 4140 Fisher Rd Columbus OH 43228

SALZMAN, CHARLES WILLIAM, veterinarian; b. Kankakee, Ill., Nov. 4, 1939; s. Willard Louis and Mary Margar (Wagner) S.; student Olivet Nazarene Coll., Bourbonais, Ill., 1957-58, Eastern Ill. U., Charlestown 1958-59; B.S. in Veterinary Medicine, U. Ill., Champaign, 1963, D.V.M., 1965; m. Janet Louis Schweigert, July 3, 1960. With Humko Corp., 1962; veterinarian North Locust Animal Hosp., Sterling, Ill., 1965-66, asso. E.E. Seavey, 1965-66; owner Aroma Park Vet. Clinic, Ill., 1969—; pres. Pets-n-Things, 1976—. Pres., Aroma Park United Meth. Ch., chmn. hunger com., 1976—, bd. dirs., 1974—; co-founder Aroma Park Little League, sec. bd., 1973-74; pres. Aroma Park Grade Sch., PTA, 1975. Mem. Am., Ill. State (mem. exec. bd., legis. com), Kankakee Valley (past pres., sec., rep. to Ill.) veterinary medicine assns. Clubs: Aroma Park Lions, Deans. Home: 3300 Waldron Rd Aroma Park IL 60910 Office: 3302 Waldron Rd Aroma Park IL 60910

SALZMAN, ROBERT MARSHALL, lawyer; b. Chgo., Jan. 23. 1942; s. Albert and Lillian (Wolovnik) S.; student U. Ill., 1962; B.A., Roosevelt U., 1966; J.D., John Marshall Law Sch., 1969; m. Marilyn Beth Wolfson, Sept. 1, 1968; 1 son, Lawrence Todd. Admitted to Ill. bar, 1969, since practiced in Chgo.; partner firm Pfeffer, Becker, Gabric & Cerveny, Ltd., 1969—; mem. faculty John Marshall Law Sch., 1970-73. Area supr. Ill. Bd. Elections, 1974—; lectr. various fraternal and civic orgns.; active Friends of Highland Park (Ill.) Library, Highland Park Hosp. Found., Highland Park YWCA, Mid-West chpt. ARC, Chgo. Hort. Soc. Recipient Am. Jurisprudence award Bancroft-Whitney Pub. Co., 1969. Mem. Ill. (workmen's compensation com. 1976—), Chgo. (workmen's compensation com. 1976—) bar assns., Ill. (young mems. com. 1975—), Chgo. trial lawyers assns., Ill. Workmens Compensation Assn. (legis. liaison), Highland Park Hist. Soc., Decalogue Soc. Mem. B'nai B'rith (founding mem. lodge 1968). Author: Workmens Compensation in the Law Office, 1976. Contbr. articles to profl. jours. and newspapers. Home: 902 Marion Ave Highland Park IL 60035 Office: Pfeffer Becker Gabric & Cerveny Ltd 79 W Monroe St Chicago IL 60603

SAMELSON, CHARLES FREDERICK, psychiatrist; b. Milw., Nov. 10, 1917; s. William and Sarah (Dubin) S.; M.D., U. Ill., 1943; m. Natalie Rudeis, May 1, 1949; children—Lawrence E., Daniel. Intern, U.S. Naval Hosp., San Diego, 1944; resident Michael Reese Hosp., Chgo., 1946-49, psychoanalytic tng. Chgo. Inst. Psychoanalysis, 1950-55; practice medicine specializing in psychiatry, Chgo., 1952—; cons., supervising psychiatrist Michael Reese Hosp., Chgo., 1952—, Manteno (Ill.) State Hosp., 1962-70, Ill. State Psychiatric Inst., Chgo., 1963-75, Schwab Rehab. Hosp., Chgo., Ill., 1963—, Holy Cross Hosp., Chgo., 1972—. Bd. dirs. Open Lands Project, 1963—, Clean Air Coordinating Com., 1969—, Save The Dunes Council, 1974—. Served to lt. USNR, 1942-46. Diplomate Am. Bd. Psychiatry and Neurology. Mem. A.M.A., Ill., Chgo. med. socs., Am., Ill. psychiatric assns. Home: 5712 S Kenwood Ave Chicago IL 60637 Office: 30 N Michigan Ave Chicago IL 60602

SAMERDYKE, FRED J., lawyer; b. Cleve., June 25, 1912; s. Peter P. and Julia E. (Wisner) S.; B.S., Case Inst. Tech., 1935; J.D., Cleve. State U., 1939; postgrad. Columbia, 1942-43, Cleve. Coll., 1939-40; m. Cecilia A. Schmitt, June 27, 1948. Admitted to Ohio bar, 1939, Ky. bar, 1952, U.S. Patent Office, 1938; patent atty. Industrial Rayon Corp., Cleve., 1935-40; mem. tech. staff and patent atty., Bell Telephone Labs., Inc., N.Y.C., 1940-45; trial and patent lawyer, Ely & Frye, Cleve., 1945-47; gen. counsel, sec., exec. v.p., U.S. Steel Homes, New Albany, Ind. and Harrisburg, Pa., 1947-55; pres. Harnischfeger Homes, Inc., Port Washington, Wis., 1955-59; partner Bosworth, Sessions & McCoy and predecessor firm, patent lawyers, Cleve., 1959—. Mem. Cleve. Bar Assn., Am., Cleve. patent law assns., Newcomen Soc., Delta Theta Phi, Tau Beta Pi. Clubs: Cleveland Yachting, Mid Day. Home: 19637 Beach Cliff Blvd Rocky River OH 44116 Office: 625 Nat City Bank Bldg Cleveland OH 44114

SAMMONS, FREDDIE WILLIS, steel co. ofcl.; b. Firebrick, Ky., July 30, 1937; s. Earl Willis and Erma Helen (Miller) S.; student Internat. Corr. Schs.; m. Katherine Faye Cantrall, Dec. 2, 1955; children—Jeffrey, Rhonda, Melinda, Gregory, Barry. Electrician, Detroit Steel Corp., 1955-64, maintenance supr., 1964-68; elec. repair supr. Hennepin (Ill.) Works, Jones & Laughlin Steel Corp., 1968—. Club: Masons. Home: Rural Route 1 Hennepin IL 61327 Office: Box 325 Hennepin IL 61327

SAMMONS, WILLIAM EDWARD, JR., judge; b. Portsmouth, O., Sept. 27, 1924; s. William Edward and Minnie Lee (Jolly) S.; student George Washington U., 1942; B.S.C., Ohio U., 1949; J.D., U. Cin., 1952; m. Elizabeth Streitenberger, Feb. 14, 1969. Admitted to Ohio bar, 1952; partner firm Sammons & Sammons, Chillicothe, 1952-62; judge Chillicothe Municipal Court, 1962—; admitted to practice before U.S. Supreme Court, U.S. Fed. Dist. Ct. of So. Ohio, U.S. Fed. Ct. Appeals. Mem. Civil Service Board, Chillicothe, 1958-59; v.p. Ross County Council on Alcoholism, 1974-75. Dem. Nat. Conv., 1956; mem. Ross County Dem. Central Com., 1953-62, sec. Ross County Exec. Com., 1953-62; mem. exec. com. Young Dems. Ohio, 1954-56. Trustee Roweton Boys Ranch; bd. dirs. Robert Gay Community Center, Ross County A.R.C.; chmn. bd. dirs. Ross County Tb Assn., 1970—. Served with USAAF, 1943-46. Mem. Am., Ohio, Ross County (pres. 1973) bar assns., Ross County Humane Soc., Ross County Hist. Soc., Am. Legion, V.F.W. (judge advocate 1952—), Ross County Conservation League (pres. 1973), 40 and 8, Am. Judicature Soc., Nat., Ohio (pres. 1976-77) municipal judges assns., Ohio U. Alumni Assn. (pres. Ross County 1965-73), North Am. Judges Association, University Cincinnati alumni assns., Civil War Round Table (pres. 1971-73), Ross County Mental Health Assn., United Comml. Travelers Am., Chillicothe Stock Car Racing Assn., Ross County Safety Council, Buckeye State Sheriff's Assn., Ross County Hist. Soc., League Ohio Sportsmen, Paint Valley Fox Hunters Assn., Ross County Law Officers Assn. (sec. 1966-69), Order Ky. Cols., Mi. Order Cootie, Tenn. Squires, Phi Delta Phi. Episcopal. Mason (32 deg., K.T., Shriner), Elk (presiding justice 1962—), Eagle, Kiwanian (2d v.p. 1977); mem. Order Symposiarchs. Clubs: Cavalier (sec. 1968—); Chillicothe Exchange (pres. 1966); Ross County Shrine (pres. 1970); Ross Investment (pres. 1972). Home: 86 Applewood Dr Chillicothe OH 45601 Office: City Hall Chillicothe OH 45601

SAMOLE, MYRON MICHAEL, lawyer, biomed. products mfg. co. exec.; b. Chgo., Nov. 29, 1943; s. Harry Lionel and Bess Miriam (Siegel) S.; student U. Ill., 1962-65; J.D. (Jewish Vocat. Service scholar), DePaul U., 1967; postgrad. John Marshall Lawyers' Inst.; m. Sandra Rita Port, Feb. 2, 1967; children—Stacey Ann, Karen Lynn, Rena Mara, David Aaron. Admitted to Ill. bar, 1967, U.S. Ct. Appeals bar, 1968; individual practice law, Chgo., 1967—; exec. v.p., gen. mgr. Fidelity Electronics, Ltd., Chgo., 1970—, also dir.; bd. dirs. Sch. Audio-Otometry. Pres. advisory bd. Prosser High Sch. ICE Program, 1975-77; bd. dir. Sager Solomon Schechter Day Sch. Parent Orgn., Northbrook, Ill. Mem. Chgo., Ill. State, Am. bar assns., Am. Trial Lawyers Assn., YMCA, Concerned Citizens for a Better Northbrook (Ill.), Phi Alpha Delta. Jewish. Clubs: Masons, Shriners. Office: 5245 W Diversey Ave Chicago IL 60639

SAMOREK, ALEXANDER HENRY, elec. engr.; b. Detroit, Mich., Feb. 14, 1922; s. Walter and Gladys (Kurys) S.; B.S., Detroit Inst. Tech., 1960; m. Matilda Louise Dusincki, May 10, 1952; 1 son, David A. Electronic instr. Radio Electronic and TV Sch., Detroit, 1946-49; electronic insp. U.S. Air Force Procurement Office, Detroit, 1950-53; chief technician Wayne Engring. and Research Inst., Wayne U., Detroit, 1954-57; elec. engr. Control Engring. Co., Detroit, 1957-60; chief engr., engring. mgr. Weltronic Co., Clare, Mich., 1960—; electronic instr. Redford High Sch., Mich., 1966. Served with USAAF, 1942-46. Mem. Soc. Automotive Engrs., IEEE, Am. Welding Soc. Lutheran. Home: 323 Markley St Clare MI 48617

SAMPAT, SUNDERDAS G., structural engr.; b. Khambhalia, India, July 29, 1934; s. Gordhandas B. and Gunvanti N. (Gajaria) S.; came to U.S., 1963, naturalized, 1971; B.Engring. with honors, Poona U., 1955; M.S. in Engring., Lehigh U., 1960; m. Rajni V. Kapadia, May 14, 1963; children—Manish, Piyush. Sr. civil engr. W.K. Shahaney & Co., Bombay, India, 1955-59; structural engr. in tng. McDowell-Wellman Co., Inc., Cleve., 1961-63; project engr. Jervis B. Webb Co., Detroit, 1964-73; sr. product engr. Chrysler Corp., Detroit, 1973-75; chief structural engr., project mgr. Mid-West Conveyor Co., Inc., Kansas City, Kans., 1975—. Registered profl. engr., Kans., Ohio, Ind., Mich., Nebr. Mem. ASCE. Hindu. Research on plastic design for multistory frames. Home: 13209 W 82d St Lenexa KS 66215 Office: Mid-West Conveyor Co 450 E Donovan Rd Kansas City KS 66115

SAMPLE, A. DOROTHY, accountant; b. Youngstown, O.; d. Harry W. and Miriam (Williams) Sample; grad. Spencerian Coll., 1927-28, Cleve. Coll., 1937-39. Sec., Apex Paper Box Co., Cleve., 1928-32, Corrigan McKinney Steel Co., 1932-34; with Riester & Thesmacher Co., Cleve., 1934—, bookkeeper, 1934-40, chief accountant, 1940-56, asst. sec., 1956-65, dir., treas., 1965—; dir., sec.-treas. The R and T Co., 1956-72, Erie Artisan Corp., 1966-72. Mem. Cleve. Credit Women's Club (pres. 1956-57), Cleve. Assn. Credit Mgmt., Am. Soc. Women Accountants. Baptist. Clubs: Zonta (pres., dir. Cleve. chpt. 1970-71), Women's City (Cleve.), White Shrine Jerusalem. Home: 3363 Warrensville Center Rd Shaker Heights OH 44122 Office: 1526 W 25th St Cleveland OH 44113

SAMPSON, SIGVED THEODORE, coop. exec.; b. Glenbeulah, Wis., Apr. 17, 1917; s. August and Mabel T. (Omness) S.; B.A., St. Olaf Coll., 1939; m. Elouise Torkelson, July 6, 1946; children—Scott, Donna. Mgr., Milltown Co-op Store, 1939-42; Denmark Co-op Services, (Wis.), 1946; with Midland Coops., Inc., Mpls., 1946—, dir. field services, 1955-57, dir. sales, 1957-64, dir. marketing, 1964-71, v.p. marketing, 1971-72, pres., gen. mgr., 1972—; dir. CF Industries, Inc., Chgo., Universal Co-ops. Inc., Nat. Council Farmer Co-ops, Washington, Alliance, O., Co-op League, Washington, Twin Ports Grocery Co., Superior, Wis., Nat. Coop Refinery Assn., McPherson, Kan. Mem. St. Anthony Village (Minn.) Bd. Edn., 1961-68, pres., 1967-68. Served with U.S. Army, 1942-45; ETO. Mem. Mpls. Sales Exec. Club, Mpls. C. of C., Sons of Norway. Lutheran (trustee 1951-58). Club: Minneapolis Athletic. Home: 3404 Maplewood Dr Minneapolis MN 55418 Office: 2021 E Hennepin Ave Minneapolis MN 55413

SAMS, ROBERT EUGENE, psychiatrist; b. Parkersburg, W.Va., July 30, 1939; s. Robert James and Irene B. (Stonestreet) S.; A.B., W.Va. U., 1961, M.D., 1965; m. Judith Ann Starcher, Dec. 15, 1963; children—Robert Steven, Patricia Ann, Erik Jason. Intern, Bayfront Med. Center, St. Petersburg, Fla., 1965-66; resident psychiatry Rollman Psychiat. Inst., Cin., 1969-71; practice medicine specializing in psychiatry, Parkersburg, W.Va., 1971—; founder Psychiat. Assos.; developer mental health unit St. Josephs Hosp., Parkersburg; cons. Western Dist. Guidance Clinic, 1971-75; clin. dir., cons., Nelsonville (Ohio) Children's Center, 1974-75. Served with USAF, 1966-68. Mem. AMA, Am., W.Va. psychiat. assns., Parkersburg Acad. Medicine. Home: Route 1 Reedsville OH 45772 Office: 3211 Emerson Ave Parkersburg WV 26101

SAMUELS, LAURENCE EDWARD, cons. engr.; b. Chgo., Sept. 5, 1935; s. Peter I. and Lena (Mills) S.; student Wilson Jr. Coll., Chgo., Ill. Inst. Tech.; m. Elneda Hill, 1957; children—Wayne, Kenneth, Alicia, Carmen, Brian. Plumbing engr. Sgt. & Lundy, 1963-71; pres. Samuels, Apea & Assos., Inc., Cons. Engrs., Chgo., 1971—. Bd. dirs. Morgan Park Civic League. Registered profl. engr., Ill. Mem. ASME, Am. Soc. Heating, Refrigeration and Air Conditioning, Ill. Soc. Profl. Engrs. Baptist. Home: 1339 W 108th Pl Chicago IL 60643 Office: 6 N Michigan Ave Chicago IL 60602

SAMUELSON, DENNIS RAY, pathologist; b. Burlington, Iowa, Jan. 4, 1940; s. Norman Russell and Josephine Katherine (McQueen) S.; B.A., U. Iowa, 1962, M.D., 1965; m. Virginia Lea Matthews, Aug. 29, 1964; children—Erik Sven, Heidi Jo. Intern Denver Gen. Hosp., 1967-70; practice medicine specializing in pathology, Denver, 1967-70, Wichita Falls, Tex., 1970-72; Macomb, Ill., Burlington, Iowa, 1972—; pathologist NuPath Profl. Corp., Macomb, 1972—; mem. staff Burlington Med. Center, 1972—, McDonough Dist. Hosp., Macomb, Community Meml. Hosp., Monmouth, Ill., Meml. Hosp., Carthage, Ill., all 1972—; dir. of labs. McDonough Dist. Hosp., Macomb, Ill., 1975—. Mem. McDonough County Bd. Health. Served with USAF, 1970-72. Recipient Ewen Murchison MacEwen Meml. prize, 1965; diplomate Am. Bd. Pathology, Am. Bd. Nuclear Medicine. Mem. Coll. of Am. Pathologists, Ill., McDonough County med. socs., Ill. Soc. of Pathologists, Am. Assn. of Physicians and Surgeons, Soc. of Nuclear Medicine, S. Central Assn. of Clin. Microbiology, Am. Coll. of Nuclear Medicine, AMA. Methodist. Clubs: Elks. Contbr. articles in field to med. jours. Home: 1300 W Adams Macomb IL 61455 Office: 525 E Grant Macomb IL 61455

SAMUELSON, MARVIN L., veterinarian; b. Oketo, Kans., July 25, 1931; s. Eben R. and Mabel (Brown) S.; B.S., Kans. State U., 1956, D.V.M., 1956; m. Judith Ann Mooney, Aug. 13, 1973. Pvt. practice veterinary medicine, San Pedro, Calif., 1958-73; prof. veterinary medicine Kans. State U., 1973—. Mem. Los Angeles County Animal Control Com., 1971-73. Served with AUS, 1956-58. Mem. Am., Kans., Calif., So. Calif. veterinary med. assns., Am. Animal Hosp. Assn., Am. Acad. Veterinary Dermatologists, Am. Assn. Veterinary Med. Eudcators. Republican. United Methodist. Home: Route 1 Manhattan KS 66502 Office: Dept Surgery Medicine Kans State U Manhattan KS 66506

SAN, NGUYEN DUY, psychiatrist; b. Langson, Vietnam, Sept. 25, 1932; s. Nguyen Duy and Tran Tuyet (Trang) Quyen; came to Can., 1971, naturalized, 1977; M.D., U. Saigon, 1960; postgrad. U. Mich., 1970; m. Eddie Jean Ciesielski, Aug. 24, 1971; children—Megan Thuloan, Muriel Mylinh, Claire Kimlan, Robin Xuanlan. Intern, Cho Ray Hosp., Saigon, 1957-58; resident Univ. Hosp., Ann Arbor, Mich., 1968-70; chief of psychiatry S. Vietnamese Army, 1964-68; staff psychiatrist Queen St. Mental Health Center, Toronto, Ont., Can., 1972-74; unit dir. Homewood San., Guelph, Ont., 1974—; cons. psychiatrist Guelph Gen. Hosp., St. Joseph's Hosp., Guelph; practice medicine specializing in psychiatry, Guelph, 1974—. Served with Army Republic of Vietnam, 1953-68. Mem. Can. Med. Assn., Can., Am. psychiat. assns., Am. Soc. Clin. Hypnosis, Internat. Soc. Hypnosis. Buddhist. Author: Etude du Tetanos au Vietnam, 1960; (with others) The Psychology and Physiology of Stress, 1969. Home: 19 Carmine Pl Guelph ON N1E 3V2 Canada Office: 150 Delhi St Guelph ON N1E 6K9 Canada

SANBORN, KENNETH EDWARD, automotive engr.; b. North Conway, N.H., Aug. 27, 1930; s. Leon Henry and Lillian May (Abbott) S.; student Tri-State Coll., 1956-59; children—Kathie, Cynthia, Lorraine. Flight instr. Tri-State Airport, Angola, Ind., 1959-60; chief pilot and flight instr. G.H. Bailey Co., Sturgis, Mich., 1960-61; automotive project test engr. Ford Motor Co., Romeo, Mich., 1962-72, design engr., Dearborn, Mich., 1972, sr. test engr., 1972—. Served with USN, 1947-56; PTO, ETO. Mem. Soc. of Automotive Engrs., Am. Security Council (dir. 1974—), Aircraft Owners and Pilots Assn. Republican. Lutheran. Home: 99 Stratford Ln Rochester MI 48063 Office: 4305 Mack Rd Romeo MI 48065

SANCHEZ, BERNARD RAYMOND, condr., educator; b. New Orleans, Sept. 18, 1935; s. William Joseph and Ione Rosalie (Serpas) S.; student La. State U., 1953-55; B.M.E., U. Louisville, 1957, B. Music, 1958, M. Music, 1960; m. Rita Lou Cullinan, June 29, 1962; children—Robin Ann, Dawn Marie. Band dir. Corydon (Ind.) Pub. Schs., 1959-60; instr. trumpet U. Louisville, 1958-60; tchr. Toledo Pub. Schs., 1960, Sylvania (Ohio) Pub. Schs., Bd. Edn., 1961-63; condr., instr. trumpet U. Toledo, 1963—, also chmn. dept. music; instr. trumpet U. Wis., Madison, 1968. Condr. Jewish Community Center Orch., Toledo, 1974—; prin. trumpet Toledo Orch., 1960-68; asst. condr. Toledo Youth Orch., 1960-67; mus. dir. U. Toledo Opera Theater, 1968—, Mini Opera Program, Toledo. Served with AUS, 1958. Mem. Am. Fedn. Musicians (local bd.), Phi Mu Alpha Sinfonia (adv., founder Toledo U. chpt.). Club: Mich. Outdoors. Home: 3336 Hazelton Oregon OH 43616 Office: 2801 W Bancroft Toledo OH 43606

SAND, RICHARD EUGENE, physician; b. Cin., Feb. 2, 1931; s. Harry Joseph and Lulu Louise (Schray) S.; B.S., U. Cin., 1953; M.D., 1957; m. Margaret Catanzaro, Feb. 21, 1975; children by previous marriage—Barbara Melissa, Jonathon Parker. Intern, U.S. Naval Hosp., Phila., 1957-58, resident, Portsmouth, Va., 1959-61; resident U. N.C. Hosp., Chapel Hill, 1959-61; chief dept. pediatrics U.S. Naval Hosp., Key West, Fla., 1961-63; practice medicine specializing in pediatrics and allergy, St. Paul, Minn., 1963—, mem. staff Children's Hosp., St. Paul, 1963—, chief of staff, 1974, co-dir. pediatric allergy clinic, 1974—; mem. staff St. Paul Allergy Clinic, 1963—, sec.-treas., 1963-76, v.p., 1976—; mem. staff St. Paul Ramsey Hosp., St. Joseph Hosp., United Hosp., Midway Hosp.; clin. instr. pediatrics U. Minn. Sch. Medicine; med. corporate mem. Blue Cross and Blue Shield of Minn., 1974-77. Bd. dirs. Am. Lung Assn. Asthma Camp, Hennepin County, 1970—. Served to lt. comdr. USN, 1957-63. Recipient awards Am. Acad. Family Physicians, 1975-77. Diplomate Am. Bd. Pediatrics, Am. Bd. Allergy and Immunology. Fellow Am. Acad. Pediatrics, Am. Coll. Allergists; mem. Am. Acad. Allergy, AMA, Northwestern Pediatric Soc., Minn. Med. Assn., Ramsey County Med. Soc., Minn., N. Central allergy socs. Lutheran. Home: 47 Evergreen Rd White Bear Lake MN 55110 Office: 565 S Snelling Ave Saint Paul MN 55116

SANDER, FRANK LAWRENCE, environmental engr.; b. Anderson, Ind., June 10, 1925; s. Frank G. and Mary (Lawrence) S.; B.S., Mich. State U., 1949; m. Madge E. Walters, Apr. 24, 1954; children—Frank T., Amy Alison, Daniel L. Chief applications engr. Detroit br. Mpls. Honeywell, Detroit, 1951-56; mech. engr. King & Park Assos., Birmingham, Mich., 1956-58; cons. engr., Royal Oak, Mich., 1958-65; mgr. environmental design Commonwealth Assos., Jackson, Mich., 1965-72; cons. environmental engr., Traverse City, Mich., 1972—. Spl. cons. Oakland U., Rochester, Mich., 1961-65. Served with USAAF, W.W. II. Mem. Civitan Internat. (dir.), Mich. Soc. Profl. Engrs., Am. Math. Assn. Registered profl. engr., Mich., N.M. Home: 3417 Scenic Hills Dr Route 1 Williamsburg MI 49690

SANDERS, ALFRED ANTHONY, environmentalist; b. Coldwater, Ohio, Feb. 8, 1952; s. Clayton John and Dolores Veronica (Fullenkamp) S.; B.S., in Environ. Health, Wright State U., 1975. Constrn. worker Tom Hunt Constrn. Co., Greenville, Ohio, 1967-69; with P.A. Leeper Co., North Star, Ohio, 1970-75; environmentalist Ashland (Ohio) City-County Health Dept., 1975—; cons. health related activities to local twp. trustees. Sec. Ashland City League Softball Assn., 1977. Mem. Nat., Ohio environ. health assns., Wright State U. Alumni Club. Roman Catholic. Home: 406 Cottage St Ashland OH 44805 Office: 110 Cottage St Ashland OH 44805

SANDERS, JERRY DON, accountant; b. Cape Girardeau, Mo., Nov. 7, 1944; s. James Roscoe and Thelma Janet (Robinson) S.; grad. Office Tng. Sch., Cape Girardeau, 1963, with jr. accounting degree; m. Connie Kay Schleinger, June 19, 1966. Stocker, checker, asst. mgr. Randall-Evans, Inc. Grocers, Houston, 1963-65; bookkeeper J-W Chevrolet, Marble Hill, Mo., 1967-69; bookkeeper, accountant, asst. sec. Inman Freight System, Inc., Cape Girardeau, 1969—. Mem. Democratic com., Scopus Twp., Mo., 1970—. Served AUS 1965-67. Baptist (ch. tng. union dir. 1968-69, 1969-70, young adult instr. 1974—). Mason (32 deg.), Eastern Star, Sword Bunker Hill. Address: Route 1 Box 113 Millersville MO 63766

SANDERS, JOHN RICHARD, educator; b. Kansas City, Kans., Sept. 23, 1937; s. Bernard Paul and Rose Catherine (Boosman) S.; B.S., Rockhurst Coll., 1955-59; M.A., U. Mo. at Kans. City, 1963; student U. N.M. 1964, Universidad Central, Quito, Ecuador, 1964; m. Madeline Mary Stewart, Aug. 11, 1962; children—Teresa, Mary Beth, Carol. Tchr. Spanish, North Kansas City Pub. Schs., 1959—; instr. Spanish, Rockhurst Coll. evening div. 1963-64. Mem. Mo. State Young Democrats, 1965-69, state del., 1968; Gladstone Democratic Club 1967-72, v.p. 1969; sec. Clay County Adminstrv. Facilities Commn., 1969-70; mem. Clay County Democratic Central Com. 1972-74. NDEA grantee, 1963. Mem. Nat. Edn. Assn. (nat. del. 1970, 72, 74), N. Kans. City Edn. Assn. (exec. bd. 1969-71), North Kans. City Polit. Action Com. for Edn. (pres. 1969-70), Greater Kan. City Dist. Tchrs. (v.p. 1971-72), Mo. N.E.A. Jud. Rev. Bd. 1975. Home: 4956 NE Chouteau Dr Kansas City MO 64119 Office: 2117 NE 48th St Kansas City MO 64118

SANDERS, NORMAN O., lawyer; b. Kansas City, Mo., Jan. 22, 1931; s. William O. and Gertrude V. (Devine) S.; B.A., LL.B., U. Mo., Kansas City, 1958; m. Shirley Ann Stasi, May 9, 1953; children—Debra, Craig, Patrick, Brian, Stacy. Admitted to Mo. bar, 1957; practiced in Kansas City, 1957—; asso. firm Popham, Popham, Conway, Sweeny & Fremont, 1957-60, Pew, Taylor, Welch & Sheridan, 1960-61; partner firm Sheridan, Baty, Markey, Sanders & Edwards, 1961-66; sr. partner firm Sheridan, Sanders, Mason & Simpson, 1966—. Cons., atty. Kansas City Area Transp. Authority, 1971—; legal adviser Kansas City Youth Ct., 1963-69. Pres., chmn. bd. dirs. De La Salle Ednl. Center; pres. Kansas City Legal Aid and Defender Soc., 1971-72, bd. dirs., 1969—; pres. Bros. Boys Assn., 1964—; mem. Mayor's Prayer Breakfast Com., 1962—, pres., 1971; pres., bd. dirs. U. Mo. at Kansas City Law Found. Recipient Lon O. Hocker Trial Lawyer award Mo. Bar, 1965; Outstanding Alumni award De La Salle Alumni Assn., 1972; named One of Outstanding Young Man of Am., 1967; Hon. col. Gov. Warren Hearnes, 1964-72. Mem. U. Mo. at Kansas City Law Sch. Alumni Assn. (pres. 1971), Phi Alpha Delta. Roman Catholic. Club: Kansas City. Home: 9400 Jarboe St Kansas City MO 64114 Office: Traders Bank Bldg 1125 Grand Ave Kansas City MO 64106

SANDERS, PARKER DAVID, agrl. adminstr.; b. Chgo., Nov. 27, 1894; s. Howard Prettymen and Mary Elizabeth (Mathias) S.; B.S. in Agrl., U. Minn., 1918; m. Isabella Gooding, Nov. 15, 1933 (dec. Aug. 1971). With Sanders Farms, Redwood Falls, Minn., 1918—. Co-chmn. Redwood Falls Municipal Swimming Pool Devel., 1954-55; asso. mem. nat. council Met. Opera; mem. Bd. Edn. Redwood Falls, 1933-42; chmn. Redwood County Rationing Bd., 1942-44; trustee, Greater Univ. Fund, U. Minn., 1948-55; charter trustee U. Minn. Found., 1962, now emeritus. Served with USNR, 1918-1919. Recipient Alumni Service award U. Minn., 1963. Mem. Redwood County Agrl. Soc. (pres. 1926-42), Am., Minn. socs., farm mgrs. and rural appraisers, Am. Soc. Agronomy, Council for Agrl. Sci. and Tech., Am. Agrl. Econs. Assn., Am. Soc. Agrl. Engrs., AAAS, St. Paul-Mpls. Com. on Fgn. Relations, Delta Kappa Epsilon. Presbyterian. Mason, Lion. Clubs: Athletic, Minikahda (Mpls.); Redwood Falls Golf (charter, pres. 1924). Home: 411 S Jefferson St Redwood Falls MN 56283 Office: 5th and Jefferson St Redwood Falls MN 56283

SANDERS, ROBERT FRANKLIN, hosp. adminstr.; b. Centralia, Ill., Mar. 8, 1933; s. Oliver Lee and Elizabeth Bell (Jones) S.; student Mercy Coll., 1961; postgrad. hosp. adminstrn. Trinity U., San Antonio, 1974; children by previous marriage—Robert Franklin II, Gary W. Dir. anesthesia Fayette County (Ill.) Hosp., Vandalia, 1962-63; asst. adminstr. Fisherman's Hosp., Marathon, Fla., 1963-65; dir. anesthesia Huber Meml. Hosp., Pana, Ill., 1965-69; adminstr. Tipton County (Tenn.) Meml. Hosp., Covington, 1964-69; adminstr. Salem (Mo.) Meml. Hosp., 1969—. Mem. Tri-State, Am., Mo. hosp. assns., U.S. Naval Inst., Am. Acad. Med. Adminstrs., Am. Financial Mgmt. Assn., Am. Mgmt. Assn., Am. Coll. Hosp. Adminstrs., Am. Soc. Hosp. Purchasing Agts., Nat. League Nursing. Editor: The Scope, 1961; editor, pub.: Manual for Supervisors, 1974. Home: 403 S Henderson Salem MO 65560 Office: Salem Meml Hosp Hwy 72 N Salem MO 65560

SANDERS, WILBUR RAY, orthodontist; b. Sioux City, Iowa, Apr. 26, 1926; s. Chris Henry and Pearl Adelade (Steen) S.; student U. Dubuque, 1944-45; B.A., Buena Vista Coll., 1947; D.D.S., U. Iowa, 1951, M.S., 1952; m. Betty Jean Davis, Mar. 26, 1948; children—Peggy Lee, Christopher Ray. Pvt. practice dentistry specializing in orthodontics, Council Bluffs, Iowa, 1954—; instr. Creighton U. Coll. Dentistry, 1954-57; asst. prof. clin. orthodontics dept. pediatrics U. Nebr. Med. Center, 1975—. Pres., S.W. Iowa Handicapped Center, 1965-68; bd. dirs. United Fund, 1965-68, Mid Am. council Boy Scouts Am., 1962—. Served with USNR, 1944-46; to capt. Dental Corps, USAF, 1952-54. Mem. Am., S.W. Iowa Dist. (pres. 1957-58) dental assns., Am. Assn. Orthodontists, Iowa Orthodontic Assn. (pres. 1969-70), Psi Omega. Republican. Unitarian. Elk. Home: 5 Alta Dr Council Bluffs IA 51501 Office: 401 Ervin Bldg Council Bluffs IA 51501

SANDERSON, RICHARD LEE, human resource devel. adminstr.; b. Decatur, Ill., May 19, 1942; s. Clarence William and LaRue Ann Ida (Cornish) S.; B.A., Mich. State U., 1964, M.A., 1967, M.B.A., 1974, Ph.D., 1978; 1 dau., Katherine Noel. Inst. sociology Graceland Coll., Lamoni, Iowa, 1965-66; buyer Procter and Gamble Co., Cin., 1968-69; mgr. personnel tng. and devel. The Hobart Corp., Troy, Ohio, 1969-71; program dir. internat. mgmt. edn. NCR Internat., Dayton, Ohio, 1971-72; mgr. mgmt. devel. PepsiCo Internat., Purchase, N.Y., 1975-76; sr. mgmt. tng. cons. U.S. Steel Corp., Pitts., 1976-77; dir. Inst. Mgmt. Devel., William Rainey Harper Coll., Palatine, Ill., 1977—. Mem. Am. Soc. Tng. and Devel., Am. Mgmt. Assn., Internat. Transactional Analysis Assn, Am. Soc. Personnel Adminstrn., Adult Edn. Assn. U.S.A., Chgo. Assn. Commerce and Industry, Palatine, Rolling Meadows (Ill.) chambers commerce. Mem. Ch. Latter Day Saints. Club: Rotary Internat. Author: Feast and Famine: An Organizational Analysis of the Michigan Grange, 1967; The Management Process: An International Perspective, 1972; Management Concepts and Practices: An Introduction, 1976; contbr. articles to profl. jours. Home: 1010 Sterling Ave Palatine IL 60067 Office: William Rainey Harper Coll Palatine IL 60067

SANDERSON, RICHARD LEWIS, assn. exec.; b. Detroit, Mar. 5, 1921; s. Lewis Clark and Ruth Blanche (Brayton) S.; student Wayne State U., 1946; M.P.A., Ill. Inst. Tech., 1971; m. Agnes Eleanor Johnson, May 19, 1941; children—Richard Lewis, Vicki Lynne Sanderson Scheele. Supervising insp. Bldg. Dept., City of Detroit, 1947-63; chief insp. Bldg. Dept., City of Livonia (Mich.), 1963-65; tech. dir. Bldg. Ofcls. and Code Adminstrs. Internat., Chgo., 1965-67, exec. dir., 1967—. Instr., U. Ill., 1971—. Founder Nat. Acad. Code Adminstrn.; trustee Govtl. Affairs Inst., Pub. Adminstrn. Service. Served with USNR, 1940-45. Mem. Am. Soc. Pub. Adminstrn., Am. Soc. Assn. Execs., Nat. Fire Protection Assn., Nat. Assn. Home Builders. Clubs: Masons (32 deg.), Shriners. Author: Codes and Code Administration, an Introduction to Building Regulations in the United States, 1969. Editor-in-chief The Building Official and Code Administrator, 1967—. Office: 1313 E 60th St Chicago IL 60637

SANDFORD, PHILLIP ARTHUR, engr.; b. Pontiac, Mich., May 17, 1927; s. Frederick Tom and Alice Ruth (Howland) S.; B.S. in Elec. Engring., U. Mich., 1950; postgrad. Gen. Electric Test Program, 1951; creative Engring. Program 1953; m. Joyce Elaine Wagner, Sept. 13, 1947; children—Harold, Kerry, Craig, Phyllis, Dale. Reigstered profl. engr., N.C. Advance devel. engr. General Electric Co., Bridgeport, Conn., 1953-54, Asheboro, N.C., 1954-61, thermal electric engr., Schenectady, N.Y., 1961-63; dir. advanced devel. engring. Norge div. Borg Warner Corp., Des Plaines, Ill., 1963-65; mgr. appliance advanced devel. Philco-Ford Corp., Phila., 1965-70, mgr. automotive climate control research and advanced engring, Connersville, Ind., 1970-72; mgr. engring. comfort products No. Electric Co., Chgo., 1972-78; sr. project engr. McDonald's Corp., Oak Brook, Ill., 1978—. Elder Presbyn. Ch., Highland Park, Ill., 1973—; mem. Comprehensive Plan Task Force, Highland Park, 1975. Served with USNR, 1945-46. Mem. IEEE. Holder 2 patents. Home: 310 Central Ave Highland Park IL 60035 Office: McDonald's Oak Brook IL

SANDIDGE, REX JOSEPH, broadcast products co. exec.; b. LaGrande, Oreg., Feb. 1, 1940; s. Joseph Luff and Muriel Helen S.; A.S., Mo. Inst. Tech., 1960; B.S., Central Mo. State U., 1966; m. Tran Thi Hai, June 2, 1970; children—Alan Roy, Susan Lynn. Test set technician Western Electric Co., Lee's Summit, Mo., 1960-62; chief technician Central Mo. State U., Warrensburg, 1966-67; electronic engr. NBC, N.Y.C., Vietnam, 1967-70; sr. technician, supr., systems engr. Page Communications Engrs., Vienna, Va., with duty in Vietnam, Libya, 1971-74; tech. instr. Ferris State Coll., Big Rapids, Mich., 1974-76; mgr. customer tng. Harris Corp. Broadcast Products div., Quincy, Ill., 1976—. Mem. Nat. Assn. Ednl. Broadcasters, Soc. Broadcast Engrs. Mem. Reorganized Ch. Jesus Christ Latterday Saints. Home: 27 Riverside Terr Quincy IL 62301 Office: 24th and Ellington Rd Quincy IL 62301

SANDONA, BRUNO, civil engr.; b. Chgo., Aug. 28, 1926; s. Mario and Pearl Santa (Fabris) S.; B.S., Ill. Inst. Tech., 1951; m. Madelyn Marinello, Aug. 15, 1953; children—Madalynne, Paula. With Johnson & Johnson, engrs. and architects, Chgo., 1950-62; partner Brankis Engring., Inc., Chgo., 1962—, v.p., 1973—. Served with USNR, 1943-46. Registered profl. engr., Ill., Wis., Iowa, Ky. Mem. ASCE, Western Soc. Engrs., Am. Legion. Moose. Home: 328 Avonelle St Chicago Heights IL 60411 Office: 53 W Jackson Blvd Chicago IL 60609

SANDQUIST, OLIVER, architect; b. Chgo., Dec. 9, 1905; s. Axel Sigfried and Selma Caroline (Fritz) S.; student Wheaton Coll., 1924-25, Armour Inst. Tech., 1927-30; m. Alice Rose Schacht, Sept. 6, 1930; 1 dau., Senny Rose. Owner, Sandquist Co., Chgo., 1931-40; chief designer Skidmore, Owings & Merrill, Chgo., 1941-44; owner Oliver Sandquist, architect, Chgo., 1945-55; partner Samuelson & Sandquist, architects and engrs., Chgo., 1955-63; owner Oliver Sandquist & Assos., architects and engrs., Chgo., 1963—. Bldg. commr. Village of Skokie (Ill.), 1956-58. Mem. AIA, Soc. Am. Registered Architects (nat. v.p. 1960), Ill. Soc. Architects (dir. 1958-61). Mem. Verdandi Ind. Order Svithiod (chmn. 1968-69). Clubs: Architects (Chgo. (pres. 1954-55, dir.), Evanston Golf. Home: 4025 Harvard Terr Skokie IL 60076 Office: 4838 Howard St Skokie IL 60077

SANDRY, MARTIN EMANUEL, psychologist; b. Phila., Sept. 1, 1937; s. Benjamin Harris and Ida Sarah (Kravitz) S.; B.A., U. Pa., 1959, M.A., 1961, Ph.D., 1974; m. Nancy Louise Jerz, Aug. 18, 1974; children—Paul, Pamela. Research asso. dept. neurology Pa. U. Med. Sch., 1960; psychologist Childrens Seashore House, Atlantic City, 1961-62, chief psychologist, research dir., 1963; research asso. Assn. Rehab. Centers, Evanston, Ill., 1964-67; pvt. practice psychotherapy, Chgo., 1967—; adminstr. Zone 11, Ill. Dept. Mental Health, 1967-68; program evauator Chgo. Read Hosp., 1968-69, clin. psychologist, 1970-74; psychologist Ravenswood Community Mental Health Center, Chgo., 1974—; dir. clin. services, mem. faculty Chgo. Inst. for Rational Living, Ltd., 1974—, also bd. dirs., 1974—. Certified psychologist, Ill. Mem. Am., Eastern, Ill. psychol. assns., Nat. Alliance for Family Life (clinical), Acad. Psychologists in Marital and Family Therapy. Fellow Inst. for Advanced Study Rational Psychotherapy. Author: Rational-emotive Theory: Relationship between Adjustment and Irrational Ideas, 1974. Contbr. articles to profl. jours. Home and office: 2503 N Halsted St Chicago IL 60614

SANDS, STANLEY HUGH, meat co. exec.; b. Lincoln, Nebr., Aug. 16, 1917; s. Albert and Pauline (Engleman) S.; B.S., U. Calif., Berkeley, 1939; m. Nancy Ann Platt, Dec. 31, 1947; children—Edward, Alan, David, Stephen, Pamela. With Standard Meat Co., Lincoln, 1939—, pres., 1956—. Pres., Govt. Research Inst., Inc., 1960-61. Mem. Lincoln Traffic Commn., 1952-53, City-County Planning Commn. Lincoln, 1963-64, Bd. Zoning Appeals Lincoln, 1963-64, Mayor's Air Pollution Com. Lincoln, 1964-65, Nebr. Centennial Com., 1967, McGovern Panel on Nat. Security, 1972; chmn. Lincoln-Lancaster County Cancer Crusade, 1960; mem. nat. council Bus. Execs. Move, 1970—; mem. Lincoln Police Rev. Bd., 1975-78. Bd. dirs. Lincoln Inst. Fine Arts for Children and Youth, 1957, Lincoln Found., 1975-78; trustee Nebr. Civil Liberties Union, 1975—. Mem. Nat. Assn. Meat Purveyors, Lincoln C. of C. (dir. 1967-68), Alpha Delta Sigma. Rotarian (dir. 1960-61). Clubs: Nebraska, University, Hillcrest; Capitol Hill (Washington). Home: 2601 Woodscrest St Lincoln NE 68502 Office: 700 Van Dorn St Lincoln NE 68502

SANDSTROM, HARVEY DEAN, artist, illustrator; b. St. Paul, Oct. 7, 1925; s. Walfred and Ruth Elvera (Anderson) S.; student Mpls. Coll. Art, 1946-50; m. Donna Rae Davidson, Sept. 9, 1951; children—Barbara, Sarah. Free lance comml. designer and illustrator, Duluth, Minn., 1950-52; art dir. Marshall & Assos., Duluth, 1952-60; design cons., free lance painter, illustrator, Duluth, 1961—; lectr. U. Wis.; cons. Sklaris Corp., Res. Mining Co., Minn. Power & Light Co., Pickands Mather & Co. Served with USN, 1943-46. Winner Fed. Migratory Bird Hunting Stamp competition, 1954-55; patentee envelope for bank drive-in window. Home and Office: Route 4 Box 504C Duluth MN 55803

SANDVIG, RALPH BERTRAM, lawyer; b. Chgo., Sept. 10, 1945; s. Bertram O. and Rose M. (Bielat) S.; B.A., North Central Coll., 1967; J.D., DePaul U., 1970; m. Saundra J. Hall, Aug. 23, 1969. Admitted to Ill. bar, 1970; asso. firm Charles O. Brizius, Chgo., 1970-71; partner Brizius, Nixon, Sandvig, attys., 1971-72; practice law, Woodridge, Ill., 1972-74; asst. to trust counsel Harris Trust & Savs. Bank, Chgo., 1973-74, trust counsel, 1975—. Treas., bd. dirs. Winston Hills Assn., 1970-71; bd. dirs. Baptist Retirement Home. Mem. Am., Ill., Chgo. bar assns. Baptist (trustee, treas.). Home: 4060 Western Western Springs IL 60558 Office: 111 W Monroe St Chicago IL 60603

SANDY, PAUL CLYDE, cons.; b. Milo, Iowa, June 24, 1918; s. Clyde Brown and Lela (Flesher) S.; student several Midwest schs. and colls., 1935-54. Engring. aide Warren County, Indianola, Iowa, 1941, asst. country engr., 1946-50, project engr., head hwy. design sect., 1951-55; project mgr. Stanley Consultants, Inc., Muscatine, Iowa, 1951-76; now cons. Officer Muscatine Service Club. Dir. Commn. on Aging. Served with AUS, 1941-46; Registered profl. engr., Iowa, Ill., Ohio, Nebr. Fellow ASCE; mem. Nat. Soc. Profl. Engrs., Am. Pub. Works Assn., Soc. Am. Mil. Engrs. (post dir.), Iowa Engring. Soc. (acting dir. 1976; Distinguished Service award 1976), Am. Road Builders Assn. (div. dir.), Iowa Hist. Soc., Muscatine County Mus. and Fine Arts Assn. Methodist. Elk. Clubs: Geneva Golf & Country, Muscatine Amateur Radio. Home: 414 Greenwood Dr Muscatine IA 52761

SANFORD, PAUL EVERETT, educator; b. Milford, Kans., Jan. 14, 1917; s. Charles Riley and Ina Bertha (Kneeland) S.; B.S., Kans. State U., 1941; M.S. (Quaker Oats fellow), Iowa State U., 1942, Ph.D., 1949; m. Helen Louise Crenshaw, Oct. 31, 1942; children—Paula Louise Sanford Schubert, Patricia Kathleen Sanford Banning, Carolyn Ruth. Sr. teaching fellow Iowa State U., Ames, 1946-47, grad. research asst., 1947-48, grad. asst., 1948-49; asso. prof. Kans. State U., Manhattan, 1949-60, prof. dept. dairy and poultry sci., 1960—. Guest lectr. P.R., 1957, Japan, 1963. Treas., pres. PTA, Manhattan, 1963-64. Republican precinct committeeman, 1974—. Chmn. bd. trustees Hosp. Assn. Kans. State U., Manhattan, 1958-60. Served with AUS, 1943-46; PTO, ETO. Eli Lilly Co. grantee, 1959-60; Comml. Solvents Corp. grantee, 1960-61; Gulf Oil Co. grantee, 1967-68; U.S. Dept. Agr. grantee, 1965-69; Pfizers Co. grantee, 1971-72; Fellow AAAS; mem. Poultry Sci. Assn., World Poultry Sci. Assn., Am. Poultry Hist. Soc. (sec. 1967-70), Animal Nutrition Research Council, United Comml. Travelers (sr. counselor 1975-76), Poultry Sci. Club Kans. State U., Broiler Soc. Japan (hon.), Nat. Assn. Coll. Tchrs. Agr., Council Agrl. Sci. and Tech., Manhattan C. of C. Presbyterian (deacon 1954-60, elder 1960-66). Home: 343 N 14th St Manhattan KS 66502

SANGHVI, MANOJ KUMAR DALICHAND, oil co. exec.; b. Morvi, India, Sept. 13, 1928; s. Dalichand Hakubhai and Navalben Jagannath (Sanghani) S.; B.S. with honors, U. Bombay, 1949, B.S. in Tech., 1951; M.S. (Fulbright fellow, Ford Found. scholar), Ohio State U., 1953, Ph.D., 1956; m. Shobhana Hiralal Shah, Apr. 1, 1958; children—Sunil, Parag, Pulin. Came to U.S., 1952. Research fellow Govt. of India Council of Sci. and Indsl. Research, Bombay, 1951-52; research fellow Ohio State U., Columbus, 1953-55, research asso., 1955-56; project chem. engr. Standard Oil Co. (Ind.), Whiting, Ind., 1956-60; economiste conseil Société Civile Amoco, Paris, France, 1960-62; chief economist Amoco (U.K.) Ltd., London, Eng., 1962-63; econ. adviser-Far East, Amoco Internat. Oil Co., N.Y.C., 1963-65; sr. tech. coordinator Amoco India, Inc., New Delhi, 1965-68; coordinator corporate planning Standard Oil Co. (Ind.), Chgo., 1968-74, sr. coordinator corporate planning, 1974—. Vis. fellow Ohio State U., 1956-57. Mem. Am. Inst. Chem. Engrs. (chmn. nat. program com., mgmt. sci. group 1972—), India League Am. (v.p., dir. 1974—), Sigma Xi, Phi Lambda Upsilon. Contbr. articles to profl. jours. Home: 1024 Heatherfield Lane Glenview IL 60025 Office: 200 E Randolph Dr Chicago IL 60601

SANGMEISTER, GEORGE EDWARD, lawyer, banker, state senator; b. Joliet, Ill., Feb. 16, 1931; s. George Conrad and Rose Engaborg (Johnson) S.; B.A., Elmhurst Coll., 1957; LL.B., John Marshall Law Sch., 1960, J.D., 1970; m. Doris Marie Hinspeter, Dec. 1, 1951; children—George Kurt, Kimberly Ann. Admitted to Ill. bar, 1960, since practiced in Joliet; partner firm McKeown, Fitzgerald, Zollner, Buck, Sangmeister & Hutchison, 1969—; pres., dir. Sauk Prairie Savs. & Loan Assn., Frankfort, Ill., 1974—. justice of peace, 1961-63; states atty. Will County, 1964-68; mem. Ill. Ho. of Reps., 1972-76, Ill. Senate, 1977—. Chmn. Will County chpt. Salvation Army; trustee Will County Family Service Agy.; bd. dirs. Joliet Jr. Coll. Found. Served with inf. AUS, 1951-53. Mem. Am., Ill., Will County bar assns., Am. Trial Lawyers Assn., Am. Legion, Frankfort (past pres.), Mokena chambers commerce, Old Timers Baseball Assn. Lion. Home: S Wolf Rd Mokena IL 60448 Office: 2455 Glenwood Ave Joliet IL 60431

SANKARAN, SURYANARAYANAN, surgeon; b. Delhi, India, Jan. 16, 1944; s. Mangudi and Meenambal (Krishnaswamy) S.; came to U.S., 1967; M.D., All India Inst. Med. Scis., 1966; m. Jayalakshmi Chandramouli, June 14, 1971; 1 dau., Anita. Intern, All India Inst. Med. Scis. Hosp., New Delhi and Detroit Gen. Hosp., 1966-68; resident Wayne State U. Affiliated Hosps., Detroit, 1968-72; asst. prof. surgery Wayne State U., Detroit, 1974-77, clin. asst. prof., 1977—. Diplomate Am. Bd. Surgery. Fellow A.C.S.; mem. AMA, Mich. State, Wayne County med. socs., MW Surg. Assn., Am. Pancreatic Study Group. Home: 2680 English St Troy MI 48098 Office: 3499 Rochester Rd Troy MI 48084

SANKEY, BRANT BURDELL, physician; b. New Castle, Pa., Nov. 7, 1908; s. Brant Elder and Lillian Grace (Mosier) S.; B.S., Allegheny Coll., 1929; M.D., Hahnemann Med. Coll., 1933; m. Helen Patterson, May 25, 1935; children—Richard, Roger. Intern, Huron Rd. Hosp., Cleve., 1933-34, resident 1934-36; practice medicine, specializing in anesthesiology, Cleve., head dept anesthesiology St. Luke's Hosp., Cleve., 1943—, asst. clin. prof. anesthesiology Case Western Res. U. Sch. Medicine, Cleve., 1959—; cons. Cleve. Safety Dept. Trustee, treas. Anesthesia Found., 1956—. Diplomate Am. Bd. Anesthesiology. Fellow Am. Coll. Anesthesiologists; mem. Am. (pres. 1955), Ohio, Cleve. socs. anesthesiologists, Acad. Anesthesiology (pres. 1968), AMA, Ohio Med. Assn., Internat. Anesthesia Research Soc. (trustee 1957—, exec. sec. 1965—), Aesculapean Soc., Med. Arts Club, Acad. Medicine Cleve. Rotarian. Club: The Country. Home: 31311 Trillium Trail Cleveland OH 44124 Office: 11311 Shaker Blvd Cleveland OH 44104

SANSBURY, RUSSELL JOSEPH, lang. specialist, therapist; b. Warsaw, Ind., Oct. 30, 1934; s. James Ralph and Rose Marian (Huddleston) S.; B.A., Manchester Coll., 1957; postgrad. Eastern Mich. U., 1961; M.A., Mich. State U., 1969; M.A., Eastern Mich. U., 1972; Ph.D., U. Mich., 1977; m. Mary Alice Gilchrist, Sept. 3, 1960; children—Rosanne, Michelle, R. Gregory, Jill. Lang. therapist Hawthorn Center, Northville, Mich., 1958-66, dir. lang. clinic, 1966—; cons. Flint (Mich.) Sch. for Deaf; MacDowell Elementary Sch., Detroit; U. Waterloo, Ontario, Canada. Mem. citizens advisory com. for Continuing Edn.; program planning com. Mich. Assn. for Children with Learning Disabilities; alumni bd. dirs., Manchester Coll. Recipient Manchester Coll. Alumni Service award. Mem. Am. Speech & Hearing Assn., Internat. Reading Assn., Council for Exceptional Children, Concerned Citizens for Mental Health, Phi Delta Kappa. Roman Catholic. Contbr. articles to profl. jours. Home: 719 Sunset Rd Ann Arbor MI 48103 Office: Hawthorne Center Northville MI 48167

SANSON, JOHN GUSTILO, pathologist; b. Ilo Ilo City, Philippines, May 27, 1933; s. Serafin A. and Milagros B. (Gustilo) S.; M.D., U. Santo Tomas, Manila, Philippines, 1958; m. Ernestina Bayona, June 10, 1953; children—Serafin, John, Gail, Jayne. Intern, U. Santo Tomas Hosp., Manila, Philippines, 1957-58; resident in pathology Mt. Sinai Hosp., Chgo., 1959-63, asst. pathologist, 1963-65; pathologist in Phila. hosps., 1965-68; asso. pathologist St. Catherine Hosp., Kenosha, Wis., 1968—; instr. pathology Chgo. Med. Sch., 1959-65; coroner's pathologist, Kenosha County, Wis. Diplomate Am. Bd. Pathology. Fellow Coll. Am. Pathologists, Am. Soc. Clin. Pathologists; mem. AMA, Wis., Kenosha Med. Socs. Contbr. articles to med. publs. Home: 4206 86th Place Kenosha WI 53142

SANSTEAD, WAYNE GODFREY, lt. gov. of N.D.; b. Hot Springs, Ark., Apr. 16, 1935; s. Godfrey A. and Clara (Buen) S.; B.A. in Speech and Polit. Sci., St. Olaf Coll., 1957; M.A. in Pub. Address, Northwestern U., 1966; Ed.D., U. N.D., 1974; m. Mary Jane Bober, June 16, 1957; children—Timothy Wayne, Jonathan Paul. Dir. debate, Luverne, Minn., 1959-60; dir. forensics, Minot (N.D.) High Sch., 1960-69; mem. N.D. Ho. of Reps., 1965-70, N.D. Senate, 1971-73; lt. gov. of N.D., Bismarck, 1973—. Del. N.D. Constl. Conv., 1972. Served with AUS, 1957-59. Coe Family Found. scholar, 1963; Eagleton scholar Rutgers U., 1969; named N.D. Outstanding Freshman Senator, A.P. Survey, 1971; N.D. Outstanding Young Educator, N.D. Jaycees, 1967; Minot's Outstanding Young Man, Minot Jaycees, 1969; named Ark. Traveler. Mem. Am. Fedn. Tchrs. (past pres. local), N.D. Edn. Assn., NEA (mem. citizenship com. 1969—), Central States Speech Assn., Am. Forensics Assn., Jaycees, ACLU, Phi Delta Kappa. Democrat. Lutheran (chmn. Western N.D. research and social action com. 1962-68). Elk, Toastmaster; mem. Sons of Norway. Home: 823 9th Ave NE Minot ND 58701 Office: State Capitol Bldg Bismarck ND 58501

SANTANGELO, MARIO VINCENT, dentist, educator; b. Youngstown, O., Oct. 5, 1931; s. Anthony and Maria (Zarlenga) S.; student U. Pitts., 1949-51; D.D.S., Loyola U. (Chgo.), 1955, M.S., 1960. Instr. Loyola U., Chgo., 1957-60, asst. prof., 1960-66, chmn. dpt. radiology, 1962-70, dir. dental aux. utilization program, 1963-70, asso. prof., 1966-70, chmn. dept. oral diagnosis, 1967-70, asst. dean, 1969-70; practice dentistry, Chgo., 1960—. Cons. Cert. Bd. Am. Dental Assts. Assn., 1967—, VA Research Hosp., 1969-75, Chgo. Civil Service Commn., 1967—; counselor Chgo. Dental Assts. Assn., 1966-69; mem. dental student tng. adv. com. Div. Dental Health USPHS, Dept. Health, Edn. and Welfare, 1969-71; cons. dental edn. rev. com. NIH, 1971-72; cons. USPHS, HEW, Region IV, Atlanta, 1973-76, Region V, Chgo., 1973—. Bd. visitors Sch. Dental Medicine, Washington U., St. Louis, 1974-76. Served to capt. USAF, 1955-57. Fellow Am. Coll. Dentists; mem. Am. Assn. Dental Schs., Odontographic Soc. Chgo., Am. (asst. sec. council dental edn. 1971—, asst. sec. commn. on accreditation 1975—), Ill., Chgo. dental assns., Am. Acad. Oral Pathology, Am. Acad. Dental Radiology, Am. Acad. Oral Medicine, Omicron Kappa Upsilon (pres. 1967-68), Blue Key, Xi Psi Phi. Contbr. articles to profl. jours. Home: 1440 N Lake Shore Dr Chicago IL 60610 Office: 211 E Chicago Ave Chicago IL 60611

SANTEE, WILLIAM MILTON, food service cons.; b. St. Marys, Kans., Aug. 14, 1922; s. Samuel Raymond and Julia (Magrath) S.; B.A., Kans. State Tchrs. Coll., 1943; m. Ruth Ann Bird, May 28, 1949; children—Michelle, Sheila Santee Rupp, Kevin William. Designer Display Props, Kansas City, Mo., 1946-47; with placement office VA, Kansas City, Mo., 1948-49; gen. mgr. Smith St. John Co., Kansas City, Mo., 1949-63; food service cons., Kansas City, Mo., 1963—. Guest lectr. Penn Valley Jr. Coll., Kansas City, Mo., 1970-75, U. Mo. Med. Center, Columbia, 1969-75, U. Kans., Manhattan, 1965-75. Bd. dirs. Rockhurst Coll., Kansas City, Mo., 1965-75, Lena River Smith's Scholarship Fund, 1970-75. Served with USAAF, 1940-45. Mem. Internat. Soc. Food Service Cons. Home: 50 E 53d St Kansas City MO 64112 Office: 4309 Madison Ave Kansas City MO 64111

SAPERSTEIN, ESTHER, state senator; b. Chgo.; ed. Northwestern U.; widow; children—Sidney, Natalie. Mem. Ill. Ho. of Reps., 1957-66; mem. Ill. Senate, 1966—, chmn. edn. com. Mem. Mayor's Com. on Human Relations, Chgo., Mayor's Juvenile Welfare Com. Chgo.; former pres. Chgo. Region P.T.A.; former sec. Juvenile Protective Assn.; mem. Citizens Adv. Council of Met. Chgo.; chmn. Ill. Commn. Status Women, 1963—; Ill. chmn. Commn. on Mental Health and Retardation, 1965—. Alderman, City of Chgo., 1975—. Bd. dirs. Jewish Community Center of Rogers Park (Ill.), Little City, Chgo. Sch. for Retarded Children, Doctors Gen. Hosp. Mem. League of Women Voters. Democrat. Jewish. Office: 1316 W Arthur Ave Chicago IL 60626

SARACENO, ANTHONY JOSEPH, chemist; b. Reggio, Italy, June 20, 1933; s. Bruno and Antonia (Tripodi) S.; came to U.S., naturalized, 1934; B.S., St. Vincent Coll., 1955; Ph.D. (fellow), U. Notre Dame, 1958; m. Edith June Landgraf, Oct. 24, 1970; 1 dau., Rochelle. Teaching asst. Notre Dame (Ind.) U., 1955-56; research chemist Gulf Oil, Pitts., 1958-61; project leader Pennwalt Corp., King of Prussia, Pa., 1961-67; with Goodyear Atomic Corp., Piketon, O., 1967—, sect. head chem. devel., 1970—. Sec., treas. Devon Strafford (Pa.) Civic Assn., 1965-67. Mem. Am. Chem. Soc., A.A.A.S., Sigma Xi. K.C. Clubs: Optimist (dir. 1968-70); Scioto Valley Investment (sec. 1975—). Contbr. articles to profl. jours. Patentee in field. Home: 731 Crestwood Dr Waverly OH 45690 Office: Goodyear Atomic Corp PO Box 628 Piketon OH 45661

SARANTOPOULOS, COSTAS, orthopaedic surgeon; b. Valtetsi, Greece, Oct. 18, 1930; s. Anthanasios Christ and Anastasia Diamantis (Lampropoulos) S.; B.S., U. Salonika, 1952, M.D., U. Athens, 1956; Ph.D., Athens U., 1965; m. Kay J. Georgelis, July 18, 1964; children—Stacy, Athan, John, Alexia. Intern, Euclid Hosp., Cleve. Hosp., 1959-60; surg. resident Jersey City Med. Center, 1960-61, orthopaedic resident Albert Einstein Med. Center, Phila., 1961-63, Kings County Hosp. Med. Center, 1963-64, orthopaedic pathology resident Temple U., Phila., 1962-63; orthopaedic surgeon Blue Cross Hosp. Athens, 1964-66, St. Elizabeth Hosp., Youngstown (Ohio) Hosp. Assn., 1967—. Cons. Easter Seal Center Crippled Children. Served to 2d lt. Greek Army. Diplomate Am. Bd. Orthopaedic Surgery. Mem. Am. Acad. Orthopaedic Surgeons, A.C.S., World Med. Assn., AMA, Am. Geriatric Soc., Am. Hellenic Ednl. Progressive Assn., Greek Am. Progressive Assn., Hippocratic Med. Soc., Ohio Orthopaedic Soc., Pan Arcadian Fedn. (pres. local chpt.), Order Knights St. Andrew of Ecumenical Patriarchate. Greek Orthodox (trustee ch.). Rotarian. Club: Hellenic U. (pres.). Contbr. articles to med. jours. Home: 12 Wildfern St Youngstown OH 44505 Office: 333 Park Av Youngstown OH 44504

SARBER, GLENN SCOTT, environ. engr.; b. Continental, Ohio, Sept. 25, 1929; s. Glenn Scott and Olive Leola (Gott) S.; B.C.E., Ohio State U., 1954; m. Caye Louise Goudy, Nov. 26, 1956; children—David Scott, Anne Louise, Elizabeth. Sr. engr. Holmquist Engrs., Phoenix, 1955-60; owner Scott Sarber Engr., Casa Grande, Ariz., 1960-64; civil specialist Sverdrup & Parcel, St. Louis, 1964-69; asst. chief civil engr. Hok-Helmuth-Obata-Kassabaum, St. Louis, 1968-73; sr. environ. design engr. Monsanto Co., St. Louis, 1973—. Bd. dirs. Grace Hall Settlement House, St. Louis, 1972—, pres., 1976-77. Mem. ASCE, Water Pollution Control Fedn., Engrs. Club St. Louis. Episcopalian. Club: Masons. Address: 6620 Clayton St Saint Louis MO 63117

SARGENT, CHARLES LEE, sanitation systems and pollution control systems mfg. co. exec.; b. Flint, Mich., Mar. 22, 1937; s. Frank T. and Evelyn M. (Martinson) S.; B.M.E., Gen. Motors Inst., 1960; M.B.A., Harvard, 1962; m. Nancy Cook, June 9, 1962; children—Wendy L., Joy A., Candace L. Reliability engr. AC Spark Plug div. Gen. Motors Corp., Flint, 1962-63; with Thetford Corp., Ann Arbor, Mich., 1962—, pres., 1974—, chmn. bd., 1974—; pres., chmn. bd. Thermasan Corp., 1969-72; dir. Stirling Power Systems Corp., Ann Arbor Bank and Trust Co. Trustee, mem. bd. edn. Lincoln Consol. Schs., Ypsilanti, Mich., 1973-77. Home: 747 Country Club Rd Ann Arbor MI 48105 Office: PO Box 1285 Ann Arbor MI 48106

SARGENT, DONALD VIRGIL, gynecologist; b. Bay City, Mich., Apr. 7, 1911; s. Edward Daniel and Nellie Ellen (Brady) S.; B.S., Loyola U., Chgo., 1932, M.D., 1936; m. Helen Marie Van Colen, Feb. 6, 1937; children—Saundra Donahue, Donald Virgil II, Michael, Pamela Richardson. Intern, St. Mary's Hosp., Saginaw, 1936-38, preceptorship, 1938-42, chmn. dept. obstetrics-gynecology, 1948-77; practice medicine specializing in gynecology, Saginaw, 1946—; cons. staff Saginaw Gen. Hosp., St. Luke's Hosp., 1948-77; mem. bd. Valley Obstetrics-Gynecology Clinic, 1965-77; asso. clin. prof. Mich. State U. Coll. Human Medicine, 1972-77. Served to lt. comdr., M.C., USNR, 1942-46. Diplomate Am. Bd. Obstetrics-Gynecology. Fellow ACS, Am. Coll. Obstetricians and Gynecologists; mem. AMA, Mich., Saginaw County med. socs., Mich. Soc. Obstetricians and Gynecologists (council). Roman Catholic. Clubs: Saginaw, Germania. Home: 4680 Ashland Dr Saginaw MI 48603 Office: 926 N Michigan Ave Saginaw MI 48605

SARGENT, EILEEN SEVERSON, ednl. adminstr.; b. Deerfield, Wis., Oct. 8, 1922; d. Martin Arthur and Lillian Myrtle (Vaage) Severson; B.S., State Coll., Whitewater, Wis., 1950; M.S., U. Wis., Madison, 1955, Ph.D., 1971; certificate advanced studies Syracuse U., 1969; m. Merle E. Sargent, Dec. 17, 1962. Tchr. rural sch., 1942-46; teaching prin. Dousman St. Graded Sch., Dousman, Wis., 1946-49; tchr. high sch., Madison, 1949-55; curriculum coordinator, reading cons. Nicolet High Sch., Milw., 1955-72; instr. Syracuse U., 1964, Marquette U., 1969; extension instr. U. Wis., Milw., 1966-69; asst. prof. Marquette U., 1972—, dir. reading and learning abilities center, 1972—. Ford fellow, 1955. Mem. Nat. (life), Wis. edn. assns., Am. Soc., Curriculum Devel., Nat. Council Tchrs. English, Internat. (conv. exhibit mgr. 1954—, past dir.), Wis. (past pres.) reading assns., Milw. Area Reading Council, Order Easter Star, Daus. of Nile, Delta Kappa Gamma, Pi Lambda Theta (life mem.; past pres. Wis.), Phi Beta Kappa. Author: How to Read a Book, 1970; The Newspaper as a Teaching Tool; also articles in field; co-editor: Chicorel Abstracts on Reading and Learning Disabilities, 1976, 77. Home: 330 E Beaumont Ave Milwaukee WI 53217 Office: 502 N 15th St Milwaukee WI 53233

SARGENT, HARRY LEE, bldg. contractor; b. Meadville, Mo., Nov. 11, 1923; s. Arthur J. and Francis E. (Cloud) S.; grad. high sch.; m. Myrtle De Renner Lawson, Oct. 17, 1970. Factory worker John Deere Tractor Corp., 1947-48; carpenter, Meadville, 1948-50; carpenter foreman Thomas Constrn. Co., St. Joseph, Mo., 1950-57; bldg. contractor, Meadville, 1957—. Alderman, City of Meadville 1958-64, 68-74. Served with USN, 1942-46. Am. Legion. Baptist. Address: Macon St Meadville MO 64659

SARGENT, KENNETH ALAN, rancher, assn. exec.; b. Murdo, S.D., Nov. 1, 1919; s. John Myers and Laura Gail (Orr) S.; student Brigham Young U., 1971-76; m. Dorothy Alice Daskam, Oct. 3, 1944; children—Dorothy Louise, Kenneth Alan, Robert Dennis, Barbara Suzanne, Kevin Scott, Patricia Lynne. Rancher, Wolsey, S.D., 1939—; rural mail carrier U.S. Postal Dept., Wolsey, 1958—, union steward, 1970-74; partner, operator KD Bar Ranch, Wolsey, 1956—; v.p. KD Bar Enterprises, Wolsey, 1974—. Treas. sch. bd. Broadland Dist. 4, Beadle County, S.D., 1951-52. Active Boy Scouts Am., Girl Scouts U.S.A. Founder, pres. James Valley Hist. Soc., 1970—. Served to sgt. USMC, 1941-45; PTO. Recipient certificate of appreciation S.D. Assn. for Retarded Children, 1963. Mem. Nat., S.D. (dist. pres. 1970-71) rural letter carriers assns., Aberdeen Area Geneal. Soc. (hon., life). Republican. Mem. Ch. of Jesus Christ of Latter-day Saints (high councilman 1972—, elder 1958—). Lion. Home: Wolsey SD 57384 Office: KD Bar Ranch Wolsey SD 57384

SARGENT, THOMAS ANDREW, educator; b. Indpls., Apr. 24, 1933; s. Thomas Edward and Inez (Secrest) S.; B.A., DePauw U., Greencastle, Ind., 1955; M.A., Fletcher Sch. Law and Diplomacy, Tufts U., 1959, M.A. in Law and Diplomacy, 1968, Ph.D., 1969; m. Cecily Constance Fox-Williams, July 10, 1965; children—Sarah Beatrice, Andrew Fox. With First Nat. City Bank, N.Y.C., 1959-64, asst. accountant, 1963-64; asst. sec. Irving Trust Co., N.Y.C., 1964-66; mem. faculty Ball State U., Muncie, Ind., 1969—, asso. prof. polit. sci., 1973—, dir. London Center, 1973-74, chmn. dept. polit. sci., 1977—, chmn. univ. senate, 1977-78; mem. Indpls. Com. Fgn. Relations, 1977—. Dir., exec. v.p. Eastern Ind. Community TV, Inc., Muncie, 1974-76, pres., 1976-77. Mem. nat. governing bd. Ripon Soc., Washington, 1976—. Served to 1st lt. USAF, 1955-58. Mem. Am. Polit. Sci. Assn., Am. Soc. Internat. Law, Am. Acad. Polit. Sci., Sigma Delta Chi, Phi Delta Theta. Republican. Methodist. Club: Muncie. Contbg. editor Ripon Forum, 1973—. Home: 2700 W Berkshire Dr Muncie IN 47304

SARGENT, WILLIAM WINSTON, anesthesiologist; b. Oshkosh, Wis., Feb. 28, 1933; s. Sprague Spencer and Lila Jane (Gjermundson) S.; B.S., U. Ill., 1955, M.D., 1957; M.S., U. Minn., 1967. Intern, Ill. Central Hosp., Chgo., 1957-58; med. fellow U. Minn. Med. Center, 1958-60, research fellow, 1965-67; staff anesthesiologist St. Anthony Hosp., Swedish Am. Hosp., Rockford, Ill., 1960-61; instr. U. Minn. Med. Center, Mpls., 1967-74, asst. prof. 1974—. Served to capt. USAF, 1961-64. Recipient Physicians Recognition award A.M.A., 1973-76. Diplomate Am. Bd. Anesthesiology. Fellow Royal Soc. Health, Am. Coll. Anesthesiologists; mem. Internat. Platform Assn. Presbyn. Address: U Minn Hosp 412 SE Union Box 321 Minneapolis MN 55455

SARICH, DENNIS PAUL, advt. agy. exec.; b. Cleve., Mar. 14, 1943; s. Paul and Kathryn (Prahin) S.; B.A., Washington U., 1966; m. Barbara Gail Love, June 7, 1966; children—Nicole Deborah, Andrew Dennis. Copywriter, Brown Shoe Co., St. Louis, 1966-68, Joseph E. Schmitt & Assos., St. Louis, 1968-69; advt. mgr. Trimfoot Co., St. Louis, 1969-70; account exec. Bemiston Advt., St. Louis, 1971-73; prodn. mgr. E.M. Reilly & Assos., St. Louis, 1973-74, creative dir., 1974—. Mem. Ad Club II of St. Louis, Nat. Acad. TV Arts and Scis., Kappa Sigma. Home: 415 Lee Ave Webster Groves MO 63119 Office: 130 S Bemiston Ave St Louis MO 63105

SARKESIAN, SAM CHARLES, educator, polit. scientist; b. Chgo., Nov. 7, 1927; s. Charles and Khatoon (Babigian) S.; B.A., The Citadel, 1951; M.A., Columbia, 1962, Ph.D., 1969; certificate African studies, Syracuse U., 1962; m. Jeannette Minasian, May 7, 1955; children—Gary Charles, Joye Simone, Guy Samuel. Enlisted in AUS, 1945, commd. 2d lt., U.S. Army, 1951, advanced through grades to lt. col., 1967; service in Germany, Korea and Vietnam; asst. prof. U.S. Mil. Acad., 1962; vis. prof. Northwestern U., 1964, Buffalo State U., 1965; ret., 1968; mem. faculty Loyola U., Chgo., 1970—, prof. polit. scis., 1974—, chmn. dept., 1974—. Pres. Rosehill Citizens Council, 1971-74. Del. elector Democratic Party, 1974. Bd. dirs. Edgewater Community Council, 1973—. Decorated Legion of Merit, Bronze Star with 2 oak leaf clusters, Combat Inf. badge. Joint grantee Russell Sage Found., 1970; travel grantee Inter-Univ. Seminar, 1971; research grantee Army Research Inst., 1974. Mem. Am. Polit. Sci. Assn., African Studies Assn. (chmn. ann. program 1974), Inter-Univ. Sem. in Armed Forces and Society (asso. chmn. 1973, exec. sec. 1968-72), Pi Sigma Alpha. Author: The Professional Army in a Changing Society, 1975; co-author: Politics and Power, 1975. Editor: The Military-Industrial Complex: A Reassessment, 1972; Revolutionary Guerrila Warfare, 1975. Home: 5948 N Hermitage Ave Chicago IL 60660

SARLEY, VINCENT CHARLES, physician; b. Chgo., Jan. 6, 1919; s. Joseph and Nettie (Friedman) S.; student Loyola U., Chgo., 1938-41; M.B., Chgo. Med. Sch., 1944, M.D., 1945; postgrad. U. Ill., 1958; LL.B., Blackstone Coll. Law, 1952; Ph.D., U. Sussex (Eng.), 1968; m. Millicent Helen Powers, Sept. 3, 1947; children—Robert Charles, Donald Joseph. Intern, Hosp. St. Anthony de Padua, Chgo., 1944-45; resident Municipal TB Sanitarium, Chgo., 1947; practice medicine, specializing in internal medicine, cardiopulmonary diseases, Chgo., 1945—; mem. attending staff, dir. endocrine clinic Ill. Masonic Hosp.; cons. staff Victory Meml., St. Therese hosps., Waukegan, Ill.; dir. med. edn. Sheridan Pavilion Hosp.; chmn. dept. medicine Charity Hosp. Assn.; bd. govs. Doctors Gen. Hosp.; cons. internal medicine Fed. Disability Program; faculty Chgo. Med. Sch., 1945—, now clin. prof., also chmn. sect. Legal medicine; chief med. officer Johns Manville Corp., Waukegon, 1970-72; med. dir. Wright-Wood Extended Care Facility, 1967-70; now corp. mgr. employee health Abbott Lab. Councilor, Chgo. Med. Soc.; vis. lectr. John Marshall Law Sch. Served to capt. M.C. U.S. Army, 1953-55. Fellow Am. Coll. Chest Physicians, Am. Coll. Legal Medicine, Inst. Medicine, Chgo., Am. Soc. Law and Medicine; mem. A.M.A., (3 recognition awards), Am. Soc. Internal Medicine, Internat. Soc. Anesthesiology, Internat. Medico-Legal Soc., Assn. Hosp. Dirs. Med. Edn., Ill. Med. Soc. (com. inter-profl. relations; del.), Chgo. Acad. Law and Medicine (founding), Am. Legion. Mason (32 deg.). Club: Garabaldi Craftsmans (sec.). Contbr. to med. publs. Home: 682 Pine St Deerfield IL 60015

SARPOLUS, MARY THERESE, vocat. instr., computer systems mgr.; b. Detroit, Dec. 5, 1954; d. Victor Sam and Dolores Theresa (Schnaubelt) S.; Assoc. Computer Sci., Marygrove Coll., 1973-77, degree, 1975; grad. Control Data Inst., 1974; postgrad. U. Mich., Flint, 1977—; Clk., computer operator DAB Industries, Troy, Mich., 1975; computer accounting analyst Clintondale Community Schs., Mount Clemens, Mich., 1975, head data processing dept., analyst, 1976—, systems mgr., 1977—, vocat. instr., 1977—. Mem. Mich. Assn. Ednl. Data Systems, Mich. Assn. Computer Users in Learning, Computer Based Instrn. Coordinators, Digital Equipment Computer Uses Soc. Home: 21217 Redmond Ave East Detroit MI 48021 Office: 35200 Little Mack St Mount Clemens MI 48043

SARTIN, BEULAH (MRS. JOSEPH ARTHUR SARTIN), county ofcl., bus. exec.; b. Clinton, Mo., Nov. 20, 1906; d. William E. and Anabel (Jones) Riead; student pub. schs.; m. Joseph Arthur Sartin, Dec. 27, 1929; 1 dau., Dixie (Mrs. Donald O. Batschelett). Tchr. pub. schs., Henry County, Mo., 1924-32; owner, operator Sartin Bookkeeping & Tax Service, Clinton, Mo., 1935—; ofcl. weather observer, 1938-44; co-owner Comml. Loan & Credit Co. Pub. adminstr. Henry County, Mo., 1963—. Chmn. Henry County Easter Seal Campaign, 1962—. Second v.p. Mo. Fedn. Democratic Women. Mem. Ind. Accountants Soc. Mo., Clinton C. of C. (dir.), Nat. Soc. Pub. Accountants, Clinton Bus. and Profl. Women (pres.), Jefferson Club Henry County (pres. 1968—). Baptist. Mem. Order Eastern Star. Club: Clinton Country (dir.). Home: 511 S 8th Clinton MO 64735 Office: 108 E Franklin Clinton MO 64735

SARVER, GARY STEVEN, clin. psychologist, educator; b. Boston, Nov. 20, 1946; s. Samuel and Judith Edith (Keesan) S.; B.A., Boston U., 1969; M.A., U. Fla., 1970, Ph.D., in Psychology, 1973; m. Ann Howland, Sept. 5, 1972; children—Andrea, Joshua. Asst. prof. psychology Ohio U., 1973—; partner Athens Psychology Clinic, Inc. Clin. Psychologists, Athens, Ohio, 1973—; cons. Athens City Schs., O'Bleness Hosp., Athens County Cts. Recipient award Ohio U., 1977; Ohio U. grantee, 1973. Mem. Am., Ohio, Southeast Ohio psychol. assns., Soc. Research Child Devel., Internat. Neurospsychol. Assn. Contbr. articles to, reviewer for profl. jours. Home and Office: 6 Berkeley Dr Athens OH 45701

SARYA, ARNOLD FRED, orthodontist; b. Allouez, Mich., May 16, 1934; s. Arne Edwin and Ethel Suzanne (Petaja) S.; M.S., U. Mo., Kansas City, 1959; D.D.S., U. Mich., 1958; m. Constance Mae Geranen, Sept. 24, 1955; children—Rebecca, Arne, Ann, John, David, Daniel. Orthodontist, Traverse City, Mich., 1960—; chmn. bd., pres. Acad. Dimension Systems, 1971-73; pres., chmn. bd. Glacier Dome and Traverse City Hockey, Inc., 1974—. Founder, bd. dirs. Traverse City Area Found., 1968—; bd. govs. Sch. Dentistry, U. Mich., 1970—. Recipient Others award Salvation Army, 1974, Alumni of Year award U. Mich., 1974. Mem. Mich. Soc. Orthodontists (pres.). Lutheran (past pres. ch.). Club: Kiwanis (pres. 1968). Home: 919 Allouez Trail Traverse City MI 49684 Office: 403 E State St Traverse City MI 49648

SATINOVER, TERRY KLIEMAN, lawyer; b. Chgo., Apr. 25, 1936; d. Charles D. and Mary (Klieman) Satinover; student Shimer Coll., 1952-54; B.A. cum laude, U. Chgo., 1955, J.D. magna cum laude (Weymouth Kirkland scholar), 1958; m. Richard Rees Fagen, June 15, 1958 (div. June 1970); children—Sharon, Ruth, Elizabeth, Michael. Admitted to Ill. bar, 1970; practice in Chicago, 1971—; partner firm Pope, Ballard, Shepard & Fowle, Chgo., 1971—; inquiry panel Ill. Atty. Registration and Disciplinary Commn. Bd. dirs. Congregation Rodfei Zedec, Charles Satinover Fund. Mem. Am. Friends Hebrew U. Order of Coif, Phi Beta Kappa. Jewish (fin. sec. congregation). Home: 5125 S Cornell St Chicago IL 60615 Office: 69 W Washington St Suite 3200 Chicago IL 60602

SATORY, JOHN JOSEPH, surgeon; b. Wabasha, Minn., Feb. 14, 1910; s. Marcus Cosmus and Josephine (Noll) S.; B.S., St. Mary's Coll., 1933, M.B., U. Minn., 1938, M.D., 1939; m. Mina C. Miencke, 1948; children—Christine Jean, John Joseph. Intern, Milw. County Gen. Hosp., 1938-39; resident Milw. County Gen. Hosp., 1939-42; practice medicine specializing in surgery, 1943—; mem. staffs Grandview Hosp., LaCrosse, Wis., chief staff, 1948-54, chief surgery, 1948-69; staff St. Francis Hosp., La Crosse, Wis.; founder, pres. dir. Grandview Clinic, LaCrosse, 1948-67; instr. surgical anatomy Marquette, U., 1940-42; preceptor U. Wis., 1960-65; instr. Mayo Sch. Med., Rochester, Minn., 1977; dir. Wis. Health Care Review, 1969-77; med. dir. LaCrosse Civil Defense, 1954-58; mem. Wis. Bd. Med. Examiners, 1968-72, pres., 1971-72; dir. LaCrosse Cancer Soc., 1952, pres., 1954. Served to maj. U.S. Army, 1942-46. Diplomate Am. Bd. Surgery. Fellow Am. Coll. Surgeons, Internat. Coll. Surgeons (regent Wis. 1975-77), Internat. Acad. Proctology. Mem. Am., Wis., LaCrosse County (pres. 1953) med. assns., Optimists. Republican. Roman Catholic. Clubs: KC, Elks. Contbr. articles to med. jours. Home: 1404 Main St LaCrosse WI 54601 Office: 815 S 10th St LaCrosse WI 54601

SATTLER, LEE ANTHONY, advt. agy. exec.; b. Regent, N.D., July 25, 1920; s. Leo Charles and Clara Marie (White) S.; student Northwestern U., 1942, Monmouth Coll., 1944, U. Ga., 1945; B.A., Fenn Coll., 1947; B.A., (hon.), Cleveland State U., 1964; m. Gertrude Louise Hoffman, June 2, 1949; children—Mary Claire, Neil Raymond, Laura Lee, Steven Charles. Gen. mgr. White Adv. Co., Cleve., 1946-53; pres. Ritchie & Sattler, Inc., Cleve., 1953—, Media Assistance Co., Cleve., 1971—. Served with USNR, 1942-46. Decorated Purple Heart medals, D.F.C., Air medals. Mem. Cleve. Advt. Club, Indsl. Marketers, Am. Legion, V.F.W. K.C. Contbr. articles on electronic and metal working to profl. jours. Created microfilm cassette projector adopted by USN Tng. Command. Home: 3193 Rumson Rd Cleveland Heights OH 44118 Office: 739 Union Commerce Bldg Cleveland OH 44115

SATTLER, THEODORE HERBERT, physician; b. Tyndall, S.D., Aug. 14, 1914; s. John I. and Paulina (Max) S.; B.A., Yankton (S.D.) Coll., 1937; B.S., U. S.D., Vermillion, 1940; M.D., Northwestern U., 1942, M.S., 1948; m. Isabel Frances Reedy, Aug. 30, 1941; children—Ann Lenore, Susan Elizabeth. Intern, Evanston (Ill.) Gen. Hosp., 1942-43; resident in internal medicine Wesley Meml. Hosp., Chgo., 1946-48; practice medicine specializing in internal medicine, Yankton, 1948—; chmn. dept. medicine Sacred Heart Hosp., Yankton, 1950—; clin. prof. medicine U. S.D., 1948-74, prof. internal medicine, 1974—, asst. dean clin. affairs, 1974-76; chmn. regional adv. group S.D. Regional Med. Program and Comprehensive Health Planning Program, 1971; mem. S.D. Health Service Agy., 1976—; med. dir. S.D. State Profl. Standards Orgn., 1977—; mem. S.D. State

Health Systems Agency, 1975—, S.D. State Health Coordination Council, 1976—. Bd. dirs. United Ch. Christ, Yankton, Yankton Coll., Yankton Carnegie Library, Higher Ednl. Facilities State of S.D. Served to maj., M.C., U.S. Army, 1943-46. Named Clin. Prof. of Year, U. S.D., 1969; recipient Alumni Achievement award for profl. excellence Yankton Coll., 1974. Diplomate Am. Bd. Internal Medicine. Fellow A.C.P. (gov. S.D. 1964-70); mem. Am., S.D. (pres. 1962) socs. internal medicine, AMA, Am., S.D. (Distinguished Service award 1958) heart assns., Am. Diabetes Assn., S.D. State (pres. 1973-74), Yankton Dist. med. assns., Sigma Xi. Clubs: Masons, Elks. Contbr. articles in field to med. jours. Home: 1701 Whiting Dr Yankton SD 57078 Office: 400 Park Ave Yankton SD 57078

SAUER, HERBERT IRVIN, epidemiologist-demographer; b. West Alexandria, O., June 13, 1910; s. Irvin Lewis and Lucy (Pontius) S.; B.A., Ohio State U., 1932; M.S. U. Mo., 1965; postgrad. Stanford, 1962; m. Esther Doris Johnson, Sept. 13, 1946; children—Charles H., Lucy H. Statistician-intake supr. Transient Bur., Columbus, O., 1933-35; asst. city supr. consumer purchases study bur. Labor Statistics, Beaver Falls, Pa., 1936; dir. social studies Tb Assn., Los Angeles, 1937-44; med. analyst, supervisory statistician Tb program USPHS, Washington, 1944-56, supervisory statistician Heart Disease and Stroke Control Program, Washington and Columbia, Mo., 1956-70; dir. health demography and statistics, also asst. prof. community health, U. Mo., 1970—. Cons. cardiovascular diseases and trace elements WHO, 1973. Served with U.S. Army, 1942-43. Fellow A.A.A.S., Am. Pub. Health Assn., Am. Heart Assn.; mem. Am. Statis. Assn., Population Assn. Am., Soc. Epidemiological Research, Gerontological Soc., Phi Beta Kappa, Sigma Xi, Alpha Kappa Delta. Contbr. articles in field to profl. jours. Home: 1635 Highridge Circle Columbia MO 65201

SAUER, MARY LOUISE, civic leader; b. Chillicothe, Ohio, June 26, 1923; d. Maurice Edward and Sarah Katherine (Kieffer) Steirhilber; B.A. in Edn., Northwestern U., 1945; postgrad. U. Mo., Kansas City, 1963-64, 70-71; m. Gordon Chenoweth Sauer, Dec. 28, 1944; children—Elisabeth Ruth, Gordon Chenoweth, Margaret Louise, Amy Kieffer. Co-chmn., Kansas City Chamber Choir, pres. Kansas City Philharmonic League, 1959-60; pres. women's com. Conservatory of Music, U. Mo., 1963-64; bd. dirs. regional auditions Met. Opera Guild, 1965-69; bd. dirs., program chmn. Nettleton Home, Kansas City, 1976-77; bd. dirs., women's council U. Mo., Kansas City, Univ. Assos. Recipient Distinguished Achievement Internat. Register Profiles award, 1976; Community Leaders and Noteworthy Americans award, Vol. Teaching Assn., 1970-74. Mem. AAUW, Am. Guild Organists, D.A.R., Northwestern U. Alumni Assn., Lyric Opera Guild, Rotary Wives Club, Kansas City Musical Club, Mu Phi Epsilon, Kappa Delta, Presbyterian. Clubs: Rockhill Tennis, Kansas City, Woman's City. Producer bicentennial pageant, Under the Liberty Tree, 1976. Home: 830 W 58th Terr Kansas City MO 64113

SAUER, WILBUR WATERMAN, optometrist; b. Chgo., Apr. 7, 1918; s. Edwin Henry and Laura Mae (Waterman) S.; B.S., U. Ill., 1944; D. Optometry, Ill. Coll. Optometry, 1948; m. Merna Mae Miller, Sept. 30, 1950; 1 dau., Judith Mae (Mrs. Harold Franklin Beck). Clinical instr. No. Ill. Coll. Optometry, 1947-48; pvt. practice optometry, Paxton, Ill., 1948—. Founder Ford Co. Hist. Soc., 1967; pres. Ill. Congress of Hist. Socs., 1970. Mem. zoning and planning, 1964-70; mem. Paxton Sch. Bd., 1960-64. Bd. dirs., Paxton Hosp., 1954-61, Ill. Hist. Soc., 1967-69. Fellow Am. Acad. Optometry; mem. Ill. Optometric Soc., Am. Optometric Assn. Methodist (mem. bd.). Mason. Home: 10 Meridian Terrace Paxton IL 60957 Office: 145 W Center St Paxton IL 60957

SAUERESSIG, ROBERT, mgmt. scientist, educator; b. Milw., Mar. 9, 1937; s. Louis Alvin and Helen (Pociopa) S.; B.S., U. Wis.-Milw., 1962; M.S., U. Wis.-Madison, 1964, Ph.D., 1969. Instr. bus. adminstrn. and psychology U. Wis., Whitewater, 1965-67, asst. prof. bus. adminstrn., 1967-69, asso. prof. mgmt., 1969-73; lectr. bus. adminstrn. and psychology, U. Md.-European div. Heidelberg, W. Ger., 1974-76; asso. prof. mgmt. U. Wis.-Whitewater, 1976—; cons. indsl. psychologist. Mem. Indsl. Relations Research Assn., Internat. Indsl. Relations Assn., Acad. Mgmt., Midwest Bus. Adminstrn. Assn., Am. Psychol. Assn. Home: 4603 Severson St McFarland WI 53558 Office: Mgmt Dept Coll Bus U Wis-Whitewater Whitewater WI 53190

SAUL, DEE C., accountant; b. Kokomo, Ind., Oct. 24, 1938; s. Don C. and Evelyn C. S.; B.S. in Bus. Adminstrn., Ind. U., 1961; m. Paula A. Nugent, Aug. 2, 1975. Auditor, J.P. Clark & Co., Punta Gorda, Fla., 1965-68, P.R. Mallory & Co., Inc., 1968-69; internal auditor Ind. Blue Cross, Indpls., 1969-70; controller St. Joseph Meml. Hosp., Kokomo, 1970-71; v.p., Ind., Hosp. Assn., Indpls., 1972-75; pres. Dee Saul & Co., Inc., Indpls., 1975—; lectr. grad. program in health adminstrn. Ind. U., C.P.A., Fla., Ind. Mem. Am. Inst. of C.P.A.s, Ind. Assn. of C.P.A.s, Hosp. Fin. Mgmt. Assn. Clubs: Economic (Indpls.). Home: 5718 Winthrop Ave Indianapolis IN 46220 Office: 1717 W 86th St Suite 300 Indianapolis IN 46260

SAUL, RICHARD CUSHMAN, pediatrician, allergist; b. Boston, Aug. 23, 1936; s. John Stanley and Shirley (Cushman) S.; A.B., Washington and Jefferson, 1957; M.D., 1961; m. Yolanda Merdinger, Jan. 1, 1967; children—Bradley, Eric, Jason. Intern, Michael Reese Hosp., Chgo., 1961-62; resident Childrens Meml. Hosp., Chgo., 1962-64, mem. med. bd. dirs., 1969-77; pvt. practice medicine specializing in pediatrics, allergy, Northbrook, Ill., 1966-76; instr. Northwestern U. Sch. Medicine, Chgo., 1966-74; asso. prof. pediatrics U. Health Sciences, The Chgo. Med. Sch., 1974, lectr., mem. deans advisory group, 1975—; med. dir. Barwell Clinic, Waukegan, Ill., com. chmn., infant and preschool child, 1974-77; cons. pediatrics U.S. Navy, 1975—; bd. dirs. Kane, Lake, Mc Henry Health Systems Agency, 1975—, Barwell Settlement, Waukegan, 1975—. Served to capt., pediatric cons., U.S. Army, 1964-66. Fellow Chgo. Inst. Medicine, Am. Acad. Pediatrics, Am. Coll. Allergists; mem. AMA, Ill. Med. Soc., Chgo. Med. Soc. Congregationalist. Developed scientific exhibit on infant feeding used by Am. Osteopathic Assn., 1972, AMA, 1973; lectr. in field to civic groups. Home: 2091 Old Briar Rd Highland Park IL 60035 Office: 1500 Shermer Rd Northbrook IL 60076

SAUNDERS, CARYLN LEE, counselor; b. Ottawa, Kans., Jan. 11, 1943; d. Caryl Newton and Mona Merle (Eaton) Saunders; B.A., U. Kans., 1965; M.A. (teaching asst.), U. Mo., Kansas City, 1969, Ph.D. (Jack C. Coffey scholar, teaching asst.), 1978; children—Amy Christine Rhoads, Heather Eileen Rhoads. Office mgr. Operation Discovery Sch., Kansas City, 1971-72; psychometrician Center Behavioral Devel., Overland Park, Kans., 1973-76; counselor Meadowlake Counseling Center, Kansas City, 1976—; intern counselor S. Kansas City Mental Health Network, Mo., 1976-77; psychotherapist Gardner Community Med. Center (Kans.), 1977—; rep. on bd. dirs. Shawnee Mission Assn. Gifted, 1976-77. Home: 5048 Reeds Rd Mission KS 66202 Office: Gardner Community Medical Center Gardner KS 66030

SAUNDERS, IVERIN, city ofcl.; b. Chgo., Aug. 13, 1928; s. Wendell Phillip and Bessie (Miller) S.; student Roosevelt U., 1948-49, Northwestern U., 1956, Wis. U., 1951-53; Cornell U., 1965; children—Steven C., Dawn M., Kimberly A., Jesse I. Case worker Chgo. Bd. Health, 1956-59; fgn. quarantine officer USPHS, 1959-64; systems accountant U.S. Postal Data Center, N.Y.C., 1964-69; data processing coordinator, Dept. Environmental Control, City Chgo., 1969—. Aquatic dir. Boy Scout Summer Camps; candidate Ill. Legislature, 1978. Served with USNR, 1945-55. Decorated Purple Heart. Recipient certificate of appreciation USPHS, 1959, WHO, 1954. Mem. Am. Legion, Disabled Am. Vets., Kappa Alpha Psi. Home: 5300 South Shore Dr Chicago IL 60615 Office: 320 N Clark St Chicago IL 60610

SAUNDERS, JOHN MATTHEW, realtor; b. Indpls., Feb. 17, 1943; s. Paul Douglas and Dora Rebecca (Polen) S.; student Purdue U., 1965; m. Marilyn Sue Bemis, July 14, 1972; children—Jeffrey Alan, Kathy Sue. Salesman, F.C. Tucker Co., Indpls., 1968-72; partner, v.p. Four Seasons, Inc., Indpls., 1972-77; pres. Mooresville Furniture Co., Inc., 1975—, Saunders Co. Investments, Indpls., 1975—, Saunders Co., Realtors, Mooresville, Ind., 1977—. Named Morgan County Realtor of Year, 1976. Mem. Morgan County Bd. Realtors (pres. 1976), Indpls. Bd. Realtors, Ind. Assn. Realtors, Nat. Assn. Realtors, Mooresville Mchts. Assn. Home: 164 Hillcrest Dr Mooresville IN 46158 Office: 9 West Main St Mooresville IN 46158

SAUNDERS, KATHERINE, univ. adminstr.; b. Teaneck, N.J.; d. Alfred R. and Katherine M. (Krall) Saunders; B.A., Trenton State Coll., 1962; M.S., U. Wis., 1966, Ph.D., 1977. Teaching asst., women's phys. edn. U. Wis., Madison, 1964-66, instr., 1966-74, dir. women's intercollegiate athletics, 1974—; founder Wis. Women's Intercollegiate Conf., 1971, sec.-treas., 1971-73; mem. Wis. Gov.'s Commn. Sports Phys. Fitness, 1975—; bd. dirs. Madison Met. YMCA, 1977—. Mem. Wis. Assn. Girls Women's Sports (past pres.). Office: U Wis Madison WI 53706

SAUNDERS, RICHARD SEAVEY, ret. piping distbg. co. exec.; b. Chgo., June 15, 1902; s. Henry T. and Harriet (Seavey) S.; B.S.C., U. Ill., 1924; postgrad. Northwestern U., 1934-40; m. Edith Guyton, Dec. 15, 1940; children—Eleanor (Mrs. J. Trenton Kostabe), Richard Guyton, Pamela (Mrs. Andrew Sabin). Sales corr. U.S. Steel Corp., Chgo., 1926; supr. Conn. Mut. Life Ins. Co., Cin., 1926-28; sales promotion Wheeling Steel Co., Chgo., 1928-30; salesman Midland Pipe and Supply Co., Chgo., 1930-32; with Saunders and Co., Chgo., after 1933, then chmn. bd.; now ret. Bd. dirs. Chgo. Credit Bur., 1956-59, Abraham Lincoln Centre. Served from lt. (j.g.) to comdr. USNR, 1942-45. Mem. Central Supply Assn. (com. chmn.), Phi Kappa Alpha, Alpha Delta Sigma. Unitarian (treas. Midwest Unitarian Universalist conf.). Home: 9534 Harding Ave Evanston IL 60203

SAVA, SAMUEL GEORGE, research inst. exec.; b. Farrell, Pa., July 12, 1931; s. George and Mary (Karavolis) S.; B.S., Slippery Rock State Coll., 1953; M.S., Westminster Coll., 1955; postgrad. 1959; postgrad. U. Md., 1959-60; D.Ed., The Am. U., 1964; LL.D., Central State U., 1975; m. Elizabeth H. Tsourounis, Feb. 19, 1966; children—Anna Lise, George Samuel. Tchr., elementary and adult edn. Farrell (Pa.) Pub. Sch. System, 1953-55; prin. Washington Sch., Farrell, Pa., 1958-59, Lyndon Hill Sch. Prince Georges County, Md., 1959-61; exec. officer, div. elementary and secondary edn. U.S. Office Edn., Washington, 1961-63, program officer div. handicapped children and youth, 1963-64, deputy dir., div. edn. personnel training, 1964-65, dir., div. higher edn. research, and div. elementary and secondary research, 1965-67; v.p. edn. and urban affairs Charles F. Kettering Found., exec. dir. Inst. Devel. Edn. Activities, Inc., Dayton, Ohio, 1967—; adj. prof. edn. Wright State U., Dayton, 1968—; cons. Office of Overseas Schs., U.S. State Dept., Washington, 1968—. Trustee, Central State U., Wilberforce Ohio. Served with USNR, 1955-58. Recipient superior service award HEW, 1965, quality performance award, U.S. Office Edn., 1966. Mem. Am. Assn. Sch. Adminstrs., Am. Edn. Research Assn., Am. Mgmt. Assn., Assn. Supervision and Curriculum Devel., Nat. Assn. Edn. Young Children, Naval Res. Officers Assn., Res. Officers' Assn., Phi Delta Kappa. Greek Orthodox. Author: Learning Through Discovery for Young Children, 1975. Contbr. to profl. publs. in field. Home: 7800 Rain Tree Rd Centerville OH 45498 Office: 5335 Far Hills Ave Kettering OH 45429

SAVAGE, AUGUSTUS ALEXANDER, newspaper editor and publisher; b. Detroit, Oct. 30, 1925; s. Thomas and Mollie (Wilder) S.; B.A. in Philosophy, Roosevelt U., 1951; postgrad. Chgo.-Kent Coll. Law, 1951-53; m. Eunice King, Aug. 4, 1946; children—Thomas James, Emma Mae. Editor, Am. Negro Mag., 1955-56, Woodlawn Booster, Chgo., 1961-65, Bull. Newspaper, 1963-65; asst. editor Ill. Beverage Jour., 1956-59; editor, pub. Westside Booster, Chgo., 1959-60, Citizen Newspapers, Chgo., 1965—; pub. The Chgo. Weekend Newspaper, 1974—. Chmn., Protest at the Polls, 1963, Coalition for a Black Mayoral Candidate, 1977. Democratic candidate U.S. Ho. of Reps., 1968, 70. Served with USAAF, 1943-46. Recipient Citizenship award Operation PUSH, 1976, Medal of Merit City of Chgo., 1976. Mem. Orgn. for S.W. Communities (pres. 1969-70), Chgo. League Negro Voters (founder, campaign mgr. 1958-59). Home: 3041 S Michigan Ave Chicago IL 60616 Office: 748 W 103d St Chicago IL 60628

SAVAGE, BARRY EMERY, lawyer; b. Jackson, Mich., Apr. 19, 1940; s. Herbert E. and Marva V. (Schultz) S.; B.A. in Econ., U. Mich., 1962, J.D., 1965; m. Joyce A. Diaz, Oct. 6, 1977; 1 son by previous marriage, Steven Vincent. Admitted to Ohio bar, 1965, Mich. bar, 1966; practice in Toledo, 1965—; with firm Brogan, Savage, Gibson & Yarbrough, Toledo; engaged in real estate investment, 1968—. Trustee, Sunshine Children's Home. Licensed real estate broker, Ohio. Mem. Mich., Toledo (chmn. unauthorized practice com. 1970-72) bar assns. Clubs: Jolly Roger Sailing (Toledo); Indian Hills Boat (Maumee, Ohio). Office: Brogan Savage Gibson & Yarbrough 228 N Erie St Toledo OH 43624

SAVAGE, CARL CLAYTON, educator; b. Golddust, Tenn., Dec. 15, 1926; s. Marvin Porter and Elsie Mary Lee (Scallions) S.; B.A., Belmont Coll., 1957; M.R.E., New Orleans Bapt. Sem., 1959; Ed.D., New Orleans Bapt. Sem., 1966; postgrad. Duke U., 1966, U. Colo., 1967-68, St. Cloud State U., 1968-71, U. Minn., 1972; m. Marilyn A. Sako; 1 son, Carl Clayton. Broadcast engr., announcer WKRM Radio, Columbia, Tenn., 1947-48; marine radio dispatcher, WJG Marine Radio Sta., Memphis, 1948-52; electronic engr. R.C.A., Memphis, 1952-54; engr., TV prodn. staff mem. WYES-TV, New Orleans, 1957-59; studio prodn. engr. WWL-TV, New Orleans, 1959-61, WLAC-TV, Nashville, 1962-63; studio prodn. supr. WYES-TV, ETV, New Orleans, 1962-63; instr. audio-visual edn. New Orleans Bapt. Sem., 1962-63; asst. dir. pub. relations, asst. prof. speech Gardner-Webb Coll., Boiling Springs, N.C., 1963-64; dir. info. services, instr. speech High Point (N.C.) Coll., 1964-67; prof. psychology Rockmont Coll., Denver, 1967-68; asso. prof. library, audiovisual edn. and learning resources services St. Cloud (Minn.) State Coll., 1968—. Non-print reviewer for Booklist, St. Cloud, 1969-73; cons. Ednl. Media Center, Montevideo, Minn., 1968-69, State Welfare and Corrections Library Services, Wilmar, Minn., 1972-74; exec. chmn. Carolinas Coll. News Seminar, 1963-66, founder, 1963; faculty Central Assn. Sem. Extension, High Point, N.C., 1965; mem. M.I. Smith Leadership Conf., of Minn., 1972—. Bloodmobile Vol. ARC, High Point, N.C., 1966. Bd. dirs. Atwood Coll. Center Council, 1973-76, pres., 1974—; trustee Camp Lebenon, Upsala, Minn., 1971-73. Served with USNR, 1945-46; ETO. Mem. ALA, Assn. Ednl. Communication and Tech., Am. Assn. Sch. Librarians, Assn. Am. Library Schs., NEA, Minn. Edn. Assn., Inter-Faculty Orgn., Minn. Library Assn., Audiovisual Communications Assn. Minn., Internat. Brotherhood Elec. Workers, St. Cloud C. of C., Phi Delta Kappa. Baptist (deacon 1950-54). Kiwanian. Writer-producer slide-tape program: The Information Lift Process, 1974; The Auditory Process, 1973. Contbr. articles to profl. jours. Home: 1220 S 11th Ave St Cloud MN 56301 Office: Learning Resources Center St Cloud State U St Cloud MN 56301

SAVAGE, EARL JOHN, educator; b. Uniontown, Pa., Feb. 28, 1931; s. Earl Edward and Emma Louise (Stetz) S.; B.S. in Biology, Waynesburg (Pa.) Coll., 1957; M.S. in Plant Pathology, W.Va. U., Morgantown, 1960, Ph.D. in Plant Pathology, 1963; m. Rosemary Ann Lazaran, July 14, 1961; 1 son, Steven Elliot. Research asst. W.Va. U., 1957-62; instr. biology, head dept. biology Lewis Coll., Lockport, Ill., 1962-63; asst. prof. U. Notre Dame (Ind.), 1963-68; asst. prof. botany Ind. U. at South Bend, 1968-70, asso. prof., 1970—, chmn. dept. biol. scis., 1971—. Cons. Bendix Corp., Mishawaka, Ind., 1964-65, Ball Band div. U.S. Rubber Co., Mishawaka, 1964—. Served with U.S. Army, 1952-54. NSF grantee, 1962-64. Mem. A.A.A.S., Am. Inst. Biol. Scis., Mycol. Soc. Am., Ind. Acad. Scis., Nat. Audubon Soc. Home: 15667 Spring Mill Dr Mishawaka IN 46544 Office: 1825 Northside Blvd South Bend IN 46615

SAVAGE, ROBERT CHARLES, ins. exec.; b. Toledo, Dec. 25, 1937; s. John N. and Kathryn (Fox) S.; B.B.A., U. Toledo, 1959; m. Susan Foeller, May 21, 1966; children—Robert John, Lisa Marie, Eric George, Michelle Kathryn. Mark Jerome. Partner, Savage Ins. Agy., Toledo, 1960—; pres. John F. Savage & Assos., Inc., Toledo. Mem. Toledo City Council, 1963, 65, 67; vice mayor, Toledo, 1967-69. Chmn. Riverside Hosp. Bldg. Commn. Vice chmn. bd. trustees Bowling Green (O.) State U.; trustee Toledo Opera Assn. Served with U.S. Army, 1961-62. Recipient U. Toledo Pacemaker award, 1965; named Outstanding Cath. Young Man of Year, 1960, Toledo Jr. C. of C. Outstanding Young Man of Year, 1964. C.L.U. Mem. Toledo Life Underwriters Assn., Million Dollar Round Table. Home: 2949 Kenwood Blvd Toledo OH 43606 Office: 4427 Talmadge Rd Toledo OH 43623

SAVAGE, ROBERT ENGLEBERT, veterinarian; b. Spencer, Iowa, June 21, 1917; s. Guy David and Hattie Ruth (Knudson) S.; D.V.M., Iowa State U., 1943; m. Josephine May Ricklefs, June 11, 1943; children—David, Susan (Mrs. Larry Eilers), John. Practice veterinary medicine, Monticello, Iowa, 1946—; dist. veterinarian Iowa Dept. Agr., 1973—. Councilman-at-large City of Monticello, 1968—. Served to capt. AUS, 1943-46. Recipient Silver Beaver award Boy Scouts Am., 1959, Iowa Woodland Owner of Year award, 1976. Mem. Am. Iowa, E. Central Iowa (pres. 1950), Eastern Iowa (pres. 1957) vet. med. assns., Iowa Polled Shorthorn Cattle Assn. (pres. 1968-69), Am. Legion, Alpha Gamma Rho. Republican. Congregationalist. Mason, Rotarian. Contbr. articles to profl. publs. Address: 200 S Chestnut St Monticello IA 52310

SAVELKOUL, DONALD CHARLES, lawyer; b. Mpls., July 29, 1917; s. Theodore Charles and Edith (Lindgren) S.; B.A. magna cum laude, U. Minn., 1939; B.S. cum laude, William Mitchell Coll. Law, 1950, J.D., cum laude, 1951; m. Mary Joan Holland, May 17, 1941; children—Jeffrey Charles, Jean Marie, Edward Joseph. Admitted to Minn. bar, 1951; adminstrv. work various U.S. govt. depts., including Commerce, War, Labor, Wage Stblzn. Bd., 1940-51; municipal judge, Fridley, Minn., 1952-54; law practice, Mpls. and Fridley, 1951—; Chmn. bd. Fridley State Bank, 1962—, Blaine State Bank; pres. Banrein, Inc., Blaine Bldg. Corp., Babbscha Co. Mem. faculty Wm. Mitchell Coll. Law, 1952-59; corp. mem. Wm. Mitchell Coll. Law, 1956—; sec. Fridley Recreation and Service Co., 1955—; treas. Gottwaldt Investment Co., 1975—. Mem. Minn. Legislature, 1967-69. Mem. Gov.'s Com. Workman's Compensation, 1965-67, Gov.'s Adv. Council on Employment Security, 1957-69. Chmn. Fridley Police Civil Service Commn., 1962-63. Served 1st lt. AUS, 1943-46. Decorated Bronze Star. Mem. Hennepin County, Minn. Am. bar assns. Am. Trial Lawyers Assn., Lawyers Guild St. Thomas More, Am. Legion, Phi Beta Kappa. Roman Catholic. K.C. (4 deg.). Clubs: Midland Hills Country, Alexandria Country, U. Minn. Alumni. Home: 916 W Moore Lake Dr Fridley MN 55432 Office: Fridley State Bank Bldg 6315 University Ave NE Fridley MN 55432

SAVIN, RONALD RICHARD, chem. co. exec.; b. Cleve., Oct. 16, 1926; s. Samuel and Ada (Silver) S.; student U. Cin., 1944-46; B.A. in Chemistry and Lit., U. Mich., 1948; postgrad. La Sorbonne (Paris, France), 1949-50; grad. Air War Coll., 1975; postgrad. Indsl. Coll. Armed Forces, 1975. m. Gloria Ann Hopkins, Apr. 21, 1962; children—Danielle Elizabeth, Andre Lianne. Vice pres. Premium Finishes, Inc., Cin., 1957-58, pres., owner, 1958—. Active Boy Scouts Am. Served with USAF, 1950-55; ETO, Korea; lt. col. Res. Mem. Soc. Mfg. Engrs. (sr.), A.I.M. (pres.'s council), Air Force Assn., Cin. Engring. Soc., Fedn. Paint Techs., Res. Officers Assn., Cin. C. of C. Clubs: Curzon House (London, Eng.); Desert Island Country (Palm Springs, Calif.). Mem. mgmt. adv. council Chem. Week Mag. Home: 7864 Ridge Rd Cincinnati OH 45237 Office: 10448 Chester Rd Cincinnati OH 45215

SAVOIE, LEONARD NORMAN, transp. co. exec.; b. Manchester, N.H., Aug. 8, 1928; s. Joseph Peter and Angelina (Desmarais) S.; B.S., Queen's U., 1952; M.B.A., U. Detroit, 1955; m. Elsie Anne Berscht, June 9, 1951; children—Deborah Anne, Judith Lynn, Andrew Peter. Indsl. engr. Kelsey-Hayes Can. Ltd., Windsor, Ont., Can., 1952-60; mgmt. cons. P.S. Ross & Partners, Toronto, Ont., 1960-64; pres., gen. mgr. Kelsey-Hayes Can. Ltd., 1964-70; pres., chief exec. officer Algoma Central Ry., Sault Ste Marie, Ont., 1970—; dir. Algoma Steel Corp. Ltd., All Canadian-Am. Investments Ltd., Pacific Atlantic Canadian Investment Co. Ltd., Thibodeau Express Ltd. Bd. dirs. United Appeal. Mem. Profl. Engrs. Ont., Engring. Inst. Can., Canadian, Sault Ste Marie chambers commerce. Clubs: Rotary, Toronto Railway, Sault Ste Marie Golf. Home: 19 Atlas St Sault Ste Marie ON Canada Office: 289 Bay St Sault Ste Marie ON Canada

SAWADISAVI, ATKAVI, surgeon; b. Bangkok, Thailand, May 19, 1942; came to U.S., 1967, naturalized, 1973; M.D., Chulalongkokn Med. Sch., Bangkok, Thailand, 1966; m. Dharmapanij; children—Eusanie, Suriya. Intern, Women's and Children's Hosp., Bangkok, 1966-67, Misericordia Hosp., N.Y.C., 1967-68; resident in surgery Albert Einstein Med. Center, Phila., 1968-69, Baroness Erlanger Hosp., Chattanooga, 1969-71, Bapt. Hosp., Nashville, 1971-73; attending surgeon Pinckneyville (Ill.) Community Hosp., 1973—, Community Hosp. of the Valleys, Perris, Calif.; cons. surgeon Sparta (Ill.) Community Hosp., Marshall Browning Hosp., Duquoin, Ill. Diplomate Am. Bd. Surgery. Fellow A.C.S., Internat. Coll. Surgeons; mem. AMA. Home: Route 2 Box 168-A1 Pinckneyville IL 62274 Office: 206 N Main St Pinckneyville IL 62274

SAWICKI, JOHN EDWARD, adminstrv. chem. engr.; b. Phila., Mar. 10, 1944; s. John Louis and Frances Theresa (Cimoch) S.; B.S. in Chem. Engring., Drexel U., 1967, M.S. (NIH trainee), 1968; Ph.D. (Memminger fellow, NDEA fellow, Univ. fellow), U. Va., 1972; m.

Geraldine Aileen Rogalski, Feb. 20, 1971; children—Christian John, Mara Beth. Sr. research officer, chem. engring. research group Council Sci. and Indsl. Research, Pretoria, Republic S. Africa, 1972-74; research devel. engr., group leader research staff, Jos. Schlitz Brewing Co., Milw., 1974—. Mem. Am. Inst. Chem. Engrs., Sigma Xi. Contbr. articles to profl. jours.; patentee in field. Home: 1722 W Bonniwell Rd Mequon WI 53092

SAWINSKI, VINCENT JOHN, educator; b. Chgo., Mar. 28, 1925; s. Stanley and Pearl (Gapinski) S.; B.S., Loyola U., 1948, M.A., 1950, Ph.D., 1962; m. Florence Whitman, Aug. 24, 1952; children—Christine Frances, Michael Patrick. Instr., asst. prof. chemistry, physiology and pharmacology Loyola U., Chgo., 1949-67; supervisory research chemist VA, Hines, Ill., 1961-66; asso. prof. chemistry, phys. sci. Chgo. City Coll., 1967-71, prof., 1971—, chmn. phys. sci. dept. Wright campus, 1971—. Served with U.S. Army, 1945-46. Fellow A.A.A.S., Am. Inst. Chemists; mem. Am. Chem. Soc., Biophys. Soc., N.Y. Acad. Sci., Nat. Sci. Tchrs. Assn., Internat. Assn. for Dental Research. Sigma Xi. Contbr. articles to profl. jours. Home: 1945 N 77th Ct Elmwood Park IL 60635 Office: 3400 N Austin Ave Chicago IL 60634

SAWYER, GLEN THOMAS, neurologist; b. Mpls., Sept. 8, 1933; s. Glen Chester and Charlotte Isabelle (Lane) S.; B.A., U. Minn., 1955, B.S., 1956, M.D., 1958; m. Roberta Louise Stephens, Sept. 5, 1959; children—Stephen Thomas, Amy Louise. Rotating intern So. Pacific Gen. Hosp., San Francisco, 1958-59; resident neurology U. Minn., 1959-62; staff neurologist VA Hosp., Mpls., 1964-69, 76—; practice medicine specializing in neurology Mpls. Clinic Psychiatry and Neurology, 1969-76; mem. exec. com. Luth. Deaconess Hosp., Mpls., 1972-73, sec. to med. staff, 1973-75, treas. med. staff, 1975-76. Served to lt. comdr. USNR, 1962-64. Diplomate Am. Bd. Psychiatry and Neurology. Fellow Am. Acad. Neurology. Methodist (chmn. adminstrv. bd. 1974). Contbr. articles to profl. publs. Home: 10631 Utica Rd Minneapolis MN 55437 Office: Neurology Sect VA Hosp Minneapolis MN 55417

SAWYER, HAROLD SAMUEL, congressman, lawyer; b. San Francisco, Mar. 21, 1920; s. Harold S. and Agnes (McGugan) S.; B.A., U. Calif. at Berkeley, 1940, LL.B., 1943; m. Marcia C. Steketee, Aug. 26, 1944; children—Stephen R., David H., Keary W., Mariya S. Admitted to Mich. bar, 1946, since practiced in Grand Rapids, Mich.; mem. firm Warner, Norcross and Judd, 1950—; pros. atty. Kent County (Mich.), 1975-76; mem. 95th Congress from 5th Mich. dist. Vice pres., dir. Grand Hotel, Mackinac Island, 1957-76; chmn. bd. Citation Cos., Inc., Grand Rapids, Kysor Indsl. Corp., Cadillac, Mich. Spl. legal counsel Gov. Romney, 1962; mem. Mich. Law Revision Commn., 1967—. Pres., bd. dirs. D. A. Blodgett Home for Children, 1950-61. Served to lt. (j.g.) USNR, 1943-45. Fellow Internat. Acad. Trial Lawyers (dir. 1964—), Internat. Soc. Barristers, Am. Coll. Trial Lawyers; mem. Am. Law Inst. Home: 11195 Summit Ave Rockford MI 49341 Office: 1 Vandenberg Center Grand Rapids MI 49502

SAWYER, JOHN, profl. football team exec.; s. Charles Sawyer; m. Ruth Sawyer; children—Anne, Elizabeth, Catherine, Mary. Pres., part owner Cin. Bengals Nat. Football League team; pres. J. Sawyer Co., Ohio, Miss., Mont., Wyo. Home: Cincinnati OH Office: 8050 Hosbrook Ct Cincinnati OH 45236

SAWYER, KATHERINE H. (MRS. CHARLES BALDWIN SAWYER), librarian; b. Cleve., July 11, 1908; d. Willard and Martha (Beaumont) Hirsh; A.B., Smith Coll., 1930; M.S. in Library Sci., Western Res. U., 1956; m. Charles Baldwin Sawyer, Aug. 19, 1933; children—Samuel Prentiss, Charles Brush, William Beaumont. With Cleve. Pub. Library, profl. librarian hosps., instns. dept., 1956-61; med. librarian St. Luke's Hosp., Pittsfield, Mass., 1965-66; library cons. Ministry of Health, Guyana, S.Am., 1966-68; curator Sophia Smith Collection, Smith Coll., 1970-71; parish librarian St. Paul's Episcopal Ch., Cleveland Heights, Ohio, 1971—. Library chmn. exec. com. Garden Center of Greater Cleve., 1959-65; chmn. Friends of Western Res. Hist. Library, 1971—. Bd. mgrs. Episcopal Ch. Home, 1954—, pres., 1961-64, trustee, 1965—; bd. govs. Western Res. U., 1957-66, bd. visitors Sch. Library Sci., 1958-68, 69—; trustee Friends of Cleve. Pub. Library, 1962-67, Christian Residences Found., 1976—; counselor Friends of Smith Coll. Library, 1962-68. Mem. ALA, Ohio Library Assn., Western Res. Hist. Soc., Archeol. Inst., Spl. Libraries Assn., Nat. League Am. Pen Women. Episcopalian (vestryman 1974-77). Clubs: Union, Kirtland Country; Intown. Co-author (talking books for blind) Gardening for Blind Persons, 1962; Beauty, Glamour and Style, 1963. Home: 17485 Shelburne Rd Cleveland OH 44118

SAWYER, ROBERT LEONARD, SR., clergyman, educator; b. Akron, Ohio, July 17, 1922; s. Thomas Willard and Estella Anna Mae (Moyer) S.; A.B., Eastern Nazarene Coll., 1945, Th.B., 1946; B.D., Nazarene Theol. Sem., 1951; Th.M., Central Baptist Theol. Sem., 1952, Th.D., 1959; m. Dorothy Madelyn Ellwanger, June 17, 1952; children—Robert Leonard, William Thomas. Ordained to ministry Ch. of the Nazarene, 1948; minister of music Beverly Ch. of the Nazarene, 1944-45, St. Paul's Ch. of the Nazarene, Kansas City, Mo., 1949-54, Oklahoma City 1st Ch. of the Nazarene, 1954-55; pastor Warwick (Ohio) Ch. of the Nazarene, 1946-49; instr. Hebrew, Nazarene Theol. Sem., Kansas City, 1952-54, vis. prof., 1967-68; prof. Bibl. langs. and lit. Bethany (Okla.) Nazarene Coll., 1954-67; chmn. div. ch. related service, prof. Bibl. langs. and lit. Mid-Am. Nazarene Coll., Olathe, Kans., 1967—. Bd. dirs. Olathe Pub. Library. Recipient Quadrennial Citation of Merit as outstanding prof. Ch. of the Nazarene, 1976. Mem. Soc. Bibl. Lit., Archeol. Soc., Am. Creation Soc., Soc. Religion, Evang., Wesleyan theol. socs., Nazarene Theol. Sem. Alumni Assn. (pres. 1968-72), Kansas City Soc. Theol. Studies. Author: Beacon Bible Commentary, Vol. II, I and II Chronicles, 1965; mem. transl. com. New American Standard Bible, 1969-71. Home: 14513 Locust Dr Olathe KS 66061 Office: Mid-America Nazarene Coll Box 1776 Olathe KS 66061

SAWYER, ROBERT MCLARAN, educator; b. St. Louis, Nov. 12, 1929; s. Lee McLaran and Harrie (Alcock) S.; B.S., S.E. Mo. State Coll., 1952; M.A., U. Ill., 1953; Ph.D., U. Mo., 1966; m. Patricia Ann Covert, Nov. 23, 1955; children—Ann Marie, Lee McLaran, Gail Louise. Tchr., Rolla (Mo.) Pub. Schs., 1955; faculty U. Mo., Rolla, 1956-67; faculty history of edn. U. Nebr., Lincoln, 1967—, chmn. dept. history and philosophy of edn., 1975—. Vis. prof. Ark. State U., Jonesboro, summer 1966. Served with U.S. Army, 1953-55. Mem. Orgn. Am. Historians, History of Edn. Soc., Am. Ednl. Studies Assn., Soc. Profs. Edn., Phi Alpha Theta, Phi Delta Kappa. Author: The History of the University of Nebraska 1929-1969, 1973. Home: 2640 S 35th St Lincoln NE 68506

SAX, EDWARD LEE, banker; b. Evergreen Park, Ill., Aug. 27, 1937; s. George D. and Rhoda (Bronstein) S.; B.A., U. Ams., Mexico City, Mexico, 1960, postgrad., 1965; m. Barbara M. Werner, Mar. 11, 1962. Exec. dir. Sax Enterprises, Inc., Miami, Fla., 1956-60; dir. Exchange Nat. Bank Chgo., 1960-62, rep., 1962-63, asst. to chmn., 1963, v.p., asst. chmn., from 1965, later sr. v.p., also dir., now chmn. exec. com.; pres. Lincolnshire Fin. Services, Miami, Fla. Mem. adv. council Navy League U.S., 1957—. Served with AUS, 1957-58. Mem. Am. Bankers Assn., Am. Econs. Soc., Phi Epsilon Pi. Club: University (Mexico City); National Exchange of Miami Beach (Fla.). Home: 910 N Lake Shore Dr Chicago IL 60611 Office: 130 S LaSalle St Chicago IL 60690

SAX, JANET BERMAN, pediatrician; b. Toledo, Feb. 6, 1924; d. Carl H. and Lillian (Shapiro) Berman; B.S., U. Mich., Ann Arbor, 1948; M.D., Western Res. U., 1953; div.; children—Steven, Richard, Leonard. Rotating intern Jefferson Davis Hosp., Houston, 1953-54; resident in pediatrics Children's Hosp., San Francisco, 1960-62; fellow in juvenile diabetes Babies and Children's Hosp., Cleve., 1963-64; practice medicine specializing in pediatrics, San Francisco, 1962-63; founding pediatrician Ohio Permanente Med. Group, Cleve., 1964—; mem. staff Kaiser Found. Hosps., 1964—; cons. Juvenile Diabetes Clinic, Rainbow Babies and Children's Hosp., 1965—, asst. clin. prof. pediatrics, 1973; asso. vis. pediatrician Mt. Sinai Hosp., 1966; sr. clin. instr. dept. community health Sch. Medicine, Case Western Res. U., 1975. Active United Torch Services of Cleve.; mem. allocations com. Health Fund Greater Cleve., 1976—, priorities determination com., 1976-77; trustee Am. Jewish Com., 1976—. Licensed pediatrician, Ohio, Tex., Calif. Diplomate Am. Bd. Pediatrics. Fellow Am. Acad. Pediatrics; mem. Cleve. Acad. Medicine, Ohio State Med. Assn., No. Ohio Pediatric Soc., Mt. Sinai Med. Soc., Am. Diabetes Assn., Diabetes Assn. Greater Cleve. Jewish. Contbr. article to New Eng. Jour. Medicine, Yearbook Pediatrics; med. editor Diabetes Newsletter Greater Cleve. Home: 18128 Scottsdale Blvd Shaker Heights OH 44122 Office: Kaiser Health Found 50 Severance Circle Cleveland Heights OH 44118

SAX, MARY RANDOLPH, speech pathologist; b. Pontiac, Mich., July 13, 1925; d. Bernard Angus and Ada Lucile (Thurman) TePoorten; B.A. magna cum laude, Mich. State U., 1947; M.A., U. Mich., 1949; m. William Martin Sax, Feb. 7, 1948. Supr. speech correction dept. Waterford Twp. Schs., Pontiac, 1949-69; lectr. Marygrove Coll., Detroit, 1971-72; pvt. practice speech and lang. rehab., Wayne, Oakland Counties, Mich., 1973—; Mem. Sci. Council Stroke Am. Heart Assn. Grantee Inst. Articulation and Learning, 1969, others. Mem. Am. Speech and Hearing Assn., Mich. Speech Pathologists in Clin. Practice, Mich. Speech and Hearing Assn. Mich. Heart Assn. (stroke com. Oakland County), AAUW, LWV. Theta Alpha Pi, Phi Kappa Phi, Kappa Delta Pi. Contbr. articles to profl. jours. Home and Office: 31320 Woodside Franklin MI 48025

SAXENA, SWARAN LAL, marketing exec.; b. Haripur, Pakistan, Jan. 18, 1934; s. Beli Ram and Ram Kali (Nanda) S.; came to U.S., 1964, naturalized, 1972; B.A., Panjab U. (India), 1955; M.S., No. Ill. U., 1966; m. Shiv Kumari Seth, July 17, 1956; children—Gunita, Ursula, Meena. Taxation inspector Excise and Taxation Dept., India, 1956-64; account exec. Market Research Corp. Am., Chgo., 1966-69; dir. research planning Burgoyne Inc., Cin., 1970-71, dir. consumer research, 1972-73; mktg. research mgr. Peter Eckrich & Sons, Inc., Ft. Wayne, Ind., 1974—; part-time mktg. instr. St. Francis Coll., Ft. Wayne, 1977-78; seminar dir. seminars on consumer research Am. Mktg. Assn., 1972, on sales mgmt., 1972, on product planning, 1973, on application marketing research, 1974, on usage of census data, 1976. Recipient Appreciation award Am. Mktg. Assn., 1972. Mem. India-Am. C. of C. (founder, chmn. 1967-74), Gita Soc. Greater Chgo. (pres. 1967-69), India Assn. Met. Chgo. (dir.-at-large 1968), Sikh Study Circle (exec. mem. 1967-68), Am. Mktg. Assn. (chpt. pres. 1977-78), Sangam Indian Assn. Club: Toastmasters. Contbr. articles in field to co. publs. Home: 3518 Springbrook Dr Fort Wayne IN 46815 Office: 3515 Hobson Rd Fort Wayne IN 46805

SAXENA, UMESH KUMAR, educator; b. Pilibhit, India, June 12, 1936; s. Ram Bahadur and Ladati (Devi) S.; came to U.S., 1964; P.G., U. Roorkee, India, 1961, B.S., 1960; M.S., U. Wis., 1965, Ph.D., 1968; m. Nirmala Sinha, Mar. 2, 1962; children—Priya, Ila, Juhi. Lectr. IIT, Delhi, India, 1962-64; asst. prof. coll. engring. and applied sci., U. Wis. at Milw., 1968-73, asso. prof., 1973—. Mem. Am. Inst. Indsl. Engrs., Ops. Research Soc. Am., Am. Soc. Quality Control, Sigma Xi. Contbr. articles to profl. jours. Office: Systems Design Dept College Engineering and Applied Science University of Wisconsin Milwaukee WI 53201

SAXTON, MARYELLEN (MRS. JERRY J. SAXTON), real estate broker; b. Gratiot County, Mich., Oct. 14, 1930; d. Harry Lee and Ethel Ellen (Hazen) Bushre; grad. high sch.; m. Lloyd Clifton Clark, Oct. 29, 1949; children—Kay Ellen (Mrs. James Deupree), Connie, Toni Sue (dec.); m. 2d, Jerry J. Saxton, Dec. 1966; stepchildren—Rosemary (Mrs. Michael Leydorf), Jimmy Lee, Mark Alan, Max James, Carol B. Insp., Fed. Mogul Corp., St. Johns, Mich., 1952-68; real estate saleswoman Harper & Young, Inc., Harrison, Mich., 1969-70; co-owner Jerry Saxton, Realtor, Harrison, Mich., 1970—. Asst. instr. fundamentals of real estate for adult edn. classes Harrison High Sch., 1970-71; sec. Fed. Mogul Employee's Credit Union, 1962-66, pres., 1966-68. Pres., P.T.A., 1965. Mem. Clare County Bd. Realtors (sec. 1970-73), Harrison C. of C. (sec. 1972-73), Harrison C. of C. Aux. (pres. 1972-73, 77—). Mem. Christian Ch. Mem. Order of Eastern Star. Home: 320 Hillcrest Ave Harrison MI 48625 Office: 152 S First St Harrison MI 48625

SAY, MARLYS MORTENSEN (MRS. JOHN THEODORE SAY), supt. schs.; b. Yankton, S.D., Mar. 11, 1924; d. Melvin A. and Edith L. (Fargo) Mortensen; B.A., U. Colo., 1949, M.Ed., 1953; adminstr. specialist U. Nebr., 1973; m. John Theodore Say, June 21, 1951; children—Mary Louise, James Kenneth, John Melvin, Margaret Ann. Tchr. Huron (S.D.) Jr. High Sch., 1944-48, Lamar (Colo.) Jr. High Sch., 1950-52, Norfolk Pub. Sch., 1962-63; Madison County supt., Madison, Nebr., 1963—. Mem. N.E.A. (life), Am. Assn. Sch. Adminstrs., Dept. Rural Edn., Nebr. Assn. County Supts. (pres.), Nebr. Elementary Prins. Assn., Am. Assn. U. Women (pres. Norfolk br.). N.E. Nebr. County Supts. Assn. (pres.), Assn. Sch. Bus. Ofcls., Nat. Orgn. Legal Problems in Edn., Assn. Supervision and Curriculum Devel., Nebr. Edn. Assn., Neb. Sch. Adminstrs. Assn. Republican Methodist. Home: 4805 S 13th St Norfolk NE 68701 Office: Courthouse Madison NE 68748

SAYAD, HOMER ELISHA, accountant; b. Rezaieh, Iran, Aug. 15, 1915 (father Am. citizen); s. Elisha E. and Najeeba Mar (Joseph) S.; B.S., U. Nottingham (Eng.), 1937; postgrad. Northwestern U., 1937-39; m. Elizabeth Foster Gentry, May 9, 1963; children—Elisha William Gentry, Helene Elizabeth Todd. Mgr. Deloitte, Plender, Griffiths & Co., Chgo., 1939-52; resident sr. partner Haskins & Sells, St. Louis, 1954—. Mem. 22d Circuit Jud. Commn., 1974—. Chmn. profl. div. United Fund Greater St. Louis, 1959-60; pres. Opera Theatre St. Louis, 1964-65. Pres. Greater St. Louis Arts and Edn. Council, 1965-71, Loretto-Hilton Repertory Theatre, Inc., 1971-74; bd. commrs. Met. Zool. Park and Mus. Dist., 1972-73; bd. dirs. The New City School, treas. 1969; bd. dirs. Adult Edn. Council St. Louis, St. Louis Symphony, William Woods Coll., St. Louis Childrens Hosp. Served with U.S. Army, 1943-46. Mem. Nat. Accounting Assn., Am. Inst. C.P.A.'s, Mo. (pres. 1969-70), Ill., N.Y. socs. C.P.A.'s. Clubs: Bellerive Country (past dir.), Noonday (treas., bd. govs. 1968-69), Racquet (gov.), St. Louis. Home: 41 Westmoreland Pl St Louis MO 63108 Office: 10 Broadway St Louis MO 63102

SAYLES, JOHN H., computer systems engr., cons.; b. Chgo., Nov. 8, 1930; s. Fred E. and Emily A. (Brown) S.; B.S., U. Ill., 1956, M.S., 1958; m. Anna Marie McKernan, 1956; children—Audrey, Gregory. Develop. engr. Lindberg Engring. Co., Chgo., 1958-63; instrumentation engr. process div. UOP Co., Des Plaines, Ill., 1963-69, computer applications project mgr., 1969-77; sr. computer systems cons. Foxboro Co. (Mass.), 1977—. Dep. dir. Arlington Heights (Ill.) CD, 1973-76. Served with USAF, 1951-54. Mem. Instrument Soc. Am. (sr.). Home: 1505 W Euclid St Arlington Heights IL 60005 Office: Foxboro Co Foxboro MA 02035

SAYLOR, HOWARD LEROY, JR., physician; b. Cogswell, N.D., July 25, 1917; s. Howard L. and Claire I. (Lyken) S.; B.S., U. S.D., 1941; M.D., Northwestern U., 1943; m. Mary Ann Peterson, Apr. 9, 1943; children—Mary Diane, Howard LeRoy III, James C. Intern, Northwestern U. Hosp., Chgo., 1943; fellow in surgery Mayo Found., Rochester, Minn., 1947-50; practice medicine specializing in surgery, Huron, S.D., 1950—; clin. instr. surgery U. S.D. Med. Sch., 1976—; mem. med. adv. com. Crippled Children's Hosp., 1976—. Mem. Gov.'s Council on Emergency Med. Service, 1968—; chmn. S.D. Welfare Commn., 1968-72; trustee Huron Coll. Served to capt. M.C., AUS, 1943-46. Recipient Presdl. citation for employment of handicapped, 1970; diplomate Am. Bd. Surgery. Fellow A.C.S. (past pres. S.D. chpt.); mem. AMA, S.D. Med. Soc., Am. Trauma Soc., Priestley Soc., Huron C. of C., Am. Legion, VFW. Republican. Clubs: Huron Country, Ducks Ultd., Sertoma, Elks, Masons, Shriners. Home: 1360 Ohio St Huron SD 57350 Office: 433 Kansas St SE Huron SD 57350

SAYRE, CHARLES HERBERT, real estate broker; b. East Letart, O., Feb. 14, 1911; s. Herbert K. and Carrie Evelyn (Roush) S.; m. Marguerite Daugherty, Sept. 24, 1931; children—Charles R., Richard M. Mgr. Smith Phillips Furniture Inc., East Liverpool, O., 1932-42; owner Sayre Furniture Co., East Liverpool, 1945-60, Sayre Real Estate, East Liverpool, 1965—. Pres. East Liverpool Bd. Realtors, 1969. Pres. United Fund East Liverpool, 1948. Mem. Community Improvement Corp.; nat. adv. bd. Am. Security Council. Served with USNR, 1944. Recipient plaque East Liverpool Women's Club, 1967, plaque Real Estate Polit. Edn., 1973-75. Mem. Ohio Assn. Realtors (trustee 1973-75), East Liverpool C. of C. (trustee 1974-75). Mem. Christian Ch. (elder). Mason (32 deg., Shriner), Kiwanian (pres. 1974-75). Republican. Club: Realtors. Address: 569 Hill Blvd East Liverpool OH 43920

SAYRE, LEE FORD, hosp. adminstr.; b. Point Pleasant, W.Va., Nov. 19, 1927; s. Perry Arthur and Lind (Rogers) S.; B.S., Morris Harvey Coll., 1952; M.H.A., Med. Coll. Va., 1966; m. Ruth Lee Winfree, Apr. 22, 1951; 1 dau., Cynthia Jo Sayre McGovern. Accountant, Columbia Gas Co., Charleston, W.Va., 1947-49; asst. adminstr. Mountain State Hosp., Charleston, 1949-64; adminstrv. resident Louis Gale Hosp., Roanoke, Va., 1965-66; dir. profl. services New Hanover Hosp., Wilmington, N.C., 1966-67; asst. adminstr. Alexandria (Va.) Hosp., 1967-69; asso. adminstr. St. Lawrence Hosp., Lansing, Mich., 1969—. Bd. dirs. local chpt. A.R.C., 1967-68. Fellow Am. Coll. Hosp. Adminstrs., Royal Soc. Health (London, Eng.); mem. Hosp. Financial Mgmt. Assn. (nat. dir. 1958-60), Tau Kappa Epsilon. Republican. Baptist. Clubs: Exchange, City, Masons, Shriner, Eastern Star. Home: 881 Ramblewood Dr East Lansing MI 48823 Office: 1210 W Saginaw St Lansing MI 48914

SAYRE, RICHARD FRANCIS, cons. engr.; b. Madison, S.D., Nov. 18, 1934; s. Lawrence Carl and Edith (Doolittle) S.; B.S. in Civil Engring., S.D. State U., 1956; m. Lois Jean Sather, June 2, 1957; children—Sue Ann, Peggy, Barbara. Engr., S.D. Dept. Transp., 1956-62; field engr. Portland Cement Assn., Sioux Falls, S.D., 1962-65; pres. R. F. Sayre & Assos., cons. engrs., Sioux Falls, 1965—. Bd. dirs. Sioux Falls River Improvement Soc. Mem. Am. Cons. Engrs. Council (state pres. 1976-78), S.D. Engring. Soc. (1st v.p. S.E. chpt. 1977). Methodist (trustee 1974-77). Home: 1817 S Jefferson Ave Sioux Falls SD 57105 Office: 738 W 10th St Sioux Falls SD 57101

SCACE, WILLIAM BUELL, business exec.; b. Chgo., May 27, 1905; s. Stephen Birch and Mae (Emmert) S.; Ph.B., U. Chgo., 1928. Mdse. tng. Sears Roebuck, 1928-31; financial cons., 1931-34; 1st lt. in command C.C.C. camp, 1935-37; co-founder Scrambled Signs Co., 1937, co. merged with Speed-Way Mfg. Co., 1939, v.p. operations and dir., 1946-51, pres., dir., 1951-65, chmn. bd., ret.; partner DeBacher and Scace, 1969—. Admitted to practice Patent Office, 1937. Served as lt. col. Signal Corps, U.S. Army; co-founder and asst. comdg. officer Army Electronic Standards Agy. and co-founder and asst. army co-dir. Army-Navy Electronic Standards Agy.; head of mission to Eng., 1946, effected joint standardization (U.S., Brit., Canadian) electronic components. Served with Signal Corps U.S. Army, lt. col. Res., ret. Awarded Legion of Merit, Army Commendation medal, Navy Commendation. Mem. Acad. Polit. Sci. (life), Armed Forces Communications Assn. (life), Res. Officers Assn. (life), Nat. Assn. Stock Car Racing, Nat. Hot Rod Assn. (charter), Ret. Officers Assn. (life), Auto Old Timers (life), Delta Sigma Pi (life). Mason. Clubs: Union League, Chicago Alumni, U.S. Auto (life mem.), 200 MPH (life). Author articles in trade papers. Set Bonneville Nat. B. modified sports car record, 1968. Home: Oak Park Arms Hotel 408 S Oak Park Ave Oak Park IL 60302

SCALES, CHARLENE MARY, counselor; b. Evansville, Ind., Apr. 8, 1935; d. Narl William and Erma Linda (Schapker) Scales; B.S., Xavier U., Cin., 1965; M.A. in History, U. Dayton (Ohio), 1969; M.A. in Counseling, U. Evansville, 1971. Tchr. parochial sch., Evansville, 1956-68; counselor, asst. dir. Newman Center, Evansville U., 1968-73, dir. female dormitory, 1970-73; rehab. counselor Goodwill Industries Central Ind., Indpls., 1975-76, dir. residential services, 1976—; mem. criteria standards survey team Ind. Assn. Rehab. Facilities. Ball State U. fellow, 1973-75. Mem. Am. Personnel and Guidance Assn., Nat., Ind. rehab. assn., Am. Rehab. Counseling Assn., Phi Delta Kappa. Democrat. Roman Catholic. Home: 7430 St Clair St Indianapolis IN 46224 Office: 1635 W Michigan St Indianapolis IN 46222

SCALES, JAMES EDWARD, counselor; b. Bklyn., Mar. 24, 1948; s. Robert and Melva Marie (Proctor) J.; B.S., Lincoln U., 1970; M.S., Kans. State U., 1976, postgrad 1976—; m. Linda Gayle Moore, May 30, 1970; 1 son, James Alexander. Personnel clk. U.S. Civil Service Commn., Fort Riley, Kans., 1975-76; personnel staffing specialist, 1976-77; placement counselor Job Service Center, Manhattan, Kans., 1977—. Served with AUS, 1970-77. Mem. Am., Kans. personnel and guidance assns., Res. Officers Assn., Assn. U.S. Army, Am. Bowling Congress, Phi Mu Alpha Sinfonia. Baptist. Home: 32 Waterway Rd Manhattan KS 66502 Office: 621 Humboldt St Manhattan KS 66502

SCALES, WENDELL PHILLIP, dentist; b. Detroit, Mar. 18, 1951; s. Erise and Esther (Hogan) S.; student Highland Park Coll., 1969-70, Wayne State U., 1970-73; D.D.S., U. Detroit, 1976; m. Lynda Joye Ashford, Aug. 5, 1972. Pvt. practice dentistry, Detroit, 1976—; mem. faculty U. Detroit Sch. Dentistry. Recipient Columbia Dentoform award U. Detroit Dental Sch., 1976, Dentsply Internat. Merit award, 1976, Francis Vedder Fixed Prosthodontic award, 1976, others. Mem. Nat., Am., Mich., Wolverine dental assns., Francis B. Vedder Soc. Fixed Prosthodontics, Acad. Gen. Dentistry, Delta Sigma Delta, Omicron Kappa Upsilon. Home: 9000 E Jefferson St Apt 21-B Detroit MI 48214 Office: 18241 Greenfield St Detroit MI 48221

SCALZO, JOSEPH RALPH, oil co. exec.; b. Newton, N.J., June 18, 1920; s. Joseph and Angiline S.; B.S. in Chem. Engring., Pa. State U., 1941; LL.B., J.D. cum laude, U. Toledo, 1948; postgrad. Columbia U. Grad. Sch. Exec. Bus. Mgmt., 1961; m. Edith Guyer, June 25, 1945; children—Joseph, Joanne, Sandra, Michael, Bonnie, Teresa. With Sun Oil Co., 1941—, asst. chief chem. engr., Toledo, 1955-57, in charge labor relations, 1957-66, mgr. employee relations and plant services, 1966—; admitted to Ohio bar, 1948; patent atty., Toledo, 1949—. Pres., Amateur Athletic Union U.S., 1974-76; mem. exec. com. U.S. Olympic Com., 1972—; U.S. rep. World Amateur Wrestling 1965—; chmn. finance cm. Internat. Wrestling Fedn., 1972—. Past pres. bd. dirs. Parkview Hosp.; bd. dirs. Torio Health Studios, Nat. YMCA, Nat. Indsl. Recreation Assn. City councilman, Toledo, 1958-60. Recipient Outstanding Alumni award U. Toledo, Helms Found. award; named to Toledo Hall of Fame, Ohio Hall of Fame; Gold medallion for service internat. wrestling. Mem. Am., Fed., Ohio bar assns., Patent Bar Assn., Nat. Mgmt. Assn., Am. Inst. Chem. Engrs., Am. Petroleum Inst., U. Toledo, Pa. State alumni assns., Delta Theta Phi, Alpha Phi Delta. Address: PO Box 920 Toledo OH 43693

SCANLON, JOHN CHARLES, physician; b. Cleve., Jan. 25, 1940; s. Charles Patrick and Mary Abigail (Dahm) S.; A.B., Xavier U., Cin., 1961; M.D., Loyola U., Chgo., 1965; m. Phyllis Catherine Steinker, May 8, 1965; children—Matthew, Lisa, Susan, Daniel. Intern, St. Vincent Charity Hosp., Cleve., 1965-66; fellow in internal medicine Cleve. Clinic, 1968-70, fellow in pulmonary disease, 1970-71; practice medicine specializing in pulmonary diseases, Lafayette, Ind., 1971-77; physician Arnett Clinic, Lafayette, Ind., 1971—; med. dir. respiratory services dept. Lafayette (Ind.) Home Hosp., 1971—, chmn. dept. medicine, 1974-76; med. dir. respiratory services dept. St. Elizabeth Hosp., Lafayette, 1971—; med. dir. respiratory technician program Ind. Vocat. Coll., Lafayette, 1972—. Served to capt. M.C., U.S. Army, 1966-67. Diplomate Am. Bd. Internal Medicine. Fellow Am. Coll. Chest Physicians. Republican. Roman Catholic. Home: 4811 Homewood Dr West Lafayette IN 47906

SCANNELL, FRANCIS X., state librarian; b. Boston, Dec. 15, 1917; s. William James and Helen (Ahern) S.; grad. Roxbury Latin Sch., 1938; A.B., Harvard U., 1942; B.S. in L.S., Columbia U.; m. Mary Donovan, Dec. 28, 1946; children—Christopher, Joel, Elizabeth, Martha. Reference librarian Boston Pub. Library, 1943-46; with Detroit Pub. Library, 1946-53; head of reader services Mich. State Library, 1953-65; head reference dept. Mich. State U., 1965-68; state librarian Mich., 1968—. Recipient citation Mich. Constl. Conv., 1961. Mem. Am. Soc. Pub. Adminstrn., Mich. Library Assn., ALA. Author: Michigan Novelists, Michigan in Books. Home: 3627 Colchester Rd Lansing MI 48906 Office: 735 E Michigan Ave Lansing MI 48913

SCARPINO, PASQUALE VALENTINE, environ. microbiologist, educator; b. Utica, N.Y., Feb. 13, 1932; s. Antonio and Mary Ann (Lia) S.; B.A. magna cum laude, Utica Coll., Syracuse U., 1955; M.S., Rutgers U., 1958, Ph.D. (USPHS fellow), 1961; m. Mary Elizabeth Riggs, June 5, 1976; 1 dau., Andrea Lia. USPHS research asst. Rutgers U., New Brunswick, N.J., 1958-61; asst. prof. biol. scis. Fairleigh Dickinson U., Madison, N.J., 1961-63; asst. prof. san. engring. U. Cin. 1963-66, asso. prof. environ. health engring., 1966-70, prof. environ. engring., 1970—. Chmn. water subcom. of Environ. Task Force, City of Cin. 1972-73; chmn. Citizen-Scientist Com. on Drinking Water Quality, City of Cin., 1975—; chmn. water com. Environ. Adv. Council of City of Cin., 1975-76. Mem. advisory council Cin. Experience, 1973-77. USPHS research grantee, 1965-68, Space Inst. grantee, 1967-69, EPA research grantee, 1969-78. Recipient Presdl. award for Excellence in Community Service U. Cin., 1975. Fellow Am. Acad. of Microbiology; mem. Am. Soc. Microbiology (chmn. com. on edn. 1970-72, chmn. com. on role of microbiology in edn. of other disciplines 1972-73), A.A.A.S., N.Y. Acad. Sci., Water Pollution Control Fedn., Internat. Assn. on Water Pollution Research, Sigma Xi. Contbr. articles to profl. jours. Home: 3843 Middleton Ave Cincinnati OH 45220 Office: 639 Baldwin Hall Dept of Civil and Environ Engineering U Cincinnati Cincinnati OH

SCEARCE, WILLIAM CARROLL, city ofcl.; b. Moultrie, Ga., Aug. 19, 1941; s. James Boyd and Lois Audry (Harrell) S.; B.S., Ga. So. Coll., 1963; M.A., U. Ga., 1967; m. Penelope Ann Leffen, Apr. 4, 1976; children—Lois Shala, W. Carroll, Helen Patricia. Recreation Center dir., Winston-Salem, N.C., 1963-64, also dist. supr. Parks and Recreation Dept.; park and recreation dir., Decatur, Ga., 1964-68; park and recreation dir., Joplin, Mo., 1968—. Mem. City Beautiful Com., Joplin, 1968—; mem. Joplin Council for the Arts, 1968—; pres. Joplin Area Assn. for Retarded Citizens, 1972-74; sec. Joplin Boys Club; bd. dirs. Joplin Area Sheltered Workshop. Mem. Mo. Park and Recreation Assn. (v.p. 1975-76), Ga. Park and Recreation Soc. (dir. 1966-68), Am. Inst. Park Execs., Nat. Recreation and Park Assn., Nat. Parks and Conservation Assn., Nat. Audubon Soc., Am. Forestry Assn. Lion. Home: 626 Jaccard Pl Joplin MO 64801 Office: 212 W Eighth St Joplin MO 64801

SCEPER, KENNETH MICHAEL, elec. engr.; b. Port Washington, Wis., Jan. 6, 1924; s. Michael Buern and Elizabeth Matilda (Aberwald) S.; B.S.E.E., Tri State Coll., 1950; m. Carol LaVerne Haines, Sept. 5, 1953; children—Kym LaVerne, Karen Ann, Kristie Jo. Design engr. Austin Co., Houston, Chgo. and Cleve., 1951-53; asso. engr. W. B. Ferguson, Cons. Elec. Engrs., Cleve., 1953-63; elec. engr. Firestone Tire and Rubber Co., Decatur, Ill., 1963-66; group leader, elec. dept. A. Epstein & Sons, Chgo., 1966-69; mgr. plant utilities Fermi Nat. Accelerator Lab., Batavia, Ill., 1969—. Served with USAAF, 1943-45. Decorated Air medal (6). Roman Catholic. Home: 2720 Wild Plum Dr Woodridge IL 60515 Office: PO Box 500 Batavia IL 60510

SCHAAF, OLUS HOYER, educator; b. nr. Nashville, O., Jan. 11, 1901; s. Leonard and Emma (Hostettler) S.; grad. Spencerian Sch. Finance, 1923; B.S. in Edn., Ashland Coll., 1931; M.A., Western Res. U., 1935; postgrad. U. Minn., 1941; m. Helen Piper, Jan. 3, 1924 (dec. Apr. 1953); 1 son, Gene Piper; m. 2d, Ellura Ropp Davis, July 12, 1954; stepchildren—Maurice Davis, Louise (Mrs. Gene Mosbarger). Elementary tchr., high sch. coach, Shreve, O., 1920-23; comml. supr. Bellfontaine (O.) High Sch., 1923-26; comml. supr. Shelby (O.) High Sch., 1928-37, prin., 1937-42; supt. schs., Shelby, 1942-43; prin. Lancaster (O.) High Sch., 1943-47, Garfield Heights (O.) High Sch., 1947-49; supt. schs., Garfield Heights, 1949-63; tchr., supr. student tchrs. Bluffton (O.) Coll., 1963-64; dir. library Ashland (O.) Coll., 1964-72. Bd. dirs. Salvation Army, Lancaster. Mem. Ohio com. North Central Assn. Colls. and Secondary Schs., Ohio High Sch. Prins. Assn. (pres. 1947-48), Am. Assn. Sch. Administrs., Nat. Assn. Secondary Sch. Prins., N.E.A., Am., Ohio library assns., Ashland County Ret. Tchrs. Assn. (pres. 1974-75). Mem. M.E. Ch. (trustee). Kiwanian (past pres.), Rotarian (past pres.), K.P. Author: Simplified Punctuation, 1952; Improved English Grammar, 1966; Pupil Personnel Record, 1960; The College Teaching Materials Center or Curriculum Library, 1972; Bowling for Fun, 1974. Home: 500 Buena Vista Ave Ashland OH 44805

SCHAAL, JOHN H., clergyman, educator; b. Kalamazoo, Apr. 28, 1908; s. Peter and Grace (Bredeweg) S.; student Hope Coll., 1926-28, Calvin Coll., 1928-30; A.B., Calvin Sem., 1933; Th.B., U. Chgo., 1944; m. Grace Workman, July 12, 1934; 1 son, Wendell J. Ordained to ministry Christian Ref. Ch., 1933; pastor Milwood Christian Ref. Ch., Kalamazoo, 1933-43, Second Christian Ref. Ch., Fremont, Mich., 1943-48; editor Christian Ref. Sunday Sch. Publs., Grand Rapids, Mich., 1945-71; dean, tchr. Bible history dept. Ref. Bible Coll., Grand Rapids, 1948-73, also dir. Dir. religious morning devotion WKZO, Kalamazoo; radio pastor WMUS, Muskegon, Mich.; pres. Christian Ref. Bd. Missions; speaker Winona Lake and Cedar Lake (Ind.) Bible Confs., Mt. Hermon (Calif.) and Story Lake (Iowa) Bible Confs.; chaplain Grand Rapids Osteo. Hosp., 1972—, Sunset Manor, 1974-77, Mary Free Bed Rehab. Center, 1977. Mem. Grand Rapids Music Soc. for Christian Schs., 1960. Bd. dirs. Christian Ref. Conf. Grounds, Children's Bible Hour. Mem. Newaygo County Ministerial Assn. (past pres.). Author: Ephesians, 1966; Better Living Through Christ, 1968; Three Letters From Prison, 1970; The Royal Roman Road, 1972. Contbr. articles to profl. publs. Home: 1137 Noble St SE Grand Rapids MI 49507

SCHABEL, DONALD ALBERT, lawyer; b. Hammond, Ind., July 22, 1927; s. Francis William and Kathleen (Conroy) S.; A.B., Ind. U., 1948; J.D. cum laude, Harvard, 1951; m. Amelia Llana Agtarap, Oct. 7, 1967; children—Victoria Eileen, Donald Albert. Admitted to N.Y. bar, 1952, Ind. bar, 1954; asso. Milbank, Tweed, Hope & Hadley, N.Y.C., 1951-53; asso. Buschmann, Krieg, DeVault & Alexander, Indpls., 1954-57, partner, 1957-60; partner Buschmann, Carr & Schabel, 1961-75; individual practice law, 1976—. Mem. cts. div. Ind. Jud. Study Commn., 1973—. Served with USNR, 1945-46. Mem. Am., Ind., Indpls. bar assns., Bar Assn. 7th Fed. Circuit, Assn. Bar City N.Y. Roman Catholic. Clubs: Columbia (Indpls.). Home: 4455 Broadway Indianapolis IN 46205 Office: 111 Monument Circle Indianapolis IN 46204

SCHAEDE, RICHARD EDWIN, physician; b. Thomasboro, Ill., Aug. 28, 1927; s. Mayo William and Opal Mae (Hutchinson) S.; B.S. in Chemistry, U. Ill., 1949, B.S. in Medicine, 1951, M.D., 1953; m. Ila Marlene Coffey, June 13, 1948; children—Pamela Sue, Janet Lynn, Mark Allen. Intern, Cook County Hosp., Chgo., 1953-54; contract physician Chanute AFB Hosp., Rantoul, Ill., 1954-55; practice medicine specializing in family practice, Rantoul, 1957-65; founder Rantoul Clinic, 1965, staff, 1965—. Faculty coronoary care Parkland Coll., 1970—; pres. staff Mercy Hosp., Urbana, 1970-73; asso. dean grad. med. edn., clin. asso. Sch. Basic Med. Scis. U. Ill., Champaign-Urbana, 1973—. Pres., Outlook Tb Sanatorium Bd., 1959-69. Mem. Rantoul Elementary Sch. Bd., 1959-73. Dir. First Nat. Bank Rantoul; mem. exec. com. Sch. Basic Med. Scis., U. Ill., 1971-72. Served with USNR, 1945-46; with USAF, 1955-57. Recipient Scholarship award Mosby Pub. Co., 1953. Diplomate Am. Bd. Family Practice. Mem. Am. Acad. Family Practice, A.M.A., Ill. State Med. Soc., Champaign County Med. Soc., Omega Beta Pi, Chi Gamma Iota. Mason, Rotarian. Researcn on cancer, 1948-49. Home: 401 Eden Park Rantoul IL 61866 Office: 320 E Sangamon St Rantoul IL 61866

SCHAEFER, CHARLES, hydraulic and mech. presses mfg. co. exec.; b. Geneva, Jan. 17, 1916; s. Charles Emil and Ida Agnes (Gurtner) S.; came to U.S., 1954, naturalized, 1959; M.S., Engr., U. Zurich, Zurich, Switzerland, 1939; m. Irene Grun, June 27, 1940; children—Edmond Charles, Arlette Irene. Supr. Swiss Govt. (K.T.A.) Mil. Def. Dept., Berne, Switzerland, 1939-43; Plant mgr. Ateliers des Charmilles, Geneva, 1943-48; v.p. mktg. and sales, Manurhin S.A. Plants in Geneva, Switzerland and Mulhouse, France, 1948-54; founder, Schaefer Sales Co. Inc., Glendale, Calif., 1957-71, ret., 1971; v.p. U.S. Industries Clearing Co., Chgo., 1973—. Named Engr. of Year, ASTM, 1970. Mem. Soc. Mfg. Engrs. Club: Verdugo (Glendale). Home: 10 N Tower Rd Oak Brook IL 60521 Office: 6499 W 65th St Chicago IL 60638

SCHAEFER, FREDERICK LEROY, JR., physician; b. Wilmington, Del., Oct. 11, 1930; s. Frederick LeRoy and Ethel Ione (Schulenberg) S.; B.A., Miami U., Oxford, Ohio, 1952; M.D., U. Cin., 1956; M.S., Ohio State U., 1963; m. Jacqueline Ann Shea, Dec. 19, 1953; children—Frederick LeRoy, III, James Michael, Katrina Marie. Intern, Cin. Gen. Hosp., 1956—57; resident in obstetrics and gynecology Ohio State U. Hosps., 1959-63; practice medicine specializing in obstetrics and gynocology, Neenah, Wis., 1963—; chief obstetrics and gynecology Theda Clark Meml. Hosp., Neenah, 1976—; cons. femine hygiene products Kimberly-Clark Corp., 1966—; pres. Wis. div. Am. Cancer Soc., 1969, chmn. service and rehab. com., mem. exec. com., 1970. Pres. Neenah-Menasha Republican Club, 1967—68. Served with USNR, 1957—59. Decorated Letter of Commendation. Diplomate Am. Bd. Obstetrics and Gynecology. Mem. Am. Coll. Obstetricians and Gynecologists (dist. sci. presentation award (1963), AMA, Wis., Winnebago County med. socs., Wis. Gynecol. Soc. Roman Catholic, Clubs: N. Shore Golf, Elks. Home 866 Bayview St Neenah WI 54956 Office: 1416 S Commercial St Neenah WI 54956

SCHAEFER, JAMES THEODORE, publisher; b. East Grand Rapids, Mich., Sept. 3, 1945; s. Walter Charles and Louise Elanore (Petersen) S.; A.A., Grand Rapids Jr. Coll., 1965; B.A., Mich. State U., 1970; m. Karen Elaine Moon, Sept. 16, 1972; children—Patrick Charles, Theodore Glenn, Daniel John. Reporter, Williamston (Mich.) Enterprise, 1966-67, Mich. State U. State News, East Lansing, 1967-68; regional editor Muskegon (Mich.) Chronicle, 1969-70; pub. Ripples mag., Ann Arbor, 1973—, editor ann. edit., 1973, 78; pub. Shining Waters Press, Ann Arbor, 1975—; co-editor O'Brien Center Newsletter, 1977—; dir. Mich. Labor Press, 1977-78. Mem. Com. of Small Mag. Editors and Pubs., Coordinating Council on Lit. Mags. Councilman, Lutheran Ch., 1973-78; editor Grapevine newsletter of Mich. dist. Am. Luth. Ch., 1975-76; chmn. Christian Service Bd., 1977-78; scheduling coordinator Luth. Standard Mag. Mich. dist. Am. Luth. Ch.; bd. dirs. O'Brien Juvenile Center, Washtenau County, 1977-78. Home: 245 Murray Ave Ann Arbor MI 48103 Office: PO Box 52 Ann Arbor MI 48107

SCHAEFER, JOHN FREDERICK, lawyer; b. Detroit, Apr. 10, 1942; s. Gilbert Frederick and Mary Cathryn (Henderson) S.; grad. Cranbrook Sch., 1961; student U. Notre Dame; B.A., Mich. State U., 1965; J.D., Detroit Coll. Law, 1968; m. Sharon Kathleen Shaefer, May 22, 1976; children—John Frederick, Kelly Leigh, Kimberly Megan. Admitted to Mich. bar, 1969; partner firm Buesser, Buesser, Snyder & Blank, attys. and counselors, Detroit, 1968-73; partner firm Williams, Schaefer, Ruby & Williams, Bloomfield Hills, Mich., 1973—; officer A.F.S. Inc. and Walker Motors Inc., dealership, Grosse Pointe Woods, Mich., 1965—; asst. prof. Detroit Coll. Law, 1972—. Mem. advanced gifts com. United Found. Torch drive, 1972; pres. alumni council Cranbrook Sch., 1972-73. Mem. Am., Oakland County (chmn. family law com. 1974-75, 75-77), Detroit (chmn. family law com. 1975-76) bar assns., State Bar of Mich. (character and fitness com. 1970—, family law com. 1972—), Detroit Coll. Law Alumni Assn., Am. Acad. Matrimonial Lawyers, Psi Upsilon. Republican. Roman Catholic. Clubs: Recess (Detroit); Birmingham Athletic; Bloomfield Hills Country. Home: 1040 Orchard Ridge Rd Bloomfield Hills MI 48013 Office: City Nat Bank Bldg Bloomfield Hills MI 48013

SCHAEFER, LAWRENCE VINCENT, educator; b. Bridgeport, Conn., July 3, 1931; s. William Joseph and Loretta Mary (Lawrence) S.; B.S., Fairfield U., 1953, M.A., 1954; M.A., Fordham U., 1961, Ph.D., 1976; dip., Internat. Inst. for Montessori Studies (Italy), 1970-71; m. Patricia Ann Scallen, Sept. 3, 1960; children—Anne L., Lawrence P., Mary J., Kristin A. Tchr., Fordham Prep. Sch., N.Y.C., 1960-67; asst. prof. European history Sacred Heart U., Bridgeport, Conn., 1967-70; headmaster Toronto Montessori Schs., Thornhill, Ont., Can., 1970-75, bd. dirs., 1974-75; adminstr. elementary sch. Montessori Found. of Minn., St. Paul, 1975-76; founder, prin. Lake Country Sch., Mpls., 1976—; lectr. Toronto Montessori Inst., 1971-75; cons. adminstrv. coordinator Milw. Montessori Sch., 1975-76; cons. Montessori Found. of Minn., 1975-76. Mem. Bishop's Commn. on Human Rights, Diocese of Bridgeport, 1968-70; mem. Norwalk Cath. Interracial Council, 1967-70; bd. dirs. The Child's Work Center, Norwalk, 1963-66, Lake Country Sch.. 1976—. Served with UsN, 1955-58. Mem. Am. Hist. Assn., Assn. Montessori Internat., N. Am. Montessori Tchrs. Assn., Minn. Alliance of Montessorians, Smithsonian Assos., Minn. Soc. Fine Arts, Minn. Geol. Soc. Democrat. Roman Catholic. Contbr. articles in field to profl. jours; designer, creator in collaboration with Jodi Abssy, Montessori ednl. materials: Time Line of the History of the Holocene Period, 1973; Time Line of American Civilizations, 1974; The Language Tree, 1974. Home: 1630 W Skillman Ave Roseville MN 55113 Office: 1601 Laurel Ave Minneapolis MN 55401

SCHAEPPI, JOSEPH JOHN, optometrist; b. St. Paul, Feb. 9, 1923; s. Joseph John and Barbara Jane (Childs) S.; student U. Minn., 1942-43, 46-49; O.D., Chgo. Coll. Optometry, 1951; m. Patricia Clair Shimek, Sept. 10, 1949; children—Dennis M., Thomas J., Patti C., Cheryl A., Lawrence J. Pvt. practice optometry, Mpls., 1951—. Served with USNR, 1943-46. Mem. Am., Minn., Mpls. optometric assns., Minn. Optometric Polit. Action Com. (treas.), Northside Comml. Club, Northside Businessmens Assn., Am. Legion. Catholic. Elk. Clubs: Golden Valley Country (Minn.), Comus Dance. Home: 6000 Wolfberry Ln Golden Valley MN 55422 Office: 1014 W Broadway Minneapolis MN 55411

SCHAFER, ALLYN JAMES, newspaper editor, publisher; b. Iowa Falls, Iowa, Dec. 15, 1937; s. Carroll James and Frances Reba (Lawler) S.; B.A., U. Iowa, 1959; m. Carolyn Joan Long, Feb. 9, 1959; children—Teresa, Scott, Deborah, Jeffrey, David. News, sports editor Eldora (Iowa) Herald-Index, 1959, part-owner, 1960-70, owner, 1970—, bus. mgr., 1966-70, editor, pub., 1970—. Pres. Project Dr. Com., 1973-76; v.p. Eldora Indsl. Devel. Corp., 1975—. Recipient leadership award Gov. State of Iowa, Outstanding Young Businessman award Eldora, Community Distinguished Service award Eldora. Mem. Iowa Press Assn. (dir.), Eldora Jaycees (pres. 1962). Republican. Roman Catholic. Rotarian (pres. Eldora 1976-77). Home: 1202 4th Ave Eldora IA 50627 Office: 1513 W Edgington Ave Eldora IA 50627

SCHAFER, MICHAEL FREDERICK, orthopedic surgeon; b. Peoria, Ill., Aug. 17, 1942; s. Harold Martin and Frances May (Ward) S.; B.A., U. Iowa, 1964, M.D., 1967; m. Eileen M. Briggs, Jan. 8, 1966; children—Steven, Brian, Kathy, David, Daniel. Intern, Chgo. Wesley Meml. Hosp., 1967-68; resident in orthopedic surgery Cook County Program Northwestern U., Chgo., 1968-72; practice medicine specializing in orthopedic surgery, Chgo., 1974—; asst. prof. orthopedic surgery Northwestern U., 1977—; asso. attending orthopedic surgeon Northwestern Meml. Hosp., 1974—; adj. staff Children's Meml. Hosp., Chgo., 1974—; cons. VA Lakeside Hosp., 1974—; mem. advisroy bd. Center for Sports Medicine, Northwestern U., 1976—; panelist Bur. Health Manpower, HEW, 1976. Served to maj., U.S. Army, 1973-74. Am. Orthopaedic Assn. fellow, 1975. Diplomate Am. Bd. Orthopedic Surgery. Mem. Am. Acad. Orthopaedic Surgeons, Am. Med. Assn., Ill., Chgo. med. socs., Internat. Soc. Study Pain. Roman Catholic. Contbr. articles to med. jours. Home: 1520 Executive Ln Glenview IL 60025 Office: 303 E Chicago Ave Chicago IL 60611

SCHAFER, THOMAS MATHIAS, aerial survey co. exec.; b. Lansing, Mich., May 19, 1939; s. Albert Mathias and Anne Gertrude (Schneider) S.; grad high sch.; m. Carol Eva Tubandt, Sept. 24, 1960; children—Joan, Andrea, Laura. Technician trainee Abrams Aerial Survey Corp., Lansing, Mich., 1957, technician, 1958, advt. mgr., 1961-63, contracting dir., 1963, v.p., dir. contracting, 1964—. Served with AUS, 1960-61. Mem. Am. Soc. Photogrammetry (dir. Great Lakes Region). K.C. Contbr. articles to surveying, engring. mags. Home: 806 E Dill Dr Dewitt MI 48820 Office: 124 N Larch St Lansing MI 48903

SCHAFF, PHILIP HAYNES, JR., advt. exec.; b. Cleve., Dec. 26, 1920; s. Philip Haynes and Jane Arms (Booth) S.; grad. Mercersburg Acad., 1938; B.A., Princeton U., 1942; m. Mary Gladding Johnson, June 19, 1948; children—Mary Gladding, Philip Douglas, Nancy Booth, Susan Haynes, Sylvester Johnson. Asso. editor employee mag. Cuneo Press, Inc., Chgo., 1946-47; with Leo Burnett Co., Inc., Chgo., 1947—, fin. v.p., 1957-58, exec. v.p. adminstrn. and finance, 1958-61, chmn. finance com., 1961-71, chmn. exec. com., 1962—, chmn. bd., 1967—; chmn. Leo Burnett Found., 1971—; trustee Burnett Profit Sharing Trust, Leo Burnett Voting Trust, Shedd Aquarium; dir. Leo Burnett Internat., Inc. Gov., Midwest Stock Exchange, 1974—. Mem. exec. bd. Chgo. area council Boy Scouts Am., 1963-70, v.p., 1968-69, communications chmn. E. Central region, 1972—; mem. adv. bd. ednl. requirements Sec. U.S. Navy, 1965-69, chmn., 1968-69; pres. Onward Neighborhood House, Chgo., 1954-57; trustee Northport Point (Mich.) Cottage Owners Assn., 1960-69; mem. alumni council Mercersburg Acad., 1960-62; chmn. Chgo. schs. and scholarship com. Princeton, 1950-52, rep. at large Princeton Alumni Assn., 1951-56, 63-69, exec. com., 1953-55, 68-69; mem. Winnetka Bd. Edn., 1964-70, v.p., 1967-69, pres., 1969-70; trustee Princeton, 1970-74, mem. exec. com., 1973-74; adv. com. Grad. Sch. Bus. Mgmt., Northwestern U., 1973—; bd. dirs. Evanston Hosp., 1972—; bd. dirs. Lyric Opera, 1976—; gov. Orchestral Assn. Chgo., 1976—. Served to capt. USAAF, 1942-46. Decorated D.F.C. with oak leaf cluster, Air medal; hon. wings Chinese Air Force. Mem. Am. Asso. Advt. Agys. (dir. 1962-65, chmn. advertiser relations com. 1962-63, mem. operations com. 1963-65), Chgo. Com., Chgo. Council on Fgn. Relations. Clubs: Princeton (pres. 1961), Mid-Am. (gov.), Commercial, Commonwealth, University, Chicago, Economic (Chgo.); Indian Hill (v.p.), Badminton (Winnetka); Northport Point (pres. 1976—). Home: 321 Sunset Rd Winnetka IL 60093 Office: Leo Burnett Co Inc Prudential Plaza Chicago IL 60601

SCHAFFER, HARWOOD DAVID, clergyman; b. Dayton, Ohio, Oct. 15, 1944; s. Phillip David and H. Ruth (Scheid) S.; B.S. in Math., Ohio State U., 196S; M.Div., Hartford Sem. Found., 1969; m. Gail Corrine Poth, June 25, 1966; children—Rosita, Virginia, Chandra. Ordained to ministry United Ch. of Christ, 1969; chaplain, tchr. Austin Sch., Hartford, Conn., 1967-71; asst. pastor S. Congl. Ch., Middletown, Conn., 1967-71; pastor Trinity United Ch. of Christ, Hudson, Kans., 1971—; area counselor 17/76 Achievement Fund of United Ch. of Christ, 1974-75; mem. Western Assn. council Kans.-Okla. Conf. United Ch. of Christ, 1971-74, 76—, sec.-treas., 1971-74, chmn. ch. and ministry com., 1976—. Bd. govs. Austin Sch., Hartford, 1970-71; mem. Stafford County Democratic Central Com., 1976—; mem. Stafford Council Overall Econ. Devel. Planning Com., 1976—, chmn., 1977. Club: Hudson Men's Community. Home:

Hudson KS 67545 Office: Trinity United Ch of Christ Hudson KS 67545

SCHAFFTER, BARRY WAYNE, engine mfg. exec.; b. Booneville, Mo., Dec. 1, 1951; s. Glenn David and Mary Frances (Aeschbacher) S.; B.S. in Engring. Mgmt., U. Mo., Rolla, 1973; m. Rebecca Ann Bestgen, Nov. 3, 1972; 1 dau., Holly Christine. Prodn. supr. tng. John Deere Waterloo (Iowa) Tractor Plant, 1973-74, sr. engring. analyst, plant engr., 1974-75, prodn. supr. John Deere Engine Works, Waterloo, 1975-76, mgr. interunit coordination marketing dept., 1976—. Mem. Soc. Automotive Engrs., Tau Beta Pi. Mem. Christian Ch. Club: John Deere Suprs. Home: 3304 Pridemore St Cedar Falls IA 50613 Office: 3801 W Ridgeway Ave Waterloo IA 50704

SCHAIBLE, C. DONELDA, ins. co. exec.; b. Ypsilanti, Mich., Mar. 31, 1920; d. Theodore E. and Charlotte (Clark) Schaible; A.B. in Social Work, U. Mich., 1942. Systems service rep. IBM, Detroit, 1942-44, spl. personnel research, N.Y.C., 1944-47; personnel asst. Washington Nat. Ins. Co., Evanston, Ill., 1948, asst. personnel dir., 1948-49, personnel dir., 1949—. Personnel cons. Ill. Shore Girl Scout Council. Mem. adv. com. Evanston Child Care Center Assn., 1967-68; adv. council Evanston Sawyer Coll. Bus., 1969-71. Mem. Am. Personnel and Guidance Assn., Chgo. Guidance and Personnel Assn. (dir. 1952-55, hospitality com. 1958-59). Nat. Vocational Guidance Assn., Ill. (mem. human resources com. 1974-76, labor relations com. 1976—), Evanston (chmn. personnel mgrs. group 1970-71) chambers commerce, No. Ill. Indsl. Assn. (personnel practices survey com. 1959-62, vice chmn. 1961), Am. Assn. U. Women, Pi Beta Phi. Republican. Methodist (ofcl. bd. 1956-59, 62-65, mem. lay personnel com. 1963-68). Home: 1567 Ridge Ave Evanston IL 60201 Office: 1630 Chicago Ave Evanston IL 60201

SCHALES, OTTO, chemist, med. adminstr.; b. Frankburt-am-Main, Germany, Dec. 27, 1910; s. Johann Ludwig and Margarete (Linck) S.; came to U.S., 1939, naturalized, 1944; B.S., U. Frankfurt, 1929, D.Sc. (Justus Liebig fellow), 1935; m. Elizabeth Anne Lloyd, May 12, 1966. Research asso. fgn. univs., 1936-39, Harvard Med. Sch., 1939-44; dir. dept. chemistry Peter Bent Brigham Hosp., Boston, 1939-44; dir. chem. research Alton Ochsner Med. Found., New Orleans, 1944-62; asst. prof. biochemistry Tulane U. Med. Sch., New Orleans, 1947-48, asso. prof., 1948-51, prof., 1951-64; dir. dept. chemistry Elyria (O.) Meml. Hosp., 1966—; v.p. North Central Labs. Inc., Elyria, 1968-74, pres., 1975—. Van't Hoff fellow, 1938; research grantee NIH, 1947-63. Fellow N.Y. Acad. Scis., A.A.A.S., Am. Assn. Clin. Chemists (pres. 1955-56); mem. Am. Chem. Soc. (chmn. div. biol. chemistry 1955-56), Am. Soc. Biol. Chemists, Soc. Exptl. Biology and Medicine, Ohio Soc. Clin. Pathologists (hon.). Contbr. articles to publs. in U.S., abroad. Home: 333 West Ave Elyria OH 44035 Office: Elyria Meml Hosp Elyria OH 44035

SCHALK, LAWRENCE ANDREW, veterinarian; b. Cin., Sept. 9, 1933; s. Clarence Lawrence and Carrie (Oser) S.; B.S. in Agr., Ohio State U., 1955, D.V.M., 1959; m. Wilma Mae Karns, June 4, 1955; children—Debra Ann, Robert Lawrence, William Allen. Practice veterinary medicine specializing in bovine and equine medicine and surgery, Mt. Victory, Ohio, 1959-60, Wakarusa, Ind., 1969-71, Rockford, Mich., 1971—. Mem. Am., Mich., Western Mich. veterinary medicine assns., Am. Assn. Equine Practitioners, Am. Assn. Bovine Practitioners, Mich. Harness Horse Assn. Clubs: Lions, Masons (Cedar Springs, Mich.). Home: 5815 18 Mile Rd Cedar Springs MI 49319 Office: 9937 Northland Dr Rockford MI 49341

SCHALLERT, RUSSELL CLARENCE, lawyer; b. Milw., Feb. 7, 1938; s. Clarence T. and Sylvia (Lewin) S.; B.S., Northwestern U., 1960; J.D., Marquette U., 1963; m. Betty Ellen Kegel, June 18, 1960; children—Elizabeth Ruth, John Benjamin Clarence, Russell Clarence. Admitted to Wis. bar, 1963, since practiced in Milw.; adminstrv. asst. to U.S. Referees in Bankruptcy for U.S. Dist. Ct. Eastern Dist. Wis., 1963-65; partner deVries, Vlasak & Schallert, 1965—. Mem. Whitefish Bay (Wis.) Sch. Bd., 1973-76. Mem. Am., Fed. (past v.p. Milw. chpt.), Wis., Milw., Milw. Jr. (past com. chmn.) bar assns., Am. Judicature Soc., Def. Research Inst., Delta Theta Phi. Lutheran. Home: 6225 N Berkeley Blvd Milwaukee WI 53217 Office: 700 N Water St Milwaukee WI 53202

SCHAMAUN, THOMAS EVERETT, optometrist; b. Bazine, Kans., Feb. 10, 1921; s. John Albert and Ruby Blyller (Anderson) S.; student U. Kans., 1940-42, 45-46; O.D., No. Ill. Coll. Optometry, 1948; m. Patricia Rae Painter, June 30, 1945; children—Linda (Mrs. Douglas A. Wyse), Gregory Thomas, Rodrick Todd, Nannette Marie. Pvt. practice optometry, Eaton, O., 1950—. Vice pres. Eaton Loan and Home Aid, Eaton Profl. Bldg., treas. Preble Lanes Inc. Served with USCGR, 1942, USNR, 1943-45. Mem. Am., Ohio optometric assns. Methodist. Clubs: Eaton Country, Masons, Lions. Home: 730 W Main St Eaton OH 45320 Office: 122 W Decatur St Eaton OH 45320

SCHAMIS, JEFFREY BERNARD, educator; b. N.Y.C., Aug. 7, 1947; s. David Daniel and Florence (Haupt) S.; A.B. with high honors, U. Rochester, 1968; postgrad. U. London (Eng.), 1966-67; M.A., U. Chgo., 1969, Ph.D., 1972, J.D., 1976. Instr. philosophy U. Chgo., 1973; instr. philosophy and humanities Kennedy-King Coll., Chgo., 1973-75; asso. firm D'Ancona, Pflaum, Wyatt & Riskind; vis. asst. prof. philosophy Northwestern U., Evanston, Ill., summer 1974. Ford fellow, 1968-72; N.Y. State Regents fellow, 1968-71; Danforth teaching fellow, 1969; Goethe Fund grantee, 1969. Mem. Am. Philos. Assn., Am., Chgo. bar assns., A.C.L.U. Home: 5436 E View Park Chicago IL 60615

SCHAPPLER, NORBERT MAURICE, librarian; b. Atchison, Kans., July 23, 1926; s. Martin Wenceslaus and Justina (Ruhlmann) S.; A.B., Conception (Mo.) Coll., 1949; student Immaculate Conception Sem., 1949-53; M.A. in L.S., Rosary Coll., River Forest, Ill., 1954. Ordained to ministry Roman Cath. Ch., 1952; librarian Immaculate Conception Sem. and Conception Abbey, 1954—; faculty Immaculate Conception Sem., 1954-61. Bd. dirs., v.p. NW Mo. Library Network, 1977—. Mem. Am., Mo., Cath. (chmn. sem. sect. 1968-70), Kansas City Theol. (pres. 1970-71) library assns., Am. Benedictine Acad. (chmn. library sect. 1965-67). Address: Conception Abbey Conception MO 64433

SCHARRES, JOHN WILLIAM, cons. engr.; b. Chgo., Sept. 3, 1912; s. John and Martha Margaret (Busse) Scharres; student Lewis Inst., 1935-40, Ill. Inst. Tech., 1940-41; m. Mary Hermes, May 1, 1954. Chief engr. E. R. Gritschke & Assos., Chgo., 1950-61, pres., 1961; Scharres & Assos., Cons. Engrs., Chgo., 1961—. Registered profl. engr., Ill. Mem. Nat., Ill. socs. profl. engrs., IEEE, Am. Soc. Heating, Refrigerating and Air Conditioning Engrs., Power Engring. Soc. Constrn. Specifications Inst., Am. Arbitration Assn. (mem. panel of arbitrators 1976—). Office: 2 Riverside Plaza Chicago IL 60606

SCHATTINGER, JAMES HENRY, mfg. co. exec.; b. Glen Cove, N.Y., Oct. 2, 1935; s. John Joseph and Margaret Florence (Kearns) S.; B.S., Mass. Inst. Tech., 1959; M.B.A. (Standard Oil scholar), Harvard, 1963; m. Joan Katherine Myers, July 22, 1961; children—Elisabeth, James. Cons. Stricker & Henning Research Assos., N.Y.C., 1959-60; mgr. comml. products div. Standard Oil of Ohio, Cleve., 1960-68; exec. v.p., mgr. Pioneer Mfg. Co., Cleve., 1968-74, pres., treas., 1974—, also dir.; dir. MacCarl Co., Products Chem. Co. Officer, dir. Council of Small Enterprises; dir. Greater Cleve. Growth Assn. Served with U.S. Army, 1954-56. Home: 3620 Tolland Rd Shaker Heights OH 44122 Office: 3057 E 87th St Cleveland OH 44104

SCHATZLEIN, ROBERT GARY, audio producer and exec.; b. Knightstown, Ind., May 10, 1953; s. George Michael and Helen Frances (Hoover) S.; student Ind. U., Bloomington, 1972-74. Exec. dir. Contemporary Talent Assos., Indpls., 1972-74; v.p. TRC Corp., Indpls., 1973-75, pres., 1975—; exec. producer TRC Prodn. Group, 1973—; dir. TRC Crop., IDEA Corp.; preceptor, instr. audio engring. and broadcast prodn. Butler U., Depauw U., Sangamon State U.; prodns. include: audio prodn. Power Passers comml. Lionel div. Gen. Mills (Advt. Age award 1977), Peddler LP for United Artists Records, comml. music for 100 maj. advertisers. Republican. Club: Advt. (Indpls.). Home: 4902 N Brouse St Indianapolis IN 46205 Office: 1330 N Illinois St Indianapolis IN 46202

SCHAUB, RUSSELL EDWARD, finance co. exec.; b. Northwood, Iowa, July 20, 1932; s. Earl D. and Margaret (Wright) S.; B.A., Iowa Wesleyan U., 1954; postgrad. U. Minn., 1960; m. Joan L. Helgeson, Dec. 19, 1954; children—Diana Jo, Kathleen Ann. Tchr. math. Center Point (Iowa) High Sch., 1955-56, high sch., Titonka, Iowa, 1956-59; mathematician Investors Diversified Services, Mpls., 1960-66; dir. data processing Sci. Computers, Mpls., 1966-67; dir. data processing and ops. research Super Valu Stores, Hopkins, Minn., 1967-74; v.p., adminstrn., gen. mgr. Midwest Data Systems subs. Celina Financial Corp., Celina, Ohio, 1974—. Danforth scholar, 1950; NSF scholar, 1959-60; named Boss of Year C. of C., 1972. Mem. Ops. Research Soc. Am., Soc. Indsl. Applied Math., Soc. Certified Data Processors, Blue Key, Lambda Chi Alpha. Republican. Methodist. Home: 5420 E State Rd 703 Celina OH 45822 Office: Insurance Square Celina OH 45822

SCHAUER, THOMAS ALFRED, ins. co. exec.; b. Canton, Ohio, Dec. 24, 1927; s. Alfred T. and Marie A. (Luthi) S.; B.Sc., Ohio State U., 1950; m. Joanne Alice Fay, Oct. 30, 1954; children—Alan, David, Susan, William. Ins. agt., Canton, 1951—; with Schauer & Reed Agy., 1951—, Kitzmiller, Tudor & Schauer, 1957—, Webb-Broda & Co., 1971—, Foglesong Agy., 1972—; pres. Independent Ins. Service Corp. Akron and Canton, Canton, 1964—; dir., Central Trust Co. Northeast Ohio, Canton Supply Co. Chmn., Joint Hosp. Blood Com., 1974. Bd. dirs. United Way, Canton, 1974, pres., 1977-78; bd. dirs. Better Bus. Bur., Canton, 1970—, Hosp. Bur. Central Stark City, 1972—, Aultman Hosp., 1971—, JMS Found., 1968—; bd. dirs. Dist. YMCA, 1974—, now v.p.; mem. distbn. com. Stark County Found., 1977—. Served with USNR, 1946-48. C.L.U., C.P.C.U. Mem. Chartered Ins. Inst. London, Nat. Assn. Mfg., Am. Soc. C.P.C.U.'s, Am. Soc. C.L.U.'s, Am. Mgmt. Assn., Assn. Advanced Life Underwriters, Am. Soc. Pension Actuaries. Clubs: Canton, Brookside Country. Home: 3755 Eaton Dr NW Canton OH 44708 Office: 801 Cleve-Tusc Bldg Canton OH 44702

SCHEANWALD, MARJORIE DIANA, clinic adminstr.; b. Toledo, Sept. 27, 1926; s. August Gottleib and Henrietta Hilda (Helbing) Scheanwald; student Saginaw (Mich.) pub. schs. Clk., Sugar Beet Products, Saginaw, 1944-46; Heavenrich's, Saginaw, 1946-56; receptionist Valley Ob-Gyn Clinic P.C., (and predecessor firms), Saginaw, 1956—, asst. sec., 1974—, also dir. Mem. Am. Assn. Med. Assts., Med. Group Mgmt. Assn., Mich. Assn. Med. Group Mgrs. Republican. Presbyterian. Home: 311 S Wheeler St Saginaw MI 48602 Office: 926 N Michigan St Box 3216 Saginaw MI 48605

SCHEETZ, AL, realtor; b. Stark County, O., Sept. 14, 1898; s. Peter and Catherine (Friedman) S.; grad. Canton (O.) Actual Bus. Coll., 1921; m. Lucille Helen Narwold, Oct. 7, 1933. With Ohio Realty Co., Canton, 1924-25; propr. Al Scheetz Agy., Canton, 1925—; appraiser and cons. for municipalities, lectr. to univs. and schs. Pres. Canton Real Estate Bd., 1947, Canton Speakers Club, 1948. Mem. adv. bd. Philomatheon Soc. for Blind. Mem. Am. Soc. Real Estate Counselors, (bd. govs. 1969-71), Ohio Assn. Real Estate Bds. (v.p. 1950). Soc. Residential Appraisers (pres. Akron chpt. 1950), Am. Inst. Real Estate Appraisers. Lion (pres. Canton 1955-56). Club: Canton. Home: 3421 22d St NW Canton OH 44708 Office: 601 Central Trust Tower Canton OH 44702

SCHEFFEL, KENNETH GEORGE, splty. chems. co. exec.; b. St. Louis, May 2, 1936; s. George and Katherine S.; A.B., U. Mo.; M.A., U. Calif.; m. Marilyn L. Hardy, June 7, 1959; children—Steven, Laurl, Sherri, Beth. Program mgr. UMC Industries, Phoenix, 1960-62; bus. devel. mgr. Dow Chem. Co., Midland, Mich., 1962-69; group product mgr. Ralston Purina Co., St. Louis, 1969-73; v.p., gen. mgr. splty. chems. C.J. Patterson Co., Kansas City, Mo., 1973-77, also dir.; pres., chief exec. officer Christian Hansens Lab., Inc., Milw., 1977—. Com. dir. Daniel Boone council Boy Scouts Am., St. Louis. Mem. Am. Mgmt. Assn., Am. Mktg. Assn., Am. Chem. Soc., Inst. Food Fedn., Synthetic Organic Chems. Mfg. Assn., Phi Kappa Psi. Republican. Methodist. Home: 18985 Glen Kebry Dr Brookfield WI 53005 Office: 9015 N Maple St Milwaukee WI 53214

SCHEFFLER, LAURA JANE, educator; b. Cumberland, Md., Apr. 6, 1942; d. John Elias and Mary Lois (Cupler) McDonald; B.S., Ohio U., 1963, M.A. in Speech Pathology, 1965; m. James Robert Scheffler, Dec. 10, 1966; 1 son, Andrew Scheffler. Speech therapist Zanesville (Ohio) City Schs., 1964-67; Portsmouth (Va.) City Schs., 1968-69, Hamilton (Ohio) City Schs., 1971-73, substitute tchr., 1976-77; speech therapist Fairfield City Schs., 1977—; instr. Ohio U., Zanesville, 1965. Certified Am. Speech and Hearing Assn. Mem. Am., Ohio speech and hearing assns. Home: 608 Millikin St Hamilton OH 45013 Office: 5050 Dixie Hwy Fairfield OH 45014

SCHEFTNER, GEROLD, dental equipment mfg. co. exec.; b. Milw., June 1, 1937; s. Arthur Joseph and Alice Agnes (Gregory) S.; student Milw. Bus. Inst., 1953, Great Lakes Naval Acad. Sch. Dental-Med. Surgery, USAF, 1955-56, USAF Inst., 1959, Marquette U., 1959-60; children—Marc A., Margaret L., Mark A., Mary L., Scot P., Michael D. Territorial rep. Mossey-Otto Co., dental retailers, Milw., 1960-63; with Den-Tal-Ez Mfg. Co., dental equipment mfg., Des Moines, 1963—, dir. foreign affairs, 1969-71, dir. far eastern affairs, 1971-72, exec. dir. internat. sales, marketing, 1973-74, v.p., gen. mgr. internat. ops., 1974—, also dir.; chmn. bd. Dentalez (Gt. Britain) Ltd., 1974—; pres. Meridian Corp., Des Moines. Dir. Iowa Dist. Export Expansion Council, 1969-73; mem. Lake Panorama (Iowa) Devel. Assn., 1972-73; chmn. Iowa World Trade Council. Mem. adv. bd. St. Charles Boys Home Bldg. Program, Milw., 1963. Served with USAF, 1955-59. Recipient presdl. mgr. of the year award Den-Tal-Ez Co., 1967; Lecture award Faculdade de Odontologia, U. Ribeiro Preto, Brazil, 1974. Mem. Am. Dental Trade Assn., Am. Dental Mfrs. Assn., Greater Des Moines C. of C. (dir. dist. export council); hon. mem. Hong Kong Dental Trade Assn., Internat. Platform Assn. Republican. Lion. Clubs: TWA Ambassador; International (Frankfurt, Germany). Research in develop. equipment and apparatus for acupuncture therapy. Office: 1201 SE Diehl St Des Moines IA 50315

SCHELKOPF, RUSSELL LEVOY, veterinarian; b. Geneva, Nebr., June 30, 1930; s. Isaac Newton and Lena Mildred (Schrock) S.; student Nebr. Wesleyan U., 1947-48; B.S., U. Nebr., 1952, M.S., 1954; Ph.D., Iowa State U., 1958, D.V.M., 1958; m. Bernice Elaine Nuss, Aug. 26, 1951; children—Michael, Charles, Steven. Veterinarian, Hall Vet. Clinic, Elburn, Ill., 1958-59; pvt. practice vet. medicine, Sycamore, Ill., 1959—. Pres., Illini Farms, Inc., Sycamore, 1970—, Anderson & Schelkopf, D.V.M., Ltd., Sycamore, 1970—; sec.-treas. Cornhusker Agr. Assos., Inc., Shickley, Nebr., 1969—; sec. Cornhusker Cattle Co., Shickley, 1971—. NSF fellow, 1954-58. Mem. Am., Ill. vet med. assns., Ill. C. of C. Home: 229 Somonauk St Sycamore IL 60178 Office: Baseline Rd Kingston IL 60145

SCHELL, RALPH RAY, mktg. cons.; b. Jasper, Mo., Jan. 12, 1943; s. Ralph Zolo and Velma Ann (Withers) S.; A.A., Sch. of the Ozarks, 1962; B.S., Kansas State Coll. at Pittsburg, 1970, M.S., 1971; m. Jan. 12, 1968; children—Michael Ray, Denise Marie. Chmn. dept. computer sci. Sch. of the Ozarks, Point Lookout, Mo., 1971-73; life underwriter Equitable of Iowa, Springfield, Mo., 1973; supr. computer ops. Carthage Marble Corp. (Mo.), 1974-75; owner, mgr. Joplin Mktg. Services (Mo.), 1976—. Served with USAF, 1963-67. Mem. Coll. and Univ. Eleven Thirty Users Group, Data Processing Mgmt. Assn. Baptist. Home: 2505 Vandalia St Joplin MO 64801

SCHENCK, DOUGLAS GARRISON, assn. exec.; b. Boston, Dec. 29, 1909; s. John Winfield and Sarah Emma (VanBuren) S.; student Lincoln U., 1929-30, Detroit Inst. Tech., 1950-53, Saginaw Valley State Coll., 1972-75; m. Madeline Goode, June 1939 (dec. Mar. 1952); children—Anita Schenck Banks, Harriet A. Schenck Kotomori, Edna C. Schenck Jones, Margaret M. Schenck Valentine; m. 2d, Charlena Howard, June 19, 1964. Reporter newspapers, 1929-38; with U.S. Pub. Housing Adminstrn., Detroit, 1949-54, U.S. Corps Engrs., Detroit dist., Great Falls, Mont., 1955-62; with U.S. Govt. Def. Contract Adminstrn., Detroit, also Saginaw, Mich., 1962-69; exec. dir. Unity Non-Profit Housing Corp., Saginaw, 1969-74; counselor, tchr. adult basic edn. Saginaw Bd. Edn., after 1974. Adv. com. Title XX Services Mich. Dept. Social Services, 1975—. Chmn. compensatory edn. council Saginaw Bd. Edn., 1964-74; sec. Municipal Planning Com., Inkster, Mich., 1950-55; exec. dir. S. Saginaw Civic Assn., 1964-70; active Boy Scouts Am., Medford, Mass., 1946-49, Saginaw, 1964-68. Chmn. bd. dirs. Cosmopolitan Community Center, Utica, N.Y., 1941-42; bd. dirs. Youth Activities West Medferd (Mass.) Community Center, 1943-49; vice chmn., treas. St. Paul's Episcopal Non-Profit Housing Corp., Saginaw, 1965-70; adv. bd. Neighborhood House, Saginaw, 1974-75; mem. Region VII Mich. State Advisory Council Aging. Recipient Community Service award South Saginaw Civic Assn., 1971, Distinguished Community award Saginaw Bd. Edn., 1976. Mem. NAACP (state, regional dir. housing 1966-71), Adult Edn. Assn. U.S.A. (chpt. pres. 1972-75), Nat. Assn. Ret. Fed. Employees, Mich. League Human Services (dir. 1974—). Elk. Home: 2934 S Washington Ave Saginaw MI 48601

SCHENCK, NORMA ELAINE (MRS. ARTHUR H. SCHENCK), sch. adminstr.; b. South Connellsville, Pa., Oct. 14, 1926; d. Gloster Dale and Etta L. (Hall) Hepler; B.S., Ind. U., 1949, M.S., 1963; postgrad. Ind. State U., 1973; m. Arthur H. Schenck, July 21, 1951; children—Lynn L., Kenneth Arthur. Sec. to chief recruitment sec. VA, Washington, 1946-47; tchr. bus. edn., St. Joseph County, Ind., 1949-50, Lakeville, Ind., 1950-53, Washington High Sch., South Bend, Ind., 1959-65; chmn. bus. edn. dept. Co-op. Office Edn., coordinator Jackson High Sch., South Bend, 1965-70; coordinator bus. edn. South Bend Community Sch. Corp., 1970—. Project dir. Career Guidance Inst., South Bend, 1973-74; tchr. Am. Inst. Banking, South Bend, 1972-73, Ind. U., South Bend, 1972-74. Mem. Nat. Suprs. Bus. Edn. (pres. 1978-79), Nat., Ind. (pres. 1978-79) bus. edn. assns., AAUW (br. pres. 1964-66, 1st v.p. Ind. div. 1975-77), Am. Soc. Tng. and Devel. (2d v.p. Michiana chpt. 1973-74), Am. Soc. Personnel Adminstrn. (pres. Michiana chpt. 1973-74), Am. Ind. (Merit award, 1973), vocat. assns., Delta Kappa Gamma, Phi Delta Kappa, Pi Lambda Theta. Home: 1354 E Huffman Dr South Bend IN 46614 Office: 635 South Main St South Bend IN 46601

SCHENCK, ROBERT ROY, hand surgeon; b. Brimfield, Ill., Sept. 19, 1931; s. Isaac Barrett and Pearl (Murnan) S.; B.A. in Chemistry, Taylor U., 1951; M.D., U. Ill., 1955; m. Audrey Rabalais, Feb. 5, 1977; children—Claudia, Lynn, Owen, Karen, Heidi, Robert. Rotating intern Akron (Ohio) Gen. Hosp., 1955-57; staff physician Door of Life Hosp., Ambo, Shoa Province, Ethiopia, 1960-61; fellow in hand surgery and hand anatomy Hosp. for Joint Diseases and Columbia U., N.Y.C., 1962; mem. attending staff Brownsville (Pa.) Gen. Hosp. and mem. Centerville Clinic, 1962-67; resident in gen. surgery Western Pa. Hosp., Pitts., 1967-69, resident in plastic surgery Presbyn. Hosp., N.Y.C., 1969-71; fellow in hand surgery Roosevelt Hosp., N.Y.C., 1971-72; asst. attending physician depts. plastic and orthopedic surgery, dir. sect. hand surgery Rush-Presbyn.-St. Luke's Med. Center, Chgo., 1972—; asst. instr. in human anatomy Columbia U., 1962, asst. in surgery, 1969-70, instr. in surgery, 1970-71; asst. prof. plastic and orthopedic surgery, dir. sect. hand surgery Rush Med. Coll., 1972—. Served with USPHS, 1957-59. Recipient Med. Photograph Blue Ribbon award CIBA, 1965. Diplomate Am. Bd. Plastic Surgery. Fellow A.C.S.; mem. Indsl. Med. Assn., Am. Soc. Plastic and Reconstructive Surgeons, Am. Soc. Surgery of Hand, Chgo. Soc. Indsl. Medicine and Surgery, Chgo., Ill. State, Christian med. socs., AMA, Holland Soc. Republican. Club: Union League. Contbr. articles to profl. publs.; writer med. films. Home: 100 E Bellevue Pl Apt 5-C Chicago IL 60611 Office: 1725 W Harrison St Chicago IL 60612

SCHENCK, WILLIAM EDWARD, electronics co. exec.; b. Mpls., June 30, 1917; s. Charles Henry and Marian (Bishop) S.; B.A., Wayne U., 1939; m. Marjorie Walker, Feb. 14, 1942; children—Charles, Marilyn, Marjorie, Christine. Cost clk. Gen. Motors Co., 1939-41; accountant, retail specialist Ernst & Ernst, 1941-47; controller Peninsular Grinding Wheel Co., 1947-52; asst. to pres. Calvert Lithographing Co., 1952-55; treas. Security Aluminum Co., Highland Park, Mich., 1955-60; gen. mgr. Hardware Co., chain stores, Detroit, 1960-69; chmn. bd. Lectron Products Inc., Troy, Mich., 1970—; cons. in field. Pres. W. Bloomfield High Sch. PTA, 1962-63; mem. Nat. UN Day Com., 1977—. C.P.A. Mem. Am. Inst. C.P.A.'s, Mich. Assn. C.P.A.'s. Republican. Presbyterian. Clubs: Orchard Lake Country (Mich.); Marco Shores Country (Fla.). Home: 6640 Commerce Rd Orchard Lake MI 48033 Office: 1800 Stephenson Hwy Troy MI 48084

SCHENK, QUENTIN FREDERICK, social worker, social psychologist, educator; b. Ft. Madison, Iowa, Aug. 25, 1922; s. Fred Edward John and Ida Margaret Caroline (Sabrowsky) S.; B.A., Willamette U., 1948; M.S., U. Wis., 1950, M.S.S.W., Ph.D., 1953; m. Emmy Lou Willson, May 23, 1970; children—Fred (dec. 1972), Patricia, Karl, Martha. Asst. prof. U. Wis., Madison, 1953-55; asso. prof. U. Mo., Columbia, 1955-61; Fulbright sr. lectr., Italy, 1959-60; prof., chmn. dept. social work U. Wis., Milw., 1961-63, dean Sch. Social Welfare, 1963-68, co dir., specialist Ford project of U. Wis. to Brazil, 1962-63, Addis Ababa, 1968-71; sec., cons. World Council Chs., Africa, 1971; prof. social welfare U. Wis., Milw., 1971—; pvt. practice social psychology, 1971—; lectr., cons. Alderman City of

Cedarburg, Wis., 1975—; mem. Cedarburg Planning Commn., Library Bd., Landmark Preservation Soc., Fiscal Control Bd. Served with USNR, 1942-46. Decorated 3 Air medals. Knapp grad. fellow, 1950. Mem. Am. Sociol. Assn., AAUP, Council Social Work Edn., Aircraft Owners Pilots Assn., Am. Legion, Cedarburg Firemans Assn., Porsche Club Am. Author: (with E.L. Schenk) Pulling Up Roots, 1978. Contbr. articles profl. jours. Home: Box 2335 W61 N439 Washington St Cedarburg WI 53012 Office: University of Wisconsin Milwaukee WI 53201

SCHENZ, ROYDEN TINDLE, architect; b. Akron, Ohio, Sept. 1, 1940; s. Royden L. and Mildred B. S.; B.S. Architecture, U. Cin., 1964; m. Magdalene Carol Turinsky, June 11, 1964; children—Royden Gregory, Denys Kimberely, Beth Ann. Asso. Tuchman & Canute, Akron, 1964-74; asso. Derr-Cornachione, Akron, 1974—. Archtl. adviser Neighborhood Redevel. Corp., Model Cities, Akron. Trustee Kvam Kinder Camp for Brain Injured. Mem. AIA (chpt. pres. 1973-74), Architects Soc. Ohio (trustee 1974-76), Lambda Chi Alpha. Catholic. Home: 456 Honeysuckle Wadsworth OH 44281 Office: 2830 Copley Rd Akron OH 44321

SCHEPER, JACK LEE, radio sta. exec.; b. Chgo., Jan. 20, 1934; s. Ernest R. and Ruth Viola (Harrison) S.; student U. Mo. at Columbia, 1955-57; m. Jacqueline Jean Hays, Sept. 8, 1961; children—Linda Ruth, Jack Lee, John Leslie. With Irwin's Men Shop, Cape Girardeau, Mo., 1946; mem. mgr. tng. program J.C. Penny Co. Cape Girardeau, 1947-50; asst. mgr. Allen's Dept. Store, Wildwood, N.J., 1957; mgr. Gidding Dept. Store, Wildwood, 1957-59; gen. mgr. radio sta. WHCO, Sparta, Ill., 1959—, host program People Speak, 1961—; supr. radio sta. KFMO, Flat River, Mo., 1975—. Active Boy Scouts Am.; dir. Civil Def., Sparta, 1960—; chmn. Sparta Community Devel. Study with So. Ill. U., 1960-63, mem. Randolph County (Ill.) Devel. Study, 1959-63; treas. Sparta Municipal Bldg. Commn., 1969—; mem. policy bd. Sparta OEO, 1969-71; mem. adv. com. Dist. 140 Sch. Bd., 1974-76; sec. Ill. State Adv. Bd. on Emergency Communication and Transp., 1975—; chmn. adv. com. Sparta City Council, 1966-70; mem. Sparta Zoning Commn., 1967-71; mem. Regional Manpower Ceta Program State of Ill. Served with USAF, 1950-54. Recipient Community Devel. award So. Ill. U., 1963; U.S. Savings Bond Service award, 1973; Radio Talkathon award Carbondale chpt. Easter Seal Soc., 1974; Broadcast Service award Optimist Club, 1974; Be Counted Again award Am. Legion, 1974; Appreciation award VA, 1971; Neighborhood award Sparta OEO, 1972; Statuette award Boy Scouts Am., 1973; Thank You award Lions Club Internat., 1973; March of Dimes Merit award, Nat. Found., 1970; Ill. Sec. of State Minuteman 76 award. Mem. Nat., Ill. assns. broadcasters, U.S., Sparta (indsl. rep. 1961—, dir. 1959—, pres. 1960, 67-69, 74-75) chambers commerce. Presbyterian (deacon, tchr.). Mason, Rotarian (pres. 1964, dir. 1959-65; Fellowship award 1964). Home: 208 S Dickey St Sparta IL 62286 Office: WHCO Box 255 Sparta IL 62286

SCHEPMAN, HENRY FREDERICK, lawyer; b. Lockwood, Mo., Sept. 26, 1898; s. William and Friedericke (Heuke) S.; student U. Chgo., 1921; A.B., U. Nebr., 1924, J.D., 1924; m. Sherlie Whitaker, Dec. 6, 1928; 1 son, John Henry. Admitted to Nebr. bar, 1924, since practiced in Falls City; sec. to Congressman Morehead 69th and 72d Congresses, county atty. Richardson County, Nebr., 1953-67, 71-75. Chmn. local unit Salvation Army, 1949-75; exec. bd. Cornhusker council Boy Scouts Am., 1959. Mem. Nebr. Ho. of Reps., 1925-27. Senate, 1929-32. Bd. control Concordia Tchrs. Coll., Seward, Nebr., 1958-68. Served with inf., U.S. Army, World War I. Mem. Am. Legion (past adj.), Nebr. County Attys. Assn. (pres. 1959-60), S.E. Nebr. (pres. 1958), Nebr., Am. bar assns., Luth. Laymen's League (pres. Nebr., Wyo. 1957, 58), Delta Theta Phi. Mem. bd. of appeals Luth. Ch.-Mo. Synod, 1956-59. Rotarian (dist. gov. 1954-55). Home: 2302 Chase St Falls City NE 68355 Office: Richardson County Bank Bldg Falls City NE 68355

SCHER, PAUL LAWRENCE, rehab. services specialist; b. Chgo., Sept. 21, 1934; s. Victor Hugo and Edith Eloise (Cohen) S.; B.A. cum laude in Govt., Harvard U., 1957; M.A., U. Chgo., 1959; M.Ed., U. Ill., 1965; m. Ann Garrison Rubin, May 14, 1972; stepchildren—Susan Rubin, Laura Rubin. Dir. Ill. Gov.'s Com. on Employment of Handicapped, 1959-63; coordinator services for blind and deaf Rehab. Edn. Center, U. Ill., Urbana, 1963-65; respiratory cons. Chgo. Christmas Seals, 1965-66; rehab. counselor Calif. Dept. Rehab., 1966-68; pvt. cons., 1968-72; rehab. services specialist nat. personnel dept. Sears Roebuck & Co., Chgo., 1972—; lectr. World Commn. on Rehab.; v.p. Market Prespectives, Inc.; vocational expert Bus. Disability Determination, Social Security Adminstrn.; del. White House Conf. Handicapped Individuals, 1977. Bd. dirs. Chgo. Lighthouse for the Blind. Recipient certificate of merit Pres.'s Commn. on Handicapped, 1962; certified Commn. on Rehab. Counselor Certification. Mem. Nat. Rehab. Assn., Am. Rehab. Counseling Assn., Am. Personnel and Guidance Assn., Nat. Alliance Businessmen (chmn. com. penal edn.), Chgo. Symphony Soc., Art Inst. Chgo., Field Mus. Natural History. Office: Dept 707 1 Sears Tower Chicago IL 60684

SCHERECK, WILLIAM JOHN, historian, cons.; b. Chgo., Dec. 22, 1913; s. Frank and Adele (Schubert) S.; student Wofford Coll., 1950-51; B.S. in Sociology, U. Wis., 1952, postgrad., 1952-53; m. Flora Blanche George, May 19, 1943; children—Linda, William John, Ralph, George. With Crawford County (Wis.) Welfare Dept., 1938-42; with State Hist. Soc. Wis., Madison, 1953—, research asst., 1954-55, field services supr., 1956-59, head Office Local History, 1960—, Wis. Council Local History, 1961—. Active Girls Scouts U.S.A., Spartanburg, S.C., 1947-48, Boy Scouts Am., Madison, 1956-58. Served to 2d lt. U.S. Army, 1942-45. Decorated Bronze star medal; recipient 1st place award S.C. State Coll. Press Assn., 1951, Crusade for Freedom awards, 1951, 1st place award for Sounds of Heritage, Am. Exhbn. Ednl. Radio and Television, 1955. Mem. Am. Legion, Ret. Officers Assn., Am. Fedn. State, County and Municipal Employees, Wis. Alumni Assn., Smithsonian Instn., Madison Civic Opera Guild, Costeau Soc., Field Mus. Natural History. Episcopalian. Author numerous publs. State Hist. Soc. Am. Contbr. articles to mags. and newspapers. Home: Route 3 4329 Harmony Dr Lodi WI 53555 Office: 816 State St Madison WI 53706

SCHERIBEL, KARL JOHN, ophthalmologist; b. Graz, Austria, Aug. 19, 1908; s. Karl and Sofie Elizabeth (Lechner) S.; student Crane Jr. Coll., Chgo., 1925-27; B.S., Loyola U., Chgo., 1930, M.D., 1931; came to U.S., 1913, naturalized, 1918; m. Feb. 14, 1942; children—Karl W., Marlene Elizabeth. Attending ophthalmologist Cook County Hosp., Chgo., 1938-58, Swedish Covenant Hosp., Chgo., 1932—; asst. attending ophthalmologist, 1967-76, attending ophthalmologist, 1976—, prof. ophthalmology Rush Presbyn. St. Lukes Med. Sch., 1976—; asst. prof. ophthalmology, Cook County Hosp., 1936-58; asst. prof. ophthalmology Abraham Lincoln Sch. Medicine U. Ill., Chgo., 1958—. Contbr. articles on ophthalmology to med. jours. Home: 3018 Hollywood St Chicago IL 60659 Office: 55 E Washington St Chicago IL 60602

SCHERICH, ESTHER ANNE, editor; b. New Haven, Dec. 15, 1943; d. Millard and Esther (Petersen) Scherich; B.A., Oreg. State U., 1966; M.A., U. Oreg., 1970, D.Arts, 1973, Ph.D., 1975. Sec. dept. English, U. Oreg., Eugene, 1966-69; research asst., 1969-70, teaching fellow English, 1970-75: manuscript editor Moody Bible Inst., 1977—. Mem. Women in Communications, Modern Lang. Assn. Am., AAUP, Am. Soc. for Eighteenth Century Studies, Kappa Delta. Republican. Episcopalian. Home: 821 N Washington Wheaton IL 60187 Office: Moody Bible Inst 820 N LaSalle St Chicago IL 60610

SCHERICH, MILLARD, clergyman, educator; b. Inland, Nebr., June 6, 1908; s. Harry Erwin and Ella March (Peterson) S.; A.B., Hastings Coll., 1930; Th.M., Iliff Sch. Theology, 1934, Th.D., 1936; postgrad. U. Idaho, summers 1940, 41, 42; M.A., Yale U., 1944, Ph.D., 1946; postdoctoral diploma U. Mich., 1957; m. Esther Marie Petersen, Sept. 30, 1942; children—Esther Anne, Millard Thomas, Mary Rebecca. Ordained to ministry Methodist Ch., 1937; pastor Kuna (Idaho) Meth. Ch., 1935-39, Nyssa (Oreg.) Meth. Ch., 1939-40; supt. schs. Kuna, 1940-42; pastor Thomaston (Conn.) Congl. Ch., 1943-44; teaching fellow Yale U., 1943-45; asst. prof. Okla. State U. at Stillwater, 1945-46, asso. prof., 1946-48, prof., head dept. philosophy, 1948-61, chmn. dept. religion, dir. instl. self study program, dir. council for academic excellence, 1957-61; pastor Corvallis (Ore.) First Presbyn. Ch., 1961-68; prof. philosophy of edn. Wheaton (Ill.) Coll., 1968-74; pastor Oak Brook (Ill.) Ch. on the County Line, 1974—. Recipient Outstanding Service certificate Okla. State U., 1971. Mem. Am. Philos. Assn., Philosophy of Edn. Soc., Assn. Higher Edn., Omicron Delta Kappa, Phi Eta Sigma, Phi Delta Kappa, Pi Gamma Mu, Kappa Delta Pi. Rotarian. Author: An Educational Philosophy of Reconciliation, 1951; Reconciliation in Educational Philosophy, 1959; American Education, an Historical Introduction, 1973. Contbr. articles to various publs. Home: 821 N Washington St Wheaton IL 60187

SCHERLING, ORLANDO KENNETH, photographer; b. Fargo, N.D., Aug. 12, 1921; s. Arvid R. and Sophia J. (Wagner) S.; student N.D. State U., 1939-41; grad. N.Y. Sch. Modern Photography, 1946; m. Sheila Kaye Walker, May 25, 1969; children—Steven, Michael, Patrick, Larry, Jerry, Randall, Kristy. Technician, Barclay Studios, Phila., 1946-48; pres., owner Scherling Studios, Inc., Fargo, 1949—. Adviser, cons. Am. Family Products, Omaha, 1972—. Recipient Nat. Service award Photographers Assn., 1956. Mem. Am. Soc. Photographers, N.D. (pres. 1952-53), Minn. photographers assns., Press Photographers Assn. Am. (Nat. Qualified award 1966), C. of C. Elk, Rotarian. Photographs selected for exhibit Nat. Traveling Loan Collection, 1955-56. Home: 1301 Oak St Fargo ND 58102 Office: 313 Broadway Fargo ND 58102

SCHERLING, RICHARD EDWARD, dept. store exec.; b. Dubuque, Iowa, June 12, 1921; s. Gustav J. and Florence (Keller) S.; B.A. in Bus. Adminstrn., U. Mich., 1942; m. Elizabeth Bailie, June 6, 1942; children—Kathryn, Richard Edward, John. With The Killian Co., Cedar Rapids, Iowa, 1946—, sales promotion mgr., 1946-49, mdse. mgr., 1950-54, gen. mdse. mgr., exec. v.p., pres., now chmn. bd., 1971—. Active A.R.C. (dir. past chmn. Linn County chpt.). Bd. dirs. St. Lukes Hosp.; chmn. bd. trustees Coe Coll. Served as officer USNR, World War II. Mem. Nat. Retail Mchts. Assn. (past chmn., bd. dirs. merchandising div.), Cedar Rapids C. of C. (past pres.), Greater Downtown Assn. (sec., dir.), Phi Delta Theta. Republican. Presbyn. Rotarian (past pres.). Club: Cedar Rapids Country. Mem. adv. com. Stores mag. Home: 300 27th St Dr SE Cedar Rapids IA 52403 Office: The Killian Co 201 3d Ave Cedar Rapids IA 52401

SCHERMERHORN, KENNETH DEWITT, mus. condr.; b. Schenectady, Nov. 20, 1929; s. Willis and Charlotte (Raes) S.; Artists Diploma, New Eng. Conservatory of Music, 1950; D.Music, Ripon Coll., 1973; m. Guadalupe Martinez, Dec. 30, 1958 (div.); children—Erica Louise, Veronica Lynn; m. 2d, Carol Neblett, 1973; 1 son, Stafan Gerrit. Asst. condr. N.Y. Philharmonic, 1959-60; mus. dir. Am. Ballet Theatre, 1957-67, N.J. Symphony, 1963-68, Milw. Symphony, 1968—. Served with U.S. Army, 1951-55. Office: 929 N Water St Milwaukee WI 53202

SCHERRER, ROBERT ALLAN, chemist; b. Sacramento, Nov. 21, 1932; s. William Richard and Betty Rose (Davis) S.; B.S., U. Calif., Berkeley, 1954; Ph.D., U. Ill., 1958; m. Marilynn Clabaugh, Sept. 4, 1954; children—Linda, Steven, Lawrence, Edward. Asso. research chemist Parke, Davis & Co., Ann Arbor, Mich., 1958-61, research chemist, 1961-66; sr. medicinal chemist Minn. Mining and Mfg. Co., St. Paul, 1966-69, research specialist, 1969-72; sr. research specialist Riker Labs. div. 3 M Co., 1972—. Mem. Am. Chem. Soc. Editor: (with Dr. M.W. Whitehouse) Antiinflammatory Agents, 1974. Mem. editorial bd. Journal of Medicinal Chemistry, 1974—. Patentee in field. Office: Riker Laboratories 3M Center 218-1 Saint Paul MN 55101

SCHERZER, MELVYN HARRY, printing co. exec.; b. St. Louis, July 26, 1915; s. Harry Louis and Clara Mae (Frey) S.; ed. Washington U., St. Louis, 1935-37; m. Irma Maguire, Feb. 9, 1944; children—Melvyn Harry, Gail Marilyn (Mrs. William Winham), Joyce (Mrs. David Shimamoto), Craig Alan, Bradley Glenn, Donald Scot (dec. Aug. 1972). With John S. Swift Co. Inc., St. Louis, 1933—, v.p., 1960—. Former bd. dirs. Salvation Army, Sales and Mktg. Execs., Vocat. Counseling and Rehab. Services, bd. dirs. Soc. Preservation of the Masonic Temple, Inc. Served with USNR, Intelligence Dept., 1942-45. Mem. Am. Assn. Indsl. Mgmt. Republican. Presbyn. Mason (33 deg., Shriner). Club: Missouri Athletic. Home: 12370 Sparrowwood Dr St Louis MO 63141 Office: 1248 Research Blvd St Louis MO 63132

SCHICK, HAROLD, city ofcl.; b. Omro, Wis., Feb. 8, 1922; s. Gottfried F. and Eva Elisabeth (Brinkman) S.; B.S., Mich. State U., 1949, M.S., 1956; postgrad. U. Mich., 1956-58; m. Jo Ann Cline, Apr. 3, 1943; 1 son, Karl Frederick. Park and recreation supt. City of LaCrosse, Wis., 1951-55; regional parks supt. State of Ore., Salem, 1959-62, state parks supt., 1962-64; dir. Fairmount Parks Commn., Phila., 1964-69; chmn. parks and recreation dept. Ohio State U., 1969-74; dir. Cleve. Met. Parks System, 1974—. Chmn., Barnabey Center for Outdoor Edn. and Natural Resources. Commr., Boy Scouts Am., 1968—, mem. exec. bd. Greater Cleve. council, 1975—, chmn. steering com. Bicentennial Jamboree, 1975-76. Mem. adv. bd. Salvation Army; mem. Pres.'s Club and campus planning adv. bd. Ohio State U.; mem. Cleve. Mayor's Lakefront Devel. Com. Served with AUS, 1943-46. Decorated Purple Heart. Mem. Nat. Recreation and Parks Assn. (chmn. exec. devel. com.), Ohio Parks and Recreation Assn. (v.p.), Am. Inst. Park Execs. (Distinguished Service award 1960), Cleve. Greater Growth Assn., Inter Museum Council, Nat. Audubon Soc., Gamma Sigma Delta. Home: 343 Royal Oak Blvd Richmond Heights OH 44143 Office: 55 Public Sq Cleveland OH 44113

SCHICK, JOSEPH SCHLUETER, educator; b. Davenport, Iowa, Mar. 23, 1910; s. Charles and Johannah (Schlueter) S.; grad. Browne and Nichols Sch., Cambridge, Mass., 1927; B.A., U. Iowa, 1931; M.A., U. Chgo., 1932, Ph.D., 1937. English instr. U. Iowa, 1935-36; prof. English, State Tchrs. Coll., Duluth, Minn., 1938-42, 45-46; lectr. Am. lit. Caserta Tech., Italy, 1945; Merit prof. English, Ind. State U., 1946-76. Served from pvt. to sgt. U.S. Army, 1942-45, cryptanalyst Signal Intelligence. Mem. Am. Assn. U. Profs., Modern Lang. Assn. Am., Iowa, Ind. hist. socs., Phi Sigma Iota, Blue Key. Author: The Early Theater in Eastern Iowa, 1939; also articles profl. jours. Exhibited paintings Swope Gallery, Terre Haute, 1953, 55. Patentee on cobber. Home: 248 S 26th St Dr Terre Haute IN 47803

SCHIEFELBEIN, BENEDICT, chemist; b. Brighton, Colo., June 17, 1943; s. Peter and Elizabeth (Hoffman) S.; B.A., U. Colo., 1965; Ph.D., Colo. State U., 1969; m. Claudine Lucille Ellis, June 8, 1968; children—Johanna Elizabeth and Virginia Lucille (twins). Research and teaching asst., dept. chemistry Colo. State U., Ft. Collins, 1965-69; sr. research staff mem. U.S. Gypsum Research Center, Des Plaines, Ill., 1969—. Mem. Fox River Grove (Ill.) Planning Commn., 1974—, chmn., 1975—; mem. Community Devel. Commn., 1975—, Fox River Grove Zoning Bd. of Appeals, 1976—. Mem. Am. Chem. Soc. (inorganic div. 1973). Contbr. articles to profl. jours. Patentee in field. Home: 420 Woodbine Lane Fox River Grove IL 60021 Office: 1000 E Northwest Hwy Des Plaines IL 60016

SCHIERER, ROBERT CHARLES, dairy co. exec.; b. Washington, Ill., Aug. 24, 1929; s. Benjamin Michael and Gay Muriel (Stivers) S.; B.S., Bradley U., 1975; m. Alice Mae Seckler, July 19, 1952; children—Timothy Lee, Tama Lynn, Ted Patrick. With Schierer's Dairy, Inc., Peoria, Ill., 1949—, sec.-treas., 1961—; dir. Metamora Industries, Inc. (Ill.). Served with Army N.G., 1951, 56. Mem. Central Ill. Dairy Tech. Soc., Peoria C. of C. Roman Catholic. Clubs: Metamora Bus. Men (pres. 1965), Kiwanis (pres. 1971); North Side Bus. Men's (Peoria); Buyers and Sellers; K.C. (4th deg.). Home: 706 W Progress St Metamora IL 61548 Office: 3530 NE Adams St Peoria IL 61603

SCHIFF, HERBERT HAROLD, shoe co. exec.; b. Columbus, O., Oct. 6, 1916; s. Robert W. and Rebecca (Lurie) S.; grad. Peddie Sch., 1934; B.B.S., U. Pa., 1938; m. Betty Topkis, June 19, 1938; children—Suzanne (Mrs. Murray Gallant), Patricia (Mrs. Richard Hershorin), Jane Ann (Mrs. Douglas J. Fleckner). With SCOA Industries Inc. (formerly Shoe Corp. Am.), Columbus, 1938—, exec. v.p., 1962-65, pres., 1965—, dir., 1955—; chmn. bd., 1968—; dir. Ohio Nat. Bank, Columbus. Mem. exec., adminstrv. coms. Am. Jewish Joint Distbn. Com.; mem. cabinet United Jewish Appeal; mem. nat. exec. bd. Am. Jewish Com. Bd. dirs. Jewish Center, Heritage House, Hillel Found. Ohio State U., United HIAS, Council Jewish Fedns. and Welfare Funds, Nat. Council Am. Jewish Joint Distbn. Com.; mem. exec. bd., past pres. United Jewish Fund and Council; trustee United Israel Appeal. Fellow, mem. exec. com. Brandeis U. Mem. Ohio Retail Mchts. (dir.), Fgn. Policy Assn. (nat. council), Newcomen Soc. N. Am., Vol. Footwear Retailers Assn. (active hon. dir.), Nat. Footwear Mfg. Assn. (past dir.), Am. Retail Fedn. (dir. vice chmn., exec. com., consumer relations com.), Am. Footwear Industries Assn. (past dir.). Mem. B'nai B'rith. Clubs: Athletic, Winding Hollow Country (Columbus); Standard (Chgo.); Presidents (Ohio State U.); Longboat Key Golf, University (Sarasota, Fla.). Home: 1620 E Broad St Columbus OH 43203 Office: 35 4th St Columbus OH 43215

SCHIFF, MARTIN, JR., lawyer; b. Akron, O., July 28, 1930; s. Martin and Edith May (Koontz) S.; A.B., Cornell U., 1952; J.D., Washington U., 1958; m. Mary Lou Bockius, July 21, 1962; children—Kurt Gregory, Karen Louise, Betsy Suzanne, Debra Lea. Admitted to Mo. bar, 1958; law asso. Husch, Eppenberger, Donohue, Elson & Cornfeld, St. Louis, 1958-65; pvt. practice, Clayton, 1965-66; partner Edwards & Schiff, 1967-70, Fordyce, Mayne, Hartman, Renard & Stribling, 1970-72; pvt. law practice, Webster Groves, Mo., 1972—. Spl. pros. atty. City of Webster Groves, 1959-61. Republican candidate for St. Louis County circuit judge, 1964. Served to lt. USNR, 1952-55. Mem. Am., St. Louis County (exec. com. 1967) bar assns., Mo. Bar (bd. govs. 1975—), Bar. Assn. Met. St. Louis, Lawyers Assn. St. Louis, Mo. Assn. Trial Attys., John Marshall Club, Webster Groves C. of C., Order of Coif, Phi Delta Phi. Presbyn. Lion. Home: 1 Gramercy Place Glendale MO 63122 Office: 30 W Lockwood Ave Webster Groves MO 63119

SCHIFF, SHELDON KIRSNER, psychiatrist; b. Bklyn., Sept. 29, 1931; s. Albert and Judith (Kirsner) S.; B.A., Washington Sq. Coll., N.Y. U., 1952; M.D., U. Chgo., 1956; m. Louise Antoinette Latsis, June 29, 1957; 1 son, Nicholas. Rotating intern Kings County Hosp., Bklyn., 1956-57; psychiat. resident Yale U. Sch. Medicine, 1957-60, also instr. psychiatry, 1962-63; chief psychiat. resident Grace-New Haven Hosp., 1959-60; asst. prof. psychiatry U. Ill. Sch. Medicine, Chgo., 1963-66; asso. prof. psychiatry Pritzker Sch. Medicine, U. Chgo., 1967-71; clin. prof. psychiatry Univ. Health Sci./Chgo. Med. Sch., 1974-76, dir. sch. intervention and tng. program, dept. psychiatry, 1970-71; practice medicine specializing in psychiatry, Chgo., 1971—; co-founder, co-dir. Woodlawn Mental Health Center, Chgo., 1963-70. Mental Health instr. City of New Haven (Conn.) Police Dept., 1959; psychiat. cons. Conn. Commn. Alcoholism, 1959-60; cons. group psychotherapy Norwich (Conn.) State Hosp., 1962-63; psychiat. cons. City of Chgo. Bd. Health, 1963-70; cons. Chgo. area plan for workers' mental health and labor edn. Roosevelt U., Chgo., 1964-65; psychiat. cons. Ill. State Psychiat. Inst., 1965-66; examiner Am. Bd. Neurology and Psychiatry, 1969; cons. Nat. Center Health Service Research and Devel., Washington, 1969; examiner N.Y. State Dept. Mental Hygiene, 1970; pres. Children's Center for Learning Capacities, Chgo., 1970—; cons. sch. mental health Muscatine-Scott County (Iowa) Sch. System, 1970-71; cons. presch. mental health Point Breeze Nursery Sch., Pitts., 1971; psychiat. cons. juveniles Ill. State Dept. Corrections, 1971; chief psychiatry Downey (Ill.) VA Hosp., 1973—. Mem. Woodlawn Urban Progress Center Adv. Bd., City of Chgo. Com. Urban Opportunity, 1964; mem. Greater Chgo. Com. Rehab., Welfare Council Met. Chgo., 1964-66; mem. systems analysis com. Ill. Mental Health Planning Bd., Ill. State Dept. Mental Health, 1966-67; mem. adv. health com. City of Chgo. Commn. Human Relations, 1966-70; chmn. Service Agys. Council on Woodlawn, Chgo., 1967-69. Served to capt., 8th Inf., M.C., AUS, 1960-62. Ill. State Dept. Mental Health grantee, 1964-65, Research Authority grantee, 1965-68; NIMH grantee, 1966-70; van Amerigen Found. grantee, 1968-69; Wieboldt Found. grantee, 1968-69; Field Found. grantee, 1968-69; Maurice Falk Med. Fund grantee, 1968-69, 70; Ia. State Mental Health Authority grantee, 1971. Diplomate Am. Bd. Neurology and Psychiatry, Nat. Bd. Med. Examiners, Pan Am. Med. Assn. Fellow Am. Psychiat. Assn. (sec. task force on poverty 1969-70), Am. Orthopsychiat. Assn. (mem. com. community mental health centers 1967-71; mem. children's mental health services com. 1968-70), Am. Pub. Health Assn.; mem. Am. Acad. Polit. and Social Sci., AAUP (pres. U. Chgo. chpt. 1967-70; mem. com. accrediting colls. and univs. 1969-71; mem. ad hoc investigating com. U. Fla. 1969), Am. Ednl. Research Assn., Am. Sch. Health Assn., N.Y. Acad. Sci., Organisation Mondiale pour l'Education Prescholaire, U.S. Nat. Com. Early Childhood Edn., World Fedn. Mental Health, Phi Chi. Contbg. author: (with S.G. Kellam) chpt. to Mental Health and Urban Social Policy: A Casebook of Community Actions (eds. L. Duhl and R. Leopold), 1968; chpt. to Procs. of 10th Ann. Conf. on Research in Med. Edn., 1971; chpt. to Handbook of Community and Social Psychology (eds. S. Golann and C. Eisdorfer), 1972. Contbr. numerous articles in field to profl. jours. Home: 6901 S Bennett Ave Chicago IL 60649 Office: 1642 E 56th St Chicago IL 60637

SCHILL, ROBERT JAMES, architect; b. Chgo., Aug. 30, 1939; s. Edward John and Mabel Edna (Harroun) S.; B.Arch., U. Ill., 1962, M.Arch., 1963; m. Janice Elaine Dahlstrom, Dec. 21, 1963; children—Carla Grace, Craig Robert, Kelvin Edward. Designer, engr.

Laz & Edwards, architects, Champaign, Ill., 1962-63, Jack C. Blackman, architect, Danville, Ill., 1963-64; asso. Richardson, Severns, Scheeler & Assos. Inc., Champaign, 1966-72, chief of prodn., 1968-72, also bd. mem.; project architect Metz, Train, Olson & Youngren, Inc., Chgo., 1972—, asso. partner, 1974—. Chmn. bd. Toddlers Campus Day Care Center, Urbana, 1970-72. Recipient citizenship award V.F.W., 1958. Mem. A.I.A. (corporate; health facilities com. Chgo. chpt. 1974—), Central Ill. Constrn. Com., Am. Concrete Inst., Nat. Fire Protective Assn., Soc. Archtl. Historians, Nat. Trust for Historic Preservation. Mem. Protestant Bible Ch. (chmn. ofcl. bd. 1969-72). Prin works include Rush Med. Coll., Chgo., Indpls. Mus. Art Complex, Undergrad. Library, U. Ill., Urbana. Home: 11 S Evanston Ave Arlington Heights IL 60004 Office: 1 E Wacker Dr Chicago IL 60601

SCHILLER, ALFRED GEORGE, veterinarian; b. Irma, Wis., Dec. 5, 1918; s. Adam and Bertha (Schiller) S.; D.V.M., Mich. State U., 1943; M.S., U. Ill., 1956; m. Carolyn Capps, Apr. 14, 1944; children—James Richard, Charles Thomas. Pvt. practice vet. medicine, Mpls., 1947-52; veterinarian U. Ill. Dept. Vet. Medicine, 1952—, acting dept. head, 1976—. Served to capt. AUS, 1943-47. Recipient Ill. Veterinarian of Yr. award, 1972. Diplomate Am. Bd. Veterinary Surgeons. Mem. Am. Animal Hosp. Assn., Ill. State Vet. Med. Assn., Am. Coll. Vet. Surgeons (pres. 1972, exec. sec. 1975—). Republican. Home: 405 Park Ln Champaign IL 61820 Office: U Ill Coll Veterinary Medicine Urbana IL 61801

SCHILLER, DONALD CHARLES, lawyer; b. Chgo., Dec. 8, 1942; s. Sidney S. and Edith L. (Lastick) S.; student Lake Forest Coll., 1960-63; J.D., DePaul U., 1966; m. Eileen Fagin, June 14, 1964; children—Ieric, Jonathan. Admitted to Ill. bar, 1966; partner firm Schiller & Schiller, Chgo., 1966—; lectr. in field; guardian and litem for minor children in contested custody cases appointed by judges Circuit Ct. Cook County, Ill., 1971—. Fellow Am. Acad. Matrimonial Lawyers (bd. mgrs. 1973—); mem. Am. (vice chmn. divorce law and procedure com. 1973—), Ill. (chmn. sect. family law 1975-76, editor Family Law bull.), Chgo. (chmn. matrimonial law com. 1976-77) bar assns., Nat. Conf. Conciliation Cts. (asso.), Decalogue Soc. Lawyers, Covenant Club Ill. Columnist matrimonial law Chgo. Daily Law Bull., 1975—. Contbr. articles to legal jours. Home: 2506 St Johns St Highland Park IL 60035 Office: 100 N La Salle St Chicago IL 60602

SCHILLER, JAMES JOSEPH, lawyer; b. Cleve., July 1, 1933; s. Jacob Peter and Helen Elizabeth (Tosh) S.; B.S. in Mech. Engring., Case Western Res. U., 1955; J.D., U. Mich., 1961; m. Sara Brooke Wilson, Oct. 24, 1964; children—Charles Alexander, Brooke VanGeem, Kristan Wilson. Admitted to Ohio bar, 1961, since practiced in Cleve.; mem. firm Zellmer & Gruber, 1973—. Co-chmn. John J. Gilligan Gubernatorial campaign, Cuyahoga County, 1970; mem. Ohio Democratic Exec. Com., 1970-74, Cuyahoga County Dem. Exec. Com., 1971—; del., mem. drafting com. Ohio Dem. Constl. Conv., 1971; dep. registrar motor vehicles Cuyahago County, 1971-75. Served to lt. (j.g.) USNR, 1955-58. Mem. Am., Ohio, Cleve. bar assns. Clubs: Cleve. City; Shaker Heights Country. Home: 3311 Maynard Rd Shaker Heights OH 44122 Office: 1400 Leader Bldg Cleveland OH 44114

SCHILLING, EDWARD GEORGE, statistician, educator; b. Lancaster, N.Y., Nov. 9, 1931; s. Edward F. and Mildred R. (Frey) S.; B.A., U. Buffalo, 1953, M.B.A., 1954; M.S., Rutgers U., 1962, Ph.D., 1967; m. Jean Catherine Bork, Sept. 5, 1959; children—Elizabeth Ann, Kathryn Jean. Instr. statistics U. Buffalo, 1957-59, 62-63, instr. mgmt. sci., 1963-64; engr. RCA, Somerville, N.J., 1959-61; teaching asst. statistics Rutgers U., New Brunswick, N.J., 1961-62, instr. statistics, 1964-67; sr. engr. Carborundum Co., Niagara Falls, N.Y., 1962-64; asso. prof. statistics Rochester (N.Y.) Inst. Tech., 1967-69; cons. statistician Lamp div. Gen. Electric Co., Cleve., 1969-74, mgr. statistics and quality systems operation, 1975—. Instr. statistics Case Western Res. U., Cleve., 1969-70; lectr. math. U. Akron, 1974; adj. asso. prof. math. Cleve. State U., 1976. Served with U.S. Army, 1955-57. Fellow Am. Soc. Quality Control (Brumbaugh award 1973), Am. Statis. Assn.; mem. Am. Soc. Testing and Materials, Inst. Math. Statistics, Am. Econ. Assn., Sigma Xi. Contbr. articles to profl. publs. Home: 1683 Rushton Rd South Euclid OH 44121 Office: Lighting Business Group Gen Electric Co Nela Park Cleveland OH 44112

SCHILLING, JOHN MICHAEL, editor; b. Hiawatha, Kans., Nov. 23, 1951; s. George Herman and Darlene Joy (Wachter) S.; student Highland Coll., 1972; B.S., U. Kans., 1974; m. Pamela Sue Hischke, Sept. 5, 1969; children—John Michael II, James Alan. Asso. editor, advt. mgr. Kansas Country Living mag. Kans. Electric Cooperatives, Inc., Topeka, 1974-75, editor, sales mgr., 1976—. Active United Way, 1975-77, Boy Scouts Am. Recipient Bruce B. Brewer Advt. Campaign award Young and Rubicam, 1974; Cooperative Editorial award Coop. Editorial Assn. 1976; George M. Haggard Meml. Journalism award Nat. Rural Electric Coop. Assn., 1976; award of Excellence, 9th dist. Am. Advt. Fedn., 1975, 76, 77. Mem. Coop. Editorial Assn. (dir.), Kans. Press Assn., Topeka Advt. Club, Topeka Press Club, Nat. Electric Cooperative Editorial Assn., Am. Inst. Cooperation, Western Rural Editorial Exchange, Midwestern Advt. Exchange, Am. Assn. Agrl. Editors, Jr. C. of C., Sigma Delta Chi. Club: Elks. Contbr. articles to consumer mags. and trade jours. Home: 2249 Indian Trail Topeka KS 66614 Office: Box 4267 Gage Center Sta Topeka KS 66604

SCHILLING, KATHERINE LEE TRACY (MRS. CLARENCE R. SCHILLING), educator; b. Mitchell, S.D., May 31, 1925; d. Ernest Benjamin and Mary Alice (Courier) Tracy; B.A., Dakota Wesleyan U., 1947; M.A., U. S.D., 1957; postgrad. U. Wyo., U. Nebr., Kearney State Coll.; m. Clarence R. Schilling, Oct. 14, 1951; 1 dau., Keigh Leigh. Tchr. elementary and secondary schs., also colls., S.D. and Nebr.; now with specially funded project for disadvantaged children Winnebago Indian reservation, Nebr. Mem. staff S.D. Girls' State, 1950-51; mem. S.D. Gov.'s Com. on Library, Neb. Gov.'s Com. on Right to Read. Recipient Outstanding Tchr. award S.D. High Sch. Speech Tchrs., 1966. Mem. NEA, Nebr., Thurston County (pres.) edn. assns., Winnebago Tchrs. Assn., Delta Kappa Gamma. Mem. Order Eastern Star. Club: Internat. Toastmistress (internat. dir. 1963-65, Mitchell Toastmistress of Year 1959). Contbr. articles to profl. jours., also poetry. Office: Winnebago Public Sch Winnebago NE 68071

SCHIMMELPFENNIG, JERRY DEAN, mfg. exec.; b. Sigourney, Iowa, May 29, 1941; s. Vernie Austin and Dorothy (McCune) S.; B.A., Iowa Wesleyan Coll., 1963; M.A., N.E. Mo. State Tchrs. Coll., 1968; m. Kathleen D. Grandall, Aug. 20, 1963; children—Tad, Matthew, Joseph. Tchr., Van Buren Community Schs., Keosauqua, Iowa, 1964-67; stockbroker, sec.-treas. Arnet-McCabe & Co., 1968-71; pres. Sci. Applications, Inc., Mt. Pleasant, Iowa, 1971—; dir. Woodside Properties, Mt. Pleasant Bank & Trust Co. Mem. Mt. Pleasant Sch. Bd., 1972-75. Mem. Am. Mgmt. Assn. Republican. Presbyterian. Office: Box 615 C H1295 Mount Pleasant IA 52641

SCHIMPFF, WAYNE HUBER, ednl. adminstr.; b. Chgo., Mar. 12, 1941; s. G. Weber and Rosalind Amelia (Klaas) S.; student North Central Coll., 1959-61; B.S., Wis. State U., 1963; M.S. in Edn., No. Ill. U., 1971; m. Gail Roberta Cech, Oct. 19, 1968. Tchr. Willow Springs (Ill.) Pub. Schs., 1964-68; naturalist Forest Preserve Dist. Cook County, Ill., 1968-70; dir. environ. edn. Open Lands Project, Chgo., 1970-76; chief naturalist Ill. Dept. Conservation, 1976—. Park ranger Ind. Dunes Nat. Lakeshore, Nat. Park Service, 1973—; sr. citizen environ. edn. coordinator Loop Colls. Chgo., 1973; asso. faculty mem., coordinator outdoor environ. edn. program Nat. Coll. Edn., Evanston, Ill., 1974—; sr. cons. environ. edn. Ill. Office of Supt. Pub. Instruction, 1972-76. Committeeman Boy Scouts Am., 1963—; instr. Am. Red Cross, 1959—. Dir. Chgo. Audubon Soc.; dir. Save the Dunes Council; pub. participation coordinator Northeastern Ill. Planning Commn., 1975—. Recipient 15 Year Service award A.R.C., 1974, Environ. Quality award EPA, 1975. Mem. Sierra Club, Nat. Wildlife Fedn., Camp Sagawau Conservation Club. Cons. to environment publs. Home: 1866 Mandel Ave Westchester IL 60153 Office: 605 State Office Bldg Springfield IL 62706

SCHIPIOUR, SHARON ANN, educator; b. Chgo., Dec. 29, 1943; d. Chester Anthony and Ann Helen (Kolodziejski) Mocny; B.E., Chgo. Tchrs. Coll., 1964; M.S. in Edn., Chgo. State U., 1977; m. Anthony William Schipiour, May 14, 1966; children—Anthony Chester, Nicholas James. Sec., United Currency Exchange, Chgo., 1956-64; collection mgr. Spiegel Co., Chgo., 1962-63; English tchr. Tilden High Sch., Chgo., 1964-74, counselor, 1974-76, tchr., 1976—. Mem. Chgo. Tchrs. Union, Am. Personnel and Guidance Assn., Tilden Tech. Alumni Assn. Roman Catholic. Clubs: Women of the Moose. Home: 7 N Edgewood St La Grange IL 60525 Office: 4747 S Union St Chicago IL 60609

SCHIPPERS, DAVID PHILIP, lawyer; b. Chgo., Nov. 4, 1929; s. David Philip and Angela Marie (Lyons) S.; J.D., Loyola U., Chgo., 1959; m. Jacquelin Joyce Liautaud, Apr. 19, 1952; children—Kathleen M., David Philip III, Antoinette M., Ann L., Colleen M., Thomas M., Kevin D., Mary A., Patrick F., Peter A. Admitted to Ill. bar, 1959; engr. Bell Telephone Co., Chgo., 1951-59; mem. firm Pope, Ballard, and others, Chgo., 1961-62; asst. U.S. Atty., Chgo., 1962-63; trial atty., organized crime and racketeering section U.S. Dept. Justice, Chgo., 1963-65, chief section, 1965-67; partner Schippers, Betar, Lamendella & O'Brien, law firm, Chgo., 1967—. Mem. Ill. Crime Investigation Com., 1969—; mem. Mayor's Com. Organized Crime Legislation, Chgo., 1964—. Recipient outstanding young man award Jr. C. of C., Northbrook, Ill., 1970, medal of excellence Loyal U. Law Alumni, 1967, Loyola U. Alumni citation, 1970. Mem. Am., Ill., Chgo. bar assns., Am. Judicature Soc., Am., Ill. trial lawyers assns., Fed. Criminal Investigators Assn., Am. Assn. Criminal Lawyers, Fed. Nat. Defender Program, Am. Arbitration Assn. Home: 1240 Church St Northbrook IL 60062 Office: 79 W Monroe St Chicago IL 60603

SCHIRRIPA, DENNIS JAMES, dentist; b. Cleve., Dec. 30, 1945; s. Joseph L. and Norma Teresa S.; B.S., John Carroll U., 1970; D.D.S., Case Western Res. U., 1974. Salesman, Form-A-Tool Co., 1964-71; lab. technician St. John's Hosp., Cleve., 1972-74; gen. practice dentistry, Medina, Ohio, 1974—; instr. Co-op Medina Joint Vocat. Sch. Chmn. Medina County unit Am. Cancer Soc., 1976-77. Mem. Ohio Acad. Dentistry for Children, Acad. Gen. Dentistry, Am. Endodontic Soc., Psi Omega (sec.). Roman Catholic. Clubs: Exec., Wedgewood Country. Address: 152 Highland Dr Medina OH 44256

SCHJELDAHL, GILMORE TILMEN, mfg. co. exec.; b. Esmond, N.D., June 1, 1912; s. Ole Cornelius and Anna (Bently) S.; student N.D. State U., 1937-43, D.Sc. (hon.), 1970; student Va. Poly. Inst., 1943-44; m. M. Charlene Hanson, Oct. 5, 1940; children—Peter C., Ann C., Peggy C., Don C., Mary C. Technician Armour & Co., 1940-43, research chemist 1945-47; tech. dir. Asso. Activities, 1947-49; pres. Herb-Shelly, Inc., 1949-54; founder Sheldahl, Inc., Northfield, Minn., 1955, pres., 1955-64, chmn. bd., treas., 1965-66, dir., 1955-69; founder, pres. Giltech Corp., Mpls., 1966-72, merged into Rainville Co., Inc., Middlesex, N.J., 1972—; chmn. bd. Rainville Co., Inc., 1972—. Served with U.S. Army, 1943-45. Decorated Bronze Star medal. Mem. Soc. Plastic Engrs., Soc. Plastic Industry. Lutheran. Patentee in machinery and adhesives. Home: 4436 Marlborough Ct Minnetonka MN 55343 Office: 200 Clay Ave Middlesex NJ 08846

SCHLACHTER, ROBERT JOHN, dentist; b. Toledo, June 3, 1923; s. Vincent Julius and Eleanor Kathern (Sattler) S.; B.S., Western Res. U., 1949, D.D.S., 1951; m. Carol Ann Wise, June 14, 1958; children—Linda (Mrs. Mark Giles). Patricia (Mrs. David LaPlante). Robert Vincent, Philip H., Teresa C. Pvt. practice dentistry, Toledo, 1951—. Comdr. Toledo Power Squadron, 1971. Served with USNR, 1942-46; PTO. Mem. Am. Dental Assn., Am. Cleft Palate Assn. Clubs: Toledo Yacht (commodore), Toledo. Home: 2702 Goddard Rd Toledo OH 43606 Office: 4207 Monroe St Toledo OH 43606

SCHLAPKOHL, EMMET KELLY, supt. schs.; b. Davenport, Iowa, July 3, 1930; s. Emmet L. and Dorothy D. (Kelly) S.; B.A., U. No. Iowa, 1955; M.A., U. Iowa, 1959, Ed.S., 1970; m. Mary C. Wilkinson, Aug. 16, 1952; children—Cynthia, Carole, Nancy. Tchr., Wellman (Iowa) Pub. Schs., 1955-57; asst. supt. Mid-Prairie Community Schs., Wellman, 1957-59; elementary prin. Washington (Iowa) Community Schs., 1959-61, high sch. prin., 1961-65, asst. supt., 1965, supt., 1966—. Chmn. Washington County Selective Service System, 1968—; chmn. J.B. Dill Student Scholarship Trust Fund; chmn. Fund drive U. No. Iowa. Pres. Washington Community Chest Bd., 1963; bd. dirs., sec. bd. YMCA, Washington, Iowa, 1965-71. Served with AUS, 1952-54. Recipient Washington Jaycees Community Distinguished Service award, 1962, Outstanding Boss award, 1971. Mem. Iowa Assn. Sch. Adminstrs., Washington County Edn. Assn. (pres. 1959-60), Am. Legion. Republican. Methodist. Mason, Rotarian (pres. 1965-66) (Washington, Iowa). Home: Green Meadows Washington IA 52353 Office: 404 W Main St Washington IA 52353

SCHLARBAUM, ROGER LEE, real estate agy. exec.; b. Mt. Auburn, Iowa, Aug. 1, 1939; s. Harley Merle and Blanche Margaret (Healy) S.; grad. high sch.; m. Joyce Lee Abernathy; children—Kevin, Scott, Lori. Farmer, Mt. Auburn, 1958-60; salesman Fuller Brush Co. br., Benton County, Iowa, 1960-61; mem. staff Abernathy Grocery Store, Vinton, Iowa, 1961-62; owner Rogers Clover Farm Grocery Store, Urbana, Iowa, 1962-67, also real estate salesman Oliphant Real Estate, Center Point, Iowa; owner, real estate broker Roger Schlarbaum Real Estate Agy., Vinton, Iowa, 1967—. Agt., Fire & Casualty Ins. Co., 1968—, Iowa Mut. Tornado Ins. Co., 1968—; co-owner Ins. Counselors, 1974—, Cummins Farm Mgmt., 1974—; co-owner, v.p. Vintex Corp., 1973—, Country Gardens, housing complex, 1974—; owner Schlarbaum's Farms, 1972—; co-owner, sec.-treas. Charger Enterprises, Inc., 1973—, all Vinton. Mem. Vinton Aquatic Club. Methodist (adv. bd.). Mason (32 deg., Shriner). Clubs: Vinton Country. Home: 1115 A Ave Vinton IA 52349 Office: 216 W 4th St Vinton IA 52349

SCHLECKER, OTTO, food cons.; b. Ulm, Germany, Oct. 22, 1921; s. Otto and Maria (Ganahl) S.; student Hotelfachschule, Munich, Germany, 1936-39; m. Hannah Krings, Apr. 13, 1949; children—Claude O., Kirk F. Came to U.S., 1961, naturalized, 1967. Apprentice, Hotel Deutscher Kaiser, Munich, 1936-39; cook Metropa, Deutsche Schlafwagen Ges., 1939; cook, chef various hotels in Europe, 1941-50; chef Mont Tremblant Hotel, Can., 1958-60; chef Waldorf Astoria Hotel, N.Y.C., 1961, Morrison Hotel, Chgo., 1961-62; cons. chef Griffith Labs., Chgo., 1962—; pres. Chef's Assos.; lectr., Auburn U., 1968, Boston Coll., 1970, Mental Health Inst., Tex., 1971. Served with German Air Force, 1943-45. Recipient Gold, Silver medals Am. Culinary Olympic Team, 1964, Silver medal Individual Culinary Olmypics, Frankfurt, Germany, 1968; Canner-Parker award, 1966, Lacroix award, 1968. Mem. Exec. Chef Assn. (founding pres.), Am. Culinary Fedn. (dir.), Soc. for Advancement Food Service Research, Inst. Food Tech., Acad. of Chefs, Internat. Food Service Cons. Contbg. editor: Culinary Rev., 1968-71, Die Kueche, 1971-72. Contbr. articles to profl. jours. Home: 712 Carpenter Ave Oak Park IL 60304 Office: 1437 W 37th St Chicago IL 60609

SCHLEMMER, ROBERT CLARK, appliance mfg. co. exec.; b. Sioux City, Ia., Feb. 11, 1921; s. John Arthur and Blanch Clara (Smith) S.; student Nat. Bus. Sch., 1939-40; B.A. in Accounting, Walton Sch. Commerce Chgo., 1951; m. Rita Mary Daldrup, May 14, 1943; 1 dau., Rachelle. Mgr., H.H. Hine, pub. accountant, Sioux Falls, S.D., 1941-43; sr. auditor T.J. Morgans, Jr., C.P.A., Sioux Falls, 1943-49; tax specialist Lybrand, Ross Bros. & Montgomery, C.P.A.'s, Chgo., 1952-55; mgr. internal auditing Maytag Co., Newton, Iowa, 1955-61, 76—, asst. controller, 1961-76, mgr. internal auditing, 1976—. Mem. adv. com. on finance Skiff Meml. Hosp., Newton, 1962-63. Headed various coms. on local sch. bond issue, Newton, 1970-71; mem. Newton City Council, 1977—. C.P.A., Ill. Mem. Newton C. of C. Republican. Roman Catholic (treas. ch. council 1971-72). Elks, K.C. Club: Newton Country. Home: 1207 S 14th Ave W Newton IA 50208 Office: 403 W 4th St N Newton IA 50208

SCHLEMMER, ROGER EDMUND, mfrs. rep.; b. Cin., June 23, 1906; s. Oliver H. and Blanche L. (Leuchtenburg) S.; M.E., U. Cin., 1929; m. Claribel Pendery, Apr. 23, 1932; 1 son, Roger Pendery. Aircraft and engine designer, stress analyst Aero. Corp. Am., Cin., 1929-33, chief engr., 1933-37; structural engr., aircraft engring. br. CAA, Kansas City, Mo., 1937-40, Washington, 1940-41, sr. aero. engr., 1941-42, chief aircraft engring. br., N.Y.C., 1942-45, Chgo., 1945-50; mech. engr. Cin. div. Bendix Aviation Corp., 1951-53, exec., engr., 1954-58; mfrs. rep., 1958-65; v.p., sec., treas. Schlemmer Assos., Inc., Cin., 1965—. Mem. Soc. Automotive Engrs., Am. Soc. for Metals, Phi Delta Theta. Presbyterian. Home: 7002 Constitution Dr Cincinnati OH 45215 Office: Schlemmer Assos 1172 W Galbraith Rd Cincinnati OH 45231

SCHLEPPI, ROBERT FREDERICK, state govt. ofcl.; b. Sept. 11, 1945; s. Vernon Chester and Margaret Louise (Humphrey) S.; B.S. in Edn., Ohio State U., 1968; M.S. in Corrections, Xavier U., Cin., 1975; m. Leah Joan Blankenship, Apr. 6, 1968; children—Jennifer Lynn, Michelle Ann. Transp. specialist Ohio Exposition Commn., 1965; successively counselor, athletic instr., boys club dir., recreation center supr. Columbus (O.) Recreation Dept., 1963-68; mem. staff Ohio Youth Commn., 1970—, asst. to dep. dir., Columbus, 1974—. Served to 1st lt. AUS, 1968-70; Vietnam. Decorated Army Commendation medal with 2 oak leaf clusters. Mem. Am. Correctional Assn. (dir.), Nat. Assn. Tng. Schs. and Juvenile Agencies, Ohio Correctional and Ct. Services Assn., Ohio Parks and Recreation Assn., Am. Cause, Ohio State U. Varsity O Assn. Lutheran. Home: 2899 Castlewood Rd Columbus OH 43209 Office: 35 E Gay St Columbus OH 43215

SCHLERETH, EUGENE PAUL, leather co. exec.; b. St. Louis, Sept. 11, 1917; s. Francis Jacob and Agnes Catherine (Stefl) S.; student St. Louis U., 1950-53; m. Dorothy Anne McDowell, Sept. 6, 1944; children—Dorothy (Mrs. Michael Hagan), Mary (Mrs. Ken Niebling), Gene, June, Kenneth. Vice pres. sales Hermann Oak Leather Co., St. Louis, 1935—. Profl. baseball player Minor League, Chgo. White Sox chain, 1940-41. Served with USAAF, 1943-46. Home: 5728 Madlar Ln Florissant MO 63034 Office: 4050 N 1st St St Louis MO 63147

SCHLERNITZAUER, DONALD ALLEN, ophthalmologist; b. Bellaire, Ohio, Jan. 5, 1942; s. Edward Anthony and Sara Elizabeth (Duvall) S.; A.B. with high honors, Cornell U., 1963, M.D., 1967; m. Pamela Joyce Trimbey, June 26, 1965; children—Amy Rose, Lori Jean. Intern, Mary Imogene Bassett Hosp., Cooperstown, N.Y., 1967-68; resident Wilmer Inst., Johns Hopkins Hosp., Balt., 1968-71; NIH spl. fellow in ophthalmic pathology Armed Forces Inst. Pathology, Washington, 1971-72; ophthalmologist Alliance (Ohio) Eye and Ear Clinic, 1974—; attending surgeon Alliance City Hosp., No. Columbiana County Community Hosp., Salem, Ohio; asst. clin. prof. ophthalmology Sch. Medicine, Case Western Res. U., 1975—; lectr. George Washington U., 1972, 73. Treas. Christ Reformed Chapel, Alliance. Served to lt. comdr. M.C., USNR, 1972-74; Recipient James Metcalf Polk prize Cornell U., 1967. Diplomate Am. Bd. Ophthalmology. Fellow Am. Acad. Ophthalmology and Otolaryngology; mem. AMA, Cleve. Ophthalmol. Soc., Ohio State, Stark County med. assns., Alpha Omega Alpha. Republican. Orthodox Presbyterian. Clubs: Alliance Country, Rotary. Co-author articles in tech. jours. Home: 619 E Milton St Alliance OH 44601 Office: 985 Sawburg Ave Alliance OH 44601

SCHLETZ, GEORGE ROBERT, accountant; b. Chgo., Sept. 30, 1937; s. George W. and Genevieve (Niedzwiecki) S.; B.S. in Commerce, DePaul U., Chgo., 1959; m. Marianne Relinski, Sept. 12, 1962; children—Julianne, Lawrence, Thomas. Staff accountant Motorola Inc., Chgo., 1959-60; accountant Peter Shannon & Co., Chgo., 1960-65; prin. G.R. Schletz, C.P.A., Chgo., 1965-71, Glenwood, Ill., 1975—; partner Hancock and Schletz, C.P.A.'s, Lansing, Ill., 1971-75; bus. advisory com. congressman Martin A. Russo. Mem. sch. bd. St. Jude the Apostle Sch., South Holland, Ill., 1973-75. C.P.A. Mem. Ill. C.P.A. Soc., Estate Planning Inst., Am. Inst. of C.P.A.'s, Computer Accountants Assn. (dir., pres. Great Lakes chpt. 1975), C. of C. of Frankfort. Roman Catholic. Clubs: Elks, Moose, Kiwanis. Home: Frankfort IL 60423 Office: 18430 S Halsted St Glenwood IL 60425

SCHLICHTER, JAKUB GERSON, physician; b. Bochnia, Austria (now Poland), Aug. 10, 1912; s. Joseph Samuel and Dora S.; came to U.S., 1943, naturalized, 1949; student Med. Sch. Vienna, 1932-38; B. Medicine, Med. Sch. Lausanne (Switzerland), 1938, M.D., 1940; m. Lois Newman, Oct. 3, 1965; 1 son, Mark D. Intern, Michael Reese Hosp., Chgo., 1945, resident in internal medicine, 1945-46, Dazion fellow in cardiology, 1944-47, research asso. cardiovascular dept., 1947-60; resident Hosp. Nestle's Lausanne, 1938-40; asst. in pathology Mt. Sinai Hosp., N.Y.C., 1943-44; asst. prof. medicine Med. Sch., Northwestern U., Chgo., 1952-77, asso. prof., 1977—; sr. attending physician in medicine Michael Reese and Weiss Meml. hosps., Chgo., 1947—; attending staff Grant and VA Research hosps., Chgo.; individual practice medicine, specializing in internal medicine, Chgo., 1947—. Served to maj., M.C., U.S. Army, 1953-54; PTO. Diplomate Am. Bd. Internal Medicine, Am. Bd. Cardiovascular Disease. Fellow A.C.P., Am. Coll. Chest Physicians, Am. Heart Assn.; mem. N.Y. Acad. Scis., AMA, Pan Am., Chgo. med. socs., Internat. Cardiol. Soc. Jewish. Contbg. author books, articles to profl. publs. Home: 3240 N Lake Shore Dr Chicago IL 60657 Office: 55E Washington St Chicago IL 60602

SCHLICKMAN, EUGENE FRANCIS, lawyer, state legislator; b. Dubuque, Iowa, Dec. 17, 1929; s. Leander J. and Helen (Juergens) S.; B.A., Loras Coll., 1951; LL.B., Georgetown U., 1956; m. Margaret M. Muraski, June 9, 1951; children—J. Andrew, Stephen E., Mary Elizabeth, Monica Ann. Admitted to D.C. bar, 1956, Ill. bar, 1957; practiced in Arlington Heights, Ill., 1963—; mem. firm Burfeind & Schlickman, Ltd., 1964—. Mem. Ill. Ho. of Reps., 1965—. Chmn. Ill. State Zoning Laws Study Commn.; chmn. Elementary and Secondary Non-pub. Schs. Study Commn., 1969-71; chmn. legislative adv. com. Northeastern Ill. Planning Commn., 1969-73. Village trustee Arlington Heights, 1959-63. Committeeman, Wheeling Twp. Republican Com., 1966-69. Named Man of Yr., Arlington Heights Jr. C. of C., 1959; recipient Outstanding Legislator award Rutgers U., 1966, award John Howard Assn., 1967, Outstanding Citizen award Des Plaines C. of C., 1976, Outstanding Legislator award Fedn. Ind. Ill. Colls. and Univs., 1976. Mem. Am., Ill., Chgo., N.W. Suburban bar assns. Club: K.C. Home: 1219 E Clarendon St Arlington Heights IL 60004 Office: 116 W Eastman St Room 205 Arlington Heights IL 60004

SCHLIENTZ, HARRY JAMES, assn. exec.; b. Montpelier, Idaho, Dec. 2, 1925; s. Harry Herbert and Rachel Mary (Budd) S.; grad. high sch.; m. Ardena Elaine Frazier, July 8, 1952; children—Harry Joseph, Mark William, Ronald James. Journeyman machinist, Union Pacific R.R., North Platte, Nebr., 1946-60; field auditor for S.W. Mo., Mo. Dept. Revenue, 1964-72; dist. mgr. Progressive Farmers Assn., Seymour, Mo., 1974-76; zone mgr. Prudential Leasing Co., Springfield, Mo.; owner, mgr. Circle Y Ranch, Arabian horses. Chmn. troop com. Ozark council Boy Scouts Am., 1964-70; founder Lincoln County (Nebr.) Humane Soc., 1948, chmn., 1948-53, 58-60; leader 4-H Club, Webster County, Mo. Chmn. Democratic Twp. Com. Findley, 1966-76; chmn. publicity Webster County Democratic party, 1972—. Served with USNR, 1944-46. Mem. V.F.W. (dist. comdr. 1971-73, dist. chief staff 1973), Neb. Arabian Horse Assn. (dir. 1954), S.W. Mo. Arabian Assn. (dir. 1971-72, pres. 1972-73). Home: RD 3 Seymour MO 65746 Office: RD 3 Seymour MO 65746

SCHLOSSMAN, JOHN ISAAC, architect; b. Chgo., Aug. 21, 1931; s. Norman Joseph and Carol (Rosenfeld) S.; student Grinnell Coll., 1949-50; B.A., U. Minn., 1953, B.Arch., 1955; M.Arch., Mass. Inst. Tech., 1956; m. Shirley Goulding Rhodes, Feb. 8, 1959; children—Marc N., Gail M., Peter C. Archtl. designer Architects Collaborative, Cambridge, Mass., 1956-57; architect Loebl, Schlossman & Bennett, Chgo., 1959-65; asso. Loebl, Schlossman, Bennett & Dart, Chgo., 1965-70, partner, 1970-75; prin. Loebl, Schlossman, Dart & Hackl, 1975-76, Loebl, Schlossman & Hackl, 1976—. Vis. lectr. Boston Archtl. Center, 1955-57, U. Ill., Chgo., 1965; chmn. Village of Glencoe (Ill.) Plan Commn., 1977—. Bd. dirs. Young men's Jewish Council, Chgo., 1959-70, mem. exec. com., 1965-70, life dir., 1970—; trustee Chgo. Sch. Architecture Found., 1970-75; bd. dirs. Chgo. Archtl. Assistance Center, 1975—, Village of Glencoe Plan Commn., 1976—. Rotch Traveling scholar., 1957. Mem. A.I.A. (v.p. Chgo. chpt. 1975, chmn. nat. com. ins. 1974-75), Alpha Rho Chi. Clubs: Tavern, Arts (Chgo.). Office: 845 N Michigan Ave Chicago IL 60611

SCHLOTT, JOHN FREDERIC, architect; b. Council Bluffs, Iowa Dec. 17, 1914; s. James Edgar and Grace Margaret (Cole) S.; B.S., Iowa State U., 1939; postgrad. Purdue U., 1939-40, U. Nebr., 1969, 72, 73; m. Ruth Margaret Ehlers, June 9, 1940; children—Michael Terry, Susan Elizabeth, Mary Anne (Mrs. Ronald Favera), James Frederic. Dir. Freddy Schlott Orch. dance orch., Council Bluffs, 1932-39; land use planner Purdue U., Lafayette, Ind., 1939-40; chief architect Nat. Homes Corp., Lafayette, 1940-41, Met. Homes Corp., Council Bluffs, 1941-42; supr. engring., modifications Glenn R. Martin Co., 1942-45, landscape architect Leo A. Day Co., 1945-46, Marshall Nurseries, 1946-59, partner, landscape architect Schlott-Farrington & Assos., 1959— (all Omaha); owner J.F. Schlott Enterprises, Council Bluffs; partner Brook Park Devel. Co., Omaha, Indian Creek Nurseries, Council Bluffs; sec., treas. Park Wild, Inc., Council Bluffs; owner, breeder angus cattle, saddle bred horses SuMar Farms, Council Bluffs, all 1974—. Mem. Council Bluffs Park Commn., 1949—, pres., 1957, 60, 63, 66, 69; mem. Council Bluffs City Planning Commn., 1951-52; v.p. trustees Hist. Gen. Dodge House, 1964—, mem. corp. bd., 1965—; mem. Hist. Pottawattami County Jail Preservation Com., 1971—, Council Bluffs River Front Steering Com., Riverfront Parks Open Space, Preservation Task Force, Riverfront Fine Arts Com., 1973—; soloist civic oratories, mus. prodns., 1945—. Bd. dirs. Council Bluffs Civic Music. Recipient Gold Seal award Nat. Landscape Exchange Competition, 1935-39; 1st pl. Chgo. Internat. Live Stock Show, 1959; Grand Champion Bull, Denver Western Live Stock Show, 1960; Am. Saddle Horse winner Iowa State Horse Show, Kansas City (Mo.) Royal, 1971; Archtl. Design award Omaha C. of C., 1970, 72. Mem. Mo. Valley Assn. Landscape Architects, Am. Soc. Landscape Architects, Am. Saddle Horse Breeding Assn., Am. Angus Assn., Tau Sigma Delta. Republican. Prin. works include: landscape design Omaha Meml. Park, 1944; Baylis Fountain, Council Bluffs, 1971; Witherspoon Mansion, Omaha, 1971; Pres. Ford Meml., Omaha, 1976. Home: 535 DeLong Ave Council Bluffs IA 51501 Office: 3715 Dodge St Omaha NE 68131

SCHLUCKBIER, GARY WALDO, agrl. engr.; b. Saginaw, Mich., Dec. 9, 1948; s. Waldo Rudolph and Loraine Agnes (Palmreuter) S.; student Ferris State Coll., 1968-69; B.S. with high honors, Mich. State U., 1972; m. Faye Ellen Brown, Aug. 22, 1970; children—Gary Wayne, Stacy Faye. Project engr. Dairy Equipment Co., Madison, Wis., 1972-74, product engr. of automated systems product line, 1974—. Served with Wis. N.G., 1972-75. Recipient Gerber award, Gerber Products Co., 1972, Ferrel award, agrl. engring. dept. Mich. State U., 1972. Mem. Am. Soc. Agrl. Engrs. (pres. student br. 1971-72). Home: 101 Walker Dr Madison WI 53714 Office: 1919 S Stoughton Rd Madison WI 53716

SCHMEDTJE, JOHN FREDERICK, histologist, educator; b. St. Louis, July 9, 1919; s. Adolph Henry and Emma Louise (Hoppe) S.; A.B., Columbia U., 1941; Ph.D., Rutgers U., 1951; m. Winifred Marie Zucchero, Aug. 11, 1956; children—John Frederick, Laura, Diane. Instr. anatomy St. Louis U. Sch. Medicine, 1951-56, Harvard U. Med. Sch., 1956-58; asst. prof. anatomy Tufts U. Sch. Medicine, Boston, 1959-66; asso. prof. anatomy Ind. U. Sch. Medicine, Indpls., 1966—. Served with AUS, 1943-47. NIH grantee, 1959-66. Mem. Histochem. Soc., Electron Microscope Soc. Am., Am. Assn. Anatomists, Am. Soc. Cell Biologists, Sigma Xi. Home: 5042 Haynes Ct Indianapolis IN 46250 Office: Dept Anatomy Ind U Sch Medicine 1100 W Michigan St Indianapolis IN 46202

SCHMELING, ROGER EMIL, constrn. co. exec.; b. Rockford, Ill., June 16, 1931; s. Elmer Albert and Florence Salena (Cope) S.; student Valparaiso U., 1949-51; B.S.A.E. Chgo. Tech. Coll., 1953; m. Mary Lou Thompson, Nov. 10, 1956; children—Anne Marie, Stephen Elmer, Laura Lucile. Vice-pres., sec. E. W. Schmeling & Sons, Inc., Rockford, Ill., 1956-70; v.p., Schmeling Constrn. Co., Rockford, Ill., 1970-71, pres., 1971—. Bd. dirs. P.A. Peterson Retirement Home, 1975-77. YMCA Camp Manito-wish, 1977—. Served with AUS, 1954-56. Mem. No. Ill. Bldg. Contractors Assn. (dir. 1960—, pres. 1962, 67), Rockford Area C. of C. (dir. 1970-77, v.p. 1971-73, 1st v.p. 1974-75, pres. 1975-76). Lutheran (trustee 1969-71, pres. 1974). Club: Forest Hills Country (bd. govs.) (Rockford, Ill.). Home: 3509 Val Mark Terr Rockford IL 61111 Office: 728 N Madison St Rockford IL 61107

SCHMELZER, PAUL WILLIAM, constrn. co. exec.; b. Madison, Wis., Jan. 11, 1922; s. Rupert John and Estelle (Endregart) S.; student Tech. and Vocat. Sch., Madison, evenings, 1940-42, Internat. Corr. Schs., 1946, 47; m. Thelma Mary Dostal, Jan. 20, 1942; children—Beverly (Mrs. Clifford Thew), Deborah (Mrs. Philip Emmling), Richard. Estimator, project mgr. Fritz Constrn. Co., Madison, 1945-57; constrn. adminstr. Flad and Assos., Madison, 1957—; partner K&S Apts., Madison; sec. K&S Devel. Co., Inc., Madison; pres. Capital City Constrn. Co., Inc., Madison. Trustee Wis. chpt. Nat. Multiple Sclerosis Soc., 1968—, past pres., past mem. regional bd., 1975—. Served with USNR, 1942-45. Mem. AIA, Constrn. Specifications Inst., Madison and Middleton (Wis.) chambers commerce, Nat. Home Builders Assn. Roman Catholic. Elk. Home: 4412 Oak Ct Monona WI 53716 Office: 6200 Mineral Point Rd Madison WI 53705 also 6333 Odana Rd Madison WI 53719

SCHMEROLD, WILFRIED LOTHAR, dermatologist; b. Munich, Germany, Dec. 30, 1919; s. Wilhelm and Frieda (Hinterwinkler) S.; M.D., U. Munich, 1945; came to U.S., 1956, naturalized, 1963; m. Gerda Ligus, 1947; 1 son, Klaus; m. 2d, Perlette Joers, 1962; children—John, Wilfred, James, Susan, Paul, Carl, Michael, Thomas, Mary. Asst., U. Munich Med. Sch., 1945; asst. UNO Hosp., Munich, 1946-50; asst. Max Planck Inst. Psychiatry, Munich, 1951; asst. U. Erlangen (Germany) Med. Sch., 1952-53; asst. dermatology Med. Sch. U. Munich, 1953-56; clin. asst. dermatology Med. Sch. U. Ill., 1957-70, instr., 1970-75, asst. prof., 1975—; pvt. practice dermatology, Wheaton, Ill., 1961—; mem. staff Central DuPage Hosp., Winfield, Ill. Diplomate Am. Bd. Dermatology. Mem. AMA, Am. Acad. Dermatology, Ill. Dermatology Soc., Chgo. Dermatol. Soc. DuPage County Med. Soc., German Med. Soc. Chgo., German Dermatology Soc. Office: 200 E Willow St Wheaton IL 60187

SCHMID, JACK ROBERT, pharmacologist; b. Chgo., Oct. 3, 1924; s. Hugo Karl and Laura Wilhelmina (Malstrom) S.; B.S., Mich. State U., 1952, M.S. 1954; Ph.D. (USPHS fellow), U. Ark., 1967; m. Jean Marilyn Beeman, Oct. 16, 1948; children—Jesse, Jane (Mrs. Douglas Parr), Jeanette (Mrs. Thomas Stutelberg), John. Pharmacologist, Mead Johnson Co., Evansville, Ind., 1954-58; tchr. Stambaugh Twp. (Mich.) Schs., 1959-62; pharmacologist specialist Riker Labs. Inc., St. Paul, 1966—. Served with USNR, 1943-45; PTO. Mem. Mich. Acad. Sci., Am. Heart Assn., Am. Chem. Soc., Western Pharmacology Soc., Internat. Soc. for Heart Research. Research cardiopulmonary effects of drugs. Home: 3987 E County Line Rd White Bear Lake MN 55110 Office: Riker Labs Inc 3M Co 3M Center Bldg 218-3 St Paul MN 55101

SCHMIDLIN, HERBERT LUCAS, mgmt. cons.; b. Maumee, O., Feb. 9, 1912; s. Frederick John and Anna Marie (Kuhlman) S.; B. Gen. Engring., U. Toledo, 1940; B.S. in Chem. Engring., Mass. Inst. Tech., 1947; m. Mildred R. Tully, Jan. 7, 1945; children—Brian T., Cynthia M., Mary-Elizabeth. Prodn. supr. E.I. duPont Co., Wilmington, Del., 1947-49; engaged in research and devel. Bay State Abrasive Co., Westboro, Mass., 1950-58; plant mgr. Manhattan Rubber Co., Neenah, Wis., 1959-74; dir. mfg., mem. mgmt. adv. bd. R M Roll Products Co. div. Raybestos-Manhattan, Inc., Clarks Summit, Pa., 1975-77; pvt. practice mgmt. consulting, Neenah, Wis., 1977—. Chmn. Algonquin council Boy Scouts Am., 1957-58; mem. com. for Lake Butte des Morts Bridge, Neenah, 1973. Served with USNR, 1942-47; PTO. Mem. Paper Industry Mgmt. Assn., TAPPI. Clubs: Butte des Morts Golf (Appleton, Wis.); Neenah-Nodaway Yacht. Patentee coated abrasives. Home: 1314 S Alicia Dr Appleton WI 54911 Office: 1615 Matthew St Neenah WI 54957

SCHMIDT, ARTHUR IRWIN, steel fabricating co. exec.; b. Chgo., Sept. 9, 1927; s. Louis and Mary (Fliegel) S.; student Colo. A. and M. Coll., 1946-47; B.S. in Aero. Engring., U. Ill., 1950; m. Mae Rosman, July 25, 1950;children—Jerrold, Cynthia, Elizabeth, Richard. Sec. Rosman Iron Works, Inc., Franklin Park, Ill., 1950—. Served with USNR, 1944-46, 51-52. Mem. N.W. Suburban Mfrs. Assn., Iron League Chgo., Am. Bowling Congress, Ill. State C. of C., Ill. Mfrs. Assn. Mem. B'nai B'rith (trustee, past pres. Lincolnwood). Home: 3601 Golf Rd Evanston IL 60203 Office: 9109 Fullerton Ave Franklin Park IL 60131

SCHMIDT, C. OSCAR, JR., machinery mfg. co. exec.; b. Cin.; s. C. Oscar and Charlotte A. (Fritz) S.; Mech. Engring., U. Cin., also B.S. in Mech. Engring.; M.B.A., Harvard; postgrad. Rutgers U.; L.H.D., Sterling Coll.; m. Eugenia Hill Williams, June 29, 1944 (dec. June 22, 1975); children—Carl O., Christoph R., Milton W., Eugene H., Juliann R. Apprentice, Am. Can Co., Cin.; mem. engring. dept. Cin. Shaper; now with Cin. Butchers' Supply Co., successively asst. to pres., v.p. prodn., v.p., gen. mgr., exec. v.p., now pres., also dir.; dir. Boss Pack Co.; pres., dir. BEC, Inc., Trussville, Ala., Winger Boss Co., Ottumwa, Iowa; dir. Cin. Refrigerator & Fixture Works, Ky. Chem. Industries, Inc., Meat Packers Equipment, Inc. of Fla., Mille Lacs Products Co.; dir., chmn. bd., treas. LeFiell Co. Active Boy Scouts Am., past chmn. Valley dist.; chmn. finance com. Nat. United Cerebral Palsy Assn.; mem. review com. United Funds Cin. Mem. Pres.'s bd. assos. Rose Hulman Inst. Tech.; trustee, past pres. Hamilton County Soc. for Crippled Children, United Cerebral Palsy of Cin.; trustee Deaconess Hosp., also mem. sch. com. Served to capt. U.S. Army, 1940-45. Recipient Distinguished Engring. Alumnus award U. Cin., 1969; Silver Beaver award Boy Scouts Am., also Harman award. Registered profl. engr., Ohio. Mem. Am. Oil Chemists Soc. (life), Am. Ordnance Assn., Engrs. Soc. Cin., Am. Assn. Indsl. Mgmt. (dir.), Air Pollution Soc., Cin. Indsl. Inst., Cin. C. of C., Meat Industry Supply and Equipment Assn. (dir., past co-chmn.), N.A.M. Nat. Metal Trades Assn. (mem. dist. council), Meat Machinery Mfrs. Inst. (past pres.), Acacia (past sec.-treas.), Heroes of '76, Cin. Hist. Soc. (life), Cin. Natural History Mus., Audubon Soc., Ohio Hist. Soc., Nat. Parks Assn., Zool. Soc. Cin., Aircraft Owners and Pilot Assn., U. Cin. Alumni Assn., Cin. Harvard Bus. Sch. Alumni (past sec.-treas.), Harvard Alumni Assn., Harvard Bus. Sch. Assn., Kappa Sigma Pi (dir., nat. sec.). Presbyterian (ruling elder, past pres. adult class, ruling elder commr., mem. eccles. order com.). Mason (Shriner), Rotarian. Clubs: Cincinnati; Wyoming Golf. Contbr. articles in field to profl. jours. Patentee in field. Home: 405 Meadow Lane Cincinnati OH 45215 Office: Box 16098 5601 Helen St Elmwood Pl Cincinnati OH 45216

SCHMIDT, CHARLES MATHEW, cons. mech. engr.; b. Charles City, Iowa, Apr. 29, 1937; s. Earl Mathew and Amy Corien (Anderson) S.; B.S., State U. Iowa, 1960; m. Carolyn May Heath, Sept. 6, 1958 (separated June 1977); children—John, Michael, Greta. Engr. chem. div. Pitts. Plate Glass, Barberton, Ohio, 1960-63; asst. chief engr. Karl R. Rohrer Assos., Akron, Ohio, 1963-65; chief engr. Noble W. Herzberg Assos., Cleve., 1965-67; pres. Schmidt Assos., 1968—; dir. Mahoning Assos., The Continental Bank. Spl. cons. engr. Pa. State U., 1971-73, Ohio Dept. Pub. Works, 1973—; judge East Ohio Energy Conservation Award Program, 1974. Village engr., Boston Heights, O., 1967-71; councilman Village of Boston Heights, 1972—. Bd. dirs. Youth Enrichment Services for Retarded Children. Registered profl. engr., Ohio, Iowa, Ky., Ill., Ind., Mich., Pa. Mem. Nat., Ohio socs. profl. engrs., ASME. Patentee in field. Home: 458 Hines Hill St Hudson OH 44236 Office: 7333 Fair Oaks St Cleveland OH 44146

SCHMIDT, FREDERICK JOSEPH, realtor; b. Johannesburg, Mich., May 12, 1938; s. Joseph Frederick and Elaine Louise (Larsen) S.; student Northwestern Mich. Coll., 1956-57, Ferris State Coll., 1957-58; m. Janice Arlene Burch, Nov. 7, 1959; children—Joseph Lorin, Frederick James, Nancy Eileen. With Schmidt Real Estate, Traverse City, Mich., 1962—, broker, partner, 1968—; sec.-treas. Landco, Inc.; partner Schmidt Land Co., S & S Mgmt. Co., J.F.K. Co. Pres. Traverse City Bd. Realtors, 1971. Served with USAF, 1958-62. Lutheran. Elk. Home: 416 Dawn Circle Dr Traverse City MI 49684 Office: 402 E Front St Traverse City MI 49684

SCHMIDT, GEORGE, engineer; b. Chicago Heights, Ill., Aug. 26, 1925; s. George and Evelyn Marie (LaVine) S.; student Concordia Theol. Sem., 1943-44, U.S. Merchant Marine Acad., 1944-45, Valparaiso U., 1947, Ray-Vogue Sch., 1950; m. Jean Ann VanBuren, Oct. 26, 1947; children—George Frederick, Paul Phillip, Gregory Joseph, Erick Charles. Draftsman Whiting Corp., Harvey, Ill., 1948-49; head methods engring. dept. Harris Hub Co., Harvey, 1949-59; chief engr. Superior Sleeprite Corp., Chgo., 1959-66; plant engr. Rheem Mfg. Co., Chgo., 1966—. V.P. South Shore Subdivision Improvement Assn., 1976-77. Served with U.S. Army, 1946-47. Mem. Am. Inst. Plant Engrs., Am. Legion. Roman Catholic. Home: 14705 Dewey St Cedar Lake IN 46303 Office: 7600 S Kedzie Chicago IL 60652

SCHMIDT, HARVEY RICHARD, elec. engr.; b. Hustisford, Wis., Apr. 30, 1945; s. Harvey George and Jeannette Gertrude (Saarloos) S.; B.S. in Elec. Engring. U. Wis., 1968; M.B.A., No. Ill. U., 1975. Project engr. Sundstrand Corp., Rockford, Ill., 1968-71, cons. minicomputer software and hardward test stand design, 1971—. Served with U.S. Army, 1969-71. NSF fellow, 1967-68. Mem. Chgo. Area Programmers of Novas and Eclipses, Phi Eta Sigma, Eta Kappa Nu, Tau Beta Pi. Methodist. Home: 1065 Palau Pkwy Rockford IL 61108 Office: D779 4747 Harrison Ave Rockford IL 61101

SCHMIDT, JEFFREY STEPHEN, dentist; b. Detroit, Sept. 7, 1942; s. Karl Fredrick and Julia (Seman) S.; D.D.S., U. Detroit, 1967; m. Meredith Ann Hall, May 15, 1965; children—Christine Meredith, Jennifer Hall. Pvt. practice dentistry, St. Joseph, Mich., 1969—; mem. dental staff, chief Mercy Hosp., Benton Harbor, 1973—; dental staff Meml. Hosp., St. Joseph, Mich., 1974-75. Served to capt. AUS, 1967-69. Mem. Am. Acad. Oral Pathology, Am. Soc. Dentistry for Children, Am. Soc. Forensic Odontology, Am., Mich. dental assns., Lakeland Valley Dental Soc., Delta Sigma Delta, Alpha Epsilon Delta. Clubs: Exchange, Berrien Hills Country. Home: 1180 Dobie Dr St Joseph MI 49085 Office: 2810 Niles Rd St Joseph MI 49085

SCHMIDT, JOHN LEO, physician; b. Cleve., May 26, 1915; s. Joseph and Esther (Friedenthal) S.; student Oberlin Coll., 1933-35; B.S., U. Ill., 1937; M.S., Western Res. U., 1944, Ph.D., 1948, M.D., 1950; m. Miriam Edith Friedman, June 28, 1942; children—Janet Susan, Barbara Ann, Diane Joy. Research asst. Gen. Biochems., Chagrin Falls, Ohio, 1937; instr. pharmacology Western Res. U., 1946-50; lab. dir. Venomin Co., Lorain, Ohio, 1946-50; with Abbott Labs., North Chicago, Ill., 1951-62; intern Cleve. Marine Hosp., 1950-51; gen. practice medicine Chgo., 1964—; mem. staffs Mary Thompson Hosp., U. Ill. Research and Edn. Hosp.; dir. Madison Sacramento Med. Clinic, Chgo., 1964-77; clin. asso. prof. anesthesiology U. Ill., Chgo., 1956-73. Cons. life scis. div. Battelle Meml. Inst., Columbus, Ohio, 1963-68. Caucus chmn. Highland Park (Ill.) Sch. Bd., high sch. dist. 113, 1961; pres. Elm Place Sch. PTA, 1960-61. Trustee Mary Thompson Hosp., 1971—. Served with USPHS, 1950-51. Fellow AAAS; mem. AMA, Am. Soc. for Pharmacology and Exptl. Therapeutics, Am. Soc. for Clin. Pharmacology and Exptl. Therapeutics, N.Y. Acad. Scis., Chgo. Inst. Medicine, Sigma Xi. Contbr. articles to profl. jours. Patentee in field. Home: 2259 Sheridan Rd Highland Park IL 60035 Office: 2949 W Madison St Chicago IL 60612

SCHMIDT, RICHARD, mfg. co. exec.; b. Kaufbeuren, Germany, July 25, 1927; s. Richard Paul and Ida (Meissgeier) S.; came to U.S., 1957, naturalized, 1965; B.S. in Mech. Engring., Rudolf Diesel Bau & Ingenieurschule der Stadt Augsburg, 1953; m. Maria Deininger, May 28, 1955; children—Richard, Angela Gudrun. Design engr. Auto Union, GmbH, Ingolstadt, Germany, 1953-57; aeronautical research engr. Army Ballistic Missile Agy., NASA, Marshall Space Flight Center, Huntsville, Ala., 1957-68; cons. Tool Steel Gear & Pinion Co., Cin., 1968-73; founding pres. Schmidt Couplings, Inc., Cin., 1973—. Co-founder, dir. Schmidt Kupplung, GmbH, Wolfenbuettel, Germany, 1965—. Served with German Luftwaffe, 1944-45. Recipient design awards for best design Design News, 1967. Mem. Soaring Soc. of Am. Contbr. publs. in field of power transmission drives and space vehicles. Patentee in field. Home: 11525 Islandale Dr Cincinnati OH 45240 Office: 4298 E Galbraith Rd Cincinnati OH 45236

SCHMIDT, RICHARD ARNOLD, physician; b. Chgo., Nov. 28, 1935; s. Gilbert Arnold and Jeanne Diane (Halowatski) S.; B.S., Ill. Coll., 1958; M.D., U. Ill., 1965; m. Nancy Anne Jackson, June 13, 1959; children—Pamela Anne, Steven Richard. Tchr. sci. Lakewood Jr. High Sch., Dundee, Ill., 1960-61; intern Hinsdale (Ill.) Hosp., 1965-66; practice medicine specializing in family practice, Ottawa, Ill., 1966—; mem. staff Ottawa Med. Center, 1966—, treas., 1974-76, also dir.; chief staff Ottawa Community Hosp., 1978. Aviation med. examiner FAA, 1965-76, crash investigator, 1966-76; pres. Fox Valley Flyers Inc., Ottawa, 1974-76, also dir. Bd. dirs. Mental Health Center of La Salle County (Ill.). Served with U.S. Army, 1958-60. Diplomate Am. Bd. Family Practice. Mem. Am. Acad. Family Practice, Am., Aerospace, La Salle County, Civil Aviation med. assns., Ottawa C. of C. (chmn. com. airport planning 1972-74). Home: 25 Oaklane Dr Ottawa IL 61350 Office: 313 W Madison St Ottawa IL 61350

SCHMIDT, RICHARD HERMAN, educator; b. Blue Earth, Minn., Aug. 2, 1916; s. Gerhard Albert and Alma Marie (Sievers) S.; student U. Minn., 1937-40, Purdue U., 1943; B.S., Okla. State U., 1946, M.S., 1947, Ed.D., 1951; m. Fredericka Pauline Letts, June 24, 1944. Instr. Oklahoma State U., Stillwater, 1947-49; asst. prof. Gustavus Adolphus Coll., St. Peter, Minn., 1949-54; adviser dept. psychology Fort Hays Kans. State Coll., Hays, 1954-55; asso. prof. psychology Western Mich. U., Kalamazoo, 1959-61, dir. profl. experiences, 1968-70, prof. psychology, 1961—. Cons. to various retail and mfg. concerns; pres. personnel Reliability Corp., Kalamazoo, 1960-62. Bd. dirs. Pretty Lake Vacation Camp, Kalamazoo, 1958-61. Served with AUS, 1942-45. Mem. Am., Mich. psychol. assns., Mich. Cons. Psychologists Assn., Phi Delta Kappa, Psi Chi, Phi Kappa Tau. Home: 2729 Mockingbird Dr Kalamazoo MI 49008

SCHMIDT, RICHARD THOMAS FRANCIS, obstetrician, gynecologist; b. Cin., Sept. 23, 1918; s. John Joseph and Elsa (Wenning) S.; B.S., Xavier U., Cin., 1940; M.D., U. Cin., 1943; m. Margaret Manchester, June 2, 1948; children—Kristen Keye, Gregory John, Stephen Bruhl, John Joseph. Intern, Univ. Hosps., Cleve., 1943-44, resident in obstetrics and gynecology, 1944-49;

research fellow, instr. obstetrics and gynecology Western Res. U., Cleve., 1949-50; practice medicine specializing in obstetrics and gynecology, Cin., 1950—; dir. dept. obstetrics and gynecology Good Samaritan Hosp., Cin., 1960—; attending obstetrician-gynecologist Cin. Gen. Hosp., 1960—; cons. obstetrician-gynecologist Christ Hosp., 1960—; instr. obstetrics and gynecology U. Cin., 1950-60, asst. prof., 1960-68, asso. prof., 1968-73, clin. prof., 1973—; cons. Nat. Center Health Statistics, 1974-76. Bd. dirs. Cin. Music Festival Assn., 1963-68. Served to capt. M.C., AUS, 1948-50. Diplomate Am. Bd. Obstetrics Gynecology. Fellow Am. Coll. Obstetricians and Gynecologists (pres. 1977-78), A.C.S. Editor: Standards for Obstetric and Gynecologic Services, 1974; contbr. articles in obstetrics and gynecology to jours. and textbooks. Office: Good Samaritan Hosp Cincinnati OH 45220

SCHMIDT, ROBERT, educator; b. Chomci, Ruthenia, May 18, 1927; s. Alfred and Lena (Konotop) S.; student Technische Hochschule Karlsruhe, 1947-49; B.S., U. Colo., 1951, M.S., 1953; Ph.D., U. Ill., 1956. Came to U.S., 1949, naturalized, 1956. Asst. prof. theoretical and applied mechanics U. Ill., Urbana, 1956-59; asso. prof. civil engrng. U. Ariz., Tucson, 1959-63; prof. engrng. mechanics U. Detroit, 1963—. Mem. Am. Soc. C.E., Am. Soc. M.E., Am. Soc. for Engrng. Edn., Am. Acad. Mechanics (founding mem.), Am. Assn. U. Profs., Indsl. Math. Soc. (pres. 1966-67, trustee 1967-69), Sigma Xi. Editor Indsl. Math., 1969—. Contbr. articles to profl. jours. Home: 18985 Pierson St Detroit MI 48219

SCHMIDT, ROBERT JACK, chiropractor; b. Hurley, S.D., Jan. 29, 1934; s. Benjamin Daniel and Elizabeth Sena (Boelson) S.; student Black Hills Tchrs. Coll., 1954; D. Chiropractic, Northwestern Chiropractic Coll., 1958; m. Betty Lou Tieszen, June 24, 1956; children—Brian Bruce, Bradley Keith. Dr. Chiropractic with Dr. Edward Tieszen Clinic, Marion, S.D., 1958-71; pres., co-owner Drs. Schmidt & Stanley Profl. Corp., Marion, 1971—. Active boys baseball. Mem. Marion City Council, 1964-71; chmn. Turner County (S.D.) Republican party, 1974, del. state convs., 1972, 74; mem. vol. fire dept., vol. ambulance service Marion. Served with AUS, 1962. Mem. Am., S.D. (v.p. 1975) chiropractic assns., S.D. Orthopedic Soc. (pres. 1973-75), Marion Bus. and Profl. Assn., Marion Community Club, Chi Omega Phi. Presbyterian (elder). Lion (pres. Marion 1967-68), Mason (32 deg., Shriner). Home: Rural Route 2 Marion SD 57043 Office: Box 37 124 N Broadway St Marion SD 57043

SCHMIDT, ROBERT MILES, surgeon; b. Milw., Dec. 8, 1937; s. Albert Charles and Margaret E. (Miles) S.; B.S., Yale U., 1960; M.D., Cornell U., 1964; m. Sally Anne Woolner, Sept. 27, 1969; children—Andrew Robert, William Matthew. Intern, Univ. Hosps. Cleve., 1964-65, asst. resident in surgery, 1965-66, 68-71, chief resident, 1971-72, USPHS fellow in biomed. engrng., 1968-70; practice medicine specializing in surgery, Milw., 1972—; mem. staff Columbia, St. Michael, Wood VA, Milw. Gen. hosps.; asst. clin. prof. surgery Med. Coll. Wis.; dir. Milw. Med. Clinic. Served with USN, 1966-68. Diplomate Am. Bd. Surgery. Fellow A.C.S.; mem. AMA, Milw. Acad. Surgery, Milw. County, Wis. State med. socs. Congregationalist. Club: Rotary. Contbr. articles to med. jours. Home: 8922 N Fielding Rd Milwaukee WI 53217 Office: 3003 W Good Hope Rd Milwaukee WI 53209

SCHMIDT, ROBERT WILLIAM, electronic control co. exec.; b. Chgo., Sept. 8, 1914; s. Andrew August and Marie (Beckman) S.; B.S. in Mech. Engring., Ill. Inst. Tech., 1936; m. Violet Danielson Schmidt, June 15, 1940; children—Carol Ann Schmidt Rebholz, Stephen Robert. Engr., Link Belt Co., Chgo., 1936-37; sales engr. Powers Regulator Co., Chgo., 1937-43; staff head of process instrumentation Kimberly Clark Corp., Neenah, Wis., 1946-51; pres., owner Copar Corp., Oak Lawn, Ill., 1951—; pres., dir. Pilotron Corp., 1951—; pres., owner Copar Internat. Corp., 1970—. Trustee Village of Indian Head Park, Ill., 1968-72. Served with USNR, 1943-46. Republican. Lutheran. Developer of corrugator cut-off control, automatic weighing, speed synch control, lineal measurement system, steel die accelerator, glue valve patents. Home: 6539 Shabbona Rd Indian Head Park LaGrange IL 60525 Office: 5744 W 77th St Oak Lawn IL 60459

SCHMIDT, WAYNE WALTER, lawyer, assn. exec.; b. St. Louis, Feb. 8, 1941; s. Warren Walter and Geneva N. (Walker) S.; Dipl. English Law, City of London (Eng.) Coll., 1963; B.A., U. N.Mex., 1964; J.D., Okla. City U., 1966; L.L.M., Northwestern U., 1974; m. Josephine R. Hanley, Aug. 29, 1970; children—Nancy Karen, Andrew Martin. Admitted to N.Mex. bar, 1966, Ill. bar, 1968, D.C. bar, 1970; dir. Police Legal Center, Internat. Assn. Chiefs of Police, Washington, 1970-73; dir. police legal adv. tng. program Northwestern U., 1968-70; operating dir. Ams. for Effective Law Enforcement, Inc., Evanston, Ill., 1973—; spl. counsel Ill. Assn. of Chiefs of Police, 1974—. County constable, Albuquerque, 1962-66. Served with AUS, 1966-67. Ford Found. fellow, 1967. Mem. Am., D.C., Ill., N.Mex. bar assns. Author: Guidelines for Police Legal Units, 1971; Legal Aspects of Criminal Evidence, 1977. Legal editor The Nat. Sheriff, 1969—; book rev. editor Jour. Police Sci. and Adminstrn., 1974—; editor Fire Dept. Personnel Reporter, 1974—. Home: 3925 Lizette Ln Glenview IL 60025 Office: 960 State National Bank Plaza Evanston IL 60201

SCHMIDT, WILLIAM GEORGE, orthodontist; b. Hailey, Idaho, Dec. 27, 1923; s. Christopher George and Agatha Katherine (Diebenow) S.; student Coll. Idaho, 1942, U. S.D., 1943-44, Carroll Coll., 1946-47; D.D.S., St. Louis U., 1951, M.S., 1953; m. Mary Louise Aholt, Aug. 2, 1952; children—Kathryn Sue, Julia Ann, Mary Margaret, Christopher George, Joseph Anthony, Helen Louise, William George. Practice dentistry specializing in orthodontics, Evansville, Ind., 1953—. Pres., Orthodontic Edn. and Research Found., 1959-61; v.p. Ind. Citizens for Ednl. Freedom, 1965-73. Bd. dirs. Little Sisters of the Poor, St. Vincent Day Care Center, SARTO Retreat Center. Served with U.S. Army, 1942-46. Recipient Distinguished Alumnus award St. Louis U., 1976. Mem. Am., Ind. (chmn. council dental care 1968-73, chmn. Blue Shield advs. 1967-73) dental assns., Am. Assn. Orthodontists, Alpha Sigma Nu, Omicron Kappa Upsilon, Delta Sigma Delta. Roman Catholic. Clubs: Serra (pres. 1958-59); Te Deum International (pres. 1961). Home: 862 S Villa Dr Evansville IN 47714 Office: 2032 Lincoln Ave Evansville IN 47714

SCHMITZ, SISTER MARY VERONE, speech pathologist; b. Alexander, N.D., Nov. 24, 1914; d. Peter and Hedwig (Hackenburg) Schmitz; B.A., Avila Coll., 1960; M.S. (Rehab. Service grantee), Marquette U., 1970. Tchr. elementary schs., Devils Lake, N.D., 1939-41, 53-54, Kansas City, Mo., 1941-52, Williston, N.D., 1952-53, Kansas City, Mo., 1954-58, Omaha, 1958-63, Kansas City, 1963-68; prin. St. Wenceslaus Sch., Omaha, 1961-63; speech pathologist, dir. Our Lady of Mercy Speech and Hearing Center, Kansas City, Mo., 1970—. Lic. speech pathologist, Mo. Mem. Am., Mo., Greater Kansas City speech and hearing assns. Home: 134 N Hardesty St Kansas City MO 64123 Office: PO Box 6679 Kansas City MO 64123

SCHMITZ, NORMAN WAYNE, retail co. exec.; b. Chgo., Nov. 16, 1937; s. Arthur John and Selma Rosiland (Danhour) S.; B.B.A., U. Wis., 1959; postgrad. Northeastern U., 1975; m. Jacqueline Jean Bikfasy, July 25, 1964; children—Jeffrey, Steven, Heather. With Carson, Pirie Scott & Co., Chgo., 1959-67, The Denver, Denver, 1967-71; v.p. Dayton's, Mpls., 1971-77; pres. John W. Heller, Inc., Edina, Minn., 1977—. Bd. dirs. Mpls. chpt. A.R.C., 1975—. Served with U.S. Army, 1959. Recipient Carson, Pirie Scott & Co. Jr. C. of C. of the Year award, 1964-65. Mem. Nat. Retail Mchts. Assn. (dir. N.Y.C. 1970—). Lutheran. Club: Interlachen Country. Home: 4301 E Lake Harriet Blvd Minneapolis MN 55409 Office: 202 Southdale Edina MN 55435

SCHMUCKER, RUBY ELVY LADRACH, nurse, educator; b. Sugarcreek, Ohio, Nov. 17, 1923; d. Walter F. and Carrie M. (Mizer) Ladrach; R.N., Aultman Hosp., Canton, Ohio, 1945; B.S. in Nursing, U. Akron, 1970, M.S. in Edn., 1973; m. Nelson E. ven. Gen. duty nurse, head nurse Aultman Hosp., 1945-47, part-time, 1950-62, instr. nursing, 1962-64, 69-74; instr. nursing Coll. Nursing, U. Akron (Ohio), 1974-76; instr. div. nursing edn. Children's Hosp., Akron, 1976—; cons. Stark-Tuscarawas Counties Student Nurses Assn., 1973-74. Health chmn. Avondale Sch. PTA, Canton, also mem. coms., 1954-70; vol. instr. home nursing courses ARC, 1959-62. Mem. Aultman Hosp. Sch. Nursing Alumni Assn., Am. Nurses' Assn., Nat. League Nursing, Am. Personnel and Guidance Assn., Am. Coll. Personnel Assn., U. Akron Alumni Assn., Alpha Sigma Lambda. Mem. Ch. of Christ. Home: 4214 Bellwood Dr NW Canton OH 44708 Office: Children's Hosp Div Nursing Edn 11 W State St Akron OH 44308

SCHNABEL, JOHN HENRY, educator; b. Evansville, Ind., Mar. 15, 1915; s. Arthur John and Myrtle L. (Walters) S.; student Phillips U., 1932-33, U. Kan., 1933-34; B.S., Evansville Coll., 1939; Mus.M., Northwestern U., 1947; Ed.D., Ind. U., 1954; m. Emily H. Wepfer, June 28, 1938; children—Jack D., Julia Belle (Mrs. Anthony Klinke), Diane (Mrs. Randy Clayton), Kathlee Mae. Dir. bands Evansville Coll., 1937-39; supr. music Carlisle-Haddon Twp. Schs., 1939-42; supr. music, dir. bands Jasper (Ind.) High Sch., 1942-49; asso. prof. music, dir. bands Panhandle A. and M. Coll., 1949-52; prin. Stratford (Tex.) Ind. Sch., 1952-53; grad. asst. Ind. U., 1953-54; vis. prof. Miami U., Oxford, O., 1954-55; dir. admissions Park Coll., Parkville, Mo., 1955-57; asso. prof. edn. So. Ill. U., Edwardsville, 1957-73, prof., 1973—, registrar, dir. admissions, 1957-67, dir. teaching learning centers, 1972—, coordinator computer based instrn. lab., 1977—; chmn. bd., chief exec. officer George G. Fetter Co., Louisville, 1970—. Oboist various symphony orchs.; mem. adv. council Ednl. Resources Information Center for Ednl. Facilities, U., Wis., Madison, 1965—. Oboist Alton (Ill.) Civic Symphony, 1957-61, also bd. dirs.; bd. dirs. Alton Meml. Hosp., 1967—. Served with AUS, USAAF, 1945. Mem. Assn. Collegiate Registrars (chmn. facilities com. 1965-67), Am. Assn. Collegiate Registrars and Admissions Officers, Am. Assn. Sch. Adminstrs., Council Ednl. Facilities Planning. Am. Assn. Higher Edn., Assn. Edn. Data Systems, Assn. Devel. Computer-based Instrnl. Systems, Phi Delta Kappa, Phi Mu Alpha, Kappa Kappa Psi. Methodist (bd. dirs.). Rotarian. Author books including: An Evaluation of Extra-Class Activities, 1966; Ten Years of University Progress, 1967. Home: 2305 Fairview Dr Alton IL 62002 Office: So Ill U Edwardsville IL 62025

SCHNACK, DERMOT JOSEPH, ednl. cons.; b. Chgo., Apr. 10, 1928; s. Damon Dwight and Elizabeth Mary (Harris) S.; student William Penn Coll., 1947; A.B., George Washington U., 1957, A.M., 1960; postgrad. NDEA Guidance Inst. Ohio State U., 1962-63, U. Mo., summer 1966; m. Nancy Ellen Young, July 6, 1957; children—Therese, Andrew, Susan and Matthew (twins). Tchr. jr. high sch., Arlington, Va., 1957-62; counselor Ohio State U., Columbus, 1963-65; ednl. cons., instr. Ohio State U. and Ohio Dept. Edn., Columbus, 1965—. Co chmn. Franklin County Forum for Handicapped Individuals, 1975-77. Served with Inf. AUS, 1950-53. Decorated Combat Infantry Badge, Bronze Star; recipient Distinguished Service award Ohio Vocational Assn., 1974, Nat. Multiple Sclerosis Soc., Franklin County, 1975. Mem. Am. Vocational Assn., Ohio Vocational Assn. (life). Am., Ohio. Central Ohio personnel guidance assns., Nat. Vocat. Guidance Assn., Phi Delta Kappa. Episcopalian. Club: Toastmasters. Home: 28 Arden Rd Columbus OH 43214 Office: 65 Front St S Columbus OH 43215

SCHNEIDER, BARRY SCHOEN, financial exec.; b. Corydon, Ind., Dec. 6, 1946; s. Paul Henry and Clematine Louise (Schoen) S.; B.S. with distinction, Ind. U., 1968; m. Marilyn Sue Stark, Dec. 18, 1965; children—Chad Shannon, Clint Patrick. Sr. accountant Ernst & Ernst, C.P.A.'s, Louisville, 1968-70; budget dir. St. Anthony Hosp., Louisville, 1971-72; dir. fiscal and mgmt. services Ky. Hosp. Assn., Louisville, 1973; asst. regional mgr. Ky.-Tenn. Humana, Inc., Louisville, 1973—. Pvt. practice C.P.A., Louisville, 1972—; hosp. cons. Financial adviser Jr. Achievement, Lanesville, Ind., 1973-74. C.P.A., Ky. Ind. Assn. C.P.A.'s grantee, 1967. Mem. Hosp. Financial Mgmt. Assn. (advanced; Distinguished Service award 1972), Ky. Soc. C.P.A.'s (chmn. health services com. 1972-73), Lanesville (Ind.) Jaycees (pres. 1975-76), Am. Inst. C.P.A.'s. Lutheran. Home: Route 1 PO Box 346A Corydon IN 47112 Office: Suite 720 9200 Shelbyville Rd Louisville KY 40222

SCHNEIDER, CURT THOMAS, atty. gen. Kans.; b. Coffeyville, Kans., Oct. 12, 1943; s. John W. and Ellen (Ferne) S.; B.S. in Bus. Adminstrn., Kans. State Coll., Pittsburg, 1965; LL.B., U. Kans., 1968; m. Barbara Gonzales, Sept. 10, 1971; 1 son, Jon. Admitted to Kans. bar, U.S. Supreme Ct. bar; chief of litigation Kans. Hwy. Commn., Topeka, 1968-72; chief of litigation Kans. Atty. Gen.'s Office, 1972-75; atty. gen. Kans., Topeka, 1975—. Mem. Kans. U. Law Soc., Kans. Peace Officers Assn., Kans. County and Dist. Attys. Assn., Kans. U., Kans. State Coll. of Pittsburg alumni assns., Nat. Assn. U.S. Army. Recipient Outstanding Young Alumni award Kans. State Coll. of Pittsburg, 1975, Outstanding Young Man in Am. award Jr. C. of C., 1976. Home: 1829 Pembroke Ln Topeka KS 66604 Office: 1st Floor State Capitol Topeka KS 66612

SCHNEIDER, ERWIN HENRY, educator; b. St. Louis, Feb. 17, 1920; s. Erwin Louis and Anna Marie (Bussee) S.; B.S., N.W. Mo. State Coll., 1942; M.S., U. Kans., 1946, Ph.D., 1956; m. Jenila Marie Adkins, Nov. 29, 1941; 1 dau., Nila Marie. Instr. music U. Kans., 1946-47; asso. prof. music Western State Coll., Gunnison, Colo., 1948-49; prof., head dept. art and music edn. U. Tenn., Knoxville, 1949-60; prof. music Ohio State U., Columbus, 1961-69, acting dir. Sch. Music, 1964-65, head div. music edn., 1965-69; prof. music and edn. U. Iowa, 1969—. Mem. Nat. Assn. for Music Therapy (pres. 1964-65, editor Bull., Yearbooks), Am. Ednl. Research Assn., A.A.A.S., Am. Psychol. Assn., Music Tchrs. Nat. Assn., Music Educators Nat. Conf., Phi Delta Kappa, Phi Mu Alpha, Phi Kappa Lambda. Editor: Tennessee Musician, 1950-51; Tennessee Music Teacher, 1958-59. Home: Iowa City IA 52240 Office: Sch Music U Ia Iowa City IA 52240

SCHNEIDER, EWALD, foundry exec.; b. Cologne, Germany, June 12, 1921; s. Ewald A. and Emilie R. (Haenseler) S.; student U. Cologne, 1946-52; m. Katharina M. Drinhausen, June 12, 1945; 1 son, Wolfgang F. Came to U.S., 1957, naturalized, 1962. Accounting apprentice Farbenfabriken Bayer AG, Germany, 1935-39, cost accountant, 1945-49, auditor, 1950-52, audit mgr. orgn. dept., 1952-57; accountant Wis. Centrifugal, Inc., Waukesha, 1957-59, asst. treas., chief accountant, 1960-65, treas., asst. sec., 1965—; trustee profit sharing and pension trusts, chmn. retirement com., adminstr. plans Wis. Centrifugal Found., Inc., 1965—. Served with inf., German Army, 1939-45. Mem. Nat. Assn. Accountants (pres. Waukesha Area chpt. 1972-73, nat. dir. 1974—), Financial Execs. Inst. Club: Waukesha Toastmasters (pres. 1965-66). Home: 3425 Hollywood Lane Brookfield WI 53005 Office: Wis Centrifugal Inc Waukesha WI 53186

SCHNEIDER, HAROLD JOEL, radiologist; b. Cin., Aug. 9, 1923; s. Henry W. and Sarah Miriam (Hauser) S.; M.D., U. Cin., 1947; m. Mary Zipperstein, Dec. 23, 1945; children—Jill, Elizabeth, Ann, Jane. Intern, Cin. Gen. Hosp., 1947-48, resident in radiology, 1953-56; resident in surgery Holzer Hosp. and Clinic, Gallipolis, Ohio, 1948-49; gen. practice medicine, Dayton, Ohio, 1949-50; asst. prof. radiology U. Ala., Birmingham, 1956-59; asso. prof. radiology U. Cin. Med. Center, 1959-69, prof., 1969—; dir. diagnostic radiology Christian R. Holmes Hosp., U. Cin. Med. Center, 1959—; cons. VA Hosp., Cin. Served to lt. USNR, 1950-52. Diplomate Am. Bd. Radiology. Mem. Am. Coll. Radiology, Radiol. Soc. N. Am., Am. Roentgen Ray Soc., Ohio, Greater Cin. radiol. socs., Cin. Acad. Medicine, Ohio Med. Soc., Assn. Am. Med. Colls., AAUP, AAAS, Am. Geriatrics Soc. Contbr. articles in field to profl. jours. Home: 7290 Elbrook Ave Cincinnati OH 45237 Office: Holmes Hosp Eden and Bethesda Ave Cincinnati OH 45219

SCHNEIDER, HAROLD WILLIAM, educator; b. Redwood County, Minn., Feb. 26, 1926; s. William Theofeld and Bertha Augusta (Mell) S.; B.A., U. Minn., 1950, postgrad., 1952-56; m. Mary Bell Willis, July 7, 1956. Teaching asst. U. Minn., 1954-56, instr. English, 1956-61; instr. English, Kans. State U., Manhattan, 1961-68, asst. prof. English, 1969—. Mem. creative writing adv. panel Kans. Cultural Arts Commn., 1969—, film adv. panel, 1971-76. Vice pres. Riley County (Kans.) Democratic Club, 1966-67. Served to master sgt. U.S. Army, 1950-52. Mem. Modern Lang. Assn., AAUP, ACLU, Phi Beta Kappa (v.p. Alpha assn. Kans. 1971-72, pres. 1973-74), Lambda Alpha Psi. Lutheran. Mng. editor Critique: Studies in Modern Fiction, 1956-61, adv. editor, 1961-64; editor Kan. Mag., 1967-68, Kan. Quar., 1968—. Contbr. articles to profl. jours. Home: 1405 Nichols St Manhattan KS 66502

SCHNEIDER, JOHN ARTHUR, chem. co. exec.; b. Saginaw, Mich., Feb. 27, 1940; s. Harvey C. and Beulah Agnes (Smiley) S.; A.B. (Gen. Motors scholar), Albion Coll., 1962; Ph.D. (NIH fellow), Mass. Inst. Tech., 1966; m. Elizabeth Louise Rose, June 15, 1963; children—Julia Suzanne, Catherine Chara. Instr. Cambridge (Mass.) Jr. Coll., 1963-66, Delta Coll., Bay City, Mich., 1967-68; group leader organic chems. devel. Dow Chem. Co., Midland, Mich., 1966—; instr. chemistry Central Mich. U., Mt. Pleasant, 1974-77. Internal v.p. Midland Area Homes, 1970. Active Boy Scouts Am. Mem. Am. Chem. Soc. (chmn. 1976), Phi Beta Kappa, Sigma Xi, Kappa Mu Epsilon, Tau Kappa Epsilon. Mem. United Ch. Christ (ch. moderator), Mason, Kiwanian (sec. Midland 1968—). Contbr. articles to profl. publs. Patentee in field. Home: 5008 Farnsworth St Midland MI 48640 Office: Dow Chem USA 1710 Bldg Midland MI 48640

SCHNEIDER, LEONARD MORTON, ednl. film maker; b. N.Y.C., Mar. 19, 1932; s. Samuel and Evelyn (Siegelbaum) S.; B.A., Coll. William and Mary, 1954; M.A., U. Kan., 1967; m. JoAnna March, May 10, 1959; children—Paul Miles, John March. Freelance motion picture cameraman, N.Y., 1962-66; motion picture dir. Centron Corp., Lawrence, Kans., 1967-69; ind. ednl. film-maker, Lawrence, Kans., 1972—; artist-painter, 1961—; one-man show at U. Kans., Lawrence, 1970, Atlanta (Ga.) Artists Club Nat. Exhbn. I, 1970, Washington and Jefferson (Pa.) U. 3rd Nat. Exhbn., 1971, 9th Nat. Exhbn., 1977. Served with Signal Corps, U.S. Army, 1954-56. Recipient Chris award Columbus (O.) Film Festival, 1972, Bronze plaque, 1973, 74, 76, Chris Statuette, 1973; Creative Excellence certificate U.S. Indsl. Film Festival, 1972, 75, Golden Eagle CINE Film Festival, Washington, 1975, Gold award IFPA Film Festival, Hollywood, 1976, Gold award Greater Chicagoland Film Festival, 1976. Ednl. films include: Rainy Day Story, 1972; Me, 1972; They, 1972; You, 1973; The American Phoenix (screenplay), 1975; Captain Dinosaur, 1975. Home: 945 Lawrence Ave Lawrence KS 66044

SCHNEIDER, LOUIS ABRAHAM, pathologist; b. N.Y.C., Oct. 4, 1913; s. Abraham and Ethel (Tracht) S.; B.S., Coll. City N.Y., 1933; M.S., N.Y. U., 1935, M.D., 1940; m. Anne L. Bass, Oct. 25, 1947. Intern, Lincoln Hosp., N.Y.C., 1940-41, resident in pathology, 1941-42; asst. med. examiner City of N.Y., 1947; asso. dir. labs. St. Joseph's Hosp., Ft. Wayne, Ind., 1948-56, dir. labs., 1956—; cons. pathologist VA Hosp., Ft. Wayne, 1955—, Whitley County Hosp., Columbia City, Ind., 1968—, Wells Community Hosp., 1972—; pres. staff St. Joseph's Hosp., 1969; asst. prof. pathology Ind. U. Med. Sch., 1965—. Served to lt. col. AUS, 1944-47. Fellow Am. Soc. Clin. Pathology, Coll. Am. Pathology, Am. Acad. Forensic Scis., Internat. Soc. Hematology; mem. Internat. Acad. Pathology, Am. Assn. Pathology. Contbr. articles in field to profl. jours. Home: 1351 W Sherwood Terr Fort Wayne IN 46807 Office: 700 Broadway Fort Wayne IN 46802

SCHNEIDER, MICHAEL JOSEPH, educator; b. Saginaw, Mich., Apr. 21, 1938; s. Michael Elias and Jane (Moffit) S.; B.S., U. Mich., 1960; M.S., U. Tenn., 1962; Ph.D. (Hutchinson Meml. fellow, John M. Coulter research fellow), U. Chgo., 1965; m. Janet Marie Potter, Nov. 24, 1967. Resident research asso. Nat. Acad. Scis., Beltsville, Md., 1965-67; asst. prof. biology Columbia U., 1968-73; asso. prof. biology U. Mich., Dearborn, 1973-77, prof. biology, chmn. dept. natural scis., 1975—. USPHS fellow, 1967-68. Mem. Am. Inst. Biol. Scis., Am. Soc. Plant Physiologists, Bot. Soc. Am., Am. Soc. Photobiology, AAAS, Scandinavian Soc. Plant Physiology, Sigma Xi. Contbr. articles to profl. publs. Home: 7397 Kingsbridge St Canton MI 48187 Office: Dept Natural Sciences U Mich Dearborn MI 48128

SCHNEIDER, RALPH WILLIAM, automobile mfg. co. exec.; b. Iroquois County, Ill., June 7, 1926; s. William F. and Louise (Wickboldt) S.; B.A. in Bus. Adminstrn., Mich. State U., 1949; m. Virginia A. Murnane, July 2, 1977; children—Steven R., Debra J., Carol L. Mgmt. trainee Chrysler Corp., Detroit, 1949-50; supr. budgets Kaiser Frazer/Kaiser Jeep Corp., Toledo, 1950-57, mgr. govt. sales and govt. products div. Kaiser Jeep Corp., 1957-67; dir. contract adminstrn. Kaiser Jeep Corp./AM Gen. Corp., South Bend, Ind., 1967-77, gen. mgr. truck div., 1977—. Pres., Redeemer Lutheran Ch. Served with U.S. Army, 1944-45. Decorated Purple Heart, Bronze Star. Certified profl. contracts mgr., Ind. Mem. Assn. U.S. Army, Am. Def. Preparedness Assn., Nat. Security Indsl. Assn., Nat. Contract Mgmt. Assn. Home: 1328 Matthews Ln South Bend IN 46614 Office: 701 W Chippewa Ave South Bend IN 46680

SCHNEIDER, ROBERT ALLEN, mktg. co. exec.; b. Cin., Apr. 8, 1940; s. Albert Edward and Evelyn Ruth (Mardis) S.; B.B.A., U. Cin., 1963, M.B.A., 1966; m. Martha Jeanne Hugenberg, Sept. 7, 1963; children—Mark Allen, David Andrew, Dirk Edward. Exec. trainee Burke Internat. Research Corp., Cin., 1967-69, v.p., 1969, sr. v.p. client service, 1971, exec. v.p., 1974, exec. v.p. corporate devel., 1976—; dir. Central Savs. Assn., Blue Ash, Ohio, 1969—. Bd. dirs. E. Walnut Hills Assembly, Cin., 1974-77. Served with U.S. Army,

1958-59. Mem. Am. Mktg. Assn. Roman Catholic. Home: 1001 Saint Gregory St Cincinnati OH 45202 Office: 1529 Madison Rd Cincinnati OH 45206

SCHNEIDER, ROBERT JOSEPH, counselor; b. Weymouth, Mass., May 11, 1941; s. Albert Joseph and Mary Catherine (LeVangie) S.; A.B., Miami U., 1972, M.S., 1977, M.Ed., 1977; m. Judie Ann Roth Weisenbarger, Sept. 18, 1966; children—David, Darrin, Christopher. Workman's compensation counselor Firestone Rubber Co., 1965-69; instr. Miami U. of Ohio, 1975-77; cons., instr. Wilmington (Ohio) Coll., 1977—; ednl. cons. on aggression in the schs.; cons., counselor residential treatment centers for pre-delinquent adolescents; facilitator for assertiveness tng. groups. Served with USNR, 1959-63. Mem. Am. Personnel and Guidance Assn., Assn. Specialists in Group Work, Am. Sch. Counselors Assn. Research on formal career planning and devel. for convicts and its effect on recidivism rate. Home: 3692 Oxford Millville Rd Oxford OH 45056 Office: 409 McGuffey Hall Miami University Oxford OH 45056 also Garfield High Sch 205 E Fair Ave Hamilton OH 45011

SCHNEITER, HARRY EDWARD, JR., physician; b. Manly, Iowa, June 1, 1926; s. Harry Edward and Ada Bernice (Raffety) S.; student Miami U., Ohio, 1943-45; B.S., U. Minn., 1946, B. Medicine, 1948, M.D., 1949; m. Joan Martindale, Sept. 15, 1945; children—John, Thomas, Christopher, Robert, Marielle. Intern, Wayne County Gen. Hosp., Eloise, Mich., 1948-49; gen. practice medicine, 1949—; cons. preceptor program Mich. State U., 1972—, clin. instr., 1976—; cons. preceptor program U. Mich., Wayne U. Med. Sch., 1972—; adj. clin. prof., Western Mich., U., 1977—, preceptor physicians asst. program, 1976—; chief of staff Allegan (Mich.) Gen. Hosp., 1960-62, 70-72, mem. staff, 1949—. Served with USN, 1943-46; U.S. Army, 1951-53. Recipient Med. Edn. Community Orientation award, 1975; Physicians Recognition award, AMA, 1976; diplomate Am. Bd. Family Practice. Fellow Am. Coll. Family Practice, Am. Acad. Family Practice; mem. AMA, Mich. State, Allegan County (sec., 1960-66, pres. 1966-68) med. socs., Rotary, Jaycees. Congregationalist. Club: Elks. Contbr. articles to med. jours. Home: 1 Williams Ln Allegan MI 49010 Office: 551 Linn Allegan MI 49010

SCHNELL, DONALD, artist; b. Mich., 1949; B.A., Central Mich. U., 1970; M.A., U. Chgo., 1972. Asso., Contemporary Art Workshop, Chgo., 1971-75; exhibited ceramics in one-man shows at Tri-Form Gallery, Chgo., 1972, U. Ill. Med. Center, 1972-76, Winter Show of Fine Arts, River Forest, Ill., 1973, 74, Contemporary Art Workshop, Chgo., 1973, 74, Chgo. Pub. Library, 1974, U. Ill., 1974, K.A.M. Art Expo 75, Chgo., 1975, Central Mich. U., 1975, U. Chgo. Sch. Social Service, 1976, Northwestern U., 1976, Tower Pl., Atlanta, 1976; pvt. practice as profl. counsellor. Asst. prof. U. Chgo. Sch. Social Services, 1974-75. Studio: 1421 W Chicago Ave Chicago IL 60622 also Cruz Bay Saint John VI 00830

SCHNELLER, JOSEPH FRANZ, furniture and art dealer; b. Neumarkt, Austria, May 30, 1923; s. Joseph and Pauline S.; came to U.S., 1923, naturalized, 1932; ed. high sch.; m. Georgia Mangos, Feb. 7, 1948 (dec. 1972); children—Joseph, Francine; m. 2d, Helen Holowell, Oct. 30, 1977. Auditor, Taylor Forge & Pipe Co., 1941-43; prodn., gen. mgr. Consol. Chrome Corp., Chgo., 1946-48; pres. Schneller Furniture Co., also Franz Joseph Galleries, Arlington Heights, Ill., 1948-73, Joseph Schneller Co., Arlington Heights; lectr. in field. Chmn. NW Suburbs Salvation Army, 1965-67. Served with Mil. Police, U.S. Army, 1943-46. Recipient Golden Cross of Honor, Gov. of Burgenland, Austria, 1972. Mem. Am.-Austrian Soc. (pres. 1971-78), Nat. Retail Furniture Assn., Burgenland Verien. Roman Catholic. Lion (pres. Arlington Heights 1964-65). Home: 212 S Dwyer Ave Arlington Heights IL 60005

SCHNEPP, KENNETH H., surgeon; b. Springfield, Ill., Mar. 5, 1905; s. William H. and Josephine R. (Lueck) S.; B.A., U. Ill., 1928, B.S., 1929, M.D., 1932; m. Lois Catron, Mar. 31, 1943; children—Deborah, Suzanne. Intern, Augustana Hosp., Chgo., 1931-34; pvt. practice specializing in surgery, Springfield, Ill., 1934—; sr. attending staff Meml. Hosp. Springfield, pres., 1965; sr. attending staff St. John's Hosp., Springfield, v.p., 1963-64; clin. prof. med. edn. Sch. Medicine, So. Ill. U. Mem. med. examining com. State Ill., 1954-74, sec., 1960, chmn., 1967; mem. Examination Inst., Fedn. State Med. Exam Bds. U.S., 1967, trustee, 1975—. Founder, Springfield Med. Library Assn., 1939, sec.-treas. 1939—; bd. mem. Springfield Day Nursery Assn., 1937-40, sec.-treas., 1938-40. Trustee Ednl. Commn. for Fgn. Med. Grads.; mem. Nat. Bd. Med. Examiners, 1969-77. Served from capt. to maj. M.C., U.S. Army, 1942-46; ETO. Fellow A.C.S. Internat. Coll. Surgeons, Am. Med. Writers Assn. (pres. 1950); mem. A.M.A., Ill., Sangamon County (sec. 1936-37, pres. 1948, founder bull. 1936, editor 1936-42, 46-47) med. socs., Ill. Surg. Soc. (pres. 1962-63), Am. Soc. Abdominal Surgeons. Elk. Clubs: Illini Country, Sangamo. Home: 123 Lawrence Ave E Springfield IL 62704 Office: 725 S 2d St Springfield IL 62704

SCHNEPPER, DONALD HERMAN, civil engr.; b. Beardstown, Ill., Feb. 10, 1922; s. Herman Gottfried and Lela (Oetgen) S.; B.A., Carthage Coll., 1943; B.S., U. Ill., 1951, M.S., 1954; m. Virginia May Wisegarver, Feb. 14, 1959; 1 dau., Ruth. Research asst. U. Ill., Urbana, 1952-54, lab. asst., 1951-52; asso. prof. scientist Ill. Water Survey, Peoria, 1954-69, profl. scientist, 1969—. Served with U.S. Army, 1943-45. Mem. Am. Water Works Assn., Am. Water Resources Assn., Internat. Assn. Hydraulic Research, Water Pollution Control Fedn., Ill. River Tech. Com. Presbyn. (elder 1971-74). Home: 121 Liberty Lane Washington IL 61571 Office: PO Box 717 Peoria IL 61601

SCHNUDA, NASR DANIEL, pathologist, educator; b. Luxor, Egypt, Dec. 20, 1933; s. Daniel and Zahia (Girgis) S.; M.B., Ch.B., Cairo U., 1958; M.S., Ohio State U., 1966; m. Sophie Fahmy, Apr. 4, 1967; children—Charles, Peter. Came to U.S., 1961. Intern Md. Gen. Hosp., Balt., 1961-62; resident pathology Allenstown (Pa.) Hosp., 1962-63, Ohio State U. Hosp., 1963-66; research fellow immunology Toronto (Ont., Can.) Western Hosp., 1967-68, electron microscopy Banting Inst., U. Toronto, 1968-71; instr. pathology Ohio State U. Sch. Medicine, 1966-67; asso. dir. Med. Pathfinder Labs., Fennville, Mich., 1971-72; asst. prof. pathology Wayne State U., Detroit, 1972-74; asso. pathologist Wyandotte (Mich.) Gen. Hosp. 1974-76, Mercy, Meml. hosps., Monroe, Mich., 1974-76; head dept. pathology and dir labs. Edgewater Hosp.-Mazel Med. Center and Rosenfield Intensive Care Inst., Chgo., 1976—. Diplomate Am. Bd. Pathology. Fellow Coll. Am. Pathologists, Am. Soc. Clin. Pathologists; mem. A.M.A., Mich., Wayne County med. socs., Mich. State Soc. Pathologists, Can. Fedn. Biol. Scis., Can. Soc. Immunology, Internat. Union Immunological Scientists, Micros. Soc. Can., Ont. Antibody Club. Research in immunology, lymphocytes, electron microscopy of blood, bone marrow, lymphoid organs in leukemias, lymphomas. Address: Edgewater Hosp 5700 N Ashland Ave Chicago IL 60660

SCHOBER, CHARLES COLEMAN, III, psychiatrist, psychoanalyst; b. Shreveport, La., Nov. 30, 1924; s. Charles Coleman and Mabel Lee (Welsh) S.; B.S., La. State U., 1946, M.D., 1949; m. Martha Elizabeth Welsh, Dec. 27, 1947 (dec.); children—Irene Lee, Ann Welsh; m. 2d, Argeree Maburl Stiles, Feb. 4, 1972; 1 son, Charles Coleman. Intern, Phila. Gen. Hosp., 1949-51; resident psychiatry Norristown (Pa.) State Hosp., 1953-56; asso. clin. dir. Pa. Hosp. Inst., Phila., 1957-59; practice medicine, specializing in psychiatry and psychoanalysis, Phila., 1960-71, St. Louis, 1973—; attending psychiatrist Pa. Hosp. Inst., Phila., 1963-68, sr. attending psychiatrist, 1968-71; staff St. Louis U. Hosp., 1973—; instr. psychiatry U. Pa. Med. Sch., Phila., 1958-62, asso. in psychiatry, 1962-70, asst. prof., 1965-71; prof., chmn. psychiatry La. State U. Med. Sch., Shreveport, 1971-73; psychiatrist in chief Confederate Meml. Med. Center and VA Hosp., Shreveport, 1971-73; prof. psychiatry St. Louis U. Med. Sch., 1973—; cons. psychiatry VA Hosp., St. Louis, 1973—; faculty Phila. Psychoanalytic Inst., 1966-71, New Orleans Psychoanalytic Inst., 1972-73, St. Louis Psychoanalytic Inst., 1973—. Served to capt. USAF, 1951-53. Decorated Air Force Commendation medal. Fellow Am. Coll. Psychiatrists, Am., Mo. psychiat. assns.; mem. ACLU, AMA, Mo., St. Louis med. socs., Am. Psychoanalytic Assn., St. Louis Psychoanalytic Soc. Contbr. articles to profl. jours. Home: 7232 Greenway Ave Saint Louis MO 63130 Office: 4524 Forest Park Saint Louis MO 63108

SCHOEDER, LLOYD BERNARD, state ofcl.; b. Darlings Springs, N.D., Mar. 23, 1918; s. Henry Peter and Evelyn Mary (Murphy) S.; student LaSalle U., 1940-44, Grad. Coll. Ins., N.Y.C., 1968; m. Marian Helen Strehlow, Oct. 23, 1940; children—Darlene (Mrs. Garth Ghering), Dean Francis, Vicki (Mrs. Roger Roehl). Self-employed accountant, auditor, Hettinger, N.D., 1940—; chief examiner N.D. Ins. Dept., 1966—; cons., sec. Hettinger Equity Elevator, 1956-65. Treas. Hettinger Hosp. Assn., 1952-66. Bd. dirs. Hettinger (N.D.) Park Bd., 1960-64. Mem. Nat., N.D. socs. pub. accountants, Mem. Nat. Soc. Fin. Examiners, Hettinger Civic Club, (pres. 1956). K.C. Club: Rod and Gun (pres. 1941-44) (Hettinger, N.D.). Home: Box 767 8th St S Hettinger ND 58639 Office: State Capitol Bismarck ND 58501

SCHOEN, LOUIS STANLEY, telephone co. exec.; b. Gladstone, Nebr., June 18, 1933; s. Edward John and Mary Louise (Miller) S.; B.A., U. Nebr., 1955; postgrad. (CBS Found. News fellow), Columbia, 1963-64, U. Kans., summer 1968, Augsburg Coll., Mpls., 1969; m. Linnah Wallace Henderson, Mar. 3, 1962; children—Linnah, Laura, Dorothy. Editor, U. Nebr. Summer Nebraskan, 1952; reporter, copy editor Lincoln (Nebr.) Evening Jour., 1952-55; news dir. KLIN Radio, Lincoln, 1955-56; state rep. for Nebr., N.D., Nat. Found. March of Dimes, 1957-59; announcer, newscaster KFYR-TV and Radio, Bismarck, N.D., 1959-61; news dir. WIMA Radio, Lima, O., 1961; reporter, pub. affairs dir. WOW-TV and Radio, Omaha, 1962-65; editorial asst. Northwestern Bell Telephone Co., Omaha, 1965-67, pub. info. supr., Mpls., 1967-71, Minn. info. supr., Mpls., 1971—. Speaker seminars on communications, human relations, orgn. for change, Christian action. Active March of Dimes, Planned Parenthood coms., 1965-67; chmn. Grass Roots Action Program, Omaha, 1965-67; mem. Community Info. Task Force, Urban Coalition Mpls., 1969-71; chmn. St. Louis Park Human Rights Commn., 1969-70; mem. nat. adv. bd., co-convenor Minn. com. Women's Ordination Now Episcopal Ch., 1974-76; founder, pres. Found. Religious Edn. on Equality. Mem. exec. com. 41st Dist. Democratic Farmer-Labor party, 1972-74; Omaha vol. coordinator Phil Sorensen for Gov. Campaign, 1966; candidate St. Louis Park Bd. Edn., 1969; chmn. vol. com. for election State Senator B. Robert Lewis, Minn. Bd. dirs. Mpls. Neighborhood Involvement Program, 1972-75, v.p., 1973-74; bd. dirs. Mpls. Urban League, 1970—, 2d v.p., 1973-75. Served with AUS, 1956-57, 61-62. Recipient Episcopal Distinguished Service Cross, 1977. Mem. Pub. Relations Soc. Am., Minn. Press Club, Environ. Control Citizens Assn., Environ. Writers Assn. Am., Minn. Soc. Profl. Journalists, Common Cause, Center for Study Dem. Instns., Assn. for Non-Smokers Rights, Mpls. Soc. Fine Arts, North Star Ski Touring Club. Episcopalian (vestryman, 1973-74, lay reader). Home: 4115 Sunset Blvd St Louis Park MN 55416 Office: 224 S 5th St Minneapolis MN 55402

SCHOENBAUM, DONALD, theatre adminstr.; b. Yonkers, N.Y., Jan. 3, 1926; s. Irving and Beatrice (Rubin) S.; student N.Y. U., 1943-44; B.A., U. So. Cal., 1947; m. Geraldine Cain, Aug. 15, 1947; children—Mark, Andrew, Robert. Ind. producer, actor, dir. for theatre and films, 1947-63; mng. dir. Trinity Square Repertory Theatre, Providence, 1964-65; mng. dir. Tyrone Guthrie Theatre, Mpls., 1965—, exec. v.p. operations, 1965—. Mem. exec. com. Office Advanced Drama Research, U. Minn., 1966—; bd. dirs. Am. Arts Alliance, Sta. KTCA-KTCI-TV, Operation de Novo. Cons. performing arts instns., 1963—. Mem. adv. com. Nat. Research Center for the Arts. Served with U.S. Army, 1944-46. Ford Found. Grantee, 1962, 65. Mem. League Resident Theatres (exec. com., pres.). Home: 705 Kenwood Pkwy Minneapolis MN 55403 Office: 725 Vineland Pl Minneapolis MN 55403

SCHOENBECK, DELBERT LOUIS, assn. exec.; b. Roselle, Ill., Dec. 29, 1931; s. Edward John and Malinda Marie (Bargamann) S.; B.S. in Bus. Adminstrn., Tri-State Coll., 1957; m. Joyce M. Kolzow, June 9, 1956; children—Kevin L., Paul J., Pamela M., Susan L. Sec., controller Pelron Corp., Lyons, Ill., 1959-65; sr. buyer Richardson Co., Melrose Park, Ill., 1965; v.p., gen. mgr. Richardson Chem. Cleaning Service subsidiary Richardson Co., Griffith, Ind., 1966-72; treas. Nat. Bur. Property Adminstrn., Inc., Chgo., 1972—; founder Uni-Prise Co., 1973, now prin., pres. Served with AUS, 1952-54. Lutheran (elder, trustee 1961—). Home: 6705 Richmond Ave Darien IL 60559 Office: 1824 Prudential Plaza Chicago IL 60601

SCHOENBERGER, SYLVIA MARY, clergyman; b. Bklyn., Apr. 8, 1928; d. Edward and Ada Bell (Drake) Carpenter; diploma Friedel-Hefley Bus. Sch., 1943-45; m. Feb. 10, 1952; children—Konrad, Kim. Ins. clk. John Hancock Ins. Co., Bklyn., 1945-47; sec. ins. dept. Edward A. Dangler, Realty, Long Island City, N.Y., 1947-52; ordained Mahdis, minister of Eckankar Ch., 1977; minister, Wausau, 1977—; ins. investigator Retail Credit Co., Wausau, 1974; dispatcher JJ Security Co., Wausau, 1976-76. Bd. dirs. Eck Info. Center, 1972—, Wausau Animal Shelter, 1970; chairlady dr. United Fund Wausau Met. Area, 1963-64. Home: 1214 McIntosh St Wausau WI 54401 Office: Eck Center 124 1/2 Washington St Wausau WI 54401

SCHOENEBERGER, WILLIAM ALPHONSE, sales exec.; b. Perham, Minn., Oct. 5, 1942; s. Alphonse W. and Marie Grace (Feyereisen) S.; B.S. in Econs., St. John's U., 1964; M.S. in Mktg., Roosevelt U., 1977; m. Joan Jeanette Nicholson, Aug. 7, 1965; children—Bill, Brian, Karla. Ter. sales mgr. Flint Labs., Mpls., 1967-70, dist. sales mgr., Kansas City, Mo., 1970-72, mktg. mgr., Deerfield, Ill., 1972-76, nat. sales mgr., 1976—. Served as capt. U.S. Army, 1964-67. Mem. Midwest Pharm. Assn., Mktg. Communication Execs. Internat., Beta Gamma Sigma. Office: One Baxter Pkwy Deerfield IL 60015

SCHOENEMAN, ROBERT BARTON, elementary sch. tchr.; b. Hawarden, Iowa, Apr. 5, 1936; s. Chester Carl and Olive Marie (Linkswiler) S.; B.Arch., U. Notre Dame; diploma Midwest Montessori Tchr. Tng. Sch., Chgo., 1967, Internat. Center Montessori Studies, Bergamo, Italy, 1972; M.A., Ohio State U., 1978; children—Carl Anthony, Sara Jane. Tchr., mem. adminstrv. staff schs. in Ind. and Calif., 1963-71; mem. faculty Montessori Tchr. Tng. Program, Ithaca, N.Y., 1971-74; adminstr., dir. elementary Montessori Sch., Elkhart, Ind., 1972-74; supr. Montessori elementary unit Escuelas Las Neredias, San Juan, P.R., also tchr. trainer, acad. coordinator Montessori Tchr. Tng. Coll. P.R., 1974-75; tchr. primary and middle sch., supr. tchrs. St. Joseph's Acad., Columbus, Ohio, 1975-78; co-dir., lectr. Columbus Montessori Elementary Tchr. Tng. Sch., 1976-78; counselor alternative to impaired driving program, Columbus, 1977; lectr. univs. and colls.; cons. to magnet schs. Dallas Ind. Sch. Dist., 1977—. NSF grantee, 1964-65. Mem. Am. Montessori Soc., Assn. Montessori Internat., N. Am. Montessori Tchrs. Assn., Am Personnel and Guidance Assn. Home: 88 Fitz-Henry Blvd Columbus OH 43214

SCHOENROCK, KENNETH FREDERICK, otolaryngologist; b. Toledo, June 25, 1920; s. Arthur Paul and Mary M. (Yeager) S.; B.S., U. Toledo, 1942; M.D., Albany Med. Coll., 1945; m. Boneta E. Belknap, June 17, 1945; children—Judith Ann, Gary Arthur, Denise Lea. Intern, Mt. Carmel Mercy Hosp., Detroit, 1945-46; resident VA Hosp., Aspinwall, Pa., 1948-50; otolaryngologist Toledo Clinic, 1950—; clin. asso. Med. Coll. Toledo. Mem. Sylvania Twp. Aux. Police. Served to capt. U.S. Army, 1946-50. Mem. Acad. Medicine Lucas County, Ohio State Med. Coll., AMA, A.C.S., Am. Acad. Ophthalmology and Otolaryngology, Am. Bd. Otolaryngology, Am. Rhinol. Soc., Royal Soc. Medicine. Clubs: Masons, Shriners. Home: 3845 Marvindale St Toledo OH 43606 Office: 4235 Secor Dr Toledo OH 43623

SCHOEPHOERSTER, LORIN KEITH, ins. co. exec.; b. Prairie du Sac, Wis., Jan. 10, 1923; s. Edwin Carl and Ruth (Preuss) S.; B.S., Marquette U., 1945; M.B.A., U. Wis., 1951; m. Lillian P. McGilvra, June 3, 1944; children—Douglas E., Linda J., Christine A. Underwriter, Farmers Mut. Group, Madison, Wis., 1948-52, dir. edn. and research, 1952-56; supr. agt. tng. Nationwide Ins. Co., Columbus, O., 1956-59; dir. edn. and research, State Auto Ins. Co., Columbus, 1959-66, v.p., 1966—. Chmn. bd. govs. Internat. Ins. Seminars; gen. chmn. Ins. Hall of Fame, 1965-71. Pres. PTA, 1953; treas. Bd. Edn., 1953-56; chmn. United Appeal, 1965. Bd. dirs. Griffith Found., chmn., 1968-71; bd. dirs. Loman Found., chmn., 1972-74; bd. dirs. Ins. Hall of Fame. Served with USNR, 1943-46. Mem. Soc. Chartered Property and Casualty Underwriters (regional v.p. 1971), Internat. Assn. Health Underwriters (v.p. 1970-73), Ohio Ins. Guaranty Assn. (vice chmn. 1973-75), Soc. Chartered Life Underwriters, Ohio Ins. Inst. (treas. 1977), Nat. Assn. Life Underwriters, Soc. Ins. Research (dir. 1968—), Ins. Co. Edn. Dirs. Soc. (dir. 1963—), Gamma Iota Sigma (life trustee). Presbyn. (trustee 1961-64). Cons. editor Handbook of Property and Liability Insurance, 1965. Editor Insurance Teaching, 1970, Research Review, 1970—, Education Exchange, 1968—, Insurance Training and Education Digest, 1975. Home: 1013 Medhurst Rd Columbus OH 43220 Office: State Auto Mutual 518 E Broad St Columbus OH 43216

SCHOESSLER, RICHARD JOHN, dentist; b. Reliance, S.D., Aug. 15, 1928; s. Henry Otto and Anna Marie (Larson) S.; D.D.S., Creighton U., 1953; m. Mary Jean Gregerson, Jan. 9, 1960; children—Richard John, Mary Ann, Sarah Jean. Pvt. practice dentistry, Pierre, S.D., 1957-61, 62—; asso. staff mem. St. Mary's Hosp., Pierre, 1959-73. Pres. PTA Council, Pierre, 1967. Bd. dirs. Internat. Hwy. 83 Assn., 1966, S.D. Cancer Soc. Served with AUS, 1952-57, 61-62; col. Res. Mem. Acad. Gen. Dentistry, Delta Dental Plan S.D. (pres. 1973), Children's Dental Soc. S.D. (pres. 1970), 3d Dist. Dental Soc. (pres. 1969), S.D. Dental Assn. (trustee 1973, pres. 1976-77), Am. Legion, Izaak Walton League. Republican. Lutheran (pres. congregation 1970-72). Clubs: Elks, Optimists (Pierre). Home: 402 N Huron St Pierre SD 57501 Office: 465 S Pierre St Pierre SD 57501

SCHOESSOW, MATHILDE M(ARTHE), librarian, musician; b. Milw., Feb. 7, 1900; d. August A.F. and Amalia Victoria (Stock) Schoessow; diploma Wis. Conservatory of Music, 1919; U. Chgo., 1937-39; M.A., U. Wis.-Madison, 1951. Tchr. piano Wis. Conservatory of Music, Milw., 1919-71, tchr. organ, 1940-71; librarian U. Wis.-Milw., 1940-70, asst. prof. library skills, 1956-70; cataloger of rare books Concordia Coll., Milw., 1970—, asst. prof., 1974—; head librarian Wisconsin Coll.-Conservatory, Milw., 1971—. Mem. Am. Guild Organists (dean Milw. chpt. 1951-53), Wis. Library Assn., Milw. Music Tchrs. Assn., U. Wis. Ret. Tchrs. Assn., Milw. Symphony Women's League, Wis. Coll.-Conservatory League, U. Wis.-Milw. Women's League, Music Library Assn., AAUP, Mac Dowell Club (accompanist 1940—), Wis. Cservatory of Music Alumni Assn. (pres. 1949-50). Lutheran (organist, choir dir. 1943—). Home: 4812 West Washington Blvd Milwaukee WI 53208 Office: 1584 North Prospect Ave Milwaukee WI 53202 also 3201 W Highland Blvd Milwaukee WI 53208

SCHOLL, EDWARD THOMAS, state senator, journalist; b. Chgo., May 18, 1937; s. Edward Joseph and Flora (Burke) S.; student Wright Jr. Coll., 1956-57, Loyola U. at Chgo., 1958-59; m. Rosemary Wright, Aug. 6, 1960; children—Michael Patrick, Cynthia Louise, and Karen Marie. With Elston Farmers Market, Chgo., 1954-55; sports and news writer Edison-Norwood Rev., Chgo., 1954-57; mng. editor Rev. Newspapers, Chgo., also Niles (Ill.), 1958-63; editor pub. Edgebrook-Lincolnwood (Ill.) Events, 1963—; mem. Chgo. City Council, 1963-73; mem. Ill. Senate, 1973—; editor Passionist Fathers Hot Line Directory, 1977. Campaign mgr. for various polit. candidates, 1960—. Mem. N.W. Traffic Safety Council, Chgo., 1958—; mem. exec. bd. Indian Boundary dist. Boy Scouts Am., 1962—, chpt. pres. Order of Arrow, 1954, dir. fund drive Northwest Chicago, 1962; mem. Ill. Bd. Vocat. Edn. and Rehab.; mem. Gov.'s Exec. com. 1969—. Bd. dirs. Park Ridge YMCA. Exec. officer 41st Ward Regular Republican Orgn., 1962—; active Cook County Young Republicans, 1960—. Mem. Ill. N.G., 1960-77. Recipient citation for outstanding service Lions Club, 1960; Outstanding Service awards Chgo. Heart Soc., 1960, 62, 63, Chgo. Cancer Soc., 1959-63, CARE, 1965; named one of 10 outstanding young men Chgo. Jr. Assn. Commerce and Industry, 1965. Mem. Ill. Press Assn., Edison Community Council (dir. 1960), Edison Park (dir. 1958—), Norwood Park, Edgebrook chambers commerce, Big Oaks, Oriole Park, Edgebrook, Bryn Mawr Higgins community assns., Norwood Citizens Assn., Friends of Lit. Roman Catholic. Clubs: Chicago Press; VFW (Park Ridge, Ill.). Author: Seven Miles of Ideal Living, 1957; March of Progress, 1960. Home: 7738 W Palatine St Chicago IL 60631

SCHOLL, JOHN DANIEL, III, economist; b. LaPorte, Ind., Dec. 4, 1948; s. John and Winifred Viola (Jourdain) S.; B.S., Purdue U., 1971, also postgrad.; M.S., Ind. State U., 1972; m. Kathleen Kay Boop, Dec. 18, 1971. Asst. dir. research Ind. Dept. Commerce, Indpls., 1973-77; v.p. G.J. Marder & Assos., Chgo., 1972—; real estate broker, Noblesville, Ind., 1974—; dir. Tri-State Engring., La Porte, Inc., G.J. Marder & Assos., Chgo. Notary pub. Hamilton County (Ind.), 1974—. Mem. Am. Econ. Assn. Republican. Roman Catholic. Author: A Staff Analysis of the State and Local Fiscal Assistance Act of 1972, 1974. Home: 19733 Allisonville Rd Noblesville IN 46060 Office: 3166 N Lincoln Suite 400 Chicago IL 60657

SCHOLTEN, LEON MARVIN, sales and service co. mgr.; b. Holland, Mich., Jan. 27, 1920; s. Alfred and Janet (Sternberg) S.; student Grand Rapids Jr. Coll., 1963; m. Adrianne Venhuizen, June 22, 1943; children—Virginia Jane, Arla Lynn. Foundry worker Bohn

Aluminum, 1940-47; poultry farmer, 1960-65; surge tester, inspl. Gen. Elec. Co., 1965-71; draftsman Hamilton Supply Co., Holland, 1965-71, gen. mgr., 1971—; irrigation cons. Mem. Laketown Twp. Sch. Bd., 1948-57; Elder Christian Reformed Ch., 1973-76. Served as sgt. F.A., AUS, 1942-45. Licensed well driller; certified pump setter, rainbird designer. Mem. Nat., Mich. (v.p.) irrigation assns., Nat. Water Well Assn., U.S., Holland C.'s of C. Home: A6068 145th St Holland MI 49423 Office: PO Box 839 783 Chicago Dr Holland MI 49423

SCHOLTZ, WERNER EGON, economist, lawyer; b. Bremen, Germany, Mar. 18, 1931; s. Ferdinand H. and Betty (Wendelken) S.; student Oberschule fuer Jungen (Germany), 1942-50; M.B.A., U. Chgo., 1966; J.D., Ill. Inst. Tech., 1971; m. Ulrike Fuchs, Jan. 6, 1961; children—Vera Cornelia, Eva Angelica. Mgr., Canadian and U.S. Gt. Lakes Service, North German Lloyd, Bremen, 1953-59; owners rep. North German Lloyd, Hamburg-Am. Line, Ernst Russ Steamship Co. (Hamburg), Chgo., 1959-69; mgr. planning and devel. Blue Cross-Blue Shield, Chgo., 1969-71, asst. v.p. marketing planning, 1971-75; pres. Ernst Russ-N.Am., Inc., 1975—; partner law firm Scholtz, Newell & Assos., Ltd. Mem. Am. Marketing Assn., Am., Ill., Chgo. bar assns., German-Am. C. of C., Chgo.-Kent, U. Chgo. alumni assns., Phi Delta Phi. Club: Rotary. Home: 17730 Larkspur Lane Homewood IL 60430 Office: 1 N LaSalle St Chicago IL 60602

SCHOMAEKER, JAMES BARTON, real estate co. exec.; b. Lima, O., Sept. 9, 1936; s. Paul Edward and Alice Ann (Siefer) S.; student St. Joseph's Coll., 1954-55; B.S., Bowling Green State U., 1958; m. Jane Frances Gerdeman, Feb. 15, 1958; children—James Barton II, Julie, Jeanne, Jeffrey, Joel. Life ins. salesman New Eng. Mut. Life Ins., Lima, O., 1958-61; owner Gooding Co., Lima, 1961—; dir. Lima Ins. Bd., 1964; dir. United Telephone Co. Ohio. Mem. budget com. United Fund, 1970—; bd. dirs. Lima YMCA, Jr. Achievement, Am. Cancer Soc. Acting fund-raising worker Ohio Republican Finance Com., 1963-70. Vice pres. Lima Better Bus. Bur., 1977-78. Served with AUS, 1959-60. Named Asso. of Yr., Lima Bd. Realtors, 1965, Realtor of Yr., 1972. Mem. Lima Bd. Realtors (pres. 1973), Ohio Assn. Realtors (v.p. 1975-76), Gallery of Homes. Clubs: Shawnee Country, K.C., Elks, Rotary. Home: 1528 Bunker Dr Lima OH 45805 Office: 406 S Cable St Lima OH 45805

SCHOMER, GARY WAYNE, paper mfg. co. exec.; b. Terre Haute, Ind., Nov. 10, 1945; s. Wayne Edgar and Anna Katherine (Walker) S.; B.S., Ind. State U., 1967, M.B.A., 1968; m. Judy Ann Miller, June 25, 1967; children—William Wayne, Debra Ann. Salesman, Ben Becker Inc., 1963-65; with Weston Paper & Mfg. Co., Terre Haute, 1965—, systems analyst, 1970-72, corp. accounting mgr., 1972-74, asst. controller, 1974—. Adviser, Jr. Achievement, 1969. Weston/Wabash Found. scholar, 1965-67; Pride City ambassador, 1970. Mem. Jr. C. of C. (recipinet Spark Plug award 1970-72), Nat. Assn. Accountants (dir. 1977), Ind. State U. Alumni Assn. (life), Alpha Tau Omega, Delta Sigma Pi. Vice chmn. adminstrv. bd. United Meth. Ch., edn. chmn., tchr., stewardship chmn. Club: Elks. Home: 6 Todd Pl Terre Haute IN 47803 Office: 2001 19th St N Terre Haute IN 47808

SCHOOLING, HERBERT WILSON, coll. chancellor; b. Pierce City, Mo., Nov. 5, 1912; s. Robert F. and Stella (Boucher) S.; B.S., S.W. Mo. State Coll., 1936; M.A., U. Md., 1940, Ed.D., 1954; m. Bess Garinger, June 1, 1939. Supt. schs., N. Kansas City, Mo., 1949-55; dir. pre-collegiate edn. U. Chgo., 1955-57; supt. schs., Webster Groves, Mo., 1957-63; dean Coll. Edn. U. Mo., Columbia, 1963-66, dean faculties, 1966-70, provost, 1968-70, interim chancellor, 1970-71, chancellor, 1971—. Mem. N.E.A., Am. Assn. Sch. Adminstrs., Nat. Soc. Study Edn. Home: 106 Burnam Rd Columbia MO 65201

SCHOPF, CLIFTON CLIFFORD, physician, hosp. adminstr.; b. Wichita, Kans., May 15, 1929; s. Clifford Henry and Opal Savilla (Bradshaw) S.; B.A., Wichita U., 1951; M.D., U. Kans., 1957; m. Jean Iyral, Dec. 19, 1948; children—Richard Clifton, David Alan, Susan Ellen. Practice medicine specializing in family practice, Clearwater, Kans., 1958-67, Wichita, 1967—; pres. med. dental staff St. Francis Hosp., Wichita, 1977—. Diplomate Am. Bd. Family Practice. Fellow Am. Acad. Family Practice. Republican. Methodist. Home: 2902 River Park Dr Wichita KS 67203

SCHORR, WILLIAM F., dermatologist; b. Fond du Lac, Wis., Dec. 19, 1930; s. Frank and Amelia S.; M.D., Marquette U. Sch. of Medicine, 1957; m. Marianne Meyers, July 16, 1955; children—Elizabeth, Thomas, Robert. Intern St. Mary's Hosp., Duluth, Minn.; resident in dermatology U. Miami Sch. of Medicine, 1960-63; practice medicine specializing in dermatology Marshfield (Wis.) Clinic, 1963-77; dir. residency tng. program, 1965-77; asso. clin. prof. U. Wis., Madison, 1975—, U. Minn., Mpls., 1972—. Panelist Fed. FDA Antimicrobial Panel II, 1975-76. Served to capt. M.C., U.S. Army, 1958-60. Diplomate Am. Bd. Dermatology. Fellow Am. Acad. Dermatology (Becker gold award 1968, Silver award 1973, bd. dirs. 1973-76), A.C.P., Soc. Investigative Dermatology; mem. Am. Dermatological Assn., Am. Fedn. for Clin. Research, A.M.A., Colegio Ibero Latino Americano de Dermatologia, Minn. (past pres.), Noah Worcester (bd. dirs. 1975), Wis. (past pres.) dermatological socs., Socieded Venezolana de Dermatologia Venereologica y Leprologia, State Med. Soc. Wis., Wood County Med. Soc. Roman Catholic. Contbr. articles to med. jours. Home: 1105 Weister Ct Marshfield WI 54449 Office: 1000 N Oak Ave Marshfield WI 54449

SCHOTTENSTEIN, HAROLD, ret. soft drink co. exec.; b. Columbus, O., Aug. 18, 1910; s. Jacob Meyer and Gertrude (Goldberg) S.; B.Sc. in Pharmacy, Ohio State U., 1931; m. Regene Gloria Wides, Apr. 7, 1946; children—James Mark, Terri Lynn, Edwin Michael. Owner, Eagle Drug Store, Columbus, 1933-36; partner Pepsi Cola Bottling Co., Columbus, 1936-62; pres., Schott Enterprises, Inc., Columbus, 1962—; sec. Niam Corp., Columbus, 1969—; pres. De Long Devel. Co., So. Devel. Co., Columbus, 1969—. Chmn., Israel Bond, 1961, 62, big gifts United Jewish Fund and Council, 1962, 63, campaign, 1964, jubilee dinner Friends of Yeshiva U., 1962; asst. treas. Heritage House, 1967—; pres. Jacob and Gussie Schottenstein Found. Served with M.C., AUS, 1942-45; ETO. Mem. Ohio Bottlers Assn. (pres. 1956), Zionist Orgn. Am., Rho Pi Phi. Jewish religion (pres. synagogue 1962-63, hon. trustee congregation 1963). Rotarian; mem. B'nai B'rith. Clubs: Winding Hollow (Columbus). Home: 544 Noe Bixby Rd Columbus OH 43213

SCHOTZ, LARRY ALLEN, elec. engr.; b. Milw., Dec. 26, 1949; s. Alex M. and Ruth (Barland) S.; A.A., Milw. Sch. Engring., 1973, B.S. in Elec. Engring., 1973. Project engr. Sherwood Electronic Labs., Chgo., 1973-74; chief engr. Lynn Industries, Chgo., 1974-75; pres. Draco Labs., Inc., Milw., 1975—; instr. U. Wis. Mil. Extension. Mem. indsl. adv. com. Milw. Sch. Engring. Mem. IEEE, Audio Engring. Soc., Sales Mktg. Execs. Milw. Recipient Hon. mention Am. Soc. Engring. Edn., 1972; Patentee vehicle intrusion alarm, solid state echo producing systems. Home: 6220 N Sunny Point Rd Milwaukee WI 53217 Office: 2010 W Bender Rd Milwaukee WI 53209

SCHOUT, ROBERT LEE, investment banker; b. Zeeland, Mich., Apr. 14, 1941; s. Herbert and Marie (Geskus) S.; B.A. in Polit. Sci. and Econs., Calvin Coll., 1964; J.D., Wayne State U., 1971; m. Janet Sorber Berg, Aug. 3, 1963; children—Michele, Melissa, Jonathan, Joel. Asst. cashier Nat. Bank, Wyandotte, Mich., 1965-67; asst. mortgage mgr. investment div. Maccabees Mutual Life, 1967-68; credit analyst, comml. and indsl. fin. div. Ford Motor Credit Co., Dearborn, Mich., 1968-69; v.p. mktg. Taubman Co., Troy, Mich., 1969—; participant Irvine Ranch Acquisition, 1977; cons. in field. Mem. Mortgage Bankers Assn. Mich., Internat. Council of Shopping Centers, Am. Mktg. Assn., Fin. Analysts Soc. Detroit, Allen Park Symphony. Republican. Contbr. articles to profl. jours. Home: 5166 Provincial Dr Bloomfield Hills MI 48013 Office: 3270 W Big Beaver Rd Troy MI 48099

SCHRADER, ARTHUR GUST, coop. exec.; b. Bryant, Wis., Aug. 24, 1908; s. Emil William and Elda Matilda (Pietz) S.; student Bus. Coll., Stevens Point, Wis., 1929-30; m. Elizabeth Maud Sansum, Oct. 6, 1945; children—Sandra, Kathleen. Gen. mgr. Antigo (Wis.) Coop. Oil Assn., 1935-65; cons. Office Econ. Opportunity, Chgo., 1966-67; mgr. cons. AID and Coop. League U.S.A., Balboa, C.Z., 1971—; dir. Midland Coops., Inc., Mpls., Peoples Bank, Antigo. Chmn. Shelter Program, Civil Def., Langlade County, 1962-71. Served with AUS, 1942-45: ETO. Mem. D.A.V. (life; post vice comdr.), V.F.W. (life). Home: 1414 7th Ave Antigo WI 54409 Office: Box J Balboa Canal Zone

SCHRADER, CHERYL ANN, univ. adminstr.; b. Waverly, Iowa, Feb. 5, 1942; d. George Arnold and Lucille Wilma (Seibel) S.; B.S. in Elem Edn., Rio Grande Coll., 1968; M.Edn. in Counseling, U. Nev., Las Vegas, 1972; postgrad. Ohio State U., Columbus, 1976-78; tchr. remedial reading Oak Hill (Ohio) Pub. Schs., 1966-67, Springfield (Ohio) City Schs., 1967-69; tchr., guidance counselor Clark County Pub. Schs., Las Vegas, Nev., 1969-74; asst. to dean Univ. Coll., U. Nev., Las Vegas, 1974-75, dir., 1975-76, grad. research asso., Ohio State U., Columbus, 1976-78; vol. counselor Planned Parenthood League, Las Vegas, 1973-74; mem. Selective Service Bd., Las Vegas, 1975-76. Mem. Clark County Counseling, Personnel Guidance Assn. (founder, pres.), Am. Coll. Personnel Assn., Nat. Assn. Women Deans Counselors, Am. Sch. Counselor Assn. Clubs: Rainbow for Girls. Home: 1007 Hunter St Columbus OH 43201 Office: Counseling Consultation Center 1739 N High Columbus OH 43210

SCHRAG, ALVIN DALE, govt. designer; b. Castleton, Kans., Feb. 1, 1938; s. John A. and Selma (Graber) S.; B.A. in Natural Sci., 1961; B.S. in Agrl. Engring., Kans. State U., 1962; m. Verna Helen Klaassen, July 24, 1964; children—Ryan, Heather. Designer, W.C. Wood Co., Guelph, Ont., Can., 1964-66; designer, quality control supr. Killbery Industries, Winnipeg, Man., Can., 1967-68; tool designer Cessna Indsl. Products div. Cessna Aircraft Co., Hutchinson, Kans., 1968-70; design draftsman Reno County, Hutchinson, Kans., 1971—. Registered profl. engr., Man. Mem. Assn. Profl. Engrs. Man. Mennonite religion. Home: Rural Route 1 Pretty Prairie KS 67570 Office: 206 W 1st St Hutchinson KS 67501

SCHRAGE, ROBERT JOSEPH, accountant; b. Breese, Ill., Oct. 14, 1936; s. Joseph Henry and Nora Katherine Middeke S.; Asso. Bus., So. Ill. U., 1961; certificate C.P.A. Tng., La Salle Extension U., 1964. Sr. accountant Benson, Lamear, Nolte & McCormack, C.P.A.'s. St. Louis, 1961-74; pres., mgr. Original Mineral Springs Hotel & Bathhouse Inc., Okawville, Ill., 1974-76, J.B.J. Services Inc., pub. accounting, Okawville, 1974—; dir. numerous corps. Mem. Okawville Bus. Assn. (sec. 1974—), Okawville Community Club, Am. Accounting Assn., Am. Inst. C.P.A.'s, Am. Paraplegic Assn. Home: 109 Mascoutah Ave Okawville IL 62271 Office: 506 Hanover St Okawville IL 62271

SCHRAM, ROY CHARLES, trailer mfg. co. exec., mayor; b. Garner, Iowa, Feb. 11, 1905; s. Edward and Flora (Hesley) S.; grad. high sch.; m. Viola J. B. Kettel, Feb. 8, 1936. Mechanic, Yellow Taxi Cab Co., Chgo., 1925-27; machine operator Century Rubber Co., Chgo., 1927-29; salesman Vacuette Co., Mpls., 1930-32; elevator operator apt. bldg., Chgo., 1933-37; owner Forest City Motor Co. (Iowa), 1937-58; owner dealership Winnebago Motor Co., Forest City, 1943-60; pres. Forest City Industries, Inc., 1958—; mayor, Forest City, 1946-76; dir. Forest City Bank & Trust Co. Mem. Forest City Devel. Co., v.p., 1956-75; chmn. Winnebago Crime Commn.; vice chmn. Iowa Research and Devel. Commn.; regional chmn. North Iowa Area Devel. Mem. exec. bd. North Iowa Area Coll. Methodist. Rotarian. Home: 108 Fairview Dr Forest City IA 50436 Office: 1246 N 4th St Forest City IA 50436

SCHRAMM, DAVID NORMAN, educator, astrophysicist; b. St. Louis, Oct. 25, 1945; s. Marvin and Betty (Math) S.; S.B. in Physics, Mass. Inst. Tech., 1967; Ph.D. in Physics, Calif. Inst. Tech., 1971; m. Melinda Holzhauer, 1963; children—Cary, Brett. Research fellow in physics Calif. Inst. Tech., Pasadena, 1971-72; asst. prof. astronomy and physics U. Tex. at Austin, 1972-74; asso. prof. astronomy and astrophysics Enrico Fermi Inst. and the Coll., U. Chgo., 1974-77, prof., 1977—, acting chmn. dept. astronomy and astrophysics, 1977—; cons. and lectr. in field. Fellow Am. Phys. Soc.; mem. Am. Astron. Soc., Astron. Soc. Pacific, Meteoritical Soc., Internat. Astron. Union, Sigma Xi. Recipient Robert J. Trumpler award Astron. Soc. Pacific, 1974; contbr. numerous articles to profl. jours.; coeditor: Explosive Nucleosynthesis, 1973; Editor: Supernovae, 1977; co-author: Advanced States of Stellar Evolution, 1977. Home: 4923 S Kimbark St Chicago IL 60615 Office: Enrico Fermi Inst U Chgo 933 E 56th St Chicago IL 60637

SCHRAMM, JAMES SIEGMUND, retail trade exec.; b. Burlington, Iowa, Feb. 4, 1904; s. Frank Edgar and Carrie Ash (Higason) S.; student Amherst Coll., 1926, L.H.D., 1961; LL.D., Coe Coll., 1954; D.F.A., Grinnell Coll., 1972; m. Dorothy Daniell, Sept. 26, 1931; children—Sieglinde Schramm Martin, Kristina Schramm Doughty. Chief exec. J.S. Schramm Co., Burlington, 1924-62. Chmn. Iowa Republican Finance Com., 1951, state chmn. and nat. committeeman, 1952-54; chmn. Iowa Arts Council, 1966-68. Served to lt. col. U.S. Army, 1942-45. Decorated Legion of Merit. Recipient Distinguished Service award U. Iowa, 1971. Mem. Nat. Retail Dry Goods Assn. (past dir.), Am. Fedn. Arts (pres. 1956-58), Century Assn. N.Y.C., Royal Soc. Arts London. Republican. Presbyterian. Club: Des Moines. Home: 2700 S Main St Burlington IA 52601

SCHRAMM, PAUL HOWARD, lawyer; b. St. Louis, Oct. 6, 1933; s. Benjamin Jacob and Frieda Sylvia (Goruch) S.; A.B., U. Mo., 1955; J.D., 1958; m. Susan Ann Susman, June 6, 1959; children—Scott Lyon, Dean Andrew, Thomas Edward. Admitted to Mo. bar, 1958, practiced in Clayton, also St. Louis, 1958—; mem. firm Schramm and Schramm, 1959-61, Schramm and Morganstern, 1970-76, Schramm, Pines & Marshall, 1977—; judge municipal ct. City of Ellisville (Mo.), 1977—. Mem. Estate Planning Council, St. Louis, 1968—. Mem. U. Mo. Law Sch. Found., 1969—; mem. music adv. com. Mo. State Council on Arts, 1971-77; pres. Kirkwood Symphony Soc., 1961. Mem. Ladue Sch. Dist. Council, 1970-74. Bd. dirs. Young Audiences, Inc., 1972-78, pres. elect, 1974-75, pres., 1975-76; bd. dirs. St. Louis Dance Concert Soc., 1969-74, sec., 1969; bd. dirs. St. Louis Jewish Family and Children's Service, 1975-77; mem. Ladue Sch. Dist. Council, 1970-74; mem. exec. com. East Ladue Jr. High Sch. Assn., 1975-76. Mem. Am., St. Louis County (chmn. lawyer reference service 1971, chmn. circuit ct. judiciary com.), Mo. bar assns., Bar Assn. Met. St. Louis (exec. com. 1976-77, chmn. St. Louis County sect. 1976-77), Am. Judicature Soc., Reed Sch. Assn. (pres. 1970-71), Phi Delta Phi, Psi Chi, Sigma Alpha Mu. Home: 2 Cedar Crest Ladue MO 63132 Office: 120 S Central Ave Clayton MO 63105

SCHRANK, HARRY PAUL, JR., librarian; b. Akron, Ohio, Oct. 21, 1927; s. Harry Paul and Julia Kathryn (Palmer) S.; B.S.C., Ohio U., 1949; postgrad. U. N.C., 1954-55; M.S., U. Ill., 1963. Expediter, jr. buyer Goodyear Tire & Rubber Co., Akron, 1949-52; security analyst Equitable Life Assurance Soc., N.Y.C., 1955-62; adminstrv. asst. to dir. libraries Ga. Inst. Tech., Atlanta, 1963-64; asst. librarian U. Akron, 1965, univ. librarian, 1965—, curator Hower House, 1974—. Vice chmn. adv. council Fed. Library Programs in Ohio, 1971-73, chmn., 1973-75; chmn. planning com. Ohio Library Coop. Inst., 1975. Trustee, Ohio Coll. Library Center, 1972-77, vice chmn. bd., 1972-75, chmn. bd., pres., 1975-77, trustee, 1977—, chmn. bd. trustees, 1977—, rep. to Council for Computerized Library Networks, 1975—, to network adv. group of Library of Congress, 1976-77. Served with USNR, 1945-46, 52-54. Mem. ALA, Ohio Library Assn., Inter-Univ. Council Ohio (chmn. 1968-69), Ohio Coll. Assn. (librarians' sect. pres. 1970-71), Spl. Libraries Assn., Am. Soc. for Info. Sci., Acad. Library Assn. Ohio, Summit County Hist. Soc. (sec. 1970-72, pres. 1972-74, trustee 1969-75), Beta Phi Mu, Theta Chi. Home: 3715 Yellow Creek Rd Akron OH 44313

SCHRAYER, MAX ROBERT, ins. exec.; b. Chgo., Nov. 17, 1902; s. Robert Max and Jennie (Weber) S.; B.S., U. Mich., 1923; m. Mildred Mayer, July 3, 1925; children—Helaine (Mrs. A.A. Freeman), Jean (Mrs. Robert L. Adler), Robert Max. Propr., Max Robert Schrayer & Assos., Chgo., 1933-42, now pres.; v.p. Asso. Agys., Inc., 1942-64, pres., 1965-75, chmn. bd., 1975—; dir. Allied Tube & Conduit Co. Gen. chmn. Combined Jewish Appeal, 1964-65, pres., 1966; v.p. Chgo. chpt. Am. Technion Soc. Bd. dirs., past pres. Better Govt. Assn.; bd. dirs. Jewish Telegraphics Agy.; vice chmn. bd. trustees Roosevelt U.; bd. dirs. Am. Joint Distbn. Com. Home: 4950 Chicago Beach Dr Chicago IL 60615 Office: 175 W Jackson Blvd Chicago IL 60604

SCHRECK, SHELDON ALLEN, city ofcl.; b. Chgo., Feb. 13, 1948; s. Solomon M. and Pauline (Brodsky) S.; B.S. in Accounting. U. Ill., 1969; M.S. in Accounting, Roosevelt U., 1974. Clk. accounting U. Ill., Chgo. campus, 1969-71, staff accountant, 1972-73, accounting officer supr., 1973-74, adminstr. research grants and contracts, 1974-75; asst. finance dir. City of Highland Park, Ill., 1975—. Served to capt. AUS. Decorated D.S.C., Purple Heart, Bronze Star. Mem. Municipal Finance Officers Assn., Ill. Municipal Finance Officers Assn., Am. Accounting Assn., Nat. Assn. Accountants, Internat. City Mgmt. Assn., Data Processing Mgmt. Assn., Assn. Govt. Accountants, Am. Soc. Pub. Adminstrn., Am. Soc. Legal History, U.S. Commn. Mil. History, Am. Com. on History of Second World War, Am. Def. Preparedness Assn., Am. Mil. Inst., Royal United Services Inst. for Def. Studies, Mil. Hist. Soc., Soc. for Army Hist. Research, Am. Hist. Assn., Orgn. Am. Historians, Assn. Computing Machinery, Assn. Systems Mgmt., Assn. Records Mgrs. and Adminstrs., Assn. Computer Programmers and Analysts, U. Ill. Alumni Assn. Office: City Hall 1707 St Johns Ave Highland Park IL 60035

SCHRECKENGAST, WILLIAM OWEN, lawyer; b. Greenwood, Ind., Oct. 14, 1926; s. Vernon Edward and Marthena O. (Mullinix) S.; LL.B., Ind. U., 1956; m. Helen Margaret Sheppard, Nov. 11, 1949; children—Pamela (Mrs. Brett Binninger), Sandra Kay (Mrs. Garry Hansford), James Owen, John Charles. Claims adjustor, supr. Gulf Ins. Co., Indpls., 1950-57; admitted to Ind. bar, 1956; since practiced in Beech Grove; partner Kitley, Schreckengast & Davis, 1957—; dir. Beech Grove Profl. Bldg. Inc., Larry Beall Shoes, Inc., Beech Grove. Democratic ward chmn. Beech Grove, 1956-58; state campaign chmn. John Walsh for sec. state, 1958. Served with AUS, 1944-46. Mem. Am., Ind. (bd. govs. 1972-73) bar assns., Am. Judicature Soc., Sigma Delta Kappa. Methodist. Mason. Home: 3780 Fairview Rd Greenwood IN 46142 Office: 4th and Main Sts Beech Grove IN 46107

SCHREIBER, GEORGE JULIUS, cordage mfg. co. exec.; b. Milw., Nov. 27, 1906; s. George and Fannie (Mack) S.; student Marquette U., U. Wis., Milw.; m. Frieda Hoefs, Sept. 20, 1930 (dec. Sept., 1969). Designer and detached millwork West Side Mfg. Co., 1927-31; mgr. budget dept. Goodrich Rubber Co., Milw., 1931-32; with John Rauschenberger Co., Milw., 1932—, now gen. sales mgr. Bd. dirs. St. Joseph Hosp., Salvation Army, Wis. Med. Found., Wis. Masonic Home, Wis. Masonic Inst. Mem. Milw. Assn. Commerce, Sales Exec. Club. Mason (33 deg.). Home: 4127 N 60th St Milwaukee WI 53216 Office: 193 N Broadway St Milwaukee WI 53202

SCHREIBER, MARTIN JAMES, lt. gov. of Wis.; b. Milw.; s. Martin Eugene and Emeline (Schreiber); student Valparaiso U., 1957-58, U. Wis.-Milw., 1958-60; J.D., Marquette U., 1964; m. Elaine R. Thaney, June 3, 1961; children—Kathryn, Martin R., Kristine, Matthew. Admitted to Wis. bar; mem. Wis. Senate, 1962-70; lt. gov. of Wis., 1970—. Ombudsman Wis. Nursing Home; chmn. Wis. Council Consumer Affairs; chmn. Wis. Am. Revolution Bicentennial Commn.; chmn. Wis. Ins. Laws Revision Com.; mem. exec. com. Nat. Conf. Lt. Govs. Active Wis. Community Care Orgn. Home: 3128 N 50th St Milwaukee WI 53216 Office: State Capitol Madison WI 53702

SCHREIBMAN, DAN A., retail exec.; b. Cin., Nov. 15; s. Jack and Cecilia (Levin) S.; student U. Cin., 1951-53, U. Denver, 1955-56; m. Roberta Sue Goldstein, Sept. 12, 1957; children—Michael S., Shelly A. Buyer, Goldsteins Dept. Stores, Celina, Ohio, 1957-72; owner, operator male fashions D. Schreibman Ltd., Celina, 1972—. Chmn. UNICEF; scoutmaster Boy Scouts Am. Served with U.S. Army, 1953-55. Mem. Nat. Am. Businessmen's Assn., Celina Retail Mchts. Assn. Am. Legion. Democrat. Jewish. Clubs: Elks, Masons, Toastmasters. Home: 1261/2 Main St S Celina OH 45822 Office: 126 Main St S Celina OH 45822

SCHREIER, JAMES WILLIAM, educator, mgmt. cons., author; b. Milw., May 18, 1946; s. Bernard J. and Edith F. (Ringler) S.; B.S. in Mktg. and Personnel, Marquette U., Milw., 1968, M.B.A., 1972; Ph.D. in Guidance and Counseling, Marquette U., 1976. Buyer, dept. mgr. Kohl's Dept. Store, Brookfield, Wis., 1962-68; mktg. researcher Colgate-Palmolive Co., Milw., 1967-68; sales dept. analyst Am. Paper & Plastics Co., Milw., 1968; teaching asst. mktg. Marquette U., 1970-72, instr. in personnel, mgmt. and computer sci. (part-time), 1971-76, asst. prof. mgmt., 1976—; asso. Lakeshore Group, Ltd., Milw., 1975-77; lectr. Small Bus. Inst., U. Wis., Milw., 1975-76; mgmt. cons. The Center for Venture Mgmt., Milw., 1973-77; mgmt. cons. Jermey D. Meyers & Assos., 1977—. Served with U.S. Army, 1968-70. Mem. Alcohol and Drug Problems Assn. of N. Am., Assn. for Bus. Simulation and Exptl. Learning, Nat. Council on Alcoholism, Soc. Advancement Mgmt., Am. Soc. Tng. and Devel., Internat. Transactional Analysis Assn., Student Assn. for Study of Hallucinogens. Roman Catholic. Author: (with John L. Komives) The Entrepreneur and New Enterprise Formation: A Resource Guide, 1973; The Female Entrepreneur, 1975; (with others) Entrepreneurship and Enterprise Development, 1975; RAISE II, A Personnel Simulation, 1975; contbr. articles on bus. edn. and drug abuse in industry to profl. publs. Home: 835 N Cass St Milwaukee WI

53202 Office: College of Business Marquette Univ Milwaukee WI 53233

SCHREIER, LEONARD, allergist, immunologist; b. Detroit, June 3, 1934; s. Alexander and Fanny (Wayne) S.; M.D., U. Mich., 1959, M.S. in Internal Medicine, 1965; m. Barbara Gay Hirsch, Aug. 11, 1956; children—Eric Marvin, Jordan Scott, Barry Andrew. Intern, Sinai Hosp., Detroit, 1959-60, resident in internal medicine, 1960-63; fellow in allergy and immunology U. Mich., 1963-65; practice medicine specializing in allergy and immunology, Detroit, 1965-66, Pontiac, Mich., 1968—; asst. clin. prof. medicine Wayne State Coll. Medicine 1976—. Served with M.C., U.S. Army, 1966-68. Diplomate Am. Bd. Internal Medicine, Am. Bd. Allergy and Immunology. Fellow Am. Acad. Allergy. Jewish. Contbr. articles to med. jours. Office: 909 S Woodward Ave Suite 16 Pontiac MI 48053

SCHREYER, EDWARD RICHARD, Canadian provincial ofcl.; b. Beausejour, Man., Can., Dec. 21, 1935; s. John James and Elizabeth (Gottfried) S.; B.A., U. Man., 1960, B. Pedagogy, 1959, M.A., 1963, B.Ed., 1962; m. Lilly Schulz, June 30, 1960; children—Lisa Kim, Karmel Joy, Jason, Toban Edward. Mem. Man. Legislature, 1958-65, Ho. of Commons, 1965-69; premier Man., Winnipeg, 1969—, minister of finance, 1969. Leader, New Democratic Party Man., 1969—. Served to 2d lt. Royal Canadian Armoured Corps, 1954-56. Roman Catholic. Home: 3069 Henderson Highway East St Paul MB Canada Office: Legislative Bldg Broadway Ave Winnipeg 1 MB Canada

SCHRIDER, SYLVIA LUANN, assn. exec., camp adminstr.; b. Thornville, Ohio, May 29, 1938; d. Bert and Vera Alice (Milbaugh) Schrider; B.S., Ohio State U., 1960; postgrad. U. N.Mex., 1968. Phys. edn. tchr. No. Local Sch. Dist., Thornville, 1960-63, Truth or Consequences (N.Mex.) Municipal Schs., 1963-64, 65-69, Estancia (N.Mex.) Schs., 1964-65; tchr. LaPorte (Ind.) Community Schs., 1969-70; field adviser, camp dir. East Lake Porter Counties, Girl Scouts U.S.A., Gary, Ind., 1971—. Recipient Appreciation Service award Girl Scouts of Cleve., 1962. Mem. Ohio State U. Alumni Assn. Roman Catholic (instr. confrat. Christian doctrine). Home: 121 S Jackson St Crown Point IN 46307 Office: 3725 Broadway Gary IN 46409

SCHRIER, ARNOLD, historian, educator; b. Bronx, N.Y., May 30, 1925; s. Samuel and Yetta (Levine) S.; student Bethany Coll., 1943-44, Ohio Wesleyan U., 1944-45; B.S., Northwestern U., 1949, M.A., 1950, Ph.D. (Social Sci. Research Council fellow), 1956; postgrad. (Learned Socs. Fgn. Area fellow), Ind. U., 1963-64; m. Sondra Weinshelbaum, June 12, 1949; children—Susan Lynn, Jay Alan, Linda Lee, Paula Kay. Asst. prof. history U. Cin., 1956-61, asso. prof., 1961-66, prof., 1966, dir. grad. studies in history, 1969-78, Walter C. Langsam prof. modern history, 1972—; vis. asst. prof. history Northwestern U., summer 1960; vis. lectr. in Russian history Duke U., summer, 1966; vis. asso. prof. history Ind. U., 1965-66; dir. NDEA Inst. in World History for Secondary Tchrs., 1965. Served with USNR, 1943-46, served to lt. USNR, 1952-54. Taft Faculty grantee, 1964, 67, 70. Mem. Am. Hist. Assn., Am. Assn. Advancement Slavic Studies, AAUP (pres. U. Cin. chpt. 1970-71), Midwest, So. confs. Slavic studies, Ohio Acad. History (pres. 1973-74), Immigration History Soc., Phi Alpha Theta. Jewish. Author: Ireland and the American Emigration, 1958, 2d edit., 1970; The Development of Civilization, 2 vols., 1962, rev. edit., 1969; Modern European Civilization, 1963; Living World History, 1964, rev. edit., 1974; Twentieth Century World, 1974; History and Life: The World and Its People, 1977. Home: 9155 Peachblossom Ct Cincinnati OH 45231 Office: History Dept Univ of Cincinnati Cincinnati OH 45221

SCHRIMPER, VERNON LEROY, mech. engr., heavy constrn. equipment mfg. co. exec.; b. Cedar Rapids, Iowa, Mar. 25, 1933; s. Clinton and Marie Lorene (Miller) S.; B.S. in Mech. Engring., Iowa State U., 1955; postgrad. Alexander Hamilton Inst., 1960-62; m. Marlene Lorene Miller, May 9, 1959; children—Michael Charles, Kenneth Andrew, Laura Maria. Mem. advt. dept. LaPlant Choate Co., Cedar Rapids, 1950-51; with engring. dept. Collins Radio Co., Cedar Rapids, 1951-54; design engr. rock crushing and asphalt mixing equipment Iowa Mfg. Co., Cedar Rapids, 1955-57, systems engr., 1957-58, devel. engr. paving equipment, 1958-61, chief research and devel. engr. of multiple new products, 1961-72, dir. engring., 1972-76, v.p. engring., 1976-78, sr. V.p. ops., 1978—. Vice chmn. maj. firms campaign United Way, 1976-77; athletic club dir. Washington High Sch., 1976-78; mem. stewardship com. St. Paul's Methodist Ch., Cedar Rapids, 1976-78; bd. dirs. United Cerebral Palsy Center, 1962-65; Jr. Achievement of Cedar Rapids, 1976-78; capt. Cedar Rapids Cancer Crusade, 1976-78. Registered profl. engr., Iowa. Mem. ASME (chmn. northeast Iowa sect. 1965-66), ASTM, Soc. Automotive Engrs., Assn. of Asphalt Paving Technologists, Assn. of Tech. Soc. in Cedar Rapids (chmn. 1960-61), Nat. Asphalt Paving Assn. (mem. quality improvement com. 1977-78), Cedar Rapids Engrs. Club (pres. 1960-61), Cedar Rapids Jr. C. of C. (v.p. 1958-64, Distinguished Service award 1964), Iowa State Alumni Assn., Knights of St. Patrick, Phi Mu Alpha, Phi Kappa Psi. Republican. Methodist. Club: Cedar Rapids Country. Patentee in field. Home: 662 Valley Brook Dr SE Cedar Rapids IA 52403 Office: 916-16th St NE Cedar Rapids IA 52402

SCHRIMPF, WILLIAM JOHN, Otolaryngologist; b. Cin., May 31, 1921; s. William John and Blanche May (Parks) S.; B.S., Xavier U., 1943; M.D., Loyola U., Chgo., 1946; M.Med.S., U. Pa., 1954; m. Margaret Freytag, June 28, 1947; children—Robert J. and Thomas M. (twins). Intern, Good Samaritan Hosp., Cin., 1946-47; chief dept. otolaryngology Colon Gen. Hosp., Panama, C.Z., 1947-48; practice medicine specializing in otolaryngology, Cin., 1953—; mem. staff Deaconess, St. Mary's, St. Francis, Cin. Gen., Good Samaritan hosps.; dir. Ohio Med. Indemnity, Inc. Mem. parish council St. Catherine Roman Catholic Ch. Served as maj. U.S. Army, 1947-50, USAF, 1950-53. Recipient Presdl. citation Xavier U., 1966. Diplomate Am. Bd. Otolaryngology. Mem. Am. Soc. Clin. Hypnosis (charter), Am. Council Otolaryngology, Am. Acad. Opthalmology and Otolaryngology, AMA, Ohio Med. Assn., Cin. Otolaryngol. Soc. (pres. 1968-69), Acad. Medicine Cin. Clubs: Western Hills Country, Centurion, K.C. Home: 2818 Cyclorama Dr Cincinnati OH 45211 Office: 199 William Howard Taft Rd Cincinnati OH 45219

SCHROEDER, COLLIN HAROLD, biochemist; b. Wausau, Wis., May 13, 1927; s. George H. and Alvina K. (Koenig) S.; B.S., Lawrence U., 1950; M.S., U. Wis., 1952, Ph.D., 1955; m. Margaret Roberts, Dec. 28, 1950; children—C. Mark, Sarah Schroeder Robbins, Anne K., Michael G. Project asso. dept. biochemistry U. Wis., Madison, 1955-60; biochemist Wis. Alumni Research Found. Inst., Madison, 1960-74, dir. research and devel. div., 1974—. Served with USNR, 1944-45. Mem. N.Y. Acad. Sci., Sigma Xi, Gamma Alpha. Patentee in field. Contbr. articles to profl. jours. Home: 4802 Bayfield Terr Madison WI 53705 Office: 3301 Kinsman Blvd Madison WI 53704

SCHROEDER, DAVID J. DEAN, psychologist; b. Hutchinson, Kans., Mar. 21, 1942; s. David John and Louise (Wedel) S.; B.A., Tabor Coll., 1964; M.S., Kans. State Tchrs. Coll. of Emporia, 1967; Ph.D., U. Okla., 1971; m. Nevonna Joyce Thomas, May 24, 1964; children—Taryn Dee, Anita Joy. Psychology technician Civil Aeromed. Inst. FAA, Oklahoma City, 1967-70, research psychologist, 1970-72; postdoctoral clin. psychology intern Norfolk (Nebr.) Regional Center and NE Mental Health Clinic, 1972-73; clin. psychologist VA Hosp., Murfreesboro, Tenn., 1973-75, VA Hosp., Topeka, 1975—; adj. asst. prof. psychology Middle Tenn. State U., 1974-75, Washburn U., 1975—. Co-chmn. steering com. Madison County (Nebr.) Alcohol Safety Action Project, Norfolk, 1973. Recipient Outstanding Performance award FAA, 1972. Fellow Aerospace Med. Assn. (asso.; mem. membership and registration coms.); mem. Southwestern, Midwestern psychol. assns., Am. Psychol. Assn., Psychonomic Soc., Assn. Aviation Psychology, Sigma Xi. Contbr. articles to profl. jours. Home: 3501 Atwood St Topeka KS 66614 Office: 2200 Gage St Topeka KS 66622

SCHROEDER, EDWARD M., lawyer; b. Chgo., Apr. 5, 1941; s. Wells H. and Dorothy (Voss) S.; B.S., Northwestern U., 1963; J.D., U. Chgo., 1966; m. Sandra J. Brantley, May 23, 1970; children—Amber Monite, Donald Kenrick. Admitted to Ill. bar, 1966, U.S. Supreme Ct. bar, 1970; asso. mem. firm Thomas, Blass, Simpson & Tyler, Chgo., 1966-70, mem. firm, 1970-76; individual practice law, Chgo., 1976—; lectr., Coll. DuPage, 1974—. Vol. fireman Lombard (Ill.) Fire Dept., 1966—; active Lombard chpt. ARC, 1969—, chmn., 1976-77; mem. Lombard Library Renovation Com., 1977—. Recipient Outstanding Alumnus award Northwestern U., 1977. Mem. Am., Ill. bar assns., Judicature Soc., Am. Assn. Vol. Firefighters. Democrat. Clubs: Rotary, Elks, Masons. Home: 1076 S Edgewood Ave Lombard IL 60148

SCHROEDER, H(AROLD) EUGENE, rancher; b. Benkelman, Nebr., Sept. 14, 1921; s. Ernest P. and Edythe (Skewes) S.; B.S., U. Nebr., 1942; m. Madeline Jackson, July 27, 1950; 1 son, Charles P. Gen. mgr. estate of F. C. Krotter, 1946-66; gen. mgr. Krotter Gravel Co., Palisade, Nebr., 1946—; mng. partner Schroeder Cattle Co., Palisade, 1951—. Cons. purebred cattle sales, 1966—; livestock show judge, 1960—. Mem. adv. council U. Nebr. Coll. Agr. Served with AUS, 1942-46; ETO. Mem. Am. (dir.), Nebr. Hereford assns., Nebr. Beef Cattle Improvement Assn., Nebr. Stockgrowers, Am. Legion, Knights Ak-Sar-Ben (ambassador), Phi Gamma Delta. Republican. Methodist. Mason, Elk. Home: Palisade NE 69040 Office: Box B Palisade NE 69040

SCHROEDER, JOHN HERMAN, coll. dean; b. Twin Falls, Idaho, Sept. 13, 1943; s. Herman John and Azalia (Kimes) S.; B.A., Lewis and Clark Coll., Portland, Oreg., 1965; M.A., U. Va., 1967, Ph.D., 1971; m. Sandra Barrow, June 16, 1965; children—John Kimes, Andrew Barrow. Mem. faculty U. Wis., Milw., 1970—, asso. prof. history, asso. dean Coll. Letters and Sci., 1976—. Recipient Edward and Rose Uhrig award for distinguished teaching U. Wis., Milw., 1974, Amoco award for teaching excellence, 1975. Mem. Orgn. Am. Historians, So., Western hist. assns., Phi Alpha Theta. Episcopalian. Author: Mr. Polk's War: American Opposition and Dissent, 1946-1948, 1973. Home: 2606 E Shorewood Blvd Milwaukee WI 53211 Office: Dept History Univ Wis Milwaukee WI 53211

SCHROEDER, LEONARD WILLIAM, chiropractor; b. Oak Park, Ill., June 10, 1921; s. Paul C. and Anna (Berndt) S.; student Valparaiso U., 1952-53; Dr. Chiropractic, Nat. Coll. Chiropractic, 1948; m. Elaine Klank, Nov. 19, 1960. Asst. instr. X-ray, Nat. Coll. Chiropractic, Chgo., 1962-75, asso. prof. dept. clin. scis., 1962—; resident dr. Chgo. Gen. Health Service, 1948-49; physician Nat. Roller Derby, 1950-52, dept. phys. medicine Hines (Ill.) VA Hosp., 1952-55; team physician Luther High Sch. N., Chgo., 1953-77; asst. trainer Chgo. Cardinal Football Club, 1958-60; pvt. practice chiropractic medicine, Oak Park, Ill., 1961—. Served with M.C. AUS, 1941-46. Fellow Internat. Chiropractic Coll.; mem. Ill. Chiropractic Soc. (dir. 1963-70, chmn. bd. 1965-70), Council on Sport Injuries (pres. 1972—), Am. Chiropractic Assn., Chi Rho Sigma, Delta Tau Alpha. Lutheran (sec. ch. 1947-48, v.p. ch. 1949-50, mem. bd. edn., 1963-65, deacon 1977). Contbr. articles to profl. jours. Home and office: 6601 W North Ave Oak Park IL 60302

SCHROEDER, RAYMOND ERNEST, educator; b. South Bend, Ind., Dec. 8, 1949; s. Marvin Klopsch and Jean Edna (Hirsch) S.; A.B., Augustana Coll., 1970; M.S., U. Ill., 1972; m. Gail Arnsdorf, Mar. 5, 1977. News dir. WVIK FM, Rock Island, Ill., 1968, program dir., 1969, gen. mgr., 1970; news photographer WAND TV, Decatur, Ill., part time 1974-77; reporter, producer WILL AM FM, Urbana, Ill., part time 1971-75; instr. radio TV, U. Ill., Urbana, 1971-77; asst. prof. communication Sangamon State U., Springfield, Ill., 1977—; bd. dirs. Illini Publ. Co., 1976-77. Mem. Urbana City Human Relations Commn., 1976-77. Mem. Ill. News Broadcasters Assn. (dir.), Soc. Profl. Journalists, Nat. Assn. Ednl. Broadcasters. Editor Newsletter, Ill. News Broadcasters Assn., 1974—. Home: PO Box 937 Riverton IL 62561 Office: Dept Communications Sangamon State Univ Springfield IL 62708

SCHROEDER, ROBERT ANTHONY, lawyer; b. Bendena, Kans., May 19, 1912; s. Anthony and Nanon (Bagby) S.; LL.B. cum laude, U. Kans., 1937; m. Janet Manning, Nov. 21, 1936; 1 son, Robert Breathitt. Admitted to Mo. bar 1937; atty. Allstate Ins. Co., Chgo., 1937-38; asso. firm Madden, Freeman, Madden & Burke, Kansas City, Mo., 1938-48; partner firm Swofford, Schroeder & Shankland, Kansas City, 1948-59; law offices Robert A. Schroeder, 1959-67; partner firm Schroeder & Schroeder, 1967—. Vice pres. Roxbury State Bank (Kans.), 1954-72, pres., 1972-77, chmn. bd., 1977—, also dir.; pres., dir. Douglas County Investment Co.; chmn. bd., dir. Hub State Bank, Independence, Mo. Vice pres. Mo. Found., 1965-70; pres. Mo. Bar Found., 1970-73. Trustee Kansas U. Law Sch. Soc.; hon. trustee Kansas City Art Inst. Fellow Am. Bar Found., Am. Coll. Probate Counsel, Kan. U. Law Soc.; mem. Nat. Legal Aid, Defenders Soc., Fed. Bar, Mo. Bar (co.-chmn. continuing legal edn. com. 1958-59, chmn. finance planning sub-com., 1958-59, mem. bd. govs. 1959-67, chmn. pub. edn. com. 1965-66, pres. 1965-66, chmn. cts. and jud. com. 1971-72, Pres.'s award 1972), Am. (state chmn. standing com. on membership 1961-62, mem. lawyer referral com. 1966-70, Ho. of Dels., 1967-71, vice chmn. bench and bar com. 1968-71, mem. bench and bar com. 1971—), Kans. (hon. life), Kansas City (pres. 1957-58, chmn. exec. com. 1957-58, judicial recommendations com. 1957-58, 69-70, pub. relations com. 1958-60, medico-legal com. 1962-64, law day com. 1964-65, chmn. lawyer welfare and placement com. 1966-72, chmn. program com. 1969-70, chmn. pre-paid legal services 1975-77, Achievement award 1976) bar assns., Greater Kansas City Kans. U. Law Sch. Alumni Assn. (pres. 1963-64), Delta Tau Delta, Phi Delta Phi (pres. 1936-37), Order of Coif. Mason. Author: Twenty-Five Years Under the Missouri Plan; Twenty-Five Years Experience with Merit Judicial Selection in Missouri. Asso. editor Kans. Law Jour., 1935-37. Office: Lathrop Bldg Kansas City MO 64106

SCHROEDER, WILLIAM CHRISTOPHER MARTIN, auto supply co. exec.; b. Chgo., Jan. 8, 1897; s. John Adolph and Corena Fredericka (Hildebrandt) S.; B.S., U. Ill., 1923; LL.B., Chgo. Law Sch., 1929; m. Olga Elizabeth Leutnegger, June 6, 1938. Accountant, Ill. Bell Telephone Co., Chgo., 1923-29, Duttine & Young, 1929-30; asso. firm Norcross & Norcross, Chgo., 1930-31; asst. comptroller Allied Motors Corp., Chgo., 1931-32; salesman central, western states B.F. Goodrich Co., Akron, Ohio, 1932-57; owner, operator Schroeder Supply Co., Galesburg, Ill., 1958—. Finance adviser Muscatine (Iowa) Luth. Homes, 1971—, bd. dirs., exec. bd., 1975—. Mem. Alpha Kappa Psi, Phi Alpha Delta, Tau Kappa Epsilon. Republican. Lutheran. Clubs: Cosmopolitan, Internat. Cultures, Masons, Shriners, K.T. Home and office: 256 Phillips St Galesburg IL 61401

SCHROER, EDMUND ARMIN, utility co. exec.; b. Hammond, Ind. Feb. 14, 1928; s. Edmund Henry and Florence Evelyn (Schmidt) S.; B.A., Valparaiso U., 1949; J.D., Northwestern U., 1952; m. Elizabeth Ruth Boeschenstein, Feb. 10, 1962; children—James, Fredrik, Amy, Lisa, Timothy. Admitted to Ind. bar, 1952; practiced in Hammond, Ind., 1952—; asso. Crumpacker & Friedrich, 1952; partner Crumpacker & Schroer, 1954-56; asso., then partner Friedrich, Petrie & Tweedle, 1957-62; partner Schroer & Eichhorn, 1963-66; partner Schroer, Eichhorn & Morrow, Hammond, 1967-77; gen. counsel, pres., chief exec. officer No. Ind. Pub. Service Co., 1977—; asst. dist. atty. No. Ind., 1954-56. Sch. bd. trustee, Munster, Ind., 1969-71, pres., 1971; Republican finance chmn., Hammond, 1958-62; del. to Ind. Rep. Conv., 1958, 60, 64, 66, 68. Mem. Am., Fed., Fed. Power, Ind. (bd. mgrs. 1969-71), Hammond (pres. 1966-67) bar assns., Am. Judicature Soc. Lutheran. Rotarian (pres. Hammond chpt. 1968). Home: 1320 MacArthur St Munster IN 46321 Office: 5265 Hohman Ave Hammond IN 46320

SCHROER, GENE ELDON, lawyer; b. Randolph, Kans., Aug. 29, 1927; s. Harry Edward and Florence Lillian (Schwartz) S.; LL.B., Washburn U., 1957; m. Edith Grace Kintner, Apr. 6, 1956; children—Kenneth, Rebecca, Connie, Sonja. Admitted to Kans. bar, 1957; practiced in Topeka, 1957—; mem. firm Jones, Schroer & Rice, Topeka, 1968—, pres., 1972—; dir. Stoffle Meat Co., Inc., Topeka. Democratic precinct committeeman, 1958—; mem. exec. com. Shawnee County Dem. Com., 1958—; mem. bd. suprs. Shawnee County Soil Conservation Dist., 1969-70, chmn. bd., 1970—. Served with AUS, 1951-53. Mem. Am., Topeka bar assns., Bar Assn. State Kans., Kans. Trial Lawyers Assn. (gov., treas. 1972-74, pres. 1974-75, Assn. Trial Lawyers Am. (sec. tort sect. 1973-74, 2d v.p. tort sect. 1974-75, 1st v.p. tort sect. 1976—, gov. 1976—), Greater Topeka C. of C. Presbyn. (elder). Mason. Home: 223 Woodlawn St Topeka KS 66606 Office: 115 E 7th St Topeka KS 66603

SCHROER, GEORGE JEROME, physician; b. Coldwater, O., Sept. 10, 1921; s. Henry Herman and Rose Elizabeth (Schlagheck) S.; B.A., Ohio State U., 1943, M.D., 1946; m. Mildred Marie Hoying, Aug. 28, 1946; children—Jerome, Thomas, William, Ann. Intern, Miami Valley Hosp., Dayton, O., 1946-47; gen. practice medicine, Sidney, O., 1949-69, Ft. Loramie, O., 1969—. Pres. First Devel., Inc., Sidney. Former trustee Ottawa Valley Hosp., Lima, O.; trustee Ohio Western Found. for Med. Care. Served to capt., M.C., U.S. Army, 1947-49. Mem. Ohio Med. Assn. (past 2d dist. counselor), Shelby County Med. Soc. (pres.). Elk, Moose. Clubs: Piqua (O.) Country; Arrowhead Country (Minster, O.). Home: 1731 Letitia Dr Sidney OH 45365 Office: 20 S Main St Fort Loramie OH 45845

SCHRUP, NICHOLAS JOHN, banker; b. Dubuque, Iowa, Sept. 28, 1929; s. Charles Joseph and Ethleen (O'Rourke) S.; B.S.S, Georgetown U., 1951; postgrad. U. Wis., 1962; m. Dorothy Ann Flanagan, Aug. 11, 1952 (div. 1967); children—John Charles, Nicholas John III; m. 2d, Jean McDonald, 1970; 1 dau., Sarah O. With Am. Trust & Savs. Bank, 1954—, asst. cashier, asst. v.p., v.p., 1954-66, sr. v.p., 1966-68, pres., 1968-73, chmn. bd., 1973—, also dir.; dir. Sunrise Golf Devel. Corp., Ft. Lauderdale, Fla.; pres. Cal-Lan Corp. Pres. Dubuque Area Health Facilities Planning Bd., 1966—. Bd. corporators, trustee Clarke Coll., Dubuque, Iowa; bd. dirs., treas. Dubuque Boys' Club, Dubuque County Cancer Soc.; bd. dirs. Dubuque United Fund, Dubuque Indsl. Bur. Served with U.S. Army, 1951-53. Mem. Am. Legion, Dubuque Shooting Soc., C. of C. Elk, K.C. Club: Dubuque Golf and Country (pres. 1969—, trustee 1970—). Home: 695 Sunset Ridge Dubuque IA 52001 Office: 9th & Main Sts Dubuque IA 52001

SCHUBERT, HELEN CELIA, pub. relations cons.; b. Washington County, Wis., May 30, 1930; d. Paul H. and Edna W. (Schmidt) Schubert; B.S., U. Wis., Madison, 1952. Dir. publicity United Cerebral Palsy Assn., Chgo.; writer Philip Lesly Co., pub. relations agy., Chgo., 1958-61; dir. dept. consumer interest, dir. Nat. Design Center, Chgo., 1963-67. Fellow Nat. Home Fashions League (dir.); mem. Women in Communications (pres. Chgo. chpt. 1969-70, regional v.p. 1970-71, Distinguished Service award 1972, dir.), Am. Women in Radio-TV, Publicity Club of Chgo. (Distinguished Service award 1966), Pub. Realtions Soc. Am., Am. Soc. Interior Designers (pub. relations affiliate), Fashion Group of Chgo., Women's Advt. Club of Chgo., Art Inst. Chgo. (life). Lutheran. Clubs: U. Wis. Alumni (life), Chgo. Press. Contbr. articles to profl. jours. Home and office: 222 E Chestnut St Chicago IL 60611

SCHUBERT, PAUL MORGAN, indsl. health engr.; b. Midland, Mich., Aug. 2, 1947; s. Frank John and Margurite Mae (Morgan) S.; M.B.A., Mich. State U., 1973, B.Ch.E., 1969. Engr., E. I. duPont de Nemours & Co., Inc., Parkersburg, W.Va., 1969-71; indsl. health engr. Mich. Dept. Pub. Health, Wayne County, Mich., Inkster, Mich., 1974—. Mem. Engring. Soc. Detroit, Am. Conf. Govtl. Indsl. Hygienists, Mich. Indsl. Hygiene Soc. Office: 1547 Middlebelt St Inkster MI 48141

SCHUCHART, JOHN ALBERT, JR., utility co. exec.; b. Omaha, Nov. 13, 1929; s. John A. and Mildred Vera (Kessler) S.; B.S. in Bus., U. Nebr., 1950; grad. Stanford U. Exec. Program, 1968; m. Ruth Joyce Schock, Dec. 2, 1950; children—Deborah J. Kelley, Susan K. Felton. With No. Natural Gas Co., Omaha, 1950-72, asst. sec., 1957-60, mgr. accounting, 1960-65, adminstrv. mgr., 1965-71; v.p., treas. Intermountain Gas Co., Boise, Idaho, 1972-75, chief fin. officer, 1973-75; fin. v.p. and treas., chief fin. officer Montana-Dakota Utilities Co., Bismarck, N.D., 1976-77, pres. and chief operating officer, 1978—, also dir. Mem. budget com. of United Way, Omaha, 1969-70; bd. dirs. Girl Scouts U.S., Boise, 1975. Served with U.S. Army, 1951-53. Recipient Scroll and Merit award Adminstrv. Mgmt. Soc., 1972. Mem. Am. (Merit award 1968), Midwest gas assns., Edison Electric Inst., N. Central Electric Assn., Fin. Execs. Inst., Delta Sigma Pi. Republican. Methodist. Clubs: Elks, Apple Creek Country. Contbr. articles on accounting to profl. jours. Home: 2009 W Grimsrud Dr Bismarck ND 58501 Office: 400 N 4th St Bismarck ND 58501

SCHUELEIN, EDWARD JUNIOR, broadcasting co. exec.; b. Enid, Okla., Sept. 9, 1921; s. Edward Peter and Bertha Louise (Klein) S.; Broadcast Engr., Central Tech. Inst., Kansas City, Mo., 1948; m. Geraldine Burnett, Feb. 25, 1946; children—Sharon (Mrs. Mike Bates), Beverly (Mrs. Jeffrey Schrimpf), Deborah, Cynthia. Instr., Central Tech. Inst., 1948-49; engr. WOAI-TV, San Antonio, 1949-51; engr. WDAF-TV, Kansas City, 1951-53; chief operating engr. KOMU-TV, U. Mo., Columbia, 1953-54; chief engr., v.p., asst. gen. mgr. KRCG-TV, Jefferson City, Mo., dir. Jefferson TV Co., 1954-66; gen. mgr. Mid Am. TV Co. (KRCG-TV), 1966-72, v.p., gen mgr., 1972—. Mem. exec. bd. Three Rivers dist. Boy Scouts Am. Served with inf. AUS, 1942-43; as 2d lt. USAAF, 1943-45. Mem. Nat. Assn. Broadcasters, Mo. Broadcasting Assn. (sec.-treas., dir. 1970-72), Jefferson City C. of C. (dir.). Lutheran. Club: Meadow Lake Acres

Country (Jefferson City). Home: 421 Castle St Jefferson MO 65101 Office: Box 659 Jefferson City MO 65101

SCHUENKE, DONALD JOHN, ins. co. exec.; b. Milw., Jan. 12, 1929; s. Ray H. and Josephine P. (Maciolek) S.; Ph.B., Marquette U., 1950, LL.B., 1958; m. Joyce A. Wetzel, July 19, 1952; children—Ann, Thomas, Mary. Admitted to Wis. bar, 1958. Spl. agt. Nat. Life of Vt., 1958-59; real estate rep. Standard Oil Co. of Ind., Milw., 1959-63; asst. gen. counsel Northwestern Mut. Life Ins. Co., Milw., 1963-65, v.p., gen. counsel, sec., 1974-76, sr. v.p. investments, 1974—. Bd. dirs. Milw. Symphony Orch., Curative Workshop, St. Camillus Health Center, Sacred Heart Sch. Theology; mem. adv. bd. YWCA of Milw. Mem. Am., Wis. bar assns., Am. Council Life Ins. Home: 7733 W Wisconsin Ave Wauwatosa WI 53213 Office: 720 E Wisconsin Ave Milwaukee WI 53202

SCHUFF, KAREN ELIZABETH, poet; b. Highland Park, Mich., June 1, 1937; d. Ernest Jack and Helen Wanda (Novak) Bishop; grad. high sch. Detroit; m. Henry Clifton Schuff, Sept. 7, 1955; children—Deborah Elaine, David Lawrence. Author collections of poems including: Barefoot Philosopher, 1968, Come, Take My Hand, 1968, Of Rhythm and Cake, 1970.

SCHUL, BILL DEAN, psychol. adminstr., author; b. Winfield, Kans., Mar. 16, 1928; s. Fred M. and Martha Mildred (Miles) S.; B.A., Southwestern Coll., 1952; M.A., U. Denver, 1954; Ph.D., Am. Internat. U., 1977; m. Virginia Louise Duboise, Aug. 3, 1952; children—Robert Dean, Deva Elizabeth. Reporter and columnist Augusta (Kans.) Daily Gazette, 1954-58, Wichita (Kans.) Eagle-Beacon, 1958-61; Kans. youth dir. under auspices of Kans. Atty. Gen., 1961-65; Kans. state dir. Seventh Step Found., Topeka, 1965-66; mem. staff Dept. Preventive Psychiatry, Menninger Found., Topeka, Kans., 1966-71; dir. cons. Center Improvement Human Functioning, Wichita, 1975—; author: (with Edward Greenwood) Mental Health in Kansas Schools, 1965; Let Me Do This Thing, 1969; (with Bill Larson) Hear Me, Barabbas, 1969; How to Be An Effective Group Leader, 1975; The Secret Power of Pyramids, 1975; (with Ed Pettit) The Psychic Power of Pyramids, 1976; The Psychic Power of Animals, 1977; Psychic Frontiers of Medicine, 1977. Bd. dirs. Recreation Commn., Topeka, Kans., United Funds, Topeka. Served with USN, 1945-46. Recipient John H. McGinnis Meml. award for Nonfiction, 1972, Am. Freedom Found. award, 1966, Spl. Appreciation award Kans. State Penitentiary, 1967. Mem. Acad. of Parapsychology and Medicine, Kans. Council for Children and Youth (pres. 1965-66), Assn. for Strenghtening the Higher Realities and Aspirations of Man (pres. 1970-71), Smithsonian Inst. Club: Lions (pres. 1957). Address: Rural Route 3 Winfield KS 67156

SCHULDENBERG, VIRGINIA MARY, educator; b. Milw., June 3, 1935; d. Armin Henry and Elsie Elizabeth (Jonen) S.; B.S. cum laude in Edn., Mt. Mary Coll., Milw., 1957; M.Ed. (NDEA grantee), U. Mo., Columbia, 1966, Ph.D. (fellow), 1970; m. Felix Feyerer, Jan. 8, 1977. Elementary tchr. Wauwatosa (Wis.) Pub. Schs., 1957-61, Dept. Def. Overseas Schs., Japan, Germany, 1961-65, Columbia (Mo.) Pub. Schs., 1966-67; behavior analyst, staff counselor, research and teaching asst. U. Mo., Columbia, 1967-70; instr. ednl. psychology E. Central Jr. Coll., Union, Mo., 1969-70; prof. counselor edn. and tchr. edn. Oakland U. Sch. Edn., Rochester, Mich., 1970—, program devel. specialist, acting dir. Tchr. Corps Projects, 1971—. Recipient Better World award Gabriel Richard Inst., 1970. Mem. Am. Personnel and Guidance Assn., Assn. Supervision and Curriculum Devel., Counselor Educators Mich. (sec.-treas. 1974-76), AAUP (negotiating team 1975), Phi Alpha Theta, Kappa Gamma Pi. Roman Catholic. Editorial bd. Jour. Counselor Edn. Supervision, 1974-76. Home: 2437 Napa Trail Waukesha WI 53186 Office: Oakland U Sch Edn Rochester MI 48063

SCHULER, JOHN WAYNE, broadcasting co. exec.; b. Moores Hill, Ind., Sept. 30, 1935; s. William Richard and Nellie Louise (Marksberry) S.; grad. high sch.; m. Barbara Wade, July 24, 1965. Factory worker Nat. Lead Ohio, 1953-60; owner, operator Schuler Service Sta., 1960-64; owner Schuler Oil Co., Aurora, Ind., 1964-70; pres., gen. mgr. radio sta WSCH, Aurora, 1970—. Mem. Nat., Ind. broadcasters assns., Aurora C. of C. Mason. Club: Valley (Indpls.). Home: Route 1 Salem Ridge Rd Aurora IN 47001 Office: Box 993 Aurora IN 47001

SCHULER, LOUIS EUGENE, lawyer; b. Griswold, Iowa, Feb. 9, 1922; s. George J. and Iona Merle (Kramer) S.; B.A., Grinnell Coll., 1943; postgrad. Drake U., 1943; J.D., U. Iowa, 1949; m. Mildred Elisabeth Heines, June 4, 1948; children—George Richard, Louis Eugene, Herbert T., Mark L., Helen E. Admitted to Iowa bar, 1949; since practiced in Clear Lake; partner firm Boyle, Schuler & Stanton; sec. Surf Land Co., Clear Lake, 1970—, also dir.; sec. Surf Conf. & Civic Center, Inc., Clear Lake, 1970—; sec. Carroll George Inc., Northwood, Iowa, 1966—, also dir. City atty. Clear Lake, 1958-70. Pres., Clear Lake P.T.A., 1968; chmn. All Vets. Social Center, Clear Lake, 1960, Gov.'s Day, Clear Lake, 1952-68. Chmn., Cerro Gordo County (Iowa) Republican Central Com., 1968-73. Served with USAAF, 1943-46. Named Clear Lake Outstanding Boss of Year, C. of C., 1964. Mem. Am., Iowa, 12th Jud. Dist. (pres. 1970), Cerro Gordo County (pres. 1971) bar assns., Am. Judicature Soc., Am. Trial Lawyers Assn., Am. Legion (post comdr. 1952), State U. Ia. Alumni Assn. (pres. 1950). Lutheran (chmn. bd. trustees ch. 1966-67). Home: 408 N Shore Dr Clear Lake IA 50428 Office: 22 N 3d St Clear Lake IA 50428

SCHULTZ, ALLEN H., lawyer; b. Chgo., Mar. 15, 1911; s. Hyman and Minnie (Goldman) S.; LL.B., J.D., DePaul U., 1932; m. Ida A. Greenberg, Oct. 13, 1940; children—Jay, Edward. Admitted to Ill. bar, 1932, since practiced in Chgo.; mem. firm Schultz & Schwartz, 1945-51, Schultz & Biro, 1954-57, Schultz, Biro & Karmel, 1957-71, Schultz & Schultz, 1973—. Mem. Am., Ill., Chgo. bar assns., Chgo. Law Inst., Decalogue Soc. of Lawyers, Pi Gamma Mu (scholastic honor soc.). Jewish. Clubs: Covenant, City. Home: 200 E Chestnut St Chicago IL 60611 Office: 221 N La Salle St Chicago IL 60601

SCHULTZ, ARTHUR WARREN, advt. exec.; b. N.Y.C., Jan. 13, 1922; s. Milton Warren and Genevieve (Dann) S.; grad. U. Chgo.; m. Elizabeth Carroll Mahan, Apr. 23, 1949; children—Arthur Warren, John Carroll (dec.), Julia Hollingsworth. With Foote, Cone & Belding Communications, Chgo., 1948—, v.p., 1957-63, sr. v.p., dir. 1963-69, gen. mgr., Chgo. office, 1967-71, exec. v.p., 1969, chmn. bd., 1970—; dir. Jewel Cos., 1973—. Dir., Chgo. Crime Commn., 1965-71, Community Fund Chgo., 1966-67; pres. Cook County Sch. Nursing, 1963-64, Welfare Council Met. Chgo., 1965-67; bd. dirs. Lyric Opera of Chgo., 1967-77, Better Bus. Bur., Chgo., 1970-77, Chgo. Council on Fgn. Relations, 1977—; trustee YWCA, 1962-74, Art Inst. Chgo., 1975—, U. Chgo., 1977—; mem. bus. adv. council Chgo. Urban League, 1971—. Served to 1st lt. USAAF, 1943-45. Mem. Am. Assn. Advt. Agys. (chmn. Chgo. council 1964-65, chmn. central region, 1970-71, dir. 1968-71, 75-76), Delta Kappa Epsilon. Clubs: Chicago, Racquet, University, Economic, Executives (Chgo.); Commercial, Commonwealth; Barrington Hills (Ill.) Country. Home: Rt 2 Meadow Hill Rd Barrington IL 60010 Office: 401 N Michigan Ave Chicago IL 60611

SCHULTZ, CHARLES WILLIAM, bus. and mgmt. cons.; b. Cedar Rapids, Iowa, Feb. 13, 1931; s. Albert Ludwig and Lydia Bell (Meyer) S.; grad. pub. schs.; B.S., 1968; m. Patricia Elaine Swenson, Dec. 21, 1969; children—Debra L., Kerry S., Roma M. Commd. ensign U.S. Navy, advanced through grades to lt., 1968; comdr. U.S. Naval Forces, Vietnam, 1965-68; recruit tng. officer, San Diego, 1969-72; ret., 1972; pres. Centurion Consultants, Alexandria, Minn., 1972—, also Profiles Alexandria. Mem. Sheriff's Posse, Douglas County, Minn., 1976—. Decorated Bronze Star medal, Silver Star medal. Mem. Nat. Small Bus. Assn., Fleet Res. Assn., Nat. Rifle Assn., Alexandria C. of C., Am. Legion. Republican. Clubs: Rotary of Alexandria, Elks. Home: 604 17th Ave W Alexandria MN 56308 Office: Marion Bldg 700 Cedar St Alexandria MN 56308

SCHULTZ, DONALD RAYMOND, chemist; b. North Tonawanda, N.Y., Nov. 2, 1918; s. Helmuth William and Eda (Kurkowski) S.; B.S., U. Mich., 1940, M.S., 1952, Ph.D., 1954; postgrad. Case Sch. Applied Sci., Cleve., 1941-42; m. Sarah Emma Toth, Sept. 25, 1942 (dec. Apr. 1967); children—Donna (Mrs. Donald Friedrich), Thomas, Winifred, Nancy; m. 2d, Eleanor Augusta Anderson, Aug. 23, 1968. Analytic chemist Penn Salt Mfg. Co., Wyandotte, Mich., 1940, McGean Chem. Co., Cleve., 1940-41; research engr. Trojan Powder Co., Sandusky, O., 1942-44, Mich. Chem. Corp., St. Louis, Mich., 1946-50; teaching fellow, research fellow U. Mich., Ann Arbor, 1950-54; sr. research chemist 3M Co., St. Paul, 1954-68, sr. patent liaison, 1968—. Prof. chemistry Bethel Coll., St. Paul, 1965-66. Vice-chmn. Indianhead council Boy Scouts Am., 1968-69, commr. Norseman dist. Viking council, 1972—, recipient numerous adult scouter awards, 1958-66; active P.T.A. Bd. dirs. St. Louis (Mich.) Fall Festival, 1948-50. Served with USNR, 1944-46. Recipient Outstanding Citizen citation Sta. WTCN, Mpls.-St. Paul, 1964. Mem. Am. Chem. Soc., Am. Inst. Chemists, A.A.A.S., Am. Legion, Sigma Xi, Phi Lambda Upsilon, Phi Kappa Phi. Lutheran (youth counselor Mo. Synod 1954-68, chmn. 1948-50, 70-72). Lion. Contbr. articles to profl. jours. Patentee boron chemistry. Home: 2592 Sumac Ridge White Bear Lake MN 55110 Office: 3M Co Research Center St Paul MN 55101

SCHULTZ, LOUIS CHARTER, dentist, educator; b. Crystal Falls, Mich., Feb. 8, 1902; s. Michael Charter and Susanna (Kresan) S.; D.D.S., U. Mich., 1926, M.S., 1942; m. Frances Keys, June 20, 1931; 1 dau., Juliana (Mrs. Robert A. Knox). Resident, Charles Godwin Jennings Hosp., Detroit, 1928-35; practice dentistry, Ann Arbor, Mich., 1935—; prof. U. Mich. Sch. Dentistry, 1935-68, prof. emeritus, 1968—, chmn. operative dept., 1941-68; lectr. U.S. Naval Dental Sch., 1962, S.Am. schs. and dental socs., summer 1966. Mem. Detroit Dental Clinic Club, Am. Acad. Restorative Dentistry (pres. 1968), Phi Sigma, Omicron Kappa Upsilon. Author: (with others) Operative Dentistry, 1966. Home: 2120 Tuomy Rd Ann Arbor MI 48104 Office: 625 Liberty St Ann Arbor MI 48108

SCHULTZ, RICHARD CARLTON, plastic surgeon; b. Grosse Pointe, Mich., Nov. 19, 1927; s. Herbert H. and Carmen (Huebner) S.; student U. Mich., 1946-49; M.D., Wayne State U., 1953; m. Pauline Zimmermann, Oct. 15, 1955; children—Richard, Lisa, Alexandra, Jennifer. Intern, Harper Hosp., Detroit, 1953-54, resident in gen. surgery, 1954-55; resident in gen. surgery U.S. Army Hosp., Fort Carson, Colo., 1955-57; resident in plastic surgery St. Luke's Hosp., Chgo., 1957-58, U. Ill. Hosp., Chgo., 1958-59, VA Hosp., Hines, Ill., 1959-60; practice medicine, specializing in plastic surgery, Park Ridge, Ill., 1961—; clin. asst. prof. surgery U. Ill. Coll. of Medicine, 1966-70, asso. prof. surgery, 1970-76, prof., 1976—, head div. plastic surg., 1970—. Mem. sch. bd., Lake Zurich, Ill., 1966—, pres., until 1972; pres. Chgo. Found. for Plastic Surgery, 1966—. Served to capt. M.C., AUS, 1955-57. Recipient research award by Found. Am. Soc. Plastic and Reconstructive Surgery, 1964-65, Robert H. Ivy award, 1969; Distinguished Sci. Achievement award Wayne U. Coll. Medicine Alumni, 1975. Fulbright scholar to U. Uppsala (Sweden), 1960-61. Fellow A.C.S.; mem. Am. Assn. Plastic Surgeons. Author: Facial Injuries, 1970, 2d edit., 1977; Maxillo-Facial Injuries from Vehicle Accidents, 1975; Outpatient Surgery, 1978. Home: 21150 N Middleton Dr Kildeer IL 60047 Office: 1600 Dempster St Park Ridge IL 60068

SCHULTZ, RICHARD DEWYL, zoo dir.; b. Jefferson City, Mo., Jan. 19, 1917; s. Carl Frederick and Molly Mabel (Cruzen) S.; B.S. in Bus. Adminstrn., Washington U., St. Louis, 1938; M.B.A., U. Chgo., 1943; m. Jean Crowder, June 18, 1959. C.P.A., Price Waterhouse & Co., St. Louis, 1938-56; controller Petrolite Corp., St. Louis, 1956-64, financial v.p., 1964-72, dir., 1969-72; dir. finance St. Louis Zool. Park, 1973-75, dir., 1975—. C.P.A., Mo. Mem. Financial Execs. Inst., Am. Inst. C.P.A.'s, Am. Assn. Zool. Parks and Aquariums, Beta Gamma Sigma, Phi Delta Theta. Episcopalian. Club: University (St. Louis). Home: 425 Breeze Wood Dr Ballwin MO 63011 Office: St Louis Zoo Park Forest Park St Louis MO 63110

SCHULTZ, RICHARD OTTO, ophthalmologist; b. Racine, Wis., Mar. 19, 1930; s. Henry Arthur and Josephine (Wagoner) S.; B.A., U. Wis., 1950, M.S., 1954; M.D., Albany Med. Coll., 1956; M.Sc., U. Iowa, 1960; m. Jane Davidson, Aug. 2, 1952; children—Henry Reid, Richard Paul, Karen Jo. Intern, Univ. Hosps., Iowa City, Iowa, 1956-57, resident physician in ophthalmology, 1957-60; chief ophthalmology sect. Div. Indian Health, USPHS, Phoenix, 1960-63; practice medicine specializing in ophthalmology, Phoenix, 1963; NIH spl. fellow in ophthalmic microbiology U. Calif. at San Francisco, 1963-64, clin. asso., 1963-64, research asso., 1963-64; asso. prof., chmn. dept. ophthalmology Marquette U. Sch. Medicine (now Med. Coll. Wis.), Milw., 1964-68, prof., chmn., 1968—; dir. Eye Inst., dir. ophthalmology Milw. County Med. Complex, Milw.; cons. Wood VA, Milw. Children's Columbia, Luth. and St. Mary's hosps. (all Milw.), Meml. Hosp., Oconomowoc. Served with USPHS, 1960-63. Diplomate Am. Bd. Ophthalmology. Fellow Am. Acad. Ophthalmology and Otolaryngology, A.C.S., Soc. Eye Surgeons; mem. Royal Soc. Medicine, Assn. Univ. Profs. Ophthalmology (trustee 1973—), Nat. Acad. Scis., Am. Acad. Ophthalmology and Otolaryngology, AMA, Am., Milw. ophthalmol. socs., Assn. Research Vision and Ophthalmology, Assn. Am. Med. Colls., N.Y. Acad. Scis., Research to Prevent Blindness, Oxford Ophthalmol. Congress (Eng.), Pan Am. Assn. Ophthalmology, State Med. Soc. Wis., Wis. Soc. Prevention Blindness, Med. Soc. Milw. County. Contbr. articles to profl. jours. Home: 690 Meadow Ln Elm Grove WI 53122 Office: 8700 W Wisconsin Ave Milwaukee WI 53226

SCHULTZ, ROGER HERMAN, educator; b. Alexandria, Minn., June 27, 1945; s. Herman John and Ruth Marie Pauline (Faehnrich) S.; B.S., Moorhead State Coll., 1967, M.S., 1974; m. Ruth Elaine Poels, June 10, 1967; children—Peter Fredrick Roger, Elizabeth Ruth Marie. Dir. speech and drama Eveleth (Minn.) High Sch., 1967-70; prodn. dir. Duluth Playhouse, 1970; asso. dir. theatre U. Minn., Duluth, 1970—; exec. producer/artist dir. Minn. Time Machine for S.W. Minn. Arts and Humanities Council, 1976; prodn. dir. Theatre L'Homme Dieu, 1977. Mem. Am. Theatre Assn., Univ. and Coll. Theatre Assn., Minn. Theatre Fedn. (bd. govs.), Speech Assn. Minn. (bd. govs., editor newsletter), Tau Kappa Epsilon. Home: 3012 E 2d St Duluth MN 55812

SCHULTZ, RONALD WARREN, laundry and dry cleaning co. exec.; b. Mpls., Dec. 24, 1923; s. Frederick G. and Mattie V. (Conrad) S.; student U. Minn., 1942-43; m. Joyce LaVon Impecoven, Aug. 18, 1945; children—Craig Frederick, Tami Lyn. Asst. mgr. Model Laundry, Rochester, Minn., 1946-52, mgr., 1952-60; v.p., gen. mgr. Lawler's Inc. div. Kahler Corp., Rochester, 1960—, dir. laundry and cleaning ops. parent orgn., 1964-72, v.p. textile care ops. parent orgn., 1972—; dir. Anderson's Men's Wear, Inc. Mem. Total Community Devel. Water and Sewer Com.; mem. Citizens Adv. Com. for Flood Control; bd. dirs. Downtown Council. Served with USAAF, 1943-46; PTO. Mem. Minn. Inst. Laundering and Cleaning (pres. 1969), Internat. Fabricare Inst., Linen Supply Assn. Am., Rochester C. of C. Presbyn. Clubs: Exchange, Rochester Golf and Country. Home: 1500 Woodland Dr SW Rochester MN 55901 Office: 217 1st Ave SW Rochester MN 55901

SCHULTZ, ROY ARLON, veterinarian; b. Council Bluffs, Iowa, Feb. 23, 1933; s. Donald Irwin and Dorothea Anne (Ehlers) S.; B.S. in Agr., Iowa State Coll., 1957; D.V.M., Iowa State U., 1960; m. Janice Marilyn Thorson, Aug. 24, 1958; children—Gary Lee, Kathryn Ann, Kent Eugene. Gen. practice veterinary medicine, Avoca, Iowa, 1960—; dir., pres. Pig Knoll, Inc.; dir. Found. for Wild Sheep. Dir. Pottawattamie County Fair Bd., 1968-72; pres. Pottawattamie County Conservation Bd., 1969-74. Served with U.S. Army, 1953-55. Recipient AK-SAR-BEN award, 1956. Mem. AMVA, Iowa, Shelby County veterinary med. assns., Iowa Acad. Veterinary Practice, Am. Assn. Swine Practitioners, Iowa State Veterinary Med. Alumni Assn. (pres.). Presbyterian. Clubs: Am. Legion, Forty and Eight, Nishwa Conservation, Eight-Ball Flying, Farm House Fraternity, Masons, Scottish Rite, Shriner. Editor Iowa State U. Veterinarian, 1959-60; co-author: Grand Slam of North American Wild Sheep, 1974. Home: 1005 Frost Ave Avoca IA 51521 Office: Box 578 Avoca IA 51521

SCHULZE, ERWIN EMIL, mfg. co. exec., lawyer; b. Davenport, Iowa, May 4, 1925; s. Erwin and Hazel (Sorensen) S.; B.A., DePauw U., 1947; LL.B., Yale U., 1950; m. Jean E. Steele, June 21, 1952; children—Suzanne Schulze Walker, William Steele, Donna Wilson, Stephen Johnson. Admitted to Ill. bar, 1950; partner Rooks, Pitts, Fullagar & Poust and predecessors, 1950-67, counsel, 1967—; exec. v.p. Standard Alliance Industries, Inc., 1965-66, pres., 1967—, also dir.; gen. counsel Standard Forgings Corp., Chgo., 1963-65, exec. v.p., 1965-67; treas., dir. Transue & Williams Steel Forging Corp., Alliance, O., 1965-66; dir. Danly Machine Corp., Ill. State Bank Chgo., AAR Corp., Midwest Stock Exchange. Mem. Joint Com. to Codify Ill. Family Law, 1958—; mem. Mayor's Adv. Council on Juvenile Delinquency, 1958-62. Served as lt. (j.g.) USNR, 1943-46; PTO. Mem. Am., Ill., Chgo. bar assns., Midwestern Air Pollution Prevention Assn. (dir., v.p. 1958-72), Air Pollution Control, Chgo. Tennis Patrons (treas. 1958-61, sec., dir. 1960-74), U.S. Lawn Tennis Assn. (chmn. men's ranking com. 1961-71), Legal Club Chgo., Phi Beta Kappa. Republican. Presbyn. (deacon, elder, trustee). Clubs: Knollwood; Chicago, Chicago Golf, Economic (Chgo.). Home: Rt 1 Box 64-A Libertyville IL 60048 Office: Oak Brook Exec Plaza 1211 W 22d St Oak Brook IL 60521

SCHULZE, JOHN HENRY, photographer, educator; b. Scottsbluff, Nebr., June 7, 1915; s. Henry George and Josephine Dorothy (Westerholt) S.; B.S., Kans. State Tchrs. Coll., Emporia, 1940; M.F.A., U. Iowa, 1948; m. Mary LaVonne Foster, Oct. 6, 1940; 1 dau., Tascha Jon. Faculty, Sch. of Art and Art History, U. Iowa, Iowa City, 1948—, prof., 1962—, also mem. Council Grad. Edn., Sch. Art.; artist in residence Washburn U., 1972, Northwest Mo. State Coll., 1972, Western Ky. U., 1973, State Coll., Geneseo, N.Y., 1973, Kansas City Art Inst., 1974, Cleve. Inst. Art, 1974, Cooper Sch. of Art, 1974; exhibited in numerous one man shows throughout U.S. and Can., 1962—; exhibited in numerous group shows throughout the world, 1961—; represented in numerous permanent and pvt. collections. Project worker photog. image and consciousness Gen. Learning Corp., Clinton, Ia., 1968; research prof., Mexico, 1968-69; teaching expt., Oaxaca, Mexico, summer 1974. Recipient citation for film The Elusive Shadow, Foothill Coll. Film Festival, 1963. Mem. Soc. Photog. Edn. (dir., membership chmn.), Mid-Am. Art Assn., Nat. Coll. Art Assn. Am. Home: 5 Forest Glen Iowa City IA 52240

SCHULZINGER, MORRIS SIMCHO, physician, religious leader; b. Serei, Lithuania, Dec. 19, 1900; s. Hyman and Bas-Sheva Sereisky; came to U.S., 1921, naturalized, 1925; B.A., Cin. U., 1925, M.A., 1927, M.B., 1928, M.D., 1929; m. Rachel Gurwitz, 1926; children—Penina Frankel, Judy Lucas, Chana Slavita. Intern, Cin. Gen. Hosp., 1928-29, resident, 1929-30; research fellow in exptl. medicine U. Cin., 1929-30; practice medicine specializing in occupational and gen. medicine, Cin., 1930—; sr. mem. staff Jewish Hosp. Cin., 1945—; guest lectr. on accident causation and prevention at numerous univs. in U.S., 1954-56, Israel, 1951-74, WHO, 1958. Founder Cin. Jewish Bible Soc., 1976, pres., 1976—; founder Am. Friends of the World Bible Centre Jerusalem, 1977, pres., 1977—; co-founder Cin. Ivriah Soc., 1921, pres., 1921-51; co-founder Cin. Jewish Vocat. Service, 1936, chmn., 1936-46; participant in Israel's Occupational Health and Safety programs, 1951—; co-founder Cin. League for Labor Palestine, 1935, pres., 1935-40; pres. Cin. Community Hebrew Schs., 1931-51; co-chmn. Cin. United Jewish Appeal, 1937. Diplomate Am. Bd. Family Physicians. Fellow Am. Acad. Family Physicians, Am. Pub. Health Assn.; mem. Ohio State Med. Assn., AMA, Am. Occupational Med. Assn. Author: The Accident Syndrome, 1956; contbr. articles on study of accidents and their prevention to sci. publs.; publisher: The Kuzari (Rabbi Yehuda Helevi-Y. Even Shmuel), 1972; Researches in Ecclesiastes and Proverbs (Meir Eiliueini), 1977. Address: 340 Reading Rd Cincinnati OH 45202

SCHUMACHER, ARNOLD CHARLES, economist; b. Hartford City, Ind., June 25, 1916; s. William and Olive (Burk) S.; B.S., Ind. U., 1939, M.A., 1940; student Northwestern U., 1940-42; m. Mary Caulk, Oct. 22, 1960. Economist, U.S. Dept. Commerce, Washington, 1942-44; economist Scudder, Stevens & Clark, Chgo., 1945-49; exec. dir. Economic Trend Lines Studies, Chgo., 1949-57; v.p., economist Chgo. Title & Trust Co., Chgo., 1957—; v.p., economst Halsey, Stuart &Co., Inc., 1971-74; sr. v.p. Lincoln Nat. Investment Mgmt. Corp., 1971—; tchr. Northwestern U., 1941, Loyola U., 1960-61; lectr. U. Chgo., 1963. Chmn., Chgo. Mayor's Com. Technol. Change, 1964. Bd. dirs. Mathers Fund, Inc. Chartered financial analyst. Mem. Chgo. Assn. Commerce and Industry (v.p. 1962-63, dir. 1962-66), Am. Econ. Assn., Am. Assn. Bus. Economists, Am. Statistical Assn., Chgo. Council Fgn. Relations, Investment Analyst Soc. Chgo. Club: University (Chgo.). Home: 140 E Franklin Pl Lake Forest IL 60045 Office: 111 W Washington St Chicago IL 60602

SCHUMACHER, BROCKMAN, educator; b. St. Louis, Aug. 26, 1924; adopted s. Dorothea Louise Brockman; B.A., U. Iowa, 1948; M.Ed., Washington U., St. Louis, 1952, Ph.D., 1969; m. Doris Goodman, July 20, 1948; children—Brockman, Andrew Jason, Douglass William. Dir. rehab. services St. Louis State Hosp., 1957-66; dir. comprehensive manpower programs Human Devel. Corp., St. Louis, 1966-68; coordinator, prof. Rehab. Counselor Tng. Program Rehab. Inst. So. Ill. U. at Carbondale, 1968—; dir. research, demonstration Halfway House Psychiat. Patients, St. Louis, 1959-62; asst. prof. social scis. Webster Coll., Webster Groves, Mo., 1966-67.

Mem. Ill. Mental Health Planning Bd., 1970-73, Ill. Bd. Mental Health Commrs., 1974—; pres. Nat. Council Rehab. Edn., 1971—. Served with USAAF, 1943-46. Recipient citation St. Louis Mental Health Assn., 1963; Services award Human Devel. Corp., 1968. Mem. Am. Rehab. Counselor Assn. (chmn. accreditation rehab. counselor tng. program 1972—), Nat. Rehab. Assn. (dir. 1971—), Nat. Assn. Non-White Rehab. Workers, Am. Psychol. Assn. Author: (with H. Dunlap) Intensive Services for the Disadvantaged, 1972; (with H. Allen) Five Vest Pocket Books on Severe Handicaps, The Physical Disabilities: A Resource Package for Counselors, Practitioners and Trainers, 1976; (with E. Bender) Medical Aspects of Disabilities, 1976. Editor: Problems Unique to the Rehabilitation of Psychiatric Patients, 1963. Home: 609 Skyline Dr Carbondale IL 62901

SCHUMACHER, GEBHARD FRIEDERICH BERNHARD, physician; b. Osnabrueck, West Germany, June 13, 1924; s. Kaspar and Magarete (Pommer) S.; M.D., U. Goettingen and Tuebingen, 1951; Sc.D. equivalent in obstetrics and gynecology, U. Tuebingen, 1962; m. Anne Rose Zanker, Oct. 24, 1958; children—Michael A., Marc M. Came to U.S., 1962. Intern, U. Tuebingen Med. Sch., 1951-52; tng. biochemistry Max Planck Inst. for Biochemistry, Tuebingen, 1952-53; tng. biochemistry and immunology Max Planck Inst. for Virus Research, 1953-54; resident obstetrics and gynecology U. Tuebingen, 1954-59, tng. internal medicine, 1959, asst. scientist in obstetrics and gynecology and biochem. research, 1959-62, dozent in obstetrics and gynecology, 1964-65; research asso. immunology Inst. Tb Research U. Ill. Coll. Medicine, 1962-63; research asso., asst. prof., dept. obstetrics and gynecology U. Chgo., 1963-64; asso. prof. dept. obstetrics and gynecology, asst. prof. dept. biochemistry Albany Med. Coll. of Union U., 1965-67; research physician, div. labs. and research N.Y. State Dept. Health, Albany, 1965-67; asso. prof. obstetrics and gynecology U. Chgo.-Chgo. Lying-In Hosp., 1967-71, chief sect. reproductive biology, 1971—, prof., 1973—. Cons. WHO, Nat. Inst. Health, other nat. and internat. orgns. Fellow Am. Coll. Obstetricians and Gynecologists; mem. Soc. Gynecologic Investigation, Am. Fertility Soc., Soc. for Study of Reprodn., Am. Acad. Reproductive Medicine, Am. Soc. Cytology, Am. Assn. Pathologists, N.Y. Acad. Sci., Deutsche Gesellschaft fur Gynakologie and Geburtshilfe, Gesellschaft fur Biologische Chemie, Gesellschaft fur Immunologie, Deutsche Gesellschaft fur Bluttransfusion, Gesellschaft Deutscher Naturforscher and Arzte. Contbr. articles to profl. jours. Home: 557 Hamilton Wood Homewood IL 60430 Office: 5841 S Maryland Ave Chicago IL 60637

SCHUMACHER, JOSEPH STUART, foundry cons.; b. Hillsboro, Ohio, June 7, 1912; s. Ernest W. and Helen H. (Hussey) S.; student Denison U., 1930-32; B.S., Ohio State U., 1935; m. Dorothy Jene Lamb, July 24, 1936; 1 son, Joseph Stuart. Metallurgist, Cin. Milacron, Cin., 1935-44; tech. dir., v.p. The Hill & Griffith Co., Cin., 1944-69; pres. J. Schumacher & Co., Cin., 1969-72, 77—; tech. dir. Internat. Minerals & Chem. Corp., Libertyville, Ill., 1972-77; dir. H.W. Dietert Co., Detroit, v.p. div. Exec. Cons. Assn., 1977—. cons. to industry; speaker to industry, 1944—. Registered profl. engr., Ohio. Fellow Inst. Brit. Foundrymen; mem. Am. Foundrymen's Soc. (chpt. chmn. 1949, award of Sci. Merit 1967, Gold medal 1974), Sigma Chi. Club: Masons. Patentee in field. Contbr. articles to profl. jours.; cons. editor The Foundry Mag., 1968—. Home: 937 Sandstone Dr Libertyville IL 60048 Office: IMC Plaza Libertyville IL 60048

SCHUMACHER, JOSEPH STUART, JR., film dir., cinematographer; b. Cin., May 6, 1942; s. Joseph Stuart and Dorothy Jean (Lamb) S.; B.A., DePauw U., 1964; B.F.A., Art Center Coll. of Design, 1968; m. Carole Elaine Gillham, May 8, 1965. Owner, operator photo studio, Los Angeles, 1966-68; photographer Patterson & Hall, San Francisco, 1968; film dir., photographer J. Walter Thompson, Co., Chgo., 1968-71; dir., cameraman Asch & Asso., Chgo., 1971-76, Sarra, Inc., Chgo., 1976-77, Jenkins-Covington, Chgo., 1977—. Recipient Silver medal, Atlanta Film Festival, 1970, Gold medal, 1971, Bronze medal, 1973; Bronze medal, U.S. TV Comml. Festival, 1972. Mem. Dirs. Guild of Am., Internat. Alliance of Theatrical Stage Employees. Democrat. Office: 909 W Diversey Pkwy Chicago IL 60614

SCHUMACHER, O. PETER, physician; b. Passaic, N.J., Oct. 13, 1927; s. Albert H. and Edith W. (Grossman) S.; A.B., Dartmouth, 1949; M.D., Johns Hopkins U., 1952; Ph.D., U. Minn., 1957; m. Margaret Flint, Sept. 8, 1951; children—Cynthia, Elizabeth, Donna. Intern, Mary Hitchcock Meml. Hosp., Hanover, N.H., 1953; fellow, asst. staff Mayo Clinic, Rochester, Minn., 1953-57; cons. in endocrinology Cleve. Clinic, 1957—, head sect. pediatric and adolescent endocrinology, 1961—; chief of medicine Camp Ho-Mita-Koda, camp for diabetic children. Mem. Men's Council St. Paul's Episcopal Ch. Served with USCG, 1945-46. Fellow A.C.P.; mem. Am. Diabetes Assn. (dir.), Am. Thyroid Assn., Am. Fertility Soc., Ohio Soc. Internal Medicine, Diabetes Assn. Greater Cleve. (past pres.), Distinguished Service citation 1970), Acad. Medicine of Cleve. Republican. Episcopalian. Editor Abstracts for Internal Medicine, 1960-70, Cleve. Clinic Quar., 1967—. Contbr. articles in field to profl. jours. Home: 2181 Middlefield Rd Cleveland OH 44106 Office: 9500 Euclid Ave Cleveland OH 44106

SCHUMACHER, RONALD RAY, real estate and chem. distbg. co. exec.; b. Bowler, Wis., Apr. 17, 1941; s. Raymond E. and Elsabeth A. (Zeinert) S.; student U. Wis., Stevens Point, 1959-62; m. Bonnie Jean Strassburg, Apr. 27, 1963; children—Lynette, Leanne, Jon, Jullie. Employed in direct sales, 1962-68; factory rep. Slant/Fin Corp., 1968-71; founder, pres., dir. Schumacher Devel. Corp., Milw., 1971—, Schumacher Constrn., Inc., Milw., 1971—; owner, Schumacher & Assos., Milw., 1971—. Mem. Wray (Colo.) Leadership Bd. Dirs., 1975-77; mem. ch. council Lutheran Ch.; chmn. Berea Stewardship Com., 1972—; pres. Berea Ch. Fellowship Orgn., 1974—. Mem. Sales and Marketing Execs. Republican. Home: 4926 N 106th St Milwaukee WI 53225 Office: 4928 N 106th St Milwaukee WI 53225

SCHUMAKER, JOHN ABRAHAM, educator; b. Marshall, Ill., July 24, 1925; s. John William and Martha Catherine (Kaufman) S.; B.S., U. Ill., 1946, M.A., 1947; postgrad. George Peabody Coll., 1950, Northwestern U., 1951, 52, 54; Ph.D., N.Y. U., 1959. Faculty, MacMurray Coll., Jacksonville, Ill., 1947-53, Grinnell (Iowa) Coll., 1953-55, Montclair State Coll., Upper Montclair, N.J., 1955-61; prof., chmn. dept. math. Rockford (Ill.) Coll., 1961—. Vis. prof. U. Vt., Burlington, summers 1962-69, 71, 73. Del., alt. del. Ams. for Democratic Action Bd., 1972-74. Mem. Met. Math. Club Chgo. (pres. 1968-69), Ill. Council Tchrs. Math. (pres. 1972-73), Math. Assn. Am. (sect. chmn. 1971-72, gov. 1974-77), Ind. Voters Ill., Phi Beta Kappa, Phi Kappa Phi, Kappa Delta Pi, Pi Mu Epsilon, Kappa Mu Epsilon, Phi Delta Kappa. Author: (with George H. Weinberg) Statistics: An Intuitive Approach, 1962, 2d edit., 1969, 3d edit., 1973. Home: 911 Woodridge Dr Rockford IL 61108

SCHUMAN, JACK, lawyer; b. N.Y.C., Nov. 10, 1926; s. Ira and Julia (Fisher) S.; B.Ch.E., Coll. City N.Y., 1949; J.D., N.Y. Law Sch., 1952; m. Doris Ann Graver, June 4, 1951; children—David J., Ira K., Robert L. Admitted to N.Y. State bar, 1953, D.C. bar, 1963, U.S. Supreme Ct. bar, 1964, N.J. bar, 1970, Ind. bar, 1976, numerous others U.S. and fgn. bars; patent atty. Bethlehem Steel Corp. (Pa.), 1954-68; div. patent counsel Johns-Manville Products Corp., Manville, N.J., 1968; individual practice, Somerville, N.J., 1969; patent atty. Western Electric Co., Princeton, N.J., 1969-75; chief patent and trademark counsel Cabot Corp., Kokomo, Ind., 1975—. Past mem. Somerset County (N.J.) Condemnation Commn. Served with AUS, 1944-46. Mem. Am., Ind., D.C. bar assns., Am. Patent Law Assn., Licensing Execs. Soc., Assn. Corp. Patent Counsel, U.S. Trademark Assn. Republican. Jewish. Home: 3762 Carmel Dr Carmel IN 46032 Office: 1020 West Park Ave Kokomo IN 46801

SCHUPP, PAUL EUGENE, educator; b. Cleve., Mar. 12, 1937; s. Paul Eugene and Venna Marie (Shinn) S.; B.A., Western U., 1959; M.A., U. Mich., 1961, Ph.D., 1966; m. Elva Ruth Stewart, Aug. 25, 1966. Asst. prof. U. Wis., 1966—67; asst. prof. mathematics U. Ill., Urbana, 1967—71, asso, prof., 1971—75, prof., 1975—; vis. mem. Courant Inst. Math. Scis., N.Y.U.; 1969—70; asso. mem. Center Advanced Study U. Ill., 1973—74. John Simon Guggenheim Meml. fellow, 1977—78. Mem. Am., London math. socs., AAUP. Author: (with R. C. Lyndon) Combinatorial Group Theory, 1977. Contbr. articles to math. jours. Home: 905 Perkins Rd Urbana IL 61801 Office: Dept Mathematics U Ill Urbana IL 61801

SCHUR, LENORA SINGER, speech therapist; b. Chgo., Mar. 30, 1930; d. Maurice and Shirley (Golden) Singer; B.S., Northwestern U., 1950; M.A. in Spl. Edn., Northeastern Ill. U., 1977; m. Robert Charles Schur, Dec. 17, 1949; children—Larry, Paul, John. Speech therapist Highwood Sch., Highland Park, Ill., 1950-52; speech and lang. therapist Chgo. Bd. Edn., 1960—. Bd. dirs. Temple Beth Israel. Delta Kappa Gamma Internat. grantee, 1977; Assn. Learning Disabilities grantee, 1965; certificate of clin. competence Am. Speech and Hearing Assn. Mem. Am. Speech and Hearing Assn., Chgo. Assn. Speech Therapists, Northwestern U. Alumni Assn., N.E. Council Interfaith Ministry. Club: Diversey Yacht. Home: 2655 W Balmoral Ave Chicago IL 60625

SCHUR, MORTON, bus. exec.; b. Chgo., July 9, 1924; s. Rubin and Sylvia (Forman) S.; B.S., DePaul U., 1949; m. Regina Miller, Jan. 26, 1947; children—Donna Gail (Mrs. Gerald Goldman), Linda. Owner Morton Schur & Co., accountants, Chgo., 1949-68; sr. partner firm Schur, Yorsark & Rabyne, Northfield, Ill., 1968—; pres. CompuData, Inc., 1968—. Pres. Road Runners, Inc., HBB Bowling Assn., LCS Meml. Found. Served with AUS, 1943-45. Mem. Ind. Accountants Assn., Nat. Accountants Soc., Jewish War Vets. Mem. B'nai B'rith (v.p., trustee). Author: Jogging. Home: 1034 Lougaker Rd Northbrook IL 60062 Office: 540 Frontage Rd Northfield IL 60093

SCHURE, RALPH MORTON, chemist; b. Chgo., Jan. 4, 1938; s. Aaron and Fannie Sawyer (Smith) S.; B.S., Roosevelt U., 1958; Ph.D. (NASA fellow), Ill. Inst. Tech., 1967; m. Ann Garver Loeffel, June 19, 1971; children—David J., Kimberly A. Cons. chemist Colburn Labs., Inc., Chgo., 1958-63; research chemist Swift & Co., Oakbrook, Ill., 1967—. Mem. Am. Chem. Soc., Ill. Acad. Sci., Sigma Xi. Mason. Contbr. articles to profl. jours. Home: 521 70th St Darien IL 60559 Office: 1919 Swift Dr Oakbrook IL 60559

SCHURICHT, ADOLPH EDWARD, assn. exec.; b. St. Louis, Apr. 17, 1912; s. Otto Edward and Charlotte Elizabeth (Trautman) S.; B.C.S., Mo. Inst. Accountancy and Law, 1940; m. Irma Caroline Lehr, Oct. 2, 1938; children—John O., Charlotte L., Robert N. Controller Banner Iron Works, St. Louis, 1943-50; chief accountant Tex. Instruments and subsidiaries, Dallas, 1951-58; partner Whitton & Co., C.P.A.'s, 1945-60; asst. controller Chance Vaught and subsidiaries, Los Angeles, 1958-65; internal auditor Aid Assn. for Lutherans, Appleton, Wis., 1965—. Instr. St. Louis U., Mo. Inst., 1945-50, U. Wis., 1966-69; chmn. Grey Iron Founders Regional Cost Com., 1947-50. Active Boy Scouts Am., United Fund. Bd. dirs. Lutheran Hospice Home, St. Louis.; bd. dirs., treas. Appleton Golden Age Club Inc.; pres. pro-tem Jr. Achievement of Appleton; treas. Outagamie unit Am. Cancer Soc.; pres. Appleton Taxpayers Assn. C.P.A., Mo., Cal., Wis. Mem. Inst. Internal Auditors (pres. St. Louis chpt. 1947, Dallas chpt. 1959), Am. Inst. C.P.A.'s, Soc. for Advancement Mgmt., Inst. Indsl. Engrs., Nat. Assn. Accountants, Soc. Certified Data Processors, Nat. Assn. Ch. Bus. Adminstrs. Lutheran (pres. Dallas council 1952). Kiwanian. Office: 222 W College Ave Appleton WI 54911

SCHURZ, FRANKLIN DUNN, JR., editor, publisher; b. South Bend, Ind., May 22, 1931; s. Franklin Dunn and Martha (Montgomery) S.; A.B., Harvard, 1952, M.B.A., 1956; m. Robin Rowan Tullis, Nov. 22, 1975. Exec. asst. South Bend Tribune, 1956-60, dir., 1961—, sec., 1970-75, asso. pub., 1971-72, editor, pub., 1972—, exec. v.p., 1975-76; pres. South Bend Tribune Corp., 1976—; v.p., treas. Herald-Mail Co., Hagerstown, Md., 1960-70, pub. Hagerstown Morning Herald and Daily Mail, 1962-70, editor, 1966-70; pres. Bloomington (Ind.) Herald-Telephone and Bedford (Ind.) Times-Mail, 1966-67; pres. WDBJ TV, Inc., Roanoke, Va., 1969-77. Mem. Md. Commn. on Phys. Fitness, 1963-70; gen. campaign chmn. United Way of St. Joseph County, 1973; trustee Housing Allowance Program, 1974—; vice chmn. Ind. Arts Commn., 1976—; trustee Am. Newspaper Pubs. Assn. Found., 1969—, treas., 1972-76; trustee Stanley Clark Sch., South Bend; mem. adv. council arts and letters U. Notre Dame, 1972—; adv. bd. Ind. U. at South Bend, 1972—; bd. regents St. Mary's Coll., Notre Dame, Ind., 1977—. Served to 1st lt. AUS, 1952-54. Recipient Presdl. award of merit Nat. Newspaper Assn., 1965. Mem. South Bend-Mishawaka Area C. of C. (v.p.), Hoosier State Press Assn. (dir. 1975—), Inst. Newspaper Controllers and Finance Officers (pres. 1971-72), Sigma Delta Chi. Presbyn. Clubs: Nat. Press (Washington); South Bend Country. Address: 225 W Colfax Ave South Bend IN 46626

SCHUSTER, CLARA SHAW, nurse, educator; b. San Francisco, Sept. 24, 1938; d. Robert H. and Lorine M. (Burnsen) Shaw; student Eastern Nazarene Coll., 1957-59; B.S. in Nursing, Cornell U. N.Y. Hosp. Sch. Nursing, 1962; M.Ed., Boston U., 1965; postgrad. Ohio State U.; m. Richard L. Schuster, Nov. 18, 1960; 1 dau., Elizabeth Lorine. Staff nurse Vis. Nurse Assn., Quincy, Mass., 1962-63; instr. Sch. Nursing, staff nurse pediatric intensive care unit Mass. Gen. Hosp., 1963-68; dir. staff devel. Martin Meml. Hosp., Mt. Vernon, Ohio, 1968-70; instr. Sch. Nursing, Riverside Methodist Hosp., Columbus, Ohio, 1971-73; instr. Sch. Nursing, Ohio State U., Columbus, 1973-76; cons. Knox County Head Start. First aid instr., vol. nurse, cons. disaster nursing, instr. Columbus div. A.R.C., 1968—, recipient recognition for service during Hurricane Agnes, 1973, Clara Barton award, 1976. Named Instr. of Year students Ohio State U., 1974, 75, 76. Mem. Am. Nurses Assn., Nat., Ohio (mem. steering com.) leagues nursing, Council for Exceptional Children, Sigma Theta Tau. Mem. Ch. of Nazarene. Producer ednl. films Ohio State U.-TV, 1973. Contbr. articles to profl. jours. Home: 600 E High St Mt Vernon OH 43050

SCHUSTER, EUGENE IVAN, art gallery exec.; b. St. Louis, Dec. 8, 1936; s. David Theodore and Anne (Kalisher) S.; B.A., Wayne State U., 1959, M.A., 1962; postgrad. U. Mich., 1959-62, (Fulbright scholar) Warburg Inst., U. London, 1962-65, Courtauld Inst., U. London and London Sch. Econs., 1962-65; m. Barbara Zelmon, June 22, 1958 (div.); children—Joseph, Sara, Adam. Lectr. art history Wayne State U., Detroit, 1959-62, Eastern Mich. U., Ypsilanti, 1960, Rackham extension U. Mich., 1961, Nat. Gallery, London, 1962-65; owner London Art Gallery, Detroit, 1965—. Pres., Nanny's Soup Kettle, Inc., Dearborn, Mich. Recipient Distinguished Alumni award Wayne State U., 1968. Mem. Founders Soc., Detroit Inst. Arts, Detroit Art Dealers Assn., Appraisers Assn. Am. Home: 2971 Moon Lake Dr West Bloomfield MI 48033 Office: London Art Gallery 321 Fisher Bldg Detroit MI 48202

SCHUSTER, RICHARD LEE, librarian; b. Tina, Mo., Mar. 24, 1933; s. Benjamin S. and Hazel Clair (Grieve) S.; A.B., Eastern Nazarene Coll., 1959, B.S., 1960; M.S. in L.S., Simmons Coll., 1965; m. Clara Shaw, Nov. 18, 1960; 1 dau., Elizabeth Lorine. Asst. librarian Eastern Nazarene Coll., Wollaston, Mass., 1963-68; head librarian Mount Vernon (Ohio) Nazarene Coll., 1968—. Served with AUS, 1953-55. Certified media specialist. Mem. Ohio Library Assn., Christian Library Assn. Home: 600 E High St Mount Vernon OH 43050

SCHUSTERMAN, LEONARD ALAN, data processing services co. exec.; b. Cleve., June 23, 1948; s. Sam William and Dorothy (Davidson) S.; student Ohio U., 1966-69; m. Toni Elaine Dellinger, July 3, 1969; children—David Samson, Lee Jacob. Sr. programmer Richman Bros. Co., Cleve., 1969-74; sr. program analyst, Nat. Systems Co., Cleve., 1974-75; project dir. Harvest Pub. Co., Cleve., 1975-76; v.p., systems coordinator Compu-logics, Mentor, Ohio, 1976—. Pres. Sprague East River N. Neighborhood Assn., 1976—. Mem. Assn. Systems Mgmt. Jewish. Home: 25152 Sprague Rd Olmsted Falls OH 44138 Office: PO Box 304 Mentor OH 44060

SCHUT, LAWRENCE JAMES, physician; b. Maple Lake, Minn., Sept. 13, 1936; s. Henry John and Hazel Jane (Dalman) S.; A.B. cum laude, Hope Coll., Holland, Mich., 1958; B.S., U. Minn., 1962, M.D., 1962; m. Loretta Fay Klemz, Dec. 31, 1954; children—Sherry, Maribeth, Ronald, David, Lawrence James. Intern, St. Lukes Hosp., Duluth, Minn., 1962-63; resident neurology U. Minn., 1963-66, clin. instr. neurology, 1968-73, clin. asst. prof. neurology, 1974-75, clin. asso. prof. neurology, 1975—; spl. fellow in neurochemistry, 1966-67; practice medicine, specializing in neurology, Mpls., 1967—; neurol. coordinator North Meml. Hosp., Mpls., 1971—; med. dir. Nat. Ataxia Found. Mem. A.M.A., Minn. Med. Assn., Hennepin County Med. Soc., Am. Acad. Neurology. Presbyterian (elder). Home: 434 Yosemite Ave N Minneapolis MN 55422 Office: 4225 Golden Valley Rd Minneapolis MN 55422

SCHUTT, PAUL LOUIS, photog. rental and supply co. exec.; b. Evanston, Ill., Aug. 5, 1937; s. Paul J. and Margaret (Dorr) S.; B.A., Northwestern U., 1958; postgrad. U. Chgo., 1958-62. Founder, pres. Helix Ltd., Chgo., 1963—; v.p. Speedotron Corp., Chgo., 1970—; pres. Color Service Inc., Chgo., 1968—, Photoart Visual Service Corp., Milw., 1971—; lectr. on underwater photography and diving. Active vol. Chgo. Shedd Aquarium. Named All-Am. Swimmer, Nat. Coll. Athletic Assn., 1956, 57. Mem. Am. Soc. Photogrammetry, Phi Kappa Psi, Pi Mu Epsilon. Home: 1310 N Ritchie Ct Chicago IL 60610 Office: 679 N Orleans St Chicago IL 60610

SCHUURMANS, THEODORE, JR., civil engr.; b. Ann Arbor, Mich., June 23, 1933; s. Theodore and Wilhelmina (Van Dreumel) S.; B.S. in Civil Engring., Mich. Tech. U., 1959; m. Frances M. Willard, Oct. 9, 1954 (div. Oct. 1969); children—Theodore M., Lawrence E., Robert J., Sandra A., Thomas S., John D.; m. 2d, Carol A. Herlik, Aug. 3, 1973; 1 stepdau., Kelly J. Resident engr. State Hwy. Commn., Green Bay, Wis., 1959-62; design engr. Robert E. Lee & Assos., engrs., Green Bay, 1962-65; engr. Joski Constrn., Green Bay, 1965-66; chief sanitation design engr. City of Green Bay, 1966-73; dir. engring. Green Bay Met. Sewerage Dist., 1973—. Sect. chmn. United Fund, 1974; pres. West High Sch. Athletic Booster Club, Green Bay, 1975. Served with USN, 1952-60. Registered profl. engr., Wis., Mich. Mem. Wis. Soc. Profl. Engrs. (pres. chpt. 1974, state dir. 1974-75, Engr. of Year in Govt. 1973, Engr. of Year 1975), ASCE (pres. br. 1972, state dir. 1973), Am. Pub. Works Assn., Am. Legion. Home: PO Box 723 Green Bay WI 54305 Office: PO Box 1015 Green Bay WI 54305

SCHWAB, DENNIS ERNEST, real estate broker; b. Eau Claire, Wis., Mar. 4, 1943; s. Walter William and Hazel Johanna (Weinke) S.; B.S. in Accounting, U. Wis.-Eau Claire, 1966; m. Gail Jean Treu, Nov. 25, 1971. Accounting instr. Fox Valley Tech. Inst., Appleton, Wis., 1966-72; owner Schwab Realty, Oshkosh, Wis., 1972—; pres. Dencur Corp., Oshkosh, 1967—; v.p. Oshkosh Bd. Realtors, 1975—. Pres. Oshkosh Bd. Realtors, 1976, Oshkosh Multiple Listing Service, 1977; state dir. Wis. Realtors Assn., 1977. Mem. Oshkosh Area C. of C. Kiwanian, K.C., Elk. Home: 1935 White Swan Drive Oshkosh WI 54901 Office: Schwab Realty 435 Alogma Blvd Oshkosh WI 54901

SCHWAB, PAUL JOSIAH, psychiatrist; b. Waxahachie, Tex., Jan. 14, 1932; s. Paul Josiah and Anna (Baeuerle) S.; B.A. with honors, North Central Coll., 1953; M.D. with honors, Baylor U., 1957; candidate Chgo. Psychoanalytic Inst., 1970-72; m. Martha Anne Beed, June 8, 1953; children—Paul Josiah, John Conrad, Mark Whitney. Intern Phila. Gen. Hosp., 1957-58; clin. asso. metabolism service Gen. Medicine br. Nat. Cancer Inst., NIH, Bethesda, Md., 1958-60; resident dept. medicine U. Chgo., 1960-62, dept. psychiatry, 1962-65, chief resident, instr. dept. psychiatry, 1964-65, lectr., 1968-74, asso. prof., 1974—, dir. psychiat. residency tng., 1976—; practice medicine, specializing in psychiatry, Chgo., 1965—; chief inpatient psychiat. service U. Chgo., 1975—; attending staff psychosomatic and psychiatric inst. Michael Reese Hosp., Chgo., 1966-71; clin. instr. dept. psychiatry U. Ill. at Chgo., 1965-66. Served to sr. asst. surgeon, USPHS, 1958-60. Diplomate Am. Bd. Psychiatry and Neurology. Fellow Am. Psychiat. Assn.; mem. Ill. Psychiat. Soc., A.M.A., DuPage County Med. Soc., Am. Psychosomatic Soc., Am. Assn. Dirs. Psychiatric Residency Tng., Alpha Omega Alpha, Phi Chi. Contbr. articles to profl. jours. Home: 725 E Highland Ave Naperville IL 60540 Office: Dept Psychiatry U Chgo 950 E 59th St Chicago IL 60637

SCHWABA, JOSEPH ROBERT, state judge; b. Chgo., Oct. 14, 1916; s. Peter H. and Joanne Germaine (Kuchnowski) S.; B.S., Northwestern U., 1938, J.D., 1941; m. Mary Christine Griffin, Sept. 12, 1942; children—Thomas, Joseph, Mary (Mrs. Timothy Bennett), Michael, Sara, Margaret, Jeanette, Patricia. Admitted to Ill. bar, 1942; since practiced in Chgo.; trial atty. Chgo. Transit Authority, 1946-71; asso. judge Circuit Ct. Cook County, Ill., 1972—; atty. Village of Summit, Ill., 1950-54; atty. dir. ins. Bur. Liquidations Ill., 1950-56. Instr. in law Police Tng. Program Wright Jr. Coll., Chgo., 1954-57. Served to lt. (s.g.), USNR, 1942-46. Mem. Fed., Am., Ill., Chgo. bar assns., Trial Lawyers Assn. Ill. Serra Club, Phi Delta Phi. K.C. Club: Lake Shore (Chgo.). Home: 2732 Woodland Dr Northbrook IL 60062 Office: Civic Center Chicago IL 60602

SCHWABAUER, ROBERT JACOB, mathematician; b. Lincoln, Nebr., Apr. 4, 1934; s. Jacob and Lydia (Klippert) S.; B.S., U. Nebr., 1958, M.S., 1960, Ph.D. (NSF grantee), 1966; m. Linda Charlene Stovall, Aug. 9, 1970; 1 son, Karl Jacob. Instr. math. U. S.D., Vermillion, 1960-62, U. Nebr., Lincoln, 1965-66; asst. prof. math. U. Okla., Norman, 1966-68, Loyola U., New Orleans, 1968-70, Va. Commonwealth U., Richmond, 1970-75; simulations analyst U.S.

Army, Ft. Leavenworth, Kans., 1975—. Mem. AAAS, Am. Math. Soc., Math. Assn. Am., Sigma Xi. Contbr. articles to math. and biol. jours. Home: PO Box 325 Leavenworth KS 66048

SCHWAIG, ROBERT HENRY, owner engring. co.; b. Richmond Heights, Mo., July 1, 1929; s. John A. and Loraine May (Pollard) S.; B.S., Mo. Sch. Mines and Metallurgy, 1951; m. Geneva L. Howard, Aug. 11, 1951; children—Kathleen, Michael, Thomas, Marianne, Jane, John, Barbara. Project engr. Merck & Co., Danville, Pa., 1951-53, with Olin Corp., St. Louis, 1953-57; owner Schwaig Engring. & Equipment Co., St. Louis, 1968—. Mem. Nat. Chem. Engring. Product Research Panel, 1970-71, 76-77. Mem. citizens com. St. Louis area Council Govts., 1974—; mem. St. Louis Circuit Ct. Grand Jury, 1964, 68. Registered profl. engr., Mo. Mem. Nat. Assn. Corrosion Engrs., St. Louis C. of C., Am. Inst. Chem. Engrs., Mfrs. Agts. Nat. Assn., Inst. Food Technologists, U.S. Coast Guard Aux., Alpha Chi Sigma. Roman Catholic. Inventor in field. Home: 6546 Itaska St St Louis MO 63109 Office: 3700 Hampton Ave St Louis MO 63109

SCHWAN, LEROY BERNARD, artist; b. Somerset, Wis., Dec. 8, 1932; s. Joseph L. and Dorothy (Papenfuss) S.; student Wis. State U., River Falls, 1951-53, Southeastern Signal Sch., Ga., 1954; B.S., U. Minn., 1958, M.Ed., 1960, postgrad., 1961-64, No. Mich. U., 1965, Tex. Tech. U., 1970; m. Patricia Ann Hageman, June 23, 1956; children—David A., Mark J., William R., Catherine L., Maria E. Head art dept. Unity Pub. Schs., Milltown, Wis., 1958-61; instr. art Fridley Pub. Schs., Mpls., 1961-64; asst. prof. art No. Mich. U., Marquette, 1964-66; asst. prof. art Mankato (Minn.) State Coll., 1966-71, asso. prof., 1971-74, tchr. off-campus grad. classes Northeast Mo. State U.; dir. Art Workshop Educultural Center, 1968; dir. art edn. Quincy (Ill.) Pub. Schs., 1974; tchr. art to mentally retarded children, Faribault, Minn., Owatonna, Minn., Mankato, Lake Owasso Children's Home, St. Paul; dir. art workshops, Mankato, 1970, St. Paul, 1972, 73, 74, 75; dir. workshops tchrs. mentally retarded Mankato, 1971, Faribault, 1972, Omaha, 1972-73, Quincy 1974; one-man shows: Estherville Jr. Coll., 1968, Mankato State Coll., 1968, 71, 73 Farmington, Wis., 1970, 71, Good Thunder, Minn., 1972, Quincy, 1975, 77, Mankato, Minn., 1975; exhibited in group shows: Pentagon, Washington, 1955, U. Minn., 1958, No. Mich. U., 1965, St. Cloud State Coll., 1967, Moorhead State Coll., 1967, Bemidji (Minn.) State Coll., 1967, MacNider Mus., Mason City, Iowa, 1969, 72, 73, 74, Gallery 500, Mankato, Minn., 1970, Rochester, Minn., 1972, Minn. Mus., St. Paul, 1973, Hannibal, Mo., 1976, Quincy, Ill., 1976; producer ednl. TV series, 1964-65. Webelos leader Twin Valley council Boy Scouts Am., 1968-69. Served with Signal Corps, AUS, 1954-56. Recipient certificate of accomplishment Sec. Army, 1955. Mem. Nat. Art Edn. Assn., Ill. Art Edn. Assn., Faculty Assn. Mankato State Coll., Cath. Order Foresters, Internat. Platform Assn., Phi Delta Kappa. Author: Art Curriculum Guide Unity Pub. Schs., 1961; Portrait of Jean, 1974; co-author: Bryant-Schwan Design Test, 1971, Bryant-Schwan Art Guide, 1973; contbr. articles to profl. jours. Home: 1444 Maine St Quincy IL 62301

SCHWANKE, MEL H., florist; b. Leigh, Nebr., Mar. 14, 1926; s. Herman J. and Anna L. (Menke) S.; grad. high sch.; m. Jo Ellen Green, May 12, 1948; children—Jo (Mrs. Curt S. Heinz), Lucinda (Mrs. Terry Gilfry), J Melvin. Apprentice, Greens Greenhouses, Fremont, Nebr., 1946-49; pres. Greens Greenhouses and Treasure House, Inc., 1975—. Mem. Bd. Edn., Fremont, Neb., 1969-72. Bd. dirs. Tri-State Nemokan Floral Conv., 1971-75. Served with USMCR, 1943-45. Decorated Purple Heart. Mem. Nebr. Florists Soc. (exec. sec-treas. 1956-77), Nemokan Florists Assn. (exec v.p. 1971—), Soc. Am. Florists (pres. 1977-79, chmn. retail div. 1973-75, dir. 1969-72), Toastmasters Club (pres. 1956-57, gov. 1959-60), Fremont C. of C. Lutheran (chmn. bd. trustees 1966-68, pres. cong. 1977-78). Kiwanian. (pres. Fremont 1965). Home: 1024 E 14th St Fremont NE 68025 Office: Bell St at 14th St Fremont NE 68025

SCHWARK, HOWARD EDWARD, civil engr.; b. Bonfield, Ill., Aug. 31, 1917; s. Edward F. and Florence M. (Schultz) S.; student St. Viators Coll., Bourbonnias, Ill., 1935-37; B.S., U. Ill., 1942; m. Arlene M. Highbarger, Sept. 28, 1940. Asst. to county supt. of hwys. Ford County, Ill., 1941-43; engr. E. I. DuPont de Nemours Co., 1942; asst. county supt. hwys. Kankakee County, Ill., 1946-52, county supt. hwys., 1952—; dir. 1st Bank of Meadowview, Kankakee Devel. Corp. Adviser county rds. FHWA. Co-chmn. Republican Finance Com., 1962-66. Pres. Kankakee Park Dist., 1959-70. Mem. tech. adv. com. to Ill. Transp. Study Commn., 1975—. Trustee, pres. Azariah Buck Old People's Home; mem. exec. bd. Rainbow council Boy Scouts Am.; bd. dirs. Soil and Water Conservation Service, 1967-74. Served with AUS, 1943-46. Recipient Distinguished Alumnus award Civil Engring. Alumni Assn. U. Ill., 1975. Mem. Nat. Assn. County Engrs., Ill. Soc. Profl. Engrs., Ill. Assn. County Supt. of Hwys. (pres. 1970), Ill. Engring. Council (pres. 1971-72), Am. Road Builders Assn. (bd. dir. county div. 1969-75, pres. county div. 1975), Kankakee Area C. of C. (bd. dirs. 1960-74), Am. Soc. Profl. Engrs., Western Soc. Engrs., Twp. Ofcls. Ill., Freelance Photographers Assn., Ill. Wildlife Fedn. Lutheran. Rotarian. Club: South Wilmington Sportsman. Home: 1051 W Vanmeter Kankakee IL 60901 Office: 750 S East Ave Kankakee IL 60901

SCHWARTZ, CRAIG JOHN, veterinarian; b. Clinton, Iowa, July 3, 1946; s. John Henry and Dorothy Jean (Meints) S.; B.S., Iowa State U., 1969, D.V.M., 1973; m. Dixie L. Keller, Apr. 10, 1965; children—Shawn D., Michelle R. Veterinarian, Animal Clinic, Hastings, Nebr., 1973-74, Shinrone Farms, Odebolt, Iowa, 1974-75, Beatrice Animal Hosp. (Nebr.), 1975—; pres. Agmacon Group Inc., 1975—; instr. SE Community Coll., Beatrice. Mem. AVMA, Nebr., Iowa veterinary med. assns. Lutheran. Clubs: Kiwanis, Eagles. Home: Route 3 Beatrice NE 68310 Office: 2108 N 6th St Beatrice NE 68310

SCHWARTZ, FRANKLIN DAVID, physician; b. Balt., May 16, 1933; s. George Henry and Anna (Snyder) S.; B.S. cum laude, U. Md., 1953, M.D. summa cum laude, 1957; m. Harriet Joan Mohline, May 25, 1971; children—Michael Howard, Ellen Sue. Intern U. Hosp., Balt., 1957-58, asst. resident in medicine, 1958-60; USPHS research fellow, U. Md., 1960-61; practice medicine specializing in nephrology, Balt., 1957-60, Washington, 1960-64, Chgo., 1964—; asso. dir. sect. nephrology U. Ill. Hosp., Chgo., 1970-71, acting chief, 1971-72, asso. chief, 1972—, attending physician U. Ill. Hosp., 1972—; attending physician St. Joseph Hosp., Chgo., 1971—, dir. sect. nephrology, 1971—; adj. physician Rush-Presbyn.-St. Luke's Med. Center, 1964-65, asst. attending physician, 1965-67, asso. attending physician, 1967-70, dir. hemodialysis unit, 1968-70, cons. physician in medicine, 1970-71; asso. chief sect. nephrology Columbus-Cuneo Carbini Med. Center, 1971—; asst. prof. medicine Abraham Lincoln Sch. of Medicine, Chgo., 1964-69, asso. prof., 1969-75, clin. prof., 1975-76, prof. clin. medicine, 1976—; mem. cons. staff Ill. Masonic Med. Center, Augustana Hosp., Martha Washington Hosp., Ravenswood Hosp., Northwest Community Hosp., Ill. Central Hosp.; mem. Renal Disease Advisory Com., State of Ill. Dept. Pub. Health, 1972—; mem. Sci. Advisory Bd., Kidney Found. of Ill., 1972—; co-dir. of hepatitis project Walter Reed Army Inst. of Research, 1962; cons. physician VA West Side Hosp., Chgo., 1972—. Diplomate Am. Bd. Internal Medicine. Mem. Ill. State, Chgo. med. socs., Am., Ill., Chgo. socs. of internal medicine, A.C.P., Internat. Soc. Nephrology, Am. Soc. Nephrology, Am. Fedn. Clin. Research, AMA, Sigma Xi. Contbr. numerous articles in field to med. jours. and chpts. in field to med. books., Home: 1110 N Lake Shore Dr Chicago IL 60611 Office: 740 N Rush St Chicago IL 60611

SCHWARTZ, GERHART ROBERT, univ. adminstr.: b. Berne, Ind., Apr. 11, 1917; s. Peter D. and Elizabeth (Nussbaum) S.; B.S., Ball State U., 1942; M.S., Ind. U., 1948, Ed.D., 1952; m. Josephine Ruth Zehr, Aug. 15, 1944; children—Robert Arthur, Susan Jo Schwartz Lavin. Asst. to registrar Ball State U., Muncie, Ind., 1939-42; tchr. speech, English Auburn (Ind.) High Sch., 1942-43; staff counselor Ind. U., Bloomington, 1946-49, asst. dir. student activities, 1949-50, acting dir. student activities, 1950-51; asst. prof. to prof. edn. Mankato (Minn.) State U., 1951-62, dean of students, 1951-62; prof. edn., dean of students Western Ill. U., Macomb, 1963—, v.p. student affairs, 1969—; mem. advisory com. on guidance, counseling and testing Minn. State Dept. Edn., 1959-62. Bd. dirs. YMCA, Mankato, Minn., 1956-63, Mankato Adult-Youth Council, 1955-60, United Fund, Mankato, 1960-63, Macomb, Ill., 1965-67. Served to lt. comdr. USN, 1943-46. Recipient Outstanding Service award bd. dirs. Mankato YMCA, 1963: Outstanding Contribution award Mankato State U., 1963. Mem. Nat. Assn. Student Personnel Adminstrs., Nat. Vocat. Guidance Assn., Student Personnel Assn. Tchr. Edn., Am. Assn. Higher Edn., Am., Ill. (treas. 1966-67, pres. 1967-68) coll. personnel assns., Am. (life), Ill. guidance and personnel assns., Blue Key Honor Fraternity, Phi Delta Kappa, Pi Gamma Mu, Pi Omega Pi, Sigma Tau Delta Alpha Phi Gamma, Theta Chi, Alpha Phi Omega, Phi Eta Sigma. Presbyterian (Elder). Clubs: Macomb Investors, Rotary Internat., Masons. Contbr. articles in field to profl. publs. Home: W Adams Rd RFD 1 Macomb IL 61455 Office: 900 W Adams St Macomb IL 61455

SCHWARTZ, JACOB JACK, govt. ofcl.; b. Bklyn., May 8, 1918; s. Abraham and Gussie (Steigman) S.; B.B.A., St. John's U., Bklyn., 1939; m. Jenette Shorr, Mar. 18, 1945; children—Robin, Stanley, Alan. Sr. cost accountant Kay Mfg. Corp., Bklyn., 1939-42; mgr., comptroller Shores Cafe, Dearborn, Mich., 1946-55; owner, operator Jack's Food Box, Oak Park, Mich., 1955-58; accountant, line supr. Detroit Ordinance Dist. (now Detroit Procurement Dist.), 1958-60, from contract price analyst to supervisory price analyst Fin. Services Div., 1960-72, acting chief, 1972-73, pricing and fin. officer, dir. contract adminstrn. directorage, 1973-75, dir. contract adminstrn., chief fin. services div., 1975-76; asst. dist. dir. SBA of Mich., Detroit, 1976—; v.p. Louis Stone Found., 1965-76. Served with USAAF, 1942-46. Recipient numerous awards, including awards Louis Stone Found., 1950-76, Govt. Contracts Assn., 1960-76, City of Detroit, 1961-62, State of Mich., 1962, U.S. Def. Supply Agy., 1964-75, Detroit Pub. Schs., 1966, Fed. Bar Assn., 1972. Mem. Govt. Contracts Assn. (v.p. 1969-71, treas., 1972-77), Engring. Soc. Detroit, Am. Def. Preparedness Assn., Allied Vets. Council (Gold award 1970). Clubs: Am. Legion, Jewish War Vets. (mem. nat. exec. com. 1976-77, Man of Year 1966). Home: 27405 Fairfax St Southfield MI 48076 Office: SBA Rm 515 477 Michigan Ave Detroit MI 48226

SCHWARTZ, ROGER ARLEN, cons. elec. engr.; b. St. Louis, Dec. 3, 1945; s. Mitchell and Esther (Kreisman) S. B.S., Washington U., St. Louis, 1971, postgrad., 1971-72. Project engr. Barnes Henry Meisenheimer & Gende, cons. engrs., St. Louis, 1974-76; cons. engr. Voss Internat. Co., St. Louis, 1976—77; project engr. Lemco Engring. Co., St. Louis, 1977—; lectr. in field. Mem. IEEE, Eta Kappa Nu. Jewish. Home: 272 Oak Moss Walk Manchester MO 63011

SCHWARTZ, RUDOLPH O., lawyer; b. Manitowoc, Wis., May 23, 1914; s. Abraham and Martha (Stein) S.; student U. Ariz., 1934-35; B.A., U. Wis., 1936, J.D., 1938; m. Carolyn Pinkus, June 11, 1946; children—Richard E., Victor R. Admitted to Wis. bar, 1938, since practiced in Manitowoc. Pres., Meml. Hosp., Manitowoc, 1952-53, Family Service, Manitowoc, 1964-66. Served to 1st lt. U.S. Army, 1942-46. Fellow Am. Bar Found.; mem. Am. (dir. probate and trust div. 1975—, chmn. real property probate and trust sect., chmn. editorial bd. 1975, editor compendium probate book 1975, jour. adv. bd.), Manitowoc County (pres. 1963-64) bar assns., State Bar Wis. (chmn. pres.'s council 1964), Am. Coll. Probate Counsel (regent Wis. 1972—), Am. Judicature Soc. Rotarian, Mason; mem. B'nai B'rith. Contbr. articles to profl. jours. Home: 939 Lincoln Blvd Manitowoc WI 54220 Office: 801 York St Manitowoc WI 54220

SCHWARTZ, SAMUEL ROBERT, microbiologist; b. Allen County, Ind., Apr. 6, 1934; s. Samuel S. and Irene Vera (Kreidt) S.; B.S. in Microbiology (Univ. Hon. scholar), Purdue U., 1956; B.S. in Geology, Ind. U., 1957; m. Sandra Jean Guenther, June 3, 1961. Supr. microbiology Parkview Meml. Hosp., Fort Wayne, Ind., 1958—; cons. in field. Mem. Am. Soc. Microbiology, Am. Soc. Clin. Microbiology, South Central Assn. Clin. Microbiology, Audubon Soc., Izaac Walton League, Acres Inc., Sigma Gamma Epsilon. Home: Box 187 13827 Schwartz Rd Grabill IN 46741 Office: Parkview Meml Hosp 2200 Randalia Dr Fort Wayne IN 46805

SCHWARTZ, THEODORE FRANK, lawyer; b. Clayton, Mo., Aug. 14, 1935; s. Ben and Mary (Roufa) S.; LL.B., Washington U., St. Louis, 1962, J.D., 1962; m. Barbara Jean Rader, Aug. 30, 1959; children—Michael David, Kenneth Rader. Admitted to Mo. bar, 1962, Calif. bar, 1974, also Supreme Ct. U.S., U.S. Cts. of Appeals (5th and 8th Circuits), U.S. Dist Cts., St. Louis, Houston, Indpls., D.C., Supreme Ct. Mo. bars; practiced in Clayton, 1962—; atty. Charles M. Shaw, 1959-63; partner Ackerman, Schiller & Schwartz, 1963-75; individual practice, 1975—. Bd. dirs. Mt. Sinai Cemetery Assn., Anti-Defamation League. Served with U.S. Army, 1957-58. Mem. Am., Mo., St. Louis bar assns., Am. Trial Lawyers Assn., Lawyers Assn., Nat. Assn. Criminal Def. Lawyers, Am. Judicature Soc. Home: 205 River Bend Dr Chesterfield MO 63017 Office: 7701 Forsyth Blvd Clayton MO 63105

SCHWARTZBERG, RALPH MORTON, lawyer: b. Negaunee, Mich., June 16, 1906; s. Harris and Sophia (Feldman) S.; J.D., U. Mich., 1928; m. Celia Kaplan, Aug. 17, 1930; children—Hugh Joel, Burton Guy. Admitted to Ill. bar, 1928, practiced in Chgo.; mem. firm Schwartzberg, Barnett, and Schwartzberg and predecessor, 1939-75, sr. partner, 1939-75; pres., dir. Buffalo Mdse. Distbn. Center, Inc.; chmn. bd. Arizill Corp. Pres., Tau Epsilon Rho Scholarship Found., 1955-75; bd. chmn. High Sch. Jewish Studies for Chgo., 1948-63, now chmn.; pres. Chgo. Allied Jewish Sch. Bd., 1946-47; v.p. Bd. Jewish Edn.; mem. ad hoc com. for Jewish Edn., 1969-72; mem. Jewish Welfare Fund Chgo. trustee Coll. Jewish Studies. Mem. Am., Ill., Chgo. bar assns., Am. Hotel and Motel Assn. (mem. internat. travel com., chmn. 1971-72), Tau Epsilon Rho (supreme chancellor 1941-46, hon. 1953—). Jewish (trustee congregation). Clubs: U. Mich.; Twin Orchard Country; Covenant of Ill.; Executives. Home: 5600 N Francisco Ave Chicago IL 60659 Died July 17, 1975.

SCHWARZ, JOSEPHINE LINDEMAN, dancer, ballet co. exec.; b. Dayton, Ohio, Apr. 8, 1908; d. Joseph and Hannah (Lindeman) Schwarz; student U. Wis., 1942, Columbia U., 1954, Ind. U., 1955; D.F.A. (hon.), U. Dayton, 1974. Appeared in Adolph Bolm's Ballet, Intime Chgo., 1925-27; co-founder Schwarz Sch. of Dance, Dayton, 1927, partner, 1977—; appeared with Wiedman Theatre Dance Co., N.Y.C., 1933-37; founder Exptl Group for Young Dancers (now Dayton Ballet Co.), 1937, dir., 1977—; adj. prof. dance Antioch Coll., U. Dayton, Wright State U., 1940's, 50's, 60's; lectr. Hunter Coll., YM-YWHA, N.Y.C.; guest choreographer Pa. Ballet Co., Wabash (Ind.) Dance Theatre, opera and theatre cos., regional ballet cos. Tri-state area; chmn. dance panel Ohio Arts Council 1967-70; founder, dir. Nat. Craft Choreography Confs., 1968-70; mem. dance adv. panels Nat. Endowment for Arts and Ohio Arts Council, 1975—. Mem. Nat. Assn. for Regional Ballet, N.E. Regional Ballet Assn. (pres. 1961, dir. 1974), Assn. Am. Dance Cos. (dir. 1967), Found. for Joffrey Ballet, Inc., Com. on Research for Dance, Am. Dance Guild, Dayton Art Inst. Contbr. articles to Dance mag. Home: 425 Dayton Towers Dr 2F Dayton OH 45410 Office: 140 N Main St Dayton OH 45402

SCHWARZ, ROBERT LESSING, advt. agy. exec.; b. Chgo., Feb. 23, 1918; s. Sol Robert and Marie (Goldstein) S.; student Northwestern Sch. Journalism, 1937-41, Ray Sch. Art, 1943, Ill. Inst. Tech., 1943-44, Ill. Inst. Tech. Sch. Design, 1955-56; m. Eleanor R. Lowenson, Oct. 5, 1941; children—David S., Steven D. Advt. mgr. Greggory, Inc., Chgo., 1937-43; asst. engr. Motorola, Inc., Chgo., 1943-49; copywriter Montgomery Ward, Chgo., 1944, supr. display publs., 1945-51; procedure editor Spiegels, Inc., Chgo., 1944; advt. mgr. Match Corp. Am., Chgo., 1951-58; owner Bertram, Blake & Russell Advt., Chgo., 1958—. Treas. Chgo. fedn. Union Am. Hebrew Congregations, 1974-75, mem. nat. membership com., 1974-75, nat. bd., 1976—, bd. exec. com., 1977-78; bd. dirs. Max Straus Center. Mem. Audit Bur. Circulation, Bus. and Profl. Advt. Assn. (editor Copy/Chgo. 1976-77). Jewish (pres. 1970-72, life trustee temple). Club: New Trier Men's Garden. Home: 4953 N Tripp Ave Chicago IL 60630 Office: 4920 Belmont Ave Chicago IL 60641

SCHWARZKOPF, LYALL ARTHUR, city govt. ofcl.; b. Waupaca, Wis., June 10, 1931; s. Arthur Charles and Dora (Venem) S.; B.A., U. Minn 1953; m. Inez Olson, Sept. 6, 1958; children—Erik Arthur, Kurt Ian, Dana Marit, Ilse Kristine. Mem. Minn. Ho. of Reps., 1963-72; city clk., Mpls., 1972—. State chmn., nat. committeeman Young Reps. Minn., 1960-63; del. Rep. Nat. Conv., 1968. Mem. Gov.'s Council on Aging, 1968-71; mem. health task force White House Conf. on Aging, 1971—; mem. health adv. com. Minn. Planning Commn., 1972-76; mem. elections adv. task force Fed. Elections Commn., 1976. Served with AUS, 1954-56. Mem. Internat. Inst. Municipal Clks. (dir. 1976—), Assn. Met. Municipalities (pres. 1977-78). Lutheran. Mason. Odd Fellow. Home: 4840 Bloomington Ave S Minneapolis MN 55417

SCHWEGLER, ROBERT CHARLES, dentist; b. Albany, Minn., Aug. 23, 1940; s. Gabriel Francis and Irene Susan (Dullingner) S.; B.A., U. Minn., 1962, B.Sc., D.D.S., 1966; m. Inez Lorene Nelson, June 18, 1966; children—Michelle Lorene, Erik Robert. Practice dentistry, Albany, 1966—. Mem. dental adv. bd. Stearns County (Minn.) Welfare Dept., 1972—. Dir., Civil Def., Albany, 1969—. Mem. adv. com. U. Minn. Dental Sch. Mem. Am., Minn. dental assns., West Central Dist., St. Cloud Dist. (treas. 1977) dental socs., Albany C. of C. (v.p. 1970), Am. Analgesia Soc., Acad. Gen. Dentistry, Minn. Acad. Practice Mgmt., Alpha Phi Omega, Xi Psi Phi. Clubs: Albany Golf (treas. 1977), Lions (pres. Albany chpt. 1970, dept. dist. gov. 1972), Elk. Address: Box 308 Albany MN 56307

SCHWIER, ROBERT WILLIAM, can co. exec.; b. Indpls., Nov. 5, 1928; s. Rolland William and Laura L. (Adney) S.; B.S., Rose Poly. Inst., 1949, M.B.A., Ind. U., 1951; postgrad. Bklyn. Poly. Inst., 1968; m. Marjorie J. Ray, Sept. 17, 1950; children—Dave William, Chris Edward, Laura Rae. Specification engr. Marathon Corp., Menasha, Wis., 1954-57; group leader Am. Can Co., Neenah, Wis., 1957-60, asst. mgr. product devel., 1960-64, mgr. graphic research, 1964-66, dir. spl. projects, corporate research and devel., Greenwich, Conn., 1966-69, dir. corp. product devel., 1969-73, lab. dir. packaging research and devel., Neenah, 1973—. Mem. research steering com. Graphic Arts Tech. Found., 1965-66. Served with USNR, 1952-54. Fellow Am. Inst. Chemists; mem. Tech. Assn. Graphic Arts. Office: American Can Co 333 N Commercial Neenah WI 54956

SCHWIETERMAN, CYRIL SYLVESTER, farm service co. exec.; b. St. Sebastin, O., July 9, 1925; s. Edward Gehard and Elenora Mary (Kramer) S.; grad. high sch.; m. Merdella Mary Borger, May 14, 1949; children—Joyce (Mrs. Kenneth Gerlach), Sharon, Michael, Barbara (Mrs. Larry Abels), Gerald, David, Connie, Jane, Sandra, Robert, Cynthia Ann, Mary Beth. Owner Cy Schwieterman Farm Drainage Co., 1946-62; pres. Cy Schwieterman, Inc., St. Henry, O., 1962—; pres. M.J.D., Inc., 1974—. Treas. St. Henry Lot Devel. Corp., 1972—, also dir. Served with USNR, 1944-46. Mem. Land Improvement Contractors Am., Ohio (pres. 1964, dir. 1961-64, 68-71), Ind. land improvement contractors assns., Am. Soc. Agrl. Engrs., Am. Soc. Testing Materials, Am. Legion. Roman Catholic. K.C. Address: Rural Route Box 312 St Henry OH 45883

SCHWIETERT, JOHN WESLEY, chiropractor; b. Sioux Falls, S.D., Apr. 7, 1923; s. Arthur Wesley and Volline Marie (Harms) S.; student Lincoln Chiropractic Coll., 1942, 46; D.Chiropractic, N.W. Coll. Chiropractic, 1949; m. Mary Theresa Davis, Jan. 1, 1949; children—David A., Cynthia J., James W. Pvt. chiropractic practice, Sioux Falls, 1949-52, Rapid City, S.D., 1952-60, 1960-73; partner Schwietert Chiropractic Clinic, Rapid City, 1973—. Chmn. ARC, Rapid City, 1966-67; mem. S.D. Pub. Health Adv. Com., 1961-68, v.p., 1966-68; S.D. committeeman K.T. Eye Found., 1970—; chmn., trustee S.D. Chiropractic Polit. Action com., 1973—; precinct committeeman Republican Party, Rapid City, 1960-61; bd. dirs. Western Health Systems. Served with USNR, 1943-46; ATO. Named Man of Year Chi Omega Phi, 1968; recipient Alumnus award N.W. Coll. Chiropractic, 1969; Key Man award Sioux Falls Jr. C. of C., 1951. Fellow Internat. Coll. Chiropractors; mem. Am. Chiropractic Assn. (state del. 1966-71, pres. house dels., 1970-71, pres. 1972-73), S.D. Chiropractors Assn. (pres. 1967-69, chmn. bd. dirs. 1969-71, Chiropractor of Year award 1967), Order DeMolay, Rapid City C. of C., Am. Council Roentgenology, Black Hills Chiropractic Soc. (pres.), Nat. Geog. Soc., Am. Forestry Assn., Nat. Audubon Soc., S.D. Wildlife Fedn., Chi Omega Phi. Clubs: Lions, K.T. (comdr. 1968-69), Masons, Shriners, Elks, Rapid City Flying (sec.-treas. 1954—), Toastmasters. Home: 216 E Saint Charles St Rapid City SD 57701 Office: 2210 Jackson Blvd Rapid City SD 57701

SCHWINGEL, WILLIAM HENRY, physician; b. Aurora, Ill., Apr. 10, 1918; s. William Henry and Rosabel K. (King) S.; student Dartmouth, 1935-37; A.B., Drake U., 1940; M.D., Loyola Sch. Medicine, 1943; m. Catherine Pearson, Dec. 19, 1943; children—Cynthia A., Katherine R. Intern, St. Luke's Hosp., Chgo., 1944; resident orthopaedics Ill. Research Hosp., Chgo., 1944-46; fellow orthopaedic surgery Northwestern U., 1948; resident orthopaedic surgery Wesley Meml. Hosp., Chgo., 1948-49; fellow orthopaedic surgery Northwestern U., 1949; practice medicine, specializing in orthopaedic surgery, Aurora, Ill., 1948—; sr. surgical staff Mercy center for Health Care Services, Aurora, bd. dirs. 1962-64, staff pres., 1964-65; cons. staff Mercyville, Aurora. Dir. Aurora Nat. Bank, 1977—. Mem. counsel staff Maramech Hill council Two Rivers dist. Boy Scouts Am., 1970-72. Bd. dirs. United Community Fund, 1969-72. Diplomate Am. Bd. Orthopaedic Surgeons. Fellow Am. Acad. Orthopaedic Surgeons, Am. Coll. Surgeons; mem. A.M.A.,

Clinical Orthopaedic Soc., Ill., Kane County med. socs. Methodist (bd. dirs. 1956—). Clubs: Aurora Country, Union League (Aurora); Union League (Chgo.). Home: 405 S Western Ave Aurora IL 60506 Office: 1240 N Highland Aurora IL 60506

SCHYMAN, SIDNEY, screw and bolt co. exec.; b. Chgo., Aug. 4, 1924; s. Joseph and Anna (Axelrod) S.; B.S., Ill. Inst. Tech., 1948; A.A., Wright Jr. Coll., 1943; m. Amy Lorraine Blatt, Sept. 5, 1948; children—Joseph, Deborah, Judith, Diane. Plant mgr. Universal Screw Co., Evanston, Ill., 1948-58; sales mgr. Anchor Bolt Co., Chgo., 1958-60; pres. Prairie State Screw & Bolt Co., Niles, Ill., 1960—. Pres., Maple Sch. P.T.A., Northbrook, Ill., 1967-68. Served with U.S. Army, 1943-45. Home: 742 Thackeray Dr Highland Park IL 60035 Office: 3685 Woodhead Dr Northbrook IL 60062

SCIAMMARELLA, CESAR AUGUSTO, civil engr.; b. Buenos Aires, Argentina, Aug. 22, 1926; s. Emilio Silvio and Maria Belen (Burrueco Mansilla) S.; came to U.S., 1957; diploma in Civil Engring., Buenos Aires U., 1950; Ph.D., Ill. Inst. Tech., 1960; m. Esther E. Norbis, Apr. 10, 1968; children—Alejandro C., Eduardo A., Federico M. Structural engr. Hormigon Elastico Inversor, Argentina, 1950-51, supr. design and stress analysis, 1951-53; spl. assignee Ing. Ducilo Co., 1953-54; tech. dir. Zofra, Inc., 1955-56; group leader reactor engring. div. AEC, Argentina, 1956-57; prof. Buenos Aires U., 1955-57; asso. research engr. Ill. Inst. Tech., Chgo., 1958-59, prof., 1972—; asso. prof., U. Fla., Gainesville, 1962-65, prof., 1965-67; prof. Poly. Inst. Bklyn., 1967-72, Argentine Army Engring. Sch., 1952-57; cons. U.S. Govt., UN, pvt. industry; dir. exptl. stress analysis lab. Ill. Inst. Tech. Mem. ASME (service award 1972), ASTM, Soc. Exptl. Stress Analysis, Gesellschaft Fur Angewadte Mathematik Und Mechanik, Sigma Xi (faculty research award, 1966). Roman Catholic. Contbr. articles in fields of applied and exptl. mechanics to profl. jours.; patentee in field. Home: 247 E Chestnut St Chicago IL 60611 Office: Ill Inst Tech MMAE Dept Chicago IL 60616

SCIOLI, FRANK PAUL, JR., educator; b. Phila., Jan. 4, 1944; s. Frank A. and Antoinette B. (Masino) S.; B.A., Temple U., 1966, M.A., 1967; Ph.D., Fla. State U., 1970; postgrad. No. Ill. U., 1973; m. Judith Francine Nisenholtz, July 3, 1967; children—Adam Drew, Anthony Douglas. Asst. prof. Drew U., 1970-71; asst. prof. polit. sci. U. Ill., Chgo., 1971-72, asso. prof., 1973—, acting head polit. sci. dept., 1973-74; cons. Village of Barrington (Ill.), 1974, City of Aurora (Ill.), 1974, NSF, 1974—. Vice chmn. Oak Park Ind. Democrats, 1972-73; vice chmn. United Dems. Oak Park, 1973-74; del. Ill. State Conv., 1974; election judge, Oak Park, 1974. NSF grantee, 1973-74, 74-75. Mem. Am., So., Midwest polit. sci. assns., Am. Soc. for Pub. Adminstrn., S.W. Social Sci. Assn., Policy Studies Orgn. Co-founder Exptl. Study of Politics Jour., 1970; editorial bd. Policy Studies Jour. Contbr. articles to profl. jours. Home: 1133 N Euclid St Oak Park IL 60302 Office: U Ill Chgo Polit Sci Dept Chicago IL 60680

SCISM, DANIEL REED, lawyer; b. Evansville, Ind., Aug. 27, 1936; s. Daniel W. and Ardath J. (Gibbs) S.; A.B. with distinction, DePauw U., 1958; J.D. with distinction (Edwards fellow), Ind. U., 1965; m. Paula Anne Sedgwick, June 21, 1958; children—Darby Claire, Joshua Reed. Reporter, Dayton (O.) Jour.-Herald, 1958-59; editor employee communications Mead Johnson & Co., Evansville, 1961; admitted to Ind. bar, 1965; since practiced in Indpls.; partner Roberts, Ryder, Rogers & Neighbours. Pres., Suemma Coleman Home, Indpls., 1973-74, bd. dirs., 1971-76; v.p. Marion County Mental Health Assn., 1970-71, bd. dirs., 1969-75; treas. Marion County chpt. Myasthenia Gravis Found., 1970, bd. dir., 1967-71. Served with U.S. Army, 1959-61, 61-62. Mem. Am., Ind., Indpls. bar assns., Ind. C. of C. (social legislation com. 1970—), Order of Coif, Phi Kappa Psi. Methodist. Clubs: Indpls. Athletic, Woodland Country. Home: 11070 Winding Brook Dr Indianapolis IN 46280 Office: Suite 2020 One Indiana Square Indianapolis IN 46204

SCOFIELD, GORDON LLOYD, mech. engr., univ. ofcl.; b. Huron, S.D., Sept. 29, 1925; s. Perry Lee and Zella Frederica (Reese) S.; B.S. in Mech. Engring., Purdue U., 1946; M.S. in Mech. Engring., U. Mo. at Rolla, 1949; Ph.D. (NSF fellow), U. Okla., 1968; m. Nancy Lou Cooney, Dec. 27, 1947; children—Cathy Lynn, Terrence Lee. Instr. in mech. engring. S.D. State Coll., Brookings, 1946-47; instr. Sch. of Mines and Metallurgy, U. Mo., Rolla, 1947-50, asst. prof., 1950-53, asso. prof., 1953-57, prof., 1957-69; prof., head mech. engring., engring. mechanics Mich. Tech. U., Houghton, 1969—; cons. to U.S. Naval Ordnance Test Sta., China Lake, Calif., 1956-71, Gen. Electric Co., summer, 1954, Douglas Aircraft Co., summer, 1962. Served with USN, 1943-46. Recipient Alumni Achievement award U. Mo., Rolla, 1975. Registered profl. engr., Mo. Mem. Soc. Automotive Engrs. (pres. 1977), ASME, Am. Soc. for Engring. Edn., Am. Inst. Aeros. and Astronautics, Sigma Xi, Phi Kappa Phi, Tau Beta Pi, Pi Tau Sigma. Clubs: Rotary. Contbr. articles on thermal radiation and engring. edn. to profl. jours. Home: 402 Vivian St Houghton MI 49931 Office: Dept of Mechanical Engring-Engring Mechanics Michigan Tech Univ Houghton MI 49931

SCOTT, ALICE HOLLY (MRS. ALPHONSO SCOTT), librarian; b. Jefferson, Ga., July 8, 1935; d. Frank David and Annie Dell (Colbert) Holly; A.B., Spelman Coll., Atlanta, 1957; M.S. in L.S., Atlanta U., 1958; postgrad. U. Chgo., 1973—; m. Alphonso Scott, Mar. 1, 1959; children—Christopher, Alison. Librarian I, Bklyn. Pub. Library, 1958-59, librarian I, Woodlawn br. library Chgo. Pub. Library, 1959-60, acting br. librarian Hall br. library, 1961-66, br. librarian Pullman br., 1967-68, Woodlawn br., 1968-74, dir. Woodson Regional Library, 1974-77, dir. community relations and spl. programs of service, 1977—. Mem. A.L.A., Ill. Library Assn., Chgo. Library Club. Office: 425 N Michigan Ave Chicago IL 60611

SCOTT, ANDREW, lawyer; b. St. Paul, Apr. 5, 1928; s. Ulric and Annamay (Gorry) S.; B.S., U. Minn., 1950, LL.B., 1952; m. Kathleen Kennedy, May 7, 1960; children—Andrea Kennedy, Lucia Kennedy. With Doherty, Rumble, and Butler, Mpls., 1952-77; prin. firm Andrew Scott, Ltd., 1978—; counsel to computer corps. including Cray Research, Inc., Dicomed Corp., Analysts Internat. Corp. Trustee Minn. Orchestral Assn., Mpls. Soc. Fine Arts, Twin City Area Ednl. TV Corp., St. Paul Acad., Summit Sch. Served with U.S. Army, 1946-47. Mem. Am. Bar Assn., Delta Kappa Epsilon, Phi Delta Phi. Roman Catholic. Clubs: Somerset; Minneapolis. Home: 1626 Edgcumbe Rd St Paul MN 55116 Office: 4125 IDS Tower Minneapolis MN 55402

SCOTT, ANNA PORTER WALL (MRS. JOHN T. SCOTT), educator, civic worker; b. Fulton, Ky.; d. Thomas M. and Jevvie R. (Patton) Porter; B.A. in Sociology, U. Ill., 1958, M.S. in Edn., 1960, M.S. in Social Work, 1965; m. John T. Scott, Sept. 5, 1959; 1 son, Harvey. Case worker Champaign County Dept. Pub. Aid, 1962-64; psychiat. social worker Danville (Ill.) Vets. Hosp., 1965-67; charter mem. faculty social sci. div. Parkland Community Coll., Champaign, Ill., 1967—. Cons. psychiat. social worker; spl. cons. to Black Students Assn., Urbana (Ill.) Sr. High Sch., 1968—. Charter mem. Mayor's Human Relations Commn., Urbana, 1968—; mem. Champaign-Urbana Symphony Guild. Pres. downstate contingent Ill. Democratic Women's Caucus; 21st congl. dist. Dem. state central Committeeman; vice chmn. Ill. Dem. Com.; mem. Dem. Nat. Com.; mem. Commn. on Future and Role of Presdl. Primaries; mem. exec. bd. Nat. Dem. State Chairpersons Assn. Served with WAC, 1944-47. Mem. Am. Sociol. Assn., AAUW, Nat. Council Negro Women, Order Eastern Star, NAACP, Amvets. Mem. Elks of World (daus., temple trustee). Home: 309 W Michigan St Urbana IL 61801 Office: 2400 W Bradley Champaign IL 61820

SCOTT, CARL CHAUNCEY, dentist; b. Scio, Ohio, Dec. 13, 1932; s. John James and Inez Margaret (Pfouts) S.; student Bethany Coll., 1950-51; B.A. in Chemistry, Kent State U., 1954; D.D.S., Ohio State U., 1962; m. Elizabeth Ann Wylie, Feb. 20, 1955; children—William, Rebecca, Jennifer. Pvt. practice dentistry, Columbus, 1962—. Instr. endodontics Ohio State U., 1962-65, 75—, lectr. practice adminstrn., 1974-76; cons. dentist Ohio Presbyn. Home, Columbus; team dentist Columbus Pacesetters; adviser Columbus Dental Hygienists Assn. Bd. dirs. Kent State U. Columbus Alumni. Served to capt. USAF, 1955-58. Mem. Ohio Dentists Polit.-Action Com., Jaguar Assn. Central Ohio, L.D. Pankey, Ohio State U. alumni assns., Chgo., Columbus dental socs., Fedn. Dentaire Internat., Am., Ohio (v.p.), Central Ohio acads. dental practice adminstrn., Carl O. Boucher Prosthodontic Conf., Fed. Prosthodontic Orgns., Am. Dental Assn., Delta Sigma Delta. Republican. Methodist. Clubs: Masons, Shriners, Lions. Home: 2780 Welsford Rd Columbus OH 43221 Office: 196 E State St Columbus OH 43215

SCOTT, CLAUDE MARSHALL, social planning orgn. adminstr.; b. Wetherford, Okla., Apr. 11, 1911; s. Claude Lester and Lucille Crutcher (Wall) S.; A.B., U. Kans., 1934; m. Ida Marie Carr, June 6, 1936; 1 dau., Janet (Mrs. Homer Duane Jennings). Social worker, Anthony, Kan., 1934-36; Harper County (Kan.) dir. welfare, Anthony, 1936-47; dir. welfare Sedgwick County, Kans., Wichita, 1947-50; exec. dir. United Way of Wichita and Sedgwick County, 1950-76. Served with U.S. Army, 1941-46; PTO. Mem. Nat. Assn. Social Workers, Assn. Certified Social Workers, Alpha Tau Omega. Methodist. Kiwanian. Home: 2331 N Yale St Wichita KS 67220

SCOTT, DAVID C., mfg. co. exec.; b. Akron, Ohio, 1915; grad. U. Ky., 1940, D.Sc. (hon.), 1971; m. Eudora A. Vance (dec. 1973); children—Sally Vincent, David C.; m. Mary M. Donohue, May 23, 1975. Owner engring. cons. firm Inst. Tech. Research, Louisville, 1940; mgr. various depts., plant Gen. Electric Co., 1945-63; v.p., group exec. several subs.'s Colt Industries Inc., Hartford, Conn., 1963-68, exec. v.p., dir. 1965-68; pres. Allis-Chalmers Corp., Milw., 1968-69, chmn. bd., pres., chief exec. officer, 1969—; dir. First Wis. Corp., First Wis. Nat. Bank Milw., Travelers Corp., Royal Crown Cola Co., Humana, Inc., Inroads Inc.; mem. Greater Milw. Com.; mem. Pres.'s Export Council; chmn. U.S. sect. Egypt-U.S. Bus. Council; dir., mem. exec. com. U.S. sect. Czechoslovak-U.S. Econ. Council; mem. U.S. sect. Iran-U.S. Bus. Council; mem. bd. dirs. U.S.-USSR Trade and Econ. Council; chmn. North Central Regional Export Council. Trustee, vice chmn. Conf. Bd.; mem. Can. Council; founding mem. Rockefeller U. Council. Home: 2100 W Dean Rd River Hills WI 53217 Office: 1205 S 70th St PO Box 512 Milwaukee WI 53201

SCOTT, ERIC ANSIL, editor, publisher; b. Sandusky, Ind., Apr. 12, 1899; s. William Henry and Florida (Fleetwood) S.; student pub. schs., Sandusky; m. Cleo Arvillia Faulkner, June 20, 1923. Masonry supt. Michael Kinder & Sons, engrs., contractors, Ft. Wayne, Ind., 1935-61; editor, pub. The Pioneer, 6th Regt. Engrs. bi-monthly mag., Ft. Wayne, 1958—. Founder Gen. Edmund L. Daley Meml. Hall and Mus., Ft. Wayne; pres. War Vets. Meml. Shrine Am. History. Served with U.S. Army, 1917-19; AEF in France. Recipient Verdun medal, 1953; Veterans Council Americanism award, 1966; Spl. Merit citation Nat. Navy Club Aux., 1974; Community Service award Lincoln Post 82, Am. Legion, 1974; Nat. Comdrs. award Disabled Am. Vets., 1977. Mem. V.F.W. (life, cited by dept. Ind. 1970, Allen County 1972), Am. Legion (hon. life), Smithsonian Instn., Nat. Hist. Soc., Soc. 3d Inf. Div. (nat. v.p. 1960-61, Ind. pres. 1958—, Audie Murphy award 1972), Vets. 6th U.S. Engrs. (nat. sec.-treas. 1958—, hon. col.), World War I. Vets. (judge advocate Ft. Wayne barracks 1963, comdr. Anthony Wayne barracks 30, 1965, 4th dist. legis. officer, 1965, comdr. 4th dist. Ind. 1967-68, nat. dep. chief of staff 1969—, historian Ind. dept. 1972-73), Allen County Vets. Council (vice-comdr. 1965, comdr. 1966-67, Patriotic award 1973), Naval Hist. Found. Republican. Address: Elrico Gardens 2122 O'Day Rd Fort Wayne IN 46818

SCOTT, ERNEST PECK, electronic co. exec., lay ch. worker; b. Cleve., May 28, 1902; s. Walter M. and Harriet D. (Peck) S.; A.B., Case Western Res. U., 1924; LL.D. (hon.), Wittenberg U., 1957; m. Meridith A. Lewis, Sept. 10, 1925; children—Ellen, Ernest, Marvin, Alcyone. Asst. chief of works control lab. Union Carbide & Carbon Co., Cleve., 1924-25; foreman Sterling Mfg. Co., Cleve., 1926-27, plant supt., 1928-29, purchasing agt., 1930-31; founder Scott Electronics, Inc., Cleve., 1931, pres., 1931-51, chmn. bd., 1952—; chief exec. officer Elimpex, Inc., Cleve., 1966—, chmn. bd., 1966—. Pres. council Messiah Luth. Ch. of Lyndhurst (Ohio), 1956-58, chmn. bldg. fund campaign, 1952-53; mem. exec. bd. Ohio Synod of Luth. Ch. Am., 1937-58, chmn. fin. com., 1942-58; v.p. Cleve. Council Churches, 1961-62, pres., 1963-64, treas., 1964-72; bd. dirs. Wittenburg U., Ohio Synod of Luth. Ch. rep., 1941-77; bd. dirs. Luth. Hosp., 1959-64. Recipient Luth. Layman of the Year award, 1957, Electronics Conf. award Cleve. Engring. Soc., 1974. Mem. IEEE, Acoustical Soc. Am., Am. Ordnance Soc., Am. Physics Soc. Lutheran. Clubs: Mid-Day, Masons (32 deg.), University, Luth. Bus. Men's (pres. 1955—). Home: 3294 Hyde Park Cleveland OH 44118 Office: 4158 Ruple Rd Cleveland OH 44121

SCOTT, FRANK MAXWELL, elec. engr.; b. McCook, Nebr., Dec. 27, 1916; s. Rex Ernest and Hazel Ruth (Barbarzette) S.; B.S. in Elec. Engring., U. Nebr., 1940; m. Edna May Lundy, June 7, 1941; children—Ronald, Linda, Suzanne. Design engr. Allis-Chalmers Co., Milw., 1940-42, engr., head motor and gen. spl. application group, 1946-50, regional specialist for heavy equipment, mgr. west central area for utility industry, Chgo., 1950-68; dept. and div. head electric utilities div. Harza Engring. Co., Chgo., 1968-73, asst. group dir., 1973-74, group dir., power and energy mgmt. group, 1974—, asso., 1973-76, sr. asso., 1976—, v.p., 1976—. Mem. Western Springs (Ill.) Plan Commn., 1956-58; pres. Western Springs Park Dist., 1958-63; nat. v.p. Camp Fire Girls, 1974-75, mem. nat. bd. dirs., 1974-76. Served to lt. col. C.E. and Gen. Staff Corps, U.S. Army, 1942-46. Decorated Bronze Star medal with oak leaf cluster, Air medal; recipient Meritorious Service medal Chgo. Heart Fund, 1958, 61, 63. Mem. Am. Nuclear Soc., ASME (v.p.), IEEE (past chmn. Chgo. sect.), Nat. Soc. Profl. Engrs., Western Soc. Engrs. (past pres.), Chgo. Engrs. Club. Congregationalist. Club: Union League (Chgo.). Contbr. articles in field to profl. jours. Home: 75 S 6th Ave La Grange IL 60525 Office: Harza Engineering Co 150 S Wacker Dr Chicago IL 60606

SCOTT, GLENN EDWARD, chamber of commerce exec.; b. Belleville, Kans., Dec. 6, 1919; s. William Merton and Ruby (Davis) S.; Mus.B., Coll. Emporia (Kans.), 1941; student N.Y. U., 1949, Ohio State U., 1950; m. Patsy Kay Rossman, Dec. 26, 1964; 1 son, Eric Rossman; children by previous marriage—Margaret Ann (Mrs. George D. Farmer), Glenn Edward, Jon Whitcomb, Lesley Carol. Tchr., Smith Center (Kans.) pub. schs., 1941; asst. mgr. Spencer Music Supply Co. (Iowa), 1945-46; tchr. Spencer pub. schs., 1946-49; asst. dir. Columbus Boy-choir Sch., Princeton, N.J., 1949-55; circulation mgr. Spencer Daily Reporter, 1955-57; exec. sec. Spencer C. of C., 1957-61; dist. mgr. U.S. C. of C., Sioux Falls, S.D., 1961-63; mgr. pub. affairs Mich. C. of C., 1963-66; exec. v.p. Mo. C. of C., 1966—; instr. Inst. Orgn. Mgmt., 1969—, mem. bd. regents, 1968—. Pres. bd. trustees Meml. Community Hosp.. Served with AUS and USAAF, 1942-45. Mem. Am. C. of C. Execs., C. of C. Execs. Mo. Republican. Methodist (trustee). Mason (Shriner), Kiwanian (pres. Spencer 1957, lt. gov. Nebr.-Iowa 1961). Home: Riviera Heights Holts Summit MO 65043 Office: 400 E High St Jefferson City MO 65101

SCOTT, HAZEL JOANNE, ednl. adminstr.; b. DuQuoin, Ill., Dec. 14, 1942; d. Albert A. and S. Lucille (Lanum) Scott; B.S., So. Ill. U., 1964, M.S., 1967, Ph.D., 1972; 1 son, Craig Alan. Tchr. elementary schs., Cahokia, Ill., 1964-67, elementary counselor, 1967-69; dormitory dir. So. Ill. U., Carbondale, 1969-72; staff psychologist Ill. State U., Normal, 1972-73, Bradley U., Peoria, Ill., 1973-75; ednl. adminstr., asst. prof. psychology U. Ill., Peoria, 1975—. Bd. dirs. Tri County Urban League, Ill. Central Health Systems Agy.; mem. prof. adv. bd. Ill. Valley Mental Health Assn., 1977, bd. dirs., 1974-77. Recipient Spl. Recognition awards Assn. Non-White Concerns in Personnel and Guidance, 1976, Am. Personnel and Guidance Assn., 1976. Mem. Ill., Am. personnel and guidance assns., Ill. Assn. Non White Concerns in Personnel and Guidance (pres.). Lutheran. Home: 3617 Rockwood Rd N Peoria IL 61604 Office: 123 Glendale Ave SW Peoria IL 61605

SCOTT, HOWARD WINFIELD, JR., temporary help service co. exec.; b. Greenwich, Conn., Feb. 24, 1935; s. Howard Winfield and Janet (Lewis) S.; B.S., Northwestern U., 1957; m. Joan Ann MacDonald, Aug. 12, 1961; children—Howard Winfield III, Thomas MacDonald, Ann Elizabeth. Mgmt. trainee R.H. Donnelly Corp., Chgo., 1958-59; sales rep. Masonite Corp., Chgo. also Madison, Wis., 1959-61; sales rep. Manpower Inc., Chgo., 1961-63, br. mgr., Kansas City, Mo., 1963-65, area mgr., Mo. and Kans., 1964-65, regional mgr. Salespower div., Phila., 1965-66; asst. advt. mgr. soups Campbell Soup Co., Camden, N.J., 1966-68; pres. PARTIME, Inc., Paoli, Pa., 1968-74; dir. mktg. Kelly Services Inc., Southfield, Mich., 1974-77, regional mgr., Detroit, 1977—. Served with AUS, 1957-58. Mem. Nat. Assn. Temporary Services (sec. 1970-71, pres. 1971-73), Sales Mktg. Execs. Detroit, Kappa Sigma. Republican. Episcopalian. Club: Econ. Detroit. Home: 7411 Old Mill Rd Birmingham MI 48010 also 1204N Sea Colony East Bethany Beach DE 19930 Office: Kelly Services Inc 16130 Northland Dr Southfield MI 48075

SCOTT, KENNETH TRESSEL, assn. adminstr.; b. New Cumberland, O., Mar. 12, 1913; s. Strawn Denney and Etta Dolores (Tressel) S.; B.S. in Edn., Kent State U., 1935; postgrad. U. Cin., 1946, 47; m. Dorothy May Walker, Aug. 8, 1943; children—Dee Dee, Kenneth Bruce. Instr. math. Joseph Welty Jr. High Sch., New Philadelphia, O., 1935-42; supr. tng. facilities VA, Cin., 1946-51; mgr. personnel Gen. Electric Co., Cin., 1951-58; owner, operator Scotty's Marina, Atwood Lake, O., 1958-62; instr. math. Indian Hills Jr. High Sch., 1963-65; nat. exec. dir. Family Motor Coach Assn., Cin., 1965—, also pub. Family Motor Coaching Mag. Served with USCGR, 1942-45. Named Ky. col., 1967, La. col., 1971. Mem. Am. Soc. Assn. Execs., Ohio Wage and Salary Assn. (chmn. bd. 1948-50), Internat. Fedn. Recreation Vehicle Users (dir.), Am. Legion (post comdr. 1951-52), Blue Key. Republican. Mason (Shriner). Author: School Memories, School Birthday Calendar, 1936. Home: 1380 Wolfangle Rd Cincinnati OH 45230 Office: 8291 Clough Pike Cincinnati OH 45244

SCOTT, MONTE MYRL, physician; b. Grand Island, Nebr., Aug. 23, 1932; s. Walter and Mildred C. (Warrick) S.; B.S. with distinction, U. Nebr., 1954, M.D., 1957; m. Marlys Anne Everts, June 20, 1954; children—Kim, Ann, Jayne. Intern, Fitzsimons Gen. Hosp., Denver, 1957-58; resident in internal medicine Letterman Gen. Hosp., San Francisco, 1958-61; mem. staff internal medicine, chief Internal Medicine Clinic, asst. chief Dept. Hosp. Clinics, Madigan Gen. Hosp., Tacoma, 1961-65; practice medicine specializing in internal medicine, endocrinology, rheumatology Platte Valley Med. Group, Kearney, Nebr., 1965-69, Wedgewood Internal Medicine Group, Lincoln, Nebr., 1970—; asso. prof. internal medicine U. Nebr. Served to maj. M.C., U.S. Army, 1956-65. Diplomate Am. Bd. Internal Medicine. Fellow A.C.P.; mem. Am., Nebr. (trustee) socs. internal medicine, Lancaster County Med. Soc., Am. Legion, Phi Beta Kappa, Sigma Xi, Alpha Omega Alpha. Republican. Lutheran. Clubs: Hillcrest Country, Elks. Contbr. articles in field to profl. jours. Home: 740 Cottonwood Dr Lincoln NE 68510 Office: 120 Wedgewood Dr Lincoln NE 68510

SCOTT, NORMAN LAURENCE, cons. engr.; b. Meadow Grove, Nebr., Oct. 17, 1931; s. Laurence Richardson and Ruth Louise (Braun) S.; B.S. in Civil Engring., U. Nebr., 1954; m. Joan Culbertson, Jan. 31, 1956; 1 son, Douglas Jay. Sales engr. R.W. Wright & Son, Ft. Lauderdale, Fla., 1956-57, mgr. Wright of Palm Beach, West Palm Beach, Fla., 1957-59; exec. sec. Prestressed Concrete Inst., Chgo., 1959-63; gen. mgr. Wiss Janney, Elstner & Assos., Northbrook, Ill., 1963-66; pres. Cons. Engrs. Group, Glenview, 1966—. Served with USAF, 1954-56. Registered profl. engr., Fla., Ill., Md. Mem. Am. Soc. C.E., Am. Concrete Inst., Prestressed Concrete Inst., Nat. Soc. Profl. Engrs., A.I.A., Structural Engrs. Assn. Ill. Mem. Community Ch. (deacon). Home: 701 Chatham St Glenview IL 60025 Office: 1701 Lake Ave Glenview IL 60025

SCOTT, THEODORE R., lawyer; b. Mt. Vernon, Ill., Dec. 7, 1924; s. Theodore R. and Beulah (Flannigan) S.; A.B., U. Ill., 1947, J.D., 1949; m. Virginia Scott, June 1, 1947; children—Anne, Sarah, Daniel, Barbara. Admitted to Ill. bar, 1950: law clk. to Judge Walter C. Lindley, U.S. Ct. Appeals, 1949-51; asso. Spaulding Glass, 1951-53, Loftus, Lucas & Hammand, 1953-58, Ooms, McDougall, Williams & Hersh, 1958-60; partner McDougall, Hersh, &Scott and predecessor, law firm, 1960— (all Chgo.). Served to 2d lt. USAAF, 1943-45; ETO. Decorated Air medal. Mem. Am., Ill., Chgo., 7th Circuit bar assns., Am. Coll. Trial Lawyers, Legal Club Chgo., Law Club Chgo., Patent Law Assn. Chgo. (past pres.), Phi Beta Kappa. Club: Union League (Chgo.); Exmoor Country (Highland Park, Ill.). Home: 1569 Woodvale Ave Deerfield IL 60015 Office: 135 S LaSalle St Chicago IL 60603

SCOTT, TIMOTHY TITUS, computer specialist; b. Hardy, Ky., Dec. 9, 1939; s. Buff and Moudie (Hatfield) S.; grad. in data processing, U.S.A. Mgmt. Engring. Training Sch., 1965; m. Mary Margaret Soltesz, Feb. 4, 1963; children—Laura Christine, Rebecca Lynn. Data processing intern U.S.A. Mobility Command, St. Louis, 1965-66; computer programmer Defense Supply Agency, Columbus, Ohio, 1966-69, staff computer specialist, 1969-72, supervisory computer systems analyst, 1972-76, supervisory computer specialist, 1976—; asst. chmn. data base mgmt. com. Defense Logistics Agency. Post advisor ADP Explorer Post, Columbus, 1970-76. Served with U.S. Army, 1958-61. Recipient awards Defense Supply Agency, 1970, 73, 74, 75, 76. Mem. Assn. of Computer Programmers/Analysts. Methodist. Clubs: Masons. Contbr. tech. articles in field. Office: PO Box 1605 Columbus OH 43216

SCOTT, WALTER EDWIN, ret. state ofcl.; b. Milw., Feb. 27, 1911; s. James Wylock and Ida (Fisher) S.; B.A., Kalamazoo Coll., 1933, M.A., 1955; M.S., U. Wis., 1965; m. Gertrude May Cox, Apr. 15, 1941. Warden, Wis. Dept. Natural Resources, Madison, 1934-36, game mgmt. supr., 1936-48, editor info. edn. div., 1948-50, asst. to dir., sec., 1950-75. Sec., Wis. Natural Resources Council State Agys., 1968-75; co-founder, past pres., sec. Wis. Natural Resources Found., 1957-77. Served with inf. CIC, AUS, 1943-46. Recipient citation Am. Motors Conservation award, 1967, citations U.S. Geol. Survey, also EPA, 1975, Outstanding Environmentalist award U. Wis., 1976. Fellow A.A.A.S.; mem. Wis. Soc. Ornithology (co-founder, past pres., custodian, spl. recognition award 1964), Citizens Natural Resources Assn. Wis. (citation 1964, co-founder), Historic Madison (co-founder, past pres.), Wildlife Soc., Soc. Am. Foresters, Soil Conservation Soc., Am. Soc. Pub. Adminstrn. (co-founder, past pres. Wis. Capital chpt.), Wildlife Trust Eng. (life), Wis. Writers Council (life), Wis. Acad. Scis., Arts and Letters (hon.; councilor 1954-76, librarian 1959-61, pres. 1964-65, citation 1966, Centennial award 1970), U. Wis.-Madison Friends of Library (pres.), Izaak Walton League Am. (citation Wis. div. 1966), Wilderness Soc., Dane County Conservation League (Distinguished Service award), Nature Conservancy, Assn. Midwest Fish and Game Commrs. (past sec.-treas.) Internat. Assn. Game Fish and Conservation Commrs. (past sec.-treas., citation 1973), Wis. Hist. Soc., Sierra Club (citation 1976). Author: Poems to Trudi, 1950; Water Policy Evolution in Wisconsin, 1965; Conservation's First Century in Wisconsin, 1967; Our Oldest Oaks-a Living Heritage, 1976. Editor: Silent Wings — A Memorial to the Passenger Pigeon, 1947. Editor The Passenger Pigeon, 1939-43, Wis. Acad. Rev., 1954-63; Wis. cons. Activities Progress Report, 1947-52; The Hickory Hill Herald, 1941-77. Home: 1721 Hickory Dr Madison WI 53705

SCOTT, WALTER O'DANIEL, educator, agronomist; b. Westmoreland, Kans., Dec. 18, 1914; s. William A. and Elizabeth (O'Daniel) S.; B.S., Kans. State U., 1939; M.S., U. Ill., 1949; Ph.D., Purdue U., 1959; m. Elizabeth Grace Brown, Aug. 24, 1940; 1 dau., Mary Elizabeth (Mrs. William L. Nack III). Asst. agrl. extension agt. Morris County, Kans., 1939-40, agrl. extension agt., 1940-44; asst. prof. agronomy Kans. State U., Manhattan, 1944-46; faculty dept. agronomy U. Ill., Urbana, 1946—, prof., 1960—. Partner, S.&A. Publs., A & L Publs., Champaign, Ill., 1972—; vis. prof. Purdue U., 1962; cons. Rockefeller Found., 1968. Fellow Am. Soc. Agronomy (Edn. award 1973, sect. chmn. 1961, dir. 1967-69), A.A.A.S.; mem. Ill. Seed Dealers Assn. (hon.), Crop Sci. Soc. Am. (sect. chmn. 1967), Am. Seed Trade Assn. (farm seed conf. 1963, soybean seed conf. 1975), Assn. Ofcl. Seed Certifying Agys. (pres. 1968-69, exec. com. 1966-71), Sigma Xi, Epsilon Sigma Phi, Gamma Sigma Delta. Republican. Presbyn. Author: (with Samuel R. Aldrich) Modern Soybean Production, 1970; (with Aldrich) Modern Corn Production, 1975. Home: 902 S Orchard St Urbana IL 61801

SCOTT, WILLIAM DYRTON, educator, realtor; b. Spartanburg, S.C., July 4, 1920; s. James Boyce and Merle (Elmore) S.; student Ohio State U., 1938-41; B.S. cum laude, U. Ariz., 1947; M.A., Bowling Green State U., 1956; postgrad. Wayne State U., 1959-60; m. Fae Elaine Huss, Apr. 6, 1946; 1 dau., Sandra Sue. Operating engr., chief copywriter So. Pacific R.R., 1941-46; newspaper staff writer Toledo Blade, 1947; sales mgr. Russ Packing Co., 1947-50; sales supr. Carnation Co., 1951-54; owner Scott Realty Co., Genoa, Ohio, 1958—; pres. Scott Realty Devel. Co., 1958—; mem. faculty U. Toledo, 1957—, asso. prof., 1965-76, prof., prof. emeritus, 1976—. Chmn., Genoa Area Sch. Bd., 1964—; founder, chmn. bd. Genoa Area Scholarship League; lectr. Toledo Mus. Art, 1960—; a founder, nat. adv. trustee acad. awards com. John W. Heisman Meml. Found. Mem. Methodist Men's League, AAUP, Alpha Kappa Psi, Sigma Tau Delta. Clubs: Toledo Press, Kiwanis. Contbr. short stories, poems, articles to popular mags.; newspaper columnist The Human Condition. Home: 7777 Scott Ct Genoa OH 43430 Office: 307 Libbey Hall U Toledo Toledo OH 43606

SCOTT, WILLIAM JOHN, atty. gen. Ill.; b. Chgo., Nov. 11, 1926; s. William Earl and Edith (Swanson) S.; student Bucknell U., 1945, U. Pa., 1946; J.D., Kent Coll. Law, Chgo., 1950; m. Dorothy Loraine Johnson, May 27, 1950; children—Elizabeth Anne, William G. Admitted to Ill. bar, 1950; individual practice law, Chgo., 1950-51; with LaSalle Nat. Bank, Chgo., 1951-53; with Am. Nat. Bank & Trust Co., Chgo., 1953-58; v.p. Nat. Blvd. Bank, Chgo., 1959-62; spl. asst. U.S. atty., 1959; exec. v.p., dir. Holiday Travel House, 1958-59, chmn. bd., 1959—, also pres.; treas. Ill., 1963-67; atty. gen. State of Ill., 1969—. First v.p. Young Republican Orgns., Ill., 1949; chmn. Cook County, 1950. Trustee MacMurray Coll., Jacksonville, Ill. Served with USNR, 1945-46. Mem. Fed., Ill., Chgo., Am. bar assns., exec. com. Nat. Assn. Attys. Gen. Delta Kappa Epsilon. Presbyterian. Club: Executives (Chgo.). Office: 500 South 2d St Springfield IL 62702

SCOTT, WILLIAM PAUL, lawyer; b. Staples, Minn., Nov. 8, 1928; A.L.A., U. Minn., 1949; B.S.L., St. Paul Coll. Law, 1952, LL.B., 1954; m. Elsie Elaine Anderson, Feb. 7, 1968; 1 son, Jason Lee; children by previous marriage—William P., Mark D., Bryan D., Scott; stepchildren—Thomas J., Terri L. Scott. Admitted to Minn. bar, 1954: atty. right of way div. Minn. Hwy. Dept., 1945-52, civil engr. traffic and safety div., 1953-55; practice law Arlington, Minn., 1955-61, Gaylord, Minn., 1963-67; sr. partner firm Scott Law Offices, and predecessors, Minn., 1967—; probate, juvenile judge Sibley County, Minn., 1956-61; Minn. pub. examiner, 1961-63. Formerly nat. committeeman Young Rep. League; Sibley County Rep. chmn., 1961. Served with USMCR, 1946-50; from 2d lt. to lt. col. USAF Res., 1950-77; liaison officer USAF Acad.; ret. Recipient George Washington Honor medal Freedoms Found., 1970, 72. Mem. Am., Minn. bar assns., Mensa, V.F.W., Am. Legion, Air Force Assn., Res. Officers Assn., U.S. Supreme Ct. Bar Assn. Mason (32 deg., Shriner). Home: Box 704 Pipestone MN 56164 Office: Park Plaza Offices Pipestone MN 56164

SCOTT, WRAY MOORE, indsl. supply co. exec.; b. Omaha, Nebr., July 9, 1901; s. William John and Harriet (Jones) S.; student pub. schs.; m. Helen Bolshaw, June 4, 1921; children—Elizabeth (Mrs. Karpf), Wray Moore II, Richard Thomas, Jane Helen (Mrs. Monte D. Mead). Journeyman steamfitter, 1922-24; organizer Wray M. Scott Plumbing and Heating Co., Inc. 1924, chmn. bd., 1971—; founder SCOCO Supply indsl. supply co., Omaha, 1947, pres., 1947—. Nebr. code adminstr. for plumbing industry NRA, 1934, mem. nat. code authority for heating, piping and air-conditioning industry, 1934, 35; pres. Omaha Constrn. Employers Council, 1948; mem. constrn. adv. council NPA, 1950-51. Mem. Mayor's Omaha City Wide Planning Com., 1945; mem. Omaha City Charter Conv., 1956. Trustee Omaha Indsl. Found., 1953-60, pres., 1960-62, chmn. sites com., 1962-64, 66-71, mem. exec. com., 1971-75; trustee Omaha Home for Boys, treas., mem. exec. com., 1953-77, chmn. bldg. com., 1954-77; bd. advisers St. Joseph's Hosp., 1960-65, pres., 1961-64; bd. dirs. State Nebr. Indsl. Research Inst., 1961-65; trustee Masonic Manor, treas., 1967—, sec. 1974—, chmn. mgmt. com., 1967—. Served with F.A., U.S. Army, 1917-18. Mem. Mech. Contractors Assn. Am. (pres. 1950, chmn. nat. indsl. relations com. 1956), Nat., Omaha (pres. 1936) small businessmen's assns., Omaha Assn. Heating, Piping Contractors (pres. 1947-60), Am. Soc. Heating, Refrigerating and Aid-Conditioning Engrs., Am. Soc. M.E. (life), Am. Ordnance Assn. (life), Nat. Aero. Assn., Nat. Assn. Plumbing Contractors, Nat. Certified Pipe Welding Bur. (chmn. bd. trustees 1952-71, chmn. emeritus 1971—). Nebr. Retail Plumbers Assn. (pres. 1931-35, 46-47, dir. 1931-35), Omaha Master Plumbers Assn. (pres. 1928-30), Omaha C. of C. (v.p. 1960-63), Omaha Mfrs. Assn. (dir. 1936-42), Navy League U.S., Am. Legion, Air Force Assn., Soc. Mil. Engrs. (life). Presbyn. Mason, Rotarian. Club: Omaha. Home: 801 S 52d St Omaha NE 68106 Office: 6161 Grover St Omaha NE 68106

SCOTT-MILLER, JAMES ROBERT, orthopedic surgeon; b. Omaha, Oct. 21, 1928; s. Emmett George and Matha Carolyn (Brown) Miller; B.A., U. Omaha, 1949; M.D., U. Nebr., 1954; m. Joanne Zander, Apr. 8, 1949; children—Pamela, James Robert, Anne, Amy. Intern Hosp. of U. Pa., Phila., 1954-55; fellow orthopedic surgery Mayo Found, Mayo Clinic, Rochester, Minn., 1955-59; resident children's orthopedic surgery Eastern N.Y. Orthopedic Hosp., Schenectady, 1957; resident children's orthopedic surgery Children's Meml. Hosp., Chgo., 1959; practice medicine specializing in orthopedic surgery, Harrisburg, Pa., 1961, 63, Omaha, 1963—; mem. staff Immanuel Med. Center, Omaha, chmn. dept. orthopedic surgery, 1975—; staff Bishop Clarkson Meml. Hosp. Omaha, Children's Meml. Hosp. Omaha, Nebr. Methodist Hosp., Omaha; asso. prof. orthopedic surgery U. Nebr. Coll. Medicine, 1972—; orthopedic cons. Meyer Children's Rehab. Inst. of U. Nebr., 1968—; chmn., bd. dirs. Orthopedic Surgery, Inc. Bd. dirs. Hattie Munroe Pavilion U. Nebr. Med. Center, 1969-74; v.p., Nebr. chpt. Arthritis Found., 1971-74. Served with M.C., AUS, 1959-61. Diplomate Am. Bd. Orthopedic Surgery. Fellow Am. Acad. Opthopedic Surgeons, A.C.S., Am. Acad. Cerebral Palsy; mem. Mid Central States, Neb. Orthopedic Socs. (sec. 1971-74, pres. 1976-77), Omaha Midwest Clin. Soc., Nebr. Med. Assn., A.M.A., Phi Rho Sigma, Alpha Omega Alpha. Republican. Presbyn. Club: Omaha, Regency Lake and Tennis (Omaha). Home: 651 J E George Blvd Omaha NE 68132 Office: 9110 W Dodge Rd Omaha NE 68114

SCOULAR, ROBERT FRANK, lawyer; b. Del Norte, Colo., July 9, 1942; s. Duane William and Marie Josephine (Moloney) S.; student Carroll Coll., 1960-61; B.S. in Aero. Engring., St. Louis U., 1964, J.D., 1968; m. Donna Lee Votruba, June 3, 1967; children—Bryan Thomas, Sean Duane. Aerodynamics engr., contract adminstr. Emerson Electric Co., St. Louis, 1964-66; admitted to Mo., Colo., N.D. bars, 1968, U.S. Supreme Ct. bar; law clk. U.S. Ct. Appeals Eighth Circuit, St. Louis, 1968-69; partner firm Bryan, Cave, McPheeters & McRoberts, St. Louis, 1969—. Dir. Corley Printing Co., St. Louis. Bd. dirs. John Marshall Republican Club, 1974-76, Bar Assn. Met. St. Louis Found., 1975-76. Recipient Outstanding Sr. award, St. Louis U., 1964; named Nat. Outstanding Civil Air Patrol Cadet, 1960. Mem. Am. (co-chmn. young lawyer sect. law day com. 1974-75, nat. dir. young lawyers sect. 1977-78, chmn. young lawyers corp. law com. 1973-74), Mo. (chmn. young lawyers sect. 1976-77, editor young lawyers sect. newspaper 1973-75) bar assns., Bar Assn. Met. St. Louis (chmn. young lawyers sect. 1975-76, exec. com. 1975—), Am. Inst. Aeros. and Astronautics, Engrs. Club St. Louis (chmn. pub. affairs com. 1972-73). Republican. Roman Catholic. Contbr. articles to profl. jours. Home: 607 Lampadaire Dr St Louis MO 63141 Office: 500 N Broadway St Louis MO 63102

SCOVILLE, MARY SYDNEY BRANCH (MRS. MERRILL SCOVILLE), social worker; b. Fulton, Mo., May 14, 1909; d. Raymond Sydney and Marian (Marquess) Branch; B.A., Western Coll. Women, 1930; M.A., U. Chgo., 1934, postgrad., 1940-41; postgrad. U. N.C., 1937, U. Cin., 1930-31; m. Merrill Scoville, Sept. 13, 1947; 1 son, Raymond Merrill. Asst. prof. econs. and sociology Western Coll., 1932-38; instr. econs. and sociology Wellesley Coll., 1938-40; asst. prof. social service adminstrn. U. Chgo., 1941-50; dir. research Edwin Shields Hewitt & Assos., Chgo., 1950-51; psychiat. caseworker Mental Health Clinic, Will County Health Dept., Joliet, 1958-59; caseworker Family Service Agy. of Will County, Joliet, 1959-70. Mem. adv. com. Consumers Union, 1940-50. Pres., Will County Community Services Council, 1962-64, mem. exec. com., 1960-70, 73—; mem. Commn. on Christian Social Concerns, 1958-68, 72—; Ill. Com. for 1970, White House Conf. Children and Youth.; mem. adv. com. Foster Grandparents, 1972-74. Bd. dirs. Sr. Service Center of Will County, 1971—. Cited by bd. dirs. Family Service Agy. of Will County, 1970, U. Chgo. Sch. Social Service Adminstrn., 1970. Mem. Nat. Assn. Social Workers, Acad. Certified Social Workers, Ill. Welfare Assn., League Women Voters (dir. 1955-58, 71-74), A.C.L.U., Will Grundy Mental Health Assn. (dir. 1971-74), UN Assn. U.S.A., United Meth. Women, Art Inst. Chgo., Joliet Artists League, Nat. Wildlife Fedn., Am. Assn. Ret. Persons, Nat. Ret. Tchrs. Assn., Western Coll., U. Cin., U. Chgo. alumni assns. Methodist. Author: Women and Wealth, 1934. Contbr. articles to profl. jours. Home: 925 Oakland Ave Joliet IL 60435

SCOVILLE, ROBERT GARVEY, lawyer; b. Hartington, Nebr., June 30, 1927; s. Ralph John and Rita Maurine (Garvey) S.; B.A., U. Nebr., 1951, J.D., 1951; m. Emile Jean Verzani, June 18, 1960; children—Robin Lynn, Lisa Anne. Admitted to Nebr. bar, 1951, Iowa bar, 1969; partner Seco Oil Equipment Co., Sioux City, 1953-63; partner firm Verzani, Beck & Scoville, Ponca, 1963-65, Ryan, Scoville & Uhlir, South Sioux City, 1965—. Sec., dir., gen. counsel Bousquet, Inc.; pres., dir. Rolling River Enterprises, Inc. Bd. dirs. Sioux City Art Center, Sioux City Community Theatre, Sioux City Rivercade Assn., Papal Vols. for Latin Am., USCG Acad. Prep. Sch. Served with CIC, AUS, 1951-53. Mem. Am., Nebr., Iowa bar assns., Am., Nebr. trial lawyers assns., Sioux City C. of C. (dir. 1961), U. Nebr. Alumni Assn. (pres. Sioux Land chpt. 1965), Phi Beta Kappa, Sigma Alpha Epsilon, Phi Delta Phi, Pi Mu Epsilon. Roman Catholic. Clubs: Century (pres. 1960), Sioux City Country. Home: 3919 Country Club Blvd Sioux City IA 51104 Office: 1913 Dakota Ave South Sioux City NE 68776

SCRENOCK, JOSEPH JOHN, II, bldg., automotive and consumer products co. exec.; b. Wallington, N.J., Nov. 18, 1918; s. Joseph John and Mary (Fallat) S.; B.S. in Chem. Engring., Cooper Union, N.Y.C., 1943; M.A. in Supervision and Adminstrn., N.Y. U., 1947; m. Elsie Newman, Mar. 30, 1941; children—Joseph John, Frances, Thomas, Catherine, Paul, Russell, Elizabeth, Esther, Lee, Robert, Ruth, Wayne. Tech. advisor Mystic Tape, Inc., Chgo., 1955-58; research and devel. dir. Print-o-Tape, Inc., Libertyville, Ill., 1958-59; pres. Poly Products, Friendship, Wis., 1959-71; research and devel. dir. Atco Rubber Products, Inc., Grand Haven, Mich., 1971-77; pres. Web Tec, Inc., 1977—; cons. to industry; tech., tutor math. and scis. Served with AUS, 1944-45. Mem. Am. Mgmt. Assn., Soc. Plastics Engrs., Am. Chem. Soc., TAPPI, Tau Beta Phi, Mu Alpha Omicron. Patentee in field. Home and office: 5255 16th Ave Hudsonville MI 49426

SCRIBNER, GILBERT HILTON, JR., real estate broker; b. Milw., June 1, 1918; s. Gilbert Hilton and Nancy (Van Dyke) S.; B.S., Yale, 1939; m. Helen Shoemaker, Mar. 22, 1941; children—Helen Eaton (Mrs. Gregory E. Euston), Nancy Van Dyke (Mrs. David W. Clarke, Jr.), William Van Dyke, II. Chmn. bd. Scribner & Co.; dir. Abbott Labs., No. Trust Co., Nortrust Corp., Quaker Oats Co., Gen. Electric Co.; trustee Northwestern Mut. Life Mortgage & Realty Investors. Pres. Civic Fedn., 1955-57; dir. Mid-Am. chpt. A.R.C., 1952-57, 67-73; dir. Northwestern Meml. Hosp. Chmn. Ill. Commn. for Constnl. Revision, 1959-61; chmn. adv. com. to Bd. commrs. of Forest Preserve, Dist. of Cook County, Ill. Trustee Northwestern U., Com. for Econ. Devel., 1967-73. Served as lt. comdr. USNR, 1941-45. Mem. Chgo. Hist. Soc. (trustee). Republican. Episcopalian. Clubs: Mid-Day, Chicago, University, Commercial (Chgo.); Indian Hill (Winnetka); Links (N.Y.C.); Shoreacres (Lake Bluff); Old Elm (Highland Park). Home: 17 Meadowview Dr Northfield IL 60093 Office: 1 First Nat Plaza Chicago IL 60603

SCRIMGEOUR, GARY JAMES, writer, educator; b. Auckland, N.Z., Jan. 15, 1934; s. Colin Graham and Caroline Lenna (Hardie) S.; came to U.S., 1957; B.A. with honors, U. Sydney (Australia), 1954; M.A. in English, Washington U., 1959; Ph.D. (Jane E. Procter fellow), Princeton U., 1968; postgrad. (Dominion scholar) Trinity Coll. Cambridge (Eng.) U., 1955. Asst. personnel officer Dexion Ltd., London, 1956-57; mem. faculty English dept. Fla. U., Gainesville, 1959-61, Rutgers U., New Brunswick, N.J., 1963-64; asst. prof. English dept. Ind. U., Bloomington, 1964-69; editor and writer for Benjamin Blom, Inc., N.Y.C., 1969-70; chief of social systems div. and head editorial office Sch. of Pub. and Environ. Affairs, Ind. U., Bloomington, 1970-74, also project dir., 1971-74; dir. Profl. Studies Associates, Bloomington, 1973—; cons. for research in alcoholism, ct. systems, hwy. safety and design of seminars to various govt. agys., schs. and social orgns., 1970—. Mem. Law and Soc. Assn., Am. Judges Assn., Am. Bar Assn., Am. Soc. for Theatre Research, ACLU, Am. Judicature Soc., Nat. Council on Crime and Delinquency, Alcohol and Drug Problems Assn., Internat. Platform Assn., Women's Equity Action League. Contbr. numerous manuals on ct. systems and alcohol safety to profl. publs. and articles on lit. criticism to lit. jours. Home: 3801 Morningside Dr Bloomington IN 47401 Office: PO Box 464 Bloomington IN 47401

SCRIPPS, CHARLES EDWARD, newspaper publisher; b. San Diego, Jan. 27, 1920; s. Robert Paine and Margaret Lou (Culbertson) S.; student William and Mary Coll., 1938-40, Pomona Coll., 1940-41; m. Louann Copeland, June 28, 1941 (div. July 8, 1947); m. 2d, Lois Anne MacKay, Oct. 14, 1949; children—Charles Edward, Marilyn Joy, Eaton Mackay, Julia Osborne. Reporter Cleve. Press, 1941; successor-trustee Edward W. Scripps Trust, 1945, chmn. bd. trustees, 1948—, v.p., dir. E. W. Scripps Co., 1946—, chmn. bd., 1953—; dir. various Scripps-Howard newspapers and affiliated enterprises, The First Nat. Bank of Cin. Mem. Scripps Clinic and Research Found., Webb Sch. Trustee, Coll. of Mt. St. Joseph. Enlisted USCG, 1942, commd. ensign, Coast Guard Res., 1944, advancing to lt. (j.g.), 1945; inactive duty, 1946-72. Mem. CAP, Cin. C. of C. (dir.), Theta Delta Chi. Home: 10 Grandin Ln Cincinnati OH 45208 Office: Central Trust Tower Cincinnati OH 45202

SCRIPPS, DOUGLAS JERRY, educator, orchestral condr.; b. Grand Rapids, Mich., Aug. 25, 1942; s. Kenneth Witvoet and Marguerite Florence (Rottier) S.; A.B., Calvin Coll., 1965; student Vienna Acad. Music, 1965-66; M.M. (univ. fellow), U. Mich., 1970; m. Betty Ann Broersma (div. 1974); children—Elisabeth Ann, Theodore Jon; m. 2d, Merilee Evelyn Collins; children—Daniel Collins, Taylor Douglas. Dir. instrumental music Grand Rapids Jr. Coll., 1967—; condr. Western Mich. Opera Assn., 1968, 69, 73, St. Clair Shores Symphony Orch., 1970-72, Kent Philharmonia, 1976—, Grand Rapids Civic Ballet, 1977, Calvin Alumni Players, 1975—; gen. mgr. Grand Rapids Symphony Orch., 1973-74, asst. condr., 1976—. Bd. dirs. Mich. Community Coll. Arts and Humanities Assn. Foster Found. grantee, 1968-70. Mem. Coll. Music Soc., Nat. Assn. Sch. Music, Mich. Orch. Assn. Home: 2349 Burchard East Grand Rapids MI 49506 Office: 143 Bostwick Grand Rapids MI 49502

SCRIPTER, FRANK C., mfg. co. exec.; b. Dansville, Mich., June 21, 1918; s. Edgar and Maggie Alice (Havens) S.; student Warren's Sch. of Cam Design, 1946; m. Dora Maebelle Smalley, Nov. 2, 1940 (dec. Sept. 1945); 1 dau., Karen (Mrs. Dee Allen); m. 2d, Elvira Elaine Taylor, Aug. 6, 1951; children—James Michael, Mark Lee, Anita Elaine, Warren Arthur, Charles Edward. Apprentice, Lundberg Screw Products Co., 1940-41; set up man Reo Motors, Inc., 1942-43; night supt. Manning Bros. Metal Products Co., 1943; with McClaren Screw Products Co., 1946-47; partner Dansville Screw Products Co., 1946-54, pres., dir. Scripco Mfg. Co., Laingsburg, Mich., 1954—. Chmn., Citizens Com. Laingsburg, 1956-58; mem. Laingsburg Community Schs., Bd. Edn., 1971—, sec., 1973-74, pres., 1974-75. Served with USNR, 1944-45. Mem. Nat. Rifle Assn. (life). Republican. Methodist. Patentee in field. Home: 9701 E Round Lake Rd Laingsburg MI 48848 Office: 9805 E Round Lake Rd Laingsburg MI 48848

SCROGIN, ROY MERLE, ret. state ofcl.; b. nr. Laddonia, Mo., Dec. 26, 1907; s. Roy W. and Rose (Lyons) S.; grad. high sch.; m. Pauline Marie Talmadge, Jan. 20, 1936 (div. Apr. 1957); children—William C., Charles M., Thomas; m. 2d, Mary Lewis, Apr. 19, 1959; 1 dau., Rose Anne. With U.S. Dept. Agr., 1935-41; with Morrison Knudsen Constrn. Co., Boise, Idaho, Ed F. Mangelsdorf & Co., St. Louis, Koss Constrn. Co., Des Moines, 1945-57; auditor Office of State Auditor, Jefferson City, Mo., 1957-65; dir. egg div. Mo. Dept. Agr., Jefferson City, 1965-73. Pres., Mo. Horse and Mule Council; Mo. chmn. Bicentennial Wagon Train Pilgrimage to Pa. Mem. Internat. Union Operating Engrs. Mo. Miniature Mule Assn. (pres.), Mo. Hist. Soc. Democrat. Home: PO Box 101 Linn Creek MO 65052

SCRUGGS, ROSEMARY JANE (MRS. NORMAN MADISON SCRUGGS), librarian; b. Culver, Ind., Aug. 14, 1919; d. Frank Harrison and Ethel Huldah (Wiseman) Taber; grad. high sch.; m. Norman Madison Scruggs, Aug. 29, 1937; children—Norma Janeen (Mrs. Mitchell Barry Resnick), Phillip David. With Culver (Ind.) Pub. Library, 1944—, head librarian, 1958—. Mem. Ind. Library Assn., Suemma Coleman Home Guild. Methodist. Mem. Order Eastern Star. Club: Culver City. Home: 311 S Main St Culver IN 46511 Office: N Main St Culver IN 46511

SCRUTCHIONS, BENJAMIN, ednl. adminstr.; b. Montezuma, Ga., Aug. 13, 1926; s. Tommie Claude and Nettie (Sanders) S.; student Howard U., 1943-44, U. Florence (Italy), 1945; A.A., Wilson Jr. Coll., 1947; B.S., Roosevelt U., 1950; M.S., De Paul U., 1952; postgrad. Chgo. Tchrs. Coll., 1953-60, U. Chgo., 1962-63, Norhtwestern U., 1972—. Tchr. Chgo. Pub. Schs., 1951-59, asst. prin., 1959-62, cons., dir. dept. community and human relations Chgo. Bd. Edn., 1966—; supt. schs., East Chicago Heights, Ill., 1962-64; cons. bds. edn. Evanston, Ill., N.Y.C., Oak Park, Ill., Harvey, Ill., Atlanta; cons. B'nai B'rith, People's Gas Chgo., N.E.A. Hon. mem. numerous P.T.A.'s, council orgns. Trustee Chgo. Credit Union. Served with U.S. Army, 1942-46. Recipient distinguished service award N.E.A., 1963, Anniversary award Alumni Assn. Roosevelt U., Ednl. Excellence Outstanding Adminstr. award Ill. Office Edn., 1975. Mem. Promethean Club, Phi Delta Kappa, Kappa Alpha Psi. Office: Chgo Bd Edn 1750 E 71st St Chicago IL 60649

SCULLY, MICHAEL EDWARD, univ. adminstr.; b. Detroit, Sept. 12, 1942; s. Robert Edward and Jean Lenore (Carmichael) S.; B.A., Parsons Coll., 1967; M.S., Ind. U., 1970. Head resident adviser/area coordinator U. Wis., Oshkosh, 1970-73 head resident adviser Western Ill. U., Macomb, 1973-76; asst. dir. housing for residence life So. Ill. U., Carbondale, 1976—. Recipient Distinguished Service award St. Jude's Children's Research Hosp., 1977. Mem. Nat. Assn. Student Personnel Adminstrs., Am. Coll. and Univ. Housing Officers, Am. Coll. Personnel Assn., Am. Personnel and Guidance Assn.

Presbyterian. Home: Route 1 Highlander Subdivision # 51 Carbondale IL 62901

SEABURY, CHARLENE A. BROWN (MRS. JOHN WARD SEABURY), civic worker; b. Evansville, Ind., July 9, 1922; d. Grant H. and Charlotte (Kirshner) Brown; B.A., U. Wis., 1944; m. John Ward Seabury, Feb. 23, 1946; children—Deborah Holloway, Charles Ward II, David Grant. Mem. Winnetka (Ill.) Bd. of Edn., 1965-71; mem. Jr. League Chgo., 1948-70, dir., 1958-60; pres. womans bd. Travelers Aid Soc. Chgo., 1956-57; chmn. exec. com. Chgo. Lyric Opera Chpts. Mem. Kappa Kappa Gamma, P.E.O. Episcopalian. Clubs: Contemporary, Woman's Athletic (dir. 1970) (both Chgo.); Lyric Opera Guild (dir. Winnetka 1963-68); Crystal Lake Yacht (dir. (Frankfort, Mich. 1969-72). Home: 936 Sunset Rd Winnetka IL 60093 also 2881 Pilgrim Hwy Frankfort MI 49635

SEABURY, JOHN WARD, business exec.; b. Oak Park, Ill., Dec. 1, 1921; s. Charles Ward and Louise (Lovett) S.; grad. Choate Sch., 1940; B.S. in Indsl. Adminstrn. and Engring., Yale U., 1943; m. Charlene Adrienne Brown, Feb. 23, 1946; children—Deborah S. Holloway, Charles Ward II, David Grant. With Marsh & McLennan, Inc., Chgo., 1946-76, asst. v.p., 1952-56, v.p., 1956-76; pres. Hanover Securities Co., 1966—; exec. dir. Seabury Found. Trustee Berea Coll., Chgo. Zool. Soc., Ch. Home (Episcopal). Chgo., Seabury-Western Theol. Sem., Lyric Opera Chgo. Served to lt. (j.g.) USNR, 1943-46. Mem. Chgo. Art Inst., Chgo. Hist. Soc., Field Mus. Natural History, Orchestral Soc. Chgo., Shedd Aquarium Soc., Chi Phi. Republican. Episcopalian. Clubs: Crystal Lake Yacht, Crystal Downs Country (Frankfort, Mich.); Univ., Yale, Tower, Economic (Chgo.); Indian Hill (Winnetka, Ill.). Home: 936 Sunset Rd Winnetka IL 60093 Office: 208 S LaSalle St Chicago IL 60604

SEACHRIST, WILLIAM EARL, plastics mfg. co. exec.; b. Columbia, Pa., Jan. 31, 1931; s. S. Earl and Madelyn Grace (Stiger) S.; A.B., Franklin and Marshall Coll., 1952; M. Govtl. Adminstrn., U. Pa., 1958; m. Marjorie L. Raab, June 20, 1953; children—Frederick E., Sibyl, David W., Eric R., Marjorie. Adminstrv. asst. to city mgr., Pottstown, Pa., 1957; city mgr., Ridgway, Pa., 1958-61; cons. on municipal govt. Commonwealth of Pa., 1959-61; v.p., gen. mgr. Cleve. Powder Metal Co., Inc., 1961-66; chmn. bd., pres., treas. Kent Industries, Inc., Kent Molded Plastics, Inc. (Ohio), 1966—; pres. Kent Research & Devel. Corp., 1971—, Seachrist Real Estate Co., Kent, 1968—, Laurel Devel. Co., 1966-69; v.p., E-Town Auto, 1965-71; dir. Kent Industries, Kent Molded Plastics, Kent Research & Devel. Corp., Orbit Mold, Seachrist Real Estate Co.; vis. lectr. bus. mgmt. Franklin and Marshall Coll.; vis. lectr. pub. mgmt. Kent State U.; vis. lectr. on ministry to professions St. Mary Sem., Cleve. Pres., Kent Area Council Christian Chs., 1969; sr. warden, vestryman Christ Ch. Episcopal, 1967-70; mem. adv. bd. Kent State U. Referral Network System; chmn. Kent-Twin Lakes United Fund Drive, 1968; bd. dirs. Akron Area Devel. Bd., 1972—, Clergy Econ. Edn. Found.; bd. overseers, trustee Franklin and Marshall Coll. Served with USN, 1954-57. U. Pa. scholar, 1952, Samuel S. Fels fellow U. Pa., 1953. Mem. Internat. Platform Assn., Am. Acad. Polit. and Social Scis., Nat. Oceanography Soc., Internat. City Mgrs. Assn., Am. Powder Metallurgy Inst., Am. Ordnance Assn., Am. Hist. Soc., Soc. Plastic Engrs., Soc. Plastics Industry. Republican. Clubs: Rotary, Masons. Author: The Role of the State Planning Agency, 1953. Home: 1655 Woodway Dr Kent OH 44240 Office: 1273 Ethan Ave Streetsboro OH 44240

SEACREST, JOSEPH RUSHTON, editor; b. Lincoln, Nebr., Feb. 3, 1920; s. Joseph Winger and Alice L. (Rushton) S.; grad. cum laude Phillips Exeter Acad., 1938; B.S., Yale, 1942; LL.B., U. Neb., 1949; m. Beatrice H. Costello, May 21, 1944; children—Eric, Theodore, Gary, Kent, Shawn. Editor Lincoln Jour., 1962—; pres. State Jour. Co., 1971—; chmn. bd., exec. v.p. Jour.-Star Printing Co.; sec. Western Pub. Co., pub. North Platte Telegraph, Star-Herald Printing Co., Scottsbluff Star-Herald; mem. exec. com., dir. KFAB Broadcasting Co. Mem. Nat. Hwy. Safety Adv. Com., 1970-73, chmn. Lincoln Met. Sts. and Hwys. Com., 1964-70; mem. Gov.'s Com. on Tourism, 1964-68, Neb. Adv. Council on Hosp. and Med. Facilities, 1968-72; past pres. Govtl. Research Inst., Lincoln Hosp. and Health Planning Council. Bd. dirs. Nebraskaland Found. Served to lt. USNR, World War II. Mem. A.P. Mng. Editors Assn., Am. Soc. Newspaper Editors, Am. Newspaper Pubs. Assn. (govt. affairs com.), Am., Nebr. bar assns., Nebr. Press Assn., Nebr. Joint Press-Bar, C. of C., Nat. Newspaper Assn., Sigma Delta Chi. Republican. Conglist. Clubs: University, Nebraska, Lincoln Country. Home: 1725 S 33d St Lincoln NE 68506 Office: 926 P St Lincoln NE 68508

SEADLE, MICHAEL STEVEN, librarian; b. Detroit, June 16, 1950; s. Peter Stephan and Ruth Mary (Stevens) S.; A.B., Earlham Coll., 1972; M.A., U. Chgo., 1973, Ph.D., 1977. Tutorial fellow Earlham Coll., Richmond, Ind., 1971-72; pub. services asst. So. Asia Reference Center Regenstein Library U. Chgo., 1976—, chmn. grad. history council, 1975-77. Mem. Phi Beta Kappa. Quaker. Home: 5254 So Dorchester Ave Apt 214 Chicago IL 60615 Office: Southern Asia Reference Center Regenstein Library Univ Chicago 1100 E 59th St Chicago IL 60637

SEAGER, GLENN MARVIN, otolaryngologist; b. Rutland, Vt., Jan. 31, 1934; s. Dan German and Bertha (Meszaros) S.; B.S., U. Vt., 1956, M.D., 1959; postgrad. U. Pa., 1963-64; m. Lila Ann Hart, Aug. 24, 1957; children—Glenn Mark, Scott Arthur, Brent Craig. Intern, Guthrie Clinic, Sayre, Pa., 1959-60; fellow Cleve. Clinic, 1960-61; resident otolaryngology U. Vt., 1962-64; instr., asst. prof. clin. otolaryngology N.Y. U. Sch. Medicine and Postgrad. Med. Sch., 1964-67; clin. asst. prof. otolaryngology U. Wash. Sch. Medicine, Seattle, 1968-69; practice medicine specializing in otolaryngology, LaCrosse, Wis., 1969—; otolaryngologist Gunderson Clinic, LaCrosse, 1969—. Bd. dirs. Chgo. Theol. Sem. Served as maj. M.C., U.S. Army, 1967-69. Fellow Am. Coll. Surgeons; mem. Am. Acad. Ophthalmology and Otolaryngology, A.M.A. (Physician Recognition award), Wis., LaCrosse County med. socs., Nat. Assn. Hearing and Speecy Agys., Am. Council Otolaryngology, A.A.A.S. Republican. Conglist. Club: Sierra. Home: Route 1 Carla Ct Stoddard WI 54658 Office: 1836 South Ave LaCrosse WI 54601

SEALEY, DAVID LEON, theatre cons.; b. Kansas City, Mo., Apr. 5, 1944; s. William Curtis and Betty Margaret (Hines) S.; B.S. in Edn., Oshkosh State U., 1968; M.F.A. in Tech. Direction, U. Iowa, 1975. Founder D.L.S. Prodns., Oshkosh, Wis., 1964, pres., chief cons., 1964—; mem. faculty U. Iowa, Iowa City, Iowa, 1972—, scenery shop foreman. Bd. dirs. Lyric Theatre, Seattle, 1970-73; dir. Inst. for Technology in Fine Arts, 1977—; cons. phys. edn. complex Oshkosh (Wis.) State U., 1966-68. Served with USCG, 1968-72. Mem. Soc. Motion Picture and TV Engrs., Nat. Standards Assn., Am. Theatre Assn., Nat. Collegiate Players, U.S. Inst. Theatrical Tech., Internat. Alliance of State and Theatrical Employees. Home: 804 1/2 9th Ave Coralville IA 52242 Office: PO Box 729 Iowa City IA 52240

SEAMAN, ANN CLARK, mktg. researcher; b. Grand Rapids, Mich., Feb. 25, 1946; d. Joseph L. and Faye E. (Cochran) S.; B.S., Miami U., Oxford, Ohio, 1968; postgrad. Western Mich. U. Jr. mktg. analyst The Upjohn Co., Kalamazoo, 1968, mktg. analyst, 1968-70, strategic planning analyst, 1970-75, salesman pharms., 1975-76; mktg. and bus. researcher Steelcase, Inc., Grand Rapids, 1976—. Mem. Am. Mktg. Assn. (dir. local chpt.). Home: 2443 Abbington St Grand Rapids MI 49506 Office: 1120 36th St Grand Rapids MI 49501

SEAMAN, GERALD ROBERT, educator; b. Pottsville, Pa., May 20, 1927; s. Aaron and Shirley (Pollock) S.; B.A., Williams Coll., 1945; M.S., Fordham U., 1947, Ph.D. (USPHS fellow), 1949; m. Leah Melnik, June 21, 1970. Instr. biochemistry Creighton Med. Sch., Omaha, 1949-59; instr. physiology U. Tex. Med. Br., Galveston, 1950-51, asst. prof., 1951-53, asso. prof., 1953-58, asso. prof. microbiology, 1959-63; prof. biol. scis. Hunter Coll., City U. N.Y., N.Y.C., 1963-66; prof. biology Roosevelt U., Chgo., 1966—, chmn. biology dept., 1972-74. Grantee, USPHS, 1950-67, Office Naval Research, 1954-56, Pardee Found., 1954-55; James W. McLaughlin fellow, 1958. Fellow A.A.A.S., N.Y. Acad. Scis.; mem. Soc. Gen. Microbiology Eng., Soc. Protozoology, Am. Soc. Cell Biology, Soc. for Exptl. Biology and Medicine. Contbr. numerous articles to sci. publs. Home: 6007 N Sheridan Rd Chicago IL 60660 Office: 430 S Michigan Ave Chicago IL 60605

SEARLE, RAY RICHARD, psychologist; b. Homewood, Ill., Dec. 28, 1916; s. Ray Russell and Carrie Agnes (Rigdon) S.; diploma Moody Bible Inst., 1936; A.A., Thornton Twp. Jr. Coll., 1938; B.A., Wheaton Coll., 1940; B.D., Princeton, 1944; Th.M., No. Bapt. Sem., 1959; Ph.D. (Grad. Council fellow), Mich. State U., 1962; m. Karen Lynn Rudolph, Aug. 9, 1969. Ordained to ministry Presbyn. Ch., 1944; pastor 1st Presbyn. Ch., Brainerd, Minn., 1944-48, Calvary Presbyn. Ch., Wichita, 1949-54, Immanuel Presbyn. Ch., Evansville, Ind., 1954-56; asst. pastor 1st Presbyn. Ch., River Forest, Ill., 1956-59; individual practice as counseling psychologist, Niles, Ill., 1962-74, Indpls., 1974—. Gen. chmn. Christ for Wichita, 1952. Mem. Am. Psychol. Assn., Am. Sci. Affiliation, Christian Assn. Psychol. Studies. Home: 3154 Lake Ct Greenwood IN 46142 Office: 18 Stonegate Dr Indianapolis IN 46227

SEARS, PAUL RAIDER, optometrist; b. Galva, Iowa, Jan. 31, 1927; s. Albert Andrew and Mary (Williams) S.; student Drake U., 1947-49; Dr.Optometry, Chgo. Coll. Optometry, 1951; m. Sonja Ismen Bellocchi, Dec. 23, 1947; children—Steven Sears, Laurie, Liana. Practice optometry, Des Moines, 1951-52, Ft. Dodge, Iowa, 1952—. Past pres. Iowa Bd. Examiners in Optometry. Served with inf. AUS, 1945-47; MTO. Named Iowa Optometrist of Yr., 1976. Mem. Am., Iowa (pres. 1973-74) optometric assns., Ill. Coll. Optometry Alumni Assn., Phi Theta Upsilon. Methodist. Kiwanian (past pres.). Club: Toastmasters. Home: 1170 N 26th St Fort Dodge IA 50501 Office: Snell Bldg Fort Dodge IA 50501

SEARSON, THOMAS EARL, psychologist; b. Deming, N.Mex., Oct. 4, 1943; s. Earl Thomas and Wilma Claire (Lykke) S.; B.A. cum laude, Hastings Coll., 1965; M.Ed., U. Ill., 1966, Ed.D., 1970; m. Jeanette Marie Stulken, Aug. 8, 1964; children—Thomas Leon, Michael Todd, Stephanie. Asst. prof. edn!. psychology Midland Lutheran Coll., Fremont, Nebr., 1970-71, edn. counseling Creighton U., Omaha, 1971-75; dir. Mid-Nebr. Com. Mental Health Center, Grand Island, 1975—; cons. in field. Mem. Am. Psychology Assn., Am. Personnel and Guidance Assn., Nat. Vocat. Guidance Assn. Lutheran. Home: 1331 N Hancock Grand Island NE 68801 Office: PO Box 1763 Grand Island NE 68801

SEATON, ROY RAY, stock broker; b. Walnut Shade, Mo., May 14, 1927; s. Ralph and Grace (Bilyeu) S.; B.S., U. Mo., 1950; postgrad. So. Methodist U., 1958; m. Lillie Mae Lee, Oct. 21, 1951; children—Jimmie Ray, Janette Lynn, John Michael. Self employed as real estate subdiv. developer, owner, operator loan co., 1950—; gen. agt. Nat. Fidelity Life Ins. Co., Kansas City, Mo., 1955-70; fin. adviser Fundamental Service Corp., Springfield, Mo., 1970—. Tchr. govt. on farm tng. to World War II vets. Asst. scoutmaster Ozark council Boy Scouts Am., 1965-68. Served with USN, 1945-46. Mem. Internat. Assn. Fin. Advisers, Nat., Mo. assns. life underwriters, Nat. Assn. Health Underwriters, Am. Legion. Baptist (deacon). Home: 5844 Roanoke St Springfield MO 65807 Office: 1736 E Sunshine St Springfield MO 65804

SEATON, SCOTT LEE, SR., architect; b. Chgo., Apr. 1, 1935; s. Charles T. and Flora M. (Coplin) S.; gen. engr. diploma Thornton Jr. Coll., 1954; B.Arch., U. Ill., 1959; m. Beverly A. Lambert, Nov. 24, 1956; children—Scott Lee, Susan, Kathryn, Sandra, Michael, Patrick, Mark, Christopher. With Holabird, Root & Burgee, Chgo., 1956, Derks & McCracken, Chgo., 1956, Glenn G. Frazier, A.I.A., Urbana, Ill., 1957-59, Clark Daily Dietz, Urbana, 1959-60; sr. architect Clark Daily Smith, Urbana, 1960-63; partner Smith Seaton Olach A.I.A., Urbana, 1963-70, Moline-Seaton, A.I.A., architect and planners, Kankakee, Ill., 1970—. Teaching asst. U. Ill., Urbana, 1957-59, asst. prof., 1966-67. Recipient Outstanding Bldg. award Decatur C. of C., 1970. Mem. A.I.A. (awards chmn. 1964-67), Gargoyle. Prin. archtl. works include Woodland Chapel Presbyn. Ch., Decatur, 1969, Urbana Civic Center, 1969, master plan for Amberg File and Index, Kankakee, 1973, East Court Village, Kankakee, 1975, Housing for Elderly, Sullivan, Ind., 1975, State of Ill. Mental Health Community Outpatient Clinic, Tinley Park, 1975, Johnson residence, Bourbonnais, Ill., 1976, Greentree I and II, Kankakee, 1978. Home: 822 Cheryl Ln Kankakee IL 60901 Office: 594 Kennedy Dr Kankakee IL 60901

SEAVER, JAMES EVERETT, historian; b. Los Angeles, Oct. 4, 1918; s. Everett Herbert and Gertrude Lillian (Sharp) S.; A.B., Stanford U., 1940; Ph.D., Cornell U., 1946; m. Virginia Stevens, Dec. 20, 1940; children—Richard Everett, William Merrill, Robert Edward. Asst. instr. Cornell U., 1940-42, 44-46; instr. Mich. State U., 1946-47; asst. prof. history U. Kans., Lawrence, 1947-52, asso. prof., 1952-60, prof., 1960—. Pres., Old West Lawrence Assn., 1972. Recipient Fulbright Hayes grant, Italy, 1953-54, Israel, 1963-64; Carnegie grantee, Costa Rica, 1966-67. Mem. Am. Hist. Assn., Am. Philol. Assn., Archeol. Inst. Am., Am. Numis. Soc., AAUP, Am. Acad. Rome, U.S. Archives of Recorded Sound. Republican. Episcopalian. Clubs: Alvamar Tennis, Alvamar Country. Author: The Persecution of the Jews in the Roman Empire, 313-438 A.D., 1952. Contbr. articles to profl. jours. Home: 600 Louisiana St Lawrence KS 66044 Office: Dept History Univ Kansas Lawrence KS 66045

SEBASTIAN, FRANKLIN WILLIAM, mech. engr.; b. Neenah, Wis., June 3, 1920; s. Franklin and Charlotte (Hartmann) S.; B.S. in M.E., Ill. Inst. Tech., 1945; m. Thelma Lucile Scott, Oct. 16, 1948; children—Franklin William, Scott Roger, Paul Allen. Staff engr. Kimberly Clark, Neenah, 1945-48, F.H. McGraw & Co., Hartford, Conn., 1948-57; project engr. K.V.P. Kalamazoo, 1957-63; sales engr. Cameron Machine Co., Dover, N.J., 1963-67; plant engr. Monasha Corp., Otsego, Mich., 1963-70; partner Continental Engring. cons., Kalamzaoo, 1970-74; sr. project engr. Plainwell Paper Co. (Wis.), 1974—. Active Fruit Belt council Boy Scouts Am. Mem. TAPPI, Chief Engrs. Kalamazoo. Clubs: Elks, Mason, Shriners. Home: 2907 Sohora St Kalamazoo MI 49004 Office: 200 Allegan St Plainwell MI 49080

SEBASTIANO, VITO, metals co. exec.; b. Chgo., June 6, 1929; s. Joseph and Jenny (Rago) S.; student Fenger Jr. Coll., 1964; m. Gloria Marie Cracco, Oct. 9, 1948; 1 son, Victor Reno. With R.H. Donnelly, Chgo., 1945-46, A & M Pipe Covers Co., 1948-49, Ill. Central R.R., 1949-50, Ingersoll Steel Co., 1951-54; with Chgo. Bridge & Iron Co., Plainfield, Ill., 1954—, buyer, storeroom supr., 1969-70, purchasing agt., 1970—. Mem. adv. com. Plainfield High Sch., mem. curriculum com., trainer coop. work tng.; mem. Plainfield Planning Commn. and Zoning Bd.; mem. Annexation Com.; coordinator Crusade for Mercy; instr. 1st aid. Served with AUS, 1946-48. Lic. beauty culturist. Mem. Plainfield Commerce Assn. (1st v.p., dir.). Home: 206 Peerless St Plainfield IL 60544 Office: Route 59 Plainfield IL 60544

SEBELIUS, CARL LOUIS, dentist; b. Norcatur, Kans., Oct. 17, 1911; s. Carl Elstrom and Minnie (Peak) S.; D.D.S., Northwestern U., 1934; M.P.H., U. Mich., 1942; m. Lucille Soper, June 28, 1936; children—Carl Louis, Jane (Mrs. Robert Oliphant), Carolyn (Mrs. David Hoglund), Susan (Mrs. Michael Shoff). Intern, USPHS Marine Hosp., N.Y.C., 1934-36; asst. dir. div. dental health Tenn. Dept. Pub. Health, Nashville, 1936-42, dir., 1942-56, 58-61; dental officer WHO, Geneva, Switzerland, 1956-58, mem. expert adv. panel on dental health, 1958-76; sec. Council Dental Health, Council Internat. Relations, asst. sec. dental health Am. Dental Assn., 1961-66; chief dental div. Ill. Dept. Pub. Health, Springfield, 1966-76; asso. prof. U. Ill. Sch. Dentistry, 1971-76. Mem. Nat. Adv. Dental Research Council, 1950-54, Task Force on Comprehensive Health Care, Nat. Commn. on Community Health Services, 1963-66; dental cons. Ill. Masonic Hosp., Chgo., 1971-76; mem. dental adv. com. Ill. Dept. Pub. Aid, 1967-76. WHO fellow to Scandinavia and Eng., 1951. Diplomate Am. Bd. Dental Pub. Health. Fellow Am. Pub. Health Assn.; mem. Internat. Dental Fedn. (sec. commn. on pub. health dental services 1962-67), Am. Dental Assn. (chmn. council on internat. relations 1961-62, pres. state and territorial dental health officers 1953-54), Am. Assn. Pub. Health Dentists (pres. 1953), Ill., G.V. Black dental socs., Xi Psi Phi (editor Quar. 1960—), Omicron Kappa Upsilon. Editor: Jour. Tenn. Dental Assn., 1953-56. Contbr. articles to profl. jours. Home: 72 W Fairview St Springfield IL 62707

SEBELIUS, KEITH GEORGE, lawyer, congressman; b. Almena, Kans., Sept. 10, 1916; s. Carl E. and Minnie (Peak) S.; A.B., Ft. Hays Kans. State U., 1941; J.D., George Washington U., 1939; m. Bette A. Roberts, Mar. 5, 1949; children—Keith Gary, Ralph Douglas. Investigator, U.S. Civil Service Commn., N.Y.C., 1939-41; admitted to Kans. bar, 1941; practiced in Norton, 1945—; city atty., Norton, 1953-68. Mem. Kans. senate, 1962-68; mem. 91st-95th congresses from 1st Dist. Kan. Served from pvt. to maj., AUS, 1941-45, 51-52. Mem. Am. Legion (state comdr. Kan.), D.A.V., V.F.W., Pi Kappa Delta, Pi Gamma Mu, Phi Kappa Phi. Methodist. Mason (33 deg.). Home: 602 W Wilberforce Norton KS 67654 Office: Longworth House Office Bldg Washington DC 20515

SEBO, STEPHEN ANDREW, elec. engr., educator; b. Budapest, Hungary, June 10, 1934; s. Emery and Elizabeth (Thieben) S.; came to U.S., 1967; M.S. in Elec. Engring., Budapest Poly. U., 1957; Ph.D. in Elec. Engring., Hungarian Acad. Scis., 1966; m. Eva Agnes Vambery, May 25, 1968. Engr. Budapest Electric Co., 1957-61; asst. prof. Budapest Poly. U., 1961-66, asso. prof., 1966-67; asso. prof. Ohio State U., Columbus, 1968-74, prof., 1974—; cons. engr. Hungarian State Power Bd., 1961-64, various utilities, 1969—. Ford Found. fellow Columbia, N.Y.C., 1967-68. Mem. IEEE (sr.), Am. Power Conf., Internat. Conf. Large High Voltage Electric Systems. Author grad. level and short-course notes. Contbr. articles to profl. jours. Research on electric power generation and transmission and high voltage technique. Developer grad. level and internat. courses on elec. power systems engring. Home: 2903 Brandon Rd Columbus OH 43221

SECH, CHARLES EDWARD, JR., chem. engring. exec.; b. St. Joseph, Mich., Feb. 4, 1922; s. Charles Edward and Bertha M. (Zimmerman) S.; B.S., U. Mich., 1944. Research engr., prodn. engr. Sharples Chems. (now div. Pennwalt Corp.), Wyandotte, Mich., 1944-49; asst. to W.L. Badger, cons. chem. engr., Ann Arbor, Mich., 1949-57, v.p., 1957-58, pres. W.L. Badger Assos., Inc., 1958-63; pres. Charles E. Sech Assos. Inc., Cin., 1963—; project mgr. Pedco, Cin., 1977—; dir. Port Huron (Mich.) Paper Co. Mem. Livingston County (Mich.) Dept. Pub. Works, 1972—. Mem. Am. Inst. Chem. Engrs., Nat., Mich. (past dir. Ann Arbor chpt.) socs. profl. engrs. Author, patentee in field. Home: 45 Creekwood Glendale OH 45246

SECHRIST, STERLING GEORGE, banker; b. Wadsworth, O., Jan. 23, 1919; s. Sterling George and Phoebe (Trew) S.; B.A. in Econs. and sociology, U. Akron, 1950; m. Marilyn Jean Ohrgren, Dec. 23, 1961; children—Sterling Anders, Kristen Trew. With Citizens Bank & Trust Co., Wadsworth, 1950—, v.p., 1962—, trust officer, 1970—, dir., 1972—, chmn. bd., 1977—. Bd. dirs. Wadsworth Devel. Corp. Chmn. ann. sustaining fund Cleve. Orch. and Blossom Music Center, 1972. Pres. Wadsworth Council, 1958-65; bd. dirs. Medina County Bd. Elections, 1955—; chmn. Medina County Republican Central Com., 1970; alternate del. Rep. Nat. Conv., 1972. Adv. com. Wayne Gen. and Tech. Coll., U. Akron, 1972; bd. dirs. Medina County YMCA, Medina County A.R.C., Wadsworth Salvation Army, Wadsworth United Fund; trustee Wadsworth-Rittman Hosp.; exec. com. Kent State U. Med. Sch. Served with AUS, 1941-44. Named Friend of Children Nat. Found Juvenile Ct Judges, 1960. Mem. Ohio Bankers Assn. (chmn. marketing and pub. relations com.), Wadsworth C. of C. (pres. 1970; Distinguished Citizens award 1960), Ohio Assn. Election Ofcls., Am. Bank Marketing Assn., Am. Bankers Assn., Am. Legion (past comdr.). Methodist (trustee). Mason (32 deg., Shriner), Rotarian. Home: 454 Crestwood Ave Wadsworth OH 44281 Office: Citizens Bank & Trust Co Wadsworth OH 44281

SECREST, RICHARD PHILLIP, printing co. exec.; b. Westerville, O., Sept. 17, 1937; s. Laurence Clark and Elizabeth Jackson (Fickel) S.; B.S., No. Ill. U., 1959; m. Brigitte Juta Sack, Jan. 12, 1966. Exec. v.p. D.C. Lithographers, 1959-61; prodn. supr. Duplex Products, Inc., 1961-63; cons. Precision Forms, Milw., 1963-64; mgr. systems quality control Star Forms, Bettendorf, Ia., 1964-66; exec. v.p. DeKalb County Press, Inc., (Ill.), 1966—; owner, Tri-Hobbies, Inc., 1968—. Served with U.S. Army, 1961. Mem. Internat. House Printing Craftsmen, Printing Industries Am., Sigma Pi, Epsilon Pi Tau. Elk. Club: Country (Kishwaukee, Ill.). Home: 134 Mattek Ave DeKalb IL 60115 Office: 121 Industrial Dr DeKalb IL 60115

SEDGEWICK, THOMAS JAMES, architect; b. Fordson, Mich., Feb. 16, 1928; s. Joseph Michael and Clara (Houde) S.; B.Archtl. Engring. U. Detroit, 1952; m. Rosemary E. Harcz, Nov. 10, 1951; children—Torey Ann, Stephen J., Gerald J., Thomas J., Mark J., Terrence A. Draftsman, Giffels & Vallet, Detroit, 1952-53, MacKenzie, Knuth & Klein, Flint, Mich., 1953-55; designer A. Charles Jones Assos., Flint, 1955-58; pres. Sedgewick, Sellers & Assoc., Inc., Flint, 1958—. Treas. Nat. Archtl. Accrediting Bd., 1974—; bd. dirs., sec., treas. Flint Downtown Devel. Authority; chmn. Genesee Twp. Planning Commn., 1966-73, Zoning Commn., 1968-73; tech. adviser, bd. dirs. Genesee Model Cities Program. Served with AUS, 1946-48. Fellow AIA; mem. Mich. Soc. Architects (a founder, past pres. Flint, gold medal for profl. achievement 1974), Mich. Bd. Registration Architects, Profl. Engrs., Land Surveyors (past chmn.), Nat. Council Archtl. Registration Bds. (chmn. Mid Central conf. 1967-68, mem. nat. bd. dirs. 1968-70, nat. 2d v.p., nat. 1st v.p. 1971-72, pres. 1972-73), Flint C. of C. (govtl. affairs com.), Wranglers.

Democrat. Roman Catholic. Home: 225 Darrow St Clio MI 48420 Office: 301 W Water St Flint MI 48502

SEE, WALTER GEORGE, combustion engr.; b. Pitts., Dec. 31, 1909; s. Theodore S. and Lois (Evens) S.; student Carnegie Inst. Tech., 1929-30, 1932-34; Ph.D. in Bus. Adminstrn. (hon.); m. Bertha Stoikowitz, Oct. 10, 1936; children—Georganne Elizabeth, Patricia Jane, Theodore Alexander. Indsl. engr. LaSalle Steel Co., Hammond, Ind., 1934-37; cons. engr. Theo. S. See & Assos., 1937-55, Walter George See & Assos., 1955—; sales and service mgr. Submerged Combustion Co., 1937-43, chief engr., 1943-46, v.p., 1947, pres., 1948-65; cons. Submerged Combustion Div. Selas Corp. Am.; Blosten Corp., Hammond, Ind., dir. Munster Steel Co., Hammond, Blosten Corp., Munster, Ind., Pureco Corp., Rosemont, Ill. Mem. adv. bd. St. Anthony Hosp., Crown Point, Ind.; mem. Crown Point Econ. Commn. Bd. dirs. N.W. Ind. chpt. A.R.C., Mid-Am. regional Red Cross Blood Program, Assissi Charitable Found., Inc. Mem. Wire Assn., Am. Iron and Steel Engrs., Am. Gas Assn. A.A.A.S., Nat. Patent Council (dir.), Liquid Petroleum Gas Assn., Ind. Mfrs. Assn., Nat. Small Businessmen's Assn., Combustion Inst., Soc. for Advancement Mgmt., Am. Ordnance Assn. Presbyterian (elder, past trustee). Rotarian. Clubs: Youche Country (Crown Point); Woodmar Country (Hammond); Ill. Athletic (Chgo.). Author articles in field. Patentee. Home: 399 Ellendale Pkwy Crown Point IN 46307

SEE, WILLIAM BERNARD, obstetrician and gynecologist; b. nr. New Florence, Mo., Jan. 20, 1915; s. Sylvester Clay and Mary Catherine Elizabeth (Norman) S.; A.A., Moberly Jr. Coll., 1935; A.B., B.S., U. Mo., 1937, M.S., 1938; M.D., Northwestern U., 1942; m. Maribeth Sapp, Aug. 9, 1936; children—Patricia, Julia, William, Thomas. Intern, Wesley Meml. Hosp., Chgo., 1941-42; resident in obstetrics and gynecology Northwestern Med. Sch. and Wesley Meml. Hosp., Chgo., 1946-48; practice medicine specializing in obstetrics and gynecology, Columbia, Mo., 1948—; mem. staff Columbia Regional and Boone County hosps.; clin. prof. obstetrics and gynecology U. Mo. Med. Sch., 1949-70; past chmn. Mo. State Maternal Welfare Com. Served to lt. comdr. USN, 1942-46. Fellow A.C.S., Am. Coll. Obstetrics and Gynecology (founding); mem. AMA, Mo., Boone County med. socs. Home: 1611 University St Columbia MO 65201 Office: 1504 E Broadway Columbia MO 65201

SEED, TERRELL MACK, radio exec.; b. Bridgeport, Ill., Jan. 23, 1944; s. Albert H. and Zelma J. (Litherland) S.; student Eastern Ill. U., 1962-64; A.S., Vincennes U., 1975; m. Judy C. Bailey, Nov. 6, 1965; children—Tracy, Trent, Trevor. Announcer, engr. Sta. WEIC, Charleston, Ill., 1962; engr., program dir. Sta. WAKO, Lawrenceville, Ill., 1965, news dir., 1967; news dir. Sta. WTAY, Robinson, Ill., 1967; engr., program mgr. Sta. WVUT-TV, Vincennes, Ind., 1968-75; program dir. Sta. WVUB, Vincennes, 1976, mgr., 1976—; instr. in broadcasting Vincennes U., 1976—. Auditor Lawrence Twp. (Ill.), 1967-72. Republican. Mem. Christian Ch. (Disciples of Christ). Home: Rural Route 1 Lawrenceville IL 62439 Office: 1029 N 4th St Vincennes IN 47591

SEEFELDT, JOHN ASMUS, ret. city ofcl.; b. Plymouth, Wis., Jan. 23, 1922; s. Walter and Rola (Asmus) S.; student Indsl. Coll. Armed Forces, 1967-68; m. Eleanor Newby, Jan. 23, 1943; children—John Allan, Jane Ann. Asst. dock supt. Bd. Harbor Commrs., Milw., 1955-63, dock supt., 1963-66, dep. port dir., 1966-69, port dir., 1969-77; dir. Badger State Mut. Casualty Ins. Co., Brookfield, Wis. Chmn., Great Lakes Task Force, 1973-74, vice chmn., 1976; commr. Great Lakes Commn., 1974—; Fed. controller Lake Mich., Lake Huron, 1969—. Served with USNR, 1942-45. Mem. Internat. Assn. Great Lakes Ports (dir.). Home: 139 N 71st St Milwaukee WI 53213

SEEHAFER, DONALD WILLIAM, radio sta. exec.; b. Marshfield, Wis., Apr. 8, 1935; s. William Rudolph and Clara Minnie (Garbisch) S.; grad. high sch.; m. Velva Jean Rasmussen, Sept. 20, 1958; children—Sandra, Karen, Mark, Debra. Announcer WDLB Radio, Marshfield, 1952-53, WPFP Radio, Park Falls, 1954; announcer, salesman WIGM Radio, Medford, 1957-59; pres. KRBI Radio, St. Peter, Minn., 1960-70; pres., gen. mgr. WOMT Radio, Manitowoc, Wis., 1970—; owner WXCO Radio, Wausau, Wis., 1973—, WGEZ, Beloit, Wis., 1976—; pres. Seehafer & Johnson Broadcasting Corp., 1959—. Mem. adv. bd. Salvation Army, Manitowoc, 1971—; gen. chmn. Manitowoc United Way, 1975—, bd. dirs., 1976—. Served with USNR, 1955-56. Recipient Distinguished Service award St. Peter Jr. C. of C., 1967. Mem. St. Peter (pres. 1969-70), Manitowoc-Two Rivers (v.p. 1975—) chambers commerce. Lutheran. Elk, Lion. Home: 1211 Tanglewood Rd Manitowoc WI 54220 Office: 410 N 10th St Manitowoc WI 54220

SEEHAUSEN, RICHARD FERDINAND, architect; b. Indpls., Mar. 17, 1925; s. Paul Ferdinand and Melusina Dorothea (Nordmeyer) S.; student DePauw U., 1943-44, Wabash Coll., 1944, State U. Iowa, 1944; B.Arch., U. Ill., 1949; m. Phyllis Jean Gates, Dec. 22, 1948; children—Lyn, Dirk. Partner, Johnson, Kile, Seehausen & Assos., Inc., architects, engrs., Rockford, Ill., 1949—, pres., 1974—. Mem. com. jail planning and constrn. standards Bur. Detention Facilities, Ill. Dept. Corrections, 1970-73; analyst Fed. Fall-Out Shelter, 1962—. Bd. dirs. Rockford Boys Club. Served with USNR, 1943-45, USAF, 1949. Mem. A.I.A. (dir. No. Ill. chpt. 1966-68, 75—, pres. chpt. 1978—), Lambda Chi Alpha. Lutheran. Mason (Shriner), Kiwanian. Club: Forest Hills Country (gov. 1970-72). Prin. works include No. Ill. U. Center, also Health Service Bldg., DeKalb, Winnebago County Courthouse, Rockford, St. Mark Luth. Ch., Rockford, Christ Meth. Ch., Rockford, 1st Presbyn. Ch., Rochelle, Ill., McHenry County Ct. House, Woodstock, Ill., Stephenson County Courthouse, Freeport, Ill., Ogle County Pub. Safety Bldg., Rochelle, DeKalb High Sch., Page Park Spl. Edn. Sch., Rockford, Social Security bldgs. in Racine, Sheboygan, Oshkosh and Janesville, Wis., Freeport YWCA Bldgs., renovation of Carroll County Ct. House. Home: 36 Briar Ln Rockford IL 61103 Office: Am Nat Bank Bldg Rockford IL 61104

SEEVERS, CHARLES JUNIOR, assn. exec.; b. Seward, Nebr., May 13, 1925; s. Ferdinand Carl and Hilda Anna (Schultz) S.; B.A., Concordia Sem., St. Louis, 1949; M.S. magna cum laude, St. Francis Coll., Ft. Wayne, Ind., 1965, postgrad., 1966; Ph.D., U. Notre Dame, 1970; m. Florine Marie Viets, June 5, 1949; children—Steven, Roger, Sandra, Jane. Ordained to ministry Lutheran Ch., 1949; asst. pastor Immanuel Luth. Ch., Balt., 1949-50; pastor St. Paul's Luth. Ch., Kingsville, Md., 1950-57, Bethlehem Luth. Ch., Richmond, Va., 1957-63; sr. pastor Zion Luth. Ch., Ft. Wayne, 1963-66; exec. dir. Assn. for Disabled of Elkhart County (formerly Elkhart County Assn. for the Retarded), 1966—. Adj. prof. psychology and spl. edn., Ind. U., South Bend, 1972-76; cons. Kans. Developmental Disabilities Div., 1972—; cons. Accreditation Council for Facilities for the Mentally Retarded, Chgo., 1972—; cons. on assessment of developmentally disabled to various states, 1974-75, Leicester, Eng., 1974-75; mem. Ind. Gov.'s Adv. Bd. Div. Mental Retardation and other Developmental Disabilities, 1973—, chmn., 1976—; mem. No. Ind. Health Systems Agy. Central Sub-Area Adv. Council, 1976—, vice chmn., 1977—. Chmn. United Way Execs., Elkhart, 1971-73. Bd. dirs. Mill Neck Manor Sch. for the Deaf, L. I., N.Y., 1950-57; mem. area vocat. edn. adv. bd., 1973-76. Eli Lilly fellow in religion and mental health, Ind. U. Med. Center, Indpls., 1964-65. Recipient Liberty Bell award Elkhart Bar Assn., 1974. Mem. Nat. Conf. of Execs. of Assns. for Retarded Children (chmn. 1974-75), Am. Psychol. Assn., Am. Assn. on Mental Deficiency, Am. Soc. Assn. Execs., Luth. Acad. for Scholarship, Phi Delta Kappa, Elkhart C. of C. (dir. 1974-76). Rotarian. Contbr. articles to profl. publs. Home: 1744 Canterbury Dr Elkhart IN 46514 Office: PO Box 398 Bristol IN 46507

SEFERT, JAY BRUCE, educator; b. Carpenter, Iowa, Jan. 12, 1908; s. William C. and Elizabeth (Lembrich) S.; B.A. cum laude, U. Minn., 1930, M.A., 1931; M.B.A., U. Wis., 1965. Instr., Minn. Sch. Bus., 1932-42; resident auditor USAF, 1942-44; agt., group supr., dist. chief audit, nat. dir. audit div. Internal Revenue Service, 1944-60; mem. faculty U. Wis., Milw., 1961-67, research fellow, 1961-63, lectr. accounting, 1963-67; mem. faculty U. Wis., Madison, 1967—, lectr. in taxation, 1967—. Mem. Nat. Accountants Assn., Inst. Internal Auditors, Fed. Govt. Accountants Assn., Phi Beta Kappa, Beta Alpha Psi, Lambda Alpha Psi, Beta Gamma Sigma, Delta Sigma Pi. Home: PO Box 469 Madison WI 53701

SEFTON, GEORGE WILLIAM, advt. agy. exec.; b. Andersen, Ind., Mar. 5, 1922; s. Earle Mohler and Kathleen (Norton) S.; student Ball State Tchrs. Coll., 1942, U. Chgo., 1946-49; m. Elizabeth M. Huie, May 4, 1946; children—Mary B., Michael W., Amelia K., Susanna M., Laurie A., Rebecca L., William D., Sarah R., David R., Kathleen R. Copywriter, prodn. mgr. dir. sales promotion and merchandising McCann-Erickson, Inc., Chgo., 1946-51; copywriter and account exec. Wesley Aves & Assos., Grand Rapids, Mich., 1951-54; partner Van Stee, Schmidt & Sefton, Grand Rapids, 1954-58, Schmidt & Sefton, Grand Rapids, 1958-63; pres. Sefton Assos., Inc., Grand Rapids, 1964—. Lectr. advt., marketing salesmanships. Mem. pres.'s bd. Aquinas Coll.; mem. Com. Cancer Soc. Bd. dirs. Youth Commonwealth. Served with AUS, World War II. Decorated Bronze Star with oak leaf cluster. Mem. Res. Officer Assn., Intermarket Assn. Advt. Agys. (pres.), Serra Internat. Club: Green Ridge Country. Home: 355 Plymouth St SE Grand Rapids MI 49506 Office: 1101 Ionia Ave NW Grand Rapids MI 49503

SEGATTO, BERNARD GORDON, lawyer; b. Joliet, Ill., July 27, 1931; s. Bernard Gordon and Rose Mary (Fracaro) S.; B.A., Beloit Coll., 1953; J.D. (Univ. scholar), U. Ill., 1958; m. Nancy L. Grady, May 2, 1959; children—Bernard Gordon III, Randall Wayne, Amy Margot. Admitted to Ill. bar, 1958; since practiced in Springfield; partner Barber & Barber, 1958—; dir. Rochester State Bank (Ill.). Pres., Little Flower Sch. P.T.A., Springfield, 1971-73; chmn. adv. bd. Griffin High Sch., Springfield, 1974—. Nat. judge adv. Daus. Union Vets. of Civil War 1861-65, 1972-73, 75—. Served with AUS, 1953-55. Recipient Real Estate award Lawyers Title Ins. Co. of Richmond (Va.), 1958. Mem. Am., Ill. (chmn. sch. law com. 1965-66, v.p. jud. adv. polls com. 1974—), Sangamon County bar assns., Am. Arbitration Assn. (arbitrator 1977—), Order of Coif, Phi Delta Phi, Sigma Chi. Roman Catholic. Rotarian. Club: Sangamo, Island Bay Yacht (Springfield). Contbr. articles to profl. jours. Home: 2600 W Lakeshore Dr Springfield IL 62707 Office: PO Box 79 Springfield IL 62705

SEGER, ROBERT MORSE, librarian; b. Detroit, Dec. 16, 1926; s. Earl Fenton and Ruth Leola (Morse) S.; B.A. in Edn., Western Mich. U., 1956; A.M. in L.S., U. Mich., 1962; m. Lois Ann Elliott, Sept. 25, 1956; children—Ellen Jean, Janet Elizabeth, Nancy Lou. Reference librarian St. Clair County Library, Port Huron, Mich., 1956-59; librarian Presque Isle County Library, Rogers City, Mich., 1960-67; dir. organizer Northland Library System, Rogers City, 1965-67; dir. Clinton (Iowa) Pub. Libraries, 1967—. Served with AUS, 1950-52. Mem. ALA, Iowa Library Assn. Presbyn. Kiwanian. Office: 306 8th Ave S Clinton IA 52732

SEGRIST, ALLEN EDWARD, counselor, educator; b. Wauseon, Ohio, Sept. 11, 1931; s. Clifford Bayes and Dorothy Frances (Goodwin) S.; B.S. in Edn., Miami U., Ohio, 1953; M.A., Ohio State U., 1956, Ph.D., 1966; m. Donna Mae Grisier, July 24, 1955; children—Donald, James, Andrew, Kurt, Anne (dec.). Tchr., Libbey High Sch., Toledo, 1956-57; counselor high sch., Shaker Heights, Ohio, 1957-60; asst. guidance supr. Ohio Dept. Edn., 1960-63; asst. dir. admissions Ohio State U., Columbus, 1963-66, practicum instr., 1963; asst. prof. Purdue U., W. Lafayette, Ind., 1966—. Served with AUS, 1953-55. David Ross research fellow, 1968-70, 71-73; Ind. Bd. Vocat. Tech. Edn. grantee, 1975-76. Mem. Ind. Personnel and Guidance Assn. (Outstanding Counselor Educator 1972, Past Pres. award 1975), Am. (dir. 1978-81), Midwest personnel and guidance assns., Am. Ednl. Research Assn. (chmn. 1976-77), Phi Delta Kappa. Contbr. articles to profl. jours. Home: 2846 Barlow St West Lafayette IN 47906 Office: Dept Edn Purdue U West Lafayette IN 47907

SEHER, RUSSELL JOHN, aluminum co. exec.; b. Cleve., Nov. 29, 1923; s. Oscar Gottlieb and Bessie Susan (Briggs) S.; student tech. high sch., Cleve.; m. Frances June Ness, Nov. 6, 1944; children—Robet John, Renee June. Draftsman, Alcoa, Cleve., 1942-47; designer Mohawk Foundry, Cleve., 1947-48; machinist Precision Mold & Die Co., Cleve., 1948-50; designer Paragon Aluminum Co., Monroe, Mich., 1951-52; chief engr. Arrow Aluminum Castings Co., Cleve., 1952—. Served with U.S. Army, 1943-45. Decorated Purple Heart. Mem. Am. Foundrymens Soc., Non-Ferrous Founders Soc. Republican. Clubs: Masons, Shriners. Home: 3855 Lake Rd E Sheffield Lake OH 44054 Office: 33659 Walker Rd Avon Lake Oh 44012

SEIBERLING, JOHN F., congressman; b. Akron, Ohio, Sept. 8, 1918; s. J. Fred and Henrietta S.; student Staunton (Va.) Mil. Acad.; grad. with honors Harvard U., 1941; LL.B., Columbia U., 1949; m. Elizabeth Behr, 1949; children—John B., David P., Stephen M. Admitted to N.Y. bar, 1950, Ohio bar, 1955; asso. firm, N.Y.C., 1949-54; specialist antitrust law Goodyear Tire & Rubber Co., Akron, 1954-70; mem. 92d-95th congresses from 14th Ohio dist. Mem. Tri-County Regional Planning Commn., Akron, 1964-70. Served to maj. AUS, 1942-46. Decorated Legion of Merit, Bronze Star; also decorations France, Belgium. Mem. Akron Bar Assn. Democrat. Address: 1225 Longworth Bldg Washington DC 20515

SEIDEL, WILLIAM CHARLES, aircraft mfg. co. exec.; b. Tipton, Kans., Dec. 23, 1932; s. William John and Ida Charlotte (Sackoff) S.; student Tri-State U., Angola, Ind., 1955-57; B.S. in Aero. Engring., Wichita U., 1961; postgrad. in Bus., Alexander Hamilton Inst., 1966; m. Alice Anne Patterson, July 16, 1976; stepchildren—Debra Brown, Rick Brown, Greg Brown, Jim Brown; children—Mark, Sandra, Steven, Krysann. Project engr. Cessna Aricraft Co., Wichita, 1957-67; chief engr. Am. Aviation Corp., Cleve., 1967-72, v.p. engring., 1972; v.p., gen. mgr. Grumman-Am. Aviation Corp., Cleve., 1972-74; v.p., gen. mgr. airborne Mfg. Co., Elyria, Ohio, 1974—; chief exec. officer, vice chmn. bd., dir. J.B. Systems, Inc., Longmont, Colo.; dir. Airborne Electrosystems, Inc., Ft. Deposit, Ala., Airborne Support Systems, Inc., Three Rivers, Mich. Served with USAF, 1951-53. Assoc. fellow Am. Inst. Aeros. and Astronautics. Lutheran. Home: 115 Denison St Elyria OH 44035 Office: 711 Taylor St Elyria OH 44035

SEIDEN, WILLIAM STANTON, electronics co. exec.; b. Evanston, Ill., Dec. 16, 1932; s. Ben Robert and Edith (Goldman) S.; B.B.A. with distinction, U. Mich., 1954; m. Jane Lipman, Mar. 5, 1960; children—Linda Helen, William Bentley, Wendy Margo. Accountant Arthur Andersen & Co., Chgo., 1956-62; v.p., sec.-treas. Pacific Coast Co., Chgo., 1962-70; sec.-treas., dir. Noranda Inc., 1967-70; v.p. finance, treas., dir. Mangood Corp., Chgo., 1971—. Bd. dirs. Lincoln Park Zool. Soc. Served to lt. (j.g.) with USNR, 1954-56. C.P.A., Ill. Mem. Am. Inst. C.P.A.'s, Ill. Soc. C.P.A.'s. Club: International (Chgo.). Home: 1504 Wincanton Dr Deerfield IL 60015 Office: 105 W Adams St Chicago IL 60603

SEIDENSTICKER, EDWARD GEORGE, educator; b. Castle Rock, Colo., Feb. 11, 1921; s. Edward George and Mary Elizabeth (Dillon) S.; B.A., U. Colo., 1942; M.A., Columbia, 1946; postgrad. Harvard U. With U.S. Fgn. Service, Dept. State, Japan, 1947-50; mem. faculty Stanford, 1962-66, prof., 1964-66; prof. dept. Japanese, U. Mich., Ann Arbor, 1966—. Served with USMCR, 1942-46. Decorated Order of Rising Sun (Japan); recipient Nat. Book award, 1970; citation Japanese Ministry Edn., 1971. Mem. Am. Oriental Soc., Assn. for Asian Studies. Author: Kafu The Scribbler, 1965; Japan, 1961. Translator: (by Murasaki Shikibu) The Tale of Genji, 1976. Home: 619 E University Ann Arbor MI 48104

SEIGNE, TALBOT DAVID, anesthesiologist; b. Dublin, Ireland, May 16, 1923; came to U.S., 1959, naturalized, 1965; s. Thomas Richard Barter and Anna Eliza (Considine) S.; M.A., B. Medicine, B. Surgery, Oxford (Eng.) U., 1948-56; m. Carole Mary Kaye, Dec. 2, 1961; children—John, Patrick, Jane, Michael, Timothy. Intern, Radcliffe Infirmary, Oxford, Eng., 1954-55, resident in obstetrics, 1955-56; resident in anesthesia Mass. Gen. Hosp., Boston, 1960-62; instr. anesthesia Harvard Med. Sch., Boston, 1962-68; cons. anesthesia Cork Health Authority, Cork, Ireland, 1968-70; attending anesthesiologist United Hosps., Detroit, 1971—. Served with British Army, 1941-45. Decorated Mil. Cross. Diplomate Am. Bd. Anesthesiology. Fellow Royal Coll. Surgeons Ireland; mem. AMA, Am., Mich. socs. anesthesiologists, Mich., Mass. med. socs., Assn. Anestetists Gt. Britain and Ireland. Address: 23714 West Warren St Apt 4 Dearborn Heights MI 48127

SEILER, ROBERT E., chief justice Mo. Supreme Ct. Office: Supreme Ct Bldg Jefferson City MO 65101*

SEILER, STEVEN LAWRENCE, hosp. exec.; b. Chgo., Dec. 30, 1941; s. Robert Lawrence and Mary Jane (Cresmer) S.; B.S. in Bus. and Pub. Adminstrn., U. Ariz., 1963; M.A. in Hosp. Adminstrn., U. Iowa, 1965; m. Pamela Jeanne Robinson, Aug. 17, 1963; children—Michele Lynn, Cheryl Ann, Allyson Brooke. Adminstrv. asst. Presbyn.-St. Luke's Hosp., Chgo., 1965-68; asst. adminstr. Lake Forest (Ill.) Hosp., 1968-71, adminstr., 1971-73, exec. v.p., 1973-76, pres., chief exec. officer, 1976—. Co-chmn. North Shore Region Hosps. Chgo. Metropolitan Crusade of Mercy, 1975, 76. Mem. Ill. Hosp. Assn. (pres. dist. 1973, dir.; treas. 1977-78), North Suburban Assn. Health Resources (dir.), Am. Coll. Hosp. Adminstrs., Lake Forest/Lake Bluff (Ill.) Jaycees (pres. 1971-72), Lake Forest C. of C. (v.p. 1974-75), Sigma Chi, Alpha Kappa Psi. Mem. Union Ch. (chmn. bd. elders 1974-76). Rotarian. Home: 298 Hilldale Pl Lake Forest IL 60045 Office: 660 N Westmoreland St Lake Forest IL 60045

SEILER, WALLACE URBAN, chem. engr.; b. Evansville, Ind., Aug. 31, 1914; s. Samuel Alfred and Anna Beatrice (Grossman) S.; student U. Evansville, 1932-34; B.S., Purdue U., 1937; postgrad., U. Mich., 1945-46; m. Charlotte Woody, Oct. 10, 1942; children—Patricia Anne, Janet Alice. With Dow Chem. Co., 1937—, engr., Midland, Mich., 1937-39, cons. research engr., Ann Arbor, Mich., 1939-49, tech. service engr., Midland, 1950-55, mgr. solvents field service, 1955-64, contract research and devel. specialist, 1964—. Mem. Am. Chem. Soc., A.A.A.S., Am. Inst. Chemists, Sigma Xi, Tau Beta Pi, Phi Lambda Upsilon. Home: 5002 Sturgeon Creek Pkwy Midland MI 48640 Office: Dow Chem Co Govt and Pub Relations Bldg 566 Midland MI 48640

SEINSHEIMER, WALTER G., arbitrator; b. Cin., Dec. 25, 1913; s. Henry A. and Cora (Fernberg) S.; m. Betty Jean Silbersock, Sept. 9, 1961; children—Walter G., Carol Goldbaum; student Mass. Inst. Tech., 1932-33, Wharton Sch., U. Pa., 1933-34, U. Cin., 1935-40. Registered profl. engr., Ohio. Indsl. engr., plant mgr., dir. H.A. Seinsheimer Co., Cin., 1934-44, S.J. Capelin Asso. Cons., N.Y.C., 1944-45; founder, pres. W.G. Seinsheimer & Asso. Mgmt. Cons., Cin., 1945-65; arbitrator labor/mgmt. disputes, 1965—; dir. Mack Shirt Corp., Automated Data Service Co. Past pres. Findlay St. Neighborhood House, Seven Hills Neighborhood, Queen City Assn.; past pres., sec. Big Bros. Assn.; past dist. fund raising chmn. ARC, United Appeal; past dir., sec. Cin. Jr. C. of C.; mem. Mayor's Field Employment Commn., Mayor's Anti-Bus Strike Com. Mem. Am. Inst. Indsl. Engrs. (past pres. Cin. chpt.), Soc. Advancement Mgmt. (past pres. Cin. chpt., past regional v.p. and gov., Profl. Mgr. citation), Tech. and Sci. Socs. Cin. (past chmn.), Engring. Soc. Cin., Indsl. Relations Research Assn. (pres.), Soc. Profls. in Dispute Resolution (charter), Nat. Acad. Arbitrators. Recipient award of merit Columbus chpt. Fed. Bar Assn., 1969. Office: 1420 Central Trust Tower Cincinnati OH 45202

SEIPEL, FERDINAND, JR., real estate broker; b. Cin., June 26, 1935; s. Ferdinand and Mildred Marie (Kenning) S.; B.S., Ohio State U., 1960; m. Janet L. Long, Aug. 3, 1963; children—Kimberly Anne, J. Scott, Renee Marie. Accountant H.E. Reichle, Inc., Toledo, Ohio, 1961-63, Peat Marwick Mitchell & Co., Toledo, 1963-64, Summit Services, Inc., Toledo, 1964-67; owner Village Realty, Waterville, Ohio, 1964—; owner, pres. Seipel Investment Co., Waterville, 1967—, Village Park Builders, Inc., Waterville, 1973—. Served with USMCR, 1953-57. Named Man of Year, Waterville Jr. C. of C., 1964. Mem. Ohio State U. Alumni Assn. (life), Ohio Bd. Realtors, Nat., Toledo assns. homebuilders, Ohio High Sch. Ofcls. Assn., Waterville C. of C. (pres. 1969). Elk, Rotarian. Club: Fallen Timbers Family Recreation (founder). Home: 483 Canal Rd Waterville OH 43566 Office: 39 S 3d St Waterville OH 43566

SEITZINGER, EDWARD FRANCIS, lawyer; b. Mapleton, Iowa, Apr. 3, 1916; s. John and Catherine Emma (Griffin) S.; student Iowa State U., 1935-36, 37-38; B.S., S.D. State U., 1943; J.D. with distinction, U. Iowa, 1947; m. Marian Bernice Westerberg, June 27, 1943; 1 dau., Pam K. Admitted to Iowa bar, 1947, since practiced in Des Moines; partner firm Buckingham, Seitzinger & Mason; asst. gen. counsel Farm Bur. Fedn. and Affiliated Cos., 1958—. Dir. Legal Aid Soc., Polk County, 1970-73. Mem. exec. com. Polk County Rep. Central Com. Bd. dirs. Luth. Home for Aging, Izaak Walton League, United Campaign for Polk County Lawyers. Served with inf., AUS, World War II. Recipient award Iowa Farm Safety Council, 1961. Mem. Iowa Def. Counsel Assn. (pres. 1964-65), Am., Iowa (gov. 1973-75), Polk County (pres. 1969-70) bar assns., Iowa Conf. Bar Assn. Pres.'s (pres. 1974-77), Fedn. Ins. Counsel (v.p. 1968-69, 74-75, gov. 1970-72), Internat. Assn. Ins. Counsel, Def. Research Inst. (dir. 1968-75, pres. 1973-74, chmn. bd. 1974-75, hon. chmn. bd. 1975-76), Lincoln Inne (pres. 1968-69). Mason (Shriner). Club: Des Moines Golf and Country. Contbr. articles to profl. jours. Home: 1223

Cummins Pkwy Des Moines IA 50311 Office: 5400 University Ave West Des Moines IA 50265

SEKULER, ROBERT WILLIAM, scientist; b. Elizabeth, N.J., May 7, 1939; s. Sidney and Marian (Siegel) S.; A.B., Brandeis U., 1960; Sc.M., Brown U., 1963, Ph.D., 1964; postgrad. Mass. Inst. Tech., 1964-65; m. Susan Pamela Nemser, June 25, 1961; children—Stacia, Allison, Erica. Center for Teaching Professions fellow Northwestern U., Evanston, Ill., 1971-75, prof. psychology, 1973—, chmn. dept., 1975—. Cons., NSF, NIH, AAAS. USPHS fellow, 1963-65; Nat. Inst. Neurol. Diseases and Stroke grantee; Eye Inst. grantee; NSF grantee; U.S. Navy contractor. Mem. Assn. Research in Vision and Ophthalmology, Optical Soc. Am., Psychonomic Soc., Eastern Psychol. Assn., Soc. Neuroscience. Editor: Vision Research Jour., 1974—, Perception and Psychophysics, 1971—, Jour. Exptl. Psychology, 1973-74, Optics Letters, 1977—. Office: Cresap Neurosci Lab Northwestern U Evanston IL 60201

SELBY, ROY CLIFTON, JR., neurosurgeon; b. Little Rock, Sept. 28, 1930; s. Roy and Ann (Bular) S.; B.Sc., La. State U., 1952; M.D., U. Ark., 1956; m. Marilyn Triffler, May 15, 1960; children—Brian Manfred, Bretta Lorraine. Intern, Montreal (Can.) Gen. Hosp., 1956-57; resident in neurosurgery U. Ill., Chgo., 1958-61; sr. fellow in neurosurgery Lahey Clinic, Boston, 1961-62; neurosurgeon Ministry Health, Malaysia, 1963-70; chmn. dept. neurosurgery Cook County Hosp., Chgo., 1970-74; practice medicine specializing in neurosurgery, Wheaton, Ill., 1974—; vis. asso. prof. neurosurgery Rush-Presbyn. St Lukes Med. Center, Chgo., 1972—. Bd. dirs. Chgo. Foundlings Home, 1972—. Named comdr. defender realm King Govt. Malaysia, 1970; diplomate Am. Bd. Neurol. Surgery. Fellow Am. Coll. Surgeons, Internat. Coll. Surgeons (Fedn. Sec. N. Central Am. 1970-74). Editorial bd. Internat. Surgery; contbr. articles and editorials to profl. publs. Home: 1303 S Elizabeth St Lombard IL 60148

SELBY, THEODORE WILLIAM, chemist; b. Nebraska City, Nebr., Oct. 19, 1928; s. Theodore Roosevelt and Marge (Bates) S.; student Wilson Jr. Coll., 1946-47, U. Ill., 1947-48; B.S., U. Detroit, 1950; M.S., Wayne State U., 1960; m. Jean Gale Campbell, Aug. 18, 1951; children—Kathleen, Mark, Shawn, Diane, Timothy, Scott, Cynthia, Rebecca, Chiara, Douglas. Self-employed, Detroit, 1949-51; chemist Ford Motor Co., Detroit, 1951; asso. chemist Gage Products, Marygrove Coll., Detroit, 1952; sr. research chemist research staff Gen. Motors Corp., Warren, Mich., 1953-64; sr. research chemist Dow Chem. Co., Midland, Mich., 1964-67, research coordinator, 1967-71; cons., pres. Saginaw Valley Inst. Materials Engring., Inc., 1971—; v.p. treas. Precision Tubing Co. Mich., 1972-76. Tech. adviser St. Josephs High Sch., Saginaw, Mich., 1968—; chmn. Midland St. Brigid Parochial Sch. Bd., 1968-71; lay pastor Community of Christ the King, 1973-76; bd. dirs. Open Door Youth Outreach of Midland. Recipient Henry Ford Meml. award, 1960; Russell S. Springer award, 1960. Fellow A.A.A.S., Am. Inst. Chemists; mem. Am. Chem. Soc., Soc. Automotive Engrs., Research Soc. Am., N.Y. Acad. Sci., ASTM, Soc. Plastics Engrs., Sigma Xi. Roman Catholic. Home: 2720 Isabella Rd Midland MI 48640 Office: 234 E Larkin Midland MI 48640

SELCK, FAYE ALBRECHT, speech pathologist; b. Hutchinson, Minn., Mar. 3, 1944; d. Emanuel Victor and Lucille Blanche (Tesch) Albrecht; B.S. summa cum laude, U. Minn., 1966; M.S., U. Wis. at Milw., 1971; m. John Edwin Selck, Mar. 20, 1965. Speech pathologist Burnsville (Minn.) Pub. Schs., 1966-67, Milw. Hearing Soc., Milw., 1970, 1971-72; teaching, research asst. U. Wis.-Milw., 1970-71; dir., chief speech pathologist Children's Clinic Archdiocese Milw., 1974-75; pvt. practice speech pathology, Milw., also cons. hosps., nursing homes, schs., 1972-74, 1975—; guest lectr. Marquette U. Chairperson TRIM (Tax Reform Immediately), 1975, chairperson for pub. relations, 1977—. Mem. Wis., Am. speech and hearing assns., Phi Beta Kappa, Pi Lambda Theta (award). Home: 6839 Wellauer Dr Wauwatosa WI 53213

SELF, HAZZLE LAYFETTE, educator; b. Clairette, Tex., Aug. 1, 1920; s. Hazzle K. and Ethel (Dowdy) S.; student Tarleton State Coll., 1940-41, 46-47; B.S., Tex. A. and M. U., 1948; M.S., Tex. Technol. Coll., 1950; Ph.D., U. Wis., 1954; m. Martha L. Smith, Oct. 16, 1943; children—Linda Ann Self Lindell, Debra Jo Self Parker, Ann Marie Self Meyer, Michael Dow. Asst. prof. Tarleton State Coll., Stephenville, Tex., 1948-52; fellow U. Wis., Madison, 1952-54, asst. prof., 1954-59; asso. prof. Iowa State U., Ames, 1959-62, prof. animal sci., 1962—. Served with AUS, 1944-45. Mem. Am. Soc. Animal Sci., Am. Forage and Grassland Council, Sigma Xi, Alpha Gamma Rho, Gamma Sigma Delta. Mem. editorial bd. Jour. Animal Sci., 1976—. Home: 2221 Clark Ave Ames IA 50010

SELF, SANDRA ADLER, educator; b. Winnipeg, Man., Can., Jan. 8, 1941; d. Alfred and Miriam (Krawitz) Adler; B.S., U. Minn., 1964; M.A., U. Mich., 1973, postgrad.; m. Daniel R. Self, Mar. 1, 1977; children—Steven Charles, Tina Marie. Instr., No. Mich. U., Marquette, 1965, Women's Job Corps, Marquette, 1966; tchr. Livonia (Mich.) Pub. Schs., 1966-78; prof. Am. Leadership Coll., Osceola, Iowa, 1977—. Internat. bd. dirs., dep. to asst. interstate promotional coordinator for Eastern U.S., Inner Peace Movement, Washington, 1976—; state officer for Mich. Internat. Astro Soul Movement, Washington, 1978—. Mem. Am. Personnel and Guidance Assn., Am. Sch. Counselor Assn., Nat., Mich. edn. assns., Phi Delta Kappa. Home: 20414 Sheffield Rd Detroit MI 48221 Office: 30500 Curtis Rd Livonia MI 48152

SELFRIDGE, CALVIN, lawyer; b. Evanston, Ill., Dec. 20, 1933; s. Calvin Frederick and Violet Luella (Bradley) S.; B.A., Northwestern U., 1956; J.D., U. Chgo., 1960. Admitted to Ill. bar, 1961; trust officer Continental Ill. Nat. Bank & Trust Co. Chgo., 1961-71; individual practice law, Chgo., 1972-76; mem. firm Howington, Elworth, Osswald & Hough, Chgo., 1976—; pres., dir. Des Plaines Pub. Co., Fame Walnut Specialties Corp., Northwest Newspapers Corp., Ozark Woodworking Corp. Pres., bd. dirs. Scholarship Fund Found., 1965—. Served with AUS, 1959. Mem. Chgo., Am., Ill. bar assns., Law Club Chgo., Legal Club Chgo., Chi Psi, Phi Delta Phi. Republican. Congregationalist. Clubs: University, Racquet (treas., gov.) (Chgo.); Balboa, Indian Hill Country. Home: 1320 N State St Chicago IL 60610 Office: 135 LaSalle St S Chicago IL 60603

SELIG, ALLAN H. (BUD), profl. baseball team exec.; b. Milw., July 30, 1934; s. Ben and Marie Selig; grad. U. Wis. at Madison, 1956. With Selig Ford, West Allis, Wis., 1959—, pres., 1966—; part owner Milw. Braves became Atlanta Braves 1965), 1963-65; co-founder Teams, Inc., 1964; co-founder Milw. Brewers Am. League baseball team, 1965, owner, pres., 1970—. Served with AUS, 1956-58. Address: care Milwaukee Brewers Milwaukee County Stadium Milwaukee WI 53214

SELIK, MARTIN, dentist; b. Detroit, Apr. 21, 1922; s. James Ike and Bessie Evelyn (Kort) S.; B.S. in Pharmacy, Wayne U., 1943; D.D.S., U. Detroit, 1950; m. Harriet S. Tenenberg, Dec. 27, 1942; children—Judith Ilene, Betsy Susan, Joel Gary, Scott Alvin. Owner, Selik Pharmacy, Detroit, 1945-46; practice of dentistry, Detroit, 1950-52, Madison Heights, Mich., 1952—. Commr., Bd. Health, Southfield, Mich., 1961—, chmn., 1967, 71; v.p. Upper Teens, Southfield, 1969, E.J. Lederle P.T.A., 1966-68. Bd. dirs. Friends of Southfield Pub. Lib. Served with USNR, 1943-45. Named 1st Citizen of Southfield, Southfield C. of C. and Southfield Eccentric, 1971. Fellow Am. Pub. Health Assn.; mem. Am., Mich. (Dental Citizen of Year award 1972), Oakland County dental assns., Detroit Dist. Dental Soc., Mich. Pub. Health Assn., Omicron Kappa Upsilon, Alpha Omega. Home: 22617 Avon Lane Southfield MI 48075 Office: 204 W Eleven Mile Rd Madison Heights MI 48071

SELIM, MOSTAFA AHMED, gynecologic oncologist; b. Cairo, June 11, 1935; s. Ahmed and Amuna (Ibrahim) S.; came to U.S., 1963, naturalized, 1975; M.B.B.Ch., Cairo U., 1959; m. Dawn Antram, Dec. 19, 1964. Intern, St. Vincent's Hosp., S.I., N.Y., 1963-64; resident Woman's Hosp., St. Luke's Hosp. Center, N.Y.C., 1964-67; fellow gynecology and oncology Roswell Park (N.Y.) Meml. Hosp., 1967-68, fellow in pelvic cancer surgery and research, 1967-68; practice medicine specializing in obstetrics/gynecology Dar El Shiefa Hosp., Cairo, 1969-70; instr. reproductive biology Case Western Res. U., Cleve., 1970-71, asst. prof., 1972-74, asso. prof., 1975—; dir. div. gynecology service Cleve. Met. Gen. Hosp., 1972—, dir. div. gynecologic oncology, 1970—, asso. obstetrician and gynecologist, 1972—. Diplomate Am. Bd. Obstetrics/Gynecology, Am. Bd. Gynecologic Oncology. Mem. ACS, Am. Coll. Obstetricians and Gynecologists, Am. Fertility Soc., Eastern Coop. Oncology Group. Author: Ovarian Cancer: Gynecologic Cancer, 1968; contbr. articles to profl. jours. Office: 3395 Scranton Rd Cleveland OH 44129

SELL, ROBERT EMERSON, elec. engr.; b. Freeport, Ill., Apr. 23, 1929; s. Cecil Leroy and Ona Arletta (Stevens) S.; B.S., U. Nebr., 1962; m. Ora Lucile Colton, Nov. 7, 1970. Chief draftsman Dempster Mill Mfg. Co., Beatrice, Nebr., 1949-53; designer-engr. U. Neb., Lincoln, 1955-65; elec. design engr. Kirkham, Michael & Assos., Omaha, 1965-67; elec. design engr. Leo A. Daly Co., Omaha, St. Louis, 1967-69; mech. design engr. Hellmuth, Obata, Kassabaum, St. Louis, 1969-70; chief elec. engr. Biagi-Hannan & Assos., Inc., Evansville, Ind., 1971-74; elec. project engr. H.L. Yoh Co., under contract to Monsanto Co., Creve Coeur, Mo., 1974—. Instr. Basic Inst. Tech., St. Louis, 1971. Registered profl. engr., Nebr., Mo., Ill., Ind., O., W.Va., Ky., Ark., Tex. Mem. Am. Soc. Heating, Refrigerating and Air Conditioning Engr., I.E.E.E. Home: PO Drawer S Bridgeton MO 63044 Office: 19016 Schuetz Rd Creve Coeur MO 63141

SELLA, ALBIN JOHN, engr., fire protection cons.; b. Nashwauk, Minn., Sept. 17, 1923; s. Albino and Helen Madaline (Piazzi) S.; student Itasca Jr. Coll., 1941-43, No. State Tchrs. Coll., Aberdeen, S.D., 1943-44, 46-47; B.S. in Civil Engring., U. Minn., 1949; m. Betty Jane Wunderlich, Sept. 12, 1953; 1 dau., Cheryl Ann. Staff engr. Nat. Bd. Fire Underwriters (became Am. Ins. Assn., Ins. Services Office), Chgo., 1950-60, suprs. engrs., 1961-68; mgr. municipal fire protection services Nat. Loss Control Service Corp., Long Grove, Ill., 1968-75; pres. Al J. Sella Assos., Galena, Ill., 1975—. Trustee Village of Hawthorn Woods (Ill.), 1972-76, mem. planning and zoning com., 1970-76, chmn. comprehensive plan com., 1973-76. Served with AUS, 1943-46. Mem. Nat. Fire Protection Assn. (fire dept. orgn. com. 1968-75, pub. fire protection com. 1972-75), Soc. Fire Protection Engrs., V.F.W. Home: Signal Ridge Rural Route 2 Box 56 Galena IL 61036

SELLAND, HOWARD MARTIN, adminstrv. systems mgr.; b. Bklyn., July 12, 1943; s. Engart Edward and Olga Eleanor (Olsen) S.; A.G.S., Jackson Community Coll., 1963; student Spring Arbor Coll., 1976—; m. Jean Ann Grossman, Nov. 16, 1963; children—Susan Lynn, Sandra Jean. Sr. systems analyst Aeroquip Corp., Jackson, Mich., 1967-68, staff asst. to data processing mgr., 1968-72, advanced systems mgr., 1972-75, data processing mgr., 1975-77, corporate adminstrv. systems mgr., 1977—. Mem. budget and allocations com. United Way. Mem. Soc. Mgmt. Info. Systems, Assn. Computing Machinery, Am. Mgmt. Assn. Clubs: Clark Lake Yacht, Jackson Ski-Touring. Home: 113 N Brown St Jackson MI 49202 Office: Aeroquip Corp 300 S East Ave Jackson MI 49203

SELLERS, ROBERT DOUGLAS, thoracic surgeon; b. Nashville, Mar. 11, 1931; s. Hugh Douglas and Martha (Eller) S.; B.A., Vanderbilt U., 1952, M.D., 1955; Ph.D., U. Minn., 1964; m. Barbara Ann Reycroft, June 14, 1954; children—Hugh Douglas II, Robert Reycroft, Martha Ann. Intern, U. Minn., 1955-56, resident, 1956-57, 59-64, instr., 1964-65, asst. prof. surgery, 1965-66; asso. prof. surgery U. Nebr., Omaha, 1966-68, prof. surgery, 1969-75, chief of thoracic surgery, 1966-75. Med. dir. Union Pacific R.R., Omaha, 1974—. Active Nebr. Heart Assn., 1967—, pres., 1974-75. Served with USNR, 1957-59. Mem. Am. Coll. Cardiology (gov. for Neb. 1972-75), A.C.S., Am. Assn. Thoracic Surgery, Soc. Univ. Surgeons, A.M.A. (Hektoon Gold medal 1957), Soc. Thoracic Surgery. Mason. Contbr. articles to profl. jours. Performed cardiovascular surgery in 3 surgical motion pictures. Home: Rural Route 2 Council Bluffs IA 51501 Office: 422 Doctors Bldg Omaha NE 68131

SELLS, ARNOLD A., ins. co. exec.; b. Toledo, May 16, 1926; s. E. Louis and Rebecca Sells; student U. Toledo, 1946-49; m. Joyce Haack, May 5, 1951; children—Elliott, Brent, Barry. Ins. Counselor John Hancock Mutual Life Ins. Co., Toledo, 1949-55; owner, pres. Arnold Sells & Assos. Inc. and predecessor firm, Toledo, 1958—; N.W. Ohio mgn. gen. agent Crown Life Ins. Co., 1961—; nominating bd. Ohio Profl. Agts. Assn., 1977; cons. in field. Troop com. chmn. N.W. Dist.-Toledo Area, council Boy Scouts Am., 1955—. Served with USN, 1944-46. Decorated Silver Star. Mem. Toledo Jewish Cemetery Assn. (dir.), Nat., Ohio assns. profl. ins. agts., Soc. Certified Ins. Counselors, United Hebrew Benevolent Assn. (chmn.), N.W. Ohio AAU Commn., VFW, Alpha Epsilon Pi. Clubs: Masons, B'nai B'rith. Home: Toledo OH 43606 Office: 2631 W Central Ave Toledo OH 43606

SELSTROM, JOHN PURCELL, JR., air force officer; b. Missoula, Mont., Mar. 16, 1951; s. John Purcell and Nina Ruth (Johnson) S.; B.S. in Bus., B. Environ. Design, U. Colo., 1974; m. Kimberly Jo Langendorfer, Apr. 5, 1975; 1 dau., Kristina Joanne. Commd. 1st lt. U.S. Air Force, 1974; squadron archtl. engr. McConnell AFB, Kans., 1974—, officer in charge planning sect., 1976—. Squadron commdr. CAP, 1973-74. Decorated Meritorious Service medal; recipient Meritorious Service award, CAP, 1971. Mem. Soc. of Am. Mil. Engrs., Air Force Assn. Republican. Methodist. Home: 8400 Travis St Wichita KS 67210 Office: 819 CESHR/DEEP McConnell AFB KS 67221

SELTENREICH, ALVIN EUGENE, state ofcl.; b. Newton, Kans., Mar. 17, 1911; s. Alexander Chris and Eugenia (Partridge) S.; diploma in Hosp. Adminstrn., Columbia, 1960; m. Willomina Maxine Hein, Aug. 8, 1937; 1 dau., Darla Jean (Mrs. Jerry Lynden Williams). Mgr., Santa Fe Laundry, Grand Canyon, Ariz., 1938-41; farmer, rancher, Fairview, Okla., 1941-56; hosp. adminstr. Gove County (Kans.) Hosp., Quinter, 1956-61; adminstr. Community Meml. Hosp., Marysville, Kans., 1961-66, Madison Meml. Hosp., Fredericktown, Mo., 1966-69, Cooper County Hosp., Boonville, Mo., 1969-74; asst. supr. med. claims dept. of social services State of Mo., 1974—. Dir. Kans. Blue Cross Bd., 1964-66. Mem. Am., Mo. hosp. assns., Am., Mo. osteo. hosp. assns., Boonville C. of C. Rotarian, Mason. Club: Rod and Gun Country. Home: 4507 Rainbow Dr Jefferson City MO 65101 Office: 221 West High Jefferson City MO 65101

SELTZER, PHILIP ALAN, chiropractor; b. Bronx, N.Y., Oct. 17, 1944; s. Irving Joseph and Elsie Marilyn (Greenhut) S.; B.S., U. City N.Y., 1965; D.C., Columbis Coll. Chiropractic, N.Y.C., 1969; M.S. in Pharmacology, St. John's U., N.Y.C., 1971; m. Anita Nancy Samek, Nov. 1, 1970; children—Sean Reid, Bret Jay. Practice chiropractic, Mass., 1969, Lansing, Mich., 1971, Ann Arbor, Mich., 1971—. Mem. Mich. Task Force on Health Personnel Licensure and Certification, 1973—; mem. Washtenaw County (Mich.) Comprehensive Health Planning Commn., 1974—; mem. Mich. Council on Roentgenology, 1971—. Bd. dirs. Huron Valley Humane Soc. Recipient Vinton F. Logan Meml. award Columbia Coll. Chiropractic, 1969, Frank E. Dean Meml. award, 1969, Distinguished Service award, 1969; D. D. Palmer Meml. award Acad. Chiropractic, 1969; Acad. Key scholar, 1965-69; diplomate Nat. Bd. Chiropractic Examiners. Mem. Columbia Coll. Physicians, Surgeons, Am. (Council Diagnosis and Internal Disorders 1970—, Council on Roentgenology 1970—; award 1969), Mich. State chiropractic assns., Washtenaw County Soc. Chiropractic Physicians (pres. 1974—), Am. Assn. Chiropractic Medicine, Beta Omega Chi. Jewish. Home: 3895 Waldenwood Dr Ann Arbor MI 48105 Office: 825 Packard St Ann Arbor MI 48104

SELTZER, PHYLLIS ESTELLE, artist, designer; b. Detroit, May 17, 1928; d. Max and Lillian (Weiss) Finkelstein; B.F.A., U. Iowa, 1949, M.F.A., 1952; postgrad. U. Mich., 1953-55, Case Western Res. U., Cleve., 1966-70; m. Gerard Seltzer, May 30, 1953; children—Kim, Hiram. Faculty U. Iowa, 1950-52, U. Mich., Ann Arbor, 1954-55, Case Western Res. U., Cleve., 1966-70; program coordinator arts and humanities Cleve. State U., 1969-71, Lake Erie Coll., Painesville, Ohio, 1970-72; art interior designer Dalton, VanDijk, Johnson, Cleve., 1973-74; pvt. practice as designer, Cleve., 1975—; exhibited group shows: Phila. Print Show, 1952, Dayton Art Mus., 1952, Cleve. Mus. Art, 1952, Walker Mus., 1961, Massilion (Ohio) Mus. Print Show, 1973, Am. Associated Artists New Talent in Printmaking Show, 1975, Cleve. Area Arts Council, Bicentennial Print Show, 1975-76, Cleve. Mus. May Show, 1973, 74, Bklyn. Print Show, 1975, Minn. Mus. Art Show, 1975, New Talent in Painting Show, 1975. Sec., Edgewater Homeowners Assn., Cleve., 1976—. Tiffany fellow, 1952; awardee Cleve. Health Dept. 1975. Mem. Am. Soc. Aesthetics, New Orgn. Visual Arts Cleve. (v.p. 1974). Designer poster Cleve. bicentennial 1975. Home and Studio: 11225 Harborview Dr Cleveland OH 44102

SELZER, CHARLES LOUIS, supt. schs.; b. Homestead, Iowa, Dec. 21, 1914; s. Louis Carl and Caroline (Shoup) S.; B.A. cum laude, Coe Coll., 1935; M.A., State U. Iowa, 1950, postgrad. 1951—; m. Louise Kippenhan, Mar. 9, 1935; 1 dau., Patricia Madelyn (Mrs. Robert Carstensen). Tchr., prin., coach Amana (Iowa) High Sch., 1935-50; supt. Amana Community Schs., 1950—; mem. Grant Wood Spl. Edn. Commn.; mem. European study tour Associated Sch. Adminstrs., 1976. Dir. Amana Telephone Co., Amana Woolens, Inc. Former justice of Peace, Iowa County; mem. Iowa County Crime Commn.; chmn. constl. com. Amana Landmark, Inc. Pres. Amana Community Chest, 1951-53; mem. adv. bd. Kirkwood Coll., Amana Service Co. Bd. dirs., mem. steering com. Amana Hist. Landmark. Mem. Am., Iowa (pres., chmn. ethics bd.) assns. sch. adminstrs., N.E.A., Iowa Edn. Assn., Amana Young Men's Bur. (hon. past pres.), Iowa County Supt.'s Assn., Joint County Area X Supts. Assn. (legislative com.), Amana Soc. (bd. dirs.), Iowa Peace Officers Assn., Amana Hist. Soc., Amana Men's Chorus, Iowa Hist. Soc. (pres. 1965-67), Iowa County Schoolmasters Assn. (past pres.), Phi Beta Kappa. Mem. Amana Ch. Soc. (trustee, elder, pres. 1971—). Elk, Mason (32 deg., Shriner), El Kahir. Clubs: Homestead Welfare (past pres., sec.), Cedar Rapids Toastmasters (hon.). Translator Amana documents, catechism and testimonies. Home: Homestead IA 52236 Office: Middle IA 52307

SEMANIK, ANTHONY JAMES, ednl. adminstr.; b. Cleve., Mar. 2, 1942; s. Anthony Joseph and Angela Theresa (Peters) S.; B.S. in Edn., Kent State U., 1965, M.Ed., 1969; m. Elaine Maria Christian, Apr. 20, 1968; TV coordinator Kent (Ohio) State U., 1969-71; dir. and TV producer High/Scope Ednl. Research Found., Ypsilanti, Mich., 1971-72; dir. Learning Resource Center, Mercy Coll. Detroit, 1972—; cons. in media prodn., 1972—; appeared in plays: American Dream, 1964, Zorba, 1974, Death of a Salesman, 1974, The Boys from Syracuse, 1975, My Three Angles, 1975, Of Thee I Sing, 1976, The Apple Tree, 1977, Mooney's Kid Don't Cry, 1977. Served with U.S. Army, 1965-67. Certified tchr., Ohio. Mem. Assn. Ednl. Communications and Tech., Mich. Assn. Media in Edn., Nat. Assn. Ednl. Broadcasters, Phi Delta Kappa. Home: 17243 Warwick Detroit MI 48219 Office: 8200 W Outer Dr Detroit MI 48219

SEMANS, WILLIAM MERRICK, dentist; b. Delaware, O., Feb. 24, 1924; s. William Oliver and Grace Elmora (Williams) S.; B.A., Ohio Wesleyan U., 1948; D.D.S., Ohio State U., 1952; m. Barbara Anne Hall, June 30, 1951; children—William Oliver III, Patricia Anne. Pvt. practice dentistry, Sandusky, O., 1952—. Pres., Sandusky (O.) Corps Salvation Army Adv. Bd., 1970-72; pres. Erie Regional Planning Commn., 1971; asst. scoutmaster Firelands Area Council Boy Scouts Am., 1965—, instl. rep., 1973—, mem. dist. com., 1973—, mem. council exec. bd., 1976—. Bd. dirs., pres. YMCA, Sandusky, O., 1966. Served with U.S. Army, 1943-46; PTO. Mem. Pierre Fauchard Acad., Am., Ohio dental assns., North Central Dental Soc., Phi Kappa Psi, Psi Omega. Presbyn. (elder 1967-69). Clubs: Yacht, Exchange (dir., pres. 1963-64) (Sandusky, O.). Home: 231 50th St Sandusky OH 44870 Office: 334 Hancock St Sandusky OH 44870

SEMBOWER, JOHN FRANKLIN, lawyer, arbitrator; b. Bloomington, Ind., July 11, 1913; s. Charles Jacob and Lois Alta (Brunt) S.; A.B., Ind. U., 1934, LL.B., 1941, J.D., 1967; postgrad. George Washington U., 1935-37, Northwestern U., 1957-58; m. Thelma Hohlt, June 20, 1936 (dec.); children—Lois Ann, Elizabeth Claire; m. 2d, Grace Mueller, Dec. 30, 1963 (dec.); children—Phyllis Mueller, Thomas D. Mueller; m. 3d. Jeanne Lawrence Schlafman, July 17, 1974. Reporter, Bloomington World, Indpls. Star, A.P., 1928-35; sec. Sen. Minton of Ind., 1935-39; faculty Ind. State Tchrs. Coll., Terre Haute, 1939-44; dir. labor relations Manhattan Dist. Atom Project (DuPont-Hanford), 1944-48; admitted to Ill. bar, 1945; Chgo. regional counsel U.S. Office of Pres., Bur. of Budget, 1948-50; litigation counsel RFC, Chgo., 1948-59; practiced law, Chgo., 1950—; arbitrator, 1948—. Professorial lectr. Northwestern U.; lectr. Loyola U., Chgo., Ind. U., Wash. State U., Lake Forest U., U. Iowa; cons. Ill. Supt. Schs. on sch. tchr. strike negotiations, 1972; mem. arbitration panels Am. Arbitration Assn., Presdl. Bd. Inquiry, Longshore Dispute, 1959, Presdl. Emergency Bd., So. Pacific Ry., 1962; adv. arbitrator U.S. AEC, Rock Island Arsenal, Iowa Ammunition, Argonne Labs., Gt. Lakes Naval, 1965—; mem. arbitration panels Fed. Mediation and Conciliation Service, Am. Arbitration Assn., Nat. Mediation Bd. Mem. alumni bd. visitors Ind. U., 1948-49. Recipient award of merit Sec. Stimson for service on Manhattan Dist., 1945. Hon. col., Miss. Mem. Am., Ill., Chgo., 7th Fed. Circuit (sec. 1951-52) bar assns., Am. Judicature Soc., Nat. Acad. Arbitrators (bd. govs.), Am. Bus. Law Assn. (pres. 1949-50), Ill. Trial Lawyers Assn., Am. Inst. Parliamentarians, Am. Soc. Med. Tech. (hon.), Beta Theta Pi, Sigma Delta Chi. Kiwanian, Elk. Club: Chicago Headline. Contbr.

articles to profl. jours. Home: 107 Warren St Calumet City IL 60409 Office: 29 S LaSalle St Chicago IL 60603

SEMMENS, RAYMOND THOMAS, hosp. educator; b. Cornwall, Eng., Apr. 30, 1946; s. James Thomas and Mary (Rawlings) S.; came to U.S., 1949, naturalized, 1966; A.A., Northwood Inst., 1968, B.B.A., 1970; postgrad. U. Evansville, 1978—; m. Christina Ann Peabody, Apr. 27, 1974; 1 child, James Bennett. Dir. admissions Northwood Inst., Cedar Hill, Tex., 1970-71, dean of students West Baden, Ind., 1971-77; coordinator human resource devel. support services St. Mary's Hosp., Evansville, Ind., 1977—; founder, pres. Am. Inst. for Leadership Studies, 1976—. Candidate for Mich. State Legislature, 1970; corp. dir. Young Americans for Freedom, Inc., 1969-71. Named hon. citizen City of Indpls., 1974; recipient commendation Gov. State of Ind., 1976. Mem. Am. Personnel and Guidance Assn., Am. Security Council, Young Republicans, Phi Sigma Beta, Phi Beta Lambda. Methodist. Clubs: Exchange, Lions, Mason. Author: Student Leadership Made Simple, 1977. Home: 632 B S Harlan St Evansville IN 47714 Office: St Mary's Hosp Washington Blvd Evansville IN 47714

SEMMES, DAVID HAMILTON, educator; b. Racine, Wis., July 12, 1931; s. Liston Roderick and Isabel (Hamilton) S.; B.S., U. Wis., 1956, M.S., 1964; postgrad. Northwestern U., 1969, 77, San Diego State U., 1976; m. Sally Ann Peterson, Jan. 8, 1955; children—Melissa, Laurie. Tchr. Phillips (Wis.) High Sch., 1957-60, Monona-Grove High Sch., Madison, Wis., 1960-63, Stoughton (Wis.) High Sch., 1963-66; faculty U. Wis. Center, Manitowoc, 1966—, asst. prof. communication arts, 1972—. Co-founder Hatrack Storytellers, readers theatre for children as motivational teaching device for reading improvement, Manitowoc, 1967—. Dir. Miss Manitowoc Pageant, 1971-74. Served with AUS, 1952-54. Mem. Circus Fans Assn. Am., Wis. Acad. Arts Scis., Am., Wis. theatre assns. Author: (with Robert Gard) America's Players, 1967. Home: 2102 Fairmont St Manitowoc WI 54220

SEN, SUNIL KUMAR, educator; b. India, Nov. 1, 1924; s. Nirmal Kumar and Prova (Mazumdar) S.; B.Sc. with honors, U. Calcutta, 1944, M.Sc., 1946, D.Phil., 1951; m. Hildegard Floercke, Aug. 22, 1955; children—Achim, Robin, Anita, Michelle. Research fellow nuclear physics Calcutta U., 1948-52; vis. physicist Liverpool (Eng.) U., 1953-56; exptl. nuclear physicist, reactor physics dept. Siemens-Schuckertwerke A.G., Erlangen, Germany, 1957-59, 60-61; spl. fellow, betatron lab. U. Sask., Saskatoon, Sask., Can., 1959-60; asst. prof. physics U. Man., Winnipeg, 1961-64, asso. prof., 1964-69, prof., 1969—. Guest prof. Institut für Strahlenund Kernphysik, Bonn (Germany) U., 1968; invited lectr. internat. summer course U. Ghent (Belgium), 1972. Recipient Heinrich-Hertz Found. award Ministry of Culture of State of Nordrhein-Westfalen, Germany, 1968. West Bengal Govt. state scholar, 1952. Fellow Am. Phys. Soc., Inst. of Physics London, Indian Phys. Soc. (life); mem. Canadian Assn. Physicists, European Phys. Soc., Nat. Geog. Soc., Sigma Xi. Club: Century (charter mem.) (Winnipeg). Contbr. articles to profl. jours. Home: 5 Sandra Bay Winnipeg MB R3T 0J9 Canada

SENDAK, THEODORE LORRAINE, state ofcl.; b. Chgo., Mar. 16, 1918; s. Jack and Annette (Frankel) S.; A.B., Harvard U., 1940; LL.B., Valparaiso U., 1958, J.D., 1970; m. Tennessee Read, Sept. 13, 1942; children—Theodore Tipton, Timothy Read, Cynthia Louise. Admitted Ind. bar, 1959; gen. practice law, Crown Point, Ind., 1959-68; atty. gen. Ind., Indpls., 1969—. Served with U.S. Army, World War II; col. Res. ret. Mem. Nat. Assn. Atty. Gens. (pres. 1977-78). Home: PO Box 359 Crown Point IN 46307 Office: 219 State House Indianapolis IN 46204

SENGPIEHL, PAUL MARVIN, state ofcl.; b. Stuart, Nebr., Oct. 10, 1937; s. Arthur Paul and Anne Marie (Andersen) S.; B.A., Wheaton (Ill.) Coll., 1959; M.A. in Pub. Adminstrn., Mich. State U., 1961; J.D., Ill. Inst. Tech.-Chgo. Kent Coll. Law, 1970; m. June S. Cline, June 29, 1963; children—Jeffrey D., Chrystal M. Adminstrv. asst. Chgo. Dept. Urban Renewal, 1962-65; supr. Ill. Municipal Retirement Fund, Chgo., 1966-71; admitted to Ill. bar, 1971; mgmt. officer Ill. Dept. Local Govt. Affairs, Springfield, 1971-72, legal counsel, Chgo., 1972-73; spl. asst. atty. gen. Ill. Dept. Labor, Chgo., 1973-76; asst. atty. gen. Ct. of Claims div. Atty. Gen. of Ill., 1976—; local govt. law columnist Chgo. Daily Law Bull., 1975—; instr. polit. sci. Judson Coll., Elgin, Ill., 1963. Mem. Ill. (vice chmn., co-editor local govt. newsletter 1976-77, chmn., editor 1977-78), Chgo. bar assns., Am. Judicature Soc., Am. Soc. Pub. Adminstrn. Republican. Baptist (vice chmn. deacons 1973-76). Home: 727 N Ridgeland Ave Oak Park IL 60302 Office: 188 W Randolph St Chicago IL 60601

SENSENBRENNER, RICHARD RAYMOND, comml. artist; b. Neenah, Wis., Sept. 4, 1942; s. Raymond Francis and Margaret I. (Gear) S.; B.F.A., Layton Sch. of Art, 1964; m. Julie Ann Neveu, June 6, 1964; children—Richard Raymond, Jeffery Lee, Scott Paul, Kevin James, Jill Marie. Comml. artist Hoffmaster Paper Co., Oshkosh, Wis., 1964-68; comml. artist Menasha Corp., Neenah, Wis., 1968-70, art dir., Chgo., 1970-72, Neenah, 1972-76; mgr. Menasha Color Packaging and Creative Art Services div. Menasha Corp., Neenah, 1977; owner, pres. Sensenbrenner Design Assos., Neenah, 1977—. Recipient awards for promotional brochures Art Direction Mag., 1974. Mem. Fox Valley Advt. Club, Fox Cities C. of C. Home: 1718 Telulah Ave Appleton WI 54911 Office: 1920 American Ct Neenah WI 54956

SENTKERESTY, JOSEPH ARTHUR, physician; b. Chgo., Sept. 6, 1935; s. Joseph and Mary Frances (Felzan) S.; student Hope Coll., 1952-55; M.D., U. Mich., 1959; m. Beverly L. Heiny, June 13, 1958; children—Diane Lynne, Nancy Anne, Sandra Kaye. Intern, Blodgett Meml. Hosp., Grand Rapids, Mich., 1959-60, resident in internal medicine, 1960-62, chief med. resident, 1964-65, mem. cons. staff in internal medicine, 1970—, chief of coronary care unit, 1973—, instr. dept. internal medicine, 1965—; practice medicine specializing in internal medicine, Grand Rapids, 1965—; cons. staff internal medicine Ferguson-Droste-Ferguson Hosp., Grand Rapids; clin. asst. prof. internal medicine Coll. Human Medicine and Grand Rapids Area Med. Edn. Center Mich. State U.; clin. cons. in cardiology Regional Med. Programs, HEW, 1968-71; lectr. Mich. Heart Assn. Served as capt. MC, U.S. Army, 1962-64. Diplomate Am. Bd. Internal Medicine. Mem. Am., Mich. (trustee 1970-75, pres. 1975-77) socs. internal medicine, AMA, Am., Mich. heart assns., Mich., Kent County med. socs. Home: 2663 Hall St SE Grand Rapids MI 49506 Office: 515 Lakeside Dr SE Grand Rapids MI 49506

SENTMAN, EVERETT EDGAR, editor; b. Wingate, Ind., Dec. 27, 1913; s. Edgar Amos and Lura (Mellott) S.; B.S. in Journalism, U. Ill., 1936; m. Frances Mara Cohn, Feb. 13, 1935; children—Sheila (Mrs. William Frederick Smith, Jr.), Susan (Mrs. Richard G. Owens). Copyreader, book reviewer, feature writer, asst. city editor Indpls. Star, 1936-41; copyreader, music reviewer Chgo. Sun, 1941-42; copyreader, music reviewer Chgo. Daily News, 1943; mng. editor World Book Ency. Childcraft, 1943-54; editor in chief Tangley Oaks Ednl. Center, Lake Bluff, Ill., 1954-74; v.p., dir. United Educators, Inc., Book House for Children, Child Devel., Inc., Tangley Oaks, Inc., 1962-74; pres. Sentman Pub. Enterprises, Lake Forest, Ill., 1974—. Mem. Assos. of Nat. Coll. Edn., Evanston, Ill.; mem. Lake Forest High Sch. Bd., 1966-68; mem. vis. com. Sch. Library Sci. Case Western Res. U., 1970-71. Mem. Chgo. Acad. Scis., Chgo. Hort. Soc., Chgo. Planetarium, Shedd Aquarium, Friends of Waukegan (Ill.) Pub. Library (life), History of Edn. Soc., Ill. Adult Edn. Assn., John Dewey Soc. (patron), Am., Chgo. (life), Ill. (life) hist. socs., Assn. for Childhood Edn., Internat., Comparative Edn. Soc., Nat. Soc. Study Edn., Art Inst. Chgo. (life), Assn. Supervision and Curriculum Devel., Am. Forestry Assn., Nat. Wildlife Fedn., Wilderness Soc., Mus. Contemporary Art (Chgo.), Mus. Modern Art (N.Y.C.), Am. Mus. Natural History, Met. Mus. Art, NEA (dept. elementary sch. prins.), Chgo. Publishers Assn., English Speaking Union, Deerpath Art League (pres. 1962-63), Soc. Fifth Line, Chgo. Press Club, Chgo. Lit. Club, Community Music Assn. Lake Forest-Lake Bluff (hon. adv. bd.), U. Ill. Alumni Assn. (life), Phi Mu Alpha. Clubs: Cliff Dwellers, Headline, Caxton, Gaslight, Quadrangle (Chgo.); National Press, Cosmos (Washington); Swedish Glee (Waukegan, Ill.). Author: The Encyclopedia—A Key To Effective Teaching, 1957. Contbr. articles popular, profl. jours. Home: 905 E Illinois Rd Lake Forest IL 60045 Office: 905 E Illinois Rd Lake Forest IL 60045

SENTMAN, FRANCES MARA (MRS. EVERETT EDGAR SENTMAN), club woman, editor; b. Chgo., Jan. 21, 1915; d. Gustave and Lillian (Strom) Cohn; student Lewis Inst., 1932-34, U. Ill., 1934-35; m. Everett Edgar Sentman, Feb. 13, 1935; children—Sheila Rose (Mrs. William Frederick Smith, Jr.), Susan (Mrs. Richard George Owens). Free-lance writer, editor, researcher, bibliographer, indexer, 1943—; planning editor United Educators, Inc., also Wonderland of Knowledge Corp., 1972-74; partner Sentman Pub. Enterprises, 1974—. Leader Girl Scouts U.S.A., 1958-59; vol. A.R.C., 1959—; sec.-treas. Lake County Fedn. Womens Clubs, 1963-66; edn. chmn. 10th dist. Ill. Fedn. Womans Clubs, 1963-66, chmn. edn. pilot project com., 1963. Lectr. on gardening, herbs, ecology. Mem. Chgo. Hort. Soc., Mus. Modern Art, Art Inst. of Chgo., Mus. Contemporary Art, Am. Hemerocallis Soc., Deer Path Art League (dir. 1955-59, 65-66), Lake Forest Community Music Assn. Aux., Art Inst. Chgo., Am. Herb Soc., Lake Forest Hospital Aux., League Women Voters. Presbyn. Club: Lake Forest Woman's (pres. 1961-63). Home: 905 E Illinois Rd Lake Forest IL 60045

SENTMAN, LEE HANLEY, III, educator; b. Chgo., Jan. 27, 1937; s. Lee H. and Esther (Dore') S.; m. Mary Alice Lerch, June 6, 1959; children—Jeanne, Charles. B.S., U. Ill., 1958; Ph.D., Stanford U., 1965. Research specialist Lockheed Missiles and Space Co., Sunnyvale, Calif., 1959-65; asst. prof. engring., U. Ill., 1965-69, asso. prof., 1969—; vis. prof. aerospace engring. U. Ariz., 1971-72; NRC Sr. Postdoctoral resident research asso. Air Force Rocket Propulsion Lab., Edwards AFB, Calif., 1972; cons. Bell Aerospace Textron, Buffalo, N.Y., 1973—. Mem. Optical Soc. Am., Am. Inst. Aero. and Astronautics, Am. Phys. Soc., Tau Beta Pi, Phi Kappa Phi, Sigma Gamma Tau, Sigma Tau, Sigma Xi, Theta Delta Chi, Western N.Y. Retriever Club. Daniel and Florence Guggenheim fellow, 1958-59; recipient W.L. Everitt Undergrad. Teaching Excellence award, 1969; U. Ill. Loyalty award, 1977. Contbr. articles in field to profl. jours. Home: 1012 S Westlawn St Champaign IL 61820 Office: 105 Transportation Bldg University of Illinois Urbana IL 61801

SEPSY, CHARLES FRANK, mech. engr.; b. Buffalo, May 19, 1924; s. Charles Steve and Elsie (Korda) S.; B.M.E., U. Tenn., 1949; M.S., U. Rochester, 1951; postgrad. Ohio State U., 1954-55; m. Betty Case, July 14, 1945; children—Scott, Saundra. Research asso. Ohio State U., Columbus, 1951-56, instr. dept. mech. engring., 1956-60, asst. prof., 1960-64, asso. prof., 1964-67, prof., research supr., 1967—; cons. Owens-Corning Fiberglas Co., Office of Civil Defense, NSF, Mathematica, Exxon. Served with USAAF, 1943-45. Named Man of Year Columbus Tech. Council, 1975. Fellow Am. Soc. Heating, Refrigerating and Air Conditioning Engrs. (Willis Carrier award 1968, Distinguished Service award 1976); mem. Am. Soc. Engring. Educators, Inst. Environ. Sci., ASME, Automated Procedures for Engring. Cons. (hon.), Tau Beta Pi, Phi Kappa Phi, Sigma Xi. Republican. Baptist. Contbr. articles on energy conservation, solar energy, heat transfer to tech. jours. Home: 3675 Rushmore Dr Columbus OH 43220 Office: 206 W 18th Ave Robinson Lab Room 1077 Columbus OH 43210

SERAFINI, JOHN, mgmt. exec.; b. Mark, Ill., Dec. 27, 1930; s. John and Pia (Marcacci) S.; student Ill. Valley Community Coll., 1977; m. Violet Chiavario, June 20, 1950; children—John, Ronald, James, Chris, Rick, Tom. Data processing mgr. General Time Corp., Westclox Div., LaSalle, Ill., 1960-62, planning and control mgr., 1962-65, controller, Precision Products Div., 1965-68, corporate dir. planning, 1968-69, operations mgr., 1969-70, v.p., gen. mgr., 1970-74, v.p., gen. mgr. Westclox div., 1974—; dir. General Time, Korea, 1970—, Gen. Time, H.K., 1970—, Gen. Time, Scotland, 1973—. Roman Catholic. Home: Route 1 Lynwood Peru IL 61301 Office: General Time Corp Westclox Div LaSalle IL

SERBO, ARTHUR KARL, pub. relations exec.; b. Chgo., July 12, 1929; s. Karl and Ann (Padlo) Szczerbowski; B.A., St. Ambrose Coll., 1953; m. Adeline Wachala, July 29, 1961; children—Susan, Steven, Ted. Sports publicity dir. St. Ambrose Coll., Davenport, Iowa, 1955-57; asst. sports editor Davenport Democrat, 1957-59; asst. pub. relations dir. Johnson Motors, Waukegan, Ill., 1959-61; asst. pub. relations dir. Ill. Tollway, Oak Brook, 1961-63; mgr. pub. relations Brunswick Corp., Skokie, Ill., 1963—. Served with USMCR, 1953-55. Mem. Pub. Relations Soc. Am., Bowling Writers Assn. Am., Chgo. Press Club. Home: 1134 Westwood Trail Addison IL 60101 Office: Brunswick Corp One Brunswick Plaza Skokie IL 60076

SEREDA, JOHN WALTER, lawyer; b. Chgo., June 27, 1918; s. Francis X. and Louise (Moson) S.; J.D., De Paul U., 1944; m. Theresa Mary Karlowicz, June 26, 1948; children—Ann Marie, John Walter, Amelia Louise. Admitted to Ill. bar, 1945; to practice Fed. Dist. Ct., U.S. Supreme Ct.; practice Chgo., 1945—, Govt. appeal agt. local bd. 66, Chgo., 1953—. Fellow Am. Acad. Matrimonial Lawyers; mem. Am., Ill., Chgo., Fed. bar assns., Advs. Soc., Judicature Soc., 7th Circuit Fed. Bar Assn., Polish Nat. Alliance, Delta Theta Phi. Elk. K.C. (4 degree). Home: 1 Cottage Lane Midlothian Country Club Grounds Midlothian IL 60445 Office: 11732 S Western Ave Chicago IL 60643 also 3728 S Paulina St Chicago IL 60609

SERSTOCK, DORIS SHAY, microbiologist, club woman; b. Mitchell, S.D., June 13, 1926; d. Elmer Howard and Hattie (Christopher) Shay; B.A., Augustana Coll., 1947; Blood Bank tng. course, Washington, 1963; postgrad. U. Minn., 1966-67, Duke, summer 1969, mycology tng. Communicable Disease Center, Atlanta, 1972; m. Ellsworth I. Serstock, Aug. 30, 1952; children—Barbara Anne, Robert E., Mark D. Bacteriologist, civil service positions, S.D., Colo., Mo., 1947-52; research bacteriologist U. Minn., 1952-53; clin. bacteriologist Dr. Lufkin's Lab., 1954-55; chief technologist St. Paul Regional Blood Center of A.R.C., 1959-65; microbiologist, then microbiologist in charge mycology lab. VA Hosp., Mpls., 1968—. Instr., Coll. Med. Scis., U. Minn., 1970—. Mem. Richfield Planning Commn., 1965-71. Recipient scholarship Am. Assn. U. Women, 1966; Ann. Distinctive Alumni medallion award Augustana Coll., 1977; named to Exec. and Profl. Hall of Fame, 1966. Mem. Minn. Planning Assn., Am., Minn. Assn. blood banks, Internat. Platform Assn. Republican Lutheran. Clubs: Richfield Women's Garden (pres. 1959), Wild Flower Garden (chmn. 1961). Author articles in field. Home: 7201 Portland Ave Richfield MN 55423 Office: VA Hospital Minneapolis MN 55417

SERVAAS, BEURT, mag. publisher; b. Indpls., May 7, 1919; s. Beurt and Lele (Neff) SerV.; A.B., Ind. U., 1940, postgrad., 1941; postgrad. (DuPont scholar) Purdue U., 1941; m. Cory Snyhorst, Jan. 7, 1950; children—Eric, Kristin, Joan, Paul, Amy. Vice pres. Vestar Corp., N.Y.C., 1948-49; chmn. bd. North Vernon Forge, Inc. (Ind.), 1957—, Ser Vaas Labs., Indpls., 1955—, Curtis Pub. Co., Indpls. 1970—, Rev. Pub. Co., Indpls., 1956—; editor, pub. Sat. Eve. Post, Indpls., 1971—; dir. Am. Fletcher Nat. Bank, Indpls., 1972—, Coll. Univ. Corp., Indpls., 1971—. Chmn. Gov.'s Commn. on Grad. Edn., 1968—; dir. health and welfare council Goodwil Industries, 1960-64. Pres. Indpls.-Marion County Council, 1962—; treas. Marion County Rep. Central Com., 1965—; pres. Marion County Tax Rev. Bd., 1965-70. Bd. dirs., mem. adv. bd. Christamore Aid Soc.; bd. dirs. Center for Independent Action, Ind. Forum. Served to lt. USNR, 1941-46. Decorated Bronze Star medal, Army Commendation medal. Mem. N.A.M., Assn. Am. Med. Colls., Ind., Marion County hist. socs., 500 Festival Assos, Phi Delta Kappa, Delta Upsilon. Presbyn. Clubs: Gyro, Columbia, Indianapolis Athletic, Meridian Hills Country (Indpls.). Home: 2525 W 44th St Indianapolis IN 46208 Office: 1100 Waterway Blvd Indianapolis IN 46202

SER VAAS, CORY SYNHORST, editor, publishing co. exec.; b. Pella, Iowa, June 21, 1924; d. John Dirk and Gertrude (Roorda) Synhorst; B.A., U. Iowa, 1946; M.D., U. Ind., 1969; m. Beurt SerVaas, Jan. 7, 1950; children—Eric, Kristin, Joan, Paul, Amy. Pres. Cory Jane Originals, Inc., N.Y.C., 1948-50; editor mag. Lionel Corp., N.Y.C., 1948-50; v.p., dir. SerVaas Labs., 1956—; v.p. Curtis Pub. Co., Indpls., 1972—; exec. editor, pub. Sat. Eve. Post, 1972—, exec. editor Holiday mag., 1972—. Mem. women's affairs com. Civic Theater, Indpls. Mem. Children's Mus. Guild, Indpls. Symphony Soc., John Herron Art Assn., A.M.A., Am. Med. Women's Assn., Theta Sigma Phi. Republican. Presbyn. Clubs: Athletic, Triangle. Author: The Magic of Chemistry, 1948; The Vitamin C Cookbook; (with Turgeon and Birmingham) Fiber and Bran Better Health Cookbook. Home: 2525 W 44th St Indianapolis IN 46208 Office: 1100 Waterway Blvd Indianapolis IN 46202

SESKIND, COLEMAN ROBERT, physician; b. Chgo., Sept. 22, 1936; s. Carl and Vera (Rose) S.; A.B., U. Chgo., 1955, B.S., 1956, M.S., 1959, M.D., 1959. Intern, San Francisco Gen. Hosp., 1959-60; postgrad. in clin. pathology NIH, 1960-62, in anat. pathology U. Chgo., 1962-63, resident in internal medicine U. Ill. Research Hosps., Chgo., 1963-65; practice medicine specializing in internal medicine and chest disease, Chgo., 1965—; attending physician, chief sect. diagnostic medicine St. Joseph Hosp., Chgo.; clin. asso. prof. medicine Northwestern U., Chgo. Served with USPHS, 1960-62. Recipient Sheard-Sanford award for med. research U. Chgo., 1959; Ford scholar, 1951-55. Fellow A.C.P., Am. Coll. Chest Physicians; mem. AMA, Ill., Chgo. med. socs., Am. Thoracic Soc., Am., Chgo. socs. internal medicine, Am. Assn. Clin. Scientists. Jewish. Contbr. articles in field to med. jours. Office: 25 E Washington St Suite 1525 Chicago IL 60602

SESSIONS, WILLIAM CRIGHTON, lawyer; b. Columbus, O., Sept. 22, 1904; s. Frank Lord and Jane (Crighton) S.; B.S., Mass. Inst. Tech., 1926; J.D., Western Res. U., 1930; m. Marian Eloise Hill, June 16, 1931; children—Elizabeth (Mrs. Thomas V. A. Kelsey), Margaret (Mrs. Frank K. Penirian). Admitted to Ohio bar, 1930, since practiced Cleve.; mem. Bosworth, Sessions & McCoy, 1941—. Mem. alumni council, ednl. council corp. devel. com. M.I.T. Mem. fiscal adv. com. Cleve. YWCA. Bd. trustees Cleve. Health Mus. Mem. Internat. Patent and Trademark Assn., Am. Judicature Soc., Am., Cleve. (pres. 1963-64) patent law assns., Am., Cleve. bar assns., Newcomen Soc., Cleve. Engring. Soc., Phi Gamma Delta. Republican. Clubs: Union, Clifton, Westwood Country, Rowfant, Rockwell Springs Trout. Home: 15710 West Shore Ct Lakewood OH 44107 Office: Nat City Bank Bldg Cleveland OH 44114

SESTRIC, ANTHONY JAMES, lawyer; b. St. Louis, June 27, 1940; s. Anton and Marie (Gasparovic) S.; B.A., Georgetown U., 1962; J.D., Mo. U., 1965; m. Carol F. Bowman, Nov. 24, 1966; children—Laura Antonette, Holly Nicole, Michael Anthony. Admitted to Mo. bar, 1965, U.S. Supreme Ct., 1970; law clk. U.S. Dist. Ct., St. Louis, 1965-66; partner firm Sestric, McGhee & Miller, St. Louis, 1966-77, Fordyce & Mayne, 1977—; spl. asst. to Mo. atty. gen., St. Louis, 1968. Mem. St. Louis Air Pollution Bd. Appeals and Varience Rev., 1966-73, chmn., 1968-73; mem. St. Louis Airport Commn., 1975-76; dist. vice chmn. Boy Scouts Am., 1970—. Bd. dirs. Full Achievement, Inc., 1970-77, pres., 1972-77; bd. dirs. Legal Aid Soc. of St. Louis, 1976—, Law Library Assn. St. Louis, 1976-78. Mem. Am. Bar Assn. (state chmn. judiciary com. 1973-75), Lawyers Assn., Am. Judicature Soc., Mo. Bar (vice chmn. young lawyers sect. 1973-76, gov. 1974—), Bar Assn. Met. St. Louis (chmn. young lawyers sect. 1974-75, exec. com. 1974—). Club: Mo. Athletic. Home: 3967 Holly Hills Blvd St Louis MO 63116 Office: 120 S Central Ave St Louis MO 63105

SETH, MAHESH KUMAR, digital systems co. exec.; b. New Delhi, India, Apr. 18, 1947; s. Madan Lal and Meena (Vohra) S.; came to U.S., 1968, naturalized, 1973; B.Tech. with honors, Indian Inst. Tech., Kharagpur, 1968; M.M.E., U. Wis.-Madison, 1969, Ph.D., 1972; m. Chander Rekha Anand, Jan. 15, 1975. Sr. research engr. Whirlpool Corp., Benton Harbor, Mich., 1972-77; pres. Digital Interface Systems, Inc., Benton Harbor, 1977—, also dir. Mem. Soc. Mfg. Engrs., ASME, Sigma Xi. Author: (with U. Rembold and J. Weinstein) Computers in Manufacturing, 1977; also articles. Home: 3233 Dody St Michigan City IN 46360 Office: 307 Colfax St Benton Harbor MI 49022

SETH, RICHARD PETER, designer; b. Khargpur, India, Mar. 27, 1940; s. Walter Barnes and Eileen Viola (Gasper) S.; student pub. schs., Peoria, Ill.; m. Dora Lee Anthony, Sept. 7, 1963; 1 son, Andrew Paul. Display artist, Carson Pirie Scott, Peoria, 1959-62, dir. display and advt., Ottawa, Ill., 1963-75; free lance display designs, Ottawa, 1975—; one-man shows: 1st Nat. Bank Ottawa, Caterpillar Co., Lake View Center, Peoria, 1973; represented in permanent collection: Continental Grain Co., Chgo., Central Tel. Co., Chgo., Jefferson Bank, Peoria, Tallman Savs. & Loan, Chgo., McDonalds Co., Oakbrook, Ill. Mem. Scholastic Arts Awards Com. North Central Ill.; art juror, Ottawa and Morris (Ill.) high sch. related activities; program dir. United Fund, Ottawa, 1975-76. YMCA Leaders fellow, 1976-77. Mem. Lakeview Center Arts and Scis., Peoria Art Guild. Home and studio: 619 Cornell St Ottawa IL 61350

SETTLE, NORMAN RUGGLES, accountant; b. Harris, Kans., Mar. 21, 1908; s. James Albert and Beatrice Emily (Norman) S.; B.S., Kans. State Coll., Pittsburg, 1927; M.A., U. Iowa, 1940; m. Lucille Anderson, June 21, 1934; 1 son, Gary. Bus. tchr. high sch., Osage City, Kans., 1927-37, Ottawa, 1937-42; project finance officer Nat. Youth Adminstrn., Hutchinson, Kans., 1942-43; with Cornell & Co., 1946-51; with Bartlett, Settle & Edgerle, C.P.A.'s, 1951—; mem. Kans. Bd. Accountancy, 1971-77. Trustee Kans. Soc. C.P.A.'s Ednl. Found. Served with USNR, 1944-46. C.P.A., Kans. Mem. Am. Inst. C.P.A.'s, Kans. Soc. C.P.A.'s (chpt. pres. 1969), Nat. Assn. State Bds. Accountancy, Sigma Tau Gamma, Pi Omega Pi. Mason (K.T.),

Rotarian. Club: Prairie Dunes Country. Home: 2510 Tyler Hutchinson KS 67501 Office: 1020 N Main St Hutchinson KS 67501

SEVERS, EUGENE RYALS, oil co. exec.; b. Des Moines, Oct. 2, 1923; s. Shafter David and Martha Miriam (Ryals) S.; B.A., Drake U., 1949, postgrad., 1949-50; m. Barbara Jean Swanson, June 25, 1949; children—Mary, Robert, Cynthia, John, Steven, Donald. Staff accountant Arthur Andersen & Co., Chgo., 1950-51; staff accountant James C. Addison Co., Des Moines, 1951-52, partner, 1952-53; pres. Macmillan Oil Co. Inc., Des Moines, 1953—. Served with U.S. Army, 1943-46; ETO. C.P.A., Iowa. Mem. Des Moines Oilmen's Club, Toastmasters Internat., Iowa Ind. Oil Jobbers, New Pioneer Gun Club, YMCA, Highland Park Businessmen's Club, Des Moines Musicians Assn., Iowa, Nat. liquid petroleum gas assns., Asso. Gen. Contractors, Aircraft Owners Pilots Assn., Phi Beta Kappa, Phi Sigma Iota. Episcopalian (treas. 1951-53). Home: 4013 29th St Des Moines IA 50310 Office: PO Box 4968 4306 2d Ave Des Moines IA 50306

SEVERSON, LLOYD JOHN, vehicle mfg. co. exec.; b. La Paz, Bolivia, Dec. 28, 1939; s. Lloyd John and Genevra Ramsdell) S.; B.S., U. Wis., 1962; m. Wendy Lou Miller, July 5, 1963; children—John Eric, Jennifer Kate. Buyer, Walker Mfg. Co., Racine, Wis., 1963-66, supr. data processing, Lake Mills, Iowa, 1966-67; data processing mgr. Streater Industries div. Litton, Albert Lea, Minn., 1967-69, 71-72; dir. MIS, EF Johnson Co., Waseca, Minn., 1969-71; dir. info. services Winnebago Industries Inc., Forest City, Iowa, 1972—. Mem. data processing curriculum adv. bd. North Iowa Area Community Coll.; finance dir. Cannon Valley council Girl Scouts U.S.A., 1968-69. Mem. Data Processing Mgmt. Assn., Assn. Systems Mgmt., Soc. Mgmt. Info. Systems., So. Minn. Data Processing Assn. Club: Masons. Home: 214 3d St N Clear Lake IA 50428 Office: PO Box 152 Forest City IA 50436

SEVERSON, ROBERT KEITH, lawyer; b. Duluth, Minn., Jan. 9, 1932; s. Kermit H. and Elin (Nyquist) S.; B.A., U. Minn., 1954; J.D., U. N.D., 1959; m. Nancy E. Browning, June 22, 1957; children—Sondra S., Mark A., Craig B. Admitted to Minn. bar, 1959; practiced in Bemidji, 1959-61, Detroit Lakes, 1964-65, Hallock, 1965—; asst. county atty. 1966—; mem. firm Olson, Kief & Severson, 1959-64; partner Erickson & Severson, 1965, Brink, Sobolik & Severson, 1966—; asst. county atty. Kittson County, 1966—. Mem. Am. Trial Lawyers Assn., Minn., 14th Dist. (pres. 1975) bar assns., Am. Judicature Soc. Mason (Shriner), Eagle, Elk. Address: Hallock MN 56728

SEWARD, ROBERT MORRIS, II, investment banker; b. Indpls., Mar. 19, 1936; s. Robert M. and Mary Ellen (Winks) S.; A.B., DePauw U., 1958; M.B.A., U. Chgo., 1963; children—Linda L., Robert M. Mgmt. com., dir. Smith Barney and Co., N.Y.C., 1959-74; pres. Seward Corp. and Seward Securities, Chgo., 1974—; exec. com. Mesirow and Co., 1977—. Served with U.S. Army, 1958. Mem. Securities Industry Assn., Bond Club N.Y. (United Fund Drive award, 1973), Bond Club Chgo. (United Fund Drive award, 1970), Econ. Club of Chgo., Phi Kappa Psi Alumni Assn. (pres.). Republican. Unitarian. Clubs: Medinah Country; Racquet of N.Y.; Chicago, Union League (Chgo.), Home: 3538 N Greenview St Chicago IL 60657 Office: 135 S LaSalle St Chicago IL 60603

SEWELL, WILLIAM CLYDE, educator; b. East St. Louis, Apr. 7, 1937; s. Nashville Clyde and Zetta Marie (Hurt) S.; student U. Ill., 1960-62, Washington U., 1962-64; B.A., So. Ill. U. at Edwardsville, 1965; Ph.D., Case Western Res. U., 1975; m. Jeanine Delores Katz, Sept. 3, 1966; children—Andrew Russell, Michael Edward. Lectr. philosophy U. Md., College Park, 1970-72; asst. prof. Mich. Technol. U. Houghton, 1972—. Served with USAF, 1955-59. Mem. Assn. Symbolic Logic, Am. Philos. Assn., Philosophy of Sci. Assn. Home: 1300 Birch St Hancock MI 49930 Office: Dept Humanities Mich Technol Univ Houghton MI 49931

SEXTON, LOGAN, mgmt. advisory co. exec.; b. Ky., June 3, 1951; s. Velman and Chelsea (Barton) S.; student (Getty scholar), Ohio No. U., 1969-70; B.S., Cleve. State U., 1974; m. Susan Jayne Gorham, Nov. 8, 1970; children—Kristan Susannah, Matthew Shelton, Autumn Elizabeth. Accountant, Fanner Mfg. Co. (Textron), Cleve., 1971-72; fin. mgr. Com. Corp., Inc., Cleve., 1972-73; adminstr. Mgmt. Advisory and Research Center, Inc., Cleve., 1973-76, treas. M.A.R.C. Inc., Pitts., 1977—, also dir. Vice pres. Jackson-Belden C. of C., 1976-77; mgr. bd. dirs. Kiwanis Internat., Massillon, Ohio. Recipient Outstanding Presentation award M.A.R.C., Inc., 1974. Mem. Massillon Area, Greater Canton chambers commerce, Nat. Assn. Accountants, Am. Acad. Med. Adminstrn., Am. Coll. Nursing Home Adminstrn., Stark County Health Planning Com., Ohio Health Care Assn. Republican. Roman Catholic. Clubs: Kiwanis, Jaycees. Home: 443 Riverview St Canal Fulton OH 44614 Office: 415 W Warrington St Pittsburgh PA 15210

SEXTON, MARGARET DURETA, speech therapist; b. Wells County, Ind., Aug. 7, 1931; d. James Helmuth and Bertha Anna (Kizer) Roberts; B.S., Ball State U., 1952, M.A., 1963; m. Gale Sexton, Nov. 21, 1950; children—Gregg Alan, Donna Sue, Sheila Rene. Speech and hearing clinician Hamilton (Ohio) City Schs., 1955-59, Kettering (Ohio) Pub. Schs., 1959-60; speech, lang. and hearing clinician Muncie (Ind.) Community Schs., 1960—; dir. Psi Iota Xi Summer Clinic, Decatur, Ind., 1964; Psi Iota Xi summer clinician Ball State U., 1965—. Mem. Muncie, Ind. State tchrs. assns., NEA, Ind., Am. (certified in clin. competency in speech pathology) speech and hearing assns., Ind. Council Suprs. Speech and Hearing, Adminstrv. Women's Club, Delta Kappa Gamma. Republican. Baptist. Club: Women of Moose. Compiler, editor curriculum for speech, lang. and hearing clinicians of Muncie Community Schs. Home: 1408 W Main St Muncie IN 47303 Office: 3201 S Macedonia St Muncie IN 47302

SEYBERT, PAUL ELNER, utility co. exec.; b. Howe, Ind., Nov. 10, 1922; s. Lyol E. and Thelma (Kain) S.; B.E.E., Purdue U., 1944; postgrad. Columbia U., 1944, Mass. Inst. Tech., 1945; m. Hilda L. Dippon, June 7, 1947; children—Paula Rae, David Kevin. Indsl. power engr. No. Ind. Pub. Service Co., Hammond, 1947-50, div. supr. indsl. power sales, Michigan City, 1950-60, dist. mgr., South Bend, 1960-63, div. mgr., Michigan City, 1963-72, div. mgr. Fort Wayne, Ind., 1972—; tchr. physics, math., elec. engring. Purdue U., Calumet Campus, 1947-50, bd. advisors Ind. U.-Purdue U., Ft. Wayne; dir. Lincoln Fin. Corp., Lincoln Nat. Bank Trust Co.; tchr. adult classes Michigan City High Sch., 1951-55; co-owner cons. firm Engring. Assos., Michigan City, 1956-60. Vice pres. Better Bus. Bur., 1960; mem. exec. bd. Boy Scouts Am., 1961-73; sec. Conv. and Tourism Bur., 1974-75; mem. Convention and Tourism Authority, 1977-78; bd. dirs. Jr. Achievement; 1st v.p. No. Ind. Econ. Devel. Assn., 1969; mem. LaPorte County (Ind.) Community Devel. Study Commn., 1971-72; pres. bd. trustees Sch. Bd., 1957-60; pres. YMCA, Miss Ind. Pageant, 1964-65; bd. dirs. Urban League of LaPorte County, United Fund, 1971. Served with USNR, 1944-46; PTO. Registered profl. engr., Ind. Mem. Ind. Soc. Profl. Engrs. (1st v.p. 1962-63), Ind. Electric Assn., Ind. Gas Assn., Downtown Ft. Wayne Assn. (dir. 1972-77), Taxpayers Research Assn. (dir. 1972-77), Michigan City C. of C. (pres. 1966-67), NCCJ. Presbyterian (elder, former trustee). Clubs: Masons (32 deg.), Jesters, Shriners (potentate 1974), Elks, Rotary (pres. 1970), Kiwanis (pres. 1957), Pottawattamie Country (pres. 1968), 100%, Summit (pres. 1977-78), Ft. Wayne Country, Quest, Mad Anthonys. Home: 2632 Covington Club Ct Fort Wayne IN 46804 Office: 114 E Wayne St Fort Wayne IN 46802

SEYMOUR, GEORGE EDWARD, psychologist; b. Newark, Feb. 27, 1939; s. George Francis and Ava Burnadette (Simon) S.; A.A., Southwestern Jr. Coll., 1965; B.A., San Diego State Coll., 1969; M.A., San Diego State U., 1973; postgrad. U. Mo., Columbia, 1974—; children—George Earl Charles, Debora Lee Ann. Instr., coordinator spl. tng. project for mentally retarded, San Diego, 1965-66; contract analyst Navy Med. Neuropsychiat. Research Unit, San Diego, 1967-69, research asso., 1969-74; research asst. psychology dept. U. Mo., Columbia, 1974—. Served with USN, 1958-62. Mem. Am. (asso.), Midwestern psychol. assns., Council for Exceptional Children (past pres.), Grad. Student Assn. U. Mo. (rep.-at-large 1974-75, pres. 1975-76). Contbr. articles to profl. lit. Home: 814 Mikel St Columbia MO 65201 Office: Dept Psychology U Mo Columbia MO 65201

SEYMOUR, KEITH GOLDIN, chem. products co. exec.; b. Fairfax, Mo., Jan. 25, 1922; s. Vern V. and Esther Althea (Goldin) S.; A.S., Kemper Mil. Sch., 1941; B.S., Iowa State U., 1943, M.S., 1950; Ph.D., Tex. A. and M. U., 1954; m. Wanda Allegra Cox, Dec. 2, 1943; children—John Kirk, Janette Ann. Farmer, Fairfax, 1946-49; chemist Dow Chem. Co., Freeport, Tex., 1953-59, research specialist, 1959-65, group leader, Midland, Mich., 1965-71, research mgr. agrl. products dept., 1971—. Chmn. Brazosport (Tex.) Area Planning Commn., 1962-64; mem. Lake Jackson (Tex.) City Council, 1964-65. Served with U.S. Army, 1943-46. Decorated Bronze Star. Fellow AAAS; mem. Am. Chem. Soc., Sigma Xi, Phi Kappa Phi. Club: Elks. Research and devel. in agrl. chem. formulations. Home: 6003 Sturgeon Creek Pkwy Midland MI 48640 Office: PO Box 1706 Midland MI 48640

SFIKAS, PETER MICHAEL, lawyer; b. Gary, Ind., Aug. 9, 1937; s. Michael and Helen (Thureanos) S.; B.S., Ind. U., 1959; J.D., Northwestern U., 1962; m. Freida Platon, Apr. 24, 1966; children—Ellen Michelle, Pamela Christine. Admitted to Ill. bar, 1962; atty. Legal Aid Bur., United Charities of Chgo., 1962-63; asso. firm Peterson, Ross, Rall, Barber & Seidel, Chgo., 1963-70, sr. partner, 1970—; instr. Sch. Law, Loyola U. Chgo., 1977—. Mem. com. on rules Ill. Supreme Ct., 1975—; arbitrator Nat. Panel of Arbitrators, 1972—; writer, lectr. program on in-house counsel practice Ill. Inst. for Continuing Legal Edn., 1975. Village prosecutor Village of LaGrange Park (Ill.), 1969-74. Recipient Maurice Weigle award Chgo. Bar Found., 1973. Fellow Am. Bar Found.; mem. Ill. Bar Found. (dir. 1975-77), Am. (chmn. publs. com. of sect. of ins., negligence and compensation law 1973-75), Ill. (gov. 1970-76, mem. assembly 1972-76), Chgo. (vice chmn. spl. task force on appointive selection 1977—) bar assns., Bar Assn. 7th Fed. Circuit (chmn. com. on meetings 1973-75). Mem. Eastern Orthodox Ch. Club: Legal (Chgo.). Contbr. articles to profl. jours. Home: 338 Dover St LaGrange Park IL 60525 Office: 200 E Randolph Dr Chicago IL 60601

SHA, WILLIAM TSENG-LU, nuclear engr.; b. Kiangsu, China, Sept. 13, 1928; s. Chin Fung and Yu Nei (Gee) S.; came to U.S., 1953, naturalized, 1960; Ph.D., Columbia U., 1963; m. Joanne Yung, July 20, 1957; children—Andrea E., Beverly E., William C. Fellow scientist Atomic Power div. Westinghouse Electric Corp., Pitts., 1960-67; sr. nuclear engr. Argonne (Ill.) Nat. Lab., 1967—, chmn. seminar com. Components Tech. div., 1975—. Bd. dirs. Chinese Student and Alumni Service, Chinese Family Camp of Midwest. Mem. Am. Nuclear Soc. Contbr. numerous articles to profl. jours.; editorial bd. Nuclear Engring. and Design. Home: 5812 Dearborn Pkwy Downers Grove IL 60515 Office: 9700 S Cass Ave Argonne IL 60439

SHABAZZ, ABDUL-ALIM, educator; b. Bessemer, Ala., May 22, 1927; s. Lewis and Mary (Roberson) Cross; A.B., Lincoln U., 1949; M.S., Mass. Inst. Tech., 1951; Ph.D., Cornell U., 1955; m. Della Café, Feb. 22, 1968; children—Markus, Suad. Asst. mathematician Cornell Aero. Lab., Buffalo, 1952-53; instr., teaching fellow Cornell U., 1953-55; mathematician metals research lab. Electro Metall. Co., Niagara Falls, N.Y., 1955; asst. prof. math. Tuskegee Inst., 1956-57; asso. prof., chmn. dept. math. Atlanta U., 1957-63; minister Muhammad Mosque 4, dir. edn. Muhammad U. Islam 4, Washington, 1963-75; dir. edn. World Community Islam in West, 1975, dir. adult edn., 1975—; mem. Imam Consultation Bd., Masjid Elijah Muhammad 2, 1976—; adj. prof. math. Union Grad. Sch., Yellow Springs, Ohio, 1975—; ednl. columnist Bilalian News, Chgo., 1975—. Mem. Census Advisory Com. on Black Population for 1980 Census, 1973—. Served with USAAF, 1946-47. Mem. Am. Math. Soc., Math. Assn. Am., Assn. Engring. Edn., Nat. Inst. Sci., AAAS, Nat. Alliance of Black Sch. Educators, Sigma Xi. Home: 8059 S Yates Blvd Chicago IL 60617 Office: 7351 Stony Island Ave Chicago IL 60619

SHACKLETON, CLARENCE JOSEPH, printing co. exec.; b. Quincy, Ill., Jan. 7, 1919; s. Joseph Emery and Clara Bernadine (Kollmeyer) S.; grad. high sch.; m. Elizabeth Ann Byerly, Feb. 4, 1942; children—Barbara Louise (Mrs. John Allen), Dianne Elizabeth (Mrs. David Beckman), David Clarence, Margaret Marie. Typographer, Jost & Kiefer Printing, Quincy, 1946-56, 57-58, Rose Printing Co., Tallahassee, Fla., 1956-57; pres. Quincy Creative Printers, Inc., 1958-71, Royal Printing Co., Quincy, 1966—. Chmn. comml. div. United Fund Drive, 1966. Served with USAAF, 1940-46. Mem. Am. Legion, United Comml. Travelers, Am. Bicentennial Soc., Quincy Typographical Union (pres. 1955, 56). Republican. Roman Catholic. Elk, Moose, Rotarian. Club: Springlake Country. Home: 9 Wilmar Dr Quincy IL 62301 Office: 514 Jersey St Quincy IL 62301

SHADE, WILLARD NORMAN, JR., design engr.; b. Willard, Ohio, Mar. 20, 1947; s. Willard Norman and Aldean Lavonne (Schafer) S.; B.M.E., Ohio State U., 1970, M.S. in Engring., 1970; m. Patricia Jane Wise, Nov. 18, 1967; children—Pamela Lynn, Rebecca Ann. Research asst. Ohio State U. Engring. Experiment Station, Columbus, 1969; process engring. asst. Owens Ill., Inc., Columbus, 1968-69; supr. research Cooper Energy Services, Mt. Vernon, Ohio, 1970-76, design engr., 1976—. Registered profl. engr., Ohio. NSF grad. trainee, 1969-70; recipient Evans Scholarship award, 1970. Mem. ASME (newsletter editor, Columbus chpt. 1975, treas., 1976, vice-chmn. 1977), Soc. for Exptl. Stress Analysis, Instrument Soc. Am., Nat. Soc. Profl. Engrs., Mutual Investment Club of Mt. Vernon, Mt. Vernon Concert Assn., Sigma Xi, Tau Beta Pi, Phi Eta Sigma, Pi Tau Sigma. Lutheran. Contbr. articles to tech. jours. Home: Route 1 Eldon Dr Mount Vernon OH 43050 Office: Cooper Energy Services N Sandusky St Mount Vernon OH 43050

SHADLE, GEORGE MILLER, physician; b. Altoona, Pa., June 21, 1921; B.S., Muskingum Coll., 1943; M.D., Temple U., 1947; M.S., U. Pitts., 1951; m. Dorothy M.; children—Graham, Gilbert, Mary Ellen, Tim; Rotating intern U. Pitts. Med. Center, 1947-48; resident pediatrics Childrens Hosp., Pitts., 1948-50. Diplomate Am. Bd. Pediatrics, Am. Bd. Preventive Medicine. Practice medicine specializing in pediatrics, Pitts., 1958-67, Columbus, Ohio, 1970—; dir. clinics Childrens Hosp., Pitts., 1950-52; pediatrician Well Child Confs., Allegheny County Pub. Health, 1950-52, asso. clin. research, 1952-55; med. coordinator Parke Davis & Co., Detroit, 1955-58; med. officer drug regulatory affairs Roche Labs., Nutley, N.J., 1967-71; pediatric cons. Ohio Dept. Health, Columbus, 1971, dept. dir., chief Maternal and Child Health Services, 1972-74, spl. asst. to dir. health, 1974-75, chief, div. Occupational Health, 1975—, also chmn. Sickle Cell Adv. Council, chmn. Pub. Employees Safety and Health Program; asst. prof. pediatrics U. Pitts. Med. Sch., 1958-67; clin. asst. prof. preventive medicine Ohio State U., 1971—, clin. asst. prof. dept. pediatrics, 1971—. Chmn., Cerebral Palsy Found. of Childrens Hosp., Pitts., 1951-54; chmn. budget com. United Fund for Detroit, 1955-58; mem. Gov.'s Occupational Health Task Force, 1975—; mem. adv. staff Ohio Com. on Trauma, 1975—; bd. dirs. Cerebral Palsy of Pitts. Mem. Am. Acad. Pediatrics (Ohio chpt.), Am., Ohio pub. health assns., Ohio Med. Assn., Columbus and Franklin County Med. Soc., Am. Confs. Govtl. and Indsl. Hygiene, Occupational Medicine Assn., Am. Indsl. Hygiene Assn., Assn. Am. Colls. and Univs., N.Y. Acad. Scis., Am. Med. Writers Assn., Am. Sch. Health Assn. Home: 124 Glen Circle Worthington OH 43085 Office: Ohio Dept Health PO Box 118 450 E Town St Columbus OH 43216

SHAEFFER, JAMES HENRY, dentist; b. Wabasso, Minn., Oct. 22, 1906; s. Henry W. and Mary (O'Neil) S.; D.D.S., Creighton U., 1928; m. Maylou E. Riedesel, Dec. 29, 1928; children—James, JoAnn (Mrs. L. Fogelman), John. Practice dentistry, Canova, S.D., 1928-30, Montrose, S.D., 1930-35, Parker, S.D., 1935—. Pres. S.D. Wildlife Fedn., 1951-52, Nat. Wildlife Fedn., 1970-71. Mem. Am., S.D. (pres. 1951-52) dental assns., Internat., Am. colls. dentists, S.D. Cancer Soc. (pres. 1955-58). Democrat. Roman Catholic. Home: 100 N Main St Parker SD 57053 Office: Post Office Bldg Parker SD 57053

SHAEVSKY, MARK, lawyer; b. Harbin, Manchuria, China, Dec. 2, 1935; s. Tolio and Rae (Weinstein) S.; came to U.S., 1938, naturalized, 1944; student Wayne State U., 1952-53; B.A. with highest distinction, U. Mich., 1956, J.D. with highest distinction, 1959; m. Lois Ann Levi, Aug. 2, 1964; children—Thomas Lyle, Lawrence Keith. Admitted to Mich. bar, 1959; legal asst. to chief judge Theodore Levin, U.S. Dist. Ct., Detroit, 1960-61; with firm of Honigman, Miller, Schwartz and Cohn, Detroit, 1961-69, sr. partner, 1969—; sec., gen. counsel Pulte Home Corp., W. Bloomfield, Mich., 1974—; dir. Schostak Bros. & Co., Inc., Southfield, Mich., 1977—; comml. arbitrator Am. Arbitration Assn., Detroit, 1974; instr. law Wayne State U. Law Sch., Detroit, 1961-64. Dir., Detroit Men's ORT, 1969—; sec., dir. Am. Friends of Hebrew U., Detroit, 1976—; trustee Jewish Vocat. Services, Detroit, 1973-76; exec. bd. Am. Jewish Com., Detroit, 1965-74. Served with U.S. Army, 1959-60. Recipient Burton Abstract fellowship award, U. Mich. Law Sch., 1958. Mem. Mich., Am., Fed. bar assns., Am. Judicature Soc., Am. Arbitration Assn., Order of the Coif, Phi Beta Kappa. Jewish. Clubs: Franklin Hills Country, Standard of Detroit. Asst. editor Mich. Law Review, 1958-59; contbr. numerous articles to profl. jours. Home: 4334 Stoneleigh Rd Bloomfield Hills MI 48013 Office: 2290 First Nat Bldg Detroit MI 48226

SHAFE, MARIE CROSS, counseling psychologist, educator; b. Crisp County, Ga., May 3, 1946; d. Otis W. and Minnie Lou (Jones) Cross; A.B., W. Ga. Coll., 1968, Ed.M., 1970; Ed.D., Ind. U., 1976; m. Charles C. Shafe, Sept. 2, 1967. Instr. gen. edn. U.S. Armed Forces Inst., Oakland, Calif., 1969; grad. asst., coordinator tchr. edn. program. W. Ga. Coll., Carrollton, 1969-70; coordinator ednl. and career exploration program Bibb County schs., Macon, Ga., 1970-71; sch. counselor Houston County schs., Warner Robins, Ca., 1971-73, No. Law Community Sch., Bedford, Ind., 1973-74; cons., intern State Dept. of Pub. Instrn., Indpls., 1974-75; cons. Indpls. pub. schs., 1976; interim prof. counseling and guidance Ind. U., Bloomington, 1976; asst. prof. applied behavioral sci., ednl. leadership Ohio U., Athens, 1976—; also cons. Bd. dirs., chmn. pub. edn. com. Athens County chpt. Am. Cancer Soc. Mem. Am. Psychol. Assn., Nat. Vocat. Guidance Assn., Am. (sec.-treas. Ind. chpt.), Ohio personnel and guidance assns., Assn. for Counselor Edn. and Supervision, Assn. of Humanistic Edn. and Devel., Phi Delta Kappa. Democrat. Presbyterian. Contbr. articles to profl. jours. Home: 129 La Mar Dr Athens OH 45701 Office: 207 McCracken Hall Ohio U Athens OH 45701

SHAFER, WILMA CLARE, educator; b. Evansville, Ind., Apr. 6, 1916; d. Alfred Bruce and Lillian (Collins) Cox; student Ind. U., 1934-36; B.A., U. Evansville, 1951; M.A., Ind. U., 1958, Ed.D., 1962; m. Ivan John Shafer, Dec. 22, 1940; children—John Allan, David Bruce (dec.). Tchr. pub. schs., Daviess County, Ind., 1936-42, 44-46, Dubois County, Ind., 1943-44, Vanderburg County, Ind., 1947-60; mem. faculty U. Evansville, 1960—, prof. edn., 1967—, dir. elementary edn. and early learning, 1970—. Mem. council Ind. Adv. Council Tchr. Certifacation and Licensing, 1960-63, 71-72; dir. Head Start Orientation, 1967, project dir., supplementary tng., 1971—. Mem. Am. Bus. Women's Assn. (pres. 1955-56), Ind. Tchr. Educator's Conf. (chmn. steering com. 1971-72), D.A.R. (chaplain, 1970-71), Am. Assn. U. Women (state pres. 1971-73), Ind. Assn. Childhood Edn. (pres. 1960-62), Ind. Assn. Tchr. Edn. (pres. 1968-69), Phi Kappa Phi, Pi Lambda Theta (v.p., 1968-72, nat. pres. 1973—), Delta Kappa Gamma, Phi Mu, Beta Sigma Phi. Mem. Daus. of Nile. Clubs: Women's Rotary, Altrusa Internat. Guest editor Educational Horizons, winter 1974. Home: 2621 Oak Hill Rd Evansville IN 47711

SHAFFER, HERBERT, JR., business exec.; b. Cin., Aug. 21, 1925; s. Herbert and Dorothy Sybil (Guckenberger) S.; B.A., Yale U., 1948; m. Mary Ann Hinsch, Apr. 27, 1957; children—Gregory, Pamela, Geoffrey. Asst. mgr. First Nat. City Bank, Tokyo, 1949-52; asst. nat. div. First Nat. City Bank, N.Y.C., 1952-55; asst. v.p. Central Bancorp., Cin., 1956-64; ltd. partner Harrison & Co., Cin., 1964-77; exec. v.p. Riverbend Group, Cin., 1977—. Chmn. Cancer Control Council, 1976—; chmn. parish council St. Francis de Sales Ch., 1977—; bd. dirs. United Cerebral Palsy Cin., 1975—. Served with U.S. Army, 1943-45. Republican. Roman Catholic. Clubs: Cin. Country, Cin. Racquet, Cin. Tennis, Miami. Home: 2546 Perkins Ln Cincinnati OH 45208 Office: 4205 Carew Tower Cincinnati OH 45202

SHAFFER, JAMES GRANT, hosp. adminstr.; b. Washington, Kans., Jan. 17, 1913; s. Bowen Ross and Myrtle Katherine (Worley) S.; B.S., Manchester Coll., 1935, D.Sc., 1973; D.Sc., Johns Hopkins, 1940; m. Esther Elizabeth Willard, Sept. 3, 1939; children—Carol (Mrs. Wesley Stieg), Susan (Mrs. John Willard), Janet (Mrs. Gregory Harsha), Nancy. Tchr., Jackson Twp. High Sch., Flint, Ind., 1935-36, Jefferson Twp. High Sch., Ossian, Ind., 1936-37; student instr. immunology and filterable viruses Johns Hopkins, Balt., 1937-40, instr., 1940-42; med. research biologist Am. Cyanamid Co., Stamford, Conn., 1942-43; asst. prof. preventive medicine Vanderbilt U. Sch. Medicine, Nashville, 1946-48, vis. prof. bacteriology, dept. biology, 1947-48; asso. prof. bacteriology and virology, U. Louisville Sch. Medicine, 1948-52; dir. labs. Louisville Children's Hosp., 1948-50, microbiologist, 1950-52; prof., chmn. dept. microbiology and pub. health Chgo. Med. Sch., 1952-60, asso. dean, prof. microbiology, 1967-74; dir. microbiology and hosp. epidemiology Luth. Gen. Hosp., Park Ridge, Ill., 1960-67, cons. hosp. epidemiology, 1967-74; dir. ednl. and profl. programs Mt. Sinai Hosp. Med. Center of Chgo., 1974—; prof. microbiology Rush U., Chgo., 1975—. Professorial lectr. microbiology U. Chgo., 1965-68; cons. VA Hosp., Hines, Ill., 1972—;

coordinator devel. of projected urban-oriented med. sch. Mt. Sinai Hosp. Med. Center and Roosevelt U., 1974—. Pres. P.T.A., Lincoln Sch., Elmhurst, Ill., 1956-57. Mem. sch. bd. dist. 46 Elmhurst Elementary Sch., 1958-67. Served to maj. AUS, 1943-46. Recipient Outstanding Alumni award Manchester Coll., 1945, Award of Merit, Chgo. Tech. Socs. Council, 1969. Fellow Am. Pub. Health Assn. (mem. action bd. 1972—), Am. Inst. Chemists, Am. Acad. Microbiology; mem. Am. Soc. Microbiology, A.A.A.S., Am. Soc. Tropical Medicine and Hygiene, Soc. Ill. Bacteriologists, Ill. Pub. Health Assn., Assn. Tchrs. Preventive Medicine, Royal Soc. Health, Alumni Assn. Manchester Coll. (pres. 1962-63), Sigma Xi, Alpha Omega Alpha, Delta Omega. Author: Amebiasis: A Biomedical Problem, 1965. Contbr. to publs. in field. Home: 605 Swain Av Elmhurst IL 60126 Office: 15th St and California Av Chicago IL 60608

SHAFFER, WALTER LOUIS, III, vending co. exec.; b. Topeka, Oct. 17, 1943; s. Walter Louis and Helen Virginia (Pensinger) S.; B.S. in Edn., U. Kans., 1965; m. Judith D. Vogelsang, Feb. 10, 1967; children—William Louis, Sherry Dianne. Tchr., Park Hill R-V Schs., Parkville, Mo., 1966-70; partner Dr. Pepper Royal Crown Bottling Co., Chillicothe, Mo., 1970—, Shaffer Vending Co., Chillicothe, 1970—; dir. Shaffer Oil, Inc., Burlington, Kan. Livingston County R-II Schs. rep. Mo. Ednl. Conf., 1973; mem. Chillicothe Bd. Parks and Recreation, 1972, pres.; county fin. chmn. Republican Congl. candidate, 1972; deacon Presbyn. Ch., 1975-77, elder, 1978—. Named an Outstanding Young Man in Am., 1974. Mem. Mo. (internal v.p. 1974), Chillicothe Jaycees (pres. 1972-73), Sigma Nu. Home: 914 Summit Chillicothe MO 64601 Office: 1201 Washington Chillicothe MO 64601

SHAHIDI, MASSOUD MIR, opthalmologist; b. Meshed, Iran, Dec. 21, 1932; s. Alireza Mir and Monir Mir Shahidi; M.D., U. Tehran, 1953; postgrad. U. Minn., 1961-63, Tulane U., 1964-67; m. Ch. Kowalski, Dec. 21, 1961; 1 son, Robert. Came to U.S., 1959, naturalized, 1969. Intern, Univ. Hosps., Tehran, Swedish Hosp., Mpls., 1959-60; resident Chgo. Eye, Ear, Nose & Throat Hosp., 1960-62; practice medicine, specializing in ophthalmology, Iran, 1953-59, McFarland Clinic, Ames, Iowa, 1968—. Fellow A.C.S.; mem. A.M.A., Am. Assn. Ophthalmology and Otolaryngology, Am. Acad. Ophthalmology, Iowa Med. Soc. Moslim. Mason, Rotarian. Home: 3213 Joy Circle Ames IA 50010 Office: 1200 Douglas St Ames IA 50010

SHAHIDI, NASROLLAH THOMAS, physician, educator; b. Meshed, Iran, Dec. 11, 1926; s. Taber and Robab (Habib) S., came to U.S., 1956, naturalized, 1970; B.S., U. Montpellier (France), 1947; M.D. mention tres honorable, Sorbonne, 1954; m. Mary Alice Vandervoort, Sept. 29, 1962; children—John, Caroline, Mark. Resident pediatrics Hopital des Enfants Malades, Paris, 1954-56; asst. resident pediatrics Balt. City Hosp., 1956-57; research fellow pediatrics Harvard Med. Sch., 1957-60, instr. pediatrics, 1960-63; asst. physician Children's Hosp. Med. Center, Boston, 1960-63; vis. prof. pediatrics Kinderspital, Zurich, Switzerland, also vis. investigator Swiss Nat. Found., 1964-66; asso. prof. pediatrics U. Wis. Center for Health Scis., also hematologist Children's Hosp., Madison, Wis., 1966-70; prof. pediatrics, dir. pediatric hematology U. Wis. Center Health Scis., Madison, 1970—. Pediatric rep. Wis. Clin. Cancer Center, 1973; cons. Madison Gen. Hosp., St. Mary's Hosp., 1966—; guest lectr., vis. prof. various profl. groups and univs. Recipient numerous pvt. and govt. grants. Diplomate Am. Bd. Pediatrics. Mem. Am., Midwest pediatric socs., Am. Soc. Hematology, Am. Soc. Pediatric Research, Central Soc. Clin. Research, Chilean Hematology Soc. (hon.), Dominican Republic Pediatric Soc. (hon.), Royal Soc. (affiliate). Contbr. articles to med. jours.; reviewer for Jour. Biol. Chemistry, Jour. Clin. Investigation, Jour. Lab. and Clin. Medicine, New Eng. Jour. Medicine; recognized for treatment of aplastic anemia. Home: 509 Ozark Trail Madison WI 53705

SHALLENBERGER, HUGH DARSIE, psychologist; b. Hershey, Pa., Apr. 5, 1935; s. Henry and Gertrude Geneva (Herrington) S.; m. Leigh Adriana Hollis, Mar. 24, 1962; children—Jenny, Hugh Darsie. A.B., Depauw U., 1957; M.A., U. Mo., Columbia, 1960, Ph.D., 1975. Served with USAF, 1961-65; asst. instr. U. Mo., Columbia, 1967-71; instr. William Woods Coll., 1971—; dir. research Fulton (Mo.) State Hosp., 1971—, asst. supt. treatment, 1976—. Mem. Am., Mo. psychol. assns., Soc. Psychol. Research. Contbr. articles to med. jours. Home: 2805 Skye Wynd Columbia MO 65201 Office: Fulton State Hosp Fulton MO 65251

SHALON, YEHUDA, chemist; b. Moiseiu, Maramuresh, Rumania, June 20, 1928; s. Solomon and Yehudith (Abush) Gruber; M.Sc.Ag., Hebrew U., Jerusalem, 1953; Ph.D. in Med. Chemistry., 1970; m. Hana Eliasoff, June 6, 1956; children—Tadmor, Ilsar, Tidhar. Research asst., dairy lab. and animal nutrition lab. Faculty Agr. Hebrew U., Rechovot, Israel, 1955-58; research asso., instr. organic chemistry Sch. Pharmacy, Jerusalem, 1963-70; analytical and research chemist Inst. Standardization of Pharms., Israeli Ministry Health, Jerusalem, 1958-63; postdoctoral fellow Worcester Found. Exptl. Biology, Shrewsbury, Mass., 1970-71; postdoctoral fellow and research asso., biochemistry dept. St. Louis U., 1971-73; chemist, dir. lipid research and prodn. Sigma Internat. Chem. Co., St. Louis, 1973—; tchr. Agrl. High Sch., Ein Karem, Jerusalem; chmn. agrl. student orgn., Rechovot, 1958-60. Served with Israeli Army, 1949-51. Mem. Am. Chem. Soc., Sigma Xi. Democrat. Patentee steroidal field. Home: 7640 Walinca Terr Clayton MO 63105 Office: Sigma Chemical Co PO Box 14508 St Louis MO 63178

SHALOWITZ, MERVIN, physician; b. Chgo., July 21, 1926; s. Isadore and Sylvia (Hammerman) S.; A.B., Johns Hopkins U., 1948; M.D., Loyola U., Chgo., 1950; m. Aileen Goldstein, July 4, 1948; children—Joel Ira, Nancy Lee, Howard Arlan, Steven David. Intern, Mt. Sinai Hosp., Chgo., 1950-51, resident in pathology, 1951-52; resident in internal medicine Hines (Ill.) Hosp., 1953-54; practice medicine specializing in internal medicine, Skokie, Ill., 1955—; clin. prof. medicine Loyola U., Maywood, Ill., 1958—; exec. dir. Intergroup Prepaid Health Services, Chgo., 1972—; corporate med. cons. Brunswick Corp., Skokie. Chmn., Ill. State Scholarship Commn., 1974-76. Fellow A.C.P.; mem. AMA, Am. Soc. Clin. Pathology, Am. Heart Assn., Inst. Medicine Chgo., Am. Soc. Internal Medicine (trustee), Am. Acad. Med. Dirs. (trustee). Contbr. numerous articles in field to med. jours. Office: 4801 Church St Skokie IL 60076

SHANAFIELD, HAROLD ARTHUR, educator; b. South Bend, Ind., Nov. 26, 1912; s. Harry Bacon and Anna (Paulsen) S.; B.A., U. Notre Dame; M.S.J., M.A., Northwestern U.; M.Ed., Chgo. State U.; m. Margaret Ann Goodman, Nov. 23, 1939; 1 son, Harold A. Copy editor Chicago Herald American, 1945-46; night picture editor Chgo. Sun-Times, 1946-47; mng. editor Elec. Dealer, Chgo., 1947-52; editor, mgr. Florists' Telegraph Delivery News, Detroit, 1952-61; asst. mng. editor Am. Med. Assn. Journal, Chgo., 1961-62; asst. dean Northwestern U., Chicago-Evanston campus, evening divs., 1962-73; with Chgo. Bd. Edn., 1973—. Vice chmn., bd. visitors Freedoms Found. at Valley Forge. Served to capt. USCGR, 1945—. Bd. dirs. Northwestern U. and Alumni Council, Am. Bus. Writing Assn., Assn. of Evening Univs., Quill and Scroll (lifetime faculty mem.), Nat. Sojourners (pres. Chgo. chpt. 1971), Ind. Soc. Chgo. (resident v.p. 1975—), Delta Mu Delta, Phi Chi Theta, Delta Sigma Pi, Sigma Delta Chi, Iota Sigma Epsilon. Mason (Shriner). Clubs: Chicago Press, North Shore Shrine (pres. 1970); Chicago Headline; Star Craft of Ill. (sec. 1972-77, pres. 1977-78). Editor Scottish Rite publs., 1976—. Home: 2448 Marcy Ave Evanston IL 60201

SHANAHAN, ELWILL MATTSON, state ofcl.; b. Salina, Kans., Sept. 22, 1912; d. August G. and Adine (Peterson) Mattson; R.N., Swedish Covenant Hosp., Chgo.; m. Paul R. Shanahan, Oct. 13, 1951 (dec. Apr. 1966); m. 2d, W. Keith Weltmer, July 11, 1977. Sec. of state State of Kans., Topeka, 1966—. Mem. pres.'s adv. council Marymount Coll., Salina. Mem. Nat. Assn. Secs. of State (pres. 1976), Topeka Am. Bus. Women's Asso., Assn. U.S. Army, Lake Wabaunsee Sportsmens Assn., Shawnee Sportsmen, Native Sons and Daus. Kans., Beta Sigma Phi (hon.). Republican. Club: Topeka Soroptimist (hon.). Home: 1320 W 27th St Topeka KS 66611 Office: State Capitol Bldg Topeka KS 66612

SHANAHAN, MICHAEL FRANCIS, computer co. exec.; b. St. Louis, Oct. 29, 1939; s. James John and Mary Agnes (Foley) S.; B.S., St. Louis U., 1961; postgrad. Washington U., St. Louis, 1964; m. Mary Ann Barrett, Aug. 24, 1963; children—Megan Elizabeth, Michael Francis, Maureen Patricia. With McDonnell Douglas Automation Co., St. Louis, 1962-73, sales mgr., 1969-71, br. mgr., 1971-72, area mgr. Southwestern area, 1972-73; v.p. marketing Numerical Control, Inc., St. Louis, 1973-74, pres., 1974—, also dir.; dir. Biomed. Systems, Inc., St. Louis. Trustee Whispering Hills, 1969, 70. Served with U.S. Army, 1961. Mem. Data Processing Mgmt. Assn., Sales and Marketing Execs. St. Louis (Distinguished Salesman award 1967), Phi Kappa Theta Alumni Assn. K.C. Home: 12751 Whispering Hills Lane St Louis MO 63141 Office: Numerical Control Inc 12115 Lackland Rd St Louis MO 63141

SHANAHAN, WILLIAM JOSEPH, mgmt. cons.; b. Chgo., Sept. 18, 1935; s. Joseph Francis and Dorothy Virginia (Ferguson) S.; B.S., Loyola U., Chgo., 1957, Ph.D., 1966; grad. Sch. Alcohol Studies Rutgers U., summer 1975; m. Patricia Ruth Mayer, Jan. 16, 1972; children—Josephine, Paul, William Joseph. Teaching asst. Loyola U., Chgo., 1960-62; instr. Mundelein Coll., Chgo., 1962-65; asst. prof. Idaho State U., Pocatello, 1965-68, asso. prof. English, 1968-70; sales rep. Globe Book Co., N.Y.C., 1970-72; editorial dir. Learning Trends, Inc. div. Globe Book Co., N.Y.C., 1972-73; mng. editor lang. arts Charles E. Merrill Pub. Co., Columbus, O., 1973-74; occupational cons. Dept. Health, Columbus, 1974-76; mgmt. cons. Labor-Mgmt. Task force Nat. Council on Alcoholism, Cin., 1976—. Instr., Am. Inst. Banking, Chgo., 1960-65; jazz trumpet player, co-leader Pocatello Big Band, 1966-70. Served with U.S. Army, 1958-59. Recipient Arion award, 1953. Mem. Modern Lang. Assn. Am. Author: (mus. comedy) The Major and the Millionaire, 1959; (with Wilbur Huck) The Modern Short Story, 1968; (with Charles Kegel) Lyric Poems on Twelve Themes, 1970; (with Robert Pierce) Copouts: Resistance to Occupational Alcoholism Programs; contbr. short stories, revs. to profl. publs. Home: 607 E Chestnut St Oxford OH 45056

SHANER, CHARLES HENRY, dentist; b. Oil City, Pa., Sept. 15, 1922; s. Charles Henry and Lucy Margaret (Reid) S.; student Clarion State Coll., 1941-42, Bucknell U., 1943; D.D.S., U. Ill., 1943; m. Janis Dickey, June 16, 1945; children—Laurel Ann, Kathy Jean, David Edward. Pvt. practice dentistry, Mount Prospect, Ill., 1948—. Chmn. dental hygiene adv. com. Harper Coll., 1968-76. Mem. Bd. Edn., Dist. 224, Barrington, Ill., 1965-68. Served with USNR, 1942-45, 51-52. Recipient 1st Ann. Distinguished Mem. award Ill. Dental Soc., 1974. Fellow Am. Coll. Dentists, Internat. Coll. Dentists; mem. Chgo. Dental Soc. (pres. 1968-69), Sigma Chi, Delta Sigma Delta. Mason (Shriner), Rotarian (dist. gov. 1973-74). Clubs: Executive Sportsmen (Chicago); Biltmore Country (Barrington, Ill.). Home: 10 Tioga Trail Barrington IL 60010 Office: 401 W Prospect Ave Mount Prospect IL 60056

SHANES, ROBERT EDWARD, ins. co. exec.; b. Keokuk, Iowa, July 17, 1927; s. John Sanford and Lurena Rose (Grinstead) S.; student Northeast Mo. U., Kirksville, 1947-48; m. Berneice Peck, May 1, 1966; 1 dau., Rose Mary; 1 dau. by previous marriage, Brenda Kay (Mrs. Buddie C. Wilson). Sec., agt. Farm Mut. Ins. Co., Memphis, Mo., 1957—, now sec., mgr. sec.-treas. Memphis Loan and Bldg. Assn., 1967—, also dir. Served with USNR, 1945-46; PTO. Mem. C. of C., Mo. Assn. Farm Mut. Ins. Cos. (pres. 1973-74, dir., bd. govs., 1968-74), V.F.W., Am. Legion. Mem. Christian Ch. Democrat. Elk. Home: Route 3 Memphis MO 63555 Office: 123 E Monroe St Memphis MO 63555

SHANKS, MARY ELMA WINDIATE, hosp. exec.; b. Pontiac, Mich., Aug. 2, 1911; d. William Alfred and Rosa (Nelsey) Windiate; student U. Ill., 1931; m. Leslie Talbot Shanks, Dec. 23, 1933; children—Nancy Sue (Mrs. John T. Kennedy), William L. With Community Nat. Bank, Pontiac, 1933-51; supr. warrent squad U.S. Internal Revenue Bur., Pontiac, 1951-55; dir. reimbursement Oakland County Bd. Auditors, Pontiac, 1955-76; reimbursement officer Northville (Mich.) State Hosp., 1976-77, Muskegon (Mich.) Developmental Center, 1977—. Mem. adv. group mental health code implementation project State of Mich. Dept. Mental Health, 1974. Mem. Nat. (v.p. 1966-67, pres. 1967-68, chmn. site com. 1974-75, ability to pay chmn. 1976-77), Mich. (chmn. 1970—) reimbursement officers assns., Greater Detroit Area Hosp. Credit Assn. (mem. inst. com. 1970—, chmn. 1971-72, pres. 1973-74, history chmn. 1974-75). Presbyn. Club: Altrusa (local past pres., bd. dirs., dist. treas. 1964-67, internat. membership chmn. 1967—, dist. gov. 1970-72, dist. dir. 1972—, internat. resolutions com. 1973—, chmn. fund-raising 1975-76). Address: 740 Wendover Blvd Muskegon MI 49441

SHANNON, GERALD TIMOTHY, mfg. co. exec.; b. Black River, N.Y., May 26, 1923; s. John Thomas and Hazel (Maxim) S.; B.S., Clarkson Coll. Tech., 1951; m. Mary T. McDonald, Oct. 23, 1954; children—Timothy, Terry, Patricia, Kathleen, Thomas. Capacitor, Gen. Electric Co., Schenectady 1951-63; exec. v.p. Universal Mfg. Co., Bridgeport, Conn., 1963-70; pres. Electro Systems, Inc., Richmond, Calif., 1970-71; pres. Modular Med. Structures, Union, N.J., 1971-72; pres. Lindsay div. Ecodyne Corp., St. Paul, 1972-77; v.p. Ecodyne Corp., Chgo., 1977—. Served with USNR, 1942-46. Mem. Water Quality Assn. (v.p.), Minn Water Conditioning Assn. (dir.), St. Paul Area C. of C. (dir.). Roman Catholic. Clubs: Rotary, Pool and Yacht, St. Croix Yacht, Mendakota Country, Met. (Chgo.); Minn. Home: 1278 Laura St St Paul MN 55118 Office: PO Box 43420 St Paul MN 55164

SHAPIN, JOHN LAWRENCE, direct mail advt. co. exec.; b. Chgo., Aug. 8, 1934; s. Tom Leon and Lucile (Rosenbush) S.; B.A. in Journalism, U. Ala., 1957; m. Margaret Ellen Levy, Apr. 10, 1960; children—Jean Ellen, Patricia Ann, Andrew John. Mgr. Midwest sales Bay State Thread Co., Chgo., 1960-63; v.p. Adams of Chgo., Inc., 1964-70, exec. v.p., 1970—. Served with U.S. Navy, 1957-60. Mem. Chgo. Assn. Direct Mktg. (dir. 1971-74, v.p. 1973-74). Club: Standard (Chgo.). Office: 333 N Michigan Ave Chicago IL 60601

SHAPIRO, ALVIN, mech. engr.; b. Jersey City, Apr. 20, 1930; s. Edward and Sophie (Green) S.; B.M.E., Bklyn. Poly. Inst., 1951; M.S., U. Cin., 1962, Ph.D., 1968; m. Sharon Ullner, June 6, 1971; children—Michael, Benjamin, Jon, Joshua, Nathaniel. Mech. research engr. Allis-Chalmers Mfg. Co., Milw., 1955-56; thermodynamic cycle analyst Gen. Electric Co., Evendale, Ohio, 1958-61; asso. prof. dept. chem. and nuclear engring. U. Cin., 1962—. Served with USNR, 1951-54. Mem. Am. Nuclear Soc., Am. Phys. Soc., Sigma Xi. Home: 1538 Corvallis Ave Cincinnati OH 45237 Office: Mail Location 163 U Cin Cincinnati OH 45221

SHAPIRO, DAVID CHARLES, dentist, state senator; b. Mendota, Ill., Feb. 16, 1925; s. Hymen and Minnie (Sprizer) S.; student Stanford, 1943-44; B.S., U. Ill. at Chgo., 1950, D.D.S., 1952; m. Norma Jean Hall, Sept. 15, 1947; children—Sarah Beth, Deborah Leah, Margaret Sue, Edward Henry, Michael Andrew, Elizabeth Ann, Daniel Hall. Pvt. practice dentistry, Amboy, Ill., 1952—; pres. Farmer's Telephone Co., Franklin Grove, Ill., 1963; dir. First Nat. Bank, Amboy. City alderman, Amboy, 1961-69; pres. Lee County Bd. Health, Dixon, Ill., 1960-69; bd. mem. Sch. Dist. 272, 1961-69; mem. Ill. Ho. of Reps. from 35th Dist., 1969-73, mem. coms. county and twp. affairs, hwys. and traffic safety, edn., chmn. sub-com. twp. affairs, vice chmn. elementary and secondary edn. com., mem. toll road adv. com., interim com. on gov.'s appointments to state toll hwy. authority, narcotic adv. council; mem. Ill. Senate, 1973—, vice chmn. edn. com., chmn. pub. employees pension laws commn., minority leader, 1977—. Dir. Amboy Pub. Hosp. Served with AUS, 1943-46. Decorated Bronze Star; named Outstanding Freshman Legislator of 76th Gen. Assembly, Outstanding Freshman Senator of 78th Gen. Assembly; recipient Outstanding Legislator award Ill. Community Coll. Trustees Assn., award of recognition Ill. Police Assn. Mem. Am., Ill. (Distinguished Mem. award 1976), Whiteside-Lee (pres. 1962—) dental socs., Ill. Assn. Bds. Health (pres. 1964), Amboy C. of C., Am. Legion. Republican. Mason, Elk, Lion. Home: 32 N Jefferson St Amboy IL 61310 Office: 4 S Jones St Amboy IL 61310

SHAPIRO, EDWARD, educator; b. Toledo, July 19, 1920; s. Benjamin and Ida (Lafer) S.; B.A., U. Toledo, 1942; postgrad. U. Mich., summer 1942; M.A., Ohio State U., 1945; M.A., Harvard U., 1947, Ph.D., 1950. Instr. econs. Wayne U., Detroit, 1947-50; financial economist Dept. Commerce, Washington, 1951; dist. economist Detroit dist. office OPS, 1952-53; owner-dir. Bus. Research Assos., Detroit, 1953-61; asso. prof. econs. U. Detroit, 1961-66, Wayne State U., Detroit, 1966-67; prof. econs. U. Toledo, 1967—; vis. prof. econs. Calif. State U. at Long Beach, 1970-71, U. East Anglia, Norwich, Eng., 1975. Served with U.S. Army, 1942-43. Mem. Am. Econ. Assn., Royal Econ. Soc., Phi Kappa Phi. Author: Macroeconomic Analysis, 4th edit., 1978; Understanding Money, 1975. Home: 2744 Farrington Rd Toledo OH 43606

SHAPIRO, MAYNARD IRWIN, physician, educator; b. Chgo., Dec. 18, 1914; B.S., U. Ill., 1937, C.M., 1939, M.D., 1940; m. Lenore M. Gold, Jan. 16, 1948, 1 dau., Juli Ann. Intern Mount Sinai Hosp., Chgo., 1939-40, resident, 1940-41; practice medicine specializing in family practice, Chgo., 1946—; active staff dept. gen. practice Jackson Park Hosp., dir. dept. phys. medicine and rehab., pres. med. staff, 1975-77, also v.p. med. administration and acad. affairs; past clin. asst. surgery, Mt. Sinai Hosp.; clin. prof. family medicine Chgo. Med. Sch. Bd. dirs. Family Health Found. Am., Inst. Sex Edn.; mem. regional adv. group Ill. Regional Med. Program; chmn. profl. adv. council Nat. Easter Seal Soc.; mem. Citizens Alliance for VD Awareness. Fellow Am Occupational Med. Assn., Acad. Psychosomatic Medicine, Am. Geriatrics Soc., Central States Soc. Indsl. Medicine and Surgery, Inst. Medicine Chgo.; mem. AMA, Ill. State (house dels.), Chgo. (council) med. socs., Chgo. Found. Med. Care (pres.), Am. (pres. 1968-69), Ill. (pres.) acads. family physicians, Pan Am. Med. Assn., Am. Congress Rehab. Medicine, Assn. Hosp. Med. Edn., Am. Acad. Med. Adminstrs., Assn. Am. Med. Colls., Soc. Tchrs. Family Medicine, Ill. Soc. Phys. Medicine and Rehab., Chgo. Soc. Indsl. Medicine and Surgery (pres.). Home: 505 N Lake Shore Dr Apt 5707 Chicago IL 60611 Office: 7531 Stony Island Ave Chicago IL 60649

SHAPIRO, ROBERT DONALD, actuary; b. Milw., Sept. 11, 1942; s. Leonard Samuel and Adeline Ruth (Arnovitz) S.; B.S. with honors, U. Wis., 1964; m. Sandra Lee Glinberg, June 21, 1964; children—Lee Evan, Stacy Ellen, Jenifer Erin. Actuarial trainee Northwestern Mut. Life Ins., Milw., 1964-65; cons. actuary Milliman & Robertson, Inc., Milw., 1965—. C.L.U. Fellow Soc. Actuaries, Conf. of Actuaries in Pub. Practice; mem. Am. Acad. Actuaries. Contbr. articles to profl. lit. Home: 110 W Krause Pl Milwaukee WI 53217 Office: 200 Executive Dr Brookfield WI 53005

SHAPIRO, SAMUEL H., lawyer, former gov. Ill.; b. Apr. 25, 1907; student St. Viator Coll., 1924: student U. Ill., 1925-29, J.D., 1929; m. Gertrude Adelman 1939. City atty., Kankakee, Ill., 1933-35; state's atty. Kankakee County, 1936-40; mem. Ill. Gen. Assembly, 1947-61: lt. gov. Ill., 1961-68, gov. Ill., 1968-69; now engaged in practice law; dir. Aetna State Bank, Chgo., Virgin Islands Dock Corp. Pres., chmn. Pub. Air, Health, Welfare and Safety Com., 1959; chmn., Mental Health Commn., 1955-63. Mem. Anti-Defamation League (nat. civil rights com.), Am., Ill., Chgo., Kankakee County bar assns., Nat. Conf. Lt. Govs. (chmn. 1962-63), C. of C., Musicians Union, Am. Legion, Amvets. Clubs: B'nai B'rith, Moose, Elks (past exalted ruler), Kiwanis, Young Democratic of Ill. (past state sec., state treas.), Kankakee Country, Covenant of Ill. Home: 1300 Cobb Blvd Kankakee IL 60901 Office: City Nat Bank Bldg Kankakee IL also 208 S LaSalle St Chicago IL 60604

SHAPTON, MARK SANDFORD, mill energy coordinator; b. Lansing, Mich., Jan. 4, 1949; s. Lee Sargent and Ruth Eleanor (Matchett) S.; B.S. in M.E., Mich. Tech. U., 1972; m. Patricia Arlene Friend, June 20, 1970; children—Mark Jacob, Daniel Lee, Tricia Valene. Maintenance engr. Penn-Dixie Cement Co., Petoskey, Mich., 1972-74; project engr. Allied Paper Corp., Kalamazoo, 1974-76; energy coordinator Nekoosa Paper Co. (Wis.), 1976—. Registered profl. engr., Mich., Wis. Mem. Am. Soc. M.E. Club: Kalamazoo Valley Chief Engrs. Home: 2510 Honeysuckle Ln Wisconsin Rapids WI 54494 Office: 100 Riverview Dr Port Edwards WI 54497

SHAPTON, WILLIAM ROBERT, mech. engr., educator; b. Lansing, Mich., June 25, 1941; s. Lee Sargent and Ruth Eleanor (Matchett) S.; B.S., Mich. State U., 1962, M.S., 1963; Ph.D. (Renton K. Brodie Research grantee), U. Cin., 1968; m. Patricia Jo Chapman, June 29, 1963; children—Heather Lee, William Sargent. Grad. teaching asst. Mich. State U., East Lansing, 1962-63; project engr. Bendix Missile Div., Mishawaka, Ind., 1963-64, sr. mech. engr. Automation and Measurement div., Dayton, O., 1964-65; asso. prof. U. Cin., 1965—. Cons. to USAF, 1968-71, AEC, 1970-72, Mound Standards Lab., 1970-72, Ford Found., 1971-74, NASA, 1972-77. Bd. dirs. Machine Tool and Mfg. Tech. Information Center, 1968-70. Mem. Am. Soc. M.E. (dir. Cin. sect. 1972-76, chmn. 1977), Soc. Automotive Engrs. (chmn. 1977-78, Teetor award 1974), Am. Soc. Engring. Edn., Am. Assn. U. Profs. Methodist. Author: (with Tobias and Koenigsberger) Advances in Machine Tool Design and Research, 1971; contbg. author: System Identification of Vibrating Structures, 1972. Home: 506 Riddle St Cincinnati OH 45231

SHARAF, MOHAMMED ABDEL-GAWWAD, educator; b. El Mansoura, Egypt, Aug. 24, 1948; s. Abdel-Gawwad Ibrahim Sharaf; came to U.S., 1974; Sc.B. with honors, Cairo U., 1971; M.Sc. in Chemistry, Am. U. in Cairo, Cairo U., 1974. Teaching fellow Cairo U., Am. U. in Cairo, 1971-74; research, teaching asst. U. Mich., Ann Arbor, 1974—. Recipient Anna Doprina award Cairo U., 1971; H. Rachaham fellow U. Mich, 1976. Mem. Egyptian Chem. Soc., Am. Chem. Soc. Home: 1929 #4038 Plymouth Rd Ann Arbor MI 48105 Office: Dept Chemistry U Mich Ann Arbor MI 48109

SHARBO, DAVID ARTHUR, psychiatrist; b. Williston, N.D., Nov. 3, 1940; s. Arthur Johnson and Esther Julia (Goodmonson) S.; B.S., U. Ia., 1962; M.D., St. Louis U., 1965; m. Karen Ruth Hubbard, Aug. 25, 1962; children—Eric David, Peter Christian. Intern, Bethesda Naval Med. Center, Bethesda, Md., 1965-66, resident, 1966-69; chief psychiatry Great Lakes (Ill.) Naval Hosp., 1969-71, Neuropsychiat. Inst., Fargo, N.D., 1971—; practiced medicine specializing in psychiatry, Fargo, 1971—; chief psychiatry St. Ansgar Hosp., Moorhead, Minn., 1971—, chief staff, 1974-75. Asst. clin. prof. dept. psychiatry U. N.D. Sch. Medicine, Fargo, 1975—; psychiatric cons. Concordia Coll., Moorhead, 1972—, St. John's Hosp. Chem. Dependency Unit, Fargo, 1973—, Cass County Welfare Dept., 1973-74. Bd. govs. Neuropsychiat. Inst. Fargo, 1975—. Served to lt. comdr. USN, 1964-71. Diplomate, Am. Bd. Psychiatry and Neurology. Fellow Am. Psychiatric Assn. (pres. N.D. Dist. br. 1975—), A.M.A., N.D. Med. Soc., Am. Orthopsychiat. Assn., Am. Acad. Psychiatry and Law. Lutheran. Home: 714 Southwood Dr S Fargo ND 58102 Office: 700 1st Ave S Fargo ND 58102

SHARKEY, THOMAS BERNARD, civil engr.; b. Middletown, O., Dec. 3, 1917; s. Bryan and Gertrude Mary (O'Donnell) S.; C.E., U. Cin., 1940; m. Norma Catherine Daley, June 7, 1947; children—Timothy J., Michael D., Patrick T., Terrence B., Dennis M., John P., Cathy A., Molly A. Structural engr. Vogt-Ivers, Cin., 1946-48; chief engr. Swan Constrn. Co., Newport, Ky., 1948-49; office engr. Duffy Constrn. Co., Cin., 1950-52; dir. engring. B.G. Danis Co., Dayton, O., 1953—. Instr., Engring. Found., Dayton, 1969-72. Mem. Montgomery County (O.) Bd. Bldg. Standards and Appeals, 1957-63, chmn., 1962. Served with U.S. Army, 1941-45. Decorated Purple Heart. Registered profl. engr., Ohio, Ind., Ky. Mem. Am. Concrete Inst., Constrn. Specifications Inst. (dir. Dayton chpt. 1974-76), 82d Airborne Div. Assn. (dir. Dayton chpt. 1974-76). K.C. Home: 5640-C Coach Dr W Kettering OH 45440 Office: 1801 E 1st St Dayton OH 45403

SHARLEY, GEORGE ELMER, photographer; b. Detroit, Apr. 26, 1922; s. Frank Arthur and Lily (Angus) S.; grad. high sch.; m. Betty Louise Noble, Mar. 25, 1967. With Craine Studio, Detroit, 1940-50, mgr., photographer, 1950-60; partner Baldwin-Chase Studio, Flint, Mich., 1960-69, owner, 1969—. Served with USAAF, 1942-45; ETO. Mem. C. of C., Am. Legion (comdr. 1954-55), Profl. Photographers Am., Mich. Photographers Soc., Genesee County Profl. Photographers Am. Episcopalian. Club: Flint Civitan (v.p. 58-59). Home: 2399 Wildwood Circle Dr Flint MI 48507 Office: 1119 W 3d Ave Flint MI 48504

SHARLIN, HAROLD ISSADORE, historian; b. Trenton, N.J., July 8, 1925; s. Solomon and Jennie (Kaplan) S.; B.S. in Elec. Engring., Drexel U., Phila., 1948; M.A. in History, Columbia U., 1953; Ph.D. in History, U. Pa., 1958; m. Tiby Mintz, June 27, 1948; children—Allan, Joshua, Shifra. Instr. elec. engring. Drexel U., 1952-56; asso. prof. econs. and history Poly. Inst. of N.Y., 1956-62; prof. history Iowa State U., Ames, 1962—; vis. scholar historians office U.S. Dept. Energy, 1977-78; Mem. Am. Hist. Assn., History of Sci. Soc. (chmn. com. undergrad. edn. 1972-75), Soc. for History of Tech., Orgn. Am. Historians. Fellow, Woodrow Wilson Internat. Center for Scholars, 1970-71; vis. scholar Energy Research and Devel. Adminstrn., 1976-77. Author: The Making of the Electrical Age, 1963; Convergent Century: The Unification of Science in the Nineteenth Century, 1966; Lord Kelvin: Dynamic Victorian, 1978; mem. editorial bd. Annals of Science, 1969—. Home: 1403 Burnett Ave Ames IA 50010 Office: Dept History Iowa State U Ames IA 50011

SHARMA, BRAHMA DUTTA, chemist; b. Khurja, India, Sept. 20, 1947; B.S., Agra U., 1966; M.S., Allahabad U., 1968; Ph.D. (vis. research fellow), Queens U., Belfast Northern Ireland, 1971; came to U.S., 1971. Research asso. dept. radiology U. Chgo., 1971-73; asst. dir. research and devel. Coe Labs., Inc., Chgo., 1973-75, dir. research and devel., 1975—; lectr. Sch. Dentistry Northwestern U., Chgo., 1975—. Mem. Am. Chem. Soc., Internat. Assn. Dental Research, Soc. Mfg. Engrs. Contbr. articles to profl. jours. Home: 2204 W 122d St Blue Island IL 60406 Office: 3737 W 127th St Chicago IL 60658

SHARMA, HARI MOHAN, pathologist, educator; b. Aligarh, India, Jan. 16, 1938; s. Ram K. and Shiv-Devi S.; came to U.S., 1971, naturalized, 1977; M.B.B.S., Lucknow U., India, 1961, M.D. in Pathology, 1965; M.Sc., Ohio State U., 1969. Research scholar pathology K.G. Med. Coll., Lucknow, India, 1961-62; intern G.M. and Asso. Hosps., Lucknow, 1962, clin. pathologist, 1963-66; med. officer health Provincial Med. Services, India, 1962-63; lectr. pathology dept. pathology bacteriology Lucknow U., 1966-67; instr. dept. pathology Ohio State U., Columbus, 1967-70, asst. prof., 1972-73, asso. prof., 1973—; mem. attending med. staff Ohio State U. Hosp., 1972—; lectr., asst. prof. dept. pathology McGill U., Montreal, Can., 1970-71; asst. pathologist Jewish Gen. Hosp., Montreal, 1970-71; asst. prof. dept. pathology Ind. U. Sch. Medicine, Indpls., 1971-72; pathology cons. VA Hosp., Dayton, Ohio, 1973—; cons. nephropathology Childrens Hosp., 1974—. Diplomate Am. Bd. Pathology. Fellow Royal Coll. Physicians Surgeons Can., Am. Coll. Clin. Pathologists, Coll. Am. Pathologists. Contbr. numerous articles to med. jours. Home: 2362 Middlesex Rd Columbus OH 43220

SHARON, ISADORE CHARLES, physician; b. Newport, Ky., July 27, 1910; s. Benjamin Louis and Annie (Berman) S.; B.Sc., U. Cin., 1932; M.D., U. Pa., 1934, M.Sc., 1937; m. Mary Ethel Holub, Mar. 16, 1952; 1 son, Robert Morris. Intern, Cin. Gen. Hosp., 1934-35; resident U. Pa. Hosp., 1935-37; pvt. practice internal medicine, 1946—; prof. internal medicine U. Cin., 1960—; dir. dept. internal medicine Deaconess Hosp., Cin., 1961-65, dir. cardiology, 1965-75; cons. VA Hosp., Cin., 1955—; dir. Med. Dental Hosp. Bur. Cin., 1957—. Trustee Jewish Family Services, 1971—, Jewish Fedn. Cin., 1972—; pres. Bur. Jewish Edn. Cin., 1972-75. Served with U.S. Army, 1941-45. Diplomate Am. Bd. Internal Medicine. Fellow A.C.P., Am. Heart Assn; mem. Cin. Acad. Medicine, Ohio State Med. Assn., AMA, Am., Ohio, Cin. socs. internal medicine, Am. Psychosomatic Soc. Club: Cin. Athletic. Asso. editor Cin. Jour. Medicine, 1957—; Contbr. articles to profl. jours. Home: 717 Avon Fields Ln Cincinnati OH 45229 Office: 374 Doctors Bldg 19 Garfield Pl Cincinnati OH 45202

SHARON, NEHAMA, immunologist, virologist; b. Tiberias, Israel, Mar. 2, 1929; d. Simon and Bracha (Weksler) Toister; came to U.S., 1966, naturalized, 1972; tchr.'s certificate, Hebrew Tchrs. Coll., 1949; M.S. in Microbiology, Hebrew U., Jerusalem, 1955, Ph.D. in Immunology, 1960; m. Aryeh Sharon, Mar. 17, 1953; 1 son, Gil. Instr., Hebrew U., Jerusalem, 1960-61; post-doctoral fellow Lobund Labs., U. Notre Dame, Ind., 1961-64, from asst. faculty fellow to vis. asso. prof., 1967-72; asst. prof. Tel-Aviv U., Israel, 1964-66; asso. prof. pathology Evanston Hosp. and Northwestern U., 1972—. Mem. A.A.A.S., Am. Soc. Exptl. Biology and Medicine, Am. Soc. Exptl. Pathology, Am. Soc. Microbiology, N.Y. Acad. Sci., Chgo. Path. Soc., Chgo. Immunology Soc., Reticuloendothelial Soc. Home: 6033 N Sheridan Rd Chicago IL 60660 Office: 2650 Ridge Ave Evanston IL 60201

SHARP, HOMER GLEN, dept. store exec.; b. Cleve., July 3, 1927; s. Homer David and Kathleen (Hawkins) S.; diploma Parsons Sch. Design, 1945; student Am. Acad. Art, 1947; m. JoAnn Harbour, Aug. 29, 1947; children—David Lee, Terry Glen. Trimmer window display Marshall Field & Co., Chgo., 1946-55, mgr. interior display, 1955-68, display dir., 1968-70, store design and display dir., 1970—, v.p. design and display div., 1971—. Served with USMCR, 1945-46. Recipient Nat. Assn. Display Industries award outstanding achievements, 1973. Mem. Chgo. Assn. Commerce and Industry, Chgo. Council Fgn. Relations, Chgo. Athletic Assn. Methodist (trustee). Office: Marshall Field & Co 111 N State St Chicago IL 60690

SHARP, PHILIP R., congressman: b. Balt., July 15, 1942; s. Riley and Florence Sharp; B.S. cum laude, Sch. Fgn. Service, Georgetown U., 1964, Ph.D. in Govt., 1974; postgrad. Exeter Coll., Oxford (Eng.) U., summer 1966; m. Marilyn Kay Augburn, 1972; 1 son, Jeremy Beck. Legis. aide to Senator Vance Hartke of Ind., 1964-69: asst. to asso. prof. polit. sci. Ball State U., Muncie, Ind., 1969-74; mem. 94th-95th Congresses from 10th Ind. Dist.; mem. Com. Interstate and Fgn. Commerce, Com. on D.C. Democrat. Methodist. Office: 1234 Longworth House Office Bldg Washington DC 20515

SHASHA, BARUCH, chemist; b. Bagdad, Iraq, Mar. 15, 1931; s. Saleh and Reena (Rabii) S.; came to U.S., 1962, naturalized, 1971; M.Sc., Hebrew U., Jerusalem, 1959, Ph.D., 1961; post-doctoral Purdue U., 1962-63; m. Doris Shamash, Feb. 6, 1958; children—Tamar, Iris, Daniel, Michelle. Asst. prof. biol. chemistry Hebrew U., Jerusalem, 1961-62; chemist No. Regional Lab. U.S. Dept. Agr., Peoria, Ill., 1963—. Served with Israeli Army, 1951-53. Recipient Merit awards Assn. Israeli Chemists, 1961, U.S. Dept. Agr., 1968. Patents, publs. in fields of carbohydrate chemistry and pesticides. Home: 4921 N Dawn Dr Peoria IL 61614 Office: No Regional Lab Peoria IL 61604

SHASKIN, MILTON, vocat. psychologist; b. Hartford, Conn., Sept. 14, 1927; s. Louis Henry and Sadie (Wolf) S.; L.P.N., Kahler Sch. Nursing, 1949; B.A., U. Minn., 1957; M.S., Mankato State U., 1970; m. Colleen Ann Knudson, May 15, 1973; children—Deborah, Daniel, David, Jessie. Surg. nurse Northwestern Hosp., Mpls., 1949-57; probation officer Mpls. Dept. Ct. Services, 1957-66; social worker Orono Sch. Dist., Mpls., 1966-67; vocat. psychologist Hennepin County Work and Tng. Div., Mpls., 1967—; instr., cons. Mankato State U., 1972-77; human relations instr. Lakewood County Coll., 1972-77. Dir., Urban Center for Minority Studies, 1976-77, Champman Edn. Center, Mpls., 1974; dist. commr. Indianhead council Boy Scouts Am., 1959-67. Served with AUS, 1944-45. Certified rehab. counselor. Mem. Am. Rehab. Counseling Assn., Minn., Am. personnel and guidance assns., Nat. Assn. Social Workers, Nat., Minn. vocat. guidance assns., Minn. Corrections Assn. Jewish. Clubs: B'nai B'rith, Prior Lake Lions. Home: 3411 The Mall Minnetonka MN 55343 Office: 15A Government Center Minneapolis MN 55416

SHAVER, JOSEPH MILTON PEARL, jewelry mfg. co. exec.; b. Rapid City, S.D., Apr. 2, 1920; s. Joseph Pearl and Nannie Minnie (Green) S.; ed. S.D. Sch. Mines, 1938; m. Inez Lenore Hofer, July 9, 1943; children—Nancy Jo, Marcia Jean, Peggy Ann. Clk. Buckingham Transp. Co., Rapid City and Denver, 1939-40; asst. mgr. N. Western Warehouse Co., Rapid City, 1940-45; mgr. Black Hills Jewelry Mfg. Co., Rapid City, 1945—. Pres. council Central PTA, 1951; committeeman Republican Precint, 1952; trustee, chmn. bd. Congregational Ch. Recipient Hire the Handicapped award, 1974. Mem. Mfg. Jewelers and Silversmiths Am (dir.), Rapid City C. of C. (dir.). Mem. United Ch. Christ. Clubs: Lions (dir.), Elks, Masons. Home: 711 Saint Charles St Rapid City SD 57701 Office: 700 Jackson Blvd Rapid City SD 57701

SHAW, DON COULTER, clergyman; b. Enid, Okla., Nov. 14, 1919; s. Roy W. and Emma (Coulter) S.; A.B., Phillips U., 1941; B.D., Garrett Bibl. Inst., Evanston, Ill., 1944; postgrad. Va. Theol. Sem., 1951-52; certificate Applied Psychiatry for Ministers, Washington Sch. Psychiatry, 1951; m. Nancy Matthews, Oct. 28, 1948 (div. 1953); 1 son, David Matthews. Ordained to ministry Episcopal Ch., 1951; Protestant chaplain-supr. Manteno (Ill.) State Hosp., 1946-48, Lorton (Va.) Reformatory, 1948-51; founder, 1st rector St. Michael and All Angels Episcopal Ch., Adelphi, Md., 1952-61; dir. information and edn. Planned Parenthood Assn., Chgo., 1961-67; exec. dir. Episcopal Charities, Diocese of Chgo., 1967-69; chmn. First Nat. Congress on Optimum Population and Environment, Chgo., 1969—; dir. vasectomy services Midwest Population Center, Chgo., 1970—; regional v.p. Negative Population Growth, Inc. Bd. dirs. Midwest Population Center, Transitional Living Process. Home: 534 Stratford Pl Chicago IL 60657 Office: 100 E Ohio St Chicago IL 60611

SHAW, DONALD HARDY, public utility exec.; b. Oelwein, Iowa, June 1, 1922: s. John Hardy and Minnie (Brown) S.; B.S., Harvard U., 1942; J.D., U. Iowa, 1948; m. Elizabeth Jean Orr, Aug. 16, 1946; children—Elizabeth Ann, Andrew, Anthony. Admitted to Iowa bar, 1948, Ill. bar, 1949; lawyer firm Sidley, Austin, Burgess and Smith, Chgo., 1948-55; v.p. fin., dir. Iowa-Ill. Gas and Electric Co., Davenport, Iowa, 1956—; dir. First Nat. Bank Davenport. Mem. Iowa State Bd. Regents, 1969—; bd. dirs. Iowa Radio-TV, 1976—; trustee St. Luke's Hosp., 1967—. Served to capt. USAAF, 1942-45. Mem. Iowa, Ill. bar assns., Delta Theta Phi. Democrat. Congregationalist. Home: 29 Hillcrest St Davenport IA 52803 Office: 206 E 2d St Davenport IA 52808

SHAW, EDWARD JAMES, physician; b. N.Y.C., Oct. 22, 1914; s. Samuel Johnson and Adele (Herndon) S.; B.A., Columbia, 1934; M.D., Yale U., 1937; m. Huguette Adele Herman, Apr. 19, 1965; children—Edward James, Emily K., Barbara A. Intern Bellevue Hosp., N.Y.C., 1937-38, resident surgery, 1938-39; resident surgery N.Y. Post Grad. Sch. and Hosp., N.Y.C., 1939-41; chief surg. services U.S. Army Sta. Hosp., Plattsburg Barracks, N.Y., 1941-42, chief gen. surg. sect. 69th Sta. Hosp., North Africa, 1942-44, comdg. officer and chief surgeon 16th Sta. Hosp., Wiesbaden, Germany, 1945-46; chief resident surgery New Rochelle (N.Y.) Hosp., 1946-47; practice medicine specializing in gen. surgery, New Rochelle, 1947-52; chief resident surgery Lawrence and Meml. Hosp., New London, Conn., 1952-53; chief resident and surgery resident Dr.'s. Hosp., N.Y.C., 1953-54, attending surgeon, 1954-65; practice medicine specializing in gen. surgery, N.Y.C., 1954-65, St. Louis, 1965-67; chief surgeon Sutter Clinic, St. Louis, 1967-71; practice medicine specializing in surgery and occupational medicine, St. Louis and Granite City, Ill., 1971—; mem. surg. staffs Luth. Hosp., St. Louis, Incarnate Word Hosp., St. Louis, Alexian Bros. Hosp., St. Louis, St. Elizabeth Hosp., Granite City, Oliver C. Anderson Hosp., Maryville, Ill. Asst. clin. prof. N.Y. Med. Coll., N.Y.C., 1954-65; asst. attending surgeon Flower Fifth Av. Hosp., N.Y.C., 1954-65; asso. attending surgeon Metropolitan and Bird S. Coler Hosp., N.Y.C., 1954-65; pres. Shaw Surg. Clinic Inc., St. Louis and Granite City, 1975—; med. dir. Am. Steel Foundries, A. O. Smith Corp., Conalco. Bd. dirs. Western Ill. Found. Med. Care. Served with AUS, 1941-45. Diplomate Am. Bd. Surgery, Am. Bd. Abdominal Surgery. Fellow Internat. Coll. Surgeons, N.Y. Soc. Colon and Rectal Surgeons, A.C.S., N.Y. Acad. Medicine; mem. A.C.S., Am. Occupational Med. Assn., Am. Geriatrics Soc., Royal Soc. Medicine, Aerospace, Pan Am., St. Louis, Mo., Madison County (Ill.), Ill. State, Am. med. assns., Mo. Surg. Soc. Assn. Mil. Surgeons of U.S., Am. Soc. Contemporary Medicine and Surgery, N.Y. Acad. Gastroenterology, Tri-Cities C. of C. Clubs: Yale of St. Louis. Home: 3105 Longfellow Blvd St Louis MO 63104 Office: 3654 S Grand Blvd St Louis MO 63118 and 1821 Edison Ave Granite City IL 62040

SHAW, ELIZABETH ORR (MRS. DONALD HARDY SHAW), lawyer, state senator; b. Monona, Iowa, Oct. 2, 1923; d. Harold Topliff and Hazel (Kean) Orr; A.B., Drake U., 1945; postgrad. pub. adminstrn. U. Minn., 1945-46; J.D., U. Iowa, 1948; m. Donald Hardy Shaw, Aug. 16, 1946; children—Elizabeth Ann, Andrew Hardy, Anthony Orr. Admitted to Ill. bar, 1949, Iowa bar, 1956; atty. Legal Aid Soc. Chgo., 1949; asso. firm Lord, Bissell and Brook, Chgo., 1950-51; practiced in Arlington Heights, Ill., 1952-56; partner firm Wood and Shaw, Davenport, Iowa, 1968-70; mem. Iowa Ho. of Reps., 1967-72; mem. Iowa Senate, 1973—, asst. minority leader, 1977-78; chmn. constl. amendments reapportionment com., 1971-72. Mem. Edn. Commn. of States. Mem. P.E.O., Am. Bus. Women's Assn., Iowa Bar Assn. (chmn. family law com.), Order of Coif, Phi Beta Kappa, Kappa Kappa Gamma. Republican. Conglist. Clubs: Davenport Country, Davenport, Outing, Federated Women's, Pilot Internat. (Davenport). Home: 29 Hillcrest Ave Davenport IA 52803 Office: Iowa State Capitol Des Moines IA 52819

SHAW, EMANUEL VICTOR, dentist; b. Zanesville, Ohio, Apr. 28, 1913; s. David Louis and Esther (Feldman) S.; B.S., Western Reserve U., 1934, D.D.S., 1937; m. Eidth M. Bailis, Sept. 18, 1971; children—Jonathan K., Richard K., Peter K. Intern, Mt. Sinai Hosp., 1937-38; pvt. practice dentistry, Cleveland Heights, Ohio, 1938-60, Cleve., 1960—. Clinician in charge out patient dept. Mt. Sinai Hosp., 1938; mem. med. adv. bd. Am. Cancer Soc., 1972—. Served to capt. AUS, 1943-46; ETO. Mem. Western Reserve Hist. Soc., Mus. Arts Assn., Cleve. Mus. Art, Inst. Music, Cleve. Health Mus., Am., Ohio State dental assns., Cleve. Dental Soc. Club: Lake Forest Country (Hudson, Ohio). Home: 3333 Warrensville Center Rd Shaker Heights OH 44122 Office: 11811 Shaker Blvd Cleveland OH 44120

SHAW, GEORGE GORDON, electron microscopist; b. St. Louis, Apr. 21, 1906; s. George Gordon and Anna M. (Lloyd) S.; student in Chemistry, Physics, Maths., Engring. Washington U., St. Louis, 1924-29; m. Pauline Mildred Cunningham, Dec. 28, 1934; 1 dau., Linda (Mrs. Donald Richard Lob). Chemist Am. Steel Foundry, Granite City, Ill., 1929-33; arbitrator Nat. Recovery Adminstrn., Kansas City, Mo., 1933-35; mfrs.' agt., Kansas City, Mo., 1935-60; sr. electron microscopist Midwest Research Inst., Kansas City, Mo., 1960—. Cons. Master Plastics Molding Corp., St. Louis, 1942-55; mem. heart research group U. Mo., Kansas City, 1957-65. Mem. Electron Microscope Soc. Am. Contbr. articles on micromechanisms of metal fatigue. Inventor electron microscopy techniques. Home: 7616 Mackey Rd Overland Park KS 66204 Office: 425 Volker Blvd Kansas City MO 64110

SHAW, JOHN ARTHUR, ins. co. exec.; b. San Antonio, June 6, 1922; s. Samuel Arthur and Ellen Agnes (Lawless) S.; student Loyola U., 1940-41, U. N.C., 1943-44; J.D., St. Louis U., 1948; m. Margaret Louise Strudell, June 9, 1951; children—John Richard, Barbara Ann, David William. Admitted to Mo. bar, 1948, since practiced in St. Louis; mem. firm Pollock, Tenney, & Dahman, 1948-51; with legal dept. Probate Ct., 1951-53; partner Pollock, Ward, Klobasa, & Shaw, 1953-63; with Reliable Life Ins. Co., Webster Groves, Mo., 1964—, asso. gen counsel, 1964-67, gen. counsel, 1967—, dir., 1968—, sr. v.p. 1969—; dir., gen counsel Old Reliable Fire Ins. Co., 1967—; dir. TRICO Service Corp., 1970—; pres., dir. Reliable Life Corp., 1974—. Active Boy Scouts Am., Glendale, Mo. Bd. dirs. Tatman Found., 1967—. Served as lt. U.S. Army, 1943-46; maj. Res. (ret.). Mem. Am. Bar Assn., Am. Judicature Soc., Mo. Bar, Bar Assn. Met. St. Louis, Cath. Lawyers Guild St. Louis, Assn. Life Ins. Counsel, Am. Council of Life Ins., Alpha Sigma Nu, Delta Theta Phi. Cath. Contbg. author: Basic Estate Planning, 1957. Editor: Missouri Probate Law and Practice, 1960. Home: 306 Luther Lane Glendale MO 63122 Office: 231 W Lockwood Ave Webster Groves MO 63119

SHAW, PATRICK, architect; b. Chgo., June 29, 1933; s. Alfred Phillips and Rue (Winterbotham) S.; student Middlesex Sch., Concord, Mass., 1947-51; A.B., Harvard, 1958, postgrad., 1958-61; m. Joanne Nagel, Jan. 19, 1968; children—Sophia Neoma, Alfred Michael. With various archtl. firms, 1960-65; pres. Shaw & Assos., architects, Chgo., 1965—. Bd. dirs., sec. Greater N. Michigan Av. Assn. Chgo., 1969—, chmn. zoning com., 1970—. Served with U.S. Army, 1952-54. Mem. A.I.A., Chgo. Hist. Soc. Clubs: Arts (Chgo.), Tavern. Prin. works include Campus Center and Residence Hall at Loyola U., Chgo., Main P.O. Bldg., Springfield, Ill., Mid-Continental Plaza office bldg., Chgo., Commerce Plaza Office Bldgs., Oak Brook, Ill. Home: 399 W Fullerton Chicago IL 60614 Office: 55 E Monroe St Chicago IL 60603

SHAW, RICHARD CLARKE, cardiothoracic surgeon; b. Salina, Kansas, July 1, 1941; s. F. Clarke and Alice M.S.; B.A., State U. Iowa, 1963; M.D., Washington U. (St. Louis), 1967; m. Mary Ann Hughes, June 15, 1963; children—David, Sandra, Brian. Intern in surgery Barnes Hosp., St. Louis, 1967-68, asst. resident in surgery, 1968-69, 1970-72, chief resident in surgery, 1972-73, sr. resident in cardiothoracic surgery, 1973-74, chief resident, 1974-75; research fellow St. Louis Children's Hosp., 1969-70; practice medicine specializing in cardiothoracic surgery, St. Louis, 1975—; asst. dir. div. cardiothoracic surgery Waldheim Dept. Surgery Jewish Hosp. of St. Louis; asst. prof. surgery Washington Sch. Medicine, 1975—. Mem. AMA, St. Louis Med. Soc., Mo. State Med. Assn., Am. Coll. Cardiology, St. Louis Thoracic Surg. Soc. Contbr. numerous articles to profl. jours. Home: 6744 Chamberlain St St Louis MO 63130 Office: 216 S Kingshighway St Louis MO 63110

SHAW, ROBERT CALVIN, supt. schs.; b. Illmo, Mo., July 1, 1929; s. William Henry and Rose (Palmer) S.; B.S., S.E. Mo. State Coll., 1950; M.Ed., U. Mo., 1954, Ed.D., 1959; m. Mary Ann Fisher, Aug. 11, 1955; children—Robert Calvin, John Curtis, Steven Lane, Stuart Kent. Tchr. math. Illmo Jr. High Sch., 1950-51; asst. to dir. adminstrn. U. Mo., summer 1955, vis. asst. prof. edn., summers 1957-62; asst. prin. David H. Hickman High Sch., Columbia, Mo., 1955-59; asst. supt. schs., Columbia, 1959-62, supt. schs., 1962—. Del., mem. planning com. Gov.'s Conf. on Edn., 1966, 69. Campaign chmn. Columbia United Fund, 1962. Bd. dirs. Central Midwestern Regional Edn. Lab.; trustee McREL Corp.; charter bd. mem. Columbia Commn. on Human Rights, 1962. Served with U.S. Army, 1951-53. Recipient citation for community service Columbia United Fund, 1960, United Fund Outstanding Citizenship award, 1962, Am. Educator medal Freedoms Found. at Valley Forge, 1969. Mem. Am.

Assn. Sch. Facilities Planners, Am. (adv. bd., Mo. primary contact for Fed. Legislation Project), Mo. (sec.) assns. sch. adminstrs., Am. Assn. for Supervision and Curriculum Devel. (adv. bd.), Am. Legion, U.S. (Distinguished Service award 1962), Columbia (named Outstanding Young Man of Year 1962) jr. chambers commerce. Methodist (past pres. bd.). Rotarian. Home: 400 Green Meadow Rd Columbia MO 65201 Office: 1002 Range Line Columbia MO 65201

SHAW, WAYNE EUGENE, sem. dean; b. Covington, Ind., May 23, 1932; s. Charles Albert and Mabel (Howard) S.; A.B., Lincoln (Ill.) Christian Coll., 1954; B.D., Christian Theol. Sem., Indpls., 1960; M.S., Butler U., Indpls., 1963; Ph.D., Ind. U., 1969; m. Janet Lee Broz, Dec. 21, 1957; children—Haydn Stewart, Scott Campbell, Barton Charles. Ordained to ministry Christian Ch., 1954; minister chs. in Ill. and Ind., 1951-66; academic dean Lincoln Christian Sem., 1974—, prof. preaching, 1966—; teaching asso. speech and theatre Ind. U., 1961-66. Grantee Ind. U., 1964. Author: Designing the Sermon, 1975; co-author: Birth of a Revolution: How the Church Can Change the World, 1974. Home: Airport Rd Lincoln IL 62656 Office: Box 178 Lincoln IL 62656

SHEA, CATHERINE BEAHAN, educator, therapy cons.; b. Flint, Mich., Mar. 27, 1940; d. Raymond Matthew and Anita Sarah (Connelly) Beahan; B.A. summa cum laude Nazareth Coll., 1965; M.A., Duquesne U., 1969; m. J. Edward Shea, June 14, 1969; children—Kathleen Anne, Kevin Beahan. Elementary tchr. Detroit Schs., 1960-66; instr. Nazareth Coll., Kalamazoo, Mich., 1967-68; student personnel adminstr., instr. Xavier Coll., Chgo., 1970-71, Elmhurst (Ill.) Coll., 1971-76; instr. Coll. of DuPage, Glen Ellyn, Ill. and therapist Gestalt Therapy Center, Elmhurst, 1976—; cons. Family Service Assn., Oak Brook Sr. Citizens, AAUW, George Williams Coll. Mem. AAUW, Am. Personnel and Guidance Assn., Am. Coll. Personnel Assn., Assn. Humanistic Psychology, Oasis Midwest Growth Center. Home: 239 E Wilson St Elmhurst IL 60126 Office: 375 W 1st St Elmhurst IL 60126

SHEA, DANIEL DENNIS, editor; b. Coronado, Calif., Aug. 2, 1930; s. Earl Clifford and Mary Anne (Taylor) S.; student (Journalism scholar) Bradley U., 1950-54, (Newspaper Guild grantee), Ind. U., 1971, (Ill. State Mil. scholar), Ill. Central Coll., 1972-75; m. Patricia Ann Sanderson, Feb. 14, 1953; children—Linda, Mary Diane (Mrs. John Vinecore), Dennis, Carol, Timothy, Donald, Thomas. With Peoria (Ill.) Jour.-Star, 1951, 52—, successively copyboy, reporter, sports writer, copy editor, editorial swingman, 1959-67, news editor, 1967—. Mem. Jour. Star Speaker's Bur., 1970—; del. Am. Newspaper Guild Conv., Vancouver, B.C., Can., 1961. Del., Ill. Democratic Conv., 1960; pres. Richwoods Dem. Club, 1961-62; ward capt. Dem. party, Peoria, 1960-64; precinct committeeman, 1960-66. Served with AUS, 1951-52. Mem. Peoria Newspaper Guild (pres. 1961). Roman Catholic. Contbr. short stories, poetry to Ill. Central Coll. Reader, 1974. Home: 3838 St Michael Ct Peoria IL 61614 Office: Peoria Jour Star 1 News Plaza Peoria IL 61614

SHEA, GERALD JOSEPH, mfg. co. exec.; b. Newport, R.I., Oct. 12, 1925; s. John M. and Emma L. (Conheeney) S.; B.E.E., Rensselaer Poly. Inst., 1950; postgrad. No. Ill. U. Grad. Sch. Bus., 1963; m. Phyllis M. Singer, Aug. 4, 1951; children—John M., Ronald R., Carolyn M. Project engr. Motorola, Chgo., 1950-61, dept. head, 1962-64; chief elec. engr., office copier div. SCM, Skokie, Ill., 1964-67; dir. engring. Underwriters Safety Device Co., Chgo., 1967—; dir. engring. Internat. Connector div. Eltra Corp., 1976—. Mem. Sch. Bd. Caucus Com. Dist 88, 1962, Country Club Highlands Homeowners Adv. Bd., 1963. Served with USAAF, 1944-45, AUS, 1951-52. Mem. I.E.E.E. (sr.), Alpha Tau Omega. Patentee in field. Office: 7300 W Wilson Ave Chicago IL 60656

SHEARD, KEVIN, educator; b. N.Y.C., Jan. 30, 1916; s. Alec Michael and Frances T. (Cox) S.; B.A., Williams Coll., 1947; M.S., U. Wis., 1949; M.B.A., Xavier U., 1955; J.D., Loyola U., Chgo., 1959; m. Ruth L. Brobst, Sept. 29, 1972; children by previous marriage—Wenda Jane, Sarah Anne, Elizabeth Margaret, Catherine Francis, Martha Joan. Instr. history Williams Coll., Williamstown, Mass., 1947-48; asst. prof. bus. adminstrn. Baldwin Wallace Coll., Berea, O., 1955-58; instr. econs. U. Ill., Chgo., 1958-59; asso. prof. bus. adminstrn. No. Mich. U., Marquette, 1959-63; prof. law Cleve. State U., 1963—. Cons. Cleveland Heights Police Acad. and Dept., 1967—. Served to maj. Coast Arty., AUS, 1940-46. Mem. Pa.-Ohio Locksmiths Assn. (hon.), Am. Inst. Parliamentarians, Cleve. Grays. Author: Academic Heraldry in America, 1962; (with Hugh Smith) Academic Dress and Insignia of the World's Universities, 1970. Home: 4152 W 49th St Cleveland OH 44144

SHEARER, ROBERT WILLIAM, educator; b. Ames, Iowa, Oct. 30, 1920; s. Phineas Stevens and Mary (Kelly) S.; B.Sc. in Chem. Engring., Iowa State U., 1942; m. Harriette E. Little, May 2, 1942; children—Steven, Carla, Barbara, James. Mgr. engring. Mallinckrodt Chem. Works, St. Louis, 1947-56; asst. gen. mgr. Mallinckrodt Nuclear Corp., St. Louis, 1956-61; asst. v.p., asst. sec. United Nuclear Corp., St. Louis, 1961-64; asso. prof., indsl. specialist Iowa State U., Ames, 1964—. Cons., Mallinckrodt Chem. Works, 1964-67. Mem. Gov.'s Com. on Fuel Supply, 1973-75; mem. Senator Clark's Task Force on Energy, 1973—. Bd. dirs. Ames Community Presch. Center, 1967—, treas., 1970-75. Mem. Am. Inst. Chem. Engrs., Am. Soc. Engring. Edn., Soc. Plastics Engrs., Soc. Plastics Industry, Plastics Edn. Found. (chmn. scholarship and grants com. 1967—), Nat. U. Extension Assn., Sigma Alpha Epsilon, Tau Beta Pi, Phi Kappa Phi, Phi Lambda Upsilon. Rotarian. Home: 2126 Greeley Ames IA 50010

SHEARMAN, ROBERT WILLIAM, assn. exec.; b. Bklyn., June 7, 1916; s. William Hugh and Florence Emily (Bell) S.; A.B., Princeton U., 1937; m. Dorothy French Dodge, July 3, 1954; children—Grace Dodge, Edith Bell. Chemist, Pitts. Plate Glass Co., Newark, 1937-39; metall. observer Bethlehem (Pa.) Steel Co., 1940-41; with gen. publicity dept. Union Carbide Corp., N.Y.C., 1946-51, 53-54, sec. metals br., 1955-57, sec. The Metall. Soc. of Am. Inst. Mining, Metall. and Petroleum Engrs., N.Y.C., 1957-66; adminstrv. sec. Am. Soc. Quality Control, Milw., 1966-71, exec. dir., 1971—. Served to capt. USAAF, 1941-46, to maj. USAF, 1951-53. Mem. Am. Chem. Soc., Am. Inst. Mining, Metall. and Petroleum Engrs., Metal Sci. Club N.Y., European Orgn. Quality Control (asso.), Internat. Acad. Quality, Am. Soc. Assn. Execs., AAAS, Council Engring. and Sci. Soc. Execs. (pres. 1973-74), Sigma Xi (asso. mem.). Club: Appalachian Mountain (Boston). Home: 7295 N River Rd River Hills WI 53217 Office: 161 W Wisconsin Ave Milwaukee WI 53203

SHEARON, KENNETH ELROY, dentist; b. Elk Point, S.D., Aug. 12, 1910; s. William King and Nancy (Good) S.; D.D.S., Northwestern U., 1939; m. Louise Timberlake, Oct. 2, 1942; children—William, James, Gerald, David. Intern St. Luke's Hosp., Chgo., 1939-41; cons. staff Presbyn.-St. Luke's Hosp., Chgo., 1941—; individual practice dentistry, Chgo., 1941—; dental surgeon Rock Island Lines, Chgo., 1952—. Sec.-treas. Dicken Grain Corp., Sycamore, Ill., 1965—. Served to lt. comdr. USNR, 1941. Mem. Am., Ill., Chgo. dental assns., Farm Bur. Home: 2241 Thornwood St Wilmette IL 60091 Office: 104 Michigan Ave Chicago IL 60603

SHEBILSKY, PAUL MARTIN WALTER, optometrist; b. Argentine, Kans., Sept. 30, 1895; s. John and Pauline Wilhelmina (Moltz) Przybylski; grad. Needles Inst. Optometry, 1923; D. Optometry, No. Ill. Coll. Ophthalmology and Otolaryngology, 1926; m. Esther Margaret Wortman, Dec. 27, 1931. Practice optometry, Fairbury, Nebr., 1923-26, Strong City, and Burlington, Kans., 1926-29, Emporia, 1929-77. Served with USNR, 1917-19. Mem. Am., Kans. optometric assns., Am. Legion, Beta Sigma Kappa. Mason, Kiwanian (pres. 1937). Club: Outlook. Editor: Kans. Optometric Journal, 1944-52. Home: 1502 Sherwood Way Emporia KS 66801

SHEEHAN, DANIEL EUGENE, bishop; b. Emerson, Nebr., May 14, 1917; s. Daniel F. and Mary Helen (Crahan) S.; student Creighton U., 1934-36, LL.D. (hon.), 1964; student Kenrick Sem., St. Louis, 1936-42; J.C.D., Cath. U. Am., 1949. Ordained priest Roman Cath. Ch., 1942; asst. pastor, Omaha, 1942-46; chancellor Archdiocese Omaha, 1949-69, aux. bishop Omaha, 1964-69, archbishop, 1969—. Pres. Canon Law Soc. Am., 1953; del. 3d-4th sessions Ecumenical Council, Rome, Italy, 1964; chaplain Omaha club Serra Internat., 1950-66. Home: 6605 Farnam St Omaha NE 68132 Office: 100 N 62d St Omaha NE 68132

SHEEHAN, LEON EARL, lawyer; b. Caledonia, Minn., Jan. 18, 1924; s. Emmet Laurence and Mathilda Louise (Horn) S.; student St. Mary's Coll., 1946-47, Loyola U., Chgo., 1947-48; LL.B., U. Wis., 1951, J.D., 1966; m. Patricia Watts, Sept. 9, 1950; children—Mary Pat (Mrs. George Dallas), Brigid A. (Mrs. Terrence Thompson). Admitted to Wis. bar, 1951; asso. Hale, Skemp, Hanson, & Schnurrer, attys., LaCrosse, Wis., 1950-58; partner Hale, Skemp, Hanson, Schnurrer & Sheehan, 1958-60; partner Moeh, Sheehan & Meyer, 1960—. Instr., Wis. Continuing Legal Edn. Series, 1966. Commr., LaCrosse City Park Bd., 1960—, pres., 1966-72; mem. LaCrosse City Plan Commn., 1966-72; pres. LaCrosse area Council P.T.A.'s, 1963; mem. LaCrosse Citizens Planning Corp. Recreation Com., 1966-67; pres. LaCrosse Confidential Exchange, 1956-58. Bd. dirs. LaCrosse County chpt. A.R.C., 1959-65, 70-75. Served with U.S. Army, 1943-45. Mem. Am., Wis. (mem. grievance dist. com. 1972-75), LaCrosse County (pres. 1976-77) bar assns., Wis. State Bar (bd. govs. 1974-78, chmn. 1977-78), Wis. Acad. Trial Lawyers. K.C. (Grand Knight 1958). Home: 120 Briarwood Ave LaCrosse WI 54601 Office: 402 1st Bank Bldg LaCrosse WI 54601

SHEEHAN, WILLIAM PHILIP, labor ofcl.; b. Falmouth, Ky., Feb. 16, 1927; s. Will Thomas and Helen Elizabeth (Finn) S.; student Xavier U., Cin., 1947-49, U. Ky., 1949-51, Ohio State U. and U. Cin. spl. courses; Bus. agt., local, Brewery Workers Union, Cin., 1955-62; exec. sec. treas. Cin. AFL CIO Labor Council, 1962—. Sec., labor edn. and research adv. com. Ohio State U., 1966—; mem. Cin. Civil Service Commn., 1974—; mem. exec. com. Citizens Council for Ohio Schs., 1974—; chmn. Health Maintenance Plan, Cin., 1974—; mem. exec. com. Community Chest and Council, Cin., 1967—; sec. ARC, Cin., 1966—; v.p. Cin. Council on Econ. Edn.; bd. dirs. Ohio Council on Econ. Edn., 1964—. Served with Inf., AUS, 1944-47. Recipient Gov.'s award for Community Action, 1974, Man of Year award Cin. Bldg. Trades Council, 1976. Mem. Internat. Assn. Machinists and Aerospace Workers, Internat. Brotherhood Elec. Workers, Ohio AFL CIO (v.p. 1974—), Cin. Hotel Employees Council (pres. 1968—). Democrat. Roman Catholic. Clubs: Cin., Ancient Order Hibernians, Friendly Sons St. Patrick. Home: 912 Seton Cincinnati OH 45205 Office: 1015 Vine St Suite 706 Cincinnati OH 45202

SHEFFIELD, LESLIE FLOYD, agrl. educator; b. Orafino, Nebr., Apr. 13, 1925; s. Floyd L. and Edith A. (Presler) S.; B.S. with high distinction in Agronomy, U. Nebr., 1950, M.S., 1964; postgrad. U. Minn., summers, 1965; Ph.D., U. Nebr., 1971; m. Doris Fay Fenimore, Aug. 20, 1947; children—Larry Wayne, Linda Faye (Mrs. Bernard Eric Hempelman), Susan Elaine. County extension agt. Lexington and Schuyler, Nebr., 1951-52; exec. sec. Nebr. Grain Improvement Assn., 1952-56; chief Nebr. Wheat Commn., State of Nebr., Lincoln, 1956-59; exec. sec. Great Plains Wheat, Inc., market devel., Garden City, Kans., 1959-61; asst. to dean Coll. Agr., U. Nebr. at Lincoln, 1961-66, supt. North Platte Expt. Sta., 1966-71, asst. dir. Nebr. Coop. Extension Service, Nebr. Agrl. Expt. Sta., Lincoln, 1971-75, asst. to vice chancellor Inst. Agr. and Natural Resources, also extension farm mgmt. specialist and asso. prof. agrl. econs., 1975—; sec.-treas. Circle 4S-L Acres, Wallace, Nebr., 1973—. Cons. econs. of irrigation in N.D., Minn., S.D. and Brazil, 1975, Sudan, Kuwait and Iran, 1976, Can., China. Served with U.S. Army, 1944-46; ETO. Recipient Hon. State Farmer award Future Farmers Am., 1955, Hon. Chpt. Farmer award, North Platte chpt., 1973; fellowship grad. award Chgo. Bd. Trade, 1964; Agrl. Achievement award Ak-Sar-Ben, 1969. NASA research grantee, 1972-77. Mem. Am. Agrl. Econs. Assn., Am., Nat., Nebr. water resources assns., Nebr. Irrigation Assn., Nebr. Assn. Resource Dists., Am. Soc. Farm Mgrs. Rural Appraisers, Lincoln C. of C. (mem. agrl. com. 1974-77), Gamma Sigma Delta, Alpha Zeta. Rotarian (dir. 1965-66). Editor: Procs. of Nebr. Water Resources and Irrigation Devel. for 1970's, 1972; contbg. editor Irrigation Age Mag., St. Paul, 1974—. Contbr. articles to various publs. Home: 3800 Loveland Dr Lincoln NE 68506 Office: 222 Filley Hall U Nebraska-Lincoln Lincoln NE 68583

SHEGRUD, DONALD MAURICE, mech. engr.; b. Dubuque, Iowa, Sept. 15, 1935; s. Maurice S. and Evelyn Rose (Howes) S.; B.S. in Mech. Engring., Finlay Engring. Coll., 1960; m. Eva Jeanne Milburn, Oct. 8, 1960; 1 dau., Sonya Sue. Customer estimating engr. Ladish Co., Cudahy, Wis., 1960-61; mech. designer J.F. Pritchard Co., Kansas City, Mo., 1961-62; new products engr. in research and devel. dept. Gustin-Bacon Mfg. Co., Kansas City, Mo., 1962-65; sales engr. Black, Sivalls, and Bryson Co., Kansas City, Mo., 1965-68; sales mgr. Continental Disc Corp., Kansas City, 1968-74, v.p. and gen. mgr., 1974—. Served with USAF, 1954-58. Registered profl. engr., Mo. Mem. ASME, Nat., Mo. socs. of profl. engrs. Roman Catholic. Clubs: North Kansas City Breakfast, Sherwood Country. Home: 3407 NW 58th Terr Kansas City MO 64151 Office: 4103 Riverside NW Kansas City MO 64150

SHEK, JOHN LEONARD, chest surgeon; b. Urumchi, China, Jan. 23, 1922; s. Peter H. and Margaret M. (Muir) S.; M.D., Nat. Med. Coll. Shanghai, (China), 1943; came to U.S., 1945, naturalized, 1954; m. Patricia Turnbull, Nov. 30, 1949; children—Peter Shuntleigh, Eugenie Victoria, John Robert. Chief of surgery Battey State Hosp., Rome, Ga., 1951-56; practice medicine specializing in surgery, Saginaw, Mich., 1956—; mem. cons. staff VA Hosp., Saginaw, Mich.; asst. clin. prof. dept. surgery Mich. State U. Med. Sch., Lansing. Mem. bd. Saginaw Symphony Orch., Saginaw Art Mus. Served to capt. M.C. Chinese Nationalist Army and U.S. Army, 1943-45. Diplomate Am. Bd. Thoracic Surgery, Am. Bd. Surgery; fellow Am. Coll. Chest Physicians, Am. Coll. Angiology; mem. AMA (Physicians Recognition award 1976-79). Republican. Methodist. Home: 11 W Hannum Blvd Saginaw MI 48602

SHELDON, GEORGE COLEMAN, feed processing co. exec.; B. Hartley, Iowa, Sept. 6, 1914; s. Joseph Orville and Lulu (Johnson) S.; B.S.C., U. Iowa, 1938; m. Helen Lois Grayson, Sept. 29, 1944; children—Barbara Ann, Richard Coleman, Georgia Ellen. Prodn. mgr. George A. Hormel, Austin, Minn. and Atlanta, 1938-48; regional sales dir. Murphy Products Co., Burlingotn, Wis., 1948-65, dir. dealer services, 1965-74; v.p., gen. mgr. West Bend Processing Co. (Iowa) 1974—. Republican. Methodist. Clubs: Masons, Kiwanis, Lions. Home: 109 4th St NW Box 125 West Bend IA 50597 Office: Box 66 West Bend IA 50597

SHELFORD, R. H., pres. Winnipeg (Man., Can.) Free Press. Office: 300 Carlton St Winnipeg MB R3C 3C1 Canada*

SHELL, CLAUDE IRVING, JR., educator; b. Pine Bluff, Ark., Oct. 15, 1922; s. Claude Irving and Ela (Hartsell) S.; B.A., Maryville Coll., 1947; M.S., U. Tenn., 1949; Ph.D., So. Ill. U., 1966; m. Mary Frances Robinson, July 27, 1952; children—Barbara Jane, Mary Louise, James Claude, William Joseph. Partner, Shell-Ross Co., 1951-54; asst. prof. bus. adminstrn. Tenn. Tech. U., 1948-51, asso. prof., 1954-57; product planner Ford Motor Co., 1957-60; asst. dir. Small Bus. Inst., So. Ill. U., 1960-65, asst. dir. placement services, 1965-66, chmn. dept. mgmt., 1966-67; prof., head dept. mgmt. Eastern Mich. U., Ypsilanti, 1967—. Cons. Ill. Div. Vocational Rehab. Mem. bd., exec. com. Visually Handicapped Mgrs. Ill., 1972—, chmn., 1974—. Served from pvt. to lt. F.A., U.S. Army, 1943-46; ETO. Mem. Acad. Mgmt., Internat. Council Small Bus., Beta Gamma Sigma, Phi Kappa Phi, Alpha Kappa Psi, Pi Sigma Epsilon, Sigma Iota Epsilon. Presbyn. (elder). Contbr. articles to profl. jours. Home: 1910 Collegewood Dr Ypsilanti MI 48197

SHELL, WILLIAM LOWELL, guidance counselor; b. Sheridan, Wyo., Mar. 1, 1949; s. Thomas Eugene and Maxine Ann (Dalzell) S.; B.S., Black Hills State Coll., Spearfish, S.D., 1972; M.S. in Edn., Wayne (Nebr.) State Coll., 1977; m. Marcia Phyllis Norman, Jan. 20, 1972. Tchr., Pine Ridge Indian Reservation, S.D., 1972, Pop John High Sch., Elgin, Nebr., 1972-74; counselor vocat. rehab. Nebr. Dept. Edn., 1974-77; behavioral counselor Ednl. Service Unit, Fremont, Nebr., 1977—; bd. dirs. Big Bros.-Big Sisters N.E. Nebr. Democratic campaign chmn. Antelope County, Nebr., 1972. Named Outstanding Big Brother, 1976. Mem. Am. Personnel and Guidance Assn., Am. Rehab. Counseling Assn., Nebr. Edn. Assn. Congregationalist. Home: 2615 Nebraska St Fremont NE 68025 Office: 2320 N Colorado Ave Fremont NE 68025

SHELL, WILLIAM ORCHARD, archtl. engr.; b. Council Bluffs, Iowa, Dec. 10, 1932; s. Kentner William and Marion Winifred (Orchard) S.; student U. Wis.-Milw., 1950-51; B.S. in Archtl. Engring., Iowa State U., 1955; m. Jeanne Yvonne Nelson, Oct. 4, 1972; children—Carlynn (Mrs. Steven Edward Bee), Rian, Marion, William. Structural engr. firm Consoer-Townsend & Assos., cons., Chgo., 1951-59; product engr. Stephens-Adamson Mfg. Co., Aurora, Ill., 1959-65; pres. Shell Consulting Engrs., Aurora, 1965-71; mgr. engring. Lusterlite Corp., metal bldg. mfr., Paris, Ill., 1971-72; systems and structure coordinator Gen. Growth Devel. Corp., shopping center developers, Des Moines, 1972-76; pres. Shell Cons. Engrs., Inc., 1976—. Owner SSS Service & Sales, Aurora, 1968-69; exec. v.p. Western Properties, Aurora, 1969-70; pres. Mid-Am. Land Co., Aurora, 1968-69. Sec. bldg. code adv. com., Aurora, 1967-71; vice chmn. bldg. code appeals bd., Aurora, 1967-71. Served with AUS, 1955-57. Registered structural engr. 25 states. Mem. Ill. (vice chmn. com. registration laws 1969-71), Nat. (v.p. chpt. 1969-71) socs. profl. engrs., Am. Concrete Inst., Am. Inst. Steel Contrn. Patentee and copyrights in field. Home and office: 4532 70th Pl Des Moines IA 50322

SHELLBERG, JERRY FRANCIS, cons. engr.; b. Griswold, Iowa, Jan. 8, 1936; s. Edwin S. and Alice C. (Quinn) S.; B.S., Iowa State U., 1957; m. Barbara L. Miller, Dec. 28, 1959; children—Julie, Jeffrey, Jeanne, Jay, Jennifer. Project engr. Iowa Hwy. Commn., Red Oak, 1957-61; city engr. City of Red Oak, 1961-65, 1965—; partner, gen. mgr. H. Gene McKeown & Assos., Red Oak, 1965—. Sec. Low Rent Housing Agy. Red Oak, 1967—; dir. Red Oak Community Sch. Dist., 1970-73, pres., 1971-72. Served with U.S. Army, 1958. Registered profl. engr., Iowa, Wis. Mem. Nat. Soc. Profl. Engrs., Iowa Engring. Soc., Red Oak C. of C., Delta Sigma Phi. Roman Catholic. Elk. Home: 1206 8th St Red Oak IA 51566 Office: 206 Coolbaugh St Red Oak IA 51566

SHELLENBERGER, THOMAS MAX, aircraft co. exec.; b. Wichita, Kans., Dec. 9, 1927; s. Thomas Mathias and Estelle M. (Bay) S.; student S.D. State U., 1945-46; student Wichita State U., 1947-49, 59-61; m. Nanci O'Connor, Feb. 14, 1950; children—Thomas Max, Debra Su. Lab. technician, Cessna Aircraft Co., Wichita, 1953-54, lab. engr., 1954-64, quality control supt., 1964-65, lab. supr., 1966—. Swimming ofcl. AAU, Wichita, 1968-70; wol. Wichita, 1971-75. Served with U.S. Army, 1945-46, 50-52. Mem. Soc. for Advancement of Material and Process Engring., ASTM, Am. Soc. for Metals, Am. Soc. for Quality Control. Republican. Mem. United Presbyterian Ch. Home: 7502 E Lincoln Wichita KS 67207 Office: 5800 E Pawnee PO Box 1521 Wichita KS 67201

SHELTON, RAYMOND FRANKLIN, hosp. adminstr.; b. Memphis, Feb. 16, 1944; s. Michael A. and Margaret (Mitchell) S.; student Harding Coll., 1962-63; B.B.A. cum laude, Memphis State U., 1967; M. Hosp. Adminstrn., U. Iowa, 1969; m. Linda Jo Climer, Aug. 9, 1969. Adminstrv. resident Union Hosp., Terre Haute, Ind., 1968-69, asst. adminstr., 1969-71, adminstr., 1971—. Bd. dir. Community Blood Program, Vigo County Mental Health Assn., Covered Bridge council Girl Scouts U.S.A. Mem. Cath. Hosp. Assn. Kiwanian. Club: Country (Terre Haute). Home: 7000 Williamsburg Ln Terre Haute IN 47802 Office: 1606 N 7th St Terre Haute IN 47804

SHELTON, ROBERT WALLACE, adminstrv. chem. engr.; b. St. Louis, Dec. 28, 1936; s. Lee William and Frances Wallace (Bulkley) S.; m. Elizabeth Becklenberg, Nov. 19, 1966; children—Trudy, Katherine, Angela. B.S. in Chem. Engring., Washington U., St. Louis, 1961, postgrad. Sever Inst. Tech., 1961-63; postgrad. Exec. Tng. Inst., Earlham Coll., 1975-76. Project engr., missiles space div. Emerson Electric Co., St. Louis, 1961-66; research engr., Linde Div. Union Carbide Corp., Speedway, Ind., 1966-69, supt. labs., 1969-73, mgr. quality control, investment casting ops., 1973-75; mgr. analytical services Stellite Div., Cabot Corp., Kokomo, Ind., 1975-77, div. mgr. quality control, 1977—. Mem. Am. Soc. Metals, Am. Soc. Quality Control, ASTM. Home: 1504 Green Acres Dr Kokomo IN 46901

SHEPHERD, HARLEY EMIL, machine tool co. exec.; b. Moline, Ill., July 7, 1931; s. William Harrison and Margaret Elizabeth (DeTaeye) S.; B.A., Augustana Coll., 1957; m. Jeanne Marilyn Neilson, Nov. 23, 1956; children—Robert Bruce, Linda Kay. Vice-pres. finance W.A. Whitney Corp., Rockford, Ill., 1965—; group controller Esterline Corp., N.Y.C., 1972—; accounting trainee Caterpillar Tractor Co., Peoria, Ill., 1957-58; accounting mgr. Clausen Works, J. I. Case, Racine, Wis., 1958-65; dir. W. A. Whitney Subsidiaries, Los Angeles, Toronto, Mexico; trustee Whitney Profit Share Trusts. Active Boy Scouts Am., Jr. Achievement. Served with U.S. Army, 1952-53. Mem. Nat. Assn. Accountants, Nat. Machine Tool Builders Assn. (mem. accounting practices com.), Nat. Rifle Assn. (life). Lutheran (treas. 1958-63). Home: 827 Tower Dr Rockford IL 61108 Office: 650 Race St Rockford IL 61105

SHEPHERD, HARRY SIMON, dentist; b. Cleve., Oct. 15, 1916; s. Kirk Emerson and Florence Maud (Potter) S.; A.B., Western Reserve U., 1937, D.D.S., 1941; m. Margaret B. Pugh, Sept. 11, 1943; children—Harry, Thomas, Richard, Betsy Ann. Intern, U. Hosp. Cleve., 1941-42; tchr. Dental Sch. Western Reserve U., 1946-57; pvt. practice dentistry, Cleve., East Claridon, Ohio, 1946—. Asst. prof. anesthesia and oral surgery Western Reserve U., 1946-57; mem. staff U. Hosp. Cleve., St. Vincents Charity Hosp., Cleve. Served with USNR, 1942-45; PTO. Mem. Am. Dental Assn., Ohio State, N.E. Ohio dental socs. Composer religious songs and choral pieces. Congregationalist (trustee). Mason. Home: 13098 Old State Rd East Claridon OH 44033

SHEPHERD, HERNDON GUINN, JR., clin. chemist; b. Schuyler, Va., Mar. 14, 1927; s. Herndon Guinn and Madeline (Coleman) S.; B.S., U. Va., 1950; M.S., Loyola U., 1958, Ph.D., 1959. Analytical chemist E.I. duPont de Nemours & Co., Richmond, Va., 1950-55; lab. dir. Mason-Barron Lab., Chgo., 1959—; clin. lectr. dept. biochemistry Loyola U., Chgo., 1960-72, adj. asso. prof., Maywood, Ill., 1972—; v.p. C & C Med. Equipment & Leasing Co., Chgo., 1967—; clin. chemist Grant Hosp., Chgo., 1965—, instr. med. tech., 1967—; instr. med. tech. Augustana Hosp., Chgo., 1967—, clin. chemist, 1975—; sec. quality control bd. Damon Corp., Needham Heights, Mass. Served with AUS, 1944-47. Recipient Distinguished Alumni award Loyola U., Chgo., 1971. Fellow Am. Inst. Chemists; mem. Nat. Registry Clin. Chemistry, Am. Assn. Clin. Chemistry (treas. Chgo. sect. 1970-73, sec. 1973-74, chmn. elect 1975-76, chmn., 1976-77, mem. nat. edn. com. 1974—), Am. Chem. Soc., Am. Soc. Clin. Pathologists, Sigma Xi. Bd. editors Lab. Medicine. Home: 3012-4 N Waterloo Ct Chicago IL 60657 Office: 4720 W Montrose St Chicago IL 60641

SHEPHERD, PATRICIA ANNE, educator; b. Braymer, Mo., Aug. 3, 1934; d. William R. and Ola LaVerne (Hankins) Shively; A.A., Christian Coll., 1954; B.S., Central Mo. State U., 1957, M.S., 1972; children—Kizan Alynn, James Matthew. Speech therapist, Nevada, Mo., 1958-65, Children's Therapy Center, Sedalia, Mo., 1967-69; tchr. North Kansas City (Mo.) Pub. Schs., 1969—; instr. Pioneer Community Coll., 1976. Mem. NEA, Mo. Edn. Assn., North Kansas City Edn. Assn. Office: 2100 NE 65th St Kansas City MO 64118

SHERAN, ROBERT JOSEPH, chief justice Minn. Supreme Ct.; b. Waseca, Minn., Jan. 2, 1916; s. Michael J. and Eleanor (Bowe) S.; B.A., Coll. St. Thomas, St. Paul, 1936; LL.B., U. Minn., 1939; m. Jean Marie Brown, Feb. 3, 1940; children—Michael, Thomas, Kathleen, John, Daniel. Admitted to Minn. bar, 1939; practice in Glencoe, 1939-42, Mankato, 1945-63; sec. to chief justice Minn. Supreme Ct., 1938-40, then asso. justice, now chief justice; spl. agt. FBI, 1942-45. Mem. Minn. Bd. Law Examiners, 1956-62, 70-73, mem. Minn. Bd. Tax Appeals, 1961-63. Mem. Minn. Ho. of Reps., 1945-49; trustee Coll. St. Thomas, 1964-73. Fellow Am. Coll. Trial Law Lawyers, Internat. Coll. Trial Lawyers, Am. Bar Found.; mem. Am., Minn. bar assns., Am. Judicature Soc., Inst. Judicial Adminstrn. Home: 1077 Sibley Meml Hwy St Paul MN 55118 Office: Minn Supreme Ct 230 State Capitol St Paul MN 55155

SHERCK, CHARLES KEITH, food co. exec.; b. Willard, O., July 27, 1922; s. Virgil Charles and Thelma Florence (Karr) S.; B.A., Miami U., 1947; m. Constance Mae Plapp, Dec. 22, 1946; children—Timothy Charles, Carol Jean. Quality assurance mgr. Am. Home Foods, Inc., Hamilton, O., 1946-50; mfg. mgr., 1950-52; quality assurance mgr. Pillsbury Co., Hamilton, 1952-57, Springfield, Ill., 1957-60, research and devel. mgr., Mpls., 1960-69, corporate research and devel. dir., 1969-77, dir. adminstrv. and tech. services, 1977—. Served to 1st lt., inf. U.S. Army, 1943-46; PTO. Mem. Inst. Food Technologists, Am. Chem. Soc., Am. Assn. Cereal Chemists (dir. 1973-75), A.A.A.S., Audubon Soc. (chpt. v.p. 1976—), Phi Eta Sigma, Sigma Alpha Epsilon, Phi Mu Alpha, Minn. Ornithology Union. Methodist (lay leader 1969-71). Patentee in field. Home: 4805 Markay Ridge Minneapolis MN 55422 Office: 311 Second St SE Minneapolis MN 55414

SHERER, WILLIAM CHARLES, sch. adminstr.; b. Dayton, O., Feb. 12, 1927; s. William Frank and Catherine Annett (Adelberger) S.; B.S., U. Dayton, 1950; M. Elementary Edn., Miami U., Oxford, O., 1956; postgrad. Wright State U., U. Wis.; m. Jean Ann Geis, June 17, 1950; children—John William, William Joseph, Timothy Charles, Joseph Edward, Thomas Raymond, Mary Ann. Tchr. and coach phys. edn. Dayton (O.) pub. schs., 1950-66, asst. prin., 1966-69; tchr. Presque Isle (Wis.) Sch., 1970-71; dist. adminstr. North Lakeland Elementary Sch., Manitowish Water, Wis., 1971—. Bus. mgr. Ohio Edn. Assn., 1953-66; owner, dir. Camp Buckatabon, Conover, Wis., 1956-72. Dir. Dayton (O.) Jewish Community Council Recreation Program, 1950-60. Served with USNR, 1945-46. Recipient merit award Ohio Assn. Health, Phys. Edn. and Recreation, 1961. Mem. Am. Camping Assn., Phi Delta Kappa. Kiwanian. Home: Box 293 Fishtrap Lake Boulder Junction WI 54512 Office: North Lakeland Elementary Sch Manitowich Waters WI 54545

SHERIDAN, JOHN ANDREW, mgmt. cons.; b. Chgo., Sept. 5, 1933; s. Kenneth Andrew and Lila K. (Wilson) S.; B.S., Loyola U., Chgo., 1955; postgrad. U. Chgo., 1955-57; m. Elizabeth Lee Weil, Oct. 5, 1968; children—Kelly, Leslie, Kevin, Lynne. Cons., Labor Relations Assos. of Chgo., Inc., 1957-59; pres. John Sheridan Assos., Inc., mgmt. cons., Des Plaines, Ill., 1959—; chmn. bd., chief exec. officer Howard Young Med. Center, Woodruff, Wis.; mem. faculty Grad. Sch. of Banking, U. Wis., Madison. Pres. Lac du Flambeau (Wis.) Elementary Sch. Bd. Edn., 1973-76; mem. facilities com. N. Central Regional Health Planning Com., 1975. Mem. Am. Mgmt. Assn., Nat. Retail Mchts. Assn. Roman Catholic. Clubs: Marco Polo (N.Y.C.); Wausau (Wis.); Minocqua (Wis.) Country. Home: Route 1 Box 276 Lac Flambeau WI 54538 Office: 1111 Touhy Ave Des Palines IL 60018

SHERIDAN, SISTER MARY FLORIANNE, nursing sch. adminstr.; b. Hymera, Ind., Dec. 27, 1908; d. William Sherman and Della May (Bledsoe) Sheridan; R.N., St. Anthony Hosp. Sch. Nursing, Terre Haute, Ind., 1938; certificate primary edn. Ind. State Tchrs. Coll., 1928, B.S., 1941; postgrad. DePaul U., 1948-49, M.S., 1954; postgrad. St. Louis U., summers 1953, 54. Elementary tchr. Terre Haute, Ind., 1929-35; nursing arts instr. St. Anthony Hosp. Sch. Nursing, Terre Haute, 1939-42; clin. instr. med., surg. nursing St. Francis Sch. Nursing, Evanston, Ill., 1942-44; joined Order of St. Francis, 1944; dir. nursing, dir. Sch. Nursing, St. Margaret Hosp., Hammond, Ind., 1946-58; dir. Sch. Nursing, St. Elizabeth Hosp., Lafayette, Ind., 1958—. Trustee St. Francis Coll., Fort Wayne, Ind., 1957—. Mem. Am., Ind. nurses assns., Nat., Ind. (v.p. 1957-60) leagues for nursing, Ind. Conf. Cath. Schs. Nursing (pres. 1964—), Nat. Council Cath. Nurses, Cath. Audio-Visual Edn. Assn., Ind. Cath. Hosp. Assn. (pres. 1965-66). Home: St Francis Convent Mount Alverno Mishawaka IN 46544 Office: 1508 Tippecanoe St Lafayette IN 47904

SHERIDAN, RICHARD GEORGE, state ofcl.; b. Detroit, Jan. 1, 1938; s. Rudolph Anthony and Lottie (Lewek) Szczotka; A.B., U. Mich., 1959; student Stanford Law Sch., 1961; M.A., U. Tenn., 1962. Credit analyst Nat. Bank Detroit, 1960; instr., research asso. U. Tenn., Knoxville, 1962-65; prof. govt. Mont. State U., Bozeman, 1965-68; state fiscal analyst Wash., 1968-73; legislative budget officer State of Ohio, Columbus, 1973—. Cons. Tenn. legislative council, 1962-65, Mont. legislative council, 1965-68, Knox County, Tenn., 1946-65; project dir. Citizens Conf. Water Resources, Mont., 1967; mem. Mont. Community Services Council, 1966-68. Fellow, recipient certificate So. Regional Tng. Program Pub. Adminstr., 1962; NSF fellow, 1965. Mem. Phi Kappa Psi, Phi Kappa Phi, Pi Sigma Alpha. Author: Urban Justice, 1965; Natural Resources Administration in Fifty States, 1966; Bibliography on Montana's Water and Related Land Resources, 1966; Conservancy Districts, 1967; Water, Water Everywhere-But, 1968. Home: 5728 Crawford Dr Columbus OH 43229

SHERIDAN, WILLIAM COCKBURN RUSSELL, bishop; b. N.Y.C., Mar. 25, 1917; s. John Russell Fortesque and Gertrude Magdalene (Hurley) S.; A.B., Carroll. Coll., 1939; M.Div., Nashotah House Theol. Sem., 1942; D.D., 1966; certificate St. Mary's Grad. Sch. Theology, 1966; S.T.M., Nashotah House Theol. Sem., 1968; m. Rudith Treder, Nov. 13, 1943; children—Elizabeth (Mrs. Allen Wilson Beeler II), Margaret (Mrs. Gerald Wilson), Mary, Peter, Stephen. Ordained deacon and priest Episcopal Ch., 1943; asst. priest St. Paul's Ch., Chgo., 1943-44; rector Gethsemane Ch., Marion, Ind., 1944-47, St. Thomas's Ch., Plymouth, Ind., 1947-72; bishop of Episcopal Diocese of No. Ind., 1972—. Vice pres. bd. trustees Nashotah House Theol. Sem.; pres. bd. trustees Howe (Ind.) Mil. Sch. Author: Journey to Priesthood, 1952; Between Catholics, 1966. Home: 2502 S Twyckenham Dr South Bend IN 46614 Office: 117 N Lafayette Blvd South Bend IN 46601

SHERIFF, ALFRED PEARSON, III, assn. exec.; b. Cadiz, O., July 2, 1927; s. Alfred P. and Edyth (Aiken) S.; B.A., Washington and Jefferson Coll., 1949; LL.B., Western Res. U., 1955; J.D., Case-Western Res. U., 1968; m. Margaret Ann Edwards, Aug. 2, 1967; children—Richard A., Thomas E., David G., Nancy G. Admitted to Ohio bar, 1956; with trust devel. div. Central Nat. Bank, Cleve., 1955-61; asst. to exec. v.p. Delta Tau Delta, Indpls., 1961-65, exec. v.p., 1965—. Bd. govs. Western Res. Sch. Law, 1960; mem. Washington and Jefferson Coll. Devel. Council, 1968-70. Mem. Am., Ohio, Cleve. bar assns., Am. Soc. Assn. Execs., Frat. Execs. Assn. (pres. 1975-76), Newcomen Soc., Summit Soc. N. Am., Delta Tau Delta, Phi Alpha Delta. Republican. Presbyn. Mason (K.T., Shriner), Rotarian. Club: Indianapolis Athletic. Home: 11825 Rolling Springs Dr Carmel IN 46032 Office: Suite 110 4740 Kingsway Dr Indianapolis IN 46205

SHERMAN, EDWARD, chemist; b. N.Y.C., Feb. 8, 1919; s. Israel and Sarah (Baron) S.; student Coll. City N.Y., 1935-36; B.S., U. Ill., 1940; postgrad. U. Ala., 1940-41; M.S., Lehigh U., 1947, Ph.D., 1949; M.B.A., Northwestern U., 1970; m. Laurel June Kaplan, Dec. 15, 1945; children—Carol Jean (Mrs. Mark Austin Cross), Patricia Ann (Mrs. William Stephen Blau). Teaching asst. U. Ala., 1940-41; jr. insp. FDA, 1941-42; research asst. Lehigh U., 1946-47, research fellow, 1947-48; research asso. Ill. Inst. Tech., Chgo., 1949-50; with Quaker Oats Co., Barrington, Ill., 1950—, mgr. research and adminstrv. services, 1972-73, mgr. planning and adminstrn., 1973-75, asst. dir. chem. research and devel., 1975—. Capt., Civil Def. Police Aux., 1955-60. Mem. Nippersink (Wis.) Community Bd., 1973—, v.p., 1976-77, pres., 1977—; chmn. Nippersink Water Trust, 1975—; mem. Randall Twp. (Wis.) Sheriff's Com., 1977—. Served to capt. USMC, 1942-46. Decorated Purple Heart, Bronze Star. Recipient Fredus N. Peters award Quaker Oats Co., 1968. Fellow A.A.A.S.; mem Am. Chem Soc., Sigma Xi, Delta Mu Delta. Mason (32 deg., Shriner). Clubs: Nippersink Community, Nippersink Lodge Country. Patentee in field. Contbr. articles to books and profl. jours. Home: RD 1 Box N94 (Nippersink) Genoa City WI 53128 Office: 617 W Main St Barrington IL 60010

SHERMAN, FRANCIS GEORGE HARRY, former bank exec.; b. Croydon, Eng., Apr. 12, 1924; s. Frank Edward and Amelia (Oddy) S.; student Hatfield Coll., U. Durham, 1942-43; B.A., Harvard, 1949, M.B.A., 1950; m. Barbara Opal Blick, May 3, 1947 (dec. 1975); children—Christopher Randolph, Dawn Madeline Ann. Came to U.S., 1947, naturalized, 1950. Sales rep. Eagle-Ottawa Leather Co., Grand Haven, Mich., 1951-55, automotive sales mgr., Detroit, 1955-58; dist. sales mgr. Rogers Pub. Co., Pitts., 1958-59; exec. v.p. Penn & Hamaker, Inc., Cleve., 1959-71, dir., 1962-71; v.p. Soc. Nat. Bank, Cleve., 1971-76. Mem. Bd. Edn., Spring Lake, Mich., 1955-58; mem. citizens com. Chagrin Falls (O.) Sch. Dist., 1964-67; chmn. coll. relations com. Harvard Bus. Sch., 1966—; bd. dirs. Chagrin Valley Artists Assn., 1966-72, pres., 1966, treas., 1968-71; instr. Minority Econ. Developers Council, 1969—, dir., 1974—. Pres. West Shore Symphony Orch., Muskegon, Mich., 1955-56; chmn. Harvard Gt. Lakes Bus. Conf., 1965. Served with RAF, 1943-47. Fellow Am. Geographical Soc.; mem. Greater Cleve. Growth Assn. (mem. internat. trade devel. com. 1969-71), Assn. Ohio Commodores (life). Clubs: Harvard Business Sch. (Cleve.) (pres. 1964-65); Racquet (Chagrin Falls, O.); Pymatuning Yacht (Jamestown, Pa.). Home: 105 Skyline Dr Chagrin Falls OH 44022

SHERMAN, GEORGE EARL, JR., mfg. co. exec.; b. St. Joseph, Mo., Dec. 14, 1924; s. George Earl and Maria Elizabeth (Olsen) S.; Gard Bus. Coll., 1942-43; Bus. Degree, Mo. Western Coll., 1946; spl. student Rockhurst Coll., 1956-57; m. Shirley Ann Petersen, Jan. 27, 1963; children—Skylar, Darren, Sharane, Sheryl, Kamala. Newspaper reporter, editor Omaha World Herald, St. Joseph Gazette, 1943-56; dir. personnel and pub. relations Noma Lites, Inc., St. Joseph, 1956-61; dir. personnel Fairchild Camera & Instrument Corp., Joplin, Mo., 1961-63; dir. employee relations City Utilities, Springfield, Mo., 1963-64; v.p. Dunham-Bush, Inc., Hartford, Conn., 1964-69; dir. labor relations and personnel Am. Safety Razor Co., Staunton, Va., 1969-71; v.p. Midland-Ross Corp., Cleve., 1971—; Am. Soc. Personnel Adminstrn. exchange personnel exec., USSR, Rumania, Yugoslavia, Berlin, 1971; mem. team for tour and productivity study Japanese industry, 1973. Nat. publicity dir. Women's Amateur Athletic Union Basketball, 1957-61; nat. dir. publicity Connie Mack World Series, St. Joseph, 1948—. Trustee Govtl. Research Inst., Cleve., Unitcast Found., Toledo. Mem. Am. Soc. Personnel Adminstrn. (v.p. 1971), Soc. Advancement Mgmt., Am. Mgmt. Assn. Roman Catholic. Clubs: Cleveland Athletic, Mid-Day (Cleve.); Country of Hudson (Ohio). Home: 2910 Old Mill Rd Hudson OH 44236 Office: Midland-Ross Corp 55 Public Sq Cleveland OH 44113

SHERMAN, JEANIE KELSO, clergyman; b. Cambridge, Mass., Sept. 28, 1909; d. George Ernest and Jeanie (Campbell) S.; Th.B., Gordon Coll., 1933; B.D., Andover Newton Theol. Sch., 1936; D.D., Sioux Falls Coll., 1967; children—John B. Dolan, Dorothy A. Bowers (Mrs. Marvin Knowles), Lottie Buchanan (Mrs. Leland Speer), Warren C. Dolan, Gladys R. Dolan (Mrs. James Danos), Kenneth B. Dolan, Paul M. Dolan, Janet M. Dolan (Mrs. Bernard Ciemiewicz). Ordained to ministry Bapt. Ch., 1936; pastor Golden Hills Union Ch., Melrose, Mass., 1935-42, Bay Rd. Chapel, Revere, Mass., 1938-42, Addison and Panto, Vt., 1942-45, 1st Bapt. Ch., Timber Lake, S.D., 1945-75, Madison, S.D., 1975—; mem. Am. Bapt. Nat. Home Mission Bd., 1966—, v.p., 1969—; mem. Am. Bapt. Profl. Leadership Task Force; v.p. Ministers Council Madison (S.D.). Treas. bd. Timber Lake Cemetery, 1958—; chmn. S.D. Am. Bapt. State Juvenile Protection Com.; pres. Am. Bapt. Home Mission Soc., 1970-72, S.D. Bapt. Conv., 1972, 1971. Recipient Rosa O. Hall award for outstanding rural work, 1952. Mem. S.D. Bapt. Women (pres. 1949-53), S.D. Bapt. Ministers (pres. 1957-59), Dewey Zieback Council Chs. (pres. 1966—), Am. Legion Aux., Am. Bapt. Homes and Hosps. Assn. (exec. com.). Mem. Order Eastern Star. Club: Home Demonstration. Home: 314 E Center St Madison SD 57042 Office: 322 E Center St Madison SD 57042

SHERMAN, JUNE MARIE ROACH, ret. vol. service coordinator, civic worker; b. White Pigeon, Mich.; d. Arthur William and Eva May (Clark) Roach; student Wayne U., 1931, Western Mich. U., 1953-54, 60-63, Mich. U., 1962; children—Nola M. (Mrs. William Benson), V. Clayton. Occupational and recreational therapist Kalamazoo State Hosp., 1947-49, coordinator vol. services, 1949-74. Founding mem., sec., Citizens Assn. for Kalamazoo State Hosp., Inc., 1959—, Kalamazoo State Hosp. Guild, 1969; chmn. com. on aging Kalamazoo County Council Chs., 1961-66; chmn. Friendly Visitors Com., 1966-68, active Kalamazoo Civic Players. Bd. dirs. Sr. Services, Inc. Recipient citation Citizen's Assn. Kalamazoo State Hosp., 1970; named Woman of Year, Kalamazoo chpt. Quota Internat., 1973; resolution Mich. Ho. of Reps., 1974; Presdl. citation, 1974. Fellow Am. Assn. Vol. Service Coordinators (charter); mem. Nat. Assn. Recreational Therapists (charter), World Fedn. Mental Health, Bus. and Profl. Women's Club (chmn. civic participation com. 1967-68), Zonta Internat. (chmn. service com. Kalamazoo), Internat. Platform Assn., Mich. Soc. Mental Health, Mich. Health and Welfare League, Assn. Retarded Children, Assn. Emotionally Disturbed Children, Council Human Relations, Mich. Mental Health Soc. (chpt. pres. 1968-70). Home: 2019 Douglas Ave Kalamazoo MI 49007

SHERMAN, KEITH MELVIN, broadcasting adminstr.; b. Waterloo, Iowa, Feb. 1, 1953; s. Melvin and Marian Jean (Kruse) S.; B.A. in Communications, Central Coll., 1975. Dir. pub. relations advt. Am. Radio Missions, Pella, Iowa, 1973-74; mgr. KCUI-FM, Central Coll., Pella, 1974-75; sports editor, Broken Bow, Nebr., 1975-77; sales rep. Messenger Printing Co., Fort Dodge, Iowa, 1977—. Recipient KCUI Key award, 1973, commendation as producer sr. citizen program Nat. Assn. Devel. Orgns., 1974. Mem. Central Coll. Inter-Varsity Christian Fellowship (pres.). Mem. Ref. Ch. in Am. (tchr. Sunday sch., 1973-74, sponsor youth group 1973-74). Address:

SHERMAN, KENNETH IRA, elec. engr.; b. Festus, Mo., Apr. 29, 1917; s. Russell Ira and Vergie Ellen (Davis) S.; B.S.E.E., Mo. Sch. Mines and Metallurgy, 1942; postgrad. Harvard U., Mass. Inst. Tech., 1943, St. Louis U., 1958; m. Icie Roberta Gautney, Mar. 20, 1959; children—Randall Dean, Lynden Craig. Asst. research engr. McDonnell Aircraft Co., St. Louis, 1946-48, sr. electronics group engr., 1959-70; radar engr. Emerson Electric Co., St. Louis, 1948-59; elec. engr. River Cement Co., Festus, 1970—. Served to lt. (s.g.) USNR, 1943-46. Mem. IEEE (sr. mem.), Instrument Soc. Am. (sr. mem.). Republican. Baptist. Co-author chpt. on generators in electronics book. Home: Route 2 Box 38 Abbey Rd Pevely MO 63070 Office: Selma Plant Festus MO 63028

SHERMAN, LESLIE ALLYN, ret. packaging engr.; b. Chesterland, O., May 16, 1911; s. Clifford C. and Zula M. (Bailey) S.; B.S., Ohio U., 1935; postgrad. Mich. State U., 1967-68; m. Flora Osborne, Feb. 9, 1935; children—Larry T., Jeffrey O., Susan K. Sherman Dolan. Chemist FDA, Cleve., 1935-40; powder and explosives chemist Kingsbury (Ind.) Ordnance Plant, U.S. Ordnance Dept., 1941-46; pharm. chemist Miles Labs., Elkhart, Ind., 1947-48; chief chemist Standard Pharm. Co., Chgo., 1949-50, Whitehall Pharm. Co., Elkhart, 1950-57; supr. packaging control lab. Miles Labs., Elkhart, 1957-70, staff packaging engr., 1971-75. Mem. Am. Chem. Soc., Am. Soc. for Quality Control, Packaging Inst., Am. Men Sci. Home: 2312 Grant St Elkhart IN 46514

SHERMAN, STANLEY NORMAN, newspaper exec.; b. Royal Oak, Mich., June 14, 1938; s. Laurel Ager and Lela Ota (Keyte) French; student Highland Park Jr. Coll., 1956-57, Detroit Bus. Coll., 1957-59; m. Serena Susan Gambee, May 1, 1971. Foreman mail room Tribune Pub. Co., Royal Oak, 1958-59, asst. mgr. bus. and classified advt. sales, 1961-64, credit mgr., 1964—, nat. advt. mgr., 1965—; asst. bus. mgr. Tribune Corp., Royal Oak, 1969-70, bus. mgr., 1970—, asst. treas., 1971—. Pres., Royal Oak Youth Assistance Com., 1973, treas., 1972—; bd. mgmt., Camp Oakland, Royal Oak YMCA; bd. dirs. Boys Club Royal Oak. Served with 25th. inf. div., U.S. Army, 1959-61. Mem. Greater Royal Oak C. of C. (pres. 1975—), Advt. Media Credit Execs. Assn., Newspaper Personnel Relations Assn., Nat. Assn. Credit Mgmt. Clubs: Red Run Golf, Rotary (pres. Royal Oak 1971-72), Elks. Office: Tribune Pub Co PO Box 311 Royal Oak MI 48068

SHERMAN, WILLIAM FREDERICK, JR., librarian; b. Evergreen Park, Ill., Dec. 19, 1938; s. William Frederick and Marie Dorothy (Streit) S.; student Oriel Coll., Oxford U., summer 1959; B.S., No. Ill. U., 1960; M.A. in L.S., Rosary Coll., 1969; m. Marilyn J. Mathis, Aug. 9, 1969; 1 son, William Anthony. Grad. asst. No. Ill. U. Library, DeKalb, 1960-61; librarian J. Sterling Morton High Sch., Cicero, 1961—. Library cons. Ill. Visually Handicapped Inst., 1963-65. Mem. Republican County Com., 1961-74; chmn. Rep. Twp. Caucus, 1977; del. Rep. State Conv., 1962, 64, 66, 68; commr. Downers Grove Park Dist., 1963-65, commr.-sec., 1965-71, pres., 1971—; pres. S.E. Assn. for Spl. Parks and Recreation, 1976—. Mem. NEA, Ill. Edn. Assn. (local pres. 1965, div. chmn. citizenship commn. 1968), Am. Fedn. Tchrs. (v.p. council 1976-77), Phi Alpha Theta, Beta Phi Mu. Roman Catholic. Home: 3311 Pomeroy Rd Downers Grove IL 60515 Office: 2423 S Austin St Cicero IL 60650

SHERMAN, WILLIAM RODERICK, educator; b. Newport, R.I., June 9, 1892; s. William Sprague and Elizabeth (Sherman) S.; A.B., Clark U., 1913, A.M., 1914, Ph.D., 1923; m. Catherine Eliza Lyman, Aug. 20, 1919; children—William Gordon, Katharine Elizabeth (Mrs. Elam L. Stewart). Prof. history and social sci. Juniata Col., 1914-15; prof. history and econs. Buena Vista Coll., 1915-17; instr. econs. Brown U., 1919-21; asst. prof. to prof. econs. DePauw U., 1921-31; head econs. dept. Hillsdale (Mich.) Coll., 1931—; vis. prof. econs. Carleton Coll., 1929-30; observer U.S. Weather Bur., 1942—. Served with C.W.S., U.S. Army, 1918-19. Recipient Thomas Jefferson award Dept. Commerce, 1975. Mem. Mich. Acad. (state pres. econs. sect. 1953-54), Am. Econ. Assn., Am. Mktg. Assn. Club: Econ. (Detroit). Home: 98 N Norwood Hillsdale MI 49242

SHERTZER, BRUCE ELDON, educator; b. Bloomfield, Ind., Jan. 11, 1928; s. Edwin Franklin and Lois Belle S.; B.S., Ind. U., 1952, M.S., 1953, Ed.D., 1958; m. Carol May Rice, Nov. 24, 1948; children—Sarah Ann, Mark Eldon. Tchr., Martinsville (Ind.) High Sch., 1952-54, counselor, 1954-56; state dir. guidance Ind. Dept. Pub. Instruction, 1956-58; asso. dir. superior student project N. Central Assn., Chgo., 1958-60; asst. prof. edn. Purdue U., W. Lafayette, Ind., 1960-62, asso. prof., 1962-66, prof., 1966—, also chmn. counseling and personnel services; vis. prof. ednl. psychology U. Hawaii, 1967; Fulbright sr. lectr. U. Reading (Eng.), 1967-68; cons. Ministry of Edn., Cyprus, 1968-69; chmn. adv. council for career edn. U.S. Office of Edn., 1976. Served with U.S. Army, 1946-47. Mem. Assn. Counselor Edn. and Supervision (pres. 1971-72), Am. (pres. 1974-75), Ind. (pres. 1963; Counselor Educator of Year award 1969) personnel and guidance assns. Author: Fundamentals of Counseling, 1974; Guidance: Program Development and Management, 1974; Fundamentals of Guidance, 1976; Career Exploration and Planning, 1976; Career Planning, 1977; contbr. numerous articles in field to profl. jours. Home: 1620 Western Dr West Lafayette IN 47906 Office: Dept Edn Purdue U West Lafayette IN 47907

SHERWIN, CHARLES STEELMAN, surgeon; b. St. Louis, Sept. 3, 1920; s. Charles Frederick and Lillie Belle (Steelman) S.; B.S., St. Louis U., 1941, M.D., 1943; m. Ruth Adele Steward, Nov. 24, 1943; children—Ann Margaret, Robert Lawrence, Paul Frederick, Mary Helen, Charles Walter. Intern, St. Louis (Mo.) U., 1943-44, resident, 1946-48; resident Barnard Free Skin and Cancer Hosps., St. Louis, 1948-49; practice medicine specializing in surgery in St. Louis, 1951—; mem. Clayton Surg. Group, Inc., 1968—; mem. staffs St. John's Mercy Hosp., Creve Couer, Mo., Cardinal Glennon Meml. Hosp. for Children, St. Louis; mem. staff St. Mary's Hosp., Richmond Heights, Mo., pres. med.-dental staff, 1972; mem. staff Bethesda Gen. Hosp., St. Louis, pres. med.-dental staff, 1975, 76; staff DePaul Hosp., St. Louis, 1977—. Instr. gen. surgery St. Louis U. Sch. Medicine, 1951-56, sr. instr., 1956-60, asst. clin. prof. surgery, 1960—. Mem. voting bd. dirs. Mo. Med. Service, 1958-74, trustee, 1968-74; mem. voting bd. dirs. St. Louis Blue Cross, 1959-75; bd. dirs. St. Mary's Hosp. Sch. Practical Nursing, 1958-64; mem. lay adv. bd. St. Mary's Health Center, 1973—; bd. trustees Bethesda Gen. Hosp., 1974. Served to lt. USNR, 1944-46. Diplomate, Am. Bd. Surgery. Fellow Am. Coll. Surgeons; mem. St. Louis Med. Soc. (mem. Council 1956-58, sec. 1959-60, pres. 1963, hon. mem. 1974—), Mo. State Med. Assn. (del. to House, 1956-77, v.p. 1965), St. Louis Surg. Soc. (gov. 1965-68). Baptist. Editor: St Louis Medicine, 1962. Home: 3971 Flora Place St Louis MO 63110 Office: 911 S Brentwood Blvd St Louis MO 63105

SHERWIN, LARRY EDWARD, chiropractor; b. White Hall, Ill., May 9, 1945; s. Perry Edward and Mabel Louise (Parks) S.; D.C., Nat. Coll. Chiropractic, Lombard, Ill., 1967; postgrad. Minn. Basci Sci. Inst., 1971; m. Debra Jean Scoggins, Oct. 2, 1971; children—Jonathan Lawrence, Michelle Renee, Jeffrey Matthew. Practice chiropractics, Winchester, Ill., 1967—. Real estate broker, Winchester, 1975—; owner farm, White Hall, Ill., 1966—. Served with AUS, 1969-70; Vietnam. Mem. Mo., Ky. State, Am. chiropractic assns., Ill. Chiropractic Soc., Ill. Pure Water Soc., Soil and Health Found., Sigma Phi Kappa. Baptist. Clubs: Kiwanis, Elks. Home: Rural Route 2 Whitehall IL 62092 Office: 32 1/2 S Main St Winchester IL 62694

SHERWOOD, LOUIS MAIER, physician; b. N.Y.C., Mar. 1, 1937; s. Arthur Joseph and Blanche (Burger) S.; A.B., Johns Hopkins U., 1957; M.D., Columbia U., 1961; m. Judith Brimberg, Mar. 27, 1966; children—Jennifer Beth, Arilh David. Research fellow dept. pathology Hartford (Conn.) Hosp., 1959; intern, Presbyn. Hosp., N.Y.C., 1961-62, asst. resident in medicine, 1962-63; clin. asso., research fellow Nat. Heart Inst., NIH, Bethesda, Md., 1963-66; NIH trainee endocrinology and metabolism Coll. Physicians and Surgeons, Columbia, N.Y.C., 1966-68; asso. medicine Beth Israel Hosp. and Harvard Med. Sch., Boston, 1968-69; chief endocrinology Beth Israel Hosp., 1968-72; asst. prof. medicine Harvard Med. Sch., Boston, 1969-71, asso. prof., 1971-72; physician in chief and chmn. dept. medicine Michael Reese Hosp. and Med. Center, Chgo., 1972—; prof. medicine div. biol. scis., also Pritzker Sch. Medicine, U. Chgo., 1972—. Bd. dirs. Physicians and Surgeons Corp., Michael Reese Med. Center, 1973—, Barren Found., 1974—; mem. bd. trustees Michael Reese Med. Center, 1974-77. Served as surgeon USPHS, 1963-66. Diplomate Am. Bd. Internal Medicine (asso.). Fellow Am. Coll. Physicians; mem. A.A.A.S., Am. Fedn. for Clin. Research, Am. Inst. Chemists, Am. Soc. Biol. Chemists, Am. Soc. for Clin. Investigation, Assn. Am. Physicians, Endocrine Soc., N.Y. Acad. Scis., Mass. Med. Soc., Central Soc. for Clin. Research, Chgo. Soc. Internal Medicine, Phi Beta Kappa, Alpha Omega Alpha. Recipient Joseph Mather Smith prize for outstanding alumni research Coll. Physicians and Surgeons, Columbia U., 1972; Sr. Class Teaching award U. Chgo., 1976, 77. Editor Beth Israel seminars New Eng. Jour. Medicine, 1968-71; editorial bd. Endocrinology, 1969-73; asso. editor Metabolism, 1970—, Gen. Medicine B Study Sect., NIH, 1975-79; editorial bd. Year in Endocrinology, 1976—. Contbr. numerous articles on endocrinology, protein hormones and calcium metabolism to jours. Office: Michael Reese Hosp and Medical Center 29th St and Ellis Ave Chicago IL 60616

SHERWOOD, SAM S(ABEAN), broadcasting exec.; b. Melrose, Minn., Oct. 11, 1930; s. George M. and Bernadeth E. (Sabean) S.; student Hamline U., St. Paul; m. Irene Novalany, Nov. 13, 1954; children—Timothy, Sandra, James, JoAnn, Samuel. With stas. WCOW, South St. Paul, 1952, WISK, St. Paul, 1954, WTCN, Mpls., 1957, KDWB, St. Paul/Mpls., 1959, KSTP, Mpls./St. Paul, 1969; mgmt. broadcast exec. Tedesco Broadcasting Co., St. Paul, 1952, Crowell Collier Broadcasting Co., Mpls./St. Paul, 1959; Valjon Inc., Mpls./St. Paul, 1968, Hubbard Broadcasting, Mpls./St. Paul, 1968, Entertainment Communications, Inc., Mpls./St. Paul, 1969—; 1st v.p. Entercom, Inc., Mpls., St. Paul, 1969—. Mem. broadcast adv. bd. U. Minn. Active local Am. Cancer Soc. drive. Served with USNR, 1948-52. Mem. Mpls. C. of C., Mpls. Downtown Council. Club: Prosperity Heights Booster (St. Paul). Home: 1358 Hazelwood St St Paul MN 55106 Office: 3470 Hwy 8 New Brighton MN 55112

SHETH, JAGDISH NANCHAND, educator; b. Rangoon, Burma, Sept. 3, 1938; s. Nanchand Jivraj and Diwaliben (Nanchand) S.; came to U.S., 1961, naturalized, 1975; B.Com. with honors, U. Madras, 1960; M.B.A., U. Pitts., 1962, Ph.D., 1966; m. Madhuri Ratilal Shah, Dec. 22, 1962; children—Reshma J., Raju J. Research asso., asst. prof. Grad. Sch. Bus., Columbia, 1963-65; asst. prof. Mass. Inst. Tech., 1965-66; asst. prof. Columbia U., 1966-69; vis. prof. Indian Inst. Mgmt. Calcutta, 1968; vis. lectr. Internat. Marketing Inst., Harvard, 1969; asso. prof. bus. adminstrn. U. Ill., Urbana, 1969-71, acting head dept., 1970-72, prof. and research prof., 1971-73, I.B.A. distinguished prof. and research prof., 1973—. Albert Frey vis. prof. marketing U. Pitts., 1974; condr. seminars for industry and govt.; cons. to industry. Recipient gold medal for 1st standing pub. exams. India, 1960. Mgmt. Program for Execs. fellow, S&H Green Stamps fellow, 1963-64. Fellow Am. Psychol. Assn.; mem. Am. Marketing Assn., Am. Statis. Assn., Am. Assn. Decision Scis., Assn. Consumer Research, Am. Acad. Advt., Psychometric Soc. Author: (with John A. Howard) The Theory of Buyer Behavior, 1969; (with S.P. Sethi) Multinational Business Operations: Advanced Readings, 4 vols., 1973; (with A. Woodside and P. Bennett) Consumer and Industrial Buying Behavior, 1977. Editor: Models of Buyer Behavior, 1974; (with Peter L. Wright) Marketing Analysis for Societal Problems, 1974; Multivariable Methods for Market and Survey Research, 1977. Contbr. articles to profl. jours. Home: 414 Brookens Dr Urbana IL 61801

SHETH, JASHWANTLAL S., cosmetics co. exec.; b. Padra, India, July 30, 1939; s. Shankerlal P. and Champaben S. (Shah) S.; came to U.S., 1970; B.S. with honors, M.S. U., Baroda, India, 1960, M.S., 1962; diploma in business La Salle Extension U., 1973; m. Hasumati P. Parikh, May 10, 1963; children—Trusha, Gopali and Shefali (twins). Sr. chemist Sara Merck, Ltd., Baroda, India, 1963-70; various supervisory-mgmt. positions with drugs and cosmetics firms, U.S., 1970-73; quality assurance mgr. Johnson Products Co., Chgo., 1973-75, dir. tech. ops., 1975—. Mem. Am. Inst. Chemists, Am. Soc. Cosmetic Chemists. Office: 8522 S Lafayette St Chicago IL 60620

SHEVERBUSH, ROBERT L., univ. adminstr.; b. Wray, Colo., Aug. 5, 1935; s. Robert L. and Emma V. (Gerber) S.; B.A., U. Colo., 1957; M.A., U. No. Colo., 1960, Ed.D., 1967; m. Gladys Joan Kremers, Aug. 22, 1964; children—Robert L., William A., John James. Dir. research, head counseling dept. Colorado Springs (Colo.) Pub. Schs., 1960-68; asst. prof. Central Mo. State U., Warrensburg, 1968-70; asso. dean counseling services U. Ill. Med. Center, Chgo., 1970-76; chmn. dept. psychology and counseling Pittsburg (Kans.) State U., 1976—. Mem. Am., Kans. psychol. assns. Home: Route 4 Box 161B Pittsburg KS 66762 Office: Room 112 Hughes Hall Kansas State Coll Pittsburg KS 66762

SHEWMAKER, MARY DIANNE, sch. counselor; b. Kennett, Mo., Mar. 3, 1945; d. Cleo B. and Arles Inez (Barham) Davis; B.A., Harding Coll., 1967; M.A., Memphis State U., 1975; m. Sherman Nelson Shewmaker, Dec. 22, 1970; 1 son, Scott. Social caseworker pub. schs., Memphis, 1968-71; psychology, social studies tchr. pub. schs., El Paso, Tex., 1972; tchr. Am. High Sch., Stuttgart, Ger., 1973; "SPAN" career coordinator Memphis City Schs., 1974-75; counselor Spencer-Owen Community Sch. System, Spencer, Ind., 1976—; youth services vol. Alternative to Jail Program. Certified tchr., Ark., Tenn., Tex., Mo., Ala.; certified counselor, Tenn., Ind. Mem. Am. Personnel and Guidance Assn., NEA, Spencer-Owen Edn. Assn. Mem. Chs. of Christ. Contbr. article to Mission Mag., 1976. Home: 4611 Middle Ct Bloomington IN 47401 Office: Hillside Ave Spencer IN 47460

SHIBLEY, FREDERIC JAMILE, glass co. exec.; b. Copperhill, Tenn., May 7, 1946; s. George Toufic and Adele (George) S.; B.S. cum laude in Marketing, U. Tenn., 1968; m. Andrea Mannal Haug, Sept. 27, 1969. Sales trainee Owens Corning Fiberglas, Raleigh, N.C., Miami, Fla., 1968-69, salesman, Cleve., 1969-72, salesman, Chgo., 1973-74, nat. marketing mgr., Toledo, 1974-77, mgr. shingle mktg. sect., 1977—; asst. mgr. Shibley's Fabric Center, Dayton, Tenn., 1972-73. Scoutmaster, Boy Scouts Am., Dayton, Tenn., 1973. Mem. Phi Sigma Kappa, Phi Kappa Phi, Delta Sigma Pi, Beta Gamma Sigma. Home: 4624 Kathy Lane Toledo OH 43623 Office: Owens Corning Fiberglas Corp 1 Levis Sq Toledo OH 43659

SHIDELER, SHIRLEY ANN WILLIAMS, lawyer; b. Mishawaka, Ind., July 9, 1930; d. William Harmon and Lois Wilma (Koch) Williams; LL.B., Ind. U., 1964; 1 dau., Gail Shideler Frye. Legal sec. Barnes, Hickam, Pantzer & Boyd, Indpls., 1953-63; admitted to Ind. bar, 1964; practiced in Indpls., 1964—; asso. firm Barnes, Hickam, Pantzer, & Boyd, 1963-70, partner, 1971—. Active fund drives Indpls. Symphony, 1968—, Indpls. Mus. Art, 1969—. Bd. dirs. bus. unit gals Indpls. Mus. Art. Mem. Am., Ind. (sec. 1975-76), Indpls. (bd. mgrs. 1968-70, 72, v.p. charge affairs 1972) bar assns., Estate Planning Council. Club: Woman's Rotary (pres. 1969-71, dir. 1968—) (Indpls.). Home: 5150 Hawthorne Dr Indianapolis IN 46226 Office: 1313 Merchants Bank Bldg Indianapolis IN 46204

SHIEL, VINCENT WYMORE, sports co. exec.; b. Atlanta, Apr. 23, 1933; s. Vincent Bernard and Ivy Jane (Wymore) S.; A.B. in Physics, Emory U., 1953; Ph.D. in Physics, Ga. Inst. Tech., 1957; m. Helen McCollough, Dec. 18, 1971; 1 son by previous marriage, S. Andrew. Systems analyst Wright Patterson AFB, Ohio, 1959-61, tech. dir. ops. research, 1961-65; pres. Outdoor Sports Hdqrs., Inc., Dayton, Ohio, 1960—. Served to lt. USAF, 1957-59. Mem. Phi Beta Kappa. Episcopalian. Club: Sycamore Creek Country. Home: 6260 Seton Hill St Dayton OH 45459 Office: PO Box 1327 Dayton OH 45401

SHIELDS, DONALD JAMES, educator; b. Paris, Ill., Oct. 28, 1937; s. John and Harriet Ann (Francis) S.; B.S., Eastern Ill. U., 1959; M.S., Purdue U., 1961, Ph.D., 1964; children—Donald Gary, Chrintina Lynn. Instr. speech Purdue U., 1963-64; asst. prof. speech communication Cornell U., 1964-65; asst. prof. speech Ind. State U., 1965-70, asso. prof., 1970—; adj. prof. Rose-Hulman Inst. Tech., 1974-77; cons. in polit. and labor communications. Deacon Presbyterian Ch., Paris, Ill. Ross-Ade fellow, 1963-64. Mem. AAUP, Speech Communication Assn., Internat. Communication Assn., Am. Forensics Assn. Democrat. Author: History of Free Speech in Decision Making, 1974; Introduction to Speech-communication, Theory and Practice, 1977. Home: Rural Route 1 Dennison IL 62423 Office: Indiana State University Terre Haute IN 47809

SHIELDS, FLOYD FRANCIS, lawyer; b. Wathena, Kans., Sept. 9, 1901; s. Elmer Francis and Caroline Augusta (Schriner) S.; A.B., U. Kans., 1925; J.D., Washburn U., 1932; m. Ella Louise Torluemke, June 23, 1933; 1 dau., Caroline Louise. Admitted to Kan. bar., 1932, Ill. bar, 1938, Mo. bar, 1953, U.S. Supreme Ct. bar, 1940; spl. counsel Kans. State Corp. Commn., Topeka, 1933-37; gen. counsel Gen. Expressways Inc. (formerly Keeshin Freight Lines Inc.), Chgo., 1937-43, 46-51; dir.-gen. transp. Aid to Russia program Imperial Govt. Iran, 1943-45; transp. specialist Office Inter-Am. Affairs U.S. Govt. S.Am., Washington, 1945; pvt. practice law Mission, Kans., 1958—; gen. counsel, dir. C.F. Emling Co., Chgo., Am. Salesmasters Ltd., Denver. Mem. Kans., Ill., Chgo., Topeka, Johnson County, Am. bar assns., Mo. Bar Integrated, Am. Judicature Soc., Phi Alpha Delta, Kappa Sigma. Episcopalian. (sec. bd. trustees). Mason (K.T., Shriner), Rotarian. Clubs: Kan. Assn. High 12 (pres. 1966-67), University (Chgo.). Home: 5325 W 60th Terrace Mission KS 66205 Office: 5822 Reeds Rd PO Box 68 Shawnee Mission KS 66201

SHIELDS, LEE ANN, speech, lang. pathologist; b. Evansville Ind., July 15, 1943; d. Curtis Willard and Sarah Francis (Brown) Sturgeon; B.S., Ind. State U., 1965, M.S., 1967; m. James Wesley Shields, Mar. 26, 1965; 1 son, Matthew James. Speech, hearing therapist Evansville-Vanderburgh Sch. Corp. (Ind.), 1965, tchr. educable mentally retarded, 1965-68, pathologist speech, hearing and lang., 1968—; speech, lang. pathologist Deaconess Hosp., Evansville, 1972—. Licensed speech pathologist Ind. Mem. Am. Speech and Hearing Assn. (certified), NEA (life), Ind., Evansville tchrs. assns., Ind. Speech and Hearing Assn. (sec.-treas. 1972-74), Kappa Kappa Iota. Address: 6600 E Chestnut St Evansville IN 47715

SHIELDS, MICHAEL ROY, computer co. exec.; b. Newark, Feb. 4, 1947; s. Roy L. and Laura Geraldine (Swart) S.; B.S., Bluffton Coll., 1969; m. Janelle Kay Erskine, Jan. 15, 1977. Tchr., Buckeye Valley Schs., Delaware, Ohio, 1969-71; mktg. mgr. trainee Burroughs Corp., Columbus, Ohio, 1971-72, mktg. rep., 1972, territory mgr., 1972, zone sales mgr., 1974-76, dist. product mgr., Indpls., 1976—. Methodist. Clubs: Carmel Racquet, Elks. Home: 579 Smokey Row Ct Carmel IN 46032 Office: 1828 Meridian St N Indianapolis IN 46202

SHIELDS, PATRICK THOMAS, property tax negotiator; b. San Antonio, Sept. 5, 1935; s. Patrick Thomas and Mary Belle (Carson) S.; B.B.A., U. Tex., 1959; m. Mary Lou Sechrist, Mar. 28, 1964; children—Llewellyn Sechrist, Patrick Terrence II. Mgr. real property taxes Sears, Roebuck & Co., Skokie, Ill., 1968—; mortgage loan officer Oak Cliff Savs. & Loan Assn., Dallas, 1962-64; Appraiser II, Office of Real Estate Assessor, Richmond, Va., 1965-68; lectr. in field. Mem. Buffalo Grove (Ill.) Planning Commn., 1973—. Served to 1st. lt., Q.M.C., U.S. Ar.ny, 1960-62. Mem. Chgo. Real Estate Bd., Internat. Assn. Assessing Officers, Nat. Assn. Review Appraisers, County Auditors Assn. Ohio. Presbyn. (deacon). Home: 1016 Whitehall Dr Buffalo Grove IL 60090 Office: 7447 Skokie Blvd Skokie IL 60076

SHIFFERMILLER, WILLIAM ERNEST, food co. exec.; b. Stamford, Nebr., Nov. 7, 1911; s. Ernest Cecil and Eliza Ray (Johnston) S.; B.S., Ohio State U., 1949; M.S., Mich. State U., 1951; M.B.A., U. Chgo., 1957; m. Vivian Anita Saville, Oct. 18, 1960. Foreman, Armour & Co., Superior, Nebr., 1929-35; div. dir. prodn. and engring. Borden Inc., Chgo., 1951-70; mgr. prodn. and engring. Kroger Co., Cin., 1970—. Served with USAAF, 1942-46. Decorated Legion of Merit, D.F.C., Air medal with clusters; research fellow Mich. State U., 1950. Mem. Am. Soc. Agrl. Engrs., Gamma Sigma Delta, Pi Kappa Alpha. Mason (32 deg., Shriner). Designer food processing plants. Home: 4951 Hawaiian Terrace Cincinnati OH 45223 Office: 1014 Vine St Cincinnati OH 45216

SHIMANSKI, GREGG THOMAS, realtor; b. LaCrosse, Wis., May 4, 1951; s. S. Thomas and Gloria Mae (Schindler) S.; student U. Colo., 1969-73; Harvard U., 1973; B.A. in Econs., U. Wis., 1974. Property mgr. Munz Investment Real Estate, Madison, Wis., 1973-76; pres. Gregg Shimanski, Realtor & Co., Inc., Madison, 1976—. Mem. Nat. Bd. Realtors, Real Estate Nat. Mktg. Inst., Omicron Delta Epsilon. Republican. Roman Catholic. Home: 4808 Dale St McFarland WI 53558 Office: 1914 Monroe St Madison WI 53711

SHIMMEL, ROBERT GILHAM, osteopathic physician; b. Jackson, Mich., Feb. 23, 1930; s. Earl Clinton and Alta Stewart (Reid) S.; B.A., Albion Coll., 1955; D.O., Chgo. Coll. Osteopathic Medicine, 1955; m. Janice Marie Evely, Oct. 12, 1957; children—Anne E., Thomas R., Amy S., Elizabeth A. Intern Chgo. Osteopathic Hosp., 1955-56, dermatology preceptor, 1956-59; pvt. practice dermatology, Lincoln Park, Mich., 1959—; clin. prof. osteopathic medicine Mich. State U.; cons. Riverside Osteopathic Hosp. Diplomate Am. Osteopathic Bd. Dermatology. Fellow Am. Osteopathic Coll. Dermatology (past pres., sec. 1969-75); mem. Am., Wayne County osteopathic assns., Mich. Assn. Osteopathic Physicians and Surgeons, Mich. Osteopathic Soc. Dermatologists (pres. 1969-75). Home: 19891 Parke Lane Grosse Ile MI 48138 Office: 3830 Fort St Lincoln Park MI 48146

SHINDELL, RICHARD MICHAEL, machinery co. exec.; b. Toledo, June 16, 1948; s. Harry and Bertha (Hattner) S.; grad. high sch. Salesman H&J Equipment Co., Toledo, 1966, sales mgr., 1967; partner H&S Equipment Co., Toledo, 1968-71; owner R. Shindell & Co., Toledo, 1971—. Promoter, producer, player various theatre pipe organ concerts, 1968—; organ cons. Toledo Symphony Orch., 1970-74. Bd. dirs., program dir. Detroit Theatre Organ, Inc., 1972—. Served with USNR, 1966. Mem. Am. Guild Organists, Am. Theatre Organ Soc., Ind. Theatre Organ Producers (charter). Home: 2228 Glenwood Ave Toledo OH 43620 Office: 3607 Marine St Toledo OH 43609

SHINDLE, WILLIAM RICHARD, musicologist; b. Van Orin, Ill., Nov. 2, 1930; s. Ira William and Elsie Virginia (Showalter) S.; Mus.B., Ill. Wesleyan U., 1959; Mus.M., Ind. U., 1963, dissertation year fellow, 1965-66, Ph.D., 1970. Music librarian State U. N.Y., Binghamton, 1964-65; mem. faculty Sch. Music Kent (Ohio) State U., 1966—, asso. prof. musicology, since 1972, summer fellow, 1974. Served with USN, 1951-55. Mem. Am. Musicol. Soc., Pa. German Soc. Author articles; editor, transcriber keyboard works. Home: 2530E Colony Park Pl Stow OH 44224 Office: School Music Kent State Univ Kent OH 44242

SHINEDLING, MARTIN MYRON, psychologist, adminstr.; b. Pateron, N.J., Oct. 13, 1936; s. Archie Edward and Ruth (Potash) S.; B.A., Cal. State U., 1965, M.A., 1967; Ph.D. (Nat. Def. Edn. Act fellow, Univ. fellow), Brigham Young U., 1971; m. Mary Annette Self, Nov. 29, 1958; children—Michelle, Dorothy, Michael, Brian. Staff psychologist CIA, Washington, 1971-72; adminstr. Gladwin (Mich.) Mental Health Clinic, 1972-75; asso. prof. Saginaw Valley Coll., Saginaw, Mich., 1973-76; dir. Planning for Living and Midwest Research and Devel. Center, 1976—. Served with U.S. Army, 1955-64. Mem. Am., Mid-Mich. (sec. 1974-75) psychol. assns. Mem. Ch. of Jesus Christ of Latter-day Saints. Home: 1003 S Adelaide Fenton MI 48430 Office: 2355 Delta Rd Bay City MI 48706

SHINEY, MARGARET LOUISE, physician; b. Hays, Kans., Nov. 27, 1926; d. Edward W. and Harriet Pearl (Dague) Shiney; A.B. cum laude, Bryn Mawr Coll., 1948; M.D., U. Kans., 1954. Intern, St. Francis Hosp., Wichita, Kans., 1954-55; gen. practice medicine, Wichita, 1955-59; splty. tng. Dayton (Ohio) VA Hosp., U. Pa. Grad. Sch. Medicine, Phila., Denver Gen. Hosp., 1960-62; staff physician dept. internal medicine Atchison, Topeka-Santa Fe Hosp., Topeka, 1962-68, chief dept. medicine, 1968—, mem. exec. com. staff, 1968—. Mem. A.M.A., Am. Med. Women's Assn., Kans., Shawnee County med. socs., Bryn Mawr Coll. Alumnae Assn. (area rep.). Home: 1617 W 26th St Topeka KS 66611 Office: 417 E 6th St Topeka KS 66607

SHINN, RICHARD FRANKLIN, JR., turkey rancher; b. Dunning, Nebr., Feb. 26, 1930; s. Richard Franklin and Evelyn M. (Burgett) S.; B.S., U. Nebr., 1951; m. Marilyn Roberta Talbot, Sept. 3, 1955; children—Douglas Brian, Michael David, Bruce Daniel, Bradley John. Partner, Shinn Turkeys, Dunning, 1954—, mgr., 1958—; bd. dirs. Norbest, Inc., Salt Lake City, 1969—, chmn., 1975-77; v.p. Nebr. Turkey Ranch, Inc., Gibbon, Neb.; pres. Nebr. Turkey Growers Co-op. Assn., Gibbon; v.p. North Fork Acres, Ltd., Salida, Colo., Sunny Day Resources, Newcastle, Wyo. Mem. chpt. adv. council Future Farmers Am., 1973-75; mem. troop exec. com. Boy Scouts Am., 1969-71; mem. Blaine County Sch. Reorgn. Com., 1974—. Mem. Hardscrabble Rural Sch. Bd., 1954-62; mem. Sandhills Pub. Schs. Bd. Edn., 1964-74, v.p., 1964-66, pres., 1966-74; mem. Halsey Rural Fire Dist. Bd., 1969-71. Served with AUS, 1952-54. Named Poultryman of Yr., Neb. Poultry Industries, 1973. Mem. Nat., Nebr. (pres. 1972, 77-78, v.p. 1977) turkey fedns., Midwest Poultry Fedn. (dir. 1973-77), Blaine County Farm Bur. (pres. 1963-66), Am. Legion, V.F.W., Kappa Sigma. Republican. Address: Dunning NE 68833

SHIPLEY, CHARLES WILLIAM, educator; b. Ottawa, Kans., Aug. 1, 1918; s. James Robert and Winifred (Shinn) S.; B.F.A., U. Kans., 1940; M.A., Northwestern U., 1949; Ph.D., Fla. State U., 1971; children—Charles William, Jane Shipley Treece. TV spokesman for nat. advertisers, 1952-68; mem. faculty So. Ill. U., Carbondale, prof. dept. radio TV, 1971—. Mem. Internat. Radio and TV Soc., Speech Communication Assn., Nat. Assn. Ednl. Broadcasters, Broadcast Pioneers. Episcopalian. Club: N.Y. Athletic. Home: Route A 1 Box 70 Cobden IL 62920 Office: Dept Radio-TV Southern Illinois University Carbondale IL 62901

SHIPLEY, GEORGE EDWARD, congressman; b. Olney, Ill., Apr. 21, 1927; s. Jesse William and Mamie (Jones) S.; grad. high sch.; m. Ann Watson, July 6, 1947; children—Lucinda Jane, George Edward, Demetri Gav. Shawn Marie. Chief dep. sheriff, Richland County, Ill., 1950-54, sheriff, 1954-58; mem. 86th-89th, 91st-92d Congresses from 23d Dist. Ill., 90th, 94th-95th Congresses from 22d Dist. Mem. V.F.W., Am. Legion. Democrat. Baptist. Mason, Elk, Moose, Odd Fellow, Lion. Home: 327 S Morgan St Olney IL 62450 Office: Old House Office Bldg Washington DC 20515

SHIPLEY, JAMES LEE, hosp. pub. relations exec.; b. New Philadelphia, Ohio, Sept. 27, 1935; s. Melvin McKinley and Sarah Ann (Smith) S.; student U.S. Army Guided Missile Sch., 1956-57, Republic Indsl. Edn. Inst., 1968, Kent State U., 1971-73. Staff announcer Sta.-WJER, Dover, Ohio, 1951-53; with Sta. WSOM-AM-FM, Salem, Ohio, 1953-66, sta. and sales mgr., 1959-66, news commentator, 1960-66; mgr. advt.-pub. relations Lyle Pub. Co., Salem, 1966-68; dir. pub. relations-communications, editor co. employee publ. Copperweld Steel Co., Warren, Ohio, 1968-73; dir. dept. community relations St. Joseph Riverside Hosp., Warren, 1973—; pub. relations adviser Trumbull County (Ohio) YMCA; bd. dirs. for pub. info. Vis. Nurses Assn.; mem. pub. relations com. Trumbull County United Way; mem. Ohio TV Steering Com.; mem. Mahoning-Shenango Area Health Edn. Network. Treas.-sec. bd. trustees Trumbull County Council on Alcoholism; bd. dirs., chmn. scholarship com. Western Res. chpt. March of Dimes; mem. com. Western Res. council Boy Scouts Am. Served with U.S. Army, 1950-60. Recipient award of Appreciation for community service Columbiana County (Ohio) Med. Soc., 1962, citation for pub. service Muscular Dystrophy Assn., 1968, 70, 1st award for excellence in patient staff and community edn. Sylvania Comml. Electronics Corp., 1976. Mem. Northeastern Ohio Hosp. Pub. Relations Assn., Pub. Relations Soc. Am. (pres. Western Res. chpt., charter mem. sect. health), Greater Cleve. Hosp. Assn. (Achievement award 1976), Amateur Trap Shooters Assn., Eastern Ohio Conservation Club. Episcopalian. Clubs: Rotary (co-chmn. info. com. local club), Elks. Home: 3190 Dunstan Dr Warren OH 44485 Office: 1400 Tod Ave Warren OH 44485

SHIPP, MAURINE SARAH HARSTON (MRS. LEVI ARNOLD SHIPP), realtor; b. Holiday, Mo., Mar. 6, 1913; d. Paul Edward and Sarah Jane (Mitchell) Harston; grad. Ill. Bus. Coll., 1945; student real estate Springfield Jr. Coll., 1962; student law LaSalle Extension U., 1959-62; m. Levi Arnold Shipp, Jan. 30, 1941; children—Jerome Reynolds, Patricia (Mrs. Rodney W. England). With Ill. Dept. Agr., Springfield, 1941-65, supr. livestock industry Brucellosis sect.; saleswoman Morgan-Hamilton Real Estate Co., Springfield, 1962-64; owner, mgr. Shipp Real Estate Agy., Springfield, 1965—. Prin. appraiser urban renewal Dept. Housing and Urban Devel., 1971-72; mem. Springfield Pub. Bldg. Commn. Bd. dirs. Springfield Travelers Aid, 1971—. Mem. Springfield Bd. Realtors, Nat., Ill. assns. real estate bds., N.A.A.C.P., Urban League, Iota Phi Lambda. Episcopalian. Mem. Order Eastern Star. Club: Bridge. Home: 31 Bellerive Rd Springfield IL 62704 Office: 1115 E Ash St Springfield IL 62703

SHIPPS, JAN, educator; b. Hueytown, Ala., Oct. 4, 1929; d. William M. and Thalia Jenkins (Bell) Barnett; B.S., Utah State U., 1961; M.A., U. Colo., 1962, Ph.D., 1965; m. Anthony W. Shipps, May 25, 1949; 1 son, Stephen Barnett. Social group worker instns. in Chgo. and Detroit, 1951-60; project coordinator (Kinsey) Inst. Sex Research, Ind. U., Bloomington, 1969-71; part-time instr. history and religious studies Ind. U.-Purdue U. at Indpls., 1971-73, asst. prof., 1973-76, asso. prof., 1976—. AAUW fellow, 1964-65; Latter Day Saints Ch. Hist. fellow, summer 1974. Mem. Nat. Hist. Soc. (adv. bd. 1975—), Am., Western, Mormon hist. assns., Orgn. Am. Historians, Social Sci. History Assn., Am. Acad. Religion. Editorial bd. Dialogue, A Jour. of Mormon Thought, 1973—; contbr. articles to religious jours. Home: 2500 E 8th St Bloomington IN 47401 Office: Ind-Purdue U at Indpls Indianapolis IN 46202

SHIRAEF, JOHN DRAGON, educator; b. Phila., Apr. 18, 1912; s. John and Rose (Kret) S. Tchr., Cass Tech. High Sch., Detroit, 1936-43; newspaperman Detroit Times, 1943-47; tchr.-lectr. on Russia, Europe, 1947—. Served with U.S. Army, 1943-44. Decorated battle star. Mem. Internat. Platform Assn. Republican. First Am. lectr. to travel to Russian villages off-limits to foreigners. Office: PO Box 451 Owosso MI 48867

SHIRE, HERBERT, dentist; b. Pitts., July 20, 1922; s. Joseph and Hattie (Pohl) S.; student Ohio State U., 1940-46; D.D.S., Temple U. Dental Sch., 1950; m. Estelle Ellen Greenberg, July 11, 1948; children—Miriam Ruth, James Robert, Susan Jill. Pvt. practice dentistry, Steubenville, O., 1950—; chief dental staff St. John Med. Center, Steubenville. Bd. dirs. A.R.C., Steubenville, 1965-69, Cancer Soc., Steubenville, 1966—, Mental Health Clinic, Steubenville, 1955-62; mem. adv. bd. Salvation Army, Steubenville, 1971—; trustee Ohio div. Am. Cancer Soc.; mem. Indian Creek Bd. Edn., Wintersville, O., 1965-67; Served with U.S. Army, 1943-45. Fellow Internat. Coll. Dentists; mem. Alpha Epsilon Pi, Alpha Omega. Elk, Mason (32 deg., Shriner); mem. B'nai B'rith, Kiwanian (pres. 1962-63). Home: 151 Woodland Park Wintersville OH 43952 Office: 531 N 4th St Steubenville OH 43952

SHIREY, WAYNE ARTHUR, lawyer; b. Daleville, Ind., Jan. 1, 1930; s. Raymond C. and Pharaba P. (Polhemus) S.; A.B. in Govt. with honors, Ind. U., 1952, J.D., 1955; m. Phyllis A. Farrow, May 25, 1963. Admitted to Ind. bar, 1956, since practiced in Muncie; partner firm Slagle & Shirey; asst. admission officer Ind. U., 1959-60; part-time instr. bus. law Ball State U., 1966-67, Del. County atty. for pub. defender, 1958; dep. pros. atty. Del. County, 1959; atty. Muncie-Del. County Met. Plan Commn., 1970-71. Mem. Del. County Election Bd., 1962-72, pres., 1966-70. Bd. dirs. Del. County Soc. Crippled, 1966—, Vis. Nurses Assn., 1968-70; mem. Ind. Probate Code Study Commn., 1975—. Fellow Am. Coll. Probate Counsel; mem. Am., Ind. bar assns., Am. Judicature Soc., Phi Beta Kappa. Methodist (chmn. bd. 1969-70). Kiwanian (pres. Del. County 1964), Mason (32 deg., Shriner). Home: Box 565 Daleville IN 47334 Office: 211 S Walnut St Muncie IN 47305

SHIRLEY, GENE HILTON, hosp. adminstr.; b. Alva, Okla., Feb. 27, 1917; s. Orvill and Lione Daisy (Bagenstos) S.; student Northwestern State Coll., 1934-36; m. Edith Geraldine Blowers, Feb. 25, 1944; children—Judy (Mrs. Bert Cody), Janice (Mrs. Gary Shaver), James O. With Central Nat. Bank, Alva, 1946-48; adminstr. Attica (Kans.) Dist. Hosp., 1961-65; adminstr. Medicine Lodge (Kans.) Meml. Hosp., 1965—. Chmn. Barber County Arthritis Found. Served with USN, 1940-46. Mem. Kans. Hosp. Assn., South Central Comprehensive Health Planning Council, Pratt Area Council Hosp. Adminstrs. Club: Elks. Home: 903 Guffey St Medicine Lodge KS 67104 Office: 710 N Walnut St Medicine Lodge KS 67104

SHIRREFFS, THOMAS GORDON, cons., ret. oil co. exec.; b. Chgo., Aug. 10, 1912; s. Gordon and Ellen (Burns) S.; student Case Sch. Applied Sci., 1934-36, Ohio State U., 1942-43, Harvard, 1954; m. Margaret Fuller, Aug. 24, 1935; children—Patricia Fuller McMurray, Thomas Gordon, Barnes Fuller. Safety dir., asst. personnel mgr. Addressograph-Multigraph Corp., Cleve., 1932-40; asst. gen. mgr. airplane div. Curtiss Wright Corp., Columbus, Ohio, 1940-44; dir. employee relations Standard Oil Co. Ohio, Cleve., 1944-68, v.p. employee relations, 1968—; v.p. BP Oil Corp., Old Ben Coal Corp., Sohio Petroleum Co., Vistron Corp., Boron Oil Co., others. Chmn. Greater Cleve. Plans for Progress Council, 1965-67; mem. ops. com. Nat. Alliance of Businessmen; mem. U.S. Marine Corps Adv. Com. for Minority Affairs, mem. spl. vocat. edn. adv. com. Cleve. Pub. Schs., 1966-67. Past pres., trustee Nat. Jr. Achievement; past pres. Cleve. Center on Alcoholism; trustee Urban League Cleve., Met. Cleve. Jobs Council; trustee, sec. Blue Cross N.E. Ohio. Recipient Achievement awards Jr. Achievement Cleve., 1956, Nat. Jr. Achievement, 1958; Inter-racial Justice award Cath. Interracial Council Cleve., 1966. Mem. First Cleve. Cavalry Vets. Assn., Ohio, Cleve. chambers commerce, Indsl. Relations Assn. Cleve., NAM, Nat. Petroleum Refiners Assn. Clubs: Country, Cleveland Skating, Mid-Day Clevelander (Cleve.); Mentor Harbor Yacht, Quail Ridge Golf and Tennis, Delray Beach (Fla.). Home: 31150 Fox Hollow Dr Pepper Pike OH 44124 also Quail Ridge Delray Beach FL Office: Midland Bldg Cleveland OH 44115

SHLENS, EDMUND, accountant; b. Hammond, Ind., May 11, 1932; s. Harold and Rebecca (Shneider) S.; B.S., Ind. U., 1953, M.B.A., 1954; J.D., U. Ill., 1958, Ph.D., 1972. Admitted to Ill. bar, 1958; prin. firm Edmund Shlens, C.P.A., Champaign, 1961-75; with Keeling & Shlens Real Estate, Champaign; lectr. in taxation field; asst. prof. Ill. State U. C.P.A., Ill. Mem. Ill. (sec.-dir.), Am. assns. attys.-C.P.A.'s, Am. Inst. C.P.A.'s. Author: Tax Ideas for Banks. Contbr. articles to profl. jours. Office: 2505 S Neil St Champaign IL 61820

SHLENSKY, RONALD, physician, lawyer; b. Chgo., Jan. 10, 1935; s. Isadore Paul and Florence (Fireman) S.; B.S., Purdue U., 1956; M.D., U. Ill., 1960; J.D., Loyola U. at Chgo., 1973; m. Evely Laser, June 17, 1962; children—Lincoln, Sheba, Aviva. Intern, D.C. Gen. Hosp., 1960-61; resident Northwestern U., 1961-62, Langley Porter Inst., San Francisco, 1962-64; practice medicine, specializing in psychiatry, Chgo., 1966—; asst. prof. psychiatry Northwestern U. Med. Sch., 1973—; admitted to Ill. bar, 1974. Chmn. bd. Forensic Psychiatry, Ltd. Mem. Gov.'s Commn. to revise Ill. Mental Health Code, 1973—; impartial psychiat. examiner Ill. Cts., 1966—. Served to capt., AUS, 1962-64. Fellow Am. Coll. Legal Medicine, Am. Psychiat. Assn.; mem. AMA, Am. Bar Assn., Am. Acad. Psychiatry and Law, Toga Soc. (pres.). Founder, editor, pub. Am. Jour. Forensic Psychiatry. Contbr. articles to legal and med. jours. Home: 165 Maple Hill Glencoe IL 60022 Office: 251 E Chicago Ave Chicago IL 60611

SHOCKLEY, DEBORAH LEIGH, psychiat. technician; b. Jefferson City, Mo., Jan. 26, 1953; d. Arthur Warren and Mary Alice (Keller) Shockley; B.S. in Edn., S.W. Mo. State U., 1975, M.S. in Guidance and Counseling (fellow), 1977. Aid counselor, research asst. Financial Aids Office, S.W. Mo. State U., 1975-77, also vol. workers various social service orgns.; psychiat. technician Springfield (Mo.) Park Central Hosp., 1977—. Mem. Am. Personnel and Guidance Assn., Am. Coll. Personnel Assn. Address: 1434 E Portland St Springfield MO 65804

SHOEMACK, HARVEY RAYMOND, mktg. center exec.; b. Cleve., Oct. 1, 1942; s. Ted and Lilian (Covitt) S.; B.S.J., Ohio U., 1965; postgrad. in communications U. Ill., 1966-67; m. Geraldine Bragman, Mar. 20, 1966; children—Todd, Brian. Publicity dir. Sta. WILL-TV, U. Ill., Urbana, 1966-67; v.p. Pub. Relations Bd., Inc., Chgo., 1967-76; pres. Internat. Mktg. Center, Ltd., Chgo., 1976—; internat. trade cons.; lectr. U.S.-Japan trade and econ. relationship. Recipient Golden Trumpet award (3) Publicity Club Chgo., 1969-70. Mem. Japan-Am. Soc. Chgo. (dir.), Internat. Trade Club Chgo. (dir. 1975—), Chgo. Council Fgn. Relations, Internat. Visitors Center, Sigma Delta Chi. Editor U.S./Japan Outlook: A Digest of American Views of Japan, 1971—; contbr. articles to profl. jours. Home: 2854 Twin Oaks Highland Park IL 60035 Office: 166 E Superior St Chicago IL 60611

SHOEMAKER, MORRELL MCKENZIE, JR., architect; b. Granville, Ohio, Aug. 25, 1923; s. Morrell McKenzie and Ruth (Doehleman) S.; B.Arch., Cornell U., 1945. Archtl. designer Mundie, Jensen & McClurg, Chgo., 1946-49; chief architect Laramore & Douglass, Chgo., 1949-53; partner McClurg, Shoemaker & McClurg, Chgo., 1953-67; partner McClurg, Shoemaker, Chgo., 1967-74, Morrell M. Shoemaker & Assos., 1975—. Registered architect, Ill., Ohio, Mich., Wis. Mem. A.I.A., Soc. Am. Registered Architects, Nat. Council Archtl. Registration Bds., Nat. Soc. Archtl. Hist., Landmark Preservation Council, Nat. Trust for Historic Preservation, Chgo. Assn. Commerce and Industry, Chgo. Natural History Mus. (life), Chgo. Hist. Soc. (life), Chgo. Orch. Assn. (life), Ill. Soc. Architects, Art Inst. Chgo. (life mem.), Ill. St. Andrews Soc., Victorian Soc. Republican. Presbyn. (elder, trustee). Clubs: Cornell of Chicago; The Cliff Dwellers. Author: Five Walks In and Around Chicago's Famous Buildings, 1969. Co-editor: The Building Estimator's Reference Book, 19th edit., 1977. Home: 1310 N LaSalle St Chicago IL 60610

SHOEMAKER, ROBERT LOUIS, audio visual co. exec.; b. Independence, Kans., Sept. 30, 1907; s. Walter Ellsworth and Blanch (Hawley) S.; A.B. in English Lit., U. Ill., 1930; student architecture Armour Inst., 1927-28; m. Helen Margaret Gerard, Oct. 9, 1942; 1 son, Theodore Merrill. Archtl. draftsman Zook & McCaughey, Chgo., 1927-28; baker Hampshire Restaurant, Hollywood, Calif., 1932; waiter Old Heidelberg Inn, Chgo., 1933-35; service mgr. Gas Appliances, Inc., Miami, Fla., 1935-37; owner The Home Appliance Store, West Palm Beach, Fla., 1937-41; mgr. aviation radio sales Lear, Inc., 1946-47; div. mgr. DuKane Corp., 1947-56; mgr. Salesmate div. Charles Beseler Co., 1957-62; v.p., co-owner Double Sixteen Co., film prodns., 1962-63; pres., owner AVACO, mfrs. reps. audio visual supplies, Winnetka, Ill., 1962—; regional mgr. LaBelle Industries, Inc., 1963—; mem. com. to establish bldg. code for sch. constrn. for audio visual use Ind. Dept. Edn., 1954-55; founder, chmn. bd. govs., mem. faculty Nat. Inst. Audio-Visual Selling, 1949-57; founder, chmn. Nat. Sound Slidefilm Contest, 1954-56; bd. dirs., mem. faculty Audio Visual Inst. Effective Communications, 1966; exec. bd., adviser archtl. com., dept. audio visual and broadcast edn. Nat. Council Chs., 1954-60. Chmn. art-antique auction Hadley Sch. Blind, 1975. Served to lt. comdr. USNR, World War II; liaison officer Office Sci. Devel./Nat. Def. Research Council, 1944. Recipient 2 awards for films The Ugly Duckling, 1955, Masha and the Bear, 1956. Mem. Soc. Motion Picture and TV Engrs., NEA (ofcl. adviser bd. dirs., dept. audio visual instruction 1953), Nat. (dir. 1953-56, Meritorious Service award 1973, Past Service award 1977), Ill. audio visual assns., Audio Engring. Soc., Am. Soc. Tng. and Devel., Sales-Mktg. Execs. Internat., Aircraft Owners and Pilots Assn., Assn. Ednl. Communication and Tech., Internat. Waiters Union, Phi Delta Theta. Club: Lions (pres. Winnetka). Producer over 100 sound slide films; 1st ednl. sound filmstrips, 1955. Author: Theory of Automated Selling, 1962; Psychology of Selling with Audio-Visual, 1969; contbr. articles to periodicals. Home: 1017 Elm St Winnetka IL 60093 Office: PO Box 45 Winnetka IL 60093

SHOGREN, ROBERT ALTON, motivation co. exec.; b. Eau Claire, Wis., Jan. 15, 1936; s. Alton Godfrey and Irene Mildred (Solberg) S.; B.A., Macalester Coll., 1958; m. Rose Helen Berger, Apr. 15, 1967. With Maritz Inc., St. Louis, 1962—, v.p., dir. creative services, 1974—. Served with U.S. Army, 1958-59. Republican. Lutheran. Club: Greenbriar Hills Country (Kirkwood, Mo.). Home: 119 Wildwood Ln Kirkwood MO 63122 Office: 1355 N Highway Saint Louis County MO 63026

SHOMBER, LARRY LEE, sch. supt.; b. Union City, O., Apr. 20, 1942; s. Marvin Bruce and Pauline Meriam (Warner) S.; B.S., Manchester Coll., 1964; M.S., St. Francis Coll., 1968; postgrad. in sch. adminstrn. Ball State U., 1968-73; m. Annemarie Richter, June 20, 1964; children—Leigh Ann, Kevin Scott. Tchr., Avilla Sch., Kendallville, Ind., 1964-67; guidance counselor Kendallville Jr. High Sch., 1967-70; prin. Rome City Elementary Middle Sch., Kendallville, 1970-74; asst. supt. Porter County Schs., Valparaiso, Ind., 1974-77, Concord Community Schs., Elkhart, Ind., 1977—. Bd. dirs. YMCA, Kendallville, 1974. Mem. Ind. Assn. Pub. Sch. Supts. (asso.), Phi Delta Kappa. Club: Kiwanis. Home: 59350 CR 11 S Elkhart IN 46514 Office: 59167 CR 13-S Elkhart IN 46514

SHOOP, GEORGE JEROME, agronomist; b. Phila., Dec. 25, 1933; s. Hamilton Wright and Helen (Johnson) S.; A.A., Ferrum Jr. Coll., 1953; B.S., Va. Poly. Inst., 1958, M.S., 1961; Ph.D., Pa. State U., 1967; m. Joe Ann Starowsky, Mar. 1, 1974; children—Elizabeth Ann, Richard Jerome. Research scientist rep. Eli Lilly & Co., Greenfield, Ind., 1966-72, Delray Beach, Fla., 1972-74, Brasil, 1973, Peoria, Ill., 1974—. Spl. dep. sheriff Hancock County, Ind., 1971-72, Palm Beach County, Fla., 1973-74. Served with AUS, 1953-55. Mem. Am. Soc. Agronomy, Weed Sci. Soc. Am., North Central Weed Sci. Soc. (dir. 1971, chmn. research com. 1977), Sigma Xi, Gamma Sigma Delta, Phi Sigma, Phi Epsilon Phi. Republican. Methodist. Mason (Shriner), Order Eastern Star. Contbr. articles to profl. jours. Home: 117 S Shore Dr Morton IL 61550 Office: 4600 W War Memorial Dr Peoria IL 61614

SHOPNECK, GEORGE, dentist; b. Boston, Oct. 23, 1919; s. Hyman and Rebecca (Paul) S.; B.S., Toledo U., 1941; D.D.S., Ohio State U., 1943; m. Hannah Offner, Dec. 3, 1944; children—Marlene Maniloff, Daryl, Craig, Jill. Pvt. practice dentistry, Toledo, 1947—; dental cons. Collingwood Park, St. Theresa's nursing homes, 1965—; instr. Whitney Sch. Dental Assts., Toledo, 1954-56; mem. dental staff St. Vincent's Hosp. Med. Center, 1974—. Vice-pres. Community Center Players, 1956-59; mem. Jewish Community Relations Com., 1966-67; bd. dirs. Jewish Community Center, 1959-61; bd. dirs., vice chaplain Toledo Meml. Assn., 1959-63; bd. dirs. Toledo Repertoire Theater, 1964, Toledo Children's Theater, 1972-73, Toledo Village Players, 1965-74. Served to capt., Dental Corps, AUS, 1943-46. Recipient Certificate of Merit, Toledo Jewish Family Service, 1974; WDHO-TV TV award, 1976. Mem. ADA, Ohio State, Toledo dental assns., Am. Legion (chaplain 1967—), Vedder and Bunning Dental Socs., Alpha Epsilon Pi, Alpha Omega (pres. Toledo chpt. 1956-57). Democrat. Clubs: Masons, B'nai B'rith, Twin Oaks Country, Tennis, Racquet (Toledo). Home: 3652 Indian Rd Toledo OH 43606 Office: 3100 W Central Ave Toledo OH 43606

SHOPNECK, SAM MILTON, realtor; b. Boston, Mar. 8, 1921; s. Hyman and Rebecca (Paul) S.; student Ohio State U., 1938-40; B.B.A., U. Toledo, 1942; children by previous marriage—James G., Robert M., Patti A. Dir. operations Westgate Shopping Center, Toledo, 1967-74; leasing agt. Westgate Office Bldg. and Westgate Exec. Park, 1969-74; real estate cons., developer shopping centers and major office bldgs. Served as pilot RAF, 1942-43, USAAF, 1943-46; PTO. Decorated Air medal. Mem. Nat. Assn. Realtors (comml. indsl. real estate div.), Ohio Assn. Realtors, C. of C. Mason. Author: Speed Putting System, 1971. Home: 3533 Kenwood Blvd Toledo OH 43606 Office: 3450 W Central St Toledo OH 43606

SHORNEY, GEORGE HERBERT, JR., music pub.; b. Oak Park, Ill., Dec. 16, 1931; s. George Herbert and Mary Louise (Wallace) S.; B.A., Denison U., 1954; m. Nancy Leith, Aug. 27, 1955; children—Cynthia Ann, George Herbert, John Leith, Scott Alfred. Asst. mgr. adjusting service Marshall Field & Co., Chgo., 1956-58; office mgr. Hope Pub. Co., Carol Stream, Ill., 1959-62, v.p., 1962-70, pres., 1970—. Chmn., Wheaton Bd. Fire and Police Commrs.; nat. donor com. Nat. Council Chs. Bd. dirs. Central DuPage Hosp., Winfield, Ill. Served with USNR, 1953-55. Mem. Ch. Music Pubs. Assn. (past pres.). Presbyterian (trustee). Clubs: Univ. (Chgo.); Soc. Alumni Denison U. (past pres.). Home: 160 W Elm St Wheaton IL 60187 Office: Carol Stream IL 60187

SHORR, JAMES WINFIELD, diversified industry exec.; b. Chgo., July 9, 1933; s. Ralph Louis and Babette J. (Zucker) S.; B.B.A. (fellow), U. Wis., 1954; M.B.A., Northwestern U., 1973; children—Karen Elizabeth, Kathryn Lynn. Mgr. sales promotion Skil Corp., 1956-59; supr. pub. relations Kraft Foods div., Kraftco, 1959-64; account exec., account supr. Daniel J. Edelman Assos., 1964-69; dir. pub. relations/sales promotion, salespower div., Manpower Inc., Chgo., 1969-72; mgr. advt. Scott Foresman & Co., Glenview, Ill., 1972-73; dir. mktg. communications Litton Microwave Cooking Products div. Litton Industries, Mpls., 1973—. Served to maj., Psychol. Warfare, U.S. Army, 1954-55; maj. USAR. Clubs: Toastmasters, Ullr Ski (pres. Twin Cities 1977-78). Home: 3630 Lancaster Ln N Minneapolis MN 55441 Office: 1405 Xenium Ln N Minneapolis MN 55441

SHORT, DONALD LEE, financial exec.; b. Piqua, O., May 29, 1936; s. Harold Leonard and Lefa Irene (Davis) S.; B.S., Miami U., Oxford, O., 1959; m. Barbara Anne Bobb, June 15, 1958; children—John Michael, Jennifer Anne. Staff accountant Ernst & Ernst, C.P.A.'s, Dayton, O., 1959-62; supr. br. accounting Hobart Mfg. Co., Troy, 1962-66; asst. controller Philips Industries Inc., Dayton, 1966-73; dir. finance Newfields Devel. Corp., Dayton, 1973-76; controller Hollander Industries, Dayton, 1976—. Instr. accounting Miami U. Extension, Piqua, 1961, 62. C.P.A., Ohio. Mem. Am. Inst. C.P.A.'s, Ohio Soc. C.P.A.'s, Nat. Assn. Accountants. Republican. Methodist. Home: 288 Shaftsbury Rd Troy OH 45373 Office: 219 Kelly Ave Dayton OH 45404

SHORT, LARRY EDWARD, educator; b. Des Moines, Feb. 16, 1934; s. Edward Alfred and Kathryn Mary (Gunn) S.; B.B.A., Tex. Tech. Coll., 1958, M.B.A. (research fellow), 1961; D.Bus. Adminstrn., U. Colo., 1971; m. Miyoko Ishida, Nov. 5, 1964; 1 dau., Katherine Michiko. Employment specialist U.S. Govt., Korea, Washington, 1960-63, tng. and devel. specialist, Okinawa, Korea, 1963-66, chief of employment, Okinawa, 1966-67, personnel dir., Denver, Okinawa, 1967-69; asso. prof. mgmt. Drake U., Des Moines, 1971—. Cons. continuing edn. for bus. and industry. Served with USNR, 1952-55. Mem. Acad. Mgmt., Soc. for Advancement of Mgmt., Am. Mgmt. Assn., Sigma Iota Epsilon, Beta Gamma Sigma, Phi Kappa Phi. Methodist. Contbr. articles to profl. jours. Home: 4700 Cody Dr West Des Moines IA 50265

SHORT, RAY L., JR., research co. exec.; b. Johnson City, N.Y., July 23, 1939; s. Ray L. and E. Norma (Schomo) S.; grad. Northwestern U., 1960; m. Louise Pike, Aug. 28, 1966; children—Marcia, Laura, Ray, Susan. Nat. sales mgr. Harwald Co., Inc., Evanston, Ill., 1961-70; pres., mng. dir. Research Tech., Inc., Lincolnwood, Ill., 1971—; chmn. bd. Lipsner-Smith Co., Ltd., Uxbridge, England. Mem. Soc. Motion Picture and TV Engrs., Ednl. Film Library Assn., Nat. Audio-Visual Assn. (internat. trade com.), Assn. Ednl. Communications and Tech. (chmn. mfrs. and producers com.). Patentee in field. Home: 700 Indian Rd Glenview IL 60025 Office: 4700 Chase Lincolnwood IL 60646

SHORT, RICHARD ROLLIN, ednl. adminstr.; b. Omaha, Nov. 7, 1927; s. Earl M. and Irene (Craven) S.; B.S., U. Nebr. 1950, M.E., 1953, Ed.D., 1962; m. Ella Mae Sizer, May 29, 1949; children—Kristine, William, Jr. High Sch. tchr. Benedict (Nebr.) Consol. Sch., 1947-49; math., counseling tchr. Lincoln Pub. Schs., 1950-53; supr. math. tchrs. U. Nebr., 1953-54; asst. sr. high prin.

Grand Island (Nebr.) Pub. Schs., 1954-57; sr. high sch. prin. Hastings (Nebr.) Pub. Schs., 1957-58, supt. schs., 1958-66; supt. schs. Maine Twp. High Schs., Dist. 207, Park Ridge-Des Plaines, Ill., 1966—; mem. Ill. State Tchr. Certification Bd., Cook County Tchr. Certification Bd. Mem. Nebr. Gov.'s Adv. Commn.; rep. White House Conf. on Children and Youth, 1960, tech. cons. for Ill. activities White House Conf., 1970; tech. adviser to Ill. Gov.'s Youth Commn.; mem. adv. com. for health edn. Nat. PTA. Trustee Lutheran Gen. Hosp., Park Ridge; bd. dirs. Jr. Achievement Chgo.; chmn. bd. dirs. Inst. Ednl. Research. Served with USNR, 1945-47. Mem. North Central Assn. Colls. and Secondary Schs. (dist. dir.). Am. Assn. Sch. Adminstrs. (adv. council), C. of C., Phi Delta Kappa, Pi Mu Epsilon, Sigma Alpha Epsilon. Presbyn. (elder 1962-64). Lion, Kiwanian. Home: 1811 Walnut St Park Ridge IL 60068 Office: Frost Adminstrn Center 1131 S Dee Rd Park Ridge IL 60068

SHORT, SAMUEL JAMES, JR., lawyer; b. El Dorado Springs, Mo., Oct. 22, 1941; s. Samuel James and Violet Ermagarde (Dimick) S.; B.S., U. Kans., 1963; J.D., U. Mo., 1967. Admitted to Mo. bar, 1967; city atty., Stockton, Mo., 1976—; owner Stockton Abstract and Title Co. (Mo.), 1970—. Dist. atty. Cedar County, Mo., 1968-72. Bd. dirs. Stockton Nursing Home, Inc. Mem. Am., Mo. bar assns., Phi Delta Phi, Delta Sigma Pi. Clubs: Stockton Country, Kansas City, Chapel Hills Golf and Country. Office: 101 Public Square Stockton MO 65785

SHORT, THOMAS JAN, lawyer; b. Napoleon, Ohio, Sept. 6, 1941; s. Earl and Verile M. (Neuhauser) S.; B.S. in Bus. Adminstrn., Bowling Green State U., 1963; J.D., Ohio State U., 1966; m. Kay L. Enck, Aug. 12, 1966; children—Patricia Kay, Michael Thomas. Admitted to Ohio bar, 1966, since practiced in Napoleon; partner firm Hoeffel, Funkhouser, Short & Hanna, 1970—; spl. counsel to atty. gen. Ohio, 1967-70; village solicitor, Deshler, Ohio, 1966—, McClure, Ohio, 1968—, Malinta, Ohio, 1972—; chief asst. pros. atty. Henry County, 1977—; pres. E.T.S. Corp. Dep. dir. Henry County Bd. Elections, 1968-73; referee Ohio Bd. Regents, 1970—; mem. fin. com. Henry County Planning Commn., 1970-72. Vice chmn. Henry County Republican Central Com., 1974-75; chmn. Henry County chpt. Nat. Found., 1969-71; v.p., bd. dirs. Henry County Tb and Health Assn., 1970-71. Recipient Pres.'s Distinguished Service award Bowling Green State U., 1963; named Outstanding Young Man, Henry County Jr. C. of C., 1969. Mem. Am., Ohio (bd. govs. real estate sect.), N.W. (pres. 1975), Henry County (pres. 1973-75) bar assns., Napoleon Area C. of C. (dir. 1970-73), Phi Beta Phi, Omicron Delta Kappa, Alpha Tau Omega. Elk (chaplain 1969-70), Rotarian (treas. Napoleon 1970). Home: Route 4 Napoleon OH 43545 Office: Hoeffel Funkhouser Short & Hanna Corner N Perry and Shelby Sts Napoleon OH 43545

SHOUP, ROBERT EARL, clergyman; b. Altoona, Pa., Jan. 27, 1918; s. John Lewis and Helen Delzina (Fasick) S.; A.B., Juniata Coll., 1940; M.Div., United Theol. Sem., 1944; M.A., Temple U., 1957; postgrad. U. Pitts., 1957-62, (NSF grantee) U. Colo., summer 1967, U. W.Va., 1969-70, Ball State U., 1971-72; Ph.D., Walden U., 1975; m. Wilma Jean Boyer, Feb. 6, 1943; children—Pamela Jane (Mrs. Arthur T. Wood, Jr.), Jack Phillip. Ordained to ministry Evang. United Brethren Ch., 1944; pastor churches, Marion, Ind., summer 1944, Windber, Pa., 1944-47, Rochester, Pa., 1957-62, North Braddock, Pa., 1962-65; served from lt. (j.g.) to lt. Chaplain Corps, U.S. Navy, 1947-57; asst. prof. Bethany (W.Va.) Coll., 1965-70; asso. prof. Huntington (Ind.) Coll., 1970-74; interim pastor Lone Pine (Pa.) Christian Ch., 1968-70; pastor First Christian Ch., Andrews, Ind., 1973-75, Federated Ch. of Lima (Ill.), 1975—. Mayor of Bethany, 1968-69; chmn. Planning Commn. Rochester (Pa.), 1963-65. Mem. Am. Sociol. Assn., Am. Anthrop. Assn., Nat. Council on Family Relations. Republican. Mem. Christian Ch. Lion. Home and office: PO Box 87 Lima IL 62348

SHOVALD, ARLENE ELIZABETH, newspaper editor; b. Stambaugh, Mich., Apr. 14, 1940; d. William Lawrence and Dorothy Mary (Scott) Mellstrom; student pub. schs., Iron River, Mich.; m. Robert Paul Shovald, June 20, 1959; children—Robert, Terri, Richard, Anne. Free-lance writer, 1959—; columnist The Reporter, Iron River, 1965—, editor, 1974—; contbr. freelance articles to Green Bay (Wis.) Press Gazette, Milw. Jour., Modern Maturity, Eagles Mag., Ideal Publs., Grit. Recipient Upper Peninsula Mich. Writer of Year award, 1977. Home: 229 5th Ave Iron River MI 49935 Office: PO Box 311 Genesee St Iron River MI 49935

SHOWALTER, STAN, criminologist; b. Syracuse, N.Y., Apr. 12, 1936; s. William Edward and Beulah Vae (Williamson) S.; B.A., Andrews U., 1962, M.A., 1966, M.A., 1974, Ed.D., 1976; m. Jeannine Wittschiebe, June 9, 1963. Teacher, Dowagiac (Mich.) Pub. Schs., 1962-66; instr. psychology Southwestern Mich. Coll., 1966-67; caseload counselor, staff psychologist, dir. psychol. services, adminstrv. asst. to warden, spl. asst. to dir. adult authority Ind. Dept. Corrections, 1967-76; lectr. criminology and criminal justice Lake Mich. Coll., 1971—, Purdue U., 1976—, Western Mich. U., 1977—; pres. Criminal Justice Assos., Inc., New Buffalo, Mich., 1977—; bd. commnrs. Berrien County Juvenile Detention Center, 1975—; sec. Chikaming Twp. Pub. Safety Commn., 1977; mem. U.S. Contingent, 5th UN Congress on Crime, Geneva, Switzerland, 1975. Fellow Menninger Found.; mem. Am. Soc. Criminology, Am. Psychol. Assn., Am. Correctional Assn., Soc. Police and Criminal Psychologists, Am. Personnel and Guidance Assn., Internat. Assn. Chiefs Police, Nat. Council Crime Delinquency, Phi Delta Kappa. Seventh-day Adventist. Clubs: Am. Philatelic Soc., Soc. Philataelic Americans. Office: PO Drawer 130 New Buffalo MI 49117

SHREVE, JAMES JOSEPH, optometrist; b. Kansas City, Mo., Dec. 11, 1922; s. Joseph Samuel and Nellie May Gladis (Albin) S.; O.D., No. Ill. Coll. Optometry, 1950; m. Betty Louise Kimzey, Jan. 12, 1952; children—Ronald Wayne, Marolyn Louise. Pvt. practice optometry, Aurora, Mo., 1950—; cons. Mo. State Chest Hosp., Mt. Vernon, 1964—. Mem. Aurora City Council, 1967-70, mayor, 1970-71. Served with AUS, 1943-46. Named Man of Year in Aurora, 1959. Mem. Am., Mo., S.W. Mo. optometric assns., Aurora C. of C., Am. Legion, United Comml. Travelers, Internat. Brotherhood Magicians. Baptist (supt. Sunday sch. 1961-66). Club: Lions. Home: 1203 Oak St Aurora MO 65605 Office: 18 E Olive St Aurora MO 65605 also 212 S Hickory St Mount Vernon MO

SHREWDER, ROY VALENTINE, lumberman, rancher; b. Fort Worth, Feb. 14, 1899; s. William Fred and Blanche (Hamilton) S.; student pub. schs., Ft. Worth; m. Dorothy Berryman, Apr. 6, 1929; children—Sarah Shrewder Tracy, Susan Shrewder Payne. Auditor, The Home Lumber & Supply Co., Ashland, Kans., 1929-40, asst. gen. mgr., 1940-50, sec.-treas., dir., 1940—, gen. mgr., 1950-66, pres., 1959-74, chmn. bd., 1975—; dir. Stockgrowers State Bank, Clark County Abstract Loan and Investment Co. Mem. Kans. Ho. of Reps., 1960-66; Republican State fin. chmn., 1967-68; chmn. exec. com. bd. trustees, past pres. bd. Coll. Emporia (Kans.); trustee Kans. Sch. Religion, Lawrence. Mem. Southwestern Lumbermans Assn. (past dir.), Kans. Peace Officers Assn. Presbyn. Clubs: Masons, Shriners, Jesters; Capitol Hill (Washington); Wichita. Home: 312 W 7th St Ashland KS 67831 also (winter) 4 Casa Blanca Estates Scottsdale AZ 85253 Office: 112 W 8th St Ashland KS 67831

SHRINER, JAMES EDWARD, advt. exec.; b. Meridian, Miss., Jan. 3, 1925; s. Clarence Elmer and Vella (Scottow) S.; B.A., U. Cin., 1947; student Berea Coll., 1943, Cornell U., 1944, U. Wis. Direct Mail Inst., 1956; m. Barbara Ann White, June 14, 1947; children—Mary Ann, Elizabeth Jane, Jennifer Lee. Food mgmt. Clark Restaurant Co., Cleve., 1947-49, S & Q Restaurant Co., Lincoln, Neb., 1950, Carders Restaurant, Chgo., 1951; retail store mgmt. S.S. Kresge Co., Chgo., 1952-55; mdse. and sales promotion, Ray-O-Vac Co., Madison, Wis., 1955-60; adv. mgr. Westclox div. General Time, LaSalle, Ill., 1961; acct. exec. H.H. Monk & Assoc., Rockford, Ill., 1961—, v.p., 1968-71, owner, 1971—. Active United Fund; dist. chmn. Boy Scouts Am., 1971, mem. exec. bd., 1971-75; mem. exec. bd. Zitelman Scout Mus. Served to lt., j.g. USNR, 1943-46. Registered agt., Patriotic Edn., Inc. Mem. Am. Mktg. Assn., Beta Theta Pi, Alpha Phi Omega. Presbyn. Mason. Clubs: Rockford Advertising (pres. 1961, dir. 1971); Rockford Country. Home: 1803 Stratford Ln Rockford IL 61107 Office: 706 N Main St Rockford IL 61101

SHRINER, RUTH SHEARER (MRS. WALTER SHRINER), social service cons.; b. Aurora, Ill.; d. Fred B. and Ivy (Chapman) Shearer; B.A., N. Central Coll., 1935; M.S., Case Western Res. U., 1937; m. Walter Shriner, Aug. 26, 1939; children—Anne Shriner Olsen, Walter Richard (dec.). Med. social worker Cook County Hosp., Chgo., 1937-41, student supr., U. Chgo., 1938-41; med. social worker Woman's Hosp., N.Y.C., 1941-42; caseworker Family & Children's Service, Evansville, Ind., 1942-43; cons. working parents, Evansville, 1943-45; social service cons., coordinator direct care programs Ill. State Dept. Pub. Health, Springfield, 1968—; guest lectr. Evansville Coll., 1944; lectr. Ill. Wesleyan Jr. Coll. Music, Springfield, 1947. Blood chmn. Sangamon County chpt. ARC, 1950-54. Recipient Ill. Kidney Found. award, 1970, Ill. Gov.'s Superior Achievement certificate, 1971. Mem. Acad. Certified Social Workers, Nat. Assn. Social Workers, Am., Ill. pub. health assns., Ill. State Med. Soc. Aux. (dir. 1950-56, 59-63), Ill. Welfare Assn., P.E.O. Home: 224 Maple Grove Springfield IL 62707 Office: 535 W Jefferson St Springfield IL 62707

SHRINER, WILLIAM CUPPY, psychiatrist; b. Terre Haute, Ind., Sept. 11, 1937; s. Walter Owen and M. Virginia (Cuppy) S.; A.B. magna cum laude, Ind. State U., 1958; M.D., Ind. U., 1962; m. Nancy McKee, Dec. 30, 1959; children—Virginia A., Walter M., Eric W. Rotating intern, Wilford Hall, USAF Hosp., San Antonio, 1962-63; resident psychiatry Ind. U. Med. Center, Indpls., 1966-69; practice medicine specializing in psychiatry, Terre Haute, 1969—; mem. staff Union Hosp., Terre Haute Regional Hosp., Clay County Hosp., Mary Sherman Hosp.; med. dir. Vigo County Adult and Child Guidance Clinic, Terre Haute, 1969-72, Katherine Hamilton Mental Health Center, Terre Haute, 1969—; adj. asso. prof. psychology Ind. State U., Terre Haute, 1971-73; clin. asst. prof. psychiatry Ind. U. Sch. Medicine and Ind. State U., 1973—. Mem. sch. community adv. com. Vigo County Sch. Corp., Terre Haute, 1971-73, pres., 1973; mem. Rose Hulman Inst. Tech. Devel. Council, 1971-76; mem. Region VII Mental Health-Mental Retardation Planning Council, 1969—; mem. Gov.'s Ad Hoc Com. to Study Mental Health Delivery System of Ind., 1975—. Served to capt. M.C., USAF, 1963-66. Mem. Am. Psychiat. Assn., AMA, Ind. Psychiat. Soc., Ind. Med. Assn., Ind. Assn. for Children with Learning Disabilities (mem. profl. adv. bd. 1972—), Vigo County Med. Soc., Ind. Council Community Mental Health Center (chmn. Ind. chpt. 1974-75). Home: 123 Woodbine Dr Terre Haute IN 47803 Office: 620 8th Ave Terre Haute IN 47804

SHRIVER, GARNER EDWARD, govt. ofcl.; b. Towanda, Kans., July 6, 1912; s. Edward Arthur and Olive (Glass) S.; AB., U. Wichita, 1934; J.D., Washburn U., 1940; D.P.S. (hon.), Friends U., Wichita. m. Martha Jane Currier, June 4, 1941;children—Kay Elaine (Mrs. Leroux), David Garner, Linda Ann (Mrs. Breeding). Instr. English and speech south Haven (Kans.) High Sch., 1935-37; admitted to Kans. bar, 1940; atty. Wichita Bd. Edn., 1951-60; mem. Kans. Legis. Council, 1955-60; mem. 87th-94th Congress from 4th Dist. Kans.; minority staff dir. U.S. Senate Vets. Affairs Com., 1977—. Mem. adv. bd. DeMolay Legion Honor. Mem. Kans. Ho. of Reps. from Sedgwick County, 1947-51, Kans. Senate from 27th Dist., 1953-61. Trustee YMCA; bd. dirs. Wichita Council Drug Abuse, Inst. Logopedics, Wichita, Starkey Developmental Center for Retarded, Wichita. Served to lt. (s.g.) USNR, World War II. Recipient Achievement award Wichita State U., Distinguished Service award Washburn U. Mem. Am., Kans., Wichita bar assns., VFW, Am. Legion, Nat. Sojourners. Republican. Methodist. Mason. Home: 5051 E Lincoln St Wichita KS 67218 Office: Russell Senate Office Bldg Washington DC 20515

SHROPSHEAR, GEORGE, surgeon; b. Chgo., Nov. 28, 1905; s. George and Ella (Baxter) S.; B.S., U. Ill., 1929, M.D. (Julius Rosenwald fellow), 1931, M.S., 1931; m. Evelyn L. Harris, Feb. 19, 1936; children—Lois (Mrs. Sidney Thompson), Doris (Mrs. Thomas J. Hawkins), George III, Joan (Mrs. John D. Yates), Norman J. Intern, Provident Hosp., Chgo., 1931-32, jr. attending surgeon, 1935-42, asso. attending surgeon, 1945-49, sr. attending, 1949—, chmn. dept. surgery, 1955-57, pres. med. staff, 1964-67; fellow gen. edn. bd. in proctology with preceptorship, Provident Hosp., 1933-36; resident surgery Cook County Hosp., Chgo., 1942-45. Med. supt. Cook County Jail, Chgo., 1960-62. Mem. Drug Abuse Council, 1971. Bd. dirs. Ill. Council Continuing Med. Edn. Diplomate Am. Bd. Surgery. Fellow A.C.S., Chgo. Surg. Soc., Am. Soc. Colon and Rectal Surgeons; mem. A.A.A.S., A.M.A. (merit certificate 1966), Ill., Chgo. med. socs., Sigma Xi. Home: 5129 S Drexel Ave Chicago IL 60615 Office: 1525 E 53d St Chicago IL 60615

SHROPSHIRE, CLYDE CALVIN, JR., architect; b. Denver, Jan. 9, 1927; s. Clyde Calvin and Jessie Ann (Murray) S.; student Fresno State Coll., 1947; B.S., Heald Engring. Coll., 1950; m. Joan Strouse, Jan. 16, 1954; children—Scott, Anne, Linda. Architect, McGuire & Shook, Indpls., 1954-60, Fleck, Quebe & Reid, Indpls., 1960-64; v.p., treas. Burkart, Shropshire, Boots, Reid & Assos., Indpls., 1964—. Served with 11th Airborne div. U.S. Army, 1945-46; PTO. Certified Nat. Council Archtl. Registration Bd., Ala., N.C., S.C. Mem. A.I.A., Ind. Soc. Architects (sec. 1966-67), Civil War Round Table Indpls. Home: 8887 Braeside S Indianapolis IN 46260 Office: 2506 Willowbrook Pkwy Indianapolis IN 46205

SHROTE, ROBERT ALLWIN, food co. exec.; b. Morganfield, Ky., Oct. 4, 1924; s. Allwin Dixon and Cora Elizabeth (Jones) S.; student DePauw U., 1942-44; B.S., U. Ill., 1947; m. Paula Esther Anslinger, Sept. 12, 1953; children—Kevin Allwin, Jennifer Sue, Curtis Kent. Sales trainee Standard Oil Co. (Ind.), Rockford, Ill., 1946-47; asst. to plant auditor Swift & Co., Evansville, Ind., 1947-56; systems engr. IBM, Indpls., 1956-59; mgr. programming and computer ops. Am. States Ins. Co., Indpls., 1959-62; mgr. systems devel. Peoples-Home Life Ins. Co., Frankfort, Ind., 1962; data processing mgr. Stokely-Van Camp, Inc., Indpls., 1962-68, asst. dir. info. systems, data processing mgr., 1968-73, staff v.p. info. systems, 1973—. Served to lt. USNR, 1943-46, 50-51. Certified data processor Data Processing Mgmt. Assn. Mem. Grocery Mfrs. Assn. (sec. adminstrv. systems com.), Assn. for Computing Machinery, Phi Gamma Delta. Methodist. Club: Masons. Home: 7139 Creekside Ln Indianapolis IN 46250 Office: 941 N Meridian St Indianapolis IN 46206

SHRUM, ALYCE JANET, guidance dir.; b. Sullivan, Ind., Jan. 3, 1920; d. Charles Richard and Stella (Ridgeway) Railsback; student Western Coll. for Women, Oxford, Ohio, 1938-40; A.B., DePauw U., 1942; M.S., Ind. State U., 1967, also postgrad.; m. James Eugene Shrum, Aug. 16, 1941; children—Janet Jean, Paricia Jane, James David. Tchr., pub. schs., Sullivan County, Ind., 1960-61, tchr. educably mentally handicapped, 1962-63; primary tchr. Ind. State U. Lab. Sch., Terre Haute, 1963-68, dir. elementary guidance, 1968-77, dir. guidance, 1977—. Mem. exec. bd., publicity chmn. adv. bd. Ind. Project for Consumer and Econ. Edn., 1975-78; finance chmn. Girls Scouts Sullivan County, 1955-59, exec. bd., 1953-59, leader, Flint, Mich., 1943-45. Recipient grants Kroger Co., 1974-75, Ind. Commn. Higher Edn., 1976-77, 77-78. Mem. Ind. Personnel and Guidance Assn. (exec. bd. 1976—, hearing bd. 1977-78), Am. Assn. Sch. Counselors, AAUP, Am. Early Childhood Edn. Assn., Am. Personnel and Guidance Assn., Ind., Am. assns. sch. counselors, Ind. Assn. Social Works Suprs., W. Central Ind. Personnel and Guidance Assn. (pres. 1976—), Ind. High Edn. Soc., Ind. Tchrs. Assn., NEA, Phi Delta Kappa, Kappa Kappa Kappa, Ind. State, Western Coll. for Women, DePauw U. alumni assns. Democrat. Clubs: Daughters of Nile, Order Eastern Star. Home: Rt 5 Box 302 Sullivan IN 47882 Office: Indiana State Univ Laboratory School 7th & Chestnut Sts Terre Haute IN 47809

SHUBIK, PHILIPPE, physician, educator; b. London, Eng., Apr. 28, 1921; came to U.S., 1949, naturalized, 1957; s. Joseph L.M. and Sara (Soloweiczyk) S.; B.M.B.Ch., Oxford (Eng.) U., 1943, D.Phil., 1949, D.M., 1971; m. Valerie Helen Reid, July 22, 1964; children—Anna, Peter, Katherine. Intern, London Hosp., 1943; demonstrator in pathology, mem. cancer research unit Sir William Dunn Sch. Pathology, Oxford U., 1947-49; instr. pathology, biologist exptl. cancer project Northwestern U. Med. Sch., Evanston, Ill., 1949-50; asst. prof. surgery Chgo. Med. Sch., 1950-53, asso. prof., 1953, prof. oncology, 1953-68, cancer coordinator, 1950-53, dir. div. oncology, 1953-66, dir. Inst. for Med. Research, 1966-68; prof. Coll. Medicine, U. Neb., Omaha, 1968—, dir. Eppley Inst. for Research in Cancer, 1968—. Mem. cancer adv. bd. Chgo. Bd. Health, 1961-68; mem. Nat. Adv. Cancer Council, 1962-66; mem. U.S.A. nat. com. Internat. Union Against Cancer, 1971—; cons. to dir. Nat. Cancer Inst., 1966-75; chmn. subcom. on environ. carcinogens Nat. Cancer Adv. Bd., 1974—. Served to maj., M.C., Brit. Army, 1944-47. Nat. Cancer Inst. grantee, 1950—. Fellow N.Y. Acad. Scis.; mem. Am. Assn. for Cancer Research (com. for environ. carcinogenesis 1971—), Am. Assn. Pathologists and Bacteriologists, Am. Soc. Cell Biology, Am. Soc. Exptl. Pathology, Am. Pub. Health Assn., Assn. Am. Cancer Insts., Environ. Mutagen Soc., Soc. Exptl. Biology and Medicine, Soc. Pathology and Bacteriology of Gt. Britain, Soc. Toxicology, Permanent Commn. and Internat. Assn. Occupational Health, Soc. Biology of Santiago (hon.), Sigma Xi, Alpha Omega Alpha. Mem. editorial bd. Cancer Research, 1956-70, Proc. Soc. Exptl. Biology and Medicine, 1960—, Internat. Jour. Cancer, 1964-66, Am. Jour. Pathology, 1967-72, Preventative Medicine, 1975—, Jour. Toxicology and Environmental Health, 1975—; mem. editorial adv. com. 2d series Atlas of Tumor Pathology; co-mng. editor Cancer Letters, 1975—. Contbr. numerous articles to med. jours. Home: 3321 S 101st St Omaha NE 68124 Office: Eppley Institute 42d and Dewey Av Omaha NE 68105

SHUEY, WILLIAM CARPENTER, govt. ofcl.; b. Emporia, Kans., July 1, 1924; s. William Harrison and Leona Mildred (Carpenter) S.; student Friends U., 1942-43, Shrivenham Am. U., England, 1945; B.S., Wichita State U., 1948; postgrad. U. Minn., 1959; M.S., N.D. State U., 1967, Ph.D., 1970; m. Rose May Wiebe, Apr. 3, 1943; children—Sharon (Mrs. Fredrick H. Schwienle III), Rebekah (Mrs. Dennis Burkholder), Rhoda May (Mrs. Richard Brumfield), Michal Marie (Mrs. Thomas Kays). Exptl. miller and baker Quality Control Lab., Gen. Mills, Inc., Wichita, Kans., 1948-51; in charge exptl. milling and phys. dough testing sect., Mpls., 1951-62; with Agrl. Research Service, U.S. Dept. Agr., Fargo, N.D., 1962—, research leader, food technologist, 1972—; faculty N.D. State U., Fargo, 1962-70, prof. cereal chemistry, 1970-75. Served with AUS, 1943-46. Mem. Am. Assn. Cereal Chemists (chmn. phys. testing methods com. 1961—, Carl Wilhelm Brabender award 1970), Nat. Assn. Advancement Sci., Assn. Operative Millers, N.D. Acad. Sci., Inst. Food Technologists, Am. Chem. Soc., Sigma Xi. Asso. editor Cereal Chemistry, 1976—. Contbr. articles to profl. jours. Home: 1533 S 5th St Fargo ND 58102 Office: Cereal Chemistry and Technology Dept North Dakota State University Fargo ND 58102

SHUFFLEBARGER, PATRICK THOMAS, stockbroker; b. Delaware, Ohio, Oct. 8, 1946; s. Harry Lynn and Jane W. (Wooton) S.; student Ohio State U., 1965-68; B.A., Miami U., Oxford, Ohio, 1970; grad. N.Y. Inst. Fin., 1970. Registerd rep. Bache & Co., Columbus, Ohio, 1971-73; asst. v.p. Fulton Reid & Staples Inc., Cleve., 1973-75; asst. v.p. Vercoe & Co., Columbus, Home: 1574 Berlin Station Rd Delaware OH 43015 Office: 17 S High St Columbus OH 43216

SHUGAR, SAMUEL ROBERT, communications exec., b. Houtzdale, Pa., July 18, 1935; s. Orville and Bernice Henrietta (Kramp) S.; A.B. in Math., Wilkes Coll., Wilkes-Barre, Pa., 1956; postgrad. Poly. Inst. Bklyn., 1965-66, No. Ill. U. 1975—; m. Edwardeen Shirley Penhallick, Sept. 3, 1960; children—Dana Renée, Tracy D'Anne, Kristin Kyle. Engring. supr. Western Elec. various locations in U.S., 1956-66; computer prins. instr. AT & T Long Lines, Cooperstown, N.Y., 1966-68; asst. mgr. staff Western Electric Co., Met. N.Y.C., 1968-73, field support mgr., Montgomery, Ill., 1973—; teaching cons. computer prins. Cooperstown Sch. Dist., Mary Imogene Bassett Hosp., 1966-68; guest lectr. Am. Mgmt. Assn., 1968-70; discussant Soc. Mgmt. Info. Systems Conf., 1970. Mem. Bound Brook (N.J.) Sch. Bd., 1971-72, v.p., 1972-73; elder, deacon Fox Valley Presbyterian Ch., Geneva, Ill. Mem. Am. Mktg. Assn., Telephone Pioneers Am. Clubs: Montgomery Amateur Radio, Masons. Contbg. author to The Burning Bush, 1974—, Western Electric Engr., 1958, 70. Office: S River St Aurora IL 60507

SHUKIN, ALEXEY, educator; b. Rostow, Russia, Nov. 30, 1927; s. Sergey S. and Maria A. (Stepanuck) S.; came to U.S., 1949, naturalized, 1954; B.S., Springfield Coll., 1954, M.S., 1956; Ph.D., U. Chgo., 1964; m. Olga Nikolsky, June 1952; children—Vitaly, Michael, Paul, Maria. USPHS-NIMH research fellow U. Chgo., 1957-60; asst. prof. psychology George Williams Coll., Downers Grove, Ill., 1960-63, asso. prof. psychology, 1964-68, prof. psychology, 1968—, chmn. grad. dept. counseling psychology, 1967—. Cons. to edn., bus. and community orgns.; pvt. practice psychotherapy, Chgo., 1962—. Walter C. Barr fellow, 1954-56; U. Chgo. fellow, 1956-57. Mem. Am., Ill. psychol. assns., A.A.U.P., World Fedn. Mental Health, InterAm. Soc. Psychology, Nat. Council on Grad. Edn. in Psychology, Council for Advancement of Psychol. Professions and Sci., A.A.A.S. Home: 118 Hiawatha Dr Clarendon Hills IL 60514 Office: 555 31st St Downers Grove IL 60515

SHULER, FRANK F., dentist; b. Janesville, Wis., April 1926; s. Frank F. and Ruth K. S.; D.D.S., Marquette U., 1952; m. Jean; children—Charles, Kathryn, Andrew, Kristine. Gen. practice dentistry, Clinton, Wis. Mem. Rock County Dept. Pub. Welfare; village trustee; mem. Wis. Gov.'s Com. Brotherhood Week; mem.

planning com. Rock County Library. Mem. ADA (pres. 1976-77), Wis. Dental Assn. (2d v.p., dir.), Wis. Assn. Professions, Acad. Gen. Dentistry, Chgo. Dental Soc., Am. Soc. Dentistry for Children, Fedn. Dentaire Internationale, Am. Legion, Kappa Sigma. Lutheran. Office: 714 Milwaukee Rd Clinton WI 53525*

SHULKIN, NEIL HOWARD, dentist; b. Chgo., Oct. 30, 1940; s. Joseph M. and Beatrice B. (Schneidman) S.; student Loyola U., Chgo., 1958-60; D.D.S., U. Ill., 1964; m. Rhoda F. Mamett, Dec. 22, 1962; children—Glenn, Arnold, Susan, Elizabeth. Individual practice dentistry, Elk Grove Village, Ill., 1964—, Deerfield, Ill., 1972—, Skokie, Ill., 1973-74; mem. staff Alexian Bros. Hosp., Elk Grove Village; dir., cons. Major-Monroe Dental Lab., Inc., Chgo., Exxcelium Corp. Charter pres. Jordan Listick Research Found., 1971-73; bd. dirs. N.W. Suburban Ill. unit Am. Cancer Soc., 1973. Mem. ADA, Acad. Gen. Dentistry, Ill., Chgo. dental socs., U. Ill. Dental Alumni Assn. (pres. 1973-74), Elk Grove Assn. Industry and Commerce (dir. 1970-74), Elk Grove Village C. of C. (charter pres. 1966-67), Alpha Omega. Jewish. Clubs: Lions (v.p. 1976-78); B'nai B'rith (dir. lodge 1973-74). Contbr. articles to profl. jours. Inventor baby toy basket, dental-tooth characterizer. Home: 1730 Birch Rd Northbrook IL 60062 Office: 1010 Grove Mall Elk Grove Village IL 60007 also 84 S Waukegan Rd Deerfield IL 60015

SHULL, CHARLES W., educator; b. Kouts, Ind., May 26, 1904; s. Samuel P. and Lorena (Kern) S.; A.B., Ohio Wesleyan U., 1926; A.M., Ohio State U., 1927, Ph.D., 1929; m. Pauline E. Scott, June 19, 1935; children—Lorena Belle (Mrs. Gerald Johnson), Harriet Elizabeth (Mrs. Kenneth Matyniak). Instr., U. Ky., 1929-30; instr. Wayne State U., 1930-36, asst. prof., 1936-43, asso. prof. 1943-50, prof. govt., 1950, prof. polit. sci., until 1969, now prof. emeritus; cons. on apportionment, orgns., govt. agys. Trustee, treas. Forney W. Clement Meml. Fund. Mem. Am. Internat. polit. sci. assns., Am. Acad. Polit. and Social Sci., AAUP, Midwest Conf. Polit. Sci. (v.p.), Hansard Soc., Mich. Acad. Sci., Arts, Letters, Am. Judicature Soc., Pi Sigma Alpha, Pi Gamma Mu, Pi Lambda Phi. Presbyn. Kiwanian (lt. gov. 1955). Author: American Experience With Unicameralism, 1937; Reapportionment of Legislature in Michigan, 1940, (with E.E. Sneeringer), 1952; Introduction to Political Science (with Roucek and Huszar), 1950; Your Government (with G.O. Comfort and R.H. Knapp), 1951; Workbook in American Government (with N.D. Grundstein), 1953; co-author American State Legislatures, 1954; State Constitutional Revision, 1961. Book rev. editor Social Science, 1947-62; bd. editors Midwest Jour. Polit. Sci., 1956-66. Contbr. to profl. jours. Address: 8900 E Jefferson St Detroit MI 48214

SHULMAN, ARTHUR DAVID, psychologist; b. Port Jervis, N.Y., June 28, 1942; s. William E. and Rose (Albert) S.; B.A., Alfred U., 1964; M.A., McMaster U., 1966; Ph.D. in Distinction, State U. N.Y., 1969; 1 dau. by previous marriage—Shanna. Vocat. and rehab. counselor Jewish Vocat. Service, Toronto, Ont., Can., 1966; asst. prof. psychology Washington U., St. Louis, 1968-74; reserach psychologist Inst. Black Studies, St. Louis, 1973-77; asso. prof. psychology Washington U., St. Louis, 1974—, dir. social psychology program, 1974—; vis. scholar Communications Studies Group, U. Coll., U. London (Eng.), 1975; vis. sr. research fellow dept. psychology U. Melbourne, Australia, 1977. HEW grantee, 1974-75, 77—. Mem. Am., Midwestern psychol. assns., Soc. Exptl. Social Psychology, Soc. Psychol. Study of Social Issues, AAAS, Am. Sociol. Assn., Gerontology Soc., Sigma Xi, Psi Chi. Contbr. articles on communication processes social psychology to profl. jours. Office: PO Box 1125 Dept Psychology Washington U Saint Louis MO 63130

SHULTZ, ELDEN EVON, accountant; b. Parshall, N.D., Oct. 5, 1923; s. Bernard Arthur and Iva (Gibbs) S.; student Western Ill. State Tchrs. Coll., 1947-48; B.A. with honors, U. Mont., 1951; m. Betty Jean Snyder, June 24, 1948; children—John, Pamela (Mrs. Rodney Sjol), Rebecca (Mrs. Dale Reak), Paula. Office mgr. Yaw-Kinney Co., Inc., Great Falls, Mont., 1951-53; office mgr. Ward Motor Co., Bismarck, N.D., 1954-57; mgr. grain and livestock ranch, also pvt. practice as pub. accountant, Parshall, 1958-72; pvt. practice as pub. accountant and agrl. income tax cons., Parshall, 1973—; sec.-treas. Farmers Union Locker Assn., Parshall. Mem. steering com. Mountrail County Rural Water Users Assn., Stanley, N.D. Sec. bd. dirs. Peoples Homes, Inc., Parshall. Licensed pub. accountant. Mem. Nat., N.D. socs. pub. accountants, Alpha Kappa Psi. Mem. United Ch. of Christ (past pres. bd. dirs.). Address: Parshall ND 58770

SHULTZ, JOHN ARTHUR, accountant; b. Kingman, Kans., Jan. 17, 1919; s. Arthur Glen and Frances Lenora (Hume) S.; student pub. schs.; m. Emma Jean Schiekofsky, Sept. 24, 1938; children—Patricia (Mrs. Earl R. Gomersall), Jack Warren, Barbara (Mrs. Donald G. Goddard). Foreman, B.W. Grant Constrn. Co., Wichita, Kans., 1938-41; mechanic Billy Jones Chevrolet Co., McPherson, Kans., 1942-43; salesman McPherson Automotive Supply, 1944-45; bookkeeper, parts man Friendly Chevrolet Co., Canton, Kans., 1946-54; pvt. practice as pub. accountant, Hutchinson, Kans., 1955—. Mem. Nat. Soc. Pub. Accountants, Pub. Accountants Assn. Kans. (pres. 1972). Lutheran. Mason (Shriner), Moose, Elk, Lion. Home: 415 E 16th St Hutchinson KS 67501 Office: 421 W 1st St Hutchinson KS 67501

SHUMAN, DAVID LEE, data processor; b. Anderson, Ind., Dec. 28, 1940; s. Lester Herman and Ruby Irene (Reavis) S.; B.A., Wabash Coll., 1962; M.S. (NSF fellow), Purdue U., 1965, postgrad., 1965-67; m. Virginia Ann Terry, Aug. 26, 1962; children—Jeffrey Lee, Bethany Ann and Kathleen Ann (twins). With Purdue U. Measurement and Research Center, West Lafayette, Ind., 1964-66; system programmer Purdue U. Adminstrv. Data Processing Center, 1967-68, mgr. programming, 1968-71, software engr., 1971-73; with First Savs. & Loan Assn., Anderson, Ind., 1973-77; data processor Ind. U.-Purdue U. at Indpls., 1977—; pvt. cons. data processing of quality control tests in mfr. telephone wire. Contbr. articles to profl. publs. Home: Route 1 Box 19A Pendleton IN 46064 Office: 1201 E 38th St Indianapolis IN 46205

SHUMAN, R(OBERT) BAIRD, educator; b. Paterson, N.J., June 20, 1929; s. George William and Elizabeth (Evans) S.; A.B. (trustees scholar), Lehigh U., 1951; M.Ed., Temple U., 1953; Ph.D. (univ. scholar), U. Pa., 1961; certificate in philology U. Vienna (Austria), 1954. Tchr., Phila. Pub. Schs., 1953-55; asst. instr. Humanities, U. Pa., 1955-57; instr. Drexel U., Phila., 1957-59; asst. prof. English, San Jose (Calif.) State U., 1959-62; asst. prof. Duke U., 1962-63, asso. prof., 1963-66, prof. edn., 1966-77; prof. English, dir. English edn. U. Ill., Urbana-Champaign, 1977—; vis. prof. Moore Inst. Art, 1958, Phila. Conservatory Music, 1958-59, Lynchburg Coll., 1965. Mem. Nat. Council Tchrs. English (state chmn. awards program 1968-69; evaluator ERIC Clearing House), Internat. Council Edn. of Tchrs., Ill. English Tchrs. Assn., Conf. English Edn. (nominating com. 1975), Internat. Reading Assn., Modern Lang. Assn., Internat. Assn. Univ. Profs. English, Nat. Soc. Arts and Humanities, Nat. Soc. Study of Edn. Democrat. Author: Clifford Odets, 1962; Robert E. Sherwood, 1964; William Inge, 1965. Editor: Nine Black Poets, 1968; An Eye for an Eye, 1969; A Galaxy of Black Writing, 1970; Creative Approaches to the Teaching of English: Secondary, 1974; Questions English Teachers Ask, 1977; Educational Drama for Today's Schools, 1978; exec. editor The Clearing House, 1976—; cons. editor Poet Lore; contbg. editor Reading Horizons, 1975—. Home: Box 1687 Champaign IL 61820

SHUMATE, CHARLES ROLANE, clergyman; b. Meridian, Miss., July 6, 1946; s. James Rolane and Evelyn (White) S.; student Meridian Jr. Coll., 1964, B.A., Anderson Coll., 1968; postgrad. Louisville Presbyn. Sem., 1968-69, Lexington Theol. Sem., 1970-74; m. Laretta Airgood, Mar. 18, 1967; children—Chara DeAnne, Chausette Dawn. Ordained to ministry Ch. God, 1970; protestant minister Bryce Canyon (Utah) Nat. Park, 1967; asso. pastor First Ch. God, Louisville, 1968-70, Eastland Pkwy. Ch. God, 1970-72; pastor First Ch. God, Kingsport, Tenn., 1972-75; dir. evangelism Bd. Ch. Extension and Home Missions, 1975—; state youth dir. Ky. Youth Ch. of God, 1969-71; Tenn. sec. Ch. God, 1972-75; chmn. youth com. Kingsport Preaching Missions, 1972, Greater Kingsport Area Crusade, 1973—. Mem. adv. bd. sr. Citizens Kingsport, 1973-74; participant Nat. Drug Abuse Tng. Seminar, Washington, 1974; mem. alumni council Anderson Coll., 1974-76; trustee, Asbury Theol. Sem., 1975. Recipient sr. award Anderson Coll., 1968; Lexington Theol. Sem., 1971-72. Mem. Kingsport Ministerial Assn. (pres. 1972), Ky. Ministers Assembly. Clubs: Civitan (chaplin Kingsport 1973-74), Amici (Anderson Coll.). Home: 1527 E 44th St Anderson IN 46013 Office: PO Box 2069 Anderson IN 46011

SHUMWAY, RICHARD KENNETH, constrn. exec.; b. Lawrenceville, Ill., Oct. 26, 1926; s. Howard Duane and Gertrude Bertha (Schmidt) S.; B.S., Tri State Coll., 1952; m. Kathleen Griffin, Dec. 25, 1949; children—John, David, Barbara, Amy. Field engr. Knowlton Constrn. Co., indsl. comml. bldg. constrn., Bellefontaine, Ohio, 1953-57; office engr. Ebasco Services, power plant constrn., Ft. Myers, Fla., 1957-59; field engr. Montgomery Ward, Chgo., 1959-66; dir. constrn. Moores Bldg. Supply, comml. bldg. constrn., Roanoke, Va., 1968; v.p. Bost, Inc., multi family housing constrn., Columbus, Ohio, 1968-76; constrn. mgr. warehousing distbn. centers Space Devel., Inc. subs. Distbn. Centers, Inc., Columbus, 1976-77; field engr. Montgomery Ward subs. Mobil Oil Co., 1977—. Served with USNR, 1943-46. Home: 10621 Riverside Dr Powell OH 43065 Office: 1310 Dublin Rd Columbus OH 43212

SHUPE, MARION CLAIRE, clergyman; b. Lacona, Iowa, May 15, 1906; s. Clyde Myron and Lizzie D. (Mitchell) S.; B.A., Simpson Coll., 1935; M.Min., Drew U., 1939, postgrad., 1939; m. Bessie Maude Vernon, May 6, 1928 (dec. 1962); 1 son, Marion Claire; m. 2d, Evelyn Marshall, 1963 (dec. 1975). Ordained deacon Meth. Ch., 1935, elder, 1939; pastor, Lucas, Iowa, 1931-35, Millbrook Ave. Ch., Dover, N.J., 1935-39, Kellogg, Iowa, 1939-42, Humeston, Iowa, 1942-49, Gatchel Ch., Des Moines, 1949-51, Winfield, Iowa, 1951-54, Brooklyn, Iowa, 1954-61, Epworth Ch., Council Bluffs, Iowa, 1961-64, Nevada (Iowa) Meth. Ch., 1964-65; sr. pastor United Meth. Ch., Nevada, Iowa, 1965-68, Bloomfield, Iowa, 1968-71; ret., 1971; interim pastor McGregor (Minn.) parish, 1972-74; visitation pastor St. John's United Meth. Ch., Davenport, 1975—; mem. bd. publs. Iowa-Des Moines Conf. Meth. Ch., 1939-51, chmn., 1963-68, mem. secretarial staff, 1951-54, sec., 1954-60, bus. mgr. youth program, 1951-54, dist. chmn. evangelism, 1961, chmn. conf. relations com. Active Boy Scouts Am., 1939-71; chmn. bd. dirs. Council Bluffs Goodwill Industries, Inc. Mem. Pi Gamma Mu, Lambda Chi Alpha. Clubs: Masons (grand chaplain 1954-57), Kiwanis, Lions, Rotary. Editor South Iowa Conf. Jour., 1956-68, Conf. Preliminary Report Book, 1963-68. Home: 3122 Harrison Davenport IA 52803

SHURR, ROGER EUGENE, dentist; b. Valparaiso, Ind., May 30, 1941; s. Harvey M. and Mary V. (Link) S.; student Valparaiso U., 1959-61; D.D.S. with honors, Ind. U., 1966; m. Judie Swartz; children—Carl, Kathleen, Laura, Scott, Laurie, Debbie. Intern Ind. U. Med. Center, Indpls., 1966-67, resident, 1967-68; gen. practice dentistry, Indpls., 1966-68; practice dentistry specializing in pedodontics, Valparaiso, 1968—; chmn. dental staff St. Anthonys Hosp., Michigan City, Ind., 1968—. Bd. dirs. YMCA, Valparaiso. NSF grantee, 1962-64. Mem. Am., Ind. (del. 1970—) dental assns., N.W. Ind. Dental Soc. (dir.), Am. Acad. Pedodontics, Am. Soc. Dentistry for Children, Ind. Pedodontic Assn., Porter County (pres. 1969-70) dental socs., Omicron Kappa Upsilon, Phi Kappa Psi, Delta Sigma Delta. Clubs: N.W. Racquet, Valparaiso Golf. Home: 2205 Wynnewood Dr Valparaiso IN 46383 Office: 809 Wall St Valparaiso IN 46383

SHURTLEFF, JOHN HOWARD, lawyer; b. Wheaton, Ill., June 27, 1928; s. Howard Freeman and Ruth Linnaea (Hawkinson) S.; B.S., U. Ill., 1950; J.D., DePaul U., 1955; m. Joan Fagerburg, Oct. 17, 1953; children—Karin, Robert Scot. Engr. Underwriters Lab., Chgo., 1950-51; admitted to Ill. bar, 1955; partner firm Keil, Thompson & Shurtleff; individual law practice specializing in patents, trademarks and copyrights, Chgo., 1955—. Pres. Riverside (Ill.) Community Fund, 1964-65; v.p. Southwest Suburban Mental Health Assn., 1969-70; 1st v.p. Community Family Service and Mental Health Assn., 1970-71, pres., 1971-73. Mem. Zoning Commn. and Bd. Appeals, Riverside, 1969—. Trustee, Riverside Pub. Library, 1974—, v.p., 1976—. Served with U.S. Army, 1952-54. Mem. Am. Bar Assn., Patent Law Assn. Chgo., Am. Chem. Soc., Soc. Plastics Engrs., Soc. Am. Magicians, Sigma Phi Delta. Republican. Methodist. Mason. Club: Riverside Swim. Home: 272 Bartram Rd Riverside IL 60546 Office: 135 S LaSalle St Chicago IL 60603

SHUTT, GEORGE MARVIN, assn. exec.; b. Auburn, Ill., Mar. 23, 1918; s. Victor J. and Ethel Irene (Collins) Shutt; B.S., U. Ill., 1939, M.S., 1941; m. Barbara Jean Laube, Jan. 31, 1942. Prof. econs., accountancy, also dir. pub. relations Blackburn Coll., Carlinville, Ill., 1941-42; editor pilot's manual, economist United Air Lines, 1942-45; prof. journalism, head dept., dir. pub. relations U. N.D., Grand Forks, 1945-46; dir. pub. relations, account exec. Waldie & Briggs Inc., Chgo., 1946-48; various positions Nat. Sporting Goods Assn., Chgo., 1948—, sec., 1949—, exec. dir., lectr. in field. Named to Sporting Goods Industry Hall of Fame, 1978. Mem. Nat. Retail Assn. (chmn. central council 1955-56), U.S. C. of C. (chmn. assn. com. 1955-56), Am. Retail Fedn. (dir., exec. com. 1955-58), Am. Soc. Assn. Execs., Greater N. Mich. Ave. Assn., Sigma Delta Chi, Kappa Tau Alpha. Republican. Methodist. Clubs: Univ. Chgo. (dir. 1968-71), Chgo. Press. Home: 505 N Lake Shore Dr Chicago IL 60611 Office: Nat Sporting Goods Assn 717 N Michigan Ave Chicago IL 60611

SHUTZ, BYRON CHRISTOPHER, mortgage banker, real estate exec.; b. Kansas City, Mo., Feb. 16, 1928; s. Byron Theodore and Maxine Eleanor (Christopher) S.; A.B. in Econs., U. Kans., 1949; m. Marilyn Ann Tweedie, Mar. 30, 1957; children—Eleanor, Byron Christopher, Collin, Allison, Lindley. Partner, Herbert V. Jones & Co., Kansas City, Mo., 1953-72, pres. Herbert V. Jones Mortgage Corp., Kansas City, Mo., 1953-72; pres. The Byron Shutz Co., Kansas City, Mo., 1973—; dir. Bus. Men's Assurance Co. Am., Traders Nat. Bank, 1st. Am. Fin. Corp., Faultless Starch-Bon Ami Co. Mem. Kansas City Sch. Dist., 1970-72; bd. dirs. Kansas City Area council Boy Scouts Am., Kansas City chpt. ARC, Downtown Inc., 1967-72, Community Services Broadcasting Inc., 1972, Family and Children Services Kansas City, 1968-74, Starlight Theatre Assn., 1968-74, Kansas City Crime Commn., 1974—, Constrn. Users Council, 1972-76; mem. Civic Council Greater Kansas City, v.p., dir., 1973-76; chmn. bd. govs. Kansas City Art Inst., 1960-62; trustee U. Kansas City, 1968—, Pembroke-Country Day Sch., 1974-76. Served to 1st. lt. USAF, 1951-53. Mem. Mortgage Bankers Assn. Am. (gov. 1966-74), Real Estate Bd. Kansas City, Mo. (dir. 1963-66, 75-78), Am. Inst. Real Estate Appraisers. Clubs: Kansas City Country, Univ., Kansas City, Mercury. Home: 1001 W 58th Terr Kansas City MO 64113 Office: The Byron Shutz Co 800 W 47th St Kansas City MO 64112

SICAM-SIMON, GRACITA ESPAÑOL, anesthesiologist; b. San Manuel, Pangasinan, Philippine Islands, Aug. 10, 1939; d. Leonardo J. and Rosario B. (Español) Sicam; M.D., Far Eastern U., 1964; m. Jorge Simon, Jr., Apr. 24, 1971; 1 dau., Jennifer Ann. Intern, Grace Gen. Hosp., Winnipeg, Man., Can., 1967-68; resident obstetrics-gynecology U. Hosp. Saskatoon (Sask., Can.), 1968-69, Boston U. Hosp., 1969-70; anesthesia resident U. Kan. Med. Center, Kansas City, 1970-71; practice medicine specializing in anesthesiology North Kansas City (Mo.) Meml. Hosp., 1972-74, Spelman Meml. Hosp., Smithville, Mo., 1974—. Home: 1020 N Woodland Dr Kansas City MO 64118 Office: PO Box 289 Smithville MO 64089

SICHERMAN, MARVIN ALLEN, lawyer; b. Cleve., Dec. 27, 1934; s. Harry and Malvina (Friedman) S.; B.A., Case Western Res. U., 1957, LL.B., 1960, J.D., 1968; m. Sue Kovacs, Aug. 18, 1957; children—Heidi Joyce, Steven Eric. Admitted to Ohio bar, 1960, since practiced in Cleve.; mng. partner Dettelbach & Sicherman, 1971—; mem. moot ct. bd. Case Western Res. Law Sch., 1958-60. Mem. Beachwood (Ohio) Civic League, 1972—, Beachwood Bd. Edn., 1978—, Beachwood Arts Council, 1977—. Mem. Am., Ohio (lectr. truth in lending 1969, lectr. bankruptcy 1972), Cuyahoga County, Cleve. (lectr. practice and procedure clinic 1965-77, chmn. bankruptcy ct. com. 1971-73) bar assns., Comml. Law League Am., Jewish Chautauqua Soc., Tau Epsilon Rho, Zeta Beta Tau. Jewish (trustee temple brotherhood 1968-76). Contbr. to legal jours.; editorial bd. Case-Western Res. Law Rev., 1958-60. Home: 24500 Albert Ln Beachwood OH 44122 Office: Ohio Savings Plaza Cleveland OH 44114

SICHERT, PAUL OTTO, automotive co. exec.; b. Jersey City, Mar. 7, 1933; s. Paul Otto and Maria Theodora (Ackerman) S.; B.S., Lehigh U., 1954; certificate Fairleigh-Dickinson U., 1957; m. Mary Irene Patterson, Jan. 17, 1961; children—Nancy Anne, Jane Elizabeth. Reporter, Bergan (N.J.) Evening Record, 1950; program prodn. relations NBC, 1950-57; supr. sales promotion and devel. Sinclair Oil Co., 1954-58; supr. sales promotion Budd Co., Troy, Mich., 1958-59, supr. market research, 1959-64, asst. mgr. advt. and pub. relations, 1964-67, corporate mgr. market devel., 1967-71, asst. to pres. for pub. affairs and asst. to chmn. for pub. affairs, 1972—. Served with U.S. Army, 1957-58. Recipient award best indsl. film: Plane-Mate. Mem. Assn. Indsl. Advertisers, Assn. Nat. Advertisers, Inst. Rapid Transit, R.R. Pub. Relations Assn., Acad. Motion Picture Arts and Scis. Clubs: Detroit Athletic, Adcraft (Detroit); Pine Lake Country; George Town. Home: 4002 Spur Hill Dr Bloomfield Hills MI 48013 Office: 3155 W Big Beaver Rd Troy MI 48084

SICKBERT, JO, painter; b. Independence, Mo., Oct. 27, 1931; d. Edward Andrew and Alma Grace (Hawthorne) Schowengerdt; student Wichita U., 1949-50, Kans. U., 1950-51; m. Wallace Jerry Sickbert, Aug. 31, 1951; children—Jan, Mike. One-woman shows: Jack O'Grady Galleries, Chgo., 1976, Johnson-Welsh Galleries, Kansas City, Mo., 1977, Albrecht Art Mus., St. Joseph, Mo., 1973, many others; group shows include: Philbrook Art Mus., Tulsa, 1975, Art Wagon Gallery, Scottsdale, Ariz., 1975, 77, others; represented in permanent collections: Albecht Art Mus., also pvt. collections. Winner Saturday Evening Post Cover Contest, 1973; Top Nat. award Biennial Art Competition, Nat. League Am. Penwomen, 1972; others. Mem. Internat. Platform Assn. Commd. painting Suffragettes, Chgo. Tribune Bicentennial Collection, 1976. Address: 10316 Beverly St Overland Park KS 66207

SICKMAN, LAURENCE CHALFANT STEVENS, art mus. ofcl.; b. Denver, Aug. 27, 1907; s. D. Vance and May Ridding (Fuller) S.; A.B. cum laude, Harvard U., 1930; Harvard-Yenching fellow, Peking, China, 1930-35; LL.D. (hon.), Rockhurst Coll., Kansas City, 1972; L.H.D., Baker U., Baldwin, Kans., 1973; Litt.D., U. Mo., 1974; H.H.D., Columbia U., 1977. Curater oriental art Nelson-Atkins Gallery Art, Kansas City, Mo., 1935-45, vice dir., 1946-53, dir., 1953-77, dir. emeritus, cons. to trustees, 1977—; lectr., resident fellow Fogg Mus., Harvard U., 1937-39; mem. exec. com. Arts in Embassies Program, Dept. State; mem. Fine Arts Exhbn. com. Expo '67, Montreal, Que., Can. Served as maj., combat intelligence, USAAF, 1942-45. Decorated Legion of Merit; knight comdr. Royal Order North Star (Sweden); recipient Charles Lang Freer medal, 1973. Mem. Chinese Art Soc. Am. (editor Archives), Am. Council Learned Socs. (com. on Far Eastern studies 1948-53), Far-Eastern Assn. (gov. 1951-53), Am. Museum Dirs., Am. Oriental Soc., Japan Soc., Far Eastern Ceramic Group, Assn. Art Mus. Dirs. U.S.A. and Can., Coll. Art Assn. (dir.), Asia Soc. N.Y. (exhbns. com.; editor Archives Asian Art), Am. Assn. Museums (council). Clubs: Rotary, Kansas City Country, River. Author: (with Alexander Soper) The Art and Architecture of China, 1968; Chinese Callgraphy and Painting, 1962; contbr. articles to profl. publs. Home: 901 E 47th St Kansas City MO 64110 Office: 4525 Oak St Kansas City MO 64111

SIDDIQI, AKHTAR HUSAIN, geographer; b. Budaun, India, Apr. 20, 1925; s. Rahat Husain and Miraj (Bano) S.; came to U.S., 1963, naturalized, 1973; B.A. with honors, Aligarh U., India; M.A., London U., 1953, Ph.D., 1959; m. Ismat Bano Hamid, Dec. 16, 1966. Lectr., A.T.U. Coll., Karachi, Pakistan, 1949-53; research officer Govt. Pakistan Planning Bd., 1954-55; sr. lectr. Dacca U., E. Pakistan, 1955-60; chief planning officer Pakistan Internat. Airlines, 1961-63; mem. faculty Ind. U., Terre Haute, 1964—, prof. geography, 1973—. Mem. Assn. Am. Geographers, Sigma Xi. Muslim. Contbr. to profl. jours. Home: 4415 Trudy's Dr Terra Haute IN 47802 Office: Dept Geography Ind State U Terre Haute IN 47809

SIDEY, EDWIN JOHN, publisher; b. Creston, Iowa, June 5, 1925; s. Keneth H. and Alice (Swanson) S.; B.S., Iowa State Coll., 1950; m. Dorothy H. Reischach, May 8, 1953 (dec. 1973); children—Kenneth Hugh, David Bruce. News editor Pierre (S.D.) Capital Jour., 1950-51; reporter Omaha World Herald, 1951-55; editor Adair County Free Press, Greenfield, Iowa, 1955—, pub., 1976—. Mem. Greenfield Sch. Bd., 1961-73, pres., 1972-73; pres. Greenfield Service Club, 1970; sec. Community Devel. Bd., 1965-77, Planning and Zoning Commn., 1965—. Served with AUS, 1943-46. Recipient Community Service award Lions, 1975. Mem. Iowa Press Assn., Nat. Newspaper Assn. Presbyterian. Home: 208 Mills St SW Greenfield IA 50840 Office: 108 Iowa St E Greenfield IA 50849

SIEBEN, JAMES GEORGE, adj. gen. Minn.; b. Hastings, Minn., Apr. 19, 1924; s. Harry A. and Irene H. (Buckley) S.; student U. Minn., Stanford U.; m. Charlotte Jean Gove, July 10, 1954; children—James, Lisa, Terrance. Served as enlisted man AUS, 1942-45; commd. 2d lt. N.G., advanced through grades to maj. gen.; served as 1st lt. U.S. Army, 1951-52; comdt. Minn. Mil. Acad.; now adj. gen. Minn. Mem. NG Assn. of U.S., Adj. Gen's Assn., Am. Legion, VFW. Decorated Silver Star medal with oak leaf cluster,

Purple Heart, Bronze Star medal, Combat Inf. badge, Minn. Commendation medal, Minn. medal for merit, others. Home: 501 W 11th St Hastings MN 55033 Office: Veterans Service Bldg Saint Paul MN 55155

SIEBENMORGEN, PAUL, physician; b. Terre Haute, Ind., Sept. 16, 1920; s. Louis and Ruby E. (Curtis) S.; B.S. in Edn., Ind. State U., 1941; M.D., Ind. U., 1944; m. Jane Maxine Waggoner, June 20, 1948; children—Paul Stephen, Elizabeth Ann, Susan Lynn. Intern, Meth. Hosp., Indpls., 1944-45; practice medicine, Terre Haute, 1947—; mem. staff St. Anthony Hosp., Terre Haute, pres. staff, 1975, instr. Hosp. Sch. Nursing, 1948-58, mem. adv. council, 1959-60; asso. clin. faculty Terre Haute center for med. edn. Sch. Medicine, Ind. U., 1973—. Pres., Vigo County Heart Assn., 1965, 66; chmn. profl. div. United Fund, Terre Haute, 1960; pres. Med. Edn. Found. Terre Haute, 1976, Vigo County Bd. Health, 1967-68, 71—; mem. Ind. Health Coordinating Council, 1977—; bd. dirs. So. Ind. Health Systems Agy., 1976—; trustee Ind. State U., 1975—, Terre Haute Regional Hosp., 1975—. Served to capt. M.C., AUS, 1945-47. Mem. AMA, Am. (charter fellow), Ind. (dist. pres. 1971; state dir. 1973—) acads. family physicians, Ind. State Med. Assn., Terre Haute Acad. Medicine (pres. 1974-75), Vigo County Med. Soc. (pres. 1970), Aesculapian Soc. Wabash Valley, Ind. State U. Alumni Assn. (pres. 1971-73), Vigo County Comprehensive Health Planning Council (sec. 1975, charter mem.), Blue Key, Alpha Phi Omega, Sigma Alpha Epsilon, Phi Rho Sigma, Kappa Delta Pi. Mem. Christian Ch. (bd. mem. ind. region 1966—, gen. bd. 1969-75, 77—, moderator Ind. region 1974-76). Clubs: Masons, Elks, Wabash Valley Lecture (pres. 1959-60). Home: 2515 N 7th St Terre Haute IN 47804 Office: 1024 S 6th St Terre Haute IN 47807

SIEBERT, DONALD EDWARD, mktg. research exec.; b. Cin., Jan. 20, 1941; s. Edward Stephan and Marion Ruth (Carroll) S.; B.S. in Psychology, Xavier U., Cin., 1964; M.B.A. in Mgmt., U. Cin., 1967; m. Barbara Jo Soat, Sept. 16, 1967; children—Michael Sean, David Edward. Project dir. Burke Mktg. Research Inc., Cin., 1967-69, sr. project dir., 1969-72, account exec., 1972-75, asso. dir. copy research, 1975-76, mktg. mgr., 1976—. Adviser, Cin. Jr. Achievement; judge, com. mem. U.S. Figure Skating Assn. Mem. Am. Mktg. Assn. Club: Queen City Figure Skating (pres. Cin. 1972-74). Home: 4040 Cottingham Dr Cincinnati OH 45241 Office: 1529 Madison Rd Cincinnati OH 45206

SIEDEL, JAMES MEREDITH, film prodn. exec.; b. Columbus, Ohio, Mar. 15, 1937; s. Frank and Alyce Louise (Van Den Mooter) S.; B.S. in Journalism, Northwestern U., 1959; m. Patricia Jean Foley, June 15, 1963; children—Thomas, Katherine. Field editor Irving Cloud Publs., 1960; researcher Storycraft Inc. Lakewood, Ohio, 1961-65, writer dir., producer film, audio-visual, 1965—, v.p. 1968-77, pres., 1977—; dir. films Recreation Land, 1973, We've Come a Long Way Together, 1976; writer, producer The Fundamentals of Advertising, 1975, The Fundamentals of Marketing, 1975, The Fundamentals of Sales Management, 1975, Pride and Progress, The Story of Cleveland, 1977. Mem. Rocky River (Ohio) City Council, 1971—. Mem. Cleve. Advt. Club, Rocky River Hist. Soc. (founder, trustee 1969—). Club: Cleve. Yachting. Author: (with Frank Siedel) Pioneers of Science, 1968, The Ohio Heritage Library, 1963. Home: 19970 Roslyn Dr Rocky River OH 44116 Office: 18630 Detroit Ave Lakewood OH 44107

SIEFKES, HERMANN W(ILLIAM), clergyman; b. Waterloo, Iowa, July 2, 1899; s. Siegfried H. and Elizabeth (Krekeler) S.; student Wartburg Acad. and Coll., 1912-18, Wartburg Theol. Sem., 1918-21, D.D., 1947; m. Elizabeth Groth, Dec. 29, 1925; children—Ulrich Luther, Elizabeth Joanne. Carolyn Barbara. Ordained to ministry Lutheran Ch., 1921; pres. Iowa Dist. Am. Luth. Ch., 1939—, chmn. Commn. Home Missions, 1940-51; 1st ranking v.p. Am. Luth. Ch., 1951-54, gen. v.p. to 1960, 1st pres. Iowa Dist. (ch. merger), 1960—; Am. Luth. Ch. rep. Commn. Orphaned Missions and Younger Chs. of Nat. Luth. Council, 1948-51; lectr. post-war confs., Europe, 1950; served Luth. World Fedn. in European Refuge cause, 1954; ofcl. visitor to assembly Luth. World Fedn., Helsinki, 1963; chmn. colloque com. Am. Luth. Ch., 1960-66, chmn. Council of Bishops, 1963-67; ofcl. visitor World Council Chs. in Evanston; founder St. Armands Key Luth. Ch., Sarasota, Fla., 1967-69; mem. div. coll. and univ. work Nat. Luth. Council, 1930-59; mem. joint union com. Am. Luth. Ch., 1950-54; mem. Nat. Luth. Council, 1948-60; now bishop emeritus Iowa Dist., Am. Luth. Ch. Recipient Churchmanship citation Wartburg Coll., 1977. Contbr. articles to religious publs. Home: 203 16th St SW Waverly IA 50677

SIEGAL, BURTON LEE, product designer cons.; b. Chgo., Sept. 27, 1931; s. Norman A. and Sylvia (Vitz) S.; B.S. in Mech. Engring., U. Ill., 1953; m. Rita Goran, Apr. 11, 1954; children—Norman, Laurence Scott. Founder, pres. Budd Engring. Corp., Chgo., 1959—, cons. in field. Winner Internat. Extrusion Design Competition, 1975. Mem. T.O.P.S. Holder 59 patents. Office: 7101 N Chicago IL 60645

SIEGEL, ELMER MARTIN, auto parts co. exec.; b. Chgo., Feb. 9, 1925; s. Jack and Lottie (Abrams) S.; student Wis. U., 1943-44; B.S., Roosevelt U., 1948; m. Rita Shapiro, Sept. 1, 1946; children—Audrey, (Mrs. Steven M. Press), Howard. Salesman, sales mgr., buyer Grand-Homan Auto Parts Co., Inc., Chgo., 1948-65, pres., 1965-75 chmn. bd., 1975—; pres. Siegal Real Estate Co. Served with U.S. Army, 1943-46; PTO. Recipient award for good bus. ethics Automotive Services Industry Assn., 1962. Mem. Automotive Wholesalers Ill., Automotive Service Industry Assn., Ill. Wildlife Assn. (outstanding contbn. award 1975). Home: 184 Aspen Ln Highland Park IL 60035 Office: 3985 Archer Ave Chicago IL 60632

SIEGEL, MICHAEL RANDOLPH, health care center exec., restaurant and nightclub owner; b. Randolph Field, Tex., June 22, 1943; s. Irving and Joyce (Rozner) S.; student U. Ill., 1961—63, Roosevelt U., 1963—65, Columbia Coll., 1965—66. Mgr., Aragon Ballroom, Chgo., 1968—71, Gang Plank Inc., Chgo., 1971—73; pres. Home Health Care Inc., Chgo., 1977—, Splty. Promotions, Inc., 1977—; vice-pres. Sie Wal Inc., Chgo.; partner Abbott Hotel; pres. Home Health Care Cons.; pub. Broadway Mag., Star Mag. Mem. Lake View C. of C. (dir.). Served with USMCR, 1968—69. Home: 601 W Diversey St Chicago IL 60614

SIEGEL, SHELDON LLOYD, coll. dean; b. Chgo., Sept. 18, 1932; s. Oscar and Min S.; B.S., U. Ill., 1954, M.S., 1956; postgrad. U. Chgo., 1960, Northeastern Ill. U., 1971-73; M.Ed., Loyola U., Chgo., 1976. Producer-dir. childrens program WILL-TV, 1954-60; writer Coronet Instructional Films, 1960-64; writer-editor/project supr. sales promotion Field Enterprises Ednl. Corp., 1964-68; registrar, dean students, tchr. Columbia Coll. of Chgo., 1968-72; dean students, dir. admissions Ill. Coll. Optometry, Chgo., 1972; tchr. grad. courses in student personnel work Loyola U. Active, Ravenswood YMCA, Leadership awards, 1973, 74. Mem. Am., Ill. assns. collegiate registrars and admissions officer, Am. Personnel and Guidance Assn., Ill. Assn. Student Financial Aid Officers, U. Ill., Loyola U. (life) alumni assns., Phi Delta Kappa, Sigma Delta Chi, Century Club. Recipient Sr. Class award for excellence in guidance and teaching Columbia Coll., 1971; Social Sci. Research Council fellow, 1957; writer numerous films in in edn., 1960-64; contbr. articles to profl. jours. Home: 2122 W Foster Ave Chicago IL 60625 Office: 3241 S Michigan Ave Chicago IL 60616

SIEGEL, TERRY LEE, elec. engr.; b. Excelsior Springs, Mo., June 9, 1947; s. Harry Jacob and Jean Frances (Summers) S.; m. Janice Elaine Diehl, Dec. 26, 1971. Elec. engr. Black & Veatch Cons., Kansas City, Mo., 1976—. Served with USAF, 1967-71. Decorated Air Force Commendation medal. Registered engr. in tng., Mo. Mem. IEEE, Mo. Solar Energy Assn. Baptist. Home: 5768 Bower St Kansas City MO 64133 Office: PO Box 8405 Kansas City MO 64114

SIEGLE, DENNIS LEE, city engr.; b. Milw., Jan. 23, 1943; s. George William and Evelyn Florence (Kessler) S.; B.C.E., U. Wis.-Platteville, 1969; m. Beth Jean Hurley, June 12, 1965; children—Corey Joel, Evan Timothy. Bridge insp. Wis. Hwy. Commn., 1966-67; traffic engr., design and field engr. City of Beloit (Wis.), 1969-73; city engr., dir. pub. works City of Fort Atkinson (Wis.), 1973—, sec. City Planning Commn., 1973—. Mem. ASCE, Nat., Wis. socs. profl. engrs., Central States Water Pollution Control Assn., Am. Pub. Works Assn., Am. Water Works Assn., Inst. Traffic Engrs. Club: Fort Atkinson Flying. Office: 101 N Main St Fort Atkinson WI 53538

SIEMENS, RICHARD ALLAN, physician; b. Newton, Kans., Jan. 1, 1930; s. Jacob John and Anna Buhler (Enns) S.; A.B., Bethel Coll., 1951; M.P.H., U. Mich., 1953; M.D., Kans. U., 1959; m. Frances Eleanor Schultz, June 8, 1954; children—Charlotte Ann, Douglas Todd. Intern, USPHS Hosp., Seattle, 1959-60; gen. practice resident Ventura County (Calif.) Hosp., 1960-61; practice medicine, Lyons, Kans., 1961—; mem. staff Dist. Hosp. 1, Lyons, chief med. staff, 1969-71; city health officer, Lyons, 1966—; county health officer, Rice County, 1974—; med. adviser Rice County chpt. Am. Cancer Soc., 1966—, Rice County chpt. Am. Lung Assn., 1976—. Bd. dirs. Lyons council Campfire Girls, 1969-71, Kans. chpt. Arthritis Found., 1971—. Served with AUS, 1953-55, USPHS, 1959-60. Mem. Am. Acad. Family Practice, AMA, Kans., Rice County (pres. 1964-66) med. socs., Phi Chi. Republican. Presbyn. (ruling elder 1963-66, 69-72). Rotarian (pres. 1965-66). Home: 916 W Noble St Lyons KS 67554 Office: 510 E Ave S Lyons KS 67554

SIERLES, FREDERICK STEPHEN, psychiatrist, educator; b. Bklyn., Nov. 9, 1942; s. Samuel and Elizabeth (Meiselman) S.; A.B., Columbia, 1963; M.D., Chgo. Med. Sch., 1967; m. Laurene Harriet Cohn, Oct. 25, 1970; children—Hannah Beth, Joshua Cobb. Intern, Cook County Hosp., Chgo., 1967-68; resident in psychiatry Mt. Sinai Hosp., N.Y.C., 1968-69, Mt. Sinai Hosp., Chgo., 1969-71; staff psychiatrist U.S. Reynolds Army Hosp., Ft. Sill, Okla., 1971-73; asso. attending psychiatrist Mt. Sinai Hosp., Chgo., 1973-74; instr. psychiatry Chgo. Med. Sch., 1973-74, dir. undergrad. edn. in psychiatry, asst. prof., 1974—; cons. in psychiatry Cook County Hosp., North Chicago (Ill.) VA Hosp. Served to maj. M.C., U.S. Army, 1971-73. Recipient Ganser Meml. award Mt. Sinai Hosp., 1970; prof. of year award Chgo. Med. Sch., 1977; NIMH grantee, 1974-78; diplomate Am. Bd. Psychiatry and Neurology. Mem. Am. Psychiat. Assn., Assn. Interns and Residents Cook County Hosp., Assn. Dirs. Med. Student Edn. in Psychiatry, Phi Epsilon Pi. Office: Chicago Medical School Bldg Chicago IL 60064

SIERON, ROBERT DONALD, chem. co. exec.; b. South Bend, Ind., Nov. 18, 1928; s. Maurice O. and Gladys (Holycross) S.; B.S., U. Notre Dame, 1950, M.S. cum laude, 1952; grad. Stanford Exec. Program, 1970; m. Ann Marie Gustafson, Sept. 27, 1952; children—Christine Ann, Paul Andrew, Barbara Elaine. Project chem. engr. Am. Oil Co., 1951-58; bus. evaluator Amoco Chem. Corp., Chgo., 1958-61, dir. market devel., 1961-65, gen. marketing mgr. polymers, 1965-66, gen. mgr. comml. devel. and planning plastics, 1966-72, mgr. custom products div., 1972-75, gen. mgr. packaging and custom products div., 1975—; v.p., dir. Amoco Plastic Products Co., Chgo., 1975—; dir. Single Service Inst. Mem. Am. Mgmt. Assn., Am. Chem. Soc., Soc. Plastics Industry, Soc. Plastics Engrs., Am. Def. Preparedness Assn., U. Notre Dame, Stanford Bus. Sch. alumni assns., Field Mus. Natural History (asso.), Art Inst. Chgo., Lyric Opera Guild. Roman Catholic. Home: 61 Graymoor Lane Olympia Fields IL 60461 Office: 200 E Randolph Dr Chicago IL 60601

SIEWERTH, BRUCE KARL, educator; b. Chgo., Sept. 16, 1940; s. Walter A. and Ethel A. (Sidenius) S.; B.S., Northwestern U., 1962, M.A., 1977; m. Sarane C. Crowther, Dec. 23, 1961; children—Ariel, Alison. Tchr., York Community High Sch., Elmhurst, Ill., 1962-64, Lake Forest (Ill.) Community High Sch., 1964-65, Evanston (Ill.) Twp. High Sch., 1965—; theatre cons. Columbus Jr. Theatre of the Arts, 1974; stage dir. Impression 68, NET-TV, TV, 1968-69, Curtain Call Inc., Glenview, Ill., 1969-72, Glenview Silver Jubilee Theatre Event, 1974, Northbrook Civic Theatre, 1974-77, Tudor Ct. Theatre, 1977. Bd. dirs. LaGrange Highland (Ill.) Community Theatre, 1962-64. Mem. Inst. Theatre Edn. (pres. 1968-70), Am., Ill. theatre assns., U.S. Inst. Theatre Tech. Author: Build Your Own Theatre, 1975. Designer, constructor Columbus (Ohio) Jr. Theatre of Arts, 1974, Evanston Twp. High Sch. Theatre, 1970. Home: 2533 Central Rd Glenview IL 60025 Office: 1600 Dodge Ave Evanston IL 60204

SIGARS, GAROLD ORLANDO, veterinarian; b. Carterville, Mo., Jan. 5, 1916; s. Lester Othelo and Lillian Pearl (Lortz) S.; student Joplin Bus. Coll., 1932-33; B.S., U. Mo., 1937; D.V.M., Kans. State U., 1946; m. Beulah Alice Brown, Dec. 18, 1937; children—Roger L., Linda S. (Mrs. Dale Linin). Asst. agt. U. Mo. Extension Service, St. Joseph, 1937-41, agt., 1941-42; individual practice vet. medicine, 1946—. Mem. Mo. State Examining Bd., 1949-58, pres., 1957-58. Adv. bd. All Am. Life Ins. Co., 1956-70. Mem. Kans. State U. Endowment Assn. Mem. Am. Soc. Vet. Allergists and Immunologists, St. Joseph (pres. 1947-49), Kansas City (pres. 1952-53), Mo. (v.p. 1954-55, mem. numerous coms.) vet. med. assns., Am. Interprofl. Inst. (pres. 1969-70). Mason (32 deg.). Home: 1 Stonecrest St St Joseph MO 64506 Office: 715 N Belt Hwy St Joseph MO 64506

SIGFUSSON, BENEDICT J., architect; b. Elmhurst, Ill., Feb. 21, 1927; s. Sigfus I. and Bertha Adina (Ericksen) S.; B.S., U. Ill., 1951; m. Mary Alice Obst, Sept. 29, 1951 (dec. Feb. 1972); children—Karen Ann (Mrs. Gregory Stuart Bates), Donna Jean, Paul Benedict; m. 2d, Audrey Ruth Saltz-Christiansen, Aug. 17, 1974. Structural designer Sargent & Lundy, Chgo., 1951-52; archtl. designer Vern E. Alden Co., Chgo., 1952-54; architect Skidmore, Owings & Merrill, Chgo., 1954-57; owner Benedict Sigfusson Assos., Chgo., 1957-67, Park Ridge, Ill., 1967—. Lectr. Sch. Architecture, Ill. Inst. Tech., Chgo., 1965-67. Parent chmn., boys swim team N.W. Suburban YMCA, 1965-66; mem. Mayor's Archtl. Rev. Bd., Mt. Prospect, Ill., 1969. Bd. dirs. Tchr.-Parent Council, Prospect High Sch., Mt. Prospect, 1970. Mem. AIA, Constrn. Specification Inst. (Chgo. chpt. pres. 1966-68). Archtl. designer Thornridge High Sch., Dolton, 1957. Home: 405 S We Go Trail Mount Prospect IL 60056 Office: 324 W Touhy Ave Park Ridge IL 60068

SIGLER, JACK EXLINE, sociologist; b. Kansas City, Mo., Feb. 26, 1926; s. Kessler Lee and Gladys Gertrude (Exline) S.; student Park Coll., 1943-44; A.B., U. Mo., 1949, M.A., 1961; M.A., Northwestern U., 1950; m. Norma Jean High, Apr. 1, 1950; children—Karl Exline, Sara Elizabeth. Owner, mgr. Sigler Chevrolet Co., Oak Grove, Mo., 1951-59; research asst. U. Mo., Kansas City, 1959-60; sr. research asso., dir. Program on Aging, Inst. for Community Studies, Kansas City, 1960-76, co-dir. Center for Aging Studies, 1977—; project dir. various govt. grants, asst. prof. sociology U. Mo., Kansas City, 1975—; lectr. Kansas City Met. Jr. Coll., 1963-64; dir. edn. and research services Swope Ridge Health Care Center, 1975—; chmn. adv. council on aging Kansas City Regional Council for Higher Edn., 1972-76; mem. tech. rev. com. State of Mo., 1967-74; mem. Gov's Task Force on the Older Missourian, 1967-73; vice chmn. Gov.'s Adv. Council on Aging, 1974—; pres. Mid-Am. Congress on Aging, 1976—. Vice pres. citizens adv. bd. Eastern Jackson County Vocat. Sch., 1967. Served with Signal Corps, AUS, 1944-46. Mem. Am. Sociol. Assn., Mo. Assn. Social Welfare (chmn. task force on aging and higher edn. 1974-76), Midwest Sociol. Soc. (treas. 1966—), Mo. Soc. Sociology and Anthropology, Gerontol. Soc., Midwest Council Social Research in Aging (coordinator 1965-76), Nat. Council on Aging, AAAS. Contbr. articles to profl. jours. Home: 2108 W Smith St Blue Springs MO 64015 Office: 5900 Swope Pkwy Kansas City MO 64130

SIGLIN, IRVIN S., physician; b. Chgo., May 28, 1916; s. Leon A. and Tillie (Hillman) S.; B.S., U. Chgo., 1938; M.D., Rush Med. Coll., Chgo., 1940; m. Shirley L. Gould, June 16, 1940; children—Irvin Steven, Martin G. Intern, Michael Reese Hosp., Chgo., 1940-41, resident internal medicine, 1941-42; resident Cook County Hosp., 1942-44; fellow Mayo Clinic, Rochester, Minn., 1944-47; mem. attending staffs Michael Reese, Weiss Meml., Ill. Masonic hosps.; instr., asst. clin. prof. medicine U. Ill., Chgo., 1948-73, asso. clin. prof., 1973—; chmn. dept. medicine Ill. Masonic Med. Center, 1971-73. Diplomate Am. Bd. Internal Medicine. Fellow A.C.P.; mem. AMA (Physician's Recognition award 1972, 75), Mayo Alumni Assn., Am. Heart Assn., Phi Beta Kappa, Alpha Omega Alpha. Contbr. articles to med. jours. Home: 701 Lake Ave Wilmette IL 60091 Office: 55 E Washington St Chicago IL 60602

SIGOLOFF, ALLEN LOUIS, youth camps exec.; b. St. Louis, May 23, 1940; s. Sidney and Ruth (Friedstadt) S.; B.S., U. Ill., 1962, postgrad., 1962-63; m. Carol Ann Altman, June 6, 1962; children—Julie Beth, Laura Jean, Shari Lynn. Dir. Camp Thunderbird for Boys, also Camp Thunderbird for Girls, Bemidji, Minn., 1965-70; pres., dir. Camp Thunderbird, Inc., St. Louis, 1970—. Served to 1st lt. U.S. Army, 1963-64. Decorated Army Commendation medal. Mem. Am. Camping Assn. (pres. St. Louis 1972-73, dir. 1974-75, chmn. pvt. ind. camp kindred program for regional conv. 1975), Zeta Beta Tau. Home: 10976 Chambray Ct Saint Louis MO 63141

SIKDAR, DHIRENDRA NATH, educator; b. Pabna, India, Nov. 1, 1930; s. Jatindra Nath and Ushalata (Maitra) S.; came to U.S., 1966; B.Sc., U. Calcutta, India, 1949, M.Sc., 1951; Ph.D., U. Wis., Madison, 1969; m. Maya Maitra, Mar. 8, 1961; children—Tuhina, Reena. Lectr. physics Darjeeling Govt. Coll., 1952; asst. prof. physics St. Paul's Coll., Calcutta, India, 1952; profl. asst. Electronic Lab., Meteorol. Office, New Delhi, 1953-56; officer-in-charge Upper Air Obs., Veraval, India, 1957-60; meteorologist-in-charge radar meteorology div. meteorology officer Bombay Internat. Airport, 1960-63; meteorologist Thumba Rocket Launching Site, Trivandrum, Internat. High Altitude Expt., Hyderabad, 1965; research and teaching asst. dept. meteorology U. Wis., Madison, 1966-69, asst. scientist Space Sci. and Engring. Center, 1970-71, asso. scientist, 1971-74; asst. prof. meteorology U. Wis., Milw., 1974-76, asso. prof. atmospheric sci., 1976—. Indian Assn. Cultivation Sci. research fellow, 1951; Nat. Oceanic Atmospheric Administration postdoctoral fellow 1969; NSF research grantee. Mem. Am. Geophys. Union, Am. Meteorol. Soc., India Meteorol. Soc., Sigma Xi. Contbr. articles to profl. jours. Home: 5339 N Lydell Ave Milwaukee WI 53217 Office: Dept Geol Scis 3409 N Downer Milwaukee WI 53201

SIKORSKI, BERNADINE CAROL, univ. adminstr.; b. Amsterdam, N.Y., Feb. 21, 1951; d. Casmier Frank and Albina Stella (Krupa) Sikorski; B.S., No. Ariz. U., 1973, M.A., 1975; postgrad. St. Louis U., 1975—. Student resident advisor Rosary Hill Coll., Buffalo, 1971; nurses aide Sunneyview Rehab. Center, Schenectady, N.Y., summer 1971; asst. dir. residence No. Ariz. U., Flagstaff, 1971-73, resident hall dir. for married housing units, summer 1972, 73, residence hall dir., coordinator for coednl. complexes, 1973-75, grad. asst. Office Student Affairs, 1974-75, orientation instr., teaching asst., 1973-74; residence hall coordinator St. Louis U., 1975-76, grad. asst. dir. project COVE, 1975-76, coordinator of internship experiences for undergrad. liberal arts students, peer-counseling coordinator, 1976—, asst. dir. housing, 1976—; instr. study skills St. Louis U., 1976—. Active Crisis Intervention, 1970-71, Head Start Program, Amsterdam, N.Y., 1969. Exxon Edn. grantee, 1975-77; recipient Hera award Alpha Omicron Pi, 1973. Mem. Assn. Coll. and Univ. Housing Officers, f Am. Personnel and Guidance Assn., Nat. Assn. Women Deans, Adminstrs. and Counselors, Nat. Assn. Student Personnel Adminstrs., Alpha Omicron Pi. Clubs: Ski, Psychology. Home: 2804 A South 59th St Saint Louis MO 63139 Office: Busch Center Room 300 Saint Louis U Grand Blvd Saint Louis MO 63108

SIKORSKI, MARTIN JEROME, II, optometrist; b. Chgo., Jan. 31, 1943; s. Harry J. and Angeline (Ziomek) S.; student U. Ill., 1961-63, Roosevelt U., 1963; O.D. cum laude, Ill. Coll. Optometry, 1966; m. Joanne C. Koral, June 5, 1965; children—Gail Lynn, Cheryl Ann, Martin Jerome, Lisa Anne, Amy Lynne. Dir. vision clinic Robert McCormick Chgo. Boys' Club, 1966-67; individual practice optometry, Glen Ellyn, Ill., 1967—; mem. clin. staff Ill. Coll. Optometry, 1966-67; guest lectr. Loyola U., Chgo., Northeastern Ill. State U., Elmhurst Coll., Coll. DuPage; visual cons. St. John's Lutheran Sch., Lombard, St. Paul Lutheran Sch., Melrose Park, Ill.; pres. Glen Ellyn Vision Center. Fellow Coll. Optometrists in Vision Devel.; mem. Jaycees, Am., Ill., West Suburban optometric assns. Tomb and Key, Beta Sigma Kappa. Roman Catholic (religious edn. tchr.). Clubs: Kiwanis (past pres. Glen Ellyn), K.C. Home: 183 Kenilworth Ave Glen Ellyn IL 60137 Office: 444 Main St Glen Ellyn IL 60137

SILBERMAN, ALLEN, psychologist; b. Houston, Mar. 28, 1943; s. Morris and Sylvia (Bellebroff) S.; B.A., Troy State Coll., 1964; M.A., Ball State Coll., 1973; Ed.D. U. S.D., 1974; m. Lillian Link, Mar. 9, 1968; 1 dau., Leslie. Social worker, City of N.Y., 1965; pvt. practice psychologist, Des Moines, 1975—. Served to capt. USAF, 1965-73; Vietnam. Decorated Bronze Star; Vietnamese Honor medal 1st class. Mem. Am., Iowa psychol. assns., Assn. Counselor Edn. Supervision, Am. Personnel Guidance Assn., Soc. Pediatric Psychology, Soc. Clin. Exptl. Hypnosis. Jewish. Home: 225 Foster Dr Des Moines IA 50312 Office: 4717 Grand Ave Suite 201 Des Moines IA 50312

SILBERMAN, EDWARD, educator; b. Mpls., Feb. 8, 1914; s. Samuel and Rose (Fisher) S.; B.C.E., U. Minn., 1935, M.S., 1936; m. Idell B. Hillman, Oct. 15, 1941; children—Marylin Silberman Condon, Cyril J., Marc D., Sheldon I. Water technician Minn. Planning Bd., St. Paul, 1936; jr. engr. TVA, Knoxville, 1937; jr. engr. U.S. Civil Aeros. Authority, Washington, 1937-40, asst. engr., 1940-46, asso. engr., 1946; dir. St. Anthony Falls Hydraulic Lab., U. Minn., Mpls., 1963-74; asst. prof. hydraulics U. Minn., 1946-51, asso. prof., 1951-57, prof., 1957—. Cons. spl. problems in hydraulics. Served to lt. col. C.E., U.S. Army, 1941-46. Fellow ASCE (sect. pres. 1963), Am. Water Resources Assn. (pres. 1969); mem. Internat. Assn.

Hydraulic Research, Soc. Am. Mil. Engrs., Am. Acad. Mechanics. Editor Procs. Third Midwestern Conf. on Fluid Mechanics, U. Minn., 1953. Contbr. tech. articles to periodicals, books. Home: 2325 Brookridge Ave Minneapolis MN 55422 Office: St Anthony Falls Hydraulic Lab Mississippi River at 3d Ave SE Minneapolis MN 55414

SILETS, HARVEY MARVIN, lawyer; b. Chgo., Aug. 25, 1931; s. Joseph Lazarus and Sylvia (Dubner) S.; B.S. cum laude, DePaul U., 1952; J.D. (Frederick Leckie scholar), U. Mich., 1955; m. Elaine Lucy Gordon, June 25, 1961; children—Hayden Leigh, Jonathan Lazarus, Alexandra Rose. Admitted to Ill. bar, 1955, N.Y. bar, 1956; mem. firm. Paul, Weiss, Rifkind, Wharton & Garrison, N.Y.C., 1955-56; asst. U.S. atty., No. Ill. Dist., 1958-60; chief tax atty. U.S. Atty.'s Office No. Dist. Ill., Chgo., 1960-62; partner Harris, Burman & Silets, Chgo., 1962—. Asst. advance tng. program Internal Revenue Service, U. Mich., 1952-53; law lectr. John Marshall Law Sch., 1962-66; gen. counsel Nat. Treasury Employees Union, 1968—. Trustee Latin Sch. Chgo.; bd. assos. DePaul U. Served with AUS, 1956-58. Mem. Bar Assn. 7th Fed. Circuit Ct. (chmn. com. criminal law and procedure 1972—), Am. (com. fed. taxation 1960—, criminal law 1963—), Fed. (treas., dir., chmn. judiciary com. 1971—, chmn. fed. rules com. 1972—, pres. elect 1977—), Chgo. (com. devel. law 1966-72) bar assns., Decalogue Soc. Lawyers. Clubs: Standard (Chgo.). Office: 7 S Dearborn St Chicago IL 60603

SILIGER, AGNES ISABELLE, psychologist; b. Memphis, Feb. 21, 1921; d. Claude Jefferson and Zulee (Dancy) Brantley; B.A., Roosevelt U., 1949; M.A., U. No. Colo., 1956; m. Fred Joseph Siliger, Feb. 19, 1966; 1 adopted son, Fred Joseph. Psychologist, Chgo. Bd. Edn., 1958; psychology instr. Phillips Evening Sch., Chgo., 1961-62; sr. psychologist Chgo. Sch. Dist. 16, 1967—; supr. interns, sch. psychology, Ill., 1965—; pres. Area A Psychologists, Chgo. Pub. Schs., 1971-72. Certified Ill. sch. psychologist, 1958, registered psychologist, Ill., 1963. Mem. Am., Ill. (chmn. com. minority concerns 1974-75) psychol. assns., Nat. Assn. Sch. Psychologists (chmn. com. minority concerns rap session Las Vegas Conv. 1974), Chgo. Assn. Sch. Psychologist (pres.), Chgo. Psychol. Club (council), Alpha Kappa Alpha, Kappa Delta Pi, Pi Lambda Theta. Contbr. article to Jour. Ill. Psychol. Assn. Home: 100 W 100th St Chicago IL 60643 Office: 10115 S Prairie St Chicago IL 60628

SILLERS, D. H., state senator, farmer; b. Calvin, N.D., Feb. 9, 1915; s. Archie and Mabel (Tuthill) S.; B.A., Concordia Coll., 1939; m. Margaret Rose Baller, Aug. 2, 1941; children—Jean M. Sillers Bardwell, D. Hal, Cynthia B., Heather P. Instr. social sci. high sch., Menahga, Minn., 1939-42; fieldman Fed. Land Bank, Washburn, N.D., 1942; owner, operator farm, Moorhead, Minn., 1946—; mem. Minn. Ho. of Reps., 1963-72, Minn. Senate, 1972—; dir. Minn. F.B. Service Co., St. Paul; pres., sec. Clay County F.B. Service Co., Moorhead, 1949-68; mem. State Planning Commn., 1967—; com. mem. Upper Midwest Research & Devel., 1960—; instr. polit. sci. Concordia Coll. Bd. dirs. Future Farmers Am. Minn. Served to lt. (j.g.) USNR, 1942-45; ETO. Recipient Goodyear Conservation award, 1956, Agr. award N.D. State U., 1974; named Minn. Soil Saver, Clay County Soil Conservation Soc., 1956. Mem. N.W. Farm Mgrs. (pres. 1961), Farm Bur., Am. Legion, VFW, Moorhead C. of C. Clubs: Masons, Rod and Gun. Address: Route 2 Moorhead MN 56560

SILLIMAN, BENJAMIN DEWAYNE, lawyer; b. Ardmore, Indian Ter., Sept. 10, 1895; s. Arthur Benjamin and Nella Mae (Whitbeck) S.; B.A., Coe Coll., Cedar Rapids, Iowa, 1917; LL.B., State U. Iowa, 1923; m. Hannah Faye Nelson, June 14, 1928. Admitted to Iowa bar, 1923; practice in Cedar Rapids, 1923—; mem. firm Silliman, Gray & Stapleton, 1938—. Dir. Morris Plan Co. Iowa, MorAm. Financial Corp., MorAm. Mortgage Co., Iowa Growth Investment Co., Lease Am. Corp., Jackson State Bank & Trust Co., Maquoteka, Iowa. Chmn., Cedar Rapids Community Chest, 1948, Iowa Assn. Community Chests, 1951. Chmn., Linn County Republican Com., 1954-58, 60-63, Iowa. Rep. Platform Com., 1962, 64. Trustee Coe Coll., 1952—, sec. bd. trustees, 1965—. Served as 2d lt. U.S. Army, World War I; to lt. col., World War II. Decorated Bronze Star; recipient Alumni award merit Coe Coll., 1967. Mem. Am., Iowa, Linn County (pres. 1952) bar assns., Am. Judicature Soc., Ret. Officers Assn., Judge Advs. Assn., Am. Legion (past post comdr.), Cedar Rapids C. of C. (chmn. pub. welfare bur. 1950-51), Phi Kappa Psi. Clubs: Mason (32 deg.), Shriners, Elks, Embassy (Des Moines). Home: 245 25th St SE Cedar Rapids IA 52401 Office: 807 Am Bldg Cedar Rapids IA 52401

SILLMAN, HERBERT PHILLIP, accountant; b. Detroit, July 18, 1927; s. David and Phyllis (Sumter) S.; B.S., U. Calif. at Los Angeles, 1949; m. Maurine R. Shapiro, Mar. 16, 1952; children—Marcie, David, Jonathon. With Harold Gilbert & Co., C.P.A.'s, Detroit, 1951-54; partner Sillman, Kleiman & Thal, C.P.A.'s, Detroit, 1954-69; nat. exec. partner J.K. Lasser & Co., Southfield, Mich., 1969—. Chmn. profl. div. Allied Jewish Campaign, Detroit, 1967-69; pres. Jewish Family and Children's Service, Detroit, 1970-73, trustee, 1964—; mem. Oak Park Sch. Dist. Bd. Edn., 1963-71, pres., 1965-69; mem. Oakland County Intermediate Bd. Edn., 1964-70, pres., 1968-70; 1st vice chmn. Southeastern Mich. Council Govts., 1969-70. Bd. dirs. Jewish Welfare Fedn., mem. exec. com. C.P.A., Mich. Mem. Am. Inst. C.P.A.'s, Mich. Assn. C.P.A.'s, Com. of 100, Phi Sigma Delta Alumni (treas. 1971—). Mem. B'nai B'rith. Home: 320 Cranbrook Ct Bloomfield Hills MI 48013 Office: 3000 Town Center Southfield MI 48075

SILVER, DAVID MAYER, univ. adminstr., historian; b. West Pittston, Pa., July 16, 1915; s. Morris Jacob and Florence (Mayer) S.; A.B., Butler U., 1937; M.A., U. Ill., 1938, Ph.D., 1938; m. Anita Cohen, May 10, 1942; children—Gregory Keith, Terence Alexander. Instr. history Butler U., Indpls., 1940-42, asst. prof., 1942-46, asso. prof., 1948-54, prof., 1954—, dean coll. liberal arts and scis., 1963—; cons. in field. Pres. Indpls. Bd. Pub. Safety, 1956-63, Indpls. Hebrew Congregation, 1963-65, 2d. Conf. Academic Deans Ind., 1971. Sr. scholar Butler U., 1936-37; grad. scholar U. Ill., 1937-38, grad. fellow, 1938-40. Mem. N. Central Assn. Academic Deans, Orgn. Am. Historians, Am. Hist. Assn., Ind. Hist. Soc., AAUP. Democrat. Jewish. Author: Lincoln's Supreme Court, 1956. Home: 8230 N Illinois St Indianapolis IN 46260 Office: Room 108 Jordan Hall Butler U 4600 Sunset Ave Indianapolis IN 46208

SILVER, NEIL MARVIN, precision components mfg. co. exec.; b. Bklyn., June 2, 1928; s. Jack and Rose (Eisenberg) S.; student U. Mich., 1945-46, 48-49; B.S., Ind. U., 1951; m. Leah Rebecca Coffman, Sept. 4, 1949; children—Pamela Sue, Carole Beth. Asst. mgr. Wolverine Parking Co., Lansing, Mich., 1951-54; treas., Capitol Parking Co., Indpls., 1955-60; controller, asst. to pres. Eberhart Steel Products, Inc., Mishawaka Tool & Die, Inc. (Ind.), 1961-63; pres., Allied Quality Products, Inc., Mishawaka, 1964-67; treas., Allied Screw Products, Inc., Mishawaka, 1968—. Bd. dirs. Ind. State Anti Defamation League, 1955-57; bd. dirs., treas. Family Service Assn. St. Joseph County, Ind.; bd. dirs., treas., pres., chmn. finance com. Family and Children's Center, Inc., Mishawaka. Served with U.S. Army, 1946-48. Mem. Soc. Mfg. Engrs., Am. Soc. Testing and Materials. Jewish religion. Mem. B'nai B'rith. Home: 2707 Leer St South Bend IN 46614 Office: 800 E Edgar Ave PO Box 543 Mishawaka IN 46544

SILVERMAN, JAMES STUART, electronic distbg. co. exec.; b. Chgo., Feb. 12, 1919; s. Paul and Rose (Schopp) S.; student Northwestern U. Sch. Bus.; m. Irene Annette Jarecki, Nov. 10, 1946; children—Karla (Mrs. Bruce Davies Conley), Leigh Peter. Pres., James S. Silverman Assos., 1946-60, Electronic Expeditors, Inc., Milw., 1960—. Pres. Electronic Industry Show Corp. Served with U.S. Army, 1941-46. Decorated Purple Heart, Bronze Star medals. Mem. Nat. Electronic Distbrs. Assn. (chmn. bd., past pres.), Electronic Distbrs. Research Inst. (pres.), Nat. Assn. Wholesalers (trustee), Electronic Distbrs. Council. Home: 2909 E Newberry Blvd Milwaukee WI 53211 Office: 6045 N Green Bay Ave Milwaukee WI 53209

SILVERMAN, MAURICE MARTIN, physician; b. Toronto, Ont., Can., Mar. 28, 1907; s. Louis and Fannie (Cohen) S.; came to U.S., 1917, naturalized, 1930; B.S., U. Mich., 1928; B.Medicine, Wayne State U., 1930, M.D., 1931; m. Helen Whitman, June 23, 1929; children—Agnes (Mrs. William Schussler), Anita (Mrs. Zalesin). Practice medicine specializing in surgery, Detroit, 1931—; mem. staff Mt. Carmel Hosp.; instr. Mercy Coll., 1936-56; med. examiner Local Draft Bd., 1941-46, med. adv., 1946—. Jewish. (pres. congregation). Mem. B'nai B'rith (pres. 1934). Contbr. articles to profl. jours. Home: 27330 Arborway Southfield MI 48075 Office: 17301 W 8 Mile Rd Detroit MI 48235

SILVERMAN, WILLIAM JOSEPH, hosp. adminstr.; b. Mpls., Sept. 4, 1916; s. Maurice and Dora (Berkuvitz) S.; m. Lynne Helen Houts, 1950; children—Sandra Lynne, Pamela Ann, James Laurence, Deborah Marie; B.A., U. Minn., 1939, M.S. in Psychometrics, 1942. Psychometrist, Minn. Civil Service, 1939-42; cons. pub. adminstrn. Pub. Adminstrn. Service, Chgo., 1946-50; adminstr. Guam Meml. Hosp., Island of Guam, 1950-52; asso. dir. Michael Reese Hosp., Chgo., 1952-59, exec. dir., 1960-70; dir. health services and facilities div. Comprehensive Health Planning, Inc., 1970-72; asst. dir. Chgo. Hosp. Council, 1970-72; dir. Cook County Hosp., Chgo., 1972—. Mem. Southside Planning Bd., Chgo., 1960-70; chmn. emergency med. services Commn. Met. Chgo., 1974-76; bd. dirs., mem. exec. com. Chgo. Community Fund, 1962-68; bd. dirs. Video Nursing, Inc., 1968-73, Hosp. Service Corp. (Blue Cross), 1970-71, Mid South Side Health Planning Orgn., 1970-71; vice chmn. bd. dirs. Ill. Regional Med. Program, 1969-70. Fellow Am. Coll. Hosp. Adminstrs., Inst. Medicine Chgo.; mem. Am., Ill. hosp. assns., Chgo. Hosp. Council (pres. 1964). Home: 25 Braeburn Dr Park Forest IL 60466 Office: 1825 W Harrison St Chicago IL 60612

SILVERNAIL, WALTER LAWRENCE, cons. rare earths, glass polishing; b. St. Louis, Sept. 8, 1921; s. Elmer Brinkman and Drusilla Mary (Coons) S.; A.B., Park Coll., Parkville, Mo., 1947; A.M., U. Mo., 1949, Ph.D. (Du Pont fellow), 1954; m. Cynthia Mercedes Shoens, July 6, 1944; children—Bruce Lawrence, Gordon William, Laura Louann. Asso. prof. chemistry Ill. Coll., Jacksonville, 1949-51, prof., 1953-56; asso. prof. chemistry Ferris State Coll., Big Rapids, Mich., 1957; research chemist Rare Earth div. Am. Potash & Chem. Corp., West Chicago, Ill., 1957-63, mgr. tech. services, 1963-73; pvt. cons. rare earths, glass polishing West Chicago, 1974—. Served with USAAF, 1943-46. Research, prodn. rare earths, thorium, glass polishing tech. Patentee in field. Address: 140 E Stimmel St West Chicago IL 60185

SILVERSTEIN, PAUL MORTON, neurologist; b. Mpls., Sept. 23, 1935; s. Robert I. and Sara (Nach) S.; B.A., U. Minn., 1956; B.S., 1960, M.D., 1960; m. Sybil Fay Schneider, June 19, 1960; children—Beth, Andrew, Julie. Intern, Hennepin County Gen. Hosp., Mpls., 1960-61; resident neurology, dept. neurology U. Minn., 1961-64; NIH fellow neuropathology Columbia Coll. Physicians and Surgeons, N.Y.C., 1964-66; practice medicine specializing in neurology, Mpls., 1966—; affiliate Mpls. Clinic Psychiatry and Neurology, 1966—; mem. staffs Meth., Mt. Sinai hosps. (Mpls.); cons. neurology Mpls. VA Hosp., 1969—; clin. asso. prof. neurology U. Minn. Hosps., 1971—. Diplomate Am. Bd. Psychiatry and Neurology. Mem. A.M.A., Minn., Hennepin County med. socs., Am. Acad. Neurology, Phi Beta Kappa, Alpha Omega Alpha. Home: 1825 Major Dr Golden Valley MN 55422 Office: 4225 Golden Valley Rd Minneapolis MN 55422

SIME, CHARLES JOHN, accountant; b. Prairie du Chien, Wis., June 15, 1905; s. Peter J. and Tourina (Sorem) S.; diploma in commerce Northwestern U., 1946; m. Mary M. Neault, July 23, 1927 (dec.); children—Mary Ada Sime Krahe, Charles John. With Acme Steel Co., Chgo., 1927-62, sales personnel adminstr., 1962; self-employed as accounting and tax practitioner, Orland Park, Ill., 1962—; v.p. Carden Pharmacy, Inc., Glenwood, Ill., 1965—; dir. Total Security Inc. Bd. dirs. Duncan Med. Center YMCA, Chgo., 1949—. Mem. Ind. Accountants Assn. Ill. (South Cook County pres. 1968-69, 1974-75, state dir. 1970—), Northwestern U. Alumni Assn. Club: Glenwood Lions (pres. 1977—). Home: 222 Brentwood Dr Chicago Heights IL 60411 Office: 14620 La Grange Rd Orland Park IL 60462

SIMMEN, ROBERT LEE, cons. elec. engr.; b. Galesburg, Ill., Aug. 1, 1927; s. Frank Wellington and Nina Lee (Vail) S.; B.S. in E.E., U. Ill., 1952; postgrad. Air U., 1957; m. Mildred Carolyn Luvall, May 11, 1963; children—Leslie Ellen, Christopher Vail. Group supr. field engring. Motorola Inc., Chgo., 1957, program mgr., 1961-63; govt. contract mgr. Gates Radio Co., Quincy, Ill., 1963-67; Navy contract adminstr., sales engr. Hallicrafters div. Northrop, Chgo., 1967-69; Navy mktg. mgr. Aerospace Optical div. ITT, Fort Wayne, Ind., 1969-72, dir. product devel., 1972-75; dir. systems Universal Telecommunications Systems Ltd., Montreal, 1976; pres. James E. Vail Co., Ft. Wayne, 1977—; mem. ad hoc com. Ft. Wayne Energy Conservation, 1977—. Served with USAAF, 1945-48. Mem. Armed Forces Communications and Electronics Assn., Assn. Old Crows, U.S. Naval Inst., Anglo Am. Tech. Exchange Soc. Lutheran. Office: 5325 Vance Ave Fort Wayne IN 46815

SIMMERMON, ROBERT DAVID, psychologist; b. Noblesville, Ind., Sept. 28, 1946; s. Carl David and Annetta Claire (Hoffmann) S.; B.S., Ind. U., 1970; M.S., Butler U., 1974; Ed.D., Ball State U., 1976; m. Judith Lynnell McGrew, June 7, 1969; children—Jill, Julie. Asst. buyer L.S. Ayres & Co., Indpls., 1970-72; coordinator state govtl. affairs Ind. Commn. Higher Edn., 1972-74; fellow counseling psychology and guidance services Ball State U., 1974-76, asst. prof. psychology, counseling psychologist, 1976—; cons. Acad. Ednl. Devel. (Washington), Muncie (Ind.) Police Dept., Athens (Greece) Testing Center; bd. dirs. Muncie Family Counseling Services, Inc.; v.p., bd. dirs. Muncie Crisis Intervention Center. Bd. dirs. Gov.'s Conf. on Occupational Edn. Project 21. Mem. Am. Personnel and Guidance Assn., Am. Psychol. Assn., Phi Delta Kappa. Office: Counseling and Psychological Services Center Ball State University Muncie IN 47306

SIMMONDS, JAMES FREDERICK, dentist; b. Muncie, Ind., May 9, 1920; s. Clendes Elzo and Mabel Jessie (Lerner) S.; D.D.S., Ind. U., 1950; m. Thelma Imogene Dawson, Mar. 15, 1949; children—Virginia Lee, Scott Willard, Christopher James. Individual practice dentistry, Anderson, Ind., 1950-66, Daleville, 1966—. Base dental officer Ind. Air N.G., Hulman Field, Terre Haute, Ind., 1957-74, state dental surgeon Hq., 1974-76, transferred to AFRES, 1976—. Civil def. officer Madison County, Ind., 1955-56. Served with U.S. Army, 1941-45; with USAAF, 1961-62. Decorated Bronze Star medal. Mem. Am. Dental Assn., Am. Legion, Nat. Guard Assn. (life). Republican. Methodist. Clubs: Hulman Officers (Terre Haute), Elks. Patentee in field. Home: Rural Route 1 Box 81 Daleville IN 47334 Office: Rural Route 1 Box 81A Daleville IN 47334

SIMMONS, CARL KENNETH, coop. exec.; b. Kingman, Ind., Dec. 5, 1914; s. Claud Elmer and Sylvia Ethyl (Myers) S.; grad. exec. devel. program Ind. U., 1959; m. Allice Lucille Weaver, Dec. 16, 1939; 1 dau., Erma Jane (Mrs. Thomas Stephen Barlow). Petroleum dept. mgr. Fountain County Coop., Veedersburg, Ind., 1936-40; dist. mgr. Ind. Farm Bur. Coop., Indpls., 1946-47; treas., mgr. Delaware County Coop., Muncie, 1940-46, 48—. Mem. Mayor's Citizens Com. Muncie, 1962. Bd. dirs. Delaware County Airport Authority, 1972—. Mem. Ind. Flying Farmers. Clubs: Mason (32 deg.), Muncie Rifle. Home: 119 E Centennial St Muncie IN 47303 Office: 901 Granville Ave Muncie IN 47305

SIMMONS, DAVID EARL, hosp. admnstr.; b. Water Valley, Miss., Feb. 25, 1929; s. Walter Bernard and Mary (Moss) S.; B.S., U. of Ill., 1956; M.A., U. of Iowa 1958; Ph.D. St. Andrew U. 1960; diploma Command and Gen. Staff Coll., U.S. Army, 1973; grad. Fed. Exec. Inst., 1977; m. Clara Smith, Sept. 9, 1956; children—Steven, Cheryl, Spencer. Admnstrv. asst. Mercy-Douglass Hosp., Phila. 1958-61: mgmt. analyst VA Hosp., Tuskegee, Ala. 1961-63: mgmt. specialist VA Central Office, Washington D.C. 1963-64, asst. to chief med. dir. 1964-65; asst. dir. trainee VA Hosp., Richmond, Va. 1965-67; asst. dir. VA Hosp. Manchester, N.H. 1967-69, VA Hosp., Northampton, Mass. 1969-72, Cleve. 1972-75; hosp. dir. VA Hosp., Erie, Pa. 1975—; dir. Health Systems Inc., Northwestern Pa., Erie, 1975—. Dir. Erie Area United Way program 1975—, Community Blood Bank of Erie, 1975—; chmn. Erie County Hosp. Authority 1975—; v.p. NAACP, Erie chpt. 1976—; pres. Booker T. Washington Ctr., Erie 1977—. Served with U.S. Army 1948-54. Recipient 2 commendations VA Hosp., Cleve., 1974, 75, 1 commendation City of Cleve. 1975, 1 commendation Cleve. Fed. Exec. Bd. 1974; 2 outstanding service awards VACO, Washington D.C. 1972, 74. Fellow Royal Soc. of Health, Am. Coll. of Hosp. Admnstrs.; mem. Am. Hosp. Assn., Assn. of Military Surgeons, Forest City Hosp. Assn. (pres. 1975), Sigma Iota Epsilon (U. IU. chpt. 1954-56), Alpha Delta Mu (charter, 1st pres. 1956-58), Kappa Alpha Psi. Democrat. Congregational. Club: Urban League. Home: 3315 Daleford Rd Shaker Hts OH 44120 Office: 135 E 38th St Blvd Erie PA 16501

SIMMONS, DONALD DUANE, psychiatrist, farmer; b. Lee's Summit, Mo., June 30, 1930; s. Herbert A. and Margaret (Larson) S.; B.S., U. Mo., 1958, M.D., 1962; m. Sherry Sue Eastin, June 2, 1962; children—Donald Steven, Morgan W. (adopted). Intern, Orange County (Calif.) Gen. Hosp., 1962-63, resident in internal medicine, 1964-65; resident in psychiatry Western Mo. Mental Health Center, Kansas City, 1962-63, 63-64, 65-67, staff psychiatrist, 1967-71; staff psychiatrist Kansas City VA Hosp., 1971—, acting chief mental clinic, 1972—; practice medicine specializing in psychiatry, Kansas City, 1971—; farmer Caldwell County, Mo. Served with M.C., AUS, 1952-53. Diplomate Am. Bd. Psychiatry and Nuerology. Mem. AMA, Mo., Jackson County med. socs., Am., Mo., Kansas City psychiat. assns., Alpha Omega Alpha. Home: 3826 S Delaware St Independence MO 64055 Office: 4301 Main St Kansas City MO 64111

SIMMONS, FRANK PETER, aerospace engring. co. exec.; b. Palmerton, Pa., June 11, 1926; s. Andrew Charles and Alice Barr (Nulty) S.; student George Washington U., 1946-49; postgrad. Mass. Inst. Tech., 1955; m. Dorothy Mae Gordon, Aug. 2, 1952; children—Gordon Scott, Gaye Lucille, Peter Craig. Research engr. Nat. Cash Register Co., Dayton, Ohio, 1950-52; mgr. spl. products Graflex, Inc., Gen. Precision Singer Components, Rochester, N.Y., 1956-57, project mgr. Comml. Controls Co. (now Friden Div. Singer), Rochester, 1957-59, staff scientist Link Div. Gen. Precision, Inc. (now Singer), Binghamton (N.Y.) Lab., 1959-60, mgr. ground support dept. Link Div., 1960-61, program mgr. advanced product center Link Div., Binghamton, 1961-63; tech. dir. anti-submarine i warfare engring. Grumman Aerospace Corp., Bethpage, N.Y., 1963-66, dir. mil. space systems, 1966-68, dir. space astronomy, 1968-72, asst. to v.p., 1968-72, bus. area mgr. satellites, 1973; dir. space sci. programs Martin Marietta Corp., Denver, 1973-74; dir. large space telescope program McDonnell Douglas Astronautics Co., St. Louis, 1974-75, dir. diversification, new products, 1975—. Recipient Appreciation certificate NASA, 1976. Mem. Sci. Research Soc. Am., Am. Astron. Soc., Inst. Radio Engrs. Author: Future Unmanned Astronomy Spacecraft, vol. 28, Sci. Tech. Series, 1972; contbr. articles to profl. publs.; initial researcher magnetic recording; patentee in field. Home: 585 Highland Dr Ballwin MO 63011 Office: PO Box 516 St Louis MO 63166

SIMMONS, FREDERICK HARRISON, physician; b. Chgo., Feb. 14, 1915; s. Lloyd H. and Rose (Patterson) S.; B.S., Ind. U., 1938, M.D., 1940; m. Mary J. Russell, Jan. 31, 1942; children—Frederick Harrison, Richard L., David. Intern, St. Vincent's Hosp., Indpls., 1940-41; resident Ind. U. Med. Center, Indpls., 1945-48; practice medicine specializing in otolaryngology, Marion, Ind., 1949—; mem. staff Marion Gen. Hosp.; attending cons. VA Hosp., Marion. Served with AUS, 1941-45. Mem. A.C.S., AMA, Am., Ind. acads. ophthalmology and otolaryngology, Am., Internat. rhinol. socs., Am. Soc. Ophthal. and Otolaryn. Allergy, Ind. Med. Assn., Am. Council Otolaryngology. Home: 2607 Beech Ln Marion IN 46952 Office: 1009 N Baldwin St Marion IN 46952

SIMMONS, JAMES PAUL, civil engr.; b. Pitts., May 1, 1952; s. James Vincent and Verna Elizabeth (Kokal) S.; B.S., U. Cin., 1975, M.S. in Civil Engring., 1976. Draftsman, quality assurance engr. Pitts. DesMoines Steel Co., Pitts., 1971-74; field engr. Turner Constrn. Co., Erie, Pa., 1976-77, estimating engr., Cleve., 1977—; teaching and research asst. dept. civil enging. U. Cin., 1975-76; v.p. James Simmons & Sons, Inc., Pitts., 1976—. Mem. ASCE, Chi Epsilon, Delta Tau Delta. Democrat. Home: 63 Mount Vernon Court Mentor OH 44060 Office: 100 Erieview Plaza Cleveland OH 44114

SIMMONS, JIMMY, dentist; b. Wink, Tex., Jan. 11, 1931; s. Charles Wilmer and Sarah (Werner) S.; B.S., U. Kans., 1955; D.D.S., U. Nebr., 1966; m. Sandra Jane Herbig, Oct. 12, 1962; children—Blake Alexander, Suzannah Leigh. Test engr. McDonnell, Douglas, St. Louis, 1958-60; test engr. Gen. Dynamics, Altas Missile project, Nebr., Iowa, Kans., Tex., 1960-62; pvt. practice dentistry, Blair, Nebr., 1966—; pres. Green Grass Growers, Inc., Waterloo, Nebr., 1972-75. Pres., Blair Pre-School, Inc., 1972-73; skipper Blair Sea Scouts, 1969-71. Served to lt. (j.g.) USNR, 1955-58. Mem. Am., Nebr. Dental assns., Blair C. of C. (mem. govt. action com. 1972-73, chmn. transportation and tourism com. 1973-75), Tri Valley Dental Soc. (pres. 1972-73), Elkhorn Valley Study Club (sec. 1972-73), Theta Chi. Republican. Clubs: Mason, Blair Aeros. Home: 410 S 15th St Blair NE 68008 Office: 17th and Lincoln Sts Blair NE 68008

SIMMONS, M. DALE, city ofcl.; b. Schuylar, Mo., Mar. 28, 1927; s. Richard W. and Lillian E. (Blodgett) S.; grad. high sch.; m. Gladys I. Church, Oct. 27, 1945; children—Jimmie D., Steven D. Laborer, 1942-43; maintainer operator City of Marshalltown, Iowa, 1952-55, 57-64, sign shop operator, 1964-70, street commr., 1970—. Charter mem., dir. Marshalltown and Marshall County Credit Union, 1961-69. Served with AUS, 1944-46. Mem. Am. Pub. Works Assn. Home: 1408 S 2d Ave Marshalltown IA 50158 Office: 312 May St Marshalltown IA 50158

SIMMONS, MERLE EDWIN, educator; b. Kansas City, Kans., Sept. 27, 1918; s. Walter Earl and Mabel Sophronia (Shoemaker) S.; A.B., U. Kans., 1939, M.A., 1941; Ph.D., U. Mich., 1952; postgrad. Harvard U., 1946-47, U. Mexico, 1945; m. Concepcion Rojas, Sept. 8, 1948; children—Martha Irene Simmons Hunt, Mary Alice. Faculty, Ind. U. at Bloomington, 1942—, prof. Spanish, 1962—, dir. grad. studies dept. Spanish and Portuguese, 1967-76, chairperson dept., 1976—; teaching fellow Harvard U., Cambridge, Mass., 1946-47. Am. Philos. Soc. grantee, 1955, 76; Am. Council Learned Socs. grantee, 1962. Mem. AAUP, Am. Folklore Soc., Am. Assn. Tchrs. Spanish and Portuguese, Conf. on Latin Am. History, Modern Lang. Assn. Am., Midwest modern lang. assns., Midwest Assn. Latin Am. Studies, Phi Beta Kappa, Phi Sigma Iota. Author: The Mexican Corrido, 1957; A Bibliography of the Romance and Related Forms in Spanish America, 1963; Folklore Bibliography for 1973, 1975; Folklore Bibliography for 1974, 1977; contbr. articles to profl. jours. Home: 4233 Saratoga Dr Bloomington IN 47401 Office: Ballantine Hall 844 Ind U Bloomington IN 47401

SIMMONS, NEVAH HOWELL, newspaperwomen; b. near Pana, Ill., May 7, 1904; d. Charles Ottis and Essie Jane (Cruce) Howell; student Bradley U.; m. Clarence Lee Simmons, July 26, 1924 (dec. Dec. 1965); 1 son, Wilber Dean. Reporter, Pana Daily Record, 1923, Canton (Ill.) Daily Register, 1923-25; supr. Postal Telegraph Co., Peoria, Ill., 1942-43; reporter Peoria Jour. Star, Inc.. 1943—, garden editor, columnist, 1957—. Mem. Garden Writers Assn. Am., Am. Hemerocallis Soc., Photog. Soc. Am. Democrat. Presbyn. Clubs: Peoria Color Camera; Photocrafters Camera (Rock Island, Ill.). Home: 6807 N Mount Hawley Rd Peoria IL 61614 Office: 1 News Plaza Peoria IL 61601

SIMMONS, PERCY SLOTSKY, timber and veneer co. owner; b. London, Dec. 27, 1906; s. Simon Slotsky and Mary (Rappaport) S.; student City London Coll., 1922-24; m. Hinda Cohen, Sept. 25, 1929; children—Rica (Mrs. Harvey K. Spivack), Nina Penelope (Mrs. Donald G. Frenkel). Came to U.S., 1938, naturalized, 1960. Owner, Simmons Co., Indpls., 1936—; purchasing agt. Fgn. Econ. Adminstrn., Washington, 1942. Dir. wine course Purdue U.-Ind. U., 1969—; mem. adv. bd. Butler U. Mus. Festival, 1968; hon. consul of France in Ind., 1956—; bd. dirs. Internat. Center Indpls., Lang. Center Indpls.; exec. bd. Am. Jewish Com., N.Y.C., 1968. Decorated officer L'Ordre National Du Merite (France). Mem. Confrerie Chevalier Des Tastevin (comdr. 1973, grand officer of grand council). Club: Athletic (Indpls.). Home: 5602 Central Ave Indianapolis IN 46220 Office: 532 Merchants Bank Bldg Indianapolis IN 46204

SIMMONS, RAY CLIFFORD, lawyer; b. Washington, Aug. 17, 1925; s. Robert Glenmore and Gladyce (Weil) S.; B.A., U. Nebr., 1949; LL.B., Nebr. Law Coll., 1950; m. Marianne Keiley, July 13, 1957; children—Michael Kelley, Elizabeth Lees. Admitted to Nebr. bar, 1950, practiced in Fremont, 1953—; law clerk for U.S. Supreme Ct. Justice Harold H. Burton, 1950-51. Mem. Nebr. Legislature, 1957-61, chmn. judiciary com., 1959-61; vice chmn. delegation Republican Nat. Conv., 1964; chmn. Nat. Young Reps., 1957; mem. Nebr. Rep. Central Com., 1958-68. Served to comdr. USNR, World War II, Korea. Mem. Nebr. State Bar (chmn. jr. bar sect. 1957), Order Coif, Phi Beta Kappa, Alpha Tau Omega (pres. 1949). Mason (Shriner). Author: Nebraska Automobile Negligence Law. Home: 525 W 19th St Fremont NE 68025 Office: 445 N Broad St Fremont NE 68025

SIMMONS, VIRGINIA LEE COWAN, educator; b. Ft. Wayne, Ind., May 17, 1921; d. James Clarence and Julia (Webster) Cowan; A.B., Ind. U., 1942, Ed.S., 1970; M.S., Butler U., 1957; postgrad. U. Wis., 1964, 65, 67; m. Eric L. Simmons, Apr. 25, 1943 (div. 1948); children—Nancy Lee Simmons (Mrs. Roy V. Green), Eric Leslie. Market research analyst McCann-Erickson, Chgo., 1944-48; retail mcht. Aquatic Galleries, Cin., 1949-52; sales, advt. Empire Tropical Fish Import Co., N.Y.C., 1952-53; with direct mail advt., Halvin Products, Bklyn., 1953-55; tchr. Indpls. Sch. 76, 1955-60; asst. prin. Sch. 61, 1960-61, asst. prin. Sch. 101, 1962-63; prin. Lew Wallace Sch. 107, 1964-72, Francis Bellamy sch. #102, 1972-74, William H. Evans Sch. 95, 1974—; program supr. audio-visual center Ind. U., Bloomington, 1961-62; lectr. Butler U., Indpls., summers 1965, 73; cons. Ind. U., summer 1969. Mem. Indpls. chpt. HOPE; coordinator gift and hobby show Indpl. Pub. Schs., 1969-76; Indpls. sch. rep. Am. Cancer Soc., 1969-74. Bd. dirs. Ind. chpt. Young Audiences, 1969—, chmn., 1976—; pres. Ind. aux. Freedoms Found., 1973-75, v.p. awards, 1975-77. Recipient Am. Educators award, 1971. Mem. NEA, Nat. Assn. Elementary sch. prins. (life), Assn. Supervision and Curriculum Devel., Internat. Reading Assn. Ind. U. Alumni Assn., Indpls. Zool. Soc. (charter), Ind. Tchrs. Assn., Bus. and Profl. Women's Clubs, Inc., Indpls. Council Adminstrv. Women Edn., Nat. Soc. Study Edn., Nat. Congress Parents and Tchrs., Butler U. Alumni Assn., Izaak Walton League, AAUW, Met. Indpls. TV Assn., Children's Mus., Art Edn. Assn. Ind. (life), Indpls. Museum of Art, Hoosier Salon patrons Assn., Ind. Artists Club, Alpha Chi Omega, Delta Kappa Gamma, Phi Delta Kappa. Methodist. Club: Indianapolis Athletic, Catherine Merrill, Century, Indianapolis Propylaeum, Indiana Schoolwomen's. Home: Box 68062 Indianapolis IN 46268 Office: William H Evans Sch 95 2801 S Pennsylvania St Indianapolis IN 46225

SIMON, DELBERT RICHARD, music educator; b. Burwell, Nebr., Aug. 7, 1927; s. Oscar Arthur and Annie Mabel (Reineke) S.; Mus.B., Simpson Coll., 1955; Mus.M., Miami U., Oxford, O., 1957; D. Musical Arts, U. Iowa, 1970; m. Betty Jeane Atkins, July 21, 1951; children—Richard Del., David Mark. Teaching fellow Miami U., 1955-57; choral and voice instr. Flint (Mich.) Jr. Coll., 1957-62; asst. prof. voice Western Wash. State Coll., Bellingham, 1962-65; teaching fellow U. Iowa, Iowa City, 1965-69, research fellow, 1968-69; prof. Sch. Music, Eastern Ill. U., Charleston, 1969—. Artist in residence Bay View (Mich.) Summer Coll. of Music, 1959-61; profl. singer in opera oratorio and concert, 1959—. Served with U.S. Army, 1945-48. Mem. Nat. Assn. Tchrs. of Singing (regional auditions chmn. 1973, 74). Home: 302 Chamberlin Dr Charleston IL 61920

SIMON, LEON AARON, furniture co. exec.; b. Fargo, N.D., Aug. 9, 1926; s. Harry Aaron and Pearl (Eisenberg) S.; grad. high sch.; m. Muriel Livon, Aug. 14, 1949; children—Phillip, Marsha Bunge, Lisa. With Simon Furniture Co., Moorhead, Minn., 1947—, pres., 1960—; v.p. Am.-Can. Investment Corp., Moorhead, 1969—, also dir.; pres. Moorhead State Bank, 1970-76, chmn. bd., 1976—, also dir.; treas. Simon Warehouse, Corp., Moorhead, 1963—, also dir.; partner Simon Bros. Properties, Moorhead, 1952—; dir. Fargo-Moorhead Retail Credit Bur., Fargo, 1973—. Active United Fund, KFME Ednl. TV; pres. adv. bd. St. Ansgar Hosp., 1965-73; bd. dirs. Concordia Coll.; bd. dirs., treas. Moorhead Urban Renewal Project, 1965-70. Served with AUS, World War II. Recipient excellence award Am. Carpet Inst., 1959; Retail All-Am. award Home Furnishings Daily, 1959; Pres.'s Regents and Founders award Concordia Coll., 1973, Soli Deo Gloria award; named Outstanding Furniture Dealer, Midwest Furniture Salesmen's Club, 1973. Mem. Shanley Grow Club (dir.), Moorhead C. of C., Sons of Norway. Jewish (dir. temple). Elk. Clubs: Fargo Country, Komus, Coterie, Moorhead Country. Home: 1203 14th St S Moorhead MN 56560 Office: Simon Furniture Co Box 939 Moorhead MN 56560

SIMON, LOU ANNA KINSEY, educator; b. Nobesville, Ind., Jan. 4, 1947; d. Melcum H. and Marcella Doris (Plain) Kimsey; B.A., Ind. State U., 1969, M.S., 1970; Ph.D., Mich. State U., 1974; m. Roy J. Simon, July 20, 1972. Grad. asst. div. student affairs Ind. State U., Terre Haute, 1969-70; office instl. research Mich. State U., East Lansing, 1970-72, instr.-asst. dir. dept. study project, 1972-73, asst. prof. office instl. research, 1974—; cons. Mich. Civil Rights Commn., Flint Police Dept., adv. bd. Mich. Project SEED. Bd. dirs. The Listening Ear of East Lansing, Crisis Intervention Center. Mem. Assn. Instl. Research, Am. Ednl. Research Assn., Am. Assn. for Higher Edn., Nat. Assn. Women Deans, Adminstrs. and Counselors, Faculty Women's Assn. (Mich. State U.), Phi Kappa Phi, Phi Delta Kappa, Alpha Lambda Delta. Home: 2814 Brentwood St East Lansing MI 48823 Office: OIR-331 Adminstrn Bldg Mich State U East Lansing MI 48824

SIMON, MARVIN, dentist; b. Omaha, Mar. 23, 1924; s. Milton and Sarah (Roitstein) S.; B.S., Creighton U. Dental Coll., 1945, D.D.S., 1946; m. Pearl Emeline Miller, Nov. 26, 1955; children—Barbara Lynn, Marc Robert, Susan Ann. Dentist, Omaha, 1946—. Developer, owner Med. Dental Plaza, Omaha, 1959—. Served with U.S. Army, 1943-44. Mem. Am., Nebr. dental assns., Pi Lambda Phi. Democrat. Judaism. Home: 2122 S 84th St Omaha NE 68124 Office: 8424 W Center Rd Omaha NE 68124

SIMON, PAUL, congressman; b. Eugene, Oreg., Nov. 29, 1928; s. Martin Paul and Ruth (Troemel) S.; student U. Oreg., 1945-46; student Dana Coll., Blair, Nebr., 1946-48, LL.D., 1965; D.Litt., McKendree Coll., (Ill.), 1965; D.C.L., Greenville Coll., 1968; LL.D. Concordia Coll., 1969, Lincoln Coll., 1969, Loyola U., Valparaiso U., 1976; m. Jeanne Hurley, Apr. 21, 1960; children—Sheila, Martin. Pub., Troy (Ill.) Tribune, 1948-66; mem. Ill. Ho. of Reps., 1954-62, Ill. Senate, 1962-69; lt. gov. Ill., 1969-73; mem. faculty Sangamon State U., 1972-73; lectr. John F. Kennedy Inst. Politics, Harvard U., 1973; mem. 94th-95th Congresses from 24th Dist. Ill. Bd. dirs. Wheatridge Found., McKendree Coll. Served with CIC, U.S. Army, 1951-53. Recipient Am. Polit. Sci. Assn. award, 1957; named Best Legislator 7 times. Mem. Luth. Human Relations Assn., Am. Legion, V.F.W., NAACP, Urban League, Sigma Delta Chi. Lutheran. Lion. Author: Lovejoy: Martyr to Freedom, 1964, Lincoln's Preparation for Greatness, 1966, A Hungry World, 1966; (with Jeanne Hurley Simon) Protestant-Catholic Marriages Can Succeed, 1967; You Want to Change the World? So Change It, 1971; (with Arthur Simon) The Politics of World Hunger, 1973; writer weekly column Sidelights from Springfield, 1955-72, P. S/Washington, 1975—; contbr. articles to periodicals, including Saturday Rev., Harper's, The New Republic. Home: Carbondale IL 62901 Office: 227 Cannon House Office Bldg Washington DC 20515

SIMON, ROBERT PAUL, architect; b. Flat River, Mo., Sept. 21, 1923; s. Ernest John and Grace (Dalton) S.; B.S. in Archtl. Engring., U. Ill., 1944; m. Beverly Ann Meyer, Aug. 23, 1968; children—William, Steven, John. Head architect Small Homes Council, U. Ill., Urbana, 1946-50; pres. Simon-Rettberg-G-F Inc., Champaign, Ill., 1950—, dir., 1977—; dir. Tile Specialists, Inc., Champaign, Ill. Chmn. Champaign Bd. Appeals, 1967—. Served with USN, 1942-46. Presbyterian. Club: Champaign County Country. Contbr. articles to profl. jours. Home: 2310 Briarhill Dr Champaign IL 61820 Office: 1 Henson Pl Champaign IL 61820

SIMON, SHIRLEY SCHWARTZ (MRS. EDGAR H. SIMON), author; b. Cleve., Mar. 21, 1921; d. Bernard H. and Sylvia (Silverman) Schwartz; student Western Res. U., 1938-40; B.A., Goddard Coll., 1973; m. Edgar H. Simon, Mar. 1, 1942; children—Allen Harold, Ruth Esther. Tchr. juvenile writing div. gen. studies Western Res. U., Cleve., 1965-68, Shaker Heights (Ohio) Adult Edn. Program, Cleve., 1968-70, John Carroll U., 1969—; instr. creative writing extended learning program Ohio U., 1972—; tchr. Children's lit. Glen Oak Sch., Gates Mills, Ohio, 1973—; speaker Cleve. Book Fair, 1963-68, Dayton (Ohio) Book Fair, 1965. Mem. Women's Nat. Book Assn., Authors Guild. Author: Molly's Cottage, 1959; Molly and the Rooftop Mystery, 1961; Cousins at Camm Corners, 1963; Best Friend, 1964, paperback edit., 1968; Libby's Stepfamily, 1966. Contbr. stories, serials and plays to Jack and Jill, Child Life, The Writer, and other nat. juvenile and tchrs. publs. Home: 3630 Cedarbrook Rd Cleveland OH 44118

SIMON, STEVEN ELLIOTT, counseling psychologist; b. Brownwood, Tex., Aug. 15, 1944; s. Max and Gertrude (Spiegler) S.; B.S., U. Fla., 1966, M.Rehab. Counseling, 1967; m. Gail Kamelhar, Apr. 22, 1967; children—Bonnie Louise, Matthew Alan. Vocat. counselor Prospect House, East Orange, N.J., 1967-69; counseling psychologist VA, 1969—, chief counseling and rehab. sect., Cleve., 1974—; mem. subcom. jobs for vets. Cleve. Fed. Exec. bd.; part-time instr. Middlesex County (N.J.) Coll., 1970; cons. in field. Vocat. Rehab. Adminstrn. grantee, 1966-67. Mem. Am. Psychol. Assn., Am. Personnel and Guidance Assn., Nat. Vocat. Guidance Assn., Am. Rehab. Counseling Assn. Home: 32664 N Roundhead Dr Solon OH 44139 Office: VA 1240 E 9th St Cleveland OH 44121

SIMONI, LEWIS EUGENE, physician, educator; b. Aliquippa, Pa., Nov. 24, 1921; s. Serafin and Amelia (Conti) S.; B.S., Geneva Coll., 1942; M.D., Marquette U., 1946; m. Anna Elizabeth Allwein, July 5, 1945; children—Christopher, Kathleen, Mark, Mary, Amy, Martha, Elizabeth. Intern, Mercy Hosp., Pitts., 1946-47; resident St. Joseph Hosp., Flint, Mich., 1949-51, dir. med. edn., 1971—; practice medicine specializing in family practice, Flint, 1951-71; attending physician Hurley Hosp., Flint, 1951-75, McLaren Hosp. Flint, 1951—, St. Joseph, 1951—; asso. prof. Mich. State U., Coll. Human Medicine; trustee St. Joseph Hosp., 1969-72. Mem. Utilization Task Force, Mich., chmn., 1975-76; mem. Am. Arbitration Advisory Subcom., 1976-77. Served as capt. M.C., U.S. Army, 1947-49. Grantee family practice tng., 1973-74 75-76, 77-78; diplomate Am. Bd. Family Practice. Fellow Am. Acad. Family Physicians; mem. AMA, Mich. State, Genesse County (pres.) med. socs., Mich. Acad. Family Practice (v.p. 1976-77), Am. Assn. for Hosp. Med. Edn., Mich. Assn. Med. Edn., Royal Soc. Health. Roman Catholic. Contbr. papers ambulatory health care. Home: G-9109 S Saginaw Rd Grand Blanc MI 48439 Office: 302 Kensington Ave Flint MI 48502

SIMONS, CLIFFORD GENE, agrl. equipment co. exec.; b. Portland, Ind., May 28, 1936; s. Clifford D. and Mary (Metz) S.; B.S. in Agrl. Engring., Purdue U., 1959; postgrad. U. Wis., 1963—; m. Oneida Louise Greer, Feb. 2, 1958; children—Gina Louise, Joni Denise, Dana Marlene, Ryan Gene; m. 2d, Lynn Louise Gregg, Nov. 23, 1973; stepchildren—Amy, Nate, Noel. Tchr. math. Gov. I.P. Gray High Sch., Portland, Ind., 1958; project engr. FMC Corp., Tipton, Ind., 1959-61; project engr. Dairy div. Sta-Rite Products, Inc., Delavan, Wis., 1961-63, chief dairy engr., 1963-65; v.p., gen. mgr. Dairy & Food Equipment div. Sta-Rite Industries, 1965-75; mgr. customer and product service J.I. Case Co., Racine, Wis., 1975—. Pres. Dewland Assn.; past pres. Delevan Elementary P.T.A. Named an Outstanding Young Man of Am., Delavan Jaycees, 1967. Registered profl. engr., Wis. Mem. Am. Soc. Agrl. Engrs., Nat., Ind., Wis. socs. profl. engrs., Am. Mgmt. Assn., Internat. Acad. Profl. Bus. Execs., Skull and Crescent, Alpha Chi Rho. Presbyterian (ruling elder, mem. session). Patentee in field. Home: 685 South Shore Dr Route 1 Box 618 Lake Geneva WI 53147 Office: 700 State St Racine WI 53404

SIMONS, RETA MARIE, psychol. counselor; b. Sask., Can., Mar. 24, 1913; d. John Dittrich and Sylvia E. (Maul) Petersen; B.A., U. Mich., 1935; M.A. with honors, 1962: m. Walter Simons, June 6, 1936; children—Jay, Dale, Cheryl. Tchr., Lakeshore High Sch., 1935; asst. prof., dir. counseling and testing Oakland (Mich.) Community Coll., 1965, 66; organizer Project Transition Detroit, 1967-71, chmn. bd., chief diagnostician, 1971-76, bd. dirs., 1976—; cons. in field. Mem. exec. bd. League Cath. Women, 1966-77; mem. Detroit Opera Com., 1965-77; active Detroit Symphony Women's Com., 1965-77, Birmingham Youth Assistance Com., 1973—. Named Dynamic Woman Birmingham, Mich., 1965; recipient plaque League Cath. Women, 1976, plaque for Project Transition Mich. Dept. Corrections. Mem. Am., Mich. personnel and guidance assns., Nat. Assn. Measurement and Guidance, Detroit Women's Econ. Club, AAUW, Mich. League for Human Services, Mich. Assn. for Specialists in Group Work, Nat. Platform Assn., Zeta Phi Eta. Clubs: Oakland Hills Country, Village Womens (named Golden Nugget Woman of Year 1973), Christ Child, Organizer live-in program for women offenders. Home: 784 Woodale Rd Birmingham MI 48010 Office: 100 Parsons St Detroit MI 48010

SIMONS, RICHARD STUART, journalist, retailer; b. Marion, Ind., July 26, 1920; s. Erwin Philip and Tillie Ethel (Bernstein) S.; A.B., Ind. U., 1942; m. Rosmarie Roeschli, Mar. 5, 1957; 1 dau., Charlotte. Editor, Winchester (Ind.) News, 1942-44, Tipton (Ind.) Daily Tribune, 1944-48; feature writer Sunday mag. Indpls. Star, 1948—; partner Richard Clothing Co., Marion, 1954-63, owner, 1963—; lectr. journalism Ind. U., 1952. Pres. Mississinewa Arts Council, 1971-72, Marion Philharmonic Orch., 1974-75; mem. Ind. Ty. Sesquicentennial Commn., 1950; adv. com. Ind. Statehood Sesquicentennial; bd. dirs. Marion Gen. Hosp. Authority, 1974—; pres. bd. dirs. Marion Gen. Hosp., 1963-64; pres. bd. trustees Marion Pub. Library, 1977—. Recipient award of merit Am. Assn. State and Local History, 1972. Mem. Ind. Hist. Soc. (trustee). Clubs: Elks, Kiwanis. Contbg. editor Popular Mechanics Picture History of Am. Transp., 1952. Contbr. articles to profl. jours. Home: 715 Berkley Dr Marion IN 46952 Office: 326 S Washington St Marion IN 46952

SIMONS, ROBERT LOUIS, physician; b. Chgo., Apr. 4, 1923; s. David B. and Kate (Silverman) S.; B.A., U. Ill., 1944, B.S., M.D., 1947; m. Florence Newman, Sept. 15, 1945; children—Hardye, John, David, Peter. Intern, Cook County Hosp., Chgo., 1948, resident in internal medicine, 1949, 1953-54; practice medicine specializing in internal medicine, Chgo.; dir. med. edn. L. A. Weiss Hosp., Chgo., 1954-60, mem. attending staff, 1954—; former mem. attending staff Cook County Hosp.; clin. asso. prof. medicine, U. Ill., Chgo. Served with U.S. Army, World War II, USAF, 1950-52; Korea. Research fellow Hektoen Inst., Chgo., 1952-54; diplomate Am. Bd. Internal Medicine. Mem. AMA, Ill. state, Chgo. med. socs., Am. Soc. Internal Editor: Bulletin L. A. Weiss Hosp.; mem. editorial bd. Legal Clinics-Trial Techniques. Home: 3150 Lake Shore Dr Chicago IL 60657 Office: 4640 Marine Dr Chicago IL 60640

SIMONSEN, RICHARD JOHN, dentist; b. Portsmouth, Eng., Aug. 20, 1945; s. Johan Wideroe and Barbara Evelyn (Hodges) S.; came to U.S., 1964; B.A., U. Minn., 1969, B.S., 1969, D.D.S., 1971; m. Elisabeth Magnus, Mar. 23, 1973; children—Joachim, Christian, Heidi. Gen. practice dentistry, Bloomington, Minn., 1975—; clin. U. Minn., Mpls., 1973-75. Mem. Am., Norwegian, Minn. dental assns., Am. Soc. Dentistry for Children, AAAS, Scandinavian Soc. Forensic Odontology, Am. Acad. Forensic Sci., Internat. Assn. for Dental Research, Am. Assn. for Dental Research, Am. Pub. Health Assn. 15947 Island View Rd NW Prior Lake MN 55372 Office: Group Health Medical Center 8600 Nicollet Ave Bloomington MN 55420

SIMONSON, GERALD WALLACE, investment co. exec.; b. St. Louis County, Minn., July 19, 1930; s. Henry and Mayme Louisa (Isaacson) S.; B.A., Macalester Coll., 1952; postgrad. U. Minn., 1954-55. Staff auditor Price Waterhouse & Co., Chgo., 1955-61; officer, dir. Community Investment Enterprises, Inc., Mpls., 1961—, pres., 1970—; dir. The Retail Group, Inc., Medtronic, Inc., Minnetonka, Inc., N.W. Teleprodns., Inc., Surrey, Inc., Flame Industries, Inc. Trustee Lutheran Deaconess Hosp., Fairview Community Hosps. Served with U.S. Army, 1952-54. Mem. Am. Inst. C.P.A.'s, Minn. Soc. C.P.A.'s. Home: 5813 Jeff Pl Edina MN 55436 Office: 7515 Wayzata Blvd Minneapolis MN 55426

SIMOTTI, GENESIO ANTHONY, landscape architect; b. Rochester, N.Y., Apr. 2, 1928; s. John and Mafalda (Maucini) S.; B.S., Mich. State U., 1952; m. Pauline Jean Russell, June 6, 1953; children—William J., Judithe J., Barbara P., Lisa R., Genessa K. Landscape architect and site planner Genesio A. Simotti & Assos., Milw., 1954—. Mem. bldg. bd. com. City of Glendale (Wis.), 1956-68, mem. bd. appeals, 1973—. Served to 1st lt. U.S. Army, 1952-54; Korea. Decorated Bronze Star; recipient Nat. Merit award Am. Assn. Nurserymen for Landscape Design, 1968, 70. Mem. Am. Soc. Landscape Architects (chmn. exam. com. Wis. chpt. 1970—), Nat. Recreation and Park Assos. Roman Catholic. Club: Kiwanis. Home: 7645 N Chadwick Rd Glendale WI 53217 Office: 726 N Milwaukee St Milwaukee WI 53202

SIMOWITZ, FREDRIC MALCOLM, neurologist; b. Augusta, Ga., Oct. 4, 1937; s. Joseph and Thelma Dorothy (Levy) S.; M.D., Med. Coll. Ga., 1962; m. Beverly Ann Seigal, Jan. 29, 1966; children—Lynn, Mark. Intern, Ohio State U. Hosp., Columbus, 1962-63; resident Sinai Hosp., Balt., 1965-66; resident in neurology U. Mich. Med. Ann Arbor, 1966-68, chief resident, 1969; instr. in neurology St. Louis U., 1969-71, sr. instr., 1971-73, clin. asst. prof. neurology, 1973—; practice medicine specializing in neurology, St. Louis, 1969—; cons. U.S. VA, 1972—, Sandoz Pharms., 1973—. Served with USN, 1963-65. Diplomate Bd. Psychiatry and Neurology. Fellow Am.-Israel Physicians; mem. AMA (Physician's Recognition award 1970—), Am. Acad. Neurology, Am. Electroencephalographic Soc., Pan-Am. Med. Assn. Jewish. Contbr. articles to med. jours. Home: 538 Chalet Ct Saint Louis MO 63141 Office: 2821 Ballas Rd Saint Louis MO 63131

SIMPSON, BRUCE LISTON, engring. co. exec.; b. Chgo., Nov. 14, 1912; s. Herbert Spencer and Edith (Moeller) S.; student Hobart Coll., 1930-33; B.S.L., Northwestern U., 1934, LL.B., 1936; m. Madeleine Edith Holmes, Apr. 17, 1937; children—Judy T. (Mrs. Henry D. Dienst), Pamela L. (Mrs. John C. Anderson), Peter Liston III. Admitted to Ill. bar, 1937; asso. Ashcraft & Ashcraft, Chgo., 1933-37; with Nat. Engring. Co., 1937—, pres., dir., 1942—, now chmn.; chmn.

Simpson Machinen A.G., Zug, Switzerland, 1966—; pres., dir. Nat. Engring. of Can., 1957—. Bd. dirs., v.p. Collier County Conservancy, Naples, Fla. Registered profl. engr., Ill. Hon. life mem. Am. Foundrymens Soc. (past pres.). Unitarian. Clubs: Union League, Chicago Yacht; Port Royal, Naples Yacht, Naples (Fla.) Royal Poinciana Golf; Dunham Woods, Wayne. Home: 2675 Treasure Lake Naples FL 33940 Office: 20 N Wacker Dr Chicago IL 60606

SIMPSON, EDWIN KERSHAW, III, educator, researcher; b. N.Y.C., Apr. 24, 1935; s. Edwin Kershaw II and Hedwig Elizabeth (Schacht) S.; B.A., Rutgers U., 1965; M.B.A., U. Dayton, 1968; Ph.D., U. Cin., 1976; m. Geraldine Winifred Macfarlane, Feb. 15, 1958; children—Eric Malcolm, Craig Kershaw. Dist. sales rep. Gen. Analine & Film, 1963-69; grad. teaching asst. U. Cin., 1970-72; instr. Miami U., Oxford, Ohio, 1972-76, asst. prof. marketing, 1976—; adj. asso. prof. Wright State U., summer 1977; cons. to industry. Served with AUS, 1957-59. Mem. Am. Marketing Assn. (pres. Dayton chpt. 1975-76, now bd. dirs., Outstanding Achievement award 1976, Nat. award for outstanding service to marketing 1976), AAUP, Beta Gamma Sigma, Pi Sigma Epsilon (nat. sec.), Mu Kappa Tau (nat. bd. dirs.). Democrat. Presbyterian. Clubs: Dayton MBA, Dayton Sales and Marketing Execs. Engaged in source credibility research. Home: 418 Aberdeen Ave Dayton OH 45419 Office: 307 Laws Hall Miami University Oxford OH 45056

SIMPSON, EVERETT JAMES, architect; b. Fairbury, Nebr., Sept. 16, 1922; s. Ralph A. and Frances A. (Chorn) S.; student Inst. Design (now Ill. Inst. Tech.), 1946; m. Sally S. Shaw, Jan. 16, 1945; children—James, Robert, Sue, Jan. Drapery salesman, window trimmer J.M. McDonald Co., Norfolk, Nebr., 1949-52; draftsman Watson & Strong, Architects, Norfolk, 1952; chief designer Howard J. Strong & Assos., Norfolk, 1953-63; partner Simpson & Strong, Architects, Norfolk, 1964-67; owner E.J. Simpson & Assos., Architects, Inc., Norfolk, 1968—. Bd. dirs. YMCA. Served with USNR, 1942-45. Decorated Purple Heart. Mem. A.I.A. (pres. Western sect. 1973-74), C. of C. (chmn. legislative affairs com. 1968-70). Methodist (supt. ch. sch. 1960-66, trustee 1967-70, chmn. 1969-70). Clubs: Rotary (pres. 1968-69), Odd Fellows (grand master Nebr. 1974-75), Elks, Norfolk Country. Home: 1001 Norfolk Ave Norfolk NE 68701 Office: 0116 S 4th Norfolk NE 68701

SIMPSON, GEORGE WILLIAM, dentist; b. nr. Oxford, Ind., Sept. 25, 1920; s. Henry E. and Ivah Clarise (Bray) S.; A.B., Ind. U., 1942, D.D.S., 1944; m. Virginia Ruth Griggs, Apr. 25, 1943; children—Ivah Susanne (Mrs. Bernard Lee Schrader). Gen. practice dentistry, Franklin, Ind., 1946-50, 53—, Indpls., 1950-52; asst. prof. dept. fixed prosthodontics Ind. U. Sch. Dentistry, 1960—. Pres., Johnson County Comprehensive Health Planning Council, 1972-73. Bd. dirs. Johnson County Bd. Health, 1972—, pres., 1973—. Served with USNR, 1942-46, 52-53. Fellow Am., Internat. colls. dentists; mem. Ind., Indpls. dental socs., ADA, Am. Prosthodontic Soc., Pierre Fauchard Acad., Omicron Kappa Upsilon. Mason. Club: Indianapolis Athletic. Home: RFD 3 Franklin IN 46131 Office: 70 W Madison St Franklin IN 46131

SIMPSON, JOHN EUGENE, utility co. exec.; b. Lovington, Ill., Jan. 6, 1919; s. John J. and Cecile (Million) S.; grad. Browns Bus. Coll., 1939; student U. Hawaii, 1945; m. Norma P. Wood, Mar. 6, 1938 (dec. 1972); children—Sharon Kaye (Mrs. Manuel Lae), John Joseph, Douglas Eugene; m. 2d, Evelyn A. Lamb, Mar. 1, 1973. Clk., George V. Penwell & Sons Co., Pana, Ill., 1936-37; jr. salesman Central Ill. Pub. Service Co., Pana, 1937-38; salesman Bateman Maxtag Co., Pana, 1938-39; with Ill. Power Co., Decatur, 1939-44, 46—, asst. purchasing agt., 1947-57, purchasing agt., 1957—. Adviser, Jr. Achievement, 1964—. Trustee Ind. Central Coll., Indpls.; pres. bd. dirs. Jr. Achievement of Decatur; mem. regional bd. and corp Nat. Jr. Achievement, 1971—. Served with USNR, 1944-46. Mem. I.E.E.E., Central Ill. purchasing Mgmt. Assn., Nat. Assn. Purchasing Mgmt. (exec. com. Pub. Utility Buyers Group). Methodist (dist. lay leader). Clubs: Masons, Decatur, Decatur Shrine. Home: 396 Oak Ln Decatur IL 62526 Office: 500 S 27th St Decatur IL 62525

SIMPSON, LYLE LEE, lawyer; b. Des Moines, Oct. 15, 1937; s. R. Clair and Martha B. (Accola) S.; B.A., Drake U., 1960, J.D., LL.B., 1963; children—Sondra Sue, Donald Scott. Asst. to dean students Drake U., 1960-62; admitted to Iowa bar, 1963; prin. Lyle L. Simpson, atty., Des Moines, 1963-64; mem. firm Beving & Swanson, 1964-68, Peddicord, Simpson & Sutphin, 1968—; dir. Am. Republic Ins. Co., Americare Growth Fund. Instr. mil. leadership Iowa Mil. Acad., 1965-68. Treas., Mental Health Coordinating Commn., 1975—. Mem. exec. bd. Polk County Republican Central Com., 1964-68. Bd. counselors Drake U. Law Sch., 1969-72; bd. dirs. Polk County Health Service Corp., 1976—, Polk County Mental Health Center, 1976—; trustee, sec. Broadlawns Polk County Hosp. Served to capt. Signal Corps, U.S. Army, 1955-68; lt. comdr. USNR. Recipient Class of 1915 award Drake U., 1960, Oren E. Scott award, 1960. Mem. Am. Humanist Assn. (humanist counselor 1974—, gen. counsel 1975—, dir. 1976—), Naval Res. Lawyers Assn., Res. Officer's Assn., Am. Acad. Trial Lawyers, Am. (coms. recent devels. real estate, condominiums, mil. lawyers and probate 1970—), Iowa (coms. mil. affairs and prison reform 1968—), Polk County (coms. ethics and grievance 1963-69) bar assns., Delta Theta Phi, Omicron Delta Kappa, Psi Chi, Tau Kappa Epsilon, Phi Eta Sigma. Mason (Shriner), Kiwanian. Clubs: Des Moines, Des Moines Golf and Country; Embassy; Morning (pres. 1964). Home: 3901 SW 28th Pl Des Moines IA 50321 Office: Suite 300 Fleming Bldg Des Moines IA 50309

SIMPSON, WILLIAM GAIL, dentist; b. LaJunta, Colo., Dec. 6, 1936; s. Alvin Gail and Cecil Ruth (Miller) S.; B.A., Union Coll., Lincoln, Nebr., 1960; D.D.S., U. Nebr., 1965; m. Thelma Lane Anders, Aug. 23, 1959; children—Steven Dean, Susan Kay, Michael Anders. Gen. practice dentistry, Kearney, Nebr., 1969—. Served with U.S. Navy, 1965-69. Mem. Am., Nebr. dental assns., Airplane Owners and Pilots Assn. Presbyterian. Clubs: Elks, Optimist. Home: 11 Lakeview Dr Kearney NE 68847 Office: 111 W 31st St Kearney NE 68847

SIMPSON, WILLIAM STEWART, psychiatrist, psychoanalyst; b. Edmonton, Alta., Can., Apr. 11, 1924; s. William Edward and Ethel Lillian (Stewart) S.; came to U.S., 1950, naturalized, 1963; B.Sc., U. Alta., 1946, M.D., 1948; m. Eleanor Elizabeth Whitbread, June 17, 1950; children—David Kenneth, Ian Stewart, James William, Bert Edward. Rotating intern U. Alta. Hosp., 1948-49, resident internal medicine, 1949-50; resident psychiatry Topeka State Hosp., fellow Menninger Sch. Psychiatry, 1950-53; asst. sect. chief Topeka State Hosp., 1953-54, clin. dir., 1954-59; chief C. F. Menninger Meml. Hosp., 1959-66, dir. edn., 1963-66; asso. dir. Menninger Sch. Psychiatry, 1966-68; clin. dir. Topeka State Hosp., 1968-72; dir. field services Menninger Found., 1972-74; chief psychiatry service, psychiat. residency tng. program Topeka VA Hosp., 1974-77; faculty mem. Menninger Sch. Psychiatry, 1953—, mem. exec. com., 1954-59, 63-72, mem. mgmt. com., 1974-77; mem. dean's com. Topeka VA Hosp., 1976-77; mem. faculty Ann. Seminar Inst. on Alcoholism, U. Wis., 1973-74; cons. Topeka State Hosp., 1967-68, Osawatomie State Hosp., 1954-68. Bd. dirs. Topeka Civic Symphony Soc., 1953-55, Topeka People to People Council, 1963-66; mem. Kans. Citizen's Adv. Com. on Alcoholism, 1973—; founder Topeka Affiliate Nat. Council on Alcoholism, 1964, pres., dir., 1964, dir. N.Y.C., 1967, v.p., 1971-73, pres., 1973-75, mem. exec. com., 1967, Bronze Key award, 1972, Silver Key award, 1975. Diplomate Am. Bd. Psychiatry and Neurology, Topeka Inst. Psychoanalysis. Recipient Achievement award U. Alta. Med. Alumni Assn., 1975. Fellow Am. Psychiat. Assn.; mem. Am. Psychoanalytic Assn., AMA, Am. Med. Soc. on Alcoholism, Kans. Psychiat. Soc., Kans., Shawnee County med. socs., Topeka Psychoanalytic Soc. Presbyterian. Club: Rotary (Topeka). Asso. editor Bull. Menninger Clinic, 1963-70. Home: 834 Buchanan St Topeka KS 66606 Office: PO Box 829 Topeka KS 66601 also 2200 Gage St Topeka KS 66622

SIMS, EUGENE RALPH, JR., indsl. engr.; b. N.Y.C., Oct. 12, 1920; s. Eugene Ralph and Rose (Simmons) S.; B.Adminstrv. Engring, N.Y. U., 1947; m. Ethel Jane Smith, June 8, 1945; children—Pamela Jeanne, Gary Wardner, Phyllis Anne. Tool, instrument maker Sperry Gyroscope Co., N.Y.C., 1939-43; research test engr. N.Y. U., 1947; cons. indsl. engr. Drake, Startzman, Sheahan, Barclay, Inc., N.Y.C., 1947-49; plant mgr. Lit Bros. Warehouse & Furniture Plant, Phila., 1949-50; project indsl. engr. Jeffrey Mfg. Co., Columbus, Ohio, 1950-51; prin. indsl. engr., mgmt. ops. research Battelle Meml. Inst., Columbus, 1951-54; corp. materials handling engr. Anchor Hocking Glass Corp., Lancaster, Ohio, 1954-56; chief indsl. engr., asso. Alden E. Stilson & Assos. Ltd., Columbus, 1956-58; pres. E. Ralph Sims, Jr. & Assos., Inc., Lancaster, 1958—, Fairhill Devel. Corp., 1966—. Mem. Ohio State Tech. Service Council, 1966-72, Lancaster Bd. Zoning Appeals, 1966-68; active Boy Scouts Am., YMCA. Served to 1st lt. USAAF, 1943-46. Registered profl. engr., Ohio, Wis., N.Y., Pa., Calif. Mem. Fairfield County Engrs. Soc., ASME, Am. Inst. Indsl. Engrs., Brit. Inst. Mech. Engrs., Inst. Mgmt. Cons. (founding mem., dir.), Assn. Mgmt. Cons.'s (past pres.), Nat. Soc. Profl. Engrs., Am. Mgmt. Assn., Air Force Assn. (charter mem.), Nat. Council Phys. Distbn. Mgmt., Psi Upsilon. Club: Masons (32 deg.). Author: Planning and Managing Material Flow, 1968; Euphonious Coding, 1967; Contemporary Comment in Retrospect, 1973; author numerous trade jour. articles; monthly column in mag.; cons. editor Materials Handling Engring. mag.; contbg. editor Production Handbook, 1958; Materials Handling Handbook, 1958; Business Management Handbook, 1967. Home: 114 Luther Ln Lancaster OH 43130 Office: 919 E Fair Ave Lancaster OH 43130 also Halterson House George Ln London England

SIMS, MARVIN HARDING, dentist; b. Nashville, Feb. 2, 1926; s. Chester Dewey and Violet Myrtle (Pettit) S.; D.D.S., U. Detroit, 1956; m. Dorothy Willodene Scott, Feb. 14, 1947. Individual dental practice, Detroit, 1956-58, Livonia, Mich., 1958-75; sec., dir. Dental Service Plans Ins. Co., 1970—. Mem. Am. Dental Polit. Action Com., 1970—, Dentist Investing in Active Legislation, 1968—. Bd. dirs. Oak Hills Home for Girls, Royal Oak, Mich., 1964-70, treas., 1964-69; bd. dirs. Delta Dental Plan of Mich., 1965-74, treas., 1966-69, pres., 1970-74, dental dir., 1975—; bd. dirs. Mich. Christian Coll., Rochester, 1976—. Served with USNR, 1944-46. Fellow Am. Coll. Dentists, Royal Soc. Health, Internat. Coll. Dentists; mem. Western (pres. 1964), Detroit Dist. (award merit 1971, pres. 1973, editorial bd. Jour. 1969-71, asst. editor 1970-71) dental socs., Am., (alternate del. 1969-73), Mich. (del. constn. conv. 1969-70) dental assns. Home: 18893 Milburn Ave Livonia MI 48152

SINCLAIR, FRANK LOUIS, educator; b. Lansing, Mich., Jan. 20, 1924; s. Arthur A. and Hattie (Schurr) S.; B.S., Mich. State Normal Coll., 1950; M.S., Mich. State U., 1955; postgrad. Wayne State U., 1958-60, U. Mich., 1964-72; m. Barbara I. Munson, Nov. 7, 1945; children—Sandra Ann Sinclair McCourt, Bonnie Lee Sinclair Rapson, Frank Jay, Arthur Munson. Sci. tchr. Fraser-Cady Pub. Schs., Fraser, Mich., 1950-51; tchr., head sci. dept. Breckenridge (Mich.) Pub. Schs., 1951-55; supervising tchr. sci. Lincoln Consol. Lab. Sch., Eastern Mich. U., Ypsilanti, 1955-64, asso. prof. biology, 1964—, dir. Kresge Environ. Edn. Center; cons. environ. edn., 1967—. Served with USNR, 1943-46. Mem. AAAS, Am. Assn. Higher Edn., Nat. Sci. Tchrs. Assn., Midwest Coll. Biology Tchrs. Assn., Mich. Acad. Sci., Arts and Letters, Conservation Edn. Assn., Mich. Environ. Edn. Assn., Kappa Delta Phi. Contbr. articles to profl. jours. Home: 5765 Country Ln Ypsilanti MI 48197 Office: Kresge Environ Edn Center 2816 Fish Lake Rd Lapeer MI 48446

SINCLAIR, ORRIETTE COINER, Republican nat. committeewoman; b. Twin Falls, Idaho, Sept. 17, 1921; d. Walter A. and Marietta Hunsberger (Detweiler) Coiner; student U. Utah, 1939-40; B.S., U. Idaho, 1943; m. James A. Sinclair, Apr. 21, 1946; children—Rose Ann Sinclair Astorquia, Judy Sinclair Imlay, Jan Sinclair Johanson, Walt. With Bur. Entomology, 1944; dep. clk. Dist. Ct., 1945; with E.W. McRoberts Securities, 1946. Past pres. high sch. P.T.A. Pres., Young Womens Republican Club, 1954-63; mem. Idaho Rep. Com., 1966-70, vice chmn., 1966; Rep. nat. committeewoman for Idaho, 1971—. Mem. Am. Legion Aux., (pres. 1975-77), P.E.O., Kappa Kappa Gamma. Toastmistress (pres. Twin Falls). Home: PO Box 249 Twin Falls ID 83301

SINCLAIR, ROBERT EWALD, physician; b. Columbus, O., Jan. 19, 1924; s. George Albert and Bertha Florence (Ewald) S.; B.A., Ohio State U., 1948, M.D., 1952; m. Mary Almyra Underwood, Mar. 31, 1945; children—Marcia Ann Sinclair, Bonnie Sue Sinclair. Intern, Mt. Carmel Hosp., Columbus, 1952-53; resident Columbus State Hosp., 1964-66, chief psychiat. resident adolescent unit, 1965-66; pvt. practice medicine, Columbus, 1953-57, Granville, 1957-64; resident neurology and psychiatry Ohio Dept. Mental Health, 1964-66; dir. student health service, prof. health edn. team physician Denison U., 1957-64; dir. student health service, prof. health edn., team physician U. Cin., 1966-70; dir. Lafene Student Health Center and Univ. Hosp., team physician Kans. State U., Manhattan, 1970—; co. physician Westinghouse Electric Corp., Columbus, O., 1953-57. Asst. zone chief Civilian Def., Columbus, 1954-57; mem. Licking County (O.) Bd. Health, 1958-59. Bd. dirs. social health com. Cin., and Hamilton County, O., 1967-70, drug abuse and edn. com., 1968-70. Served with USNR, 1943-46. Mem. Am., Ohio med. assns., Kans., Riley County med. socs., Columbus Acad. Medicine, Licking County Med. Soc., Nat. Athletic Trainers Assn., Ohio Coll. (editor Newsletter 1968-70, pres. 1970-71), Central Coll. (pres. 1972—) health assns., Delta Tau Delta, Nu Sigma Nu, Nu Sigma Nu Alumni Assn. (pres. 1953-54) Lutheran. Home: 300 Fordham Rd Manhattan KS 66502 Office: Lafene Health Center Kansas State U Manhattan KS 66502

SINCLAIR, WARREN KEITH, physicist; b. Dunedin, N.Z., Mar. 9, 1924; s. Ernest W. and Jessie E. (Craig) S.; came to U.S., 1954, naturalized, 1959; B.Sc., U. Otago (N.Z.), 1944, M.Sc., 1945; Ph.D., U. London, 1950; m. Elizabeth J. Edwards, Mar. 19, 1948; children—Bruce W., Roslyn E., Allen. Radiol. physicist U. Otago, 1945-47; radiol. physicist U. London, Royal Marsden Hosp., 1947-54; prof., chmn. dept. physics U. Tex., M.D. Anderson Hosp., 1954-60; sr. biophysicist Argonne (Ill.) Nat. Lab., 1960—, div. dir., 1970-74, asso. lab. dir., 1974—; prof. radiation biology U. Chgo., 1964—; mem. Internat. Commn. on Radiation Units and Measurements, 1969—, Internat. Commn. on Radiol. Protection, 1977—; dir. Nat. Council on Radiation Protection and Measurements, 1967—, pres., 1977—; sec. gen. 5th Internat. Congress Radiation Research, 1974. Served with N.Z. Army, 1942-43. Nat. N.Z. scholar, 1942-45. Fellow Inst. Physics; mem. Am. Assn. Physicists in Medicine (pres. 1961-62), Radiation Research Soc. (council 1964-67, pres. 1978—), Brit. Inst. Radiology (council 1953-54), Internat. Assn. Radiation Research (council 1966-70, 74—), Radiol. Soc. N.Am., Biophys. Soc., Soc. Nuclear Medicine. Club: Innominates (U. Chgo.). Contbr. numerous articles to profl. jours., also chpts. to books. Home: 1419 87th St Downers Grove IL 60515 Office: 9700 S Cass Ave Argonne IL 60439

SINENENG, ROLANDO SUNPONGCO, physician; b. Philippines, May 3, 1943; s. Felipe T. and Estella T. (Sunpongco) S.; came to U.S., 1967; A.A., U. Philippines, 1961, M.D., 1967; m. Leda J. Laureta, June 25, 1971; children—Rolando L., Philip B. Intern, St. Michael Hosp., Milw., 1967-68; resident in medicine and liver diseases N.J. Coll. Medicine Hosp., 1968-72; fellow gastroenterology Bridgeport (Conn.) Hosp., 1972-73; staff gastroenterologist VA Hosp., Dayton, Ohio, 1974; practice medicine specializing in gastroenterology, Dayton, 1975—; mem. staff Miami Valley Hosp., Good Samaritan Hosp.; clin. asst. prof. medicine Wright State U. Med. Sch., Dayton. Diplomate Am. Bd. Internal Medicine. Mem. Ohio, Montgomery County med. socs., Philippine Med. Assn. Roman Catholic. Home: 5294 Brooklawn Ct Dayton OH 45429 Office: 2661 Salem Ave Dayton OH 45406

SING, ERIC JOHN, educator; b. Agra, India, Oct. 9, 1936; s. Walter Mashi and Lilly (Singh) S.; came to U.S., 1963, naturalized, 1971; M.S., Agra U., 1957; Ph.D., U. Allahalead, 1962. Research asso. N.W. Inst. for Med. Research, Chgo., 1964-69; research asso., asso. prof. dept. obstetrics and gynecology, U. Chgo., 1969-74, Northwestern U., 1977—. Abstractor, Chem. Abstracts Service, Columbus, O., 1964—. Fellow Harry S. Truman Library Inst.; mem. Am. Oil Chemists Soc., A.A.A.S., Royal Inst. Chemistry (London) (asso.), Fedn. Am. Scientist, N.Y. Acad. Scis. Republican. Episcopalian. Contbr. articles to profl. jours. Home: 5500 South Shore Dr Chicago IL 60637

SINGER, DEREK STAUGHTON, TV exec.; b. N.Y.C., May 25, 1929; s. A. Alexander and Olive Catherine (Lathbridge) S.; B.A., N.Y. U., 1952; M.A., Johns Hopkins U., 1953; Ph.D., U. Md., 1972; m. Ruth Chaikin Sorensen, July 9, 1954; children—Victoria, Alex, Theodore, Jason. Dir. relief and nutrition programs CARE, Inc., Colombia and Bolivia, 1954-56; adminstr. overseas devel. AID and Peace Corps, Asia, Latin Am. and Africa, 1956-66; ednl. cons. UN, Washington Asia, Latin Am., Africa, 1966-73; research and devel., producer, writer WTTW, Chgo. Pub. TV, 1973—; asst. prof. Northeastern Ill. U., Roosevelt U. Asso. Wilmette United Fund, 1975; vice chmn., bd. mem. Lakeshore Unitarian Soc. Recipient Meritorious Service award AID, 1961. Served with USMC, 1946. Mem. UN Assn. (local and state v.p.), Nat. Acad. TV Arts and Scis., Soc. Internat. Devel., Am. Soc. Pub. Adminstrn., Phi Beta Kappa. Democrat. Contbr. articles on TV, higher edn. and world devel. to periodicals. Exec. producer, prodn. coordinator 2 TV spls., As We See It series. Home: 15 Crescent Pl Wilmette IL 60091 Office: 5400 N Saint Louis Ave Chicago IL 60625

SINGER, EDWARD J., mfrs. rep.; b. Superior, Wis., Sept. 29, 1914; s. Samuel N. and Lena H. (Dorf) S.; A.B., George Washington U., 1941; m. Sylvia E. Rivkin, Oct. 12, 1945; children—Myra J. Singer Neviaser, Norma E. Singer Portnoy. With Reconstrn. Fin. Corp., 1934-53, asst. sec. RFC Mortgage Co., 1941, sec., 1941-43, asst. sec. Defense Homes Corp., 1941-42, asst. sec. War Damage Corp., 1941-43, asst. sec. Rubber Devel. Corp., 1943-44, sec. RFC Price Adjustment Bd., 1943-53, asst. sec. Disaster Loan Corp., 1944-45, asst. sec. Mortgage Co., Fed. Nat. Mortgage Assn. and War Damage Corp., 1944-53, asst. sec. RFC, Washington, 1945-53; pres. Edward J. Singer Assos., Cleve., 1953—. Address: 2670 Green Rd Shaker Heights OH 44122

SINGH, BALJIT, educator; b. Budaun, India, Oct. 1, 1929; s. Sardar Baboo and Kartar (Kaur) S.; came to U.S., 1957, naturalized, 1966; B.A., Agra U., 1951; M.A., Aligarh U. (India), 1953; postgrad. (Ford Found. fellow), U. Pa., 1957-58; Ph.D., U. Md., 1961; m. Barbara Leona Hassler, Aug. 11, 1962; children—Balkrishna, Balram. Lectr. polit. sci. U. Baroda (India), 1953-55; research fellow Indian Sch. Internat. Studies, New Delhi, 1955-57; research asst. Embassy of India, Washington, 1958; asst. prof. polit. sci. Mich. State U., East Lansing, 1961-62, 63-65, asso. prof., 1965-71, prof., 1971—, asst. dean Coll. Social Sci., 1967—; asst. prof. polit. sci. Wayne State U., Detroit, 1962-63. Served to 2d lt. Indian Army, 1954-58. Asia Found. fellow, 1961. Mem. Internat. Studies Assn., Am. Polit. Sci. Assn., Mich. Acad. Sci., Arts and Letters (program chmn. history and polit. sci. sect. 1966), Pi Sigma Alpha, Delta Phi Epsilon. Author: (with Ko-Wang Mei) The Theory and Practice of Modern Guerrilla Warfare, 1971; Indian Foreign Policy: An Analysis, 1975. Contbr. articles to profl. jours. Home: 2400 Tulane Dr Lansing MI 48912 Office: Coll Social Sci Michigan State U 205 Berkey Hall East Lansing MI 48824

SINGH, MADAN MOHAN, mining engr.; b. Quetta, Pakistan, Nov. 8, 1933; s. Mohan and Inder (Kaur) S.; came to U.S., 1956, naturalized, 1967; AISM, Indian Sch. of Mines and Applied Geology, 1956; M.S., U. Ill., 1957; Ph.D., U. Pa., 1961; m. Sartaj Inder Kaur, Aug. 19, 1964. Research engr. Gulf Research & Devel. Co., Harmasville, Pa., 1961-63; asst. prof. mining engring. Pa. State U., Univ. Park, 1963-66, also dir. Rock Minerals Lab., 1963-66; mgr. soil and rock mechanics Ill. Inst. Tech., Chgo., 1966-74; v.p. mining Found Scis., Inc., Lombard, Ill., 1974-75; pres. Engrs. Internat., Inc., Downers Grove, Ill., 1976—; cons. to U.S. Bur. of Mines, 1964-66, Morton Salt Co., 1967-68, Atlantic Richfield Co., 1964-65; elected to U.S. Nat. Com. on Tunneling Tech., 1974-76, U.S. Nat. Com. Rock Mechanics, 1977. Mem. Soc. of Petroleum Engrs., Internat. Soc. Rock Mechanics, ASTM (chmn. com. 1968-78), Soc. of Mining Engrs., Am. Underground Assn., Ill. Mining Inst., AAAS, ASCE, Brit. Tunneling Soc., Sigma Xi. Contbr. numerous articles on mining engring. to profl. jours. Home: 1105 Barberry Ct Downers Grove IL 60515 Office: 2514 Wisconsin Ave Downers Grove IL 60515

SINGLETON, MARVIN AYERS, physician, real estate broker, bus. exec.; b. Baytown, Tex., Oct. 7, 1939; s. Henry Marvin and Mary Ruth (Mitchell) S.; B.A., U. of the South, 1962; M.D., U. Tenn., 1966. Intern, City of Memphis Hosps., 1966-67; resident in surgery Highland Alameda City Hosp., Oakland, Calif., 1967-68, resident in otolaryngology U. Tenn. Hosp., Memphis, 1968-71; Am. Acad. Otolaryngology and Ophthalmology fellow in otolaryngic pathology Armed Forces Inst. Pathology, Washington, 1971; fellow in otologic surgery U. Colo. at Gallup (N.Mex.) Indian Med. Center, 1972; practice medicine specializing in otolaryngology and allergies, Joplin, Mo., 1972—; founder, operator Home and Farm Investments, Joplin, 1975—, Video Systems, Joplin, 1977—; staff mem. Freeman Hosp., St. John's Hosp., Joplin; cons. in otolaryngology Parsons (Kans.) State Hosp. and Tng. Center, Mo. Crippled Children's Service, Santa Fe R.R. Served with USNG, 1966-72. Diplomate Am. Bd. Otolaryngology, Am. Bd. Otorhinolaryngology. Fellow A.C.S., Am. Acad. Otolaryngology and Ophthalmology, Am. Acad. Ophthalmologic and Otolaryngologic Allergy, Am. Coll. Otorhinolaryngologists, Am. Assn. Clin. Immunology and Allergy; mem. AMA, Mo. State, So., Jasper County med. assns., Council of Otolaryngology, Mo. State Allergy Assn., Ear, Nose and Throat Soc. Mo., Joplin C. of C., Sigma Alpha Epsilon, Phi Theta Kappa, Phi Chi. Episcopalian. Clubs: Kiwanis, Elks. Contbr. articles in field to profl.

jours. Home: Five Mile Ranch Route 2 Box 138 Seneca MO 64856 Office: 114 W 32d St Joplin MO 64801

SINHA, PRAMILLA, obstetrician and gynecologist; b. Punjab, India, Nov. 9, 1937; d. Ramesh Chander and Savitri (Devi) Saxena; came to U.S., 1966; M.D., Govt. Med. Coll., Patiala, India, 1959; m. Surendra K. Sinha, Dec. 4, 1960; children—Sujata, Samir. House obstet. intern, Patiala, India, 1960-61; asst. lady surgeon Gwalior M.P., India, 1962-66; rotating intern S.I. Hosp., 1966-67, resident in obstetrics and gynecology, 1967-68; resident in obstetrics and gynecology Highland Park (Mich.) Gen. Hosp., 1968-70; resident in gen. surgery Oakwood Gen. Hosp., Dearborn, Mich., 1970-71; staff physician in obstetrics and gynecology Met. Hosp., Detroit, 1972—. Diplomate Am., Canadian bds. obstetrics and gynecology. Fellow A.C.S., Royal Coll. Surgeons of Can., Am. Coll. Obstetrics and Gynecology. Home: 17567 Lincoln Dr Southfield MI 48706 Office: Metropolitan Hospital 1800 Tuxedo Ave Detroit MI 48206

SINK, ALVA GORDON (MRS. CHARLES A. SINK), civic worker; b. Rose Twp., Mich.; d. Nathaniel J. and Ella M. (Highfield) Gordon; student Eastern Mich. U., summers 1914, 18; A.B., U. Mich., 1923; m. Charles A. Sink, June 18, 1923 (dec.). Tchr. pub. schs., Rose Center, Mich., 1914-17, Hickory Ridge, Mich., 1917-18, Holly, Mich., 1918-19, Canfield Pvt. Sch., Ann Arbor, Mich., 1919-22. Bd. dirs. Faculty Women's Club, 1940-42; dir. Washtenaw County chpt. A.R.C., 1943-48, 53-59, in charge First Aid and Accident Prevention, 1941-61; pres. Mich. House and Senate Club, 1929-30, U. Mich. Alumnae Club, 1931-33, Sara Browne Smith Group Alumnae Club, 1957-59, Woman's Soc. Congl. Ch., 1946-48; regent Sarah Caswell Angell chpt., D.A.R., 1955-57. Recipient Red Cross citation, 1959; Alumnae Council award U. Mich., 1971; Alva Gordon Sink Group of U. Mich. Alumnae named in her honor. Trustee Women's City Club, 1954-57. Mem. French Huguenots, A.A.U.W., Ann Arbor Art Assn., P.E.O. Clubs: Art Study, Garden, Faculty Women, Women's Republican (Ann Arbor); Presidents, Emeritus (pres. 1975-76) (U. Mich.) Home: 1325 Olivia Ave Ann Arbor MI 48104

SINNER, JAKE, heating, air conditioning co. exec.; b. Lincoln, Nebr., Oct. 11, 1920; s. August and Anna Margaret (Krumm) S.; ed. pub. schs., Lincoln; m. Dorothy Hill, July 12, 1941; children—Gary Lee (dec.), Joyce Ann Eisenman. With Cornhusker Heating & Air Conditioning Co., Lincoln, 1954—. Served as chief warrant officer inf., U.S., Army, 1942-46, CE, 1950-54. Mem. Lincoln Heating and Air Conditioning Assn. (pres. 1961-62), Lincoln Builders Bur. (dir. 1971), Sheet Metal Air Conditioning Nat. Assn., Am. Inst. Plant Engrs., Am. Soc. Heating, Air Conditioning and Refrigeration Engrs., Footprinters Assn., Am. Hist. Soc. Germans from Russia (internat. v.p.), Am. Forward Soc., Welfare Soc., VFW, DAV, Am. Legion. Democrat. Mem. United Ch. Christ. Home: 3115 Kucera Dr Lincoln NE 68502 Office: 2959 Cornhusker Hwy PO Box 81712 Lincoln NE 68501

SINNINGER, DWIGHT VIRGIL, research engr.; b. Bourbon, Ind., Dec. 29, 1901; s. Norman E. and Myra (Huff) S.; student Armour Inst., 1928, U. Chgo., 1942, Northwestern, 1943; m. Coyla Annetta Annis, Mar. 1, 1929. Electronics research engr. Johnson Labs., Chgo., 1935-42; chief engr. Pathfinder Radio Corp., 1943-44, Rowe Engring. Corp., 1945-48, Pioneer Electric & Research Corp., Forest Park, Ill., 1948-56, Hupp Electronics div. Hupp Corp., 1956-58; pres. Senn Custom, Inc., Oak Park, Ill.; dir. research Pioneer Electric & Research Corp., Forest Park, Ill., 1958-65; dir. Rowe Engring. Corp. Registered profl. engr., Ill. Mem. A.I.M., Inst. Radio Engrs., Instrument Soc. Am., Armed Forces Communications Assn. Holder several U.S. patents. Home: PO Box 1 Oak Park IL 60303 Office: 7542 Adams St Forest Park IL 60130

SINOR, DENIS, orientalist; b. Kolozsvar, Hungary, Apr. 17, 1916; s. Miklos and Marguerite (Weitzenfeld) S.; B.A., U. Budapest, 1938; M.A., U. Cambridge (Eng.), 1948. Asst., Institut des Hautes Etudes Chinoises, U. Paris, 1941-45; attaché de recherches Centre de la Recherche Scientifique, Paris, 1946-48; lectr. Cambridge U., 1948-62; prof. Uralic and Altaic studies and history Ind. U., Bloomington, 1962—, distinguished prof., 1975—; chmn. dept. Uralic and Altaic studies, 1963—; dir. U.S. Office of Edn. Uralic and Inner Asian Lang. and Area Center, 1963—, dir. research projects, 1969-70; dir. Asian Studies Research Inst., 1967—. Guggenheim fellow, 1968-69; D. hon. causa, U. Szeged, 1971; recipient grants Am. Council Learned Socs., 1962, Am. Philos. Soc., 1963. Fellow Korosi Csoma Soc. (hon.); mem. Am. Oriental Soc. (pres. 1975-76), Permanent Internat. Altaistic Conf. (sec. gen. 1960—), Royal Asiatic Soc. Gt. Britain and Ireland (hon. sec. 1952-62), Societas Uralo Altaica (v.p. 1964—), Assn. Asian Studies (chmn. devel. com. Inner Asian studies 1973—), Am. Oriental Soc. (chmn. Inner Asian regional com. 1968—), Tibet Soc. (pres. 1967-69), Mongolia Soc. (chmn. bd. 1964—), Internat. Union Orientalists (past sec.), Am. Hist. Assn., Société Asiatique, Société de Linguistique, Deutsche Morgenlandische Gesellschaft. Clubs: United Oxford and Cambridge U. (London); Cosmos (Washington). Served with Forces Françaises de l'Interieur, 1943-44, French Army, 1944-45. Author: Introduction à l'étude de l'Eurasie Centrale, 1963; History of Hungary, 1959; Inner Asia, 1969; Modern Hungary, 1977; Inner Asia and Its Contact With Medieval Europe, 1977; contbr. articles to profl. jours.; editor Jour. Asian History, 1967—. Home: 5581E Lampkins Ridge Bloomington IN 47401 Office: Uralic Altaic Studies Dept Ind Univ Bloomington IN 47401

SIOMOPOULOS, VASILIS KONSTANTINOS, psychiatrist; b. Paramythia, Greece, June 23, 1938; s. Konstantinos V. and Aspasia M. (Kajanji) S.; came to U.S., 1964; M.D. (Bros. Zosima scholar), Athens U., 1962; m. Magda Georgacopoulou, Feb. 23, 1964; children—Christina, Anna. Intern, West Suburban Hosp., Oak Park, Ill., 1964-65; resident psychiatry Ill. State Psychiat. Inst., Chgo., 1965-68, research trainee, 1968-69, staff psychiatrist, 1969—. Cons., Adult and Guidance Clinic, St. Francis Hosp., Evanston, Ill., 1972—, Day Center, Ravenswood Hosp., Chgo., 1972—; asst. clin. prof. psychiatry U. Ill., Abraham Lincoln Sch. Medicine, 1972—. Mem. Am. Psychiat. Assn. A.M.A., Ill. Psychiat. Soc., Chgo. Med. Soc., A.A.A.S. Research, publs. in field. Home: 1710 Riverside Ct Glenview IL 60025 Office: 1601 W Taylor St Chicago IL 60612

SIPES, GERALD EUGENE, chemist; b. Scottsburg, Ind., Jan. 15, 1939; s. George Stanley and Lillia Pearl (Sipes) S.; A.B., Ind. Central U., 1961; M.S., U. Ill., 1963, Ph.D., 1969. Analytical chemist R.J. Reynolds Tobacco Co., Winston-Salem, N.C., 1969-70, Swift and Co., Oak Brook, Ill., 1970-71; chemist Chas. Martin Insps. Petroleum, Argo, Ill., 1972-73, dir. labs, 1973—. Mem. Am. Chem. Soc., ASTM, Am. Oil Chemists Soc., Soc. Applied Spectroscopy, Sigma Xi. Home: 1444 Carriage Ln Westmont IL 60559 Office: PO Box 402 Argo IL 60501

SIPIERA, PAUL PETER, JR., educator; b. Chgo., Nov. 30, 1948; s. Paul P. and Frances A. (Blazejack) S.; B.A., Northeastern Ill. U., 1971; M.S., Northeastern Ill., 1975. Instr. geology and astronomy Aurora (Ill.) Coll., part-time 1974-77; research asso. Center for Meteorite Studies, Ariz. State U., Tempe, summers 1974, 75, 76; instr. geology and phys. sci. Harper Coll., Palatine, Ill., 1974—; research asso. Field Mus. Natural History, Chgo., 1976—; sci. cons. Young Peoples Sic. Ency. for Children's Press, 1977-78. Recipient Research award Ill. State Acad. Sci., 1975, 77; Nininger Meteorite Research award, 1975; Harper Coll. grantee, 1976-77. Mem. The Meteoritical Soc., Ill. State Acad. Sci., Chgo. Acad. Sci., Sigma Xi, Phi Alpha Theta. Roman Catholic. Contbr. articles in field to profl. jours. Home: 5635 S Newland Ave Chicago IL 60638 Office: William Rainey Harper Coll Dept Geology and Phys Sci Algonquin and Roselle Rds Palatine IL 60067

SIPPY, RODNEY EDWARD, dentist; b. Chgo., Feb. 2, 1934; s. Everett Tunis and Helen Marie (Rydell) S.; student Purdue U., 1952-54; B.S., U. Ill., 1956, D.D.S., 1960; m. Marilyn Joyce Landis, June 13, 1954 (dec. June 1971); children—Deborah Lynn, Linda Darlene; m. 2d, Polly Palmer Lloyd, Apr. 13, 1974; children—Joseph William, Mellisa Palmer. Practice dentistry, LaGrange, Ill., 1960—; mem. attending staff Community Meml. Gen. Hosp., 1966—, sec. dental staff, 1962-65, chmn. dental staff, 1965-77; mem. staff Hinsdale San., 1968-70; chief dental service Suburban Cook County Tb Sanatorium, 1961-70; clin. instr. dept. prosthetics U. Ill. Coll. Dentistry, 1960-61. Adviser, Tri-County Dental Assts. Soc., Oak Brook, Ill., 1968-69, 73-74. Fellow Royal Soc. Health, Am. Coll. Dentists; mem. Am. Dental Assn., Ill., Chgo., West Suburban (pres. 1977-78) dental socs., Pierre Fauchard Acad., Am. Soc. Preventive Dentistry, Acad. Gen. Dentistry, Fedn. Dentaire Internationale, U. Ill. Alumni Assn. (dir. 1967-71, pres. 1974-75), Far West Study Club, West Suburban C. of C., Delta Sigma Delta. Republican. Clubs: Mason (32 deg.), Shriners, Illini, Progressive (sec. 1970-71, treas. 1968-69, pres. 1974-75). Home: 1324 Laurie Lane Burr Ridge IL 60521 Office: 4727 Willow Springs Rd LaGrange IL 60525

SISLER, MAYNARD LEE, physician, ret. naval officer; b. Massillon, Ohio, Aug. 12, 1923; s. George Turner and Audrey Augusta (Athey) S.; student Washington Missionary Coll., 1939-40, Shepherd State Tchrs. Coll., 1941; B.S., Northwestern U., 1953, M.D., 1956; m. Sandra Ellen Byrd, Mar. 24, 1977; children by previous marriage—Suzanne, Judith, Kathleen, Mary Elizabeth, Maynard Lee, Leandra; 1 stepdau., Kim Wilburn. Intern, Passavant Meml. Hosp., Chgo., 1956-57; resident U.S. Naval Hosp., St. Albans, N.Y., 1958-61; practice medicine specializing in internal medicine, 1957—; commd. lt. M.C., U.S. Navy, 1957, advanced through grades to comdr., 1968; gen. med. officer U.S. Naval Acad., 1957-58; mem. staff U.S. Naval Hosp., Memphis, 1961-63; head gen. medicine U.S. Naval Hosp., San Diego, 1963-66, head sick officer quars., 1968-69; chief of medicine U.S. Naval Hosp., Corpus Christi, 1966-68, ret., 1969; asso. with Med. Group, Internal Medicine Assos., Palm Springs, Calif., 1969-70, Dunmire-Cash Clinic, Kennett, Mo., 1970-73; dir. Saturday Clinic, Parma, Mo., 1973-74. Served with USN, 1941-50. Recipient Freedoms Found. award, 1963, 66, 67; Stitt award U.S. Naval Hosp., San Diego, 1966; diplomate Am. Bd. Internal Medicine. Fellow ACP; mem. Mo. State, Dunklin County med. socs., Royal Soc. of Medicine of London. Author: A Large Slice of Life, Carved Into Poetry, 1974; contbr. numerous poems and essays to various newspapers and mags.; editorial editor Dunklin County Press, 1974—. Home: 217 College Ave Kennett MO 63857

SISMAN, FLORENCE E., export shipping co. exec.; b. Alpena, Mich., May 3, 1916; d. Thomas and Katherine (Nelson) McClatchey; B.A., Mich. State U., 1930; D.Sc., Cleary Coll.; m. Buell A. Sisman, Oct. 29, 1932 (dec. Dec. 1950). Owner, pres. Kennelly & Sisman, Detroit, 1962—. Chmn., Tb and Health Soc., Detroit, 1967; asst. chmn. Project Hope, 1967-69. Mem. Soc. Women Engrs., World Trade Engrs., Soc. Packaging and Handling Engrs. Clubs: Everglades (Palm Beach, Fla.); Grosse Point Yacht (Mich.); Round Table, Lockmoor, Womens City, Economic, Spirit of Detroit Racing Assn. (commodore), Detroit Yacht (Detroit). Home: 17840 E Jefferson St Grosse Point MI 48214 also Ocean Towers Palm Beach FL and Chateau Benefrat Sol Mio Cannes France Office: 563 Lycaste St Detroit MI 48211

SISSON, EVERETT ARNOLD, diversified industry exec.; b. Chgo., Oct. 24, 1920; s. Emmett B. and Norma (Merbitz) S.; A.B., Valparaiso U., 1942; postgrad. Yale, 1944; m. Roberta E. Blauman, Mar. 20, 1943; children—Nancy Lee Genz, Elizabeth Anne Levy. Sales mgr. Ferrotherm Co., Cleve., 1946-51, Osborn Mfg. Co., Cleve., 1951-56; dir. sales Patterson Foundry & Machine Co., E. Liverpool, O., 1956-58; mgr. sonic energy products Bendix Corp., Davenport, Ia., 1958-60; pres., chief exec. officer, dir. Lamb Industries, Inc., Toledo, O., 1960-65, Lehigh Valley Industries, Inc., N.Y.C., 1965-66, Am. Growth Industries, Inc., Chgo., 1966—, Workman Mfg. Co., Chgo., 1966-69, Am. Growth Devel. Corp., Chgo., 1968—, Am. Growth Mgmt. Corp., Oak Brook, Ill., 1970—, Oak Brook Club Co., 1969—; chmn. Hausske Harlen Furniture Mfg. Co., Peru, Ind., 1976—; dir. Luth. Mut. Life Ins. Co., Waverly, Iowa, Libco Corp., Lincolnwood, Ill. Pres. council, Mayfield Heights, O., 1952-57. Adviser to bd. trustees Valparaiso U., 1960-69; bd. regents Cal. Luth. Coll. Served to capt. USAAF, 1943-46. Fellow Cal. Luth. Coll.; mem. Am. Mgmt. Assn., Cleve. Engring. Soc., President's Assn., Tau Kappa Epsilon. Club: Oak Brook. Home: 1405 Burr Ridge Club Dr Burr Ridge IL 60521 Office: 16th St and Spring Rd Oak Brook IL 60521

SISSON, HAROLD LEROY, dentist; b. Waterloo, Iowa, Mar. 2, 1907; s. Leroy Wallace and Martha Melvina (Snow) S.; student U. No. Iowa, 1925-28; D.D.S., State U. Ia., 1932; m. Helen Irene Boeddeker, Aug. 8, 1934; children—Phyllis Marie (Mrs. John L. Kestel, Jr.), Mary Helen (Mrs. Stephen F. True), Virginia Ruth, Joseph Harold. Gen. practice dentistry, Waterloo, 1932-73. Astronomer counselor Boy Scouts Am., 1962—; commr. Waterloo Park Commn., 1957, 60-66; mem. Urban Renewal bd., 1959-76; vice chmn. C.E. Flood Control Project, 1959-70, chmn., 1970-76; mem. lay sch. bd. Columbus High Sch., 1966-70, chmn., 1969-70. Served with U.S. Army, 1942-46. Mem. Am. (life), Ia. (life) dental assns., Waterloo (pres. 1940-41), Waterloo Dist. (sec. 1936-42, pres., 1948) dental socs., Soc. Mayflower Descs., Gt. Plains Astron. Soc. (sect. pres. 1958), Waterloo C. of C., Am. Legion, Omicron Kappa Upsilon. Elk. Home: 405 E Dale St Waterloo IA 50703

SITTARD, HERMAN JOSEPH, journalist; b. New Ulm, Minn., June 17, 1919; s. Cornelius and Margaret Ellen (Milch) S.; B.A., U. Minn., 1947; m. Lillian Ruth Russell, June 12, 1948; children—Margaret (Mrs. Michael Schwingle), Susan, Paul, Stephen, Michael, Robert, Patricia, Christopher. War corr. St. Paul Dispatch-Pioneer Press, South Pacific and Far East, 1943-45; reporter, columnist, photographer Rochester (Minn.) Post-Bulletin, 1947-51; editor Richfield News, Bloomington News, Mpls., 1951; asst. editor Cath. Digest Mag., St. Paul, 1951-56; picture editor Mpls. Star, 1956, edn. reporter, 1956-60, spl. projects reporter, 1960-61, gen. assignment reporter, 1961-64, editor Star World Affairs program, 1959-62; dir. pub. information Hennepin County Govt., Mpls., 1964-73; pres. Herm Sittard & Assos., Profl. Communicators, St. Paul, 1974—. Lectr. journalism U. Minn., Mpls., 1960—. Bd. dirs. Vols. Am., Minn. Served to capt. U.S. Army, 1943-45. Decorated Bronze Star, Bronze Arrowhead. Recipient 1st place award Editor and Publisher mag., 1960, Mike Halloran award Mpls. Star, 1956, 58, Page One award Newspaper Guild, 1964, award A.P., 1950. Mem. Nat. Assn. Pub. Information Officers (pres. 1968-70), Am. Newspaper Guild (local sec.-treas. 1947-48), Citizen's League, Nat. Assn. County Information Officers (pres. 1968-70, regional dir. 1970-72), Nat. Assn. Counties (bd. dirs. 1968-70), Pub. Relations Soc. Am. (exec. com. govt. sect. 1974—, Midwest regional chmn. 1974—), Sigma Delta Chi, Guild Cath. Choirmasters and Organists (chpt. pres. 1955-56), Am. Guild Organists (chpt. exec. bd. 1954-57). Roman Cath. (choirmaster 1954—). Clubs: Minnesota Press (bd. dirs. 1969-71, chmn. edn. com. 1969-71), Rochester Music (pres. 1949-50), St. Paul Rostrum (treas. 1952-53), St. Paul Athletic. Editor: Hennepin Today, 1968. Composer: That Christmas Long Ago, 1956. Home: 691 Lincoln Ave St Paul MN 55105 Office: 691 Lincoln Ave St Paul MN 55105

SITTLER, EDWIN CONRAD, mgmt. co. exec.; b. Keokuk, Iowa, Apr. 12, 1907; s. Joseph and Katherine (Wirtz) S.; B.S., U. Iowa, 1929; m. Lois Monks, Feb. 3, 1973; children by previous marriage—Susan, Edwin, Virginia, Penelope. Research engr. Frigidaire div. Gen. Motors Corp., Dayton, Ohio, 1929-36; research engr., asst. sales mgr. Liebel Flars Heim, Cin., 1936-42; supt. Chgo. Intensive Treatment Center, 1942-45; asst. sanitarian USPHS assigned to Chgo. Bd. Health, 1942-45; v.p., Sittler Corp., pres. Sittler Sales Engring. Corp. (both Chgo.), 1945—; dir. DuPage Trust Co., Glen Ellyn, Ill. Mem. Triangle, Scabbard and Blade, Tau Beta Pi. Conglist. Clubs: Glen Oak Country (Glen Ellyn). Contbr. articles to profl. jours. Patentee in field. Home: 976 Dartmouth Dr Wheaton IL 60187 Office: 18 N Ada St Chicago IL 60607

SITTLER, LELAND LOYD, realtor; b. Hallam, Nebr., Jan. 22, 1925; s. Elmer J. and Sophia (Mueller) S.; student U. Nebr., 1942-43; m. Camille Elizabeth Rice, Nov. 11, 1949; 1 son, Douglas Kirk. Owner, mgr. petroleum jobber bus., Martell, Nebr., 1950-53, milk transport bus., Lincoln, Neb., 1951-61; partner tobacco candy jobber bus., Omaha, 1953-56, dairy equipment & supply store, Lincoln, 1958-61; owner, mgr. Caribbean Motor Lodge, Estes Park, Colo., 1961-64, Lee Sittler Off-Sale Beverages, Lincoln, 1964—; real estate salesman Lincoln, 1966—, farm sales mgr., 1967—; real estate salesman Town & Country Realty, Lincoln, 1972—. Served with USNR, 1945-46. Mem. Nebr. Realtors Assn., Lincoln Bd. Realtors, Nebr. Licensed Beverage Assn., Am. Legion, Eastern Nebr. and Western Iowa Exchange Counselors. Home: 1601 Surfside Dr Lincoln NE 68528 Office: 5615 O St Lincoln NE 68510

SIU, KENNETH KWONG CHEE, surgeon; b. Hong Kong, Sept. 7, 1928; s. Hon Kit and Kam Ching (Choy) S.; came to U.S., 1953, naturalized, 1970; M.B., B.S., U. Hong Kong, 1952; m. Mary Elizabeth Faber, Aug. 22, 1956; children—Ravenna Kay, Stephen Marcus, Deborah Jean, Rebecca Mary, Yvette Elizabeth. House surgeon Queen Mary Hosp., Hong Kong, 1952; clin. asst. in medicine U. Hong Kong, 1953; rotating intern St. Thomas Hosp., Akron, Ohio, 19S3-54; resident in surgery Md. Gen. Hosp., Balt., 1954-57, chief resident in surgery, 1957-58, resident in pathology Women's Hosp., Balt., 1958-59; acting sr. surgeon Nethersole Hosp., Hong Kong, 19S9-61, asst. surgeon, 1964-66, sr. surgeon, head dept. surgery, 1966-68; practice medicine specializing in surgery, Balt., 1962-64, Jefferson City, Mo., 1970—; active staff Meml. and St. Mary's Hosps., 1970—, pres. med. staff, 1978-79. Bd. dirs. Jefferson City Family YMCA, 1969-76, pres., 1975-76, trustee, 1977—; chmn. Five Rivers dist. Boy Scouts Am., 1974-76; mem. exec. bd. Great Rivers council, 1974—. Recipient Scouter's award Boy Scouts Am., 1972, Scouter's Key, 1973, Wood Badge, 1974; diplomate Am. Bd. Surgery. Fellow Internat. Coll. Surgeons, A.C.S., Royal Coll. Surgeons of Edinburgh (Scotland); mem. Cole County (Mo.) Med. Soc. (pres. 1973-74), Mo. State, Am., So., Brit. med. assns., Mo. Surg. Soc., Christian Med. Soc. Methodist. Clubs: Rotary, Shriners; Masons (Jefferson City). Home: 1009 Fairmount Blvd Jefferson City MO 65101 Office: 915A Leslie Blvd Jefferson City MO 65101

SIY, PEPE, elec. engr.; b. Philippines, June 30, 1942; s. Tiong Kang and Hua (Tan) S.; came to U.S., 1966; Ph.D., U. Akron, 1973; m. Preeya Lorchirachoonkul, July 18, 1972; children—Teddy, Eunice. Instr., Mapua Inst. Tech., Manila, Philippines, 1965-66; programmer U. Calif., Berkley, 1967-68; grad. asst. U. Akron, 1969-73; project engr. Burroughs Corp., Detroit, 1973—. Mem. IEEE, Sigma Xi, Eta Kappa Nu. Research on handwritten character recognition, 1974-75, signature verification, 1976—. Home: 7742 Amboy St Dearborn Heights MI 48127 Office: 14300 Tireman St Detroit MI 48228

SIZELOVE, CARY LEON, agrl. engr.; b. Woodward, Okla., Dec. 31, 1941; s. Ivo Leon and Mary Alma (Holmes) S.; B.S. in Agrl. Engring., Panhandle A. and M. Coll., 1963; student Okla. State U., 1963-66; m. Lisbeth Ann Douglas, Aug. 14, 1964; children—Rose Mary, Cary Leon, Douglas Wayne. Feed lot layout engr. A.O. Smith Harvestore, Arlington Heights, Ill., 1966-68; design engr. Wood Bros., Inc. Oregon, Ill., 1969-71; chief engr. DMI Inc., mfrs. farm machinery, Goodfield, Ill., 1971—. Served with U.S. Army, 1960-61. Registered profl. engr., Ill. Mem. Am. Soc. Agrl. Engrs., Soc. Automotive Engrs. Home: 307 Gloria Dr Eureka IL 61530 Office: PO Box 65 Goodfield IL 61742

SJOERDSMA, RICHARD DALE, musician; b. Grand Rapids, Mich., July 1, 1941; s. Andrew and Wilhemina Hendrika (Wynsma) S.; A.B., Calvin Coll., 1962; M.Mus., U. S.D., 1965; Ph.D., Ohio State U., 1970; m. Linda Lou Roelofs, Nov. 22, 1960; children—Debra Jane, Ronda Jo, Pamela Joy. Music tchr. Dakota High Sch., New Holland, S.D., 1962-65; teaching asst. in voice, opera Ohio State U., 1965-68; asso. prof. music, chmn. dept. Carthage Coll., Kenosha, Wis., 1968—; profl. singer, tenor, opera, oratorio, concert, appearing throughout Midwest and Europe; several European concert tours; adjudicator high sch. solo-ensemble clinics, Wis. Bd. dirs. Kenosha Symphony Assn. Recipient Mary H. Osborne award Ohio State U., 1967; Deutscher Akademischer Austauschdienst, 1968. Mem. Nat. Assn. Tchrs. Singing (asso. editor bull.), Met. Opera Guild, Music Library Assn., Fine Arts Philatelist. Home: 7418 2d Ave Kenosha WI 53140

SKAGGS, WILLIAM T., chem. engr.; b. Centralia, Mo., Apr. 10, 1949; s. Lory T. and Betty (Wade) S.; B.S. in Chem. Engring., Auburn U., 1971; postgrad. Washington U., St. Louis, 1972—; m. Darlene L. Wallis, Aug. 31, 1974. Environ. engr., group leader Research 900 div. Ralston Purina Co., St. Louis, 1971-74, environ., microscopy lab. supr., 1975-76, mgr. 1976—. Mem. Am. Inst. Chem. Engrs., Water Pollution Control Fedn., Air Pollution Control Assn., Am. Water Works Assn. (asso. referee), Assn. Ofcl. Analytical Chemists. Mem. Christian Ch. Home: 444 Applestone Dr Ballwin MO 63011 Office: 900 Checkerboard Sq Saint Louis MO 63188

SKARAN, RAYMOND O., former broadcasting exec.; b. Grand Meadow, Minn., May 5, 1919; s. Olaf and Tillie (Myhre) S.; student Austin (Minn.) Jr. Coll., 1946. Photo interpreter Agrl. Adjustment Adminstrn., 1940; free lance motion picture producer, dir. and cinematographer, 1945-65; continuity writer KAUS radio, Austin, Minn., 1948; TV program mgr. KROC-TV, Rochester, Minn., 1954; pvt. practice as cons. in planning, designing, bldg., staffing and adminstrn. TV stas., 1952-67; TV program mgr. WKBT, LaCrosse, Wis., 1954-65. Active Am. Cancer Soc. Served with Signal Corps, U.S. Army, 1940-45; served with M.I., U.S. Army, 1948-52; Korea. Mem. Nat. Geog. Soc., Am. Legion, Nat. Assn. TV Program Execs., Nat. Assn. Ednl. Broadcasters, Assn. Profl. Broadcasting Edn., Am. Mgmt. Soc., Mil. Intelligence Res., Am. Mus. Natural History, Am. Soc. Personnel Adminstrs., Minn. Soc. Adminstrs. Nursing Care

Facilities, Pub. Personnel Assn., Pub. Relations Soc. Am., Am. Nursing Home Assn., Minn. Assn. Health Care Facilities, Internat. Platform Assn., Westinghouse Confs. Pub. Service, Nat. Trust Historic Preservation, Minn. Hist. Soc., Smithsonian Assos., Norwegian-Am. Mus. (asso.), Norsk Slektshistorisk Forening, Nat. Archives (asso.). Lutheran. Lectr. on Americanism and Communism, 1945-65. Home: PO Box 93 Grand Meadow MN 55936

SKARE, ROBERT MARTIN, lawyer; b. Fargo, N.D., Jan. 13, 1930; s. Martin Samuel and Verna Adelle (Forseth) S.; student St. Olaf Coll., 1947, 48; B.S., U. Minn., 1951, LL.B., 1954; m. Marilyn Hutchinson, Aug. 28, 1954; children—Randolph, Robertson, Rodger, Richard. Admitted to Minn. bar, 1954, Fed. bar, 1956; clk. to justices Minn. Supreme Ct., 1953-54; asso. Best & Flanagan, Mpls., 1956-60, partner, 1960—, mng. partner, 1970—; city atty. Golden Valley, Minn., 1963—; dir. J.N. Johnson Co., Inc., Mpls.; adv. dir. Northwestern Nat. Bank of Mpls.; v.p., gen. counsel Lutheran Brotherhood Mut. Funds. Mem. adv. com. hwy. planning Met. Council Mpls., St. Paul and suburbs, 1968-69; mem. Citizens League Mpls.; regent Golden Valley Luth. Coll., 1973—; bd. govs. Met. YMCA Greater Mpls.; asso. St. Olaf Coll., Northfield, Minn.; bd. dirs., sec.-treas. Phi Alpha Found., Sigma Alpha Epsilon; del. bd. trustees Fairview Hosp., 1971—; bd. dirs., bd. mgmt. U. Minn. YMCA, 1971-76; nat. pres., bd. dirs. Luth. Human Relations Assn. Am., 1973—, Laurelwood Assn., Aspen, Colo. Served to 1st lt. CIC, AUS, 1954-56. Recipient citizenship award City of St. Louis Park, Minn., 1960; Lilly Found. grantee Denver U., 1969. Mem. Minn., Am. bar assns., Minn. Alumni Assn., U.S. Ski Assn., Sigma Alpha Epsilon. Lutheran (ch. pres. 1966). Clubs: Minneapolis, Golden Valley (Minn.) Golf. Home: 109 Paisley Ln Golden Valley MN 55422 Office: 4040 IDS Tower Minneapolis MN 55402

SKATZES, DAWERANCE HORACE, ret. educator; b. Delaware, Ohio, Aug. 21, 1914; s. Carl Henry and Eulalia (Strickler) S.; B.S., Ohio U., 1951, M.Ed., 1954; postgrad. Ohio State U., 1958-59, 67-73, Muskingum Coll., 1965-66; m. Ruth Helen Jones, Apr. 1, 1941 (div. June 1949); children—Thelma Ruth Skatzes Moore, Elta Anne Skatzes Hower, Carl Alvin, Neatha Elaine Skatzes Bostick, August Brent; m. 2d, Mildred M. Stillion, Feb. 18, 1975. Transient laborer, 1932-36; enrollee Civilian Conservation Corps, Price, Utah, 1936-37; unit clk. Soil Conservation Service, Price, 1938-41; field office mgr. Hunt & Frandsen, Gen. Contractors, Elko, Nev., 1942-44; boiler operator, supt. bldgs. and property Delaware (Ohio) City Schs., 1946-49; tchr. South Zanesville (Ohio) High Sch., 1951-54, 58-59; supt. Wills Local Sch. Dist., Old Washington, Ohio, 1954-58, Somerset (Ohio) Sch., 1959-60; prin. Adamsville (Ohio) Elementary Sch., 1960-61, supt., 1960-61; supt. Quaker City (Ohio) Sch. Dist., 1961-62; prin. Valley High and Elementary Sch., Buffalo, Ohio, 1962-66; tchr. Columbus City Schs., 1967-74. Mayor, Old Washington, Ohio; Democratic candidate state rep., 1960-74. Served with U.S. Army, 1945. Mem. Ohio Council Econ. Edn., Nat. Soc. Study of Edn., Am. Assn. Sch Adminstrs., Nat. Council Tchrs. of Math., Acad. Polit. and Social Sci., Ohio Hist. Soc., Internat. Platform Assn., Am. Legion, Am. Def. Preparedness Assn., Amvets (adj.), 37th Div. Vets. Assn., Ohio Def. Corps, Kappa Delta Pi. Clubs: Eagles, Elks, Moose. Home: Old Washington OH 43768

SKEEL, ROBERT LEE, constrn. co. financial exec.; b. Freeport, Ill., June 17, 1935; s. Floyd Ellis and Rachel Viola (Sandruck) S.; student Bowling Green (O.) State U., 1953-56; B.S., Rockford (Ill.) Coll., 1960; m. Janet Marie Kohler, Sept. 15, 1956; children—Andrea Rae, Linda Kathryn, Jennifer Marie. Accountant Atwood Vacuum Machine Mfg. Co., Rockford, 1956-59, Hanson Equipment Co., South Beloit, Ill., 1959-66; account supr. R. E. Van Sickle, C.P.A., Rockford, 1966-67; accountant-controller Robert Hallen, Inc., Rockford, 1967-74, Rockford Metal structures, Inc., Rockford, 1974—. Pres. Forest Hills Coop. Nursery Sch., Rockford, 1961; pres. Maud E. Johnson Sch. Assn. Inc., Rockford, 1962; pres. Maud E. Johnson Sch. P.T.A., 1968; chmn. sect. youth involvement Mayor's Com. for 40th Ann. Gov's Conf., 1971; mem. Citizen's Twenty-Seven Mem. Govt. Study Com., 1972. Bd. dirs. Rockford Area Council of P.T.A.'s., 1969-70, pres., 1970; bd. dirs. Council for Community Services, Rockford, 1970-72, chmn. youth services coordinating com. delinquency prevention program, 1971-72; bd. dirs. Forward Rockford Inc., 1970-73, chmn. youth task force, 1970-71, pres., 1971; bd. dirs. Booker T. Washington Community Center, Rockford, 1973; mem. steering com. Forward Rockford Congress, also co-chmn. panel planning com., 1970; mem. steering com. Congress for Community Progress, also co-chmn. panel planning com., 1970. Recipient citation Gov. Ill., 1971. Mem. Nat., Am. assns. accountants, Rockford Area C. of C. (grad. Community Leadership Sch. 1970, vice chmn. Clean Rivers and Streams Help Project, 1971, rep. to lay com. Open Schs Program 1971 chmn. public facilities com. 1975-76), Am. Contract Bridge League, Alpha Tau Omega. Home: 3620 Cardinal Lane Rockford IL 61107 Office: 10540 N 2nd St Rockford IL 61111

SKELTON, ARCH MASON, lawyer; b. Higginsville, Mo., Apr. 23, 1932; s. Arch M. and Harriett (Oglesby) S.; student William Jewel Coll., 1950-52; A.B., Mo. U., 1957, LL.B., 1958; m. Lee Ann Hill, Aug. 10, 1957; children—Samuel Arch, Melinda Lee, Susan Hill. Admitted to Mo. bar, 1958; asso. atty Mann Walter Powell Burkart & Weathers, Springfield, Mo., 1958-59, Chinn & White, 1959, Chinn, White & Dickey, 1960-63; partner White, Dickey & Skelton, 1963-65, Skelton & Bonacker, 1965-68, (all Springfield); individual practice, Springfield, 1968-72, 74—; partner Skelton & Forehand, 1972-74. Active Springfield United Fund, 1958-65; pres. Springfield Speech and Hearing Center, 1961-64; exec. bd. Ozark Empire council Boy Scouts Am., 1962-70, leadership tng. chmn., 1962, chmn. Frontier Dist., 1963-66, v.p., 1967. Pres., Greene County tng. chmn., 1962, chmn. Frontier Dist., Young Democrats, 1961-62, mem. 1960-64, chmn. County Dem. Com., 1962-64, Dem. nominee 7th Congl. dist., 1966, del. nat. conv., 1968, statewide coordinator primary election campaign Sen. Edward V. Long, 1968; chmn. Jackson Day, 1965-70, 75. Recipient 10,000 Outstanding Young Man of Year award U.S. Jr. C. of C., 1964. Served with AUS, 1953-55. Mem. Am., Mo., Green County bar assns., Mo., Am. trial lawyers assns., Am. Judicature Soc., Springfield Jr. C. of C. (Outstanding young man of Year 1964, 1st v.p. 1962), Mo. State Jr. C. of C., Phi Delta Phi, Kappa Alpha. Methodist. Mason (Shriner), Elk. Home: 3057 White Oak Dr Springfield MO 65804 Office: 2200 E Sunshine St Springfield MO 65804

SKELTON, ISAAC NEWTON, IV, state senator Mo.; b. Lexington, Mo., Dec. 20, 1931; s. Isaac Newton and Carolyn (Boone) S.; A.B., U. Mo., 1953, LL.B., 1956; m. Susan B. Anding, July 22, 1961; children—Ike, Jim, Page. Admitted to Mo. bar, 1956; practiced in Lexington; pros. atty. Lafayette County, Mo., 1957-60; spl. asst. atty. gen. Mo., 1962-65; dir. Wellington Bank; mem. Mo. Senate from 28th dist., 1970—. Chmn., Lafayette County Tom Eagleton for Senator campaign, 1968. Active Cub Scouts. Trustee Wentworth Mil. Acad. Mem. Phi Beta Kappa, Sigma Chi. Democrat. Mem. Christian Ch. Clubs: Masons, Shriners, Elks. Home: 712 Highland St Lexington MO 64067 Office: Box 130 Lexington MO 64067

SKEWES, MORT B., lawyer; b. nr. Luverne, Minn., Nov. 9, 1909; s. George Edwin and Emma (Hagedorn) S.; B.A., U. Minn., 1930, LL.B., 1932; m. Mildred Pettes, Dec. 28, 1935; children—Mary Skewes Fisher, William F. Admitted to Minn. bar, 1932; gen. practice law, Luverne, 1934—; sr. mem. firm Skewes, Klosterbuen & Connell; municipal judge, Luverne, 1935-39; county atty., 1939-59; dir. Northwestern State Bank of Luverne, v.p., 1958—; sec.-dir. A. R. Wood Mfg. Co., Norwood Products Co., Luverne Fire Apparatus Co., Siouxland Broadcasting, Inc., Luverne Farm Store, Northco Ventilating Co. Mem. Gov.'s Com. on Mental Health; past mem. Southwestern Minn. Mental Health Center; past treas., bd. dirs. Ind. Sch. Dist. 671 Luverne, 1959-72; bd. dirs. Maplewood Cemetery Assn.; past pres. Luverne Library Bd.; bd. regents, sec. Augustana Coll., Sioux Falls, S.D., 1975—. Mem. Minn. County Attys. Assn. (past pres.), Minn. Bar Assn. (bd. govs., past council and chmn. real estate sect.), Augustana Fellows, CenCoad, Sigma Nu. Republican. Methodist. Clubs: Masons, Shriners, Rotary (past pres.), Luverne Country, Cardinal, U. Minn. M. Home: 601 N E Park Luverne MN 56156 Office: A Skewes Bldg Luverne MN 56156

SKILLINGS, RALPH E., clin. psychologist; b. Troy, Ohio, Sept. 4, 1946; s. Charles Lewis and Helen Esther S.; B.S., Owosso Coll., 1968; M.A., Ball State U., 1971; Ph.D., U. Pitts., 1977; m. Karen L. Bowie, June 22, 1973. Grad. asst. secondary, adult and higher edn. Ball State U., Muncie, Ind., 1970-71; instr. psychology State U. N.Y. Agrl. Tech. at Alfred, Olean extension, 1972-73, asst. prof., 1973-74; instr. psychology Houghton (N.Y.) Coll., 1971-73; asst. prof., 1973-74; counseling intern U. Pitts. Counseling Center, 1975; staff psychologist Newaygo County Mental Health Center, White Cloud, Mich., 1977—. Bd. dirs. Congregational Homes, Pitts., 1976-77; treas. Newaygo County Interagy. Council, 1977-78. Owens fellow, 1975-76. Mem. Houghton Coll. Alumni Assn. (pres. Pitts. chpt. 1975-76), Am. Personnel and Guidance Assn., Am. Counselor Edn. and Supervision Assn., Am. Psychol. Assn. Republican. Home: 109 E Pine St Fremont MI 49412 Office: 1052 Wilcox Ave White Cloud MI 49349

SKINNER, CHARLES SCOFIELD, mgmt. cons.; b. Cleve., Feb. 10, 1940; s. Harry Harrison and Margaret Charlotte (Scofield) S.; B.S., Cornell U., 1964, M.M.E., 1969; M.B.A., Case Western Res. U., 1976; m. Nancy Lee Cleveland, Sept. 20, 1974; 1 son, Jeffrey Charles. Indsl. mktg. engr. Exxon Corp., Pelham, N.Y., 1964-65, Chevrolet div. Gen. Motors Corp., Cleve., 1963; v.p., partner Booz Allen & Hamilton, Inc., Cleve., 1969—. Regional chmn. Undergrad. Secondary Schs. Com. Northeastern Ohio, 1963. Served to capt. U.S. Army, 1965-68. Decorated Air medal with 26 oak leaf clusters. Registered profl. engr., N.Y., Ohio. Mem. Am. Mgmt. Assn., Am. Mktg. Assn., ASME, Soc. Automotive Engrs., Soc. Mining Engrs., Scabbard and Blade. Club: Cornell. Contbr. articles in field to profl. jours. Home: 763 Valley Brook Circle Sagamore Hills OH 44067 Office: 8801 E Pleasant Valley Rd Cleveland OH 44131

SKINNER, WILLIAM EDWIN, savs. and loan exec.; b. Sidell, Ill., May 1, 1922; s. Elmer S. and Olive A. (Ayres) S.; student U. Ill., 1941-42, 46-47; m. Helen Flesor, Jan. 15, 1947; children—Gregory G., Esther L. (Mrs. Bradley Boyer). With Gus Elesor & Co., Tuscola, Ill., 1946-54, mgr., until 1965; with 1st Fed. Savs. and Loan Assn., Tuscola, 1965—, sec., treas., mgr., 1970-75, exec. v.p., 1975—, also dir. Bd. dirs. Tuscola Youth Center, 1970-71. Served with USNR, 1942-46. Mem. Ill. Savs. and Loan League (dir. 1975—), Ill. Council Savs. and Loans (1st pres., dir. 1975-76), Tuscola C. of C. (dir. 1970-72), Alpha Sigma Phi. Presbyn. (elder 1950-75). Mason, Rotarian. Club: Am. Business. Home: 401 N Main St Tuscola IL 61953 Office: 504 S Main St Tuscola IL 61953

SKINNER, WILLIAM LANGDON, forging co. exec.; b. Oneida, N.Y., Nov. 19, 1937; s. Joseph Langdon and Marion Josephine (Rich) S.; student U.S. Air Force Acad.; B.S.C.E. (Sr. Honor Soc.), U. Mich., 1961; m. Julie Ann Kempf, June 28, 1962; children—Eric William, Michael Joseph, John Craigin. Sales corr. Armco Steel Corp., Indpls., 1961-62, sales engr., Chgo., 1962-63; sales engr. Ontario Corp., Muncie, Ind., 1964-67, plant mgr., 1967-70, sales mgr., 1970-73, v.p. mktg., 1973—. Personnel dir. Child Guidance Clinic, 1966-72; troop com. Boy Scouts Am.; sr. warden, treas. Grace Episcopal Ch., 1969-76. Served with USAF, 1956. Registered profl. engr., Mich.; recipient Gold medal Canadian Gymnastic Championships, 1958; named All-American Gymnast, 1959. Mem. Am. Soc. for Metals, Forging Industry Assn. (chmn. sales promotion com.), Alliance of Metalworking Industries, Muncie-Delaware County C. of C., Am. Mktg. Assn. (dir. Ind. chpt. 1975). Republican. Episcopalian. Clubs: Delaware Country, Muncie Tennis, Ambassador, 1,000,000 Mile, Alpha Tau Omega. Exec. producer Forging the Pivotal Industry, 1976. Home: 301 Winthrop St Muncie IN 47304 Office: 1200 W Jackson St Muncie IN 47303

SKLENICKA, GEORGE WAYNE, food co. exec.; b. Chgo., July 4, 1939; s. George Anthony and Betty (Chalpeck) S.; student U. Ill., 1957-58; B.S. in Bus. Adminstrn., Bradley U., 1962; m. Judith Mary Gagain, Jan. 18, 1964; children—George, Gary, Amy. With Price Waterhouse & Co., 1962-63, sr. accountant, 1965-70; controller Vienna Sausage Mfg. Co., Chgo., 1970—. Served with AUS, 1963-65. Mem. Am. Inst. C.P.A.'s. Home: 1075 Cherry Ln Lombard IL 60148 Office: 2501 N Damen Ave Chicago IL 60647

SKOOG, RALPH EDWARD, lawyer; b. Topeka, Dec. 17, 1929; s. Ralph O. and Anna C. (Haley) S.; B.S., Kans. State U., 1952; J.D., Washburn U., 1959; m. Beth Henry, Nov. 19, 1953; children—Eric S., Peter R., Carl E., Curt A., Edward. Engr., geologist Howard, Needles, Tammen & Bergendoff, Topeka, 1954-59; partner Cook, Flatt & Skoog, cons. engrs., Topeka, 1960-63; admitted to Kans. bar, 1959; partner firm Dickinson, Crow & Skoog, 1962-71, Crow & Skoog, 1971-74, Skoog & Reed, 1974—; treas., gen. counsel Steel Fixture Mfg. Co., Topeka, 1971—; lectr. Washburn U., 1971—; Mem. Kans. Ho. of Reps., 1961-65, 67-69; pres. Community Resources Council, 1970-71; mem. fin. com. Republican State Com., 1971-72; mem. Rep. State Com., 1973-74; mem. Kans. Rep. Exec. Com., 1976—; Rep. chmn. Kans. 2d Congl. Dist., 1976—; pres. Dist. Citizens Adv. Com., 1976-77; bd. dirs. Topeka Inst. Urban Affairs, 1966-74. Served to 1st lt. AUS, 1952-54. Registered profl. engr., Kans. Mem. Geol. Soc., ASCE, Nat. Soc. Profl. Engrs., Kans. State U. Alumni Assn. (internat. pres. 1967-69, gov. 1970-74), Am., Kans. bar assns., Kans. Trial Lawyers Assn. (bd. govs.), Phi Alpha Delta, Sigma Tau, Sigma Alpha Epsilon, Phi Kappa Phi, Sigma Gamma Epsilon. Congregationalist. Home: 235 Greenwood Ave Topeka KS 66606 Office: 434 Topeka Ave Topeka KS 66603

SKOWRONSKI, FRED STANLEY, banker; b. Chgo., Oct. 27, 1918; s. Joseph and Bernice (Toczek) S.; grad. Ill. Coll. Commerce, 1937-38; grad. Wright Jr. Coll., 1938-40; student Am. Inst. Banking, 1950-51; m. Lois Elaine Lundgren, Nov. 19, 1941; children—Barbara Yvonne, Joan Elaine (Mrs. Victor Tippet), Therese Shirley, Rita Marie. With Mfrs. Nat. Bank Chgo., 1948—, asst. cashier, 1963—, asst. v.p., 1974—; mgr., treas. Mfrs. Nat. Safe Deposit Co., 1963—. Served to 1st sgt. USAAF, 1942-45. Recipient Chgo. Clearing House honor award Am. Inst. Banking, Class of 1951; meritorious citations Italian Am. War Vets., Ill. Vets. Commn., Jewish War Vets., Marine Corps League, Mil. Order Purple Heart, Paralyzed Vets. Am., also numerous others citations. Mem. Am. Inst. Banking, Combined Vets. Assn. Ill. (comdr. 1967), Cath. War Vets. (meritorious award), Ill. Safe Deposit Assn., Holy Name Soc., Air Force Assn., Polish Legion Am. Vets. (nat. treas., 1950—, comdr. 1947, treas. Ill. 1949—), DAV (meritorious award), Amvets (meritorious award), Polish Nat. Alliance, Polish Roman Cath. Union, Polish Alma Mater Am. (dir. 1976—). Elk, Kiwanian (dir.). Home: 5229 W Melrose St Chicago IL 60641 Office: 1200 N Ashland Ave Chicago IL 60622

SKROWACZEWSKI, STANISLAW, condr., composer; b. Lwow, Poland, Oct. 3, 1923; s. Pawel and Zofia (Karszniewicz) S.; diploma faculty philosophy, U. Lwow, 1945; diploma faculties composition and conducting, Acad. Music Lwow, 1945, Conservatory at Krakow (Poland), 1946; L.H.D., Hamline U., 1963, Macalaster Coll., 1973; m. Krystyna Jarosz, Sept. 6, 1956. Came to U.S., 1960. Composer, 1931—; first symphony and overture for orch. written at age 8, played by Lwow Philharmonic Orch., 1931; pianist, 1928—, violinist, 1934—, conductor, 1939—; permanent conductor and music dir. Wroclaw (Poland) Philharmonic, 1946-47, Katowice (Poland) Nat. Philharmonic, 1949-54, Krakow Philharmonic, 1955-56, Warsaw Nat. Philharmonic Orch., 1957-59, Minn. Orch., 1960—; guest conductor Europe, S.A., U.S., 1947—. Recipient nat. prize for artistic activity, Poland, 1953; first prize Santa Cecilia Internat. Concours for Conductors, Rome, 1956. Mem. Union Polish Composers, Internat. Soc. Modern Music, Nat. Assn. Am. Composers-Conductors, Am. Music Center, Nat. Soc. Lit. and Arts. Composer: 4 symphonies; Prelude and Fugue for Orchestra (conducted 1st performance Paris), 1948; Overture 1947 (2d prize Symanowski Concours, Warsaw 1947), 1947; Cantiques des Cantiques, 1951; String Quartet (2d prize Internat. Concours Composers, Belgium 1953), 1953; Suite Symphonique (first prize gold medal Composers Competition Moscow, 1957), 1954; Music at Night, 1954; English Horn Concerto, 1969; also music for theatre, motion pictures, songs and piano sonatas. Address: Minn Orch 1111 Nicollet Mall Minneapolis MN 55403

SKRZYPEK, MICHAEL ALLEN, service engr.; b. Chgo., June 3, 1948; s. Albert and Julia (Biela) S.; B.A., Northeastern U., 1974; m. Judith Anne Rosen, Aug. 18, 1974. Field service engr. Datagraphix, San Diego, 1971-72; prodn. mgr. Container Corp. Am., Chgo., 1974-77; sr. field service engr. Datapoint, Chgo., 1975-77; regional field service mgr. Dymo Retail Systems, Boston and Westchester, Ill., 1977—. Served with USNR, 1967-71. Club: Moose. Home: 3212 Birchwood Dr Hazelcrest IL 60429 Office: 1127 S Mannheim Rd Westchester IL

SKUBITZ, JOE, congressman; b. Frontenac, Kans., May 6, 1906; s. Joseph and Mary (Youvan) S.; B.S., Kans. State Coll., 1929, M.S., 1934; student Washburn Law Sch., Topeka, 1938; LL.B., George Washington U., 1946; m. Mary Jess McClellan, Sept. 27, 1930; 1 son, Dan Joseph. Mem. 88th-95th Congresses from 5th Dist. Kans. Recipient citation outstanding work in govt. Kans. State Coll., Pittsburg, 1961. Republican. Home: 7704 Glennon Dr Bethesda MD 20034 also 306 W Webster Pittsburgh KS 66762 Office: Rayburn House Office Bldg Washington DC 20515

SKURAUSKIS, MICHAEL JOSEPH, buyer; b. Oak Park, Ill., Oct. 27, 1948; s. Anthony John and Elizabeth Fay (Henich) S.; B.S. in Chemistry, Elmhurst Coll., 1973; m. Pamela Kay Baermann, July 26, 1968; 1 son, Jon Robert. Technician process engring. Richardson Co., Melrose Park, Ill., 1969-72; chemist coatings lab., U.S. Gypsum Co., Des Plaines, Ill., 1973-75, chemist joint systems lab., 1975, chemist texture coating lab., 1976-77, corp. raw material buyer, Chgo., 1977—. Recipient service award Joint Edn. Symco Com., Chgo. Paint and Coatings Assn. and Chgo. Soc. for Coatings Tech., 1976. Mem. Chgo. Soc. for Coatings Tech. Home: 85 S Lodge Ln Lombard IL 60148 Office: 101 S Wacker Dr Chicago IL 60606

SKWERES, THOMAS WALTER, sales and marketing exec.; b. Chgo., May 11, 1929; s. Marion John and Sophie (Rataiczyk) S.; student Wright City Coll., 1947-49, Northwestern, 1949-55; m. Charmaine Liska, Oct. 28, 1950; children—Thomas Allan, Pamela Charmaine, Patricie Ann. Prodn. mgr. Reincke Meyer & Finn, 1953-55; v.p. account exec. Hanson & Stevens, 1955-62; v.p. sales Ross & White Co., 1962—. Marketing and advt. cons., pub. relations writer, 1962—. Served with U.S. Army, 1951-53. Mem. Eta Iota Psi. Home: 5613 Snowdrop Lisle IL 60532 Office: 50 W Dundee Wheeling IL 60090

SKWERSKI, ARTHUR PETER, advt. exec.; b. Chgo., Apr. 11, 1938; s. Arthur Edward and Lottie E. (Ganek) S.; B.S., U. Ill., 1960; postgrad. Loyola U., Chgo., 1969-71; m. Jacquelyn Pledger, July 19, 1969; 1 son, Peter Kenneth. Sales promotion supr. Victor Comptometer Corp., Chgo., 1962-67; indsl. advt. mgr. Imperial-Eastman, Chgo., 1967-76; mgr. indsl. sales promotion and advt. valve and fittings div. Gould Inc., Chgo., 1977—. Home: 810 N Euclid Ave Oak Park IL 60302 Office: 6300 Howard St Chicago IL 60648

SKWERSKI, JACQUELYN PLEDGER, editor; b. Chgo., Mar. 20, 1937; d. Jack Moss and Gladys (Ricks) Pledger; B.S., Purdue U., 1959; M.A., Ind. U., 1964; m. Arthur P. Skwerski, July 1969; 1 son, Peter Kenneth. Substitute tchr. Bloomington (Ind.) Met. Sch. System, 1960-61; editor, author ednl. filmstrips Soc. for Visual Edn., Chgo., 1961; editor primary textbooks Benefic Press, Chgo., 1961-63; editor Gas News, Peoples Gas Light & Coke Co., Chgo., 1963-66, pub. relations asst., 1966-70; pub. relations specialist Peoples Gas Co., Chgo., 1970-71; pres. Jackie Pledger & Assos. Pub. Relations, Sales Promotion, Advt. Agy., 1971-77; news editor Leader Post Newspapers, Chgo., 1977—. Pub. relations adv. com., bd. dirs. Chgo. Girl Scout Council. Mem. Women in Communications, Theta Sigma Phi (pres. Chgo. chpt. 1970-71). Baptist. Address: 810 N Euclid Ave Oak Park IL 60302

SLACK, WILLIAM JOHN, coll. adminstr.; b. Syracuse, N.Y., Nov. 9, 1944; s. William George and Florence Barbara (Meister) S.; A.B., St. Lawrence U., 1966; M. Ed., 1972; m. Mary T. Sherwin, Aug. 8, 1970; 1 dau., Elizabeth Copeland. Sr. master Brewster Acad., Wolfeboro, N.H., 1966-70; adminstrv. intern St. Lawrence U., Canton, N.Y., 1970-72; coordinator campus activities Monmouth (Ill.) Coll., 1972-73; fine arts coordinator Coe Coll., Cedar Rapids, Iowa, 1973—, asso. dean students, 1975—. Founder, dir. Wolfeboro Fine Arts Festival, 1967-70. Mem. Nat. Assn. Student Personnel Adminstrs., Assn. Coll. Unions Internat., Assn. Coll., Univ. and Community Arts Adminstrs. Episcopalian. Home: 935 20th St SE Cedar Rapids IA 52403

SLAGER, RICHARD FOREMAN, orthopedic surgeon; b. Columbus, Ohio, May 24, 1928; s. Foreman Ward and Mary Catherine (Mace) S.; B.A., Ohio State U., 1953; M.M.Sc., 1959, M.D.; m. Elaine Foster Huber, June 29, 1951; children—Susan Elaine, Richard Ramey, Robin Lynn, Debra Ann. Intern, Mt. Carmel Hosp., Columbus, 1953-54; resident in orthopedic surgery Ohio State U. Hosp., Columbus, 1956-60; pvt. practice medicine specializing in orthopedic surgery, Columbus, 1960—; chmn. continuing edn. com. Mt. Carmel Hosp., 1976. Chmn. Sch. Levy Com., 1976; pres. Upper Arlington Boosters, 1973. Served to lt. comdr., M.C., USNR, 1954-56. Fellow A.C.S.; mem. Am. Acad. Sports Medicine, Scoliosis Research Soc., Am. Acad. Orthopedic Surgery, Clin. Orthopedic Soc., Tri State Orthopedic Soc. Methodist. Clubs: Torch, Rotary (pres. 1974-75) (Upper Arlington). Editor Bull. Am. Acad. Orthopedic Surgery. Home: 1926 Collingswood Rd Columbus OH 43221 Office: 1300 Dublin Rd Columbus OH 43221

SLAGLE, HARRY RICHARD, obstetrician, gynecologist; b. Pitts., Dec. 22, 1935; s. Harry C. and Helen M. (Chadwick) S.; B.A., Coll. Wooster, 1957; M.D., Hahnemann Med. Coll., 1961; m. Kay E. Vigrass, Aug. 23, 1958; children—Scott R., Robyn K. Intern, Harrisburg (Pa.) Hosp., 1961-62, resident in obstetrics and gynecology, 1962-65; practice medicine specializing in gynecology, Wooster, Ohio; mem. staff Wooster Community Hosp. Served to capt. USAF, 1965-67. Diplomate Am. Bd. Obstetrics and Gynecology. Fellow Am. Coll. Obstetricians and Gynecologists; mem. Wayne County Med. Soc., Ohio State Med. Assn., Cleve. Obstetrics and Gynecology Soc., Mid-Ohio Race Physicians, Motor Racing Safety Soc. Republican. Club: Downtown Rebounders. Home: 650 Beechwood Dr Wooster OH 44691 Office: 1874 Cleveland Rd Wooster OH 44691

SLANKARD, J(AMES) EDWARD, obstetrician and gynecologist; b. Pittsburg, Kans., Oct. 11, 1928; s. James Alfred and Hazel Rachel (Nimmo) S.; B.A., U. Kans., 1949, M.D., 1954; m. Camille Cheryl Marsh, Mar. 8, 1975; children by previous marriage—James Andrew, Myra Kay, Carrie Elizabeth. Rotating intern Bethany Hosp., 1958-59; gen. practice medicine, Kansas City, Kans., 1959-60; fellow in gen. surgery Alton Ochsner Med. Found., New Orleans, 1960-61, in obstetrics and gynecology, 1961-64; Am. Cancer Soc. fellow M.D. Anderson Hosp. and Tumor Inst., Houston, 1968; practice medicine specializing in obstetrics and gynecology, Kansas City, Mo., 1964—; staff St. Luke's Hosp.; courtesy staff Research Hosp.; cons. Kansas City Gen. Hosp., U. Mo. (Kansas City). Med. dir. Planned Parenthood of Western Mo., 1965-69; bd. dirs. Jackson County unit Am. Cancer Soc., 1969—. Served with AUS, 1946-49. Diplomate Am. Bd. Obstetrics and Gynecology. Fellow A.C.S.; mem. Am. Coll. Obstetrics and Gynecology, Kansas City, Continental gynecol. socs., AMA, Mo., So. med. assns., Jackson County Med. Soc., Kansas City S.W. Clin. Soc., Central Assn. Obstetrics and Gynecology, Royal Soc. Medicine, Pan Pacific Surg. Assn. Episcopalian. Clubs: Masons, Saddle and Sirloin, Carriage. Office: Plaza Medical Bldg 4320 Wornall Rd Kansas City MO 64111

SLATER, JAMES WILLIAM, lawyer; b. Waterbury, Conn., Oct. 5, 1943; s. Clifford Eldridge and Jane (Casmirro) S.; B.A. with honors, U. Conn., 1966; J.D., Georgetown U., 1969; m. Janet M. Genovese, June 18, 1966; 1 dau., Casye Lyn. Admitted to Ohio bar, 1970; engaged in internat. indsl. relations Goodyear Internat. Corp., Akron, 1969-71; mem. firm Alpeter, Diefenbach, Davies, Koerber & Nostwich, Akron, 1971-73; corp. atty. White Motor Corp., Cleve., 1973-75; mem. firm Christoff & Slater, Cleve., 1975—. Mem. mgmt. com. Nat. Vol. Parole Aide Program, 1973; bd. dirs. Small Enterprise Devel. Assn. Mem. Am. (co-chmn. vol. parole aide com., young lawyers sect. 1972-73), Ohio (gov. young lawyers sect. 1972-73), Akron (chmn. young lawyers sect. 1972) bar assns. Democrat. Episcopalian. Rotarian. Club: Akron City. Home: 1586 Bob White Trail Stow OH 44224 Office: 100 Erieview Plaza Cleveland OH 44114

SLATER, RAYMOND E.O., mfg. co. exec., cons. engr.; b. Springfield, Mo., June 27, 1913; s. Edgar Otis and Rosa S. (Mosser) S.; B.S., Iowa State Coll., 1936; postgrad. LaSalle Extension U., 1937-41; degree in Indsl. Engring., Iowa State U., 1942; m. Eleanor Johnson, Jan. 30, 1937; children—Janet Rae Slater Darwin, Marian Joan Slater Swaine. Asst. prodn. mgr. Chgo. Vitreous Enamel Co., 1936-37; asst. mgr. spl. services div. Ernst & Ernst, Chgo., 1938-42, mgr. mgmt. services, 1943-50; pres. Asso. Bus. Services, Inc., St. Louis, 1946-50; owner Slater Engring. Assos., St. Louis, 1950—; comptroller Hawthorn Co., New Haven, Mo., Glasgow, Mo. and St. George, Utah, 1960-64, v.p., comptroller, 1964-73; comptroller H. Wenzel Tent & Duck Co., St. Louis, 1959-72; controller New Haven (Mo.) Mfg. Co., 1960-73, also dir.; controller Am. Waterproofing Co., New Haven, 1959-73, Judson Group, 1970-73; dir. bus. devel. recreation groups Kellwood Co., New Haven, 1973-75; sec. First Mo. Devel. Fin. Corp., 1969-70, pres., 1971—, also dir.; chmn. bd., chief exec. officer Zero Mfg. Co., Washington, Mo., 1974-77. C.P.A., Ill., Mo.; registered profl. engr. Ill., Iowa, Mo. Mem. Fin. Execs. Inst., Ill. Soc. Profl. Engrs., ASME, Am. Inst. C.P.A.'s, Am. Mgmt. Assn., Adminstrn. Mgmt. Soc. (chpt. sec. 1947-50), Nat. Assn. Accountants, Ill. Soc. C.P.A.'s, Nat. Assn. Registered Profl. Engrs., Mo. Soc. Registered Profl. Engrs. Home: 18 York Dr St Louis MO 63144

SLATER, WILLIAM ADCOCK, psychiat. social worker; b. Nan Tung, Kiang Su, China, July 26, 1933 (parents Am. citizens); s. Paul Raymond and Daisy (Butcher) S.; student Phillips U., 1955-58; B.A., U. Wichita, 1958; M.S.W., U. Denver, 1960; m. Karen C. Crutchfield, Sept. 4, 1956; children—Kathleen Ann, Bryan Paul. Probation officer Hennepin County Dept. Ct. Services, Mpls., 1960-63, program dir., 1963-65, dir. social services, 1965-67; clin. dir. St. Cloud (Minn.) Children's Home, 1967-70; exec. dir. Gillis Home for Children, Kansas City, Mo., 1970—; student supr. U. Minn., Mpls., 1965-67, St. John's Coll., St. Cloud, 1967-70. Served with U.S. Army, 1955-57. Mem. Nat., Mo. assn. social workers, Nat. Council Crime and Delinquency, Minn. Assn. Child Caring Agy., Child Welfare League Am. (treas. S.W. regional conf. 1975, nat. council 1977—), Mo. Assn. Children's Residential Agys. (treas., dir. 1973-75). Mem. Disciples of Christ. Home: 9328 Woodson St Overland Park KS 66207 Office: 8150 Wornall Rd Kansas City MO 64114

SLATON, PAUL GEORGE, optometrist; b. Vienna, Austria, Oct. 25, 1923; s. Emil and Wilhelmine (Schladnich) Eckstein; came to U.S., 1946, naturalized, 1948; O.D., Ill. Coll. Optometry, 1949; m. Susan Weiss, Oct. 23, 1950 (dec. 1974); children—Eric, Ellen. Pvt. practice optometry, Hopkins, Minn., 1952—. Mem. Hopkins Planning Commn., 1967-73, Hopkins City Council, 1975—. Mem. State Bd. Optometry, 1964-65. Served with U.S. Army, 1946. Fellow Brit. Optical Assn.; mem. Am. (chmn. informatic com. 1968), Minn. (pres. 1963, editor jour. 1959-62; Optometrist of Year award 1964) optometric assns., Am. Acad. Optometry. Jewish. Mason, Rotarian; mem. B'nai B'rith. Author: Optometric Assistants Notebook, 1970. Home: 121 7th Ave N Hopkins MN 55343 Office: 905 Professional Bldg Hopkins MN 55343

SLAUGHTER, CARL RAY, physician; b. Little Rock, Jan. 29, 1933; s. Wilbur Logan and Florence Elizabeth (Ray) S.; B.S. in Medicine, M.D., U. Ark., 1959; m. Barbara Jewell Viar, Apr. 8, 1955; children—Mark Carl, Stanley Logan. Intern, Hillcrest Med. Center, 1959-60; resident in surgery Ellis Fischell State Cancer Hosp., Columbia, Mo., 1960—; resident in obstetrics and gynecology Kans. U. Med. Sch., 1960-64; practice medicine specializing in obstetrics and gynecology, N. Kansas City, Mo., since 1964; mem. staff N. Kansas City, Liberty Meml. hosps.; clin. instr. Kans. U. Med. Center; dir. Profl. Bldg. North. Mem. Mayor Kansas City Com. for Advancement. Served with USAF, 1951-53. Mem. AMA, Am. Coll. Obstetricians and Gynecologists, Mo., Clay County (exec. com.) med. socsl, Kans City, Gynecol. Soc. Republican. Methodist. Club: Nat. Travel. Contbr. med. jours. Home: 1001 N Woodland Dr Kansas City MO 64118 Office: 2700 Hospital Dr North Kansas City MO 64116

SLAUGHTER, ROBERT LESLIE, advt. exec.; b. Cleve., Feb. 19, 1933; s. Edwin M. and Florence L. (Black) S.; student Wayne State U., 1951-53, 57-58, U. Mich., 1971; m. Jean E. Little, June 1, 1968; children—Robert Leslie, Susan, Laurie, James. Asso. dir., then dir. Mich. Republican Com. and affiliates, 1960-64; account exec. N.W. Ayer & Son, Detroit and San Francisco, 1965—; pres. Slaughter & Assos., Inc., Dearborn, Mich., 1966—. Mem. Dearborn (Mich.) City Beautiful Commn.; citizens adv. com., past pres. Players Guild of Dearborn; presdl. elector, 1976; bd. dirs. Dearborn Police Res. Served with USAF, 1953-57. Mem. Am. Arbitration Assn., Bus. and Profl. Advt. Assn., Mich. Advt. Agy. Council (chmn. 16th dist. Mich.). Republican. Methodist. Club: Elks. Home: 441 S Melborn St Dearborn MI 48124

SLAUGHTER, RUDIE WRIGHT, elec. coop. exec.; b. Kennett, Mo., Oct. 31, 1907; s. George B. and Nancy Elizabeth (Wright) S.; grad. high sch.; m. Margaret Evelyn Blankinship, Mar. 23, 1930; children—Rudie Wright, Victor B., Elizabeth Ann (Mrs. Dan Neely), Margaret (Mrs. Richard Adamson), Allen. Pres. Pemiscot-Dunklin REA Coop., Hayti, Mo., 1970—, M & A Electric Power, Poplar Bluff, Mo., 1973—, Federated Electric, Springfield, Mo., 1973—; v.p. Asso. Electric, Springfield, 1973—. Pres. Assn. Mo. Electric Coops., 1971-73. Mem. Mo. U. Extension Council, 1970-75; chmn. Soil and Crops Conf., Kennett, 1963. Pres. Senath (Mo.) Bd. Edn., 1949-52; mem. Dunklin Republican Com., 1964-74. Mem. Dunklin County Farm Bur. (pres. 1968-70). Baptist (deacon, trustee). Club: Lions (pres. 1963-64). Home: RFD 1 Box 241 Senath MO 63876

SLAYTON, RANSOM DUNN, elec. products co. engr.; b. Salem, Nebr., Mar. 10, 1917; s. Laurel Wayland and Martha Ellen (Fisher) S.; B.S. with distinction, U. Nebr., 1938; postgrad. Ill. Inst. Tech., 1942, DePaul U., 1945-46; m. Margaret Marie Ang, Sept. 25, 1938; children—R. Duane, David L., Sharon J. Slayton Manz, Karla M. Slayton Fogel, Paul L. With Western Union Telegraph Co., Lincoln, Nebr., 1937-38, St. Paul, 1938-40, Omaha, 1940, Chgo., 1940-45; asst. prof. elec. engring. Chgo. Tech. Coll., 1945-46; with Teletype Corp., Chgo. and Skokie, Ill., 1946—, elec. engr., dept. chief, 1950-59, project supr., sr. engr. research and devel., 1959—; radio instr. Am. TV Labs., Chgo., 1943. Active vol. civic orgns., numerous ch. offices. Named Pub. Relations Speaker of Year, Western Electric/Teletype, 1976. Mem. IEEE (sr.; chmn. founder com. IEEE Communications Soc. 1970-71, parliamentarian 1972—, recipient soc. meritorious service award 1976). Editor: IEEE mag. Trans. on Communication Tech., 1964-69; contbr. articles to profl. publs. Patentee in field. Home: 1530 Hawthorne Ln Glenview IL 60025 Office: 5555 Touhy Ave Skokie IL 60076

SLEDGE, BARNETT JENKINS, mech. engr.; b. Memphis, Aug. 1, 1914; s. Turner Elmore and Ethel Elizabeth (Jenkins) S.; B.S. in Mech. Engring., U. Tenn., 1936, postgrad. in structrual engring., 1950; m. Rachael Pauline Davis, May 28, 1928; children—Barnett Jenkins, Thomas Davis, Elizabeth Ann. With Champion Papers, Canton, N.C., and Hamilton, Ohio, 1936—, supt. maintenance engr. and construction, 1945-60, chief engr., 1966—, dir. internat. engring., 1968—. Served to col. USAR, 1936-40, 45-66, C.E. U.S. Army, 1940-45. Mem. ASME, Paper Industry Mgmt. Assn., TAPPI. Episcopalian. Home: 985 Sunview Dr W Hamilton OH 45013 Office: General Engineering Champion Papers Knights Bridge Hamilton OH 45020

SLEEMAN, JOHN PAUL, chem. coatings mfg. co. ofcl.; b. Cleve., May 19, 1920; s. John J. and Mildred A. (Blubaugh) S.; student pub. schs., Cleve.; m. Mary L. Gerba, Apr. 27, 1946; children—Sandra J. Swyrydenko, Robert W.D., Gary J.P., Linda E. With Arco Paint Co., Cleve., 1938-61, quality control mgr., 1947-51, supr. lacquer mfg. dept., 1951-61; quality control mgr. Midland div. Dexter Corp., Cleve., 1961—, formulator, 1961-63, group leader research and devel., 1963—. Served with U.S. Army, 1942-45; ETO. Mem. Cleve. Soc. for Coatings Tech. (pres. 1971-72), Fedn. Socs. for Coatings Tech., Nat. Paint Coatings Assn. Republican. Methodist. Home: 18171 Logan Dr Walton Hills OH 44146 Office: 9001 Kinsman Rd Cleveland OH 44104

SLEEMAN, MARY (MRS. JOHN PAUL SLEEMAN), librarian; b. Cleve., June 28, 192 d. John and Mary Lillian (Jakub) Gerba; B.S., Kent State U., 1965; m. John Paul Sleeman, Apr. 27, 1946; children—Sandra Sleeman Swyrydenko, Robert, Gary, Linda. Supervising librarian elementary schs. Nordonia Hills Bd. Edn., Northfield, Ohio, 1965—; children's librarian Twinsburg Pub. Library, 1965-66. Mem. A.L.A., Ohio Sch. Librarians Assn., N.E.A., Summit County Librarians Assn., North Eastern Ohio Tchrs. Assn. Methodist. Home: 18171 Logan Dr Walton Hills OH 44146 Office: 115 Ledge Rd Northfield OH 44067

SLEICHTER, CHARLES GEORGE, JR., orthodontist; b. Luray, Kans., July 2, 1922; s. Charles George and Louise Estelle (Wilson) S.; D.D.S., State U. Iowa, 1945; M.S., U. Ill., 1953; m. Shirley Maxeen Holtorf, Apr. 25, 1943; children—Charles George III, John Mark. Pvt. practice dentistry, specializing in orthodontics, Iowa City, 1954—; mem. staff Mercy Hosp., Iowa City; pres. River Vue Devel. Corp., Iowa City, 1968-73; bd. dirs., sec. Towncrest Profl. Offices, Inc., 1969-75; pres. Fairport Marina, 1968-73; partner Arthur Street Properties, 1973—; mem. faculty State U. Iowa, 1954-68, prof., acting head dept. orthodontics, 1966-68; cons. USPHS, 1954-55. Vol. exec. Hawkeye council Boy Scouts Am.; mem. com. planning and zoning City of Iowa City, 1956. Mem. Schleswing (Ia.) Bd. Edn., 1947. Bd. dirs. YMCA, Iowa City, 1960, Iowa City Devel. Corp., 1960, Community Givers, 1962. Served with USCGR, 1947-48; with USPHS, 1947-53. Diplomate Am. Bd. Orthodontics. Fellow Am. Coll. Dentists; mem. Angle Soc. Orthodontists, Am. Assn. Orthodontists, ADA. Mason (Shriner). Contbr. articles to profl. publs. Home: 302 Highland Dr Iowa City IA 52240 Office: 1041 Arthur St Suite B Iowa City IA 52240

SLEIGHT, JUSTIN LEROY, ophthalmologist; b. Clinton County, Mich., Aug. 11, 1922; s. Rolan W. and Bernice G. (Beckwith) S.; A.B., Albion (Mich.) Coll., 1943; B.M., Northwestern U., 1945, M.D., 1946; m. Marjorie Jean Wardell, June 23, 1945; children—Kenneth Roland, Barbara (Mrs. James Meininger), Carolyn J. (Mrs. Brian La Beau), Stephen D. Intern, Hurley Hosp., Flint, Mich., 1945-46; resident ophthalmology McMillan Hosp., Washington U., St. Louis, 1949-51; pvt. practice ophthalmology, Lansing, Mich., 1951-66; partner Lansing Ophthalmology Profl. Corp., 1966—; mem. staffs Sparrow, St. Lawrence, Ingham med. hosps.; supervising ophthalmologist for State Mich., 1970-73; asst. clin. instr. surgery Mich. State U. Med. Sch., 1970—. Vice pres., dir. Ind. Liberty Life Ins. Co., 1964—. Bd. dirs. Urban League Lansing, 1967-69; trustee Albion Coll., 1963-69. Served with AUS, 1946-48. Diplomate Am. Bd. Ophthalmology. Fellow Am. Acad. Ophthalmology and Otolaryngology. Mem. AMA, Mich. (ho. dels. 1966-75, pres. 1970), Ingham County med. socs., Greater Lansing C. of C. (dir.) 1962-67. Methodist (trustee 1967-71). Home: 3001 Westchester Rd Lansing MI 48910 Office: 2909 E Grand River Ave Lansing MI 48912

SLEIGHT, NORMAN REED, ins. co. exec.; b. Clinton County, Mich., Feb. 15, 1920; s. Rolan W. and Bernice G. (Beckwith) S.; A.B., Albion Coll., 1940; postgrad. Ia. State Coll., Ohio State U.; m. Alethea E. Paul, June 3, 1942; children—Douglas R., Susanne (Mrs. Gary Fuller). Group leader Manhattan Project, Ia. State Coll., 1942-46; agt. State Farm Ins. Cos., St. Johns, Mich., 1946-53, Ohio dir., Columbus, 1953-60, Ohio dep. regional v.p., Newark, 1960-61, regional v.p., 1961—. Pres., Griffith Found. for Ins., 1971-73, chmn., 1973—. Bd. dirs. Ohio Citizens Council; past pres., mem. bd. United Appeal Licking Co.; trustee Licking County Meml. Hosp., 1965-71, pres., 1968-70; trustee Mid-Ohio Health Planning Fedn., 1970-74, v.p., 1974—; bus. adv. council Coll. Adminstrv. Sci., Ohio State U., 1976—. C.L.U. Mem. Assn. C.L.U. (pres. Columbus chpt. 1957-58), Gen. Agts. and Mgrs. Assn. (dir. 1955-58), Newark Area C. of C. (exec. bd. 1962-65. 68-71, pres. 1972-73), Gamma Iota Sigma, Omicron Delta Kappa, Phi Lambda Upsilon, Alpha Chi Sigma, Kappa Mu Epsilon. Presbyn. (elder). Rotarian (dir. Newark 1965-72, pres. 1972). Home: 685 Snowdon Dr Newark OH 43055 Office: 1440 Granville Rd Newark OH 43055

SLEIGHT, STUART DUANE, veterinarian, educator; b. Lansing, Mich., Oct. 19, 1927; s. Rolan Wallace and Bernice Gertrude (Beckwith) S.; D.V.M., Mich. State U., 1951, M.S., 1959, Ph.D., 1961; m. Geraldine Ann Biergans, Sept. 12, 1950; children—Marcia Louise, William Stuart, Catherine Ann, James Francis. Veterinarian, Columbus Vet. Hosp. (Wis.), 1951-58; asst. instr. Mich. State U., 1958-61, asst. prof., 1961-65, asso. prof., 1965-68, prof. dept. pathology, 1968—. NIH grantee, 1966-70. Mem. Am. Vet. Med. Assn., Am. Coll. Vet. Pathologists (diplomate), Sigma Xi, Phi Kappa Phi, Alpha Gamma Rho. Roman Catholic. K.C. Contbr. articles to profl. jours. Home: 6250 Skyline Dr East Lansing MI 48823

SLEMMONS, ROBERT SHELDON, architect; b. Mitchell, Nebr., Mar. 12, 1922; s. M. Garvin and K. Fern (Borland) S.; B.A., U. Nebr., 1948; m. Dorothy Virginia Herrick, Dec. 16, 1945; children—David (dec.), Claire, Jennifer, Robert, Timothy. Draftsman, Davis & Wilson, architects, Lincoln, Nebr., 1947-48; chief designer, project architect Office of Kans. State Architect, Topeka, 1948-54; asso. John A. Brown, architect, Topeka, 1954-56; partner Brown & Slemmons, architect, Topeka, 1956-69; v.p. Brown-Slemmons-Kreuger, architects, Topeka, 1969-73; owner Robert S. Slemmons, A.I.A. & Assos., architects, Topeka, 1973—. Cons. Kans. State Office Bldg. Commn., 1956-57; lectr. in design U. Kans., 1961. Bd. dirs. Topeka Civic Symphony Soc., 1950-60. Served with USNR, 1942-48. Mem. A.I.A. (Topeka pres. 1955-56, Kans. dir. 1957-58), Topeka Art Guild (pres. 1950), Kans. Council Chs. (dir. 1961-62), Greater Topeka C. of C., Downtown Topeka, Inc. Presbyn. (elder, chmn. trustees). Kiwanian (pres. 1966-67). Prin. archtl. works include: Kans. State Office Bldg., 1954, Topeka Presbyn. Manor, 1960-74, Luther Pl Apts. for Sr. Citizens, 1975. Office: 1515 1 Townsite Plaza Topeka KS 66603

SLICHTER, CHARLES PENCE, physicist, educator; b. Ithaca, N.Y., Jan. 21, 1924; s. Sumner Huber and Ada (Pence) S.; A.B., Harvard U., 1946, M.A., 1947, Ph.D., 1949; m. Gertrude Thayer Almy, Aug. 23, 1952; children—Sumner Pence, William Almy, Jacob Huber, Ann Thayer. Research asst. Underwater Explosives Research Lab., Woods Hole, Mass., 1943-46; mem. faculty U. Ill. at Urbana, 1949—, prof. physics, 1955—, prof. physics Center for Advanced Study, 1969—; Morris Loeb lectr. Harvard U., 1961; dir. Polaroid Corp., 1975—; mem. Nat. Sci. Bd., 1975-78; mem. Pres. Sci. Adv. Com., 1964-69, Com. on Nat. Medal Sci., 1969-74. Mem. corp. Harvard U. Recipient Langmuir award Am. Phys. Soc., 1969; Alfred P. Sloan fellow, 1957-63. Mem. Nat. Acad. Scis., Am. Acad. Arts and Scis., Am. Philos. Soc. Author: Principles of Magnetic Resonance, 1963; contbr. articles to profl. jours. Home: 3012 Valley Brook Dr Champaign IL 61820 Office: Dept Physics U Ill Urbana IL 61801

SLIFKIN, SAM CHARLES, cons.; b. Milw., July 28, 1918; s. Isadore Jacob and Tillie (Benin) S.; B.S. in Chemistry, U. Wis.-Madison, 1942; m. Nancy Gail Fausch, Feb. 11, 1956; children—William, Michael, Carolyn. Head products devel. Ozalid div. Gen. Aniline and Film Corp., Johnson City, N.Y., 1942-49; v.p. Tecnifax Corp., Holyoke, Mass., 1949-50; cons. diazotype and reprography, 1951-71; pres. Splty. Coatings, Inc., Plymouth, Mich., 1964-72; cons. Ozalid Group Holdings, Ltd., 1972-77; pres. Slifkin Co., Ann Arbor, Mich., 1978—. Fellow Am. Inst. Chemists; mem. Am. Chem. Soc., Soc. Photog. Scientists and Engrs., Tech. Assn. Graphic Arts, T.A.P.P.I., Royal Photog. Soc. (asso.), Photog. Soc. Am. (asso.), Soc. Plastic Engrs., N.Y. Acad. Sci., Am. Saddle Horse Assn. Mich. (dir.), Phi Beta Kappa, Phi Lambda Upsilon, Pi Mu Epsilon. Contbr. articles to profl. jours. Address: 1303 Park Pl Plymouth MI 48170 Office: 119 Huron View Blvd Ann Arbor MI 48017

SLOAN, GOVER GENE, physician; b. Galatia, Ill., Nov. 3, 1929; s. Grover Monroe and Nova (Durham) S.; B.A., So. Ill. U., 1949; M.D., U. Ill., 1954; m. Betty Stout, June 19, 1964; children—Stephen Anders, Bruce Edward, Elizabeth Ann, Warren Gene, Bertram Ashley. Intern, Ill. Central R.R. Hosp., Chgo., 1954-55; practice medicine specializing in family practice, Carrier Mills, Ill., 19S7—; mem. staff Doctors Hosp., Harrisburg, Ill.; dir. Bank Harrisburg, 1973—. Trustee Southeastern Ill. Community Coll., 1974, sec., 1977—; mem. Egyptian Health Dept. Bd., 1959—; bd. dirs. Saline County Tb Bd., 1975—. Served as capt. M.C., U.S. Army, 1955-57. Diplomate Am. Bd. Family Practice. Mem. Am., So. Ill. med. assns. assns., Ill. State, Saline Pope Hardin County med. socs. Democrat. Club: Elks, 40 & 8. Home: 9 Country Club Ct Harrisburg IL 62946 Office: Box 157 Carrier Mills IL 62917

SLOAN, JAMES PARK, educator, novelist; b. Greenwood, S.C., Sept. 22, 1944; s. James Park and Alice Catherine (Gaines) S.; B.A., Harvard U., 1968; m. Jeanette Carol Pasin, July 25, 1968; children—Eugene Blakely, Anna Jeanette. Mem. faculty English dept. U. Ill., Chgo. Circle Campus, 1972—, chmn. the program for writers, 1976—. Lectr. to univ. and civic groups; book reviewer Chgo. Tribune. Served with U.S. Army, 1964-67. Decorated Army Commendation medal; Vietnamese medal of honor; recipient Cliff Dwellers award, 1977. Author: War Games (Best First novel Great Lakes Colls. Assn.; Peggy McPhaul award Midwestern Writers), 1971; The Case History of Comrade V. (Friends of Lit. award), 1972. Contbg. editor Am. Pen. Quar., 1974—. Office: Univ Ill Chicago Circle Campus Chicago IL 60680

SLODKI, SHELDON JOSHUA, physician; b. Chgo., Aug. 18, 1932; s. Irving and Goldie (Sklar) S.; B.S., U. Ill., 1954, M.D., 1956; m. Nancy Vandernald, May 9, 1966; children—Jeanie, Naomi, Vivian, David, Jacob, Joshua. Intern, Cook County Hosp., Chgo., 1956-57, resident internal medicine, 1957-59, resident in pediatrics, fellow in cardiology, 1959-60, chief resident, 1961; practice internal medicine specializing in cardiology, Chgo., 1963—; mem. staff Louis A. Weiss Meml. Hosp., Mt. Sinai Hosp., N.E. Community Hosp., Chgo.; asst. prof. medicine and cardiovascular research Chgo. Med. Sch., 1962-67, asso. prof., 1967—; asso. dir. Cermak Meml. Hosp., 1961-72; cons. cardiology Ridgeway Hosp., 1963—, Martha Washington Hosp., 1965—, River Edge Hosp., 1965—, Christ Community Hosp., 1965—, Holy Cross Hosp., 1967—, N.E. Community Hosp., 1970—; cons. gen. medicine Augustana Hosp., 1970—, Ill. Central Hosp., 1971—, London Meml. Hosp., 1971—; lectr. Loyola Univ. Hosp., Chgo., 1970—. Diplomate Am. Bd. Internal Medicine. Fellow A.C.P., Am. Coll. Cardiology; mem. AMA, Am. Heart Assn., Am. Fedn. Clin. Research, Am. Coll. Chest Physicians, N.Y. Acad. Sci., Sigma Xi. Club: Safari. Home: 8905 Lemont Rd Downers Grove IL 60515 Office: 25 E Washington St Chicago IL 60602

SLOGGY, WILLIAM E., library adminstr.; b. Montreal, Que., Can., Sept. 4, 1919; s. Lee Harrison and Ellen (McCay) S. (parents Am. citizens); B.A., U. Minn., 1952, B.S. in L.S., 1954; m. Dorothea Anne Darling, June 29, 1946; children—William LeRoy, John Edward, Samuel Lee, Daniel Harrison. Reference librarian pub. library, Duluth, Minn., 1954-56; head librarian pub. library, Kaukauna, Wis., 1956-60; dir. N.W. Wis. Library System, Ashland, 1960—. Bd. dirs. Ashland Found. Served with U.S. Army, 1941-45; PTO. Mem. A.L.A., Wis. Library Assn., Common Cause. Clubs: Rotary, Eagles, Elks, Odd Fellows. Home: 805 MacArthur St Ashland WI 54806 Office: 502 W 2d St Ashland WI 54806

SLOMINSKI, LEO FRANK, machine mfg. co. exec.; b. Saginaw, Mich., June 20, 1909; s. Michel A. and Valentine (Brzeczkiewicz) S.; grad. high sch.; m. Eleonore Rita Konieczka, Nov. 29, 1941. With Gen. Motors Corp., Saginaw, 1927-45; with Allied Tool & Die Co., mfr. spl. and exptl. automotive precision machines, Saginaw, 1945—, pres., 1959—. Tchr. machine shop Saginaw High Sch., 1941. Mem. 7 man U.S. Trade Mission to USSR, 1971. Mem. Nat. Tool and Die and Precision Machining Assn. (v.p. 1973-75, pres. 1975—). Home: 1740 N Center Rd Saginaw MI 48603 Office: 3545 Janes Rd Saginaw MI 48605

SLONAKER, EDWARD LEE, city mgr.; b. Dayton., Ohio, Jan. 11, 1924; s. Albert J. and Emma M. (Apple) S.; student Tex. Western Coll., 1944; m. Mildred Eileen Lohman, July 27, 1946; children—Susan E., James E. Dep. clk. Montgomery County (Ohio) Cts., 1946-51; owner, operator E.L. Slonaker, Contractor, West Carrollton, Ohio, 1951-59; street commr., village adminstr. Village of West Carrollton, 1959-62, city mgr., police chief, 1962-67, city mgr., 1962—; chief West Carrollton Aux. Police, 1957. Vice pres. West Carrollton Girls Activity Bd., 1958; rep. Boy Scouts Am., 1956-58; treas. Montgomery County Community Action Agy., 1970-72; civil def. dir., West Carrollton; mem. citizens adv. com. Miami U., Middletown, Ohio. Served with AUS, 1943-46. Decorated Purple Heart, Combat Inf. medal. Mem. Montgomery County Mayors and City Mgrs. Assn. (v.p. 1966, sec.-treas. 1976—), Area City Mgrs. Assn. (pres. 1970), VFW, Am. Soc. Pub. Adminstrn. (v.p. 1972), Internat., Ohio (dir. 1976-77) city mgmt. assns., Miami Valley Council Govts. Lutheran. Clubs: Masons, Lions (pres. West Carrollton 1960), Order Eastern Star. Home: 17 Ironwood Dr West Carrollton OH 45449 Office: 41 E Central Ave West Carrollton OH 45449

SLOTSKY, LAWRENCE S., business exec.; b. Sioux City, Iowa, Jan. 15, 1921; s. William C. and Katherine G. S.; B.S., U. Iowa, 1942; m. Charlotte R. Liebling, May 1, 1946; children—Jeffrey, Donald, Marilyn. Office, credit mgr. Liebling Furniture Co., St. Joseph, 1946-52; exec. v.p. Credit Bur. of Sioux City and Woodbury County, Iowa, 1952, now pres., gen. mgr.; pub. The Daily Reporter, 1952; sec.-treas., mgr. Sioux City Parking Devel., Inc., 1954—. Pres. Jewish Fedn. of Sioux City, 1965-67; chmn. United Jewish Appeal, 1965, Iowa Civil Rights Commn., 1969-70; asso. gen. chmn. United Campaign, Sioux City, 1970, gen. chmn., 1971—; pres. United Way of Siouxland, 1977—; bd. dirs. Better Bus. Bur., Salvation Army, St. Lukes Med. Center; trustee Sioux City Art Center, 1976—; pres. Mt. Sinai Temple, 1969-71. Served with USAAF, 1943-45. Decorated D.F.C., Air medal with five oak leaf clusters. Mem. Asso. Credit Bur. Iowa (pres.), Asso. Credit Bus. Am. (dir.). Home: 3625 Nebraska St Sioux City IA 51104 Office: Commerce Bldg Sioux City IA 51101

SLOTVIG, PHILIP LEROY, rehab. counselor; b. Glenwood City, Wis., July 16, 1938; s. Ole K. and Mary L. (Wold) S.; A.A., Waldorf Jr. Coll., 1958; B.A., Augsburg Coll., 1960; M.S., St. Cloud State U., 1972; m. Kathleen E. Eide, Aug. 15, 1959; children—Mark, Paul. Rehab. counselor Div. Vocat. Rehab., Mankato, Minn., 1967-68, sr. counselor, Mpls., 1975-76, career counselor, 1976—; vocat. adj. coordinator Ind. Sch. Dist. #16, Mpls., 1968-75. Certified rehab. counselor. Lutheran. Home: 9070 Fillmore St NE Minneapolis MN 55434 Office: 6500 Brooklyn Blvd Minneapolis MN 55429

SLUSHER, SHIRLEY BROWN, librarian; b. Covington, Ky., May 28, 1923; d. Calloway and Elsie Mae (Burford) Brown; B.B.A. magna cum laude, U. Evansville (Ind.), 1953; M.L.S., U. Wis.-Milw., 1973; m. Claude Hylton Slusher, Aug. 26, 1950; children—Alice Rose, Clara Ruth, Barbara Anne, Robert Claude. Process cost accountant Am. Viscose Corp., Roanoke, Va., 1943-50; accountant Unit Crane & Shovel Corp., New Berlin, Wis., 1973-75; info. sci. specialist Rexnord, Inc., Milw., 1975—. Sec. health, phys. edn. and recreation com. Waukesha (Wis.) YWCA, 1967-70; mem. City of Waukesha Library Bd., 1977—. Mem. Spl. Libraries Assn., ALA, Am. Mgmt. Assn., League of Women Voters, Alpha Omicron Pi, Pi Gamma Mu. Presbyterian. Home: 1008 Lemira Ave Waukesha WI 53186 Office: Rexnord Inc PO Box 2022 Milwaukee WI 53201

SLUSS, RAY C., publishing co. exec.; b. Louisville, O., Sept. 30, 1926; s. Howard J. and Anna M. (Kurtz) S.; A.B., Ashland Coll., O., 1948; M.A., Ohio State U., 1951; m. Ellen Ann Stoffer, June 1, 1947; children—Michael, Mollie, Andrew. Tchr., prin. high sch., elementary schs., Ashland County (O.), 1946-51; textbook rep. Row, Peterson & Co., Evanston, Ill., 1951-62; dir. promotion Harper & Row Pubs., Evanston, 1962-63, midwest sales mgr., 1963-68, nat. sales mgr., 1969-70, v.p., pub. sch. dept., 1970-75, also dir.; nat. sales mgr., sch. dept. Rand McNally, Skokie, Ill., 1975—. Mem. Winnetka (Ill.) Caucus Com., Winnetka, 1967. Mem. Assn. for Supervision and Curriculum Devel., Assn. Am. Pubs., Internat. Reading Assn., Profl. Bookmen Am. Republican. Methodist (treas. 1973-76, lay leader 1977—). Home: 1156 Ash St Winnetka IL 60093 Office: 8255 Central Park Skokie IL 60076

SLYKHOUSE, ROGER ALLEN, civil engr.; b. Grand Rapids, Mich., June 16, 1929; s. Gerrit John and Emma Louise (Ozinga) S.; B.S., U. Mich., 1950, M.S., 1954; m. Mildred Gloria Bursey, Apr. 6, 1957; children—Roger Allen, Gary Bursey, Holly Jane. Jr. engr. U.S. Bur. Reclamation, Denver and Hungry Horse, Mont., 1950; civil and staff engr. community devel. sect. Arabian Am. Oil Co., N.Y.C., 1954-55, The Hague, 1955, Dhahran, Saudi Arabia, 1955-58; civil engr. J & G. Daverman Co., Grand Rapids, Mich., 1958-59; cons. civil engr. Roger A. Slykhouse, Cons. Engr., 1959-64, 76—; prin. Weeber & Slykhouse Cons. Engrs., 1964-76. Mem. Grand Rapids Charter Revision Commn., 1970-73; mem. Mich. plat adv. com. Dept. Treasury, 1967—; mem. Kent County Soil Erosion and Sedimentation Control Bd., 1975—; pres. Oakleigh Middle Sch. PTA, Grand Rapids, 1970-72; pres. Union High Sch. Parent Tchrs. Student Assn., 1975-76; exec. bd., properties com. chmn. W. Mich. Shores council Boy Scouts Am.; mem. Kent County Republican Exec. Com., 1973-75, 76—; bd. dirs. Western Mich. Environ. Action Council, 1968-72, 76—. Served with USAF, 1951-53. Named Engr. of Year, W. Mich. chpt. Mich. Soc. Profl. Engrs., 1972. Fellow ASCE (br. pres. 1964-65); mem. Mich. Water Pollution Control Assn., Joint Engrs. Council Western Mich. (pres. 1968-69), Grand Rapids Engrs. Club. Clubs: Masons, Kiwanis (pres. Grand Rapids 1976-77), Grand Rapids Riding (dir. 1973-76), Army-Navy of Grand Rapids (pres. 1977—). Home and Office: 2221 W Leonard St Grand Rapids MI 49504

SMALE, JOHN GRAY, mfg. exec.; b. Listowel, Ont., Can., Aug. 1, 1927; s. Peter J. and Vera Gladys (Gray) S.; B.S. in Bus., Miami U. (Ohio), 1949; m. Phyllis Anne Weaver, Sept. 2, 1950; children—John Gray, Catherine Anne, Lisa Beth, Peter McKee. With Vick Chem. Co., N.Y.C., 1949-51, Bio-Research Inc., N.Y.C., 1952-52; pres., dir. Procter & Gamble Co., Cin., 1952—. Trustee Kenyon Coll. Served with USNR, 1945-46. Clubs: Commercial, Commonwealth Cin. Country, Queen City (Cin.); Zanesfield Rod and Gun. Office: Procter and Gamble Co PO Box 599 Cincinnati OH 45201

SMALL, DONALD DAVID, educator; b. Hammond, Ind., Dec. 30, 1932; s. Victor Peter and Wanda (Rubinska) S.; M.S., Ind., U., 1963, Ed.D., 1967; m. Sergine Anne Oliver, June 6, 1970 (dec. 1974); children—(by previous marriage)—David Arthur, Elaine Diane. Asso. prof. Coll. Edn., Western Ky. U., 1967-68; asso. prof. edn. U. Toledo, 1968-77, prof., 1977—, dir. honors programs in edn., chief instr. karate programs, 1969—. Chmn., nat. com. on English methods, conf. on English edn., 1967—; cons. in grammar and linguistics to numerous Ohio sch. dists. under Title III Elementary and Secondary Edn. Act. Mem. steering com. Students of Toledo Organized for Peace, 1970—; bd. dirs. Toledo Mental Hygiene Center, 1977—. Served with AUS, 1955-57. Mem. A.A.U.P., Am. Fedn. Tchrs., Nat. Council Tchrs. English, Am. Ednl. Studies Assn., Assn. Supervision and Curriculum Devel., English Assn. Ohio, U.S. Power Squadrons, Am. Karate System (charter), AAU (exec. com. Karate nat. com. 1973—). Club: Bayview Yacht. Author numerous books and articles on edn. Home: 2807 Goddard Rd Toledo OH 43606

SMALL, RICHARD DONALD, travel co. exec.; b. West Orange, N.J., May 24, 1929; s. Joseph George and Elizabeth (McGarry) S.; A.B. cum laude, U. Notre Dame, 1951; m. Arlene P. Small; children—Colleen, Richard Donald, Joseph, Mark, Brian. With Union-Camp Corp., N.Y.C., Chgo., 1952-62; pres. Alumni Holidays, Inc., Studentaire Travel, Inc., Chgo., 1962—; pres. AHI Internat. Corp., Chgo. Mem. Chgo. Assn. Commerce and Industry (edn., visitors bur., transp. coms.), Am. Soc. Travel Agts. Club: University (Chgo.) Home: 505 N Lake Shore Dr Chicago IL 60611 also 1111 Crandon Blvd Key Biscayne FL 33149 Office: 11 E Adams St Chicago IL 60603

SMALL, SHEILA EVELYN, ednl. assn. adminstr.; b. Boston, Apr. 26, 1934; d. Meyer and Rose (Levine) Goldstein; A.A., George Washington U., 1954, B.A., 1957; M.S., U. N.Y. at Plattsburgh, 1975; m. Arthur Harold Small, May 5, 1957; children—Allison, Marc. News, features dir. Radio Sta. KCGO, Cheyenne, Wyo., 1969-71; instr. Provincial Jr. Coll., Taichung, Taiwan, 1971-73; instr. Clinton Community Coll., Plattsburgh, 1973-76; facilitator Ohio Congress Sch. Adminstr. Assns., 1976—, editor Congress Comments, 1976—; free lance writing to Sunday supplements features, greeting cards. Mem. Am. Personnel and Guidance Assn. Home: 1093 Loch Ness Ave Worthington OH 43085 Office: 750 Brooksedge Blvd Westerville OH 43081

SMALLEY, JAMES ADDISON, Realtor; b. Mt. Auburn, Iowa, Apr. 26, 1930; s. Edwin Royal and Florence Iva (Willson) S.; student Oakland U., 1965—; m. Lillie Kathryn Ledbetter, Aug. 6, 1955; 1 son, Edwin Royal. Served as enlisted man U.S. Army, 1948-51, now lt. col., C.E., U.S. Army Res.; pres. Smalley Inc., Realtors, Rochester, Mich., 1955—; pres. The J.E.L. Corp.; tchr. real estate investments Oakland U.; instr. Real Estate Investments and Taxation U. Mich., Ann Arbor. Trustee, mem. adminstrv. bd. St. Paul's United Meth. Ch., 1955—. Mem. Nat. Assn. Realtors, Mich. (pres. Exchange Comml. Group 1969-73) Assn. Realtors, Rochester Bd. Realtors (pres. 1961-65, Realtor of Year 1965), Soc. Exchange Counselors (bd. govs.), Ind. Fee Appraisers, C. of C. (v.p. 1965-74), Am. Legion Res. Officers Assn. (life). Clubs: Masons (32 deg.), Moslem Temple Shrine (pres. 1961), Rochester Shrine, Elks, Gt. Oaks County. Home: 896 Allston Dr Rochester MI 48063 Office: 2660 S Rochester St Rochester MI 48063

SMALLWOOD, JOHN EDGAR, mgmt. cons.; b. Hampton, Iowa, Aug. 27, 1926; s. Benjamin Richard and Della Sarah (Combs) S.; student Mich. State U., 1944, Bowling Green State U., 1947; A.B., Albion Coll., 1951; m. Mary Ellen Goll, May 24, 1947; children—John Mark, Mary Carol. With Union Steel Products Co., 1951-55; with Whirlpool Corp., Benton Harbor, Mich., 1955-74, supr. cost estimating and financial analysis, 1961-64, dir. econ. and marketing research, 1965-74; v.p., dir. econ. and mktg. research Mgmt. Horizons Inc., Columbus, O., 1974—. Lectr., tchr. Northwestern U., 1966, Mich. State U., 1970, Lake Mich. Coll., 1972. Served with Signal Corps, U.S. Army, 1944-46. Author: The Product Life Cycle: A Key to Strategic Marketing Planning; Exploiting the Price-Demand Curve; Superflation Management; Distribution Demographics; Multiple Future Planning; Profitability and Productivity Trends in Retailing. Home: 267 Pinney Dr Worthington OH 43085 Office: Mgmt Horizons Inc 450 W Wilson Bridge Rd Worthington OH 43085

SMART, BRADFORD DYER, psychol. cons.; b. Hartford, Conn., July 3, 1944; s. Walter Elden and Dorothy (Alvord) S.; A.B., Miami U., 1966; M.S., Purdue U., 1968, Ph.D., 1970; m. Mary Joan Hudson, Aug. 17, 1967; children—Geoffrey Hudson, Kathryn Bradford. Psychol. cons. Humber, Mundie & McClary, Milw., 1970; v.p., Mgmt. Psychologists, Inc., Chgo., 1970-72; pres. Smart & Assos., Inc., Chgo., 1973—; instr., Purdue U., 1968-70, U. Wis., 1970, Northwestern U., 1971-74; vol. cons. Chicagoland YMCA, 1972—. Asso. bd. dirs. Chgo. Lung Assn. Mem. Am., Midwest, Ill. psychol. assns. Contbr. articles to profl. jours. Home: 21937 N Andover Rd Kildeer IL 60047 Office: 150 N Wacker Dr Chicago IL 60606

SMART, DAVID BARTON, food co. exec.; b. Boston, July 21, 1929; s. Harry L. and Dorice Chase (Elkins) S.; student Tufts U., 1947-48; B.A., Marietta Coll., 1951; M.A. (Cordell Hull fellow), Vanderbilt U., 1953; m. Susan Jean Tresch, Nov. 16, 1957; children—Kendall, Bruce, Laura, Karen. Copywriter, Gen. Electric Co., Schenectady, N.Y., 1953-57; account supr. Marsteller, Inc., Chgo., 1957-60; account exec. Needham, Harper & Steers Co., Chgo., 1960-64; v.p., account supr. Gardner Advt. Co., St. Louis, 1964-69; dir. food enterprises div. Ralston Purina Co., St. Louis, 1969—; guest lectr. Milw. Mktg. Assn., 1959, Greenville Coll., 1965, So. Ill. U., 1966, Met. St. Louis Fed. Assn., 1976, Internat. Food Editors Conf., 1971. Vice pres. PTA, University City, Mo., 1969-70; com. chmn. Cub Scouts Am., 1969; Jr. Achievement project leader, 1955-56. Mem. Nat. Restaurant Assn., Internat. Foodservice Mfrs. Assn., Marietta Coll. Alumni Assn. (pres. Chgo. 1961-62), Phi Alpha Theta, Omicron Delta Kappa, Pi Delta Epsilon. Home: 768 Straub Rd Ballwin MO 63011 Office: Checkerboard Square St Louis MO 63188

SMART, GUY ALEXANDER, accountant, managerial cons.; b. Shelby County, N.C., Sept. 21, 1903; s. Lawson Henderson and Mary Tullalah Jane (Ward) S.; student U. Akron, 1940-46, Walsh Coll., 1970-74; m. Maxine Lucille Darner, Jan. 30, 1972; children by previous marriage—Lois Elizabeth, Guy Cooper; stepdau., Mary Elizabeth Little. With Republic Steel Corp., 1922-68, div. property accountant Union Drawn div., Massillon, Ohio, 1933-68; pvt. practicing tax cons., pub. accountant and managerial cons., Massillon, Ohio, 1968—; instr. U. Akron, Washington High Sch. Vice-chmn. Massillon Republican Central Com.; active Boy Scouts Am.; bd. dirs. Massillon Boys Club. Recipient Service awards YMCA, 1964, also United Fund. L.P.A., Ohio. Mem. Pub. Accountants Soc. Ohio (treas. Stark County chpt.; Distinguished award 1971), Nat. Soc. Pub. Accountants, Am. Trial Lawyers Assn. Presbyterian (tchr. Bible Class). Clubs: Masons, Shriner, Order of Eastern Star, Optimist (pres. 1974-75, Outstanding Leadership award 1974-75). Home: 1629 Tremont Ave SW Massillon OH 44646 Office: PO Box 534 Massillon OH 44646

SMART, HAROLD DEARBORN, educator; b. Detroit, Dec. 18, 1926; s. Harold Dearborn and Margaret Sutherland (Shields) S.; B.S. in Edn., Wayne State U., 1950; M.F.A., Cranbrook Acad., Bloomfield Hills, Mich., 1960; m. Winifred Jean Milne, July 4, 1952; children—Graeme, Cameron, David. Dir. recreation Haven Sanitarium, Rochester, Mich., 1948-50; instr., supr. art Brookside Sch., Bloomfield Hills, 1950-71; chmn. art dept. Cranbrook Schs., 1972—; dir. Lost Trail Camp, Sula, Mont., 1966-72, Lost Trail Wilderness Adventures, 1972-76, Cranbrook Summer Camp, 1977—. Exec. council Mich. Art Edn. Assn., 1976—. Trustee Bloomfield Art Assn.; bd. dirs. Tri-County Arts Council, Cranbrook Dads Club. Served with USNR, 1944-46. Mem. Nat. Assn. Ind. Schs., Ind. Schs. Assn. Central States (dir.), Nat. Art Edn. Assn., Mich. Alliance for Arts Edn. (dir.), Ind. Schs. Assn. Greater Detroit (v.p.), Am. Camping Assn. Exhibited art Detroit Inst. Arts, 1955-60, Cranbrook Acad. Galleries, 1960. Home: 100 Tamarack Way Bloomfield Hills MI 48013

SMART, IRENE BALOGH, lawyer, judge; b. Cleve., Mar. 24, 1921; d. John and Elizabeth (Szaszak) Balogh; B.S., Wittenberg U., 1942; student Phys. therapy Harvard Med. Sch., 1943; LL.B., William McKinley Sch. Law, 1955; m. Charles Eugene Smart, May 17, 1945; children—Charles Eugene II, Mary Smart Radebaugh (dec.), Jennifer Lynn. Phys. therapist Cleve. Clinic, 1943-44; asst. supr. phys. therapy John Hopkins Hosp., Balt., 1944-45; phys. therapist Sunbeam Sch. for Crippled Children, Cleve., 1945-46; head phys. therapy Mercy Hosp., Canton, Ohio, 1946-47; admitted to Ohio bar, 1956; mem. firm Smart & Smart, Canton, 1956-78; mem. Ohio Ho. of Reps., 1973-78; judge Canton Municipal Ct., 1978—. Mem. urban devel. commn. City of Canton, 1957-58; council-at-large City of Canton, 1959-72. Mem. Stark County (Ohio) Central Com. Democratic party; mem. Federated Dem. Women of Ohio, Dem. Women's Club. Trustee United Cerebral Palsy Assn., 1966—, v.p., 1972-75; trustee Ohio War Orphans Scholarship Bd., 1973-78. Recipient Alumni award Wittenberg U., 1973; Mayors Citation for outstanding performance in urban renewal, 1972; Citations, Canton City Council, 1972; Conservation award Am. Sportsman Club, 1974; Outstanding Service award Ohio Profl. Firefighters, 1976; Meritorious Service award Fraternal Order of Police, 1976. Mem. Ohio Bar Assn., AAUW, Delta Zeta. Presbyn. Mem. Order Eastern Star. Home: 3807 Third St NW Canton OH 44708 Office: City Hall Room M31 Canton OH 44702

SMEDAL, ERLING ARNOLD, ophthalmologist; b. McFarland, Wis., Mar. 26, 1899; s. Harald Aslakson and Aasne Eivindsdatter (Evans) S.; B.S., U. Wis., 1922; M.D., U. Chgo., 1925; postgrad. Rush Med. Coll., 1931-32; m. Erma Kathleen Houston, July 29, 1931. Intern, Cook County Hosp., Chgo., 1924-25; gen. practice medicine, Viroqua, Wis., 1926-31; practice medicine specializing in ophthalmology, Mansfield, Ohio, 1932—; mem. staff Mansfield (Ohio) Gen. Hosp.; adv. bd. First Nat. Bank, Mansfield. Served to maj. AUS, 1918, 1942-46. Diplomate Am. Bd. Ophthalmology. Fellow Internat. Coll. Surgeons, Am. Acad. Ophthalmology and Otolaryngology; mem. Am., Ohio ophthalmol. socs., AMA, Ohio, Richland County med. socs., Am. Legion, Amvets, Ohio State Geneal. Soc., Order Crown of Charlemagne in U.S.A. Mason. Club: Tucson Nat. Golf. Author: Smedal Family History and Genealogy, 1966. Address: 456 W Park Ave Mansfield OH 44906

SMEDSRUD, MILTON ELVIN, agrl. assn. ofcl.; b. Fergus Falls, Minn., Mar. 23, 1932; s. S.E. and Sophi S. (Larson) S.; student Moorhead State Coll., 1951-52; m. Villamsen, Feb. 18, 1956; children—Greg, Jeff. Gen. agt. Life Investors Ins. Co., Cedar Rapids, Iowa, 1956-76; founder Communicating for Agr., Inc., Fergus Falls, 1972, pres., 1972—; pres. Smedsrud Ins., Fergus Falls, 1970—; farmer, Otter Tail, Minn., 1932-51. Served with USAF, 1952-56. Mem. VFW, Am. Legion, Assn. Life and Health Underwriters. Lutheran. Clubs: Elks, Eagles. Home: Stalker Lake Dalton MN 56324 Office: Law Office Center Fergus Falls MN

SMEESTER, JOSEPH GLENN, beverage distbr.; b. Quinnesec, Mich., Sept. 14, 1928; s. Jule and Fay (Rector) S.; student Nat. Radio Inst., 1951-52; m. Dolores Francis Bierstaker, May 25, 1951; children—Joseph, Jeanna. Partner Smeester Bros. Trucking, beer and wine distbr., Iron Mountain, Mich., 1946—; pres. Four Season Beer Distbg. Inc., 1955—. Served with USNR, 1950-54. Home: River Hills Rd Kingsford MI 49801 Office: 1330 S Jackson St Iron Mountain MI 49801

SMELSER, MARGARET LEE, real estate broker; b. Marion, Ind., Oct. 6, 1928; d. Lemley George and Ruth Elizabeth (Fisherbuck) Himelick; student Ind. No. U., 1963-64; m. Warren Duane Smelser, Sept. 5, 1948; children—Rosilyn Smelser Vice, Robert Lee. Telephone operator, Gaston, Ind., 1946; bookkeeper Marion Plywood, 1964; saleswoman Puckett Realty, Marion, 1965; self-employed real estate broker, Marion, 1966—. Mem. Nat. Assn. Real Estate Bds., Ind. Real Estate Assn., Marion Bd. Realtors (auditing com. 1970-72), Women's Council Real Estate (by laws com. 1972), DeMolay Mother's Circle. Presbyterian. Club: Christian Women's. Home and office: 123 SE St Marion IN 46952

SMELSER, WARREN DUANE, realtor, craftsman; b. Muncie, Ind., Sept. 10, 1920; s. Oliver C. and Violet M. (Chesworth) S.; grad. high sch.; m. Margaret Lee Himelick, Sept. 5, 1948; children—Rosilyn (Mrs. B. E. Vice), Robert Lee. Patternmaker Engle King Pattern Works, Columbus, Ind., 1952-55; partner Precision Pattern Works, Muncie, 1955-59; wood patternmaker Fisher Body, Marion, Ind., 1959—; real estate salesman Puckett Realty Co., Marion, 1965-67, W.D. Smelser, realtor, Marion, Ind., 1967—. Served with USNR, 1942-45; PTO. Mem. Nat. Assn. of Real Estate Bds., Marion Area Bd. of Realtors, Ind. Assn. of Realtors, Pattern Makers League N. Am., (rec. sec. Muncie br. 1956-58, 63). Presbyn. (deacon 1965-68). Mason. Address: 123 South E Marion IN 46952

SMID, ARTHUR CHARLES, pediatrician; b. Omaha, May 30, 1924; s. Jerry Joseph and Josephine (Stolarik) S.; B.S. in Medicine, Creighton U., Omaha, 1946, M.D., 1948; M.S. in Pediatrics, U. Minn., 1957; m. Mary Ellen McGrath, Aug. 31, 1946; children—Patti, Arthur, Jonathan, Mary Beth, David. Intern, U.S. Naval Hosp., Gt. Lakes, Ill., 1948-49; gen. practice medicine, Chicago Heights, Ill., 1949-51; fellow in pediatrics Mayo Clinic, Rochester, Minn., 1953-56; practice medicine specializing in pediatrics, Naperville, Ill., 1956—; mem. staff Edward and Copley hosps.; dir. Bank of Naperville, First Security Bank Fox Valley. Bd. dirs. Benet Acad., 1967-74, chmn., 1971-74; mem. pres.'s adv. council Ill. Benedictine Coll., 1965—. Served with AUS, 1942-46; with M.C., USNR, 1948-49, 51-53. Diplomate Am. Bd. Pediatrics. Mem. Am. Acad. Pediatrics, AMA, Ill. Med. Soc., Mayo Clinic, U. Minn., Creighton U. alumni assns.,

Ret. Officers Assn. (life), Phi Rho (life). Roman Catholic. Clubs: K.C., Rotary. Home: 551 White Oak Dr Naperville IL 60540 Office: 25 S Washington St Naperville IL 60540

SMITH, ALFRED NORBERT, surgeon; b. Waterloo, Iowa, Jan. 1, 1921; s. John C. and Rose (Hennigan) S.; B.S., Loras Coll., 1942; M.D., U. Iowa, 1944; m. Mary Louise Wyman, Jan. 11, 1947; children—Clyde, Phillip, Charlotte, David, Kathryn, Theresa. Intern, U.S. Naval Hosp., Long Beach, Calif., 1944-45; resident in surgery VA Hosp., Des Moines, 1946-49, VA Hosp., Fayetteville, Ark., 1949-50; practice medicine specializing in surgery, Des Moines, 1957—; thoracic surgery ward officer Va Hosp., Wadsworth, Kans., 1950-51; chief surgery Va Hosp., Knoxville, Iowa, 1951-53; asst. chief surgery Va Hosp., Des Moines, 1953-57; chief thoracic surgery Broadlawns Gen. Hosp., Des Moines, 1960—; chief staff NW Hosp., 1967, Mercy Hosp., 1976; chmn. Iowa Found. Med. Care Area IV, 1976. Served to lt. j.g. USNR, 1944-47. Recipient Des Moines Health Center Service award, 1973. Mem. AMA, Iowa, State, Polk County med. socs., Iowa Acad. Surgery, Am. Soc. Contemporary Medicine and Surgery. Contbr. articles to med. jours. Home: 2550 Heliotrope Dr Des Moines IA 50315 Office: 1407 Woodland St Des Moines IA 50309

SMITH, ALFRED RUSSELL, lawyer; b. Akron, Ohio, Feb. 1, 1936; s. Lawrence Junior and Alta Lucinda (McGilton) S.; B.A., Ohio State U., 1959, J.D., 1961; m. Regina Diane Morris, Aug. 5, 1961; children—Melanie Angela, Benjamin Lawrence, Matthew Alfred. Admitted to Ohio bar, 1961; practiced in Akron, 1962—, Cuyahoga Falls, Ohio, 1965-69; adjuster State Farm Ins. Co., Akron, 1961; asst. pros. atty. Summit County, Akron, 1963-64; mem. firm Laybourne, McClenathen and Smith, Akron, 1969—; spl. counsel for atty. gen. State of Ohio, 1965-68; spl. counsel for City of Akron, 1965-69. Mem. Task Force of Summit County Criminal Justice Commn., 1971-72. Served with AUS, 1962. Mem. Am., Ohio (mem. negligence law com. 1969—), Akron bar assns., Ohio Acad. Trial Lawyers (governing trustee 1972, pres. 1977—), Am. Trial Lawyers Assn., Am. Judicature Soc., Phi Delta Phi, Kappa Sigma (pres. Alpha Sigma Chpt. 1959). Home: 1386 Briar Hill Dr Akron OH 44313 Office: 1101 Centran Bldg Akron OH 44308

SMITH, ALICE BYRD APPLETON (MRS. JUSTIN V. SMITH), civic worker; b. Berwyn, Ill., July 9, 1907; d. Ernest and Ethyl (Messer) Appleton; student Lombard Coll., 1925-26; m. Richard Crawford, Apr. 9, 1927 (div. June 1956); children—Carroll, Richard, Rodney; m. Justin V. Smith, Aug. 27, 1958. Pres. Women's Symphony Assn., Mpls., 1960-61, Center Opera Assn., Mpls., 1965-67; sec. Minn. Opera Co., Mpls., 1968-69, pres., 1973; mem. Mpls. Inst. Arts, 1954—; mem. Friends of the Inst., 1956—. Bd. dirs. Walker Art Center, 1974—; corporate trustee Northwestern Hosp.; trustee T.B. Walker Found., 1972-76. Recipient award by Pres. Roosevelt for A.R.C. service, 1946. Mem. Pi Beta Phi, Lambda Phi Delta. Republican. Conglist. (deaconess 1964-66). Home: 4915 Regents Walk Excelsior MN 55331

SMITH, ALTON CARL, SR., educator, former city ofcl.; b. Novi, Mich., Jan. 21, 1931; s. Alton Presley and Alzona (Gray) S.; diploma Eastern Bible Inst., 1952; Asso. Sci., Flint Community Jr. Coll., 1959; A.B., U. Mich. at Flint, 1961, M.S., U. Mich., 1963, M.A., 1969; m. Gladys Marie Farrand, June 26, 1952 (dec. 1975); children—Barbara Joanne, Alton Carl, Brenda Jean, Beverly Joy, Bonnie Janine; m. 2d, Norma Youngs McGee; stepchildren—Rachel Leona McGee, Joyce Ann McGee Nestler. Ordained to ministry Assemblies of God Ch., 1954, minister, 1952-56; with IBM, 1956-60; minister edn. Riverside Tabernacle, Flint, 1960-62; tchr. pub. schs., Flint, 1962-69; instr. Central Mich. U., Mt. Pleasant, 1969-70; prin. Byron (Mich.) Area Schs., 1970-73, tchr., 1973-76; appointed missionary-educator West African Advanced Sch. Theology, Togo, West Africa, 1976—; commr. City of Flint, 1964-68, chmn. finance com., 1966-68; mem. Fenton Twp. Zoning Bd. Appeals, 1973-74; mem. Fenton Twp. Planning and Zoning Bd., 1974-76. Mem. N.E.A., Mich. Edn. Assn., Genesee County Hist. Soc. Contbr. numerous articles to denominational publs. Home: care Div Fgn Missions Gen Council Assemblies of God 1445 Boonville Ave Springfield MO 65802

SMITH, ANDREW WARREN, educator; b. Johnstown, Pa., May 16, 1932; s. Andrew W. and Agnes Blair (Cranston) S.; B.S., Ind. State Coll., 1954; M.Mus., U. Mich., 1961, Ph.D., 1970; student Internat. Summer Academie, Mozarteum, Salzburg, Austria, 1961, 63, U. Innsbruck, 1963-64, U. Vienna, State Acad. Music, Vienna, 1964-65; m. Nancy Jane Kroehl, Aug. 14, 1965; children—Andrew Thomas, David Howard. Organist, choirmaster various chs., 1948—, also organ cons.; supr. elementary music, Ford City, Pa., 1958-62; high sch. choral dir., Ford City, 1962-63; asso. prof., coordinator music edn., adminstrv. asst. to chmn. Moorhead (Minn.) State U., 1968—. Served with U.S. Army, 1954-57. Mem. Music Educators Nat. Conf., Am. Guild Organists. Mason (Shriner). Organist for 1964 Winter Olympic Games, Protestant Chapel, Innsbruck, Austria. Home: 1020 1st St N Fargo ND 58102

SMITH, ARTHUR ALLAN, lawyer; b. Detroit, May 22, 1931; s. Arthur M. and Barbara (Allan) S.; student Mich. State U., 1949-52; LL.B., U. Va., 1955, J.D., 1970; m. Lois Crutchfield, June 14, 1955; children—Mark A., Scott A., Amy A. Admitted to Mich. bar, 1956; practiced in Detroit and Dearborn, 1957—; asst. U.S. atty. Eastern Dist. Mich., 1957-59; partner Smith, Poplar & Kalis, Dearborn, Mich., 1971—. Tchr. bus. law Lawrence Inst. Tech., 1962-66. Chmn. bd. YMCA, Dearborn, Mich., 1965-69; vice chmn. Indian Affairs Commn., State Mich., 1968-72; pres. Dearborn C. of C., 1977-78. Mem. Rep. State Central Com., 1969-71. Served to 1st lt. Mil. Police Corps, AUS, 1955-57. Mem. Fed. Bar Assn. Detroit (pres. 1970-71), Fed., Am., Mich., Dearborn, Detroit bar assns., Am. Trial Lawyers Assn., Central States Archeol. Soc. Rotarian. Home: 408 S Vernon Dr Dearborn MI 48124 Office: 728 Parklane Towers West Dearborn MI 48126

SMITH, ARTHUR APPLEBY, physician and surgeon; b. Springfield, Mo., Sept. 16, 1931; s. Harold Byron and Lucille Helen (Appleby) S.; B.A., S.W. Mo. U., 1952; M.S. in Biochemistry, U. Ark., 1954; M.D., St. Louis U., 1958; m. Stella Elizabeth Baber, May 30, 1952; children—Michael Arthur, Barbara Ann, James Edward, Cynthia Sue. Intern, St. Louis City Hosp., 1958-59, resident in obstetrics and gynecology, 1959-62; practice medicine specializing in obstetrics and gynecology, Belleville, Ill., 1962—; instr. obstetrics and gynecology Barnes Hosp.; pres. Arthur A. Smith M.D. Service Corp.; mem. Ill. State Maternal Mortality Com., 1971—. Diplomate Am. Bd. Obstetrics and Gynecology. Fellow A.C.S., Am. Coll. Obstetrics and Gynecology; mem. St. Clair County, St. Louis, Ill. med. socs., AMA. Methodist. Home: 206 Country Club Ln Belleville IL 62273 Office: 306 E 8th St O'Fallon IL 62269

SMITH, BARRY WARD, lawyer; b. Detroit, Dec. 27, 1920; s. Barry Albert and Ethel Ida (Ward) S.; B.A., Detroit Inst. Tech., 1942; J.D., U. Detroit, 1948; m. Joan Arlene Schneeman, Aug. 16, 1947; children—Barry Robert, Barbara Joan. Admitted to Mich. bar, 1948; practiced in Detroit, Dearborn, Mich., 1954—; practice, Dearborn, 1954-63; partner Cozadd, Shangle & Smith, 1964—. Sec. Lawyers Title Agy. of Mich., Detroit, 1947-51; exec. v.p. Met. Fed. Savs. & Loan Assn., Detroit, 1951-53; dep. corp. counsel City of Dearborn, 1953-54. Mem. Dearborn City Planning Commn., 1953; pres. Dearborn Pub. Devel. Corp., 1960—; vice-chmn. Dearborn Bd. Canvassers, 1965—. Served as lt. (j.g.) USNR, 1943-46. Mem. State Bar Mich., Detroit, Dearborn (pres. 1963) bar assns., Dearborn Orchestral Soc. (pres. 1970). Episcopalian. Kiwanian. Home: 840 Beechmont St Dearborn MI 48124 Office: 1427 Parklane Towers East 1 Parklane Blvd Dearborn MI 48126

SMITH, BERTRAND LEE, JR., publisher; b. Indpls., Aug. 14, 1906; s. Bertrand Lee and Catherine A. (Campbell) S.; grad. high sch., Cin.; m. Margaret Louise Shawhan, May 11, 1929 (dec. 1964); one son, Bertrand Lee III; m. 2d, Helen Maloney Lockwood, Apr. 8, 1969. Engaged as bookseller Bertrand Smith's Acres of Books, Inc., Cin., 1929—, gen. mgr., 1935-60, pres., chmn. bd., 1960-71, pres. emeritus, 1971—; cons. pub. and instnl. libraries. Served with U.S. Army, 1926-30. Mem. Am. Booksellers Assn., Antiquarian Booksellers Assn. Am., Antiquarian Booksellers Assn. Great Britain, Am. Bibliog. Soc. Republican. Clubs: Mason, Queen City, Optimists, Literary; Grolier (N.Y.). Address: The Edgecliff 2200 Victory Pkwy Cincinnati OH 45206

SMITH, BOLLING BARTON, univ. adminstr.; b. Catonsville, Md., Aug. 24, 1924; s. Hawthorne and Hattie Beatrice (Thomas) S.; B.S., Morgan State U., 1950, postgrad., 1962; postgrad. Towson State Coll., 1963, Am. U., 1964-65, Nat. Aero. and Space Inst., 1964; m. Susan Beatrice Goodson, Feb. 27, 1960; children—Millicent Victoria, Bolling Barton. Sci. tchr., dept. head Balt. City Schs., 1954-64; lectr. NASA Lewis Research Center, Cleve., 1964-66; dir. spl. and ednl. programs James A. Lovell Space Center, Milw., 1966-70, also ednl. cons., 1965; coordinator community ednl. programs U. Wis.-Milw., 1970-75; dir. Equal Opportunity Program, Sch. Nursing, U. Wis.-Madison, 1975—; ednl. cons. Wis. Electric Power Co., 1968, U. Wis. Extension, 1968. Mem. adv. com. Milw. Urban League, 1973—; mem. social action com. Episcopal Diocese Milw., 1972—; mem. cultural adv. com. Milw. Pub. Mus., 1972—; bd. dirs. Milw. Theol. Inst., Dane County Mental Health Center. Served with AUS, 1943-46. Mem. Nat. Sci. Tchrs. Assn., NAACP (exec. com. Madison), Urban League, Wis. Futures Soc., Assn. Black Profls. U. Wis. at Milw. (mem. steering com. 1973—). Home: 6213 Piedmont Rd Madison WI 53711 Office: Equal Opportunity Program Sch Nursing U Wis Madison WI 53706

SMITH, BRUCE, mag. editor; b. Chgo., May 21, 1942; s. James Bruce and Jane (Ericsson) S.; B.A. in Journalism, U. Calif. at Los Angeles, 1962. Editor, Chgo. FM Guide, 1962-64; feature editor Instns., Chgo., 1964-65; editor Food Service Mktg., Madison, Wis., 1966-75, also v.p. editorial devel., editorial dir. Food Service Chain Exec., Food Service Distbn. News; editor, pub. Mktg. Decisions for Food Service Industry, Chgo., 1975—; pres. Bruce Smith Co., Chgo., 1975—; pres. Instl. Food Editorial Council, 1971—. Recipient Editorial awards Nat. Fisheries Inst., 1967, 68, Nat. Assn. Coll. and Univ. Food Service Dirs., 1972. Mem. Internat. Food Service Mfrs. Assn., Internat. Wine and Food Soc., Soc. Advancement Foodservice Research, Newberry Library Assos. Clubs: Caxton, Whitehall, Press (Chgo.). Author: A Directory of Systems Capability, 1972; Towards the Establishment of a Great American Cuisine, 1974. Contbr. articles to profl. jours. Address: 1825 N Lincoln Plaza Chicago IL 60614

SMITH, BURNELL RAYMOND, sch. supt.; b. Garber, Iowa, Dec. 21, 1937; s. Carter Harrison and Hildegard Marie (Clefisch) S.; B.S., Upper Iowa Coll., 1959; M.A., Drake U., 1965; Ph.D., U. Iowa, 1971; m. Sharon Elaine Pensel, Dec. 22, 1961; children—Kathleen Marie, Laura Elaine. Tchr., Bellevue Community Sch. Dist., 1961-64; prin. North-Linn Sch. Dist., Troy Mills, Iowa, 1964-67; asst. supt. Marion (Iowa) Ind. Sch. Dist., 1967-70; supt. Riverdale Sch. Dist., Port Byron, Ill., 1971-73; supt. Monroe (Wis.) Pub. Schs., 1973—; mem. Black Hawk Area Spl. Edn. Exec. Bd., 1972-74. Mem. Am. Assn. Sch. Adminstrs. (life), Wis. Assn. Sch. Dist. Adminstrs., NEA, Phi Delta Kappa. Home: 923 4th St Monroe WI 53566 Office: 1510 13th St Monroe WI 53566

SMITH, CHARLES CARROLL, JR., state ofcl.; b. Chgo., Oct. 12, 1944; s. Charles Carroll and Anna May (Hawekotte-Smith) S.; B.S., Loyola U., 1967; M.A., Sangamon State U., 1973; m. Mary Ann Kenny, Mar. 19, 1977. Spl. agt. in charge Chgo. field office Def. Intelligence Agy., 1969-71; adminstrv. asst. Auditor of Accounts, State of Ill., 1971-73; adminstrv. asst. to Sec. of State of Ill., 1973-74; dir. corp. devel. Rippel Archtl. Metals, Chgo., 1974-77; asst. dep. sec. of state, Ill. Served with U.S. Army, 1967-68; capt. Res. Mem. Am. Soc. Pub. Adminstrn., Ill. Assn. Chiefs Police. Roman Catholic. Clubs: Sangamo (Springfield) Lake Shore (Chgo.). Home: 420 W Melrose Chicago IL 60657 Office: 188 W Randolph Chicago IL 60601

SMITH, CHARLES CLYDE, electronic components mfg. co. exec.; b. Evansville, Ind., Oct. 21, 1926; s. Clyde Frank and Mathilda Rosalie (Pirnat) S.; student Ohio U., 1944-45, Tex. A. and M. U., 1945; B.S. in Elec. Engring., Purdue U., 1950; m. Elizabeth Joan Frederick, May 19, 1951; children—Stephanie Gay, Kevin Clyde. With CTS Corp., 1950—, v.p. CTS of Elkhart (Ind.) div. 1968-77, corp. v.p., gen. mgr. div., 1977—. Troop committeeman, sec. Boy Scouts Am., Elkhart, 1968-70; chmn. vocat. edn. adv. com. Elkhart Community Schs., 1965-68; bd. dirs. Elkhart County Jr. Achievement, 1976—. Served with AUS, 1945-46. Clubs: Elkhart Indsl., Elks, K.C. Home: 3010 E Lake Dr S Elkhart IN 46514 Office: 1142 W Beardsley Ave Elkhart IN 46514

SMITH, CHARLES WARREN, educator; b. Palmerton, Pa., Sept. 5, 1936; s. Stanley Aquilla and Luella Mae (Ziegenfus) S.; B.M. with honors, U. Wyo., 1958; M.A., N.Y. U., 1965; postgrad. Eastman Sch. Music, 1967-68, U. N.C., 1970; D.Mus. Arts, George Peabody Coll., 1974; m. Janet Lucille Bass, Aug. 24, 1957; children—Randall Allan, Bradley Taylor, Bryan Keith, Roger Andrew. Music tchr., supr. pub. schs., Wyo., Mont., N.J., N.Y., 1957-68; asst. prof. music Madison Coll., Harrisonburg, Va., 1968-69; asst. prof. Wake Forest U., Winston-Salem, N.C., 1969-75; asso. prof. Southeast Mo. State U., Cape Girardeau, 1975—; prin. flutist in numerous symphony orchs. Recipient Prize winning award certificate Am. Guild Musical Artists, 1958; Academia award Wake Forest Univ. Students, 1974. Mem. Am. Guild Musical Artists, Am. Fedn. Musicians, ASCAP, Southeast Composers League, Music Educators Nat. Conf., Nat. Assn. Rudimental Drummers, Coll. Music Theory Soc., Am. Soc. Univ. Composers, Phi Mu Alpha Sinfonia. Composer numerous published music. Home: Route 1 Gordonville MO 63752 Office: Dept Music Southeast Mo State Univ Cape Girardeau MO 63701

SMITH, CLARENCE WILLIAM, civil engr.; b. Clay County, Kans., Sept. 27, 1915; s. Archie W. and Mary E. (Edison) S.; B.S. in Civil Engring., Kans. State U., 1946; m. Philena Merten, Jan. 14, 1939; children—Philip, Jan, Nan. Constrn. engr. J.A. Tobin Constrn. Co., Kansas City, Kans., 1938-43; field engr. Kans. Hwy. Commn., 1943-46; engr. Jewell County, Kans., 1946-50, 73—, Rural Electric Coop Mgmt., Kans. and Ill. 1950-62; engr. Republic County, Kans., 1962—, Cloud County, Kans., 1966-73. Named Kans. County Engr. of the Year, 1973. Mem. Kans. Engring. Soc., Nat. Soc. Profl. Engrs., ASCE, Kans. County Engrs. Assn., Nat. Assn. County Engrs. (regional v.p. 1970-72, 1st v.p. 1972-73, pres. 1973-74, Rural Engr. of Year 1976), Am. Roadbuilders Assn. Clubs: Lions, Elks. Home: 2410 K St Belleville KS 66935 Office: PO Box 307 Belleville KS 66935

SMITH, CLIFFORD NEAL, writer, educator; b. Wakita, Okla., May 30, 1923; s. Jesse Newton and Inez Lane (Jones) S.; B.S., Okla. State U., 1943; A.M., U. Chgo., 1948; postgrad. Columbia U., 1960; m. Anna Piszczan-Czaja, Sept. 3, 1951; children—Helen Inez Smith Snow. Selector, U.S. Displaced Persons Commn., Washington and Munich, Germany, 1948-51; auditor Phillips Petroleum Co., Caracas, Venezuela, 1951-58; planning analyst Mobil Internat. Oil Co., N.Y.C., Mobil Oil A.G., Deutschland, Hamburg, Germany, 1960-61, Mobil Internat. Oil Co., N.Y.C., 1963-65; asst. to v.p. for Germany, Mobil Inner Europe, Inc., Geneva, 1961-63; asst. prof. No. Ill. U. Sch. Bus., DeKalb, 1966-69, prof. internat. bus., part-time 1970—; writer, lectr. Mem. at large exec. com. Friends Com. on Nat. Legis., 1968-75; mem. regional exec. com. Am. Friends Service Com., 1969-76; v.p. Riverside Democrats, N.Y.C., 1959-61. Recipient Distinguished Service medal Ill. Geneal. Soc., 1973, award for outstanding service to sci. genealogy Am. Soc. Genealogists, 1973. Mem. S.R., SAR, Soc. Descs. Colonial Clergy, Soc. Advancement Mgmt., Ill. Genealogic Soc. (dir. 1968-69), Phi Eta Sigma, Beta Alpha Psi, Sigma Iota Epsilon. Mem. Soc. of Friends. Club: American of Hamburg (v.p. 1962-63). Author: Federal Land Series, Vol. 1, 1972, Vol. 2, 1973; Encyclopedia of German-American Genealogy, 1975; American Genealogical Resources in German Archives, 1977; contbr. articles to profl. jours. Address: 594 W Lincoln Hwy DeKalb IL 60115 also Peter-Mueller-Strasse 53 Munich-Allach Federal Republic of Germany also Box 117 Route 1 McNeal AZ 85617

SMITH, DAVID BERNARD, agrl. engr.; b. Little Rock, Apr. 6, 1942; s. Marvin Ross and Maggie Mae (Legett) S.; B.S., Miss. State U., 196S, M.S., 1970; Ph.D., U. Mo., 1975; m. Annette Brent, June 7, 1970; children—Allan, Nathan. Research engr. Agrl. Research Service, U.S. Dept. Agr., Mississippi State, Miss., 1963-71, Columbia, Mo., 1971—. Mem. Am. Soc. Agrl. Engrs. (vice chmn. field plot research equipment com. 1975, chmn. 1976, vice chmn. agrl. chem. application com. 1977, chmn. 1978), Entomol. Soc. Am. (chmn. sect. spl. com. entomology-engring. cooperation), Mo. Acad. Sci., Nat. Entomol. Soc., Sigma Xi, Gamma Sigma Delta, Tau Beta Pi, Alpha Epsilon. Baptist (deacon). Contbr. articles to profl. jours. Patentee in field. Home: 2502 Highland Dr Columbia MO 65201 Office: U Mo Bldg T-12 Columbia MO 65201

SMITH, DAVID HARRY, designer; b. Battle Creek, Mich., May 21, 1946; s. David Hicks and Marguerite Louise (Rand) S.; A.A., Kellogg Comml. Coll., 1966; B.A., Mich. State U., 1969; m. Lucile Vanch Fruin, Aug. 28, 1971. Publs. designer, coordinator Wittenberg U., Springfield, Ohio, 1969-78; dir. univ. publs. Western Mich. U., Kalamazoo, 1978—; pub. relations coordinator Springfield Arts Council, 1972-73. Bd. dirs. Springfield Civic Theatre, 1971-75, sec., 1972-74; bd. dirs. Springfield Civic Opera, 1971-77, v.p. bd., 1973-77, choreographer, set designer, 1970-77. Mem. Am., Mich. dance masters, Council Advancement and Support of Edn. (award for designing Wittenberg's Presdl. Inauguration program 1976). Home: 3905 Kimberly Dr Springfield OH 45503

SMITH, DILLON, television editorialist; b. Pitts., June 30, 1941; s. Robert M. and Mary Cecelia (Dillon) S.; B.J., Northwestern U., 1963, M.S., 1964, J.D., 1967; m. Loretta Bowler, Jan. 28, 1967; children—Kevin, Lisa, Colleen, Kerry. Admitted to Ill. bar, 1967. News reporter, producer WTIC-TV-Radio, Hartford, Conn., 1967-69; newswriter, producer NBC News, Chgo., 1969; asst. editorial dir. WMAQ-TV, Chgo., 1970-72, editorial dir., 1972—; chmn. Nat. Broadcast Editorial Conf., 1972; faculty Medill Sch. Journalism, Northwestern U., 1974—. Recipient Silver Gavel award Am. Bar Assn. 1976; Nat. Headliner award, 1972, 73, Broadcast Media awards, 1972, 73, Chgo. Emmy awards, 1975, 76. Mem. Nat. Broadcast Editorial Assn. (v.p. 1976—), Nat. Assn. TV Arts and Scis. (Chgo. chpt.), Am., Chgo. bar assns. Home: 101 Orchard Pl Mount Prospect IL 60056 Office: WMAQ-TV Merchandise Mart Chicago IL 60654

SMITH, DONALD ARCHIE, aerospace co. exec.; b. Dayton, Ohio, Feb. 23, 1934; s. Archie Ford and Catherine Rosella (Rabold) S.; B.A. in Sci., Harvard U., 1956; certificate in nat. security mgmt., Indsl. Coll. Armed Forces, 1971; m. Joan Sandra Speedie, May 18, 1955; children—Douglas Alan, Keith Cameron, Deirdre Lynn, Neal Ramsey. Nuclear research and project engr. N.Am. Aviation, Columbus, Ohio, 1956-62; financial software specialist, internal auditor Nat. Cash Register, Dayton, 1962-63; mgr. systems engring. N.Am. Aviation, Columbus, 1963-67; mgr. bus. planning, marketing services and pub. relations N.Am. Rockwell, Columbus, 1967-72, mgr. internat. sales and marketing, 1968-73; mgr. bus. devel. and strategic planning Rockwell Internat. Corp., Columbus, 1973-76, program mgr. Condor weapon system, 1976-77, dir. guided bomb programs, 1977—; industry chmn. mil. specifications and standards review com. Airarmament, 1972—; operations research cons., 1962-64; instr. math. Sinclair Coll., Dayton, Ohio, 1961-63; U.S.-U.K. Bipartite Com. on Nuclear Weapons, 1958-61. Pres., bd. trustees Players Theatre of Columbus, 1975—; dist. commr. Boy Scouts Am., 1970-73; cubmaster Cub Scouts, 1965-70; squadron comdr. Civil Air Patrol, 1976; chmn. com. on racism Columbus Pub. Schs., 1972; civic fund raiser. Recipient nat. award Jr. Achievement. Inc., 1954, letters of commendation govt. agencies, Am. Def. Preparedness Assn., awards Boy Scouts Am. Mem. Royal Inst. Navigation, Nat. Mgmt. Assn., Am. Inst. Aeros. and Astronautics, Nat. Rifle Assn. (life), S.A.R. Republican. Methodist. Clubs: Harvard of Central Ohio, Rockwell Flying (gen. mgr.), Masons, Shriners. Home: 1426 Yorktown Rd Columbus OH 43227 Office: 4300 E 5th Ave Columbus OH 43216

SMITH, DONALD BURTWIN, mktg. exec.; b. Nobel, Ont., Can., Sept. 12, 1917; s. Claude H. and Grace (Sinsabaugh) S. (parents Am. citizens); came to U.S., 1919; A.B., Denison U., Granville, Ohio, 1939; m. Margaret, Feb. 27, 1976; 1 dau., Alicia; children by previous marriage—Hollace Ann Smith Turl, Vernon A., Kimberly. Advt. mgr. Magic Chef, 1945-57; dir. advt. promotion and pub. relations Lewyt Corp., 1947-54; dir. advt. and promotion Servel, 1954-56; sr. account exec. Leo Burnett Co., Inc., Chgo., 1956-60; exec. v.p. Tobias, O'Neil & Gallay Advt. Agy., Chgo., 1960-64; pres., owner Smith Mktg. Services, Chgo., 1964—; cons., lectr. Nat. Found. Funeral Service, Nat. Selected Morticians and Casket Mfrs. Assn. Served to 2d lt. USAAF, 1942-45. Recipient 1st awards Bus. Paper Assn., Outdoor Advt. Assn. and 100 Best Ads of Year, 1954. Mem. Nat. Sales Promotion Execs. Assn. (bd. dirs., past v.p.), Am. Mktg. Assn., Market Research Assn. Episcopalian. Club: Masons. Author syndicated articles on funeral service, death and dying; contbr. articles to trade press. Home: 6112 N Campbell St Chicago IL 60659 Office: 2609 W Peterson St Chicago IL 60659

SMITH, DONALD CALLISTUS, computer services exec.; b. New Albany, Ind., May 26, 1942; s. Callistus John and Geneva Margaret (Buechler) S.; B.A., Ind. U., 1964; m. Mary Katherine Russell, Jan. 4, 1963; children—David, Matthew, Christopher. Mgr. nfo. Services Bus. Div., Gen. Electric, Louisville, 1969-74; regional v.p. Compuserve Network, Louisville, 1974-76; v.p. Sheldon Enterprises, Louisville, 1976—, also dir. Fulton Data Joint Venture, Atlanta, 1976—; dir. Louisville Trust Bank; cons., dir. Fulton Nat. Bank

(Atlanta). Com. dir. United Way, 1971. Served with USAF, 1960-66. Recipient Paladin award, 1968; Gen. Electric Outstanding Achievement award, 1973-74; Marion Kellogg award, 1974. Mem. Am. Mktg. Assn. (v.p. 1975-77), Data Processing Mgmt. Assn., Printing Industries Assn. of South, Econ. Resource Mgmt. Assos. Democrat. Roman Catholic. Clubs: Louisville Bonsai (pres. 1975), Kiwanis (v.p. 1970-73). Landscape designer for several maj. archtl. works, Ind., Ky., Ga. Home: Scottsville Rd Pinecliffe Floyds Knobs IN 47119 Office: 3 Riverfront Plaza Louisville KY 40202

SMITH, DONALD DEAN, bus. exec.; b. Lewistown, Ill., June 25, 1926; s. Donald Mansfield and Gladys (Dawson) S.; B.S., Bradley U., Peoria, Ill., 1954; m. Priscilla Dean Wightman, Apr. 1, 1954; children—Todd Morrison, Susan Kimberly, Debra Dean. Rep., ICS, 1954-57, dist. sales mgr., 1958-65; nat. sales mgr. Britannica Inst., 1966-68, Chgo. Tech. Coll., 1969-71; owner, pres. Todd Co., Lombard, Ill., 1972—; dir. I.B. Systems, Hasco, Inc.; lectr. motivation and tng. Served with U.S. Army, World War II; PTO. Mem. U.S. Masters Track and Field Assn., AAU, Steel Plate Fabricators Assn, Sigma Chi. Unitarian. Current nat. and world champion in masters 800 meter run, joint world record holder 4 by 400 relay, nat. record holder 1500 meter run. Home: 1061 Daniel Ct Lombard IL 60148 Office: 1113 S Main St Lombard IL 60148

SMITH, DONALD GLEN, educator; b. Streator, Ill., Feb. 4, 1919; s. John Ward and Edith Francis (Horn) S.; B.Agr. with highest honors, U. Ill., 1947, postgrad. law school, 1947-49; M.S. in Agr. Econs., 1961; m. Eleanor Kathryn Watford, Oct. 9, 1943; children—Stephen Craig, David Jay. Fieldman, Northeastern Ill. Farm Bus. Farm Mgmt. Service, Elgin, 1949-52; farm mgr., asst. trust officer, asst. cashier First Trust and Savs. Bank of Kankakee (Ill.), 1952-58; mgr. U. Ill. Trust Farms, Urbana, 1958—; asso. prof. agrl. econs. U. Ill., Urbana, 1966—. Mem. exec. bd. Arrowhead council Boy Scouts Am., Champaign, Ill., 1972—, chmn. council camping com., 1972-74, Merit award, 1972, Silver Beaver award, 1973, vigil mem. Order of the Arrow, 1973, scouting v.p., 1974—. Served to maj., inf. U.S. Army, 1941-46; PTO. Mem. Ill. Soc. Profl. Farm Mgrs. and Rural Appraisers (pres. 1959), Soil Conservation Soc. Am. (pres. No. Ill. chpt. 1966), Am. Soc. Farm Mgrs. and Rural Appraisers (pres. 1971, Outstanding Service award, 1965, Highest award 1973). Sr. author: Professional Farm Manager's Handbook on Services, 1958; Professional Rural Appraisal Manual, 1965, 4th edit., 1975. Home: 607 Sunnycrest Ct Urbana IL 61801

SMITH, DONALD ROY, state ofcl.; b. Elmhurst, Ill., Nov. 13, 1926; s. George C. and Florence (Straus) S.; student Loyola U., 1946-49, John Marshall Law Sch., 1949-50; m. Dorothy J. Covington, May 17, 1952; children—Brian, Marilyn, Virginia, Kevin, Karen. Mem. DuPage County Bd. Rev., Wheaton, Ill., 1950-54, chief dep. treas., 1954-58, treas., 1958-61, supr., 1961-64; chief fin. officer State of Ill., Springfield, 1964-77, state treas., 1977—. Served with USNR, 1944-46. Mem. Municipal Finance Officers Assn., Am. Soc. for Pub. Adminstrn., Nat. Assn. State Treasurers. Roman Catholic. K.C. Home: 2313 Black Hawk St Springfield IL 62702 Office: Capital Bldg Springfield IL 62706

SMITH, DUDREY CRAIG, computer engr.; b. Weatherford, Tex., Aug. 7, 1945; s. Richard Farmer and Alice Jean (Gebo) S.; student Grand Rapids Jr. Coll., 1963-66; B.S., Grand Valley State Coll., 1973; M.S. in Math., U. Mich., 1974, M.S. in Computer Info. and Control Engring., 1976; m. Martha Joanne Tuthill, Dec. 16, 1972. Software engr. Lear Siegler, Inc., Grand Rapids, 1976—; guest lectr. Aquinas Coll., Grand Valley State Coll., 1976. Served with U.S. Army, 1967-71. Decorated Bronze Star; academic scholar Grand Valley State Colls., 1971-73; Rackham scholar U. Mich., 1973-74; Rackham teaching fellow U. Mich., 1975-76. Mem. Math. Assn. Am., IEEE. Home: 417 Alger SE Grand Rapids MI 49507 Office: 4141 Eastern SE Grand Rapids MI 49508

SMITH, E. BERRY, TV sta. exec.; b. Daytona Beach, Fla., Feb. 21, 1926; s. Samuel Rogers and Rosemary (Berry) S.; B.S. in Bus. Adminstrn., Butler U., 1949; m. Mary Terese Hoffmann, Apr. 3, 1948; children—Kevin B., Martin J. With Sta. WIRE, Indpls., 1949-53; dir. pub. relations Franklin Fin., Hartford City, Ind., 1953-56; with CBS, Inc., Detroit, 1956-57; v.p., gen. mgr. WFIE-TV, Evansville, Ind., 1957-60, WFRV-TV, Green Bay, Wis., 1960-62, WLKY-TV, Louisville, 1962-64; pres., gen. mgr., WTVW-TV, Evansville, 1964—. Mem. citizens adv. panel Ind. Dept. Pub. Instruction; mem. communications adv. bd. Wabash Valley Jr. Coll., Henderson (Ky.) Community Coll.; pres. Met. Evansville C. of C., 1977; bd. dirs. R.E.S.C.U.E., Inc., 1976-77, Welborn Hosp. Served with U.S. Army, 1944-46. Mem. Ind. (pres. 1968-69), S.W. Ind. (pres.) broadcasters assns. Clubs: Evansville Country, Petroleum, Evansville Kennel. Home: 391 Park Plaza Dr Evansville IN 47715 Office: 477 Carpenter St Evansville IN 47701

SMITH, EDWARD BYRON, bank exec.; b. Chgo., 1909; student Yale U., 1932; married. With No. Trust Co., Chgo., 1932—, exec. v.p., 1949-57, pres., 1957—, chmn. bd., chief exec. officer, 1963—; chmn. Nortrust Corp., Chgo.; war savs. staff Office of Procurement Material, U.S. Dept. Treasury, 1942-43; dir. Ill. Tool Works, Commonwealth Edison Co. Served to lt. USN, 1943-45. Home: 1133 Lake Rd Lake Forest IL 60045 Office: No Trust Co 50 S LaSalle St Chicago IL 60675

SMITH, EUGENE VALENTINE, chem. co. exec.; b. Ossian, Ind., Jan. 7, 1924; s. Keith R. and Clona M. (Valetine) S.; B.S. with distinction, Purdue U., 1948; m. Maxine Louise Byerly, May 19, 1945; children—Penelope Ann Smith Scheidt, Rebecca Jo Smith Schinderle. Mech. engr., plant engr. Stanolind Oil and Gas Co., Midwest, Wyo., 1948-54; sr. project engr. Amoco Chems. Corp., Brownsville, Tex., 1954-57, asst. chief plant engr., Texas City, Tex., 1957-61, ops. supr., Texas City and Joliet, Ill., 1961-65, supt. ops., Joliet, 1965-71, tech. dir., 1972—. Trustee Jesse Walker United Meth. Ch., Joliet, 1968—, pres., 1972-74; mem. Will Grundy Mfg. Environ. Control Commn., 1965—; bd. dirs. Crystal Lawn Homeowners Assn., 1971-74. Served to 1st lt. USAAF, 1943-45. Registered profl. engr., Tex. Mem. Will-Grundy Mfg. Assn., Joliet C. of C., ASME (nat.) (pres. Texas City chpt. 1963), Am. Inst. Chem. Engrs. (dir. Joliet sect. 1976—), Am. Legion, Pi Tau Sigma, Tau Beta Pi (hon.). Republican. Home: 2504 Chevy Chase Dr Joliet IL 60435 Office: PO Box 941 Joliet IL 60434

SMITH, EUGENE WILLIAM, educator; b. West Bend, Wis., Aug. 11, 1923; s. William Albert and Ruth Ottilia (Frings) S.; B.S., Marquette U., 1950, M.S., 1951; m. Joy Emilie Loudon, Feb. 19, 1965; children—Renee Ruth, Ann Rachelle. Faculty, Aquinas Coll., Grand Rapids, Mich., 1951—, asso. prof. biology-bacteriology, 1961—. Research biologist Mich. Blueberry Growers Assn., 1967—. Served with USAAF, 1943-45. Mem. Bot. Soc. Am., Mycol. Soc. Am., A.A.U.P., Phi Sigma, Beta Beta Beta. Home: 12234 Bailey Dr Lowell MI 49331 Office: 1607 Robinson Rd Grand Rapids MI 49506

SMITH, EVERETT WARE, banker; b. Quincy, Mass., Aug. 25, 1913; s. Edward Hale and Blanche Everett (Ware) S.; grad. Moses Brown Sch., Providence, 1932; B.S., Yale, 1936; m. Ruth Howe Tyler, July 15, 1938; children—Pamela (Mrs. Alan K. Henrikson), Karen Howe (Mrs. Thomas E. Malican), Nathaniel Tyler and Jonathan Hale (twins). Trust officer New Eng. Trust Co., Boston, 1945-48; asst. financial v.p. Boston and Me. R.R., 1948-51, treas., 1951-54; with New Eng. Mchts. Nat. Bank, Boston, 1954—, sr. v.p., 1959-64, vice chmn., 1964-68, also dir.; chmn. Union Commerce Bank, 1968-69; pres. Cleve. Trust Co., 1969-73, chmn., 1973—; pres. Cleve. Trust Corp., 1974—; trustee Cleve. Trust Realty Investors; dir. N.Am. Coal Co., Midland Mut. Ins. Co., Higbee Co., Nat. Bankamericard, Inc. Bd. govs. Asso. Industries Cleve.; Pres. New Eng. Council, 1964-66; v.p. planning and allocations United Torch Services; trustee, mem. finance com. Mus. Arts Assn. Pres., chmn. trustees Winsor Sch., 1958-63; trustee, treas. Abbot Acad., 1964-70; trustee Gov. Dummer Acad., 1964-75; trustee Govtl. Research Inst., pres., 1977-78; bd. dirs. Nat. Conf. Christians and Jews. Served to lt. col. USMC, 1934-46; PTO. Mem. Assn. Res. City Bankers, Robert Morris Assos., Phi Gamma Delta (trustee). Clubs: Country (Brookline, Mass.); Union, Yale (Cleve.); Chagrin Valley Hunt; Kirtland Country; Pepper Pike. Home: Old Mill Rd Gates Mills OH 44040 Office: Cleveland Trust Co E 9th and Euclid Ave Cleveland OH 44101

SMITH, F. JOSEPH, musicologist, educator; b. Superior, Wis., Mar. 19, 1925; s. Robert Glen and Clare (Farrell) S.; M.A., Catholic U., 1955; Ph.D., U. Freiburg (Ger.), 1960; m. Gertrude Ann Kass, 1966; children—Adrienne Ruth, Laurel Elizabeth. Vis. prof. Duquesne U., Pitts., 1963-64; researcher U. Freiburg, 1964-65; asso. prof. philosophy Emory U., Atlanta, 1965-67; prof. music Kent (Ohio) State U., 1967; vis. prof. U. Bucharest (Romania), 1978-79; editor Music and Man, Jour. Musicological Research, Gordon and Breach, N.Y.C.-London, Paris, 1973; cons. fine arts, music therapy. Mem. Am. Musicological Soc., Am. Husserl Conf. (hon.), Internat. Musicology Soc., Phi Beta. Author numerous books in field; contbr. articles in music, philosophy, religion to profl. jours. Home: 6134 N Maplewood Ave Chicago IL 60659

SMITH, F. NEIL, constrn. adminstr.; b. Stockton, Calif., Nov. 19, 1938; s. Floyd N. and Margie C. (Craig) S.; B.S., London Coll., 1964, M.S., 1966; m. Martha L. Matheson, June 19, 1958; children—Sabrina, Todd, Blair. Supr. indsl. relations groups Kaiser Engrs., Oakland, Calif., 1964-68; asst. to v.p., gen. mgr. pressurized water reactor div. Westinghouse, Corp., Pitts., 1968-72; mgr. projects Fluor Power, Los Angeles, 1972-73; v.p. Gen. Energy Resources, Inc., Irvine, Calif., 1973-75; mgr. constrn. Gibbs & Hill, Omaha, 1975—. Pres. (WEDCO) Am. Mgmt. Assn., 1970—, chmn., 1971-72. Mem. Am. Nuclear Soc., Atomic Indsl. Forum, Pacific Coast Electric Assn., Rocky Mountain Elec. League, N.W. Electric Light, Power Assn. Home: 10069 Ohio St Omaha NE 68134 Office: 8420 W Dodge Rd Omaha NE 68114

SMITH, FRANK EDWARD, II, publishing exec.; b. Easton, Pa., Oct. 1, 1912; s. Frank Edward and Ella (Heavener) S.; B.S., Pa. State Coll., 1934; M.A., N.Y. U., 1946; m. Lena J. Popenciu, Sept. 16, 1950; 1 dau., Nancy Joan. Dir. employee activities Riegel Paper Co., Milford, N.J., 1938-43; nat. field rep. ARC, 1943-45; recreation dir. Gen. Electric Co., Erie, Pa., 1947-50; with C.J. LaRoche Advt. Agy., N.Y.C., 1950-52, McFadden Pub. Co., 1952-54; mgr. Buttenheim Pub. Co., Cleve., 1954-61; with Indsl. Pub. Co., Cleve., 1961-77, pub. dir., 1962-77; editor Changing Sch. Market, pub. Sch. Product News, 1962-77; columnist Ednl. Dealer Mag., Peter Li, Inc., 1977—; faculty Ind. U. Nat. Inst. Audio Visual Selling, 1969—. Chmn., Civic Assn. Edn. Com., Mentor, 1966-67. Served with U.S. Mcht. Marine, 1945-47. Mem. Nat. Sch. Supply and Equipment Assn. (membership com. 1968—, publicity com. 1969—, long range planning com. 1976—, Pub. Relations award 1971), Nat. Audio Visual Assn. (chmn. publicity com. 1970-71, profl. devel. bd. 1974—, pub. relations com. 1976—, Commerative award 1973), Edn. Industries Assn. (dir. 1972-74, sec.-treas. 1974-75), Phi Delta Kappa, Kappa Delta Pi. Club: Masons. Home: 720 Tinkers Ln Northfield OH 44067 Office: 614 Superior Ave W Cleveland OH 44113

SMITH, FRANK RAY, aerospace mfg. co. exec.; b. Waco, Tex., Aug. 18, 1924; s. Frank Carruthers and Osie Helen (Womack) S.; B.A. in English with honors, U. Tex., 1948, M.A. in English, 1949, Ph.D. in English, 1956; m. Patricia Mattingly, Oct. 1, 1948; children—Patricia Kathleen, Ramona Louise, Rebecca Jo. Instr. English U. Tex., 1949-50, 52-53; asst. prof. dept. humanities Air Force Inst. Tech., Dayton, Ohio, 1953-56, asso. prof., 1956-59, prof., head dept., 1959-62; editor Douglas Aircraft Co., Santa Monica, Calif., 1962, sect. head, 1962-64, br. mgr., 1964-65, mgr., 1965-69; corporate mgr., tech. info. McDonnell Douglas Corp., St. Louis, 1969—; cons. in field. Served with U.S. Army, 1943-46. Fellow Sec. Tech. Communication (past pres.), Am. Soc. Engring. Edn. Contbr. articles in field to profl. jours. Editor in chief: Technical Communication, 1977—. Home: 910 Milldale Dr Ballwin MO 63011 Office: PO Box 516 Saint Louis MO 63166

SMITH, FREDDYE LEE, sch. counselor; b. Oklahoma City, Oct. 16, 1938; d. Frederick Douglass and Leeoshia Marguerite (Harris) Moon; B.A., Fisk U., 1959; M.A., U. Chgo., 1965; m. Stanford Lee Smith, July 1, 1961; children—Karyn Lynita, Stanford Brandon. Tchr., Chgo. Bd. Edn., 1960-61, 63-65, 66-69, counselor, 1969—; tchr. Gary (Ind.) Bd. Edn., 1961-62; guest lectr. Malcolm X Coll., Chgo., 1973; cons., counselor Catalyst for Youth, Inc., 1970-76. Mem. adv. bd. Community Mental Health Council, 1974—. Mem. Am., Ill., Chgo. personnel and guidance assns., Am. Assn. Tchrs. French, Coalition of Adolescent Services, Council Coll. Attendance, Ill. Council Ednl. Services, Experiment in Internat. Living, League Black Women, Chgo. Fisk Club, North Avalon Community Orgn. Home: 7958 S Kimbark Ave Chicago IL 60619 Office: 7629 S Constance Ave Chicago IL 60649

SMITH, GEORGE CLIFFORD, V, electronics co. exec.; b. Cin., July 14, 1944; s. George Gilmore and Thelma (Thaubald) S.; B.F.A., U. Cin., 1977; m. Marilyn Petering, Feb. 21, 1970; 1 son, Christopher Martin. Disc jockey Sta. WCIN, Cin., 1965, Sta. WUBE, Cin., 1966; engr. Sta. WLW-T-TV, Cin., 1967; chief engr. TV, U. Cin., 1966-77, instr. TV, 1970-77; pres. Smithall Electronics, Cin., 1967—; cons. on broadcasting equipment to colls., univs.; dir. Looking Glass Enterprises, Last Moving Picture Co. Tech. dir. Peoples Jr. High Sch., 1970-73; production mgr., Wyo. Corral Show, 1960-68. Mem. Soc. Audio Engrs., Soc. Motion Picture TV Engrs. Patentee design for computer driven plexiglass dance floors for discotheques. Home: 2386 Grandin Rd Cincinnati OH 45208 Office: 2001 Vine St Cincinnati OH 45210

SMITH, GEORGE WOLFRAM, physicist, educator; b. Des Plaines, Ill., Sept. 19, 1932; s. Murray Sawyer and Alice Lucile (Wolfram) S.; B.A., Knox Coll., 1954; M.A., Rice U., 1956, Ph.D., 1958; m. Mary Lee Sackett, Sept. 7, 1956; children—Dean, Grant. Welch Found. fellow Rice U., 1958-59; sr. research physicist Gen. Motors Research Labs., Warren, Mich., 1959-76, deptl. research scientist, 1976—; lectr. physics and astronomy Cranbrook Inst. Sci., Bloomfield Hills, Mich., 1963—; tchr. Lawrence Inst. Tech., 1963-65; vice chmn. Gordon Research Conf. on Orientational Disorder in Crystals, 1976, chmn., 1978. Mem. Mich. Regtl. Civil War Roundtable, 1965—, pres., 1971-72; active Boy Scouts Am., Sci.-Engring. Fair Met. Detroit. Recipient Knox Coll. Achievement award, 1977. Fellow Am. Phys. Soc.; mem. Phi Beta Kappa, Sigma Xi, Phi Delta Theta, Alpha Delta. Contbr. articles to sci., tech. jours. Patentee temperature measuring device, liquid crystal device technology. Home: 1882 Melbourne St Birmingham MI 48009 Office: Physics Dept Gen Motors Research Warren MI 48090

SMITH, GERALD JAMES, clin. psychologist; b. Chgo., Feb. 4, 1943; s. Edward James and Josephine Marie (Strenk) S.; B.S., Loyola U., Chgo., 1966, Ph.D., 1974; postgrad. Marquette U., 1966-68; postdoctoral student psychotherapy Chgo. Med. Sch., 1974-76; m. Denise Marie Dahl, July 27, 1968; children—Edward Dahl, Lisa Marie. Program dir. youth care program Children and Family Services, Lockport, Ill., 1974; asso. prof., chmn. dept. psychology Lewis U., Lockport, 1968-76; pvt. practice, Calumet City, Ill., 1976—; co-founder, 1974, past pres. Ill. Sch. Profl. Psychology, Chgo.; lectr. Chgo. Coll. Osteo. Medicine. Mem. Am., Midwestern, Ill. (chmn. standards and tng. com.) psychol. assns., Am. Soc. Psychologists in Pvt. Practice, Blue Key, Psi Chi, Phi Kappa Theta. Roman Catholic. Home: 536 Marquette Ave Calumet City IL 60409 Office: 80 River Oaks Center Suite 808 Calumet City IL 60409

SMITH, GLENN LEE, chem. co. exec.; b. St. Louis, Apr. 7, 1929; s. Clifford Edward Peter and Genevieve Mary (Heesen) S.; B.M.E., U. Cin., 1952; M.B.A., Am. Internat. Coll., 1962; m. Elaine Rose Radloff, June 4, 1949; children—Richard Erwin, Barbara Ann. With Aeroproducts div. Gen. Motors Corp., Vandalia, Ohio, 1947-51; constrn. engr. Monsanto Co., Addyston, Ohio, 1952-53, devel. engr., Dayton, Ohio, 1953-54, sr. engr., engring. supr., Springfield, Mass., 1957-62, gen. mfg. supt., plant engr., Addyston, 1962-69, mgr. dist., product adminstr., dir. mfg., 1969-77, Plastics div., St. Louis, 1973—. Elder, Bonhomme Presbyn. Ch., Chesterfield, Mo., 1973-76; pres. Glan Tai Homeowners Assn., Manchester, Mo., 1973-74, trustee, 1973-76; com. chmn., scoutmaster Boy Scouts Am., 1972-77. Served to lt. USNR, 1954-57. Named Distinguished Engring. Alumnus, U. Cin., 1976; registered profl. engr., Ohio, Mass. Mem. ASME. Republican. Presbyn. Home: 13 Swindon Ct Manchester MO 63011 Office: 800 N Lindbergh Blvd Saint Louis MO 63166

SMITH, GLENN PARKHURST, musician; b. Oswego, Ill., Feb. 26, 1912; s. Royce Edward and Amy Effie (Parkhurst) S.; Mus.B., Wheaton Coll., 1934; Mus.M., Northwestern U., 1949; m. Marie Constance Allen, Dec. 29, 1936; children—Beverly Jean, Marjorie Anne, David Allen, Jacqueline Marie. Trombonist, Chgo. Civic Symphony, 1934-35; tchr. music pub. schs., Kans., Ill., 1935-50; prof. trombone Sch. Music, U. Mich., Ann Arbor, 1950—; adjudicator, clinician; editor solo and emsenble lit. for brass instruments. Mem. Internat. Trombone Assn. (chmn. research com.), Nat. Assn. Coll. Wind and Percussion Instrs. (past state chmn.), U. Mich. Band Alumni Assn. (hon. life), Music Educators Nat. Conf., Mich. Music Educators Assn., Hist. Soc. Mich., Pi Kappa Lambda. Republican. Mem. Reformed Ch. Am. Contbr. articles to profl. jours. Home: 312 Doty Ave Ann Arbor MI 48103 Office: Sch Music U Mich Ann Arbor MI 48109

SMITH, GLENN WILLIAM, pub. accountant; b. Major County, Okla., Dec. 10, 1908; s. Frank Henry and Pearl V. (Brown) S.; student Oklahoma City U., Hills U., 1927-30, Internat. Accounting Soc., 1930; m. Billie Jeanne Redman, Apr. 2, 1944; children—Richard G., Timothy W. Jr. accountant Bonicamp & Young, Enid, Okla., 1930-33; treas., chief accountant Central Appliance Co., also controller Midwest Maytag Co., Enid, 1933-35; sr. accountant John P. Bonicamp, Wichita, 1935-42; civilian chief accountant USAAF, Air Transport Command, 1942-45; gen. partner Bonicamp, Keolling & Smith, C.P.A.'s, Wichita, 1945-63, Bonicamp, Koelling, Smith & Farrow, 1964-69; partner Peat Marwick Mitchell & Co., 1969-71; individual C.P.A. practitioner, 1971-73; partner Smith & Russell, 1973—. Chmn., Wichita Cancer Campaign Com., 1956-58; treas., chmn. Cloudridge Community Center, 1956-66; chmn. explorer post Boy Scouts Am., 1957-58; treas. K-9 patrol Wichita Police Dept., 1956-69; treas. Wichita Crime Commn., 1969-72; mem. Tony Manhardt Inst. Speech Tng.; mem. awards jury Freedoms Found., Valley Forge, 1961. C.P.A., Kans.; hon. adm. Nebr. Navy, 1961; hon. citizen Tex., 1961; hon. mayor San Antonio, Ft. Worth, 1961; recipient Cosmopolitan Club awards, 1951, 63; others. Mem. Kans. Soc. C.P.A.'s (dir. 1957-59, pres. 1960-61, chmn. bd. 1962-64, chmn. nominating com. 1963-64, co-chmn. audit procedures com. 1969-70), Am. Inst. C.P.A.'s (mem. council 1961-62, auditing procedures com. 1965-66), Am. Assn. Oil Well Drilling Contractors, Am. Inst. Accountants (mem. council), Wichita Tennis Assn. (past treas.), C. of C., Kans. Ind., Mid-Continent oil and gas assns., Am. Accounting Assn. Methodist (auditor 1948—). Clubs: Petroleum, Toastmasters (chpt. sec.-treas. 1958, pres. 1959—), Crest View Country, Cosmopolitan Internat. (gov. Mo.-Kans. fedn. 1956-57, internat. pres. 1960-61, chmn. bd. 1962-63, chmn. past pres.'s council 1962-64); Air Capitol Cosmopolitan (past hon. pres.). Contbr. articles to profl. mags. Home: 8234 Limerick St Wichita KS 67206 Office: 901 Union Center Bldg Wichita KS 67202

SMITH, GLENN WILLIS, univ. adminstr.; b. Lincoln, Nebr., Feb. 6, 1931; s. Russell Blair and Mabel Luella (Combellic) S.; B.Sc., U. Nebr., 1955, M.A., 1968; m. Janet Irene Tiekotter, June 18, 1953; children—H. Bradley, David G. Staff accountant Ernst & Ernst, Chgo., 1955-57; sr. accoumtant Peat, Marwick, Mitchell & Co., Lincoln, Nebr., 1957-61; controller, sec. Benner Tea Co.. Burlington, Iowa, 1961-63; with U. Nebr., 1963-68, asst. v.p. adminstrn. Lincoln, 1968—, vis. asst. prof. accounting, 1976-77; controller U. Minn., Mpls., 1977—. Del., Lancaster County (Nebr.) Republican. Conv., 1974, 76; bd. dirs. United Way of Lincoln/Lancaster County, 1976. Served with USMC, 1949-50, 51-52. C.P.A. Mem. Am. Assn. Higher Edn., Am. Inst. C.P.A.'s (discussion leader profl. devel. course), Am. Mgmt. Assn., Assn. Systems Mgmt. Neb. Soc. C.P.A.'s, Delta Sigma Pi. Presbyterian. Home: 6805 Indian Hills Rd Edina MN 55435 Office: Univ Minnesota Morrill Hall 100 Church St SE Minneapolis MN 55455

SMITH, HAMLIN HENRY, JR., realtor; b. Rensselaer, Ind., Jan. 21, 1929; s. Hamlin Henry and Edna Pearl (Romine) S.; grad. high sch.; m. Phyllis Joan Hall, May 21, 1950; children—Karen Kay, Michael Dale. With Jasper County (Ind.) Rural Electric Membership Corp., 1947-51, Lowell Holt & Co., Rensselaer, 1951-54; office mgr. Security Loan Co., Rensselaer, 1954-57; v.p., treas. Blue Agy., Inc., ins., Rensselaer, 1957-70; pres. Consol. Inc., ins., Rensselaer, 1970—. Owner Smith Realty Co., Rensselaer, 1959—; cons. to local govt. Treas. Rensselaer Community Recreational Devel. Corp.; mem. Rensselaer Park Bd. Justice of peace, 1963-67. Served with U.S. Army, 1953-54. Mem. Ind. Assn. Realtors, Nat. Assn. Real Estate Bds., Ind. Ins. Agts. Ind., Nat. Ind. Ins. Agts., Rensselaer C. of C. (v.p. 1964), Ill. Harness Horsemans Assn., Ind. Trotting and Pacing Horse Assn., Am. Legion. Clubs: Mason, Eagles. Home: 903 Thompson St Rensselaer IN 47978 Office: 116 W Washington St Rensselaer IN 47978

SMITH, HARLAN ELLIOTT, lawyer; b. Mpls., July 21, 1932; s. Rollin Kelliher and Helen (Halverson) S.; A.A., U. Minn., 1952; B.S., 1959, J.D., 1961; m. Carol Jeanne Sandquist, Feb. 2, 1953; children—Victor Harlan, Deborah Jeanne, Cheryl Lynn. Admitted to Minn. bar, 1961; practiced in Mpls., 1961-70, Walker, Minn., 1971—; chief counsel Legal Aid Soc. Mpls., 1961-70; dir. Leech Lake Indian Reservation Legal Services, 1968-70; partner firm Peterson, Tupper & Smith, Walker, 1971-76, Tupper, Smith & Seck, 1976—; village atty.,

Walker, 1971—; teaching asst. U. Minn. Law Sch., 1961-70; cons. OEO, 1965—. Bd. dirs. Mpls. Met. YMCA, Mpls. Area Campfire Girls. Served with AUS, 1953-56. Recipient Distinguished Service award U. Minn., 1961. Fellow Am. Acad. Matrimonial Lawyers; mem. Am., Minn. bar assns., Nat. Legal Aid and Defender Assn., Gamma Eta Gamma. Mem. Democrat-Farm Labor party. Presbyn. Home: Box 188 Walker MN 56484 Office: Box 160 Walker MN 56484

SMITH, HARRY ELMER, physician; b. Indpls., Apr. 25, 1903; s. John Daniel and Emma Alice (Pitcher) S.; student Butler U., 1928-29, Ind. Coll. Phys. Therapy, 1931, Eclectic Med. Coll., 1932-33; A.B., Ind. U., 1942, Sc.D., 1967; M.D., Chgo. Coll. Medicine and Surgery, 1947; M.S., Lincoln Jefferson U., 1950; D.Sc., Philathea Coll., 1967; m. Agnes Lucille Cooling, Oct. 20, 1940; children—Stephen Craig, Richard Douglas, Kathy Adair, Beverly Gifford. Pharm. asst. R.C. Lagenaur Drug Co., 1936-38; med. asst. to William E. Tenney, 1934-36; prof. urology Ind. U., 1935-45; tchr. McCormick Med. Coll., 1938-42, dean, 1948-52, acting pres., 1952-57; tchr. Chgo. Coll. Medicine and Surgery, 1942-47, tchr. biochemistry and physiology, med. dir. Direct Lab., Buffalo, 1959-65; med. dir. Scrip Pharm., Inc., Peoria, 1965—. Fellow Internat. Med. Assn.; mem. Assn. U. Chemists, Am. Assn. Med. and Physiol. Research, Nat. Med. Soc. Methodist (pres. bd. trustees). Clubs: Masons, K.T., Shriners (past illustrious master council, potent master 3 times). Contbr. articles to profl. jours. Address: 819 N Butler St Indianapolis IN 46219

SMITH, HELEN CATHARINE, author; b. Chgo., June 7, 1903; d. J.A. and DeEtte (Gericke) Miller; B.A., U. Calif. Los Angeles, 1926; postgrad. U. Wis., 1954-56; M.S., Christian Coll., 1962, Ph.D., 1965, Ed.D., 1967, D.D., 1969; Ph.D., U. Remo, 1976; m. H.C. Smith, June 7, 1932; children—Glen Dean, DeEtta Ellen (Mrs. Gerald L. Amdahl), George Dale. Tchr. 2d grade Maple Lawn Sch., Clinton, Wis.; legal sec. law office, Janesville, Wis.; legal sec. to city atty., Evansville, Wis., 1933-72; v.p., dir. Blue Moon poetry mag., 1952-57. Chmn. Fidelia Van Antwerp Folk-Lore Collection, 1961—. Jade Ring winner for short story Wis. Regional Writers Assn., 1957, 1st pl. award for article Herdman Meml. Competition of British Press, 1957, John Francis Sims Meml. award for poetry, 1955, leadership citation Wis. Regional Writers' Assn., 1956, 1st award essay contest Raconteurs, 1961, Laurel wreath, gold medal Pres. Philippines, named Hon. Poet Laureate (Am.-Visayan), 1967; named to Contemporary Poets Hall of Fame, 1969; 1st place for sonnet Fleetwood (Eng.) Music and Arts Festival, 1972. Fellow Intercontinental Biog. Assn.; mem. Nat. League Am. Pen Women, Nat. Poetry Day Com., Nat. Soc. Lit. and Arts, Nat. Ret. Tchrs. Assn., Fla. Poetry Soc., Wis. Regional Writers Assn. (life mem., sec. 1949-55, dir. 1949-57, life dir. 1957—), Wis. Regional Artists Assn., Wis. Fellowship Poets, Wis. Acad. Scis., Arts and Letters, State Hist. Soc. Wis., Am. Lit. Assn. (life), Council Wis. Writers (life), UN Assn., Evansville Writers Club (pres. 1972-73), AAUW, Centro Studie Scambi Internazionali, Accademia Internazionale Leonardo da Vinci, Accademia Internazionale di Pontzen, Baconian Soc., Internat. Poetry Soc., United Poets Laureate, World Poetry Soc., Phi Beta Kappa (sustaining), Alpha Psi Omega, Sigma Iota Xi. Author: Laughing Child, Books I, II, III, 1945, 46, 47; Off the Rocord, 1949; From the Countryside, 1952; Stars in My Eyes, 1954; Windfalls, 1955; Valediction for Man, 1963; Chiaroscuro, 1963; Applesauce, 1965; Mirrors of Faith, 1969; But Not Yet, 1973; (essays) You Can't Cry All the Time, 1975; (poetry) Full Circle, 1975; HCS Sketchbook, 1977. Editor: Evansville Anthology of Verse, 1952. No. Spring, anthology, 1956. Contbr. numerous mags., newspapers. Original manuscripts in permanent collection U. Ky. Libraries. Founded Helen Smith Lit. award, 1974, Art award, 1976. Home: 409 Lincoln St Evansville WI 53536

SMITH, HERBERT EUGENE, univ. dean; b. English, Ind., July 12, 1929; s. Charles Franklin and Eva Gertrude (Froman) S.; B.S., Ind. U., 1952, M.S., 1954, Ed.D., 1964. Dir. student personnel services for regional campuses Ind. U., Bloomington, 1964-66, dir. student activities, 1966-69, asst. dean for student services, 1969—. Pres., pub. Self Instructional Reading Services, Inc., Bloomington, 1975—. Game chmn. Ind. Shrine Bowl high sch. all stars, Indpls., 1967, 68. Bd. dirs. Monroe County (Ind.) Cancer Soc., 1970—, YMCA, Bloomington, Ind., 1968—; chmn. bd. dirs. WIUS Radio, Ind. U., Bloomington, 1964—. Served with USAF, 1949-56. Mem. Nat. Assn. Student Personnel Adminstrs., Am. Coll. Personnel Assn., Optimists, Phi Delta Kappa, Delta Upsilon (trustee ednl. found. 1973—, ednl. dir., 1963—). Mason (Shriner, pres. 1965, Jester), Order DeMolay. Clubs: Columbia (Indpls.); Bloomington Country. Producer numerous ednl. TV programs, study films. Home: 800 N Smith Rd Bloomington IN 47401

SMITH, HOWARD WESLEY, engr.; b. N.Y.C., Nov. 24, 1929; s. Albert Edwin and Rose Maria (Fabri) S.; B.S., Wichita State U., 1951, M.S., 1958; Ph.D., Okla. State U., 1968. Registered profl. engr., Kans. Jr. engr. Boeing Co., Wichita, Kans., 1950-52, stress analyst, 1952-55, structures engr., 1956-58, group supr., 1959-63, structures res. mgr., Seattle, 1965-68, staff engr., 1969-70; asso. prof. U. Kans., Lawrence, 1970-74, asso. dean, 1974-76, prof., 1977—. Rocketry leader Douglas County (Kans.) 4-H Club, 1976-77. Fellow Am. Inst. Aeros. and Astronautics (asso.); mem. Soc. Exptl. Stress Analysis, Air Force Hist. Found., Mid-Am. Engring. Guidance Council, Soc. Am. Mil. Engrs., Kans. Acad. Sci., Am. Soc. Engring. Edn. (exec. council aero div.), Phi Kappa Phi. Named Outstanding Faculty Advisor of Year, Am. Inst. Aeros. and Astronautics, 1973; Outstanding Campus Activity Coordinator, Am. Soc. Engring. Edn., 1973-74; Tasker Howard Bliss medal Soc. Am. Mil. Engrs., 1974. Contbr. articles to profl. jours. Home: 1612 Crescent Rd Lawrence KS 66044 Office: Aerospace Engring Dept U Kans Lawrence KS 66045

SMITH, HUESTON MERRIAM, cons. indsl. engr.; b. Almeta, Tex., Dec. 19, 1912; s. Harry Merriam and Ruth Alice (Vasconcellos) S.; B.S. in Elec. Engring., U. Mo., 1938; m. Edith Adele Fort, Dec. 12, 1970; 1 son, Joseph Hueston. Asst. engr., Mo. Pub. Service Commn., 1938-40; indsl. engr. Union Electric Co., St. Louis, 1947-50; chief engr. Fruin-Colnon Co., St. Louis, 1950-54; pres., Smith-Zurheide & Associates, Inc., cons. engrs., St. Louis, 1954-65; sr. v.p. Thatcher & Patient, Inc., St. Louis, 1965-69; exec. v.p. Milling Design, Inc., St. Louis, 1965-69; prin. Hueston M. Smith & Associates, Inc., cons. engrs., St. Louis, 1969—; mem. advisory bd. Cons. Engr. Mag., 1958-77; city engr. Frontenac, Mo., 1957-59. Chief of police, City of Frontenac, 1952-54. Served to col. C.E., U.S. Army, 1940-46; PTO. Decorated Bronze Star; registered profl. engr., Mo., Tex., Kans., Ark. Mem. Cons. Engrs. Council of U.S. (pres. 1960-61, dir. 1963-64), Cons. Engrs. Mo. (pres. 1956-57, dir. 1962-63), Mo. Soc. Profl. Engrs. (Outstanding Achievement award 1962), Soc. of Am. Mil. Engrs., Res. Officers Assn. of U.S., Ret. Officers Assn., Mo. Real Estate Assn., Nat. Rifle Assn., U. Mo. Alumni Assn., Eta Kappa Nu. Clubs: Masons, Mo. Athletic. Editorial bd. Building Construction Mag., 1960-74. Home: 711 E Monroe Ave St Louis MO 63122 Office: 8460 Hwy 66 St Louis MO 63119

SMITH, HUGH BYRON, dentist; b. Waverly, Ohio, Jan. 6, 1901; S. George B. and Dora M. (Donahoe) S.; student U. Mich., 1922-23; D.D.S., Ohio State U., 1926; m. Jessie Adelaide Merkle, Nov. 29, 1933; children—Jessica. Dentist, Columbus, Ohio, 1926-71; dental cons., Columbus, 1971—; dental regional cons. Aetna Life and Casualty Ins. Co., Columbus, 1971—; mem. Ohio Dental Bd., 1945-52, sec., 1945-52. Mem. bd. Park of Roses, Columbus, 1961-71; trustee Florence Crittenton Services, Columbus, 1961-74, treas., 1962-74. Fellow Internat. Coll. Dentists, Peirre Fouchard Acad.; mem. Am. (life), Ohio dental assns., Psi Omega, Alpha Tau Omega. Clubs: Masons (32 deg.), Shriners; Maener Chore, Columbus Rose, Scioto Country (Columbus); Zanesfield Trout and Gun. Home: 3126 Carisbrook Rd Columbus OH 43221 Office: 1900 E Dublin Granville Rd Columbus OH 43229

SMITH, IAN MURRAY, oral surgeon; b. Toronto, Ont., Can., Mar. 11, 1924 (parents Am. citizens); s. Percy Thomas and Margaretta (Carrigan) S.; student DePaul U., 1942, U. Chgo., 1942-44, U. Ill., 1944-46; B.S., U. Detroit, 1948, D.D.S., 1952, M.S., 1955; postgrad. U. Mich., Wayne State U., 1952-55; m. Barbara Jean Moran, Aug. 15, 1953; children—Kathleen, Karen, Ian Murray, Patrick. Resident oral surgery Detroit Receiving Hosp., 1952-55; chief oral surgery Wright Patterson AFB, 1955-57; practice dentistry specializing in oral surgery, Wyandotte, Mich., 1957—; staff oral surgeon Wyandotte Gen. Hosp., Seaway Hosp., Trenton, Mich., Outer Dr. Hosp., Allen Park, Mich.; mem. teaching staff Detroit Gen. Hosp. Dir. Sailmasters of Mich.; instr. U.S. Power Squadron, 1960—, U.S. Coast Guard Aux., 1975—; pres. Sacred Heart Sch. Parent Tchrs. Orgn., 1970-71; mem. Sacred Heart-Grosse Ile Parish Council, 1972; pres. Down River br. Mich. Cancer Soc., 1977-78. Served with U.S. Army, 1942-45; to capt. USAF, 1955-57. Mem. Detroit Acad. Oral Surgeons (pres.), ADA, AMA, Wayne County Med. Soc., Internat., Am., Gt. Lakes, Mich. socs. oral surgeons, Southwestern Dental Club, Blue Key, Psi Omega, Nu Sigma Nu. Clubs: Grosse Ile Yacht (dir. 1966-69), Grosse Ile Golf and Country, Grosse Ile Tennis; Offshore Cruising, River Isles Yachting, Detroit River Yachting, Grosse Ile Islanders; Great Lakes Cruising (Chgo.). Home: 28315 Elba Island Dr Grosse Ile MI 48138 Office: 1811 Fort St Wyandotte MI 48192

SMITH, JAMES DOUGLAS, architect; b. Chgo., May 14, 1943; s. Lyman Douglas and Hallie Marie (Sanders) S.; B.Arch. with honors (Lydia Bates scholar 1964-66, Schlaeder Meml. scholar 1966-67, Deeter-Ritchey-Sipple fellow 1967, A. Epstein meml. scholar 1967-68), U. Ill., 1968; certificate with honors Ecole des Beaux Arts, Fontainbleau, France, 1967; m. Anita Louise Metzger, June 24, 1967; 1 dau., Elisa Marie. Planner, Northeastern Ill. Planning Commn., Chgo., 1966, Dept. Devel. and Planning, Chgo., 1968-69; archtl. designer A. Epstein Internat., Chgo., 1969-72; architect-planner, partner Smith-Kureghian & Assos., Chgo., 1972-77; city architect City of Gary (Ind.), 1977—; planning dir. Indsl. Council/N.W. Community, Chgo., 1972; urban planning cons. Nathan-Barnes & Assos., Chgo., 1972—. Precinct del. 44th Ward Assembly, Chgo., 1973—, chmn. services com., 1973-74, chmn. steering com., 1974—, campaign area chmn., 1974-76. Named an Outstanding Young Man Am., 1974. Mem. AIA (sec. planning com. 1972-75), Prestressed Concrete Inst., Nat. Council Archtl. Registration Bds., Chgo. Assn. Commerce and Industry, Gargoyle Soc., Scarab, Sigma Tau. Home: 1215 W Wellington St Chicago IL 60657 Office: 401 W Broadway Gary IN 46402

SMITH, JAMES FRANKLIN, educator; b. Ishpheming, Mich., Sept. 11, 1923; s. Claude and Tiami (Mitchell) S.; B.S., No. Mich. U., 1950; M.A., U. Mich., 1951, postgrad., 1953, 56, 57, 62; specialist in Edn. degree U. Mich., 1966; m. Elizabeth Ann Buswell, Sept. 6, 1947; children—Peggy, Barbara, Joan, Rebecca. Tchr., Madison Heights (Mich.) pub. schs., 1951-52, 56-57; tchr., dir. adult edn., coordinator coop. occupational tng. Lake Shore Pub. Schs., St. Clair Shores, Mich., 1952-56, vis. tchr. sch. social work, 1957—, now dir. spl. ednl. services. v.p. 1968-69. Served with AUS, 1943-46; ETO. Mem. Mich. Assn. Vis. Tchrs., Macomb County Vis. Tchrs. Assn. (pres. 1958-59), Mich., Macomb County (pres. 1972-73) assns. adminstrs. spl. edn., Lake Shore Am., (treas. 1973-74) assns. sch. adminstrs., Mich. Assn. Professions. Rotarian (pres. St. Clair Shores 1962-63). Home: 23030 Euclid St St Clair Shores MI 48082 Office: 23100 Thirteen Mile Rd St Clair Shores MI 48082

SMITH, JAMES THOMPSON, electronic mfg. co. exec.; b. Middletown, Del., July 9, 1924; s. Harry and Mary Alice (McCluskey) S.; B.S., U.S. Naval Acad., 1945; B.S., Mass. Inst. Tech., 1948; m. Jean Riddle Truss, Sept. 21, 1946; children—James Thompson, Richard R., Margaret T. Elec. engr. G & I div. Magnavox Electronics Co., Ft. Wayne, Ind., 1955-56, chief engr. adminstrn., 1956-58, product mgr. anti-submarine warfare systems, 1958-61, gen. mgr. Magnavox Research Lab., Torrance, Calif., 1961-63, gen. mgr. Urbana (Ill.) ops., 1963-65, v.p., gen. mgr. ASW ops., Ft. Wayne, 1965-72, sr. v.p., 1974—, also dir. Served as lt. USNR, 1945-54. Mem. Electronic Industries Assn. (gov. 1974—), Ft. Wayne C. of C., U.S. Naval Acad. Alumni Assn., Assn. Old Crows, Nat. Security Indsl. Assn. Clubs: Army and Navy, Summit, Wildwood Racquet. Home: 3207 Maxim Dr Fort Wayne IN 46805 Office: 1313 Production Rd Fort Wayne IN 46808

SMITH, JAMESON WARREN, microscopist; b. Montgomery, Ala., Dec. 6, 1944; s. Jameson Willigham and Margaret (Farris) S.; student U.S.C., 1963-65, McCrone Research Inst., 1974; m. Mary Ann Kathryn Morganti, Aug. 24, 1968; 1 son, Jameson Michael. Field technician Cleve. Mus. Nat. History, 1966-67; microscopy technician Ferro Corp. Tech. Center, Cleve., 1967-71, microscopy supr., Independence, Ohio, 1971—. Cubmaster, Cub Scout Pack, 1976-77. Recipient awards in field, ASTM, 1971, 72, 73. Mem. Electron Microscopy Soc. Am., No. Ohio Electron Microscopy Soc., Mineral. Soc. Cleve. Republican. Baptist. Home: 7338 Parma Park Blvd Parma OH 44130 Office: 7500 E Pleasant Valley Rd Independence OH 44131

SMITH, JEANNE KELLENBERGER, speech pathologist; b. Park Ridge, Ill., Sept. 23, 1910; d. William Gaild and Georgia Mae (Esmond) Kellenberger; B.A., U. Iowa, 1933, M.A., 1937; m. Clyde H. Smith, Apr. 18, 1941; 1 dau., Mary Jeanne. Speech clinician pub. schs., Mankato, Minn., 1934-35, Beaver Dam, Wis., 1935-36; dir. speech and hearing program, Racine, Wis., 1937-39, Davenport, Iowa, 1939-41; speech and hearing cons. dept. otolaryngology Univ. Hosp., Iowa City, 1953—, asso. prof. U. Iowa, 1966—; cons. Augustana Coll. summer program, 1973—. Fellow Am. Speech and Hearing Assn.; mem. Am. Cleft Palate Assn. (mem. council 1972-75, mem. parent edn. com. 1973, edn. found. pub. edn. com. 1974-75, honors and awards com. 1975), Iowa Speech and Hearing Assn. (edn. com. 1977—), Council Speech, Hearing and Lang. Disorders Iowa (mem. council 1974-77). Alexander Graham Bell Assn., Am. Audiology Soc., Kappa Kappa Gamma. Roman Catholic. Contbr. articles to profl. jours. Office: Dept Otolaryngology Univ Hosp Iowa City IA 52242

SMITH, JESSE LEE, civil engr.; b. Milan, Tenn., July 30, 1918; s. Oliver Price and Carrie Lee (Williamson) S.; B.S., U. Cin., 1949; m. Gloria Jean Cahall, June 1, 1942; children—Randall Lee, Steven Price, Kathleen Louann. Asst. chief engr. HC Nutting Co., Cin., 1949-52; gen. supt. Walt Kunz Co., Cin., 1952-55; partner McGill & Smith, cons. engrs., Amelia, Ohio, from 1955, now pres. Explorer adv., scoutmaster, inst. rep. Boy Scouts Am., 1958-68; mem. Hamersville Bd. Edn., 1963-67, pres., 1966-67; mem. Western Brown Bd. Edn. Trustee, Clermont Christian Assembly. Served to capt. USAAF, 1941-45. Decorated D.F.C. with oak leaf cluster, Air medal with four oak leaf clusters. Registered profl. engr., W.Va., Ky., Ohio; surveyor Ohio, Ky. Mem. Nat., Ohio socs. profl. engrs., Water Pollution Control Fedn., Am. Water Works Assn., Cons. Engrs. of Ohio. Mason (32 deg., Shriner). Home: Box 296 Rural Route 2 Hamersville OH 45130 Office: 119 W Main St Amelia OH 45102

SMITH, JESSOP, mech. products mfg. co. exec.; b. Cleve., Oct. 23, 1933; s. Vincent Kinsman and Anne Thomas (Jessop) S.; B.S., Kent State U., 1960; m. June Evelyn Dickinson, Sept. 7, 1956; children—Kimberly Jessop, Scott Vincent. Vice pres. mfg. Aquarium Systems, Inc., Eastlake, Ohio, 1964-68, also dir., 1964—; v.p. Marine-Electro-Mech., Inc., Wickliffe, Ohio, 1968-71; pres. Triple-S Devel. Co., Inc., Wickliffe, 1976—. Bd. dirs. Cleve. Center on Alcoholism, 1975—; trustee Cleve. Zoo, 1977. Served with AUS, 1956-58. Mem. ASME, English Speaking Union (dir. Cleve. br. 1974—, v.p.), Great Lakes Offshore Powerboat Racing Assn. (trustee 1975—, treas. 1977), Internat. Wine and Food Soc. (dir. Cleve. br. 1975—, pres. 1977), Alpha Tau Omega. Republican. Episcopalian. Clubs: Kirtland Country, Union (Cleve.), Chagrin Valley Hunt, Mentor Harbor Yachting. Patentee in field. Home: Rd Gates Mills Address: County Line Rd Box 268 Gates Mills OH 44040 Office: 1450 E 289th St Wickliffe OH 44092

SMITH, JOHN HENRY, obstetrician, gynecologist; b. Worthington, Ind., Mar. 12, 1908; s. Henry Herold and Margaret Dixson (Allen) S.; A.B., Rice U., 1929; M.D., U. Ind., 1939; m. Catherine, Jan. 1, 1936; children—John Henry, Frank Schuyler. Resident physician Grady Meml. Hosp., Atlanta, 1946-49; instr. U. Ind. Sch. Medicine, Bloomington, 1940-42; practice medicine specializing in obstetrics and gynecology, Rockford, Ill., 1949—; clin. asso. Rockford Sch. Medicine, 1974, U. Ill. Sch. Medicine, 1974. Served with M.C., AUS, 1942-46. Diplomate Am. Bd. Obstetrics and Gynecology. Mem. Am. Coll. Obstetricians and Gynecologists, A.C.S. Home: 1826 Old Wood Rd Rockford IL 61107 Office: 1415 E State St Rockford IL 61108

SMITH, JUSTIN VANDER VELDE, lumber and coal co. exec.; b. Mpls., Oct. 25, 1903; s. Ernest F. and Julia A. (Walker) S.; B.A., Princeton U., 1925; postgrad. Cambridge (Eng.) U., 1926; m. Alice B. Appleton, Aug. 27, 1958; children—Kathleen, Barlow. Pres., Hennepin Lumber Co., Mpls., 1926-36, Foote Lumber and Coal Co., Mpls., 1940—; sec. Red River Lumber Co., Mpls., 1936-50. Sec., T. B. Walker Found., Mpls., 1936-72, pres., 1972-76, trustee, 1936-76; bd. dirs. Walker Art Center, Mpls., 1940—, Minn. Symphony Assn., 1950-60, Guthrie Theater Found., Mpls., 1960—. Mem. Mpls. Bd. Realtors. Republican. Congregationalist. Clubs: Mpls.; Woodhill Country (Wayzata, Minn.); Skyline Country (Tucson); Princeton of N.Y.C. Author novel: Marriage A La Mode, 1947. Home: 4915 Regents Walk Excelsior MN 55331 Office: 1121 Hennepin Ave Minneapolis MN 55403

SMITH, KEITH ALLEN, electronics co. exec.; b. Kansas City, Mo., July 9, 1928; s. Levi Byron and Martha Miller (Buree) S.; B.S. in Mech. Engring., U. Mo., 1948-50, 54-57; m. Tori Desmond, Mar. 27, 1977; children—Gregory Luke, Daniel Cameron. Engr., Allied Chem. Corp., Solvay Process, Baton Rouge, 1957-58; engring. supr. U.S. Army C.E., Los Angeles, 1958-62; cons. engr. Ralph M. Parsons Co., Los Angeles, 1962; lead engr. Gen. Dynamics, Pomona, Calif., 1963-66; founder, v.p. R.T. Fuller Corp., Pomona, 1966-67; engring. specialist Philco Ford Corp., Palo Alto, Calif., 1967-68; v.p. Dietzgen Electronics/Melabs, South San Francisco, 1964-72; mfg. mgr. Systron Donner, Sunnyvale, Calif., 1972-74; founder, pres. Student's Review, Los Altos, Calif., 1972—; bus. cons. S & N Assos., Monterey, Calif., 1972. Served with USN, 1950-51. Decorated Air Medal (3). Mem. ASME. Club: Elks. Contbr. articles to profl. jours. Inventor in field. Home and office: 4205 Clark St Kansas City MO 64111

SMITH, KENNETH POWER, corp. exec.; b. South Bend, Ind., May 23, 1914; s. James and Isabella (Power) S.; A.B., U. Ill., 1939; m. Winifred Jeanette Flood, July 1, 1939; children—Kenneth Power, Carolyn Jane George, Robert Pershing. Accountant, Ind. & Mich. Electric Co., 1939-41, Studebaker Corp., 1941-43; staff accountant Touche, Niven & Co., C.P.A.'s, 1943-45; asst. chief accountant Standard Ry. Equipment Mfg. Co., Hammond, Ind., 1945-57, controller, 1957-60, now Stanray Corp., Chgo., v.p. fin., 1960-67; pres. John Gillen Co., 1967-71; v.p., treas. dir. Chgo. Extruded Metals Co., 1971—; dir. Anchor-Harvey Components, Inc., Tuthill Pump Co., Columbia Tool Steel Co. Mem. adv bd. Salvation Army; pres. bd. trustees Washington and Jane Smith Home. Mem. Newcomen Soc., Phi Delta Theta. Mason. Episcopalian. Clubs: Economic (Chicago); Union League, Hinsdale Golf. Home: 611 Woodland Ave Hinsdale IL 60521 Office: 600 Hunter Dr Oak Brook IL 60521

SMITH, LARRY JAY, realtor, developer; b. Chgo., Apr. 2, 1936; s. Jack L. and Sydell (Blinder) S.; B.A. in Econs., Wharton Sch. Finance, U. Pa., 1957; m. Nancy Beth Sherman, Oct. 20, 1957; children—S. Scott, Jason G. Pres. Am. Realty Corp., Chgo., 1961-67; exec. v.p. Romanek-Golub & Co., Chgo., 1967—; lectr. in field. Pres. Jr. Real Estate Bd. Chgo., 1967. Served to lt. AUS, 1958. Mem. Inst. Real Estate Mgmt., Realtors Nat. Mktg. Inst., Phi Epsilon Pi. Clubs: Standard, Mason, Shriners (Chgo.). Contbr. articles to publs. Office: 625 N Michigan Ave Chicago IL 60611

SMITH, LAUREN ASHLEY, clergyman, lawyer; b. Clinton, Iowa, Nov. 30, 1924; s. William Thomas Roy and Ethel (Cook) S.; B.S., U. Minn., 1946; J.D., U. Minn., 1949; B.D., McCormick Theol. Sem., 1950, M.Div., 1971; postgrad. U. Chgo., 1948-49; m. Barbara Ann Mills, Aug. 22, 1947; children—Christopher Allin, Laura Nan, William Thomas Roy. Ordained to ministry Presbyn. Ch., 1950; minister Presbyn. chs., Fredonia, Kans., 1950-52, Lamar, Colo., 1952-57; newspaper editor, Pine Bluff, Ark., 1957-58; admitted to Colo. bar, 1957, Iowa bar, 1959, Ill. bar, 1963; practiced in Clinton, 1959—; dep. atty. Clinton County, 1969—; free-lance journalist and newspaper columnist (under pseudonym Christopher Crow), 1958—; U.S. bur. chief Press and News of India, Clinton, 1977—; pastor Clinton Community Congregational Ch., United Ch. Christ, 1974—; moderator Presbytery, Pueblo, Colo., 1955-56; legal counsel Presbytery S.E. Iowa, 1961—; pres. Clinton Council Chs., 1962-63; mem. Harvard U. Council on Religion and Law, 1977—; v.p. Clinton County ARC, 1961-65, pres., 1965; pres. Valley Dist. council Boy Scouts Am., 1964-65; founder, chmn. Clinton Council on Internat. Affairs. Bd. dirs. Clinton County Mental Health Clinic. Mem. Am., Iowa, Ill., Clinton County (pres. 1972) bar assns., Nat. Dist. Attys. Assn., Iowa County Attys. Assn., St. Andrew Soc., Clinton Ministerial Assn., Nat. Presbyn. Charismatic Communion, UN Assn. (dir. Iowa div.), Ark. Press Assn., Internat. Platform Assn., Acacia. Author: Forma Dat Esse Rei, 1974. Home: 1610 N 3d St Clinton IA 52732 Office: Wilson Bldg Clinton IA 52732

SMITH, LAWRENCE NORVAL, meat packing co. exec.; b. Alden, Kans., Sept. 12, 1920; s. Chris Clark and Eleanor Susan (Colwell) S.; m. Helen Geneva Fox, Aug. 5, 1939; children—Geneva Ferne Smith Barrington, Lawrence Allie, Steven Craig, Eddie Lee. With Winchester Packing Co., Hutchinson, Kans., 1940—, supt., 1950-72, v.p., plant mgr., 1972—, also dir. Bd. dirs. Hutchinson Safety Council, 1958-63. Served with AUS, 1945-46. Mem. Hutchinson C.

of C. Republican. Home: 708 W 22d Hutchinson KS 67501 Office: 521 S Main Hutchinson KS 67501

SMITH, LEONARD RICHARD, physician; b. Chgo., Dec. 19, 1924; s. Isidore and Clare (Wales) S.; student Northwestern U., 1941-43, U. Wis., 1946; B.S., U. Ill., 1948, M.D., 1950; m. Janice Grant, Nov. 21, 1954; children—Lendy, Jamie. Intern, Cook County Hosp., Chgo., 1950-51; resident U. Ill., Chgo., 1951-54, Michael Reese Hosp., Chgo., 1954-55; practice medicine specializing in orthopedic surgery, Chgo., 1955—; pres. Leonard R. Smith, M.D., S.C., 1968—; pres., chief of staff Roosevelt Meml. Hosp., 1965—; dir. Schwab Rehab. Hosp., 1972—; asst. prof. orthopedic surgery Stritch Sch. Medicine, Loyola U., 1959—; fellow dept. bone and joint surgery Northwestern U. Med. Sch.; cons. orthopedics Dept. Labor, No. Dist. of Ill.; dir. 322 Oakdale Corp., Modigraphics Corp. Active Civic Club of Chgo.; active gov. com. employment of handicapped; pres., dir., Easter Seal Soc. of Chgo., 1965-67, v.p. ho. of dels., 1970-71; med. and profl. com. Arthritis and Rheumatism Found of Chgo., 1965-68; pres. Chgo. Phys. Therapy Center. Served with AUS, 1943-46. Fellow Internat. Coll. Surgeons, Am. Acad. Orthopedic Surgery; mem. Sigma Alpha Epsilon. Clubs: Bryn Mawr Country, Standard (Chgo.). Home: 320 Oakdale St Chicago IL 60657 Office: 30 N Michigan Ave Chicago IL 60602

SMITH, LOREN MITCHELL, wire mfg. co. exec.; b. Cleve., Jan. 30, 1943; s. Robert H. and Janet (Lebby) S.; B.S., Miami U., Ohio, 1964; M.B.A., Northeastern U., 1974; m. Gloria Goetze, June 15, 1976; children—Bradley, David. Sales engr., Standard Pressed Steel, 1964-66; with Texas Instruments, Attleboro, Mass., 1966-75, product mgr., 1972-73, div. gen. mgr., 1973-75; v.p., gen. mgr. Augat Co., Attleboro, 1975-76; pres. Monona Wire Corp. (Iowa), 1976—. Home: 411 Main St N Monona IA 52159 Office: Hwy 18 Monona IA 52159

SMITH, LOUIS ADRIAN, lawyer; b. Lansing, Mich., Apr. 22, 1939; s. John Paul and Marjorie (Christmas) S.; B.A. in Communication Arts cum laude, Mich. State U., 1962; J.D. (univ. scholar), U. Mich., 1965; m. Karen Terry Emens, Feb. 5, 1966; children—Timothy Paul, Patrick Louis, Elizabeth Karen. Mem. labor relations staff Gen. Motors Corp., Detroit, 1963-65; admitted to Mich. bar, 1965; practiced in Lansing, 1965-75, Traverse City, Mich., 1975—; partner firm Fowler & Smith, 1965-67; partner fir, Doyle, Smith, Whitmer & Carruthers, 1967-75, pres., 1970-75; part-owner Estes Furniture Co., Lansing, Luke Enterprises, Lansing; co-founder Thomas M. Cooley Sch. Law, Lansing, 1st v.p., sec., 1972-75, pres., 1975—. Bd. dirs., also a founder Mich. Montessori Internat. Sch., Okemos, Mich. Mem. Am., D.C., Ingham County (dir. 1972—), Fed. bar assns., Am. Judicature Soc., Am. Trial Lawyers Assn., State Bar of Mich., Nat. Assn. Accountants, Phi Delta Phi. K.C. Office: 607 Bay St Traverse City MI 49684

SMITH, LUCRETIA LUTTIE, clergywoman; b. Richmond, Va., Dec. 28, 1909; d. Earl and Ira (Reeves) Winchester; ed. Ill. Theol. Sem.; m. Charles B. Marshall, Sept. 16, 1924 (div. Mar. 1929); 1 dau., Constance Marshall (Mrs. McSpadden); m. 2d, Elucious M. Smith, Apr. 19, 1930. Ordained to ministry Ch. of Christ, 1932; pastor Lily of Valley Spiritual Ch., Chgo., 1937—, founder Lily of Valley Progressive Center, Chgo., 1941. Pres., Chgo. Local Ministers and Laymen's Council Met. Spiritual Chs. of Christ, Inc., 1935—, 1st v.p. Met. Spiritual Chs. of Christ, Inc., 1975-77. Named hon. citizen Boys' Town, Neb., 1952; recipient Civic award Chgo. 100, 1971. Mem. Chgo. and No. Dist. Assn. Club Women (chaplain), Nat. Council Colored Women's Club, Chgo. Urban League (3d v.p. council religious leaders), Phyllis Wheatley Assn. Office: 257 W 48th Pl Chicago IL 60609

SMITH, MARILYN FOX, sch. adminstr.; b. Phila., Aug. 10, 1936; d. Walter J. and Marie T. (Schenkel) Fox; B.A., Rosemont Coll., 1958; M.S., No. Ill. U., 1974; m. William G. Smith, Dec. 27, 1958; children—Cheryl T.,. J. Gregory. Tchr., Holy Child Acad., Sharon Hill, Pa., 1958-59; personal sec. to theology prof. St. Joseph's Coll., Phila., 1959-61; tchr., Lexington, Ky., 1964-65; with Holy Family Parish, Rockford, Ill., 1966-68; student tchr. Guilford High Sch., Rockford, Ill., 1971; faculty Counseling Lab., No. Ill. U., DeKalb, 1973; developer Office of Health Careers Counseling, Rockford Sch. Medicine, U. Ill., 1975-76, asst. dir. office student affairs, 1976—. Mem. Am. Personnel and Guidance Assn., Delta Epsilon Sigma. Home: 2623 Cerro Vista Dr Rockford IL 61107 Office: 1601 Parkview St Rockford IL 61101

SMITH, MARJORIE MAE OSTREICH, speech pathologist; b. Long Branch, N.J., Feb. 17, 1949; d. Leonard L. and Ellen Sarah (Stein) Ostreich; student Adelphi U., 1967-68, Ithaca Coll., 1968-69; B.S., U. Mich., 1970, M.S., 1971; m. Dustan Terry Smith, Sept. 5, 1971; children—Carey Phillip, Jordan Seth. Speech pathologist Loyola U. Med. Center, Maywood, Ill., 1971-72; dir. speech dept. Oak Park (Ill.) Hosp., 1972-74; cons. Oak Park Speech and Hearing Center, 1974-76, Green Oak Terrace Nursing Home, Park Ridge, Ill., 1977—. Mem. Am. (certificate clin. competence in speech pathology), Ill., Chgo. speech and hearing assns., Women's Am. ORT (chpt. pres. 1977—). Home: 2131 Habberton St Park Ridge IL 60068

SMITH, MARY LUCY, educator; b. Richland, Ga., Dec. 12, 1940; d. Charles and Odessa Lucille (Mathis) Martin; B.A., St. Xavier Coll., 1973; postgrad. Governor State U., 1973-75; m. Betrand Smith, Aug. 29, 1964. Tchr., Crispus Attucks Elementary Sch., Chgo., 1973—. Mem. profl. women aux. Provident Hosp., 1973-77, corr. sec., 1975-76, installation chmn., 1977; mem. civic aux. Planned Parenthood, Chgo., 1975—, social chmn., 1976-77, corr sec., 1977. Address: 9722 S Yale Ave Chicago IL 60628

SMITH, MICHAEL ROLAND, engring. co. exec.; b. Grantsburg, Wis., Oct. 23, 1938; s. Charles D. and Bernice Ann (Hjort) S. Dist. sales mgr. trainee Rose Chem. Products Co., Columbus, Ohio, 1965-66; co-founder, co-operater Chardon Labs., Inc., Columbus, 1966—, also Weatherator Engring. Co. div., 1976—. Chmn. coordinator Jr. Achievement, 1976-77. Served with USCG, 1960-64. Recipient Contbns. award Distbv. Edn. Clubs Am., 1976-77. Mem. Chem. Splty. Mfg. Assn., Internat. San. Supply Assn., Aircraft Owners and Pilots Assn., Pi Sigma Epsilon. Republican. Lutheran. Clubs: Sales Exec. Columbus (dir.), Masons, Highlands Golf, Hideway Hills, Flying Nobles. Home: 8948 Chevington Chase St Pikerington OH 43147 Office: 539 Stimmel Rd PO Box 1004 Columbus OH 43216

SMITH, MILBOURN LILE, consulting engr.; b. Hope, Ark., Jan. 13, 1936; s. Roy N. and Francis M. (Douglas) S.; B.S. in Civil Engring., Tex. A & M U., 1960; M.S. in Environ. Engr., U. Tex., 1968; m. Judy V. Watkins, Feb. 24, 1956; children—Laurie Lynn, Lisa Diane, Leslie Jean. Dir. solid wastes demonstration projects U.S. Bur. of Solid Wastes Mgmt., 1967-70; dir. solid wastes systems engr. Continental Can Co., Chgo., 1970-76; cons. engr. M.L. Smith Environ. Co., Oakbrook, Ill., 1976—; cons. in field. Served with USMC, 1954-62, USPHS, 1964-70. Registered profl. engr., Tex., Wis. Mem. U.S. Pub. Health Service Commd. Officers Assn., ASCE, U.S. C. of C. Methodist. Author: (with others) Recycling & Disposal of Solid Wastes, 1973. Home: 261 Pleasant Dr Glenwood IL 60425 Office: 2625 Butterfield Rd Oakbrook IL 60521

SMITH, MILDRED TAYLOR, psychologist; b. Arcadia, Kans., Nov. 22, 1911; d. James Newton and Nora Ellen (Rollen) Taylor; A.A., Horner Conservatory Music, 1928; B.S., Kans. State Coll., 1932; A.B., Marymount Coll., 1958; M.Ed., Xavier U., 1962; m. Linus B. Smith, Apr. 1, 1932 (dec.); 1 dau., Mildred A. Grade sch. tchr., Kans., 1928-32; ednl. asso. Social Hygiene Soc., Cin., 1958-61; dean/headmistress Fairfax Hall, Coll. Prep. Sch., Waynesboro, Va., 1961-65; project dir. William A. Mitchell Center, Cin., 1965-68, exec. dir., psychologist, 1968—. Mem. personnel com., search com. Cin. Met. YWCA, 1976—; mem. mgmt. and adv. bds. Edgecliff Coll., Cin., 1976—. Fellow Am. Orthopsychiat. Assn., Am. Pub. Health Assn., Soc. Pub. Health Educators, Royal Soc. Health (London); mem. Nat., Ohio rehab. counseling assns., Southwestern Ohio Rehab. Assn., Ohio Pub. Health Assn., Am., Ohio, Southwestern psychol. assns., Mental Health Assn. Cin., Internat. Union for Health Edn., Ohio Assn. Community Mental Health Adminstrs., DAR, AAUW (past pres. Ohio div. 1971-73), Delta Kappa Gamma. Club: Women's City. Home: 2401 Ingleside Ave River Terr Cincinnati OH 45206 Office: 2517 Burnet Ave Cincinnati OH 45219

SMITH, MILTON REYNOLDS, biochemist; b. Chgo., Mar. 15, 1934; s. John Milton and Lorraine (Reynolds) S.; B.A., Knox Coll., 1956; M.S., U. Ariz., 1958, Ph.D., 1963; m. Suana Eleanor Sells, Aug. 27, 1955 (dec.); 1 son, Dirk Macon; m. 2d, Gretchen Sue Tidd, Apr. 3, 1976. Instr. chemistry Ind. Central Coll., Indpls., 1967-71; sr. biochemist Eli Lilly & Co., Indpls., 1963—. Active Cub Scouts, Boy Scouts, Indpls. Symphony Orch., Civic Theater. U.S. Dept. Agr. grantee, 1958-60. Fellow Am. Inst. Chemists; mem. N.Y. Acad. Sci., Am. Chem. Soc., A.A.A.S., Sigma Xi, Phi Lambda Upsilon, Beta Beta Beta, Tau Kappa Epsilon. Presbyn. Patentee in field. Home: 7603 Vintage Ct Indianapolis IN 46226 Office: Eli Lilly Co 307 E McCarty St Indianapolis IN 46206

SMITH, NEAL EDWARD, congressman; b. Hedrick, Iowa, Mar 23, 1920; s. James N. and Margaret M. (Walling) S.; student U. Mo., 1945-46, Syracuse U., 1946-47; LL.B., Drake U., 1950; m. Beatrix Havens, Mar. 23, 1945; children—Douglas, Sharon. Farmer, Iowa, 1937—; admitted to Iowa bar, 1950; practiced in Des Moines, 1950—; atty. 50 sch. bds. in Iowa, 1953—; asst. county atty. Polk County, Iowa, 1951; mem. 86th-92d congresses from 5th Dist. Iowa, 93d-95th Congresses from 4th Dist. Iowa. Chmn. Polk County Bd. Social Welfare, 1954-56; pres. Young Democratic Clubs Am., 1953-55. Served with AUS, World War II. Decorated Air medal with 4 oak leaf clusters, Purple Heart. Mem. Am. Bar Assn., Farm Bur., Farmers Union., DAV. Mason. Office: House Office Bldg Washington DC 20515

SMITH, NEIL EDWARD, constrn. and real estate exec.; b. Stillwater, Minn., July 20, 1930; s. Sheldon Edward and Ellen Irene (Swanson) S.; B.A., Hamline U., 1956; J.D., William Mitchell Coll. Law, 1962; banking credit So. Meth. U., 1969; m. Betty Jean Sallee, July 24, 1954; children—Jeffrey, Randy, Michael. Asst. cashier First Nat. Bank, Stillwater, 1958-62; trust officer Central Nat. Bank, Des Moines, 1962-66; v.p., trust officer, dir. First Nat. Bank, Mt. Vernon, Ill., 1966-70, Central Bank & Trust Co., Owensboro, Ky., 1966-70, Edgar County Bank Paris, Ill., 1966-70, Security Bank & Trust Co., Cairo, Ill., 1966-70; v. p. Silver Enterprises, St. Paul, 1970-75; pres. Chippewa Homes of Minn., Stillwater, 1977—, Growth Equity, Inc., Stillwater, 1977—; mem. Ill. Bd. Banks and Trust Cos., 1968-69. Served with USAF, 1950-54. Mem. Am., Iowa, Ill. bar assns., Nat. Assn. Realtors, St. Paul Bd. Realtors, C. of C. Stillwater. Methodist. Club: Elks. Home: 704 W Pine St Stillwater MN 55092 Office: 5340 N Stillwater Blvd Stillwater MN 55082

SMITH, NORVEL E., business exec.; b. Kansas City, Kans., Mar. 17, 1901; s. Archie Webb and Hannah (Bright) S.; student Finley Engring. Coll., 1927; m. Wilhelmina Pace, June 24, 1967. Pres., dir. Universal Constrn. Co., Kansas City, Kans., 1931—, Universal Holding Co., Kansas City, 1946—, Security Investment Fund, Topeka, 1937—, Hotel LaSalle Co., Kansas City, Mo., 1948—, Smith-Universal Constrn. Co. Okla., Oklahoma City, 1950—; v.p., dir. Universal Bridge Co., Kansas City, Kans., 1947—; partner Shopian Plaza Hotel, Kansas City, Mo., 1948, Smith-Universal Co., Kansas City, Mo., 1951—; dir. Security Benefit Life Ins. Co., Topeka, Kans., Balt. Bank, Kansas City, Mo. Vice chmn. Nat. UN Day. Trustee Kansas City Mus.; adv. trustee Research Hosp., Kansas City. Mem. Builders Assn. Kansas City, Asso. Gen. Contractors Am., Jackson County Hist. Soc. (trustee), Am. Legion (hon. trustee). Club: Kansas City (Mo.); Saddle and Sirloin (Leawood, Mo.); 611 (treas., dir.), Owl (Kansas City, Mo.); Terrace (Kansas City, Kan.); Indian Hills Country (Prairie Village, Kan.). Home: 1514 N 21st St Kansas City KS 66102 Office: 29 Greystone Ave Kansas City KS 66103

SMITH, OTHA WILLIAM, JR., wholesale co. exec.; b. Omaha, Aug. 31, 1925; s. Otha William and Alice Hattie (Clark) S.; grad. high sch.; m. Audra Ellen Barnes, June 27, 1943; children—Michael Eugene, Pamela Jo, Rocella Ann (dec.). Co-owner Smith & Clark Trucking Co., Breckenridge, Colo., 1947-49; dept. mgr. Gamble Skogmo, Inc., Fremont, Nebr., 1952-67; dist. mgr. 20th Century Mfg. Co., Mpls., 1968—. Pres. bd. Nebr. Softball Assn. Corp., 1965—; commr. State Nebr., Amateur Softball Assn., 1967—. Served with Signal Corps U.S. Army, World War II. Mem. Am. Legion (comdr. 1955-56). Lion. Address: 1840 N C St Fremont NE 68025

SMITH, PAUL KEITH, mech. engr.; b. Muncie, Ind., Feb. 7, 1931; s. Curtis Russell and Sylvia (Deich) S.; m. Helen Elizabeth Schick, Aug. 26, 1961; children—Jennifer, Andrew. B.S., Purdue U., 1961. Registered profl. engr., Mich., Iowa. Project engr. Borg Warner Corp., Decatur, Ill., 1961-68; engring. supr. Babcock & Wilcox Co., Barberton, Ohio, 1968-72, Bechtel Assos. Profl. Corp., Ann Arbor, Mich., 1972—. Mem. Am. Nuclear Soc. Home: 2613 Patricia Ct Ann Arbor MI 48103

SMITH, PAUL MILTON, JR., psychologist; b. Raleigh, N.C., Aug. 10, 1920; s. Paul Milton and Ella Louise (Turner) S.; B.A., St. Augustines Coll., 1941; M.A., U. Ill., 1950; Ed.D., Ind. U., 1957; m. Eleanor Jane Lewis, Dec. 27, 1972; children—Cheryl Delores, Paul Byron. Mem. faculty S.C. State Coll., 1959-60, N.C. Central U., at Durham, 1960-69; adj. prof. Tchrs. Coll. Columbia U., N.Y.C., 1969-70, also asso. dir. ERIC Info. Center on Disadvantaged Inst.; prof. psychology and Afro Am. studies, U. Cin., 1970—. Served with USMC, 1943-46. Mem. Assn. Black Psychologists, Am. Personnel and Guidance Assn., Nat. Council Black Studies, NAACP. Club: Masons. Home: 2930 Scioto St #313 Cincinnati OH 45219 Office: 114 Old Commons U Cin Cincinnati OH 45221

SMITH, PAUL ROLAND, artist; b. Colony, Kans., Sept. 12, 1916; s. Russell O. and Mary M. (Smith) S.; B.S., Pittsburg (Kans.) State Coll., 1941; M.F.A., U. Iowa, 1951; m. Tyrola C. Wold, Mar. 10, 1946; children—Patricia L., Edmond Erickson, Cris R., Jill J., Cheryl L. Instr. art Ft. Scott (Kans.) Jr. Coll., 1946-47, Ft. Hays (Kans.) State Coll., 1947-49; faculty art U. No. Iowa, 1951-65; faculty, chmn. dept. Hamline U., St. Paul, 1965—; juror nat., regional art competitions, 1955—; one-man shows include: AAA Galleries, N.Y.C., 1954, Des Moines Art Center, 1958, Wright Mus., Beloit, Wis., 1959, Mulvane Mus., Topeka, 1971, Krasner Gallery, N.Y.C., 1973-74, 76-77; represented in pub., pvt. collections; mem. sculpture selection com. Nat. Endowment Arts, Minn., 1973—; dir. visual arts div. Minn. Arts Council, 1970-74. Trustee Minn. Mus. Art, 1969-75, exec. com., 1972-75. Served to maj. C.E., AUS, 1941-46. Recipient numerous art awards. Mem. Artists Equity Assn. (pres. 1964-68), Coll. Art Assn. (program chmn. Mid-Am. conf. 1968), AAUP, Kappa Pi. Home: Box 352 Nisswa MN 56468

SMITH, PETER LANG, USAF officer; b. Paterson, N.J., Mar. 25, 1930; s. Peter and Louise (Lang) S.; B.Ed. with honors U. Nebr., 1965; M.S., U. So. Calif., 1968; m. Vera Marie Elkins, Nov. 2, 1954; 1 son, Dana Lang. Enlisted U.S. Air Force, 1951, commd. 2d. lt., 1953, advanced through grades to col., 1974; aircraft comdr. SAC KC-97 and KC-135, Castle AFB, Calif., 1962-63, instr. SAC combat crew tng. crew, 1963-70, ops. officer, also comdr. rescue helicopter unit Korea, 1971-72; comdr. SAC air refueling squadron, Westover AFB, 1972-73; dep. comdr. ops. 384th. Air Refueling Wing, McConnell AFB, Kans., 1973—. Decorated Air medal. Mem. Mensa. Clubs: Masons, Shriners. Home: 8509 Travis Dr Wichita KS 67210 Office: 384th Air Refueling Wing McConnell AFB KS 67220

SMITH, PRISCILLA DEAN, constrn. co. exec.; b. Hammond, Ind., Nov. 25, 1935; d. David Dean and Mary Eleanor (Morrison) Wightman; ed. Shimer Coll., Mt. Carroll, Ill., 1953; m. Donald Dean Smith, Apr. 1, 1954; children—Todd Morrison, Susan Kimberly, Debra Dean. Trainee, Todd Co., Peoria, Ill., 1959-64, v.p., Lombard, Ill., 1965-71; asst. to pres. Hasco Tank Erectors, Inc., Lombard, 1971-72, pres., 1972—, chmn. bd., 1976—; dir. I.B. Systems, Inc., Hinsdale, Ill. Mem. Steel Plate Fabricators Assn. Unitarian. Home: 1061 Daniel Ct Lombard IL 60148 Office: 20 W 603 Glen Ct Lombard IL 60148

SMITH, REGAN GRANVILLE, educator; b. Kalamazoo, Aug. 13, 1938; s. Granville B. and Frances Marion (Little) S.; B.A., Kalamazoo Coll., 1960; postgrad. U. Denver, 1963, So. Colo. State Coll., 1964; A.M., U. Ill. at Urbana, 1970, Ph.D., 1970; m. Lillian Sanders, July 27, 1968; children—Phillip M., Steven A., Ethan J., Robert J. Dir., Civic Theater, Marshall, Mich., 1961; houseparent Colo. State Children's Home, Denver, 1961-63; cottage counselor Lookout Mountain Sch. for Boys, Golden, Colo., 1963-64; probation officer Dist. Ct., Juvenile Div., Pueblo, Colo., 1964-65, Probate Ct., Juvenile Div., Calhoun County, Marshall, Mich., 1965-67; instr. sociology U. Ill. at Urbana, 1968-69; asst. prof. sociology U. Wyo., Laramie, 1970-72; asst. prof. sociology/anthropology program Sangamon State U., Springfield, Ill., 1972-75, asso. prof., 1975—, chmn. sociology/anthropology program, 1973—. Mem. Citizen's Adv. Com. to Juvenile Justice, Sangamon County, Springfield, Ill., 1973—. NIMH grantee, 1967-70. Mem. Am. Sociol. Assn., Soc. for Study Social Problems, Nat. Council on Crime Delinquency, Soc. Study Symbolic Interaction (corr. sec., treas.), Midwest Sociol. Soc. (recruiting chmn.). Home: 1410 N 3d St Springfield IL 62702

SMITH, RICHARD BUTLER, clergyman, educator; b. Laurel, Miss., Sept. 26, 1923; s. George Washington and Winnie Mae (Sellers) S.; diploma Clarke Coll., 1945; B.A., Miss. Coll., 1947; B.D., New Orleans Bapt. Theol. Sem., 1960, Th.D., 1968; m. Nina Lucile Hutchison, Mar. 1, 1942; children—Peggy Ann (Mrs. Donnie Lee Collins), Carol (Mrs. Roy David Ambrose), George Richard, John Wayne, Warren Butler. With Memphis Union Sta., 1942-44; ordained to ministry Bapt. Ch., 1942; pastor Leesburg Ch., Morton, Miss., 1944-47, Hardy (Miss.) Ch., 1947-59, Fairview Ch., Indianola, Miss., 1959-61; Inner-City Parish, New Orleans, 1962-64, First Ch., Winslow, Ariz., 1964-72; asso. prof. philosophy and theology Oakland City (Ind.) Coll., 1972—, dean students, 1975—, dir. MANPOWER, 1975—, chmn. div. religious studies, 1976—; lectr., counselor; curriculum writer Sunday Sch. Bd., So. Bapt. Conv., Nashville, 1969; exec. bd. Ariz. So. Bapt. Conv., Phoenix, 1968-71; curriculum writer Gen. Assn. Gen. Bapt. Ch., 1973. Chmn. personnel Office Econ. Opportunity, Winslow, 1969-70. Chmn. bd. dirs. Navajo County Guidance and Counseling Clinic, Winslow, 1965-72, No. Ariz. Comprehensive Guidance and Counseling, 1969-72; trustee Ariz. Bapt. Children's Home, Phoenix, 1968-71. Mason (32 deg.). Home: 431 W Oak St Oakland City IN 47660

SMITH, ROBERT EARL, coll. adminstr.; b. Dallas, May 15, 1936; s. Robert A. and Lillie (Harrell) S.; A.A., Central Coll., McPherson, Kans., 1955; B.S., Greenville Coll., 1957; M.S. (Univ. fellow), So. Ill. U., 1958; Ph.D., Fla. State U., 1973; m. Joanna M. Riggs, Aug. 30, 1957; children—Charles Edward, Cynthia Kay. Prof. phys. edn., baseball coach Taylor U., Upland, Ind., 1958-61; dir. phys. edn., coach Greenville (Ill.) Coll., 1961-69, dir. phys. edn., coach, asst. to pres., 1971—; asst. baseball coach Fla. State U., Tallahassee, 1969-71. Named Coach of Yr., Nat. Assn. Intercollegiate Athletics, 1969. Mem. U.S. Baseball Fedn. (sec.-treas. 1974—), Nat. Assn. Intercollegiate Athletics (pres. baseball coaches assn. 1976-78), Am. Assn. Coll. Baseball Coaches (research com. 1974, clinic com. 1974), Ill. Assn. Health, Phys. Edn. and Recreation, Greenville Coll. Alumni Assn. (pres. 1965-68). Kiwanian. Home: 503 Shannon Dr Greenville IL 62246

SMITH, ROBERT JACK, educator; b. New Haven, Apr. 9, 1930; s. Norman Nathaniel and Dorothy (Resnikoff) S.; stepson Lillian Riemer Smith; B.A., Yale, 1951, M.A., 1955; Ph.D., U. Pa., 1963; m. Doris Arlene Noel, July 4, 1960; children—Stephanie Rachelle, Rebecca Norene, Elisa Lauren. Research anthropologist Eastern Pa. Psychiat. Inst., Phila., 1958-61, NIMH project Osawatomie (Kans.) State Hosp., 1961-63; asst. prof. anthropology Western Mich. U., Kalamazoo, 1963-66, asso. prof., 1966-72, prof., 1972—, chmn. Latin-Am. studies program, 1964-70, mem. faculty senate, 1965-70; vis. prof. anthropology Inst. Technologico y de Estudios Superiores de Monterrey, Mexico, summer 1968; researcher, Trinidad, W.I., 1957-58, 70-71, Guatemala, 1966, 67, Mich., 1974. Mem. Kalamazoo County Bd. Health, 1976—, chmn., 1977—. Fellow Am. Anthrop. Assn., Soc. for Applied Anthropology; mem. Latin Am. Studies Assn., Midwest Assn. for Latin Am. Studies, Am. Ethnol. Soc., AAUP, Soc. Med. Anthropology, Central States Anthrop. Soc. Contbr. articles to profl. jours. Home: 1104 Highgate Rd Kalamazoo MI 49007

SMITH, ROBERT JAMES, designer, pub.; b. Chgo., Oct. 23, 1918; s. Edward W. and Emma (Olson) S.; student Chgo. Tech. Coll., 1936, U. Ill., 1937-39, U. Chgo., 1943, Elmhurst Coll., 1949; m. Ruth Marion Hall, Feb. 8, 1942; children—Gregory Hall, Gerald Edward, Marilyn Emily Smith Lovett, Brian Woodley. Partner, designer Craft Patterns internat. home workshop newspaper feature, Elmhurst, Ill., 1947—; pres. Crafts Products Co., Elmhurst and St. Charles, Ill., 1965—; owner Craft Clocks & Gifts, Elmhurst, 1967—. Committeeman Republican party Addison Twp., 1965-72; pres. bd. York High Sch., Elmhurst, 1955-61. Served with Manhattan Dist. Engrs., 1943-46. Mem. Delta Kappa Epsilon. Methodist. Designed and invented instruments for AEC pioneering modern, quick-reading, portable Geiger counter and deep hole proble. Home: 6 No 91 Denker Rd Saint Charles IL 60174 Office: Route 83 and North Ave Elmhurst IL 60126 also 2200 Dean Saint Charles IL 60147

SMITH, ROBERT KEITH, photographer, educator; b. Baraboo, Wis., Jan. 20, 1943; s. Melvin Charles and France Margaret (Walker) S.; B.S., Wis. State U.-Whitewater, 1965; M.S., U. Wis.-Stout, 1970; specialist St. Cloud State U., 1975; m. Jane Marie Grunwaldt, July 11,

1969; children—Heather Annamarie, Heidi Annamarie. Peace Corps assignment, Venezuela, 1965-69; asst. prof. dept. communication media Bemidji (Minn.) State U., 1969—, chmn. dept., 1975—, audio-visual dir., 1975—. Owner, operator Image Photography, Bemidji, 1971—. Bemidji State U. grantee, 1972-74. Mem. Assn. Ednl. Communications and Tech., Profl. Photographers Am., Minn. Profl. Photographers Assn., A.A.U.P., Minn. Edn. Assn. Methodist (youth edn. com. 1974). Author: (with Barry Prichard) Seeing Itasca-State Park, 1974; (with Larry Aitken) Wanda-Kee Wadin, 1971. Home: 1401 Beltrami Ave Bemidji MN 56601

SMITH, ROBERT LEONARD, plastic co. exec.; b. Newton, Iowa, Nov. 20, 1916; s. William Walter and Nellie (Van Dusseldorp) S.; B.S., Iowa State U., 1939; m. Katharine Margaret Wulfing, June 17, 1939; children—Walter Wulfing, Katharine Louise. Procedure writer Montgomery Ward & Co., Chgo., 1939-41; with Thombert, Inc., Newton, Ia., 1946—, pres., 1950—. Pres. Mid-Iowa council Boy Scouts Am., 1969-71; chmn. Planning Commn., Newton, Iowa, 1962-66; mem. adv. council Center for Indsl. Research and Service, Iowa State U., 1968-70. Mem. mfrs. adv. com. Iowa Coll. Found., 1969-74. Served to maj. U.S. Army, 1941-46. Recipient Silver Beaver award Boy Scouts Am., 1952, Silver Antelope award, 1971, Distinguished Eagle award, 1971. Mem. Iowa Mfrs. Assn. (vice chmn. S.E. Iowa region 1971-74), Polyurethane Mfrs. Assn. (pres. 1973-74), Newton C. of C. (pres. 1968), Newton High Sch. Alumni Assn. (pres. 1963). Presbyn. (elder 1949—). Clubs: Mason, Eastern Star, Kiwanis, Industries (pres. 1967), Newton Country. Home: 1123 S 12th Ave W Newton IA 50208 Office: 316 E 7th St N Newton IA 50208

SMITH, ROGER ORBIN, filter mfg. co. exec.; b. Moline, Ill., Aug. 14, 1935; s. Glenn Orbin and Florence Marion (Engstrom) S.; B.A., Augustana Coll., 1957; m. Norma June Nordberg, Sept. 26, 1959; children—Jana, Sharilyn. Pres. Smith Filter Corp., Moline, 1965—; v.p. Air Filtration Center Inc., Moline, Ill., 1969—, Vanda Smith Inc., Indpls., 1968—. Mem. Aircraft Owners and Pilots Assn., Quad City Airmen's Assn. (pres. 1971—, gen. chmn. Aerorama 1972), Toastmasters Club. Kiwanian (pres. Moline chpt. 1974—. Lutheran. Home: 1902 Parkway Dr Bettendorf IA 52722 Office: 1601 2d Ave Moline IL 61265

SMITH, ROLAND EMERSON, accountant; b. Kalkaska, Mich., Jan. 9, 1918; s. Ernest C. and Sybil M. (Planck) S.; student Mich. State U., 1935-36; B.A., Olivet Coll., 1939; certificate Walsh Coll., 1942; m. Lois F. Frontjes, Feb. 11, 1950; 1 son, Richard. Accountant, Coopers & Lybrand, Detroit, 1942-46, Chgo., 1946-52; partner, accountant Moore, Smith & Dale, Detroit and Southfield, Mich., 1952—. C.P.A., Mich., Ill. Mem. Am. Inst. C.P.A.'s, Mich. Assn. C.P.A.'s. Mem. Ch. of Jesus Christ of Latter day Saints. Clubs: Franklin Racquet, Torch Lake Yacht. Home: 751 Hawthorne Dr Bloomfield Hills MI 48013 Office: 24700 Northwestern Hwy 206 Southfield MI 48075

SMITH, SHELBY, lt. gov. Kansas. Office: Office of the Lt Gov State House Topeka KS 66612*

SMITH, TERRY J., lawyer; B. Detroit, Mar. 7, 1938; s. Russell Albert and Anna Marie (Chape) S.; B.A. with high honors, Mich. State U., 1960; LL.D., U. Chgo., 1965. Admitted to Mich. bar, 1965; research asso. to Chief Judge pro tem John W. Fitzgerald, Mich. Ct. Appeals, 1965-67; mem. firm Deming and Smith, Grand Ledge, Mich., 1965-72, Smith and Smith, 1973-76, Smith Bros., 1976—; dir. Am. Bank of Grand Ledge; v.p., dir. Blaney Park, Inc., 1969-76; city atty. Grand Ledge, 1977—. Mem. Eaton County Social Services Bd., 1970-76, Mich. State Boundries Commn., 1970—; bd. dirs. Grand Ledge Community Chest, 1969-75, v.p., 1970-73. Mem. Am., Eaton County (pres. 1968-69) bar assns., State Bar Mich., Grand Ledge C. of C. (dir.) 1968—, pres. 1971-72), Grand Ledge Jaycees. Club: Rotary. Home: 221 E Scott St Grand Ledge MI 48837 Office: 207 E Jefferson St Box 56 Grand Ledge MI 48837

SMITH, TRENT WHITMER, plastic surgeon; b. Columbus, Ohio, Apr. 7, 1913; s. Harvey H. and Almetta W. S.; A.B., Ohio State U., 1933, M.D., 1937; postgrad. Washington U., 1946-47; m. Eileen Marie Ebert, Sept. 29, 1939; children—T. Wynn, Muguet Smith Jones. Intern, St. Luke Hosp., Cleve., 1937-38; resident Ohio State U. Hosp., Columbus, 1947-48; practice medicine, Loveland, Ohio, 1939-40, Cin., 1940-42; practice medicine specializing in plastic surgery, 1948—; clin. prof. medicine Ohio State U., 1947—; pres. staff Children's Hosp., Columbus, 1957-58. Served to maj. USAF, 1942-46. Fellow Am. Bd. Otolaryngology, Am. Assn. Cosmetic Surgeons (pres. 1976-77), Am. Acad. Facial, Plastic and Reconstructive Surgery (pres. 1973-74), A.C.S., Am. Acad. Ophthalmology and Otolaryngology; mem. Am., Ohio med. assns., Columbus Acad. Medicine, Columbus Surg. Soc., Columbus Eng. Soc. Republican. Episcopalian. Clubs: Rocky Fork Headley Hunt, Faculty, Univ. Contbr. articles to med. jours. Home: 46 N Parkview Ave Columbus OH 43209 Office: 327 E State St Columbus OH 43215

SMITH, VIRGINIA DODD (MRS. HAVEN SMITH), congresswoman; b. Randolph, Iowa, June 30, 1911; d. Clifton Clark and Erville (Reeves) Dodd; A.B., U. Nebr., 1936; m. Haven N. Smith, Aug. 27, 1931. Nat. pres. Am. Country Life Assn., 1951-54; nat. chmn. Am. Farm Bur. Women, 1954-74; dir. Am. Farm Bur. Fedn., 1954-74, country Women's Council; world dep. pres. Asso. Country Women of World, 1962-68; mem. Dept. Agr. Nat. Home Econs. Research adv. com., 1960-65; mem. Crusade for Freedom European Inspection tour, 1958. Del. Republican Nat. Conv., 1956, 72. Mem. bd. govs. Agrl. Hall of Fame, 1959—. Mem. Nat. Livestock and Meat Bd., 1955-58, Nat. Commn. Community Health Services, 1963-66; adv. mem. Nebr. Sch. Bds. Assns., 1949; mem. Nebr. Territorial Centennial Commn., 1953; mem. Gov.'s Commn. Status of Women, 1964-66; chmn. Presdl. Task Force on Rural Devel., 1969-70; mem. 94th Congress from 3rd dist. Nebr. Vice pres. Farm Film Found., 1964-74. Apptd. admiral Nebr. Navy. Recipient Award of Merit, D.A.R., 1956; Distinguished Service awards U. Nebr., 1956, 60; award for best pub. address on freedom Freedom Found., 1966; Eyes on Nebr. award Nebr. Optometric Assn., 1970; Internat. Service award Midwest Conf. on World Affairs, 1970; Woman of Achievement award Nebr. Bus. and Profl. Women, 1971; selected as 1 of 6 U.S. women Govt. France for 3 week goodwill mission to France, 1969; Outstanding 4H Alumni award Iowa State U., 1973, 74. Mem. Am. Assn. U. Women, Delta Kappa Gamma (state hon. mem.), Beta Sigma Phi (internat. hon. mem.), Chi Omega, P.E.O. (past pres.). Methodist. Clubs: Business and Professional Women, Order of Eastern Star. Good Will ambassador to Switzerland, 1950. Home: Chappell NE 69129

SMITH, WALLACE PAUL, educator; b. Cleve., July 10, 1923; s. Paul C. and Helen (Poland) S.; B.A., Baldwin-Wallace Coll., 1948; M.A., Northwestern U., 1952. Tchr. drama Medina (Ohio) High Sch., 1948-52, Lakewood (Ohio) High Sch., 1952-57; dir. auditorium activities Evanston (Ill.) Twp. High Sch., 1957—, coordinator program for gifted, 1972—, coordinator research and curriculum devel., 1973-75; cons. HEW; v.p. Evanston Symphony Orch., 1964-68; dir. Secondary Sch. Theatre Conf., 1963-65, Ill. Demonstration Center for Gifted Arts Students; mem. Ill. Sesquicentennial Com. on Arts, 1968; mem. artists-in-sch. panel Nat. Endowment for Arts, 1974; treas. Ill. Alliance for Arts Edn., 1974-75; pres. Am. Council on Arts in Edn., 1976-77. Trustee, Am. Council on Arts in Edn., 1975. Served with AUS, 1943-45; PTO. Recipient regional award of excellence Am. Coll. Theatre Festival, 1973, nat. award excellence, 1973. Fellow Am. Ednl. Theatre Assn.; mem. Am. Theatre Assn. (v.p. 1969-70, pres. 1971), Ill. Art Edn. Assn. (Outstanding Contbn. award 1976), Phi Delta Kappa, Alpha Sigma Phi, Pi Kappa Delta, Theta Alpha Phi. Contbr. articles to profl. jours. Home: 100 E Walton Pl Apt 31F Chicago IL 60611 Office: 1600 Dodge St Evanston IL 60204

SMITH, WILLIAM JACOB, II, bank examiner; b. Huntington, W. Va., May 15, 1946; s. William Jacob and Opal (Cyrus) S.; student Ohio State U., 1964-65; B.B.A., Morehead State U., 1969; certificate Am. Inst. Banking, 1973; postgrad. Stonier Grad. Sch. Banking, Rutgers U., 1978—; m. Patricia Rose Ball, June 16, 1973; 1 dau., Stephanie Suzanne. Law enforcement officer Village of Chesapeake (Ohio), 1967-69; trainee examiner FDIC, Columbus, 1969-70, jr. asst. examiner, 1970-71, sr. asst. examiner, 1971-73, examiner, 1974—. Mem. Chesapeake Vol. Fire Dept., 1959-70. Republican. Baptist (ch. sch. supt. 1976-77). Club: Masons. Home: 5064 Tillamook Trail Lima OH 45805 Office: Suite 2600 One Nationwide Plaza Columbus OH 43215

SMITH, WILLIAM ROBERT, utility co. exec.; b. Mount Clemens, Mich., Nov. 11, 1916; s. Robert L. and Elsie (Chamberlain) S.; B.S., Detroit Inst. Tech., 1947; postgrad. Detroit Coll. Law, U. Mich. Grad. Sch. Bus. Adminstrn.; m. Ann Sheridan; children—William R., Laura Ann. Indsl. engr. Detroit Edison Co., 1934-60; mgr. econ. devel. East Ohio Gas Co., Cleve., 1960—; v.p. T.S.T. Corp. Vice pres. Cleve. Ballet; v.p. fin. Real Property Inventory Met. Cleve.; councilman City of Pepper Pike (Ohio); bd. dirs. Animal Protective League; mem. trustees' devel. council St. Luke's Hosp. Served with USAAF, 1942-45. Registered profl. engr., Mich., Ohio. Fellow Am. Indsl. Devel. Council; mem. Ohio, Cleve. chambers of commerce, Am. Gas Assn. (econ. devel. com.), Assn. Ohio Commodores, Soc. Indsl. Realtors, Cleve. Engring. Soc., Delta Theta Tau. Presbyn. Home: 27750 Fairmount Blvd Pepper Pike OH 44124 Office: 1717 E 9th Cleveland OH 44114

SMITH, WRAY CAMERON, clergyman; b. Springfield, O., Mar. 27, 1922; s. Charles Lewis and Amelia (Walter) S.; A.B., Wittenberg U., 1944; B.D., Hamma Div. Sch., 1946, postgrad., 1946-48, M.Div., 1972; D.D., Wittenberg U., 1968; m. JoAnn E. Carson, Aug. 2, 1947; children—Mark Cameron, Timothy Wray. Ordained to ministry Luth. Ch., 1946; asst. minister chs., Dayton, O., 1946-48; minister, Mansfield, O., 1948—. Lectr. Nat. Register Protestant Ams.; counsellor Sci. Marriage Found.; mem. exec. bd. Ohio Synod Luth. Ch. Am., chmn. acting dir. com. on Christian edn., dean, lectr. Luth. Summer Sch. Mem. Mansfield Recreation Bd., Mansfield Bicentennial Congress. Bd. dirs. athletic club YMCA; founder, bd. dirs. Good Shepherd Home, Ashland, O.; chmn. Sheriff's Adv. Com. Mem. Internat. Platform Assn., Am. Security Council, Luth. Pastor's Assn. (chmn. leadership devel. com., dir. radio broadcasting), Mansfield C. of C. Blue Key, Pi Delta Epsilon, Theta Chi. Clubs: Exchange (pres.), Westbrook Country. Author articles profl. jours. Author: Jesus Interprets The Ten Commandments, 1966. Home: 1020 Laurelwood Rd Mansfield OH 44907 Office: 525 Cook Rd Mansfield OH 44907

SMITHWICK, FRED, JR., hosp. adminstr.; b. Washington, June 24, 1934; s. Fred and Genevieve (Davis) S.; A.A., Montgomery Coll., 1953; B.A., George Washington U., 1955, M.A., 1974. Asst. to pres. Dwoskin, Inc., Atlanta, 1956-63; dir. mktg. Moderncote, Inc., New Castle, Ind., 1963-70; v.p. Riverside Meth. Hosp., Columbus, Ohio, 1973—; dir. Washington Wallcoverings, Inc.; lectr. health care adminstrn. Ohio State U., George Washington U.; chmn. adv. com. Sch. Licensed Practical Nurses, Columbus Pub. Schs. Mem. Royal Soc. Health (Gt. Britain), Am. Hosp. Assn., Am. Coll. Hosp. Adminstrs., Ohio Hosp. Assn. Methodist. Clubs: Touchdown (Washington), Masons; Porta Bella Yacht and Racquet (Boca Raton, Fla.). Office: 3535 Olentangy River Rd Columbus OH 43214

SMOCK, MARTHA FLORENCE (MRS. CARL FRANCIS SMOCK), mag. editor; b. Kansas City, Mo., Nov. 3, 1913; d. James Vincent and Maybelle Frances (Snell) McNamara; student Kansas City Jr. Coll.; m. Carl Francis Smock, Jan. 25, 1935; children—Stephanie (Mrs. John Thomas), Katherine (Mrs. Andrew Wales). With Unity Sch. of Christianity, Unity Village, Mo., 1933—, editor Daily Word, non-sectarian devotional mag., 1944—. Author: Meet It With Faith, 1966; Halfway Up The Mountain, 1971; Turning Points, 1976. Home: 6408 High Dr Shawnee Mission KS 66208 Office: Unity Village MO 64063

SMOLDT, CHARLES ELDON, farmer; b. Indpls., Nov. 5, 1937; s. Eldon Charles and Frances (Willoughby) S.; B.S., Iowa State U., 1959; m. Darlene Ann Willms, Dec. 7, 1958; children—Cynthia L., David C. Farm mgr. Henderson Investment Co., Cedar Rapids, Iowa, 1959-63; mortgage loan appraiser Prudential Ins. Co., Monticello, Iowa, 1963-66; engaged in farming, custom feeding, Grundy Center, Iowa, 1966—. Dir. Grundy Center Schs., 1976—; dir. Area Edn. Agency, 1975—; trustee First Baptist Ch., Grundy Center, 1971—. Mem. Agrl. Council Am., Profl. Farmers Am., Am. Farm Bureau Fedn., Alpha Zeta. Home: Route 1 Box 51 Grundy Center IA 50638

SMOLLER, SANFORD JEROME, ballet co. adminstr.; b. Pitts., Feb. 13, 1937; s. Paul and Mildred (Rosenthal) S.; B.A., U. Calif., Los Angeles, 1962; M.A. (Woodrow Wilson fellow), Columbia U., 1964; Ph.D., U. Wis., 1972; m. Merry Sue Thompson, Aug. 20, 1959; children—Jonathan, Deborah, Pamela. Instr. English, Dickinson Coll., 1964-67; lectr., asst. prof. English, U. Wis. Centers, 1968-70, film coordinator, Madison, 1970-72; tour mgr., gen. mgr. Wis. Ballet Co., Madison, 1976-78; reader Coll. Entrance Exam. Bd., 1966-69. Served with USN, 1955-57. Danforth Found. tchr. grantee, 1967. Mem. Modern Lang. Assn., Phi Beta Kappa. Author: The Arts in the Inner City: A Selection of References, 1969; Adrift Among Geniuses: Robert McAlmon, Writer and Publisher of the Twenties, 1975; editor: Pa. AAUP Newsletter, 1965-67. Home: 322 Glenway St Madison WI 53705

SMOOT, THURLOW, lawyer; b. Glendive, Mont., Dec. 30, 1910; s. Marvin A. and Ivah (Cook) S.; J.D., U. Colo., 1933. Admitted to Ohio bar, 1933; practice in Cleve., 1933-37, 47—; atty., later trial examiner NLRB, 1937-47. Served with U.S. Army, 1942-45; ETO. Mem. Am. (chmn. labor relations law sec. 1967, sect. del. to Ho. Dels. 1970-71), Cleve., Ohio, Cuyahoga County bar assns., Nat. Trial Lawyers Assn., Ohio Acad. Trial Lawyers. Home: 12700 Lake Ave Lakewood OH 44107 Office: 2141 Illuminating Bldg Cleveland OH 44113

SMUCKER, SILAS JONATHAN, agrl. cons.; b. Goshen, Ind., Dec. 31, 1904; s. Jesse E. and Anna (Yoder) S.; A.B., Goshen Coll., 1930; M.S., Purdue U., 1932; m. Esther Veronica Meck, Sept. 4, 1934; children—George, Glenn. Technical advisor U.S. Dept. Agr., Morristown, N.J., 1934-44, Rensselaer, Ind., 1945-60; tech. adviser tropical agr. U.S. Dept. State, Haiti, 1960-62, Laos, 1963-68; agrl. cons., Goshen, 1969—. Chmn. Jasper County (Ind.) chpt. A.R.C., 1957-60. Mem. Am. Fgn. Service Assn., Soil Conservation Soc. Am., Ind. Acad. Sci., Gideons Internat. Author bull. Conservation of Soil, Life, and Community Living, 1951. Address: 1304 S 14th St Goshen IN 46526

SMULL, NED WILLITS, physician, univ. ofcl.; b. St. Francis, Kans., Jan. 4, 1925; s. Charles Ward and Hollis (Harrison) S.; A.B., U. Kans., 1948, M.D., 1951; m. Lois Jane Miller, Apr. 13, 1949; 1 dau., Sarah Jane. Intern U. Kans. at Kansas City, 1951-52, resident, 1952-54; practice medicine specializing in pediatrics, Kansas City, 1954-57, 58-63; dir., prof., chmn. dept. pediatrics Children's Mercy Hosp., Kansas City, Mo., 1962—; asst. dean U. Mo.-Kansas City, 1970-74; vice provost for health scis., 1974—. Trustee Barstow Sch., Kansas City, 1964—, pres., 1969-70. Served with USAAF, 1943-46. John and Mary Markle scholar, 1957. Mem. Am. Pediatric Soc., Am. Acad. Pediatrics, Phi Gamma Delta, Nu Sigma Nu. Clubs: University, River. Home: 33 Compton Ct Shawnee Mission KS 66208 Office: 24th and Gillham Rd Kansas City MO 64108

SMUTNY, JOAN FRANKLIN (MRS. HERBERT PAUL SMUTNY), educator; b. Chgo.; d. Eugene and Mabel (Lind) Franklin; B.S. Northwestern U., M.A.; m. Herbert Paul Smutny; 1 dau., Cheryl Anne. Tchr., New Trier High Sch., Winnetka, Ill.; mem. faculty, founder, dir. Nat. High Sch. Inst., Northwestern U. Sch. Edn., Chgo., 1958-67; mem. faculty, founder dir. high sch. workshop in critical thinking and edn., chmn. dept. communications Nat. Coll. Edn., Evanston, Ill., 1967—, exec. dir. high sch. workshops, 1970—, founder, dir. Woman Power Through Edn. Seminar, 1969—, dir. Right to Read seminar in critical reading, 1973—, seminar gifted high sch. students, 1973, dir. new dimensions for women, 1973, dir. Thinking for Action in Career Edn. project, 1974—; co-dir., instr. seminars in critical thinking Ill. Family Service, 1972—. Writer ednl. filmstrips in lang. arts and lit. Soc. for Visual Edn., 1960—; mem. speakers bur. Council Fgn. Relations, 1968—; mem. adv. com. edn. professions devel. act U.S. Office Edn., 1969—; writer, cons. Radiant Ednl. Corp., 1969—; cons. A.L.A., 1969—, coordinator of career edn. Nat. Coll. Edn., 1976—; dir. Future Tchrs. Am. Seminar in Coll. and Career, 1970—; cons. for research and devel. Ill. Dept Vocat. Edn., 1973—; cons. in career edn. U.S. Office Edn., 1976—; mem. Leadership Tng. Inst. for Gifted, U.S. Office Edn., 1973—; dir. workshops for high sch. students. Mem. Soc. Arts and Letters, A.A.U.P., Mortar Bd., Pi Lambda Theta, Phi Delta Kappa (chpt. v.p.). Editor, contbr. Maturity in Teaching, 1962. Writer ednl. filmstrips The Brother's Grimm, 1960, How the West Was Won, 1960, Mutiny on the Bounty, 1960, Dr. Zhivago, 1964, Space Odessey 2001, 1969, Christmas Around the World, 1973. Home: 633 Forest Ave Wilmette IL 60091

SMUTZ, DOROTHY DRING, pianist, music educator; b. Kansas City, Mo.; d. Johnson and Emma L. (Mack) Dring; studied with Walter Goff, Sterling, Colo., Dr. Ernest R. Kroeger, St. Louis, E. Robert Schmitz, San Francisco, Paul Badura-Skoda, U. Wis.; postgrad. Kroeger Sch. Music, 1926-28; m. Harold Turk Smutz, Oct. 27, 1930 (dec. Sept. 1976); 1 son, Robert Allen. Radio, TV appearances, also concerts, recitals; soloist St. Louis Philharmonic, St. Louis Little Symphony, St. Louis Symphony orchs.; harpsichordist St. Louis Bach Soc., 1940-44; piano, clavichord, seminars and master classes for tchrs., 1946—; debut Town Hall, N.Y.C., 1949; guest artist, forum leader Okla. Music Tchrs. Assn., 1950; guest artist, workshop cons. Okla., Nebr., Kans. music tchrs. assns.; mem. faculty, adjudicator Nat. Guild Piano Tchrs.; lectr., guest artist various assns. convs.; dir. tchrs. clinic and workshop, So. Ill. U., 1963; guest artist, condr. workshop music dept. Coll. William and Mary, 1973; mem. piano faculty St. Louis Conservatory Music, 1974—; analyst J.S. Bach Seminars. Mem. Am. Piano Tchrs. Assn., Mo. (exec. bd.), Nat. (mus. theory com. 1962-64, adjudicator West Central div.) music tchrs. assns., St. Louis Piano Tchrs. Round Table, Suburban Community Concerts Assn. (exec. bd. 1951-57), Mu Phi Epsilon. Presbyterian. Home: 619 Hollywood Pl Webster Groves MO 63119

SMYD, EDWIN STANLEY, dentist; b. Chgo., Aug. 1, 1907; s. Anthony and Michaelena (Podrzycki) S.; A.A., YMCA Coll. Arts and Scis., Chgo., Ill., 1930; B.S.D., Northwestern U., then D.D.S., 1935; m. Mae Brychta, Jan. 18, 1936. Dentist primarily occupied with research in dental physiology and application of engring. scis. to refine dental clinic procedures, practice concentrated in restorative dentistry, Detroit, 1936—; spl. lectr. U. Mich. Postgrad. Sch. Dentistry, 1946. Lectr., photog. exhibitor featuring hist. and documentary data from past civilization. Fellow Am. Coll. Dentists; mem. Am. Dental Assn., Internat. Assn. for Dental Research, Fed. Dentaire, A.A.A.S., Omicron Kappa Upsilon. Contbr. articles to profl. jours., chpts. to books. Home: 607 Pemberton Rd Grosse Pointe Park MI 48230 Office: 7815 E Jefferson Ave Detroit MI 48214

SMYTH, MARY ELLEN, medical supply co. exec.; b. Lander, Wyo., July 2, 1935; d. Fred and Mary (Kosanovich) Savage; B.A. with honors, U. Wyo., 1956, M.A., 1960; m. W. Patrick Smyth, June 20, 1964; children—Timothy Murphy and Kevin Anthony (twins). Tchr. secondary schs. in Colo., 1956-59; instr. U. Wyo., 1959-60, 63-64; instr. speech Pa. State U., 1960-63; tchr. high sch. in Ill., 1964-70; bus. mgr. Orthopaedics Corp., Oak Park, Ill., 1973—. Summer theatre stock appearances, 1959-70; TV show hostess, 1962; speech cons., 1974—. Mem. Ill. Com. on Media. Vice pres. aux. MacNeal Hosp., 1973-74; program dir. aux. Oak Park Hosp., 1973-74, pres., 1976—; mem. Ill. Adv. Com. on Edn. Mem. Speech Communication Assn., Ill. Speech Assn., Chgo. Council Fgn. Relations, Common Cause, AAUW (dir. Ill. div., pres. Riverside br. 1972-74, del. nat. conv. 1973; mem. AAUW-LWV del. to China 1976), Phi Beta Kappa, Pi Beta Phi (pres. Chgo. West Suburban chpt. 1973-74), Phi Kappa Phi, Kappa Delta Pi, Theta Alpha Phi. Contbr. articles to publs. Address: 7600 Augusta St River Forest IL 60305

SNADER, JACK ROSS, edn. co. exec.; b. Athens, Ohio, Feb. 25, 1938; s. Daniel Webster and Mae Estella (Miller) S.; B.S., U. Ill., 1959; m. Sharon Genevieve Perschnick, Apr. 4, 1959; children—Susan Mae, Brian Ross. Salesman, Wm. S. Merrell div. Richardson-Merrell, Cin., 1959-61, product mgr., 1961-63, asst. tng. mgr., 1963-64, sales promotion mgr. 1964-65; nat. account mgr. Xerox Corp., N.Y.C., 1965-66, product mgr., 1966-67; dir. Profl. Communications Assos. div. Sieber & McIntyre Inc., Chgo., 1967-69; pres. Systema Corp., Chgo., 1969—. Mem. Chgo. Crime Commn., 1976—; mem. Chgo. Law Enforcement Week Com., 1976—. Mem. Nat. Soc. Performance and Instrn., Am. Soc. Tng. and Devel., Chgo. Assn. Commerce and Industry, Assn. Mgmt. Consultants, Soc. for Applied Learning Tech. Clubs: Masons, Shriners, Tower. Home: 647 Ambleside Dr Deerfield IL 60015 Office: 150 N Wacker Dr Chicago IL 60606

SNAPP, ROBERT EARL, educator; b. Greeneville, Tenn., Apr. 8, 1924; s. Robert Earl and Martha (Myers) S.; certificate music Cin. Conservatory Music, 1945; B.S., U. Cin., 1945, M.Mus. Edn., 1951; m. Margery Zumbiel, June 12, 1945; children—Jean Ann, Cheryl Lynn. Dir. instrumental music Deer Park Pub. Schs., Cin., 1945-47; music cons. Knoxville (Tenn.) Pub. Schs., 1947-48; dir. music Lebanon (O.) Pub Schs., 1948-51; dir. instrumental music Walnut Hills High Sch., Cin., 1951-55; head of artists and repertoire Chime Record Co., Cin., 1955-60; dir. music Indian Hill Pub. Schs., Cin., 1960—; leader Earl Snapp Orch., Cin., 1951-61; minister music Pleasant Ridge Presbyn. Ch., Cin., 1954—; condr. Earl Snapp Chorale, 1955-60, Earl Snapp Symphonic Band, 1959—, Cin.

Symphonette Orch., 1960—. Mem. Am. Soc. Composers, Authors and Pubs., Nat. Band Assn., N.E.A., Ohio Edn. Assn., Southwestern Ohio Tchrs. Assn. (sec. 1946), Music Educators Nat. Conf., Ohio Music Edn. Assn. (dist. pres., mem. state bd. control 1950-52, 54-55), Choral Conductors Guild Am. (charter), Am. Guild Organists, Presbyn. Assn. Musicians, Cin. Musicians Assn., Acacia, International Platform Association, also mem. Kappa Kappa Psi, Cincinnatus Soc., Phi Delta Kappa. Republican. Presbyn. Club: Kenwood Country. Home: 8150 Shawnee Run Rd Cincinnati OH 45243

SNAWDER, KENNETH DAVID, dentist; b. Valley Station, Ky., Dec. 5, 1934; s. Nelson Edward and Carrie Elizabeth (Hibbs) S.; B.S., Georgetown Coll., 1962; D.M.D., U. Ky., 1967; m. Carolyn Virginia Marshall, July 26, 1957; children—Lisa Anne, Kenneth David. Intern, James Whitcomb Riley Children's Hosp., Indpls., 1967-68, resident, 1968-69; chmn. dept. pedodontics U. Louisville, 1969-76; part-time practice dentistry specializing in pedodontics, Jeffersonville, Ind., 1969-76, full-time practice, 1976—; cons. to hosps., rehab. centers; lectr. in field. Lic. dentist, Ky., Ind., Ga., Ill., New South Wales, Australia. Diplomate Am. Bd. Pedodontics. Mem. ADA, Internat., Am., SE, Ind., Ky. socs. dentistry for children, Ky. Dental Soc., Ind. Dental Assn. Contbr. articles to profl. jours. Home: 200 N Howard St Clarksville IN 47130 Office: 207 Sparks Ave Jeffersonville IN 47130

SNEED, RUBY BLAKE, realtor; b. Chgo., July 20, 1918; d. Sanders and Lola Belle (Fitzpatrick) Ray; grad. Kennedy-King Coll., 1938; student U. Chgo., 1955-57, Drake U., 1959-60, LaSalle U., 1965-67; m. David A. Blake, Sept. 25, 1958 (dec. Jan. 1970); 1 dau., Lola Belle Sneed Campbell; m. 2d, Herbert Ray Sneed, Aug. 1972. Supr. finance and statistics dept. Dept. Pub. Welfare Cook County, Western dist. office, 1943-58; owner, operator Equal Opportunity Housing Center-S. Ray & Blake Realty Co., Harvey, Ill., 1967—; mgr. Ebenezer-Primm Towers Homes for Sr. Citizens, Evanston, Ill. Owner L&R Lettershop, Harvey, Ill., 1967-69. Mem. Harvey LWV, 1969—; housing chmn. South Suburban NAACP, 1969—; mem. Harvey Area Leadership Resource Forum, 1970—; office mgr. Women in Community Services, Springfield, Ill., 1964-66; mem. various human relations coms. Mem. real estate exam. com. Ill. Dept. Registration and Edn., 1973—. Chmn. bd. dirs. Found. for Freedom and Democracy in Community Life, Evanston, Ill., 1971—; trustee Ill. Freedom Residence Com., 1965—; bd. dirs. Ill. Human Rights Commn., 1964-66. Recipient citations Women in Community Service, 1965, Leadership Council Met. Open Communities, 1973. Mem. Evanston-North Shore, S. Suburban, Ill., Nat. Homewood-Flossmor bds. realtors, Dearborn Real Estate Bd. (legis. chmn., 1971—), Nat., Ill. (legislative rep.) assns. realtors, Equal Opportunity Brokers Assn. Mem. A.M.E. Ch. Home: 1001 Emerson St Evanston IL 60201 Office: 108 W 154th St Harvey IL 60426 also 1932 Maple Evanston IL 60201

SNEERINGER, ELDON WOERTH, assn. exec.; b. Wyandot County, Ohio, Sept. 29, 1922; s. Alfred Truman and Grayce Pearl (Hauff) S.; B.A., Ohio State U., 1945; M.Pub. Adminstrn. (Volker fellow), Wayne State U., 1949; m. Jean Marie Foster, Sept. 24, 1955; children—James Richard, Nancy Jean. Local govt. analyst Ohio C. of C., Columbus, 1947-48; sr. research asso. Citizens Research Council Mich., Detroit, Lansing, 1948-56; asst. dir. Mfrs. Assn. Flint, Mich., 1956-61; mgr. research and taxation dept. Mich. State C. of C., Lansing, 1961-66; sec., dir. research Mich. Mfrs. Assn., Lansing, 1966—. Research analyst Mich. Commn. on Legis. Apportionment, 1964-65, 71-72; cons. Congl. Redistricting in Mich., 1964; project dir. Welfare Adminstrn., Mich. Little Hoover Commn., 1950-51. Mem. Mich. Gov.'s Task Force on Single Bus. Tax, 1976-77; vice chmn. edn. and research Ingham County Republican Com., 1966-70, 72-74; trustee Ingham Med. Hosp., 1973—, vice chmn., 1977. Recipient Pub. Service award Mich. Dept. Edn., 1974. Mem. Orgn. Execs. Mich. (past pres., dir. 1975-76), Phi Beta Kappa, Pi Sigma Alpha. Republican. Lutheran. Club: City (Lansing). Author: (with Charles W. Sholl) Reapportionment of the Michigan Legislature, 1952. Home: 4458 Arbor Dr Okemos MI 48864 Office: Stoddard Bldg Lansing MI 48933

SNELL, BRUCE MOREY, JR., state judge; b. Ida Grove, Iowa, Aug. 18, 1929; s. Bruce Morey and Donna Marie (Potter) S.; A.B., Grinnell Coll., 1951; J.D., State U. Iowa, 1956; m. Anne Fischer, Feb. 4, 1956; children—Rebecca Jane, Bradley Steven. Admitted to Iowa bar, 1956, N.Y. bar, 1959; judge Iowa Ct. Appeals. Mem. Am., Iowa, N.Y. bar assns., Am. Judicature Soc., Order of Coif, Phi Delta Phi. Republican. Methodist. Clubs: Mason (Shriner), Kiwanian. Home: 310 Burns St Ida Grove IA 51445 Office: 209 Taylor St Ida Grove IA 51445

SNELL, JOEL CHARLES, educator; b. Omaha, July 15, 1943; s. Charles Norris and Doris Maudlin (Wallin) S.; B.A., U. Omaha, 1966; M.A., U. Nebr., 1970; postgrad. S.D. State U., 1971-74; m. Jennifer Sue Horrum, June 7, 1968; children—Nathan Mikael-Edward, Jason Joel. Research asst. Nebr. Psychiat. Inst., Omaha, 1965; interviewer Nebr. Dept. Roads, Omaha, 1966, Transcentury Corp., Omaha, 1967; research asst. U. Nebr., Omaha, 1967, teaching asst., 1966-68; counselor, dept. labor Nebr. Employment Service, Omaha, 1968-69; asst. prof. dept. sociology Dana Coll., Blair, Nebr., 1969—; environ. cons. U.S. C.E., 1974-75; research cons. Dept. Criminal Justice, 1975; partner Dell Research, Blair, 1973—. Am. Luth. Ch. fellow, 1974-75. Mem. Am. Sociol. Assn. Unitarian-Universalist. Author: (with William O. Wakefield) Everyday Sociology, 1970, numerous others including (with Vincent Webb) Criminal Justice Manpower in LEAA Region VII, Current States and Future Prospects; (with Donald Kisicki) Alternative Futures; (with R. Gary Dean) The Dana Report: Socio-Economic Forcast to 2020; editorial bd. Instructional Psychology, 1974-75, Edn., 1975—; contbr. to publs. in field. Home: Cottonwood Marina Rural Route 1 Blair NE 68008

SNELL, WALTER WILBERT, farmer; b. St. John, Kans., Oct. 26, 1922; s. Walter Monroe and Bertha (Adcock) S.; student Spartan Sch. Aeros., 1946; m. Andora Lucile Strickland, June 26, 1944; children—Sharrie Ann Wartell, Susan Denice (Mrs. Donald Duane Harden). Aircraft, engine mechanic Aviation Service, Wichita, Kans., 1946-47, Janesville, Wis., 1947-48; with Boeing Corp., Wichita, 1948; farmer, nr. Garden City, Kans., 1948—. Bd. dirs. Com. on Daming Ark. River. Served with USAAF, 1943-45. Recipient Conservation Service citation Nat. Wildlife Fedn., 1971. Mem. Kans. Wildlife Fedn. (Pres.'s award for outstanding service 1969, pres. 1972-77). Clubs: Sand and Sage Rifle and Pistol; Finney County Parks Fish and Game. Address: 626 E Mary St Garden City KS 67846

SNIDER, DONALD GENE, nursing home ofcl.; b. Detroit, Apr. 4, 1952; s. Virgil and Velma (Farris) Smith; A.A. in Accounting, Highland Park Coll., 1972; B.S., Wayne State U., 1975; m. Sandra Elaine Dazier, Feb. 15, 1975; 1 dau., Jasmine Renee. Personnel dir. Wilshire Inc., 1971-75; ins. cons. Equitable Life Assurance Co., U.S., 1976; now adminstr. nursing home. Mem. office hunger and malnutrition, Detroit. Mem. Alpha Phi Alpha (pres. 1975—). Mason. Home: 23020 Webster St Oak Park MI 48236

SNIDER, ROBERT WAYNE, educator; b. Roaring Spring, Pa., Dec. 16, 1928; s. Claude Kagarise and Sara Elizabeth (Gingrich) S.; B.A., Bryan Coll., 1950; M.Div., Grace Theol. Sem., 1953, Th.M., 1955; M.A., Ind. U., 1961; m. Hyla Mae, Aug. 15, 1959; children—Lisa Michelle, Jacqueline Lea, Jennifer Lynn. Ordained to ministry Nat. Fellowship of Grace Brethren Chs., 1957; instr. history Grace Coll., Winona Lake, Ind., 1954-55, asst. prof., 1955-57, asso. prof., 1957-61, prof., head dept., 1961—, dean of men, 1954-59. Precinct committeeman Republican Party, 1968—; del. state Rep. conv., 1970, 72, 74, 76, 78. Recipient awards Optimist of Year, 1964-65, 69-70, Tchr. of Excellence Alva J. McClain, 1968. Mem. Am., Ind. hist. assns., Kascinsko County Hist. Soc., Ind. Acad. Social Scis., Nat. Trust Hist. Preservation, Conf. on Faith and History. Club: Warsaw Optimist. Office: Grace Coll Winona Lake IN 46590

SNIPES, ALFRED HAYWOOD, architect; b. Cameron, N.C., Jan. 17, 1909; s. Alfred Marshall and Bessie Inez (McLaurin) S.; student Richmond (Va.) Bus. Coll., 1931-32, Duke, 1928-29, N.C. State Coll., 1929-30; B.Arch., Cath. U. Am., 1942; m. Annie Laurie Trevvett, Nov. 25, 1936; children—Laure Anne (Mrs. Charles N. McKinnon Jr.), Alfred Haywood. Various positions in constrn., 1926-30; with U.S. Govt., 1930-45; with various archtl. firms, Va., N.Mex., Mo., 1945-50; individual archtl. practice, Poplar Bluff, Mo., 1951—. Mem. constrn. and design adv. council Three Rivers Jr. Coll., Poplar Bluff, 1967—. Active various community drives; mem. Health Coordinating Council Mo., 1977—; bd. govs., bd. dirs. Eye Research Found. Mo., 1972-75; bd. dirs., v.p. Mo. Easter Seal Soc. for Crippled Children and Adults. Recipient numerous awards including Distinguished Service and Appreciation award Lions Internat., 1965. Mem. AIA, Mo. Assn. Registered Architects. Baptist. Lion (chmn. state sight conservation com. 1965-75, chmn. eye tissue bank and clinic 1965-75). Prin. works include schs., chs., hosps., bank bldgs. Home and office: Westwood Hills Country Club Rd Route 7 Box 426 Poplar Bluff MO 63901

SNOOK, ORRIE MCVEY, dentist; b. Independence, Kans., Jan. 17, 1929; s. Orrie Vernon and Emma (McVey) S.; A.A., U. Kans., B.A., 1953; D.D.S., U. Mo., 1957; m. Marcia Clare Speer, June 10, 1956; children—Karen Elizabeth, David Michael, Jennifer Lynn, Amy Diane. Pvt. practice dentistry, Mission, Kan., 1957-61, Kirksville, Mo., 1961—. Served with AUS, 1946-47. Mem. N.E. Dist. Dental Soc. (pres. 1969), Mo., Am. dental assns., Pi Kappa Alpha. Republican. Methodist. Mason, Shriner, Kiwanian. Club: Kirksville Country. Home: Rural Route 4 Kirksville MO 63501 Office: 302 N High St Kirksville MO 63501

SNORTLAND, HOWARD J., supt. pub. instruction State of N.D. Office: State Capitol Bismarck ND 58505*

SNOWDEN, HERBERT NORRIS, JR., ins. co. exec.; b. Trenton, N.J., June 28, 1923; s. Herbert Norris and Evelyn Keeler (Tomlinson) S.; A.B., Ohio State U., 1947; postgrad. Columbia, 1948-49; m. Gladys Keller, Aug. 24, 1946; 1 son, Herbert Norris III. Instr. history Ohio State U., Columbus, 1949; claim mgr., actuary Nationwide Ins. Co., Columbus, 1950-57; founder, pres. Educator & Exec. Ins. Cos., Columbus, 1957-75; pres. Am. Realty Title Assurance, 1975—; pres., dir. E&E Fund; dir. Nat. Mortgage Co. Bd. dirs. Ohio Ins. Fedn.; bd. dirs., treas. Ohio Ins. Inc.; dir. RFI Realty Trust; trustee Riverside Meth. Hosp., Griffith Found. of Ohio State U., Meth. Theol. Sem. Served with USNR, 1943-46; PTO. Mem. AAAS, Am. Acad. Polit. Sci., NEA, Am. Mgmt. Assn., Am. Forestry Assn., Nat. Assn. Ind. Insurers, Am. Assn. Sch. Adminstrs., Ohio Edn. Assn., S.A.R. Home: 1990 Chatfield Rd Columbus OH 43221 Office: 4400 N High St Columbus OH 43214

SNYDER, BERNARD SHAW, oral surgeon; b. Sarahsville, Ohio, Sept. 8, 1927; s. Marsh Allen and Mary Elizabeth (Shaw) S.; D.D.S., Ohio State U., 1951, M.S., 1956; m. Barbara Jane Hoppes, July 2, 1949; children—Douglas Alan, Pamela Jane. Intern dentistry Nat. Naval Med. Center, Bethesda, Md., 1951-52, U.S. Naval Hosp., Great Lakes, Ill., 1952; resident oral surgery Ohio State U. Hosps., Columbus, 1954-56; pvt. practice oral surgery, Columbus, Ohio, 1956—; asso. prof. oral surgery Ohio State U. Coll. Dentistry, Columbus, 1956—; mem. staff Univ., Grant, Children's, Doctor's, Riverside, St. Anthony hosps. (all Columbus). Mem. supervisory bd. Paul C. Hayes Tech. Sch., Grove City, Ohio, 1967—. Served with AUS, 1945-47, with USNR, 1951-54. Diplomate Am. Bd. Oral Surgery. Fellow Am., Internat. colls. dentists; mem. Ohio Dental Assn. (past pres.), Omicron Kappa Upsilon, Psi Omega. Republican. Methodist. Clubs: Rotary, Faculty, Pres.'s (Ohio State U.); Scioto Country (Columbus). Home: 3400 Stonehenge Ct Columbus OH 43221 Office: 141 S 6th St Columbus OH 43215

SNYDER, BROCK ROBERT, lawyer; b. Topeka, Kans., Sept. 18, 1935; s. Ralph Ernest and Helen Dorothy (Fritze) S.; B.S., U. Kans., 1957; J.D., Washburn U., 1964; m. Carol Lee Cunningham, June 5, 1957; children—Lori, Holli, Staci. Admitted to Kans. bar, 1964; since practiced in Topeka; partner firm Edison, Lewis, Porter Haynes, Topeka. Lectr. Kans. Bar Rev. Bd. dirs. Campfire Girls, Topeka Legal Aid Soc., Kans. Legal Services. Served with USMC, 1957-61. Mem. Am., Topeka (chmn. pub. relations com.) bar assns., Bar Assn. State of Kans., Phi Alpha Delta. Clubs: Counselors, Topeka. Home: 729 High St Topeka KS 66606 Office: 1300 Merchants National Bank Topeka KS 66612

SNYDER, CHARLES RICHARD, clin. psychologist, educator; b. Omaha, Dec. 26, 1944; s. Charles Fritz and Shirley Mae (Schuldt) S.; B.A. in Psychology, So. Meth. U., 1967; M.A. in Clin. Psychology (NDEA fellow), Vanderbilt U., 1968, Ph.D. in Clin. Psychology (NDEA fellow 1968-69, NIMH fellow 1970), 1971; m. Rebecca Lee Wright, Dec. 14, 1975; children—Staci, Shannon. Asst. supr. clin. practicum Vanderbilt U., 1970, colloquium dir., 1971; lectr. in psychology Belmont Coll., summer 1971; asst. prof. psychology U. Kans., 1972-76, asso. prof., dir. clin. psychology program, 1976—; fellow in med. psychology Langley Porter Neuropsychiat. Inst., 1972. Mem. Am., Midwestern, Southeastern, Western psychol. assns., Sigma Xi, Psi Chi. Author: Comparisons, 1974; (with H. L. Fromkin) The Psychology of Uniqueness, 1978; contbr. articles to profl. publs.; cons. editor Jour. Cons., Clin. Psychology, Jour. Counseling Psychology, Personality and Social Psychology Bull., 1976—. Office: Psychology Dept Fraser Hall U Kans Lawrence KS 60045

SNYDER, CONWAY ALLEN, elec. co. exec.; b. Ortonville, Minn., July 28, 1933; s. Allen Joseph and Ethel Josephine (Voltz) S.; student Macalester Coll., 1951-52, Humboldt Inst., 1955-57; m. JoAnn Ladd, Oct. 3, 1953; children—Allen J., Claudia A., Jeffrey S., Debra J. With Onan Corp., Mpls., 1952—, gen. traffic mgr., 1965-72, dir. purchases, 1973—. Mem. staff Onan Assessment and Devel. Center, 1973—; mem. Eagle bd. rev. Indianhead council Boy Scouts Am., 1973—. Served with AUS, 1953-55. Mem. Nat. Assn. Purchasing Mgmt. Methodist (chmn. fin. 1970-72). Clubs: Masons, Shriners, Order Eastern Star. Home: 878 Edgewater Ave W Saint Paul MN 55112 Office: 1400 73d Ave NE Minneapolis MN 55432

SNYDER, DAVID WILLIAM WILSON, hosp. adminstr.; b. Muncy, Pa., Sept. 30, 1924; s. Brady Raymond and Mae Agnes (Scott) S.; M.B.A., Strayer Coll. Accountancy, Washington, 1952; m. Mary Etta Derrick, Apr. 19, 1949 (div.); children—Jay, David William Wilson, Cindy, Sonya. Accountant, Eastern Airlines, Washington, 1949-52; accountant, asst. adminstr., adminstr. Muncy Valley Hosp., 1952-63; asst. adminstr. Soldiers and Sailors Meml. Hosp., Wellsboro, Pa., 1964-66; adminstr. Lodi (Ohio) Community Hosp., 1966-77, Wellington (Ohio) Community Hosp., 1978—. Bd. dirs. Northeastern Pa. Heart Assn., 1965-66. Served with AUS, 1943-46. Mem. Am. Coll. Hosp. Adminstrs., Am. Hosp. Assn. Rotarian. Home: 212 Bank St Lodi OH 44254 Office: Wellington Community Hosp Dickson St Wellington OH 44090

SNYDER, DONALD RICHARD, biologist; b. Ravenwood, Mo., Jan. 12, 1943; s. William Harold and Mary Mildred (Trullinger) S.; B.S. in Secondary Edn., N.W. Mo. State U., 1965; M.S., Syracuse U., 1970; m. Peggy Diann Lillard, May 24, 1975; Tchr. biology W. Nodaway High Sch., Burlington Junction, Mo., 1965-66, Richmond (Mo.) High Sch., 1966-72, Kirkwood (Mo.) High Sch., 1972-73; asst. prof. biology Lewis & Clark Community Coll., Godfrey, Ill., 1973-77, asso. prof., 1977—. Recipient Conservation Edn. award Boy Scouts Am., 1972. Mem. AAAS, Biology Assn. Tchrs. St. Louis (sec. 1973-74), Am. Inst. Biol. Scis., Nat. Wildlife Fedn., Nat. Assn. Biology Tchrs., AAUP, Ill. Assn. Community Coll. Biologists (regional dir. 1975-76, sec.-treas. 1976-77, pres. 1977-78), Phi Sigma Epsilon. Methodist. Home: 705 Stamper Ln Godfrey IL 62035

SNYDER, HERBERT HOWARD, mathematician, educator; b. Ravenswood, W.Va., Feb. 26, 1927; s. Harvey Lester and Wilma Clare (Howard) S.; A.B., Marietta Coll., 1949; M.A., Lehigh U., 1951, Ph.D., 1965; Ph.D., U. S. Africa, 1971; m. Rebbeca Knight Bush, June 16, 1966; 1 dau., Jennifer. Devel. engr. ITT Labs., Nutley, N.J., 1953-63; mem. math. faculty N.J. Inst. Tech., 1963-64, Lehigh U., 1964-65, Drexel U., 1965-66; mem. math. faculty So. Ill. U., Carbondale, 1966—, prof., 1972—. Trustee Ind. Technol. U. Served with Q.M.C., U.S. Army, 1945-46. Fellow Washington Acad. Scis.; mem. Am. Math. Soc., Ill. (chmn. sect. applied math. and mechanics), Ind., Iowa acads. sci. Republican. Presbyterian. Editor: Handbuch der Elektrotechnik, 2d edit., 1972—; editorial bd. Ill. Acad. Sci. Transactions, 1969-71; contbr. articles to profl. jours. Patentee in field. Home: RFD A-1 Box 7 Cobden IL 62920 Office: So Ill U-Carbondale Math Dept Carbondale IL 62901

SNYDER, HOWARD ERROL, surgeon; b. Winfield, Kans., Mar. 15, 1903; s. Howard Lincoln and Glenoril Elizabeth (Dawson) S.; student U. Kans., 1921-23; A.B., Southwestern Coll., 1926; M.D., Jefferson Med. Coll., 1927; m. Mary Viola Essex, Feb. 25, 1962; children—Howard Martin, Edward Jarvis. Intern, Pa. Hosp., Phila., 1927-29, Harriet Lane-Johns Hopkins Hosp., Balt., 1929; apprentice to Dr. H.L. Snyder, 1929-40; practice medicine specializing in surgery, Winfield, 1929-42, 45—. Mem. bd. edn. Winfield Pub. Schs., 1939-41; chmn. com. control cancer Kans. Med. Soc., 1939-42, 46-50; pres. Kans. div. Am. Cancer Soc., 1949-50, dir., 1952-58; commr. Joint Commn. Accreditation Hosps., 1958-66. Served with M.C., U.S. Army, 1942-45. Diplomate Am. Bd. Surgery, Am. Bd. Thoracic Surgery. Mem. Kans. Med. Soc., AMA, Western (treas. 1953-56), Central (council 1954-56) surg. assns., Am. Assn. Surgery Trauma, Am. Assn. Thoracic Surgery, Soc. U.S. Med. Cons. World War II, Excelsior, Kansas City surg. socs., A.C.S., S.W. Surg. Congress (v.p. 1952), 2d Aux. Surg. Group, Am. Legion, VFW. Republican. Methodist. Club: Elks. Contbr. articles to profl. jours. Home: Rt 5 Winfield KS 67156 Office: 1317 Wheat Rd Winfield KS 67156

SNYDER, JEAN MACLEAN (MRS. JOEL MARTIN SNYDER), writer; b. Chgo., Jan. 26, 1942; d. Norman Fitzroy and Jessie (Burns) Maclean; B.A., U. Chgo., 1963; m. Joel Martin Snyder, Sept. 4, 1964; children—Jacob Samuel, Noah Scot. Research asso. in charge exhibits and publs. programs of com. on cutaneous health and cosmetics AMA, Chgo., 1963-68; home safety specialist Dept. Pub. Info. Nat. Safety Council, Chgo., 1968-70; dir. pub. relations Planned Parenthood Assn., Chgo., 1970; free lance writer, 1970—. Club: Esoteric Women's (pres. 1961-62). Contbr. articles to nat. mags. Home: 5627 S Dorchester Ave Chicago IL 60637

SNYDER, JOSEPH QUINCY, chemist; b. Joplin, Mo., Aug. 7, 1920; s. Joseph Lyman and Mary Elizabeth (Church) S.; B.S., U. Okla., 1942, M.S., 1951, Ph.D., 1954; m. Bona Bell Osborne, Jan. 28, 1942; children—Helen Hoyt Harter, Joseph Quincy, John R., David R. Instr., U. Okla., Norman, 1946-48, spl. instr., 1951-55; research chemist, asst. dir. research S.R. Noble Found., Ardmore, Okla., 1948-51; dir. mfg. and research Dan Cu Chem Co., Oklahoma City, 1955; research specialist Monsanto Co., St. Louis, 1956—. Active Boy Scouts Am., Boys' Club, Jr. Achievement, El Dorado, Ark., St. Louis, 1956-63; founding mem., first pres. St. Charles (Mo.) County Men's Republican Club, 1968. Served to lt., AUS, 1942-45. Decorated Bronze Star. Merck fellow, 1952-53; Kerr-McGee scholar, 1946-47; Mem. Am. Chem. Soc., Am. Inst. Chem. Engrs., AAAS, Alpha Chi Sigma, Sigma Xi, Phi Lambda Upsilon. Home: 1151 Tompkins St St Charles MO 63301 Office: 800 N Lindbergh St St Louis MO 63166

SNYDER, MARY ALICE DEXHEIMER (MRS. GUY MAXWELL SNYDER), photo processing co. exec.; b. Sedalia, Mo., Mar. 22, 1921; d. Harry Melvin and Hazel Inez (Gorrell) Dexheimer; bus. adminstrn. Central Bus. Coll., Sedalia, 1939-41; m. Guy Maxwell Snyder, Dec. 31, 1952; children—Giana Marie, Aric Nelson. Sec., office mgr. Inter-State Studio (named changed to Inter-State Processing Co., Inc. 1951), Sedalia, 1941-43, plant mgr., 1943-52, personnel mgr., exec. v.p., 1952—, exec. v.p., personnel mgr. several sales subsidiaries, 1967—. Pres. Horace Mann Elementary PTA, Sedalia, 1965-66, Smith-Cotton High Sch. PTA, Sedalia, 1972-73; an organizer Parent-Tchr.-Student Assn., Smith-Cotton High Sch., 1972; pres. Sedalia City PTA Council, 1969-72; rep. to Mo. PTA Convs., 1963-71. Mem. Am. Bus. Women, Christian Bus. and Profl. Women's Club. Baptist (sec. Sunday sch. 1964—). Home: Route 2 Sedalia MO 65301 Office: 601 W 16th St Sedalia MO 65301

SNYDER, MERLE LAVERNE, elec. engr.; b. Anthony, Kans., Mar. 21, 1917; s. Don Richard and Florence (Ford) S.; student Kans. State Tchrs. Coll., 1946-47, Kans. State Engring. Coll., 1947-49; m. Paula Mae McDaniel, Nov. 23, 1941; children—Jeanne Ann (Mrs. Johnnie W. Breckenridge), Kent Edward. Gen. engr., scientist U.S. Bur. Mines, Amarillo, Tex., 1953-56; elec. engr. Litwin Engring. Refinery & Petrochem. Design Co., Wichita, Kans., 1956-60; elec. engr. USAF, McConnell AFB, Wichita, 1960-69; indsl. engr. Def. Contracts Adminstrn., 1969—; pres., chmn. bd. 5B Plastics, Inc.; pres. Plastics Machinery Research, Inc.; process cons. Wichita Plastics, Inc. Bd. examiners CSC, 1964-68. Served with USNR, 1942-45. Registered profl. engr., Kans. Mem. Am. Inst. Plant Engrs. Mason. Home: 100 E Lincoln St Derby KS 67037 Office: Mid Continent Airport Wichita KS 67209

SNYDER, MICHAEL DENNIS, EDP adminstr., clergyman; b. Iowa City, Iowa, Nov. 9, 1942; s. Dennis George O'Brien and Catherine Irene (Brown) S.; B.S. magna cum laude, Mankato State U., 1970; m. Rose Marie Kasper, May 17, 1969; 1 son, Patrick Michael. Accounting clk. Peavey Co., Omaha, 1965-66, programmer, Mpls., 1966-67; tech. cons. data processing Jostens, Owatonna, Minn., 1967-71, systems mgr. corp. finance, 1971-76, group systems mgr., 1977—; ordained deacon Episcopal Ch., 1976; clergyman, several mission congregations, 1976—. Served with USAF, 1961-65. Mem. Minn. Honeywell Users Group (pres. 1974-75, dir. 1973-76). Republican. Episcopalian. Home: 506 16th St SE Owatonna MN 55060 Office: 148 E Broadway Owatonna MN 55060

SNYDER, RALPH HOWARD, automotive repair co. exec.; b. Manly, Iowa, July 16, 1923; s. Ralph Harnden and Gertrude Francis (Wendt) S.; student Iowa State U., 1941-43, 46; Brigham Young U., 1943-44; m. Opal Dorothy Peterson, Jan. 19, 1947; children—Donald Carleton, Douglas Eugene, Steven Leroy (dec.). Shop foreman Olds-Cadillac Agy., Estherville, Iowa, 1946-50; exptl. engr. Boeing Aircraft Co., Wichita, Kans., 1950-53; founder Snyder's Garage, Wichita, 1953—. Cons. with instrs. of local auto vocational classes in various high schs. Active Boy Scouts Am., 1959-68. Chmn. Democratic precinct com., 1969-71. Served with USAAF, 1943-46. Mem. Automotive Council. Presbyn. (trustee 1971—). Clubs: Masons, Shriners, Lions. Club: Bella Vista (Ark.) Country. Home: 1933 S Ridgewood St Wichita KS 67218 Office: 3419 E Harry St Wichita KS 67218

SNYDER, ROBERT DONALD, supt. schs.; b. St. Louis, Apr. 16, 1921; s. Eugene Theodore and Pearle V. (West) S.; A.B., Harris Tchrs. Coll., 1942; M.A., Washington U., 1946; Ed.D. (fellow in edn. 1952-53), Harvard, 1955; m. Betty Lou Thompson, Aug. 21, 1944; children—Susan Dee, Sally Jean. Tchr. math. Hanley Jr. High Sch., University City, Mo., 1945-46; supervising prin. Normandy Schs., St. Louis County, 1946-50; supt. Mason Ridge Sch. Dist., St. Louis County, 1950-54; supt. Parkway Sch. Dist., 1954-59; supt. Wayzata, Minn. Pub. Schs., 1959—; mem. bd. for certification adminstrs. Minn. Dept. Edn.; dir. Mark Twain Summer Inst., 1959; lectr. St. Louis U., 1947—, Washington U., 1948, 49, 54; grad. lectr. Mankato State Coll., U. Minn. Chmn. St. Louis Human Rights Inst., 1955-56, St. Louis Council on Human Relations, 1952, 55—; dir. St. Louis White House Conf. on Edn.; pres. Glendale Civic Assn., 1958; chmn. Greater Mpls. Sch. Study Council, 1961-62; dir. Twin City Ednl. Research Devel. Council, Nat. Sch. Facilities Council, pres. Minn. Sch. Facilities Council, 1973—; chmn. Gov.'s Adv. Council on Reading, 1973—; ex-officio mem. Wayzata Bd. Edn.; dir. Minn. Continuing Edn. Com., 1977-79; mem. Minn. Profl. Standards Com.; team chairperson Nat. Council Accreditation of Tchr. Edn. Dir. Horace Mann Ins. Co. Democratic nominee to U.S. Congress, 1948, 50. Served in pilot tng. AUS, 1942-43. Named Hon. Ky. Col., 1950; recipient Jr. C. of C. distinguished service award St. Louis County, 1955. Mem. N.E.A. (life), Am. Assn. Sch. Adminstrators (mem. nat. resolutions com., v.p. nat. planning com. 1978-79), St. Louis Suburban Tchrs. Assn. (pres. 1957-58), Mo. State Tchrs. Assn., Minn. Edn. Assn., Minn. Congress Parents and Teachers (chmn. coll. cooperation, mem. state bd. mgrs., mem. resolutions com.), Minn. Assn. Sch. Adminstrs. (dir. 1978-80), Minn. P.T.A. (state bd. mgrs. 1973—, dir. Right to Read project 1973—), Am. Legion (state trustee), Minn. Lake Conf. Assn. (pres.), Phi Delta Kappa, Sigma Tau Gamma. Presbyn. Clubs: Masons, Shriners, Rotary (dir.), Harvard. Contbr. numerous articles to profl. jours. Home: 1700 Holdridge Circle Wayzata MN 55391 Office: Wayzata Pub Schs Wayzata MN 55391

SNYDER, ROBERT EMILE JAMES, univ. dean; b. Hillsboro, Ill., July 29, 1922; s. Alden Eugene and Florence G. (Baxter) S.; B.A., U. Ill., 1944; M.A., U. Iowa, 1947, Ph.D., 1964; children—Lawrence, Alden. Sales mgr. radio sta. KOKX, Iowa, 1947; owner, mgr. radio sta. KXIC, Iowa, 1947-51; owner, mgr. radio sta. WKID, Ill., 1951-54; sales mgr. KCRG-TV, 1954-55; instr. mktg. U. Iowa, 1958-64, asst. prof., 1964-65; asso. prof. Roosevelt U., Chgo., 1965-67, acting chmn. market dept., 1968, asso. dean Coll. Bus. Adminstrn., 1968—; real estate broker, 1955-69; owner Bob Snyder Agy., 1955-69. Cons. U.S. Steel, Gary Tube Works, 1968, Am. Tel. & Tel., 1967-69, Foote, Cone & Belding, Chgo., 1967-77, Branham Co., 1968, Yoder Feeds, Frytown, Ia., Bendix Corp., Davenport, Iowa, 1967, WTVG, Joliet, 1970, Farm Credit Banks, 1971; textbook cons. Allyn & Bacon, 1965-66, Prentice Hall, 1966; sales cons. Canteen Corp., Chgo., 1968-69, Cal. Chem., Ft. Madison, Iowa, 1966. Chmn. March of Dimes, Champaign County, Ill., 1954; active Boy Scouts Am., Cub Scouts Am., 1954—. Served with AUS, 1942-46; PTO. Named Top Prof., Roosevelt U., 1968-69; recipient Silver Beaver award Boy Scouts Am., 1964. Mem. Am. Market Assn., Audit Bur. Chgo., Am. Acad. Advt., Broadcast Advt. Club, Bus. Profs. Advisory Assn. Order of Arrow, Alpha Delta Sigma, Sigma Delta Chi, Alpha Kappa Psi. Rotarian. Home: 400 E Randolph Chicago IL 60601 Office: 430 S Michigan Ave Chicago IL 60605

SNYDERS, JEANETTE AGNES, editor; b. Chgo., Mar. 1, 1928; d. Andrew Joseph and Martha Marie Ri (Ruitenberg) S.; B.S., Coll. St. Francis, 1976. Data processing mgr. 7-Up Bottlers, Chgo., 1953-66; systems analyst Alberto Culver Co., Melrose Park, Ill., 1966-67; editor Hitchcock Pub. Co., Wheaton, Ill., 1967-74; project editor Auerbach Pubs., Inc., Pennsauken, N.J., 1977—; pres. System Cons. Entrepreneurs. Mem. Assn. Systems Mgmt. (Distinguished Service award 1976, pres., chmn. div. council), Ill. Women's Press Assn. (writing awards), Bus. and Profl. Women's Club Lockport. Republican. Roman Catholic. Club: Altrusa (pres.) (Joliet, Ill.). Home: PO Box 237 Lockport IL 60441

SOBEL, BURTON ELIAS, educator, physician; b. N.Y.C., Oct. 21, 1937; s. Lawrence J. and Ruth (Schoen) S.; A.B., Cornell U., 1958; M.D. magna cum laude, Harvard U., 1962; m. Susan Konheim, June 19, 1958; children—Jonathan, Elizabeth. Intern Peter Bent Brigham Hosp., Boston, 1962-63, resident, 1964-66; clin. asso., cardiology br. NIH, Bethesda Md., 1968-71; asst. prof. med., U. Cal. at San Diego, La Jolla, 1971-72, asso. prof. med., also dir. Myocardial Infarction Research Unit, also dir. Coronary Care, 1972-73; asso. prof. medicine Washington U.-Barnes Hosp., St. Louis, 1973-75, prof., 1975—, dir. cardiovascular div., 1973—, program dir. Specialized Center Research in Ischemic Heart Disease, 1975—, Principles in Cardiovascular Research, 1975—. Cons. U.S. Naval Hosp., San Diego, 1971-73, Geomet Inc., Los Angeles, 1972-73. Served to lt. comdr. USPHS, 1964-68. Recipient Research Career and Devel. award, USPHS, 1972. Fellow A.C.P.; mem. Am. Heart Assn. (pub. com., 1970-73, clin. and basic sci. councils, 1971-73), Am. Coll. Cardiology (pub. com., 1972-73), Assn. Univ. Cardiologists, Am. Soc. Clin. Investigation, Assn. Am. Physicians, Am. Physiol. Soc., Cardiac Muscle Soc., Western Soc. for Clin. Research, Soc. for Exptl. Biology and Medicine, Am. Fedn. for Clin. Research, Alpha Omega Alpha. Asso. med. editor The Heart Bull., 1971-72; editor Clin. Cardiology, 1971-74, mem. circulation bd., 1971—; editorial bd. Am. Jour. Cardiology, 1976—; editorial bd., asso. editor Jour. Clin. Investigation, 1977—; editorial bd. Circulation Research, 1974—, Annals of Internal Medicine, 1976—. Home: 444 Baker Ave Webster Groves MO 63119 Office: Barnes Hosp 660 S Euclid Av St Louis MO 63110

SOBEL, WALTER HOWARD, architect, engr.; b. Chgo., July 25, 1913; s. Karl B. and Blanche K. (Klein) S.; student (Bentley scholar) Northwestern U., 1930-31; B.S. in Arch. (AIA medalist), Ill. Inst. Tech., 1935; m. Betty Debs, Oct. 2, 1943; children—Susan Sobel Kaufman, Richard, Steven, Nancy, Robert. Partner, Walter H. Sobel-J. Stewart Stein, 1945-60; prin. firm Walter H. Sobel and Assos., Chgo., 1960—; archtl. cons. on courthouses throughout U.S.A.; instr. archtl. registration refresher course; works include courthouses, religious bldgs., schs., and businesses. Vice pres. Wilmette (Ill.) Family Service Center, 1962-64, pres., 1965; mem. Wilmette Planning Commn.; v.p. Wilmette United Fund, 1965-66; mem. Wilmette Council Comml. Renewal; mem. exec. mansion com. State of Ill., 1966—; bd. dirs. Abraham Lincoln Centre, 1968—, Hull House Assn., 1968—. Served to lt. (s.g.), USNR, 1942-45; PTO. Decorated Purple Heart. Registered profl. engr., Ill.; registered architect Del., Ill., Ind., Miss., Md., Mo., Mich., N.Y., Ohio, Pa., S.C., Va., Wis. Fellow AIA (pres. Chgo. chpt., medal 1965); mem. Nat. Trust Hist. Preservation, Landmarks Preservation Council Chgo., Am. Judicature Soc., Ill. Architects-Engrs. Council (past chmn.), World Futures Soc., Ill. Assn. Professions (pres. 1970). Editor: (with others) The American Courthouse: Planning and Design for the Judicial Process, 1973. Contbr. articles on courthouse design and planning to law and archtl. jours. Home: 507 Lake Ave Wilmette IL 60091 Office: 2 N Riverside Plaza Chicago IL 60606

SOBY, BIRGER KRISTOFFER, constrn. co. exec.; b. Kensington, Minn., June 29, 1906; s. Olaf and Karen (Wedum) S.; student Park Region Luther Coll., 1922-24, LaSalle Ext. U., 1925-26; m. Lucile W. Peterson, Jan. 5, 1933; children—Odny L., Dayton E., John D. Timekeeper, John Dieseth Co., Fergus, Minn., 1927-29, pres., 1964— (purchased corp. 1968; changed name to Soby Constrn., Inc. 1968); dir, chmn. bd. Security State Bank; dir. West Central Airways, Inc., M-R Sign Co., Empire Broadcasting Stas., Inc., Fergus Falls Indsl. Devel. Corp., Indsl. Park of Fergus Falls, Life Stocks of Minn.; chmn. bd. dirs. Jenoff, Inc., 1969—. Chmn. Fergus Falls City Planning Commn., 1958-66, 69-73; pres. Fergus Falls YMCA, 1969-70; bd. dirs., treas. Fergus Falls Area Jr. Coll. Found., 1966—. Recipient award Bicentennial Salute to Small Bus. in Minn., 1976, Man of Year award Asso. Gen. Contractors Minn., 1976. Mem. C. of C. (dir. 1963-65), Minn. Surveyors and Engrs. Soc., Asso. Gen. Contractors Am. (dir.), Nat. Arbitration Assn. (panel of arbitrators), Maplewood State Park Assn. (dir. 1960—), Nat. Rifle Assn. (dir. 1947-53), Minn. Rifle and Revolver Assn. (pres. 1946-48), Asso. Gen. Contractors Minn. (dir. 1956-65, pres. 1965), Otter Tail County Hist. Soc. (life), Aircraft Owners and Pilots Assn., Pilots Internat. Assn., Voyageurs Nat. Park Assn., Minn. State Automobile Assn., Minn. Zool. Soc., Ducks Unlimited (sponsor), Sons of Norway, Modern Woodmen of Am. Republican. Lutheran (pres. council 1952, 63). Clubs: Masons, Shriners, Elks, Rotary (pres. 1969-70), Fergus Falls Fish and Game (pres. 1945-46); C-400 (Concordia Coll.) (Pres.'s award 1974). Home: 545 W Summit Ave Fergus Falls MN 56537 Office: Hwy 210 E Fergus Falls MN 56537

SODERBERG, FREDERICK ALEXANDER, mfg. co. exec.; b. Braham, Minn., Dec. 28, 1915; s. Fred and Sallie Victoria (Monson) S.; A.A., U. Minn., 1938; m. Virginia Mae Wilson, May 29, 1940; children—Thomas Frederick, Gloria Lynn. Pres., Northwest Optical Service, St. Paul, 1945-58, Soderberg Optical Service, St. Paul, 1958-74; chmn. bd. dirs. Soderberg, Inc., St. Paul, 1974—; dir. Aquarius Contact Lens Co., Indpls. Chmn. St. Paul Police Study Commn., 1964-65; bd. dirs. St. Paul Goodwill Industries; trustee House of Hope Ch., St. Paul. Mem. Nat. Assn. Ind. Optical Wholsalers (pres. 1958), Optical Labs. Assn., Contact Lens Mfg. Assn., Better Vision Inst., Upper Midwest Council for Better Vision. Republican. Presbyterian. Clubs: Town and Country, Northoaks Country, Decathalon, Pools Yacht, Royal Order of Jesters. Home: 6 Evergreen Rd Saint Paul MN 55110 Office: 200 Finch Bldg Saint Paul MN 55101

SODERLUND, HAROLD ARTHUR, radio TV advt. rep. co. exec.; b. Lincoln, Nebr., Jan. 23, 1913; s. Axel D. and Anna E. (Johnson) S.; A.B., U. Nebr., 1935; m. Ethel Bash Perkins, Nov. 3, 1936; children—Sandra (Mrs. Arthur Soons), Jan Allen, Janis B. (Mrs. Robert Kruse), Cecily (Mrs. Michael Frazier). Partner, Universal Advt. Co., Lincoln, 1933-37, Outdoor Display Advt., Omaha, 1947-49; advt. mgr. Sheridan County Star, Rushville, Nebr., 1937, Nebr. Hardware Mcht., Lincoln, 1937; salesman Von Hoffman Corp., 1938-41, Burroughs, 1941-42; civilian moblzn. adviser Office Civilian Def., Omaha, 1942-44; account exec. Buchanan Thomas Advt. Agy., 1944; sales mgr. KFAB Broadcasting Co., 1944-57; owner, mgr. K000 Radio Sta., 1957-58; pres. The Soderlund Co., radio TV representation, Omaha, 1957—. Sunday sch. supt. Congl. Ch., 1952; publicity chmn. Community Chest, Omaha, 1952; instl. rep. Boy Scouts Am., Omaha. Mem. Nat. Assn. Broadcasters (sales mfrs. exec. com. 1947), Omaha Advt. Club (pres. 1952), Omaha Better Bus. Bur. (dir. 1952), Delta Sigma Rho, Alpha Tau Omega, Masons (32 deg.), Omaha Club, Happy Hollow Club. Recipient certificate meritorious service U.S. Office Civiian Def., 1944, Silver medal award Am. Advt. Fedn., 1971; named Omaha Advt. Man of Year, 1961, 9th dist. Advt. Man, 1962. Home: 2502 Garden Rd Omaha NE 68124 Office: 302 Exec Bldg 1624 Douglas St Omaha NE 68102

SODON, JAMES RICHARD, communications cons.; b. St. Louis, Jan. 21, 1942; s. James Edward and Opal Lucilvia (Doss) S.; B.A., William Jewell Coll., 1964; M.A., U. Ark., 1966; postgrad. So. Ill. U., Edwardsville, 1966-67, So. Ill. U., Carbondale, 1968-71; m. Wanda Beryl Tripp, Aug. 31, 1963; children—Meekee, Lara. Minister, Trimble (Mo.) Bapt. Ch., 1963-65; tchr. North Platte (Mo.) High Sch., 1964-65; minister Winslow (Ark.) Bapt. Ch., 1965-66; tchr. Mehlville (Mo.) High Sch., 1966-67; prof. English, St. Louis Community Coll., 1967—; instr. English, So. Ill. U., 1970-71; pvt. practice cons., St. Louis, 1969—, free-lance writer, 1969—; bd. dirs. Greenways Sch., St. Louis, 1972-74; book reviewer Glencoe Press, Beverly Hills, Calif., 1969—, Mo. State Library, 1977—. Div. rep. United Fund, St. Louis, 1967-68; trustee City View Place, St. Louis, 1974—. Fulbright exchange prof., Eng., 1975-76. Mem. Nat., Mo. edn. assns., AAUP, Mo. Assn. Community and Jr. Coll., Soc. Tech. Communications. Baptist. Home: 7319 Chamberlain Saint Louis MO 63130 Office: 3400 Pershall Rd Saint Louis MO 63135

SOFORENKO, ALBERT ZELIG, ednl. adminstr.; b. Boston, Mass., May 5, 1931; s. Charles and Genevieve (Fox) S.; B.S., U. R.I., 1954; M.S., U. Conn., 1960; Ph.D., Ohio State U., 1964; m. Evelyn Marie Haupt, Aug. 26, 1956; children—David, Cheryl, Deborah, Randal, Sara. Dir. tng. Waterford County Sch. for Emotionally Disturbed, 1957-60, Orient (Ohio) State Sch. for Mentally Retarded, 1960-64; asst. supt. Central Wis. Colony and Tng. Sch., Madison, 1964-68; supt. Hartford (Conn.) Regional Center for Mentally Retarded, 1968-73; supt. Orient State Inst., 1973—; faculty U. Wis., 1964-68, U. Hartford, Central Conn. State Coll., 1968-73; adj. prof. Ohio State U., 1973—. Exec. bd. Central Ohio council Boy Scouts Am., 1973—; adv. bd. Waterford County Sch., 1971—. Named State Employee of Year, Conn. State Employees Assn., 1971; citation for service Conn. Gen. Assembly, 1971; HEW fellow, 1962-64. Fellow Am. Assn. Mental Deficiency, Hartford Assn. Retarded Children (dir.). Jewish (trustee temple). Clubs: Masons, Shriners, Rotary (toastmaster 1966-68). Contbr. articles to profl. publs. Home: Box 125 Orient OH 43146

SOHL, JOHN FRANKLIN, automobile delivery exec.; b. Phila., June 8, 1915; s. William Andrew and Mabel E. (King) S.; B.E., Drexel U., 1940; student Charles Morris Price Sch. Advt., 1941-42; m. Rose Anne Avellino, Feb. 15, 1944; 1 son, Brandon Allen. Pres., Advertisers Service, Phila., 1946-60, Sohl Mfg. Co., Phila., 1948-60; pres., founder Auto Driveaway Co., Chgo., 1952—. Pres., Hazel Crest-Homewood Republican Club, 1964-66; precinct chmn. Breman Twp. Rep. Com., Cook County, Ill., 1964-68; mem. Hazel Crest Plan Commn., 1962—, Hazel Crest Zoning Bd., 1962-68. Clubs: Rotary; Poor Richard (Phila.); Traffic (Chgo.). Home: 2718 Larkspur Ln Hazel Crest IL 60429 Office: 310 S Michigan Ave Chicago IL 60604

SOHL, STANLEY DUANE, museum dir.; b. Naperville, Ill., Nov. 5, 1924; s. Aaron W. and Mable E. (Fauss) S.; B.F.A., U. Nebr., 1949, postgrad.; m. Norma Jean Fischer, Aug. 19, 1949; children—Duane, Jeanine, Glen, Martha, Mark. Instr. art and journalism depts. U. Nebr., Lincoln, 1948-54; mem. staff Nebr. State Hist. Soc., 1949-54; dir. Kans. State Hist. Soc., Topeka, 1954—; cons. Truman, Eisenhower museums, Wichita Hist. Assn., Fort Leavenworth Mil. Mus., West Tex. State Mus.; past pres. Mountains-Plains Mus. Conf.; past chmn. Mid-Am. Mus. Conf. Mem. adv. council Menninger Found. Served with USAF. Mem. Kans. Mus. Assn., Am. Assn. State and Local History, Am. Assn. Museums (exec. bd., regional rep., council mem.), Photog. Soc. Am. (asso.), Westerners (Kans. Corral), Kappa Alpha Mu. Editor Mountains-Plains Mus. Conf. Ann. Proc., 1969—; contbr. numerous articles to profl. and popular mags. Home: 5428 W 19th St Topeka KS 66604 Office: 120 W 10th St Topeka KS 66612

SOHN, HERBERT, physician; b. N.Y.C., May 23, 1927; s. Maurice I. and Anna (Perlman) S.; B.A., U. Va., 1950; M.D., Chgo. Med. Sch., 1955; m. Rayna Barbara Mayer, June 23, 1971; children—Andy, Douglas, Marc, Tracy, Dana. Intern, Bellevue Med. Center, N.Y.C., 1955-56; resident in urology Univ. Hosp., Cleve., 1956-60; physician Strauss Surg. Group, Chgo., 1960—, chief urology, 1968—; asst. prof. surgery U. Ill., 1973—; mem. staff Louis A. Weiss Hosp., Chgo., Cook County (Ill.) Hosp. Trustee, Chgo. Med. Sch.; bd. govs. Am. Cancer Soc. Chgo. Served with USN, 1945-46. Am. Urol. Soc. traveling fellow, 1956. Mem. Chgo. Urol. Soc. (past pres.), Chgo. Med. Soc., Ill. Med. Soc. (vice chmn. polit. action com.), Alumni Assn. Chgo. Med. Sch. (past nat. pres.), AMA, Am. Urol. Assn. Jewish. Splty. editor Chgo. Medicine, 1976—. Office: 4640 N Marine Dr Chicago IL 60640

SOKOL, DAVID MARTIN, art historian; b. N.Y.C., Nov. 3, 1942; s. Harry and Ruth (Waldman) S.; A.B., Hunter Coll., 1963; M.A., N.Y. U., 1966, Ph.D. (Univ. scholar), 1970; m. Sandra H. Schorr, June 15, 1963; children—Adam, Andrew. Lectr. in art Bronx Community Coll., 1965-66; instr. in art history Kingsborough Community Coll., 1965-68, asst. prof., asst. chmn. dept. art history, 1968-71; asso. prof. art history U. Ill., Chgo. Cirle, 1971—, chmn. dept. history of architecture and art, 1977—. Trustee Village of Oak Park (Ill.), 1977—. Mem. AAUP, Coll. Art Assn. Am., Am. Studies Assn. (nat. council), F. L. Wright Home, Studio Found. Club: Masons (N.Y.C.). Author: American Architecture and Art, 1976; John Quidor: Painter of the American Myth, 1973; contbr. numerous articles, revs. to profl. jours. Home: 330 S Taylor Ave Oak Park IL 60302 Office: U Ill Dept History of Architecture and Art Chicago IL 60680

SOKOL, ROBERT JAMES, obstetrician, gynecologist, educator; b. Rochester, N.Y., Nov. 18, 1941; s. Eli and Mildred (Levine) S.; B.A. with highest distinction in Philosophy, U. Rochester, 1963, M.D. with honors, 1966; m. Roberta Sue Kahn, July 26, 1964; children—Melissa Anne, Eric Russell, Andrew Ian. Intern, Barnes Hosp., Washington U., St. Louis, 1966-67, resident in obstetrics and gynecology, 1967-70, asst. in obstetrics and gynecology, 1966-70, research asst., 1967-68, instr. clin. obstetrics and gynecology, 1970; Buswell fellow in maternal fetal medicine Strong Meml. Hosp., U. Rochester, 1972-73, asst. prof., asso. obstetrician and gynecologist, 1972-73; fellow in maternal fetal medicine Cleve. Met. Gen. Hosp., Case Western Res. U., Cleve., 1974-75, asso. obstetrician and gynecologist, 1973—, asst. prof. obstetrics and gynecology, 1973-77, asst. program dir. Perinatal Clin. Research Center, 1973—, acting dir. obstetrics, 1974-75, co-dir., 1977—, asso. prof., 1977—; mem. profl. adv. bd. Educated Childbirth, Inc., 1976—. Mem. pres.'s leadership council U. Rochester, 1976—. Served from capt. to maj. M.C., USAF, 1970-72. Diplomate Nat. Bd. Med. Examiners, Am. Bd. Obstetrics and Gynecology. Mem. Am. Coll. Obstetricians and Gynecologists, AMA, Royal, Cleve. acads. medicine, Cleve. Ob-Gyn Soc., Soc. Perinatal Obstetricians, Phi Beta Kappa Alpha Omega Alpha. Republican. Jewish. Contbr. articles and chpts. to med. jours. and books; researcher computer applications in perinatal medicine, fetal cardiacphysiology and fetal neurophysiology. Home: 20120 Scottsdale Blvd Shaker Heights OH 44122 Office: Cleve Met Gen Hosp Perinatal Clin Research Center 3395 Scranton Rd Cleveland OH 44109

SOKOLIK, STANLEY LEWIS, mgmt. cons.; b. St. Louis, Aug. 8, 1928; s. Herman Morris and Ruth (Arber) S.; B.S., Washington U., St. Louis, 1950, M.B.A., 1951; Ph.D., Ohio State U., 1955; m. Paulette Anderman, June 21, 1953; children—Sandra R. Sokolik Arundale, Marcia L., Merle A., Ruth A. Asst. prof. mktg. Washington U., St. Louis, 1954, Wayne State U., Detroit, 1955-58; dir. personnel Ernst Kern Co., Detroit, 1958-59; dir. tng. Federal's, Inc., Detroit, 1959-63; mgmt. cons., Detroit, St. Louis and Springfield, Ill., 1963—; asst. prof. mgmt. U. Detroit, 1963-67; asso. prof. bus. adminstrn., chmn. dept. So. Ill. U., Edwardsville, 1967-69; asso. prof. mgmt., dir. orgn. devel. program U. Mo., St. Louis, 1969-70; prof. adminstr. Sangamon State U., Springfield, Ill., 1970-74; dir. planning, Office Sec. State Ill., Springfield, 1974-75; prin. Profl. Cons. Assos., Springfield, 1976—; dir. Comml. State Corp., Comml. State Life Ins. Co. Mem. Acad. Mgmt., Orgn. Devel. Network, Am. Soc. Personnel Adminstrn., Beta Gamma Sigma. Jewish. Club: B'nai B'rith (pres.). Author: The Personnel Process, 1970. Home: 132 Oakmont Dr Springfield IL 62704 Office: 2140 S Walnut St Springfield IL 62704

SOKOLNICKI, ALFRED JOHN, educator; b. Milw., May 21, 1918; s. Ignacy and Sophie (Brodaczvnski) S.; Ph.B., Marquette U., 1942, M.A., 1947; L.H.D., Alliance Coll., 1961; m. Mildred Downer, June 9, 1951. Instr., Marquette U. Sch. Speech, 1945-53, asst. prof., 1953-58, asso. prof., 1958-62, prof., 1962—, adminstrv. asst. to dir. Sch. Speech, 1961-69, dean, 1969—. Founder, exec. dir. Mazur Polish Dancers of Milw., 1940—; mem. Milw. Folk Council, 1937—. Decorated Polonia Restituta medal (Poland). Served with AUS, 1942-45; ETO. Fellow Am. Speech and Hearing Assn.; mem. Acad. of Aphasia, Speech Communication Assn., Internat. Assn. Legopedics and Phoniatrics, Wis. Acad. Scis., Arts and Letters, Wis. Speech and Hearing Assn., Central States Speech Assn., Polish Inst. Arts and Scis. in Am., Indsl. Communication Council, Phi Delta Kappa, Alpha Sigma Nu. Contbr. articles to profl. jours. Home: 3411 S Illinois Ave Milwaukee WI 53207

SOKOLOV, SHERWIN LEONARD, psychologist, social worker; b. Newark, June 7, 1935; s. Meyer and Annie Sokolov; B.S., U. Mich., 1956; M.A., Wayne State U., 1961; m. Barbara Elaine Schanz, Aug. 25, 1957; children—Judith, Mark, Cheryl. Psychologist, Mich. Epilepsy Center, Detroit, 1957-61; sr. psychologist Oakland County Juvenile Ct., Pontiac, Mich., 1961—; chief counselor Royal Oak (Mich.) Municipal Ct., 1962-67; staff mem. Clin. Resources, Inc., Clarkston, Mich., 1972—. Cons. in field, 1964—. Mem. drug abuse treatment adv. com. St. Joseph Hosp., Pontiac, 1970—. Bd. dirs. Mich. Out-Patient Clinics Assn.; trustee Mich. Psychologists Pub. Affairs Com. Mem. Am., Mich., Oakland County psychol. assns., Sigma Xi, Psi Chi. Contbr. articles to profl. jours. Home: 21280 Constitution Dr Southfield MI 48076 Office: 5885 Ortonville Rd Clarkston MI 48016

SOLBERG, NELLIE FLORENCE COAD, artist; b. Sault Ste. Marie, Mich.; d. Sanford and Mary (McDonald) Coad; B.A., Minot State Tchrs. Coll., 1930; M.A., N.D. State U., 1963; postgrad. Wash. State U., 1960, Wyo. U., 1964, St. Cloud (Minn.) Coll., 1971; m.

Ingvald Solberg, Aug. 24, 1930; children—Jeanne Elaine (Mrs. Clarence Unruh), Walter Eugene, Kay Louise (Mrs. Arthur Link). Tchr., Bismarck (N.D.) Elementary Schs., 1954-63, art dir. high sch., 1963-72; art instr. Bismarck Jr. Coll., 1964-67; one-woman shows: Minot State Coll., 1963, Dickinson State Coll., 1964, Jamestown Coll., 1964, U. N.D., Valley City State Coll., Bismarck Jr. Coll., 1963, 65, 68, 69, N.D. State U., 1970, 74, Linha Gallery, Minot, N.D., 1972, 74-77, Bank of N.D., 1972-74, 76-77; group shows Gov. John Davis Mansion, 1960, Concordia Coll., Moorhead, Minn., 1965, N.D. Capitol, 1968, 69, Gov. William Guy Mansion, 1971, Internat. Peace Gardens, 1969; mem. Indian Culture Found., 1964—, numerous others; cons. Bismarck Art Assn. Gallery, 1973—; dir. N.D. Petroleum Art Show, 1962, 64, Statewide Religious Arts Festival, Bismarck, 1969—; dir. State Treas.'s Gallery, 1977, N.D. State Capitol, Bismarck, 1973—; co-dir. Indian Art Show, Nat. Congress Am. Indians, Bismarck, 1963. Mem. Civic Music Assn., 1942—; religious arts com. Conf. Chs., 1973. Recipient 3d pl. graphics Five State Show, Pierre, S.D., 1968; Purchase award S.D. Arts Council, 1968. Mem. Bismarck (charter, Honor award 1960, pres. 1963-64, 71-72), Jamestown art assns., Linha Gallery (Minot), Nat. League Am. Pen Women (pres. N.D. 1964-66, pres. Medora br. 1972—), Mpls. Soc. Fine Arts, Am. Crafts Council, AAUW, P.E.O. (chpt. pres. 1967-69), Order Eastern Star, Republican Wives Club, Republican Women 1st Ladies Club, Sigma Sigma Sigma. Presbyn. Home: 925 N 6th St Bismarck ND 58501 Studio: 1021 N 6th St Bismarck ND 58501

SOLBERG, PAUL BERNARD, data processor; b. Bessemer, Mich., Dec. 20, 1936; s. Melvin Ford and Ellen Marie (Karyula) S.; student Spencerian Coll., Milw., 1957-59; m. Karen Florence Osten, Sept. 26, 1960; children—Dale Paul, Dean Michael (twins), Diana Lynn. Data processing analyst AC Electronics, Oak Creek, Wis., 1959-69; systems mgr. Elmbrook Meml. Hosp., Brookfield, Wis., 1969-71; systems services mgr. SSM Mgmt. Services, Milw., 1971-76, dir. EDP Service, 1976—; mem. Waukesha County Computer Selection Com. Served with AUS, 1956. Mem. Coop. Health Care Users, Upper Midwest NCR Users, Assn. Systems Mgmt. Mem. Assembly of God. Home: 14410 W Oklahoma St New Berlin WI 53151 Office: 6610 N Teutonia St Milwaukee WI 53209

SOLBRIG, INGEBORG HILDEGARD, educator; b. Weissenfels, Ger., July 31, 1923; d. Reinhold Johannes and Hildegard (Ferchland) Solbrig; came to U.S., 1961, naturalized, 1966; B.A. summa cum laude, San Francisco State U., 1964; M.A., Stanford U., 1966, Ph.D., 1969. Chemist, Schoeller Co., Osnabrück, Ger., 1951-58, Stazione Zoologican and Ditta Mercedes, Naples, Italy, 1958-61; asst. prof. German, U. R.I., Kingston, 1969-70, U. Ky., Lexington, 1972-75; asso. prof. German U. Iowa, Iowa City, 1975—. Recipient Gold medal Austrian Hammer-Purgstall Soc. Cultural and Econ. Relations with Near and Middle East, 1974; Old Gold fellow, 1977; fellow Austrian Ministry Edn., 1968-69; tuition grantee, dissertation fellow Stanford U., other research grants. Mem. Internat. Assn. German Studies, Modern Lang. Assn., Am. Assn. Tchrs. German, Am. Comparative Lit. Assn., Am. Soc. German Lit. in 16th-17th Centuries, Am. Council Study Austrian Lit., Goethe Gesellschaft, Deutsche Schillergesellschaft, Arthur Schnitzler Soc., AAUP. Author: Hammer-Purgstall und Goethe, 1973. Prin. editor; Rilke Heute, 1975; editor, translator: Reinhard Goering, Seabattle/Seeschlacht, 1977. Author poems, articles, revs. Home: 228 S Summit St Apt B 2 Iowa City IA 52240 Office: Dept German Univ Iowa Iowa City IA 52242

SOLEM, G(EORGE) ALAN, zoologist, mus. curator; b. Chgo., July 21, 1931; s. George Oliver and Lillian Taylor (Kinloch) S.; B.S. magna cum laude, Haverford Coll., 1952; M.A., U. Mich., 1954, Ph.D., 1956; children—Anders Eric, Kirsten Marie. Asst. curator lower invertebrates Field Mus. Natural History, Chgo., 1957-58, curator lower invertebrates, 1959-70, curator invertebrates, 1971—; research asso., dept. biol. scis. Northwestern U., Evanston, Ill., 1970—; lectr., com. evolutionary biology U. Chgo., 1971—. Trustee, Barrington (Ill.) Pub. Library Dist., 1970-76. Several NSF grants. Fellow AAAS; mem. Phi Beta Kappa. Author articles, catalogues and children's books in field. Office: Field Museum Natural History Roosevelt Rd at Lake Shore Dr Chicago IL 60605

SOLER, NILDA M., lawyer; b. San Juan, P.R., Apr. 2, 1945; d. Carlos R. and Matilde R. (Zeno) S.; B.A. cum laude, Tulane U., 1967; M. Urban Planning, U. Ill., 1969; J.D. cum laude, DePaul U., 1976. Urban intern HUD, Chgo., 1969-70, urban planner, 1970-71, community planning and mgmt. rep., 1971-72, dir. planning and codes br., 1972-73; head tech. and adv. planning services Ill. Dept. Local Govt. Affairs, 1973-76; admitted to Ill. bar, 1976; mem. firm Ancel-Glink, Diamond & Murphy, Chgo., 1977—. Mem. Am., Ill., Chgo. bar assns., Am. Soc. Planning Ofcls. (dir.), Nat. Trust Historic Preservation, Am. Soc. Pub. Adminstrn. Roman Catholic. Home: 1629 W Belle Plaine Ave Chicago IL 60613 Office: 111 W Washington St Suite 1857 Chicago IL 60602

SOLIDAY, MAUREEN HARTER (MRS. DONALD M. SOLIDAY), civic worker; b. Sioux City, Iowa, Nov. 15, 1925; d. Charles Melvin and Mary (Hassenger) Harter; student State U., Iowa, 1943-44, Morningside Coll., 1946-48; m. Donald M. Soliday, June 17, 1948 (div. 1975); children—Jeffrey P., Karen, Melissa, Heidi, Amanda, Jay B., Joel P., Rebecca, Sarah, Jon A., Jeremy B., Joshua L., Jason M. Mem. West Des Moines and Polk County One Vote Com., 1952-56; chmn. fund drive Mercy Hosp., 1955-56; pub. relations chmn. Catholic Women's League 1958-62; active AAU, 1958—, asst. dir. Iowa spl. olympics com., 1969-71, state dir., 1972—, mem. nat. adv. com., 1969—; nat. chmn. Jr. Olympic Luge Com., 1972—, mem. adv. bd. Iowa Assn. Swim Clubs, 1966—, treas., 1970—; founding mem. Stillwell Jr. High Sch. P.T.A., West Des Moines, 1960—; exec. dir. Iowa Spl. Olympics, Inc., 1975—. Mem. Polk County Democratic Central Com., 1969—, Polk County Dem. Women's Club, 1957—; candidate for Ho. of Reps., 1968. Bd. dirs. Polk County chpt. Easter Seal Drive, 1961-62, Polk County Soc. Crippled Children and Adults, 1961-66; bd. dirs., sec. Concerned Christians Assn., Des Moines, 1967-68; bd. dirs. Polk County Human Rights Com., 1969-70; mem. U.S. Olympic Luge Com., 1976—. Named U. Iowa Mother of Year, 1974. Roman Catholic. Home and office: 1133 16th St West Des Moines IA 50265

SOLLEY, THOMAS TREAT, museum ofcl.; b. N.Y.C., Sept. 4, 1924; s. John Beach and Katherine (Lilly) S.; B.A., Yale, 1950; M.A., Ind. U., 1966, postgrad., 1966-68; children—Evan L., Robert L., Katherine H., Virginia H. Archtl. projects engr. Eli Lilly & Co., Indpls., 1951-61; pvt. archtl. practice, Indpls., 1961-64; asst. dir. Ind. U. Art Mus., Bloomington, 1968-71, dir., 1971—. Advt. trustee Children's Mus. of Indpls. Served with AUS, 1943-46. Mem. Assn. Art Mus. Dirs. Office: Art Museum Indiana U Bloomington IN 47401

SOLOMON, CHESTER DOUGLAS, steel co. exec.; b. Monticello, Iowa, Dec. 6, 1924; s. David Sol and Dora (Marmis) S.; student U. Dubuque, 1942-43, U. Iowa, 1946-47; m. Charlotte Lynn Schwartz, Mar. 23, 1947; children—Mark Jay, Steven Lee, Cynthia Kay. Pres., sec., Dubuque Gases and Steel Co. (Iowa), 1954—, dir. Chmn. Dubuque Transit Bd., 1973—; mem. Clarke Coll. Devel. Council, Dubuque, 1975—; trustee Finley Hosp., Dubuque, 1974—; bd. dirs. Dubuque Symphony Orch. Served with AUS, 1943-46. Recipient Philanthropic Service award Nat. Jewish Hosp., 1971. Mem. Assn. Steel Distributors (vice chmn. govt. relations com., mem. small bus. legisl council, chmn. Midwest region 1978, nat. dir. 1978). Republican. Jewish. Clubs: Dubuque Golf and Country, B'Nai Brith (past pres.). Home: 1030 Arrowhead Dr Dubuque IA 52001 Office: 120 Railroad Ave Dubuque IA 52001

SOLOMON, HERBERT, optometrist; b. Chgo., June 7, 1923; s. Arthur and Faye (Hoffman) S., student Herzl Jr. Coll., High Point (N.C.) Coll., 1943; D.Optometry, D.Ocular Sci., Ill. Coll. Optometry, 1946; m. Phoebe Boas Baumgarten, Apr. 30, 1966; children—Sheryl Mae, Jeffrey Philip, Ellen Ronna, Craig, Ross, Karen. Practice optometry, Chgo., 1946—; dir. Eye Clinic, Bethany Methodist Hosp., Chgo.; v.p. Visual Service Corp., 1970—; visual cons. Chgo. Pub. Schs., The Vatican. Vice pres. Vision Conservation Inst. Ill.; del. health careers council Ill., Interprofl. Council Ill. Pres., Skokie (Ill.) Civic Theatre, 1952. Served to 1st lt. USAAF, 1942-46. Decorated D.F.C. with oak leaf cluster, Air medal with 5 oak leaf clusters, Fellow Am. Acad. Optometry; mem. Am., Ill. (chmn. com. visual care aging 1968-70, low vision care 1970-71, pathology 1971-72, optometric technicians 1972-74, v.p. edn. 1975-77) optometric assns., North Suburban Optometric Soc. (1st v.p. 1973-74, pres.-elect 1974-75), Coll. optometrists Vision Devel., Better Vision Inst., Am., Ill. socs. prevention blindness, Nat. Eye Research Found., Jewish War Vets., Am. Legion. Jewish. Lion. Author: A Syllabus of Optics, 1947; co-author The Complete Guide to Eye Care, Eyeglasses and Contact Lenses, 1977. Contbr. articles to profl. jours. Home: 1020 Bluff Rd Glencoe IL 60022 Office: 30 N Michigan Ave Chicago IL 60602 also 6201 N California Ave Chicago IL 60659

SOLOMON, IZLER, symphony condr.; b. St. Paul, Jan. 11, 1910; s. Harry Thomas and Eva (Levin) S.; student Mich. State Coll., 1928-31; studied violin, St. Paul and Kansas City to 1924, N.Y. and Phila., 1924-28, Europe, summer 1928; Mus.D., Pacific U., Anderson Coll., Franklin (Ind.) Coll.; LL.D., Ind. Central Coll.; Mus.D., Butler U., 1966, Ind. U., 1972; m. Sorelle Melamed, Nov. 26, 1931 (dec. Dec. 1959); children—Joseph (dec.), David; m. 2d, Elizabeth Westfeldt, Feb. 26, 1961 (div. 1971). Instr. violin, Mich. State Coll., 1931-36, organized and conducted local orchestra; condr. Ill. Symphony Orch., Chgo., 1936; condr. Woman's Symphony Orch., Chgo., and presented with this orgn. 26 weekly broadcasts for the Libby-Owens Ford Glass Co., 1940-41; guest condr. Buffalo Philharmonic and Detroit Civic orchs., 1936, Les Concerts Symphoniques de Montreal, NBC Symphony, 1939-42, Phila. Orchestra, 1940; mus. dir. and condr. Columbus (Ohio) Philharmonic Orch., 1941-49; became prof. music Ohio U., 1947; resident condr. Buffalo Philharmonic Orch., 1952-53; condr. New Orleans summer Pops Symphony, 1943-44; guest condr. Detroit Orch., 1945, Vancouver (B.C.) Symphony Orch., 1945, Buffalo Philharmonic Orch., 1946, Chgo. Grant Park Symphony, 1945, 46, 47, Hollywood Bowl Symphony, 1946-47, NBC Symphony, 1947, Palestine Philharmonic Orch., 1948, Israel Philharmonic, 1948-49 (U.S. tour 1951, 58), Boston Symphony, 1959, Berlin Philharmonic Orch., 1965; music director and conductor Brandeis Festival of Creative Arts, 1955, Aspen Music Festival, 1956-62; now permanent post music dir., condr. Indpls. Symphony Orch.; music dir., condr. Flagstaff Music Festival, 1966—. Recipient of several awards for distinguished service to Am. Mus. Recordings for RCA Victor and MGM Record Co. Home: 6437 C Park Central Dr W Indianapolis IN 46260 Office: Clowes Meml Hall 4600 Sunset Ave Indianapolis IN 46208

SOLOMON, NEIL WALKER, ins. co. exec.; b. Culbertson, Nebr., Apr. 26, 1927; s. Ralph Edward and Alma (Walker) S.; B. Music Edn., U. Nebr., 1951; C.L.U., 1962; m. Barbara Phyllis Stephens, May 19, 1957; children—Stephen Walt, Cynthia Ann. Nat. field sec. Phi Gamma Delta, 1951-53; mgr. Alliance, Nebr. C. of C., 1953-56; salesman N.Y. Life Ins. Co., 1956-59; with Occidental Life Ins. Co. Calif., 1959—, gen. agt. Lincoln, Nebr., 1959—; pres. Jerry Solomon C.L.U. & Assos., 1970—, Ins. Adminstrs. Co., 1969—, Greenville Retirement Village, 1970—; v.p. Western Cattle Co., Bob Stephens & Assos., Inc. Bd. dirs. Lancaster County chpt. ARC; trustee St. Johns Mil. Sch. Served with AUS, 1946-47. Mem. Lincoln Assn. C.L.U.'s (pres. 1963-64), Life and Qualifying Millon Dollar Round Table, Nebr. Assn. Life Underwriters, Lincoln Estate Planning Council (sec.), Lincoln C. of C., V.F.W., Am. Legion, Phi Gamma Delta (v.p. bd. archons). Republican. Mason (Shriner), Rotarian, Elk. Clubs: University, Country, Nebraska (Lincoln). Contbr. to ins. jours. Composer mus. comedies, songs. Home: 2752 Manse Ave Lincoln NE 68502 Office: 1200 First Nat Bank Bldg Lincoln NE 68508

SOLOMON, O. DAVID, ophthalmologist; b. Mezokovaczhaza, Hungary, Mar. 20, 1932 (came to U.S. 1937, naturalized 1945); s. Joseph and Emmy (Klein) S.; A.B., Johns Hopkins U., 1954; M.D., U. Pitts., 1958; postgrad. in ophthalmology Harvard U., 1959-60; m. Louise Joann Lichter, June 14, 1955; children—Jeffrey (dec.), Abby, Jodi, Joel. Intern, Mound Park Hosp., St. Petersburg, Fla., 1968-59; resident in ophthalmology Mt. Sinai Hosp., Cleve., 1959-62, dir. contact lens clinic, 1967—, also dir. ophthalmic assts. program, 1972—, v.p. med. staff, 1974-76; practice medicine specializing in ophthalmology, Cleve., 1962—; research cons. Center for Materials, Case Western Res. U., Cleve., 1972—, also mem. faculty. Mem. Am., Ohio State, Cuyahoga County, Mt. Sinai (trustee, pres. 1976-78) med. assns., Cleve. Med. Library Assn., A.C.S., Cleve. Ophthalmol. Soc. (sec.-treas. 1963—, v.p. 1974-75, pres. 1975-76), Am. Acad. Ophthalmology and Otolaryngology, Contact Lens Assn. Ophthalmology, Am. Assn. Ophthalmology, Phi Delta Epsilon (trustee, regional gov. 1965—). Contbr. articles to profl. publs. Home: 20525 Byron Rd Shaker Heights OH 44122 Office: 3609 Park East Beachwood OH 44122

SOLOMON, RICHARD HUMPHREY, fire protection engr.; b. Bloomington, Ill., June 2, 1933; s. Robert Clinton and Mildred Marie (Clark) S.; B.S., Ill. Inst. Tech., 1955; m. Jane Joann Henderson, Oct. 9, 1955; children—Karen, Diane. Asst. chief engr. Ins. Services Office Ill., Chgo., 1955-66; owner, operator Richard H. Solomon & Assos., cons. fire protection engring., 1967—; dir. bldg. and zoning City of Naperville (Ill.), 1971; lectr. in field. Mem. Ill. Fire Commn., 1972—, chmn., 1975—; chmn. City of Naperville Bldg. Rev. Bd., 1974-76; adv. bd. Ill. Supt. Pub. Instrn., 1964-70; tech. adv. bd. DuPage County (Ill.), 1966—. Served with USNR, 1956-57. Western Actuarial Bur. scholar, 1951-55. Registered profl. engr. Ill., Ky. Mem. Wis.-No. Ill. Firemen's Assn. (hon.), Nat. Fire Protection Assn. (chmn. bldg. heights and areas 1976—), Ill. (chmn. ethics and practice com. 1968), Nat. socs. profl. engrs., Internat. Assn. Fire Chiefs, Bldg. Ofcls. and Code Adminstrs., Internat. Soc. Fire Protection Engrs. (chmn. engring. edn. com. 1972—). Republican. Congregationalist. Moose. Home: 356 S Loomis St Naperville IL 60540

SOLOMON, TED JOSEPH, educator; b. Bismarck, N.D., May 28, 1932; s. Ted J. and Elizabeth M. (Yeasley) S.; B.A., Macalester Coll., 1954; S.T.B., Boston U., 1957; M.A., U. Chgo., 1961, Ph.D., 1966; m. Marian Grace Loomer, Oct. 24, 1953; children—Robert I., Richard L., Rebecca J. Prof. philosophy St. Andrew's Presbyn. Coll., Laurinburg, N.C., 1962-66; prof. religion Fla. Presbyn. Coll., St. Petersburg, 1966-69; prof. philosophy Iowa State U., Ames, 1969—. Chmn., Iowa Am. Friends Service Com., 1972-74. Del., Democratic State Conv., 1970, 72, 74. Recipient Danforth Tchr. award, 1965. Mem. Assn. Asian Studies, Am. Acad. Religion, AAUP, Soc. Sci. Study Religion. Methodist. Mason, Kiwanian. Contbr. articles to philos. and religious jours. Home: Route 4 North Dakota Rd Ames IA 50010

SOLTI, SIR GEORG, conductor; b. Budapest, Hungary, Oct. 21, 1912; s. More and Theres (Rosenbaum) S.; ed. Budapest Music High Sch.; m. Hedi Oechsli, October 29, 1946; m. 2d, Anne Valerie Pitts, Nov. 11, 1967. Musical asst. Budapest Opera House, 1930-33, condr., 1934-39; pianist (refugee), Switzerland, 1939-45; gen. music dir. Bavarian State Opera, Munich, Germany, 1946-52, Frankfurt (Germany) Staats Theater, 1952-60; mus. dir. Royal Opera House Covent Garden, London, 1961-71, Chgo. Symphony Orch. 1969—; pianist Concours Internat., Geneva, 1942; guest condr. various orchs.; condr. Salzburg Festival, Edinburgh and Glyndebourne festivals, Vienna State Opera, Paris Opera, Vienna Philharmonic, Berlin, London, N.Y. Philharmonic orchs., Amsterdam, Concertgebouw, orchs. in San Francisco, Hollywood, Los Angeles, St. Louis, Ravinia (Ill.) Park, Chgo., Chgo. Lyric Opera. Decorated Great Cross of German Republic; comdr. Order Brit. Empire; knight Order Brit. Empire, comdr. Legion Honor (France); recipient grand prix du Disque Mondiale, 1959, 62, 63, 64, 66, 70, 77. Address: 220 S Michigan Ave Chicago IL 60604

SOMERS, EMMANUEL, pathologist, lab. dir.; b. Cania, Greece, Jan. 20, 1931; s. Nicholas and Angela (Marakakis) Psomatakis; came to U.S., 1958, naturalized, 1968; M.D., U. Salonika (Greece), 1954; m. Katherine Kouromichali, June 21, 1954; children—Michael, Angela, Nicholas, Mary Ann, Elizabeth. Asst. pathologist Michael Reese Hosp., Chgo., 1963-65; asso. pathologist St. Margaret Hosp., Hammond, Ind., 1965-69; asso. pathologist, St. Mary's Hosp., Kankakee, Ill., 1970-76, chief pathologist, dir. labs., 1976—; cons. pathologist Manteno (Ill.) Mental Health Center, 1971—; asst. prof. pathology U. Ill. Sch. Medicine, Chgo., 1972—. Served to capt., M.C., Greek Army, 1955-57. Fellow Coll. Am. Pathologists, Am. Soc. Clin. Pathologists; mem. AMA, Ill. State Med. Soc. Greek Orthodox. Home: 139 Graymoor Ln Olympia Fields IL 60461

SOMERS, GERALD A., librarian; b. Marshalltown, Iowa, Dec. 4, 1921; s. Richard Arthur and Edna Mae (Lieberon) S.; student Knox Coll., 1945-46; B.L.S., U. Chgo., 1948; m. Gloria Ann Graeszel, Nov. 26, 1955; children—Scott James, Steven Craig, Cynthia Ann. Br. head Milw. Pub. Library, 1949-56; dir. Eau Claire (Wis.) Pub. Library, 1956-61, Green Bay Pub. Library, 1961-67, Brown County Library, 1968—. Exec. dir. Nat. Library Week in Wis., 1964. Served with USAAF, 1941-45; ETO. Mem. Wis. Library Assn. (treas. 1957-58, v.p. 1964-65, pres., 1965-66, Librarian of Year 1972). Methodist. Home: 1808 Carroll Ave Green Bay WI 54304 Office: 515 Pine St Green Bay WI 54301

SOMERS, JOHN EDWARD, physician, educator; b. East Twas, Mich., Apr. 2, 1932; s. Stanley Edward and Edys Evelyn (Owen) S.; B.S., U. Mich., 1953, M.D., 1957; m. Antoinette Tamburro, Sept. 11, 1954; children—Evelyn, John, Russell, James, Elizabeth. Intern, USPHS Hosp., S.I., N.Y., 1957-58; asst. resident neurology U. Mich. Med. Sch., Ann Arbor, 1958-59, resident, 1959-60, clin. instr., 1960-61; clin. asso. med. neurology NIH, Bethesda, Md., 1961-63; faculty U. Mo. Sch. Medicine, Columbia, 1963-69, 74—, clin. asso. prof. neurology, 1974—; practice medicine specializing in med. neurology, Columbia, 1969—; mem. staffs Boone County, Columbia Regional hosps., Columbia, St. Mary's, Charles E. Still hosps., Jefferson, Mo., Audrain Med. Center, Mexico, Mo. Served with USPHS, 1957-58, 61-63. Mem. Am. Acad. Neurology, N.Y. Acad. Scis., Mo., So., Boone County med. socs., Assn. for Study Headache, Am. Geriatric Soc., AAAS, Phi Beta Kappa, Phi Kappa Phi, Alpha Omega Alpha. Home: Rural Route 3 Columbia MO 65201 Office: 11 S Williams Columbia MO 65201

SOMERS, ORVILLE HAROLD, hosp. data processor; b. S. Lyon, Mich., Feb. 17, 1937; s. Harold and Mina Pearl (Bariger) S.; B.S., Ferris State Coll., 1959; m. Deloris Ann Wade, Mar. 25, 1961; children—Jeffrey, Michelle. Sr. programmer Fisher Body div. Gen. Motors Corp., Warren, Mich., 1959-66; data processing mgr. Evans Products Co., Plymouth, Mich., 1966-68; dir. info. systems St. Joseph Mercy Hosp., Ann Arbor, Mich., 1968—. Active Little League, South Lyon, Mich., 1971-75. Mem. St. Joseph Mercy Hosp. Speakers Bur., Am. Hosp. Assn., Electronic Computing Hosp. Orgn., Am. Accounting Assn., Hosp. Info. Systems Assn. (pres. 1974, trustee 1973, 75), Assn. for Computing Machinery, Assn. Record Mgrs. and Adminstrs., Spl. Interest Groups on Bus. Data Processing, Biomed. Computing, Data Communications, Delta Sigma Pi. Baptist. Home: 9555 Rushton South Lyon MI 48178 Office: 5301 E Huron Dr Ann Arbor MI 48106

SOMERS, PATRICIA ANN, guidance counselor, ednl. adminstr.; b. Lansing, Mich., Apr. 22, 1949; d. Arthur John and Stella Rose (Hendges) Somers; B.A. with honors, Mich. State U., 1971; M.A. with high honors, U. Ill., 1973; postgrad. Ohio State U.; m. Mark M. Willett, June 5, 1969; 1 dau., Susan B. Anthony. Recruiter ACTION: Peace Corps/VISTA, 1972; research asso. U. Ill., 1972-73; teaching asso. Ohio State U., 1973; state compliance coordinator NOW, Ohio, 1973-75; personnel specialist women's unit Ohio Dept. Adminstrv. Services, 1974; research coordinator Women's Resource and Policy Devel. Center, Columbus, Ohio, 1975-76; dir. career and life and work planning Denison U., Granville, Ohio, 1976—; tchr. workshops, cons. in field. Democratic candidate city and county offices, Champaign, Ill., 1972, 73; mem. Columbus Area Leadership Program, Licking County (Ohio) Fair Housing Commn. Wodrow Wilson instr., 1977. Mem. NOW (Susan B. Anthony Sisterhood award Ohio chpts. 1975), Am. Soc. Personnel Adminstrn., Midwest Coll. Placement Assn., Indsl. Relations Research Assn., Columbus Area Coll. Placement Consortium, Nat. Assn. Student Personnel Adminstrn., Am. Personnel and Guidance Assn., United Ostomy Assn. Unitarian. Office: Slayter Hall Denison Univ Granville OH 43023

SOMMERER, KARL THEODOR, photographer, educator; b. Munich, West Germany, July 16, 1931; s. Georg and Maria Franziska (Elsner) S.; diploma Agrl. Sch., Balingen, Germany, 1949-51; m. Gisela Kaete Moessinger, May 22, 1953; children—Juergen, Ursula. Technician Photolab, Sudbury, Ont., Can., 1955-56; photographer CKSO-TV, Sudbury, 1957-59, cinematographer, 1966-68; mgr. Color-Lab., Sudbury, 1960-65; faculty Cambrian Coll., Sudbury, 1969—, asst. master photography, 1970-76, master, 1976—; freelance photographer, 1950—. Named Can. Profl. Photographer of the Year, 1973. Mem. Profl. Photographers of Am., Craftsman Photog. Arts, Master Photog. Arts. Home: 1505 Gary Ave Sudbury ON P3A 4G2 Canada Office: 1400 Barrydowne Rd Cambrian College Sudbury ON Canada

SOMMERFELD, CARL JOHN, dentist; b. Forest Park, Ill., Sept. 21, 1908; s. Oscar Emil and Anna Johana (Reinhardt) S.; D.D.S., U. Ill., 1932; m. Evelyn Emma Seegers, Dec. 19, 1935 (dec.); children—Carla Joyce, Evan Eroll, Charlotte Anne; m. 2d, Charlotte Farr, Dec. 20, 1969. Pvt. practice dentistry, Forest Park, Ill., 1932-77; dec., Mar., 1977. Served to capt. AUS, 1943-46. Club: Kiwanis (pres. 1951-52). Home: 217 Maison Court Elmhurst IL 60126 Office: 7422 Madison St Forest Park IL 60130

SOMMERS, HERBERT MYRON, physician, educator; b. Colorado Springs, Colo., Sept. 4, 1925; s. Herbert Manitou and Edna Earl (McReynolds) S.; student U. Colo., 1943, 46-48; B.S., Northwestern U., 1949, M.D., 1952; m. Sarah Mason Shute, Apr. 30, 1955 (div. 1977); children—Mark Stuart, Lee Scott, Keith Eric, Todd Craig. Intern, Chgo. Wesley Meml. Hosp., 1953-54, resident surgery and pathology, 1954-58; practice medicine, specializing in pathology, Chgo., 1958—; attending pathologist Chgo. Wesley Meml. Hosp., 1958-68, Passavant Meml. Hosp., Chgo., 1968—; instr. pathology Northwestern U. Med. Sch., Chgo., 1957-61, asso., 1961-62, asst. prof., 1962-66, asso. prof., 1966-71, prof., 1971—. Served with AUS, 1943-46. Chgo. Heart Soc. grantee, 1968-69. Diplomate Am. Bd. Pathology. Mem. Am. Assn. Pathologists and Bacteriologists, Am. Soc. Exptl. Pathology, Am. Soc. Clin. Pathology (council on microbiology 1967-77, vice chmn. council 1969—, chmn. microbiology resource com.), Coll. Am. Pathologists, Am. Soc. Microbiology, A.A.A.S., Ill. Soc. Microbiology. Club: Wilmette (Ill.) Sailing. Co-author: Infectious Disease. Contbr. articles to profl. jours. Home: 643 Walden Rd Winnetka IL 60093 Office: 303 E Chicago Ave Chicago IL 60611

SOMMERSCHIELD, HAROLD STANLEY, clin. psychologist; b. Chgo., Feb. 18, 1938; s. William Stanley and Evelyn S.; B.A., U. Mich., 1960; B.D., No. Bapt. Theol. Sem., 1966; Ph.D., Mich. State U., 1969; m. Shirley Ruth Earl, Aug. 18, 1962; children—Stephen, Karin, Kristin, Kammelynn. Intern, Traverse City (Mich.) State Mental Hosp., 1965, Dearborn (Mich.) VA Hosp., 1967, Lansing (Mich.) Child Guidance Clinic, 1968, Ann Arbor (Mich.) VA Hosp., 1969; sch. diagnostician Eaton County (Mich.) Bd. Edn., 1966; clin. psychologist Bay Area Guidance Center, Bay City, Mich., 1969-73; clin. psychologist Genesee Psychiat. Center, Flint, Mich., 1973—; psychol. cons. rehab. project Delta Coll., 1970; instr. psychology Central Mich. U., 1971; cons. Nat. Council Alcoholism, Flint, 1977. Certified cons. psychologist and marriage counselor. Mem. Am., Mich. psychol. assns. Contbr. articles to psychol. jours. Home: 1222 Pomona Ct Fenton MI 48430 Office: 2110 W Hill Rd Flint MI 48507

SOMSEN, HENRY NORTHROP, lawyer; b. New Ulm, Minn., Aug. 12, 1909; s. Henry Northrop and Meta Augusta (Koch) S.; B.A., U. Minn., 1932; J.D., 1934; m. Anne Elizabeth Duncan, Sept. 12, 1936; children—Pennell Somsen Huhn, Stephen Duncan. Admitted to Minn. bar, 1934; practiced in New Ulm, 1934—, mem. firms Somsen, Dempsey, Johnson & Somsen, 1934-40, Somsen & Dempsey, 1940-46, Somsen & Somsen, 1946-55, Somsen & Dempsey, 1964-71, Somsen, Dempsey & Schade, 1971—; adminstrv. asst. U.S. Senator Joseph H. Ball, 1940-43; dir. New Ulm Industries, Inc., 1952—, pres., 1968-77; dir. Am. Artstone Co., 1955—, v.p., 1965—; dir. Farmers & Mchts. State Bank of New Ulm, 1954—, v.p., 1970—; dir. Cottonwood Land Co., 1955—, pres. 1970—; dir. State Bond & Mortgage Co., State Bank of Klossner, Minn., Forest Hills, Inc., State Bond & Mortgage Life Ins. Co. Pres., New Ulm Community Concert Assn., 1947—, New Ulm Industries Found., 1968—; nat. committeeman Young Reps., 1936, 40, regional dir., 1936; vice chmn. Rep. State Central com., 1936; sec. Young Rep. Nat. Fedn., 1936; trustee Minn. Parks Found., 1967—, Episcopal Diocese of Minn., 1975—, Shattuck Sch., 1971-72; bd. dirs. Minn. Council of State Parks, 1956—, pres., 1973-74; bd. dirs. New Ulm Meml. Found., 1958—, Union Hosp., 1959-77, Highland Homes, Inc., 1970—. Served to capt. AUS, 1943-46. Named Paul Harris fellow Rotary Found., 1971. Mem. Am. Arbitration Assn. (panel of arbitrators 1967—), U. Minn. Alumni Assn. (dir. 1970-73), Ninth Jud. Dist. Bar Assn. (pres. 1951), C. of C. (dir. 1947-49, 58-61), Nat. Collegiate Players, Psi Upsilon, Phi Delta Phi. Episcopalian (sr. warden 1960-61). Clubs: Masons, Mpls. Athletic; Mpls.; New Ulm Country. Bd. editors Minn. Law Rev., 1932-33. Home: 20 Camelsback Rd New Ulm MN 56073 Office: State Bond Bldg New Ulm MN 56073

SONDEREGGER, JOHN FORSTER, chem. co. exec.; b. Chgo., July 3, 1931; s. Hans H. and Edith M. (Aagaard) S.; student Ill. Inst. Tech., 1949-50; B.S. in Bus. Adminstrn., Drake U., 1957; m. Beatrice E. Morris, June 22, 1957; children—David A., Stephen M. Auditor Arthur Young & Co., Chgo., 1957-59; v.p., controller Internat. Minerals & Chem. Corp., Libertyville, Ill., 1959—. Mem. functional unit camps and confs. Chgo. Presbytery. Served with USMCR, 1952-54. C.P.A., Ill. Mem. Am. Inst. C.P.A.'s, Ill. Soc. C.P.A.'s, Fin. Execs. Inst., Beta Gamma Sigma, Alpha Kappa Psi (chpt. pres. 1955-56). Presbyterian (elder 1971—). Home: 422 E Maude St Arlington Heights IL 60004 Office: IMC Plaza Libertyville IL 60048

SONE, MIGUEL ANGEL, JR., pharm. co. exec.; b. Distrito Federal, Mexico, Sept. 2, 1925; s. Miguel Angel and Francisca Sone (Ruizadame) Sone; B.S., Universidad Nacional Autonoma de Mexico, 1943, M.S., 1944; m. Guadalupe Gomez, July 13, 1963; 1 son, Maurice Albert. Quality control supr. Continental Can Co., Chgo., 1955-59; sr. quality engr. ITT Kellogg, Chgo., 1960-61; quality control gen. foreman Chgo. Rawhide Co., 1961-62; mgr. quality control Grayhill, Inc., LaGrange, Ill., 1962-73; program mgr. quality assurance info. systems Abbott Labs., North Chicago, Ill., 1973-77; dir. quality assurance Searle Diagnostics Inc., Des Plaines, Ill., 1977—. Mem. adv. bd. Cyrus H. McCormick Sch., pres., 1972-74; del. Dist. 19 Chgo. Bd. Edn., 1972-74, mem. adv. council bilingual edn., 1973-75. Served with AUS, 1944-46. Mem. Am. Soc. Quality Control (Joe List award, 1973), Chgo. Chamber of Commerce and Industry. Home: 2843 Troy St S Chicago IL 60623 Office: 200 Nuclear Dr Des Plaines IL 60018

SONG, JOSEPH, physician; b. Pyong Yang, Korea, May 11, 1927; s. Ha Chu and Wha Soon (Koh) S.; came to U.S., 1952; M.D., Seoul Nat. U., Korea, 1950; M.S., U. Tenn., 1956; M.D., U. Ark., 1965; m. Kumsan Ryu, Apr. 12, 1958; children—Patricia, Michael, Jeff. Intern, John Gaston Hosp., Memphis, 1952-53; resident U. Tenn. Inst. Pathology, Memphis, 1953-56; pathologist-in-charge State Cancer Project, R.I., 1956-59; asso. pathologist Providence (R.I.) Lying-In Hosp., 1959-61; asso. prof. pathology U. Ark., Little Rock, 1961-64; chief pathologist Mercy Hosp., Des Moines, 1965—; clin. prof. pathology Creighton U. Sch. Medicine, Omaha, 1969. Bd. dirs. Community Blood Bank, Des Moines. Recipient Martin Luther King Med. Achievement award SCLC, 1972. Fellow A.C.P.; mem. Am. Assn. Pathologists and Bacteriologists, Am. Soc. Clin. Pathologists, Coll. Am. Pathologists, Am. Cytology Soc., Am. Assn. for Cancer Research. Clubs: Des Moines, Des Moines Gold and Country. Author: The Human Uterus, 1964; Pathology of Sickle Cell Disease, 1971; Circulating Cancer Cells, 1975. Home: 7208 Benton Dr Des Moines IA 50322 Office: 6th and University Des Moines IA 50314

SONGER, HERBERT LEE, JR., ednl. adminstr.; b. Little Rock, Apr. 9, 1943; s. Herbert L. and Eva May (Phipps) S.; B.S., Ft. Hays (Kans.) State U., 1966, M.S., 1970; m. Sheryl Lynn S., Mar. 27, 1967; 1 dau., Jennifer Lynn. Counselor, instr. Ft. Hays U., 1970-71; dir. counseling Marymount Coll., Salina, Kans., 1971-75, dean students, 1976—; exec. dir. Salina Drug Council, 1971; bd. dirs. Kans. ACT Program, 1976—. Bd. dirs. Salina Youth Care Home, 1972—. Served with U.S. Army, 1966-68. Mem. Kans. Psychol. Assn., Am., Kans. personnel and guidance assns., Nat., Kans. assns. student personnel, Phi Delta Kappa, Phi Chi. Presbyterian. Clubs: Lions, Elks. Home: 803 Pentwood Dr Salina KS 67401 Office: Marymount Coll E Iron and Marymount Rd Salina KS 67401

SONNINO, CARLO BENVENUTO, mfg. co. exec.; b. Torino, Italy, May 12, 1904; s. Moise and Amelia S.; Ph.D., U. Milano (Italy), 1927, LL.B., 1928; m. Mathilde Girodat, Jan. 21, 1949; children—Patricia, Frederic, Bruno. Dir. research Italian Aluminum Co., Milan, 1928-34; pres. Laesa Cons. Firm, Milano, 1934-43; tech. adviser Boxal, Fribourg, Switzerland, 1944-52, Thompson Brand, Rouen, France, 1972-76; materials engring. mgr. Emerson Electric Co., St. Louis, 1956-72; prof. metall. engring. Washington U., St. Louis, 1960-68, U. Mo. at Rolla, 1968—; cons. Monsanto Chem. Co., other major firms U.S., Europe. Decorated knight comdr. Italian Republic. Fellow Am. Soc. Metals, ASTM (hon.), Alpha Sigma Mu. Patentee process for synthetic cryolite; mfr. 1st aluminum cans in world, 1940; patentee in field metallury corrosion. Home: 7206 Kingsbury Blvd Saint Louis MO 63130 Office: Emerson E and S div Emerson Electric Co 8100 W Florissant St Saint Louis MO 63136

SONS, LESTER GEORGE, newspaper exec.; b. Harvey, Ill., June 7, 1931; s. William Henry and Gladys Lydia (Steinko) S.; B.A., U. Mich., 1954; student No. Ill. U., 1975-77; m. Meya H. Arosemena, Aug. 19, 1961. Reporter, S. Bend (Ind.) Tribune, 1956-57; with Chgo. Heights (Ill.) Star Publs., 1957—, editor, 1974-75, exec. editor, 1975—. Served with AUS, 1954-56. Recipient various profl. awards Nat., No. Ill. Newspaper assns., Ill. Press Assn. Mem. U. Mich. Alumni Assn., Sigma Delta Chi, Kappa Tau Alpha. Club: Chgo. Headline. Roman Catholic. Contbr. to instructional textbooks. Home: 17806 Larkspur Ln Homewood IL 60430 Office: 1526 Otto Blvd Chicago Heights IL 60411

SOOD, JAGDISH CHAND, elec. engr.; b. Amritsar, India, June 30, 1942; s. Fateh Chand and Indra S.; m. Suman Mohindra, Aug. 30, 1970; children—Serena, Neeta, Jiten; came to U.S., 1969, naturalized, 1974; B.E.E., Jadavpur U. India, 1968; M.S. in Indsl. Engring., Ill. Inst. Tech., 1973, M.B.A., 1976. Registered profl. engr., Ill. Sectional officer elec. Central Pub. Works Dept., Govt. of India, Nagpur, 1963-64, Calcutta, 1964-68; asst. lectr. Kenya Poly. Inst., Nairobi, 1969; plant engr. Western Electric Co., Chgo., 1969—. Mem. IEEE. Office: Western Electric Co Hawthorne Works Dept 4931 Chicago IL 60623

SOOD, MANMOHAN KUMAR, educator; b. Manpur Nagaria, India, Apr. 17, 1941; s. Prem Nath and Gunvanti (Sood) S.; came to U.S., 1970; B.Sc., Panjab U., India, 1960, B.Sc., 1961, M.Sc., 1963; M.Sc., U. Western Ont., Can., 1968, Ph.D., 1969; m. Joginder Kaur, 1965; children—Sanjay, Rishi. Tech. asst. Dept. Industries, Chandigarh, India, 1963-64; research asso. U. Western Ont., Can., 1969-70, sec. India-Can. Student Assn., 1966-68; asst. prof. dept. earth sci. Northeastern Ill. U., Chgo., 1970-73, asso. prof., 1973—, chmn. dept., 1974—. Commonwealth Edison grantee, Northeastern Ill. U. grantee, 1973. Mem. AAAS, Internat. Assn. Advancement Earth and Environ. Scis. (founding sec. 1972-75, editor Environ. Resource 1973-74), Indian Geologists Assn. (fgn. corr.). Contbr. articles to sci. lit.

SOORYA, NARENDIR TOLARAM, psychiatrist; b. Karachi, Pakistan, May 10, 1939; s. Tolaram Khemchand and Savitri S.; came to U.S., 1964, naturalized, 1976; I.Sc. certificate D.J. Sci. Coll., 1958; M.D., Dow Med. Coll., Karachi, 1964; m. Sarla Rangwani, July 16, 1967; children—Geeta, Nitin, Sandeep. Intern, Deaconess Hosp., St. Louis, 1965-68; staff psychiatrist Central State Hosp., Milledgeville, Ga., 1968-71; child psychiatrist Washington U. program Malcolm Bliss Mental Health Center, St. Louis, 1971-72, instr. univ., 1973-74, child psychiatrist Malcolm Bliss Mental Health Center, 1973-74, asst. clin. dir. children's services, 1973-74, dir. tng. and research children's services, 1974—, also asst. clin. prof. St. Louis U. Sch. Medicine; mem. staff Luth. Med. Center, Deaconess Hosp. Diplomate Am. Bd. Psychiatry and Neurology in Adult and Child Psychiatry. Mem. Am., Eastern Mo. psychiat. socs., St. Louis Med. Soc. Office: 6651 Chippewa St Saint Louis MO 63109

SOPHER, MERVYN DAVID, internist; b. Calcutta, India, Feb. 3, 1921; s. David Abraham and Grace (Elisa) S.; came to U.S., 1957; naturalized, 1962; M.D., Calcutta Med. Coll., 1944; m. Doris Marcuson, June 14, 1959; children—Deborah, Elizabeth. Intern, Montagu Hosp., Mexborough, Eng., 1949-51, resident, 1951-57, Mt. Sinai Hosp., Cleve., 1957-59; practice medicine specializing in internal medicine, 1959—; mem. staffs Sunny Acres, Highland View, Mt. Sinai, Suburban hosps., Cleve.; asst. clin. prof. medicine Case Western Res. U., 1973. Served with Indian Army, 1944-47. Diplomate Am. Bd. Internal Medicine. Fellow Royal Soc. Medicine, Cleve. Chest Soc., Ohio Thoracic Soc.; mem. AMA, Cleve. Acad. Medicine, Ohio State Med. Assn., Am. Assn. History of Medicine. Democrat. Jewish. Home: 3339 Norwood Rd Shaker Heights OH 44122 Office: 2460 Fairmount Blvd Cleveland Heights OH 44106

SOPKO, THOMAS CLEMENT, lawyer; b. Warren, Ohio, Mar. 21, 1945; s. Clement R. and Mary M. (Sroka) S.; B.S. in History, Xavier (Ohio) U., 1967; J.D. (univ. scholar), U. Notre Dame, 1970; m. Joyce Ann Deffenbaugh, Aug. 5, 1967; children—Amy Lynn, Kathleen Ann. Admitted to Ind. bar, 1970; since practiced in South Bend; asso. firm Edward N. Kalamaros & Assos., 1970-75; partner firm Hardig & Sopko, South Bend, 1975—; dep. pros. atty. St. Joseph County (Ind.), 1976-77; atty. Town of Osceola (Ind.), 1976—. Chmn. profl. div. United Way of St. Joseph County; bd. dirs. St. Joseph County unit Am. Cancer Soc. Served to capt. AUS, 1971. Mem. Am., Ind., St. Joseph County bar assns., Notre Dame Quarterback Club, Notre Dame Alumni Club, Phi Alpha Theta. Home: 15585 Winding Brook Dr Mishawaka IN 46544 Office: 419 W Jefferson St South Bend IN 46601

SOPKOVICH, NICHOLAS JOSEPH, dentist; b. Youngstown, Ohio, June 1, 1909; s. Joseph B. and Anna M. (Duritza) S.; B.S., U. Pitts., 1932, D.D.S., 1932; m. Catherine Brincko, July 18, 1936; children—Nicholas, Joann Sopkovich Zgonc, Thomas. Asst. instr. oral surgery Georgetown U. Dental Sch., Washington, 1933; practice gen. dentistry, Farrell, Pa., 1933-34, Youngstown, 1934—; dentist Youngstown Parochial Schs., 1945-47; pres. dental staff St. Elizabeth Hosp., 1951-54. Mem. Am. (del. 1965-66), Ohio (del. 1952-73) dental assns., Corydon Palmer, Pierre Fauchard dental socs., Fedn. Dentaire Internationale, Internat. Coll. Dentists, Greek Catholic Union, Delta Sigma Delta (life). Byzantine Cath. (chmn. bldg. campaign). Clubs: Elks (life), K.C. (4th deg.), Kiwanis (past v.p. Canfield), U. Pitts. Mahoning Valley. Home: 4372 Raccoon Rd Canfield OH 44406 Office: 502 Home Savs & Loan Bldg Youngstown OH 44503

SOPO, ROBERT WILLIAM, church music dir.; b. London, Ont., Can., July 7, 1951; s. Charles William and Margaret S.; B.A., U. Western Ont., 1976, Asso. Music, 1972. Church organist London (Ont.) Seventh-Day Adventist Ch., 1973; pvt. instr. music. Mem. Royal Canadian Coll. Organists, Ont. Registered Music Tchrs. Assn., Internat. Harpsichord Soc., Choristers Guild, Canadian, Ont. psychol. assns., AAAS, Hymn Soc. Am., Canadian Assn. Music Therapy. Recorded: The Heaven's Are Telling, 1973. Home: 2101 1570 Adelaide St N London ON N5X 2L7 Canada

SORAH, BAXTER LEE, JR., labor union exec.; b. Lee County, Va., June 9, 1920; s. Baxter Lee and Laura Mae (Tignor) S.; degree McClungs' Bus. Coll., Greensboro, N.C., 1942; postgrad. Detroit Inst. Tech., 1950-52; certificate trade union program Harvard U., 1949; m. Eunice G. Gabel, Aug. 19, 1944; children—Sandra, Terry, Janice, Dian, Margaret, Charles, John Scott. Trackman, So. Ry. System, St. Charles, Va., 1940; chief clk.-organizer So. System div. Brotherhood Maintenance of Way Employees, Greensboro, 1940-47, administrtv. asst to pres. Grand Lodge, 1948-70, internat. sec.-treas., 1970—; mem. R.R. Retirement Bd., 1970—; treas. Maintenance of Way Polit. League, 1970—. Served as flight officer USAF, 1942-45; PTO. Decorated Bronze Star. Mem. AFL-CIO Sec.-Treas.'s Assn. Club: Lions. Office: 12050 Woodward St Detroit MI 48203

SORELL, VICTOR ALEXANDER, art historian; b. Mexico City, Mexico, Oct. 31, 1944; s. Adi Agathon and Dora Elsa (Wassermann) S.; naturalized, 1972; B.A., Shimer Coll., 1966; M.A., U. Chgo., 1969, postgrad, 1970—; m. Aida Nasarita Guzman, June 25, 1976. Tchr., mil. instr. Jr. Mil Acad., Chgo., 1968-69; art historian, dept. art Chgo. State U., 1969—, chmn. dept. art, 1975—; tchr. Beverly Art Center, Chgo., 1977—; mem. adv. bd. Chgo. Mural Group; program adminstr. Park Forest (Ill.) Art Center, 1978—; Mayoral appointee Chgo. Council Fine Arts, 1976—. Served with Canadian Army, 1960-63. Ill. Humanities Council grantee, 1976; Internat. Design Conf., Aspen faculty fellow, 1975. Mem. Coll. Art Assn. Am., Midwest Art History Soc., Nat. Soc. Lit. and Arts, Am. Crafts Council, Am. Studies Assn. (membership chmn. local chpt. 1975), Am., Brit. socs. aesthetics. Co-editor Abrazo, MARCH jour., 1976—; Office: Dept Art Chicago State Univ Chicago IL 60628

SORENSEN, MOURITS AXEL, psychologist; b. Bemidji, Minn., July 8, 1921; s. Valdemar Axel and Anna (Rygg) S.; B.S., Bemidji State Coll., 1949; M.A., Washington U., St. Louis, 1951; Ed.D., U. N.D., 1964; m. Catherine Ann Heatherman, Feb. 3, 1973; children—Mourits Alan, Soren Christian, Sanna Mourita. Pub. sch. tchr., Minn., N.D., 1949-60; faculty No. Ill. U., DeKalb, 1960-67; psychologist Upper Miss. Mental Health Center, Inc., Bemidji, 1967—. Chmn., N.W. (Minn.) Developmental Disabilities Council, Bemidji, 1973-74; mem. adv. bd. Brainerd State Hosp., 1973—. Served with USAAF, 1940-46. Decorated D.F.C. Mem. Am. Psychol. Assn., Am. Assn. for Mental Deficiency. Club: Elks. Contbr. articles to profl. jours. Home: Route 5 Box 197-B Bemidji MN 56601 Office: 722 15th St PO Box 646 Bemidji MN 56601

SORENSEN, PETER FENSHOLT, JR., educator; b. Chgo., Oct. 11, 1933; s. Peter Fensholt and Ellen (Fensholt) S.; B.A., Roosevelt U., 1958, M.A., 1961; Ph.D. (fellow 1968-69), Ill. Inst. Tech., 1971; m. Nancy Evans, Nov. 2, 1963. Asst. dir. orgnl. analysis Continental Casualty Co., Chgo., 1960-64; adminstr. research and devel. Continental Nat. Am. Group, Chgo., 1964-66; dir. grad. studies adminstrn. and orgnl. behavior George Williams Coll., Downers Grove, Ill., 1968—. Served with AUS, 1955-57. Mem. Acad. Mgmt., Am., Ill., Midwest sociol. assns., Indsl. Relations Research Assn., AAUP. Contbr. articles to profl. jours. Author: Perspectives on Organization Behavior, 1973, 2d edit., 1974; Intervention: The Management Use of Organizational Research, 1975. Home: 1053 W Ogden Ave Apt 342 Naperville IL 60540 Office: 555 31st St Downers Grove IL 60515

SORENSON, MARION WESLEY, educator; b. Salt Lake City, Dec. 29, 1926; s. Marion Wesley and Louise (Davis) S.; B.S. with honors, U. Utah, 1959, M.S., 1960; Ph.D., U. Mo., 1964; m. Simone Rachel Chatelanat, Nov. 18, 1948; children—Chantal, Michael, Cindy (Mrs. Dwight Sutherland). Asst. prof. zoology U. Mo., 1964-70; asso. prof. biol. scis. U. Mo., Columbia, 1970—. Served with AUS, 1945-46. Mem. Am. Soc. Mammalogists, Ecol. Soc. Am., Am. Mus. Natural History, Am. Inst. Biol. Scis., AAAS, Am. Assn. Zoologists, Animal Behavior Soc., Sigma Xi. Home: RFD 1 Columbia MO 65201

SORENSON, PAUL MORRIS, farmer, farm orgn. exec.; b. Kennedy, Minn., Feb. 12, 1912; s. Olof Nels and Anna (Helseth) S.; grad. N.W. Sch. Agr., 1932; m. Dorothy Marie McIlraith, Apr. 18, 1936; children—Janice Sorenson Stroom, Alice Sorenson Sedenquist, Betty Sorenson Treumer, Paula. Farmer, Hallock, 1930—; pres.; mem. Kittson County Agr. Soc., 1950—. Chmn. bd. supr. Thompson Twp. Kittson County; bd. dirs. Kittson County Meml. Hosp. Recipient Valley Farmer and Homemaker award Red River Valley Winter Show, Crookston, Minn., 1967. Mem. Kittson County (dir.), Minn. crop improvement assns., Kittson County Twp. Officers Assn. (dir., pres.), Internat. Platform Assn. Lutheran (deacon 1941-48). Clubs: Masons, Shriners, Lions (pres. 1965-66). Address: Hallock MN 56728

SORET, MANUEL GONZALEZ, pathologist; b. Havana, Cuba, Oct. 15, 1914; s. Manuel A. and Luscinda (Soret) G.; D.V.M., U. Havana, 1939; m. Virginia Ledesma, Dec. 9, 1940; children—Manuel, Virginia (Mrs. E.T. Rowland). Dir. biol. labs., Havana, 1940-46; asst. prof. vet. pathology and immunology U. Havana, 1946-49; asst. v.p. vet. sci. U. Miami (Fla.), 1949-50, asso. prof., 1950-52, research asso. prof., 1952-59; research virologist Upjohn Co., Kalamazoo, 1959-69, pathologist, 1970—. Dir. Mani Soret Chevrolet, Decatur, Mich., K. Woodworth Chevrolet, Union City, Mich. Recipient Carlos Finlay medal, 1952. Mem. Internat. Acad. Pathology, Nat. Registry Microbiologists, N.Y. Acad. Scis., Am. Soc. Microbiology, Electron Microscopy Soc. Am. Home: 1826 Charter St Kalamazoo MI 49002 Office: 301 Henrietta St Kalamazoo MI 49001

SORGE, JAY WOOTTEN, lawyer; b. Detroit, July 27, 1917; s. Ervin H. and Harriet Louise (Wootten) S.; student Washington and Lee U., 1935-36; A.B., U. Mich., 1940, J.D. (editorial staff law rev.), 1942; m. Mary Jane Peterson, June 19, 1943; children—Jay Wootten, Susan Jane Sorge Anderson, David E. Admitted to Mich. bar, 1942, since practiced in Detroit; partner firm Hill, Lewis, Adams, Goodrich & Tait, 1953—; lectr. corp. law Wayne State U., 1954-55; dir. Karnut Products Co.; sec., dir. Squirt-Detroit Bottling Co., Charles A. Parcells & Co., Huron City Co.; v.p., sec., dir. Georgian Ct. Am., Inc., Vitality Unltd., Inc. Pres., Friends of Grosse Pointe Pub. Library, 1954-56; sec. William Lyon Phelps Found., 1947—; trustee Fund for Henry Ford Hosp. Served to lt. USCGR, 1942-45. Mem. Am., Mich., Detroit bar assns., State Bar Mich. (chmn. corp. com. 1954-56), Mich. Law Sch. Lawyers Club. Republican. Episcopalian. Clubs: Detroit, Renaissance, Country (Detroit). Home: 88 Touraine Rd Grosse Pointe Farms MI 48236 Office: 100 Tower Renaissance Center Suite 3200 Detroit MI 48243

SORIANO, DANILO BUENAFLOR, neurosurgeon; b. Manila, P.I., May 15, 1938; s. Restituto F. and Leonisa (Buenaflor) S.; B.S., U. Phillippines, 1957, M.D., 1962; m. Lydianila S. San Pedro, Sept. 5, 1964; children—Brian, Perry, Jennifer. Intern, St. Francis Hosp., Pitts., 1962-63; teaching fellow, resident in neurosurgery U. Pitts., 1964-66; asst. instr. neoranatomy Albert Einstein Coll. Medicine, 1966-67, neurosurgery, 1968-69, instr. neurosurgery, 1969-70; chief of neurosurgery Queens Hosp. Center, N.Y., 1970-73; asst. prof. neurosurgery State U. N.Y., Stony Brook, 1972; asst. prof. neurosurgery Rush Med. Coll., Chgo., 1976—; chief of neurosurgery Hempstead Gen. Hosp., 1972-74; cons. neurosurgeon Palos Community, Holy Cross, Central Community, Christ hosps. Recipient William C. Menninger award; NIH research fellow. Diplomate Am. Bd. Neurosurgery. Fellow A.C.S.; mem. Am. Assn. Neurol. Surgeons, Congress Neurol. Surgeons, Internat. Coll. Surgeons, AMA, Chgo.,

Ill. med. socs., Central Neurosurg. Soc., Soc. Functional Neurosurgery, Mensa, U.S. Chess Fedn., Phi Kappa Phi, Phi Sigma. Republican. Roman Catholic. Contbr. articles profl. jours. Research on spinal cord physiology, spasticity, pain. Composer: I Endure (Voice and Piano), 1960; Silangan Quartet (2 Violins, Viola, Cello), 1976. 1st violinist S.W. Symphony Orch.; mem. Chamber Music Players. Office: 10522 S Cicero St Oak Lawn IL 60453

SORKIN, ALEX, optometrist; b. Chgo., Aug. 6, 1937; s. Sidney and Nettie (Horwitz) S.; B.S., Ill. Coll. Optometry, 1963, Dr. Optometry, 1964. Mem. faculty Ill. Coll. Optometry, 1964-66; gen. practice optometry, Chgo., 1964-66, Champaign, Ill., 1972—; researcher and lectr. contact lens design and fitting; supr. research clinic Wesley-Jessen, Inc., Chgo., 1969-72; attending staff dept. ophthalmology Cook County Hosp., Chgo., 1971-72; optometry officer med. service corps U.S. Army, U.S. Army Hosp., Nurnberg, Bavaria, Germany, 1966-68. Judge Chgo. Pub. Schs. Sci. Fair, 1965, 66; classical music annotator Sta. WTWC-FM, 1973—. Chmn. sect. on eye photography Nat. Eye Research Found., 1969-72, traveling lectr., 1969—, vice chmn. sect. keratoscopy, 1973—; bd. dirs. Cancer Co-op., 1977—. Mem. Am., Ill. optometric assns. Contbr. articles to profl. jours. Home: 1210 W Union St Champaign IL 61820 Office: 605 S Wright St Champaign IL 61820

SOROKAC, JOSEPH ANTHONY, psychologist; b. Wilkes-Barre, Pa., May 21, 1940; s. Joseph Anthony and Anna (Vasilko) S.; B.S., Villanova U., 1963; M.A., U. Detroit, 1965; postgrad. Wayne State U., 1967-68; m. Cheri Lynn Sado, July 12, 1969; 1 dau., Elizabeth Marie. Teaching fellow U. Detroit, 1963-65; clin. psychologist Wayne County Gen. Hosp., Eloise, Mich., 1965-77, Met. Regional Psychiat. Hosp., Eloise, 1977—; lectr. social sci. Lawrence Inst. Tech., Southfield, Mich., 1972-75; instr. psychology U. Windsor (Ont., Can.), 1969-70, Henry Ford Community Coll., Dearborn, Mich., 1976—; part time teaching Wayne County Community Coll., Providence Hosp. Sch. Nursing, Oakland Community Coll., Marygrove Coll., 1971-73; vocat. rehab. tester State of Mich., Livonia, 1972-76; vol. abstractor Psychol. Abstracts, 1971—. Mem. Am. (asso.), Midwestern (asso.), Mich. psychol. assns., Sociedad Interamericana de Psicologia. Roman Catholic. Home: 30109 Lyndon Ave Livonia MI 48154 Office: Met Regional Psychiat Hosp Eloise MI 48132

SORRELL, ROY WAYNE, health care co. exec.; b. Hancock County, Ind., July 21, 1938; s. Roy Herman and Carrie Bell (Florence) S.; B.S.B.A., Ball State U., 1963; postgrad. Hillsdale Coll., 1969; m. Barbara Ann Malik, July 31, 1965; children—Suzanne Marie, Roy Wayne, Jeanette Christine. Accountant, Dana Corp., Marion, Ind., 1963, corp. finance supr., Toledo, 1963-71; founder, chmn. bd., pres., dir. Professionnel, Inc., Toledo, 1971—. Served with USN, 1956-59. Mem. Nat. Fedn. Ind. Bus., Nat. Small Bus. Assn., Nat. C. of C., Soc. For Preservation, Encouragement of Barbershop Quartet Singing Am. (Outstanding Achievement award 1976, v.p. 1977-78, dir. 1976-79). Republican. Roman Catholic. Home: 5223 Bridlington Dr Toledo OH 43623 Office: 2926 Republic Blvd S Toledo OH 43615

SOTER, CONTANTINE SOTIRIOS, radiologist; b. Rachova, Greece, June 30, 1922; s. Sotirios K. and Evangeline (Angeletopoulos) Soteropoulos; came to U.S., 1952, naturalized, 1956; M.D., U. Athens (Greece), 1948; m. Constance Trampas, May 2, 1954; children—Susan, Desirée. Intern, Ill. Masonic Hosp., Chgo., 1952-53, resident in radiology, 1953-56; mem. staff Ill. Masonic Hosp.; chmn. dept. radiology and nuclear medicine NW Community Hosp., Arlington Heights, Ill.; pres. O'Hare Indsl. Clinic. Mem. councilor bd. St. John the Baptist Greek Orthodox Ch., Des Plaines, Ill. Served with Nat. Greek. Army, 1948-51. Diplomate Am. Bd. Radiology, Am. Bd. Nuclear Medicine, Fellow Am. Coll. Radiology; mem. AMA, Radiol. Soc. N.Am., Soc. Nuclear Medicine, Chgo. Radiol. Soc. (sec., pres.-elect), Chgo., Ill. med. socs., Hellenic Med. Soc. (pres. Chgo. chpt.). Contbr. articles on radiology to med. jours. Home: 3455 Whirlaway Dr Northbrook IL 60062 Office: 800 W Central Rd Arlington Heights IL 60005

SOTEROPULOS, GUST STEVE, project engr.; b. Ottumwa, Iowa, May 6, 1923; s. Steve and Elaine (Patratos) S.; B.S., Iowa State U., 1945; postgrad. Cornell U., 1945; m. Vivian Pontikes, Nov. 4, 1950; children—Constance, Gust Dean. Engr., trainee Owens-Corning Fiberglas Corp., Kansas City, Mo., 1946-47; asst. chief engr. Ottumwa Iron Works, 1947-50; project engr. John Deere Ottumwa Works, 1951—. Served to ensign USNR, 1942-46. Recipient McGraw-Hill Master Design award, 1966, Design in Steel award, 1973. Mem. Am. Soc. Agrl. Engrs., Ottumwa C. of C., Sigma Phi Epsilon. Episcopalian (sr. warden). Mason. Club: Ottumwa Country (dir.). Home: 345 E Alta Vista Ottumwa IA 52501 Office: Vine St Ottumwa IA 52501

SOUBY, ARMAND MAX, JR., research project mgr.; b. Murfreesboro, Tenn., Jan. 12, 1917; s. Armand Max and Susan Isabel (Smith) S.; B.S. in Chem. Engring. summa cum laude, Vanderbilt U., 1938; m. Catherine Elizabeth Walters, Nov. 15, 1947; children—Susan Elizabeth, Anne Rose, Margaret Ruth, Myra Catherine. Research engr. Humble Oil & Refining Co., Baytown, Tex., 1939-58, research sect. head, 1959-64; research asso. Esso Research and Engring. Co., Baytown, 1965-71; mgr. lignite research project U. N.D., Grand Forks, 1972—. Registered profl. engr., Tex., N.D. Fellow AAAS, Am. Inst. Chemists; Mem. Am. Inst. Chem. Engrs., Am. Chem. Soc., N.D. Soc. Profl. Engrs., Tau Beta Pi, Phi Kappa Sigma. Democrat. Episcopalian. Elk, Rotarian. Contbr. articles to profl. jours. Patentee in field. Home: 1018 Shakespeare St Grand Forks ND 58201 Office: Box 8052 Univ Sta Grand Forks ND 58202

SOUBY, JAMES MARTIN, JR., assn. exec.; b. Kansas City, Mo., Oct. 17, 1916; s. James Martin and Bertha Elizabeth (Weitzel) S.; B.A. magna cum laude, Vanderbilt U., 1938; LL.B., Yale U., 1941; m. Lois Teresa Anderson, Dec. 3, 1942; children—Stephanie (Mrs. John Perry), James Martin III, Marietta, Charles. Admitted to Calif. bar, 1941; practiced in San Francisco, 1941-42; mem. firm McCutchen, Olney, Mannon & Greene; gen. atty., commerce counsel A., T. & S.F. Ry., Chgo., 1946-61; chmn., counsel Western Ry. Traffic Assn., Chgo., 1961-70; pres., chief exec. officer Western Railroad Assn., Chgo., 1970—; dir. Mercantile Nat. Bank, Chgo. Served to lt. USNR, 1942-46. Mem. Am. Bar Assn., Pacific (pres. 1950), Western (dir. 1974-75) ry. clubs, Am. Soc. Traffic & Transp., Nat. Def. Transp. Assn., Nat. Freight Traffic Assn., Transp. Assn. Am., ICC Practitioners Assn., Vanderbilt U. Alumni Assn. (dir. 1963-67), Sierra Club, Phi Beta Kappa, Phi Delta Theta, Omicron Delta Kappa. Clubs: Traffic, Union League, Chicago, Metropolitan; Exmoor Country (Highland Park, Ill.). Home: 1115 W Deerpath Rd Lake Forest IL 60045 Office: 222 S Riverside Plaza Chicago IL 60606

SOUCEK, DONALD HENRY, dentist; b. Cleve., Feb. 13, 1935; s. Henry J. and Margaret (Hajostek) S.; student John Carroll U., 1953-56; D.D.S., Case Western Res. U., 1960; m. Louise Rosalie Maxim, Aug. 30, 1958; children—Cynthia Ann, David Andrew, Sharon Lynn. Intern, Univ. Hosp., Cleve., 1960-61; practice dentistry, Parma, Ohio, 1961—; courtesy staff St. John's Hosp., Cleve., 1962—, St. Augustine Manor, Cleve., 1976—. Mem. ADA, Cleve., Ohio dental assns., Am. Dental Soc. Anesthesiology, Internat. Anesthesia Research Soc., Holy Name Soc., Delta Sigma Delta. Roman Catholic (usher). Club: K.C. Columnist newspaper Seven Hills News. Co-inventor Rendell-Baker Soucek Pediatric Anesthesia Masks. Home: 1580 Driftwood Dr Cleveland OH 44131 Office: 1834 Snow Rd Parma OH 44134

SOUDER, MARK EDWARD, retail furniture exec.; b. Ft. Wayne, Ind., July 18, 1950; s. Edward Getz and Irma (Fahling) S.; B.S., Ind. U., Ft. Wayne, 1972; M.B.A., U. Notre Dame, 1974; m. Diane Kay Zimmer, July 28; 1 dau., Brooke Diane. Mgmt. trainee Crossroads Furniture Co., Houston, 1974; mktg. mgr. Gabberts Furniture & Studio, Mpls., 1974-76; mktg. mgr., exec. v.p. Souder's Furniture & Studio, Grabill, Ind., 1976—; columnist Allen County Times. Publicity chmn. Grabill County Fair, 1977; chmn. Quayle for Congress Com., 2d Ward, Ft. Wayne, 1976; chmn. Allen County Win with Whitcomb Com., 1976. Mem. Midwest Home Furnishings Assn. (dir.), Ft. Wayne, Grabill (dir.) chambers commerce, Allen County Hist. Soc., Alumni Assn. Ind. U. at Ft. Wayne (dir.), Alumni Assn. U. Notre Dame, Am. Canal Soc., Young Americans for Freedom. Republican. Mem. Apostolic Christian Ch. Home: 13733 Ridgeview Ct Grabill IN 46741 Office: State at Main Grabill IN 46741

SOUDER, PAUL CLAYTON, banker; b. Greencastle, Ind., Dec. 2, 1920; s. Dewey C. and Julia (Dowell) S.; A.B., DePauw U., 1941; grad. Harvard Grad. Sch. Bus. Adminstrn., 1943, Grad. Sch. Banking, Rutgers U., 1951; m. Doris E. Elliott, Sept. 27, 1941; children—Douglas Paul, Julie Jan. Sr. v.p., dir. Comml. Credit Corp., 1941; credit mgr. Mich. Nat. Bank, 1946, asst. v.p., 1947-52, v.p. Saginaw bd. dirs., 1952-62, sr. v.p., dir., 1962-70, exec. v.p., 1970-72, pres., dir., 1972—; chmn. bd., dir. MNB-Valley, 1st Nat. Bank of East Lansing; dir. Auto-Owners Ins. Co., Wickes Corp., Mich. Nat. Bank, Mich. Nat. Corp., Detroit & Mackinac R.R. Co., Jameson Corp., Lake Huron Broadcasting Corp., Homeowners Mut. Ins. Co., Auto Owners Life Ins. Co., Owners Ins. Co., W.F. McNally Co., Inc. Trustee Mich. Wildlife Found., Mich. Week, Delta Wesley Found., Mich. State U. Devel. Fund; bd. dirs., v.p. Frank N. Anderson Found.; bd. dirs. Woldumar Nature Center; co-gen. chmn. devel. fund Saginaw Valley Coll.; mem. Lansing Bicentennial Exec. Com.; past dir. Saginaw Symphony Assn. Served from ensign to lt. comdr. USNR, 1942-46. Recipient Distinguished Service awards; named Saginaw's Outstanding Young Man. Mem. Robert Morris Assos., Am., Mich. bankers assns., Ind. Petroleum Assn. Am., Mich. Oil and Gas Assn., Greater Saginaw C. of C. (past dir.). Methodist. Clubs: Saginaw; Detroit Banker's, Economic (Detroit); Otsego Ski; Country of Lansing. Author: Financing Oil Production in Michigan, 1951. Home: 2800 Maurer Rd Charlotte MI 48813 Office: Mich Nat Bank Lansing MI 48904

SOUDERS, FLOYD RAYMOND, book pub. co. exec.; b. Cheney, Kans., Dec. 8, 1905; s. Linnaeus Rudolph and Iva May (Sears) S.; grad. Friends U., 1929, hon. degree, 1976; grad. Wichita State U., 1930; m. Norma Harriet Keith, Aug. 13, 1931. Tchr. Cheney High Sch., 1930-32; supt. schs., 1932-36, 39-41; editor-pub. Cheney (Kan.) Sentinel, 1941-71; farmer, nr. Cheney, 1924—. Mem. Kans. Ho. Reps., 1946-47; councilman City of Cheney, 1940-42; mem. Kans. Bd. Edn., 1952-57, 64-69; mem. Sedgwick County-Wichita Planning Commn., 1969-71, chmn., 1971; mem. Sedgwick County Sch. Planning Bd., 1961-64, chmn. bd., 1961-64; mem. South Central Kans. Health Planning and Econ. Devel. Bds. Bd. dirs. Friends U. Recipient various conservation awards; Alumni Recognition award Wichita State U., 1970. Mem. Kans. State Hist. Soc. (pres. in 1968), Native Sons and Daus. Kans., State Fair Assn. Republican. Methodist. Mason. Home: 128 N Marshall St Cheney KS 67025 Office: PO Box 527 Cheney KS 67025

SOUERS, LOREN EATON, lawyer; b. Canton, Ohio, Jan. 29, 1916; s. Loren Edmunds and Ilka (Gaskell) S.; A.B., Denison U., 1937; J.D., Case Western Res. U., 1940, postgrad., 1954-55; m. Mildred Mae McCollum, June 21, 1941; children—Sue Souers James, Loren. Admitted to Ohio bar, 1940, U.S. Supreme Ct. bar, 1960; asso. firm Black, McCuskey, Souers & Arbaugh, Canton, 1940—, partner, 1946—; dir. Continental Steel Corp., Kokomo, Ind., Harter Bank & Trust Co., Harter Ban Corp. Ind.; cons. Ohio Supreme Ct. Continuing Com. Admissions, 1957-59; mem. Ohio Bd. Bar Examiners, 1959-64; citizens adv. com. to State Library System, 1966-69. Pres., McKinley area council Boy Scouts Am., 1954-57, mem. exec. com. region IV, 1956-68, nat. council, 1954-71; mem. Canton City Council, 1948-49; del. Rep. Nat. Conv., 1948; Rep. city campaign mgr., 1951, 53; mem. Ohio Bd. Edn., 1956-60, v.p., 1958-60; mem. Canton City Bd. Edn., 1962-72, pres., 1965, 68, 71; mem. Canton Recreation Bd., 1964-72, Canton Planning Commn., 1972—; bd. mgrs. Canton YMCA, 1965—; trustee Stark County Law Library Assn., 1947-76, pres., 1972-76; trustee Canton Welfare Fedn., 1965-71, Denison U., 1967—, Ohio Bar Found., 1968-75; trust com. Hoover Found., North Canton, Ohio; mem. vis. com. Case Western Res. U. Law Sch., 1967-77. Served from pvt. to capt., inf., AUS, 1942-45; ETO. Decorated Fourragere (Belgium); recipient research prize in econs. Denison U., 1937, Distinguished Service award Canton Jaycees, 1950, Silver Beaver award Boy Scouts Am., 1957. Fellow Am. Bar Found.; mem. Am., Ohio (pres. jr. bar sect. 1947-48, exec. com. 1976—), Stark County (pres. 1965-66) bar assns., Am. Legion, Canton Jaycees (pres.), Canton C. of C. (v.p. 1959-60), Phi Delta Theta, Phi Delta Phi, Omicron Delta Kappa, Tau Kappa Alpha, Pi Delta Epsilon. Baptist (endowment com. Ohio Bapt. Conv. 1963-75). Clubs: Masons (32 deg.); The Canton; Brookside Country (Canton). Contbr. to profl. publs.; lectr. on legal subjects. Home: 135 19th St NW Canton OH 44709 Office: Harter Bank Bldg Canton OH 44702

SOUGHERS, RICHARD KEITH, veterinarian; b. Sullivan County, Ind., Jan. 27, 1934; s. Harry Archie and Donna (Gouckenour) S.; student Ind. State U., 1952-54, Ohio State U., 1954-55; D.V.M., Ohio State U., 1961; m. Peggy Sue Angleton, Nov. 14, 1954; children—K. Richard, Tara Kathleen. Practice vet. medicine and surgery, Mooresville, Ind., 1961—. Agrl. subcom. of Haiti Com., Episcopal Diocese of Indpls., 1972-76; vestryman, former jr. and sr. warden St. Mark's Episcopal Ch. Served with U.S. Army, 1954-57. Mem. Central Ind., Ind., Am. vet. med. assns., Phi Zeta. Democrat. Club: Elks. Home: 30 West St Mooresville IN 46158 Office: PO Box 171 Mooresville IN 46158

SOUKUP, ELOUISE MARILISS, assn. exec.; b. Hastings, Nebr., Oct. 15, 1926; d. Robert George and Gretchen Eloise (Guildner) Hoff; student U. So. Calif., 1945-48; B.A., U. Nebr., 1973; m. Leo Soukup, Jr., Mar. 22, 1948; children—Leo, Mariliss Suzanne Soukup Erickson. Bus. mgr., co-owner Leo Soukup Cleaners, Beatrice, Nebr., 1955—; controller C.D. Hoff, Inc., Hastings, Nebr., 1976—; curator edn. Nebr. State Hist. Soc., Lincoln, 1974-77. Vice chmn. Gage County Republican Party, 1964; bd. dirs. Beatrice (Nebr.) YWCA, 1965-67; bd. dirs. Nebr. Gov.'s Commn. Status of Women, 1977—. Mem. Am. Hist. Assn., Am. Soc. State and Local History, Nebr. Mus. Conf., Internat. Fabricore Inst., Nebr. Writers Guild, AAUW, DAR, Pi Alpha Theta. Home: Route 2 Beatrice NE 68310 Office: 517 W 2d St Hastings NE 68901

SOUKUP, JOHN, ret. physician and surgeon; b. Chicago, Ill., Dec. 29, 1900; s. Anthony M. and Rosa (Vanecek) S.; B.S., Northwestern, 1924, M.D., 1925; m. Rowena Drake, June 20, 1925 (dec. 1950);children—John, Robert; m. 2d, Theresa Isherwood, Sept. 15, 1951. Intern Roseland Community Hosp., 1924-25. Chgo. Lying-in Hosp., 1926; instr., Northwestern U., 1927-37; chmn. dept. obstetrics Roseland Community Hosp., Chgo., 1937-64, chief of staff, 1961-63, consulting staff, now emeritus staff; mem. staff VA Hosp., Marion, Ill., 1973-76. Diplomate Am. Bd. Obstetrics and Gynecology. Mem. Chgo. Gynecol. Soc. Presbyterian. Elk, Kiwanian. Club: Porcupine. Home: Apt I-4 Cambridge Manor Apts Herrin IL 62948

SOULAK, JOSEPH HAROLD, publishing co. exec.; b. Adams, Wis., Mar. 25, 1932; s. Harold Joseph and Mary I. (Turski) S.; A.B., Providence Coll., 1960; postgrad. Boston U., 1960, Roosevelt U., 1969; m. Leanora Galante, Sept. 1, 1956 (div. Oct. 1971); 1 dau., Deborah; m. 2d, Judith A. Sharpe, Oct. 1975. Sports editor Lakeland Pubs., Grayslake, Ill., 1960-62, news editor, 1962-64, mng. editor, 1964-65; news editor Pawtuxet Valley Times, West Warwick, R.I., 1964; mgr. pub. relations Bastian-Blessing Co., Chgo., 1966-68; publs. mgr. Ryerson Steel, Chgo., 1969; dir. news services Ency. Brit., Inc., Chgo., 1969-75; pub., editor South Milw. Voice-Jour., Cudahy Free-Press, Suburbanite (all South Milw.), 1975—; editor PR/Chicago, 1969-75; sec. Wis. Spectacle of Music, Inc.; mem. Wis. Jr. Miss, Inc.; columnist, writer Waukegan (Ill.) News Sun, 1969-75. Mem. Lake County Safety Commn., 1961-65; mgr. pub. relations for Ill. Senator, 1964-75. Served with USN, 1952-56; Korea. Mem. Pub. Relations Soc. Am., S. Milw. Assn. Commerce (dir., pres. 1976—); Chgo. Press Club. Home: 1332 Manitoba South Milwaukee WI 53172 Office: 723 Milwaukee Ave South Milwaukee WI 53179

SOULE, EDWARD BENNETT, lawyer, council exec.; b. Kansas City, Kans., Nov. 1, 1940; s. Howard Stewart and Olive Louise (Bennett) S.; A.B., Washburn U., 1962, J.D., 1965; m. Judith Elnora Stuenkel, June 5, 1965; children—Steven Edward, Sharon Elizabeth. Admitted to Kans. bar, 1965; practiced in Topeka, 1965-74; exec. dir. Kans. Council on Crime and Delinquency, Topeka, 1974—. Instr. polit. sci. Washburn U., Topeka, 1964—; instr. Clark's Sch. Bus., Topeka, 1967—. Pres. Topeka Family Service and Guidance Center, 1970-72, dir., 1967-72. Mem. Head Start Policy Council, Topeka, 1972-74; chmn. Topeka Recreation Commn., 1973. Served with AUS, 1967. Mem. Am., Topeka (sec. 1972-74) bar assns., Bar Assn. of State of Kans., Jayhawker Club (pres. 1970-71), Capitol Civitan Club (pres. 1969-70), Alpha Delta Alumni Assn. (dir. 1969-74), Delta Theta Phi. Conglist. (deacon). Contbr. articles to profl. jours. Home: 1824 W 27th St Topeka KS 66611 Office: 112 W 6th St Suite 509 Topeka KS 66603

SOULEN, ROBERT WILLIAM, architect; b. Milw., Dec. 20, 1925; s. Harry Beneverus and Margaret Sylvia (Augustyn) S.; B.Arch., U. Mich., 1950; certificate Am. Hosp. Assn. Inst. Hosp. Design, 1969; m. Margaret Ann Ehalt, Feb. 12, 1966; children—(by previous marriage) Richard, Michael, Carol. With Chas. W. Conklin, architect, 1950-51; supt. bldgs. and grounds Mansfield Tire & Rubber Co. (Ohio), 1951-53; asso. Herbert S. Jones, Mansfield, 1953-60, partner, 1960-63; sr. partner Soulen & Assos., Mansfield, 1963—; mem. Richland County Regional Planning Commn., 1963—, pres., 1971-72, chmn. zoning and subdiv. subcom., 1971-74. A founder Richland County Mus., 1965, co-curator, 1966-68; bd. dirs. Richland County Red Cross, 1967-69; mem. Christian Bus. Men's Com., 1974—, vice-chmn., 1977—. Mem. AIA, Architects Soc. Ohio, Ohio Geneal. Soc. (pres. 1964), Richland County Auto Club (dir. 1978—). Republican. Congregationalist (trustee 1962-69, deacon 1974-76, lay minister 1977—). Clubs: Rotary (pres. 1970-71, dist. exec. com. 1973—, dist. gov. 1975-76), Elks, U. Mich. Alumni (pres. 1958). Prin. archtl. works include Mansfield Gen. Hosp., The Geriatric Center, Farmers Savs. & Trust Co., Rehab. Center N. Central Ohio, Lumbermen's Mut. Ins. Co. Home Office. Home: 582 W Andover Rd PO Box 3634 Mansfield OH 44907 Office: 3 N Main St Mansfield OH 44902

SOURS, CALVIN DEAN, veterinarian; b. Marble Rock, Iowa, May 7, 1919; s. Clifton Eugene and Vera Mabel (Bower) S.; D.V.M., Iowa State U., 1941; m. Wanda Charlotte Cooper, Mar. 7, 1942; children—Carol Frances, Roy Cooper. Gen. practice veterinary medicine, Brooklyn, Iowa, 1941-42, Nora Springs, Iowa, 1943, 46-73, Rockford, Iowa, 1973—. Mem. Soldiers and Sailors Relief Commn., 1948-56; school bd. Nora Springs, 1948-51, councilman, Nora Springs, 1954-58; pres. N. Iowa Area Community Coll. Found., Mason City, 1970—. Served with Veterinary Corps, U.S. Army, 1943-46. Mem. Am., Upper Iowa (program chmn. 1956-57, sec., treas. 1958-59, pres. 1960-61), Iowa (meat inspection com., life membership award, 1976) veterinary med. assns. Republican. Club: Roclkford Country. Home: 502 Riverview Dr Rockford IA 50468 Office: 106 E Main St Rockford IA 50468

SOUTHALL, CAREY THOMAS, univ. adminstr.; b. Gainesville, Fla., Sept. 21, 1921; s. Carey Thomas and Fannie Mae (Pierce) S.; student U. Fla., 1941-43, B.S., 1948, M.A., 1950, Ed.D. (fellow 1953-55), 1955; student Duke U., 1943; m. Lola Jean Rose, July 8, 1948; children—Carole, Carey, Katherine. Social studies tchr. Gainesville (Fla.) High Sch., 1949-51; research asso. U. Fla., Gainesville, 1953-55; supr. student teaching East Tex. State Coll., Commerce, 1955-57; dir. secondary student teaching Tex. Tech., Lubbock, 1957-64; prof. edn., dir. edn. field experiences Coll. Edn., U. Mo., Columbia, 1964—. Served with USMC, 1943-46, USAF, 1951-53. U. Mo. faculty grantee, 1969, 70. Mem. Tex. Assn. Student Teaching (pres. 1961-62), Mo. Assn. Student Teaching (pres. 1965-66), Mo. State Tchrs. Assn., Phi Delta Kappa, Kappa Delta Pi. Contbr. articles to profl. jours. Home: 709 Bluff Dale Dr Columbia MO 65201

SOUTHERN, WALTER ARTHUR, lab. librarian; b. Milw., Apr. 30, 1919; s. Louis Walter and Ella Marie (Mockrud) S.; B.A., U. Wis., 1942; M.A., U. Mich., 1943; postgrad. U. Chgo.; grad. Indsl. Mgmt. Inst. of Lake Forest (Ill.) Coll., 1958. With Dearborn Chem. Co., 1948-49, U.S. Steel Corp., 1946-48, Engring. Socs. Library, 1945-46; mgr. info. services Abbott Labs., North Chicago, Ill., 1949—. Mem. adv. bd. Ill. State Library, 1953-58, John Crerar Library, Chgo., 1959-61. Fulbright fellow, London, 1953-54. Mem. Am. Soc. Info. Scis., Assn. Spl. Libraries Information Bur. (London), Med. Library Assn., Spl. Libraries Assn. Contbr. articles profl. jours. Home: 99 S Butrick St Waukegan IL 60085 Office: 1400 Sheridan Rd North Chicago IL 60064

SOUTHWELL, EUGENE ALLEN, psychologist; b. San Diego, Apr. 9, 1928; s. Daniel and Nora (Valleroy) S.; A.B., Coll. of Pacific, 1951; M.A., U. Iowa, 1961, Ph.D., 1961; m. Gloria J. Powers, Jan. 7, 1957; children—William Glen, Kim Marlene, Kirk Daniel. Asst. prof. psychology U. Chgo., 1961-64; asso. prof. psychology, chmn. dept. Ind. U., Gary, 1964—; dir. Southwell Inst., Olympia Fields, Ill., 1967—; practice clin. psychology, Olympia Fields, 1961—. Served with USAAF, 1945-47. Mem. Am., Midwest, Ill. psychol. assns., N.Y. Acad. Scis., Sigma Xi. Author: (with M. Merbaum) Personality: Readings in Theory and Research, 1964, 3d edit., 1978; (with H. Feldman) Abnormal Psychology; Readings in Theory and Research, 1969. Home: Park Forest IL 60466 Office: 2601 W Lincoln Hwy Olympia Fields IL 60461

SOVIK, EDWARD ANDERS, architect; b. Honan, China, June 9, 1918 (parents Am. citizens); s. Edward Anderson and Anna (Tenwick) S.; B.A., St. Olaf Coll., 1939; student Art Students League

N.Y., 1939-40, Luther Theol. Sem., 1940-42; B.Arch., Yale, 1949; m. Genevieve Elaine Hendrickson, June 29, 1946; children—Rolf, Martin, Peter. With Northfield Architects, Inc., 1949-53; pres Sovik, Mathre, Sathrum, Quanbeck Inc., and predecessor firms. Tchr. art St. Olaf Coll.; lectr. on ch. design at various confs., schs., univs. U.S. del. Internat. Conf. Church Bldg., Bossey, Switzerland, 1959; chmn. Interfaith Research Center; mem. steering com. Internat. Congresses on Religion and Architecture, N.Y.C., 1967, Brussels, Belgium, 1970, Jerusalem, 1973. Mem. com. ch. and culture Nat. Council Chs. in U.S.A. Bd. dirs. Liturg. Conf., 1969—, sec., 1969-71; pres. Interfaith Research Center; bd. dirs. Luth. Social Services Minn., 1962-68. Served to maj. USMCR, 1942-45; maj. Res. Decorated D.F.C., Purple Heart. Fellow AIA; mem. Guild for Religious Architecture (dir. 1961-71, past pres.), Minn. Soc. Architects (pres. 1977). Lutheran. Author: Architecture for Worship, 1973. Contbr. numerous articles to mags.; encys., anthologies. Patentee in furniture design. Former chmn. editorial bd. Faith and Form; chmn. editorial com. N.W. Architect, 1971—; asso. editor Worship. Works include churches, instns. Home: 711 Summit Ave Northfield MN 55057 Office: 205 S Water St Northfield MN 55057

SOWER, CHRISTOPHER ELIAS, sociologist, educator; b. Ludington, Mich., June 1, 1912; s. David E. and Dorothy (Shafford) S.; B.S., Ashland Coll., 1934; M.A., Ohio State U., 1936, Ph.D., 1948; m. Virginia Judy, Oct. 2, 1937; children—Charles, John, Margaret, William. Sociologist, U.S. Govt., 1941-46; club supr. A.R.C., Europe, 1943-45; asst. prof. to prof. sociology Mich. State U., E. Lansing, 1946—; cons. in field. Fulbright scholar, Ceylon, 1955-56; mem. UN Mission on Community Devel. to Ceylon, 1961-62. Mem. Mich. Gov.'s Conservation Study Com., 1963. Mem. Am., Rural, Mich. sociol. assns. Author: (with others) Community Involvement, 1957; contbr. articles profl. jours. Home: 4330 Hulett Rd Okemos MI 48864 Office: Dept Sociology Michigan State Univ East Lansing MI 48824

SOWERS, RONALD LEE, lawyer; b. Dover, Mo., Apr. 20, 1938; s. John Lee and Mary Catherine (Dysart) S.; B.A., U. Notre Dame, 1960, J.D., 1965; m. Launa Rose Stayer, June 11, 1960; children—Julie, Jennifer, Jill Susan. Admitted to Ind. bar, 1965; mem. firm Torborg, Miller, Moss, Harris & Sowers, Ft. Wayne, Ind., 1965—; pres., dir. C. & W. Devel. Co., Ft. Wayne, Ind., 1972—; dir. Allen Mortgage Co., Ft. Wayne, Ind., 1973—. Mem. Selective Service Bd., Ft. Wayne, 1972-75. Dir., Marine Corps Toys for Tots Program, Ft. Wayne, Ind., 1965-68; bd. dirs. Aboite Community Assn., 1972-75, v.p. bd. dirs. Mental Health Assn. of Allen County, 1967-68; chmn. bd. Saint Anne Home for the Aging, 1971-73, pres. 1971-73; mem. businessmen com. St. Francis Coll. Served to 1st lt. USMC, 1960-62; lt. col. Res. Mem. Internat., Am., Ind., Allen County (specialization and recertification com. 1974—, pub. relations com. 1974—). Fed. Circuit, bar assns., Ind., Allen County trial lawyers assns., Judicature Soc., Am. Trial Lawyers Assn. (trial techniques com. sect. ins., negligence and compensation law 1976—), Am. Arbitration Assn. (arbitrator 1970—), Notre Dame Alumni Law Assn. (dir. 1966-67, 69—), Fraternal Order of Police. Republican. Roman Catholic. Club: U. Notre Dame (pres. 1967-69, dir. 1971—) (Ft. Wayne). Home: 1630 W Goldspur Dr Fort Wayne IN 46804 Office: 1800 Fort Wayne National Bank Bldg Fort Wayne IN 46802

SPADE, LEE IRVING, psychologist; b. Muncie, Ind., Aug. 25, 1928; s. Carl Irving and Helen Kline (Morrisey) S.; B.S., U. Cin., 1950; B.S. in Edn., Butler U., 1964; M.A., Ohio State U., 1968, Ph.D., 1973; m. Ruth Marie Heisel, Oct. 10, 1953; children—Pamela, Cynthia, Margaret. Employed as indsl. salesman, 1953-63; tchr. phys. sci. Westerville (O.) High Sch., 1964-67; sch. psychologist Delaware (Ohio) City Schs., 1967-70; teaching fellow Ohio State U., Columbus, 1970-71; dir. psychol. services Madison County Pub. Schs., London, Ohio, 1970-71; clin. psychologist Children's Mental Health Center, Columbus, 1971-75; dir. behavioral sci. edn. Grant Hosp. Family Practice Center, 1975—; pvt. practice as psychologist, Columbus, 1972—. Served with AUS, 1950-52. Recipient award for recognition of services Ohio Psychol. Assn., 1972. Mem. Am., Central Ohio (treas. 1970-72) psychol. assns., Soc. Tchrs. Family Medicine. Home: 6754 Berend St Worthington OH 43085 Office: 1631 NW Profl Plaza Columbus OH 43220

SPADY, RICHARD JAY, agrl. co. exec.; b. Hastings, Nebr., July 18, 1929; s. John and Alberta Elaine (Perkins) S.; B.S., U. Nebr., 1956, M.A. in Agrl. Econs., 1958; m. Norma Eilene Wolf, June 14, 1958; children—Sarah, John, Stephen, Thomas. Profl. baseball player, Bklyn. Dodgers System, 1948-56; land mgr. Nebr. Game and Parks Commn., Lincoln, 1958-59, area mgr., 1959-63, acquisition agt., 1962-63, chief land mgmt., 1963-69, asst. dir., 1969-74; mgr. farm and trust McKinley & Lanning Co., Hastings, 1974-75, partner, 1975—; dir. First Nat. Bank Hastings. Gov.'s rep. Fed. Pub. Land Law Rev. Commn., 1965-70. Trustee Hastings Coll., 1972—, Mary Lanning Meml. Hosp., Hastings, 1975—. Mem. Soil Conservation Soc. Am., Wildlife Soc., Wildlife Fedn., Soc. Farm Mgmt. and Rural Appraisers, Assn. Profl. Ballplayers. Clubs: Elks, Kiwanis. Home: 1330 Heritage Dr Hastings NE 68901 Office: 122 N Hastings Ave Hastings NE 68901

SPAETH, HERBERT HELLMUT, mktg. cons.; b. Bandjermasin, Indonesia, Aug. 28, 1930; s. Erwin Alfred and Elisabeth (Fanderl) S.; came to U.S., 1956, naturalized, 1972; diploma in indsl. mgmt. Nuernberg Bus. Coll. (W. Ger.), 1952. Exec. asst. Acme Mfg. Co., Detroit, 1958-72; dir. internat. realtions Acme Murray-Way Internat. Co., Detroit, 1973-75; specialist internat. mktg., cons. to indsl. legal and investment firms, Ferndale, Mich., 1975—. Active Mich. Interfaith Full Employment Com. Mem. Am. Mgmt. Assn. Home: 770 Withington St Ferndale MI 48220

SPAHR, JON RAY, lawyer; b. New Castle, Ind., Sept. 20, 1939; s. Marvin M. and Virginia (Allaback) S.; B.S. in Bus., Miami U., Oxford, Ohio, 1961; J.D., Ohio State U., 1964; m. Mary Jane Barr, Aug. 24, 1963; children—Jennifer, Julie, Joel. Admitted to Ohio bar, 1964, So. Ohio Dist. U.S. Fed. Dist. Ct., 1965; partner firm McDonald, Robison, Spahr & Noecker, Newark, Ohio, 1967—; solicitor Village of Hebron (Ohio), 1965-70. Mem. devel. fund. com. Ohio State U., 1972—; Newark Boosters Club, 1970—, Big Bros. Assn., 1971—; adviser League Women Voters, 1972—. Bd. dirs. Newark Drug Forum, Family Services Assn., United Way, Chi Rho House (all Newark), Newark Library, 1975—. Recipient Outstanding Young Man award Newark Area Jr. C. of C., 1972. Mem. Am., Ohio, Licking County bar assns. Presbyterian (elder). Clubs: Elks, Newark Maennerchor. Home: 240 Quentin Rd N Newark OH 43055 Office: 63 N 3d St Newark OH 43055

SPAID, DONALD LEWIS, city ofcl.; b. Fort Wayne, Ind., Oct. 28, 1932; s. Orieon Meeker and Gwendolyn Louise (Dorey) S.; A.B., Butler U., 1955; m. Sue Ann Hartley, Aug. 7, 1955; children—Craig Edward, Ted Hartley, Nancy Jane, Timothy Allen. Dir. Madison (Ind.) County Plan Commn., 1958; sr. planner Marion County Met. Plan Commn., Indpls., 1959-62, prin. planner, 1963-69; dep. dir. div. planning and zoning City of Indpls., 1969-75; planning coordinator City of St. Paul, 1975-77; dir. community devel. City of St. Louis, 1977—; adj. prof. St. Louis U., 1977—; instr. Ind. U., Indpls., 1973-74. Bd. dirs. Community Interfaith Housing Corp., Indpls., 1974-75, N.W. Youth Athletic Assn., Indpls., 1966-74. Served to capt. USAF, 1956-58. Mem. Am. Inst. Planners (chpt. pres. 1970-72, chpt. Honor award 1972). Christian Ch. (trustee 1974-75). Home: 2545 Clifton Ave Saint Louis MO 63139 Office: 1015 Locust St Suite 1201 Saint Louis MO 63101

SPAIGHTS, ERNEST, ednl. psychologist, univ. adminstr.; b. St. Petersburg, Fla., Sept. 4, 1935; s. Marcellus and Sally (Sims) S.; B.S., Central State U., 1960; M.A., Ohio State U., 1962, Ph.D., 1971; m. Ethel Ann Woods, July 1, 1958; 1 son, Ernest Van. Social case worker Franklin County Dept. Pub. Assistance, Columbus, Ohio, 1960-61; tchr. Columbus Pub. Schs., 1960-61, coordinator freshman edn., 1963-65; asst. prof. ednl. psychology U. Wis.-Milw., 1965-68, asso. prof., 1968-71, spl. asst. to chancellor, 1968-70, asst. chancellor, 1970—, prof., 1971—. Bd. dirs. Milw. YMCA, 1973-77. Named Outstanding Adminstr. of Year, 1975; recipient Edward and Rosa Uhrig award, 1967, Distinguished Service award Wis. chpt. NCCJ, 1970. Served with Signal Corps, U.S. Army, 1954-57. Mem. Milw. Urban League (dir. 1969-71), Wis. Heart Assn. (dir. 1972-74), Milw. Advt. Council (dir. 1972—), NCCJ (regional dir. 1971—), YMCA (dir. Milw. 1973—), Am., Wis. psychol. assns., Am. Ednl. Research Assn., Am. Personnel and Guidance Assn., AAUP, N.Y. Acad. Sci., other orgns. Contbr. articles to profl. publs. Home: 4137 N Lake Dr Shorewood WI 53211 Office: Chapman Hall Room 116A Milwaukee WI 53201

SPAIN, RICHARD WELLS, glass mfg. co. exec.; b. Terre Haute, Ind., Aug. 5, 1914; s. Robert Turner and Julia Blanche (May) S.; B.S., Rose-Hulman Inst. Tech., 1936; m. Betty Jane Conley, June 22, 1940; 1 son, Carl Robert. Foreman warehouse and shipping dept., glass container div. Owens-Ill., Inc., Terre Haute, 1936, combustion engr. batch and furnace dept., 1937, Columbus, Ohio, 1938-41, supr., 1942-47, sr. project engr. glass furnace design, operation and glass prodn. problems gen. engring. dept., Alton, Ill., 1947-53, chief engr. corporate tech., Toledo, 1953—. Active Jr. Achievement, Alton, 1952-53. Mem. Am. Ceramic Soc., Nat. Inst. Ceramic Engrs., Sigma Nu. Author: Better Glass Making, 1958. Home: 2666 Secor Rd Toledo OH 43606 Office: PO Box 1035 Toledo OH 43666

SPALDING, AL, realtor; b. Akron, Ohio, July 30, 1928; s. F. Ross and Margaret (Younker) S.; student Kent State U., 1950-53, Cleve. Coll., 1955-57; m. Mary H. Pickett, Mar. 21, 1952: children—Lisa Anne, Laura Jean, Anne Renee. Real estate appraiser Summit County Auditor's office, 1953-59; sec. Frank Krause, Inc., Akron, 1959-61; pres. Spalding Realty Co., Akron, 1961—; pres. Brunswick Mgmt. Co. Instr. Am. Inst. Savs. and Loans, 1962-63, Soc. Real Estate Appraisers, 1965—; guest lectr. U. Akron Community Coll., Kent State U., U. Okla., U. Rochester (N.Y.), U. Conn., Malone Coll., Canton, Ohio. Trustee Loyola of Lakes; sec. Akron Area Regional Devel. Bd. Served with USMCR, 1946-49, 50-51. Mem. Am. Soc. Appraisers (sr.; chpt. pres. 1962-63), Akron Area Bd. Realtors (chmn. comml. and indsl. appraisal com., bd. dirs., pres. 1970), Nat., Ohio assns. real estate bds., Soc. Real Estate Appraisers (sr. residential appraiser; past chpt. pres.; sr. real estate analyst), Am. Soc. Real Estate Appraisers (state dir. 1963-65), Soc. Indsl. Realtors. Clubs: Athletic, Akron City. Home: 594 Upper Merriman Dr Akron OH 44303 Office: 207 Ohio Bldg Akron OH 44308

SPANIOL, ROLAND DEAN, coll. adminstr.; b. Streator, Ill., June 17, 1931; s. Raymond Henry and Venus Arlene (Lawrence) S.; B.S., Ill. State U., 1953, M.S., 1956; postgrad. U. Ill., 1960-62, certificate data processing, 1965; Ph.D., U. Iowa, 1967; postgrad. (IBM Mgmt. Sci. fellow), U. Ind., 1968; m. Lois Josephine Gaspardo, June 12, 1952; children—Alan Dean, Michael Roland, Bill Eugene, Jane Marie, Jack Phillip, Lee Raymond. Tchr. bus. subjects Lostant (Ill.) High Sch., 1953-57, Pekin (Ill.) High Sch., 1957-60; instr. computer courses Eastern Ill. U., Charleston, 1960-65, 66-68, dir. computer services for instr., research and adminstrn., 1968—; instr. U. Iowa, Iowa City, 1965-66. Workshop tchr. Ill. Assn. Registrars, 1971-72, Data Processing Mgmt. Assn., 1973; computer cons. with various secondary schs., pvt. and pub. univs., 1966—; research cons. State of Ill., 1972—; curriculum cons. for Jr. coll. computer curriculum, 1970—. Adult scouter Boy Scouts Am., Charleston, Ill., 1966—. Recipient Research grant Eastern Ill. U. Faculty, 1966. Mem. NEA, Assn. for Ednl. Data Systems, Data Processing Mgmt. Assn. (mem. research grants com. 1970-72, chpt. pres. 1966-67, regent, pres. Edn. Found. 1975—), Beta Gamma Sigma, Delta Phi Epsilon. Elk. Contbr. articles to profl. jours. Home: 1040 7th St Charleston IL 61920

SPANKUS, JACK DEAN, orthopedic surgeon; b. Milw., Dec. 2, 1927; s. Harry Otto and Marie (Moeller) S.; B.S., Marquette U., 1950, M.D., 1953, M.S. in Surgery, 1960; m. Marcia Ann Hempe, June 19, 1959; children—Mark Dean, John Daniel, Martha Ann. Intern, VA Hosp., Houston, 1953-54; resident orthopedic surgery Columbia Hosp., Milw., 1954-55, VA Hosp., Wood, Wis., 1957-60, Milw. Children's Hosp., 1958-59; practice medicine specializing in orthopedic surgery, Milw., 1960—; staff Deaconess Hosp., Milw., 1960—, chief orthopedic surgery, 1969-74, v.p. med. staff, 1969-73; staff Luth. and St. Mary's hosps., Milw.; cons. Milw. County Gen. Hosp., VA Hosp., Wood; asst. clin. prof. Med. Coll. Wis., Milw., 1960—. Served to capt. USAF, 1955-57. Fellow A.C.S., Am. Acad. Orthopedic Surgeons; mem. Milw. Orthopedic Residents Alumni Club (sec.-treas. 1968-70), AMA, Med. Soc. Wis., Wis., Milw., Clin. orthopedic socs., Med. Soc. Milw. County, Milw. Acad. Medicine. Clubs: Tripoli Country; Milw. Athletic. Contbr. articles to profl. jours. Office: 2040 W Wisconsin Ave Milwaukee WI 53233

SPANNAUS, WARREN R., atty. gen. Minn.; b. St. Paul, Dec. 5, 1930; s. Albert and Anna S.; ed. U. Minn., U. Minn. Law Sch.; m. Marjorie Clarkson; children—Christine Ann, David. Admitted to Minn. bar; spl. asst. atty. gen. State of Minn., 1963-65, now atty. gen.; mem. staff Senator Walter F. Mondale, 1965-66, campaign dir., 1966; finance dir. Minn. Democratic-Farmer-Labor State Central Com., 1967, state chmn., 1967-69, chmn. Midwestern Regional Conf. Attys. Gen., 1972-73. Bd. dirs. Sch. Social Devel., Mpls. Served with USNR, 1951-54. Mem. Minn. Bar Assn. Home: 2619 Robbins St Minneapolis MN 55410 Office: State Capitol St Paul MN 55155

SPANO, JOHN JOSEPH, pub. relations exec.; b. N.Y.C., Sept. 10, 1919; s. John and Anna S.; B.J., U. Mo.; M.A., Webster Coll.; m. Lois D. Heisinger, Feb. 9, 1947; children—Martha Ann, John Joseph, Susan Jeanne. Reporter, New Orleans States, 1947-50; rewriteman St. Louis Star Times, 1950-51, Houston Press, 1950-53; staff St. Louis Globe-Democrat, 1953-59, day city editor, 1956-59; pub. relations staff McDonnell Douglas Corp., St. Louis, 1959; pub. relations rep. pub. relations dept. Monsanto Co., St. Louis, 1959-66, mgr. community relations, 1966-67, mgr. information services, 1967-72, corporate mgr. news media relations, 1972-73; dir. pub. relations and advt. Monsanto Polymers & Petrochems. Co. and Monsanto Chem. Intermediates Co., St. Louis, 1973—. Mem. Webster Groves (Mo.) Sch. Dist., 1970—. Bd. mgrs. Webster Groves YMCA. Served to lt. USNR, 1942-46. Mem. Pub. Relations Soc. America (accredited; pres. St. Louis chpt.), Am. Acad. Polit. and Social Scis., Sigma Delta Chi, Kappa Tau Alpha. Club: Press of Metropolitan St. Louis (dir.), Media, Bath and Tennis. Home: 1417 Norman Pl Warson Woods MO 63122 Office: 800 N Lindbergh Blvd St Louis MO 63166

SPARBERG, MARSHALL STUART, gastroenterologist; b. Chgo., May 20, 1936; s. Max Shane and Mildred Rose (Haffron) S.; B.A., Northwestern U., 1957; M.D., 1960; m. Nancy Carol Zimmerman, Dec. 27, 1958. Intern, Evanston (Ill.), Hosp., 1960-61; resident in internal medicine Barnes Hosp., St. Louis, 1961-63; fellow U. Chgo., 1963-65; practice medicine specializing in gastroenterology, Chgo., 1967—; asst. prof. medicine Northwestern U. Med. Sch., 1967-72, asso. prof., 1972—; instr. Washington U., St. Louis, 1961-63, U. Chgo., 1963-65. Pres. Fine Arts Music Found., 1974-76; bd. dirs. Lyric Opera Guild, 1974—. Served with USAF, 1965-67. Named Outstanding Tchr. Northwestern U. Med. Sch., 1972. Mem. AMA, A.C.P., Am. Gastroent. Assn., Chgo. Med. Soc., Chgo. Soc. Internal Medicine, Chgo. Soc. Gastroenterology (v.p.). Democrat. Jewish. Author: Ileostomy Care, 1969; Primer of Clinical Diagnosis, 1972; contbr. numerous articles to profl. jours. Office: 700 N Michigan Ave Chicago IL 60611

SPARGER, CHARLES FORREST, physician and surgeon; b. Goree, Tex., Sept. 25, 1924; s. Marvin Wheeler and Rosa Nell (Perrien) S.; student N. Tex. U., 1941-43; B.S., Tex. Christian U., 1945; M.D., Southwestern Med. Coll., Tex. U., 1947; Intern, St. Elizabeth's and Gallinger hosps., Washington, 1947-48; gen. practice resident All Saints Episcopal Hosp., Ft. Worth, Tex., 1948-49, resident in surgery USPHS Hosp., New Orleans, 1953-56, resident in thoracic surgery USPHS Hosp., S.I., N.Y., 1956-58; fellow in cardiovascular surgery Bailey Clinic and Hahnemann Hosp., Phila., 1958-59; asst. chief surgery USPHS Hosp., S.I., N.Y., 1956-58, 59-62; chief thoracic surgery USPHS Hosp., S.I., N.Y., 1959-62; chief gen. and thoracic surgery USPHS Hosp., Gallup, N. Mex., 1962-66; asst. chief Emergency Health Services, USPHS, Washington, 1967-68; chief surgery and vascular surgery VA Hosp., Butler, Pa., 1968-69; instr. coronary care Frank Phillips Coll., 1975-76; practice medicine specializing in endoscopy, thoracic and gen. surgery, Poplar Bluff, Mo., 1977—. Served with USNR, 1943-45, USPHS, 1947-68. Diplomate Am. Bd. Gen. Surgery. Fellow Am. Coll. Surgeons, Am. Coll. Chest Physicians, Am. Coll. Angiology. Democrat. Baptist. Clubs: Rotary, Toastmasters Internat. Home: Box 1130 Poplar Bluff MO 63901 Office: 217 Oak St Poplar Bluff MO 63901

SPARKMAN, THOMAS CARROLL, physician; b. Poplar Bluff, Mo., Nov. 2, 1931; s. Thomas Eichelberger and Gertrude Pauline (Gardner) S.; student David Lipscomb Coll., Nashville, 1949-50, Harding Coll., Searcy, Ark., 1950-51; B.S., S.E. Mo. State Coll., 1957; M.D., Baylor U., 1962; m. Elizabeth Ann Jackson, Oct. 31, 1952; children—Thomas Kendall, Randall Bradley. Intern Jefferson-Davis City County Charity Hosp., Houston; gen. practice medicine, Cape Girardeau, Mo., 1963—. Mem. Pres.'s Council Harding Coll. Served with AUS, 1954-56. Diplomate Am. Bd. Family Practice. Mem. Am. Geriatric Soc., AMA, Mo. Med. Assn., Am. Acad. Gen. Practice, Cape County Med. Soc. (treas. 1964-65), Cape Girardeau C. of C., Alpha Kappa Kappa. Mem. Ch. of Christ. Home: 1629 Oxford Dr Cape Girardeau MO 63701 Office: 15 Doctors Park Cape Girardeau MO 63701

SPARKS, BILLY SCHLEY, lawyer; b. Marshall, Mo., Oct. 1, 1923; s. John and Clarinda (Schley) S.; A.B., Harvard, 1945, LL.B., 1949; student Mass. Inst. Tech., 1943-44; m. Dorothy O. Stone, May 14, 1946; children—Stephen Stone, Susan Lee, John David. Admitted to Mo. bar, 1949; partner Langworthy, Matz & Linde, Kansas City, Mo., 1949-62, firm Linde, Thomson, Van Dyke, Fairchild & Langworthy, 1962—. Mem. Mission (Kans.) Planning Council, 1954-63; mem. Kans. Civil Service Commn., 1975—. Mem. dist. 110 Sch. Bd., 1964-69, pres., 1967-69; mem. Dist. 512 Sch. Bd., 1969-73, pres., 1971-72; del. Dem. Nat. Conv., 1964; candidate for representative 10th Dist., Kans., 1956, 3d district, 1962; treas. Johnson County (Kans.) Dem. Central com., 1958-64. Served to lt. USAAF, 1944-46. Mem. Kansas City C. of C. (legis. com. 1956—), Am., Kansas City bar assns., Mo. Bar, Law Assn. Kansas City, Harvard Law Sch. Assn. Mo. (past dir.), Nat. Assn. Sch. Bds. (mem. legislative com. 1968-73), St. Andrews Soc. Mem. Christian Ch. (trustee). Clubs: Harvard (v.p. 1953-54) (Kansas City, Mo.); Milburn Golf and Country. Home: 8517 W 90th Terr Shawnee Mission KS 66212 Office: Columbia-Union Nat Bank Bldg Kansas City MO 64106

SPARKS, ROBERT DEAN, gastroentologist, found. exec.; b. Newton, Iowa, May 6, 1932; B.A., U. Iowa, 1955, M.D., Coll. of Medicine, 1957; Dr. (h.c.), Creighton U., 1978; m. Shirley L. Nichols, Sept. 5, 1954; children—Steven, Ann, John. Intern, Charity Hosp. La., New Orleans, 1957-58; resident Charity Hosp. La. in New Orleans Tulane U. Service, 1958-59, fellow in internal medicine, 1959-62; asst. in medicine Tulane U., 1958-59, instr. in medicine, 1959-63, asst. prof. medicine, 1963-64; asso. prof., 1964-68, prof., 1968-72, asst. dean curricular and hosp. affairs, 1964-66, coordinator regional and affiliated clin. programs, 1966-67, dir. of div. grad. and postgrad. med. studies, 1967-68, acting dean, 1967-68, vice dean, 1968-69, chief section gastroentology dept. medicine, 1968-72, dean, 1969-72; vice pres. U. Nebr. and chancellor U. Nebr. Med. Center, 1972-76, prof. medicine Coll. of Medicine, 1972-76; program dir. W.K. Kellogg Found., Battle Creek, Mich., 1977—; asst. vis. physician Charity Hosp. of New Orleans, 1959-63, vis. physician, 1963-70, head Tulane U. Service, 1968-72, sr. vis. physician, 1970-72; asso. internist Ill. Central R.R. Hosp., 1959-72; asso. staff internist DePaul Hosp., New Orleans, 1961-72, chief gastroentology service VA Hosp., New Orleans, 1966-68; mem. med. staff Bishop Clarkson Meml. Hosp., Omaha, 1972-76; med. staff U. Hosp., Omaha, 1972-76; cons. staff Community Hosp., Battle Creek, 1977—. Mem. interagy. adv. com. New Orleans Area Health Planning Council, 1967-72; vice chmn., 1967-70, chmn., 1970-72, bd. dirs., 1970-72; asst. dir. La. Regional Med. Program, 1967-68, mem. regional adv. group, 1970-72. Diplomate Am. Bd. Internal Medicine. Fellow Am. Coll. of Physicians; mem. AAAS, Am., Calhoun County, Mich. med. socs., Health Edn. Media Assn. (bd. dirs., chmn. of the bd. emeritus), Am. Fedn. for Clin. Research, Am. Assn. Med. Colls. (adv. com. for feasibility study on multimedia in health edn., 1973-74, Distinguished mem. 1974—), Am. Gastroenterology Assn., Am. Soc. Internal Medicine, Am. Med. Soc. on Alcoholism (co-chmn. region VI 1973-75), Assn. Acad. Health Center, La. Heart Assn. (student research com. 1964-70, chmn. 1966-70, govt. relations com. 1968-70, bd. dirs. 1968-71), Am. Cancer Soc. (La. div., service com. 1967-72, bd. dirs. 1968-72, sec. 1969-71, chmn. 1971-72, exec. com. 1969-72), Cancer Assn. of Greater New Orleans (research adv. com. 1968-72), La., Orleans Parish med. socs., Nu Sigma Nu, Omaha C. of C. (pres. adv. bd. 1976). Club: Rotary Internat. Contbg. editor Biomed. Communications, 1975—, editorial advisory bd., 1977—; editorial advisory com. Preventive Medicine, 1977—; contbr. numerous articles to profl. jours. Home: 144 Waupakisco Beach Battle Creek MI 49015 Office: WK Kellogg Found 400 North Ave Battle Creek MI 49016

SPARKS, (THEO) MERRILL, entertainer, translator, poet; b. Mount Etna, Iowa, Oct. 5, 1922; s. David G. and Ollie M. (Hickman) S.; student U. Besançon (France), 1945; B.A., U. So. Calif., 1948; postgrad. U. Iowa, 1948-51, Columbia U., 1951-52. Entertainer as singer, pianist, Los Angeles, Midwest, Fla., N.Y., N.J. areas, 1953—. Served with AUS, 1942-46. Co-recipient P.E.N. transl. award, 1968, Cross of Merit with Vernon Duke for cantata Order of St. Brigida, Rome, 1966. Mem. Am. Fedn. Musicians, Authors Guild, Am. Guild

Authors and Composers, Modern Poetry Assn. Composer songs including Sleepy Village, 1942, A Heart of Gold, 1956, Anima Eroica, 1971, An Italian Voyage, 1976; poems pub. in mags. including Western Rev., Choice, South & West, N.Y. Rev. Books; poems included in: Arts of Russia, Primer of Experimental Poetry; co-editor, co-translator (with Vladimir Markov) Modern Russian Poetry, 1966. Address: Mount Etna IA 50855

SPARROW, EDWARD, chemist; b. Franklin, La., Mar. 11, 1922; s. Adam and Evelyn (Ambrose) S.; B.S., Xavier U., 1949, M.S., 1954; student U. Pitts., 1954-55; m. Juanita Meade Childress, Oct. 15, 1957. Chemist, Naval Supply Center, U.S. Naval Sta., Norfolk, Va., 1955-62; chemist, chief Chem. and Material Lab., Quality Control Div., Newark (Ohio) Air Force Sta., 1962—; instr. gen. inorganic chemistry Va. State Coll., 1961-62. Served with AUS, 1943-45. Mem. Am. Chem. Soc., AAAS, ASTM, Am. Conf. Govtl. Indsl. Hygienists, Am. Indsl. Hygiene Assn., Omega Psi Phi, Indsl. Mgmt. Club Newark. K.C. Home: 35 N Buena Vista St Newark OH 43055 Office: Newark Air Force Sta Newark OH 43055

SPATTA, CAROLYN LEE DAVIS, coll. adminstr.; b. Gauhati, Assam, India, Jan. 20, 1935; d. Alfred Charles and Lola Mildred (Anderson) Davis; B.A., U. Calif. Berkeley, 1964; M.A., U. Mich., 1968, Ph.D., 1974; m. John Robert Spatta, June 2, 1957 (div. 1963); children—Robert Alan, Jennifer Lynn. Instr. geography Schoolcraft Coll., Livonia, Mich., 1968-74; asst. to pres., sec. of coll. Oberlin (Ohio) Coll., 1974—. Mem. Ohio planning com. Nat. Identification of Women project, Office of Women in Higher Edn., Am. Council on Edn., 1977—; mem. Oberlin Open Space Commn., 1975-77; mem. platform com. Ann Arbor Democratic Com., 1970, steering com. Ann Arbor Citizens for Good Schools, 1968-70; pres. Tenaya Guild, John Muir Hosp. Aux., Walnut Creek, 1959-62. NDEA fellow, 1966-67, 67-68. Mem. Am. Assn. Geographers, Assn. Asian Studies, Am. Assn. Higher Edn. Home: 162 S Cedar St Oberlin OH 44074 Office: Cox Administration Bldg Oberlin Coll Oberlin OH 44074

SPAUN, WILLIAM BECKER, lawyer; b. Atchison, Kans., Aug. 22, 1913; s. Floyd and Bertha (Becker) S.; J.D., U. Mo., Kansas City, 1936; m. Sidney Clyde Collins, Sept. 13, 1930 (dec.); 1 dau., Theon Spaun Martin; m. 2d, Mary Louise Robinson, Aug. 5, 1948; children—William Becker, Mary Lou Spaun Montgomery, Robert R., Sarah Jean, Shirley Anne. Admitted to Mo. bar, 1937; U.S. Supreme Ct., 1960; practice law, Hannibal, 1937—; charter mem. World Peace Through Law Center, participant Washington conf., 1965. Regional fund chmn. ARC, 1961, nat. staff mem., 1943-44, nat. vice chmn. fund campaigns, 1963-64, local chpt. chmn., 1977—; govt. appeal agt. SSS, 1968-72, chmn., 1972—. Recipient award for meritorious personal service WW II from ARC. Fellow Am. Coll. Probate Counsel, Harry S. Truman Library Inst. (hon.); mem. Am., Tenth Jud. Circuit (pres. 1958-60) bar assns., Mo. Bar (chmn. Law Day 1961, asso. editor jour. 1942-43), Am. Judicature Soc., Scribes. Republican. Home: 2929 McKinley St Hannibal MO 63401 Office: 500 Broadway Hannibal MO 63401 also PO Box 1169 Hannibal MO 63401

SPEAR, RAYMOND EARLE, supt. schs.; b. Sharon, Mass., June 6, 1931; s. Carleton Jarvis and Edith Dolores (Irons) S.; B.Ed., Plymouth (N.H.) Tchrs. Coll., 1955; M.A., U. Mich., 1959, Ed.S., 1968; m. Freida Odette Turner, Aug. 3, 1955; children—Carol Lynn, Scott Turner. Tchr. Hayward (Calif.) Sch. Dist., 1956-57, U. Mich., 1957-59; prin. Cherry Hill Sch. Dist., Inkster, Mich., 1959-62; prin. Northville (Mich.) Pub. Schs., 1962-65, asst. supt., 1965-67, supt., 1967—; vis. lectr. U. Mich. Served with USAF, 1952-56. Mem. Am., Mich. assns. sch. adminstrs., Mich. Assn. Professions, Phi Delta Kappa. Club: Northville Rotary (pres., treas., dir.). Home: 986 Grace Northville MI 48167 Office: 303 W Main St Northville MI 48167

SPECHT, CHARLES ALFRED, mfg. exec.; b. Passaic, N.J., July 30, 1914; s. Alfred F. and Marian A. (Clarke) S.; B.B.A., Rutgers U., 1938; postgrad. N.Y.U., 1939-40; m. Gertrude A. Morris, Sept. 14, 1940;children—Sara Ann, Sandra Morris. Clk., bookkeeper Am. Surety Co., N.Y.C., 1933-37; credit analyst Irving Trust Co., 1937-42; staff accountant Price Waterhouse & Co., 1942-44; chief accountant DeLaval Steam Turbine Co., Trenton, N.J., 1944-45; works controller Joy Mfg. Co., Franklin, Pa., 1945-50; controller Chas. Pfizer & Co., Inc., Bklyn., 1950-52, dir., 1952-55, also pres. fgn. trade subsidiaries, 1952-55; pres., dir. Horizons Titanium Corp., 1955-57; financial analyst Lazard Freres & Co., N.Y.C., 1955-56; v.p., dir. Horizons, Inc., 1955-56; pres., dir., chief exec. officer Minerals & Chems. Phillipp Corp., 1956-63; pres., dir., mem. exec. com. MacMillan Bloedel Ltd., Vancouver, B.C., 1963-68; pres., chief exec. officer, dir., mem. exec. com. Consol. Packaging Corp., Chgo., Ill., 1968-73, cons., 1973—; dir. Interpace Corp., Horizons Research, Inc., Hazeltine Corp., Am. Investment Co.; instr. Rutgers U., 1940-45. Mem. Financial Execs. Inst. Clubs: University (N.Y.C.); Vancouver (B.C., Can.); Union League, Economic (Chgo.); Englewood (N.J.). Home: 628 Armada Rd Venice FL 33595 Office: 535 N Michigan Ave Chicago IL 60611

SPECKMAN, GLENN HOY, physician; b. Indpls., Feb. 19, 1928; s. Henry Lee and Anna Egli (Lewis) S.; A.B., DePauw U., 1950; M.D., Ind. U., 1953; m. Linda Sue Dixon, Dec. 19, 1974; children—David, Betsy, Jay, Jon, Shelly, Michael. Intern, Meth. Hosp., Indpls., 1953-54; gen. practice medicine, Indpls., 1954—; chief of staff Community Hosp., 1978—; mem. staffs Meth. and St. Francis hosps. Served with USNR, 1955-57. Fellow Am. Acad. Family Practice, Am. Geriatric Soc.; mem. AMA, Ind., Marion County med. socs., Am. Profl. Practice Assn., Sigma Nu, Nu Sigma Nu, Train Collectors Assn. Republican. Mem. Christian Ch. Clubs: Masons (32 deg.), Shriners, Moose, Sertoma (Indpls.). Home: 8036 Cheswick Dr Indianapolis IN 46219 Office: 5508 E 16th St Indianapolis IN 46218

SPECTER, MELVIN H., lawyer; b. E. Chicago, Ind., July 12, 1903; s. Moses and Sadie (Rossuck) S.; A.B., U. Mich., 1925; J.D., U. Chicago, 1928; m. Nellie Rubenstein, Feb. 1, 1927; children—Lois, Michael Joseph. Admitted to Ind. bar, 1928; individual practice law, East Chicago, Ind. 1928—. Bd. dirs. ARC (chpt. chmn. 1940-46), Community Chest Assn., Salvation Army Adv. Bd., pres., 1930-35; bd. dirs. Vis. Nurse Assn., pres., 1943-44; bd. dir. Twin City Recreation Center, v.p. 1957-58; bd. dirs. East Chgo. Boys Club, 1958—; trustee East Chicago Pub. Library, 1956—, pres., 1957—; pres. Anselm Forum, 1957-58; chmn. Brotherhood Week NCCJ, East Chicago, 1958-61; exec. bd. Twin City council Boy Scouts Am.; city chmn. U. Chgo. Alumni Found. Fund, 1951-55. Awarded James Couzen Medal for Inter-collegiate debate, U. Mich., 1924; citation for distinguished pub. service, U. Chgo. Alumni Assn., 1958. Citizenship award Community Chest Assn., 1965. Mem. Am. Ind. (del.), East Chicago (pres. 1942-44) bar assns., Am. Judicature Soc., Acad. Polit. Sci., Comml. Law League Am., Community Concert Assn. (dir. 1950-55), Am. Library Assn., Ind. Library Trustees Assn., Wig and Robe Frat., Phi Beta Kappa, Delta Sigma Rho. Elk (exalted ruler 1945), K.P., Kiwanian (dir. 1946, 49-51, 52-55, pres. 1961); mem. B'nai B'rith. Home: 4213 Baring Ave East Chicago IN 46312 Office: 815 W Chicago Ave East Chicago IN 46312

SPECTOR, SAMUEL, pediatrician; b. Bklyn., Mar. 11, 1914; s. William Zeidel and Rose (Krapko) S.; B.S., Columbia, 1934; M.D., L.I. Coll. Medicine, 1937; m. Lillian Hutchinson, July 24, 1943; children—Judith Ann, Susan Yancey (Mrs. Dale Wegelin), Michael Lew. Intern, Beth El Hosp., Bklyn., 1937-38, Kingston Ave. Hosp., Bklyn., 1938; resident Willard Parker Hosp., N.Y.C., 1939-41; resident pediatrics U. Mich. Hosp., Ann Arbor, 1941-42; instr. pediatrics U. Mich., 1942-43; asst. prof. pediatrics Case Western Res. U., Cleve., 1946-51, asso. prof., 1951-60, prof., 1960-70; dir. pediatrics research and devel. Children's Hosp. Akron, 1967-70; prof. pediatrics U. Chgo., 1970—, chmn. dept., 1973—; dir. pediatrics Wyler Children's Hosp. U. Chgo. Hosps. and Clinics, 1970—; dir. La Rabida Children's Hosp. and Research Center, Chgo., 1974—. Bd. dirs. Home for Destitute Crippled Children, Chgo., 1974—. Served to lt. M.C., USNR, 1944-46. Recipient McClintock award U. Chgo., 1971. Diplomate Am. Bd. Pediatrics. Mem. Am. Acad. Pediatrics (mem. com. newborn and fetus 1962-66), Soc. Pediatric Research, Chgo. Pediatric Soc., Soc. Human Genetics, Am. Pediatric Soc., Sigma Xi, Alpha Omega Alpha. Contbr. articles to profl. jours. Home: 5201 S Cornell Ave Chicago IL 60615

SPEER, DAVID JAMES, pub. relations exec.; b. Mpls., Apr. 30, 1927; s. Ray Patterson and Grace Elizabeth (Kane) S.; B.A. in Polit. Sci., U. Minn., 1950. Sports reporter Mpls. Tribune, 1945-50; night radio editor AP, Mpls., 1950-51; partner Speer's Publicity Service, Mpls., 1950-59; pres. Sullivan and Speer, Inc., pub. relations counsel, Mpls., 1959-61; sr. v.p. Padilla, Sarjeant, Sullivan & Speer, Inc., Mpls., 1961-71, pres., 1971—, pub. relations Mpls., N.Y.C., Los Angeles, 1961—. Pub. relations dir. Minn. State Fair, 1961-68, St. Paul Winter Carnival Assn., 1952-70; bd. dirs. Mpls. Red Cross, also pub. relations chmn.; mem. steering com. Minn. NAACP Legal Def. Fund. Served with USN, 1945-46. Mem. Pub. Relations Soc. Am. (chpt. pres. 1967, mem. midwest jud. panel 1967-71), U. Minn. Liberal Arts Alumni Assn. (past pres.), Psi Upsilon (pres. 1967). Club: Minn. Press (dir. 1965-66). Home: 1400 Alpine Pass Golden Valley MN 55416 Office: 224 W Franklin Ave Minneapolis MN 55404

SPEER, GEORGE SCOTT, psychologist; b. Oak Park, Ill., Sept. 24, 1908; s. George Scott and Dorothy May (Niver) S.; student U. Wis., 1927-28; A.B., Central YMCA Coll., 1934; S.M., U. Chgo., 1936; m. Jean Mainland, July 24, 1936; children—Mary Catherine, George Scott. Research asst. Mooseheart Lab. for Child Research (Ill.) 1935-36; psychologist Berkshire Indsl. Farm, Canaan, N.Y., 1936-37, Sangamon County Child Guidance Service, Springfield, Ill., 1937-40; asst. prof. psychology, dean of students Central YMCA Coll., Chgo., 1940-45; prof., dir. Inst. Psychol. Services, Ill. Inst. Tech., Chgo., 1945-74, prof. emeritus, cons., 1974—; cons. psychologist for phys., bus. and indsl. orgns., 1938—; lectr. Northwestern U., 1948—. Chmn., Oak Park (Ill.) Bd. Fire and Police Commrs., 1960-73. Diplomate in counseling and guidance Am. Bd. Examiners in Profl. Psychology. Fellow Am. Psychol. Assn.; mem. Nat. Vocat. Guidance Assn. (v.p. 1947-49), Chgo. Guidance and Personnel Assn. (v.p. 1948-49, pres. 1949-50), Ill. Assn. Prof. Psychologists, Am., Midwestern psychol. assns., Internat. Reading Assn., Internat. Assn. Counseling Services (pres. 1974), Am. Assn. Mental Deficiency, Chgo. Soc. Personality Study, AAUP, Am. Soc. Engring. Edn., Nat. Soc. Research and Devel., Am. Personnel and Guidance Assn., Sigma Xi. Contbr. articles on psychol. and engring. to sci. jours. Home: 225 S Euclid Ave Oak Park IL 60302 Office: Ill Inst Tech 3300 S Michigan Ave Chicago IL 60616

SPEIDEL, GEORGE, zoo adminstr.; b. Brookfield, Ill., Jan. 23, 1912; s. Paul and Pauline (Moeck) S.; ed. Chgo. pub. schs.; D.Sci. (hon.), Marquette U., 1975; m. Mary Susan Bean, June 24, 1939; 1 son, George Speidel. With Brookfield (Ill.) Zoo, 1930-45; dir. Racine (Wis.) Zoo, 1945-47; dir. Milw. Zoo, 1947—; cons. zoo constrn.; lectr. Tex Tech. Coll. Chmn. Milw. Christmas Seal Dr., 1964, 65. Trustee, Salvation Army, bd. dirs., 1971. Recipient Distinguished Service award Am. Inst. Park Execs., 1962; Service award Milwaukee County Tb Assn., 1964, 65; Vocat. Recognition award Milw. Rotary Club, 1967; Community Service award Neville-Dunn Legion Post, 1972; Man of Yr. award Milw. Conv. and Visitors Bur., 1973. Fellow Am. Assn. Zool. Parks and Aquariums (pres. 1953-54, dir., Distinguished Service award 1967), Nat. Park and Recreation Soc. (trustee 1970-73, dir. 1959-62); mem. Wis. Park and Recreation Soc., Wis. Moose Breeders Assn., Wis. Zoo Assos. (chmn. 1971), Wis. Humane Soc. (dir. 1971), Internat. Union Dirs. Zool. Gardens, Wild Animal Propagation Trust (trustee). Address: 10001 W Bluemound Rd Milwaukee WI 53226

SPEIGEL, IRVING JOSHUA, surgeon; b. Ft. William, Ont., Can., Aug. 16, 1915; s. Jeremiah and Dora (Slobed) S.; came to U.S., 1937, naturalized, 1942; M.D., U. Toronto (Ont.), 1937; m. Rosalynde Green, June 25, 1942; children—Virginia S., Jonathan G., Petra. Rotating intern Mt. Sinai Hosp., Cleve., 1937-38; asst. resident neuropsychiatry State Hosp., Howard, R.I., 1938-39; asst. resident neurosurgery Boston City Hosp., 1939-40; sr. resident neurol. surgery St. Luke's Hosp., Chgo., 1940-41; chief resident neurol. surgery Cook County Hosp., Chgo., 1941-42; chief resident neurology and neurol. surgery Neuropsychiat. Inst., Chicago, 1942; asst. in neurology and neurol. surgery U. Ill. Med. Sch. and Research and Ednl. Hosp., Chgo., 1942-43, instr. neurology and neurol. surgery, 1946—, asso. in neurology and neurol. surgery, 1950-55; asso. prof. neurol. surgery Chgo. Med. Sch., 1955—; cons. neurol. surgeon Edgewater Hosp.; sr. attending neurol. surgeon Michael Reese Hosp., Chgo.; cons. Weiss Meml., Belmont Community, Provident, S. Chicago Community S. Shore, Am., Jackson Park, Martha Washington hosps. Served with AUS, 1943-46. Diplomate Am. Bd. Neurol. Surgeons, Internat. Bd. Surgery. Fellow Internat. Coll. Surgeons (chmn. com.); mem. AMA, Ill., Cook County, Chgo. med socs., Chgo. Neurol. Soc., Neurosurg. Soc. Am. (pres. 1957), Am. Assn. Neurol. Surgeons, Congress Neurol. Surgeons, Assn. Mil. Surgeons U.S., Central, Ill., Interurban neurosurg. socs., Royal Soc. Medicine. Clubs: Adventurer's, Standard, Safari Internat, Shikar-Safari, Adventures, Bull Valley Hunt. Contbr. articles to med. jours. Home: 1420 N Lake Shore Dr Chicago IL 60610 Office: 55 E Washington St Chicago IL 60602

SPEIR, KENNETH GUINTY, lawyer; b. Peabody, Kans., June 22, 1908; s. John and Bessie (Guinty) S.; student Colo. Coll., 1926-28; LL.B., Kans. U., 1931; m. Helen Sills, Jan. 1, 1935; children—Helen Ann, Patricia Jane, Elizabeth Eve. Admitted to Kans. bar, 1931, N.Mex. bar, 1932, U.S. Supreme Ct. bar, 1943; practiced in Albuquerque, 1932-34, Newton, Kans., 1934—; county atty. Harvey County (Kans.), 1939-41; Judge 9th Jud. Dist. Kans., 1941-44; dir. Central Securities, Inc., Acra-Plant, Inc., 1st Fed. Savs. & Loan Assn. of Newton; counsel Hesston Corp.; gen. counsel Excel Industries, Inc., Legg Co., Inc., Midland Nat. Bank, Newton. Mem. Kans. Bd. Health, 1950-51. Served as lt. col. USMCR, 1942-46. Mem. Am., N.Mex., Kans., Harvey County bar assns., Am. Legion, VFW. Republican. Lutheran. Home: 1411 Hillcrest St Newton KS 67114 Office: PO Box 546 809 Main St Newton KS 67114

SPEISER, WARREN HENRY, dentist; b. Bridgeport, Conn., Sept. 2, 1923; s. Reinhold C. and Florence Christine (Peterson) S.; student Muhlenberg Coll., 1942-44; D.D.S., Washington U., St. Louis, 1948, M.S., 1962; m. Eileen Catherine Lupo, Feb. 7, 1948; children—James Warren, Sally Christine, Barbara Suzanne. Dentist, Bridgeport, 1949-51; dentist specializing in prosthodontics, Florissant, Mo., 1966—; asso. prof. Washington U., 1965-71, lectr. Sch. Dentistry, 1977—; cons. in prosthodontics VA Hosp., St. Louis, 1969-71. Bd. dirs. Am. Cancer Soc., St. Louis, 1971-72. Served to lt. USNR, 1948-54; to lt. col. USAF, 1956-64. Decorated Air Force Commendation medal. Diplomate Am. Bd. Prosthodontics. Fellow Am. Coll. Prosthodontics, Am. Coll. Dentists, Midwest Soc. Prosthodontists, Royal Soc. Health; mem. ADA, St. Louis, Mo. dental assns., Delta Sigma Delta, Omega Kappa Upsilon. Home: 26 Brookwood Rd Saint Louis MO 63137 Office: 885 Saint Francois St Florissant MO 63031

SPELIOS, ANDREW JAMES, instl. adminstr.; b. Chgo., Sept. 2, 1922; s. James and Diane (Perdikis) S.; student Western Ill. U., 1949-50, M.S., 1955; student Loyola U., 1954-55; m. Patricia L. Sheahan, Jan. 3, 1953; children—Timothy, Michael, Catherine, Mary. Dir. therapies Research Hosp., Galesburg, Ill., 1953-59; asst. supt. Ill. Soldier's and Sailors' Children's Sch., Normal, Ill., 1959-63, supt., 1963—. Regional chmn. Inter-Agy. Com. on Children and Adolescents, Champaign, Ill., 1967—; mem. adv. council Parks and Recreation Bd., Normal, 1965-68; mem. Normal (Ill.) Central Area Devel. Com., 1972—. Mem. adv. bd. St. Joseph's Hosp., Bloomington, Ill., 1968—; mem. edn. adv. com. Assn. Commerce and Industry of McLean County, 1973—. Served with AUS, 1943-46. Mem. Child Care Assn. Ill. (v.p. central region 1972). Rotarian (pres. 1969-70). Home: 600 E Lincoln St Normal IL 61761 Office: Illinois Soldiers' and Sailors' Children's School Normal IL 61761

SPELLMAN, GEORGE GENESER, internist; b. Woodward, Iowa, Sept. 11, 1920; s. Martin Edward and Corinne (Geneser) S.; B.S., St. Ambrose Coll., 1940; M.D., State U. Iowa, 1943; m. Mary Carolyn Dwight, Aug. 26, 1942; children—Carolyn Anne Spellman Rambow, George G., Mary Alice Spellman Gross, Elizabeth Marie, John Martin, Loretta Suzanne. Intern, Providence Hosp., Detroit, 1944; resident in internal medicine State U. Iowa, Iowa City, 1944-46; practice specializing in internal medicine, Mitchell, S.D., 1948-50, Sioux City, Iowa, 1950—; instr. Coll. Medicine U. S.D., 1975-77; mem. staff St. Joseph Mercy Hosp., 1950—, chief of staff, 1963; mem. staff St. Vincent Hosp., 1950—, chief of staff, 1954, 77; 7 mem. staff St. Luke's Med. Center; clin. asso. prof. medicine State U. Iowa; instr. schs. nursing St. Vincent Hosp., Luth. Hosp.; co-founder, pres. Siouxland Mental Health Assn., 1968-75; bd. dirs. St. Vincent Hosp., Marian Health Center. Served to capt., M.C., U.S. Army, 1946-48. Decorated knight of St. Gregory (Vatican); diplomate Am. Bd. Internal Medicine. Fellow A.C.P.; mem. AMA, Am. Acad. Scis., Iowa State, Woodbury med. socs., Am., Iowa socs. internal medicine, Am., Iowa thoracic socs., Am., Iowa heart assns., Am. Geriatric Soc., Alpha Omega Alpha. Contbr. articles to med. jours. Home: 3849 Jones St Sioux City IA 51104 Office: 505 Badgerow Bldg 4th and Jackson Sts Sioux City IA 51101

SPELTS, RICHARD ERRETT, JR., banker, bus. exec.; b. Gregory, S.D., Jan. 1, 1919; s. Richard Errett and Flo R. (Ray) S.; B.S., U. Nebr., 1941; A.B., Hastings Coll., 1948; m. Dorothy Tipton, Apr. 11, 1942; children—Connie (Mrs. Gary Brouilette), Susan (Mrs. James Russell). Pres., 1st Nat. Bank of Grand Island (Nebr.), 1975—; chmn. bd. Bankshares of Nebr., Inc., 1972—; pres. United Bank Services Co., Grand Island, 1973—; exec. v.p., dir. Spelts of Nebr., Inc.; officer, dir. Spelts-Schultz Lumber Co., Mid-Am. Co., Spelts Lumber Co. (Kearney, Nebr.), Spelts-Swanson Implement Co. (Kearney), Spelts Lumber Co. (Valentine, Nebr.); dir. MEI Corp. (Mpls.) and subsidiaries, Investors Life Ins. Co. Nebr. (Omaha), Northwestern Pub. Service Co. (Huron, S.D.), Hamilton Internat. Corp. (Detroit). U.S. del. UNESCO Conf., Venice, Italy, 1970; Presdl. envoy Kingdom of Tonga Centennial, 1975; bd. dirs. Grand Island United Fund, Hall County Crippled Children's Soc., Hall County ARC, Am. Cancer Soc.; mem. nat. council, dir. Overland Trails council Boy Scouts Am.; chmn. Golden Age Village of Hall County Housing Authority; pres. Greater Grand Island Devel. Corp.; chmn. Nebr. Republican Party, 1955-59; mem. Rep. Nat. Com., 1955-59, Rep. Nat. Fin. Com., 1963-65; del. at large Rep. Nat. Conv., 1960; campaign treas. Sen. Carl T. Curtis, 1966, mgr., 1972; asst. floor leader Rep. Nat. Conv., 1964; dir. Truth Squad of Rep. Nat. Com., 1964; chmn. Grand Island City Planning Commn., 1955-60. Trustee U. Nebr. Found.; mem. adv. council U. Nebr.; trustee Nebr. Tax Research Council, Inc., 1962-63, Nebr. Ind. Coll. Found., 1965-71, Grand Island Charitable Found., Grand Island Indsl. Found., Central Nebr. Tech. Found. Served as lt. (j.g.) USNR, 1944-46. Named outstanding young man Grand Island Jr. C. of C., 1952; recipient alumni service award U. Nebr., 1958, Mr. Grand Island award Grand Island C. of C., 1963; Am. Cancer Soc. award, 1965; community service award KMMJ Radio, 1967. Mem. Am. Soc. Agrl. Engrs., Newcomen Soc. N.Am., Am. Legion, Nebr. Assn. Commerce and Industry (dir.), U.S. (mem. Aircade 1967), Nebr. (pres. 1962-63), Grand Island (pres. 1964) chambers commerce, Hastings Coll. Alumni Assn. (pres. 1955), Asso. Industries Neb., U. Nebr. Regional Alumni (pres. 1958). Presbyn. (elder). Mason (Shriner), Elk, Rotarian (pres. 1962-63). Home: 2203 W Charles St Grand Island NE 68801 Office: 1st National Bank PO Box 1387 Grand Island NE 68801

SPENCE, BEATRICE MARIE, chiropractor; b. Gate, Okla., Dec. 17, 1907; d. Clyde and Rebecca Jane (Neville) Spry; D. Chiropractic, Colvin Chiropractic Coll., 1928; Ph.D., Logan Chiropractic Coll., 1944; postgrad. Inst. Chiropractic Hypnosis, 1971; m. Apr. 19, 1932; children—Clyde Lowell, Neal Barnes. Pvt. chiropractic practice, Garnett, Kans., 1929-32, Leavenworth, Kans., 1945—. Mem. Am. Chiropractic Assn., Kans. Chiropractic Assn., Leavenworth City Taxpayers Assn., Am. Assn. Ret. Persons, Internat. Platform Assn. Republican. Eagle; mem. Order Eastern Star. Patentee in field. Research on raw fruits and vegetables nutrients as the foundation of health. Home: 917 6th Ave Leavenworth KS 66048

SPENCE, JOHN D(ANIEL), univ. ofcl.; b. Lethbridge, Alta., Can., May 18, 1915; s. Benjamin Abner and Clara May (Fullerton) S.; came to U.S., 1915, naturalized, 1943; A.B., Grinnell Coll., 1938; m. Phyllis Saxton Johnson, Feb. 4, 1939; children—Susan Kathleen Spence Horton, John-Daniel. With Container Corp. Am., 1938-54, v.p., 1949-54; Lanzit Corrugated Box Co., 1954-64; dir. devel. Rockford (Ill.) Coll., 1964-65, v.p. devel., 1965—, acting pres., 1977—. Mem. adv. bd. Forest Preserve Commn., 1974—; mem. land adv. council Winnebago County Forest Preserve, 1975—; chmn. Stevenson Dells Adv. Council, 1976—; trustee Keith Country Day Sch.; former trustee Children's Home Rockford, until 1976; bd. dirs. John Howard Assn., until 1974, Pecatonica Prairie Path, 1975—. Mem. Ill. (com. for respect law enforcement 1967-72), Rockford (dir. 1966-72) chambers commerce. Republican. Presbyterian. Clubs: Univ. (Chgo.); Lions. Home: 6710 Woodcrest Pkwy Rockford IL 61109 Office: 5050 E State St Rockford IL 61101

SPENCER, ALVIN DELANO, research engr.; b. Brenham, Tex., Sept. 28, 1944; s. Walter Chester and Pearl Onella (Alcorn) S.; B.S. in Mech. Engring., U. Wash., 1967; postgrad. Iowa State U., 1968—; m. Brenda Maurine Dunlap, Nov. 23, 1974; children—Chad William and Richard Titus (twins). Summer student Deere & Co., Moline, Ill., 1966, research engr., 1972—; design engr. John Deere Indsl. Equipment Works, Moline, 1967-69; sci. and engring. program U.S. Army Engr. Strategic Studies Group, Washington, 1971; design engr. John Deere Tractor Works, Dubuque, Iowa, 1971-72. Mem. crime and delinquency com. Model Cities Group, Rock Island, Ill., 1968-69; adviser Jr. Achievement, 1973—. Served with AUS, 1969-71.

Recipient Excellence of Design award Design Rev., 1969. Mem. Am. Soc. Agrl. Engrs., Soc. Automotive Engrs., Prudent Soc. Investment (pres.). Episcopalian. Home: 2712 4th St Ct East Moline IL 61244 Office: 3300 River Dr Moline IL 61265

SPENCER, DALE RAY, lawyer, editor; b. Pocatello, Idaho, Oct. 21, 1925; s. Howard Harris and Eleda (Eastman) S.; student Idaho State U., 1944-45; U. N.Mex., 1945-46; B.J., U. Mo., 1948, M.A., 1955, J.D., 1968: m. Lillian Joy Hodkins, Dec. 21, 1947; children—Melinda Sue, Jennifer Joy. Mem. faculty U. Mo., Columbia, 1950—, prof. journalism, 1971—, lectr. in communications law, 1958—; admitted to Mo. bar, 1969; founder, 1st pres. Mo. Assembly of Faculty in Higher Edn. Bd. dirs. Wonderland Camp for Handicapped Children, 1973—. Served with USN, 1943-46. Recipient Joyce Swan Distinguished Faculty award, 1967. Mem. Mo., Am. bar assns., Investigative Reporters and Editors, Sigma Delta Chi (nat. v.p. 1951-53), Kappa Xau Alpha, Kappa Alpha Mu. Club: Kiwanis. Editor Columbia Missourian, 1950-73. Home: 917 LaGrange St Columbia MO 65201 Office: School Journalism U Mo Columbia MO 65201

SPENCER, GEORGE EDWARD, surgeon; b. Cleve., Jan. 16, 1922; s. George Edward and Jessie Louise (Fairbank) S.; B.S., U. Mich., 1943; M.D., 1945; m. Jean Marie Toth, Apr. 24, 1945; children—George Edward, Geoffrey T. Intern, Charity Hosp. of La., New Orleans, 1945-46; resident in orthopedic surgery U. Hosps. Cleve., 1948-52; instr. Case Western Res. U., Cleve., 1952-55, asst. prof., 1955-64, asso. prof., 1964-73, prof., 1973—. Mem. med. adv. bd. Muscular Dystrophy Soc., 1967—. Bd. dirs. Acad. Medicine Cleve., 1968-71. Served with USNR, 1946-48. Diplomate Am. Bd. Orthopedic Surgery (examiner 1963—). Fellow A.C.S. (gov. 1973—); mem. Am. Acad. Orthopedic Surgery (chmn. com. on injuries, 1969-72), AMA, Cleve. Orthopedic Club (pres. 1970—), Ohio Orthopedic Soc., Am. Orthopedic Assn., Am. Acad. Orthopedic Surgeons, Orthopaedic Research Soc. Clubs: Chatauqua Lake Yacht (Lakewood, N.Y.). Mem. editorial bd. Emergency Care and Transportation of the Injured, 1971. Home: 22575 Canterbury Ln Shaker Heights OH 44122 Office: 11201 Shaker Blvd Cleveland OH 44104

SPENCER, JAMES CALVIN, educator; b. Detroit, Oct. 21, 1941; s. Donald Arthur and Beulah Nell (Hamilton) S.; B.A., Calif. State U., Los Angeles, 1966; M.A. (NDEA fellow), State U. N.Y. at Buffalo, 1970, Ph.D. (grad. fellow), 1973; m. Carol Johanna Brown, Dec. 18, 1965; children—James Calvin, Anne Elizabeth. Teaching asst. State U. N.Y. at Buffalo, 1967; instr. Genesee (N.Y.) Community Coll., 1971; asst. prof. philosophy and religion Cuyahoga Community Coll., Parma, Ohio, 1971-77; asso. prof., 1977—; cons. articulation, degree programs Case Western Res. U., 1973. Mem. Parma Area Fine Arts Council, Ashland County Hist. Soc.; sponsor Ashland Symphony Orch.; precinct committeeman Liberal party, Buffalo, 1967-71, Democratic party, 1976; chmn. Supt.'s Citizens Adv. Com. Mapleton Sch. Dist., 1977—. Mem. Internat. Phenomenological Soc., Am. Philos. Assn., Am. Acad. Religion, Les Amis du Vins, Mansfield Art Center. Democrat. Unitarian-Universalist. Home: 760 County Rd 601 Polk OH 44866 Office: 11000 Pleasant Valley Rd Parma OH 44130

SPENCER, JOSEPH STEWART, mfg. co. exec.; b. Kilbirnie, Scotland, Apr. 26, 1922; s. Hugh Morrison and Mary (MacInnes) S.; A.B., Harvard U., 1948; M.B.A., Columbia U., 1950. Tax accountant, asst. to treas., asst. treas. Union Spl. Corp., 1950-66, sec.-tres., 1966—. Served with AUS, 1942-45. Mem. Machinery and Allied Products Inst. (fin. council), Ill. C. of C., Ill. St. Andrew Soc., Chgo. Assn. Commerce and Industry. Presbyterian. Home: 1360 Lake Shore Dr Chicago IL 60610 Office: 400 N Franklin St Chicago IL 60610

SPENCER, MERLIN CLIFFORD, educator; b. Lake City, Iowa, Sept. 10, 1939; s. Clifford Cecil and Alice Mildred (Deuel) S.; B.S., Iowa State U., 1960; M.B.A., Ind. U., 1961, D.B.A., 1964; m. Jacqueline Bell, Jan. 8, 1972; children—Heather Sabrina, Ansley Monique. Asst. prof. marketing U. Kans., 1964-67; U. Mo., Kansas City, 1967-71, asso. prof., 1972-77; pres. Spencer Profl. Cons., Kansas City, Mo., 1966; univ. assoc. Lawrence-Leiter & Co., Kansas City, 1966—; v.p. corp. devel. Topsy's Internat., 1971-72; exec. dir. Nat. Educators Found., 1971-72; pres. Constituency Response, Inc., Kansas City, 1977—; cons. in field. Bd. dirs. Prime Health of Kansas City, 1975-77; chmn. Mo. State Environment Improvement Authority, 1964—; cons. Clay County Devel. Commn., 1977—. Mem. Citizens Assn. Kansas City, Mo. (bd. dirs. 1977), Am. Marketing Assn., Sales and Marketing Execs. Kansas City, Nat. Platform Speakers Assn., Internat. Relations Club, Friends of Art, Philharmonic Men's Club, Kansas City Hist. Soc. Republican. Episcopalian. Home: 4113 NW Claymont Dr Kansas City MO 64116 Office: 5100 Rockhill Rd Kansas City MO 64110

SPENCER, RALPH GEORGE, ednl. adminstr.; b. Brewster, Nebr., Apr. 26, 1923; s. Harry Bert and Edith Idora (Waters) S.; B.A., Chadron State Coll., 1947; M.Ed., U. Colo., 1955; certificate as edn. specialist U. Nebr., 1977; m. Mary Eva Coleman, June 3, 1951; children—Ruth Ellen, Steven George, Michael John. Prin., tchr. Brewster High Sch., 1944-49, Keya Paha County High Sch., Springview, Nebr., 1949-56; dir. guidance services Sidney (Nebr.) Pub. Schs., 1956—. Organist, Presbyn. Ch., Sidney. Recipient Doer award Cornhusker Counselor Assn., 1974; named Nebr. Outstanding Counselor of Yr., Nebr. Personnel and Guidance Assn., 1975. Mem. Am., Nebr. personnel and guidance assns., NEA, Nebr., Sidney (past pres.) edn. assns., Sidney Men's Chorus (past pres.), Phi Delta Kappa. Republican. Club: Kiwanis (past pres.) (Sidney). Editor, pub. Cornhusker News Views, 1973-74. Home: 1306 Dodge St Sidney NE 69162 Office: 1122 19th St Sidney NE 69162

SPENCER, STANLEY RAYMOND, mech. engr.; b. Albion, Mich., Mar. 5, 1930; s. Raymond George and Mae Lulla (Davis) S.; student Washington U., St. Louis, 1949-51; B.S. in Mech. Engring., U. Kans., 1953; m. Eve Bannister McRoberts, June 7, 1958; children—Stanley Raymond, Robert Davis, Elizabeth Anne. Engr. in tng. works 9, PPG Industries Inc., Crystal City, Mo., 1953-56, methods engr. works 9, 1956-59, chief indsl. engr., 1959-63, chief plant engr., 1963-69, chief engr. works 14, Mt. Zion, Ill., 1969—. Com. chmn. Explorer post 320, Lincoln Trails council Boy Scouts Am., 1972—, unit commr. Lincoln Trails council, 1973—. Served with Anti-Aircraft, U.S. Army, 1954-56. Mem. ASME (sec. local chpt. 1977—), Am. Inst. Indsl. Engrs. (pres. Land of Lincoln chpt. 1964-65), Am. Inst. Plant Engrs., Decatur C. of C., Tau Kappa Epsilon. Lutheran. Home: 454 Hackberry Dr Decatur IL 62521 Office: PO Box R Mount Zion IL 62549

SPENCER, TEMPLE (TIM) KEITH, writer, film producer; b. Ft. Wayne, Ind., June 26, 1931; s. Robert Theodore and Salome Irene (Skinner) S.; student U. Evansville (Ind.), 1959-61; m. Anna K.E. Klein, May 24, 1956; children—Kristina, Kristopher. With radio sta. WEOA, Evansville, 1959-61, radio sta. KJCK, Junction City, Kan., 1961-65; with sta. WEHT-TV, Evansville, 1965-74, dir. news and pub. affairs, 1965-74; owner Free Lance Assos., Evansville, 1974-77, Temple Communications, Portland, Mich., 1977—. Served with AUS, 1953-59. Recipient Alfred P. Sloan awards, 1968, 69, Gilmore award for editorials, 1972., named Outstanding TV Writer, Nat. Safety Council, 1969. Mem. Internat. Platform Assn., Sigma Delta Chi. Home and office: 230 Kent St Portland MI 48875

SPENCER, THOMAS H., agrl. machinery mfg. co. exec.; b. Independence, Iowa, Feb. 1, 1915; s. Elmer D. and Harriet (Irving) S.; B.S., Bradley U., 1939; m. Margaret R. Brown, Mar. 26, 1944; children—Mary Lauren, r James E. With Caterpillar Tractor Co., East Peoria, Ill., 1936—, heat treat supt., 1948-52, asst. chief metallurgist, 1952-55, heat treat mgr., 1955, plant metallurgist, 1955-57, quality control mgr., 1957-70, mfg. and materials devel. mgr., 1970—. Gen. chmn. Greater Peoria United Fund, 1965; treas. Community Health Found. Central Ill., 1967; commr., chmn. Greater Peoria Airport Authority, 1975—; mem. Mayor's Commn. on Poverty, 1968-69. Mem. Automation Research Council, Am. Soc. for Metals (mem. exec. com. 1950-65, nat. steelmaking com. 1970-71), Soc. Automotive Engrs. (chmn. Peoria chpt. 1966-67, chmn. iron and steel tech. com. 1966-76), Am. Welding Soc., Am. Soc. Quality Control, Metall. Soc. Am. Inst. Mining, Metall. and Petroleum Engrs., Soc. Mfg. Engrs. Contbr. articles to tech. jours. Patentee method for forming a composite welded article, 1963, track pin bushing, 1966. Home: Route 2 Southport Rd Peoria IL 61614 Office: 600 W Washington St East Poeria IL 61630

SPENCER, WILLIAM ARTHUR, univ. ofcl.; b. Huntington, Ind., Jan. 30, 1921; s. Lowell G. and Edith Evangeline (Augustine) S.; A.B., Ind. U., 1942; m. Jo Ann Whipple, May 26, 1951; children—Nancy, Thomas, Kevin. Reporter, New Enterprise, Corinth, N.Y., 1947; asst. dir. pub. relations Armour Research Found. of Ill. Inst. Tech., Chgo., 1948-52; dir. office info. services N.Y. U., N.Y.C., 1952-66; univ. relations officer Ind. U., Indpls., 1966-70; asst. to chancellor Ind. U.-Purdue U., Indpls., 1970—. Served to capt. AUS, 1943-46. Decorated Combat Infantryman's Badge, Bronze Star. Mem. Am. Coll. Pub. Relations Assn. (conf. chmn. Gt. Lakes dist.). Pub. Relations Soc. Am. (chpt. pres. 1970, Nat. Edn. com. 1974), Sigma Delta Chi, Theta Chi. Presbyn. Club: Devon Country, Indianapolis Press. Contbr. articles to profl. jours. Home: 4910 Winston Dr Indianapolis IN 46226 Office: 355 Lansing St Indianapolis IN 46202

SPENSLEY, GEORGE THOMAS, lawyer; b. Chgo., Mar. 29, 1905; s. Walter Franklin and Charlotte (Dechert) S.; LL.B., DePaul U., 1927; m. Irene Mungovan, Dec. 18, 1936. Admitted to Ill. bar, 1927, since practiced in Chgo. Mem. Am., Ill., Chgo. bar assns., Am. Judicature Soc., Sigma Delta Kappa. Home: 810 Vine Ave Park Ridge IL 60068 Office: 105 W Madison Chicago IL 60602

SPERO, KEITH ERWIN, lawyer; b. Cleve., Aug. 21, 1933; s. Milton D. and Yetta (Silverstein) S.; B.A., Western Res. U., 1954, LL.B., 1956; m. Carol Kohn, July 4, 1957 (div. 1974); children—Alana, Scott, Susan; m. 2d, Karen Weaver, Dec. 28, 1975. Admitted to Ohio bar, 1956; asso. firm Sindell, Sindell & Bourne, Cleve., 1956-57; asso. firm Sindell, Sindell, Bourne, Markus, Cleve., 1960-64; partner firm Sindell, Sindell, Bourne, Stern & Spero, 1964-74, firm Spero & Rosenfield, Cleve., 1974-76; pres. firm Spero, Rosenfeld & Bourne Co., Cleve., 1977—; tchr. bus. law U. Md. Overseas div., Eng., 1958-59; lectr. Case-Western Res. U., 1965-69; instr. Cleve. Marshall Law Sch. of Cleve State U., 1968—; mem. nat. panel arbitrators Am. Arbitration Assn. Served as 1st lt., JAGC, USAF, 1957-60; capt. Res., 1960-70. Mem. Am., Ohio, Cleve., Cuyahoga bar assns., Ohio (pres. 1970-71), Am. acads. trial lawyers, Order of Coif, Assn. Trial Lawyers Am. (state committeeman Ohio 1971-75, bd. govs. 1975—, sec. family law litigation sect. 1975-76, vice chmn. 1976-77, chmn. 1977-78), Phi Beta Kappa, Zeta Beta Tau, Tau Epsilon Rho. Jewish (trustee, v.p. congregation). Club: Masons. Author: The Spero Divorce Folio, 1966. Home: 2 Bratenahl Pl Bratenahl OH 44108 Office: Terminal Tower Cleveland OH 44113

SPERO, LESLIE WAYNE, wholesale distbn. and linen service exec.; b. Youngstown, Ohio, July 3, 1926; s. Harry and Sadie (Weiskopf) S.; student Ohio State U., 1943; B.A. summa cum laude, U. Calif. at Los Angeles, 1948; postgrad. Harvard U., 1965; m. Elaine Grossfield, Jan. 25, 1952; children—Rand Kevin, Laurie Diane. Purchasing agt. United Service Co., Youngstown, 1949, v.p., dir., 1953-68, chmn. bd., pres., 1968—; v.p., dir. United Paper Service Co., Youngstown, 1953-68, chmn. bd., pres., 1968—; v.p., dir. Nat. Textile Co., Youngstown, 1953-68, chmn. bd., pres., 1968—; dir. Dollar Savs. & Trust Co., Youngstown. Div. chmn. Community Chest, Youngstown, 1960-61, now mem. budget com.; pres. Community Relations Council, 1963, Am. Jewish Com., 1963-65, Child Guidance Center; bd. dirs. Nat. Found. March of Dimes, Youngstown, 1963; pres. Jewish Fedn. Youngstown, 1965-66; bd. dirs. Butler Gallery Am. Art, 1965-66, Heritage Manor; v.p., bd. dirs. Joint Bd. Children and Adult Mental Health Center, 1966—; trustee Bellfaire Home. Served to lt. (j.g.) USNR, 1944-46. Mem. Ohio Linen Supply Assn. (pres. 1965-66), Linen Supply Assn. Am. (dir.), U. Calif. Alumni Assn. (treas. 1949-50), C. of C., Phi Beta Kappa, Zeta Beta Tau (sec. 1947-48), Phi Eta Sigma. Clubs: Elks, Squaw Creek Country (gov. 1966), Rotary. Home: 3013 Logan Way Youngstown OH 44505 Office: 310 North Ave Youngstown OH 44502

SPERRY, FREDERICK EDWARD, univ. adminstr.; b. Milw., Aug. 11, 1936; s. Edward Joseph and Victoria Rose (Korek) S.; B.S., Marquette U., 1958; postgrad U. Wis., Milw., 1975-79; m. Barbara Jean Rhody, Nov. 18, 1961; children—Frederick J., Kathryn E., Robert J. With U. Wis., Milw., 1960—, asso. dir. admissions and records, 1969-75, dir. admissions, 1975—. Mem. Wis. Assn. Collegiate Registrars and Admissions Officers (pres.), Wis. Micrographics Assn. (past pres.), Am. Assn. Collegiate Registrars and Admissions Officers, Phi Kappa Phi. Roman Catholic. Lectr. on microfilming, U.S., Can. Home: 1519 Lake Bluff Blvd E Shorewood WI 53211 Office: PO Box 749 Milwaukee WI 53201

SPERRY, STUART MAJOR, educator; b. N.Y.C., Feb. 22, 1929; s. Stuart Major and Doris Mackenzie (Laidlaw) S.; A.B., Princeton U., 1951; A.M., Harvard U., 1955, Ph.D., 1959; m. Sophie Alma Zeytoon, June 11, 1966. Faculty, Ind. U., Bloomington, 1958—, prof. English, 1970—; vis. asso. prof. English, U. Calif. at Riverside, 1968-69. Served with arty. U.S. Army, 1951-53. Decorated Bronze Star with V, Purple Heart; recipient essay prize Wordsworth Bicentenary Colloquium Competition, 1970. Mem. Modern Lang. Assn., AAUP. Author: Keats the Poet, 1973; editorial bd. Keats-Shelley Jour., 1977—. Home: 908 S High St Bloomington IN 47401 Office: Dept English Ind U Bloomington IN 47401

SPEYER, FRED B., scientist; b. Kalamazoo, Feb. 28, 1916; s. Alfred and Cora (Burow) S.; B.A., Kalamazoo Coll., 1939, M.S., 1940; Ph.D., Internat. U., 1964; children—Alfred W. (dec.), Kip. With Dow Chem. Co., 1934-35, 40-41; chemist Upjohn Co., 1939-40; chief chemist Shellmar div. Continental Can Co., 1943-45, Am. Resinous Chem. Co., 1945-49, Gen. Mills Chem. Div., 1949-53; product devel. specialist Pierce & Stevens Co., 1953-55; supr. Splty. Coatings Union Oil Co. of Calif., 1955-59; supr. chem. product devel. Bendix Corp., 1959-62; supr. materials engring. Avco Corp., Lowell, Mass., 1962-65; prin. engr. TRW, Inc., Cleve., 1965—; dir. Cons. Research Assos. Mem. Am. Chem. Soc., Soc. Plastics Engrs., Sigma Xi. Republican. Christian Scientist. Patentee in field. Home: 24101 Lake Shore Blvd Euclid OH 44123 Office: 23555 Euclid Ave Euclid OH 44117

SPHIRE, RAYMOND DANIEL, anesthesiologist; b. Detroit, Feb. 12, 1927; s. Samuel Raymond and Nora Mae (Allen) S.; B.S., U. Detroit, 1948; M.D., Loyola U., Chgo., 1952; m. Joan Lois Baker, Sept. 5, 1953; children—Suzanne M., Raymond Daniel, Catherine J. Intern, Grace Hosp., Detroit, 1952-53, Harvard Anesthesia Lab., Mass. Gen. Hosp., 1953-55; attending anesthesiologist Grace Hosp., 1955-72, dir. dept. inhalation therapy, 1968-70; sr. attending anesthesiologist, dir. dept., dir. dept. respiratory therapy Detroit-Macomb Hosps., 1970—; clin. asst. prof. Wayne State U. Sch. Medicine, 1967—; clin. prof. respiratory therapy Macomb County Community Coll., Mt. Clemens, Mich., 1971—. Examiner, Am. Registry Respiratory Therapists, 1972—; insp. Joint Rev. Com. Respiratory Therapy Edn., 1972—; med. adviser Mich. Soc. Respiratory Therapists, 1973—. Served with AUS, 1944-45; as 1st lt. M.C., USAF, 1952. Diplomate Am. Bd. Anesthesiology. Fellow Am. Coll. Anesthesiologists, Am. Coll. Chest Physicians; mem. AMA, Am., Wayne County (pres. 1967-69), socs. anesthesiologists, Am. Assn. Respiratory Therapists, Soc. Critical Care Medicine. Clubs: Detroit Athletic, Country of Detroit, Otsego Ski, Severance Lodge. Co-author: Operative Neurosurgery, 1970. Home: 281 Lake Shore Rd Grosse Pointe Farms MI 48236 Office: 119 Kercheval St Grosse Pointe Farms MI 48236

SPICER, HAROLD OTIS, educator; b. Gosport, Ind., Dec. 10, 1921; s. Otis R. and Hattie Grace (Wampler) S.; A.B., DePauw U., 1947, M.A., 1949; Ph.D., Ind. U., 1962; m. Hilda Jane Templeton, June 21, 1946; children—Sheryl Lynne Spicer Ecenbarger, Sylvia Jean, Stephen Michael. Teaching asst. DePauw U., 1947-49, asst. prof., 1957-63; instr. Western Ill. U., 1949-55, asst. prof., 1955-57; asso. prof. English, Ind. State U., Terre Haute, 1963-73, prof., 1973—; lectr. English, Ind. U. Extension Center at Indpls., 1960-63; news dir. Sta. WWKS-FM, Macomb, Ill., 1955-57; editorial dir., office pub. relations DePauw U., 1957-60. Publicity man Community Concerts Assn., Macomb, Ill., 1952-56, Crippled Children's Soc., Greencastle, Ind., 1957-60. Served with USNR, 1942-46. Recipient Danforth Tchr. award 1959-60; Ind. U. fellow, 1955, 60. Mem. AAUP, Modern Lang. Assn., Modern Humanities Research Assn., Ind. Coll. English Assn., Nat. Council Coll. Publs. Advisers (nat. head dist. chmn. 1964-65; editor Coll. Press Rev. 1965-67), Soc. Profl. Journalists, Lambda Chi Alpha, Sigma Delta Chi (Man of Year award 1968). Christian Scientist. Author: News Writing, 1964; contbr. to 3d edit. Halkett and Lang Dictionary Anonymous and Pseudonymous Literature; asso. editor Ind. English Jour., 1974—. Home: 706 Highwood Ave Greencastle IN 46135 Office: 206 Parsons Hall Ind State U Terre Haute IN 47809

SPICER, JOHN AUSTIN, space scientist; b. Rock Springs, Wyo., Sept. 25, 1930; s. Ernest Marvin and Ruth (Stevens) S.; student Mass. Inst. Tech., 1949-51; B.S., U. Wyo., 1956, M.S., 1957; Ph.D., U. Freiburg (Germany), 1962; m. Erika Marianne Grundig, Aug. 19, 1961; children—Cynthia, Michael, Marilynn. Physicist, Marshall Space Flight Center, Huntsville, Ala., 1957-59; mathematician Goodyear Aerospace, Litchfield Park, Ariz., 1962-63; sr. engr. Aerojet Gen. Corp., Azusa, Calif., 1963-64; research specialist N.Am. Aviation, Downey, 1964-66; asso. scientist Chrysler Space div. Chrysler Corp., New Orleans, 1966-68; sr. research mathematician U. Dayton (Ohio) Research Inst., 1968-70; ops. research analyst McCalls Printing Co., Dayton, 1970-71; mathematician Air Force Flight Dynamics Lab., Wright Patterson AFB, Dayton, 1971-72, program mgr., physicist Air Force Avionics Lab., 1972—. Served with Signal Corps, AUS, 1951-53. Mem. Am. Math. Soc., IEEE (chmn. aerospace and electronics group Dayton sect. 1968-69), Tensor Soc., Ops. Research Soc. Am. Home: 4172 Meadowsweet Dr Dayton OH 45424 Office: AF Avionics Lab Wright Patterson AFB Dayton OH 45433

SPICER, SAMUEL GARY, lawyer; b. Dickson, Tenn., Jan. 8, 1942; s. Clark and E. Maybelle (Hogin) S.; A.B., Adrian Coll., 1964; M.B.A., Wayne State U., 1965; J.D., Detroit Coll. of Law, 1969; m. Katherine Stettner, May 12, 1972; children—Victoria, Gary, Matthew. Admitted to Tenn. bar, 1969, Mich. bar, 1969; with personnel dept. Gen. Motors Corp., Pontiac, Mich., 1964-66; with trust dept. Nat. Bank of Detroit, 1966-69; accountant Price Waterhouse and Co., Detroit, 1969-71; mem. firm Spicer and Littman, P.C., Detroit; dir. Hoke Enterprises, Inc., Tayler Internat. Inc. Elder, mem. fin. com. Fort St. Presbyn. Ch. Served with USAR, 1966-72. Mem. Am., Mich., Tenn., Detroit bar assns. Clubs: Detroit Athletic, Adrian Coll. Alumni (dir.). Home: 1300 Lafayette St E Apt 2507 Detroit MI 48209 Office: 200 Renaissance Center Suite 3720 Detroit MI 48243

SPIEGELBERG, HARRY LESTER, paper co. exec.; b. New London, Wis., Apr. 24, 1936; s. Harry Henry and Gladys Louise (Kalt) S.; B.S. in Chem. Engring., U. Wis., 1959; M.S., Inst. Paper Chemistry, 1963, Ph.D. (NSF fellow), 1966; m. Bonnie Faye Ludden, Jan. 23, 1960; children—Susan, Sharon, Stephen, Scott. Engr., Kimberly Clark Corp., Neenah, Wis., 1959-61, research chemist, 1965-67, project leader, 1967-68, supt. new concepts lab., 1968-70, mgr. new concepts research, 1970-73, dir. research and devel., 1973—; instr., U. Wis., 1957-59. Chmn., Gordon Research Conf., 1971. Bd. dirs. Children's Theatre. Served with C.E., AUS, 1959. Mem. Alpha Chi Sigma, Tau Beta Pi, Delta Sigma, Phi Kappa Phi. Congregationalist. (chmn., sr. deacon, trustee). Contbr. to Consolidation of the Paper Web, 1965. Home: 2017 N Eugene Appleton WI 54911 Office: Kimberly Clark W Neenah WI 54956

SPINK, FRANK HAIL, JR., city ofcl.; b. Kansas City, Mo., Sept. 9, 1918; s. Frank Hail and Margaret Cecila (Gilchrist) S.; B.A., U. Kans.; postgrad. Command and Gen. Staff Coll., Ft. Leavenworth, Kans., 1944, Indsl. Coll. of Armed Forces, Washington, 1952; m. Anne Marie Vernson, Aug. 5, 1942; children—Frank Hail III, Anne M. Ryan, John J. Exec. v.p. Bunting Hardware Co., Kansas City, 1952-68; dir. fire and emergency preparedness City of Kansas City, 1969—. Bd. dirs. ARC, Nat. Council Pres.'s Support of Guard and Res. Served to maj. gen. USAF. Mem. Greater Kansas City C. of C. (chmn. mil. affairs com.), Am. Royal Assn., Liberty Meml. Assn., Air Force Assn. (dir. Harry S. Truman chpt.), Mil. Order World Wars (comdr. Kansas City chpt.), Armed Forces Council Greater Kansas City (pres.), Builders Hardware Assn., Nat. Assn. Fire Chiefs, Res. Officers Assn., Club Pres.'s Round Table (pres. 1967), Sigma Phi Epsilon. Rotarian (past club pres.). Club: Homestead Country. Contbr. articles to trade jours, nat. mags. Home: 1234 Huntington Rd Kansas City MO 64113 Office: 414 E 12th St Kansas City MO 64106

SPINO, FRANK JOHN, dentist; b. Cleve., June 11, 1937; s. Dominic A. and Lucy (De Baltzo) S.; student Otterbein Coll., 1955-57; B.A., Case-Western Res. U., 1959, D.D.S., 1963; m. Arline Grace Stanbury, May 7, 1960; children—Susan Laurel, Thomas Jeffrey. Gen. practice dentistry, Solon, Ohio, 1965—. Served to capt. USAF, 1963-65. Recipient Outstanding Service award Delta Sigma Delta, 1963; named Outstanding Young Man of Am., Jaycees, 1970; recipient Outstanding Service certificate USAF Surgeon Gen.'s Office SAC, 1965. Mem. Am. Acad. Gen. Dentistry, ADA, Ohio, Cleve. dental socs., Delta Sigma Delta. Clubs: Rotary (pres. Solon 1970), Solon Jaycees (v.p. 1966-67), Boosters (Solon and Chagrin Falls, Ohio), A.F.S.-Chagrin Valley, YMCA, Chagrin Valley Country, Otterbein Coll. O, Centurion, Case-Western Res. Dental Sch. Scholars. Home: 33199 Fairmount Blvd Pepper Pike OH 44124 Office: 6370 SOM Center Rd Solon OH 44139

SPIOTTA, RAYMOND HERMAN, editor; b. Bklyn., Feb. 24, 1927; s. Michael Joseph and Olga Elizabeth (Schmidt) S.; B.M.E., Pratt Inst., 1953; m. Marie Theresa Attanasio, Apr. 17, 1949; children—Michael, Ronald, Mark, Sandra. Mfg. engr. Arma div. Am. Bosch Arma Corp., Garden City, N.Y., 1948-53; mng. editor Machinery mag., N.Y.C., 1953-65; editor Machine and Tool Blue Book, Wheaton, Ill., 1965-74, exec. editor, 1974—. Mem. DuPage (Ill.) area council Boy Scouts Am., 1966-73. Served with A.C., USNR, 1944-48. Mem. Indsl. Mgmt. Soc., Numerical Control Soc., Soc. Bus. Press Editors, Am. Bus. Press, Am. Inst. Indsl. Engrs., Soc. Am. Value Engrs. Roman Catholic. Contbr. articles to profl. jours. Home: 26W354 Blackhawk Dr Wheaton IL 60187 Office: Hitchcock Bldg Wheaton IL 60187

SPIRO, BERNARD, dentist; b. Russia, Jan. 18, 1896; s. Israel and Ethel (Newman) S.; came to U.S., 1906, naturalized, 1912; D.D.S., Loyola U., Chgo., 1916; m. Goldie Gold, Feb. 12, 1918 (dec.); 1 dau., Pearl Penninah (Mrs. Adolph M. Maller). Pvt. practice dentistry, Chgo., 1918—. Founder, Hebrew U., Jerusalem; founding mem. Israel Inst. Tech., Haifa; mem. Am. for a Music Library in Israel; chmn. dental div. Jewish United Fund of Met. Chgo., 1960-62, State of Israel Bonds, 1955-77; mem. bd. Jewish edn. Jewish Theological Seminary of N.Y., Hebrew Theological Coll. of Chgo. Bd. dirs. State of Israel Bonds, Am. Friends of the Hebrew U. Served with USNR. Recipient Certificate of Merit, Alpha Omega Internat. Dental Fraternity, 1962, Man of Yr. award 1969, Meritorious award medal, 1971; Ben Gurian award State of Israel, 1961, 71; State of Israel Achievement award, President's Citation award, State of Israel, S.Y. Agnon Gold medal Hebrew U. Jerusalem, 1973; Dr. Bernard Spiro chair for vis. prof. established Hebrew U., 1975. Mem. Am. Ort Fedn., ADA, Ill., Chgo. dental socs., Am. Legion, Zionist Orgn. Chgo., NCCJ, Am.-Israel Cultural Found., Weizmann Inst. Sci. in Israel, Loyola U. Alumni Assn. Mason; mem. B'nai B'rith. Club: Covenant Club Ill. (Chgo.). Home: 2800 N Lake Shore Dr Chicago IL 60657 Office: 55 E Washington St Suite 1717 Chicago IL 60602

SPIRO, HARRY, dentist; b. Lida, Russia, Apr. 29, 1898; came to U.S. 1906, naturalized 1912; s. Israel and Ethel (Newman) S.; D.D.S., Chgo. Coll. Dental Surgery, 1921; m. Rose Ruth Jacobson, Sept. 25, 1918; children—Alvin Piermont, Seymour Selby, Bette Ann (Mrs. Richard Bloom). Pvt. practice dentistry, Chgo., 1921—. Conducted postgrad. courses Tufts U., Boston, 1949-51; lectures, postgrad. courses and clinics at dental colls., dental socs., study clubs U.S. and Canada. Recipient Ambassador of Goodwill award Fla. Dental Soc., 1939. Mem. Am., Ill., Chgo., Englewood dental socs. Mason (lodge master 1928). Inventor, developer of numerous prosthetic dentistry devices and techniques. Home: 3600 N Lake Shore Dr Chicago IL 60613 Office: 25 E Washington St Chicago IL 60602

SPIRO, JAMES (DEMETRI) MICHAEL, lawyer; b. Chgo., Jan. 1, 1920; s. Michael M. and Mary (Kubelka) S.; A.B., U. Chgo., 1941; J.D., DePaul U., 1948; m. Leila Wetzel, June 10, 1948. Jr. exec. Bauer & Black div. Kendall Co., Chgo., 1941-43, 46-47; admitted to Ill. bar, 1947, U.S. Dist. Ct., 1948, Supreme Ct. U.S., 1950, U.S. Ct. Mil. Appeals, 1954; pvt. practice law, Chgo., 1947-49, 69—; exec. Am. Bar Assn., Chgo., 1949-69; sec.-treas. Spiros Bros. Corp., Chgo., 1972—; spl. projects cons. Nat. Strategy Info. Center, N.Y.C., 1974—, v.p., 1969-74; exec. v.p. Anthony Kane Assos., Inc., Chgo., 1970-72; faculty Roosevelt U., Chgo., 1950, City of Chgo. Jr. Coll., 1952-62. Served with AUS, 1943-45, 51-52; now brig. gen. Res. Decorated Bronze Star medal. Mem. Am., Ill., Chgo. bar assns., Hellenic Bar Assn., Am. Judicature Soc., Judge Advocates Assn., Scribes. Contbr. articles to profl. jours. Home: 2021 W Hunt Ave Chicago IL 60620 Office: 134 N LaSalle St Chicago IL 60602

SPITZ, WERNER URI, physician; b. Stargard, Pomerania, Germany, Aug. 22, 1926; s. Siegfried and Anna Judith (Faktor) S.; came to U.S., 1959, naturalized, 1970; student U. Geneva (Switzerland), 1946-50; M.D., Hebrew U., Jerusalem, 1954; m. Anne R. Keates, Sept. 23, 1961; children—Rhona Judith, Jonathan David, Daniel Joseph. Intern, Tel-Hashomer Govt. Hosp., Israel, 1953-54, resident, 1954-58; resident Hadassah U. Med. Sch., 1958-59; fellow in forensic pathology U. Md., 1959-61; asso. prof. forensic pathology Free U. Med. Sch., West Berlin, Germany, 1961-63; asst. med. examiner State of Md., 1963-68, dep. chief med. examiner, 1969-72; chief med. examiner Wayne County, Detroit, 1972—; asso. prof. pathology U. Md., 1966-72, Johns Hopkins, 1966-72, Wayne State U. Sch. Medicine, 1972—; cons. Johns Hopkins Applied Physics Lab., 1970—, VA Hosp., Allen Park, Mich., 1973—. Pres., Mich. Medico-legal Research and Ednl. Assn., Inc., 1975—. Served to lt. M.C., Israeli Army, 1955-58. Fellow Coll. Am. Pathologists, Am. Soc. Clin. Pathologists; mem. AMA, Am. Acad. Forensic Scis., Nat. Assn. Med. Examiners, Soc. Exptl. Biology and Medicine, Mich. Soc. Pathologists, Brit. Acad. Forensic Scis. Author: Medicolegal Investigation of Death, 1973. Editor: Jour. Legal Medicine, Heidelberg, 1970, Excerpta Medica, 1975—, Am. Jour. Forensic Scis., 1975—. Contbr. articles to profl. jours. Home: 50 Stonehurst St Grosse Pointe Shores MI 48236 Office: 400 E Lafayette Ave Detroit MI 48226

SPITZER, JOHN ANDREW, retail co. exec.; b. Grafton, Ohio, Feb. 1, 1917; s. George G. and Harriet N. (Neufer) S.; B.S. in Accounting, Ohio State U., 1939; m. Helen C. Casper, Aug. 1, 1942; children—Alan, Randy, Douglas, Karen, Kevin. Mgr., Spitzer Hardware, Spitzer Motors, Grafton, 1939-42, Spitzer Motors Elyria, Inc. (Ohio), 1945-53; chmn. bd. Spitzer Mgmt., Inc., automobile dealerships, fin. cos., constrn. firms, real estate devel., Elyria, 1953—. Mem. Lorain County (Ohio) Fair Bd., 1948-55; exec. com. Lorain County council Boy Scouts U.S.A., 1949-53; v.p. Culver (Ind.) Mil. Acad. Fathers Assn., 1964-67; mem. pres.'s adv. bd. Ashland (Ohio) Coll.; trustee Lorain County Community Coll., Elyria. Served to capt. USAAF, 1942-45. Recipient numerous Quality Dealer awards, automobile mfrs. Mem. Am., Ohio, Fla. automobile dealers assns., Nat., Ohio hardware dealers assns., Ohio State U. Alumni Assn. Home: Brentwood Lake Village OH 44044 Office: 150 E Bridge St Elyria OH 44035

SPITZER, RANDY LEE, hardware store exec.; b. Elyria, Ohio, Nov. 2, 1947; s. John A. and Helen C. (Casper) S.; B.S. in Accounting and Bus. Mgmt., Ashland Coll., 1970. Vice pres., mgr. Spitzer Hardware & Supply Co., Akron, O., 1965-71, v.p., dir., 1971—; v.p., gen. mgr. Spitzer Akron, Inc., automobile dealership, 1971—; pres. Spitzer Buick Co., 1975—; dir. Spitzer Columbus Inc. Tchr. Wellington (Ohio) High Sch., 1970-71. Mem. Nat., Ohio hardware dealers assns., Akron Area Automobile Dealers Assn., Phi Delta Theta. Home: 2168 Beech Tree Dr Uniontown OH 44685 Office: 745 E Market St Akron OH 44305

SPIVEY, DONALD, historian; b. Chgo., July 18, 1948; s. Alex Gayles and Roberta (Spivey) Gayles Smith; B.A. with distinction, U. Ill., 1971, M.A., 1972; Ph.D., U. Calif., Davis, 1976; m. Diane Marie Collins, Aug. 28, 1971; 1 dau., Sahar Adama. Lectr. history U. Calif., Davis, 1975-76; asst. prof. history Wright State U., Dayton, Ohio, 1976—; research and cultural dir. African-Am. Studies Inst., Dayton, 1977—. Mem. Assn. for Study Afro-Am. History and Life, Am. Hist. Assn., Internat. Psychohistory Assn., Orgn. Am. Historians, Southwestern Social Sci. Assn., Omega Psi Phi. Author: Schooling for the New Slavery: Black Industrial Education, 1868-1915, 1978. Home: 3738 Cornell Woods Dr Dayton OH 45406 Office: Dept History Wright State U Dayton OH 45431

SPLITTSTOESSER, WALTER EMIL, educator; b. Claremont, Minn., Aug. 27, 1937; s. Waldemar Theodore and Opal Mae (Young) S.; B.S. with distinction (univ. fellow), U. Minn., 1958; M.S., S.D. State U., 1960; Ph.D., Purdue U., 1963; m. Shirley Anne O'Connor, July 2, 1960; children—Pamela, Sheryl, Riley. Plant breeder U. Minn., 1956-58; weed scientist S.D. State U., 1958-60; plant physiologist Purdue U., Lafayette, Ind., 1960-63, Shell Oil, Modesto, Calif., 1963-64; biochemist U. Calif., Davis, 1964-65; prof., head, vegetable crops div. U. Ill., Urbana, 1965—; vis. prof. Univ. Coll., London, Eng., 1972; biologist Parkland Coll., Champaign, Ill., 1974. NIH fellow, 1964-65. Recipient J.H. Gourley award Am. Fruit Grower and Am. Soc. Hort. Sci., 1974. Mem. Weed Sci. Soc. Am., Am. Soc. Hort. Sci. (rev. editor Jour. 1969—), Am., Japanese, Scandinavian socs. plant physiologists, Sigma Xi, Alpha Zeta, Gamma Sigma Delta, Delta Theta Sigma, Phi Kappa Phi. Rev. editor Hort. Sci., Analytical Biochemistry, 1969—. Contbr. articles to profl. jours. Home: 2006 Cureton Urbana IL 61801 Office: Vegetable Crops Bldg U Ill Urbana IL 61801

SPODEK, BERNARD, educator; b. Bklyn., Sept. 17, 1931; s. David and Esther (Lebenbaum) S.; B.A., Bklyn. Coll., 1952; M.A., Columbia U. Tchrs. Coll., 1955, Ed.D., 1962; m. Prudence Moy Far Debb, June 21, 1957; children—Esther Yinling, Jonathan Chou. Tchr. nursery, kindergarten and primary grades Beth Hayeled Sch., N.Y.C., 1952-56, elementary grades N.Y.C. Bd. Edn., 1956-57, nurser-kindergarten Early Childhood Center, Bklyn. Coll., 1957-60; asst. prof. elementary edn. U. Wis., Milw., 1961-65; prof. early childhood edn. U. Ill., 1965—; dir. NDEA Insts., 1965-66, 67. Childcraft fellow, 1960-61. Mem. Assn. Supervision and Curriculum Devel. (head task force on presch. edn. 1966-68), Assn. Childhood Edn. Internat., Am. Ednl. Research Assn., AAUP, Nat. Assn. Edn. Young Children (book rev. editor Young Children 1972-74, pres. 1976—), Nat. Soc. Study Edn., Profs. Curriculum. Author books, the latest being: Teaching in the Early Years, 1972; Early Childhood Education, 1973; Teacher Education, 1974; editor: Preparing Teachers of Disadvantaged Young Children, 1966; (with Herbert J. Walberg) Studies in Open Education, 1975, Early Childhood Education: Issues and Perspectives, 1977; contbr. articles to profl. publs. Home: 1123 W Charles St Champaign IL 61820 Office: 302 Education Bldg U Ill Urbana IL 61801

SPOHN, WILLIAM BOYD, land devel. exec.; b. Des Moines, Dec. 27, 1920; s. William Bacon and Maude Mae (Boyd) S.; m. Patricia Marie Curran, Mar. 9, 1941; children—Sandra (Mrs. Claire Evert Brooks), Patricia (Mrs. Kerry Scott Nelson), Teresa Mae, Nancy Jane (Mrs. Benjamine Clyde Dilliner). Auto parts distbn. mgr. Delevan Engring., Des Moines, 1945-48; cons. supt. Colby Constrn. Co., Des Moines, 1948-58, gen. mgr., 1958-73; gen. mgr. Sherwood Forest Co., land devel., Des Moines, 1962—; v.p. Colby Trust Services Co., land devel., Des Moines, 1974—. Cons. to various land devel. trusts. Served with USNR, 1942-45. Mem. Am. Mgmt. Assn., Urban Land Inst. Home: 6804 Reite Ave Des Moines IA 50311 Office: 6581 University Ave Des Moines IA 50311

SPOHR, ARNOLD, artistic dir., choreographer; b. Rhein, Sask., Can., Dec. 26, 1927; ed. Winnipeg Tchrs. Coll., 1942-43; LL.D. (hon.), U. Man., 1970. Piano tchr., 1946-51; prin. dancer Royal Winnipeg Ballet, 1947-54, artistic dir., 1958—, dir., tchr. Sch. of Royal Winnipeg Ballet, 1958—; television choreographer, performer CBC, 1955-57; choreographer Rainbow Stage, 1957-60; dir. dance dept. Nelson Sch. Fine Arts, 1964-67; artistic dir. dance dept. Banff Sch. Fine Arts, 1967—; bd. dirs. Canadian Theatre Centre; vice chmn. Bd. Dance Can. Choreographer, Ballet Premier, 1950, Intermede, 1951, E Minor, 1959, Hansel and Gretal, 1960, also 18 musicals for Rainbow Stage. Recipient Can. Council Molson prize for outstanding contbn. to arts, 1970, Order of Can., 1970, Centennial medal Govt. of Can., 1967. Home: 289 Portage Ave Winnipeg MB R3B 2B4 Canada

SPOLYAR, LUDWIG JOHN, univ. adminstr.; b. Detroit, Feb. 5, 1931; s. Ludwig and Leona Anna (Tomay) S.; B.A., San Jose State Coll., 1952; M.A., Mich. State U., 1955, Ph.D., 1959; m. Kirsten Elizabeth Staff, Sept. 6, 1958; children—Elizabeth Ann, Charles Anthony, John Ludwig. Counselor, Long Beach (Calif.) State Coll., 1959-60; asso. dean students Fullerton (Calif.) State Coll., 1960-62; mgr. Associated Students, U. Wash., Seattle, 1962-67; dir. student activities U. Minn., Mpls., 1967-71, dir. campus assistance center, 1971—. Served with USAF, 1952-54. Licensed psychologist, Minn., Wash. Mem. Am. Psychol. Assn., Am., Minn. personnel and guidance assns., Am., Minn. coll. personnel assns., Am. Assn. Higher Edn., Nat. Assn. Student Personnel Adminstrs., Phi Delta Kappa. Roman Catholic. Home: 1505 E River Rd Minneapolis MN 55414 Office: 107 TNM U Minn Minneapolis MN 55455

SPONSELLER, EUGENE, psychologist; b. Canton, Ohio, Feb. 4, 1921; s. Donald and Nettie (Gordon) S.; B.S., Kent State U., 1943, M.Ed., 1956; postgrad. Akron U., 1958-59, Western Res. U., 1962; m. Betty M. Foust, June 7, 1942; children—Terry L., Kathy Dee Gribble. Tchr., coach Navarre (Ohio) High Sch., 1947-52; tchr., coach counselor, psychologist Perry schs., Canton, 1952-61; psychologist, then chief psychologist Canton City Schs., 1961-75, coordinator Child Diagnostic Center, 1975—. Dir. Human Engring. Inst., Canton, 1968-69; faculty Walsh Coll., Canton, summer 1973. Served with AUS, 1943-46. Mem. Nat., Ohio assns. sch. psychologists, Nat., Ohio edn. assns., Canton Profl. Educators Assn., Phi Delta Kappa. Home: 1391 Indian Hill Dr Bolivar OH 44612 Office: 618 High Ave NW Canton OH 44703

SPOONER, SUE ELIZABETH, educator; b. Indpls., Feb. 14, 1939; d. Hugh J. and Dorothy Cooper (Genung) Baker; B.S., Purdue U., 1960, Ph.D., 1975; M.S., U. Wis., Madison, 1961; m. John Alfred Spooner, June 30, 1962; 1 son, Jon Kevin. Counselor, instr. Colo. Coll., Colorado Springs, 1962-63; counselor Univ. Counseling Center, U. Wis., Madison, 1961-62, research asso. Tchr. Placement Bur., 1965-67, asst. dir. Office of High Sch. Relations, 1967-70; exec. dir. Sycamore Girl Scout Council, Lafayette, Ind., 1970-72; student personnel intern Office of Registrar, Purdue U., W. Lafayette, Ind., 1972-74, asst. to dir. Univ. Placement Service, 1974-75, vis. asst. prof. counseling and personnel services Dept. Edn., 1975-76; asst. prof. counselor edn. Coll. Edn. U. Wis., Oshkosh, 1976—; cons. YWCA, Girl Scouts USA, pub. sch. systems, colls., univs. Certified psychologist, Ind. Mem. Am. Psychol. Assn., Am. Wis., E. Central personnel and guidance assns., Am., Wis. coll. personnel assns., Midwest Assn. Student Personnel Educators, Nat., N. Central, Wis. assns. counselor educators and suprs. Contbr. articles to Jour. Coll. Student Personnel, Jour. Counseling Psychology, Nat. Assn. Student Personnel Adminstrs. Home: 805A Anchorage Ct Oshkosh WI 54901 Office: Dept Counselor Edn U Wis Oshkosh WI 54901

SPOONER, WILLIAM AUSTIN, mgmt. cons.; b. Madison, S.D., Mar. 20, 1918; s. William Tracy and Abigail Pauline (Connell) S.; B.S., Calif. Inst. Tech., 1940; M.B.A., Harvard U., 1956; m. Rita Therese Nicholson, Sept. 7, 1946; children—William Austin, Eileen T. Spooner O'Brien. Commd. ensign U.S. Navy, advanced through grades to comdr., 1956; ret., 1963; bus. operations mgr. F-111 Systems programs Litton Industries, Inc., 1963-65; controller Rocket Research Corp., Seattle, 1966; supr. missiles mgmt. systems Columbus div. Rockwell Corp., 1965-70; pres., chief exec. officer William A. Spooner Assos., Inc., Columbus, Ohio, 1970—; dir. Superior Plating Co.; speaker on mgmt. planning to community and trade assns. Mem. IEEE, Ind. Profl. Cons. Assn., Planning Execs. Inst. Roman Catholic. Home: 1746 Pin Oak Dr Columbus OH 43229 Office: 1900 E Dublin Granville Rd Columbus OH 43229

SPOTT, SAAD, elec. engr.; b. New Castle, Pa., Nov. 1, 1921; s. Hassan Habib and Mariam (Salah) S.; B.E.E., Ill. Inst. Tech., 1961; m. Massika Sebat, Aug. 5, 1956; children—Alan, Michele. Registered profl. engr., Ind. Jr. engr. No. Ind. Pub. Service Co., Hammond, 1948-49, engr., 1949-50, jr. test engr., 1950-52, test engr., 1952-62, substa. engr., 1962-65, sr. substa. engr., 1965-69, sr. elec. engr., 1969-74, gen. standards elec. engr., 1974—; lectr. Purdue U., Calumet, 1965-76. Mem. IEEE (sr.), Am. Nuclear Soc., Am. Legion. Club: Masons. Home: 9228 Cottage Grove Ave Highland IN 46322

SPRAGUE, BERNARD, judge; b. Hastings, Nebr., May 1, 1932; s. Leon A. and Helen M. (McNeny) S.; B.S., U. Denver, 1956, LL.B. cum laude, 1958; m. Barbara Mary Flanagan Aug. 6, 1955; children—Michael, Kathleen, Patrick, Ann. Admitted to Nebr. bar, 1958; practice in Red Cloud, 1958-60, 63-72; asst. U.S. atty., 1960-63; atty. Webster County, 1966-72; dist. county judge, 1972-77; dist. judge 10th Jud. Dist. Nebr., 1977—. Mem. Nebr. Democratic Central Com., 1958-60; del. Nebr. Dem. Conv., 1958-62; mem. Red Cloud High Sch. System, 1965-66. Served with USMCR, 1952-55. Mem. Nebr. Dist. County Judges Assn. (pres. 1975-76), Am. Legion, VFW, DAV, Order St. Ives, Omicron Kappa Delta, Delta Tau Delta, Phi Delta Phi. Roman Catholic. Club: Elks. Home: 840 W 7th St Red Cloud NE 68970 Office: Webster County Ct House Red Cloud NE 68970

SPRAGUE, DAVID STANLEY, univ. adminstr.; b. Osakis, Minn., Aug. 6, 1934; s. Stanley P. and Margaret Harriet (Johnson) S.; B.S., Dakota State Coll., 1960; M. Ed., S.D. State U., 1963; Ed.D., U. S.D., 1969; m. Betty Lou Moberg, May 25, 1963; children—Clark John, Travis David. Tchr. Lynd (Minn.) High Sch., 1960-62; prin. Russell (Minn.) High Sch., 1962-63; dir. testing, asst. to grad. dean S.D. State U., Brookings, 1963-67; dir. counseling St. Cloud (Minn.) State U., 1969-72, v.p. student life and devel., 1972-77; cons. in field. Deacon 1st. Presbyn. Ch. St. Cloud, 1976—; active Democratic party. Served with U.S. Army, 1954-56. NDEA fellow, 1967-69; Bur. Indian Affairs grantee, 1968. Mem. Minn. (pres. 1977-78), Am. (dir. commn. II 1977—) coll. personnel assns., Am. Personnel and Guidance Assn., Nat. Assn. Student Personnel Adminstrs. (asst. regional v.p. 1977-78). Club: Elks. Home: 33 Jeffrey Ct Saint Cloud MN 56301 Office: Atwood Center Saint Cloud State U St Cloud MN 56301

SPRATT, DORIS LOUISE, bus. scientist; b. Indpls., Mar. 26, 1933; d. William Henry and Edna Rebecca S.; B.A. cum laude, Bob Jones U., 1954, M.A., 1956; postgrad. Anderson Bus. Coll., 1963. Instr. in Christian edn. Bob Jones U., Greenville, S.C., 1954-62; dean, coordinator curriculum Alverson-Draughon Bus. Coll., Huntsville, Ala., 1963-67; instr. bus., student adviser Porter Coll., Indpls., 1967-70; instr., student adviser, coordinator curriculum Hammel-Actual Coll., Akron, Ohio, 1970-72; head secretarial dept., chief instr. Columbus (Ohio) Bus. U., 1972—. Mem. Ohio Bus. Tchrs. Assn., Evang. Tchr. Tng. Assn., Awanas and Pine Hills Missionary Fellowship. Baptist. Home: 5955 Parliament Dr Columbus OH 43213 Office: 4807 Evanswood Dr Columbus OH 43229

SPRATT, GENE, publishing co. exec.; b. Ottawa, Kans., June 11, 1924; s. Eugene and Sadie (Crumley) S.; B.A., Kans. State U., 1946; m. Naomi Sanders, Mar. 15, 1950; children—Marc Millard, Lindsey Leroy. Editor, Am. Poultry Jour., Chgo., 1948-51; publs. editor Kans. Bd. Agr., Topeka, 1948-51; dep. dir. U.S. Treasury savs. bonds div. for Kans., 1951-68; mem. staff lt. gov. John Crutcher for gov., 1968; editor Kans. Transporter Mag., Kans. Motor Carriers Assn., Topeka, 1968-74; pres. Storytell Co., Topeka, 1975—. Guest lectr., instr. pub. relations Washburn U., Topeka, 1949-50. Mem. Trucking Industry Pub. Relations Coordinating Com., Washington, 1970-74. Mem. Topeka Pub. Relations Soc. (treas. 1974-75), Kans. State U. Alumni Assn., Sigma Delta Chi, Tau Kappa Epsilon. Kiwanian. Address: 207 Woodlawn Potwin Pl Topeka KS 66606

SPRECHER, LINDA JANE, marketing exec.; b. San Diego, Oct. 19, 1951; d. Marvin Edward and Margaret Fern (Phillips) Sprecher; B.S. in Mktg., No. Ill. U., 1973. Mktg. analyst Kohler Co., Kohler, Wis., 1973—. Advisor, Jr. Achievement, Kohler. Mem. Am. Mktg. Assn., Wis. State Hist. Soc. Roman Catholic. Home: 419 High St Kohler WI 53044 Office: 44 High St Kohler WI 53044

SPRENGEL, DONALD PHILIP, educator; b. Chgo., Aug. 5, 1938; s. Andrew Cyril and Margaret Mary (Kirkpatrick) S.; B.S., Loyola U., Chgo., 1960; A.M., St. Louis U., 1962; Ph.D., U. N.C., Chapel Hill, 1966; m. Annette Jean Rysiewski, June 13, 1964; children—Andrew Thomas, Jean Michele. Asst. prof. U. Ia., 1965-69; prof. urban affairs St. Louis U., 1969—, asso. univ. research adminstr., 1975—; cons. in field. Mem. Midwest regional Am. Assembly on State Legislatures, 1967—, Mid-Am. regional Am. Assembly on State and Urban Crisis, 1970—. Ford Found. legis. intern, 1962-63. Named Am. Assn. Sch. Adminstrs./NEA Distinguished Prof., 1968. Mem. Am., Midwest, Mo. polit. sci. assns., Am. Soc. Pub. Adminstrn., Pi Gamma Mu, Pi Sigma Alpha. Author: Gubernatorial Staffs, 1969; Comparative State Politics, 1971; co-author: The American Metropolis, 1975. Home: 58 Sun Valley St St Louis MO 63141

SPRICK, LARRY PAUL, agrl. engr.; b. Fremont, Nebr., Sept. 15, 1939; s. Paul Christian and Helen (Wolff) S.; B.S. in Agrl. Engring., U. Nebr., 1962; m. Mary Louise Harris, Sept. 7, 1968; children—Patricia Ann, Amy Marie. Design engr. Simonsen Mfg. Co., Quimby, Iowa, 1963—. Asso. mem. Am. Soc. Agrl. Engrs. Home: 1009 Geneseo St Storm Lake IA 50588 Office: Quimby IA 51049

SPRING, HENRY CARL, savs. and loan exec.; b. Gnaden Hutten, Ohio, Aug. 10, 1903; s. Frederick Simon and Mary Anna (Feller) S.; student Ohio U., 1926; m. Thelma Christine Packer, June 30, 1933; children—Daniel, June (Mrs. Roy Rice), Bette Ann (Mrs. Robert Wills), Marilyn Jean (Mrs. Robert Miller), Robert. Pres., owner H.C. Spring Electric, Inc., Uhrichsville and New Philadelphia, Ohio, 1926—; dir. Indian Village Savs. & Loan Assn., Gnaden Hutten, 1926—, pres., 1945—; dir., pres. bd. Tusco Mfg. Co., Gnaden Hutten, 1949—; owner Buckeye Hotel Uhrichsville. Vice pres. World's Christian Endeavor Union, 1930, pres. Ohio Christian Endeavor Union, 1934-36; pres. Tuscarawas County Hist. Soc., 1967-72; incorporator Trumpet in the Land, outdoor drama. Named Man of Year, Twin City C. of C., 1968; Tuscarawas County Old Timers Baseball Hall of Fame, 1970. Mem. Uhrichsville C. of C. (organizer, pres. 1946), Tuscarawas County C. of C. (v.p. 1962). Mem. Moravian Ch. (elder, trustee). Mason (32 deg.), Lion. Home: 703 N Dawson St Uhrichsville OH 44683 Office: 114 E High St New Philadelphia OH 44663

SPRINGBORN, BRUCE ALAN, psychologist, retail co. exec.; b. Geneva, Ill., Nov. 21, 1936; s. Carl Frederick and Mabel Nellie (Lintner) S.; B.A., Northwestern U., 1958; M.A., U. Mich., 1959, Ph.D., 1963; m. Rosemary Kelly, Dec. 19, 1964. Registered psychologist, Ill. Sr. staff specialist in manpower planning and devel., program coordinator Gen. Motors Corp., Detroit, 1962-68; asso. A.T. Kearney Mgmt. Cons., Chgo., 1968-70, mgr. human resources devel., 1976-77; corp. dir. personnel R.R. Donnelley & Sons, Chgo., 1970-74; corp. dir. orgn. and individual devel. Quaker Oats Co., Chgo., 1974-76; v.p. personnel Marshall Field & Co., Chgo., 1977—. Bd. dirs. Child and Family Services, Chgo., 1977—. Mem. Am. Psychol. Assn., Am. Soc. Personnel Adminstrn. Contbr. author: Introduction to Manufacturing Management, 1969; articles in Industry Week, Plan and Print, Indsl. Psychologist. Home: 225 Francis Ln Barrington IL 60010 Office: 25 E Washington Blvd Chicago IL 60602

SPRINGBORN, ROSEMARY KELLY (MRS. BRUCE ALAN SPRINGBORN), editor, publisher, cons.; b. South Bend, Ind., June 2, 1932; d. Edward Joseph and Hazel Jeannette (Thompson) Kelly; B.S., Purdue U., 1953; postgrad. Northwestern U., 1958-59, U. Mich., 1960; m. Bruce Alan Springborn, Dec. 19, 1964. Mng. editor Brewers Digest, Siebel Pub. Co., Chgo., 1955-58; sr. tech. writer Bendix Corp., Ann Arbor, Mich., 1960-63; editor-in-chief, books div. Soc. Mfg. Engrs., Dearborn, Mich., 1965-69; dir. contracts, copyrights and subsidiary rights Harper & Row, Pubs., Inc., N.Y.C., 1969-73; mng. editor Research and Devel. Tech. Pub. Co., Barrington, Ill., 1973-75; editor-in-chief TPC Tng. Systems div. Tech. Pub. Co., Barrington, 1975-78; pres. Kelly-Springborn Assos., Inc., Barrington, 1978—. Mem. Am. Inst. Plant Engrs., Soc. Women Engrs., Am. Soc. Tng. and Devel., Ill. Tng. and Devel. Assn., Nat. Soc. Performance and Instruction, Am. Assn. Engring. Edn., Am. Vocat. Assn., Internat. Visual Literacy Assn. Am. Tech. Edn. Assn. Editorial advisory bd. Tng. mag. Home and office: 225 Francis Lane Barrington IL 60010

SPRINGER, JAMES JEROME, ins. co. exec.; b. Chgo., Apr. 19, 1932; s. Anton Andrew and Alice Agnes (Hahn) S.; B.S. in Bus. Adminstrn. (scholar), Lewis U., 1954. Actuarial clk. Sterling/Constitution Ins. Co., Chgo., 1954-56; key clk. Bankers Life & Casualty Co., Chgo., 1956-60; statis. supr. Fed. Life Ins. Co., Chgo., 1960-67, records mgr., home office, 1967—; speaker Inst. for Graphic Communications, 1977, numerous others. Certified records mgr. Mem. Assn. of Records Mgrs. (chpt. mem. of year 1974, 77, Regional award of merit 1977, editor bull. 1968-72, pres. 1973-74), Nat. Micrographics Assn. (chpt. dir.). Contbr. articles on bus. mgmt. to profl. jours. Office: 3703 E Lake St Glenview IL 60025

SPRINGER, JOSEPH PERRY, physician; b. Elmwood, Wis., June 27, 1916; s. Frank Albert and Vera Jenine (Doughty) S.; A.B., U. Wis., 1943, M.D., 1948; m. Charlene Ann Warner, Dec. 24, 1945; children—Sally, Joseph, Barbara, Stephen. Intern, St. Joseph's Hosp., Phoenix, 1948-49; resident Colo. State Hosp., Pueblo, Colo., 1949-51; pvt. practice medicine, Elmwood, Wis., 1951-57, Durand, 1971—; asst. prof. Tufts Med. Sch., Mound Bayou, Miss., 1969; dir. student health dept. Stout State U., Menomonie, Wis., 1970-71; staff physician Hosp. Ship HOPE, Conakry, Republic of Guinea, Africa, 1964-65; civilian physician Civilian Hosp., DaNang, Viet Nam, 1966; med. staff Dr. Torres Hosp., Siapan, Mariana Islands, 1974. Bd. dirs. Durand Unified Sch. Dist., 1964-69. Served with USMCR, 1941-42. Recipient certificate for humanitarian service AMA, 1967, certificate of appreciation Republic of Viet Nam, 1966, physician's recognition award AMA, 1971. Diplomate Am. Bd. Family Practice. Mem. Am., Wis., Tri-County med. assns., Am. Acad. Gen. Practice, Delta Kappa Epsilon., Nat. Jogging Assn. Club: Durand Lawn Tennis. Home: 1127 Oakwood Dr Durand WI 54736 Office: Star Route Durand WI 54736

SPROGER, CHARLES EDMUND, lawyer; b. Chgo., Feb. 18, 1933; s. William and Minnette (Weiss) S.; B.S., B.A., (David Himmelblau scholar), Northwestern U., 1954; J.D., 1957. Admitted to Ill. bar, 1957; since practiced in Chgo.; asso. Ehrlich & Cohn, 1958-63, Ehrlich,Bundesen, Friedman & Ross, 1963-71; partner firm Ehrlich, Bundesen, Broecker & Sproger, 1971—. Mem. adv. com. for curriculum Ill. Inst. For Continuing Legal Edn., Chgo., 1971—. Fellow Am. Acad. Matrimonial Lawyers (chmn. Law Day U.S.A. 1975); mem. Ill. (chmn. Council of Family Law 1970-71), Chgo. (mem. matrimonial law com. 1968—) bar assns., Decalogue Soc., Phi Alpha Delta. Editor Family Lawyer, 1962-63. Contbr. articles to legal publs. Home: 2901 S King Dr Chicago IL 60616 Office: 69 W Washington St Chicago IL 60602

SPROWL, CHARLES RIGGS, lawyer; b. Lansing, Mich., Aug. 22, 1910; s. Charles Orr and Hazel (Allen) S.; A.B., U. Mich., 1932, J.D., 1934; m. Virginia Lee Graham, Jan. 15, 1938; children—Charles R., Robert A., Susan G., Sandra D. Admitted to Ill. bar, 1935, pvt. practice, 1934—; practice as partner in firm of Taylor, Miller, Magner, Sprowl & Hutchings; dir. Paul F. Beich Co., Busch & Schmitt, Inc., Simmons Engring. Corp., Petersen Aluminum Corp., A.H. Ross & Sons Co. Mem. Bd. Edn. New Trier Township High Sch., 1959-65, pres., 1963-65; chmn. Glencoe Zoning Bd. of Appls., 1965-76; bd. dirs. Glencoe Public Library, 1953-65, pres., 1955-56; bd. dirs. Northwestern U. Settlement Assn., pres., 1963-70; bd. dirs. Cradle Soc., Juvenile Protective Assn., 1943-53; trustee Highland Park Hosp., 1959-69. Mem. Chgo. (mem. bd. mgrs. 1949-51), Ill., Am. bar assns., Am. Coll. Trial Lawyers, Soc. Trial Lawyers. Delta Theta Phi, Alpha Chi Rho. Presbyn. Clubs: Law (pres. 1969-70), Legal (pres. 1953-54), University, Monroe, Skokie Country. Home: 558 Washington Ave Glencoe IL 60022 Office: 120 S LaSalle St Chicago IL 60603

SPRUNGER, KEITH LAVERNE, educator; b. Berne, Ind., Mar. 16, 1935; s. Arley and Lillian (Mettler) S.; A.B., Wheaton Coll., 1957; M.A., U. Ill., 1958, Ph.D., 1963; m. Aldine Mary Slagell, June 13, 1959; children—David, Mary, Philip. Tchr., Berne High Sch., (Ind.), 1958-60; prof. history Bethel Coll., North Newton, Kan., 1963—. Recipient E. Harris Harbison award Danforth Found., 1972; grantee Am. Philos. Soc., 1967, 69-70, Social Sci. Research Council, 1969-70, Am. Council Learned Soc., 1967, 76-77. Mem. Am. Hist. Assn., Am. Soc. Ch. History, Am. Assn. U. Profs., Conf. on Faith and History. Author: The Learned Doctor William Ames, 1972. Editor: Voices Against War, 1973; asso. editor: Fides et Historia, 1973. Home: 2412 College Ave North Newton KS 67117 Office: Bethel Coll North Newton KS 67117

SSEKASOZI, ENGELBERT, educator; b. Kampala, Uganda, East Africa, Nov. 7, 1938; s. Francis Xavier and Ann Mary (Nabitaka) Matovu; came to U.S., 1961, naturalized, 1968; B.A., Knoxville Coll., 1965; M.A., U. Tenn., 1966; postgrad. La Salle Extension U., 1969-77; Ph.D., U. Kans., 1976; children—Josaphat, Francis, Charles. Grad. asst. dept. philosophy U. Tenn., Knoxville, 1965-66; teaching fellow U. Kans., Lawrence, 1966-68, asst. instr. philosophy, 1973-75, asst. inst. dept. Western civilization, 1974-75; asst. prof. philosophy Knoxville Coll., 1968-70; asst. prof. philosophy Grambling (La.) State U., 1969, asso. prof., 1972-73; prof. philosophy Makerere U., Kampala, 1970-71, asst. prof., acting head dept. philosophy Lincoln (Mo.) U., 1975—. Mem. Am. Philos. Assn., Phi Beta Sigma. Home: Jefferson City MO Office: Dept Philosophy Lincoln U Jefferson City MO 65101

STACK, NICOLETE MEREDITH MCGUIRE (MRS. CHARLES M. STACK), author; b. Des Moines, Feb. 22, 1899; d. Patrick Henry and Frances (Lynch) McGuire; student U. Colo., Highland Park Coll., Franconia Floating U.; m. Edward Randolph Meredith, Feb. 8, 1921 (dec. Dec. 1934); m. 2d, Charles Monroe Stack, July 29, 1940 (dec. July 1945). Free-lance writer; author books for young people. Mem. Ia. Bd. Social Welfare, 1935-40. Two books named Catholic Y Peoples books of year. Mem. Nat. League Am. Pen Women, Mo. (past pres.), St. Louis writers guilds, Marquis Biog. Library Soc. Author: Two to Get Ready, 1953, Braille edit., 1977; Pierre of the Island, 1954 (also in Braille and in large type); Rainbow Tomorrow (plaque Mo. Writers Guild 1957), 1956; Welcome Love, 1959; Milestone Summer, 1962; King of the Kerry Fair, 1960; (pseudonymn Kathryn Kenny) 8 mystery books for girls, 1961-66; Catholic Men of Science, 1966; Corky's Hiccups, 1966; Ladislaus and Annabella, 1966; Rudy Biplane, 1966; 3 Mysteries, Robin Kane Series (pseudonyn Eileen Hill), 1965-67; The Vain Little Train, The Little Donkey Piccolo, Katrina's Doll Family, 1967; A Friend for Katie, 1968; Who Made That Noise?, 1969; Mystery of Missing Heiress, 1970; Flight to Camelot, 1971; Turquoise Woman, 1972; others including Blacksmith and the Princess, Princess and Bronze Bell of Peking, Princess of the Outer World. Home: 8 Colonial Village Jamestown House Webster Groves MO 63119

STACKELBERG, OLAF PATRICK, mathematician, acad. adminstr.; b. Munich, Germany, Aug. 2, 1932; s. Curt F. and Ellen (Biddle) vonStackelberg; B.S., Mass. Inst. Tech. ,1955; Ph.D., U. Minn., 1963; m. Cora E. Sleighter, Sept. 4, 1954; children—John S., Peter O., Paul E. Asst. prof. math. Duke U., Durham, N.C., 1963-68, asso. prof., 1968-76; prof., chmn. math. dept. Kent (Ohio) State U., 1976—; Alexander von Humboldt fellow U. Stuttgart (Germany), 1965-66; vis. asso. prof. math. U. Ill., Urbana, 1969-70, London (Eng.) U., 1974; mem. vis. staff math. Wesleyan U., Middletown, Conn., summers 1965-76. Served with Chem. Corps, U.S. Army, 1956-58. Editor, Duke Math. Jour., 1971-74; contbr. articles to math. jours. Home: 5924 Horning Rd Kent OH 44240

STACKHOUSE, DAVID WILLIAM, JR., mfrs. rep.; b. Cumberland, Ind., Aug. 29, 1926; s. David William and Dorothy Frances (Snider) S.; B.S., Lawrence Coll., Appleton, Wis., 1950; m. Shirley Pat Smith, Dec. 23, 1950; 1 son, Stefan Brent. Indsl. designer Globe Am. Co., Kokomo, Ind., 1951-53; product designer, chief engr. L.A. Darling Co., Bronson, Mich., 1954-66; contract mgr. Brass Office Products, Indpls., 1966-73; mfrs. rep., Nashville, Ind., 1973—. Precinct committeeman Republican Party; mem. Bronson Park Bd., 1963-65; dist. commr. Boy Scouts Am., 1961-63; chmn. ARC Blood Drive, 1964. Served with USNR, 1944-46; PTO. Certified pesticide applicator; certificate in basic seamanship USCG Aux. Mem. Bldg. Owners and Mfrs. Assn. (past pres. Indpls. chpt.), Brown County Bd. Realtors, Nat., Ind. State rifle assns., Am. Wine Soc. (past regional pres., certificate of appreciation), Brown County Humane Soc., Brown County Hist. Soc., Beta Theta Pi. Anglican. Clubs: Lions, Kiwanis (past v.p.), Masons, Shriners. Patentee interior structural systems. Home: Rural Route 3 Box 324 Nashville IN 47448

STADE, CHARLES EDWARD, archtl. co. exec.; b. Des Plaines, Ill., June 28, 1923; s. Chris E. and Martha (Drexler) S.; B.S., U. Ill., 1946; M.F.A., Princeton, 1948; certificate Beaux Art Inst. Design, N.Y.C., 1948; French Govt. traveling scholar, 1948; m. Annette B. Grewe, Nov. 7, 1972; 1 dau., Ramsey. With W.J. McCaughey, architect, Park Ridge, Ill., 1945-48, K. Kessler, architect, Princeton, N.J., 1948; owner Charles Edward Stade & Assos., architects, Park Ridge, 1948—; various designs in permanent exhibit Am. Soc. Ch. Architecture. Served with USAAF, 1942-43. Recipient numerous AIA awards, 1956, 57, 61-63, 65, gold cup for excellence in masonry architecture, 1972, award of merit in outstanding lighting design, 1973; Crosby Butler prize, 1948; medal Prix-de-Emulation, Groupe Am., 1948; Nat. award for excellence in design GRA, 1974. Palmer fellow, 1946; Princeton fellow, 1947. Fellow Am. Soc. Ch. Architecture (past pres.); mem. Constrn. Specifications Inst., Gargoyle, Alpha Rho Chi. Past archtl. editor Your Church Mag., from 1956. Contbr. articles to mags., newspapers. Important works include Valparaiso (Ind.) U. Chapel. Home: 1020 S Knight St Park Ridge IL 60068 Office: 819 Busse Hwy Park Ridge IL 60068

STADEM, CLIFFORD JENNINGS, physician; b. Mpls., July 30, 1925; s. Fridtjof Christen and Helga (Jacobson) S.; B.S., U. Minn., 1948, B.M., 1950, M.D., 1951; m. Gladys May Davis, July 31, 1948; children—Karl, Paul, Rebecca, Mark, Hugh. Intern, Mpls. Gen. Hosp., 1950-51; physician Twin Valley (Minn.) Med. Center, 1951-67, Crookston (Minn.) Clinic, 1967-75, Northwestern Clinic, Crookston, 1975—. Bd. dirs. Northwestern Mental Health Center, Crookston, 1957-67, 71—. Mem. Twin Valley Sch. Bd., 1957-60. Mem. AMA, Minn., Red River Valley (pres.) med. socs. Mason, Lion. Home: 729 Park Ln Crookston MN 56716 Office: 220 S Broadway Crookston MN 56716

STADLER, ERVIN ANTHONY, accountant; b. Cin., Feb. 22, 1912; s. John William and Margaret (Bernzott) S.; A.B., Xavier U., 1933; postgrad. in accounting U. Cin., 1933-37; m. Rosemary Elizabeth McCarren, May 8, 1937; children—Paul, Suzanne Stadler Thompson, Richard, Thomas, James, John. Accountant, Rouse, Favret & Co., C.P.A.'s, 1934-55, partner 1950-55; partner Haskins & Sells, C.P.A.'s, Cin., 1955-74. Mem. Ohio Bd. Accountancy, 1972-77, pres., 1977. C.P.A., Ohio, Ky., N.Y., La., N.C. Mem. Am. Inst. C.P.A.'s, Ohio Soc. C.P.A.'s (chpt. pres. 1955-56), Nat. Assn. Accountants, Am. Accounting Assn., Beta Alpha Psi. Roman Catholic. Clubs: Cin. (treas. 1959-60), Clovernook Country (treas. 1954-55). Home: 5536 E Galbraith Rd Cincinnati OH 45236

STAEHLE, ROGER WASHBURNE, metall. engr.; b. Detroit, Feb. 4, 1934; s. Haswell E. and Carrie (Washburne) S.; B.S., Ohio State U., 1957, M.S., 1957, Ph.D., 1965; children—Elizabeth J., Eric W., Sara L., Catherine E. Researcher, U.S. Navy and U.S. AEC, Washington, 1957-61; research asso. Ohio State U., Columbus, 1961-65, prof. metall. engring., 1965—; cons. numerous bus. firms; chmn. U.S.A. Corrosion Del. to USSR, 1975, U.S.A.-Japan Seminar on Passivity of Iron Base Alloys in Hawaii, 1975, corrosion adv. com. Electric Power Research Inst., shipboard incinerator materials devel. Nat. Materials Adv. Bd., NRC, adv. panel, metall. dir. Nat. Bur. Standards; organizer internat. confs. Recipient Coll. Engring. awards for achievement Ohio State U., 1966, 69; Internat. Nickel prof. corrosion sci. and engring., 1971-76. Fellow Am. Soc. Metals; mem. Electrochem. Soc. (chmn. corrosion div.), Nat. Assn. Corrosion Engrs., Am. Nuclear Soc., Am. Inst. Metall. Engrs., Am. Soc. Testing Materials, Am. Soc. Engring. Edn. (award for innovative teaching), Fedn. Materials Socs. (chmn. com. on conservation materials in nat. economy), Sigma Xi, Tau Beta Pi, Phi Eta Sigma, Phi Zeta. Editor: Corrosion Jour., 1973—; Advances in Corrosion Science and Technology, 7 vols.; Handbook on Stress Corrosion Cracking and Corrosion Fatigue of Metals, 1977; contbr. tech. articles to profl. jours. Office: 116 W 19th Ave Columbus OH 43210

STAFFORD, WARREN SYLVESTER, lawyer; b. nr. Springfield, Mo., Feb. 18, 1928; s. Curtis and Eula Belle (Johnson) S.; student S.W. Mo. State U., 1948-50, 51-53; J.D., U. Mo. at Kansas City, 1958; m. Juanita Jane Brooks, Aug. 13, 1954; children—Jane Lynn, Zachary Randall. Account engr. Frisco Ry., St. Louis, 1953-54; auditor Fed. Res. Bank, Kansas City Mo., 1955; office mgr. Victor Adding Machine Co., Kansas City, Mo., 1956-58; admitted to Mo. bar, 1958; asso. mem. firm Neale, Newman, Bradshaw & Freeman, Springfield, Mo., 1958-64, partner, 1964-74; sr. partner Taylor, Stafford & Gannaway, 1974—. Active Boy Scouts Am. Served with USNR, 1946-48, 50-51. Mem. Am., Mo. bar assns., Greene County Bar Assn., Internat. Assn. Ins. Counsel, Def. Research Inst., Order Bench and Robe, Jr. C. of C. (various offices), Phi Delta Phi. Presbyn. Home: 2639 S Luster St Springfield MO 65804 Office: Tenth Floor Plaza Towers Springfield MO 65804

STAFNE, ERIC EDWARD, dentist; b. Rochester, Minn., Apr. 7, 1935; s. Edward Christian and Adeline (Middelstadt) S.; student Carleton Coll., 1953-55; B.A., U. Minn., 1958, B.S., 1960, D.D.S., 1960, M.S.D., 1965; m. Dorie Jean Supplee, July 8, 1961; children—Mark Eric, Melanie Ross. Practice dentistry specializing in periodontics, St. Paul, 1965—; asst. prof. periodontics U. Minn. Sch. Dentistry, 1965-70, asso. prof., 1970—. Served to capt. Dental Corps, USAF, 1960-62. Fellow Internat., Am. colls. dentists; mem. ADA, Minn., St. Paul Dist. (treas. 1967-71, pres. 1975-76) dental assns., Am. Acad. Periodontology, Midwest Soc. Periodontology, Minn. Acad. Gnathological Research, Minn. Assn. Periodontists (pres. 1972-73), Am. Soc. Preventive Dentistry, Am. Cancer Soc. (v.p. Ramsey county unit 1974-75, dir. Minn. div. 1977—), Omicron Kappa Upsilon. Home: 960 Lydia Dr Saint Paul MN 55113 Office: 706 Lowry Med Arts Saint Paul MN 55102

STAHL, HENRY GEORGE, lawyer; b. Fremont, Ohio, Apr. 18, 1902; s. John Burton and Florence B. (Fisher) S.; student Tiffin U., 1925, Miami U., 1923, Bowling Green U., 1924; Ohio No. U., 1926; read law with father; m. Gertrude M. Elmers, Mar. 6, 1926; children—Joyce E. (Mrs. Howard Bruce Thompson), Florence E. (Mrs. Kenneth Harmon), John B. Admitted to Ohio bar, 1926, since practiced in Fremont; mem. firm Stahl, Stahl & Stahl, 1926-51; as H. G. Stahl, 1951—; probate judge, Sandusky County, 1932, 33. Mem. Sandusky County C. of C. (past pres.), Am., Ohio, Sandusky County (past pres.) bar assns., Am. Judicature Soc. Clubs: Masons (past dist. dep.), Elks (past dist. dep.), K.P. (past dist. dep.). Home: 1710 McPherson Blvd Fremont OH 43420 Office: 802 Court St Fremont OH 43420

STAHL, JOEL SAUL, plastic-chem. engr.; b. Youngstown, Ohio, June 10, 1918; s. John Charles and Anna (Nadler) S.; B.Chem. Engring., Ohio State U., 1939; postgrad. Alexander Hamilton Inst., 1946-48; m. Jane Elizabeth Anglin, June 23, 1950; 1 son, John Arthur. With Ashland Oil & Refining Co. (Ky.), 1939-50, mgr. spl. products, 1946-50; pres. Cool Ray Co., Youngstown, 1950-51, Stahl Industries, Inc., Youngstown, 1951—, Stahl Internat., Inc., Youngstown, 1969—, Stahl Bldg. Systems, Inc., Youngstown, 1973—. Active Boardman Civic Assn., Boy Scouts Am., Community Chest, ARC. Named Ky. col., 1967. Mem. Regional Export Expansion Council, Soc. Plastics Engr., Soc. Plastics Industry, Internat. Platform Assn., Ohio Soc. N.Y., Tau Kappa Epsilon, Phi Eta Sigma, Phi Lambda Upsilon. Republican. Christian Scientist. Mason (Shriner), Rotarian. Clubs: Toastmasters (pres. 1949); Berlin Yacht (North Benton, O.); Circumnavigators. Patentee insulated core walls, plastic plumbing wall. housing in continous process. Contbr. articles to profl. jours. Home: 746 Golf View Ave Youngstown OH 44512 Office: Dollar Bank Bldg 9th Floor Youngstown OH 44503

STAHL, RAYMOND EARL, chemist; b. Chgo., Feb. 21, 1936; s. Arthur Daniel and Gladys Hazel (Lockwood) S.; Ph.B., Northwestern U., 1971. Lab. technician, coatings formulator DeSoto Co., Chgo., 1956-62; group leader metal finishes research and devel. Morton Chem. Co., Chgo., 1962-66; tech. dir. Am. Indsl. Chems., Chgo., 1966-67; sr. chemist, research chemist, sr. research chemist, research asso. packaging research and devel. De Soto Co., Chgo., 1967-73; staff scientist Midland-Dexter Co., Waukegan, Ill., 1973—; cons. chem. coatings. Served with AUS, 1954-56. Fellow Am. Inst. Chemists, Am. Inst. Physics; mem. Am. Chem. Soc., Am. Phys. Soc., Math. Assn. Am., Am. Statis. Assn., Ill. State Acad. Sci., AAAS, Am. Self Def. Preparedness Com., Société de Chimie Industrielle, Fedn. Paint Socs., Smithsonian Assos., Nat., Ill. rifle assns., Am. Reloaders Assn. Contbr. articles to profl. orgns. Developer comml. coatings. Home: 440 Westmoreland Dr Apt 8 Vernon Hills IL 60061 Office: E Water St Waukegan IL 60085

STAHL, THOMAS BURTON, lawyer; b. Fremont, O., Apr. 5, 1904; s. John Burton and Florence Belle (Fisher) S.; student Miami U., 1922-23, U. Toledo, 1923-24; J.D., Ohio State U., 1927; m. Harriett May Beatty, Nov. 4, 1936; children—John Thomas, James Philip. With Thomas Maxwell Print Shop, Fremont, 1921-22; clk. Child's Clothing Store, 1922, atty. John B. Stahl, 1922-26; admitted to Ohio bar, 1926; mem. firm. Stahl, Stahl & Stahl, attys., 1927-52; practice law, 1952—; judge Court Common Pleas, Sandusky County, O., 1936-37. Pres., law librarian Sandusky County Law Library Assn., 1935—. Precinct committeeman Republican party, 1932-75; treas. Sandusky County Republican Com., 1965-75. Mem. Am., Ohio, Sandusky County bar assns. Presbyn. Mason (32 deg., Shriner), Elk. Clubs: Fremont Country, Catawba Island. Home: 720 Garrison St Fremont OH 43420 Office: 615 Croghan St Fremont OH 43420

STAHL-BERKOWITZ, PHYLLIS BARBARA, writer; b. Milw., Sept. 30, 1940; d. Nathan Loeser and Pearl Marion (Stahl) Berkowitz; student U. Mich., 1958-59, Simmons Coll., 1960-63; children—Daniel Clark Schnur, Jonathan Henry Schnur. Asst. editor Wis. Jewish Chronicle, Milw., 1972-74; free-lance writer, Milw., 1974—. Co-founder Milw. Met. Coop. Nursery Sch., 1968-72; chairperson Young Women's Com. and bd. mem. Milw. Jewish Fedn., 1969-76; founder Milw. Children's Mus. Home: 4440 N Prospect Ave Milwaukee WI 53211

STAHLHEBER, RUDOLPH B., counselor, educator; b. Pinckneyville, Ill., May 15, 1934; s. Rudolph James and Alice Ann (Ogilvie) S.; B.S. in Edn., So. Ill. U., 1956, M.S. in Edn., 1959, Specialist in Guidance and Counseling, 1963; postgrad. U. Louisville, 1965, Western Ill. U., 1967, No. Ill. U., 1967, U. Wis., Stout, 1968-70; m. Roberta M. Needham, Dec. 22, 1956; children—Jeanne, Brent Robert. Tchr. pub. schs., Vergennes, Ill., 1956-58, Murphysboro, Ill., 1958-60; dir. guidance Mascoutah (Ill.) High Sch., 1960-65, Black Hawk Coll., Moline, Ill., 1965-68; student services adminstr., asst. dir. Advotech 18 Vocat.-Tech. and Adult Edn. Dist., New Richmond, Wis., 1968-72; coordinator counseling and appraisal, prof. student devel. and services Richland Community Coll., Decatur, Ill., 1972—; part time instr. Belleville (Ill.) Jr. Coll., 1961-63, So. Ill. U., 1959-60. Active Macon County Council of Community Services. Gen. Elec. Career Edn. and Guidance fellow U. Louisville, 1965; NDEA grantee, 1961. Mem. Am., Ill. (pres. Area 12 Chpt.) personnel and guidance assns., Am. Coll. Personnel Assn., Phi Delta Kappa. Methodist. Contbr. articles to Ill. Guidance and Personnel Newsletter, 1962, Wis. Student Personnel Assn. Newsletter, 1969. Home: 183 35th Ct Decatur IL 62521 Office: 100 N Water St Decatur IL 62523

STAHLHUT, EMIL OSCAR, hosp. adminstr.; b. Edwardsville, Ill., Feb. 2, 1918; s. Paul and Ida (Holt) S.; B.A., Elmhurst Coll., 1939; M.A., Northwestern U., 1948; m. Jane Sherman, Feb. 14, 1941;

children—Carolyn (Mrs. Gerald Frank), Barbara (Mrs. Melvin Thake), Margaret (Mrs. Michael Webster), Mary. Social worker Family Service Bur., United Charities, Chgo., 1941-42, 46; registrar VA Hosp., Hines, Ill., 1946-49; asst. adminstr. Mt. Sinai Hosp., Chgo., 1949-50; adminstr. Jackson County Pub. Hosp., Maquoketa, Ia., 1950-53; adminstr. Abraham Lincoln Meml. Hosp., Lincoln, Ill., 1953—, project dir. health maintenance orgn., 1971-74, exec. officer Abraham Lincoln Health System, 1974—. Mem. exec. com. Central Ill. Health Planning Council, Springfield, 1970-72, treas., 1970-72; mem. com., health care planning So. Ill. U. Sch. Medicine, 1970-71; mem. com. for Logan County Health Dept. 1970, 72; mem. com. planning hosp. based ambulances Logan County, 1972; mem. hosp. licensing bd. Ill. Dept. Pub. Health, 1960-74; mem. adv. council Ill. Dept. Children and Family Service, 1966-74; personnel grievance panel Ill. Dept. Personnel, 1971—. Charter pres. Logan County Assn. Mental Health, 1960; mem. exec. com. Peoria Regional Blood Center (Red Cross), 1969-73, chmn., 1972; charter pres. United Fund Lincoln, 1961. Served to capt. AUS, 1942-46. Fellow Am. Coll. Hosp. Adminstrs.; mem. Ill. Hosp. Assn. (trustee 1960-66, 71-77). Rotarian (pres. 1957-58, Toastmaster (pres. 1955). Weekly columnist hosp. and health activities Lincoln Courier, 1967—. Home: 147 9th St Lincoln IL 62656 Office: 315 8th St Lincoln IL 62656

STAHMANN, FRED SOEFFNER, educator, physician; b. Spanish Fork, Utah, Aug. 24, 1909; s. Benjamin Robert and Lydia Ann (Soeffner) S.; B.A., U. Utah, 1931; M.D., Northwestern U., 1935; m. Mary Emma Thompson, Dec. 17, 1938; children—Robert, Fred, Mary. Intern, St. Lukes Hosp., Chgo., 1934-35; resident in obstetrics-gynecology, 1935-37; practice medicine specializing in obstetrics-gynecology, Peoria, Ill., 1937-42, Sioux Falls, S.D., 1946-74; staff Sioux Valley Hosp., 1946—, chief of staff, 1949-50; staff McKennan Hosp., Sioux Falls, 1946—; cons. VA Hosp., Sioux Falls, 1950-74; faculty Sch. Medicine, U. S.D., Sioux Falls, 1955—, asso. prof. obstetrics-gynecology, 1955—. Mem. dist. council Boy Scouts Am., 1949-51; service chmn. Am. Cancer Soc., Minnehaha County, 1971-73. Served to maj. M.C., AUS, 1942-46. Diplomate Am. Bd. Obstetrics and Gynecology. Mem. Central Assn. Obstetricians and Gynecologists, Am. Coll. Obstetricians and Gynecologists (founding mem.), S.D. Soc. Obstetrics and Gynecology (pres. 1954). Republican. Presbyterian. Clubs: Rotary, Masons, Shriners. Contbr. articles to profl. jours. Address: 401 E 27th St Sioux Falls SD 57105

STAHR, HENRY M., analytical chemist; b. White, S.D., Dec. 10, 1931; s. George C. and Kathryn E. (Smith) S.; B.S., S.D. State U., 1956; M.S., Union Coll., 1961; Ph.D., Iowa State U., 1976; m. Irene F. Sondey, July 27, 1953; children—Michael, John, Mary, Patrick, Mathew. Analytical chemist Gen. Elec. Co., Hudson Falls, N.Y., 1956-64; sr. scientist Philip Morris Research, Richmond, Va., 1964-69; asst. prof. Iowa State U., 1969—. Bd. dirs. Isaac Walton League, Ames, Iowa, 1969-71; pres. K.C., Ogden, Iowa, 1974-77; vice-comdr. Am. Legion, Ogden, 1975-77; bd. dirs. Ogden Community Sch. Dist., 1976; active Boy Scouts Am. Mem. Am. Chem. Soc., Electro-chem. Soc., Instrument Soc. Am., Soc. Applied Spectroscopy, Am. Microchem. Soc., Nat. Safety Council, Assn. Ofcl. Chemists, Veterinary Toxicologists, Internat. Soc. Food Tech., Nutrition Council, Sigma Xi, Gamma Sigma Delta. Asso. referee Chlorinated Hydrocarbons in Whole Blood, 1972-77, also Sodium Flouroacetate, 1975-77. Managerial Award for Outstanding Patent, Gen. Electric Co., 1961; requested participant in Thinlayer Chromatography Symposium, 1974-75; participant in World Food Conf., Iowa State U., 1976. Home: 802 Locust St Ogden IA 50212 Office: Rm 1636 Veterinary Diagnostic Lab Iowa State U Ames IA 50011

STAIB, ROBERT BURNS, electric utility exec.; b. Monongahela, Pa., May 7, 1921; s. Frank A. and Dorothy (Rearick) S.; B.S. in Elec. Engring., Carnegie-Mellon U., 1942; postgrad. Ohio State U., 1959, U. Mich., 1962; m. Virginia Kerr, Sept. 10, 1940; children—Robert Burns, Carol Sue. With Ohio Edison Co., 1946—, supt. elec. equipment constrn., Akron, Ohio, 1965, spl. assignment, 1965, mgr. prodn. and transmission constrn. dept., 1965—. Served to capt. Signal Corps, AUS, 1943-46; ETO. Decorated Purple Heart. Republican. Lutheran. Mason. Club: Akron City. Home: 687 Garnette Dr Akron OH 44313 Office: 76 S Main St Akron OH 44308

STAKER, RODD DAVID, structural engr.; b. Lansing, Mich., June 27, 1943; s. James Melville and Helen Schlack (Avis) S.; student U. Colo., 1961-62; B.S., U. Kans., 1966; postgrad. U. Mo., 1975—; m. Martha Delia Leahy, Sept. 6, 1969; children—David Matthew, Daniel Christopher, Bridget Suzanne. Structural engr. Burns & McDonnell Engring. Co., Kansas City, Mo., asst. structural engr., 1969, resident engr., 1970-72, project structural engr., 1974—; dir. Burns & McDonnell Credit Union. Served to lt. USNR, 1966-69. Registered profl. engr., Mo. Mem. Nat. Soc. Profl. Engrs., Mo. Soc. Profl. Engrs., ASCE, Kans. Gamma Alumni Assn. (dir. 1974—), Sigma Phi Epsilon (alumni dir. 1969—, pres. 1974-75). Editor: Gammaramma, 1974—. Home: 646 W 70th St Kansas City MO 64113 Office: PO Box 173 Kansas City MO 64141

STALBAUM, MERRILL, ex-state legislator, surveyor; b. nr. Waterford, Wis., Apr. 24, 1911; s. John Martin and Amanda (Ebert) S.; grad. high sch.; m. Lucille Hanson, July 15, 1944; 1 son, John. Farmer, Waterford, 1928-57; surveyor, Waterford, 1959—; town clk., Norway, 1937-67; mem. Wis. Assembly, 1961-73. Lutheran. Address: Route 1 Waterford WI 53185

STALEY, AUGUSTUS EUGENE, III, advt. exec.; b. Decatur, Ill., Sept. 12, 1928; s. Augustus Eugene Jr. and Lenore (Mueller) S.; grad. Cheshire Acad., 1945; student Northwestern U., 1946-49. Copywriter, Hill Blackett & Co., 1948-49; account exec. Ruthrauff and Ryan, Inc., 1950-52; advt. dir. A.E. Staley Mfg. Co., 1952-58; v.p. Dancer-Fitzgerald-Sample, Inc., 1958-61; v.p. Arthur Meyerhoff Assos., Inc., 1961-62; exec. v.p. Don Kemper Co., Inc., Chgo., 1962-69; pres. S.M.Y., Inc., Chgo., 1969—, Advt. Contractors Inc., N.Y.C., 1970-74, Atwood Richards, Inc., N.Y.C., 1970-74. Served from pvt. to sgt. AUS, 1948-58. Clubs: Tavern, Athletic Assn. (Chgo.); Williams (N.Y.C.); Masons, Elks. Home: 209 E Lake Shore Dr Chicago IL 60611 Office: 230 N Michigan Ave Chicago IL 60601

STALEY, CHARLES WESLEY, minister; b. Kansas City, Mo., July 24, 1917; s. Arthur B. and Cassie Ella (Barton) S.; B.S., Okla. Bapt. U., 1953; M.Ed., Kans. State Tchrs. Coll., 1965; m. Ann Marie McGlaughlin, Dec. 26, 1944; 1 dau., Carol Ann. Ordained to ministry Bapt. Ch., 1940; pastor, Glasgow, Mo., 1939-41, Brunswick, Mo., 1941-44, Kans City, Mo., 1944-45, Wichita, Kans., 1945-48, Stroud, Okla., 1948, Healdton, Okla., 1948-52, Larned, Kans., 1954-58; asso. chaplain Larned State Hosp., 1954-58; dist. staff mem. Kans. Bapt. Conv. in N.W. Kans., Topeka, 1958-62; instl. chaplain Norton (Kans.) State Hosp., 1963-66; pastor Phillipsburg, Kans., 1961-66, First Bapt. Ch., Vinton, Iowa, 1966-74; prof. Coe Coll., Cedar Rapids, Iowa, 1975—; founder The Bapt. Preacher, nat. jour. for Bapt. ministers, Kansas City, Mo., 1943, The Career-Work Service Group, 1975. Recipient Communicators award Syracuse U., 1973, Distinguished Service to Community Citation, Internat. Biog. Centre, Cambridge, Eng., 1976. Mem. Internat. Platform Assn., Ministerial Assn., Media Assn. Ch. Communicators (dir. 1975-76). Democrat. Contbr. articles to profl. jours.; patentee. Home and office: 807 W 15th St Vinton IA 52349

STALKER, KENNETH WALTER, cons. engr.; b. St. John, Kans., Oct. 3, 1918; s. Walter Richard and Bertha (Bissett) S.; B.A., U. Colo., 1941; LL.B., LaSalle U., 1952; m. Eva Leona Teagarden, Feb. 7, 1947. Mfg. engr. Gen. Electric Co., Lynn, Mass., 1950-52; mgr. mfg. engring. and process devel. Aircraft Engring. Group, Gen. Elec. Co., Cin., 1952-59, chief cons. engr. process advanced tech., 1965—; mgr. engring. Goodman Mfg. Co., Chgo., 1959-64; editorial adv. bd. Nat. Acad. Sci.; lectr. U. Ark. Precinct committeeman Cook County (Ill.) Republican Party, 1962-64. Recipient managerial award Gen. Electric Co., 1956, William L. Badger Meml. award, 1970. Mem. ASME, Soc. Mfg. Engrs., Soc. Automotive Engrs. Clubs: Masons, Shriners. Contbr. articles to trade jours. Patentee in field. Home: 929 Oregon Trail Cincinnati OH 45215 Office: General Electric Co Mail Drop M82 Cincinnati OH 45125

STALLARD, RICHARD ELGIN, dentist; b. Eau Claire, Wis., May 30, 1934; s. Elgin Gale and Caroline Frances (Betz) S.; student Macalester Coll., 1952-54; B.S., U. Minn., 1956, D.D.S., 1958, M.S., 1959, Ph.D., 1962; m. Jaxon Shirley Sandlin, May 2, 1974; children by previous marriage—Rondi Lynn, Alison Judith; 1 son, Elgin Sandlin. Co-dir. periodontal research Eastman Dental Center, Rochester, N.Y., 1962-65, asst. dir., head, dept. oral biology and pathology, 1968-70; prof. chmn. dept. periodontology U. Minn., Mpls., 1966-68; asst. dean, dir. clin. research center Boston U., 1970-74, prof. anatomy, 1970-74; dental dir. Group Health Plan, Inc., Bloomington, Minn., 1975—. Mem. Am. Acad. Periodontology (pres. 1974), Am. Dental Assn., Am. Coll. Dentists, Internat. Coll. Dentists, Sigma Xi, Omicron Kappa Upsilon. Home: 4810 Lakeview Dr Edina MN 55424 Office: Group Health Medical Center 8600 Nicollet Ave Bloomington MN 55420

STALLARD, WAYNE MINOR, lawyer; b. Onaga, Kans., Aug. 23, 1927; s. Minor Regan and Lydia Faye (Randall) S.; B.S., Kans. State Tchrs. Coll., Emporia, 1949; J.D., Washburn U., 1952; m. Wanda Sue Bacon, Aug. 22, 1948; children—Deborah Sue, Carol Jean, Bruce Wayne. Admitted to Kans. bar, 1952 pvt. practice Onaga, Kans., 1952—; atty. Community Hosp. Dist. No. 1, Pottawatomie and Jackson Counties, Kans., 1955—; Pottawatomie County atty., 1955-59; city atty. Onaga, 1953—; atty Unified School Dist. 322, Pottawatomie County, Kans., 1966—. Bd. dirs. N. Central Kans. Guidance Center, Manhattan, 1974—; atty. Rural Water Dist. No. 3, Pottawatomie County, Kans., 1974—. Fund dr. chmn. Pottawatomie County chpt. Nat. Found. for Infantile Paralysis, 1953-54. Served from pvt. to sgt., 8th Army, AUS, 1946 to 47. Mem. Am., Pottawatomie County, Kans. bar assns., Onaga Businessmen's Assn., Am. Judicature Soc., City Attys. Assn. Kan. (dir. 1963-66), Phi Gamma Mu, Kappa Delta Pi, Delta Theta Phi, Sigma Tau Gamma. Conglist. Mason (Shriner); mem. Order Eastern Star. Address: Onaga KS 66521

STALLINGS, JAMES OTIS, III, plastic surgeon; b. Memphis, Jan. 11, 1938; s. James Otis, II and Mabel R. (Haygood) S.; B.S., Miss. Coll., 1958; M.D., U. Pa., 1962; M.S. (NIH fellow), U. Iowa, 1968. Diplomate Am. Bd. Otolaryngology, Am. Bd. Plastic Surgery. Intern, U. Pa. Hosp., 1962-63; resident gen. surgery VA Hosp., Iowa City, Iowa, 1963-64, Mercy Hosp., Mason City, Iowa, 1964-65; resident otolaryngology Univ. Hosp., Iowa City, 1965-68; resident plastic surgery Inst. Reconstructive Plastic Surgery, N.Y. U. Med. Center, 1970-72; practice medicine, specializing in otolaryngology and plastic surgery, West Des Moines, Iowa, 1972—; dir. Plastic Surgery Inst., 1972—; teaching asst. plastic surgery N.Y. U. Sch. Medicine, 1970-72. Mem. AMA, Iowa, Polk County med. socs. Author: A New You: How Plastic Surgery Can Change Your Life, 1977; contbr. articles to med. jours. Home: 3131 Fleur Dr #603 Des Moines IA 50315 Office: 1025 Ashworth Rd 528 Univac Bldg West Des Moines IA 50265

STAMBAUGH, EDGEL PRYCE, chemist; b. Blaine, Ky., Aug. 31, 1922; s. Ray A. and Nova B. (Boggs) S.; B.S., Ohio State U., 1950, M.S., 1951; m. Joan Marie Snider, July 7, 1950; 1 son, Michael Pryce. Research chemist NL Industries, Sayreville, N.J., 1951-56; project leader Nat. Distillers Inc., Cin., 1957-59; research leader Battelle Meml. Inst., Columbus, Ohio, 1956-57, 59—. Served with AUS, 1942-46. Fellow Am. Inst. Chemists; mem. Am. Inst. Mining, Metall. and Petroleum Engrs., Am. Chem. Soc. Patentee in field. Home: 921 Evening St Worthington OH 43085 Office: 505 King Ave Columbus OH 43201

STAMBERGER, EDWIN HENRY, farmer, civic leader; b. Mendota, Ill., Feb. 16, 1916; s. Edwin Nicolaus and Emilie Anna Marie (Yost) S.; grad. high sch.; m. Mabel Edith Gordon, Oct. 6, 1937; 1 son, Larry Allan. Farmer seed corn and livestock, machinery devel., nr. Mendota, 1939—; dir. Mendota Co-op. & Supply Co., 1949-67, pres., 1958-67. Mem. Mendota Watershed Com., 1966-73, 77—; asst. in devel. Mendota Hosp., Mendota Lake; bd. dirs. LaSalle County Mental Health Bd., 1969-74; chmn. bldg. com. Mendota Luth. Home, 1972-73; mem. revue and comment com., subregion and region Ill. Central Comprehensive Health Planning Agy., 1974-76; bd. dirs. U. Ill. County Extension, 1963-67, chmn., 1966-67; bd. dirs. Soil and Water Dist., 1968-73, vice-chmn., 1971-73. Mem. Soil Soc. Am., Smithsonian Assos., Mental Health Assn., People to People, Internat. Platform Assn., Mendota C. of C. (Honor award 1974). Lion (dir. 1965-67). Lutheran (mem. ch. council 1958-64, chmn. 1964, treas. N.W. Conf. men, 1966-68, trustee bible camp). Club: Mendota Sportsmans. Goodwill farm tours, Europe, Africa, Australia and New Zealand, Central and S.Am., Russia, Hungary, NATO countries, India, Scandinavia. Address: Rural Route 1 Sabine Farm Mendota IL 61342

STAMER, DWANE STOWE, farm implement co. exec.; b. Mt. Olive, Ill., July 8, 1933; s. Chris G. and Alva (Stowe) S.; student Ill. Western Coll., 1952; m. Wilma J. Climer, Dec. 31, 1955; children—Kirk R., Greg A. Owner, pres. Stamer Implement Co., Litchfield, Ill., 1955—. Served with U.S. Army, 1953-55. Mem. Nat. Farm and Power Equipment Dealers Assn. (nat. dir.), Miss. Valley Farm Equipment Assn. (past pres.). Republican. Lutheran. Home: Rural Route 3 Litchfield IL 62056 Office: 1 Stamer Dr Litchfield IL 62056

STAMETS, WILLIAM, mech. engr.; b. Bellevue, Pa., May 24, 1919; s. William Kerr and Lillie Mae (Smith) S.; B.M.E., Cornell U., 1942, M.M.E., 1949; m. Ramona Hinton, June 12, 1975; children—Lillian, John, William, C. North, Paul. Vice pres., dir. William K. Stamets Co., Pitts., 1942-59; cons. engr., Columbiana, Ohio, 1959-70; engring. cons. Sperry Rand Corp., Huntsville, Ala., 1971-72; prin. engr. Babcock & Wilcox Co., Mt. Vernon, Ind., 1972—; instr. Cornell U., 1947-49; asso. prof. Jefferson County Tech. Inst., Steubenville, Ohio, 1970; lectr. engring. U. Evansville (Ind.), 1973—; mem. indsl. adv. bd. Ind. State U. Div. Engring. Tech., Evansville, 1975—. Served to lt. USNR, 1943-46. Recipient Appreciation certificate Design Engring. Conf., Chgo., 1974, 76; registered profl. engr., N.Y., Ohio, Ind. Mem. ASME, Am. Acad. Mechanics, Soc. Exptl. Stress Analysis. Republican. Methodist. Designer nuclear reactors, pressure vessels, sawmills and steel mill equipment; contbr. articles to profl. jours. Home: 6815 Springdale Dr Evansville IN 47712

STAMM, WILLIAM, city ofcl.; b. Milw., Nov. 7, 1916; s. Jacob Herman and Flora Elizabeth (Kappeler) S.; grad. high sch.; m. Etelka Ann Wittmann, June 4, 1938; 1 dau., Charlene Anita (Mrs. Carl J. Wussow, Jr.). With Milw. Fire Dept., 1940—, capt., 1950-59, bn. chief, 1959-62, dep. chief, 1962-70, chief, 1970—. Bd. dirs. Deaconess Hosp., Milw., Blue Coats Found., Inc., local chpt. ARC, America de Los Amigos, Muscular Dystrophy, Pres.'s Masonic Home Bd. Mem. Internat. Assn. Fire Chiefs chmn. met. com.), Internat. Assn. Fire Fighters, Nat. Fire Protection Assn., Internat. Assn. Fire Service Instrs., Milw. Fire Bell. Mason (Shriner), Eagle. Club: Milw. Athletic. Home: 3830 N 85th St Milwaukee WI 53222 Office: 711 W Wells St Milwaukee WI 53233

STAMOS, THEODORE JAMES, clin. psychologist; b. Oskaloosa, Iowa, May 1, 1933; s. James and Sophia (Zaffiras) S.; student Ball State Coll., 1951-52, N.Y.U., 1952-53; B.A., U. Iowa, 1957, M.S.W., 1959, Ph.D., 1974; m. Roberta Lea Stamos, May 26, 1977; children by previous marriage—Jacqueline, James. Staff Hastings (Minn.) State Hosp., 1959-61, Mental Hygiene Outpatient Clinic of VA Center, St. Paul, 1961-63; exec. dir. Dakota County Mental Health Center, South St. Paul, Minn., 1963-73; pvt. practice, 1960—; staff Mississippi Valley Clinic, Hastings, Minn., 1973—, Zeller Inst. for Living, Hastings, 1974—; guest lectr. group psychotherapy U. Minn., 1963, clin. faculty instr., 1965—; chmn. east Met. Regional Mental Health-Mental Retardation coordinating com., 1968—; sec. Minn. Assn. of Mental Health Programs, 1968—. Mem. mental health adv. com. to Gov. of Minn., 1963—, Gov.'s State Com. on Study Suicide, 1967. Served with USAF, 1953-55. Mem. Am. Group Psychotherapy Assn., Am. Assn. Marriage counselors, Am. Psychol. Assn., Nat. Assn. Social Workers, Minn. Group Psychotherapy Soc. (pres.), Acad. Certified Social Workers. Independent. Mem. Greek Orthodox Ch. Mason. Home: 5000 Abbott Ave South Minneapolis MN 55410 Office: Zeller Inst for Living 12421 Point Douglas Dr Hastings MN 55033 also Interstate Med Center Hwy 61 W Red Wing MN 55066

STAMP, WILLARD JAY, optometrist; b. Salem, Ohio, Oct. 25, 1932; s. J. Richard and Leora H. (Hoopes) S.; student Kent State U., 1950-52; D. Optometry cum laude, Ohio State U., 1955; grad. Command and Gen. Staff Coll.; m. Patricia Lou Davis, June 23, 1957; children—Joel Willard, Alan Jay. Pvt. practice optometry, Akron, Ohio, 1955-56, Salem, 1958—. Served from pvt. to 1st lt. AUS, 1956-58; now lt. col. Res. Mem. Am., Ohio (zone pres. 1970) optometric assns., Am. Pub. Health Assn., United Comml. Travelers, Ohio State U. Alumni Assn., Salem High Sch. Alumni Assn. (pres. 1970, dir.), Vision League Ohio, Res. Officers Assn., Columbiana County Pub. Health League, Internat. Platform Assn., Salem C. of C., Epsilon Psi Epsilon (alumni bd. dirs. 1958-66). Methodist. Clubs: Sevakeen Country (Salem), Masons, Shriners, K.T., Lions (pres. 1967), Elks. Home: 29805 Buck Rd Sevakeen Lake Salem OH 44460 Office: 389 N Ellsworth Ave Salem OH 44460

STANBERY, ROBERT CHARLES, veterinarian; b. Conneaut, Ohio, Apr. 5, 1947; s. Robert James and Ruth Virginia S.; student Miami U., Oxford, Ohio, 1965-67; D.V.M., Ohio State U., 1971; m. Constance Ann Coutts, July 24, 1971; 1 son, Scott Andrew. Veterinarian, Lexington (Mass.) Animal Hosp., 1971-74, Avon Lake Animal Clinic Inc. (Ohio), 1974-76; pres., treas. Bay Village Animal Clinic Inc. (Ohio), 1976—. Mem. AVMA, Ohio Vet. Med. Assn., Animal Hosp. Assn. Cleve. Acad. Vet. Medicine, Lorain County Vet. Assn. Fundamentalist Christian. Home: 351 Bellaire Rd Avon Lake OH 44012 Office: 627 Clague Rd Bay Village OH 44140

STANCIL, ANEMARI, psychologist; b. Grayling, Mich., Jan. 6, 1942; d. Thomas and Georgiana S.; B.S., Central Mich. U., 1972, M.A., 1974; children—Geoffrey, Gregory. Certified psychol. examiner, Mich., 1976; social worker, Mich., 1977. Intern, Gratiot County Community Me tal Health, Alma, Mich., 1973; staff psychologist Huron County Mental Health, Norwalk, Ohio, 1974; behavioral cons. N.E. Mich. Mental Health, Alpena, 1975; staff psychologist Sanilac County Mental Health, Sandusky, Mich., 1976—; instr. R.A.P. Female Identity and Growth Seminar, 1976; coordinator E.V.E.N., Sanilac County; coordinator Rape Counseling Services, Sanilac County, 1976—; instr. psychology dept. St. Clair County Community Coll., 1976—. Mem. Mich. Assn. Profl. Psychologists (v.p.), Blue Water Psychol. Assn., Kappa Delta Pi (sec.-treas. 1971-72), Psi Chi (sec. 1971-72). Home: PO Box 217 Grayling MI 49738

STANFORD, JOHN DAVID, food processing equipment mfg. co. exec.; b. Salem, Ill., Sept. 12, 1946; s. William Thomas and Melba (Hagar) S.; B.S., Georgetown Coll., 1969; m. Donna Maxine Green, Aug. 14, 1971; 1 son, Shane. With Bettendorf Stanford Co., Salem, 1969—, pres., 1970—, owner, 1973—; dir. Best Sales Co., Let's Travel Co. Trustee Kaskaskia Coll. Mem. Georgetown Coll. Assos., Am. Soc. Bakery Engrs., Bakery Equipment Mfg. Assn. Democrat. Baptist. Clubs: Mo. Athletic, Rotary, Toastmasters. Office: PO Box 90 Salem IL 62881

STANICK, WALTER JOHN, dentist; b. St. Louis, Oct. 8, 1927; s. Stanley and Rose S.; student U. Wyo., 1946; A.B., Washington U., St. Louis, 1950, D.M.D., 1956; postgrad. Tufts U., Temple U.; m. Patricia Jean Hazelwood, Dec. 18, 1965; 1 dau., Nancy Marie. Pvt. practice dnetistry, St. Louis, 1958—; faculty Washington U. Sch. Dental Medicine, 1977—. Bd. dirs. Greater St. Louis Council Boy Scouts Am., St. Louis County YMCA. Served with AUS, 1956-58. Mem. Am., Mo. dental assns., Greater St. Louis Dental Soc., Fedn. Dentaire Internationale, St. Louis Dental Research Group. Clubs: Masons, Shriners, Rotary, Elks. Home: 16 Muirfield Ln St Louis MO 63141 Office: 777 S New Ballas Rd St Louis MO 63141

STANISIC, MILOMIR MIRKOV, mathematician, educator; b. Bujacic, Serbia, Aug. 19, 1914; s. Mirko Vule and Ana Milovana (Bujisic) S.; came to U.S., 1949, naturalized, 1955; Diploma Ing., Tech. U., Hannover, Ger., 1946, Dr. Ing., 1949; Ph.D. in Math., Ill. Inst. Tech., 1958; m. Oct. 2, 1954; children—Ana, Michael, Susana. Researcher, faculty mem. dept. mechanics Tech. U., Hannover, 1949-50; research scientist Armour Research Found. of Ill. Inst. of Tech., Chgo., 1950-56; prof. engring. scis. Purdue U., West Lafayette, Ind., 1956-66, prof. aeros. and astronautics, 1967—; vis. prof. Johns Hopkins U., Balt., 1966-67; cons. scientist Gen. Electric Co., Boeing Aircraft Co., Lockheed Co., Picatinny Arsenal. Served with Yugoslavian Army, 1934-45. Mem. Am. Math. Soc., Am. Physics Soc., Soc. for Natural Philosophy, AAUP. Mem. Free Serbian Orthodox Ch. Research in wing in supersonic flow, thermoelasticity, magnetic flow, turbulence, motion of heavy masses, nonlinear phenomena. Office: 801 Princess Dr West Lafayette IN 47906

STANLEY, C. MAXWELL, cons. engr.; b. Corning, Iowa, June 16, 1904; s. Claude Maxwell Stanley, Sr., and Laura Esther (Stephenson) S.; B.S. in gen. engring., U. Iowa, 1926, M.S. in hydraulic engring., 1930; L.H.D., Iowa Wesleyan Coll., 1961; D. Humanities, U. Manila, 1970;; m. Elizabeth M. Holthues, Nov. 11, 1927; children—David M., Richard H., Jane S. Buckles. Structural designer Byllesby Engring. and Mgmt. Corp., Chgo., 1926-27; part time dept. grounds and bldgs.

U. Iowa, 1927-28; hydraulic engr. Mgmt. & Engring. Corp., Dubuque, Iowa and Chgo., 1928-32; cons. engr. Young & Stanley, Inc., 1932-39; partner Stanley Engring. Co. 1939-66; pres. Stanley Consultants, Inc., 1966-71, chmn. bd., 1971—; pres. HON Industries, 1944-64, chmn. bd., 1964—; pres. Stanley Cons., Ltd., Liberia, 1959-71, now dir.; mng. dir. Stanley Cons., Ltd., Nigeria, 1960-67, now dir.; pres. Atlas World Press Rev., 1975—; dir. New Directions. Mem. council World Assn. World Federalists, chmn., 1958-65; exec. council World Federalists U.S.A., 1947—, pres., 1954-56, 64-66; chmn. Strategy for Peace Confs., 1962—, Confs. on UN of Next Decade, 1965—. Pres. Stanley Found., 1956—; mem. Pres.'s Commn. Personnel Interchange, 1976—. Trustee, Iowa Wesleyan Coll., 1951—, chmn., 1963-65; bd. dirs. U. Ia. Found., 1966—, pres., 1971-75; bd. dirs. UN Assn., 1970—. Recipient Distinguished Service award U. Iowa, 1967, Hancher-Finkbine medallion, 1971. Fellow ASCE (Alfred Noble prize 1933, Collingwood prize 1935), IEEE, ASME, Am. Cons. Engrs. Council (chmn. com. fellows); mem. Iowa Engr. Soc. (hon. mem., pres. 1949; John Dunlap prize 1943, Marston award 1947, Distinguished Service award 1962), Nat Planning Assn., Am. Inst. Cons. Engrs. (councilor 1973-75), Nat. Soc. Profl. Engrs. (award for outstanding service to engring. profession 1965), Am. Water Works Assn. Republican. Methodist. Rotarian (Paul Harris award 1976). Author: Waging Peace 1956; The Consulting Engineer, 1961; also articles in profl. jours. Home: 115 Sunset Dr Muscatine IA 52761 Office: Stanley Bldg Muscatine IA 52761

STANLEY, FERDA ETHELDA, labor union ofcl.; b. Chgo., Sept. 6, 1920; d. Oscar D. and Mysan Skinner (Williams) Stanley; B.A. in Edn., Ball State U., 1957, M.A. in L.S. and Audio-Visual Supervision, 1961; div.; children—John, James, Stephanie (Mrs. T. Teagardin). Elementary sch. tchr., 1957—, reading instr. Title 1 Program, 1970—; labor union ofcl., 1962—, pres. Anderson (Ind.) Fedn. Tchrs., Am. Fedn. Tchrs., AFL-CIO, 1972—; mem. exec. bd. Ind. Fedn. Tchrs., 1975—, also chairperson human rights com. NDEA grantee English, 1968. Mem. Assn. for Childhood Edn., Women's Polit. Caucus, Urban League, Bus. and Profl. Women's Club (pres. Anderson 1967), Pi Lambda Theta. Christian Scientist (reader 1961-63, clk. 1964-67). Home: 3923 Main St Anderson IN 46014 Office: 2025 Hillcrest Dr Anderson IN 46012

STANLEY, JAMES GORDON, engring. mktg. exec., writer; b. Birmingham, Ala., Feb. 13, 1925; s. Joseph Gordon and Amy I. (Crocker) S.; B.S., U. Ala., 1949; m. children—Cynthia Ruth, Pamela Anne, Gordon Bruce, James Alan, Joseph Christopher; m. 2d, Patricia Ann Peuvion, 1969. Instr., Miss. State U. Extension, Jackson, 1956; tech. rep. S.E., Price Brothers Co., Dayton, 1957-59; project mgr., dept. mgr. Brown Engring. Co., Kennedy Space Center, Fla. and Huntsville, Ala., 1959-64; dir. engring., reliability Bendix Launch Support Div., 1964-67; mgr. reliability, systems engr. Dow Chem. Co., Kennedy Space Center, 1967-71, mgr. engring. mktg. Houston, 1971-73, contract research mgr., Midland, Mich., 1973—; free lance writer. Served to lt. (j.g.) USNR), 1943-66. Mem. Cocoa Beach C. of C., Phi Gamma Delta. Democrat. Baptist. Elk. Home: 2560 Arbutus Ct Midland MI 48640 Office: Dow Chem Bldg 566 Midland MI 48640

STANLEY, JOHN HARLAN, physician; b. Massena, Iowa, May 7, 1936; s. Harlan Coleman and Amy Lucille (Anstey) S.; B.A., St. Ambrose Coll., 1958; M.D., U. Iowa, 1965; m. Karon R. Lorenz, Aug. 13, 1960; children—Susan, Christopher. Intern, Broadlawns Hosp., Des Moines, 1965-66; resident adult, child psychiatry U. Ia., 1966-70; community psychiatry Johnson County Mental Health Center, Overland Park, Kan., 1970-72; individual practice medicine specializing in child and adolescent psychiatry, Kansas City, Mo., 1970—. Cons. child psychiatry Gillis, Ozanam boys' homes, 1971—; mem. adv. bd. Johnson County (Kan.) Assn. Children with Learning Disabilities, 1972—. Cub scout leader Kaw council Boy Scouts Am., 1972—. Served with AUS, 1960-62. Mem. Am. Assn. Psychiat. Services for Children, Am. Psychiat. Assn., Am. Orthopsychiat. Assn., Mo., Jackson County med. socs., Phi Rho Sigma. Republican. Roman Catholic. Home: 5307 W 100th St Overland Park KS 66207 Office: 4400 Broadway Kansas City MO 64111

STANLEY, JOHN ROBERT, obstetrician-gynecologist; b. Indpls., Apr. 23, 1924; s. Foster Lee Roy and Eva Lorine (Snyder) S.; M.D., Ind. U., 1947; m. Mary Kathryn Detrick, Feb. 1, 1947; children—Dolores Ann Stanley Hodnett, David Lee, Daniel Vernon, Douglas Arthur. Intern, Ind. U. Med. Center, Indpls., 1947-48; surgery preceptor, Muncie, Ind., 1948-50; resident in pathology Ball Meml. Hosp., Muncie, 1950-51; gen. practice medicine, Muncie, 1951-60; with city health officer Muncie, 1951-55; resident in obstetrics-gynecology Ind. Med. Center, 1960-64; practice medicine specializing in obstetrics-gynecology, Muncie, 1964—; past pres. clin. staff Ball Meml. Hosp., Muncie Acad. Medicine; bd. sub area council Health Service Agy. Chmn. Planned Parenthood, E. Central Ind.; past pres. Del. County Cancer Soc. Served with AUS, 1944-46. Diplomate Am. Bd. Obstetrics-Gynecology. Fellow Am. Coll. Obstetrics-Gynecology; mem. AMA, Del. Blackford Med. Soc. (past pres.), Ind. State Med. Assn., Ind. Obstetrical-Gynecol. Soc. Republican. Episcopalian. Clubs: Muncie Tennis and Country, Masons, Elks. Home: 400 Brentwood Ln Muncie IN 47304 Office: 1111 W Jackson St Muncie IN 47305

STANLEY, JOSEPH RICHARD, educator; b. Huntington County, Ind., Mar. 17, 1936; s. John Charles and Bessie Ellen (Fritz) S.; B.S., Huntington Coll., 1959; M.S., St. Francis Coll., 1969; m. Joanna Sue Drake, Aug. 26, 1972. Tchr., coach Sparta Twp. Schs., Cromwell, Ind., 1959-60, Springfield Twp. Schs., LaGrange, Ind., 1960-63, Blue Creek Local Schs., Paulding, Ohio, 1963-64; tchr., head bus. edn. dept. Bellmont High Sch., Decatur, Ind., 1964—. Mem. Adams, Jay and Wells County Bd. Realtors, Ind. Auctioneers Assn. Home: 104 Marshall Decatur IN 46733 Office: 1000 E North Adams Dr Decatur IN 46733

STANLEY, MORRIS BURNS, tax lawyer, automobile co. exec.; b. Lizard Hill, McClure, Va., May 19, 1920; s. Roley Stephenson and Imogene (Smith) S.; student Md. State Tchrs. Coll. at Frostburg, 1937-39; A.B. magna cum laude, Lincoln Meml. U., 1941; M.A., Emory U., 1942; J.D., Harvard, 1948; LL.M., Wayne State U., 1959; m. Alice Yvonne Keller, July 24, 1943; children—Karen Helene, Burns Stephen. Seasonal ranger Nat. Park Service, Shenandoah Nat. Park, 1940-42; chief bus. and occupation tax div. State W. Va., 1948-49; admitted to W.Va. bar, 1949; asst. atty. gen. in charge of taxes State of W.Va., Charleston, 1949-51; tax exec., office of gen. counsel Ford Motor Co., Dearborn, Mich., 1951—; adj. prof. Wayne State U., Detroit, 1957—; lectr. in tax field. Mem. adv. group to Commr. Internal Revenue, 1976. Mgr. heavyweight boxers Sonny Banks and H. Cody Jones, 1961-65; hypnotist. Served with USMCR, 1942-45; col. ret. Mem. W.Va., Fed., Am. bar assns., Tax Execs. Inst. (internat. pres. 1975—), Council of State Chambers Commerce (chmn. com. state taxation 1973-74), Greater Detroit C. of C. (chmn. state tax com. 1971-74), Mich. C. of C. (co-chmn. tax evaluation com. 1971—), Iota Alpha Sigma. Departmental editor state and local taxes Jour. Taxation, 1967-73. Contbg. author Annual Survey of Michigan Law, 1958—. Home: 10031 Island Dr Grosse Ile MI 48138 Office: Office of Gen Counsel Ford Motor Co Am Rd Dearborn MI 48121

STANLEY, RICHARD HOLT, cons. firm exec.; b. Muscatine, Iowa, Oct. 20, 1932; s. Claude Maxwell and Elizabeth Mabel (Holthues) S.; B.S. in Mech. Engring., Iowa State U., 1955, B.S. in Elec. Engring., 1955; M.S. in San. Engring., State U. Iowa, 1963; m. Mary Joanne Kennedy, Dec. 20, 1953; children—Lynne Elizabeth, Sarah Catherine, Joseph Holt. With Stanley Consultants, Muscatine, 1955—, exec. v.p., 1968-71, pres., 1971—, also dir.; dir. HON Industries, Muscatine. Mem. adv. council Center Indsl. Research and Sci., Ia. State U., Ames, 1967-69, chmn., 1969, mem. adv. council Engring. Coll., 1969—. Bd. dirs. Muscatine United Way, 1969-75; v.p., bd. dirs. Stanley Found., 1956—, pres. bd. dirs. Eastern Iowa Community Coll., Bettendorf, 1966-68. Named Sr. Engr. of Yr., Joint Engring. Com. of Quint Cities, 1973. Registered profl. engr., numerous states. Fellow Am. Cons. Engrs. Council (Ia. pres. 1967, pres. 1976-77); mem. Nat. Soc. Profl. Engrs., Am. Nuclear Soc., ASME, IEEE, ASCE, Iowa Engring. Soc. (John Dunlap-Sherman Woodward award, pres. 1973-74), Am. Soc. Engring. Edn., Ia. Acad. Sci., Am. Nuclear Soc., Muscatine C. of C. (pres. 1972-73), Tau Beta Pi, Phi Kappa Phi. Presbyterian. (elder). Rotarian. Home: 601 W 3d St Muscatine IA 52761 Office: Stanley Bldg Muscatine IA 52761

STANMAR, MARGARET MARY VIDAS, physician; b. Chgo., Mar. 12, 1915; d. Klement E. and Gertrude (Byon) Vidas; student Mundelien Coll., 1932-35, Lewis Inst., 1935; M.D., Chgo. Med. Sch., 1939; m. Stanley Stanmar, June 23, 1938; children—Greg, Reg, Michele (Mrs. David Neill). Intern Grace Gen. Hosp., Windsor, Ont., Can., 1939-40, resident East Moline State Hosp., 1940-42; gen. practice medicine, LaSalle, Ill., 1942—; staff Illinois Valley Community hosps., LaSalle and Peru, St. Margaret's Hosp., Spring Valley, Ill. Fellow Am. Acad. Gen. Practice; mem. AMA, Am. Med. Womens Assn., LaSalle Country (past sec.-treas., pres. 1959-60), Ill. med. socs., LaSalle Bus. and Profl. Women's Club (pres. 1950), Hammond Organ Soc., Zonta (past pres. LaSalle). Home: 1608 St Vincent St LaSalle IL 61301 Office: 555 2nd St LaSalle IL 61301

STANTON, JEANNE FRANCES, lawyer; b. Vicksburg, Miss., Jan. 22, 1920; d. John Francis and Hazel (Mitchell) Stanton; student George Washington U., 1938-39; B.A., U. Cin., 1940; J.D., Salmon P. Chase Coll. Law, 1954. Admitted to Ohio bar, 1954; chief clk. Selective Service Bd., Cin., 1940-43; instr. USAAF Tech. Schs., Biloxi, Miss., 1943-44; with Procter & Gamble, Cin., 1945—, legal asst., 1952-54, head advt. services sect. legal div. Trade Practices Dept., 1954-73, mgr. advt. services, legal div., 1973—. Team capt. Community Chest Cin., 1953. Mem. AAAS, Am., Ohio (chmn. uniform state laws com. 1968-70), Cin. (sec. law day com. 1965-66, chmn. com. on preservation hist. documents 1968-71) bar assns., Vicksburg and Warren County, Cin. hist. socs., Internat. Oceanographic Found., Otago Early Settlers Assn. (asso.), Intercontinental Biog. Assn., Cin. Lawyers, Cin. Women Lawyers (treas. 1958-59, nominating com. 1976). Club: Terrace Park Country. Home: 2302 E Hill Ave Cincinnati OH 45208 Office: 306 E 6th St Cincinnati OH 45202

STANTON, JOHN WILLIAM, congressman; b. Painesville, Ohio, Feb. 20, 1924; s. Frank M. and Mary (Callinan) S.; B.A., Georgetown U., 1949; m. Margaret Smeeton, Dec. 3, 1966; 1 dau., Kelly Marie. Pres. J. W. Stanton, Inc., Painesville, 1949-63; commr. Lake County, Ohio, 1956-64; mem. 89th-95th Congresses 11th Dist. Ohio. Served to capt. AUS, 1942-46. Decorated Bronze Star medal with 1 oak leaf cluster, Purple Heart. Mem. Painesville Jr. (charter), Painesville (pres. 1952-55) chambers commerce, Am. Legion, Elk, K.C. (4 deg.). Republican. Roman Catholic. Club: Painesville Exchange (pres. 1951). Home: 7 N Park Pl Painesville OH 44077 Office: Rayburn Bldg Washington DC 20515

STAPLER, HARRY BASCOM, educator, pub.; b. N.Y.C., Mar. 10, 1919; s. Henry Bascom and Gertrude (Haupert) S.; B.A., Coll. Wooster (Ohio), 1950; m. Normalee Waggoner, May 16, 1961. Reporter, Daily Record, Wooster, 1940-41, 47-50, also photographer; reporter AP, Detroit, 1950, regional sports editor, 1951-53; sports reporter Detroit News, 1953-58; editor Fostoria (Ohio) Rev. Times, 1958-60; bus. reporter Lansing (Mich.) State Jour., 1960-62; pub., editor, founder East Lansing (Mich.) Towne Courier, 1962-73, pres., 1966-73; pub., editor, founder Meridian Towne Courier, Okemos, Mich., 1965-73; pub., editor Williamston (Mich.) Enterprise, 1966-73; instr. journalism Ferris State Coll., 1974—, dir. journalism program, 1977—; mng. editor Competency Forum, 1977—; v.p. Suburban Newspapers of Mich., 1969-73. Served with USNR, 1941-46. Recipient John Field Journalism Edn. award Mich. Interscholastic Press Assn., 1973. Mem. East Lansing C. of C. (dir. 1973), Gladwin Blue Lake and Emerald Valley Assn. (pres. 1971-73), Univ. Internat. (v.p. 1970-72). Republican. Presbyn. Rotarian. Author: The Student Journalist and Sportswriting, 1974; Your Future in Pro Sports, 1977. Home: Apt 302 D 521 Fuller Big Rapids MI 49307

STAPLES, LAWRENCE FLINT, physician; b. Grasmere, N.H., Spet. 24, 1922; s. Clarence Lawrence and Mary Louise (Harris) S.; B.S., U. N.H., 1949, M.S., 1950; M.D., U. Iowa, 1956; m. Marilyn Elaine Hauser, Dec. 22, 1945; children—Alan, Bruce, Marylou. Intern, Iowa Meth. Hosp., Des Moines, 1956-57; resident U. Iowa Hosps., Iowa City, 1957-60; practice medicine specializing in internal medicine, Des Moines, 1960—; dir. med. edn. Iowa Meth. Hosp., 1960-69, pres. med. staff, 1974-76, chief dept. internal medicine, 1968—; med. dir. Northwestern Bell Telephone Co., 1973—; clin. asso. prof. State U. Iowa Med. Sch.; adv. com. nursing Grandview Coll., Des Moines. Bd. dirs. Des Moines Symphony. Served with AUS, 1940-45. Diplomate Am. Bd. Internal Medicine. Fellow A.C.P., Am. Coll. Cardiology, Am. Coll. Chest Physicians; mem. AMA, Am. Soc. Internal Medicine, Am. Occupational Med. Assn., Iowa, Polk County med. socs. Lutheran. Clubs: Wakonda, Embassy, Des Moines Racquet. Contbr. articles to med. jours. Home: 3509 Caulder St Des Moines IA 50321 Office: 1221 Center St Suite 17 Des Moines IA 50309

STAPLES, ROBERT ALFRED CHARLES, computer engr.; b. Saint John, N.B., Can., Apr. 8, 1937; s. Alfred Graham and Olga Clinton (von Richter) S.; came to U.S., 1970; B.Sc. in Elec. Engring., U. N.B., 1949; M.B.A., McGill U., 1968; m. Iona Marie Griffin, Sept. 6, 1958; children—David, Laurie. Student engr. N.B. Telephone Co., 1957-59; computer contract engr. Bailey Meter Co., Ltd., Wickliffe, Ohio, 1960-66; mgr. digital systems marketing Bailey Meter Co., Ltd., Montreal, 1967-69, computer product mgr., Wickliffe, 1970—; lectr. McGill U., 1966-68. Lord Beaverbrook scholar, 1954-59; Jack Bridone fellow, 1959. Registered profl. engr., Que. Mem. Am. Nuclear Soc. Episcopalian. Club: Euclid Curling. Contbr. articles tech. jours. Patentee in field. Home: 8801 Rockwood Ct Mentor OH 44060 Office: 29801 Euclid Ave Wickliffe OH 44092

STAPLETON, ROBERT J., indsl. devel. exec.; b. Ft. Wayne, Ind., Jan. 9, 1922; s. Clarence Albert and Eva Elizabeth (Grashoff) S.; A.B., Valparaiso U., 1946; M.S., U. Wis., 1947; postgrad., U. Mich., 1943; m. Marilyn Jeane Stinchfield, Sept. 7, 1946; children—Jan Elizabeth, Jill Leigh, Robert Guy. Indsl. devel. rep. Commonwealth Edison Co., Chgo., 1947-55; mng. dir., sec. Clinton Devel. Co. (Iowa), 1955-63; mgr. Cordova (Ill.) Indsl. Park, No. Natural Gas Co., 1963-69; exec. dir. Elgin (Ill.) Econ. Devel. Commn., 1969-71; exec. dir. Jobs div. IVAC, LaSalle, Ill., 1971-77; exec. v.p. Scioto Econ. Devel. Corp., Portsmouth, Ohio, 1977—; pvt. practice as indsl. devel. cons., 1955—. Past pres., dir. Ill. Devel. Council. Served to lt (j.g.), USNR, 1942-46; capt. Res. ret. Certified indsl. developer. Mem. Res. Officers Assn., Naval Res., Assn. Am. Soc. Planning Ofcls., Am., Gt. Lakes States Area devel. councils, Nat. Assn. Corp. Real Estate Execs., Urban Land Inst., Indsl. Devel. Research Council, Portsmouth C. of C., Valparaiso U. Lettermen's Assn., Wis. Alumni Assn. Republican. Lutheran. Clubs: Rotary, Elks Country. Home: Box 1513 Old Post Rd Portsmouth OH 45662 Office: 6th and Court Sts Portsmouth OH 45662

STARK, HOWARD, pharmacist; b. San Antonio, Mar. 23, 1933; s. Joseph L. and Jeanette (Krashin) S.; B.S. in Pharmacy, U. Mo., 1958; m. Maxine Kreitman, Dec. 6, 1959; children—Dana Hope, Kimberle Ann. Student pharmacist Drs. Bldg. Pharmacy, Kansas City, Mo., 1955-58, chief pharmacist, 1958-61, v.p., pharmacist, 1961-66; owner Stark's Profl. Pharmacy, Kansas City, Mo., 1966—; mem. adv. bd. for pharmacy Blue Cross and Blue Shield, 1968—. Served with AUS, 1953-55. Recipient Man of Year award Mo. Pharm. Assn. also Alumni Assn. U. Mo. Sch. Pharmacy, 1974; Alumni Achievement award U. Mo., Kansas City, 1976. Mem. Am. Pharm. Assn., Am. Coll. Apothecaries (past pres. Greater Kansas City chpt., nat. chmn. indsl. relations, ins. and 3d party coms., nat. pres. 1975-76, chmn. bd. 1976-77), U. Mo. at Kansas City Sch. Pharmacy Alumni Assn. (dir., pres.), Greater Kansas City Pharmacist Assn. (dir.), Alpha Zeta Omega. Clubs: B'nai B'rith, Beth Shalom Men's (Kansas City). Home: 9641 Riggs St Overland Park KS 66212 Office: 6700 Troost St Kansas City MO 64131

STARK, JACK ALAN, psychologist; b. Hastings, Nebr., Sept. 20, 1946; s. Arlen O. and Virginia (Dryden) S.; B.A., St. Francis Coll., 1968; M.A., U. Nebr., 1970, Ph.D., 1973; m. Shirley Theis, Aug. 1, 1970; children—John, Nicholas. Counseling psychologist, pub. schs. Lincoln, Nebr., 1970-73; asst. prof. psychology U. Nebr., Omaha, 1973—, asst. prof. med. psychology Med. Sch., 1973—; instr. Creighton U., 1975—. Licensced psychologist, Nebr.; NDEA fellow, 1968-70. Mem. Nebr. Psychol. Assn. (exec. council), Epilepsy League Nebr., Nat. Assn. Retarded Citizens, Nat. Rehab. Counselors Assn., Rehab. Assn. Nebr. (dir.; com. chmn.), Rehab. Counseling Assn. Nebr., Soc. Pediatric Psychology, Am. Assn. Edn. Severely and Profoundly Handicapped, Acad. Psychologists in Marital and Family Therapy. Democrat. Roman Catholic. Contbr. articles to profl. jours. Home: 306 Heavenly Dr Omaha NE 68154 Office: Dept Psychiatry Med Center Univ Nebr Omaha NE 68131

STARK, LOUIS EDWARD, welding research engr.; b. Youngstown, Ohio, Sept. 15, 1918; B.S., Mass. Inst. Tech., 1947; m. Mary E. Hoye, July 15, 1944; children—Phoebe Ann, Louis E., Sarah Jane. Welding sect. head metals research labs. Union Carbide Corp., Niagara Falls, N.Y., 1947-56; supr. welding and melting research Reactive Metals, Inc., Niles, Ohio, 1957-70; sr. welding engr. Babcock & Wilcox Co., Alliance, Ohio, 1970—. Served with AUS, 1942-46. Mem. Am. Soc for Metals, Am. Welding Soc. Contbr. articles to profl. jours. Patentee in field. Home: 3454 White Beech Ln Youngstown OH 44511 Office: 1562 Beeson St Alliance OH 44601

STARK, PATRICIA ANN, sch. psychologist; b. Ames, Iowa, Apr. 21, 1937; s. Keith Curtis and Mary Louise (Johnston) Moore; B.S., Southern Ill. U., Edwardsville, 1970, M.S., 1972; Ph.D., St. Louis U., 1976; m. Edward Milton Stark, June 12, 1959. Counselor alcoholics Bapt. Rescue Mission, East St. Louis, Ill., 1969; Gateway Rehab. Center, 1972; intern. sch. psycnologist Henry Stark Counties Spl. Edn. Dist., Kewanee, Ill., 1972-73; instr. psychology Lewis and Clark Community Coll., Godfrey, Ill., 1973-74, (developer complete child care degree program), coordinator child care services, 1974—, asst. prof., 1976—. School Fellowship, 1970-71, 1971-72. Mem. Ill., Midwestern psychol. assns., Nat. Assn. Sch. Psychologists, Am. Psychol. Assn., Assn. Specialists in Group Work, Am. Personnel and Guidance Assn., Nat. Honor Soc. in Psychology, Psi Chi. Contbr. articles to profl. jours., producer, director videotape presentations. Home: 8808 Bunkum Rd Caseyville IL 62232 Office: Lewis and Clark Community Coll Godfrey IL 62035

STARK, PHILLIP CARL, realtor, developer; b. Madison, Wis., Nov. 17, 1925; s. Paul E. and Julia (Polk) S.; B.B.A., U. Wis., 1948; m. Mary Jane Marty, June 28, 1952; children—David K., Jeffrey P., Thomas F. With The Stark Co., Madison, Wis., 1948—, partner, 1963-67, mng. partner, 1967—; dir. Anchor Savs. & Loan Assn., Dane County Title Co. Pres. Madison YMCA, 1956-57; chmn. Dane County chpt. A.R.C., 1958-59. Mem. Madison Housing Authority, 1953-58. Chmn. bd. dirs. Madison C. of C., 1977. Served with inf., AUS, 1944-45; ETO. Decorated Silver Star, Purple Heart; named Young Man of Year Madison Jr. C. of C., 1953, one of Wis.'s 5 outstanding young men, 1957, Madison realtor of year, Madison Bd. Realtors, 1970, Wis. realtor of year, 1974. Mem. Madison Bd. Realtors (pres. 1954), Wis. Realtors Assn. (pres. 1972). Presbyn. (elder). Clubs: Masons, Shrine, Rotary, Blackhawk Country (Madison, Wis.). Home: 6346 Landfall Dr Madison WI 53705 Office: 117 Monona Ave Madison WI 53703

STARK, ROBERT JAMES, JR., packing co. exec.; b. N.Y.C., Apr. 11, 1920; s. Robert James and Lucia (Rhyne) S.; B.A., Amherst Coll., 1941; m. Martha K. Lamb, Aug. 5, 1944 (dec. 1976); children—Martha Louise (Mrs. R. W. Clifford), Lucia Burnham (Mrs. C.W. Scott), Polly Robertson, Robert Bruce; m. 2d, Stella X. Gilbert, Feb. 5, 1977. Salesman, Graybar Electric Co., N.Y.C., 1941, 45-50; with Crane Packing Co., Morton Grove, Ill., 1952—, asst. sales mgr. seal div., 1952-57, asst. to pres., 1954-57, sales mgr. seal div., 1957-63, asst. v.p. seal sales, 1963-65, v.p. 1965—, dir., 1968—; v.p. Crane Packing, Ltd., Hamilton, Ont., Can., 1956—, also dir.; dir. John Crane Western, Inc. Active Northbrook (Ill.) United Fund, 1955-60, pres. 1959; mem. Dist. 28 Sch. Bd. Northbrook, 1961-68. Served to lt. USNR, 1941-45, lt. comdr., 1950-52; PTO. Mem. Am. Mgmt. Assn., Research Inst. Am., Am. Ordnance Assn., Ill. C. of C., No. Ill. Ind. Assn. (pres. 1973), Phi Kappa Psi. Republican. Episcopalian. Clubs: Garden of Gods (Colorado Springs); Sunset Ridge Country (Northfield, Ill.). Home: 1854 Somerset Ln Northbrook IL 60062 Office: 6400 W Oakton St Morton Grove IL 60053

STARK, SANFORD BRUCE, accountant; b. Morganton, Ark., Apr. 7, 1938; s. Johnson W. and Judith C. (Van Nada) S.; B.S., Wichita State U., 1968, B.A., 1968; m. Betty Sue Stark, May 30, 1957; 1 dau., Rebecca. Auditor, Moberly, West, Jennings & Shaul, Wichita, Kans., 1964-68; sr. auditor Elmer Fox & Co., Wichita, 1968-70; audit mgr. Cohen Kirkpatrick & Co., Springfield, Mo., 1970-71; pvt. practice accounting, Branson and Mountain Grove, Mo., 1971—. C.P.A., Kans., Mo. Mem. Am. Inst. C.P.A., Mo. Soc. C.P.A. Club: Rotary. Home: Branson N Branson MO 65616 Office: PO Box 219 Branson MO 65616

STARK, THOMAS ISAAC, educator; b. Saginaw, Mich., Dec. 26, 1930; s. Jacob Henry and Dorothy May (Chapman) S.; student Bay City Jr. Coll., 1948-50; B.A., U. Mich., 1952; B.S., U. Chgo., 1960, M.A., 1962, postgrad., 1967—; m. Patricia Ann Bilzi, June 11, 1955; 1 dau., Rachael Marie. Mathematician, Systems Research, U. Chgo., 1956-58; instr. Ill. Inst. Tech., Chgo., 1958-59, Purdue U., Calumet City, Ind., 1959-60, Inst. for Computer Research, U. Chgo., 1962; prof. philosophy and humanities Chgo. City Coll., 1962—; cons.

DePaul U., 1975. Served with AUS, 1952-54. Recipient Tchr. of Year award Loop City Coll., 1967, Distinguished Service award, 1972; U. Mich. Regents scholar, 1950. Mem. Am. Philos. Assn., Medieval Acad. Am., Ill. Assn. Devel. Teaching Philosophy (v.p. 1976-77), Ill. Philos. Assn., AAAS, Phi Theta Kappa. Home: 5510 S Woodlawn Ave Chicago IL 60637

STARKEY, ROBERTA NEIL JOHNSTON (MRS. JOHN DOW STARKEY), educator; b. Eskota, Tex., June 13, 1921; d. Clarence Beaman and Fannie Irene (Hassell) Johnston; B.S., Tex. Technol. Coll., 1942, Ed.D., 1961; M.A., Eastern N.Mex. U., 1956; m. John Dow Starkey, Nov. 3, 1943; children—David Joe, Bill Clarence, Marilyn Elaine. Tchr. various schs., 1942-44; tchr. Clovis (N.M.) Lincoln-Jackson Elementary Sch., 1956-59; tchr. Mil. Heights Elementary Sch., prof. Roswell Community Coll., 1961-63; asst. prof. U. Wyo., Laramie, 1964-67; asso. prof. elementary edn. No. Ill. U., DeKalb, 1967-70, now prof. Mem. summer faculty Eastern N.Mex. U., 1961-63. Active Girl Scouts U.S.A. Mem. AAUW (Laramie pres. 1965-67, editor state bulletin 1958-60), N.E.A. (sectional chmn. 1959), Internat. Reading Assn. (state chmn. 1966-67), Am. Personnel and Guidance Assn. (exec. bd. 1975-76), Assn. Humanistic Edn. and Devel. (nat. pres. 1974-75), Student Personnel Assn. for Tchr. Edn. (nat. editor newsnotes 1968-72, pres. 1974-75), Nat. Soc. Coll. Tchrs. Edn., Ill., N.Mex. ednl. assns., Ill. Assn. for Study of Perception (v.p. 1975-76), Delta Kappa Gamma (pres. 1966-67, Phi Lambda Theta (pres. Beta Delta chpt.), Democrat. Methodist (chmn. bd. edn. 1959-61). Editor: Assn. Study of Perception newsletter. Home: Route 2 DeKalb IL 60115

STARKEY, WALTER LEROY, mech. engr.; b. Mpls., Oct. 5, 1920; s. Harry N. and Rena B. (Towne) S.; B.M.E., U. Louisville, 1943; M.S., Ohio State U., 1947, Ph.D., 1950; m. Bonna B. Preston, Dec. 17, 1949; children—David Harry, John Mark. Instr., U. Louisville, 1943-46; instr. Ohio State U., Columbus, 1947-49, asst. prof., 1950-54, asso. prof., 1954-58, prof. mech. engring., 1958—; chmn. bd. Jadco, Inc. Fellow ASME (Machine Design award 1976); mem. Am. Soc. Engring. Edn. Author: Motorhome Facts, 1973; contbr. tech. articles to profl. jours. Home: 7000 Coffman Rd Dublin OH 43017 Office: Mech Engring Dept Ohio State U Columbus OH 43210

STARNER, GLENN LESLIE, univ. adminstr.; b. Woodbine, Iowa, Nov. 6, 1923; s. Jess F. and Lillian (Hanson) S.; B.S., No. Iowa U., 1948; student U. Iowa, 1949; M.S., Drake U., 1952; student U. Ill., 1960; Ph.D., Mich. State U., 1969; m. Kathryn Jeanne Klousia, Dec. 25, 1944; children—Dennis, Katha, Carrie. Teacher, Casey (Iowa) High Sch., 1949-51; prin. New Sharon (Iowa) High Sch., 1951-53; prin. Bremen High Sch., 1953-63; asso. dean students Central Mich. U., 1963—. Vice-chmn. Mt. Pleasant (Mich.) City Housing Commn., 1976—. Served with USAAF, 1943-45. Mem. Am. Personnel and Guidance Assn., Assn. Humanistic Edn. and Devel., Mich. Coll. Personnel Assn., Nat. Assn. Student Personnel Adminstrs., Phi Delta Kappa, Kappa Delta Pi. Republican. Methodist. Club: Lions. Home: 1034 South Dr Mount Pleasant MI 48858 Office: Central Mich U Office of Student Affairs Mount Pleasant MI 48859

STARNES, JAMES WRIGHT, lawyer; b. East St. Louis, Ill., Apr. 3, 1933; s. James Adron and Nell (Short) S.; student St. Louis U., 1951-53; LL.B., Washington U., St. Louis, 1957; m. Helen Woods Mitchell, Mar. 29, 1958; children—James Wright, Mitchell A., William B. II. Admitted to Mo., Ill. bars, 1957; asso. Stinson, Mag, Thomson, McEvers & Fizzell, Kansas City, Mo., 1957-60, partner, 1960—; partner Mid-Continent Properties Co., 1959—, Fairview Investment Co., Kansas City, 1971-76, Monticello Land Co., 1973—; sec. Packaging Products Corp., Mission, Kan. Bd. dirs. Mo. Assn. Mental Health, 1968-69; bd. dirs. Kansas City Assn. Mental Health, 1966—, pres., 1969-70; bd. dirs. Heed, 1965-73, 77—, pres., 1966-67, finance chmn. 1967-68; bd. dirs. Kansas City Halfway House Found., exec. com., 1966-69, pres., 1966; bd. dirs. Joan Davis Sch. for Spl. Edn., 1972—, v.p., 1972-73, pres. elect, 1974-76; bd. dirs. Sherwood Center for Exceptional Child, 1977—. Served with arty. AUS, 1957. Mem. Am., Kansas City bar assns., Kansas City Lawyers Assn. Presbyterian (deacon). Mem. adv. bd. Washington U. Law Quar., 1957—. Home: 10712 Glenwood Overland Park KS 66211 Office: 2100 Ten Main Center Kansas City MO 64105

STARR, EDWARD CARYL, librarian; b. Yonkers, N.Y., Jan. 9, 1911; s. Edward Charles and Mary Hamilton (Reid) S.; A.B. cum laude, Colgate U., 1933; B.S., Columbia Univ. Sch. Library Service, 1939; M.Div., Colgate-Rochester Div. Sch., 1940; m. Hilda Ruth Thomforde, Aug. 31, 1940; children—Caroline May (Mrs. Norman C. Wehmer), E(dward) Jonathan. Curator, Samuel Colgate Baptist Hist. Collection, Colgate U., 1935-48; librarian Crozer Theol. Sem., Chester, Pa., 1948-54; curator Am. Baptist Hist. Soc., 1948-55; ordained to ministry Bapt. Ch., 1952; curator combined Samuel Colgate Bapt. Hist. Collection and Am. Bapt. Hist. Soc., Colgate Rochester Div. Sch., 1955-76. Archivist, Am. Bapt. Chs. in U.S.A., Colgate Rochester Bexley-Crozer Theol. Sem. Mem. Am. Soc. Ch. History, Am. Archivists, Am. Assn. Theol. Librarians, Phi Beta Kappa. Republican. Editor, compiler A Baptist Bibliography, 1947-76. Contbr. articles to periodicals. Home: 3215 Brookshire Dr Florissant MO 63033

STARRETT, THOMAS ALLEN, dynamite equipment mfr.; b. Chgo., Dec. 18, 1916; s. James William and June (Rockcastle) S.; grad. Elgin Acad., 1935; Chem. Engr., U. Ill., 1939; m. Joyce Lorayne DeWitt, Dec. 10, 1939; children—Thomas Allen, Karen Lynne. Vice pres. Starrett Machine & Engring. co., Chgo., 1939-44; chem. engr. Ill. Watch Case Co., Elgin, 1944-46; works mgr. Consol. Silver Refining Co., Chgo., 1946-47; partner James W. Starrett Co., Algonquin, Ill., 1947-58, pres., owner, 1958—; pres., owner Republic Mfg. Co., Algonquin, 1958—, Starrett Products Co., Algonquin, 1958—. Registered profl. engr., Ill. Mem. Ill. Aux. State Police, 1951—; mem. lay adv. bd. St. Joseph Hosp. Mem. Am. Def. Preparedness Assn. (life), Elgin Assn. Commerce, U. Ill. Alumni Assn., Nat. Rifle Assn. (life), Ill. Rifle Assn. Moose, Rotarian (past pres.; dist. treas. 1975-76). Club: Chicagoland Sports Car (mem. Midwest council). Home: 321 Marquerite St Elgin IL 60121 Office: Heager's Bend Subdivision Algonquin IL 60102

STARSHAK, MICHAEL JOHN, accountant; b. Chgo., Oct. 14, 1941; s. Norbert P. and Edna (Reiter) S.; B.A. cum laude, Loras Coll., 1963; m. Patricia L. McDonald, July 18, 1964; 1 son, Michael John. With Price Waterhouse & Co., Chgo., 1963-72, audit mgr., 1969-72; v.p. fin. and adminstrn. Rollins Burdick Hunter Co., Chgo., 1972—, also dir., mem. exec. com. C.P.A., Ill. Mem. Am. Inst. C.P.A.'s, Ill. Soc. C.P.A.'s. Clubs: Chgo. Athletic Assn.; Park Ridge Country. Office: 10 S Riverside Plaza Chicago IL 60606

STASZAK, LAWRENCE ROBERT, electronics co. exec.; b. Toledo, June 25, 1941; s. Zigmond Robert and Ann Irene (Mioduzewski) S.; B.S. in Elec. Engring., U. Toledo, 1966; postgrad Mich. State U., 1966-67; m. Gloria R. Frey, Mar. 22, 1969; children—Terasa Marie, Todd Michael. With Sparton Electronics Div., Jackson, Mich., 1966—, profject engr., 1969-74, mktg. rep., 1974-75, mgr. advanced programs and product devel., 1975—. Mem. IEEE, Naval Helicopter Assn., Am. Radio Relay League, Assn. Old Crows, Cricket Soc., Am. Def. Preparedness Assn. Republican. Roman Catholic. Home: 3853 Kirkwood St Jackson MI 49203 Office: 2400 Ganson St E Jackson MI 49202

STATES, ALFRED ZIMMER, chiropractic orthopedist; b. Clarinda, Iowa, Oct. 12, 1929; s. Coy Vaughn and Lucille Wilhelmina (Boone) S.; B.A., U. Nebr., 1951; D.C., Nat. Coll. Chiropractic, Chgo., 1954; m. Sarah Marie Felton, May 9, 1953; children—Deborah L., Jeffrey A., Derek V., Mark W., David N., Alfred A., Randall J., Valerie A., Cynthia D., Jennifer L., Ryan P. Practice chiropractic, Chicago Heights, Ill., 1963-73, Flossmoor, Ill., 1973—; mem. chiropractic com. Nat. Bd. Chiropractic Examiners, 1967-71; v.p., examiner Am. Bd. Chiropractic Orthopedists, 1975-76; postgrad. lectr. Nat. Coll. Chiropractic, 1966—, bd. dirs. dept. of chiropractic. Served with AUS, 1955-57. Fellow Internat. Coll. Chiropractors; mem. Am. Council Chiropractic Orthopedics (pres. 1975-76), Am. Chiropractic Assn., Ill. Chiropractic Soc., Gamma Lambda, Acacia, Delta Tau Alpha. Mem. Ch. of Jesus Christ of Latter-day Saints. Mason. Contbg. author: Spinal and Pelvic Technics, 1967. Address: 2817 Flossmoor Rd Flossmoor IL 60422

STATHAKIOS, JAMES, clergyman; b. Samos, Greece, May 3, 1942; s. Stamatios and Aggelina (Karavokyrou) S.; B.Th., Patmias Sem., Patmos, Greece, 1961; postgrad. Holy Cross Greek Orthodox Theol. Sch., Boston, 1961-63; Case Western Res. U., 1966-69; m. Stella Alexandrou, Dec. 27, 1964; children—Tommy, James. Came to U.S., 1961, naturalized, 1967. Med. research technician, mem. faculty Case Western Res. U., Cleve., 1965-69; ordained to ministry Greek Orthodox Ch., 1969; pastor Monessen (Pa.) Parish, 1969-74; pastor Sts. Constintine and Helen Greek Orthodox Ch., Detroit, 1974—; corr. sec. Council of Eastern Orthodox Chs. Met. Detroit, 1975—. Mem. Hellenic Profl. Assn. Am. Clubs: Masons, Shriners, Rotary, K.T.; Orthodox Square of Am. (Greater Pitts.). Home: 18200 Kilbirnie Ave Lathrup Village MI 48076 Office: 4801 Oakman Blvd Detroit MI 48204

STATLAND, HARRY, internist; b. St. Louis, Dec. 16, 1917; s. Samuel V. and Ida (Chalk) S.; M.D., U. Kans., 1939; m. Suzanne T. Ginsberg, Feb. 26, 1957; 1 dau., Mary Beth. Intern, U. Kans. Hosp., Kansas City, 1939-40; resident Boston City Hosp., 1941-42, Mass. Gen. Hosp., Boston, 1949-50; practice medicine specializing in internal medicine, Kansas City, Mo., 1946—; asst. medicine Peter Bent Brigham Hosp., Boston, 1968-69; mem. staffs Menorah Med. Center and Research Hosp., Kansas City; asso. prof. medicine U. Kans. Sch. Medicine, 1951—, U. Mo. Med. Sch. at Kansas City, 1972—. Served with U.S. Army, 1942-46. Decorated Legion of Merit. Diplomate Am. Bd. Internal Medicine. Fellow A.C.P.; mem. AMA, Am. Internist Soc., Am. Diabetes Assn., Am. Soc. Nephrology Internat. Nephrology Soc., Jackson County Med. Soc. (pres. 1965-66), ACLU, Wild Life Assn., Alpha Omega Alpha. Jewish. Club: B'nai B'rith. Author: Fluids and Electrolytes in Practice, 1954, 3d edit., 1963. Contbr. articles to profl. jours. Home: 1016 W 69th Terr Kansas City MO 64113 Office: 6724 Troost St Kansas City MO 64131

STATLER, CHARLES DANIEL, investment banker; b. Cape Girardeau, Mo., Aug. 22, 1938; s. Floyd L. and Nell M. (Maxwell) S.; B.S., S.E. Mo. State U., 1960; postgrad. So. Ill. U., 1960-61; m. Deanna G. DeWitt, July 1, 1967 (div.); children—Stacy, Chaney. Dir. agys. New Am. Life Ins. Co., 1965-67; v.p. Roosevelt Nat. Investment Co., Springfield, Ill., 1968-76, sr. v.p., 1976—; v.p., dir. Roosevelt Nat. Equity Corp.; v.p., dir. agys. Roosevelt Nat. Life Ins. Co.; dir. tng. United Life Assurance Soc.; dir. Roosevelt Nat. Life of Ind. Served with AUS, 1961-62. Named #2 Pork Chef, State of Ill., 1971; certified fin. planner. Mem. Internat. Assn. Financial Planners, Tau Kappa Epsilon (internat. investment bd.). Mason. Home: 67 Pine Cove Springfield IL 62707 Office: PO Box 5147 Springfield IL 62705

STAUB, BARRY ALAN, bus. services co. exec.; b. Miami Beach, Fla., May 2, 1943; s. Allen Alexander and Mildred (Beren) S.; B.A., U. Okla., 1965; m. Jocelyn Levin, June 19, 1966; children—Elyse Rolyn, Michelle Lynn. Dir. marketing Misco Industries, Wichita, Kans., 1969-73, Leisure Living Inc., Wichita, 1973-75; pres. Misco Textile Rentals Inc., Wichita, 1975—. Active United Way; bd. dirs. Wichita Wagonmasters, Wichita Area Devel. Inc., NCCJ. Mem. Confrerie des La Chaine de Rottisseures. Republican. Jewish. Home: 1802 Farmstead Wichita KS 67208 Office: 257 N Broadway Wichita KS 67202

STAUB, JAMES RICHARD, chiropractor; b. Peoria, Ill., Apr. 22, 1938; s. John and Dorothy Christine (Benson) S.; student Bradley U., 1956-60, U. Wis., 1972; D.Chiropractic, Palmer Coll. Chiropractic, 1972; student Columbia Coll.; m. Sandra Lee Herman, Dec. 21, 1958; children—Gary James, Gregory Alan. Asst. to mgr. A & J Lumber Co., Peoria Hts., Ill., 1956-60; with Central Ill. Light Co., Peoria, 1961-69; pvt. practice chiropractic, Valparaiso, Ind., 1972—. Recipient certificate of merit Palmer Coll. Chiropractic Clinic, 1972. Mem. Valparaiso Bus. and Profl. Couples Club (chmn. 1974-75), Internat., Am., Ky., Ind., Porter County (v.p. 1975-76), N.W. Dist. Ind. (sec. 1975-76), Christian chiropractic assns., Palmer Coll. Alumni Assn. (Ind. pres. 1974-77), Internat. Acad. Preventive Medicine, N.W. Ind. Comprehensive Health Planning Council, Phi Mu Alpha. Home: 1705 Peachtree Dr Valparaiso IN 46383 Office: 1402 Evans Ave Valparaiso IN 46383

STAUDER, RAYMOND GEORGE, elec. engr.; b. St. Louis, Jan. 23, 1924; s. George A. and Rose (Weidlinger) S.; student U. Idaho, 1943; B.S. in Elec. Engring., St. Louis U., 1950, postgrad., 1951; m. Regina Adelaide Stevison, June 24, 1950; children—Mary Alice, Carla Ann, Thomas Joseph, Daniel Edward, Suzanne Jane. Clk, Stix Baer &Fuller, 1941-42; payroll and labor cost Nixdorff Krein Mfg. Co., 1942-43; calibration engr. methods, processing engr. Emerson Electric Co., 1950-51; transformer design and devel. engr. Moloney Electric Co., 1952-71, former supr. elec. design engring. St. Louis div. Central-Moloney, Inc.; materials engr. TVA, 1971—. Mem. Transfiguration Council Youth Activities, Sch. Bd. Served with USNR, 1943-46. Registered profl. engr., Mo. Mem. Legion of One Thousand Men, IEEE, IEEE Power Group, St. Louis U. Alumni Assn. Home: 14907 Rutland Circle Chesterfield MO 63017 Office: Tenn Valley Authority Bank of Crestwood Bldg 9705 Hwy 66 St Louis MO 63126

STAUFFER, RICHARD GARY, ednl. adminstr.; b. Vestaburg, Mich., July 15, 1927; s. Clair C. and Mildred (Tupper) S.; B.S., Central Mich. U., 1948; M.A., U. Mich., 1954; Hu.D. (hon.), Am. Coll. Quito (Ecuador), 1970; m. Willa M. Kirkendall, Feb. 25, 1949; children—Christine Lee, Robin Shelley, Jeffrey Todd, Jonathan Clair. Tchr., athletic dir. coach, Vicksburg (Mich.) Community Schs., 1948-54; asst. prof. phys. edn., coach, asso. dir. admissions Alma (Mich.) Coll., 1954-59; co-founder, trustee, 1st v.p. Northwood Inst., Midland, Mich., 1959-74, vice chmn., 1974—; mem. Devel. Coop. Ednl. Programs Mgmt., 1959—; dir. Devel. Nat. Automotive Edn. Center Northwood, 1971-73. Clubs: Mid Country, Detroit Athletic. Mem. Christian Ch. (elder). Office: Northwood Inst Midland MI 48640

STAUFFER, THOMAS GEORGE, restaurant exec.; b. Akron, Ohio, Mar. 4, 1932; s. Caldwell E. and Rose C. (Ortcheidt) S.; B.S., Case-Western Res. U., 1954; m. Lois Campsey, June 18, 1960. Exec. v.p., dir. Stouffer Corp., Cleve., 1955—; pres. Stouffer Hotels. Trustee hospitality mgmt. Ashland Coll. Mem. Am. Hotel and Motel Assn. (adv. council), Nat. Restaurant Assn. (dir.). Mason (Shriner). Home: 1044 Roy Dr Lakewood OH 44107 Office: 1375 Euclid Ave Cleveland OH 44115

STAUNTON, GARDNER SEAVER, sales co. exec.; b. Orange, N.J., Feb. 19, 1902; s. Edward Paul and Helen (Seaver) S.; C.E., Rensselaer Poly. Inst., 1923; m. Lydia Grace Turner, May 10, 1930; children—Richard Turner, Joy Seaver. Metall. engr. Am. Malleable Casting Assos., Albany, N.Y., 1923-25; supt. foundries Laconia Car Co. (N.H.), 1925-28; supr. DuPont Pathe Film Corp., Parlin, N.J., 1928-29, with spl. sales, N.Y.C., 1930-32, sales mgr., 1933-35; sales mgr. Ternsted div. Gen. Motors Corp., Detroit, 1935-42; sales mgr. brass mill div. Western Cartridge Co., Alton, Ill., 1942-44; sales mgr. Bendix Aviation Corp., South Bend, Ind. and Elmira, N.Y., 1944-46; pres., owner G.S. Staunton & Co., Birmingham, Mich., 1947—; trustee, dir. Staunton Industries, Inc., 1968—. Mem. Engring. Soc. Detroit, Sigma Alpha Epsilon, Chi Phi. Clubs: The Recess, Pine Lake Country. Holder patents on air conditioner filters and paint spray masking. Home: 18 Barbour Ln Bloomfield Hills MI 48013 Office: 4327 Delemere Ct Royal Oak MI 48073

STAZEN, PAUL JOSEPH, periodontist; b. Barberton, Ohio, Oct. 19, 1946; s. Paul and Frances Katherine (Guyris) S.; B.A., Kent State U., 1967; D.D.S., Ohio State U., 1971, M.S., 1975; m. Deborah Ann Bernardo, May 5, 1973. Resident in periodontics Dwight Eisenhower Gen. Hosp., Augusta, Ga., 1973-75; pvt. practice periodontics, Warren, Ohio, 1975—; asst. prof. periodontics Case Western Res. U., Cleve., 1973—. Served with AUS, 1971-73. Mem. Am., Ohio dental assns., Corydon-Palmer Dental Assn., Am., Ohio acads. periodontics, Midwest Soc. Periodontics, Am. Assn. Prevention Oral Disease, Ohio State U. Alumni Assn. (mem. bd. govs. 1975—), Beta Beta Beta, Psi Chi, Blue Key. Home: 770 Shadowood Ln Warren OH 44484 Office: 3915 E Market St Warren OH 44484

STEAD, JAMES JOSEPH, JR., securities co. exec.; b. Chgo., Sept. 13, 1930; s. James Joseph and Irene (Jennings) S.; B.S., DePaul U., 1955, M.B.A., 1957; m. Edith Pearson, Feb. 13, 1954; children—James, Diane, Robert, Caroline. Asst. sec. C. F. Childs & Co., Chgo., 1955-62; exec. v.p., sec. Koenig, Keating & Stead, Inc., Chgo., 1962-66; 2d v.p., mgr. midwest municipal bond dept. Hayden, Stone Inc., Chgo., 1966-69; sr. v.p., nat. sales mgr. Ill. Co. Inc., 1969-70; mgr. instl. sales dept. Reynolds and Co., Chgo., 1970-72; partner Edwards & Hanly, 1972-74; v.p., instnl. sales mgr. Paine, Webber, Jackson & Curtis, 1974-76; v.p., regional instl. sales mgr. Reynolds Securities, Inc., 1976—. Instr. Municipal Bond Sch., Chgo., 1967—. Served with AUS, 1951-53. Mem. Sec. Traders Assn. Chgo., Nat. Security Traders Assn., Am. Mgmt. Assn., Municipal Finance Forum Washington. Clubs: Executives, Union League, Municipal Bond, Bond (Chgo.); Olympia Fields Country (Ill.); Wall Street (N.Y.C.). Home: 20721 Brookwood Dr Olympia Fields IL 60461 Office: 208 S LaSalle St Chicago IL 60604

STEAHLY, VIVIAN EUGENIA EMRICK, educator, author, cons.; b. Wapakoneta, Ohio, July 10, 1915; d. Daniel and Katharine (Bush) Emrick; B.S., Ohio State U., 1936, B.A. cum laude, 1936; M.A., U. Cin., 1941; m. Frank Lester Steahly, Oct. 17, 1936 (dec. May 1967); 1 son, Lance Preston. Tchr. Latin, French, English, Grant High Sch., Georgetown, Ohio, 1936-39; instr. English, Seaford (Del.) High Sch., 1942-43; instr. English, U. Tenn., Knoxville, 1948; tchr. Latin, French, English, Winfield (W.Va.) High Sch., 1955-58; asst. prof. English, French, Morris Harvey Coll., Charleston, W.Va., 1958-66, chmn. dept. modern langs., 1962-64, asst. prof. edn., 1964-65; asst. prof. English, Ohio State U., 1967—; editing cons. W.Va. U. bd. govs., W.Va. Dept. Edn., 1966-67. Free-lance writer, book reviewer, monologuist; tech. writing cons. Mem. Modern Lang. Assn., AAUS, Ohio Acad. Sci., Am. Assn. Higher Edn., Ohio State U. Assn., U. Cin. Alumni Assn., Scholaris, Phi Beta Kappa, Pi Lambda Theta, Eta Sigma Phi. Republican. Presbyterian. Author: Fanny Burney; Seven Steps to Sensible Structure and Style; I Always Wanted to Live in the Chicken Yard; The Gift and Other Tales; Stories For Little People. Home: 206 Stinebaugh Dr Wapakoneta OH 45895 Office: Ohio State U Lima OH 45804

STEARNS, DAN HUNTER, curator; b. Lawrence County, Mo., July 13, 1909; s. Udell and Pernie Otis (Hunter) S.; student Joplin Bus. Coll., 1929-30; m. Thelma Lucille Duke, May 26, 1940; children—Lana Stearns Kern, Michael A., Linden G., Brent, Jan D. Operator, mgr. Stearns Food Store, Mt. Vernon, Mo., 1932-36; bookkeeper Lawrence County Treas. Office, 1938; asst. to mortician, salesman Fossett Funeral Home, Mt. Vernon, 1939-42; mgr., operator farm, Mt. Vernon, 1942-46; owner, operator Stearns Elec. Contracting Service, Mt. Vernon, 1946-67; electrician Mo. State Chest Hosp., Mount Vernon, 1967-75; accountant Yellowstone Nat. Park, 1975; curator, dir. Lawrence County Hist. Soc. Mus., Mt. Vernon, 1976-77. 4-H Club leader, counsel mem., 1937-40. Mem. Lawrence County Hist. Soc. (pres. 1969-77). Democrat. Presbyn. (elder 1942-77). Author: (with others) A Brief History of Lawrence County Mo. 1845-1970, 1970; (with others) A History of Lawrence County Missouri, 1975. Home: 210 N Main St Mount Vernon MO 65712

STEBBINS, MELVIN EUGENE, psychologist; b. Omaha, July 11, 1930; s. Carl Schultz and Ruth (Andersen) S.; B.A., Colo. State Coll., 1956; M.A., U. Iowa, 1959, Ph.D., 1964; m. Myra Joan White, July 21, 1951; children—Christi, Michael, Susan, Barbara. Tchr., Cedar Rapids, Iowa, 1956-60; counselor Iowa City, 1960-63; counselor, educator Baylor U., Waco, Tex., 1963-64; counseling psychologist, dir. counseling, guidance and psychol. services Bradley U., Peoria, Ill., 1964-69; clin. dir. Children and Adolescent Services Zeller Zone Center, Ill. Dept. Mental Health, 1969-72, regional coordinator children and adolescent services, 1972-75, staff psychologist, case supr. med. students and residents, 1975—; psychol. cons. Ill. State Dept. Pub. Instn., Ill. State Dept. Mental Health, Fulton County (Ill.) Health Dept. Bd. dirs. Boys Club Am., Neighborhood House Assn. Served with USAF, 1950-54. Mem. Am. Psychol. Assn. Address: PO Box 3175 Peoria IL 61614

STECK, ROBERT CARL, physician, state ofcl.; b. Herrin, Ill., Jan. 7, 1910; s. Lewis Washington and Lelia (Felts) Steckenrider; M.D., U. Ill., 1942; m. Patricia Lee Dick, Mar. 12, 1949; children—Mary Jane, Susan Lee, Carla Jean, Patricia Gail, Robert Lewis. Intern, St. Margaret's Hosp., Hammond, Ind., 1942-43; pvt. practice medicine, 1943-50; cons. Ill. Dept. Pub. Welfare, 1950; supt. Anna (Ill.) State Hosp., 1950-65; region 5 adminstr. Ill. Dept. Mental Health, 1964—; adj. prof. Rehab. Inst., So. Ill. U.; rehab. cons. Nat. dir. Boy Scouts Am., 1959-60, 61-63; bd. dirs. Union County United Fund, 1958—, Russell Tuthill Found., 1957—. Certified mental hosp. adminstr. Mem. AMA, Am. Psychiat. Assn., Nat. Rehab. Assn., Ill. Welfare Assn., Am. Soc. Pub. Adminstrn., Phi Beta Pi. Presbyn. Mason (K.T., 32 deg., Shriner). Address: 1000 N Main St Anna IL 62906

STECKLER, WILLIAM ELWOOD, judge; b. Mt. Vernon, Ind., Oct. 18, 1913; s. William Herman and Lena (Menikheim) S.; LL.B., Ind. Law Sch., 1936; J.D., 1937; LL.D., Wittenberg U., Springfield, Ohio, 1958; H.H.D., Ind. Central Coll., 1969; m. Vitallas Alting, Oct. 15,

1938; children—William Rudolph, David Alan. Admitted to Ind. bar, 1936, practiced in Indpls., 1937-50, mem. firm Key & Steckler; pub. counselor Pub. Service Commn., State Ind., 1949-50; judge U.S. Dist. Ct. So. Dist. Ind., 1950—, now chief judge. Served as seaman USN, 1943. Mem. Am., Fed., Ind., Indpls. bar assns., Am. Judicature Soc., Nat. Lawyers Club, Jud. Conf. U.S., Am. Legion, Order of Coif, Sigma Delta Kappa. Democrat. Lutheran. Mason (33 deg., Shriner). Club: Indianapolis Athletic. Home: Rural Route 2 Box 149 I Trafalgar IN 46181 Office: Federal Bldg Indianapolis IN 46204

STECKLOW, JAMES PATRICK, cons.; b. Bklyn., Apr. 30, 1915; s. Samuel and Lena (Landsberg) S.; student Case Inst. Tech., 1947; m. Nellie Grey Carter, June 14, 1941; children—John E., Ronald J., Larry C., Judy, Richard L. Jr. draftsman Daniel & Wallen, N.Y.C., 1938-40; layout draftsman Foster Wheeler, N.Y.C., 1940; piping draftsman Carbide & Carbon, S. Charleston, W.Va., 1940-41; design mech. engr. H.K. Ferguson, Cleve., 1941-42, 45-46; design engr. Vincent Eaton, Cleve., 1946-48; now profl. cons. engr., Westlake, Ohio. Served with USNR, 1943-45. Mem. Cleve. Cons. Engrs. Council. Patentee in field. Home: 8558 Broadview Rd Broadview Heights OH 44147 Office: 24700 Center Ridge Rd Westlake OH 44145

STEDMAN, ERVIN FRANK, personnel mgmt. co. exec.; b. St. Louis, July 27, 1937; s. E. Frank and Lydia Ella (Vogt) S.; A.A., Harris Tchrs. Coll., 1958; B.S., U. Mo., 1972; m. Patricia Sue Williams, Aug. 23, 1958; children—Beth, David, Daniel, Dean. With Maritz Motivation Co. div. Maritz Inc., Fenton, Mo., 1963—, asst. mgr., 1965-66, mgr., 1967-69, dir., 1969-72, v.p. adminstrn., 1972-75, v.p. ops., 1975—; dir. Glenn Meadows Ltd. Served with U.S. Army, 1960-63. Mem. Adminstrv. Mgmt. Soc. (dir. systems), Internat. Word Processing Assn. (pres. St. Louis chpt. 1977, internat. dir. 1976, 77), U. Mo. St. Louis Alumni Assn., Creve Coeur Khoury League. Republican. Lutheran. Office: 1355 North Highway Dr Fenton MO 63026

STEDMAN, ROBERT KIMBELL, patent licensing corp. and tennis club exec.; b. Chgo., June 28, 1930; s. Cresswell Edward and Elizabeth (Kimbell) S.; student Coll. William and Mary, 1950-51; B.B.A., U. Miami, 1952-53; m. Judy Amelia Wiehe, June 6, 1959; children—Scott Emmett, Karen Kimbell. Chmn. bd. U.S. Acoustics Corp., Ft. Lauderdale, Fla., 1956—, Internat. Perlite Products, S.A., Panama, 1971—; pres. Naperville Racquet Club, Ltd. (Ill.), 1972—; dir. Danum, S.A., Caracas, Venezuela, Environ. Controls Systems, Inc., St. Charles, Ill. Mem. Alpha Kappa Psi, Pi Kappa Alpha. Club: Hinsdale (Ill.) Golf. Home: 627 S Elm St Hinsdale IL 60521 Office: 1011 E Benton St Naperville IL 60540

STEELE, CLARENCE HART, otolaryngologist, allergist; b. Sabetha, Kans., Feb. 21, 1914; s. Clarence C. and Lucretia W. (Hart) C.; A.B., U. Kans., 1936, M.D., 1940; m. Yvonne Maddern, Feb. 8, 1941; children—Clarence Hart, Lucretia Lynne. Intern, Kansas City Gen. Hosp., 1940-41; resident in otolaryngology Tulane U., New Orleans, instr., 1943-48; instr. U. Kans., 1948-51; active staff dept. otolaryngology Ochsner Clinic, New Orleans, 1943-48; chief dept. otolaryngology St. Margaret Hosp., Kansas City, Kans., 1950—, also pres. Ear, Nose and Throat, Kansas City, Kans., 1973—. Diplomate Am. Bd. Otolaryngology. Fellow Am. Coll. Allergists, Am. Acad. Ophthalmology and Otolaryngology, Am. Soc. Ophthalmol. and Otolaryngol. Allergy, Kansas City Soc. Ophthalmology and Otolaryngology, A.C.S.; mem. AMA, Kans., Wyandotte County med. socs., Phi Kappa Psi, Phi Beta Pi. Presbyterian. Clubs: Terr., Victory Hills Country (Kansas City, Kans.). Contbr. articles to sci. jours. Home: 8009 Nebraska Ave Kansas City KS 66112 Office: 255 Brotherhood Bldg Kansas City KS 66101

STEELE, DANIEL LEE, computer programmer; b. Wenatchee, Wash., Jan. 1, 1941; s. Danton Gibbs and Blanche Marion (Wynhoff) S.; B.S., U. Mo., 1962, M.A., 1969. Computer programmer, engring. sect. Mo. Hwy. Dept., Jefferson City, 1969—. Served with USN, 1962-66. Mem. Math. Assn. Am., Amateur Athletic Union, Am. Contract Bridge League, VFW, Am. Legion, Mensa. Methodist. Home: 416 Brooks St Jefferson City MO 65101 Office: Surveys and Plans Hwy Bldg Jefferson City MO 65101

STEELE, DARRELL STANLEY, veterinarian; b. Treynor, Iowa, Sept. 30, 1917; s. Carroll Chester and Hazel Lydia (Redman) S.; D.V.M., Kans. State U., 1939; m. Betty Jean Guyot, Feb. 1, 1936; children—Richard, Suzanne. Dir. small animal biol. products Pitman Moore Co., Zionsville, Ind., 1939-41; practice veterinary medicine specializing in small animals, Mpls., 1947—; pres. Minn. Veterinary Exam. Bd. Trustee North Methodist Ch., Mpls., 1959-63, chmn. ofcl. bd., 1961-63. Served with U.S. Army, 1941-47. Mem. Am., Minn. veterinary med. assns., Am., Met. (pres. 1956-57), animal hosp. assns., Midwest Small Animal Assn. (pres. 1958-59, Distinguished Service award 1960). Clubs: Midland Hills Country (pres. 1959-60), Masons, Shriners. Home: 584 Westwood Village Saint Paul MN 55113 Office: 1332 Marshall St NE Minneapolis MN 55413

STEELE, EMMETT MITCHELE, music educator, condr.; b. Waverly, Iowa; s. Emmett M. and Mildred D. (McInroy) S.; B.A., U. of No. Iowa, 1949; student Juilliard Sch. Music, 1950; M.M., Eastman Sch. Music, 1953; further studies Sorbonne, Mozarteum; pvt. studies Pierre Monteux, Andre de Ribaupierre, Walter Hendl, Lorvo von Matacic, Leon Barzin, Milton Preves. Faculty Kemper Mil. Coll., 1953-54, North Central Coll., 1954-57, Cosmopolitan Sch. Music, Chgo., 1957-64, U. Ill., 1959-65, Park Forest (Ill.) Conservatory, 1960—, Inst. Musica Viva Lausanne, Switzerland, 1965—; mem. faculty Chgo. Conservatory Coll. 1967—, now dean, v.p. bd. trustees, head music history and lit. dept.; string adviser North Chicago (Ill.) Schs., 1957-59; string supr. Nat. Music Camp; condr., founder Concerts Symphoniques; condr. Chgo. Suburban Symphony, Emmett Steele Chorale, Handel Choral Soc.; officer Inter-Continental Records and Musica Viva Records; organizer, dir. Brush Hill Music Theatre; violist in Quintet Musica Viva-resident quintet Chgo. Conservatory Coll., 1967—; concert mgmt. Gosta Schwark, Copenhagen, Denmark; owner, pres. Internat. Art Assos., Ltd.; dir. Emmett Steele Gallery, Inc. Named nat. patron, Phi Beta, 1963. Mem. Condrs. Club N.Y., AAUP, Soc. Am. Musicians, Phi Mu Alpha, Alpha Phi Omega. Author: The Materials of Music. Home: 1439 Brassie Ave Flossmoor IL 60422

STEELE, HILDA HODGSON, home economist; b. Wilmington, Ohio, Mar. 24, 1911; d. George and Mary Jane (Rolston) Hodgson; certificate Wilmington Coll., 1932, B.S., 1935; M.A. in Home Econs. Edn., Ohio State U., 1941; postgrad. Ohio U., 1954, Miami U., 1959; m. John C. Steele (dec. Jan. 1973). Tchr., Brookville (Ohio) Elementary Sch., 1932-37; tchr. home econs. Lincoln Jr. High Sch., Dayton (Ohio) Pub. Schs., 1937-40, coordinator home econs. dept., traveling exptl. home econs. tchr., 1940-45, supr. home econs., 1945—. Mem. Ohio Farm Electrification Com., 1964-66. Mem. town and country br. career com. Miami Valley br. YMCA, 1948-59. Adv. bd. Dayton Sch. Practical Nursing, 1951—; adv. com. Dayton Miami Valley Hosp. Sch. Nursing, 1951-63; jr. adv. com. Montgomery County chpt. ARC, 1940—; mem. com. United Appeal, 1970—. Mem. Dayton area Nutrition Council, Am. (del. 1961), Ohio (chmn. elementary and secondary edn. com. 1947-51, co-chmn. ann. conv. 1961, 77), Dayton Met. (pres. 1949-50, 60-61) home econ. assns., Nat., Ohio edn. assns., Ohio Council Local Adminstrs., Dayton Sch. Adminstrs. Assn. (pres. 1960-61), Elec. Women's Round Table, Dayton City Sch. Mgmt. Assn. (charter), Vocat. Edn. Assn. Mem. Ch. of Christ. Mem. Order Eastern Star. Club: Zonta (pres. Dayton 1950-52). Research in pub. sch. food habits, 1957. Home: 1443 State Route 380 Xenia OH 45385 Office: 348 W 1st St Dayton OH 45402

STEELE, OLIVER LEON, seed co. exec.; b. Ill., Apr. 8, 1915; s. Blondee Wood and Mary (Eagle) S.; student Ill. State Normal U., 1934-35; B.S., Ill. Wesleyan U., 1940; postgrad. U. Ill., 1945-48; D.Sc. (hon.), Ill. Wesleyan U., 1967; m. Ruth Marie Holbert, June 21, 1941; children—David, Dennis, Nancy. Research asso. Michael-Leonard Seed Co., 1936-40; mgr. research dept. Funk Seeds Internat., 1940-52, asso. research dir., 1952-57, research dir., 1957—, v.p., 1963—. Mem. AAAS, Soc. Agronomy, Bot. Soc., Genetics Soc., Genetic Assn. Presbyn. (elder). Rotarian. Home: 804 Broadway St Normal IL 61761 Office: 1300 W Washington St Bloomington IL 61701

STEELE, ROBERT ELMER, pharm. exec.; b. Tomah, Wis., July 31, 1924; s. Ray Phillip and Vera Eunice (Griswold) S.; B.S., U. Wis., 1947; m. Arlys Lorraine Johnson, June 6, 1945; children—James, John, Jacquelyn, Jerome, Jenny. Pharmacist Pederson Drug Store, Tomah, 1947-51; pres Steele Drugs, Inc., Tomah, 1951—; dir. Spence McCord Drug Co., Tomah Savs. & Loan Assn. Mem. Wis. Pharmacy Internship Bd., 1966—; mem. Wis. Bd. Pharmacy, 1958-63, pres., 1962-63; mem. U.S. Assay Commn., 1975. Dist chmn. Nixon for Pres., 1968; state chmn. Pharmacists for Nixon, 1972; mem. Tomah Police and Fire Commn.; pres. bd. dirs. Handi-shop Industries; bd. dirs. Tomah Meml. Hosp. Served with USAAF, 1942-45. Decorated Air Medal with 5 oak leaf clusters; recipient mortar and pestle award Wis. Pharm. Assn., 1965, pharmacy citation U. Wis., 1972; named boss of year Tomah Jr. C. of C., 1958; recipient distinguished service award Tomah C. of C., 1971, Monroe County Woodland conservation award, 1970. Mem. Am., Wis. (pres. 1964-65, chmn. bd. 1966) pharm assns., Nat. Assn. Retail Druggists, U. Wis. Pharmacy Alumni Assn. (pres. 1968), Tomah C. of C. (pres. 1970-72), Am. Legion, V.F.W., Kappa Psi, Rho Chi. Lutheran. Mason (Shriner). Home: 303 Superior Ave PO Box 568 Tomah WI 54660 Office: 1004 Superior Ave Tomah WI 54660

STEEN, EDWIN BENZEL, biologist, author; b. Wheeling, Ind., July 23, 1901; s. Henry Wylie and Lora May (Benzel) S.; student Mo. Valley Coll., 1919-20; A.B., Wabash Coll., 1923; A.M., Columbia U., 1926; Ph.D., Purdue U., 1938; m. Harriet Ellen Lewis, July 23, 1927; children—Marjorie Alice (Mrs. Dayton D. Dickinson), Philip Lewis. Instr. zoology Wabash Coll., Crawfordsville, Ind., 1923-25, acting head dept., 1926-27; grad. asst. N.Y. U., 1926; instr. zoology U. Cin., 1927-31; instr., also asst. in agrl. expt. sta. Purdue U., 1931-38; instr. biology Coll. City N.Y., 1938-41; asst. prof. Western Mich. U., Kalamazoo, 1941-46, asso. prof., 1946-52, prof. biology, 1952-72, prof. emeritus, 1972—, head dept., 1963-65. Mem. Mich. Bd. Examiners in Basic Scis., 1960-63. Bd. dirs. Kalamazoo chpt. Mich. Soc. Mental Health, 1958-65. Mem. AAAS, Am. Inst. Biol. Scis., N.Y. Acad. Sci., Mich. Acad. Sci., Arts and Letters, Sigma Xi. Author: (with Ashley Montagu) Anatomy and Physiology, 1959; Dictionary of Abbreviations in Medicine, 1960; Dictionary of Biology, 1971; (with J.H. Price) Human Sex and Sexuality, 1977; also lab. manuals in anatomy and physiology. Contbg. editor: Taber's Cyclopedic Medical Dictionary, 1973, Acronyms and Initialisms Dictionary, 1965. Home: 2011 Greenlawn Ave Kalamazoo MI 49007 Office: Western Michigan University Kalamazoo MI 49008

STEEN, LOWELL HARRISON, physician; b. Kenosha, Wis., Nov. 27, 1923; s. Joseph Arthur and Camilla Marie (Henriksen) S.; B.S., Ind. U., 1945, M.D., 1948; m. Cheryl Ann Rectanus, Nov. 20, 1969; children—Linda C., Laura A., Lowell Harrison, Heather J., Kirsten M. Intern, Mercy Hosp.-Loyola U. Clinics, Chgo., 1948-49; resident in internal medicine VA Hosp., Hines, Ill., 1950-53; practice medicine specializing in internal medicine, Hammond, Ind., 1953—; pres., chief exec. officer Whiting Clinic; mem. sr. staff St. Catherine Hosp., E. Chicago, Ind.; bd. commrs. Joint Commn. Accreditation of Hosps. Served with M.C., AUS, 1949-50, 55-56. Mem. AMA (trustee 1975), Ind. Med. Assn. (pres. 1970, chmn. bd. 1968-69), Ind. Soc. Internal Medicine (pres. 1963), Lake County Med. Soc., A.C.P., Am. Geriatric Soc. Methodist. Home: 8800 Parkway Dr Highland IN 46322 Office: 2450 169th St Hammond IN 46323

STEEN, ROBERT HOAGLAND, food co. exec.; b. Port Chester, N.Y., Jan. 30, 1921; s. Percy Knapp and Marjorie (Van Scoy) S.; B.S., U. Md., 1945; m. Dec. 15, 1961; children—William V., Robert, Patricia, Susan. Mgr. night operations CBS Shortwave radio, N.Y.C., 1944-45; producer, dir. ABC Radio/TV Network, N.Y.C., 1945-50; asst. mgr. radio-TV dept. Warwick & Legler, N.Y.C., 1950-56; sr. producer Foote, Cone & Belding, N.Y.C., 1956-62; dir. TV prodn. Compton McCann, Erickson, Inc., Chgo., 1962-69; mgr. creative coordination advt. and marketing service dept. Quaker Oats Co., Chgo., 1969-72; v.p. marketing Communications Dynamic Marketing Programs, Glenview, Ill., 1972-73; v.p. IDC Services/Teleproof, Chgo., 1973-75; v.p. mktg. V.I.P. Prodns., Arlington Heights, Ill., 1975—. Served with AUS, World War II. Home: 920 Hawthorne Ln Northbrook IL 60062 Office: VIP Prodns 750 W Algonquin Rd Arlington Heights IL 60005

STEENROD, EMERSON J., surgeon; b. Pitts., Feb. 5, 1907; s. Evan J. and Mathilda M. (Ludwig) S.; B.S., U. Pitts., 1929, M.D., 1933; M.S. in Surgery, U. Minn., 1938, fellowship surgery, Mayo Clinic, 1934-38; m. Dorien Ethel Reid, Sept. 3, 1938; children—Patricia Dorien, Robert Emerson. Surgeon, Ellsworth Municipal Hosp., Iowa Falls, Iowa. Served as lt. comdr., USNR. Recipient citation for work abroad U.S.S. Solace, World War II. Fellow: A.C.S., Internat. Coll. Surgeons; mem. Hardin County, Iowa med. socs., Pan-Pacific Surg. Assn. Alumni Assn. Mayo Clinic, Sigma Alpha Epsilon, Phi Beta Pi, Episcopalian (sr. warden). Mason (Shriner, past Master), Rotarian (past pres.). Author articles. Home: 111 Foster Blvd Iowa Falls IA 50126

STEFANELLI, JOHN ROBERT, ednl. adminstr.; b. Gary, Ind., Sept. 23, 1936; s. Frank A. and Sylvia (Cifaldi) S.; B.S., Ball State U., 1958; M.A., Roosevelt U., 1964; m. Carolyn Gritton, Aug. 23, 1958; children—John R., Martin J., Frances P. Tchr. elementary, high schs., Gary, 1958-67, asst. prin. Beckman Jr. High Sch., 1967-69, Gary West Side High Sch., 1969-72, prin. Horace Mann High Sch., 1972—. Guest lectr. Ind. U., 1965-72. Bd. dirs., co-owner Mother Goose Nursery Sch. and Kindergarten, 1964—. Recipient 1st Outstanding Young Educator award Gary Jr. C. of C., 1964. Mem. NEA, Ind. Tchrs. Assns., Am. Fedn. Tchrs., Ball State, Roosevelt U. alumni assns., Nat. Assn. Secondary Sch. Prins., Phi Delta Kappa, Sigma Tau Gamma. Contbr. articles to profl. jours., local newspapers. Home: 3648 Fillmore St Gary IN 46408

STEFFAN, LLOYD JOHN, physician; b. Fond du Lac, Wis., Apr. 7, 1918; s. John L. and Frances A. (Kalt) S.; student Lawrence U., 1938-40, Northwestern U., 1940-41; M.D., George Washington U., 1944; m. Sirley J. Hafemeister, Apr. 25, 1947; children—John, Mary (Mrs. Alfred Harney), Michael, Ann Kathryn (Mrs. Michael Baumgartner), Peter. Intern, U.S. Naval Hosp., Great Lakes, Ill., 1944-45; gen. practice medicine, Plymouth, Wis., 1946—; partner Plymouth Clinic, 1946—; mem. staff Plymouth Hosp. Health officer City of Plymouth, 1952—. Vice pres., dir. Dairy State Bank, Plymouth, 1959—. Served with USNR, 1942-46. Mem. AMA, Am. Acad. Family Practitioners, Wis. Med. Soc., Wis. Soc. Obstetrics and Gynecology. Roman Catholic. Club: Sheboygan Country. Home: 824 Riverview Dr Plymouth WI 53073 Office: 1000 Eastern Ave Plymouth WI 53073

STEFFEN, CURT, gynecologist and obstetrician; b. Hamburg, Germany; M.D., U. Kiel, Germany, 1918; degree pub. health, Hamburg, 1931; 1 son, Alf. Resident Univ. Hosps., Berlin and Hamburg, 1918-23; pvt. practice limited to obstetrics and diseases of women, Hamburg, 1923-37; chief gynecologist Clinics of State Social Ins. Hamburg; cons. to Labor Ministry, Berlin, Bd. of Health and Cts. of Hamburg and to Spa of Pistyan, Czechoslovakia, 1925-1933; founder first free cancer detection clinic for women, in the world; lectr. State Peoples Univ., Hamburg, 1927-33; intern Michael Reese Hosp., Chgo., 1937-38; staff surgeon Peoria State Hosp., 1939-42; med. staff Swedish Am. Hosp., 1942—; practice medicine specializing in gynecology and obstetrics, Rockford, 1942—. Life mem. Am. Com. on Maternal Welfare. Served with German Navy, 1914-18. Certified as specialist in obstetrics and gynecology German Specialty Bd., 1923. Diplomate Internat. Bd. Surgery. Fellow Internat. Coll. Surgeons (life), Am. Coll. Obstetricians and Gynecologists (founder); mem. World Med. Assn. (founder), AMA. Author articles in German and Am. med. jours. Home: 523 Indian Terr Rockford IL 61103 Office: 119 N Church St Rockford IL 61101

STEFFEN, FRANCIS JEROME, librarian, educator; b. Platteville, Wis., Nov. 18, 1931; s. Frank Louis and Florence Catherine (Klar) S.; B.A., Loras Coll., 1953; postgrad. St. Francis Sem., 1953-57; M.L.S., U. Wis., 1968. Ordained priest Roman Catholic Ch., 1957; asso. pastor St. Stanslaus Ch., Berlin, Wis., 1957, Sacred Hearts Ch., Sun Prairie, Wis., 1957-64; librarian, instr. Latin and religion Holy Name Sem., Madison, Wis., 1964—. Mem. Madison Area Library Council, 1969—, bd. dirs., 1969-70; treas., 1975-76; chmn. Diocese Madison Music Commn., 1967—; chaplain Madison Dominic Club, 1968—. Mem. Wis. Cath. Library Assn. (chmn. 1973-75), Wis. Assn. Sch. Librarians (pres. 1970-71, editor WASL Communique 1973-74), Wis. Assn. Audio-Visual Instruction, Cath., Wis. library assns., ALA. Address: 3577 Holy Name Sem High Point Rd Madison WI 53711

STEFFENSEN, POUL VILHELM, adminstrv. mech. engr.; b. Copenhagen, Denmark, Mar. 26, 1922; s. Carl Christian Vilhelm Frederik and Anna (Svenson) S.; came to U.S., 1951, naturalized, 1955; B.S. in Mech. Engring., Marine Engring. Acad., Copenhagen, 1944; m. Elie Pedersen, July 18, 1951; children—Paul, Carl. Mech. engr. Sumner Sollitt Co., Chgo., 1957-63; mech. engr. Mid-Am. Engrs. Inc., Chgo., 1963-65; mgr. design engring. Commonwealth Assn., Chgo., 1965-71; sr. mech. engr. Consoer Townsend & Assos., Chgo., 1971-75; sr. environ. engr. P & W Engrs. Inc., Chgo., 1975-78; project mgr. Henningson, Durham & Richardson, Omaha, 1978—. Mem. bd. Danish Old People's Home, Chgo., 1964, pres., 1970-73; dir. Danish Am. Lang. Found. Decorated Knight of Order of Dannebrog (Denmark). Mem. Am. Soc. Mech. Engrs., Tech. Assn. Pulp Paper Industry, Am. Scandinavian Found., Rebuild Nat. Park Soc., Smithsonian Nat. Assn., Field Museum, Danish Am. Athletic Club (hon., pres. 1960-65), Chgo. Chamber Orch. Assn., Dansk Samvirke. Home: 10308 P St Omaha NE 68127 Office: 8404 Indian Hills Dr Omaha NE 68114

STEFFEY, WILLIAM GARNETT, city mgr.; b. Albion, Neb., Jan. 17, 1914; s. Irvin Harvey and Mary (Horne) S.; B.S. in Engring., U. Tenn., 1937; postgrad. N.Y. U., 1950; M.A. in Govt. Adminstrn., George Washington U., 1962; postgrad. Am. U., 1962—; m. Barbara Hennigan, Nov. 29, 1957; 1 dau., Melinda Mary. Commd. 2d lt. C.E., U.S. Army, 1937, advanced through grades to lt. col., 1950; tchr. advanced engring. Engr. Sch., Ft. Belvior, Va., 1947-50; tchr. engring. Paraguayan Nat. War Coll., Asuncion, 1954-57, engring. cons. to minister pub. works Paraguay, 1954-57; ret., 1961; city mgr. Tazewell, Va., 1961-65, Lewiston, Ida., 1965-71; Addison, Ill., 1971—. Tchr. higher math. Bluefield (W.Va.) State Coll., 1963-64. Decorated Grand Master Nat. Order of Merit. Pres. of Paraguay, 1957; recipient certificate appreciation for civic responsibility Gov. Va., 1963; named hon. citizen Lexington, Ky., 1968, hon. citizen, Lewiston, 1971. Mem. Internat. City Mgrs. Assn., Am. Pub. Works Assn., Permanent Internat. Assn. Nav. Congresses, Soc. Am. Mil. Engrs., Nat. Municipal League, Nat. League Cities, Ill. Municipal League, Assn. Ida. Cities, Acad. Polit. Sci., Am. Acad. Arts and Scis., Am. Acad. Polit. and Social Scis., Am. Soc. Pub. Adminstrn., Ret. Officers Assn., Pub. Personnel Assn., Internat. Platform Assn., Lambda Chi Alpha, Alpha Chi Sigma. Mason (32 deg., Shriner). Rotarian. Clubs: Wayfarers (N.Y.C.); Lehigh Acres (Fla.) Country. Home: 231 Wood Dale Rd Addison IL 60101 Office: City Hall 130 Army Trail Rd Addison IL 60101

STEFFY, DAVID LOUIS, hosp. adminstr.; b. Indpls., June 4, 1943; B.S., Ohio State U., 1965; M.S., U. So. Calif., 1971. Mgr. clinic Ohio State U. Hosps., Columbus, 1966-68, asso. adminstr., 1972-73, adminstr., 1973-74, dir., 1974—; adminstrv. asst. Kaiser Found. Hosp., Bellflower, Calif., 1968-70; research asso. Sch. Pub. Health, U. Calif. at Los Angeles, 1970-71; asst. adminstr. Cin. Gen. Hosp., 1971-72; asst. prof. Ohio State U., 1976—. Served with Armed Forces, 1965-66. Mem. Am. Pub. Health Assn., Ohio Hosp. Assn. (coms.). Contbr. articles to profl. jours. Home: 4455 Hayden Falls Dr Columbus OH 43220 Office: 410 W 10th Ave Columbus OH 43210*

STEFKA, RICHARD STEPHAN, mktg. analyst; b. Cleve., Apr. 22, 1951; s. Steve Joseph and Grace Ann (Gedgaud) S.; B.B.A. in Mktg., Cleve. State U., 1973, also postgrad.; m. Brigitte G. Pietzonka, Aug. 28, 1971. Asst. to pres. Juno Inc., Cleve., 24 1973-74; mktg. asst., acting mktg. mgr. Automatic Sprinkler Corp. div. ATO Inc., Broadview Heights, Ohio, 1974-76; mktg. analyst The Cleve. Trust Co., 1976—. Mem. Am. Mktg. Assn., Nat. Assn. of Bus. Economists. Clubs: U.S. Power Squadrons. Home: 10769 Waterfall Rd Strongsville OH 44136 Office: 900 Euclid Ave Cleveland OH 44101

STEGEMEYER, F. LEE, mag. editor; b. Cin., July 15, 1929; s. Philip E. and Pearl Elizabeth (Hover) S.; B.S., U. Ala., 1957, M.A., 1958; m. Patricia Dawn Nickens, Aug. 4, 1962; children—Sarah Renee, Susan Elizabeth, Sandra Lee, Sharon Jean, Stephen Kyle. Journalism instr. U. Ala., University, 1956-59; pub. Oakdale (La.) Jour. and Kinder (La.) Progress, 1960-61; radio news editor AP, New Orleans, 1961-62; telegraph editor, asst. news editor Cin. Enquirer, 1962-69, columnist on stamps and coins, 1962—; editor Tobacco Reporter, Cin., 1969—. Mem. Terrace Park (Ohio) Fire Dept. and Life Squad, 1947—, fire chief, 1969—. Served with AUS, 1954-56. Recipient Sigma Delta Chi award as outstanding student, 1958. Episcopalian. Author: Type Faces and Styles Workbook, 1956. Home: 801 Princeton Dr Terrace Park OH 45174 Office: Western Printing 424 Commercial Sq Cincinnati OH 45202

STEGER, JOHN FRANCIS, dentist; b. Waterloo, Iowa, Mar. 18, 1939; s. Gilbert Theodore and Bernice Catherine (Freymann) S.; B.S. cum laude, Loras Coll., 1961, teaching certificate, 1962; D.D.S., U. Ia., 1966; m. Karla Jean Krapfl, Aug. 25, 1962. Practice dentistry,

Dubuque, Iowa, 1968—; instr. Instr. dept. preventive dentistry U. Iowa, 1971-73; pres., Stark Enterprise, Inc., Dubuque, 1970—; sec.-treas. Dubuque Dental Assos. Co-chmn. advanced dental gifts United Fund drive, 1972; campaign dir. advanced dental gifts United Fund, 1973; bd. dirs. United Fund, 1974. Served with USPHS, 1966-68. Mem. Tri State Dentistry for Children (pres. 1972-74), Am. Soc. Preventive Dentistry, Am., Iowa (Bronze citation 1973) dental assns., Dubuque County (sec. 1974-75, now v.p.) and dist. dental socs., Dubuque Traveling and Business Men's Assn., Gt. River Rd. Assn., Dubuque County Conservation Soc., Psi Omega. Elk. Clubs: Old Gold (U. Iowa). Recipient 1st Pl. award Ia. Peace Oratorical, 1959, 4th Pl. award Nat. Peace Oration, 1959. Home: 3345 Foothill Rd Dubuque IA 52001 Office: 1890 JF Kennedy Rd Dubuque IA 52001

STEIDL, RICHARD MEREDITH, pathologist; b. Marion, N.D., Jan. 5, 1927; s. Martin Terence and Tressie (Keller) S.; B.S., N.D. State U., 1949; B.A., U. N.D., 1950, B.S., 1951; M.D., Albany Med. Coll., 1953; m. Virginia Whitley, Sept. 25, 1954; children—Scott Meredith, James Douglas. Intern, Presbyn.-St. Luke's Hosp., Chgo., 1953-54; resident in anatomic pathology U. Minn., 1957-59, in clin. pathology, 1959-61; practice medicine specializing in pathology, Mpls., 1963—; mem. staffs Mercy, Unity, Glenwood Hills hosps.; instr. clin. pathology and phys. medicine and rehab. U. Minn., 1961-62, asst. prof., 1962-63; dir. labs. Glenwood Hills Hosp., Mpls., 1963-65, Mercy Hosp., Anoka, 1965-74; pres. Doctors Diagnostic Labs., Mpls., 1974—. Bd. dirs. Met. Youth Symphonies, 1971-74, pres. bd. dirs., 1973-74. Served with USNR, 1944-46. Recipient Merit award City of Mpls. Com. on Urban Environment, 1976. Diplomate Am. Bd. Pathology. Mem. Coll. Am. Pathologists, Am. Soc. Clin. Pathologists, Am. Soc. Cytology, Internat. Acad. Cytology, Am. Coll. Nuclear Medicine, Minn., Hennepin County med. socs., AMA. Democrat. Congregationalist. Inventor microbiol. incubator. Home: 5030 Woodlawn Blvd S Minneapolis MN 55417 Office: 100 University Ave SE Minneapolis MN 55414

STEIGER, AARON ARMIN, electronic mfg. co. exec.; b. Grodek, Austria, Sept. 19, 1909; s. Louis and Sarah (Braun) S.; A.B., Western Res. U., 1930; LL.B., Western Res. U., 1932; m. Donna Jarboe, Sept. 4, 1949 (div. 1974); 1 dau., Cheryl. Admitted to Ohio bar, 1932; individual practice law, Cleve., 1932-40; v.p. Nat. Metal Products Co., Cleve., 1941-45; pres. Tel-A-Sign Inc., Chgo., 1948-67, Sign Corp. Am., Chgo., 1970—, Signcor Leasing Corp., Chgo., 1971—; v.p., Benco Industries Inc., Chgo., 1975—, also dir. Active Jewish United Fund, NCCJ. Mem. Point of Purchase Advt. Inst. (outstanding merchandising award 1962), Mktg. Communications Execs., Phi Beta Kappa, Sigma Alpha Mu, Sigma Delta Chi, Phi Delta Gamma, Tau Kappa Alpha. Clubs: Federated Advt., Chgo. Headline, Standard, Ravisloe Country, Execs., Masons, B'nai B'rith. Contbr. articles to industry, profl. jours. Home: 100 E Bellevue Pl Chicago IL 60611 Office: 919 N Michigan Ave Chicago IL 60611

STEIGER, WILLIAM ALBERT, congressman; b. Oshkosh, Wis., May 15, 1938; s. Carl Emil and Ruth (Storms) S.; B.S., U. Wis., 1960; m. Janet Dempsey, Aug. 10, 1963; 1 son, William Raymond. Mem. Wis. Assembly, 1961-66; mem. 90th-95th Congresses from 6th dist. Wis. Mem. corp. Joslin Diabetes Found.; trustee People-to-People. Named one of 5 Outstanding Young Men in Wis., 1964. One of 10 Outstanding Young Men in Am., U.S. Jr. C. of C., 1968. Episcopalian. Contbr. articles to profl. jours. Home: PO Box 1279 Oshkosh WI 54901 Office: 1111 Longworth House Office Bldg Washington DC 20515

STEIGERWALD, RICHARD FRANK, chem. co. exec.; b. Cleve., July 30, 1924; s. Peter John and Meta Katherine (Nunn) S.; student Ill. Inst. Tech., 1943-44, John Carroll U., 1946-47; B.Ch.E., U. Detroit, 1950, M.B.A., 1952; m. Joan Katherine Becka, Jan. 28, 1956; children—Richard S., Cynthia J., Lisa Anne, John P., Kurt R. Jr. engr. Harshaw Chem., Cleve., 1947-49; engr. Indsl. Rayon, Cleve., 1951-53; sr. engr., part owner Marspon Industries, Bethany, Ohio, 1953-54; with Diamond Shamrock Corp., Cleve., 1954—, sr. engr. corporate planning, 1970—. Served with AUS, 1943-46. Decorated Bronze Star medal. Registered profl. engr., Ohio, W.Va. Roman Catholic. Home: 9401 Stoney Creek Ln Parma Heights OH 44130 Office: Diamond Shamrock Bldg 1100 Superior Ave Cleveland OH 44115

STEIN, ADLYN ROBINSON (MRS. HERBERT ALFRED STEIN), jewelry co. exec.; b. Pitts., May 8, 1908; d. Robert Stewart and Pearl (Geiger) Robinson; Mus.B., Pitts. Mus. Inst., U. Pitts., 1928; m. F. J. Hollearn, Nov. 14, 1929 (dec.);children—Adlyn (Mrs. Brandon J. Hickey), Frances (Mrs. Thomas M. Kidd); m. 2d, Allen Burnett Williams, Dec. 5, 1955 (dec.); m. 3d, Herbert Alfred Stein, Nov. 28, 1963; 1 dau., Rachel Lynn. Treas., R. S. Robinson, Inc., Pitts., 1947—. Mem. Pitts. Symphony Soc., Tuesday Musical Club, Pitts.; mem. women's com. Cleve. Orch. Mem. D.A.R. Republican. Episcopalian. Clubs: Duquesne, University, South Hills Country (Pitts.); Rolling Rock (Ligonier); Lakewood Country, Clifton (Cleve.). Home: 22200 Lake Rd Cleveland OH 44116 Office: Clark Bldg Pittsburgh PA 15222

STEIN, DAVID JEROME, fin. co. exec., fin. cons.; b. Fairbury, Ill., Aug. 10, 1934; s. Frank F. and Doris Eleanor (Elliott) S.; B.S. in Agrl. Econs., U. Ill., 1959; grad. degree in Credit and fin. mgmt. Dartmouth Coll., 1968; m. Roberta Frieda Riecks, June 5, 1955; children—Cheryl Ann, Dennis Ray, David Jay, Cindy Lou, Sandra Sue. Field credit mgr. Internat. Harvester Credit Corp., Dixon, Ill., 1959-61, credit supr., Lansing, Mich., 1961-64; retail credit dir. F.S. Services, Inc., Bloomington, Ill., 1964-67; regional fin. services mgr. Monsanto Co., St. Louis, 1967-69, dist. sales mgr., Kansas City, 1969-71; asst. regional mgr. farm mortgages Mut. of N.Y. Life Ins. Co., Kansas City, Mo., 1971-72, asst. to v.p., N.Y.C., 1972-74; fin. cons. and comml. mortgage broker, Peoria, Ill., 1974—; pres. Med. Condominiums, Inc., Peoria, 1975—; propr., mgr. Karmelkorn Shoppe, Peoria, 1975—, Galesburg, Ill., 1975—; trustee Doris Stein Land Trust, 1976—; exec. v.p., gen. mgr. Roy Demanes Industries, Inc., Peoria, 1977—; sec. Ill. Valley Savs. & Loan Assn., 1977—; pres. Med. Park Physician's Center Condominium Assn., 1975;. Elder of ch. council First English Lutheran Ch., Peoria, 1974—, chmn. evangelism and worship com., 1974, tchr. adult edn., 1973. Served with U.S. Army, 1953-55. Recipient Exec. award Grad. Sch. fin. Mmgt., 1968. Republican. Club: Willow Knolls Country. Home: 906 W Kensington Dr Peoria IL 61614 Office: 1916 N Knoxville Ave Peroia IL

STEIN, HERBERT ALFRED, contractor; b. Warren, Ohio, Mar. 27, 1898; s. Fred David and Nancy (Troxel) S.; B.S., U. Pitts., 1924; m. Adlyn K. Robinson, Nov. 28, 1963; 1 dau., Rachel Lynn. Pres., H. A. Stein Co., Herb Stein, Inc., Feas, Inc., Hiram of Tyre, Inc., 1954—; dir. Dollar Savs. Bank, Niles, Ohio. Named to Nat. Football Hall of Fame, 1967. Mem. Phi Delta Theta. Republican. Presbyn. Clubs: Duquesne; Rolling Rock; South Hills Country (Pitts.); Lakewood Country (Cleve.); Clifton (Lakewood, Ohio). Home: 22200 Lake Rd Cleveland OH 44116 Office: 317 Clark St Cleveland OH 44109

STEIN, HERMAN DAVID, educator; b. N.Y.C., Aug. 13, 1917; s. Charles and Emma (Rosenblum) S.; B.S.S., Coll. City N.Y., 1939; M.S., Columbia U., 1941, postgrad. Sch. Social Work, 1945-47, D.S.W., 1958; m. Charmion Kerr, Sept. 15, 1946; children—Karen Gelender, Susan Deborah, Naomi Elizabeth. Case worker, dir. pub. relations, Jewish Family Services, N.Y.C., 1941-45; mem. faculty Columbia U. Sch. Social Work, N.Y.C., 1945-47, 50-64, prof., 1958-64, dir. research center, 1959-62; dean sch. applied social scis., Case Western Reserve U., Cleve., 1964-68, provost social and behavioral scis., 1967-71, provost of Univ., 1969-72, v.p., 1970-71, prof., 1972—; vis. prof. U. Hawaii, 1971-72; fellow Center Advanced Study Behavioral Scis., Palo Alto, Calif., 1974-75; mem. com. human resources Nat. Acad. Scis., 1972-74; chmn. adv. coms. NIMH, 1958-71; lectr. Sch. Social Work, Smith Coll., Northampton, Mass., 1950-63; chmn. Mayor's Commn. Crisis in Welfare, Cleve., 1968; cons. UN Childrens Fund, 1962—. Mem. Council Social Work Edn. (pres. 1966-69), Internat. Assn. Schs. Social Work (pres. 1968-76), Nat. Assn. Social Workers (chmn. commn. internat. social welfare, 1964-66), Internat. Council Social Welfare (exec. com. 1976—). Mem. editorial bd. Adminstration in Social Work, 1976—; author Curriculum Study of Columbia U. Sch. Social Work, 1960; editor (with Richard A. Cloward) Social Perspectives on Behavior, 1958; Planning for the Needs of Children in Developing Countries, 1965; Social Theory and Social Invention, 1968; The Crisis in Welfare in Cleveland, 1969; co-author: The Characteristics of American Jews, 1965; contbr. articles to profl. jours.; Commonwealth fellow 1941; recipient distinguished service award Council Social Work Edn., 1970. Office: 436 Pardee Hall Case Western Reserve U Cleveland OH 44106

STEIN, KATHARINE ANNE BRZEZINSKI, psychol. counselor; b. Chgo., May 30, 1947; d. Casimir Frank and Anna Maria (Para) Brzezinski; B.A., So. Ill. U., 1970, M.A., 1973; postgrad. U. Nebr., Lincoln; m. Michael Carl Stein, Nov. 18, 1967. Counselor Univ. Counseling Center, So. Ill. U., Carbondale, 1972-73; counseling psychologist, instr. psychology Madison Coll., Harrisonburg, Va., 1973-75; psychol. counselor U. Nebr., Lincoln, 1975—. Mem. Am. Personnel and Guidance Assn., Am. Coll. Personnel Assn. Author: A Referral Service for Aid to Transient Women, 1972; Is There Life After Graduation, 1977. Home: 902 N 29th St Lincoln NE 68503 Office: Counseling Center 1300 Seaton Hall Univ Nebr Lincoln NE 68518

STEIN, S. LARRY, real estate broker; b. Kansas City, Mo., May 3, 1930; s. William B. and Mary (Snitz) S.; B.A. with honors, U. Mich., 1951; J.D., U. Mo., 1954; m. Floralou Israel, July 2, 1951; children—Susan, Thomas, Lisa. Admitted to Mo. bar, 1954; claim adjuster Ahlvin & Nelson, attys., Kansas City, Mo., 1952-54; exec. v.p. Beerman-Stein Realty Co., Dayton, Ohio, 1954-58; pres., chmn. bd. Larry Stein Realty Co., Dayton, 1958—; dir. No. Union Holdings Corp., Fin. Land Corp., Capital Facilities, Inc.; spl. commr. Fed. Lands Commn. Trustee Dayton River Corridor Dist.; chmn. bd. City Wide Devel. Corp., 1977—. Mem. Soc. Indsl. Realtors (pres. Ohio chpt. 1976), Nat. Inst. Real Estate Brokers, Nat. Assn. Realtors, Ohio Assn. Real Estate Bds., Dayton Area Bd. Realtors (dir., named realtor of year 1976), Zeta Beta Tau, Phi Alpha Delta. Clubs: Dayton Racquet, Meadowbrook Country. Home: 3111 Winter Haven Ave Dayton OH 45415 Office: 40 W 4th St Dayton OH 45402

STEIN, YALE, lawyer; b. Chgo., Mar. 14, 1920; s. Max and Yetta (Oberman) S.; LL.B., John Marshall Law Sch., 1948, J.D., M.P.L.,., 1949; m. Ruth Goldstein, June 26, 1952; children—Ava, Mark. Admitted to Ill. bar, Fed. bar, U.S. Supreme Ct bar; agt. U.S. Treasury Dept., 1951-52; spl. cons. Spl. Big 9 Crime Investigating Com., Chgo. City Council, 1952; pvt. practice law, Ill., 1952—. Appeal agt. SSS, 1965-72, mem. appeal bd., 1972-76. Served with AUS, 1943-46. Decorated Purple Heart, Bronze Star; Menninger Found. fellow. Mem. Am., Fed., Ill., Chgo., N. Suburban bar assns., Am. Trial Lawyers Assn., Appellate Lawyers Assn. Ill., Am. Judicature Soc., World Assn. Lawyers, Internat. Assn. Lawyers and Judges, Nat. Assn. Criminal Def. Lawyers, Am. Lawyers Assn., Internat. Platform Assn., Art Inst. Chgo., Bar Assn. 7th Fed. Circuit, VFW, chmn. Ill. dept.), Mil. Order Purple Heart, Am. Legion, Amvets. Clubs: Moose, Execs. (Chgo.), Starcraft Soc. Office: 5102 W Oakton St Skokie IL 60076

STEINBAUER, ROBERT ANDRUS, educator; b. Niles, Mich., May 20, 1926; s. Perley J. and Myrta E. (Andrus) S.; B.Mus., U. Mich., 1949, M.Mus., 1950; D.Mus. (Nat. Fedn. Music Clubs scholar 1956-57), Ind. U., 1959; m. June L. Young, Sept. 7, 1947; children—Jeffrey Robert, Martha June. Head music dept. S.C. Sch. for Blind, Spartanburg, 1951-53; head piano dept. Drury Coll., Springfield, Mo., 1953-59; head keyboard dept. Wichita (Kans.) State U., 1959-69, U. Nev., Las Vegas, 1969-70; prof. music, head music dept. Kans. State U., Manhattan, 1970—; grad. faculty U. Mich., Ann Arbor, Ind. U., Bloomington. Lectr., clinician, recitalist, adjudicator. Mem. Bicentennial Commn., Manhattan, 1972—. Bd. dirs. Manhattan Arts Council, 1972—, Music Service Guild, Manhattan, 1970—. Served with inf. AUS, 1944-46. Recipient Ind. Young Artist's award, 1947. Mem. C. of C. (v.p. 1974—), Sinfonia, Lambda Chi Alpha. Rotarian. Editor Kans. Music Review, 1965-69. Home: 2916 Princeton Pl Manhattan KS 66502

STEINBERG, DORA ELLEN (MRS. ROY DAVID STEINBERG), librarian; b. Newburg, Mo., Mar. 31, 1906; d. John Jacob and Dora Charlotte (Delashmit) Brown; B.S., U. Mo., 1940; M.S., Central Mo. State U., 1964; m. Roy David Steinberg, Nov. 29, 1941; children—David Lee. Tchr., librarian Newburg (Mo.) Schs., 1923-38, 40-42, 47-55, 71—; tchr. Pub. Schs., Caryle, Ill., 1938-40, Waynesville, Mo., 1955-60; sch. library supr. Waynesville-Ft. Leonard Wood Sch., Ft. Leonard Wood, Mo., 1961-71. Cons. library media to various libraries and school in several states; instr. library sci. U. Mo., Columbia, 1967-72; asso. Ency. Briannica Edn. Corp., Mo., 1971-74. Mem. Nat., Mo. edn. assns., Am., Mo. library assns., Democrat. Baptist. Mem. Order Eastern Star. Home: PO Box 176 Newburg MO 65550

STEINBERG, GLENN DAVID, real estate developer, urban planner; b. Chgo., Mar. 9, 1941; s. Jay Zola and Muriel (Kallis) S.; ed. Francis W. Parker Sch., Chgo.; B.A., U. Ill., 1966; M.City Planning, U. Pa., 1968; postgrad. Northwestern U. Law Sch., 1968-69, Grad. Sch. Mgmt., 1974—, m. Judith Sue Pellar, June 27, 1965; children—Ellen Lisa, Peter Alan. Urban planner Skidmore, Owings & Merrill, Chgo., 1969-71; predevel. coordinator Urban Investment & Devel. Co., Chgo., 1971—; guest lectr. Sch. Architecture, U. Ill., Chgo., 1973—, Harvard Grad. Sch. Design, 1976-77; co-chmn. Ill. Environ. Adv. Com. of Internat. Council Shopping Centers, 1973—. Mem. men's council Mus. Contemporary Art; mem. adv. bd. park art com. Friends of Parks, 1977—; bd. dirs. Urban Gateways, Chgo., 1975—, Young Men's Jewish Council, Chgo., 1973-75, Landmarks Preservation Council, Chgo., 1970-72, Ill. Planning and Conservation League, 1970-74. Registered real estate broker. Mem. Am. Inst. Planners, Am. Soc. Planning Ofcls., Met. Housing and Planning Council, Tau Sigma Delta. Editor Planning Comment, 1967-68. Office: Suite 800 845 N Michigan Ave Chicago IL 60611

STEINBERGER, ROBERT, orthopedic surgeon; b. Detroit, July 17, 1938; s. Eugene and Fannie (Raskin) S.; B.S., Wayne State U., Detroit, 1960, M.D., 1966; m. Lyn Carol, Jan. 2, 1965; children—Brita Ilene, Robert Anders. Intern, Henry Ford Hosp., Detroit, 1966-67, resident in orthopedic surgery, 1967-71; practice medicine specializing in orthopedic surgery, Jackson, Mich., 1974—; staff Foote Meml. Hosps.; pres. Jackson Orthopaedics, P.C. Served to maj. M.C., USAF, 1971-74. Diplomate Nat. Bd. Med. Examiners, Am. Bd. Orthopaedic Surgery. Fellow Am. Acad. Orthopaedic Surgeons, A.C.S.; mem. Mich., Jackson County med. socs., Detroit Orthopaedic Acad. Club: Jackson Town. Home: 1340 Austscot St Jackson MI 49203 Office: 500 Lansing St Jackson MI 49201

STEINBRINK, JOHN PAUL, editor, author; b. Chgo.; s. Paul Ralph and Christine (Wolter) S.; M.B.A., U. Chgo., 1960; student Northwestern U., 1941-42; m. Myra G. Gold, 1947; children—Diane, Roger, Jill. Art and prodn. mgr. Sci. Research Assos., Chgo., 1947-52, asst. sales mgr., 1953-60, dir. field services, 1960-61, marketing cons., 1961-62; editor Dartnell Corp., Chgo., 1962-65, editorial dir., 1965—. Served to 1st lt., USAAF, 1942-45. Mem. Sales Mktg. Execs. Internat. (nat. chmn. career guidance com. 1974—, author Forum 1973—), Sales/Mktg. Execs. Chgo. (dir., sec. 1965-67), Ill. Found. for Distributive Edn. (bd. govs. 1973—), Niles Art Guild, Pi Sigma Epsilon. Author: Selling Success, 1961; (with Walter C. Lane) DuPont Marketing Training, 1969; Compensation of Salesman, 1976, 78; Executive Compensation, 1976, 78. Author, editor: Dartnell Sales/Marketing Newsletter, 1962—. Editor: Dynamic Sales Leadership (J.V. Fort) 1964; How to Comply with the Equal Employment Opportunity Act (Joseph Lawson), 1966; Collective Bargaining Guide for School Adminstrs. (Hill & Quinn), 1970; How to Conduct Successful Sales Meetings, (Jack Kielty), 1969; How to Plan and Manage Sales Territories (Charles C. Schlom), 1973; Dartnell 10-Point Sales Training Program (Charles C. Schlom), 1973, How to Make Sales Meetings Come Alive (George B. Anderson), 1974; How to Increase Sales and Profits Through Salesman Performance Evaluation (Frank Eby), 1975; How to Participate Profitably in Trade Shows (Konikow), 1976; contbr. article to profl. jour. Home: 8510 Shermer Rd Niles IL 60648 Office: 4660 Ravenswood Ave Chicago IL 60640

STEINDLER, MARTIN JOSEPH, chemist; b. Vienna, Jan. 3, 1938; Ph.B., U. Chgo., 1947, B.S., 1948, M.S., 1949, Ph.D., 1952; married; 2 children. Research asso. U. Chgo., 1952-53; with Argonne (Ill.) Nat. Lab., 1953—, sr. chemist, 1974—, asso. dir. chem. engring. div., 1978—; cons. advisory com. on reactor safeguards Nuclear Regulatory Commn.; mem. Atomic Safety and Licensing Bd. Panel. Mem. Am., Brit. chem. socs., AAAS, Am. Nuclear Soc., Sigma Xi. Author numerous articles, reports on nuclear science, chemistry, safety. Patentee. Office: 9700 S Cass Ave Argonne IL 60439

STEINEGER, JOHN FRANCIS, lawyer, state senator; b. Kansas City, Kans., Sept. 13, 1924; s. John F. and June (Wear) S.; A.B., U. Kans., 1947, J.D., 1949; m. Margaret Leisy, Dec. 2, 1949; children—John Francis, III, Cynthia, Melissa, Christian. Admitted to Kans. bar, 1949, Fed. bar, 1949; with solicitors office U.S. Dept. Labor, Washington, 1949-50; legal advisor U.S. Dept. State, Europe and Middle East, 1950-55, pub. affairs officer Middle East, 1955-57; probate judge protem, Kansas City, 1957-58; practice law, Kansas City, Kans., 1960—; chief dep. county atty., Kansas City, 1958-60; sr. mem. firm Steineger & Holbrook; mem. Kans. Senate, 1964—, now minority leader. chmn. Gov.'s Prairie Park Commn., Spl. Ecology Commn. of Legislature. Mem. Gov.'s Com on Exec. Reorgn. Bd. dirs. Kansas City Ballet. Served to lt. USNR, 1943-46. Named One of Twenty Five Outstanding State Senators, Eagleton Inst. Politics Rutgers, 1972. Mem. Am. Bar Assn., Bar Assn. Kans., Nat. Housing Conf., Phi Delta Theta, Phi Delta Phi. Democrat. Episcopalian. Home: 6400 Valley View Rd Muncie KS 66111 Office: 2 Gateway Plaza Kansas City KS 66101

STEINER, BRADFORD EZRA, physician; b. Calcutta, India, Nov. 28, 1917; s. Ezra Bradford and Elizabeth (Geiger) S.; B.S., Wheaton Coll., 1939; M.D., U. Ill., 1943; m. Martha Ellen Milbourn, Dec. 25, 1942; children—Natalie A., Cheryl E. (dec.), Douglas M., Suzanne E., Mark E. Intern, Cook County Hosp., Chgo., 1943-44; resident Evang. Hosp., Chgo., 1946; med. missionary Evang. Alliance Mission, North India, 1947-58, med. supt. Almora Tb San.; med. supt. Landour Community Hosp.; resident surgeon VA Hosp., Hines, Ill., 1952-53, 57-58; pvt. practice internal medicine, 1958—; mem. staff Meml. Hosp., Elmhurst; sch. physician Dist. 87 Cook County, 1958—. Served with USN, 1944-46. Diplomate Am. Bd. Family Practice; licentiate Med. Council Can. Fellow Internat. Coll. Surgeons, Am. Acad. Family Physicians; mem. AMA, Ill., DuPage County med. socs., Assn. Surgeons India, Royal Soc. Tropical Medicine and Hygiene, Am. Soc. Tropical Medicine and Hygiene, Am. Soc. Abdominal Surgeons, Am. Geriatrics Soc., Christian Med. Soc., Am. Sci. Affiliation, Home: Elmhurst IL 60126 Office: 240 E North Ave Northlake IL 60164

STEINER, IVAN, JR., ins. cons.; b. Ossining, N.Y., Jan. 1, 1912; s. Ivan and Merle (Holter) S.; B.A., Coll. Wooster, 1933; m. Lillian C. Gisinger, Dec. 27, 1939; children—Amy L. (Mrs. Anthony J. Pryor), Michael S., Sara A. (Mrs. William M. Marks), Deborah (Mrs. Martin T. Weber, Jr.), Jeffrey, Andrew. With W. C. Myers & Co., gen. ins. agy., Wooster, Ohio, 1936—, successively solicitor, jr. partner, 1940, sr. partner, 1948—; merged with W.G. Whitaker & Son, 1970, pres. Whitaker-Myers Ins. Agy. Inc., 1970-77, chmn. bd., 1977; ins. cons. in pvt. practice, Wooster, 1978—; v.p., dir. Wayne Recreation, Inc.; dir. Comml. Banking and Trust Co., Medal Brick & Tile Co.; instr. ins. Community Coll., U. Akron, 1956-57. Mem. Govs. Ins. adv. com. Fire and Casualty Ins. Bd., 1960-63; vice chmn. all-industry com. for revision agts. licensing manual Ohio Ins. Dept., 1960-61. Mem. Wooster Municipal Civil Service Commn., 1967-73. Chmn. bd. trustees Wooster YMCA; mem. cultural events com. Coll. of Wooster. Served from pvt. to 1st sgt. AUS, 1943-46; ETO. Chartered Property Casualty Underwriter, 1955. Mem. Wayne County Ind. Ins. Agts. Assn. (pres. 1957), Ohio Assn. Ins. Agts. (pres. 1959, chmn. legis. policy com. 1960-61, exec. com., 1965—, chmn. edn. com. 1957, 65, 66, chmn. long range planning team 1973, dir.; Paul Revere Trophy 1965), Nat. Assn. Ins. Agts. (chmn. spl. acquisition cost allowance com. 1959-60), Nat. Soc. Chartered Property Casualty Underwriters (mem. seminar bd., pres. Akron-Canton chpt., regional dir. N. Central dist. 1965-68, regional v.p. 1968, chmn. com. revise soc.'s constn. and by laws, mem. long range planning bd. 1970-74, chmn. 1973-74), Am. Risk and Ins. Assn., Ins. Inst. Am. (diploma-asso. risk mgmt.), Ins. Soc. Phila., Wooster C. of C. (pres. 1954-55), Internat. Platform Assn., 8th Armored Div. Assn., VFW. Democrat. Zion Lutheran (trustee). Clubs: Masons (32 deg.), Shriners, Elks, Rotary (pres. Wooster 1968-69), Century, Julie Fe Country. Contbr. to trade jours. Home: 257 W Henrietta St Wooster OH 44691

STEINER, PHILIP G., ret. toy mfg. co. exec.; b. Balt., Apr. 20, 1901; s. Sigmond S. and Emma (Lowenbach) S.; B.A., U. Mich., 1923; m. Desiree H. Harris, Jan. 20, 1935; children—Philip Harry, Richard Harris. Salesman, Cin. Soap Co., 1923-29; pres. Tom Collins Jr. Co., Cin., 1923-60; v.p. Kenner Products Co., Cin., 1947-72. Pres. Jewish Welfare Fund, Cin., 1955, 61; bd. dirs. NCCJ, 1956-67; pres. Sheltering Oaks Hosp., Cin., 1960-67; mem. distbn. com. Greater Cin. Found. Recipient Herbert H. Lehman award, 1967, Guardian of Menorah award B'nai B'rith, 1968, Citation award Nat. Conf. Christians and Jews, 1970. Club: Losantville Country (pres. 1954-56). Home: 2444 Madison Rd Cincinnati OH 45208 Office: 317 E 8th St Cincinnati OH 45202

STEINER, ROBERT LIVINGSTON, writer, educator, cons.; b. Charlevoix, Mich., Aug. 12, 1923; s. Albert M. and Therese Rose (Livingston) S.; B.A. magna cum laude, Dartmouth Coll., 1947; M.A. in Econs., Columbia, 1948; m. Christine May Johnson, Dec. 27, 1959; children—Therese, Carl, Lorraine, Robert C. With Kenner Products Co., Cin., 1948-72, v.p., advt., 1960-68, gen. mgr., 1968-70, pres., 1970-72; adj. prof. mktg. Grad. Coll. Bus. Adminstrn., U. Cin., 1974—; dir. Clopay Corp. Mem. bd., v.p. Charter Com., Cin. and Hamilton County, Ohio; bd. dirs. Robert Krohn Livingston Meml. Camp, Cin.; trustee Cin. TV Ednl. Found. WCET Channel 48. Served with USAAF, World War II. Decorated Air Medal with 5 clusters. Mem. Toy Mfrs. Am. (dir. 1967-68), Am. Mktg. Assn. (chmn. productivity measurement com.), Acad. of Advt. (chmn. econ. role of advt. panel), Am. Econ. Assn. Jewish. Clubs: Southwest Ohio Sportsmen; University, Hyde Park Tennis (Cin.). Author: Visions of Cablevision, 1972. Contbr. articles mags. Home: 2731 Johnstone Pl Cincinnati OH 45206 Office: 317 E 8th St Cincinnati OH 45202 also Coll Bus Adminstrn U Cin Mail Location Cincinnati OH 45221

STEINFELD, MANFRED, furniture mfg. co. exec.; b. Josbach, Germany, Apr. 29, 1924; s. Abraham and Paula (Katten) S.; student U. Ill., 1942; B.S. Commerce, Roosevelt U., 1948; m. Fern Goldman, Nov. 13, 1949; children—Michael, Paul, Jill. Research analyst State Ill., 1948-50; v.p. Shelby Williams Industries, Inc., Chgo., 1954-63, pres., 1964-72; chmn. bd., 1973—; dir. Amalgamated Trust & Savs. Bank, Met. Bank of Addison (Ill.), Albany Bank & Trust. Trustee Roosevelt U., Chgo. Served to 1st lt. AUS, 1942-45, 50-52. Decorated Bronze Star, Purple Heart; named Small Bus. Man of Year Central Region, 1967. Pres., Roosevelt U. Bus. Sch. Alumni Council. Mem. Beta Gamma Sigma. Clubs: Standard, Bryn Mawr Country. Home: 13000 Lake Shore Dr Apt 34D Chicago IL 60610 Office: Mdse Mart Room 1348 Chicago IL 60654

STEINHARDT, MILTON JOSEPH, psychiatrist; b. Poland, July 15, 1905; s. Abraham Haskell and Zelda (Shafran) S.; came to U.S., 1920, naturalized, 1923; B.A., Wayne State U., 1928, M.D., 1932; m. Freda Freedenson, Dec. 23, 1937; children—Frederick, Judith (Mrs. John Patrick MacDonald), Daniel. Intern, Jewish Hosp., Cin., 1932-33; resident medicine Sea View Hosp., N.Y.C., 1934-35; resident psychiatry Wayne State U.-Receiving Hosp. Detroit, 1960-63; gen. practice medicine, Detroit, 1936-42, specializing in allergy, Detroit, 1945-60, specializing in psychiatry, Detroit and Oak Park, 1960—; cons. psychiatry staff Grace Hosp., Detroit; teaching staff Sinai Hosp.-Wayne U. Med. Sch., 1950—. Mem. community relations council com. Jewish Community Council Detroit, 1957—. Served with M.C., AUS, 1942-45. Decorated Bronze Star medal (2). Fellow Am. Coll. Allergists, Am. Acad. Allergy, Am. Soc. Psychosomatic Medicine, Am. Psychiat. Assn.; mem. AMA, Mich., Wayne County med. socs., Mich. Allergy Soc. (pres. 1959-60), Maimonides Med. Soc. Detroit (pres. 1958-59), A.C.P. (life), Mich. Soc. Psychiatry. Address: 24760 Manistee St Oak Park MI 48237

STEINHAUS, HENRY RICHARD, nursing home exec.; b. N.Y.C., Jan. 28, 1921; s. Jacob and Ida (Orstein) S.; B.S., U. Mo., 1941; B.S. in Pharmacy, Kansas City U., 1953; m. Bettye Rose Levine, Nov. 26, 1941; children—Linda Carol (Mrs. A.R. Levine), Susan Ellen (Mrs. Robert A. Bloom), David M. Pres., dir. Doctor's Bldg. Pharmacy, Inc., Kansas City, Mo., 1955-71, Sr. Estates Convalescent Center, 1958-62, Victoria Estates Convalescent Center, Kansas City, 1963-76, Profl. Nursing Homes Am., Inc., 1966-69; chmn. bd., pres. Health Related Services, Inc., Prairie Village, Kans., 1971—; pres. Windsor Estates of Kokomo (Ind.), 1967—; treas., dir. Windsor Estates of Camdenton (Mo.), 1969—; treas. Sedgwick Convalescent Center, Golden Plains Convalescent Center, Hutchinson, Kans.; exec. v.p. Monterey Life Systems, Inc., 1969-71; dir. Community Equities, Kansas City. Cons., developer nursing homes in midwest, 1958-71; nat. speaker on geriatrics, 1963—; lectr. pharmacy U. Mo. at Kansas City, 1964-65. Chmn. Joan Davis Sch., Kansas City, 1972-74. Bd. dirs. U. Mo. at Kansas City Sch. Pharmacy Found., 1965-68, Jewish Vocational Guidance Services, 1966; past bd. dirs. Nat. Council Christians and Jews, Nat. Council Health Care Facilities. Served with AUS, 1944-46. Fellow Am. Coll. apothecaries; mem. Am. Mo. nursing home assns. Jewish (pres. congregation). Mason. Contbr. numerous articles to profl. publs. Home: 4201 W 90th St Prairie Village KS 66207 Office: 7930 State Line Prairie Village KS 66208

STEINHILBER, JACK DANIEL, lawyer; b. Oshkosh, Wis., Sept. 14, 1931; s. Elmer G. and Rose B. (Wingeier) S.; B.S., U. Wis., 1953, LL.B., 1955. Admitted to Wis. bar, 1955, since practiced in Oshkosh; mem. firm Chaney, Steinhilber & Nesbitt, 1965—; mem. Wis. Senate, 1970-74, asst. majority leader, 1973-74; asst. dist. atty. Winnebago County, Oshkosh, 1956, dist. atty., 1957-64; mem. Wis. State Assembly, 1966-70. Chmn., Republican State Conv., 1974, Rep. Senate Campaign Com., 1972. Mem. Wis. Dist. Attys. Assn. (sec.-treas. 1963, pres. 1964), Winnebago, Wis., Am. bar assns., Artus Econ. Soc., Phi Alpha Delta, Kappa Sigma. Republican. Lutheran. Elk. Office: 219 Washington Ave Oshkosh WI 54901

STEINIGER, (IRENE) MIRIAM LARMI, child devel. specialist; b. Weirton, W.Va., Dec. 20, 1916; d. (Kustaa) Edward and Aune Ellen (Raitanen) Larmi; B.S. in Edn., Ohio State U., 1936; M.A., Miami U. (Ohio), 1964; Ed.D., U. Cin., 1975; m. Erich W. Steiniger, June 6, 1941; children—Erika, Fredrik, Anthony, Karsten, Theron. Tchr., Ohio Sch. for Deaf, Columbus, 1937-41, 44-46; tchr. English and lit. Mason (Ohio) High Sch., 1955-56; tchr. elementary schs., Hamilton, Ohio, 1956-59, tchr. of deaf, Hamilton Pub. Schs., 1959-63, speech and hearing therapist, 1963-70; tchr.-cons. for neurologically handicapped, Hamilton, 1970-72; cooperating tchr. Tchr. Tng. Program, Miami U., Hamilton, 1970-72; vis. asst. prof., adj. vis. prof. U. Cin., 1972-75, asst. prof., 1975—; asst. dir. presch. programs Cin. Center for Devel. Disorders, 1975—; tching. cons. Perceptual Motor Workshops, Miami U., 1970, 71; dir., planner tchr. tng. projects and workshops Hamilton City Schs., 1965, 68, 69, 71. Vice pres. Talawonda Bd. Edn., Oxford, Ohio, 1968-72; pres., chmn. coms. LWV, Oxford; ednl. com. Butler County Mental Hygiene Assn.; leader Girl Scouts U.S.A., Dan Beard council Boy Scouts Am.; Sunday sch. tchr. Lutheran Ch.; mem. CORVA. Martha Holden Jennings Found. grantee, 1968. Mem. Butler County (pres. 1969, legis. chmn. 1964—, dir. 1964—), Ohio, Nat. councils exceptional children, Am. (certified), Cin., Ohio, Nat. speech and hearing assns., Tri-County (certificate of appreciation 1974), Ohio, nat. assns. for children with learning disabilities, Nat. Ohio, Cin. Assns. for Edn. of Young Children, Day Care and Child Devel. Council Am., Inter-Univ. Council for Exceptional Children, AAUP, Delta Kappa Gamma. Democrat. Contbr. writing to Piagetian research book. Home: 208 Beechpoint Dr Oxford OH 45056 Office: Cin Center Developmental Disorders Pavilion Bldg 3300 Elland Ave Cincinnati OH 45229

STEINMETZ, JOHANNA (MRS. GARY PEARSON CUMMINGS), TV reporter and producer; b. Trenton, N.J., July 2, 1941; d. Edward George and Dorothy Grace (Sainsbury) Steinmetz; student Internat. Christian U., Tokyo, 1961-62; B.A. cum laude, Lawrence U., 1963; postgrad. Stockholm U., 1967; m. Gary Pearson Cummings, Apr. 18, 1970; children—Ian Christian Dane, Pearson Forrest. Aide, Japanese Mission to UN, N.Y., 1963-65; free lance journalist, Tokyo, 1966; stringer Time, Inc., others, Stockholm, part-time, 1967-68; feature writer Chgo.'s Am., 1968-69; radio-TV columnist Chgo. Today newspaper, 1969-73; freelance writer, 1973-76; reporter, producer WTTW-TV Evening News, Chgo., 1976-78; producer WTTW-TV, 1978—; critic-at-large WBBM Radio, 1973—; contbg. editor Chicagoan mag., 1973-74, theater columnist, 1974. Recipient Nat. Headliner award, 1972. Home: 641 Michigan Ave Evanston IL 60202 Office: WTTW News 5400 N St Louis Ave Chicago IL 60625

STEINMETZ, WILLIAM RONALD, constrn. co. exec.; b. South Bend, Ind., Feb. 3, 1926; s. William John and Clara Alice (Peters) S.; B.M.E., Purdue U., 1949; m. Shirley Joan Proudfit, May 8, 1954; children—Janet Ellen, William Ronald. With Midland Engring. Co., Ind., South Bend, 1949—, v.p., 1954-61, pres., 1961-74, chmn. bd., 1974—. Served with USN, 1943-46. Recipient Industry award Nat. Roofing Contractors Assn., 1976, Midwest Roofing Contractors Assn., 1976, Ind. Roofing Contractors Assn., 1971 (past pres. all assns.). Roman Catholic. Clubs: Rotary (past dist. gov.), Union League Chgo., South Bend Country (past pres.). Home: 225 S Sunnyside St South Bend IN 46615 Office: PO Box 1019 South Bend IN 46624

STEINREICH, OTTO SELICK, surgeon; b. N.Y.C., Mar. 13, 1914; s. George and Ida (Mayer) S.; A.B., U. N.C., 1934; M.D., Med. Coll. Va., 1938; m. Helen Natalie Bane, June 19, 1938; children—Michael Martin, Steven Carl. Intern, Newark City Hosp., 1939-41; resident surgery St. Thomas Hosp., Akron, Ohio, 1946-48; practice medicine specializing in surgery, Akron, 1948—; med. staff St. Thomas Hosp., dir. med. edn.; mem. staff Akron Gen. Hosp., Akron City Hosp., Akron Children's Hosp. Bd. dirs. Jewish Welfare Fund, Jewish Family Service, Akron Jewish Center. Served to capt. M.C. AUS, 1941-46. Diplomate Am. Bd. Surgery. Fellow A.C.S., Internat. Coll. Surgeons; mem. AMA, Council Coordinators Grad. Med. Edn. Northeastern Ohio Univs. Coll. Medicine Phi Sigma Delta, Phi Lambda Kappa. Jewish (pres. congregation). Contbr. articles to profl. jours. Home: 433 Delaware Ave Akron OH 44303 Office: Saint Thomas Hosp Akron OH 44310

STEINZEIG, SHERMAN MILLARD, physician; b. Ka Mo., Nov. 3, 1925; s. Morris and Lillian (Sandhaus); B.S., U. Kans., 1949, M.D., 1952. Intern, Albert Einstein Med. Center, Phila., 1952-53; resident internal medicine U. Kans. Med. Center, 1953-56, Nat. Heart Inst. fellow in cardiology, 1956; practice medicine specializing in cardiology, Kansas City, Kans., 1956—; instr. medicine U. Kans., 1956-57, asso., 1957-60, asst. clin. prof., 1960-73, adj. clin. prof., 1976—; chief dept. medicine St. Margaret Hosp., Kansas City, 1960-70; cons. cardiology Bethany Med. Center, Kansas City, 1962; med. dir. Bethany Hartford Coronary Care Unit, 1970—. Served with U.S. Army, 1944-66. Diplomate Am. Bd. Internal Medicine. Fellow A.C.P., Am. Coll. Cardiology; mem. AMA, Kans. (chmn. com. regional med. programs 1969-70), Wyandotte County (pres. 1969) med socs., Kans., Kaw Valley (v.p. 1973-74) heart assns., Kansas City Soc. Internists (pres. 1973), Wyandotte County Vis. Nurses Assn. (chmn. med. adv. com. 1970), Met. Area Med. Council (sec.-treas. 1970), U. Kans. Med. Alumni (pres. 1971-72), Phi Chi. Contbr. articles to profl. jours. Home: 4407 W 71 St Prairie Village KS 66102 Office: 155 S 18th St Kansas City KS 66102

STEIOFF, ARTHUR FRANCIS, chem. engr.; b. Cin., Dec. 9, 1907; s. Henry Ferdinand and Flora Barbara (Rein) S.; Chem. E., U. Cin., 1934. With Brighton Corp., Cin., 1935-74, chief engr., 1935-74; process and design engr. A.M. Kinney, Inc., Cin., 1974—. Cons. chem. engr. Mem. Engring. Soc. Cin., Am. Inst. Chem. Engrs., Am. Soc. Metals, Fedn. of Socs. for Coatings Technology. Patentee in field. Author: The Story of Alkyd Resins, 1959 (booklet). Contbr. to Treatise on Coatings (Myers and Long), 1967. Home: 615 Evening Star Ln Cincinnati OH 45220 Office: 2900 Vernon Pl Cincinnati OH 45219

STELLA, FRANK DANIEL, food service equipment co. exec.; b. Jessup, Pa., Jan. 21, 1919; s. Facondino and Ciarina (Pennoni) S.; B.B.A., U. Detroit, 1937-41; m. Martha T. Yetzer, Sept. 20, 1941; children—Daniel F., Mary Anne, William J., Philip, Marsha James, Stephen. Instr., U. Detroit, 1947-60; pres. F.D. Stella Products Co., Detroit, 1946—; gen. partner Fairlane Club, Dearborn, Mich., 1972; dir. Peoples Fed. Savs. of Detroit, 1971—; instr. orgn. and mgmt. Coll. Commerce and Fin., U. Detroit. Exec. v.p. Willoway Center for Performing Arts, Birmingham, Mich., 1973; co-chmn. Family Orch. Hall, Detroit, 1973; mem. N. Rosedale Park Civic Assn., Detroit, 1950; mem. St. John's Hosp. Guild, Detroit, 1960; chmn. income tax bd. rev. City of Detroit, 1967; mem. Mich. Employment Securities Commn., 1964-65; mem. Presdl. Commn. on Fed. Statistics; 1970-71; mem. Nat. Voluntary Service Adv. Council, 1974, chmn., 1974—; mem. Mich. Higher Edn. Facilities Commn., 1975—; pres. Mich. Republican Heritage Groups Council; mem. fin. com. Mich. Rep. Party, Southeastern Mich. Rep. Party; trustee U. Detroit, 1970—, mem. exec. com., 1970—, devel. chmn., 1970—; trustee Maryglade Coll., 1965-73; mem. exec. bd. advisers Mt. Carmel Mercy Hosp. and Med. Center, Detroit, 1970—; bd. dirs. Detroit Bd. Commerce, 1970—, v.p., 1975—; trustee Nat. Shrine Immaculate Conception, Washington, 1977; bd. dirs. Music Hall, 1977, Italian Am. Found., Washington, 1977. Served to maj. USAAF, 1941. Recipient Columbus Day Italo-Am. Man of Year award, 1976; Ethnic of Year award Ethnic Bicentennial Council, 1975; Ethnic Man of Year award, Phila., 1976; Tower alumni award U. Detroit, 1977; Michelangelo award Boystown of Italy, 1977. Mem. U. Detroit Alumni Assn. (pres. 1967-68), Friends of Maryglade Coll. (chmn. adv. bd. 1950), Titan Club, Wholesale Distbrs. Assn., Econs. Club Detroit, Food Service Exec. Assn., Nat. Restaurant Assn., Amicus Club (pres. 1968—), Italian Boy Towns, Boys' Club Met. Detroit, Menninger Found., Young Pres.'s Orgn., Am. Legion, Air Force Assn., Internat. Platform Assn., Founders Soc., Guest House, Smithsonian Inst., Friends of Folger Library, Italian C. of C., Alpha Kappa Psi (past pres. Beta Theta chpt., life mem., recipient distinguished alumni award). Rotarian, Elk., K.C. Clubs: Detroit Golf; Detroit Athletic; Capitol Hill (Washington). Home: 19180 Gainsborough Rd Detroit MI 48223 Office: 7000 Fenkel Ave Detroit MI 48238

STELLMAN, SAMUEL DAVID, educator; b. Detroit, Nov. 11, 1918; s. Solomon D. and Fannie (Wiseblum) S.; B.Health and Phys. Edn., U. Toronto, 1943; M.S.W., Ohio State U., 1958, Ph.D., 1963; m. Lillian Mandlsohn, July 11, 1943; children—Steven Dale, Leslie Robert. Asso. dir. Columbus (Ohio) Jewish Center, 1950-62; asso. prof. social work Ohio State U., Columbus, 1963-68; prof. social work, chmn. social work extension U. Wis., 1968—, dir. Criminal Justice Inst., 1974—; exec. dir. Anti-Poverty Program, Franklin County, Ohio, 1965-66; cons. Nat. Jewish Welfare Bd., 1956-72, U.S. OEO, 1964-73. Mem. Columbus Community Relations Commn., 1966-68. Bd. dirs. Wis. Family Life Assn., Milw. Jewish Community Council. Served with Canadian Army, 1943-46. Recipient Distinguished Service award U. Wis., 1973. Mem. Am. Corrections Assn., Adult Edn. Council U.S., Council Social Work Edn., Nat. Council Crime and Delinquency, Wis. Criminal Justice Edn. Assn. (dir.). Home: 1545 W Fairfield Ct Glendale WI 53209 Office: 3270 N Marietta Ave Milwaukee WI 53201 also Bayview Continuing Edn Center Madison WI 53706

STELZNER, GLENN WILBERT, physician; b. Muscatine, Iowa, Sept. 18, 1909; s. John and Bessie (Knapp) S.; B.A., U. Iowa, 1933, M.D., 1936; m. Ruth Elizabeth Schroder, June 18, 1934; children—Paul B., Karen I. (Mrs. William Hawley), Judith A. (Mrs. Douglas R. MacQueen), Gretchen R. Rotating intern Grant Hosp., Columbus, Ohio, 1936-37; gen. practice medicine and surgery, Newcomerstown, Ohio, 1937-43, Coshocton, Ohio, 1946—; mem. med. staff Coshocton County Meml. Hosp., chief of staff, 1969-70; teaching anatomy and physiology Coshocton City Hosp. Sch. Nursing, 1946-47. Coshocton City Health Commr., 1946—; registrar vital statistics, Coshocton, 1946—. Served with M.C., AUS, 1943-45; ETO. Mem. Coshocton County Med. Soc. (pres. 1950), Ohio Med. Assn., AMA, Am. Legion, 40 and 8. Presbyterian. Mason (Shriner, K.T.), Elk (life mem.), Rotarian (pres. 1943). Home: 18 Ridgewood Dr Coshocton OH 43812 Office: 118 N 7th St Coshocton OH 43812

STEMAN, ROBERT EDWARD, lawyer; b. Cin., Apr. 12, 1908; s. Louis J. and Lillie (Trarbach) S.; A.B., Miami U., Oxford, Ohio, 1931; J.D., U. Cin., 1933; m. Josephine Lambert, Oct. 28, 1944; children—Sara S. (Mrs. David A. Whittaker), Susan (Mrs. Ethan B. Stanly), E. Conrad, Sharon Lambert (Mrs. Jerome C. Earl). Admitted to Ohio bar, 1933; practice law, Cin., 1933-41, 46—; spl. counsel Cin. Bd. Edn., 1949—, city Cin., 1965—, city North College Hill, 1955-61; mem. firm Peck, Shaffer & Williams. Served to lt. comdr. USNR, 1942-45. Recipient Freedoms Found. George Washington honor medal, 1972. Mem. Am., Ohio, Cin. bar assns., Mil. Order World Wars (judge adv. gen. 1965-69, comdr.-in-chief, 1970-71), Navy League, English Speaking Union, Phi Delta Theta (pres. chpt. trustees). Mem. Mil. Hospitaler Order St. Lazarus of Jerusalem. Clubs: Queen City, Cin. Tennis (Cin.). Home: 13 Bull Run Dr Oxford OH 45056 Office: First Nat Bank Bldg Cincinnati OH 45202

STEMEN, GREGORY DONALD, TV ofcl.; b. Columbus, Ohio, Mar. 11, 1949; s. Arthur Donald and Eileen (Scholl) S.; A.B., Ohio State U., 1971, postgrad., 1972-73, 75; M.A., Mich. State U., 1972. Grad. adminstrv. asso. Ohio State U., Columbus, 1972-74, coordinator Ohio State awards, Inst. for Edn. by Radio-TV, 1974-76, asst. dir. Ohio State awards, 1975-77, TV spl. projects unit mgr. Ohio State U. Telecommunications Center, 1974-76; unit mgr., asst. producer-dir. Sta. WOSU-TV, Columbus, 1977—. Deacon, chmn. communications Trinity United Church of Christ, 1974—. Mem. Nat. Assn. Ednl. Broadcasters, Nat. Acad. TV Arts Scis., Am. Film Inst., Kappa Kappa Psi (life). Clubs: TBDBITL Alumni (treas. 1976—, treas. active band 1976—), Ohio State and Franklin County Alumni Club, Mich. State U. Alumni Assn. Home: 293 Hennessey Ave Worthington OH 43085 Office: 2400 Olentangy River Rd Columbus OH 43210

STEMPEL, JOHN EMMERT, educator, journalist; b. Bloomington, Ind., May 6, 1903; s. Guido Hermann and Myrtle (Emmert) S.; A.B., Ind. U., 1923, postgrad., 1926-27; M.S. in Journalism, Columbia U., 1928; m. Mary Roberts Farmer, Aug. 30, 1928; children—John Dallas, Thomas Ritter. Reporter, Bloomington Evening World, 1917-19; instr. journalism, dir. publicity, Lafayette Coll., Easton, Pa., 1923-26; part time instr. journalism, Ind. U., 1925-27; asso. editor Bloomington Star, 1926-27; news editor Columbia U. Alumni News, 1927-30; staff N.Y. Sun, 1929-36; news and mng. editor Easton Express, 1936-38; prof. journalism, chmn. dept. Ind. U., 1938-68, prof. emeritus, 1968—; acting ednl. adviser Def. Information Sch., 1968-69. Recipient Bronze medal Columbia Sch. Journalism; Distinguished Alumni Service award Ind. U., 1972; named Ind. Newspaper Man of Yr., 1968; named to Ind. Journalism Hall of Fame, 1970. Mem. Assn. Edn. for Journalism, Internat. Typog. Union, Greater Bloomington C. of C. (acting exec. v.p. 1977), Phi Kappa Psi, Sigma Delta Chi (past nat. pres.). Democrat. Episcopalian. Mason. Clubs: Rotary (past dist. gov., ex-chmn. Rotary Internat. Mag. com., publ. com.); Indpls. Press; University (Ind. U.). Compiled (with N.P. Poynter) The Indiana Daily Student Style Book, 1923 (revised several times). Author textbook. Contbr. to journalism publs. Home: 924 Atwater Ave Bloomington IN 47401

STENERSON, ORVILLE, educator; b. Dodge, N.D., July 9, 1918; s. Erick and Christina (Knutson) S.; B.A., Concordia Coll., 1956; M.A., U. N.D., 1966; m. Beatrice Marie Nygaard, June 21, 1959; children—John Orville, Daniel Erick. Tchr. English, Dodge High Sch., 1956-57; tchr. social sci. and English, Hettinger (N.D.) High Sch., 1959-66; instr. philosophy, chmn. humanities dept. Bismarck (N.D.) Jr. Coll., 1966—. Dist. v.p. Am. Luth. Ch. Men, 1963-64; mem. N.D. Council for Humanities and Pub. Issues, 1973—. Research asst. N.D. Republican party, 1966-68; precinct chmn. Burleigh County Rep. party, 1974—. Mem. Bismarck Jr. Coll. Edn. Assn. Home: 604 E Turnpike Ave Bismarck ND 58501

STENSTROP, ERNEST, architect; b. Chgo., Mar. 29, 1927; s. Carl Peter and Emma Federicka (Jensen) S.; B.A., U. Ill., 1951; m. Lois Lillian Lavelle, May 9, 1953; children—Linda Sue, Leslie Ann; m. 2d, Margaret K. Ewald, Dec. 4, 1971; 1 dau., Victoria Kay. Archtl. designer Chgo. Park Dist., 1953-64; designer, project architect Lawrence Monberg Assn., archtl. firm, Kenosha, Wis., 1964-65; project mgr. A.M. Kinney Assn. Inc., archtl. engring. cons., Skokie, Ill., 1965-68; project mgr. real estate and constrn. div. IBM Corp., Chgo., 1968—. Served with AUS, 1945-47. Mem. AIA (com. architects in industry), Park Ridge Art League (pres. 1970-71). Mason. Home: 416 E Hawthorne Ave Arlington Heights IL 60004 Office: One IBM Plaza Chicago IL 60610

STENVIG, CHARLES S., mayor; b. Mpls., Jan. 16, 1928; s. Selmer and Myrtle (Lee) S.; B.A., Augsburg Coll., 1951; postgrad. Juvenile Officers Inst., U. Minn., 1960; m. Audrey L. Thompson, Aug. 6, 1951; children—Terri, Tracy, Todd, Thomas. With Mpls. Police Dept., 1955-69; mayor, Mpls., 1969-74, 76—. Vice pres. Internat. Conf. Police Assn., 1966-69. Served with AUS, 1946-47. Recipient Reverence for Law award Eagles, 1969, Nat. Gold medal of merit VFW, 1972. Mem. Police Officers Fedn. Mpls. (pres. 1965-69), VFW (nat. security com.), Am. Legion, Sons of Norway. Methodist. Clubs: Masons, Shrine. Home: 5604 35th Ave S Minneapolis MN 55417 Office: 127 City Hall Minneapolis MN 55415

STENZ, LAWRENCE HERBERT, mech. engr., engring. co. exec.; b. Milw., Mar. 11, 1930; s. Arthur J. and Caroline A. (Bunzel) S.; certificate Milw. Sch. Engring., 1956; Archtl. Engring. degree U. Wis., 1956; m. Patricia Helen Lipski, Apr. 26, 1952; children—Gary A., David J., Greg L., Timothy J., Jeffrey L., Lawrence A. Mech. designer Gates, Weiss, Kramer, Inc., Milw., 1954-57, Schutte, Phillips, Mochon, Inc., Milw., 1957-61; chief engr., pres. Stenz Assos., Inc., Milw., 1961—. Cons. to Hist. Soc., Greenfield, Wis., 1966—. Active in local politics. Served with USMC, 1948-51; Korea. Decorated Purple Heart. Registered profl. engr., Wis. Mem. Am. Soc. San. Engrs., Greenfield Jaycees (sec. 1959-67, Key Man award 1965, Community Service award 1966), Wis. Jaycees (Robert Olen Meml. award 1965), Greenfield, Met. Milw. chambers commerce, numerous sportsman's and gun clubs. Roman Catholic. Home and Office: Route 3 Box 334 Minocqua WI 54548

STEP, HANNAH SCHEUERMANN, guidance counselor; b. Nuremberg, Ger., July 22, 1932; d. Max and Hilda (Kaufman) Scheuermann; B.S., U. Nebr., Omaha, 1954; M.S., Butler U., Indpls.,

1976; m. Eugene L. Step, Dec. 27, 1953; children—Steven, Michael, Jonathan. Tchr., Ft. Knox, Ky., 1954-57, Indpls. pub. schs., 1957-58; pvt. practice psychol. and guidance counseling, Indpls., 1976—; vol. Women's Center, Ind. U. - Purdue U., 1976—. Mem. allocations com. Indpls. United Way, 1976-77; bd. dirs. Indpls. Children's Bur., Hooverwood Guild. Mem. Am. Personnel and Guidance Assn., Am. Assn. Sex Educators, Counselors and Therapists. Address: 1131 Pimbury Ct Indianapolis IN 46260

STEPAN, ALFRED CHARLES, JR., chem. mfg. exec.; b. N.Y.C., Apr. 17, 1909; s. Alfred Charles and Charlotte (Corbett) S.; B.A., U. Notre Dame, 1931, LL.D., 1963; postgrad. Northwestern U., 1931-33, Armour Inst. Tech., 1933-34; m. Mary Louise Quinn, Feb. 10, 1934; children—Marilee (Mrs. Richard Wehman), Alfred III, Quinn, Stratford, Charlotte (Mrs. Joseph Flanagan), Paul, John. Founder, Stepan Chem. Co., 1932, pres., 1932-73, chmn., chief exec. officer, 1973—; dir. 1st Nat. Bank of Winnetka. Bd. dirs. Chgo. Cath. Charities, Ravinia Festival Assn., Lyric Opera of Chgo.; pres. Opera Sch. Chgo.; vis. com. humanities U. Chgo.; trustee U. Notre Dame, Chgo. Orchestral Assn. Republican. Clubs: Chicago, Arts, Commercial (Chgo.); Glen View (Golf, Ill.); Bob O'Link Golf, Exmoor Country (Highland Park, Ill.); Everglades, Bath and Tennis, Seminole Golf (Palm Beach, Fla.). Home: 76 Woodley Rd Winnetka IL 60093 also 212 Via Palma Palm Beach FL Office: Edens and Winnetka Northfield IL 60093

STEPAN, FRANK QUINN, chem. co. exec.; b. Chgo., Oct. 24, 1937; s. Alfred Charles and Mary Louise (Quinn) S.; A.B., U. Notre Dame, 1959; M.B.A., U. Chgo., 1963; m. Jean Finn, Aug. 23, 1958; children—Jeanne, Frank Quinn, Todd, Jennifer, Lisa, Colleen, Alfred, Richard. Salesman Indsl. Chems. div. Stepan Chem. Co., Northfield, Ill., 1961-63, mgr. internat. dept., 1964-66, v.p. corporate planning, 1967-69, v.p., gen. mgr. Indsl. Chems. div., 1970-73, pres., 1974—, also dir.; dir. Kona Communications, Inc. Trustee Loyola Acad.; mem. liberal arts council Notre Dame U., South Bend, Ind., 1972—. Served to 1st lt. AUS, 1959-61. Clubs: Economic (Chgo.); Exmoor (Highland Park, Ill.). Home: 200 Linden St Winnetka IL 60093 Office: Stepan Chem Co Edens and Winnetka Sts Northfield IL 60093

STEPEK, DANIEL THOMAS, lawyer; b. Highland Park, Mich., Jan. 26, 1944; s. Frank Thomas and Agnes (Sasinowski) S.; B.A., Wayne State U., 1967, J.D., 1969; m. Susan Beasley, Sept. 11, 1965; 1 son, Peter Daniel. Admitted to Mich. bar, 1969, since practiced in Mt. Clemens; mem. firm Daner, Freeman, McKenzie & Matthews, Mt. Clemens, 1970—. Bd. dirs. Macomb County Legal Aid Bur., 1972—. Mem. Am., Macomb County (dir.) bar assns., State Bar Mich. (regional chmn. 1971, council mem. 1971—, chmn. young lawyers sect.; mem. bd. commrs. 1977—, rep. assembly 1977—), Delta Theta Phi. Home: 134 Moross Mt Clemens MI 48043 Office: 1 S Gratiot Ave Mt Clemens MI 48043

STEPHAN, JAMES WILBER, ret. hosp. cons., educator; b. Cleve., July 27, 1911; s. Walter George and May (Storer) S.; B.A., Colgate U., 1933; M.B.A., U. Chgo., 1934; postgrad. Western Res. U., 1933-34; m. Margaret C. Ross, Oct. 1, 1937; children—James Ross, Walter George, Gordon Ross. Asst. personnel dir. Cleveland St. Ry. Co., Ohio, 1934-36; personnel dir. Cleve. City Hosp., 1936-37; project dir. CSC, Cleve., 1937-38; asst. dir. New Haven Hosp., 1939-43; dir. Aultman Hosp., Canton, Ohio, 1943-46; prof. program in hosp. and health care adminstrn. U. Minn., Mpls., 1946-76; cons. James A. Hamilton Assos., Inc., Mpls., 1947-76, pres., 1966-74, chmn. bd., 1974-76; vis. prof. various univs., U.S., Sao Paulo, Brazil, Chile, Mexico; mem. WHO Mission To Nicaragua, 1973; mem. adv. com. on hosp. effectiveness HEW, 1968. Mem. Citizen League Mpls., 1947—. Fellow Am. Coll. Hosp. Adminstrs.; mem. Am. Assn. Hosp. Consultants (pres. 1968-70), Minn. Hosp. Assn. (pres. 1970-71), Internat. Hosp. Fedn., Assn. U. Programs in Hosp. Adminstrn. Contbr. articles to profl. lit. Home: 230 Valley View Pl Minneapolis MN 55419

STEPHENS, BEULAH JANE, guidance counselor; b. Grabill, Ind., May 8, 1930; d. William Henry and Wilma Liechty (Beer) Bertsch; B.A., Heidelberg Coll., 1954; M.A., St. Francis Coll., 1967; postgrad. Ball State U., 1956-57, Purdue U., 1953, LaVerne Coll., 1974; m. James Agustus Stephens, Sept. 12, 1959; children—Theresa Jane (dec.), Thomas James, Holly Jane (dec.). Home demonstration agt. co-op. Extension Service Purdue U., Plymouth, Ind., 1954-56; dietician Ball State U., Muncie, Ind., 1956-57; dir. Christian edn. St. John's United Ch. of Christ, Fort Wayne, Ind., 1957-60; home economist Food Mktg. Corp., Fort Wayne, 1960-62; home economist, dir. Project Spark, Fort Wayne Urban League, 1963-65; extension worker Fort Wayne pub. schs., 1966-67, tchr., 1967-69, guidance counselor, 1969—. Youth fellowship, student council advisor, tailoring instr. Regional Vocat. Center; state pres. Internat. Farm Youth Exchange; deaconess United Ch. of Christ, 1978; mem. nat. host com. Ind. Internat. 4-H Youth Exchange Assn. Internat. Farm Youth Exchange student from Ind. to Ger., 1952. Mem. Scottsville Civic Assn. (dir. 1970-71), NEA, Am. Sch. Counselors Assn., Am., Ind. personnel guidance assns., Am. Home Econs. Assn., Hesperian Literacy Soc. (sec. 1953). Office: 2825 Fairfield Ave Fort Wayne IN 46807

STEPHENS, JERRY OSCAR, lawyer; b. Warren, Ohio, Sept. 26, 1928; s. Oscar Alverton and Alice Josephine (Heeg) S.; B.A., Denison U., 1950; J.D., Ohio No. U., 1952; m. Mildred A. Spicer, Aug. 22, 1972; children—Karen, Jay, Julie, Ben. Admitted to Ohio bar, 1952; pvt. practice law, Youngstown, O., 1954—. Served with C.I.C., AUS, 1952-54. Mem. Am., Ohio, Mahoning County bar assns., Lawyer-Pilots Bar Assn., Nat. Assn. R.R. Trial Counsel, Internat. Assn. Ins. Counsel. Elk, Rotarian. Home: 1052 Genessee St Youngstown OH 44511 Office: Union National Bank Bldg Youngstown OH 44503

STEPHENS, JOHN FIRTH, chem. engr.; b. Covington, Ky., Dec. 22, 1910; s. John Tupman and Emma LaPorte (Firth) S.; B.S., U. Tenn., 1935; m. Julia Edna Graper Lancaster, Dec. 24, 1939. Coop. engring. student Tenn. Eastman Corp., Kingsport, 1930-34; lab. asst. TVA, Knoxville, Tenn., 1934; sales engr. Warren Candies, Inc., Knoxville, 1935-36; chemist Am. Bemberg Corp., Elizabethton, Tenn., 1937-42; line foreman, volunteer ordnance works Hercules Powder Co., Tyner, Tenn., 1942-44; sr. chemist Clinton Engring. Works, Tenn. Eastman Corp., Oak Ridge, 1944-46; indsl. hygienist Carbide & Carbon Chem. Corp., Oak Ridge, 1946-49; asst. indsl. hygienist City Bur. Indsl. Hygiene, Detroit, 1949-51; sr. indsl. hygienist Gen. Motors Corp., Warren, Mich., 1951-67, research engr., indsl. hygiene dept., 1967-76; indsl. hygiene cons., 1976—. Mem. planning com., air pollution control conf. Oakland U., Rochester, Mich., 1966-77; pres. Lorland Civic Assn., Inc., Detroit, 1967-68; mem. bd. connectional outreach Detroit Conf. United Meth. Ch. Diplomate Am. Acad. Indsl. Hygiene. Fellow Am. Inst. Chemists; mem. Am. Indsl. Hygiene Assn., Am. Chem. Soc., Engring. Soc. Detroit, Mich. Indsl. Hygiene Soc., Delta Sigma Phi. Clubs: Econ. of Detroit; Fairlane (Ingleside). Republican. Author: (with others) Air Pollution Manual, Part I, Evaluation, 2d edit., 1972. Home and office: 14970 Lindsay St Detroit MI 48227

STEPHENS, PAUL ALFRED, dentist; b. Muskogee, Okla., Feb. 28, 1921; s. Lonny and Maudie Janie (Wynn) S.; B.S. cum laude, Howard U., 1942, D.D.S., 1945; m. Lola Helena Byrd, May 7, 1950; children—Marsha (Mrs. Ronald Monah), Paul Alfred, Derek M. Instr. dentistry Howard U., Washington, 1945-46; gen. practice dentistry, Gary, Ind., 1947—; dir. Summit Labs., Indpls.; chmn. bd. Miracle Products, Inc., Gary. Sec., Gary Ind. Sch. Bldg. Corp., 1967—; pres. Bd. Health, 1973—; mem. Ind. State Bd. Dental Examiners, 1975—. Mem. adv. bd. Ind. U.-Purdue U. Calumet campus, 1973. Bd. dirs. Urban League N.W. Ind. Served with AUS, 1942-44. Fellow Acad. Gen. Dentistry (pres. chpt. 1973, nat. chmn. dental care com. 1977), Am. Coll. Dentists; mem. C. of C., Nat., Am., N.W. Ind. (dir., pres. 1976-77) dental assns., Am. Soc. Anesthesia in Dentistry, Am. Acad. Radiology, Alpha Phi Alpha. Baptist. Home: 1901 Taft St Gary IN 46404 Office: 2200 Grant St Gary IN 46404

STEPHENS, ROBERT HOOD, lawyer; b. Springfield, Ill., Jan. 18, 1937; s. Robert Allan and Helen Hood (Solenberger) S.; B.A., Colo. Coll., 1959; J.D., Stanford, 1962; m. Linda Ruth Bartscht, May 8, 1965; 1 son, Robert Hursh. Admitted to Ill. bar, 1963, practiced in Springfield, 1963—; asst. state's atty. Sangamon County, Springfield, Ill., 1963-65; mem. firm Brown, Hay and Stephens, 1965—; dir. Central Individual Mausoleum Co., Springfield. Sec., Jr. Achievement of Sangamon Valley, Ill., 1971; mem. Springfield Fire Adv. Council, chmn., 1975; trustee Lincoln Land Community Coll., 1970—, chmn., 1972-73; bd. dirs. Aid to Retarded Citizens Sangamon and Menard Counties, 1975—, Ill. Community Coll. Trustees Assn., 1975—. Mem. Am., Ill., Sangamon County bar assns., Vachel Lindsay Assn. (dir. 1965—), Phi Gamma Delta, Phi Delta Phi. Republican. Conglist. Home: 65 Andover Dr Springfield IL 62704 Office: 700 First National Bank Bldg Springfield IL 62701

STEPHENS, THOMAS MARON, educator; b. Youngstown, Ohio, June 15, 1931; s. Thomas and Mary (Hanna) S.; B.S., Youngstown Coll., 1955; M.Ed., Kent State U., 1957; D.Ed., U. Pitts., 1966; m. Evelyn Kleshock, July 1, 1955. Asso. prof. edn. U. Pitts., 1966-70; prof. edn., chmn. dept. exceptional children Ohio State U., 1970—. Mem. Higher Edn. Consortium for Spl. Edn., chmn., 1976-77. U.S. Office of edn. fellow, 1964-65. Mem. State Dirs. for Gifted (pres. 1962-63), Council Exceptional Children (gov.), Council Children with Behavioral Disorders (pres. 1972-73). Author: Directive Teaching of Children with Learning and Behavioral Handicaps, 2d edit., 1975; Implementing Behavioral Approaches in Elementary and Secondary Schools, 1975; Teaching Skills to Children with Learning and Behavioral Disorders, 1977; Directive Teaching of Language, Reading, Arithmetic and Social Skills: A Handbook, 1977; Prescription for Teaching Social Behavior, 1978. Dir. of Jour. Sch. Psychology, 1965-75; asso. editor Exceptional Children Jour., Behavior Disorder Jour. Contbr. articles profl. jours. Home: 1753 Blue Ash Pl Columbus OH 43229

STEPHENSON, I(SAAC) WATSON, III, pilot; b. Hartford, Conn., May 1, 1933; s. Isaac Watson and Molly (George) S.; grad. Adm. Farragut Acad., 1952, Spartan Coll. Aeros., 1954; m. Susan Lindsay, Nov. 26, 1966; 1 son, Isaac Watson IV. Founder Monterey Air Transport (Calif.), 1954, pres., 1954-56; with Bahamas Airways, Nassau, 1958-59; capt. Aerotron Radio, Tulsa, 1959-61; sales rep. Marinette & Menominee Box Co., Marinette, Wis., 1961-62; salesman Indian Aviation, Inc., Menominee, Mich., 1962; chief pilot, ops. mgr. Stephenson Air Taxi, Menominee, 1962-63; owner Carib-Pacific Aviation, Menominee, 1963-65; with Island Air, St. Thomas, Virgin Islands, 1965-67; pilot, dir. maintenance V.I. Airways, St. Croix, Virgin Islands, 1967; pilot, sales rep. Fontana Aviation, Iron Mountain, Mich., 1967-77. Pres. Menominee Hangar Co., 1961-67. Commodore, Area I Boy Scouts Am. Sea Explorers, 1973-74. Served with AUS, 1956-58. Mem. Menominee County Hist. Soc. (dir. 1970—), Aircraft Owners and Pilots Assn., U.S. Seaplane Pilots Assn. (dir. 1972—), Nat. Aeros. Assn., Lake Michigan Yachting Assn., N. Am. Yacht Racing Union. Clubs: M&M Yacht (commodore 1971-72), Rotary. Columnist, "Waterfront News,", and Wings N'Things Menominee Herald Leader, 1969-76. Contbr. photographs and articles on aviation and yachting to newspapers and mags. Home: 1818 1st St Menominee MI 49858

STEPHENSON, JAMES OLIVER, chem. co. exec.; b. Ft. McKinley, Philippines, July 7, 1933; s. James Oliver and Lois (Gregory) S.; B.S., U. Mo., 1955; M.B.A., N.Y. U., 1962; m. Katherine Gay Krughoff, Jan. 13, 1962; children—Suzanne, James Oliver. With Richardson Merrell, Inc., N.Y.C., 1960-63, Hooker Chem. Co., N.Y.C., 1964-68; pres. Corporate Planners, San Francisco, 1968-72; dir. planning and acquisitions Peabody Internat., N.Y.C., 1972-75; gen. mgr. acquisitions Mallinckrodt, Inc., St. Louis, 1975—. Served as lt., arty., AUS, 1955-57. Mem. Assn. Corporate Growth N.Y.C., Nat. Soc. Corporate Planning, Corporate Planners Assn. Club: River Bend Tennis Assn. Home: 59 River Bend Dr Chesterfield MO 63017 Office: 675 Brown Rd Saint Louis MO 63134

STEPHENSON, RALPH LAWRENCE, environ. engr.; b. Wichita, Kans., Dec. 12, 1939; s. Chester Delbert and Neva Maxine S.; B.S. in Civil Engring., U. Kans., 1963, M.S. in Environ. Engring., 1964; m. Earlene Williams, Sept. 25, 1974; 1 dau., Seana Elizabeth. Civil engr. Wichita Water Dept., 1964-65; asst. chief Water Supply div. Kansas City (Mo.) Water Dept., 1965-67; design group leader Smith & Loveless div. Union Tank Car Co., Lenexa, Kans., 1967-70; chief environ. engr. Butler, Fairman & Senfert, Indpls., 1970-77; chief environ. engr. M.D. Wessler & Assos., Indpls., 1977—, also sec. Constable Sedgwick County (Kans.), 1962-64. Registered profl. engr., Ind., Mo. USPHS grantee, 1963. Mem. Water Pollution Control Fedn., Am. Water Works Assn., ASCE (service award 1976). Democrat. Designer of water and sewerage systems for communities in Ind., Mo., Kans. Contbr. articles in field to profl. jours. Home: 7909 Hoover Ln Indianapolis IN 46260 Office: 535 Turtle Creek Executive Center Indianapolis IN 46227

STEPP, DONALD LEWIS, assn. exec.; b. Cin., July 14, 1937; s. Tilden Earl and Olga (Trivett) S.; student Columbus Coll. Art and Design, 1960-61; m. Nancy Lynn Shuman, May 3, 1957; 1 son, Terry Lee. Staff, Timken Roller Bearing Co., Columbus, Ohio, 1960-61; advt. mgr. Lennox Heating & Air Conditioning Co., Marshalltown, Iowa, 1962-71; staff Homs, Blitz & Strauss, Miami, Fla., also freelance designer, 1971-72; advt. mgr. Ames Lawn & Garden Tools Co., Parkersburg, W. Va., 1972; mktg. mgr. Nat. Retail Hardware Assn., Indpls., 1973—. Served with USNR, 1954-59. Republican. Lutheran. Clubs: Masons (32 deg.), Advt. Indpls. Home: 7811 Kimlough Dr Indianapolis IN 46240 Office: 770 N High School Rd Indianapolis IN 46224

STERGIOS, PAUL JAMES, lawyer; b. Ramsey, Ohio, Sept. 10, 1931; s. George and Evangeline (Sharkavos) S.; B.S., Ohio State U., 1953, J.D. summa cum laude, 1960; m. Miletsa Miric, June 13, 1959; 1 son, Pericles G. With Mead Corp., Dayton, Ohio, 1955-58; admitted to Ohio bar, 1961; practiced in Canton, 1961-63, Massillon, 1963—; mem. firm Christoff & Stergios, Massillon, 1963—; dir. State Bank Co., Midwestern Equipment, Inc., Screen Heating Transformers, Inc. Chmn., Massillon City Planning Commn., 1971-75; councilman-at-large, Massillon, 1976—; mem. exec. com. Stark County (Ohio) Democratic Com., 1972—. Trustee Doctors Hosp., Massillon, Massillon chpt. ARC, 1972-73. Served with AUS, 1953-55. Mem. Am., Ohio, Massillon, Stark County bar assns., Am. Trial Lawyers Assn., Order Am. Hellenic Progressive Assn. Home: 1241 Burd St NE Massillon OH 44646 Office: Suite 301 Giltz Bldg 121 Lincoln Way E Massillon OH 44646

STERLING, LEROY FARWELL, educator; b. Williamsport, Pa., Dec. 25, 1929; s. Leroy Peck and Ethel Virginia (Rielly) S.; B.S., U. Ill., 1955; M.S., 1956, Ph.D., 1960; m. Ann Childs Carter, Aug. 25, 1953; children—Donald, Charles, Elizabeth. Asso. prof. health edn. Central Mich. U., Mount Pleasant, 1959-65, prof. health edn., 1969—; asso. prof. phys. edn. U. Fla., Gainesville, 1965-69. Served with USAF, 1948-49, 51-52. Fellow Am. Coll. Sports Medicine; mem. Blue Key, Phi Epsilon Kappa, Phi Delta Kappa, Kappa Delta Pi, Eta Sigma Gamma. Presbyn. Lion. Home: 1423 Ridge Rd Mount Pleasant MI 48858

STERN, CLARENCE A., historian, educator; b. McCluskey, N.D., Jan. 6, 1913; s. Adam M. and Minnie (Krieger) S.; A.B. salutatorian, Eastern Mich. U., 1934; M.A., Wayne State U., 1938; postgrad. LaSalle Extension U., 1947-49; Ph.D., U. Nebr., 1958; m. Kathleen Gober, Feb. 20, 1946. Tchr. social sci. Ecorse (Mich.) Pub. Schs., 1934-37; tchr. history and social sci. Detroit Pub. Schs., 1937-42, River Rouge (Mich.) Pub. Schs., 1954-55; asst. prof. history and polit. sci. Coll. Engring., Lawrence Inst. Tech., Detroit, 1946-50; asst., dept. history U. Nebr., 1951-53; asso. prof. history polit. sci. Wayne (Nebr.) State Coll., 1958-65; asso. prof. constl. and polit. party history, U.S., Europe, U. Wis., Oshkosh, 1965—, asso. prof. history U. Wis., Fond du Lac, 1975—. Ford Found. Am. Polit. Sci. Assn. grantee U. Ind., 1962. Mem. AAUP (pres. chpt. 65), Am. Hist. Assn., Orgn. Am. Historians, Am. Polit. Sci. Assn., ACLU, Wis. Civil Liberties Union (acad. freedom com. Pi Alpha Theta, Pi Gamma Mu, Kappa Delta Pi. Author: Republican Heyday: Republicanism Through the McKinley Years, 1962, 69; Resurgent Republicanism: The Handiwork of Hanna, 1963, 68; Golden Republi The Crusade for Hard Money, 1964, 70; Protectionist Republicanism: Republican Tariff Policy in the McKinley Period, Home: 1625 Elmwood Ave Oshkosh WI 54901 PO Box 2294 Oshkosh WI 54901

STERN, RICHARD ALAN, psychologist, camp dir.; b. Chgo., Nov. 18, 1947; s. Richard Eisendrath and Babette (Kaplan) S.; B.A. in Psychology, U. Mich., 1968; M.A. in Psychology, Temple U., 1972. Psychology intern Ill. State Psychiat. Inst., 1972-73; therapist, case-worker Jewish Children's Bur. Chgo., 1974-76; dir. older adolescent program Lawrence Hall Sch. for Boys, Chgo., 1976—; owner, dir. Camp Sullivan, Eagle River, Wis., 1975—; pvt. practice family and individual psychotherapy, Chgo., 1974—; lectr. psychology Loyola U., Chgo., 1973. Treas. Rogers Park Community Center, 1975—. Registered social worker, Ill. Mem. Am. Psychol. Assn. (asso.), Am. Camping Assn. Asso. editor The Mich. Daily, 1967-68. Contbr. book rev. to periodicals. Home: 7439 N Ashland Ave Chicago IL 60626 Office: 4833 N Francisco Ave Chicago IL 60625

STERNBERG, RICHARD IRA, psychologist; b. Bklyn., Dec. 25, 1948; s. Jay and Ray S.; B.A., Yeshiva U., 1970; M.A., City Coll. N.Y.; Ph.D., Calif. Sch. Profl. Psychology, 1976. Mem. grad faculty City Coll. N.Y., 1972-74; psychol. intern, psychologist, program evaluation cons. Fresno (Calif.) Community Hosp., 1974-76; clin. and forensic psychologist Center For Forensic Psychiatry, Ann Arbor, Mich., 1976—; instr. Eastern Mich. U., 1977-78; pvt. practice psychology, Ann Arbor, 1976—; certified psychologist, Mich., sch. psychologist, N.Y.; N.Y. State Regents scholar, 1970-72. Mem. Am., Calif. psychol. assns., Yeshiva Coll. Alumni Assn. (exec. bd. 1970-72), City Coll. Alumni Assn., Calif. Sch. Profl. Psychology Alumni Assn. Editorial rev. bd. Am. Psychologist, 1977—, Nat. Register of Health Service Providers in Psychology, 1976—. Home: 1 320 Wisteria Dr #B-4622 Ann Arbor MI 48104 Office: PO Box 2060 Center Forensic Psychiatry Ann Arbor MI 48104

STERR, AMBROSE MELVIN, dentist; b. Lomira, Wis., July 8, 1918; s. Melvin and Mayme (Hesprich) S.; B.S., Marquette U., 1938, D.D.S., 1942; m. Lois Ann Scheer, Feb. 1, 1947; children—William, Tom, James, John, Jennifer, Richard, Lisa, Marcia. Practice dentistry, DePere, Wis., 1946—; chief of dental staff St. Vincents Hosp. Dist. chmn. Rotary Found., 1970-73. Served from lt. to maj., Dental Corps, AUS, 1942-46. Decorated Bronze Star medal. Paul Harris fellow Rotary Internat. Fellow Internat. Coll. Dentists; mem. Am. Soc. Preventive Dentistry (dir. Wis. chpt.), Am. (del.), Wis. (pres. 1974-75, dir.) dental assns., Fox River Valley (pres.), Brown Door Kewanee (pres.) dental socs., Acad. Gen. Dentistry, Am. Soc. Dentistry for Children, Chgo. Dental Soc. (asso.), Greater Milw. Dental Assn., Holy Name Soc., Am. Legion. K.C. (4 deg.), Rotarian (pres., gov. dist. 1976-77). Club: Oneida Country. Home: 823 N Broadway DePere WI 54115 Office: 412 Charles St DePere WI 54115

STETSON, JOHN BENJAMIN BLANK, anesthesiologist, educator; b. Chgo., Mar. 18, 1927; s. Louis Blank and Dorothy (Cohen) S.; student U. Chgo., 1941-43, 45-46; M.D., Harvard U., 1951; m. Gwyneth Evans, Dec. 22, 1966; children—Diana S., Dana L., Jonathan O. Intern, U. Utah Hosp., 1951-52; resident Mass. Gen. Hosp., Lowell Gen. Hosp., 1952-54; instr. anesthesiology U. Mich., 1954-57; practice medicine specializing in anesthesiology, Johnson City, Tenn., 1957-59; instr. anesthesiology Harvard Med. Sch., Children's Hosp., 1959-65; asst. prof., dir. vital function lab. U. Ind. Med. Sch., 1965-67; asso. prof., asso. dir. dept. anesthesiology Ohio State U. Sch. Medicine, 1967-68; dir. clin. pharmacology, acting med. dir. Strasenburgh Labs., Rochester, N.Y., 1968-70; asso. anesthesiologist Strong Meml. Hosp., U. Rochester (N.Y.), 1970-76; dir. clin. research Arnarstone Labs., Inc., Mt. Prospect, Ill., 1976-77; prof. Rush Med. Coll., 1977—; cons. Roswell Park Meml. Inst., Buffalo, 1968—. Served with USNR, 1943-45. FDA grantee, 1973-76, Jackson Johnson research fellow in biochemistry Washington U., St. Louis, 1947—; diplomate Am. Bd. Anesthesiologists. Fellow Am. Coll. Anesthesiologists; mem. Canadian Anaesthetist's Soc., Assn. Anaesthetists Gt. Britain and Ireland, Internat. Anesthesia Research Soc., Soc. Critical Care Medicine, Pan Am. Med. Assn., Am. Soc. Anesthesiologists (past chmn. history and archives com.). Republican. Unitarian. Editor: Cardiovascular Problems, 1963; Ventilation in Anesthesiology, 1965; Metabolism In Anesthesiology, 1967; Prolonged Tracheal Intubation, 1970; (with P. R. Swyer) Neonatal Intensive Care, 1976; contbr. articles to profl. jours. Office: Rush-Presbyterian-St Lukes Med Center Chicago IL 60612

STEUER, THOMAS MICHAEL, pub. relations exec.; b. Karlsruhe, Germany, Apr. 8, 1937; s. Ulrick B. and Edith (Rosenthal) S.; came to U.S., 1937, naturalized, 1944; B.A., Ind. U., 1959; m. Leah Lipis, Aug. 31, 1958; children—Michael E., Daniel B., Andrew D. Account exec. Daniel J. Edelman & Assos., Chgo., 1959-61, Pub. Relations Bd., Chgo., 1961-65; account supr. Harshe-Rotman & Druck, Chgo., 1966-71; pres. Compass 4 Pub. Relations, Chgo., 1971-73; pres., chief exec. officer Pub. Relations Center, Inc., Chgo., 1973—; pub. relations counselor, 1971—. Bd. dirs. The Thresholds, Chgo., 1964-74. Recipient Golden Trumpet awards Pub. Relations Soc. Am., 1968, 72. Mem. Pub. Relations Soc. Am. Jewish. Home: 1086 Ridgewood Dr Highland Park IL 60035 Office: 233 E Erie St Suite 2500 Chicago IL 60611

STEVENS, ANITA EILEEN, librarian; b. Decatur, Ill., July 24, 1943; d. Elmer Hubert and Josephine Elizabeth (Spittler) Fawley; B.S., Ill. State U., Normal, 1965, M.Ed., 1976; m. Milton Gray Stevens, Jan. 25, 1964. Tchr. pub. schs., Decatur, Ill., 1964-70, librarian, 1970—. Past vol. RAPP crisis phone; Decatur Meml. Hosp. Aux., 1971-74; mem. adminstrv. bd., council on ministries and bd. discipleship United Meth. Ch. Mem. Decatur, Ill. edn. assns., Ill. Library Assn., NEA, Kappa Delta Pi. Methodist (del. ann. conf. 1976). Home: 12 Maple Ct Decatur IL 62526 Office: 3789 Water St N Decatur IL 62526

STEVENS, EDWIN DANIEL, state legislator; b. Raleigh, N.C., May 2, 1943; s. Ross Oliver and Rose Elizabeth (Askew) S.; B.S., U. Mich., 1965, M.A., 1968; J.D., Thomas M. Cooley Law Sch., 1977; m. Karen Diane Colby, Jan. 22, 1966; children—Joseph Oliver, Kirsten Ross. Tchr. Whitmore Lake (Mich.) Pub. Schs., 1965-67; pres. Summer Sci., Inc., Ann Arbor, Mich., 1967-73; pres. real estate firm; dir. Sci. Land Co.; mem. Mich. Ho. Reps., 1975—, now asst. minority floor leader; cons. Community Systems Found.; founder Summer Sci. Camp. Trustee Atlanta (Mich.) Community Sch. Bd., 1972-73; legislative analyst Mich. Ho. Reps., 1973. Recipient sci. tchr. award, Edison Found., 1967. Mem. State Bar Mich., Atlanta (Mich.) C. of C. (v.p. 1972-73). Club: Lions. Home: State St Atlanta MI 49709 Office: Box 405 Atlanta MI 49709

STEVENS, GARY GROSSMAN, radio broadcasting exec.; b. Buffalo, Apr. 5, 1940; s. Leslie I. and Gertrude (Mattis) Grossman; student U. Miami, 1958-61; m. Frances Johnson, Nov. 11, 1966; children—Kristin, Victoria, Christopher. Radio personality WFUN, Miami, 1960-61, WIL, St. Louis, 1961-63, WKNR, Detroit, 1963-65, WMCA, N.Y.C., 1965-68; pres. Interprogram, Ltd., Lugano, Switzerland, 1968-70; gen. mgr. KRIZ, Phoenix, 1970-74; corp. v.p. Doubleday Broadcasting, N.Y.C., 1973-76, sr. v.p., 1976-77, pres., 1977—; v.p., gen. mgr. KDWB, St. Paul, 1973—; dir. Radio Advt. Reps., Inc. (Westinghouse); chmn. Internat. Radio Programming Conf., Toronto, Ont., Can. Mem. Minn. Press Council, 1977—; trustee Twin Cities Area Pub. TV Corp., 1977—. Served with USAF, 1962. Recipient VIP award Advt. Club Phoenix, 1971; named Nation's Top Contemporary Radio Personality, Billboard mag., 1966-67. Clubs: Arizona; Decathlon; Edina Country. Home: 5305 Kingsberry Dr Edina MN 55436 Office: 152 Radio Dr St Paul MN 55119

STEVENS, HAROLD RUSSELL, physician; b. Detroit, Nov. 18, 1930; s. Harold Russell and Etheleen Mae (Stone) S.; A.B., Albion Coll., 1951; M.D., U. Mich., 1955; m. Shirley Ann Sias, Sept. 30, 1950; children—Kirk Russell, Martha Lee. Intern Toledo Hosp., 1955-56, resident in anesthesiology 1960-62, attending anesthesiologist, 1962—, med. dir. respiratory therapy, 1966—, research asso. Inst. Med. Research, 1965-70; practice medicine specializing in anesthesiology, respiratory therapy, Toledo, 1962—; med. dir. respiratory therapy U. Toledo, 1971—, prof. respiratory therapy, 1974—; clin. asso. Med. Coll. Toledo, 1971—; dir. anesthesiology Mercy Hosp., Toledo, 1968—, med. co-dir. respiratory therapy, 1969—; dir. intensive care unit Toledo Hosp., 1975—. Health councilor Community Planning Council Northwestern Ohio, 1970-71. Trustee Maumee Valley Found. Served to capt. M.C., USAF, 1957-59. Diplomate Am. Bd. Anesthesiology. Mem. Acad. Medicine Toledo and Lucas County (councilor 1970-71), Am., Ohio med. assns., Am. Assn. Respiratory Therapy, Internat. Anesthesia Research Soc., Am., Toledo (pres. 1971) socs. anesthesiologists, Phi Beta Kappa, Alpha Omega Alpha. Mason (32 deg., Shriner). Contbr. articles to profl. jours. Home: 2149 Emkay Dr Toledo OH 43606 Office: 3939 Monroe St Toledo OH 43606

STEVENS, HOWARD PETER, cons. psychologist; b. Key West, Fla., Nov. 14, 1941; s. Howard Bernard and Alice (Reagan) S.; m. Sally Sullivan, May 15, 1965; children—Howard Arthur, Brian David. B.A., U. Dayton (Ohio), 1964, M.A., 1966. Intern, Dayton Psychiat. Hosp., 1966; licensed psychologist, Ohio. Staff psychologist U. Dayton Psychol. Services, 1967-73; cons. civil service City of Dayton, 1969-70; dir. law enforcement project Montgomery County, Ohio, 1973-74; cons. selection validation Monsanto Co., Goodyear Corp., Duriron, Dayton, 1967-72; v.p. SSS Cons., Inc., Dayton, 1973—. Mem. bd. Ta-Wa-Si, 1974; founder, chmn. bd. Ohio Inst. Photography. Mem. Am., Ohio psychol. assns., Am. Soc. Tng. Devel. Author: The College Game and How to Play It, 1967; author self-devel. monographs. Home: 1101 Greenridge Dr Kettering OH 45429 Office: SSS Consulting 2600 Far Hills Ave Dayton OH 45419

STEVENS, JOANNE, guidance counselor; b. Indpls., Ind., Nov. 4, 1939; s. Asa Neiley and Elizabeth (Boyd) Stevens; B.S. (Hanover fellow), Hanover Coll., 1961; M.S., Ind. U., 1965; postgrad. U. Edinburgh, 1970. Instr. Indpls. Pub. Schs., 1961-63, 65-67; asst. dean of women Nat. Music Camp, 1963-68; asst. program office, 1971-76; guidance counselor, dir. Arlington Heights (Ill.) Pub. Schs., 1967-69; guidance counselor Palatine High Sch. Dist. 211, 1969—. Active Best Off Broadway Community Theatre Group, 1976—; dir. chancel choir St. Mark's Lutheran Ch., Mount Prospect, 1976—; mem. adv. bd. Interlochen Center for Arts, 1971-72, 77—. Recipient William C. Mc Cormack award Indpls. 2d Presbyn. Ch., 1957. Mem. Am. Choral Dirs. Assn., P.E.O., Ill. Guidance and Personnel Assn., Nat., Ill. edn. assns., Am. Sch. Counselors Assn., Am. Coll. Personnel Assn., Ill. Guidance Personnel Assn., Ind. U. Alumni Assn., Hanover Coll. Alumni Assn., Am. Personnel and Guidance Assn. Presbyterian. Home: 809 N Wilke Rd Apt B Arlington Heights IL 60005 Office: 1100 W Schamburg Rd Schamburg IL 60193

STEVENS, MILDRED JULIUS (MRS. ROBERT LOUIS STEVENS), physician; b. Burdick, Kans., Apr. 21, 1923; d. Carl Anderson and Sene (Nelson) Julius; student Bethany Coll., 1941-42; B.S., Kans. U., 1945, M.D., 1947; m. Robert Louis Stevens, Apr. 4, 1947; children—Laura Bea, Victor Louis, Rhoads Elliott, Leah Jane, James David. Intern, St. Margaret's Hosp., Kansas City, Kans., 1947-48; pvt. practice, Garnett, Kans., 1948—; mem. staff Anderson County Hosp., chief of staff, 1961, 65, 73. Mem. Kans., Anderson County (pres. 1961, 65, 73) med. socs., AMA, World Med. Assn., Alpha Omega Alpha. Republican. Presbyterian. Author: Memories of Salem, 1974; Memories of Hebron, 1974; This I Believe, 1975; From Now On . . . (pen and ink sketches), 1977. Home: 346 W 4th St Garnett KS 66032 Office: 202 W 4th St Garnett KS 66032

STEVENS, ROBERT EUGENE, librarian; b. Mattoon, Ill., Mar. 15, 1928; s. William Franklin and Helen Murial (DeVore) S.; B.S., Eastern Ill. U., 1965; m. Mary Ellen Chapman, Nov. 25, 1948; children—Karol Ann, Kathie Lynn. Librarian, info. specialist U.S. Indsl. Chems. Co. div. Nat. Distbg. Corp., Tuscola, Ill., 1960—; night supr. Coles Publs., Mattoon, Ill., 1969—. Active United Fund campaign, Charleston, Ill., 1969—, youth reform and rehab. Human Relations Council. Bd. dirs. Big Bros., Coles County, 1974-76. Served with USNR, 1949-53. Mem. Ill. C. of C., Ill. Spl. Libraries Assn. Methodist (bd. dirs. 1972-74). Elk. Home: 2512 Village Rd Charleston IL 61920 Office: W Rt 36 Tuscola IL 61953

STEVENS, SUE CASSELL, chemist; b. Roanoke, Va.; d. Edward B. and Dora (Fox) Stevens; A.B., Goucher Coll., 1930; M.A., Columbia U., 1931, Ph.D., 1940. Research biochemist N.Y. Skin and Cancer Hosp., N.Y.C., 1932-35; biochemist Fifth Ave. Hosp., N.Y.C., 1935; research chemist Coll. Phys. and Surg., Columbia U., 1935-39; research chemist N.Y. Orthopaedic Hosp., N.Y.C., 1940-41; Cal. Milk Products Co., Gustine, 1941-43; research dairy chemist Golden State Co. Ltd., San Francisco, 1943-46. Swift & Co., Chgo., 1946-47; dir. research and quality control Steven Candy Kitchens, Chgo., 1947-48; asso. prof. chemistry, biology MacMurray Coll., 1948-49; chief biochemist VA Center, Dayton, Ohio, 1949-52, research biochemist, 1952-56; supr. research lab. VA Hosp., Lincoln, Nebr., 1956-65; dir. endocrine chemistry lab. Jewish Hosp. of St. Louis, 1965—; asst. prof. pathology Washington U. Sch. Medicine, 1967—; cons. clin. chemistry device classification panel Bur. Med. Devices, FDA, 1977—. Fellow Am. Inst. Chemists. AAAS; mem. Am. Chem. Soc., Am. Assn. Clin. Chemists (chmn. Midwest sect. 1965, councilor 1973), AAUW, Am. Soc. Quality Control (treas. St. Louis sect. 1973, sec. St. Louis 1974-75), Am. Soc. Clin. Pathology, N.Y. Acad. Scis., Sigma Xi, Sigma Delta Epsilon (nat. pres. 1964). Home: PO Box 4854 Field Sta St Louis MO 63108 Office: Jewish Hosp of St Louis 216 S Kingshighway St Louis MO 63110

STEVENSON, ADLAI EWING, III, lawyer, U.S. senator; b. Chgo., Oct. 10, 1930; s. Adlai Ewing and Ellen (Borden) S.; grad. Milton Acad., 1948; A.B., Harvard, 1952, LL.B., 1957; m. Nancy L. Anderson, June 25, 1955; children—Adlai Ewing IV, Lucy W., Katherine R., Warwick L. Admitted to Ill. bar, 1957; law clk. Ill. Supreme Ct., 1957-58; asso. firm Mayer, Friedlich, Spiess, Tierney, Brown & Platt, Chgo., 1958-66, partner, 1966-67; mem. Ill. Ho. of Reps., 1965-67; treas. State of Ill., Springfield, 1967-70; U.S. senator from Ill., 1970—. Served to capt. USMCR, 1952-54. Mem. Am., Ill., Chgo. bar assns., other assns, Home: Rural Route 1 Hanover IL 61041 Office: US Senate Washington DC 20510

STEVENSON, FORREST CAMP, JR., marriage counselor; b. Deming, N.Mex., July 4, 1922; s. Forrest Camp and Fern (Norris) S.; A.B., Park Coll., 1945; M.A., U. Detroit, 1964; M.R.E., Central Bapt. Sem., 1949, B.D., 1950, D.R.E., 1959; m. Bernice Freda Wells, June 3, 1952; children—Rita Fern, Paul Forrest, Eric Jon. Dean, Calvary Coll., Kansas City, Mo., 1955-64; pvt. practice marriage counseling, Allen Park, Mich., 1964-74; pres. Personality Dynamics, Inc., Southfield, Mich., 1974—. Served with U.S. Army, 1952-55. Decorated Bronze Star medal. Mem. Am. Assn. Marriage and Family Counselors, Am. Psychol. Assn., Interprofessional Assn. on Marriage, Divorce and the Family. Home: 11349 Culver Rd Brighton MI 48116

STEVENSON, FRANCES ELIZABETH LEWIS (MRS. JOHN E. STEVENSON, JR.), sorority exec.; b. Farmington, Mich., Sept. 6, 1923; d. Peirce and Amy (Fee) Lewis; B.A., Albion Coll., 1945; postgrad. Northwestern U., 1946-47; m. John E. Stevenson, Jr., Feb. 6, 1950; children—Vanstan L., Lynn, Kelland D. Reporter, Ludington (Mich.) Daily News, 1943-45; copy desk Battle Creek Enquirer News, 1944; decorator's cons. J.L. Hudson Co., 1945-46; field sec. Delta Gamma, Columbus, Ohio, 1947-49, editor, 1949-56, 1961-66, dir. communications and info., 1967—. Bd. dirs. Ohio Soc. for Prevention of Blindness, 1963-69; chmn. Panhellenic Editors Conf., 1969-71; adviser Pre-Sch. Vision Screening Clinic, Columbus, 1969—. Frances Lewis Stevenson hon. fellow, 1961-62. Mem. Columbus Acad. Mothers Assn., P.E.O. (chpt. pres. 1964-65, 1969-70), Mortar Bd., Phi Beta Kappa, Kappa Pi, Alpha Phi Gamma, Delta Gamma. Republican. Methodist. Home: 2395 Abington Rd Columbus OH 43221 Office: 3250 Riverside Dr Columbus OH 43221

STEVENSON, JOHN DANIEL, constrn. engr.; b. Rockville, Ind., Mar. 31, 1926; s. William D. and Edna G. (Gilligan) S.; B.S. in M.E., Purdue U., 1950; m. Jean C. Day, June 27, 1949; children—William Allan, Charles Daniel. Sales engr. The Trane Co., 1950-52; design engr. Bevington Taggart & Fowler, 1952-57; project mgr. Ammerman Davis & Stout, Indpls., 1957-59; pres. Mussett Nicholas & Stevenson, Inc., Indpls., 1959-69, M & E Engrng. Service, Inc., Indpls., 1969—, also chmn. bd. Served with USNR, 1944-46. Registered profl. engr., Ind., N.Y., Tex., Fla., Ill., Ohio; holder Nat. Engrng. Certificate; named Engr. of Distinction Joint Council Engrs., 1974. Mem. Am. Soc. Heating and Refrigeration Engrs., Inst. Food Technologists, Constrn. Specification Inst., Thistle Class Assn. (regional v.p.), Sigma Chi. Club: Dolphin (bd. dirs.). Home: 3002 Horse Hill W Dr Indianapolis IN 46224 Office: 311 W Washington St Indianapolis IN 46204

STEVENSON, T(HOMAS) H(ULBERT), historian, polit. scientist; b. Cleve., Sept. 7, 1919; s. Thomas and Mary Elizabeth (Hulbert) S.; A.B., Oberlin Coll., 1941; A.M., U. Chgo., 1945, Ph.D. (Ency. Britannica medieval history fellow), 1964; m. Dorothy Ann Ruggles, May 19, 1950; children—Mary Anne, James Randolph. Instr. history and govt. William Woods Coll., Fulton, Mo., 1947-48; research asst. in behavioral sci. Stanford U., 1955; lectr. municipal govt. U. Santa Clara (Calif.), 1955-56; asst. to pres. Found. Vol. Welfare, San Francisco, 1956-57; instr. history, govt., French, Mich. Tech. U., Houghton, 1958-59; asst. prof. history Wayne (Nebr.) State Coll., 1965-66, asso. prof., 1966-70, acting chmn. div. social sci., 1968, researcher, cons., lectr., 1970—. Co-author: Political Science, 1951, Japanese edit., 1977; World Politics, 1962; author: Politics and Government, 1973; editor: Building Better Volunteer Programs, 1958; editorial cons. Found. Vol. Welfare, 1959-60; transl. cons. Am. Behavioral Scientist, 1960-61; contbr. to books and jours. in field. Home: 711 Logan St Wayne NE 68787

STEVENSON, THOMAS MOODY, criminologist; b. Chgo., Feb. 21, 1920; s. Earle Dodds and Florence (Ezzell) S.; student Morgan Park Jr. Coll., 1938-39, Central YMCA Coll., Chgo., 1939-40, Roosevelt Coll., Chicago, 1948-51; LL.B., Blackstone Coll. Law, Chgo., 1951; m. Mary Ellen Mosher, Jan. 26, 1952; children—Thomas Moody II, Lynda Ellen. Research chemist Berry Asphalt & Petroleum Products, Waterloo, Ark., 1938-40; rate expert I.C.R.R., Chgo., 1940-41; spl. investigator Ill. Dept. Conservation, Chgo., 1948-50; dep. sheriff Cook County, Chgo., Ill., 1949; asst. dir. security Montgomery Ward & Co., Chgo., 1951-56; gen. mgr., dir. Interstate Service Corp., Chgo., 1956-60; v.p., dir. Mut. Labs., Inc., Chgo., 1956-60; pres., chmn. bd. Stevenson & Assos., Inc., Chgo., 1960—, Stevenson Syndicated Businesses, Inc., 1962—, Stevenson Investments, Inc., 1965—, Stevenson & Weiss, Ltd., 1973—; owner Thomas-Moody Co., Chgo., 1944—, Grayce Pub. Co., Chgo., 1963—. Security cons. indsl. assns., 1963-65; polygraph cons. Nat. Police Testing Labs., Inc., 1946-51; cons. dep. sheriff Lake County (Ind.), 1975—; exhibited numerous art works including oil painting Art Inst. Chgo., 1958. Asst. to ward com., precinct capt. Republican Party, Chgo., 1948-50, asst. campaign mgr. U.S. Congressman Fred E. Busby, 1948. Served with USAAF, to lt., inf. AUS, 1941-44. Licensed pvt. investigator, detection of deception examiner, Ill. Recipient commendation for contbns. to advancement modern law enforcement Tex. Law Enforcement Found., 1958; hon. mem. Nat. Police Hall of Fame. Mem. Spl. Agts. Assn., Am. Assn. Commodity Traders, Am. Polygraph Assn., Ill. Polygraph Soc., Ky. Sheriffs' Assn. (hon. life), Am. Assn. Criminology (officer; hon. life, Merit award for distinguished achievement in pub. service 1963), Asso. Detectives Ill., Am. Acad. Registered Crimologists (hon. life; officer), Internat. Police Congress, Nat. Sheriffs Assn., Nat. Pilots Assn., Aircraft Owners and Pilots Assn., Assn. to Advance Ethical Hypnosis, Internat. Assn. Chiefs Police, Asso. Guard and Patrol Assn. Clubs: U.S. Polo, Lions. Author: How to be a Store Detective, 1965. Designer, builder undersea search and rescue craft, ground effects machine. Home: 7600 W 134th Pl Cedar Point Park Cedar Lake IN 46303 also 3152 Palisades Dr Merrionette Park IL 60655 Office: 8020 S Chicago Ave Chicago IL 60617

STEVICK, BILL MAZE, lawyer; b. Topeka, June 8, 1920; s. James F. and Vera May (Maze) S.; B.B.A., Washburn U., 1947; LL.B., 1950; m. Lois Meyer Johnson; children by previous marriage—James Dexter, Jacquelyn Marie, Ronald Glen, Craig William. Admitted to Kans. bar, 1950, Mo. bar, 1961; pvt. practice law, 1950—; municipal judge Lee's Summit, Mo., 1964-66. Dir. Div. Vital Statistics, Kans. Bd. Health, 1952-54; gen. counsel Kans. Employment Security Div., 1955-56; commr. Workmen's Compensation Kans., 1956-59. Chmn. Kans. Safety Council, 1958-59; chmn. com., Internat. Assn. Indsl. Accident Bds. Comms., 1959; chmn. Citizens Com. Indsl. Devel., Topeka, 1959; pres. City Council PTA, Topeka; campaign dir. United Funds, Lee's Summit and Jackson County (Mo.), 1962-63, campaign chmn. Eastern Jackson County, 1964-65; pres. Jackson County Health and Welfare Planning Council, 1968; mem. Richards-Gebaur Air Force Base Community Council, 1968; mem. Sch. Adv. Com., Lee's Summit, 1968; mem. adv. com. County Ct. Children's Instns. Served to maj., AUS, 1941-46; lt. col. Res. Decorated 4 Battle Stars, Victory Medal. Mem. Mo. Bar Assn., Mil. Order World Wars, Am. Legion, VFW, Delta Theta Phi. Home: 704 Thunderbird Dr Harrisonville MO 64701 Office: 7 E 3d St Lee's Summit MO 64063

STEWART, BRUCE HUBBARD, physician; b. Flint, Mich., Nov. 3, 1929; s. Samuel Sidney and Louise Gunn (Burroughs) S.; B.A., U. Mich., 1951, M.D., 1954; m. Alice Virginia Persons, June 12, 1952; children—Bruce H., John Persons. Intern, Univ. Hosp., Ann Arbor, Mich., 1954-55, resident, 1955-56, 58-61; asst. prof. surgery U. Mich., 1962-64; sr. staff mem. dept. urology Cleve. Clinic Found., 1964—, chmn. dept. surgery, 1972—, bd. govs., 1976—, trustee, 1977. Mgr., Little League Baseball. Served with USAF, 1956-58; Japan. Mem. AMA, Am. Urol. Assn., Am. Assn. Clin. Urologists, Am. Assn. Genito-Urinary Srugeons, A.C.S., Am. Fertility Soc. (pres.), Société Internationale d'Urologie, Transplantation Soc. N.E. Ohio (pres.), Cleve. Urology Soc. (pres.). Republican. Presbyterian. Clubs: Country, Cleve. Racket, Torch. Author: Operative Urology, 1976. Editorial bd. Urology Digest, 1968—, Fertility and Sterility, 1968-76, Stedman's Illustrated Med. Dicy., 1976—; contbr. articles to profl. jours. Home: 12 Cotswold Ln Moreland Hills OH 44022 Office: 9500 Euclid Ave Cleveland OH 44106

STEWART, DAVID RHEES, physician; b. Boston; s. John Dunham and Henrietta (Rhees) S.; A.B., Harvard U., 1960; M.D., U. Rochester, 1964; m. Mary Louise Evans, June 30, 1962; children—Jeffrey, Elizabeth, Kathryn. Intern, Yale U., 1964-65; resident in surgery Peter Bent Brigham Hosp., Boston, 1967-68, Boston Children's Hosp., 1968-79, Mass. Gen. Hosp., 1969-72, Royal Manchester (Eng.) Children's Hosp., 1972-73; asst. prof. surgery and pediatrics U. Utah, 1973-76; asso. prof. surgery and pediatrics U. Kans., Kansas City, 1976—, also chief pediatric surgery. Trustee, 1st Congl. Ch., Salt Lake City, 1974-76. Served with USN, 1965-67. Mem. Am. Pediatric Surgery Assn., A.C.S., Am. Acad. Pediatrics, Brit., Pacific assns. pediatric surgeons, Assn. Acad. Surgery. Contbr. articles to profl. jours. Home: 10 Navajo Trail Lake Quivira KS 66106 Office: Med Center U Kans Kansas City KS 66103

STEWART, DONALD EDWARD, surgeon; b. Duluth, Aug. 7, 1911; s. Alex and Amelia (Charrier) S.; student Duluth Jr. Coll., 1930-32; B.S., U. Minn., 1935, M.B., 1937, M.D., 1938, M.S. in Surgery, 1949; m. Phyllis Ann Saxine, May 12, 1941; children—Anita, Donald, Beth, Mary Threse. Intern Med. Center, Jersey City, 1937-38; resident Eitel Hosp., Mpls., 1938-39; gen. practice medicine, Grand Rapids, Minn., 1939-41; resident in surgery U. Minn. and VA Hosp., Mpls., 1946-49; practice medicine specializing in gen. and thoracic surgery, Crookston, Minn., 1949—; mem. staffs Riverview Hosp., Crookston, Minn.; clin. asso. U. N.D. Med. Sch.; clin. asso. prof. surgery U. Minn. Pres. Crookston Pub. Library, 1958-60, Polk County (Minn.) Library Bd., 1960-62. Served with U.S. Army, 1941-45; ETO. Recipient Am. Cancer Soc. Nat. Divl. award, 1969, Good Neighbor award Radio Sta.-WCCO, 1970; diplomate Am. Bd. Surgery. Mem. Red River Valley Med. Soc., Minn. State Med. Assn. (chmn. cancer com. 1965—), A.C.S. (Nat. Divisional award 1968, Cancer Commn. 1965—, pres. Minn. chpt. 1972-73), Am. Cancer Soc. (pres. Minn. chpt. 1968-70, nat. dir. 1970-76), Minn. Surg. Soc. (bd. dirs. 1965-73, pres. 1971-72), Am. Thoracic Soc., AMA, Phi Beta Pi. Democrat. Roman Catholic. Clubs: Elks, Lions, K.C. Home: 518 N Ash St Crookston MN 56716 Office: 220 S Broadway Crookston MN 56716

STEWART, DONALD EUGENE, mech. engr.; b. Wyandotte County, Kans., Apr. 29, 1924; s. Thomas Jefferson and Minnie Sophia (Heinrichs) S.; B.A. in Math., U. Mo., Kansas City, 1960; B.S. in Engrng. Scis., Calif. Christian U., Los Angeles, 1974, M.S. in Engrng. Mgmt., 1976; m. Marjorie Jean Bloomfield, Oct. 5, 1946; 1 dau., Eileen Cheryl. Project engr. Colgate Palmolive Co., Kansas City, Kans., 1948-62; sales and field engr. Bublitz Machinery Co., North Kansas City, Mo., 1962-66; materials handling engr. Allis Chalmers Co., Independence, Mo., 1966-74; sr. engr. John Deere Co., Dubuque, Iowa, 1974—. Adviser, Jr. Achievement, 1974-77. Served with U.S. Army, 1943-45; ETO. Recipient Engrng. Achievement award Midwest Maintenance Inst., 1960; Achievement award Heart of Am. Engrng. and Sci. Club. Mem. ASME, Am. Inst. Plant Engrs., Soc. Mfg. Engrs., Nat. Mgmt. Assn., Alpha Phi Omega (life mem.). Episcopalian. Club: Masons. Contbr. articles to profl. publs. Home: 170 Copper Kettle Ln East Dubuque IL 61025 Office: John Deere Co Hwy 386 Dubuque IA 52001

STEWART, DOUGLAS A., packaging co. exec.; b. Bronx, N.Y., Sept. 12, 1940; s. Arnold J. and Dorothy G.; B.B.A. in Finance, Manhattan Coll., 1962; m. Linda G. Sahagian, May 8, 1971; children—Debra Arlene, Phillip Douglas, Gregory Lynn. Sales rep. Hazel Atlas Glass subs. Continental Can Co., N.Y.C., 1962-64, Brockway Glass Co., N.Y.C., 1964-65; purchasing agent Chesebrough-Pond's, Inc., N.Y.C., 1965-68; sales mgr. Sheffield Tube Corp., N.Y.C., 1968-71, mgr. Western Operations, Chgo., 1971-73, v.p. mktg., Broadview, Ill., 1973—. Mem. Am. Mktg. Assn., Metal Tube Pkg. Council of N. Am., Pkg. Inst. (Chgo. chpt.), Drug, Chemical & Allied Trades Assn., Chgo. Drug & Chemical Assn., Cosmetic Toiletry and Fragrance Assn. Clubs: City (Chgo.). Home: 1001 N Fair Oaks Ave Oak Park IL 60302 Office: 2850 Eisenhower Expwy Broadview IL 60153

STEWART, GEORGE DANIEL, JR., dentist; b. Ashland, Ohio, June 6, 1929; s. George Daniel and Grace Elizabeth (Roland) S.; student Ashland Coll., 1947-48; D.D.S. cum laude, Ohio State U., 1958; m. Esther Ferdina Langlois, Dec. 24, 1950; children—Daniel Thomas, Jeffrey Lee, Patrick Kyle. Practice gen. dentistry, Wooster, Ohio, 1958—. Served with USAF, 1948-52. Mem. Am., Ohio (del. 1973), Stark County, Akron dental assns., Am. Dental Soc. Anesthesiology, Acad. Gen. Dentistry, Wooster Dental Group, Ohio State Alumni Assn. Mason (Shriner), Lion (chmn. 1965). Home: 1049 Mayflower Dr Wooster OH 44691 Office: Dental Arts Bldg 621 Quinby Ave Wooster OH 44691

STEWART, JACK MELVIN, indsl. engring. cons.; b. Oneida, N.Y., Feb. 20, 1926; s. Ephraim J. and Frieda (Holz) S.; B. in Mech. Engring., Syracuse U., 1946, M.S. in Indsl. Engring., 1950; m. Tudy Newman, June 26, 1955; children—Eileen, Leslie, Ralph. Research engr. Martin Co., Balt., 1946-47; indsl. engring. supr. Syracuse Ornamental Co. (N.Y.), 1947-49; instr. indsl. engring. Syracuse (N.Y.) U., 1949-50; asst. mfg. engring. mgr. Gen. Electric Co., Syracuse, 1950-53; v.p. Wheeler Assos., Inc., engring. cons., Cleve., 1953-57; pres. Research for Industry, Inc., Cleve., 1962—, Indsl. Technol. Assos., Inc., Cleve., 1957—. Active Greater Cleve. council Boy Scouts Am., 1971—; mem. adv. bd., chmn. orgns. State of Israel Bonds, 1969—; Republican precinct committeeman, Cleve., 1971—; mem. Republican Central Com., Cleve., 1971—; trustee Fairmount Temple, Cleve., 1973—, Am. Red Magen David, 1976—, Ben Gurion U., 1977—; trustee Fairmount Temple Brotherhood, pres., 1971—. Mem. ASME, Internat. Material Mgmt. Soc., Am. Foundrymen's Soc., Am. Def. Preparedness Assn., Syracuse U. Alumni (nat. v.p. 1965-69), Sigma Xi, Zeta Beta Tau, Tau Beta Pi, Pi Mu Epsilon. Clubs: Masons, Shriners. Contbr. numerous articles on indsl. engring. to profl. publs. and tech. handbooks. Home: 28326 Belcourt Rd Pepper Pike OH 44124 Office: 2108 Payne Ave Cleveland OH 44114

STEWART, JAMES FRANKLIN, urologist; b. Marietta, Ohio, Jan. 19, 1930; s. John M. and Mayme O. (Shankland) S.; A.B., Ohio U., 1952; M.D., U. Cin., 1956; m. Ruth Sandner, Aug. 27, 1955; children—James Franklin, Thomas, Amy. Intern, Cin. Gen. Hosp., 1956-57, gen. surgery resident, 1957-58; resident urology Louisville Gen. Hosp., 1964-67; gen. practice medicine, Middletown, Ohio, 1958-64; practice medicine, specializing in urology, Middletown, 1967—; staff Middletown Hosp., 1958-64, 67—, v.p. med. staff, 1974, pres. med. staff, 1975-78. Pres. Middletown PTA, 1967-69, 74-75; active Boy Scouts Am.; chmn. devel. com. Middletown Audubon Soc., Sebald Park Interpretive Area, 1970—. Bd. dirs. Am. Cancer Soc., Middletown, 1968—, v.p., 1977—. Diplomate Am. Bd. Urology. Fellow A.C.S.; mem. Butler County Med. Soc. (pres. 1963-64), Ohio Med. Assn. (del. 1970—), AMA (sec. council on urology 1973-77, vice chmn. 1977—), Am. Urologic Assn. (del. from Ohio to exec. com. N. Central sect. 1977—), Am. Assn. Clin. Urologists, Beta Theta Pi. Home: 516 Curryer Rd Middletown OH 45042 Office: 100 S Breiel Blvd Middletown OH 45042

STEWART, JOHN DONALD, physician; b. Chatham, Ont., Can., Feb. 1, 1934; s. John Keith and Yvonne Marie (Robidoux) S.; M.D., U. Toronto, 1958. Intern, St. Michael's Hosp., Toronto, Ont., Can., 1958-59; resident Henry Ford Hosp., Detroit, 1960-65; sr. houseman Churchill Hosp., Oxford, Eng., 1959-60; practice medicine specializing in cardiology, Kitchener, Ont., 1966—; chmn. dept. medicine Kitchener-Waterloo Hosp., 1969-73; pres. Waterloo Motor Inn. Ltd., 1973-75; med. dir. Waterloo County chpt. Ont. Heart Found., 1970—. Fellow Royal Coll. Physicians; asso. fellow Am. Coll. Cardiology; mem. Ont., Can. med. assns., Kitchener-Waterloo Acad. Medicine, Phi Chi. Club: Granite. Office: 900 King St W Kitchener ON Canada

STEWART, RICHARD ALLAN, sch. counselor; b. Fairmont, W.Va., Nov. 12, 1931; s. Cecil F. and Flossie (Yoho) S.; B.A., Fairmont State Coll., 1955; M.Ed., U. Mo., 1957; m. Mary Jane Hillman, Aug. 17, 1957. Tchr., Springfield Local Schs., Ontario, Ohio, 1956-58; counselor Westlake (Ohio) City Schs., 1958-72; elementary counselor West Muskingum Schs., Zanesville, Ohio, 1972-73; counselor East Knox Schs., Mt. Vernon, Ohio, 1973—. Vice pres. Mt. Vernon Mental Health Assn. Served with M.C., AUS, 1952-54. Recipient grant State U. N.Y., Buffalo, 1965. Mem. Am., Ohio personnel and guidance assns., Am., Ohio sch. counselors assns., Nat. Vocat. Guidance Assn., NEA, Ohio, North Central Ohio, E. Knox edn. assns., Phi Delta Kappa. Clubs: Optimist, Kiwanis, Elks. Home: 1219 N Mulberry St Mount Vernon OH 43050 Office: Box 128 Howard OH 43028

STEWART, RONALD GEORGE, educator; b. Del Rio, Tex., Sept. 22, 1932; s. Elvis Gus and Lila Christine (Parker) S.; B.S., Tex. Tech. U., 1954; M.S., Ill. Inst. Tech., 1967; Ph.D., Northwestern U., 1974; m. Frances Ann Howard, Mar. 16, 1957; children—Jeff, Diana, Meri. Rancher, livestock feeder, Del Rio, 1948-62; partner Cullum & Jones Assos., Del Rio and Quemado Valley, Tex., 1954-60; tchr. high sch., Del Rio, 1960-65; adult edn. instr. OEO, Del Rio, 1960-65; prof. sociology Harper Coll., Palatine, Ill., 1967—. Research cons. Alpha, Inc., 1971; reviewer for proposed texts Coll. div. Scott Foresman & Co., Glenview, Ill., 1973—. Mem. Hoffman Estates (Ill.) Youth Commn., 1969—; developer rationale for youth outreach worker program, Hoffman Estates, Ill., 1972-73; conductor survey of Schaumburg Twp. (Ill.) to determine community needs and prevailing attitudes toward recreation and ednl. facilities, 1971. NDEA grantee, 1965; NSF fellow, 1966-67. Mem. Am., Midwest, S.W., Ill. sociol. assns., Phi Gamma Delta. Author intro. to text Understanding Society. Contbr. articles to profl. jours. Home: 318 Rosedale Ln Hoffman Estates IL 60195 Office: Harper Coll Palatine IL 60067

STEWART, WILLIAM OSCAR, sch. adminstr., polit. exec.; b. Chgo., Feb. 8, 1925; s. James and Marvella (Brewer) S.; B.S., Tenn. State U., 1950; M.A., DePaul U., Chgo., 1967; certificate in collective bargaining and negotiating, U. Ill., 1968; m. Corinne Lucas, June 27, 1974. Asst. prin. John Farren Elementary Sch., Chgo., 1974—, dir. Sch. Social Center, 1968—. Active A.R.C. Capt. 17th Precinct 3d ward Regular Republican Orgn., 1952—, chmn. suprs. 3d ward, 1958—, candidate for alderman, 1962, candidate for committeeman, 1964, 72; pres. 3d ward Young Reps., 1954-64; v.p. Cook County Young Reps., 1957-64, chmn. civil rights com., 1956-60; 1st Negro sec. Ill. Young Reps., 1958-62; regional dir. Citizens for Percy for Gov., 1964; vice chmn. Ill. Rep. State Central Com., 1968—. Bd. dirs. Joint Negro Appeal. Named Outstanding Young Rep. Pres. S. Side Cook County Young Reps., 1958; recipient citation for Outstanding Work in Politics, Tenn. State U., 1962, citations for Great Guy award Radio Sta. WGRT, 1968, WJPC, 1974. Mem. Chgo. Tchrs. Union (trustee), Toastmasters Internat., Nat. Congress Parents and Tchrs. Assn., Urban League, NAACP, Chgo. Fedn. Labor AFL-CIO Council, Ill. Fedn. Tchrs., U.S. Jr. C. of C. (life), Nat. Tenn. State U. Alumni Assn. (life), Kappa Alpha Psi. Office: Ill Rep State Central Com 219 E 45th St Chicago IL 60653

STEYER, RAYMOND JAMES, II, computer programmer; b. Downers Grove, Ill., Aug. 11, 1950; s. Raymond James and Jeane Olga (Wensch) S.; B.A. in Math. and Physics, Beloit (Wis.) Coll., 1972. Sr. programmer No. Trust Co., Chgo., 1972-75; v.p. software dept. Child Inc., Lawrence, Kans., 1975-77, also dir; sr. analyst/programmer Zurich Ins. Co., Chgo., 77; programmer technician Montgomery Ward, Chgo., 1977—. Mem. Math. Assn. Am., Assn. Computing Machinery. Home: 215 Griffing Ave Woodstock IL 60098 Office: 1 Montgomery Ward Pl Chicago IL 60671

STICKLE, DAVID WALTER, state ofcl.; b. Boston, Apr. 18, 1933; s. Harold Edwards and Lucille Margaret (Magee) S.; B.S., Tufts U., 1955; M.S., Northeastern U., Boston, 1968; M.P.H., U. N.C., 1969, D.P.H., 1971; m. Mary DeLong, July 29, 1972. Chem. technician Nat. Research Corp., Boston, 1957-58; med. technician U.S. Dept. Agr., Boston, 1958-59; bacteriologist Mass. Dept. Pub. Health, Boston, 1959-63, bacteriologist in charge of spl. serology, 1963-68; chief clin. lab. improvement program Minn. Dept. Health, Mpls., 1971—, asst. dir. div. med. labs., 1975-76, acting dir., 1976—; adj. asst. prof. U. Minn., 1977. Mem. Am. Soc. Microbiology, Am. Pub. Health Assn., Conf. Pub. Health Lab. Dirs., Minn. Assn. Blood Banks. Contbr. articles in field to profl. jours. Office: 717 Delaware St Minneapolis MN 55440

STICKLEY, JAMES JOHN, oral surgeon; b. Iowa City, Iowa May 26, 1933; s. Carl and Maye (Moses) S.; student U. Iowa, 1951-53D.D.S., 1960; student Coe Coll., 1955-56; postgrad. Boston U., 1960-61; m. Marianna Jean Feldtang, Dec. 22, 1956. Intern, Mount Carmel Mercy Hosp., Detroit, 1961-62, resident in oral surgery, 1962-63; practice dentistry specializing in oral surgery, Cedar Rapids, Iowa, 1963—; chief of staff oral surgery Mercy Hosp., 1965, 68, 75-76, St. Lukes Hosp., 1965, 68, 75-76 (both Cedar Rapids). Bd. dirs., v.p. Cedar Rapids Symphony Assn.; bd. dirs. 10th St. Assn., 5th Ave. Assn. Served with inf. AUS, 1953-55. Mem. ADA, Iowa Dental Assn., Linn County (pres.), Cedar Rapids dental socs., Am., Iowa (award 1960, sec., treas. 1966-69, pres. 1973-74), Midwest, Internat. socs. oral surgeons, Cedar Rapids C. of C. Clubs: Executive, Cedar Rapids Country (Cedar Rapids); Whitehall (Chgo.); Classic Car Am. (dir. Iowa region 1968-69); Sports Car Am. (treas. Iowa region 1968—); Am. Bugatti; Rolls Royce Enthusiasts (London, Eng.); Rolls Royce Owners (Harrisburg, Pa.); Bugatti Owners, Bentley Drivers (Eng.); Sturgeon Bay (Wis.) Yacht; U.S. Yacht Racing Assn. Home: 1364 Elmhurst Dr NE Cedar Rapids IA 52402 Office: 1030 5th Ave SE Cedar Rapids IA 52402

STIEHL, CHARLES WILLIAM, surgeon; b. South Milwaukee, Wis., Apr. 23, 1924; s. Carl Ernst and Marjorie (Simon) S.; B.S., Northwestern U., 1942, B.M., M.D., 1947; m. Sarah D. Harding, Dec. 20, 1945 (div. Oct. 1957); children—Patti (Mrs. Michael Boris), Carl Harding, Sarah Ann; m. 2d, Edith Ann Mauer, Nov., 1967; 1 dau., Edith Ann. Intern, Columbia Hosp., Milw., 1947-48; resident St. Mary's Hosp., Milw., 1948-49; physician and surgeon Algoma (Wis.) Clinic, 1950-66; chief surgery Algoma Meml. Hosp., 1964—; med. dir. Heil Co., Milw. owner Von Stiel Wine, Inc., Algoma, 1961—; pres. S & M Real Estate Corp., Algoma, 1958—. Mem. Sch. Bd., 1954-58. Served with USNR, 1942. Mem. Wis., Kewaunee County (past pres.) med. socs., Wis. Coll. Emergency Physicians (pres.), Acad. Indsl. Medicine, Beta Theta Pi, Nu Sigma Nu. Lutheran. Originator Von Stiehl natural cherry wine, stabilization natural cherry wine, aging wrap. Home: 518 Glenview Av Oconomowoc WI 53066 Office: 2740 W Forest Home Milwaukee WI

STIER, RONALD LEE, elec. wire and cable mfg. co. exec.; b. Richmond, Ind., Aug. 6, 1937; s. Robert Lawrence and Mary Mildred (Cunningham) S.; student St. Meinrad Coll., 1964-70; student elec. engring. Internat. Corr. Schs., 1970-74; B.S. in Indsl. Mgmt., Aurora Coll., 1974; m. Donna Jean Foultz, Apr. 4, 1964; children—Kimberly, Denise, Ronald. Product engr. Belden Corp., Richmond, Ind., 1964-68, product devel. engr. Tech. Research Center, 1968-71, mktg. specialist, 1971-74, mktg. mgr., 1974—. Mem. St Andrews Parish Council, Richmond, pres., 1975—. Served with AUS, 1961-64. Mem. Electronics Industry Assn. (co-chmn. Young Exec. group Central div.), Richmond Amateur Radio Assn. (pres.), Nat. Cable TV Assn., Security Equipment Industry Assn. (dir.), Electronics Internat. Adv. Panel, Computer Design Adv. Panel, Amateur Radio Relay League. Republican. Roman Catholic. Club: K.C. Contbr. articles electronics jours. Patentee in field. Home: 3605 Backmeyer Rd Richmond IN 47374 Office: PO Box 1327 Richmond IN 47374

STIFFLER, PAUL WEIR, med. microbiologist; b. Buffalo, N.Y., June 24, 1943; s. Samuel Henry and Margaret Beatrice (McCulloch) S.; B.S. in Biology and Chemistry, Bowling Green (Ohio) State U., 1965, M.A. in Biology, 1967; Ph.D. in Microbiology and Pub. Health, Mich. State U., 1971; m. Lois Jean Steel, June 18, 1967; children—Andrew William, Scott Gregory. Research asso. microbiology Michael Reese Hosp. and Med. Center, Chgo., 1972-73; USPHS fellow clin. microbiology tng. program Pritzker Sch. Medicine U. Chgo., 1973-75; microbiologist Mason-Barron Labs. Inc., Chgo., 1975—. Cons. Grant Hosp. of Chgo., Augustana Hosp., Chgo. Mem. Am. Soc. Microbiology, South Central Assn. Clin. Microbiology, Sigma Xi. Contbr. articles to profl. jours. Mem. editorial bd. Lab. Medicine, 1978. Home: 2063 Burr Oak Highland Park IL 60035 Office: 4720 W Montrose St Chicago IL 60641

STIKA, ELAINE ANNA, advt. exec.; b. Kenosha, Wis., July 3, 1924; d. Alexander and Paulina L. (Janota) Stika; student Kenosha Coll. Commerce, 1943, Mgmt. Center Marquette U., Milw., 1960, Kenosha Center U. Wis., DePaul U., 1963, Kenosha Tech. Inst., 1970. Asst. to mgr. market list div. sales dept. Macwhyte Wire Rope Co., Kenosha, 1943-49, asst. to advt., sales promotion, pub. relations, mktg. mgr., 1949-65, advt. and sales services adminstr., 1966-73, adminstr. marketing services, 1974—. Sec., treas. Kenosha Civic Council, 1955—; mem. Kenosha County Health Planning Commn., 1969—; loaned exec. United Way, 1976—. Bd. dirs. Kenosha County United Fund, 1966-72, Kenosha County council Girl Scouts U.S.A., 1962-68; bd. dirs. Kenosha County Blood Bank, 1964—, v.p., 1968-70, pres., 1971-74; br. adv. bd. Wis. Tb and Respiratory Disease Assn., 1970—. Mem. Milw. Assn. Indsl. Advts., Constrn. Equipment Advts., Kenosha Bradford Alumni Assn. (bd. dirs. 1968-75, v.p. 1970-71, pres. 1971-73), Kenosha Advt. Club (dir. 1959-70, v.p. 1961-62, pres. 1963-64), Sigma Alpha Sigma (dir. 1953—, v.p. 1960-62, pres., 1962-64), Kenosha County Hist. Soc. Home: 926 48th St Kenosha WI 53140 Office: Macwhyte Wire Rope Co 2906 14th Ave Kenosha WI 53140

STILES, ELIZABETH CONNELLY, coll. adminstr.; b. Chgo.; d. Harrington John and Barbara Cassilda (Mayer) Connelly; B.A., St. Xavier Coll., 1941; M.Ed., Chgo. State U., 1964; children—Elizabeth Ann, Barbara Carol, Patricia Jean. Personnel counselor and research Western Electric Co., Chgo., 1942-50; tchr., counselor Mother McAuley High Sch., Chgo., 1958-62, Oak Lawn (Ill.) Community High Sch., 1962-68; dir. financial aid and placement Moraine Valley Community Coll., Palos Hills, Ill., 1968—; cons. HEW. Miseracordia scholar, 1938-41. Mem. Am. Assn. Community and Jr. Colls., Midwest, Ill. (v.p.) assns. fin. aid adminstrs., Chgo. Council Fgn. Relations, Placement Assn. Community Colls. and Employers (sec.), Kappa Gamma Pi. Office: 10900 S 88th Ave Palos Hills IL 60465

STILES, JAMES FULLER, III, water treatment co. exec.; b. Evanston, Ill., Nov. 28, 1918; s. James Fuller and Ruth Marion (Jenkins) S.; grad. Lake Forest Acad., 1936; B.A., Williams Coll., 1940; postgrad. in law Northwestern U., 1941; m. Helen Alma Ferry, June 21, 1941; children—James Fuller IV, Susan Ruth (Mrs. Ralph R. Basile), Douglas William, Donald A., Judith H., Richard E., Pamela J., Paul G. Partner, Stiles Bros. Plating, Zion, Ill., 1945-57; with Stiles Bros., Inc., Waukegan, Ill., 1947-57, pres., 1947-52; dir., 1947-52; pres. Stiles Ferry, Inc., Zion, 1952—, dir., 1952—; pres. Stiles-Radel, Maywood, Ill., 1960-69, dir., 1960-69; pres., dir. Stiles-Kem Corp., Zion, 1962—; dir. Met. Pro Water Treatment Corp. Bd. dirs. Salvation Army, 1951—. Served to capt. USMC, 1941-45. Mem. World Council of Bus., Water Conditioning Found., Chgo. Pres.'s Orgn., C. of C. Republican. Methodist. Mason (Shriner), Rotarian (pres. 1946—). Club: Skokie Country (Glencoe, Ill.). Home: 500 Adams Ave Glencoe IL 60022 Office: 3301 Sheridan Rd Zion IL 60099

STILES, JAMES RICHARD, guidance counselor; b. Lowell, Mich., Mar. 2, 1938; s. Arthur H. and Marian Elizabeth (Everhart) S.; B.S., Central Mich. U., 1962; M.A., Western Mich. U., 1965; Ed.S., Mich. State U., 1971; m. Dawn Anne Derhammer, June 10, 1961; children—Katherine, Daniel, Mark, Kari Sue. Instr. Battle Creek (Mich.) Central High Sch., 1962-66, coach wrestling and cross country, 1962-66; counselor, tchr. Lansing (Mich.) Everett High Sch., 1966-71, coach wrestling, 1966-71; counselor, guidance dir. Lansing Hill High Sch., 1971—; cons. in field. Served with USNR, 1956-58. Recipient Outstanding Counselor Mich. award Mich. Sch. Counselors Assn., 1976. Mem. Am., Mich. personnel and guidance assns., Nat. Mich. vocat. guidance assns., Am., Mich. sch. counselors assns., Nat. Mich., Lansing edn. assns., Nat. Jogging Assn., BMW Owners Assn. Methodist. Home: 3818 Churchill Ave Lansing MI 48910 Office: 205 Urban Planning Bldg Mich State U East Lansing MI 48824

STILLER, CHARLES EDWARD, telephone co. exec.; b. Ky., Sept. 10, 1928; s. Charley Edward and Ruth Ethel (Denton) S.; student Evansville Coll., 1956; courses Internat. Corr. Schs., 1942; m. Aloma Darlene Jacobi, Feb. 14, 1948; children—Terry, Jack Tensley, Cristy Lane, Kimber Leigh. Apprentice, Bucyrus Erie, Evansville, Ind., 1945, tng. instr., 1945-54; ins. underwriter Western and So. Life Ins. Co., 1955-59; mem. staff marketing dept. Ind. Bell Telephone Co., Evansville, 1959-66, dir. advt. and sales promotion, 1966—; owner Stiller Advt. Agy., Evansville, Adsco Wynns Distbrs., Tennyson, Ind.; dir. Burch, Inc. Served with USNR, 1945-47. Mem. Ind. Bell Comml. Employees Assn. (so. chmn. 1960-66), Met. Evansville C. of C. (chmn. agrl. devel. com. 1971). Club: Evansville Advt. Home: Rural Route 1 Tennyson IN 47637 Office: 7701 US 41 N Evansville IN 47711

STILWELL, WILLIAM RHOADES, anesthesiologist; b. Peoria, Ill., Aug. 14, 1923; s. Harold Irving and Marjorie Frances (Rhoades) S.; A.B., Wabash Coll., 1945; M.D., Ind. U., 1949; m. Helen Louise Hale, Oct. 7, 1951; children—Nancy Lee, Sarah Ellen. Intern, Indpls. Gen. Hosp., 1949-50, resident in anesthesiology, 1950-52; staff anesthesiologist Reid Meml. Hosp., Richmond, Ind., 1952-54, 56—, chief surgery, 1963-64, chief anesthesia, 1970-73, 75—, chief of staff, 1974-75. Served to lt. M.C., USN, 1952-54. Diplomate Am. Bd. Anesthesiology. Fellow Am. Coll. Anesthesiologists; mem. AMA, Ind. State Med. Assn., Am., Ind. socs. anesthesiology, Internat. Anesthesiology Research Soc., Wayne Union County Med. Soc. (pres. 1977-78), Am. Diabetes Assn. (dir., v.p. E. Central Ind. chpt.), Forest Farmer Assn., Phi Beta Kappa, Sigma Xi, Kappa Sigma, Nu Sigma Nu. Presbyterian. Club: Forest Hills Country (Richmond, Ind.). Home: 2607 S C Place Richmond IN 47374 Office: 1400 Chester Blvd Richmond IN 47374

STIMPSON, CLINTON FRANK, III, mfg. co. exec.; b. Detroit, Nov. 14, 1936; s. Clinton Frank and Rachel S.; B.S.E., U. Mich., 1959, M.B.A., 1960; m. Catherine Elizabeth Corey, Sept. 17, 1966; children—Marguerite Rachel, Robert Clinton. Engr., Vickers div. Sperry Rand, Troy, Mich., 1960-64; sales engr. Bin Dicator Co., Detroit, 1964-68, project engr., Port Sanilac, Mich., 1968-71; gen. mgr. Conveyor Components Co., Croswell, Mich., 1971—, corporate sec. parent co. Material Control Inc. Mem. Instruments Soc. Am. Home: 3210 Shoreview St S Port Huron MI 48060 Office: 130 Selter St Croswell MI 48422

STIMSON, JAMES CRAIG, mktg. exec.; b. Des Moines, Mar. 24, 1949; s. James Eldon and Shirley Ann (Hardman) S.; A.A., Grand View Coll., 1969; B.A., U. Iowa, 1972; m. Barbara Jean Knudtson, June 22, 1974. News editor KIOA Radio, Des Moines, 1969-70; asst. sports dir. KCRG Radio and TV, Cedar Rapids, Iowa, 1970-72; pub. relations rep. Winnebago Industries, Inc., Forest City, Iowa; 1972-75; pub. relations asst. The Bankers Life, Des Moines, 1975-77; mktg. comm. mgr. Red Jacket Pumps, Davenport, Iowa, 1977—. Mem. Pub. Relations Soc. Am. (sec.-treas. Iowa chpt.) Home: Route 1 LeClaire IA 52753 Office: 500 E 59th St Davenport IA 52808

STINE, EARLE JOHN, JR., physician; b. Saginaw, Mich., Feb. 21, 1932; s. Earle John and Ione Genevieve (Best) S.; A.B., Albion Coll., 1954; M.D., Wayne State U., 1958; m. Bernita Evelyn Emerson, Aug. 27, 1954; children—Renee Evelyn, Mark Earle, John Emerson. Rotating intern, resident gen. surgery Bon Secours Hosp., Grosse Pointe, Mich., 1958-61; group practice Pigeon (Mich.) Clinic, 1961-62; pvt. practice gen. medicine and surgery Marcus (Iowa) Clinic, 1962-65, Ida Grove (Iowa) Clinic, 1965-75; resident in nuclear medicine U. Iowa, 1975-76, resident in diagnostic radiology, 1976-78; med. missionary, Nicaragua, 1966, Honduras, 1969; chief of staff Horn Meml. Hosp., 1968-70. City health officer, Ida Grove, 1965-75; asst. med. examiner Ida County, Iowa, 1965-75; mem. Ida County Bd. Health, 1969-75; mem. Iowa Council Drug Abuse, 1970—; med. adviser to World Gospel Mission (Marion, Ind.). Pres. Ida Grove Bd. Edn., 1969-72. Chmn. bd. trustees Vennard Coll. (University Park, Iowa). Mem. AMA, Iowa, Ida County (pres.) med. socs., Am. Soc. Abdominal Surgeons, Christian Med. Soc., Gideons Internat., Am. Acad. Family Practice. Methodist (chmn. adminstrv. bd.; conf. del. 1973, 74; chmn. council ministries 1974-75). Home: 2412 E Court St Iowa City IA 52240

STINE, ROBERT HOWARD, physician; b. Bethlehem, Pa., Nov. 1, 1929; s. Harry Raymond and Mabel E. (Newhard) S.; B.S., Moravian Coll., Bethlehem, 1952; M.D., Jefferson Med. Coll., Phila., 1960; m. Lois Elaine Kihlgren, Oct. 22, 1960; children—Robert E., Karen E., Jonathan N. Intern, St. Luke's Hosp., Bethlehem, 1960-61, resident in surgery, 1961-62; resident in pediatrics State U. N.Y. Hosp., Syracuse, 1962-64; resident in allergy Robert A. Cooke Inst. Allergy, N.Y.C., 1964-65; practice medicine specializing in allergy, Peoria, Ill., 1965—; mem. staff St. Francis, Proctor Community hosps., Meth. Med. Center; pres. Robert H. Stine, M.D., S.C., 1972—; instr. U. Ill. Coll. Medicine, 1965-71, Rush-Presbyn.-St. Luke's Hosp., 1971—; mem. teaching staff medicine and pediatrics St. Francis Hosp.; cons. staff Meth. Hosp. Served as officer USNR, 1952-56. Fellow Am. Acad. Allergy, Am. Assn. Certified Allergists, Am. Acad. Pediatrics; mem. AMA, Chgo., Peoria med. socs., Chgo. Allergy Soc., Christian Med. Soc. Republican. Presbyterian. Home: 105 Hollands Grove Ln Washington IL 61571 Office: 710 E Archer Ave Peoria IL 61603

STITT, JAMES RAYMOND, cons. welding engr.; b. Youngstown, Ohio, Oct. 25, 1906; s. Harry Edwin and Mary (McKee) S.; B.S., Pa. State Coll., 1930; m. Edith Hope Schenck, Dec. 21, 1935; children—Ethel Louise Stitt Ekland, Robert Harry, Richard Charles. Organizer, tchr. first curriculum in welding engring. Ohio State U., Columbus, 1938-44; welding research engr. R.C. Mahon Co., Detroit, 1945-67, mgr. tech. services dept., 1967-72; owner J.R. Stitt & Assos., Madison Heights, Mich., 1972—. Registered profl. engr. Mem. Engring. Soc. Detroit, Am. Welding Soc., Am. Soc. Metals, ASTM, Am. Soc. Nondestructive Testing, Soc. Exptl. Stress Analysis. Patentee in field. Home: 10 Woodside Park Pleasant Ridge MI 48069 Office: 32500 Concord Dr Madison Heights MI 48071

STIVER, MYRTLE PEARL, nurse, bus. exec.; b. Osprey Twp., Ont., Can., Nov. 9, 1908; d. Henry and Abbie Olga (Smith) Stiver; R.N., Toronto Western Hosp., 1932; certificate Pub. Health Nursing, U. Toronto, 1940; B.S. in Nursing, Columbia, 1947. Individual practice nursing, Toronto, Ont., 1932-39; staff nurse Victorian Order Nursing,

Toronto, 1940-41; staff nurse Toronto Dept. Health, 1941-43; nurse cons. Ont. Dept. Health, 1943-48; dir. pub. health nursing Ottawa Dept. Health, 1948-52; gen. sec.-treas. Canadian Nurses Assn., Montreal, 1952-60, hon. life mem., 1966—, exec. dir., Ottawa, 1960-63; exec. sec.-treas. Canadian Nurses' Found., 1963-64; co-owner Croft, Canadian handcraft shop, Baysville, Muskoka, Ont., 1963-75. Mem. nat. nursing adv. com. Victorian Order Nurses Can., 1952-63, Can. Civil Def., 1952-62; mem. dental med. services adv. bd. Canadian govt., 1955-62; mem. vocational adv. com. Dist. Muskoka Bd. Edn., 1969—. Bd. dirs. Canadian Citizenship Council. Recipient Centennial medal Govt. Can., 1968. Fellow Am. Pub. Health Assn.; mem. Bus. and Profl. Women's Club (v.p. Bracebridge 1969-71, pres. 1971-73), Zonta Internat. (pres. Ottawa 1961-63), Venerable Order St. John Jerusalem (comdr. sister), Ont. Pub. Health Assn. (hon. life mem.). Baptist (deacon). Club: University Women's (Toronto, Montreal). Author: (with Christine Livingston) Patient Care in the Home, 1965. Address: Moosewood Baysville Muskoka ON P0B 1A0 Canada

STOCKMAN, DAVID ALLEN, Congressman; b. Ft. Hood, Tex., Nov. 10, 1946; s. Allen Robert and Carol Alberta (Bartz) S.; B.A. cum laude in History, Mich. State U., 1968. Spl. asst. to Congressman John Anderson of Ill., 1970-72; exec. dir. House Republican Conf., 1972-75; mem. 95th Congress from 4th Mich. Dist., mem. Interstate and Fgn. Commerce com., House Adminstrn. com., select com. on population, chmn. Rep. Econ. Policy Task Force. Fellow Harvard U. Inst. Politics, 1974. Address: 1021 Longworth House Office Bldg Washington DC 20515 also 325 S Main St Adrian MI 49221 2912 S State St Saint Joseph MI 49085

STODDER, PAGE WATSON TIMOTHY, investment banker; b. Elizabeth, N.J., Nov. 27, 1929; s. John David and Helen Adelia (Watson) S.; A.B., Holy Cross Coll., 1951; postgrad. U. Chgo. Sch. Bus., 1955-58; m. Charlotte Hawley Hunter, Oct. 26, 1956; children—Suzan Carter, Timothy Jay. With Blyth & Co., Inc., Chgo., 1954—, v.p., 1969-72; first v.p. Blyth Eastman Dillon & Co., Inc., 1972-74; v.p. corporate fin. Drexel Burnham & Lambert Inc., 1974—. Pres., North Dearborn Assn., 1972, treas., 1974—; trustee Chgo. Urban Transp. Dist., 1969-74; exec. com. 42d Ward Regular Rep. Orgn., 1969, bd. dirs. 1969. Served as lt. (j.g.) USNR, 1951-54. Clubs: Bond, University (Chgo.). Home: 50 W Schiller St Chicago IL 60610 Office: 230 W Monroe St Chicago IL 60606

STOEBER, LEO OTTO, pneumatic conveying systems mktg. exec.; b. Belleville, Ill., Dec. 12, 1919; s. Herman John and Clara Ann (Goepfert) S.; B.S., U. Ill., 1948; m. Esther Lucille Nitzel, July 28, 1943; children—Jonathan, Jerome, Nancy (dec.), Thomas. Farm machinery mktg. J.I. Case Co., 1948-53; with Nat. Elec. Contractors, 1953-54, Delco Products, 1955-56; design and mktg. of pneumatic conveying systems Dunbar Kapple, Inc., Normal, Ill., 1957—; mfrs. rep. Served to capt. USAAF, 1939-45. Address: 20 Knollcrest Ct Normal IL 61761

STOELTING, VERGIL KENNETH, anesthesiologist; b. Freelandville, Ind., Feb. 10, 1914; s. Andrew Philip and Ethel B. (Jones) S.; B.S., Ind. U., 1936, M.D., 1936; m. Bernice Blanche Marcus, Sept. 5, 1936; children—Robert K., Ann Stoelting Sputh. Intern, Ind. U. Hosps., 1936, Waterbury (Conn.) Hosp., 1937; resident U. Wis. Hoosps., 1943-44, U. Iowa Hosps., 1946-47; practice medicine specializing in anesthesiology; dir. anesthesiology Ind. U. Hosps., 1947—; mem. staffs VA, Wishard Meml., Meth., Community hosps., Indpls.; prof. anesthesiology Ind. U., 1947—. Diplomate Am. Bd. Anesthesiology. Fellow Am. Coll. Anesthesiologists; mem. Am., Ind. State, Indpls. soc. anesthesiologists, Ind. State, Am. med. assns., Univ. Anesthesiologists, Acad. Anesthesiology, Sociedade Brasileira de Anestesgiologia, Flying Physicians Ind., Aerospace Med. Assn., Aircraft Owners and Pilots Assn., Flying Physicians Assn., Phi Chi. Republican. Contbr. articles to med. jours. Home: 4706 Laurel Circle Indianapolis IN 46200 Office: 1100 W Michigan St Indianapolis IN 46202

STOETZER, GERALD LOUIS, lawyer; b. Detroit, Apr. 6, 1914; s. Albin August and Ida (Kuhlman) S.; A.B., Valparaiso U., 1935; J.D., U. Mich., 1938; m. Helen Muriel Simons, Aug. 16, 1941; children—Gerald Louis, James Brian, Susan Hart (Mrs. Ronald J. Bockelman). Admitted to Mich. bar, Fed. bar, 1938, U.S. Supreme Ct., 1955; partner firm Clark, Klein, Brucker & Waples, Detroit, 1938-60, Clark, Klein, Winter, Parsons & Prewitt, Detroit, 1961—; lectr. U. Mich. Law Sch. Inst. of Continuing Legal Edn., 1964—. Sec., 14th Congl. Dist. (Mich.) Republican Party, 1950-54. Pres., Monteith Sch. PTA, Grosse Pointe, Mich., 1956, Brownell Jr. High Sch., Grosse Pointe, 1962; mem. Grosse Pointe Symphony Orch. Served with AUS, 1942-46. Decorated Bronze Star. Mem. Judge Advs. Assn., Mich. Assn. Professions, State Bar of Mich. (chmn. corp., fin. and bus. law sect. 1965-68), Am., Detroit bar assns., Fine Arts Soc. Detroit, Order of Coif, Lawyers Club, Internat. Platform Assn., Wisdom Soc. Hall of Fame, Pi Gamma Mu. Delta Theta Phi, Phi Delta Theta. Lutheran. Clubs: University; Hidden Valley (Gaylord, Mich.); Lochmoor (Grosse Pointe Woods, Mich.); The Players (v.p. 1969). Home: 1949 Littlestone Rd Grosse Pointe Woods MI 48236 Office: First Fed Bldg Detroit MI 48226

STOFFLE, CARLA JOY, librarian, univ. adminstr.; b. Pueblo, Colo., June 19, 1943; d. Samuel Bernard and Virginia Irene (Berry) Hayden; A.A., So. Colo. State Coll., 1963; B.A. with distinction, U. Colo., 1965; M.L.S., Kent U., 1969; m. Richard William Stoffle, June 12, 1964; children—Brent William, Kami Ann. Peace Corps vol. tchr. secondary sch., Barbados, W.I., 1965-67; library intern U. Kent Library, Lexington, Ky., 1967-69; head govt. pub. dept. Eastern Kent U. Library, Richmond, Ky., 1969-72; reference librarian in charge of library instrn. U. Wis. at Parkside, Kenosha, 1973-76, head pub. services div., 1973-76, asst. dir. library, learning center and coordinator pub. services, 1976-77, exec. asst. to chancellor, 1977—; participant 15 panels and workshops on library instrn.; tchr. study skills, 1974; study team leader Council on Library Resources Acad. Library Devel. Program, 1977-78. U. Wis. System Undergrad. Teaching Improvement grantee, 1977-78. Mem. ALA, Wis. Library Assn. (library edn. com. 1975, pub. relations com. 1977—), Wis. Assn. Acad. Librarians (Task Force on Instrn. in Acad. Library, Com. on Edn. in Library 1976—, chmn. 1976), Midwest Fedn. Library Assns. Author: (with Rebekah Harleston) Administration of Government Documents Collections, 1974; contbr. articles to profl. jours.; editor Library Instrn. New Communique, 1973-76; book reviewer Library Jour., 1969. Home: 455 Melvin Ave Racine WI 53402 Office: U Wis-Parkside Library Learning Center Kenosha WI 53140

STOJANOVIC, GEORGE DJORDJE, surgeon; b. Belgrade, Yugoslavia, July 2, 1929; s. Mihajlo and Milica (Vracevic) S.; M.S., Med. Sch. Belgrade, 1957; m. Mirjana Marjanovic, Apr. 28, 1963; children—Michael, Robert. Came to Can., 1963, naturalized, 1968. Resident, McGill U., Montreal, Que., Can., 1963-67; sr. surgeon, Bottrop, West Germany, 1960-63; practice medicine specializing in surgery, Windsor, Ont., Can.; Western Hosp. Centre, Hotel Dieu, Grace, Met. hosps. (all Windsor). Served with Yugoslavian Army, 1967-68. Fellow Royal Coll. Surgeons Can.; mem. Ont., Canadian med. assns., Coll. Physicians and Surgeons Can., Essex Med. Soc., Windsor Acad. Surgeons. Home: 3715 Huntington Windsor ON N9E 3N4 Canada Office: 700 Tecumseh E Windsor ON N8X 2S1 Canada

STOKES, HENRY DUERRE, JR., dentist; b. St. Paul, Dec. 14, 1926; s. Henry Duerre and Marie Belle (Lambert) S.; B.S., U. Minn., 1950, D.D.S., 1952; m. Evelyn Dixen Sorensen, Dec. 27, 1945; children—Cynthia Lee (Mrs. Patrick Boyd Dufour), Henry Duerre III, Matthew Arnold. Gen. practice dentistry, Cambridge, Minn., 1952—; mem. staff Cambridge Meml. Hosp. Chmn. adv. com. Riverside Jr. Coll., Cambridge, 1971—. Chmn., Isanti County Planning Commn., 1965-73; Republican chmn. 8th Congls. Dist., 1963-67, Isanti County, 1970—; del. Rep. Nat. Conv., 1964. Served with AUS, 1944-47, USNR, 1950-53. Mem. Cambridge Bus. Assn. (chmn. 1957-58). Mason. Home: 410 SW 2d St Cambridge MN 55008 Office: 135 SW 2d St Cambridge MN 55008

STOKES, LOUIS, congressman; b. Cleve., Feb. 23, 1925; s. Charles and Louise (Stone) S.; student Western Res. U., 1946-48; J.D., Marshall Law Sch., Cleve., 1953; LL.D. (hon.), Wilberforce U., 1969; Shaw U., 1971; m. Jeanette Francis, Aug. 21, 1960; children—Shelley, Louis C., Angela, Lorene. Admitted to Ohio bar, 1954, practiced in Cleve.; mem. firm Stokes, Character, Terry and Perry, 1966—; mem. 91st-95th congresses from 21st Dist. Ohio, mem. budget com., appropriations com., select com. King/Kennedy Assassinations; lectr. in field. Served with AUS, 1943-46. Recipient numerous awards for civic activities. Mem. Am., Ohio (past chmn. criminal justice com.) bar assns., Nat. Assn. Def. Lawyers Criminal Cases (dir.), Fair Housing (dir.), Urban League, Citizens League, John Harlan Law Club, ACLU, Kappa Alpha Psi. Democrat. Club: Plus (Cleve.). Office: 2455 Rayburn House Office Bldg Washington DC 20025

STOKES, ZOE MAXINE CHRISTIAN, univ. adminstr.; b. Calcutta, India, May 10, 1941; d. Raymond Earl and Ellen J. (Davis) Christian; B.A. in German, U. Mo.-Columbia, 1965; M.S. in Counseling, U. Mo.-St. Louis, 1971. Asst. to head resident of hall U. Mo.-Columbia, 1964-65; academic adviser Coll. Arts and Sci., U. Mo.-St. Louis, 1965-67, academic adviser Sch. Bus. Adminstrn., 1967-70, sr. academic adviser, 1972-77, dir. academic advising and asst. dir. undergrad. studies, 1977—. Mem. Am. Personnel and Guidance Assn., Am. Coll. Personnel Assn., U. Mo.-St. Louis Alumni Assn. (dir. 1977—). Club: U. Mo.-St. Louis Faculty Women (v.p. 1977-78). Home: 321-F Chapel Ridge Saint Louis MO 63042 Office: U Mo Saint Louis MO 63121

STOLL, DONALD HAROLD, elec. mfg. co. engr.; b. Lincoln, Ill., Nov. 23, 1937; s. Harold Eugene and Eda Anna (Boerger) S.; B.S., U. Ill., 1959; postgrad Union Coll., Schenectady, 1975-76; m. Doris Irene Henrichsmeyer, June 8, 1958; children—Donald Harold, Diane Carol. With Gen. Electric Co., Morrison, Ill., 1959—, sr. design engr., 1969-72, mgr. product engring., 1972-75, sr. application engr., 1975—. Cleve. Air Soc. scholar, 1958. Mem. Fort Wayne Assn. Gen. Electric Engrs., Engrs. and Suprs. Assn., Elfun Assn. Lutheran. Patentee in field. Home: Route 2 Morrison IL 61270 Office: West Wall St Morrison IL 61270

STOLL, JOHN HENRY, clergyman, educator; b. Oxford, Pa., Feb. 22, 1925; s. Ralph Henry and Lula Irene (Beckley) S.; student Wheaton (Ill.) Coll., 1942-45; B.A., Manchester Coll., 1949; M.Div., Grace Sem., Winona Lake, Ind., 1949, Th.M., 1960; postgrad. U. Mo., 1962-64; Ph.D., U. Notre Dame (Ind.), 1975; m. Irma Aurich, Oct. 22, 1977; children by previous marriage—Kenneth, Jane, Kevin, Carolyn. Tchr. Wheaton Coll., 1949-51; prof. Cedarville (Ohio) Coll., 1951-57; ordained to ministery Baptist Ch., 1949; pastor Grace Chapel, West Liberty, Ohio, 1957-61; v.p., acad. dean Calvary Bible Coll., Kansas City, Mo., 1961-66; prof. philosophy of religion, chmn. dept. religion Grace Coll., Winona Lake, Ind., 1966-75; psychotherapist Christian Counseling Center, Mpls., 1977—. Bd. dirs. Camp Forest Springs, Westboro, Wis. Mem. AAUP, Ohio Hist. Soc., Evang. Theol. Soc., Am. Sci. Assn., Christian Camping Internat. Author: Old Testament-Poetry and Prophecy, 1969; The Book of Habbakuk, 1972; A Christian and His Life, 1977. Home: 1618 Amy Ln Minneapolis MN 55430

STOLL, JULIANA IMPERIAL, chemist; b. Manila, Apr. 19, 1924; d. Felix Samson and Dionisia Detera (Stedje) Imperial; came to U.S., 1946, naturalized, 1953; student U. Philippines, 1938-41; B.S., U. Puget Sound, 1947; postgrad. U. Wash., 1947; m. Joseph S. Stoll, Dec. 27, 1947; children—Denise R., Tina M. Asst. prof. Philippine Women's U., Manila, 1949-50; jr. chemist Uniroyal Inc., Painesville, Ohio, 1951-56, sr. chemist, 1956-76, chief chemist, 1976—. Roman Catholic. Research in determination of total solids by refractive index in nitrile latex. Home: 670 Riverside Dr Painesville OH 44077 Office: PO Box 460 Painesville OH 44077

STOLL, RICHARD FREDERICK, mgmt. cons.; b. Ann Arbor, Mich., Oct. 19, 1920; s. George Vincent and Marie Magdalene (Rentschler) S.; B.S., U. Mich., 1946, M.S., 1950; m. Phyllis Jean Wood, Aug. 9, 1941; children—Michael, Richard Frederick, George, Charles, Mary, Anne. Cost analyst U. Mich., Ann Arbor, 1950-53; exec. sec., editor Methods-Time Measurement Assn., Pitts., Ann Arbor, 1953-66, internat. sec. Methods-Time Measurement Internat. Directorate, Ann Arbor, 1957-66; Kellogg dir. continuing edn. U. Mich. Sch. Pub. Health, 1966-68; exec. dir., editor Internat. Material Mgmt. Assn., Washington and Ann Arbor, 1968-74; adminstrv. dir. Mich. Assn. Registered Med. Programs, 1974; mgmt. cons., 1975—. Instr. Inst. Research in Productivity, Waseda U., Tokyo, 1957; lectr. indsl. engring. U. Mich., 1965. Served with AUS, 1944-46. Mem. Am. Soc. Assn. Execs., Orgn. Execs. Mich. Club: Kiwanis. Home: 5000 Queen Oaks Dr Chelsea MI 48118

STOLL, THOMAS VINCENT, mgmt. and merger cons.; b. Milw., Sept. 14, 1923; s. Peter F. and Elsa D. (Weissleder) S.; B.B.A., Marquette U., 1951, student, 1946-51; m. Ann F. Pekar, Jan. 8, 1949; children—Thomas G., William E., Patrice M., Richard P., Donald J. Div. accountant A.O. Smith Corp., Milw., 1951-53; controller, treas. Milprint Inc., Milw., 1953-65; v.p. planning-fin. Philip Morris Indsl. Operating Co., Philip Morris, Inc., Milw., 1965-69; exec. v.p., treas., dir. Milprint Inc., Milw., 1969-73; pres. Thomas V. Stoll & Co. Inc., mgmt. and merger cons., 1973—. Troop leader Boy Scouts of Am., 1939-69, merit badge counselor, 1961-69. Served with USAAF, 1943-46. Roman Catholic. Home: 17765 Bonnie Ln Brookfield WI 53005 Office: 161 W Wisconsin Ave Milwaukee WI 53203

STOLL, WILLARD LEWIS, engr.; b. Corning, N.Y., Apr. 13, 1922; s. Willard Frank and Hazel Mildred (Stanton) S.; student Elmira Coll. Veterans Extension Center, 1946-47; B. Ae.E., U. Detroit, 1951; m. Cecelia Mary Syzdek, May 3, 1946; children—James Lewis, Susan Katherine, Daniel Willard. Stock expediter Ingersoll-Rand Co., Painted Post, N.Y., 1940-42; pre-engring. student asst. Elmira (N.Y.) Coll., 1946-47; engring. asst. Drake-Groves-Winkelman Constrn. Co., Elmira, 1947; coop engring. student U. Detroit, 1948-52; gen. foreman, staff asst. Kaiser Motors, Willow Run, Mich., 1952-53; process engr. Huron Engring. Corp., Roseville, Mich., 1953; material rev. engr. Continental Aviation and Engring. Co., Detroit, 1953-57; project engr. Teledyne-CAE, Toledo, 1956—. Scoutmaster, chmn. troop com., instl. rep. Boy Scouts Am., 1958—; cadet squadron advisor Civil Air Patrol, 1976—. Served with USN, 1942-46. Mem. Soc. Automotive Engrs. (mem. com.), Am. Inst. of Aero. and Astronautics, Am. Def. Preparedness Assn. Roman Catholic. Clubs: Monroe Rod and Gun, Mgmt.

STOLLER, WILLIAM LEWIS, educator; b. Schenectady, June 8, 1934; s. Guy William and Frances (Berlin) S.; B.A., Syracuse U., 1960, Ph.D., 1965; m. Rita Astride Vija Zarins, Dec. 22, 1961. Asst. prof. psychology Ind. U., Kokomo, 1967-72, asso. prof., 1972—. USPHS grantee; summer Faculty fellow. Mem. AAUP, AAAS, N.Y., Ind. acads. sci., Am. Psychol. Assn., Psychonomic Soc. Contbr. articles to profl. jours. Home: 2503 Bradford Ave Kokomo IN 46901

STOLPIN, DOROTHY FLORENCE MITCHELL (MRS. WILLIAM STOLPIN), registered stock rep.; b. Flint, Mich., June 12, 1917; d. Roger Earl and Neva Marie (Ketrow) Mitchell; A.S., Flint Jr. Coll., 1938; student Mich. State Coll., 1938, Washington U., summer 1938, Internat. Corr. Schs., 1948-50, Wis. Coll. Music, 1950-53; diploma in higher accounting Baker Bus. U., 1956, B.A. in Bus. Adminstrn., U. Mich. at Flint, 1967; certificates N.Y. Inst. Finance, 1956, 57, Investment Bankers Assn. Am., 1962, Gen. Motors Inst., 1969, 72; m. William Stolpin, Dec. 24, 1938; children—William Roger, Roger Mitchell. Pharm. trainee Hurley Hosp. Pharmacy, Flint, Mich., 1935-36; pvt. piano tchr., 1930-45; clk. Colony Shop, Whitefish Bay, Wis., 1952, Plimpton Music Shop, Whitefish Bay, 1952; rep. Fahnestock & Co., stock brokerage house, Flint, 1956—. Mailing chmn. Flint Community Players, 1961-68; mem. Greater Flint Arts Council; active Boy Scouts Am., Girl Scouts U. Solton. Fellow Harry S. Truman Library Inst.; mem. Am. Anthrop. Soc., AAUW, League Women Voters, Am. Mgmt. Assn., Women Stockbrokers Assn., Flint Inst. of Arts Founders Soc., Univ. (Mich.) Hist. Soc. of Archaeol. Soc. Mus. Soc., Soc. Am. Archaeology, Mich. Hist. Soc., Internat. Graphoanalysis Soc., Internat. Platform Assn., UN Assn. U.S., Postal Commemorative Soc. Genesee County Hist. Mus. Soc., Mich. Archaeol. Assn., Nat. Soc. Lit. and Arts, Mo. Archael. Soc., Mich. State U. Com. One Thousand, Flint Coll. and Cultural Devel. Assn., Marquis Biog. Library Soc., Musical Performing Arts Assn., Alumni Bus. Soc. Flint Coll. U. Mich., U. Mich. Alumni Assn. (life mem. permanent endowment fund), Pi Mu, Alpha Chi Omega (life). Club: Zonta (treas. 1961, dir. 1965-67); President's (Ann Arbor). Composer: Four Ducks On A Pond. Home: 140 E Carpenter Rd Flint MI 48505 Office: 346 S Saginaw St Flint MI 48502

STOLPIN, WILLIAM ROGER, mech. engr., artist; b. Flint, Mich., June 25, 1942; s. William and Dorothy Florence (Mitchell) S.; B.M.E., Gen. Motors Inst., 1965; m. Kathleen Diane Poyner, Aug. 14, 1970; 1 dau., Krishna Ann. Project engr. Buick Motor div. Gen. Motors Corp., Flint, 1969-73, reliability engr., 1973—; exhibited Left Bank Gallery, 1977; represented in permanent collection Nat. Air and Space Mus., Washington. Community mem. bd. edn. ad hoc com. on adult edn., 1975-77; bd. dirs. Flint Community Players, 1969-76; vice chmn. Greater Flint Arts Council, 1976-77; exec. bd. Friends of Modern Art, 1973; active Flint Inst. Art, 1972—. Named first in graphics Internat. Platform Assn. Art Show, 1969, hon. mention, 1976. Asso. fellow Brit. Interplanetary Soc.; mem. Am. Fedn. Arts, Internat. Platform Assn. (bd. govs.), Soc. Automotive Engrs., Am. Inst. Aeros. and Astronautics, Left Bank Gallery, Flint Artists Market, Mich. Archeol. Soc., Nat. Space Inst., World Future Soc. Home: 134 E Carpenter Rd Flint MI 48505 Office: Buick Motor Div Gen Motors Corp Flint MI 48550

STOLTZ, DANIEL LEWIS, metall. engr.; b. Princeton, Ind., Dec. 9, 1937; s. Eurus Vernon and Marjory (Mowe) S.; B.S., U. Ill., 1961; M.S., U. Fla., 1970, Ph.D., 1972; m. Orleen Faye Corn, Oct. 2, 1965; children—Daniel Lee, David Lewis, Douglas Lyle. Metall. engr. Delco Moraine div. Gen. Motors Corp., Dayton, Ohio, 1961-62; research metall. engr. Battelle Meml. Inst., Columbus, Ohio, 1962-66; grad. research asst., predoctoral asst. U. Fla., 1966-72; project engr., sr. supr. metall. and finishes sect. Materials Engring. dept. Bendix Corp., Kansas City, Mo., 1972—. Sports coordinator, basketball and soccer coach St. John LaLande Sch., 1974—; v.p. St John LaLande Sch. PTA, 1975—; asst. mgr. Little League Baseball, Blue Springs, Mo., 1974-75, asst. coach Pop Warner Football League, 1976—. Registered high sch. ofcl. basketball and football, Mo., Kans., 1973-75. Mem. Am. Soc. Metals (mem. exec. com. 1974-76, vice-chmn. 1976-77, chmn. 1977), Am. Vacuum Soc., ASTM, AAAS, Microbean Analysis Soc., U. Fla. Alumni Assn., Sigma Xi, Omicron Delta Kappa, Alpha Sigma Mu (pres. 1971-72), Epsilon Lambda Chi. Contbr. articles to profl. jours.; patentee in field. Home: 506 Wedgewood Dr Blue Springs MO 64015 Office: 2000 E Bannister Rd PO Box 1159 Kansas City MO 64141

STONE, ALAN, paperboard and corrugated box, plastic and packaging machinery mfg. co. exec.; b. Chgo., Feb. 5, 1928; s. Norman H. and Ida (Finkelstein) S.; B.S.E., U. Pa., 1951; m. Joan Ehemann, Dec. 27, 1962; children—Christie Anne, Joshua M. With Stone Container Corp., Chgo., 1951—, area mgr., 1969-72, mktg. v.p., 1972—. Sr. v.p. Jewish Vocat. Service, 1977; chmn. Vocat. Research Council. Mem. Beta Alpha Psi, Phi Eta Sigma, Zeta Beta Tau. Jewish (trustee, v.p. Sinai synagogue). Clubs: Standard, Bryn Mawr Country, Tavern (Chgo.). Home: 233 E Walton St Chicago IL 60611 Office: 360 N Michigan Ave Chicago IL 60601

STONE, DONALD DIAMOND, investment co. exec.; b. Chgo., June 25, 1924; s. Frank J. and Mary N. (Miller) Diamondstone; student U. Ill., 1942-43; B.S., DePaul U., 1949; m. Catherine Mauro, Dec. 20, 1970; children—Richard, Jeffrey. Pres., Poster Bros., Inc., Chgo., 1950-71, Revere Leather Goods, Inc., Chgo., 1953-71; owner Don Stone Enterprises, Chgo., 1954—; v.p. Horton & Hubbard Mfg. Co., Inc. div. Brown Group, Nashua, N.H., 1969-71, Neevel Mfg. Co., Kansas City, Mo., 1969-71. Served with U.S. Army, 1943-46. Club: Bryn Mawr Country. Home: 209 E Lake Shore Dr Chicago IL 60611 Office: 875 N Michigan Ave Suite 4012 Chicago IL 60611

STONE, FARILYN, real estate exec.; b. Rantoul, Ill., Sept. 29, 1909; d. Orin Edson and Helen (Holsman) Crooker; student Butler U., evenings 1951-63; grad. Nat. Sch. Fashion Design, 1953; m. Walter Fred Stone, June 28, 1931 (dec. Oct. 1942); 1 son, Walter Fred. Partner, Frank's Sales & Service, auto dealer Princeton, Ind., 1945-51; asst. office mgr. Johnson Chevrolet Co., Indpls., 1951-56; head billing dept. Vonnegut Hardware Co., Indpls., 1956-63; exec. sec. C.S. Ober, Indpls., 1963—; instr. bus. courses Ind. Coll. Bus. and Tech., evenings 1963-73; pres. Balsam Ct. Apts., Inc., Pkwy. Apts., Inc., Indpls., 1966-75; treas. Ober Bldg. Corp., Indpls., 1973—. Sec., Mapleton Fall Creek Neighborhood Assn., Inc., 1965-75; mem. 1st Congregational Ch., Indpls., 1952—, clk., 1977—. Named Sec. of Day, Radio Sta. WIFE, 1971; certified property mgr. Mem. Bus. and Profl. Women's Club (2d v.p. 1970-73), Am. Theatre Organ Soc. (treas. 1973—), Exec. Women Internat. Club: Order Eastern Star. Home: 4303 Washington Blvd Indianapolis IN 46205 Office: 38 N Pennsylvania Indianapolis IN 46204

STONE, FRANK FAIRBANKS, educator; b. Bellows Falls, Vt., Feb. 26, 1909; s. Frank Hubbard and Edith Mary (Westney) S.; grad. New Eng. Conservatory Music, 1927-31; B.A., Hiram Coll., 1933; M.A., Hartford Sem. Found., 1940; M.Divinity, Union Theol. Sem., 1944; postgrad. (St. Bartholomew's fellow), Gen. Theol. Sem., 1943-44;

M.S.T. (Jacobus fellow), Hartford Sem. Found., 1945, Th.D., 1950; postdoctoral La. Tech. U., 1959-60. Asst. to dean adminstrn., tutor Hartford (Conn.) Sem. Found., 1947-59; asso. prof. history Bethel Coll., McKenzie, Tenn., 1960-63; prof. philosophy and religion, chmn. dept. Sch. of Ozarks, Point Lookout, Mo., 1963-76, prof. emeritus, 1976—. Area cons. in religious edn., Hartford, 1947-59, Southwest Mo., 1963—. Mem. Am. Acad. Religion, AAUP, Center for Study Democratic Instns., Religious Edn. Assn., Soc. for Sci. Study Religion, Internat. Platform Assn. Home: Point Lookout MO 65726

STONE, GAYLE VAUGHN, psychologist; b. Abilene, Tex., Aug. 20, 1943; s. Victor Von and Christene Moselle (Pack) S.; B.A., Northwestern Coll., 1965; Ph.D., U. Minn., 1970; m. Priscilla Ruth Elftmann, Dec. 26, 1964; children—Larisa Marie, Gregory Vaughn. Trainee, Vocat. Rehab. Adminstrn., 1966, VA, 1967-70; psychologist, Lebanon (Pa.) VA Hosp., 1970-71; counseling psychologist Wood (Wis.) VA Center, 1971—. Lectr., Pa. State U., 1971, U. Wis., Waukesha, 1972, Marquette U., Milw., 1972-74; asst. prof. Med. Coll. Wis., 1971—. Mem. Am. Psychol. Assn., Am. Personnel and Guidance Assn. Home: 124 N 85th St Wauwatosa WI 53226 Office: 5000 National Ave Wood WI 53193

STONE, GEORGE STEINGOETTER, broadcasting exec.; b. Belleville, Ill., Apr. 5, 1920; s. George H. and Bessie (Dew) S.; student Western Military Academy, 1935-37; student Shurtleff Coll., 1937-38; m. Helen M. Ehrmann, Aug. 29, 1944; children—Mary Elizabeth, Anne Helen. Radio announcer King-Trendle Broadcasting Corp., Grand Rapids, Mich., 1941-44; announcer, newscaster, music commentator NBC, Chgo., 1944-66; program dir. Zenith Radio Corp.-WEFM, 1966-70, gen. mgr., 1970-73; gen. mgr. GCC Communications Chgo. Inc., 1973—. Bd. dirs. Chgo. Chamber Orch. Assn., 1961—, pres., 1962-69, hon. pres., 1969—; bd. dirs. Youth Guidance-Youth Service, 1957-71, pres., 1968-70; governing mem. Chgo. Symphony Orch. Assn.; adv. bd. Young Friends of Arts. Mem. Chgo. Unltd. (chmn. bd.), Nat. Acad. TV Arts and Scis. (gov. Chgo.), Broadcast Pioneers, Nat. Assn. Broadcasters, UN Assn. U.S.A. (mem. space communications adv. com. Ill. div.). Republican. Presbyterian. Clubs: Merchants and Manufacturers, Executives; Glen Lake Yacht (dir.) (Glen Arbor, Mich.). Home: 3204 Wilmette Rd Wilmette IL 60091 Office: GCC Communications Chgo Inc 120 W Madison Chicago IL 60602

STONE, J. W., sch. adminstr.; b. Fortescue, Mo., Nov. 6, 1927; s. Perry Allen and May (Murrah) S.; B.S., N.W. Mo. State Coll., 1956; M.A., U. Mo. at Kansas City, 1957, also postgrad. Farmer, Fortescue, Mo., 1944—; instr. Craig (Mo.) R-III High Sch., 1957-59; supt. schs., Holt County, Oregon, Mo., 1959-61, Craig R-III Sch. Dist., 1961—. Del. to Hungary, USSR, Internat. Edn. Soc., 1968. Dist. dir. A.R.C., 1954—; mem. bd. Heart Assn., Crippled Children's, March of Dimes, Tb Soc., 1954—; mem. Town Bd., Fotescue, Mo., 1962—; vice chmn. Wesley Found., N.W. Mo. State U., 1970—; mem. regional empire com. bd. Girl Scouts, 1973—; mem. com. Mo. Council Pub. Higher Edn., 1973; regional dir. Mo. Vocational Rehab., 1967—. Mem. 6th Congl. Dist., 1960—, 6th Congl. Legislative Dist., 1960—, Mo. Republican State Com., 1964—; chmn. Holt County Rep. Central Com., 1954—; mayor, Fortescue, 1972—. Dir. Office of Econ. Opportunity Corp.; sec.-treas. N.W. Mo. Econ. Opportunity Corp., Maryville, Mo., chmn. bd., 1969—; v.p. Mo. Council Chs., 1948-50; dir. Camps and Conf. Mo. W. Conf., United Meth. Ch., 1965—, mem. bd. adminstrv. finance, 1972—; U.S. del. World Meth. Council Meeting, Dublin, 1976; Maryville dist. trustee Meth. Ch., 1960—. World del. Meth. Conf., Oslo, Norway, 1961; del. United Meth. Ch. Mo. West Conf. to World Meth. Council Evangelism, Jerusalem, Israel, 1974; world del. representing U.S. on Christian Edn., Tokyo, Japan, 1958; U.S. del. Comparative and Internat. Edn. Soc., Round-the-World, 1970, South Am., 1971. Served with AUS, 1950-52. Mem. N.E.A., Nat., Mo. State assns. sch. adminstrs., Mo. State, Holt County (past pres.) tchrs. assns., Pi Omega Pi, Kappa Delta Pi, Tau Kappa Epsilon. Methodist (dist. lay leader 1968—). Mason (32 deg., Shriner); mem. Order Eastern Star. Home: Fortescue MO 64452 Office: Craig MO 64437

STONE, JAMES HIRAM, oil co. exec.; b. N.Y.C., Dec. 20, 1925; s. Jacob Chauncey and Isabel (Greenbaum) S.; B.A., Williams Coll.; postgrad. in geology Tex. A & M U., 1950; m. Elizabeth Asbury, June 28, 1951; children—Suzanne, Andrew, Thomas, Margaret. Owner, operator Stone Oil Co., Cin., 1951—, chmn. bd., chief exec. officer, 1975—; dir. Isted Am. Exchange Corp., Westone Corp. Trustee Bellurmire Coll.; bd. dirs. New Orleans Crime Commn., 1976—. Served to capt. U.S. Marine Corp., 1943-46. Mem. Ind. Petroleum Assn. Am., New Orleans, Lafayette geol. socs. Republican. Episcopalian. Clubs: Los Angeles Rams Football (dir.), Cin. Country, Queen City (Cin.); Lake Placid (N.Y.); Cricuet, Palm Bay (Miami, Fla.); Petroleum, Plimsoli, New Orleans Country (New Orleans). Office: 3100 Fountain Sq Plaza Cincinnati OH 45202

STONE, JOHN BROUGHMAN, sch. adminstr.; b. Hanover, Ind., Aug. 29, 1918; s. Charles H. and Fay E. (Broughman) S.; student Purdue U., 1937; B.S., Ball State U., 1942, M.A., 1949, postgrad., 1973-74; m. Mabel A. Coleman, Aug. 13, 1941; children—John Kenton, Craig Coleman. Coach, tchr., Marion (Ind.) High Sch., 1945-60, athletic dir., sch. adminstr., 1960-65; prin. Mt. Vernon (Ind.) High Sch., 1965-68; prin. Rochester (Ind.) Community High Sch., 1968-75, North Miami High Sch., Denver, Ind., 1975—. Mem. Ind. Bd. Edn., 1969—. Served with AUS, 1941-45; ETO. Republican. Presbyterian (elder 1955—). Kiwanian. Club: Exchange (pres. 1964-65). Home: Box 117 Barrett Rd Rochester IN 46975 Office: North Miami High Sch Denver IN 46926

STONE, MORTON BERTRAND, pub. relations agy. exec.; b. N.Y.C., Aug. 16, 1929; s. Joseph and Susan (Rowitz) S.; B.A., U. Okla., 1950; m. Sybil H. Liebman, Nov. 22, 1953 (div.); children—Beth Amy, Matthew Laurance. Sci. editor Drug Topics mag., N.Y.C., 1951-54; pub. relations mgr. Pfizer Co., N.Y.C., 1954-56; dir. pub. relations Roche Labs., Nutley, N.J., 1957-58; v.p. Fuller Miele Inc., N.Y.C., 1958-62; pres. Morton B. Stone & Assos., Chgo., 1962—. Cons. to div. dental health USPHS, 1971-73. Bd. dirs. Citizens Against Noise, Chgo., 1972—, Better Boys Found., Chgo., 1974-75, Nat. Found. for Prevention Oral Disease, 1974—. Mem. Publicity Club Chgo. (v.p. 1974-75, bd. dirs. 1971-75), Am. Acad. Periodontology (hon.), Sigma Delta Chi. Editor Pharmacists Mgmt. mag., 1971-72. Home: 2001 Sherman Ave Evanston IL 60201 Office: 3553 W Peterson Ave Chicago IL 60659

STONE, NICHOLAS LOUIS, ret. air force officer, recreational and social service adminstr.; b. Berlin, May 25, 1930; s. William Gus and Mdrgaret Louise (Budgereit) S.; came to U.S., 1939, naturalized, 1939; B.A., Syracuse U., 1962; M.S., U. Colo., 1966; m. Laura Ann Mitchell, Jan. 10, 1958; children—Teresa Ann, William Matthew. Enlisted in U.S. Air Force, 1951, advanced through grades to lt. col., 1971; dir. of budget for 15th Air Force, Calif., 1968-71; dir. of mgmt. analysis for 8th Air Force, Westover AFB, Mass., 1966-68; chief mgmt. analyst SAC, 8th Air Force, Chicopee, Mass., 1966-68, 15th Air Force, Riverside, Calif., 1968-71; ret., 1971; purchasing mgr. Nat. Homes Corp., W. Lafayette, Ind., 1971-73; fiscal officer Ill. State Fair, Springfield, 1973-74, asst. mgr., 1973-76, dir., 1976—. Mem. exec. bd. Land of Lincoln council Boy Scouts Am., 1976—. Decorated Legion of Merit. Mem. Am. Mgmt. Assn., Air Force Assn., Ret. Officers Assn., Am. Legion, Adminstrv. Mgmt. Assn. Republican. Lutheran. Clubs: Elks, Rotary, Optimists. Home: 2909 Arlington Springfield IL 62704 Office: PO Box 567 Springfield IL 62705

STONE, PAUL, lawyer, lawyer, state legislator; b. Newton, Ill., Sept. 21, 1915; s. Claude Lee and Ruth (Stewart) S.; B.S., U. Ill., 1940, J.D., 1942; m. Thelma Lucille Jones, Feb. 5, 1939; children—Elaine (Mrs. James Kirk), Paul Lee, Michael L., Marsha (Mrs. James Daniel). Admitted to Ill. bar, 1942; practiced in Sullivan, Ill., 1942—; mem. firm Stone & Stone, Sullivan; mem. Ill. Ho. of Reps., 1950-51, 66—. Mem. Ill. State U. Found., 1962-66, Western Ill. U. Found., 1962-66; mem. Univ. Civil Services Merit Bd., 1962-66; chmn. bd. govs. State Colls. and Univs. Ill., 1964-66; chmn. bd. Ill. Tchrs. Coll., 1962-64. Recipient Outstanding Legislator award Fedn. of Ind. Coll. and Univs. and Young Dems. of Ill., 1972, Social Justice award United Auto Workers, 1972; named Alumnus of Month U. Ill. Law Sch., 1973, Outstanding Legislator award Ill. Community Coll. Trustees Assn., 1974. Mason, Kiwanian. Home: 1 Harbor Dr South Shores Sullivan IL 61951 Office: 112 N Main St Sullivan IL 61951

STONE, PAUL DOUGLAS, chem. engr.; b. Ottawa, Kans., Feb. 7, 1940; s. Paul Edwin and Ollie Francis (Zook) S.; B.S. in Chem. Engring., U. Kans., 1963; M.S. in Chem. Engring., U. Fla., 1967; postgrad. Mich. State U., U. Mich.; m. Betty Jane Hardage, Aug. 12, 1961; children—Deborah Jane, Trisha Denise. With Dow Chem. Co., Midland, Mich., 1968—, beginning as sr. materials engr., successively sr. pilot plant project leader, sr. area engr. maintenance tech. center, group leader materials and corrosion research and devel., 1968-76, group leader Halogens Research Lab., 1976—. Loaned exec. United Community Fund; pres. Adams Grade Sch. Parent Tchr. Orgn., 1974-76. Served to capt. USAF, 1963-68. Registered profl. engr., Mich. Mem. Am. Inst. Chem. Engrs. (chmn. Mid-Mich. sect.), Nat. Assn. Corrosion Engrs., Am. Chem. Soc., Aircraft Owners and Pilots Assn., Nat. Eagle Scout Assn. Democrat. Methodist. Home: 5613 Whitehall St Midland MI 48640 Office: 768 Bldg Dow Chem Co Midland MI 48640

STONE, ROBERT NORTON, lawyer; b. Mpls., Oct. 10, 1930; s. Sol William and Ruth Cerna (Hersch) S.; B.S.L., U. Minn., 1954, J.D., 1956; m. Nancy Atlas, June 28, 1953; children—Karen, Gary, Gregg. Admitted to Minn. bar, 1956, U.S. Supreme Ct. bar, 1960; partner firm William H. DeParcq, 1956-64, Scallen, Stone, Evidon & Harder, 1964-65, Rothman & Stone, 1965-67, Stone & Stone, 1967-69, Rothman, Stone & Fallon, 1969-71, Rerat, Crill, Foley & Boursier, 1972-75, Rerat Law Firm, P.A., 1976—, all Mpls. Commr., City Hopkins, Minn., 1968—; referee Hennepin County Dist. Ct., 1965. Mem. Nat. Lawyers' Com. for Johnson & Humphrey, 1964. Served with USAF, 1951-52. Fellow Law Sci. Acad. Am.; mem. A.F.T.R.A., Nat. Panel Arbitrators, Am., Hennepin County (chmn. legal med. com. 1972-73), Minn. bar assns., Minn. (bd. govs. 1964-73, pres. 1971-72), Am. (bd. govs. 1971-74) trial lawyers assns., Am. Arbitration Assn., Democratic Farmer Labor party. Mem. B'nai B'rith. Club: Variety of NW (Mpls.). Home: 14901 Wychewood Rd Minnetonka MN 55343 Office: 656 IDS Center Minneapolis MN 55402

STONE, THOMAS HASKEL, co. exec.; b. Chgo., Mar. 13, 1942; s. Saul and Esther (Winokur) S.; B.A. in Anthropology, Northwestern U., 1964, grad. Sch. Bus. Adminstrn., 1966; m. Donna Cohn, July 26, 1964; children—Kimberly Ellen, Thomas Haskel. Exec. v.p. dir. Saul Stone & Co., Chgo., 1965—; treas., dir. V.J. Benincasa Co., Chgo., 1967—; exec. v.p., dir. Stone Commodities Corp., Chgo., 1970—, Sioux Livestock Co., 1975—, Gervais Meat Co. Inc., 1975—, Stonarco, Inc., Chgo., 1975—; sec., dir. Benco Pet Foods, Inc., Benco Internat., Inc., 1974—; dir. Bartow Food Co. Mem. Chgo. Bd. Trade, 1966-71; mem. Chgo. Merc. Exchange, 1963—, mem. clearing house, cattle, pork, finance and quotations coms., 1965—; mem. Internat. Monetary Market, 1972—; mem., bd. dirs. Minn. Grain Exchange, 1972—. Mem. Field Mus. Natural History, Art Inst. Chgo.; patron Ravinia Festival Assn. Clubs: Executive, Metropolitan (Chgo.). Office: 222 S Riverside Plaza Chicago IL 60606

STONE, W. CLEMENT, ins. exec.; b. Chgo., May 4, 1902: s. Louis and Anna M. (Gunn) S.; student Detroit Coll. Law, 1920, Northwestern U., 1930-32; LL.D., Monmouth Coll., 1963; H.H.D., Interlochen Arts Acad., 1964; Litt.D., Coll. Chiropractic, Lombard, 1969; H.H.D. (hon.), Whitworth Coll., 1969, S.W. Baptist Coll., 1970, Lincoln Coll., 1970; LL.D., Whittier Coll., 1973; D. Pub. Service, Salem Coll., 1974; m. Jessie Verna Tarson; children—Clement, Donna, Norman. Chmn. bd., dir. Combined Am. Ins. Co., Dallas; chmn. bd. Combined Ins. Co. Am., Chgo.: pres., dir. Combined Life Ins. Co. N.Y., Albany; chmn. bd. Combined Opportunities, Inc., Chgo.; chmn. bd., chief exec. officer, dir. Combined Ins. Co. Wis., Fond du Lac, Wis., pres., treas., dir. Combined Registry Co.; organizer Combined Mut. Casualty Co., 1940, pres. 1940-47; dir. Alberto-Culver Co.; chmn. bd. Hawthorn Books, N.Y.C., Success Unltd., Chgo., Hughes Engring., Santa Ana; dir. Commerce & Industry Ins. Co., N.Y.C. Chmn. bd. Chgo. Boys Club; mem. Com. Preservation White House; mem. nat exec. com. Boys Club Am.; chmn. bd. W. Clement and Jessie V. Stone Found. Trustee George Williams Coll.; bd. govs. Chgo. Heart Assn.; bd. dirs., mem. Lyric Guild, Lyric Opera Chgo.; pres., trustee Religious Heritage Am., hon. trustee So. Baptist Coll., trustee Urol. Research Found., Coll. Medicine U. Utah; chmn. trustees Interlochen Arts Acad. and Nat. Music Camp. Recipient Horatio Alger award, 1963; Church Layman of the Year award, 1968. Mem. Chgo. Planetarium Soc., Chgo. Assn. Health Underwriters Chgo., Am. Life Ins. Assn., Soc. Midland Authors, United Shareholders Am. (mem. nat. policy adv. com.), Art Inst. Chgo., Northwestern U. Alumni Assn., Ill. C. of C., Ins. Fedn. Ill., Chgo. Edml. TV Assn. (trustee), Insts. Religion and Health (chmn. bd.), Alpha Kappa Psi. Presbyn. Mason. Clubs: Chicago Press, John Evans, Executives, Michigan Shores Country. Author: (with Napoleon Hill) Success Through a Positive Mental Attitude: (with Norma Lee Browning) The Other Side of the Mind; The Success System that Never Fails. Editor, pub. Success Unltd. mag. Office: 5050 Broadway Chicago IL 60640

STONE, WILLIAM ROYAL, graphic designer, typographer; b. Cin., Dec. 12, 1925; s. Royal Amidon and Ruth Sherman (Andrews) S.; B.A., Antioch Coll., 1949; postgrad. Graphic Inst., Stockholm, Sweden, 1949, Sch. Graphic Studies, Stockholm, 1949; m. Nancy Pierce Young, July 28, 1947; children—John, Emily. Founder, pres. Sequoia Press, Kalamazoo, 1950-71, dir. design Sequoia Design Group Communication Technics Center, Inc., Kalamazoo, 1971-73; sr. graphic designer Franklin Mint, Franklin Center, Pa., 1973-74; dir. design and typography Embossing Printers, Inc., Battle Creek, Mich., 1974—. Instr. layout and design Western Mich. U., 1967. Mem. edn. com. Kalamazoo Art Center, 1971-72; art dir., designer Dimensions mag. Simpson Lee Paper Co., 1957-72, World Graphics mag. Kimberley Clark Corp., 1961-63; work represented in numerous profl. jours. Mem. Soc. Typog. Arts, Typophiles, Am. Inst. Graphic Arts. Democrat. Unitarian. Home: 2219 Sycamore Ln Kalamazoo MI 49008 Office: Embossing Printers Inc Box 1025 Battle Creek MI 49016

STONECIPHER, ELDO HUGH, automotive mfg. exec.; b. DePauw, Ind., May 31, 1910; s. L.A. and Charlotte (Jones) S.; B.S. in Mech. Engring., Purdue, U., 1932; Dr. Laws (hon.), Franklin (Ind.) U.; m. Edna Steffen, May 6, 1934 (dec.); children—Sue Carol, Judith Lynn, m. 2d, Mrs. William Oswalt, Aug. 17, 1973; step-children—Phillip Oswalt, Mrs. Kelly. With Arvin Industries, Inc., Columbus, Ind., 1932—, dir. and plant mgr., 1944-50, mgr. Greenwood, Franklin and Seymour, Ind. divs., 1950-55, v.p., gen. mgr. automotive div., 1955-60, pres., chief exec. officer, 1960-70, chmn. bd., 1970—; dir. emeritus Franklin Bank & Trust Co., Am. Fletcher Corp., Mem. future planning commn., Franklin, 1947. Faculty adviser sch. bus. Ind. U. Bd. dirs. Johnson County Tb Assn. Mem. Franklin and Columbus (past dir.), Ind. (v.p., dir.) chambers commerce, Ind. Mfrs. Assn. (dir.), Beta Gamma Sigma, Phi Kappa Alpha. Presbyn. (elder). Mason (Shriner). Clubs: Columbia; Hillview Country (past pres., dir.); Harrison Lake Country (past pres.); Rotary (past pres. Franklin and Columbus). Home: Rural Route 9 N Harrison Lake Columbus IN 47201 Office: Arvin Industries Inc 13th and Big 4 Rural Route Columbus IN 47201

STONEHILL, MAURICE LEWIS, glass co. exec.; b. Marshalltown, Iowa, Oct. 17, 1901; s. Joseph and Pearl (Zukav) S.; student U. Minn., 1920-22; m. Marjorie Handel, Nov. 23 1932. Pres., Stonehill Creameries, Cleve., 1929-60, Colston Optical Co., Cleve., 1954-61; chmn. bd. Jeannette Corp. (Pa.), 1960—; chmn. bd. E.B. Brown Optical Co., Cleve., 1968—. Pres. council, fellow Brandeis U. Jewish (trustee temple). Club: Presidents (Ohio State U.). Home: 19601 Van Aken Blvd Cleveland OH 44122 Office: 1549 E 30th St Cleveland OH 44114

STONER, JAMES EDWARD, data processing co. exec.; b. Fremont, Ohio, Jan. 24, 1930; s. Russell Ferman and Datha Viola (Wheeler) S.; grad. Davis Bus. Coll., 1949; student Bowling Green State U., 1948-49, U. Wis., 1957-58, Northwestern U., 1960-61; m. Elizabeth Warner, July 10, 1951; children—Susan, William, Michael, Russell. Auditor, ops. officer Croghan Colonial Bank, Fremont, 1949-63; v.p., dir. First Nat. Bank, Bowling Green, Ohio, 1963-65; pres., chief exec. officer, dir. Fin. Computer Services, Inc., Fremont, 1965-75; v.p. ADP Banking & Thrift Services, Fremont, 1975—; v.p., dir. Payment Systems, Inc., N.Y.C., 1968-69; acting chief exec. BancSystems Assn., Rocky River, Ohio, 1969-70, trustee, 1968—, chmn., 1971-72. Mem. adv. com. on tech. Bowling Green State U. Wood county chmn. fund raising Girl Scouts U.S.A., 1963; active Boy Scouts Am., various community drives. Bd. dirs. YMCA, Jr. Achievement. Served with AUS, 1951-53. Recipient Author's award Auditgram, Nat. Assn. Bank Auditors and Controllers, 1964; Jaycees Spoke award. Mem. Pres. Assn., Bank Adminstrn. Inst. (pres. Toledo chpt. 1965-66), Nat. Assn. Bank Servicers (dir. 1972-73), C. of C. (trustee, finance chmn. 1972-74). Episcopalian (sr. warden, treas. 1966-68, mem. diocesan commn. on ministry 1969-74). Clubs: Country, Masons. Home: 59 Pinewood Dr Fremont OH 43420 Office: 2201 Commerce Dr PO Box 471 Fremont OH 43420

STONER, MAX DOYLE, accountant; b. West Unity, Ohio, Mar. 26, 1927; s. Beryl Vincent and Francis Ruth (Davis) S.; B.S., Ohio State U., 1950; m. Donna Craig, Oct. 1, 1950; children—Michael D., Susan L., Diane C. Salesman telephone Farm Bur. Coop., Columbus, Ohio, 1950; trainee City Nat. Bank, Columbus, 1950-51; accountant Brandt & Lee Co., Columbus, 1952-64; practice accounting, Worthington, Ohio, 1964—; pres. J. Plaza Inc., Worthington, 1966—. Treas., King Ave. United Methodist Ch., 1964—; fin. adviser Childhood League Inc. Served with USNR, 1946-47, 51-52. C.P.A., Ohio. Mem. Columbus, Worthington chambers commerce, Ohio Soc. C.P.A.'s. Republican. Clubs: Univ. Columbus, Masons. Home: 3336 Kirkham Rd Columbus OH 43221 Office: 6902 N High St Worthington OH 43085

STONER, RAYMOND ROSS, indsl. valve and control mfg. co. exec.; b. Mpls., Jan. 10, 1924; s. Raymond Everett and Grace Elizabeth (Robertson) S.; student U. Minn., 1941, Calif. Inst. Tech., 1943-44; m. Margaret Lorraine Bredeson, Aug. 4, 1943; children—Ann Stoner Kussman, Susan Stoner Legatt. Mechanical draftsman Mpls. Moline Power Implement Co., 1941-42; with DeZurik Corp., Sartell, Minn., 1942—, v.p. engring. Indsl. div. chmn. St. Cloud (Minn.) area United Way, 1971, campaign vice-chmn., 1972, gen. campaign chmn., 1973. Served with U.S. Army, 1942-46. Mem. ASME, Am. Mgmt. Assn. Presbyn. Club: Lions (pres.) (Sartell, Minn.). Home: Pine Point Route 2 St Cloud MN 56301 Office: DeZurik Corp Sartell MN 56377

STONER, RICHARD BURKETT, engine mfg. co. exec.; b. Ladogo, Ind., May 15, 1920: s. E.N. and Florence B. (Burkett) S.; B.S., Ind. U., 1941; J.D., Harvard, 1947: m. Virginia Austin, Feb. 22, 1942; children—Pamela, Richard, Benjamin, Janet, Rebecca, Joanne. Admitted to Ind. bar, 1947; with Cummins Engine Co., Inc., Columbus, 1947—, various adminstrv. and exec. positions, 1947-66, exec. v.p., gen. mgr., 1966-69, vice chmn. bd., 1969—; dir. Kirloskel Cummins Ltd., Am. Fletcher Nat. Bank & Trust Co., Pub. Service Ind., Am. Fletcher Bank Switzerland S.A., Am. United Life Ins. Co. Democratic nat. committeeman, 1966—. Bd. dirs. Christian Found; bd. dirs., vice chmn. Cummins Engine Found.; bd. dirs., pres. Irwin-Sweeney-Miller Found.; trustee Ind. U.; chmn. Ind. Forum, Inc. Served as capt., finance dept. AUS, World War II. Mem. Ind. C. of C. (dir.), MAPI (exec. com.), Sigma Nu. Democrat. Mem. Disciples of Christ. Club: Indianapolis Athletic. Home: 2770 Franklin St Columbus IN 47201 Office: 301 Washington St Columbus IN 47201

STONESTREET, RUTH HORNING, speech and lang. pathologist; b. Evansville, Ind., Apr. 12, 1947; d. Joel Ralph and Kathryne Josephine (Davis) Horning; B.S., Miss. U. for Women, 1969, M.S., 1971; m. William Garland Stonestreet, Jr., Nov. 27, 1971; 1 son, William Garland III. Speech pathologist Sanders Sch. for Cerebral Palsy, Jackson, Miss., 1969-70; instr., clin. supr. speech pathology Brescia Coll., Owensboro, Ky., 1971-73; supr. cons. staff cons. on speech, lang. and hearing, dept. mental health Macomb-Oakland Regional Center, Mt. Clemens, Mich., 1973-75; speech-lang. pathologist Macomb Intermediate Sch. Dist., Mt. Clemens, 1975—. Recipient Outstanding Contbn. award Macomb-Oakland Regional Center, 1975. Mem. Am. (certified in speech pathology), Mich., Macomb-St. Clair speech and hearing assns., Council for Exceptional Children, Am. Assn. for Mental Deficiency. Democrat. Presbyterian. Author: Clinical Guide for Students in Speech Pathology, 1972; Language and Speech Development Training Manual: A Guide for Training the Mentally Retarded, 1975; Language and Speech Guidelines for Activities of Daily Living, 1976. Home: 340 Woodside Ct Rochester MI 48063 Office: 44001 Garfield Rd Mount Clemens MI 48044

STOPHER, PETER ROBERT, civil engr.; b. Crowborough, Sussex, Eng., Aug. 8, 1943; s. Harold Edward and Joan Constance (Salmon) S.; came to U.S., 1968; B.Sc., U. Coll. London, 1964, Ph.D., 1967; m. Valerie Anne Alway, Apr. 11, 1964; children—Helen, Claire. Research officer Dept. Hwy. and Transp., Greater London Council (Eng.), 1967-68; asst. prof. civil engring. Northwestern U., Evanston, Ill., 1968-70, asso. prof., 1973—, dir. research Transp. Center, 1975—; asst. prof. civil engring. McMaster U., Hamilton, Ont., Can., 1970-71; asso. prof. Cornell U., Ithaca, N.Y., 1971-73; transp. adviser Nat. Inst.

Transport and Rd. Research, S. Africa, 1977; cons. to Paul C. Box Assos., 1969, H.W. Lochner Inc., 1969-70, Planning Research Corp., 1972-73, World Bank, 1972-74, Gen. Motors Research Labs., 1973-75, Charles River Assos., 1975—, J.E. Leisch & Asso., Inc., 1975-76, Commonwealth Bur. Roads (Australia), 1975, Arthur Young & Co., 1976, ABT Assos., 1976—. Recipient Fred Burgraaf award Hwy. Research Bd., 1969. R.B. Hounsfield prize and scholar, 1964-66. Mem. Transp. Research Bd., Transp. Research Forum (acad. v.p. 1973-74, program v.p. 1974-75, exec. v.p. 1975-76), ASCE, Am. Statis. Assn., Regional Sci. Assn., Inst. Civil Engrs., Royal Statis. Soc., Inst. Hwy. Engrs. Home: 115 Lockerbie Ln Wilmette IL 60091 Office: Dept Civil Engring Northwestern U Evanston IL 60201

STORBECK, HELEN IRENE, service organization exec.; b. Peabody, Kans., Jan. 20, 1927; d. Gilbert Arthur and Gladys Glessner (Burton) Manka; A.A. Colo. Woman's Coll. 1947; A.B. U. of Kans. 1949; student Ciudad Universitaria of Mex. City 1947, SW Coll. of Winfield 1978—; m. Dean Robert Storbeck, Aug. 7, 1949; children—Todd Robert, Chris Burton, Scott Nelson. Secy., asst. to editor U. of Kans. Alumni Assn., Lawrence, 1948-50; office mgr. Dwellette Modular Homes, Wichita, Kans., 1950; exec. secy. for project engr. Boeing Co., Wichita 1950-51; state pres. PEO philanthropic-ednl. organization Winfield, Kans. 1977-78. Secy. Cowley County (Kans.) TB Assn. 1954-60; mem. bldg. com. First United Meth. Ch., Winfield, 1965-67; mem. special com. for new high sch. Winfield, 1970-71, hosp. auxiliary 1960—, com. for evaluation of cooperating Winfield colls. 1974-75. Mem. MW Genealogical Soc., Nat. Sons and Daughters of Kans., Nat. Assn. of Parliamentarians, Sigma Nu. Republican. Methodist. Clubs: Hypatia Study, Sorosis Study, United Meth. Women. Author: Genealogical Record of Henry Jacob Manka Family, 1833-1965, 1965; Nonken Family Record 1821-1967, 1967; Genealogical Record of Christian Stauffer Kraft and Philip Kraft Family 1816-1970, 1970; Winfield Rotary Club, Fifty Golden Years, 1968; editor United Methodist Women newsletter 1974-77. Address: 219 Park St Winfield KS 67156

STORCE, FRANK ROBERT, optical exec.; b. Chgo., Apr. 2, 1938; s. Stanley Stephen and Pauline Anna (Szacik) S.; B.A., U. of Ill., 1960. Various positions Wesley-Jessen, Inc., Chgo., 1963-76; div. mgr. House of Vision Instrument Co., Chgo., 1976; mgr. Wesley-Jessen, Inc., 1977—. Served with U.S. Army, 1960-62. Mem. Nat. Eye Research Found., Nat. Pvt. Pilots Assn. Roman Catholic. Clubs: St. Peter's Social. Home: 1312 N Bosworth Chicago IL 60622 Office: 37 S Wabash Chicago IL 60603

STORCK, JOHN NORMAN, librarian; b. Fairbury, Ill., Feb. 22, 1916; s. Norman Lee and Rebecca (Cooke) S.; B.A., L.I. U., 1951; M.L.S., Pratt Inst., 1952; m. Elizabeth M. Gabbert, Dec. 2, 1944; children—John W.P., Thomas C.J., Victoria E. Corr. Crane Co., Chgo. and N.Y., 1936-48; asst. L.I. U. Library, Bklyn., 1948-52; librarian Upper Sandusky (Ohio) Pub. Library, 1952-56; head librarian Massillon (Ohio) Pub. Library, 1956-65; dir. Lime (Ohio) Pub. Library, 1965—. Served with AUS, 1943, U.S. Mcht. Marine, 1944-46. Mem. ALA, Ohio Library Assn. (dir. 1965-69). Illustrator: (with others) Life, Land and Water in Ancient Peru (Paul Kosok), 1965. Author: (with others) A Survey of the Public Libraries of Mercer County, Ohio, 1967; A Study of the Extension Services in the Ohio Valley Area Libraries of Ohio, 1971; the Libraries of Miami County, Ohio, 1971; A Study of the Libraries of the Western Ohio Regional Library Development System, 1973; contbr. to Ency. Americana. Office: 650 Market St Lima OH 45801

STORMS, EVEREK RICHARD, church editor; b. Everek, Turkey, Oct. 19, 1914 (parents Canadian citizens); s. Dorwin J. and Nancy (Good) S.; B.A., McMaster U., Hamilton, Ont., Can., 1946; M.A., Winona Lake Sch. Theology, 1949; LL.D., Bethel Coll., 1974; m. Irene Welch, Aug. 18, 1945; children—James, Nancy Tiers. Elementary sch. tchr., Ont., 1933-58; prin., Kitchener, Ont., 1958-73; prof. ch. history and missions Emmanuel Bible Coll., Kitchener, Ont., 1949-55; editor Gospel Banner, Elkhart, Ind., 1952-69, asso. editor Emphasis, Ft. Wayne, 1969-73, editor, 1974—. Lay preacher Missionary Church, mem. publs. bd. 1952—. Mem. Gideons Internat. Christian Writers Can. (founder 1954, pres. 1954-56, 62-63), Kitchener Tchrs. Fedn. (pres. 1955), Can. Coll. Tchrs., mem. Men Tchrs. Waterloo County (pres. 1960-61), Internat. Platform Assn. Author: Gems That Are Different, 1944; What God Hath Wrought, 1948; History of the United Missionary Church, 1958. Contbr. Ency. Canadiana. Office: 336 Dumfries Ave Kitchener ON N2H 2G1 Canada

STOTT, ALFRED FRANK, aero. engr., coll. pres.; b. Grand Rapids, Mich., Oct. 4, 1911; s. Tally F. and Louise (Fouts) S.; B.S. in Aero. Engring., Hancock Coll., 1932; D.Sc. (hon.), Ind. No. U., 1969; m. Martha Jane Allyn, June 26, 1937; children—James Lee, Allyn T., Carol Lynn Stott Conroy, Laura Louise Stott Otto. Asst. chief engr., Milw. Parts Corp., 1932-35; v.p., dean engring. Aero U., Chgo., 1935-59; asst. dir. tng. U.S. Army Air Corps Tech. Tng. Command, 1939-44; founder aero. engring and aviation adminstrn. sch. Aero-Space Inst., Chgo., 1959, pres., 1959—; cons. to airframe industry, 1958—; cons. to various tech. schs., 1958—. Registered profl. engr., Ill. Fellow Am. Inst. Aeros. and Astronautics (sec. Chgo. sect. 1948-53), Soc. Licensed Aircraft and Engine Technologists; mem. Profl. Racing Piolts Assn., Air Force Assn., Ill. Jr. Acad. Sci. (sec. 1968-70, chmn. aviation div. 1957-71), Am. Assn. of Specialized Colls. (vice chmn. 1970-71), Chgo. Assn. of Commerce and Industry (mem. edn. and aviation com. 1968—). Club: Masons. Home: 4044 Woodland Ave Western Springs IL 60558 Office: 160 E Grand Ave Chicago IL 60611

STOTTS, LARRY HENDERSON, educator; b. Mpls., Aug. 17, 1935; s. West Dodd and Florence (Henderson) S.; student Grinnell Coll., 1953-55; B.A., Macalester Coll., 1958, M.Ed., 1961; postgrad. U. Minn., 1969-70; m. Patricia Ann Holland, Aug. 16, 1958; children—Lora Ann, James Holland, Andrew Roger Holland. Tchr., Kerkhoven, Minn., 1958-60; tchr. Edina (Minn.) High Sch., 1961—, drama dir., 1966—, Nat. Thespian adviser, 1966—; participant Minn. Heritage for Tomorrow, 1976-77, Nat. Humanities Faculty's Master Tchrs. in Humanities Program, 1977-78. Dir. Edina Community Theater, 1965-66. John Hay fellow, 1973; recipient Tchr. of Year award, Edina West, 1976. Mem. NEA, Minn. Edn. Assn., ANTA, Children's Theater Assn., Minn. Humanities Council (v.p., pres. elect). Congregationalist. Mason. Home: 4205 W 42d St Minneapolis MN 55416 Office: 6754 Valley View Rd Edina MN 55435

STOTZER, HAROLD FREDERICK, banker; b. Archbold, Ohio, June 20, 1898; s. Henry William and Laura (Dorshimer) S.; A.B., U. Mich., 1920; m. Grace D. Miller, Sept. 8, 1920; children—Robert, Dr. Don. With Farmers & Mchts. State Bank, Archbold, 1945—, pres., 1968—; dir. Beatrice Foods Co., Chgo., 1945-71, Dinner Bell Foods, Defiance, Ohio. Chmn. Ohio Small Bus. Com., 1950-54; mem. Ohio Devel. Council, 1960-71. Mem. Archbold Sch. Bd., 1926-46; rep. Ohio Legislature, 1947-55. Served with USN, 1918-19. Mem. Ohio Hardware Assn. (pres. 1936-37), U. Mich. Band Alumni (exec. com.), Ohio Commodores, Lambda Chi Alpha. Methodist. Mason (32 deg., Shriner), Elk, Rotarian. Home: 203 Murbach St Archbold OH 43502 Office: 301 N Defiance St Archbold OH 43502

STOUDER, GREGORY DALE, optometrist; b. Ft. Wayne, Ind., Dec. 4, 1928; s. Herbert Albion and Maude Esther (Powell) S.; student Ind. U., 1950; B.S. in Optometry, No. Ill. Coll. Optometry, 1953, D. Optometry, 1954; m. Susan Brown McNabb, Dec. 29, 1954; children—Deborah, David, Ann, Amy. Individual practice optometry, Ft. Wayne, 1956—. Organizing dir., v.p. Ft. Wayne Fed. Savs. & Loan Assn.; v.p. S.W. Investment Corp. Donor, Ind. U. Found. Served with AUS, 1954-56. Mem. Am., Ind., North Eastern Ind. (past pres.) optometric assns., Ft. Wayne C. of C., United Comml. Travelers, Izaac Walton League, Ind. U. Alumni Assn., Tomb and Key Frat., Demolay (life). Republican. Baptist. Mason (Shriner), Lion. Home: 715 Nightfall Rd Fort Wayne IN 46819 Office: 2811 Lower Huntington Rd Fort Wayne IN 46809

STOUGHTON, STEPHEN H., state legislator; b. Shelbyville, Ind., Apr. 14, 1944; s. Homer C. and Doris D. (Robison) S.; B.S., Ind. U., 1966; m. Edy Comfort, Apr. 22, 1967; children—Jason Thomas, Craig Michael, Christopher Stephen. Mktg. analyst Ford Motor Co., 1966-67; exec. dir. Ind. Constrn. Industry Advancement Program, 1971-73; v.p. Indpls. Bd. Realtors, 1973—; mem. Ind. Ho. of Reps. from Marion County Dist. 43, 1973—. Vice chmn. Indpls. Housing Com.; mem. Greater Indpls. Progress Task Force Govt. Financing. Pres. jr. officers council USAF, 1968. Served to capt. USAF, 1967-71. Decorated Air Force Commendation medal. Mem. Ind., Indpls. chambers commerce, Indpls. Art Mus., Marion County Assn. Retarded Citizens. Republican. Office: Investors Trust Bldg Indianapolis IN 46204

STOUP, ARTHUR HARRY, lawyer; b. Kansas City, Mo., Aug. 30, 1925; s. Isadore and Dorothy (Rankle) S.; student Kansas City (Mo.) Jr. Coll., 1942-43; B.A., J.D., U. Mo., 1950; m. Kathryn Jolliff, July 30, 1948; children—David C., Daniel P., Rebecca Ann, Deborah E. Admitted to Mo. Bar, 1950; pvt. practice law, Kansas City, Mo., 1950—; mem. firm Stoup & Bohm. Trustee U. Mo. at Kansas City Law Found. Served with USNR, 1942-45. Recipient Alumni Achievement award U. Mo.-Kansas City Alumni Assn., 1975. Mem. Kansas City (pres. 1966-67), Mo. (bd. govs., 1967-76, v.p. 1972-73, pres. 1974-75), Am. (mem. ho. of dels.) bar assns., Lawyers Assn. Kansas City, Mo. Assn. Trial Attys., Assn. Trial Lawyers Am. (dir. 1973—, v.p.), Mobar Research Inc., Phi Alpha Delta Alumni (justice Kansas City area 1955-56, William H. Pittman hon. award Lawson chpt. 1974), Tau Kappa Epsilon. Mem. B'nai B'rith. Clubs: Optimist (pres. Ward Pkwy. 1961-62, lt. gov. Mo. dist. internat. 1963-64); Sertoma. Home: 9002 Western Hills Dr Kansas City MO 64114 Office: Home Savs Bldg Kansas City MO 64106

STOUT, CHESTER BERNARD, librarian, curator; b. Jacksonville, Tex., May 31, 1918; s. Chester Bernard and Besse (Smith) S.; student W. Tenn. Bus. Coll., 1936-37, Tulane U., 1952-54; B.S., Auburn U., 1960; M.S., La. State U., 1963; M.A., Central Mo. State U., 1967; Ph.D., Case Western Res. U., 1976; m. Shirley Mae Carradine, June 13, 1953; children—Chester, Wayne, Sandra. Enlisted USN, 1937; librarian U.S. Submarine Base, Pearl Harbor, 1940; asst. library services U.S. Antarctic Expdn., 1955-57; instr. Naval R.O.T.C., Auburn U., 1957-61; ret., 1961; instr., asst. librarian Central Mo. State U., 1963-68; librarian, curator McKinley Meml. Library, Niles, Ohio, 1969—; micrographics cons. Active Boy Scouts Am., YMCA. Mem. ALA, Ohio, Northeastern Ohio (sec.) library assns, NEA, Fleet Res. Assn., Am. Legion, Vets. Fgn. Wars, Phi Delta Kappa, Omicron Delta Epsilon. Mason (Shriner); Mem. Order Eastern Star. Contbr. articles to profl. jours. Home: 67 Helen St Niles OH 44446 Office: 40 N Main St Niles OH 44446

STOUT, DONALD EVERETT, real estate developer and appraiser; b. Dayton, Ohio, Mar. 16, 1926; s. Thorne Franklin and Lovella Marie (Sweeney) S.; B.S., Miami U., 1950; m. Gloria B. McCormick, Apr. 10, 1948; children—Holly Sue, Scott Kenneth. Mgr. comml.-indsl. div. G.P. Huffman Realty, Dayton, 1954-58; leasing agt., mgr. Forest Park Plaza, Dayton, 1959-71; developer 1st transp. center for trucking in Ohio; pres. devel. cos. Sunderland Falls Estate, Wright Gate Indsl. Mall, Edglo Land Recycle and Grande Tierra Corp., Dayton, Eastwood Lake Lodge and Marina; now pres. Donald E. Stout, Inc.; appraiser FHA, Dept. Transp., utility cos. Served with AUS, 1944-45, USN, 1945-46. Named The Outstanding Real Estate Salesman in Dayton, Dayton Area Bd. Realtors, in Ohio, Ohio Bd. Realtors, 1961. Licensed real estate broker, Ohio, U.S. Virgin Islands. Mem. Dayton Area Bd. Realtors (founder; 1st pres. salesman div. 1959, dir. 1959-60), Nat. Assn. Real Estate Bds., Dayton Soc. Real Estate Appraisers (sr. real estate appraiser, dir. 1959-60, pres. 1964), Soc. Indsl. Realtors, Appraisal Inst., C. of C., Phi Delta Theta. Clubs: Masons (32 deg.), Shrine, Dayton Racquet. Contbr. articles to profl. jours. Home: 759 Plantation Ln Dayton OH 45419 Office: 505 Riverside Dr Dayton OH 45405

STOVER, DENNIS WAYNE, san. engr.; b. Centralia, Ill., Oct. 27, 1942; s. Paul Willis and Alvera Louise (Sprehe) S.; B.S. in Civil Engring., U. Mo. at Rolla, 1966, M.S. in San. Engring., 1967; m. Sharon Lee Conrad, Aug. 26, 1965; children—Teresa L., Cynthia L., Jennifer R. Engr., Ill. Dept. Pub. Health, Carbondale, 1967-70; regional mgr. regulatory and service work div. water supplies Ill. EPA, Marion, 1970—; mem. advisory bd. water and wastewater programs Southeastern Ill. Coll. Registered profl. engr., land surveyor, sanitarian, Ill. Mem. Am. Water Works Assn. (dist. rep.), ASCE, Nat. Soc. Profl. Engrs. Ill. Soc. Profl. Engrs. (chpt. pres., co-chmn. water quality com.), So. Ill. Water Works Operators Assn., Dist. Assn. County Supts. Hwys., Am. Acad. Environ. Engrs. (diplomate). Presbyn. Home: 1711 Julianne Dr Marion IL 62959 Office: 2209 W Main St Marion IL 62959

STOVER, HARRY MANNING, refractory exec.; b. Los Angeles, June 9, 1926; s. Harry Manning and Gladys Martha (Cryer) S.; student U. N.M., 1945; B.S., U. So. Cal., 1947; m. Winifred Nation, Dec. 17, 1949; children—Harry Manning II, Eric, Carina. Chief engr. Raymond Internat. Venezuela, 1948-51; chief project engr. Standard Vacuum Oil Co., Indonesia, 1951-54; v.p. A.P. Green Refractories Co., Mexico, Mo., 1954-71, exec. v.p., 1971-72, pres., dir., 1972—, chief exec. officer, 1974—; pres., dir. Bigelow Liptak Corp., Southfield, Mich., E. J. Bartells Co., Renton, Wash.; group v.p., dir. United States Gypsum Co., 1976—. Bd. dirs. Refractories Inst., Pitts. Served as ensign USNR, 1944-46. Mem. Mo. C. of C., Am. Ceramic Soc. Episcopalian. Clubs: Chicago, Garden of the Gods. Contbr. articles to profl. jours. Home: 2367 Woodpath Highland Park IL 60035 Office: 101 S Wacker Dr Chicago IL 60606

STOVER, ROBERT DAVID, chiropractor; b. West Point, Nebr., July 13, 1945; s. Raymond Martin and Marjorie Elizabeth (Mugge) S.; student Midland Luth. Coll., 1963-65; D.Chiropractic, Nat. Coll. Chiropractic, 1969; m. Susan Jane Swan, June 8, 1968; children—Michelle Marie, Laura Suzanne. Intern, Chgo. Gen. Health Service, 1969-70; resident roentgenology Northwestern Coll. Chiropractic out-patient clinic, Mpls., 1970-71; asso. Black Hills Chiropractic Center, Rapid City, S.D.; 1972-73; pvt. practice Stover Chiropractic Clinic, West Point, 1973—. Served with AUS, 1971-72. Mem. West Point C. of C., Am. Chiropractic Assn., Nebr. Chiropractic Physician Assn., Sigma Phi Kappa. Club: Optimist. Home: 237 S Farragut St West Point NE 68788 Office: 129 E Grant St West Point NE 68788

STOWE, WILLIAM EARL, orgn. exec.; b. Buchanan, Mich., Apr. 25, 1923; s. Kenneth Earl and Anna Marie (Keller) S.; B.S., U. Colo., 1949; postgrad. U. Denver, 1953-55; m. Pauline Malovrh, Mar. 17, 1951; children—Michael William, Diana Sue. Revenue agt. Colo. Dept. Revenue, Denver, 1953-62; financial analyst Martin-Marietta Corp., Denver, 1962-68; corporate tax mgr. Samsonite Corp., Denver, 1968-71, mgr. tax dept. Ill. State C. of C., Chgo., 1971—. Mem. steering com. Replacement Revenue Sources-The Economics of Replacing Ill. Personal Property Tax, 1972, Impact of Fgn. Trade on Ill. Economy, 1973, Equity Through Administrative and Judicial Review of Original Assessments, 1974-76, Ill. div. U. Colo. Second Century Fund, 1977; cons. Ill. Legis. Joint Subcom. to Study Property Tax Reforms, 1974—, lectr. on current problems in taxation for Ill. bus., legis. and profl. groups, 1971—. Served to cpl. AUS, 1943-46. Mem. Nat. Tax Assn.—Tax Inst Am. (mem. property tax com. 1972—), Chgo. Tax Club (chmn. publs. com. 1976-77), Inst. Orgn. Mgmt., Phi Kappa Tau. Presbyterian (trustee 19—). Toastmaster. Office: Ill State C of C 20 N Wacker Dr Chicago IL 60606

STOXEN, PAUL BENNETT, chiropractor; b. Rockford, Ill., Feb. 17, 1925; s. Paul Fred and Bertha Jane (Bennett) S.; D.C., Nat. Coll. Chiropractic, 1950, N.D. cum laude, 1950; m. Lydia Marie Porter, Jan. 11, 1946; children—Douglas Bennett, James Edward. Practice chiropractics specializing in spinal conditions, Chgo., 1950-64, Evergreen Park, Ill., 1964—. Served with USNR, 1943-46. Mem. Evergreen C. of C., Am. Legion. Kiwanian, Mason (Shriner, Highlander of Year 1971), Elk. Club: Chgo. Exec. Home: 12801 S 86th Ave Palos Park IL 60464 Office: 9503 S Homan Av Evergreen Park IL 60642

STRACHAN, BRIAN CLARK, aerospace engr.; b. Toronto, Ont., Can., Dec. 27, 1942; s. William and Mildred Isobel (Clark) S.; came to U.S., 1952, naturalized, 1960; B.S. in Aerospace Engring., U. Cin., 1966; m. Pamela Sue McClary, Mar. 19, 1966; children—Deborah, Darin. Aerospace engr. Naval Ship Research and Devel. Center, Washington, 1966-69; engr. transient analysis, then engr. cycle analysis aircraft engine group Gen. Electric Co., Evendale, Ohio, 1969-77, mgr. installed performance programs, 1977—. Adv. council Forest Park (Ohio) Sch. Bd., 1970-72; sec. Forest Park Planning Comm., 1972-73; vice chmn. Forest Park Bd. Zoning Appeals. 1975—; councilman Forest Park City Council, 1973—, vice mayor, 1975—; trustee Ohio-Ky.-Ind. Regional Council Govts., 1973—. Recipient Community Service award Gen. Electric Co., 1972. Mem. ASME, Am. Inst. Aeros. and Astronautics, Nat. League Cities, Ohio Municipal League, Tau Beta Pi. Republican. Author research reports. Home: 11349 Lincolnshire Dr Forest Park OH 45240 Office: Gen Electric Co Interstate 75 Evendale OH 45215

STRACHAN, WILLIAM JOHN GORDON, assn. exec.: b. Galveston, Tex., Aug. 16, 1915: s. James and Beatrice Rosamond (Owen) S.: B.J., U. Tex., 1936: m. Melba Vivian Guthrie, Mar. 15, 1939: children—James Dean, John Gordon, Michael David. Editorial staff Childress County (Tex.) News, 1936-37, Galveston News, 1937-39, Brownsville (Tex.) Herald, 1940-42: mem. pub. relations staff Santa Fe R.R., Galveston, 1942-44: traveling rep., Los Angeles, 1944-53, spl. rep., Chgo., 1953-58: dir. pub. relations Ill. Mfrs. Assn., Chgo., 1958-72, dir. transp., 1974—; exec. dir. Ill. Mfrs. Assn. Financial Mgmt. Assn. 1969—; sec.-treas. Ill. Territory Mfrs. Traffic League, 1974—. Republican precinct capt., 1960-73; chmn. 50th ward Rep. Exec. Com., Chgo., 1970-71. Mem. Nat. Assn. Accountants, Sigma Delta Chi. Presbyn. (ruling elder 1962—). Clubs: Headline (pres. 1961-62), Press (Chgo.). Home: 1833 W Norwood St Chicago IL 60660 Office: 135 S LaSalle St Chicago IL 60603

STRACKE, WLN, singer, actor; b. Lorraine, Kans., Feb. 20, 1908; s. Robert Norbert and Anna (Rodenburg) S.; student Lake Forest Coll., (1929-32, Am. Conservatory Mus., 1945-47; L.H.D., Lincoln (Ill.) Coll., 1969; m. Genevieve Adrienne McMahon, May 1, 1942 (div. Jan. 1966); children—Barbara Ellen, Jane Elizabeth. Began singing career on sta. WLS, Chgo., 1931, appearing as soloist on programs including Hymns of All Churches, Chgo. Theatre of the Air, Nat. Barn Dance; appearances with Chgo. Repertory Group, 1938-42; extensive concert appearances singing folk songs with guitar, 1945—; singing actor on Chgo. network TV programs including Studs' Place, Hawkins Falls, Animal Playtime, NBC Children's Theatre; founder, pres. Old Town Sch. Folk Music, Chgo., 1957—, also dir.; founder Old Town Folklore Center, 1963; mus. cons. Ill. Sesquicentennial Commn., toured Japan with Lincoln exhibit. sponsored by U.S. Dept. Commerce, 1969. Served with AUS, 1942-45; ETO. Mem. Chgo. Hist. Soc. (corr.), Chgo. Civil War Round Table (hon.). Author: (with Norman Luboff) Songs of Man, 1965, Cantata Freedom Country 1967; composer numerous, hist. songs about Chgo. and Ill. Office: 909 W Armitage St Chicago IL 60014

STRADER, JOHN JACOB, former co-owner radio sta.; b. Cin., Dec. 4, 1923; s. John Jacob and Jean Morton (Abbott) S.; student Coll. Music Cin., 1939-40; m. Joan Ganne, Oct. 20, 1944; 1 dau., Jacqueline (Mrs. Don Michael Darragh). With WSAI, Cin., 1939-40, WKRC, Cin., 1942-43, WCPO, Cin., 1943-45, WCKY, Cin., 1946; co-owner WVAW, FM radio sta., Cheviot, Ohio, 1947-48. Mem. Am. Theatre Organ Soc. (chpt. chmn. 1961-63), Sons and Daus. Pioneer Rivermen, Cin. Music Hall Assn. Home: 3650 Clifton Ave Cincinnati OH 45220

STRAFFON, RALPH ATWOOD, urologist; b. Croswell, Mich., Jan. 4, 1928; s. Lloyd Atwood and Verle R. (Rice) S.; M.D., U. Mich., 1953; m. Cary Arden Higley, Feb. 13, 1954; children—David, Daniel, Jonathan, Peter, Andrew. Intern, Univ. Hosp., Ann Arbor, 1953-54, resident in surgery, 1954-56, urology, resident, 1956-59; staff mem. dept. urology Cleve. Clinic, 1956-63, head dept. urology, 1963—; practice medicine specializing in urology Cleve., 1959—. Served with U.S. Army, 1946-48. Diplomate Am. Bd. Urology. Fellow A.C.S.; mem. Am. Assn. Genitourinary Surgeons, AMA, Cleve. Acad. Medicine, Am., Cleve. urol. assns., Clin. Soc. Genitourinary Surgeons, Soc. Univ. Urologists, Frederick A. Coller Surg. Soc., Am. Soc. Nephrology, Transplantaion Soc., Soc. Pelvic Surgeons, Soc. Pediatric Urology, Am. Fertility Soc., Am. Assn. Clin. Urologists, Société Internationale d'Urologie. Contbr. articles to med. jours. Home: 2839 Winthrop Rd Shaker Heights OH 44120 Office: 9500 Euclid Ave Cleveland OH 44106

STRAG, GERALD ANTHONY, psychologist; b. Englewood, N.J., Apr. 20, 1942; s. Harry and Mary Catherine (Kniep) S.; B.S., U. Miami, 1965, M.Ed., 1967; Ed.D., U. Ga., 1970; m. Thurza Marie Whitaker, Dec. 18, 1965; 1 son, Benjamin Whitaker. Tchr., Fulton County Bd. Edn., Atlanta, 1965-66, Dade County Bd. Edn., Miami, Fla., 1967-68; asst. prof. U. No. Iowa, Waterloo, 1970-72; dir. adolescent services Mental Health Inst., Independence, Iowa, 1972-74; counseling-clin. psychologist St. Francis Hosp., Waterloo, 1974-76; counseling-clin. psychologist Black Hawk Psychiat. Assos., 1976—. Psychol. cons. Quakerdale Group Homes, Waterloo, 1974—. Mem. Am., Iowa psychol. assns., Iowa Mental Health Assn., Am. Assn. Marriage and Family Counselors, Phi Delta Kappa. Democrat. Roman Catholic. Elk. Home: 308 Sunset Rd Waterloo IA 50701 Office: 537 Black Bldg Waterlo IA 50703

STRAHLER, CLYTLE EVELYN, librarian, educator; b. Dayton, Ohio, June 17, 1907; d. Ezra Frederick and Bertha (Daniels) Strahler; A.B., Wittenberg Coll., 1934; B.S. in L.S., U. Ill., 1938. Asst. children's dept., high sch. dept., sch. br. asst. Dayton and Montgomery County Pub. Library, 1925-31, br. librarian, sch. librarian, 1932-49, head, tng. class activities and 1st asst. reference dept., 1949-56, coordinator personnel services, 1956-62; asst. head librarian Wittenberg U., Springfield, Ohio, 1962-64, chief reader services, 1964-66, asst. dir. univ. libraries, 1967, asso. dir. libraries, 1968-75, asso. prof., 1962-70, prof., 1971-75, prof., asso. dir. univ. libraries emerita, 1975—. Mem. Am., Ohio library assns., Dayton, Cin. councils on world affairs, Am. Assn. U. Profs., Springfield Urban League, Beta Phi Mu. Home: 5340 Brendonwood Lane Dayton OH 45415 Office: Wittenberg U Springfield OH 45501

STRAHLER, VIOLET RUTH, educator, author; b. Dayton, Ohio, Sept. 30, 1918; d. Ezra Frederick and Bertha (Daniels) Strahler; A.B., Wittenberg U., 1944; M.A., Miami U., 1959, Ed. D., Ind. U., 1972. Tchr. sci. and math. Miamisburg (Ohio) High Sch., 1944-51; tchr. sci., counselor Dayton pub. schs., 1951-66, tchr., cons. secondary instrn. and curriculum, 1967-69; supr. sci., math., curriculum publs., 1969-72, exec. dir. for curriculum services, instrn. dept., 1972—; indsl. scientist, summers 1944-58, vis. instr. sci. and edn. Miami U., Oxford, Ohio, summers 1959-61. Mem. planetarium com. Dayton Mus. Natural History, 1961-63. Ford Found. fellow; 1952-53. Fellow Ohio Acad. Sci. (chmn. sect. on edn. 1950-51, editor Jr. Acad. Newsletter 1951-53), Nat. Sci. Tchrs. Assn. (alternate dir. 1956-58), NEA, Am. Chem. Soc., Nat. Assn. for Research in Sci. Teaching, Nat. Soc. for Study Edn., Am. Edn. Research Assn., Ohio Edn. Assn., Assn. for Supervision and Curriculum Devel., Am. Assn. Sch. Adminstrs., Phi Delta Kappa, Delta Kappa Gamma (chmn. research com. 1962-64). Club: Altrusa. Author jr. high sch. sci. text books; Contbr. articles to profl. jours. Home: 5340 Brendonwood Ln Dayton OH 45415 Office: Service Bldg Bd Edn 4280 North Western Ave Dayton OH 45427

STRAIN, EDWARD RICHARD, psychologist; b. Indpls., Apr. 12, 1925; s. Edward Richard and Ernestine (Kidd) S.; student DePauw U., 1943-44; A.B., Butler U., 1948; Ph.D., Duke, 1952; m. Marsha Ellen Beeler, 1972; children—Douglas MacDonald, Elizabeth Stacy, Chadwick Edward, Sarah Abigail. Clin. psychologist Ohio State Med. Center, Columbus, 1952-53, Ind. U. Med. Center, Indpls., 1953-56; pvt. practice cons. psychology, Indpls., 1956—. Lectr. dept. psychology Butler U., Indpls., 1958-68. Pres. Marion County (Ind.) Mental Health Assn., 1967-69; 500 Festival asso., Indpls., 1961—; pres. Perry Twp. (Ind.) Rep. Club, 1968-69. Founder, bd. dirs. Downtown Sr. Citizens Center, Indpls., 1958-62. Served with USNR, 1943-46. Mem. Lambda Chi Alpha. Episcopalian (vestryman, sr. warden). Clubs: Masons, Rotary, Indpls. Athletic. Home: 911 Briarpatch Ln Greenwood IN 46142 Office: 517-19 Illinois Bldg 17 W Market St Indianapolis IN 46204

STRAND, ALAN LAWRENCE, mgmt. psychologist; b. Chgo.; s. Axel E. and Ruth (Tyler) S.; B.S., U. Ill., also M.A. in Psychology; Ph.D., Ill. Inst. Tech.; m. Anita Charlene Bray; children—Tyler, Lauren, Mark, Ruth. Instr., asst. research scientist Ill. Inst. Tech., Chgo.; mgmt. cons. Booz, Allen & Hamilton, Chgo.; mgr. planning Packaging div. Union Carbide Corp., Chgo.; v.p. Roy Doty & Assos., Inc., psychol. cons., Chgo.; now pres. Strand, Gill & Assos., Inc. Police commr. Evergreen Park, Ill. Bd. dirs. Mental Health Society Greater Chicago. Served to lt. (j.g.) USNR; PTO, MTO. Mem. Am., Ill. psychol. assns., S.A.R., Sigma Xi. Research in personnel assessment and devel.; test developer and pub. Address: 1301 W 22d St Oakbrook IL 60521

STRAND, MERLIN ARTHUR, optical co. exec.; b. Mpls., Apr. 21, 1920; s. Carl Arthur and Emily Grace (Bennis) S.; student U. Minn., evenings 1941, Internat. Corr. Schs., 1950; hon. M. Ophthalmic Optics, Am. Bd. Opticians, 1953; m. Margaret Lorraine Anderson, June 15, 1939; children—Merlin Arthur, David Philip, Linda Kathryn. Salesman, Stillman's Grocery, Mpls., 1935-38; optician Minn. Optical Co., 1938-44; with Britton Motor Freight Co., Mpls., 1941-42; salesman Am. Republic Ins. Co., Mpls., 1948-50; with Benson Optical Co., Mpls., 1946—, v.p., mgr. instrument div., 1970—, v.p. Western regional sales, 1972—. Served with USNR, 1944-45. Mem. N. Central States Exhibitors Assn. (pres. 1970-71), Am. Legion. Lutheran (pres. council 1947-50). Mason (Shriner). Home: 9100 Upton Ave S Bloomington MN 55431 Office: 6600 France Ave S Minneapolis MN 55435

STRANG, DONALD WILLIAM, JR., hotel, restaurant exec.; b. Lakewood, Ohio, Jan. 5, 1938; s. Donald William and Jeannette (Canfield) S.; B.S., Cornell U., Ithaca, N.Y., 1960; m. Karen Kline, Apr. 20, 1957; children—Donald William III, David Eugene, Peter Wayne, Allison Jeanette. Pres., Strang Mgmt. Corp., 1960—; pres. Dr. Don's Inc., Don-Clar Corp.; pres., owner Howard Johnson Motor Lodge, Skokie, Ill., Don's Lighthouse Inn, Don's Butcherblock, Don's Fishmarket; dir. Nat. Franchise Council, Howard Johnson Co., Nucorp, Inc. Trustee West Shore Concert series of Cleve. Orch. Mem. Greater Chgo. Hotel-Motel Assn. (dir.), N.E. Ohio Restaurant Assn. (dir.), Young Presidents Orgn., Skokie C. of C. (past pres., dir.), Beta Theta Pi. Rotarian. Home: 17820 Lake Rd Lakewood OH 44107 Office: 8905 Lake Ave Cleveland OH 44102

STRANG, WILLIAM CHARLES, psychiatrist; b. Bedford, Ind., Nov. 26, 1912; s. Howard Arthur and Rowenna Catherine (Kauffman) S.; B.S., Ind. U., 1935, M.D., 1937; m. Janet Rae Martin, Jan. 23, 1941; children—William, Joyce, Thomas, Priscilla. Intern, Ind. U. Med. Center, Indpls., 1937-38, resident in psychiatry, 1954-57; staff physician Evansville (Ind.) State Hosp., 1938-40; med. officer to asst. med. dir. U.S. Civil Service, Med. Div., Washington, 1940-54; chief of men's service LaRue Carter Meml. Hosp., Indpls., 1957-60, asst. supt., 1960-63; individual practice medicine, specializing in psychiatry, Indpls., 1963—; asst. prof. psychiatry Ind. U., Indpls., 1962—; dir. Wesley Otterbein Corp., Indpls. Bd. dirs. Marion County Child Guidance Clinics, 1971-74. Diplomate Am. Bd. Psychiatry and Neurology. Mem. Marion County Med. Soc., Ind., Am. med. assns., Ind., Am. psychiat. assns. Republican. Methodist. Clubs: Riviera, Masons. Home: 7760 Cree Trail Indianapolis IN 46250 Office: 1815 N Capitol Ave Suite 407 Indianapolis IN 46202

STRASBURG, LENARD EUGENE, newspaper publisher; b. Humboldt, Iowa, Apr. 17, 1929; s. Ralph L. and Jennie (Lankjer) S.; B.A., U. Iowa, 1952; m. Dorothy Jean Wagner, Apr. 10, 1952; children—Stephanie, Susan, Sarah, Ellen. Sports editor, Manchester (Iowa) Press, 1952, news editor, 1953-73, partner, 1959-67; pres., pub. Manchester Pub. Co., 1967—; dir. Pinicon Pub. Co., Independence, Iowa, 1973—, pres., 1976-77. Recipient Distinguished Service award Manchester Jaycees, 1960; named Most Progressive Businessman, Manchester C. of C., 1968. Mem. Nat. Newspaper Assn., Iowa Press Assn., U. Iowa Alumni Council, Sigma Delta Chi. Methodist. Clubs: Lions, Manchester Golf and Country, Masons. Home: 840 N Franklin St Manchester IA 52057 Office: 109 E Delaware St Manchester IA 52057

STRASHEIM, LORRAINE ANNETTE, univ. adminstr.; b. Lincoln, Nebr., Feb. 5, 1930; d. Alexander C. and Marie Strasheim; B.S. in Edn. (Regents scholar), U. Nebr., Russian, Ind. U., 1964. Tchr. English and Lati (Nebr.) Pub. Schs., 1951-53; tchr. Latin, Shawnee Mission (Kans.) Schs., 1953-55; tchr. Latin, English, Germ Lincoln Pub. Schs., 1955-65; tchr. Latin and Russian, Ind. U. Lab. Sch., 1965-66; cons. Ind. Lang. Program, Ind. U., Bloomington, 1966-68, dir., 1968-72, coordinator Sch. 1972—; incorporator, bd. dirs. Central States Lang. Edn. Conf., 1969-74, editor, 1970-72, conf. chmn., 1973. Recipient Barber prize U. Nebr. dept. classics, 1950, Nat. Lang. Leadership citation N.Y. State Assn. Fgn. Lang. Tchrs., 1975; Fulbright scholar Am. Acad. in Rome and Vergilian Sch. at Cumae, 1958. Mem. Am. Council on Teaching Fgn. Langs. (exec. council 1973-76, pres. elect 1978), Am. Assn. Tchrs. German, Am Slavic and East European Langs., Assn. for Supervision and Curriculum Devel., Pi Lambda Theta. Author: (with Virginia Garibaldi) A Visual Aids Handbook for Foreign Language Teachers, 1967; (with Clemens L. Hallman) Foreign Language in Indiana, 1968; editor, Target: Methods, 1967; Language Laboratory Teaching, 1968; contbr. articles on fgn. langs. to profl. jours. Home: 703 Gourley Pike #42 Bloomington IN 47401 Office: M21 Memorial E Ind U Bloomington IN 47401

STRASSHOFER, ROLAND HENRY, JR., lawyer; b. Cleve., May 21, 1924; s. Roland Henry and Margaret Avis (Norris) S.; student Univ. Coll., Eng., 1949; A.B., Case Western Res. U., 1948, LL.B., 1950; children—Craig Thomas, Lesley Ann, Heidi Lynn, Carol Rae. Admitted to Ohio bar, 1950, to practice before U.S. Supreme Ct., 1957; atty. SEC, 1950-51, Goodyear Tire & Rubber Co., 1951-53, Pennell, Carlson & Rees, 1953-63, Brown & Strasshofer, 1963-67, Ford, Whitney & Haase, 1970-75, Bremer, Thompson, Morhard, Coyne & Strasshofer, 1975—; dir. Anderson-Bolds, Inc.; mem. nat. labor panel Am. Arbitration Assn., Fed. Mediation and Conciliation Service. Republican candidate Ohio Legislature, 1958. Trustee Hillcrest Hosp., Mayfield Heights, Ohio, 1967—; pres. Cleve. Meml. Med. Found., 1966-69, trustee, 1963—; asso. in law Am. Coll. Legal Medicine. Served with USCG, 1943-46; ETO. Mem. Am. Soc. Hosp. Attys., Am., Fed., Ohio, Cleve. (trustee 1973-77) bar assns., Phi Delta Phi, Delta Kappa Epsilon. Episcopalian (vestryman 1975—). Clubs: Singers (pres. 1962-64), Cleve. Skating, City. Home: 2865 Coleridge Rd Cleveland Heights OH 44118 Office: East Ohio Bldg Cleveland OH 44114

STRATOUDAKIS, JAMES PETER, psychologist; b. Stamford, Conn., Feb. 21, 1949; s. James and Rose Stratoudakis; B.A., Fairfield U., 1971; M.S., DePaul U., 1973; Ph.D., Mich. State U., 1976; m. Carol Jay Colello, Aug. 14, 1971. Coordinator of info., asst. prof. Internat. Rehab. and Spl. Edn. Network, Mich. State U., 1976—; psychotherapist Battle Creek (Mich.) Sanitarium, 1975-77; pvt. practice, East Lansing, 1977—; Mem. Am. Personnel and Guidance Assn., Am. Psychol. Assn., Assn. for Advancement of Psychology, Mich. Psychol. Assn. Office: IRSEN Mich State Univ D-201 W Fee Hall East Lansing MI 48824 also Profl Psychol Consultants Inc 5000 Northwind Dr Suite 220 East Lansing MI 48823

STRATTON, OLIN WILLMER, supt. schs.; b. Hettick, Ill., Feb. 21, 1921; s. Joseph W. and Bessie (Stewart) S.; B.S., So. Ill. U., 1947, M.S., 1949; m. Elaine Miller, Dec. 25, 1947; children—Candace Lou, Jeffrey William, John Noel. Tchr., prin. Shipman (Ill.) Elementary Sch., 1941-42; tchr., coach Highland (Ill.) High Sch., 1947-56, tchr., asst. prin., 1956-58; supt. Highland Community Schs., 1958—. Mem. Ill. Gov.'s Task Force on Edn., Adv. Com. State Supts. of Pub. Instns.; past pres. Southwestern Supts. Forum. Mem. Latzer Meml. Library Bd., State Life Safety Code Com.; past pres. Weinheimer Meml. Bd. Served with USAAF, 1942-45. Mem. Nat., Ill. edn. assns., Am. (exec. com., v.p.), Ill. (past pres., bd. dirs.) assns. sch. adminstrs., Ill. Guidance and Personnel Assn., Highland C. of C. (past pres.). Conglist. Mason. Club: Optimist. Home: 800 Dolphin Dr East Highland IL 62249 Office: 1800 Lindenthal St Highland IL 62249

STRAUB, JOSEPH JOHN, obstetrician and gynecologist; b. Dubuque, Iowa, Aug. 7, 1915; s. Joseph W. and Grace E. (Flynn) S.; student Columbia U., 1933-36; M.D., U. Iowa, 1940; m. Ann Welsh, May 29, 1943; children—Mary Ann Straub Burns, Joseph John, Michael J. Intern Detroit Receiving Hosp., 1940-41; resident in obstetrics and gynecology U. Iowa Hosp., 1946-49; practice medicine specializing in obstetrics and gynecology, Sioux City, Iowa, 1950-52, Dubuque, 1952—; mem. active staff, past. chmn. dept. obstetrics, past pres. staff Mercy Med. Center, Finley, Xavier hosps. Served to lt. comdr. M.C., USNR, 1941-46. Named Boss of Year, Am. Bus. Women's Assn., 1976. Diplomate Am. Bd. Obstetrics and Gynecology. Mem. ACS, Am. Coll. Obstetricians and Gynecologists, Internat. Coll. Surgeons, AMA, Iowa, Dubuque County (past pres.) med. socs., Iowa (past pres.), Milw. obstet. socs., Dubuque C. of C. (past dir.). Roman Catholic. Clubs: Rotary, Dubuque Golf and Country. Home: 1290 Arrowhead Dr Dubuque IA 52001 Office: 807 Dubuque Bldg Dubuque IA 52001

STRAUSS, ALFRED CARMICHAEL, cement co. exec.; b. N.Y.C., Oct. 13, 1932; s. Alfred Amiel and Lorraine (Carmichael) S.; B.S., U. N.C., 1954; J.D., U. Mich. Law Sch., 1959; m. Barbara Elizabeth Scully, Apr. 12, 1958; children—Patricia, Michael, Christopher. With Lehigh Portland Cement Co., 1959—, v.p. adminstrn., 1969-71, v.p. N. Central region, Mpls., 1971—. Bd. dirs. Indsl. Devel. Corp. Lehigh Valley. Served with USMCR, 1954-56. Mem. N.Y. State Bar Assn., Pi Kappa Phi, Delta Theta Phi. Presbyterian. Home: 1566 Rhode Island St Golden Valley MN 55427 Office: 12300 DuPont Ave S Burnsville MN 55337

STRAVINSKY, SOULIMA, composer, pianist; b. Lausanne, Switzerland, Sept. 23, 1910; s. Igor and Catherine (Nossenko) S.; came to U.S., 1948, naturalized, 1955; student Ecole Normale de Musique, Paris, France, 1929-31; m. Françoise Blondlat, Dec. 30, 1947; 1 son, John. Pianist in Europe, Africa, N. and S.Am., 1932-75; tchr. piano, 1940-75; prof. U. Ill., Urbana, 1950-77, prof. emeritus, 1977—. Served with French Army, 1939-40. Decorated chevalier l'Ordre des Arts et des Lettres. U. Ill. grantee for mus. publs., 1961; Center for Advanced Studies grantee, 1974. Composer: Six Sonatinas, 1967; Piano Variations, 1973; Music Alphabet, 1973; Chantefables, 1975. Home: 910 W Oregon St Urbana IL 61801

STRAWHECKER, PAUL JOSEPH, assn. exec.; b. Omaha, Oct. 31, 1947; s. John Leslie and Leone Francis (Kalamaja) S.; student St. Joseph's Sem., 1963-67, Blessed John Neumann Coll., 1967-68; B.A., Creighton U., 1970, student Law Sch., 1971-73; postgrad. U. Nebr., 1974—; m. Margaret Ellen Baumann, Aug. 31, 1974. Research specialist Mayor's Office, City of Omaha, 1970, spl. asst. to mayor, 1971, mgr. spl. programs, 1972-73; dir. spl. resources Father Flanagan's Boys Home, Boys Town, Nebr., 1974—, treas. Credit Union, 1975; writer Am. Soc. Planning Ofcls.; owner The Wooden Spoon Ltd., Omaha. Bd. dirs. U.C.S. Vol. Bur., 1973, Keep Omaha Beautiful, 1972-73; chmn. Met. Area Planning Agency Council Ofcls. Goals Com. for Human Services, 1976. Mem. Internat. City Mgmt. Assn. (speaker 1971), Phi Kappa Psi. Roman Catholic. Home: 123 N 39th St Omaha NE 68131 Office: Administration Bldg Boys Town NE 68010 also 2537 S 132d St Omaha NE

STRAYER, GORDON BYERS, pub. relations exec.; b. Moose Jaw, Sask., Can., June 23, 1923; s. Carl J. and Nina Naomi (Carr) S.; student Bradley Poly. Inst., 1942. U. Chgo., 1943-44; B.A., Iowa State Tchrs. Coll., 1949; M.A., U. Iowa, 1951; m. Faye Adel Hyde, June 4, 1948; children—Hilary, Scott. News editor U. Iowa, Iowa City, 1950-53, editor, 1953-57, asst. dir., exec. editor, 1957-62, acting dir., 1962-64, dir. pub. information univ. relations, 1964-75, dir. health center information and communication, 1975—. Served with AUS, 1943-46; ETO. Mem. Am. Coll. Pub. Relations Assn. (dist. dir. 1963-64, nat. trustee 1966-71, nat. sec. 1969-71), Pub. Relations Soc. of Am. (chpt. pres. 1973), Argonne Univs. Assn. (information com. 1968-71), North Central Assn. Coll. and Secondary Schs. (publs. com. 1969-72), Iowa-Ill. Pub. Relations Council, Iowa City C. of C., Sigma Delta Chi, Phi Delta Kappa, Omicron Delta Kappa. Unitarian. Mason, Kiwanian. Clubs: Triangle, University Athletic (Iowa City). Contbr. articles to profl. jours. Home: 1 Forest Glen Iowa City IA 52240

STRECKER, SHERRY, city ofcl.; b. Arcadia, Kans., June 29, 1932; d. Raymond Cecil and Emma (Pearce) Strecker; student Kans. State Coll., 1961. Bookkeeper, billing clk. Mackie Clemens Fuel Co., Pittsburg, Kans., 1951-55; police dispatcher records clk. Pittsburg Police Dept., 1955-59; clk.-typist Pittsburg Fin. Dept., 1959-62, dep. city clk., 1963-64, city clk., 1964-73, city commr., 1973—, pres. bd. commrs., 1977—; mgr. Centennial Abstract Co., Inc. Licensed abstractor. Mem. City Clks. Assn. Kans., Internat. Inst. Municipal Clks., Am. Bus. Womens Assn. (charter pres.), Pittsburg Bd. Realtors, City Clks. Assn. Kans. (past pres.), Pittsburg C. of C., S.E.K. Humane Soc. Crawford County (founder; pres. 1974-75), Pitts. Altrusa Club (past pres.), Altrusa Internat. Mem. Order Eastern Star. Mem. Christian Ch. (deaconess, sec. to bd., elder). Home: 406 Fieldcrest Dr Pittsburg KS 66762 Office: 109 E 4th St Pittsburg KS 66762

STREED, DONOVAN PALMER, electronics co. exec.; b. Preston, Minn., Mar. 8, 1925; s. Daniel and Esther Juliet (Evenson) S.; student pub. schs.; m. Monica Eldora Venne, June 20, 1946; children—Donovan A., Barbara Streed Butler, Peter A., Daniel H. Mechanic Northwest Airlines, Mpls., 1942-43; watchmaker Pederson Jewelry, Mpls., 1946-51; lab. machinist U. Minn., Mpls., 1951-53; pres. Streed Electronics, Shakopee, Minn., 1953—. Park adviser Scott County, Minn., 1971-74. Served with USNR, 1943-46. Mem. Minn. Watchmakers Assn., Airplane Owners and Pilots Assn. Office: Box 213 Rural Route 2 Shakopee MN 55379

STREELMAN, ROBERT FRANK, dentist; b. Grand Rapids, Mich., Dec. 13, 1926; s. Harold Franklin and Crystal Olive (Stevens) S.; student Emmanuel Missionary Coll., 1944-45, Grand Rapids Jr. Coll., 1946; B.S., Ball State Tchrs. Coll., 1950; D.D.S., U. Mich., 1955; m. Merriam Irma Wiltjer, June 3, 1951; children—Richard, Robin, Jeffrey, Steven, Karen. Gen. practice dentistry, Wyoming, Mich., 1955—. Chmn., Sch. Millage drive, 1966, 67, 69, 70; mem. Bd. Edn. Wyoming, Mich., 1971—, v.p., 1973-75, pres., 1975-77; tchr. Grand Rapids Jr. Coll., 1973-77. Chmn., Mich. Dental Polit. Action Com., 1973—; bd. dirs. Tb, Health and Emphysema Soc. West Mich., 1963—, pres., 1971-73; bd. dirs. State Mich. Tb and Respiratory Disease Assn., 1966-71. Served with AUS, 1945-46. Mem. Western Mich. (pres. 1969), Kent County dental socs., Wyo. Jaycees. Seventh Day Adventist (dir.) Rotarian (pres. 1965-66). Leader 3 missionary trips of physicians, dentists, optometrists, youths, Haiti, 1968, 69, 70. Developer dental exhibit for Grand Rapids Mus., 1977. Home: 1272 Cricklewood St Wyoming MI 49509 Office: 2459 28th St SW Wyoming MI 49509

STREETT, ROBERT WELLS, printing co. exec.; b. St. Louis, Aug. 22, 1938; s. Rolla Wells and Mary Lee (Kennard) S.; A.B., Brown U., 1961; m. Elizabeth Stewart Bertelson, Sept. 2, 1967; children—Rebecca Robards, Elizabeth Kennard. Mktg. rep. Stephens Bus. Forms, St. Louis, 1965-74; pres. Postal Instant Press St. Louis, 1974—. Bd. dirs. Central Inst. of the Deaf. Served with USN, 1961-65. Episcopalian. Club: St. Louis Country. Home: 6420 Cecil Ave Clayton MO 63105 Office: 20 South Central Ave Suite 200 Clayton MO 63105

STREICH, ARTHUR HAROLD, business exec.; b. Mpls., Apr. 22, 1925; s. Herman Henry and Rose (Anderson) S.; B.A. in Journalism, Macalester Coll., 1952; m. Arlene June Ostlund, Aug. 30, 1947; children—Jennifer (Mrs. Michael Hallam), Jack, Paula Jo. Partner, S&E Pubs., St. Paul, 1952-55; asst. sec. Northwestern Lumbermans Assn., 1955-57; gen. mgr. Nat. Electronics Conf., 1957-59; pub. relations exec. Mullen & Assos., Inc., Mpls., 1959-60; investment adviser Dempsey Tegeler & Co., Inc., Mpls., 1960-63; regional sales mgr. Dreyfus Corp., 1963-68; regional v.p. Anchor Corp., Chgo., 1968-69; regional v.p. wholesale sales and mgmt. Dreyfus Sales Corp., Chgo., 1969-72; regional v.p. Crosby Corp., Chgo., 1972-73; regional sales mgr. John Nuveen & Co., Chgo., 1973-74; owner Gen. Sales & Mktg. Services Co., Lake Zurich, Ill., 1974—. Republican candidate mayor, St. Paul, 1952. Served with USNR, 1942-46. Mem. Nat. Assn. Security Dealers (registered prin.). Republican. Mem. Evang. Free Ch. Address: 1201 Geneva Ln Lake Zurich IL 60047

STRENG, PAUL BENEDICT, univ. supr.; b. Howell, Mich., Jan. 8, 1949; s. Richard and Victoria Matilda (Starkey) S.; student Ferris State Coll., 1969-70; B.A. in Telecommunications, Mich. State U., East Lansing, 1976; m. Cynthia Kay Grimes, July 17, 1976. Dir. closed circuit TV, St. Lawrence Hosp., Lansing, Mich., 1971-73; media coordinator dept. psychiatry Mich. State U., 1973-76, supr. instrnl. devel. dept. psychiatry, 1976—; cons. Ingham County Sheriff's Dept. Rehab. Program, Traverse City (Mich.) State Hosp., Riverside Center, Mich. Dept. Mental Health, Mich. Dept. State Police. Arson investigator Howell Fire Dept., 1972, tng. officer, 1974, asst. chief, 1977. Mem. Mich. Firemen's Assn. (bd. control), Mich. Fire Chiefs, Mich. Fire Service Instrs., Mich. Fire Inspectors Soc., Phi Sigma Epsilon. Presbyterian. Home: 307 W Brooks St Howell MI 48843 Office: Dept Psychiatry Mich State U East Lansing MI 48824

STRESEN-REUTER, FREDERICK ARTHUR, II, mining co. exec.; b. Oak Park, Ill., July 31, 1942; s. Alfred Procter and Carol Frances (von Pohek) S.-R.; B.A., Lake Forest Coll., 1967. Mgr. advt. Stresen-Reuter Internat., Bensenville, Ill., 1965-71; sr. mktg. coordinator Internat. Minerals & Chem. Corp., Mundelein, Ill., 1971—; lectr. mktg. U. Ill., 1977, Am. Mgmt. Assn., 1978; cons. mktg. to numerous feed cos., 1973—; cons., writer Wis. Vocat. Tech. and Adult Edn. System, 1976—. Exec. chmn. floor com. Presentation Ball, Chgo., 1974—. Recipient certificate appreciation Chgo. Soc. Paint Tech., Chgo. Paint and Coatings Assn., 1975, certificate excellence Chgo. 77 Vision Show, 1977, Silver Aggy award, 1977, spl. jury gold medal V.I., N.Y. Internat. film festival awards, 1977. Mem. Nat. Feed Ingredients Assn., Nat. Agrl. Mktg. Assn., Am. Feed Mfrs. Assn. (citation 1976), Lake Forest Sailing Soc., World Expeditionary Assn., USCG Aux. (officer), U.S. Naval Inst. Episcopalian. Home: Thaxmeade Farm 2500 W Everett Rd Lake Forest IL 60045 Office: 421 E Hawley St Mundelein IL 60060

STRIBLING, JAMES KEITH MARSHALL, wholesale co. exec.; b. St. Louis, July 29, 1939; s. G. Carroll and Jane F. (Forder) S.; B.A., Westminster Coll., 1962; m. Barbara J. Noblin, June 3, 1967; children—James K.M., Richard A., Tommy A. With McDonnell Douglas Aircraft, St. Louis, 1965-66; sales trainee Nat. Cash Register Co., St. Louis, 1966, sr. sales rep., 1966-69, account mgr. maj. retail account, 1969-72; store mgr. Wetteran Inc., Washington, Mo., 1972-73, asst. to gen. mgr. Non-Foods div., 1973—. Democratic committeeman, Warren County, 1972-73. Served to 1st lt., USAF, 1962-65. Mem. C. of C. Home: Route 2 Terre DuLac Bonne Terre MO 63628 Office: 701 Main St Desloge MO 63601

STRICKLER, PAUL E., investment co. exec.; b. Adams County, Decatur, Ind., Apr. 23, 1916; s. Clarence Gilbert and Golda Gazetta (Shoaf) S.; student pub. schs. Decatur; m. Kathryn Rose Pyle, Sept. 2, 1939; children—Cassandra Sanderson, Paula Fuller, Deborah Lee, Cynthia Strickler. Pres., Adams County Trailer Sales, Inc., Decatur, 1946—, Strickler Investments, Inc., 1963—; pres. Alpine Acres, 1970-74; chmn. bd. Decatur Bank & Trust Co. Trustee Anderson Coll., 1971—, exec. com. com., 1973—; mem. adv. bd. Huntington (Ind.) House, 1973-76; trustee Ch. of God, Decatur, 1958-60, 65-70. Mem. Ind. Mobile Home Assn. (bd. govs.), Decatur Econ. Devel. Commn. (pres. 1971—), Decatur, Bluffton chambers commerce, Anderson Coll. Bus. and Profl. Mens Assn. Club: Optimist. Home: Route 3 Decatur IN 46733 Office: 803 13th St N Decatur IN 46733

STRIETER, JAMES FREDERICK, optometrist; b. Hinsdale, Ill., Sept. 26, 1929; s. Theophilus William and Martha Augusta (Henn) S.; student Valparaiso U., 1948-51; B.S., Ill. Coll. Optometry, 1953, O.D., 1954; m. Margaretha Katharina Demling, Jan. 16, 1956; children—Barbara, Mark, Christopher. Pvt. practice optometry, Collinsville, Ill., 1956—; founder, pres. Ophthalmos, Inc., mfr. visual sci. products, Collinsville, Ill., 1967—. Mem. Planning Commn. Collinsville, 1971-72. Served with AUS, 1954-56; now lt. col. Res. Diplomate Contact Lens Practice. Fellow Am. Acad. Optometry, Royal Soc. Health; mem. Mil. Optometrists Assn., Am., Ill. (v.p. 1963-67, 69-71, Distinguished Service award 1972, Optometrist of Year 1975) optometric assns., S.W. Ill. Optometric Soc. (pres. 1961-63), Collinsville C. of C. (dir., v.p. 1968-73). Lutheran (dist. bd. dirs. 1968-76, elder 1960-63, 72— sec. congregation 1969-70). Club: Lions (pres. 1970-71). Patentee in visual sci. field. Home: 537 E Lake Dr Edwardsville IL 62025 Office: 724 Saint Louis Rd Collinsville IL 62234

STRIGLOS, NICK G., office equipment co. exec.; b. DeKalb, Ill., July 21, 1935; s. Gus and Jean (Mitchell) S.; B.A., Northwestern U., 1958; m. Patricia Joan Grant, June 25, 1959; children—Scott G., Jamie D., Patricia E. Pres. Striglos Office Equipment Co., Decatur, Ill., 1960—, Contemporary Properties, Inc., Decatur, 1973—; v.p. Community Research, Decatur, 1968-71. Mem. zoning bd. appeals Decatur, 1971—; pres. Decatur (Ill.) Merchant St. Mall Assn., 1969—. Episcopalian. Clubs: Decatur; Decatur Country. Home: 26 S Shores Dr Decatur IL 62521 Office: 124 E Prairie St Decatur IL 62523

STROBECK, CHARLES LEROY, real estate exec.; b. Chgo., June 27, 1928; s. Roy Alfred and Alice Rebecca (Stenberg) S.; A.B., Wheaton Coll., 1949; m. Janet Louise Halverson, June 2, 1951; children—Carol, Nancy, Beth, Jane, Jean. Asso., Sadler & Co., real estate, Chgo., 1949-63, partner, 1959-63; pres. Strobeck, Reiss & Co., real estate, Chgo., 1964—. Pres., South Loop Devel. Co., 1970—. Trustee, Wheaton Christian High Sch., 1968—, pres. bd., 1970—; bd. dirs. Chgo. Youth Centers; trustee Wheaton San. Dist., 1975-79. Served with AUS, 1950-51. Mem. Inst. Real Estate Mgmt. (chpt. pres. 1969) nat. pres. 1970), Am. Soc. Real Estate Counselors, Chgo. Real Estate Bd. (1st v.p. 1966, chmn. admissions com. 1969-71), Nat. Assn. Christians Schs. (dir., treas.), Union League Club Chgo. (dir. 1968-71, treas. 1972-73, 2d v.p. 1973-74, 1st v.p. 1974-75, pres. 1975-76), Chgo. Bldg. Owners and Mgrs. Assn. (dir.), Lambda Alpha. Mem. Coll. Ch. Wheaton (chmn. bd. elders 1971-72). Clubs: Chicago Golf, Mid-America, Union League, Realtors Forty, Realty, Downtown Brokers. Home: Hawthorne Ln Wheaton IL 60187 Office: 134 S La Salle St Chicago IL 60603

STROBEL, GEROLD CARL, state hwy. dept. exec.; b. Jefferson County, Nebr., Sept. 12, 1921; s. John George and Minnie Louise (Weishahn) S.; B.S. in Civil Engring., U. Nebr., 1947; m. Florence M. Bock, Jan. 9, 1945; children—Cory Thomas, James Carl, Debra Lynelle Strobel Fischer. Bridge structural designer Nebr. Dept. Roads, Lincoln, 1947-53, bridge engr., 1953-59, roadway design engr., 1959-60, dep. state engr. designs, ops., devel., 1960-72, dep. state engr. ops., 1972—. Served to capt. C.E. U.S. Army, 1942-46. Recipient Certificate of award James F. Lincoln Arc Welding Found., 1970; registered profl. engr., Nebr. Mem. ASCE, Am. Assn. State Hwy. and Transp. Ofcls. (25 Yr. award of Merit), Am. Rd. and Transp. Builders Assn. Lutheran. Home: 1164 S 47th St Lincoln NE 68510

STROBL, FRED ANTON, elec. engr.; b. Vienna, Austria, May 12, 1942; s. Friedrich and Helene (Konetschny) S.; Journeyman in Bus., Trade Sch. for Bus. Adminstrn., Austria, 1956-59; m. Maria I. Tuna, Sept. 27, 1963; 1 son, Manfred. Came to U.S., 1966. Chief technician Fidelity Electronics, Ltd., Chgo., 1966-67; design. engr. Accurate Electronics, Chgo., 1967-69, chief engr., 1969-73, gen. mgr., 1974—. Served with Austrian Army, 1961-62. Office: 2635 S Wabash Ave Chicago IL 60616

STRODEL, ROBERT CARL, lawyer; b. Evanston, Ill., Aug. 12, 1930; s. Carl Frederick and Imogene (Board) S.; B.S., Northwestern U., 1952; J.D., U. Mich., 1955; m. Mary Alice Shonkwiler, June 17, 1956; children—Julie Ann, Linda Lee, Sally Payson. Admitted to Ill. bar, 1955; U.S. Supreme Ct. bar, 1970; mem. firm Davis, Morgan & Witherell, 1957-59; pvt. practice, 1959-69; prin. Strodel & Kingery, Assos., Peoria, Ill., 1969—; asst. state's atty. Peoria, Ill., 1960-61; instr. bus. law Bradley U., Peoria, 1961-62; lectr. Belli seminars Denver, 1969, Miami, 1970, 73, Portland, 1971, St. Louis, 1972, others. Gov. appointee Ill. Dangerous Drugs Adv. Council, 1970-73; gen. chmn. Peoria-Tazewell Easter Seals, 1963, Cancer Crusade, 1970; pres. Peoria Civic Ballet, 1969-70; mem. Mayor's Commn. on Human Relations, 1962-64. Chmn. City of Peoria Campaign Ethics Bd., 1975. Sec., Peoria County Republican party, 1970-74; campaign chmn. Gov. Richard Ogilvie, Peoria County, 1972, Sen. Ralph Smith, 1970. Bd. dirs. Crippled Children's Center, 1964-65, Peoria Symphony Orchestra, 1964-68. Served with CIC, AUS, 1956-57. Named Outstanding Young Man Peoria, Peoria Jr. C. of C., 1963. Mem. Am., Ill. trial lawyers assns., Am., Ill. (Lincoln awards for legal writing 1961, 63, 65) bar assns. Mason (Shriner). Home: 3908 N Pinehurst Ct Peoria IL 61614 Office: 1st Nat Bank Bldg Peoria IL 61602

STROM, JERRY ERNEST, frozen food co. exec.; b. Glendale, Calif., Jan. 11, 1943; s. Edward Pershing and Vera Iola (Barber) S.; grad. in accounting U.N.D., 1965, M.B.A., 1966; m. Darlene Frances Bender, Oct. 1, 1970; children—Kelly, Kevin. Accountant, Haskins & Sells, Portland, Oreg., 1966-67; controller N.D. Hwy. Dept., Bismarck, 1967-72; dep. dir. dept. adminstrn. State of N.D., Bismarck, 1972-73; exec. v.p. Dakota Bake-N-Serv, Inc., Jamestown, N.D., 1973—. C.P.A., N.D. Mem. Am. Inst. C.P.A.'s, N.D. Soc. C.P.A.'s, Am. Accounting Assn., Am. Mgmt. Assn., Tau Kappa Upsilon, Beta Alpha Psi. Home: 900 7th Ave NW Jamestown ND 58401 Office: Airport Rd Box 688 Jamestown ND 58401

STROM, JOHN STANLEY, banker; b. Mpls., Mar. 10, 1933; s. Elmer Stanley and Marie (Oberg) S.; B.A., St. Olaf Coll., 1955; M.B.A., U. Minn., 1974; m. Nancy Elizabeth Fandrem, Nov. 25, 1960; children—Elizabeth, Claudia, Kathryn. Cashier, First Southdale Nat. Bank, Mpls., 1958-67; v.p., dir. mgmt. systems N.W. Bancorp., Mpls., 1967—. Mem. adv. bd. Upper Midwest Am. Indian Center Newcomer Program, 1970-75; bd. dirs. Edina ABC Found., 1977—. Served to capt. as pilot USAF, 1955-58. Mem. Inst. Mgmt. Scis. (pres. upper Midwest chpt. 1973-74). Lutheran (mem. council 1969-72). Home: 5005 Arden Ave Minneapolis MN 55424 Office: 1200 NW Bank Bldg Minneapolis MN 55480

STROM, LOUIS JOHN, patent lawyer; b. Omaha, Jan. 6, 1925; s. Elmer T. and Eda (Hanisch) S.; student U. Omaha, 1946-48; B.S., U. Nebr., 1950; J.D., Creighton U., 1959; m. Bonnie Yates, June 15, 1957; children—Paul, Robert, Eric. Admitted to Nebr. bar, 1959; engr. No. Natural Gas Co., Omaha, 1950-55, cons., 1959-64; partner Henderson, Strom & Sturm, 1964—. Lectr. law Creighton U.; instr. engring. law U. Nebr., Omaha, 1970. Served with U.S. Army, 1943-45. Mem. Am., Nebr., Omaha bar assns. Rotarian. Home: 3022 S 106th St Omaha NE 68124 Office: Woodmen Tower Omaha NE 68102

STROMAN, CONNIE ELIZABETH, social agy. exec.; b. Edgemont, S.D., Mar. 14, 1917; d. Ruel Homer and Lela Mena (Barton) Stalcup; student Nebr. Wesleyan U., 1934-35, Lincoln Sch. Commerce, 1955; m. J. Oakland Sidell, Nov. 17, 1940; children—Susan (Mrs. Roger D. Brandt), Joel Ruel; m. 2d, Vincent J. Stroman, Sept. 5, 1970. Govt. relations rep. Sperry and Hutchinson Co., N.D. and S.D., 1961-66; mdse. cons. J.P. Stevens Co., 1966-67; women's dir. radio sta. KMMJ, Grand Island, Nebr., 1967-69; exec. dir. Grand Island United Way, 1969—. N.D. rep. Nat. Commn. on Status of Women, Washington, 1963-64. Mem. Nat. Assn. Parliamentarians, Grand Island C. of C. (pres. women's div. 1970), Bus. and Profl. Women's Club, LWV. Republican. Methodist. Clubs: Grand Island Women's, Grand Island Toastmistress. Home: 1324 North Huston St Grand Island NE 68801 Office: 2020 W 7th St Grand Island NE 68801

STROMBERG, ROLAND NELSON, historian; b. Kansas City, Mo., July 5, 1916; s. Clarence Roland and Harriet (Ridgell) S.; A.B., U. Kansas City, 1939; M.A., Am. U., 1946; Ph.D., U. Md., 1952; m. Mary R. Gray, June 10, 1939; children—Eric, Juliet. With U.S. Dept. Justice, 1940-45; instr., then asst. prof., asso. prof., prof. U. Md., College Park, 1949-66; prof. So. Ill. U., Carbondale, 1966-67; prof. history U. Wis., Milw., 1967—, acting chmn. dept. art history, 1977-78. Rockefeller Found. grantee, 1957-58; recipient Distinguished Alumnus award U. Mo., Kansas City, 1966; fellow Woodrow Wilson Internat. Center for Scholars, 1974. Mem. Am. Hist. Assn., Soc. History of Edn., Soc. Historians of Am. Fgn. Relations. Author: Collective Security and American Foreign Policy, 1963; An Intellectual History of Modern Europe, 1966, 75; After Everything, 1975; Religious Liberalism in Eighteenth Century England, 1954; Heritage and Challenge of History, 1971; A History of Western Civilization, 1963, 2d edit., 1969; Realism, Naturalism, Symbolism, 1968; Arnold J. Toynbee, 1972. Home: 7033 N Fairchild Circle Fox Point WI 53217 Office: Bolton Hall U Wis Milwaukee WI 53201

STROMINGER, DONALD B., physician, educator; b. N.Y.C., May 11, 1928; s. William and Esther (Rosenthal) S.; B.A., Yale, 1948; postgrad. N.Y. Med. Coll., 1949-51; M.D., Washington U., St. Louis, 1953; m. Marleah Sprague Hammond, Dec. 21, 1951; children—Linda R., Dale Hammond, Mark Randall. Intern, St. Louis Children's Hosp., 1953-54, asst. resident, 1954-56, chief resident, 1956-57; preceptor allergy Washington U. Clinics, St. Louis, 1960-65; med. dir. Children's Consultation Services, Inc., St. Louis; asst. pediatrician St. Louis Maternity Hosp., McMillan Hosp.; mem. staff Barnes Hosp.; mem. vis. staff St. Luke's Hosp., St. John's Hosp.; instr. clin. pediatrics Sch. Medicine Washington U., 1960, asst. prof., 1971-75, asso. prof., 1975—. Chmn. Cystic Fibrosis Nat. Center Com., Cystic Fibrosis Found., Atlanta, 1973-75, chmn., 1976—. Pres. St. Louis Little Symphony, 1974—. Served with USAF, 1956-60; Germany. Cystic Fibrosis grantee, 1964—. Diplomate Am. Bd. Pediatrics, Am. Bd. Allergy and Immunology. Fellow Am. Acad. Pediatrics, Am. Coll. Chest Physicians, Am. Acad. Allergy, Am. Assn. Clin. Immunology and Allergy, Am. Coll. Allergy; mem. Am. Assn. Certified Allergists, Am. Thoracic Soc. (sec. pediatric assembly 1970), Soc. Med. Cons. to Armed Forces, N.Y. Acad. Scis., Pan Am. Med. Assn. (mem. sect. on Allergy), Am. Lung Assn. of Eastern Mo. (dir. 1974—), Am. Heart Assn. (mem. council on cardio-pulmonary diseases), Alph Omega Alpha. Club: Yale (Nat. rep. 1969-70, bd. govs. 1969—, sec. 1971-74, treas. 1975—). Contbr. articles to profl. jours. Home: 701 Yale Ave St Louis MO 63130 Office: 4989 Barnes Hosp Plaza St Louis MO 63110

STRONG, MARK LAVON, civil engr., land surveyor; b. Garrett, Ind., July 26, 1950; s. Harry Leslie and Lois Jean (Tomlinson) S.; B.C.E., Tri-State Coll., 1972; m. Melanie Lou Carnahan, June 14, 1970; children—Nathan, Ryan, Eric. Jr. engr. Turnbell-Green & Assos., Fort Wayne, Ind., 1973, project mgr., 1973-76, sec.-treas., 1976-77, v.p., sec.-treas., 1977—, also dir. Registered profl. engr. and land surveyor, Ind. Mem. ASCE, Nat., Ind. socs. profl. engrs., Chi Epsilon. Republican. Mem. Ch. of Christ. Home: 3925 Union Chapel Rd Fort Wayne IN 46825 Office: 519 Tennessee Ave Fort Wayne IN 46805

STRONG, RICHARD ALLEN, safety engr., writer; b. Detroit, Apr. 11, 1930; s. Winfried and Jane Liddle (Cleveland) Gilbert; B.Sc. in Aero. and Astro. Engring., U. Mich., 1964; M.A., Central Mich. U., 1975; m. Rosa Maria Amaya, Aug. 18, 1957; children—Harold Allen, Edward Gilbert, Randall Ethan, Marisa Ann. Aircraft mechanic Mich. Flyers, Detroit, 1948, Naval Air Res., 1948-54; clk. Cadillac Motors, Detroit, 1948-54; enlisted in USAF, 1955, advanced through grades to maj., 1974; instr. pilot, 1957, nav. tng. pilot, 1958-61, project officer USAF Space Systems Div., 1964-65, foward air controller, 1966, engr. System Safety Engr. Space and Missile Systems div., 1967-69, aero engr., 1969-71, br. chief, Aero. Systems div. Wright-Patterson AFB, 1973-74, ret., 1974; sr. system safety engr. Global Graphics, Fort Worth, Lockheed Missile and Space Co., Sunnyvale, Calif., 1975; propr. Star-Tchr. Systems, Strongmobile Systems, Safety Analysis Systems, Sychic Sci. Systems, Dayton, Ohio, 1974—; lectr., cons. in field. Decorated Silver Star, D.F.C., Air medal Mem. System Safety Soc., Soc. Flight Test Engrs., Exptl. Aircraft Assn., Am. Soc. Psychical Research, Intertel, Mensa, Air Force Assn. Roman Catholic. Editor Jour. Psychic Sci., 1977—. Home: 7514 Belle Plain Dr Dayton OH 45424 Office: 4950th Test Wing Safety Office Wright Patterson AFB OH 45433

STRONG, WILLIAM LEE, mfg. co. exec.; b. Jacksonville, Fla., Sept. 17, 1919; s. William M. and Hedwig C. (Ulm) S.; A.B. in Econs., Occidental Coll., 1942; M.B.A., Harvard U., 1947; m. Betty Jean Stream, Dec. 13, 1941; children—William Lee, Thomas B., Robin E. Budget dir. Byron-Jackson div. Borg-Warner Corp., Los Angeles, 1954-56, controller, 1956-57; budget dir. Consol. Freightways, Inc., Menlo Park, Calif., 1957-60, treas., chief fin. officer, 1960-62; v.p. fin., treas., dir. Packard-Bell Electronics Corp., Los Angeles, 1962-65; treas. Allis-Chalmbers Mfg. Co., Milw., 1965-68; v.p., treas. Continental Can Co., Inc., 1968-75; sr. v.p., chief fin. officer Firestone Tire & Rubber Co., Akron, Ohio, 1976-77, exec. v.p., dir., 1978—; dir. U.S. Life Corp.; mem. adv. bd. Mfrs. Hanover Trust Co., N.Y.C.; guest lectr. various grad. bus. schs., other groups. Trustee, Fin. Execs. Research Found. Served to lt. comdr. USN, 1942-54; PTO. Mem. Am. Mgmt. Assn. (fin. planning council), Treas. Club N.Y., Council Fin. Execs., Conf. Bd., Fin. Execs. Inst., Phi Gamma Delta, Harvard Bus. Sch. Club (N.Y.), Portage Country Club (Akron). Home: 1033 Bunker Dr Akron OH 44313 Office: 1200 Firestone Pkwy Akron OH 44317

STROOP, HENRY RODGER, architect; b. Holland, Mich., Feb. 13, 1922; s. Henry and Lucille (Vanden Berg) S.; student U. N.H., 1943; B.S., Chgo. Tech. Coll., 1947; m. Virginia Ruth Potter, Apr. 20, 1946; children—Doyle, Kenton, Mark, Marlin, Sheldon, Glenn. Architect, L.C. Kingscott & Assos., Kalamazoo, 1948-56; partner Kammeraad-Stroop, Holland, 1956-59; pres. Kammeraad, Stroop, Vanderleek, Inc., Holland, 1969—. Mem. Sterling, Rock Falls (Ill.) Planning Commn., 1954-55; chmn. bldg. bd. rev. City of Holland, 1975—. Served with AUS, 1942-46; ETO. Mem. AIA (chpt. pres. 1968-69), Holland Area Hist. Assn., V.F.W., Am. Legion, Friends of Art, Holland Exchange (pres. 1966-67). Ref. Ch. Am. Club: Holland Country. Home: 943 Bluebell Dr Holland MI 49423 Office: 355 Settlers Rd Suite 3-A Holland MI 49423

STROPE, RICHARD RUSSELL, hosp. adminstr.; b. Venus, Nebr., Sept. 29, 1927; s. William W. and Dora (Ickler) S.; B.A. in Hosp. Adminstrn., U. Minn., 1976; m. Romona Rose Koza, June 10, 1951; children—Mark A., Marla L. Lab. technician St. Anthony Hosp., Hays, Kans., 1950-53; chief lab. technician St. Joseph's Mercy Hosp., Centerville, Iowa, 1954-66, personnel dir., 1967-69, adminstr., 1969—, also dir. Served with AUS, 1946-47. Presbyn. Elk, Rotarian. Home: 805 S 10th St Centerville IA 52544 Office: 708 S Main St Centerville IA 52544

STROTZ, ROBERT HENRY, univ. pres.; b. Aurora, Ill., Sept. 26, 1922; s. John Marc and Olga (koerfer) S.; student Duke U., 1939-41; B.A., U. Chgo., 1942, Ph.D., 1951; LL.D., Ill. Wesleyan U., 1976; m. Helen Berry, July 24, 1961; children—Vicki, Michael, Frances, Ellen, Ann. Mem. faculty Northwestern U., Evanston, Ill., 1947—, prof. econs., 1958—, dean Coll. Arts and Scis., 1966-70, pres. univ., 1970—; chmn., dir. Fed. Res. Bank Chgo.; dir. Ill. Tool Works Inc., Norfolk & Western Ry. Co., Peoples Gas Co., U.S. Gypsum Co., Mark Controls Corp. Bd. dirs. McGaw Med. Center of Northwestern U., Nat. Merit Scholarship Corp., Northwestern Meml. Hosp.; trustee Mus. Sci. and Industry, Field Mus. Nat. History. Served with U.S. Army, 1943-45. Fellow Econometric Soc.; mem. Am. Econ. Assn., Econometric Soc. (mem. council 1961-67), Am. Statis. Assn., Royal Econ. Soc. Clubs: Old Elm, Comml., Econ., Execs., Univ., Standard, Tavern (Chgo.); Glen View (Ill.); Bohemian (San Francisco). Mng. editor Econometrica, 1953-68; econometrics editor Internat. Ency. Social Scis., 1962-68; editor Contributions to Economic Analysis, 1955-70. Home: 639 Central St Evanston IL 60201 Office: 633 Clark St Evanston IL 60201

STROUD, WILLIAM ARTHUR, banker; b. Ocala, Fla., Dec. 28, 1920; s. William A. and Nellie (Beckham) S.; student U.S. Army Air Corps Flight Sch., 1942; m. Peggy Brooks, Dec. 3, 1946; 1 son, Kimbol B. Sta. mgr. U.S. Airlines, St. Petersburg, Fla., 1946-48; v.p. marketing 1st Nat. Bank, Mansfield, Ohio, 1948-66; pres. First Knox Nat. Bank, Mt. Vernon, Ohio, 1966—; chmn. NB5 Fin. Services, 1975-76. Instr., Ohio Sch. Banking, Ohio U., 1964—. Pres., Area Devel. Found., 1969-72; finance chmn. 4-H Nat. Found., 1970, chmn. Mayor's Task Force Com., 1969-72; county chmn. U.S. Savs. Bonds, 1967—; v.p. Martin Meml. Hosp., 1974—; pres. Civic Improvement Corp., 1970-76, Community Improvement Corp., 1974-76; mem. bus. adv. council Ohio State U., 1974; chmn. for Knox County, Kenyon Coll. Devel. Trustee Martin Meml. Hosp., Mt. Vernon Parking Co., Kenyon Coll., YMCA, Columbus Regional Automated Funds Transfer System. Served to maj. USAAF, 1942-46. Decorated Silver Star medal, D.F.C. with oak leaf cluster, Air medal with 5 oak leaf clusters. Mem. Am. (mem. exec. com. and marketing savs. 1966-71), Ohio (chmn. group six 1973—, chmn. council of adminstrn. 1975-76, v.p. 1976-77) bankers assns., Mt. Vernon C. of C. (trustee). Clubs: Old Homestead, Mt. Vernon Country, Rotary. Home: 8 Highland Ct Mount Vernon OH 43050 Office: 1 S Main St Mount Vernon OH 43050

STROUP, CHARLES LOUIS, JR., utilities exec.; b. Pittsburg, Kans., Mar. 16, 1935; s. Charles Louis and Bernice Harmon (Tonnies) S.; B.S., U. Kans., 1957; m. Peggy Sue Martin, July 20, 1963; children—Bradley Martin, Kimberly Ann. Staff mem. U. Kans. Extension Service, Lawrence, 1960-61; editor Central States Constrn. mag., Topeka, reporter Pittsburg Sun, 1961-64; exec. dir. Kans. Municipal Utilities, Inc., McPherson, 1964-66, 69—; research and products mgr. pipe div. Certain-teed Products Corp., McPherson, 1966-69. Chmn., Kan. Council on Electricity and Environment, 1972-75; mem. PRIDE steering com. Kans. Community Devel. Program, 1971—; pres. McPherson County Bd. Logopedics, 1973—. Served with USAF, 1957-60. Mem. Am. Pub. Gas Assn. (nat. dir. 1971—), Am. Pub. Power Assn. (nat. dir. 1972-73), Mid-West Electric Consumers Assn. (dir.), U. Kans. Alumni Assn. (mem. devel. com. 1971—), Delta Tau Delta. Republican. Methodist (pres. adminstrv. bd. 1975—). Elk. Home: 315 Penn St McPherson KS 67460 Office: Box 1225 McPherson KS 67460

STROUP, THOMAS BENTON, county ofcl.; b. Bloomfield, Mo., Sept. 13, 1919; s. Harvey Daniel and Nellie Maud (Keating) S.; B.S., U. Mo., 1941, M.S., 1967; postgrad. Colo. State U., 1950, 51, 56; m. Geraldine M. McLane, June 25, 1949; children—Judy Kay Stroup Lockwood, Jana Leigh Stroup Putnam, Joyce Alane. Asst. supt. Farm Security Adminstrn., Pemiscot County, Mo., 1941-42; asst. county agt. U.S. Dept. Agr., Extension Service, Scott County, Mo., 1947-48, balanced farming agt., New Madrid and Scott Counties, Mo., 1948-60, county extension agt., Scott County, 1961, area asso. dir., Bootheel area, Benton, Mo., 1965—. Rural real estate appraiser; cons. to real estate appraisers. Chmn. City of Benton (Mo.) planning commn., 1975. Served with USNR, 1941-45. Recipient Distinguished Service award, Mo. County Agts. Assn., 1961, Nat. County Agts. Assn., 1962; Service award for appreciation of leadership, Cape Girardeau C. of C., 1971. Mem. Benton C. of C. (pres. 1950), Mo. County Agts. Assn. (sec.-treas. 1960), Nat. County Agrl. Agts. Assn., Mo. Extension Agts. Assn., Epsilon Sigma Phi. Methodist. Mason. Home: 11 Bland St Benton MO 63736 Office: PO Box 187 Benton MO 63736

STROZIER, CHARLES BURNETT, historian; b. Athens, Ga., Feb. 16, 1944; s. Robert M. and Margaret (Burnett) S.; B.A., Harvard U., 1966; M.A., U. Chgo., 1967, Ph.D., 1971; m. Carol A. Kelly; children—Michael, Matthew, Christopher. Asst. prof. history Sangamon State U., Springfield, Ill., 1972-76, asso. prof., 1976—; research candidate Chgo. Inst. Psychoanalysis; project dir. Lincoln's Thought and the Present, Nat. Endowment Humanities. Mem. Am.

Hist. Assn. (exec. officer group for use of psychology in history). Editor Psychohistory Rev., 1974—; contbr. articles in psychohistory to profl. jours. Home: Rural Route 1 Box 51 Edinburg IL 62531 Office: Sangamon State U Springfield IL 62708

STRUBLE, JAMES ROBERT, mech. engr.; b. Salina, Kans., June 2, 1935; s. James Lester and Kathryn L. (Brick) S.; student Kans. State U., 1953; B.S. in M.E., Wichita State U., 1963; postgrad. Tex. Christian U., 1965; m. Sue Jean Wallace, Oct. 30, 1954 (div. June 1967); children—Jennifer K., Stephanie L., Julienne J.; m. 2d, Earletta K. Divelbess, June 18, 1971. Pvt. practice as mech., elec. and structural engr., Struble & Co., cons. engrs., McPherson, Kans., 1965—; contact engr. Boeing Co., Wichita, Kans., 1956-63; design and lead engr. McDonnell Aircraft, St. Louis, 1963-64, Gen. Dynamics Corp., Fort Worth, 1964-65; research and devel. engr. Salina Mfg. Co., 1965-66; project engr. Shaver & Co., Salina, 1966-68; group engr., asst. project engr. Beech Aircraft Co., Salina, 1968-72; mgr. engring. Certainteed Machinery Corp. McPherson, 1974-77; mech. engr. Bucher & Willis Cons. Engrs., Architects & Planners, Salina, 1977—. Republican precinct committeeman, 1968-70. Registered profl. engr., Kans., Tex. Mem. Profl. Engrs. in Pvt. Practice. Mason (Shriner). Home: 1719 Sycamore St Salina KS 67401 Office: W North St Salina KS 67401

STRUEH, PAUL EDWARD, physician; b. Evansville, Ind., June 3, 1920; s. Edward and Mary (Martin) S.; B.S., U. Chgo., 1942, M.D., 1945; postgrad. U. Ill., 1948-51; m. Ruth Hadis Hurt, June 23, 1945; children—Robert E., William P., Joy LeeAnn. Intern, Presbyn. Hosp., Chgo., 1945-46; practice medicine ltd. to otolaryngology, Evansville, 1951—. Served with AUS, 1946-48 Diplomate Am. Bd. Otolaryngology. Fellow Am. Acad. Ophthalmology and Otolaryngology; mem. AMA, Ind., Vanderburgh County med. assns., Ind. Acad. Ophthalmology and Otolaryngology, Am. Council Otolaryngology. Clubs: Masons (Shriner), Kiwanis. Home: 1207 Harrelton Ct Evansville IN 47715 Office: 220 SE 7th St Evansville IN 47713

STRUKOFF, RUDOLF STEPHEN, musician; b. Rostov, Russia, July 18, 1935; s. Stephen and Olga (Flemming) S.; came to U.S., 1951, naturalized, 1957; B.Mus. Edn., Andrews U., 1960; Mus.M., Mich. State U., 1964, Ph.D., 1970, post-doctoral in higher edn. adminstrn., 1974-76; m. Donna Lee Hill, May 31, 1959; children—Rudolf Stephen, Robbin Stanley, Regan Stuart. Vocal music dir. Mountain View (Calif.) Acad., 1960-61, Milo (Oreg.) Acad., 1961-63, Grand Ledge (Mich.) Acad., 1965-66; voice instr. Mich. State U., East Lansing, 1963-64; asst. prof. music Ind. State U., Terre Haute, 1966-69; asso. prof. music Andrews U., Berrien Springs, Mich., 1969-75; prof. music Govs. State U., Park Forest South, Ill., 1977—. Choral dir. First Presbyn. Ch., Benton Harbor, Mich., 1959-60; bass soloist First Bapt. Ch., Lansing, Mich., 1963-66; minister music Central Presbyn. Ch., Terre Haute, Ind., 1966-69. Named Singer of Year, Nat. Assn. Tchrs. Singing Mich., 1966. Mem. Am. Choral Dirs. Assn., Nat. Assn. Tchrs. Singing, Am. Choral Found., Nat. Assn. for Am. Composers and Condrs., ASCAP, Music Educators Nat. Conf., AAUP, Pi Kappa Lambda. Composer: Childhood Sketches, a Song Cycle of Seven Contemporary Poems for Mezzosoprano and Piano, 1965, The Greatest of These, 1969; Moods in Blue for Harp and Flute, 1972. Home: 740 N Main St Berrien Springs MI 49103

STRUTZ, CARL E., ret. research co. exec., conservationist; b. Holmes, N.D., Sept. 27, 1910; s. Robert Edward and Emma (Kahl) S.; B.A., Jamestown Coll., 1937; m. Ruth Marion Compaan, Apr. 10, 1950; 1 dau., Joan Lynne. With R.E. Strutz & Sons Co., Jamestown, N.D., 1937-75, pres., 1958-75. Recipient Feather of Distinction award Game Bird Breeders Assn. jour., 1964; Wildlife Conservation award Sears Roebuck Found. and Nat. Wildlife Fedn., 1965. Mem. Internat. Wild Waterfowl Assn. (dir., sec. treas. 1963—, Outstanding Mem. Year award 1963, Outstanding Achievement award 1970), Am. Pheasant and Waterfowl Soc. (Pearson award 1965, Master Waterfowl Breeder award 1966), N.D. Wildlife Fedn. (pres. 1956—), Audubon Soc., Alaska Conservation Soc., Whooping Crane Conservation Soc., Mus. Nat. History, N.D. chpt. Wildlife Soc., Wildfowl Trust Eng., Smithsonian Assos. Methodist. Club: Lions. Contbg. author: Home Grown Honkers, 1970; Keeping and Raising Wild Ducks in Captivity, 1973. Pioneer in techniques of raising rare species of wild geese; first to raise Aleutian Can. goose, 1966. Home: PO Box 1075 Jamestown ND 58401

STRYKER, MARIAN ANDERSON, ret. ednl. adminstr.; b. Green Springs, Ohio, May 6, 1909; d. James Arthur and Elnora (Lynch) Anderson; A.B. in English, Modern Lang., Hope Coll., 1931; student Tiffin Bus. U., 1931-32; m. John Alvin Stryker, Oct. 15, 1936 (dec. 1946); children—John Alvin II, James William, David Philip. Sec. law office, Muskegon, Mich., 1932-33; sec. to sec. state Mich. Adminstrv. Bd., Lansing, 1933-36; corr. Grand Rapids (Mich.) Herald, 1953-58; alumni exec. sec. Hope Coll., Holland, Mich., 1947-74, also alumni editor, 1949-74. Pres. Holland Concert Assn., 1970-72; sec. Holland Arts Council, 1973-75, trustee, 1975—. Mem. Am. Alumni Council (treas. dist. 1959-63, editorial achievement award 1961). Club: Holland Century (pres. 1966-67). Home: 105 W 26th St Holland MI 49423

STRYZINSKI, ROBERT JOSEPH, univ. adminstr.; b. Oak Park, Ill., Mar. 7, 1938; s. Edward Max and Helen Marie (LeBeouf) S.; B.S., Butler U., 1960; m. Norma Jean Jostes, Mar. 31, 1960; children—Deborah, Michael, Ronald, Daniel, Rick, Kathryn, Donna. State budget analyst Ind. State Budget Agency, Indpls., 1961-65, dep. budget dir., 1965-74; budget analyst Hughes Aircraft Co., Tucson, 1974-75; bus. mgr., treas. Vincennes (Ind.) U., 1975—; budget cons. Ind. Ho. of Reps., 1976. Mem. Butler B-Men's Assn. (pres. 1970-71), Nat. Assn. Coll. and Univ. Bus. Officers. Club: Elks. Home: 110 Beech St Vincennes IN 47591 Office: 1002 N First St Vincennes IN 47591

STUART, JAMES FORTIER, music educator; b. Baton Rouge, Dec. 22, 1928; s. Evander Morgan and Jeanne (Fortier) S.; Mus.B., La. State U., 1950, B. Music Edn., 1950, Mus.M., 1954; Mus.D., U. Rochester, 1968. Soloist with major opera cos. and symphonies, N.Y.C., Boston, Phila., Atlanta, New Orleans, 1950-70; leading tenor Am. Savoyards, 1957-60, Martyn Green Gilbert & Sullivan Co., 1961-67; asst. prof. voice, dir. opera Boston U. and Boston Conservatory, 1964-68; prof. music, dir. opera Kent (Ohio) State U., 1968—, founder, artistic dir. Kent Light Opera Co., 1969—; pres. Stuart Prodns., Ltd., Cleve., 1974—. Musical cons. Internat. Hospitality Mgmt., Inc., Cleve., 1974. Home: 135 Forest Dr Kent OH 44240

STUART, ROBERT ALLAN, lawyer; b. Sheridan, Wyo., Mar. 11, 1917; s. Robert Bland and Lillian Grace (Mason) S.; student U. Wyo., 1934-35; A.B., U. Mich., 1938, J.D., 1941; m. Elizabeth Louise Pexton, Feb. 14, 1942; children—Elizabeth Anne (Mrs. John F. Linxwiler), Mary Louise, Robert Allan. Admitted to Wyo. bar, 1941, Ill. bar, 1941, U.S. Supreme Ct. bar, 1950, mem. firm Brown, Hay & Stephens, Springield, Ill., 1941—; v.p., sec., dir. Town Gas Co. Ill.; dir. various small corps. Instr. Lincoln Coll. Law, Springfield, 1948-53. Mem. Gov. Torts Law Commn., 1960-64, Gov.'s Adv. Council to Dept. Local Govt. Affairs, 1968-73. Mem. youth commn. YMCA, 1948-65; pres. Boys Farm Found., Springfield, 1964-66; mem. nat. council Boy Scouts Am., 1958-74; pres., Springfield Park Dist., 1954-75; mem. Springfield Regional Plan Commn., 1969-75, bd. dirs. Springfield Auditorium Authority, 1965-71; bd. dirs. Abraham Lincoln council Boy Scouts Am., 1948-74, Ill. Park and Recreation Found., 1968-72, Nat. Recreation Found., 1975—. Served to 1st lt. CIC, AUS, World War II. Recipient Silver Beaver award Boy Scouts Am., 1958. Mem. Ill. Assn. Park Dist. (dir. 1954—), Nat. Recreation and Park Assn. (dir 1968—), Sangamon County, Ill., Met. St. Louis, Am. (nat. sec., v.p. younger mem. sect. 1950-53) bar assns., Sigma Chi. Clubs: Masons (33 deg.), Shrine, Lions. Home: 2100 Wiggins Ave Springfield IL 62704 Office: 700 1st Nat Bank Bldg Springfield IL 62701

STUART, WALTER STANLEY, JR., consumer products mfg. co. exec.; b. St. Louis, Sept. 18, 1939; s. Walter Stanley and Barbara (Osborne) S.; student Beloit Coll., 1957-59; B.S., Ind. U., 1962; M.B.A. with honors, 1965; m. Judith M. Anderson, May 18, 1963; children—Michael Carl, Matthew David, Mark Stephen. Mem. product mgmt. staff Gen. Foods Corp., White Plains, N.Y., 1965-67; project dir. advanced methods group N.W. Ayer Co., Phila., 1968-69, v.p., mgmt. supr., Chgo., 1970-73; v.p. corp. mktg. devel. Ball. Corp., Muncie, Ind., 1973-74, v.p., gen. mgr. consumer products div., 1974—; instr. mktg. Roosevelt U., Chgo., 1968, Rutgers U., 1969. Pres. Indian guide program YMCA, Delaware County, Ind., 1974-75; bd. dirs. Delaware County Jr. Achievement, 1976—; mem. legis. council Ind. U. Alumni Assn., 1975—. Mem. Am. Mktg. Assn., Ind. U. Sch. Bus. Alumni Assn. (past pres., mem. exec. council 1973—), Ill. St. Andrew Soc. Chgo., Assn. Nat. Advertisers, Ind. Soc. Chgo., Art Inst. Chgo., Beta Gamma Sigma, Phi Delta Theta, Alpha Delta Sigma, Delta Sigma Pi. Clubs: Univ., Tavern, Arts (Chgo.); Delaware Country, Muncie (Muncie); Columbia (Indpls.). Author: Guidelines for Successful New Product Test Marketing, 1976. Home: 3556 Johnson Circle Muncie IN 47304 Office: 345 S High St Muncie IN 47302

STUART, WILLIAM EDWARD, banker; b. Cin., Oct. 18, 1933; s. Albert Boynton and Winifred Alice (Burns) S.; A.B. cum laude in Econs. and Bus. Adminstrn., Drury Coll., 1964; basic and standard certificate (Scholarship award), Am. Inst. Banking, 1968; certificate of systems analysis St. Louis U., 1971; grad. Stonier Sch. Banking, Rutgers U., 1975; m. Martha Ann Allgeyer, July 13, 1963; children—Beth Ann, David Andrew. Vice-pres., treas. Baker-Stuart Oil Co., St. Louis, 1954-63; mem. employee audit dept. Tower Grove Bank & Trust Co., St. Louis, 1964-66, asst. sec.-treas., chmn. automation com., 1967-68, asst. v.p. bookkeeping dept., 1969-71, v.p. ops., 1972-77; pres. First State Bank Union (Mo.), 1977—. instr. Grad. Sch. Banking, Madison, Wis., 1976—; dir. Fin. Computing Corp. Mo., 1974-75. Mem. civilian adv. bd. St. Louis County Spl. Sch. Dist., 1977. Mem. Am. Inst. Banking, Assn. Time-Sharing Users (pres. St. Louis chpt.), Am. Mgmt. Assn., Phi Gamma Mu. Mem. United Ch. Christ. Office: Oak and Springfield Sts Union MO 63084

STUBBE, ANNE MARIE, artist, poet; b. Gleason, Wis., Mar. 13, 1911; d. Walter A. and Mary (Below) Schenk; student U. Wis., 1967-76; m. Ervin Stubbe, Aug. 15, 1940; children—Patrick Stubbe, Robert Stubbe, Kay Stubbe. Dir. Wis. Regional Writers, Madison, 1966-75; judge S.D. Poetry Contest; chmn. Wausau (Wis.) Festival of Arts, Poetry, 1964-71. Jade Ring 1st Prize, 1965; 3d prize Nat. Fedn. State Poetry Socs., 1967, 1st prize, 1976; recipient numerous awards for poetry, paintings. Mem. Wis. Valley Art Assn. (sec. treas. 1966-67), Wis. Fellowship Poets (pres. 1974-76), Wausau Poetry Soc. (founder), Wis. Regional Writers Assn., Wis. Acad. Sci., Arts and Letters. Democrat. Lutheran. Poems published in numerous anthologies and mags. Home: 905 S 6th Ave Wausau WI 54401

STUBBLEFIELD, ERVIN ANDREW, mcht.; b. St. Louis County, Mo., Apr. 11, 1933; s. Andrew Ervin and Lillian Irene (Rahlman) S.; student Mo. U., 1951-52; m. Mary Jean Ambruster, June 14, 1953; children—Andrew Lee, Doris Jean. Co-owner dairy farm, nr. Cuba, Mo., 1953-56; cement finisher C. Sansone Constrn., St. Louis, 1956-73; owner Western Auto Store, Cuba, 1973—; dir. Crawford Electric Coop., Bourbon. Mem. Mo. U. Extension Council for Crawford County, 1969-73. Dir. Bd. Edn., Crawford R-2 Schs., 1964-67; mem. Rep. Central Com. Crawford County, 1970—. Presbyn. (former deacon, elder). Home: Box 109 Star Route Cuba MO 65453 Office: 402 N Washington St Cuba MO 65453

STUBER, PAUL JOHN, chem. engr.; b. Miller City, Ohio, Feb. 1, 1915; s. Claude Clifford and Nora Naomi (Mullett) S.; B.Chem. Engring., Ohio State U., 1942, M.Chem.Engring., 1948; m. Leona M. Thomas, June 8, 1940; children—Thomas, Sue Stuber Lively, Paula Stuber Gronemeyer. Devel. engr. Monsanto Co., St. Louis, 1942-46, prodn. supr., 1946-51, engring. mgr., 1959-71, devel. mgr., applications engr., Chgo., 1972-76, St. Louis, 1976—. Mem. Am. Inst. Chem. Engrs. Contbr. articles to profl. jours. Home: 25 Steeple Hill Ballwin MO 63011 Office: Corporate Sq Office Park Box 14547 St Louis MO 63178

STUCKO, JOHN VINCENT, ins. co. exec.; b. Chgo., May 24, 1941; s. August Raymond and Martha Bernadette (Kasluga) S.; B.A. in Communications, Notre Dame, 1964; M.A. in Communications, Mich. State U., 1976; m. Elizabeth Ann Alexander, Mar. 19, 1967; children—Mary Kathleen, Michael Denis. With Farm Bur. Ins. Group, Lansing, Mich., 1967—, pub. relations advt. coordinator, 1970-73, advt. mgr., 1973-77, mgr. advt. and sales promotion, 1977—. Served with U.S. Army, 1964-67. Mem. Toastmasters Internat., Am. Advt. Fedn. (Mich. legis. chmn. 1977), Lansing Ad Club (dir. 1976—), Life Ins. Advertisers Assn., Advt. Research Found., Lansing Advt. Club. Home: 1228 Garfield St Lansing MI 48917 Office: 7373 W Saginaw Lansing MI 48909

STUCKY, MILO ORLANDO, educator; b. Moundridge, Kans., Aug. 13, 1912; s. Daniel J. and Anna (Stucky) S.; B.S., McPherson Coll., 1933; M.A., U. Wash., 1940; student U. Colo., 1937, 51; Ed.D., U. Kans., 1959; m. Mabel Gaering, June 10, 1937; children—Nicholas G., Anna C., Constance M., Eric D. Tchr. rural sch. McPherson County, Kans., 1933-35; tchr., prin. Bloom Rural High Sch., 1935-42; supt. schs., Florence, 1942-44; prin. Buhler (Kans.) Rural High Sch., 1944-62; prof. edn. Sch. Edn. U. Kans., Lawrence, 1962—, chmn. dept., 1969—. Ednl. cons. Ford Found. Central Am., 1967-68, Orgn. of Central Am. States, 1970—; vis. lectr. Tubingen (Germany) U., also Vlissingen (Holland) Tech. Inst., 1972. Exec. com. Kans. Study Edn. for Citizenship, 1949-52; mem. Kans. Life-Adjustment Comm., 1954—, chmn., 1953; mem. Kans. Commn. for the Improvement of Secondary Edn., 1953—; mem. nat. com. N. Central Assn. Secondary Schs. and Colls., 1968. Mem. Kans. State Tchrs. Assn. (v.p. 1950). Kans. State High Sch. Activities Assn. (legis. council, 1955—), Nat., Kans. assns. secondary school prins., AAUP, Am. Assn. Sch. Adminstrs., NEA, Kans. Adminstrs. Club: Kans. Educators Club, Phi Delta Kappa. Mennonite. Home: 506 Pioneer Rd Lawrence KS 66044

STUDZINSKI, DENIS RAY, accountant; b. Chgo., July 19, 1952; s. Raymond and Stephanie Alice (Pelczarski) S.; B.S., De Paul U., 1975. Accounting clk. Martin J. Callaghan & Co., accountants, Chgo., 1968-73; staff gen. accountant Transo Envelope div. Arvey Corp., Chgo., 1973-75, gen. accounting supr., 1975-76, staff cost accountant, 1976-77; office services mgr., accountant Ben Franklin Ins. Agy. div. City Products Corp., Des Plaines, Ill., 1978—. Mem. Nat. Assn. Accountants, Nat. Soc. Pub. Accountants. Home: 8322 O'Connor Dr River Grove IL 60171 Office: 1700 S Wolf Rd Des Plaines IL 60018

STUERMAN, LINDA KAY, educator, counselor; b. Brookings, S.D., Apr. 9, 1949; d. Hugo Fredrick William and LaVonne Roberta (Tjossem) S.; B.C.S., S.D. State U., 1972, M.Ed., 1977. Florist, designer Watson Flowers, Brookings, 1969-71; designer Larsen Design, Sioux Falls, S.D., 1972; mgr., buyer The Showcase, Brookings, 1973-75; instr. art Brookings Middle Sch., 1975—; inter counselor 3d Judicial Circuit Ct. Services, Brookings, 1976-77, Girls Group Home, Sioux Falls, 1977—. Originator, adviser Brookings Youth Art Club. Mem. Am. Personnel and Guidance Assn., Brookings Assn. Arts Council, Alpha Xi Delta, Bus. and Profl. Womens Club. Methodist. Office: 601 4th St Brookings SD 57006

STUERMANN, LEONARD HENRY, coll. adminstr.; b. Washington, Mar. 4, 1926; s. Leonard Henry and Augusta Margaret (Nau) S.; B.C.S., Benjamin Franklin U., 1949; postgrad. Boston U., 1955, U. Ky., 1963, U. Omaha, 1964-65, U. Wis., 1969-70; m. Doris C. Schmidt, June 25, 1955. Accountant, Marinus Koster, C.P.A., Washington, 1945-54; auditor Gen. Accounting Office, Chgo., 1954-55; office mgr. Laborers Health and Welfare Adminstrn., Boston, 1955-56; auditor Dept. Army, Chgo., 1956-57; comptroller Milw. Area Tech. Coll., 1957—. Mem. Assn. Sch. Bus. Ofcls. U.S. and Can. (registered sch. bus. ofcl.), Wis. Assn. Vocat., Tech. and Adult Edn., Student Fin. Aid Adminstrs., Am. Mgmt. Soc. Clubs: Kiwanis, Masons, Shriners. Home: 7318 Wellauer Dr Wauwatosa WI 53213 Office: 1015 N 6th St Milwaukee WI 53203

STUHLMAN, ROBERT AUGUST, veterinarian; b. Cin., Apr. 9, 1939; s. Robert A. and Marion June (Hannig) S.; student U. Cin., 1962-63; D.V.M., Ohio State U., 1968; M.S. in Lab. Animal Medicine, U. Mo., 1971; m. Liliane Jeannine Pierre, Nov. 12, 1960; children—Robert A., Michael A., Lisa M. Research asso., dept. veterinary medicine and surgery, U. Mo., Columbia, 1968-71, asst. dir. dept. lab. animal medicine, 1971-75, instr. dept. pathology, 1971-75; veterinary med. officer Research Service Veterans Hosp., Columbia, Mo., 1972-75; dir. Lab. Animal Resources Wright State U. Sch. Medicine, Dayton, Ohio, 1975—, asso. prof. dept. pathology, 1975—, mem. deans staff, 1975—; cons. in lab. animal care Research Service VA Center, Dayton, Ohio, 1975—; participant 3rd Brooklodge Workshop on Spontaneous Diabetes in Lab. Animals, 1974. Served with USAF, 1957-62. Nominated for Established Investigator award Am. Diabetes Assn., 1974; U.S. Pub. Health grantee, 1974—. Mem. Am. Assn. for Lab. Animal Sci., Am. Coll. Lab. Animal Medicine, Am. Veterinary Med. Assn., Am. Soc. Lab. Animal Practitioners, Phi Zeta. Contbr. articles on diabetes in lab. animals to profl. jours. Home: 2111 Granada Dr Dayton OH 45431 Office: Wright State Univ School Medicine Laboratory Animal Resources Dayton OH 45431

STUHR, ROBERT LEWIS, pub. relations cons.; b. Tabor, Iowa, Oct. 10, 1917; s. John R. and Elsa J. (Strange) S.; B.A., Drake U., 1939; M.A., U. Iowa, 1940; Ph.D., Northwestern U., 1961; m. Ruth P. Jones, Sept. 21, 1946; children—John, Margaret. Dir. pub. relations and devel. Drake U., Des Moines, 1947-59; partner Gonser Gerber Tinker Stuhr, devel. cons., Chgo., 1959—; asso. dir. Econ. Club Chgo., 1959-68, exec. dir., 1968—, mem. exec. com., 1968—; dir. First Security Bank Chgo. Served to capt., inf. AUS, 1941-46. Decorated Bronze Star medal; recipient Distinguished Alumni award Drake U., 1960. Mem. Pub. Relations Soc. Am., Internat. Pub. Relations Soc., Council Advancement and Support Edn., S.A.R., Phi Beta Kappa, Sigma Delta Chi, Sigma Alpha Epsilon, Omicron Delta Kappa, Phi Eta Sigma. Clubs: Univ. (Chgo.); Westmoreland Country (Wilmette, Ill.). Editor Bull. on Pub. Relations and Devel. for Colls., 1959—, Bull. on Pub. Relations and Devel. for Prep Schs., 1959—, Bull. on Pub. Relations and Devel. for Hosps., 1959—. Contbr. to various mags. Home: 3033 Iroquois Rd Wilmette IL 60091 Office: 105 W Madison St Chicago IL 60602

STUKEL, JAMES JOSEPH, engineer, educator; b. Joliet, Ill., Mar. 30, 1937; s. Philip and Julia (Mattivi) S.; B.S. in Mech. Engring., Purdue U., 1959; M.S., U. Ill., Champaign-Urbana, 1963, Ph.D., 1968; m. Mary Joan Helpling, Nov. 27, 1958; children—Catherine, James, David, Paul. Research engr. W. Va. Pulp and Paper Co., Covington, Va., 1959-61; asst. prof. U. Ill., Urbana, 1968-71, asso. prof., 1971-75, prof., 1975—, dir. office coal research and utilization, 1974-76, dir. office energy research, 1976—; exec. sec. MW Consortium on Air Pollution, 1972-73; chmn. bd. dirs., 1973-75; mem. adv. bd. regional studies program Argonne (Ill.) Nat. Lab., 1975-76; mem. adv. com. Energy Resources Center, U. Ill., Chgo., 1975-76; mem. coal study panel Energy Resources Commn., State of Ill., 1976; cons. in field. Pres. parish council Holy Cross Ch., Urbana, Ill., 1967-68. Mem. ASCE (State-of-the-Art of Civil Engring. award 1975), ASME, AAAS, Sigma Xi, Phi Kappa Phi, Pi Tau Sigma. Contbr. articles to profl. jours. Home: 2504 Bedford Champaign IL 61820 Office: 3219 CEB Univ Ill Urbana IL 61801

STULL, DANIEL, mortgage banker; b. Wadsworth, Ohio, Nov. 17, 1942; student Akron (Ohio) U., 1960; certificate in mktg. Kent (Ohio) State U., 1965; certificate in mgmt. U. Denver, 1965; certificate in teaching Moody Bible Inst., 1973; grad. N.Y. Inst. Fin., 1973; student Law Sch., La Salle Extension U., 1973-76. Ordained to ministry Ch. of World Brotherhood, 1972, trustee, 1972—; pres. Stull & Co., Cleve., 1974—; pres. Stull & Co. (Europe), Geneva, Switzerland, Nationwide Supply, Inc.; pub. Stull Fin. News and Stull Golden Rule Observer; pub., author: (with Henry Stull) How & Where to Obtain Capital; How to Earn $50,000 Yearly; How to Become a Mortgage or Financial Broker; also editor condensed reports; officer or dir. Nationwide Supply, Inc., Premier Advt. & Supply Co., Skipper's Discount Co., Trader's Import Co.; pres., dir. Aaban Modelling Agy., Aaban Pub. Co., Aaban Travel Agy., Amvestco, Inc., Branch Office, Inc., Crown Corp., Investors Internat., Inc. Mem. Internat. Moneybrokers Assn. (v.p.), Mortgage Bankers Assn. Internat. (v.p.). Home: Penthouse 2B Carlyle Towers Lakewood OH 44107 Office: 79 Wall St New York City NY 10005 also Union Bldg Cleveland OH 44115

STULL, DAVID WILLIS, psychologist; b. Omaha, July 9, 1943; s. Willis Clifford and Evelyn Pauline (Bishop) S.; B.S. in Music and Ednl. Psychology (Tuition scholar), Kearney (Nebr.) State Coll., 1965, M.S. in Ednl. Psychology, 1969; m. Norma C. Smith, Aug. 26, 1962; children—Todd, Jana, Corey. Psychologist, Elm Creek (Nebr.) Pub. Schs., 1965-69; psychologist Mid-Nebr. Community Mental Health Center, Grand Island, Nebr., 1969—, chmn. adult out-patient service, 1972—, chief of staff, 1976—. Cons./psychologist Grand Island VA Hosp., 1973-74; instr. vocat. rehab. Nebr. Law Enforcement Sch., 1970—; mem. Grand Island Pub. Sch. Evaluation Team. Vice pres. Central Nebr. Goodwill Industries, 1969-74; pres. West Lawn Sch. PTA, 1973-75, Grand Island City PTA, 1975-76; adviser Parents Without Partners, 1972-74; Nebr. del. Nat. Bapt. Conv. on Key '73. Bd. dirs. Friendship Halfway House for Alcoholics, 1969-71. Recipient Outstanding Musician awards Lions Internat., Grand Island Pub. Schs., 1961. Mem. Am., Nebr. psychol. assns., Liederkranz Soc.

Home: 1903 W Division St Grand Island NE 68801 Office: Box 1763 Baumann Dr Grand Island NE 68801

STULL, HENRY, banker, author, fin. and tax cons., clergyman; b. Seville. Ohio; student Akron U. Community Coll., 1960, 63, 64, Kent State U., 1966; certificate in sales mgmt. U. Denver, 1965; certificate in teaching with results Moody Bible Inst., 1974. Ordained to ministry Ch. of World Brotherhood, 1972, trustee, 1972—; v.p., chmn. bd. Stull and Co., N.Y.C., 1968—; v.p. Stull and Co. (Europe), Geneva; pub. Stull Financial News, N.Y.C., Stull Golden Rule Observer, Stull Business Directory; chmn., v.p. Nationwide Supply, Inc., n.y.c. notary pub., 1963—68. Mem. Internat. Mail Order Assn. (dir.), Internat. Moneybrokers Assn. (pres. and dir.) Mortgage Bankers Assn. Internat. (pres. and dir.), Internat. Tax Consultants (dir.), Internat. Import/Export Assn. (dir.), Barter Exchange Assn. (pres.), Internat. Lectrs. Assn. (dir.). Club: Stull Writers (pres.). Home: Penthouse 2A Carlyle Towers Lakewood OH 44107 Office: 615 Union Bldge Cleveland OH 44115 also 79 Wall St New York City NY 10005

STUMP, HARL GENE, surgeon; b. Shattuck, Okla., July 9, 1939; s. Harley H. and Jeanette L. (Slaughter) S.; B.S., McPherson Coll., 1961; M.D., U. Kans., 1965; m. LaVena I. Murray, June 16, 1962; children—Stephen B., Phillip B. Intern, Wesley Med. Center, Wichita, Kans., 1965-66; resident in gen. surgery St. Joseph Hosp., Denver, 1968-72; practice medicine specializing in gen. surgery, Hays, Kans., 1972—; attending staff physician St. Anthony Hosp., Hadley Regional Med. Center. Diplomate Am. Bd. Surgery. Fellow A.C.S. Republican. Methodist. Home: 3208 Willow St Hays KS 67601 Office: 2717 Canal St Hays KS 67601

STUMP, JOHN EDWARD, veterinary anatomist; b. Galion, Ohio, June 3, 1934; s. Clarence Willard and Mabel Katherine (Pfeifer) S.; D.V.M. summa cum laude, Ohio State U., 1958; Ph.D., Purdue U., 1966; m. Patricia Anne Auer, Aug. 7, 1955; children—Karen, James. Pvt. practice veterinary medicine, Bucyrus, Ohio, 1958-61; instr. veterinary anatomy Purdue U., W. Lafayette, Ind., 1961-66, asst. prof., 1966-70, asso. prof., 1970-76, prof., 1976—; anatomy cons. Nat. Bd. Veterinary Med. Examiners. Mem. Lafayette (Ind.) Bd. Health, 1973—, Lafayette Animal Control Commn., 1976—. Recipient Borden award for highest academic average in veterinary medicine Ohio State U., 1958; Autotutorial Excellence award Student AVMA, 1974; Norden Distinguished Tchr. (in a veterinary medicine) award Purdue U., 1977, Outstanding Teacher award Purdue Alumni Found., 1978. Mem. Am., Ind. veterinary med. assns., Ind. Acad. Veterinary Medicine, World, Am. (pres. 1977-78) assns. veterinary anatomists, Am. Assn. Anatomists, Assn. Am. Veterinary Med. Colls., Ind. Acad. Sci., Sigma Xi, Phi Zeta. Republican. Presbyterian. Club: Kiwanis (pres. Lafayette chpt. 1972). Home: 2515 Oswego Ln Lafayette IN 47905 Office: Dept Anatomy Sch Veterinary Medicine Purdue U West Lafayette IN 47907

STUMPE, WARREN ROBERT, mfg. co. exec.; b. Bronx, July 15, 1925; s. William A. and Emma J. (Mann) S.; B.S., U.S. Mil. Acad., 1945; M.S., Cornell U., 1949; M.S. in Indsl. Engring., N.Y. U., 1965. m. Jean Marie Mannion, June 5, 1952; children—Jeffrey R., Kathy, William E. Commd. 2d lt. C.E., U.S. Army, 1945, advanced through grades to capt., 1954; 65th Engr. Bn., 1945-48; asst. prof. mechanics U.S. Mil. Acad., 1951-54; resigned, 1954; col. Res. assigned to dep. chief of staff R&D Dept. Army, Washington, 1974—; dep. gen. mgr., gen. engring. div. AMF, Stamford, Conn., 1954-63; exec. v.p. Dortech, Inc., Stamford, 1963-69; dir. systems mgmt. group Mathews Conveyor div. REX, Darien, Conn., 1969-71, dir. research and devel. Rexnord, Milw., 1971-73, v.p. corporate research and tech., 1973—. Founder, pres. No. Little League, Stamford, 1965-69; pres. Turn of River Jr. High Sch. PTA, Stamford, 1967-68; mem. Nat. Com. Employer Support Guard and Res.; mem. exec. bd. Inst. Mineral and Solid Fuel Tech. U. Wis. Bd. dirs. Milw. Sch. Engring. Registered profl. engr., N.Y., Fla., Wis. Mem. Am. Mgmt. Assn., Soc. Am. Mil. Engrs., Am. Water Pollution Control Fedn., Bridgeport Engring. Inst. (bd. assos. 1960-71), Process Equipment Mfrs. Assn., Indsl. Research Inst., West Point Soc. N.Y. (career adv. bd.), West Point Soc. Wis., Tau Beta Pi. Club: Ozaukee Country. Contbr. articles to profl. jours. Home: 2555 W Hemlock Rd Glendale WI 53209 Office: PO Box 2022 Milwaukee WI 53201

STUMPF, LOWELL C(LINTON), artist-designer; b. Canton, Ill., Dec. 8, 1917; s. Oral Baxter and Marie (Dawson) S.; grad. Chgo. Acad. Fine Arts; student L'Ecole de Beaux Arts, Marseille, France, 1945; m. Jacqueline Jeanne Charlotte Andree Lucas, Sept. 5, 1945; children—Eric Clinton, Roderick Lowell. Staff artist Internat. Harvester Co., Chgo., 1939-42, Nugent-Graham Studios, Chgo., 1945-47; free lance artist, designer, Chgo., 1947—. Served with AUS, 1942-45; NATO USA, ETO. Mem. Artist Guild Chgo., Internat. Platform Assn. Contbr. sci. and tech. illustrations, maps to Compton's Pictured Ency., Rand McNally & Co., World Book Year Book, Field Enterprises Sci. Yearbooks, Childcraft Ann. and Library, World Book Dictionary. Home: 7N161 Medinah Rd Medinah IL 60157 Office: 203 N Wabash Ave Chicago IL 60601

STUMPF, WALTER NICHOLAS, farm equipment engr.; b. Nashua, Minn., May 1, 1933; s. Nicholas John and Anna Mae (Bullis) S.; B.S., U. Minn., 1960; postgrad. U. Wis., 1961-62, Purdue U., 1968-72; m. LaVonne Jerome, Aug. 30, 1958; children—Patrick, Catherine, Joan, Mary, Elizabeth. With farm equipment div. Allis-Chalmers, 1960-73, new product planning rep. farm and indsl. equipment, 1966-68, mgr. quality assurance, LaPorte, Ind., 1971-73; mgr. quality assurance Gradall div. Warner & Swasey, New Philadelphia, O., 1973-75; mgr. quality control Indsl. Truck div. Clark Equipment Co., 1975-76; mgr. quality assurance constrn. and mining equipment group Westinghouse Air Brake Co., 1976—. Active Boy Scouts Am. Served to sgt., AUS, 1952-55. Registered profl. engr., Minn., Ind. Mem. Am. Soc. Agrl. Engrs. (past vice chmn. Wis. sect.), Am. Soc. Quality Control (sec. Peoria sect.), Milw. Archdiocese Council Cath. Men (past pres.). Roman Catholic. Club: WABCO Squares (pres.) (Peoria). Home: 5110 N Dawn Dr Peoria IL 61614 Office: Westinghouse Air Brake Co Peoria IL 61639

STUNARD, EUGENE WALTER, real estate appraiser; b. Chgo., Mar. 7, 1933; s. Louis and Harriet (Kurdas) S.; B.S., U. Ill., 1955; m. Joan Ann Stabach, June 22, 1955; children—Laura, Vicki, Walter. Regional appraiser Prudential Ins. Co. Am., Chgo., 1957-68; partner Real Estate Appraisal Corp., Oak Brook, Land Econ. Research Corp., Oak Brook, Ill., 1968; owner Real Estate Appraisal Co., Chgo., 1968—, pres. Appraisal Research Counselors, Ltd., Chgo., 1974—; instr. real estate appraisal Triton Coll., River Grove, Ill., 1966—; Am. Inst. Real Estate Appraisers, Chgo., 1974—. Village commr. Oak Park (Ill.) Plan Commn., 1973-76. Mem. real estate adv. com. Triton Coll., 1967—. Served with AUS, 1955-57. Mem. Am. Inst. Real Estate Appraisers, Appraisal Inst. Can., Soc. Real Estate Appraisers, Chgo. Real Estate Bd., Chgo. Mortgage Bankers and Chgo. Assn. Commerce and Industry, Lambda Alpha, Phi Eta Sigma, Delta Upsilon. Home: 155 Harbor Dr Chicago IL 60601 Office: 400 E Randolph Dr Chicago IL 60601

STUPEC, GERTRAUD L. BLEY, chemist; b. Lansing, Mich., June 3, 1937; d. Alfred and Marie Margot (Barkow) Bley; B.S., Mich. State U., 1959. Chemist, CPC Internat., Argo, Ill., 1959-67, Wilson & Co., Chgo., 1967-69; research chemist Beatrice Foods Co., Chgo., 1969—. Sec., Illini Nines Air Derby, 1970. Mem. Inst. Food Technologists, Am. Meat Sci. Assn., Mich. State Alumni Assn., Amateur Fencers League Am. Home: 7628 Knottingham Ln Downers Grove IL 60515 Office: 1526 S State St Chicago IL 60605

STURDIVANT, FREDERICK DAVID, educator; b. Whitewright, Tex., Oct. 17, 1937; s. Wyatt A. and Juanita S. (Phillips) S.; B.S., San Jose State Coll., 1959; M.B.A., U. Oreg., 1960; Ph.D., Northwestern U., 1963; m. Patricia A. Robinson, Dec. 22, 1959; children—Kaira, Lisha, Brian. Asst. prof. mktg. U. So. Calif., 1964-67; asso. prof. U. Tex. at Austin, 1967-70; asso. prof. Harvard U., 1970-72; M. Riklis prof. bus. and its environment Ohio State U., 1972—; prin. Mgmt. Analysis Center, Cambridge, Mass., 1969—; dir. Progressive Corp., Cleve., State Savs. Bank, Columbus, Ohio, Actmedia, N.Y.C. Mem. task force mktg. and low-income consumers Dept. Commerce, 1967-70; cons. Senator Charles Percy, 1968; mem. adv. council to lt. gov. State of Tex., 1969-70. Mem. Am. Mktg. Assn., Assn. Consumer Research, Southwestern Social Sci. Assn., Beta Gamma Sigma. Democrat. Author: (with others) Competition and Human Behavior, 1968; The Ghetto Marketplace, 1969; (with others) Managerial Analysis in Marketing, 1970; Growth Through Service: A History of American Hospital Supply Corporation, 1970; The Credit Merchants: A History of Spiegel, Inc., 1973; Business and Society: A Managerial Approach, 1977; (with L. Robinson) The Corporate Social Challenge: Cases and Commentaries, 1977. Contbr. articles to numerous jours. Home: 2500 Stonehaven Ct S Columbus OH 43220

STURDIVANT, JACK EDWARD, orthodontist; b. Madrid, Iowa, Jan. 26, 1929; s. George Randal and Lillian Irene (Fountain) S.; student Midwestern U., Wichita Falls, Tex., 1951-54; D.D.S., U. Iowa, 1959, M.S., 1961; m. Jacqueline Louise Brown, Dec. 26, 1951; children—Niki Ann, Jeffrey Jack, Lisa Ann, Jana Ann. Practice dentistry, Kalona, Iowa, part time 1959-61; practice orthodontics Ames, Iowa, 1961—. Tchr. orthodontics Iowa State U., Ames, 1966-67; chmn. Story County (Iowa) Dental Health, 1969—. Served with USAF, 1950-54. Recipient Mosby Scholastic Book award, 1956; Gold Foil Operators award Dental Sch. U. Iowa, 1959. Mem. Christian Med. Soc., Am., Iowa dental assns., Iowa, Am. orthodontic assns., Iowa socs. preventive dentistry, Ames Dental Study Club, Am. Assn. Oral Myo Therapists, Psi Omega. Republican. Mem. Evang. Free Ch. Home: Route 4 Oakwood Rd Ames IA 50010 Office: 1220 Duff Ave Ames IA 50010

STURGELL, CHARLES LEE, motel exec.; b. Monett, Mo., Feb. 1, 1928; s. Marcius and Hattie (Bolin) S.; student Draughons Bus. U., 1944; m. Martha Sue McLean, June 10, 1949; 1 dau., Vicki Lee. Owner, operator Skyline Motel, Springfield, Mo., 1959-68; with Howard Johnson's Motor Lodges, Springfield, 1962—, exec. v.p., gen. mgr. Topeka, Springfield, Kansas City East, Mo., 1962—, exec. v.p., gen. mgr. Mobile, Ala., 1968—, pres. nat. operators council Howard Johnson Co.; pres., gen. mgr. Kansas City East, Kansas City SW, San Francisco North, Mpls. Airport, Mpls. South, Tulsa, Okla.; v.p., gen. mgr. McLean Enterprises, Springfield, from 1968, now exec. v.p., gen. mgr.; pres., gen. mgr. Sho-Me Motor Lodges, Inc. Bd. dirs. Ozark Playgrounds Assn., Joplin, Mo. Served as staff officer U.S. Mcht. Marine, 1945-47. Mem. Mo. (dir.), Springfield motel assns. Lutheran Address 2610 N Glenstone St Springfield MO 65803

STURGIS, JOHN CANTWELL, farmer, banker; b. Utica, N.Y., Nov. 22, 1919; s. William and Margaret (Cantwell) S.; ed. St. George's Prep. Sch., night schs.; m. Loretta M. Howard, Oct. 26, 1946; children—Loretta E. (Mrs. Robert T. Jacobs), Sharon, William, Charles, Michael, Maxwell, Peter David. Mem. credit dept. J.P. Morgan & Co., N.Y.C., 1938-40, 46-48; asst. sec. Chem. Bank-N.Y. Trust Co., N.Y.C., 1948-51; v.p., dept. head Continental Ill. Nat. Bank, 1951-70; pres., chief exec. officer, dir. Chgo. Wesley Meml. Hosp. (now Northwestern Meml. Hosp., 1970-72, chmn. exec. com. Northwestern Meml. Hosp., 1972-76; interim pres., chief exec. officer Milw. Children's Hosp.; dir. Edward Hines Lumber Co., 1st Nat. Bank, Wilmette, So. Mineral Corp., Bank of Burlington (Wis.). Trustee Northwestern U.; bd. dirs. Northwestern Meml. Hosp.; life dir. Children's Meml. Hosp., Chgo.; bd. dirs., exec. com. Meml. Hosp., Burlington. Served to 1st lt. AUS, 1940-46. Clubs: Chicago; Indian Hill (Winnetka, Ill.) Lake Geneva Country. Home: Panacea Farm Box 124 Lyons WI 53148 Office: 1700 W Wisconsin Ave Milwaukee WI 53201

STURM, ROBERT NELSON, JR., microbiologist; b. Cin., Mar. 19, 1945; s. Robert Nelson and Alice Louise (Girty) S.; B.S. in Bacteriology, U. Cin., 1967, M.S., 1969; m. Laura Ann Wichman, Feb. 1, 1969; children—John David, Nelson Ross. Tech. staff dept. environ. water quality research Procter & Gamble, Cin., 1970-73, group leader toxicology, 1973-75, sect. head toxicology, environ. safety, 1975—; dir. D. & B. Guest Shoppes Inc. Capt., Loveland (Ohio) Community Fire Dept. and Life Squad, 1972-76; v.p. Loveland Indsl. Corp., 1973-76; mem. city council, Loveland, 1973-76. Trustee Ohio-Ky.-Ind. Regional Planning Authority, 1973-76; chmn. Loveland Indsl. Devel. Com., 1975—. Served to lt. USNR, 1968—. Mem. Nat. Pilots Assn., Aircraft Owners and Pilots Assn., Am. Radio Relay League, Sigma Xi, Alpha Tau Omega. Contbr. articles on microbial metabolism, environ. scis., and toxicology to profl. jours. Home: 1714 Nimrod St Loveland OH 45140 Office: Procter & Gamble Co Ivorydale Tech Center Cincinnati OH 45217

STURM, WILLIAM JAMES, adminstrv. nuclear physicist; b. Marshfield, Wis., Sept. 10, 1917; s. Jacob and Catherine (Coughlin) S.; B.S., Marquette U., Milw., 1940; M.S., U. Chgo., 1942; Ph.D. (AEC fellow and Univ. fellow), U. Wis., 1949; m. Arleen L. Weide, Aug. 20, 1951; children—Diana Patrice, Elissa Monique. Research asst. Metall. Lab., Manhattan Project U. Chgo., 1942-43; jr. physicist Argonne (Ill.) Nat. Lab., 1943-46, group leader, 1945-47, asso. physicist, 1946-47, cons. physicist, 1949-51, asso. physicist, 1956-59; physicist Oak Ridge (Tenn.) Nat. Lab., 1951-53, sr. physicist, 1953-56; mem. faculty Internat. Sch. Nuclear Sci. & Engring., 1960-66; mem. staff Office Coll. and Univ. Cooperation, 1965-66, asst. dir. applied physics div., 1967—; participating physicist, first self-sustaining nuclear chain reaction, U. Chgo. Recipient Commemorative medal Am. Nuclear Soc., Nuclear Pioneer award Soc. Nuclear Medicine. Contbr. articles to profl. jours. Home: 5400 Woodland Ave Western Springs IL 60558 Office: Argonne National Lab 9700 S Cass Ave Argonne IL 60439

STURR, THOMAS FRANCIS, architect; b. Chgo., Aug. 30, 1935; s. Anthony Thomas and Estelle (Rimkus) S.; B.Arch., U. Detroit, 1958; postgrad. Ill. Inst. Tech., 1958-59; m. Dolores Barbara Kuchar, Jan. 25, 1958; children—Mark, Kurt, Tomas, Eric, John. With various archtl. firms, 1958-65; with Perkins & Will, Chgo., 1965-69; partner Thomas F. Sturr & Asso., Oak Park, Ill., 1969-71; pres. Sturr Young Asso. Ltd., Oak Park, Ill., 1971-76, also dir. Mem. Oak Park (Ill.) Mall Planning Com., 1973-74. Mem. Oak Park Zoning Bd. Appeals, 1965-69; trustee Village of Oak Park, 1969-73. Mem. Constrn. Specifications Inst. Roman Catholic. Home: Route 1 Scenic Lake Dr Pentwater MI 49449

STUTSMAN, ALBERT CHESTERFIELD, physician; b. Roanoke, Va., Apr. 2, 1905; s. Charles Albert and Clara (White) S.; m. Helen Eades, Dec. 21, 1940; children—Melissa Jane, Nancy Eades, Albert Chesterfield. Asst. prof. emeritus in otolaryngology Washington U. Med. Sch., St. Louis. Diplomate Am. Bd. Otolaryngology. Mem. AMA, So. Med. Assn., Mo., St. Louis, St. Louis County med. socs., Am. Broncho-Esophagological Soc., Am. Acad. Ophthalmology and Otolaryngology. Presbyterian. Club: Univ. St. Louis. Home: 19 Kingsbury Pl St Louis MO 63112 Office: 141 Meramec St N St Louis MO 63105

STUTSMAN, WARREN EARL, asso. realtor; b. Deputy, Ind., Sept. 27, 1940; s. W. Warren and M. Marie (Howell) S.; B.S., Bob Jones U., 1966; m. Joy Ann Robinson, Aug. 18, 1962; children—Jennifer Lynn, Janelle Ann. Auditor, Arthur Andersen & Co., Indpls., 1966-69, dir. of office adminstrn., 1969-72; dir. fin. Indpls. Baptist Temple & Indpls. Baptist Schs., Inc., 1972-77; asso. realtor F.C. Tucker Co., Inc., Indpls., 1977—. Sec. Indpls. Bapt. Schs., Inc., 1971-77, treas., 1971-77; deacon Indpls. Bapt. Temple, 1968-70, 72, chmn. bd. trustees, 1972, jr. high dept. Sunday sch. supt., 1969-77. Mem. Met. Indpls. Bd. Realtors, Farm and Land Inst., Bob Jones U. Alumni Assn., Econ. Club of Indpls. Home: 2210 Brewer Dr Indianapolis IN 46227 Office: 2152 E S County Line Rd Indianapolis IN 46227

STYFFE, EDWIN HOWARD, JR., printing co. exec.; b. Bklyn., Nov. 12, 1937; s. Edwin H. and Anna (McDermott) S.; B.S., St. Louis U., 1959; m. Myra Janet Foulke, Oct. 3, 1964; 1 son, John Edwin. Asst. to exec. dir. Mo. Republicans Unltd., St. Louis, 1959-60, exec. dir., 1960-64; account mgr. Thomas W. Parry & Assos., St. Louis, 1964, account dir., 1964-68, v.p., 1968-72, partner, 1970-72; v.p. Hanson & Parry Assos., Inc., St. Louis, 1972-74; asst. to the chmn. Corley Printing Co., St. Louis, 1974-76, exec. v.p., 1976-77, pres., 1977—. Trustee St. Louis U. High Sch. Mem. St. Louis U. Sch. Bus. and Adminstrn. Alumni Assn. (pres. 1967-71), Delta Sigma Pi. Home: 1882 Cedarmill Dr Chesterfield MO 63017 Office: 9804 Page Blvd St Louis MO 63132

SUBA, ANTONIO RONQUILLO, surgeon; b. Philippines, Apr. 25, 1927; s. Antonio Mesina and Valentina Cabais (Ronquillo) S.; came to U.S., 1952, naturalized, 1961; M.D., U. St. Thomas, Philippines, 1952; m. Sylvia Marie Karl, June 16, 1956; children—Steven Antonio, Eric John, Laurinda Ann, Gregory Karl, Timothy Mark, Sylvia Kathleen. Intern, St. Anthony's Hosp., St. Louis, 1952-53; resident St. Louis County Hosp., St. Louis, 1953-57; trainee Nat. Cancer Inst., Ellis Fischel State Cancer Hosp., Columbia, Mo., 1957-59; chief surg. services U.S. Army, Bremerhaven, Germany, 1959-61; practice medicine specializing in surgery, St. Louis, 1961—. Diplomate Am. Bd. Surgery. Fellow A.C.S.; mem. AMA, Pan-Pacific, Mo. State surg. assns., St. Louis Surg. Soc., Am. Assn. Hand Surgery. Club: K.C. Contbr. articles to med. jour. Home: 12085 Heatherdane Saint Louis MO 63131 Office: 141 S Meramec St Clayton MO 63105

SUBRAMANIAN, BALA RAMANATHAN, mgmt. cons.; b. Broach, India, Sept. 14, 1944; s. Ramanathan Ramaswamy and Vedambal (Anatharaman) Iyer; came to U.S., 1969, naturalized, 1977; L.M.E., Govt. Poly., 1962; M.S., U. Dallas, 1970; Ph.D., N. Tex. State U., 1977; m. Elizabeth Laiwah Tsang, Feb. 23, 1974. Charge-hand Nat. Rayons Corp., Kalyan, India, 1962-63; tech. asst. Voltas Ltd., Bombay, India, 1963-68; quality control officer Shakti Insulated Wires, Bombay, 1968; design engr. Collins Radio, Richardson, Tex., 1969-70; quality control engr. Varo Semi-Conductors, Inc., Garland, Tex., 1973; dist. rep. Bur. Nat. Affairs, Inc., Washington, 1974-76; pres. Synergism, Inc., Chgo., 1976—. Mem. Am. Soc. Quality Control, Bombay Productivity Council (life), Planning Execs. Inst., Mid-west Planning Assn., Sigma Iota Epsilon. Club: Health (Chgo.). Home: 3520 N Lake Shore Dr #8E Chicago IL 60657 Office: 24 N Wabash Ave Chicago IL 60602

SUDERMAN, ELMER FRANCIS, educator; Isabella, Okla., Sept. 19, 1920; s. Daniel and Margaret (Becker) S.; B.A., Tabor Coll., 1944; M.A., U. Kans., 1948, Ph.D. (U. fellow), 1961; postgrad, summers Bethel Coll., 1943, 44, Okla, State U., 1945, Iliff Sch. Theology, 1953; m. Norma Mae Unrau, Aug. 27, 1946; children—Amy, James, Prin., Hillsboro (Kans.) Grade Sch., 1944-46; asst. instr. English, U. Kans., 1946-49, 58-59; instr. English, Bethel Coll., North Newton, Kans., 1949-51; asst. prof. English, Baker U., Baldwin, Kans., 1955-58, acting dept. chmn., 1955-57; asst. prof. Kans. State Tchrs. Coll., Emporia, 1959-60; asst. prof. English, Gustavus Adolphus Coll., St. Peter, Minn., 1960-63, asso. prof., 1963-66, prof., 1966—; vis. prof. English, Bluffton (Ohio) Coll., summer 1962, 67, U. S.D., summer 1963, 65, Earlham Coll., 1964-65, Kans. U., summer 1968, Kans. State Tchrs. Coll., summers 1969, 1970, 71, 72, 73. Mem. Modern Lang. Assn., Nat. Council Tchrs. English, Am. Studies Assn., Minn. Dakotas Am. Studies Assn. (pres. 1968-69), Modern Lang. Assn. Editor Minn. English. Author: What Can We Do Here, 1974. Contbr. poems, short stories, sermons, articles to numerous mags. Home: 717 W Traverse Rd St Peter MN 56082

SUDERMAN, JAKE PETER, sr. citizens home exec.; b. Regina, Sask., Can., Dec. 30, 1929; s. Peter and Sara (Klassen) S.; evang. tchr. tng. diploma Winkler Bible Inst., 1951; grad. U. Man. Sch. Social Work, 1954; m. Elizabeth Ann Peters, Aug. 30, 1952; children—Betty Lou (dec.), Sara Jane, Marilyn. With Sask. Govt. Welfare and Rehab., Regina, 1948-53; social group worker Logan Neighbourhood House, Winnipeg, Man., 1954-55; supr. care services Province Man., 1960-64; exec. dir. Lions Manor, sr. citizens residence, Winnipeg, 1964—; dir. Christian Press, Fellowship Book Centre, Donwood Manor, nursing home, Man. Health Orgn., Inc., Big Bend Resorts Ltd., Winnipeg. Bd. dirs. Concordia Hosp. Mem. Canadian, Man. assns. social workers, Man. Inst. Registered Social Workers, Canadian Assn. Gerentology, Canadian Council Social Devel. Home: 485 Roberta Ave Winnipeg MB R2K OK7 Canada Office: 320 Sherbrook St Winnipeg MB R3B 2W6 Canada

SUDHEIMER, RICHARD HAROLD, systems engr.; b. Waconia, Minn., Sept. 16, 1933; s. Edward Andrew and Lydia Martha (Zeman) S; B. Aero. Engring., U. Minn., 1956; postgrad. Ohio State U., 1964-68; m. Barbara Louise Bowman, Nov. 30, 1957. Asso. devel. engr. Honeywell Corp., Mpls., 1956-57; aerospace engr. U.S. Air

Force, Wright Patterson AFB, Ohio, 1960-67, supv. aerospace engr., 1967-70, ops. research analyst, 1970-76, systems study engr., 1976—. Served with USAF, 1957-60. Registered profl. engr., Ohio; Stanford Sloan fellow, 1970-71. Mem. Am. Inst. Aeros. and Astronautics, Am. Def. Preparedness Assn., Air Force Assn., Assn. Old Crows, Toastmasters Internat. Lutheran. Contbr. articles to profl. jours. Home: 4358 Carlo Dr Kettering OH 45429 Office: ASD/XRO Wright Patterson AFB OH 45433

SUDILOVSKY, OSCAR, physician, educator; b. Rosario, Argentina, Nov. 8, 1933; s. Malquiel and Esther (Busel) S.; B.S., Nat. Coll., Tucuman, Argentina, 1949; M.D., U. Littoral, Argentina, 1959; Ph.D., Case Western Res. U., 1972. Licensed Argentina, 1959, Ohio, 1976; m., 1961; 4 children. Intern, Hosp. Nacional del Centenario, Rosario, 1957-58; resident Mt. Sinai Hosp., Cleve., 1962-64; USPHS fellow in pathology and oncology U. Kans. Med. Center, 1964-67; with dept. pathology U. Littoral, 1959-62, also chief tissue culture lab.; with dept. pathology, instr. Case Western Res. U., 1967-70, asst. prof., 1970-76, dir. autopsy service, 1971-76, asso. prof., 1976—, dir. Tissue Culture lab., 1976—; fellow McArdle Lab. for Cancer Research, 1969-71; adj. staff cons. in pathology div. research Cleve. Clinic, 1975—. NIH Spl. Research fellow, 1967-69, 69-71; recipient Gold Medal award Nat. Coll., Tucuman, 1949. Mem. Am. Assn. Cancer Research, Am. Assn. Pathologists, Am. Soc. Clin. Pathologists, Internat. Acad. Pathology, N.Y. Acad. Sci., Tissue Culture Assn., Sigma Xi. Contbr. articles in field to profl. jours. including Science, Cancer Research, Analytical Biochemistry and others. Address: 2085 Adelbert Rd Cleveland OH 44106

SUDIMACK, JOSEPH, JR., physician; b. Bayonne, N.J., May 15, 1928; s. Joseph H. and Miriam (Tarasevick) S.; B.A., Ohio State U., 1949, M.Sc., 1952, M.D., 1956; children—Joseph III, James M., Jeffrey S., Miriam J., John R., Amy Jo, Jennifer Jo; m. Linda M. Sudimack, Dec. 22, 1973. Intern, Lankenau Hosp., Phila., 1956-57; practice gen. medicine, Warren, Ohio, 1959—; pres. staff Trumbull Meml. Hosp.; mem. staff St. Joseph's Hosp., Warren. Dist. physician Republic Steel Corp., Mahoning Valley Dist., Ohio, 1960—; coroner Trumbull County, 1960—. Bd. dirs. Trumbull County Heart Assn. Served with USNR, 1957-59. Fellow Indsl. Med. Assn., Am. Occupational Med. Assn.; mem. Ohio Med. Assn. (del.), Trumbull County Med. Soc. (past pres.), Trumbull County Acad. Gen. Practice (past pres.), Ohio Coroners Assn., Nat. Football Found., Ohio State U. Alumni Assn. (pres. Trumbull County), Republican Congl. Club, Sigma Xi, Sigma Nu. Republican. Clubs: Elks, Presidents, Faculty (Ohio State U.); Trumbull Country. Home: 8625 Deer Creek Ln Warren OH 44484 Office: 121 Center St W Warren OH 44481

SUEDHOFF, CARL JOHN, JR., lawyer; b. Fort Wayne, Ind., Apr. 22, 1925; s. Carl John and Helen (Lau) S.; B.S., U. Pa., 1948; J.D., U. Mich., 1951; m. Carol Mulqueeney, Apr. 10, 1954; children—Thomas Lau, Robert Marshall, Mark Mulqueeney. Admitted to Ind. bar, 1951; asso. mem. firm Hunt & Mountz, Fort Wayne, 1951-54; partner Hunt, Suedhoff, Borror, Eilbacher & Lee and predecessor firms, 1955—. Sec.-treas., dir. Inland Chem. Corp., Fort Wayne, 1952—; pres., dir. Lau Bldg. Co., Fort Wayne, 1951—, S.H.S. Realty Corp., Toledo, 1960—; sec. dir. Inland Chem. P.R., Inc., San Juan, P.R., 1972—; others. Mem. Allen County Council, 1972-76, pres., 1974-76; mem. Allen County Tax Adjustment Bd., 1973-74. Bd. dirs. YMCA, Fort Wayne, 1961-63. Served with AUS, 1943-45. Mem. V.F.W. (comdr. 1958-59), Am. Ind., Allen County bar assns., Beta Gamma Sigma, Phi Delta Phi, Psi Upsilon. Republican. Lutheran. Clubs: Univ. Michigan (pres. 1965-66), Friars, Fort Wayne Country. Office: 625 Lincoln Towers Bank Fort Wayne IN 46802

SUELLENTROP, JOHN FRANCIS, bank exec.; b. Colwich, Kans., May 29, 1922; s. John A. and Cathryn T. (Neuhold) S.; student St. GregorV's Coll., 1937-42; m. Marigene Wegeng, Sept. 29, 1947; children—Ann, Thomas, Daniel (dec.), Jeanne, James, Rosemary, Mary Nell. With State Bank of Colwich, 1946—, pres., 1969—. Vice chmn. Kans. Newman Coll. Bd., 1977—; trustee St. Gregory's Coll., Shawnee, Okla. Served to 2d lt. AUS, 1942-46. Mem. Kans. Ind. Bankers (pres. 1975-77), Am., Kans. bankers assns., Ind. Bankers Assn. Am. Democrat. Roman Catholic. Clubs: Serra of Wichita, K.C. Home: 124 S 7th St Colwich KS 67030 Office: 200 E Wichita St Colwich KS 67030

SUESS, HEATHER FAYE, psychologist; b. Cleve., Dec. 12, 1948; d. Alvin M. and Rose (Robins) Suess; B.A., U. Mich., Ann Arbor, 1972. Research psychologist Manpower Research and Data Analysis Center, Office Asst. Sec. of Def., Washington, 1973-75; pvt. practice in counseling, Springfield, Va., 1975, in group counseling, Ann Arbor, Mich., 1975—. Mem. Assn. Humanistic Psychology, Am. Personnel and Guidance Assn., Assn. Specialists in Group Work, NOW.

SUFFETY, HAMED WILLIAM, lawyer; b. Port Huron, Mich., July 26, 1926; s. Albert and Sadie Ruth (Konieczka) S.; A.A., Bay City Jr. Coll., 1948; LL.B., U. Detroit, 1953; m. Dorothy Marie Davy, July 15, 1950; children—Debra M., Hamed William. Admitted to Mich. bar, 1953, since practiced in Saginaw. Mem. Saginaw County Democratic Com., 1962-68. Served with AUS, 1944-46. Club: Saginaw Country. Home: 110 Golfview Dr Saginaw MI 48603 Office: 2604 W Genesee St Saginaw MI 48602

SUGAR, MARILYN SUSMAN, counselor, educator; b. Everett, Mass., Dec. 1, 1942; d. Eliot and Helen (Silver) Epstein; A.B., Brandeis U., 1964; M.A., Washington U., 1967; Ph.D., St. Louis U., 1972; m. Joel Sugar, Sept. 3, 1973; 1 son, Andrew Susman. Tchr. second grade Ladue (Mo.) Pub. Schs., 1964-66; elementary sch. counselor, Pub. Schs. Clayton, Mo., 1968-72; asst. prof. U. Fla., Gainesville, 1972-73; vis. asst. prof. U. Mo., St. Louis, 1973-74; program coordinator parent and child enrichment Pub. Schs. Melville (Mo.), 1974-75; asst. prof. Loyola U. at Chgo., 1975—. Mem. Am. Personnel and Guidance Assn., Am. Sch. Counselors Assn., Assn. Counselor Educators and Suprs. Home: 412 Greenwood St Evanston IL 60201 Office: 820 N Michigan Ave Chicago IL 60211

SUHOWATSKY, STEPHEN JOSEPH, bronze mfg. co. exec.; b. Troy, N.Y., Feb. 7, 1939; s. Stephen Alexander and Mary (Hasko) S.; B.S., Delta State U., 1964; M.B.A., U. Pa., 1966; m. E. Gale Hartness, Aug. 10, 1969; children—Stephanie Mary, Allison Gale, Jennifer Cerise. Asst. to treas. Eagle Picher Industries Inc.-Cin., 1966-69; v.p. adminstrn., treas. Markey Bronze Corp., Lima, Ohio, 1969—; pres. Masten Corp. & Apex Bearings Co. div. Markey Bronze Corp., Lima, 1973—. Mem. YMCA. Elk. Home: 750 Kiowa Trail Lima OH 45806 Office: 908 1st Nat Bank Bldg Lima OH 45801

SUJECKI, JOY MARY, hosp. med. service adminstr.; b. Milw., Nov. 29, 1935; d. John Henry and Helen Eleanor (Bronikowski) Jakubowski; B.S. in Med. Tech., Marquette U., 1957; postgrad. Central Mich. U., 1975—; children—Ellen, Michael, Laura, Paul, Carol, Nancy, Thomas. Med. technologist Milw. Luth. Hosp., 1957; med. technologist in physicians office, Milw., 1958-59; med. technologist St. Luke's Hosp., Milw., 1961-62; med. technologist Trinity Meml. Hosp., Cudahy, Wis., 1969-75, lab. mgr. and supr., 1975—. Den leader Cub Scouts Am., Milw., 1968—. Mem. Am. Soc. Clin. Pathology, Am. Soc. Med. Technologists, Wis. Assn. Med. Technologists (edn. chmn. 1976-77), Am. Cancer Soc. (dir. south unit 1975—). Roman Catholic. Asso. editor Our Lady of Lourdes News, 1974-75. Home: 2943 S 43rd St Milwaukee WI 53219 Office: 5900 S Lake Dr Cudahy WI 53110

SUKHWAL, BHERU LAL, educator; b. Palana Kalan, Udaipur, India, June 18, 1929; s. Bhuri Lal and Narayani Bai (Upadhyay) S.; came to U.S., 1964; B.A., Agra U., 1957; B.Ed., U. Rajasthan, Jaipur, India, 1958, M.A. in Geography, 1960; M.A. (Fgn. student scholar), U. Oreg., 1966; Ph.D., U. Okla., 1969; m. Lilawati Sharma, Mar. 10, 1955; children—Aditya, Archna. Tchr., dir. edn., Ajmer, Rajasthan, 1954-60, sr. tchr. geography, dir. edn., 1960-64; map librarian univs. Oreg., Okla., 1964-69; asso. prof. geography U. Wis.-Platteville, 1969—, Faculty research grantee, 1971; vis. prof. U. Rajasthan, Jaipur, India, 1975, U. Madras, 1977; sr. research fellow Am. Inst. Indian Studies; NEDA grantee, 1968-69. Life mem. Am. Geog. Soc., Assn. Geography Tchrs. India, Geog. Soc. India; mem. Assn. Am. Geographers, Internat. Geog. Union, Wis., Nat. councils geog. edn., Gamma Theta Upsilon. Author: India: A Political Geography, 1971; A Systematic Geographic Bibliography on Bangladesh, 1973; Theses and Dissertations in Geography of South Asia, 1973; South Asia: A Systematic Geographic Bibliography, 1974. Contbr. articles to profl. jours. Home: 630 W Madison St Platteville WI 53818

SUKUMARAN, KIZHAKEPAT PISHAROTH, anesthesiologist; b. Kollengode, India, Oct. 10, 1938; s. Chakrapani Pisharoth and Kochu (Pisharasyar) Pisharoty; came to U.S., 1972; M.D., U. Kerala (India), 1964; m. Kamala Sukumaran; children—Harry S., Suma. Intern, Calicut Med. Coll., Hosp., Kerala, 1954-65; resident in anesthesiology Epsom (Surrey, Eng.) Dist. Hosp., United Liverpool (Eng.) Hosps., Walton and Wiston Hosp., Liverpool, 1967-70; med. officer govt. service, India, 1965-67, house officer, 1967-70; sr. registrar Nat. Health Service, Liverpool, 1970-71; staff anesthesiologist Kristinehamn (Sweden) Hosp., 1972; fellow Mt. Sinai Sch. Medicine, N.Y.C., 1972, Dalhousie U., Halifax, N.S., Can., 1972-74; staff, chief dept. anesthesia St. Mary's Hosp., Saginaw, Mich., 1977—; cons. staff St. Luke's Hosp., Saginaw, 1975—; lectr. Mich. State U.; practice medicine specializing in anesthesiology and critical care, Saginaw. Diplomate Royal Coll. Surgeons, Royal Coll. Physicians, Am. Bd. Anesthesiology. Fellow Royal Coll. Surgeons Ireland; mem. AMA, Am. Soc. Anesthesiologists. Home: 3590 Hickory Ln Saginaw MI 48603 Office: St Mary's Hosp S Jefferson Ave Saginaw MI 48603

SUKUP, EUGENE GEORGE, mfg. exec.; b. Venus, Nebr., May 11, 1929; s. Louis and Dorothy Amelia (Buerkley) S.; student pub. schs.; m. Mary Elizabeth Bielefeld, Feb. 24, 1952; children—Charles Eugene, Steven Eugene. Farmer, Hampton, Iowa, 1946-51; owner, farm mgr., Dougherty, Iowa, 1951—; pres. Sukup Mfg. Co., Sheffield, Iowa, 1963—, Sukup Enterprises Inc., Sheffield, 1968—. Mem. Sheffield-Chapin Community Sch. Bd., 1967—; mem. County Extension Council, 1962-65; pres. Sheffield Community Club, 1972; bd. regents Waldorf Coll., Forest City, Iowa, 1977—. Mem. Iowa Mfrs. Assn., Farm Bur. Republican. Lutheran (ch. council 1970-72, pres. 1971). Patentee in field. Home: Dougherty IA 50433 Office: North Rd Sheffield IA 50475

SULICH, FREDERICK JOSEPH, grocery chain exec.; b. Chgo., Jan. 25, 1942; s. William S. and Sally V. (Kratovil) S.; B.S., U. Ill., 1963; m. Joan Barbara Tury, Nov. 23, 1963; children—Adam William, Kenneth Albert, Dawn Marie. Sr. auditor Ernst & Ernst, Chgo., 1963-67; internal auditor Jewel Cos., Melrose Park, Ill., 1967-69, asst. corporate cash mgr., 1969-73, cash mgr. Jewel Food Stores, Melrose Park, Ill., 1973-74; mgr. financial reporting White Hen Pantry, Elmhurst, Ill., 1974—. C.P.A., Ill. Am. Inst. C.P.A.'s. Office: 666 Industrial Dr Elmhurst IL 60126

SULLIVAN, ANTONY THRALL, found. exec.; b. New Haven, Nov. 7, 1938; s. Francis Joseph and Hazel Mae (Thrall) S.; B.A., Yale, 1960; M.A., Columbia U., 1961; Ph.D. (Sophie Davis Tucker fellow, H.B. Earhart fellow, Center for Near East and North African Studies fellow, Dept. History fellow), U. Mich., 1976; m. Marjory Elizabeth Kuhn, May 5, 1962; children—Sandra Lincoln, David Thrall. Instr. history Internat. Coll., Beirut, 1962-67; counselor U. Mich., Ann Arbor, 1968-69; asst. to program officer Relm and Earhart Found., Ann Arbor, 1969-71, program officer, asst. sec., 1971—; vis. prof. history Hillsdale (Mich.) Coll., 1977—. Mem. budget com. United Fund Ann Arbor, 1973-75; mem. steering com. Council Mich. Founds., 1973-75. Mem. Am. Hist. Assn., French Colonial Hist. Assn., Middle East Studies Assn., Soc. French Hist. Studies, Philadelphia Soc., Alliance Francaise d'Ann Arbor (exec. com.), Phi Kappa Phi. Republican. Episcopalian. Club: Huron Valley Swim. Home: 908 Westwood Ann Arbor MI 48103 Office: 904 1st Nat Bldg Ann Arbor MI 48108

SULLIVAN, AUDLEY NOEL, travel co. exec.; b. Alma, Nebr., Aug. 13, 1903; s. William and Hattie (Hedden) S.; B.S., U. Nebr., 1924; m. Solveig Winslow, Aug. 3, 1945; children—Patricia, Noel, Sharon. Asst. to pres. Monticello Coll., Godfrey, Ill., 1940-49, v.p., 1955-58; v.p. Tamblyn and Brown Inc., N.Y.C., 1950-55; chmn./treas. Internat. Travel Advisers Inc., Alton, Ill., 1958—; pres. Internat. Retirement Cons.'s, Alton, 1975—. Chmn. Community Chest campaign Greater Alton-Wood River, Ill., 1944; bd. dirs. Alton Civic Orch., 1960—. Recipient Distinguished Service award Monticello Coll., 1958, Spl. Achievement award Trans World Airlines, 1972. Mem. Inst. Certified Travel Cons.'s, Kappa Sigma. Republican. Unitarian. Clubs: Lockhaven Country, Inter-Am., Kiwanis (pres. Alton 1946); Media (St. Louis). Author: Retirement When? How? Where?, 1976. Home: 2306 Fairview Dr Alton IL 62002 Office: 413 E Broadway St Alton IL 62002

SULLIVAN, DAVID STAFFORD, clin. psychologist; b. Oak Park, Ill., Dec. 11, 1943; s. Orville A. and Voris A. (Stafford) S.; B.A., No. Ill. U., 1965, M.A., 1968, Ph.D., 1974; m. Sharon Eenigenburg, May 30, 1964; 1 son, David. Asso. prof. psychology Wheaton (Ill.) Coll., 1969-75; pvt. practice clin. psychology N. Park Clinic, Park Ridge, Ill., 1974—; chief psychol. cons. Comprehensive Accounting Co., Aurora, Ill., 1975—; pres. Winners Sports Service, Bklyn., 1972—; pres. Stafford Pub. Co., Bklyn., 1973—. Chmn. bd. mgrs. Ryall YMCA-DuPage Club, Glen Ellyn, Ill., 1975—. Certified clin. psychologist, Ill. Mem. Am., Ill. psychol. assns., Nat. Register Mental Health Service Providers, Am. Assn. Marriage and Family Counselors, Acad. Psychologists in Marriage and Family Therapy, Sigma Xi. Author (under pen name Donald Sullivan): (with Hank Adams) Thoroughbred Racing: Predicting the Outcome, 1974, The S/A Advanced Method for Throughbred Handicapping, 1975, Harness Racing: Predicting the Outcome, 1975, The S/A Advanced Method for Harness Handicapping, 1976; editor, author (under pen name Donald Sullivan): Winners Sports Service Football Newsletter, 1971—; contbg. editor (under pen name Donald Sullivan): The Sullivan-Adams Racing Newsletter, 1976—; contbr. articles in field to profl. psychol. jours. Office: 650 Busse Hwy Park Ridge IL 60068

SULLIVAN, GERARD, psychodramatist, psychotheologist; b. Yonkers, N.Y., Oct. 31, 1927; s. Simon Joseph and Julia Agnes (McCaffery) S.; student Capuchin Sem., 1949, 54, Moreno Acad., 1972; m. Sheila Lynn Miller, Mar. 12, 1977. Ordained preist Roman Catholic Ch., 1953; asst. pastor Our Lady of Sorrows Ch., N.Y.C., 1954-60; staff psychodramatist Southdown Inst., Aurora, Can., 1973-74; coordinator personal growth systems St. Anthony Hosp., Columbus, Ohio, 1974—. served with U.S. Army, 1970. Mem. Am. Soc. Psychodrama and Group Psychotherapy, Am. Personnel and Guidance Assn., Spiritual Serenity Soc. (pres. 1978). Home: 9074 Mink St Pataskala OH 43062 Office 1450 Hawthorne Ave Columbus OH

SULLIVAN, MARK DAVID, communications co. exec.; b. Chgo., Dec. 2, 1934; s. John Martin and Amelia Marie (Stauder) S.; B.A., Northwestern U., 1958. Various exec. positions Jack Morton Prodns., Inc., Dallas, and Chgo., 1959-64; v.p., exec. producer Michael John Assos., Inc., N.Y.C., 1965-66; ind. producer, cons., Dallas, and N.Y.C., 1962-71; exec. producer Wilding div. Bell and Howell Co., Southfield, Mich., 1971-75; exec. producer Sandy Corp., Southfield (formerly Bill Sandy Co., Inc., Detroit), 1975—. Served with AUS, 1954-57. Named alumnus of the year Phi Kappa Psi N.Y. Alumni Assn., 1971. Mem. Actors' Equity Assn., Internat. Platform Assn., Hotel Sales Mgmt. Assn., Meeting Planners Internat., Phi Kappa Psi (pres. 1972-74, quarter century commn. 1975—). Home: 35081 Drakeshire Pl Farmington MI 48024 Office: 16025 Northland Dr Southfield MI 48075

SULLIVAN, THOMAS LEE, nursing home adminstr.; b. Peoria, Ill., May 3, 1942; s. Terrence William and Winifred Ann (Bowers) S.; R.N., Alton Meml. Hosp. Sch. Nursing, 1963; m. Dorothy Louise Huebner, Oct. 10, 1964; children—Thomas Lee, Catherine Louise, Joseph Daniel, Theresa Elizabeth. Staff nurse St. Joseph's Hosp., Bloomington, Ill., 1963-64, St. Francis Hosp., Peoria, 1964-65; nurse I, Peoria State Hosp., 1965-66, nurse II, 1966-67, supr. I, 1967-71; adminstr. Galena Park Home, Peoria Heights, Ill., 1971—, also adminstr. Galena Park Terrace, Peoria Heights, 1973—. Mem. sub-com. on long term care Tri-County Health Planning, 1974—; mem. St. Thomas Grade Sch. Bd., Peoria Heights. Served with U.S. Army, 1968. Mem. Peoria Multiple Sclerosis Assn. (dir. 1975—), Tri-Agy.-Provider Council Region 1B. Club: K.C. Home: 3910 N Columbus St Peoria IL 61614 Office: 5533 N Galena Rd Peoria Heights IL 61614

SULLIVAN, WARREN GERALD, diversified industry exec.; b. Chgo., Sept. 8, 1923; s. Gerald Joseph and Marie (Fairrington) S.; student U. Wis., 1943; A.B., U. Ill., 1947; J.D., Northwestern U., 1950; m. Helen Ruth Young, Aug. 21, 1948 (div. May 1974); children—Janet Marie, Warren Douglas, William Carroll; m. 2d, H. Louise Curtis, July 27, 1974. Admitted to Ill. bar, 1950, Conn. bar, 1971; lawyer Ill. Dept. Revenue, Chgo., 1950-52; mem. firm Naphin, Sullivan & Banta, Chgo., 1952-60; asst. gen. counsel labor Avco Corp., Greenwich, Conn., 1969-70, v.p. adminstrn. and personnel 1971-75; v.p. indsl. relations Gen. Dynamics Corp., St. Louis, 1975—; dir. Asbestos Corp. Ltd., Stromberg Carlson Corp.; lectr. Chgo. Bar Assn., 1956-69, U. Wis., Mgmt. Inst., 1964-65. Served with AUS, Mil. Intelligence Service, 1942-45; ETO. Mem. Am., Conn., Chgo. (vice chmn. labor law com. 1964-65, chmn. 1966-69) Bar assns., Am. Judicature Soc., Indsl. Relations Soc., Am. Soc. Personnel Adminstrs., Econ. Club Chgo., Delta Tau Delta, Phi Delta Phi. Clubs: University (Chgo.); St. Louis; Beelcrive Country. Contbr. articles to profl. jours. Home: Hanley Towers 900 S Hanley Clayton MO 63105 Office: Pierre Laclede Center Saint Louis MO 63105

SULSBERGER, JOHN DIEHL, ret. dentist; b. Woodsfield, Ohio, Feb. 28, 1908; s. John Jacob and Louise Catherine (Diehl) S.; D.D.S., Ohio State U., 1931; M.S. in Dentistry, Northwestern U., 1932; m. Elizabeth M. Henneberg, Sept. 12, 1935; 1 son, John Diehl (dec.). Practice gen. dentistry and oral surgery, Zanesville, Ohio, 1932-76; mem. dental div. med. staff Bethesda and Good Samaritan hosps., Zanesville, 1938-76, chief staff, 1942. Chmn. dental program Pub. Schs. Zanesville, 1945—. Mem. Am., Ohio, Muskingum Valley (pres. 1941) dental assns., Psi Omega. Club: University (Zanesville). Home: 2801 Dresden Rd Zanesville OH 43701

SUMERFORD, KENNETH SCOTT, chemist; b. Springfield, Mo., Jan. 10, 1948; s. Milton Scott and Martha Lucille (Orr) S.; B.S., S.W. Mo. State U., 1970; M.B.A., 1973; m. Donna Elaine Copelin, Jan. 29, 1972; 1 dau., Angela. Mgr. toy dept. Venture Stores, 1974; chemist Caterpillar Tractor Co., East Peoria, Ill., 1974—; chmn. bd. dirs. K & D Sumerford Enterprises, Inc., 1975-78. Mem. Am. Mgmt. Assn. Republican. Baptist. Home: 6102 N Idlewhile Peoria IL 61614

SUMMERS, CHARLES L., physicist, engr.; b. Kansas City, Kans., Feb. 24, 1933; s. Samuel and Sarah (Karo) Summers. B.S., Mass. Inst. Tech., 1954; M.A., Columbia U., 1958. Research asst. Columbia U., 1959-62; space scientist Geophys. Corp. Am., Bedford, Mass., 1963-64; mem. tech. staff TRW Systems, Houston, 1966-70; mem. program staff ATT, Kansas City, Mo., 1970—; instr. physics Coll. City N.Y., 1962, U. Kans., 1965. Mem. Am. Phys. Soc., Sigma Pi Sigma, Mason. Home: 1307 W 85th St Kansas City MO 64114

SUMMERS, H. MEADE, JR., lawyer; b. St. Louis, Mar. 12, 1936; s. H. Meade and Josephine Elizabeth (Hicks) S.; A.B., Brown U., 1958; J.D., U. Mich., 1961; m. Bonnie Barton, Sept. 2, 1960; children—H. Meade, Elizabeth Barton. Admitted to Mo. bar, 1961, U.S. Supreme Ct. bar; practiced in St. Louis, 1961—; asso. firm Thompson & Mitchell, St. Louis, 1960-67. Chmn., Mo. Adv. Council on Hist. Preservation, 1973-78; mem. exec. com. Am. Revolution Bicentennial Commn. of Mo., 1973-76; mem. Thomas Hart Benton Meml. Homestead Commn., 1976-77, bd. dirs., v.p., co-founder Mo. Heritage Trust, Inc., 1976—; mem. Old Post Office Landmark Com., St. Louis, 1969—; mem. exec. com. St. Louis-St. Louis County Commn. on Equal Ednl. Opportunities, 1968-74; chmn. legis. com. City of Ladue (Mo.), 1976—; bd. dirs. Landmarks Assn. St. Louis, 1969—, pres., 1972-73; mem. St. Louis County Hist. Bldgs. Commn., 1971—; bd. advisers Churchill Sch., St. Louis, 1977—. Mem. Am., Mo., St. Louis County, St. Louis Met. (spl. com. on jud. refrom 1975-76), Nat. Trust Historic Preservation, State Hist. Soc. Mo., Mo. Hist. Soc., St. Louis Met. C. of C. (edn. com. 1964-74, chmn. com. 1972-74), Beta Theta Pi, Phi Delta Phi. Club: Rotary. Home: 42 Woodcliffe Rd Ladue MO 63124 Office: 7777 Bonhomme St Saint Louis MO 63105

SUMMERS, JAMES DESMOND, JR., publishing co. exec.; b. Mt. Clemens, Mich., Aug. 24, 1923; s. James Desmond and Estella H. (Van Haelen) S.; B.S., Northwestern U., 1948; postgrad. Chgo. Federated Advt. Club, 1949, U.S. Armed Forces Indsl. Coll., 1956, Northeastern Ill. State U., 1968—; m. Lois Christine Kingwill, Dec. 26, 1947; children—Scott K., James Desmond III, Stuart, Andrew. Export advt. mgr. Inter-Am. Orange Crush Co., Chgo., 1948-49; promotion mgr. Philco Distbrs., Inc., Chgo., 1949-50; account exec. Chek-Chart Corp., Chgo., 1950-51; advt. mgr. Ampro Corp., Chgo., 1951-52, Simpson Electric Co., Walsh Press and Die and Size Control divs. Am. Gage & Machine Co., 1953-55; owner, mgr. Jim Summers & Assos., pubs. rep., Northfield, Ill., 1955-73; midwest sales mgr. Palmerton Pub. Co., 1973—. Mem. sales adv. bd. Am. Bus. Press, Inc. Mem. parents adv. com. Eureka (Ill.) Coll., 1970-74; chmn. troop com. Boy Scouts Am., Wilmette, Ill., 1973. Republican precinct capt. New Trier Twp. (Ill.), 1968-69. Served to comdr. USNR, 1941-43; PTO. Mem. Assn. Pubs. Reps., Acacia, Sextant, Delta Phi Epsilon. Contbg. author Casket and Sunnyside mag., 1971—,

Dealerscope-Midwest, 1972-73. Home: 1463 W Balmoral Chicago IL 60640 Office: 307 N Michigan Ave Chicago IL 60601

SUMMERSETT, KENNETH GEORGE, psychiatric social worker, educator; b. Marquette, Mich., Mar. 9, 1922; s. Frank Elger and Ruth H. (Fairbanks) S.; B.S., No. Mich. U., 1948, M.A. in Sociology, 1964; M.S.W., Wayne State U., 1951; student U. Pudget Sound, 1942-43; m. Vivian M. Wampler, June 17, 1950; children—Nancy M., Kenneth R., Mark G. With Mich. Dept. Mental Health, 1950—, successively Marquette (Mich.) Child Guidance Clinic, 1950-52, chief psychiat. social worker Battle Creek (Mich.) Child Guidance, 1952-54; dir. social services Newberry (Mich.) State Hosp., 1954-66, dir., cons. social services, 1966-73, adminstrv. dir. community psychiatry, 1973—; mental health exec., 1975—, dir. community services div., 1975—; extension prof. sociology dept. No. Mich. U., 1962-70; lectr. sociology Lake Superior State Coll., 1968—. Mem. Upper Peninsula Mental Health Planning Com., 1964-65, Mich. Task Force Com. Mentally Retarded, 1964-65, Upper Peninsula Mental Health Com. for Comprehensive Health Planning, 1972-75, Mich. Dept. Mental Health Legis. Planning Com. Release Planning, 1975—. Bd. dirs. Eastern Upper Penninsula Mental Health Clinic, v.p., 1970-72; bd. dirs. Luce County Extension Program, sec. bd., 1972-75. Served with AUS, 1943-46. Certified marriage counselor. Mem. Nat. Assn. Social Workers (chmn. upper Peninsula chpt. 1957-59, 64-65, vice chmn. 1972-73), Acad. Certified Social Workers, Theta Omicron Rho. Clubs: Lions (pres. 1959-60), Elks (maj. projects chmn. 1968-70). Author various articles pub. in profl. jours. Home: 217 W Truman Blvd Newberry MI 49868 Office: Newberry State Hosp Newberry MI 49868

SUMNICHT, FRANCIS HENRY, learning innovation center exec.; b. Appleton, Wis., Dec. 25, 1921; s. Henry August and Rose Marie (Honeck) S.; B.S., Marquette U., 1948; m. Patricia Beth Gambsky, Feb. 4, 1964; children—Nancy Lee, Vern, Christopher, Shawn, Eric, Heidi. Advt. and display mgr. Sears Roebuck, Appleton, 1948-51; sec., founder Advance Industries Inc., electronics, Appleton, 1951-70; postmaster, Appleton, 1956-72; sec., founder A-1 Builders, Inc., Appleton, 1954—; partner Sumnicht Supply Co., Appleton, 1951-71; pres., dir. Children's Learning Innovation Center, Inc., Appleton, 1973—. Mem. E. Central Wis. Regional Planning Commn., 1974-75; treas. History Alive Inc., hist. mus. found., 1973—; co-founder nat. Pray for Peace movement, 1948. Sec., Outagamie County Republican Com., 1951-55; Wis. chmn. Young Republicans, 1952. Bd. dirs. Sumnicht Charitable Found., 1968—, Outagamie County Hist. Soc., 1948—. Served with USCGR, 1942-46. Mem. Am. Mgmt. Assn., Soc. Advancement Mgmt. (regional v.p. 1971-74), Am. Soc. Personnel Adminstrn., VFW, Am. Legion, Catholic War Vets. K.C. Clubs: Butte des Morts Country. Home: 325 W Michigan St Appleton WI 54911 Office: 319 W Michigan St Appleton WI 54911

SUN, ALBERT YUNG-KWANG, neurochemist; b. Amoy, China, Oct. 13, 1932; s. Peh-Cheng and Sui-Ho Kao W.; came to U.S., 1959, naturalized, 1972; B.S., Nat. Taiwan U., 1957; M.S., Oreg. State U., Ph.D., 1967; m. Grace Yan-Chi Cheung, May 9, 1964; 1 dau., Aggie Yee-Chun. Postdoctoral research asso. biochemistry Case Western Res. U., Cleve., 1967-68; sr. research scientist Lab. Neurochemistry, Cleve. Psychiat. Inst., 1968-74; research prof. biochemistry Sinclair Comparative Medicine Research Farm U. Mo., Columbia, 1974—. Grantee Nat. Inst. Alcohol Abuse and Alcoholism, 1974—, Nat. Inst. Neurol. and Communicative Disease and Stroke, 1975—. Mem. A.A.A.S., A.C.S., Biochem. Soc., Am. Soc. Neurochemistry, Am. Soc. Neurosci., Am. Gerontol. Soc., N.Y. Acad. Sci., Internat. Soc. Neurochemists, Am. Soc. Biol. Chemists Internat. Soc. Study of Pain, Phi Sigma, Phi Lambda Upsilon. Research alcohol-membrane interaction, roles of phospholipids in membrane function. Home: 1400 Truman Dr Columbia MO 65201 Office: Sinclair Comparative Medicine Research Farm U Mo Route 3 Columbia MO 65201

SUNDARAM, SHANMUGHA K., surgeon; b. Kottayam, India, July 21, 1938; s. Kanniah P.C. and Saraswathi Chettiar; came to U.S., 1964; I.S.C., Kerala U. (India), 1956, M.D., 1961; m. Padma Sarada Pillai, May 4, 1964; children—Kannan, Anand, Ravi. Intern, Med. Coll. Hosp., Trivandrum, India, 1961-72, Mac Neal Meml. Hosp., Berwyn, Ill., 1964-65; resident Trumbull Meml. Hosp., Ohio, 1965-66, Mt. Sinai Hosp., Chgo., 1966-70; practice medicine, specializing in surgery, Bolingbrook, Ill., 1972—; mem. staff Hinsdale (Ill.) Sanitorium and Hosp., Good Samaritan Hosp., Downers Grove, Ill., Loretto Hosp., Chgo.; instr. anatomy Med. Coll. Trivandrum (India), 1963-64; clin. instr. Mt. Sinai Hosp., Chgo., 1969-70. Fellow A.C.S., Internat. Coll. Surgeons. Home: 6911 Lyman St Downers Grove IL 60515 Office: 402 W Boughton Rd Bolingbrook IL 60439

SUNDBERG, COLLINS YNGVE, funeral dir.; b. DeKalb, Ill., May 29, 1911; s. Axel and Sophia (Collin) S.; student Worsham Coll. Mortuary Sci., 1937-38; m. Norma E. Johnson, June 20, 1942. Partner, Sundberg Funeral Home, Rockford, Ill., 1952—; pres. Col-Nor Corp., Rockford, 1961—. Pres. Winnebago County Humane Soc.; active Goldie B. Flaberg Center for Children. Served with USNR, 1942-45. Mem. Nat., Ill., No. Ill. funeral dirs. assns., Am. Vets. (comdr. Rockford post), Rockford C. of C., Rockford Hist. Soc., Swedish Hist. Soc. Am. Legion, VFW. Republican. Lutheran. Mason (Shriner), Moose, Odd Fellow. Clubs: Navy of U.S.A. (Rockford), Pyramid (Rockford), John Ericsson (past pres.), Rock River Kennel (past pres., dir.) (Rockford); Forest Hills Country. Home: 5431 Einor St Rockford IL 61108 Office: 215 N 6th St Rockford IL 61107

SUNDBERG, DARRYLL, land devel. co. exec.; b. Ishpeming, Mich., Dec. 16, 1948; s. Leo Leslie and Charlotte Genevieve (LaFreniere) S.; B.S.E.E., Mich. Tech. U., 1971, B.S.C.E., 1974, M.S.C.E., 1978; m. Susan Emily Hill, Oct. 9, 1971. Office engr. Brumm Constrn. Co., Inc., 1975-77; v.p. Mink, Inc., Ishpeming, 1977—. Mem. IEEE, ASCE, Am. Concrete Inst. Roman Catholic. Home: 138 Excelsior St Ishpeming MI 49849 Office: PO Box 896 126 E Hewitt Ave Marquette MI 49855

SUNDBERG, NORMA ELIZABETH JOHNSON (MRS. COLLINS Y. SUNDBERG), funeral dir.; b. Rockford, Ill.; d. Conrad Walfred and Olga (Pierson) Johnson; student Brown's Bus. Coll., 1928-30; m. Collins Y. Sundberg, June 20, 1942. Partner Sundberg Funeral Home, Rockford, Ill., 1952—; sec.-treas. ColNor Corp., Rockford, 1961—. Mem. Winnebago County Women's Republican Club, 1948—, v.p., 1956, 57; active Goldie B. Flaberg Center for Children. Mem. Nat., Ill. funeral dirs. assns., Swedish Hist. Soc., Jenny Lind Soc., Am. Legion Aux., Humane Soc. Aux., Humane Soc., Women of Moose. Lutheran. Mem. Order Eastern Star, Order White Shrine of Jerusalem, Daus. of the Nile. Clubs: Zonta (bd. dirs. 1962-64), Rockford Woman's; Forest Hills Country. Home: 5431 Einor St Rockford IL 61108 Office: 215 N 6th St Rockford IL 61107

SUNDBY, ELMER ARTHUR, educator; b. Eau Claire, Wis., Nov. 23, 1928; s. Russell Walter and Nettie Mathilda (Johnson) S.; B.A., No. Central Coll., 1952; M.A. (Ford Found. fellow), Vanderbilt U., 1959, Ph.D., 1962; m. Marilyn Edruth Koeller, Mar. 21, 1953; children—Steven, Scott, Mark. Prof., chmn. psychology North Central Coll., 1956-72; prof., chmn. psychology, U. Wis.-Eau Claire, 1972—. Fulbright lectr. Chiengmai U., Thailand, 1965-66; vis. prof. Nat. Coll. Edn., 1969. Served with AUS, 1946-48. Mem. Am., Midwest, Ill. psychol. assns., Pi Gamma Mu. Methodist (trustee). Home: 3603 Pine Pl Rd Eau Claire WI 54701

SUNDSTROM, ERNEST DALE, mech. engr.; b. Mud Butte, S.D., Apr. 15, 1930; s. Carl John and Elsie Marie (Johnson) S.; B.S. in Mech. Engring., S.D. Sch. Mines and Tech., 1958; m. Iola Hope Erickson, June 4, 1955 (div. 1976); children—Nancy, Dale, Linda, James. Power plant results engr. Mont.-Dakota Utilities Co., Mandan, N.D., 1958-64, Colo.-Ute Electric Assn., Hayden, Colo., 1964-65; utilities design engr. Monsanto Co., St. Louis, 1965-72; sr. power plant design engr. Commonwealth Assos. Inc., Jackson, Mich., 1972-73, engring. mgr., 1974—; instr. steam power plant supervisory program U. Wis., 1977. Pres. Immanuel Lutheran Ch., Mandan, 1960-64; bd. dirs. Mont.-Dakota Utilities Credit Union, 1961-64. Served with U.S. Army, 1951-53; Korea. Registered profl. engr., Mich., Ohio, N.D. Mem. ASME, Am. Legion. Home: PO Box 672 Jackson MI 49204 Office: 209 E Washington Ave Jackson MI 49201

SUNG, C. B., multi-industry co. exec.; b. Shanghai, China, Feb. 1, 1925; s. Tsing-Ching and Hsu-Ying (Ma) S.; B.S., Chiao-Tung U., China, 1945; M.S., Mass. Inst. Tech., 1948; M.B.A., Harvard, 1950; m. Beulah C.H. Kwok, June 4, 1953; children—Dean, Wingate. Came to U.S., 1947; naturalized, 1954. From engr. to dept. chief Nanking-Shanghai Ry. Systems Adminstrn., China, 1945-47; devel. engr. instrumentation Ruge-de Forest, Inc., 1950-52; engr. research labs. Bendix Corp., 1952-62, asst. gen. mgr., 1962-64, gen. mgr., dir., 1964-67, corporate v.p. engring. and research, Detroit, 1967-69, v.p., group exec. advanced tech. group, Southfield, Mich., 1969-72, v.p., group exec. advanced concepts group, 1972-74; pres., chief exec. officer CMA Inc., Cleve., 1974—; chmn. bd. Airborne Mfg. Co., Elyria, Ohio, 1975—; chmn. bd., pres. Cleve.-CAE Metal Abrasive, Ltd., Welland, Ont., Can., 1976—; dir. Cleve. Metal Abrasive Inc., Galileo Electro-Optics Corp., Codata Corp., ETEC Corp. cons. in field. Mem. vis. com. Engring. Coll. U. Mich., Carnegie-Mellon U., Oakland U. Mem. Am. Mgmt. Assn., Soc. Automotive Engrs., Sigma Xi. Patentee in field. Home: 2 Bratenahl Pl Cleveland OH 44108 Office: Exec Offices CMA Inc Euclid Office Plaza Cleveland OH 44132

SUNLEAF, ROGER WENDELL, lawyer; b. Bellevue, Iowa, May 26, 1938; s. Arthur Wendell and Virginia Eleanor (Anderson) S.; B.A., U. Iowa, 1959, J.D., 1963; m. Rose Marie DeGear, Oct. 23, 1965. Admitted to Ia. bar, 1963; mem. firm McFarlin & McFarlin, Montezuma, Iowa, 1964-65; partner McNeil & Sunleaf, 1966—. Chmn., Poweshiek County Republican Central Com., 1970-74. Mem. Poweshiek County (pres., 1969-74), Iowa bar assns., Iowa (bd. govs. 1976—), Am. trial lawyers assns. Rep. Elk. Home: 906 E Washington St Montezuma IA 50171 Office: 105 N 4th St Montezuma IA 50171

SUNSTEIN, MICHAEL ALLEN, constrn. co. exec.; b. Chgo., June 4, 1942; s. Cass Herman and Shirley Jeanne (Blum) S.; B.A., Shimer Coll., 1964; m. Dennet Ann Sheridan, Sept. 30, 1961; children—Lisa, Robert, Julie, Vicki, Jason, Megan. Salesman Vinco Industries Inc., Chgo., 1965-66, v.p. mktg., 1966-68; salesman Kaufman & Broad Homes Inc., Chgo., 1968-69, sales mgr., 1969-70, v.p. mktg. and sales, Freehold, N.J., 1970-72, asst. div. mgr., 1972-74, pres. div., chief exec. officer, Detroit, 1974—; instr. mktg. Monmouth County (N.J.) Coll., Toms River, 1973-74. Recipient Plaque and watch Coventry Square Homeowners Assn., 1973. Mem. Home Builders Assn. (dir. state). Rotarian (hon.). Home: 5715 Andover Rd Troy MI 48084 Office: 470 N Woodward Ave Birmingham MI 48011

SURACE, GENE ALLEN, county ofcl.; b. Lorain, Ohio, Dec. 7, 1946; s. Dominic and Helen (Balint) S.; B.S. in Social Studies, Kent (Ohio) State U., 1970; M.S. in Personnel Counseling, Jacksonville (Ala.) State U., 1974. Substitute tchr. Lorain city schs., 1970-71; econ. devel. coordinator Lorain City Hall, 1975; acting dir. Lorain County Econ. Devel. Com., 1975—. Served with U.S. Army, 1971-73. Mem. Am. Personnel and Guidance Assn. Nat. Employment Counselors Assn., Nat. Vocat. Guidance Assn., Nat. Assn. Counties, Council Urban Econ. Devel., Italian Am. War Vets., Fraternal Order Police Assos. Ohio. Democrat. Roman Catholic. Home: 545 E Erie Ave Lorain OH 44052 Office: 200 W Erie Ave 5th Floor City Hall Lorain OH 44052

SURDAM, ROBERT MCCLELLAN, banker; b. Albany, N.Y., Oct. 28, 1917; s. I. Burke and LeMoyne (McClellan) S.; grad. Deerfield (Mass.) Acad., 1935; B.A. cum laude, Williams Coll., 1939; m. Mary Caroline Buhl, July 8, 1946; children—Peter Buhl, Robert McClellan, Mary Caroline. With Nat. Bank of Detroit, 1947—, v.p., 1954-60, sr. v.p., 1960-64, exec. v.p., 1964-68, pres., 1968-72, chmn., 1972—; dir. Internat. Bank of Detroit, Bundy Corp., Western Am. Bank (Europe) Ltd., Burroughs Corp. Mem. Assn. Res. City Bankers. Clubs: Detroit, Detroit Athletic, Country of Detroit, Yondotega (Detroit); Grosse Pointe; Links (N.Y.C.); Metropolitan (Washington). Home: 396 Provencal Rd Grosse Point Farms MI 48236 Office: PO Box 116 Detroit MI 48232

SURPRENANT, THOMAS TERRY, librarian; b. Troy, N.Y., May 3, 1942; s. Thomas Leo and Rita Marie (Sloyan) S.; B.S. in History and English, Siena Coll., 1964; M.S. in L.S., Catholic U. Am., 1967; M.S. in Audiovisual Media, U. Wis., 1975, postgrad. in L.S., 1975—; m. Carol Francis Vincent, Nov. 10, 1963; children—Andre, Brett, Aimee, Geoffrey. Library asst. Applied Physics Lab., Johns Hopkins, Silver Spring, Md., 1964-65; librarian Electromagnetic Compatability Analysis Center, Ill. Inst. Tech., Chgo., 1965-69; asso. prof. library sci., also librarian Northland Coll., Ashland, Wis., 1969—. Cons. Wilmarth Sch., Ashland, Wis., 1972-73, Meml. Med. Center, Ashland, 1972-73, Ashland High Sch., 1971-73. Title I Gildden (Wis.) Pub. Schs., 1971-73. Mem. Am., Wis. library assns. Home: 1330 Vilas Ave Madison WI 53715

SURRELL, HELEN MYRA WEBB (MRS. JACK SURRELL), social worker; b. Charleston, Ark.; d. Roy L. and Essie M. (Waters) Webb; A.B., Ark. State Coll., 1947; M.S.W., Wayne State U., 1962, postgrad., 1964-65, U. Detroit Law Sch., 1968—; m. Jack Surrell, Dec. 19, 1959. Tchr., Eliza Miller High Sch., Helena, Ark., 1947-50, Drew County High Sch., Monticello, 1950-51; with Barthwell Drug Stores, Inc., Detroit, 1951-52, Henry Ford Hosp., Detroit, 1952, J.L. Hudson, Detroit, 1952-54; caseworker foster homes Children's Aid Soc., Detroit, 1954-60; with Wayne County Juvenile Ct., Detroit, 1962—, unit dir. field work instrn., intensive casework and tng. unit, and supr. trainee program, 1967-76, chief social worker, 1976—, referee adoption releases and consents, part time, 1967-72, program dir., psychiat. social work supr. Pub. Act 54, 1973-74, adminstrv. asst. to dir. ct. and clinic services, 1974—. Vice pres. alumni exec. bd. Wayne State U. Sch. Social Work, 1967-69, editor alumni publ., 1967-68. Recipient various awards. Nat. Inst. Mental Health scholar, 1960-62. Mem. Nat. Assn. Social Workers, Nat. Council Crime and Delinquency, Mich. Soc. Mental Health, Am. Bar Assn. (student mem.), Social Workers Club Met. Detroit, Acad. Certified Social Workers, Internat. Platform Assn., Delta Sigma Theta. Home: 14870 Piedmont Ave Detroit MI 48223 Office: 1025 E Forest Ave Detroit MI 48207

SURRELL, MATTHEW ANTHONY, hosp. adminstr., physician; b. Newberry, Mich., Aug. 21, 1910; s. Matthew A. and Alvina M. (Beaulieu) S.; A.B., Olivet Coll., 1931; M.D., U. Mich., 1935; grad. Army Command and Gen. Staff Sch., Ft. Leavenworth, Kans.; m. Agnes Grace Costello, July 2, 1932; children—Stephen E., Matthew J., James A. Intern Henry Ford Hosp., Detroit, 1935-36; practice medicine, Newberry, Mich., 1936-40, 50-66; clin. dir. Newberry State Hosp., 1947-50, med. dir. mentally retarded service, Served from lt. to col. M.C., AUS, 1941-46. Decorated Legion of Merit, Bronze Star medal, Army commendation medal; Croix de Guerre with gold star (France). Mem. Ret. Officers Assn., Am. Legion, VFW. Elk. Home: 416 W Ave B Newberry MI 49868 Office: Newberry State Hospital Newberry MI 49868

SUSKIND, RAYMOND ROBERT, physician; b. N.Y.C., Nov. 29, 1913; s. Alexander and Anna (Abramson) S.; A.B., Columbia Coll., 1934; postgrad. U. Edinburgh (Scotland), 1938-39; M.D. (Mitchell prize), State U. N.Y., 1943. Diplomate Am. Bd. Dermatology; m. Ida Blanche Richardson, Dec. 27, 1944; children—Raymond Robert, Stephen Alexander. Intern, Cin. Gen. Hosp., 1944, resident in dermatology, 1944-46, 48-49; research asst. bacteriology N.Y. U., 1934-36; research fellow to asso. prof. preventive medicine and indsl. health U. Cin. Coll. Medicine, 1948-62, instr. to asso. prof. dermatology, 1948-62, dir. and Schmidlapp prof. environ. health Kettering Lab., 1969—, prof. medicine, 1969—; prof., head div. environ. medicine, prof. dermatology U. Oreg., 1962-69; mem. Cin. Air Pollution Bd., 1972-76, chmn., 1974-75; mem. Nat. Inst. Environ. Health Scis. Task Force for Research Planning in Environ. Health Scis., 1975—; mem. adv. com. on biology and medicine Los Alamos Sci. Lab., 1976—; cons. in occupational medicine Surgeon Gen. Dept. Navy, 1975—, Navy Environ. Med. Center, 1976; cons. FDA, 1976—; mem. sci. adv. bd. ad hoc study group biol. and climate effects research EPA, 1977—; cons. in field. Fellow Am. Dermatol. Assn.; mem. Am. Occupational Medicine, Soc. Occupational and Environ. Health, N.Y. Acad. Scis., Dermatology Found., Soc. Investigative Dermatology, A.C.P., Sigma Xi., Alpha Omega Alpha. Contbr. chpts. to books, articles in field to profl. jours. Office: Kettering Lab U Cin Coll Medicine 3223 Eden Ave Cincinnati OH 45267

SUSMAN, BERNARD MARVIN, real estate developer; b. Chgo., Apr. 6, 1924; s. Eli Walter and Bess (Shaffer) S.; student Ill. Inst. Tech., 1941-43; B.S., Roosevelt U., 1948; m. Caryl Rose Hollender, May 3, 1953; children—Sue Ellen, John David, William Joseph. Real estate negotiator Landau & Pearlman, 1948-53; owner Bernard M. Susman & Co., Chgo., 1953—; dir. Carlyle JMB, Inc., Carlyle 74 Mgrs., Inc. Pres. Big Bros. of Met. Chgo., 1972-73, Parkview Home, 1973-75; bd. dirs. Council for Jewish Elderly, 1973—. Served with USAAF, 1943-46. Mem. Internat. Council Shopping Centers. Clubs: Standard, Northmoor Country. Home: 1300 Westmoor Trail Winnetka IL 60093 Office: 134 N LaSalle St Chicago IL 60602

SUSSKIND, TAMAR YOUNINAH, educator; b. Bklyn., Aug. 28, 1930; d. Irving and Rose Leah (Bookchin) Liftman; B.A., U. B.C., 1950; postgrad. Bklyn. Coll., 1951-54; M.S., Oakland U., 1970; m. Norman Lee Suskind, June 15, 1952 (div. 1973); children—David L., Robert D., Judith Anne. Chief chemist Etched Products Co., N.Y.C., 1952-54, Levco Metal Finishers, N.Y.C., 1954-56; chief chemist Park Nameplate Co., N.Y.C., 1956-60, cons., 1960-64; lab. instr. Oakland U., Rochester, Mich., 1960-61; prof. chemistry Oakland Community Coll., Auburn Heights, Mich., 1965—. Recipient teaching award Mfg. Chemists Assn., 1977. Mem. Am. Chem. Soc. (mem. com. on chemistry in 2-yr. coll., div. chemistry edn. 1974—), A.A.A.S., Am. Inst. Chemists. Home: 758 McGill Dr Rochester MI 48063 Office: 2900 Featherstone Rd Auburn Heights MI 48057

SUTCLIFFE, GRENVILLE GEORGE, mfg. co. exec.; b. St. Louis, May 27, 1944; s. Eugene Grenville DeCantwell and Hazel Louise (Duffendack) S.; B.S. in Bus. Adminstrn., U. Mo., 1971; m. Dianne E. Steed, Nov. 25, 1972; 1 dau., Katherine Mae. Vice pres. Husky Corp., Pacific, Mo., 1962-65, v.p., 1971—; dir. Am. Security Bank, Pacific, Mo., Petroleum Equipment Inst. Served with Spl. Forces U.S. Army, 1965-68. Decorated Purple Heart. Mem. Soc. Automotive Engrs., Exptl. Aircraft Inst., Am. Petroleum Inst., Nat. Assn. Petroleum Equipment Rebuilders (pres. 1972-77). Patentee pollution control devices. Home: Route 2 Box 189A Village Ridge MO 63088 Office: 1 Dailey Industrial Park Pacific MO 63069

SUTER, WILLIAM ALVA, lawyer; b. Pana, Ill., Apr. 29, 1934; s. Weldon R. and Beatrice E. (Mercer) S.; B.A., U. Ill., 1955, LL.B., 1957; children—William Anthony, Ty Amling. Admitted to Ill. bar, 1959, Washington D.C. bar, 1960; trust officer trust dept. First Nat. Bank, Springfield, Ill., 1958; partner Whitley, Suter & Heiss, Decatur, Ill., 1958—. Served with USMC, 1957-58. Mem. Am. Judicature Soc., Ill. Bar Assn., Sigma Nu, Phi Delta Phi. Home: 2410 S 34th St Decatur IL 62521 Office: 363 S Main St Decatur IL 62523

SUTHERLAND, GEORGE HENRY, educator; b. Edmonton, Alta., Can., Nov. 25, 1947; s. James Robert and Norah Margaret (Hutton) S.; came to U.S., 1970, naturalized, 1977; B.Sc., U. Alta., 1969; M.Eng., McMaster U., 1970; Ph.D., Stanford U., 1973; m. Judy Carlene Johnson, Aug. 30, 1969; 1 son, Eric John. Asst. prof. mech. engring. Ohio State U., Columbus, 1973—; dir. Advanced Design Methods Lab., 1977—; cons. various indsl. firms. Registered profl. engr., Ohio; recipient various scholarships, fellowships and awards, 1964-73; recipient Ronald W. Thompson Meritorious Service award Ohio State U., 1975. Mem. Am. Soc. Engring. Edn. (local chpt. chmn. 1974-75), ASME (newsletter editor 1977-78), Lambda Chi Alpha (bd. trustees). Methodist. Clubs: Columbus Ski. Contbr. tech. articles on machine design to profl. jours. Home: 2740 Oakridge Ct Columbus OH 43221 Office: 206 W 18th St Columbus OH 43210

SUTHERLAND, RONALD ROY, planetarium adminstr.; b. Pitts., Dec. 28, 1931; s. Roy Elmer and Dellia (Abbiatti) S.; B.S., U. Pitts., 1956; grad. U.S. Army Transp. Sch., 1956, U.S. Army Chem., Biol. and Radiol. Warfare Sch., 1957. Planetarium astronomer Buhl Planetarium, Pitts., 1958-60, asst. to dir., 1960-62; asst. dir. McDonnell Planetarium, St. Louis, 1962-66, planetarium dir., 1966—. Pres., Technamics Co., St. Louis, 1970—. Astronomy subject dir. St. Louis Area council Boy Scouts Am. Served with AUS, 1956-58. Mem. Royal, St. Louis astron. socs., Nat. Geog. Soc., Mo. Acad. Sci., Pacific Planetarium Assn., Planetarium Assn. Can., Adult Edn. Council St. Louis, Am. Mus. Natural History, Smithsonian Assos. Home: 6307 Winona St St Louis MO 63109 Office: McDonnell Planetarium St Louis MO 63110

SUTTER, ELIZABETH HENBY (MRS. RICHARD A. SUTTER), civic leader; b. St. Louis, May 15, 1912; d. William Hastings and Alvina (Steinbreder) Henby; A.B., Washington U., 1931; m. Richard A. Sutter, June 15, 1935; children—John Richard, Jane Elizabeth, Judith Ann (Mrs. William Hinrichs). Nat. chmn. com. on mental health AMA Aux., 1960-62, v.p., 1962-63, 64-64, pres., 1965-66, editor Direct Line newsletter, 1967-74, now life mem.; asso. editor Facet's, 1973—; mem. adv. bd. Deaconess Hosp. Sch. of Nursing, St. Louis; trustee John Burroughs Sch., 1958-61, v.p. 1959, devel. commn., 1960-61; mem. Historic Bldgs. Commn. St. Louis County, 1959—, chmn., 1973-78; sec., treas. Sutter Clinic, Inc., St. Louis, Sutter Mgmt., Inc., Downtown Med. Bldg., Inc.; bd. dirs. Conv. and

Visitors Bur. Greater St. Louis, 1976—. Mem. planning bd. Health, Hosp. Health, Welfare Council Met St. Louis, 1955-64; pres. Aux. Central States Soc. Indsl. Medicine and Surgery, 1960-61; pres. St. Louis County Med. Soc. Aux. 1948-49, Mo. Med. Soc. Aux., 1952-53; sec. St. Louis County Health and Hosp. Bd., 1956-60, chmn., 1961; bd. dirs. Tb Soc. St. Louis, exec. com., 1956—, v.p., 1960-61; pres. Tb and Health Soc. of St. Louis, 1962-65; former mem. adv. council vol. services Nat. Assn. Mental Health; dir. Am. Cancer Soc., St. Louis, exec. com. 1954-64; mem. Community Cancer Council, 1975; bd. dirs. Mental Health Assn. St. Louis, 1960-61; mem. Practical Nursing Edn. Council, chmn. exec. com., 1959-60; mem. Nat. Def. Adv. Com. Women in Services, 1969-71, vice chmn. 1971; mem. bd. govs. Washington U. Alumni, 1970-71, 74—; mem. bd. Health Systems Agy. Greater St. Louis, 1976—; mem. East-West Gateway Coordinating Council Task Force on Historic Preservation, 1975—; mem. University City Historic Preservation Com., 1977—. Named one of 10 Women of Achievement in good citizen category St. Louis Globe-Democrat, 1961; recipient St. Louis County Med. Soc. award of merit, 1964; Alumna of Year award Gamma Phi Beta St. Louis, 1966; Distinguished Alumni citation Washington U., St. Louis, 1968, Distinguished Alumni Service citation, 1977. Mem. Mo. Hist. Soc. St. Louis Symphony Soc., Mo. State Med. Assn. Womans Aux. (hon. life). Presbyterian (chmn. finance com. Women's Assn. 1954-60). Contbr. articles to med. publs. Home: 7215 Greenway Dr St Louis MO 63130

SUTTER, RICHARD ANTHONY, surgeon; b. St. Louis, July 20, 1909; s. John Henry and Molly (Schuchman) S.; A.B., Washington U., 1931, M.D., 1935; m. Elizabeth Henby, June 15, 1935; children—John Richard, Jane Elizabeth, Judith Ann Sutter Hinrichs. Intern, St. Louis City Hosp., 1935-36; preceptor, Otto Sutter, M.D., St. Louis; founder, dir. Sutter Clinic, Inc., St. Louis, 1946—; lectr. in indsl. medicine and rehab. in preventive medicine, Sch. Medicine, Washington U.; med. dir. St. Louis Internat. Airport; med. advisor Union Electric Co., St. Louis Globe Democrat. Bd. dirs. St. Louis Convention Bur., Downtown St. Louis, Inc., Herbert Hoover Boys Club Ill., Mo. Progressive Airport Creation Task Force; elder, bd. trustees First Presbyn. Ch. of St. Louis. Served to lt. col. U.S. Army, 1941-45. Decorated Bronze Star. Diplomate Am. Bd. Preventive Medicine. Mem. AMA, Mo. State, So. Med. Assns., St. Louis County Med. Soc. (hon.), Royal Soc. Health, Permanent Commn. and Internat. Assn. Occupational Health, Am. Acad. Occupational Medicine, Am., Central States occupational medicine assns., Am. Coll. Preventive Medicine, Am. Pub. Health Assn., Aerospace Med. Assn., Air Medics Med. Assn., Nat., Mo. Rehab. Assns. Clubs: Mo. Athletic, St. Louis, St. Louis Beta Theta Pi (Man of Year, 1974), Faculty of Washington U., Washington U. Club, Rotary (St. Louis), Am. Legion (hon. surgeon Fred W. Stockham Post). Advanced aviation med. examiner FAA; contbr. articles in field of occupational medicine and geriatrics to profl. jours. Home: 7215 Greenway Ave Saint Louis MO 63130 Office: 819 Locust St Downtown Med Bldg Saint Louis MO 63101

SUTTER, WILLIAM PAUL, lawyer; b. Chgo., Jan. 15, 1924; s. Harry Blair and Elsie (Paul) S.; A.B., Yale U., 1947; J.D., U. Mich., 1950; m. Helen Yvonne Stebbins, Nov. 13, 1954; children—William Paul, Helen Blair. Admitted to Ill. bar, 1950, Fla. bar, 1977; asso. firm Hopkins, Sutter, Mulroy, Davis, & Cromartie, and predecessor firm, Chgo., 1950-57, partner, 1957—; mem. Ill. Supreme Ct. Atty. Registration Commn., 1975—. Precinct capt. New Trier Twp. (Ill.) Rep. Party, 1960-68; asst. area chmn. New Trier Rep. Orgn., 1968-72. Chmn. Winnetka Caucus Committee, 1966-67. Trustee Gads Hill Center, pres., 1962-70, chmn., 1971—. Served to 1st lt. AUS, 1943-46. Fellow Am. Bar Found., Am. Coll. Probate Counsel; mem. Am. (ho. dels. 1972—, chmn. com. on income estates and trusts, taxation sect. 1973-75), Ill. (bd. govs. 1964-75, pres. 1973-74), Chgo. (chmn. probate practice com. 1963-64), bar assns., Am. Law Inst., Am. Judicature Soc., Ill. LAWPAC (pres. 1977—), Chgo. Assn. Commerce and Industry (govt. affairs div.), Am. Arbitration Assn., Order of the Coif, Phi Beta Kappa, Phi Delta Phi, Chi Psi. Episcopalian. Clubs: Law, Legal, Economic (Chgo.). Contbr. articles on estate planning and taxation to profl. jours. Home: 96 Woodley Rd Winnetka IL 60093 Office: 1 First National Plaza Chicago IL 60603

SUTTLES, RAYMOND HERSCHEL, publishing co. exec.; b. Indpls., May 31, 1923; s. Raymond H. and Maude (Thompson) S.; student Occidental Coll., 1943-44; B.S., U. So. Calif., 1946, postgrad., 1954-55; m. Patricia Ann Horkheimer, Oct. 19, 1955; children—Steven Arthur, Kathleen Mary (Mrs. Richard L. Nehmer), Nancy Lynn. Customer Service engr. Douglas Aircraft Co., Santa Monica, Calif., 1955-59; missile service engr. Gen. Dynamics/Astronautics, San Diego, 1959-60; mktg. analyst Kintel div. Cohu Electronics, San Diego, 1960-61; co-owner Ednl. Materials Service, La Jolla, Calif., 1962-69; promotion dir. Educators Progress Service, Inc., Randolph, Wis., 1969-74, pres., 1974—. Asst. dist. commr. San Diego County council Boy Scouts Am., 1966-69, inst. rep., 1969—; treas. St. Gabriels's Ch. Corp., Randolph, 1970—; pres. Randolph Centennial Corp. Served to lt. (j.g.) USN, 1941-54. Mem. Phi Kappa Tau. Clubs: Kiwanis (lt. gov. 1971-72; Fox Lake Golf (sec. treas.) (Wis.). Editor: Supplement to Educators Grade Guide to Free Teaching Aids, 1959-76, Educators Guide to Free Tapes, Scripts and Transcriptions, 1970-75. Home: 427 W Main St Madison WI 53703

SUTTON, CHARLES F(REDERICK), physician; b. Jackson Center, Ohio, Apr. 29, 1903; s. Charles W. and Bertha (Davis) S.; A.B., Milton Coll., 1925; M.S., Battle Creek Coll., 1928; M.D., Rush Med. Coll., U. Chgo., 1936; M.P.H., Columbia U.; m. Constance Aileen Bennett, June 22, 1926. Intern, Ill. Central Hosp., Chgo., 1935-36; gen. med. practice, Chillicothe, Ill, 1936-41; asst. chief div. local health services Ill. State Dept. Pub. Health, Springfield, Ill., 1946-48, chief of div., 1948-73; cons. pub. health-preventive medicine, 1973—. Served as 1st lt. to maj., M.C., AUS, 1941-46; sr. surgeon to med. dir. USPHS, 1950-68. Diplomate Am. Bd. Preventive Medicine and Pub. Health. Fellow Am. Pub. Health Assn., Am. Coll. Preventive Medicine; mem. AMA, Ill., Sangamon County med. socs.; Ill., Pub. Health Assn., Am. Assn. Pub. Health Physicians, Amvets. Home: 1544 W Cook St Springfield IL 62704

SUTTON, JAMES MATTHEW, graphics and electronics co. exec.; b. St. Louis, Mar. 8, 1948; s. Jean and Dorothy Anne (Varga) S.; B.S. in Agronomy, Colo. State U., 1970, M.S., in Bus., 1973. Cash soybean merchandiser Archer Daniels Midland Co., Fremont, Nebr., 1973-74; agrl. economist to Minsitry Agr., Suva, Fiji Islands, S. Pacific, 1975; cons. agronomist Inter-Am. Labs., Ogallala, Nebr., 1976—; owner, mgr. Sutton Graphics, Ogallala, 1977—. Asso. dir. CSU Alumni Found. Mem. Nat., Internat. wildlife fedns., Internat. Oceanographic Found., Am. Mus. Natural History, Denver Mus. Natural History, Cousteau Soc., Nat. Audubon Soc. Baptist. Research in retailing and direct selling. Address: PO Box 206 Ogallala NE 69153

SUTTON, LOUISE WEIBERT, poet; b. Evansville, Ind., Apr. 22, 1920; d. Asa August and Rhoda Alice (Kell) Weibert; student pub. schs., Evansville; m. Walter Lee Sutton, Nov. 1, 1947; children by previous marriage—Dorothy, Patricia, Carol; children—Edward, Myrtle, Asa, Susan Mary, Donald, Anne, Gwen, Daisy, Madonna. Collections of poems include: Through Lens of Poetry, 1967, Songs From the April Hills, 1968, The Voice of Verse, 1968, A Pen of Stars, 1969, The Emerald Quill, 1969; contbr. poetry to numerous mags., newspapers; editor, tchr. poetry; illustrator poetry and religious mags. Mem. Internat. Acad. Poets (founder), NAPA, Lone Indian Fellowship. Home and Office: 203 S Bosse Ave Evansville IN 47712

SUZUKI, JON BYRON, microbiologist, periodontist, educator; b. San Antonio, Tex., July 22, 1946; s. George and Ruby (Kanaya) S.; B.A. in Biology, Ill. Wesleyan U., 1968; Ph.D. magna cum laude in Microbiology, Ill. Inst. Tech., 1971; D.D.S., Loyola U., 1978; m. Cynthia Onaga, Aug. 16, 1969. Med. technologist Ill. Masonic Hosp. and Med. Center, Chgo., 1966-67; instr. of lab. in histology and parasitology Ill. Wesleyan U., Bloomington, 1967-68; med. technologist Augustana Hosp., Chgo., 1968-69; research asso. and instr. microbiology Ill. Inst. Tech., Chgo., 1968-71; research asso. U. Chgo. Hosps., 1970-71; clin. microbiologist St. Luke's Hosp. Center, Columbia Coll. Physicians and Surgeons, N.Y.C., 1971-73; asso. med. dir. Paramed. Tng. and Registry, Vancouver, B.C., Canada, 1973-74; dir. of clin. labs. Registry of Hawaii, 1973-74; chmn. continuing med. asst. edn. U. Hawaii, Honolulu, 1974; lectr. in microbiology Loyola U. Med. Center, Maywood, Ill., 1974—; vis. scientist to Moscow (USSR) State U., 1972, summer; lectr. Internat. Congress of Allergology, Tokyo, Japan, 1973; lab. dir. Dept. Health, Hawaii. Water safety instr. ARC, Honolulu, 1973—. Recipient president's medallion Loyola U. of Chgo., 1977; named Alumni of the Year, Wesleyan U., 1977. Mem. Am. Inst. Biol. Scis., Internat. Soc. of Biophysicists, Internat. Soc. of Endocrinologists, Ill. Acad. Sci. (chmn. microbiology session of 65th ann. meeting 1972), AAAS, Am. Dental Assn., Am., Internat. assns. dental research, Am. Acad. Microbiology, Nat. Aeronautics and Space Adminstrn. Bd., Am. Soc. Microbiology, Soc. for Indsl. Microbiology, AAUP, N.Y. Acad. Scis., Sigma Xi, Beta Beta Beta. Club: Blue key. Author: Clinical Laboratory Methods for the Medical Assistant, 1974; contbr. numerous articles on research in microbiology and endocrinology to sci. jours. Home: 6007 N Sheridan Rd Suite 30-J Chicago IL 60660 Office: Loyola Univ School of Dentistry 2160 South 1st Ave Maywood IL 60153 also Dept Periodontics Univ Washington SC-62 Seattle WA 98195

SVEBAKKEN, GENE LEROY, social worker; b. Waukon, Iowa, Jan. 18, 1940; s. Roy Nelson and Ester (Colsch) S.; B.A., Luther Coll., 1961; M.S.W., U. Mo., 1964; m. Kathleen Adel Amundson, June 8, 1963; children—Kristine, Peter, Hans. Social worker Howard County Dept. Social Welfare, Cresco, Iowa, 1961-62, Clayton County Dept. Social Welfare, Elkader, Iowa, 1964-65; social work supr. State Iowa, Elkader, 1965-66; dir. dept. social services Story County, Nevada, Ia., 1966-69; tng. specialist State Dept. Social Services, Des Moines, from 1969; dir. social service Iowa Annie Wittenmeyer Home; field instr. U. Iowa Sch. Social Work; part time faculty Marycrest Coll., Davenport; now exec. dir. Bethany Home, Moline, Ill. Pres. Rock Island County Community Services Council; adv. bd. Lutheran Welfare Western Ill.; chmn. Alternatives to Detention Adv. Bd. of Rock Island County Probation Office. Mem. Nat. Assn. Social Workers (v.p. Quad City chpt., Social Worker of Yr., Quad City chpt. 1976), Ill. Child Care Assn. (dir.). Lutheran. Rotarian. Home: 2739 E High St Davenport IA 52803 Office: 220 11th Ave Moline IL 61265

SVENDSEN, ELINE MARGUERITE, educator; b. Decatur, Ill., Feb. 7, 1924; d. Niels and Johanne (Moller) S.; B.A., Millikin U., 1945; M.A., Columbia U., 1948; M.S. (Gen. Electric fellow), Purdue U., 1959. Tchr. math. Decatur (Ill.) High Sch., 1945-67; instr. math. Lakeland Coll., Mattoon, Ill., 1968—. NSF fellow, 1957, 64, 69, 73. Mem. NEA, Ill. Edn. Assn., Nat., Ill. councils tchrs. of math., Math. Assn. Jr. Coll. Tchrs., Ill. Assn. Math. Tchrs. in Jr. Coll. (pres. elect), AAUW, Delta Kappa Gamma. Lutheran. Home: 20 Elm Ridge Mattoon IL 61938 Office: Lakeland Coll S Route 45 Mattoon IL 61938

SWAIM, JOHN FRANKLIN, physician; b. Bloomingdale, Ind., Dec. 24, 1935; s. Max DeBaun and Edna Marie (Whitely) S.; B.S. cum laude, Ind. State U., 1960; M.D., Ind. U., 1963; m. Esther Joan Dooley, Sept. 7, 1957; children—John Franklin II, Parke Allen, Pamela Ann. Intern, USAF Hosp., Travis AFB, Calif., 1963-64; gen. med. officer USAF Hosp., Williams AFB, Ariz., 1964-66, Maryvale Community Hosp., Phoenix, 1965-66; comdg. officer 559th Med. Service Flight, Vietnam, 1966-67; practice medicine, Rockville, Ind., 1967—; owner, dir. Parke Clinic, Rockville, 1969—, Kingman Community Health Center, 1971—, Clinton br. Parke Clinic, 1972—, Cayuga Community Health Center, 1974—, Russelville Community Health Center, 1975—; mem. staffs Vermillion County Hosp., Clinton, Ind., Union Hosp., Terre Haute, Ind.; med. dir. Rockville Tng. Center, 1969—; med. dir. Newport Army Ammunition Plant, 1968—, Holiday Nursing Home, Clinton, 1975—, Planned Parenthood Clinic, Clinton, Ind., 1976—; coroner Parke County, 1974—. Owner farm, nr. Rockville, 1965—; pres. Parke Investments, Inc., Rockville, 1971—. Active various community drives; area rep. Ind. Heart Assn., 1969-70; cubmaster Boy Scouts Am., Rockville, 1969-71; mem. alumni adv. council Ind. State U., Terre Haute, 1969-71. Bd. dirs. Kathrine Hamilton Mental Health Center, Terre Haute, 1972—. Served to capt. M.C., USAF, 1963-67. Decorated Bronze Star medal. Mem. Am., Ind. (chpt. pres. 1969, 73) acads. gen. practice, Am. Thoracic Soc., Parke-Vermillion County Med. Soc. (sec. 1968, pres. 1972), V.F.W., Ind. Med. Assn. (pres. 5th dist. chpt. 1973), Rockville C. of C. Republican. Mason (Shriner). Contbr. article to profl. jour. Home: 1007 Eastwood Dr Rockville IN 47872 Office: Parke Clinic Anderson St Rockville IN 47872

SWAIM, LLOYD MILTON, paper co. exec.; b. Tangier, Ind., Nov. 15, 1913; s. Jacob D. and Anna C. (English) S.; B.S., Purdue U., 1935, M.S., 1940; m. Evelyn Ann Govert, June 14, 1941; children—Lloyd Earl, Robert John, Mary Ann, Thomas Joseph. Tchr., prin. Griffith (Ind.) High Sch., 1935-42; indsl. engr., asst. plant indsl. engr. Nat. Tube Co., Gary, Ind., 1942-45; div. supt., chief indsl. engr., P. R. Mallory Co., Inc., Indpls., 1945-55; mgr., central indsl. engr., asst. to v.p. Am. Can Co., Neenah, Wis., N.Y.C., 1955-65; dir., v.p. ops. Appleton Coated Paper Co. (Wis.), 1965-71; v.p. mfg. Appleton Papers div. NCR, 1971-76, sr. v.p. mfg., 1976—, also dir. Mem. Soc. for Advancement Mgmt. (chpt. pres. 1958-59), Work Factor Assos. Midwest (dir. 1963-67), Am. Inst. Indsl. Engrs. (dir. 1960), Appleton C. of C. (projects, div. vice chmn. 1967, dir. 1970—), TAPPI, Am. Mgmt. Assn. Republican. Club: Butte Des Morts Golf. Home: 1082 Reed St Neenah WI 54956 Office: 825 E Wisconsin Ave Appleton WI 54911

SWAIN, TIMOTHY WHITZEL, II, lawyer; b. Peoria, Ill., Mar. 13, 1939; s. Timothy Whitsel and Katherine Cynthia (Altorfer) S.; A.B., U. Ill., 1961, J.D., 1963; m. Avalyn Berry, May 9, 1965; children—Devan Elizabeth, Kathryn Alicia, Timothy Whitzel III, Kristan Melissa. Admitted to Ill. bar, 1963; mem. firm Swain, Johnson & Gard, Peoria, 1965—. Spl. asst. atty. gen., 1969—. Campaign coordinator Senator Percy, Peoria County, 1972. Trustee Lakeview Center for Arts and Scis., Neighborhood Settlement House, Peoria; bd. dirs. Peoria Jr. Achievement. Mem. Senator Percy's Service Acad. Selection Bd., 1973—. Mem. Ill. Def. Counsel. Served with 101st Airborne Div., AUS, 1963-65. Decorated Combat Infantryman's badge, Bronze Star. Mem. Peoria County (chmn. legislative com., 1972-73), Ill., Am. bar assns., Am., Ill. trial lawyers assns., Am. Right of Way Assn., U. Ill. Alumni Assn. (life), Skull and Crescent, Toastmasters (pres. 1967), 101st Airborne Div. Assn. (life). Baptist (deacon). Clubs: Peoria Country, Peoria Illini. Home: 111 E Morningside Dr Peoria IL 61614 Office: Savings Center Tower Peoria IL 61602

SWALLOW, PETER THOMAS, packaging co. exec.; b. Detroit, Mar. 4, 1933; s. Leslie Thomas and Loretta (Schmitt) S.; B.S., U. Detroit, 1954, M.B.A., 1956; m. Judith Diane Maskell, May 25, 1956; children—David Thomas, Mary Ellen. With Chrysler Corp., 1951-55, Kieffer Paper Mills, 1955-56; mng. partner Swallow & Assos., packing designers, Lathrup Village, Mich., 1956—; pres. Argent Property Corp., Detroit, 1965—; chmn., v.p. Creative Foam Corp., Fenton, Mich., 1969—; v.p. Expanded Plastics, Inc., Drew Foam of Mich. Chmn. Lathrup Village Action Com., 1966—. Mem. alumni bd. U. Detroit High Sch. Mem. Beta Gamma Sigma. Home: 18833 Sunnybrook St Lathrup Village MI 48076 Office: 511 Beach St Fenton MI 48430

SWAN, GEORGE SAMUEL, independent oil producer; b. Balt., Aug. 9, 1914; s. William R. and Carolyn E. (Lamp) S.; grad. McDonogh (Md.) Sch. 1932; student U. Md., Johns Hopkins, U. Va.; m. Pauline E. Womack, 1937; children—Nancy (Mrs. David S. Williams), Patricia (Mrs. Van Sanstrom), Susan (Mrs. Andrew R. Spence), George S. Asst. office mgr., plant cashier Chevrolet Motor Co., 1932-36; oil scout Tex-Jersey Oil Corp., Tyler, Tex., 1937-39; ind. oil producer, Saginaw, Michigan, 1939—. Past mem. bd. dirs. Saginaw div. ARC; bd. dirs. Cancer Soc. Mem. Mich. Oil and Gas Assn. (dir.), Ind. Petroleum Assn. Am. (pub. info. com.), Pi Kappa Alpha. Episcopalian (past sr. warden. vestryman). Clubs: Saginaw (past pres.), Kiwanis (past pres.) (Saginaw); Detroit; Otsego Ski (Gaylord, Mich.); Lost Tree (North Palm Beach, Fla.). Home: Cottage Grove Route 1 Roscommon MI 48653 also 11701 Turtle Beach Rd Lost Tree Village North Palm Beach FL 33408 Office: Second Nat Bank Bldg Saginaw MI 48607

SWAN, HERBERT SIEGFRIED, communications mfg. exec.; b. Montclair, N.J., Jan. 2, 1928; s. Herbert S. and Alma (Oswald) S.; grad. Phillips Exeter Acad., 1945; A.B. in Econs. and Bus. Adminstrn., Lafayette Coll., 1949; m. Roberta J. Whitmire, July 2, 1960; 1 dau., Roberta Allyson. Advt. supr. tv receiver dept. Gen. Electric Co., Syracuse, N.Y., 1954-55; copywriter Bresnick Co. advt. agy., Boston, 1955-58; sr. copywriter, J.T. Chirurg Advt. Agy., Boston, 1958-59; advt. mgr. agrl. chems., indsl. minerals div. Internat. Minerals & Chem. Corp., Skokie, Ill., 1959-61; editor Motorola Newsgram, direct indsl. advt. mgr. Motorola, Chgo., 1962-68; dir. pub. info. Motorola Communications & Electronics, Schaumburg, Ill., 1968-71, mgr. indsl. advt. and sales, 1971-73, mgr. field merchandising, 1973—. Served with USAF, 1950-54. Mem. Community Radio Watch (nat. coordinator 1967-68). Home: 48 Little Cahill Rd Cary IL 60013 Office: 1300 E Algonquin Rd Schaumburg IL 60172

SWAN, PATRICIA BRINTNALL, nutritionist; b. Hickory, N.C., Oct. 21, 1937; d. Philip Earle and Lucille (Farmer) Brintnall; B.S., U. N.C., 1959; M.S., U. Wis., 1961, Ph.D., 1964; m. James Byron Swan, Apr. 23, 1962; children—Kathryn Ann, Deborah Lee. Research asst., research fellow U. Wis., 1959-64; research fellow U. Minn., 1964-65; asst. prof. nutrition, 1965-69, asso. prof., 1969-73, prof., 1973—. Mem. Am. Inst. Nutrition, British Nutrition Soc., Soc. Nutrition Edn. Home: 1525 Berne Rd Minneapolis MN 55421 Office: U Minn Dept Food Science St Paul MN 55108

SWAN, WALLACE KENT, govt. ofcl.; b. Kearney, Nebr., June 13, 1942; s. Kenneth Dean and Regina Joy (Young) S.; B.A., U. Idaho, 1964; M.A., U. Minn., 1969; m. Alice Ramona Kyvig, Sept. 24, 1967; children—Gregory Dean, Eric William. Intern, Village of Edina, Minn., 1966-67; research fellow U. Minn., Mpls., 1967; adminstrv. analyst Minn. Dept. Pub. Welfare, St. Paul, 1967-72, planner, 1972-74, dir. regional devel., 1974; planning/evaluation dir. Hennepin County Welfare Dept., Mpls., 1975—. Nat. Endowment Humanities grantee program pub. adminstrs. Princeton U. Mem. Am. Soc. for Pub. Adminstrn. (sec. Twin Cities chpt. 1974-75, pres. 1976-77, mem. bd. 1977—), Am. Polit. Sci. Assn., Am. Pub. Welfare Assn., Minn. Social Service Assn., Phi Beta Kappa, Pi Gamma Mu, Phi Kappa Phi. Contbr. articles to profl. jours. Home: 583 W Shryer Roseville MN 55113

SWANEY, GORDON EDMUND, food co. exec.; b. Chillicothe, Ohio, Nov. 5, 1925; s. Arvel George and Helen (Weigand) S.; student Ohio Wesleyan U., 1943-44; B.S., Ind. U., 1947; m. Irene Olewnick, Aug. 9, 1952; children—Allyn, Laura, Rebecca. Sales promotion mgr. La Choy Food Products, Archbold, Ohio, 1947-50, asst. gen. sales mgr., 1950-52, mktg. mgr., 1952-57, dir. sales and mktg., 1957-62, gen. mgr., 1962-69; corp. v.p., asst. gen. mgr. grocery div. Beatrice Foods Co., Chgo., 1969, sr. group mgr., 1969—; dir. Farmers & Mchts. State Bank, Archbold, 1969—, Beatrice Foods, Ltd., Middlesex, Eng., 1964-76. Bd. dirs. Detwiler Meml. Hosp., Wauseon, Ohio, 1963-72; trustee Tri-State U., Angola, Ind., 1977—. Served as pilot USNR, 1943-45. Recipient Bowes Mktg. award Ind. U. 1947. Mem. Am. Legion (comdr. 1948), Phi Delta Theta. Roman Catholic. Clubs: Rotary, Lions (pres. 1960-61), Otsego Ski. Home: 306 Buckeye St Archbold OH 43502 Office: 901 Stryker St Archbold OH 43502

SWANK, JOHN LINDLEY, realtor; b. Eaton Rapids, Mich., Aug. 16, 1926; s. Wallace C. and Coral L. (Lindley) S.; B.A., Mich. State U., 1947; M.Ed., U. Colo., 1952; m. Jean Mae Williams Stark, Dec. 29, 1961; children (by previous marriage)—Robert Jon, Victoria Barbara. Elementary tchr., Longmont, Colo., 1950-52, Grosse Pointe, Mich., 1952-53, Midland, Mich., 1953-54; loan officer, chief appraiser Midland Fed. Savs. & Loan Assn., (Mich.), 1954-69; owner Swank's Appraisal and Real Estate Service, Midland, 1970—. Tchr. bus. Delta Coll., University Center, Mich., 1973—. Mem. bd. rev. City of Midland, 1959-60; pres. Mich. Eye Bank, 1974-75. Mem. Midland Bd. Realtors (pres. 1977—). Club: Lions. Home: 55 S Sandow Rd Midland MI 48640 Office: 2809 Ashman St Midland MI 48640

SWANN, JAMES, JR., banker; b. Eureka, Ill., Jan. 11, 1927; s. James Cayton and Minnie (Faubel) S.; B.S., Bradley U., 1953; m. Margaret Ann Troehler, Oct. 27, 1956. Pub. accountant Arthur Andersen & Co., Chgo., 1953-62, mgr. financial div., 1959-62; asst. dir. tech. div. Bank Adminstrn. Inst., Park Ridge, Ill., 1962-68; asst. v.p. audit div. 1st Nat. Bank Chgo., from 1968, now v.p. Served with USMC, 1944-48. C.P.A.; chartered bank auditor, certified internal auditor. Home: 388 N WinHaven Dr Elgin IL 60120 Office: One First National Plaza Chicago IL 60670

SWANN, MARGARET ANN TROEHLER, pub. health nurse; b. Euclid, Ohio, Sept. 4, 1930; d. Ted and Margaret (Hayes) Troehler; student Elgin Community Coll., 1952-53; B.S., Wayne State U., 1955; m. James J. Swann, Oct. 27, 1956. Staff nurse U. Hosp., Cleve., 1951, Sherman Hosp., Elgin, Ill., 1952-53, Harper Hosp., Detroit, 1953-54; teaching supr. Sherman Hosp., Elgin, Ill., 1955; exec. dir. Community Nursing Service of Proviso Twp., Bellwood, Ill., 1955-75. Vol. nurse ARC. Adv. bd. Triton Coll. Sch. Practical Nursing. Mem. West Suburban Homemakers (dir.), Coordinating Council of Proviso, Am., Ill. pub. health assns., Mt. Sinai Hosp. Sch. Nursing, Wayne State U. alumni assns., Sigma Theta Tau. Home: 388 N Win Haven Dr Elgin IL 60120

SWANSON, ARTHUR P., architect; b. Chgo., Nov. 25, 1906; s. Paul William and Ida (Mord) S.; B.S., Ill. Inst. Tech., 1929; m. Jean M. Lillyquist, Feb. 4, 1939; children—Paul W., Lynn Virginia (Mrs. Thomas Wilson), Carol Jean (Mrs. David Robbin), Christine Mary, Carl John. With N. Max Dunning Co., Chgo., 1929-32, Douglas Aircraft Co., Chgo., 1941-42; pvt. practice architecture, Des Plaines, Ill., 1932-41, Chgo., 1943-59, Skokie, Ill., 1959-66, Rosemont, Ill., 1966—; v.p. O'Hare Inn, Chgo., 1959-71. Registered architect, Ill. Mem. AIA, Western Srs. Golf Assn. (dir.). Clubs: Chicago Athletic Assn., Architects (past pres.) (Chgo.); Bobolink Golf; Quail Ridge (Fla.). Prin. works include O'Hare Inn, Des Plaines, 1959, Win Schuler Restaurants, Mich., 1960—, O'Hare East Office Bldg., Rosemont, 1966, Gen. Mills Office Bldg., Internat. Harvester, Ft. Wayne, O'Hare Internat. Transp. Center Office Bldg., Rosemont, 1968, Nat. Assn. Ind. Insurers Office Bldg., Des Plaines, 1971. Home: 1454 Estate Ln Glenview IL 60025 Office: 9501 W Devon Ave Rosemont IL 60018

SWANSON, DONALD WARREN, bicycle co. exec.; b. Wasco, Ill., Mar. 20, 1933; s. Wallace Austin and Louise Martha (Gerdau) S.; B.S., U. Ill., Urbana, 1960; m. JoAnne F. Gricunas, Oct. 14, 1956; children—Deanne Marie, Jill Louise. Sr. auditor Peat, Marwick, Mitchell & Co., Chgo., 1960-65; accountant Schwinn Bicycle Co., Chgo., 1965-66, office mgr. Midwest div., Elk Grove Village, Ill., 1966-68, controller div., 1968—, asst. sec.-treas. div., 1970—; pres. Swanson Mgmt. and Investment Co., Geneva, Ill., 1973—; treas. Geneva Investment Group (Ill.), 1976—. Chmn. finance com. Geneva Meth. Ch., 1972—, Geneva Meml. Community Center, 1974—, chmn. finance com. Geneva Bd. Edn. Dist. 304, 1977—. Served with U.S. Army, 1954-56. Mem. U. Ill. Alumni Assn., Nat. Assn. Accountants, Am. Accounting Assn., Fin. Execs. Inst. Club: Executives (Chgo.). Home: 119 Nebraska St Geneva IL 60134 Office: 2101 Arthur Ave Elk Grove Village IL 60007

SWANSON, EDWARD, librarian; b. Thief River Falls, Minn., Feb. 10, 1941; s. Eugene Nathaniel and Leone Marie (Peterson) S.; B.A., Macalester Coll., 1964; M.A., U. Minn., 1969. Asst. to librarian Macalester Coll., 1964-66, asst. circulation librarian, 1966-68; head newspaper div. Minn. Hist. Soc., St. Paul, 1968, head tech. services dept., 1969—. Lectr., Coll. St. Catherine, St. Paul, fall 1968. Bd. dirs., sec. Friends St. Paul Pub. Library, 1973—; bd. dirs. World Affairs Center, U. Minn., Twin City Boy Choir. Mem. ALA, Minn. Library Assn. (editor Bull. 1968-71, pres. 1972-73, dir. 1971-74), Twin Cities Manuscript Soc. (pres. 1972-74). Republican. Contbr. articles to profl. jours. Home: 1065 Portland Ave St Paul MN 55104 Office: 690 Cedar St St Paul MN 55101

SWANSON, EDWIN LEROY, sales exec.; b. Chgo., Mar. 14, 1938; s. Edwin Sevelius and Ethel Lillian (Telander) S.; B.S., Northwestern U., 1959, M.A., 1960; m. Barbara Ann Buehler, Apr. 28, 1962; children—Janet Barbara, Paul Edwin. Faculty, dept. radio-TV Northwestern U., Evanston, Ill., 1960-61; faculty, dir. closed circuit TV, Nat. Coll. Edn., Evanston, 1960-61; account exec., writer Gilbert Altschul Prodns., Chgo., 1961-65; account exec. Modern Talking Pictures, Inc., Chgo., 1965-72, sales mgr., 1972—, v.p., 1975—. Dir., program chmn. Chgo. Film Council, 1972-77, pres., 1977—; dir. U.S. Indsl. Film Festival, Chgo., 1972—; mem. caucus nominating com., Northbrook, Ill., 1971. Served with USAF, 1959-60. Recipient Gold Key award Pub. Relations News, 1976. Mem. Pub. Relations Soc. Am., Sales Mktg. Execs. Internat., Mktg. Communications Execs., Milw. Advt. Club. Presbyn. (elder 1972—). Home: 936 Cedar Ln Northbrook IL 60062 Office: 2020 Prudential Plaza Chicago IL 60601

SWANSON, FERN ROSE (MRS. WALTER E. SWANSON), educator; b. Kalmar Twp., Olmsted County, Minn., July 5, 1900; d. Henry E. and Susie (Hastings) Rose; student Winona (Minn.) Normal Coll., 1918-20; B.S., St. Cloud (Minn.) State Coll., 1955, M.S., 1958; m. Walter E. Swanson, June 24, 1928. Tchr. high sch. English, Latin, Eyota, Minn., 1920-21; tchr. jr. high sch. English, Appleton, Minn., 1921-22; tchr. elementary schs., Harmony, Minn., 1922-23; tchr. high sch. English, Latin, Augusta, Wis., 1923-24, South Haven, Minn., 1924-26; tchr. elementary, high sch. dramatics, Waterville, 1926-27; tchr. elementary schs., South Haven, 1927-41, 43-51, Silver Creek, Minn., 1941-43; tchr. elementary schs., Annandale, Minn., 1951-53, prin., 1953-67; tchr. elementary reading, Belgrade, Minn., 1967-71. Organizer, South Haven council Girl Scouts U.S.A., 1927, leader, 1927-30. Mem. Minn. Elementary Sch. Prins. Assn. 25 Year Club, NEA, Minn. Edn. Assn., Nat. Council Tchrs. English, Central Minn. Reading Council (past dir.), Internat., Minn. reading assns., D.A.R., Ladies of Grand Army Republic (pres. Minn. dept. 1974-77), Minn. Hist. Soc., Delta Kappa Gamma (past pres. Upsilon chpt.). Home: 541 Fairhaven Ave South Haven MN 55382

SWANSON, LESLIE CHARLES, writer, photographer, publisher; b. Moline, Ill., Aug. 21, 1905; s. Victor Ansfrid and Agnes Hilda (Wyman) S.; B.A., 1928; m. Gladys C. Huddleston, Aug. 10, 1940 (div. 1958); children—Vicki Swanson Wassenhove, Wendy; m. 2d, Mildred Clara Hyler, Oct. 7, 1972; stepchildren—Gary, Gerald, Sandra. State editor Davenport (Iowa) Times, 1929-45; free lance writer and photographer, Moline and Rock Island, Ill., 1945-60; contbr. articles to newspapers and mags.; pub. author Americana Books, Moline, 1960—; books include: Covered Bridges in Illinois, Iowa, and Wisconsin, 1960; Old Mills in the Mid-West, 1962; Canals of Mid-America, 1963; Rural One-Room Schools of Mid America, 1976. Pianist, mem. Tri-City Musical Soc., 1926—. Address: 824 20th Ave Moline IL 61265

SWANSON, PATRICIA ANN, library adminstr.; b. Sioux City, Ia., Mar. 18, 1936; d. Vernon W. and Clara May (Smith) Strain; B.A., U. No. Iowa, 1958; M.A., U. Minn., 1968; m. Sherman W. McKinley, June 28, 1958; 1 dau., Sandra Elaine; m. 2d, Thomas N. Swanson, Dec. 20, 1968; children—Tara Lynn, Karla Jean. Tchr. librarian East High Sch., Sioux City, Iowa, 1958-60; English tchr. high sch., Geneva, Iowa, 1960-61; head librarian pub. library, Hampton, Iowa, 1964-66; adminstr., library cons. N. Iowa Library Extension, Iowa State Traveling Library, Mason City, 1966-73; adminstr. North Central Regional Library System, 1973—. Mem. ALA, Am., Iowa, library assns., AAUW. Mem. Christian Ch. Mem. P.E.O. Home: 906 S Garfield Mason City IA 50401 Office: 500 College Dr Mason City IA 50401

SWANSON, PAUL EUGENE, veterinarian; b. Sikta, Kans., July 29, 1925; s. Thomas Felton and Leila (Gofroth) S.; B.S., Kans. State Tchrs. Coll., 1948; D.V.M., Kans. State U, 1952; m. Maxine Elizabeth Bradley, Jan. 4, 1968; children—Kandace Lianne, Paul Eugene II. Owner, Swanson Trailer Sales, Manhattan, Kans., 1948-66; pres., veterinarian Swanson Small Animal Hosp., Inc., Joplin, Mo., 1952—; pres. Joplin Miracle Water Co., 1975—; pres. Pier I Imports Stores, 1975; owner Shoal Creek Constrn. Co., Joplin, 1971—; owner Around Town Center, 1972—, pres. Around Town Realty, 1972—. Mem. Joplin Health Welfare Bd., 1954-67. Served with U.S. Army, 1942-44. Mem. AVMA, Mo., Southwestern veterinary med. assns., Realtors Assn., Joplin Bd. Realtors. Methodist. Clubs: Elks, Masons, Shriners. Home: Route 2 Box 144 Lot 10 Joplin MO 64801 Office: 2800 Rangeline St Joplin MO 64801

SWANSON, PAUL JOHN, JR., educator; b. Crawfordsville, Ind., May 10, 1934; s. Paul John and Helen (Bath) S.; student DePauw U., 1952; B.S. in Accountancy, U. Ill., 1959, B.S. in Econ. and Fin., 1960, M.S. in Fin., 1962, Ph.D., 1966. Grad. teaching asst. U. Ill., Urbana, 1960-65, grad. research asst., 1964-65; asst. prof. finance U. Cin., 1965-67, asso. prof., 1967—, prof.-in-charge dept. quantitative analysis, 1967-68. Cons. local bus. and govt. agencies. Served with AUS, 1956-58. Mem. Nat. Def. Exec. Res., Inst. Mgmt. Scis. (past pres. Miami Valley chpt.), Ops. Research Soc. Am., Am., Midwest finance assns., Fin. Analysts Soc., Inst. Chartered Fin. Analysts, Am. Statis. Assn., Delta Chi, Delta Sigma Pi. Republican. Presbyterian. Home: 3441 Telford St Cincinnati OH 45220

SWANSON, PAUL REGINALD, clergyman, educator; b. Moline, Ill., June 10, 1928; s. Herbert C.M. and Regina A.N. (Rosenberg) S.; A.B., Augustana Coll., Rock Island, Ill., 1950; M.Div., Augustana Theol. Sem., 1955; S.T.M., Andover-Newton (Mass.) Theol. Sch., 1958; Ph.D. (Danielsen fellow), Boston U., 1962; m. Cordelia Kathleen Morrison, May 25, 1957; children—Jonathan Paul, Rosanne Cordelia. Ordained to ministry Lutheran Ch., 1955; pastor in Page City, Kans., 1955-56; chaplain Mass. Gen. Hosp., Boston, 1957-62; faculty pastoral care Luth. Sch. Theology, Chgo., 1962—; dir. Marriage and Family Counseling Service Christ Hosp., Oak Lawn, Ill., 1975—; pres. Council Chs. Rock Island (Ill.) and Scott County (Iowa), 1965-66. Chmn. bd. Rock Island County Council Alcoholism, 1955-56; v.p. Rock Island County Mental Health Assn., 1966. Fellow Judge Baker Guidance Center, Boston, 1957-58; Marriage Counseling fellow Marriage Council Phila., 1969-70. Diplomate Am. Assn. Pastoral Counselors; certified psychotherapist Council Nat. Register Health Service Providers in Psychology, 1975. Fellow Coll. Chaplains of Am. Protestant Hosp. Assn.; mem. Assn. Clin. Pastoral Edn. (chaplain supr. clin. pastoral edn.), Am. Assn. Marriage and Family Counselors (clin. mem.). Home: Box 1230 41 Aspen Rd Ogden Dunes Portage IN 46368 Office: 1100 E 55th St Chicago IL 60615

SWANSON, RANDALL COVER, safety cons.; b. Stillwater, Minn., Oct. 15, 1903; s. Edward N. and Harriet (Cover) S.; B.S., U. Minn., 1926; postgrad. Ohio State U., 1927; m. Karine Dokken, June 24, 1935; children—Karen (Mrs. Theodore Bolles), Neil E., Kenneth R. Agrl. instr., Oak Hill, Ohio, 1926-27, Stanley, Wis., 1927-30; prin. Dunn County Sch. Agr., Menomonie, Wis., 1930-33; county agrl. agt. Outagamie County, Appleton, Wis., 1934-39, Milwaukee County, Wis., 1939-43; mem. faculty, farm safety specialist U. Wis., 1943-67; now pres. Sunnyside Seed Farms, Inc., Farm and Forest Enterprises, Inc., Middleton, Wis. Mem. Pres.'s Occupational Safety Conf., 1957. Named man of year, Appleton, Wis. Jr. C. of C., 1937, hon. Wis. farmer, Future Farmers Am., 1956; recipient award, Milw. Jour., 1967, Fellow Am. Soc. Agrl. Engrs. (hon.); mem. Nat. safety Council (dir.), Nat. Inst. Farm Safety (pres., exec. sec.), Alpha Zeta, Alpha Gamma Rho, Epsilon Sigma Phi. Republican. Lutheran. Elk. Club: West Side Business Men's (Madison, Wis.). Home: 937 Waban Hill Madison WI 53711 Office: Route 1 Middleton WI 53562

SWANSON, ROBERT MARTIN, hosp. adminstr.; b. Bell, Calif., Oct. 14, 1940; s. Harold M. and Elsie Lorraine (Allison) S.; A.B., Long Beach (Calif.) State Coll., 1963; M.A., U. Iowa, 1965; Ph.D., U. Calif., Los Angeles, 1970; m. Patricia Ann Roberts, Dec. 20, 1962. Dir., Office of Mental Health Research, U. Iowa, Iowa City, 1966-70; research dir. Health Planning Council, St. Paul, 1970-73; exec. dir. Kansas City (Mo.) Health Plan, 1973-76; asst. dir. St. Louis U. Hosps., 1976—; dir. Organizational Research & Devel. Corp., Kansas City, 1973—; adj. prof. Webster Coll., St. Louis, 1975—; spl. cons. to Kansas City (Mo.) Health Dept., 1975-76; tech. cons. Health Services Adminstrn., HEW, 1973-75; coordinator St. Louis Community-Univ. Conf., 1977; mem. health affairs task force Mo. Catholic Conf., 1977. Named Adm. in Nebr. Navy, 1971; State of Iowa grantee, 1969. Mem. Nat. Assn. for Hosp. Devel., Advt. Club Greater St. Louis, Nat. Beagle Club, Basset Hound Club Am., Zeta Beta Tau. Republican. Roman Catholic. Contbr. articles on health services to profl. jours. Home: 320 Meramec Station Rd Manchester MO 63011 Office: 1325 S Grand Blvd St Louis MO 63104

SWANSTONE, FLOYD TRUMAN, veterinarian; b. Boonville, Mo., July 1, 1925; s. Truman Hickox and Grace Magdalene (Oerly) S.; student Central Meth. Coll., 1942-44, Northwestern U., 1944-45; B.S., U. Mo., 1948, D.V.M., 1954; m. Alice Estelle Hyers, Oct. 11, 1948; children—Helen Elizabeth, Sharon Ann (Mrs. William L. Long III), Linda Sue, Shirley Jean. Instr. agr. extension U. Mo., 1948-50; practice vet. medicine, Plattsburg, 1954-55, Boonville, 1955—; owner, mgr. Swanstone's Vet. Hosp., Boonville, 1956-75, Swanstone's Dog Kennels, Boonville, 1959—; real estate broker. Served to lt. (j.g.) USNR, 1943-46. Mem. Am., Mo., West Central Mo. vet. med. assns., U. Mo. Alumni Assn., C. of C., V.F.W., Internat. Platform Assn., Am. Legion. Mem. Christian Ch. (elder 1976-77, pres. Christian men's fellowship 1968—). Mason (Shriner), Odd Fellow, Eagle. Club: Boonville Rod and Gun. Home: Rural Route 1 Boonville MO 65233 Office: Rural Route 2 Boonville MO 65233

SWANSTROM, KATHRYN RAYMOND, conv. mgmt. exec.; b. Milw., Sept. 5, 1907; d. William Hyland and Jessie Viola (Bliss) Raymond; student Bryant and Stratton Bus. Coll., 1927-28; m. Luther D. Swanstrom, Aug. 27, 1937; 1 son, William Hyland Raymond. Caterer, Racine, Wis., 1926; field rep., asst. mgr. Master Reporting Co., 1936-52; dir. sec. Diesel-Ritter Corp., 1942-46; pres. Kay C. Raymond Assos., 1952—; v.p., treas. Kenneth G. MacKenzie Assos., 1954—. Asst. sec. nat. com. U.S.A. 3d World Petroleum Congress, 1950-51. Sec. Ridge Civic Council, 1940-60; sec. Police Traffic Safety Com., Mayor's Com. Keeping Chgo. Clean. State chmn. legislation Ill. Congress Parents and Tchrs. Rep. state central committeewoman, 1938-44, asst. ofcl. reporter Rep. Nat. Conv., 1940-48. Mem. Anti-Cruelty Soc., AIM, Soc. Mayflower Descs., D.A.R., Nat. Geog. Soc., ASTM, Ladies Oriental Shrine N. Am., Founders, Patriots (nat. councillor), Aux. Ancient Honorable Arty. Co. of Boston (nat. pres. 1977—), John Alden Kindred, Internat. Platform Assn., Hugenot Soc., Pi Omicron (nat. pres. 1950-54). Republican. Episcopalian. Clubs: Beverly Hills Woman's Crescendo. Address: 9027 S Damen Ave Chicago IL 60620 also 3 Old Hill Farms Rd Westport CT 06880

SWANSTROM, THOMAS EVAN, retail co. exec.; b. Green Bay, Wis., May 17, 1939; s. Alfred Enoch and Elizabeth (Thomas) S.; student, U. Notre Dame, 1957-59; B.A., U. Wis., 1962, M.A., 1963; postgrad. Am. U., 1963-65. Economist, U.S. Dept. Labor, Washington, 1963-66; dir. research Population Reference Bur., Washington, 1966-68; economist Sears Roebuck & Co., Chgo., 1968-70, market analyst, 1970-72, catalog research mgr., 1972-74, mgr. econ. and sales forecasting, 1974—. Mem. Am. Mktg. Assn., Am. Statis. Assn., Nat. Assn. Bus. Economists. Home: 1107 W George St Chicago IL 60657 Office: D/720 Sears Tower Chicago IL 60684

SWARD, JON MICHAEL, psychologist; b. Larned, Kans., May 10, 1944; s. Carl Ernest and Alice (Nilsen) S.; B.S. cum laude, Sterling Coll., 1967; M.A. (Nat. Rehab. Counseling Study fellow), Mich. State U., 1969; postgrad. Kans. State U. Psychologist, Ingham County Juvenile Ct., Lansing, Mich., 1968; clin. psychologist Larned State Hosp., 1968-69; psychologist, exec. dir. Sunflower Mental Health Center, Concordia, Kans., 1970—. Instr., Cloud County Community Coll., Concordia. Campaign coordinator Frizzell for Gov., 1970; mem. speakers bur. Kans. Young Republicans, 1970-71. Mem. Kans., Western Kans. psychol. assns., Profl. Counselors Assn., Internat. Platform Assn., Am. Mental Health Counselors Assn., Concordia C. of C., Jr. C. of C., Pi Gamma Mu. Baptist. Moose. Home: Route 3 Concordia KS 66901 Office: 520B Washington St Concordia KS 66901

SWART, HANNAH WERWATH, museum curator; b. Milw., Mar. 21, 1913; d. Oscar and Hannah (Seelhorst) Werwath; student Milw. Downer Coll., part-time 1931-34, U. Wis., 1933-36, Milw. Sch. Engring., 1933-46; m. George Jerry Swart, Oct. 7, 1937; children—Greta Toni, JoHannah Werwath Nicholai, George Jerry Jr., Paul Oscar. Head dept. records, registrar coll. engring. Milw. Sch. Engring., 1931-51, mem. corp., 1952—, also cons. dept. alumni affairs; curator Hoard Hist. Mus., Fort Atkinson, Wis., 1967—. Mem. Wis. Gov.'s Bicentennial Commn. Bd. dirs. Girl Scouts Am. Recipient Bronze Statue, Girl Scouts U.S.A., Nat. Thanks badge, 1967. Mem. State Hist. Soc. Wis. (past pres. women's aux., life mem.), Watertown (hon. life), Fort Atkinson (program chmn.) hist. socs., Wis. Acad. Scis., Arts and Letters (councilor-at-large). Clubs: Tuesday, Quarter Century. Author: Footsteps of our Founding Fathers, 1963; Biography of General Henry Atkinson, 1964; Margarethe Meyer Schurz, 1967; Koshkonong Country: A History of Jefferson County. Home: Rural Route 3 Box 27 Fort Atkinson WI 53538 Office: Hoard Historical Museum Merchants Ave Fort Atkinson WI 53538

SWARTHOUT, HERBERT MARION, ins. exec.; b. Sioux Falls, S.D., Aug. 29, 1900; s. Earl Beagle and Jennie Laura (Aldrich) S.; student Nebr. U., 1920-21, Washington U., 1922; grad. Am. Coll. Life Underwriters, 1942; m. Lila Ellen Sosamon, Dec. 21, 1926; 1 dau., Joan Sosamon (Mrs. Robert Paul Wahlstedt). In life ins. bus., 1928—, specializing in estate planning; rep. Mut. Benefit Life Ins. Co. of N.J., 1947—; founder Uniformed Services Benefit Assn., exec. sec., 1959-75; pres. Herrick Fin. Services, Inc. Active YMCA; pres., gen. chmn. Heart Am. Meml. Torch Ceremony, 1963-64. Mem. Nebr. U. Alumni Assn. (past pres. Kansas City chpt.), Life Underwriters Assn. Kansas City, Million Dollar Round Table (life), Nat. Assn. Life Underwriters, Am. Soc. C.L.U.'s, S.R. (pres. Kansas City 1956—, pres. Mo. soc. 1958-59), Assn. Advanced Life Underwriters, Kansas City Art Inst. Mem. Christian Ch. (deacon). Mason (K.T., Shriner, Jester), Rotarian. Clubs: Kansas City, Advertising and Sales Executives, Carriage, Eleven-Eleven (Kansas City, Mo.). Contbr. articles to profl. jours. Speaker on estate planning. Home: 850 W 55th St Kansas City MO 64113 Office: 1221 Baltimore Ave Kansas City MO 64105

SWARTOUT, CHARLES WILLIAM, mgmt. cons.; b. St. Louis, Feb. 26, 1915; s. William Cornelius and Agnes Sybil (Dole) S.; B.S., U. Mich., 1937; m. June Kathryn Wiley, July 19, 1942; children—William Roy, Carol Alice. Devel. engr. Linde Air Products Co., Buffalo, 1937-42; chief engr. Mallinckrodt, Inc., St. Louis, 1946-55, ops. mgr., 1955-62; gen. mgr., personnel div., 1962—, v.p., 1964-77; mgmt. cons., St. Louis, 1977—. Vice chmn. Gateway dist. St. Louis Area council Boy Scouts Am.; active St. Louis area United Way, Jr. Achievement. Bd. dirs. Opportunities Industrialization Center, St. Louis; adv. com. St. Louis Community Coll.; fin. com. Mo. Bapt. Hosp. Served to maj. AUS, 1942-46. Recipient Silver Beaver Award, Boy Scouts Am., 1973. Fellow Am. Inst. Chem. Engrs.; mem. Am. Assn. Indsl. Mgmt. of Mo. (dir.), Industries of Mo. (dir.), Pharm. Mfg. Assn., NAM, Mfg. Chemists Assn., Am. Chem. Soc., Am. Soc. for Personnel Adminstrn., Am. Meteorol. Soc. Presbyn. Club: Media. Patentee liquid oxygen explosives and flame piercing of rock. Home: 217 Calverton Rd Saint Louis MO 63135 Office: 675 Brown Rd PO Box 5840 Saint Louis MO 63134

SWARTWOUT, JOSEPH RODOLPH, physician; b. Pascagoula, Miss., June 17, 1925; s. Thomas Roswell and Marshall (Coleman) S.; student Miss. Coll., 1943-44; M.D., Tulane U., 1951; m. Dorothy Ann York, June 10, 1948; children—Susan, Richard Milton, James Edward, Charles John, Laura. Intern Touro Infirmary, New Orleans, 1951-52; asst. obstetrics and medicine Tulane U., 1952-53, instr., 1955-60; Nat. Found. fellow Harvard, 1953-55; asst. medicine Peter Bent Brigham Hosp., Boston, asso. obstet. research Boston Lying-in Hosp., 1953-55; asst. prof. U. Pitts., 1960-61; asso. prof. Emory U., Atlanta, 1961-66; asso. prof. obstetrics and gynecology U. Chgo., 1967—; med. dir. outpatient dept. Chgo. Lying-In Hosp. Bd. dirs. Ill. Family Planning Council, Abortion Rights Assn. Ill. Served with USNR, 1943-46. Fellow Am. Coll. Obstetricians and Gynecologists, Council Clin. Cardiology Am. Heart Assn., Am. Acad. Reproductive Medicine; mem. Orleans Parish Med. Soc., Chgo. Heart Assn., Population Assn. Am., AAAS, Planned Parenthood Assn., N.Y. Acad. Scis., Soc. Gynecol. Investigation, Am. Pub. Health Assn. Home: 3039 Scott Crescent Flossmoor IL 60422 Office: 5841 S Maryland Ave Chicago IL 60637

SWARTZ, EDWARD MORTON, dentist; b. Chgo., June 11, 1938; s. Aaron and Frances (Marc) S.; B.S., U. Chgo., 1960; D.D.S., U. Ill., 1963; m. Doreen Minus, Aug. 11, 1962; children—Arden, Alan, Heidi. Practice dentistry, Niles, Ill., 1965—. Served with AUS, 1963-65. Mem. Am. Dental Assn., Am. Analgesia Soc., N.W. Acad. Applied Dental Econs., Acad. Gen. Dentistry (past editor Ill. Pulse), Niles C. of C. Club: Rotary. Contbg. author: Bloom's Textbook Histology. Contbr. articles profl. publs.; author lectrs. relative analgesia in modern dentistry. Home: 818 Prairie Lawn Rd Glenview IL 60025 Office: 7942 W Oakton St Niles IL 60648

SWARTZ, HARRY LEO, farm mgr. and appraiser; b. Mansfield, Ill., May 8, 1921; s. Francis Edward and Eva Opal (Swinney) S.; student U. Ill., 1939-40, 46-47; m. Sylvia L. Twedt, June 19, 1941; children—Patricia (Mrs. Darrell Brown), Robert Lee. Owner, Swartz Agrl. Service, farm mgmt., appraisals, real estate and cons., Champaign, Ill., 1960—. Agrl. cons. Comml. Bank of Champaign. Pres., Champaign County Forest Preserve 1976—; mem. Champaign County Zoning Commn., 1970-73. Bd. dirs., vice chmn. Champaign County Devel. Council Found., chmn. land trusteeship and meml. endowment com., 1973—. Served with M.C., AUS, 1942-46. Mem. Ill. Inst. Farm and Land Brokers (pres. 1960-61), E. Central Ill. Soc. Profl. Farm Mgrs. and Rural Appraisers (pres. 1969-70), Champaign County Agr. Club (sec. 1974-75), Champaign C. of C. (chmn. agrl. com. 1968-69). Baptist. Kiwanian (chmn. agrl. com. 1969-70), Moose. Home: 27 Spring Lake Mahomet IL 61853 Office: 1 Comml Bank Plaza Champaign IL 61820

SWARTZENDRUBER, HARLAN LEE, textile products exec.; b. Harper, Kans., Nov. 23, 1922; s. Ray Henry and Maude Agnes (Driskell) S.; student pub. schs.; m. Melba Jean Boatright, June 4, 1943; children—Vicki Lee (Mrs. Carter), Jill Ann (Mrs. Larry White). Chmn. bd., dir. Wichita Canvas Supply; pres., dir. Comml. Properties, Inc.; v.p., dir. Legg Co., Inc., Halstead, Kans.; partner S & R Properties, Okla. and Kans.; dir. Del City Wire Co., Inc., Oklahoma City. Served with AUS, World War II; ETO. Club: Crestview Country (Wichita). Home: 101 Ridgecrest St Wichita KS 67218 Office: 2943 S Kansas St Wichita KS 67216

SWARTZLANDER, GARELD WILLIAM, electronics engr.; b. Milan, Ohio, Jan. 4, 1908; s. Clarence Henry and Mary Amelia (Paul) S.; student, Tri-State Bus. U., Toledo, 1926, Port Arthur (Tex.) Radio Coll., 1935; m. Iva Lucille Rafferty, July 1, 1930; children—David Lee, Janet Arlene Swartzlander Althoff. With Wabash R.R. Ann Arbor div., 1926-33; self-employed radio engr., Gibsonburg, Ohio, 1935-37, police radio constrn. engr., chief engr., various cities, 1937-57; chief engr., cons. engring., WFRO radio station, Fremont, Ohio, 1945-48; chief engr. Swartzlander Radio Ltd., Fremont, 1957—; cons. in field. Dir. United Fund, Fremont, 1977—. Mem. Assod. Police Communications Officers (mem. Frequency Allocations Com.), Amateur Radio Relay League, Sandusky Valley Amateur Radio Club (trustee), IEEE (life). Lutheran. Clubs: Rotary, Hi Twelve, Shriners (Fremont, pres. 1969), Fraternal Order Police. Home: 120 S Granville Blvd Fremont OH 43420 Office: 1524 Oak Harbor Road Fremont OH 43420

SWEARINGEN, GERALD BRENT, optometrist; b. Kansas City, Kans., Nov. 5, 1946; s. Gerald Jack and Amanda Mildred (Sapp) S.; A.A., S.W. Bapt. Coll., 1966; B.S., So. Coll. Optometry, 1969, D.Optometry, 1969; m. Marilyn Ann Courdin, July 19, 1969; children—Erica Ann, Brent Courdin, Andrea Celeste. Pvt. optometric practice, Lamar, Mo., 1969—. Sec. bd. dirs. Dale Phipps Ford-Mercury, Inc. Mem. Am., Mo. (dir. 1976-78), S.W. Mo. (v.p. 1970-72, pres. 1976-77) optometric assns., Lamar C. of C. Republican. Baptist (deacon). Rotarian (v.p. 1977-78). Home: Route 4 Lamar MO 64759 Office: Box 191 802 Gulf St Lamar MO 64759

SWEARINGEN, JOHN ELDRED, oil exec.; b. Columbia, S.C., Sept. 7, 1918; s. John Eldred and Mary (Hough) S.; B.S., U. S.C., 1938; M.S., Carnegie-Mellon U., 1939; Eng.D., S.D. Sch. Mines and Tech., 1960; LL.D., Knox Coll., 1962, DePauw U., 1964, U. S.C., 1965, Ill. Coll., 1968, Butler U., 1968, Samford U., 1973, Calumet Coll., 1976; D.L.H., Nat. Coll. Edn., 1967; Dr. Bus. Mgmt., Ind. Inst. Tech., 1973; m. Bonnie L. Bolding, May 18, 1969; children (by previous marriage)—Marcia Lynn (Mrs. F.G. Pfleeger), Sarah Kathryn (Mrs. T.E. Origer), Linda Sue. Chem. engr. research dept. Standard Oil Co. (Ind.), Whiting, Ind., 1939-47; various positions Amoco Production Co., 1947-51, gen. mgr. prodn. Standard Oil Co. (Ind.), Chgo., 1951, dir., 1952—, v.p. prodn., 1954-56, exec. v.p., 1956-58, pres., 1958-65, chmn. bd., 1965—, chief exec. officer, 1960—; dir. Chase Manhattan Corp., N.Y.C., First Nat. Bank Chgo., Am. Nat. Bank & Trust Co. Chgo., Am. Petroleum Inst. Bd. dirs. Northwestern Meml. Hosp., 1965—, Hwy. Users Fedn. for Safety and Mobility, 1969-75, McGraw Wildlife Found., 1964-75; bd. dirs. Automotive Safety Found., 1959-69, chmn., 1962-64; trustee Carnegie-Mellon U., 1960—, DePauw U., 1966—, Orchestral Assn. Chgo., 1973—; mem. adv. bd. Hoover Inst. War Revolution and Peace, 1967—. Decorated Order of Jaj (Iran), Commendatore Dell'Ordine Del Merito Della Repubblica Italiana. Fellow Am. Inst. Chem. Engrs.; mem. Nat. Petroleum Council (chmn. 1974-76), Nat. Acad. Engring., Am. Inst. Mining and Metall. Engrs., Am. Chem. Soc., Phi Beta Kappa, Sigma Xi, Omicron Delta Kappa, Tau Beta Pi. Clubs: Chicago, Commercial, Racquet, Mid-America, Economic, Executives (Chgo.); Glen View (Golf, Ill.); Old Elm (Lake Forest, Ill.); Links (N.Y.C.); Bohemian (San Francisco); Eldorado Country (Palm Springs, Calif.). Home: 1420 Lake Shore Dr Chicago IL 60610 Office: 200 E Randolph Dr Chicaogo IL 60601

SWEARINGIN, JOHN DAVID, farmer; b. Carrollton, Mo., June 27, 1948; s. Clyde Willis and Nellie Alpha Delila (Lemasters) S.; B.S. cum laude (honors scholar), U. Mo., 1970, M.S., 1971; m. Peggy Sue Francis, May 27, 1973. Sec.-treas. Swearingin Bros. Farms, Inc., Carrollton, Mo., 1970—; adv. mem. to bd. dirs. Mo. Farm Bur., 1977—. Mem. Carroll County Pork Producers (dir. 1974—), Mo. Farm Bur., Am. Soc. Agrl. Engrs., Tau Beta Pi, Alpha Epsilon, Gamma Sigma Delta, Pi Mu Epsilon. Baptist (chmn. deacons 1974—, asst. moderator, youth dir. 1974—). Home: Route 5 Carrollton MO 64633

SWEDO, JOHN LAWRENCE, JR., electron microscopist; b. Detroit, Feb. 28, 1939; s. John and Helen M. (Mamula) S.; B.S., Detroit Inst. Tech., 1963. Electron microscopist, 1963—; with Oreg. Regional Primate Research Center, Beaverton, 1965-66; with Edsel B. Ford Inst., Detroit, 1963-65, 1966—. Mem. Mich. Electron Microscopy Forum (treas. 1969-70), Electron Microscopy Soc. Am., Polish Nat. Alliance, Kappa Sigma Kappa. Roman Catholic. Contbr. articles to profl. jours. Home: 18904 Runyon St Detroit MI 48234 Office: 2799 W Grand Blvd Detroit MI 48202

SWEENEY, JOSEPH PATRICK, broadcasting co. exec.; b. Kokomo, Ind., Apr. 20, 1925; s. James B. and Anna (Cunningham) S.; student Sprayberry Acad. Radio, 1950-52; m. Patricia A. Smith, July 4, 1959; children—Cheryl, Michael, Maureen. With Delco Radio div. Gen. Motors Corp., Kokomo, 1952-62, electronics products trouble shooter, 1952-56, reliability engring. tester, 1956-62; founding pres. Fidelity Broadcasting Co., Inc., Rochester, Ind., 1962—, also subs. stations WFKO, Kokomo, WVTL, Monticello, Ind., WFDT, Columbia City, Ind., WROI, Rochester. Elk, Kiwanian. Home: Rural Route 6 Box 45 Rochester IN 46975 Office: 116 W 9th St Rochester IN 46975

SWEET, HENRIETTA MARY DORSEY, ceramics artist and educator; b. St. Louis, Dec. 5, 1911; d. Nicholas Brice and Lillian Helen C. (Heinecke) Dorsey; B.S. in Bus. Mgmt., Webster Groves Coll., 1934; B.A., Layton Sch. Arts, 1967; m. Arthur Earl Sweet, Dec. 9, 1934; 1 foster son, Raymond J. Dept. head Stix Baer Fuller of St. Louis, 1929; purchasing agt. Sears Roebuck & Co., St. Louis, 1930-34; color cons. Sweet Decorating Co., St. Louis, 1934-45; owner, operator, tchr. Sweets Ceramic Studio, Mukwonago, Wis., 1961—. Active 4-H; bd. dirs., mem. sch. bd. Stone Sch., Mukwonago, Wis., 1944-48, dir. United Consol. Elementary Sch., 1948-54, treas., 1954-64. Recipient Lit. award 4-H award Waukesha County (Wis.) 4-H, 1959, 25 Yr. Service award, 1969. Mem. Badger (Service award 1972), Greater Milw. ceramic assns., 4-H Exec. Bd. League, Waukesha County Home Demonstration Club (treas. bd.). Democrat. Lutheran. Home and Office: Route 1 Box 52 Mukwonago WI 53149

SWEET, JACK DARRELL, lawyer, banker; b. S. Lyon, Mich., Aug. 9, 1929; s. Reynold Milo and Bessie May (Havershaw) S.; B.A., Mich. State U., 1951; J.D., U. Mich., 1957; m. Margaret Dickson Owens, Jan. 14, 1956. Admitted to Ill. bar, 1957, Mich. bar, 1957; atty. Chgo. Title & Trust, 1957-58; regional mgr. Burton Abstract & Title, Flint, Mich., 1959-62; builder, developer, Grand Blanc, Mich., 1962-65; mortgage banker Guardian Mortgage Co., Grand Blanc, Mich., 1965—; dir. First Security Bank, Grand Blanc, Mich., 1974—, Pacesetter Corp., Grand Rapids, Mich., 1977—. Served with USAF, 1952-56. Mem. Am. Bar Assn., Mortgage Bankers Assn. of Mich., Mortgage Bankers Assn. of Dallas. Clubs: Flint Golf, Warwick Hills Golf and Country, Univ., Country of Sarasota (Fla.); Los Rios Country (Dallas). Home: 6503 Carriage Hill Dr Grand Blanc MI 48439 Office: G8455 S Saginaw St Grand Blanc MI 48439

SWEET, PHILIP WHITFORD KIRKLAND, JR., banker; b. Mt. Vernon, N.Y., Dec. 31, 1927; s. Philip Whitford Kirkland and Katharine (Buhl) S.; A.B., Harvard U., 1950; M.B.A., U. Chgo., 1957; m. Nancy Frederick, July 23, 1950; children—Sandra Harkness, Philip Whitford Kirkland, III, David A.F. With No. Trust Co., Chgo., 1953—, sr. v.p. bond dept., 1968-74, exec. v.p. bank, 1974-75, pres., dir., 1975—; pres., dir. Nortrust Corp., 1975—. Vestryman, Ch. of Holy Spirit, Lake Forest, Ill., 1971-74; chmn. bus. div. Chgo. Heart Assn., 1974-76; mem. bus. adv. council Chgo. Urban League; mem. Ill. com. United Negro Coll. Fund, Northwestern Assos.; alderman, Lake Forest, 1972-74; bd. dirs. Johnston R. Bowman Health Center for Elderly, U. Chgo. Council on Grad. Sch. Bus.; trustee Lake Forest Improvement Trust. Mem. Assn. Res. City Bankers. Clubs: Bankers, Econ., Attic, Bond, Chgo., Commonwealth (Chgo.); Onwentsia, Shoreacres, Old Elm. Home: 990 Ringwood Rd Lake Forest IL 60045 Office: 50 S LaSalle St Chicago IL 60675

SWEEZY, JOHN WILLIAM, polit. mgr.; b. Indpls., Nov. 14, 1932; s. William Charles and Zuma Frances (McNew) S.; B.S. in Mech. Engring., Purdue U., 1956; M.B.A., Ind. U., 1958; student Butler U., 1953-54, U. Ga., 1954-55, Ind. Central Coll., 1959; m. Carole Suzanne Harman, July 14, 1956; children—John William, Bradley E. Design, test engr. Allison div. Gen. Motors Corp., Indpls., 1953-57; power sales engr. Indpls. Power & Light Co., 1958-69; dir. pub. works City of Indpls., 1970-72; chmn. Marion County Republican Central Com., 1972—; mng. partner MCLB Co., Indpls., 1972—; dir. Lorco Engring., Indpls. Chmn. 11th Dist. Rep. Com., 1970, 73—; alt. del. Rep. Nat. Conv., 1968, del., 1972; mem. Warren Schs. Citizens Screening Com., 1958-72. Served with AUS, 1953-55. Mem. Sigma Iota Epsilon. Home: 166 N Gibson Indianapolis IN 46219 Office: 47 E Washington St Indianapolis IN 46204

SWENEY, ARTHUR BARCLAY, educator; b. Champaign, Ill., Apr. 30, 1923; s. Merle Arthur and Edith I. (Sendenburgh) S.; B.S., U. Ill., 1947, M.S.W., 1949; Ph.D., U. Houston, 1958; m. Martha Royce, June 7, 1944 (div. May 1961); children—Ann, Deirdre, Michael; m. 2d, Raquel Zaldivar, Oct. 20, 1961; children—Rachel, Rebecca, Robert, Raymond, Richard. Program dir. Ripley House, Houston, 1949-50; dir. Rusk Settlement, Houston, 1950-53; lectr. U. Houston, 1956-58, sch. social worker, 1954-58; research asso. U. Ill., 1958-60, asst. prof., 1960-62; asso. prof. Tex. Tech. U., 1962-65, prof., 1965-68; prof., adminstr., dir. Center Human Appraisal, Wichita State U., 1968—. Cons. Big Spring State Hosp., Nat. Tng. and Testing, Rexall Chem., Skelly Oil, Cessna Aircraft, Beech Aircraft, U.S. Army, USAF; v.p. Mgmt. Research and Devel. Inst.; pres. Test Systems Inc. Served with Signal Corps, AUS, 1943-46. Mem. Soc. Multivariate Exptl. Psychology, Psychometric Soc., Am., Southwestern psychol. assns. Author: Fear Anxiety Profile, 1963; Defense Mechanism Index, 1964; Response Analysis, 1963; Response to Power Measure, 1970; Chromatic Differential Scale, 1970; Motivation Recruitment Model, 1976; Leadership: The Management of Power and Obligation, 1977. Home: 4300 Janesville St Wichita KS 67220

SWENSON, ALFRED THOMAS, architect; b. Mpls., July 12, 1935; s. Alfred C. and Beatrice (Kauffman) S.; student Carleton Coll., 1953-55; B.Arch., Ill. Inst. Tech., 1960, M.Arch., 1968; m. Pao-Chi Chang, Mar. 3, 1962. Sr. designer, C.F. Murphy Assos., Architects, Chgo., 1960-66; research dir. Pub. Bldg. Commn. of Chgo., 1968-73; prin. Swenson & Chang, Architects, Chgo., 1973—; asso. prof. architecture Ill. Inst. Tech., 1966—. Mem. AIA, AAUP, Ill. Soc. Architects, Alpha Chi Rho. Club: Arts Club Chgo. Sr. archtl. designer Chgo. Civic Center Bldg., 1965; prin. archtl. works include IBM Office Bldg., Lafayette, Ind., Superframe Project. Home: 5530 South Shore Dr Chicago IL 60637 Office: 18 S Michigan Ave Chicago IL 60603

SWENSON, COURTLAND SEVANDER, educator; b. Akron, Iowa, July 2, 1936; s. Clifford Sevander and Selma Lillian (Swanson) S.; B.F.A., U. S.D., 1958, M.Mus., 1962; postgrad. U. Ill., 1968-69; postgrad. U. Würzburg (Ger.); m. Bonnie Jan Hull, Aug. 23, 1966; children—Callan Sevander, Corey McAllister. Tchr. music Sibley (Iowa) Pub. Schs., 1958-60; faculty U. S.D., Vermillion, 1960—, prof. music, 1973—; instr., chmn. fine arts Ramey AFB, P.R., 1971-72; musical dir. Black Hills Playhouse, 1963—; cons. music, Guatemala, 1976-77. Prin. percussionist Sioux City (Ia.) Symphony, 1964-71; prin. timpanist Sioux Falls (S.D.) Symphony, 1973—. Bd. dirs. Arnie B. Larson Shrine to Music of Antique Instruments, 1970-75. Named Best Tchr. U. S.D., 1967. Mem. AAUP, Nat. Assn. Rudimental Drummers, Percussive Arts Soc., Lambda Chi. Home: 334 N Plum St Vermillion SD 57069

SWERHONE, PETER EDWARD, hosp. exec.; b. Canora, Sask., Can., May 30, 1931; s. Daniel and Marie (Zabinsky) S.; B.A., B. Commerce, U. Sask., 1953; diploma hosp. adminstrn., U. Toronto, 1955; m. Genevieve Miller, Dec. 27, 1956; children—Lorna M., Danielle K., Michelle A., Edward D.P., Patricia M. Adminstrv. asst. Calgary Gen. Hosp., 1953-56; asst. adminstr. Notre Dame Hosp., North Battleford, Sask., 1957-58; asst. adminstr. Winnipeg Gen. Hosp., 1958-63, adminstr., 1963-67, exec. dir., 1967-72; pres. Health Scis. Centre, Winnipeg, 1972—; asso. prof. pub. health U. Man., 1967—; vis. prof. U. Alta., 1967—; mem. survey team Canadian Council Hosp. Accreditation, 1970—. Dir. United Health Ins. Corp., Winnipeg, 1970—, mem. exec. bd., 1973—. Dir. Med. Products Inst., Inc., Man., 1973—. Dir., pres. Red River Exbn., Winnipeg, 1960-67. Bd. dirs. Holy Family Nursing Home, Winnipeg, chmn. bd., 1976—. Fellow Am. Coll. Hosp. Adminstrs. (gov. 1972—, gold medal for excellence in hosp. adminstrn. 1976); mem. Canadian (dir. 1968—, pres. elect 1972-73), Man. (pres. 1966-67, dir. 1962-66) hosp. assns., Assn. Canadian Teaching Hosps. (pres. 1971), Hosp. Research and Devel. Inst. (dir. 1967—). Editorial bd. Health Devices, 1970—. Home: 306 Laidlaw Blvd Winnipeg MB R3P 0K5 Canada Office: Health Scis Centre 800 Sherbrook St Winnipeg MB R3A 1M4 Canada

SWICK, MYRA AGNES, accountant; b. Chgo., Dec. 5, 1945; d. Arthur T. and Marcella M. (Pankiewicz) Swick; B.B.A. cum laude, Loyola U., Chgo., 1967. Mem. audit staff Ernst & Ernst, Chgo., 1967-72; controller Shorr Paper Products Co., Aurora, Ill., 1972-73; staff accountant Otto Hillsman & Co., Ltd., Chgo., 1973—. C.P.A., Ill. Mem. Am. Inst. C.P.A.'s, Nat. Assn. Accountants, Ill. Soc. C.P.A.'s, Am. Womans Soc. C.P.A.'s (pres. 1976-77), Am. Soc. Women Accountants (pres. Chgo. chpt. 1974-75), Chgo. Soc. Women C.P.A.'s, Beta Alpha Psi, Beta Gamma Sigma. Contbr. accounting articles to profl. publs. Office: 20 N Wacker Dr Chicago IL 60606

SWICKARD, KENNETH RAY, chiropractor; b. Jerico Springs, Mo., May 25, 1941; s. Finis Elton and Mildred Leona (Long) S.; D. Chiropractic, Cleve. Chiropractic Coll., 1963; m. Sara Sue Eder, Nov. 5, 1960; children—Mark Andrew, Bruce Edward, Diana Sue, David Mathew, Janice Rene. Founder, Swickard Chiropractic Clinic, North Kansas City, Mo., 1963-75, Kansas City, Mo., 1975—; prof. spinal anatomy Cleve. Chiropractic Coll., 1964-69. Named chiropractor of year Beta Chi Rho, 1972, distinguished pres. award Kiwanis Internat., 1973. Mem. Internat., Mo. (dir. 1972) chiropractors assns., Cleve. Chiropractic Coll. Alumni Assn. (dir. 1969-75), Beta Chi Rho. Kiwanian (pres. North Kansas City 1972-73). Home: 18703 Mission Ave Stilwell KS 66085 Office: 6317 NE Antioch Rd Suite 302 Kansas City MO 64119

SWIERCZEWSKI, JOHN ADAM, SR., microbiologist; b. Waterbury, Conn., Sept. 11, 1940; s. Adam T. and Balbina (Czaplicki) S.; B.S., Norwich U., 1962; M.S., U. Conn., 1964; m. Janice Kaminski, June 16, 1962; children—John Adam, Heidi Ann, Christine Michelle. Dir. clin. microbiology Mercy Hosp., Gary, Ind., 1966-71; dir. clin. microbiology Nat. Health Labs., Arlington, Va., 1971-72; dir. clin. microbiology Mercy Hosp., Muskegon, Mich., 1972—. Lectr. microbiology med. tech. program Purdue U., Ind. U., Gary, 1967-71; vis. lectr. Valparaiso (Ind.) U., 1970-71; instr. med. lab. tech. program Ferris State U., Muskegon, 1972—. Active Boy Scouts Am. Served to capt., AUS, 1964-66; Germany. Mem. Am. Soc. Microbiology, Nat. Registry Microbiologists Am. Acad. Microbiology (bd. dirs. 1977—), Sigma Phi Epsilon. Contbr. articles to profl. jours. Home: 2885 Seabolt Ave Muskegon MI 49445 Office: Mercy Hosp 1500 E Sherman Blvd Muskegon MI 49443

SWIFT, A. DEAN, retail trade exec.; b. 1918; B.A., U. Ill., 1940; married. With Sears, Roebuck & Co., 1940—, store mgr., 1949-64, product mgr., 1964-69, v.p. so. territory, 1969-73, pres., 1973—, also dir.; dir. Commonwealth Edison Co., First Chgo. Corp., Sears Roebuck Acceptance Corp., Allstate Ins. Co., Homart Devel. Co. Address: Sears Roebuck & Co Sears Tower Chicago IL 60606

SWIFT, JOHN LIONEL, civil engr.; b. Rochester, N.Y., Jan. 19, 1947; s. Stanley Melven and Ethel Eleanor (Hyde) S.; B.S. in Civil Engring., Heald Engring. Coll., 1969; m. Martha Aida Hernandez, July 19, 1969; children—John Paul, Mark Stuart. Hwy. design engr. Capitol Engring. Assos., Painesville, Ohio, 1969-75; sr. civil engr. Polytech, Inc., Cleve., 1975—; cons. profl. surveyer State of Ohio for Polytech, Inc., 1975—. Bd. dirs. The Lake County (Ohio) Regional Transit Authority, 1975—. Registered profl. surveyor, Ohio. Mem. Nat. Soc. Profl. Engrs., ASCE, Profl. Land Surveyors of Ohio. Democrat. Baptist. Club: Mentor Racquet. Home: 613 W Walnut St Painesville OH 44077 Office: 1836 Euclid Ave Cleveland OH 44115

SWIFT, MORDEN L., mdse. exec.; b. Chgo., Oct. 9, 1924; s. Jack and Reah (Leib) Steinberg; B.S., DePaul U., 1949; m. Dolores Monica Marcin, Dec. 18, 1966. Buyer Spiegel, Inc., Chgo., 1949-64; v.p. Ekco Products Import Co., N.Y.C., 1964-66; v.p. J & H Internat. Corp., Chgo., 1966-67; pres. Grinold Auto Parts, Inc., Hartford, Conn., 1968-69; div. dir. Topco Asso., 1970—. Fund raising com. Community Chest, Chgo., 1962-63, ARC, 1961-62. Served with AUS, 1943-46. Mem. Housewares Clubs Chgo., N.Y., Furniture Club Am., Wadsworth Athenaeum, Hartt Opera Guild, Mark Twain Meml. Jewish. Home: 525 Hawthorne Pl Chicago IL 60657 Office: 7711 Gross Point Rd Skokie IL 60076

SWIGERT, ALICE HARROWER (MRS. JAMES MACK SWIGERT), civic worker; b. Montrose, Pa., Dec. 18, 1908; d. Lewis Titcomb and Margaret (Ayars) Harrower; student U. Tenn., 1927-29; m. James Mack Swigert, July 7, 1931; children—Oliver, David Ladd, Sally Harper (Mrs. Swigert Hamilton). Sec. to profs. Harvard Law Sch., Cambridge, Mass., 1932-35; pub. relations U. Chgo. Press, 1935-36. Mus. panoramas chmn. Cin. Symphony Orch. Womens Com., 1963-65; founder, treas. Citizens Crusade, 1967-77; vol. Childrens Convalescent Hosp., 1969-75. Trustee emeritus Cin. Speech and Hearing Center; founder, trustee New Life for Girls, 1968—; mem. adv. council Presbyn. Homes, 1972-75, 3 Arts Scholarship Fund, 1971-75. Mem. D.A.R., Chi Omega. Republican. Presbyterian. Clubs: Cincinnati Womans, Cincinnati Country, Queen City, Town. Home: 196 Green Hills Rd Cincinnati OH 45208

SWIRNOFF, MICHAEL ALLEN, lawyer; b. Marshfield, Wis., Sept. 6, 1936; s. Irwin E. and Rose (Abromowitz) S.; B.A. magna cum laude, U. Minn., 1958; LL.B., Harvard U., 1961; m. Sandra G. Zidel, Aug. 9, 1958; children—Wendy J., David B. Admitted to Minn. bar, 1961; mem. firm Popham, Haik, Schnobrich, Kaufman & Doty, Mpls., 1961-64, Mullin, Swirnoff & Weinberg, Mpls., 1973—; instr. Street & Deinard, 1975—; adj. prof. law U. Minn., 1973—; instr. William Mitchell Coll. Law, 1973—. Bd. dirs. Twin Cities Internat. Program for Youth Leaders and Social Workers, Inc., 1966—, pres., 1969-72. Mem. Am., Minn., Hennepin County bar assns., Phi Beta Kappa. Home: 1635 W 26th St Minneapolis MN 55405 Office: 1200 Nat City Bank Bldg Minneapolis MN 55402

SWISHER, JOHN EDGAR, JR., realty exec.; b. Ann Arbor, Mich., June 23, 1919; s. John Edgar and Elizabeth (Kirkpatrick) S.; A.B. in Bus. Adminstrn., Mich. State U., 1940; m. Harriet Dean, June 21, 1941; children—John E. III, Samuel D., Sallie (Mrs. Colin Durie). Pres., Swisher Realty Co., Ann Arbor, 1947—; dir. Ann Arbor Bank & Trust, Am. Bankcorp. Lectr. real estate appraising U. Mich., Ann Arbor, 1961-66. Chmn. Planning Commn., Ann Arbor, 1953-57, Bd. Rev., Ann Arbor, 1967-70, bd. dirs. Forest Hill Cemetery. Served with USNR, 1944-46; ETO. Mem. Ann Arbor Bd. Realtors (past pres.), Am. Soc. Real Estate Counselors, Internat. Real Estate Fedn. (bd. dirs., past pres.), Nat. Inst. Real Estate Brokers (past gov.), Psi Upsilon. Clubs: Ann Arbor Golf and Outing (Mich.). Home: 9957 Algonquin Pinckney MI 48169 Office: 208 E Washington St Ann Arbor MI 48108

SWOVICK, MELVIN JOSEPH, chemist; b. Altoona, Pa., Jan. 20, 1926; s. Walter Joseph and Magdalen Mary (Krish) S.; student U. Detroit, 1943-45, Med. Sch., Marquette U., 1945-47, Lawrence Inst. Tech., 1971-72; B.S. with honors in Chemistry, Detroit Inst. Tech., 1974; m. Maria Elizabeth Galatz, Nov. 23, 1968; 1 son, Michael Wayne. Med. technician, histopathy technician VA Hosp., Altoona, Pa., 1954-55; technician Allied Chem. Corp., Buffalo, N.Y., 1955-60; devel. chemist Nopco Chem. Co., Linden, N.J., 1960-64; analytical chemist Schwarz Bio Research, Orangeburg, N.Y., 1964-65; analytical chemist Reichhold Chemicals Inc., Elizabeth, N.J., 1965-66, Ferndale, Mich., 1966—; tchr. clin. medicine Bon Secours Hosp., Grosse Pointe, Mich., 1974—; tchr. Austin Cath. Prep. Sch., Detroit, 1975—. Active Boy Scouts Am., 1969-73. Mem. Detroit Soc. for Coatings Tech., Am. Chem. Soc. Democratic. Roman Catholic. Club: Verein der Oesterreicher, Carpathia. Home: 345 Folkstone Ct Troy MI 48098 Office: 707 Woodward Heights Blvd Ferndale MI 48220

SWYGERT, LUTHER MERRITT, judge; b. Miami Co., Ind., Feb. 7, 1905; s. Irven W. and Catherine (Hoover) S.; LL.B., magna cum laude, Notre Dame U., 1927; LL.D. (hon.), Valparaiso U., 1964, Notre Dame U., 1969; m. Mildred Kercher, Oct. 10, 1931 (dec.); children—Robert L. (dec.), Michael I.; m. 2d, Mrs. Gari Pancoe, July, 1969. Admitted to Ind. bar; in law practice, 1927-31; dep. pros. atty., Lake County, Ind. 1931-33; asst. U.S. atty., No. Dist. of Ind., 1934-43; U.S. dist. judge No. Dist. of Ind., 1943-61, chief judge, 1954-61; U.S. Ct. of Appeals, Seventh Circuit, 1961—, chief judge, 1970-75. Mem. Am., Ind., 7th Circuit, Fed., Chgo. bar assns. Home: 4 Shore Dr Dune Acres Chesterton IN 46304 Office: 219 S Dearborn St Chicago IL 60604

SYLORA, HERME O., urologist; b. Dumaguete City, Philippines, Apr. 13, 1936; s. Pin Liong and Che Tee (Ong) Sy; came to U.S., 1971; M.D., U. Santo Tomas, Manila, 1960; m. Mary T. Libi, Feb. 14, 1962; children—James, John, Roxanne. Rotating intern Mercy Hosp., Buffalo, 1961-62; resident in surgery Sisters Charity Hosp., Buffalo, 1962-66; hosp. dir. Holy Child Hosp., Dumaguete, 1966-71; resident in urology U. Chgo. Hosps. Clinics, 1971-74; practice medicine specializing in urology, Palos Heights, Ill., 1974-75, Evergreen Park, Ill., 1975—. Diplomate Am. Bd. Surgery, Am. Bd. Urology. Fellow A.C.S. Contbr. articles to med. jours. Home: 608 Prestwick Dr

Frankfort IL 60423 Office: 9450 S Francisco Ave Evergreen Park IL 60642

SYLVANOVICH, W. RICHARD, physician; b. Warsaw, Poland, Dec. 21, 1937; s. Wladyslaw R. and Maria A. (Rudzinska) S.; came to U.S., 1968, naturalized, 1973; M.D., Acad. Medicine, Warsaw, 1962; m. Anna Kwiecinski, Dec. 3, 1966; children—Monica A., Sonia C. Intern, St. Johns Mercy Hosp., St. Louis, 1968-69, resident in medicine, 1970-72, dir. Gastrointestinal Diagnostic Lab., 1974-77, chief gastroenterology, 1977—; fellow in gastroenterology U. Mo., Columbia, 1972-74, instr. medicine, 1974-77; practice medicine specializing in internal medicine and gastroenterology, St. Louis, 1974—. Diplomate Am. Bd. Internal Medicine. Mem. AMA, A.C.P., Am. Soc. for Gastrointestinal Endoscopy, Am. Gastroenterology Assn., St. Louis Med. Soc. Home: 480 Briarwyck Dr Ballwin MO 63011 Office: 615 S New Ballas Rd St Louis MO 63141

SYLVESTER, GLEN MORRIS, tree service co. exec.; b. Goshen, Ind., Apr. 5, 1944; s. Clarence F. and Marjorie (Briggs) S.; B.S., Ind. U., 1970; m. Walda L. Estrup, Dec. 18, 1971; children—Tasha, Carolyn, Eleanor, Charles. Tel. salesman Richardson Homes Corp., Elkhart, Ind., 1970-73; salesman Steury Corp., Goshen, 1973-74, v.p. mktg., 1974-77, nat. sales mgr., 1974-77; pres. Goshen Tree Expert Service, 1977—. Served with USAF, 1964-67. Home: 54705 Holly Dr Elkhart IN 46514 Office: 17406 US 20 Goshen IN 46526

SYMNS, RICHARD DEAN, research engr.; b. Atchison, Kans., Sept. 29, 1951; s. Perrin Kent and Barbara E. (Stinebaugh) S.; B.S., Kans. State U., 1972; M.S., Ill. Inst. Tech., 1977. Process engr. Argo plant Corn Products CPC Internat., Inc., Argo, Ill., 1974-75, prodn. engr., 1976, research engr. pilot plant Moffett Tech. Center, Argo, 1977; pilot plant mgr. Am. Maize Products Co., Hammond, Ind., 1977—: grad. teaching asst. Kans. State U., 1973-74. Mem. Assn. Operative Millers, Am. Assn. Cereal Chemists, Am. Inst. Chem. Engrs., Am. Soc. M.E., Mensa Soc. Republican. Presbyterian. Office: American Maize Products Co 113th St and Indianapolis Blvd Hammond IN 46326

SYMONS, CLAYTON HAROLD, ednl. adminstr.; b. Detroit, Oct. 16, 1925; s. Harold S. and Ella M. S.; B.S., No. Mich. U., 1949; M.A., U. Mich., 1952, Edn. Specialist, 1972; m. C. Jean DeCaire, June 19, 1945; children—James, William, Mary, Michael, Patricia. Math. tchr. Onaway (Mich.) Pub. Schs., 1949-50, high sch. prin., 1950-52; supt. Merritt (Mich.) Consol. Schs., 1952-56; high sch. prin. LeRoy (Mich.) Community Schs., 1956-57, supt., 1957-62; supt. Covert (Mich.) Pub. Schs., 1962-64, Milan (Mich.) Area Schs., 1964—; participant IDEA fellows program Kettering Found., 1975, 76. Pres. council local Roman Catholic Ch., 1972-74, treas. council, 1974-76, lector, 1966—, lay minister, 1970—. Served in USN, 1943-46. Recipient Community Service award Milan Jaycees, 1969. Mem. Am., Mich. (region pres. 1968-69, state council 1968-71, mem. edn. program com. 1973-74, legis. com. 1974—), Washtenaw (pres. 1976-77, chmn. legis. com. 1975-76) assns. sch. adminstrs., Wayne County Bus. Ofcls., Mich. Congress Sch. Adminstrs., Washtenaw County Sch. Officers Assn. Club: Rotary (past dir.; mem. dist. found. scholarship com. 1971—). Home: 123 E Michigan St Milan MI 48160 Office: 920 North St Milan MI 48160

SYNCHEF, RICHARD MICHAEL, lawyer; b. Chgo., Jan. 12, 1950; s. Barry Maurice and Rena Ruth (Jacobson) S.; B.A. with honors, U. Wis., 1972; J.D., Northwestern U., 1975. Admitted to Ill. bar, 1975; mng. partner firm Synchef & Synchef, Chgo., 1975—. Active Democratic gubernatorial campaigns, 1972, 76, candidate for del Dem. Nat. Conv., 1976. Mem. Am. (adminstrv. law sect. communications com.), Ill. (civil practice sect.), Chgo. bar assns., ACLU, Sierra Club, Ind. Voters Ill., Ams. for Dem. Action, Shorin Ryu Karate Assn., Phi Eta Sigma. Contbr. to U. San Francisco Law Rev. Home: Apt 1002 5815 N Sheridan Rd Chicago IL 60660 Office: Suite 1664 221 N LaSalle St Chicago IL 60601

SYVERSON, LESLIE ARTHUR, physician; b. Emmons, Minn., May 24, 1927; s. John Melvin and Minnie Theodore (Berkvam) S.; B.A., U. Minn., 1950, M.D., 1955; m. Lela M. Pertl, June 30, 1950; children—Patti J., Bonnie L., Ann R. Intern, St. Mary's Hosp., Duluth, Minn., 1955-56; practice medicine specializing in family practice, Fergus Falls (Minn.) Clinic (name now Fergus Falls Med. Group), 1958—; mem. bd. dirs. Min-Dak Health Service Agy., Minn. Health Coordinating Council; asst. clin. prof. dept. family practice community health U. Minn. Med. Sch.; area cons. Minn. Dept. Vocat. Rehab.; dir. Western Minn. Savs. & Loan. Served with M.C., USAF, 1956-58. Diplomate Am. Bd. Family Practice. Republican. Mem. United Ch. Christ. Home: 628 W Maple Ave Fergus Falls MN 56537 Office: 615 S Mill St Fergus Falls MN 56537

SZABO, STEVEN, ednl. adminstr.; b. Detroit, July 28, 1929; s. John and Rose (Poisguy) S.; B.Ed., U. Toledo, 1951; M.Ed., Wayne State U., 1960; Ph.D., U. Ill., 1969; m. Madelyn Molnar, Jan. 27, 1951; children—Catherine, Christine, Carol, Colette, Constance, Clarissa, Carla. Tchr., Catawba Island Elementary Sch., Port Clinton, Ohio, 1951-53, Pickett Elementary Sch., Toledo, 1955-56; math. tchr. Cass Tech. High Sch., Detroit, 1956-62; research asso. in curriculum lab. U. Ill., Urbana, 1962-73; curriculum coordinator, math. chmn. Joliet (Ill.) Twp. High Sch., 1974—; dir. ESEA Title III Computer Programming Project, 1975-76. NSF inservice and summer study grantee Wayne State U., 1958-59. Mem. Math. Assn. Am., Nat. Council Tchrs. Math., Kappa Delta Pi, Pi Mu Epsilon. Author: Goals, 1967; Plane Geometry: An Approach Through Isometries, 1971; (with H. E. Vaughan) A Vector Approach to Euclidean Geometry, Volumes I and II, 1971. Home: 2306 Black Rd Joliet IL 60435

SZALAJKA, WALTER STANLEY, educator; b. Detroit, Sept. 15, 1942; s. Walter Joseph and Stella (Gawlik) S.; B.A., St. Mary's Coll. Minn., 1964; M.S., U. Notre Dame, 1970, Ph.D. (NSF fellow), 1972. Tchr., Helias High Sch., Jefferson City, Mo., 1964-66, O'Rafferty High Sch., Lansing, Mich., 1966-67, St. Francis High Sch., Wheaton, Ill., 1967-68; asso. prof., chmn. dept. math. and computer sci. Lewis U., Lockport, Ill., 1972—. Mayor Daley Youth Found. scholar, 1960. Mem. Am. Math. Soc., Math. Assn. Am., Nat. Council Tchrs. Math, Ill. Council Tchrs. Math, Nat. Geog. Soc. Roman Catholic. Home: 610 Preston Dr Bolingbrook IL 60439 Office: Dept Math Lewis Univ Lockport IL 60441

SZATHMARY, LOUIS ISTVAN, II, restaurateur; b. Rakospalota, Hungary, June 2, 1919; s. Louis Istvan and Irene (Strauss) S.; Ph.D., U. Budapest, 1944; m. Sadako Tanino, May 9, 1960; 1 dau., Magda. Came to U.S., 1951, naturalized, 1963. Chef, New Eng. Province Jesuits, Manresa Island, Conn., 1952-55; exec. chef Mut. Broadcasting System, N.Y.C., 1955-58; plant supt. Reddi Fox, Inc., Conn., 1958-59; exec. chef Armour & Co., Chgo., 1959-64; chef, owner Bakery Restaurant, Chgo., 1964—; owner Louis Szathmary Assos.; pres. Lou D'or, Inc.; pres. Transworldtaste, Inc. Food columnist Chgo. Daily News. Bd. govs. Nat. Space Inst. Mem. Chgo. Acad. Scis. (trustee) Nat. Restaurant Assn., Soc. Profl. Mgmt. Cons., Japan-Am. Soc., Council on Hotel, Restaurant and Instl. Edn., Instl. Food Editorial Council, World Inst. of Chefs London (Western Hemisphere v.p. 1963-67), Screen Actors Guild, Acad. Chefs U.S.A. Clubs: Grolier (N.Y.C.); Caxton, Cliff dwellers, Chicago Press. Author: The Chefs Secret Cookbook; American Gastronomy; The Chefs New Secret Cookbook; author, editor Cookery Americana, 16 vols. Office: 2218 N Lincoln Ave Chicago IL 60614

SZEBEDINSZKY, JANOS EMIL, publisher; b. Budapest, Hungary, July 11, 1942; s. Jenö and Amalia (Krause) S.; came to U.S., 1949, naturalized, 1965; B.S. in Chemistry, Indiana U. of Pa., 1968; postgrad. anthropology Brandeis U., 1969, State U. N.Y. at Binghamton, 1970-74. Research chemist Jones & Laughlin Steel Corp., Pitts., 1963-68, pub., editor, 1972—; mng. editor Triad Mag., Chgo., 1973-74; pub. Around Publishing, Mentone, Ind., 1974—; geochem. cons., 1968-71; linguistic analyst, 1970-73. NSF grantee, 1968-69. Mem. Koskiusko County (Ind.) Graphic Design Council. Socialist. Lutheran. Designer 1984 Calendar, 1984 Almanac. Home: 224 W Washington Ave Mentone IN 46539 Office: PO Box 541 Mentone IN 46539

SZEMLER, G(EORGE) J(OHN), historian; b. Szombathely, Hungary, Aug. 17, 1928; s. Francis Weber and Marie (Szemler) Szendy; came to U.S., 1950, naturalized, 1954; Lic.Phil., U. Innsbruck, 1950, Ph.D., 1969; A.M., Creighton U., 1956; Ryerson fellow U. Chgo., 1957-59; m. Barrie Redfearn, Feb. 2, 1957; children—John Francis, Jessica Marie, Jennifer Rose. Tchr. Latin and history Farther Flanagan's Boys Home, Boys Town, Nebr., 1951-56; instr. Greek and Roman history Mundelein Coll., 1951-61; asst. prof. to prof. ancient history Loyola U., Chgo., 1961—, adj. prof. classics, 1971—; historian, asst. dir. Phokis-Doris Archaeol. Expdn. in Greece, 1975—. Served with M.I., AUS, 1952-53. Mem. Am. Inst. Archaeology, Am. Philol. Assn., Am. Hist. Assn., Assn. Ancient Historians, Assn. Guillaume Budé, Consociatio Internatinalis Musicae Sacrae, Cambridge, Canadian philol. assns. Author: Handbook for Students of Roman History, 1970; The Priests of the Roman Republic, 1972. Contbr. articles to Numen, Rhein Mus., Hermes, Pauly Wissowa Realencyclopädie, Anzeiger für Altertumswissenschaft. Home: 9501 Monticello St Evanston IL 60203 Office: 6525 N Sheridan Rd Chicago IL 60626

SZOKE, GEORGE LESLIE, educator; b. Sofia, Bulgaria, Aug. 19, 1927; s. Emil and Anna (Dimitrijevics) S.; came to U.S., 1956, naturalized, 1962; Dipl.Eng., Tech. U. Budapest, 1951; M.S., U. Akron, 1963; m. Yvette Goldberger, Aug. 16, 1952; 1 son, Thomas R. Supr. foundry works Magyar Radiator Gyar, Budapest, Hungary, 1950-51; research group leader Thermotech. Research Inst., Hungary, 1951-56; lectr. Tech. U. Budapest, 1953-56; analytical research engr. Babcock & Wilcox Co. Research Center, Alliance, Ohio, 1957-63; asst. prof. math. U. Akron (Ohio), 1963—; mem. curriculum com. Akron Pub. Schs., 1976-77. Recipient awards Hungarian Govt., 1954, U. Akron Evening Student Council, 1975. Mem. Math. Assn. Am., Pi Mu Epsilon. Author: Elementary Functions, 1968; Algebra and Trigonometry, 1970; contbr. articles to profl. jours. Home: 565 Garnette Rd Akron OH 44313 Office: U Akron Dept Math and Statistics Akron OH 44325

SZWARC, WLODZIMIERZ (WILL RAYMS), educator; b. Kowel, Poland, Apr. 9, 1924; s. Maksym and Raja (Frenkel) S.; came to U.S., 1970, naturalized, 1975; M.S., Wroclaw U., 1952, Ph.D., 1960; Dozent, Main Sch. Planning and Statistics, Warsaw, 1967; m. Maria Bass, July 17, 1954 (div. 1976); children—Michael, Richard. Instr., Tech. U., Wroclaw, 1951-S3, asst. prof., 1953-61, adj. prof., 1961-67, asso. prof., 1967-69; vis. prof. Carnegie-Mellon U., Pitts., 1970-71; vis. prof. U. Wis., Milw., 1971-72, prof. ops. research, mgmt. sci., 1972—. Cons. Inst. Inner Trade, Warsaw, 1959-68, Elec. Inst., Wroclaw, 1961-62, Inst. of Inner Trade, Budapest, 1963-64, Transp. Inst., Wroclaw, 1967-69. Mem. Ops. Research Soc. Am., Inst. Mgmt. Scis. Asso. editor: Naval Research Logistics Quar. (U.S.A.), Opsearch (India). Contbr. 50 articles to profl. jours. Home: 2455 N Maryland St Milwaukee WI 53211

SZWEDA, JOHN ALEXANDER, cardiologist, internist; b. Chgo., Nov. 19, 1926; s. John B. and Aleksa (Rozanski) S.; Pre-med. degree, Loyola U., Chgo., 1948, M.D., 1952; m. Alice Jean Osberg, Sept. 6, 1952; children—Barbara M., Alice M., Theresa M., John D., Luke I., Margaret M., Matthew B., Bridget M. Intern, Milwaukee County Hosp., 1952-53; gen. practice medicine, Beaver Dam, Wis., 1953-57; resident in internal medicine and cardiology, Henry Ford Hosp., Detroit, 1957-60; practice medicine specializing in cardiology, Beaver Dam, 1960—; chief of staff St. Joseph's Hosp., Beaver Dam, 1965, chief of medicine various years 1960-72; chief of staff Lutheran Hosp., Beaver Dam, 1970, chief of medicine various years 1960-72; chief of medicine Community Hosp., Beaver Dam, various years 1972—; cons. in field; participant preceptee and summer student programs Beaver Dam; cons. Waupun Meml. Hosp. Active Family Life Movement; bd. dirs. St. Peters Sch., 1967, religion and ethics tchr., various years 1960-70. Served with U.S. Army, 1945-47. Diplomate Am. Bd. Internal Medicine. Fellow A.C.P.; mem. AMA, Madison Acad. Internal Medicine, Am. Soc. Internal Medicine, Wis. (bd. dirs. 1971-73, speakers bur.), Am. heart assns., Dodge County Med. Soc. Roman Catholic. Contbr. research papers to med. jours. Home: 1300 N Center St Beaver Dam WI 53916 Office: 130 Warren St Beaver Dam WI 53916

TAAFFE, GORDON, health care exec.; b. Atlanta, Aug. 22, 1916; s. Roderick Arthur and Susan Stewart Fairbanks T.; B.S., Tulane U. of South, 1948; M.A., U. So. Calif., 1952; Ed.D., Wayne State U., 1968. Research asso. U. So. Calif., Los Angeles, 1950-54; social scientist Rand Corp., Santa Monica, Calif., 1954-55; research asso. John Tracy Clinic, Los Angeles, 1955-60; asso. prof. U. Calif. at Los Angeles, 1960-63; counselor students U. Detroit, 1963-68, adj. prof. psychology Grad. Sch., 1964-70; dir. research Blue Shield of Mich., 1968—. Served with AUS, 1941-45; PTO. HEW grantee research on cognative domain lipreading, 1967-68. Mem. Am. Psychol. Assn., Am. Assn. Pub. Health, Mich. Pub. Health Assn., Council for Advancement Psychol. Professions and Scis. Home: 28390 13 Mile Rd Farmington Hills MI 48018 Office: 600 Lafayette E Detroit MI 48226

TABAK, HENRY H., biochemist; b. Drohobych, Poland, Oct. 20, 1924; s. Joachim Chaim and Fannie (Borg) T.; came to U.S., 1938, naturalized, 1943; B.S., City U. N.Y., 1949; M.S., U. Ky., 1952; Ph.D. (USPHS fellow), U. Wis., 1964; m. Pauline Newsome, Dec. 21, 1951; children—Gay Sonja Tabak Howard, Valerie Bridget. Teaching, research asst. U. Ky., Lexington, 1950-51, U. Mich., Ann Arbor, 1952-54, U. Wis., 1962-64; research biochemist U.S. Pub. Health Hosp., NIMH, NIH, Lexington, Ky., 1954-55; research microbiologist, biochemist advance waste treatment processes R. A. Taft Sanitary Engring. Center, USPHS, Cin., 1955-68; research biochemist Nat. Environ. Research Center, EPA, Cin., 1968—. Lectr. meetings Internat. Biodegradation Sumposia, Socs. Indsl. Microbiology, Chemistry and Bio-Engring. Served with AUS, 1943-45; ETO. Decorated Bronze Star medal, Silver Star medal. Mem. Am. Soc. Microbiology, Am. Chem. Soc., Soc. Indsl. Microbiology, Mycological Soc. Am., Scientific Research Soc. Am., Sigma Xi. Contbr. articles to profl. jours. Home: 2448 Concord Green Dr Coventry Farms Cincinnati OH 45244 Office: EPA Nat Environmental Research Center 26 W St Clair St Cincinnati OH 45268

TABER, MARGARET RUTH STEVENS (MRS. WILLIAM J. TABER), educator, engr.; b. St. Louis, Apr. 29, 1935; d. Wynn Orr and Margaret (Feldman) Stevens; B. Elec. Engring., Fenn Coll (now Cleve. State U.) 1958, B. Engring. Sci., 1958; postgrad. Western Res. U., 1959-64; M.S. in Engring., U. Akron, 1967; Ed.D., Nova U., 1976; m. William J. Taber, Sept. 6, 1958. Engring. trainee Ohio Crankshaft Co., Cleve., 1954-57, devel. engr., 1958-64, tng. dir., 1963-64; instr. elec.-electronic engring. tech. Cuyahoga Community Coll., Cleve. 1964-67, asst. prof., 1967-69, asso. prof., 1969-72, prof., 1972—, acad. unit leader engring. techs., 1977—; lectr. Cleve. State U., 1963-64. Bd. dirs. West Blvd. Christian Ch., deaconess, 1974-77, elder, 1977—. NSF grantee, 1970, 71, 72, 73. Registered profl. engr., Ohio. Mem. IEEE, Soc. Women Engrs. (sr.), Am. Bus. Women's Assn. (ednl. chmn. 1964-66), Nat. Rifle Assn. Am., Am. Soc. for Engring. Edn., Ohio Assn. Two Year Colls., Audio-Tutorial Congress, Tau Beta Pi (hon.). Author: (with Frank P. Tedeschi) Solid State Electronics, 1976. Home: 4028 E 53d St Cleveland OH 44105 Office: Sci and Tech Bldg 2900 Community Coll Ave Cleveland OH 44115

TABER, MERLIN ARTHUR, educator; b. Anamosa, Iowa, Nov. 24, 1926; s. Melvin Louis and Esther (Wilcox) T.; B.A., William Penn Coll., 1948; M.S.W., U. Iowa 1953, Ph.D. in Sociology, 1962; m., Marilyn Flynn, 1972; children from previous marriage—David, Sara, Rachel. Social worker, tng. cons., Iowa, 1951-56; faculty U. Iowa, 1956-64; prof. social adminstrn. U. Ill.-Urbana, 1964—, asso. dir. grad. sch. social work. Cons. VA, Ill. Inst. Social Policy, Cath. Charities, Iowa Children's Home and Aid Soc. Fellow Am. Sociol. Assn.; mem. Nat. Assn. Social Workers. Author: The Community Professional: A Handbook for Planning and Action, 1971—. Contbr. articles in field to profl. jours. Home: 301 W High St Urbana IL 61801 Office: U Il Urbana IL 61821

TABOR, PURVIS F(RANCIS), grain mcht.; b. Sullivan, Ill., Jan. 18, 1908; s. Jesse B. and Nina Mae (Smith) T.; student Marquette U., Coll., Bus. Adminstrn., 1925-28; m. Roberta June Morris, Sept. 11, 1937; children—Sarah Elizabeth, Nina. Dir. Tabor & Co. (formerly Grain Co.), 1950—, now chmn. bd.; chmn. bd., dir. Coeval, Inc., 1958—. Dir. Archer Daniels Midland Co. Hon. trustee Millikin U. Mem. St. Louis Mchts. Exchange, Chgo. bds. trade, Decatur Assn. Commerce. Presbyn. Clubs: Mid-Am., Monroe (Chgo); Decatur, Decatur Country (past pres.); Thunderbird Country (Palm Springs, Calif.). Home: 24 South Shores Dr Decatur IL 62521 Office: 4666 Faries Pkwy Decatur IL 62526

TABORN, JOHN MARVIN, educator; b. Carrier Mills, Ill., Nov. 7, 1935; s. John and Bertha (Allen) T.; B.S., So. Ill. U., 1956; M.Ed., U. Ill., 1958; Ph.D., U. Minn., 1970; grad. Mgmt. Devel. Program, Harvard Grad. Sch. Bus. Adminstrn., 1970; m. Marjorie Carol Campbell, Apr. 4, 1964; children—John Gregory, Craig Marvin. Vocational counselor Cook County Dept. Welfare, Chgo., 1958-62; psychiat. rehab. counselor Ill. Dept. Mental Health, 1962-64; sr. counselor/psychologist Mpls. Rehab. Center, 1964-65; dir. adult basic edn. Mpls. Pub. Schs., 1965-67, sch. psychologist, 1967-69; coordinator Mpls. Schs./U. Minn., 1969-70; asst. to dean coll. edn. U. Minn., 1971—, staff devel. cons., 1971-72, asso. prof. Afro-Am. studies and psychoedn. studies, 1972—. Cons. State of Mich., State of Minn., No. Ill. U. Bd. dirs. Minn. Dept. Human Rights, Mpls. Urban League. Served as officer USNR, 1959-62. Mem. Am., Minn. psychol. assns., Nat. Alliance Black Educators, Am. Assn. U. Profs., Nat. Assn. Black Psychologists, Kappa Alpha Psi. Mem. A.M.E. Ch. Home: 6925 Olympia St Minneapolis MN 55427 Office: U Minn Minneapolis MN 55455

TABRI, ADIB FARID, phys. scientist; b. Jerusalem, Palestine, July 24, 1928; s. Farid Farah and Theodora (Moubarak) T.; came to U.S., 1949, naturalized, 1959; B.S., Wilmington Coll., 1953; m. Valentina Bokatsch, Feb. 1954; children—Carmen Olivia, Edward Adib, Charles Farid. Research chemist The Christ Hosp., Cin., 1953-56; analytical chemist The Dow Chemical Co., Midland, Mich., 1956-57; research biochemist, The Christ Hosp., Inst. Med. Research, 1957-61; research chemist USPHS, Cin., 1961-70; research chemist Office of Enforcement, EPA, Cin., 1970-77, phys. scientist Environ. Research Info. Center, 1977—; mem. exec. devel. program, 1975—. Vice pres. Arab-Am. Assn., Cin., 1967-73. Mem. Am. Chem. Soc., Am. Water Works Assn. Republican. Presbyterian. Contbr. articles to profl. jours. Home: 10672 Indian Woods Dr Cincinnati OH 45242 Office: 26 W St Clair Cincinnati OH 45268

TACKE, ARTHUR WILLIAM, ophthalmologist; b. Milw., Sept. 27, 1921; s. Arthur Bernard and Esther Emily (Jeske) T.; B.A., Valparaiso U., 1942; M.D., Marquette U., 1946; m. Roberta Jean Hines, Sept. 9, 1950; children—David, Margret. Intern, U.S. Naval Hosp., Bethesda, Md., 1946-47; resident Presbyn. Hosp., Chgo., 1949-51; pvt. practice ophthalmology, Milw., 1951—; mem. staff St. Joseph's, Milw. Children's, Milwaukee County hosps.; med. dir. Lumano Med. Dispensary, Zambia, 1958-65; instr. U. Ill. Med. Sch., 1949-51; asst. clin. prof. ophthalmology Med. Coll. Wis. 1956—. Sec. bd. Wis. Luth. High Sch. Assn., 1963; mem. exec. com. for N. Rhodesia, Wis. Evang. Luth. Synod, 1956-66. Served with USNR, 1943-49. Mem. Am. Acad. Ophthalmology and Otolaryngology, Am., Pan Am. assns. ophthalmology, Soc. Eye Surgeons, AMA, Milwaukee County, Wis. med. socs., Milw. Ophthalmic Soc. (past pres.), Chgo. Ophthal. Soc., Am. Assn. Ophthalmology, State Med. Soc. Wis. (co-chmn. sect. ophthalmology), Ferrari Club Am., Phi Chi. Home: 2205 W Greenwood Rd Milwaukee WI 53209 Office: 777 Glencoe Ct Milwaukee WI 53217

TAFT, FRANCES PRINDLE, art educator; b. New Haven, Dec. 12, 1921; d. William Edwin and Mildred (Bradley) Prindle; B.A. (Janet Warren Shaw Meml. scholar), Vassar Coll., 1942; M.A., Yale U., 1948; m. Seth Chase Taft, June 19, 1943; children—Frederick I., Thomas P., Cynthia B., Seth Tucker. Biol. research technician Yale U. Med. Sch., 1942; chmn. liberal arts dept. Cleve. Inst. Art, 1953—, prof. art history, acting dean, 1974-76; free-lance lectr. art history. Trustee, Cleve. Mus. Art, Vassar Coll., Western Res. Acad., Laurel Sch. Served with USNR, 1942-45; instr. naval communications. Mem. Phi Beta Kappa. Home: 6 Pepper Ridge Rd Cleveland OH 44124 Office: Cleve Inst Art East Blvd Cleveland OH 44106

TAGATZ, GEORGE ELMO, obstetrician, gynecologist, educator; b. Milw., Sept. 21, 1935; s. George Herman and Beth Elinore (Blain) T.; A.B., Oberlin Coll., 1957; M.D., U. Chgo., 1961; m. Susan Trunnell, Oct. 28, 1967; children—Jennifer Lynn, Kirsten Susan, Kathryn Elizabeth. Rotating intern Univ. Hosps. of Cleve., 1961-62, resident in internal medicine, 1962-63; resident in obstetrics and gynecology State U. Iowa, 1965-68; sr. research fellow in endocrinology U. Wash. dept. obstetrics and gynecology, 1968-70; asst. prof. obstetrics and gynecology U. Minn. Med. Sch., 1970-73, asso. prof., 1973-76, prof., 1976—, asst. prof. internal medicine, 1970-73, dir. div. reproductive endocrinology, 1974—. Served with M.C., U.S. Army, 1963-65. Diplomate Am. Bd. Obstetricians and Gynecologists (lectr. endocrinology postgrad. course 1975-76, examiner bd. reproductive endocrinology 1976-77), Minn. Obstetrical and Gynecol. Soc., Hennepin County (Minn.), Minn. State med. socs., AMA, Endocrine Soc., Internat. Soc. Advancement Humanistic Studies in Gynecology, Am. Fertility Soc., Central Assn. Obstetricians and Gynecologists, U. Iowa Obstetric and Gynecologic Alumni Soc. Contbr. articles to profl.

publs.; ad hoc editor Am. Jour. Obstetrics and Gynecology, 1976, Fertility and Sterility, 1976, Chest, 1976. Home: 6708 Sioux Tr Edina MN 55435 Office: PO Box 395 Mayo Meml Bldg 420 Delaware St SE Minneapolis MN 55455

TAGATZ, GLENN EDWIN, ednl. psychologist, educator; b. Milw., Jan. 27, 1934; s. Edwin Christian and Sidonia Adelaide (Friedrichs) T.; B.S., Wis. State U., 1956; M.S., U. Wis.-Milw., 1959; Ph.D., U. Wis.-Madison, 1963; m. Jeanette Alma Sabin, Aug. 10, 1957; 1 son, Bradford G.C. Tchr. lang. arts and social studies Milw. pub. schs., 1956-60; asst. prof. ednl. psychology Wis. State U., Oshkosh, 1963-65; asso. prof. psychology Ind. State U., Terre Haute, 1965-68; asso. prof. edn. Marquette U., Milw., 1968-69, prof. ednl. psychology, 1971—, chmn. dept. ednl. psychology, 1971-72: pres. Internat. Personnel Services, Inc., 1974-76; cons. in field. Mem. U.S. Atty. Gen.'s Task Force Minority Group Hiring Practices in Law Enforcement Agys., 1971—. Served with U.S. Army, 1961-62. Wis. Research and Devel. Center for Cognitive Learning fellow, 1965-67; NSF grantee, 1974-75. Mem. Am. Psychol. Assn., Am., Wis. ednl. research assns., Phi Delta Kappa, Psi Chi. Elk. Author: Child Development and Individually Guided Education, 1976. Contbr. articles to profl. jours. Home: 166 N 93d St Milwaukee WI 53226

TAGGART, GORDON HARRY, baby furniture broker: b. LaCrosse, Wis., Aug. 12, 1903; s. Harry and Ida (Smith) T.; student Wis. State U., 1924-25, Notre Dame U., 1925-26; m. Aleda Amble, Jan. 15, 1943; 1 dau., Diane Mary. Mgr. N.Am. Life Ins. Co., 1929-40; sales mgr. Nat. Surveys, Los Angeles, 1940-44; free lance writer news media, Phoenix, 1945-54; gen. sales mgr. Moulded Products Co. toy mgrs., 1955-60; gen. sales mgr. Infanseat Co. mfrs. baby products, Eldora, Ia., 1960-70; marketing cons. mfg. products for consumer appeal; self employed broker toys, juvenile mdse., 1970—. Mason, Elk. Club: OX 5 (LaCrosse, Wis.). Author: Rymes of A G.I., 1945; On Silent Wings, 1966; Tag-Lines, 1970; Fruit from the Money Tree (Vignettes for Salesmen), 1973. Home and office: 1332 Winnebago St LaCrosse WI 54601

TAHLER, ROBERT, mktg. cons. co. exec.; b. Bklyn., Feb. 9, 1946; s. Sidney and Shirley (Yablonsky) T.; B.B.A., City Coll. N.Y., 1967; M.B.A., Long Island U., 1970; student Bklyn. Coll., 1968-69; m. Bdrbara Sue Reingold, Mar. 9, 1968; children—Rori Ann, Ali Felice. Media buyer Ogilvy & Mather Advt. Co., N.Y.C., 1967-68, mktg. coordinator, 1970-75; tchr. Bd. Edn., N.Y.C., 1968-70; pres. M.D. Dimensions Inc., Springfield, Ill., 1975—; cons., lectr. in field; adj. mem. faculty mgmt. dept. Sangamon State U., Springfield. Mem. NEA, Alpha Delta Sigma (past pres. City Coll. chpt.). Jewish. Home: 3221 Ellendale Dr Springfield IL 62704 Office: #1 Horace Mann Plaza Springfield IL 62715

TAKEMORI, AKIRA EDDIE, pharmacologist; b. Stockton, Calif., Dec. 9, 1929; s. Matsutaro and Haruko (Teshima) T.; A.B., U. Calif. at Berkeley, 1951; M.S., U. Calif. at San Francisco, 1953; Ph.D., U. Wis., 1958; m. Valerie Williams, June 22, 1958; children—Tensho, Rima. Instr., State U. N.Y. at Syracuse, 1959-61; asst. prof., 1961-63; asst. prof. U. Minn., 1963-65, asso. prof., 1965-69, prof. pharmacology, 1969—; cons. NIH; review panel new drug regulation HEW, 1970-74. Bd. dirs. Minnihon Arts Center. Served with AUS, 1953-55. Recipient Am. Cancer Soc. Postdoctoral fellowship, 1958-59; Alan Gregg fellowship, 1971; Nat. Acad. Scis. Internat. Travel award, 1962-65. Mem. Am. Soc. Pharmacology and Exptl. Therapeutics, AAAS, AAUP, Am. Chem. Soc., Soc. Exptl. Biology and Medicine, Japanese Pharmacol. Soc., Sigma Xi. Buddhist. Contbr. numerous articles to sci. jours. Home: 5237 Wooddale Ave S Minneapolis MN 55424 Office: 105 Millard Hall U Minn Minneapolis MN 55455

TALABA, LINDA (CUMMENS), artist, lectr., poet; b. Detroit, July 15, 1943; d. Laszlo and Irma Leona (Fairles) Talaba; B.F.A., Ill. Wesleyan U., 1965; M.F.A., So. Ill. U., 1973; m. John Albert Cummens, Aug. 28, 1964; 1 son, Michael Sean. One-woman shows: Coachman Gallery, Bloomington, Ill., 1965, Vircil Wheaton Gallery, Detroit, 1966, Green's Gallery, Birmingham, Mich., 1966, Finger Gallery, Pontiac, Mich., 1966, Rosenzweig Residence, Bloomfield, Mich., 1967, Pety Residence, Clarkston, Mich., 1961, Ill. Wesleyan U., 1965, Renee Galleries, Detroit, 1968, Doctors' Med. Arts Center Gallery, Carbondale, Ill., 1970, The Breakaway Gallery, Marion, Ill., 1973, Lewis Towers Gallery, Loyola U., 1975; group shows include: Detroit Artists Market Gallery, 1969, Distaff Side Exhbn., So. Ill. Women's Art Coop., 1973, Ill. Wesleyan U., 1974, St. John's U., Can., 1976; represented in permanent collections: Henry Ford Found., Albion U., Ill. Wesleyan U., Detroit Inst. Arts, Canadian Arts Council, Leopold Schepp Found.; mem. art faculty Shawnee Community Coll., Ullin, Ill., 1970; univ. exhibits designer, mem. art faculty So. Ill. U., 1970-72; tchr. sculpture, metalsmithing Springfield (Ill.) Art Asso., 1974-76; vis. lectr. Lincoln Land Community Coll., Springfield, 1975-76; vis. lectr., mem. art faculty Sangamon State U., Springfield, 1975-76. Nat. Scholarships, Inc. grantee, 1972; Smithsonian Instn. Research grantee, 1976; recipient Boston Mus. Printmakers prize, 1965; Royal Oak Art Assn. award for sculpture, 1966; Lutheran Brotherhood Nat. Competition Purchase prize, 1967; Ball State U. Nat. Show award sculpture, 1975; Ill. State Mus. Crafts Biennial award, 1975. Mem. Women's Caucus for Art, Ill. State Mus. Hist. Soc., Am. Crafts Council, Soc. Concerned Scientists, Detroit Artists Market, Coll. Art Assn., Phi Kappa Phi, Delta Phi Delta. Illustrator: Lakeland's Paradise, 1961, The Black Book, 1964-65. Home: 825 S Glenwood St Springfield IL 62704

TALBOT, RICHARD CHARLES, coop. exec.; b. Grand Island, Nebr., July 11, 1930; s. Charles and Hannah Isabelle (Lee) Talbot; student U. Minn., 1963; m. Ardith Ann Snell, Oct. 17, 1954; children—Richard Daryl, Robert Charles. Truck driver, 1953-54; office clk. Williams Bros., Hastings, Nebr., 1954-59; rackman Williams Bros., Hudson, Ia., 1960-65; with Coop. of Hudson (Iowa), 1963-67; mgr. Lawn Hill Coop., New Providence, Iowa, 1967-72; mgr. Sutherland (Iowa) Farmers Coop., 1972-74, Portland Coop. Co., Mason City, Iowa, 1974—. Served with AUS, 1950-53. Mem. Am. Legion. Republican. Mem. Soc. Friends. Lion. Club: Toastmasters (Hastings). Address: Box 653 Nora Springs IA 50458

TALBOTT, THOMAS HOWARD, mfg. co. exec.; b. Kansas City, Mo., Mar. 4, 1940; s. William B. and June K. (Boyce) T.; B.A. in Econs., U. Mo., Kansas City, 1963, M.B.A. (fellow), 1965; m. Linda E. Hood, Mar. 5, 1965. With Mobil Oil Corp., 1965-73, staff analyst, N.Y., 1967-68, asst. to div. controller, Boston, 1968-69, div. supr. systems and indsl. engring., 1969, div. mgr. planning, systems and controls, Kansas City, Mo., 1969-73; project mgr. bus. planning and devel. C.J. Patterson Co., Kansas City, Mo., 1973-74, dir. fine food ops., 1974-75, asst. to pres., 1975-76, v.p. adminstrn., 1976—, dir., 1977—. Hon. fellow Harry S. Truman Library Inst., 1976; active United Fund, 1969, Friends of Art, Philharmonic Assos.; adviser Jr. Achievement, 1973. Victor Wilson Scholar, 1958-62. Mem. U. Mo. Kansas City Alumni Assn., Omicron Delta Kappa, Phi Kappa Phi, Tau Kappa Epsilon. Presbyterian. Clubs: Univ., Woodside Racquet. Home: 411 W 60th Terrace Kansas City MO 64113 Office: 3947 Broadway Kansas City MO 64111

TALBOTT, VERNON GLENN, labor relations educator; b. Keokuk, Iowa, Jan. 16, 1930; s. Vernon G. and Maxine (King) T.; B.A., U. Ill., 1951, postgrad., 1951-53; m. Nancy Inman Freeland, Sept. 8, 1957; 1 dau., Melissa. Quality control engr. Decatur Pump Co. (Ill.), 1968; with York div. Borg-Warner Corp., Decatur, 1960-68, 68-73, personnel dir., 1968-73. Instr. quality control courses; lectr. Inst. Labor and Indsl. Relations, U. Ill. at Champaign, 1973-77, asst. prof., 1977—; project dir. labor-mgmt. com. implementation project, 1974—; arbitrator, cons. in collective bargaining, 1974—. Mem. bd. Decatur Pub. Sch., 1969—; chmn. steering com. Prairie Jr. Coll., Decatur, 1966-69, Maconland Jr. Coll. 1971; pres. French Sch. PTA, 1971-73. Bd. dirs. Jr. Achievement, Decatur. Served with AUS, 1953-55. Mem. Am. Soc. Quality Control (nat. adminstrv. devel. com. 1968—, judge nat. saddoris com. 1965—, adminstrn. div. sec. elect 1969—, dir. central Ill. sect. 1972—), Am. Mgmt. Assn., Am. Statis. Assn., Indsl. Relations Research Assn., Indsl. and Personnel Relations Assn., U. Ill. Alumni Assn., C. of C. (chmn. edn. com. 1968-69). Home: 505 Fielding Ct Decatur IL 62522 Office: 504 E Armory Ave Champaign IL 61820

TALIANA, LAWRENCE EDWIN, educator; b. Mt. Vernon, Ill., Feb. 27, 1929; s. Paul Thomas and Anastasia (Ulrich) T.; B.S., So. Ill. U., 1951, M.S., 1952; Ph.D., Purdue U., 1958; m. Phyllis Owen, Sept. 21, 1953; children—Lawrence Owen, Lisa Ellen. Counselor, chief counselor Purdue U. Counseling and Testing Center, 1954-57; surp. testing service So. Ill. U. at Carbondale, 1957-59, asso. prof. psychology and guidance So. Ill. U. at Edwardsville, 1959-67, prof. psychology and psychol. services, 1967—, coordinator acad. student counseling, 1962-65, acting chmn. dept. psychology, guidance and spl. edn., 1965, asst. to chancellor for acad. affairs, 1969-71, asst. v.p. planning and devel., 1971-72. Vis. prof. Ore. System Higher Edn., 1965-66. Cons., Social Security div. U.S. Dept. Health, Edn. and Welfare, 1962-66. Ill. Div. Vocational Rehab., 1959—, Ill. Dept. Guidance Services, 1961-66, State Supt. Pub. Instrn. Title III, 1970-75, 3d Circuit Ct. Ill., 1973—. Mem. Edwardsville Human Relations Commn., 1963-64, Ill. Mental Health Planning Bd., Council Univs., 1972-75. Served with M.C., AUS, 1952-54. Mem. A.A.A.S., Am., Midwestern, Ill. (chmn. acad. sect.) psychol. assns., Am., Ill. (past treas.) personnel and guidance assns., Soc. Personality Assessment, Nat. Register Health Service Providers in Psychology, Am. Ednl. Research Assn., Edwardsville C. of C. (dir. 1971-75), Sigma Xi. Home: 1312 Randle St Edwardsville IL 62025

TALLEY, HAYWARD LEROY, broadcasting co. exec.; b. Springfield, Ill., Nov. 3, 1923; s. Roy and Reta (Hayward) T.; student Shurtleff Coll., 1946-47, U. Chgo., 1943; B.S., U. Ill., 1948; m. Emma Mae Chandler, Sept. 2, 1950; children—Brian Chandler, Kevin Milby. Instr., Eastern Signal Corps Schs., Fort Monmouth, N.J., 1944-45; chief engr. WOKZ, radio, Alton, Ill., 1948-50; pres. Talley Broadcasting Corp., gen. mgr. Radio Sta. WSMI, Litchfield, Ill., 1950—; pres. Talley Broadcasting Co., Fort Madison, Iowa, 1960—, N. Central Ia. Broadcasting Co., Mason City, 1963—. Mem. Litchfield Indsl. Adv. Com., 1968-69. Served with AUS, 1943-46. Mem. Broadcast Pioneers, Am. Mgmt. Assn., Ill. Broadcasters Assn., Nat. Assn. Broadcasters, Internat. Platform Assn., Litchfield C. of C. Methodist (chmn. ofcl. bd. 1961-63, 65-66, lay leader 1966-67). Mason, Rotarian. Home: 1414 N Harrison St Litchfield IL 62056 Office: WSMI Bldg Litchfield IL 62056

TALLEY, JAMES CHARLES, hosp. adminstr.; b. New Rochelle, N.Y., Nov. 29, 1926; s. Charles and Caroline (Schmidt) T.; A.B. in Econ., Yale, 1947; M.Hosp. Adminstrn., U. Minn., 1952; m. Patricia Leeson McIntosh, Feb. 11, 1962. Asst. adminstr. Butterworth Hosp., Grand Rapids, Mich., 1952-53; adminstr., Tipton County Meml. Hosp., Tipton, Ind., 1955—. Served with AUS, 1953-55. Mem. Am. Hosp. Assn. Kiwanian. Home: 316 S Main St Tipton IN 46072 Office: 1000 S Main St Tipton IN 46072

TALLEY, MELVIN GARY, coll. adminstr.; b. Westchester, Pa., Feb. 26, 1945; s. Melvin G. and Alberta M. (Faddis) T.; B.S., Pa. State U., 1967; grad. N.Y. Fin. Inst., 1968; m. Jolene Keller, Dec. 19, 1969; children—Kristin Jolene, Mark Gary. Registered rep. DeHaven & Townsend, Crouter & Bodine, Phila., 1967-68; pres. Brown Mackie Coll., Salina, Kans., 1972—; dir. Hilton Hotel, Claymont Savs. and Loan Assn. Bd. dirs. St. Francis Boys' Homes. Served with U.S. Army, 1968-69. Mem. Assn. Ind. Colls. and Schs. (dir.), Kans. Assn. Pvt. Career Schs. (pres.). Presbyterian. Clubs: Rotary, Masons, Shrine. Home: 215 Greenway Salina KS 67401 Office: 126 S Santa Fe Salina KS 67401

TALLMAN, CLIFFORD WAYNE, supt. schs.; b. Columbus, Ohio, June 13, 1932; s. Frank Albert and Ella Louise (Ott) T.; B.S., Capital U., 1954; M.A., Ohio State U., 1960; postgrad. U. Alaska, 1956, Ohio State U., 1957-60, Bowling Green State U., 1961-65, U. Toledo, 1962, Kent State U., 1968-75, Akron U., 1971-72; m. Ruth Anne Fletcher, Apr. 6, 1958; children—Martin Wayne, David Edwin, Kathryn Anne. Tchr., Grove City (Ohio) High Sch., 1954-56; adminstr.-tchr. Southwestern City Schs., Grove City, 1956-60; supt. Scipio-Republic (Ohio) Schs., 1960-63; supt. Columbus Grove (Ohio) Schs., 1963-65; supt. Jackson Local Schs., Massillon, Ohio, 1965-73; supt. Brecksville (Ohio) city schs., 1973—. Cons. AMA Conv. on Schs., Physicians, 1963; athletic dir. Seneca County; chmn. Seneca County Health Com., 1960-63; chmn. Ohio Right to Read program, 1970-73. Served with U.S. Army, 1954-56, USNR, 1950-54. I.D.E.A. fellow, 1969; F.E.E. fellow, 1971. Mem. Am., Buckeye assns. sch. adminstrs., NEA, Ohio Edn. Assn., Ohio Historic Assn., Central, Ohio (pres.) tchrs. assns., Cuyahoga County Supts. Assn., Phi Delta Kappa, Ben Hur. Lutheran. Lion. Home: 8457 Vera Dr Brecksville OH 44141 Office: 6638 Mill Rd Brecksville OH 44141

TALLMAN, JACK LEVERETT, automobile agy. exec.; b. Decatur, Ill., May 14, 1926; s. Jessie Leverett and Gail Louise (Frede) T.; student James Millikin U., 1944, U. Ill., 1946-48, U. Colo., summer 1947, Gen. Motors Inst., 1950; m. Marilyn Wilber, Dec. 11, 1948; children—Jill, Joy. Gen. mgr., v.p., sec. J.L. Tallman, Inc., Decatur, 1948—; Cadillac distbr., 1956-65; gen. mgr., pres. Tallman Cadillac, Inc., Decatur, 1965—; an organizer Soy Capital Bank, Decatur, 1956; dir. Northtown Bank of Decatur. Capt. fund drive, United Fund, 1957, 60, 66, YMCA, 1959, Millikin U., 1967; mem. Decatur Meml. Hosp. Devel. Council, 1970-73. Served with USAAF, 1944-46. Recipient nat. 1st prize, primary, Antique Auto Club Am., 1964, nat. sr. 1st prize, 1965, 69, 75; nat. 1st prize Classic Car Club Am., 1959, 64, 68, 74, sr. nat. 1st prize, 1965, 67, 69, 74, 76; 1st place award sr. classic Ill. State Fair, 1952, 54, 55, 57, 58, 59, 60, 63, 64, 67, 68, 71, 72, 75. Mem. Ill. Automobile Trade Assn. (ins. trustee 1965-73), Ill. Automotive Trade (dir. 1959-64), Central Ill. Automotive Trade (pres. 1954, 55, 56, dir. 1956-70), Central Ill. Horseless Carriage Club (organizer, dir. 1952-59, pres. 1953-55), Cadillac Distbrs. and Dealers (council rep. 1962, 66, 68, 71, 75, 76), Cadillac LaSalle Car Club (organizer 1959, dir. 1959-72). Presbyn. (deacon 1962-65). Kiwanian (dir. 1960-64). Clubs: Decatur, Decatur Country. Restorer and rebuilder of antique and classic automobiles. Home: 12 Montgomery Pl Decatur IL 62522 Office: 2020 N Oakland St Decatur IL 62526

TALLMAN, RUSSELL WARRICK, ednl. cons.; b. Ames, Iowa, Aug. 22, 1891; s. Francis Boone and Annette (McKim) T.: A.B., Highland Park Coll., 1916: B.S., Des Moines Coll., 1918; M.A., U. Iowa, 1923, Ph.D., 1925; m. Carrie Nadine Wilson, Aug. 28, 1920. Supt. schs., Coin, Iowa, 1916-17, 1919-20: statistician U. Iowa, 1924-25; prof., head dept. edn. and psychology, chmn. grad. faculty Western State Coll., Colo., 1925-30, v.p., 1928-30; pres. Motivation Charts, Inc., Jewell, Iowa, 1930-52; owner Zippo Bar-Charts, Jewell, 1952-69. Dir. Iowa Emergency Edn., 1934-40; cons. Civilian Conservation Corps, 1934-40; dir. workers edn. tchr. tng., Iowa, Kans., Mo., 1934; Iowa adminstr. Nat. Youth Adminstrn., 1936-40; dir. field service, cons. Iowa State Tchrs. Assn., 1940-41; field rep. Western div. Nat. Policy Commn., Washington, 1942-43; dir. supr. tng., asst. to comdg. officer U.S. Army Air Force, Des Moines, 1944-46; chief employee devel. br. tng. officer War Assets Adminstrn., Omaha, 1946-47; tng. specialist, cons. for bus., industry and edn., 1947—; mem. Gov.'s Ednl. Planning Commn. for Iowa; edn. adviser Iowa AFL-CIO. Served with U.S. Army, 1918. Certified trainer Civil Service Commn. Fellow AAAS, Iowa Acad. Sci.; mem. NEA, Nat. Soc. Study Edn., Phi Delta Kappa. Republican. Mem. Federated Ch. Co-author: Guideline-Problem series syllabus and workbook for Principles of Education; Author: Live and Learn?—Learn and Live!. Contbr. articles to profl. publs. Inventor graph chart forms. Home: 418 S Main St Jewell IA 50130

TALSO, PETER JACOB, physician, educator; b. Ishpeming, Mich., Sept. 22, 1921; s. Jacob and Jennie (Mattson) T.; student No. Mich. Coll. Edn., 1939-41; A.B., Wayne U., 1943, M.D., 1945; m. Evelyn M. Lucynski, Dec. 18, 1943; children—Jennifer, Cassandra, Kathryn Ann, Peter. Intern, U. Chgo. Clinics, 1945-46, asst. resident in medicine, 1948-50, instr., chief resident in medicine, 1950-51; asst. prof. medicine U. Chgo., attending physician Albert Merritt Billings Meml. Hosp., Chgo., 1951-52; asst. chmn., asst. prof. medicine Stritch Sch. Medicine, Loyola U., asso. attending physician Mercy Hosp., Chgo., 1952-55, asso. prof., asst. chmn., 1955-58, prof., asst. chmn. medicine, 1958-63, prof., chmn. dept., 1963-69; sr. attending physician Mercy Hosp., 1955-65; attending physician St. Joseph Hosp., 1965—, also Cook County Hosp., Chgo.; clin. asso. prof. medicine U. Chgo., 1976—; med. dir., ex-officio mem. bd. dirs. Little Company of Mary Hosp., Evergreen Park, Ill.; cons. Hines VA Hosp.; dir. Hypertension Clinic, Fantus Clinic of Cook County Hosp., Chgo. Bd. govs. Chgo. Heart Assn., 1955—; mem. Ill. Psychiat. Tng. and Research Authority, 1957—; adv. council on mental retardation to Gov. Ill., 1964—; bd. dirs. St. Joseph's Carondelet Child Center, 1971—, Cath. Charities, Chgo., Taxtician Found., Chgo. Served to capt. M.C., AUS 1946-48. Diplomate Am. Bd. Internal Medicine. Fellow A.C.P., Am. Coll. Cardiology; mem. Central Soc. for Clin. Research, Chgo. Inst. Medicine, Ill., Chgo. socs. internal medicine, Am., Chgo. med. assns., Ill. Med. Soc., Am. Fedn. for Clin. Research, Central Soc. for Clin. Research, Am. Soc. Nuclear Medicine, Am. Soc. Human Genetics, Am. Acad. Med. Dirs., Am. Med. Soc. on Alcoholism, N.Y. Acad. Sci., Sigma Xi, Alpha Omega Alpha. Roman Catholic. Club: Executive (Chicago). Home: 10359 S Longwood Dr Chicago IL 60043 Office: 2800 W 95th St Evergreen Park IL 60642

TAMAN, MAHMOUD SHAWKY, psychiatrist; b. Shebin El-Kom, Egypt, Jan. 6, 1933; s. Abdel-Rahman and Fathia (Yahya) T.; m. Rafia El-Nashar, Mar. 20, 1961; children—Sahar, Mona, Tarik; came to U.S., 1971, naturalized, 1976; M.D., Alexandria U., Egypt, 1957; diploma in psychol. medicine Royal Coll. London (Eng.), 1969. Rotating intern Alexandria U. Hosp., 1957-58; resident gen. medicine Kobba Gen. Hosp., Cairo, 1958-61, resident psychiatry Banstead Hosp., Surrey, Eng., 1966-69; sr. resident High Croft Hosp., Birmingham, Eng., 1969-71; staff psychiatrist and physician in charge alcoholic and drug abuse treatment unit Mental Health Inst., Clarinda, Iowa, 1971-72, chief psychiatrist, 1972-73; pvt. practice psychiatry, Chippewa Falls, Wis., 1973—; med. dir. Chippewa County Guidance Clinic; pres. Chippewa Valley Clinic, 1973—. Mem. AMA, Chippewa County Med. Soc. (pres.), Am. Psychiat. Assn., Royal Coll. Psychiatrists (Eng.). Club: Rotary of Chippewa Falls. Home: 411 E Wisconsin St Chippewa Falls WI 54729 Office: 705 Bay St Chippewa Falls WI 54729

TAMASY, ROBERT JULIUS, newspaper editor; b. Giessen, Germany, July 4, 1948; s. Julius N. and Helen R. (Katona) T.; student Houston (Tex.) Bapt. Coll., 1966-67; B.A., Ohio State U., 1970, M.A., 1971; m. Sally Jo White, July 20, 1974; 1 dau., Amy. Editor, Grove City (Ohio) Record & Weekly Observer, 1971-76, 76—; asst. city editor Daily Intelligencer, Doyleston, Pa., 1976; instr. agrl. news writing Ohio State U., 1977. Recipient Story of Yr. award Buckeye Press Assn., 1975. Home: 3192 Monterey Dr Grove City OH 43123 Office: 69 Grant Ave Grove City OH 43123

TAMMINGA, DAVID JACOB, architect; b. Chgo., Aug. 28, 1924; s. Jacob Douwe and Anna (Roorda) T.; B.S., Ill. Inst. Tech., 1949, M.S., 1951; m. Helen Rita Stanley, Sept. 19, 1967. Instr. dept. architecture Ill. Inst. Tech., Chgo., 1949-52; draftsman Childs & Smith, Inc., architecture engring., Chgo., 1952-60, project architect, asst. v.p., 1960-65; v.p., mng. agt. and bd. mgmt., 1965-70; v.p., project dir. Welton Becket & Assos., architects, Chgo., 1970-76; architect Burnham & Hammond, Architects-Engrs., Chgo., 1976—. Served with AUS, 1943-46. Mem. AIA. Prin. archtl. works include: Employers Ins. of Wausau Home Office Bldg., 1967, George S. Parker Sr. High Sch., Janesville, Wis., 1967, Solid State Sci. Bldg., Argonne Nat. Lab., Argonne, Ill., 1968, Kemper Ins. Bldg., Long Grove, Ill., 1972. Club: Apollo Musical (dir. 1959-63, 67-69) (Chgo.). Home: 111 East Chestnut St Apt 49H Chicago IL 60611 Office: 53 W Jackson St Chicago IL 60604

TANASICHUK, MURRAY ARTHUR, physician; b. Rossburn, Man., Can., Sept. 17, 1928; s. John and Aqaphia (Hinkevitch) T.; M.D., U. Man., 1952, postgrad., 1957-58; M.Sc., U. Minn., 1960; m. Vera Zaslavetz, June 28, 1964; 1 dau., Kristi Ann. Came to U.S., 1958. Intern Winnipeg (Man.) Gen. Hosp., 1951-52, Misericordia Gen. Hosp., 1952; resident in anesthesiology St. Boniface Hosp., Winnipeg, 1957-58, U. Minn. Hosp., Mpls., 1958-60; gen. practice medicine, Grandview, Man., 1952-57, specializing in anesthesiology, St. Paul, 1963-74; anesthesiologist Calgary (Alta., Can.) Gen. Hosp., 1960-61, Anesthesia Assos. of Mpls., 1961-63, St. Lukes Hosp., 1963-74, St. Paul, Anesthesia Services, Ltd., St. Paul, 1963-74, Fairview Anesthesiology Ltd., Mpls., 1974—. instr. U. Minn., Mpls., 1961-63. Mem. Doctors Emergency Med. Personnel, St. Paul, 1965—. USPHS research grant, 1960. Diplomate Am. Bd. Anesthesiology. Mem. Am., Minn., Cal. med. assns., Am. (sci. exhibit 1961), Minn. socs. anesthesiologists. Mem. Ukranian Orthdox Ch. Home: 1811 Summit Ave St Paul MN 55105 Office: 2312 S 6th St Minneapolis MN

TANCEK, ANNA EVELYN, physician; b. Cleve.; d. Frank and Barbara (Heisz) Tancek; A.B., Flora Stone Mather Coll., 1917; M.D., Case Western Res. U., 1931. Tchr. langs. and Americanization work. Cleve., 1913-25; with Standard Oil Co., Cleve., 1918, U.S. Army Ordnance, 1919; appraiser Hydraulic Pressed Steel Co., Cleve., 1919; tchr. high sch., Cleve., 1920-25; intern Womans Hosp., Cleve., 1931-32; practice medicine, Cleve., 1932-67; clinic physician Pub. Health, Pediatrics, Cleve., 1959-71. Fellow Royal Soc. Health. Home: 1618 Newman Ave Lakewood OH 44107

TANDON, JAGDISH SINGH, pollution control co. exec.; b. New Delhi, India, Apr. 3, 1940; s. Mool C. and Vidya V. (Somra) T.; came to U.S., 1961, naturalized, 1973; B.Sc., U. Delhi, 1961; M.S., U.

Minn., 1963, postgrad., 1963-67; m. Monika Dettmers, May 12, 1967; 1 son, Hans Peter. Mgr. mech. collector div. Aerodyne Corp., Hopkins, Minn., 1968-69; dir. control systems div. Environ. Research Corp. div. Dart Industries, St. Paul, 1969-70; gen. mgr. pollution control systems div. George A. Hormel & Co., Coon Rapids, Minn., 1970-77; pres. Am. Envirodyne div. Pettibone Corp., Chgo., 1977—; instr. U. Minn. Inst. Tech.; vis. scientist Nat. Center Atmospheric Research, Boulder, Colo. Mem. ASCE, Air Pollution Control Assn., Am. Foundry Soc. Contbr. pollution control articles to profl. lit. Home: 1344 Southwind Dr Northbrook IL 60062 Office: 2541 N Keeler Ave Chicago IL 60639

TANDON, RAJIV, car rental co. exec.; b. Allahabad, India, May 9, 1944; s. Jagdish Bihari and Vimla Devi (Mehrotra) T.; came to U.S., 1969; B.Tech. with honors, Indian Inst. Tech., 1966; M.S. in Ops. Research, U. Minn., 1972, M.B.A., 1972, postgrad, 1976; m. Priti Khanna, Sept. 21, 1969; children—Ribhu, Veeti. Mgmt. trainee Kumardhubi Engring. Works, Kumardhubi, Bihar, India, 1966-67, prodn. control officer, 1967-69; ops. research analyst Nat. Car Rental Systems, Inc., Mpls., 1971-72, mgr. ops. research, 1972-75, dir. fin. analysis, 1975-77; corporate v.p. Mgmt. Info. Services, Mpls., 1977—; teaching asst. U. Minn., 1970-71, instr., 1971. Mem. Inst. Mgmt. Scis. (sec. Upper Midwest chpt. 1975-76, v.p. 1976-77, pres. 1977—), Ops. Research Soc. Am., Am. Inst. Decision Scis., Am. Mgmt. Assn., Am. Fin. Assn. Hindu. Home: 8109 Rhode Island Ave S Bloomington MN 55438 Office: 5501 Green Valley Dr Minneapolis MN 55437

TANEGA, JOSE RESMA, elec. engr.; b. Manila, July 31, 1940; s. Anselmo F. and Estela T. (Resma) T.; came to U.S., 1970, naturalized, 1975; B.S. in Elec. Engring., Mapua Inst. Tech. 1967; m. Conchita M. Salaan, Oct. 2, 1970; children—Joey, Cheryl, Cliff, Jason. Elec. estimator Aluminum Products unit Reynolds Aluminum, Manila, 1962-67; acting plant mgr. Impact Corp. Ltd., Manila, 1968-70; asst. telephone engr. GTE Inc., Automatic Electric, North Lake, Ill., 1970-72; elec. designer Castle Engring., Chgo., 1972-74, Macdonald Engring., 1974-76; elec. design engr. Moffett Tech. Center, CPC Internat. Inc., Argo, Ill., 1976—. Mem. IEEE, Philippine Engrs. Scis. Orgn., Nat. Rifle Assn. Roman Catholic. Contbr. articles in field. Home: 2614 W 23d Pl Chicago IL 60608 Office: Moffett Technical Center CPC Internat Inc Box 345 Argo IL 60501

TANG, SING CHIH, scientist; b. Shanghai, China, Oct. 6, 1935; s. Si Siang and Pauline (Wang) T.; came to U.S., 1959; naturalized, 1971; B.S., Nat. Taiwan U., 1956; Ph.D. (fellow), U. Mich., 1963; m. Kin Ling Chow, Aug. 29, 1964; children—Wayne, Terry, Gale. Research scientist Ford Motor Co., Dearborn, Mich., 1963-65, sr. research engr., 1965-72, prin. research engr., 1972-77, staff scientist, 1977—. Mem. ASME, ASCE, Sigma Xi. Contbr. articles in field of applied mechanics to various engring. jours. in U.S. and abroad. Home: 12519 Beacon Hill Dr Plymouth MI 48170 Office: Rotunda Dr Dearborn MI 48121

TANG, THOMAS TZE-TUNG, physician, educator; b. Peking, China, Nov. 11, 1920; s. San and Tsun-yin (Kuo) T.; A.B., Nat. Central U., China, 1944; B.S., St. Mary's Coll., 1949; M.S., George Washington U., 1951, Ph.D., 1954, M.D., 1958; m. Georgeen Hartmann, Nov. 3, 1959; 1 son, Tom. Came to U.S., 1945, naturalized, 1961. Intern Washington (D.C.) Hosp. Center, 1958-59; resident Mt. Sinai Hosp., N.Y.C., 1959, Mt. Alto VA Hosp., Washington, 1960; pathologist VA Hosp., Madison, Wis., 1963-65, Milw. Children's Hosp., 1965—; instr. U. Wis., Madison, 1963-65; asst. prof. Marquette Sch. Medicine, Milw., 1965—; mem. staff Milw. Children's Hosp. Diplomate Am. Bd. Pathology, Am. Bd. Nuclear Medicine. Fellow Coll. Am. Pathologists, Am. Soc. Clin. Pathology; mem. Soc. Nuclear Medicine, AMA, Sigma Xi. Home: 18295 Lamplighter Ct Brookfield WI 53005 Office: 1700 W Wisconsin Ave Milwaukee WI 53233

TANGORA, MARTIN CHARLES, mathematician; b. N.Y.C., June 21, 1936; s. Albert and Virginia (Martin) T.; B.S., Calif. Inst. Tech., 1957; M.S., Northwestern U., 1958, Ph.D., 1966; m. Linda F. Perry, June 16, 1973. Mem. tech. staff Aerospace Corp., 1962-64; instr. Northwestern U., 1966-67; instr. U. Chgo., 1967-69; temporary lectr. U. Manchester (Eng.), 1969-70; asst. prof. U. Ill., Chgo., 1970-72, asso. prof., 1972—. Bd. dirs. Landmarks Preservation Council and Service Ill., 1971—, pres. service, 1971-72, pres. council, 1976. Fulbright scholar U. Paris, 1959-60; Sci. Research Council sr. vis. fellow, Oxford, 1973-74; NSF grantee, fellow. Mem. Am. Math. Soc., Math. Assn. Am., Sigma Xi, Tau Beta Pi. Home: 4636 Magnolia Ave Chicago IL 60640 Office: Dept Math Univ Ill Chicago IL 60680

TANGWALL, RAYMOND HOLGER, radiologic technologist; b. Duluth, Minn., Nov. 11, 1935; s. Arthur and Edna (Gallagher) T.; Medex, U. N.D., 1972; grad. Mayo Clinic Coll. Med. Tech., 1953; m. Melody Meyer, June 29, 1974; children by previous marriage—Randy, Ramona, Robin, RaeAnn. Physician asst., radiologic technologist Community Meml. Hosp., Sidney, Mont., 1954-57, Williston (N.D.) Clinic, 1957-71, McIntosh County Meml. Hosp. and Ashley (N.D.) Clinic, 1971—. Clk., Ashley Park Dist., 1971-74, v.p., 1971—. Named Williston Outstanding Young Man of Year, 1970. Mem. Am., N.D. (pres. 1968) socs. radiologic technologists, Kotana Med. and X-Ray Soc., Am. Acad. Physicians Assts., Am. Med. Technologists, Am. Registry Radiologic Technologists, Williston Jaycees (past pres., Outstanding Jaycee of Year 1970). Elk, Moose, Mason. Address: 503 1st St Ashley ND 58413

TANKUS, HARRY, engring. exec.; b. Bialystok, Poland, Aug. 23, 1921; s. Isador and Sima (Siegal) T.; came to U.S., 1929; grad. engring. Armour Tech., 1942; student U. Ill., 1946-47; grad. mgmt. course U. Chgo., 1966; m. Lila Beverly Lee, Sept. 9, 1947; children—Rolana, Ilyce. Came to U.S., 1929, naturalized, 1929. Insp. dept. head Buick div. Gen. Motors, Melrose Park, Ill., 1942-44; specification engr. Crane Packing Co., Chgo., 1947-53; chief engr., 1953-62, asst. v.p. engring., Morton Grove, 1962-64, asst. v.p. sales, 1964-71, v.p. product sales, 1971-75, pres., 1975—, also dir. Bd. dirs. Oakton Coll. Ednl. Found., 1977—. Served with AUS, 1944-46, ETO. Decorated Purple Heart; registered profl. engr., Ill. Fellow Am. Soc. Lubrication Engrs. (pres. 1975-76); mem. Soc. Automotive Engrs. (chmn. seal program aerospace conf. 1965), ASME, Am. Soc. Metals (certificate of recognition 1965), Western Soc. Engrs., Am. Soc. Tool and Mfg. Engrs., AAAS, Am. Ordnance Assn., Nat. Conf. on Fluid Power (chmn. 1970, bd. govs. 1970—), Nat. Assn. Corrosion Engrs., ASTM (chmn. subcom. carbongraphite 1965), Chgo. Natural History Mus. (asso.). Clubs: Masons, Shriners, Moose. Author articles in field. Patentee in field. Home: 415 Sunset Dr Wilmette IL 60091 Office: 6400 Oakton Morton Grove IL 60053

TANNEBAUM, SOL, optometrist; b. Brest-li-tovsk, Poland, Apr. 2, 1924; s. Martin and Rose (Tenenbaum) T.; brought to U.S., 1929, naturalized, 1948; B.S., Roosevelt U., 1957; O.D., Ill. Coll. Optometry, 1948; postgrad. U. Ind., 1959, Ohio State U., 1958, Pa. State Coll. Optometry, 1955, Govs. State U.; m. Marilynn Etta Barshay, June 25, 1949; children—Ross, Lisa. Practice optometry, Olympia Fields, Ill., 1954; clin. asso. Ill. Coll. Optometry, Chgo., 1970—; asso. editor Jour. Am. Optometric Assn., 1966—; vis. prof. European Coll. Optometry, 1973. Chmn. visual health com. Park Forest Health Council, 1961—, South Suburban Pub. Sch. Coop., 1966—; mem. bd. Suburban-Cook-DuPage County Health Systems Agy. Bd. dirs. Camp Lions for Visually Handicapped State Ill., Lake Villa, 1963-64. Family Counseling Service South Cook County, 1966-69, Health Careers Council Ill., 1967-72. Served with USNR, 1945. Mem. Am., Ill. (editor jour. 1969-71, mem. child vision care com. 1973) optometric assns., Assn. Optometric Editors, Optometric Hist. Soc. (trustee), Assn. Optometric Educators. Lion. Contbr. profl. jours. Home: 2620 Oakwood Dr Olympia Fields IL 60461 Office: Olympia Fields Profl Bldg 2555 W Lincoln Hwy Olympia Fields IL 60461

TANNEHILL, JOHN CHARLES, engring. educator; b. Salem, Ill., Oct. 14, 1943; s. John Bell and Pearl Hanna (Trulin) T.; B.S., Iowa State U., 1965, M.S., 1967, Ph.D., 1969; m. Marcia Kay George, Jan. 28, 1967; children—Michelle, Johnny. Aerospace engr. NASA Flight Research Center, Edwards, Calif., 1965; mem. tech. staff Aerospace Corp., El Segundo, Calif., 1967; NASA-ASEE fellow NASA Ames Research Center, Moffett Field, Calif., 1970, 71; asst. prof. Iowa State U., Ames, 1969-74, asso. prof. aerospace engring., 1974—; chmn. bd. Engring. Analysis, Inc., Ames, 1976—. NSF trainee, 1965-68; Iowa State U. Research Found. fellow, 1968-69; NASA fellow, 1970-71. Fellow Am. Inst. Aeros. and Astronautics (asso.); mem. Am. Soc. Engring. Edn., Sigma Xi, Sigma Gamma Tau, Tau Beta Pi. Contbr. articles to profl. jours. Home: 2963 Monroe Dr Ames IA 50010 Office: Dept of Aerospace Engring Iowa State U Ames IA 50011

TANNER, RICHARD THOMAS, educator; b. Hillsboro, Oreg., Nov. 2, 1936; s. Robert Edward and Alba Oleanna (Thomson) T.; B.S., Oreg. Coll. Edn., 1958; M.S., Oreg. State U., 1962; Ph.D., Stanford, 1968; m. Sarah Cole Johnson, June 24, 1962; 1 son, Thomas Cole. High Sch. tchr., Oreg., Mont., East Africa, 1958-63; asst. prof. Oreg. State U., 1968-72, dir. Rachel Carson Project, 1971-72; prof. environ. edn. Central Wash. State Coll., Randle, 1972-76; prof. environ. edn. Iowa State U., 1977—; cons. environ. and energy edn., 1969—. Served with U.S. Army, 1959-67. Recipient Fulbright award, 1962. Mem. Nature Conservancy, Wilderness Soc., East Africa Wild Life Soc., Nat. Sci. Tchrs. Assn., Nat. Council Social Studies, Sierra Club, Foresta Inst., Phi Delta Kappa. Author: Ecology, Environment, and Education, 1974; Of Democracy, Truth, and Courage, 1976. Contbr. articles to profl. jours. Home: Rural Route 1 Boone IA

TAO, LIANG NENG, engineer, educator; b. Shanghai, China, June 27, 1927; s. Hsieun-Mo and Li-Chien (Chen) T.; came to U.S., 1949, naturalized, 1967; B.S., Chaio Tung U., China, 1949; M.S., U. Ill., 1950, Ph.D., 1953; m. Micheline C. Chao, June 8, 1957; children—Amy Rose, Leonard Michael, Cynthia Mary. Research engr. Worthington Corp., Harrison, N.J., 1953-55; asst. prof. mechs., Ill. Inst. Tech., Chgo., 1955-59, asso. prof., 1959-61, prof., 1961—; cons. in field. Recipient Outstanding New Citizen of Met. Chgo. award, Citizen Council Met. Chgo., 1967. Mem. AAUP, A.S.M.E., Soc. Engring. Science, Am. Inst. Aero. and Astronautics, Sigma Xi, Pi Mu Epsilon. Contbr. articles to profl. jours. Home: 6950 N Kilpatrick Ave Lincolnwood IL 60646 Office: 3300 S Federal St Chicago IL 60616

TARANIK, JAMES VLADIMIR, geologist; b. Los Angeles, Apr. 23, 1940; s. Vladimir James and Jeanette Downing (Smith) T.; B.Sc. in Geology, Stanford U., 1964; Ph.D., Colo. Sch. Mines, 1974; m. Colleen Sue Glessner, Dec. 4, 1971; children—Debra Lynn, Danny Lee. Chief remote sensing Iowa Geol. Survey, Iowa City, 1971-74; prin. remote sensing scientist Earth Resources Observation Systems Data Center, U.S. Geol. Survey, Sioux Falls, S.D., 1975—; adj. prof. geology U. Iowa, 1971—; vis. prof. civil engring. Iowa State U., 1972-74; adj. prof. earth sci. U. S.D., 1976—. Served with C.E., U.S. Army, 1965-67. Decorated Bronze Star medal. NASA prin. investigator, 1973; NDEA fellow, 1968-71. Fellow Geol. Soc. Am.; mem. Am. Assn. Petroleum Geologists, Soc. Mining Engrs., Am. Inst. Profl. Geologists (certified), Soc. Exploration Geophysicists, Am. Soc. Photogrammetry (certified), Am. Inst. Aeros. and Astronautics, AAAS, Sigma Xi. Developer remote sensing program and remote sensing lab. for State of Iowa, ednl. program in remote sensing for Iowa univs.; contbr. to profl. jours. Home: 4301 Oak Ridge Ave Sioux Falls SD 57103 Office: EROS Data Center U S Geol Survey Sioux Falls SD 57198

TARPEY, ELIZABETH ANNE, counselor; b. Haskell, Okla., July 15, 1938; d. Herschel Andrew and Ann Mae Reichman (Hobbs) McCaslin; B.S., Okla. State U., 1957; M.S., So. Ill. U., 1967, Ednl. Specialist, 1973; Ph.D., St. Louis U., 1977; children—Stephen Paul, Bruce William. Tchr. evening div. pub. schs., Edwardsville, Ill., 1965-70; acad. advisor So. Ill. U., Edwardsville, 1966-73, counselor, instr., 1973—; career edn., communications skills tng. workshop cons., St. Louis, DeKalb, Ill., Park Ridge, Ill., Venice, Ill. Div. Adult, Vocat. and Tech. Edn. grantee State Ill. to develop Career Edn. Readiness Test, 1974-77. Mem. Am. Personnel and Guidance Assn., Am. Coll. Personnel Assn., Kappa Delta Pi, Ill. Edn. Assn. Mem. Christian Ch. (Disciples of Christ). Home: 408 W Union St Apt 2 Edwardsville IL 62025 Office: Gen Studies Div So Ill U Edwardsville IL 62026

TARSINOS, LOUIS DEMETRIOS, urologist; b. Athens, Greece, Dec. 13, 1927; s. Demetrios E. and Bess G. (Xirogiannis) T.; came to U.S., 1956, naturalized, 1961; M.D. U. Athens, 1952; m. Dolores Stolz, Jan. 12, 1957 (dec.) 1 son, James; m. 2d, Electra Maria Milonas, Dec. 6, 1970; children—Athena, Thalia, Pericles. Intern. Alexian Bros. Hosp., Elizabeth, N.J., 1956; resident in gen. surgery Allentown (Pa.) Hosp. Assn., 1957; resident in urology Martland Med. Center, Newark, 1958-61; practice medicine specializing in urology, Princeton, Ill. and Spring Valley, Ill., 1961—; former chief staff Perry Meml. Hosp., St. Margaret's Hosp.; cons. urologist Kewanee (Ill.) Pub. Hosp., Mendota Hosp., Streator, Ill.; asst. clin. prof. urol. surgery U. Ill.-Peoria Sch. Medicine. Diplomate Am. Bd. Urology. Fellow A.C.S.; mem. Chgo., Iowa urol. socs., Am. Urol. Assn. (N. Central sec.), Pan Pacific Surg. Assn., Am. Geriatric Soc., Am. Fertility Soc., Am. Acad. Cin. Pathologists. Greek Orthodox. Clubs: Bureau Valley Country; Union League of Chgo.; Elks. Home: Rural Route 3 Princeton IL 61356 Office: 682 E Peru St Princeton IL 61356 also 200 W St Paul St Spring Valley 61362

TATHAM, CLIFFORD BLENN, ednl. adminstr.; b. Pittsburg, Kans., Sept. 5, 1932; s. James Robert and Bonnie Lavonne (Willis) T.; B.A., U. Kans., 1960, Ed. S., 1971; M.A., U. Hawaii, 1964; m. Elaine LaValle Johnson, Aug. 20, 1960; children—Eirene Cheryl, Christopher Eric. Psychometrist, Counseling and Testing Center, U. Hawaii, Honolulu, 1961-64; counselor, residence dir. Franklin (Ind.) Coll., 1964-66; asst. prof. psychology Ottawa (Kans.) U., 1966-71; research and evaluation specialist McREL, Kansas City, Mo., 1971-73; coordinator research projects Sch. Nursing, Research Hosp. and Med. Center, Kansas City, Mo., 1973-75; sr. research asso. Customer Satisfaction Research Inst., 1976—. Served with USNR, 1952-56. Mem. Am. Psychol. Assn., Assn. Instl. Research, Am. Ednl. Research Assn., Phi Delta Kappa. Mason. Contbr. articles to profl. jours. Home: 701 N Walker St Olathe KS 66061 Office: 4901 College Blvd Shawnee Mission KS 66211

TAUB, ROBERT GOLDE, physician; b. Chgo., Sept. 16, 1928; s. Samuel J. and Thelma (Golde) T.; B.S., Northwestern U., 1947, M.D., 1951; M.S. in Ophthalmology, U. Minn., 1955; m. Sheila Mae Kaplan, June 15, 1952; children—Jay Preston, Susan Jane, Jodie Lynn. Ophthalmology fellow Mayo Clinic, Rochester, Minn., 1952-55; intern Michael Reese Hosp., Chgo., 1952-55; resident Mayo Clinic, Rochester, 1952-55; practice medicine, specializing in ophthalmology, Chgo., 1955—; mem. dept. ophthalmology Med. Sch., Northwestern U., Chgo., 1955—, instr., 1955-57, asso. in ophthalmology, 1957—; mem. staff Columbus Hosp., Chgo., Childrens Meml. Hosp., Chgo., Cuneo Hosp., Chgo. Cons. research div. Armour Co., 1955-59. Sch. trustee Michigan City, Ind., 1970—, pres. bd. trustees, 1974-77; bd. dirs. Nat. Eye Research Found., Chgo. Diplomate Am. Bd. Ophthalmology. Fellow A.C.S.; mem. A.M.A. (physicians recognition award 1969), Mayo Eye Alumni Assn. (pres.), Ind. Acad. Ophthalmology, Ill., Chgo. med. socs., Sigma Xi, Phi Beta Kappa, Alpha Omega Alpha. Jewish religion. Club: Illinois Athletic (Chgo.). Contbr. articles to profl. jours. Home: 113 Valentine Ct Michigan City IN 46360 Office: 6 N Michigan Ave Chicago IL 60602

TAUBE, WILLIAM HAROLD, lawyer; b. Kankakee, Ill., Jan. 17, 1934; s. Harold Herman and Cleo Almeda (Rich) T.; B.S., Memphis State U., 1961; J.D., Vanderbilt U., 1963; m. Joanne Joyce Carter, Dec. 12, 1953; children—John William, Janette Elizabeth. Admitted to Tenn. bar, 1963, Ill. bar, 1964; mem. firm. Gray, McIntire & Petersen, Kankakee, 1963-68, Ackman, McKnelly, Reagan & Taube, 1968-71, Taube & Judd, 1971-76, Taube & Phipps, 1976—; corp. counsel City of Kankakee, 1965—; spl. asst. state's atty., 1969. Mem. legislative com. Ill. Municipal League, 1971—, vice chmn., 1974, chmn., 1975—. Mem. commercial panel Am. Arbitration Assn., 1975—. Bd. dirs. Kankakee County Heart Fund. Served with USN, 1952-56. Mem. Am., Ill., Kankakee County bar assns., Am. Judicature Soc., Am. Legion, Nat. Inst. Municipal Law Officers (nominating com. 1972-73, resolutions com. 1974, chmn. ordinance and ordinance enforcement com. 1975, Ill. Chmn. 1975—). Mason (Shriner), Elk. Clubs: Kankakee Country (dir.), Kankakee County Hundred. Republican. Conglist. Home: 796 S Greenwood Ave Kankakee IL 60901 Office: 258 E Court St Kankakee IL 60901

TAUSSIG, LEONARD MICHAEL, testing lab. exec.; b. Chgo., Aug. 5, 1925; s. Louis and Carrie (Ascherman) T.; B.S., Ill. Inst. Tech., 1950; m. Shirley Kaufman, Jan. 30, 1949; children—Lisa, Cara. Research metallurgist Internat. Harvester, Chgo., 1950-51; chief metallurgist Magnaflux Corp., Chgo., 1951-54; founder, pres. Taussig Assos., Inc., metall. testing lab., Chgo., 1954—. Instr. evening div., metall. engring. dept. Ill. Inst. Tech., 1957-58. Bd. financial advisers The Lambs, 1966-68. Served with AUS, 1943-46. Registered profl. engr., Ill. Mem. Am. Soc. Testing and Materials (vice chmn. com. on surg. materials 1968-70), Am. Welding Soc., Am. Soc. for Metals, Am. Soc. for Non-destructive Testing, Standards Engring. Soc. (chmn. 1960-62), Am. Council Ind. Labs. (chief rep. 1972-76). Jewish (mem. temple exec. bd. 1970-72, v.p. 1972—). Club: Ravinia Green Country (exec. bd. 1976—). Home: 8824 N Kenneth Terr Skokie IL 60076 Office: Taussig Assos Inc 6955 N Hamlin Ave Chicago Il 60645

TAY, CHENG HIN, anesthesiologist; b. Rangoon, Burma, Mar. 24, 1938; s. Soo Hong and Shiok Kyin (Ho) T.; came to U.S., 1971, naturalized, 1977; M.B.B.S., Inst. Medicine, Rangoon, Burma, 1965; m. Jenny Peh, June 19, 1968; children—Nora PoPo, Ann Belinda. Rotating intern Columbia Cuneo Med. Center, Chgo., 1971; resident in anesthesiology U. Ill. Med. Center, Chgo., 1972-75; anesthesiologist Asso. Anesthesiologists, Peoria, Ill., 1975—; active staff Meth. Med. Center; mem. courtesy staff St. Frances Med. Center, Proctor Community Hosp., 1975—; clin. asso. anesthesia Peoria Sch. Medicine, 1975-77, clin. asst. prof. surgery (anesthesia), 1977—. Mem. AMA, Am. Soc. Anesthesiologists, Gen. Med. Council (Eng.), Ill. State, Peoria med. socs. Home: 111 E Coventry Ln Peoria IL 61614 Office: 416 St Mark Ct Suite 508 Peoria IL 61603

TAYLOR, BETTYE JEAN, educator; b. Birmingham, Ala., Feb. 23, 1934; d. Willie James and Annie Mae (Hood) P.; B.A., Detroit Inst. Tech., 1968; M.A., Wayne State U., 1974; postgrad. U. Detroit, 1975-76; m. William Taylor, Sept. 17, 1960. Social worker Wayne County Social Service, Detroit, 1968-70; tchr. Highland Park (Mich.) High Sch., 1970-71; tchr. Detroit Bd. Edn., 1971—. Sec., Young Democrats Club, Detroit, 1958-60. Mem. Am., Mich. personnel and guidance assns., Nat. Rehab. Assn., Mich. Rehab. Counseling Assn., Detroit Fedn. Teachers, YWCA of Met. Detroit, Delta Sigma Theta. Democrat. Home: 19400 Redfern St Detroit MI 48219 Office: 2001 W Warren St Detroit MI 48203

TAYLOR, CURTIS LEE, city ofcl.; b. Milw., Oct. 8, 1929; s. Herbert Charles and Emily Margaret (Anderson) T.; B.S., U. Wis., Stevens Point, 1954; m. Barbara Louise Nottleson, June 16, 1951; children—Kim Louise, Wendy Sue, Thomas Lee. Tchr., coach Bd. Edn. Stevens Point, 1954-55; recreation dir. City of Stevens Point, 1955-59; dir. recreation City of Rochester, Minn., 1959-67, supt. parks and recreation, 1967—. Instr., Rochester State Jr. Coll., 1971-72. Mem. Gov.'s Com. on Leisure Activity, 1962-66; chmn. recreation safety Olmsted County Safety Council, 1963-66; pres. Gamehaven council Boy Scouts Am., 1971-72. Served with USNR, 1948-49. Recipient Sportsmanship award YMCA, 1971, certificate of recognition C. of C., 1971. Mem. Internat. City Mgrs. Assn., Nat. (council of presidents, dist. adv. com.), Minn. (pres. 1971, award for outstanding service to profession 1971) park and recreation assns. Republican. Lutheran (chmn. bd. trustees, pres.). Kiwanian. Contbr. articles to profl. jours. Home: 828 10 1/2 St SW Rochester MN 55901 Office: 403 E Center St Rochester MN 55901

TAYLOR, D(ARL) CODER, architect, engr., planner; b. Ft. Wayne, Ind., July 18, 1913; s. Frank A. and Edith M. (Zook) T.; B.Arch., Carnegie Inst. Tech., 1935; student U. Wash., 1933; m. Audrey Helen Larkin, June 6, 1944; children—Barbara Helen (Mrs. Albert R. Schreiber), Thomas Coder, Julia Marie. Draftsman and designer various archtl. firms 1935-39; partner Zook & Taylor, architects, 1939-42, Holsman, Klekamp & Taylor, Chgo., 1948-52, Yost & Taylor Kenilworth, Ill., 1952-60; pres. Coder Taylor Assos., Inc., 1960—. Trustee, Sherman Garden Apts. Trust, 1946-52. Mem. Glenview Plan Commn.; chmn. Glenview Appearance Commn., 1968-72. Served to lt. comdr., Civil Engr. Corps, USNR, 1942-45. Registered architect, Ill., Mich., Wis., Ind., Iowa, Colo., Fla., N.J., Nat. Council Archtl. Registration Bds.; registered profl. engr., Ill. Recipient various awards for archtl. works. Fellow AIA (pres. Chgo. chpt.); mem. Architects Assn. Ill., Am. Soc. for Ch. Architecture, Ill. Assn. Redevel. Authorities, Am. Arbitration Assn. (nat. panel arbitrators), Scarab. Tau Sigma Delta, Sigma Phi Epsilon. Methodist. Club: North Shore Country and Curling (Glenview). Contbr. articles to profl. jours. Prin. works include: Municipal Bldg., St. Charles, 1939, Sherman Garden Apts., Evanston, Ill., 1948, Amana Refrigeration, Inc., Amana, Iowa, 1956, 1200 unit family housing Kinchloe AFB, Mich., 1958-63, 530 unit family housing U.S. Naval Tng. Center, Gt. Lakes, Ill., 1960, Indak Mfg. Co., Northbrook Ill., 1957-59, 62, Gibson Community Hosp. Annex, Gibson City, Ill., 1963; 1020 Grove, Evanston, Ill., 1965; Glenview Pub. Library, 1968; Wilmette Park Dist. Recreation, 1973-75; Des Plaines Pub. Library, 1974; Wilmette Village Hall, 1975; Alpha Phi Internat. Hdqrs., 1975, Wilmatte Park Dist. Recreation Complex, 1976, Barrington Area Library, 1977. Home: 727 Redwood

Ln Glenview IL 60025 Office: 500 Green Bay Rd Kenilworth IL 60043 also 1200 Central Ave Wilmette IL 60091

TAYLOR, DONALD ROBERT, distbg. co. exec.; b. Detroit, Oct. 4, 1931; s. Herbert F. and Mary (Jekot) T.; Asso. in Sci., Lawrence Tech. Inst., 1961; m. Dorothy Ruth Curtis, June 28, 1958; children—Dean, Diane, Dwayne, Donna. Service mgr. Earle Equipment Co., Detroit, Mich., 1959-63, dir. of parts service, 1963-67, exec. asst., 1967-70, v.p. and gen. mgr., 1970—; mem. Miosha Standards Com., 1973-76. Served with USMC, 1952-54; Korea. Mem. Engring. Soc. of Detroit, Soc. of Automotive Engrs., Mich. Equipment Dealers Assn. (dir. 1972—). Lutheran. Club: Fairlane. Office: PO Box 305 Romulus MI 48174

TAYLOR, EDMUND EUGENE, metrologist; b. Eaton, Ind., May 30, 1924; s. Howard and Guila Beatrice (Barley) T.; student pub. schs. Electronic inspection Farnsworth TV & Radio Co., Marion, Ind., 1943; radio facsimile devel. RCA, Indpls., 1944; owner, chief engr. Taylor Elec. Lab., Indpls., 1943—; with P.R. Mallory & Co. Inc., Indpls., 1944—, metrologist elec. standards lab., 1945—. Treas., Mid-E. Civic League, Indpls., 1968—. Curator, historian, archivist Ed Taylor Radio Mus., Indpls., 1973—. Mem. Marion County (Ind.) Hist. Soc., Instrument Soc. Am., Antique Wireless Assn., Ind. Hist. Radio Soc. (treas. 1971—), Antique Radio Club Am., Can. Vintage Wireless Assn., Indpls. Radio Club, Am. Guild Organists, Am. Theatre Organ Soc. Patentee in field. Home: 245 N Oakland Ave Indianapolis IN 46201 Office: 3029 E Washington St Indianapolis IN 46206

TAYLOR, FLORENCE MARIE, author; b. New Smithville, Pa.; d. Franklin Newton and Clara Jennie (Kistler) T.; B.A., Butler U. Mem. staff personnel dept. Diamond Chain Co., Indpls.; reporter Fairchild's Publs., N.Y.C.; local corr. Universal Trade Press Syndicate, N.Y.C., 1944-56; free-lance author, 1935—; author poetry: Night of Stars, 1956; contbr. poems to N.Y. Times, N.Y. Jour. Am., Think Mag., Washington Star; contbr. articles to various mags. Named Poet Laureate of Ind., Fedn. Poetry Clubs, 1945-46. Home: 5300 W 96th St Indianapolis IN 46268

TAYLOR, FRANK DESMOND, engring. co. exec.; b. Belper, Eng., May 6, 1926; s. Frank and Cissie (Fletcher) T.; ed. pub. schs., Eng.; m. Annie Rebecca Glover, June 9, 1945; children—Gregory Fletcher, Andrew Fletcher, Timothy John. Came to U.S., 1968. Chief engr. Short Bros. & Harland, Belfast, Eng., 1954-58; chief engr. Plessey Co., Swindon, Eng., 1958-64, gen. mgr. Hydraulic div., 1964-68; v.p., gen. mgr. Sundstrand Corp., Rockford, Ill., 1968-70, group v.p., 1970—; dir. United Bank of Ill., Rockford. Bd. dirs., mem. exec. bd. Boy Scouts Am. Home: 2627 Norwood Dr Rockford IL 61107 Office: 2210 Harrison Ave Rockford IL 61101

TAYLOR, GENE, congressman: b. nr. Sarcoxie, Mo., Feb. 10, 1928; student S.W. Mo. State Coll., Springfield, 1945-46; m. Dorothy Wooldridge, July 26, 1947; children—Linda Kay, Larry Eugene. Mayor, Sarcoxie, 1954-60; automobile dealer, Sarcoxie, 1958-73; mem. 93d-95th Congresses from Mo. Republican nat. committeeman, 1966-72. Trustee Mo. So. Coll., Joplin. Mem. Mo. N.G., 1948-49. Mem. Mo., Sarcoxie chambers commerce. Methodist. Clubs: Masons, Shriners, Lions. Home: Fairlane Meadows Sarcoxie MO 64862 Office: 1114 Longworth House Office Bldg Washington DC 20515

TAYLOR, HENRY OLIVER, JR., paper products co. exec.; b. Jacksonville, Fla., Dec. 22, 1924; s. Henry Oliver and Elizabeth Stormes (Heagy) T.; student Carroll Coll., 1946-47, Jacksonville U., 1947-48; B.A., Vanderbilt U., 1950; m. Anne Frances Locke, Dec. 31, 1949; children—Henry Oliver III, Lise Anne. Plant supt. Container Corp. Am., Chattanooga, 1952-57; plant mgr. Mead Corp., Miami, Fla., 1957-62; plant and office mgr., Chgo., 1962-65; pres. Corr-Pak Corp., McCook, Ill., 1965—, also prin. owner. Served with inf. and air corps AUS, 1942-45. Republican. Methodist. Clubs: Downers Grove Golf, Great Books, Meadows Swim. Home: 5804 Primrose Ln Lisle IL 60532 Office: Route 66 and Indiana Harbor Belt RR McCook IL 60525

TAYLOR, HERMAN LAMON, lawyer; b. Knox County, Ill., Jan. 18, 1902; s. James Allen and Martha (Varnold) T.; A.B. magna cum laude, Knox Coll., 1926; J.D. cum laude, U. Chgo., 1932; m. Berniece Pollock, Sept. 24, 1931; children—Jean Ann (Mrs. James S. Johns), William Miles. Rural sch. tchr. Knox County, 1920, 22; coach, high sch. prin. Rio (Ill.) Consol. Sch. System, 1926-30; admitted to Ill. bar, 1932; asso. McCulloch & McCulloch, Chgo., 1932-41; with Essington, McKibbin, Beebe & Pratt, 1941-65, partner, 1948-65; asso. Lord, Bissell & Brook, Chgo., 1965-69; partner McCulloch, Veatch & Taylor, 1969—. Mem. Flossmoor (Ill.) Zoning Bd. Appeals, 1959-74, chmn., 1961-74; mem. Flossmoor Planning Commn., 1961-74. Bd. dirs. Greater Chgo. Churchmen, 1960—, pres., 1966-67; bd. dirs., finance com., exec. com. Ch. Fedn. Greater Chgo., 1957—. Recipient Alumni Achievement award Knox Coll., 1971; named Layman of Year, Greater Chgo. Churchmen, 1961. Mem. Am., Ill., Chgo. bar assns., Judicature Soc., Am. Arbitration Assn. (mem. nat. panel arbitrators 1965—), Elec. Assn. Chgo. (dir. 1973-75), Knox Coll. Alumni (Chgo. pres. 1954-55), Lambda Chi Alpha. Republican. Mason, Kiwanian. Clubs: Beverly Hills University, Beverly Cotillion (pres. 1942, 43); Executives (Chgo.); Flossmoor (Ill.) Country. Home: 1610 Brassie Ave Flossmoor IL 60422 Office: 72 W Adams St Chicago IL 60603

TAYLOR, JACK PAUL, supt. schs.; b. Wapakonata, Ohio, Jan. 27, 1931; s. George T. and Frieda (Moeller) T.; B.S., Bowling Green State U., 1953, M.S., 1954; Ph.D., Ohio State U., 1966; m. Berneda Florence Ruck, Dec. 27, 1953; children—Thomas Roberts, Carole Jane. Sr. social studies instr., guidance Perrysburg (Ohio) Schs., 1954-56; high sch. prin. Liberty Center Schs., 1956-59; supt. schs., Crestline, Ohio, 1959-62, Xenia, Ohio, 1964-67; supt. of schs., Saginaw, Mich., 1967-76, Shaker Heights, Ohio, 1977—; coordinator Sch. Mgmt. Inst. (Columbus, Ohio); vis. prof. Central State U.; cons. grad. faculty Ohio State U. Pres., Future Tchrs. Ohio, 1952; mem. Library Bd., Crestline, 1959-62; mem. Human Relations Commn., Mayor's Com. Concern; chmn. Nat. Consortium on Ednl. Evaluation. Mem. exec. com. Young Republicans Ohio, 1950-54. Bd. dirs. United Fund, Jr. Achievement, YMCA; pres. Saginaw Symphony Assn.; trustee United Appeal Crestline. Recipient Worth McClure award Am. Assn. Sch. Adminstrs., 1964; E.E. Lewis award in edn. Ohio State U., also Frontier's Internat. service award of year, 1973. Mem. Xenia Area C. of C. (dir.), Distributive Edn. Clubs Am. (past nat. v.p.), Mich. Middle Cities Edn. Assn. (pres.), Bowling Green State U. Alumni Assn. (trustee), Ohio Soc. N.Y., Delta Tau Delta, Omicron Delta Kappa, Pi Sigma Alpha, Phi Delta Kappa. Mem. United Ch. Christ. Rotarian. Club: Edliners (pres.) (Ohio State U.). Home: 21875 S Woodland Rd Shaker Heights OH 44122

TAYLOR, JAMES ROBERT, chemist; b. Dubuque, Iowa, Apr. 3, 1923; s. Fredrick Karl and Helen Elizabeth (Webster) T.; B.S., U. Dubuque, 1947; m. Betty Jane Thoma, June 19, 1944; children—Robert, David, Richard. Chemist, Swift & Co., Oakbrook, Ill., 1948-52, research chemist 1952-65, 1969-73, supr. routine chemistry, 1969-72, sect. head analytical services, 1973—. Served with U.S. Army, 1943-45, 1951, 1952. Decorated Bronze Star with oak leaf cluster. Mem. Am. Oil Chemist Soc., Am. Chem. Soc., ASTM, Lombard Hist. Soc. Republican. Episcopal. Contbr. articles to profl. jours. Home: 560 S Fairfield Lombard IL 60148 Office: 1919 Swift Dr Oak Brook IL 60148

TAYLOR, JANE URBAN, market researcher; b. Sacramento; d. Clarence Urban and Virginia (Doron) Taylor; certificate studies U. Valencia (Spain), 1960; B.A., Northwestern U., 1962; student ((Fulbright grant) U. Madrid (Spain), 1962-63; M.A. (Univ. fellow), U. Ill., 1964; M.B.A., U. Chgo., 1971. Market analyst, med. writer Davee Koehnlein & Keating, Chgo., 1964-69; mgr. client services, pharm. market research IMS Am. Ltd., Chgo.-DesPlaines, Ill., 1969-71, free-lance drug market research, 1971—; writer abstracts, transl. AMA, Chgo., 1965-71; bus. mgr., treas., Natresources, Inc., Chgo., 1971-73; mgr. marketing analysis G.D. Searle & Co., Chgo., 1973—. Mem. Am. Marketing Assn., Council Fgn. Relations, Art Inst. Chgo., Phi Beta Kappa. Club: Columbia Yacht. Home: 210 E Pearson St Chicago IL 60611 Office: G D Searle Co PO Box 5110 Chicago IL 60680

TAYLOR, JAY ROBERT, mktg. exec.; b. Waterbury, Conn., May 5, 1935; s. William Oliver and Mary Elizabeth (Plummer) T.; Asso. Sci. in Mech. Engring., New Haven Coll., 1959; B.B.A., Northwestern U., 1972, M.B.A., 1973; m. Rebecca Lee, Feb. 28, 1962; 1 dau., Lauren Elizabeth. Vice pres. mktg. signal products div. Amerace Corp., 1977—. Chmn. bd. fin. Town of Morris (Conn.), 1959-64. Served with AUS, 1957-58. Mem. Am. Mktg. Assn., IEEE. Republican. Roman Catholic. Patentee in field. Home: 725 Trailside Dr Lake Zurich IL 60047

TAYLOR, JOHN LLOYD, museum dir.; b. Muskegon, Mich., May 24, 1935; s. William Burton and Grace (Kidder) T.; student U. Denver, 1954-55; A.A., Muskegon Community Coll., 1959; B.A., So. Ill. U., 1960, M.A., 1965; postgrad. Courtauld Inst. Art, London U., 1962. Asst. dir. Hackley Art Gallery, Muskegon, 1958-59; exhbn. coordinator art dept. Southern Ill. U., Carbondale, 1959-60, 63-64, head Univ. Galleries, 1964-65; dir. Madison (Wis.) Art Center, 1965-67; dir. exhbns. and collections Milw. Art Center, 1967-72; dir. Art History Galleries, U. Wis., Milw., 1972-74; curator Sidney Kohl Collection, Milw., 1974-76; dir. Fine Art Galleries, U. Wis., Milw., 1976—, asso. prof., 1972-74, lectr., 1976—; adviser visual arts Summerfest, Milw., 1970-72. Served with AUS, 1956-57. Nat. Endowment Arts fellow, 1972, 74. Mem. Am. Assn. Museums (chmn. accreditation and vis. coms.), Internat. Council Museums, Midwest Museums Conf., Wis. Fedn. Museums, Coll. Art Assn. Am., Internat. Inst. Conservation Historic and Artistic Works, Archives Am. Art. Editor and introduction: Alberto Giacometti: The Complete Graphics, 1970; contbg. editor Mid West Art, 1971—; contbr. articles to profl. jours. Office: Fine Arts Galleries U Wis Milwaukee WI 53201

TAYLOR, KENNETH ROBERT, surgeon; b. Noble, Ill., Mar. 17, 1906; s. William Otis and Lilly Belle (Meredith) T.; grad. So. Ill. State U., 1928; M.B., Chgo. Med. Sch., 1938, M.D., 1939; postgrad. Ill. Postgrad. Med. Sch., 1938-40; m. Ruth J. Summers, Dec. 24, 1935; children—Kenneth William, Meredith Lee. Intern, West Side Hosp., Cook County County Hosp., Chgo., 1938-39; owner, operator North Av. Hosp., Chgo., 1936-58, chief surgeon, 1939-58; chief surgeon Riverview Amusement Park, Chgo., 1940-57, Morton Salt Co., 1943—; operator, gen. surgeon Jackson Hosp., Olney, Ill., 1949-53; mem. attending staff Am. Hosp., Chgo., 1960—. Pres., Taylor Oil and Minerals Corp., Chgo., 1958—. Mem. med. parents loyalty fund com. Duke, 1962—, fund raiser, 1962—; fund raiser, promotional work So. Ill. U., S.E. Mo. State Coll. Pres., bd. dirs. Ill. Post Grad. Med. Sch. Served to capt., M.C., AUS, 1943-46; ETO. Recipient Wisdom award honor Wisdom Hall Fame, 1971. Mem. A.M.A., Ill., Chgo. med. socs., Assn. Mil. Surgeons U.S., Am. Soc. Abdominal Surgeons. Republican. Mem. Congl. Christian Ch. Lion (Wicker Park charter mem.; pres. 1949-50). Home: Taylor Ln Rural Route 2 Noble IL 62868

TAYLOR, LARRY LEE, sch. adminstr.; b. Homer, Ill., Mar. 21, 1937; s. Virgil Charles and Ethel Telitha (Wright) T.; B.S., Eastern Ill. U., 1959; M.S., U. Ill., 1964; m. Shirley Ann Burton, Dec. 21, 1957; children—Kimberly Ann. Speech correctionist Dixon (Ill.) pub. schs., 1959-64, dir. spl. edn., 1964-65; exec. dir. Truman Sch. for Retarded Children, Dixon, 1964-65; head tchr., coach Grand Detour Sch., Dixon, 1965-67; prin. Lincoln Sch., Dixon, 1967—. Bd. dirs. Truman Sch. for Handicapped, Dixon Petunia Festival, 1968-70. Mem. Nat., Ill. edn. assns., Nat. Assn. Elementary Sch. Prins., Ill. Elementary Sch. Prins. Assn., Sigma Alpha Eta (pres. 1958). Methodist (asst. supt. personnel Sunday sch. 1969-71). Lion. Author: Speech Fun Through Pictures. Home: 324 Prospect St Dixon IL 61021 Office: 510 Lincoln Ave Dixon IL 61021

TAYLOR, LOGAN, machine co. exec.; b. Tamaroa, Ill., Aug. 25, 1917; s. James B. and Rosa Lee (Logan) T.; ed. pub. schs.; m. Lida L. Lisenby, Feb. 24, 1943; 1 dau., Cynthia (Mrs. Stephen Rice). Exec., Taylor Bros. Welding and Machine Works, Inc., Tamaroa, Ill., 1936—, also sec., 1968—. Mem. First Christian Ch. Home: Box 44 E Main St Tamaroa IL 62888 Office: E Main St Tamaroa IL 62888

TAYLOR, MARY JOAN (MRS. EDWARD MCKINLEY TAYLOR, JR.), lawyer; b. Kenton, Ohio, Dec. 24, 1926; d. Maurice A. and Martina (Dolan) McMahon; student St. Mary Springs Coll., 1944-45; Asso. Degree in Bus. Adminstrn. Frankin U., 1946-49; J.D. with high distinction, Ohio No. U., 1951; postgrad., U. Wyo., 1954-56; m. Edward McKinley Taylor, Jr., Apr. 23, 1952; 1 dau., Mary Margaret. Admitted to Ohio bar, 1951; gen practice law, Kenton, 1951-52, Wichita Falls, Tex., 1953—; mem. law firm Taylor and Taylor, Dayton, Ohio, 1957—; law librarian Franklin U., 1948-49. Mem. Ohio Bar Assn., Montgomery County Law Library Assn., Ohio No. U. Alumni Assn. (sec. Miami Valley 1958-60), Ieta Tau Lambda, Kappa Beta Pi. Club: Soroptomist. Home: 7417 N Main St Dayton OH 45415

TAYLOR, MELVIN A., graphic arts co. exec.; b. Eureka Twp., Mich., Feb. 14, 1930; s. James George and Marie C. (Christiansen) T.; grad. high sch.; m. Marjorie A. Anderson, Sept. 4, 1948; children—Gregory M., Melodee A. Printer, Banner Pub. Co., Belding, Mich., 1948-54, advt. mgr., 1954-65, bus. and sales mgr., 1961-65; corp. treas., plant mgr. graphic arts Three Rivers Press Corp. (Mich.), 1965—, bus. mgr., 1965—. Lutheran. Mason, Rotarian, Elk. Home: 312 Walnut St Three Rivers MI 49093 Office: 112 Prutzman St Three Rivers MI 49093

TAYLOR, MORRIS, analytical chemist; b. St. Louis, July 10, 1922; s. Henry Clay Nathaniel and Georgia Leanna (Kenner) Taylor; B.S. in Chemistry, St. Louis U., 1952; m. Millie B. Fudge, July 17, 1948 (dec. Jan. 2, 1969); children—Morris, Jr., Carla Maria; m. 2d Veonnia J. McDonald, Aug. 4, 1973; children—Dorcas Lynnea, Demetrius Sirrom. Research chemist Universal Match Corp., Ferguson, Mo., 1952-54; mfg. chemist Sigma Chem. Co., St. Louis, 1954; clin. chemist 5th Army Area Med. Lab., St. Louis, 1955-56; with Dept. Agr.-Agrl. Research Service Meat and Poultry Inspection Lab., St. Louis, 1956—, supervisory chemist, 1967-76, chemist-in-charge, 1976—. Mem. Draft Bd. III, 5 years; rating panel mem. Bd. U.S. Civil Service Examiners for Eastern Dist. Mo., Madison and St. Clair Counties, Ill., 1969—; reviewer for Assn. Ofcl. Analytical Chemists; collaborator FDA Labs. on Analytical Methods. Mem. Am. Chem. Soc. (certified), Assn. Ofcl. Analytical Chemists, St. Louis U. Alumni Chemist Assn., Omega Psi Phi (charter mem. Omicron Sigma chpt.). Recipient Suggestion award by Dept. Agr. Animal-Plant Health Inspection Service Sci. and Tech. Services Meat and Poultry Inspection Lab. for use of hydrogen generators in lab. to reduce hazard of tanks of hydrogen; participant in group award for analytical proficiency Dept. Agr. Home: 4464 Clarence St St Louis MO 63115 Office: Room 942 1114 Market St St Louis MO 63101

TAYLOR, RALPH ORIEN, JR., developer, builder, investor; b. Kansas City, Mo., Jan. 6, 1919; s. Ralph Orien and Genevieve (Sturgeon) T.; student U. Kansas City, 1936-38; B.S., U. Mo., 1940; m. Betty Boswell, Dec. 7, 1940 (dec. 1959); children—Bradley, Nancy. Partner Sturgeon & Taylor, 1940-42; owner Sturgeon & Taylor, Inc., Kansas City, Mo., 1942—, chmn. bd., 1959—; pres. Sturgeon & Taylor Investment Co., Inc., 1949—, chmn. bd., 1959—; pres. Sturgeon & Taylor Devel. Co., 1950—, chmn. bd., 1959—; pres., chmn. bd. Sturgeon & Taylor Realty Co., Inc., 1955—; pres., chmn. bd. Park Estates, Inc., Tiger Constn. Co., Inc., Charm Homes, Inc., Bengal Homes, Inc., Westbrooke Hotels, Inc., Sturgeon & Taylor Co., Joint Venture. dir., mem. exec. com. Patrons State Bank & Trust, Olathe, Kan. Mem. adv. council U. Mo. Sch. Forestry. Served as lt. comdr. USNR, World War II. Recipient Bronze Star medal. Mem. Home Builders Assn. Greater Kansas City (dir., pres.), Johnson County (Kans.), Kansas City (Mo.) real estate bds., Nat. Assn. Home Builders (life dir.), Phi Delta Theta. Clubs: Kansas City, Indian Hills Country; Lauderdale Yacht, Ft. Lauderdale. Home: 3505 W 71st St Prairie Village KS 66208 Office: 6909 Nall Ave Prairie Village KS 66208

TAYLOR, RAYMOND ELLORY, materials scientist; b. Ames, Iowa, Oct. 19, 1929; s. Alva A. and Maude Marguarite (Crow) T.; B.S., Iowa State U., 1951; M.S., U. Idaho, 1957; Ph.D., (N. Am. fellow), Pa. State U., 1967; m. Elfa Mae Shaffer, Apr. 27, 1952; children—Wayne Alva, David Leo. Research chemist, supr. Gen. Electric Co., Richland, Wash., 1951-57; sr. research N. Am. Rockwell Group., Canoga Park, Calif., 1957-64; asso. sr. research Purdue U., West Lafayette, Ind., 1967-74, sr. researcher, head Properties Research Lab., 1974—. Com. chmn. Boy Scouts Am., 1970-75. NSF grantee. Mem. ASTM, Sigma Xi, Phi Lambda Upsilon. Contbr. articles to profl. jours. Home: 618 Essex St West Lafayette IN 47906 Office: 2595 Yeager Rd West Lafayette IN 47906

TAYLOR, RICHARD FRENCH, veterinarian; b. Shelbina, Mo., May 5, 1936; s. Richard French and Willie Ben (Maupin) T.; B.S. in Agr., U. Mo., Columbia, 1962, D.V.M., 1962; m. Joyce Lee Thoeni, Sept. 3, 1960; children—Leigh Anne, Rick, Lisa Jan. Gen. practice veterinary medicine, Fayette, Mo., 1962—; sr. partner Howard County Veterinary Service, Fayette, 1972—. Bd. dirs., chmn. antique veterinary equipment Mo. Veterinary Med. Found.; mem. Fayette RIII Bd. Edn. Served with U.S. Army, 1958. Mem. Am., Mo., W. Central, Northeast veterinary med. assns., Soc. for Theriogenology, Am. Assn. Bovine Practitioners, Am. Assn. Swine Practitioners, U. Mo. Alumni Assn., U. Mo. Veterinary Alumni Assn., Phi Eta Sigma, Alpha Zeta, Gamma Sigma Delta, Phi Zeta. Democrat. Baptist. Office: Howard County Veterinary Service Hwy 5 and 240 N Fayette MO 65248

TAYLOR, ROBERT MALCOLM, physician; b. Detroit, Sept. 13, 1924; s. Malcolm Edgar and Mary Estelle (Trevarthen) T.; student U. Vermont, 1943, Washington U., St. Louis, 1944; M.D., Wayne U., 1948; m. Lorna Elaine Mundt, June 21, 1947; children—Robert Malcolm, Jr., Jill Anne, Sara Jo. Intern, Harper Hosp., Detroit, 1948-49; resident in internal medicine Crile VA Hosp., Cleve., 1950-53; internist Burns Clinic, Petoskey, Mich., 1955—, v.p., 1964-68, 71-74, dir., 1971-74. Mem. Emmet County Rep. Com., 1958-64; del. Mich. Rep. Convention, 1960; elder Presbyterian Ch., Petoskey. Served as capt. M.C., U.S. Army, 1949-50, 53-54. Fellow Am. Coll. Chest Physicians; mem. AMA, Mich. (internal medicine del.), No. Mich. med. socs., A.C.P., Am., Mich. (pres. elect 1977) socs. internal medicine. Clubs: Birchwood Country (Harbor Springs, Mich.), DeMoley. Home: Box 500 Birchwood Farm Estate Harbor Springs MI 49740 Office: Burns Clinic Petoskey MI 49770

TAYLOR, SAMUEL GALE, III, physician; b. Elmhurst, Ill., Sept. 2, 1904; s. Samuel Gale, Jr. and Anna Jeffrey (Mead) T.; B.A., Yale, 1927; M.D., U. Chgo., 1931; m. Eleanor Roberts, June 1, 1938; children—Constance (Mrs. William Blackwell), John Winthrop, Samuel Gale IV. Intern, Highland Park Hosp., Chgo., 1931; intern Cook County Hosp., Chgo., 1932-33, resident, 1933-35, research fellow metabolic diseases, 1935-40, attending physician, mem. tumor bd., 1963-66; asso., instr., asst. prof. medicine Rush Med. Coll., Chgo., 1933-42, prof. medicine, 1971-77, emeritus, 1977—, dir. Cancer Center Planning Program, 1972-74; asso. dir. Rush Cancer Center, 1975-77; asso. prof. medicine U. Ill. Coll. Medicine, Chgo., 1942-65, mem. Tumor Council, 1948-72, dir. steroid therapy div. Tumor Clinic, 1950-71, prof. medicine, 1965-74, emeritus, 1974—; dir. sect. med. oncology, dept. medicine Presbyn.-St. Lukes Hosp., 1954-71, asso. attending physician, 1961-65, sr. attending, 1965—, cons., 1971—; chmn. tumor bd. West Side VA Hosp., 1967-72, cons. staff, 1966-72; asst. attending physician Henrotin Hosp., 1935-36, sr. attending physician, 1936-45; asst. attending physician Presbyn. Hosp., 1941-50; asso. attending physician Lake Forest (Ill.) Hosp., 1945-55, cons. staff, 1955—. Mem. Bd. Health, Lake Forest, 1946-58; chmn. med. adv. com. Chgo. Vis. Nurses Assn., 1955-65; pres. Ill. Cancer Council, 1972-74; dir. Ill. Cancer Council Comprehensive Cancer Center Program, 1974-77. Dir., S.G. Taylor Chain Co., Inc. Trustee, cancer cons. Nat. Cancer Inst.; mem. adv. com. Cancer Control Program, HEW, 1956-60; liaison mem. cancer commn. A.C.S., 1956-73; cancer adv. com. Ill. Dept. Pub. Health, 1976—. Diplomate Am. Bd. Internal Medicine. Fellow A.C.P. (chmn. com. on cancer 1959-73); mem. Am., Pan Am. med. assns., Ill., Chgo. med. socs., Central Soc. for Clin. Research, James Ewing Soc., Am. Radium Soc., Chgo. Soc. Internal Medicine, Am. Soc. Clin. Oncology, AAAS, Am. Soc. Cancer Research, Am. Cancer Soc. (dir.-at-large, Distinguished Service award), Inst. Medicine of Chgo., Am. Diabetes Assn., N.Y. Acad. Scis., AAUP, Chgo. Soc. Internal Medicine, Am. Coll. Radiology (Commn. on Cancer 1960-76), Sigma Xi. Episcopalian. Clubs: Wausaukee; University; Onwensia. Contbr. articles Episcopalian. Clubs: Wausaukee; University; Onwensia. Contbr. articles to profl. jours., also chpts. to books. Home: Athlestane WI 54104 Office: 37 S Wabash Ave Chicago IL 60603

TAYLOR, THOMAS FRANKLIN, lawyer; b. Effingham, Ill., July 14, 1934; s. Harold J. and Elsa K. (Kuglar) T.; B.S., U. Ill., 1955, J.D., 1957. Admitted to Ill. bar, 1960; partner Taylor & Taylor, attys., Effingham, Ill., 1960—; v.p., now pres. Effingham Title Co., 1960—. U.S. Fed. magistrate, 1971-74; city atty., Effingham, 1961—. Precinct committeeman Democratic Party, 1968-76. Mem. exec. bd. Effingham United Fund, 1970-71, Lincoln Trails council Boy Scouts Am. Served to 1st lt. AUS, 1957-59. Mem. Am., Ill., Effingham County (pres. 1964, 74) bar assns., Ill. Land Title Assn. (bd. dirs. 1962-63, treas. 1964, 69). Mason (Shriner), Elk. Home: Box 668 Effingham IL 62401 Office: 120 E Washington St Effingham IL 62401

TAYLOR, VAUGHN KEMP, psychologist, ednl. adminstr.; b. Dayton, Ohio, May 1, 1931; s. Guy Elza and Marion Earline (Kemp) T.; m. Shirley Ann Krieger, July 25, 1953; children—Vaughn Craig, Deborah Sue, Julia Ann. B.S., U. Dayton, 1953; M.Ed., Wittenberg U., 1960; postgrad. Miami U., 1959-64; Ph.D., Ohio State U., 1970. Grad. asst. Ohio State U., 1968-69; tchr. Northwestern Local Schs., Ohio, 1953-58; tchr., counselor Dayton Bd. Edn., 1958-68; counselor pub. schs., Columbus, Ohio, 1968-69; mem. adminstrv. staff Ohio State Med. Sch., 1969-72, adj. asso. prof. preventive medicine, 1970-73; adminstr. continuing edn., health careers Clark Tech. Coll., 1971-73; prin. Kiser High Sch., Dayton, 1973—; pvt. practice psychol. counseling, 1970—; instr. edn. Wittenberg U., 1970-73. Coordinator profl. div. United Way Clark County, 1971-72; mem. com. to study Springfield Pub. Schs., 1971-72; pres. Tri-County Council, 1969-73; bd. dirs. Delta Dental Plan Ohio, 1971-72, Clark County Heart Assn. Mem. Am., Ohio psychol. assns., Nat. Assn. Secondary Sch. Prins., Phi Delta Kappa. Mem. United Ch. of Chris. Club: Lions. Home: 516 Heiss Ave Dayton OH 45403

TAYLOR, WALTER PORTER, warehouse co. exec.; b. Asheville, N.C., Feb. 12, 1910; s. Walter P. and Mary Katharine (Henderson) T.; student Williams Coll., 1932; m. Polly Gable, June 20, 1953; children—Nancy, Sally. Asst. gen. mgr. Cin. Mdse. Warehouses, Inc., 1936-40; v.p. Lawrence Warehouse, Altanta, 1940-43; v.p. N.Y. Terminal Warehouse Co., Chgo., 1946-49; Allied Distbn., Inc., Chgo., 1950-53; pres., treas., dir. Affiliated Warehouse Cos., Inc., Chgo., 1953—. Served to lt. Signal Corps USNR, 1943-46. Mem. Nat. Council Phys. Distbn. Mgmt., Beta Theta Pi. Clubs: Chgo. Traffic, Chgo. Transp., San Francisco Press. Home: 2052 Lincoln Park W Chicago IL 60614 Office: 222 W Adams St Chicago IL 60606

TAYLOR, WILLIAM MENKE, elec. wiring harnesses co. exec.; b. Logansport, Ind., May 24, 1918; s. William T. and Ethel M. (Menke) T.; student in bus. adminstrn. LaSalle Coll., 1936-40; A.A.F., Elec. Spl. Sch., Lincoln, Nebr., 1942; m. Betty L. Flory, May 8, 1944; children—William M., Alan R. Cost accountant Essex Wire Corp., Logansport, 1935-50, salesman, 1950-55, plant mgr., 1955-56; sales mgr., plant mgr. Airdesign Corp., Norristown, Pa., 1956-60; sales mgr. Dill Products, Inc., Norristown, 1960-73; pres. Tay-Mor Industries Inc., Logansport, 1973—; instr. aircraft elec. systems. Served with USAF, 1942-45. Named Ky. Col. Mem. Soc. of Automotive Engrs. Republican. Clubs: Logansport Country, Elks, Masons. Home: 2825 Perrysburg Rd Logansport IN 46947 Office: PO Box 64 Logansport IN 46947

TAYLOR, WINNIFRED JANE, psychologist; b. Akron, Ohio, Aug. 27, 1925; d. Edwin Dain and Jessie Pearl (Keeran) Fletcher; B.S., U. Akron, 1962, M.S., 1965, Ph.D., 1971; m. John Idris Taylor, June 22, 1943; children—John Frederick Taylor, Timothy David Taylor, Kathryn Sue Taylor Cline. Tchr., Akron and Barberton, Ohio, 1959-65; sch. psychologist Akron Pub. Sch., 1965-74; pvt. practice family counseling and psychology, Clinton, Ohio, 1969-74; asst. prof. counselor edn. U. Wis., Superior, 1974—. Recipient Freedom Found. award for Teaching, 1965-66. Mem. Nat. Assn. Sch. Psychologists, Am., Wis. personnel and guidance assns., Am. Soc. Adlerian Psychology, Am. Edn. Research Assn., Am. Sch. Counselors Assn., Assn. Humanistic Psychology, Douglas County Mental Health Assn., Am. Soc. Individual Psychology. Contbr. articles to profl. jours. Home: 3d and Lake Ave Lake Nebagamon WI 54849 Office: U Wis Dept Edn Adminstrn and Counseling Superior WI 54880

TEAGER, JOHN CARLYLE, chem. co. exec.; b. Dakota City, Nebr., Dec. 19, 1932; s. Mark Carlyle and Eva Matilda (Johnson) T.; B.S. in Bus. Adminstrn., U. Nebr., 1960; m. Patricia Ann Friest, Nov. 29, 1957; children—John, Lisa Ann, Mary Pat. Rate auditor, Maytag Co., Newton, Iowa, 1960-62; buyer Collins Radio Co., Cedar Rapids, Iowa, 1962-65; adminstrv. specialist Fisher Controls Co., Marshalltown, Iowa, 1965-71; purchasing mgr. Hach Chem. Co., Ames, 1971—; owner Teager's Art & Frame Shoppe, Marshalltown, 1972—. Served with USN, 1957-60; Korea. Mem. Profl. Picture Framers Assn., Purchasing Mgmt. Assn. Republican. Home: 1511 Brentwood Terr Marshalltown IA 50158 Office: 100 Dayton Ave Ames IA 50010

TEAGER, PATRICIA ANN, nurse; b. Eldora, Iowa, Oct. 31, 1935; d. Amos Edwin and Verdelle Henrietta (Amundson) Friest; B.S.N., U. Iowa, 1957; m. John Carlyle Teager, Nov. 29, 1957; children—John, Lisa Ann, Mary Pat. Exec. dir. Dist. 4 Nebr. Nurses Assn., Lincoln, 1958-59; evening supr. Mercy Hosp., Marshalltown, Iowa, 1966-69; instr. Marshalltown Community Sch. Nursing, 1969-75, dir., 1975—. Mem. Nat. League Nursing, Iowa Nurses Assn., AAUW, Delta Kappa Gamma. Democrat. Home: 1511 Brentwood Terr Marshalltown IA 50158 Office: 3 4th Ave S Marshalltown IA 50158

TEASDALE, JOSEPH PATRICK, gov. Mo.; b. Kansas City, Mo., Mar. 29, 1936; s. William B. and Adah Maurine (Downey) T.; student St. Benedicts Coll., 1954-55; B.S. in Lit., Rockhurst Coll., 1957; LL.B., St. Louis U., 1960; m. M. Theresa Ferkenhoff, Oct. 13, 1973; 1 son, William D. Admitted to Mo. bar, 1960; asst. U.S. atty., 1962-66; pros. atty. Jackson County (Mo.), 1966-72; gov. Mo., Jefferson City, 1977—. Served with USAFR, 1961-67. Named Outstanding Man of Year, Jr. C. of C., 1969. Mem. Nat. Dist. Attys. Assn., Kansas City Bar Assn. Democrat. Roman Catholic. Mem. editorial staff St. Louis U. Law Jour., 1958-60. Home: 100 Madison St Jefferson City MO 65101 Office: Capitol Bldg Room 216 Jefferson City MO 65101

TEDESCHI, JOHN ALFRED, historian, librarian; b. Modena, Italy, July 17, 1931; s. Caesar George and Piera (Forti) T.; came to U.S., 1939, naturalized, 1944; B.A., Harvard U., 1954, M.A., 1960, Ph.D., 1966; m. Anne Wood Christian, Sept. 8, 1956; children—Martha, Philip, Sara. Bibliographer, European history and lit., Newberry Library, Chgo., 1965—, curator rare books and manuscripts, head dept. spl. collections, 1970—; lectr. history U. Chgo., 1969-71; vis. prof. U. Ill., Chgo., 1972-73. Served with U.S. Army, 1954-56. Recipient grants Am. Philos. Soc., 1961, Nat. Endowment Humanities, 1967; Old Dominion fellow Harvard U. Center for Renaissance Studies, Florence, Italy, 1967-68; fellow Inst. Research in Humanities, U. Wis., Madison, 1976-77. Mem. Am. Soc. Reformation Research (pres. 1972), Renaissance Soc. Am. (exec. bd, 1971—), Am. Hist. Assn. Editor series Corpus Reformatorum Italicorum, 1968—; editor-in-chief Bibliographie Internat. de L'Humanisme et de la Renaissance, 1975—; contbr. articles to profl. jours. Home: 5021 S Woodlawn Ave Chicago IL 60615 Office: 60 W Walton St Chicago IL 60610

TEEFY, PAUL DONALD, ins. agy. exec.; b. Iowa City, Jan. 16, 1926; s. John and Anna (Miller) T.; student Gustavus Adolphus Coll., 1944-46, U. Minn., 1946; B.S., State U. Iowa, 1949; m. Geraldine Oberkofler, Aug. 5, 1950; children—Margaret, Kathleen (dec.), Maureen, Patricia, Kevin (dec.), Elizabeth, Martha, Colleen. Salesman, Styleline Greeting Card Co., 1949-50; clk. Honeywell Co., Mpls., 1950, indsl. engr., 1951-56; dist. mgr. sales Woodmen Accident & Life Co., Mpls., 1956-65; owner Teefy Ins. Agy., Mpls., 1950—, Aldrich-Clark Agy., 1977—; pres., treas., Teefy Assos. Inc., Richfield Minn., 1968—. Finance chmn. Incarnation Ch., Mpls., 1975-77; precinct chmn. Republican party, 1976—. Served with Supply Corps, USNR, 1943-46. Mem. Ind. Agts. Am., Health Underwriters Mpls. (pres. 1958), Mpls. Assn. Life Underwriters, VFW (chaplain post 1491 1976-77), Am. Legion. Roman Catholic. Clubs: Lions, K.C., Amicus. Home: 4001 Colfax Ave S Minneapolis MN 55409 Office: 319 W 48th St Minneapolis MN 55409

TEEGARDEN, KENNETH LEROY, clergyman; b. Cushing, Okla., Dec. 22, 1921; s. Roy Albert and Eva B. (Swiggart) T.; student Okla. State U., 1938-40; A.B., Phillips U., 1942, M.A., 1945, D.D., 1963; B.D., Tex. Christian U., 1949, D.D., 1976; D.D., Bethany Coll., 1974; LL.D., Lynchburg Coll., 1975; L.H.D., Culver-Stockton Coll., 1975; m. Wanda Jean Strong, May 28, 1944; children—David Kent, Marshall Kirk. Ordained to ministry Christian Ch. (Disciples of Christ), 1940; pastor in Chandler, Okla., 1944-47, Texas City, Tex., 1947-48, Healdton, Okla., 1948-49, Vernon, Tex., 1949-55, Ft. Smith, Ark., 1955-58; exec. minister Christian Ch. in Ark., 1958-65, asst. to pres., Indpls., 1965-69, exec. minister in Tex., 1969-73, gen. minister, pres., Indpls., 1973—. Mem. governing bd. Nat. Council Chs., 1973—; del. 5th Assembly of World Council Chs., Nairobi, Kenya, 1975; rep. Nat. Council Chs. in Exchange of Ch. Leadership with Soviet Union, 1974. Named Distinguished Alumnus, Tex. Christian U., 1973, Phillips U., 1975; Outstanding Citizen, Vernon, Tex., 1954. Author: We Call Ourselves Disciples, 1975. Home: 7232 Highburry Dr Indianapolis IN 46256 Office: 222 S Downey Ave Indianapolis IN 46219

TEEL, ROBERT LEE, retail trade co. exec.; b. Kansas City, Mo., Mar. 7, 1925; s. William Henry and Mary Ophelia (Biddlecome) T.; B.A. in Econs., U. Kans., 1950; m. Sue Newcomer, Oct. 3, 1952; children—Leslie Sue, Robert Lee II. Founder, owner Unfinished Shop, Fairway, Kans. and Kansas City, Mo., 1955—, Robert L. Teel Co., Kansas City, 1958—, Woodcraft Products, Kansas City, 1963—. Active YMCA; mem. U.S. Olympic Swimming Com., 1972-76. Bd. dirs., v.p. Homes Assn. of Country Club Dist., Prairie Village, Kans., 1975-77. Served with USNR, 1943-46, 50-54. Mem. Amateur Athletic Union U.S. (life, regional chmn. 1969-70, nat. chmn. age group swimming com. 1970-72, pres. Mo. Valley Assn. 1971-72), Mchts. Assn. Fairway (pres. 1955-65), Am. Helicopter Soc., Mensa, Phi Kappa Psi. Clubs: Trap and Skeet Gun, Western Riding, Golf, Astronomy, Yacht, Tennis, Photography, Flying, Amateur Radio, Navy. Home: 7637 Tomahawk Rd Prairie Village KS 66208 Office: Robert L Teel Co PO Box 303 Shawnee Mission KS 66201

TEELE, DORIS CORINNE, real estate broker; b. Springfield, Ill., Feb. 13, 1926; d. John Raymond and Corinne (Burch) Headrick; student Lincoln Land Community Coll., 1970, 71, 73; B.A. in Mgmt., Sangamon State U., 1975; m. Paul Edward Teele, Nov. 27, 1945; children—Cheryl Suzette, Stephan Paul. Real estate salesman Al Sokolis, Springfield, Ill., 1955-57, James D. Call, Realtor, Springfield, 1960-64, Charles Dunseth, Realtor, Springfield, 1964-66; owner Doris Teele, Realtor, Springfield, 1958-60, 66—; owner D'Eleet Residential Rentals, Springfield, 1970—. Chmn. coalition of urban devel. com. Franklin Park Assn., 1975-76. Served with USMCR, 1945. Mem. Women Marines Assn., Family Motor Coach Assn., Land of Lincoln Coachmen (sec.), Marine Corps League, Lincoln Meml. Gardens, Springfield Art Assn., Ill. Assn. Realtors (Make Am. Better com. 1977), Luth. Ch. Women, Springfield Bd. Realtors (program chmn. 1967, chmn. Make Am. Better com. 1977-78), Alpha Omega. Lutheran (mem. evangelism com. 1974-75). Home: 4004 Hazelcrest Rd Springfield IL 62703 Office: 430 W Edwards St Springfield IL 62704

TEGEDER, ROBERT MARTIN, credit union exec.; b. Mpls., Nov. 2, 1912; s. William J. and Hildegarde (Ruegg) T.; B.A. in Bus. Adminstrn., Notre Dame U., 1930-34; m. Barbara Norblom, Sept. 23, 1936; children—Robert Martin, James David, Barbara (Mrs. Charles Bahn). Treas. Fr. Hennepin Credit Union, Mpls., 1962—. Chmn. Fort St. Charles Restoration Com., 1972—. Served with AUS, 1944-45. Mem. U.S. Natural History Soc., Minn., Hennepin County hist. socs., Fort Snelling Meml. Com., Com. for Preservation of Abandoned Mil. Posts. K.C. (4th deg., sec. Mpls. council 1938—, comptroller Nicollet assembly 1940—). Home: 5867 139th St W Apple Valley MN 55124 Office: 2745 Park Ave S Minneapolis MN 55407

TEI, TAKURI, accountant; b. Korea, Feb. 25, 1924; s. Gangen and Isun (Song) T.; came to U.S., 1952, naturalized, 1972; diploma Concordia Theol. Sem., 1959; B.D., Eden Theol. Sem., 1965; M.Ed., U. Mo., 1972; m. Maria M. Ottwaska, Dec. 1, 1969; 1 dau., Sun Kyung Lee. Partner, Madeleine Ottwaska & Assos., St. Louis, 1968—; pres. TMS Tei Enterprises Inc., Webster Groves, Mo., 1969—; instr. Forest Park Community Coll. Mem. Am. Coll. Enrolled Agts. (pres. 1976—), Am. Accounting Assn., Am. Taxation Assn., Assn. Asian Studies, NAACP. Democrat. Lutheran. Home and office: 7529 Big Bend Blvd Webster Groves MO 63119

TEICH, RALPH DONALD, bus. exec.; b. Chgo., May 24, 1925; s. Curt and Anna (Niether) T.; grad. Lake Forest Acad., 1943; B.S., Northwestern U., 1949; m. Joan Martha Laurine (div. Sept. 1965); children—Deborah, Lawrence, Cheryl; foster children—Fred W. Anderson, Robert Amirante, Gail Lynn Deloney; m. 2d, Elizabeth Perrizo, Jan. 20, 1968. Vice pres. Curt Tech & Co., Inc., Chgo., 1949-76; pres. R-Dit Enterprises, Inc., 1976—; Vice pres. Lake Forest Property Owners Assn., 1972—, past deacon, v.p. Luth. Ch. of Holy Spirit; past dir., v.p., pres., interstate bd. govs. Mid-Am. Ballet Found.; past dir., trustee numerous founds. and trusts, active local and nat. historic preservation groups. Mem. Am. Friends Austria (dir.), Field Mus. Natural History (life), Nat. History Mus., Chgo. Hist. Soc., Balzekas Mus. Lithuanian Art, Lake Forest Hist. Soc., Gleassner House, English Speaking Unions, U.S. Power Squadron. Clubs: Executives, University (Chgo.); Michigan Shores (Wilmette, Ill.); Wantagan Swedish Glee, Variety. Mason (32 deg. Shriner). Home: 700 S Ridge Rd Lake Forest IL 60045 Office: PO Box 169 Lake Forest IL 60045

TEMIN, HOWARD MARTIN, educator; b. Phila., Dec. 10, 1934; B.A., Swarthmore (Pa.) Coll., 1955, D.Sc. (hon.), 1972; Ph.D., Calif. Inst. Tech., 1959, postdoctoral fellow, 1959-60; D.Sc. (hon.), N.Y. Med. Coll., 1972, U. Pa., 1976, Hahnemann Med. Coll., 1976, Lawrence U., 1976. Asst. prof. oncology U. Wis., Madison, 1960-64, asso. prof., 1964-69, USPHS research career devel. award Nat. Cancer Inst., 1964-74, prof. oncology, 1969—, Wis. Alumni Research Found. prof. cancer research, 1971—, Am. Cancer Soc. prof. viral oncology and cell biology, 1974—; mem. virology study sect. NIH, 1971-74, spl. virus cancer program tumor virus detection segment working group Nat. Cancer Inst., 1972-73, report rev. panel Nat. Acad. Scis., 1975—. Recipient Warren Triennial prize Mass. Gen. Hosp., 1971, Spl. Commendation, Wis. Med. Soc., 1971, Pap award Papanicolaou Inst., Miami, Fla., 1972, Bertner award M.D. Anderson, Houston, 1972, U.S. Steel Found. award in molecular biology Nat. Acad. Scis., 1972, Waksman award Theobald Smith Soc., 1972, Am. Chem. Soc. award in enzyme chemistry, 1973, Modern Medicine award for distinguished achievement, 1973, Griffuel prize Assn. Devel. Recherche Cancer, Villejuif, 1973, G.H.A. Clowes Lectureship award Am. Assn. for Cancer Research, 1974, Gairdner Found. Internat. award Toronto, 1974, Albert Lasker award in basic med. research, 1974, Nobel prize for physiology or medicine, 1975, Lucy Wortham James award in basic research Soc. Surg. Oncologists, 1976, Alumni Distinguished Service award Calif. Inst. Tech., 1976; New Horizons for Radiologists lectr. Radiol. Soc. N.Am., 1968, Harry Shay Meml. lectr. Fels Inst., Phila., 1973, Dyer lectr. NIH, 1974, Harvey lectr., 1974. Fellow Am. Acad. Arts and Scis.; mem. Nat. Acad. Sci. Asso. editor: Jour. of Cellular Physiology, 1966—, Cancer Research, 1971-74; mem. editorial bd. Jour. of Virology, 1971—, Intervirology, 1972-75, Archives of Virology, 1975—, Procs. Nat. Acad. Scis., 1975—. Office: McArdle Lab 450 N Randall St U Wis Madison WI 53706

TEMPLE, DONALD ERNEST, dermatologist, allergist; b. Chgo., May 21, 1933; s. Samuel Leonard and Matilda Eve (Riff) T.; B.S. cum laude, Harvard, 1954; M.D., U. Chgo., 1958; m. Sarah Rachel Katz, Sept. 20, 1957; children—Michael A., Matthew D., Madeline B. Intern, Michael Reese Hosp., Chgo., 1958-59; resident U. Chgo. Hosps. and Clinics, Chgo., 1959-62; practice medicine specializing in dermatology and allergies, Permanente Med. Group, Santa Clara, Calif., 1964-65, Chgo., 1965-73, Glen Ellyn, Ill., 1972—; staff Louis A. Weiss Hosp., Chgo., 1965-75, Luth. Gen. Hosp., Park Ridge, Ill., 1970—, Central DuPage Hosp., Winfield, Ill., 1973—; clins. asst. Dept. Dermatology Boston U. Sch. Medicine, 1963-64; clin. instr. dermatology Stanford (Calif.) U. Sch. Medicine, 1964; clin. asst. prof. dermatology Abraham Lincoln Sch. Medicine, U. Ill., Chgo., 1972—; clin. asst. prof. allergy Stritch Sch. Medicine, 1977—, Loyola U. Hosp. 1977—. Served with AUS, 1962-64. Diplomate Am. Bd. Dermatology, Am. Bd. Allergy and Immunology. Fellow Am. Acad. Allergy, Am. Coll. Allergists, Am. Acad. Dermatology, Am. Assn. Certified Allergists; mem. Chgo. Soc. Allergy, Chgo. Dermatological Soc., Soc. Investigative Dermatology, DuPage-McHenry Lung Assn. (dir. 1975—). Contbr. articles to profl. jours. Home: 2819 Floral Dr Northbrook IL 60062 Office: 454 Pennsylvania Ave Glen Ellyn IL 60137

TEMPLEMAN, CHARLES FRANK, pub. co. exec.; b. Allendale, N.J., Sept. 7, 1922; s. Charles S. and Ina (Van Horn) T.; B.A., Montclair State Coll., 1943; M.A., Columbia, 1947; postgrad. Rutgers U., 1947-50; m. Betty Lou Albers, Oct. 11, 1947; children—Lucinda, Kurt, Greg. Tchr. bus. adminstrn. Passaic Valley Regional High Sch., Little Falls, N.J., 1946-52; field rep. South-Western Pub. Co., Cin., 1952-55, asso. editor Balance Sheet, 1955-59, editor, 1959-76, mgr. secondary sch. dept., 1966-76, asst. v.p., 1967-76, v.p. govtl. affairs, 1976—; tchr. bus. adminstrn. adult edn., Norwood, Ohio, 1960-62. Served with AUS, 1943-45; ETO. Decorated Purple Heart, Bronze Star, Silver Star. Mem. Nat., Cath., Eastern bus. edn. assns., Nat. Assn. Secondary Sch. Prins., Am. Vocational Assn. (nat. adv. council), Am. Assn. Sch. Adminstrs., Delta Pi Epsilon. Presbyn. (deacon, elder). Clubs: Lamplighter's Dance (pres. 1962). Home: 6184 Woodlark Dr Cincinnati OH 45280 Office: 5101 Madison Rd Cincinnati OH 45227

TEMPLETON, JOHN ALEXANDER, II, diversified co. exec.; b. Chgo., Mar. 31, 1927; s. Phillip Henry and Florence (Moore) T.; B.S., Ind. U., 1950; m. Norma Jane Frazier, Aug. 10, 1949; children—Lori, Linda, Leslie, Sally. Agt., Conn. Mut. Life Ins. Co., Terre Haute, Ind., 1949-51; part owner Miller, Templeton, Scott Ins. Agy., Terre Haute, 1951-64; with Templeton Coal Co., Inc., Terre Haute, 1964—, pres., 1972—; pres. Firman Equipment Corp., Terre Haute, 1958—; Sherwood Templeton Coal Co., Inc., 1968—; chmn. bd. Plumb Supply Co., Des Moines, 1965—; dir. Calvert & Youngblood Coal Co., Inc., Mchts. Nat. Bank Terre Haute. Mem. exec. council Ind. U. Alumni Council, 1953-56. Bd. dirs. Union Hosp., Inc., 1969—, v.p. bd., 1974—; bd. dirs. Ind. State U. Found.; trustee U. Evansville. Served with AUS, 1946-48. Mem. Lynch Coal Operators Reciprocal Assn. (dir.), Ind. Coal Assn., Interstate Coal Conf., Ind. Assn. Ins. Agts. (pres. 1959). Methodist (ch. lay leader 1970—). Mason (Shriner), Elk. Club: Aero.

TEMPLIN, ROBERT LEWIS, JR., judge; b. Westchester, Pa., June 29, 1921; s. Robert Lewis and Helen (Dowlin) T.; A.B., U. Mich., 1943; LL.B., Detroit Coll. of Law, 1954; postgrad. Northwestern U., 1963; m. Enid Mobbs, Nov. 24, 1949. Various positions Ford Motor Co., Dearborn, Mich., 1948-58, admitted to Mich. bar, 1955; practiced in Pontiac, Mich., 1958-59, Birmingham, Mich., 1964-66; sr. asst. pros. atty., Pontiac; 1959-64; judge 6th Circuit Ct., Pontiac, 1967—. Past mem. Republican Exec. Com. Oakland County, Mich.; del., alternate del. Rep. convs., 1963-65. Mem. lay adv. bd. Providence Hosp. Served to 1st lt. USAAF, 1943-45. Decorated Air medal with 2 oak leaf clusters. Mem. State Bar Mich., Oakland County Bar Assn., Am. Legion. Mason (Shriner). Home: 3800 Lakeland Ln Bloomfield Hills MI 48013 Office: Court Tower Pontiac MI 48053

TEN BROEKE, JAMES ENGBERT, dermatologist; b. Wichita Falls, Tex., May 30, 1940; s. Hendrik Jan and Blanche Violet (Druet) Ten B.; B.A., Rice U., 1962; M.S., M.D., Baylor U., 1967; m. Susan K. Zerkle, June 29, 1963; children—Sharon Elizabeth, Catherine Ann. Intern, U. Iowa Hosps., Iowa City, 1967-68, resident in dermatology, 1970-73; practice medicine specializing in dermatology, Iowa City, 1973—; clin. asst. prof. dermatology U. Iowa, Iowa City, 1973—. Served with M.C., U.S. Army, 1968-70. Diplomate Am. Bd. Dermatology. Fellow Am. Acad. Dermatology; mem. Iowa Dermatol. Soc. (pres.), AMA (Physicians' Recognition award 1977—), Iowa State, Johnson County med. socs., Alpha Omega Alpha. Home: 3 Princeton Ct Iowa City IA 52240 Office: 2423 Towncrest Dr Iowa City IA 52240

TENDICK, JOHN PHILLIP, cons. engr.; b. St. Louis, Aug. 29, 1922; s. John Edward and Genevieve (Roeslein) T.; B.S., U. Mo., 1944; m. Ruth M. Paulson, Jan. 13, 1945; children—Jacquelin (Mrs. John A. Schafer), John Phillip, James, David, Charles. Engr., AEC, 1944-45; engr. Westinghouse Co., 1945-53; mgr. Westinghouse Elec. Supply Co., Madison, Wis., 1954-55, Milw., 1956-57; founder, pres. J.P. Tendick & Assos., Inc., cons. engrs., Brookfield, Wis., 1958—. Pres. East Side Community Orgn., Duluth, 1953, 54; mem. Frost Woods Community Planning Commn., Madison, 1954, 55; pres. Cottage-Swanson PTA, Brookfield, 1957-58; mem. Brookfield Sch. Bldg. Com., 1958, 59; chmn. annexation com. City of Brookfield, 1960, 63. Mem. ASME (pres. 1943), Illuminating Engrs. Soc. (membership chmn. 1966), Cons. Engrs. Council. Home: 17645 Evergreen Ct Brookfield WI 53005 Office: 17260 W North Ave Brookfield WI 53005

TEN EYCK, GEORGE ROBERT, agrl. engr.; b. Corning, Kans., June 17, 1925; s. George Edward and Estella Bernice (Gallaher) Ten E.; B.S., Kans. State U., 1951, M.S., 1970; m. Alice Marie Schlagowsky, Sept. 19, 1956; children—Barbara Ann, Robert Andrew. Self-employed farm operator, Walton, Kans., 1951-65; irrigation research engr. Kansas State U., Manhattan, 1964-69, supt. experiment field, 1969—. Pres., Farmers Grain Coop., Walton, 1958-59, sec., 1959-64. Mem. community com. Agrl. Stabilization Conservation Service, 1954-58; trustee Walton Twp., Walton, 1953-55. Served with USMCR, 1943-46, 51. Mem. Am. Soc. Agrl. Engrs., Accacia, Sigma Tau. Mason, Lion. Address: 410 N Nutting St St John KS 67576

TEN EYCK, JAMES EDWARD, optometrist; b. Detroit, Mich., Oct. 30, 1926; s. Herbert Augustus and Gertrude Mabel (Lowry) Ten E.; student St. Norbert's Coll., 1944, Wayne State U., 1949-51; D.Optometry, Chgo. Coll. Optometry, 1954; m. Patricia Ann Sroka, June 24, 1950; children—Pamela, Kenneth, Michael, Susan. Practice optometry, asso. Dixon Eye Clinic, North Platte, Nebr., 1954-68; pvt. practice optometry, 1969—. Councilman, City North Platte, 1964. Served with AUS, 1944-46. Mem. Am., Nebr. optometric assns., Community Playhouse, Elk. Home: 1020 E 2d St North Platte NE 69101 Office: 111 N Dewey St North Platte NE 69101

TEN EYCK, ROBERT LANCASTER, JR., psychologist; b. Hartford, Conn., Nov. 13, 1944; s. Robert Lancaster and Anne Laurie (Van Hook) Ten E.; B.A., DePauw U., 1966; M.S., Fla. State U., 1968, Ph.D., 1970; m. Hannah Jo Hofherr, Aug. 12, 1967; 1 son, Peter Philip. Resident in clin. psychology, U. Ill. Coll. Medicine, Chgo., 1969-70; chief psychologist, Children's Service, Larve Carter Meml. Hosp., Indpls., 1970-73, dir. Internship Tng. in Clin. Psychology, 1973—; instr. Dept. Psychiatry, Ind. U. Sch. Medicine, 1970-73, asst. prof., 1973—; psychol. cons. Goodwill Industries of Central Ind., 1970—; cons. Ind. Counseling and Pastoral Care Center, 1970—, Domestic Relations Counseling Bur. of Marion County Superior and Circuit Cts., 1976—. Bd. dirs. Ind. Counseling and Pastoral Care Center, pres., 1975—. USPHS Pre-doctoral Research fellow, 1968-69. Mem. Ind. (chmn. legislative affairs com. 1974—, chmn. sci. fair com. 1974-75, chmn. profl. and sci. affairs 1975-76), Am., Midwestern, Ind. (pres. div. profl. psychology 1977-78), Central Ind. psychol. assns., AAAS, Sigma Xi, Psi Chi, Sigma Alpha Epsilon (treas. 1965-66). Contbr. articles to profl. jours. Home: 9446 Nora Ln Indianapolis IN 46240 Office: 1315 W 10th St Indianapolis IN 46202

TENNEY, MARK WILLIAM, environ. engring. cons.; b. Chgo., Dec. 10, 1936; s. William and Frieda (Sanders) T.; B.S., Mass. Inst. Tech., 1958, M.S., 1959, Sc.D., 1965; m. Jane E. Morris, June 1, 1974; children by previous marriage—Scott, Barbara. Design engr. Greeley & Hansen, Engrs., Chgo., 1959-61; asso. prof. civil engring. U. Notre Dame, 1965-73; pres. TenEch Environ. Cons., Inc., South Bend, Ind., 1973—. Served with C.E., AUS, 1959-60; lt. col. Res. USPHS research fellow, 1961-64. Diplomate Am. Acad. Environ. Engrs. Fellow ASCE; mem. Nat. Soc. Profl. Engrs., Water Pollution Control Fedn., AAAS, Am. Water Works Assn., Sigma Xi, Chi Epsilon, Phi Delta Theta. Clubs: Ill. Athletic; Lake Macatawa Yacht; Summit. Contbr. articles to profl. jours. Home: 15668 Springmill Dr Mishawaka IN 46544 Office: 52580 US 31 N South Bend IN 46637

TENOLD, LYLE OBERT, supt. schs.; b. Kensitt, Iowa, June 8, 1925; s. Gaylord C. and Grace Norma (Medgaarden) T.; B.S.C., U. Ia., 1951; M.A., U. No. Colo., 1958; m. Patricia Maxine Folven, May 18, 1957; children—Lee, Pamela, Gay. Supt. schs., Iowa and Minn., 1958-67; supt. schs. Carroll County, Ia., 1967—. Served with AAC, 1943-46. Mem. Am., Iowa assns. sch. adminstrs., N.E.A., Delta Phi Epsilon, Am. Legion. Mason, Elk. Address: 1311 N Main St Carroll IA 51401

TENTONI, STUART CHARLES, psychologist; b. Chgo., June 17, 1949; s. Robert A. and Vivian (Ginsberg) T.; B.S., Wis. State U. at Oshkosh, 1970; M.S., U. Wis. at Oshkosh, 1971; Ph.D., N. Tex. State U., 1974; m. Priscilla Jane Diehl, Jan. 8, 1972; 1 son, Christian. Psychometrist, Testing Center, U. Wis. at Oshkosh, 1971; teaching asst. Coll. Edn., N. Tex. State U., 1973-74; cons. psychologist Behavior & Mgmt. Cons. Inc., Milw., 1974-76; clin. psychologist Kettle Moraine Hosp., Oconomonoc, Wis., 1977—. Registered psychologist, Ill.; licensed psychologist, Wis. Mem. Am., Midwestern psychol. assns., Am. Personnel and Guidance Assn., Kappa Delta Pi, Phi Delta Kappa, Psi Chi. Lutheran. Home and office: 2727 S 72d St West Allis WI 53219

TENZER, MARILYN MEARS, mfg. co. exec.; b. Chgo., June 17, 1946; d. Frank Hanford and Esther R. (Mason) Mears; student Ripon (Wis.) Coll., 1964-66; B.A., U. Okla., 1968; m. Lee E. Tenzer, Oct. 22, 1971; 1 dau., Kathryn Lyn. Pub. relations asst. N.W. Ayer, 1968; research analyst Leo Burnett, 1969-71; market analyst Kraft Foods, Chgo., 1971-75; sales mgr. U.S. Testing Co., Chgo., 1975-76; mgr. mktg. research Container Corp. Am., Carol Stream, Ill., 1976—. Mem. Am. Mgmt. Assn., AAUW, DAR, Market Research Assn. Home: 301 41st St Downers Grove IL 60515 Office: 400 E North Ave Carol Stream IL 60187

TEPLE, EDWIN RUSSELL, lawyer; b. Bloomsburg, Pa., June 20, 1913; s. James E. and Helen (Masteller) T.; A.B., Ohio No. U., 1933; J.D. summa cum laude, Ohio State U., 1936; m. Roberta Mills, June 11, 1937; children—Susan Kay (Mrs. Chester P. Guyer), Lynda Lee (Mrs. Frank Amel Warner, Jr.), Deborah Anne (Mrs. Keith Stincic). Admitted to Ohio bar, 1936; staff atty. Social Security Bd., 1936-39, CAB, 1939-41; asst. regional atty. FSA, 1941-43; regional atty. War Manpower Commn., 1943-44; regional staff HEW, 1947-53; practiced in Willoughby, Ohio, 1953—; asso. firm Quinn, LaPorte & Ipavec, Cleve., 1953-76; labor arbitrator, 1957—; lectr. law Case Western Res. Law Sch., 1952—; pres. Century Fed. Credit Union, 1950-56. Pres., Consumers League Ohio, 1960-71; pres. Internat. Soc. for Labor Law and Social Legislation, 1966—. Bd. dirs. Nat. Consumers League, 1963-73. Served from lt. (j.g.) to lt. USNR, 1944-46. Mem. Am. Arbitration Assn. (chmn. Cleve. regional council 1969-71), Labor Law Trust Group, Nat. Acad. Arbitrators (regional chmn. 1964, 66, 72, bd. govs. 1972-75, chmn. com. devel. arbitrators 1975—), Am. (chmn. internat. labor law com. 1974-77), Ohio, Lake County bar assns., Order of Coif, Alpha Phi Gamma, Delta Theta Phi. Democrat. Presbyterian (elder, chmn. Christian edn. com. 1956-66). Author: (with others) Labor Relations and the Law, 1953; (with others) The Employment Relation and the Law, 1957; Arbitration as a Method of Resolving Disputes, 1972. Home: 7093 South Ln RD 3 Willoughby OH 44094 Office: 38052 Euclid Ave Willoughby OH 44094

TEPPER, NEAL GARY, mental health counselor; b. Bklyn., Mar. 12, 1951; s. Leon and Bernice Rhoda (Fisher) T.; B.A., State U. N.Y., Potsdam, 1972; M.A., U. N.D., 1973. Group therapist St. Mike's Hosp., Grand Forks, N.D., 1972-73; tchr. courses Center Teaching and Learning, U. N.D., 1973-75, grad. teaching asst. dept. counseling and guidance, 1974-77, intern counselor Counseling Center, 1975-77; practicum guidance counselor Red River High Sch., Grand Forks, 1973-74; mental health clinician IV, Meml. Mental Health and Retardation Center, Mandan, N.D., 1977—. Mem. Am. Personnel and Guidance Assn., N. Central Assn. Counselor Educators Assns. Home: 423 W Century Apt 302 Bismarck ND 58501 Office: PO Box 369 Mandan ND 58554

TEREZIS, NICK LOUIS, surgeon; b. Wheeling, W.Va., Jan. 14, 1932; s. Louis N. and Helen (Karras) T.; student U. Va., 1949-51; B.S. in Chemistry, U. W.Va., 1953; M.D., U. Pitts., 1956; m. Diana M. Bellas, Oct. 12, 1961; children—Cynthia, Teresa, Nicholas. Intern, Ohio State U. Hosp. Med. Center, 1956-57; resident U. Pitts. Health Center, also VA Hosp., Pitts., 1957-62, 1962-63; individual practice medicine, specializing in gen. and thoracic surgery, Steubenville, O., 1963—; teaching fellow in surgery U. Pitts., 1957-63. Chmn. Am. Cancer Soc. of Jefferson County. Served to capt. MC AUS, 1958-60. Diplomate Am. Bd. Surgery. Fellow A.C.S., Am. Coll. Chest Physicians; mem. Jefferson County Med. Assn. (pres. 1977-78), Pitts. Surg. Soc. Kiwanian. Home: 505 Braebarton Blvd Steubenville OH 43952 Office: 141 Brady Circle W Steubenville OH 43952

TERHUNE, MARIE AMREIN, speech lang. pathologist; b. Chgo., Feb. 16, 1922; d. Andrew Paul and Anna Emily (Machalitzsky) Amrein; B.S., Northwestern U., 1950; m. Richard T. Terhune, Dec. 30, 1950; children—Anne Terhune-Loomis, Richard T. Speech therapist New Trier High Sch., Winnetka, Ill., 1950-52; speech lang. pathologist Bensenville (Ill.) Elementary Schs., 1958—. Served with US Navy, 1943-46. Mem. Am. (certificate of clin. competence), Ill., DuPage County speech and hearing assns., NEA, Ill., Bensenville edn. assns., Delta Kappa Gamma. Presbyterian (elder). Office: Tioga School Addison and Memorial St Bensenville IL 60106

TERRA, DANIEL JAMES, chem. co. exec.; b. Phila., June 8, 1911; s. Louis J. and Mary (DeLuca) T.; B.S., Penn State U., 1931; m. Adeline Evans Richards, Aug. 7, 1937; children—Penny Jane (dec.), James D. Founder, Lawter Chems., Inc., Chgo., 1940, chmn., chief exec. officer, 1964—, also dir.; dir. McLouth Steel Corp., 1st Nat. Bank & Trust Co. Evanston, Stewart-Warner Corp. Past v.p., mem. exec. com. United Republican Fund Ill., now pres. Bd. dirs. Easter Seal Soc., Chgo. Lyric Opera, Evanston Hosp. Assn., Chgo. Crime Commn.; trustee Chgo. Orchestral Assn., Dickinson Coll., Ill. Inst. Tech., Roycemore Sch.; adv. council Northwestern U. Grad. Sch. Mgmt., mem. Pres.'s Council Nat. Coll. Edn.; exec. com. Ill. Inst. Tech. Research Inst.; mem. Chgo. Commn., Assos. of Northwestern U.; mem. grand council Am. Indian Center Chgo.; citizens bd. U. Chgo.; mem. univ. council Pa. State U.; mem. Am. arts com. Art Inst. Chgo. Recipient Winthrop Sears medal Chem. Industry Assn., 1972, Distinguished Alumnus medal Pa. State U., 1976. Mem. Ill. Mfrs. Assn. (dir.). Clubs: Westmoreland Country (Wilmette, Ill.); Kenilworth; Capitol Hill (Washington); Metropolitan, Chicago, Comml., Casino, Mid-America (Chgo.); Lauderdale Yacht (Fort Lauderdale, Fla.); Nat. Arts of N.Y.; Links (N.Y.C.). Home: 528 Roslyn Rd Kenilworth IL 60043 also 19 Isla Bahia Dr Ft Lauderdale FL 33361 Office: 990 Skokie Blvd Northbrook IL 60062

TERRELL, CHARLES JOSEPH, aluminum casting foundry exec.; b. Tipton, Ind., Jan. 14, 1908; s. Benjiman Joseph and Hazel (Ogle) T.; student Ball State U., 1926-27; m. Harriet Elizabeth Johnson, Dec. 24, 1928; children—Joanne Terrell Lyons, Joyce Terrell Timmons, Jane Terrell Thompson. Lab. technician Gen. Motors Corp., Anderson, Ind., 1941-43; supt. Apex Elec. Mfg. Foundry, Cleve., 1943-45; asst. supt. Nat. Bronze & Aluminum Foundry, Cleve., 1945-46; owner Washington Aluminum Castings Co., Washington Court House, Ohio, 1946—, pres., 1955—. Mem. nat. adv. bd. Am. Security Council, 1971—; mem. Liberty Lobby Bd. Policy, 1972—. Mem. Bass Fisherman Sportsman's Soc., Fishing Club Am. Republican. Baptist. Club: Nat. Travel. Patentee flower urn. Home: 740 Van Deman St Washington Court House OH 43160 Office: 1011 Mead St Washington Court House OH 43160

TERRELL, VELMA HOUSTON, counselor; b. New Roads, La., May 9, 1946; d. Ulysses and Mary Magaline (Milton) Houston; B.S., So. U., Baton Rouge, La., 1968; M.A., U. Minn., 1972, postgrad., 1973—; m. Henry Willie Terrell, Nov. 7, 1970; 1 dau., Joy Denise. Social studies tchr. Livingston and Acadia parishes, Crowley, La., 1968-70; math. tchr. Ascension High Sch., Donaldsonville, La., 1970-72; social studies tchr., Mpls., 1972-75; guidance counselor Park Center High Sch., Osseo, Minn., 1975—; coordinator Black studies Anthony and Ramsey Jr. High Sch., Mpls., 1972-75; coordinator career edn. Park Center High Sch., 1975—. Soloist, Greater Sabathani Minn. Gospel Stars. Mem. Am., Minn. personnel and guidance assns., Am. Sch. Counselor Assn., Minn., Osseo fedns. tchrs., So. U. Alumni Fedn. Baptist. Home: 7309 Chowen Ave N Brooklyn Park MN 55443 Office: 7300 Brooklyn Blvd Brooklyn Park MN 55443

TERRILL, ROSCOE VERL, former govt. ofcl.; b. Hudson, Mich., Nov. 9, 1903; s. Jerome Jr. and Florence (Ferris) T.; student Grand Valley Coll., 1970-72; m. Pauline Dorothy Ladd, Jan. 1, 1928; children—Merlin, Paul, Donna (Mrs. Kenneth Dale Northuis), Lowell John. City engr., Coldwater, Mich., 1935-43; supt. grounds Willow Run, Mich., 1943-45; city mgr. Grand Haven, Mich., 1945-68; supr. Ottawa County, 1958-73. Dir. cons. firm John Kistler & Assos., Grand Haven. Life mem. Internat. City Mgrs. Assn. (pres. Mich. 1958), Am. Pub. Works Assn., Mensa. Mason, Rotarian. Home: 111 S Hopkins St Grand Haven MI 49417 Office: 202 S Beechtree St Grand Haven MI 49417

TERRY, M. DONALD, transp. co. exec.; b. Chgo., Feb. 4, 1939; s. Gordon M. and Fredrica (Gordon) T.; student U. Ill., 1956-58; B.B.A., Milton Coll., 1960; m. Lois Sherman, Nov. 22, 1961; children—Howard, Roger, Sydnei Beth. With Rothery Storage & Van Co., Elk Grove Village, Ill., 1960—, exec. v.p., 1970-72, pres., 1972—; pres. DeLuxe Leasing, Inc., 1971—, Allied Overseas Shippers, Inc., 1975—. Mem. Execs. Guild Ltd. (chmn. bd.), Des Plaines Tomorrow Corp. (1st v.p.), Am. Movers Conf., Movers and Warehousemens Assn. Am., Ill. Movers Tariff Bur., Movers Assn. Greater Chgo., Elk Grove, Des Plains, U.S. chambers commerce and industry. Jewish. Clubs: Early Ford V8 of Am., Milestone Soc., Buick of Am., Buick of Ill., Elks. Office: 1525 Chase Ave Elk Grove Village IL 60007

TERRY, PERCY, JR., tool and die co. exec.; b. Shreveport, La., Apr. 18, 1919; s. Percy and Marianne (Woodall) T.; student Centenary Coll., 1941-42, U. Mich., 1945-46, Walsh Coll., 1946-48; m. Margaret Ellen Schroeder, Dec. 1, 1945; 1 son, Kim Woodall. Office mgr. Glendale Machine & Tool Co., 1948-49; office mgr. Springfield Detail & Machine Parts Co., 1949-56; treas., gen. mgr., dir. Springfield Tool & Die, Inc., Dearborn, Mich., 1956—. Mem. devel. com. Henry Ford Community Coll., 1956, mem. library planning com., chmn. sch. naming com., 1964-72; mem. bus./industry/edn. adv. com. Wayne County Schs., 1971-75. Served with USAAF, 1936-45. Mem. Detroit Tooling Assn., Am. Ordnance Assn., U. Mich. Alumni Club (pres. 9th dist.; Recognition award 1974). Lutheran. Rotarian. Clubs: Western Golf and Country (Detroit); University of Michigan (Dearborn) (bd. govs., pres.); University (Ann Arbor); Palmetto Dunes Golf (Hilton Head Island, S.C.). Home: 206 N Mildred St Dearborn MI 48128 Office: 2005 Westwood St Dearborn MI 48123

TERVO, WALTER PAUL, assn. exec.; b. South Range, Mich., Aug. 28, 1914; s. Matt and Selma (Kilpela) T.; B.S., Mich. Tech. U., 1935; m. Dorothy Lillian Martin, Sept. 4, 1937; children—Nancy K. Tervo Cook, James Martin. With Mich. Dept. State Hwys. and Transp., Lansing, 1936-63; asst. to constrn. engr. Mich. Asphalt Paving Assn., Lansing, mng. dir., 1964—. Recipient Alumni award Mich. Tech. U., 1971. Registered profl. engr., Mich. Mem. Mich. Engring. Soc., Mich. Soc. Profl. Engrs., Nat. Soc. Profl. Engrs., Transp. Research Bd., Assn. Asphalt Paving Technologists, State Assn. Execs. in Nat. Asphalt Pavement Assn. Home: 4351 Oakwood Dr Okemos MI 48864 Office: 705 Washington Sq Bldg Lansing MI 48933

TERWILLIGER, ROY WILLIAM, banker; b. Winfred, S.D., June 20, 1937; s. Harold C. and Alice Lee T.; B.S., U. S.D., 1960; M.A., U. Iowa, 1961; m. Mary Lou Abner, July 13, 1963; children—Kathryn Mary, Michael Roy, Susan Mary. Asst. to village mgr. Village of Golden Valley (Minn.), 1963; sec. Greater S.D. Assn., Huron, 1964-65; exec. sec., treas. S.D. Bankers Assn., Huron, 1965-68; exec. dir. Am. Bankers Assn., N.Y.C. and Washington, 1968-74; sec.-treas. Internat. Montary Conf., Washington, 1969-74; chmn., pres. Suburban Nat. Bank, Eden Prairie, Minn., 1975—; cons. Internat. Realty & Investments, Inc., Washington. Served with U.S. Army, 1961-63. Decorated Army Commendation medal. Mem. Am. Bankers Assn. Republican. Congregationalist. Clubs: Rotary, Elks, Masons, Shriners. Home: 6512 Navaho Trail Edina MN 55435 Office: 1080 Eden Prairie Center Eden Prairie MN 55343

TERWOORD, JAMES ANTHONY, bottling co. exec.; b. Berea, Ohio, Mar. 6, 1947; s. Anthony Francis and Adeline Blanche (Yanke) T.; B.B.A., Ohio U., 1969; M.B.A., Youngstown (Ohio) State U., 1976-78; m. Cher Waldeck, June 1, 1974. Staff accountant Arthur Andersen & Co., Cleve., 1973-75; controller Youngstown Coca-Cola Bottling Co., 1975—. Co. rep. United Appeal. Served as officer USMC, 1970-73. C.P.A., Ohio. Mem. Ohio Soc. C.P.A.'s, Am. Inst. C.P.A.'s, Nat. Assn. Accountants. Republican. Roman Catholic. Clubs: Youngstown Athletic. Home: 1148 N Highland Ave Girard OH 44420 Office: 531 E Indianola Ave Youngstown OH 44502

TESCHNER, JOHN STEPHEN, judge; b. Shorewood, Wis., Jan 29, 1935; s. Paul August and Helen Jane (Bovington) T.; B.S., So. Ill. U., 1957; J.D., U. Wis., 1965; m. Margaret Cassandra Cronin, Mar. 23, 1963; children—Cassandra Ann, John Stephen. Admitted to Wis. bar, Ill. bar; auditor Amsted Industries, 1961-63; teaching asst. U. Wis. Law Sch., Madison, 1964-65; practice law, Wheaton, Ill., 1965—; asso. firm Popejoy, Bowman, Unverzagt & Nelson, 1965-68; partner Bowman, Unverzagt & Teschner, 1968-70; Teschner, Benda, Botti & Fawell, 1971-74, Teschner & Botti, 1974-75; asso. judge 18th Jud. Circuit, 1975-77, judge Circuit Ct., 1977—; atty. for villages Oakbrook and Clarendon Hills, Ill.; spl. asst. atty. gen. Ill. Republican precinct committeeman, 1966-74. Served to capt. USAF, 1958-61. Mem. Am., Ill., Wis., DuPage County (dir., chmn. continuing legal edn. com.) bar assns. Home: 214 Kenmore St Elmhurst IL 60126 Office: DuPage County Courthouse Wheaton IL 60187

TESCHNER, PAUL AUGUST, lawyer, educator; b. Green Bay, Wis., June 20, 1925; s. Paul August and Helen (Boyington) T.; student U. Wis., 1943-44; B.B.A., Northwestern U., 1949; D.J. with distinction, Ind. U., 1953; m. Barbara Malmstone, June 12, 1948; children—Karen Janette, Paul August III, Tammy, Jane (Mrs. Anastasia Ferensen). Teaching asso. Northwestern U. Sch. Law, Chgo., 1953-54; admitted to Ind., Ill. bars, 1953-54; employee Pope & Ballard, Chgo., 1954-57; partner firm Pope, Ballard, Uriell, Kennedy, Shepard & Fowle, Chgo., 1958-72; sr. partner Teschner & Teschner, Chgo., 1972-75; chief exec. officer Teschner Profl. Corp., Chgo., 1975—; instr. tax, constl. and bus. law Elmhurst Coll. Evening Div., 1960-73; adj. prof. legal ethics Ind. U. Sch. Law, Bloomington, 1975-76; lectr. in field. Sec., mem. Village of Hinsdale (Ill.) Zoning Bd. of Appeals, 1966—, Zoning Commn., 1966-71; mem. Ill. Master Plan Com. on Legal Edn., 1968-69. Served with AUS, 1943-46. Decorated Bronze Star with oak leaf cluster. Mem. Am. (com. on standards tax practice of tax sect. 1966-75), Ind., Ill. (com. on specialization 1968-71, 73—, chmn. legal edn. and admission to bar com. 1970-72, assembly del. 1972—, com. profl. ethics 1973—), Chgo. (com. fed. taxation 1958-67, com. legal edn. 1955—, chmn. com. 1967-68, 76-77), also unauthorized practice com., specialization com., chmn. specialization com. 1976—) bar assns., World Assn. Lawyers (founder, life), Am. Judicature Soc., Am. Soc. for Legal History, Selden Soc., Internat. Platform Assn., Order of Coif, Phi Delta Phi, Beta Alpha Psi. Clubs: Monroe (founding life), Chicago Athletic Assn. Author: Essays Before Watergate, 1977. Contbr. articles to profl. jours. Home: 316 E 6th St Hinsdale IL 60521 Office: 39 S LaSalle St Chicago IL 60603

TESKA, ROBERT BENTS, urban planner; b. Madison, Wis., Oct. 23, 1934; s. Joseph J. and Jessie E. (Bents) T.; B.S. in Civil Engring., U. Wis., 1957, B.S. in City Planning, 1958; M.S. in City Planning, U. Ill., 1961; m. Diane S. Lesinski, June 23, 1962; children—Tracy, Michael, David. Sr. asso. Barton-Aschman Assos., Inc., Chgo., 1961-68, Washington, 1968-71, v.p., Chgo., 1971-75; prin. Robert B. Teska Assos., Evanston, Ill., 1975—; mem. faculty Northeastern Ill. U., William Rainey Harper Coll.; mem. Evanston Plan Commn., 1964-68; chmn. Evanston Bus. Dist. Redevel. Commn., 1976—; lectr. in field. Served to lt. C.E., U.S. Army, 1958-60. Recipient 1st prize Interam. Planning Soc., 1970. Mem. Am., Inst. Planners, ASCE, Am. Soc. Planning Ofcls., Urban Land Inst., Coastal Soc., Chgo. Assn. Commerce Industry, Lambda Alpha. Congregationalist. Author column Land Use Mgmt. Trends, Chicagoland Devel. Mag., 1974—; contbr. articles to profl. jours.; planner: Barrington (Ill.) Area (Environ. Monthly citation 1973), Lincoln (Nebr.) Center (Design and Environment award for excellence 1975, Progressive Architecture citation 1976, Am. Soc. Landscape Architects Merit award 1976). Registered profl. engr., Ill. Office: State Nat Bank Plaza 1603 Orrington St Evanston IL 60201

TESS, BERNARD RICHARD, microbiologist; b. Chgo., Aug. 20, 1936; s. Stanley and Marie (Rozewicki) T.; B.S., Loyola U., 1958; Ph.D., U. Ill., 1963; m. Eileen Frances Whalen, July 2, 1966; children—David, James, Lisa, Jennifer. Instr., U. Ill., Urbana, 1958-61, fellow, 1962-63; research asso. Abbott Labs., North Chicago, Ill., 1964-67; microbiologist Mercy Hosp. and Med. Center, Chgo., 1967—; clin. asso. pathology dept. Abraham Lincoln Sch. Medicine, U. Ill., 1970-75, clin. asst. prof., 1975-76. USPHS fellow, 1962-63. Mem. Am., Ill. socs. microbiology, Tissue Culture Assn., AAAS, Am. Soc. Clin. Pathology, S. Central Assn. for Clin. Microbiologists, Chgo. Area Virus Club, Sigma Xi. Contbr. Articles to profl. jours. Home: 6232 W 91st St Oak Lawn IL 60453 Office: Mercy Hosp Stevenson at King Dr Chicago IL 60616

TEWS, DONALD WILLIAM, ednl. counselor; b. Ottumwa, Iowa, Aug. 9, 1939; s. William J. and Leona Lucile (Marks) T.; B.A. in Polit. Sci., U. Iowa, 1967, M.A. in Counseling, 1970; postgrad. Emporia Kans. State Coll., 1972, U. Mo., Kansas City, 1973; m. Christy Iona Zahrt, Aug. 29, 1967 (div. Mar. 1975); 1 dau., Gail Melanie. Adult edn. adminstr. Kirkwood Community Coll., Cedar Rapids, Iowa, 1968-69; coll. counselor Monmouth (Ill.) Coll., 1970-71; counselor Johnson County Community Coll., Overland Park, Kans., 1971-75; ednl. counselor St. Mary Coll., Leavenworth, Kans., 1976—. Served in U.S. Army, 1962-65; Vietnam. Certified profl. counselor Profl. Counselors Assn.; tchr.'s certificate, Kans. Mem. Am., Kans. personnel and guidance assns., Nat. Vocational Guidance Assn., Pub. Offender Counselor Assn. (Kans. coordinator 1977—), Kans. Vocational Guidance Assn., VFW, Phi Delta Kappa. Home: 518A Shawnee St Leavenworth KS 66048 Office: Kans State Penitentiary PO Box 2 Lansing KS 66043

THADA, NARONGSAK KIATIKAJORN, physician; b. Saraburi, Thailand, Dec. 12, 1944; s. Amneuy Kiatikajorn and Ooy Kiatikajorn Thada; came to U.S., 1970; naturalized, 1974; M.D., Mahidol U., Thailand, 1969; m. Napaporn Charoenpong, July 25, 1971; children—Monakan and Chatchapol (twins). Intern, Vajira Municipal Hosp., Thailand, 1969-70, Fordham Hosp., Bronx, N.Y., 1970-71; resident in medicine Bronx-Lebanon Hosp. Center, Bronx, N.Y., 1971-73, fellow in hematology, 1973-75; practice medicine specializing in internal medicine and hemato-oncology, Hays, Kans., 1975—; staff St. Anthony and Hadley Regional Med. Center, 1975; vice chief of staff St. Anthony Hosp., Hays, 1977. Diplomate Am. Bd. Internal Medicine. Mem. A.C.P., Kans. State, Central Kans. med.

socs. Buddhist. Club: Smoky Hill Country. Home: 3104 Olympic Ln Hays KS 67601 Office: 1201 Fort St Hays KS 67601

THADEN, RONALD THEODORE, area extension farm mgmt. exec.; b. Milbank, S.D., Apr. 18, 1941; s. Theodore and Grace (Hippen) T.; B.S., S.D. State U., 1967, M.S., 1973; m. Linda Muriel Lucas, Aug. 9, 1969; children—Scott, Thomas. Research asst. S.D. State U., Brookings, 1969-73; county extension agt. Extension Service, U.S. Dept. Agr., Philip, S.D., 1973-76, area farm mgmt. specialist extension service, 1976—. Served with USNR, 1967-69. Mem. Am. Soc. Agronomy, Soc. Range Mgmt., Farm House Frat. Home: 1224 4th St NW Watertown SD 57201 Office: 1600 W Kemp Ave Watertown SD 57201

THAIN, JOHN GRIFFITHS, lab. adminstr.; b. Hayes, Middlesex, Eng., Sept. 27, 1937; s. Charles J. and Dilys D. (Griffiths) T.; came to U.S., 1958; student Acton Tech. Coll., 1955-58, Ind. U., 1958-63, U. New Haven, 1970-73; m. Jacqueline M. Hart, Nov. 3, 1962; children—Jeremy Guy, Richard Gary, Jennifer Ann. Lab. asst. Castrol Ltd., Hayes, Middlesex, U.K., 1953-58; lab. technician Miles Labs., Inc., Elkhart, Ind., 1958-61, coordinator mfg. records, 1961-67, coordinator packaging devel. and labelling, 1967-72, adminstr. regulatory affairs and inspections, 1972-74, supr. records and auditing, 1974-75, mgr. coprorate quality assurance-tng. services, 1976—. Episcopalian. Home: 59527 Ridgewood Dr Goshen IN 46526 Office: 1127 Myrtle St Elkhart IN 46514

THAMES, CLEMENT BEAL, JR., lawyer, judge; b. Hearne, Tex., Mar. 29, 1931; s. Clement Beal and Katy (Ely) T.; B.S. in Geology, U. Tex., 1953, M.A., 1957; m. Carolyn Bratton, May 31, 1952 (div. Feb. 1963). children—Joseph Walton, William Henry, Lisa Ann, m. 2d, Ethyl Delores Fish Myrum, Sept. 22, 1965; 1 dau., Katherine Louise, step-children—Marsha Myrum, Dale Harold Myrum. Admitted to N.D. bar, 1967, since practiced in Bismarck; geologist Pan Am. Petroleum Corp., Denver and Bismarck, N.D., 1957-60; prin. consulting geologist, Bismarck, 1960—; partner firm Pearce, Anderson, Thames & Durick, Bismarck, since 1967—; alt. municipal judge City of Bismarck, 1972-76, municipal judge, 1976—; guest lectr. geology Bismarck Jr. Coll., 1958-59; lectr. Am. Inst. Banking, 1972, 77. Mem. Am. Inst. Profl. Geologists (certified profl. geologist; certified petroleum geologist), Am. Assn. Petroleum Geologists, N.D. Geol. Soc. (pres. 1968), Am. Judges Assn., N.D. Assn. Municipal Judges (v.p.), Am., N.D., Burleigh County bar assns., Soc. Mining Engrs. (v.p. N.D. sect.), Dakota Petroleum Club, Am. Assn. Petroleum Landmen. Elk. Home: 1213 Eastwood St Bismarck ND 58501 Office: PO Box 400 Bismarck ND 58501

THARP, DONALD RHEA, educator, dentist; b. Greencastle, Ind., Oct. 17, 1937; s. Harry Maurice and Gladys Marie (Keller) T.; B.A., Butler U., 1961; D.D.S., Ind. U., 1964; m. Gail Maureen O'Brien, Aug. 10, 1963; 1 dau., Maureen Rae. Practice dentistry, Greencastle, 1966-73; faculty Ind. U. Sch. Dentistry, Indpls., 1973—. Chmn., Greencastle Kiwanis Found., 1971-72. Served with USNR, 1964-66. Mem. Am., Ind. dental assns., Indpls. Dist. Dental Soc., Am. Legion, Delta Sigma Delta. Republican. Home: 7 Round Hill Rd Danville IN 46122 Office: Sch Dentistry Ind U Indianapolis IN 46202

THATCHER, HUGH KNOX, JR., physician, surgeon; b. Indpls., May 16, 1910; s. Hugh Knox and Mary Elsie (Staneart) T.; A.B., Butler U., 1930; M.D., Ind. U., 1934; m. Mary Lou Briles, May 14, 1938; children—Sandra Sue Gillum, David H., Jane A. Intern, resident Indpls. City Hosp., 1934-36; practice medicine specializing in surgery, Indpls., 1936-42, 46—; mem. staff Meth. Hosp., pres., 1974-75; mem. staff Winona Hosp., St. Vincent's Hosp. Chmn. Ind. State Hosp. Licensing Council, 1972—; mem. med. adv. com. Vis. Nursing Assn., 1968—; mem. joint liaison com. to bd. dirs. Meth. Hosp., 1976—. Served to maj. M.C., AUS, 1942-46; PTO. Fellow Am. Acad. Family Practice (charter); mem. Marion County Med. Soc. (dir. 1966-67, pres. 1967-68), Alumni Assn. Butler U. (dir. 1947-49), Ind. Med. Assn. (treas. 1972-75). Mason (Shriner). Home: 11318 Dona Dr Carmel IN 46032 Office: 1010 E 86th St #24 Indianapolis IN 46240

THAYER, CHARLES BENNETT, veterinarian; b. Maplewood, N.J., Aug. 21, 1922; s. George Dickinson and Dorothy (Bennett) T.; B.S., Rutgers U., 1944; D.V.M., Kan. State U., 1947; m. Deloris Huber, Feb. 26, 1967; children—Stephen, Cynthia, Jeffrey, Laurie; stepchildren—Penelope, John. Gen. practice veterinary medicine, Aurora, Ill., 1947-48, Sussex, N.J., 1948-50, Iowa City, Iowa, 1952-57; plant mgr. Fort Dodge Labs., Okmulgee, Okla., 1950-52; dir. animal care U. Iowa, Iowa City, 1957—. Mem. Iowa City Parks and Recreation Commn., 1976—, Iowa City River Front Commn., 1976. Served with AUS, 1943-47. Mem. Am., Iowa, Eastern Iowa (pres. 1962) veterinary med. assns., Am. Soc. Lab. Animal Practitioners (pres. 1969), Am. Assn. Lab. Animal Sci. (dir. 1968-71, chpt. pres. 1964), Delta Phi. Republican. Presbyn. (elder 1974-75, deacon 1965-68). Clubs: Iowa City Optimist (bd. dirs. 1974-75, v.p. 1976); Hawkeye Sailing (commodore 1972); U. Iowa Faculty (sec. 1974, treas. 1975—); Iowa City Community Theatre (dir. 1972). Home: 7 Montrose Ave Iowa City IA 52240 Office: Univ Iowa Iowa City IA 52242

THAYER, KEITH EVANS, educator; b. Lime Springs, Iowa, Feb. 5, 1928; s. Carl Henry and Mary (Evans) T.; B.A., Cornell Coll., 1951; D.D.S., U. Iowa, 1955, M.S., 1956; m. Nancy Jane Delahooke, June 27, 1953; children—James Carl, Gregory Keith, Scott Evans, Bradley John. Faculty, U. Iowa Dental Sch., Iowa City, 1956—, head fixed prosthodontics dept., 1960—, prof., 1963—, acting head dept. removable prosthodontics, 1970-72. Fulbright vis. prof. U. Singapore, 1968-69; cons. VA Hosp. Served with AUS, 1947-48. Fellow Internat. Coll. Dentists; mem. Am. Dental Assn. (con. Vietname edn. project), Internat. Assn. Dental Research, Fedn. Dentaire Internat., Am. Prosthodontic Soc., Sigma Xi, Psi Omega, Omicron Kappa Upsilon. Methodist. Mason, Lion. Home: Longview Knoll Route 6 Iowa City IA 52240

THAYER, WILLIAM VANCE, mathematician; b. Pitts., Apr. 17, 1942; s. Arthur George and Eva Rebecca (Smith) T.; B.S., Defiance Coll., 1964; M.S., U. Toledo, 1970; postgrad Utah State U., 1972, U. Akron, 1966; m. Elaine Mendelson, Aug. 8, 1976; children—Edward Chris, Kim Marie, Robert Clinton. Tchr. math. high sch., Wooster, Ohio, 1964-66, Defiance Coll. (Ohio), 1966-70, Barber-Scotia Coll., Concord, N.C., 1970-71, Queens Coll., Charlotte, N.C., 1971, Sedgefield Jr. High Sch., Charlotte, N.C., 1971-72, Verde Valley Sch., Sedona, Ariz., 1973-74, Lindenwood Coll., St. Charles, Mo., 1975; asst. prof. St. Louis Community Coll. at Forest Park, St. Louis, 1975—, John Burroughs Sch., St. Louis, 1974—. NSF grantee, 1968. Mem. Math. Assn. Am., Soc. Indsl. and Applied Math., Nat. Council Tchrs. Math, Research in Math. Edn. Spl. Interest Group. Home: 819B Longacre St University City MO 63132 Office: 755 Price Rd St St Louis MO 63124

THEIMER, AXEL KNUT, educator; b. St. Johann in Tirol, Austria, Mar. 10, 1946; s. Otto and Iris Maria (Zerzawy) T.; came to U.S., 1969; B.A., St. John's U., 1971; M.F.A., U. Minn., 1974. Mem. Vienna Boys Choir, Vienna, Austria, 1956-61; dir. Chorus Viennensis, Vienna, 1967-69; asst. prof. music, dir. choral and vocal activities St. John's U., Collegeville, Minn., 1969—. Vocal soloist Mozart Festivals, Pueblo, Colo., 1971, 75, Alverno Coll., Milw., 1972, Northrup Meml. Auditorium, Mpls., 1973, U. Minn., 1973; clinician/dir. choral and vocal workshops; performing mem. Thursday Musical Mpls. Mem. Am. Choral Found., Am. Choral Dirs. Assn., Coll. Music Soc., Internat. Music Council, Minn. Music Tchrs. Assn., Music Tchrs. Nat. Assn., Am. Ch. Music Assn. Address: St John's U Collegeville MN 56321

THEIVAGT, JAMES GORDON, pharm. co. exec.; b. Bloomington, Ill., May 9, 1928; s. Lafe Edward and Rita Lucille (Brown) T.; B.S., U. Ill., 1952; m. Alice Joyce Hoffman, Sept. 14, 1953; children—Sandra (Mrs. Donald Good), James, Debra, Timothy, John. With Abbott Labs., N. Chicago, Ill., 1952—, supr. analytical lab., 1972—. Mem. Dist. 76 Sch. Bd., 1961-64, sec., 1963-64. Served with AUS, 1946-48. Mem. Acad. Pharm. Scis., Am. Inst. Chemists, Am. Pharm. Assn., Am. Chem. Soc., Aircraft Owners and Pilots Assn. Contbr. articles to profl. jours., encys. Home: 3516 Rock Pkwy Waukegan IL 60085 Office: 1400 Sheridan Rd North Chicago IL 60064

THELLMANN, EDWARD LOUIS, powder metallurgist; b. Cleve., May 16, 1927; s. Louis and Augusta (Marton) T.; B.S., Cleve. State U., 1959; certificate in metallurgy Fenn Coll., 1963; m. Catherine Ann McCarthy, May 9, 1970; children—Mark, Leah, Kenn, Kim. Project engr. Horizons, Inc., Cleve., 1951-57; process engr. Kennecott Titanium Devel. Corp., Beford, Ohio, 1957-60; mgr. powder metallurgy Gould Labs. div. Gould Inc., Cleve., 1960—. Mem. Village of Walton Hills (Ohio) Planning Commn., 1975—. Served with USN, 1945-46. Recipient John C. Vaaler award Chem. Processing Mag., 1966. Mem. Am. Soc. Metals (Materials Awards Competition award 1967), Am. Def. Preparedness Assn., Am. Powder Metallurgy Inst. (chmn. local chpt. 1974-75). Clubs: Walton Hills Lake (chmn. 1967-68), Walton Hills Men's (chmn. 1975-76). Contbr. articles to profl. jours.; patentee in field. Home: 18307 Orchard Hill Dr Walton Hills OH 44146 Office: 540 E 105th St Cleveland OH 44108

THEOBALD, HENRY EDWARD, real estate and ins. agy. exec.; b. Chgo., Dec. 18, 1915; s. Henry George and Agnes Marie (Mueller) T.; B.S., Northwestern U., 1953, M.B.A., 1954; grad. Realtors Inst.; diploma in risk mgmt.; m. Yvonne Breaux, Apr. 7, 1946; 1 son, Bruce Charles. Asst. dean, asst. prof. bus. adminstrn. tchr. ins. Northwestern U., Evanston, Ill., 1954-60; ins. mgr. Crane Co., Chgo., 1960-61; corp. ins. mgr. Union Tank Car Co., Chgo., 1961-63; owner Henry E. Theobald & Co., real estate and ins., Evanston, Ill., 1963—. Chmn. Wildcat dist. Northeast Ill. council Boy Scouts Am. Served with USAAF, 1943-46. C.L.U., C.P.C.U.; certified real estate broker, property mgr., real estate appraiser. Mem. Psi Upsilon, Alpha Kappa Psi, Beta Gamma Sigma, Delta Mu Delta. Republican. Presbyn. (trustee ch. 1969-71, elder 1976-79). Kiwanian (dir. 1974-76). Mason (Shriner). Clubs: Fortnightly, Chasse. Home: 2606 Grant St Evanston IL 60201 Office: 2006 Central St Evanston IL 60201

THIELEN, LOWELL GEORGE, advt. and pub. relations agy. exec.; b. Mpls., Feb. 22, 1932; s. Leo John and Rosalie Ann (Nathe) T.; B.A., St. Thomas Coll., 1954; postgrad. Bank Mktg. and Pub. Relations Sch., Northwestern U., 1967; m. Kathleen Ann Fuchs, June 24, 1961; children—Stephen Lowell, Michelle Kathleen. With Marquette Nat. Bank, Mpls., 1955-68, dir. pub. relations, 1966-68; pres. Lowell G. Thielen & Asso., Inc., Mpls., 1968—. Past dir. Toll Cryogenics, Inc. Campaign dir. March of Dimes, 1969, chpt. chmn., Mpls., 1971; campaign dir. Am. Cancer Soc., 1965. Served with AUS, 1956-58. Recipient award March of Dimes, 1971, Am. Cancer Soc., 1969, Dakotas-Minn.-Man. dist. Optimist Internat., 1970; Distinguished Service award City of Greater Mpls., 1969. Mem. Sales and Mktg. Execs. Mpls. (dir. 1969-71), Pub. Relations Soc. Am. (also Mpls. chpt.), Greater Mpls. C. of C. (chmn. membership com. 1967-69), Mpls. Downtown Council (mem. promotion bd. 1964-67), Advt. Club Minn., Mpls. Minute Men (dir. 1969-70, sec. 1970). Clubs: Minn. Press, Decathlon Athletic, Optimist Internat. (dist. gov. 1969-70, dir. 1967-72, pres. Breakfast Optimist of Mpls. 1966). Home: 5219 14th Ave S Minneapolis MN 55417 Office: 715 Foshay Tower Minneapolis MN 55402

THIELING, JOHN RICHARD, accountant; b. St. Paul, Mar. 29, 1944; s. Raymond R. and Lucille A. (Dietz) T.; B.S., Ind. U., 1970; m. Patricia Ann Maldonis, Aug. 23, 1969; children—Amy Katherine, Jennifer Lee, Erik David. Accountant, Inland Steel Co., East Chicago, Ind., 1967-70; partner McQueen & Thieling, Plymouth, Ind., 1970—. Dist. commr. Boy Scouts Am., 1973; chmn. Marshall County chpt. March of Dimes, 1976; mem. Ind. Estate Planning Council. C.P.A., Ind. Mem. Am. Inst. C.P.A.'s (Sells certificate of hon. mention), Ind. Assn. C.P.A.'s (High Grad. award). Clubs: Kiwanis, Elks. Home: Rural Route 3 Box 137 Plymouth IN 46563 Office: PO Box 280 Plymouth IN 46563

THIERS, WERNER AUGUST, owner welding shop, orgn. exec.; b. McGregor, Ia., June 4, 1907; s. Bernhard Dietrich and Lena Magdalene (Miller) T.; grad. high sch.; m. Ada Myrtle Bachtell, Jan. 17, 1928; children—Allene (Mrs. Bernard Liegel), Verna (Mrs. Charles Roelke), Carol (Mrs. Robert Niendorf), Barbara (Mrs. Stanley Ingraham). Welder, A.O. Smith Co., Milw., 1928-46; owner Thiers' Welding, Mazomanie, Wis., 1946—. Treas. sch. bd., Mazomanie, 1949-52; vice chmn. Wis. Council Local History, 1977—. Mem. Wis. Blacksmiths and Weldors Assn. (sec.-treas. 1965-71), Mazomanie Hist. Soc. (pres. 1965—). Mason, Lion (pres. 1974). Editor Wis. Blacksmiths and Weldors Newsletter, 1965-71, Modern Blacksmith, nat. newsletter, 1974—. Address: 502 W Hudson St Mazomanie WI 53560

THIES, FLOYD LEVI, sch. counselor; b. Java, S.D., Nov. 11, 1937; s. Levi Robert and Kate (Brockel) T.; B.A., No. State U., Aberdeen, S.D., 1960, M.A., 1965; student Mankato (Minn.) State U., 1977; m. Beverly J. Clausen, Aug. 20, 1961; 1 dau. Tamara T. Tchr. sci., high sch., Groton, S.D., 1960-64; prin. high sch., Langford, S.D., 1964-66; supt. pub. schs., Farmer, S.D.; middle sch. counselor, Algona, Iowa, 1968—. Mem. Kossuth County Republican Central com. N.S.F. fellow. Mem. Nat. Councilor Year Round Edn., Am. Personnel Guidance Assn., Iowa Dept. Spl. Edn., Iowa Edn. Assn. (exec. bd.), Kappa Delta Pi, Phi Delta Kappa. Republican. Lutheran. Home: PO Box 333 Algona IA 50511

THIESSEN, EDGAR P., educator; b. Kiel, Wis., Oct. 23, 1913; s. Fred and Meta (Langemak) T.; B.Mus. Edn., VanderCook Coll. Music, 1956, M.Mus. Edn., 1965; m. Ethel E. Sy, Oct. 26, 1936; children—Prudence (Mrs. Palmer J. Smith), Sandra (Mrs. James L. Wise), Terry. Tchr. pub. schs., Wis., 1941-55; mem. faculty Lakeland Coll., Sheboygan, Wis., 1951—, asso. prof., 1975—; mem. faculty Silver Lake Coll., Manitowoc, Wis., 1971—, now asso. prof. Dir. Kiel (Wis.) Mcpl. Band, 1934—. Mem. City Council New Holstein, 1969-76; trustee VanderCook Coll. Music, 1975—. Mem. Am. Wis. (past pres.) bandmasters assns. Nat. Band Assn. (state chmn., 1974-76), Music Educators Nat. Conf., Am. Fedn. Musicians, Phi Beta Mu. Composer, arranger band music. Home: 2218 Prospect St New Holstein WI 53061 Office: Dept Music Silver Lake Coll Manitowoc WI 54220

THILL, RICHARD EUGENE, geophysicist; b. St. Paul, June 16, 1934; s. Alphonse James and Marie Irene (Labelle) T.; student Macalester Coll., 1953-54; B.A., U. Minn., 1958, M.S., 1967; m. Patricia Ann Pasket, Mar. 25, 1966; children—Steven Daniel, Jeffrey Scott, Brian Kevin. Curator geol. collections U. Minn., 1962; geophysicist U.S. Bur. Mines, St. Paul, 1963—; instr. geology dept. Macalester Coll., St. Paul, 1959-60. Recipient Invention award U.S. Bur. Mines, 1971. Mem. Soc. Exptl. Stress Analysis (chmn. Twin City subsect.), Am. Geophys. Union, Twin Cities Geologists Club. Contbr. articles to profl. jours.; patentee in field. Office: PO Box 1660 Twin Cities MN 55111

THIMOTHEOSE, KADAKAMPALLIL GEEVARGHESE, psychol. counselor; b. Kerala, India, Nov. 7, 1936; s. K.G. and Varghese (Mariamma) Varghese; came to U.S., 1976; M.S. in Ednl. Psychology, U. Kerala, 1966, M.A. in Sociology, 1969, M.A. in History, 1975, Ph.D., 1975; m. P.I. Mariamma, May 20, 1968; children—Geebee, Sonia. Lectr. ednl. psychology, head dpet. Tng. Coll., U. Kerala, 1966-76, faculty univ., 1969-76, hon. dir. Anada Nilayam Orphanage and Widow Center, 1966-76; psychol. counselor Metro Substance Abatement Center, Detroit, 1976—, Ford Hosp., Detroit, 1977—; dir. inservice tng. and social services Alexandrine Drug Rehab. Program, Detroit, 1977—; alcoholism therapist Talc Clinic, Detroit, 1977—. Mem. adv. bd. Trivadrum Med. Coll. Hosps., 1972-76. Certified social worker, Mich.; certified tchr. Mich., Ga.; accredited social psychologist, Mich. Mem. Am. Personnel and Guidance Assn., Am. Assn. Rehab. Counselors, Am. Black Psychol. Assn. Author book on ednl. psychology. Home: 489 Peterboro St Apt 13 Detroit MI 48201

THISTLETHWAITE, PAUL CALVIN, educator; b. Indpls., Nov. 9, 1945; s. Paul Eugene and Berniece Mardelle (Brown) T.; B.S., Ball State U., 1968, M.B.A., 1969; Ph.D., U. Mo. at Columbia, 1975; m. Lindia Lee Schulenberg, Aug. 25, 1968; 1 son, Craig Eric. Grad. asst. mktg. and statistics Ball State U., 1968-69; instr. mktg. So. Ill. U., 1969-70; grad. asst. U. Mo. at Columbia, 1970-73; asst. prof. mktg. Western Ill. U., 1973-77, asso. prof. mktg., 1977—. Mem. Am., So., Midwest mktg. assns., Ill. Retail Mchts. Assn., Midwest Bus. Adminstrn. Assn. Republican. Methodist (jr. high youth leader 1974-75). Contbr. articles to profl. jours. Home: 1185 Stacey Ln Macomb IL 61455 Office: Dept Mktg Finance Western Ill U Macomb IL 61455

THOM, ELROY MILTON, veterinarian; b. Fergus Falls, Minn., May 1, 1926; s. Reinhardt and Marybelle (Orendorff) T.; B.S., U. Minn., 1951, D.V.M., 1953; m. Shirley Hansen, Dec. 3, 1961; children—William, Joseph, Mary Ellen. Veterinarian, Elbow Lake, Minn., 1953-61, Eureka, S.D., 1961-73; veterinary med. officer U.S. Dept. Agr., Sioux Falls, S.D., 1973—. Served in USN, 1944-47; PTO. Mem. AVMA, Minn. Veterinary Med. Assn. Home: 1401 E 49th St Sioux Falls SD 57103 Office: US Dept Agriculture 1401 E 49th St Sioux Falls SD 57103

THOMAN, JOHN HERMAN, engr.; b. Ft. Madison, Iowa, Apr. 6, 1945; s. John Herman and Kathaleen Elizabeth (Hughes) T.; student U. Iowa, 1963-65; B.S. in Indsl. Tech., U. No. Iowa, 1970; m. Dianne Ruth Neu, Nov. 4, 1967; children—Todd John, Kimberly Jo. Engring. asst. Chamberlain Corp., Waterloo, Iowa, 1967-69; machine designer Doerfer Corp., Cedar Falls, Iowa, 1969-72; automation process engr. Square D. Co., Lincoln, Nebr., 1972-73; engring. mgr. Instrumentation Splty. Co., Lincoln, 1973—; advisor Coll. Engring. U. Nebr. Mem. Soc. Plastics Engrs., ASME. Home: 3730 Spruce St Lincoln NE 68516 Office: 4700 Superior St Lincoln NE 68504

THOMAN, MARK EDWARD, physician; b. Chgo., Feb. 15, 1936; s. John Charles and Tasula Mark (Petrakis) T.; A.A., Graceland Coll., 1956; B.A., U. Mo., 1958, M.D., 1962; m. Sandra Kay Halvorson, June 22, 1975; children—Marlisa Rae, Susan Kay, Edward Kim, Nancy Lynn, Janet Lea, Edward Charles Douglas, David Mark. Intern, U. Mo. at Columbia, 1962-63; resident in pediatrics Blank Meml. Children's Hosp., Des Moines, 1963-65, chief resident, 1964-65, lt. comdr. USPHS, Washington, 1965-66, cons. in toxicology, 1966-67; chief dept. pediatrics Shiprock (N.Mex.) Navajo Indian Hosp., also dir. N.D. Poison Info. Center, 1967-69 also practice medicine, specializing in pediatrics Quain & Ramstad Clinic, Bismarck, N.D., 1967-69; dir. Iowa Poison Info. Center, Des Moines, 1969—; pvt. practice pediatrics, Des Moines, 1969—; med. examiner, accident investigator FAA, 1976; dir. Cystic Fibrosis Clinic, 1973—; dir. Mid-Iowa Drug Abuse Program, 1972-76; mem. med. adv. bd. La Leche Leauge Internat., 1965—; pres. Medic-Air Ltd., 1976—. Bd. dirs. Polk County Pub. Health Nurses Assn., Des Moines Speech & Hearing Center. Served with USMCR, 1954-58. Recipient N.D. Gov.'s award of merit, 1969; Cystic Fibrosis Research Found. award, 1975, Am. Psychiat. Assn. Thesis award, 1962. Mem. AMA (del.), Iowa State Med. Assn., Soc. Adolescent Medicine, Inst. Clin. Toxicology, Internat. Soc. Pediatrics, Am. Acad. Pediatrics, Am. Bd. Pediatrics, Cystic Fibrosis Club, Am. Acad. Clin. Toxicology (trustee 1969—), Am. Assn. Poison Control Centers. Republican. Mem. Reorganized Latter-Day Saints Ch. Clubs: Flying Physicians, Aircraft Owners and Pilots Assn., Nat. Pilots Assn., Hyperion Field and Country. Editor-in-chief AACTION. Home: 6896 NW Trailridge Dr Des Moines IA 50323 Office: 1426 Woodland Ave Des Moines IA 50309

THOMAS, ALBERT WILLIAM, investment co. exec.; b. N.Y.C., Jan. 12, 1927; s. Albert W. and Florence (Greene) T.; B.S., Northwestern U., 1950; N.D., Bernadean U., 1973; div.; children—Peter Alan, Paulette. Advt., account exec., 1954-60; ins. broker, 1960-65; became pres., dir. Security Dynamics Investment Corp., Chgo., 1965; broker Archer Commodities, Inc., Chgo.; pres., dir. Mid Am Adv. Service, Chgo. Mem. Huna Research Assos. Mem. Mid-Am. Commodity Exchange. Adv. bd. Edward Parish Dance Found. Served with AUS, 1944-46. Mem. Internat. Naturopathic Assn., Mensa, Exptl. Aircraft Assn., Internat. Assn. Cancer Victims and Friends, Art Inst. Chgo., Aircraft Owners and Pilots Assn., Alpha Kappa Psi. Mason (Shriner). Contbr. articles to profl. pubs. Home: 1157 W Farwell St Chicago IL 60626 Office: Archer Commodities Inc 175 W Jackson Blvd Chicago IL 60604

THOMAS, BILL, journalist, author; b. Elizabethtown, Ky., Nov. 11, 1934; s. William Roy and Elizabeth (Crabtree) T.; A.B., Western Ky. U., 1958; m. Phyllis Newkirk, Dec. 6, 1965; children—David, Dianne, Billy, Lisa, Alan. Reporter, photographer Park City Daily News, Bowling Green, Ky., 1955-58; staff writer UP Internat., Louisville, 1959-62; feature writer Cin. Enquirer, 1962-63, travel editor, 1964-66; freelance photojournalist and author, 1966—; author: Tripping in America, 1974; Eastern Trips and Trails, 1975; Mid-America Trips and Trails, 1975; The Swamp, 1976; Lakeside Recreation Areas, 1977; The Complete World of Kites, 1977; American Rivers, 1978. Recipient Geographics Publs. award, 1976. Mem. Authors Guild, Audubon Soc., Wilderness Soc., Outdoor Writers Assn. Am., Soc. Am. Travel Writers, Am. Soc. Mag. Photographers, Sierra Club. Address: Route 4 Box 387 Nashville IN 47448

THOMAS, BRUCE LORREY, charitable assn. exec.; b. Boston, Apr. 4, 1930; s. Frank Bryan and Louise Anna Julia (Lorrey) T.; B.A., U. Mass., 1953; M.S.W., U. Conn., 1957; m. Sara Alice Folger, Mar. 18,

1961; children—Richard Folger, Alice Lorrey. Caseworker, Family and Children's Service, Pitts., 1957-59; sr. clin. social worker VA Neuropsychiat. Hosp., Pitts., 1959-63; exec. dir. Western Pa. Multiple Sclerosis Soc., Pitts., 1963-68; exec. dir. United Way of Central Washington County, Washington, Pa., 1968-76, Trumbull County Community Chest and United Way of Trumbull County, Warren, Ohio, 1976—; Vol. group chmn. social agys. sect. United Fund Allegheny County, Ptts., 1966-67; mem. citizens participation com. Washington County Planning Commn., 1971-76; field work placement inst. Grad. Sch. Social Work, U. Pitts., 1971-72; mem. Washington County Health Task Force for Long Term Care, 1972-76; treas. Wesley Town, Inc., 1973-76. Bd. dirs., past pres. Washington County-Greene County Community Action Corp. Served with AUS, 1953-55. Mem. Nat. Assn. Social Workers (pres. S.W. Pa. chpt. 1966-69), Acad. Certified Social Workers, NAACP, Washington County History and Landmarks Soc., Washington C. of C. (co-chmn. legislative action com. 1971). Presbyn. (elder 1966—). Rotarian. Home: 2866 Crescent Dr NE Warren OH 44483 Office: 415 Washington St NW Warren OH 44482

THOMAS, BRUCE ROBERT, physicist, educator; b. Guthrie Center, Iowa, Jan. 1, 1938; s. Roger A. and Gladys (Congdon) T.; B.A., Grinnell (Iowa) Coll., 1960; Ph.D., Cornell U., 1965; m. Alice A. Miller, Sept. 11, 1960; children—Lise, Valerie, Megan. Asst. prof. physics Grinnell Coll., 1965-67; asst. prof. physics Carleton Coll., Northfield, Minn., 1967-71, asso. prof., 1971-77, prof., 1977—; gastdozent Institut Angewandte Physik U. Heidelberg (W.Ger.), 1974-75. Mem. Am. Phys. Soc., Am. Assn. Physics Tchrs. Office: Carleton Coll Northfield MN 55057

THOMAS, CARL EDWARD, clergyman; b. Detroit, June 21, 1930; s. Carl August and Beatrice M. (Williams) T.; A.B., Wittenberg U., 1952; B.D., Hamma Sch. Theology, 1955; M.S.W., Ohio State U., 1961; D.D., Wittenberg U., 1968; m. Patricia Ann Moore, June 25, 1955; children—Susan Marie, Deborah Anne. Ordained to ministry Luth. Ch., 1955; asst. exec. dir. Oesterlen Home for Children, Springfield, Ohio, 1955-63; asst. pastor Fifth Luth. Ch., Springfield, 1955-63; sec. for agys., instns. Bd. Social Ministry, Luth. Ch. Am., N.Y.C., 1963-66, exec. sec., 1966—. Chmn., Luth. Resources Commn., Washington, 1969—; mem. gen. bd. Nat. Council Chs., 1969—; del. World Council Chs. Assembly, Uppsala, Sweden, 1968; adviser Luth. World Fedn. Assembly, Evian, France, 1970; exec. dir. Luth. Social Services of Mich., 1973—. Mem. Acad. Certified Social Workers, Acad. Polit. Sci. Clubs: Economic (Detroit); Detroit Athletic. Home: 1315 Balfour Rd Grosse Pointe MI 48230 Office: 484 E Grand Blvd Detroit MI 48207

THOMAS, CLIVE ALWYN, city ofcl., loan and investment co. exec.; b. Goehner, Nebr., July 24, 1913; s. Lloyd Harold and Ann (Priefert) T.; grad. Chillicothe (Mo.) Bus. Coll., 1935; m. Ruth Maxine Chrestensen, Sept. 4, 1938; children—Gary Alan, Shelley Jan. Asst. loan mgr. Securities Acceptance Corp., Lincoln, Nebr., 1937-40; gen. mgr. Capitol Credit Corp., Lincoln, 1940-42; chief interviewer Cornhusker Ordnance Plant, Grand Island, Nebr. 1942-45; mgr. City Investment Co., Scottsbluff, Nebr., 1945-68; sec.-treas., gen. mgr. City Investment Corp., Scottsbluff, 1946—; pres., gen. mgr. City Loan & Investment Co., Scottsbluff, 1968—; mayor Scottsbluff, 1964-74; dir. Nile Valley Bldg. and Loan Assn., 1970—. Chmn. bd. budgets and admissions Scottsbluff Community Chest, 1956-57; 1st v.p. St. Mary's Hosp., 1971—, bd. govs., 1973—, pres. governing bd., 1977—. Commr. Scottsbluff County, 1975—, chmn., 1977—; mem. Gov.'s Devel. Disabilities Adv. Bd., Gov.'s Supreme Ct. Nominating Com., 1975—. Mem. Scottsbluff Greater C. of C. (pres. 1958), Neb. League Municipalities (chmn. large cities sect. 1967, exec. bd. 1968, pres. 1971-72), Republican (headed Nebr. Mayors for Nixon 1972). Methodist. Lion (pres. 1951-52). Mason (Shriner). Elk (state pres. 1967-68, grand inner guard 1969). Home: 2809 5th Ave Scottsbluff NE 69361 Office: 1607 1st Ave Scottsbluff NE 69361

THOMAS, DANIEL ANTHONY, therapist; b. Knoxville, Jan. 6, 1951; s. Dominic Anthony and Taide (Albertelli) T.; B.A., Marquette U., 1973; M.A., Bowling Green U., 1975. Therapist, Family Counseling Agy., Joliet, Ill., 1975—; former mem. bd. dirs. Joliet Alcoholic Halfway House; instr. Joliet Jr. Coll. Mem. Am. Psychol. Assn., Ill. Psychol. Assn., Am. Personnel Guidance Assn., Biofeedback Research Soc., Ill. Biofeedback Soc., Sigma Phi Epsilon. Home: 5518 E Lake Dr #A Lisle IL 60532 Office: 168 Ottawa St N Joliet IL 60431

THOMAS, DAVID BENEDICT, mfg. co. exec.; b. Pipestone, Minn., Feb. 17, 1939; s. Clarence B. and Mildred R. (Luety) T.; student St. John's U., Collegeville, Minn., 1957-59; B.B.A. in Finance and Accounting, U. Notre Dame, 1962; postgrad. U. Detroit, 1964; m. Carolyn A. Smith, June 22, 1968; children—John B., Cynthia A. Staff accountant Price Waterhouse & Co., Peoria, Ill., 1964-66, sr. accountant, 1966-69; comptroller Edward Hines Co., Peoria, 1969-70, treas., 1970-72, dir., 1971-72; controller L.R. Nelson Corp., Peoria, 1972-74, v.p. adminstrn., 1974—. Dir. C.B. Thomas Co., Pipestone, Minn., 1968—. Served to 1st lt. AUS, 1962-64. C.P.A., Ill. Mem. Nat. Assn. Accountants, Am. Inst. C.P.A.'s, Ill. Soc. C.P.A.'s, Peoria Assn. Commerce (mem. com. 1971-73), Notre Dame Club Peoria (treas. 1965-66). Club: Peoria Country. Home: 660 Miller Rd Peoria Heights IL 61614 Office: 7719 N Pioneer Ln Peoria IL 61614

THOMAS, DOMINICK ANTHONY, psychiatrist; b. Herkimer, N.Y., Feb. 19, 1917; s. Joseph and Mary (Zongrone) T.; B.S., Royal Lyceum Visconti, Rome, Italy, 1938; M.D., Royal U. Parma (Italy), 1945; postgrad., Menninger Sch. Psychiatry, Topeka, 1958; children—Joseph, Daniel. Intern, Kanawha Valley Hosp., Charleston, W.Va., 1947-48; resident Marcy (N.Y.) Psychiat. Inst., 1946-47; fellow Menninger Sch. Psychiatry, Menninger Found, 1948-49; sect. chief dept. psychiatry Inst. Eastern Tenn., Knoxville, 1951-56; clin. dir. Upper Miami Valley Guidance Center, mental health clinic, Piqua, Ohio, 1958-61; practice medicine, specializing in psychiatry, Piqua, 1958—, Dayton, Ohio, 1971—; chief, dept. psychiatry Dettmer Hosp., Troy, Ohio, 1958-69, now cons.; founder, med. dir., chmn. bd. Dartmouth Behavioral Scis. Center, Dayton, 1971—; asst. clin. prof. psychiatry Wright State Med. Sch., Dayton; cons. div. forensic psychiatry State of Ohio, Lima State Hosp. for Criminally Insane, 1965-75. Fellow Am. Acad. Forensic Scis., Menninger Found., Royal Soc. Health (London); mem. AMA, Ohio State Med. Assn., Montgomery County, Miami County med. socs., Am., World psychiat. assns., Internat. Soc. Clin. and Exptl. Hypnosis, Am. Acad. Psychiatry and Law, N.Y. Acad. Scis., Am. Acad. Clin. Psychiatrists. Roman Catholic. Clubs: Dayton Racquet; Piqua Country. Home: 7880 Normandy Ln Dayton OH 45459 Office: 1620 Winters Bank Tower Dayton OH 45402

THOMAS, DON R., psychologist; b. Fredericktown, Mo., Mar. 5, 1939; s. Roy Vernon and Nina Elizabeth (Smallen) T.; m. Carolyn Erickson, Dec. 31, 1971; children—Marilyn, Jeffrey, Donya, Matthew. B.S., U. Ill., 1967, Ph.D., 1972. Program mgr. Englemann-Becker Follow Through Model, Urbana, Ill., 1968-70, asso. dir. Behavior Analysis Follow Through Program, Lawrence, Kans., 1971-73; chief psychologist Minn. Learning Center, Brainerd, 1973, dir., 1973—. Coordinator, Dept. Pub. Welfare Task Force Competency Based Certification of Profls. Using Aversive Treatment Procedures, Minn., 1976-78. Mem. Am. Psychol. Assn., Assn. Advancement of Behavior Therapy, Minn. (pres. 1975-76), Midwestern assns. for behavior analysis, Minn. Psychol. Assn. Recipient Psi Chi Research award, U. of Ill., 1967. Co-Author: Teaching; A Course in Applied Psychology, 1971; Teaching 1: Classroom Mgmt., 1975; Teaching 2: Cognitive Learning and Instruction, 1975. Home: 432 Tyrol Dr Brainerd MN 56401 Office: Minnesota Learning Center Box 349 Brainerd MN 56401

THOMAS, EDWARD PAUL, allergist, internist; b. Hattiesburg, Miss., July 26, 1920; s. Simon S. and Rosa A. (Henry) T.; student Butler U., 1937-40; M.D., Meharry Med. Coll., 1944; m. Ruby Leah Thomas, May 6, 1944; children—Paul A., Bradford E., Leeland M., Leah Anne. Intern Homer G. Phillips Hosp., St. Louis, 1945; practice medicine specializing in allergies and internal medicine, Indpls.; med. staff Meth. Hosp., Indpls. Served to lt. comdr., M.C., USNR, 1954-56. Mem. Am. Coll. Allergy, Am. Coll. Chest Physicians, Am. Acad. Allergy, Omega Psi Phi, Chi Delta Mu. Home: 1520 Thomas Wood Trail Indianapolis IN 46260 Office: 3450 N Illinois St Indianapolis IN 46208

THOMAS, FRED BROADDUS, physician; b. Irvine, Ky., Aug. 10, 1940; s. Fred and Hazel (Broaddus) T.; B.A., Ohio State U., 1962, M.D., 1965; m. Linda Kay Abbuhl, Sept. 8, 1962; children—Tracy, Timothy, Freddie B. Intern, Ohio State U. Hosp., Columbus, 1965-66, resident in medicine, 1966-68, chief med. resident, 1968-69, fellow gastroenterology, 1969-71, faculty, 1973—, asso. prof. medicine, 1976—, dir. div. gastroenterology, 1974—, dir. gallstone research Project Treatment Center, 1977—; practice medicine specializing in gastroenterology, Columbus, 1973—. Served to maj. USAF, 1971-73. Diplomate Am. Bd. Gastroenterology. Fellow A.C.P.; mem. AMA, Am. Gastroent. Assn. Contbr. articles to profl. jours. Home: 3660 Kennybrook Ln Columbus OH 43220 Office: 410 W 10th St Columbus OH 43210

THOMAS, GARTH E., data processing exec.; b. Fostoria, Ohio, Aug. 6, 1942; s. Charles E. and Helen M. (Roper) T.; B.S., Ohio State U., 1964; M.S., Xavier U., 1970; m. Jean Thomas, Sept. 16, 1961; children—Timothy, Douglas, Jeffrey, Jennifer. Mgr. systems programming Ohio State U. Hosps., 1966-71; mgr. tech. support U. Mich., Ann Arbor, 1971—. Asst. scoutmaster Troop 78, Boy Scouts Am., 1965-76. Mem. Am. Mgmt. Assn., Am. Phys. Soc. Clubs: Ann Arbor Town, Moose. Home: 9602 Waters Rd Ann Arbor MI 48103 Office: 1005 Greene St Ann Arbor MI 48109

THOMAS, GORDON LAWRIE, educator; b. Kent, Eng., Dec. 4, 1914; s. Reginald Haslam and Amy (Lawrie) T.; came to U.S., 1924, naturalized, 1938; A.B., Albion Coll., 1936; M.A., Mich. State U., 1941; Ph.D., Northwestern U., 1952; m. Phyllis Marie Lenzner, June 21, 1941; children—David Alan, Kathleen Marie (Mrs. Richard H. Field). Tchr. English and speech Fenton (Mich.) High Sch., 1936-39; grad. asst. Mich. State U., 1939-41, instr. dept. speech, 1945-52, asst. prof., 1952-56, asso. prof., 1956-60, prof., 1960-68, prof. communication, 1968—, asso. chmn. dept. communication, 1968-70, asso. dean continuing edn. Coll. Communication Arts, 1970-73, sec. acad. governace, 1973—; instr. English and speech, asst. registrar U. Miami, Coral Gables, Fla., 1941-42. Mem. Gov.'s Adv. Com. on Local Govt., 1966-67, Gov.'s Spl. Commn. on Urban Problems, 1970—; treas., dir. Mich. Conf. Mayors, 1965-68, pres., 1971-72; mem. City Council, East Lansing, Mich., 1959-61, mayor, 1961-71. Served with USAAF, 1942-45. Mem. Mich. Municipal League (trustee 1965—, pres. 1965-66), Nat. League Cities (bd. dirs., mem. exec. com.), Mich. Speech Assn. (exec. sec. 1977—), Pi Kappa Delta, Delta Sigma Rho, Phi Kappa Phi. Mem. United Ch. of Christ (moderator 1967). Author: (with David Potter) the Colonial Idiom, 1970. Home: 334 N Hagadorn Rd East Lansing MI 48823

THOMAS, IRWIN ROSS, supt. schs.; b. Atlantic, Iowa, Aug. 31, 1927; s. Jay Ralph and Anna (Hansen) T.; B.S., NW Mo. State U., 1949; M.A., NE Mo. State U., 1953; specialist certificate U. Mo., 1958; U. Iowa, 1960, U. Nebr., 1961; m. Nina Lou Gilliland, May 27, 1951; children—David R., Deborah Ann. Tchr. pub. schs., Oregon, Mo., 1949-51, Rock Port, Mo., 1951-53; supt. schs., Nemaha, Neb., 1953-54, Elmo, Mo., 1954-56, Oregon, Mo., 1956-62, Carrollton, Mo., 1962—. Served with AUS, 1945-47. Mem. Am., Mo. (exec. com. 1971-75) assns. sch. adminstrs., Mo. Tchrs. Assn., Phi Delta Kappa, Kappa Delta Pi, C. of C. (past pres.). Methodist. Clubs: Masons, Shriners, Kiwanis (past pres.), Lions (pres. 1967-68, zone chmn. 1969-70). Home: 1408 N Main St Carrollton MO 64633

THOMAS, JAMES SAMUEL, bishop; b. Orangeburg, S.C., Apr. 8, 1919; s. James and Dessie Veronica (Mark) T.; A.B., Claflin Coll., Orangeburg, 1939, B.D., 1953; B.D., Gammon Theol. Sem., Atlanta, 1943; M.A., Drew U., 1944; Ph.D., Cornell U., 1953; LL.D., Bethune Cookman Coll., 1963, Simpson Coll., 1965, Morningside Coll., 1966; L.H.D., Cornell Coll., 1965, Ohio Wesleyan U., 1967; m. Ruth Naomi Wilson, July 7, 1945; children—Claudia, Gloria Jean, Margaret Yvonne, Patricia Elaine. Ordained to ministry Methodist Ch., 1942; pastor in Orangeburg Circuit, 1942-43, York, S.C., 1946-47; chaplain S. C. State Coll., 1944-46; prof. Gammon Theol. Sem., 1947-53; asso. dir. Meth. Bd. Edn., 1953-64; bishop of Ia. area Meth. Ch., 1964—. Cons. on Negro colls. Danforth Found., 1957-60; vis. prof. Perkins Sch. Theology, So. Meth. U., summer 1958. Trustee Claflin Coll., Simpson Coll., Morningside Coll., Gammon Theol. Sem., Clark Coll., Cornell Coll., Ia. Wesleyan Coll. Mem. Phi Kappa Phi, Phi Delta Kappa, Kappa Delta Pi. Home: 3005 Patricia Dr Des Moines IA 50322 Office: 1019 Chestnut St Des Moines IA 50309

THOMAS, JERRY K., cons. engr.; b. Turton, S.D., Nov. 7, 1925; s. Howard A. and Anna M. (Sondergard) T.; B.C.E., with distinction, U. Minn., 1948; m. Beverly F. Dickinson, May 17, 1947; children—David A., Linda J. With Staven Engring. Co., Rapid City, S.D., 1948-65, v.p., 1961-65; partner, owner Thomas & Lockwood, cons. engrs., Rapid City, 1965-73, pres., 1973-76; pres. Thomas, Erickson, Dominicak & Crow Cons. Engrs., 1976—. Served with USNR, 1944-46. Mem. Am. Soc. C.E., S.D. Engring. Soc., Cons. Engrs. Council S.D. (pres. 1968, nat. dir. 1970-71), Rapid City C. of C., Greater S.D. Assn., Chi Epsilon. Methodist (chmn. trustees 1971-72). Clubs: Optimist, High Twelve, Knife and Fork (Rapid City), Masons, Shriners, K.T. Home: Canyon Lake Heights Route 4 Box 1004 Rapid City SD 57701 Office: 2222 Jackson Blvd Rapid City SD 57701

THOMAS, JOHN MEREDITH, educator; b. Arkansas City, Kans., Jan. 28, 1930; s. Arthur and Pearl (Buck) T.; Mus.B. with honors, Southwestern Coll., 1951; M.Mus., Wichita State U., 1956; m. Connie Sue Wiegand, June 10, 1956 (dec. Sept. 7, 1974); children—Catherine Anne, Michael Arnold, John Arthur; m. 2d, Mariko Oku, Aug. 14, 1976; children—Daniel, Paul, Thomas. Asst. prof. organ Greenville (Ill.) Coll., 1956-61; grad. asst. organ U. Ill., 1959, 1962-63; organist, dir. St. Paul's United Ch. Christ, Wausau, Wis., 1966-69, Frame Meml. Presbyn. Ch., Stevens Point, 1970—; asst. prof. organ U. Wis., Stevens Point, 1963—; organ cons. Guest recitalist Am. Guild Organists Convs., 1955, 65; violinist Stevens Point Civic Symphony, 1963-68, 76—; mem. Univ. Faculty String Quartet, 1963-66; organist, recitalist Sta. KFUO, 1958. Active Boy Scouts Am., instnl. rep., 1966-68, asst. scoutmaster, 1971—. Asso. Danforth Found., 1966—. Served with AUS, 1953-54. Recipient Nat. Luth. Fellowship, 1962-63. Asso. mem. Am. Guild Organists (founder Wis. River chpt. 1964, dean 1964-66), Church Music Interest Agy. (founder, dir.). Lutheran. Composer: Once to Every Man and Nation, 1955. Home: Route 3 PO Box 578 Stevens Point WI 54481

THOMAS, JOSEPH E., psychologist; b. India, Feb. 11, 1937; s. Ipe and Kunjamma Thomas; m. Chinnamma Kavatt, Nov. 23, 1964; children—Joseph, Kurian, Elizabeth. B.A., Kerala U. (India), 1957, M.A., 1960, Ph.D., 1969. Mem. faculty dept. psychology Kerala U. 1963-72; postdoctoral internship in clin. psychology Northwestern U. Med. Sch., 1971-72, mem. faculty dept. psychiatry, 1972—; psychologist Univ. Health Center, Trivandrum, India, 1964-68; psychologist dept. psychiatry U. Chgo., 1972-74; dir. inpatient psychiat. services Mental Health Center La Salle County, Ottawa, Ill., 1974; psychologist Northwestern Meml. Hosps., Chgo., 1974—. Sec. Student Christian Movement of India, Bangalore, 1957-58; treas. St. Thomas Orthodox Ch., Chgo., 1973. Mem. Am. Psychol. Assn., Assn. Advancement Behavior Therapy. Contbr. articles to profl. jours. Home: 9440 N Oriole Morton Grove IL 60053 Office: Rehab Inst Chicago 345 E Superior St Chicago IL 60611

THOMAS, JOYCE MARGUERITE P., counselor; b. St. Louis, 1926; d. Booker and Helene (Johnson) Pickens; B.S. in Edn., Lincoln U., 1948; M.S. in Edn., St. Louis U., 1966, Ph.D. in Counselor Edn., 1978; m. Joseph B. Thomas Jr., Oct. 7, 1950 (dec. 1975). Clk., Govt. Service, St. Louis, 1951-53; elementary tchr., St. Louis Pub. Schs., 1954-65; counselor diagnostic center St. Louis Pub. Schs., 1966-68, coordinator of counseling, 1969-70, evaluator div. evaluation and research, summer sch. 1970; gen. coordinator Model Cities Ednl. Program, St. Louis Pub. Schs., 1970-74; instr. human relations Harris Tchrs. Coll., now Harris Stowe Coll., St. Louis, 1974-76, counselor, instr., 1976—, cons. in field; counselor in service Banneker Central-Vashon Dist. St. Louis Pub. Schs. Bd. dirs. Ferrier-Harris Home for Aged; active YWCA, Apptd. mem. State Advisory Council Comprehensive Psychiat. Services Dept. Mental Health, Mo., 1977. Recipient pub. service awards St. Louis Police Dept., 1967, 68, 69, 70, 76. Mem. Am. Personnel and Guidance Assn., Am. Coll. Personnel Assn., Assn. Humanistic Edn. and Devel., Assn. Black Psychologists, St. Louis Urban League, NAACP, St. Louis Mental Health Assn. (exec. bd.), Delta Sigma Theta (past pres. St. Louis U. Alumnae chpt.). Roman Catholic. Home: 440 Plaza Square Apt 701 Saint Louis MO 63103 Office: 3026 Laclede Ave Saint Louis MO 63103

THOMAS, JUERGEN ERICH, neurologist; b. Berlin, Germany, Feb. 4, 1924; s. Erich and Ilse (Maahs) T.; grad. Knight's Acad. Liegnitz (Germany), 1942; student med. schs. U. Berlin, 1942, U. Graz (Austria), 1943, U. Breslau (Germany), 1944; M.D., U. Goettingen (Germany), 1949; M.S. in Neurology, U. Minn., 1959. Came to U.S., 1954, naturalized, 1961. Intern, Waldkrankenhaus, Berlin, 1950, resident in neurology, 1951, resident in internal medicine, 1953; resident in neurosurgery U. Zurich (Switzerland), 1952; resident in psychiatry Kansas City (Mo.) Gen. Hosp., 1954-55; research asst. electroencephalography U. Ill., Chgo., 1956; resident in neurology Mayo Clinic, Rochester, Minn., 1956-59, cons., 1959—. Asso. prof. neurology U. Minn. at Rochester, 1969—; prof. neurology Mayo Med Sch., 1974—. Diplomate Am. Bd. Neurology. Mem. Am. Assn. Electromyography and Electrodiagnosis (pres. 1967, dir. 1962-72), AMA, Minn. Med. Assn., Am. Acad. Neurology, Am. Neurol. Assn. Contbr. articles to med. jours. Home: 410 6th Ave SW Rochester MN 55901 Office: Mayo Clinic Rochester MN 55901

THOMAS, KENNETH EUGENE, univ. adminstr.; b. Oxford, Kans., Aug. 7, 1925; s. Charle H. and Belle (Boatler) T.; B.A., Southwestern Coll. at Winfield (Kans.), 1951; M.S., Kans. State U., 1952; Ph.D., U. Wis., 1961; m. Betty Marie Reynolds, Mar. 22, 1946; 1 dau., Linda Suzanne. Program mgr. Sta. KJCK, Junction City, Kans., 1952-53; asst. mgr. Sta. KSAC, Kans. State U., Manhattan, 1953-54, mgr., 1954-62, prof., dir. communications, 1962—; owner, pres. Midwest Research Assos., Manhattan, 1953—; v.p. Lindal Homes, Inc., 1962—. Served with U.S. Mcht. Marine, 1943-45, AUS, 1945-47; PTO, ETO. Kellogg Found. fellow, 1959-61. Mem. Nat. Assn. State Univs. and Land Grant Colls. (exec. com. pub. relations), Manhattan C. of C. (dir. 1968), Rural Sociologists Am., Am. Assn. Agrl. Editors, Am. Legion, VFW, Pi Kappa Delta, Pi Gamma Mu, Alpha Epsilon Rho, Epsilon Sigma Phi. Presbyterian (trustee). Clubs: Rotary, Elks, Manhattan Country. Home: 3000 Montana Ct Manhattan KS 66502 Office: Dept Communications Kans State U Manhattan KS 66502

THOMAS, LEWIS EDWARD, chem. engr.; b. Lima, Ohio, May 18, 1913; s. Lewis Edward and Ilma Kathryn (Siebert) T.; B.S., Ohio No. U., 1935; M.S., Purdue U., 1937, postgrad., 1937-40; m. Elinda Patricia Grafton, Dec. 21, 1939; children—Linda (Mrs. John R. Collins), Stephanie (Mrs. Andrew Pawuk), Kathryn (Mrs. James N. Ramsey), Deborah (Mrs. James Masker). Asst. prof. chemistry Va. Mil. Inst., Lexington, 1940-45; devel. engr. Sun Oil Co., Toledo, Ohio, 1945-49, lab. supr., 1950-69, div. supr., 1969-73, lab. mgr., 1973—. Dir. First Fed. Savs. & Loan, Toledo. Pres. Harvard Elementary Sch. PTA, 1953-54; mem. Mayor's Indsl. Devel. Com., Toledo, 1963-66. Precinct committeeman, mem. Lucas County Republican Central Com., 1958—. Trustee Toledo Pub. Library, 1966-70, pres., 1969-70; trustee U. Toledo, 1967—, vice chmn. bd., 1971-75; trustee Toledo Lucas County Pub. Library, 1970—, pres., 1973-74; adv. bd. St. Charles Hosp., 1972—. Named Chem. Engr. of Yr., Toledo Tech. Council, 1961, 63; Toledo area Engr. of Yr., 1976. Registered profl. engr., Ohio. Mem. Nat., Ohio (chmn. state conv. 1975) socs. profl. engrs., Am. Inst. Chem. Engrs., Am. Chem. Soc. (pres. Toledo chpt. 1960), Nat. Mgmt. Assn. (trustee Toledo chpt. 1962-70, nat. dir. 1968-70), Tech. Socs. Toledo (pres. 1968-69), Assn. Governing Bds. Univs. and Colls., Ohio Acad. Sci. (adv. bd. engring. sect. 1972—), Sigma Xi (asso.), Tau Beta Pi, Nu Theta Kappa, Pi Kappa Alpha. Episcopalian (lay reader). Clubs: Explorers, Toastmasters. Home: 4148 Deepwood Lane Toledo OH 43614 Office: PO Box 920 Toledo OH 43693

THOMAS, SISTER M. EVANGELINE, ednl. adminstr.; b. Carbondale, Pa.; d. John W. and Lida M. (Coggins) Thomas; A.B., Marymount Coll., 1932; M.A., Catholic U. of Am., 1934, Ph.D., 1936. Prof. history, chmn. dept. Marymount Coll., Salina, Kans., 1936-68, dean of students, 1941-48, 56-57, chmn. artist series, 1941—, dir. coll. relations and spl. projects, 1962—. Mem. exec. com. Coop. Coll. Devel. Program, 1966—. Mem. Salina Cultural Arts Commn., 1966-70; bd. dirs. St. John's Hosp., Salina, 1978—; archives project dir. Leadership Conf. Women Religious, 1976. Mem. Kans. Hist. Soc., Kan. Tchrs. History (pres. 1962), Am. Cath. Hist. Assn. (exec. bd. 1962-66), AAUW (exec. bd. 1966—, v.p. Salina br. 1968-74), Am. Hist. Assn., Orgn. Am. Historians, Kans. State Hist. Soc. (exec. bd. 1956—, v.p. 1977-78), Am. Oral Historians, Council Advancement and Support Edn., Salina C. of C. (edn. com., community affairs com.). Author: Nativism in Old Northwest, 1936; Footprints on the Frontier, 1948. Contbr. to Cath. Youth Ency., New Cath. Ency. Contbr. chpts. to book, articles to publs. Home: 116 S 9th St Salina KS 67401 Office: Medaille Center 148 N Oakdale St Salina KS 67401

THOMAS, MELVIN HAROLD, accountant; b. Chgo., Oct. 2, 1947; s. Melvin Harold and Mildred (Ross) T.; A.A., Central YMCA Coll., Chgo., 1973; B.S., Northwestern U., 1975; M.B.A., Purdue U., 1977.

Cost accountant Intercraft Industries Corp., Chgo., 1971-74; plant accountant W. R. Grace & Co., Chgo., 1974; financial accountant John Morrell & Co., Chgo., 1974-75; sr. accountant Blaw Knox Corp., steel co., East Chicago, Ind., 1975-76; accounting mgr. BHIB Bell & Howell Schs. div. Bell & Howell Corp., 1976—. Instr. Bus. Acads. Inc., Chgo., 1975. Notary pub., Ill. Mem. Am. Mgmt. Assn., Am. Accounting Assn., Nat. Assn. Accountants, Planning Execs. Inst., Assn. Systems Mgmt., Assn. M.B.A. Execs., Nat. Soc. Pub. Accountants, Alpha Phi Alpha (financial sec. chpt. 1969-71). Home: 8621 S Champlain Ave Chicago IL 60619 Office: 209 W Jackson Blvd Chicago IL 60606

THOMAS, NORMAN MARVELL, beverage distributing co. exec.; b. Cairo, Ill., Oct. 4, 1936; s. William Henry and Claudia (Campbell) T.; B.A., Philander Smith Coll., 1964; postgrad. Purdue U., 1972-73; M.B.A., U. Chgo., 1978; m. Jacqueline Smith, June 5, 1960; children—Michael, Michelle. Sorter, Western Electric Co., Chgo., 1957-62; patrolman Chgo. Police Dept., 1962-63; tchr. elementary grades Little Rock Bd. Edn., 1964-65; spl. rep. Joseph Schlitz Brewing Co., Balt., 1965-66, project, mgr. market devel., Milw., 1970-73, mgr. program devel., 1973-74; mktg. rep. Mobil Oil Corp., Phila., 1967-68, area mgr., 1969-70; gen. sales mgr. Miller Distbg. Co., Chgo., 1974-75; pres. Thomas-Randall Distbrs., Inc., Chgo., 1975—. Bd. dirs. Hyde Park YMCA, Chgo., 1976—. Served with USMC, 1958-60. Mem. Chgo. Beer Wholesalers Assn., Associated Beer Distbrs. Ill., Cosmopolitan C. of C. (dir. 1975—), Execs. Merchandising Club. Baptist. Home: 612 Old Forge Ct Park Forest IL 60644 Office: 941 E 99th St Chicago IL 60628

THOMAS, O. PENDLETON, rubber co. exec.; b. Forney, Tex., June 14, 1914; s. William Pendleton and Lottye (Trail) T.; B.S., East Tex. State U., 1935, LL.D. (hon.), 1972; M.B.A., U. Tex., 1941; m. Anne Swindell; children—William Pendleton II, Alexander Cole, James Trail. With Sinclair Oil Corp., N.Y.C., 1945-69, pres., 1964-69, chief exec. officer, 1968-69, also dir.; chmn. exec. com. Atlantic Richfield Co., N.Y.C., 1969-71, also dir.; chmn. bd., chief exec. officer, dir. B.F. Goodrich Co., Akron, Ohio, 1971—; dir. Superior Oil Co., Armco Steel Corp.; trustee Mut. Life Ins. Co. N.Y. Bd. govs. ARC. Served as lt. USNR, 1942-45. Recipient Distinguished Grad. award U. Tex. Coll. Bus. Adminstrn., 1964; Distinguished Alumnus award U. Tex., 1969. Mem. Am. Petroleum Inst. (hon. dir.), Conf. Bd. (trustee), UN Assn. (econ. policy council), Rubber Mfrs. Assn. (mem. exec. com.), Bus. Roundtable (exec. com., policy com.). Clubs: Round Hill (Greenwich, Conn.); River, Links (N.Y.C.); Blind Brook (Portchester, N.Y.); Augusta (Ga.) Nat. Golf; Union (Cleve.); Sharon Golf, Portage Country (Akron); Pepper Pike (O.). Office: B F Goodrich Co 500 S Main St Akron OH 44318

THOMAS, PATRICIA GRAFTON (MRS. LEWIS EDWARD THOMAS), educator; b. Michigan City, Ind., Sept. 30, 1921; d. Robert Wadsworth and Elinda (Opperman) Grafton; student Stephens Coll., 1936-39, Purdue U., summer 1938; B.Ed. magna cum laude, U. Toledo, 1966; postgrad. (fellow) Bowling Green U., 1968; m. Lewis Edward Thomas, Dec. 21, 1939; children—Linda L. (Mrs. John R. Collins), Stephanie A., (Mrs. Andrew M. Pawuk), I. Kathryn (Mrs. James N. Ramsey), Deborah (Mrs. James E. Masker). Tchr., Toledo Bd. Edn., 1959—, tchr. lang. arts Byrnedale Sch., 1976—. Dist. capt. Planned Parenthood, 1952-53, ARC, 1954-55; mem. lang. arts curriculum com. Toledo Bd. Edn., 1969, mem. grammar curriculum com., 1974. Mem. Toledo Soc. Profl. Engrs. Aux., Helen Kreps Guild, AAUW, Phi Kappa Phi, Kappa Delta Pi (chpt. pres. 1976—), Pi Lambda Theta, Delta Kappa Gamma (chpt. v.p. 1968-70). Republican. Episcopalian. Home: 4148 Deepwood Lane Toledo OH 43614 Office: 3645 Glendale St Toledo OH 43614

THOMAS, ROBERT JAY, state ofcl.; b. July 18, 1942; s. Fred and Veda (Brehm) T.; B.S., No. Ill. U., 1964, M.S., 1973; m. Elizabeth Stacey, Nov. 2, 1968; 1 son, Robert Fawell. With Ill. Youth Center DuPage, Naperville, 1964-74; supt. Ill. Youth Center, St. Charles, 1974—. Lectr. George Williams Coll., Downers Grove, Ill., 1973-74. Mem. adv. bd. Coll. DuPage, 1972-75. Mem. Am. Correctional Assn., Nat. Assn. Tng. Sch. Supts., Nat. Assn. Wardens and Supts., Nat. Inst. Crime and Delinquency, John Howard Assn. Episcopalian. Home and office: Illinois Youth Center St Charles IL 60174

THOMAS, WALTON DOWDELL, surgeon; b. Montgomery, Ala., July 7, 1919; s. Jonathan Render and Mabel (Randall) T.; B.A., Yale, 1941; M.D., Columbia, 1944; M.S. in Surgery, U. Minn., 1949; m. Jane Magin, July 5, 1944; children—Gregory Walton, Leslie Gram, Jan Magin, Clay Randall. Intern Roosevelt Hosp., N.Y.C., 1944, resident surgeon, 1945; resident surgeon Mayo Clinic, Rochester, Minn., 1946-50; individual practice surgery, Milw., 1950-66; founder, mng. partner Milw. Med. Clinic, 1966—; asso. clin. prof. Marquette U., 1960—. Mem. council Boys Club, Milw., 1967—. Served with M.C., USNR, World War II, 1953-55. Diplomate Am. Bd. Surgery. Mem. Milw. Surg. Soc. (pres. 1975), Milw. Acad. Surgery, Milw. Acad. Medicine, Wis. Surg. Soc., Wis. Surg. Travel Club. Clubs: Milwaukee Country (pres. 1972-75), Milwaukee Town. Home: 7829 N Regent Rd Milwaukee WI 53217 Office: 3003 W Good Hope Rd Milwaukee WI 53209

THOMAS, WILLIAM, JR., pathologist; b. Uniontown, Pa., Feb. 17, 1926; s. William and Catherine (Tibbs) T.; B.S. magna cume laude, Springfield Coll., 1951; M.D., Boston U., 1955; m. Elizabeth Ann Driessen, Sept. 17, 1960; children—William C., John J., Christopher P. Intern Detroit Receiving Hosp., Hosp., 1955-56; resident Cin. Gen. Hosp., 1956-60, Henry Ford Hosp., Detroit, 1960-61; practice medicine specializing in pathology, 1961; asst. pathologist Bridgeport (Conn.) Hosp., 1961-64; asso. dir. pathology Michael Reese Hosp., Chgo., 1964-65; asso. pathologist Mt. Sinai Hosp., Chgo., 1965-66, vice-chmn. pathology dept. 1966—; asst. prof. pathology Chgo. Med. Sch., 1965-67, asso. prof., 1967-71, prof., 1971-74; asso. prof. pathology Rush Med. Sch., 1975—; asst. insp. Coll. Am. Pathology, 1974—; cons. alcohol counselor program Gov.'s State U., 1977—. Vice pres. bd. dirs. Haymarket House, 1977—; bd. dirs. Chgo. Met. Council on Alcoholism, 1973—; mem. Ill. Citizen's Adv. Com. on Alcoholism, 1974—. Served with USMC, 1945-46. Recipient Certificate of Recognition Chgo. Met. Council on Alcoholism, 1976. Fellow Am. Soc. Clin. Pathologists, Coll. Am. Pathologists, Chgo. Inst. Medicine; mem. AMA, Chgo. Soc. Med. History, Ill. Alcoholism and Drug Dependence Assn., AAUP, Chgo. Pathological Soc., Chgo. Med. Soc., Ill. Med. Soc., Ill. Soc. Pathologists, Sigma Xi, Alpha Omega Alpha. Roman Catholic. Home: 1727 Wilmette Ave Wilmette IL 60091 Office: Mt Sinai Hosp California Ave at 15th St Chicago IL 60608

THOMAS, WILLIAM JAMES, engring. co. exec.; b. Wadena, Minn., Feb. 22, 1934; s. James Maurice and Idabelle Louella (Ehrky) T.; student St. Paul Vocational Sch., 1951-52; m. Thelma Ilene Jacobson, Aug. 4, 1967; children—Robin Gail, William James, Kathy Jane, Carolle Ann, Jay William; stepchildren—Wendy, Tara, Steffany, Timothy. Tool and die foreman Wright Products, Inc., St. Paul Park, Minn. and Rice Lake, Wis., 1952-59; tool and die designer Telex Amco, Inc., Mankato, Minn., 1959-62; pres. Thomas Engring. Co., Inc., Mpls., 1962—; pres. Progressive Stampings, Inc. (formerly Bergquist Mfg. Co.). Served with AUS, 1959. Mem. Am. Metal Stamping Assn. (dir. 1972-76), Twin City Tool and Die Assn., Metal Fabricators Assn., Soc. Mfg. Engrs. Home: 7012 Tupa Dr Edina MN 55435 Office: 8900 70th Ave N Minneapolis MN 55428

THOMAS, WILLIAM RICHARD, ednl. adminstr.; b. Elberta, Mich., June 1, 1911; s. William Richard and Fannie (Hoglebarger) T.; student Benzie County Normal Sch., 1930-31, Ferris Inst., 1931-33; B.A., U. Mich., 1935; teaching certificate Central Mich, U., 1939; M.A., Mich. State U., 1969. Supt., tchr. schs., Elberta, Mich., 1942-58; prin. Benzie County Normal Sch., Frankfort, Mich., 1958-60; supt. schs. Benzie County, Beulah, Mich., 1961-65; elem. sch. cons., adminstrv. asst. Traverse Bay Area Intermediate Sch. Dist., Traverse City, Mich., 1965-74. Co-owner W.R. Thomas Sons, Elberta, 1942-77. Mem. Mich. Edn. Assn. Republican. Methodist (mem. ofcl. bd. 1950—, trustee 1960—, lay leader). Mason. Home: 755 Washington Ave Elberta MI 49628

THOMASON, JACQUELINE, guidance counselor; b. Sylacauga, Ala., Apr. 26, 1954; d. Lurie and Deleane Della (Boyd) Thomason; B.A. (scholarship 1972-76), Talladega (Ala.) Coll., 1976; M.A. (United Negro Coll. Fund grantee 1976-77), Ohio State U., 1977. Tchr., Knoxville Kindergarten, Talladega, 1971-72; asst. playground dir. Knoxville Recreation Dept., summer 1972; vol. counselor North Central Mental Health Clinic, Columbus, Ohio, 1976-77; asst. to dir. U. Akron Edgewood Community Services Center, 1977—; research asst. Talladega Coll., 1976. Sunday Sch. tchr. Talladega Mt. Zebulon Ch. of God, 1968-72, pres. young adult choir, 1968-72, Florina and Loula Lasker scholar, 1976; recipient Outstanding Acad. Achievement award Talladega Coll., 1973. Mem. NEA, Am. Personnel and Guidance Assn., Talladega Coll., Ohio State U. alumni assns., Phi Delta Kappa, Alpha Chi. Address: 795 S Arlington St Akron OH 44306

THOMASSON, MARY LOU WAHLERT, radiologist; b. St. Louis, July 1, 1926; d. Ernest Henry and Myrtle Ruth (Jenkins) Wahlert; A.B., Washington U., 1946, M.D., 1951; m. Robert Edgar Thomasson, June 17, 1947; children—Mary Sue Thomasson McSwain, Jeffrey Lee. Intern, St. Louis City Hosp., 1951-52, resident in radiology, 1952-55; practice radiology Luth. Hosp., St. Louis, 1955-60, St. Francois Med. Center, Florissant, Mo., 1960—, Mo. Bapt. Hosp., St. Louis, 1963-65, DePaul Hosp., St. Louis, 1969-76; instr. St. Louis U., 1955-61; pres. St. Francois Med. Center, 1977. Diplomate Am. Bd. Radiology. Mem. St. Louis Med. Soc., Mo. Med. Assn., St. Louis Radiol. Soc., Am. Coll. Radiology, Radiol. Soc. N. Am., St. Louis, St. Charleshist. socs., Soc. Preservation of Old Mills, Gamma Phi Beta. Club: Eastern Star. Home: 935 Terrill Farms Rd St Louis MO 63124 Office: 525 St Francois Med Center Florissant MO 63031

THOMOPOULOS, NICK TED, educator; b. Chgo., Aug. 21, 1931; s. Nick and Marie (Augustinos) T.; B.S., U. Ill., 1953, M.A., 1959; Ph.D., Ill. Inst. Tech., 1966; m. Elaine Cotsirilos, May 24, 1964; children—Marie, Melina, Diana. Corporate supr. ops. research Internat. Harvester Co., Chgo., 1959-66; sr. scientist Ill. Inst. Tech. Research Inst., Chgo., 1966-68, asso. prof., 1968—; cons. in U.S., Europe and Japan. Author: (with T. Prenting) Assembly Line Systems, 1974; contbr. articles to profl. jours. Home: 53 Regent Dr Oak Brook IL 60521 Office: 3300 S Federal St Chicago IL 60616

THOMPSON, ALFRED ARNOLD, former judge; b. Lisbon, N.D., Sept. 25, 1918; s. Martin Olaus and Nettie (Martin) T.; B.S., N.D. Agrl. Coll., 1940, postgrad., 1941; postgrad. Valley City State Tchrs. Coll., 1942; LL.B., U. N.D., 1951; m. Betty Jean Connell, July 14, 1945; children—Karen Shelley, Charles Martin, Eric Rolfe. Tchr. pub. schs. N.D., 1941-43, 46-48; admitted to N.D. bar, 1951; asst. state's atty. Burleigh County, 1951-53; partner firm Register & Thompson, 1953-55; ind. practice, Bismarck, N.D., 1955-60; partner firm Thompson & Lundberg, Bismarck, 1960-65, firm Thompson, Lundberg & Nodland, Bismarck, 1965-73; judge N.D. Dist. Ct., 1973-77. Mem. N.D. Game and Fish Adv. Bd., 1963-73; pres. Missouri Valley council Boy Scouts Am., 1964-65; mem. legal adv. bd. Izaak Walton League Am., 1961-71. Served with intelligence AUS, 1943-46. Recipient Silver Beaver award Boy Scouts Am., 1963, Wood Badge award, 1962. Mem. Burleigh County, (past pres.), N.D. bar assns, Sons Norway. Mason (Shriner). Club: Plainsman (Bismarck). Home: N River Rd Bismarck ND 58501

THOMPSON, BARBARA STORCK, state ofcl.; b. McFarland, Wis., Oct. 15, 1924; d. John Casper and Marie Ann (Kassabaum) Storck; B.S., Wis. State U., 1956; M.S., U. Wis., 1959, Ph.D., 1969; L.H.D. (hon.), Carroll Coll., 1974; m. Glenn T. Thompson, July 1, 1944; children—David C., James T. Tchr. pub. schs. West Dane County, Mt. Horeb, Wis., 1944-56; instr. Green County Tchrs. Coll., Monroe, Wis., 1956-57; coordinator curriculum Monroe Pub. Schs., 1957-60; instr. U. Wis., Platteville, 1960; supr. schs. Waukesha (Wis.) County Schs., 1960-63, supt. schs., 1963-65; prin. Fairview Elementary Schs., Brookfield, Wis., 1962-64; adminstrv. cons. Wis. Dept. Pub. Instrn., Madison, 1964-72, state coordinator, 1971-72; instr. U. Wis., Madison and Green Bay, 1972; supt. pub. instrn. State of Wis., Madison, 1973—. Mem. White House Conf. Children, 1970, Gov.'s Com. State Conf. Children and Youth, 1969-70, Manpower Council, 1973—. Bd. dirs. Vocational, Tech. and Adult Edn., 1973—, Ednl. Communications, 1973—, Higher Edn. Aids, 1973—, Agy. Instructional TV, 1975—. Recipient State Conservation award Madison Lions Club, 1956; Waukesha Freeman award, 1961. Mem. Nat. Council Adminstrv. Women in Edn. (named Woman of Year 1974), Nat. Council State Cons. in Elementary Edn. (pres. 1974-75), Wis. Assn. Sch. Dist. Adminstrs., Assn. Supervision and Curriculum Devel., Wis. Assn. Supervision and Curriculum Devel., Southwestern Wis., Southeastern Wis. (mem. exec. council 1972-73) assns. supervision and curriculum devel., Dept. Elementary Sch. Prins., Wis. Elementary Sch. Prins. Assn., Nat., Wis. (pres. local chpt. 1970-71, life mem.), So. Wis. edn. assns., Wis. Ednl. Research Assn., Dept. Elementary-Kindergarten-Nursery Edn., Assn. Childhood Edn. Internat., Assn. Childhood Edn., Council Chief State Sch. Officers, Edn. Commn. of States, Nat. Council State Cons. in Elementary Edn. (pres. 1974-75), Delta Kappa Gamma. Author: A Candid Discussion of Critical Issues, 1975. Mem. editorial bd. The Education Digest, 1975—. Contbr. articles to profl. jours. Home: 1 Springwood Circle Madison WI 53717 Office: 126 Langdon St Madison WI 53702

THOMPSON, DALE MOORE, banker; b. Kansas City, Kans., Nov. 19, 1897; s. George Curl and Ruth Anna (Moore) T.; A.B., cum laude, U. Mich., 1920; m. Dorothy Allen Brown, July 2, 1921; 1 son, William Brown. Trainee, City Bank of Kansas City (Mo.) (now United Mo. Bank, N.A.), 1920-22, asst. cashier, 1922-27, asst. v.p., 1927-30, v.p., 1930-34; v.p. City Bond & Mortgage Co. Kansas City, 1934-43, exec. v.p., 1943-48, pres., 1948-68, chmn. bd., 1968-74, hon. chmn. bd., 1974—, also dir.; chmn., trustee Central Mortgage & Realty Trust, 1972-76; v.p. Regency Bldg. Co., Kansas City. Lectr. Northwestern U. Sch. Mortgage Banking, also Stanford, 1954-62. Mem. Mo. Govs. Com. on Arts. Chmn. Kansas City campaign United Negro Coll. Fund, 1958-59; mem. Mo. State Bd. Edn., 1966—; pres. Kansas City Philharmonic Assn., 1944-54. Trustee, U. Kansas City, Kansas City Philharmonic Assn. Conservatory Music Kansas City, Kansas City Art Inst., Kansas City Children's Mercy Hosp.; treas. Kansas City Truman Med. Center. Served with USN World War I. Recipient citation Kansas City C. of C., 1954, Archbishop's Community Service citation, 1954, citation Nat. Conf. Christians and Jews, 1965. Mayor's citation, 1955. Mem. Mortgage Bankers Assn. Am. (pres. 1962-63, Distinguished Service award 1966), U. Mich. Alumni Assn. (past dir.), Phi Beta Kappa (pres. Kansas City 1946-49), Trigon, Phi Kappa Psi. Mem. Christian Ch. Clubs: River, University, Indian Hills Country (Kansas City); Monterey Peninsula Country (Pebble Beach, Calif.). Home: 221 W 48th St Kansas City MO 64112 Office: United Mo Bank Bldg Kansas City MO 64106

THOMPSON, DOROTHY BROWN, writer; b. Springfield, Ill., May 14, 1896; d. William Joseph and Harriet (Gardner) Brown; A.B., U. of Kansas, 1919; m. Dale Moore Thompson, July 2, 1921; 1 son, William B. Began writing professionally, 1931; contributed verse to nat. magazines and newspapers including Saturday Review, Sat. Eve. Post, Va. Quar. Rev., Poetry, Commonweal, Good Housekeeping and others, author research articles for various historical jours.; poems pub. in over two hundred collections and textbooks; magazines and textbooks pub. in Eng., Australia, New Zealand, Canada, Sweden; twenty-five in Braille. Leader poetry sect. Writers' Conf., U. Kan., 1953-55, McKendree Coll., 1961, 63, Creighton U., Omaha, 1966; lectr. writers' conf. U. Kan., 1965, Am. Poets Series, Kansas City, Mo., 1973; mem. staff Poets Workshop, Central Mo. State U., 1974; poet-in-schs. residency for Mo. State Council of Arts, 1974—. Received Mo. Writers' Guild Award, 1941, Poetry Soc. Am., nat. and local awards. Mem. Diversifiers, Poetry Soc. Am., Nat. Soc. Colonial Dames. Mem. Christian Ch. Clubs: Woman's City, Filson (Louisville). Author: Subject to Change (poems), 1973. Address: 221 W 48th St Kansas City MO 64112

THOMPSON, ERNEST EDWARD, clergyman; b. Reidsville, Ga., Oct. 8, 1919; s. Columbus Monroe and Annie (Ryals) T.; B.S., Ga. Tchrs. Coll., 1941; postgrad. U. Edinburgh, Scotland, 1945; M.A., Butler U., 1950, B.D., 1949; m. Sarah Darsey, June 30, 1943; children—Barbara Ann (Mrs. Michael Jon Duch), Sarah Jo (Mrs. Ralph M. Norwood), Pamela, Ernest Edward. Secondary sch. tchr., Ga., 1939-42; ordained to ministry Christian Ch., 1941; pastor Sixth St. Christian Ch., Middletown, Ind., 1948-49; asst. minister Peachtree Christian Ch., Atlanta, 1949-51; minister First Christian Ch., Macon, Ga., 1951-56, Central Christian Ch., Elkhart, Ind., 1956-62, Third Christian Ch., Indpls., 1962—. Mem. recommendations com. Internat. Conv. of Christian Chs.; Disciples of Christ rep. to Gen. Assembly of Nat. Council of Chs., Boston, 1954; chmn. program com. World Conv. Christian Chs., San Juan, P.R., 1965; mem. gen. bd. Christian Ch., 1973—. Bd. dirs. Bibb County unit Am. Cancer Soc., 1953-56. Trustee Christian Coll. of Ga., Christian Theol. Sem., Indpls. Served from 2d lt. to capt., AUS, 1942-46. Chaplain (col.) Ind. N.G. Decorated Bronze Star medal, Army Commendation medal, Meritorious Service medal; Ind. Commendation medal, 1975. Mem. Ind. Christian Ministers Assn. (pres, 1957-58), Ind. Assn. Christian Chs. (state bd.), Internat. Platform Assn., Acad. Parish Clergy, Mil. Chaplains Assn. (life mem.), Theta Phi. Mason (32 deg.). Clubs: Civitan (Macon, Ga.); Exchange (Elkhart, Ind.); Kiwanis (Indpls.). Home: 6046 Andover Rd Indianapolis IN 46220 Office: 5220 E Fall Creek Parkway North Dr Indianapolis IN 46220

THOMPSON, FREDRICK BLAINE, county ofcl.; b. Thayer County, Nebr., Jan. 18, 1927; s. Fredrick Everett and Flora Marie (Salisbury) T.; grad. high sch.; m. Erla Mae Butts, June 10, 1946; children—Gary Lee, Cheryl (Mrs. Larry Dixon McCaslin). Maintenance supt., engrs. aid Neb. Dept. Rds., Sidney, 1947-66; partner J.D. Olinger Co., rd. constrn., Sidney, 1965-66; hwy. supt. Cheyenne County, Neb., Sidney, 1966—. Mem. Neb. Bd. Pub. Rds., Classifications and Standards, 1971—; Fed. Aid Secondary Com. on County Hwys., 1973—; coordinator Cheyenne County Hwy. Traffic Safety Commn., 1974—. Mem. adv. council Western Neb. Tech. Coll., 1971—. Served with USNR, 1945-46. Mem. Neb. Assn. County Engrs. Hwy Supts. and Surveyors (pres. 1972), Neb. Panhandle Dist. County Hwy. Supts. (pres. 1971-72), Nat. Assn. County Engrs., Am. Rd. Builders Assn., Cheyenne County C. of C. United Methodist. Mason, Elk. Home: 1105 Rose St Sidney NE 69162 Office: 920 Jackson St Sidney NE 69162

THOMPSON, GEORGE GREENE, educator; b. Bucklin, Kans., Mar. 17, 1914; s. Otis Kenrick and Georgia (Beach) T.; B.A., Fort Hays (Kans.) State Coll., 1937, M.S., 1938; Ph.D., State U. Iowa, 1941; m. Evelyn Schuller, Oct. 25, 1940; 1 son, Kenrick Steven. Asst. prof. psychology So. Ill. U., Carbondale, 1941-42; asst. prof. psychology Syracuse U., 1942-46, asso. prof., 1946-49, prof., 1949-59; prof. psychology Ohio State U., Columbus, 1959—; spl. research asso. psycho-acoustic lab. Harvard, 1943-45; mem. review com. research grants div. NIMH, 1964-67. Fellow Am. Psychol. Assn.; mem. Soc. Research in Child Devel., Am. Ednl. Research Assn., A.A.A.S., Sigma Xi. Author: Child Psychology, 2d edit., 1962; (with F.J. Di Vesta) Educational Psychology, 1971; (with R.G. Kuhlen) Psychological Studies of Human Devel., 3d edit., 1971; (with E.F. Gardner) Social Relations and Morale in Small Groups, 1957. Editor: Social Development and Personality, 1971. Cons. editor Jour. Genetic Psychology, 1959—, Genetic Psychology Monographs, 1959—, Jour. Ednl. Psychology, 1958—. Home: 203 W Southington Ave Worthington OH 43085

THOMPSON, HAROLD, ins. co. exec.; b. Winnipeg, Man., Can., Aug. 18, 1922; s. Harry and Hrodny (Finnson) T.; B. Commerce with honours, U. Man., 1944; m. Beatrice May Shipman, Sept. 21, 1946; children—Patricia Lynn, Gordon Douglas. With Monarch Life Assurance Co., Winnipeg, 1946—, actuary, 1952-59, asst. gen. mgr., 1959-62, v.p., dir. sales, 1962-66, v.p., asst. gen. mgr., 1966-68, v.p. adminstrn., 1968-70, exec. v.p., 1970, pres., chief exec. officer, 1971—. Pres. Man. div. Canadian Cancer Soc., 1967—. Mem. Winnipeg C. of C. Club: Manitoba (Winnipeg). Home: 53 Aldershot Blvd Winnipeg MB R3P 0C9 Canada Office: 333 Broadway Ave Winnipeg 1 MB Canada

THOMPSON, HOWARD ELLIOTT, educator; b. West Allis, Wis., July 30, 1934; s. Leonard Adolph and Hulda Axe ina (Granstrom) T.; B.S., U. Wis., 1956, M.S., 1958, Ph.D., 1964; m. Judith M. Gram, June 30, 1956; children—Linda Kay, Karen Marie, James Howard, John Leonard, Ann Elizabeth. Mathematician, ops. research analyst A.O. Smith Corp., Milw., 1957-61; asst. prof. Sch. Bus. U. Wis., Madison, 1964-67, asso. prof., 1967-69, prof., 1969—, Mary Rennebohm prof., 1975—. Vis. prof. Ohio State U., 1970-71; cons. various utilities and utility commns., 1968—, Wis. Atty. Gen., 1973-74. Mem. Am. Fin. Assn., Am. Econs. Assn., Operations Research Soc. Am., Inst. Mgmt. Scis., Am. Inst. Decision Scis., Math. Assn. Am., Pi Mu Epsilon, Beta Gamma Sigma, Alpha Iota Delta. Author: Aplications of Calculus in Business and Economics, 1973; A Brief Calculus with Applications to Business and Economics, 1976. Contbr. articles to profl. jours. Home: 6302 Bradley Pl Madison WI 53711 Office: Commerce Bldg Univ Wis Madison WI 53706

THOMPSON, JAMES ROBERT, gov. Ill.; b. Chgo., May 8, 1936; s. J. Robert and Agnes Josephine (Swanson) T.; student U. Ill., Washington U., St. Louis; LL.B., No. U., 1959; m. Jayne Anne Carr, June 19, 1976. Admitted to Ill. bar; prosecutor, Cook County States Atty.'s Office, Chgo., 1959-64; asso. prof. Northwestern U. Law Sch., 1964-69; chief dept. law enforcement and pub. protection Atty. Gen.'s Office, 1969-70; asst. U.S. atty. No. Dist. Ill., 1970-71, U.S. atty., 1971-75; gov. Ill., 1976—. Author: Cases in Common on Criminal

Procedure; Cases in Common on Criminal Law; Criminal Law and Its Administration. Home: Exec Mansion Springfield IL 62701 Office: 207 State House Springfield IL 62706

THOMPSON, JAMES ROREM, physician; b. Fergus Falls, Minn., June 15, 1933; s. Carl Otmer and Margaret (Rorem) T.; B.A., U. Minn., 1955, B.S., 1956, M.D., 1959; m. Darlene Ann Olson, July 20, 1958 (div. Aug. 1976); children—Beth, Sara, Brian; m. 2d, Dorothy L. Johanneson, Dec. 6, 1976. Intern St. Luke's Hosp., Duluth, Minn., 1959-60; resident Mayo Clinic, Rochester, Minn., 1963-66; practice medicine, specializing in ophtholomology Bemidji (Minn.) Clinic Ltd., 1966—; mem. staff Bemidji Hosp.; instr. ophtholmology Sch. Medicine, U. Minn., Mpls., 1968—. Diplomate Am. Bd. Ophtholmology. Home: Bemidji MN 56601 Office: 6th and Beltrami St Bemidji MN 56601

THOMPSON, JAMES TEMPLE, dairy processing mfg. co. exec.; b. Seymour, Ind., Jan. 29, 1922; s. James Ralph and Helen Louise (Temple) T.; B.S., Purdue U., 1943; m. JoAnn Gray, Mar. 27, 1949; children—James Thomas, Robert David, Ann Louise. With Thompson Dairy Co., Seymour, 1946—, pres., 1963—. Pres., Seymour Sch. Bd. Served with AUS, 1943-46, 51-52. Recipient awards Boys' Club. Mem. Ind. Dairy Products Assn. (pres.), Internat. Assn. Ice Cream Mfg. (pres.), Midwest Dairy Products, Milk Industry Found. Presbyterian. Clubs: Elks, Country of Seymour. Home: 1111 North Dr Sunset Pkwy Seymour IN 47274 Office: 201 Tipton St E Seymour IN 47274

THOMPSON, JOHN BROWN, physician, educator; b. Eugene, Oreg., Mar. 18, 1929; s. Kenneth Guy and Alta Mae (Brown) T.; A.B. in Chemistry, Willamette U., 1951; M.D., U. Oreg., 1956; children—Sheri, Mark. Intern Salt Lake Gen. Hosp., Salt Lake City, 1956-57; resident Denver VA Hosp., 1957-60; practice medicine specializing in gastroenterology, Oklahoma City, 1962-75, Fargo, N.D., 1975—; instr. medicine U. Okla. Sch. Medicine, Oklahoma City, 1962-67, asst. prof., 1967-72, asso. prof., 1972-75, co-dir. Nat. Inst. Health Gastroenterology Traineship Program, 1967-71, co-dir. VA Research and Edn., 1968-72; prof. medicine U. N.D. Dept. Medicine, Fargo, 1975—, chief div. gastroenterology, 1975—; chief gastroenterology sect. VA Hosp., Oklahoma City, 1966-74, Fargo, N.D., 1975—. Served with USAF 1960-62. Diplomate Am. Bd. Internal Medicine. Fellow A.C.P.; mem. Am. Gastroenterological Assn., N.Y. Acad. Scis., Am. Fedn. Clin. Research, N.D., Am. med. assns., N.D. Med. Found., First Dist. Med. Soc. N.D. Contbr. articles to profl. jours. Home: Sleepy Hollow Horace ND 58047 Office: VA Hosp N Elm and 21st St Fargo ND 58102

THOMPSON, KENRICK STEVEN, sociologist; b. Syracuse, N.Y., May 1, 1946; m.; B.A., Ohio State U., 1967, M.A., 1970, Ph.D., 1974. Spl. research asst. Ohio State U., summer 1968, teaching asst. dept. sociology, 1968-70, teaching asso., 1972-74; asst. prof. dept. sociology No. Mich. U., Marquette, 1974—; extension tchr. K.I. Sawyer AFB, Mich., Mich. Dept. Corrections, Marquette Br. Prison. Mem. Am., North Central sociol. assns., Midwest Sociol. Soc., Nat. Council on Family Relations, Am. Soc. Criminology, Soc. for Study Social Problems, AAUP, Mich. Assn. U. Profs. Named Outstanding Young Man of Am., U.S. Jaycees, 1977; contbr. articles to profl. jours. Home: 611 Mesnard St Marquette MI 49855

THOMPSON, LYLE FRANCIS, advt. exec.; b. South Milwaukee, Wis., May 9, 1929; s. Clarence L. and Emily (Martinek) Nowack; student U. Wis., 1947-48; m. Helen M. Taberman, Apr. 6, 1963. Mng. editor Tri-Town News and Greenfield Guardian, Hales Corners, Wis., 1961-63; advt. mgr. Controls Co. Am., Milw., 1963-68; v.p. Andrews, Advt., Inc., Milw., 1968-73; corp. partner Thompson/Gardner & Assos., Inc., Milw., 1973—. Vice pres. South Shore Ins. Agy., Milw. Gen. chmn. Milw. Graphic Communications Month, 1968. Mem. Milw. Assn. Indsl. Advertisers (pres. 1968-69, internat. dir. 1970-71, regional v.p. 1971-72), Sales Promotion Execs. Assn. (Milw. pres. 1967-68, internat. dir. 1967-71), Milw. Press Club, U.S. Ski Assn. (nat. com. chmn. 1968-70, nat. dir. 1969-70), Internat. Fedn. Sports (dir. pub. relations). Clubs: South Shore Yacht; Vagabond Ski Milw. (pres. 1965-66). Home: 2583 S Superior St Milwaukee WI 53207 Office: 8705 N Port Washington Rd Milwaukee WI 53217

THOMPSON, MARGARET M., educator; b. nr. Falls Church, Va., Aug. 1, 1921; d. Lesley L. and Madeline (Shawen) Thompson; B.S., Mary Washington Coll., U. Va., 1941; M.A., George Washington U., 1947; Ph.D., U. Ia., 1961. Tchr., supr. phys. edn. Staunton (Va.) City Schs., 1941-44; tchr. jr. high sch. phys. edn., Arlington County, Va., 1944-47; instr. womens phys. edn. Fla. State U., Tallahassee, 1947-51; instr., asst. prof., asso. prof. phys. edn. Purdue U., Lafayette, Ind., 1951-65; asso. prof. phys. edn. U. Mo., Columbia, 1965-68, prof., 1968-71, dir. Cinematography and Motor Learning Lab. Dept. Health and Phys. Edn., 1965-71; prof. phys. edn. U. Ill., Champaign-Urbana, 1971—. Mem. Am., Ill. assns. health, phys. edn. and recreation, Nat., Midwest assns. phys. edn. for coll. women, Nat. Found. Health, Phys. Edn. and Recreation, Nat. Assn. Higher Edn., AAUP, Internat. Assn. Phys. Edn. and Sports for Coll. Women, Pi Lambda Theta. Author: (with Barbara B. Godfrey) Movement Pattern Checklists, 1966; (with Chappelle Arnett) Perceptual Motor and Motor Test Battery for Children, 1968; (with Barbara Mann) An Holistic Approach to Physical Education Curriculum: Objectives Classification System for Elementary Schools, 1977, Gross Motor Inventory, 1976; also film strips. Contbr. articles to profl. jours. Home: 3 Wildwood Ln Mahomet IL 61853 Office: 211 Freer Gymnasium Dept Phys Edn U Ill Urbana IL 61801

THOMPSON, MELVIN LEROY, hydrologist; b. Litchfield, Nebr., Apr. 11, 1924; s. James Wrenwick and Effie Jane (Lamb) T.; B.S.C.E., U. Nebr., 1949; m. Velma Lucille Baade, Sept. 27, 1944; 1 dau., Marcia Emily. Hydraulic engr. U.S. Geol. Survey, Riverton, Wyo., 1949-51, hydraulic engr. investigations, St. Louis, 1951-55, engr.-in-charge, Norton, Kans., 1955-58, chief sub.-dist., Topeka, 1958-68, dist. supervisory hydrologist, chief hydrologic surveillance unit, Lawrence, Kan., 1968—. Faculty Kans. U., Lawrence, 1967-76; instr. radio communication Douglas County Amateur Radio Club, Lawrence, 1975—. Bd. dirs., founders Melvin L. and Velma L. Scholarship Fund, engring. edn. Served to 1st lt., AC, AUS, 1943-46; CBI. Decorated Air medal, Bronze Star with two oak leaf clusters. Registered profl. engr., Kans. Mem. Kan. Engring. Soc., Nat. Soc. Profl. Engrs., Douglas County (Kans.) Amateur Radio Club (news editor 1973, treas. 1974—), Kans. U. Outland Club. Lutheran. Rotarian (treas. 1976—). Dir. Water Resources Data, annual Kans. publ., 1967-77. Home: 514 Millstone Dr Lawrence KS 66044 Office: 1950 Ave A Campus West U of Kans Lawrence KS 66045

THOMPSON, OSCAR JUNIOR, minister, ednl. adminstr.; b. Canton, Ohio, July 23, 1922; s. Oscar and Emma Mae (Moorman) T.; B.A., Findlay Coll., 1948; postgrad. Ohio No. U., 1956; postgrad. Kent State U., 1960-62; M.A., U. Akron, 1967; m. Beverly Jane Arnold, July 21, 1946; children—Rodney Lee, Kenneth Lynn, Ned Brian. Pastor, Chs. of God in Ney, Ohio, 1948-51, Lima, Ohio, 1951-57, Smithville, Ohio, 1957—; pub. sch. tchr. Lima, 1957-58; tchr., prin. Burbank Sch., N. Central Sch. System, Wayne County, Ohio, 1958—; prin. Smithville Elementary Sch., 1964—. Mem. Bd. Pub. Affairs Smithville, 1967-68, Village Council Smithville, 1968-70; mayor Smithville, 1970—; officiater, State Baseball Tournaments, 1973, 74. Mem. exec. com. Republican party, 1970—. Served with M.C., AUS, 1943-46. Mem. Wayne County Tchrs. Assn. (pres. 1965), Wayne County Ofcls. Assn., Ohio High Sch. Athletic Assn., Ohio Elementary Sch. Prins. Royal Arcanum, Lion. Home: 273 Parkview Circle Smithville OH 44677 Office: 156 N Milton St Smithville OH 44677

THOMPSON, PAUL LELAND, artist; b. Buffalo, Iowa, May 20, 1911; s. Buell and Flora Elizabeth (Steen) T.; student Cal. Sch. of Fine Arts, 1932-34, Corcoran Sch. of Art, 1944-45; m. Phyllis McGregor, June 15, 1953; 1 dau., Leslie Ruth. One-man shows Internat. Galleries, Washington, 1946, M. Knoedler Co. Inc., 1954, Unitarian Ch., Plainfield, N.J., 1975; exhibited group shows Seattle Art Mus., 1937, Honolulu Acad. of Art, 1933, Corcoran Biennial Nat. Painting Exhbn., 1945, San Francisco Palace of Legion of Honor, 1948, San Francisco Art Mus., 1948, NAD Nat. Watercolor Exhbn., 1956, Hunterdon County Art Center, Clinton, N.J., 1968; executed two murals Shiloh Baptist Ch., Plainfield, N.J.; represented in permanent collections Barry's Art Gallery, Scotch Plains, N.J., The Heritage Gallery, Cin. Recipient Soc. Washington Artists prize, 1946; Washington Times Herald award, 1947. Mem. Artists Equity N.Y., Artists Equity of N.J., N.J. Watercolor Soc., Somerset Art Assn., Cin. Art Club. Home: 220 Lorraine Av Cincinnati OH 45220 Office: 3412 Telford St Cincinnati OH 45220

THOMPSON, PHEBE KIRSTEN, physician; b. Glace Bay, N.S., Can., Sept. 5, 1897; d. Peter and Catherine (McKeigan) Christianson; M.D., C.M. Dalhousie U., Halifax, N.S., 1923; m. Willard Owen Thompson, M.D., June 21, 1923 (dec. Mar. 1954); children—Willard Owen, Frederic, Nancy, Donald. Came to U.S., 1923, naturalized, 1937. Intern Children's Hosp., Halifax, N.S., 1922-23; asst. biochemistry, dept. applied physiology Harvard Sch. Pub. Health, 1924-26; asst. and research fellow in medicine thyroid clinic, Mass. Gen. Hosp., Boston, 1926-29; asst. in metabolism dept. (endocrinology) Rush Med. Coll. of U. Chgo. and The Central Free Dispensary Chgo., 1930-46; asso. with husband in practice medicine, Chgo., 1947-54; mng. editor Jour. Clin. Endocrinology and Metabolism, 1954-61, cons. editor, 1961-64; editor Jour. Am. Geriatrics Soc., 1954—; cons. editor Endocrinology, 1961-64; free-lance editor and writer. Recipient Thewlis award Am. Geriatrics Soc., 1966; certificate of appreciation Am. Thyroid Assn., 1966. Fellow Am. Med. Writers' Assn. (adv. com. 1955-60, v.p. Chgo. 1962), Am. Geriatrics Soc., Gerontological Soc.; mem. Endocrine Soc., AAAS, Am. Genetic Assn., Am. Pub. Health Assn., Ill. Acad. Scis., life mem. Art Inst. Chgo., Chgo. Hist. Soc. Clubs: University; Harvard; Canadian (corr. sec. 1968-73; mem. bd. 1973-76). Address: 2337 N Commonwealth Ave Chicago IL 60614

THOMPSON, RENOLD DURANT, mining and shipping co. exec.; b. Cleve., July 28, 1926; s. James R. and Gertrude G. (Meyers) T.; B.A., Dartmouth, 1946; B.S., Case Inst. Tech., 1948; m. Shirley Ann Sprague, June 24, 1949; children—Renold Durant, Bradley S., Patricia S. Metallurgist Steelworks div. Am. Steel and Wire div. U.S. Steel Corp., 1948-52; with Oglebay Norton Co., Cleve., 1952—, v.p. vessel and mining operations, 1970-72, sr. v.p., 1972-73, exec. v.p. ops., 1973—; dir. Eveleth Taconite Co., Lubrizol Corp., Central Nat. Bank of Cleve., Cleve. Metal Stamping Co., Licking River Terminal Co., Oglebay Norton Co., ONCO Eveleth Co., Pringle Transit Co., Oglebay Norton Taconite Co., ON Coast Petroleum Co., Tex. Mining Co., Travis Mfg. Co., Saginaw Mining Co., Superior Land Co.; mem. mgmt. com. Eveleth Expansion Co. Served with USNR, 1944-46. Mem. Am. Inst. Mining, Metall. and Petroleum Engrs., Am. Iron Ore Assn. (dir., mem. exec. com.), Am. Iron and Steel Inst., Greater Cleve. Growth Assn., Eastern States Blast Furnace and Coke Oven Assn., LakeCarriers' Assn. (trustee, advisory com.), Lake Superior Indsl. Bur. (dir.), Water Transp. Assn. (trustee, exec. com., budget and fin. com., steering and policy com.). Clubs: Cleve. Athletic, Mid-Day, Tavern, Union (Cleve.); Duquesne (Pitts.); Mayfield Country (South Euclid, Ohio); Pepper Pike (Hunting Valley, Ohio); Propeller U.S. Home: 14883 Hillbrook Dr Hunting Valley Chagrin Falls OH 44022 Office: 1200 Hanna Bldg Cleveland OH 44115

THOMPSON, RICHARD ARTHUR, machine products co. exec.; b. Elkhart, Ind., May 11, 1926; s. Charles Arthur and Harriette Ellen (Splady) T.; B.S. in Bus., Mktg., Ind. U., 1950; m. Virginia Dare Bentz, Feb. 14, 1953; 1 dau., Suzann Ellen. Mgr. Thompson Auto Supply Co., Elkhart, 1950-64; plant mgr. Thompson Mfg. Co., Inc., Elkhart, 1955—, also exec. sec., 1959-77, pres., 1977—; mgr. Charles D. Hoyt Co., Inc., Mishawaka, 1958-75, pres., 1977—. Dir. United Way, 1973-76. Served with AUS, 1944-45. Mem. Elkhart Jaycees, Sigma Phi Epsilon (sec. 1948-49, v.p. 1949-50, alumni bd. 1952-54). Republican. Episcopalian (every mem. canvas chmn. 1969-73, clk. vestry 1971, jr. warden 1972). Elk, Lion. Home: 15 St Joseph Manor Elkhart IN 46514

THOMPSON, RICHARD NEIL, lawyer; b. Newman Grove, Nebr., Nov. 20, 1933; s. Oscar T. and Gladys M. (Olson) T.; student Wayne State Coll., Nebr., 1951-52; B.S. in Law, U. Nebr., 1955, J.D., 1957; m. Dorothy M. Bilson, Aug. 15, 1957; children—Pamela Sue, Richard Neil, Beth Ann. Admitted to Nebr. bar, 1957, asso. firm Cline, Williams, Wright, Johnson & Oldfather, Lincoln, Nebr., 1957-60, mem. firm, 1960-70, Thompson & Sweet, Lincoln, 1970-75; individual practice law, Lincoln, 1975—; sec., dir. Spencer Foods, Inc. (Iowa), 1972—. Bd. dirs. Lincoln Symphony Assn., 1975—; trustee Westminster Ch. Found., 1975—, chmn. investment com., 1975—. Served with AUS, 1950-58. Mem. Lincoln, Nebr., Am. (com. fed. regulation securities, 1969—) bar assns., Lincoln C. of C., Phi Delta Phi, Pi Delta Kappa, Phi Gamma Delta. Presbyterian. Clubs: Lincoln U., Lincoln Country, Palmas del mar, Bankers of San Juan. Home: 2909 Bonacum Dr Lincoln NE 68592 Office: 968 NBC Center Lincoln NE 68508

THOMPSON, RICHARD THOMAS, coll. adminstr.; b. Kenmore, N.Y., Oct. 11, 1939; s. Donald Whittington and Dorothy Jean (Porter) T.; B.A., Eastern Mich. U., 1961, M.A., 1963; m. Nancy Ann Streeter, Aug. 29, 1959; children—Elizabeth Jean, Richard Thomas, David Bryant. Tchr., Warren (Mich.) Consol. Schs., 1961-65; instr. English, Macomb (Mich.) Community Coll., 1965-66, Oakland (Mich.) Community Coll., 1966-67; asst. prof. counseling Oakland Community Coll., 1967-68, dept. head, asst. prof. developmental edn., 1968-69, dept. head, asso. prof. foundational studies, 1969-70, dean Highland Lakes campus, 1970-75, provost Orchard Ridge campus, 1975—. Staff mem. Gov.'s Youth Leadership Conf., 1969—; mem. Huron Valley Human Relations, 1969—, Huron Valley Fine Arts Council, 1977—; bd. dirs. Oakway Symphony Orch. Wall St. Jour. fellow, 1963. Mem. Oakland Community Coll. Faculty Assn. (pres. 1968-69), Mich. Acad. Arts and Scis., Am., Mich. personnel and guidance assns., Mich. Sch. Pub. Relations Assn., Am. Coll. Personnel Assn., Oakland Area Counselors Assn., Farmington Area C. of C., Phi Delta Kappa, Alpha Psi Omega. Home: 625 E Commerce St Milford MI 48042 Office: 27055 Orchard Lake Rd Farmington MI 48018

THOMPSON, ROBERT ALLAN, engring. and edn. cons.; b. Cleve., June 10, 1937; s. Roy Henry and Viola (Nehls) T.; B.S., Case Inst. Tech., 1958; postgrad. Cleve. State U., 1958-59; m. Louise Saari Thompson, Nov. 27, 1970. Research engr. Sohio Satellite Tracking Sta., Standard Oil Research Lab., Cleve., 1958-63, dir., 1964-65; tchr. Cleve. Bd. of Edn., 1958-65; dir. Warrensville Heights Planetarium and Space Sci. Program, 1964-65; tchr. Spl. Programs Faculty, Case Inst. Tech., 1965; dir. planning phase sci. div. Cleve. Supplemental Ednl. Center, 1965-66; dir. James A. Lovell Regional Space Center, Milw., 1967-73. Lectr., U. Wis., Milw., 1968-71. Chmn. secondary Math. curriculum com. Cleve. pub. schs., 1963-64; mem. Wis. Aerospace Edn. Com., 1968-71; sec. Friends of Space Center, 1968-75. Named one of 10 Outstanding Young Men, Cleve. Jr. C. of C., 1961. Registered profl. engr. Mem. IEEE (sr.; chmn. membership, exec. coms. Cleve. sect. 1965-66), AAAS, Am. Inst. Aeros. and Astronautics (chmn. Wis. sect. 1969-70), Brit. Interplanetary Soc. (fellow), Cleve. Engring. Soc. (profl.), Cleve. Astron. Soc. (exec. com. 1966-67), Case Alumni Assn. Kiwanian (Key Club Leadership plaque 1961). Presbyterian. Author: Cynosure-A New Reality, 1974. Contbr. to Above and Beyond, Ency. Aviation and Aerospace Scis. Home: 1954 Seneca St Euclid OH 44117 Office: 2650 Lakeview Apt 4001 Chicago IL 60614

THOMPSON, RONALD WADE, ret. metal mfg. co. exec.; b. Montpelier, Ohio, Oct. 24, 1897; s. Martin Stopher and Mina (Eckerfield) T.; B.Chem. Engring., Ohio State U., 1920; m. Delorous Levine Shanks, May 26, 1942; children—Ronald Wade, William Oxley, Thomas Evans, John Richard. Open hearth helper United Alloy Steel Canton, Ohio, 1920; with Interlake Iron, Chgo., 1920-62, various positions to plant mgr., Toledo, 1941-43, gen. works mgr., Chgo., Cleve., 1943-48, v.p. operations, 1948-51, pres., chief exec. officer, 1951-60, chmn., chief exec. officer, 1960-62. Served with F.A., U.S. Army, 1918. Clubs: Union Fifty, Mid-Day, Chagrin Valley Country, Pepper Pike (Cleve.); Presidents (Ohio State U.). Home: 13720 Shaker Blvd Cleveland OH 44120

THOMPSON, ROY HENRY, physician; b. Cleve., Dec. 7, 1906; s. Harry Epler and Gertrude E. (McBride) T.; M.D., Ohio State U., 1932; m. Viola Alverta Nehls, June 8, 1935; 1 son, Robert Allan. Intern Cleve. St. Alexis Hosp., 1933; chief med. insp. Ohio and W.Va. CCC camps, 1933-39; postgrad. Cook County Hosp., 1939; fellow Cleve. Clinic, 1946; resident Sta. Hosp., Ft. Hayes, Columbus, Ohio, 1940-43; practice medicine, specializing in radiology, Cleve., 1945—; chief radiology Doctors Hosp., Cleve., 1946-52; chief radiology Womans Gen. Hosp., Cleve., 1952-74; hon. mem. med. staff, asso. radiologist VA Hosp., Cleve., 1974—; asst. prof. radiology Med. Sch., Case-Western Res. U., 1974—. Mem. supplementary sci. adv. com. Cleve. Bd. Edn. Bd. dirs. Univ. Circle YMCA. Served from capt. to lt. col. M.C., AUS, 1940-45, ret. col., 1967. Diplomate Am. Bd. Radiology. Fellow Cleve. Med. Library Assn., Cleve. Radiol. Soc.; mem. Am., Ohio, Cleve. med. assns., Radiol. Soc. N.Am., Brit. Inst. Radiology, Am. Coll. Radiology, Soc. Nuclear Medicine (sponsor local technologist chpt. 1967-72), Ohio, Cleve. radiol. socs., Cleve. Acad. Medicine, Indian Hills Community Assn. Presbyn. Mason (Shriner), Kiwanian (past pres. Univ. Circle Club). Home: 1954 Seneca Dr Cleveland OH 44117 Office: VA Hosp 10701 East Blvd Cleveland OH 44106

THOMPSON, RUSSELL ALDEN, physician; b. Hutchinson, Minn., Aug. 13, 1917; s. Thomas Apolonius and Sena (Hansen) T.; student U. Minn., 1936-37, B.S., 1952, M.D., 1954; m. Jo Ann Cash, Sept. 5, 1953; children—Ann, Thomas, John, Barbara; m. 2d, Mary Kruse Hiniker, Sept. 10, 1974. Intern St. Mary's Hosp., Duluth, Minn., 1954-55; gen. practice medicine, Cosmos, Minn., 1955-59; resident Ophthal. Study Council, Waterville, Maine, 1960; practice specializing in ophthalmology, Mpls., 1959-62, Willmar, Minn., 1963—, Hutchinson, Minn., 1977—; asso. M.A. McCannel, Mpls., 1959-62; chief staff Meeker County Hosp., Litchfield, Minn., 1955-59; mem. staff Rice Meml. Hosp., Willmar, Hutchinson Community Hosp. Active Willmar United Fund, 1966-69; mem. Bd. Edn. New London, Minn., 1969-74, chmn., 1973-74. Served with USAAF, 1942-45. Decorated Air medal with 6 oak leaf clusters. Mem. Audubon Soc., Minn. Ornithologist Union, Friends of Earth Soc., Wilderness Soc., Save the Redwoods League, Nature Conservancy, Minn. Assn. Ophthalmologists, AMA, Minn. Med. Assn., Mid-Minn. Med. Soc., Royal Soc. Health, Internat. (life), Nat. (life) wildlife fedns., Ducks Unlimited, Sierra Club, East African, South African wildlife socs., Phi Rho Sigma. Clubs: Masons, Elks, Order Eastern Star. Home: 1000 SW 14th Ave Willmar MN 56201 Office: 115 E Litchfield St Willmar MN 56201 also Hutchinson Med Complex Hutchinson MN 55350

THOMPSON, SIDNEY A., investment banker; b. Trail, Minn., Nov. 5, 1939; s. Gilbert A. and Violet G. (Evenson) T.; student San Diego Jr. Coll., 1959-60; m. Charlene E. Thompson, Jan. 20, 1962; children—Blair, Jill, Mark Anthony. Asst. v.p. sales State Auto and Casualty Underwriters, Des Moines, 1960-62; promoter Nat. Properties Corp., Des Moines, 1962-64; ins. salesman, Mpls., 1964-72; stockbroker Marquette Securities, Inc., Mpls., 1972-76; v.p., prin., Pagel, Inc., Mpls., 1976—; pres. Ainsco, Inc., 1974—, Kimball Minn., Inc., 1976—. Chmn., Minnetonka Village Little League, 1972-77. Served with USN, 1956-60. Mem. Twin City Traders Assn. Club: Elks. Democrat. Home: 2433 Marcy Ln Minnetonka MN 55343 Office: 625 Marquette Ave Minneapolis MN 55402

THOMPSON, STANLEY MILFORD, mktg. exec.; b. Mt. Horeb, Wis., May 13, 1920; s. Melvin Tosten and Adeline (Oimoein) T.; B.S., U. Wis., 1943, M.S., 1953; m. Gail Elizabeth Peterson, May 25, 1946; children—Stanley Martin, Stephen Theobald, Eric Douglas, Martha Ann. Instr. agr. pub. schs., Wonewoc, Wis., 1943-46, Beaver Dam, Wis., 1946-53, Argyle, Wis., 1953-56; sales rep. Cargill, Inc., Rochester, Minn., 1956-59, terminal mgr., 1959-65, regional sales mgr., 1965-75, marketing mgr., 1975—. Chmn. council Boy Scouts Am., 1961-65; mem. Cargill Polit. Action Com., 1977—; advisor Jr. Achievement, Mpls., 1972-73. Served with USMC, 1943-46. Decorated Purple Heart; recipient Hon. Future Farmers degree State of Wis., 1951. Mem. Water Quality Assn., Nat. Hide Assn. (dir. 1970-71), Salt Inst. (chmn. agr. com. 1976-77). Lutheran. Clubs: Masons, Shriners. Home: 16516 Grays Bay Blvd Wayzata MN 55391 Office: Cargill Inc PO Box 9300 Minneapolis MN 55440

THOMPSON, THEODORE SEVRIN, dentist; b. Erskine, Minn., July 16, 1922; s. Thomas Aslak and Anne (Medveit) T.; B.A., U. Minn., 1950, B.S., D.D.S., 1952; m. Annacile Parrish, Mar. 2, 1946; children—Thomas Craig, Pamela Ann. Gen. practice dentistry, Austin, Minn., 1952—; mem. staff St. Olaf Hosp., Austin. Chmn., Mower County Cancer Soc., 1954-56; pres. Austin YMCA, 1966-68; bd. dirs. Minn. Dental Alumni Assn., 1974-77. Served with AUS, 1943-46. Fellow Internat. Coll. Dentists; mem. Am., Minn. (chmn. com. orgn. and structure 1971, com. on sci. and ann. session 1976—) dental assns., Southeastern Dist. (pres. 1970), Austin (pres. 1956-58) dental socs., Austin Dental Study Club (pres. 1969), Austin C. of C., Sons of Norway, Delta Sigma Delta. Lutheran (pres. 1968). Lion (pres. Austin 1962). Home: 2415 8th Ave SW Austin MN 55912 Office: 1431 Oakland Ave W Austin MN 55912

THOMPSON, THOMAS GEORGE, accountant, educator; b. Madison, Wis., Oct. 18, 1943; s. John X. and Mabel Lucille (Cretney) T.; A.A. in Accounting, Madison Area Tech. Coll., 1966; B.B.A., U. Wis., 1970. Owner, T.G.Thompson, accountant, Madison, 1964-69; sr. partner Thomas G. Thompson and Assos., Madison, 1970-73; pres.

T.G. Thompson & Assos., S.C., Madison, 1973—; instr. Madison Area Tech. Coll., 1970—. Founder, Madison Art Supply Co., 1965-66; dir. several corps. C.P.A., Wis. Mem. Nat. Assn. Accountants, Wis. Soc. C.P.A.'s, Am. Soc. Tax Accountants, Nat. Soc. Pub. Accountants, Verona High Sch. Alumni Assn. (pres. 1971-74), Madison Area Tech. Coll. Alumni Assn. (pres. 1967). Conglist. Address: 2821 Wannona Way Madison WI 53713

THOMPSON, TOMMY GEORGE, lawyer, state legislator; b. Elroy, Wis., Nov. 19, 1941; s. Allan and Julie (Dutton) T.; B.S., U. Wis., 1963, J.D., 1966; m. Sue Ann Mashak; children—Kelli Sue, Tommi Noel, Jason. Admitted to Wis. bar, 1966; practiced in Elroy, 1966—, Oxford, Wis., 1967—; mem. Wis. Ho. of Reps., 1966—, now asst. minority leader, past mem. joint finance, vets. affairs coms., now mem. adminstrv. rules com., judiciary, ins. and banking coms., assembly orgn., criminal justice and pub. safety com., rules com. Past mem. County Bd. Suprs. Past mem. N.G.; capt. Res. Mem. Jr. C. of C. Republican. Roman Catholic. Club: Lions. Home: 609 Academy St Elroy WI 53929 Office: Dippen Bldg Mauston WI 53948

THOMPSON, VERA EILEEN KRAMER (MRS. JOHN MAURICE THOMPSON), nurse; b. Watsontown, Pa., Oct. 7, 1918; d. Harvey Markle and Florence Agnes (Huffman) Kramer; R.N., Williamsport Hosp. Sch. Nursing, 1939; B.S., Columbia, 1951; M.A. in Counseling, George Washington U., 1958; m. John Maurice Thompson, Jan. 29, 1953. Commd. ensign U.S. Navy, 1942, advanced through grades to comdr., 1957; head, standards and tng. sect. Bur. Medicine and Surgery, Washington, 1954-59; asst. chief nursing service, Oakland, Calif., 1959-61; coordinator surg. hosp., San Diego, 1962-64; ret., 1964; dir. nursing Chgo. Wesley Meml. Hosp., 1966-71, v.p. nursing care and nursing edn., 1971-74; adminstr. Wesley-Passavant Sch. Nursing, Northwestern Meml. Hosp., 1972—; asso. prof. Northwestern U. Med. Sch., Chgo., 1968—. Fellow Inst. of Medicine (sec.); mem. Am., Ill. nurses assns., Nat., Ill. leagues for nursing, Am. Hosp. Assn., Pi Lambda Theta, Kappa Delta Pi. Episcopalian. Club: Lake Shore (Chgo.). Home: 111 E Chestnut St Chicago IL 60611 Office: 244 E Pearson St Chicago IL 60611

THOMPSON, VERNON DALE, educator; b. St. Joseph, Mo., Apr. 10, 1936; s. Robert Allen and Violet Marie (Kirkendoll) T.; B.S. in Civil Engring., The Citadel, 1959; M.S. in Civil Engring., U. Mo. at Rolla, 1970; m. Letha Marie Keck, Dec. 22, 1959; children—Scott Vernon, Mark Allen. Commd. officer U.S. Army, advanced through grades to lt. col., 1975; engr. Basic Sch., Airborne/Ranger Sch., 1959-60; co. comdr. 175th Engr. Co., Germany, 1960-63; canaverial engr., dist. asst. resident engr., Vietnam, 1965; adviser, Korea, ops. officer. exec. officer 44th Engr. Bn., Ft. Stewart, Ga., 1966-68; ops. officer, exec. officer 575th Engr. Bn., Vietnam, 1968-69; ops. officer 27th Engr. Bn., 45th Engr. Group, 1968-69; facilities engr., Frankfurt, Germany, 1970-72; dir. facilities engring. U.S. Army Engr. Command, N.Y.C., 1973-74; with Hdqrs. V Corps, 1974-75; prof. mil sci. Mich. Tech. U., Houghton, 1975—. Decorated Bronze Star medal with oak leaf cluster, Air medal with 2 oak leaf clusters. Mem. ASCE, Assn. U.S. Army, Assn. Citadel Men (Life). Club: Rotary. Office: Mich Tech U Hougton MI 49931

THOMPSON, WILLIAM NEIL, educator; b. Atlanta, Ill., Dec. 6, 1920; s. Ray Eugene and Ida Florence (Crihfield) T.; B.S., U. Ill., 1941, M.S., 1942, Ph.D., 1952; postgrad. (Farm Found. fellow), U. Chgo., 1947-48; m. Geraldine Alice Pech, Jan. 31, 1942; children—William Ray, John David, Julia (Mrs. Paul Z. Han). Instr., asst. prof. U. Ill., 1946-53; agriculturist TVA, Knoxville, Tenn., 1954-55; mem. faculty U. Ill. at Urbana, 1955-64, 66—, prof. agrl. econs., 1966—, asso. dir. internat. agrl. programs, 1973—. Chief party, adviser adminstrn. Njala Univ. Coll., Sierra Leone, 1964-66; cons. TVA, AID; spl. internat. agr. assignments in Sierra Leone, India, Pakistan, Nepal, Thailand, Saudi Arabia. Served with AUS, 1943-46: ETO, PTO. Recipient Outstanding Service award U. Ill. Coll. Agrl. Alumni Assn., 1959. Mem. Am. Econ. Assn., Am. Agrl. Econs. Assn., Am. Soc. Farm Mgrs. and Rural Appraisers (v.p. 1964), Soc. Internat. Devel., African Assn. Advancement Agr. Mem. Ch. Disciples of Christ. Author: Building Institutions to Serve Agriculture, 1968; Mission Overseas, A Handbook for U.S. Families in Developing Countries, 1969; A Method of Assessing Progress of Agricultureal Universities in India, 1970; The Punjab Agricultural university An Assessment of Progress to 1970, 1970; NIDA: A Case Study in Institution Development, 1974. Home: 2118 Bristol Rd Champaign IL 61820 Office: Internat Agrl Programs Univ Ill Urbana IL 61801

THOMSON, EDWARD WILSON, JR., printing co. exec.; b. Coshocton, Ohio, Sept. 8, 1931; s. Edward Wilson and Helen (Currie) T.; B.A., Denison U., 1953; m. Mary Jane Chenoweth, June 12, 1954; children—Bruce, Jane, Ann. Gen. mgr. Braun-Brumfield Inc., Ann Arbor, Mich., 1967-72; pres. Thomson-Shore Inc., Ann Arbor, 1972—; founder, pres. Thomson-Shore Pub., Inc., Detroit, 1977—. gen. partner TSK Investments. Office: 2040 Delaware Dr Ann Arbor MI 48103

THOMSON, LESTER GARLAND, veterinarian; b. Sparta, Wis., Apr. 13, 1937; s. Charles Scott and Frances Ruth (Wieland) T.; B.S., U. Ill., 1959, D.V.M., 1961; student Western Ill. U., 1955-57; m. Judith Kay Carson, Feb. 2, 1965; children—Scott, Todd, Lesli, Brett. Regional veterinarian Ill. Dept. Agr., Clinton, 1970-73, asst. adminstr. Bur. Meat and Poultry Insp., Springfield, 1973—. Elder, trustee Jefferson Street Christian Ch., Lincoln, Ill. Served to maj. U.S. Army, 1961-70. Mem. Ill., Central Ill. veterinary med. assns., Ill. Farm Bur., Omega Tau Sigma. Home: 9 Rigg Dr Lincoln IL 62656 Office: Emmerson Bldg Annex State Fairgrounds Springfield IL 62706

THOMSON, RALPH JOHN, data processing corp. mktg. exec.; b. Salt Lake City, Aug. 15, 1937; s. Ralph and Ruth (Watts) T.; A.B. with honors, U. Utah, 1962; A.M., Fletcher Sch. Law and Diplomacy, Tufts and Harvard Univ., 1963, M.A.L.D., 1964, Ph.D., 1968; m. Julienne Allen, June 14, 1962; children—Brook, Kim, Heidi-Noel, Tracy-Ciel. Asst. to dean Fletcher Sch. of Law and Diplomacy, 1963-66; asst. prof. govt. Boston U., 1968-72, co-dir. overseas grad. program in internat. relations, 1968-72; mgt. govt. programs and ednl. services Control Data Corp., Mpls., 1972-73, regional mgr. edn. services USSR and Eastern Europe, 1973-74, dir. internat. edn. services, 1974-75, gen. mgr., spl. rep. to govts., 1975—; dir. govt. programs Control Data Inst., 1972-73. Mem. bd. curriculum devel. Internat. Bur. Informatics and Internat. Computer Center, Rome, 1973-74; cons. UN, NATO, U.S. Dept. State, Dept. Def. Active Boy Scouts Am. Woodrow Wilson fellow, 1962-63, 65-67; Zellerbach fellow, 1963-65. Mem. Am. Polit. Sci. Assn., Am. Assn. Advancement of Slavic Studies, Inter-Am. Soc., Atlantic Assn., Sigma Chi, Pi Sigma Alpha. Home: 3903 Huntingdon Dr Minnetonka MN 55343 Office: 8100 34th Ave MN 55440

THOMSON, ROBERT JAMES, utility exec.; b. Detroit, Dec. 16, 1927; s. Harold E.J. and Irene (Silsbee) T.; A.B. in Bus. Adminstrn., Mich. State U., 1951, M.B.A., 1967; m. Doris L. Mullen, Sept. 19, 1953; children—Gregory, Susan, Jeffrey, Arthur. Mgr. firm Arthur Andersen & Co., Detroit, 1951-58; with Southeastern Mich. Gas Co., Port Huron, 1958—, v.p., 1961-72, pres., 1972—; also dir.; pres. Southeastern Mich. Gas Enterprises, Inc., Port Huron, 1977—; dir. Mich. Nat. Bank, Port Huron. Bd. dirs. United Way St. Clair County, 1974—, campaign chmn., 1974; trustee Port Huron Dist. Found., 1972—; bd. dirs. Indsl. Devel. Corp., Port Huron, 1972—, pres., 1976—; pres. St. Martin Luth. Ch., Port Huron, 1976—. Served with USN, 1946-47. C.P.A., Mich. Mem. Internat. Mgmt. Council (chmn. advt. com., 1972-73), Am. Inst. C.P.A.'s, Mich. Assn. C.P.A.'s, Am. Gas Assn., Am. Mgmt. Assn., Mich. State U. Advt. Mgmt. Program Club, Greater Port Huron-Marysville C. of C. (v.p. 1973-75, bd. dirs.). Clubs: Detroit, Port Huron Golf, Elks. Home: 3355 Lomar Dr Port Huron MI 48060 Office: 405 Water St Port Huron MI 48060

THONE, CHARLES, congressman; b. Hartington, Nebr., Jan. 4, 1924; J.D., U. Nebr., 1950. Admitted to Nebr. bar, 1950, U.S. Supreme Ct. bar, 1956; asst. state atty. gen. Nebr., 1951-53; asst. U.S. atty., 1953-55; adminstrv. asst. to Senator Roman L. Hruska of Nebr., 1955-59; mem. 92d-95th Congresses from 1st Nebr. dist. Chmn. Lincoln (Nebr.) Human Rights Commn., 1967-68. Chmn. Republican State Com., Nebr., 1959-61. Mem. Am., Nebr., Lincoln bar assns., U. Nebr. Alumni Assn. (pres. 1964-65), Phi Alpha Delta. Address: 1515 Circle Dr Lincoln NE 68506

THONE, JAMES O., veterinarian; b. Herman, Nebr., Sept. 27, 1926; s. Elmer L. and Edna E. (Matthews) T.; student Dana Coll., 1943-45; D.V.M., Iowa State U., 1949; m. Leone I. Christenson, May 5, 1950; children—John, Brent, Dennis, Sarah. Practice vet. medicine, Blair, Nebr., 1949—. Recipient Outstanding Citizen award Tri-County Saddle Club and Rodeo Assn., 1973. Mem. AVMA, Am. Assn. Swine Practitioners, Am. Bovine Practitioners Assn., Nebr., Intermountain, S.W. Iowa vet. assns., Dana Coll. Century Club, Papio Valley Preservation Assn. Lutheran (sec. council 1970-73). Mason (Shriner, K.T.). Home: 902 S 19th St Blair NE 68008 Office: 904 S 19th St Blair NE 68008

THONG, SIONG-HOAT, anesthesiologist; b. Phnom-Penh, Cambodia, Nov. 4, 1937; s. Kang and Yen Chai (Ngoan) T.; came to U.S., 1967, naturalized, 1971; M.D., Nat. Def. Med. Center, 1965; m. Karen Man-Hua Sun, May 2, 1967; children—Samul, Ida. Intern, Augustana Hosp., Chgo., 1967-68; resident in anesthesiology St. Elizabeth Hosp., Youngstown, Ohio, 1968-70, Ind. Med. Center, Indpls., 1970-71; practice medicine specializing in anesthesiology, Ft. Wayne, Ind., 1972—; clin. instr. in anesthesiology Ind. U. Med. Center, 1971-72. Diplomate Am. Bd. Anesthesiology. Mem. AMA, Am., Ind. socs. anesthesiologists. Home: 8418 Fantasia Way Fort Wayne IN 46815 Office: 5800 Fairfield Ave Fort Wayne IN 46807

THORDARSON, T.W., ednl. adminstr.; b. Gardar, N.D.; s. Grimur and Ingibjorg (Hanson) T.; grad. State Tchrs. Coll., 1912; B.S., State U. N.D., 1916, M.S., 1925; Rockefeller Found. fellow for spl. study Ohio State U. and Stanford, 1938; LL.B., La Salle U., 1950; LL.D., Concordia Coll., Moorhead, Minn., 1956; m. Kathryn Olafson, Dec. 10, 1917; 1 dau., Sally K. Admitted to N.D. bar, 1950, also admitted to U.S. Supreme Ct. bar; county agt. Barton Co., Kans., 1919-20; agrl. cons. Montgomery Ward & Co., Chgo., 1920, N.W. br. gen. advt. and sales mgr. St. Paul, 1921-22; colonization organizer N.P. R.R., 1923; Fed. Land Bank Appraiser, 1933; head vets. agrl. tng., alumni sec., prof. gen. extension N.D. State U., 1923-35, founder and state dir. div. supervised study, 1935—; founder, dir. N.D. State Film Library, Lyceum Entertainment Service and Tape Recs. Service; organizer first N.D. state wide testing and guidance service; farm mgr.; golf course owner; state chmn. 16 mm. films U.S. bond sales for N.D., 1942-45; cons. in Iceland for U.S. Dept. State on invitation of Iclandic govt., 1956; mem. People to People Tour study agr. in Japan, Hong Kong, Taiwan, P.I., S.Am., 1966; conducted comparative edn. study in Eng., France, East Germany, Russia, 1967. Served as commd. officer Armed Forces, 1917-19. Bldg. at N.D. State U. named Thordarson Hall for him. Mem. Am. Assn. Sch. Adminstrs., N.E.A., N.D. Edn. Assn., Internat. Platform Assn., Am. Scandinavian Found., Am. Legion, N.D. Bar, Optimist Club, Alpha Zeta, Pi Gamma Mu. Mason (Shriner). Club: Concordia. Co-author: Basic Mathematics, 1959. Contbr. articles to farm and ednl. jours. Editor Education Bulletin. Home: 1303 9th St S Fargo ND 58102

THORESEN, PAUL WALTER, psychologist; b. Milw., Oct. 19, 1941; s. Norman Royal and Dorothy Ann (Zelinske) T.; B.S. cum laude, Loras Coll., 1963; M.S., U. Wis., 1965; Ph.D., Marquette U., 1968; m. Margaret Mary Cawley, Sept. 7, 1964; children—Beth Anne, David, Kevin, Karen. Chief psychologist Kiwanis Children's Center, Milw., 1968-69; asst. prof. psychiatry Med. Sch. Ind. U., Indpls., 1970—. Dir. consultation and edn. Midtown Community Mental Health Center, Indpls., 1973-74, chief psychologist, 1974—; pvt. practice, 1970—. Mem. Suicide Prevention Service Tng. Com. Marion County, 1975—. Bd. dirs. Horizons Orgn. for Profl. Growth, 1973—, Downtown Pastoral Counseling Service, 1974-75. Recipient Vol. Achievement award Marion County Mental Health Assn., 1974, 75, 76. Mem. Am., Ind. Central Ind., psychol. assns., Ind. Counseling and Pastoral Care Center. Democrat. Roman Catholic. Home: 4717 N Graceland Ave Indianapolis IN 46208 Office: Midtown Community Mental Health Center 1505 N Delaware St Indianapolis IN 46202

THORESON, RICHARD WALLACE, educator; b. Mpls., Jan. 27, 1931; s. Milo and Corinne (Cady) T.; B.A., U. Minn., 1954, M.A. 1958; Ph.D., U. Mo., 1963; m. Carol Ann Schmeling, July 21, 1952; children—Wallace B., Bonita L. Asst. prof. edn. U. Wis.-Madison, 1963-66; asso. prof. U. Mo. at Columbia, 1966-69, prof. edn. 1969—, dir. grad. studies in rehab. counseling, 1969-72, dir. rehab. and alcoholism counseling, 1973—, also dir. employee assistance program; vis. prof. Sch. Edn. U. Reading (Berkshire, England), 1972-73. vice pres. Phoenix House Half-Way House, 1976. Social and Rehab. Service spl. postdoctoral research fellow, 1972-73. Fellow Am., Mo. psychol. assns.; mem. Midwest Psychol. Assn., Mo. Rehab. Assn. (pres. 1970), Am. Rehab. Counseling Assn. (pres. 1972), Alcohol and Drug Problems Assn. N.Am., AAUP, AAAS, Am. Personnel and Guidance Assn. (dir. 1971-72). Unitarian-Universalist. Contbr. articles to profl. jours. Home: 611 Westridge Dr Columbia MO 65201 Office: Coll Edn U Mo Columbia MO 65201

THORMAN, DONALD JOSEPH, editor, publisher; b. Oak Park, Ill., Dec. 23, 1924; s. Harry C. and Adolphine M. (Levermann) T.; B.A., DePaul U., 1949, L.H.D. (hon.), 1976; M.A., Loyola U., Chgo., 1951; student U. Fribourg (Switzerland), 1950, Fordham U., 1950-51, U. Notre Dame, 1956-57; m. Barbara Lisowski, Feb. 22, 1952; children—Margaret, Judith, James, Elizabeth, David, Daniel, Damian. Editor, Christian Family, 1949; instr. Loyola U., 1950-54; editor U.S. Catholic, Chgo., 1952-56, Ave Maria, Notre Dame, Ind., 1956-62; dir. devel., pub. Spiritual Life Inst. Am., Ariz., 1962-63; cons., pres. Cath. Communications Cons., 1963-65; pub. Nat. Cath. Reporter Pub. Co., Inc., Kansas City, Mo., 1965—, editor, 1971—, pres., 1975—. Editor, pub. newsletter Successful Marriage, 1973—; cons. in field. Nat. bd. govs. NCCJ. Served with USMCR, 1943-46. Recipient Outstanding Alumni award DePaul U., 1972. Mem. Am. Mgmt. Assn., Am. Mktg. Assn., Advt. and Sales Execs. Club, Kansas City Direct Mktg. Assn. (pres. 1969-70), Cath. Press Assn. (dir. 1958-60), Internat. Transactional Analysis Assn., Nat. Cath. Social Action Conf. (pres. 1958-59), Direct Mail Mktg. Assn., Nat. Council on Family Relations (chairperson pub. relations 1976), Nat. Cath. Devel. Conf., Alpha Sigma Nu, Pi Gamma Mu. Club: Overseas Press (N.Y.C.). Author: The Emerging Layman, 1962; Christian Vision, 1965; American Catholics Face the Future, 1968; Power to the People of God, 1970; also numerous articles in religious and secular mags. Home: 5408 Baltimore St Kansas City MO 64112 Office: Box 281 Kansas City MO 64141 Died Nov. 30, 1977.

THORN, JAMES ELWOOD, lawyer; b. LuVerne, Iowa, May 28, 1935; s. James Bernard and Velma Viola (Ramus) T.; student Wartburg Coll., 1956-59; B.A., State U. Iowa, 1962, J.D., 1963; m. Mary Cecelia Shimek, Aug. 21, 1959; children—James, Patricia, Thomas, Charles. Admitted to Ia. bar, 1963; asso. Ross, Johnson, Stuart, Tinley, & Peters, Council Bluffs, 1963-68; partner Johnson, Stuart, Tinley, Peters & Thorn, Council Bluffs, 1968—. Mem. Council Bluffs Recreation Commn., 1965, chmn., 1968-70; chmn. Council Bluffs Low Rent Housing Study Com., 1965. Pres., Pottawattamie County Young Democrats, 1964. Bd. dirs. Health Planning Council of Midlands, 1970. Served with USMC, 1953-56. Mem. Ia., S.W. Ia., Pottawattamie County bar assns., Iowa Def. Counsel Assn. Lutheran (ch. council 1967-70). Home: 41 Spencer Circle Council Bluffs IA 51501 Office: 501-510 Park Bldg Council Bluffs IA 51501

THORNBURG, RUSSELL CHARLES, photgrapher, writer; b. Akron, Ohio, June 27, 1953; s. Edwin James and Irma Marie (Wallace) T.; grad. U. Akron, 1977. Chef, Lujan's Restaurant, Akron, 1971-72, Talmadge, Ohio, 1973; machinist Harrington Machine Co., Akron, 1973-74; editor Horizon Newspaper, 1976; investigator, guard, N. Am. Bur. Investigators, Revenna, Ohio, 1976—; free-lance photographer, Akron, 1973—, free-lance writer, 1976—; asst. photo editor U. Akron Buchtelite, 1976-77; instr. in field. Notary public Summit, Portage (Ohio) Counties, 1974—. Served with USAF Res., 1974-76. Recipient advisor's award, Arnold Air Soc., 1976; membership award, Soc. Am. Military Engrs., 1976. Mem. Am. Defense Preparedness Assn., AAAS, Soc. Am. Military Engrs., Arnold Air Soc., Soc. Physics Students, Am. Security Council (nat. adv. bd.). Clubs: Math, Geology, Physics (U. Akron). Home: 2386 Lakeside Dr Lakemore OH 44250

THORNBURY, JOHN ROUSSEAU, physician; b. Cleve., Mar. 16, 1929; s. Purla Lee and Gertrude (Glidden) T.; A.B. cum laude, Miami U., Oxford, Ohio, 1950; M.D., Ohio State U., 1955; m. Julia Lee McGregor, Mar. 20, 1955; children—Lee Allison, John McGregor. Intern Hurley Hosp., Flint, Mich., 1955-56; resident U. Iowa Hosps., Iowa City, 1958-61; instr., asst. prof. radiology U. Colo. Med. Center, Denver, 1962-63; practice medicine, specializing in radiology, Denver, 1962-63, Iowa City, 1963-66, Seattle, 1966-68, Ann Arbor, Mich., 1968—; mem. staff U. Hosp., Ann Arbor; asst. prof. radiology U. Iowa Hosps., 1963-66, U. Wash. Hosp., Seattle, 1966-68; asso. prof. radiology U. Mich. Med. Center, 1968-71, prof. radiology, 1971—. Served to capt. M.C., USAF, 1956-58. Diplomate Am. Bd. Radiology. Fellow Am. Coll. Radiology; mem. AMA, Mich., Washtenaw County med. socs., Soc. Uroradiology (pres. 1976-77), Assn. U. Radiologists, Radiol. Soc. N.Am., Am. Roentgen Ray Soc., Rocky Mountain Radiol. Soc., Phi Beta Kappa, Delta Tau Delta, Omicron Delta Kappa, Phi Chi. Republican. Presbyterian. Asso. editor Yearbook of Radiology, 1971—. Home: 3040 Foxcroft Ann Arbor MI 48104 Office: Univ Hosp Ann Arbor MI 48104

THORNE, C(ECIL) MICHAEL, pathologist; b. Georgetown, Guyana, May 13, 1929; s. Alfred Athiel and Violet (Ashurst) T.; student Queen's Coll., Guyana; A.B., Lincoln U., 1952; M.D. Mainz (Germany) U., 1957; m. Sandra Janette Marsh, Dec. 23, 1965; children—Timothy Michael, Christine Michelle, Christopher Michael, Jonathan Gilbert, Victor Marsh. Came to U.S., 1951, naturalized, 1965. Intern, Springfield (Mass.) Hosp., 1958-59, resident, 1959-62; resident Western Mass. Hosp., Westfield, 1962-63; asst. prof. Ohio State U., 1963-67, clin. asst. prof., 1968—; pathologist Licking County Meml. Hosp., Newark, Ohio, now dir. labs. Past chmn. bd. dirs. Licking County chpt. A.R.C.; cons. Central Ohio blood program A.R.C.; pres. Licking County br., trustee Central Ohio chpt. Am. Heart Assn. Fellow Am. Coll. Pathologists, Am. Soc. Clin. Pathologists; mem. Am., Ohio med. assns., Licking County Med. Soc., Am., Ohio (trustee, pres. elect) assns. blood banks, Ohio, Central Ohio (sec.-treas., past pres.) socs. pathologists, Acad. Clin. Lab. Physicians and Scientists, Newark Area C. of C. (dir.). Rotarian. Home: 1327 Burg St Granville OH 43023 Office: 1320 W Main St Newark OH 43055

THORNE, JOSEPH CECIL, JR., savs. and loan exec.; b. Willmar, Minn., Sept. 26, 1917; s. Joseph Cecil and Clara Matilda (Johnson) T.; grad. Mpls. Bus. Coll., 1936; extension student U. Minn., 1939-60; m. Marie E. Mercier, Jan. 19, 1952. Gen. credit mgr. retail div. Thompson Yards, Weyerhaeuser Co., 1956-62; pub. relations dir., mgr. home improvement loan dept. First Fed. Savs. & Loan Assn., Mpls., 1962-67, v.p. charge loan activities, 1967—. Tchr., Savs. and Loan Inst. classes. Past treas., dir. Greater Mpls. Area Bd. Realtors; past dir. Mpls. Builders Assn. Pres., bd. dirs. Hennepin County unit Am. Cancer Soc. Served with USAAF; maj. Res. ret. Mem. Mortgage Bankers Assn. (dir.), Soc. Residential Appraisers (asso.), Am. Legion. Clubs: Toastmasters (past pres.) (Mpls.); Minnetonka Country (Excelsior, Minn.). Home: 6802 36th Ave N Crystal MN 55427 Office: 77 S 7th St Minneapolis MN 55402

THORNE, REGINALD KENNETH, financial cons.; b. Wales, U.K., Apr. 14, 1939, came to U.S., 1964; s. Reginald James and Doreen Ethyl (Royal) T.; B.Sc. in Chem. Engring., U. Birmingham (Eng.), 1962; M.B.A. in Finance, Case Western Reserve U., 1970; m. Patricia Ann Canfield, Oct. 14, 1967; children—Elizabeth, David, John. Process engr. British Petroleum, Wales, 1962-64; comml. devel. mgr. Lubrizol Corp., Cleve., 1964-68; asst. v.p. firm Fulton, Reid & Staples, Cleve., 1968-72; gen. mgr. Thorne & Assos., Mentor, Ohio, 1972—; sec., dir. Fluid Regulators Corp., Painesville, Ohio, 1974—; v.p., sec., dir. Island Transport Service Inc., St. Croix, U.S. Virgin Islands, 1976—, Island Transport, Stevedoring Corp., St. Croix, 1976—. Trustee Lake County Community Improvement Corp., Mentor, 1974—, sec., 1975-77, pres., 1977—. Mem. Am. Inst. Chem. Engrs., N. Am. Soc. Corp. Planning. Clubs: Madison Country, Mentor Heisley Racquet. Home: 8814 Norwood Dr Mentor OH 44060

THORNHILL, WILLIAM THOMAS, banker; b. Washington, Oct. 14, 1926; s. William Joseph and Gartha Fay (Duncan) T.; student Md. U., 1947; B.C.S., Strayer Coll., 1949, M.C.S., 1950; student Am. U., 1950-51, Richmond U., 1961; m. Janet Marie Eustace, Nov. 23, 1957 (div.); children—Thomas William, Karen Marie; m. 2d, Barbara Jean Allen, Dec. 20, 1969 (div.); m. 3d, Rosemary T. Di Costanzo, Mar. 6, 1976. Sr. auditor Ernst & Ernst, Balt. and Washington, 1950-53; fgn. supervisory auditor Standard-Vacuum Oil Co., White Plains, N.Y., 1953-60; mgmt. trainee Bank Va., Richmond, Va., 1960-61; audit supr. C.I.T. Financial Corp., N.Y.C., 1961-62; v.p. U.S. Indsl. Corp. and U.S. Indsl. Leasing Corp. subsidiaries U.S. Industries, Inc., N.Y.C., 1962-63, asst. controller U.S. Industries, Inc., 1963-65, gen. mgr. 6 Continents Travel Service subsidiary, 1964-65; exec. controller Central Charge Service, Inc., Washington, 1965-67, treas., asst. sec., 1966-67; asst. v.p. First Nat. Bank, Chgo., 1967-70, v.p., 1970—. Served with AUS, 1944-46. Mem. Am. Accounting Assn., Am. Mgmt. Assn. (past mem. finance planning council), Nat. Assn. Accountants, Inst. Internal Auditors, Assn. for Systems Mgmt., Optimist, Am. Legion, Nat. Retail Mchts. Assn. (controller's congress), Phi Theta Pi. Frequent speaker and writer on bus. mgmt.

Home: 220 Pine Crest Circle Barrington IL 60010 Office: One First Nat Plaza Chicago IL 60670

THORNTON, EDMUND BRAXTON, mining co. exec.; b. Chgo., Mar. 9, 1930; s. George A. and Suzanne (Woodward) T.; A.B., Yale U., 1954; children—Jonathan Butler, Thomas Volney, Amanda Braxton, Susan Oakes. With No. Trust Co., Chgo., 1957-59; asst. sec., treas. Ottawa Silica Co. (Ill.), 1959-61, v.p. corp. devel., 1961-62, pres., chief exec. officer, dir., 1962-75, chmn., chief exec. officer, 1975—. Dir. Nat. Indsl. Sand Assn. Adviser, Ill. Nature Preserves Commn., 1969—, chmn. Ill. Historic Sites Adv. Council, 1969-75; bd. advisers Nat. Trust Historic Preservation, 1970—; chmn. Nat. Parks Centennial Commn., 1972-73; trustee Nat. Recreation and Parks Assn., 1973—. Bd. dirs., v.p., exec. com. United Republican Fund Ill., 1962-74; trustee Ottawa YMCA, 1974—. Served to 1st lt. USMCR, 1950-58. Mem. Arctic Inst. N.Am., LaSalle County Hist. Soc., Am. Def. Preparedness Assn., Ill. Mfrs. Assn. (dir. 1969—, vice chmn. 1975-76, chmn. 1976), Ill. C. of C. (dir.), Delta Kappa Epsilon. Congregationalist. Clubs: Chgo., Adventurer's, Univ. (Chgo.); Capitol Hill (Washington). Home: PO Box 1 Ottawa IL 61350 Office: Boyce Memorial Dr Ottawa IL 61350

THORNTON-TRUMP, WALTER EDMOND (TED), manufacturer, inventor; b. Edmonton, Alta., Can., Aug. 8, 1918; s. Walter Edward and Olga Wilhelmena Lyntine (Lund) T.; m. Bernice Ruth Boale, Mar. 18, 1942; children—William Hamilton, Alexander Beverly, Belva Lynn, Anne Louise; came to U.S., 1970, naturalized, 1977; student U. B.C., Vancouver, Can., 1939-41. Pres., Trump, Ltd., Oliver, B.C., 1944-64, Trump Hydraulics, Ltd., Toronto, Ont., Can., 1964-70, Trump, Inc., Plattsmouth, Nebr., 1970—; pres. Trump Engrs., Inc. Mem. Soc. Automotive Engrs., Rotary Club (past pres.). Patentee Fire Dept. "Snorkel" aerial device, Cherry Picker, Power Co. Bucket Trucks, Hot Water aircraft ramp deicing, also 12 basic hydraulic machines. Home: 108 Bellevue Dr Beaver Lake Plattsmouth NE 68048 Office: Hwy 73-75 Box 368 Plattsmouth NE 68048

THORPE, ALBERT, real estate broker; b. Ironwood, Mich., July 2, 1929; s. Albert and Marie Ann (Haugen) T.; student pub. schs.; m. Betty Joan Stafford, Oct. 18, 1953; children—Vicki L., Wendy L., Steven A., Timothy. Salesman, dealer J.R. Watkins Co., Scott and Renville counties, Minn., 1954-59; registered rep. Jamison & Co., mem. N.Y. Stock Exchange, Mpls., 1959; real estate salesman L.F. Lowe, Northfield, Minn., 1960-64; partner Lowe & Thorpe Realtors, Northfield, 1964-69; owner Al Thorpe Realty, Northfield, 1969—. Mem. Northfield Planning Commn., 1964-72, pres., 1970-72. Bd. dirs. Northfield Indsl. Corp., 1972—. Recipient Distinguished Service award Rice County Bd. Realtors, 1970. Mem. Minn. Assn. Realtors (chmn. membership com. 1974-75), Rice County Bd. Realtors (pres. 1965). Lutheran (deacon 1957-59, 62-68). Lion (2d v.p. 1974-75). Home: 920 E 5th St Northfield MN 55057 Office: 504 Division St Box 255 Northfield MN 55057

THORPE, SAMUEL L., JR., oral surgeon; b. Cleve., Nov. 19, 1921; s. Samuel L. and Eunice (Brown) T.; B.S., Western Res. U., 1950; D.D.S., Howard U., 1955; Ph.D., U. Mich.; m. Lenore M. Tucker, June 11, 1959; 1 dau., Shelly Marie. Practice dentistry, Detroit, 1957—; asst. prof. allied health dept. Wayne County Community Coll.; cons. Detroit Med. Found.; dir. dental services Mich. Health Maintenance Orgn. Plan, Inc. Served with AUS. Decorated Purple Heart. Fellow Am. Coll. Dentists; mem. Nat. Dental Soc., AAAS, Am. Dental Assn. Home: 9000 E Jefferson Ave Detroit MI 48214 Office: 2200 Walker Cisler Bldg Detroit MI 48201

THORREZ, CAMIEL EARL, mfg. co. exec.; b. Concord, Mich., Nov. 12, 1948; s. Henry Camiel and Phyllis Joan (Nivison) T.; B.S. in Mech. Engring., Mich. Tech. U., 1970; m. Anne Marie Tarbox, Aug. 30, 1969; children—Christiana, Heather, Holly, Diana, Henry. Machine operator Concord (Mich.) Mfg. Co., 1964-69, tool designer, 1971-72, plant mgr., 1972—; plant engr., coop. trainee transmission and axle div. Ford Motor Co., Livonia, Mich., 1969-70; tool designer Allied Chucker and Engring. Co., Jackson, Mich., 1970-71; pub., owner Concord News, 1974—; dir. Concord Mfg. Co., C. Thorrez Industries, Induction Heating Systems Co. Bd. dirs. Concord Community Sch. Bd., 1972—, sec. 1973-75, 76—; mem. career advisory coms. Concord Pub. Schs., Jackson Community Coll., Jackson Career Center; founder Thorrez Found., 1972, pres. 1972-75, adminstr., 1975—. Kellogg Found. fellow, 1973-75; Mem. Albion Montessori Assn., Mich. C. of C. (pvt. enterprise com. 1976—), ASME (treas. 1969), Soc. Mfg. Engrs. (pres. 1969), Concord Heritage Assn. (charter, treas. 1971-73). Club: Concord Lions (dir. 1972). Roman Catholic. Home: 126 Hanover St Concord MI 49237

THORSEN, ROBERT, lawyer; b. Winnetka, Ill., July 8, 1912; s. Henry T. and Catherine (Henrich) T.; B.S.L., Northwestern, 1932; LL.D., U. Chgo., 1934; m. Frances Adele Pierce, Apr. 28, 1935; children—Frances Adele, Robert Lloyd, Richard Pierce. Admitted to Ill., Mo. bars, 1935; br. atty. Nat. Bond Investment Co., St. Louis, 1935-37; asso. with Edward P. Madigan, 1937-40; partner Madigan & Thorsen, Chgo., 1941—; sec. Kerr-Wireryte Co., Kerr Wire Products Co.; asst. sec., dir. Tee-2-Green Corp.; v.p., asst. sec., dir. McCormick Commodities Inc. Mem. Am., Ill., Chgo. bar assns., Chgo. Bd. Trade, Chgo. Real Estate Bd., Chgo. Assn. Commerce and Industry. Clubs: University Executives, Westmoreland Country (past pres.), John Henry Wigmore Club (past pres.). Home: 145 Bertling Ln Winnetka IL 60093 Office: Suite 2680 One First Nat Plaza Chicago IL 60603

THORSON, MILTON ZENAS, paint and varnish co. exec.; b. Thorsby, Ala., Oct. 26, 1902; s. Theodore T. and Emma (Hokanson) T.; student Am. Inst. Banking, extension courses U. So. Cal.; m. Grace Kirksey, July 30, 1967. Chief teller Tenn. Valley Bank, Decatur, Ala., 1919-28; teller Security First Nat. Bank, Los Angeles, 1928-29; with Red Spot Paint & Varnish Co., Inc., Evansville, Ind., 1929-60, chmn. exec. bd., dir., 1961-75; chmn. bd., dir. Owensboro Paint & Glass Co. (Ky.), Red Spot Paint & Glass Co., Paducah, Ky. Mem. Regional Export Expansion Council, U.S. Dept. Commerce. Mem. Audubon Soc. Republican. Contbr. tech. articles profl. jours. Home: 6219 Newburgh Rd Evansville IN 47715 Office: 110 Main St Evansville IN 47708

THROCKMORTON, RAY IAMS, JR., farm equipment ofcl.; b. Manhattan, Kans., Mar. 9, 1924; s. Ray Iams and Marcia (Story) T.; B.S., Kans. State U., 1949; m. Mildred Arlene Terrar, Aug. 4, 1946; children—Ray Iams III, Richard Terrill, Mildred Anne. Sales Internat. Harvester Co., Wichita, Kans., 1949-54, product planning rep., Chgo., 1954-60, supr. crop products planning research, 1960-64, supr. farm equipment product planning research, 1964-70, supr. all agrl. and indsl. equipment product research, 1970—, also supr. product research-crop prodn. Active Boy Scouts Am., 1963—. Served with USNR, 1943-45. Mem. Am. Soc. Agrl. Engrs., Soc. Automotive Engrs., Kans. State U. Alumni Assn. (treas. 1964), Sigma Chi. Episcopalian. Mem. editorial bd. Compaction of Agricultural Soils, 1971. Patentee in field. Home: 357 Harris Ave Clarendon Hills IL 60514 Office: International Harvester 401 N Michigan Ave Chicago IL 60611

THROOP, JAMES WARREN, process engr.; b. Goodrich, Mich., Aug. 26, 1931; s. Warren E. and Mildred (Wolfe) T.; B.M.E., Gen. Motors Inst., 1959; M.S., Mich. State U., 1962; m. Dorothy Lewis (dec.); children—James, Linda Throop Marsh, Cynthia Throop Hufnagel; m. 2d, Ann W. Kinney, Aug. 10, 1968. Supr. plant engring. Fisher Body div. Gen. Motors Corp., Grand Blanc, Mich., 1958-60; instr. agrl. engring. Mich. State U., East Lansing, 1960-62; asst. prof. process engring. Gen. Motors Inst., Flint, Mich., 1962-66, asso. prof., 1966-68, prof., 1968—, Rodes prof., 1976-77; NSF cons., India, 1970. Mem. ASME (profl. devel. com.), Soc. Mfg. Engrs. (metalworking fluids com.), Am. Soc. Metals, Tau Beta Pi. Unitarian. Author: (with T. Judson) Theory and Practice of Material Removal, 1968; contbr. articles to profl. jours. Home: 6636 Waterford Hill Terr Waterford MI 48095 Office: 1700 W 3d Ave W Flint MI 48502

THURINGER, CARL BERNARD, surgeon; b. Norman, Okla., Dec. 22, 1922; s. Joseph Mario and Bess LeMarr (Cronim) T.; student St. Johns U., 1942; M.S., U. Okla., 1943, M.D., 1946; m. Mary Ann Hall, June 24, 1945; children—Linda, Brian, Anne, Elizabeth. Intern, St. Anthony Hosp., Oklahoma City, 1946-47; pvt. practice medicine specializing in surgery, St. Cloud, Minn., 1953—; chief surgery St. Cloud Hosp. Served as capt. M.C., U.S.Army, 1947-48. Diplomate Am. Bd. Surgery. Mem. A.C.S., Mayo Alumni Assn., Minn. Surg. Soc., St. Cloud C. of C., AMA, Stearns County Med. Soc. Republican. Roman Catholic. Clubs: Exchange; Elks. Home: 104 Dunbar Rd St Cloud MN 56301 Office: 13 and St Germaine Sts St Cloud MN 56301

THURSTON, FRED STONE, printing co. exec.; b. Oak Park, Ill., Apr. 1, 1931; s. Fred Stone and Marie (Stemen) T.; student Eastern Ill. State Coll., 1948-50; B.A., N.M. Highlands U., 1954; postgrad. U. Chgo. Exec. Program, 1975-76; m. Barbara Coy Carnes, Nov. 6, 1954; children—Fredric Kent, Bruce Edward, Janice Marie. Asst. plant mgr. UARCO, Inc., Watseka, Ill., 1955-63; asst. to pres. Joe Daley & Sons, Inc., Los Angeles, 1963-64; mgr. manifold forms Diamond Internat. W.G.A.D., San Francisco, 1964-65; gen. mgr. Uniform Printing & Supply div. Courier Citizen Co., Chgo., 1965-69; dir. mfg. forms div. Control Data Corp., Phila., 1969-70; pres., gen. mgr. Printing Service, Inc. subsidiary Am. Standard, Detroit, 1970-71; exec. v.p., gen. mgr. Workman Bus. Forms div. John Blair & Co., Chgo., 1971-72; exec. v.p., mktg. mgr. Forms Corp. Am., Spring Grove, Ill., 1972—. Vice pres. Iroquois County (Ill.) Young Republicans, 1960-61. Served to capt. AUS, 1951-53. Certified forms cons. Mem. Mensa, Sigma Tau Gamma. Republican. Home: 1238 Wildwood Ct Libertyville IL 60048 Office: PO Box 278 Route 12 Spring Grove IL 60081 also 2474 Dempster Suite 203 Des Plaines IL 60016

THURSTON, ROBERT WARD, mech. engr., contractor; b. Grand Rapids, Mich., Aug. 11, 1926; s. Gilbert Ward and Ida (Snook) Thurston; stepson Grace (Fuller) Thurston; B.S.M.E. in Design Engring., Mich. State U., 1949; m. Lois Marie Morton Bowe, July 8, 1967; 1 stepdau., Barbra Eileen. Mfg. and devel. engr. Duo Therm Corp., Lansing, Mich., 1948-51, Western Electric Co., Indpls., 1952-54, Bell Telephone Labs., Murray, Hill, N.J., 1954-56, Stewart Warner Corp., Indpls., 1956-57, P. R. Mallory and Co., Indpls., 1957-60, Am. Foundry div. Chrysler Corp., Indpls., 1962-63; mgr. product engring. Jenn-Air Corp., Indpls., 1960-62; sr. magnetic tape engr. Radio Corp. Am., Indpls., 1963-67; chief engr. LeRoy M. Russell and Assos., Indpls., 1967—; pres. Robert W. Thurston and Co., Indpls., 1971—, Collingswood Homes, Indpls., 1977—, Leisure Living I, Inc., Indpls., 1977—, Collingswood, Inc., Indpls., 1977—. Served with USAAC, 1945, to 2d lt. USAF, 1951-52. Registered profl. engr., Ind. Mem. Constrn. Specification Inst. Republican. Christian Scientist. Clubs: Masons, Police Athletic League, Shriners, Order Eastern Star, Exchange. Home: 10404 Collingswood Ln Indianapolis IN 46256 Office: 70 E Oak St Zionsville IN 46077

THYGERSON, KENNETH JAMES, assn. exec.; b. Chgo., Oct. 1, 1945; s. R. James and Doris L. (Niemann) T.; B.S. with highest distinction, Northwestern U., 1967, Ph.D., 1973; m. Darlene Kay Vernon, June 24, 1967; children—Keith David, Kent James. Instr. mgmt. Northwestern U., Chgo., 1968-70; economist U.S. League Savs. Assns., Chgo., 1970—, chief economist, dir. econs. dept., 1975—; cons. in field; instr. exec. devel. schs. Am. Savs. and Loan Inst., 1970—. Trustee Trinity Lutheran Ch., 1975-77. NDEA fellow, 1967-70. Mem. Am. Statis. Assn. (pres. Chgo. chpt. 1974-75, mem. council 1974-75), Am. Econ. Assn., Am. Fin. Assn., Nat. Assn. Bus. Economists, Am. Real Estate and Urban Econs. Assn. (dir. 1977-80), Phi Sigma Kappa, Delta Sigma Pi. Beta Gamma Sigma. Author: The Effect of Government Housing and Mortgage Credit Programs on Savings and Loan Associations, 1973; Tax Management for Savings and Loan Executives, 1977; Mortgage Portfolio Management, 1978; contbr. articles to profl. jours. Home: 9547 Avers Ave Evanston IL 60203 Office: US League Savs Assns 111 E Wacker Dr Chicago IL 60601

TICHENOR, EDWARD JOHN, motor co. exec.; b. LaCrosse, Wis., July 1, 1942; s. Leslie Stuart and Georgina Elizabeth (Malay) T.; B.S. with honors, U. Wis.-La Crosse, 1964, M.S. with honors, 1967; m. Mary Anne Slawik, Oct. 9, 1965; children—John Edward, David Kyle, Patricia Elizabeth, Joseph Paul, Jennifer Lynn. Accountant, Midway Ford Co., St. Paul, 1965, then various sales mgmt. positions, gen. mgr., 1970—, v.p., 1977—; dir. Am. Loan & Thrift Co., Slawik Ins. Agency, Roading Leasing Inc., Northstar Automotive Co.; lectr. in field. Recipient Accountants Award Excellence, Ford Motor Co., also Sales Mgrs. Award Excellence. Mem. Nat. Automobile Dealers Assn., Twin Cities Ford Dealers Group (sec. 1976—), Minn. at Metro Auto Dealers Assn., Midway YMCA Judo Club (pres. 1967—). Home: 2865 Neal Ave Afton MN 55001 Office: Midway Ford Co 1850 University Ave St Paul MN 55104

TICHENOR, ROBERT WOODROW, physician; b. St. Louis, Sept. 1, 1914; s. Robert Anderson and Willie Mae (Wooley) T.; B.S., St. Louis Coll. Pharmacy, 1939; A.B., Washington U., St. Louis, 1941, M.D., 1943; m. Letitia Bernice Youngman, May 20, 1935; children—Trebor Jay, Bruce Harding. Intern, resident St. Louis City Hosp., 1944-45; practice medicine, Sappington, Mo., 1946—; mem. staff St. Joseph, St. Anthony hosps. Served to 1st lt. M.C., AUS, 1945-46. Fellow Am. Acad. Family Physicians; mem. St. Louis (past pres.), Mo., Am. acads. family physicians, Pan-Am., Am. (recognition award for continuing med. edn. 1972), So., Mo., St. Louis med. assns., St. Louis German Shepherd Club (past pres.), Am. Kennel Club (conformation judge), German Shepherd Dog Club Am. (past dir.). Club: Washington University. Home: 175 Misty Manor Rd Fenton MO 63026 Office: 11521 Gravois St Sappington MO 63126

TICHENOR, WILLIAM GEILEY, savs. and loan exec.; b. Terre Haute, Aug. 28, 1917; s. William Taylor and Ause (Geiley) T.; B.S., Ind. State U., 1939; m. Margaret L. Brown, May 4, 1971; 1 son, William Taylor. With Internat. Harvester Co., 1939-41; with Ind. Savs. & Loan, Terre Haute, 1941—, now pres.; dir. Spirit of Terre Haute, Inc., Croy Crest, Inc., Ind. Savs. & Loan. Mem. Terre Haute C. of C., Ind. Savs. and Loan League (past dir.), Terre Haute Bd. Realtors (past sec.-treas.). Clubs: Kiwanis, Shriners, Elks. Office: 100 7th St S Terre Haute IN 47808

TICKEL, WILLIAM ERNEST, JR., city ofcl.; b. Laredo, Tex., Dec. 23, 1928; s. William Ernest and Marie Victoria (Wilkinson) T.; student Eastern N. Mex. U., 1956-57; B.G.E., U. Nebr., 1961; m. Mittie Gordon Boyett, Mar. 11, 1950; children—William E., Victoria I. Enlisted U.S. Air Force, 1947, advanced through grades to maj.; mem. staff hdqrs. SAC, 1961-64, hdqrs. U.S. European Command, 1964-67, hdqrs. 7th Air Force S.E. Asia, 1967-68; ret., 1968; cons. EDP and mini-computer devel.; mgr. data processing City of New Ulm, Minn., 1976—; cons. Bus. Machines and Computers Inc.; dir. Transystems, Inc. Decorated Bronze Star. Mem. Data Processing Mgrs. Assn., Assn. Computing Machinery. Republican. Roman Catholic. Club: Am. Legion. Home: Rural Route 3 Box 184 New Ulm MN 56073 Office: City Hall New Ulm MN 56073

TICKEMYER, GARLAND ELIJAH, educator; b. Longwood, Mo., Jan. 1, 1913; s. George Lester and Mary Catherine (Johnson) T.; B.A., U. Mo., Kansas City, 1943, M.A. in Edn., 1944; M.A. in Philosophy, U. So. Calif., 1957; Ph.D., U. Tex., 1963; m. Hazel Vernita Roberson, Mar. 6, 1936; children—Garland Lee, David Kent. Sec. Transcontinental & Western Airlines, Kansas City, Mo., 1932-34; ordained to ministry Reorganized Ch. of Jesus Christ of Latterday Saints, 1934; minister, Wichita, Kans., 1934-38; asst. to pres. Reorganized Ch. of Jesus Christ of Latter-day Saints, 1938-46, pres. Los Angeles Stake, 1946-59, regional adminstr. Tex., 1959-61, pres. Central Mo. Stake, 1961-63, pres. Blue Valley Stake, 1963-66, chmn. archtl. adv. com., 1961—, chmn. orgn. and rules com. for World Confs., 1964-69; prof. philosophy Central Mo. State U., Warrensburg, 1966—. Pres., Chapel Hill Devel., Inc., 1972—, G.E.T. Homesites, Inc., 1973—; pres. Blue Hills Devel., Inc., 1978—; v.p. Inheritance, Inc., 1973—, Gateway, Inc., 1974—; pres. Nat. Inheritance, Inc., 1976—. Bd. dirs. Mo. Council of Chs., 1962-67, mem. exec. com., 1963-66. Mem. Am. Philosophy Soc., Philosophy of Edn. Soc., Quorum of High Priests (pres. 1958-72), S.A.R. (chaplain Mo. chpt. 1944). Lion (charter pres. Independence club 1939). Author: Story Illustrations for Church and Home, 1961; The Old Testament Speaks to Our Day, 1961; The Good News, 1962. Home: Rural Route 1 Patrick Rd Warrensburg MO 64093

TIDSTROM, FRED LEWIS, dentist; b. Ashland, Wis., Jan. 19, 1929; s. George Lewis and Emma Gunda (Christopherson) T.; B.S., Gustavus Adolphus Coll., 1951; D.D.S., U. Minn., 1955; m. Ellen Ann Enright, Aug. 28, 1954; children—Erik, Kyle, Janna, Fred, Dana. Practice dentistry, Ashland, Wis., 1957—; mem. dental staff, bd. dirs. Meml. Med. Center, Ashland, vice chmn. bd., 1974-75; preceptor Marquette U. Sch. Dentistry; life mem. century club U. Minn. Sch. Dentistry. Pres., also treas. Chequamegon Bay United Fund, 1966-67; mem. Lake Superior council Boy Scouts Am., 1958-73. Mem. Ashland Unified Sch. Bd., 1968-71, v.p., 1969-70, active 5 sch. referendums, 1970; mem. Savon Lutheran and Presbyterian Chs., Ashland. Served with USNR, 1955-57; comdr. Res. ret. Recipient Silver Beaver award, Scoutmasters key, Boy Scouts Am., both 1970; named Ashland Citizen of Year, 1977. Fellow Acad. Gen. Dentistry; mem. ADA, No. Wis. Dental Soc. (past pres.), Nat. Rifle Assn. (life), Ashland C. of C. (dir. 1962-65). Clubs: Ashland Gun, Elks. Home: 600 W 14th St Ashland WI 54806 Office: Lakeview Dental Bldg 615 W Front St Ashland WI 54806

TIECKE, RICHARD WILLIAM, assn. exec., oral pathologist; b. Muscatine, Iowa, Apr. 5, 1917; s. Harry Frederick and Nell Eola (McKibben) T.; B.S., U. Iowa, 1940, D.D.S., 1942, M.S., 1947; postgrad. U. Chgo., 1947-49. Jr. pathologist, asst. pathologist, dep. chief oral pathology div. Armed Forces Inst. Pathology, 1949-54; asso. prof. pathology Georgetown U., 1949-54; prof. pathology, head oral pathology, asso. cancer coordinator Northwestern U. Sch. Dentistry Chicago, 1954-62; prof. dept. oral pathology U. Ill., 1962—; research fellow Hektoen Inst. Med. Research, Cook County Hosp., Chgo.; dir. research inst. Am. Dental Assn., Chgo., 1968-71, asst. exec. dir., 1971—; cons. U.S. Naval Hosp., Great Lakes, Ill., VA Research Hosp., VA West Side Hosp., Pub. Health Hosp., Chgo., City Chgo. Bd. Health, Surgeon Gen. USPHS, head and neck cancer detection Nat. Center Chronic Disease Control-USPHS, Nat. Cancer Inst. NIH; cons. to Surgeon Gen. Army, 1969—. Served from 1st lt. to col. AUS, 1942-54; now col. Res. ret. Diplomate Am. Bd. Oral Pathology (dir., past pres.). Fellow Am. Acad. Oral Pathology (past pres.), Am. Coll. Dentists; mem. Am. Dental Assn. (asst. sec. Council Dental Therapeutics 1962-68), Ill., Chgo. dental socs., Internat. Assn. Dental Research, Psi Omega, Omicron Kappa Upsilon. Author: Physiologic Pathology of Oral Disease, 1959; Oral Pathology, 1964; Atlas on Oral Cytology, 1969; also research articles. Home: 179 E Lake Shore Dr Chicago IL 60611

TIEDE, CHARLES RICHARD, lawyer; b. Walkerton, Ind., Oct. 18, 1929; s. Charles Louis and Margaret Leatha (Gunn) T.; B.S., Ball State U., 1951; J.D. (Edwards fellow), Ind. U., 1956; m. Julie Verona Godo, Oct. 6, 1956; children—Karen, Franklin, Kathryn, Julianne, Margo. Admitted to Ind. bar, 1956; atty. Ind. Bell Telephone Co., Indpls., 1956-59; practice law, Wabash, Ind., 1959-63; founder, pres. Frances Slocum Bank & Trust Co., Wabash, 1963-67, dir., 1963—; partner Plummer, Tiede Magley Metz & Downs, Wabash, 1967—. Atty. North Manchester Town Bd., Met. Sch. Dist., Vocational Sch. Bd. Co-dir. Wabash Centennial. Treas., bd. dirs. Honeywell Found., Wabash. Served with AUS, 1951-53. Recipient Distinguished Service award Wabash Jr. C. of C., 1963. Mem. Am., Ind. bar assns., Wabash C. of C. (pres. 1962), Order of Coif, Phi Delta Theta, Phi Sigma Epsilon. Democrat. Lutheran. Home: 560 Valley Brook Ln Wabash IN 46992 Office: 21 W Canal St Wabash IN 46992

TIEMANN, JEROME NOEL, storage co. exec.; b. Parshall, N.D., Aug. 24, 1926; s. O.G. and Alma (Frerking) T.; B.B.A., U. Mo., 1950; m. Kathryn Heil, June 10, 1951; children—Becky Carol, Susan Kaye. With U.S. Cold Storage Corp., 1950-70, sales mgr., Chgo., 1952-58, asst. mgr., Kansas City, Mo., 1958-63, v.p., Kansas City, Mo., 1963-70; v.p. marketing Am. Consumer Industries, N.Y.C., 1964-70; v.p. McCormick Distilling Co., Weston, Mo., 1970-75; pres. Kansas City Cold Storage Corp., 1975—. Trustee Kansas City Coll. Osteopathic Medicine; adv. trustee Research Hosp., Kansas City, Mo. Served with USNR, 1944-47. Mem. U. Mo. Columbia (dir.), St. Paul's Coll. (dir.) alumni assns. Clubs: Allied Food of Kansas City (v.p. 1967-68), Am. Royal (dir.), Saddle and Sirloin of Kansas City (pres. 1968). Home: 5013 NW Coves Dr Kansas City MO 64151 Office: Kansas City Cold Storage Corp 500 E 3d St Kansas City MO 64106

TIEN, HSIN CHEN, psychiatrist; b. Peking, China, July 13, 1929; s. Fang Cheng and Wenn Juun (Chou) T.; came to U.S., 1947, naturalized, 1963; B.S. cum laude, Adrian Coll., 1951; M.D., U. Mich., 1955, M.S., 1959, postgrad. certificate electroencephalography, 1960; postgrad. Mich. State U., 1961-64, M.S., 1966; m. Audrey Roberts, Jan. 9, 1958; children—Davrell, Gareth, Aled, Tudor. Intern, Riverside Hosp., Toledo, 1955-56; resident psychiatry Ypsilanti (Mich.) State Hosp., 1956-59; child psychiatrist Lansing (Mich.) Child Guidance Clinic, 1959-61; coordinator, lectr. postgrad. tng. Mich. Soc. Neurology and Psychiatry, Am. Psychiat. Assn., 1965-69; pvt. practice psychiatry, neurology and electroencephalography, Lansing, Mich., 1959-69; dir. dept. electroencephalography St. Lawrence Hosp., Lansing, 1961-72; dir. Mich. Inst. Psychosynthesis, Lansing, 1969—. First chmn. Human Relations Commn., East Lansing, 1963. Diplomate Nat. Bd.

Med. Examiners, Am. Bd. Psychiatry and Neurology. Mem. Internat. Assn. for Social Psychiatry, Am. Assn. for Social Psychiatry, Am. Soc. Electrotherapy (pres., founder 1975—), Mich. Fedn. Physicians and Dentists (sec. 1975—), AMA, IEEE, Am. Psychiat. Assn., Am. Electroencephalography Soc., Mich. Soc. Neurology and Psychiatry. Founder, editor-in-chief World Jour. Psychosynthesis, 1969—. Contbr. to publs. in psycholinguistics. Home: 801 N Glenhaven Ave East Lansing MI 48823 Office: 820 N Capitol Ave Lansing MI 48906

TIERNAN, THOMAS ORVILLE, chemist; b. Chattanooga, July 22, 1936; s. Thomas Martin and Ida (Harris) T.; B.Sc., U. Windsor, Ont., Can., 1958; M.S., Carnegie Inst. Tech., 1960, Ph.D. (Ethyl Corp. fellow), 1966; m. Marlene Clare Gerstner, Feb. 11, 1961; 1 dau., Margaret Ann. Research chemist API Research Project 44, Carnegie Inst. Tech., Pitts., 1958; research asso. Oak Ridge Nat. Lab., 1959; research chemist Ohio State U. Research Found., Dayton, 1960-61; research chemist Aerospace Research Labs., USAF, Wright-Patterson AFB, Ohio, 1961-67, group leader high energy kinetics research, 1967-75; prof. chemistry Wright State U., Dayton, 1975—, also dir. Brehm Lab.; pres., chmn. bd. Spectronics, Inc., 1975—. Mem. Alumni Admissions Council, Carnegie Inst. Tech. (now Carnegie-Mellon U.), 1967-75, chmn., 1970-75. Recipient Profl. awards USAF, 1962, 65, 68; Outstanding Profl. Achievement award Engring. and Sci. Found. of Dayton, 1976. Fellow Am. Inst. Chemists; mem. A.A.A.S., Am. Chem. Soc., Am. Phys. Soc., ASTM, Am. Soc. Mass Spectrometry (charter), Sigma Pi Sigma. Contbr. numerous articles to profl. jours., chpts. to books. Patentee in field. Home: 6532 Senator Ln Dayton OH 45459 Office: Brehm Lab Wright State U Dayton OH 45431

TIERNEY, JOHN FRANCIS, mfg. co. exec.; b. Newark, N.J., Mar. 27, 1939; s. John Paul Clair (McLaughlin) T.; B.S. in Physics, Seton Hall U., 1966; m. Judith Ann Mackay, Aug. 27, 1966; children—Brian, Kyle. Engr., Sperry Co. Norwalk, Conn., 1965-66; dept. mgr. Gulton Industries Metuchen, N.J., 1966-71; plant mgr. N.L. Industries Muskegon, Mich., 1971-74; pres. Geepres Wringer Co. Muskegon, 1974—; chmn. Geerpres Wringer Co. Ltd. U.K., Reditch, Eng. Pres. Goodwill Industries Muskegon, 1973—; mem. bd. United Way, Muskegon, 1972—, Outstanding Citizenship award, 1974-75; mem. bd. Seaway Festival, 1972-75, pres. 1975; chmn. Community Services Bldg. Com., 1975-76. Recipient Muskegon Jaycees Distinguished Service award, 1973. Mem. W. Mich. Mfrs. Assn. (mem. bd. 1973-75), Am. Mgmt. Assn., Am. Inst. of Mgmt. Republican. Club: Rotary. Home: 730 Franklin St N Muskegon MI 49445 Office: PO Box 658 Muskegon MI 49443

TIERNEY, JOHN PATRICK, wholesale co. exec.; b. Bloomington, Ind., July 12, 1926; s. John Leo and Mae Christene (Stark) T.; B.S. in B.A., U. Notre Dame, 1949; m. Joyce Romayne Oesch, Dec. 26, 1948; children—Mike, Pat, Tom, Tim, Jim. Br. mgr. Great Lakes Distbg., South Bend, Ind., 1950, br. mgr., 1951-59; v.p. Wabash Wholesale, Inc., Logansport, Ind., 1959-62, pres., 1963—, also; dir. sec., treas. Asphalt Supplies, Inc., Logansport, Ind., also dir. Del. Ind. Democratic State Conv., 1974. Bd. dirs. Cass County United Fund, 1965-67. Mem. Nat. Bldg. Materials Distbrs. Assn., Air Force Assn. Clubs: Rotary (dir. 1957), Kiwanis (dir. 1961), Elk, K.C., Moose, Logansport Country. Home: 117 Orchard Hill Logansport IN 46947 Office: PO Box 508 Logansport IN 46947

TIERNON, CARLOS HERSCHEL, mfg. co. engring. exec.; b. Hartshorn, Mo., Dec. 15, 1930; s. Charles John and Delphia Ann (Riley) T.; B.S., also Metall. Engr., U. Mo. at Rolla, 1954; m. Joan Marie Mercer, Aug. 26, 1953; children—Theodore Carlos, Timothy Lee, Thomas Joseph, Terry Alan. Engr., Deister Concentrator Co., Inc., mfr. mineral concentrating and coal washing equipment, Fort Wayne, Ind., 1956-64, asst. chief engr., 1964-69, v.p. engring., 1970—. Served with AUS, 1954-56. Recipient Fort Wayne Mayor's Citation for rescue of mother and child from fire, 1970. Mem. Am. Inst. Mining Engrs., Am. Ceramic Soc., Canadian Inst. Mining and Metallurgy Engrs., United Comml. Travelers, Fort Wayne C. of C., Sigma Nu. Republican. Mem. Missionary Ch. (pres. men's missionary fellowship 1972). Mem. Gideons Internat. (camp pres. 1972—). Home: 810 W Oakdale Dr Fort Wayne IN 46807 Office: 901 Glasgow Ave Fort Wayne IN 46801

TIETZ, GARY ALBERT, librarian; b. St. Joseph, Mo., Mar. 29, 1945; s. George and Verna (Butler) T.; B.S., N.W. Mo. State U., 1967; M.A., Mo. U., 1968; m. Sally Darlene Despain. With Am. Electric Co., St. Joseph, 1968-71; librarian Central High Sch., St. Joseph, 1972—. Adviser Jr. Achievement, 1970-71; active Boy Scouts Am. Mem. Mo. State Tchrs. Assn., Assn. Am. Geographers, Kappa Delta Pi, Pi Gamma Mu. Home: 2301 Faraon St St Joseph MO 64501 Office: 26th and Edmond Sts St Joseph MO 64501

TIFFANY, JOSEPH CALVIN, II, surgeon; b. Grand Rapids, Mich., Aug. 12, 1939; s. Joseph Calvin and Dorothy Elizabeth (Yeakey) T.; A.B., Northwestern U., 1961, M.D., 1965; m. Ruth Pauline Luiten, June 15, 1968; children—Dawn Marie, Joseph Calvin. Intern, Cook County Hosp., Chgo., 1965-66; resident in surgery Mayo Grad. Sch. Medicine, Rochester, Minn., 1966-68, Allegheny Gen. Hosp., Pitts., 1969-71, Ross Clinic, Inc. Merrillville, Ind., 1974—. Served with U.S. Army, 1972-74. Diplomate Am. Bd. Surgery. Fellow A.C.S.; mem. AMA, Lake County Med. Soc., Ind. Med. Assn. Republican. Presbyterian. Home: 3550 W 90th Ct Merrillville IN 46410 Office: 6111 Harrison St Merrillville IN 46410

TIFFANY, NORMAN OLCOTT, educator, computer co. exec.; b. Los Angeles, June 28, 1925; s. Willis Norman and Enid Pearl (Olcott) T.; A.B., U. So. Calif., 1949, M.A., in Math., 1951; m. Nancy Ann Moritz, June 8, 1953; children—Christopher Lynn, Patricia (Mrs. Ronald G. Johnson), Matthew Caleb. Instr. math., physics Moravian Coll., Bethlehem, Pa., 1950-52, Alfred (N.Y.) U., 1952-55, Wayne State U., Detroit, 1955-57. Detroit Inst. Tech., 1955-57; mathematician Bendix Research Labs., Southfield, Mich., 1955—, mgr. computer facility, 1971—. Adv. com. data processing Oakland (Mich.) Community Coll., 1962—. Served with USNR, 1943-45. Mem. Multi Lakes Conservation Assn., Assn. for Computing Machinery. Home: 2248 S Commerce Rd Walled Lake MI 48088 Office: Bendix Center Southfield MI 48076

TIGERMAN, STANLEY, architect; b. Chgo., Sept. 20, 1930; s. Samuel Bernard and Emma Louise (Stern) T.; student Mass. Inst. Tech., 1948-49; B.Arch., Yale, 1960, M.Arch., 1961; children—Judson Joel, Tracy Lee. Apprentice G.F. Keck, 1949-50; designer S.O.M., 1957-59; draftsman Paul Rudolph, 1959-61; chief design Harry Weese, 1961-62, Tigerman & Koglin, prin. Stanley Tigerman & Assos., Chgo., 1964—. Prof. architecture U. Ill., Chgo., 1966-72; vis. lectr. various univs. Mem. alumni bd. Yale, 1964-65, adv. bd. Sch. Architecture, 1975—. Served with USN, 1950-54. Fellow Alpha Rho Chi medal Yale, A.I.A. Recipient regional and nat. design awards. Graham Found. grantee, 1965. Fellow A.I.A. (chmn. com. on design 1975-76). Clubs: Arts (Chgo.); Yale (N.Y.C.). Home: 910 Lake Shore Dr Chicago IL 60611 Office: 233 N Michigan Ave Chicago IL 60601

TIGRAK, MEHMET FAUT, structural engr.; b. Istanbul, Turkey, Aug. 26, 1911; s. M. Suleyman and Hediye (Harputlu) T.; Diploma, Mil. Coll., Habiye-Istanbul, 1932, Diploma Mil. Engring., 1934; Certificate, U. Berlin (Germany), 1938; student Technische Hochschule, Berlin, 1938-39; B.S., U. Ill., 1942, M.S., 1943, Ph.D., 1945; m. Mary Louise Evans; children—William M.U., James A.F., Hediye Louise. Came to U.S., 1958, naturalized. With Turkish Army Corps Engrs., 1934-51, resigned as sr. maj., 1951; tech. dir. Turk Yapi Ltd. Co., Ankara, Turkey, 1951; dept. head Metcalf, Hamilton, Grove, Kansas City, Mo., 1951-53; principle engr. project co-ordinator Hamilton Co., Kansas City, Mo., 1953-54; owner, operator Tigrak Cons. Engr. Co., Tigrak Constrn. Co., Ankara, 1954-58; prin. partner, mgr. Tigrak & Kolbasi, engrs.-contractors, Ankara, 1956-58; asso. in charge structure Clark, Daily, Dietz & Assos., 1958-62; v.p. charge structure and hwy. div. Clark, Dietz & Assos., engrs.-inc., Urbana, Ill., 1962-66, v.p. charge fed. and r.r. projects, 1966—. Recipient Honorable Mention award for Findlay Bridge (Shelbyville, Ill.), U.S. Army C.E., 1969. Registered profl. engr., Ill., Ind., Mo., Ky., Tenn., Wis., Turkey; registered structural engr., Turkey, Ill., Ky.; Certified fallout shelter analyst. Fellow ASCE (life); mem. Ill. Assn. Professions, Nat. Ill. socs. profl. engrs., Am. Concrete Inst. Am. Ry. Engring. Assn., Soc. Am. Mil. Engrs., AAAS, Chamber Architects and Engrs. Turkey, Sigma Xi, Chi Epsilon, Phi Kappa Epsilon. Mason (32 deg., Shriner). Home: 23 Briarcliff Rural Route 1 Mahomet IL 61853 Office: 211 N Race St Urbana IL 61801

TILLERY, STEPHEN MATTHEW, lawyer; b. Wood River, Ill., Mar. 9, 1950; s. Donald Lee and Ada Victoria (Waters) T.; B.A., Ill. Coll., 1972; J.D., St. Louis U., 1976; m. Katherine Jean Thompson, Aug. 19, 1972. Student law clk. U.S. Dist. Ct., Eastern Dist. Ill., 1976; admitted to Ill. bar, 1976; law clk. 5th Dist. Ct. Appeals of Ill., Mt. Vernon, 1976-77; asso. firm Kassly, Bone, Becker and Carlson, Belleville, Ill., 1977—; instr. law St. Louis U., 1977—. SAR fellow, 1968. Mem. Am., Ill., St. Clair County bar assns., Am., Ill. trial lawyers assn., Am. Judicature Soc., Phi Beta Kappa. Presbyterian. Home: 45 Fourscore Dr A D Belleville IL 62223 Office: 7705 W Main Belleville IL 62223

TILLOTSON, RAYMOND JENNISON, rancher; b. Shields, Kans., Mar. 1, 1904; s. Warren Jackson and Bessie (Jennison) T.; B.S., Kans. State U., 1929; M.S., Iowa State U., 1931; m. Amy C. Jones, Aug. 28, 1929; children—Don R., Paul J., Betty (Mrs. Kenneth L. Milford), Peggy (Mrs. Edwin J. Tajchman). Rural service engr. Kans. Gas & Elec. Co., Newton, 1929-30; asst. agrl. engr. Soil Conservation Service, U.S. Dept. Agr., Iowa, Mo., Kans., 1934-43; owner, operator ranch, Shields, Kans., 1944—. Mem. dist. bd. Lane County Soil Conservation, 1944-69, chmn., 1949-55; mem. Extension Council Bd., 1966-70, chmn., 1967-70. Mem. Am. Soc. Agrl. Engrs., Am. Soc. Range Mgmt., Kans. Livestock Assn., Kans. Wheat Growers Assn., Lane County Farm Bur. (dir. 1962-66), Kans. Master Farmer (pres. 1971), S.W. Kans. Gem and Mineral Soc. (pres. 1971-72, show chmn. 1977), Kans. Anthrop. Soc. (dir. 1974-76), Lane County Hist. Soc. (pres. 1956-57, dir. 1958-77). Methodist. Mason, Rotarian. Home: Shields KS 67874

TILTON, RICHARD WALLIS, trade assn. exec.; b. St. Joseph, Mo., Oct. 1, 1934; s. Raymond Marcus and Hazel Viola (Wallis) T.; m. Carol Jean Schiltz, Aug. 5, 1954; children—Renee Lynn, Julie Ann, Darcie Lee; A.B. in Bus. and Econs., N.W. Mo. U., 1956. Sales and mktg. rep. Shell Oil Co., St. Louis, 1956-59; sch. supply salesman Mead Corp., Little Rock and Salt Lake City, 1960-64, regional sales mgr., Kalamazoo, 1964-66, v.p. sales, Dayton, Ohio, 1966-74; exec. dir. Gen. Mdse. Distbrs. Council, Dayton, 1974—. Elder, Presbyn. Ch., 1963-64, 68-69, 72-73, 76—; bd. dirs. Brentwood, Mo., Little Rock, Ark., Salt Lake City, Utah Jr. chambers commerce, 1958-64. Mem. Sales Execs. Club (dir. 1965-66, 71-73), Am., Chgo. socs. assn. execs., Nat. Assn. Wholesale Distbrs. Home: 7012 Cherbourg Pl Dayton OH 45459 Office: 5250 Far Hills Ave Suite 221 Dayton OH 45429

TIMM, JEROME JOSEPH, dentist; b. Michigan City, Ind., July 20, 1924; s. Edward Clement and Magdalen Pauline (Wagner) T.; student Ind. U., 1946-48; D.D.S., Loyola U., Chgo., 1952; m. Helen Marie Meers, Nov. 14, 1953; children—Ann Therese, Christopher John, Carol Victoria, Edward Jerome, Mary Elizabeth. Practice gen. dentistry Michigan City, 1952—; staff dentist Crippled Children Clinic No. Ind., 1971—; mem. staff St. Anthony Hosp., chmn. dental staff, 1968-69; mem. staff Meml. Hosp. Bd. dirs., v.p. Meals on Wheels; bd. dirs. Vis. Nurse Assn. of LaPorte County; pres. Marquette High Sch. Booster Club and Found. Served with AUS, 1943-46. Fellow Royal Soc. Health; mem. Fedn. Dentaire Internat., ADA, St. Joseph Young Men's Soc., Fraternal Order Police, Am. Endodontic Soc., Am. Assn. Hosp. Dentists, Michigan City C. of C., Serra Internat. (dist. dep. gov. 1962-63. pres. 1960-61, 69-70). Republican. Roman Catholic. K.C. Club: Pottowattomie Country. Home: 208 Robin Trail Michigan City IN 46360 Office: 1232 E Michigan Blvd Michigan City IN 46360

TIMM, ROGER ALFRED, economist; b. Council Bluffs, Iowa, Apr. 8, 1943; s. Alfred Willard and Elsie Magdelene (Limburg) T.; B.A. in Econs. and Polit. Sci., Drake U., 1965; M.A. in Econs., U. Wis., 1966; m. Loretta Jean Boyd, May 23, 1970; children—Roger Alfred II, Peter W. Budget analyst, programmer Fed. Res. Bank, Omaha, 1969-70; systems analyst Physicians Mut. Ins. Co., Omaha, 1970-72, adminstrn. mgr., 1973-74; systems and data processing mgr. Lozier Mfg. Co., Omaha, 1974-75; sr. project mgr., economist Kansas City Power & Light Co. (Mo.), 1975—. Mem. Iowans for Muskie Com., 1972; finance com. Iowa Democratic Party, 1971-72; Western Iowa chmn. Clark for Sen., 1972; mem. Gladstone (Mo.) Planning Commn. Served with USMC, 1966-68. Deocrated Bronze Star, Silver Star, Purple Heart. Certified data processor. Mem. Assn. Systems Mgmt., Adminstrv. Mgmt. Soc. Lutheran. Home: 1705 NE 68th St Gladstone MO 64118 Office: PO Box 679 Kansas City MO 64141

TIMMERMAN, JAY CARL, dermatologist; b. Blue Island, Ill., Oct. 10, 1935; s. Henry Carl and Elizabeth June (Snider) T.; B.A., U. Iowa, 1956, M.D., 1960; m. Barbara Claire Wick, June 23, 1956; children—Barbara Jayne, Elizabeth Irene. Intern, St. Elizabeth Hosp., Youngstown, Ohio, 1960-61; gen. practice medicine, Mt. Pleasant, Iowa, 1961; resident in dermatology Univ. Hosp., U. Iowa, Iowa City, 1963-66; practice medicine specializing in dermatology, Iowa City, 1966—; clin. asst. prof. dermatology U. Iowa, 1975—. Served with U.S. Army, 1961-63. Diplomate Am. Bd. Dermatology and Pathology (jointly certified with spl. competence in dermatopathology.) Fellow Am. Acad. Dermatology; mem. Am. Soc. for Dematologic Surgery, Iowa (past pres. 1970, sec.-treas. 1967-69), Chgo. dermatol. socs., Alpha Omega Alpha. Clubs: Masons. Contbr. articles to profl. jours. Home: 5 Glendale Terr Iowa City IA 52240 Office: 2423 Towncrest Dr Iowa City IA 52240

TIMMONS, GEORGE GRANT, assurance co. exec.; b. Des Moines, Apr. 22, 1934; s. Kenneth Eugene and Vera Louise (Taylor) T.; ed. Life Underwriters Tng. Council, Drake U., 1956; student Purdue U., 1966; m. Mary Marlene Coday, May 29, 1954; children—Becky, Cindy, Julie, Randy. With Inter-State Assurance Co., Des Moines, 1955—, field sales supr., 1961-64, dir. health sales, 1964-65, regional supr., 1965-67, regional v.p., 1967-69, v.p. agy., 1969-71, agy. v.p., also agy. dir., 1971—; pres. Future Security, Inc., 1976—. Instr., Sales Technique Inst., Des Moines, 1969. Active United Campaign, Des Moines, 1968. Bd. dirs. YMCA Indian Guides. Served with Iowa N.G., 1952—. Decorated Meritorious Service ribbon. C.L.U. Mem. Iowa (pres. 1969), Central Iowa (dir. 1970) health underwriters, Iowa Noncommd. Officers Assn. (dir.). Mem. Christian Ch. Mason (Shriner). Clubs: Bohemian. Wakonda Golf and Country. Home: 3303 SW 35th St Des Moines IA 50321 Office: 420 Keosauqua Way Des Moines IA 50308

TIMMONS, GERALD DEAN, pediatric neurologist; b. Rensselaer, Ind., June 1, 1931; s. Homer and Tamma Mildred (Spall) T.; A.B., Ind. U., 1953, M.D., 1956; m. Janet Patricia Wilson, June 28, 1953; children—Jane Christina, Ann Elizabeth, Mary Catherine. Intern, Lima (Ohio) Meml. Hosp.; resident Ind. U. hosps., Indpls., 1957-59, 61-62; practice medicine, Indpls., 1963-64, Akron, Ohio, 1964—; instr. neurology dept. Ind. U. Med. Sch., Indpls., 1962-64; chief pediatric neurology Akron Children's Hosp., 1964—, chief staff, 1976-77; mem. staff Met. Gen. Hosp., Cleve.; spl. course instr. Kent State U., 1969-70, Ohio U., 1970-71, U. Akron, 1971-72; chief subcouncil of Neurology North Eastern Ohio Coll. Medicine. Med. dir. Akron Cerebral Palsy, Inc., 1965—, Ohio Cerebral Palsy, Inc., 1966—; mem. med. adv. com. United Services for Handicapped, Akron, 1966—. Trustee Montgomery Inst., Akron, 1966-74. Served to capt. USAF, 1959-61. Diplomate Am. Bd. Psychiatry and Neurology with spl. competence in child neurology. Mem. Ohio, Summit County med. socs., A.M.A., Am. Acad. Pediatrics, Am. Acad. Neurology, Child Neurology Soc., Am. Maternal and Child Health Assn. (trustee Ohio chpt. 1968—, nat. orgn. 1970—), Phi Beta Pi. Republican. Methodist. Mason. Clubs: Rotary, Cascade (Akron). Contbr. articles to med. jours. Home: 841 Merriman Rd Akron OH 44303 Office: 300 Locust St Akron OH 44308

TINEN, JOHN VICTOR, bldg. and constrn. co. exec.; b. Berwyn, Ill., Jan. 24, 1922; s. John Victor and Jane (Mills) T.; B.S. in Bus. Adminstrn., Northwestern U., 1946; m. Lois J. Heicher, Jan. 23, 1943; children—Susan J. (Mrs. Charles W. Morton), Diane (Mrs. William F. Wood), Mary, Brian. Auditor, Arthur Andersen & Co., C.P.A.'s, Chgo., 1946-49; asst. treas. Hafner Mfg. Co., Chgo., 1950-51; partner W.J. Tinen & Co., C.P.A.'s, Chgo., 1951-54; regional accounting dir. U.S. P.O., Chgo., 1955-56; controller Howard Foundry, Chgo., 1957-60; exec. v.p. W.N. Handy Co., Springfield, Mo., 1961-63, pres., 1963—; pres. Ozark Concrete Co., (Mo.), 1969—; chmn. bd. Fly Ash Sales Co., Springfield, Mo., 1963—, Handy Trucking Co., Springfield, 1974—. Served with USAAF, 1943-46; PTO. C.P.A., Ill., Mo. Ky. col. Mem. Am. Inst. C.P.A.'s, Mo. Soc. C.P.A.'s, Beta Alpha Psi. Club: Hickory Hills Country (Springfield). Home: 2721 S Glendale Springfield MO 65804 Office: 1948(C) S Glenstone Springfield MO 65804

TINGLEY, DONALD FRED, educator; b. Marshall, Ill., Mar. 13, 1922; s. James Frederick and Ruth Catherine (McDonald) T.; B.S., Eastern Ill. U., 1947; M.A., U. Ill., 1948, Ph.D., 1952; m. Eleanor Jeanne Cress, May 23, 1944; 1 dau., Elizabeth Catherine. With U.S. Steel Co., Gary, Ind., 1940-42; hist. research editor Ill. State Hist. Library, 1952-53; prof. history Eastern Ill. U., 1953—. Chmn., Citizens for Kennedy, 1960; staff Senator Eugene McCarthy, Democratic Nat. Conv., 1968; McGovern coordinator, 1972; Democratic precinct committeeman, 1962-74. Served with USNR, 1943-46. Recipient Distinguished Faculty award Eastern Ill. U., 1971. Mem. Ill. State Hist. Soc. (pres. 1971-72, chmn. bd. 1972-73), Orgn. Am. Historians, Am. Hist. Assn., Assn. for State and Local History, Sigma Tau Gamma. Methodist. Club: Charleston Country. Author: Essays in Illinois History, 1968; The Emerging University, 1974; also hist. articles and revs. Home: 98 Harrison St Charleston IL 61920

TINKHAM, MATTHEW HOSMER, JR., lawyer; b. Detroit, June 4, 1920; s. Matthew Hosmer and Dora J. (Foss) T.; B.A., Mich. State U., 1941; J.D., U. Mich., 1948; m. Dorothy J. Todd, July 3, 1942; children—Todd M., Lynn A. Admitted to Mich. bar, 1948, U.S. Supreme Ct. bar, 1957. Fed. Dist. Ct. bar, 1948; practice law, Wayne, Mich., 1948—; sr. partner firm Tinkham, MacDonald, Jahr & Steffen, Wayne, 1970—. Trustee Nankin (Mich.) TWP., 1953-55; mem. Charter Commn. City of Wayne, 1960, City Council, Wayne, 1972-75. Served with USAAF, 1941-46; ETO. Fellow Am. Coll. Probate Counsel; mem. State Bar of Mich. (chmn. sect. probate and trust, chmn. grievance Panel), Am., Detroit bar assns., Suburban Bar (pres. 1956-57). Conglist. Mason, Rotarian (trustee Wayne Found. 1952—). Home: 37033 Forest St Wayne MI 48184 Office: 34629 Michigan Ave W Wayne MI 48184

TINNING, FRED C., educator; b. Detroit, Aug. 15, 1936; s. James C. and Susan G. (Smith) T.; B.A., Mich. State U., 1959, M.A., 1961, Ph.D. (HEW fellow), 1973; m. Janet E. Marshall, Mar. 9, 1963; children—Marie Cathryn, Jean Alison, Laura Anne. Rehab. counselor State of Mich., Detroit, 1961-65; dist. adminstr. rehab. div. Mich. Dept. Edn., Detroit, 1965-69; grad. fellow med. edn. Mich. State U., E. Lansing, 1970-71, instr., asst. to dean Coll. Osteo. Medicine, 1972, asst. dean Office of Academic Affairs, 1972-75, asst. dean Office of Planning, 1975—, prof. community medicine, prof. personnel counseling and ednl. psychology, 1973—; acting dean, cons. N.J. Coll. Medicine and Dentistry; cons. Fla. Osteo. Med. Assn., N. Tex. State Coll. Osteo. Medicine. Merck Found. grantee, 1974. Mem. Am. Ednl. Research Assn., Am. Assn. Med. Colls., Am. Osteo. Assn., Nat., Mich. (dir. 1965-69) rehab. assns., Am., Mich. (award for excellence in field of rehab. 1972) personnel and guidance assns., Am. Rehab. Counseling Assn., Am. Assn. Colls. Osteo. Medicine. Clubs: Varsity, Fellowship of Christian Athletes (faculty advisor), Christian Med., President's. Author: Simulation in Medical Education, 1974; co-author fed. tng. manuals HEW, 1970-71; co-editor Mich. Personnel and Guidance Assn. Jour., 1972-73. Home: 1867 Ann St East Lansing MI 48832 Office: 310 E Fee Hall Mich State U East Lansing MI 48824

TIPEI, NICOLAE, elec. and mech. engr.; b. Calarasi, Romania; s. Sever and Elena (Gherghiceanu) T.; came to U.S., 1972; grad. electromechanic engr. Poly. Inst. Bucharest (Romania), 1936, D.Eng., 1968; m. Letitia Radulescu, Apr. 27, 1941; 1 son, Sever. Instr. engring. Poly. Inst. Bucharest, 1936-46, asst. prof., 1946-64, prof. emeritus, 1964-71; chief engr. Romanian Airlines, 1937, Romanian Rys. Locomotive Workshops, 1938; owner, engr. Nicolae Tipei & Co., 1939-43; research worker, corr. mem. Romanian Acad., 1949-71; chief engr. IRMC, Bucharest, 1945-48; sr. research engr. Gen. Motors Tech. Center Research Labs., Warren, Mich., 1972—. Served with Romanian Air Force, 1936, 43. Recipient Prize for Sci. Activity, Govt. Romania, 1956. Mem. Am. Inst. Aeros. and Astronautics, Soc. Applied Math. Mechanics (W.Ger.). Author: Theory of Lubrication, 1962; Lagare in Alunecare (Sliding Bearings), 1961; contbr. numerous articles to profl. jours. Home: 1403 E 5th St Royal Oak MI 48067 Office: 12 Mile and Mound Rd Warren MI 48090

TIPPIN, GEORGE RICHARD, social worker; b. St. Louis, Sept. 27, 1931; s. George Irwin and Jean (Wallace) T.; B.A., Hastings Coll., 1956; M.S.W., U. Denver, 1962; m. Helen Cecil Jones, Jan. 31, 1954; children—George William, Marilyn Cecil, Janet Kay, Kenneth Richard. Case Worker Hastings State Hosp., Ingleside, Nebr., 1956-60; social worker, central psychiat. inst. Colo. State Hosp., Pueblo, 1962-63, dir. geriatric release program, 1963-68, chief social worker admission evaluation program, 1968-71; dir. social service dept. Hastings Regional Center, Ingleside, 1971—, dir. mental retardation unit, 1974—. Cons. to various govt. agys. Mem. Nat. Assn. Social Workers (v.p. 1966, treas. 1968), Acad. Certified Social Workers, Lambda Chi Alpha. Presbyn. (deacon). Home: 2210 W 12th St Hastings NE 68901 Office: Hastings Regional Center Hastings NE 68901

TIPSHUS, EDWARD CHESTER, data processing specialist; b. Chgo., Nov. 13, 1929; s. Blase Frank and Tekli (Songaile) T.; B.S., U.S. Naval Acad., 1954; M. Pub. Adminstrn., Am. U., 1968; m. Sandra Leah Bell, June 2, 1962; children—Lisa Ann, John Blase. Served as enlisted man U.S. Marine Corps, 1947-50, commd. 2d lt., 1954, advanced through grades to lt. col., 1969; various assignments in artillery and infantry command and staff, U.S. and overseas, 1954-68; asst. dir. Automated Services Center, Okinawa, 1968-69; dir. automated resources support, Hdqrs. USMC, 1969-70, dir. Automated Services Center, 1971-72; ret., 1972; mgr. data processing ops. dept. Chemical Abstracts Service, Columbus, Ohio, 1972—. Decorated Bronze Star with V, 3 Air Medals, Navy Commendation Medal with V, Vietnamese Gallentry Cross with Silver Star. Mem. U.S. Naval Inst., U.S. Marine Corps Assn., U.S. Naval Acad. Alumni Assn., Ret. Officers Assn., Assn. for Computing Machinery. Republican. Club: Worthington Hills. Home: 8315 Fairway Dr Worthington Hills OH 43085 Office: Box 3012 Columbus OH 43210

TIPTON, CLYDE RAYMOND, JR., community urban redevel. co. exec.; b. Cin., Nov. 13, 1921; s. Clyde Raymond and Ida Marie (Molitor) T.; B.S., U. Ky., 1946, M.S. (Haggin fellow), 1947; m. Marian Gertrude Beushausen, Aug. 6, 1942; children—Marian Page Cuddy, Robert Bruce. Research engr. Battelle Meml. Inst., Columbus, Ohio, 1947-49, sr. tech. adviser, 1951-62, coordinator corporate communications, 1969-73, v.p. communications, 1973-75; mem. staff Los Alamos (N.Mex.) Sci. Lab., 1949-51; dir. research Basic, Inc., Bettsville, Ohio, 1962-64; asst. dir. Battelle Pacific N.W. Labs., Richland, Wash., 1964-69; trustee, pres. Battelle Commons Co., 1975—. Secretariat, U.S. del. 2d Internat. Conf. Peaceful Uses Atomic Energy, Geneva, Switzerland, 1958; cons. AEC, Tokyo, 1959, New Delhi, India, 1959-60, Rio de Janeiro, Brazil, 1961. Bd. dirs. Pilot Dogs, Inc., Central Ohio United Negro Coll. Fund, Columbus Jr. Theatre of Arts, Columbus Assn. Performing Arts, CARE, Central Ohio Resource Bd.; bd. dirs. Greater Columbus Arts Council, pres., 1977; exec. com. Columbus Conv. and Visitors Bur. Served with USAAF, 1943. Mem. AAAS, Am. Mgmt. Assn., Am. Soc. Metals, Nat., Ohio socs. profl. engrs., Urban Land Inst., Ohio Acad. Sci., Sigma Xi, Alpha Chi Sigma. Editor: The Reactor Handbook, vol. 3, 1955, vol. 1, 1960, Jour. Soc. Nondestructive Testing, 1953-57. Patentee plutonium-aluminum alloys. Home: 2155 Cheshire Rd Columbus OH 43221 Office: 35 E Chestnut St Columbus OH 43215

TITCHENAL, OLIVER RAY, packaging co. exec.; b. Parker, Ariz., Mar. 18, 1920; s. Charles Elmer and Dora (Kieth) T.; student Fullerton Calif. Jr. Coll., 1937-38; m. Florence Mae Rabourn, Mar. 21, 1948 (div. 1973); children—Stephen Ray, Douglas Wayne, Jeffery Scott. Tooling engr. Douglas Aircraft Co., Santa Monica, Calif., Tulsa, 1938-48; mgr. sales engring. St. Regis Paper Co., Los Angeles, San Francisco, 1948-56, chief engr., 1956-60, gen. mgr. packaging machinery div., 1960-63, dir. packaging engring., 1963-65; asst. dir. research, converted products PKG div. Dow Chem. Co., Midland, Mich., Cleve., 1965-71; founder exec. v.p. Basic Packaging System Inc., Avon Lake, Ohio, 1971—, also dir. Served with USMC, 1944-46. Mem. Am. Assn. Mech. Engrs., Packaging Inst. Registered profl. engr., Calif. Patentee in field. Home: 143 Shakespeare St Avon OH 44011 Office: 583 Miller Rd Avon Lake OH 44012

TITKO, JERRY L., podiatrist; b. Hemlock, Ohio, Feb. 2, 1941; s. Peter E. and Anna M. (Marolt) T.; student Ohio State U., 1958-59; D. Podiatric Medicine, Ohio Coll. Podiatric Medicine, 1963; div.; children—J. Russell, Kristin Kimberly. Intern Cleve. Foot Clinic, 1963-64, Youngstown (Ohio) Foot Clinic, 1964; pvt. practice podiatry, Hamilton, Ohio, 1964—; clin. instr. Ohio Coll. Podiatric Medicine, 1974—. Mem. Am., Ohio, So. Ohio podiatry assns., Acad. Hosp. Podiatry, Internat. Acad. Preventive Medicine, Am. Pub. Health Assn., Acad. Ambulatory Foot Surgery (charter), Ohio Acad. Foot Surgery (charter), Hamilton Investment Club (pres. 1971, 74, 75), Hamilton Jr. C. of C. (v.p. 1967). Presbyterian. Home: 1103 Buckhead Dr Fairfield OH 45014 Office: 25 N F St Hamilton OH 45013

TITLE, MONROE M., hosp. adminstr.; b. Bklyn., Oct. 6, 1918; s. Joseph and Helen (Sonenberg) T.; B.S., Coll. City N.Y., 1939; M.Social Work, U. Mich., 1941; m. Rena Offutt, Sept. 6, 1972; children by previous marriage—Diane Auster, Gerald Edward. Adminstr. Brent Gen. Hosp., Detroit, 1953-64; adminstr. Woodside Med. Nursing Home, Pontiac, Mich., 1964-65; adminstr. Park Community Hosp., Detroit, 1965-66; adminstr. North Detroit Gen. Hosp., 1966—. Cons., Burton Mercy Hosp., 1961-74, Dearborn Med. Center Hosp., 1959-64; instr. Wayne State U. Applied Mgmt. and Tech. Center, 1967—, chmn. nursing home adminstrn. program, 1972—; sr. extension lectr. Mich. State U., 1972—. Fellow United Found., 1940-41. Fellow Am. Coll. Hosp. Adminstr., Am. Coll. Nursing Home Adminstrs.; mem. Am. Hosp. Assn., Hamtramck C. of C. (dir. 1970—). Contbr. articles on hosps. and nursing homes to profl. jours. Home: 8515 Winchester St Sterling Heights MI 48078 Office: 3105 Carpenter St Detroit MI 48212

TIU, ALFONSO LI, internist, cardiologist; b. Cebu, Philippines, Feb. 16, 1943; s. Ching Quiat and Chuti (Li) T.; came to U.S., 1966; A.A. with high honors, U. San Carlos, Cebu City, Philippines, 1960; M.D. with honors, Cebu Inst. Medicine, 1965; m. Lou Divina Taclob, Aug. 25, 1966; children—Chuti Lynn, Alphonse Patrick, Carmelita Anne. Intern, St. Michael Hosp., Milw., 1966; resident in internal medicine Mt. Sinai Hosp., 1967; resident in internal medicine, cardiology fellowship Tulane U. Med. Program, New Orleans, 1968-70; cardiology fellowship Springfield (Mass.) Med. Center, 1970; practice medicine specializing in internal medicine and cardiology, West Allis, Wis., 1971—; med. cons. Allis Chalmers Med. Dept. Diplomate Am. Bd. Internal Medicine. Fellow Am. Coll. Internat. Physicians; mem. AMA, A.C.P., Am. Soc. Internal Medicine, Am. Heart Assn., Med. Soc. Milw. County, State Med. Soc. Wis., Physician's Martial Arts Assn. Roman Catholic. Office: 10617 W Oklahoma Ave West Allis WI 53227

TOBIN, CALVIN JAY, architect; b. Boston, Feb. 15, 1927; s. David and Bertha (Tanfield) T.; B.Arch., U. Mich., 1949; m. Joan Hope Fink, July 15, 1951; children—Michael Alan, Nancy Ann. Designer, draftsman Arlen & Lowenfish, architects, N.Y.C., 1949-51; with Samuel Arlen, N.Y.C., 1951-53, Skidmore, Owings & Merrill, N.Y.C., 1953; architect Loebl, Schlossman & Bennett, architects, Chgo., 1953-57; v.p. Loebl, Schlossman & Hackl, 1957—. Chmn., Jewish United Fund Bldg. Trades Div., 1969; chmn. AIA and Chgo. Hosp. Council Com. of Hosp. Architecture, 1968-76. Chmn. Highland Park (Ill.) Appearance Rev. Commn., 1972-73; mem. Highland Park Plan Commn., 1972-73; mem. Highland Park City Council, 1974—. Bd. dirs. Young Men's Jewish Council, 1953-67, pres., 1967; bd. dirs. Jewish Community Centers Chgo. Served with USNR, 1945-46. Mem. A.I.A. (2d v.p. Chgo. chpt.), Pi Lambda Phi. Jewish. Archtl. works include Michael Reese Hosp. and Med. Center, 1954—, Prairie Shores Apt. Urban Redevel., 1957-62, Louis A. Weiss Meml. Hosp., Chgo., Chgo. State Hosp., Central Community Hosp., Chgo., Gottlieb Meml. Hosp., Melrose Park, Ill., Water Tower Pl., Chgo., also numerous apt., comml. and community bldgs. Home: 814 Dean Ave Highland Park IL 60035 Office: 845 N Michigan Ave Chicago IL 60611

TOBIN, MICHAEL E., stock exchange exec.: B.S. in Econs., U. Pa., 1948; m. Mona Tobin; children—Michael E., Allegra, Corey. Cons., RCA, Ebasco Service, Inc.; sr. cons. Arthur Young & Co., N.Y.C., 1956-59, Midwest dir. cons. services, Chgo., 1959-68; pres. Midwest Stock Exchange, 1968—. Active in Community Fund Chgo., Welfare Council Met. Chgo. Address: 120 S LaSalle St Chicago IL 60603

TODD, ALVA CRESS, educator, elec. engr.; b. Ligonier, Ind., July 30, 1917; s. Frederick White and Bessie Pearl (Cress) T.; B.S. in Elec. Engring., Purdue U., 1947, M.S., 1949, Ph.D., 1957; m. Mary Elizabeth Schelle, Apr. 17, 1941; children—Richard Schelle, Carol Jean (Mrs. Everett A. Biegalski), Joanne Frances (Mrs. Louis E. Horton), Elizabeth Ann (Mrs. Scott R. Lowry). Broadcast engr. radio sta. WSBT, South Bend, Ind., 1936-40, radio sta. WBAA, Lafayette, Ind., 1940-42; elec. engr. U.S. Signal Corps, Washington, 1942; instr., research engr. Sch. Elec. Engring., Purdue U., 1947-53, asst. prof., 1953; dir. engring. Fournier Inst. Tech., Lemont, Ill., 1953-55; sr. engr. Farnsworth Electronics Co., Ft. Wayne, Ind., 1955-56; pvt. practice, Lafayette, 1956-57; research engr. Ill. Inst. Tech. Research Inst., 1957-60; mgr. active electronic warfare div. Hallicrafter Co., 1960-61; mem. faculty Ill. Inst. Tech., 1961-62; prof. elec. engring., 1962-67; founder, pres. Midwest Coll. Engring., 1967—; sr. partner Todd Assos., Villa Park, Ill., 1961—. Served to lt. USCGR, 1942-46. Registered profl. engr., Ind., Ill. Sr. mem. IEEE; mem. Armed Forces Communications and Electronics Assn., AAAS, Nat. Fire Protection Assn., Nat. Soc. Profl. Engrs., Am. Soc. Engring. Edn., Soc. Broadcast Engrs., Sigma Xi, Tau Beta Pi, Eta Kappa Nu. Patentee in field. Home: 827 S Summit Ave Villa Park IL 60181 Office: Midwest Coll Engring 440 S Finley Rd Lombard IL 60148

TODD, DAVID WARREN, surgeon; b. Newark, July 6, 1937; s. David G. and Mabel (Flanders) T.; A.B., Johns Hopkins, 1959; M.D., Tufts U., 1963; postgrad. Mayo Grad. Sch., 1964-68; M.S. in Surgery, U. Minn., 1968; m. Gunnel U. Ericsson, June 18, 1964; children—David Eric, Daniel Warren, Steven Timothy, Rebecca Emily. Intern Mountainside Hosp., Montclair, N.J., 1963-64; resident Mayo Clinic, 1964-68; practice medicine specializing in surgery, Fargo, N.D., 1971—; mem. staffs Fargo Clinic, St. Luke's Hosp.; courtesy staff St. John's Hosp., Dakota Hosp. Asst. clin. prof. U. N.D., Fargo, 1975—. Served to maj., M.C., AUS, 1968-71; Germany. Fellow A.C.S.; mem. AMA. Contbr. numerous articles to profl. jours. Home: 118 Woodcrest Dr S Fargo ND 58102 Office: 737 Broadway Fargo ND 58102

TODD, GARY IRL, radio exec.; b. Walla Walla, Wash., May 8, 1937; s. William Irl and Ruby Alice (Waddington) T.; grad. high sch.; m. Linda May Wolfe, June 21, 1958; children—Teresa Rene, Gary Irl, Scott Robert. Promotion dir. KIMN Radio, Denver, 1965-66; KOL Radio, Seattle, 1967-68; program dir. WIBC Radio, Indpls., 1968—. Mem. Mayor's Stadium Task Force, 1970—; mem. new events com. 500 Festival Assn., 1970; capt. 150th birthday fund dr. Ind. U., 1970—; mem. pub. relations adv. com. Cath. Youth Orgn., 1970—; radio chmn. Easter Seals, 1969-70, chmn. central Ind.; radio chmn. Ind. Hemophilia Found., 1970—; crusade chmn. Am. Cancer Soc., 1972, bd. dirs. Marion County unit, 1971—; chmn. Central Ind. Christmas Seal Campaign; bd. dirs. Indpls. Christmas Com., 1975-76, Lawrence N. Progress, Inc., 1976-77. Recipient Nat. award of merit Am. Assn. Blood Banks, 1970; Distinguished Service award Indpls. Jr. C. of C., 1971, Speedway Jr. C. of C., 1970; Service to Mankind award Castleton Sertoma, 1976; named Outstanding Young Hoosier, Ind. Jr. C. of C., 1972; Gary Todd Day proclaimed by mayor of Indpls., 1970. Office: 2835 Illinois St Indianapolis IN 46208

TODD, JACKSON DEAN, oral surgeon; b. Bedford, Ind. Sept. 23, 1929; s. Theodore Price and Iona (Cox) T.; A.B. in Zoology, Ind. U., 1951, D.D.S., 1955; m. Sally Katherine Tinkle, June 30, 1957; children—Kimberly Ann, Jeffrey Dean. Intern, Ind. U., 1955-56, resident in oral surgery, 1956-58; practice oral surgery, Marion, Ind., 1959—; mem. staff Marion Gen. Hosp., Wabash County Hosp., Wabash, Ind.; asso. prof. oral surgery Ind. U. Sch. Dentistry; cons. oral surgery VA Hosp., Marion. Mem. Citizens Adv. Com. for Marion Coll., 1970—. Mem. Ind. Dental Assn. (chmn. dental law com. 1974-75), Ind. Soc. Oral Surgeons (pres. 1972-73), Gt. Lakes Soc. Oral Surgeons (mem. exec. com. 1971—, pres. 1976-77), Ind. (mem. council for hosp. dental services 1966-70), Grant County (pres. 1966-67) dental socs., Grant County Ind. U. Alumni Assn. (pres. 1968-69), Acad. Internat. Dentistry, Wabash Valley Dental Soc. (pres. 1976-77), Am. Soc. Oral Surgeons, Omicron Kappa Upsilon. Republican. Presbyterian (past deacon, past trustee). Clubs: Indiana University Varsity; Meshingomesia Country (Marion, Ind.), Masons. Home: 602 Berkley Dr Marion IN 46952 Office: 444 Wabash Ave Marion IN 46952

TODD, JOHN ODELL, ins. co. exec.; b. Mpls., Nov. 12, 1902; s. Frank Chisholm and Mary Mable (Odell) T.; A.B., Cornell U., 1924; C.L.U., Am. Coll., 1933; m. Katherine Sarah Cone, Feb. 21, 1925; children—John Odell, George Bennett. Spl. agt. Equitable Life Assurance Soc., Mpls., 1926-28; ins. broker, Mpls., 1928-31; spl. agt. Northwestern Mut. Life Ins. Co., Mpls., 1931-38, Evanston, Ill., 1951—; partner H.S. Vail & Sons, Chgo., 1938-43, Vail and Todd, gen. agts. Northwestern Mut. Life Ins. Co., 1943-44; sole gen. agt., Chgo., 1944-51; pres. Todd Planning and Service Co., life ins. brokers, 1951—; founder prin. John O. Todd Orgn. Inc., Exec. Compensation Specialists and Cons., 1970—; faculty lectr. C.L.U. Insts., U. Conn., 1952-53, U. Wis., 1955-57, U. Calif., 1956, U. Hawaii, 1966; host interviewer ednl. Films Series of the Greats, 1973-74. Pres. Evanston (Ill.) 1st. Ward Non-Partisan Civic Assn., 1956-57; trustee Evanston Hist. Soc., 1973-76. Recipient Golden Plate award Am. Acad. Achievement, 1969; named Ins. Field Man of Year, Ins. Field Pub. Co., 1965. Mem. Nat. Assn. Life Underwriters (John Newton Russell award 1969), Assn. Advanced Life Underwriters (pres. 1963-64), Am. Coll. Life Underwriters (trustee 1957-78), Chgo. Life Underwriters Assn. (dir. 1938-41), Northwestern Mut. Spl. Agts. Assn. (pres. 1955-56), Life Agy. Mgrs. Assn. (dir. 1945-48), Northwestern Mut. Assn. Agts. (pres. 1957-58), Chgo. Life Trust Council, Psi Upsilon, Sphinx Head. Republican. Clubs: Evanston Univ.; Glen View; Mpls. Author: Taxation, Inflation and Life Insurance, 1950; The Beneficiary in Life Insurance, 1948; Ceiling Unlimited, 1965; contbg. author to text Huebner Foundation, 1951.

TODD, MARY ELIZABETH (MRS. ALVA CRESS TODD), ednl. adminstr.; b. Lafayette, Ind., Aug. 26, 1920; d. Christian Frederick and Anna Marie (Mahlke) Schelle; diploma Ind. Bus. Coll., 1940; m. Alva Cress Todd, Apr. 17, 1941; children—Richard Schelle, Carol Todd Biegalski, Joanne Todd Horton, Elizabeth Ann Todd Lowry. Sec., Sears Roebuck & Co., Lafayette, 1940, Riley Pountry Farm, Lafayette, 1940-41; treas. Todd Assos., engrs., Villa Park, Ill., 1961-67; bus. mgr., treas. Midwest Coll. Engring., Lombard, Ill., 1967—, trustee, 1973—. Mem. Meml. Hosp. Guild, Elmhurst, Ill., 1963—. Mem. Nat. Assn. Coll. and Univ. Bus. Officers, Lombard C. of C., Delta Sigma Kappa. Home: 827 S Summit Ave Villa Park IL 60181 Office: 440 S Finley Rd Lombard IL 60148

TODD, MARYSNOW STONE (MRS. ZANE G. TODD), educator; b. Owensville, Ind., Apr. 6, 1920; d. Clarence Edgar and Mary Pearl (Knowles) Stone; student Lockyear Bus. Coll., 1945-46, Ind. Central Coll., 1958-62; m. Zane G. Todd, Feb. 8, 1950; 1 dau., Betty (Mrs. William Hudson). Bookkeeper, Mo. Valley Bridge & Iron Co., Evansville, Ind., 1942-45, McCrory's Stores, Indpls., 1947-51; asst. editor Research and Rev. Publs., Inc., Indpls., 1951-55, asso. editor, 1956-58; tchr. Perry Twp. schs., Indpls., 1968—. Counselor in edn., 1965-67. Mem. com. Ind. Symphony Soc., 1960—; area leader Am. Cancer Soc., 1966; mem. Winchester Civic Assn., 1962—, Ind. Hist. Soc., 1959—; volunteer A.R.C., 1970-72; mem. Lions Aux., 1956—. Bd. dirs. Muscular Dystrophy Assn., 1969. Mem. Soc. Comml. Journalists, Internat. Platform Assn. Republican. Presbyn. Clubs: Riviera, Meridian Hills Country, Indianapolis Athletic. Contbr. articles to ins. jours. Home: 1941 Remington Dr Indianapolis IN 46227

TODD, THOMAS CARMEL, supt. schs.; b. Dothan, Ala., Jan. 9, 1929; s. Alda Thomas and Ada Estelle (Tharp) T.; m. Barbara Irene Sheen, May 15, 1973; children—Tom, Teri, Kimberly, Tamara; B.S., Troy (Ala.) State Tchrs. Coll., 1955; M.S., Fla. State U., 1957. Teaching prin., Liberty County, Fla., 1955; elementary prin., Clearwater, Fla., 1958-63; supt. schs., Bay County, Fla., 1966-72; exec. asst. to commr. edn. State of Fla., 1972-75; supt. div. elementary and secondary edn., State of S.D., Pierre, 1975—; owner, operator retail furniture store, 1963-73. Mem. Am. Assn. Sch. Adminstrs., Council of Chief State Sch. Officers, Phi Delta Kappa, Kappa Delta Phi. Clubs: Elks, Rotary. Home: 218 Neltom Dr Pierre SD 57501 Office: Div Elementary and Secondary Edn New State Office Bldg Pierre SD 57501

TODD, ZANE GREY, utility exec., elec. engr.; b. Hanson, Ky., Feb. 3, 1924; s. Marshall Elvin and Kate (McCormick) T.; student Evansville Coll., 1948-49; B.S. summa cum laude, Purdue U., 1951; postgrad. U. Mich., summer 1965; m. Marysnow Stone, Feb. 8, 1950. Fingerprint classifier FBI, 1942-43; electric system planning engr. Indpls. Power & Light Co., 1951-56, spl. assignments supr., 1956-60, head elec. system planning, 1960-65, head substa. engring., 1965-68, head distbn. engring., 1968-70, asst. to v.p., 1970-72, v.p., 1972-74, exec. v.p., 1974-75, pres., 1975-76, chmn. bd., pres., 1976—; also dir.; gen. mgr. Mooresville Pub. Service Co., Inc. (Ind.), 1956-60; dir. Mchts. Nat. Bank. Mem. adv. bd. St. Vincent Hosp.; bd. dirs. United Hosp. Services, Central Ind. Health Systems Agy., Greater Indpls. Progress Com., Environ. Quality Control Inc. mem. sci. adv. bd. Indpls. Center for Advanced Research; mem. adv. bd. Christian Theol. Sem. Served with AUS, 1943-47. Recipient Distinguished Alumnus award Purdue U., 1976. Fellow IEEE (past chmn. com. application probability methods, chmn. power systems engring. com.); mem. Indpls. (dir.), Ind. (dir.), Mooresville (past pres.) chambers commerce, Ind. Soc. Profl. Engrs., Ind. Electric Assn. (dir., chmn. 1976—), Eta Kappa Nu, Tau Beta Pi. Rotarian. Clubs: Indianapolis Athletic, Meridian Hills Country, Columbia. Contbr. to tech. jour. Originator probability analysis of power systems reliability. Home: 1941 Remington Dr Indianapolis IN 46227 Office: 25 Monument Circle Indianapolis IN 46204

TODES, KENNETH, hotel exec.; b. St. Louis, Oct. 5, 1924; s. Maurice and Fay (Feldman) T.; A.B., Vanderbilt U., 1945; m. Cecily Bell, Oct. 8, 1959; children—Anne Conde, Pierre, Paul. Pvt. practice as architect, Clayton, Mo., 1965-71; owner Mark Twain Hotel, St. Louis, 1971—. Served with AUS, 1945-46. Mem. A.I.A. (asso.), English-Speaking Union, Irish Georgian Soc. Republican. Club: University (St. Louis). Home: 4976 Pershing Pl St Louis MO 63108 Office: 116 N 8th St St Louis MO 63101

TODOROFF, ALBERT, editor, pub.; b. Chgo., May 30, 1912; s. Alexander and Elizabeth (Martin) T.; A.B., DePauw U., Greencastle, Ind., 1934; m. Mary Jane Stangland, Oct. 1, 1938 (div. Apr. 1967); children—Bonnie Sue (Mrs. Charles Lettow), Laura Jean; m. 2d, Fay Rehm Novakovich, Aug. 25, 1967; 1 dau., Ann Fay. Asso. editor Grocery Trade Tips, Chgo., 1935-37, The Co-Operative Merchandiser, 1937-41; editor, Meat Merchandising, 1941-47; editor Meat Plant Mag., St. Louis, Mo., 1947—, pub., 1957—; pres. Upright, St. Louis, 1970—; exec. sec. Frozen Food Locker Inst., 1949-50; lectr. frozen foods, meat locker plants throughout country. Recipient Meat Processors Industry award, 1956. Mem. St. Louis Bus. Mag. Editors Council, Soc. Bus. Paper Editors, Sigma Delta Chi. Republican. Mem. Disciples of Christ Ch. Mason (K.T., Shriner). Author: How to Build and Operate a Locker Plant, 1945; Store Tested Ideas for Meat Men, 1947; How to Wrap Foods for Freezing, 1949. Home: 11908 Kendon Dr Des Peres MO 63131 Office: 8678 Olive Blvd St Louis MO 63132

TOEDMAN, GORDON REED, editor; b. Enid, Okla., Feb. 17, 1933; s. Neil L. and Marjorie (Reed) T.; B.A., Kans. U., 1956; m. Nancy Owsley, Nov. 22, 1958; children—Loree Ellen, Gordon Reed, Robert Tate. Asso. editor Mid-West Truckman Topeka, 1958-64, editor, 1964—; pres. The Neil L. Toedman Agy., Inc., 1964—. Served with AUS, 1956-58. Mem. Topeka Insurors, Highway Users, Delta Sigma Pi, Phi Kappa Sigma. Elk. Home: 2924 Sunnymede Ct Topeka KS 66611 Office: 1101 Topeka Ave Topeka KS 66612

TOEDTMAN, JAMES CHRISTIAN, advt. and publishing exec.; b. Miamisburg, Ohio, Sept. 19, 1914; s. Henry C. and Henrietta E. (Lucas) T.; A.B., Capital U., 1936; postgrad. Ohio State U., U. Dayton, Dayton Art Inst.; m. Ella Barnes Smith, Aug. 17, 1940; children—James S., Craig B., Carol A. Newspaperman Columbus (Ohio) Dispatch, 1932-36; with Gen. Motors Corp., Dayton, 1936-42, Monsanto Co., Dayton, 1942-46; with D'Arcy Advt. Co., Cleve., 1947-58, 64-67, sr. account exec., 1947-57, v.p., 1957-67; sr. v.p. H.D. McKinney Co., Cleve., 1958-64; sr. v.p. Lieberman Assos., Inc., Allentown, Pa., 1967-69; pres. Berea Pub. Co. (Ohio), 1958-70; v.p., sec. W.N. Gates Co., 1971—, pres., 1973—. Cons. graphic arts U.S. Dept. Commerce, Far East, 1974, Yugoslavia, 1975, South Africa, 1977. Bd. dirs. SW Gen. Hosp., Berea, 1969-77; pres., bd. dirs. Ohio Chamber Orch., 1974-76. Recipient award for advt. Am. Bus. Press, 1957; award for world understanding United World Federalists, 1967; Berea C. of C. award, 1971, Community Service award Baldwin Wallace Coll., 1972, SW Hosp., 1977; service awards U.S. Dept. Commerce, 1974, 75. Mem. Council World Affairs. Clubs: Cleve. Athletic; Nat. Press (Washington). Home: 188 Manning Dr Berea OH 44017 Office: 10 Beech St Berea OH 44017 also 662 Hanna Bldg Cleveland OH 44114

TOEPFER, CAROLINE ELIZABETH THROCKMORTON, clin. psychologist, behavior modification dir.; b. Newark, Feb. 17, 1944; d. Chester and Caroline Amanda (Lange) Throckmorton; m. James R. Toepfer, June 13, 1964; 1 son, Neil. B.A., Kent (Ohio) State U., 1965, M.A., 1967, Ph.D., 1969. Intern, Portage County (Ohio) Welfare Dept., 1966-68, psychologist, 1966-68; intern Univ. Hosps., Case Western Res. U., 1968; prof. psychology Slippery Rock (Pa.) State Coll., 1969-74; dir. Inst. Behavior Modification, 1973—; pvt. practice clin. psychology, Youngstown, Ohio, 1974—. Mem. Am. Psychol. Assn., Assn. Advancement Psychology, Acad. Cons. Psychologists (v.p.), Biofeedback Soc. Ohio, Psi Chi. Cleve. Found. scholar,

1962-65; NIMH research fellow, 1967-69. Author: Readings in Applied Psychology and Human Problems, 1970; Environmental Psychology, 1972; producer film: Individualized Instruction Through Contingency Management, 1972. Contbr. articles to psychol. jours. Home: 330 Bradley Ln Youngstown OH 44504 Office: 1350 Fifth Ave Youngstown OH 44504

TOEPFER, LOUIS ADELBERT, univ. pres.; b. Sheboygan, Wis., Aug. 31, 1919; s. Albert and Laura (Reed) T.; B.A., Beloit Coll., 1940; LL.B., Harvard, 1947; m. Alice Mary Willy, Aug. 7, 1942; children—Thomas Michael, Anthony, Daniel, Andrew, John. Asst. dean Law Sch. Harvard, 1947-56, soc., 1956-59, vice dean, 1959-66, dir. admissions, 1947-66, mem. faculty, 1959-66, dean, prof. law Case Western Res. U., Cleve., 1966—, pres., 1971—. Mem. Ct. Nisi Prius. Served with USNR, 1942-46. Mem. Ohio, Cleve. bar assns., Phi Beta Kappa. Home: Route 3 Chagrin Falls OH 44022 Office: Pres' Office Case Western Reserve U Cleveland OH 44106

TOGUCHI, FRED SHINICHI, architect; b. Stockton, Calif., Sept. 6, 1922; s. Shinpon and Yoshi (Maeshiro) T.; A.A., U. Calif., Berkeley, 1942; B.Arch., Washington U., St. Louis, 1945; m. Betty Tsuneko Hidekawa, Mar. 9, 1945; children—Frederick Scott, Joseph Shinji, David Seiji. With Outcalt Guenther Assos., Architects, Cleve., 1947-52, Levin and Toguchi, Cleve., 1953-55; with Outcalt, Guenther, Rode, Toguchi, Bonebrake, Cleve., 1956-61; prin. Fred Toguchi Assos., Cleve., 1962—. Asst. prof. architecture Western Res. U., 1958-68; cons. in planning Little Italy Redevel. Assn., 1969. Mem. Mayor's Adv. Com., Cleve., 1967—, Fine Arts Adv. Com., Cleve., 1967—; mem. Bd. Zoning Appeals, Cleveland Heights, Ohio, 1968—, chmn., 1976—; mem. Greater Cleve. United Appeal, 1960—. Trustee, chmn., mem. exec. com. Inner City Protestant Parish; trustee Mental Health Rehab. and Research, Inc., Univ. for Young Americans. Recipient Nat. Archtl. Design award HEW, 1969, A.I.A. Design awards, 1969, Design award Progressive Architecture mag., Nat. Design award Plywood Assn., Design awards Architects Soc. Ohio, 1966, 67, 69, 71, 73-77, also Design awards for partition designs Mills Co., Cleve., local design awards and graphic awards for advertisements in nat. publs. Mem. A.I.A. (dir. Cleve. chpt.), Architects Soc. Ohio, Greater Cleve. Growth Assn., Group 66 Cleve. Illustrator book: The Land Speaks (Donald Faulkner), 1965; archtl. works include Mather Coll., 1959, 64, Adelbert Coll., 1963, 68, undergrad. housing Western Res. U., Firelands Campus Phase II Bowling Green State U., Gilmour Acad. master planning, Burke Lakefront Airport, 1959, expansion, 1970, Mayfield Regional Library, 1971; planner-architect for retail center Univ. Circle, Cleve., Arts Center, Ashtabula, Ohio, 1973, State Office Bldg., Cleve., 1974, Kenneth C. Beck Center for Cultural Arts, Lakewood, Ohio, Capital Improvement Program for Cuyahoga County Bd. Mental Retardation. Home: 2416 Demington Dr Cleveland Heights OH 44106 Office: 12000 Shaker Blvd Cleveland OH 44120

TOLER, HAYWARD CURT, psychologist; b. Taft, Calif., May 26, 1944; s. Hayward Curt and Marilyn M. (Jones) T.; B.S., Calif. State U., Humboldt, 1968, M.A., 1969; Ed.D., Ind. U., 1975; m. Susan M. Marqua, Feb. 6, 1974. Psychologist, U.S. Penitentiary, Terre Haute, Ind., 1975—; asst. adj. prof. criminology Ind. State U., 1976—. Mem. Am. Psychol. Assn., Am. Assn. Correctional Psychologists, Am. Personnel and Guidance Assn. Contbr. articles to profl. jours. Research on insomnia and counselor edn. Home: Rural Route 2 Box 18B Spencer IN 47460 Office: U S Penitentiary Terre Haute IN 47801

TOLES, EDWARD BERNARD, judge; b. Columbus, Ga., Sept. 17, 1909; s. Alex and Virginia Frances (Luke) T.; A.B., U. Ill. at Urbana, 1932, postgrad. law, 1932-34; J.D., Loyola U., Chgo., 1936; m. Susan Evelyn Echols, Jan. 24, 1944; 1 son, Edward Bernard. Admitted to Ill. bar, 1936; practiced in Chgo., 1936-69; asst. atty. U.S. Housing Authority, 1939-40; asst. gen. counsel, war corr. Chgo. Defender, ETO, 1943-45; U.S. bankruptcy judge No. Dist. Ill., Chgo., 1969—. Recipient Services as War Corr. award U.S. War Dept., 1947; Barrister of Year award Nat. Bar Assn., 1960, C.F. Stradford award, 1970; Edward H. Wright Meritorious Services to the Bar award Cook County (Ill.) Bar Assn., 1962; Ode to Excellence, Services to Lawyers award Omega Psi Phi, 1963. Mem. Am., Fed., Nat., Chgo. (bd. mgrs. 1969-70), Cook County (pres. 1960-62), 7th Circuit, World Peace Through Law bar assns., Am. Judicature Soc., Nat. Conf. Bankruptcy Judges., Alpha Phi Alpha. Democrat. Conglist. (trustee 1960-63). Author: Chicago Negro Judges, 1959; Negro Federal Judges, 1960; Negro Lawyer in Crisis, 1966; Black Lawyers and Judges in the U.S., 1970. Editor Cook County Bar News, 1961-63. Columnist, Bench and Bar, Nat. Bar Assn. Bull., 1968-75. Home: 4800 Chicago Beach Dr Chicago IL 60615 Office: US Courthouse Chambers 1604 219 S Dearborn St Chicago IL 60604

TOLLAKSEN, ROBERT EARL, mental health cons., psychotherapist; b. Chgo., Jan. 2, 1932; s. Earl and Mary Angeline (Davis) T.; student Am. Conservatory Music, 1949-51; B.S., U.S. Naval Acad., 1955; postgrad. U. Hawaii, 1958-59; M.Div., Lutheran Sch. Theology, 1962; postgrad. U. Chgo., 1962-63; M.A., Roosevelt U., 1966; m. Carol Jean Knapp, Aug. 11, 1962; children—Steven Scott, Jeffrey Mark, Kiri Lynn. Psychologist transitional care program Elgin (Ill.) State Hosp., 1966-67; chief adolescent unit Ridgeway Hosp., Chgo., 1967-68; dir. consultation and edn. services Riverwood Community Mental Health Center, St. Joseph, Mich., 1968—; field work instr. social work Andrews U., Berrien Springs, Mich., 1974—; bd. dirs. Samaritan Counseling Center, Benton Harbor, Mich., 1973—, Berrien County chpt. Mich. Soc. Mental Health, 1970—. Served to lt. (j.g.) USN, 1955-59. Registered psychol. examiner, certified social worker, Mich. Mem. Community Mental Health Assn. Mich. (pres. 1973-75), Am. Group Therapy Assn., Am. Psychol. Assn. (asso.). Home: 2951 W Glenlord Rd Stevensville MI 49127 Office: Riverwood Community Mental Health Center 2611 Morton Ave St Joseph MI 49085

TOLLEFSON, JOHN EDWARD, fertilizer co. exec.; b. Glendive, Mont., Nov. 10, 1922; s. John and Hannah (Peterson) T.; student St. Olaf Coll., 1940-42; m. Mary Louise O'Brien, Apr. 4, 1947; children—John Michael, William Brien, Kevin Thomas, Randi Martha, Elizabeth Irene. Pres. Fieldcrest Fertilizer, Madison, Minn., 1951—, also Campbell, Minn. div., 1960—; pres. Viking Fertilizer, Alexandria, Minn., 1972—; owner Fieldcrest Farms, Madison, 1961—. Chmn., Minn. Agronomy Council, 1968-70. Councilman city of Madison, 1966-70. Served with USAAF, 1942-45. Mem. Am. Legion, C. of C. (pres. 1968), Minn. Plant Food Assn. (dir. 1960—). Home: 118 E 8th St Madison MN 56256 Office: 210 5th Ave S Madison MN 56256

TOLMAN, SUZANNE NELSON, psychologist; b. Omaha, Nov. 8, 1931; d. Raymond LeRoy and Lottie (Kerns) Nelson; B.A. with distinction in Spanish, U. Nebr., Omaha, 1951; M.A., U. Nebr., Lincoln, 1952, Ph.D., 1957; m. Dan Edward Tolman, June 8, 1957; 1 dau., Kimberly Suzanne. Research asst. U. Nebr., Lincoln, 1951-52; tchr. Omaha Pub. Schs., 1952-53, counselor, high sch. instr. history and English, 1953-59; instr. psychology U. Nebr., Omaha, 1957-59; social service worker Mayo Clinic, Rochester, Minn., 1959-60; instr. psychology U. Tampa, 1962-63; sch. psychologist Sch. Dist. 535, Rochester, 1966—. Bd. dirs. Jefferson PTA, Rochester, 1966-68; bd. dirs., sec. Family Consultation Center, Rochester, 1970-76; bd. dirs. Olmsted County (Minn.) Council Coordinated Child Care, 1971-75, pres., 1973-75; bd. dirs. Olmsted County Assn. Mental Health; pres. condr.'s com. Rochester Symphony, 1977-78. Mem. Minn., Rochester edn. assns., Minn. Sch. Psychologists, Am. Psychol. Assn., AAUW, Zumbro Valley Dental Aux. (pres. 1970-71), Phi Delta Kappa, Alpha Lambda Delta, Alpha Delta Kappa, Psi Chi, Chi Omega. Presbyterian. Club: Order Eastern Star. Home: 2709 Merrihills Dr Rochester MN 55901 Office: Ind Sch Dist 535 Rochester MN 55901

TOMAN, ANDREW JOHN, physician; b. Chgo., Feb. 21, 1905; s. John and Bertha (Sefcik) T.; student U. Chgo., 1923; B.S., U. Ill., 1927, M.D., 1929; m. Emily M. Serhant, June 3, 1939; 1 son, John II. Intern Cook County Hosp., Chgo., 1930-31, resident, 1931-32; med. supr. House of Correction, Chgo., 1932-52; instr. med. and surg. nursing St. Anthony de Padua Hosp. Sch. of Nursing, Chgo., 1936; mem. staff Hosp. St. Anthony de Padua, 1932—, McNeal Meml. Hosp., Berwyn, Ill., Oak Park (Ill.) Hosp.; med. dir. Armour & Co., Chgo., 1953-57; pub. health dir. City of Berwyn (Ill.) Health Dept., 1957-60; Coroner Cook County (Ill.), 1960-76. Served to comdr. M.C., USNR, 1942-46. Mem. A.M.A., Ill. State, Chgo. (com. emergency med. service) med. socs., Cook County Traffic Safety Commn., Chgo. Civil Def. Corps, Am. Cancer Soc., Inst. Medicine Chgo., Spl. Agts. Assn., Ill. Police Assn., Nat. Assn. Coroners, Ill. State Coroners Assn., Am. Acad. Forensic Scis., Nat. Assn. County Ofcls., Chgo. Soc. Med. Jurisprudence, Am. Legion, V.F.W., Am., Ill., Middle West pub. health assns., Pitts. Inst. Legal Medicine, A.C.S. (com. on trauma), Cook County Hosp. Internes Assn., Art Inst. Chgo. (life), Phi Beta Pi. Elk, Moose, Lion, Mason (Shriner). Club: Bohemia. Home: 287 Southcote Rd Riverside IL 60546

TOMARAS, PETER THEOPHANIS, motel-restaurant exec.; b. Champaign, Ill., Sept. 10, 1934; s. Peter F. and Julia Ellen (Creighton) T.; diploma cum laude Shattuck Sch., 1951; B.A. in Econs., U. Ill., 1956; m. Katherine Ralli, Sept. 4, 1955; children—Peter Anthony, Natalie Marie. Propr. Paradise Inn Motel and Restaurant, Champaign, 1956-61, mgr., 1961-67, gen. mgr., 1967—. Treas., V Pende Corp., Champaign, 1966—, Redbloom Corp., Bloomington, Ill., 1971—, Josi Norm Corp., Normal, Ill., 1975—; pres. R & T Ltd., DeKalb, Ill., 1976—, Restaurant Concepts, Inc., Champaign. Mem. tourism adv. com. state Ill., 1965-67. Served with AUS, 1957. Mem. Ill. (dir.), Champaign-Urbana (founder, 1st pres.) hotel and motel assns., Champaign-Urbana-Danville Restaurant Assn. (founder), Ill. Innkeepers Assn. (pres. 1964), Chgo. and Ill. Restaurant Assn. (pres. 1974). Rotarian (pres. 1974-75). Contbr. articles to Am. Rifleman, Rotarian, Cirascope mags., newspapers. Address: 5 Eton Ct Champaign IL 61820

TOME, PHILIP LEWIS, furniture co. exec.; b. Warren, Pa., May 17, 1937; s. Philip E. and Edna E. (Learn) T.; student Pa. State U., 1955-57; m. Barbara Ann Heinz, Nov. 22, 1958; children—Julie, Kathy, Philip, Michael, Nancy. With Taylor Woodcraft, Inc., Malta, Ohio, 1968—, products mgr., 1968, mfg. mgr., 1968-71, v.p. mfg., 1971—; dir. Brodhead-Garrett Co. Exec. com. Morgan County Health Planning Council, 1972—; trustee S.E. Ohio Health Planning Assn., 1973—; bd. dirs. Buckeye Hills-Hocking Valley Regional Devel. Dist., 1977—; bd. dirs. Muskingum Comprehensive Mental Health Center, 1974—; asso. trustee Bethesda Hosp. Home: 661 N Big Oak RD 3 Malta OH 43758 Office: Box 245 Malta OH 43758

TOMKINS, FRANK SARGENT, physicist; b. Petoskey, Mich., June 24, 1915; s. Charles Frederick and Irene Eugenie (Gouin) T.; B.S., Kalamazoo Coll., 1937; Ph.D. (Parke-Davis fellow), Mich. State U., 1941; m. Mary Ann Lynch, Jan. 6, 1964; 1 son, Frank Sargent. Physicist, Buick Aviation Engine Div., Melrose Park, Ill., 1941-42; scientist Manhattan Project U. Chgo., 1943-45; sr. scientist Argonne (Ill.) Nat. Lab., 1945—, group leader, 1944—; cons. Bendix Corp., Cin., 1963-69. John Simon Guggenheim fellow Laboratoire Aime-Cotton, Bellevue, France, 1960-61; Sci. Research Council fellow Imperial Coll., London, 1975; recipient Argonne Universities Assn. Distinguished Appointment, 1975-76. Fellow Optical Soc. Am. (William F. Meggers award 1977); mem. Am. Phys. Soc., Societe Francaise de Physique, AAAS, Sigma Xi, Research Soc. Am. Contbr. articles to sci. jours. Home: 11714 S 83rd Ave Palos Park IL 60464 Office: 9700 S Cass Ave Argonne IL 60439

TOMKO, MICHAEL ANTHONY, rehab. counselor; b. Finleyville, Pa., Nov. 26, 1935; s. William and Carolin (Kuna) T.; B.A., Westminster Coll., 1957; M.Ed., U. Pitts., 1969; Ed.D., U. Cin., 1973; m. Teresa A. Caserta, Apr. 26, 1961; children—Gina Marie, Michele Ann. Asst. dir. Vocat. and Ednl. Services, Harmarville Rehab. Center, Pitts., 1964-69; asst. prof. U. Cin. Coll. Medicine, 1969-73; pvt. practice rehab. counselling, Cin., 1973—. Served with AUS, 1958-60. Mem. Ohio (dir. 1972-74), South Western Ohio (pres. 1973) rehab. assns., Ohio Rehab. Counseling Assn. (pres. 1975—). Mason. Author: An Analysis of Personality Profiles Obtained in the MMPI by Deaf and Hard of Hearing Adolescents, 1973; Sexual Problems of Patients with Spinal Injuries: An Annotated Bibliography, 1973. Contbr. articles to profl. jours. Home: 7953 Heatherglen St Cincinnati OH 45230 Office: 401 Provident Bank Bldg 632 Vine St Cincinnati OH 45202

TOMPKINS, ARTHUR WILSON, JR., ins. co. exec.; b. Huron, S.D., Oct. 4, 1925; s. Arthur Wilson and Dortha (Christopher) T.; M.B.A., U. Pa., 1949; B.S., U. Ill., 1948; m. Connie Thomassen, June 19, 1948; children—Chris, David, Connie, Bruce, Winifred. Agt., State Farm Ins. Co. Cal., 1949-50, asso. dist. agt., Calif., 1951-52, agy. supr., Richmond, Va., 1952-53, asst. state dir., 1953-54, regional dir., Bloomington, Ill., 1955, regional agy. v.p., 1955-66, agy. v.p., 1966-72, regional v.p. Ill., 1972—. Served with USAAF, 1944-45. C.L.U. Mem. Life Ins. Agy. Mgmt. Assn., Sigma Alpha Epsilon. Mason (Shriner). Home: 1320 E Washington St Bloomington IL 61701 Office: 2309 E Oakland Ave Bloomington IL 61701

TOMPKINS, CARL OSCAR, physician; b. Byers, Kans., Feb. 20, 1922; s. Elmer Lee and Jetta (Alton) T.; B.A., Friends U., 1948; M.D., U. Kans., 1951; m. Violet Van Brocklin, June 14, 1942; children—Gregory Giles, Carolyn Marie, Christa Ellene. Intern Wesley Hosp., Wichita, Kans., 1951-52; practice gen. medicine Hillsboro, Kans., 1952-53, Newton, Kans., 1953—; mem. med. staff Bethel Hosp., Newton, pres., 1958; staff mem. Coroner, Harvey County, Kans., 1958—; county health officer, 1963-75. Vice chmn. South Central Kans. Comprehensive Health Planning Council, 1969-72, chmn., 1972-75. Served with USCGR, 1942-45. Mem. A.M.A., Harvey County, Kans. med. socs., Am. Acad. Family Practice, Nat. Assn. Coroners, Am. (state del. to nat. governing council), Kans. (chmn. health officers sect. 1965—, pres. 1968—) pub. health assns., Kansas Obstet. Soc. Methodist. (chmn. commn. Christian social concerns). Home: 5 Rollin Hills Co Newton KS 67114 Office: 316 Oak St Newton KS 67114

TONEY, DORIS CARPENTER, sch. counselor; b. Columbia, S.C., Mar. 29; d. George Freeman and Agnes Elizabeth (Counts) Carpenter; B.S., S.C. State Coll., 1959; M.A., Governors State U., 1972; m Louis Toney, Oct. 28; children—Valerie Patricie, Stephanie Elizabeth. Tchr. pub. schs., Florence County, S.C., 1959-60, Spartanburg, S.C., 1960-62, Lexington, S.C., 1962-63, Gadsden, S.C., 1963-65, Posen, Ill., 1966-68; tchr. Harvey (Ill.) Sch. Dist. 147, 1968-71, elementary sch. counselor, 1972—; organizer parent discussion groups; condr. career workshops. Mem. Nat., Ill. edn. assns., Am., Ill. personnel and guidance assns., Am. Sch. Counselors Assn., Minister's Wives Alliance. Mem. A.M.E. Ch. Home: Markham IL 60426

TONEY, MYRNA MAE, educator; b. Richland, Center, Wis., Oct. 22, 1937; d. Henry and Margaret (Jewell) T.; B.S., Wis. State U., Platteville, 1963, M.S., 1967; Oh.D. (Delta Kappa Gamma scholar), U. Wis., Madison, 1971. Tchr. Oak Ridge Rural Sch., Muscoda, Wis., 1957-61, Jefferson Elementary Sch., Richland Center, Wis., 1961-63, 68-70, Wilson Sch., Beaver Dam, Wis., 1963-66, Boscobel, Wis., 1966-68; asst. prof. edn. Ill. State U., Normal, 1971-75, clin. prof. Tchr. Edn. Center, Peoria, 1971-74; dir. McLean County Tchr. Edn. Center, Bloomington, Ill., 1974-76; specialist dept. ednl adminstrn. U. Wis., Madison, summer 1974, asso. prof., 1976-77; spl. asst. to state supt. and liaison to non-pub. schs. Office of State Supt., Wis. Dept. Pub. Instrn., Madison, 1977—. Mem. AAUW, Delta Kappa Gamma, Kappa Delta Pi. Author: (with M.M. Toney and L.E. Deiterle) Working with the Prospective Teacher, 1976; Planning, Conducting and Evaluating Conferences, 1976. Contbr. articles to profl. jours. Home: 905 S Whitney Way Apt 6 Madison WI 53702 Office: Office of State Supt Wis Dept Pub Instrn Madison WI 53702

TOOL, RICHARD HENDRICKS, accountant; b. nr. Newton, Iowa, Aug. 16, 1938; s. Floyd Earl and Bernice Viola (Hendricks) T.; B.S. in Bus. Adminstrn., Drake U., 1960; M.B.A., Roosevelt U., 1975; m. Margaret Jean Miller, Oct. 9, 1965; children—Tracy, Debra. Sr. auditor Lybrand, Ross Bros. & Montgomery, C.P.A.'s, Chgo., 1960-64; staff accountant Abbott Labs., North Chicago, Ill., 1964-67, mgr. corp. gen. accounting, 1967-69, div. controller, 1969-70, asst. to corp. controller, 1970-74; mgr. corp. project and property accounting Daubert Chem. Co., Oak Brook, Ill., 1973-74, accounting mgr., 1974—. Gov. mem. Lake County Family YMCA. C.P.A., Ill. Mem. Am. Inst. C.P.A.'s, Nat. Assn. Accountants (dir. 1974—), Beta Gamma Sigma. Lutheran (mem. ch. council, chmn. long-range planning task force). Home: 225 E Ellis Libertyville IL 60048 Office: 1200 Jorie Blvd Oak Brook IL 60521

TOPOUZIAN, LEVON KRIKOR, physician; b. Alexandria, Egypt, June 29, 1926; s. Krikor and Brigitte (Croubalian) T.; student Victoria Coll., 1938-45; B.S., U. Paris, 1947, M.D. with honors, 1955; m. Nancy Goodchild, Sept. 22, 1958; 1 son, Krikor Levon. Came to U.S., 1956, naturalized, 1962. Intern gen. surgery, Paris, 1953-54, Chgo. Wesley Meml. Hosp., 1956-57; resident Northwestern U., Cook County Hosp. orthopaedic surgery training program, 1957-61; fellow orthopaedics Boston City Hosp.; practice medicine specializing in orthopaedic surgery, Chgo., 1961—; mem. Strauss Surg. Group Assn.; mem. staff Louis A. Weiss Mem. Hosp., chmn. dept. orthopaedic surgery, 1970—, also dir. orthopaedic residency tng. program; staff orthopaedic dept. Cook County Hosp., chief of service children's orthopaedics, 1966—; asst. prof. dept. orthopaedic surgery Northwestern U., 1970—; mem. med. disciplinary bd. State of Ill., 1976—. Diplomate Am. Bd. Orthopaedic Surgeons. Fellow A.C.S.; mem. AMA, Ill., Chgo. med. socs., Am. Acad. Orthopaedic Surgeons, Am. Rheumatism Assn., Internat. Coll. Surgeons, Société Internationale de Chirurgie Orthopédique et de Traumatologie. Contbr. articles to profl. jours. Office: 4640 Marine Dr Chicago IL 60640

TOPPER, TIMOTHY HAMILTON, educator; b. Kleinburg, Ont., Can., May 20, 1936; s. Garnet Stanley and Ida (Hamilton) T.; B.A., U. Toronto, 1959; Ph.D., U. Cambridge (Eng.), 1962; m. Joyce Alice Kobil, Sept. 6, 1958; children—Timothy, Anne, Jane. With dept. civil engring. U. Waterloo, Ont., 1962—, prof., 1969—, chmn. dept., 1972—; vis. prof., dept. theoretical and applied mechanics U. Ill., Urbana, 1966, 68. Pres., Tijan Devel. Ltd., Kitchener, Ont., 1969—, T.H. Topper Ltd., Kitchener, 1971-76; dir. Domtera, Kitchener. Mem. Am. Soc. Metals, Am. Soc. Testing Materials, Soc. Automotive Engrs., Profl. Engrs. Ont. Home: 65 Westmount Rd N Apt 602 Waterloo ON Canada Office: Dept Civil Engring U Waterloo Waterloo ON Canada

TORLINE, (MARTIN) EUGENE, oil, restaurant, real estate co. exec.; b. Wichita, Kans., July 20, 1926; s. John Albert and Beatrice Imogene (Root) T.; B.A., Wichita State U., 1950; m. Cecilia Ann Sturn, July 6, 1963; children—John Eugene, Elizabeth Marie, Joan Catherine, James Martin. Cons. geologist, partner Morgan & Torline, Wichita, 1951-68; v.p. Acme Oil Corp., Wichita, 1953-68, pres., 1968—; pres. Casey Jones Junction Restaurants, Wichita, 1968—; pres., chmn. bd. Variant Corp., Wichita, 1969—. Asso. bd. dirs. Kans. Newman Coll., Wichita, 1974—; mem. sch. bd. St. Patricks Sch., Wichita, 1977—. Served with USMCR, 1944-46. Mem. Kans. Geol. Soc. (editor bull. 1952-68), Am. Assn. Petroleum Geologists. Clubs: K.C., Breakfast Optimists (pres. Wichita 1958), Toastmasters Internat. (gov. dist. 22 1965), Midway Cosmopolitan. Democrat. Roman Catholic. Contbr. articles to trade mags. Home: 1801 Heiserman St Wichita KS 67203 Office: 6235 W Kellog St Wichita KS 67209

TORNOW, WALTER WILLIAM, computer corp. exec.; b. West Berlin, Aug. 23, 1942; s. Fritz and Erna (Schwersenz) T.; came to U.S., 1958, naturalized, 1963; B.A. with honors, U. Minn., 1965, M.A., 1968, Ph.D. (Univ. fellow), 1970; m. Ellen Louise Zamansky, Aug. 2, 1964; children—Jason Scott, Jeffry Allen. Dir. corp. personnel research Control Data Corp., Mpls., 1970—. Mem. Am. Psychol. Assn. Home: 8209 Northwood Pkwy New Hope MN 55427 Office: 8100 34th Av S Minneapolis MN 55440

TORNQUIST, LEROY JOHN, lawyer, educator; b. Chgo., Apr. 2, 1940; s. William John and Gertrude L. (Johnson) T.; B.S., Northwestern U., 1962, J.D., 1965; m. Janet Mossberg, Aug. 31, 1963; children—William, Lisa, Jon. Admitted to Ill. bar, 1965; with Williams, McCarthy, Kinley and Rudy, Rockford, Ill., 1965-66; atty. King, Robin, Gale and Pillinger, Chgo., 1966—, of counsel, 1971—; faculty bus. law Rockford Coll., 1966-67; asst. prof. law Loyola U. Sch. Law, Chgo., 1971-75, asso. prof., 1975—, also asso. dean Sch. Law; spl. counsel, dir. Urban Ventures, Inc., 1970; govt. appeal agt. SSS, 1968-70. Alderman, City of Park Ridge (Ill.), 1971-74; chmn. procedures and regulations com. Park Ridge City Council, 1971-74, chmn. Park Ridge Zoning Bd. Appeals, 1975—; mem. Cook County Bd. Sch. Trustees. Mem. Am., Ill. State, Chgo. bar assns., Am. Soc. Internat. Law. Author: (booklet) Materials for Trial Advocacy, 1972. Home: 410 S Fairview Park Ridge IL 60068 Office: 135 S LaSalle St Chicago IL 60603

TORRES, JOSE DIMAS, univ. adminstr.; b. Luquillo, P.R., Mar. 25, 1932; s. Antonio and Maria Socorro (Labawld) T.; B.A. cum laude, Inter-Am. U. P.R., 1957; M.P.A. (Commonwealth of P.R. fellow), Syracuse U., 1959; Ph.D., Ohio State U., 1973; m. Patricia Ann Zaccaria, Apr. 18, 1959; children—Peter, Michelle Marie, Mary Elizabeth, Patrick, David, Gwendolyn, Christopher. Mgmt. ofcl. office personnel U.S. Tech. Assistance Program (Point IV Program), Office of Gov., Commonwealth of P.R., 1959-62; teaching asst. Ind. U., South Bend, 1963; NDEA lectr. Knox Coll., summer 1965; instr. Ohio U., Athens, 1965-69; research asso. Mershon Center for Studies

Nat. Security Policies, Ohio State U., 1970-71; dir. dept. gen. studies Hocking Tech. Coll., Nelsonville, O., 1973-75, dir. office instl. research, 1975—. Chmn., Athens County area Youth for Understanding-Internat. Program for Exchange High Sch. Students, 1972—; mem. edn. com. Human Relations Commn. Athens, 1972-73; supr. Spanish House for Women, Ohio U., 1966-68; P.R. rep. Confs. on States Merit System, HEW, Washington, summer 1961; intern pub. affairs Govt. N.J., 1971; mem. Citizens for Better Health Orgn., Athens, 1968-69. Nominated candidate Athens County Central Com., Democratic party, 1974. Served with AUS, 1951-53. Mem. Am. Polit. Sci. Assn., Am. Soc. for Pub. Adminstrn., Latin Am. Studies Assn., Midwest Latin Am. Studies Assn., Am. Acad. Polit. Sci., Ohio Coll. and Univ. Planning Assn., Phi Alpha Theta, Gamma Phi. Roman Catholic. K.C., Lion. Clubs: Athens Tennis; Lancaster (Ohio) Indoor Tennis. Home: 15 Grand Park Blvd Athens OH 45701 Office: Route 1 Nelsonville OH 45764

TORRES, ROGER LUIS, geotech. engr.; b. Cochabamba, Bolivia, Jan. 17, 1935; s. Jose Luis and Marie Irene (Vargas) T.; came to U.S., 1962; naturalized, 1972; Engring. Diploma, U. Oruro, 1960; postgrad. Northwestern U., Ill. Inst. Tech., Colo. State U. Geotech. engr. Harza Engring. Co., Chgo., 1962-74, 75—; Engring. Cons., Inc., Denver, 1974-75. Mem. Prof. Engr. for States of Ill., Colo., ASCE. Roman Catholic. Home: 6042 N Maplewood Dr Chicago IL 60659 Office: 150 S Wacker Dr Chicago IL 60606

TORRINGTON, WILLIAM PAUL, pharm. mfg. cons.; b. N.Y.C., Feb. 29, 1908; s. Paul and Margarit (Weiss) T.; m. Mildred Barth, Dec. 18, 1932; 1 dau., Rosemarie Albers. Engr. Intercontinent Gas Corp., Gas Fuel Corp., 1929-37; chief engr. Process Corp., 1937-42; asst. to pres. Mead Johnson & Co., Evansville, Ind., 1942-48, v.p. mfg., 1948-59, dir., 1957-74, exec. v.p., 1959-73, vice chmn. bd., 1968-73, cons., 1973—. Vice pres., dir. Evansville Vanderburgh County Bldg. Authority, 1961-70. Mem. Ind. Mfrs. Assn. (dir. 1958-64), S.A.R. Clubs: Columbia; Key Biscayne Yacht; Evansville Country. Home: 2317 E Gum St Evansville IN 47714 Office: 2404 Pennsylvania St Evansville IN 47721

TORT, CARLOS LEONARDO, pub. co. exec.; b. N.Y.C., May 22, 1914; s. Ricardo Carlos and Emma Louise (Torgerson) T.; B.S. in Journalism, U. Buenos Aires; m. Maria del Carmen Buscarini, Aug. 4, 1969; stepchildren—Enrique, Jorge, Fernando. Research mgr. J. Walter Thompson Co., Buenos Aires, Argentina, 1940-47; asst. editor Spanish ed. Popular Mechanics Mag., Chgo., 1947-49; owner, mgr. Spanish-Portuguese Transp. Bur., Chgo., 1949-60; owner, mgr. Trans-World Transp., Chgo., 1960—; pres. exec. dir. Carlos Tort Internat., Inc., Chgo., pubs. Industries Lacteas, Panadero Latin Americano and El Hospital trade jours., 1971—. Home: 1304 W Lunt Ave Chicago IL 60626 Office: 4753 N Broadway Chicago IL 60640

TOSCANO, JAMES VINCENT, arts adminstr.; b. Passaic, N.J., Aug. 8, 1937; s. William V. and Mary A. (DeNigris) T.; A.B., Rutgers U., 1959; M.A., Yale, 1960; m. Sharon Lee Bowers; children—Shawn, Lauren, David Brendan. Lectr., Wharton Sch., U. Pa., 1961-64; chief opinion analyst Pa. Opinion Poll, 1962-64; mng. dir. World Press Inst., Macalester Coll., St. Paul, 1964-68, exec. dir., 1968-72, dir. devel., 1972-74, also dir. Internat. Center, 1964-72; v.p. for resource devel. and pub. affairs Mpls. Soc. Fine Arts, 1974—; dir. Southside Newspaper, Mpls. Bd. dirs., exec. com. Minn. Citizens for Arts; chmn. improving student behavior com. St. Paul Pub. Schs.; bd. dirs. Planned Parenthood St. Paul, 1965-72; sec. bd. dirs. World Press Inst., 1972—. Clubs: Univ., Skylight (St. Paul). Author: The Chief Elected Official in the Penjerdel Region, 1964; author, editor: (with Philip Jacob and others) The Integration of Political Communities, 1964. Home: 1982 Summit Ave St Paul MN 55105

TOSHACH, DANIEL WILKIE, architect; b. Saginaw, Mich., June 28, 1928; s. Clarence Eneas and Charlotte Sellers (Hassett) T.; grad. Phillips Exeter Acad., 1946; B.A., Yale U., 1950, B.Arch., M.Arch., 1953; children (by previous marriage)—Charlotte, Mary, Daniel, Pamela, Katrina; m. 2d, Clarice Oversby, July 30, 1965; children—Duncan, Paul Beard. Architect-in-tng. various archtl. offices, Midland and Saginaw, 1953-57; individual practice architecture, Saginaw, 1957-61; prin. Prine Toshach Spears, Architects and Engrs., Inc., Saginaw, 1961-73, Toshach Assos., Architects and Engrs., Inc., Saginaw, 1973-77; pres. Toshach & Sobczak, Asso. Architects, 1977—. Chmn. adv. com. on archtl. tech. Delta Community Coll., 1965—. Bd. fellows Saginaw Valley Coll. Mem. Saginaw County Met. Planning Commn., 1966—, vice chmn., 1971-76, chmn., 1976-77. Mem. AIA (pres. Saginaw Valley chpt. 1961, merit award 1966, 72), Mich. Soc. Architects (dir. 1964-65), Council Ednl. Facilities Planners, Mich. Archtl. Tech. Council, Nat. Council Archtl. Registration Bds. Rotarian. Club: Saginaw (pres. 1976-77). Designer Trinity Luth. Ch., Midland, Mich., Univ. Luth. Ch., East Lansing, Mich., Swan Valley High Sch., Saginaw, Career Opportunities Center, Saginaw, 2d Nat. Bank of Saginaw. Office: 122 N Washington Ave Saginaw MI 48607

TOSI, DONALD JAMES, educator; b. Martins Ferry, Ohio, Oct. 14, 1940; s. Henry Louis and Rose Marie (Purpura) T.; B.S., Steubenville Coll., 1963; M.Ed., Toledo U., 1965; Ph.D., Kent State U., 1968; m. Josephine P. DeBlasis, Apr. 11, 1964; children—Francesca, Nicole, Alicia. Asst. prof. Western Mich. U., 1968-70; asso. prof. Ohio State U., Columbus, 1970-74, prof. counseling, 1974—; asso. clin. instr. psychiatry Riverside Meth. Hosp., Columbus; cons. in field; pvt. practice psychotherapy, Columbus, 1971—. Licensed psychologist, Ohio. Mem. Am. Psychol. Assn., Am. Soc. Clin. Hypnosis, Am. Personnel and Guidance Assn. Author: Youth Toward Personal Growth, 1974. Contbr. numerous articles to profl. jours. Home: 1216 Nantucket St Columbus OH 43220

TOSI, OSCAR I., educator; b. Trento, Italy, June 17, 1929; s. Mario and Ethel (Manescu) T.; came to U.S., 1962, naturalized, 1973; D.Sc. cum laude, Nat. U. Buenos Aires, 1951; Ph.D., Ohio State U., 1965. Asso. prof. physics Nat. U. Buenos Aires, 1952-62; asst. prof. acoustics Mich. State U., East Lansing, 1966-68, asso. prof., 1968-71, prof., 1971—, dir. Speech and Hearing Lab., 1970—, asst. dean (research) Coll. Communication Arts and Scis., 1972-76. Expert witness voice identification in fed., state cts., U.S. and Can.; founder, dir. Internat. Assn. Voice Identification, Inc., Lansing, 1971—; mem. com. on evaluation sound spectrograms Nat. Acad. Scis., 1976—. Recipient Certificate of Appreciation, Mich. State Police, 1971; award Spanish Assn. Phoniatrics and Logopedics, 1973. Mem. Internat. Collegium Phonology, Internat. Assn. Phoniatrics and Logopedics, Acoustical Soc. Am. (staff mem. tech. com. speech communication 1974-77), Am. Speech and Hearing Assn., Am. Assn. Tchrs. Physics, Internat. Assn. Phonetics, Opera Guild Greater Lansing (founder 1973), Italian Am. Club of Lansing. Author: Physics for Medical Students, 1962; Voice Identification, 1971; contbr. chpts. to Theory of Speech Production and Acoustic Phonetics, 1972, The Problem of Voice Identification and Elimination, 1974, Pausometry, 1974. Contbr. articles in field to profl. jours. Research dir. voice identification project U.S. Dept. Justice, 1968-71. Home: 221 Bessemaur East Lansing MI 48823 Office: 247 Auditorium Michigan State Univ East Lansing MI 48824

TOTH, FERENC JOHN, mgmt. cons. co. exec.; b. Nagykanizsa, Hungary, June 9, 1939; s. Ferenc and Stephanie (Lick) T.; came to U.S., 1957, naturalized, 1966; B.S., U. Wis., Stout, 1963; m. Nancy Marie Lang, Apr. 16, 1966; children—Jennifer Nancy, Steven Zoltan, Caroline Margaret. Indsl. engr. Ford Motor Co., Chgo., 1965-66, Remington Arms Co., Park Forest, Ill., 1966-68, S.C. Johnson & Son, Inc., Racine, Wis., 1968-75; sr. indsl. engr. Pullman Standard Co., Hammond, Ind., 1975-77; pres. Indsl. Engring. Mgmt. & Research, Inc., South Holland, Ill., 1977—. Dir. Racine Soap Box Derby, 1972-73. Served with U.S. Army, 1963-65. Mem. Am. Mgmt. Assn., Am. Inst. Indsl. Engrs. Episcopalian. Club: Lions (Munster, Ind.). Home: 7905 Harrison Ave Munster IN 46321 Office: 145 Taft Dr South Holland IL 60473

TOTH, RICHARD MICHAEL, chiropractor; b. St. Louis, Feb. 19, 1950; s. Michail John and Olivia Ray (Jurgens) T.; B.S., in Physiotherapy, Van Norman U., 1971, D. Physiotherapy, 1974; D. Chiropractic, Logan Coll. Chiropractic, 1973. Extern Logan Coll. Chiropractic, St. Louis, 1971-73, sr. extern, 1972, head clin. pathology dept., 1972-73, sr. unit dir., 1973; pvt. practice chiropractic St. Louis, 1973—; sec. Career Guidance Center Inc., St. Louis, 1972—. Active Get Out and Vote Campaign, 1969-70. Diplomate Nat. Bd. Chiropractic Examiners, Nat. Bd. Phys. Therapy Examiners. Fellow Am. Council Applied Clin. Nutrition; mem. Logan Coll. Alumni Assn., Nat. Assn. Phys. Therapists, Am., Mo., St. Louis Met. chiropractic assns., Nat. Health Fed. Mem. Ch. Religious Sci. (Sunday sch. tchr.). Mason (Shriner). Mem. Order of DeMolay. Home: 3809 Keats Dr St Louis MO 63134 Office: 8420 Delmar St St Louis MO 63124

TOTO, PATRICK DANIEL, dentist, educator; b. Niles, Ohio, Jan. 6, 1921; s. Vincent J. and Smeralda E. (Mazza) T.; student Denison U., 1938-40; B.S., Kent State U., 1943; D.D.S., Ohio State U., 1948, M.Sc., 1950; m. Eleanor P. Mitrikeff, Sept. 1, 1945; children—James Robert, Michael George, Robert Daniel. Practice dentistry, specializing in oral pathology, Chgo., 1950-68, Maywood, Ill., 1968—; prof., chmn. oral pathology Loyola U. Sch. Dentistry, Chgo., Ill., 1950—, coordinator research and grad. studies, 1974—. Cons. VA Hosp., Hines, Ill., Indsl. Biotest Lab., Northbrook, Ill., 1971—, Alberto Culver Co., Melrose Park, Ill., 1971—. Served with AUS, 1943-44, USNR, 1944-45. Diplomate Am. Bd. Oral Pathology, Am. Bd. Oral Medicine. Fellow Am., Internat. colls. dentistry; mem. ADA, Internat. Assn. Dental Research, A.A.A.S., Am. Acad. Oral Pathology, Am. Soc. Gerontology, N.Y. Acad. Sci. Contbr. articles to profl. jours. Home: 433 Gillett Ave Waukegan IL 60085 Office: 2160 S First Ave Maywood IL 60153

TOTTEN, PAUL RAYMOND, real estate exec.; b. Greenwood, Ind., Aug. 29, 1924; s. Joseph L. and Flossie Mable (McCormick) T.; grad. high sch.; grad. Ind. Realtors Inst., 1973; m. Carla Jean Porter, Apr. 17, 1953; 1 dau., Deborah Jo. Account exec. Indpls. Times, 1954-63; propr. Blue Ribbon Realty Co., Inc., Greenwood, 1963—. Mem. Greenwood Plan Commn., 1960-73; pres. Greenwood Bd. Zoning Appeals, 1968-73. Bd. dirs. Central 9 Vocat. Bldg. Trades, Inc., Greenwood, 1972-73. Served with AUS, 1943-46. Decorated Bronze Star; named Man of Year, City of Greenwood, 1967; named Real Estate Man of Year, Suburban Multi-List Exchange, 1971; recipient Meritorious Service award City of Greenwood, 1969. Mem. Nat., Ind. (v.p. 7th dist. 1973-77), assns. realtors, Greenwood Jaycees (pres. 1963—), Greenwood C. of C. (pres. 1966). Democrat. Methodist. Home: 767 Brookview Dr Greenwood IN 46142 Office: 1028 US Hwy 31 S Greenwood IN 46142

TOUCHMAN, WILLIAM STANLEY, chem. engr.; b. Troy, Ohio, May 1, 1915; s. Stanley Nelson and Emma Norene (Roeser) T.; B. Chem. Engring., Ohio State U., 1937; m. Nancy Jane Whitehead, June 15, 1941; children—Gregor William, Deborah Isabel Touchman Ford, Victoria Jean. Devel. engr. Surface Combustion Corp., Toledo, 1937-39; pattern maker Troy Pattern Works, 1939-42; project engr. Antioch Foundry Delco Remy div. Gen. Motors Corp., Yellow Springs, Ohio, 1942-45; engr., cons. Kearney & Trecker Corp., Milw., 1946-50; chief engr. Vacumatic Carburetor Co. (now Miles Instrument Co.), Milw., 1950-51; research engr. Morris Bean Co., Yellow Springs, 1951-56; sr. mech. engr. Ohio Labs. United Shoe Machinery Corp., Xenia, 1956-60; mech. design engr., project leader Senior mech. engr., NCR Corp., Dayton, 1960-73; pres. Firm, Inc., Dayton, 1973—. Registerd profl. engr., Wis. Mem. ASME. Patentee plaster mixing machine, gasoline mileage indicator, portable record sensing and recording apparatus and numerous others. Home and office: 5087 Cloudsdale Dr Kettering OH 45440

TOURTELOT, JOSEPH LOWRY, mfrs. rep.; b. Oak Park, Ill., July 14, 1910; s. Elie C. and Katherine M. (Tobin) T.; student U. Ill., 1928-31; m. Irene M. Victor, May 7, 1938; children—Katherine M. (Mrs. William Vincent), Jeanne L. (Mrs. Thomas J. Welsh), Joseph Victor, Mary Anne (Mrs. Roger Dennis Ball), Susan I., Barbara A. With Fred I. Tourtelot Co., River Forest, Ill., 1931—, v.p., 1945-50, pres., 1950—; pres. Oaks Electric Control Co., Chgo., Tourtelot Broadcasting Co., KDES, Palm Springs, Calif.; dir. Oak Park Trust & Savs. Bank. Mem. adv. bd. Catholic Charities Chgo. Bd. dirs. Oak Park Hosp. Trustee Oak Park Hosp. Mem. Theta Delta Chi. Clubs: Oak Park Country; Chicago Athletic Assn.; Butler Nat. Golf; La Quinta Country. Home: 907 Lathrop Ave River Forest IL 60305 Office: 7716 Madison St River Forest IL 60305

TOUTANT, WILLIAM JOSEPH, assn. exec.; b. Detroit, Dec. 10, 1946; s. Hubert Carl and Lillian Marie (Macaluso) T.; A.A., Macomb County Community Coll., 1967; B.A., Central Mich. U., 1969; M.A., Ball State U., 1973; postgrad. U. Mich., 1976—; m. Dawn Caroline Clements, June 16, 1973; 1 son, Mark William. Tchr., Buckley (Mich.) Community Schs., 1969-70; youth program coordinator United Cerebral Palsy Assn., Detroit, 1974-77, social devel. program coordinator, 1977—. Served with USAF, 1970-74. Mem. Am. Personnel and Guidance Assn., Nat. Assn. Social Workers, Mich. Assn. Profl. Psychologists. Home: 30217 Utica Rd Roseville MI 48066 Office: 15 E Kirby St Detroit MI 48202

TOWERS, MICHAEL DOUGLAS, coll. adminstr.; b. Enterprise, Oreg., Aug. 8, 1944; s. Kenneth Ebert and Shandon Aileen (Gettings) T.; B.S., Eastern Oreg. Coll., 1966; M.A., Wichita State U., 1968; postgrad. U. Nebr., 1972-75; m. Emily Ann Lucas, Aug. 21, 1966; children—Shahn Lucas, Allison Aileen. Instr. history Westmar Coll., 1968-72; asst. prof. history, 1972-75, dir. devel., 1975—. Mem. Plymouth County Civil Service Commn., 1973-74. Mem. Council for Advancement and Support of Edn., Am. Hist. Assn., Blue Key, Phi Alpha Theta, Theta Delta Phi. Democrat. Presbyterian. Clubs: Sertoma Internat., Elks. Home: 317 Central Ave SW LeMars IA 51031 Office: Westmar Coll LeMars IA 51031

TOWLE, KELSO CHURCHILL, newspaper exec.; b. Haverhill, Mass., Nov. 18, 1928; s. W. Wilder and Georgiana (Schaub) T.; student Rochester Inst. Tech., 1950-51; A.B., Washington U., St. Louis, 1952; m. M. Jane Dodge, Apr. 21, 1956; children—Jeffrey K., Courtney E. Office clk. So. Illinoisan, Herrin, 1952-53, office mgr., Carbondale, 1953-55, bus. mgr., 1955-57; dir. office ops. Lindsay-Schaub Newspapers, Inc., Decatur, 1957-58; bus. office mgr. Herald & Rev., Decatur, 1958-64, gen. mgr., 1964-76, pres., dir., 1971—, pub., 1976—; dir. Lindsay-Schaub Newspapers, Inc. Mem. adv. bd. Salvation Army, 1965—, chmn., 1967-68; bd. dirs. United Way, 1972-75; bd. dirs. Decatur chpt. ARC, 1972—, sec., 1977—. Mem. Decatur C. of C. (dir. 1962-65, v.p. 1966-67, pres. 1967-68), Ill. State Hist. Soc., Ill. Mus. Soc., Nat. Audubon Soc. Congregationalist. Clubs: Masons, Rotary (2d v.p. 1977). Home: 203 Silver Dr Decatur IL 62521 Office: PO Box 311 601 E William St Decatur IL 62525

TOWNER, JOHN HARDING, realtor; b. Bangor, Maine, July 15, 1922; s. Wayland Dean and Betty (Mills) T.; B.S., Mich. State U., 1948; M.S., U. Ill., 1951; m. Judith E. Dellorto Dec. 16, 1976; children—Alan Edward, Robert Lee, Patricia Ann. Sales dir. Am. Comml. Builders, Park Forest, Ill., 1951-57; owner Town & Country Realty, Inc., Richton Park, Ill., 1957-61; chmn. bd., dir. Thorn Creek Realty, Inc., Chicago Heights, Ill., 1961-75; exec. v.p. Continental Real Estate Inc., Elmhurst, Ill., 1971-74. Instr. real estate Prairie State Coll., Chicago Heights, 1965—. Mem. sch. bd. dist. 163, Park Forest, 1952-58. Bd. dirs. Harvey (Ill.) Meml. YMCA, 1965-70. Served with USAAF, 1942-45. Mem. Ill. Assn. Real Estate Bds. (dist. v.p. 1969-70, dir. 1977—, Service medallion 1968), S. Suburban Bd. Realtors (Realtor of Year 1968, pres. 1967-68, 75), Ill. Realtors Inst. (bd. govs.), Phi Delta Kappa, Sigma Chi. Moose. Club: Lakes of Four Seasons Country (past pres., bd. dirs., Crown Point, Ind.). Home: 428 Springfield St Park Forest IL 60466 Office: 276 W 14th St Chicago Heights IL 60411

TOWNER, LAWRENCE WILLIAM, historian, librarian; b. St. Paul, Sept. 10, 1921; s. Earl Chadwick and Cornelia (Mallum) T.; B.A., Cornell Coll., Mt. Vernon, Iowa, 1942, L.H.D., 1965; M.A., Northwestern U., 1949, Ph.D. (Hearst Found. fellow), 1955, L.H.D., 1965; LL.D., Lake Forest Coll., 1965; m. Rachel Eleanor Bauman, Nov. 28, 1943; children—Wendy Kay Towner Yanikovski, Kristin Anne Towner Moses, Lawrence Baumann, Elizabeth Gail, Peter Mallum, Michael Chadwick. History master Chgo. Latin Sch., 1946-47; instr., asst. prof. history Mass. Inst. Tech., Camridge, 1950-55; asso. prof. history Coll. William and Mary, Williamsburg, Va., 1955-62; librarian and dir. Newberry Library, Chgo., 1962—, pres., 1975—. Vis. prof. Northwestern U., summer 1957, 68—; dir. Inst. for Hist. and Archival Mgmt., Radcliffe Coll., Harvard U., 1959; Center for Study History of Liberty In Am. fellow Harvard U. 1961-62. Chmn. Williamsburg Area Interracial Study Group, 1960-61; mem. Ill. Humanities Council, 1974—, chmn., 1976-78; mem. adv. bd. Who's Who in Am.; trustee Grinnell (Iowa) Coll., 1966-72, Chgo. Latin Sch., 1970-72, Mus. Contemporary Art, 1972-75; mem. council Eleutherian Mills-Hagley Found., 1976—, Fedn. Pub. Programs in Humanities, 1977—. Served to 1st lt., pilot AUS, 1943-46. Mem. Am. Hist. Assn. (mem. council 1973-75), Orgn. Am. Historians, Am. Antiquarian Soc., Colonial Soc. Mass., Mass. Hist. Soc., Bibliog. Soc. Am., Modern Poetry Assn. (trustee, pres.). Clubs: Grolier; Cosmos, Caxton, Econ., Tavern, Arts. Author: An Uncommon Collection of Uncommon Collections: The Newberry Library, 1970, 76; (with A.N.L. Munby) The Flow of Books and Manuscripts, 1969. Editor: William and Mary Quar.: A Mag. of Early Am. History, 1955-62, A Summary View of the Rights of British America by Thomas Jefferson, 1976; bd. editors Jour. Am. History, 1965-68, America, History and Life, 1965—. Home: 65 E Bellevue Pl Chicago IL 60611 Office: 60 W Walton St Chicago IL 60610

TOWNLEY, ARTHUR JAMES, dentist; b. Jackson, Mich., May 25, 1926; s. Arthur James and Metha (Pelham) T. Asso. Sci., Jackson Jr. Coll., 1948; B.S., U. Detroit, 1950, D.D.S., 1957; m. Rita Louise Howard, Sept. 19, 1964; children—Daniel, Susan, Arthur James, Jane. Practice gen. dentistry Mich. Center, Mich., 1957—. Lectr. Am. art pottery. Served with USAF, 1943-45. Mem. Am. Dental Assn., Mich. State Dental Soc. Lutheran. Rotarian. Club: University of Detroit Century (charter mem.). Home: 10696 Hewett Brooklyn MI 49230 Office: 4515 Page Ave Michigan Center MI 49254

TOWNLEY, CHARLES ORLEFF, physician; b. Mpls., Dec. 30, 1916; s. Claude J. and Lottie (Chase) T.; B.S., Capital U., Columbus, Ohio, 1941; M.D., Ohio State U., 1944; m. Naomi Welsh, Feb. 22, 1941 (div. 1963); children—Jeffrey, Mark, Susan, Jon, Jill, Kim, Julie. Intern, Henry Ford Hosp., 1944-45, resident, 1945-46, 48-50; practice medicine, specializing in orthopedic surgery, Port Huron, Mich., 1950—. Served with AUS, 1946-48. Diplomate Am. Bd. Orthopedic Surgery. Mem. AMA, Mich., St. Clair County (pres. 1958) med. socs., A.C.S., Am. Acad. Orthopedic Surgery, Internat. Coll. Surgeons, Latin Am. Orthopedic Soc., Clin. Orthopedic Soc., Assn. Bone and Joint Surgery. Inventions, research, publs. and lectures in orthopedic field. Home: 3204 Shoreview Dr Port Huron MI 48060 Office: 1037 Water St Port Huron MI 48060

TOWNLEY, NORMAND THOMAS, physician; b. Ashley, Ohio, May 26, 1933; s. Cecil Marquis and Violet Rosella (Bishop) T.; B.S., Capital U., 1955; M.D., Ohio State U., 1959; m. Magdalene Marie Schulze, July 9, 1955; children—Steven, Rhea, Lisa, Amy, Ann. Intern Toledo Hosp., 1959-60; resident in anesthesiology Ind. U. Med. Center, Indpls., 1960-62; clin. asso. NIH, Bethesda, Md., 1962-64; practice medicine specializing in anesthesiology, Kokomo, Ind., 1964-66, Indpls., 1966—; instr. Ind. U. Med. Sch., Indpls., 1965—; pres. med. staff Winona Meml. Hosp., Indpls., 1966—, chief staff, 1970-72. Spl. cons. to med. safety cons., 1970—. Served with USPHS, 1962-64. Diplomate Am. Bd. Anesthesiology. Fellow Am. Coll. Anesthesiologists; mem. A.M.A., Ind., Marion County med. socs., Ind. Soc. Anesthesiologists (pres. elect 1973), Alpha Omega Alpha. Contbr. articles profl. jours. Research in influence of halothane on digitalis induced toxicity, influence of halothane on renal function. Home: 6211 Harbridge Rd Indianapolis IN 46220 Office: 3266 N Meridian St Indianapolis IN 46208

TOWNSEND, ALDEN MILLER, geneticist; b. Tulsa, Mar. 4, 1942; s. Albert McMillan and Mary Margaret (Miller) T.; B.S., Pa. State U., 1964; M.Forestry, Yale, 1966; Ph.D., Mich. State U., 1969; m. Ruth Anne Bushfield, June 8, 1968; children—Jeffrey Bushfield, David Alden. Forester U.S. Forest Service, Estacada, Ore., 1964-66; grad. asst. Mich. State U., E. Lansing, 1966-69; research geneticist Nursery Crops Research Lab., U.S. Dept. Agr., Agrl. Research Service, Delaware, Ohio, 1970—. Scoutmaster Boy Scouts Am., Delaware, 1970-73, com. mem., merit badge counselor, 1973—. Served with AUS, 1965. Yale U. grad. scholar, 1965-66. Mem. Am. Genetic Assn., Internat. Soc. Arboriculture, Metropolitan Tree Improvement Alliance, Central States Tree Improvement Conf., Xi Sigma Pi, Gamma Sigma Delta. Clubs: Optimists, Toastmasters. Contbr. articles to profl. jours. Home: 245 Grandview Av Delaware OH 43015 Office: Nursery Crops Research Lab PO Box 365 Delaware OH 43015

TOWNSEND, CARL GODFREY, mathematician, educator; b. Camp Crook, S.D., Oct. 4, 1935; s. Earl Johnson and Mescal Eunice (Burch) T.; B.S. summa cum laude, Rocky Mountain Coll., Billings, Mont., 1959; M.A., Wash. State U., Pullman, 1961, Ph.D., 1965; m. Marie Ester Ryan, Apr. 2, 1956. Draftsman, Asso. Engrs., Billings, Mont., 1957-59; instr. math. Wash. State U., Pullman, 1962-65; asso. prof. math. So. Ill. U., Carbondale, 1965—; vis. prof. math. Rajshahi U., Bangladesh, 1970-71, Rangoon (Burma) Arts and Sci. U., 1971-73, Taiwan (Taipei) Nat. Normal U., 1972. Served with U.S. Army, 1953-55. NDEA fellow, 1959-62; Fulbright prof., 1970-71; U.S. Dept. State grantee, 1971-73. Mem. Am. Math. Assn., AAUP, Sigma Xi, Pi

Mu Epsilon. Home: Rural Route 1 PO Box 225 Makanda IL 62958 Office: Dept Math So Ill U Carbondale IL 62958

TOWNSEND, EARL CUNNINGHAM, JR., lawyer, author; b. Indpls., Nov. 9, 1914; s. Earl Cunningham and Besse (Kuhn) T.; student DePauw U., 1932-34; A.B., U. Mich., 1936, J.D., 1939; m. Emily Macnab, Apr. 3, 1947; children—Starr (Mrs. John R. Laughlin), Vicki, Julia, Earl Cunningham III, Clyde. Admitted to Ind. bar, 1939, Mich. bar, U.S. Supreme Ct. bar, Bar of 4th, 5th, 7th, 9th U.S. Circuits; sr. partner firm Townsend & Townsend, 1939-69, Townsend Hovde and Townsend, Indpls., 1969—; v.p., founder, treas. Am. Underwriters, Inc., Am. Interins. Exchange, 1965-70; also practice in Roscommon, Mich.; mem. Ind. Supreme Ct. Com. Indiana Pattern Jury Instructions, 1975—. dep. prosecutor Marion County, Ind., 1942-44; radio-TV announcer Stas. WIRE, WFBM, WFBM-TV, 1940-50; owner Tropical Isle Palm Tree Farms, Key Biscayne, Fla. Seminar lectr. in trial practice U. Mich., Notre Dame U., Ind. U. Founder, life trustee Roscoe Pound Am. Trial Lawyers Found., Cambridge, Mass. Basketball ofcl., Big Ten Conf., 1941-48. Life trustee Indpls. Mus. Art, mem. finance, endowment and bldg. coms.; bd. dirs. Ind. State Mus., Higgins Lake Property Owners Assn., 1971—; trustee Cathedral High Sch.; co-founder Meridian St. Found. Recipient Ind. U. Writers Conf. award, 1960; named Sagamore of Wabash; hon. chief Saginaw-Chippewa Tribe. Fellow Meth. Hosp. Assn. Fellow Ind. Coll. Trial Lawyers, Internat. Acad. Trial Lawyers, Internat. Soc. Barristers; mem. Ind. Trial Lawyers Assn. (pres. 1963-64), Am., Ind. State, Indpls. bar assns., Am. Trial Lawyers assn. (v.p. Ind. 1959-60, bd. govs. 7th judicial circuit 1966-68), Bar Assn. 7th Fed. Circuit, Trowel and Brush Soc. (hon.), U. Mich. Pres.'s Club, U. Mich. Victors Club (charter), Key Biscayne C. of C., Delta Kappa Epsilon, Phi Kappa Phi. Methodist. Mason (32 deg.). Clubs: The Players; Univ. of Mich. (local pres. 1950); Columbia; Key Bicayne Yacht. Author: Birdstones of the North American Indian, 1959; contbr. articles to legal jours. Home: 5008 N Meridian St Indianapolis IN 46208 Office: 150 E Market St Indianapolis IN 46204

TOWNSEND, EDWIN BYRON, III, accountant; b. Parkersburg, W.Va., Dec. 4, 1941; s. Edwin Byron, Jr. and Zora Hazel (Williamson) T.; B.S. in Bus. Adminstrn., W.Va. U., 1963; m. Janet Elizabeth Sidell, Sept. 1, 1962; children—Edwin Byron IV, Kevin Andrew. Staff accountant Waller & Woodhouse, C.P.A.'s, Norfolk, Va., 1965-67; controller Gen. Hosp. Virginia Beach, Va., 1967-69, Gen. Foam Plastics Corp., Norfolk, Va., 1969-71; pub. accountant, Marietta, Ohio, 1971—. Asst. chmn. Williamstown (W.Va.) Community Chest drive, 1973, chmn., 1974, v.p., 1975, pres., 1976; treas. Williamstown Community Assn., 1974—. Served with USNR, 1963-65. Mem. Am. Legion. Mason, Elk. Methodist. Home: 413 Williams Ave Williamstown WV Office: 286 Front St Marietta OH 45750

TOWNSEND, HAROLD GUYON, JR., pub. co. exec.; b. Chgo., Apr. 11, 1924; s. Harold Guyon and Anne Louise (Robb) T.; A.B., Cornell U., 1948; m. Margaret Jeanne Keller, July 28, 1951; children—Jessica, Julie, Harold Guyon III. Advt. salesman Chgo. Tribune, 1948-51; gen. mgr. Keller-Heartt Co., Clarendon Hills, Ill., 1951-62; pub. Santa Clara (Calif.) Jour., 1962-64; pres., pub. Dispatch-Tribune newspaper Townsend Communications, Inc., Kansas City, Mo., 1964—; dir. United Mo. Bank of Blue Valley. Chmn., Suburban Newspaper Research Commn., 1974—; dir. Certified Audit Bur. of Circulation, 1968-72. del. Rep. Nat. Conv., 1960; chmn. Mission Hills Rep. Com., 1966-77; bd. dirs. Kansas City Jr. Achievement, 1966-68, Kansas City council Girl Scouts U.S.A., 1969-71, Kansas City council Boy Scouts Am., 1974, Kansas City chpt. ARC, Kansas City Starlight Theater, Clay County (Mo.) Indsl. Commn.; treas., trustee Park Coll., Parkville, Mo., Northland Med. Found. Mem. adv. com. North Kansas City Hosp. Served with inf. AUS, World War II. Mem. Kansas City Advt. and Sales Club, Kansas City Press Club, Suburban Press Found. (pres. 1969-71), Suburban Newspapers Am. (pres.), Kansas City Printing Industries Assn. (dir.), North Kansas City C. of C. (dir., pres.), Sigma Delta Chi, Pi Delta Epsilon, Phi Kappa Psi. Clubs: University (treas. 1977); Indian Hills Country; Hinsdale (Ill.) Golf. Home: 6321 Norwood Rd Mission Hills KS 66208 Office: 7007 NE Parvin Rd Kansas City MO 64117

TOWNSEND, HOWARD GARFIELD, JR., entomologist; b. Rochester, N.Y., Sept. 10, 1938; s. Howard Garfield and Mildred Leona (Hunt) T.; B.S., Cornell U., 1960; M.S., Va. Poly. Inst., 1963; Ph.D., Pa. State U., 1970; m. Janet Gaylan Slate, June 5, 1964; children—Lori Ann, David Gary. Research asst. dept. entomology Va. Poly. Inst., Blacksburg, 2960-63; experimentalist dept. entomology N.Y. Agrl. Expt. Sta., Geneva, 1963-65; instr. dept. entomology Pa. State U., 1965-70; research entomologist State Fruit Expt. Sta. of S.W. Mo. State U., Mountain Grove, 1970—. Dist. commr. Ozarks council Boy Scouts Am., 1974-75, v.p., 1975-77, Order of Arrow adviser, 1971-75, recipient vigil honor, 1969, award of merit, 1974, silver beaver award, 1975. Mem. Entomol. Soc. Am., Mo. Acad. Sci., Mo., Ark. hort. socs., Mountain Grove Jr. C. of C. Club: Rotary (pres. 1974). Contbr. articles to profl. jours. Home: 707 Barkley Dr Mountain Grove MO 65711 Office: State Fruit Experiment Sta Mountain Grove MO 65711

TOWNSEND, J. RUSSELL, JR., ins. exec.; b. Cedar Rapids, Iowa, Nov. 21, 1910; s. J. Russell and Mabel (Ferguson) T.; B.S., Butler U., 1931; M.B.A., U. Pa., 1933; m. Virginia Holt, Aug. 1, 1938; 1 son, John Holt. Field asst. Equitable Life Ins. Co. Iowa, 1933-50, gen. agt., 1950-69, gen. agt. emeritus, 1969—; asso. prof. ins. Butler U., Indpls., 1933—; cons. Ind. Dept. Ins., 1948-50; mem. Ind. Ho. of Reps., 1946-48, Ind. Senate, 1956-64; lectr., writer ins. field. Served with USNR, 1942-46; lt. comdr. Res. ret. Chmn. Indpls. Bicentennial Com., 1975-76; pres. Indpls. Jaycees, 1940. Recipient 25-year teaching award Am. Coll. C.L.U.'s, 1960. Mem. Indpls. Chpt. C.L.U.'s (past pres.), Ind. Life Underwriters Assn. (past v.p.), Ret. Officers Assn. (pres. Indpls. chpt.), Ind. Soc. Assn. Execs., Naval Res. Assn., Navy League U.S., Am. Soc. C.L.U.'s, AAUP, Am. Soc. Risk and Ins., Ind. Acad. Sci., Sales and Marketing Execs. Council, U.S. Naval Inst. Republican. Presbyterian. Clubs: Columbia, Meridian Hills Country, Indpls. Literary, Kiwanis (lt. gov. Ind. dist. internat. 1975-76), Indpls. Press, Ft. Harrison Officers, Masons, Sojourners (Indpls); Army and Navy (Washington); Crystal Downs Country (Frankfort, Mich.) Contbr. articles to trade mags. Home: 8244 N Pennsylvania St Indianapolis IN 46240 Office: Board Trade Bldg Indianapolis IN 46204

TOWNSEND, JAMES EDWARD, circuit judge; b. Boyne City, Mich., Apr. 7, 1925; s. Glen Cecil and Esther Margaret (Angstrom) T.; A.B., U. Mich., 1949, LL.B., 1951; grad. Nat. Coll. State Judiciary, 1976; m. Corinne Janette Calkins, Aug. 30, 1947; children—Susan Lee, Steven Glen, Margaret Helen, Mary Ellen. Admitted to Mich. bar, 1951, since practiced in Holland; partner firm Ten Cate, Townsend & Cunningham, 1959-72; city atty., Holland, 1952-62; atty. Saugatuck Village, 1961-71, Douglas Village, 1962-72; atty. Saugatuck Twp., 1965-72, Holland Sch. Dist., 1965-72, Hope Coll., 1968-72; circuit judge 20th Jud. Circuit Mich., 1973—; instr. bus. law Hope Coll., 1953. Dir., atty. Ottawa Savs. & Loan Assn., 1969-72; lectr. Center Adminstrn. Justice, 1975—. Chmn. Greater Holland United Fund drive, 1960, bd. dirs., 1960-71, pres., 1962; chmn. Chippewa dist. Boy Scouts Am., 1961-64, pres. Grand Valley council, 1967-70. Mem. Ottawa County Bd. Suprs., 1952-62. Trustee Mich. United Fund, 1962-72; pres. Greater Holland Community Found., 1967-73; bd. dirs. Ottagan Alcoholic Rehab., 1971—; mem. community council Hope Coll., 1959-60, 72—. Served with AUS, 1943-45. Decorated Bronze Star medal; recipient Silver Beaver award Boy Scouts Am., 1964; Distinguished Service award Holland Jaycees, 1954, 61; Grand Valley Scout Reservation Ranger's home named James E. Townsend Ranger's Home, 1970. Mem. Mich. (pres. pub. corp. law sect. 1969-70), Ottawa County (pres. 1958-60) bar assns., Mich. Municipal Attys. Assn. (pres. 1960-61), Am. Judicature Soc., Mich. Judges Assn. (exec. bd.). Office: Ottawa County Bldg Grand Haven MI 49417

TOWNSEND, PAUL HENSON, ret. mfg. exec.; b. Clermont, N.J., Dec. 19, 1889; s. Eli and Frances (Dryburgh) T.; B.A. honoris causa, Yale, 1918; m. Clarissa Marie Davis, Sept. 3, 1920; children—Ann (Mrs. Rodney Wood), Paul H. Tchr. grade schs. Cape May Co., N.J., 1908-10, 13-14; clk. Huron Portland Cement Co., 1919, supt. plants, ships, 1920-39, gen. mgr., 1938-53, v.p., 1942-53, dir., 1944—, pres., 1953-59, chmn. bd., 1959-66; v.p., dir. Detroit Chem. Works, 1937-63, Fed. Motor Truck Co., 1944-49, Nat. Gypsum Co., 1958-64. Dir. adv. com. Great Lakes Protective Assn., 1940-58. Served as capt., 315th F.A., U.S. Army, World War I. Recipient Purple Heart. Mem. Lake Carriers Assn. (dir.), Detroit Bd. Commerce, Detroit Engring. Soc., N.J. Hist. Soc., Detroit Soc. Geneal. Research, Newcomen Soc., Cape May Geog. Soc., Atlantic County Hist. Soc., Mich. Audubon Soc., Newcomen Soc., Alpha Delta Phi. Mem. Grosse Pointe Meml. Ch. Clubs: Propeller, Detroit, University, Yacht (Detroit); Seventy Five; Alpena; Hunter's Creek. Home: 112 Longford Dr Rochester MI 48063

TOWNSEND, THORNTON LEWIS, journalist; b. Larned, Kans., Nov. 14, 1931; s. Russell Thomas and Ethel Mabel Patrick (Welsh) T.; student U. Kansas City, 1948-49, Universidad de las Americas, Mexico, 1953-55; U. Mo., 1963, Brookings Instn., Wichita State U., 1967; m. Wynema Lea Cameron, Dec. 11, 1966; stepchildren—Richard Lamar Shaffer, Marque Michele Shaffer. Editor sports Streator (Ill.) Times-Press., 1964-65, Pittsburg (Kans.) Headlight and Sun, 1965-66; urban affairs reporter Wichita (Kans.) Eagle-Beacon Pub. Co., 1967-68; exec. editor AOPA Pilot Mag., Washington, 1971-73; editor Airport World, Washington, 1973-74; aviation editor Wichita Eagle-Beacon Pub. Co., 1975—; founder Nat. Aviation Theft Bur., 1974. Rep. U.S. Postal Service Mailers Tech. Adv. Com., 1973-74. Served with AUS, 1956-59, USMC, 1950-53, USAF, 1949, 63-64. Mem. Soc. Nat. Assn. Publs. (chmn. govt. relations com. 1973-74), Aviation Space Writers' Assn. (recipient Earl D. Osborn award 1974, gen. aviation writing award 1977), Aircraft Owners and Pilots Assn., Mo. Pilots Assn., Nat. Aviation Club, Sigma Delta Chi. Home: 241 N Oliver St Wichita KS 67208 825 E Douglas St Wichita KS 67201

TOWNSEND, WILLIAM BEACH, welfare agy. exec.; b. Cleve., Mar. 16, 1910; s. Henry Burton and Helen (Malley) T.; B.A., Western Res. U., 1932, M.A., 1948; m. Colette Marie Sheehan, Dec. 28, 1937; 1 son, Eric Beach. Employment supr. Cleve. Asso. Charities, 1933-40; exec. dir. Cleve. Soc. Crippled Children, 1940—; adminstr. of Heman Rehab. Inst. Registrar of Camp Cheerful, 1940—; cons. to aux. Soc. for Crippled Children, 1942—; cons. Lakewood (Ohio) Draft Bd., 1948— (fed. commendation award for 15 years service); adv. bd. Cuyahoga Assn. Retarded Children; budget com. Health Council; mem. occupational planning com. Ohio Citizens Council for Health and Welfare; v.p. Madonna Hall, 1954-56; pres. Cath. Youth Orgn., 1938-42; trustee Cath. Child Guidance Bur., 1956—; gov. Lakewood Safety Council; pres. Citizens Juvenile Council; dir. Council Retarded Child, 1952-55, Cleve. Health Council, 1947—, Council Human Relations, 1955—. Treas. Mayor's Com. Employment of Handicapped, 1944—; adviser F.S.R.C., Rehab. Internat., United Torch Services-Speakers' Bur. Agy.; nat. trustee Nat. Council for Handicapped; mem. Buckeye-Woodland Community Congress, No. Ohio Area Coordinating Com., United Torch Exec. Adv. Com., 1975—; sec.-gen. Stop the Arms Race. Served with Transp. Corps, AUS, 1945-46; PTO. Recipient distinguished service award and Man of year award Cleve. Jr. C. of C., 1943; 25-Year commendation U.S. Selective Service, 1973; 1st Ann. Dedicated Service award Nat. Council for Handicapped, 1975; proclamation Mayor of Lakewood, 1975; proclamation of congratulations City of Cleve., 1975; resolution of commendation Ohio Ho. of Reps., 1975. Mem. Council for Exceptional Children, Nat. Conf. Social Work, Am. Camping Assn. (sec. Ohio sect.), Ohio Rural Health Assn., Easter Seal Execs. Assn., Western Res. U. Alumni Assn., Early Settlers Assn., Advt. Fedn. Am., Cleve. Counsellors Assn. (pres.), Para-Progressives (hon.), Am. Legion, Cleve. Advt. Club, Nat. Publicity Council, Internat. Soc. Welfare of Cripples (U.S. del. Stockholm Conv. 1951), Cleve. C. of C., Lake Erie Jr. Mus., Ohio Assn. Workers for Blind, Rehab. Internat., Cleve. Council World Affairs, Greater Cleve. Growth Assn., Fedn. for Community Services (rep. assembly), Friends Cleve. Zoo, Cleve. Health Mus., Nat., Ohio (exec. bd. 1958—) rehab. assns., United Cerebral Palsy Assn., Cleve. Citizens League, Cleve. Mus. Art, Am. Acad., Am. Mus. Natural History, New Eng. Soc. Western Res. (life), Phillis Wheatley Assn., Western Res., Lakewood hist. socs., League Ohio Sportsmen, Frostville Mus., Cleve. Inst. Music, Human Soc. U.S., Nat. Council Cath. Men, Internat. Platform Assn., New Eng. Soc. Western Reserve, Smithsonian Instn., Am. Acad. Polit. and Social Sci., Council Rehab. Center Execs., Defenders of Wildlife. Roman Catholic. Clubs: City, Mid-Day; Auto, Rotary (Cleve.). Home: 1107 Nicholson Ave Lakewood OH 44107 Office: 11001 Buckeye Rd Cleveland OH 44104

TOZZER, JACK CARL, civil engr., surveyor; b. Marion, Ohio, Jan. 5, 1922; s. Carl Henry and Henrietta (Schellenbaum) T.; B.C.E., Ohio No. U., 1944; children—Brent Jack, Hal Jack; m. Aleta C. Lehner, July 14, 1974. Partner firm Tozzer & Assos. Ltd., Marion, 1948—; engr. Marion County, Ohio, 1964—; city engr. Marion, 1959, Galion, Ohio, 1960—. Cons. civil engr. Mem. consultants bd. Coll. Engring. Ohio No. U., 1970, recipient Order of Engr., 1971; v.p. Marion Community Improvement Corp.; mem. Marion County Regional Planning Commn. Served with USNR, 1944-46. Registered profl. engr., Ohio, Fla., registered surveyor, Ohio. Fellow ASCE; mem. Nat. Soc. Profl. Engrs., Marion C. of C., Cons. Engrs. Ohio, Profl. Land Surveyors Ohio, Ohio, Marion County (past dir.) hist. socs., Delta Sigma Phi. Lutheran (past trustee). Elk. Home: 307 Forest Lawn Blvd Marion OH 43302 Office: 299 Clover Ave Marion OH 43302

TRACHSEL, FRED RICHARD, dental lab. exec.; b. Black River Falls, Wis., Feb. 10, 1933; s. Fred Jacob and Mildred Margarite (Anderson) T.; student dental trade schs.; m. Ramona Ruthe Senske, Sept. 22, 1956; children—Gregory, Brian, Jonathan. Dept. head Oralcraft Dental Lab., Rochester, Minn., 1957-63; pres. Trachsel Dental Studio, Inc., Rochester, Minn., 1963—. Adv. bd. Rochester Area Vo-Tech. Sch., 1973—. Served with USNR, 1952-56. Mem. Nat., Minn. (dir. 1970-71, 75—) dental lab. assns., Nat., Rochester chambers commerce, Nat. Fedn. Ind. Small Businesses. Mem. United Ch. of Christ (pres. 1965-68, mem. bd. Christian edn. 1969-70). Home: 2025 18th Ave SW Rochester MN 55901 Office: 1202 1/2 7th St NW Rochester MN 55901

TRACY, MARY ELIZABETH, librarian; b. Joliet, Ill., Aug. 18, 1922; d. Charles Joseph and Catherine (Fay) Tracy; B.A. cum laude, Coll. St. Francis, 1944; M.A., Rosary Coll., 1958. Tchr., librarian Joliet pub. schs., 1944-52, 54-61, Am. schs., Bremerhaven and Frankfurt, Germany, 1952-54; librarian Central Campus Joliet Twp. High Sch., 1961—. Sec., v.p., and mem. adv. bd. Alumnae of the Coll. of St. Francis. Mem. Am., Ill. Library Assns., Ill. Assn. Sch. Librarians, Ill. Audio-Visual Assn., Will County Library/Media Assn. (pres. 1976), Joliet Jr. Cath. Woman's League (pres. 1950-51). Home: 1010 Glenwood Ave Joliet IL 60435 Office: 201 E Jefferson St Joliet IL 60432

TRACY, WILLIAM THOMAS, univ. adminstr.; b. Milw., Sept. 23, 1934; s. William Carroll and Dorothy Helen (Smith) T.; B.S., Marquette U., 1957, M.Ed., 1962, Ed.D., 1969; children—Thomas, Maureen, Eileen, Kathleen, Lynn. Tchr., counselor, pub. schs. Milw., 1957-64; asst. dean U. Wis., Madison, 1964-65; dir. admissions U. Wis., Milw., 1965-67; dir. continuing edn. Marquette U., Milw., 1967—, prof. ednl. adminstrn., 1969—. Served with AUS, 1954-56. Recipient Distinguished Service award Nat. assn. Bds. Edn., 1975. Mem. Nat. U. Extension Assns., Assn. Continuing Higher Edn., N.Am. Assn. Summer Sessions, Wis. Cath. Conf., Am. Assn. Higher Edn., Phi Delta Kappa. Roman Catholic. Editorial bd. Nat. Assn. Bds. Edn., 1973-77. Home: 2835 Kilbourn St W Milwaukee WI 53208 Office: 1217 Wisconsin Ave W Milwaukee WI 53233

TRAEGER, BARBARA SHIELDS (MRS. JOHN E. TRAEGER), pub. relations exec.; b. Pitts., Oct. 19, 1932; d. Marshall Charles and Margaret Helen (Ward) Shields; B.A. in English, Ripon Coll., 1954; postgrad. U. Chgo., 1971; m. John E. Traeger, Apr. 30, 1971; children by previous marriage—Cynthia, Charles R., Henry. Dir. pub. relations Chgo. unit Am. Cancer Soc., 1964-65; asst. bur. pub. info. Am. Hosp. Assn., Chgo., 1966-68; dir. pub. relations U. Chgo. Hosps. and Clinics, 1968-72; dir. pub. relations Evanston (Ill.) Hosp., 1972—, also Glenbrook Hosp. Recipient excellence award, Am. Inst. Graphic Arts, 1971, 76, recognition of achievement Nat. Publs. Assn., 1975, MacEachern award, 1972, 73, 74, 75, award Type Dirs. Club, 1970, excellence award Modern Publicity, 1972. Mem. Assn. Am. Med. Colls., Am. Soc. Hosp. Pub. Relations Dirs. (accreditation com.), Acad. Hosp. Pub. Relations (seminar chmn. 1974, dir. 1976, pres.-elect 1977), Ill. Hosp. Assn. (ann. mktg. com.), Press Council of McGaw Med. Center of Northwestern U., North Shore Pub. Relations Soc., Pub. Relations Soc., Chgo. Hosp. Council, Pub. Relations Assn. (mktg. com.). Club: Publicity (Chgo.). Home: PO Box A 3197 Chicago IL 60690 Office: 2650 Ridge Ave Evanston IL 60201

TRAFIMOW, JORDAN HERMAN, orthopaedic surgeon; b. Chgo., Nov. 4, 1935; s. Jack and Florence (Silver) T.; B.S., U. Ill., Chgo., 1957, M.D., 1958; m. Alice Emma Lewis, July 11, 1959; children—David, Alan, Janet. Intern, Kings County Hosp., Bklyn., 1958-59; resident Akron Gen. Hosp., 1962-63; Cleve. Met. Gen. Hosp., 1963-64, Cleve. VA Hosp., 1964-65, Columbus (Ohio) Children's Hosp., 1965-66; orthopaedic surgeon Los Angeles Permanente Med. Group, 1966-69, Elmhurst (Ill.) Clinic, 1969—; attending orthopaedist Hines VA Hosp., 1974—; asst. prof. Loyola U. Med. Sch., 1972—. Served with AUS, 1960-62. USPHS fellow, 1959-60. Mem. Am. Acad. Orthopaedic Surgeons. Jewish religion (v.p. congregation 1973-74). Home: 380 Webster St Elmhurst IL 60126 Office: 172 Schiller St Elmhurst IL 60126

TRAINOR, JOHN FELIX, educator; b. Mpls., Dec. 1, 1921; s. James Patrick and Myra Catherine (Pauly) T.; B.A., Coll. St. Thomas, 1943; M.A., U. Minn., 1950; Ph.D., Wash. State U., 1970; m. Margaret Dolores Pudenz, July 3, 1965 (dec. 1977); children—John Anthony, Patrick James. Instr. high sch. Mpls., 1946-47; v.p. Trainor Candy Co., Mpls., 1949-56; instr., asst. prof. econs. Rockhurst Coll., Kansas City, Mo., 1956-62; instr. Wash. State U., Pullman, 1966-67; asst. prof. Moorhead (Minn.) State Coll., 1967-70, asso. prof. econs., 1971—. Served to lt. (j.g.) USNR, 1943-46; ETO. Mem. Am., Minn. (pres. 1976-77) econ. assns., Assn. Social Econs., AAUP, Minn. Acad. Scis., Interfaculty Assn., NEA, Minn. Edn. Assn., Omicron Delta Epsilon. Democrat. Roman Catholic. Author: (with Frank J. Kottke) The Nursing Home Industry in the State of Washington, 1968. Home: 1333 4th Ave S Moorhead MN 56560 Office: Dept Econs Moorhead State U Moorhead MN 56560

TRANEL, DANIEL DAVID, counselor; b. East Dubuque, Ill., Sept. 15, 1932; s. Edward Henry and Lucille Barbara (Kieffer) T.; B.A., Loras Coll., 1953; Ph.D., Loyola at Chgo., 1970. Tchr., Loyola U., Chgo., 1970-71; dir. Counseling-Learning Insts., Chgo., 1970—; mem. C.A. Curran Assos., Chgo., 1973—. Mem. Soc. Human Relations Research (pres. 1971—), Am. Personnel and Guidance Assn., Phi Delta Kappa. Author: (with C.A. Curran and J.P. Rardin) Counseling-Learning: A Whole-Person Model For education, 1972. Home: 107 Webster St Apple River IL 61001 Office: Dominican Edn Center Sinsinawa WI 53824

TRANEN, MARTIN WILLIAM, accountant; b. N.Y.C., Dec. 24, 1919; s. Charles and Celia (Rachlin) T.; B.B.A., Coll. City N.Y., 1940; m. Dolores Jane Plotkin, Sept. 26, 1948; children—Shelley, Bruce, Amy. Sr. accountant Alexander Bernfield & Co., C.P.A., Chgo., 1946-52; individual practice C.P.A., Chgo., 1953-60; sr. partner Goettsche, Tranen & Co., Chgo., 1961—. Cons., and/or dir. William Greiner Cos., Chgo., F.J. Littell Machine Co., Chgo., Weil Pump Co., Chgo., Carol Buick, Inc., Evanston, Ill. Served with USAAF, 1942-46. Mem. Am. Inst. C.P.A.'s, Ill., N.Y. socs. C.P.A.'s, Am. Meteorol. Soc., Am. Geophys. Union. Clubs: Standard (Chgo.); John Evans (Evanston). Home: 265 South Ave Glencoe IL 60022 Office: 4711 Golf Rd Skokie IL 60076

TRAPANI, ANDREW PATRICK, orthodontist; b. Aurora, Mo., Sept. 7, 1944; s. Patrick D. and Helen C. (Chapman) T.; M.S. in Oral Biology, Loyola U., Chgo., 1971; D.D.S., U. Ill., 1969; m. Arleen Carol Widowski, Aug. 27, 1966; children—David Andrew, Amy Colette, Justin Scott. Asso., Drs. Braun and Fleming, Olympia Field, Ill., 1973-74, Dr. Arai, Park Ridge, Ill., 1974-77; pvt. practice orthodontics, Dundee, Ill., 1974—; instr. Dental Coll., U. Ill.; instr. anatomy and orthodontic depts. Coll. Dentistry Loyola U.; cons. orthodontist Sherman Hosp., Elgin, Ill. Chmn. Dundee Days Parade Com., 1974-77; treas. Sleepy Hollow P.T.A.; v.p. Sleepy Hollow Service Club. Served to capt. Dental Corps, U.S. Army, 1971-73. Recipient certificate of achievement Am. Acad. Oral Medicine. Mem. ADA, Ill., Fox Valley dental assns., Am., Midwest, Ill. assns. orthodontists, Elgin Dental Soc. (dir.), U. Ill. Alumni Assn., Loyola Alumni Assn., Dundee Jr. C. of C., Omicron Kappa Upsilon. Roman Catholic. Clubs: Lions, St. Catherine's of Sienna Men's. Home: 861 Willow Lane Sleepy Hollow IL 60118 Office: 825 Village Quarter Rd Dundee IL 60118

TRAPP, CHARLES FRANCIS, mfg. co. exec.; b. Bayonne, N.J., July 1, 1918; s. Charles Francis and Margaret Mary (Campen) T.; B.S., Carnegie-Mellon U., 1940; grad. Advanced Mgmt. Program, Harvard, 1957; m. Carrie Louise Kinzer, Sept. 20, 1941. Sales engr. Westinghouse Corp., Youngstown, Ohio, 1946-52, area sales mgr., Detroit, 1952-55; v.p. Formsprag Co., mfr. mech. transmission products, Warren, Mich., 1955-69, pres. and chief exec. officer, 1969-76; pres., chief exec. officer Indsl. Power Transmission div. Dana

Corp., Warren, 1977—. Served to maj., C.E., AUS, 1941-45. Mem. Soc. Automotive Engrs., Engring. Soc. Detroit, Beta Theta Pi. Episcopalian. Clubs: Detroit, Country of Detroit; Rotary (Grosse Pointe). Home: 11 Waverly Ln Grosse Pointe Farms MI 48236 Office: 23601 Hoover Rd Warren MI 48090

TRASK, LAURENCE MARION, pub. co. exec.; b. Oneonta, N.Y., Nov. 7, 1935; s. Millard Rathbun and Laura Pamela (Woodlands) T.; B.S. in Pub. Relations Journalism, Bowling Green (Ohio) State U., 1957; m. Jeanne Frances Anderson, Nov. 10, 1957; children—Cynthia, Laurence Marion, Michael, Richard. Asst. continuity dir. sta. WIMA TV, Lima, O., 1958-59; with Constrn. Digest, Columbus, Ohio, 1959—, Eastern mgr., asso. editor, 1961-73, v.p., 1973—. Pres. Laurence M. Trask, Pub. Relations, Dublin, Ohio, 1973-75; mem. tech. adv. com. Agrl. Tech. Inst. Ohio State U.; mem. steering com. Ohio Transp. Engring. Conf. Served to capt., AUS, 1957-58. Mem. Ohio Equipment Distbrs. Assn. (exec. sec. 1970-75), Ohio Motorcycle Dealers Assn. (exec. sec. 1974-77), Ohio Land Improvement Contractors (exec. sec. 1972-77), Nat. Safety Council (exec. com. sect. constrn. 1972-77), Dublin Area C. of C. (charter), Mercedes Benz Club Am. (dir. sect.), Antique Motorcycle Club Am., Pub. Relations Soc. Am., Aviation/Space Writers Am., Phi Delta Theta. Contbg. author: Places To Fly, 1967. Contbr. numerous articles to trade publs., popular mags., Sunday supplements. Home: 8371 Trails End Dr Dublin OH 43017 Office: 39 S High St Dublin OH 43017

TRAUGOTT, MICHAEL WOLFE, ednl. adminstr., polit. scientist; b. Providence, June 26, 1944; s. Fritz J. and Lucia L. (Scola) T.; B.A., Princeton, 1965; M.A., U. Mich., 1967, Ph.D., 1974; m. Santa Mary Algeo, May 13, 1967; children—Elisabeth Santa, Christopher Michael. Asst. study dir. U. Mich. Inst. for Social Research, Ann Arbor, 1966-70; asst. dir. Hist. Archive, 1970-76, study dir. Center for Polit. Studies, 1974—; dir. ICPSR Archive, 1976—. Cons. elections ABC, 1968—; instr. U. Essex, Eng., 1973, 74. Recipient Philo Sherman Bennett prize Princeton, 1965. Mem. AAAS, Am. Assn. Pub. Opinion Research, Am., Midwest polit. sci. assns., Pi Sigma Alpha. Home: 3204 Sunnywood Dr Ann Arbor MI 48103

TRAUM, EMIL FRANK, educator; b. Detroit, Dec. 18, 1920; s. Joseph and Sophie (Helfrich) T.; B.S., Wayne State U., 1943, M.Ed., 1949; Ph.D., U. Mich., 1970; m. Sarah Anne McCormick, June 25, 1955; children—Frank McCormick, Carolyn DeCou. Indsl. edn. teaching fellow Cass Tech. High Sch., Detroit, 1940-42; tchr. gen. drafting Neinas Jr. High Sch., 1946-55; head indsl. edn. dept. Jefferson Jr. High Sch., 1955-62, Edwin Denby High Sch., Detroit, 1963—; supervising faculty Wayne State U., Detroit, 1948—; cons. Timken Axle Co., 1948. Deacon, elder First Presbyn. Ch., Detroit, 1965-70. Served to lt. (j.g.) USNR, 1943-46; ETO. Mem. Am. Council on Indsl. Arts Tchr. Edn., Phi Delta Kappa. Club: Detroit Boat. Author: Closed Circuit Television and Programmed Learning Used as Instructional Media for the Performance of Measurements in Industrial Education, 1970. Contbr. articles to profl. periodicals. Home: 1216 Harvard Rd Grosse Pointe Park MI 48230 Office: 12800 Kelly Rd Detroit MI 48224

TRAVERS, THOMAS JOSEPH, metal products co. exec.; b. Boston, Jan. 13, 1918; s. Daniel A. and Mary H. (McGarry) T.; A.B. cum laude, Boston Coll., 1939, M.S., 1941; m. Katherine O'Leary, June 29, 1946; children—Thomas Joseph, Stephen, Maureen, Daniel, Richard, Robert. Mgmt. services rep. Ernst & Ernst, Boston, 1946-49; labor relations dir. Comml. Shearing, Inc., Youngstown, Ohio, 1949-61, v.p., 1961-75, chmn. bd., 1975—, also sec., dir.; mgr. European ops. Diekirch, G.D. of Luxembourg, 1963-65; dir. Comml. Hydraulics S.A., Diekirch Luxembourg, Comml. Hydraulics Ltd., Bedford, Eng., Eurocast S.A., Grevenmacher, Luxembourg, Dollar Savs. and Trust Co., Youngstown. Trustee, Indsl. Info. Inst., Youngstown Community Corp., Youngstown Hosp. Assn. Mem. Mfrs. Assn. Eastern Ohio and Western Pa. (dir., pres. 1975), Nat. Fluid Power Assn. (dir.), Am. Soc. Corporate Secs. Clubs: Youngstown, Youngstown Country. Home: 230 N Cadillac Dr Youngstown OH 44512 Office: 1775 Logan Ave Youngstown OH 44501

TRAVIS, DEMPSEY JEROME, mortgage banker; b. Chgo., Feb. 25, 1920; s. Louis and Mittie (Strickland) T.; B.A., Roosevelt U., 1949; certificate in Mortgage Banking, Central YMCA Community Coll., 1963; D.Econs. (hon.), Olive Harvey Coll., 1974, D.B.A. (hon.), Daniel Hale Williams U., Chgo., 1976; m. Moselynne Hardwick, Sept. 17, 1949. Pres. Travis Realty Co., 1949-53, Sivart Mortgage Corp., 1949—, Freeway Mortgage & Investment Co., 1961—, Dempsey J. Travis Security & Investment Co., Chgo., 1961—; dir. Sears Bank & Trust Co. Pres., Dearborn Real Estate Bd., 1957-59, 70-72, Urban Research Inst., 1969—; mem. Presdl. Task Force on Urban Renewal, Washington, 1970—, Ill. Ins. Consumers Adv. Panel, 1970—, Mayor's Adv. Com. on Bldg. Code Amendments, 1970—, Chgo. Com. on Urban Opportunity, 1971-75; mem. Mayor's Commn. Preservation Chgo. Hist. Bldgs.; mem. constructive adv. com. Fed. Energy Adminstrn., 1974-75; mem. Presdl. Task Force on Inflation, 1974; mem. Mayor's Council Manpower and Econ. Advisers, 1974-75; chmn. HUD/PUSH Nat. Housing Task Force, 1975. Trustee Wesley Meml. Hosp.; bd. dirs. Central YMCA Community Coll., 1969—; bd. govs. Chgo. Assembly; mem. adv. bd. Nonprofit Housing partnership; mem. bd. Nat. Housing Conf., Inc., Washington. Served with Ordance Corps, AUS, 1942-46. Certified property mgr. Mem. Mortgage Bankers Assn. Am., Fed. Nat. Mortgage Assn. (adv. bd. 1971-72), United Mortgage Bankers Assn. Am. (founder 1961, pres. 1961-74), Chgo. Mortgage Bankers Assn., Nat. Real Estate Brokers (1st v.p. Dallas 1959-60), Am. Soc. Real Estate Counselors, Internat. Platform Assn., Inst. Real Estate Mgmt., Beta Gamma Sigma, Lambda Alpha. Clubs: Economic, Forty, Execs., Met., Cliff Dwellers (Chgo.). Author: Don't Stop Me Now, 1970; A 100-Year Odyssey on Black Housing: Chicago, 1900-2000, 1977. Fin. editor Dollars and Sense mag. Home: 8001 S Champlain Ave Chicago IL 60619 Office: 840 E 87th St Chicago IL 60619

TRAVIS, FIONA HENDERSON, dance therapist; b. Pitts., Apr. 3, 1940; d. Findlay White and Helen Anderson (Liddell) Henderson; B.A., Muskingum Coll., 1962; M.A., Ohio State U., 1973, Ph.D., 1977; m. Alan Craig Travis, Aug. 18, 1962; children—Todd Alan, Craig Steven. Tchr., French, Worthington (Ohio) High Sch., 1962-64; tchr. creative dance Columbus (Ohio) YWCA, 1965; dir./tchr. Developmental Sch. Dance, Columbus, 1970—; dance therapist, day treatment therapist N. Central Community Mental Health Center, Columbus, 1974—; pvt. practice of movement therapy, Columbus, 1977—; lectr., cons. in field. Bd. dirs. Columbus YWCA, 1968-69. Mem. Assn. Specialists Group Work (charter), Am. Dance Therapy Assn., Am. Personnel and Guidance Assn. Republican. Presbyterian. Home: 1810 N Devon Rd Columbus OH 43212 Office: 4700 Reed Rd Columbus OH 43221

TRAVIS, RANDALL HOWARD, physiologist, educator; b. Curdsville, Ky., July 11, 1924; s. Charles Spaulden and Celestine (Eaty) T.; B.S., U. Chgo., 1947; M.D., Western Res. U., 1952; m. Priscilla Beryl Korabeck, June 16, 1950 (div.); children—Randall Howard, Laura Jane; m. 2d, Ilona Marie Engel, 1974. Intern, resident Univ. Hosp., Cleve., 1952-55; fellow in medicine Western Res. U., Cleve., 1955-56, fellow in physiology, 1956-59, instr. physiology and medicine, 1959-64, asst. prof., 1964-69, asso. prof., 1969—; cons. in endocrinology VA Hosp., 1959—. Served with USMCR, 1943-46. Mem. Endocrine Soc., Central Soc. for Clin. Research, AAUP. Contbr. articles to profl. jours. Home: 2425 N Park Blvd Cleveland Heights OH 44106 Office: Cleveland Metropolitan Gen Hosp Cleveland OH 44109

TRAWICK, LEONARD MOSES, educator; b. Decatur, Ala., July 4, 1933; s. Leonard M. and Frances Whitmire (Earle) T.; B.A., U. of the South, 1956; M.A., U. Chgo., 1957; postgrad. U. Dijon (France), 1957-58; Ph.D., Harvard U., 1961; m. Kerstin Hildegarde Ekfelt, July 16, 1960; children—Eleanor Frances, Matthew Leonard. Asst. prof. English, Columbia U., N.Y.C., 1961-69; asso. prof. English, Cleve. State U., 1969-73, prof., 1973—; poet. Served in U.S. Army, 1958-59. Mem. Modern Lang. Assn. Author: Backgrounds of Romanticism, 1967; contbr. articles, revs. and poems to lit. jours. Office: Dept English Cleve State U Cleveland OH 44115

TRAXEL, WILLIAM LOUIS, ophthalmologist; b. Maysville, Ky., Mar. 17, 1939; s. William Louis and Clara Ellen (Brashears) T.; B.A., Northwestern U., 1961; M.D., Vanderbilt U., 1965; postgrad. U. Mich., 1970-72; m. Mary Ann Walker, July 9, 1966; children—Richard Louis, Benjamin Frederick. Intern, Vanderbilt U., Nashville, 1965-66, resident in internal medicine, 1966-67; resident in ophthalmology U. Mich., 1970-72; practice medicine specializing in ophthalmology, Poplar Bluff, Mo., 1973—; mem. staff Doctor's Hosp., Kneibert Clinic. Served to lt. comdr. USN, 1967-69; flight surgeon. Mem. Am. Acad. Ophthalmology, Am., Mo. assns. ophthalmology. Methodist. Contbr. articles to profl. jours. Home: 47 Tomard Trail Poplar Bluff MO 63901 Office: 666 Lester St Poplar Bluff MO 63901

TRAXLER, BOB, congressman; b. Kawkawlin, Mich., July 21, 1931; B.A. in Polit. Sci., Mich. State U., 1953; LL.B., Detroit Coll. Law, 1959; m. Mary Bissounette; children—Tamara, Brad. Admitted to Mich. bar; prosecutor Bay County, Mich., 1960-62; mem. 93d-95th congresses from 8th Mich. dist., mem. Appropriations Com. Mem. Mich. Ho. of Reps., 1962-73, Mem. Am., Mich. bar assns., Bay County Mental Health Soc. Episcopalian. Home: 341 Killarney Beach Bay City MI 48706 Office: Ho of Reps Washington DC 20515

TRAXLER, EUGENE RICE, mech. engr.; b. Akron, Ohio, Sept. 6, 1912; s. Claude King and Treasure Irene (Hotchkiss) T.; A.B., Kent State U., 1933; B.S. in Mech. Engring., Ohio State U., 1936, M.S. in Engring., 1946; m. Alice Louise Grove, July 14, 1945. With B.F. Goodrich Co., Akron, Ohio, 1935-75, head field engring. group for conveyor belting, 1950-75; cons. belt conveyor work, 1975—; cons. Brad. Assos. Inc., Akron, 1978—. Registered profl. engr., Ohio. Mem. ASME, Am. Inst. Mining Engrs. Republican. Mem. Christian Ch. (Disciples of Christ). Clubs: Wampum Investment. Holder 5 patents; contbr. articles to profl. jours. Home: 3066 Kent Rd Apt 205-B Stow OH 44224 Office: 799 N Main St Akron OH 44310

TRAYNOR, MACK VINCENT, JR., internist; b. Devils Lake, N.D., May 31, 1925; s. Mack Vincent and Betty (Dostert) T.; B.A., U. N.D., 1946, B.S., 1947; B.M., Northwestern U., 1949, M.D., 1950; M.S., U. Minn., 1960; m. Rita C. Roach, June 22, 1957; children—Mack Vincent III, Cathy, James, Peggy, Pat. Intern, St. Joseph's Hosp., Chgo., 1949-50; resident in medicine St. Joseph's Hosp., 1952-53, Mayo Clinic, Rochester, Minn., 1953-57; chief of staff St. Luke's Hosp., Fargo, N.D., 1969-72, chief of medicine, 1972—; prof. medicine U. N.D.; adj. prof. medicine N.D. State U. Served to comdr. M.C., USNR, World War II and Korea. Diplomate Am. Bd. Internal Medicine. Fellow A.C.P.; mem. N.D. Med. Assn., 1st Dist. Med. Soc., AMA, Am. Rheumatism Assn. Roman Catholic. Clubs: Elks, K.C., Fargo Country. Home: 1310 9th St S Fargo ND 58102 Office: Box 2067 Fargo ND 58102

TREADWAY, DONALD RAY, lawyer; b. Kearney, Nebr., June 24, 1933; s. Gerald G. and Hazle J. (Trindle) T.; B.S. in Bus. Adminstrn., U. Nebr., 1957, J.D., 1962; m. Gretchen A. Lecron, Sept. 15, 1957; children—Ann, Thomas, Steven. With marketing dept. Continental Oil Co., 1957-59; admitted to Nebr. bar, 1962, since practiced in Fullerton; partner Brower, Treadway & Bird, 1962—; Nance County atty., 1957—. Mem. State Code of Ethics Bd., 1969—, chmn., 1973—; mem. pres.'s adv. council U. Nebr., 1971—; chmn. U. Nebr. Task Force on Rural Health, 1974—. Chmn. County Republican Com. 1967-72. Served with AUS, 1953-55; Korea. Mem. Nebr. State Bar Assn. (mem. exec. com. young lawyers sect. 1966-69, chmn. sect. 1969, dir. continuing legal edn. non-profit corp. 1973—), Phi Delta Phi, Phi Gamma Delta, Phi Tau Gamma. Methodist. Home: 106 N Johnson St Fullerton NE 68638 Office: Fullerton Nat Bank Bldg Fullerton NE 68638

TREADWAY, WILLIAM EUGENE, lawyer, educator; b. Bloomington, Ind., Dec. 20, 1901; s. Eugene Theodore and Minnie May (Byerly) T.; A.B., Ind. U., 1924; J.D., George Washington U., 1927; S.J.D., U. Mich., 1933; m. Joyce Winona Asher, July 20, 1927; 1 son, David Armand. Admitted to Ind. bar, 1927, Kans. bar, 1942; gen. law practice Spencer and Indpls., Ind., 1927-41; pros. atty., Owen County, Ind., 1927-29; gen. atty. A.T. & S.F. Ry., Topeka, Kans., 1945-71; lectr. Washburn U. Law Sch., 1946-71, prof., 1971—. Sec. Ind. Commn. on Interstate Cooperation, 1938-41. Pres. bd. trustees Topeka Pub. Library, 1962-70. Judge advocate gen. Kans. Nat. Guard, 1947-62. Mem. Indiana Ho. of Reps., 1934-38. Served from capt. to lt. col. AUS, 1941-45. Mem. Am., Kans., Topeka bar assns., Am. Legion, Nat. Guard Officers Assn., S.A.R. (pres. Topeka chpt. 1958-59). Am. Judicature Soc., Samuel Johnson Soc. Kans. (pres. 1969-70), Kan. Hist. Soc. (pres. 1972-73), Delta Theta Phi, Phi Kappa Phi. Conglist. Mason. Rotarian. Author chpts in books, articles in field. Editor: Kansas Bar Jour., 1947-63. Home: 3500 Avalon Ln Topeka KS 66604 Office: Washburn U Law School Topeka KS 66621

TREANOR, JOHN ZIMBECK, religious broadcasting co. exec.; b. Boone, Iowa, June 18, 1912; s. Elmer John and Iva Mae (Zimbeck) T.; student Grand Island Bus. Coll., 1933-36; m. Ida Roine Speed, Sept. 19, 1936; children—Sally Ann (Mrs. Elmer L. Kliewer), Susan Kay (Mrs. Harmon D. Stinnett). Accountant, head miscellaneous vouchers unit Soil Conservation Service, U.S. Dept. Agr., 1936-54; accountant, adminstrv. dir. Back to the Bible Broadcast, Lincoln, Nebr., 1954—, treas., 1969—. Served with USNR, 1944-46. Home: 6725 Colby St Lincoln NE 68505 Office: PO Box 82808 Lincoln NE 68501

TREANOR, RICHARD CLIFFORD, physician; b. Chgo., June 14, 1926; s. Bernard and Margaret (Clifford) T.; student Wright Jr. Coll., 1943-44, 46-47; M.D., U. Ill., 1952; m. Helen June Hudon, Aug. 8, 1953; children—Kathi, Terri, Peggy, Paul, Michael, John, Sharon, Thomas. Intern, Cook County Hosp., Chgo., 1952-53; resident in internal medicine Hines (Ill.) Hosp., 1953-56; gen. practice medicine, Arlington Heights, Ill., 1956—; asso. med. dir. Universal Oil Products, Des Plaines, Ill., 1956-66, med. dir., 1966—; mem. staff Holy Family Hosp., NW Community Hosp. Mem. Bd. Health Arlington Heights, 1960-67; health dir. Village of Kildeer, 1964—. Pres., Northwest Suburban Microfilming, 1970—; founder EMICARD physician med. microfilm info. service, 1972—. Served with USAAF, 1944-46. Mem. Chgo. Assn. Commerce and Industry, AMA, Chgo., Ill. med. assns., Chgo. Heart Assn., Indsl. Med. Assn., AMA. Roman Catholic. Club: K.C. (4 deg.). Home: 21539 Boschome Dr W Kildeer IL 60047 Office: 1430 N Arlington Heights Rd Arlington Heights IL 60004

TREECE, ELEANOR MAE WALTERS (MRS. JAMES WILLIAM TREECE, JR.), nursing cons., author; b. Mansfield, Ohio, Feb. 11, 1921; d. Clarence Samuel and Helen LaDonna (Marmet) Walters; grad. Mansfield Bus. Tng. Sch., 1939; diploma in missions Nyack Coll., 1944; R.N., Manfield Gen. Hosp. Sch. Nursing, 1948; B.A., Ashland Coll., 1952; M.Ed., U. Minn., 1962, Ph.D., 1967; m. James William Treece, Jr., Apr. 11, 1954. Asst. instr. Mansfield Gen. Hosp. Sch. Nursing, 1949, asst. evening supr. hosp., 1950-51, asst. to dir. nurses, 1951-52, instr. Sch. Nursing, 1952-53; asst. dir. nursing service Meml. Hosp., Casper, Wyo., 1953-54; office nurse Dental Clinic, Casper, 1954-56; instr. practical nursing Casper Coll., 1956; pvt. duty nurse, Casper, 1957-58; dir., instr. Mpls. Vocational Sch. Practical Nursing, 1958-61; instr. St. Paul Bible Coll., 1965-67, St. Mary's Jr. Coll., Mpls., 1965-66; adminstrv. head St. Paul unit S.D. State U., 1967-68; curriculum coordinator Arthur B. Ancker Meml. Sch. Nursing. St. Paul-Ramsey Hosp. and Med. Center, 1968-71; nursing cons., Mpls., 1971—. USPHS spl. nurse trainee, 1961-62; USPHS predoctoral fellow, 1963-65. Mem. Internat. Platform Assn., Am. Ednl. Research Assn., Am. Assn. Higher Edn., Am., Minn. nurses assns., Nat., Minn. leagues nursing, Am., Minn. vocational assns. Co-author: Elements of Research in Nursing, 1973; author: Internship in Nursing Education: Technoterm, 1974. Address: 1809 E 41st St Minneapolis MN 55407

TREECE, JAMES WILLIAM, JR., sociologist; b. Parkerton, Wyom., July 12, 1924; s. James William and Myrtle (Chaney) T.; diploma Barnes Sch. Commerce, 1948; certificate N.Y. Sch. Modern Photography, 1958; B.R.E. (Paul and Priscilla Johnson scholar), St. Paul Bible Coll., 1962; B.A., Bethel Coll., 1965; M.A., U. Minn., 1967, postgrad.; m. Eleanor Mae Walters, Apr. 11, 1954. Mgr. shipping, receiving Sears Roebuck & Co., Casper, Wyo., 1954-58, stock work, Mpls., part-time 1958-67; instr. sociology St. Paul Bible Coll., 1965-66, S.D. State U. at St. Paul, Minn., 1967-68, Arthur B. Ancker Meml. Sch. of Nursing, St. Paul, 1967-70; asst. prof. sociology Bethel Coll., St. Paul, 1969-74; instr. Ednl. Study Assn., St. Paul, 1971—; free lance photographer, 1952—; one-man shows in photography Hennepin County Hist. Soc., 1974, Minn. Archeol. Soc., 1974. Lectr. social problems. Served with AUS, 1944-46. Recipient Snapshot of Year award Newspaper Snapshot Awards, 1961; Union Bd. Govs. Photo Contest award U. Minn., 1966. Mem. Internat. Platform Assn., Am. Sociol. Assn. (registration chmn., planning com. Midwest sect. 1971), Nat. (membership chmn. 1970-71, 72-74), Minn. leagues for nursing, Hennepin County Hist. Soc. Congregationalist. (mem. stewardship com. 1971, bd. of benevolence 1972—). Author: (with Eleanor Mae Treece) Elements of Research in Nursing, 1973, 2d edit., 1977. Home: 1809 E 41st St Minneapolis MN 55407

TREGER, HARVEY, social worker, educator; b. Chgo., July 5, 1924; s. Sam and Lillian (Ertrachter) T.; B.S., Roosevelt U., 1948; M.A., Sch. Social Service Adminstrn. U. Chgo., 1956; certificate Summer Sch. Alcohol Studies Yale U., 1957; certificate child care program Chgo. Inst. Psychoanalysis, 1963; m. Shirley Gladys Feldman, Oct. 24, 1954. Fed. probation officer U.S. Dist. Ct., No. Ill., 1957-65; prof. social work and criminal justice U. Ill., Chgo., 1965—; originator, project dir. police-social work teams, Maywood, Ill., 1974-77, Niles, Ill., 1971-73, Wheaton, Ill., 1970-73; chmn. state and nat. police social work confs. Recipient John Howard award, 1973; Key to City, Kansas City, Mo., 1976; Ill. Law Enforcement Commn. grantee, 1970, 70-73, 75, 74-77. Fellow Am. Orthopsychiat. Assn.; mem. Ill. Acad. Criminology (pres. 1969-70, Morris J. Wexler award 1974), Nat. Assn. Social Workers (Social Worker of Yr., Chgo. Area, 1977). Author: The Police Social Work Team, 1975; film project dir.: The Police Social Work Team, 1977 (Helen Cody Baker award). Home: 1501 Maple Ave Apt 804 Evanston IL 60201 Office: 4246 ECB Box 4348 Chicago IL 60680

TREIMAN, EDWARD M., elec. engr.; b. Toledo, Iowa, July 29, 1910; s. Samuel E. and Dorothy (Walker) T.; B.S. in E.E., Iowa State Coll., 1933, E.E., 1943; m. Selma White, June 24, 1942; children—Paul, Rosalind, Ann. With Western Electric Co., Chgo. and New York, engring., research and transcontinental line experimentations, 1933-37; asst. purchasing agt. Allied Machinery Corp., Feb.-Sept. 1937; with Internat. Western Electric Co., 1938-39; mng. dir. Nat. Electric Light Assn., 1946-52; cons. engr., Chgo., 1952—. Sec. St. Lawrence Commn. of U.S., 1944-46, Second Nat. Radio Conf., 1945. Commd. 1st lt., Signal Corps, U.S. Army, 1937, later capt.; served in U.S. and France. Mem. Am. Inst. Elec. Engrs., Edison Electric Inst., NAM, Tau Beta Pi, Delta Upsilon. Republican. Clubs: Union League, Univ., Recess (N.Y.C.); Univ. (Chgo.). Address: 2918 W Fargo St Chicago IL 60645

TREISTER, MICHAEL ROY, orthopaedic and hand surgeon; b. Cleve., Dec. 3, 1943; s. Bert Allen and Marjorie (Roseman) T.; student Franklin and Marshall Coll., 1961-63; M.D., Washington U., St. Louis, 1967; m. Dana Fern Shepard, June 18, 1967; children—Jeremy Stewart, Nathaniel Simon. Intern, Wesley Meml. Hosp., Chgo., 1967-68; resident in orthopaedic surgery Northwestern U.-Cook County Hosp., 1968-71; practice medicine specializing in orthopaedic and hand surgery, Chgo., 1974—; mem. staff Augustana, Henrotin, Norwegian-Am., St. Elizabeth, St. Mary, Thorek, and Walther Meml. hosps.; asso. prof. orthopaedic surgery Ill. Coll. Podiatric Medicine; pres. Treister Orthopaedic Services, Ltd.; v.p. Midwest Modern Med. Bill Specialists, Inc., N.W. Chgo. Rehab. Center, Ltd., Central Chgo. Orthopaedic X-ray Services, Ltd.; sec. Dana Aviation. Served as maj. USAF, 1972-73. Diplomate Am. Bd. Orthopaedic Surgery. Fellow Philippine, Western Pacific orthopaedic assns.; mem. Am. Trauma Soc. (founding), Dominican Traumatology Soc. (hon.), Orthopaedic Research Soc., Chgo. Found. Med. Care (dir.), Chgo. Med. Soc. (chmn. grievance com., vice chmn. peer rev. com.). Jewish. Club: Covenant (Chgo.). Office: 25 W Chicago Ave Chicago IL 60610

TREMBLE, STELLA CRAFT, author, editor, poet; b. Frenchburg, Ky.; d. Levi and Mary (Sexton) Craft; student State Tchrs. Coll., Charleston, 1922, Ypsilanti Tchrs. Coll., 1928; D.Litt., Free U. Asia, 1968; D.Hum., Acad. of Culture, Hull, Eng., 1968; D. Liberal Arts, World U. (Hong Kong); m. Walter Shirley Tremble, Nov. 26, 1925. Tchr. elementary schs., Ashmore, 1922-23, Joliet, 1923-25, Charleston, 1926-34, Royal Oak, Mich., Mattoon, Ill., 1947-50. Author: The Silver Chain, 1953; Thorns and Thistledown, 1954; Wind in the Reed, 1957; Crystal Prism, 1958; Loom and Lyre, 1961; The Prairie Poet Anthology, Vol. II, 1961; Telescope of Time, 1962; Happy Holidays, Vols. I-II, 1963, Vol. II, 1974 (2d place Nat. Fedn. Press Women 1964), Vol. II, 1974; Songs of the Prairie, 1964, 2d edit., 1965; In His Day, 1966; Goodbye, Little Country School, 1966; Bells of Autumn, 1967; From Isles of Silence, 1968 (Mate Palmer award 1969); Center and Circumference, 1968; Paths to Parnassus, 1969; Unmeasured Moments, 1972; Clod and Cloud, 1974; Veering Weathervane, 1975; Peddler's Pack, 1977; editor, compiler, pub. 35 anthologies; profl. activities include poetry analyst, sec.-treas. Am. Poetry League, 1958-64, pres., 1964—; nat. exec. adviser Am. Poets Fellowship Soc., 1964—, life pres., 1965—. Mem. bd. Nat. Poets Shrine, Hollywood, World Poetry Days Activities; regional dir. Internat. Scambi, Rome. Recipient Book of Year award Am. Poets

Fellowship Soc., 1958, gold cup, 1965; 1st prize Nat. Fedn. Press Women (for The Crystal Prism), 1960, George Washington medal Freedoms Found., 1963, Distinguished Alumni award Eastern Ill. U., 1974, numerous other awards. Mem. Ill. Woman's Press Assn. (3d v.p. 1967), Ill. State Pen Women (chmn. letters 1967—), Nat. League Am. Penwomen (pres. br.) D.A.R. (chpt. regent, chpt. chaplain, vice chmn. youth work Ill. 1966—), Ill. Poetry Soc. (founding pres. 1973-76), United Poets Soc. Am. (v.p.), Ill. State Poetry Soc. (founding pres. 1971-74), Cosmosynthesis Poetry League Australia (life), Am. Poets, Poets Laureate Internat. Pub., editor: The Am. Poet (2d Mate Palmer award 1964), 1966, 67; founder, editor Prairie Poet, United Poets (mags.); editor Prairie Poet Anthology, 1961, 65, 67; From Sea to Sea in Song (Am. Poetry League anthology), 1965, 66, 67. Home: 902 10th St Charleston IL 61920

TRENNT, EVELYN LADENE, educator; b. Miller, Nebr.; d. William Carl and Alura (Chartraw) Trennt; B.A., U. Omaha, 1942; M.A., U. Ill., 1946. Tchr. math. Gaza (Iowa) High Sch., 1942-43, Walnut (Iowa) High Sch., 1943-45; instr. math. Springfield (Ill.) Jr. Coll., 1946-53; tchr. math. Milw.-Downer Sem., 1953-55; asso. prof. math. Monticello Coll., Godfrey, Ill., 1955-71; prof. math. Lewis and Clark Community Coll., Godfrey, 1971—. Judge math. div. ann. State Sci. Exposition of Ill. Jr. Acad. Sci., 1958—. Mem. Nat., Ill. (mem. bd. 1960-61) councils tchrs. math., Math. Assn. Am., AAUP, Alton Bus. and Profl. Women's Club, Sigma Pi Phi, Pi Mu Epsilon. Home: 1012 Richard Dr Godfrey IL 62035

TRENT, ALTHEA, realtor; b. Savannah, Okla., Aug. 29, 1916; d. James Francis Rogers and Dorothy (Lewis) Templeton; student Ind. U., 1961-62; m. Theodore Anderson, Aug. 3, 1935, (div. 1948); 1 dau., Phyllis Jean Anderson (Mrs. Trowbridge Calloway III); m. 2d Henry D. Trent, Jan. 11, 1954. Mgr. Lincoln Hwy. Inn, Mishawaka, Ind., 1940-60; broker B & F Realty Inc., Elkhart, Ind., 1962-65, sales mgr., 1965-69, v.p., treas., 1969—. Mem. Elkhart Bd. Realtors (treas. 1968), Ind. Real Estate Assn., Nat. Assn. Real Estate Brokers, Nat. Fedn. Bus. & Profl. Women's Clubs. Republican. Episcopalian. Clubs: Elks (treas. Lady Elks 1969-70), Four Lakes Country (Adamsville, Mich.). Home: 25787 Laverne Ct Elkhart IN 46514 Office: 1300 Cassopolis St Elkhart IN 46514

TRENT, DONALD MUDRA, scientist; b. Oskaloosa, Ia., June 15, 1922; s. Thomas Wesley and Ruby Leona (Mudra) T.; student Central Coll., 1946-47, Ia. State U., 1948-49; m. Mary Lou Dixon, Aug. 30, 1946; children—Carol Suzanne, Timothy William. Jr. techician Maytag Co., Newton, Ia., 1949-50, sr. technician, 1950-51, process engr., 1951-56, supr. lab., 1956-65, sr. chemist, 1965—. Served with AUS, 1941-46. Decorated Bronze Star medal, Purple Heart medal. Fellow Am. Inst. Chemists; sr. mem. Soc. Plastic Engrs.; mem. Am. Soc. Metals, Nat. Mgmt. Assn., ASTM. Republican. Conglist. Club: Maytag Mgmt. Home: Box 153 RR 1 Newton IA 50208 Office: Maytag Co Newton IA 50208

TRENT, NELLIE JANE, psychologist; b. St. Louis, July 5, 1921; d. Richard Wesley and Helen Elizabeth (Kuhn) Mellow; A.B., Wellesley Coll., 1943; M.A., Washington U., St. Louis, 1944; m. John Brabson, Apr. 9, 1946; children—Elizabeth (Mrs. Peter D.W. Heberling), John Brabson. Tchr., Mary Inst., St. Louis, 1944-46; grad. asst. psychology Washington U., 1963-65; psychologist Kirkwood (Mo.) Sch. Dist., 1965-75; psychologist spl. services East Ladue Jr. High Sch., St. Louis, 1975—; lectr. psychology Meramec Community Coll., St. Louis, 1969-70; lectr. spl. edn. St. Louis U., 1970. Founder, pres. Greater St. Louis Women's Assn. of Freedoms Found. at Valley Forge, 1968; residential chmn. St. Louis and St. Louis County United Fund, 1968; v.p. Wellesley Coll. Class of '43, 1973—. Founder, pres. bd. Ladue Chapel Nursery Sch., 1957; mem. long range planning com. Ladue Chapel; bd. dirs. Campbell House, Girls Home, Multiple Sclerosis Soc. St. Louis. Recipient Wellesley Coll. award of year, 1968; Liberty Bowl, Freedoms Found., 1968. Mem. Am. Psychol. Assn., Nat. Assn. Sch. Psychologists (charter), Assn. Children with Learning Disabilities, Council Exceptional Children, Am. Personnel and Guidance Assn., St. Louis Jr. League (dir. 1950-53), Mo. Hist. Soc. (pres. women's assn. 1963-64, trustee soc. 1968-71), Kirkwood Community Tchrs. Assn. (dir. 1970-75), Mo. State, Ladue Community assns., Nat. Soc. Colonial Dames in Mo. (dir. 1967-69). Presbyn. (deaconess). Clubs: Wellesley Coll. of St. Louis (pres. 1960), St. Louis, Woman's (St. Louis). Contbr. article to publs. Home: 70 Fair Oaks St St Louis MO 63124 Office: 9701 Conway Rd St Louis MO 63124

TRESCOTT, MARTHA FRANCES MOORE, historian, minister; b. Dallas, Nov. 1, 1941; d. Murray Winn and Frances Marie (McConnell) Moore; student U. Ark., 1960-61; B.S., Southern Methodist U., 1964, postgrad, 1964-66, M.A., 1972, postgrad, 1977; postgrad Perkins Sch. Theology, 1966; m. Paul B. Trescott, Dec. 18, 1971; stepchildren—Jeffrey A., Jill V., Andrew B. Chemist, Southwestern Med. Sch., U. Tex., Dallas, 1964-67; tchr. sci. and math. Ursuline Acad., Dallas, 1966; mem. ch. staff Lovers Lane Meth. Ch., Dallas, 1966; literature chemist, searcher Lone Star Gas Co. research and devel. library, Dallas, 1968; lit. researcher, info. scientist, indsl. info. services Sci. and Engring. Library, Southern Meth. U., Dallas, 1968-75; founder, owner Research in Literature of Industry, Dallas, 1973-77; lic. for ministry, Disciples of Christ, 1976; asst. campus minister Ill. Disciples Found., Urbana, 1976—. Mem. Com. on Aging Champaign County; bd. dirs. Sisters in Service Champaign County. NSF grantee, 1972-74; Rovensky fellow, 1976-77. Mem. U. Ill. Religious Workers Assn., NOW, Soc. History of Tech., Women in Technol. History (founder, sec.), History of Sci. Soc., Econ. History Assn., Bus. History Conf., Am. Hist. Assn., Am. Chem. Soc. (history of chemistry div.), Soc. Indsl. Archeology, Coll. Profl. Christian Ministers in Ill and Wis., Nat. Trust for Historic Preservation, Chi Omega, Phi Alpha Theta, Alpha Lambda Delta. Home: 406 Green St E Apt 101 Urbana IL 61801 Office: 403 Wright St S Champaign IL 61820

TRETHEWEY, WILLIAM CHARLES, glass products mfg. co. exec.; b. Eugene, Ore., Dec. 7, 1920; s. Richard D. and Delphine Aurora (Mailhot) T.; m. Kathryn Thompson Clark, Nov. 11, 1945; children—Polly, Penny, Beth Ann, William Joseph. Service technician Woolley Instrument Service, Portland, Oreg., 1946-48; instrument technician Harshaw Chem. Co., Cleve., 1948-52; instrument engr. Owens Corning Fiberglas, Newark, Ohio, 1953-60, mgr. instrument dept., 1960-70; v.p. PHD Assos., Dover, Mass., 1970-72; tech. dir. control systems Anchor Hocking Corp., Lancaster, Ohio, 1973—. Served with USNR, 1942-45. Fellow Instrument Soc. Am., Republican. Episcopalian. Home: 176 Skyline Dr Lancaster OH 43130 Office: W Fair Av Lancaster OH 43130

TREUTER, CHARLES RICHARD, retail co. exec.; b. Houston, May 19, 1942; s. Richard Oscar and Nellie (Vernon) T.; A.A., Schreiner Inst., 1962; B.S., U. Houston, 1963; m. Lillie Gay, Feb. 16, 1968; children—Shannon Marie, Robert Wayne. With S.S. Kresge Co., various locations, 1963—, mgr. Louisville, 1972-73, dist. mgr., Detroit, 1973—. Mem. Retail Mchts. Assn., Phi Theta Kappa. Republican. Lutheran. Kiwanian. Home: 17074 Raccoon Trail Strongsville OH 44136 Office: 41425 Joy Rd Plymouth MI 48170

TREVAN, GEORGIA ETHA OLIVER, educator, ednl. adminstr.; b. Forsyth County, N.C., Sept. 8, 1909; d. George Washington and Laura Louise (Craver) Oliver; student U. Chgo., 1959-60; B.Gen. Studies, Roosevelt U., 1970; postgrad. DePaul U., 1973, Loyola U., Chgo., 1973, Ill. State U., 1973-74; m. George Clarence Trevan, June 29, 1947. With Ill. Dept. Labor, Chgo., 1941-72, claims dep., 1945-49, vocat. counselor, 1950-67, vocat. supr., 1967-72; tchr., work tng. coordinator Bloom High Sch., Chicago Heights, Ill., 1972—; nat. judge Distributive Ednl. Clubs Am., 1976. Panelist, Ill. Gov.'s Conf. on Youth, 1965, YWCA, 1971; chmn. bd. dirs. Beatrice Caffrey Youth Service, 1956-59. Recipient certificate of appreciation Ill. Youth Commn., 1964, Beatrice Caffrey Youth Service, 1966, Prairie State Coll., 1971, Westchesterfield Community Assn., 1974, Distributive Edn. Clubs Am., 1976, award Chicago Heights Youth Com., 1977. Mem. Am. Personnel and Guidance Assn., Nat. Vocat. and Guidance Assn., Nat. Ret. Tchrs. Assn. Democrat. Office: Bloom High School 10th St and Dixie Hwy Chicago Heights IL 60411

TREVARTHAN, FRED, III, assn. exec.; b. Clinton, Ind., Sept. 23, 1939; s. Fred and Ruth L. (McCracken) T.; B.S., Ind. State U., 1963; m. Zona Elizabeth Jones, June 30, 1962; children—Denise, Kenneth. Speech therapist pub. schs., Ill., 1964-69, Marshall (Ill.) Community Schs., 1964-66, Martinsville (Ill.) Sch. Dist., 1966-67, Kankakee (Ill.) Sch. Dist. III, 1967-69; dir., therapist Easter Seal Soc., Kankakee, 1969—. Cons. child care program Bradley-Bourbonnais High Sch., 1971—. Methodist (chmn. finance com. 1970-71, asso. lay leader 1971-73). Home: 334 S Evergreen St Kankakee IL 60901 Office: 895 S Washington Ave Kankakee IL 60901

TREYZ, JOSEPH HENRY, librarian; b. Binghamton, N.Y., Nov. 23, 1926; s. Joseph Henry and Edna Belle (Leonard) T.; B.A., Oberlin Coll., 1950; postgrad. Harvard U., 1951; M.L.S., Columbia U., 1952. Circulation asst. N.Y. Acad. Medicine Library, 1950-51; cataloger Columbia Libraries, N.Y.C., 1951-53, Stevens Inst. Tech., Hoboken, N.J., 1953-54; adminstrv. asst. Yale Library, 1955, asst. head catalogue dept., 1955-61; head new campuses program U. Calif., La Jolla, 1961-65; asst. dir. U. Mich. Library, Ann Arbor, 1965-71; dir. libraries U. Wis., Madison, 1971—; univ. rep. Consumer Reaction Survey Team for Cataloging in Source, 1959; cons. Library Tech. Project for Catalog Card Reprodn. Study, 1961; condr. survey tech. services Fordham U. Libraries, 1967-69, Brandeis U. Libraries, 1970-71; mem. Wis. Gov.'s Com. on Library Devel., 1973—. Bd. dirs. Wis. Center for Theatre Research. Served with AUS, 1945-46. Mem. Universal Serials and Book Exchange (v.p. 1976, pres., chmn. bd. dirs. 1977), ALA (councilor 1970-74, 77—, chmn. various coms. 1967-69 recipient Melvil Dewey medal 1970, dir. 1976—) Assn. Research Libraries (commn. orgn. materials, bd. dirs. 1975—), Assn. Coll. and Research Libraries (chmn. editorial bd. Choice, 1968-70), Wis. Library Consortium (pres. 1975-76), Wis. Assn. Acad. Libraries (chmn. 1973-74), Council Wis. Librarians (chmn. 1975-76), Wis. Library Assn. (bd. dirs. 1973-74, mem. White House Conf. com. 1977—), Madison Area Library Council (v.p. 1973-74), Mich. Library Assn. (chmn. tech. services sect. 1968-69), N.Y. Tech. Services Librarians (pres. 1959-60), Am. Soc. Info. Sci., Bibliog. Soc. Am. Methodist. Clubs: Masons, Shriners, Signature (sec.-treas. 1969-70), Univ. (Madison). Author: Books for College Libraries, 1967; also articles. Home: 843 Farwell Dr Madison WI 53704

TRIBBIE, THOMAS LEYSHON, lawyer; b. Cambridge, Ohio, Dec. 17, 1926; s. Earl Henderson and Mary Alpha (Leyshon) T.; B.A., Ohio State U., 1950, J.D., 1952; m. Marjorie K. Caldwell, Aug. 8, 1954; children—Melinda, Deborah, Stephen, Terri. Admitted to Ohio bar, 1952, since practiced in Cambridge; partner firm Tribbie, Scott & Moorehead, 1967—, solicitor Village of Byesville, Ohio, 1956-64, 66-70; pros. atty. Guerney County, 1961-69. Trustee Guernsey Meml. Hosp., Cambridge, 1967—, v.p., 1971-73, pres., 1973-75. Served with AUS, 1945-46. Mem. Am., Ohio, Guernsey County (pres. 1960) bar assns., Nat. Dist. Attys. Assn., Am. Legion, V.F.W. Republican. Presbyn. Mason (hon. 33 deg., Shriner). Home: RD 3 Cedar Hills Cambridge OH 43725 Office: 139 Court House Sq Cambridge OH 43725

TRIEZENBERG, RYER, realtor-developer; b. Evergreen Park, Ill., Apr. 6, 1925; s. Herman G. and Gertie (Smit) T.; student DePaul U., 1946-47; Northwestern U., 1947, Roosevelt Coll., 1947-49, YMCA Inst., 1948-51; m. Sarah M. Yff, Aug. 27, 1946; children—Marianne (Mrs. Robert Lenters), Herman Lee, Marcia (Mrs. Jack DeBaar), Ryer G. Adminstrv. asst. Teninga & Co., Realtors-Developers, Chgo., 1946-51; owner Triezenberg & Co., Palos Heights, Ill., 1951—; sec.-treas. Westgate Devel. Co.; dir. Navajo Devel. Co.; sec.-treas. Ridgeland Water Service Co.; dir. Royal Acres Nursing Home. Mem. Evergreen Park Plan Commn., 1958; mem. Evergreen Park Elementary Sch. Bd., 1952-58; dir. Crestwood Indsl. Commn., 1973—. Trustee Christian Counselling Found., Evergreen Park Library Bd. 1958-70; mem. adv. bd. Little Co. of Mary Sch. Nursing, 1959-63. Served with USMCR, 1943-46. Mem. Ill. Real Estate Bd., Southwest Suburban Bd. Realtors, Chgo. Real Estate Bd. (bd. govs. 1958-61, chmn. brokers div. 1960-61), Nat. Assn. Real Estate Bds. Mem. Christian Reformed Ch. Home: 7700 W McIntosh Dr Orland Park IL 60462 Office: 12750 S Harlem Ave Palos Heights IL 60463

TRIMMER, ROBERT WHITFIELD, chemist; b. Binghamton, N.Y., Dec. 13, 1937; s. Charles Moore and Dorothy James (Kirk) T.; A.B., Hope Coll., 1960; postgrad. Universitat Erlangen-Nurnberg (Germany), 1963; Ph.D., Rensselaer Poly. Inst., 1973; m. Telma Berberian, July 24, 1965; children—Roberta Dorothy, Derek. Asst. research chemist Sterling Winthrop Research Inst., Rensselaer, N.Y., 1964-69; supr. lab. product devel. Miles Labs., Elkhart, Ind., 1973-76, pharm. research chemist, 1977—. Mem. Elkhart (Ind.) Symphony Soc., 1973—. Served with AUS, 1961-63. Mem. Am. Chem. Soc., Knickerbocker Hist. Soc. (trustee 1971—), Chem. Soc. (London), A.A.A.S., St. Andrews Soc. of Albany (N.Y.), Am. Sci. Affiliation and Organic Reaction Catalysis Soc. Ref. Ch. Am. Home: 23357 Delany Ln Elkhart IN 46514 Office: 1127 Myrtle St Elkhart IN 46514

TRINE, RALPH DONALD, steel fabrication mfg. co. exec.; b. Albion, Mich., Nov. 21, 1941; s. Donald Clyde and Reva (Hattie Hinkle) T.; B.S., Tri State U., 1961; M.S., Mich. State U., 1963, M.B.A., 1965; m. Sheri Ann Gaertner, July 3, 1966; children—Carri, Ralph Donald II, Barry. Computer systems scientist IBM, Detroit, 1966-67; gen. mgr. T & S Equipment Co., Albion, 1967—, also dir.; dir. Vestil Mfg. Co. Mem. Albion Indsl. Devel. Corp. (pres.), Am. Soc. M.E., Mich. C. of C. Republican. Methodist. Clubs: Duck Lake Country, Minges Creek Racquet. Home: 1110 Locust St Albion MI 49224 Office: 710 Cass St W Albion MI 49224

TRIPP, MARIAN BARLOW LOOPE, pub. relations exec.; b. Lodgepole, Nebr., July 26, 1921; d. Lewis Rockwell and Cora Dee (Davis) Barlow; B.S., Iowa State U., 1944; m. James Edward Tripp, Feb. 9, 1957; children—Brendan Michael, Kevin Mark. Writer, editor Dairy Record, St. Paul, 1944-45; head product promotion div. pub. relations dept. Swift & Co., Chgo., 1945-55; account exec. pub. relations dept. J. Walter Thompson Co., N.Y.C., 1955-66, v.p. mgmt. and supervision, Chgo., 1966-73, v.p., dir. consumer affairs, 1973-75; pres. Marian Tripp Communications Inc., Chgo., 1976—. Bd. dirs. Chgo. Conv. and Tourism Bd., 1973-75. Mem. U.S. of C. (consumer affairs com.), Pub. Relations Soc. Am., Womens Advt. Club Chgo., Am., Ill. home econs. assns., Chgo. Home Economists in Bus. Episcopalian. Home: 100 E Bellevue Pl Chicago IL 60611 Office: 100 Walton Pl E Chicago IL 60611

TRIPPET, CHARLES KIGHTLY, telephone co. exec.; b. Princeton, Ind., Apr. 14, 1913; s. Sanford and Edith (Kightly) T.; A.B., Wabash Coll., 1936; m. Isabel Key, Sept. 28, 1940; children—Susan, Bruce, Tresa Lynn. Ins. agt. Trippet Ins. Agy., Princeton, 1937—; dir. Princeton Telephone Co., 1947—, treas., 1953-66, pres., 1966—; dir. Gibson County Bank. Trustee Oakland City Coll.; bd. govs. Associated Colls. Ind. Served to 1st lt. U.S. Army, 1942-46. Decorated Bronze Star. Mem. Ind. Telephone Assn. (dir. 1956—, pres. 1977—), U.S. Ind. Telephone Assn. (dir. 1969—), Am. Legion, VFW. Democrat. Methodist. Clubs: Princeton Rotary (pres. 1954-55), Athletic, Petroleum, Masons, Shriners. Elks. Home: 306 W Spruce St Princeton IN 47670 Office: PO Box 324-315 N Hart St Princeton IN 47670

TROJAK, THERESE ANNE (MRS. EDWARD V. TROJAK), banker; b. Chgo., Nov. 17, 1929; d. Robert Roger and Anne Marie (Loula) Du Monte; corr. course Chg. Sch. Nursing, 1950-51; student N. Central Tech. Inst. Adult Edn., 1971; m. Edward V. Trojak, June 13, 1953; children—Gregory Edward, Maureen Ann. With State Bank Phillips (Wis.), 1950-55, 61—, comml. and savs. teller, 1962—, bookkeeper and bank officer, 1970—. Sec. Ladies Drum and Bugle Corps, 1951-53; treas. So. Price County chpt. A.R.C., 1966-68, mem. bloodmobile com., 1968; chmn. reunion day Lugerville Sch. P.T.A., 1969—, treas., 1962-63, sec.-treas., 1970—, chmn. publicity, 1962—, pres., 1963-65, 68-70; chmn. Friendship Campaign for Retarded Children, 1972; instr. snowmobile safety Wis. Dept. Natural Resources, 1972—. Acting sec. Price County adv. com. New Concepts Found., 1972-73. Mem. V.F.W. (treas. ladies aux. 1967—, chmn. membership com. 1967—, chmn. rehab. com. 1974—, dist. poppy and publicity chmn. 1976-77, dist. sec. 1977-78), Cath. Daus. Am. Roman Catholic (mem. adult choir 1942-53). Home: Luger Route Box 174 Phillips WI 54555 Office: Drawer 67 Phillips WI 54555

TROLDAHL, OATHER FRANKLIN, newspaperman; b. Hanska, Minn., June 21, 1936; s. Oscar Carl and Ruth Victoria (Peterson) T.; student Mankato State Coll., 1956-58; m. Ann B. Williamson, Aug. 24, 1956; children—Todd, Kim, Dawn. Editor, owner Janesville (Minn.) Argus, 1959-70; partner, v.p., gen. mgr. Waseca (Minn.) Daily Jour., 1968—; owner Waseca Travel Service, 1969—. A founding dir. Minn. Newspaper Assn. sponsored printing skills sch., Canby, Minn., 1968; v.p. Waseca Cable TV, 1973—. Chmn. stock soliciting dr. Waseca Devel. Corp., 1971. Mem. Waseca County Republican Com., 1971; bd. dirs. Waseca Hockey Assn., 1975-77. Served with AUS, 1954-56. Recipient awards in gen. excellence Minn. Newspaper Assn. Mem. 2d Dist. Editorial Assn. (pres. 1967), Waseca C. of C. (pres. 1974). Clubs: Masons Shriners, K.T., Rotary (charter pres. Janesville 1965, pres. Waseca 1977), Lakeside Country (dir. 1975-77, citation 1976). Home: Route 3 Sunset Shore Waseca MN 56093 Office: 203 3d Ave NW Waseca MN 56093

TROMBLA, WILLIAM GILBERT, JR., educator; b. Manitowoc, Wis., Jan. 9, 1934; s. William Gilbert and Elsa Rose (Schrieber) T.; B.A., Lakeland Coll., 1962; M.A., No. Colo. U., 1967; m. Nancy Carol Nelson, Aug. 18, 1962; children—David Allen, Leigh Anne. Tchr., Pulaski (Wis.) Community Sch., 1962-64, tchr.-counselor, 1964-73; sch. counselor, guidance dir. Westfield (Wis.) Area Schs., 1973—. Mem. articulation steering com. Madison Area Tech. Coll., 1977; mem. Chem. Dependency United Services Bd., 1977; mem. mental health com. Unified Services Bd., 1974-76; mem. subject matter adv. com. Northeastern Wis. Tech. Inst., Green Bay; state coordinator Nat. Career Guidance Week, 1974—; v.p. Westfield Community Chest. Served in USMR, 1953-57. Certified profl. counselor Wis. Dept. Pub. Instrn.; certified secondary sch. tchr., Wis. Mem. NEA, Wis., Westfield edn. assns., Am., Wis. personnel and guidance assns., Nat. Vocat. Guidance Assn., Am., Wis. sch. counselors assns., Wis. Career Guidance Assn. (an organizer 1976). Roman Catholic. Club: Lions (past pres. Pulaski; sec. Westfield 1974—). Home: Route 1 Box 167F Westfield WI 53964

TRONE, PETER DONALDSON, summer camp and sch. adminstr.; b. Inpls., Oct. 27, 1929; s. Donaldson Greene and Mary Almeda (Daum) T.; student Butler U., 1947-50, Rollins Coll., 1950-51; m. Beverly J. Geariety, Aug. 18, 1974; 1 stepson, Bradd J. Geariety. Counselor, Culver (Ind.) Ednl. Found. Woodcraft Camp, 1949-61, asst. camp dir., 1962-68, dir., 1969—; mgr. Don Trone's, Inc., Culver, 1953-60, v.p., 1960—. Football ofcl., 1955—; treas. Culver Pub. Library, 1959-69; mem. Culver Town Plan Commn., 1959-67, pres., 1960; mem. Culver Bd. Zoning Appeals, 1967—, Local Election Bd., 1958—; active Boy Scouts Am. Served with AUS, 1951-53. Mem. Culver C. of C. (sec. 1955-65), Culver Summer Schs. Alumni Assn. (sec. 1963-68, dir.), Am. Camping Assn. (dir. Ind. sect. 1975—), Ind. High Sch. Athletic Assn., St. Joseph Valley Athletic Ofcls. Assn. (v.p. 1968). Republican. Presbyn. Clubs: Maxinkuckee Yacht (commodore Culver, 1970); Columbia (Indpls.). Author: Camp Directors Manual, 1970; Editor, pub. Camp Sailing and Boating Manual, 1968. Home: 425 College Ave Culver IN 46511 Office: Culver Woodcraft Camp Culver IN 46511

TROUP, GEORGE BARNETT, steel co. exec.; b. Buffalo, July 7, 1920; s. Albert James and Clara (Smeader) T.; B. Metall. Engring., Rensselaer Poly. Inst., 1942; postgrad. N.Y. U., 1943; m. Ruth Rockefeller, Dec. 24, 1943; children—Nancy Jean, Barbara Jane. Material and process engr. Westinghouse Electric Corp., Buffalo, 1946-49; chief metallurgist Instrument div. Am. Optical Co., Buffalo, 1949-54; v.p., gen. mgr. Lubri-Case, Inc., N.Y.C., 1954-60; asst. to v.p. Bliss & Lauchlin, Inc., Oak Brook, Ill., 1960-73; metall. engr. La Salle Steel Co., Hammond, Ind., 1973—; pres. Econo Bar Co. Mem. Oak Brook Polit. Devel. Com., 1967; bd. govs. Brook Forest, Ill., 1967—, pres., 1968. Served to capt. USAAF, 1942-46. Registered profl. engr., Pa., Ill. Mem. Soc. Automotive Engrs., Am. Soc. for Metals. Contbr. articles to profl. jours. Clubs: Oak Brook Athletic Assn. (dir. 1968), Midwesterners. Home: 16 Concord Dr Oak Brook IL 60521 Office: 1412 E 150th St Hammond IN 46320

TROUPE, LAUREL ANTOINETTE, educator; b. Chgo., Nov. 24, 1944; d. Adam Joseph and Lucille Jennie (Moore) Zimmerman; A.Applied Sci., Olive Harvey City Coll., 1972; B.A. with honors, Chgo. State U., 1973; M.S. in Edn., Chgo. State U., 1975; 1 son, Floyd D. Troupe, Jr. Lab. technician Met. San. Dist. of Chgo., 1967-71; psychologist S.T.E.A., Inc., Mental Health Program, Chgo., 1974-76, program cons., 1976—; family counselor Chgo. Youth Centers, Chgo., 1976-77; family therapist The Depot Family Counseling Center, Chgo., 1975—; research asso. Governors State U., Park Forest South, Ill., 1977—; adult edn. instr. for sr. citizens Kennedy King Coll., 1975-76. Recipient Certificate of Merit, Chgo. State U., 1972-73; Merit Award for program adminstrn., Chgo. Youth Centers, 1976. Mem. Assn. Black Social Workers, Am. Personnel and Guidance Assn., Far S.W. Mental Health Council, Concerned Citizens Council, Am. Sch. Counselors Assn., Nat. Vocat. Guidance Assn., Assn. for Non-White Concerns. Home: 11058 S Esmond St Chicago IL 60643 Office: Chgo State U 95th and King Dr Chicago IL 60628

TROWBRIDGE, KAREN SUE, mech. engr.; b. Vermontville, Mich., Nov. 12, 1950; d. Vernon Clifford and Mary Delilah (Viele) T.; B.S. with honors in Mech. Engring., Mich. State U., 1972. Maintenance engr. Johnson & Johnson Corp., Chgo., 1972-73, control supr. facilities and equipment, 1973-75; project engr. Procter & Gamble Corp., Lima, Ohio, 1975, production mgr., 1976—. Vol., VA Hosp., Battle Creek, Mich., 1969; troop leader Girl Scouts U.S.A. Beckman Sch. for Retarded, 1969-72; chmn. campus blood drive ARC, 1971-72; advisor Jr. Achievement program, 1975—. Recipient Award for Contributions to Community and Industry Chgo. YWCA, 1974. Mem. ASME, Pi Tau Sigma, Gamma Sigma Sigma. Club: Venture (pres. 1976). Home: 2275 N Cable St Lima OH 45807 Office: PO Box 1900 Lima OH 45802

TROXEL, ALBERT DELONE, JR., dentist; b. Portsmouth, Ohio, Dec. 25, 1925; s. Albert Delone and Emily Miriam (Hadfield) T.; B.S., Johns Hopkins, 1949; D.D.S., Ohio State U., 1955; m. Mary D. Stevens, Jan. 19, 1961; 1 dau., Mary Kathleen (Mrs. Ronald McGrew). Practice dentistry, Columbus, Ohio, 1955—, Mt. Sterling, Ohio, 1962-67. Dir. Woodbridge Land Co., Mt. Sterling, treas., 1964—; dir. Captain's Cove Marina, Inc., Portsmouth, Ohio, pres., 1969—; dir. Deer Creek Devel. Co., Mt. Sterling, treas., 1964—. Precinct committeeman Republican party, Mt. Sterling, 1962—, mem. central and exec. com. Madison County, 1962-68. Served with inf., AUS, World War II; ETO; col., chief dental surgeon Ohio N.G. Decorated Bronze Star medal with oak leaf cluster, Combat Infantryman's badge. Fellow Royal Soc. Health; mem. Am., Ohio dental assns., Columbus Dental Soc. Methodist. Rotarian. Home: Box 111 Route 3 Mt Sterling OH 43143 Office: 4480 Refugee Rd Columbus OH 43227

TROXEL, JAY CORWIN, real estate analyst, cons.; b. Flint, Mich., Jan. 23, 1917; s. Harley Anthony and Ilah Pearl (Jay) T.; A.B., U. Mich., Ann Arbor, 1938, M.B.A. with distinction, 1939; m. Eloise Hurst, Sept. 2, 1939. Valuator FHA, Detroit, 1939-43, underwriter, Detroit, 1943-44, adminstrv. officer, Washington, 1944-46; real estate analyst, cons., Flint, Mich., 1946—. Instr. real estate U. Mich., 1948. Mem. Davison Township (Mich.) Housing Commn., 1974-75. Recipient Robert H. Armstrong award Appraisal Jour., 1964. Mem. Am. Inst. Real Estate Appraisers, Soc. Real Estate Appraisers (sr. real estate analyst 1963—, pres. chpt. 1952). Contbr. articles to Appraisal Jour., Real Estate Appraiser. Editorial bd. Appraisal Jour., 1966-67. Home: 2280 Old Hickory Blvd Davison MI 48423

TROXELL, JOHN FRANKLIN, veterinarian; b. Shelbina, Mo., Nov. 25, 1935; s. Clarence Delmar and Eleanor Delano (Smock) T.; B.S., U. Mo., 1963, D.V.M., 1963; m. Mary Elizabeth Shively, July 9, 1964; children—Jason Franklin, Grant Alan. Practice vet. medicine, also cons. to VA Hosp., Martinsburg, W.Va., 1966-68; practice vet. medicine Humane Soc. Mo., St. Louis, 1968; practice vet. medicine, Homewood, Ill., 1968—. Pres., dir. Flossmoor Pet Hosp., Ltd. (Ill.), 1968—; owner Glenwood Village Pet Clinic, Glenwood, Ill.; dir. radio program on vet. edn. WCGO, Chicago Heights, Ill., 1970. Bd. dirs. South Suburban Ilumane Soc. Served with USNR, 1953-54; served to capt., AUS, 1964-66. Mem. Am., Chgo. vet. med. assns., Toastmasters Internat., Am. Legion, Gamma Sigma Delta, Alpha Zeta. Republican. Methodist. Rotarian. Office: Route 54 and 196th St Homewood IL 60430

TROY, MATTHEW MICHAEL, real estate co. exec.; b. Dublin, Ireland, July 31, 1938; s. Mathew Edward and Mary Ann (Byrne) T.; came to U.S., 1949, naturalized, 1964; grad. Realtors Inst., Ind. U., 1973; postgrad. Nat. Inst. Real Estate Brokers, 1972-75; m. Barbara Lynn Kriesel, Jan. 6, 1968; children—Patrick M., Matthew T., Erin L. Vice pres. Credit Bur. LaPorte County, Michigan City, Ind., 1964-69; pres. Eisner and Troy Real Estate, Inc., Michigan City, 1970-73; pres. New England Investment Corp., Michigan City, 1969—; pres. Real Estate Service Corp., Michigan City, 1973—. Pres., Michigan City Bd. Realtors, 1972-73, dir., 1974-76; dir Multiple Listing Service of Michigan City, 1973-74; pres. Michigan City Vocat. Bldg. Trades, Inc., 1973-74, dir., 1975—. Commr. Michigan City Human Rights Commr., 1975-77; adv. bd. Michigan City Legal Aid Soc., 1975-77; area mgmt. broker LaPorte and Stark Counties, FHA/HUD, 1976-77. Served with USMC, 1955-60. Recipient Realtor of Year award Michigan City Bd. Realtors, 1973, Outstanding Community Service to Vocat. Trades State award, 1974. Mem. Nat., Ind. (dir. 1975-77) assns. realtors, Nat. Inst. Real Estate Brokers, Ind. Real Estate Commn., Inter-City Relocation Service, Michigan City C. of C. (chmn. membership com. 1973-74), Michigan City Jaycees. Toastmaster. Clubs: Hibernians, Exchange (v.p. 1970-72) Home: 7197 125th St N La Porte IN 46350 Office: US Hwy 20 and Longwood Dr Michigan City IN 46360

TROY, WILLIAM NORMAN, advt., pub. relations agy. exec.; b. Cleve., July 12, 1927; s. William F. and Norma Winifred (Higgins) T.; B.A. in English, Western Res. U., 1951; m. Jean A. Baird, July 11, 1953; children—Bartley John, Norma Janice, Terence Francis, Timothy Norman. Editor, Trade Mags., Inc., 1951-53, McGraw-Hill Pub. Co., 1953-57; mgr. indsl. publicity Griswold-Eshleman Co., 1957-63; v.p. WYSE Advt., 1963-67; pres. William Troy & Co., Cleve., 1967-73; v.p. Watts, Lamb, Kenyon & Herrick, Cleve., 1973—. Served with AUS, 1945-47. Cleve. Playhouse fellow, 1944. Mem. Pub. Relations Soc. Am. Home: 7560 Hollycroft Ln Mentor OH 44060 Office: 19201 Villaview Rd Cleveland OH 44119

TROYER, ALVAH FORREST, JR., plant breeder, adminstr.; b. La Fontaine, Ind., May 30, 1929; s. Alvah Forrest and Lottie Eunice Waggoner T.; B.S., Purdue U., 1954; M.S., U. Ill., 1956; Ph.D., U. Minn., 1964; m. Joyce Ann Wigner, Sept. 22, 1950; children—Anne (Mrs. Charles Sherwood), Barbara, Catherine, Daniel. Research sta. mgr. Pioneer Hi-Bred Internat., hybrid corn, 1958-64, research coordinator No. stas., 1965-77, Eastern stas., 1971-77; dir. research and devel. Pfizer Genetics, Inc., St. Louis, 1977—. Served with Arty., to M. Sgt., AUS, 1951-52; Korea. Mem. A.A.A.S., Sigma Xi, Lambda Chi Alpha. Mason. Pioneer devel. large volume hybrids. Home: 153 Hawaiian Dr Mankato MN 56001 Office: Box 877 Mankato MN 56001

TROYER, DANA ORION, ophthalmologist; b. Chgo., July 13, 1920; s. George Delton and Kathryn S. (Sommers) T.; M.D., Northwestern U., 1944; m. Verna M. Burkholder, Jan. 30, 1947; children—Don Lawrence, Robert Martin, Frederick John. Intern, St. Joseph's Hosp., Chgo., 1943-44; resident in ophthalmology Tulane U., New Orleans, Ill. Eye and Ear Infirmary, Chgo., 1950-52; practice medicine specializing in ophthalmology, Bloomington, Ill., 1952-55, Goshen, Ind., 1956—: pres. Goshen Hosp., 1966, mem. staff. Mem. Elkhart County Med. Soc. (pres. 1975), Ind. Acad. Ophthalmology (v.p. 1972), Chgo. Ophthalmol. Soc., Mennonite Med. Assn. Mennonite. Club: Maplecrest Country (Goshen). Home: 1727 S 13th St Goshen IN 46521 Office: 201 E Clinton St Goshen IN 46526

TROYER, LEROY S., architect, planner; b. Middlebury, Ind., Nov. 23, 1937; s. Seth S. and Nancy D. (Miller) T.; student Ind. U., 1964-66; B.S., U. Notre Dame, 1971; m. Phyllis Joy Eigsti, May 24, 1958; children—Terry Lee, Ronald Jay, Donald Ray. With Yutzy Constrn. Co., Middlebury, 1954-59; archtl. draftsman, designer Robert E. Foltz, A.I.A., South Bend, 1959-71; sr. partner LeRoy Troyer & Assos., architects, planners, landscape architects, Mishawaka, 1971—. Vice pres. Environic Found. Internat., 1973-75. Supr. St. Joseph County Soil Conservation Dist., 1974—. Adv. bd. Mishawaka Salvation Army, 1974-75; bd. dirs. YMCA Camp Eberhart. Recipient AIA award for restoration Bonneyville Mills, Elkhart County, Ind., 1975; named Outstanding Young Man of Yr., Mishawaka (Ind.) Jr. C. of C., 1974. Mem. A.I.A. (chpt. treas. 1975-76, v.p., pres. elect No. Ind. chpt. 1977), Ind. Soc. Architects (dir. 1977—), Am. Inst. Planners, Am. Soc. Planning Ofcls., South Bend-Mishawaka Area C. of C. Mennonite (trustee 1974-77). Lion. Home: 3019 Essex Dr South Bend IN 46615 Office: 112 Lincolnway E Mishawaka IN 46544

TROYER, THOMAS FRANKLIN, real estate broker; b. Walnut Creek, Ohio, Jan. 5, 1910; s. Albert M. and Jessie A. (Syler) T.; B.S. in Edn., Kent State U., 1933; m. Dorothea M. Viall, Nov. 25, 1933; 1 son, Thomas Lynton. Tchr., Ohio Pub. Schs., 1928-43; chief design draftsman, chief prodn. engr. Fageol Products Co., Kent, Ohio, 1944-57; became owner Troyer Realty, Kent, 1958, now co-owner. Real estate fee appraiser, 1964—; author, poet. Recipient Distinguished Service award City of Stow (Ohio), 1976; named Realtor of Year, Portage County Bd., 1966. Mem. Portage County Bd. Realtors (pres. 1964, dir.), Nat., Ohio (trustee), assns. real estate bds., Izaak Walton League, Stow (Ohio) Bus. Men's Club, Stow C. of C. (dir. 1967—, pres. 1970-71), Am. Bird Watching Soc. (charter), Internat. Platform Assn., Kent State U. Alumni Assn., Internat. Clover Poetry Assn. Republican. Conglist. (chmn. bd. trustees 1947-50, deacon 1962-64). Rotarian (dir. 1967—, pres. Stow chpt. 1972-73). Club: Men's Garden of Am. (past pres. Kent chpt.). Home: 4174 Kent Rd Stow OH 44224 Office: 4299 Kent Rd Stow OH 44224

TROZZOLO, ANTHONY MARION, chemist; b. Chgo., Jan. 11, 1930; s. Pasquale and Francesca (Vercillo) T.; B.S. Ill. Inst. Tech., 1950; M.S., U. Chgo., 1957, Ph.D., 1960; m. Doris C. Stoffregen, Oct. 8, 1955; children—Thomas, Susan, Patricia, Michael, Lisa, Laura. Asst. chemist, Chgo. Midway Labs., 1952-53; asso. chemist Armour Research Found., Chgo., 1953-56; mem. tech. staff Bell Laboratories, Murray Hill, N.J., 1959-75; Charles L. Huisking prof. chemistry U. Notre Dame, 1975—; visiting prof. Columbia U., N.Y.C., 1971. AEC fellow, 1951; NSF fellow, 1957-59; Phillips lecturer, U. Okla., 1971; P.C. Reilly lecturer, Notre Dame, 1972; C. L. Brown lecturer, Rutgers, 1975; Sigma Xi lecturer, Bowling Green, 1976; M. Faraday lecturer, No. Ill. U., 1976. Mem. Am. Chem. Soc., AAUP; fellow N.Y. Acad. Sciences, AAAS, AIC; Sigma Xi. Roman Catholic. Asso. editor Jour. Am. Chem. Soc., 1975-76; editor Chem. Reviews, 1977—; patentee; contbr. articles in field to profl. jours. Home: 1329 E Washington St South Bend IN 46617 Office: U Notre Dame Notre Dame IN 46556

TRUDEAU, ROBERT WAYNE, banker; b. Ironwood, Mich., Nov. 13, 1941; s. Archie Arthur and Lempi Selma T.; B.S., Northland Coll., Ashland, Wis., 1965; M.B.A., Mich. State U., 1966; m. Ann Tapio, June 1, 1963; children—Todd, Laurie. Trainee mktg. mgmt. Gen. Electric Co., N.Y.C., 1966-67; mgr. mktg. research and planning The Ansul Co., Marinette, Wis., 1967-70; mgr. mktg. planning and services A.O. Smith Corp., Kankakee, Ill., 1971-73; dir. savs. and mktg. Detroit & No. Savings, Hancock, Mich., 1973—; prof. mktg. Governors State U., Park Forest, Ill., 1972-73, Mich. Tech. U., 1974. Served with U.S. Army, 1959-61. Mem. Copper County C. of C., Savs. Instns. Mktg. Soc. Am. (certificate of excellence in advt. 1976), Am. Mktg. Assn. Club: Elks. Home: 105 Chippewa Trail Dollar Bay MI 49922 Office: 400 Quincy St Hancock MI 49930

TRUDO, FREDERICK JOSEPH, microcomputer co. exec.; b. Cheboygan, Mich., Mar. 1, 1941; s. George A. and Ella A. (Chasse) T.; student Ferris State Coll., 1959-60; B.M.E., Gen. Motors Inst., 1964; M.M.E., U. Mich., 1965; m. Marlene Dana, Apr. 8, 1961; children—Dana, Michael, Valerie, Kristen. Project engr. Buick Motor div. Gen. Motors Corp., Flint, Mich., 1965-69; co-founder, v.p., dir. Process Computer Systems, Inc., Flint, 1969—. Gen. Motors Edn. fellow, 1964; named young engr. of year Flint chpt. Mich. Soc. Profl. Engrs., 1975. Mem. Soc. Automotive Engrs., Nat., Mich. socs. profl. engrs., Am. Mgmt. Assn., Greater Flint Pilots Assn. (sec., dir.), Flint Area C. of C., Tau Beta Phi. Roman Catholic. Home: 10200 Moon Rd Saline MI 48176 Office: 750 N Maple Rd Saline MI 48176

TRUE, MARION (MRS. LAURENCE M. TRUE), civic worker; b. Franklin, N.H., Feb. 16, 1902; d. Ichabod S. and Mary K. (Dunlap) Williams; B.S. in Chemistry, U. N.H., 1923; m. Laurence M. True, Sept. 3, 1927 (dec.); children—Lavinia (Mrs. Paul H. Plough, Jr.), David, Gilbert, Melbern, Katharine (Mrs. Douglas Logan). Tchr. Sanborn Sem., 1923-24, Braintree High Sch., 1924-27. Active Cleve. Girl Scouts, 1942-69, mem. bd. dirs., mem. regional com. 1951-61, mem. group services council, 1943-61, vice chmn., 1943-58, mem. exec. bd., 1955-58; mem. personnel com. Welfare Fedn. of Cleve., 1954-56; mem. Com. on Older Persons; chmn. Com. on Homes for Aged; alumni dir. U. N.H., 1964-70; pres. Aux. Bapt. Home Ohio; trustee, house chmn., sec. of bd. Judson Park, chmn. work com. Aux., 1973—, co-chmn. gift shop, 1976—; trustee First Baptist Ch., 1958-61, 64-70, 74-76, vice chmn. bd., 1975, chmn. bd., 1976, mem. cabinet, 1970-73, 74-77, stewardship com., 1972-74. Recipient Alumni Meritorious award 1961; Thanks badge, Lake Erie Girl Scouts. Mem. Nat. Soc. New Eng. Women (pres. Cleve. colony, v.p.) New Eng. Soc. Western Res. Daus. Am. Colonists (v.p., vice chmn. 1975-76), ASME (woman's aux.), Alpha Xi Delta. Clubs: College dir.); Canterbury Golf. Home: Jordan-Gardner Tower 2181 Ambleside Rd Cleveland OH 44106

TRUEBLOOD, CARL YATES, banker; b. Decatur, Ill., Jan. 15, 1924; s. Archie William and Mary Amy (Howell) T.; student Millikin U., 1942-43, 45-46; B.S. in Edn. with honors, Eastern Ill. Coll., 1949; postgrad. So. Ill. U., 1956, U. Wis., 1961; m. Sarah Catherine Curtin, June 24, 1961. Cashier 1st Trust & Savs. Bank, Taylorville, Ill., 1953-61; dir. Bussey 1st Nat. Bank, Urbana, Ill., 1961—, v.p., 1961-69, pres., 1970-74; pres. Nat. Bank Urbana, 1975—; dir. 1st Nat. Bank Rantoul (Ill.). Past pres. Champaign County Bankers Fedn. Served with AUS, 1943-45, to 1st lt., 1951-53. Roman Catholic. Lion (past pres. Urbana), Elk. Club: Urbana Golf and Country (past pres.). Home: 23 Sherwin Circle Urbana IL 61801 Office: 2001 Philo Rd Urbana IL 61801

TRUEMPER, VERNON JACOB, packaging film mfg. co. exec.; b. St. Louis, Dec. 6, 1922; s. William Steven and Madolyn Carolyn (Cagna) T.; student Harris Tchrs. Coll., 1941-42; B.S., Iowa State U., 1949; m. Deloris Maxine Kephart, Aug. 18, 1948; children—Gerald, Steven, Craig. With Allied Chem. & Dye Corp., St. Louis, 1949-53; with E.I. du Pont de Nemours & Co., Inc., Clinton, Iowa, 1953—, personnel supr., 1975—. Mem. budget rev. com. Clinton United Fund, 1966-71. Pres. Camanche Community Sch. Dist. Bd. Edn., 1957-75. Served with USAF, 1941-46. Decorated Air medal with 5 oak leaf clusters. Mem. Am. Inst. Chem. Engrs. (charter), Clinton Engring. Club, Kappa Sigma. Roman Catholic (trustee ch. 1969). K.C. Home: 1316 Anthony Pl Camanche IA 52730 Office: PO Box 451 Clinton IA 52732

TRUETTNER, JEAN, soc. exec.; b. Milw., June 14, 1922; d. Oscar R. and Norma (Seitz) T.; student Downer Coll., 1940-41. Sec., A. O. Smith Corp., Milw., 1942-56; office mgr. Am. Soc. Quality Control, Milw., 1956-69, membership and services mgr., 1969—. Mem. Am. Soc. Quality Control (sr.). Republican. Roman Catholic. Home: 9110 W Lisbon Ave Apt 3 Milwaukee WI 53222 Office: Am Soc Quality Control 161 W Wisconsin Ave Milwaukee WI 53203

TRUHLSEN, STANLEY MARSHALL, physician; b. Herman, Nebr., Nov. 13, 1920; s. Henry and Lola Mollie (Marshall) T.; A.B., U. Nebr., 1941, M.D., 1944; m. Ruth Haney, June 2, 1943; children—William, Nancy, Stanley M., Barbara. Intern, Albany (N.Y.) Hosp., 1944-45; resident Barnes Hosp., St. Louis, 1948-51; practice medicine, specializing in ophthalmology, Omaha, 1951—; mem. staff U. Nebr., Clarkson, Immanuel, Childrens, Methodist hosps.; pres. med. staff Immanuel Hosp., 1961, Clarkson Hosp., 1972-73; prof. ophthalmology U. Nebr. Coll. Medicine, 1974—; dir. Nebr. Blue Shield, Health Planning Council Midlands, 1972-75, Clarkson Hosp., 1974-76, Nebr. Soc. Prevention Blindness; trustee Omaha Home of Boys, Brownell Talbot Sch., 1966-69, Omaha Citizens Assembly, 1972—. Served with AUS, 1946-48. Fellow A.C.S.; mem. Am. Ophthal. Soc. (asst. editor transactions 1973—), Am. Acad. Ophthalmology and Otolaryngology (asso. editor transactions 1968-75, editor 1975—), Nebr. Acad. Ophthalmology (pres. 1975), Assn. Research in Vision and Ophthalmology, Omaha Med. Soc. (pres. 1973), Sigma Xi, Alpha Omega Alpha, Sigma Nu, Phi Rho Sigma. Republican. Mason (Shriner). Clubs: Rotary, Omaha, Omaha Country (pres. 1977-78). Home: 10086 Fieldcrest Dr Omaha NE 68114 Office: Doctors Bldg Omaha NE 68131

TRUMBLE, EUGENE FLETCHER, pub. relations exec.; b. Montevideo, Minn., Nov. 8, 1925; s. Eugene Fletcher and Elna Louisa (Gust) T.; B.J., U. Mo., 1950, B.A., 1950; m. Betty Oberlander Jaynes, Nov. 30, 1950; children—Susan (Mrs. Richard M. Chappell, Jr.), Janet (Mrs. Hooman Amiri), Mark, Cynthia, David, John. Program dir. U.S. Jr. C. of C., Tulsa, 1953-55; staff dir. Citizens Com. for Hoover Report, N.Y.C., 1955-56; account exec. Campbell-Mithun Advt., Mpls., 1956-60; dir. pub. relations Apache Corp., Mpls., 1960-66; pres. Trumble & Assos., Inc., Mpls., 1966—. Vice chmn. nat. dist. adv. council SBA, 1972—. Asst. nat. dir. Nixon-Lodge Vols., 1960; Midwest dir. Nixon Campaign Com., 1968; mem. Minn. Republican State Central Com., 1970. Trustee Sumner T. McKnight Found., 1963—, U. Minn. Landscape Arboretum, 1976—. Served with AUS, 1943-46. Recipient Feature Story of Yr. award U. Mo., 1950. Mem. Pub. Relations Soc. Am., Tau Kappa Epsilon, Sigma Delta Chi. Presbyn. Clubs: Minneapolis, Minn. Press, Hazeltine Nat. Golf. Home: 2025 Audubon Dr Chaska MN 55318 Office: 520 Baker Bldg Minneapolis MN 55402

TRUNNELL, EUGENE ERLE, psychoanalyst, psychiatrist; b. Novinger, Mo., Dec. 8, 1925; s. Eugene Erle and Mahala Livinston (Robb) T.; M.D., Washington U., St. Louis, 1952; grad. Western New Eng. Inst. Psychoanalysis, 1963; m. Joan Utara, Jan. 30, 1954; children—Rebecca Susan, Matthew Thomas, Nancy Robb, Paul Robert. Fellow Menninger Sch. Psychiatry, 1953-55, advanced fellow in psychiatry, 1955-57, mem. permanent staff, 1957-62; resident psychiatry Topeka State Hosp., 1953-55; mem. sr. staff Austin Riggs Center, Stockbridge, Mass., 1963—; cons. psychiatry Jefferson Barrack VA Hosp., 1972—; clin. asst. prof. dept. psychiatry St. Louis U., 1972—; mem. faculty, tng. and supervising analyst St. Louis Psychoanalytic Inst., 1974—. Served with inf. AUS, 1944-46. Home: 4915 Pershing St St Louis MO 63108 Office: 4524 Forest Park St Louis MO 63108

TRUSTY, THOMAS FRANCIS, ins. co. exec.; b. Ft. Dodge, Iowa, Apr. 9, 1931; s. Howard Francis and Mary Henrietta (Maguire) T.; student St. John's U., 1949-50; student Iowa State U., 1954-58; m. Mary Yavonne McDonald, Nov. 15, 1950; children—Thomas J., Catherine M., Mark H., Beth Ann, Lisa M. Data processor Hormel Packing Co., Ft. Dodge, 1950-54; data processing tech. Iowa State U., Ames, 1954-58; sr. systems analyst John Deere & Co., Ankeny, Iowa, 1958-69; sr. v.p. info. systems Am. Republic Ins. Co., Des Moines, 1969—. Mem. data processing adv. com. Ankeny (Ia.) Community Coll., 1972-78; adv. to Des Moines/Polk County Joint Data Processing Center, 1970; pres. Ankeny Library Bd., 1976. Served with USAF, 1951-53. Mem. Greater Des Moines C. of C., Assn. of Systems Mgmt., Data Processing Mgmt. Assn. (chpt. pres. 1968-69, Achievement award 1972). Roman Catholic. Clubs: Des Moines, Hyperion Golf and Field. Home: 308 NW Beechwood St Ankeny IA 50021 Office: 601 6th Ave Des Moines IA 50034

TRUTTER, JOHN THOMAS, telephone co. exec.; b. Springfield, Ill., Apr. 18, 1920; s. Frank L. and Frances (Mischler) T.; A.B., U. Ill., 1942; postgrad. Northwestern U., U. Chgo.; m. Edith English Woods, June 17, 1950; children—Edith English II, Jonathan Woods. With Ill. Bell Telephone Co., Chgo., 1946-55, 58—, gen. traffic mgr. 1959-62, asst. v.p. pub. relations, 1962-65, asst. v.p. suburban ops., 1965-67, gen. mgr. north suburban ops., 1967-69, v.p. pub. relations, 1969-71, v.p. operator services, 1971—; mem. personnel relations staff Am. Tel. & Tel. Co., N.Y.C., 1955-58; dir. State Nat. Bank Evanston (Ill.). Lectr. gen. semantics. Mem. City of Evanston Zoning Amendment Bd., 1968-70; exec. v.p., dir. Internat. Visitors Center, Chgo. 1971-72, mem. adv. bd., 1973—; mem. regional bd. NCCJ, Chgo., 1963—, v.p., chmn. exec. com., 1969-73, presiding co-chmn., 1973—, nat. trustee, 1967—; active Met. Crusade Mercy, 1968-72; mem. adv. bd. Citizenship Council Met. Chgo., 1969—; mem. exec. bd., chmn. Operation Reach, Chgo. Area council Boy Scouts Am., 1969-75; trustee Ill. Children's Home and Aid Soc., 1970—, v.p., 1975—; trustee Hull House Assn., pres., 1972-74; bd. dirs., exec. com., pres. United Cerebral Palsy Greater Chgo., 1972—, chmn., 1977—; v.p., nat. campaign chmn. United Cerebral Palsy Assns., 1977—; bd. dirs. Nat. Cerebral Palsy Found., 1977—, Chgo. Council Fgn. Relations, 1968-74; bd. dirs. Nat. Minority Purchasing Council, 1976—, treas., 1976-77; task force chmn. Chgo. United Inc. mem., dir. Chgo. Crime Commn., 1976—; bd. dirs. Lyric Opera Chgo., 1976—, Constl. Rights Found., 1975—, Vol. Interagy. Assn., 1976-77, North Communities Health Plan; trustee U. Ill. YMCA. Served to lt. col AUS, 1942-46; CBI. Decorated Legion of Merit. Mem. Sangamon County Hist. Soc. (pres. 1961-62), Pub. Relations Soc. Am., Alpha Sigma Phi (Nat. award Delta Beta Xi). Clubs: Mid-America, Tavern (bd. govs.), Economic (Chgo.). Co-author: Handling Barriers in Communications, 1957; The Governor Takes a Bride, 1977. Contbr. articles to profl. jours. Home: 630 Clinton Pl Evanston IL 60201 Office: 225 W Randolph St Chicago IL 60606

TRUX, HUGO RONASZEKI, metrology engr.; b. Budapest, Hungary, May 15, 1919; s. Hugo R. and Janka (Fallbohmer) T.; B.S., Hungarian Army Tech. Mil. Acad.; m. Andrea Ortvay, Aug. 12, 1944; children—Hugo, Andrew. Investigator-analyst Research Assos., Cleve., 1957-64; head metrology Aerospace div. Clevite, Cleve., 1964-65; head metrology Clevite Research Center, Cleve., 1965-66; sr. quality engr. underwater propulsion Ocean Systems div. Gould, Cleve., 1967—. Served to lt. Hungarian Army. Deocrated Order of Merit, Fighting Cross (2). Mem. Cleve. Engring. Soc., Am. Def. Preparedness Assn., Am. Soc. Quality Control, CIC Assn. Patentee in metrology. Home: 15706 Munn Rd Cleveland OH 44111 Office: 18901 Euclid St Cleveland OH 44117

TRYON, RICHARD RUNDEL, JR., bus. exec.; b. Cleve., May 6, 1932; s. Richard Rundel and Gertrude Delicia (Williams) T.; B.A. in Econs., Kenyon Coll., 1954; m. Anne Elizabeth Colwell, Feb. 26, 1955; children—Elizabeth Anne, Richard Rundell III, Amy Colwell. With Kroger Co., Columbus, Ohio, 1955-56; personnel adminstrn. Battelle Meml. Inst., Columbus, 1956-58; with Colwell Co., Champaign, Ill., 1958—, v.p. research and devel., 1964-75, pres., 1975—; pres. Colwell Systems, Ltd., Montreal, Can., 1969—, Leisure Time Rentals, Inc., Champaign, 1972—; chmn. bd. Matrix Pubs., 1975. Pres. Champaign-Urbana Symphony, 1969—; treas. Champaign County Rehab. Center, 1970-72; treas. Nat. Acad. Arts, 1974-76, chmn. bd., 1977—. Served with USAF, 1954-55. Mem. Graphic Communications Computer Assn. of Printing Industry Am. (dir., pres. 1973-75). Episcopalian (treas.). Rotarian. Club: Champaign Country. Developer Peg-Log accounting system for drs., 1965, also numerous computer systems for comml. applications, including one for automatic prodn. of stationery composition. Home: 2 Moraine Ct Champaign IL 61820 Office: 201 Kenyon Rd Champaign IL 61820

TSAI, STEPHEN WEILUN, scientist; b. Peiping, China, July 6, 1929; s. Stephen and Lily (Li) T.; B.E., Yale, 1952, D.Eng., 1961; m. Iris Lee, June 20, 1954; children—Ming-hsi, Ming-hao. Proj. engr. Foster Wheeler Corp., N.Y.C., 1952-58; researcher Philco-Ford Corp., Newport Beach, Calif., 1961-66; prof. engring. Washington U., St. Louis, 1966-68; scientist Air Force Materials Lab., Wright-Patterson AFB, Ohio, 1968—. Mem. Am. Inst. Aero. and Astronautics, ASME, Research Soc. Am., Am. Inst. Physics, Rho Psi, Tau Beta Pi, Sigma Xi. Editor-in-chief Jour. Composite Materials, 1966—. Contbr. articles to profl. jours. Home: 3033 Locust Camp Rd Dayton OH 45419 Office: Air Force Materials Lab Wright-Patterson AFB OH 45433

TSAI, YOU-WEN, surgeon; b. Chu-nan, Taiwan, Oct. 11, 1936; s. Lan and Tseng-Mei (Hilatate) T.; came to U.S., 1966, naturalized, 1976; M.D., U. Taiwan, 1963; m. Kuei-Yin Chen, June 19, 1965; children—Cynthia, Sandra. Intern, Grace Hosp., Detroit, 1966-67, resident in surgery, 1967-71, surg. fellow, 1971-72, staff surgeon, 1972—, mem. teaching staff, 1972—. Diplomate Am. Bd. Surgery. Fellow A.C.S.; mem. Mich. Med. Assn., Detroit, Midwest, Pan-Pacific surg. assns. Contbr. articles in field to profl. jours. Home: 4052 Wentworth St Troy MI 48098 Office: 18500 W 12 Mile Rd Southfield MI 48076

TSANG, PETER HING-SHYA, chemist; b. Meishien, Kwangtung, China, July 20, 1942; s. Yuk-Fai and Lie-Er (Chang) T.; came to U.S., 1963, naturalized, 1976; B.S., Hong Kong Bapt. Coll., 1963; M.A., Sul Ross State U., 1965; Ph.D., U. Houston, 1969; m. Marian Sih-Ming Djou, Aug. 16, 1970; children—Byron FaEng, Jennifer Farnsie. Teaching fellow U. Houston, 1965-69, Welch Found. reseach fellow, research asso. U. Houston, 1969; project scientist Aerospace Systems div. Bendix Corp., Ann Arbor, Mich., 1969-72, sr. project chemist, project supr. Research Labs., Southfield, Mich., 1972—; lectr. chemistry Lawrence Inst. Tech., 1974—. Recipient I.R. 100 award Indsl. Research mag., 1974. Mem. Am. Chem. Soc., Am. Inst. Chemists, N.Y. Acad. Scis., Nat. Ski Patrol Systems, Sigma Xi, Alpha Chi Sigma. Contbr. articles to profl. jours. Home: 20261 LaCross St Southfield MI 48076

TSAO, KEH CHENG, educator; b. Kiangsu, China, Apr. 20, 1923; M.S., Ill. Inst. Tech., 1956; Ph.D., U. Wis., 1961. Research asso. and asst. U. Wis., 1957-61; research asso. Argonne Nat. Lab., summers 1963-65; asso. prof. S.D. Sch. Mining and Tech., 1961-67; vis. asso. prof. U. Wis., Milw., 1967-68, asso. prof., 1968-72, prof., 1972—. Mem. ASME, AAAS, Am. Soc. E.E., N.Y. Acad. Scis., Sigma Xi. Contbr. articles to profl. jours. Office: Coll Engring and Applied Sci 3200 N Cramer St Milwaukee WI 53201

TSAY, CHING SOW, physician; b. Taipei, Taiwan, Jan. 25, 1939; s. Shui Sheng and Len (Chang) T.; came to U.S., 1967, naturalized, 1976; M.D., Kao-Hsiung Med. Coll., Taiwan, 1964; m. Zei-Tsu Chen, Jan. 18, 1964; children—Michael, Cindy, Alice. Intern, St. Vincent's Med. Center of Richmond, S.I., N.Y., 1967-68; resident anesthesia, St. Joseph Hosp., Joliet, Ill., 1968-69, Washington Hosp. Center, Washington, 1969-71; practice medicine, specializing in anesthesiology, 1971—; chief anesthesiology VA Hosp., Kansas City, Mo., 1971—; instr. anesthesia dept. U. Kan. Med. Center, 1971—. Diplomate Am. Bd. Anesthesiology Fellow Am. Coll. Anesthesiologists; mem. Am., Kans., Kansas City socs. anesthesiologists. Home: 9601 Beverly St Overland Park KS 66207 Office: 4801 Linwood St Kansas City MO 64128

TSCHAPPAT, DONNA BELLE, coll. ofcl., pub. relations exec.; b. Chgo., Oct. 25, 1936; d. Robert William and Rena Louise (Morgan) Tschappat; A.A., William Woods Coll., 1956; B.S., U. Houston, 1958; postgrad. U. Colo., 1961. Tchr. Wheatridge High Sch., Jefferson County (Colo.) pub. schs., 1958-62; coordinator of field services William Woods Coll., Fulton, Mo., 1962-68, asst. dean of students, 1968-72, dir. pub. relations and alumnae affairs, 1972—. Instr. adult edn. program Denver pub. schs., summer, 1959. Mem. Fulton (Mo.) Plan Town Council and Housing Com., 1971-73; William Woods Coll. rep. for Callaway County United Fund Drive, 1972—, publicity chmn., 1974. Recipient Order of the Green Owl award William Woods Coll. Alumnae Assn., 1969, Soc. Centennial Fellows medallion William Woods Coll., 1972. Mem. Callaway County League of Women Voters (dir. 1972-75), Am. Alumni Council, U. Houston Alumni Fedn., Fulton Area C. of C. (pres. 1975, dir. 1972-76), AAUW (pres. 1966-69, world problems area rep. 1969-70), William Woods Nat. Alumnae Assn. (dir. 1966—), Bd. Assos. Fulton Colls., Phi Kappa Phi, Phi Theta Kappa, Kappa Delta Pi, Delta Gamma (Delta Omega chpt. adviser 1977—). Mem. Christian Ch. Clubs: Callaway County Alumnae, Denver William Woods Coll. Alumnae (chmn. 1959-61). Address: William Woods College Fulton MO 65251

TSCHETTER, ROBERT ALAN, mgmt. cons.; b. Sioux Falls, S.D., Dec. 24, 1935; s. William and Mildred Anne (Wagenhals) T.; B.S., U. S.D., 1957; M.H.A., U. Minn., 1962; m. Judith Ellen Fitzsimmons, Dec. 27, 1958; children—Robert Alan, Jr., William Wood. Adminstrn. resident Baylor U. Med. Center, Dallas, 1961-63, asst. adminstr., 1963-66; v.p., mng. officer health and med. div. Booz, Allen & Hamilton, Mgmt. Cons., Chgo., 1966—, also dir. Treas., pres. Montessori Soc. Lake Forest, Ill., 1968-70; mem. citizens' bd. Ill. Masonic Med. Center, 1975; bd. dirs. Evanston (Ill.) Hosp. Served with AUS, 1957-59. Certified Inst. Mgmt. Cons. Fellow Am. Assn. Hosp. Cons.; mem. Am. Hosp. Assn., Am. Pub. Health Assn., Am. Coll. Hosp. Adminstrs., Am. Assn. Hosp. Planning. Clubs: Bath and Tennis (Lake Forest, Ill.); University (Chgo.). Home: 496 E Illinois Rd Lake Forest IL 60045 Office: 135 S LaSalle St Chicago IL 60603

TSCHETTER, WESLEY GENE, state ofcl.; b. Mitchell, S.D., Sept. 26, 1947; s. Emil J. and Barbara (Hofer) T.; B.S. in Agrl. Engring., S.D. State U., 1969; M.B.A., U. S.D., 1971. Legis. research dir. Internat. Farm Youth Exchange, Israel, 1969; sr. budget analyst Gov.'s Bur. Budget, State of S.D., Pierre, 1971-72; fiscal analyst Legis. Research Council, State of S.D., 1972-75, dir., 1975—. Trustee S.D. Employees Retirement System. Mem. Western States Legis. Fiscal Officers Assn., Am. Soc. Agrl. Engrs., S.D. Hist. Soc., Nat. Conf. State Legislature (mem. legis. modernization and improvement com.), Pierre Jaycees (treas. 1973-74), Farm House, Sigma Tau, Alpha Epsilon. Mennonite. Contbr. article on retirement system consol. to State Govt. Home: 111 S Poplar Apt 4 Pierre SD 57501 Office: Legis Research Council Capitol Bldg Pierre SD 57501

TSCHIRKI, ROBERT DEAN, supt. schs.; b. Hancock County, Iowa, Aug. 31, 1937; s. Chris J. and Mildred A. (Hagen) T.; B.A., U. No. Iowa, 1958; M.A., U. Iowa, 1964; Ph.D., Iowa State U., 1972; m. Joan Alice Plummer, Dec. 26, 1956; children—Rhonda Rae, Lona Kay, Christopher Robert. Tchr., coach high schs., Iowa, 1958-65; prin. sr. high sch., Spencer, Iowa, 1965-68; asst. supt. secondary edn., Marshalltown, Iowa, 1968-73; supt. schs., Newton, Iowa, 1973-75, Burnsville, Minn., 1975—. Speaker in field, participant symposia, workshops; participant World Devel. Seminar, 1970, 71; chmn. evaluation teams N. Central Assn., 1968—; mem. adv. council U. No. Iowa, 1967-72; mem. gen. adv. com. Des Moines Area Community Coll., 1974-75; adv. council St. Thomas Acad., 1976—. Named Outstanding Young Educator, 1968. Danforth fellow, 1976. Mem. Minn., Am. assns. sch. adminstrs., Nat. Sch. Pub. Relations Assn., Nat. Acad. Sch. Execs. (state acad. lectr. 1977-78), Phi Delta Kappa. Episcopalian. Club: Rotary. Home: 104 Krestwood Dr Burnsville MN 55337 Office: 900 W 128th St Burnsville MN 55337

TSEN, CHO CHING, educator; b. Chekiang, China, Oct. 12, 1922; s. Chung Po and Huang Yuh (Chun) T.; came to U.S., 1954, naturalized, 1972; B.S., Chekiang Nat. U., 1944, M.S., 1946; Ph.D., U. Calif. at Davis, 1958; m. Po Kwei Chen, July 19, 1952; children—Vivian, Andrew, Lawrence, Caroline. Research chemist Taiwan (China) Sugar Expt. Sta., 1946-50; asso. prof. Taiwan Provincial Coll., 1950-54; scientist Grain Research Lab., Winnipeg, Man., Can., 1958-67; research group leader Am. Inst. Baking, Chgo., 1967-69; prof. dept. grain sci. and industry Kans. State U., Manhattan, 1969—. Hon. cons. Nat. Council Sci., Taiwan, 1974—; cons. Wheat Assos., 1968-69, Am. Soybean Assn., 1972-73, L.M. Johnson Grain Co., Lauhoff Grain Co., 1975—. Bd. dirs. Truman Med. Research Lab., Kansas City, Mo., 1974—. Recipient Agr. Student award Chinese Agr. Soc., 1944; Best Coll. Tchr. award Taiwan Provincial Coll., 1954; Excellent Service award Taiwan Bakery and Cannery Assn., 1972; Distinguished Merit award Taiwan Flour Millers Assn., 1972; Putnam Food Processing award, 1977. Mem. Am. Assn. Cereal Chemists (sect. chmn. 1956-66), Inst. Food Technologists, Am. Soc. Bakery Engrs., Am. Chem. Soc., Sigma Xi. Contbr. articles to profl. jours. Editor: Triticale: First Man-made Cereal, 1974. Editor Cereal Sci. Today, 1965-67. Patentee in field. Home: 1415 Meadow Ln Manhattan KS 66052

TSIEN TSUEN-HSUIN, educator; b. Kiangsu, China, Dec. 1, 1909; s. Wei-Chen and Chuan-Shih (Hsu) T.; came to U.S., 1947, naturalized, 1959; B.A., U. Nanking (China), 1932; A.M., U. Chgo., 1952, Ph.D., 1957; m. Wen-ching Hsu, Aug. 31, 1936; children—Ginger, Gloria, Mary. Chief Shanghai office, also editor Nat. Library of Peking, 1937-47; mem. faculty U. Chgo., 1949—, prof. Chinese lit., 1964—, curator Far Eastern Library, 1947—; vis. prof. Asian studies U. Hawaii, 1959. Chmn. com. E. Asian libraries Assn. Asian Studies, 1966-68. Bd. dirs. Chinese Student and Alumni Services, 1957—, pres., 1960-62. Recipient award Chinese Ministry Edn., 1943, award Am. Council Learned Socs., 1968-69, NSF, 1977-78, Nat. Endowment for Humanities, 1978-79. Mem. Am. Oriental Soc., ALA, Assn. Asian Studies. Author: Written on Bamboo and Silk: The Beginnings of Chinese Books and Inscriptions, 1962; History of Chinese Writing and Writing Materials (in Chinese), 1975; China: An Annotated Bibliography of Bibliographies, 1978. Editor: (with H.W. Winger) Area Studies and the Library, 1966, (with David T. Roy) Ancient China: Studies in Early Civilization, 1977. adv. editor Tsing Hua Jour. Chinese Studies, 1959—. Contbr. articles to profl. jours. Home: 1408 E Rochdale Pl Chicago IL 60615

TSUANG, MING TSO, psychiatrist, educator; b. Tainan, Taiwan, Nov. 16, 1931; s. Ping Tang and Chhun Kuei (Lin) T.; came to U.S., 1971; M.D., Nat. Taiwan U., Taipei, 1957; Ph.D. in Psychiatry (Sino-Brit. Fellowship Trust scholar), Inst. Psychiatry, U. London (Eng.), 1965; m. Snow Huei S. Ko, Nov. 24, 1958; children—John, Debby, Grace. Intern Nat. Taiwan U. Hosp., 1956-57, resident in psychiatry 1957-61, asso. prof. psychiatry, staff psychiatrist, 1968-71; vis. asso. prof. psychiatry Washington U. Sch. Medicine, St. Louis, 1971-72; asso. prof. psychiatry, staff psychiatrist U. Iowa Coll. Medicine, Iowa City, 1972-75, prof., 1975—. Clin. tchr., lectr. to residents, med. students; cons. psychiatrist VA Hosp., Iowa City, 1972—. Bd. dirs. Midwest Formosan Christian Found., 1974, pres. 1975-76. Research Fellow Chinese Nat. Council Sci. Devel., 1966-70; NIMH grantee, 1973—. Mem. Psychiat. Research Soc., Am. Psychopathol. Assn., Behavior Genetics Assn., AMA, Am. Psychiat. Assn., Sigma Xi. Author: A Study of a Pair of Sibs Both Hospitalized for Mental Disorder, 1965. Contbr. numerous articles in field to profl. jours. Spl. research on schizophrenia, mania and depression, with follow-up and family studies. Home: 350 Hutchinson Ave Iowa City IA 52240 Office: 500 Newton Rd Iowa City IA 52242

TSURUOKA, CATHERINE BOULGER, psychologist; b. Mpls., Mar. 19, 1917; d. Francis James and Mary (Armstrong) Boulger; m. George Tsuruoka, Nov. 3, 1945; B.A., Coll. St. Catherine, 1938; M.S., U. Minn., 1941. Occupational analyst U.S. Employment Service, Washington, 1942-43, chief Aptitude Tests Unit, 1943-47; psychologist aviation psychology br. U.S. Dept. Navy, Washington, 1947-48; v.p. Design Promotion Inc., Evanston, Ill., 1964—. Mem. Am. Psychol. Assn., Psi Chi, Kappa Gamma Pi, Pi Lambda Theta, Alpha Pi Epsilon. Contbr. Jour. Consulting Psychology. Home: 1416 Hinman Ave Evanston IL 60201

TUCKER, BARBARA (BEBE LOU MUEHLE) (MRS. RICHARD WALTER TUCKER), arts patron, fashion cons.; b. Des Moines; d. Louis John and Harriett (Shilke) Muehle; student Drake U. Music Sch.; B.S., Iowa State U.; m. Richard Walter Tucker; 1 dau., Pamela Helen. Fashion writer W.T. Grant, N.Y.C., 1946-47, Kresge Newark, Newark, 1947-50, Best & Co., N.Y.C., 1950-51; millinery designer Chez Nous, Detroit, 1954-57; instr. fashion design Detroit Bd. Edn., 1960-63; fashion lectr. John Robert Powers Sch., Detroit, 1965-68; fashion coordinator Armo Co. of N.Y., 1968-72, Hoechst Fibers, 1972-75; v.p. Richard Tucker & Co., Detroit, 1969—. Mem. speakers bur. United Found., Detroit, 1967; mem. Met. Opera Com., Detroit, 1962—; v.p., workshop chmn. Am. Symphony Orch. League Women's Council, 1966-70, nat. pres., 1971-73, instr. mgmt. course, 1975, 76; pres. Jr. Women's Assn. for Detroit Symphony, 1957. dirs. Womens Assn. Detroit Symphony Orch., 1960—, pres., 1963, bd. dirs. Orch., 1969—, legis. chmn., 1977; bd. dirs. Womens Com. Tb and Health Soc., 1967—, Womens Com. for Project Hope, 1966—, Nat. Guild Community Schs. Arts, 1975—; mem. nat. women's bd. Northwood Inst., 1972—; bd. dirs., sec. Mich. Orch. Assn., state pres., 1976—; trustee nat. bd. Nat. Guild Community Schs. for Arts. Mem. Am., Mich. home econs. assns., Founders Soc. Detroit Inst. Arts, Fashion Group Detroit (sec. 1973—), Theatre Arts Detroit, Internat. Platform Assn., Alpha Gamma Delta. Home: 3335 Burning Bush Rd Birmingham MI 48010

TUCKER, CAROLYN COSTON (MRS. JOHN D. TUCKER, SR.), pub. relations exec.; b. Indpls., June 17, 1927; d. James W. and Mildred C. (Chandler) Coston; B.A., DePauw U., 1949; m. John D. Tucker, Sr., Oct. 8, 1949; children—John David, Tracy Lee. Dir. pub. edn. Crossroads Rehab. Center, Indpls., 1961—. Chmn. women's div. Republican Fin. Com. for Greater Indpls. Recipient Salute to Women Who Work, C. of C., 1964; Golden Quill award Woman's Press Club Ind., 1968. Mem. Pub. Relations Soc. Am. (sec. Hoosier chpt. 1968—), Am. Women in Radio and TV, Am. Hosp. Assn. Pub. Relations Soc., Jr. League Indpls. Home: 6160 Afton Crest Indianapolis IN 46220 Office: 3242 Sutherland Ave Indianapolis IN 46205

TUCKER, CLARINE SMITH, historian, genealogist; b. Gilmer, Tex., Sept. 4, 1923; d. David Franklin and Myrtis Rossie (Castle) Smith; student Dodd Jr. Coll. for Girls, Shreveport, La., 1941-42, N. Tex. State U., 1942-45; m. Huel Clive Tucker, June 6, 1948. Tchr., Gilmer, Tex., 1945-48; active in real estate, Tex., 1957—; historian and genealogist, Centerville, Ohio, 1958—. Recipient Service award St. Louis Geneal. Soc., 1971; named Queen, E. Tex. Yamboree, Gilmer, 1940. Mem. DAR (geneal. records chmn. 1976, lineage chmn. 1977), Mo. Hist. Soc., St. Louis (life), Tex., S. Central Ohio, Miami Valley geneal. socs., Tex. Forestry Assn., Beta Sigma Phi. Baptist. Club: Dayton Dance-Tonians. Contbg. author: Early Smiths of Georgia, 1970; Shipp Family in America, 1976; Tracing Family Trees in 11 States, 1970. Address: 19 Mimosa Dr Centerville OH 45459

TUCKER, DENNIS KEITH, instrument analyst; b. Danville, Ill., Apr. 9, 1951; s. Robert Keith and Carol Rose (Henschen) T.; A.S., Danville Jr. Coll., 1971; student U. South Fla., 1971-72; B.S. in Biology, Ill. State U., Normal, 1973; m. Barbara Dale Clay, Dec. 16, 1972; children—Heather Dale, Christopher Keith. Devel. technician Lauhoff Grain Co., Danville, 1973-76; instrument analyst A. E. Staley Mfg. Co., Decatur, Ill., 1976—. Aux. policeman City of Georgetown (Ill.), 1972-74. Mem. Staley Tech. Soc. Republican. Developed gas chromatographic method of determining residual hexane in corn and soybean oil. Home: 2688 S 34th St Decatur IL 62521 Office: 2200 Eldorado St PO Box 151 Decatur IL 62525

TUCKER, EARL LEONARD, forging co. exec.; b. Painesville, Ohio, Apr. 17, 1918; s. DeWitt Clinton and Ellen (Pritschau) T.; B.B.A., Western Res. U., 1942, M.B.A., 1955; m. Anna Louise Baker, June 14, 1941; children—Sally Anne, David Earl, Richard Lloyd. Accountant, TRW, Inc., Cleve., 1938-43; cost auditor U.S. Gen. Accounting Office, Cleve., 1946-47; controller Joseph Dyson & Sons, Inc., Eastlake, Ohio, 1947—, sec.-treas., 1977—; instr. Western Res. U., 1947—. Served with USAAF, 1943-46. Mem. Newcomen Soc., Am. Mgmt. Assn., Citizens League, Indsl. Fastener Inst., Nat. Assn. Accountants, Ohio Soc. C.P.A.'s, Am. Inst. C.P.A.'s, Cleve. Council World Affairs. Mem. United Ch. of Christ. Republican. Home: 1034 Nela View Cleveland Heights OH 44112 Office: 33300 Lakeland Blvd Eastlake OH 44094

TUCKER, FRANK LEON, utilities exec.; b. Paducah, Ky., Jan. 3, 1931; s. Elbert Leon and Nell Annie (Freeman) T.; student U. Ky., 1951-52, Murry State U., 1952-55, Sangammon State U., 1976-77; m. Judy Bond, Aug. 2, 1958; children—Brian Patrick, Dwain Shannon. Foreman, gen. foreman, project coordinator various constrn. cos., 1958-71; supt. sewers City of E. St. Louis (Ill.), 1971-72; plant mgr. Water Pollution Control Center, E. St. Louis, 1972-75; supt. Morrisonville (Ill.) Sewage Treatment Plant, 1975-76, Kincaid Sewage Treatment Plant, 1975—, Taylorville (Ill.) San. Dist., 1975—; instr. wastewater plant operation Lincoln Land Community Coll., Springfield, Ill., 1975—. Recipient Certification of Competency, Ill. Mem. Mid-Central States (sec., treas. 1976, pres. 1977—), Central States water pollution control assns., Ill. Assn. Water Pollution Control Operators (Ill. Operator of Year award 1978), Water Pollution Control Fedn. Democrat. Baptist. Clubs: Masons, Shriners, Odd Fellows. Developed info. collection form for nat. pollutant discharge elimination system monthly report. Home: PO Box 83 Morrisonville IL 62546 Office: PO Box 298 Taylorville IL

TUCKER, FRED C., JR., realtor and developer; b. Indpls., Oct. 25, 1918; s. Fred C. and Bernice (Caldwell) T.; grad. Lawrenceville Sch., 1936; A.B., DePauw U., 1940; student law, Harvard, 1940-41; m. Ermajean MacDonald, Sept. 2, 1944; children—Fred C. III, Lucinda Ann. Pres. F.C. Tucker Co. Inc., Indpls., 1946—; dir. Ind. Nat. Bank, Jefferson Nat. Life Ins. Co., Jefferson Corp.; prin. officer, dir. real estate and development cos. Mem. Fed. Savs. and Loan Adv. Council, 1975-76. Mem. nat. council YMCA, 1967; dir. Indpls. Met. YMCA, pres., 1964-65; Ind. chmn. Crusade Freedom, 1954-55. Trustee DePauw U., 1968—; trustee Arthur Jordan Found. Indpls., 1964—, chmn., 1977—; trustee Indpls.-Marion County Bldg. Authority. Served as lt. USNR, World War II. Mem. Nat. Inst. Real Estate Brokers (nat. pres. 1966), Indpls. Real Estate Bd. (pres. 1961), Nat. Assn. Real (dir., nat. pres. 1972) Am. Arbitration Assn., Am. Soc. Realtors Estate Counselors, Rep. Vets, Ind., Central Ind. DePauw Alumni Assn. (past pres.), Indpls. C. of C. (dir., pres. 1973-74), Am. Legion, Delta Tau Delta (nat. pres. 1975-76). Methodist. Clubs: Meridian Hills Country, Crooked Stick, Indianapolis Athletic, Columbia, Rotary (Indpls.); Royal Poinciana (Naples, Fla.). Home: 6141 Sunset Ln Indianapolis IN 46208 Office: One Indiana Sq Indianapolis IN 46204

TUCKER, HUEL CLIVE, elec. engr.; b. Rhonesboro, Tex., May 3, 1921; s. Uriah Taylor and Vera Ella (Mitchell) T.; B.S., Tex. A. and M. U., 1953, postgrad. (Tex. Power and Light fellow), 1953-54; m. Clarine Smith, June 6, 1948. With Monsanto Co., 1954-71, research engr., Texas City, Tex., 1954-59, research specialist, 1959-65, engring. specialist, 1965-68, engring. specialist, St. Louis, 1968-71; group leader Monsanto Research Corp., Dayton, Ohio, 1971—. Served with USMCR, 1941-45. Decorated Purple Heart medal, Bronze Star medal. Mem. I.E.E.E., Tex. Forestry Assn., St. Louis (treas. 1970), Tex., Miami Valley, Ga. geneal. socs., Phi Eta Sigma, Tau Beta Pi, Phi Kappa Phi. Baptist. Patentee in field. Home: 19 Mimosa Dr Centerville OH 45459 Office: 1514 Nicholas Rd Dayton OH 45418

TUCKER, JOHN DAVID, stone co. exec.; b. Fairland, Ind., Jan. 9, 1923; s. Fred B. and Claire (Conner) T.; student Tulsa U., 1943, Colo. U., 1947; B.A., DePauw U., 1948; m. Carolyn Costin, June 17, 1927; children—John D., Tracy Lee. With Tucker Stone Co., Inc. (formerly Taylor-Tucker Stone Co., Inc.), 1949—, sec.-treas., 1949-54, pres., 1954—; pres. Tucker Stone Co. of Bloomington, Inc., 1959—; pres. Fairland Nat. Bank, 1960-62, chmn. bd., 1963—; pres. 4-R-Quarries, Inc., 1962—; pres., chief exec. officer Ind. Limestone Co., Inc., 1974—, vice chmn. bd., chief exec. officer, 1974-76; dir. Wide World Devel. Bd. dirs. Aero. Commn. Ind., 1953-61. Republican precinct committeeman, 1950-54. Served USAAF, 1942-45, ETO. Mem. Cut Stone Assn. Ind. (pres.), Ind. Limestone Inst. (v.p., dir.), Quarriers Assn. Ind. Limestone (vice chmn.), Delta Kappa Epsilon. Methodist. Club: Maxin Kuckee Country. Home: 6160 Afton Crest Indianapolis IN 46220 Office: Box 72 Bedford IN 47421

TUCKER, JOHN THOMAS, aviation service co. exec.; b. St. Louis, June 21, 1933; s. Raymond Roche and Edith L. (Leiber) T.; student Washington U., 1951-53, Spring Hill Coll., 1953-54; m. Lucy Claire

George, Jan. 28, 1956; children—Patricia, Timothy, Susan, John, Elizabeth. Vice pres. ops. Remmert Werner, Inc., 1958-68; pres. Butler Aviation Co., 1968-71, Midcoast Aviation Services, Inc., St. Louis, 1971—; dir. Butler Aviation Internat., Internat. Aero Products., Mooney Aircraft Corp., Midcoast Aviation. Mem. adv. council Nat. Bus. Aircraft Assn. Served to capt. USMC, 1953-58. Mem. Nat. Aviation Transp. Assn. (dir.). Clubs: University (St. Louis); Metropolitan, Wings (N.Y.C.); St. Louis, Monday (St. Louis); Nat. Aviation (Washington). Home: 19 Huntleigh Woods St Louis MO 63131 Office: Lambert Field St Louis MO 63145

TUCKER, THEODORE JON, lawyer; b. Allegan, Mich., Apr. 26, 1939; s. Irving J. and Dorothea (Neerken) T.; B.A., Albion Coll., 1961; LL.B., Wayne State U., 1964; m. Elaine Ianni, Aug. 31, 1963; children—Theodore Jon II, James David. Admitted to Mich. bar, 1964; with Weiner and Wade, Three Rivers, Mich., 1964-68; partner Weiner, Wade and Tucker, Three Rivers, 1969—; village atty. Constantine Village 1968—, White Pigeon Village, 1973—, Centreville Village, 1973—. Mem. St. Joseph County Planning Commn., 1969-71, Three Rivers City Commn., 1971-73; vol. Community Chest. Treas., Three Rivers Republican party, 1967-70; bd. dirs. St. Joseph County YMCA; bd. dirs. Three Rivers Hosp., 1975—, pres., 1977—. Mem. Mich., St. Joseph County (pres. 1969) bar assns., Greater Three Rivers C. of C. (dir.), Three Rivers Jr. C. of C. (pres. 1966-67), Sigma Nu. Methodist. Clubs: Rotary (pres. 1978), Elks. Home: 706 Flower St Three Rivers MI 49093 Office: 211 Portage Ave Three Rivers MI 49093

TUCKER, THOMAS RANDALL, engine co exec.; b. Indpls., Aug. 6, 1931; s. Ovie Allen and Oris Aleen (Robertson) T.; A.B., Franklin Coll., 1953; m. Evelyn Marie Armuth, Aug. 9, 1953; children—Grant, Roger, Richard. Grad. asst. U. Minn., 1953-54; dir. admissions, registrar Franklin Coll., 1954-57; trainee Cummins Engine Co., Inc., Columbus, Ind., 1957-58; supr. community relations, 1958-61, mgr. community relations, 1961-64, mgr. pub. relations, 1964-68, dir. pub. relations, 1968-72, dir. corp. and community relations, 1972-75, dir. pub. relations, 1975—. Mem. Bd. Sch. Trustees Bartholomew County, Ind., 1966-72, pres., 1968-69; pres. Bartholomew County A.R.C., 1961-64, Retirement Found. Bartholomew County, 1958-61; chmn. Bartholomew County Sch. Reorgn. Com., 1964-65; mem. Bartholomew County Health Planning Com., 1970-71; chmn. legislative com. Ind. Sch. Bd. Assn., 1970-71; mem. selection com. Congressman Lee Hamilton's Services Acad., 1965—. Treas. Bartholomew County Republican Central Com., 1960—, precinct committeeman, 1959-69; moderator Columbus Citizens' Forum. Bd. dirs. Bartholomew County Hosp. Found., 1966-70, pres., 1968; trustee Franklin Coll. Recipient Distinguished Service award Columbus (Ind.) Jr. C. of C., 1965; named One of Five Outstanding Young Men, Ind. Jr. C. of C., 1965. Mem. Pub. Relations Soc. Am. (chpt. v.p. 1971), Columbus C. of C., Kappa Tau Alpha, Phi Delta Theta, Sigma Delta Chi. Lutheran. Rotarian. Club: Harrison Lake Country. Home: 4380 N Riverside Dr Columbus IN 47201 Office: 1000 5th St Columbus IN 47201

TUDOR, CHARLES DORSEY, lawyer; b. Webb City, Mo., May 11, 1917; s. Charles Finis and Jessie Valeria (Watson) T.; A.B., U. Mo., 1938, J.D., 1940; m. Grace Elizabeth Walsh, June 27, 1944; 1 son, Charles Anthony. Admitted to Mo. bar, 1940; practiced in Webb City, 1945-56, Joplin, 1956—; asst. county atty. Jasper County, 1951-53, 64-66; asst. atty. gen. State of Mo., 1956-63; dir. United Mo. Bank of Joplin, Mid-Western Mfg. Co., Joplin. Bd. dirs. Boys Club, Joplin, 1956-68, Joplin Pub. Library, 1962-71, 73—; bd. dirs. Border Library System, 1965-71, pres., 1965-71. Served to lt. col. AUS, 1940-45. Recipient Bishop's medal Episcopal Diocese of W. Mo. 1971. Mem. Mo. Library Trustees Assn. (pres. 1971, mem. exec. council 1966-71). Episcopalian (mem. diocesan exec. council Diocese W. Mo. 1966-70, 72-76, mem. exec. steering com. 1967-70). Elk, Kiwanian. Home: 2932 E 17th St Joplin MO 64801 Office: Frisco Bldg Joplin MO 64801

TUFTY, LYLE HOLLES, agrl. engr.; b. Volga, S.D., Mar. 26, 1931; s. Chester Alfred and Alma Eleanor (Johnson) T.; B.S. in Agrl. Engring., S.D. State U., 1960; m. LaVonne L. Madsen, Sept. 18, 1949; children—Ladonna Joye (Mrs. David Lieb), Lyle Rickie, Lynnette Renee. Farmer, Brookings, S.D., 1952-56; design engr. Gravely Tractors, Dunbar, W.Va., 1960-62; project engr. Rolfes Mfg. Co., Boone, Ia., 1962-63; tool design engr. Chamberlain Corp., Waterloo, Ia., 1963-64; project engr. Universal Mfg. Co., Hudson, Ia., 1964-66; project engr. Owatonna Mfg. Co. (Minn.), 1966-69, chief engr. indsl. products, 1969-72; chief engr. agrl. products Melroe div. Clark Equipment Co., Bismarck, N.D., 1972—. Tchr. flight tng., 1958—. Served with USNGR, 1948-50. Mem. Am. Soc. Agrl. Engrs., Indsl. Equipment Mfrs. Council, Aircraft Owners and Pilots Assn. Lutheran (deacon 1965-66). Elk, Kiwanian. Patentee steering control skid-steer loader, speed change hitch for attachments to skid-steer loader. Home: 2501 East Blvd Bismarck ND 58501 Office: Melroe Div Clark Equipment Co 323 Airport Rd Bismarck ND 58501

TUGGLE, WILLIAM PHILIP, lawyer; b. Chgo., June 26, 1922; s. William H. and Vionett V. (Prince) T.; certificate Wilson Jr. Coll., 1939-41; student U. Ill., 1941-42; J.D., De Paul U., 1948; m. Audrey L. Bables, Aug. 26, 1966; 1 son, William Philip III. Admitted to Ill. bar, 1949; since practiced in Chgo.; partner firm Staradford, Lafontant, Fisher & Cousins, Chgo., 1970-71; gen. counsel Health and Hosps. Governing Commn., Chgo., 1971—. Vol. instr. polit. sci. Malcom X Jr. Coll., 1970—. Served with AUS, 1942-46; PTO. Mem. Am. Soc. Hosp. Attys., Am. Trial Lawyers Assn. Home: 4940 S East End Ave Chicago IL 60616 Office: 1900 W Polk St Chicago IL 60612

TULIS, ALLEN JOSEPH, chem. engr.; b. Cicero, Ill., Jan. 28, 1929; s. Anton Francis and Antoinette Amalia (Drtilek) T.; B.S. in Chem. Engring., Ill. Inst. Tech., 1955, B.S. in Math., 1958, M.S. in Chem. Engring., 1963, postgrad., 1972—; m. Elinore Cathaline Maass, May 20, 1951. With Quakers Research Labs., Chgo., 1948; experimentalist Chgo. Vitreous Enamel Corp., Chgo., 1949-51; chem. engr. Inst. Gas Tech., Chgo., 1952-57; sr. chem. engr. Ill. Inst. Tech. Research Inst., Chgo., 1957—. Session chmn. Internat. Pyrotechnics Seminar, 1972, 76. Served with AUS, 1951-52. Mem. Am. Inst. Chem. Engrs., Am. Chem. Soc., Am. Inst. Aeronautics and Astronautics, Am. Def. Preparedness Assn., Air Force Assn., Combustion Inst. Contbr. to publs. in field. Home: 174 N Country Club Dr Addison IL 60101 Office: 10 W 35th St Chicago IL 60616

TULLIS, RICHARD BARCLAY, communications and info. handling equipment mfg. co. exec.; b. Western Springs, Ill., July 12, 1913; s. Lauren Barclay and Izelah (Gilmore) T.; A.B., Principia Coll., Elsah, Ill., 1934; m. Chaille Handy, Aug. 17, 1935; children—Sarah (Mrs. Charles de Barcza), Barclay J., Garner H. With Miller Printing Machinery Co., Pitts., 1936-56, pres., 1952-56; with Harris Corp., Cleve., 1956—, exec. v.p., 1957-61, pres., 1961-72, chief exec. officer, 1968—, chmn., 1972—, also dir.; dir. Cleve. Electric Illuminating Co., Nat. City Bank Cleve.; trustee First Union Real Estate Investments, Cleve. Trustee Principia Coll., Elsah, Ill., Case-Western Res. U., Cleve., Musical Arts Assn., Cleve. Home: 13515 Shaker Blvd Cleveland OH 44120 Office: 55 Public Sq Cleveland OH 44113

TUMA, ARTHUR TENNYSON, physician; b. Dickinson, N.D., May 13, 1913; s. John and Mary (Zahradnik) T.; B.S., Dickinson State Tchrs. Coll., 1936; M.S., Mont. State U., 1948; M.S., U. Nebr., 1953; M.D., Creighton U., 1957; m. Kathleen O'Connell, Sept. 25, 1942; children—Arthur D., Edwin D., Darcy O. Navigator, Pan Am. Ferries, Army Transport Command and Trans World Airlines, Washington, 1942-47; physicist AEC, Ames, Ia., 1948-49; radiol. physicist U. Nebr. Coll. Medicine, 1949-61, instr., 1950-61; intern Nebr. Meth. Hosp., 1957-58; resident U. Nebr. Coll. Medicine, 1958-61; asst. prof. radiobiology U. Miss. Sch. Medicine, radiologist VA Hosp., Jackson, Miss., 1961-63; practice medicine, specializing in radiology, Poplar Bluff, Mo., 1963—; chief of staff Poplar Bluff Hosp. Mem. Adv. Com. on Radiation Legislation Neb., 1958-60, Miss., 1961-63. Served with USNR, 1939-40, Diplomate Am. Bd. Radiology. Fellow Am. Geriatrics Soc. (founding); mem. Am. Coll. Radiology, A.M.A., Soc. Nuclear Medicine, U.S. Mil. Engrs., Mo. State, Tri-County (treas. 1964-66, v.p. 1966-67, pres. 1968) med. socs., Radiation Research Soc., Am. Coll. Nuclear Medicine (charter), Radiol. Soc. N. Am., Mo. Radiol. Soc. Address: 1601 Big Bend Rd Poplar Bluff MO 63901

TUNEBERG, RICHARD KENT, dentist; b. Ida Grove, Iowa, June 9, 1925; s. Herbert Dewey and Alveda Elizabeth (Larson) T.; student Iowa State U., 1946-48; D.D.S., Northwestern U., 1952; m. Lois LaVerne Carlson, Oct. 10, 1952; children—Lee, Perry, James, Vance, Ann, Chad. Practice dentistry, Des Moines, 1952-56, Rockford, Ill., 1956—; owner, dir. Deerpath Farms, Belvidere, Ill., 1959—; mem. dental staff Swedish-Am. Hosp., Rockford. Served with AUS, 1946-47. Mem. Am. Dental Assn., Ill., Winnebago County dental socs., Am. Acad. Oral Radiology, Am. Soc. Children's Dentistry, Am. Soc. Preventive Dentistry, G.V. Black Soc.-Northwestern U. (charter), Am., Ill. farm burs. Mem. Evang. Free Ch. (chmn. 1973-75, 77-78), Clubs: John Evans of Northwestern U.; Chgo. Farmers. Home: 1321 Williamsburg Rd Rockford IL 61107 Office: 4040 Morsay Dr Rockford IL 61107

TUNG, THEODORE HSCHUM, economist; b. Peking, China, Aug. 28, 1934; s. Ren Tze and Chuang (Lin) T.; came to U.S., 1959; naturalized, 1971; B.A., Taiwan U., 1956; M.B.A., U. Okla., 1962; Ph.D., U. Pa., 1965; m. Patricia Hsu, Dec. 24, 1966; children—Candice Hsulin, Roderick Hschum. Asst. prof., research project dir. Colo. State U., 1964-66; asst. prof. Wharton Sch. U. Pa., 1966-68; sr. economist Bank of N.Y., N.Y.C., 1968-71; v.p. Continental Ill. Nat. Bank and Trust Co., Chgo., 1971—; lectr. in field. Mem. Nat. Assn. Bus. Economists. Author: (with W. Isard) General Theory-Social, Political, Economic and Regional, 1969. Contbr. articles to profl. jours. Home: 1232 Arthur Rd Naperville IL 60540 Office: 231 S LaSalle St Chicago IL 60693

TUNKS, FREDERICK EDWARD, editor; b. Center Point, Iowa, Feb. 2, 1928; s. Frederick Charles and Lovon Ann (Robertson) T.; B.S. in Tech. Journalism, Iowa State U., 1953; m. Ruth Ann Beckman, June 14, 1953; children—Brian, Lynne, Karen. News editor Independence (Iowa) Newspapers, 1953-54, Monticello (Iowa) Express, 1954-59; markets editor, news editor, mng. editor Feedstuffs, Miller Pub. Co., 1976—, chmn. photography, graphic and editorial coms., 1960—. Chmn. promotion com. New Hope (Minn.) Indsl. Commn., 1969-70. Served in USN, 1946-49. Mem. Nat. Agri-Mktg. Assn., Am. Bus. Press, Livestock Merchandising Inst. (trustee), Sigma Delta Chi, Alpha Zeta, Alpha Gamma Rho. Republican. Presbyterian. Clubs: Lions (Monticello); Downtown Kiwanis (Mpls.); Hopewood Internat. Friendship (New Hope); Dairy Shrine (Life). Lyricist religious song, 1976. Home: 8416 39th Ave N New Hope MN 55427 Office: 2501 Wayzata Blvd Minneapolis MN 55440

TUNNICLIFF, PHILIP HUNTER, cons. engr.; b. Island City, Iowa, Oct. 11, 1918; s. Nathaniel Hunter and Annabelle Elizabeth (Lucas) T.; student Cornell Coll., 1937-39, Iowa State U., 1940-41; m. Nancy Eleanor Jackson, Apr. 12, 1947; children—Scott Douglas and Kim Hunter (twins). Engr., land surveyor Tunnicliff Surveyors & Engrs., Inc., Davenport, Iowa, 1946—, pres., 1953—. Served with AUS, 1942-46, 50-52; maj. C.E. ret. Decorated Bronze Star medal. Registered profl. engr., Iowa, Ill. Mem. Nat. Soc. Profl. Engrs., Soc. Am. Mil. Engrs., Davenport C. of C., Res. Officers Assn. (local pres. 1966), Sigma Nu. Moose, Rotarian (mem. membership com. 1970). Home: 4909 Fairhaven Rd Davenport IA 52807 Office: 710-711 Putnam Bldg Davenport IA 52801

TUPPER, KENT PHILLIP, lawyer; b. Huron, S.D., July 24, 1931; s. Ezra Lynn and Mildred Virginia (Nason) T.; B.A., U. Minn., 1956; J.D., William Mitchell Coll. Law, St. Paul, 1963; m. Joan McGinley, Dec. 18, 1954; children—Kent Michael, Kay Maria. Indsl. psychologist Chrysler Corp., 1956; ins. claims adjuster and supr. Hardware Mut. Ins. Co., 1957-63; admitted to Minn. bar, 1963, also U.S. Supreme Ct.; pvt. practice, Mpls., 1963-67; dir. legal services project Leech Lake Indian Reservation, 1967-69, chmn. legal services bd., 1969—; partner firm Tupper Smith and Seck Ltd., Walker, Minn., 1969—. Tchr. comml. law Am. Inst. Banking, 1972; part-time instr. Indian studies Bemidji (Minn.) State Coll., 1973—; cons. Native Am. Tech. Assistance, Tri-State Indian Community Action Project; evaluator legal services project OEO. Chmn., Shingobee Twp. Democratic Farmer Labor party, 1972, del. Minn. State Conv., 1972. Served with USMC, 1951-53. Mem. Minn., Cass/Hubbard County (pres. 1970—), 15th Dist. bar assns., Am. Legion, Smithsonian Assos., Tupper Family Assn. Am. Episcopalian. Home: PO Box 146 Walker MN 56484 Office: PO Box 160 Walker MN 56484

TURCHYN, ANDREW, librarian; b. Chernytsia, Ukraine, July 17, 1912; s. Mykola and Maria (Chrzanowska) T.; grad. Cath. Theol. Acad., Lviv, 1938; Ph.D., Munich U., 1949; M.A. in L.S., U. Mich., 1953; M.A., Ind. U., 1960; m. Olha Salamacha, June 7, 1951 (dec. Nov. 1964); children—George A., Nicholas B., Leo R. Came to U.S., 1950, naturalized, 1956. Tchr. in Poland and Ukraine, 1938-44; editor Christian Voice, Munich, Germany, 1949-50, sr. cataloger Ind. U. Library, Bloomington, 1953-59, asso. head catalog dept., 1959-68, librarian, Slavic and East Asian collections, 1966-69, librarian for Slavic studies, 1969—, vis. lectr. Grad. Library Sch. Ind. U., 1969-72, asso. prof., 1972-75, prof., 1975—. Ind. state chmn. Ukrainian Nat. Republican Fedn., 1968—; v.p. Ind. Rep. Nationalities Council, 1972-74. Mem. ALA (past chmn., mem. exec. com. Slavic and East European sect.), Shevchenko Sci. Soc., Am. Assn. for Advancement Slavic Studies, Ukrainian Hist. Assn., A.A.U.P. Contbr. articles, book revs. to newspapers and periodicals. Home: 3205 Browncliff Ln Bloomington IN 47401

TURCOTTE, JEREMIAH GEORGE, physician, educator; b. Detroit, Jan. 20, 1933; s. Vincent Joseph and Margaret Campau (Meldrum) T.; B.S. with high distinction, U. Mich., 1955, M.D. cum laude, 1957; m. Claire Mary Lenz, July 5, 1958; children—Elizabeth Margaret, John Jeremiah, Sara Lenz, Claire Meldrum. Intern, U. Mich. Med. Center, 1957-58, resident, 1958-60, 61-63; practice medicine specializing in gen. surgery and transplantation, Ann Arbor, Mich., 1963—; mem. faculty dept. surgery U. Mich., Ann Arbor, 1963—, instr., 1963-65, asst. prof., 1965-68, asso. prof., 1968-71, prof., 1971—, chmn. dept. surgery, head sect. gen. surgery, 1974—; mem. sci. adv. bd. Mich. Kidney Found., 1965—. Recipient Henry Russell award Regents U. Mich., 1970. Diplomate Am. Bd. Surgery. Fellow ACS; mem. Internat. Transplantation Soc., Soc. Surgery Alimentary Tract, Am. Soc. Transplant Surgeons, Frederick A. Coller Soc., Am. Trauma Soc., Am., Central, Western surg. assns., Soc. Univ. Surgeons, Transplantation Soc. Mich. (pres. 1973-75). Roman Catholic. Contbr. articles to profl. jours. Home: 769 Heatherway St Ann Arbor MI 48104 Office: 1405 E Ann St Ann Arbor MI 48109

TUREK, ARTHUR FRANK, dentist; b. Faribault, Minn., July 17, 1922; s. Joseph James and Mary Ann (Budin) T.; student St. John's U., 1939-41; D.D.S., U. Minn., 1944; m. Ruth Louise Blumenberg, Feb. 12, 1944; children—Thomas M., Deborah (Mrs. Kenneth Picha). Practice dentistry, Olivia, Minn., 1946-47, Le Center, Minn., 1947—. Treas. Le Center Community Club, 1950-55, pres., 1966. Chmn. Bd. Edn. Sch. Dist. 392, Le Center, 1964-73; chmn. Le Center Housing and Redevel. Authority, 1972—. Served to capt., Dental Corps, AUS, 1943-46; PTO. Mem. So. Dist. (Minn.) Dental Soc. (pres. 1972-73), Am., Minn. dental assns., Minn. Prosthodontic Soc., Izaak Walton League, Am. Legion (dist. comdr. 1957, dept. vice comdr. 1959), VFW (post comdr. 1952), Psi Omega. K.C. Home: 260 N Waterville St Le Center MN 56057 Office: 34 N Park St Le Center MN 56057

TUREK, ROBERT WALTER, assn. exec.; b. Chgo., May 11, 1928; s. Walter and Frances (Skora) T.; student St. Joseph's Coll., 1946-49, DePaul U., 1953-55; m. Erna Boehringer, Nov. 21, 1956; children—James Robert, John Robert, Elizabeth Ann. Illumination engr. Commonwealth Edison Co., Chgo., 1952-66; exec. v.p. Chgo. Lighting Inst., 1968—, Electric Assn., 1971—, Elec. Apparatus Service Assn., 1971, Elec. Inst. Chgo., 1972—; instr. illumination design Chgo. Lighting Inst., 1968-72, Harrington Inst. Interior Design, 1968-72. Mem. Chgo. Com. on High-Rise Bldgs., 1974, Ill. Energy Conservation Code Com. Served with F.A., AUS, 1951-52. Mem. Am. Legion, Illuminating Engring. Soc., Little Wheels, Internat. Assn. Elec. Leagues, Smithsonian Assos., Am. Soc. Assn. Execs., Chgo. Assn. Commerce and Industry. Contbr. articles to profl. jours. Home: 814 E Cherry Ln Arlington Heights IL 60004 Office: 125 S Clark St Chicago IL 60603

TUREK, STEPHEN, coputer scientist; b. St. Louis, Nov. 18, 1941; s. Raymond and Helen Rose (Puzniak) T.; Ph.D., U. Mo., 1972; m. Tarvi Ann Hermann, Aug. 7, 1965. Instr., U. Mo., 1969-73; programmer LTV Aerospace Co., 1973-74; sci. programmer Senturion Scis. Co., Tulsa, 1974-75; systems analyst Kansas City (Mo.) Municipal Ct., 1975—. Mem. Math. Assn. Am., Phi Delta Kappa. Republican. Home: 7328 Walnut St Kansas City MO 64114 Office: 1101 Locust St Kansas City MO 64107

TURNER, ALLEN MARK, lawyer; b. Chgo., June 27, 1937; s. Myer H. and Madeline G. (Gross) T.; B.B.A., U. Wis., 1958; J.D., U. Chgo., 1961; m. Lynn Sharon Bernberg, Mar. 22, 1959; children—Jennifer Ellen, Christopher Marshall Richard. Admitted to Ill. bar, 1961; since practiced in Chgo.; mem. firm Portes & Green, 1961-64, Pritzker & Pritzker, 1965—; dir., gen. counsel Hyatt Internat. Corp., 1965—; dir., sec., gen. counsel Agrow Industries, Inc., 1965—; dir. McCalls Pub. Co. Lectr. philosophy Chgo. Sch. for Gifted, 1960-61; instr. Chgo. Police Acad., 1966-68. Bd. dirs. Jewish Welfare Fund Met. Chgo., Am. Jewish Com., Jewish Student Service Com., com. on Goodman Theater, Art Inst. Chgo., Chgo. Theater Group; chmn. adv. bd. Victory Gardens Theater. Jewish Fedn. Chgo. travel grantee, 1965. Recipient Glasser award, 1969. Mem. Am., Chgo. bar assns. Club: Standard (Chgo.). Home: 521 Stratford Pl Chicago IL 60657 Office: 2 First Nat Plaza Chicago IL 60670

TURNER, AMOS, engring-constrn. co. exec.; b. Tel Aviv, Israel, Feb. 18, 1926; s. Alex and Helen (Turner) T.; B.S. in Elec. Engring., Munich (Germany) Inst. Tech., 1949; M.S. in Elec. Engring., Ill. Inst. Tech., 1955; m. Edith Singer, June 11, 1954; children—Helene, Nancy, David. Came to U.S., 1950, naturalized, 1955. Elec. project engr. MacDonald Engring. Co., Chgo., 1955-59; chief elec. engr. Meissner Engring. Co., Chgo., 1959-62; with Hoyer-Schlesinger-Turner, Chgo., 1963—, v.p., treas., 1963—. Registered profl. engr., Ill., Ark., Pa., Calif., Okla., Nebr., Minn., Ala., Ind., Mich., Ky., La., Wis. Mem. Nat., Ill. socs. profl. engrs., IEEE (chmn. Chgo. sect. indsl. group 1964—), Am. Inst. Iron and Steel Engrs., Tau Beta Pi, Eta Kappa Nu. Office: 300 W Adams St Chicago IL 60606

TURNER, ARTHUR EDWARD, coll. adminstr.; b. Hemlock, Mich., Jan. 31, 1931; s. Alvin S. and Grace E. (Champlain) T.; B.S. (Silliman scholar), Alma (Mich.) Coll., 1952; M. Ed., Wayne State U., 1954; extension studies Central Mich. U., U. Mich.; LL.D., Ashland Coll., 1968; H.U.D., Colegio Americano de Quito, Ecuador, 1968; m. Johann M. Jordan, May 10, 1953; children—Steven Arthur, Michael Scott, Kathryn Jo. Admissions counselor Alma Coll., 1952-53, dir. admissions, alumni relations, 1953-59; Presbyn. lay minister, 1956-59; organizer Eastminister Presbyn. Ch., Alma, 1956; co-founder Northwood Inst., Alma, 1959, with campuses at Midland, Mich., Cedar Hill, Tex., West Baden, Ind., Quito, Ecuador (extension center), and Bloomfield Hills Acad., Bloomfield Hills, Mich., 1st pres., 1959-74, chmn., chief exec. officer, 1974—, also trustee. Trustee Nat. council Boy Scouts Am. Recipient People of Peru award, 1966; named One of Ten Outstanding Young Americans, 1965. Mem. Alpha Psi Omega, Phi Phi Alpha. Mason (33 deg., Shriner), Rotarian. Clubs: Internat. (Washington); Detroit; Midland Country. Home: 4608 Arbor Dr Midland MI 48640 Office: Northwood Inst Midland MI 48640

TURNER, CHARLES JOSEPH, educator; b. Jacksonville, Fla., Apr. 21, 1926; s. Henry Selkirk and Louise (Fendrich) T.; A.B., Wheaton Coll., 1946; M.Ed., Harvard, 1952; Ed.D., Columbia, 1954; m. Sarah E. Traverse, Apr. 25, 1964; 1 son, George. Tchr. pub. schs., Jacksonville, Fla., 1947-51; asso. dir. research Richmond (Va.) Pub. Schs., 1954-59; prof. edn., chmn. dept. Glassboro (N.J.) State U., 1966-69; prof. edn. reading clinic So. Ill. U., Edwardsville, 1969—. Project dir. U.S. Office Edn. grant, 1964-66. Served with AUS, 1946-47. Mem. AAUP (local v.p. 1968-69), Internat. Reading Assn. (placement com. 1968-70), Am. Ednl. Research Assn., NEA. Author: Differential Identification of Successful Students, 1966; also articles. Home: 609 Sunset Dr Edwardsville IL 62025

TURNER, DEAN SCHILLER, oil co. exec.; b. Youngstown, Ohio, Dec. 16, 1912; s. Edward Henry and Grace (Schiller) T.; B.S., in Metallurgy, Westminster Coll., 1931-35; postgrad. Youngstown Coll., 1935-37; m. Sally E. McBain, June 29, 1940; children—Marilyn Ruth (Mrs. Rune Carlson), William S. With Carnegie Illinois subsidiary U.S. Steel Co., Youngstown, 1933-46, supt. wage and salary, 1933-37, tng. dir., 1939-46; with Standard Oil of Ohio, Cleve., 1946—, sr. personnel asst. refining div., 1946-47, sr. tng. specialist corp. tng. and devel., 1967—. Indsl. mgmt. instr. Baldwin Wallace Coll., 1967—. Pres., Cleve. Film Council, 1953-57; chmn. Bay Village Service Commn., 1970—; chmn. West Shore bd. mgrs. YMCA, 1971; trustee Met. Cleve. Area YMCA, 1973—, chmn. fall conf., 1968-71; mem. sales adv. com Cuyahoga Community Coll., 1969—; active West Shore Family Service, 1957-65, chmn., 1964-65. Recipient Refining div. award Am. Petroleum Inst., 1969. Kiwanian (charter mem., past pres.). Home: 26100 Lake Rd Bay Village OH 44140

TURNER, EDWARD CLARK, bishop; b. Buenos Aires, Argentina, Mar. 26, 1915; s. Edward and Eva Helen (Clark) T.; came to U.S., 1922; A.B., Northwestern U., 1937; B.D., Seabury-Western Theol. Sem., Evanston, Ill., 1940, D.D., 1954; m. Virginia Hunter, Nov. 19, 1938; children—John Bowen, Mary, David Hunter, James Clark. Ordained priest Episcopal Ch., 1940; assigned missions St. John, Okanogan, St. Paul, Omak, Trinity, Oroville and Tranfiguration, Twisp, Wash., 1940-44; rector Ch. Ascension, Pueblo, Colo., 1944; bishop coadjuster Diocese Kans., Topeka, 1956, diocesan, 1959. Pres. Pueblo City-County Bd. Health, 1953-56. Chmn. bd. dirs. Parkview Episcopal Hosp., Pueblo, bd. dirs. Pueblo chpt. A.R.C., Pueblo Family Service Soc., Stormant-Vail Hosp., Topeka; trustee Seabury-Western Theol. Sem. Home: Bethany Pl Topeka KS 66612

TURNER, GLENN EVERETT, supt. schs.; b. Plymouth, Neb., Aug. 10, 1903; s. William A. and Mary (Gerth) T.; student Cotner Coll., 1921-22, Nebr. Wesleyan U., 1922; A.B., U. Nebr., 1933, A.M., 1948, Ph.D., 1959; m. Elizabeth Loos, Dec. 26, 1933; 1 son, Roger. Tchr. pub. schs., Jefferson County, Nebr., 1922-23, Swanton, Nebr., 1923-24; supt. schs., Garrison, Nebr., 1927-28, Rokeby, Nebr., 1929-40; dir. Nebr. Nat. Youth Adminstrn., 1940-42; supt. schs., Lancaster County, Nebr., 1942—. Pres. Lancaster County Activities Assn., 1932-33, Lincoln (Nebr.) Inter-Civic Council, 1950-51; bd. dirs. Lincoln-Lancaster County Tb Assn., Nebr. State Sch. Bd. Assn., Kiwanis Found. of Lincoln. Recipient Nash Nat. Conservation award, 1953, Merit award DAR, 1965, Kiwanis Vocat. Guidance award, 1966. Mem. N.E.A. (life), Nat. Geog. Soc., Neb. Acad. Scis. (life), Neb. State Hist. Soc., Neb., Am. assns. sch. adminstrs., Lincoln C. of C. (dir.), Nebr. State, Lancaster County (pres. 1930-31) edn. assns., Govtl. Research Inst., Internat. Platform Assn. Republican. Congregationalist. Clubs: Masons, Shriners; Kiwanis (lt. gov. Nebr.-Iowa div. 1965); Order Eastern Star (patron 1969); Lincoln Dinner (sec.-treas. 1951-63), Hiram (pres. 1971), Knife and Fork (pres. 1948-49) (Lincoln). Home: 5030 Washington Lincoln NE 68506 Office: 3234 S 13th St Lincoln NE 68502

TURNER, HAROLD EDWARD, educator; b. Hamilton, Ill., Nov. 22, 1921; s. Edward Jesse and Beulah May (White) T.; A.B., Carthage Coll., 1950; M.S., U. Ill. at Urbana, 1951, Ed.D. (George Peabody fellow), 1956; m. Catherine Skeeters, Apr. 5, 1946; children—Michele (Mrs. William Warren), Thomas, Barbara, Krista. Tchr., Taylorville (Ill.) Jr. High Sch., 1951-52, Moline (Ill.) Jr. High Sch., 1952-54; dir. elementary edn. Jefferson County, Colo., 1955-57, prin. Jefferson County High Sch., 1957-60; asst. prof. edn. North Tex. State U., Denton, 1960-63; asst. supt. curriculum Sacramento City Schs., 1963-66; asso. prof., chmn. dept. curriculum and instrn. U. Mo. at St. Louis, 1966-69, prof., 1971—. Vis. prof. Adams State Coll., Alamosa, Colo., 1959; adjunct prof. N.Y. U., 1965; cons. in field to various sch. dists., Tex., Mo.; spl. cons. Mo. State Dept. Edn., 1973. Served with USNR, 1942-46. Mem. Nat., Mo. (exec. sec. 1967—, pres. elect 1976-77) assns. supervision and curriculum devel., Greater St. Louis Curriculum Dirs., John Dewey Soc. (chmn. meetings 1973—), Profs. Supervision, Nat. Soc. Study Edn., Soc. Profs. Edn., Mo. State Tchrs. Assn., Greater St. Louis White House Conf. Edn., Phi Delta Kappa. Presbyn. (elder). Mason. Author: (with Adolph Unruh) Supervision for Change Innovation, 1970. Contbr. articles in field to profl. jours. Home: 12184 Gladshire St Bridgeton MO 63044 Office: School of Education Univ of Missouri 8001 Natural Bridge Rd St Louis MO 63121

TURNER, HERMAN NATHANIEL, JR., educator, mathematician; b. St. Louis, Nov. 6, 1925; s. Herman Nathaniel and Rosie Mae (Williams) T.; B.S., Bradley U., Peoria, Ill., 1951; m. Helen Lorraine Quarles, Mar. 1, 1975; children by previous marriage—Anthony, Mark, Herman Nathaniel III, Erik. Cartographic aide Aero. Chart and Info. Center, St. Louis 1953-54; mathematician White Sands Proving Ground, N.Mex., 1954-55; tchr. math., Caruthersville, Mo., 1961-62, Phila., 1956-59, East Moline, Ill., 1965-66, N.W. High Sch., St. Louis, 1968—. Served with USMC, 1944-46. Certified math. tchr., Mo., Ill., N.Y., Pa., N.J. Mem. Math. Assn. Am., Am. Math. Soc., Am. Fedn. Tchrs. Democrat. Presbyterian. Club: East Moline Kiwanis. Home: 4709 Lee Ave St Louis MO 63115 Office: Northwest High School 5140 Riverview Blvd St Louis MO 63120

TURNER, L. BOWMAN, sheet metal co. engr.; b. Newark, Ohio, Aug. 28, 1918; s. Aaron and Bertha Florence (Kreager) T.; B.S., Capital U., 1940; M.A., Ohio State U., 1941; m. Genieva Sheppard, May 16, 1943; children—Beverly Turner Lofquist, Carol Turner Ryerson. Engr., Waco Aircraft Co., Troy, Ohio, 1942-44; engr. Jeffrey Mfg. Co., Columbus, Ohio, 1946-51; engr. N. Am. Aviation Corp., Columbus, 1951-52; engr. plant engring. Westinghouse Electric Corp., Columbus, 1952-66; engr. research and devel. United Sheet Metal div. United McGill Corp., Westerville, Ohio, 1966—, chief engr., 1968—. Mem. staff air conditioning design engring. course U. Wis. Extension, Madison, 1973. Registered profl. engr., Ohio, Ill., Mich., Calif., Ky. Mem. Nat. Soc. Profl. Engrs., Am. Soc. Heating, Refrigeration and Air Conditioning Engrs. (mem. tech. com. 1968-76), Pi Mu Epsilon. Methodist (Sunday sch. supt. 1963-66, chmn. fin. com. 1971-72, mem. choir 1955—). Patentee in field. Home: 4978 Taunton Way Columbus OH 43228 Office: 200 E Broadway Westerville OH 43081

TURNER, MARY RUTH, lawyer; b. Joliet, Ill., July 12, 1944; d. Arthur and Ruth M. (Denson) T.; B.S., Ind. U., 1965, M.S., 1966; J.D., Loyola U., Chgo., 1976. Admitted to Ill. bar, 1976; asso. firm Seyfarth, Shaw, Fairweather & Geraldson, Chgo., 1976—. Mem. operations com. United Crusade of Met. Chgo. Mem. Am., Ill., Cook County, Chgo. bar assns., Chgo. Women's Bar Assn., Urban League. Office: 55 E Monroe St Suite 4200 Chicago IL 60603

TURNER, MICHAEL SETH, broadcast co. exec.; b. San Diego, July 28, 1948; s. Charles Irwin and Lee (Yomin) T.; B.S., San Diego State U., 1970; M.S., Iowa State U., 1971. Teaching asst. radio/TV San Diego State U., summer 1970; instr. speech/radio/TV U. Nebr. at Omaha, 1971-72; asso. mgr. sta. KFJM/KFJM-FM, U. N.D., Grand Forks, 1972—. Chmn. pub. relations, also bd. dirs. Pine to Prairie council Girl Scouts U.S., 1973—. Recipient Operation Threshhold award U.S. Jaycees, 1975, News Tip award N.D. A.P. 1976, 77. Rotary internat. study exchange student, Philippines, 1978. Mem. Grand Forks (dir. 1973-74), N.D. (pub. relations chmn. 1974-75, v.p. 1975-76) jaycees, Nat. Assn. Ednl. Broadcasters, Speech Communication Assn., Soc. Profl. Journalists, N.D. AP Broadcasters. Mem. B'nai B'rith (pres. lodge, 1st. v.p. Dakota council 1977—). Home: 315 1/2 Cornell St Grand Forks ND 58201 Office: Box 8116 KFJM Radio Sta Grand Forks ND 58202

TURNER, RICHARD, coll. pres.; b. New Bedford, Mass., July 28, 1932; s. Louis Alexander and Margaret (Mather) T.; m. Jane Wymond Beebe, June 25, 1955; children—Louis Hamilton, David Alexander; A.B., Princeton U., 1955, M.F.A. (Fulbright fellow), 1958, Ph.D., 1959. Instr. art history U. Mich., 1959-60; asst. prof., prof. art and archeology Princeton U., 1960-68; prof. art Middlebury (Vt.) Coll., 1968-74, dean faculty, 1970-74; pres., prof. art Grinnell (Iowa) Coll., 1974—. Trustee, Hazen Found. Mem. Coll. Art Assn., Renaissance Soc. Am., Phi Beta Kappa. Fellow, Am. Council Learned Socs., 1963-64, Harvard U. Center for Italian Renaissance Studies, 1963-64; Author: The Vision of Landscape in Renaissance, 1966. Home: 1600 Park St Grinnell IA 50112

TURNER, RICHARD CLARK, lawyer, state ofcl.; b. Avoca, Iowa, Sept. 30, 1927; s. Joe W. and Elizabeth (Clark) T.; B.A., State U. Iowa, 1950, J.D., 1953; m. Charlotte Forsen, Nov. 30, 1956; children—Joe W. II, Amy Elizabeth, Mark Howard. Admitted to Iowa bar, 1953; partner Turner & Turner, Avoca, 1953-54; asst. county atty., 1954-56; practice law, Council Bluffs, Iowa, 1956-67; atty. gen. Iowa, Des Moines, 1966—. Town clk., Avoca, 1953-60; mem. Iowa Senate, 1961-65. Served with USAAF, 1945-47. Mem. Am., Iowa, S.W. Iowa, Polk County Pottawattamie County bar assns., Am. Trial Lawyers Assn., Iowa Acad. Trial Lawyers, Am. Judicature Soc., Nat. Assn. Attys. Gen., Am. Legion, 40 and 8. Republican. Presbyn. Home: 1054 21st St West Des Moines IA 50265 Office: State Capitol Bldg Des Moines IA 50318

TURNER, ROBERT HOMER, architect; b. Indpls., Apr. 16, 1938; s. Homer Milton and Mary Mildred (Summers) T.; B.S., U. Cin., 1964; postgrad Ball State U.; m. Charlene Anne Flynn, Sept. 11, 1959; 1 dau., DeAnna Lynn. Pvt. practice architecture, Indpls., 1964—; archtl. adviser on changes in chs. for handicapped. Mem. AIA, Ind. Soc. Architects, Jordon Family YMCA. Methodist. Elk. Clubs: Kokomo Toastmasters (pres. 1969-70); Dolphin, Dads (Brebref Prep. Sch.) (Indpls.). Home and office: 10156 N Park Av Indianapolis IN 46280

TURNER, ROBERT RUST, dental equipment mfg. co. exec.; b. Denison, Iowa, Dec. 12, 1921; s. Robert F. and Florence Belle (Rust) T.; ed. U. Iowa m. Joyce Elaine Swaney, June 21, 1947; children—Dan W., Robert S., Elizabeth L., Gail E. Expediter C.E., U.S. Army, Sausalito, Calif., 1946-47; salesman, 1949-53; agt. Standard Oil Co., 1954-58; salesman sporting goods firm, Pa., 1959-60; with Den-Tal-Ez Mfg. Co., Des Moines, 1961—, also dir. Served with AUS, 1941-45. Home: 1100 E 2d Ave Indianola IA 50125 Office: 1201 SE Diehl St Des Moines IA 50315

TURNER, STEPHEN HONEYWELL, mktg. research co. exec.; b. Madison, Wis., May 24, 1940; s. Vernon C. and Jacqueline (Honeywell) T.; B.A., U. S.D., 1964, M.A., 1966; m. Ann M. Raebel, July 14, 1964; children—Randall, Molly, Clay. Sr. project dir. Amoco Oil Co., Chgo., 1968-72; mgr. consumer research Theo Hamm Brewing Co., St. Paul, 1972; mgr. custom research Coca-Cola U.S.A., Atlanta, 1972-75; exec. v.p. Creative Research Assos., Chgo., 1975—. Mem. Am. Mktg. Assn., Am. Assn. Pub. Opinion Researchers. Democrat. Club: Exec. Chgo. Contbr. articles in field to profl. jours. Home: 1 S 621 Bender Ln West Chicago IL 60185 Office: 180 N Michigan Ave Chicago IL 60601

TURNER, THOMAS ALLEN, automobile co. exec., mayor; b. Nashville, Oct. 19, 1931; s. George Edgar and Laura Barton (Johnson) T.; B.B.A., U. Mich., 1955, M.B.A. with high distinction, 1956; m. June Alice Rohrman, Sept. 5, 1953; children—Mark Allen, Judi Lynn. With Ford Motor Co., Dearborn, Mich., 1956—, mktg. product plans mgr. Lincoln-Mercury div., 1968-69, mgr. N.Am. programs, 1969-70, dir. mktg. research, 1970-71, dir non-automotive mktg., 1971-73, gen. mgr. indsl. engine operations, 1973-77, supply and distbn. mgr. parts and service div., Livonia, Mich., 1977—; instr. accounting Henry Ford Community Coll., 1956-61; mayor protem City of Plymouth, 1975-77, mayor, 1977—. Mem. Plymouth (Mich.) Bd. Edn., 1973-74; v.p. Plymouth-Canton Devel. Commn., 1973-75. Mem. Am. Mktg. Assn., Beta Alpha Psi, Phi Kappa Phi, Beta Gamma Sigma. Republican. Presbyterian (ruling elder 1961—, chmn. trustees Detroit presbytery 1972-76). Home: 1300 Linden St Plymouth MI 48170 Office: 29500 Plymouth Rd Livonia MI 48150

TURNER, WILLIAM LEE, lawyer; b. Kansas City, Mo., Sept. 13, 1930; s. William and Marie (Gude) T.; B.S., U. Kans. 1958, LL.B., 1960, J.D., 1968; m. Katie L. Carroll, June 6, 1953; children—Garry L., Stacy M. Admitted to Kan. and Mo. bar, 1960, U.S. Supreme Ct., 1973; asso. firm Gage, Hodges, Moore, Park & Kreamer (name changed in 1964 to Gage, Hodges, Park & Kreamer and in 1968 to Gage, Hodges, Kreamer & Varner and in 1975 to Gage & Tucker), Kansas City, Mo., 1960-63, jr. partner, 1963-64, sr. partner, 1965—, chief, trial div., 1968—. Mem. Mayor's Corps of Progress, Kansas City, Mo. Campaign mgr. Western Mo., Edward L. Dowd for Gov., 1972, now mem. Gov.'s Adv. Council. Served with USAF, 1950-57. Mem Am., Kansas City, Independence bar assns., Lawyers Assn., Am. Legion, Phi Alpha Delta. Club: University. Home: 925 Red Rd Independence MO 64055 Office: 1000 Bryant Bldg Kansas City MO 64106

TURPIN, JOHN CLYDE, educator; b. Ogden, Utah, Feb. 16, 1944; s. Clyde Wilford and Joyce Ethlind (Christensen) T.; B.S., Weber State Coll., 1967; M.Ed., Brigham Young U., 1970; Ed.D., U. Toledo, 1973; m. Barbara Lynn Hawkins, June 17, 1972; children—Michael John, Jennifer Lynn. Tchr., paraprofl., then mem. social studies team Roy (Utah) High Sch., 1965-67; teaching missionary Ch. Jesus Christ of Latter-Day Saints, Berkley, Oakland and San Jose, Calif., 1967-69; research and teaching asst. Brigham Young U., 1969-70; grad. asst. U. Toledo, 1970-73; vis. instr. Bowling Green U., 1971-73; asst. prof. psychology of edn., guidance, career decision and values edn. Baldwin Wallace Coll., 1973—; cons. in field. Mem. Am. Personnel and Guidance Assn., Assn. Supervision and Curriculum Devel., Ohio Coll. Personnel Assn., Assn. Mormon Counselors and Psychotherapitst, Phi Delta Kappa. Republican. Mormon. Author: Building Human Relations Skills—Helps for Teachers, Parents and Leaders, 1977. Home: 9274 Willow Ln Olmsted Falls OH 44138 Office: Div Edn Baldwin Wallace Coll Berea OH 44017

TURRIFF, CLARENCE JOSEPH, chem. co. exec.; b. Green Bay, Wis., Apr. 22, 1920; s. Charles Henry and Dorinda (Quatsoe) T.; B.S., St. Norbert Coll., 1941; m. Gladys Cecelia Hoenslaar, Apr. 30, 1942; children—Barbara Ann (Mrs. Frederick Shiple III), Thomas Joseph, Susan Clare, Terry Lynn, Mary Lee. Buyer, McKesson & Robbins, Inc., Chgo., 1946-48; br. mgr. McKesson Chem. Co., Chgo., 1948-53, dist. mgr., 1953-58; pres., chief exec. TAB Chem. Inc., Chgo., 1958—; dir. 1st Nat. Bank Western Springs. Served to maj. AUS, 1941-46. Mem. Chgo. Drug and Chem. Assn. (dir. 1963—, pres. 1970). Republican. Roman Catholic. Club: LaGrange (Ill.) Country (gov.). Home: 102 Rugeley Rd Western Springs IL 60558 Office: 4801 S Austin Ave Chicago IL 60638

TURSKI, BEN, dentist; b. Madison, Ill., Mar. 4, 1919; s. Faustyn and Natalia (Banach) T.; D.D.S., St. Louis U., 1954; m. Wanda Gregorgwicz, Jan. 21, 1943; children—Ronald Ben, Patrick Alan. Practice dentistry, East St. Louis, Ill., 1954—; clin. instr. St. Louis U. Sch. Dentistry, 1954-56. Served as capt. USAAF, 1942-45; PTO. Decorated Distinguished Flying Cross, Air medal with 6 oak leaf clusters. Recipient State of Ill. citation for meritorious service, 1944. Mem. ADA, St. Clair Dist., East St. Louis (pres. 1964) dental socs. Roman Catholic. Home: 469 Collinsville Ave East St Louis IL 62201 Office: 469 Collinsville Ave East St Louis IL 62201

TUSCHMAN, JAMES MARSHALL, steel co. exec., lawyer; b. Toledo, Nov. 28, 1941; s. Chester and Harriet (Harris) T.; B.S. in Bus., Miami U., Oxford, Ohio, 1963; J.D., Ohio State U., 1966; m. Ina S. Cheloff, Sept. 2, 1967; children—Chad Michael, Jon Stephen, Sari Anne. Admitted to Ohio bar, 1966, since practiced in Toledo; partner firm Shumaker, Loop & Kendrick, 1966—; spl. asst. atty. gen., Ohio, 1974—; chmn. bd., sec. Tuschman Steel Co., Toledo, 1969-76; vice chmn. bd. Kripke Tuschman Industries, Inc., 1977—; chmn. bd., sec. Toledo Steel Supply Co., 1969—; pres. Tuschman Realty & Investment Co.; partner Starr Ave. Co., Toledo. Trustee Darlington House, Jewish Home for Aged; bd. govs. Jewish Community Center. Mem. Am. (com. law and medicine), Ohio, Toledo bar assns., Nat. Assn. R.R. Trial Counsel, Def. Research Inst., Soc. Hosp. Attys., Zeta Beta Tau, Phi Delta Phi. Jewish (trustee, treas. temple). Clubs: Glengary Country, Toledo. Home: 5240 Coldstream Rd Toledo OH 43623 Office: 500 Libbey-Owens-Ford Bldg Toledo OH 43624

TUTINS, ANTONS, electronics engr.; b. Ludza, Latvia, May 2, 1933; s. Francis and Veronika (Seipulniks) T.; came to U.S., 1950, naturalized, 1963; B.S. in Elec. Engring., Ill. Inst. Tech., 1970; M.B.A., U. Chgo., 1974; m. Raita Snebergs, July 8, 1961; 1 son, Robert. Mfg. mgr. Communications div. Motorola Inc., Chgo., 1964-73; applications engring. supr. Knowles Electronics Inc., Franklin Park, Ill., 1973-77, product engring. mgr., 1977—. Served with USN, 1955-57. Mem. Audio Engring. Soc., Chgo. Audio and Acoustical Group (pres. 1977-78), IEEE, Motorola Engring. Club (pres. 1970-71), Am. Latvian Cath. Assn. (sec. 1975—). Roman Catholic. Home: 1338 Briar Ct Des Plaines IL 60018 Office: 3100 N Mannheim Rd Franklin Park IL 60131

TUTT, CHARLES LEAMING, JR., ret. univ. dean; b. Coronodo, Calif., Jan. 26, 1911; s. Charles Leaming and Eleanor (Armit) T.; B.S., Princeton U., 1933, M.E., 1934; D.Engring., Norwich U., 1967; m. Pauline Barbara Shaffer, Aug. 16, 1933; children—Charles Leaming IV, William Bullard. Student engr. Buick Motor div. Gen. Motors Corp., Flint, Mich., 1934-36, engr. chassis unit sect., 1936-38, spl. assignment engr., 1938-40; asst. prof. mech. engring. Princeton U., 1940-46; staff asst. ASME, N.Y.C., 1940-44; asso. editor Product Engring. mag. McGraw-Hill Pub. Co., N.Y.C., 1944-46; asst. to pres. Gen. Motors Inst., Flint, 1946-50, adminstrv. chmn., 1950-60, dean engring., 1960-69, dean acad. affairs, 1969-74. Mem. adv. com. Sloan Panorama of Transp., Flint, 1965—. Trustee Norwich U., Northfield, Vt., 1964-76; mem. Engring. Found. Bd., N.Y.C., 1963-75, chmn., 1967-73; mem. bd. Engrs. Council for Profl. Devel., 1975—. Fellow ASME (v.p. 1964-66, pres. 1975-76); mem. Soc. Mfg. Engrs. (dir. 1972—), Am. Soc. Engring. Edn., Soc. Automotive Engrs., Princeton Engring. Assn., Mich. Soc. Profl. Engrs., Am. Assn. Higher Edn., Soc. Cin. State Va., Sigma Xi, Delta Tau Delta, Tau Beta Pi. Clubs: Flint City, Flint Rainbow, Univ. (Flint); Princeton (N.Y.C.); Rotary. Contbr. numerous articles to profl. jours. Home: 3401 Westwood Pkwy Flint MI 48503

TUTTLE, GEORGE ALBERT, liaison engr.; b. Newark, Jan. 27, 1924; s. Harold Story and Ruth Naiomi (Heiser) T.; B.S., U.S. Mil. Acad., 1944; M.S. in Mech. Engring., U. Mich., 1949; grad. U.S. Army War Coll., 1962; m. Margaret Henrietta Beckman, Apr. 8, 1948; children—Edgar George, Neil Alan. Commd. lt. U.S. Army, 1944, advanced through grades to col., 1966; various positions from combat comdr. to sr. adviser to Philippine Mil. Assistance Group; instr. engring. drawing U.S. Mil. Acad., 1949-51; chief of labs. Detroit Arsenal, 1955-59; comdg. officer Joint U.S. Republic of Germany Tank Program, Detroit, ret., 1968; liaison engr. Lycoming div. Avco Corp., Detroit area, 1968—. Decorated Combat Inf. badge, Bronze Star medal with 4 oak leaf clusters, Legion of Merit. Mem. Soc. Automotive Engrs., Assn. U.S. Army, Am. Def. Preparedness Assn., Armor Assn., Assn. Grads. U.S.Mil. Acad., Assn. Grads. U.S. Army War Coll., Grosse Pointe Power Squadron. Methodist. Clubs: Chrysler Yacht; Grosse Pointe Woods Boat (vice commodore, 1976). Contbr. articles to mil. and tech. publs. Home: 2051 Oxford Rd Grosse Pointe Woods MI 48236

TUTTLE, JACK LYMAN, veterinarian; b. St. Louis, Sept. 24, 1947; s. George Austan and Helen Louise (Lyman) T.; B.S., U. Ill., 1969, D.V.M., 1973, M.Ed., 1978; 1 son, Christopher Ryan. Gen. practice veterinary medicine, Chgo., 1973-75; small animal extension veterinarian U. Ill., 1975—, instr., 1975-77, asst. prof., 1978—. Mem. AVMA, Ill., Eastern Ill. veterinary med. assns., Am. Assn. Extension Veterinarians, Am. Soc. Veterinary Ethology, U. Ill. Alumni Assn., Alpha Kappa Lambda, Omega Tau Sigma, Phi Zeta, Kappa Delta Pi, Phi Delta Kappa. Home: 1106 Holiday Dr Champaign IL 61820 Office: 256 Large Animal Clinic Urbana IL 61801

TVEDTEN, HAROLD WILLIAM, veterinarian; b. Milw., Oct. 21, 1946; s. Leonard Reginald and Ruth Elizabeth (Peatow) T.; B.S., U. Mich., 1968; B.S., Mich. State U., 1970, D.V.M., 1971, M.S., 1973, Ph.D., 1975; m. Gretchen Legrid Flo, June 8, 1972; 1 dau., Elizabeth Lynn. Veterinarian, Easthaven Animal Hosp., Ann Arbor, Mich., 1971-72; Upjohn postdoctoral fellow Mich. State U., East Lansing, 1972-73, NIH postdoctoral fellow, 1973-74, clin. pathologist, also asst. prof. veter. clin. pathology, 1975—. Diplomate Am. Coll. Veter. Pathologists and Veter. Clin. Pathologists. Mem. Am. Coll. Veter. Pathologists, Am., Mich. (dir. 1975—), Mid-State (pres. 1976) veter. med. assns., Am. Soc. Veter. Clin. Pathologists. Home: 15227 Peacock Rd Haslett MI 48840 Office: Dept Pathology Mich State U East Lansing MI 48824

TVRDIK, TIMOTHY CHARLES, JR., dentist; b. Omaha, Mar. 6, 1939; s. Timothy Charles and Marybelle (Pipal) T.; D.D.S., Creighton U., 1964; m. Kathleen McDermott, Sept. 3, 1960; children—Mark, Michael, Gregory, Stephen, Katie. Dentist in pvt. practice Omaha, 1966—. Served with Dental Corp, USNR, 1964-66. Mem. Am. Dental Assn. Home: 9305 Pauline St Omaha NE 68124 Office: 5025 Grover St Omaha NE 68106

TWEEDIE, LEONARD CHRISTIE, container co. exec.; b. Chgo., May 4, 1932; s. David and Isabel (Heddle) T.; B.A., Coe Coll., 1953; m. Eathel Darnell, Feb. 19, 1954; children—Sherry Lynn, Jack, Douglas. Mgmt. trainee Am. Boxboard Co., Chgo., 1955-58; regional sales mgr. packaging div. Olin Corp., Joliet, Ill., 1958-68; regional mgr. Time Container, Chgo., 1968-69; gen. mgr. Menasha Corp., Chgo., 1969-70, Neenah, Wis., 1970-74, pres. Hartford Container subsidiary, 1972—, also v.p. and gen. mgr. container div., 1976—. Cubmaster, 1955-59, 74—, scoutmaster, 1959-60; pres. PTA, 1974-75. Served with USAF, 1953-55. Mem. T.A.P.P.I., Soc. Packaging and Handling Engrs., Rotary Internat., Tau Kappa Epsilon. Presbyn. Mason, Elk; mem. Order Eastern Star (asso. patron). Home: 1226 Lynrose Ln Neenah WI 54956 Office: PO Box 367 Neenah WI 54956

TWEEDY, ROBERT HUGH, equipment co. exec.; b. Mt. Pleasant, Ia., Mar. 24, 1928; s. Robert and Olatha (Miller) T.; B.S. in Agrl. Engring., Ia. State U., 1952; m. Genevieve Strauss, Aug. 15, 1969; children—Bruce, Mark; 1 stepdau., Mary Ellen Francis. Sr. engr. John Deere Waterloo Tractor Works, Waterloo, Ia., 1953-64; mktg. rep. U.S. Steel Corp., Pitts., 1964-69; mgr. product planning agrl. equipment div. Allis-Chalmers Corp., Milw., 1969-76, mgr. strategic bus. planning Agrl. Equipment Group, 1976—. Chmn. agrl. research com. Farm and Indsl. Equipment Inst., Chgo., 1974-76, mem. safety policy adv. com., 1972—; mem. farm conf. Nat. Safety Council, Chgo., 1973—. Fellow Am. Soc. Agrl. Engrs. (v.p. 1974—, gen. chmn.

hdqrs. bldg. project 1968-70); mem. Soc. Automotive Engrs. Mason. Patentee in field. Home: 1340 Bonnie Ln Brookfield WI 53005 Office: Allis-Chalmers Corp PO Box 512 Milwaukee WI 53201

TWELLS, DOUGLAS SINCLAIR, automotive parts mfg. co. exec.; b. Ferndale, Mich., June 6, 1924; s. Robert and Margaret (MicKillop) T.; student Ohio State U., 1942; grad. naval aviator U.S. Naval Tng. Coll., 1944; m. Nancy M. MacBurnie, Mar. 19, 1948; children—Bruce Stuart, Leslie Jean, Margaret Jane. Mgr. mfg. engring. Prestolite div. Eltra Corp., 1950-65; engr. div. staff equipment Essex Wire Corp., Detroit, 1965-73; mgr. facilities engring. Halley Carburetor div. Colt Industries, Warren, Mich., 1973-75; dir. mfg. services Electro-Wire Products Inc., Troy, Mich., 1976—. Served with USNR, 1942-45. Mem. ASME. Home: 7241 Flamingo Rd Algonac MI 48001 Office: Suite 222 2855 Coolidge Rd Troy MI 48084

TWELLS, JOHN LAWRENCE, replacement parts co. exec.; b. Flint, Mich., Feb., 1934; s. Robert and Margaret Shaw (MacKillop) T.; B.B.A., U. Toledo, 1957; postgrad. Marquette U., 1968; m. Mary Jane Jentzen, Nov., 1961; children—Linda, John Lawrence, Robert William. Terr. mgr., nat. accounts rep. Motorcraft/Autolite div. Ford Motor Co., Dearborn, Mich., 1950-63; regional sales mgr. MOPAR div. Chrysler Corp., Detroit, 1963-67; asst. gen. mgr. NAPA Genuine Parts Co., Atlanta, 1967-68; gen. mgr. John MacKillop & Co., Inc., Milw., 1968—; mgr. replacemnt parts Baker Material Handling Corp., a joint venture of Linde AG (W.Ger.) and United Technologies Corp., Cleve., 1976—; lectr. in field. Deacon, Immanuel Presbyterian Ch., Milw., 1974-76. Served with U.S. Army, 1957-59. Mem. Am. Ordnance Assn., Am. Legion, VFW. Republican. Club: Rotary (Cleve.). Contbr. articles on microfiche, inventory control, personnel selection, motivation and evaluation to profl. jours. Home: 31123 Wolf Rd Bay Village OH 44140 Office: 8000 Baker Ave Cleveland OH 44102

TWESME, RUSSELL WILLIS, supt. schs.; b. Ettrick, Wis., Aug. 24, 1916; s. Edward Nickolai and Norah Sophia (Johnson) T.; B.S., Wis. State U., 1954; M.S., U. Wis., 1958, postgrad., 1960-68; m. Evelyn Yahr, June 9, 1940; children—Edward, John, James. Tchr. rural and elementary schs., Trempealeau and Jackson County, Wis., 1936-42; prin. Melrose (Wis.) Elementary Sch., 1950-54, Watertown (Wis.), Jr. High Sch., 1954-58; prin. Watertown High Sch., 1958-63, asst. supt., 1963-65; supt. schs., 1965-71, asst. supt. bus. services, 1971—. Mem. Vocational and Adult Edn. Bd. Watertown. Mem. Watertown Edn. Assn. (past pres.), Watertown Tchrs. Edn. Assn., NEA, Wis. Edn. Assn., Wis. Assn. Sch. Dist. Adminstrs., Am. Assn. Sch. Adminstrs., Kappa Delta Pi, Phi Delta Kappa. Lutheran. Rotarian, Elk. Club: Watertown Country. Home: 1012 S 8th St Watertown WI 53094 Office: 415 S 8th St Watertown WI 53094

TWIST, CHARLES RUSSELL, lawyer, assn. exec.; b. Los Angeles, July 8, 1943; s. Dwight Ellsworth and Marjorie (Braude) T.; B.A., U. Chgo., 1966, postgrad. fellow in humanities, 1966-67, now postgrad. in bus.; J.D., U. Iowa, 1970; m. Nancy Flasch, Aug. 24, 1968; children—Matthew Morse, Elizabeth Battell. Admitted to Iowa bar, 1970, Ill. bar, 1976; dir. dept. profl. standards Am. Bar Assn., Chgo., 1971—. Mem. exec. com. U. Chgo. Alumni Cabinet, 1974—. Mem. Am., Iowa bar assns. Home: 175 E Delaware Pl Chicago IL 60611 Office: 1155 E 60th St Chicago IL 60637

TWITCHELL, ROBERT CORT, educator; b. Phila., Mar. 10, 1938; s. John Ingraham and Dorothy Adelle (Huesselman) T.; student Grinnel Coll., 1956-58; B.S. No. State Coll., Aberdeen, S.D., 1962; M.A., U. S.D. at Vermillion, 1964; postgrad. Mich. State U., East Lansing, 1964-66, 68-69; m. Mary Catherine Finger, Apr. 19, 1962; children—John Andrew, Anthony James. Tchr., Wall (S.D.) High Sch., 1962-63; teaching asst. theater U. S.D. at Vermillion, 1963-64; mem. Performing Arts Co., Mich. State U., East Lansing, 1964-66, 68-69; instr. theater arts, also choreographer, dir. U. Wyo. at Laramie, 1966-67; asst. prof. theater, also choreographer, dir. U. S.D. at Vermillion, 1967, asso. prof., 1973—. Judge plays, regional and state level; conductor dance and mime workshops, pub. schs. S.D.; gen. cons. in music and theater, S.D.; participant state tours with major musical prodns.; guest speaker in creative dramatics and children's theater; choreographer, dir. Black Hills (S.D.) Playhouse, 1964, 65, 70, 71, 72, 73, 74, 75, 76, bd. dirs., 1976—. Served with AUS, 1958-59. Grantee scholar to study with Hanya Holm, Colo. Coll., Colorado Springs, 1960, 61. Mem. Am. Theatre Assn. Rotarian. Home: 18 N University St Vermillion SD 57069

TWYMAN, JAMES ELLIOTT, ednl. cons.; b. Washington, Aug. 7, 1935; s. James Albert and Marion (Elliott) T.; B.A. (La Vergne Noyes scholar), Northwestern U., 1957, M.A., 1960. Probation officer Family Ct. of Cook County, Chgo., 1960-61; asst. editor World Book Ency., Field Enterprises Ednl. Corp., Chgo., 1965-66, area studies editor, 1966-68; instr. social scis. St. Xavier Coll., Chgo., 1968-70, asst. prof. social scis., 1970-74, chmn. sociology-anthropology dept., 1972-74, dir. Social Work Field Tng. Program, 1970-73; lectr. anthropology Loyola U., Chgo., 1969-73; ednl. cons., 1974—. Served to 1st lt. AUS, 1961-64. Recipient Outstanding Service award Tinley Park Mental Health Center, 1971; award Wanderer Forum Found., 1977. Mem. Theta Chi. Roman Catholic. Author: College Social Customs, 1959; Walking Down State Street, 1976; The Fork in the Road, 1977. Contbr. to various periodicals. Home and office: 1534 W Pratt Blvd Chicago IL 60626

TYAGI, NARENDRA SINGH, surgeon; b. Nangola, India, Jan. 12, 1945; s. Tilak Ram and Jagwati (Tyagi) T.; M.D., All India Inst. Med. Scis., New Delhi, 1966; m. Shashi Tyagi, June 26, 1970; children—Rachana, Renuka, Ashutosh. Intern Ellis Hosp., Schenectady, N.Y., 1968; resident in gen. surgery St. Joseph Mercy Hosp., Pontiac, Mich., 1970-73; dir. Pontiac Med. Scis. Research Labs., 1973-74; dir. intensive care unit Oakland Med. Center, Pontiac, 1973-74; active attending physician St. Joseph Mercy Hosp., Pontiac, 1973—; dir., v.p. Pontiac Emergency Care Group. Chmn. ad-hoc com. Bharatiya Temple, 1975, sec. bd. trustees, 1976. Recipient C. Walton Lilliehei award Pontiac Med. Sci. Research Lab., 1971, Charles G. Johnston award Detroit Surg. Assn., 1971-72; Frederick A. Coller award Mich. chpt. A.C.S., 1972. Diplomate Am. Bd. Surgery. Fellow A.C.S., Internat. Coll. Surgeons; mem. Mich. State, Oakland County med. socs., Am. Coll. Emergency Physicians. Developer sling suture technique for use in tracheal surgery. Home: 2060 Joanne Dr Troy MI 48084 Office: 909 Woodward Ave Pontiac MI 48053

TYLER, ARNOLD JAMES, ret. ednl. adminstr.; b. Kendallville, Ind., Sept. 10, 1920; s. John Roy and Dessie May (Whiteman) T.; B.S., Ind. State U., 1946, M.S., 1951, postgrad., 1951-56; m. Dorothy Frances Nusbaum, Dec. 29, 1941; children—James, Thomas, William, Arnold James. Tchr., Winchester (Ind.) High Sch., 1945-46, Marshall (Ill.) Twp. High Sch., 1946-48, Marshall Community Unit Dist. High Sch., also Jr. High Sch., 1948-52, supr. elementary schs., 1952-62; supt. New Lenox (Ill.) Sch. Dist. 122, 1962-77. Active Big Bros. of Will County (Ill.). Served with AC, AUS, 1942-45. Mem. Will County Sch. Adminstrn. Orgn. (pres. 1969), Lincoln Way (Ill.) Area Adminstrv. Orgn. (pres. 1970), New Lenox Assn. Commerce (pres. 1966-67, 70), Ind. State U. Alumni Assn. (dir. 1964-67), Ill. Assn. Sch. Adminstrs., VFW, Ind. State U. I-Mens Assn. Methodist. Club: Lions (cabinet sec. chpt. 1967). Home: 3211 N 14th St Terre Haute IN 47804

TYLER, HELEN (MRS. TRACY F. TYLER), social worker; b. Fulda, Min., Oct. 3, 1918; d. Sanke and Ida (Johnson) Behr; B.S., Mankato State Tchrs. Coll., 1940; M.A. in Psychiat. Social Work, U. Minn., 1950; m. Willard P. Comstock, May 27, 1942 (dec. June 1945); children—Patricia Ann; m. 2d, Tracy F. Tyler, Nov. 17, 1950; adopted children—Fletcher W., Ralph S. Tchr. 1st grade Alden, Minn., 1940-41, Waterville, Minn., 1941-42; jr. clk.-typist U.S. Naval Air Sta., Corpus Christi, Tex., 1942; vis. tchr. Mpls. Pub. Schs., 1948-58, cons. in social work, 1958-68, asst. dir. for sch. social work, 1969—, also chmn. human relations com. 1963—. Mem. edn. com. Mpls. Mayor's Com. on Human Relations, 1964—; mem. edn. task force Hennepin County Econ. Opportunity Com., 1964—; pres. bd., co-chmn. Midwest Sch. Social Work Conf., 1970; mem. adv. bd. Hennepin County Community Health and Welfare Council Agys., Vol. Service Bur., Holiday Bur., Children's Dental Services, Pub. and Parochial Child Welfare. Fellow Am. Orthopsychiat. Assn.; mem. Nat. Assn. Social Workers (dir., sec. Minn. chpt.), Acad. Certified Social Workers, Council for Exceptional Children, NEA, Minn. Edn. Assn., Midwest Sch. Social Work Assn. (dir.), Minn. Adminstrs. Spl. Edn., Minn. Sch. Social Workers Assn. (dir.), Mpls. Assn. Retarded Children, City of Mpls. Adminstrn. Assn., Nat. Conf. Social Welfare, Minn. Welfare Assn., Delta Kappa Gamma (past pres. chpt.), Phi Delta Kappa. Clubs: Quota (corr. sec. 1965-66, chmn. service com. 1964-65), Faculty Women's (U. Minn.). Home: 1564 Fulham St St Paul MN 55108 Office: Spl Edn Services Center Minneapolis MN 55413

TYLER, LLOYD JOHN, lawyer; b. Aurora, Ill., May 28, 1924; s. Lloyd J. and Dorothy (Curtis) T.; B.A., Beloit Coll., 1948; J.D., U. Mich., 1951; m. Inez Chappell Busener, Feb. 25, 1970; children—(by previous marriage) Barbara Voorhees, John R., Benjamin C., Robert B., Amy C. Admitted to Ill. bar, 1951; mem. partner Tyler, Peskind & Solomon, Aurora, 1965—. Served with USAAC, 1943-46. Fellow Am. Bar Found.; mem. Ill. Bar Found. (dir. 1968-72, pres. 1972-75), Ill. Bar Assn. (gov. 1970-76, 1st v.p. 1977—), Soc. Trial Lawyers. Contbr. articles to profl. jours. Home: 701 Fargo Blvd Geneva IL 60134 Office: PO Box 1425 Aurora IL 60507

TYLER, WILLIAM HOWARD, JR., advt. exec.; b. Elizabethton, Tenn., May 21, 1932; s. William Howard and Ethel (Schueler) T.; student Ia. State U., 1950-52, U. Ia., 1952; A.B., U. Mo., 1958, B.J., 1958, M.A., 1966; m. Margery Ann Moss, Aug. 31, 1957; children—William James, Daniel Moss. Advt. mgr. Rolla (Mo.) Daily News, 1958-59; instr. U. Mo. Sch. Journalism, 1959-61; copywriter D'Arcy Advt. Co., St. Louis, 1961-64, v.p., copy dir., 1964-67; creative supr. Gardner Advt. Co., St. Louis, 1967-69; v.p., creative dir. D'Arcy-MacManus-Masius, St. Louis, 1969-77; sr. v.p., creative dir. Larson Bateman, Inc., Santa Barbara, Calif., 1977—. Bd. adjustment DesPeres (Mo.) City Govt., 1976-77. Served to 1st lt. USMCR, 1952-55. Mem. Mo. Newspapers Advt. Mgrs. Assn. (v.p. 1959), U. Mo./Columbia Alumni Assn. St. Louis (pres. 1969), Nat. U. Mo. Alumni Assn. (dir. 1969-70), Mensa, Kappa Tau Alpha, Alpha Delta Sigma, Phi Delta Theta. Episcopalian. Home: 1054 San Antonio Creek Rd Santa Barbara CA 93111 Office: 1421 State St Santa Barbara CA 93102

TYNES, MORRIS HARRISON, clergyman; b. Lynchburg, Va., May 12, 1923; s. Joseph Walter and Lucy (Rich) T.; B.S., N.C. Agrl. and Tech. U., 1944; postgrad. U. Mich., summer, 1946; B.D., Yale Div. Sch., 1947; D.D., Western Theol. Sem., 1958; m. Lillian Marguerite Payne, June 4, 1949; children—Lillian Marguerite, Sharon Rose, Morrisine Marie. Ordained to ministry Baptist Ch., 1945; dean theology Va. Theol. Sem. and Coll., Lynchburg, 1947-49; pastor 8th St. Bapt. Ch., Lynchburg, 1947-49, Mt. Zion Bapt. Ch., Staunton, Va., 1949-53; pastor Monumental Bapt. Ch., Chgo., 1953-66; pastor 1st Ch. of the Master, Chgo. Theol. Sem., 1967—, also Greater Mt. Moriah Bapt. Ch., Chgo., 1968—. Adminstrv., also program cons. Dept. Human Services, Chgo.; dir. Churches United, Inc., 1976—. Chaplain, Ill. Gen. Assembly, 1958; pres. United Christian Fellowship, 1958-62; mem. adv. bd., social service dept. Chgo. Ch. Fedn., 1954-59, mem. com. on racial policy, 1955-58; chmn. adv. bd. Gen. Bapt. Ill. Conv., 1959; mem. bd. dept. Christian life and work Nat. Council Chs., 1960. Spl. asst. to pres. Community Family Center Stores, 1973—. Mem. reviewing com. Chgo. Community Fund, 1954-58; mem. bd. guidance dept. Chgo. Urban League, 1954-57; v.p., mem. exec. com. Chgo. br. NAACP, 1954-57, bd. dirs., 1971—; chmn. Christian action com. U. Chgo., 1955-59; chmn. exec. com. Chgo. Conf. for Brotherhood, 1965, pres., chmn. exec. com., 1968—; mem. adv. bd. DuSable Mus., 1972—; bd. dirs. Children's Center for Learning Capacities, 1974—, South Shore Center on the Lake, 1976—; mem. Ill. Bd. Elections, 1975; spl. asst. to mayor Chgo. Recipient Mersick award for excellence in pub. speaking Yale, 1946. Mem. Alpha Phi Alpha. Mason (32 deg., Shriner). Home: 6900 S Bennett Ave Chicago IL 60649 Office: 640 N LaSalle St Chicago IL 60610

TYREE, LEWIS, JR., cryogenic engr., inventor; b. Lexington, Va., July 25, 1922; s. Lewis and Winifred (West) T.; student Washington and Lee U., 1939-40; S.B., Mass. Inst. Tech., 1947; m. Dorothy A. Hinchcliff, Aug. 21, 1948; children—Elizabeth Hinchcliff (Mrs. Barry Taylor), Lewis Tyree III, Dorothy Scott. Cryogenic engr. Joy Mfg. Co., Michigan City, Ind., 1947-49; v.p. Hichcliff Motor Service, Chgo., 1949-53; cons. engr. Cryogenic Products, Chgo., 1953—, Liquid Carbonic Corp., 1960—. Served to 1st lt. C.E., AUS, 1943-46. Mem. Am. Soc. M.E. (cryogenic com. 1965-68), Am. Soc. Heating, Refrigeration and Air-Conditioning Engrs. Republican. Episcopalian. Club: Hinsdale Golf. Patentee in field. Home: 145 Briarwood Ave N Oak Brook IL 60521 Office: PO Box 1342 Oak Brook IL 60521

TYRMAND, LEOPOLD, author; b. Warsaw, Poland, May 16, 1920; s. Mieczyslaw and Maria (Manski) T.; student L'Academie des Beaux-Arts in France, 1938-39; m. Mary Ellen Fox, Aug. 6, 1971. Lit. journalist Cath.-Liberal Press, Poland, 1949-57; asso. dir. Rockford (Ill.) Coll. Inst., 1976—. Mem. Internat. PEN Club. Recipient various Polish lit. awards; Ford Found. fellow, 19—; Author: Notebooks of Dilettante, 1970; The Rosa Luxemburg Contraceptives Cooperative, 1972; contbr. to Am. lit. mags. Home: 315 Roland Ave Rockford IL 61107 Office: Rockford Coll Inst Rockford IL 61101

TYRRELL, THOMAS CARROLL, physician; b. Chgo., July 13, 1912; s. William C. and Mary J. (Kelly) T.; B.S., St, Louis U., 1933, M.D., 1937; m. Sallie Major, Sept. 25, 1944; children—Thomas Carroll, Michael, Timothy, Patrick. Intern, St. Louis City Hosp., 1937-41; practice medicine and surgery, Calumet City, Ill., 1937—; instr. surgery Strich Sch. Medicine, Chgo. Founder, dir., chmn. bd. 1st State Bank Calumet City. Bd. dirs. Lake County Med. Soc. Found.; mem. citizens bd. St. Margaret Hosp., Hammond, Ind. Served to 1st lt. M.C. AUS, 1941. Mem. A.M.A. (del. 1970—). K.C. Lion. Home: 1066 Forest Hills St Calumet City IL 60409 Office: First State Bank 925 Burnham Ave Calumet IL 60409

TYRRELL, TOM GEORGE, supt. schs.; b. Iroquois, S.D., Nov. 2, 1933; s. Pierce and Hennrietta Marie (Marsh) T.; B.A., Huron Coll., 1958; M.A., No. State Coll., Aberdeen, S.D., 1962; postgrad. U. S.D., 1969, 74; m. Rose Marie Welsh, May 21, 1955; children—Bruce A., Brenda E., Brian Lee, Brent Thomas, Steven Patrick. Tchr., coach Willow Lake High Sch., 1958-60, Frederick High Sch., 1960-62; prin. Rosholt High Sch., 1962-65; supt. Veblen Pub. Sch., 1965-69, Waubay Pub. Schs., 1969-70; asst. dir. Title 1, State of S.D., Pierre, 1970-73; supt. schs. White River (S.D.) Sch. Dist. #29, 1973—. Served with USNR, 1951-54. Mem. S.D. Sch. Adminstrs. Assn., Am. Legion (boys state staff 1964-74). Club: Lions (sight for needy 1969-75, tailtwister 1974—). Home: Box 224 White River SD 57579

TYSL, GLORIA JEANNE, coll. dean; b. Chgo., Apr. 17, 1931; d. Anton O. and Myrtle Geraldine (Voborsky) T.; B.A., Mt. Mary Coll., 1960; M.A., DePaul U., 1967; NSF fellow Ill. Inst. Tech., 1967; Ph.D., Ind. U., 1976; Carnegie fellow Inst. Academic Deans, 1976. Tchr., Sacred Heart Acad. Lisle, Ill., 1952-66; teaching asst. Ind. U., Bloomington, 1967-69; prof. history Ill. Benedictine Coll., Lisle, 1969—, dean of faculty and instruction, 1974—; mem. exec. bd., v.p. Asso. Colls. Chgo. Area; mem. academic panel Council West Suburban Colls. Mem. Am. Assn. Academic Deans, Am. Assn. Colls., Am. Assn. Higher Edn., AAUP, Am. Council on Edn., Am. Hist. Soc., Conf. on Brit. Studies, Cath. Hist. Assn., Cath. Ednl. Assn., English Hist. Soc. (London), Inst. Hist. Research (London), Nat. Assn. Deans and Coll. Adminstrs., N. Central Assn. Academic Deans, Pi Gamma Mu, Phi Delta Kappa. Roman Catholic. Home: 234 E Mayfield Ln High Point Hoffman Estates IL 60195 Office: Office of Dean Ill Benedictine Coll Lisle IL 60532

TZANGAS, GEORGE JOHN, lawyer; b. Canton, Ohio, Oct. 1, 1930; s. John M. and Mary (Christian) T.; student Kent State U., 1948-50; B.S.C., Ohio U., 1952; J.D. (Univ. scholar), Washington and Lee U., 1956; m. Venus Mouskondis, Aug. 31, 1952; children—Marianne Tzangas Weiss, John Daniel, Byron George. Office mgr. Minerva (Ohio) plant U.S. Ceramic Tile Co., 1956-58; admitted to Ohio Supreme Ct. bar, 1957; individual practice law, Canton, 1957—; dir. numerous cos. Bd. dirs. numerous charitable corps.; co-founder, pres. World Wide Orthodox Renewal for Christ, Inc., Canton; trustee Canton Scholarship Found. Mem. Ohio State, Stark County bar assns., Ohio Acad. Trial Lawyers, Assn. Trial Lawyers, Assn. Trial Lawyers Am., Am. Arbitration Assn., Phi Alpha Delta. Greek Orthodox. Author: Secrets of Life, 1971; (as John Christian) Have You Talked to Him?, 1974. Home: 4864 Edinderry Dr NW Canton OH 44708 Office: 454 Citizens Savs Bldg Canton OH 44702

UCHENDU, VICTOR CHIKEZIE, educator; b. Nsirimo, Nigeria, Jan. 1, 1932; s. Aburonye Isaac and Sabina Ogbuisi (Enyidiya) U., B.Sc., U. London, 1962; M.A., Northwestern U., 1963, Ph.D. (Rockefeller Found. fellow), 1965; m. Caroline Urasi Onuoha, Dec. 22, 1959; children—Carolyn Ijeoma, Chimela Victor, Clarita Uchechi, Chike, Chinturu Chinwe. Asst. prof. Stanford (Cal.) U., 1966-69; research asso. Makerere U., Uganda, 1966-67; research asso. U. Ghana, 1967-68; sr. lectr. Makerere Inst. Social Research, Uganda, 1969-70, reader anthropology and dir., 1970-71; dir. African Studies Center, prof. anthropology U. Ill., Urbana, 1971—. Cons. UNESCO, govt. and pvt. founds. Mem. vis. com. Afro Am. studies dept. Harvard, 1974-76. Fellow Am. Anthropol. Assn.; mem. African Studies Assn. (v.p., 1975, pres. 1976), Assn. Applied Anthropology, Internat. African Inst. Britain, Royal Anthropol. Inst. Britain and Ireland, Assn. Current Anthropology. Rotarian. Author several books. Contbr. to profl. jours. Home: 2401 Barberry Dr Champaign IL 61820 Office: 1208 W California St Urbana IL 61801

UDEHN, CARLYSLE DAVID, dentist; b. Moline, Ill., Dec. 31, 1921; s. Axel David and Nellie Cecelia (Safe) U.; B.A., U. Iowa, 1949; B.S., U. Ill., 1951, D.D.S., 1953; m. Catharine Isabelle Belding, June 4, 1949; children—David Duane, Kenneth James, Kathleen Ann. Practice dentistry, Alexis, Ill., 1953-54, Cambridge, Ill., 1954-57, Moline, 1957—. Sec. Rock Island County bd. health; adj. instr. oral diagnosis and oral pathology U. Iowa Coll. Dentistry. Served with AUS, 1942-45. Decorated Purple Heart. Mem. Am. Dental Assn., Rock Island Dist. Dental Soc., Am. Acad. Gen. Dentistry, U. Iowa, U. Ill. alumni assns., VFW. Home: 3111 38th St Moline IL 61265 Office: 551 18th Ave Moline IL 61265

UECKER, ARTHUR HENRY, milk co. exec.; b. Stewart, Minn., Dec. 18, 1915; s. Albert F. and Martha (Klitzke) U.; student dairy sch. course U. Minn., 1939; m. Gladys Viola Christensen, June 15, 1940; children—James Curtis, Thomas Lee, Mark Bruce. Asst., Webster Coop. Creamery Assn., 1935-38; asst. Meriden Creamery Assn., 1938-41, gen. mgr., 1941-66; gen. mgr. So. Dairy Assn., 1966-69; gen. mgr. Asso. Milk Producers, Inc., Owatonna, Minn., 1969-73, Blair, Wis., 1973—; sec., mgr. Steele County Creameries Assn., Dairy Quality Improvement Assn. Lutheran (council 1948-51). Mason, Elk, Eagle. Club: Exchange (Owatonna). Address: Blair WI 54616

UECKER, JAMES CLYDE, engr.; b. Freeport, Ill., Jan. 26, 1942; s. Warren E. and Mary Elizabeth (Hawkins) U.; B.C.E., U. Ill., 1965; m. Barbara Jean Montford, June 30, 1962; children—Jennifer, Jason. Registered profl. engr., Ill. Asst. city engr., Elgin, Ill., 1965-70, dir. engring. and inspection, 1970-72; asso. Alstot, March and Assos., Des Plaines, Ill., 1972-74; pres. J. C. Uecker & Assos., Inc., Elgin, Ill., 1974—. Mem. council Messiah Luth. Ch., 1970-73; bd. mgrs. Elgin YMCA, 1976—, pres. bd., 1977—. Trustee Midwest Coll. Engring. Mem. Ill. Soc. Profl. Engrs. (sec.-treas. 1974-76, v.p. 1976-77, nat. dir. 1977—), ASCE, Am. Pub. Works Assn., Am. Water Works Assn., Ill. Inst. Traffic Engrs., Fox Valley Kiwanis Club (dir. 1975-77). Home: 200 S Edison St Elgin IL 60120 Office: 450 Shepard Dr Elgin IL 60120

UECKER, MARVIN FREDERICK, ins., real estate agy. exec.; b. Lena, Ill., Nov. 5, 1925; s. Albert William and Olga Anne (Klug) U.; student U. Dubuque, 1946-48; B.B.A., U. Wis., 1950; m. Rachael Lucille Glanz, June 18, 1955; 1 child, Jan E. Ins. agt. Marvin F. Uecker, 1950-52, ins. broker, 1952-75; founder Marvin F. Uecker, Inc., ins., real estate, Lena, 1975, pres., 1973—; dir. Lena Continental Manor. Served with AUS, 1944-46; PTO. Decorated Bronze Star medal; recipient Dean Goodnight award Iron Cross Soc., U. Wis. at Madison, 1950. Mem. Ill. Assn. Profl. Ins. Agts. (dir. 1973-79, 1st v.p. 1977-78), Beta Alpha Psi. Lutheran (elder). Lion (dir. Lena 1951-55, sec., treas. 1951-52, pres. 1953-54). Clubs: Germania; Lena Golf (dir. 1954-71, sec., treas. 1962, 70, pres. 1958-59, 63-64, 69). Home: 502 Center St Lena IL 61048 Office: 109 Railroad St Lena IL 61048

UEMURA, JOSEPH NORIO, educator; b. Portland, Oreg., July 3, 1926; s. Seijiro and Hana (Morishita) U.; B.A., U. Denver, 1946; Th.M., Iliff Sch. Theology, 1949; Ph.D. (Warren fellow, John Hay Whitney fellow), Columbia, 1958; m. Maye Mitsuye Oye, Sept. 10, 1949; children—Wesley Makoto, Charissa Keiko. Asst. prof. Westminster Coll., Salt Lake City, 1953-56, asso. prof., 1956-59; prof. philosophy, chmn. dept. Morningside Coll., Sioux City, Iowa, 1959-66, Hamline U., St. Paul, 1966—. Council Philos. Studies fellow Carnegie Fedn., 1969; Nat. Endowment for Humanities fellow Brown U., summer 1974. Recipient Merrill E. Burgess Excellence in Teaching award, 1969. Mem. Am. Interprofl. Inst., Am. Philos. Assn., ACLU, Japanese-Am. Citizens League, Phi Beta Kappa, Omicron Delta Kappa. Methodist. Editor: Morningside Rev., 1963-66; Hamline Rev., 1968-71. Contbr. articles to profl. jours. Home: 1641 Stanbridge Ave St Paul MN 55113

UFFELMANN, HANS WERNER, philosopher, educator; b. Kassel, Germany, July 24, 1933; s. Wilhelm and Anna (Fremder) U.; A.A., Sacramento Jr. Coll., 1954; B.A., U. Calif. at Davis, 1960; M.A., Northwestern U., 1963, Ph.D., 1967; m. Marilynn Bishop Morrissey, Aug. 20, 1960; children—Glenn Kirk, Darryl Kirk. Instr. philosophy Northwestern U., Evanston, Ill., 1960-63; prof. philosophy U. Mo., Kansas City, 1963—, chmn. dept. philosophy, 1974—. Cons. NIH, A.A.A.S. Active Indian Guides. Served with Med. Service Corps. AUS, 1954-57. Recipient award for excellence in undergrad. teaching Standard Oil Ind., 1968. Mem. Am. Philos. Assn., Am. Assn. for Behavioral Scis. and Med. Edn., Hastings Center, Inst. Soc., Ethics, and Life Scis., A.C.L.U., Omicron Delta Kappa. Club: Woodside Racquet. Contbr. articles to profl. jours. Home: 629 W 61st Terr Kansas City MO 64113

UGAJIN, KAZUO, neurosurgeon; b. Tokyo, Japan, Feb. 22, 1928; s. Goichi and Hide (Yatabe) U.; came to U.S., 1961, naturalized, 1966; M.D., Keio U., Tokyo, 1952, Ph.D. in Neurophysiology, 1959; m. Margaret Joan Bennett, Aug. 7, 1976; 1 son, Michael Kazuo. Intern, Keio U. Hosp., Tokyo, 1952-53, resident in surgery, 1953-54, in neurol. surgery, 1957-61; intern, St. Peter's Gen. Hosp., New Brunswick, N.J., 1954-55, resident in surgery, 1955-56; resident in surgery Bellevue Hosp., N.Y.C., 1956-57; resident in pathology with neurol. research, Middlesex Gen. Hsop., New Brunswick, 1961-63; resident in neurosurgery, Iowa Hosp., Iowa City, 1963-67; mem. staff Meml. Hosp., St. Joseph, Mich., 1973—, chief of surgery, 1977; mem. staff Mercy Hosp., Benton Harbor, Mich., 1973—; neurosurg. cons. St. Joseph's Hosp., South Bend, Ind., 1976—. Recipient Humanitarian award, V.J. Sarte Nat. Hydrocephalus Found., 1975. Diplomate Am. Bd. Neurol. Surgery. Fellow A.C.S.; mem. Am. Assn. Neurol. Surgeons, Congress Neurol. Surgeons, AMA, Berrien County, Mich. State med. socs., Club: Econ. of Southwestern Mich. Co-author sect. of book, 1956, transl. into Japanese, 1958; contbr. articles to neurosurg. jours. Home: 2216 Lake View Ave Saint Joseph MI 49085 Office: 1901 Niles Ave Saint Joseph MI 49085

UHL, KEITH EDWARD, lawyer; b. Mapleton, Iowa, May 27, 1946; s. Ariel Ambrose and Muriel Valentine (Stratton) U.; B.A. with honors, U. S.D., 1968; J.D. with honors (Scottish Rite grad. fellow), George Washington U., 1972; m. Nancy Ann Norman, June 24, 1972. Legis. asst. Congressman Ben Reifel, U.S. Ho. of Reps., Washington, 1968-71; admitted to D.C., Iowa bars, 1972; practiced in Des Moines, 1972—; asst. U.S. atty. So. Dist. Iowa, U.S. Dept. Justice, Des Moines, 1972-76, spl. prosecutor Wounded Knee non-leadership cases, 1975-76; mem. firm Scalise, Scism, Gentry Brick & Brick, 1976—. Served as 1st lt. AUS, 1973. Mem. Am. (vice chmn. young lawyer's com. criminal justice 1973—; joint com. legal status of prisoners 1974-76), Iowa (chmn. young lawyer's disaster relief com. 1972-75; young lawyer's ethics seminar Drake U. Law Sch. 1974, young lawyer's exec. council 1975—, chmn. spl. com. on criminal law 1976—), D.C. bar assns., Am., Iowa trial lawyers assns., Phi Delta Phi, Phi Delta Theta (pres. S.D. Alpha 1966), Omicron Delta Kappa, Pi Sigma Alpha, Phi Eta Sigma (pres. S.D. chpt. 1965). Republican. Methodist. Mason. Home: 3103 Elmwood Dr Des Moines IA 50312 Office: 909 Fleming Bldg Des Moines IA 50309

UHR, CLINTON WILLIAM, JR., venture capital co. exec.; b. San Antonio, Feb. 15, 1943; s. Clinton William and Ethel Priscilla (Dolch) U.; B.S. in Elec. Engring., U. Tex., 1966, M.S., 1968, M.B.A., 1969. Engr., Tracor Co., Austin, Tex., 1966-69; loan officer Citibank, N.Y.C., 1969-72; v.p. Heizer Corp., Chgo., 1972—; dir. Nortec Electronics Co., 1974—. Mem. Assn. M.B.A. Club: Tower (Chgo.). Home: 1560 N Sandburg Terr Apt 4106 Chicago IL 60610 Office: 20 N Wacker Dr Suite 4100 Chicago IL 60606

UHRIN, MICHAEL, ednl. adminstr.; b. Cambridge, Ohio, Nov. 21, 1944; s. George and Elizabeth U.; student Hiram Coll., 1966-67, Penn Ohio Jr. Coll., 1964; m. Pearlene E. Lancaster, Jan. 15, 1966; children—Michele Renee, John Michael. Data processing operator Goodyear Aerospace Corp., Akron, Ohio, 1964-66; dir. data processing Shaker Heights (Ohio) City Schs., 1966-69; regional sales mgr. Nat. Scanning Inc., Columbus, Ohio, 1970—; mgr. computer services South Western City Schs., Grove City, Ohio, 1977-78; pres. ACE Software, Inc., Grove City, 1978—; pres., owner Accounting Cons.'s for Edn. Cubmaster, com. chmn. Boy Scouts Am. Mem. Internat. Assn. Ednl. Data Systems, Ohio Ednl. Data System (past pres., dir.). Home: 2507 Park Ridge Dr Grove City OH 43123 Office: 2180 Stringtown Rd Grove City OH 43123

UICKER, JOSEPH BERNARD, mech. engr.; b. State College, Pa. Mar. 29, 1940; s. John Joseph and Elizabeth Josephine (Flint) U.; B.S. in Mech. Engring., U. Detroit, 1963, M.S., 1965; m. Janet Ann Ballman, Sept. 22, 1973; children by previous marriage—Patricia Marie, Suzanne Marie. With Smith, Hinchman & Grylls Assos. Inc., Detroit, 1964—, asst. dir. health facilities div., 1973-75, corp. dir. mech. engring., 1975—, asso., 1971-78, v.p., 1978—. Served with C.E. U.S. Army, 1966-67. Registered profl. engr., Mich., N.C. Mem. ASME, Soc. Am. Mil. Engrs., Am. Soc. Heating, Refrigeration, Air Conditioning Engrs., Nat. Soc. Profl. Engrs., Engring. Soc. Detroit. Home: 20820 Rampart Circle Apt 207 Southfield MI 48034 Office: 455 W Fort St Detroit MI 48226

UIHLEIN, HENRY HOLT, refrigeration mfg. co. exec.; b. Milw., Aug. 17, 1921; s. Herman Alfred and Claudia (Holt) U.; B.A., U. Va., 1946; m. Marion Struss, June 13, 1942; children—James Christopher, Richard A., Philip John, Henry Holt. Pres., gen. mgr. Ben Hur Mfg. Co., Milw., 1947-62; pres. Ouictrez Inc., Fond duLac, Wis., 1955-60; pres., gen. mgr., dir. U-Line Corp., Milw., 1962—; pres., dir. Jensen Service Co., 1962—. Bd. dirs. Herman A. Uihlein Found., Inc., 1955—. Served with USMC, 1943-45. Christian Scientist. Clubs: Milw., Athletic, Milw. Country. Contbr. articles to profl. jours. Home: 8500 Green Bay Ct N Milwaukee WI 53209 Office: 8900 55th St N Milwaukee WI 53223

UJIKI, GERALD TOSHIMI, surgeon; b. Honokaa, Hawaii, June 5, 1937; s. Masao and Masaye (Hirayama) U.; B.A., Northwestern U., 1959, M.D., 1962; m. Nenon Lynette Merrell, June 1, 1968; children—Michael Bryant, Amy Elizabeth. Intern, Wesley Meml. Hosp., Chgo., 1962-63; resident in gen. surgery Northwestern U., Chgo., 1965-70, asst. prof. surgery, 1974—; attending physician Northwestern Meml. Hosp.; attending surgeon VA Lakeside Hosp. Served to lt. comdr., USNR, 1963-65. Am. Cancer Soc. jr. fellow, 1967-68. Mem. AMA, Ill., Chgo. med. socs., Assn. Acad. Surgery, Chgo. Surg. Soc., Soc. Surgery of Alimentary Tract, Collegium Internationale Chirurgiae Digestium. Home: 534 Stratford Pl Chicago IL 60657 Office: 700 N Michigan Ave Chicago IL 60611

ULLMAN, PIERRE LIONI, educator; b. Nice, France, Oct. 31, 1929; s. Eugene Paul and Suzanne (Lioni) U. (parents Am. citizens); B.A., Yale, 1952; diploma en estudios Hispánicos, U. Salamanca (Spain), 1955; M.A., Columbia, 1956; Ph.D., Princeton, 1962; m. Mary Meade McDowell, June 9, 1956; children—Katherine Meade Parker, Susan Randolph. Master, Choate Sch., Wallingford, Conn., 1956-57, St. Bernard's Sch., 1957-58; instr. Rutgers U., 1961-63; asst. prof. U. Cal. at Davis, 1963-65; asso. prof. U. Wis. at Milw., 1965-68, prof. Spanish, 1968—; vis. prof. U. Minn., 1970-71, U. Mich., summer 1975. Signatory convocation First Internat. Congress on Archpriest of Hita, Madrid, Spain, 1972, First Internat. Congress on Celestina, 1974. Served with AUS, 1952-54. Mem. Modern Lang. Assn., Midwest Modern Lang. Assn., Am. Assn. Tchrs. Spanish and Portuguese, Wis. Assn. Fgn. Lang. Tchrs., Am. Assn. Tchrs. Esperanto, Universal Esperanto Assn. (asso. judge lit. contests 1975—), AAUP, Esperanto Soc. Wis., Sigma Delta Pi. Author: Mariano de Larra and Spanish Political Rhetoric, 1971. Adv. editor Papers on Lang. and Lit., 1966—; Estudos Ibero-Americanos (Brazil), 1975—. Contbr. articles, book revs. to profl. jours. Office: Dept Spanish and Portuguese Univ Wis Milwaukee WI 53201

ULLOM, CHARLES BAUMANN, ednl. adminstr.; b. Charles City, Iowa, Sept. 1, 1939; s. John P. and Mayme H. U.; B.A., U. No. Iowa, 1961, M.A., 1964; postgrad. Colo. State U., 1969, Nova U., 1976—; m. Ellen A. Swinton, Aug. 30, 1959; children—Scott Charles, Brian John. Tchr., Plainfield (Iowa) Community Sch., 1961-64; coordinator distributive edn. Algona (Iowa) Community Sch., 1964-68; instr., coordinator Iowa Lakes Community Coll., Estherville, Iowa, 1968-69, chmn. bus., 1969-76, adminstrv. asst., 1976—; cons. in field. Mem. Iowa Assn. Sch. Adminstrs., Am., Iowa vocat. assns., Delta Pi Epsilon. Lutheran. Home: 204 Harrison St Emmetsburg IA 50536 Office: 101 1/2 N 6th St Estherville IA 51334

ULLRICH, HELEN STINE, mus. ofcl.; b. Morris, Ill., Nov. 5, 1900; d. Fred W. and Julia Cecelia (Moran) Stine; student Ill. State Coll., 1919, Internat. Corr. Schs.; m. John H. Ullrich, Oct. 17, 1920; children—Barbara (Mrs. William McArdle), Elinore (Mrs. Charles Hansen), Lois (Mrs. William Kindelspire). Tchr. schs., Morris, 1918-20, 41-45; co-owner, sec. Ullrich Dairy, Morris, 1932-48; bookkeeper Ullrich Gravel Co., Morris, 1948-54; Ullrich Antiques, Morris, 1950—; mgr., co-owner Ullrich Recreation Hall, Morris, 1956-61; writer syndicated newspaper column, 1941-51; hostess radio talk show, 1954-73; co-owner, mgr., curator Ill. Valley Mus., Morris, 1962—. Mem. Morris Hosp. Aux., 1968—; chmn. Bicentennial, 1974-75. Precinct committeewoman Republican party, 1950-58. Mem. Grundy County (plaque 1971, pres. 1965-72), Ill. Valley (pres. 1964—) hist. socs., Bus. and Profl. Women. Presbyn. Mem. Order Eastern Star. Author: From the Head and Foot of a Square Dancer, 1960; This is Grundy County, 1969; Fox Tales, 1973. Home: 835 Southmor Morris IL 60450

ULLYOT, MARIANNE WILLIAMS, pianist; b. Dallas, Nov. 14, 1940; d. Russel Stanley and Mary L. (Gebhardt) Williams; B.A., Radcliffe Coll., 1962; artists' diploma Longy Sch. Music, Cambridge, Mass., 1967; M.F.A., U. Minn., 1970, D.Mus.Arts, 1976; m. James Richard Ullyot, Sept. 17, 1967; children—James Russel, Kathryn Lee. Tchr., Longy Sch. Music, 1964-66; teaching asst. U. Minn., 1967-69; tchr. dept. music St. Paul Acad., Summit Sch., 1976—; performed in ann. Schubert Club concerts, ann. solo recitals U. Minn., also O'Shaugnessy Auditorium; adjudicator for music contests, Minn. Mem. Nat., Minn. music tchrs. assns., Am. Liszt Soc. Republican. Presbyterian. Author: The First Book of Musical Instruments, 1970. Home: 63 Otis Ave Saint Paul MN 55104

ULMER, GEORGE ELBURN, design engr.; b. Barry County, Mo., Jan. 10, 1930; s. George Clarence and Eula Mae (Hankins) U.; student Crowder Coll., 1966; B.S. in Agrl. Engring., U. Ark., 1969; m. Ruby Jewell Sanders, Dec. 14, 1950; children—Edward, Jimmie, Patricia, Pamela, Brenda. Employed in heavy constrn., 1950-61; design engr. Miller-Newell Engrs. Ltd., Newport, Ark., 1969-71, design engr., office mgr., Cassville, Mo., 1971—. Mem. Am. Soc. Agrl. Engrs. Club: Rotary. Home: Route 1 Cassville MO 65625 Office: 710 West St Cassville MO 65625

ULMER, RICHARD LEE, agronomist-geneticist; b. Geneva, Nebr., Oct. 21, 1943; s. Friedhold and Geneice Mary (Meyer) Ulmer; B.S., U. Nebr., 1968, M.S., 1970, Ph.D., 1973; m. Beverly Kay Refior, Apr. 1, 1967; 1 son, David. Instr., U. Nebr. at Lincoln, 1971-73; group leader corn products research Anheuser-Busch, Inc., St. Louis, 1973—. Mem. Am. Soc. Agronomy, Crop Sci. Soc. Am., Am. Assn. Cereal Chemists, AAAS, Gamma Sigma Delta, Alpha Zeta. Contbr. articles to profl. jours. Home: 5708 Hempline Rd St Louis MO 63129 Office: Anheuser-Busch Inc 1101 Wyoming St St Louis MO 63118

ULRICH, DAVID MACK, dentist; b. Columbus, Ohio, Mar. 24, 1932; s. Harold Ellis and Ruth (Mack) U.; D.D.S., Ohio State U., 1957; m. Marilee Ann Long, July 12, 1958; children—Bradley David, Lisa Marie. Practice gen. dentistry, Dayton, Ohio, 1957—. Pres. Combined Health Dist., 1972-73, 76—; chmn. Health Planning Councils Health Planning Com. Miami Valley, 1973—; pres. Dayton Dental Soc. Services Orgn., Inc., 1974-75. Trustee United Health Found. Fellow Internat. Coll. Dentists; mem. Dayton-Am. Soc. Dentistry for Children (pres. 1969-70), Dayton Dental Soc. (pres. 1971-72), Ohio Dental Assn. (chmn. council on pubs. 1972-74), Delta Upsilon, Psi Omega. Republican. Methodist. Home: 5235 Mad River Rd Dayton OH 45429 Office: 1800-02 S Brown St Dayton OH 45409

UMANS, ALVIN ROBERT, fixture mfg. co. exec.; b. N.Y.C., Mar. 11, 1927; s. Louis and Ethel (Banner) U.; student U. Rochester, 1944-45; m. Nancy Jo Zadek, June 28, 1953; children—Kathi Lee, Craig Joseph. Sales mgr. Textile Mills Co., Chgo. Chgo., 1954-56; regional sales mgr. Reflector Hardware Corp., Melrose Park, Ill., 1956-58, nat. sales mgr., 1959-62, v.p., 1962-65, pres., treas., dir., 1965—; dir. Concepts, Inc., Mpls.; chmn. Garcy Corp., Chgo., v.p., dir. Midland Industries, Inc., Wichita, Kans.; v.p., dir. Goer Mfg. Co., Inc., Charleston Heights, S.C.; pres., treas., dir. Spacemaster Corp., Chgo.; dir. Banner Press, N.Y.C.; v.p., dir. Servicomex S.A., Mexico; dir. Fine Arts Broadcasting, Inc., Chgo.; pres., treas. Spacemaster-Garcy Corp., Chgo. Bd. dirs. Mt. Sinai Hosp. Med. Center, Chgo., 1972—, Milton & Rose Zadek Fund, 1965—. Served with U.S. Army, 1945-46. Mem. Nat. Assn. Store Fixture Mfrs. (dir. 1969-70), Young Pres. Orgn., Chgo. Pres. Orgn. Clubs: Standard (Chgo.); Green Acres Country (Northbrook, Ill.). Home: 285 Green Bay Rd Glencoe IL 60022 Office: 1400 N 25th Ave Melrose Park IL 60160

UMBEHOCKER, KENNETH SHELDON, pub. relations assn. exec., clergyman; b. Mpls., Sept. 23, 1934; s. Kenneth and Mildred Adeline (Johnson) U.; B.A., Vanderbilt U., 1956; L.Th., Seabury-Western Theol. Sem., 1959; grad. U. Ga. Mgmt. Inst., 1973. Ordained to ministry Episcopal Ch., 1959; pastor chs., Hallock, Minn., Virginia, Minn., 1959-65; field rep. Am. Cancer Soc., Mpls., 1965-67; dept. mgr. Rochester (Minn.) Area C. of C., 1967-74; exec. dir. Fargo (N.D.) Parking Authority & Downtown Bus. Assn., 1974—; priest asso. Gethsemane Episcopal Cathedral, Fargo, 1974—; ch. cons. in communications, adminstrn., 1967—. Dir. Rochester (Minn.) United Fund, 1970-72. Recipient Distinguished Service Award Rochester Jaycees, 1970; named Young Man of Year Rochester, Minn., 1970; Seabury fellow Seabury-Western Theol. Sem., 1972. Mem. Am. C. of C. Execs., Internat. Downtown Execs. Assn., Clubs: Mason, Elks, Eagles, Rochester Kiwanis (dir. 1974), Rotary Internat. Home: 901 8th Ave N Fargo ND 58102 Office: Suite 410 1st Nat Bank Bldg Fargo ND 58102

UNDERHILL, WILLIAM GEORGE, physician; b. Pontiac, Mich., June 19, 1933; s. Leonard Irwin and Ida G. (Downes) U.; M.D., U. Mich., 1958; m. Darlene Ann Brokaw, May 8, 1954; children—Kim, Valerie, John, James. Intern, Saginaw (Mich.) Gen. Hosp., 1958-59, asso. staff, 1966-72; practice gen. medicine, Saginaw, 1959—; mem. sr. staff St. Lukes Hosp., Saginaw, 1961-72. Med. cons. Chesapeake and Ohio R.R., 1959-72. Mem. Delta Sigma Phi, Phi Rho Sigma. Clubs: Pioneer, Germania (Saginaw). Home: 8 Five Oaks St Saginaw MI 48603 Office: 1500 Gratiot St Saginaw MI 48602

UNDERKOFLER, THOMAS ARTHUR, oral surgeon; b. Ledyard, Iowa, Mar. 12, 1918; s. Jess Christopher and Leone (Murray) U.; student Iowa State Coll., 1935-37; D.D.S., State U. Iowa, 1942; m. Virginia Esther Craven, Aug. 30, 1941; children—Richard, Janice (Mrs. Gary Herbert Brown), Robert, Thomas, Peggy. Intern oral surgery U. Iowa Hosp., demonstrator U. Iowa Dental Sch., Iowa City, 1942-43; pvt. practice dentistry Marshalltown, Iowa, 1964—; lectr., cons. in field. Mem. Iowa State Bd. Dentistry, 1975—; examiner Central Regional Testing Service, 1976. Pres. St. Mary's Sch. Bd., 1969; active Boy Scouts Am. Served with Dental Corp, AUS, 1943-46. Mem. Marshalltown Jr. C. of C. (dir. 1949), Iowa Dental Study Club (founder, pres. 1951-52), Midwest Gnathastatic Research Group (sec., treas. 1957—), Pierre Fauchard Acad. K.C., Elk. Home: 609 W Linn St Marshalltown IA 50158 Office: 106 W Linn St Marshalltown IA 50158

UNDERWOOD, BRUCE, miniature racing engine mfg. co. exec.; b. Chgo., Sept. 27, 1910; s. Wallace Blaine and Frieda Christina (Bast) U.; grad. Caterpillar Apprentice Sch., 1932; student Bradley U., 1944-45; m. Edith Fondelia Griswold, Oct. 7, 1974; children by previous marriage—Janice May Underwood Russell, Jeannette Louise Underwood Watts. With Caterpillar Tractor Co., E. Peoria, Ill., 1928-47; staff engr. Fairbanks Morse & Co., Three Rivers, Mich., Beloit, Wis., 1947-51; process engr. aircraft engine div. Ford Motor Co., Chgo., 1951-53; project engr. environ. test sect. S.W. Research Inst., San Antonio, 1953-54; project engr. Peter Smith Heater Co., Detroit, 1954-55; prin. technologist Battelle Meml. Inst., Columbus, Ohio, 1955-64; precision technologist The Laurel Corp., Columbus, 1964-69; machinist Columbia Research & Devel. Corp., Columbus, 1969-71; machinist service dept. Adco Container Service, Columbus, 1971; factory serviceman Columbia Research & Devel. div. Ludlow Industries, Columbus, 1974-75; owner, operator Model Power Co., Columbus, 1944-47, 55—. Mem. Am. Ordnance Assn., Soc. Automotive Engrs., Acad. of Model Aeronautics, Am. Miniature Race Car Assn. (Assistance Appreciation awards 1963, 71), Internat. Miniature Race Car Assn. (Assistance Appreciation award 1963), Nat. Model Tractor Puller Assn. Clubs: Moose, The Underwood Family Orgn. Miniature race car equipped with Model Power Co. engine "Yellow Jacket" set world's record, 1969. Home and Office: 931 Minerva Ave Columbus OH 43229

UNDERWOOD, DENNIS JAMES, ednl. counselor, social worker; b. Alma, Mich., Dec. 31, 1944; s. Edward Lee and Erma Lucille (Cummings) U.; M.A., Oakland U., 1974; postgrad. Wayne State U., 1975—. Tchr. sci. Huntsville (Ala.) City Schs., 1969-71; sr. probation officer Oakland County Circuit Ct., Pontiac, Mich., 1971-75; therapist, Detroit, 1975—; acad. advisor-testing specialist Detroit Inst. Tech., 1976—; instr. Henry Ford Community Coll., Dearborn, Mich., 1976—; co-dept. coordinator Detroit Coll. Bus., 1974-75. Served with U.S. Army, 1967-69. Certified secondary tchr., Ala., Mich., Utah; social worker, Mich. Mem. Am., Mich. personnel and guidance assns., Am., Mich. assns. specialists in group work, Assn. for Humanistic Edn. and Devel., Nat. Assn. Social Workers, AAUP, Mensa. Home: 8619 Pierson St Detroit MI 48228 Office: 2727 2d St Detroit MI 48201

UNDERWOOD, GARY DALE, advt. agy. exec.; b. Steubenville, Ohio, June 27, 1943; s. Ernest and Elexandria (Mercer) U.; diploma in comml. art Art Inst. Pitts., 1963; student Columbus Coll. Art and Design, 1964-65; m. Sophia Callas, Nov. 29, 1963; 1 son, Matthew Dean. Art dir., designer John Bircher Advt., Newark, Ohio, 1963-65, Shaw-Barton, splty. advt., Coshocton, Ohio, 1965-70; art dir. Robert A. Sherman & Asso., advt., Warren, Ohio, 1970-72; v.p., creative dir. Gapstur Advt., Inc., Ashland, Ohio, 1972—. Served with AUS, 1966-72. Mem. Columbus Soc. Communicating Arts (award 1972, 73, 74, 75, 76). Elk. Home: 1269 Columbus Circle Ashland OH 44805 Office: 1126 Cottage St Ashland OH 44805

UNDERWOOD, PAUL STAATS, educator; b. Rocky Ridge, Ohio, Dec. 6, 1915; s. Michael Beal and Margaret Pearl (Staats) U.; student Ohio No. U., 1933-35, U. Cin., 1936; m. Mary Lou Perkins, Sept. 13, 1941; children—Michael, Sidney, Arthur. Reporter, Cin. Enquirer, 1937-44, columnist fgn. affairs, 1965-67; reporter-editor A.P., Cleve., N.Y.C., London, Eng., 1944-56; copy editor, writer, fgn. corr. N.Y. Times, N.Y.C., Belgrade, Yugoslavia, Warsaw, Poland, 1956-65; prof. journalism Ohio State U., Columbus, 1967—, asst. dir. Sch. Journalism, 1970—. Mem. Internat. Press Inst., Interam. Press Assn., Assn. for Edn. in Journalism, Am. Assn. for Advancement Slavic Studies, Overseas (citation N.Y.C. 1966), Nat. (Washington) press club. Author: Getting to Know Eastern Europe, 1966. Home: 5050 Olentangy River Rd Columbus OH 43214

UNGER, ROBERT MICHAEL, dentist; b. Chgo., Nov. 25, 1923; s. Robert and Mary Elizabeth (Janisch) U.; student De La Salle Inst., 1941, Loyola U., 1941-43; D.D.S., Chgo. Coll. Dental Surgery, Loyola U., 1946; m. Dorothy Marion Kinnavy, Apr. 30, 1949; children—Margaret, Marilyn, Robert, James, Richard, Joseph, Dorothy. Pvt. practice dentistry Chgo., 1948—; head dental dept. J.F. Kennedy Jr. Sch. Exceptional Children, 1955-70; cons. in field; bd. dirs. Ill. Dental Service Corp., 1976-80. Served to capt., Dental Corps, AUS, 1946-48. Fellow Am., Internat. colls. dentists; mem. Ill. (pres. 1972-73), Englewood (pres. 1965-66) dental socs., Loyola U. Dental Alumni Assn. (pres. 1972-73), Am. Dental Assn. (1st v.p. 1973-74), Acad. Gen. Dentistry (v.p. Chgo. 1975-76, pres. 1976-78), Odontographic Soc., Guild St. Appoliona, Fedn. Dentaire Internat., Pierre Fouchard Acad., Redemptorist Club Chgo., Am. Friends Austria. K.C. (4 deg.). Home: 6017 W 55th St Chicago IL 60638 Office: 2656 W 63d St Chicago IL 60629

UNRUH, MILTON CHARLES, heavy equipment co. exec.; b. Great Bend, Kans., Jan. 2, 1930; s. Frank H. and Esther Viola (Siebert) U.; student Bethel Coll., 1947-48; B.S., Kans. State U., 1952; m. Lillian Marilyn Coray, Apr. 14, 1962; children—Lorelle Marie, Bruce Charles. Auditor, Continental Oil Co., Ponca City, Okla., 1952-58; internal auditor Union Tank Car Co., Chgo., 1958-59; office mgr. Hobart Mfg. Co., Chgo., 1959-63; mgr. accounting systems Clark Equipment Co., Niles, Mich., 1963-69, mgr. systems auditing, 1969-72, mgr. spl. projects, 1972-75, regional bus. mgr., 1975—. Mem. Am. Accounting Assn., Nat. Assn. Accountants (communications dir. 1971-72). Presbyn. (elder 1972-74). Home: 806 S Lincoln Ave Niles MI 49120 Office: 128 E Front St Buchanan MI 49107

UPTON, LUCILE MORRIS (MRS. EUGENE V. UPTON), writer; b. Dadeville, Mo., July 22, 1898; d. Albert G. and Veda (Wilson) Morris; student Drury Coll., 1915-16, S.W. Mo. State U., 1917-20; m. Eugene V. Upton, July 22, 1936 (dec. July 1947). Pub. sch. tchr., Dadeville Mo., 1917-19, Everton, Mo., 1920-22, Roswell, N.Mex., 1921-23; tchr. creative writing Adult Edn. div. Drury Coll., 1947-52; reporter Denver Express, 1923-24, El Paso (Tex.) Times, 1924-25,

Springfield (Mo.) Newspapers, Inc., 1926-64, writer weekly hist. column, 1964—. Mem. Springfield City Council, 1967-71, Springfield Hist. Sites Bd., 1972—. Named Woman of Achievement Woman's div. Springfield C. of C., 1967. Mem. Mo. Writers Guild (past pres.), State Hist. Soc. Mo., Greene County (Mo.), White River Valley hist. socs. Congregationalist. Author: Bald Knobbers, 1939; (booklet) Battle of Wilson's Creek, 1950; contbr. short stories, articles to mags., newspapers. Home: 1305 S Kimbrough Springfield MO 65807

UPTON, WENDELL WARD, mgmt. cons.; b. Sylvarena, Miss., July 8, 1934; s. Nathaniel Kidd and Martha Evelyn (Ward) U.; B.A. in Marketing summa cum laude, Mich. State U., 1959, M.B.A. in Mgmt., 1972; children—Paul Alan, Beverly Gay, Todd David. Supr. market research Cummins Engine Co., Columbus, Ind., 1959-62; mgr. merchandising Hercules Engine div. White Motor Corp., Canton, Ohio, 1962-64; mgr. market analysis Trailmobile div. Pullman, Inc., Chgo., 1964-66; asst. to v.p. corp. planning Central Nat. Bank, Cleve., 1966-67; pres., owner Wendell Upton & Assos., mgmt. cons., Cleve., 1967-69, Clawson, Mich., 1969-74; pres. Upton Mgmt. Services, Inc., Troy, Mich., 1974—. Instr. Wayne State U. Applied Mgmt. and Tech. Center, 1968—, Walsh Coll., Troy, 1976. Served as info. and edn. specialist AUS, 1954-56. Mem. Am. Mktg. Assn. (dir. 1972—), Troy C. of C. Home: 5121 Buckingham Pl Troy MI 48098 Office: Suite 218 2855 Coolidge Rd Troy MI 48084

URBAN, DEWEY EMANUEL, dentist; b. Perryville, Mo., Apr. 24, 1913; s. Walter Edgar and Nettie Lee (Bush) U.; A.B., Washington U., St. Louis, 1935; D.D.S., St. Louis U., 1938, also postgrad.; postgrad. Tufts U., Temple U., Loyola U. Chgo.; m. Ione Beatrice Laux, June 1, 1938. Formerly in gen. practice dentistry, Perryville, Mo., oral surgery, San Diego, Cal.; now gen. practice dentistry, Sikeston, Mo. Served with AUS, 1940-45. Fellow Royal Soc. Health (Eng.); mem. Am., Mo. dental assns., Southeast Dental Soc. (past pres.), Acad. Gen. Dentistry (gov. Mo. chpt.); charter mem. Internat. Coll. Implantology, Internat. Assn. Anethesiologists. Presbyn. (elder). Mason (Shriner). Contbr. articles to profl. jours. Home: 920 Moore Sikeston MO 63801 Office: 215 Tanner Sikeston MO 63801

URBAN, DOLORES JEAN, utility co. exec.; b. Lebanon, Ind., Aug. 29, 1940; d. Paul M. and Mary C. (MacIntyre) Urban; B.S. in Edn., Ball State U., 1962. Programmer, Meth. Publishing House, Nashville, Tenn., 1964-68; sr. programmer state of Ind., Indpls., 1968-69, systems analyst, 1969-70; systems analyst Citizens Gas & Coke Utility, Indpls., 1970-72, sr. systems analyst, 1972-74, systems mgr., 1974—. Served with U.S. Army, 1962-64. Mem. Assn. for Systems Mgmt. (v.p. Indpls. chpt. 1977-78), Indpls. C. of C. Home: 9457 San Miguel Dr #A Indianapolis IN 46250 Office: 2020 N Meridian St Indianapolis IN 46202

URBAN, DONALD A., surgeon; b. Zanesville, Ohio, June 14, 1914; s. Frank Pierce and Lelia Mabel (Lighthizer) U.; B.A., Ohio State U., 1936, M.D., 1940; m. Flora Conrad Avera, Jan. 20, 1945; children—Lelia Elizabeth, Flora Caroline, Donald Avera. Intern, City Hosp. Akron (Ohio), 1940-41; fellow in gen. surgery Mayo Clinic, Rochester, Minn., 1944-44, 47; practice medicine specializing in gen. surgery, Zanesville, 1947—; past chief of staff Good Samaritan and Bethesda hosps., Zanesville. Served to maj. M.C., U.S. Army, 1944-47. Diplomate Am. Bd. Surgery. Fellow A.C.S.; mem. Muskingum County (Ohio) Med. Soc. (past pres.), Ohio State Med. Assn., AMA. Republican. Methodist. Home: 3003 Dresden Rd Zanesville OH 43701 Office: 2762 Bell St Zanesville OH 43701

URBOM, WARREN KEITH, judge; b. Atlanta, Nebr., Dec. 17, 1925; s. Clarence A. and Anna Myrl (Ireland) U.; A.B., Nebr. Wesleyan U., 1950; J.D., U. Mich., 1953; m. Joyce Crawford, Aug. 19, 1951; children—Kim Marie Urbom Rager, Randall, Allison Lee, Joy R. Admitted to Nebr. bar, 1953. Mem. firm Baylor, Evnen, Baylor, Urbom & Curtiss, Lincoln, 1953-70; U.S. dist. judge, 1970—, chief judge Dist. of Nebr., Lincoln, 1972—. Del., Gen. Conf., United Meth. Ch., 1962, 76; pres. Lincoln YMCA, 1965-67; chmn. bd. govs. Nebr. Wesleyan U. Mem. Am., Nebr., Lincoln bar assns., Am. Coll. Trial Lawyers, Masons, Shriners. Home: 4510 Van Dorn St Lincoln NE 68506 Office: 100 Centennial Mall N Federal Bldg Lincoln NE 68508

USHER, DAVID, pollution control co. exec.; b. Detroit, Dec. 29, 1929; s. Charles and Hannah (Komisaruk) Uschkatz; grad. Admiral Farragut Acad., 1946; m. Althea Marie Dienne, June 7, 1954; children—Lisa, Ellen, Amy, Charles. Partner Emanon Record Co., 1948—50; pres. Dee Gee Record Co., 1951—54; record producer Chess Producing Co., 1958—60; v.p. Usher Oil Service, Detroit, 1960—; pres. Mich. Tank Cleaning Co., Detroit, 1960—, pres. Marine Services Corp., Detroit, 1961—, Marine Pollution Control Co., Detroit, 1967—. Served with USCG, 1950. Mem. Oil Spill Control Assn. Am. (pres. and founder), Hazardous Materials Control Research Inst. (pres.), Nat. Def. Transp. Assn., Soc. Am. Military Engrs. Club: Rotary. Home: 16400 N Park Dr Southfield MI 48075 Office: 8631 W Jefferson St Detroit MI 48209

USHER, NEWELL ELSWORTH, computer edn. co. exec.; b. Lawrence, Kan., July 17, 1933; s. Samuel Elsworth and Lora Lucille (Myers) U.; B.A. in Math., So. Ill. U., 1962; postgrad. U. Chgo. Grad. Sch. Bus., 1963; m. Gerry Kay Acuncius, Feb. 17, 1957; 1 dau., Dannette Kay. With applied math. dept. McDonnell Automation Center, St. Louis, 1956-62; mathematician IIT Research Inst., Chgo., 1962-66; mgmt. cons., Chgo., 1966-67; sr. cons. info. services and computer scis. dept. Standard Oil (Ind.), Chgo., 1967-74; instrn. mgr. Newell E. Usher Assos., Inc., computer cons. and edn., Chicago Heights, Ill., 1969-76; owner Newell Usher Co., 1976—; founder, pres., also chmn. bd. Internat. Computer Edn. Corp., Chicago Heights, Ill., 1971-74; founder, editorial dir. Computer Educator Corp., 1974-75. Instr. data processing mgmt. Roosevelt U., 1970-71; cons., mem. data processing curriculum adv. com., also instr. exptl. research in computer fundamentals, Central YMCA Community Coll., Chgo., 1972-73, chmn. applied scis. dept., 1974—; speaker profl. and community groups on computers. Served with AUS, 1953-55. Mem. Assn. for Computer Machinery (newsletter editor, also dir. Chgo. chpt. 1970-72), Data Processing Mgmt. Assn., Soc. Mgmt. Info. Systems. Home: 720 Enterprise Rd Chicago Heights IL 60411 Office: 1540 Halsted St Box 460 Chicago Heights IL 60411

UTECHT, ALOISE JOSEPH, psychologist; b. Hamtramck, Mich., June 10, 1924; s. John Ignace and Agnes (Wawrzyniak) U., Ph.B., U. Detroit, 1950; M.A., U.Pa., 1952; postgrad. Wayne State U., 1952-53; Ph.D. (Univ. teaching fellow), U. N.D., 1960; m. Ederina DiBiaggio, Sept. 7, 1957; children—Steven, Michael. Dir. Hazel Park Youth Protection Com., Mich., 1954-57; clin. psychologist Children's Center of Wayne County, Detroit, 1960-65; asso. dir. psychology Hawthorn Center, Northville, Mich., 1965—; practice cons. psychologist, Southfield, Mich., 1965-70, Plymouth, Mich., 1970—; Lectr. psychology U. Detroit, 1954-57, 62-68. Mem. bd. Guardian Angel Home Soc., 1963-69, Cath. Youth Orgn., 1967-69 (Detroit). Served with AUS, 1943-46. Decorated Bronze Star (2). Mem. Am., Mich. psychol. assns., Common Cause. Home: 16299 Edgewood Dr Livonia MI 48154 Office: 18471 Haggerty Rd Northville MI 48167

UTGAARD, MERTON BLAINE, music camp exec.; b. Maddock, N.D., Nov. 2, 1914; s. Peter Wesley and Agnes Katherine (Knatterud) U.; B.A., Valley City State Coll., 1940; Mus.M. Edn., U. Minn., 1947; Ed.D., U. No. Colo., 1950; m. Noella G. Michon, July 30, 1940; children—Michael Kent, Karen Ann (Mrs. Ernest Rolston), Mark Cevin. Mem. faculty, dir. bands U. S.D., 1949-53, Ball State U., 1953-57, No. Ill. U., 1957-60; lectr. music edn. Brandon (Man., Can.) U., 1964-70; founder, dir. Internat. Music Camp, Bottineau, N.D., 1956—. Del. World Band Congress, Luxembourg, 1972. Mem. N.D. Com. 100 for Higher Edn., 1962—; N.D. Bicentennial Commn., 1973—. Served with USAAF, 1943-45. Recipient citations Gov. N.D., 1966, Nat. Band Assn., 1971. Mem. Am. Bandmasters Assn. Nat. Band Dirs. Assn., Bottineau County Concert Assn., Nat. Fedn. Music Clubs (award 1974), Music Educators Nat. Conf. Home: Highview Estates Bottineau ND 58318 Office: Box 328 Bottineau ND 58318

UTGAARD, STUART BRADY, mgmt. cons., poultry co. exec.; b. New Richmond, Wis., May 9, 1945; s. Stanley Brady and Evelyn Winifred (Johnson) U.; B.A., St. Olaf and Augsburg Coll., 1967; M.A., U. Minn., 1969; m. Sharon Lynn Christenson, June 17, 1967; children—Christopher Brady, Erica Lynn. Adminstrv. asst. to v.p. mktg. Minneagasco, Mpls., 1969-71; v.p. Northstar Industries, Mpls., 1971—; chief exec. officer Utgaard's Hatchery & Poultry Farm, Star Prairie, Wis., 1969—. Trustee Master Eye Found., 1973-77. Served with N.G., 1969. Licensed real estate broker, Minn. Mem. Soc. for Corporate Growth, N. Am. Soc. Corporate Planning, MW Poultry Fedn., Am. Mgmt. Assn. (guest lectr.). Lutheran. Clubs: Mpls. Probus (past pres.), Masons, (past master Wis.). Home: 2496 E Brookview Dr St Paul MN 55119 Office: 4570 W 77th St Minneapolis MN 55435

UTZ, CAROLYN MAY GLOVER (MRS. STANLEY MINOR UTZ), musician, educator; b. Portsmouth, Va.; d. Edward Eben and Jessie F. (Stephens) Glover; B.S., Ohio State U., 1934, M.A., 1938; m. Stanley Minor Utz, Sept. 28, 1943; children—Stanley Minor II, Carolyn Gloria. Clk., Census Bur., Washington, 1942-43; semi-confidential clk. War Dept., 1943-44; string bass player Columbus (Ohio) Philharmonic Orch., 1944-49, Springfield (Ohio) Symphony, 1949-54; occasional string bass player Ohio Wesleyan U. Orch., 1949-63, Denison U. Orch., 1950-60; string bass player Columbus Symphony Orch., 1951-76, guest condr., 1975; library asst. in catalog dept. Ohio State U. Libraries, 1955-64; instrumental music tchr. N.C. Coll., 1934-36, Ky. State Coll., 1936-39; instrumental music, speech, gen. edn. methods, ednl. psychology tchr. Edward Waters Coll., Jacksonville, Fla., 1940-42; vocal music tchr. Monroe Jr. Hi, 1965-68, chmn. music dept., also fine and cultural arts dept., 1968—; condr. Top Teen Orch., 1971—, All City Jr. High Sch. Orch., 1975. Mem. Columbus council Nat. Council Negro Women (v.p. 1965-68), Columbus Fedn. Musicians, Nat., Ohio edn. assns., Columbus, Central Ohio tchrs. assns., Music Educators Nat. Conf., Nat. Congress Parents and Tchrs., Ohio State Alumni Assn., Columbus Top Ladies of Distinction (v.p. 1971-74, pres. 1974—, nat. 3d v.p. 1974—), Alpha Kappa Alpha (pres. Columbus 1964-68), Columbus Women's Music Club. Home: 7086 Landsdowne St Worthington OH 43085

UVEGES, ALFRED CHARLES, dentist; b. Rivesville, W. Va., Jan. 23, 1934; s. John and Elizabeth (Toth) U.; B.S., Fairmont State Coll., 1956; D.D.S., Case Western Res. U., 1960; m. Mary Lou Shurmer, Aug. 18, 1960; children—Ruth, Alfred Charles II, Beth Ann, Cathy. Instr. dentistry U. Md., Balt., 1967-68; pvt. practice dentistry Fairveiw Park, Ohio, 1968—; cons. in field. Active Boy Scouts Am., pres. Riveredge P.T.A., 1970-71. Mem. adv. com. Berea Bd. Edn. Served with Dental Corp., USN, 1960-68, comdr. Res. Mem. Am., Ohio dental assns., WestShore Dental Study Club, Cleve. Dental Soc., Phi Beta Kappa, Delta Sigma Delta, Tau Beta Iota, Lambda Delta Lambda, Zeta Beta Phi. Mem. United Ch. Christ. Clubs: Berea Midpark, Amateur Athletic Union Swim (pres. 1974). Home: 617 Grayton Rd Berea OH 44017 Office: 21851 Center Ridge Rd Rocky River OH 44116

UZE, IRVING, auto parts distbg. co. exec.; b. Chelsea, Mass., June 21, 1918; s. Philip and Ann (Conners) U.; M.A., New Eng. Conservatory Music, 1938; m. Rosalynn Siegel, Apr. 6, 1941; children—Martin A. (dec.), Beth Ellen, Vicki Jean. Asst. mgr. parts dept. Noyes Buick Co., Boston, 1937; with Esco Supply Co., Waterloo, Iowa, 1944-60; owner ESCO Corp., 1961—; pres., treas. sec. Central States Warehouse Distbrs., Waterloo, 1961—; pres. Banvir Corp., Waterloo, 1964—, Royal Oaks Devel. Corp., 1971—. Served with USNR, 1942-44. Mem. Automotive Warehouse Distbrs. Assns., Automotive Parts and Accessories Assns., Splty. Equipment Mfg. Assn., Performance Warehouse Assn., Nat. Tire Dealers Assn., Iowa Automotive Wholesalers. Jewish. Clubs: P.G.I. Country (Punta Gordo, Fla.); Sunnyside Country, Masons (32 deg.), Shriners. Home: 390 Sheridan Rd Waterloo IA 50701 Office: 106 E 11th St Waterloo IA 50703

UZELAC, GEORGE, JR., steel co. exec.; b. Gary, Ind., Sept. 26, 1942; s. George and Ann Marie (Stofega) U.; student Ind. U., 1961-70; children—Stacey Lynn, Todd Allen. Research asst. Sch. Bus., Ind. U. N.W., Gary, 1968-70; dir. govt. tax research Gary C. of C., 1969-72; pres. Info. Research Assos., Inc., Merrillville, Ind., 1972-76; tax rep. U.S. Steel Corp., Gary, 1976—; cons. Ind. Commn. on Tax and Fin. Policy, Town of Schererville (Ind.), Town of Dyer (Ind.), Town of St. John (Ind.), Govt. of Lake County (Ind.). Served with USAF, 1963-67; Vietnam. Mem. Am. Mgmt. Assn., Greater Gary C. of C., Lake County Community Devel. Com., Lake County Research Bur. Mem. Serbian Orthodox Ch. Author: Crime Within Our Society, 1971; A Comparative Review of Seven Indiana Public School Systems, 1971. Office: 1 N Broadway Gary IN 46402

VAAL, JOSEPH JOHN, JR., psychologist; b. St. Louis, Nov. 19, 1947; s. Joseph John and Dorothy Jane (Collett) V.; B.A., Lawrence U., 1969; M.A. in Psychology, Western Mich. U., 1971; m. Mary Irene Grubb, Jan. 30, 1971; 1 dau., Lauren Elizabeth. Tchr. spl. edn. KVISD Title VI Program, Kalamazoo, 1970, Mannheim Pub. Schs. Franklin Park, Ill., 1971; sch. psychologist Wheaton (Ill.) pub. schs., 1971—; adj. instr. Grad. Sch., Nat. Coll. Edn., Evanston, Ill., 1972—. Mem. Am. Psychol. Assn., Nat. Assn. Sch. Psychologists, W. Suburban Sch. Psychologists Assn., Arnold Air Soc. Republican. Methodist. Home: 1422 A Woodcutter Ln Wheaton IL 60187 Office: Wheaton Pub Schs 130 W Park St Wheaton IL 60187

VACHHER, PREHLAD SINGH, psychiatrist; b. Rawalpindi dist., Pakistan, Nov. 30, 1933; s. Thakar Singh and Harbans Kaur (Ghai) V.; came to U.S., 1960, naturalized, 1968; B. Medicine, B.Surgery, Panjab (India) U. Med. Coll. Amritsar, 1956; m. Margaret Begley, Oct. 4, 1963; children—Paul, Sheila, Mary Ann, Eileen, Mark. Intern Worcester (Mass.) City Hosp., 1960-61; resident in psychiatry Rochester (N.Y.) State Hosp., 1962-64, Phila. Gen. Hosp., 1964-65; practice medicine specializing in psychiatry Livonia, Mich., 1966—; staff psychiatrist Trenton (N.J.) State Hosp., 1965-66, Wayne County Gen. Hosp., Eloise, Mich., 1966-68; dir. community psychiatry Northville (Mich.) State Hosp., 1968-72; mem. staff Mercywood Hosp., Ann Arbor, Mich., 1970—; cons. psychiatrist St. Joseph Mercy Hosp., Ann Arbor, Mich., 1975. Mem. Am. Psychiat. Assn., Canton C. of C.

(v.p. 1972-73, pres. 1973-74). Clubs: Rotary; Econ. of Detroit. Research in use of packed red blood cells in treatment of hepatic cirrhosis. Home: Plymouth MI 48170 Office: Vachher Psychiat Center 32300 Schoolcraft St Livonia MI 48150

VAFI, HOUSHANG, psychiatrist; b. Teheran, Iran, Mar. 6, 1936; M.D., Teheran U., 1960; m. Mary Antonia, Aug. 5, 1964; children—Joseph Anthony, Roxane Maria, Lillian Nicole. Resident in psychiatry Washington U., St. Louis, 1962-65; head dept. neuropsychiatry Ahwaz (Iran) U. Med. Sch., 1966-68; clin. dir. Malcolm Bliss Mental Health Center, St. Louis, 1969-71; chief psychiatrist St. Joseph Hosp., St. Charles, Mo., 1975—. Bd. dirs. St. Louis Montessori Acad. Home: Box 669 Route 1 Glencoe MO 63038 Office: 1360 S 5th St St Charles MO 63301

VAGH, AMRISHKUMAR SURYAPRASAD, physicist; b. Visnagar, India, Jan. 19, 1936; s. Suryaprasad Bapalal and Manglagauri Suryaprasad (Jani) V.; came to U.S., 1968, naturalized, 1974; M.Sc., Gujarat U., 1961; Ph.D. with distinction, S. P. U., 1966; m. Kokila S. Desai, May 18, 1954; 1 son, Avinash. Lectr. Sardar Patel U., 1966-68; postdoctoral fellow State U. N.Y., Buffalo, 1968-69; asst. prof. State U. N.Y., Buffalo, 1969-70, chmn. phys. sci. div., asst. prof. Coop. Community Coll., 1970-71; sr. research physicist, 1971-74; sr. research physicist Ball State U., Muncie, Ind., 1974-75; research physicist NASA, Lewis Research Center, Cleve., 1976—; sr. research fellow Univ. Grant Commn., Govt. India, 1968. Mem. Am. Phys. Soc., Am. Carbon Soc. Contbr. articles to profl. jours. Home: 728 Main St Cincinnati OH 45202

VAGNIERES, ROBERT CHARLES, architect; b. Chgo., Oct. 2, 1932; s. Alfred and Elsa (Krueger) V.; B.Arch., U. Ill., 1955; m. Dorothy Lee Wandrey, June 13, 1953; children—Robert, Krista, Ross, Pam. Draftsman, Robert Soellner, Architect, Park Forest, Ill., 1957-59; asso. mem. firm Joel Robert Hillman, Architect, Chgo., 1959-71; partner Hillman Vagnieres & Assos., Chgo., 1972-75; owner, prin. Robert C. Vagnieres Architect Ltd., Olympia Fields, Ill., 1975—. Served to lt. C.E., U.S. Army, 1955-57. Mem. AIA. Club: Olympia Fields Country. Architect: Chgo. City Centre, 1976, Sheraton Plaza Hotel, Chgo., 1971, Homewood-Flossmoor (Ill.) High Sch., 1977. Home and office: 99 Graymoor Ln Olympia Fields IL 60461

VAIL, JOE FRANKLIN, mktg. co. exec.; b. Indpls., Mar. 24, 1928; s. Frank Albert and Trixie May (Hawley) V.; B.S., Purdue U., 1951; m. Delores Ann Knotts, Dec. 21, 1968; 1 son, Kevin Joe. Treas., Apex Corp., Indpls., 1953-60; owner, operator Bus. Service Co., Indpls., 1961-63; partner Pulse Publs., Indpls., 1963-64; pres. Unique, Inc., Indpls., 1965-70; owner, operator Mid-Am. Advt. Co., Indpls., 1970-73; pres. Mid-Am. Mktg., Inc., Indpls., 1973—. Mem. Chgo. Assn. Direct Mktg.; Nat. Fedn. Ind. Bus., Am. Bus. Club. Clubs: John Purdue, Masons. Editor, pub.: Land Opportunity Review, 1970—. Author: Keys to Wealth, 1971; Your Fortune in Mail Order, 1972; How to Get Out of Debt and Live Like a Millionaire, 1977. Home: 1340 N Eustis Dr Indianapolis IN 46229 Office: 1150 N Shadeland Ave Indianapolis IN 46219

VAIL, ROGER STANLEY, retail dept. store exec.; b. nr. Bowling Green, Ohio, Apr. 15, 1942; s. Robert S. and Bertha L. (Maidment) V.; B.A., Bowling Green State U., 1964; M.B.A., 1969; m. Sharon Kay Klotz, Aug. 19, 1962; children—Michelle, Melissa. Accountant, Ernst & Ernst, Toledo, Ohio, 1964-67; treas., controller Fred W. Uhlman & Co., Bowling Green, 1967—, v.p., 1972-75, pres., 1975—, also dir. Bd. dirs. Credit Bur. Toledo, 1975—. C.P.A., Ohio. Mem. Am. Inst. C.P.A.'s, Ohio Soc. C.P.A.'s, Young Pres.'s Orgn., Beta Alpha Psi, Jr. C. of C. Clubs: Exchange. Home: 1249 Brownwood Dr Bowling Green OH 43402 Office: 126 N Main St Bowling Green OH 43402

VAIL, THOMAS VAN HUSEN, publisher, editor; b. Cleve., June 23, 1926; s. Herman Lansing and Delia (White) V.; A.B. cum laude in Polit. Sci., Princeton U., 1949, H.H.D., Wilberforce U., 1964; L.H.D., Kenyon Coll., 1969, Cleve. State U., 1973; m. Iris Jennings, Sept. 15, 1951; children—Siri, Thomas Van Husen, Lawrence J.W. Reporter, Cleve. News, 1949-53, polit. editor, 1953-57; bus. editor Cleve. Plain Dealer, 1957-61, v.p., 1961-63, pub., editor, 1963—, pres., 1970—, also dir.; pres., dir. Art Gravure Corp., Ohio, AP, 1968-74; mem. U.S. Adv. Commn. on Info., Nat. Adv. Commn. on Health Manpower, Pres.'s Commn. Observance 25th Anniversary UN. Dir., past pres. Cleve. Conv. and Visitors Bur.; chmn. Nat. Brotherhood Week, 1969; bd. dirs. Greater Cleve. Growth Assn.; mem. distbn. com. Cleve. Found.; trustee Cuyahoga unit Am. Cancer Soc., Cleve. Clinic Found., No. Ohio region NCCJ, Downtown Cleve. Corp. Served to lt. (j.g.) USNR, 1944-46. Recipient Nat. Human Relations award NCCJ, 1970, Man of Yr. award Sales and Mktg. Execs. of Cleve. Clubs: Cleve. Athletic, Union (Cleve.); Kirtland Country (Willoughby, Ohio); Cypress Point (Pebble Beach, Calif.); Nat. Press (Washington). Home: Hunting Valley Chagrin Falls OH 44022 Office: 1801 Superior Ave Cleveland OH 44114

VAILE, HORACE SNYDER, mgmt. cons.; b. Logansport, Ind., Feb. 2, 1896; s. George Rawson and Flora (Snyder) V.; B.S., Purdue U., 1920, E.E., 1926; m. Jeanne M. Scott, June 18, 1928; children—Horace Snyder, Edward Scott. Indsl. marketing counsellor McGraw-Hill Pub. Co., Chgo., 1920-28; asst. to v.p. Ill. Steel Co., Carnegie Steel Co., Tenn. Coal. Iron & R.R. Co., 1928-31; asst. v.p. U.S. Steel Corp., N.Y.C. 1932-37; comptroller Marshall Field & Co., Chgo., 1937-38; mgmt. cons. operating under own name, 1938—; dir. Permacor-Altair Inc., Oak Lawn, Ill. Served as lt. F.A., A.E.F., 1917-19. Life trustee, past pres. Illinois Fed. Real Estate Acad.; Ind. Soc., Chgo. Mem. Soc. Colonial Wars, S.A.R., Iron Key, Alpha Tau Omega, Eta Kappa Nu, Sigma Delta Chi. Republican. Presbyn. Mason. Clubs: Curling (Chgo.); Epham Yacht (past commodore) (Wis.); Exmoor Country (Highland Park). Home: 112 Maple Ave Highland Park IL 60035 Office: 11 S LaSalle St Chicago IL 60603

VAILE, JEANNE SCOTT (MRS. HORACE S. VAILE), civic worker; b. Winnipeg, Man., Can.; d. William and Margaret (MacLean) Scott; student U. Manitoba, 1920-23; teaching certificate Manioba Normal Coll., 1924; m. Horace Snyder Vaile, June 18, 1928; children—Horace E. Scott. Came to U.S., 1927, naturalized, 1930. Historian Ill. Fedn. Republican Women, 1956-58, corr. sec., 1958-60, v.p., chmn. state legislation, 1960-62; dir., founder Highland Park Women's Rep. Club, 1957-59; chmn. Women's Rep. Club, 13th Congl. Dist. Ill., 1954-60; Rep. State Central committeewoman 13th Congl. Dist., 1954-60; mem., sec. legislative Commn. Study Adoption Laws Ill., 1957-59; dir. Woman's Nat. Rep. Club Chgo., 1958-76, sec., 1961-65; mem. White House Conf. on Children and Youth, 1960. Bd. dirs. Highland Park Bd., Northwestern U. Settlement, 1938—, Highland Park-Ravinia Bd., Infant Welfare Soc., Chgo., 1938—; pres. Woman's Aux., Highland Park Hosp., 1942-44; capt. 1st team Am. Lady Curlers, Scotland, 1955. Mem. exec. com. Lake County Tb Assn., 1955—, pres. 1959-60; bd. dirs. Highland Park Community Chest, 1956-68; exec. com. Ill. Tb and Respiratory Diseases Assn., 1957—, sec., 1961-62, v.p., 1962-63, chmn. program and devel. com. 1962-64, 1st v.p., 1966-68, pres., 1968-70; Ill. rep. dir. Nat. Tb and Respiratory Disease Assn., N.Y.C., 1972-74, mem. qualification and contract com., 1972-73; gov. Task Force on Tb Problems in Ill., 1970-71; chmn. ad hoc com. Tb Problems in Ill., 1971-73; gov. Mississippi Valley Conf. Tb, 1965-

bd. dirs. Highland Park Welfare Council, 1965-68. Mem. Ill. Lung Assn. (life, exec. com. 1975), Sr. Ladies Internat. Curling Club (charter mem.). Clubs: Exmoor Country; Chicago Curling. Home: 112 Maple Ave Highland Park IL 60035

VAISVIL, FRED ANTHONY, coll. adminstr.; b. Chgo., Oct. 21, 1931; s. Frank J. and Bernice (Lauraitis) V.; B.A., U. Ill., 1949; M.A., U. Chgo., 1961; Ed.D., Nova U., 1976; m. Joann E. Zaturski, June 13, 1959; children—Wayne, Christopher, Sandra, Mark. Tchr., High Sch. Dist. 214, Arlington Heights, Ill., 1957-67, vocat. counselor, 1961-67; dir. placement and student aid William Rainey Harper Coll., Palatine, Ill., 1967-73, dir. placement and career devel., 1973—; cons. Bell & Howell Scholarship; mem. Coll. Entrance Exam. Bd.; mem. Gould Scholarship Com.; chmn. Eugenia Chapman Scholarship Com. Mem. adv. com. N.W. Mental Health Assn.; active Wheeling Township Community Council, Chgo. Govtl. Relations Com., Cook County Council of Govts., 1965-67. Served with U.S. Army, 1954-56. Recipient Outgoing Presdl. plaque Ill. Assn. Fin. Aid Adminstrs., 1972; NDEA summer inst. guidance and counseling, 1964. Mem. Am., Ill., N.W. Suburban personnel and guidance assns., Coll. Placement Council, Midwest Coll. Placement Assn., Placement Assn. Community Colls. and Employers, Phi Delta Kappa. Roman Catholic. Clubs: Rotary, The Right. Contbr. articles to Ill. Guidance and Personnel Quar., Heuristic, Jour. Coll. Placement, 1975—. Home: Route 1 Box 200A Prairie View IL 60069 Office: Algonquin and Roselle Rds Palatine IL 60067

VALENTINE, BARRY, bishop; b. Shenfield, Essex, Eng., Sept. 26, 1927; s. Harry John and Ethel Margaret (Purkiss) V.; B.A., St. John's Coll., Cambridge (Eng.) U., 1949, M.A., 1952; B.D., McGill U., 1951; L.Th., Montreal Diocesan Theol. Coll., 1951, D.D., 1970; D.D., St. John's Coll., Winnipeg, Man., 1969; m. Mary Currell Hayes, Oct. 4, 1952; children—John Nugent, Lesley Claire, Guy Richard Neville, Michael Hayes. Ordained to ministry Anglican Ch.; curate Christ Ch. Cathedral, Montreal, 1952; incumbent Chateauguay-Beauharnois, 1954; dir. religious edn. Diocese of Montreal, 1957-61; rector St. Lambert Ch., 1961-65; exec. officer Diocese of Montreal, 1965-66, archdeacon, 1966-68; dean of Montreal and rector Christ Ch. Cathedral, 1968-69; coadjutor bishop of Rupert's Land (Winnipeg), 1969-70, bishop, 1970—; chancellor St. John's Coll., Winnipeg, 1970. Office: 66 Saint Cross St Winnipeg MB R2W 3X8 Canada*

VALENTINE, BOB LEON, microbiologist; b. Dry Prong, La., Feb. 5, 1929; s. James Ellis and Beatrice (Brown) V.; B.A., La. Coll., 1954; M.S., La. State U., 1956; Ph.D., Purdue U., 1963; m. Georgeann Murphey, Sept. 3, 1955; 1 son, James Joseph. With Miles Labs., Elkhart, Ind., 1956-61; asso. prof. Miss. State U., Starkville, 1963-67; corp. dir. product integrity Sherwood Med. Industries, St. Louis, 1967—. Chmn. bd. dirs. St. Martins Sch. for Children, St. Louis, 1972-73. Served with USN, 1947-51. Mem. Am. Soc. Microbiology, AAAS, Health Industry Mfg. Assn. (chmn. med. sci. sect. 1975—). Office: 11802 Westline Industrial Dr St Louis MO 63141

VALENTINO, PAUL JON, transp. co. exec.; b. Chgo., Jan. 1, 1942; s. John and Eileen (Johnson) V.; grad. high sch.; m. Paula Edyth Deacon, Mar. 3, 1962; children—Kelly Ann, Marc Jon. With Universal Oil Products Co., Des Plaines, Ill., 1964-76, purchasing agt., 1968-71, mgr. transp., 1971-75; nat. fleet sales mgr. Roto Lincoln-Mercury Inc., Arlington Heights, Ill., 1976-77; fleet sales mgr. Elmhurst Lincoln-Mercury, Inc. (Ill.), 1977—. Served with USAF, 1960-64. Mem. Nat. (chmn. car rental com., 1973-74), Midwest (v.p., 1972-74) passenger traffic assns., Nat. Assn. Fleet Adminstrs. (sec., 1973-74), Am. Mgmt. Assn., Automotive Fleet and Leasing Assn. Home: 1016 S Highland Ave Arlington Heights IL 60005 Office: 150 W Grand Ave Elmhurst IL 60126

VALINSKY, MARK STEVEN, podiatrist; b. Chgo., May 24, 1951; s. Harry and Beckie (Baker) V.; student Ohio State U., 1969-71, State U. N.Y. at Buffalo, 1971-72; B.S., D. Podiatric Medicine, Ill. Coll. of Podiatric Medicine, 1976. Gen. practice surg. podiatry, Oak Park, Ill., 1977—; biol. photographer. Mem. Mayor's Council Sr. Citizens and Handicapped. Certificate of service, Nat. Assn. for Human Devel., 1977. Mem. Ill., Am. podiatry socs., Biol. Photographers Assn., Smithsonian Inst. Jewish. Club: Am. Karate Assn. Office: 715 W Lake St Suite 220 Oak Park IL 60301

VALIS, WILLIAM VICTOR, lawyer; b. Cleve., Nov. 23, 1943; s. William John and Anna Frances (Chaplic) V.; A.B. in Econs., St. Vincent Coll., 1965; J.D., Case Western Res. U., 1968; m. Barbara Ann Yeckley, May 21, 1966; children—Kimberly Ann, Kevin William. Admitted to Ohio bar; supr. fin. dept. lamp div. Gen. Electric Corp., Nela Park, Ohio, 1968-69; law clk. for judges of Common Pleas Ct. of Cuyahoga County, Ohio, 1969-71; real estate counsel to Developers Diversified, Beachwood, Ohio, 1971; mem. firm Reminger and Reminger Co., Cleve., 1971-77, partner, 1977—; arbitrator, Am. Arbitration Assn.; panel chmn. Common Pleas Ct. Cuyahoga County Arbitration; bd. dirs. Ins. Office of Cleve., Inc.; legal cons. Cleve. Heights Housing Service; instr. bus. law, Cleve. Acad. Profl. Secs., 1969-71. Liaison Fairfax Community Congress to Cleve. Heights Community Congress. Mem. Ohio State, Am. Bar Assns. Home: 2932 Clarkson Rd Cleveland Heights OH 44118 Office: 731 Leader Bldg Cleveland OH 44114

VALTOS, WILLIAM, advt. agy. exec.; b. Scranton, Pa., Aug. 18, 1937; s. James Anthony and Mary (Rukat) V.; student U. Scranton; m. Maria Rosario Cecilia Tolentino Vallarta, Sept. 2, 1959; children—William, Catherine, Anthony, Michael. Copy chief R.H. Macy & Co., N.Y.C., 1959-61; copy chief, v.p., prin. Rockmore, Garfield & Shaub, Inc., 1961-65; creative dir., v.p. Clinton E. Frank, Inc., N.Y.C., 1965-70, v.p., creative dir., Chgo., 1970-75; v.p., creative dir. D'Arcy, MacManus & Masius, Inc., 1975—. Served with USAF, 1955-59. Home: 420 High Ridge Rd Barrington IL 60010 Office: 200 E Randolph Chicago IL 60601

VALUSEK, JOHN EMIEL, psychologist; b. Mt. Clemens, Mich., May 14, 1930; s. Stephan and Anna (Lauchik) V.; B.S., Mich. State Normal Coll., 1952; M.A., U. Mich., 1957, Ph.D., 1963; m. Barbara DeCoppette Bell, Jan. 27, 1951; children—Valerie Ann, John Eric, Jay Evan. Tchr. spl. edn., Flint, Mich., 1952-56; instr. Sch. Edn., U. Mich., Ann Arbor, 1956-59; asst. prof. Western State Coll., Gunnison, Colo., 1959-61; pvt. practice as psychologist, Wichita, Kans., 1961—, cons., lectr., 1968—; mem. psychology staff Coop. Urban Tchr. Edn. Program, Wichita, 1969—. Campaign adviser, atty. gen. election State of Kan., 1968, gubernatorial election, 1970. Mem. Am., Kans., Wichita psychol. assns. Presbyn. (elder 1964). Author: (with others) Learning To Learn, 1961; Some Ways of Thinking About Human Behavior, 1971; Jottings, 1972; People Are Not For Hitting, 1974. Home: 3629 Mossman St Wichita KS 67208 Office: 3100 McCormick St Wichita KS 67213

VAN ANDEL, BETTY JEAN, household products co. exec.; b. Mich., Dec. 14, 1921; d. Anthony and Daisy (Van Dyk) Hoekstra; A.B., Calvin Coll., 1943; m. Jay Van Andel, Aug. 16, 1952; children—Nan Elizabeth, Stephen Alan, David Lee, Barbara Ann. Elementary sch. tchr., Grand Rapids, Mich., 1943-45; service rep. and supr. Mich. Bell Telephone Co., Grand Rapids, 1945-52; dir.-stockholder Amway Corp., Grand Rapids, 1972—. Treas., LWV, 1957-60; chmn. Eagle Forum, Mich., 1975—. Mem. Nat. Trust Hist. Preservation, St. Cecelia Music Soc., Smithsonian Assos. Republican. Club: Women's City of Grand Rapids. Home: 7186 Windy Hill Rd SE Grand Rapids MI 49506 Office: PO Box 172 Ada MI 49301

VAN ANDEL, JAY, mfg. and sales co. exec.; b. Grand Rapids, Mich., June 3, 1924; s. James and Nella (Vanderwoude) Van A.; student Pratt Jr. Coll., 1945, Calvin Coll., 1942, 46, Yale, 1943-44; hon. doctorate in bus. No. Mich. U.; m. Betty J. Hoekstra, Aug. 16, 1952; children—Nan, Stephen, David, Barbara. Formerly engaged in aviation, restaurant, mail order businesses; co-founder Ja-Ri Corp., 1949, now chmn. bd.; co-founder Amway Corp., Ada, Mich., 1959, chmn. bd., 1964—; chmn. bd. Amway of Can., Ltd., 1964—, Amway Australia, Pty. Ltd., Amway France, Amway U.K., Ltd., Amway Germany, Amway Hong Kong, Nutrilite Products, Inc., Amway Malaysia, Amway Mgmt. Co., Inc.; dir. Mich. Nat. Bank, Grand Rapids and Lansing, Van Andel & Flikkema Motor Sales, Grand Rapids, Amway Distbrs. Assn. U.S.; dir., treas. Amway Distbrs. Assn. Can. Chmn. bd. Citizens Choice, Washington; bd. dirs. World Affairs Council; chmn. Mich. Republican Fin. Com.; trustee Hillsdale Coll., Calvin Coll. Found., Mich. Research Council: bd. dirs. Nat. Chamber Found., Bus.-Industry Polit. Action Commn., Ferguson-Droste-Ferguson Hosp. Served to 1st lt. AC, AUS, 1943-46. Recipient Religious Heritage Man of Yr. award, 1972; Mktg. Man of Yr. award, 1975; Alumni of Yr. award Calvin Coll. Mem. U.S. (v.p., dir.), Mich. (chmn. 1974, dir.), Grand Rapids (dir.) chambers commerce, Am. Fedn. Small Businesses (dir.), Soap and Detergent Assn. U.S.A. (chmn. bd.). Mem. Christian Reformed Ch. (elder). Clubs: Peninsular, Cascade, Lotus (dir., v.p.) (Grand Rapids); Economic (Detroit); Cat Cay (Bahamas); La Mirador (Switzerland); Capitol Hill (Washington); Macatawa Yacht (Holland). Home: 7186 Windy Hill Rd Grand Rapids MI 49506 Office: 7575 E Fulton St Ada MI 49355

VAN ARSDELL, RONALD DORR, physician; b. Lexington, Ky., Apr. 2, 1929; s. Roger Allen and Henrietta Estelle (Jacobs) Van A.; student Atlantic Union Coll., S. Lancaster, Mass., 1946-49; B.A., Andrews U., Berrien Springs, Mich., 1950; postgrad. Walla Walla (Wash.) Coll., 1950-52; M.D., Howard U., 1956; m. Jeannette Evelyn Drake, Aug. 19, 1956; children—Kent, Brent, Lance. Intern, Loma Linda U., 1956-57; gen. practice medicine, Bourbon, Mo., 1957-59, Joliet, Ill., 1965—; missionary doctor, Thailand, 1959-64; faculty Chgo. Med. Sch., 1970—. Mem. adv. com. Andrews U. Mem. A.M.A., Ill., Will Grundy County med. socs., Am. Coll. Emergency Physicians, Alpha Omega Alpha. Home: Route 3 Division St Lockport IL 60441 Office: 2000 Glenwood St Joliet IL 60435

VAN ARSDELL, STEPHEN COTTRELL, accountant; b. Champaign, Ill., Aug. 28, 1950; s. Paul Marion and Sophia Wilsford (Smith) Van A.; B.S., U. Ill., 1972, M.A.S., 1973. Research asst. Financial Accounting Standards Bd., Stamford, Conn., 1973-74, tech. asst. to chmn., 1974-75, cons., 1976; accountant Haskins & Sells, Chgo., 1975-76, 76—; instr. CPA review course DePaul U., Chgo., 1976. Haskins and Sells grantee, 1972-73; C.P.A., Ill. Mem. Am. Inst. C.P.A.'s, Am. Accounting Assn., Ill. State Soc. C.P.A.'s, Phi Kappa Phi, Beta Alpha Psi, Beta Gamma Sigma, Sigma Iota Epsilon. Office: 200 E Randolph St Chicago IL 60601

VAN BEVER, ROGER ADOLPH, supr. edn.; b. Detroit, Dec. 18, 1924; s. Adolph and Marie Louise (Couvreur) Van B.; A.B., Wayne State U., 1949, B.S. in Edn., 1950, M.Ed., 1954, Ed.D., 1974; m. Jean Marie Van De Walle, Apr. 11, 1950; children—Steven R., Susan E. Tchr. sci. Detroit Pub. Schs., 1950-63, asst. prin. elementary sch., 1963-69, program coordinator, 1964-68, supr. sci. edn. elementary schs., 1969—, supr. edntl. broadcasting, tchr. tng. specialist, 1969-70. Instr. Wayne State U., 1955-59; cons. in field. Served with AUS, 1943-46. Mem. Nat., Mich. Met. Detroit (pres. 1976-77) sci. tchrs. assns., Phi Delta Kappa. Author: Discovering Science Series, K-6, 1970; Time Without Clocks, 1970. Home: 480 Elizabeth Ct Grosse Pointe Farms MI 48236

VAN BIJLEVELT, HENDRIK KAREL, computer co. exec.; b. Taruntung, Indonesia, Mar. 10, 1940; s. Johan George and Johanna Barbara (Boedart) Van B.; came to U.S., 1973; student Tech. U., Voorburg, Holland, 1954-58, Royal Acad. Naval Engring., Vlissingen, Holland, 1958-62; m. Edith Louise Verwoord, May 30, 1970; 1 son, Michiel Christiaan. Apprentice to 2d engr. Royal Interocean Lines, Hong Kong, 1962-67; project mgr. heating, ventilating and air-conditioning systems Van Swaay Co., The Hague, Holland, 1967-69; sales mgr. L.P.G. Den Hartog, The Hague, 1969-70; computer ops. support engr. Control Data Corp., Holland, 1970-72, Mpls., 1972—; tchr. CDC computer refrigeration systems. Mem. Free Netherlands Com., 1968. Republican. Inventor job time monitor. Home: 735 Blue Gentian Rd Mendota Heights MN 55120 Office: 7401 Bush Lake Rd Edina MN 55435

VAN BLARICOM, ROBERT PERRY, indsl. co. exec.; b. Salem, Ohio, Aug. 19, 1910; s. Stephen N. and Maude (Griselle) V.; student Ohio State U., 1929-33; m. Janice Kirk, May 16, 1936; children—Nan, Katrina (Mrs. Richard Inar Jensen), J. Kirk, Daniel T. With Durametallic Corp., 1935—, v.p., dir. mktg., Kalamazoo, 1961—. Mem. Am. Inst. Chem. Engrs., Sigma Alpha Epsilon (nat. pres. 1971-73). Methodist. Mason. Home: 527 Lodge Ln Kalamazoo MI 49009 Office: 2104 Factory St Kalamazoo MI 49001

VAN BUSKIRK, CARROLL CHARLES, city ofcl.; b. Avard, Okla., Oct. 30, 1927; s. Charles and Cora (Mikels) Van B.; B.S., Okla. State U., 1951; m. Haldis Barstad, June 6, 1953; children—Linda Rae, Steven Charles, Kent Jonathan. With Home Stake Co's, 1953-56; gen. mgr. Bison Oil Co., Inc., 1956-69; city mgr., Independence, Kans., 1969—. Kiwanian. Home: 2112 N 8th St Independence KS 67301 Office: City Hall Independence KS 67301

VAN BUSKIRK, EDMUND LINFORD, ophthalmologist; b. Ft. Wayne, Ind., Oct. 15, 1907; s. Edmund Michael and Mary Louise (Schwartz) Van B.; A.B., Albion Coll., 1929; B.S., Ind. U., 1932, M.D., 1933, M.D. cum laude, 1935; m. Dorothy E. Deming, Jan. 30, 1930; children—Nancy (Mrs. James W. Treacy), Joan (Mrs. James W. Tanner), E. Michael. Intern Meth. Hosp., Ft. Wayne, 1933, St. Vincent's Hosp., Indpls., 1933-34; resident in opthalmology Ind. U. Med. Center, 1934-36; practice medicine specializing in ophthalmology Arnett Clinic, Lafayette, Ind., 1936-77, pres. Arnett Clinic and Hosp., Inc., 1949, 55, 61, 62, 63; pvt. practice, Lafayette, 1977—; mem. staff St. Elizabeth, Lafayette, Home, Purdue U. Student Health hosps., Lafayette. Cons. Selective Service Bd. Ind., 1943-46; pres. West Lafayette Bd. Health, 1940-75. Diplomate Am. Bd. Ophthalmology. Fellow A.C.S., Am. Acad. Ophthalmology and Otolaryngology; overseas fellow Royal Soc. Medicine; mem. Soc. Eye Surgeons, Ind. Acad. Ophthalmology and Otolaryngology, Indpls. Soc. Ophthalmology and Otolaryngology, Chgo. Ophthal. Soc., Am. Soc. Human Genetics, Pan-Am. Assn. Ophthalmology, N.Y. Acad. Sci. Assn. for Research in Vision and Ophthamology, Contact Lens Assn. Ophthalmology, Inc., Ind. Med. Assn. (chmn. conservation of vision com. 1967). Elk. Clubs: Lafayette Country, Ind. Skeet. Editorial bd. Ind. State Med. Jour., 1939-44. Contbr. articles to profl. jours. Home: 1301 Ravinia Rd West Lafayette IN 47906 Office: 2600 Greenbush St Lafayette IN 47902

VANCE, ARTHUR LESLIE, banker; b. Cleve., Dec. 20, 1925; s. Charles Wallace and Julia (McFarland) V.; student Kent State U., 1946-48; J.D., Cleve. State U., 1952; m. Marilyn E. Murrell, July 31, 1948; children—Wendy A., Arthur M. Trust officer Lawyers Title Ins. Corp., Cleve., 1950-68; asst. to supt. of schs., Shaker Heights, Ohio, 1968-70; asst. v.p. Union Commerce Bank, Cleve., 1970-73, Society Nat. Bank, 1973-76, Shaker Savs. Assn., 1976—. Trustee Nat. Fedn. Settlements, 1960-65, Fedn. Community Planning, 1970—; mem. pres.'s adv. bd. SBA, Cleve., 1972—; mem. vis. com. social and behavioral scis. Case Western Res. U., Cleve. Served with USAAF, 1943-46. Mem. Am. Bankers Assn., Alpha Phi Alpha. Clubs: Cleve. City, Cleve. Racquet; Chargin Valley Hunt. Home: 16960 Chillicothe Rd Chagrin Falls OH 44022 Office: Shaker Savs Assn 20133 Farnsleigh Rd Shaker Heights OH 44122

VANCE, HERBERT A., pub.; b. Brooklyn, Aug. 29, 1901; s. William and Jane (Brown) V.; B.S., St. Lawrence U., Canton, N.Y., 1924; m. Dorothy J. Jones, Dec. 18, 1942; children—Herbert A., Jr., William Colkin. Statistician Bankers Trust Co., N.Y.C.; sec., treas. Ault & Wiborg Co., Cin.; gen. mgr. R.H. Donnelley Corp., N.Y.C.; chmn. bd., dir., pub. Vance Pub. Corp., dir. Hartford Plaza Bank, Chgo. Trustee Lincoln (Ill.) Coll. Served as comdr., U.S. Navy, 1943-46. Recipient U.S. Treas. Award, War Finance, 1945, Alumni citation St. Lawrence U. Clubs: St. Lawrence University; Racquet, Union League, Chicago (Chgo.); Farmington Country (Charlottsville, Va.); Knollwood Country, Onwentsia (Lake Forest, Ill.). Home: 791 Hawthorne Ln Lake Forest IL 60045 Office: 300 W Adams St Chicago IL 60606

VANCE, JOAN EMILY JACKSON (MRS. NORVAL E. VANCE), educator; b. Anderson, Ind., Feb. 25, 1925; d. Virgil S. and Hannah (Hall) Jackson; B.S., Ball State U., 1947, M.A., 1955; m. Norval E. Vance, Aug. 17, 1955; 1 son, Bill E. Tchr. art and phys. edn. Winchester (Ind.) High Sch., 1948-50, 50-52, Wheatfield (Ind.) Elementary and High Sch., 1952-54; tchr. Eaton (Ind.) Elementary and High Sch., 1954—; tchr. elementary art, Elwood, Ind., 1954—, bilingual-bi-cultural migrant sch., summers 1969—; exhibited in group shows at Erica's Gallery, John Herron. Anderson Fine Art Center, state shows, street fairs. Mem. council Hoosier Salon, Indpls. Mus. Art. Recipient First prize Anderson Fine Arts Center show, 1975. Mem. Nat., Western art edn. assns., Ind. Art Tchrs. Assn. (mem. council), Anderson Art League (pres. 1967-68, 76—) Anderson Soc. Artists (v.p.), Elwood Art League (pres. 1960-70), Brown County Gallery, Brown County Guild, Delta Kappa Gamma, Delta Theta Tau. Home: Route 1 Box 48 Frankton IN 46044 Office: Elwood Community School 1630 Main St Elwood IN 46036

VAN CONANT, DARREL LEE, systems specialist; b. Detroit, Dec. 8, 1934; s. Ivy L. and Myrtle Lois (Clark) V.; student Wayne State U., 1956-57, U. Mich., 1957; B.S. in Math., Mich. State U., 1958; M.B.A., Eastern Mich. U., 1973; m. Linda Marie Oppenhuizen, June 15, 1963; children—Susan, Peter, Ruth, Matthew. Tchr. math high schs. Marysville, Mich., 1959-60, Fremont, Mich., 1960-62, Warren, Mich., 1962-63; systems engr. IBM, Lansing, Mich., 1963-64; systems analyst Consumers Power Co., Jackson, Mich., 1964-74; systems specialist Burroughs Corp., Detroit, 1974—. NSF fellow, summer 1963. Mem. Assn. Computer Machinery, Toastmasters Club (exec. bd., chpt. pres. 1968). Mem. Christian Reformed Ch. (sec. deacons 1969-71). Home: 15251 Farmbrook Plymouth MI 48170 Office: 707 W Milwaukee Av Detroit MI 48202

VAN CURLER, DONALD EDWARD, architect; b. Pontiac, Mich., Apr. 13, 1931; s. Raymond and Cornelia (Vanderzyl) Van C.; B.Arch., U. Mich., 1960; m. Charlotte Kunzli, Apr. 14, 1956; 1 dau., Claudine. Mem. tool design dept. P.R. Mallory & Co., Indpls., 1951-52; draftsman, designer Charles M. Valentine Architect, Marysville, Mich., 1954-55; draftsman Wyeth & Harmon, Inc., Port Huron, Mich., 1955-56; designer James H. Livingston Architect, Ann Arbor, Mich., 1956-59; partner Hammett Assos. in Architecture, 1959-61; practice as Donald E. Van Curler, Architect, 1961—; partner Old Orchard Assos., real estate developers, Flying Dutchman Mgmt. Co. Inc.; pres. Flying Dutchman Motor Inn, Inc. Pres. Ann Arbor Research Inst., Modular Bldg. Research Found. Served with AUS, 1952-54. Registered architect, Mich., Ind., Ohio, Pa., Ill., Ga., Ky., Miss., Wis., Tenn., Ala., Tex., S.C. Mem. Soc. Am. Registered Architects, AIA, Nat. Rifle Assn., Soc. Archtl. Historians, Mich. Soc. Architects, Phi Kappa Phi, Tau Sigma Delta. Republican. Baptist. Important works include restaurants, apt. bldgs. shopping centers, municipal bldgs. Home: 120 Packard St Ann Arbor MI 48104 Office: 2000 Hogback Ann Arbor MI 48104

VANDEBERG, JOHN THOMAS, mgr., chemist; b. Great Falls, Mont., Aug. 27, 1939; s. Harvey J. and Ruth M. (Rollings) Vandeberg; B.A., Carroll Coll., Helena Mont., 1962, M.S., Loyola U., Chgo., 1966, Ph.D., 1969; m. Donna M. Hoff, Sept. 7, 1963; children—Simone, Colette. Mgmt. Devel., U. Chgo., 1970. Chemist, DeSoto Inc., DesPlaines, Ill., 1964-66, research chemist, 1966-68, sr. research chemist, 1968-69, tech. mgr., analytical chemistry, 1969-73, mgr. research service dept., 1973—. Pres., Soc. Applied Spectroscopy, Chgo., 1974-75; chmn. sci. advisory com., Oakton Community Coll., 1975-77; chmn. Chemistry Advisory Com., Loyola U., 1977—; ASTM Task Group chmn., 1973—; chmn. infrared spectroscopy com. Chgo. Soc. for Coating Tech., 1976—. Mem. AAAS, Am. Chem. Soc., Soc. for Applied Spectrosocopy, Am. Soc. Testing Materials, Fedn. of Soc. for Coating Tech., Sigma Xi, Forest Grove Racquet and Swim Club. Recipient Roon Found. award, 1965; Societies for Coatings Tech. award, 1968; author: Infrared Spectroscopy—Its Use In The Coatings Industry, 1969; contbr. articles in field. Home: 415 W Oakwood Dr Barrington IL 60010 Office: 1700 Mt Prospect Rd DesPlaines IL 60018

VAN DE LEUV, JOHN HENRI, physician; b. Batavia, Dutch East Indies, Oct. 1, 1926; s. Henri Richard and Wilhelmina Cornelia (Kleef) Van de L.; Candidaats Medicine, U. Amsterdam, Holland, 1947, postgrad., 1947-51; B.Sc., Sir George Williams Coll., 1953; M.D., McGill U., 1957; m. Johanna N. Van Beekum, Aug. 3, 1951; children—Jacqueline, Mark, Monique, Erik. Came to U.S., 1962, naturalized, 1967. Intern, Detroit Meml. Hosp., 1957-58, resident obstetrics and gynecology, 1958-59; gen. practice medicine, Port Coquitlam, B.C., Can., 1959-62, Oxford, Mich., 1962-73; chmn. outpatient care com. St. Joseph Mercy Hosp., Pontiac, Mich., 1970-73, mem. exec. com., chief div. emergency care, 1971-73; pres. Physicians Emergency Care Group, 1968-73; pres. Wyandotte (Mich.) Emergency Physicians, 1974—; dir. emergency dept. Wyandotte Gen. Hosp., 1975—. Mem. exec. com., chmn. com. emergency facilities Oakland County Emergency Med. Services; chmn. critical care com. Wayne County Emergency Med. Services, 1975-77, mem. exec. com., 1975—; mem. Task Force Regional Emergency Med. Services Southeast Mich.; chmn. Down River Hosp. Com. on Emergency Med. Service and Disasters. Mem. Am. Coll. Emergency Physicians (dir. 1968-73, cons., editorial bd. jour. 1974—, chmn. hosp. com. 1974—, pres. elect Mich. chpt. 1976-77), A.M.A., Am. Acad. Family Physicians, Mich. State, Oakland County (alt. del. 1970-71, chmn. com. emergency med. services, Wayne County med. socs. Editor McGill Med. Jour., 1956-57, Quart. Report and Jour. Am. Coll. Emergency Physicians, 1969-72. Home: 75 Chippewa Trail Lake Orion MI 48035 Office: Emergency Dept Wyandotte Gen Hosp Wyandotte MI 48192

VAN DE MARK, PAUL LAVERNE, personnel exec.; b. Sterling, Ill., May 31, 1922; s. Fred Vernon and Maureen (Maxfield) Van De M.; B.A., Northeastern Ill. U., 1976; m. Mar jorie Boyle, Apr. 12, 1944; children—Jon Douglas, Carol Ann Van De Mark Hillary, Rebecca Sue. Position classifier USAF, Dayton, Ohio, 1946-60, personnel officer, 1960-63; personnel officer Air Force Systems Command, Chgo., 1963-65, Def. Logistics Agy., Dept. Def., Chgo., 1965—; spl. assignment on contract adminstrn. nat. planning group Dept. Def., 1965, regional coordinator Stability of Civilian Employment/Priority Placement Program, 1965—. Bd. dirs. N.W. Suburban Headstart Program, 1973; mem. personnel policy forum Bur. Nat. Affairs, 1975—. Served with USAF, 1943-45. Mem. Chgo. Profl. Devel. Assn. (pres. 1972). Recipient Meritorious Civilian Service awards USAF, 1964, Def. Logistic Agy., 1966. Home: 601 S Mt Prospect Rd Des Plaines IL 60016 Office: O'Hare Internat Airport PO Box 66475 Chicago IL 60666

VAN DEMARK, ROBERT EUGENE, orthopedic surgeon; b. Alexandria, S.D., Nov. 14, 1913; s. Walter Eugene and Esther Ruth (Marble) Van D.; S.B., U. S.D., 1936; A.B., Sioux Falls (S.D.) Coll., 1937; M.B., Northwestern U., 1938, M.D., 1939; M.S. in Orthopedic Surgery, U. Minn., 1943; m. Bertie Thompson, Dec. 28, 1940; children—Ruth Elaine, Robert, Richard. Interne Passavant Meml. Hosp., Chgo., 1938-39; fellow orthopedic surgery, Mayo Found., 1939-43; 1st asst. orthopedic surgery Mayo Clinic, 1942-43; orthopedic surgeon Sioux Falls (S.D.), 1946—; attending orthopedic surgeon McKennan Hosp., pres. med. staff, 1954, 70, attending orthopedic surgeon Sioux Valley Hosp., pres. staff, 1951-52; clin. prof. orthopedic surgery U. S.D., 1953—; med. dir. Crippled Children's Hosp. and Sch.; chief hand surgery clinic VA Hosp., Sioux Falls. Served from lt. to maj. AUS, 1943-46. Diplomate Am. Bd. Orthopedic Surgery. Fellow A.C.S. (pres. S.D. chpt. 1952, 1953); mem. Am. Assn. Med. Colls., Assn. Orthopaedic Chmn., Am. Acad. Orthopedic Surgery, Clin. Orthopedic Soc., Am. Assn. Hand Surgery, Assn. Mil. Surgeons U.S., Am. Acad. Cerebral Palsy, S.D. Med. Assn. (pres. 1974-75), Sioux Falls Dist. Med. Soc., S.A.R., 500 1st Families Am., Sigma Xi, Phi Chi. Lutheran. Clubs: Optimist; Minnehahn Country. Editor S.D. Jour. Medicine. Contbr. to med. jours. Home: 320 S Prairie St Sioux Falls SD 57104 Office: 1701 S Minnesota Ave Sioux Falls SD 57105

VANDENBERG, KENNETH WAYNE, power plant adminstr.; b. Otley, Iowa, Feb. 5, 1933; s. John P. and Margret (Klein) V.; student Central Coll., Pella, Iowa, 1951-52; B.S., Iowa State U., 1955; m. Arla Jane VanDoorninck, June 10, 1955; children—Mark, Eric, Jack. Technologist, Shell Chem. Corp., Houston, 1955-57; plant supt. Iowa Power & Light Co., Des Moines, 1957—. Mem. Des Moines Bus. and Indsl. Mgmt. Club, Iowa Engring. Soc., Nat. Soc. Profl. Engrs., Am. Inst. Chem. Engrs. Mem. United Ch. Christ. Kiwanian. Home: 1109 NW 4th St Ankeny IA 50021 Office: Iowa Power & Light Co 823 Walnut St Des Moines IA 50303

VANDEPORTAELE, DANIEL D., educator; b. Staden, Belgium, May 16, 1931; s. Maurice and Martha (Decaestecker) V.; A.B., Ypres; St. Vincent's Coll., 1949; Ph.B., Bruges Inst. Philosophy, 1951; M.A., Louvain, Belgium, 1957; Ph.D., U. Chgo., 1968; m. Rogelia A. Napalit, June 18, 1965; 1 dau., Arlene. Came to U.S., 1963, naturalized, 1966. Sr. instr. dept. sociology St. Louis U., Baguio City, P.I., 1959-63; research asst. Population Research and Tng. Center, U. Chgo., 1964-67; asst. prof. sociology Roosevelt U., 1967-68, asst. prof. sociology Ill. Inst. Tech., Chgo., 1968-73, asso. prof., 1973—, acting chmn. sociology dept., 1970-71, chmn. dept., 1971-75; vis. prof. Office for Population Studies, U. San Carlos, Cebu City, Philippines, 1976-77. Cons. forecasting office Ill. Bell Telephone Co., summer, 1966. Mem. Population Assn. Am., Philippine Sociol. Assn., Internat. Soc. for Technology Assessment, AAAS, Am. Sociol. Assn., Internat. Union Sci. Study Population. Author: A Population Study of Suburban Chicago, Ill., 1966. Contbr. articles in field of demography to profl. jours. Home: 3100 S Michigan Ave Chicago IL 60616

VANDERGRIFT, JAMES BARRETT, indsl. rubber distbn. co. exec.; b. Pitts., Aug. 2, 1941; s. James George and Alice (Mossman) V.; B.S.B.A., Pa. State U., 1964; m. Jane Hanna, Mar. 18, 1972; 1 son, Tuck. Mem. staff sales and advt. promotions Armstrong Cork Co., Lancaster, Pa., 1966-71; eastern sales rep. rigid plastics div. Crown Zellerbach Corp., Devon, Pa., 1971-73; pres. Hanna Rubber Co., Kansas City, Mo., 1973—; v.p. Hanna Real Estate Devel. Corp. Mem. Kansas City Philharmonic, Friends of Art, Pa. State Alumni Assn., Kansas City Builders Assn., Nat. Right to Work Com. Presbyterian. Club: Rotary (Kansas City, Mo.). Collector classic English and Am. automobiles and transp. artifacts. Home: 1017 W 57th St Kansas City MO 64113 Office: 1512 Main St Kansas City MO 64108

VANDER JAGT, GUY ADRIAN, congressman; b. Cadillac, Mich., Aug. 26, 1931; s. Harry and Marie (Copier) Vander J.; B.A., Hope Coll., 1953; B.D., Yale, 1957; LL.D., U. Mich., 1960; m. Carol Doorn, Apr. 4, 1964; 1 dau., Virginia Marie. Minister, Tustin Presbyn. Ch., 1949-52, Cadillac Congl. Ch., 1957; admitted to Mich. bar, 1960; asso. firm Warner, Norcross & Judd, Grand Rapids, Mich., 1960-64; Mem. Mich. Senate, 1965-66; mem. 89th-95th Congresses from 9th Mich. Dist., mem. ways and means com., chmn. Nat. Republican Congl. Com. Named One of 5 Most Outstanding Young Men in Mich., Mich. Jr. C. of C., 1956. Mem. Mich., Wexford County, Grand Rapids bar assns. Republican. Mason, Rotarian (hon.). Office: 2334 Rayburn House Office Bldg Washington DC 20515

VANDER KAM, CORNELIUS, bldg. supply co. exec.; b. Grand Rapids, Mich., Sept. 11, 1930; s. Gerrit and Jeanette (Buys) Vander K.; student U. Mich.; m. Frances A. Vanden Berg, Oct. 16, 1953; children—Barbara, Steven, Thomas, Rick. Advt. mgr. Young Calvinist Fedn., 1950-55; pres. Edcor Foam Plastics, 1965-67, Capitol Products of Grand Rapids, Inc. (Mich.) 1960—. Treas. bd. trustees Unity Christian Sch., 1967-70, Grandville Christian Sch., 1976—; trustee Pine Rest Found., 1976—. Served with USNG, 1950-56. Republican. Mem. Christian Reformed Ch. Home: 5900 Wilson St SW Grandville MI 49418 Office: 440 Kirtland St SW Grand Rapids MI 49507

VANDER KOLK, KENNETH JAY, obstetrician-gynecologist; b. Zeeland, Mich., Aug. 10, 1928; s. William A. and Johanna (Freriks) Vander K.; B.S., U. Mich., 1950, M.D., 1953; m. Arloa Jean Vander Velde, June 26, 1951; children—Ronald Dale, Kathy Jo, Judy Kay, James Alan. Intern, St. Mary's Hosp., Grand Rapids, Mich., 1953-54; practice medicine specializing in family practice, Petoskey, Mich., 1954-55; resident in obstetrics and gynecology Butterworth Hosp., Grand Rapids, 1957-60, mem. staff, 1960—, dir. obstetrics-gynecology edn., 1966—; practice medicine specializing in obstetrics and gynecology, Grand Rapids, 1960—; asso. prof. Mich. State U. Sch. Human Medicine, 1973—; Mem. central med. adv. bd. Salvation Army; bd. dirs. Planned Parenthood. Mem. consistory Central Ref. Ch., 1975—. Served with MC, USAF, 1955-57. Diplomate Am. Bd. Obstetrics and Gynecology. Fellow Am. Coll. Obstetricians and Gynecologists; mem. AMA, Mich., Kent County med. socs., Am. Assn. Maternal and Infant Health, Central Assn. Obstetricians and Gynecologists, Mich. Soc. Obstetricians and Gynecologists, Central Travel Club Obstetricians and Gynecologists, U. Mich. Alumni Assn. (gov. 1973—). Club: Blythefield Country. Home: 7183 Davies Dr Rockford MI 49341 Office: 21 Michigan St NE Grand Rapids MI 49503

VANDER MOLEN, ROBERT LAVERNE, JR., educator, poet; b. Grand Rapids, Mich., Apr. 23, 1947; s. Robert LaVerne and Marjorie R. (Mollo) Vander M.; B.A. in Advt., Mich. State U., 1971; M.F.A. in English, U. Oreg., 1973. Instr. in English, Grand Rapids Jr. Coll., 1975—; poetry books include: The Lost Book, 1968; Variations, a Poem, 1970; The Pavilion and Other Poems, 1974; Along the River and Other Poems, 1978; Circumstances, 1978. Recipient R.L. Newberger Writing award, Oreg., 1973, Dyer-Ives Found. Poetry award, Mich., 1975; fellow MacDowell Colony, N.H., 1973. Mem. Asso. Writing Programs, 10 Mile River Poets Coop., MacDowell Colony. Home: 2215 Ducoma Dr Grand Rapids MI 49504 Office: Apt 603 68 Ransom St NE Grand Rapids MI 49503

VANDERPOOL, WARD MELVIN, mgmt. and mktg. cons.; b. Oakland, Mo., Jan. 20, 1915; s. Oscar B. and Clara (McGuire) V.; M.E.E., Tulane U.; m. Lee Kendall, July 7, 1935. Vice pres. charge sales Van Lang Brokerage, Los Angeles, 1934-38; mgr. agrl. div. Dayton Rubber Co., Chgo., 1939-48; pres., gen. mgr. Vee Mac Co., Rockford, Ill., 1948—; pres., dir. Zipout, Inc., Rockford, 1951—, Wife Save Products, Inc., 1959—; chmn. bd. Zipout Internat., Kenvan Inc., 1952—, Shevan Corp., 1951—, Atlas Internat. Corp.; pres. Global Enterprises Ltd., Global Assos. Ltd.; chmn. bd. Atlas Chem. Corp., Merzart Industries Ltd.; trustee Ice Crafter Trust, 1949—; dir. Atlas Chem. Internat. Ltd., Shrip Tool Internat. Ltd. Mem. adv. bd. Nat. Security Council. Mem. Internat. Swimming Hall of Fame. Mem. Nat. (dir. at large), Rock River (past pres.) sales execs., Sales and Mktg. Execs. Internat. (dir.), Am. mgmt. assn., Rockford Engring. Soc., Am. Tool Engrs., Internat. Acad. Aquatic Art (dir.), Am. Inst. Mgmt. (pres. council), Am. Ordnance Assn., Internat. Platform Assn., Ill. C. of C. Clubs: Mason, Shriners, Elks, Rockford Swim, Forest Hills Country, Exec., Elmcrest Country, Pyramid, Dolphin, Marlin. Home: 374 Parkland Dr SE Cedar Rapids IA 52403 Office: Boz 242A Auburn St Rd Rockford IL 61103 also 101 Richmond St W Suite 602 Toronto ON Canada

VANDERSTEEN, PAUL RICHARD, dermatologist; b. St. Paul, Sept. 2, 1936; s. Rudolph Richard and Mabel Clare (Tybering) V.; B.S. summa cum laude, Hamline U., 1958; M.D., U. Minn., 1962; m. Bette Jean Nelson, June 16, 1963; children—David, Daniel, Peter, Rachel. Intern, Mpls. Gen. Hosp., 1962-63; resident in dermatology, Mayo Clinic, Rochester, Minn., 1967-70, practice gen. medicine, Minot, N.D., 1965-67; staff Med. Arts Clinic, Minot, 1965-67; practice medicine specializing in dermatology, Fargo (N.D.) Clinic, 1970—; fellow in dermatology, Mayo Clinic, 1967-70; clin. asso. prof. dermatology, U. N.D.; clin. asst. prof. dermatology, U. Minn. Med. Sch. Mem. St Paul Jr. C. of C., Coll. Ct. of Honor. Served with USPHS, 1963-65. Recipient L.A. Brunsting award for outstanding research in dermatology, 1970. Fellow Am. Acad. Dermatology; mem. 1st Dist. Med. Soc., Am., N.D. State med. assns., Minn. Dermatological Soc., N.C., Noah Worcester dermatological socs., Soc. Investigative Dermatology, Dermatologic Therapy Assn., Dermatology Found., Beta Beta Beta, Kappa Phi. Republican. Lutheran. Club: Eagles. Contbr. numerous articles in field. Home 155 S Woodcrest Dr Fargo NE 58102 Office: Fargo Clinic 737 Broadway Dr Fargo ND 58102

VANDER VELDE, JOHN JACOB, librarian; b. Emporia, Kans., Aug. 12, 1936; s. Jacob and Clara Joy (Coverdill) Vander V.; certificate with honors Yale U., 1960; B.A. (Curli-Q Hon. scholar), Kans. State Tchrs. Coll., Emporia, 1967, M.L.S., 1968; postgrad. in German and Russian langs. Clk., Vander Velde Bros. Grocery, Emporia, 1950-58; linguistic and adminstrv. specialist USAF, Lackland AFB and Goodfellow AFB, Tex., Okinawa and Taiwan, 1959-65; asst. cataloger William Allen White Meml. Library, Kans. State Tchrs. Coll., 1966-68; cataloger-bibliographer Farrell Library, Kans. State U., Manhattan, 1968-69, acquisitions librarian, 1969-77, spl. projects librarian, editorial cons., 1977—; pvt. piano tchr., Emporia, 1956-58. Editor Kans. State U. Library Bibliography Series, 1971—; ann. indexer Mil. Affairs, 1970—. Served with USAF, 1959-65. Hon. citizen W. Tex. Boys Ranch, Tankersly. Mem. ALA, Kans. Library Assn. (past chmn. intellectual freedom com., sec.-treas. coll. and univ. libraries sect. 1975-76), Music Library Assn., Assn. Coll. and Research Libraries, Kans. State U. Library Staff Assn. (editor Farrell Footnotes quarterly bull. 1969-70, pres. 1968, 72), Kans. State U. Hist. Soc., Kans. Museums Assn., Riley County Hist. Soc., Alumni Assn. Kans. State Tchrs. Coll., Beta Phi Mu (sec. Beta Epsilon chpt. 1974-76). Presbyterian. Home: 3129 Lundin Dr Manhattan KS 66502 Office: Kans State U Library Manhattan KS 66502

VANDER WERF, DONALD GEORGE, county data processing ofcl.; b. Colton, S.D., Dec. 27, 1934; s. Chris and Alice (Zuiderhof) Vander W.; B.S., Calvin Coll., 1969; m. Norma Fae DeRuiter, Mar. 8, 1958; children—Pamela, Michael, Rebecca. Programmer Pacific Mut. Life Ins. Co., Los Angeles, 1958-61; programmer analyst Long Beach (Cal.) Unified Sch. Dist., 1961; sr. systems analyst Univac div. Sperry Rand Corp., Grand Rapids, Mich., 1963-70; dir. edn. Cascada Data, Inc., Grand Rapids, 1970-74; sr. systems analyst Amway Corp., Ada, Mich., 1974; data processing coordinator County of Kent, Grand Rapids, 1974—. tchr. computer programming Grand Rapids Jr. Coll.; cons. in field. Served with AUS, 1957-58, 61-62. Mem. Christian Ref. Ch. (past pres. deaconate; treas.; chmn. finance com., elder). Author programming manual. Home: 9354 Hanna Lake Ave Caledonia MI 49316

VANDERWIER, TAMSEN RAINER FITZGERALD, chem. co. ofcl.; b. Kalamazoo, Feb. 6, 1929; d. James Elliott and Helene (Minogue) Rainer; student Grand Rapids Jr. Coll., 1947-48; m. Gordon E. Fitzgerald, Feb. 10, 1951 (div. 1966); children—Steven C., Kathleen M., Carol Ann, Elizabeth L.; m. 2nd. Donald A. Vanderwier, Dec. 29, 1967 (div. 1971). With Mich. Bell Telephone Co., Grand Rapids, 1948-51, Fields Ednl. Enterprises, Grand Rapids, 1964-66, Bowman Assos., Grand Rapids, 1966-68; with Amway Corp., Ada, Mich., 1968—, mgr. pub. relations, 1973—. Vice pres. Grand Rapids chpt. Mich. Soc. Mental Health, 1973-77; adv. bd. Coll. IV, Grand Valley State Colls., Allendale, Mich. Mem. Pub. Relations Soc. Am. (v.p. West. Mich. chpt. 1974-75, Spl. Achievement award East Central dist. 1973), Direct Selling Assn. (chmn. communications com. 1977), Epsilon Sigma Alpha (pres. 1949-51). Conglist. Home: 1656 Wayside Dr SE Grand Rapids MI 49506 Office: 7676 E Fulton Rd Ada MI 49355

VAN DUZER, FRANKLIN KENNETH, real estate co. exec., food products co. exec.; b. Menlo, Iowa, Feb. 3, 1919; s. Thomas Ralph and Ethel Beatrice (Mount) V.; m. Sharon Marie Eide, Dec. 7, 1973; children—Julie (Mrs. James B. Elting), Marilyn (Mrs. Steven W. Johnson); stepchildren—Richard, Dennis, David, Valerie. Farmer, Mason City, Iowa, 1946—; pres. Ris-Van Fertilizer Co., Belmond, Iowa, 1958-62; pres. Legreid Fertilizer Co., Mason City, 1962-64; pres. Ris-Van Realty & Ins. Co., Clear Lake, Iowa, 1964—; partner Clear Lake Grain Co., 1972—. Dir., Guardsman Life Ins. Co., Des Moines, Community State Bank, Clear Lake, North Central Iowa Pork Producers, Inc., Clear Lake. Served with Paratroopers, AUS, 1942-46. Decorated Purple Heart medal, Bronze Star medal. Mem. North Central Ia. Bd. Realtors (pres. 1973), Clear Lake C. of C. (v.p. 1969), Am. Legion, VFW. Lutheran. Elk, Lion. Home: Lakeview Dr Ventura IA 50482 Office: 10 S 4th St Clear Lake IA 50428

VAN DYKE, WILLIAM ELBERT, utility co. exec.; b. Sedalia, Mo., Oct. 31, 1927; s. Frank Benjamin and Mary Irene (Sims) VanD.; B.S. in Elec. Engring., U. Mo., 1950, M.B.A., 1962; m. Patricia Joan Opp, Oct. 1, 1950; children—Beverly Joan, Melody Ann, Jeffrey Ray, Alan Frank. With Mo. Pub. Service Co., Kansas City, Mo., 1950—, field engr., 1950-51, indsl. engr., 1951-62, sales mgr., 1966-68, v.p., sales, 1968—. Past pres. Eastern Jackson Co. Jr. Achievement. Bd. dirs. Greater Kansas City Jr. Achievement, Nat. Food and Energy Council. Registered profl. engr., Mo. Mem. I.E.E.E. (elec. heating com.), Mo. Farm Electrification Council (dir., past pres.), Mo.-Kans. Elec. Assn. (past pres., dir.), Mo. Valley Elec. Assn. (market exec. officer). Methodist (past chmn. bd.). Rotarian (past pres.). Home: 603 E 3d St Lee's Summit MO 64063 Office: 10700 E Highway 50 Kansas City MO 64138

VAN EENENAAM, ROBERT DALE, dentist; b. Holland, Mich., Aug. 7, 1928; s. Charles Richard and Bernice (Vanden Brink) Van E.; B.A., Hope Coll., 1950; D.D.S., U. Detroit, 1954; m. Mary Catherine Johnson, June 13, 1953; children—Jeffrey Alan, Ann Patrice. Practice gen. dentistry, St. Joseph, Mich., 1956-59, Kalamazoo, 1959—. Mem. Athletic Bd. Portage No. High Sch., 1973—. Chmn. reelection campaign Wayne Sackett to Mich. Ho. of Reps., 1970. Served with Dental Corps USNR, 1954-56. Mem. Kalamazoo Valley, Mich. State dental socs., Am. Dental Assn., Psi Omega. Republican. Presbyn. (elder 1968-70). Elk, Lion, Kiwanian (pres. 1968). Home: 2711 Coachlite Portage MI 49081 Office: 3907 S Westnedge Kalamazoo MI 49008

VANEK, MIROSLAV, architect; b. Chgo., Apr. 17, 1927; s. Bretislav and Bozena (Klouda) V.; student Mich. State Coll., 1945; B.S. in Architecture, U. Ill., 1952; m. Camille B. Stepanek, May 17, 1952; children—Gary Miro, Paul Otto. Constrn. supt. Skidmore, Owings & Merrill, 1952-55; constrn. supt., chief draftsman Nicol & Nicol, Chgo., 1955-61, partner, v.p., 1964-69; mem. archtl. firm Pratt & Vanek, 1961-64; pres. Nicol & Nicol, Inc., 1969-73; pres. Nicol Nicol Chaney & Vanek, Inc., Chgo., 1973—; treas., dir. Quintan Enterprises, Inc., Evergreen Park, Ill., 1961—. Mem. Ill. Partners for Americas, serving as cons. architect on schs. for multi-handicapped children for São Paulo, Brazil. Mem. men's lay bd. Sch. Little Flower; chmn. Eisenberg Chgo. Boys Club. Served with USAAF, 1945-47. Mem. AIA, Am. Sokol Orgn. Constrn. Specifications Inst., Sch. Facilities Inst., Chgo. Assn. Commerce and Industry, Czechoslovak Soc. Am. Moose, Lion. Club: Architects (pres.) (Chgo.). Home: 24 E Harding Ave LaGrange Park IL 60525 Office: 332 S Michigan Ave Chicago IL 60604

VAN ETTEN, DONALD DEAN, surgeon; b. Orange City, Iowa, Mar. 10, 1934; s. Amos Donald and Ruth Luella (Cambier) Van E.; B.A., Hope Coll., 1956; M.D., U. Iowa, 1960; m. Verla Jean Vanderbush, June 21, 1957; children—Julie Kay, Kristen Jill, Karen Jo, Jeffrey Kent. Intern, then resident in gen. surgery Butterworth Hosp., Grand Rapids, Mich., 1960-65; missionary surgeon, Bahrein, 1966-69; practice medicine specializing in surgery, 1969—; partner Park Clinic, Mason City, Iowa, 1969—. Bd. dirs., pres. Alcoholism Coordinating Center, North Iowa Med. Center, Fellow A.C.S.; mem. Cerro Gordo County, Ia. med. socs., A.M.A., Christian Med. Soc. Kiwanian. Mem. Christian Ref. Ch. (consistory). Home: 18 Lakeview Dr Mason City IA 50401 Office: 116 N Washington St Mason City IA 50401

VAN GOOR, KORNELIUS, dermatologist; b. Hawthorne, N.J., Sept. 15, 1922; s. Andrew and Clara (Van Dyke) Van G.; B.S., Calvin Coll., 1943; M.D., U. Md., 1950, postgrad., 1951-54; m. Madeline Koster, June 27, 1947; children—Drew, James Edward, Judith Kay, Robert. Intern, Iowa U. Hosp., Iowa City, 1950-51; resident, U. Mich., Ann Arbor, 1951-54; practice medicine specializing in dermatology, Grand Rapids, Mich., 1954—; teaching asst., Mich. State U.; pres. Ole Taco, Inc. Served with inf. AUS, 1943-46. Mem. AMA, Mich. State, Kent County (del. to Mich. State Med. Soc., sec., treas., 1961-63) med. socs., Am. Acad. Dermatology, Mich. State Dermatol. Soc. Research, publs. on metabolism, pharmacology and therapeutic uses of gold compounds. Home: 2265 Onekema Dr SE Grand Rapids MI 49506 Office: 26 Sheldon St SE Grand Rapids MI 49503

VANGOR, DONALD WILLIAM, physician; b. Joliet, Ill., Jan. 26, 1938; s. Andrew John and Elizabeth Ann (Christofer) V.; B.S. in Pharmacy cum laude, U. Ill., 1958, M.D. cum laude, 1962. Intern, Milw. County Gen. Hosp., 1962-63; gen. practice medicine, Dells Clinic, Wisconsin Dells, Wis., 1966-69; mem. staff Divine Savior Hosp., Portage, Wis., 1969; mem. staff St. Clare's Hosp., Baraboo, Wis., 1967—, chief med. staff, 1973—; partner Med. Assos., Baraboo, 1971—; dir. Sauk County (Wis.) Emergency Med. Services, 1971—. Mem. South Central Areawide Emergency Services Council, 1973. Served to capt. M.C., USAF, 1963-66. Fellow Am. Acad. Family Practice; mem. A.M.A., Am. Profl. Practice Assn., Am. Acad. Family Physicians, Internat. Acad. Proctology, Med. Soc. State Wis., Sauk County Med. Soc. (pres. 1973), U. Ill. Alumni Assn. (life), Civil Aviation Med. Assn., Phi Delta Chi, Rho Chi, Phi Rho Sigma, Pi Kappa Epsilon. Lutheran. Rotarian. Club: Baraboo Country. Home: Route 1 Wisconsin Dells WI 53965 Office: 703 14th St Baraboo WI 53913

VAN HEMERT, DALE EDWIN, civic worker; b. Pella, Iowa, Nov. 10, 1926; s. William Simon and Thelma Beatrice (Secress) Van H.; student Drake U., 1972—; m. Arleen Ruth Tuttle, Apr. 15, 1950; children—Belinda Lou (Mrs. Leroy John Stephenson), Duane Leslie. Linotype operator Waverly Democrat, Iowa, 1944-48, Des Moines Register & Tribune, 1949—; treas. Iowa Assn. of Deaf, Des Moines, 1950-60, pres., 1960-70, 1st v.p., 1973-77 (award 1972). Trustee Iowa Assn. of Deaf Found. Fund, 1960-70. Mem. Nat. Assn. of Deaf, Nat. Fraternal Soc. of Deaf, Iowa Conf. for Hearing Impaired. Lutheran (sec. 1962—). Club: Des Moines Silent (sec. 1958-68). Home: 3316 Bel-Aire Rd Des Moines IA 50310

VAN HEULE, THOMAS JOSEPH, mfg. co. exec.; b. Chgo., Aug. 15, 1932; s. Emil Joseph and Vina Mary (Snowden) Van H.; B.B.A., Northwestern U., 1957; m. Nancy Jean Schulte, Dec. 29, 1956; children—Thomas Joseph, Patricia, Robert. Computer programmer Continental Casualty Co., Chgo., 1957-59; supr. programming and systems Honeywell, Inc., Chgo. and Detroit, 1959-67; sr. mgmt. cons. Peat, Marwick, Mitchel & Co., Chgo., 1967-70; mgr. info. systems Superior Concrete Accessories, Inc., Franklin Park, Ill., 1970-74, ops. mgr., 1974-76; mgr. mgmt. info. services Hammond Organ Co., Chgo., 1976—. Committeeman Boy Scouts Am. Served with AUS, 1951-53. Mem. Assn. Computing Machinery, Bull Terrier Club Am., Ft. Dearborn Bull Terrier Club (pres. 1971-72), Chi Phi. Roman Catholic. Home: 100 Woodbine Wilmette IL 60091 Office: 4200 Diversey St Chicago IL 60639

VAN HORN, LOUIS HAROLD, realtor; b. Greenville, Mich., Apr. 4, 1928; s. Adrian L. and Mildred (Davis) Van H.; Asso. Scis., Grand Rapids Jr. Coll. 1956, student, 1965; student Mich. State U., 1956-57, U. Mich. Extension, 1958; m. Christina F. Bogden, Oct. 15, 1969 (dec.

Jan. 1977); children—Sheila Kay, David Louis. Owner, Koncrete Tile Co., Burbank, Calif., 1946-48; salesman Donald Beardslee Real Estate, Greenville, 1948-50; with Gibson Refrigerator Co., 1952-53; mem. planning and scheduling dept. Gen. Motors 1952, Grand Rapids, 1953-54; builder, realtor, Greenville, 1955—; dir. Realtor Computer Services, subsidiary Nat. Assn. Real Estate Bds., 1971—, v.p., 1972—. City assessor, Greenville, 1958-60; mem. Greenville Zoning Bd., 1958-66, Greenville Planning Commn., 1970—; Montcalm County chmn. Republican Party, 1976—. Served with U.S. Army, 1950-52. Decorated Combat Infantry badge. Mem. Montcalm County Bd. Realtors, Farm and Land Brokers (pres. Mich. chpt. 1, 1971), Nat. Inst. Farm and Land Brokers (regional v.p. 1971-72, chmn. spl. services com. 1974, chmn. subcom. computers on real estate 1970, gov. 1975-77). Patentee instant pontoon bridge. Address: 311 W Washington St Greenville MI 48838

VAN HORNE, PIETER HAMMOND, lawyer; b. Chgo., Dec. 26, 1941; s. David E. and Marjorie N. (Peterson) van H.; student Williams Coll., 1959-61; B.A., Parsons Coll., 1963; J.D., Northwestern U., 1966; postgrad. Wayne State U.; m. Priscilla S. Kruse, Aug. 21, 1965; 1 dau., Jennifer Paige. Admitted to Mich. bar, 1967; atty. Penn Central Transp. Co., Detroit, 1966-71; asso. McInally, Rockwell & Brucker, profl. corp., Detroit, 1971-73, dir., shareholder McInally, Rockwell, Brucker, Newcombe & Wilke, profl. corp., Detroit, 1974-77; propr. Pieter Van Horne, Esq., 1977—; dir., counsel J. Broder Assos., Inc., Detroit, 1972—, Resistance Welder Corp., Bay City, Mich., 1973—. Guest lectr. U. Detroit Urban Law Clinic, 1969-70. Com. chmn. U.S. Senator Robert Griffin re-election 14th Congressional Dist., 1972, mem. re-election com. for Mich. Rep. William Bryant, 1972, 74. Bd. dirs., sec. Alexandrine House, Inc., drug treatment facility. Recipient certificate merit Fed. Defender Program, 1966, certificate of outstanding service Phi Alpha Delta, 1966; named Outstanding Young Man Grosse Point Jaycees, 1974, senator Jr. Chamber Internationale, 1975. Mem. Am., Detroit bar assns., State Bar Mich., Am. Trial Lawyer Assn., Am. Judicature Soc., U.S., Mich., Grosse Pointe Jaycees. Methodist (ch. sch. tchr., counsellor 1969-73, mem. adminstrv. bd. 1970-73, chmn. pastor parish relations com. 1970-73, youth fellowship counsellor 1973—). Home: 791 Lincoln St Grosse Pointe MI 48230 Office: 4472 City Nat Bldg Detroit MI 48226

VAN HORNE, WILLIAM EARL, internat. trade exec.; b. Hamilton, Ohio, Jan. 8, 1924; s. William Earl and Margaret Emily (Stevenson) V.; B.S. in Elec. Engring., Purdue U., 1948; M.B.A., U. Pa., 1950; m. Suzanne Ames Fitzgerald, June 24, 1950; children—William Earl, Thomas Fitzgerald. Indsl. electronics salesman Honeywell, Inc., 1950-52; sales mgr. Indsl. Nucleonics Corp., Columbus, Ohio, 1952-59; founder Keinath Instrument Co., 1960, pres., 1960-68; v.p. Brun Sensor Systems, Inc., Columbus, 1968-75; pres. Franklin/Far East div. Internat. Trade Group of Ohio, Inc., 1975—. Mem. Condr.'s Com. Columbus Symphony Orch. Served to 1st lt. USAAF, 1943-46. Mem. IEEE, Instrument Soc. Am., Ohio Hist. Soc., Soc. Ohio Commodores, Torch Club, Beta Gamma Sigma, Tau Bata Pi. Club: Rotary. Contbr. numerous articles to profl. and popular pubs. Patentee in field. Home: 1576 Guilford Rd Columbus OH 43221 Office: 100 E Broad St Columbus OH 43215

VAN HOUSEN, EDWARD IRVIN, banker; b. St. Paul, Mar. 4, 1922; s. William Ross and Ovidia (Iverson) Van H.; B.B.A., U. Minn., 1943; M.B.A., Harvard, 1947; m. Dorothy Puelicher, Sept. 13, 1947; children—Sandra Ann (Mrs. Yanke), Barbara Ann, Peter Ross, Patricia Ann. With Marshall & Ilsley Bank, 1947—, v.p., 1957-70, sr. v.p., 1970-72, exec. v.p., 1972—; dir. Richter-Schroeder Co., First Nat. Leasing Co., Wenthe Davidson Engring Co., Milw., Utility Products Co., Acme-Machell, Inc., Blower Application Co. (all Milw.). Chmn. bd. dirs. United Way Greater Milw.; bd. dirs. St. Joseph's Hosp.; trustee Lawrence U., Citizen's Governmental Research Bur., Milw. Served to lt. (j.g.) USNR, 1943-46. Mem. Wis. Bankers Assn. (credit council), Robert Morris Assos. (dir. Chgo. chpt. 1956-58), Nat. Ski Patrol, Kappa Sigma. Republican. Presbyn. (dir. 1957-60, treas. 1958-60). Kiwanian. Clubs: Milwaukee, Milwaukee Country; Heiliger Huegel Ski (pres. Holy Hill, Wis. 1962-63). Home: 9090 N Range Line Rd Milwaukee WI 53217 Office: 770 N Water St Milwaukee WI 53201

VAN HOUTEN, VERNE WILLIS, clin. psychologist; b. Modesto, Calif., Nov. 17, 1943; s. Paul and Margaret (Sankey) Van H.; B.A., Calvin Coll., 1967; M.A. (Mich. Dept. Edn. fellow), Central Mich. U., 1969; m. Janice Ruth Mead, Aug. 23, 1968; children—Kimberly Joy, Jason Paul. Sch. psychologist IaIsabella County (Mich.) Intermediate Sch. Dist., 1968-69; vocat. rehab. counselor Vocat. Rehab. Services, Grand Rapids, Mich., 1970; clin. psychologist Allegan County (Mich.) Community Mental Health Services, 1970-72, West Shore Mental Health Services, Muskegon, Mich., 1972—; cons. Muskegon County Community Mental Health Services' Partial Hospitalization Program. Bd. dirs. Muskegon Christian Sch., 1974-77, v.p., 1976-77. Served with U.S. Army, 1969. Mem. Community Mental Health Assn. Mich., Am. Psychol. Assn., Mich. Assn. Profl. Psychologists, Mich. Soc. Mental Health (dir. 1976-77). Mem. Christian Reformed Ch. Home: 1335 Brookwood Dr Muskegon MI 49441 Office: 2525 Hall Rd Muskegon MI 49442

VANIK, CHARLES A., congressman; b. Cleve., Apr. 7, 1913; s. Charles Anton and Stella (Kvasnicka) V.; A.B., Western Res. U., 1933, LL.B., 1936; m. Beatrice Marian Best, Feb. 2, 1945; children—Phyllis, John. Admitted to Ohio bar, 1936, since practiced in Cleve.; asso. judge Cleve. Municipal Ct., 1947-54; mem. 84th-90th Congresses, 21st Dist. Ohio, 91st-95th Congresses, 22d Dist. Ohio. Mem. City Council, 1938-39; mem. Ohio Senate, 1940-41; mem. Cleve. Bd. Edn., 1941-42. Trustee Cleve. Library, 1946. Served as lt. USNR, 1942-45, N. Africa, Sicily and Okinawa. Mem. Cleve., Cuyahoga bar assns. Home: 16815 Eldamere Ave Cleveland OH 44128 Office: Leader Bldg Cleveland OH 44114 also House Office Bldg Washington DC 20515

VAN KAMPEN, ROBERT DONALD, investment co. exec.; b. Chgo., Dec. 16, 1938; s. Robert Cornelius and Darthy Agnes (Ruisch) Van K.; B.A., Wheaton Coll., 1960; m. Judith Marlee Crouse, June 25, 1960; children—Kimberly, Kristen, Karla. Rep., John Nuveen & Co., Chgo., 1961-66; v.p., dir. Julien Collins & Co., Chgo., 1966-67; founder, dir. Van Kampen, Wauterlek & Brown, Inc., Chgo., 1967—; founder, dir. Van Kampen Sauerman & Co., 1975—. Served with Finance Corps, AUS, 1960-61. Mem. Investment Bankers Assn. Am., Chgo. Tax Exempt Bond Club. Home: 28 W 100th St St Charles Rd West Chicago IL 60185 Office: 208 S La Salle St Chicago IL 60604

VAN KIRK, MAURICE MELVIN, agrl. assn. exec.; b. Holyoke, Colo., Nov. 26, 1917; s. James W. and Laura Ellen (Sheets) Van K.; B.A., Hastings Coll., 1938; m. Lucille Maxine Guthrie, June 30, 1940; children—Sherrill (Mrs. Richard D. Blaha), Mary Louise (Mrs. William Cushing). Advt. salesman North Platte (Nebr.) Telegraph, 1938-40, Scottsbluff (Nebr.) Star-Herald, 1940-43; pub., mng. editor Chadron (Nebr.) Record, 1947-57; editor, Scottsbluff (Nebr.) Daily Star-Herald, 1960-66; editor Nebr. Agr., information dir. Nebr. Farm Bur. Fedn., Lincoln, 1969—. Served with AUS, 1943-46; ETO. Republican. Methodist. Home: 1409 W Avon St Lincoln NE 68505 Office: Terminal Bldg Lincoln NE 68501

VAN LEEUWEN, JERRY BERNARD, psychologist; b. Grand Rapids, Mich., Jan. 24, 1937; s. Samuel Cornelius and Lucille Estelle (MacMeal) Van L.; A.A., Grand Rapids Jr. Coll., 1963; B.A., Aquinas Coll., 1967; M.A., Western Mich. U., 1968, Ed.S. in Counseling, 1972; Ph.D. in Clin. Psychology, Western Colo. U., 1973; m. Barbara Helen Workman, Aug. 20, 1966; children—Lesley Marie, Elizabeth Ann. Med. technologist Blodgett Meml. Hosp., Grand Rapids, 1959-62; dir. lab. Lakeside Lab., Grand Rapids, 1962-67; psychologist Mich. Dept. Mental Health Regional Consultation Center, Grand Rapids, 1967-70; exec. dir. Adv. Center for Teens, Wyoming, Mich., 1969-77; asso. Human Resource Assos., 1977—; psychol. cons. Wyoming Police Dept., 1974—; instr. psychology Grand Rapids Jr. Coll., 1974—; mem. adv. com. splty. program alcohol and drugs Western Mich. U., Kalamazoo, 1973—; mem. council State Tech. Inst. and Rehab. Center. Mem. City of Wyoming Revenue Sharing Com., 1974—; chmn. Mich. Week, Wyoming, 1974, 75. Served with USAF, 1955-58. Mem. Inst. Rational Living, Am. Assn. Marriage and Family Counseling, Mich. Soc. Mental Health (com. on mentally ill and emotionally handicapped children and youth), Am., Mich., West Shore personnel and guidance assns., Community Mental Health Assn., Mich. Soc. Study of Adolescents. Home: 6674 Woodbrook SE Grand Rapids MI 49508 Office: Suite 303E Waters Bldg Grand Rapids MI 49503

VAN LEUVEN, ROBERT JOSEPH, lawyer; b. Detroit, Apr. 17, 1931; s. Joseph Francis and Olive (Stowell) Van L.; student Albion Coll., 1949-51; B.A. with distinction Wayne State U., 1953; J.D., U. Mich., 1957; m. Holly Goodhue Porter, Dec. 31, 1976; children—Joseph Michael, Douglas Robert, Julie Margaret. Admitted to Mich. bar, 1957, since practiced in Muskegon; partner firm Hathaway, Latimer, Clink & Robb, 1957-68, partner McCroskey, Libner & Van Leuven, 1968—. Bd. dirs. Muskegon Children's Home, 1965-75. Served with AUS 1953-55. Fellow Am. Coll. Trial Lawyers; mem. Am. Bar Assn., State Bar Mich. (past mem. council negligence law sect.), Mich. Assn. Professions, Am. Arbitration Assn., Muskegon Urban League, Delta Sigma Phi. Club: Muskegon Country. Home: 1727 Forest Park Rd Muskegon MI 49445 Office: 1440 Peck St Muskegon MI 49443

VAN LIEROP, PETER, clergyman, counseling dir.; b. Chgo., Apr. 11, 1918; s. Johannes Bernard Henderik and Johanna Kathrina (Hamel) van L.; student Royal Athenaeum of Ghent (Belgium), 1930-36, Ghent Nat. U., Belgium, 1938-40, U. Mich., 1941-42; B.A. in Biology, Hope Coll., 1946; M.Div., Pitts. Theol. Sem., 1949; M.Ed., U. Pitts., 1949, Ph.D., 1955; M.A. in Counseling, Columbia U., 1961; Th.M., Princeton Theol. Sem., 1967; m. Eleanor Catherine Creswell, June 19, 1943; children—Peter Creswell, J. Bernard H., Eleanor J., Martha J., Andrea Margaret. Ordained to ministry United Presbyterian Ch.; missionary to Korea, Fgn. Missions Bd. Presbyn. Ch. in U.S.A., 1949 and after; instr. Bible and Christian lit. N. Japan Coll., Sendai, 1951-52; founder Kyung An High Sch., Andong, Korea, 1954, prin., 1954-56; founder Sung-Ro Won Home for ret. Bible women, Andong, Korea, 1953, Good Samaritan Clinic, Andong, 1953; instr. in Bible, Kyung An Bible Inst., Andong, 1952-54, 55-56; prof. Christian edn. and psychology of religion Yonsei U., Seoul, Korea, 1956-76; acting gen. sec. Korea Student Christian Movement, 1957-59; lectr. Presbyn. Sem., Seoul Nat. U., Seoul Women's Coll.; chmn. United Presbyn. Mission in Korea, 1963, 76; founder Christian edn. dept. Yonsei U., Seoul, chmn., 1965-69, 74-76, also dir. clin. pastoral tng. program at United Grad. Sch. Theology, 1973-76; v.p. Korea Human Relations Tng. Assn., 1972-76; dir. Alpha Counseling Services, Villa Park, Ill., 1977—. Bd. dirs. Kyung Shin High Sch., Seoul, 1958-76, Pierson Bibl. Sem., Seoul, 1960-76, Agape House Coffee House Ministry, Seoul, 1972-76, Korea Bible Soc., 1962-64, Korea Student Christian Fedn., 1959-66. Served with M.C., U.S. Army, 1942-45; ETO. Recipient Human Rights award Korea Bar Assn., 1963. Mem. Am. Personnel and Guidance Assn., Assn. Mental Health Clergy, Assn. Counselor Edn. and Supervision, Assn. Psychol. and Ednl. Counselors in Asia (standing com. 1976—), Kappa Delta Pi. Republican. Author: Christian Education: Theory and Practice, 1961; Pastoral Counseling, 1977; contbr. numerous articles on Christian edn. to profl. publs.; instrumental in establishment of 120 Bible clubs and ch. schs. in Korea. Home: 726 N Lincoln Ave Villa Park IL 60181 Office: Alpha Counseling Services 723 N Addison Ave Villa Park IL

VAN METER, DAVID, JR., veterinarian; b. Monroeville, Ind., Sept. 3, 1923; s. David and Agnes Orr (Dunn) Van M.; student Blackburn Coll., 1942-43, Ill. State Normal U., 1943-44; D.V.M., Mich. State U., 1951; m. Alvena E. Kanning, July 20, 1946; children—Suzanne, Jeanette, Jon David (dec.), Sherri, Lori. Pvt. practice vet. medicine, Owenton, Ky., 1951-52, Wakarusa, Ind., 1952-60, Albion, Ind., 1960—. Pres., County Council, 1963-66; chmn. United Fund, 1970; treas. County Extension Bd., 1970-72; mem. State Bd. Animal Health, 1970—, chmn., 1974-76; pres. Noble County Comprehensive Health Com., 1971-72; chmn. Noble County Long Range Planning Commn., 1971-72. Pres. town bd. Albion, 1968-72. Served with USNR, 1943-46. Mem. Am., N.E. (pres. 1964-65), Ind. (pres. 1970-71) vet. med. assns., Mich. State U. Vet. Alumni Council, Bovine Practicioners C. of C. Democrat. Lutheran (elder 1971-75). Rotarian. Home: 918 E Main St Albion IN 46701 Office: Route 1 Albion IN 46701

VAN MILLIGEN, ALFRED CORNELIUS, chem. co. exec.; b. Chgo., Sept. 21, 1922; s. Cornelius and Helen T. (Gilleran) Van M.; student Northwestern U., 1940-42, 46-49, Loyola U., 1967; m. Hedwig P. Pienczykowski, Sept. 21, 1946; children—Cornelius, Patricia, James, David, Joyce, Michael. Asst. chief accountant Triplex Corp. Am., Pueblo, Colo., 1947-50; chief accountant, 52-69; controller Cardox div. Chemetron Corp., Chgo., 1969-70, asst. group controller, gases and related products group, 1970-74, controller indsl. gases div., 1974—. Treas. Lansing Interfaith Human Relations Council, 1967-71. Served to capt. AUS, 1942-46. Mem. Nat. Assn. Accountants, Am. Legion. Roman Catholic (council chmn. 1970-73). K.C. Home: 18030 Escanaba St Lansing IL 60438 Office: 111 E Wacker Dr Chicago IL 60601

VANNEMAN, EDGAR, JR., lawyer, city ofcl.; b. El Paso, Ill., Aug. 24, 1919; s. Edgar and Fern (Huffington) V.; B.S., Northwestern U., 1941, J.D., 1947; m. Shirli Thomas, Apr. 28, 1951; children—Jill, Thomas Edgar. Admitted to Ill. bar, 1947; atty. Campbell, Miller, Carroll & Paxton, Chgo., 1947-49. C. & N.W. Ry., 1949-62, asst. gen. solicitor, 1955-62; gen. atty. Brunswick Corp., 1962—. Alderman City of Evanston, 1957-65, mayor, 1970-77; chmn. Cook County Council Govts., 1972-74. Chmn. Ecumenical Inst., 1959-61. Pres. Ill. Young Republicans, 1955-57. Served as maj. USAAF, World War II. Editorial bd. Ill. Law Review, 1946-47, Jour. Air Law and Commerce, 1946-47. Home: 715 Monticello Pl Evanston IL 60201 Office: 1 Brunswick Plaza Skokie IL 60076

VAN NORMAN, WILLIS ROGER, clinic exec.; b. Windom, Minn., June 17, 1938; s. Ralph Peter and Thelma Pearl (Bare) Van N.; A.A., Worthington Jr. Coll., 1958; B.S., Mankato State Coll., 1960; m. Irene Anna Penner, Sept. 7, 1959; children—Eric Jon, Brian Mathew, Karin Ruth. Tchr. chemistry, St. Peter, Minn., 1961; tchr. Byron, Minn., 1962, spl. edn. Rochester, Minn., 1963-65; instr. pilots ground sch. Rochester Jr. Coll., 1968-69; with Mayo Clinic, Rochester, Minn., 1962—, developer biomedical computer systems, 1974—; instr. Gopher Aviation, 1968-71. Mem. Mankato State Alumni Assn. (dir.), Minn., Nat. ednl. assns. Methodist. Founder, mgr. Van Norman's Flying V Ranch, 1972—. Home: Route 3 Box 25 St Charles MN 55972 Office: Mayo Clinic Rochester MN 55901

VAN NOSTRAND, DAVID MICHAEL, surgeon, b. Rochester, N.Y., Dec. 29, 1936; s. Manning Eugene and Thyra A. (Gundlach) V.; B.A., Grinnell Coll., 1958; M.D., Boston U., 1962; m. Catharine Marie Herr, July 16, 1960; children—Laura Susan, Catherine Louise, Maren Thyra. Intern, St. Luke's Hosp., Duluth, Minn., 1962-63; resident Hennepin County Gen. Hosp., Mpls., 1963-65, VA Hosp., Mpls., 1965-68; practice medicine specializing gen. surgery, St. Cloud, Minn., 1968—; mem. staffs Paynesville (Minn.) Community Hosp., Milaca (Minn.) Hosp., St. Michael's Hosp., Sauk Center, Minn., St. Gabriel's Hosp., Little Falls, Minn., Meeker County (Minn.) Hosp., Central Minn. Surg. Center, St. Cloud, Monticello-Big Lake (Minn.) Hosp. Vice-pres. YMCA, St. Cloud, 1977—; bd. dirs. Nat. YMCA, 1970—, Camp Olson, Longville, Minn., 1970—. Served to capt. Air N.G., 1963-69. Diplomate Nat. Bd. Med. Examiners; recipient Physicians Recognition award AMA, 1977. Fellow A.C.S.; mem. Minn. Surg. Soc., Aerospace Med. Assn. Contbr. articles to med. jours. Home: 1220 N 13th St St Cloud MN 56301 Office: 106 Doctors Park St Cloud MN 56301

VAN NUYS, JOHN DIXON, physician; b. Chgo., Sept. 15, 1925; s. George Thomas and Marion Esther (Dixon) Van N.; B.S., U. Notre Dame, 1950; M.D., Loyola U., 1955; m. Ann Duginski, May 16, 1959; children—Thomas, Julia, Peter, Timothy, Steven. Intern, Cook County Hosp., Chgo., 1955-56, resident, 1956-57; gen. practice medicine, Chgo., 1957-59; resident ear, nose and throat U. Ill., Hines VA Hosp., 1959-62; practice medicine specializing in ear, nose and throat, Waukegan, Ill., 1962—; mem. attending staff Victory Meml., St. Therese hosps., Waukegan, Ill., 1962—; cons. Zion Benton, Condell Meml. hosps., 1963—; mem. asso. staff Lake Forest Hosp., 1965—; clin. asso. U. Ill., 1963—; mem. governing bd. Victory Meml. Hosp., 1975—. Served with USNR, 1944-46. Diplomate Am. Bd. Otolaryngology. Fellow ACS, Am. Acad. Facial Plastic and Reconstructive Surgery; mem. AMA, Am. Acad. Ophthalmology and Otolaryngology, Am. Trauma Soc., Ill. State, Lake County med. socs. Roman Catholic. Clubs: Serra (pres. 1970), Notre Dame (pres. 1969), Elks (Waukegan, Ill.). Home: 511 Cambridge Lane Lake Bluff IL 60044 Office: 609 Greenwood Ave Waukegan IL 60085

VAN ORDSTRAND, HOWARD SCOTT, physician; b. Wichita, Kans., Mar. 21, 1911; s. Winfield Scott and May Louise (Hellums) Van O.; A.B., U. Wichita, 1932; M.D., U. Kans., 1933, M.D., 1935; m. Carlotte Louise Baker, Sept. 8, 1939; children—John, Mary. Intern, U. Kans. Hosp., Kansas City, 1935-36; fellow in medicine Cleve. Clinic Found., 1936-40; postgrad. tng. Trudeau Sanatorium, Saranac Lake, N.Y., 1939; founder, head dept. pulmonary disease Cleve. Clinic Found., 1940-73, sr. physician, head sect. environ. health, dept. pulmonary disease, 1973—; nat. pulmonary cons. to surgeon gen. Air Force, 1969-73, cons. AEC, 1956—, USPHS, 1966—; mem. coal mine health research adv. com. HEW, 1975—. Served with UAS, 1944-47. Recipient alumnus year award, U. Kans. Med. Sch., 1968. Diplomate Am. Bd. Internal Medicine. Mem. Am. Coll. Chest Physicians (pres. 1974), Cleve. Chest Soc. (pres. 1958), Am. Thoracic Soc., Am. Soc. Internal lMedicine, Am. Fedn. Clin. Research, Central Soc. Clin. Research, Am., Ohio State med. assns., Am. Legion. Baptist. Club: Mayfield Country. Contbr. numerous articles to profl. jours. Home: 21849 Parnell Rd Shaker Heights OH 44122 Office: 9500 Euclid Ave Cleveland OH 44106

VAN PELT, PHILIP FRISBEE, writer, pub. relations exec.; b. Evanston, Ill., Oct. 5, 1928; s. Willis and Virginia Darling (Frisbee) Van P.; A.B., The Citadel, 1949; m. Carlotta Marberry, Feb. 23, 1963; 1 dau., Susan Rosemary. Sales corr. Uniform Printing & Supply Co., Chgo., 1950-51; casualty underwriter trainee Hartford Accident & Indemnity Co., Chgo., 1954-56; casualty underwriter Nat. Fire Ins. Co., Chgo., 1956-57, asst. editor Nat. Underwriter, 1957; editor publs., spl. rep. pub. relations Ry. Progress Inst., Chgo., 1958-61; editor Onalaska (Wis.) Record-Times, 1961; editorial assignments Chgo. Daily Law Bull., 1961-64; editor Ry. Purchases and Stores, asso. editor Ry. Age, Chgo., 1964-65; editor Vol. Firefighter/Fire Chief mag., Chgo., 1965-67; Western editor Traffic World, Chgo., 1967-70; service exec. Pub. Relations Bd., Inc., Chgo., 1970-73, account supr., 1973-75, v.p., editorial dir., 1975-76, editor Leasing mag., 1971-73; mgr. editorial services Huwen & Davies, Inc., Chgo., 1976; free lance writer, Evanston, Ill., 1976—. Instr. English, Northwestern U., evenings 1959-60. Served to 1st lt. AUS, 1951-53. Decorated Combat Inf. badge, Purple Heart, Silver Star; recipient George Washington Honor medal Freedoms Found., 1953. Composer: Going to Wyoming, Happy Hanukkah, 1973, Going Back to Omaha, 1974. Home: 493 Sheridan Rd Evanston IL 60202

VAN PRAAG, ALEX, JR., cons. engr.; b. Little Falls, Minn., Jan. 29, 1896; s. Alexander and Rachel (Davis) Van P.; student James Millikin U., 1913-15; B.S. C.E., U. Ill., 1917; m. Bernice I. Metzger, Dec. 27, 1926; children—Roger C., James N. Asst. engr. Miller, Holbrook & Warren, Decatur, Ill., 1919-20; asst. to chief san. engr., Ill. Dept. Pub. Health, 1920-22; mem. firm Warren & Van Praag, Inc., Decatur, cons. engrs., architects, 1922—, pres., 1952-68, chmn. bd., 1968—; treas., dir. Midwest Computer Service, Decatur, 1958-64; dir. First Nat. Bank Decatur, 1955—. Mem. Ill. Bd. Pub. Health Advisers, Springfield, 1962-69; mem. Ill. Bldg. Authority, 1961-65; mem. Pres.'s Citizens Adv. Com. U. Ill., 1961—; mem. adv. com. St. Mary's Hosp., Decatur, 1963-68. Bd. dirs. United Fund Decatur and Macon County, Ill., 1966-69; trustee Millikin U., 1961-70. Served with U.S. Army, 1917-19; AEF. Recipient Loyalty award U. Ill. Alumni Assn., 1964; Alumni Merit Loyalty award Millikin U., 1973; Distinguished Alumnus award Civil Engring. Alumni Assn. U. Ill., 1975; registered profl. engr., Ill., Ind., Ohio, Iowa, Ky., Mo., N.D., Tenn., Wis. Mem. Am. Soc. C.E. (life), Nat. (past pres.), Ill. (past pres. hon.) socs. profl. engrs., Am. Cons. Engrs. Council, Cons. Engrs. Council Ill., Ill. Registered Land Surveyors Assn., Am. Soc. Testing and Materials, Am. Rd. Builders Assn., Am. Water Works Assn., Water Pollution Control Assn. Central States, Decatur Assn. Commerce, Ill. C. of C. (chmn. water resources com. 1959-60, mem. econ. devel. com. 1964—), U. Ill. Alumni Assn., Am. Legion. Presbyn. Elk. Clubs: Decatur. Home: 402 Southmoreland Pl Decatur IL 62521 Office: 253 S Park St Decatur IL 62523

VAN RAAPHORST, DONNA L., educator; b. Detroit, Dec. 5, 1943; d. Leonard Francis and Eleanor Margaret (Schnur) Van R.; student Henry Ford Community Coll., 1963-65; B.S., Eastern Mich. U., 1967, M.A., 1969; postgrad. Kent State U. Tchr. history Saline (Mich.) Sch. System, 1967-70; asst. prof. history Cuyahoga Community Coll., Parma, Ohio, 1972-77, asso. prof., 1977—. Nat. Endowment for the Humanities fellow, 1973. Mem. Am., So. hist. assns., Orgn. Am. Historians, Ohio Acad., Western Reserve Hist. Soc., Historians Greater Cleve., Women Historians Greater Cleve. (treas. 1975-77, pres. 1977—), Community Coll. Social Sci. Assn., Ohio Historians Media Group, No. Ohio Womens Consortium. Author: (with others) From Then to Now, 1975; I Won't Give Up, I Can't Give Up, I'll Never Give Up. Home: 2107 Glenbury St Lakewood OH 44107 Office: 11000 Pleasant Valley Parma OH 44130

VAN RIPER, SUE ELLEN FOUKE (MRS. EDWARD L. VAN RIPER, JR.), psychometrist; b. Indpls., Dec. 19, 1943; d. Myron Tyler and Jean Ellen (Storen) Fouke; B.A., DePauw U., 1965; M.S. (grad. fellow), Butler U., 1968; m. Edward L. Van Riper, Jr., Aug. 12, 1967; 1 son, Edward Stewart. Fourth grade tchr. Noblesville (Ind.) Pub. Schs., 1965-67, 68-70, psychometrist, tchr. jr. high sch. spl. edn. 1970-71; 4th grade tchr. Indpls. Pub. Schs., 1967-68; psychometrist Hamilton County Spl. Services Coop., Carmel, Ind., 1971—; psychometric coordinator Hamilton Madison Boone Tipton Spl. Services Coop., 1976—. Sales cons. Yarn Shoppe, Etc., Zionsville, Ind., 1971—. Sec. profl. group Jr. League Indpls., 1973-74; active Christamore Aid Soc. Mem. Nat. Assn. Sch. Psychologists, Council Exceptional Children. Democrat. Methodist. Club: Dramatic (Indpls.). Home: 4740 Washington Blvd Indianapolis IN 46205 Office: 420 E Main St Carmel IN 46032

VAN RYZIN, SISTER MARTINA, coll. dean; b. Appleton, Wis., June 10, 1923; d. Clarence H. and Lucille (Schabo) Van Ryzin; B.A., Holy Family Coll., 1946; M.S., Marquette U., 1956; Ph.D., U. Wis., 1960. Elementary sch. tchr., Plymouth, Kellnersville, Wis., 1943-44, 46-53; high sch. tchr. math., Kellnersville, 1946-52, Cath. Meml. High Sch., Waukesha, Wis., 1953-55; math. instr. Silver Lake (formerly Holy Family) Coll., Manitowoc, Wis., 1960—, chmn. math. dept., 1960—, acad. dean, 1970—. Radiol. def. officer Civil Def., Manitowoc County, 1967—, radiol. monitor instr., 1962—. Mem. Nat. Council Tchrs. Math., Math. Assn. Am., History Sci. Soc., Manitowoc County Hist. Soc., Assn. Academic Affairs Adminstrs., North Central Assn. Academic Deans. Address: Silver Lake Coll 2406 S Alverno Rd Manitowoc WI 54220

VANSANT, CARL ALLEN, engring. cons.; b. Clinton, Mo., Feb. 14, 1938; s. Emmett Allen and Mary Elinor (Howell) V.; B.S., U. Mo. at Rolla, 1960; M.S., Purdue U., 1963; m. Margaret Joan Chiabotta, June 15, 1958; children—Lori Elizabeth, John Ayres. Engr., Tex. Instruments, Dallas, 1962-63; phys. metallurgist U.S. AEC, Germantown, Md., 1963-65; systems analyst Operations Research Inc., Silver Spring, Md., 1965-68; systems analyst Vertex Corp., Kensington, Md., 1968-69; energy systems cons., Kensington, 1969-70; systems engr. Value Engring. Co., Alexandria, Va., 1970-71; systems engr. Black & Veatch Cons. Engrs., Kansas City, Mo., 1972—. Served with AUS, 1963-65. Alcoa Found. fellow, 1960-61; NSF fellow, 1961-62. Registered profl. engr., Mo., Md., D.C. Mem. Phi Kappa Phi, Tau Beta Pi, Sigma Gamma Epsilon, Alpha Sigma Mu. Lutheran. Patentee in field. Author: Strategic Energy Supply and National Security, 1971. Contbr. articles to profl. jours. Home: 10901 Harrison St Kansas City MO 64131 Office: 1500 Meadow Lake Pkwy Kansas City MO 64114

VAN SANT, JOANNE FRANCES, coll. dean and ofcl.; b. Morehead, Ky., Dec. 29, 1924; d. Lewis L. and Dorothy (Greene) Van Sant; B.A., Denison U., 1946; M.A., Ohio State U., 1953; LL.D., Albright Coll., 1975. Instr. health and phys. edn. Mayfield (Ky.) High Sch., 1946-48, Denison U., 1948; instr. health and phys. edn. Otterbein Coll., 1948-52, asst. prof., 1952-55, asso. prof., 1955—, dean of women, 1952-60, 62-64, v.p. for student affairs, dean of students, 1964—. Mem. Am., Ohio (chmn. coll. sect. 1963-64) assns. health, phys. edn. and recreation, Ohio Coll. Assn., Nat., Midwest assns. for phys. edn. coll. women, AAUW (dir. 1951-62, 73—), Ohio Assn. Women Deans, Adminstrs. and Counselors (treas., exec. bd. 1972-73), Nat., Ohio assns. student personnel adminstrs., Cap and Dagger, Alpha Lambda Delta, Theta Alpha Phi, Torch and Key. Presbyterian (elder 1967-69, trustee Central Coll. Ch. Retirement Center, 1973, sec. 1973—, trustee 1975-77). Clubs: Zonta Internat. (1st v.p. 1976—), Walnut Valley Boat, Westerville Women's Music (dance chmn. 1968-74, 76—). Home: 9100 Oakwood Pl Westerville OH 43081 Office: Otterbein Coll Westerville OH 43081

VANSCOY, BEATRICE IONA, accountant; b. Duck River, Tenn., Feb. 18, 1914; d. Robert Estle and Jennie Marvin (Baxter) Harvill; student U. Calif., Los Angeles, 1944-46, Cuyahoga Community Coll., 1962-63; m. Raymond Russell Vanscoy, Oct. 17, 1963; 1 dau. by previous marriage—Jennie Ruth Sager. Bookkeeper, Bank of Am., Los Angeles, 1944-50; tchr., accountant Bailin & Brover, Cleve., 1950-55; property accountant Cleve. Ryan Industries, 1956-60; accounting office mgr. Power Brake Service, Cleve., 1960-63; accounting trustee Roach-Reid, Cleve., 1963-70; accountant, office mgr. Brown Insulating, Cleve., 1971-75; pvt. practice accounting and bookkeeper tax work, Cleve., 1960—. Sec. Rep. Primary Bd., Dickson, Tenn., 1935-36. Mem. VFW. Club: Bus. Women's (past pres.). Home: 66 Crosby St Berea OH 44017 Office: 6275 PO Box Cleveland OH 44101

VAN STRATEN, GERRIT STANLEY, cons. engr.; b. Balt., July 6, 1932; s. Albert and Dorothy Belle (Patterson) Van S.; diploma Balt. Poly. Inst., 1950; student Johns Hopkins, 1950-53; B.S. in Mech. Engring., Ohio State U., 1959. Mech. engr. Frank, Lingberg & Maki, Columbus, Ohio, 1956-61; project engr. N.Am. Aviation, Columbus, 1961-66; practice profl. engring. Van Straten Engrs., Columbus, 1966-69; partner, profl. engr. Van Straten & Edwards Engrs., Columbus, 1970—; exec. v.p. Tectonics, Inc.; partner Energy Ltd. Mem. U.S. Bicentennial Commn. from Ohio; mem. Ohio Gov.'s Task Force Energy Conservation. Chmn. bd. trustees Republican Glee Club, Columbus, 1973-76, 78, pres., 1977; bd. dirs. Franklin County (Ohio) Republican Forum, 1974-75, sec., 1976, v.p., 1977, 78. Bd. dirs., treas.-sec. T.I.P. Corp., Columbus. Served with AUS. Registered profl. engr., Ohio, Pa., N.Y., W. Va., Md., Del., N.C., Fla., Ky., Mass., Iowa, Ill., Ind., Tenn., Mich., Ga., Va. Mem. Illuminating Engring. Soc., Constrn. Specification Inst., Nat., Ohio socs. profl. engrs., Am. Soc. Heating, Refrigerating and Air Conditioning Engrs. (dir. 1974-75; regional chmn. energy com. 1973-75, sec. Columbus chpt. 1976-78), Cons. Engrs. Council Am., Nat. Council Engring. Examiners, Am. Soc. Plumbing Engrs., Assn. Energy Engrs., Navy League U.S., Ohio State U. Alumni Assn. (life), Rathcamp Matchcover Soc., Long Beach Matchcover Club, Phi Kappa Psi. Lutheran (mem. steering com. ch. orgn. 1957; fin. sec. 1957-61; elder 1973-75, rep. ecumenical council 1973-75, ch. pres. 1976—). Kiwanian (club pres. 1970-71; div. chmn. 1972, 74, 75, 76, 77, del. internat. conv. 1968, 70-71, 74, 76, Kiwanian of Year 1973). Home: 1731 Shanley Dr Apt 11 Columbus OH 43224 Office: 1500 West Lane Ave Columbus OH 43221

VAN TASSEL, LEO M., univ. adminstr.; b. Howard City, Mich., Jan. 28, 1912; s. Louis M. and Lillian (Ranshaw) Van T.; A.C., Grand Rapids Jr. Coll., 1933; A.B., Western Mich. U., 1936; M.A., U. Mich., 1942; postgrad. Columbia, 1949; m. Evelyn Loveridge, Nov. 5, 1938; 1 dau., Marilyn. High sch. tchr., Fennville, Mich., 1936-41, Midland, Mich., 1941-45; pub. accountant Ernst & Ernst, Detroit, 1945-46; prof. accounting No. Mich. U., Marquette, 1946-49, v.p., 1949—, treas. Univ. Found., 1960-68, devel. fund, 1968—. Mem. Central, Nat. assns. bus. officers, NEA, Mich. Edn. Assn., Assn. Sch. Bus. Ofcls., Delta Sigma Phi. Mason (Shriner). Home: 710 W Kaye St Marquette MI 49855

VAN TIEGHEM, ALBERT RICHARD, SR., accountant; b. Moline, Ill., Sept. 1, 1927; s. Clement N. and Martha N. (DeRammalaere) VanT.; student Augustana Coll., 1951-55; m. Ruth Elaine Lambrick, Oct. 2, 1948; children—Nancy (Mrs. Gary Frye), Carol (Mrs. Stephen Haines), Diane (Mrs. Stephen Dryden), Albert Richard, Robert Allen. With Farmall Works, Internat. Harvester Co., Rock Island, Ill., 1946-57, factory ledger accountant, 1955-57; sec.-treas. Moline Iron Works, 1957-61; prin. Albert R. VanTieghem, Ltd., accountants, East Moline, Ill., 1961—. Tchr., Blackhawk Jr. Coll., 1961-63, Moline Inst. Commerce, 1961-63. Treas., East Moline Vis. Nurses Assn., 1964-66; coach Little League Baseball, 1965-68. Bd. dirs., officer numerous local civic orgns. Served with USNR, 1945-46, 50-51. Mem. Nat. Soc. Pub. Accountants (gov. 1969-73, 1st v.p. 1974-75, pres. 1975-76), Ind. Accountants Assn. Ill. (state dir. 1964-67, pres. Western chpt. 1965-66), Upper Rock Island County C. of C. (pres. 1969-70, 71-72). Rotarian. Home: 512 29th Ave East Moline IL 61244 Office: 605 17th Ave East Moline IL 61244

VAN TIEM, FLORENTINE URBAN STEWART (MRS. RICHARD L. VAN TIEM), bus. exec.; b. Detroit, Sept. 15, 1928; d. Joseph Stephen and Helen (Reinowski) Urban; A.B., Wayne U., 1948; m. John Slagle, June 15, 1950 (dec.); 1 son, John Gerard (dec.); m. 2d, Dr. Maitland Newman Stewart, May 4, 1957 (div. 1965); children—Joseph Gerald, Victoria Helen; m. 3d, Richard L. Van Tiem, Apr. 22, 1972. Copywriter and publicity dir. of the W. B. Doner Co., 1948; account exec. Wolfe, Jickling, Dow & Conkey, 1948-51; exec. v.p. Ruse & Urban, Inc., 1951-55; pres. Splty. Bakers Services, Inc., 1954—; owner Scope Advt. Agy., 1955—, Christopher Gerard & Asso., 1963—, Hilltop Farm Products Inc., 1968—, Specialized Investment Co., 1968—, Victoria Farms, Inc., 1968—. Bd. dirs. Ednl. Found., trustee Louis K. Buell Scholarship and Award Found. Recipient numerous awards including Crusade for Freedom, Capital V Viscountess. Mem. Catholic Theatre Detroit, Navy League, Am. Inst. Mgmt., Am. Bakers Assn., Am. Women Radio and TV, Women's Advt. Club, Fashion Group, Detroit Symphony Orch. Women's Assn., Theta Sigma Phi. Republican. Roman Catholic. Clubs: Pilot, Western Golf and Country, Women's City, Young Republicans, Bakers of Chicago, Edgewood Country; Lapeer Golf and Country, Great Oak Country. Home: 1779 Brocker Rd Metamora MI 48455 Office: 280 N Washington St Oxford MI 48051

VAN TIEM, PHILLIP MICHAEL, hosp. ofcl.; b. Grosse Pointe, Mich., Oct. 4, 1935; s. August Gerard and Margaret Mary (Power) Van T.; B.A., Mich. State U., 1963; postgrad. Wayne State U., 1972-73, U. Detroit, 1974-76; M.A. pub. adminstrn., Central Mich. U., 1978; m. Darlene Miriam Roff, Apr. 4, 1964; children—Bradford, Adrienne. With Gen. Motors Acceptance Corp., 1963-68, credit mgr., 1965-68; comml. sales rep. Goodyear & Rubber Co., 1968-69; mgr. accounts receivable Lansing (Mich.) Gen. Hosp., 1969-70; mgr. patient accounting Sinai Hosp., Detroit, 1971-72, St. John Hosp., Detroit, 1972—. Bd. dirs. Lansing Gen. Hosp. Credit Union, 1969-70, treas., 1970; chmn. supervisor com. Sinai Hosp. Credit Union, 1971-72. Vol. social worker Family to Family Movement, 1965-71; mem. vol. program Mich. Dept. Social Services, 1965-71; chmn. publicity Grosse Pointe Park Civic Assn. Served with AUS, 1958-60. Recipient hon. mention for suggestion Mich. Hosp. Assn., 1972. Mem. Hosp. Fin. Mgmt. Assn. (membership com. 1975-77), Patent Accounting Mgmt. Assn. (awards chmn. 1977-78). Roman Catholic. Home: 1310 Kensington Rd Grosse Pointe MI 48230 Office: 22101 Moross Rd Detroit MI 48236

VAN TIL, WILLIAM, author, educator; b. Corona, N.Y., Jan. 8, 1911; s. William Joseph and Florence Alberta (MacLean) Van T.; B.A., Columbia, 1933, M.A., Tchrs. Coll., 1935; Ph.D., Ohio State U., 1946; m. Beatrice Barbara Blaha, Aug. 24, 1935; children—Jon, Barbara, Roy. Tchr. N.Y. State Tng. Sch. for Boys, 1933-34; instr. dept. univ. schs. Coll. Edn., Ohio State U., 1934-36, asst. prof., 1936-43, on leave, 1943-45; researchist, writer Consumer Edn. Study N.E.A., 1943-44; dir. learning materials Bur. Intercultural Edn., 1944-47; prof. edn. U. Ill., 1947-51; prof. edn., chmn. div. curriculum and teaching George Peabody Coll. Tchrs., Nashville, 1951-57; prof. edn., chmn. dept. secondary edn. N.Y.U., 1957-66, head div. secondary and higher edn., 1966-67; Coffman Distinguished prof. edn. Ind. State U., 1967-77, prof. emeritus, 1977—; lectr. Mexico, New Zealand, Australia, Asia, 1974. Mem. Ill. Interracial Commn., 1948-51; moderator Nashville sch. desegregation meetings, 1955-57; adv. bd. Jour. Tchr. Edn., 1956-59; co-organizer Nashville Community Relations Conf., 1956; cons. Phelps-Stokes Fund project, 1958-62; staff of P.R. edn. survey, 1958-59, Iran tchr. edn. survey, 1962, V.I. edn. survey, 1964. Recipient awards N.J. Collegiate Press Assn., 1962, N.J. Assn. Tchrs. English, 1962; Centennial Achievement award Ohio State U., 1970. Mem. John Dewey Soc. (v.p. 1957-60; acting pres. 1958-59, pres. 1964-66, Service award 1977), Assn. Supervision and Curriculum Devel. (dir. 1950-54, 57-61, pres. 1961-62, chmn. rev. council 1972-73), Nat. Soc. Coll. Tchrs. Edn. (pres. 1967-68), United Educators (chmn. bd. educators 1969-77), Asso. Orgns. for Tchr. Edn. (adv. council 1967-73, chmn. issues tchr. edn. 1972-73), Am. Ednl. Studies Assn. (editorial bd. 1970-77). Author: The Danube Flows Through Fascism: Economic Roads for American Democracy; The Making of a Modern Educator: Modern Education for the Junior High School Years; Education: A Beginning; One Way of Looking at It; The Year 2000: Teacher Education; Another Way of Looking at It; also articles, revs., editorials. Editor: Forces Affecting Am. Edn.; Curriculum: Quest for Relevance; Issues in Secondary Education. Co-editor: Democratic Human Relations, Intercultural Attitudes in the Making, Education in American Life. Adv. editor Houghton Mifflin, 1964-70. Columnist Ednl. Leadership, Contemporary Education, Kappan. Contbr. to Saturday Rev., Woman's Day, Parents and numerous other publs. Home: Lake Lure Rural Route 32 Box 316 Terre Haute IN 47803

VAN VLEET, WILLIAM BENJAMIN, JR., lawyer, ins. co. exec.; b. Milw., Dec. 4, 1924; s. William Benjamin and Irene (Peppey) Van V.; student Lawrence Coll., 1943-44; J.D., Marquette U., 1948; m. Marilyn Nilles, Dec. 26, 1946; children—Terese (Mrs. Edward Svetich), Susan (Mrs. Paul Waldo), William Benjamin III, Monica, Mark. Admitted to Wis. bar, 1948, Ill. bar, 1950; gen. counsel George Rogers Clark Mut. Casualty Co., Rockford, Ill., 1948-59; gen. counsel Pioneer Life Ins. Co., Rockford, 1950-59, v.p., gen. counsel, 1959-68; dir., exec. v.p., gen. counsel Pioneer Life Ins. Co. of Ill., Rockford, 1968—. Mem. Boylan Central Cath. High Sch. Council of Adminstrn., 1965-72; mem. Diocesan Bd. Edn., Rockford, 1970-77, pres., 1970-73; v.p. Nat. Assn. Bds. Edn., 1972-74, pres., 1974-76; dir. Nat. Catholic Edn. Assn., 1975—. Served to lt. (j.g.) USNR, 1944-46. Mem. Am., Ill., Wis. bar assns. Roman Catholic. Home: 811 Coolidge Pl Rockford IL 61107 Office: 127 N Wyman St Rockford IL 61101

VAN WINKLE, CHARLES KELLOGG, lawyer, banker; b. Howell, Mich., Feb. 18, 1917; s. Don William and Annabel Lee (Kellogg) Van W.; LL.B., U. Mich., 1940, J.D., 1940; m. Mary Elizabeth Barth, Dec. 28, 1939; children—Peter Barth, Mary Elizabeth, Margaret Ann (Mrs. Robert Joseph Gajda), Sara Louise. Admitted to Mich. bar, 1941; mem. firm Van Winkle & Van Winkle, Howell, 1941, firm Van Winkle, Van Winkle & Konopka, P.C., Howell, 1976-78, Van Winkle & Van Winkle, P.C., 1978—; former sr. v.p., dir. First Nat. Bank, Howell; dir. Brighton State Bank (Mich.), 1953—, sr. v.p., 1975—. City atty., Howell, 1945-65; village atty., Pinckney, Mich., 1946-58; city atty., Brighton, 1948-52. Livingston County Circuit Ct. commr., 1942-46; home service chmn. A.R.C., 1942-46. Mem. sch. bd., Howell, Mich., 1948-56. Past bd. dirs. Kenny-Mich. Rehab. Found. Mem. Mich. State., Livingston County bar assns., Howell C. of C. (dir. 1946-48), Sigma Alpha Epsilon. Presbyn. (trustee 1950-53). Home: 130 Inverness Rd Howell MI 48843 Office: 105 E Grand River Howell MI 48843

VAN WINKLE, TILFORD WAYNE, mfg. co. exec.; b. Merrimac, Iowa, May 31, 1905; s. Doss and Victoria (Lillyblade) Van W.; student pub. schs., Jefferson County, Iowa; m. Goldie Esther Sinn, Dec. 25, 1924 (div. June 1955); children—Lola (Mrs. Robert Triska), Harold, Leland; m. 2d, Ellen Isadora Bender, Apr. 15, 1971. Farmer, Jefferson County, Iowa, 1926-30; owner Van Winkle Well Drilling, Salem, Iowa, 1930-56, Freeman Decorating Co., Des Moines, 1956-59; pres. V & H Mfg. Co., Salem, Iowa, 1960—. Democrat. Episcopalian. Club: Commercial (pres. 1940-45) (Salem). Inventor excavating machine, board extractor. Home: 502 S Pine Dr Mt Pleasant IA 52641 Office: Depot St Salem IA 52649

VARDARIS, RICHARD MILES, educator; b. Lakewood, Ohio, Nov. 28, 1934; s. George Kalos and Florence (Read) V.; B.A. cum laude (NSF fellow), Case Western Res. U., 1962; postgrad. U. Iowa, 1962-63; M.S., U. Oreg., 1967, Ph.D., 1968; m. Kay A. Vatter, June 12, 1970; children—Paul Stephen, Matthew Read. Asst. prof. psychology Kent State U., 1967-71, asso. prof., 1972—, dir. div. biomed. scis., chmn. neurosci. program com., dir., sr. scientist Neurosci. Lab., 1971—, U. fellow, 1971; research asso. prof. neurobiology Northeastern Ohio Univs. Coll. Medicine. NIH grantee, 1972-73, 74—. Mem. Soc. Neurosci., AAAS, Am., Midwestern psychol. assns., Brit. Brain Research Assn. (hon.), European Brain and Behavior Soc. (hon.), Psychonomic Sci., Phi Beta Kappa, Sigma Xi. Reviewer for various sci. jours.; editor's cons. Scott, Foresman & Co., 1973—. Contbr. articles to profl. jours. Home: 3175 Bird Dr Ravenna OH 44266 Office: Kent Hall Kent State U Kent OH 44242

VARGHESE, JOSEPH EATVILA, rehab. counselor; b. Kalangore, Kerala, India, Aug. 20, 1932; s. Junjummen Ghee and Hannah (Ghee) V.; came to U.S., 1970; B.A., U. Madras, 1958, M.A., 1959; M.A., Eastern Mich. U., 1973; Ed.D., Wayne State U., 1978. Research fellow U. Kerala, 1960-63; gen. sec. Christian Welfare Service, Kerala, 1964-65; state welfare officer for handicapped State of Kerala, 1968-69; dir. disabled student services U. Mich., Ann Arbor, 1974—; staff counselor Life Skills Inc., Dearborn, Mich., 1977—. Independent candidate for Parliament seat from Trivandrum (India), 1967. Certified social worker, Mich.; certified rehab. counselor. Mem. Am. Personnel and Guidance Assn., Am. Rehab. Counseling Assn. Office: Life Skills Inc 23400 Michigan Ave Suite 528 Dearborn MI 48124

VARICHAK, RICHARD WARREN, educator; b. Hibbing, Minn., May 4, 1931; s. George and Mae Cecilia (Severson) V.; student Hibbing Jr. Coll., 1950-51; B.S., U. Tex., 1958, M.Ed., 1960; m. Dessie Wynoka Carter, June 15, 1955; children—Thomas James, Vikki Lynne, Donald Gene, Pamela Gail. Instr. zoology U. Tex., 1959-60; athletic dir., coach, instr. Evant (Tex.) High Sch., 1960-62; prin., coach Darrouzett High Sch., Tex., 1962-63; instr., coach, athletic dir. Hibbing (Minn.) Community Coll., 1963—. Instr. phys. edn. Wyoming U., 1969-70. Served with USN, 1951-55. Candidate for Minn. Tchr. of Year, 1968-69. Mem. A.A.H.P.E.R., Minn., Hibbing (pres. 1967-68) state jr. coll. faculty assns. Elk. Club: Hibbing Exchange (sec. 1968-69). Home: 325 Mesabi Dr Hibbing MN 55746

VARKEY, BASIL, pulmonary physician, educator; b. Quilon, India, Feb. 28, 1941; s. Antony V. and Mariamma (Varghese) V.; M.B.B.S., Trivandrum Med. Coll., 1963; m. Sheela Angela Ben, Aug. 17, 1968; children—Anita, Jay Basil. Intern, Saint Michael Hosp., Milw., 1966-67; resident Trumbull Meml. Hosp., Warren, Ohio, 1967-68; resident VA Hosp., Wood, Wis., 1968-70, fellow in pulmonary disease, 1970-72, staff physician, 1972-73, asst. chief pulmonary sect., 1974, acting chief pulmonary sect., 1975, med. dir. respiratory therapy sect., 1975—, chief pulmonary disease sect., 1976—; asst. prof. internal medicine Med. Coll. of Wis., 1973-77, asso. prof., 1977—; cons. pulmonary medicine Milwaukee County Med. Complex; advisor health occupations Milw. Area Tech. Coll. Recipient Plaque of Honor, Commn. on Sci. Medicine State Med. Soc. of Wis.; Spl. Performance award VA; diplomate Am. Bd. Internal Medicine (subsplty. bd. pulmonary disease). Fellow Royal Coll. Physicians Can., Am. Coll. Chest Physicians (pres. Northlands chpt.); mem. Wis. Respiratory Disease Assn., Am. Thoracic Soc., Am. Fedn. for Clin. Research. Contbr. articles to profl. jours. Home: 2335 Tilton Ct Brookfield WI 53005 Office: 5000 W National Ave Wood WI 53193

VARNER, CHARLEEN LAVERNE MCCLANAHAN (MRS. ROBERT B. VARNER), educator, nutritionist, adminstr.; b. Alba, Mo., Aug. 28, 1931; d. Roy Calvin and Lela Ruhama (Smith) McClanahan; student Joplin (Mo.) Jr. Coll., 1949-51; B.S. in Edn., Kans. State Coll. Pittsburg, 1953; M.S., U. Ark., 1958; Ph.D., Tex. Woman's U., 1966; postgrad., Mich. State U., summer, 1955, U. Mo., summers, 1952, 62; m. Robert Bernard Varner, July 4, 1953. Apprentice county home agt. U. Mo., summer 1952; tchr. Ferry Pass. Sch., Escambia County, Fla., 1953-54; tchr. biology, home econs. Joplin (Mo.) Sr. High Sch., 1954-59; instr. home econs. Kans. State Coll. Pittsburg, 1959-63; lectr. food, nutrition Coll. Household Arts and Scis., Tex. Woman's U., 1963-64, research asst., NASA grantee, 1964-66; asso. prof. home econs. Central Mo. State U., Warrensburg, 1966-70, adviser to Colhecon, 1966-70, adviser to Alpha Sigma Alpha, 1967-70, 73, mem. bd. advisers Honors Group, 1967-70; prof., head home econs. dept. Kans. State Tchrs. Coll., Emporia, 1970-73; prof., chmn. home econs. dept. Benedictine Coll., Atchison, Kans., 1973-74, Baker U., Baldwin City, Kans., 1974-75; owner, operator Diet-Con Dietary Cons. Enterprises Topeka, 1973—. Mem. Joplin Little Theater, 1956-60. Mem. NEA, Mo., Kans. state tchrs. assns., AAUW, Am., Kans., Mo. dietetics assns., Am., Mo., Kans. home econs. assns., Mo. Acad. Sci., AAUP, U. Ark. Alumni Assn., Alumni Assn. Kans. State Coll. of Pitts., Am. Vocat. Assn., Assn. Edn. Young Children, Sigma Xi, Beta Sigma Phi, Beta Beta Beta, Alpha Sigma Alpha, Delta Kappa Gamma, Kappa Kappa Iota, Phi Upsilon Omicron. Methodist (organist). Home: Main PO Box 1009 Topeka KS 66601

VARNER, DURWARD BELMONT, found. exec.; b. Cottonwood, Tex., Jan. 1, 1917; s. Harry S. and Martha (Griffin) V.; B.S., Tex. A. and M. U., 1940; M.S., U. Chgo., 1949; LL.D., Saginaw Valley Coll. and Olivet Coll., 1969; L.H.D., Oakland U., 1970; LL.D., Nebr. Wesleyan U. and Mich. State U., 1970; m. Paula Price, Sept. 14, 1940; children—Thomas A., Judy (Mrs. J. Arthur Seaman), Susan. Asst. to pres. Fed. Land Bank, Houston, 1940-41; asst. dean students Tex. A. and M. U., 1946-47; asst. prof. agrl. econs. Mich. State U., 1949-52, dir. Coop. Extension Service, 1952-55, v.p., 1955-59; chancellor Oakland U., Rochester, Mich., 1959-70; chancellor U. Nebr., Lincoln, 1970-71, pres., 1971-77; chmn. bd. U. Nebr. Found., 1977—. Dir. Beatrice Foods, Inc., Williams Cos., Woodmen Accident and Life Ins. Co. Mem. Joint Com. on U.S.-Japan Cultural and Ednl. Cooperation, 1971—. Mem., chmn. Omaha bd. Fed. Res. Bd. Kansas City, 1974—; chmn. bd. dirs. Mid-Am. Arts Alliance, 1974—; trustee W.K. Kellogg Found., 1975—. Served from 2d lt. to lt. col. AUS, 1941-45; ETO. Mem. Lincoln C. of C., Nebr. Acad. Scis. Rotarian. Home: 3901 S 27th St Lincoln NE 68502

VARNER, ROBERT BERNARD, educator, youth counselor; b. Ellsworth, Kans., May 31, 1930; s. Bernard Lafayette and Leota (Campbell) V.; B.S., Kans. State Coll. at Pittsburg, 1952; M.S., U. Ark., 1959; postgrad. (grantee) U. Kan., 1972-73; m. Charleen LaVerne McClanahan, July 4, 1953. Tchr., coach high sch. Joplin, Mo., 1955-63; head social sci. dept. R.L. Turner High Sch., Dallas County, Tex., 1963-66; tchr., coach Warrensburg (Mo.) Pub. Schs., 1966-70, Lowther Jr. High Sch., Emporia, Kans., 1970-72; counselor Topeka Youth Center, 1973—. Youth dir. Farmers Br. Recreation Center, Dallas County, 1964-66; dir. city recreation program, Warrensburg, 1967. Served with USNR, 1952-54. Mem. NEA, Sigma Tau Gamma, Phi Delta Kappa. Methodist. Home: Main PO Box 1009 Topeka KS 66601

VARNEY, THEODORE ROOSEVELT, book store exec.; b. Manhattan, Kans., Mar. 11, 1906; s. Joseph Guy and Grace Ernestyne (O'Brien) V.; B.S., Kans. State U., 1929; m. Wilma Helene Hahn, July 10, 1931; children—Theodore William, Helen Ruth Varney Burst. Mgr. University Book Store, Inc., Manhattan, 1929-36, pres., 1936-45, owner, pres., 1946—; pres. Varney's Inc., investment co., Manhattan, 1970—. Mem. Manhattan City Planning Bd., 1968-71. Bd. dirs. United Fund, Manhattan, 1951-53, Riley County chpt. ARC, 1947-52, 61; v.p., chmn. Manhattan Band Bd., 1968; bd. dirs. Westminster Found., Manhattan, 1958-61, treas., 1959-61. Served to lt. col. AUS, 1941-46. Mem. Manhattan C. of C. (dir. 1936-37, 39, 51-52, pres. 1952), Nat. Coll. Store Assn. (trustee 1961-63, 69), Kans. Res. Officers Assn. (v.p. 1939), Am. Legion. Presbyn. (elder 1947-51, 52). Elk, Rotarian (dir. 1972-73, editor Bull., 1971). Home: 211 N 18th St Manhattan KS 66502 Office: 1305 Anderson Ave Manhattan KS 66502

VARNOLD, CECIL BURL, twp. ofcl.; b. Maquon, Ill., Mar. 14, 1912; s. James Martin and Nellie Mae (Smith) V.; m. Ellouise Lorraine Ronesela Conner, Oct. 14, 1943; children—Paul Martin, Richard Mark, Charles Burdette. Rd. commr. Maquon Twp. (Ill.), Maquon, 1939-47, 71-77; owner, operator Varnold Found. & Erection Co., Maquon, 1947-66. Mem. Ill. Assn. Twp. and County Ofcls., Taxpayers Fedn., Internat. Union Operating Engrs. Republican. Methodist. Clubs: Masons, Shriners. Home: PO Box 155 Maquon IL 61458

VARWIG, HARRY JULIUS, architect; b. St. Louis, Nov. 21, 1936; s. Harry William and Anna Matilda (Rosenkoetter) V.; student Northeast Mo. State Coll., 1954-55; B.Arch., Washington U., St. Louis, 1961; m. Ruby JoAnn Womble, June 18, 1960; children—David Lee, Scott Allen. Draftsman, Carl E. Etz, architect, 1955-60, job capt., 1958-62, project architect, 1962-69; asso. architect Carl E. Etz & Assos., architects, 1963-65; architect, v.p., partner Etz & Assos., Inc., 1965-69; job capt. Hosp. Designers, Inc., St. Louis, 1969-73, project architect, 1970-73, asso. architect, 1973—, v.p., 1973—. Mem. Mo. Council Registered Architects. Home: 840 Amersham Dr Town and Country MO 63141 Office: 717 Office Pkwy St Louis MO 63141

VARY, JAMES PATRICK, physicist; b. Savanna, Ill., May 23, 1943; s. Willis Leavenworth and Ethice Kathryn (Mc Cabe) V.; B.S., Boston Coll., 1965; M.S., Yale U., 1967, M.Philosophy, 1968, Ph.D., 1970; m. Audrey M. Zarba, June 11, 1966; children—William, Brian. Vice-pres. Compute A Mark Corp., Cleve., 1968—; research asso. Center for Theoretical Physics, Mass. Inst. Tech., 1970-72; asst. physicist Brookhaven Nat. Lab., Upton, N.Y., 1972-74, asso. physicist, 1974-75; asst. prof. physics Iowa State U., asso. physicist Ames Lab., 1975-77, asso. prof., dir. nuclear theory program, physicist Ames Lab., 1977—. Vice pres., bd. dirs. Montessori Family Center, Roxbury, Mass., 1970-71. Mem. Am. Phys. Soc., Sigma Pi Sigma, Sigma Chi. Contbr. articles to profl. jours. Home: 1121 Clark Ave Ames IA 50010 Office: Physics Dept Iowa State U Ames IA 50011

VASILS, ALBERT, artist, illustrator; b. Siberia, Russia, May 3, 1915; s. Augusts and Pauline (Kronitis) V.; came to U.S., 1954, naturalized, 1960; B.F.A., Mich. State U., 1962, M.A., 1963; postgrad. Sch. Arts and Crafts, Eng., 1952-53. Free lance illustrator of books, 1960—; graphics illustrator of film animation Mich. State U., East Lansing, 1960—; one-man shows of include: Duncan Galleries, N.Y.C., 1972, 74, 76; various colls. and univs. in Mich., 1962-68; group shows include: Mich. State U., 1963; Detroit Art Inst., 1965, Lansing Community Coll., 1968, Central Mich. U., 1966, Flint Art Inst. (Mich.), 1968, Duncan Galleries, Paris, 1974-77; represented in permanent collections: Nat. Gallery of Art, Washington, Mich. State U., East Lansing Library, also schs. Recipient numerous awards including: Du Prix de Paris, France, 1977, The Creativity '72' award Certificate of Distinction, Art Direction Mag., 1972, Palmes de Oro al Merito Belgo-Hispanico, Assn. Belgo-Hispanico, 1974. Mem. Am. Fedn. of Arts, Smithsonian Assos., Assn. of Belgo-Hispanica, Academia de Ciencias Humanisticus y Relaciones. Home: 511 Charles St East Lansing MI 48823 Office: Michigan State Univ Instructional Media Center East Lansing MI 48824

VASSALOTTI, LOUIS ANGELO, county ofcl.; b. Akron, Ohio, Jan. 7, 1947; s. Louis Joseph and Angeline Kathryn (Verderico) V.; degree in data processing U. Akron, 1971; m. Susan Lynn Ulrich, May 16, 1970; children—Louis Christopher, Kari Lynn. Computer operator City of Akron, 1970-71, programmer, 1971-72, programmer analyst, 1972-73, systems analyst, 1973-75; data processing coordinator Summit County (Ohio), Akron, 1975—; mem. 4 county data processing steering coms.; dep. adminstr. all county data processing; initiator co-op. program in data processing with U. Akron; speaker, demonstrator to various orgns., clubs, schs. Served with U.S. Army, 1968-69. Mem. Computer Security Inst., Am. Mgmt. Assn., Data Processing Mgmt. Assn. Democrat. Roman Catholic. Club: K.C. Home: 251 Mission Dr Akron OH 44301 Office: 72 S High St Akron OH 44308

VASSILIADES, ANTHONY EPAMINONDAS, paper co. exec.; b. Chios, Greece, Nov. 26, 1933; s. Epaminondas and Cornelia (Manolakis) V; naturalized, 1961; B.S., Wagner Coll., 1956; M.S., Syracuse U., 1958; Ph.D., Poly. Inst. Bklyn., 1962; m. Constance Vallas, Jan. 27, 1957; children—Cornelia, Peter. Asst. prof. Wagner Coll., S.I., N.Y., 1960-65, asso. prof. chemistry, 1965-66; asso. dir. research Champion Internat. Corp., Chgo., 1966-68, dir. research, 1968-70, v.p., dir. research and devel., 1970—, cons., 1960-66. Mem. Am. Chem. Soc., N.Y. Acad. Sci., Soc. Plastics Engrs., Omicron Delta Kappa, Sigma Chi. Contbr. articles to profl. jours. Home: 8738 Tanager Woods Dr Cincinnati OH 45242 Office: Knightsbridge Hamilton OH 45020

VATTEROTT, JOSEPH HENRY, motel chain owner; b. St. Louis, Mo., Aug. 23, 1909; s. Charles Francis and Margaret (Harvey) V.; grad. pub. schs.; m. Margaret R. Flaherty, June 5, 1935; children—Michael J., Thomas P., Mary Honora, Joseph Henry. Chmn. bd. dirs. Joseph H. Vatterott Mgmt. Co., owner, operator Holiday Inn Franchise, St. Louis, 1955—, Collinsville, Ill., 1972—; pres. Joseph H. Vatterott Realty & Bldg. Co., Clayton, Mo., 1964—; owner, opr. Airport Lumber Co., Florissant, Mo., 1940—; dir. Florissant Bank, St. Louis Union Trust Co. Bd. dirs. Municipal Theatre Assn., Child Center of Our Lady Grace, Daus. of St. Paul; mem. exec. com. United Way of Greater St. Louis; chmn. lay bd. De Paul Community Health Center; mem. pres.'s council St. Louis U.; trustee Vatterott Found. Recipient St. Louis award, 1963; Human Relations award Am. Jewish Com., 1977; Fleur de Lis medal St. Louis U. decorated Knight of Malta, Pope Pius XII, Knight of Holy Sepulchre. Mem. Home Bldrs. Assn. Greater St. Louis (past pres.), Internat. Assn. Holiday Inns (past pres.). Home: 13321 Pine Creek Dr Chesterfield MO 63017 Office: 10 S Brentwood Blvd Clayton MO 63105

VAUGHAN, ANDREW THOMAS, educator; b. West New York, N.J., June 2, 1921; s. Thomas Martin and Emma Elizabeth (Jozseffy) V.; student Miami U., 1939-43; B.S. in Edn., Otterbein Coll., 1945; M.A., Columbia, 1957, Ed.D., 1958; m. Doris M. Minton, Aug. 7, 1943. Tchr., Loveland, Ohio, 1945, Fairfield, Ohio, 1946-51, Leonia, N.J., 1952-55; prof. health edn. So. Ill. U., Carbondale, 1958—. Cons. Nat. Soc. for Better Environment, Republic of Philippines, 1973, Nat. Health Adminstrn., Republic of China, 1973; USIS guest lectr., Malaysia, Singapore, S. Korea. Mem. Delta Tau Delta, Phi Kappa Phi, Phi Delta Kappa, Kappa Delta Pi. Club: Jackson Country. Author: A Study Guide for Healthful Living, 1962. Home: Rural Route 2 Misty Lake Murphysboro IL 62966 Office: Dept Health Edn So Ill U Carbondale IL 62901

VAUGHAN, LAWRENCE EDWARD, educator; b. Brunswick, Nebr., Aug. 4, 1922; s. J. Gordon and Beatrice (Van Kirk) V.; B.A., Nebr. Wesleyan U., 1946; M.A., Northwestern U., 1953; Ed.D., U. Neb., 1959; m. Ruth Norton, Aug. 21, 1942; 1 son, Victor. Tchr. elementary schs., Cook County, Ill., 1949-52; tchr. jr. high sch., Hastings, Nebr., 1952-54, Lincoln, Nebr., 1954-55; tchr., counselor Lincoln S.E. High Sch., 1955-57; asst. prof. Nebr. Wesleyan U., Lincoln, 1957-60, asso. prof., 1960-62, prof. edn., 1962—, head edn. dept., 1962—, chmn. profl. edn. div., 1962-77. Served with AUS, 1943-46; PTO. Mem. N.E.A., Nebr. Schoolmasters Club, Nebr. Assn. Tchr. Educators (sec.-treas. until 1976), Nebr. Assn. Colls. Tch. Edn. (pres. 1976-77), Phi Delta Kappa, Psi Chi, Kappa Delta Pi, Pi Gamma Mu, Theta Chi. Kiwanian (past lt. gov.; gov. Nebr.-Iowa dist. 1977-78; life fellow Kiwanis Internat. Found.). Club: Capital City (past pres.) (Lincoln). Home: 5945 Leighton Ave Lincoln NE 68507

VAUGHAN, RICHARD HENRY, banker; b. Mpls., Sept. 21, 1927; s. James A. and Katherine (Wyman) V.; B.A., Dartmouth Coll., 1950; M.B.A., Amos Tuck Sch., 1951; grad. Stonier Grad. Sch. Banking, 1963; m. Mary Wurtele, Aug. 4, 1950; children—Peter Wurtele, Angus MacDonald, Charlotte Lindley, Carol Wyman. With Northwestern Nat. Bank, Mpls., 1951-71, exec. v.p., 1968-71, also dir.; pres., dir. Northwest Bancorp, 1971—; dir. N.W. Nat. Bank, St. Paul, Northwest Growth Fund, 1967-76, Northwest Computer Services, Inc., Banc Northwest and Upper Midwest Council. Chmn. spl. gifts Mpls. United Fund, 1967-68; mem. Fed. Advisory Council, 1977; trustee Highcroft Country Day Sch., Mpls., 1963-67, Minn. Outward Bound Sch., Mpls., 1964-68, Blake Schs., to 1975, Carleton Coll., Smith Coll. Republican. Mem. Minneapolis Club, Woodhill Country Club. Office: Northwest Bancorp 1200 Northwestern Bank Bldg Minneapolis MN 55480

VAUGHN, CHARLES GEORGE, coll. dean; b. Marshfield, Wis., Nov. 14, 1915; s. Charles George and Dora (Wilcott) V.; student U. Wis., 1936-41; B.S., U. Dayton, 1961; M.S., Miami U., Oxford, Ohio, 1964; m. Noel Janet Wyandt, July 9, 1971; children—Charles George, Jeffrey James, Barbara Jean. Commd. 2d lt. U.S. Army Air Force, 1941, advanced through grades to lt. col., 1964; ret., 1964; dean student personnel Sinclair Community Coll., Dayton, Ohio 1964—. Mem. ednl. adv. com. Dayton Urban League, Dayton Human Relations Council; mem. evaluation com. Ednl. Opportunity Center; chmn. residence com. YMCA, 1965-73, bd. dirs. 1971-73. Mem. Miami Valley Personnel and Guidance Assn. (past pres.), Am. Coll. Personnel Assn., Nat. Vocat. Guidance Assn., Assn. for Measurement and Evaluation. Democrat. Home: 244 Hadley Ave Dayton OH 45419 Office: 444 3d St W Dayton OH 45402

VAUGHN, CHARLES GORDON, dermatologist; b. Graceville, Minn., Feb. 26, 1926; s. Timothy Charles and Bertha Marie (Haack) V.; B.S., U. Minn., 1944, M.B., 1946, M.D., 1947; m. Mary Ellen Madden, Aug., 1957; children—John, Charles, Peter. Intern, Gen. Hosp., Mpls., 1948-49; U. Minn. Hosp., Mpls., 1953-56; practice medicine specializing in dermatology, 1956; mem. staffs United, St. Joseph's, Bethesda, Midway St. Paul-Ramsey hosps. (all St. Paul); clin. prof. dermatology U. Minn., 1970—; med. dir. Degree of Honor Ins. Co., St. Paul, 1957—. Served to maj. U.S. Army, 1950-52. Mem. AMA, Minn., Ramsey County med. socs., Am. Acad. Dermatology. Roman Catholic. Home: 200 Mt Curve Blvd St Paul MN 55105 Office: 1812 Am Nat Bank Bldg St Paul MN 55101

VAUGHN, CHARLES ROBERT, lawyer; b. Olney, Ill., Feb. 17, 1922; s. Charles S. and Elsie B. (Ray) V.; B.S., James Millikin U., 1943; LL.B., U. Ill., 1948; m. Elizabeth Ann Gassmann, Dec. 4, 1943; children—Ann (Mrs. Robert Martin), Carol (Mrs. Robert Schafer), Charles B., Kathleen (Mrs. John Longueville), John R., Allen Z., Ray W., Mary G., Frank E. Admitted to Ill. bar, 1948; practice law, Olney, Ill., 1948—; dir. First Nat. Bank, Olney. States atty., Richland County, Ill., 1952-64, 68—, asst. states atty., 1948-52. Alt. del. Republican Nat. Conv., 1964. Served with USMCR, 1943-46. Mem. Am. Legion, VFW, Ill. State Attys. Assn., Ill., Richland County bar assns. Roman Catholic. Elk. Home: 507 N Boone St Olney IL 62450 Office: Courthouse Olney IL 62450

VAUGHN, CLARENCE BENJAMIN, oncologist; b. Phila., Dec. 14, 1928; s. Albert and Aretha (Johnson) V.; B.S., Benedict Coll., 1951; M.S., Howard U., 1955, M.D., 1957; Ph.D., Wayne State U., 1965; m. Sarah Campbell, Sept. 25, 1953; children—Steven, Annette, Carl, Ronald. Intern, D.C. Gen. Hosp., Washington, 1957-58; fellow medicine and allergy, resident, Freedman's Hosp., Washington, 1958-59; NIH fellow, 1961-62; NIH spl. research fellow, Wayne State U., Detroit, 1952-64, lab. instr., 1963-67; research physician Milton A. Darling Meml. Center, Mich. Cancer Found., Detroit, 1964-70, clin. dir., 1970-72; dir. div. oncology Providence Hosp., Southfield, Mich., 1973—; cons. med. staff, dept. medicine Kirwood Gen. Hosp., Detroit, 1967—, Oakwood Hosp., Dearborn, Mich., 1968—; cons. staff, dept. medicine Detroit Meml. Hosp., 1970, Crittenton Hosp., Rochester, Mich., 1972; courtesy staff Grace Hosp., Detroit, 1973, S.W. Detroit Hosp., 1973; jr. attending Hutzel Hosp., Detroit, 1975—; lab. asst. chemistry Benedict Coll., Columbia, S.C., 1945-51; grad. asst. Howard U., Washington, 1951-52, research asst., 1952-53; chemist Dept. Interior, Washington, 1953-55; lab. instr. Wayne State U., 1963-67, asst. prof. oncology, 1967—, asso. dept. biochemistry, 1967—; med. service liaison office between USAF and Wayne State U., 1960—. Pres. Wayne County unit Am. Cancer Soc. Served to lt. col. USAF, 1959-61. Decorated Air Force Commendation medal; recipient Aerospace Physician award Air Force Res., 1974, Outstanding Flight Surgeon award, 1975. Fellow Am. Coll. Clin. Pharm.; mem. Am. Cancer Soc. (dir. 1973—), Air Force Assn., Am. Chem. Soc., A.C.P., A.A.U.P., A.M.A., Am. Radium Soc., Am. Soc. Clin. Oncology, Assn. Mil. Surgeons U.S., Detroit Cancer Club, Detroit Physiol. Soc., Mich. Med. Soc., Mich. Assn. Med. Edn., Nat. Med. Assn., N.Y. Acad. Scis., Oakland County Med Soc., Res. Officers Assn. U.S., S.W. Oncology Study Group, Wayne County Med. Soc., Sigma Xi, Alpha Kappa Mu, Beta Kappa Chi, Phi Lambda Upsilon. Contbr. articles to profl. jours. Home: 19410 Canterbury Rd Detroit MI 48221 Office: 16001 W Nine Mile Rd Southfield MI 48075

VAUGHN, JACK LEE, veterinarian; b. Helena, Mo., June 7, 1934; s. Maynard Harte and Hazel Marie (Christy) V.; B.S., U. Mo., 1958, D.V.M., 1958; m. Julie Ann Ramm, June 1, 1975; children—Maynard, David, Judy, Daphne, Pamela. Farmer, 1952—; large animal veterinarian, Columbia, Mo., 1958-63, mixed practice, 1963-67, specialist in small animals, 1967—; dir. Mo. Veterinary Supply Co. Mem. Columbia, Central Mo., Mo. veterinary med. assns., AVMA. Republican. Baptist. Clubs: Forrest Hills Country, Rotary. Home: Route 2 Columbia MO 65201 Office: 400 Nebraska Ave Columbia MO 65201

VAUGHN, LAWRENCE (LARRY) EUGENE, JR., assn. exec.; b. Hannibal, Mo., Feb. 14, 1944; s. Lawrence Eugene and Marjorie Gwendolyn (White) V.; diploma Carolina Sch. Broadcasting, 1963; m. Leona Marie Tate, Feb. 8, 1964; children—Link, Lance. Staff announcer Sta. WIST Radio, Charlotte, N.C., 1962-63; news dir. Sta. KWRT Radio, Boonville, Mo., 1963-65; program dir. WDAN Radio, Danville, Ill., 1965-69; sgt. Danville Police Dept., 1969-74; sales mgr. Sta. KCBJ-TV, Columbia, Mo., 1974-75; dir. info. Assn. Mo. Electric Coops., Jefferson City, 1975-77, mgr. coop. advt., 1977—; lobbyist Mo. legislature; Mo. agt. Federated Rural Electric Ins. Corp. Mayor City of Holts Summit (Mo.), 1977—; bd. dirs. Mid-Mo. Council Govts. Recipient 1st pl. award spl. projects Nat. Rural Electric Coop. Assn., 1976, spl. award pub. service Mo. Dept. Agr., 1977, Humanitarian award C.A.P., 1977. Mem. Mo. Broadcasters Assn. (spl. award pub. service broadcasting 1976), Pub. Relations Soc. Am., Pub. Utility Communicators Assn., Mo. Pilots Assn., C.A.P. Democrat. Baptist. Clubs: St. Louis Advt., Lions. Home: Route 3 Box 16 Holts Summit MO 65043 Office: 2722 E McCarty St Jefferson City MO 65101

VAUGHN, RICHARD ADELBERT, dentist; b. Hamtramck, Mich., Mar. 1, 1935; s. John Oliver and Mildred (Smith) V.; B.S., U. Detroit, 1957, D.D.S., 1961; postgrad. U. Pitts., 1961-64; m. Brenda Farrington, Feb. 18, 1956 (div.); children—Belinda, Richard, Carla; m. 2d, Esther Livingston, Mar. 23, 1974; stepchildren—Ronald Livingston, Andrea Livingston. Practice of dentistry, specializing in oral and maxillofacial surgery, Detroit, 1964— instr. oral surgery U. Pitts., 1962-63; instr. oral and maxillofacial surgery Detroit Gen. Hosp., 1964—, trustee, 1971—, chmn. superintending com., 1972—. Mem. Detroit Mayor's Com. Human Resources, Devel. Med. Subcom., Com. Study Med. Care of Indigent; mem. Spl. Admissions Com. U. Detroit Sch. Dentistry. Treas., Cub Scouts, Boy Scouts Am., 1966-67, asst. Webelo instr., 1967-68, scoutmaster, 1968-69. Trustee, mem. exec. bd. Detroit Med. Center, 1972. Mem. Gt. Lakes Soc. Oral Surgeons, Am., Nat., Mich., Detroit Dist. (chmn. children's dental health week 1970-71) dental assns., Wolverine Dental Soc. (pres. 1968-69). Am. Dental Soc. Anesthesiology, Detroit Acad. Oral Surgeons, U. Detroit Black Dental Alumni Assn. (chmn. 1974—), U. Detroit Nat. Alumni Assn. (dir. 1973—). Clubs: Economic, Century (trustee) (Detroit). Home: 1333 Strathcona Dr Detroit MI 48203 Office: 13724 Woodward Highland Park IL 48203

VAYHINGER, JOHN MONROE, clergyman, educator; b. Upland, Ind., Jan. 27, 1916; s. Paul J. and Harriett E. (Palmer) V.; A.B., Taylor U., 1937; B.D., cum laude, Drew Theol. Sem., 1940; M.A., Columbia U., 1948, Ph.D., 1956; M.A., Drew U., 1951; m. Ruth Catherine Imler, Sept. 17, 1939; children—John Earl, Karen Lynn. Ordained to minstry Meth. Ch., 1941; pastor Meth. Chs., Ind., N.Y., Conn., Colo., 1938-58; head, dept. psychology W. Va. Wesleyan Coll., Buckhannon, 1949-51; chief clin. psychologist Adult and Child Guidance Clinic, South Bend, Ind., 1951-58, Ind. U., 1953-58; prof. pastoral psychology and counseling Garrett Theol. Sem., Evanston, Ill., 1958-64; prof. psychology of religion and pastoral counseling Iliff Sch. Theology, Denver, 1964-67; prof. psychology and pastoral care Anderson (Ind.) Sch. Theology. Bd. dirs. Ind. Council Chs., Life Psychiat. Center, Denver. Seved with AUS, 1944-47. Diplomate Am. Bd. Examiners in Profl. Psychology. Fellow Am. Orthopsychiat. Assn.; mem. N.Y. Ann. Conf. Meth. Ch., Am. Psychol. Assn., Am. Assn. Marriage and Family Counseling, Am. Assn. Pastoral Counselors, Am. Group Psychotherapy Assn., Colo., Ind. psychol. assns., Am. Assn. U. Profs., Assn. Mil. Chaplains, Acad. Religion and Mental Health, Nat. Congress of Parents and Tchrs., Ind. Congress of Parents and Tchrs., Christian Assn. for Psychol. Studies. Inst. of Pastoral Care, Am. Sci. Affiliation. Author (with others) Casebook of Pastoral Counseling, 1962, In the Beginning of Divorce, 1971. Home: 1235 Favorite St Anderson IN 46013 Office: 1123 E 3d St Anderson IN 46011

VAZIRI-NAZAR, HABIB, psychiatrist; b. near Esphahan, Iran, Aug. 7, 1934; s. Mohamadiali and Batool (Entekhabi) V.; came to U.S., 1963; M.D., Tehran U., Iran, 1960, Bd. in Gen. Psychiatry, 1963; m. Rashi Entekhabi, Mar. 19, 1960; children—Haleh, Sholeh. Med. dir. Rczzi Hosp., Tehran, Iran, 1960-63; intern, St. Joseph Mercy Hosp., Flint, Mich., 1963-64; resident Eastern State Hosp., Williamsburg, Va., 1964-66; resident Lafayette Clinic, Detroit, 1966-68, head adolescent service, 1968-74; dir. Dept. Mental Health, St. Joseph Mercy Hosp., Pontiac, Mich., 1972—. Asst. prof. Wayne State U., Detroit, 1968—; pres. staff Woodside Hosp., Pontiac, 1974. Named Best Tchr. Year, Wayne State U. Dept. Psychiatry, Detroit, 1972. Diplomate Am. Bd. Psychiatry and Neurology. Mem. A.M.A., Am., Mich. psychiat. assns., Wayne County, Oakland County med. socs. Author: (with H. Rezal) Organic Brain Syndrome, 1961. Contbr. articles to profl. jours. Home: 6743 Vachon Dr Birmingham MI 48010 Office: 21415 Civic Center Dr Southfield MI 48010

VEACH, DARRELL ALVES, engring. co. exec.; b. Lexington, Ky., Dec. 21, 1928; s. Darrell Goldman and Gladys Elizabeth (Stanhope) V.; B.S., U. Ky., 1951, postgrad. 1955-57; m. Maureen Mefford, Oct. 19, 1957; children—Darrell C., Cynthia K. Gen. field engr. Portland Cement Assn., 1957-63; v.p. Engineers Assos., cons. engrs., Evansville, Ind., 1963—. Mem. Democrats for Better Govt. Bd. dirs. ARC. Served to 1st lt., Corps Engrs., U.S. Army, 1951-54. Recipient Ind. Jr. Engr. of Year award, 1963, Alumnus of Year U. Ky., 1963. Mem. ASTM, Am. Concrete Inst., Nat. Soc. Profl. Engrs., ASME, ASCE, Am. Legion, Evansville Rose Soc., Alpha Tau Omega. Episcopalian (vestryman, 1968—). Elk, Optimist, Mason (Shriner). Home: 4000 Jennings Ln Evansville IN 47712 Office: 425 3d Ave Evansville IN 47708

VECCHIO, PETER JAMES, food co. exec.; b. Mt. Pleasant, Pa., July 3, 1947; s. Peter and Mary Margaret (Daly) V.; B.B.A., Marshall U., 1969; m. Linda Lou Snyder, Mar. 15, 1968; 1 son, Peter James. Grocery sales rep. H.J. Heinz Co., Pitts., 1969-72, dist. staff asst., 1973-74, area mgr. Cin., 1974-76, broker-mgr. Central region, 1976-77; pres., chmn. bd. Sno Mountain Co., Cin., 1977—. Trustee Bevis Athletic Assn., 1976. Served with U.S. Army, 1969-71; Vietnam. Decorated Bronze Star. Mem. Nat. Frozen Food Assn., Cin. Grocery Mfrs. Reps. Roman Catholic. Home: 3315 Grovewood Dr Cincinnati OH 45239 Office: Hilltop Plaza Center 8212 Hamilton Ave Cincinnati OH 45231

VEECK, WILLIAM LOUIS, sports exec.; b. Chgo., Feb. 9, 1914; s. William L. and Grace (De Forrest) V.; student Kenyon Coll.; m. Eleanor Raymond, Dec. 8, 1935 (div. 1949); m. 2d, Mary Frances Ackerman, Apr. 29, 1950; 9 children. Treas., asst. sec. Chgo. Cubs Profl. Baseball Team, 1933-41; pres., owner profl. baseball teams Milw. Brewers (Am. Assn.), 1941-45, Cleve. Indians, 1947-49, St. Louis Browns, 1951-53, Chgo. White Sox, 1959-61, 76—; sports announcer NBC-TV, 1957-58; pres., owner Suffolk Downs, Boston, 1969-71. Served with USMCR, 1943-45. Roman Catholic. Author: (with Ed Linn) Veeck-As in Wreck, 1962, The Hustler's Handbook, 1965, Thirty Tons a Day, 1972. Office: Comiskey Park Dan Ryan at 35th St Chicago IL 60616*

VEENHUIS, PHILIP EDWARD, physician; b. Kalamazoo, Aug. 4, 1935; s. Claude Albert and Placide Mary (Steger) V.; B.A., Kalamazoo Coll., 1957; M.D., U. Mich., 1961; m. Joanne Elizabeth Williams, Aug. 8, 1959; children—Mark Edward, Suzanne Marie. Intern, James Decker Munson Hosp., Traverse City, Mich., 1961-62; resident Lafayette Clinic, Detroit, 1962-65; practice medicine specializing in psychiatry, Wauwatosa, Wis., 1967—; asso. prof., acting chmn. dept. psychiatry Med. Coll. Wis., 1973-75, dir. continuing edn. dept. psychiatry, 1977—. Served with USNR, 1965-67. Fellow Am. Psychiat. Assn.; mem. AMA. Office: 1220 Dewey St Wauwatosa WI 53213

VEENKER, CLAUDE HAROLD, educator; b. George, Iowa, July 31, 1919; s. Ralph C. and Fannie (Casjens) V.; B.A., U. No. Iowa, 1943; M.A., U. No. Colo., 1953; D.Health and Safety, Ind. U., 1957; m. Elizabeth Louise Higgins, Jan. 1, 1944; children—Jo Lee, Vicki Susan. Tchr., Osage (Iowa) High Sch., 1946-47, Mason City (Iowa) Pub. Schs., 1947-55; teaching. asst. Ind. U., 1955-56, vis. lectr., 1956-57; asst. prof. Purdue U., Lafayette, Ind., 1957-61, asso. prof., 1961-66, prof., 1966—, chmn. health edn. sect., 1961-77. Chmn. health edn. test project Ednl. Testing Service, Princeton, 1965-74; cons. bur. research coop. research br. U.S. Office Edn., 1966-68; cons. healthful sch. environment AMA, NEA, Washington, 1969; mem. Ind. Council on Sch. Health, 1971—, Ind. Adv. Com. on Drug Edn., 1969-74, Ind. Gov.'s Regional Com. on Mental Health, 1966-67. Served to 1st lt. USMCR, 1943-46. Decorated Purple Heart. Fellow Am. Sch. Health Assn., Am. Pub. Health Assn. (governing council 1974-76, mem. sch. health sect. council 1970-73); mem. Am. Alliance for Health, Phys. Edn. and Recreation (exec. council sch. health div. 1964-67, chmn. sch. health service sect. 1959-60), Mid-Am. Coll. Health Assn., Ind. Assn. Health Educators (pres. 1970), Phi Delta Kappa, Eta Sigma Gamma. Methodist. Editor, contbr. author: Synthesis of Research in Selected Areas of Health Instruction, 1963; mem. editorial bd. Jour. Health, Phys. Edn. and Recreation, 1961-62, 64-66. Contbr. articles to profl. jours. Home: 224 E Knox Dr West Lafayette IN 47906 Office: Lambert Bldg Purdue University Lafayette IN 49707

VEENSTRA, H. ROBERT, cons. engr.; b. Leighton, Iowa, Oct. 21, 1921; s. Henry and Gretta (Vandehaar) V.; B.S. in Civil Engring., Iowa State U., 1947; m. Norena D. Grandia, Sept. 9, 1944; children—Henry Robert, Cynthia L., John N., Mark A. Design engr. Stanley Engring. Co., Muscatine, Iowa, 1947-49, sect. head, 1949-51, project engr., 1951-57, supervising engr., 1957-61; partner Veenstra & Kimm, Engrs. and Planners, West Des Moines, 1961—. Served to capt. AUS, 1942-46. Mem. Nat. Soc. Profl. Engrs. (past nat. dir.), Iowa Engring. Soc. (Anson Marston award 1962), ASCE, Am. Congress on Surveying and Mapping, Cons. Engrs. Council Iowa (past treas., pres.), ASTM, Am. Water Works Assn., Water Pollution Control Fedn., Cons. Engrs. Council, Theta Xi. United Methodist. Mason. Contbr. articles to profl. jours. Office: 300 West Bank Bldg 1601 22nd St West Des Moines IA 50265

VEIT, IRWIN, elec. distbg. co. exec.; b. Chgo., July 14, 1930; s. Lawrence Leo and Jennie (Kudesh) V.; B.S., U. Ill., 1952; m. Alice Joyce Levy, Aug. 12, 1956; children—Lynne Judith, Hope Ellen. With Bright Elec. Supply Co., Chgo., 1952—, pres., 1959—. Mem. Midwest Elec. Distbrs. Assn. (dir.), Illuminating Engring. Soc. (dir., sec.-treas. Chgo. sect. 1971, pres. 1973-74, lighting progress com. 1971, mem. Nat. Tech. Conf. 1971). Home: 5229 Jarvis St Skokie IL 60076 Office: 701 W Jackson Blvd Chicago IL 60606

VELAER, CHARLES ALFRED, ret. educator; b. Kansas City, Mo., Jan. 25, 1932; s. Charles Alfred and Edna (Bothwell) V.; B.S., Roosevelt U., 1957; M.S., Ill. Inst. Tech., 1960; m. Caryl Ruth Sonnenburg, Nov. 17, 1962; children—Ruth Anne, Charles Alfred. Instr., asst. prof. Roosevelt U., Chgo., 1957-68, asso. prof. physics, 1968-74, ret., 1974; cons. New Horizons Pub., Inc., Chgo. Served with Signal Corps, AUS, 1950-54. Mem. Am. (cons. rosarian 1971—), English, Chgo. Regional (dist. pres. 1966-67, dir. 1968—) rose socs., Am. Inst. Physics. Home: 9636 S Brandt Ave Oak Lawn IL 60453

VELINSKY, BARBARA LYNN MIHELIC, community services orgn. dir.; b. St. Joseph, Mo., Feb. 16, 1947; d. John Joseph and Barbara Lucille (Pacini) Mihelic; B.A., U. Nebr., Lincoln, 1968, M.S. in Guidance Counseling, Omaha, 1971; m. Frank J. Velinsky, Dec. 29, 1973; 1 son, Jason. Caseworker, Douglas County (Nebr.) Social Services, Omaha, 1968-70; sec., child care aide tng. program U. Nebr., Omaha, 1971; planning asst. United Community Services of Midlands (now United Way), Omaha, 1971-72, planning asso., 1972-77, asst. dir. allocations and agy. relations, 1977—, exec. dir. United Way Council Bluffs (Iowa), 1977—. Mem. Nebr. Welfare Assn. (chpt. pres. 1975-76, mem. bd. 1976-77). Home: 14062 Drexel Circle Omaha NE 68137 Office: 1805 Harney St Omaha NE 68102

VENEZIA, ANTONIO JOSEPH, orthodontist; b. New Orleans, Dec. 20, 1932; s. Antonio J. and Zulime (Agnelli) V.; student Memphis State U., 1949-51; D.D.S., U. Tenn., 1954; M.S. in Orthodontics, Northwestern U., 1962; postgrad. U. Md., 1957, Inst. Dental Research Walter Reed Med. Center, 1960; m. Joan Loretta Reid, Dec. 24, 1971; children—Steven Michael, Valerie Kim, Natalie Claire, Christopher Jay, Terrence Joseph Wiley, Jennifer Daniel. Commd. 2d lt. U.S. Army, 1954, advanced through grades to lt. col.; cons. in orthodontics and pedodontics to surgeon-gen. U.S. Army, Europe, ret., 1967; pvt. practice orthodontics, Chgo., Floosmoor, and Lansing, Ill., 1967—; mem. faculty Northwestern U. Grad. Sch. Orthodontics, Chgo., 1971, now asst. prof. Guest lectr. grad. orthodontic dept. U. Detroit. Fellow Chgo. Inst. Medicine, Am. Coll. Dentists; mem. Am. Dental Assn., Am. Soc. Orthodontics, Edward H. Angle Soc. Orthodontists, Odontological Soc. Chgo., G.V. Black Soc., Richard Doggert Dean Odontological soc. (hon.), Sigma Phi Epsilon, Delta Sigma Delta. Contbr. numerous articles to profl. jours. Home: 653 Pheasant Trail Frankfort IL 60423 Office: 3235 Vollmer Rd Floosmoor IL 60422 also 845 N Michigan Ave Suite 943-W Chicago IL 60602 also 18333 Burnham Ave Lansing IL

VENIT, WILLIAM BENNETT, elec. products co. exec.; b. Chgo., May 28, 1931; s. George Bernard and Ida (Schaffel) V.; grad. high sch.; m. Nancy Jean Carlson, Jan. 28, 1956; children—Steven Louis, Aprilann. Sales mgr. Coronet, Inc., Chgo., 1952-63, pres., chmn. bd., 1963-74; pres., chmn. bd. Roma Wire Inc., Chgo., 1971-74; pres. Wm. Allen Inc., Chgo., 1972-74; pres., chmn. bd. William Lamp Co., Inc., William Wire Co., Inc., 1974—; spl. cons. Mac Kinney Co., Hanover Park, Ill., Hartlaub Legs Inc., Mc Sherrystown, Pa., 1978—. Served with Q.M.C., AUS, 1949-52. Mem. Mfr. Agt. Club, Chgo. Lamp and Shade Inst. (dir.). Home: 4850 N Monticello Ave Chicago IL 60625 Office: 715 N Kedzie Ave Chicago IL 60622

VENKATAKRISHNA, V. BELLUR, educator; b. Mysore State, India, Apr. 6, 1934; s. Bellur and Bellur (Venkatalaxamma) Venkataramaiah; came to U.S., 1966, naturalized, 1977; diploma Nat. Dairy Research Inst., India, 1957; B.A., Utkal U., India, 1959; FAO fellow, India, 1962, Denmark, 1963; diploma (Royal Danish Govt. scholar), Royal Vet. and Agrl. Coll., Copenhagen, 1965; Ph.D., Kans. State U., 1972; m. Kirsten Marie Rusholt, Aug. 19, 1968; children—Ravi, Chand. Shift mgr. Bangalore Dairy, India, 1957-63; with Danish dairy industry, 1965-66, Am. dairy and egg processing industry, summers 1967-69; temp. instr. econs. Kans. State U., 1968-70; asst. prof. mktg. Ball State U. Coll. Bus., Muncie, Ind., 1970-75, asso. prof., 1975-77; prof. mktg. No. Mich. U., Marquette, 1977—. Participant, Ford Motor Co. project for acad. community, 1972-74. Mem. Am. Econ. Assn., Am. Mktg. Assn., Acad. Internat. Bus., Am. Statis. Assn., Midwest Bus. Adminstrn. Assn. Chgo. Council Fgn. Relations, Omicron Delta Epsilon, Delta Sigma Pi. Home: 1201 Mc Clellan Marquette MI 49855 Office: Dept Mgmt and Mktg Sch Bus and Mgmt No Mich Univ Marquette MI 49855

VENNERS, THEODORE, realtor; b. Nidda, Germany, Apr. 29, 1948; s. John and Hilda V.; came to U.S., 1950, naturalized, 1958; student S.D., State U., 1968. Exec. sec. S.D. Republican Party, Pierre, 1968; exec. asst. to Gov. Farrar, S.D., 1968-70; pres. Black Forest, U.S.A., Rapid Forest, S.D., 1970—; prin. Ted Venners Real Estate, Rapid City, S.D.; dir. Black Forest Devel., Inc. & Subs. Bd. dirs. YMCA; dir. Sunday Clothes Fine Arts Assn.; pres. Young Republicans S.D. State U.; founder, pres. Western S.D. German Club. Mem. Black Hills, Nat. realtors assns., Greater S.D., Black Hills Badlands & Lakes assns., Rapid City C. of C. (state, local govt. com.). Lutheran. Club: Cosmopolitan. Home: 1182 Parkwood Rd Rapid City SD 57701 Office: PO Box 8002 Rushmore Mutual Life Bldg Rapid City SD 57709

VENNING, COREY, educator; b. Spanish Fork, Utah, July 4, 1924; d. Robert A. and Blanche E. (Rockhill) Brown; M.A., U. Chgo., 1948, Ph.D., 1968; children—Robert, Ruth, Alan. Research analyst U.S. Dept. State, Washington, 1948-49, fgn. service officer, Bombay, India, 1949-52, Athens, Greece, 1952-54: instr. polit. sci. Loyola U. Chgo., 1965-68, asst. prof., 1969-75, asso. prof., 1975—. Mem. Am. Polit. Sci. Assn., Internat. Studies Assn., Univ. Coll. Women Ill. Republican. Author: (under name Tracy E. Hyde) The Single Grandmother, 1974. Home: 1632 Chase St Chicago IL 60626 Office: Loyola U 820 N Michigan Ave Chicago IL 60611

VENTLING, JACK LESTER, chiropractor; b. Davis City, Iowa, Oct. 19, 1935; s. Lester Kenneth and Marie Margaret (Bronson) V.; B.A., Simpson Coll., 1958; M.S.C., London Coll. Applied Sci., 1959; Ph.D., St. Andrew's U. (Eng.), 1960; D.C., Cleveland Chiropractic Coll. of Los Angeles, 1968; m. Patricia Anne Mills, July 12, 1973; children—Stephanie K., Derek F., Eric W. Personnel officer Union Bank of Los Angeles, 1965-68; practice chiropractic, Poland, Ohio, 1968—. Dir. Youngstown Chiropractic Clinic, Poland, 1968—; dean div. basic sci. Cleveland Chiropractic Coll. of Los Angeles, 1965-68; Trustee Life Chiropractic Coll. Served to capt. USAF, 1961-65. Certified for evaluation of permanent disability. Mem. East Ohio Chiropractic Soc. (pres. 1974-76), Ohio State Chiropractic Assn. (Dedicated Chiropractor of Yr. 1974, chmn. peer rev. com. 1977—, rep. assemblyman to Internat. Chiropractors Assn.; 2d v.p.), Am. Chiropractic Assn., Parker Chiropractic Research Found., Amvets, VFW, Beta Beta Beta, Beta Chi Rho, Epsilon Sigma, Sigma Alpha Epsilon, Pi Delta Kappa. Elk. Club: Saxon. Home: 78 Newport Dr Boardman OH 44512 Office: 44 N Main St Poland OH 44514

VENTO, BRUCE FRANK, congressman: b. St. Paul, Oct. 7, 1940; s. Frank A. and Ann V. (Sauer) V.; B.A., Wis. State U., River Falls, 1965; postgrad. U. Minn., 1966—; m. Mary Jean Moore, Oct. 24, 1959; children—Michael, Peter, John. Tchr. sci., social studies Mpls. pub. schs., 1965—; mem. Minn. Ho. of Reps. from St. Paul 66A Dist., 1971-76, asst. majority leader, vice chmn. jud. com., 1973-76; mem. 95th Congress from 4th Minn. Dist. Mem. legis. rev. com. Minn. Commn. on Future. Del., Democratic Farm Labor party Central Com., 1972—, chmn. Ramsey County Com., 1972—. NSF grantee, 1967-68. Mem. Minn. Fedn. Tchrs., Beta Beta Beta, Kappa Delta Phi. Home: 1534 Atlantic St St Paul MN 55106 Office: 1330 Longworth House Office Bldg Washington DC 20515 also 316 N Robert St St Paul MN 55101

VENTO, ELIO GAETANO, obstetrician-gynecologist; b. Rome, Dec. 3, 1924; s. Umberto and Elisabetta (Gualano) V.; came to U.S., 1952, naturalized, 1958; M.D., U. Rome, 1951; m. Anita Rose DiSilvestro, Aug. 9, 1952; children—Elio Marco, Annette Marie. Intern, Columbus Hosp., Chgo., 1952-53; resident in obstetrics and gynecology Lutheran Deaconess Hosp., Chgo., 1955-56, St. Anne's Hosp., Chgo., 1956, W. Suburban Hosp., Oak Park, Ill., 1959-61; practice medicine specializing in obstetrics and gynecology, Oak Park; mem. staff W. Suburban Hosp., Oak Park, St. Anne's Hosp., Chgo., Loyola Hosp., Maywood; asst. prof. Rush Med. Sch., Chgo.; clin. asst. prof. Loyola U. Med. Center, Maywood. Diplomate Am. Bd. Obstetrics and Gynecology. Fellow Am. Coll. Obstetricians and Gynecologists; mem. AMA, Ill. State, Chgo. med. socs. Home: 1115 N Rossell St Oak Park IL 60302 Office: 6609 W North Ave Oak Park IL 60302

VENUGOPAL, MUTHUGOUNDER, physician; b. Annur, India, June 6, 1940; s. Muthugounder and Angammal Venugopal; came to U.S., 1967; M.B., B.S., Stanley Med. Coll., Madras, India, 1965; m. Carol Lander, June 27, 1968; 1 son, Suresh. Intern, St. Luke's Hosp., N.Y.C., 1967-68; resident in surgery Meml. Hosp., Charleston, W.Va., 1968-72; surgeon Blue Earth (Minn.) Med. Center, 1972—. Diplomate Am. Bd. Surgery. Fellow A.C.S.; mem. AMA, Minn. Surg. Soc. Home: 617 S Moore St Blue Earth MN 56013 Office: 520 S Galbraith St Blue Earth MN 56013

VERBAL, CLAUDE ARTHUR, automotive co. engr.; b. Durham, N.C., Nov. 12, 1942; s. Sidney John and Mary Gladys (Dennis) V.; B.S., N.C. State U., 1964; m. Dorothy Mae Simmons, Apr. 24, 1974; children—Robin, Randall, Dru. Project engr. Buick Motor Div., Gen. Motors Co., Flint, Mich., 1964-67, sr. project engr., 1971-72, test engring. supr., 1972-74, staff project engr., 1947-76, asst. supt. quality control, 1976-77, supt. quality control, 1977—. Bd. dirs. Flint Econ. Devel. Corp., 1975—, pres., 1976—; mem. Flint Environ. Action Team and Found. Bd., 1975—. Mem. Nat., Mich. socs. profl. engrs., Soc. Automotive Engrs., Am. Soc. Quality Control, ASME. Baptist. Clubs: Lions (pres.), Masons, Shriners. Home: 1800 Valley Ln Flint MI 48503 Office: Factory 12 905 Hamilton Ave Flint MI 48550

VER BURG, JOHN ROBERT, accountant; b. Inwood, Iowa, June 18, 1936; s. Bert and Pearl Ranzella (Remmerde) Ver B.; grad. Davenport Coll. Bus., Grand Rapids, Mich., 1961; Asso. Sci., Aquinas Coll., 1967; m. Eleanor Scholten, Mar. 28, 1958; children—G. Robert, David Lee, Philip John, Brent Alan, Mark Aron. Sales corr. Mich. Fleet Equipment Co., Grand Rapids, 1960-64; comptroller W.J. Dykstra Co., Grand Rapids, 1964-73; owner John R. Ver Burg, accountant, Grand Rapids, 1973—; founder, pres. Heritage Book Publs., Inc. Founder, pres. Evangelism Reachout, Inc., 1972—. Bd. dirs. Grand Rapids Right to Life Com.; co-organizer, bd. dirs. Final Phase Evangelism, Inc., 1970—, Corr. Bible Studies, Inc., 1973—. Served with AUS, 1954-57. Mem. Nat. Soc. Pub. Accountants, Accountants Assn. Mich. Home: 6823 Mildred Ave SE Grand Rapids MI 49508 Office: 6631 Division Ave S Grand Rapids MI 49508

VERBY, JOHN EDWARD, physician; b. St. Paul, May 24, 1923; s. John Edward and Amy (Martin) V.; B.A., Carleton Coll., 1944; B.S., U. Minn., 1946, M.B., 1947, M.D., 1948; m. Jane E. Crawford, 1946; children—John Edward III, Steven, Ruth, Karl. Rotating intern Mpls. Gen. Hosp., 1947-49; semi-profl. baseball player, New Ulm, Mankato, Minn., 1941-49; gen. practice medicine, Litchfield, Minn., 1949-51, 53-54; family practice medicine, partner Olmsted (Minn.) Med. Group, 1954-68; asso. prof. dept. family practice and community health U. Minn. Med. Sch., 1969-73, prof. dept. family practice, 1973—, asst. head dept. family practice and community health, 1971—, dir. rural physician asso. program, 1971—; chief staff Olmsted Community Hosp., Rochester, Minn., 1958; vis. prof. gen. practice Welsh Nat. Med. Sch., Cardiff, 1977-78. Pres., organizer Rochester (Minn.) Youth Baseball Assn., Inc., 1958; pres. Holmes Elementary Sch. P.T.A., Rochester, 1958; active YMCA, Rochester. Bd. dirs. Internat. Mag. Gen. Medicine. Served with USNR, 1944-45; served to 1st lt. M.C., AUS, 1951-53, Korea. Matteson Athletic scholar award Carleton Coll., 1944. Diplomate Am. Bd. Family Practice (charter). Fellow Am. Geriatric Soc., Am. Acad. Family Physicians (charter); mem. Am. Med. Soc. Vienna, Austria (life), Minn. Acad. Gen. Practice (chpt. pres. 1960), A.M.A., Minn. State Med. Assn., Zumbro Valley, Hennepin County med. socs., Philo Mathean Literary Soc. Methodist (chmn. bd. trustees 1966-68). Author: Medical Exam Board Review in Family Practice, 1972; (with Jane Verby) How to Talk to Doctors, 1977. Contbr. articles to profl. jours. Home: 9609 Washburn Rd Bloomington MN 55431 Office: Dean's Office U Minn Med Sch Minneapolis MN 55455

VERCLER, JOHN ROBERT, sales engr.; b. Pontiac, Ill., Feb. 18, 1945; s. John Edwin and Josephine Naomi (Kinsinger) V.; B.S. in Agrl. Engring., U. Ill., 1967. Sales engr. Bodine Electric Co., mfr. fractional horsepower electric motors, Chgo., 1967-74; service specialist F.S. Services, Inc., distbr. agrl. supplies, Bloomington, Ill., 1974—. Home: 1424 E College Ave Apt 5 Normal IL 61761 Office: 1701 Towanda Ave Bloomington IL 60108

VERDUN, MICHAEL DOUGLAS, counselor; b. Beardstown, Ill., Feb. 6, 1947; s. Frances L. and Darlene (Sarff) V.; B.A., Huron Coll., 1969; M.Ed. Idaho State U., 1972, Ed.D., 1974; m. Claudia Kaye Warren, Aug. 21, 1970; 1 dau., Marianne Kaye. Tchr., high sch., Hitchcock, S.D., 1969-70; caseworker Dept. Pub. Welfare, Huron, S.D., 1970-71; intern Idaho State U. at Pocatello, 1972-74; co-supr. mental health unit Bannock Meml. Hosp., Pocatello, 1973-74; chief supr. five county area Dept. Social Services, Dept. Welfare, Mitchell, S.D., 1974-76; counselor Red Lake (Minn.) Sch. Dist., 1976—. Co chmn. adv. commn. to dist. ct. Mitchell, 1975-76. Mem. Am. Personnel and Guidance Assn. Roman Catholic. Home: 2419 Park Ave Apt 4 Bemidji MN 56601 Office: Red Lake Jr High Sch Reed Lake MN 56671

VERDUN, RUDOLPH JAMES, electronics service co. exec.; b. White Plains, N.Y., Feb. 5, 1945; s. Norman Rodley and Virginia Etta (Futch) V.; student pub. schs., Flint, Mich.; m. Ollie Mae Collins, Mar. 5, 1977. Prodn. foreman Mich. Saw and Tool Co., Flint, 1963-71; pres. El-Tech Radio and TV, Inc., Flint, 1971—. Democrat. Roman Catholic. Home: 5810 Baldwin Blvd Flint MI 48505 Office: 657 E Pierson Rd Flint MI 48505

VERMILLION, GEORGE HEATON, city ofcl.; b. Kansas City, Mo., Apr. 29, 1924; s. John Fred and Mabel Ellen (Roseberry) V.; B.A., U. Wichita, 1950; A.A., Independence Jr. Coll., 1948; postgrad. Central Mo. State U., 1974-78; m. Barbara Ann Hoffman, Aug. 10, 1948; children—David H., Debra Ann, Douglas B. Program coordinator Cessna Aircraft Co., Wichita, Kans., 1950-59; sr. contract adminstr. AiResearch Mfg. Co., Phoenix, 1959-62; project adminstr. N.Am. Aviation, Tulsa, 1962-64; mgr. contract adminstrn. Benson Mfg. Co., Kansas City, Mo., 1964-69; sr. adminstr. Magnavox Corp., Urbana, Ill., 1969-71; dir. personnel City of Independence (Mo.), 1971—. Bd. dirs. Scottsdale council Boy Scouts Am., 1961-62. Served with U.S. Naval Air Corp, 1942-46; PTO. Mem. Nat. Pub. Employer Labor Relations Assn., Internat. Personnel Mgmt. Assn. (dir. Kansas City chpt. 1976—), Am. Legion, U. Wichita Alumni Assn. Home: 16717 E 29th St Independence MO 64055 Office: 103 N Main St Independence MO 64050

VERNIER, DOUGLAS LEE, educator; b. Detroit, Dec. 27, 1943; s. Floyd L. and Marie L. (Jenkins) V.; B.A., U. Mich., 1966, M.A., 1968; m. Gayle Y. Rittenger, Aug. 19, 1967; children—Melanie Ann, Adam Ray. Announcer, transmitter engr. WAAM, Ann Arbor, Mich., WKNR, Detroit, 1964-65; newsman WKNR, Detroit, 1966; sales mgr. WCBN, Ann Arbor, 1964-66; night sch. instr. electronics Henry Ford Community Coll., Dearborn, Mich., 1967; dir. advt., sales promotion WJBK, Detroit, 1967; instr. speech Washtenaw Community Coll., Ypsilanti, Mich., 1968; gen. mgr. WMOT, instr. broadcasting Middle Tenn. State U., Murfreesboro, 1968-72; dir. pub. radio stas. KHKE, KUNI, asst. prof. (dir. broadcasting) U. No. Iowa, Cedar Falls, 1972—. Mem. radio adv. com. Iowa Pub. Broadcasting Network, 1972—; founding mem. Mayor's Com. on CATV, Cedar Falls, 1974; mem. radio devel. com. Corp. for Pub. Broadcasting, 1974—; mem. feasibility com. Iowa Pub. Radio Network, 1975; cons. pub. radio devel., engring. and sta. expansion. Mem. Nat. Assn. Ednl. Broadcasters, Speech Communications Assn., Alpha Phi Gamma. Photographer, producer Inevitably (recipient several awards including U.S.A. Council on Non-theatrical Internat. Events Eagle award 1969). Home: 3904 Oak Park Circle Waterloo IA 50701 Office: KHKE/KUNI U No Iowa Cedar Falls IA 50613

VERNON, CARL ATLEE, JR., wholesale co. exec.; b. Topeka, Aug. 15, 1926; s. Carl Atlee and Capitola (Jarboe) V.; B.S., Yale, 1947; m. Marion Leila Colton, May 7, 1950; children—Mary Catherine, Matthew Fowler, Susan Elizabeth. With Fleming Cos., Topeka, 1947—, dir. grocery, frozen food merchandising, 1961-66, dir. info. services, 1966-74, corp. v.p., 1972, corp. v.p. regional systems, 1974—. Chmn. Shawnee County (Kans.) chpt. A.R.C., 1957-58. Served with Supply Corps, USNR, 1944-46. Mem. Assn. Yale Alumni, Chi Phi (past officer). Republican. Episcopalian (vestryman 1961-63, jr. warden 1968-70). Clubs: Topeka Allied Food (founder, pres. 1961); Yale of Topeka; Topeka Country (dir. 1973-77). Office: Fleming Cos Two Townsite Plaza Topeka KS 66601

VERSACE, JOHN, automotive engr.; b. Washington, May 14, 1925; s. Cosimo and Candelora (Pustorino) V.; B.S., U. Md., 1951, M.S., 1953; Ph.D., Ohio State U., 1955; m. Rita Marie Maloney, Apr. 7, 1956; children—Devin G., Candelora, Elizabeth I., Mary C. Engr., WTTG-TV, Washington, 1948-51; human factors specialist Chrysler Corp., Detroit, 1955-62; exec. engr. safety research Ford Motor Co., Dearborn, Mich., 1962—. Served with USNR, 1943-46. Mem. Am. Psychol. Assn., Am. Statis. Assn., Soc. Automotive Engrs. (chmn. human factors engring. com. 1962, mem. automotive council 1976—).

Home: 4785 Ranch Ln Bloomfield MI 48013 Office: PO Box 2053 Dearborn MI 48121

VETTER, DALE BENJAMIN, educator; b. Henry County, Ill., Aug. 11, 1908; s. John and Esther (Soliday) V.; A.B, North Central Coll., 1930; A.M., Northwestern U., 1935, Ph.D., 1946; m. Frona A. Tonkinson, Mar. 28, 1932; children—Sharon, Ione, Judith, Rebecca. Prin. Hooppole High Sch., 1932-35; tchr. Harrison Pub. Sch., 1936-37; teacher-librarian Riverside-Brookfield High Sch., 1937-41; tchr. English, Ill. State Normal U., 1941—. Exec. com. Midwest English Conf., 1962—. Mem. Am. Assn. U. Profs., Mod. Lang. Assn. Am., Northwestern U. Alumni Assn., Ill. English Assn., Augustan Reprint Soc., Friends of Milner Library, Newberry Library (fellow). Unitarian. Author articles, Bull. of Friends of Milner Library, Ill. State Normal Bull., Modern Language Notes. Home: 214 W Willow St Normal IL 61761 Office: Illinois Normal University Normal IL 61761

VETTER, DAVID AUGUSTIN, savs. and loan exec.; b. Portsmouth, Ohio, Oct. 2, 1919; s. Louis Joseph and Madeline Norine (Augustin) V.; student Xavier U., 1937-38; grad. Ind. U., Sch. Savs. and Loan, 1952; student Ohio Savs. & Loan Acad., 1954-56; m. Marcella Louise Ladd, Nov. 25, 1941; children—David Michael, Stephen Gregory, Dennis Ladd, Mary Ann, Nancy Louise, Catherine Susan, Paul Augustin. With Citizens Savs. & Loan Assn. Co., 1938—, asst. sec., 1948-55, sec., 1955-57, v.p., 1957-63, pres., 1963—, also dir.; dir. Fed. Home Loan Bank, Cin., 1975—. Chmn., City Planning Adv. Com., 1960-68, Central City Devel. Com., 1967-70, City Portsmouth Workable Program Com., Urban Renewal, 1960-69; mem. Notre Dame High Sch. Bd., 1962-68, Diocese Columbus Sch. Bd., 1965-68; mem. Gov.'s Housing and Community Devel. Commn., 1971-73. Bd. dirs. Community Chest, United Fund, 1958-64, YMCA, Ohio U., Portsmouth, Meth. Retirement Center; pres. Portsmouth Area Growth Found., 1973—; bd. dirs. Am. Automobile Assn. So. Ohio, pres., 1972; trustee Shawnee State Gen. and Tech. Coll. Served to 2d lt. AUS, 1942-46. Recipient award for outstanding service to area Southeastern Ohio Regional Council, 1968, Portsmouth Area Distinguished Citizen of Year award Jr. C. of C., 1969. Mem. U.S. (legis. com. 1971-73), Ohio (1st v.p. 1971, pres. 1972) savs. and loan leagues, Savs. Instn. Mktg. Soc. Am., C. of C. (dir.). Republican. Roman Catholic. Rotarian. Home: 3120 Forest Ave Portsmouth OH 45662 Office: 507 Chillicothe St Portsmouth OH 45662

VEVERKA, JOSEPH FREDERICK, physician; b. Mpls., May 17, 1933; s. Joseph Edward and Margaret Elizabeth (Englund) V.; B.A. (scholar), Johns Hopkins, 1955; M.D., McGill U., 1959; m. Erlene Louise Fullington, May 12, 1962; children—Constance, Bonnie, Christopher, Jeffrey. Intern, Royal Victoria Hosp., Montreal, Que., Can., 1959-60; gen. practice resident Sacramento County Hosp., Sacramento, Calif., 1962-63, Broadlawns Polk County Hosp., Des Moines, 1963-64; gen. practice medicine, Prairie City, Ia., 1964—; pres. elect for chief staff Broadlawns Polk County Hosp., Des Moines, 1971-72; dir. med. edn. Luth. Hosp., Des Moines, 1971; instr. interns Luth. Hosp., Broadlawns Polk County Hosp., Des Moines. Served with USNR, 1960-62. Diplomate Am. Bd. Family Practice. Fellow Am. Acad. Family Physicians; mem. AMA, Iowa, Jasper County, Polk County med. socs., Omicron Delta Kappa, Alpha Delta Phi. Republican. Methodist. Mason. Home: 407 N Marshall St Prairie City IA 50228 Office: PO Box 324 Prairie City IA 50228

VIAR, JACK BYRON, health center adminstr.; b. Kansas City, Kans., Sept. 28, 1935; s. Fred Walker and Aletha Lucille (Kiplinger) V.; student Baker U., 1953-55; B.S., Central Mo. State U., 1959; M.S.W., Mo. U., 1964; m. Virginia Hall Walk, Apr. 3, 1959; children—Julie Ann, Andrew Jay, Amy Lynn. Dir. E. Central Mo. Mental Health Center, Mexico, 1957-73; dir. Tri-County Mental Health Center, No. Kansas City, Mo., 1973—. Chmn., Mexico Community Chest, 1971-73; bd. mem. Mental Health Services Corp., Kansas City. Bd. dirs. Mexico Vocational-Tech. Sch., 1971-73. Served with USAF, 1961. Mem. Nat. Assn. Social Workers (vice chmn. 1972-73), Nat. (Mo. chmn. 1971-73, legis. chmn. 1975), Met. (chmn. 1975) councils community mental health centers, Mo. Coalition Community Mental Health Centers (legis. chmn. 1975), Kappa Sigma. Republican. Methodist. Home: 202 NW 43d Terr Kansas City MO 64116 Office: 2900 Hospital Dr North Kansas City MO 64116

VICHER, EDWARD ERNEST, educator; b. Chgo., Nov. 12, 1914; s. John James and Bessie Rose (Benes) V.; M.S., U. Ill., 1937, Ph.D., 1942, B.S. in Pharmacy, 1935; m. Pauline Hakala, Dec. 2, 1950; children—John and Jerry (twins). Asst. bacteriology U. Ill. Coll. Pharmacy, Chgo., 1935-39, instr. bacteriology Coll. Medicine, 1939-49, asst. prof. bacteriology, 1949-57, asso. prof., 1957-69, prof., 1969—, asso. head dept. microbiology, 1976—, mem. faculty Grad. Coll., 1957—; cons. microbiology U. Ill. Hosps., 1946-70, VA Hosp., Hines, Ill., 1946-56, VA Hosp., West Side, Chgo., 1954-55, Toni Co., personal care div. Gillette Co., St. Paul, 1948-70; pvt. practice as pharmacist, Chgo., 1970—. Bd. dirs. Internat. Inst. Biochem. and Biomed. Tech., 1975—. USPHS grantee, 1961-62. Mem. Am. Pharm. Assn. (Chgo. br. sec. 1937-42), Chgo. Med. Mycological Soc. (pres. 1962-63), AMA, Am., Ill. socs. microbiology, Med. Mycological Soc. of Ams., Sigma Xi, Phi Kappa Phi, Rho Chi, Phi Rho Sigma. Home: 734 N Harvey Ave Oak Park IL 60302 Office: 835 S Wolcott Ave Chicago IL 60612

VICK, TIMOTHY DOUGALL, geologist, educator; b. Rochester, N.Y., Dec. 5, 1945; s. William Lyon and Louise Elizabeth (Stockard) V.; B.A., Beloit Coll., 1969; M.A.T., U. Wis., River Falls, 1974; m. Jean Louise Inglis, Aug. 19, 1968. Beloit Coll. intern, N.Y. Times, 1967-68; reporter Beloit Daily News, 1968-69, Rhindelander (Wis.) Daily News, 1969-71; tchr. earth scis., pub. schs. Rosemount, Minn., 1973-75; tech. supr. geology Carleton Coll., Northfield, Minn., 1975-76, tech. dir. geology, 1976—, Mellon teaching fellow, 1976-77. Served with USAR, 1970-75. Mem. Nat. Assn. Sci. Tchrs., Nat. Assn. Research in Sci. Teaching, Nat. Assn. Geology Tchrs., Northfield Arts Guild, Audubon Soc. Home: 915 Linden St N Northfield MN 55057 Office: Dept Geology Carleton Coll Northfield MN 55057

VICKERY, EUGENE LIVINGSTONE, physician; b. Fairmount, Ind., Nov. 27, 1913; s. Lee Otis and Grace (Hawkins) V.; B.S. with distinction, Northwestern U., 1935, M.B., Northwestern U., 1940, M.D., 1941; m. Millie Margaret Cox, Dec. 21, 1941; children—Douglas Eugene, Constance Michelle Anita Sue, Jon Livingstone. Intern Evanston (Ill.) Hosp., 1940-41; pvt. practice medicine, Lena, Ill., 1946—; chmn. med. records com. Freeport Meml. Hosp., 1954-64, sec. staff, 1964-67, chairman credentials com., 1964-69, v.p. staff, 1967-69, chief staff, 1969-71, chmn. constn. and bylaws com., 1971—; mem. staff St. Francis Hosp.; local surgeon Ill. Central R.R. Health officer, Lena, Ill., 1948—; mem. Stephenson County Bd. Health, 1966-75, v.p., 1969-75; mem. peer rev. policy com. No. Ill. Found. Med. Care. Mem. Lena Sch. Bd., 1951-54; mem. Lena Library Bd., 1958-62; med. dir. Civil Def., rural Stephenson County, Ill., 1961-70; mem. exec. bd. Blackhawk Area council Boy Scouts Am., recipient Silver Beaver award Nat. Council, 1968, Distinguished Eagle award Nat. Council, 1977, mem. nat. council, 1971—; bd. dirs. Stephenson County unit Am. Cancer Soc. Served from 1st lt. to maj. AUS, 1941-46. Decorated Legion of Merit; recipient Lena Community Service award, 1972. Mem. Stephenson County, Ill. (chmn. med.-legal council) med. socs., AMA, Am., Ill. (chmn. bd. dirs., v.p. 1977) acads. family physicians, Assn. Mil. Surgeons U.S., Blackhawk Area Ind. Practice Assn. (exec. com.), Blackhawk Area Med. Assn. (dir.), AAAS, Ill. Soc. Med. Research, Ill. Assn. of Professions (dir., v.p.), Am. Numis. Assn., Soc. of Medallists, Nat. Rifle Assn., Ill. Gun Collectors Assn., Arctic Inst. N.Am., Am. Legion, Phi Beta Kappa. Republican. Mem. Evang. Free Ch. Lion. Club: Apple Canyon. Contbr. articles to numis. publs. Home: 602 Oak St Lena IL 61048 Office: 202 S Schuyler St Lena IL 61048

VICTOROFF, VICTOR MORTON, psychiatrist; b. Jersey City, June 8, 1918; s. Irving and Minnie (Florman) V.; M.D., N.Y. U., 1944; m. Virginia Wegman, Sept. 25, 1947; children—Mark Alan, V. Michael, Jeffrey, Gregory, Debra, Brian. Intern, Bellevue Psychiat. Hosp., N.Y.C., 1944-45; postgrad. Montefiore Hosp., Bronx, N.Y., 1947; asso. to Joseph L. Fetterman, M.D., Cleve., 1947-53; practice medicine specializing in neuropsychiatry, Cleve., 1953—; mem. staff Huron Road Hosp., East Cleveland, Ohio, 1947—, chief div. psychiatry, 1973—; mem. staff Doctor's Hosp., 1947—, Woman's Hosp., 1948—, Windsor Hosp., 1947—, Euclid Gen. Hosp., 1960—. Pres., med. dir. Victor M. Victoroff, M.D. and Assos., Inc. Chmn. Ohio Gov.'s Citizen's Task Force on Mental Health and Mental Retardation, 1971-73. Recipient citation Acad. Medicine Cleve. and Cuyahoga County, 1961. Mem. Acad. Medicine of Cleve. (peer norms com. 1977—), Ohio Psychiat. Assn. (pres. 1967, pres. Edn. and Research Found. 1968-69, commendation plaque 1972), Cleve. Soc. Neurology and Psychiatry (commendation and certificate 1972). Home: 1821 N Park Blvd Cleveland OH 44106 Office: 2231 Taylor Rd Cleveland OH 44112

VIGNIERI, CHARLES JOSEPH, meat packing co. exec.; b. Chgo., Oct. 7, 1924; s. Frank and Rosario (Saporito) V.; student pub. schs., Kenosha, Wis.; m. Lorraine Vander Warn, June 29, 1946; children—Allan, Susan, Dennis, Richard, Patricia, Joseph, Thomas, Daniel, Mark. With Frank Vignieri & Sons, Kenosha, 1936-54; with Kenosha Beef Internat., 1954—, pres., 1960—; pres. Birchwood Meat & Provision, Inc., Kenosha, 1960—; dir. Kenosha Savs. & Loan Assn. Sec., Milw. Meat Council, 1965-67; guest lectr. Carthage Coll., Kenosha, 1970-75, bd. assos., 1970—. Co-chmn. March of Dimes Campaign, Kenosha, 1964; chmn. Paris-Kenosha County Plan Commn., 1965; co-founder, chmn. Kenosha Youth, Inc., 1968-70. Bd. dirs. United Way, Kenosha, 1966-68, 72-75, campaign gen. chmn., 1972, pres., 1973-74; mem. adv. bd. Dominican Sisters of Bethany, Kenosha, 1963-71. Served with AUS, 1943-46; PTO. Mem. Kenosha C. of C. (dir. 1965-68), Nat. Ind. Meat Packers Assn. (dir. 1965-77, v.p. central div. 1974-77, 1st v.p. 1978—). Roman Catholic (trustee, treas. 1952-66, parish chmn. archibishops fund appeal, 1952-66). Elk, Rotarian (dir. 1965-70, pres. 1967-68). Contbr. articles to profl. jours. Home: 4001 5th Pl Kenosha WI 53142 Office: PO Box 639 Kenosha WI 53141

VIJ, GURBACHAN SINGH, civil engr.; b. Multan, Pakistan, June 13, 1937; s. Lajpat Rai and Kushlya Devi (Mehndru) V.; came to U.S., 1969, naturalized, 1974; B.S. in Engring., Punjab U., India, 1955, M.Sc. in Engring., 1967; M.Engring., Cleve. State U., 1974; m. Gurbakhsh Kaur Saluja, May 26, 1962; children—Harvinder, Raminder. Asst. prof. Punjab Engring. Coll., Chandigarh, India, 1959-62; exec. engr. Central Pub. Works Dept., Delhi, India, 1962-68; engr. Erdman & Anthony, Cons. Engrs., Rochester, N.Y., 1969-72, McDowell Wellman Engring. Co., Cleve., 1972-73; sr. design engr. Dow Chem. U.S.A., Strongsville, Ohio, 1973—. Registered profl. engr., N.Y., N.J. Mem. ASCE, Am. Concrete Inst. Mem. Sikh Religious Soc. Home: 7857 List Ln Parma OH 44130 Office: 14955 Sprague Strongsville OH 44136

VILAS, FAITH LEHMAN, civic worker; b. Gettysburg, Pa., Dec. 13, 1924; d. Samuel Franz and Irene (Granville) Lehman; B.A., Wellesley Coll., 1946; m. Jack Vilas, Jr., Nov. 26, 1947 (div. Apr. 29, 1969); children—Faith, Jack. Chemist, Pure Oil Co., 1946-48; tchr. Girls Latin Sch., 1948-50, pres. Alumnae Assn., 1950-52; chmn. bd. mem. tng. course Welfare Council Met. Chgo./U. Chgo., 1959-61; pres. bd. dirs. Jr. League Chgo., Inc., 1963-65; bd. dirs. Vis. Nurses Assn., 1965—; pres. Aux. Cook County Hosp., 1970-71; pres. bd. dirs. Vis. Nurses Assn. Chgo., 1972-74; regional fund chmn. Wellesley Coll., 1974-77; v.p. bd. dirs. United Community Services, Evanston, Ill., 1974—; mem. fin. and allocations com. United Way Suburban Chgo., Zone IV, 1976—; mem. operating effectiveness com. Community Fund Chgo., 1976—. Republican. Episcopalian. Club: Woman's Athletic Chgo. Home: 708 Michigan Ave Evanston IL 60202

VILLANUEVA, ANTONIO DEL ROSARIO, research scientist; b. La Union, Philippines, Oct. 17, 1926; s. William Martinez and Pia Guerrero (del Rosario) V.; came to U.S., 1946, naturalized, 1954; B.S., Detroit Inst. Tech., 1961; M.A., Central Mich. U., 1977; m. Carmen Emilia Perez, Sept. 5, 1954; children—Yvette, Suzanne. Research asst. Ind. U. Med. Center, Indpls., 1953-54, 1956-57; research asso., research scientist, dir. calcified tissue lab. Henry Ford Hosp., Detroit, 1959—; cons. in field. Served with arty. U.S. Army, 1950-52. Co-recipient Hektoen Gold medal AMA, 1963. Mem. AAAS, Am. Soc. Clin. Pathology, Nat. (charter mem., chmn. awards com.), Mich. socs. of histotech., Am. Soc. Med. Tech., P.A.C.E. Sci. Assembly (mem. subcom.). Contbr. numerous articles to profl. jours.; developer 2 biol. dyes; editor Jour. of Histotech., 1977. Home: 13101 Oak Park Blvd Oak Park MI 48237 Office: Henry Ford Hosp Detroit MI 48202

VINCE, ROBERT, educator; b. Auburn, N.Y., Nov. 20, 1940; s. George John and Betty (Colavito) V.; B.S., U. Buffalo, 1962; Ph.D., State U. N.Y. at Buffalo, 1966; m. Maureen Veronica Ramsey, Aug. 26, 1961; children—Susan Maureen, Sharon Mary. Asst. prof. med. chemistry U. Miss., Oxford, 1966-67; asst. prof. U. Minn., Mpls., 1967-71, asso. prof., 1971-76, prof., 1976—. Vis. scientist Roche Inst. Molecular Biology, 1974-75. Recipient Lunsford Richardson Research award, 1966, Research Career award Nat. Cancer Inst., 1972-76. Mem. Am. Chem. Soc., Am. Pharm. Assn., AAAS, Am. Assn. Cancer Research, Am. Soc. Biol. Chemists, Sigma Xi, Rho Chi. Contbr. 45 articles to profl. jours. Patentee antibiotics and antiviral agts. Home: 1723 Yorkshire Ave St Paul MN 55116 Office: Coll Pharmacy Univ Minn Minneapolis MN 55455

VINCENZ, STANISLAW ALEKSANDER, geophysicist, educator; b. Oskrzesince, Poland, Feb. 4, 1915; came to U.S., 1961, naturalized, 1971; s. Stanislaw Andrzej and Helena (Loeventon) V.; B.S., Imperial Coll., U. London, 1937, D. Imperial Coll., 1939, Ph.D., 1952; m. Margit Annemarie Schwarz, June 3, 1949; 1 son, Felix. Demonstrator in geophysics Imperial Coll., London, 1948-49, asst. lectr., 1949-52, research asst., 1952-53; head geophysics div. Indsl. Devel. Corp., Kingston, Jamaica, W.I., 1953-61; asso. prof. geophysics St. Louis U., 1961-67, prof., 1967—; vis. scientist U. Tex. at Dallas, 1965; sr. vis. fellow U. Colo., 1976; Nat. Acad. Sci. exchange scientist to Polish and Czechoslav acads. sci., 1976. NSF grantee, 1963—, U.S. Geol. Survey grantee, 1973-76. Fellow Royal Astron. Soc. London; mem. Am. Geophys. Union, Soc. Exploration Geophysicists, European Assn. Exploration Geophysicists, AAAS, Soc. Geomagnatism and Geoelectricity Japan, Nat. Geog. Soc., St. Louis Met. br. Am. Geophys. Union (pres. 1974-75), Astron. Soc. St. Louis, Sigma Xi. Roman Catholic. Contbr. articles to revs. to sci. publs. Home: 805 Pine Tree Ln Webster Groves MO 63119 Office: St Louis U PO Box 8099 Laclede Sta St Louis MO 63156

VINEYARD, JERRY DANIEL, geologist; b. Dixon, Mo., Mar. 26, 1935; s. Henry and Bessie Florence (Giesler) V.; A.B., U. Mo., 1958, A.M., 1963; m. Helen Louise Anderson, Nov. 24, 1960; children—Monica Lynne, Vanessa Anne. Faculty Met. Jr. Coll., Kansas City, Mo., 1961-63; geologist Mo. Dept Natural Resources, Rolla, 1963—, chief information services, 1965—. Cons. to Time-Life Books, Inc.; conferee U.S.-Yugoslav Project on Karst Hydrology, 1975. Served with USNR, 1958-60. Recipient Outstanding Service award in pub. ofcl. category Sierra Club, 1974. Fellow Nat. Speleological Soc. (dir. 1961-70 certificate of merit 1967); mem. Nature Conservancy (dir. 1971—), A.A.A.S., Geol. Soc. Am., Assn. Mo. Geologists, Am. Inst. Profl. Geol. Scientists (pres. Mo. chpt. 1970-71). Baptist (trustee 1974—). Editor: Mo. Speleology, 1960-62, Nat. Speleological Soc. Bull., 1963-70, Mo. Mineral News, 1963-74. Home: Route 1 Box 41A Saint James MO 65559 Office: PO Box 250 Rolla MO 65401

VINKE, HARRY WILLIAM, lumber co. exec.; b. South Holland, Ill., Oct. 14, 1899; s. John L. and Maggie (Gouwens) V.; student Chgo. Met. Bus. Coll., 1915-16; m. Anna Jaynes, Sept. 3, 1921; children—John Louis, Harry William, James Paul. Pres., Wausau Lumber Co., South Holland, 1940—, South Holland Trust & Savs. Bank, 1942-49, also dir., 1940—; dir. South Suburban Savs. & Loan, Harvey, Ill., chmn. bd., 1946-50. Mem. First Ref. Ch. (trustee). Lion. Home: 15915 S Park St South Holland IL 60473 Office: 236 161st Pl South Holland IL 60473

VINKE, JOHN LOUIS, lumber co. exec.; b. Harvey, Ill., July 9, 1924; s. Harry William and Annie (Jaynes) V.; B.A., Coll. of Wooster, 1948; m. Kathryn Mae De Young, June 19, 1946; children—Jill Kathleen, John Louis, Craig Alan, Robert Jaynes, Mary Beth. With Wausau Lumber Co., South Holland, Ill., 1948—, v.p. adminstrv. services, 1953—; v.p. Lansing Lumber & Supply Co., 1964-73; pres., South Holland Loan Assos., 1967—, Illiana Warehouse, Inc., Dixmoor Realty, 1973—; dir. 1st Nat. Bank, Dolton, Ill. Village trustee South Holland, 1951-76. Served with AUS, 1943-46; ETO. Decorated Silver Star, Bronze Star medal, Combat Infantryman's badge. Mem. South Cook and North Will County Geneal. and Hist. Soc., South Holland Hist. Soc., Lumber Trade Assn. Chgo. (v.p.), Am. Legion (comdr. 1954-55). Mem. Ref. Ch. Club: Lions (pres. 1955-56). Home: 525 E 160th Pl South Holland IL 60473 Office: 236 E 161st Pl South Holland IL 60473

VINSON, ARNOLD WILLIAM, psychologist; b. Memphis, Tenn., Feb. 9, 1941; s. William and Margaret (Chairs) Vinson; B.A., Calif. State U. at Los Angeles, 1969; M.A., Brown U., 1971; Ph.D., U. Minn., 1973. Certified Sch. Psychologist, 1972; Licensed Psychologist, Minn. Sch. psychologist, Sacramento, Calif., 1973-74; asst. prof. ednl. psychology Howard U., Washington, 1974-75; mental health psychologist, Rochester, Minn., 1975—; mem. ind. psychology practice Tavin Psychol. Services, Inc., St. Paul, 1977—. Mem. Am., Minn. psychol. assns., Minn. Psychologists in Pub. Practice Orgn. (tng. and edn. com. 1975—), Minn. Assn. Sch. Psychologists, Soc. Personality Assessment, Assn. Black Psychologists, Minn. Assn. Edn. Young Children. Author: Journal of Personality Assessment, 1975. Home: 1530 S 6th St Apt C-1203 Minneapolis MN 55454 Office: Suite 238 Griggs-Midway Bldg St Paul MN 55104

VIRDEN, MAXINE FERRELL (MRS. ROBERT MILES VIRDEN), ret. occupational therapist; b. Webster City, Iowa, July 22, 1916; d. Walter Jason Roger and Maye Addo (Thompson) Ferrell; student Am. Bus. U., 1935, Drake U., 1935-36, U. Calif. at Los Angeles, 1936-37; B.S., Iowa State U., 1940; certificate occupational therapy U. Ill., 1946; grad. ceramic workshop John Herron Art Sch., Indpls., 1951; m. Robert Miles Virden, May 22, 1955. Dir. art dept. Hertzberg Craftsman, Des Moines, 1940-45; occupational therapist aide U.S. Army Hosp., Brigham City, Utah, 1945-46; occupational therapist VA Hosp., Des Moines, 1946-76, dir. occupational therapy, 1946-76, ret., 1976. Mem. Health Careers Council Ia., 1963-67; mem. Iowa Gov.'s Com. on Status Women, 1964. Mem. Am. (del. 1948-54, mem. bd. mgmt. 1951-53), Iowa (v.p. 1947, pres. 1961-63) occupational therapy assns., Phi Kappa Phi, Delta Phi Delta, Omicron Nu, Alpha Delta Pi. Home: 3108 26th Place Des Moines IA 50310

VISNAPUU, HERK, architect; b. Tartu, Estonia, Apr. 26, 1920; s. Eduard and Lilli (Tarri) Y.; student Nomme Jr. Coll., Estonia, 1938-40, Tech. U., Tallinn, Estonia, 1942-43, Tech. Inst., Stockholm, Sweden, 1947-48; A.B., Oberlin Coll., 1950; B.Arch., Western Res. U., 1953; m. Malle Oder, Apr. 14, 1973; children by previous marriage—Lilli, Andres. Came to U.S., 1948, naturalized, 1957. Architect, City Stockholm, 1945; with Ernst Gronwal, Stockholm, 1946, Ancher, Gate & Lindgren, Stockholm, 1947, H.K. Ferguson Co., Cleve., 1950-51, Garfield, Harris, Robinson, Schafer, Cleve., 1954-56; partner Visnapuu & Gaede Architects & Planners, Cleve., 1956-74; pres. Visnapuu & Assos., Inc., Architects and Planners, 1974—. Mem. fine arts adv. com. City of Cleve.; active Cleve. Mus. Art, YMCA. Bd. dirs. Estonian Nat. Com. U.S.A., Estonian Relief Com., Henrik Visnapuu Lit. Found. Recipient nat. award Ch. Archtl. Guild Am., 1962; merit certificate Ohio Prestressed Concrete Inst., 1963; Honor award Architects Soc. Ohio, 1965; Honor award Greater Cleve. Growth Assn., 1971. Registered architect, Ohio, Pa., Ill., Mass., Ind. N.Y., Mich., Fla., Man., Can. Mem. AIA, Royal Archtl. Inst. Can., Korp Sakala (Estonian frat.), Epsilon Delta Rho. Lutheran. Rotarian. Archtl. work exhibited locally and nationally and pub. in nat. archtl. and trade mags. Home: 2886 Kingsley Rd Shaker Heights OH 44122 Office: Keith Bldg Euclid Ave Cleveland OH 44115

VISSER, JOHN EVERT, univ. pres.; b. Orange City, Iowa, Apr. 24, 1920; s. Arthur J. and Frances (Te Paske) V.; B.A., Hope Coll., 1942; M.A., U. Iowa, 1947, Ph.D., 1957; Dr. Honoris Causa, Universided Industrial de Santander, Bucaramanga, Columbia, 1968; m. Virginia Jean Schuyler, May 29, 1946; children—Betty Jean, Mary Frances, Nancy Ann, Martha Ellen. Asst. prof. history Hope Coll., Holland, Mich., 1949-56; asst. registrar Western Mich. U., Kalamazoo, 1956-57; asst. dean Ball State U., Muncie, Ind., 1957-58, exec. asst. to pres., prof. history, 1962-67; dean Grand Rapids (Mich.) Jr. Coll., 1958-62; pres. Emporia (Kans.) State U., 1967—; treas. Am. Assn. State Colls. and Univs., 1971-75. Served with AUS, 1942-46. Mem. Am. Assn. Higher Edn., Kans. Assn. Sch. Adminstrs., Nat. Assn. Intercollegiate Athletics (exec. com.), Phi Delta Kappa, Phi Alpha Theta, Blue Key. Presbyterian. Club: Rotary. Home: 1522 Highland St Emporia KS 66801

VITALE, JOSEPH ANTHONY, frozen food co. exec.; b. St. Paul, June 11, 1943; s. Joseph and Constance (Frattalone) V.; student bus. adminstrn. U. Minn., 1961-64; m. Janice A. Goodland, Aug. 10, 1963; children—Lisa, Gina, Dana, Jody. Treas. Venetian Inn Inc., St. Paul, 1963-71, v.p., 1971—; pres. Vitales Italian Foods Co., St. Paul, 1973—; dir. Minn. Food Expo Inc. Mem. Planning Commn. Village of Little Canada, Minn., 1976—. Mem. Minn. Restaurant Assn. Roman Catholic. Clubs: Kiwanis (pres. N. Star 1975-76), Unico (treas. St. Paul 1976-77). Home: 2612 Edgerton St St Paul MN 55113 Office: Vitales Italian Foods 2814 Rice St St Paul MN 55113

VITE, FRANK ANTHONY, realtor; b. Aurora, Ill., Feb. 9, 1930; s. Frank A. and Rose (Cosentino) V.; grad. Marmion Mil. Acad., 1948; student Sch. Mgmt., U. Notre Dame, 1958; D.B.A. (hon.), Hillsdale Coll., 1972; m. Barbara Ann Decio, Oct. 23, 1954; children—Bradley Scott, Mark Steven, Michael Lee, Leslie Ann, Lisa Ann. Plant engr. Lyon Metal Products, Aurora, 1951-52, purchasing agt., 1953-54; became sales mgr., exec. v.p., owner, dir. Skyline Homes, Inc., Elkhart, Ind., 1954; pres., owner B&F Realty, Inc., No. Ind. Appraisal Co., Inc., Golden Falcon Homes, Inc.; real estate broker; dir. 1st Nat. Bank, Elkhart, Ind. Trustee Hillsdale (Mich.) Coll.; bd. dirs. Ind. Commn. Higher Edn. Served with AUS, 1952-53, Korea. Mem. Elkhart Bd. Realtors, Nat. Sales Execs. Assn., Ind. Real Estate Assn., Nat. Inst. Real Estate Brokers, Holy Name Soc. Republican. K.C. (4 deg.), Knight of Malta, Elk. Home: 23236 Shorelane Elkhart IN 46514 Office: 1300 Cassopolis St Elkhart IN 46514

VITEK, RICHARD KENNETH, scientific co. exec.; b. Chgo., Feb. 1, 1935; s. Martin and Mildred (Veverka) V.; A.B., Albion Coll., 1956; M.S., U. Mo., Rolla, 1958; m. Marilyn W. Young, June 23, 1956; children—Christine, Debra, Evelyn. Analytical chemist AEC, Nat. Lead Co., Cin., 1957; asst. instr. chemistry, U. Mass., Amherst, 1958-59; research chemist Allied Chem. Corp., Morristown, N.J., 1959-64; dir. mktg. Aldrich Chem. Co., Inc., Milw., 1964-68; pres. CAMAG Inc., New Berlin, Wis., 1968—, also dir.; lectr., instr., cons. in field; dir. Trans-Sales, Inc., Bio-Metal Analysis, Inc. Mem. ch. bd. deacons. Mem. Am. Chem. Soc., AAAS, Ind. Businessman's Assn. Wis., Milwaukee Astron. Soc., Astron. League. Republican. Club: N.Y. Chemist. Contbr. articles to profl. jours. Home: 3367 S 122d St West Allis WI 53227 Office: 16229 W Ryerson Rd New Berlin WI 53151

VITIELLO, MICHELE, lumber co. exec.; b. Ferryville, Tunisia, Feb. 13, 1947; s. Nicola and Caterina (Sammartano) V.; came to U.S., 1967, naturalized, 1969; B.A. cum laude in Psychology, Oakland U., 1974, M.S. in Mgmt., 1975; m. Cheryl Lynn Darlington, Dec. 28, 1973. Programmer, Church's Lumber Yards, Utica, Mich., 1970-73, programming mgr., 1973-75, EDP mgr., 1975-77, v.p. mgmt. information systems, 1977—. Served with U.S. Army, 1968-70; Vietnam. Decorated Army Commendation medal, Bronze Star medal. Mem. Data Processing Mgmt. Assn., Inst. Mgmt. Scis., Inst. Certification Computer Profls. (certified). Home: 44081 Kings Gate Dr Apt 2 Sterling Heights MI 48078 Office: 7669 Auburn Rd Utica MI 48087

VITKO, JOHN PETER, lawyer; b. Virginia, Minn., Sept. 7, 1931; s. Leo and Frances (Zennie) V.; A.A., Virginia Jr. Coll., 1951; B.S., U. Minn., 1953, J.D., 1955; m. Mary Ann LePage, June 28, 1952; children—Jeffrey J., Elizabeth J., Susan L., Jennifer A., Stacy M. Admitted to Minn. bar, 1955; since practiced in St. Paul, partner firm Blomquist, Vitko, Neimeyer & Mooney, 1955-75; partner firm Dorsey, Windhorst, Hannaford, Whitney & Halladay, 1975—; pres., dir. Viking Growth Fund, 1962-63; exec. v.p., dir. Pioneer Investments, Inc., 1961-64; sec., dir. Splty. Mfg. Co., St. Paul. Vice.-chmn. Partners in Excellence Dr., U. Minn. Law Sch., 1968; bd. dirs. William Boss Found., St. Paul Unity Fund, ARC. Mem. Minn., Ramsey County, Am. bar assns., Phi Delta Phi. Clubs: St. Paul Torch (pres. 1965-66), Internat. Assn. Torch Clubs (1st v.p. 1968, pres. 1969-70), St. Paul Athletic; North Oaks Country. Contbr. articles to profl. jours.; editorial bd. Minn. Law Rev., 1951-52. Home: 45 Island Rd North Oaks MN 55110 Office: W-1468 First Nat Bank Bldg Saint Paul MN 55101

VIVONA, DANIEL NICHOLAS, chemist; b. Chgo., Apr. 13, 1924; s. Daniel and Mary Rose (Lamonico) V.; student Chgo. City Coll., 1941-42, 46; B.A., U. Maine, 1951; M.S., Pa. State U., 1953; postgrad. Purdue U., 1953-56; m. Helen Mary Belanger, Sept. 14, 1950; 1 son, Daniel Maurice. Instr. chemistry Purdue U., Lafayette, Ind., 1955-56; with Minn. Mining and Mfg. Co., St. Paul, 1956—, sr. chemist, 1969—. Served with USAAF, 1942-45. Decorated Air medal with oak leaf clusters, D.F.C. Dow Corning fellow, 1952-53. Mem. Am. Chem. Soc., Phi Beta Kappa. Democrat. Roman Catholic. Club: Toastmasters. Home: 3253 Kraft Circle North Lake Elmo MN 55042 Office: Minnesota Mining and Mfg Company 235-1E St Paul MN 55101

VLAHOS, GEORGE EFTHYMIOS, educator; b. Arbouna, Greece, June 18, 1936; s. Efthymios G. and Maria E. (Demopoulos) V.; B.S., U. Ill., 1964; M.S., So. Ill. U., 1967; Ph.D., U. No. Colo., 1974. Co-mgr. store Sure Save Food Marts, Chgo., 1955-60; asst. prof. math. Eureka (Ill.) Coll., 1966-72, chmn. div. sci. and math., 1969-72, asso. prof., head dept. math., 1974—; adminstrv. asst., vets. coordinator U. No. Colo., Greeley, 1973-74, grad. fellow in research and statis. methodology, 1972-74; curriculum cons. Project Upward Bound, 1975—; dir. metric workshops for tchrs., 1975—; computer programmer, analyst physics dept. U. Ill., 1963-64; statis. cons. U. No. Colo., Eureka Coll., 1972—. Chmn. tri-county area United Hellenic Voters Ill., 1975—, also mem. polit. action com. Served with U.S. Army, 1960-62. NSF grantee, 1968-70, State Ill. scholar, 1963-64, Mem. Am. Statis. Assn., Math. Assn. Am., Internat. Council on Edn. for Teaching, Am. Edn. Research Assn., Am. Inst. Decision Scis., Edn. Commn. of States, Nat. Council Tchrs. Math., AAUP, Ill. Council Tchrs. Math., Pi Mu Epsilon, Sigma Zeta. Greek Orthodox. Club: Krikos, Inc. Reviewer, Jour. Exptl. Edn., 1973-74. Home: PO Box 184 Eureka IL 61530

VOCKEL, RICHARD LANDIS, petroleum co. exec.; b. Harrisburg, Pa., Aug. 8, 1920; s. Stewart Meldred and Miriam Lucille (Landis) V.; B.S. in Mech. Engring., Lehigh U., 1941; m. Barbara Louise Somers, June 27, 1942; children—Constance Lindsay Vockel Ching, Richard Landis, Robert Somers. Mem. tech. service staff Standard Oil Co. (Ohio), 1941-43; with Waverly Oil Works Co., Newark, Ohio, 1946-75, v.p., dir., 1955-65, pres., dir., 1965-75; pres., dir. Waverly Oil, Inc. (subs. Witco Chem. Corp.), Newark, 1975—; vice chmn. bd. exec. com. Central Trust Co.; pres., dir. Granville Resources Corp.; dir. Nat. Transit Pipe Line Co., 1975—; mem. Nat. Petroleum Council, 1960-69. Mem. Granville Sch. Bd., 1960-69, pres., 1966-69; mem. Granville Village Council, 1972-73; vice chmn. Granville charter commn., 1963. Served to 1st lt. USAF, 1943-46. Mem. Ind. Petroleum Assn. (dir. exec. com.), Ohio Oil Gas Assn. (past pres.). Republican. Episcopalian. Clubs: Moundbuilders Country, Duquesne, Masons, Elks. Home: PO Box 457 725 Burg St Granville OH 43023 Office: 1627 Bryn Mawr Dr Newark OH 43055

VODA, FREDERICK ALLEN, coll. adminstr.; b. Port Huron, Mich., Sept. 9, 1934; s. Louis R. and Lillian M. (Eamon) V.; B.A., Mich. State U., 1957; M.Ed., Wayne State U., 1959; Ed.D., U. Mo., 1973; m. Elaine G. Shimer, Mar. 23, 1956; children—Kathryn L., Derek A. Tchr., Fitzgerald Pub. Schs., Warren, Mich., 1957-60, also instr. South Macomb Community Coll., Warren, 1959-60; tchr., communication coach Pinellas County (Fla.) Schs., 1960-61; counselor, tchr., dean Lake Park High Sch., Medinah, Ill., 1961-66; counselor fin. aid, housing and student activities Sauk Valley Coll., Dixon, Ill., 1966-68; fin. aid, student activities, research and devel. ofcl. Highland Community Coll., Freeport, Ill., 1969-75; asst. supt., v.p. Iowa Lakes Community Coll., Estherville, Iowa, 1975—; cons. St. Vincent's Home for Children (Freeport), St. Francis Home for Exceptional Children (Freeport), No. Ill. U. (DeKalb), Iowa Dept. Pub. Instrn. County chmn. Stephenson County Heart Assn., 1974. Served with USN, 1952-54; Korea. NDEA fellow U. Ohio, 1962, U. Mo., 1968-69; recipient commendation Office of Edn., 1968, Ill. Community Coll. Bd., 1968. Mem. Am. Psychol. Assn., Am. Personnel and Guidance Assn., Am. Coll. Personnel Assn., NEA, Iowa Sch. Adminstrs. Assn., Phi Delta Kappa, Delta Phi Epsilon. Clubs: Estherville Rotary (bd. dirs. 1977), Estherville Golf and Country, Community Concert, Elks. Home: N 532 W 9th St Estherville IA 51334 Office: 101 1/2 N 6th St Estherville IA 51334

VODERBERG, KURT ERNST, mfg. co. exec.; b. Rendsburg, Germany, Apr. 8, 1921; s. Max Henry and Margarethe (Siedel) V.; came to U.S., 1925, naturalized, 1929; B.S. in Mech. Engring., Ill. Inst. Tech., 1943; postgrad. Northwestern U., 1944-45; m. Louise Collier, May 21, 1948 (div.); children—Paul, John, Mary Beth, Jill; m. 2d, Sophie Dufft, Sept. 5, 1969. Asst. master mechanic Danly Machine Co., 1943-47; pres. Dynamic Mach. Co., Chgo., 1947-75, Dynamic Machinery Sales Co., Chgo., 1975—; cons. Japanese machine tools, 1965—. Committeeman, North Shore council Boy Scouts Am., 1961—. Registered profl. engr., Ill. Mem. Soc. Mfg. Engring., Tool and Die Inst., Ill. Soc. Profl. Engring., Chgo. Assn. Commerce and Industry, German Altenheim (dir.). Lutheran. Clubs: Masons, Am. Turners, Michigan Shores. Patentee in field. Home: 1440 Sheridan Rd Wilmette IL 60091 Office: 1800 N Rockwell Ave Chicago IL 60647

VOEGEL, KATHLEEN WALLIS, historian; b. Evansville, Ind., Oct. 3, 1953; d. Charles Wheeler and Jane Maxine (Berry) Wallis; B.A., B.S., Purdue U., 1975, M.A., 1977; m. William W. Voegel, Aug. 9, 1975. Teaching asst. history Purdue U., Lafayette, Ind., 1975-77; tchr. Am. history Clinton Prairie Jr.-Sr. High Sch., Ind., 1977—. Mem. Tippecanoe County-Purdue U. Bicentennial Com., 1975-76. Mem. Am., Ind. hist. assns., Am. Home Econs. Assn., Nat. Council Family Relations, Clinton County Hist. Soc., Purdue U. Alumni Assn., Phi Alpha Theta, Kappa Delta Pi. Republican. Methodist. Home: 700 St Marys Ave Frankfort IN 46041 Office: Route 6 Clinton Prairie High Sch Frankfort IN 46041

VOELLER, JOHN GEORGE, III, mech. engr.; b. Denver, Jan. 18, 1949; s. John George and Catherine Eunice (Higgins) V.; B.M.E., Ga. Inst. Tech., 1971; m. Sheila Kay Marriott, June 10, 1972. Field service engr. Westinghouse Electric Corp., N.Y.C., 1971-73, Atlanta, 1973-74; pipe stress analysis engr. Black & Veatch, Kansas City, Mo., 1974-75, computer applications engr., 1975—; info. cons. on consumer product reliability. Mem. ASME (asso.), AAAS, Consumer Aid Assn. Club: Home Computer. Home: 10850 Rosehill Rd Overland Park KS 66210 Office: 1500 Meadow Lake Pkwy Kansas City MO 64114

VOELPEL, RAY CARNELL, real estate broker; b. Morton, Ill., Feb. 14, 1922; s. Rae Marion and Ruth Imogene (Grieder) V.; B.S. in Bus. Adminstrn., Marquette U., 1949; postgrad. Law Sch., U. Wis., 1951; m. Joyce Marie Burns, May 10, 1952; children—Mark, Thomas, David. Dist. sales mgr. Am. Can Co., Indpls., 1951-64; real estate broker, sales trainer F.C. Tucker Co., Inc., Indpls., 1964-78. Bd. dirs. Devonshire VIII Civic Assn., Indpls.; sec. ch. council Lutheran Ch. of Good Shepherd, Indpls. Recipient Distinguished Salesman award Sales and Mktg. Execs. Indpls., 1972. Real estate Broker, Ind. Mem. Nat. Assn. Realtors, Realtors Nat. Mktg. Inst., Ind. Assn. Realtors, Met. Indpls. Bd. Realtors. Club: Executive Sales. Home: 6929 Daneby Circle Indianapolis IN 46220 Office: 1810 E 62d St Indianapolis IN 46220

VOEPEL, KARL HEINZ, agrl. chem. co. exec.; b. Bad Wildungen, W. Ger., May 2, 1931; s. Heinrich and Minna (Meister) V.; came to U.S., 1974; Ph.D., Marburg U., 1960; m. Renate Klingenburg, May 22, 1958; children—Kai, Christina, Jens. Various managerial positions Bayer AG, Leverkusen, W. Ger., 1960-74; mfg. dir. pesticides, gen. mgr. Chemagro div. Mobay Chem. Corp., Kansas City Mo., 1974—. Clubs: Blue Hills Country, Hasso Guestfalia. Patentee chem. compounds, intermediates. Home: 12504 Overbrook St Leawood KS 66209 Office: PO Box 4913 Kansas City MO 64120

VOET, LEO FRANCIS, hosp. adminstr.; b. Eureka, Kans., Sept. 28, 1940; s. Alphonse Bernard and Velma Marie (Lau) V.; B.S., Kans. State U., 1962; m. Barbara Anne Wheeler, July 18, 1964; children—Kimberley Anne, Joseph Michael. Staff auditor Arthur Andersen & Co., Kansas City, Mo., 1962-65; sr. accountant Baird, Kurtz & Dobson, Joplin, Mo., 1965-68; controller St. John's Med. Center, Joplin, 1968-74; asst. adminstr., controller Mo. Baptist Hosp., St. Louis, 1974—. Trustee Village of Sunnyvale (Mo.), 1970-74, sec.-treas., 1970-74. C.P.A., Mo. Mem. Am. Inst. C.P.A.'s, Hosp. Fin. Mgmt. Assn., Fin. Execs. Inst., Kans. State Alumni Assn., Hosp. Assn. Met. St. Louis, (chmn. centralized data processing com.). Home: 12746 Fee Fee Rd Creve Coeur MO 63141 Office: 3015 N Ballas Rd St Louis MO 63131

VOGE, WILFRED ALLAN, sanitary engr.; b. Racine, Wis., Sept. 28, 1938; s. Verne William and Genivieve Rose (Larson) V.; student U. Wis., 1974, U. Ill., 1975, Internat. Corr. Schs., 1965; m. June Marie Gilbert, Sept. 17, 1966; children—William, Douglas, Wayne, Warren, Sue, Jay, Wesley, Ryan. With Beloit Corp. (Wis.), 1961-65, designer Beloit Passavant Corp., Birmingham, Ala., 1967-71; engr. Peabody Welles Co., Roscoe, Ill., 1971—. Mem. Water Pollution Control Fedn. (asso.), Waste Water Equipment Mfg. Assn. Home: Route 1 Beloit WI 53511 Office: 11765 Main St Roscoe IL 61073

VOGEL, ARTHUR ANTON, clergyman; b. Milw., Feb. 24, 1924; s. Arthur Louis and Gladys Eirene (Larson) V.; student U. of South, 1942-43, Carroll Coll., 1943-44; B.D., Nashotah House Theol. Sem., 1946; M.A., U. Chgo., 1948; Ph.D., Harvard, 1952; S.T.D., Gen. Theol. Sem., 1969; D.C.L., Nashotah House, 1969; D.D., U. of South, 1971; m. Katharine Louise Nunn, Dec. 29, 1947; children—John Nunn, Arthur Anton, Katharine Ann. Ordained deacon Episcopal Ch., 1946, priest, 1948; teaching asst. philosophy Harvard, Cambridge, Mass., 1949-50; instr. Trinity Coll., Hartford, Conn., 1950-52; mem. faculty Nashotah House Theol. Sem., Nashotah, Wis., 1952-71, asso. prof., 1954-56, William Adams prof. philosophical and systematic theology, 1956-71, sub-dean Sem., 1964-71; bishop coadjutor Diocese of West Mo., Kansas City, 1971-72, bishop, 1972—. Rector, Ch. St. John Chrysostom, Delafield, Wis., 1952-56; dir. Anglican Theol. Rev., Evanston, Ill., 1964-69; mem. Internat. Anglican-Roman Cath. Consultation, 1970—; mem. Nat. Anglican-Roman Catholic Consultation, 1965—, Anglican chmn., 1973—; mem. Joint Commn. on Ecumenical Relations of Episcopal Ch., 1957—; mem. gen. bd. examining chaplains Episcopal Ch., 1971-72; del. Episcopal Ch., 4th Assembly World Council Churches, Uppsala, Sweden, 1968, and others. Vice chmn. bd. dirs. St. Luke's Hosp., Kansas City, Mo., 1971, chmn. 1973—. Research fellow, Harvard, 1950. Mem. Am. Philos. Assn., Metaphys. Soc. Am., Soc. Existential and Phenomenological Philosophy, Catholic Theol. Soc. Am. Author: Reality, Reason and Religion, 1957; The Gift of Grace, 1958; The Christian Person, 1963; The Next Christian Epoch, 1966; Is the Last Supper Finished?, 1968; Body Theology, 1973; The Power of His Resurrection, 1976. Contbr. profl. jours. Home: 524 W 119th Terr Kansas City MO 64145 Office: 415 W 13th St Kansas City MO 64105

VOGEL, BYRON WILLIAM, advt. co. exec.; b. Fairmont, Minn., May 15, 1917; s. William Horace and Grace Elaine V.; Asso. Engring, U. Minn., 1938; m. Arlene Beth Larson, Dec. 26, 1941; children—William Byron, Virginia Anette. Pres., Vogel Outdoor Advt. Inc., Rochester, Minn., 1969—, Vogel Investment Properties, 1964—, Outdoor Advt. Northern States, 1973—. Chmn. United Way fund drive, Olmsted County. Served with U.S. Army, 1941-45. Mem. Minn. Gov.'s Council Beautification Environment. Mem. Outdoor Advt. Assn. Am. (nat. dir.), Minn. Advt. Club, VFW. Methodist. Clubs: Bear Fax, Rochester Country. Home: 1317 2d St NW Rochester MN 55901 Office: 505 17th Ave NW Rochester MN 55901

VOGEL, CARL EDWARD, property adminstrn. exec.; b. Chgo., Oct. 21, 1919; s. Eugene E. and Madeline (Kelm) V.; student Wilson Jr. Coll., Chgo., 1937-39, Northwestern U., 1940-41; m. Frances Stevens Terrell, Mar. 17, 1945; children—Cynthia, Susan, Meredith, Kirkland. With Nat. Bur. Property Adminstrn., Inc., Chgo., 1939—, chmn. bd., exec. v.p., 1958-63, chmn. bd., pres. 1963—; chmn., bd., pres. Kirkland Corp., Chgo., 1969—. Active in local fund-raising drives. Served to 1st lt. USAAF, 1942-46. Mem. Chgo. Assn. Commerce and Industry, Internat. Assn. Assessing Officers, Nat. Tax Assn. Clubs: Executives, Ill. Athletic, Mid-America (Chgo.); North Shore Country (Glenview). Home: 720 Glenayre Dr Glenview IL 60025 Office: 1824 Prudential Plaza Chicago IL 60601

VOGEL, DAVID AGNEW, patent lawyer; b. New Castle, Ind., Dec. 27, 1925; s. Karl Conrad and Josephine (Agnew) V.; B.S. in Chem. Engring., Purdue U., 1945, M.S., 1948; LL.B., Chgo. Kent Coll. Law, 1951; student John Marshall Law Sch., 1953-54; M.B.A., Ill. Inst. Tech., 1977; m. Josephine Farrell, May 29, 1952; children—David Agnew, Walter C. Farrell, Sarah J., Ellen A. Instr. in chemistry Purdue U., 1947-48; admitted to Ill. bar, 1951, U.S. Supreme Ct., 1957; patent lawyer Chgo., 1951—; partner firm Prangley, Clayton & Vogel, 1954-57, Smith, Prangley, Baird & Clayton, 1957-58, Prangley, Baird, Clayton, Miller & Vogel, 1958-69, Prangley, Clayton, Mullin, Dithmar & Vogel, 1969-72, Prangley, Dithmar, Vogel, Sandler & Stotland, 1972-77, Vogel, Dithmar, Stotland, Stratman & Levy, 1977—; partner Gurnee Apts., 1969—, Big Oaks Assos., 1970—; dir., sec. Gravi-Mechanics Co., 1974—; dir., treas. H.S.V. Corp., 1970-73; dir. Acoustic Fiber Sound Systems, Inc. Vice pres. Young Republicans Ill., 1953-55; past sec., trustee Chgo.-Kent Coll. Law, mem. adv. bd. Chgo.-Kent Coll. Law-Ill. Inst. Tech., 1969—, chmn., 1970—; trustee Kendall Coll., 1969—, vice chmn. bd., 1970—. Mem. Am. Chem. Soc., Chgo.-Kent Alumni Assn. (pres. 1963-64), Am., Ill., Chgo. bar assns., Am., Chgo. patent law assns., Am., Ill. trial lawyers assns., AAAS, Sigma Xi, Tau Beta Pi, Omega Chi Epsilon, Phi Lambda Upsilon, Tau Kappa Epsilon, Phi Alpha Delta. Republican. Methodist (chmn. ofcl. bd. 1958-60, pres. bd. trustees 1960-61). Club: Masons. Home: 1136 Long Valley Rd Glenview IL 60025 Office: 105 W Adams St Chicago IL 60603

VOGEL, FRANCIS XAVIER, educator; b. Arcola, Ill., July 17, 1933; s. Henry Aloysius and Bernice (Brown) V.; B.S., Eastern Ill. U., 1955, M.S., 1956; Ph.D., Northwestern U., 1967; m. Constance Mary Zewen, Apr. 18, 1959; children—Mary Constance, Caroline Florence. Tchr., Staley Sch., Springfield, Ill., 1956-57; reading tchr., dir. reading program Skiles Sch., Evanston, 1958-62, asst. prin., 1960-62; prin. Central Sch., 1962-67; asst. prof. Fla. State U., Tallahassee, 1967-68; asst. prof. elementary edn., coordinator suburban community Tchr. Edn. Center, Northeastern Ill. U., Chgo., 1968-70, asso. prof., 1970-74, prof., 1974—, coordinator centers Coll. Edn., 1970—. Vis. asso. prof. Northwestern U., 1972-73; cons. sch. dists. in various states. Mem. Dist. 34 Pub. Schs. Caucus, Glenview, Ill., 1971-72. Served with AUS, 1957-58. Grantee U.S. Office Edn., 1966, 68, 71, State of Ill., 1964, 65, 66. Mem. Am. Edn. Research Assn., AAUP, Phi Delta Kappa. Contbr. articles to profl. pubs. Home: 1206 Hutchings St Glenview IL 60025 Office: 5500 N St Louis St Chicago IL 60625

VOGEL, RAYMOND STEFAN, research chemist; b. St. Louis, Jan. 27, 1918; s. Stefan and Freda Louise (Buchroeder) Vogel; B.S., Wash. U., 1961; m. Vera Rose Woelfer, Aug. 3, 1957. Analyt. chemist Mallinckrodt Co., St. Louis, 1943-57, supr. Uranium div. Weldon Spring, Mo., 1957-63, research spectrographer, 1963-66; dir. Heath Instrumentation Research Center, Urbana, Ill., 1966-70; asst. dir. Environ. Research Lab., U. Ill. at Urbana, 1970-76, asso. research chemist Inst. Environ. Studies, research asso. Coll. Vet. Medicine, 1976—. Mem. Am. Chem. Soc., Soc. Applied Spectroscopy (chmn. conv. com. 1974), Fedn. Analytical Chemistry and Spectroscopy Socs. (mem. governing bd. 1974), ASTM, Sci. Apparatus Makers Assn., Photographic Soc. Am., Sierra Club. Recipient Presdl. citation, Manhattan Project, 1948. Contbr. numerous articles to sci. jours. Patentee instrumentation for microspectroscopy, x-ray detector systems, radiant energy modulation. Home: 11 Concord Ln Urbana IL 61801 Office: Coll Vet Medicine U Ill Urbana IL 61801

VOGEL, THOMAS TIMOTHY, surgeon; b. Columbus, Ohio, Feb. 1, 1934; s. Thomas Andrew and Charlotte (Hogan) V.; A.B., Holy Cross Coll., 1955; M.S., Ohio State U., 1960, Ph.D., 1962; M.D., Georgetown U., 1965; m. Darina Kelleher, May 29, 1965; children—Thomas, Catherine, Mark, Nicola. Intern, Georgetown U. Hosp., Washington Gen. Hosps., 1965-66; resident in surgery Ohio State U. Hosps., Columbus, 1966-70; practice medicine specializing in surgery, Columbus, 1971—; trustee Region X Peer Rev. Systems, Inc. Trustee St. Vincent's Children Center, Columbus. Hartford fellow Ohio State U., 1968-69. Mem. AMA, A.C.S., Am. Physiol. Soc., Franklin County Acad. Medicine, Ohio State Med. Assn., Assn. Academic Surgery, Am. Trauma Soc., Sigma Xi. Roman Catholic. Club: Whitehall-Bexley Rotary. Contbr. articles in field to profl. jours. Home: 247 S Ardmore Rd Columbus OH 43209 Office: 621 S Cassingham Rd Columbus OH 43209

VOGET, FRED WILLIAM, anthropologist; b. Salem, Oreg., Feb. 12, 1913; s. Fred A. and Faye (Isham) V.; B.A., U. Oreg., 1936; Ph.D., Yale U., 1948; m. Mary K. Mee, May 6, 1942; children—Antoinette, Jane, Colleen. Asst. prof. anthropology McGill U., Montreal, 1948-52; prof. U. Ark., Fayetteville, 1952-61, U. Toronto, 1961-65, So. Ill. U., Edwardsville, 1965—. Served with U.S. Army, 1942-46. Can. Council grantee, 1964; Fulbright Research award to Ger., 1971. Fellow Am. Anthrop. Assn., Soc. Applied Anthropology (exec. com. 1974-76); mem. Current Anthropology, Sigma Xi. Author: Osage Indians, 1974; A History of Ethnology, 1975. Home: 106 Osage Edwardsville IL 62025 Office: Dept Anthropology So Ill U Edwardsville IL 62026

VOGT, JAMES ROBERT, nuclear chemist; b. Saginaw, Mich., Oct. 22, 1937; s. George and Minnie (Dodenhoff) V.; m. Corazon Riel Hastings, Dec. 14, 1974; children—Nelson, Pamela, Douglas; B.S., U. Mich., 1962; Ph.D., U. Ky., 1966. Sr. nuclear chemist Battelle Meml. Inst., Columbus, Ohio, 1966-68; sr. radiochemist U. Mo. at Columbia, 1968-69, nuclear sci. research mgr., 1969-73, asso. prof. nuclear engring., asso. dir. Environ. Trace Substances Research Center, 1973—. Mem. Am. Nuclear Soc., Am. Chem. Soc., ASTM, AAAS, Sigma Xi. Club: Forest Hills Country. Contbr. articles to sci. jours. Home: 1389 S El Chaparrel Ave Columbia MO 65201 Office: Environ Trace Substances Research Center Route 3 Columbia MO 65201

VOIGT, WESLEYAN KENT, communications adminstr.; b. Detroit, June 6, 1942; s. Wesleyan Feagan and Ruth Marie (Bowman) V.; B.S., Wayne State U., 1964, M.A., 1967, postgrad. 1970-77; m. Terrie Marie Hershiser, Oct. 3, 1970; 1 dau., Tobi Marie. Announcer, Sta. WEXL, Detroit, 1959-61; news dir. Sta. WOMC-FM, Detroit, 1961-65; tchr. of social scis. Warren Consol. Schs. Warren, Mich., 1965-67, dist. ednl. media coordinator, 1967-71; dir. Macomb/St. Clair Regional Ednl. Media Center, Mount Clemens, Mich., 1971—; guest prof. Saginaw Valley State Coll., Saginaw, Mich., 1975-76; free lance narrator for various films and commercials, 1959—. Mem. Nat. Assn. of Ednl. Broadcasters, Mich. Assn. for Media in Edn., Assn. for Ednl. Communication and Tech. Presbyterian. Club: Optimist. Home: 2620 Coral St Troy MI 48098 Office: 44001 Garfield Mount Clemens MI 48044

VOIT, ROGER JOSEPH, banker; b. Albany, Minn., Apr. 6, 1939; s. Roman P. and Marcella (Woeste) V.; grad. high sch.; m. Jeanette Urbashich, June 15, 1963; 1 son, Ross. With First State Bank, Albany, 1957-66, asst. cashier, 1962-66; asst. cashier Stearns County Nat. Bank, Albany, 1966-69, cashier, 1969—, dir., 1969—, v.p. 1970—. Treas., Albany Vol. Dept., 1970. Mem. Albany C. of C. (treas., dir.), St. Joseph Soc. (treas.). Clubs: Albany Lions (past pres.), Albany Sportsmen (dir. 1957-67). Address: Albany MN 56307

VOLIVA, BENJAMIN HARRISON, JR., chem. engr.; b. Monroe County, Ind., July 15, 1936; s. Benjamin Harrison and Margaret Elizabeth (Capshew) V.; B.S., Purdue U., 1958; m. Sharon Lee Grossman, July 23, 1966; children—Annette L., Alan L., Andrea E., Cheryl L., Benjamin Harrison III. Project engr. research and devel. dept. R.R. Donnelley & Sons Co., Chgo., 1958-70, environ. control dept., 1971-76, implementation engring. dept., 1977—. Area fin. chmn. South County council Girl Scouts U.S., 1976. Served with Chem. Corps, U.S. Army, 1958-59, to lt. col. Res. Mem. Soc. Mfg. Engrs., Chgo. Paint and Coatings Soc., South Suburban Geneal. and Hist. Soc. (pres. 1976-77), Republican. Club: Kiwanis (v.p. Riverdale-Dolton 1977). Researcher splty. printing inks, 1960-70, catalysts for air pollution control, 1971-73, incorporation heat recovery with pollution control equipment, 1974—. Home: 10 W Sibley Blvd Dolton IL 60419 Office: 2223 S Martin Luther King Dr Chicago IL 60616

VOLKER, WILLIAM HENRY, educator; b. Cin., Oct. 12, 1931; s. William Albert and Blanche Angela (Ehemann) V.; B.S., Cin. Coll. Pharmacy, 1953; M.S., U. Cin., 1958; postgrad. (NSF research participant) Ohio State U., 1960; m. Frances Barbara Elston, June 23, 1962; children—William M., Thomas L., John M., Barbara M. Faculty Bethesda Hosp. Sch. Nursing, Cin., 1959-61, St. Elizabeth Hosp. Sch. Nursing, Covington, Ky., 1962-68; faculty biology Villa Madonna/Thomas More Coll., Fort Mitchell, Ky., 1958—, asso. prof. biology, 1968—, dir. field biology sta., 1967-72, chmn. dept. biology, 1968-75. Cons. Chase Pharmacy, Cin., 1966—; liaison with schs. nursing, colls. pharmacy, other health career groups; participant Argonne Lab. and U.S. Dept. Interior programs, 1968—; mem. conf., Ind. U., Bloomington, 1964, Miami U., Oxford, Ohio, 1975-76. Mem. bd. edn. St. Teresa Sch., Cin., 1972—. Served with AUS, 1953-55. U. Cin. assistantships, 1955-56, 57-58. Mem. AAAS, Am. Soc. Microbiology, Am. Pub. Health Assn., Ohio Acad. Sci., Sigma Xi. Home: 4735 Glenway Ave Cincinnati OH 45238 Office: Thomas More Coll Biology Dept Fort Mitchell KY 41017

VOLKMER, HAROLD LEE, Congressman; b. Jefferson City, Mo., Apr. 4, 1931; grad. St. Louis U.; LL.B., U. Mo., 1955; m. Shirley Ruth Braskett; children—Jerry Wayne, John Paul, Elizabeth Ann. Admitted to Mo. bar, 1955; individual practice law, Hannibal; pros. atty. Marion County, 1960-66; mem. Mo. Ho. of Reps., 1966-76, chmn. Judiciary com.; mem. 95th Congress from 9th Mo. Dist., mem. Judiciary com., Agr. com.; asst. atty. gen. Mo. Mem. Mo., 10th Jud. Circuit bar assns. Clubs: K.C., Hannibal Lions. Recipient two awards for meritorious pub. service in Gen. Assembly, St. Louis Globe-Democrat. Office: 1228 Longworth House Office Bldg Washington DC 20515

VOLKMUTH, DONALD HAROLD, printing co. exec.; b. St. Cloud, Minn., May 22, 1931; s. Anton and Clara Sabina (Zapf) V.; grad. high sch.; m. Patricia Mary O'Brien, June 4, 1955; children—Mark, Beth, Lynn, Paul. With Volkmuth Printers, Inc., St. Cloud, 1958—, now pres., chmn. bd. dirs.; dir. Northwestern Bank and Trust. Pres. St. Cloud Opportunities. Mem. fellows com. St. John's U., Collegeville; chmn. indsl. div. United Fund, St. Cloud, 1974. Served with AUS, 1952-54. Mem. St. Cloud C. of C. (dir. 1970-74, v.p. 1977—), St. Cloud's Printer's Assn. (pres. 1968), V.F.W., Am. Legion. Roman Catholic (pres. ch. council). Home: 1722 Woodland Rd Saint Cloud MN 56301 Office: East Hwy 23 PO Box 1007 Saint Cloud MN 56301

VOLZ, PAUL ALBERT, educator; b. Ann Arbor, Mich., Mar. 26, 1936; s. Albert Carl and Frieda Clara (Larmee) V.; B.A., Heidelberg Coll., 1958; M.S., Mich. State U., 1962, Ph.D., 1966; postgrad. Ind. U., 1966-68. Asst. prof. biology Purdue U., Indpls., 1968-69; prof. mycology Eastern Mich. U., Ypsilanti, 1969—; resident research asso. NASA, Johnson Space Center, Houston, 1971-73; vis. prof. mycology and research Nat. Taiwan U., Taipei, 1974—; prin. investigator microbial ecology evaluation device NASA, 1971-74. Am. Soc. Engring. Edn. faculty fellow, 1969-71. Mem. Am. Inst. Biol. Scis., Am. Soc. Microbiology, Mycological Soc. Am., AAAS, Mich. Acad. Sci., Arts and Letters, Assn. for Tropical Biology, Am. Fern Soc., Electron Microscopy Soc. Am., Am. Mus. Natural History, Internat. Soc. for Human and Animal Mycology, Med. Mycological Soc. Ams. Contbr. articles to profl. jours. Home: 1805 Jackson Ave Ann Arbor MI 48103 Office: Dept Biology Eastern Mich U Ypsilanti MI 48197

VON ACHEN, JON KURT, architect; b. Kansas City, Kans., Mar. 2, 1939; s. Kenneth Otto and Dorothy Elizabeth (Paffen) von A.; student U. Kans. at Lawrence, 1957-58, M. Arch., 1966; B. Arch., U. Ill. at Champaign, 1962; postgrad. Sch. Planning Lab. Stanford, 1967; m. Pennie Lynn Hutton, June 23, 1967; 1 dau., Megan Jean. Draftsman archtl. services U. Kans., 1962-64; draftsman Kenneth O. von Achen Architects, 1966-68, project architect, 1968-71; v.p. Kenneth O. von Achen Chartered Architects, 1971—. Mem. Carpenters Operations com. Kansas City Plan, 1972-78; mem. Joint Carpenters' Apprenticeship Com. Greater Kansas City, 1971—; mem. Lawrence-Douglas County Planning Commn., 1977—. Mem. bd. edn. sch. dist. #491, 1967-68; chmn. Eudora (Kans.) City Planning Commn., 1972—. Bd. dirs. Lawrence Boys Club. Mem. Eudora (pres. 1968-69), Kans. (state. v.p. 1970-71), U.S. (dir. 1971-72) Jaycees, Jr. Chamber Internat. (senator), U.S. Jaycees Pres. Club, Builders' Assn. Greater Kansas City, Kan. State Hist. Soc., Scarab, Sigma Tau Delta, Alpha Tau Omega. Republican. Works include schs., banks, libraries, comml. and pvt. bldgs. Home: Rural Route #2 Eudora KS 66025 Office: PO Box 530 Eudora KS 66025

VON BARGEN, WAYNE JAMES, ednl. adminstr.; b. Chgo., Sept. 9, 1946; s. James Earl and Grace Mary (Dunkel) Von B.; B.S., Ill. Inst. Tech., 1969, M.S., 1970, Ph.D., 1972; m. Cathleen Nora Whisler, Apr. 19, 1969. Clinician, Chgo. Reading and Speech Clinic, 1968-70; cons. psychologist LaSalle County Mental Health Center, Ottawa, Ill., 1970-71; psychologist Valparaiso U., 1971-77, asst. dir. Univ. Counseling Center, 1972-77, part-time asst. prof. psychology, 1972-77; dir. psychophys. therapy Mental Health Center, Fort Wayne, Ind., 1977—; pvt. practice psychology, 1976—. Mem. Am., Ind., Midwestern psychol. assns., Biofeedback Soc. Ind. Contbr. articles to profl. jours. Home: 5030 Twilight Ln Fort Wayne IN 46815 Office: Mental Health Center 909 E Blvd Fort Wayne IN 46805

VON BERG, LOIS HELENE, univ. adminstr.; b. Albert Lea, Minn., Oct. 6, 1932; d. John Phillip and Helene Annette (Oliver) Von B.; B.A., U. No. Iowa, 1955; M.A., U. No. Colo., 1962; postgrad. Springfield Coll., 1966. Tchr. high sch., Madelia, Minn., 1955-56; tchr. jr. high sch., Clinton, Iowa, 1956-59; tchr. high sch., Rochester, N.Y., 1959-61; counselor Douglas High Sch., Ellsworth AFB, S.D., 1962-64; dir. guidance Sch. Nursing, Rochester, Minn., 1964-67; asst. dir. fin. aids State Coll., St. Cloud, Minn., 1967-69; asst. dir. fin. aid U. Wis., Stout, Menomonie, Wis., 1969-71, dir. fin. aid, 1971—; mem. adv. council State Higher Ednl. Aids Bd., 1976-78. Mem. Am. Personnel and Guidance Assn., Am. Coll. Personnel Assn., Nat., Midwest, Wis. assns. student fin. aid adminstrs., Assn. U. Wis. Faculties (del. assembly 1972-74), Rochester C. of C. (edn. com. 1965-67), Bus. and Profl. Women's Club (treas. 1968-69), Delta Kappa Gamma (v.p. 1972-76). Home: 511 16th St Menomonie WI 54751

VON BERLICHINGEN, MAXIMILIAN ADELBERT, structural engr.; b. Denmark, July 23, 1914; s. Graf Goetz and Frafin Anna von der (Schulenberg) von Berlichingen; LL.B., Chgo. Law Sch., 1934, LL.M., 1935, B.Sc., Albertus and Webster U., 1940, M.Sc., 1941, D.Sci., 1943; B.Sc./Arch., Minerva Sch. Applied Scis., 1963; Ph.D. in Engring., Calif. Western U., Santa Ana, 1978; m. Marget Lerch; children—Carla, Ingeborg, Albert, Renee. Structural engr. M.W. Kellogg Co., N.Y.C., 1945-48, Asso. Engrs. Inc., Springfield, Mass., 1948-50, Gilbert & Barker Mfg. Co., 1950-51; dir. of research and chief engr. Houses div. Harnischfeger Corp., 1950-56; v.p. and chief engr. Great Lakes Homes Inc., 1956-58; structural engr. City of Green Bay, Wis., 1961—; cons. in field; major works include: Asphalt Tile plant for S.Am.; design of bldgs. for S. Am. earthquake areas; oil refinery equipment for Standard Oil Co.; design of 1st. movable large gas operated electric plant, Okla.; various harbour works, bridges and pumping stations. Served with USAAF, Registered profl. engr., Wis., other states, Can. Mem. Nat., Wis. socs. of profl. engrs., Forest Products Research Soc., Nat. Council of State Bds. of Engring. Examiners, Stuben Soc. of Am. (vice chmn.). Republican. Lutheran. Clubs: Masons (32 deg.), Shriners. Contbr. numerous articles on research on wood and cellulose materials to tech. jours.; patentee in field. Address: PO Box 901 721 S Monroe Ave Green Bay WI 54301

VON BESSER, KURT WOLF FREDERICK, chem. products co. exec.; b. N.Y.C., Nov. 25, 1936; s. Verne and Jeannette (Streibaugh) von B.; B.B.A., Lake Forest Coll., 1957; m. Gerlinde Petritsch, July 25, 1966; children—Kurt Friedrich, Kristin Wynn, Kiera Linda. Vice-pres. Middle West Display & Sales, Inc., 1958-65; pres. Middle West Mktg. Co., Chgo., 1965—, Safety Systems, Inc., Chgo.; mfr. Besser ski bindings; exec. v.p. A & T Ski Co., Seattle, 1976—. Vice-pres. German-Am. Democratic Orgn., 1970-71; chmn. democratic com. German Am. Nat. Congres, 1971. Democrat. Club: Corinthian Yacht, Chicago Yacht. Developed and formulated chem. weapon formulation known as mace, 1965, developed fogging device for tear gas fog, 1970. Patentee ski bindings. Office: 216-226 S Hoyne St Chicago IL 60612

VONDRACEK, JOHN JOSEPH, supt. schs.; b. Verdigre, Nebr., June 3, 1930; s. George J. and Marie (Holan) V.; B.A., Wayne State Teacher's Coll., 1957; M.E., U. Nebr., 1971, grad. adminstrv. specialist, 1976; m. Rosalie Burkhardt, Apr. 6, 1953; children—Kathryn (Mrs. Kirk Fox), Susan, Debra (Mrs. John Gibson), John Joseph, Barbara. Supt. Arthur County High Sch., Arthur, Nebr., 1962-65; supt. schs. Lynch (Nebr.) Pub. Schs., 1965-73, Oxford (Nebr.) Community Schs., 1973—. Served with USAF, 1952-56. Roman Catholic. K.C., Rotarian (pres. Oxford 1976-77). Home: 104 Colorado St Oxford NE 68967 Office: Oxford School Oxford NE 68967

VONDRUSKA, JAMES FRANCIS, veterinarian; b. Chgo., Feb. 8, 1940; s. James J. and Helen B. (Wortner) V.; student Loyola U., 1958-59; D.V.M., Ohio State U., 1964; postgrad. Northwestern U., 1969-72; m. Joan Elizabeth Broxham, July 4, 1964; children—James Francis, Juliet Elizabeth. Zoo veterinarian Chgo. Zool. Park, Brookfield, Ill., 1964; research veterinarian U.S. Army, Edgewood, Md., 1965-66; pvt. practice as veterinarian, Oak Lawn, Ill., 1967, Lombard, Ill., 1967-68; staff veterinarian Indsl. Bio-Test Labs., Inc., Northbrook, Ill., 1968-73; research scientist Searle Labs., Skokie, Ill., 1973-77; research veterinarian Quaker Oats Co., Barrington, Ill., 1978—. Ofcl. veterinarian Am. Kennel Club shows, 1968-74; judging ofcl. Chgo. Archdiocesean Sci. Program, 1968-72; cons. IIT Research Inst., N. Ill. Jr. Acad. Sci. Mem. sch. bd., St. Louise de Marillac, 1971-72. Served to capt. AUS, 1965-66. Diplomate Am. Coll. Lab. Animal Medicine. Mem. Am. Vet. Med. Assn., Am. Assn. Lab. Animal Sci., Am. Soc. Vet. Clin. Pathology, Am. Assn. Indsl. Vets., Nat. Geog. Soc., Smithsonian Assos., Phi Kappa Theta, Phi Zeta. Club: Dairyman's Country (Boulder Junction, Wis.); Internat. Sports Core (Oak Brook, Ill.). Home: 5145 Grand Ave Western Springs IL 60558 Office: Quaker Oats Co 617 W Main St Barrington IL 60010

VON LANG, FREDERICK WILLIAM, librarian; b. Scranton, Pa., May 6, 1929; s. Frederick William and Carrie (Brundage) Baron von Lang zu Leinzell; B.S., Kutztown State Coll., 1951; M.S. in L.S., Syracuse U., 1955; m. Ilsabe von Wackerbarth, July 12, 1960; children—Christoph, Karl Philip. Librarian, Broughal Jr. High Sch., Bethleham, Pa., 1951; asst. librarian Bethlehem Pub. Library, 1952-55; asst. librarian Enoch Pratt Free Library, Balt., 1956-66; library dir. Lehigh County Community Coll., Allentown, Pa., 1966-73; library dir. Auburn (Maine) Pub. Library, 1973-77; dir. St. Joseph (Mo.) Pub. Library, 1977—. Founding mem., exec. bd., treas. Friends Bethlehem Pub. Library, 1964-70; mem. exec. bd. Northampton County Assn. for Blind, 1970-72; bd. dirs. St. Joseph Hist. Soc., St. Joseph Mental Health Soc. Edn. counselor Lehigh Valley br. Luth. Brotherhood, 1972-73. Mem. Pa. (treas., mem. exec. bd. Lehigh Valley chpt. 1967-70, chmn. community and jr. coll. sect. 1970-71), Maine (legis. com.), New Eng., Mo. library assns., ALA (mem. council, fed. relations coordinator to Maine Library Assn.), Bethlehem Jr. C. of C. (past editor, chmn. publs.), S.A.R. (past sec.-treas. bd. mgrs. Valley Forge chpt.), Maine Soc. Mayflower Descs., Soc. Colonial Wars in State Maine, Huguenot Soc. Maine Bradford Family Compact, Beta Phi Mu. Lutheran. Clubs: Masons, K.T., Shriners, Elks, Kiwanis. Asso. editor Genealogisches Handbuch des in Bayern immatrikulierten Adels, Vol. 4, 1953. Home: 2524 Lucille Ave St Joseph MO 64506 Office: 10th and Felix Sts St Joseph MO 64501

VONNAHMEN, FRANCIS HENRY, dentist; b. Alton, Ill., Oct. 24, 1924; s. Henry Anthony and Teresa Ann (Daley) V.; student U. Ill., 1942-43, Stanford U., 1944; D.D.S., St. Louis U., 1948; m. Patricia Ann Poterack, Dec. 27, 1948; children—Patrick, Michael, Barbara. Commd. officer U.S. Army, 1948, advanced through grades to lt. col.; ret., 1967; gen. practice dentistry, Alton, 1967—. Active YMCA, 1973. Served with AUS, 1942-44. Decorated United Nations medal. Mem. Am. Dental Assn., Ill., Madison Dist. dental socs., Ret. Officers Assn., Xi Psi Phi Roman Catholic. Lion, Eagle. Home: 5325 River Aire Dr Godfrey IL 62035 Office: 305 W Elm St Alton IL 62002

VON STEIN, PETER, state ofcl.; b. N.Y.C., Aug. 6, 1934; s. William George and Charlotte (McAleer) von S.; A.B., Brown U., 1956; m. Geraldine K. Woehler, Aug. 3, 1963; children—Stephanie, Michele, Eric. Reporter, A.P., Indpls., 1960-64; dep. sec., State Ind., 1965-66; asst. to corrections commr., State Ind., 1967, 68—; v.p. Bio-Dynamics, Inc., Indpls., 1970—, dir., 1972—; pres. Diagnostic div., 1972—. Served with AUS, 1957-59. Mem. Delta Upsilon. Democrat. Home: 8383 N Illinois St Indianapolis IN 46260 Office: 9115 Hague Rd Indianapolis IN 46250

VON TISH, JOHN JOSEPH, counselor; b. Summitt, N.J., July 26, 1946; s. John Joseph and Shelia Winiford (Murphy) vonT.; B.A., U. Dubuque, 1968; M.A., U. Wis., 1970; m. Mary Ann Priller, Apr. 21, 1973. Dir. guidance Sch. Dist. Hartford (Wis.), 1969—. Leader, Boy Scouts Am.; bd. dirs. United Fund, 1977. Gen. Electric fellow U. Louisville, 1971. Mem. Wis. (past pres.), Am. (rep. nat. conv. 1976), sch. counselors assns., Wis. Elementary Sch. Counselors Assn. (past pres.), Wis., Am. personnel guidance assns., NEA, Wis. Edn. Assn., Assn. Specialists Group Work, Wis. Assn. Counselor Edn. Supervision, Phi Delta Kappa, Kappa Delta Pi. Roman Catholic. Home: 118 Martin Dr Hartford WI 53027 Office: 60 Mill St Hartford WI 53027

VON WYSS, MARC ROBERT, cement co. exec.; b. Zurich, Switzerland, Feb. 12, 1931; s. George H. and Mariejenny A. (Burckhardt) von W.; came to U.S., 1971; grad. in mech. engring. and aerodynamics Fed. Inst. Tech., Zurich, 1956; m. Marina V. Gygi, Sept. 4, 1963; children—George M., Martin C. Control systems design engr. Svenska Aeroplan AB, Joenkoeping, Sweden, 1957-60; control systems design engr., asst. dept. head Contraves AG, Zurich, 1961-65; sr. v.p. Holderbank Mgmt. & Cons. Ltd., Holderbank, Switzerland, 1966-71; pres., chief exec. officer Dundee Cement Co. (Mich.), 1971—. Office: PO Box 122 Day Rd Dundee MI 48131

VOSMEIER, LEONARD FRANCIS, printing co. exec.; b. Richmond, Ind., Nov. 29, 1925; s. Leonard Henry and Ruth M. (Miller) V.; A.B., Ind. U., 1950; m. Monabelle Romaine Brockmyer, Aug. 26, 1950; children—Valerie, Mark, Mary (dec.), Ned, Matthew. Vice-pres. Mulhaupt Printing Co., Inc., Ft. Wayne, Ind., 1951-55; pres., Ft. Wayne (Ind.) Printing Co., Inc., 1955—; dir., treas. Mulhaupt Printing Co., Inc. Div. chmn. United Way, 1974; co-chmn. patriotism com. Bicentennial Com., 1974-76. Served to col. AUS, 1943-46. Recipient Ind. Commendation medal Mil. Dept. Ind., 1969. Mem. Res. Officers Assn. (pres. 1967, 76), VFW, DAV, Mil. Order World Wars, Am. Legion, Fort Wayne Printing House Craftsman, Allen County-Fort Wayne Hist. Soc., C. of C., Phi Kappa Theta. Republican. Roman Catholic. Clubs: Olympia Country (pres. 1973-75), Serra (Ft. Wayne) (pres. 1976-77). Home: 2705 Whitegate Dr Fort Wayne IN 46805 Office: 340 E Berry St Fort Wayne IN 46802

VOSS, EDWARD WILLIAM, JR., immunologist; b. Chgo., Dec. 2, 1933; s. Edward Willaim and Lois Wilma (Graham) V.; AB., Cornell Coll., 1955; M.S., Ind. U., 1964, Ph.D., 1966; m. Virginia Hellman, June 15, 1974; children from previous marriage—Cathleen, Valerie. Asst. prof. microbiology U. Ill., Urbana, 1967-71, asso. prof., 1971-74, prof., 1974—. Served with U.S. Army, 1956-58. NIH fellow, 1966-67; NSF fellow, 1975-77, grantee, 1967—. Mem. AAAS, Am. Assn. Immunologists, Am. Assn. Biol. Chemists, N.Y. Acad. Scis., Nat. Geog. Soc., Jacques Cousteau Soc., Sigma Xi. Adv. editor Immunochemistry, 1975—. Contbr. articles to profl. jours. Home: 2207 Bourdreau Circle Urbana IL 61801 Office: 217 Burrill Hall Dept Microbiology Univ Ill Urbana IL 61801

VOSS, JAN (MRS. CONRAD JOHNSON), pub. radio exec.; b. Exira, Iowa, Nov. 18, 1922; d. George Carl and Evelyn (Rendleman) V.; m. Conrad Johnson, 1955; children—Dawn, Lisa, Scott. Traffic dir., broadcaster, Radio KJAN, 1952-53; dir. women's activities KVTV, 1953-57; asso. producer, broadcaster TV sales WMT-TV, WMT-radio, 1957-64; nat. consumer relations Schaper Mfg. Co., Mpls., 1964-65; TV dir., producer-broadcaster, merchandising coordinator WMT-TV, 1965-70; sch.-community relations dir. Grant Wood Area Edn. Agy. (Benton, Cedar, Iowa, Johnson, Jones, Linn, Washington Counties), 1970-76; asso. head devel. KCCK-FM, pub. radio, 1977—. Mem. pub. information com. Iowa chpt. Am. Cancer Soc. Mem. Linn County, Iowa sch. pub. relations assns., Am. Women in Radio and TV (past nat. v.p., past pres. Hawkeye-Iowa chpt.), Women in Communications. Lutheran (communications bd.). Clubs: Order of Eastern Star, Beethoven. Author: Poems My Mother Taught Me, 1970; Quo Fata Vocant, 1972. Home: 1300 O Ave NW Cedar Rapids IA 52405 Office: Kirkwood Community Coll Cedar Rapids IA 52406

VOSS, OMER GERALD, farm equipment co. exec.; b. Downs, Kans., Sept. 14, 1916; s. John and Grace (Bohlen) V.; A.B., Ft. Hays (Kans.) State Coll., 1937; J.D., U. Kans., 1939; m. Annabelle Katherine Lutz, June 20, 1940; children—Jerrol Ann, Omer Gerald. With Internat. Harvester Co., 1936—, v.p. farm equipment div., 1962-66, exec. v.p., dir., 1966—, vice chmn., dir., 1977—; admitted to Kans. bar, 1939; dir. Ill. Tool Works, No. Trust Co., Beatrice Foods Co.; trustee ADELA Investment Co. S.A. Chmn., pres. Nat. 4-H Council. Served with USAAF, 1943-46. Clubs: Chgo.; Comml.; Westmoreland Country. Home: 9359 N Ridgeway Ave Evanston IL 60203 Office: 401 N Michigan Ave Chicago IL 60611

VOTH, HAROLD MOSER, psychiatrist, psychoanalyst; b. Newton, Kans., Dec. 29, 1922; s. Albert Cornelius and Margret (Unruh) V.; B.S., Washburn U., Topeka, 1943; M.D., Kans. U., 1947; m. Patsy Ruth Gardner, Mar. 9, 1946; children—Eric, Gregory, Nicholas. Intern San Diego County Gen. Hosp., 1947-48; resident Menninger Sch. Psychiatry, 1948-50; sr. psychiatrist and psychoanalyst Menninger Found., Topeka, 1957—; asso. chief psychiatry for edn. Topeka VA Hosp., 1975—; cons. surg. gen. USN. Fellow Am. Coll. Psychoanalysts, Am. Psychiat. Assn. Recipient Wm. C. Menninger Outstanding Tchr. award, 1970; Author: Psychotherapy and the Role of the Environment, 1973; The Castrated Family, 1977. Home: 745 Westchester Rd Topeka KS 66606 Office: Menninger Found Topeka KS 66601

VOURAX, MYRON ANTHONY, mus. dir.; b. Detroit, Aug. 8, 1931; s. Anthony Myron and Harriet Evangeline (Anagnos) V.; B.A., Earlham Coll., 1959; postgrad. So. Ill. U., 1960-64; m. Ruth Eleanor Reynolds, Oct. 24, 1959 (div.); children—Celeste Evangeline, Anthony Allen. Exhibits preparator Univ. Mus., So. Ill. U., Carbondale, 1960-64; dir. Nature and Sci. Mus., Winston-Salem, N.C., 1964-71; dir. Conner Prairie Pioneer Settlement, Noblesville, Ind., 1971—. Mus. and live animal exhibit cons. in Va., N.C. Served with USAF, 1951-55. Mem. Am. Assn. Museums, Am. Assn. State and Local History, Midwest Mus. Conf., Ind. Hist. Soc., Internat. Oceanographic Found., Assn. Ind. Museums, S.E. Mus. Conf. Office: 30 Conner Ln Noblesville IN 46060

VRETTAS, ARTHUR THOMAS, guidance counselor; b. Rock Springs, Wyo., July 2, 1942; s. Thomas Arthur and Helen (Scocos) V.; B.S., Mich. State U., 1965; M.A., John Carroll U., 1969; m. Elana Titones, June 12, 1976. Tchr., counselor Cleve. Pub. Schs., 1965-69; dir. guidance U.S. Naval Sta. Schs., P.R., 1969-70; brokerage cons. Conn. Gen. Life Ins. Co., Southfield, Mich., 1970-71; Title I math coordinator Detroit Pub. Schs., 1971-74; author, cons. E.D.R. Corp., Shaker Heights, Ohio, 1972-76; counselor East Cleveland pub. schs., 1974—; author, project dir. Inst. Contemporary Curriculum Devel. Mem. Am. Personnel and Guidance Assn., John Carroll U. Educators' Alumni Assn. (pres.), Phi Delta Kappa. Greek Orthodox. Home: 4060 Harwood Rd South Euclid OH 44121 Office: 15320 Euclid Ave East Cleveland OH 44112

VUCKOVICH, DRAGOMIR MICHAEL, neurologist; b. Bileca, Yugoslavia, Oct. 27, 1927; s. Alexander J. and Anka (Ivanisevich) V.; came to U.S., 1957; naturalized, 1962; M.D., U. Birmingham, Eng., 1953; m. Brenda Mary Luther, Aug. 23, 1958; children—John, Nicholas, Adrian. Jr. resident in pediatrics Birmingham Children's Hosp., 1954-55; resident med. officer Princess Beatrice Hosp., London, 1955; house physician Hosp. for Sick Children, London, 1955; resident physician Nat. Hosp., London, 1956-57; rotating intern Columbus Hosp., Chgo., 1957-58; resident in neurology and pediatrics VA Research Hosp., Northwestern U. Med. Sch., Chgo., 1958-59, Wesley Meml. Hosp., Chgo., 1959-60, Children's Hosp., 1960-62; practice medicine specializing in neurology, Chgo., 1962—; asso. attending neurologist Children's Hosp., Chgo., 1968—; head, neurology psychiatry Columbus Hosp., Chgo., 1968—, head of electroencephalography dept., 1969—; head, pediatric neurology Loyola U., Chgo., 1970—, asso. prof., neurology and pediatrics, 1970-77, prof., 1977—. Served with Royal Yugoslav Army, 1942-44. Diplomate Am. Bd. Psychiatry and Neurology, Am. Bd. Pediatrics, Pan Am. Med. Assn. Fellow Am. Acad. Pediatrics, Royal Soc. Health; mem. Am. British med. assns., Am. Acad. Neurology, Am. Med. Electroencephalographic Assn., Royal Coll. Surgeons, Royal Coll. Physicians. Serbian Orthodox. Clubs: Ill. Athletic, Beefeaters, Les Gourmet. Contbr. articles to med. jours. Home: 755 Kipling Pl Deerfield IL 60015 Office: 104 S Michigan Ave Chicago IL 60603

VUKAS, RONALD, assn. exec.; b. Elmshorn, Germany, Feb. 3, 1946; s. Vasilye and Maria (Kopanica) Vukasinovic; B.S. in Mgmt., No. Ill. U., 1968; m. Sandra Jean Carlson, Apr. 5, 1969; children—Michele, Dean, Christopher. Bus. research analyst U.S. Steel Supply Co., Chgo., 1968-70; controller Inst. Real Estate Mgmt., Chgo., 1970-75, exec. v.p., 1975—. Served with AUS, 1968-74. Mem. Am. Mgmt. Assn., Nat. Assn. Accountants, Am. Soc. Assn. Execs., Nat. Accounting Assn., Am. Statis. Assn. Home: 6700 Powell St Downers Grove IL 60515 Office: 430 N Michigan Ave Chicago IL 60611

VUKIN, WALTER JOHN, transp. equipment co. exec.; b. Lorain, Ohio, June 25, 1918; s. John and Pauline (Burich) V.; student Ohio State U., 1936-37, Fenn Coll., 1942-43, Western Res. U., 1943-44, 44, Coll. Advanced Traffic, Detroit, 1948-49, Mich. State U., 1957, Detroit Inst. Tech., 1958-59; m. Leocadia L. Leshinski, Aug. 3, 1940; 1 dau., Nancy Lee. With W.&L.E. Ry., 1937-42, chief rate clk., 1940-42; with Fruehauf Corp., Detroit, 1945—, asst. gen. traffic mgr., 1956-61, dir. traffic, 1961—; mem. adv. bd. Am. Airlines Freight System, 1972-78, Central Ter. Shippers, 1970-78. Mem. pres.'s adv. bd. Siena Heights Coll. Served with USAAF, 1942-45. Mem. Motor City Traffic Club Detroit (exec. com. 1949—), Mich. (dir., chmn. mem. com. 1966—, pres. 1977), Eastern Mich. (membership chmn. 1962), Nat. Freight traffic assns., Assn. ICC Practitioners, Nat. Def. Transp. Assn. (pres. Detroit chpt. 1966—, nat. v.p. 1968-69, 76-78), Traffic Club N.Y., Truck-Trailer Mfrs. Assn. (chmn. traffic com. 1974-78), Nat. Indsl. Traffic League (hwy. transp. com. 1962—, containerization and tofc com. 1970-78), Traffic Clubs Internat., Passenger Traffic Club Detroit, Traffic Club Detroit, Am. Soc. Traffic and Transp. (certified), Greater Detroit C. of C. (transp. com.). Home: 2119 Country Club Dr Grosse Pointe Woods MI 48236 Office: 10900 Harper Ave Detroit MI 48232

VUMBACO, JOSEPH ANTHONY, pub. utilities mgr.; b. Meriden, Conn., May 20, 1947; s. Rocco Joseph and Mildred Katherine (Bartley) V.; B.S., in M.E., Rose Poly. Inst., 1969; M.B.A., U. Hartford, 1975; m. Linda Mae Maddox, June 19, 1970. Research and devel. engr. Collins Radio Corp., Dallas, 1969-70; exec. asst. elec. div. Dept. Pub. Utilities, Wallingford, Conn., 1971-75, asst. gen. mgr., chief engr., 1975-76; gen. mgr., supt. Hibbing (Minn.) Pub. Utilities, 1976—; owner Vumbaco & Assos. Engring. Consultants. Registered profl. Engr., Conn. Mem. Minn. Municipal Utilities Assn. (bd. dirs., 1st v.p.), ASME, Am. Pub. Power Assn., Nat., Minn. socs. profl. engrs., Am. Water Works Assn., Am. Pub. Gas Assn. Club: Hibbing Kiwanis. Office: Hibbing Public Utilities 19th St and 6th Ave E Hibbing MN 55746

WABER, JAMES THOMAS, educator; b. Chgo., Apr. 8, 1920; s. James Warren and Anna May (Cline) W.; B.S., Ill. Inst. Tech., Chgo., 1941, M.S., 1943, Ph.D., 1946; m. Santon Fotheringham, May 12, 1951; children—Lauriene, Sue Berenaise, Gay Ellen (dec.), John James. Research asst. prof. chemistry Ill. Inst. Tech., 1946; staff mem., sect. leader Los Alamos Sci. Lab., 1947-66; prof. materials sci. and engring., nuclear enging. Northwestern U., Evanston, Ill., 1967—; cons. Los Alamos Sci. Lab. Recipient Sr. U.S. Scientist award Alexander von Humbolt Found., 1975, Profl. Achievement award Ill. Inst. Tech. Alumni Assn., 1967, Willis Rodney Whitney award Nat. Assn. Corrosion Engrs., 1961. Fellow Am. Phys. Soc., Inst. Metallurgists (Gt. Britain); mem. Am. Inst. Mining and Metall. Engrs., Am. Soc. Metals. Editor; Compounds of Interest in Nuclear Reactor Technology, 1964; Energy Bands in Metals and Alloys, 1967; Magnetism in Alloys, 1972; contbr. aticles to sci. jours.; patentee in field. Office: 2145 Sheridan Rd Evanston IL 60201

WACHAL, DAVID EUGENE, accountant; b. Windom, Minn., May 23, 1939; s. Louis Leon and Virginia Eva (Rickert) W.; B.A., Mankato State U., 1962; m. Merry Dee Cummings, Aug. 13, 1960; children—Michael David, Susan Dee. Staff accountant Arthur Andersen & Co., Mpls., 1962-67, audit mgr., 1967-73; v.p.-controller Ellerbe Inc., Bloomington, Minn., 1973-77; v.p. finance Am. Crystal Sugar Co., Moorhead, Minn., 1977—. Mem. Plymouth (Minn.) Zoning Bd., 1968-72; capt. N.D. wing CAP, 1977—. Served with AUS, 1957-58. C.P.A., Minn. Mem. Am. Inst. C.P.A.'s, Minn. Soc. C.P.A.'s, Plymouth Jaycees (pres. 1966-67), Aircraft Owners and Pilots Assn. Club: Twin City Cloud 7 Inc. (treas. 1968-74) (Mpls.). Home: 79 N Woodcrest Dr Fargo ND 58102 Office: 101 N 3d St Moorhead MN 56560

WACHOWSKI, THEODORE JOHN, radiologist; b. Chgo., Nov. 20, 1907; s. Albert and Constance (Korzeniewski) W.; B.S., U. Ill., 1929, M.D., 1932; m. Barbara F. Benda, June 1, 1931; 1 son, Ted James. Intern, resident in radiology, asso. radiologist U. Ill. Hosps., 1931-67; clin. prof. radiology U. Ill., 1949—; radiologist Copley Meml. Hosp., Aurora, Ill., 1935-77, Loretto Hosp., Chgo., 1941-48; practice medicine specializing in radiology, Wheaton and Carol Stream, Ill., 1975—. Mem. Radiol. Soc. N.Am. (pres. 1969, Gold medal, 1969), Am. Coll. Radiology (pres. 1963, Gold medal 1969), Ill., Kane County med. socs., AMA, Am. Roentgen Ray Soc. Republican. Club: Glen Oak Country. Contbr. articles to profl. jours. Home: 101 Tennyson Dr Wheaton IL 60187 Office: 387 Schmale Rd Carol Stream IL 60187

WACHTMAN, DONALD CARL, computer systems engr.; b. Napoleon, Ohio, Aug. 24, 1934; s. Ferdinand Peter and Mary Elsie (Otte) W.; B.S. in Edn. summa cum laude, Capital U., 1961; postgrad. in history and govt. Ohio State U., 1961-62; m. Carolyn Louise Herath, June 30, 1962; children—Stephen, Timothy, Andrew. Office mgr. Coll. Classics, Columbus, Ohio, 1957-62; tchr. Worthington (Ohio) High Sch., 1962-63; with F & S Lazarus Dept. Store, Columbus, 1963-74, mgr., 1969-71, dir. computer services, 1971-74; computer systems engr. Electronic Data Systems, Dallas, 1974—. Mem. alumni bd. Capital U., 1975—. Served with AUS, 1955-57. Mem. Capital U. Alumni Assn. Lutheran (pres. congregation 1976-77). Clubs: Capital University Men's Luncheon, Capital Crusader Athletic (pres. 1971—) (Columbus). Home: 9685 Grandview Ave Pickerington OH 43147 Office: High-Town Sts Columbus OH 43215

WACKER, FREDERICK GLADE, JR., mfg. co. exec.; b. Chgo., July 10, 1918; s. Frederick Glade and Grace Cook (Jennings) W.; grad. Hotchkiss Sch., 1936; B.A., Yale, 1940; student Gen. Motors Inst. Tech., 1940-42; m. Ursula Comandatore, Apr. 26, 1958; children—Frederick Glade III, Wendy, Joseph Comandatore. With AC Spark Plug div. Gen. Motors Corp. 1940-43, efficiency engr., 1941-43; with Ammco Tools, Inc., North Chicago, Ill., 1947—, pres., chmn. bd., 1948—; founder, 1954, since pres., chmn. bd. Liquid Controls Corp., North Chicago; partner Francis I. duPont & Co., N.Y.C., 1954-70; dir. Midwest Nat. Bank Lake Forest, 1964-71, Zenith Life Ins. Co., Hydro-Air Engring., Inc., 1973—; condr. Freddie Wacker and His Orch., 1955-70; orch. has appeared on TV and radio, recorded for Dolphin Records, Cadet Records. Mem. World Bus. Council, 1971—; chmn. Chgo. chpt. Young Presidents Orgn., 1965-66. Bd. govs. United Republican Fund Ill. Trustee Lake Forest Acad., 1956-71, Chgo. chpt. Multiple Sclerosis Soc., Warren Wilson Coll.; bd. govs. Lyric Opera Chgo., dir., 1963-66. Served to lt. (j.g.) USNR, 1943-45. Mem. N.A.M., Sports Car Club Am. (pres. 1952-53), Waukegan-North Chgo. C. of C. (dir. 1965-68), Chief, Exec.'s Forum, Chgo. Pres.'s Orgn. (pres. 1972-73), Pres.'s Forum, Am. Motorcycle Assn., Soc. Automotive Engrs., Chgo. Fedn. Musicians, Ill. Mfrs. Assn. (dir. 1966—, chmn. bd. 1975), Automotive Orgn. Team (life mem., dir. 1976—). Presbyn. Clubs: Chicago, Racquet (pres. 1960-61), Casino, Chicago Yacht, Metropolitan, Mid-America (Chgo.); Shoreacres (Lake Bluff); Onwentsia (Lake Forest, Ill.); N.Y. Yacht. Home: 1600 Green Bay Rd Lake Bluff IL 60044 Office: 2100 Commonwealth Ave North Chicago IL 60064

WACKER, MAXWELL NATHAN, obstetrician and gynecologist; b. Russia, Mar. 18, 1907; s. Nathan and Dena (Pearlman) Wachowsky; came to U.S., 1922, naturalized, 1923; B.S., U. Ill., 1931, M.D., 1934; m. Zena Bateman, Aug. 19, 1931; children—Doris Wacker Wolin, Denise. Intern Mt. Sinai Hosp., Chgo., 1933-34; preceptorship in obstetrics and gynecology Cook County Hosp., Chgo., 1942-51; practice medicine specializing in obstetrics and gynecology, Chgo., 1934—; attending staff Mt. Sinai, St. Joseph, Edgewater hosps.; chmn. dept. obstetrics and gynecology Mt. Sinai Hosp., 1965-68; clin. asso. prof. obstetrics and gynecology Chgo. Med. Sch. Diplomate Am. Bd. Obstetrics and Gynecology. Fellow A.C.S., Internat. Coll. Surgeons, Am. Coll. Obstetricians and Gynecologists (founding), AMA; mem. Chgo. Gynecol. Soc. Contbr. articles to med. jours. Home: 3750 N Lake Shore Dr Chicago IL 60613 Office: 30 N Michigan Ave Chicago IL 60602

WADDELL, JAMES RICHARD, veterinarian; b. Milw., Apr. 22, 1932; s. James Frost and Irene Elaine (Straka) W.; B.S., U. Mo., 1957, D.V.M., 1959; m. Shirley Ann Manning, Jan. 28, 1961; children—Margaret Ann, John Jouett, Barbara Jane, Rebecca Lynn. Practice vet. medicine, Lancaster, Mo., 1959-66, Grinnell, Iowa, 1966-67; vet. med. officer Animal Plant Inspection Service, Vet. Service, U.S. Dept. Agr., Sedalia, Mo., 1967—; veterinarian, Sedalia, 1959—. Served with AUS, 1952-54. Mem. Nat. Assn. Fed. Veterinarians, Am., Mo., West Central Mo. (v.p. 1971, pres. 1973) vet. med. assns. Address: 2416 S Quincy St Sedalia MO 65301

WADDICK, WILLIAM ANTHONY, lawyer; b. Chgo., Dec. 7, 1931; s. William Anthony and Mary Elizabeth (Dolan) W.; student Xavier U., 1949-51; B.S. cum laude, U. Notre Dame, 1957; J.D., Ind. U., 1961; m. Clara Maria Taylor, June 13, 1964; children—Maria B., Julia L., Patricia A., Brenda J., Linda J. Admitted to Ind. bar, 1961; mem. firm. Kunz & Kunz, Indpls., 1961—, partner, 1963—. Served with USAF, 1951-54. Mem. Ind., Indpls. bar assns., Ind. Trial Lawyers Assn., St. Thomas More Soc. (pres. 1970-71), Phi Delta Phi. Roman Catholic. Republican. K.C. Clubs: Heather Hills Country (Indpls.), Indianapolis Athletic. Home: 2 Songbird Ct Carmel IN 46032 Office: 320 N Meridian St Indianapolis IN 46204

WADDINGTON, EDWARD HOLMES, architect; b. Kansas City, Mo., July 25, 1928; s. Chester Sprague and Daisy Orilla (Stewart) W.; B.Arch., Washington U., St. Louis, 1949; m. Zetta Margaret Gunnels, Jan. 29, 1960 (div. Nov. 1966); children—Tauni Howell, Tad Stewart-Holmes. With Bank Bldg Corp., 1951-53, Bloomsdale Bank Bldg. & Equipment Corp., 1953; practice architecture, Kansas City, Mo., 1953—; pres., dir. Tad, Inc., Tauni, Inc.; gen. partner in multi-family apt. devels. Mem. Constrn. Specifications Inst., Scarab, Theta Xi. Presbyn. Optimist. Important works include banks, health centers. Home: 3838 N Cherry Ln Kansas City MO 64116 Office: 3836 N Cherry Ln Kansas City MO 64116

WADDINGTON, RAYMOND BRUCE, JR., educator; b. Santa Barbara, Calif., Sept. 27, 1935; s. Raymond Bruce and Marjorie Gladys (Waddell) W.; B.A., Stanford U., 1957; Ph.D., Rice U., 1963; postdoctoral (Univ. fellow in Humanities) Johns Hopkins U., 1965-66; m. Linda Gayle Jones, Sept. 7, 1957; children—Raymond Bruce, Edward Jackson. Instr. English, U. Houston, 1961-62; instr. U. Kans., 1962-63, asst. prof., 1963-65; asst. prof. English lit. U. Wis., Madison, 1966-68, asso. prof., 1968-74, prof., 1974—. Huntington Library fellow, 1967, 75; Inst. Research in Humanities fellow, 1971-72; Guggenheim fellow, 1972-73; Nat. Endowment for Humanities fellow, 1977; Newberry Library fellow, 1978; Am. Philos. Soc. grantee, 1965. Mem. Modern Lang. Assn., Milton Soc. Am., Friends of Bemerton. Club: Logos. Author: The Mind's Empire, 1974; co-editor: The Rhetoric of Renaissance Poetry, 1974; editorial bd. Sixteenth Century Jour., 1975—, Lit. Monographs, 1974—. Home: 4010 Paunack Ave Madison WI 53711 Office: 600 N Park St Madison WI 53706

WADE, GORDON STANFIELD, librarian; b. Mpls., Dec. 13, 1936; s. Warren Benjamin and Helen (Freyschlag) W.; B.A., U. Minn., 1958, M.A., 1963; m. Penelope Barels, June 24, 1967; 1 son, David Barels. Bookmobile librarian Hennepin County Library, Mpls., 1960-62, documents librarian, 1962-63; head librarian Carroll (Iowa) Pub. Library, 1963—; teaching asst. Library Sch., U. Minn., 1960. Book reviewer Library Jour., 1973—; mem. librarian's adv. council Northwest Regional Library System, 1974—. Bd. dirs., treas. Films for Iowa Library Media Services, 1973-75; bd. dirs. Carroll Arts Council, 1976—. Served with AUS, 1960-63. Mem. Iowa Library Assn. Republican. Presbyn. (ruling elder 1968-70, clk. session 1970). Home: 1326 N Adams St Carroll IA 51401 Office: 118 E 5th St Carroll IA 51401

WADE, JAMES G., publisher, editor; b. Canton, Ohio, Jan. 15, 1945; s. James and Iva (Little) W.; student Mt. Union Coll., Alliance, Ohio; m. B. Maxine Twaddle, Feb. 14, 1967. Dist. mgr. Steubenville (Ohio) Herald Star, 1961-68; mgr. circulation Alliance (Ohio) Rev., 1968-76; dir. circulation Casa Grande (Ariz.), 1976; owner Wintersville (Ohio) Citizen, 1976—. Office: 734 Main St Wintersville OH 43952

WADSWORTH, GERALD J., machinery co. exec.; b. nr. Grand Blanc, Mich., May 19, 1918; s. William S. and Aethel O. (Beebe) W.; grad. Gen. Motors Tech. Sch., 1940; postgrad. Mich. State Coll., 1943; m. Ruth A. Ackerman, Jan. 10, 1941; children—Jon F., Jo Ann (Mrs. Stephen R. Donahue). Toolroom foreman A.C. Spark Plug Co., Flint, Mich., 1941; toolmaker Indsl. Metal Products Corp., Lansing, Mich., 1942-51, foreman, 1951-52, supt., 1952-68, proposal engr., 1968-69, chief sales engr., 1969-76, advanced planning engr., 1969-76, pres., gen. mgr., 1976—, dir. apprentice tng. program, 1952-68, chmn. joint apprenticeship com., 1974—. Served with AUS, 1944-46. Mem. Am. Bowling Congress, Am. Mus. Natural History, Indsl. Execs. Republican. Presbyn. Elk. Home: 2810 Delta River Dr Lansing MI 48906 Office: 3417 W St Joseph Rd Lansing MI 48917

WADZINSKI, LEROY ANTHONY, cheese co. exec.; b. Marathon City, Wis., Dec. 1, 1928; s. Raymond and Genevieve (Volhard) W.; student parochial sch.; m. Violet Lucille Horn, June 26, 1948; children—Terry, Sue, Judy, Debra, Lori, Michael. Mgr., Mayflower Cheese, Dancy, Wis., 1949-51, Pittsville Creamery, 1951-53; owner Lone Elm Dairy, Junction City, 1953-58; partner Junction City Milk Products, 1958-66; pres. Ravenna Cheese Co. (Nebr.), 1967—, L.A.W., trucking, 1968—, Mid Whey Inc., 1969—, Navasota Cheese Co. (Tex.); v.p. Oxford Cheese Co. (Nebr.), 1976—; v.p. Ravenna Bldg. Corp.; dir. Ravenna Industries. Vice-chmn. Planning Commn. Ravenna, 1971. Named Nebr. Small Businessman of Year, 1972. Mem. Neb. Cheesemakers Assn. (v.p. 1971—), Nebr. Dairy Industries (pres. 1975, dir.), Am. Dairy Assn. (pres. Nebr., 1974-76). Republican. Roman Catholic. Forrester, Lion. Home: 910 Verona Ave Ravenna NE 68869 Office: Lincoln Ave Ravenna NE 68869

WAETJEN, WALTER BERNHARD, univ. pres.; b. Phila., Oct. 16, 1920; s. Walter E. and Marguerite D. (Dettmann) W.; B.S., State Coll., Millersville, Pa., 1942; M.S., U. Pa., 1947; Ed.D., U. Md., 1951; m. Betty Walls, Sept. 28, 1945; children—Walter Bernhard, Kristi (Mrs. Richard Jenkins), Daniel G. Tchr., Sch. Dist. of Phila., 1945-48; research fellow U. Md., 1948-50, asst. prof., 1950-55, asso. prof., 1955-57, prof., 1957-65, dir. Bur. Ednl. Research and Field Services, 1962-65, gen. dir. Interprofl. Research Commn. on Pupil Personnel Services, 1963-65, v.p. adminstrv. affairs, 1965-70, v.p. gen. adminstrn., 1970-73; pres. Cleve. State U., 1973—; dir. Union Commerce Bank, Gray Drug. Bd. dirs. United Torch, Cleve. Scholarship Programs, Inc., Cleve. Internat. Program, Cleve. Commn. on Higher Edn., Cleve. Council World Affairs, Ohio World Trade Center, Boy Scouts Am., Nat. ARC, Downtown Cleve. Corp. Mem. NEA, Assn. for Supervision and Curriculum Devel., Soc. for Research in Child Devel., AAAS, Am. Edn. Research Assn. W.T. Grant Found. fellow, 1960-61; Patty Hill Smith Meml. lectr. U. Louisville, 1964. Club: Mason (33 deg.). Author: (with Jean D. Grambs) Sex: Does It Make a Difference?, 1971; editor, contbr. Learning and Mental Health in the School, 1966. Home: 14706 Larchmere Blvd Shaker Heights OH 44120 Office: Cleve State U Cleveland OH 44115

WAFER, JOHN ALBERT, elec. engr.; b. Akron, Ohio, July 5, 1935; s. Albert Eugene and Vera Ball (Grover) W.; student Ohio U., 1957; B.S. in Elec. Engring., Villanova U., 1959-61. Elec. engr. Adamson United Co., Akron, 1958, Nat. Rubber Machinery Co., Akron, 1958-60; project elec. engr. Lee Tire & Rubber Co., Conshohocken, Pa., 1960-62; staff elec. engr. Goodyear Tire & Rubber Co., Akron, 1962—. Mem. IEEE (past sect. chmn. rubber and plastics com.), ASTM, Am. Numismatic Assn. (life), Token and Medal Soc., Lighter Than Air Soc. Methodist. Clubs: Coin (v.p.) (Akron), Warren Heights. Home: 1339 Broad Blvd Cuyahoga Falls OH 44223 Office: 1144 E Market St Akron OH 44316

WAGENHEIM, JOEL STEVEN, bus. exec.; b. Atlantic City, Aug. 1, 1943; s. Joseph and Bette M. (MacDonough) W.; student Temple U., 1961-63, Ohio State U., 1969-70. Founder, pres. Consol. Services, Columbus, Ohio, 1969-77, chmn., 1977—; founder, pres. In Crowd, Inc., 1977—; owner Jo-Lin Farms, 1973—. Served with U.S. Army, 1965-68. Mem. Arabian Horse Assn. Home: 6666 Davis Rd Hilliard OH 43026 Office: 246 E Sycamore St Columbus OH 43216

WAGENKNECHT, THEODORE WILLIAM, JR., radiologist; b. Chgo., Dec. 18, 1926; s. Theodore William and Lillian Marie (Arnesen) W.; B.S., U. Ill., 1946, M.D., 1948; m. Verda Hamann, Oct. 31, 1947 (dec.); children—Jon Theodore, Karl Theodore, Kay Marie, Lynn Marie, Ann Marie; m. 2d, Sharon Rexroth, Aug. 12, 1973; children—Eric Theodore, Celenda Marie. Intern, Ancker Hosp., St. Paul, 1948-49, resident in surgery, 1951-53; gen. practice medicine, Appleton, Minn., 1949-51; resident in radiology VA Hosp., Dallas, 1955-57; asso. radiologist St. Mary's Hosp., Streator, Ill., St. James Hosp., Pontiac, Ill., 1958-60; chief radiologist St. James Hosp., 1960-66, St. Mary's Hosp., 1961—. Chmn. Com. to Save City Park, 1962; bd. dirs. Streator YMCA, YWCA, 1961; mem. fin. com. Eagle Ln Theatre. Served to capt. USAF, 1953-55. Diplomate Am. Bd. Radiology. Mem. La Salle County Med. Soc., Am. Coll. Radiology, Radiol. Soc. N. Am., Am. Heart Assn., Met. Area Radiation Therapists, Soc. Nuclear Medicine, Am. Coll. Nuclear Medicine. Republican. Clubs: Rotary, Ivy Racquet, Streator County. Home: Ridge Pl Streator IL 61364 Office: 131 S Vermillion St Streator IL 61364

WAGESTER, EUGENE KENNETH, cons. civil engr.; b. Mich., June 25, 1940; s. Kenneth G. and Ada (Reisner) E.; A.S., Ferris State Coll., 1960; B.S., Mich. State U., 1966; m. Wanda Jean Dobbins, Apr. 20, 1963; children—Suzanne, Kenneth. Draftsman R.W. Petrie & Assos., Inc., Benton Harbor, Mich., 1960-63, project engr., 1966-67; chief engr. Hough Brothers Inc., Sunfield, Mich., 1967-75; owner, mgr. Wagester Engring. Co., Sunfield, Mich., 1975—. Mem. Town Council Sunfield, 1976—. Registered profl. engr., Mich., Ind., N.C., Vt. Mem. ASCE. Home: 28 1st St Sunfield MI 48890 Office: PO Box 37 Sunfield MI 48890

WAGMAN, FREDERICK HERBERT, librarian; b. Springfield, Mass., Oct. 12, 1912; A.B. summa cum laude, Amherst Coll., 1933, L.H.D., 1958; A.M., Columbia, 1934, Ph.D., 1942; LL.D., Alderson-Broaddus Coll., 1967; Litt. D., Luther Coll., 1969; m. Ruth Jeannette Wagman. Instr. in extension German Columbia, 1933-35; Ottendorfer Meml. fellow N.Y.U., 1935-36; teaching fellow Amherst Coll., 1936-37; instr. German U. Minn., 1937-42; successively head planning unit, head regulations and tng. sect., regulations officer U.S. Office Censorship Postal div., 1942-45; acting dir. personnel and adminstrv. service, then asst. dir. reference dept., dir. processing dept., dep. chief asst. librarian, dir. adminstrn. Library of Congress, Washington, 1945-53; dir. U. Mich. Library, 1953—; Cons. UN Library, 1959-62, Hebrew U. Jerusalem, 1969-70. Vice chmn. Commn. Obscenity and Pornography, 1968-70. Bd. dirs. Council

Library Resources, Inc., 1956—; bd. regents Nat. Library Medicine, 1967-71; pres. Midwest Region Library Network, 1975-76. Mem. Am. (pres. 1963-64), Mich. (pres 1960) library assns., Mich. Acad. Sci., Arts and Letters (librarian), Phi Beta Kappa, Phi Kappa Phi. Club: University. Author: Magic and Natural Science in German Baroque Lierature, 1942. Address: 818 Harlan Hatcher Grad Library Ann Arbor MI 48104

WAGNER, ALVIN LOUIS, JR., profl. real estate appraiser, cons.; b. Chgo., Dec. 19, 1939; s. Alvin Louis and Esther Jane (Wheeler) W.; student U. Ill., 1958-59; B.A., Drake U., 1962; postgrad. Real Estate Inst., Chgo., 1960-65; m. Susan Carole Fahey, Aug. 14, 1965; children—Alvin Louis III, Robert Percy. Asst. appraiser Oak Park (Ill.) Fed. Savings & Loan Co., 1955-60; v.p. real estate sales A. L. Wagner & Co., Flossmoor, Ill., 1961-63; real estate loan officer, chief appraiser Beverly Bank, Chgo., 1963-67; asso. real estate appraiser C. A. Bruckner & Assos., Chgo., 1967-70; founder, profl. real estate appraiser and cons. A. L. Wagner & Co., Flossmoor, 1970—. Mem. faculty Am. Inst. Real Estate Appraisers, Chgo., 1974—; instr. real estate appraising Prairie State Coll., Chicago Heights, Ill., 1970—; mem. adv. com. Real Estate Sch., 1972—; community prof. Gov.'s State U., 1977—, founding mem. real estate adv. bd. Mem. Rich Township (Ill.) Personal Services Commn., 1973—; v.p., drive chmn. Flossmoor Community Chest, Crusade of Mercy, 1974-75, pres., 1975-76. Auditor, Rich Township, 1973-77. Governing bd. Glenwood (Ill.) Sch. for Boys, 1973—; chmn. bus. edn. occupational adv. com. Homewood-Flossmoor High Sch., 1977. Mem. Am. Inst. Real Estate Appraisers (mem. governing council 1974-75, Profl. Recognition award 1977), Chgo. Assn. Commerce and Industry, Chgo., Homewood-Flossmoor real estate bds., Nat., Ill. assns. realtors, Homewood-Flossmoor Jaycees, Phi Delta Theta (pres. chpt. 1960), Chgo. Phi Delta Theta Alumni Club (pres.), Omega Tau Rho. Rotarian. Club: Flossmoor Country. Mem. editorial bd. Appraisal Journal, 1975—; contbr. articles to real estate jours. Home: 927 Park Dr Flossmoor IL 60422 Office: 2709 Flossmoor Rd Flossmoor IL 60422

WAGNER, FRANK EUGENE, economist, educator; b. Guilford, Conn., July 9, 1933; s. Frank F. and Helene (Graf) W.; B.A., U. Kansas City, 1958; M.A., U. Mo. at Kansas City, 1960; Ph.D., Syracuse U., 1967; m. Jane E. Trewhella, Aug. 17, 1955; children—Mark E., Kimberly Jane. Asst. prof. econs. U. Mo. at Kansas City, 1962-67, asso. prof., 1967-73, prof., 1973—, chmn. dept., 1973-76. Vis. Fulbright prof. Universidad Autonoma de Guadelajara, 1969-70. Served with AUS, 1953-55. Mem. Am. Econs. Assn., A.A.U.P., Am. Acad. Polit. and Social Scis., Home: 6418 Main St Kansas City MO 64133 Office: Dept Econs Univ Mo Kansas City MO 64110

WAGNER, JOYCE AILEEN, journalist; b. Aurora, Ill., Nov. 23, 1941; d. Julius Jeppesen and Laura (Timmerman) Wagner; attended U. Mo., 1959-61. Editor, Warrenville (Ill.) News, summer 1960; reporter Downers Grove (Ill.) Graphic, 1961, Bailey Publs., Independence, Mo., 1962; TV editor K.C. Kansan, Kansas City, Kans., 1963-65; TV editor, columnist Kansas City (Mo.) Star, 1965-77; pub., editor City mag., 1977—. Mem. Nat., Mo. press women's assns. Address: City Magazine Suite 636 20 W 9th St Kansas City MO 64105

WAGNER, LOREN LAVERNE, diversified mfg. co. exec.; b. Lancaster, Pa., Mar. 19, 1936; s. Irvin Elmer and Marie Ellen (Grove) W.; A.A. in Bus. Adminstrn., Goldey Beacom Sch. Bus., 1956; B.S. in Bus. Adminstrn., Elizabethtown Coll., 1959; postgrad. Temple U., 1963-67; m. Kathryn Regina Swigart, June 7, 1958; children—Lori, Londa. Field rep. G.A.C. Finance, Lancaster, Pa., 1959-60; marketing research analyst New Holland Sperry, (Pa.), 1960-65, sr. project analyst, 1965-68; mktg. research mgr. Valmont Industries, Valley, Nebr., 1968-72, dir. corp. planning and research, 1973-74, v.p. corp. planning and research, 1974—, also dir. Vice pres. Chapel Hill Recreation Assn., 1971-72. Mem. Am. Mktg. Assn. (chpt. pres. 1971-72). Baptist (chmn. bd. trustees 1971—). Home: 21708 Harney St Elkhorn NE 68022 Office: Valmont Industries Valley NE 68064

WAGNER, PERCY EVAN, real estate counselor; b. Chgo., Mar. 14, 1894; s. Louis Christopher and Mary (Gantzert) W.; Ph.B., U. Chgo., 1916; m. Elizabeth McGeeney, July 31, 1920; children—Betty Joy, Mary Louise Wagner Forrester. Partner, Wagner Bros., Chgo., 1915-30; pres. Midway State Bank, Chgo., 1928-31; chief valuator FHA, Chgo., 1933-35, zone rental mgr. Middle Western states, 1935-40; owner Am. Home Builders, Chgo., 1940-51; lectr. U. Ala., Northwestern U. Mag. Inst. Tech., U. So. Calif., U. Wis.; dean Real Estate Inst., Central YMCA Schs., 1940-75, dean emeritus, 1975—; dean Stanford, 1954; instr. U. Mich., Purdue U.; pres. Park Forest South Investments, Inc. (Ill.); real estate counselor. Chmn. examining com. Ill. Dept. Registration and Edn., 1950, now edn. cons.; chmn. Flossmoor (Ill.) Planning Commn., 1956—. Recipient Testimonial plaque DuPage Bd. Realtors, 1960. Mem. Am. Inst. Real Estate Appraisers (pres. 1960), Nat. Assn. License Law Ofcls. (past dir.), Inst. Real Estate Mgmt., Soc. Residential Appraisers, Am. Soc. Real Estate Counselors, Internat. Real Estate Fedn., Nat. Assn. Real Estate Bds. (v.p. 1962, chmn. license law com., resolutions com.), Chgo. Real Estate Bd. (pres. 1963), Omega Tau Rho, Phi Kappa Psi, Lambda Alpha. Clubs: Homewood Rotary, Masons; South Shore Country (Chgo.); Flossmoor Country. Author: Condominium—How It Works, 1967; (with Harry Grant Atkinson) Management and Policies of Real Estate Brokerage. Contbr. articles to Appraisal Jour. Home: 1518 Braeburn Rd Flossmoor IL 60422 Office: 29 W Randolph St Chicago IL 60601

WAGNER, PHILIP IRA, cardiologist; b. Berwyn, Ill., June 4, 1931; s. Arthur Mattern and Lucille Clarissa (Boush) W.; B.A., Kalamazoo Coll., 1953; M.D., U. Ill., 1957; m. Florence Park, Aug. 1, 1973; children—Leslie, Kent, Ross. Intern King County Hosp., Seattle, 1957-58; resident Portland (Wash.) VA Hosp., 1958-60; resident in cardiology 1960-61; fellow in cardiology U.S. Naval Hosp., San Diego, 1963-64, chief cardiopulmonary lab., 1964-69, head cardiopulmonary tech. sch., 1964-69, chief cardiology, 1968-69; practice medicine specializing in cardiology, Chgo., 1969-73, Kalamazoo, Mich., 1973—; mem. staffs. Edgewater Hosp., Chgo., 1969-73; head cardiology and CCU, dir. cardiac catheterization lab. Borgess Hosp., Kalamazoo, 1973—, chmn. sect. cardiology, 1975-76, dir. cardiovascular lab., 1975-76, dir. coronary care unit, 1973; asst. clin. profl. coll. human medicine, Mich. State U., 1975—; advisor Emergency med. com. S. Central Mich. Health Planning Council, Inc., 1975—. Served to comdr. USN, 1961-69. Diplomate Am. Bd. Internal Medicine. Fellow Am. Coll. Cardiology, Am. Coll. Angiology; mem. Am., Mich. heart assns., AMA, Mich. Med. Soc., Kalamazoo Acad. Medicine, Am., Mich. socs. internal medicine. Contbr. articles in field to med. jours. Home: 1748 Waite Ave Kalamzoo MI 49008 Office: 1717 Shaffer St Suite 202 Kalamazoo MI 49001

WAGNER, RICHARD GORDON, orthodontist; b. Primghar, Iowa, Nov. 26, 1926; s. James A. and Iva F. (O'Donnell) W.; D.D.S., U. Iowa, 1951, M.S. in Orthodontics, 1952; m. Dorothy Y. Van Dyke, Sept. 17, 1949; children—Richard Wayne, David Van. Practice dentistry, specializing in orthodontics, Sioux City, 1953—. Head profl. div. United Fund, 1969, head advanced gifts div., 1970-71; adult leader Fellowship Christian Athletes, 1973—. Mem. Sioux City Community Schs. Dist. Bd., 1973-77. Served with USAF, 1952-53. Recipient Outstanding Service award Sertoma, 1957; Distinguished Service award Sioux City Jr. C. of C., 1961. Mem. Sioux City Dental Soc. (pres. 1959—), Iowa Orthodontic Soc. (pres. 1968-69, 74—), Am. Assn. Orthodontists (trustee representing Iowa), Iowa Alumni Assn. Sioux City (co-chmn. 1971—). Clubs: Sertoma (pres. 1959-60), North High Booster (co-chmn. 1972) (Sioux City). Home: 3917 Sylvian Way Sioux City IA 51104 Office: 620 Sioux City Fed Plaza Bldg Sioux City IA 51101

WAGNER, ROBERT EARL, veterinarian; b. Glidden, Iowa, Dec. 12, 1920; s. Frank Earl and Lola Floy (Horton) W.; D.V.M., Iowa State U., 1943; m. Virginia Mae Buddin, Jan. 24, 1942; children—Robert Earl, Jeri L., Curtis J., Roxanne M., Janet R., Kevin J. Gen. practice of vet. medicine, Glidden, 1943-44, Titonka, Iowa, 1944-45, Coon Rapids, Iowa, 1945-54, Glidden, 1954-65; vet. med. officer Vet. Services, Animal and Plant Health Inspection Service, U.S. Dept. Agr., Glidden, 1965-69, Kearney, Nebr., 1969-76, dist. veterinarian-in-charge, Mo., 1976—, grad. vet. adminstr. Devel. Program, 1974. Mayor, Glidden, 1959-60; mem. sch. bd. Glidden-Ralston Community Sch., 1967-69; chmn. troop com. Boy Scouts of Am., 1960-64; pres. Glidden Booster Club, 1956-57. Bd. dirs. Glidden United Fund, 1957-59; bd. dirs. Glidden Devel., Inc., 1960-67, pres., 1962-65. Served AUS, 1942-43. Mem. Nebr. Vet. Med. Assn., Am. Legion. Presbyn. (elder 1962—). Mason (Shriner), Elk; mem. Eastern Star. Club: Cosmopolitan Internat. (Kearney). Home: 721 Leonard Dr Jefferson City MO 65101 Office: 901 Missouri Blvd Jefferson City MO 65101

WAGNER, WILLIAM BURDETTE, educator; b. Oswego, N.Y., Apr. 27, 1941; s. Guy Wesley and Gladys Matilda (Redlinger) W.; B.A. with highest honors, Mich. State U., 1963; M.B.A. (NDEA fellow), Ohio State U., 1965, Ph.D. (NDEA fellow), 1967; m. Cathryn Nettie Warfel, Mar. 22, 1969; 1 son, Geoffrey David. Asst. prof. bus. U. Toledo, 1968-69; asst. prof. U. Mo. at Columbia, 1969-75, asso. prof., 1975—. Cons. transp., mfg. and service related firms; coll. coordinator book program for minorities McDonnell Douglas, 1972—. Vice-chmn. acad. awards com. John W. Heisman Meml. Found., 1974-76, chmn., 1976—. Recipient Spl. Civic Service award McDonnell Douglas Corp., 1977; elected to Mystical Seven (service hon. soc.) U. Mo., 1976. Mem. Am. Soc. Traffic and Transp. (bd. govs. Mo. 1971-73, 76-78, pres. 1974-75), So. Mktg. Assn., Southwestern Fedn. Adminstrv. Disciplines, Delta Sigma Pi, Beta Gamma Sigma, Omicron Delta Epsilon. Contbr. articles to profl. jours. Home: 2401 Bluff Blvd Columbia MO 65201 Office: Room 324 Middlebush Univ Mo Columbia MO 65201

WAHL, EMIL DEWEY, business exec.; b. Bismarck, N.D., Mar. 28, 1935; s. Emil C. and Lydia Ione (Pepple) W.; B.S., U. N.D., 1957, M.S., 1962; postgrad. U. Mich., 1964-65; Ph.D., Purdue U., 1971; m. Mary Jean Engler, June 10, 1962; 1 dau., Linda Kay. Tech. asst. Nat. Lead Co. of Ohio, Mt. Healthy, 1957; instr. chem. engring. U. N.D., Grand Forks, 1959-62, asst. prof., 1962-64; research asst. U. Mich. Sch. Pub. Health, Ann Arbor, 1965-66; chem. engr. Eli Lilly Co., Lafayette, Ind., 1966-69; research asst. Purdue U., W. Lafayette, Ind., 1970-71, asst. prof., 1971-75; asso. supt. long range planning and devel. Ind. Dept. Pub. Instrn., Indpls., 1975-76; pres. Mgmt., Adminstrv. and Profl. Services Co. (MAPSCo), Indpls., 1976—. Served with AUS, 1957-59. Mem. A.A.A.S., Am. Assn. Higher Edn., Am. Chem. Soc., Am. Ednl. Research Assn., Am. Soc. Microbiology, Am. Inst. Decision Scis., Am. Soc. Tng. and Devel., SAM, Sigma Tau, Phi Delta Kappa. Elks. Club: Optimist (Indpls.). Contbr. articles to profl. jours. Home: PO Box 19297 Indianapolis IN 46219 Office: 8130 E 21st St Suite G Indianapolis IN 46219

WAHL, MARY EVELYN GARLICK (MRS. KENNETH ROBERT WAHL), home economist; b. South Lyon, Mich., Feb. 1, 1940; d. Arthur Francis and Phyllis (Jackson) Garlick; B.S., Mich. State U., 1961, M.S., 1964; m. Kenneth Robert Wahl, June 13, 1964; children—Michael Kenneth, Mark Kevin. Tchr. homemaking Caro (Mich.) High Sch., 1962; tchr. homemaking and math. Laingsburg (Mich.) Community Sch., 1964; tchr. homemaking Douglas MacArthur High Sch., Saginaw, Mich., 1964-65; extension home economist Mich. State U., Midland, Bay and Saginaw counties, 1965—. Del. on Internat. Farm Youth Exchange, Italy, 1961. Water safety instr. A.R.C.; trustee Mich. 4-H Found., 1974—. Mem. Am., Mich. home econs. assns., Nat. (Distinguished Service award 1976), Mich. (pres. 1975) assns. extension home economists, Mich. State U. Alumni Assn., AAUW, Bay City Pan-Hellenic Assn., Soc. for Nutrition Edn., Omicron Nu, Sigma Delta Epsilon, Epsilon Sigma Phi, Delta Gamma. Presbyn. Home: 3357 Old Kawkawlin Rd Bay City MI 48706 Office: Bay County Bldg Bay City MI 48706

WAHL, NORMAN STEPHEN, cons. mech. engr.; b. Cin., Jan. 23, 1924; s. William Kenneth and Norma (Steidel) W.; B.S. in M.E., U. Cin., 1955; A.S. in Marine Biology, U. Miami, 1948; m. Phyllis Chritine Miller, Dec. 31, 1965; children—Rochelle Rene, Amy Lynn, Stephen Michael. Pres., Wahl & Assos., Portsmouth, and Cin., 1955-57; design engr. Ziel Blossom & Assos., Cin., 1957-66; chief engr. Chester Products Co., Inc., Hamilton, Ohio, 1966-70; design engr. Ziel Blossom & Assos., Cin., 1971-75; v.p., gen. mgr. Mech. Constrn. Co., Inc., Portsmouth, Ohio, 1975—. Served with USN, 1940-45; PTO. Decorated Silver Star, Purple Heart. Mem. Am. Soc. Refrigeration and Air Conditioning Engrs., Am. Soc. San. Engrs. (certificate excellence, 1969), Nat. Soc. Profl. Engrs. (merit certificate, 1970), Am. Soc. Plumbing Engrs., Ohio Soc. Profl. Engrs., Ohio Assn. Pub. Health, Water Pollution Control Fedn. Presbyn. Clubs: Cin., Nat. Oceanosphere Assn., Rotary, Mason. Home: Box 199 Rt 5 Portsmouth OH 45266 Office: 2302 8th St Portsmouth OH 45266

WAHLQUIST, ERIC, water meter co. exec; b. Stockholm, Sweden, June 17, 1913; s. Ragnor and Elbba H. (Wahlquist) W.; B.B.A., B.S. in Elec. Engring., NKI Tech. Coll., 1941-44; m. Eivor Maria Phillipson, Dec. 24, 1935; children—Gunilla Maria (Mrs. Carl E. Warden Jr.), Erik Lennart. Came to U.S., 1950, naturalized, 1956. Pres., Sweda Cash Register Inc., Chgo., 1950-56; bus. cons., 1956-58; pres. Tex. Hydraulics Inc., Austin, 1958-64; with Badger Meter Mfg. Co., Milw., 1964-71, v.p., 1965-71; pres. Badger Meter Internat., Milw., 1964-71; v.p. internat. div. Milw. Electric Tool Corp., Brookfield, Wis., 1971—; chmn. bd., pres. Badger Del Peru, Lima, 1965—; mng. dir. W. Gottlob Volz, Stuttgart, Germany, 1966—. Served to 1st lt. Swedish Army, 1942-43. Named Ky. col., Hon. VIP, Lufthansa Airlines. Mem. A.I.M., Milw. Soc., Internat. Assn. Water Pollution Research Am. Mgmt. Assn. (mem. presidents council). Republican. Lutheran. Mem. Royal Order (Vikings. Clubs: Airways (N.Y.C.); Milwaukee World Trade. Home: 13335 Watertown Plank Rd Apt 306 Elm Grove WI 53122 Office: 13135 W Lisbon Rd Brookfield WI 53005

WAHRMAN, WILLIAM FRANK, beverage co. exec.; b. Los Angeles, Sept. 18, 1925; s. Frank C. and Edna (Bagwell) W.; student Long Beach Jr. Coll., 1942-43, U. Iowa, 1945-47; m. Deborah Ann Page, July 12, 1947; children—Ann, Mark. Salesman, Dr. Pepper Bottling Co., Denison, Iowa, 1948-63, mem. marketing adv. bd., 1961; pres. Denison Bottling Co., 1963—. Mem. Denison Planning Commn., 1963-70, Denison Community Sch. Bd., 1967-70. Served with USCGR, 1943-45. Mem. Iowa Bottlers Carbonated Beverages (past pres.), Denison Indsl. Bur., C. of C. (past pres.). Republican. Presbyn. Mason (Shriner). Club: Optimist (past pres.). Home: 39 Pleasant St Denison IA 51442 Office: 421 S Main St Denison IA 51442

WAIR, FRED LEE, human services cons.; b. East St. Louis, Ill., Oct. 6, 1939; s. Ezell and Annie Laura (Haynes) W.; B.S., So. Ill. U., 1963, M.S., 1968; postgrad. St. Louis U., Washington U., St. Louis; m. Thelma Jean Mothershed, Dec. 25, 1965; 1 son, Scott Frederick. Tchr. biology De Andreis High Sch., St. Louis, 1963-64; tchr. gen. sci. Clark Jr. High Sch., East St. Louis, Ill., 1964-68; dormitory dir., counselor, instr. Ky. State U., Frankfort, 1968-69; acad. counselor So. Ill. U., Edwardsville, 1969-72; mental health adminstr. Metro-East Health Services Council, East St. Louis, 1972-75; program dir. for aging Urban League, East St. Louis, 1975-76; dir. program devel. and evaluation Family Planning Council, Clayton, Mo., 1976-77; human services cons., East St. Louis, 1977—. Bd. dirs., v.p. Both Cities Devel. Corp., 1974; bd. dirs. Mental Health Center St. Clair County, Children, Family and Youth Advocacy Council, Belleville, Ill.; v.p. Children Youth and Family Advocacy Bd. Mem. AAUP, Am. Personnel and Guidance Assn., East St. Louis Artists Guild, Phi Delta Kappa, Kappa Delta Pi, Alpha Phi Alpha. Home and Office: 752 Pershing St PO Box 608 East St Louis IL 62201

WAITE, DAVID ANTES, tile mfg. co. exec.; b. Evansville, Wis., Jan. 13, 1923; s. John Howard and Madeline Elizabeth (Antes) W.; B.B.A., U. Wis., 1949; m. Carol Frances Moore, Oct. 8, 1955; children—Judith, Jeffrey, Daniel, Elizabeth, Patrick. Sales mgr. Waukesha Cement Tile Co. (Wis.), 1949-61, v.p., 1955-61, pres., gen. mgr., 1961—; dir. Waukesha Savs. and Loan Assn., 1968—. East dist. chmn. Boy Scouts Am., Waukesha, 1952-53; chmn. bldg. fund dr. YWCA, 1960-61. Bd. dirs. YMCA, Waukesha, 1954-57, United Fund, Waukesha, 1955-57. Served to 2d lt. USAAF, 1943-46. Recipient Man of Year award Waukesha Jr. C. of C., 1957, Outstanding Service award YWCA, 1962. Mem. Am. (pres. 1971, dir.), Wis. (pres. 1972) concrete pipe assns., Waukesha C. of C. (dir. 1955-60), Sigma Alpha Epsilon. Presbyn. (founding elder 1966-69). Optimist (v.p. Waukesha). Home: N11 W28723 Northview Rd Waukesha WI 53186 Office: 2000 S West Ave Waukesha WI 53186

WAITE, WILLIAM EUGENE (GENE), assn. exec.; b. Shelbyville, Mo., Apr. 18, 1934; s. John William and Lulu Marie (Pollard) W.; student Lincoln Christian Coll., 1952-55, Central Christian Coll., Moberly, Mo., 1957-58, Drury Coll., 1974; m. JoAnne Blankenship, Mar. 30, 1958; children—Stanley, Bradley. Student minister Christian Ch., rural Mo., 1953-58; minister Bland, Mo., 1958-61, St. Louis, 1961-63, Crane, Mo., 1963-69; exec. dir. United Cerebral Palsy S.W. Mo., Springfield, 1969—. Chmn. Regional Com. for Developmental Disabilities, 1970-73; mem. Gov.'s State Adv. Bd. for Mentally Retarded and Developmental Disabilities, 1974—; mem. Community Health Com. of Planning Council, 1972-74; regional chmn. White House Conf. Handicapped Individuals, 1976. Bd. dirs. Springfield Sheltered Workshop for Handicapped, 1969-77. Mem. Assn. Profl. Workers for Cerebral Palsy, Royal Neighbors Am. Home: Springfield MO 65807 Office: Springfield MO 65804

WAKEFIELD, KENNETH MCGREGOR, physician; b. Gladstone, Man., Can., Jan. 27, 1924; s. John Albert and Anne Margaret (McGregor) W.; came to U.S., 1950; M.D., U. Man., Winnipeg, 1948; m. Lois Isabel, LaPlant, June 23, 1959; children—John, Charles, Dawn. Intern, St. Boniface (Man.) Gen. Hosp.; physician Hollenberg Clinic, Winnipeg, Man., 1948-49; gen. practice medicine, Gackle, N.D., 1950-51, Cooperstown, N.D., 1951—; mem. staffs St. Lukes Hosp., St. Johns Hosp., Dakota Hosp., Fargo, N.D.; preceptor programs U. N.D. Med. Sch., from 1972, asst. prof. family practice, 1977—; asso. dir. Family Practice Center, Fargo. Pres. N.D. Mental Health Assn., 1965-67. Diplomate Am. Bd. Family Practice. Fellow Am. Family Practice; mem. Am., N.D. med. assns., 1st Dist. Med. Soc. of N.D. Home and Office: Cooperstown ND 58425

WAKEFIELD, WILLIAM ORAN, JR., sociologist, educator; b. Omaha, Apr. 29, 1943; s. William Oran and Martha V. (Kinnison) W.; B.A. in Psychology and Sociology, Omaha U., 1965; M.A. in Sociology, U. Nebr. at Omaha, 1967; Ph.D. in Sociology, S.D. State U., 1976; m. Sandra L. McKinnon, Apr. 9, 1971. Instr. sociology Dana Coll., Blair, Nebr., 1967-68, chmn. dept., 1969-73; research asst. in sociology S.D. State U., Brookings, 1973-74; asst. prof. dept. criminal justice U. Nebr. at Omaha, 1974—. Dir. fed. grant Law Enforcement Assistance Adminstrn., 1971-73. Profl. musician; prin. percussionist Omaha Symphony Orch., 1960-75; pvt. tchr. music. Mem. Am. Sociol. Assn., Mid-West Sociol. Soc., Nebr. Sociologists Assn., Council on Social Work Edn., Community Coll. Social Sci. Assn., AAUP (sec.-treas. chpt. 1969-73), Omaha Jr. C. of C. (civil rights com. 1969), Alpha Kappa Delta, Omicron Delta Kappa, Pi Kappa Alpha. Mason. Contbr numerous articles to profl. jours. Home: 923 Hillcrest Dr Omaha NE 68132

WALBAUM, ROBERT CRUM, lawyer; b. Springfield, Ill., Nov. 13, 1933; s. George Crum and Mary Emma (Taylor) W.; student Bradley U., 1951-53; B.S., U. Ill., 1955; J.D., Washington U., St. Louis, 1960; m. Anita Ann Parent, Aug. 6, 1960; children—John Taylor, Charles Robert. Admitted to Ill. bar, 1961; staff Chgo. Title & Trust Co., Chgo., 1960-61; asst. state's atty. for Sangamon County, Ill., 1961-63; practice law, Springfield, Ill., 1963—; asst. city atty. City of Springfield, 1963-64, city atty., 1964-69; tech. adviser Ill. Dept. Law Enforcement, 1969-74; atty. Village of Pleasant Plains, Ill., 1969—. Mem. Sangamon County Bd., 1963-75, former chmn.; chmn. 1971 Lincoln Day Luncheon, Springfield; active Ill. Mus. Soc., YMCA, Springfield Mental Health Assn., Springfield Child and Family Service, Lyric Opera of Chgo. Guild. Republican precinct committeeman, 1968—; pres. Sangamon County Young Rep. Club, 1966-67. Vice pres., bd. dirs. Washington St. Mission, Springfield; bd. dirs. Goodwill Industries, YWCA, Springfield. Served with AUS, 1955-57. Mem. Am., Ill., Sangamon County bar assns., Springfield Art Assn., U. Ill. Alumni Assn., Springfield Am. Bus. Club, Phi Alpha Delta. Episcopalian. Clubs: Illini Country, Sangamo (Springfield). Home: 1049 Woodland Ave Springfield IL 62704 Office: 1231 S 8th St Springfield IL 62705

WALCH, WILLIAM NICHOLAS, mfrs. agt.; b. Detroit, July 30, 1922; s. Albert John and Antoinette Anna (Looman) W.; B.M.E., U. Detroit, 1950; m. Mary Louise Kappel, Sept. 15, 1951; children—William Nicholas, Michael Louis, Kathleen Mary, Timothy Joseph, Patrick Joseph. Supr. plumbing and heating installation Sears, Roebuck & Co., Detroit, 1950-53; sales engr. Detrex Chem. Industries, Inc., Cin., 1953-58; sales engr. Permutit Co., Kansas City Mo., 1958-61, Cin., 1961-65; sales engr. J.R. McCutcheon & Assos., 1965-69; pres. Ecology Equipment, Inc., Cin., 1969—. Served with AUS, 1943-46; ETO. Registered profl. engr., Kans. Mem. Am. Water Works Assn., Water Pollution Control Fedn. Republican. Roman Catholic. Home: 6565 Salem Rd Cincinnati OH 45230 Office: 3737 Mt Vernon Ave Cincinnati OH 45209

WALCOFF, LAWRENCE, broadcaster; b. N.Y.C., Jan. 26, 1932; s. Harry and Rose (Knobel) W.; A.A., Jersey City Jr. Coll., 1951; B.A., N.Y. U., 1954; M.A., U. Iowa, 1959; m. Judith Kay Reich, Aug. 28,

1955; children—Steven Harris, David Allan, Linda Ann. Program dir. univ. radio stas. State U. Iowa, 1956-62; asst. dir. sch. services WQED-WQEX, Pitts. ETV, 1962-67; dir. spl. projects Nat. Instructional TV, Bloomington, Ind., 1967-76; asso. exec. dir. Agy. for Instructional TV, Bloomington, 1976—; adj. faculty ednl. communications U. Pitts., 1965-67. Served with AUS, 1954-56. Recipient Emmy for outstanding instructional children's programming Nat. Acad. TV Arts and Scis., 1974. Mem. Nat. Assn. Ednl. Broadcasters. Jewish. Home: 1509 Clairmont Pl Bloomington IN 47401 Office: 1111 W 17th St Bloomington IN 47401

WALCOTT, ROGER EUGENE, librarian; b. Grand Rapids, Mich., July 21, 1923; s. Leslie Ernest and Iva May (Follette) W.; B.A., U. Mich., 1947, B.L.S., 1948, M.L.S., 1955; m. Marjorie May De Young, July 25, 1947; children—Nancy (Mrs. Vern A. Yetman), Thomas Roger, Pamela Sue (Mrs. Jesse Miller). Mem. staff Grand Rapids Pub. Library, 1935-42; circulation asst. Flint (Mich.) Pub. Library, 1948-49; librarian Hall-Fowler Meml. Library, Ionia, 1949-52; city librarian Ferndale Pub. Library, 1952-60; dir. libraries Grand Rapids Jr. Coll., 1960-66; library dir. Herrick Pub. Library, Holland, Mich., 1966—; cons. Lake Michigan Community Coll., 1960, Kelloggsville (Mich.) Jr. High Sch., 1964. Served with USAAF, 1943-46. Recipient City of Ferndale citation, 1960. Mem. ALA, Mich. Library Assn., Adult Edn. Assn. Mason, Kiwanian. Home: 335 Maple Ave Holland MI 49423 Office: 300 River Ave Holland MI 49423

WALDBAUER, GILBERT PETER, educator; b. Bridgeport, Conn., Apr. 18, 1928; s. George Henry and Hedwig Martha (Gribisch) W.; student U. Conn., 1949-50; B.S., U. Mass., 1953; M.S., U. Ill., Urbana, 1956, Ph.D., 1960; m. Stephanie Margot Stiefel, Jan. 2, 1955; children—Gwen Ruth, Susan Martha. Instr. entomology U. Ill., 1958-60, asst. prof., 1960-65, asso. prof., 1965-71, prof., 1971—, prof. agrl. entomology Coll. Agr., 1971—. Cons. Ill. Natural History Survey. Served with AUS, 1946-47; PTO. Agrl. Research Service U.S. Dept. Agr. grantee, 1966-71; Nat. Geog. Soc. grantee, 1972-74; NSF grantee, 1976-79. Mem. AAAS, Am. Soybean Assn., Animal Behavior Soc., Entomol. Soc. Am., Sigma Xi, Phi Kappa Phi. Contbg. author: Insect and Mite Nutrition, 1972; Introduction to Insect Pest Management, 1975. Contbr. numerous articles to profl. jours. Home: 1806 Maynard Dr Champaign IL 61820 Office: Dept of Entomology 320 Morrill Hall U of Ill Urbana IL 61801

WALDBILLIG, RONALD JOSEPH, retail food co. exec.; b. Dubuque, Iowa, Oct. 29, 1941; s. Carl August and Kathryn (Scholtes) W.; student Indians Hills Community Coll., 1967-68; m. Marcella Rae Miles, Aug. 24, 1968; children—Laura, Brian, Olivia. With Nabisco, Dubuque, Iowa, 1963-67; with Hy-Vee Food Stores Inc., Chariton, Iowa, 1968—, asst. data processing mgr., 1969—. Served with USMC, 1960-63. Mem. Assn. for Systems Mgmt. Roman Catholic. Club: K.C. Home: 633 Auburn Ave Chariton IA 50049 Office: 1801 Osceola Ave Chariton IA 50049

WALDEMAR, DAVID LEE, librarian; b. Rochester, Minn., May 30, 1934; s. Oswald Matt and Dorothy Mildred (White) W.; A.A., Rochester Jr. Coll., 1954; B.A., U. Minn., 1956, M.A., 1957; m. Carla Miriam Bryce, Mar. 11, 1956 (div. Sept. 1977); children—Lydia, Bryce, Martha. Branch librarian Milw. Pub. Library, 1957-60; reference asst. Mpls. Pub. Library, 1960-65; head librarian Excelsior (Minn.) Library, 1965-69, St. Louis Park (Minn.) Library, 1969-70, Richfield Library, 1970-72; head reference service Hennepin County Library, Mpls., 1972-74; head librarian Golden Valley (Minn.) Library, 1974—, acting North Area librarian, 1976-78. Caucus chmn. Democratic-Farm-Labor Party, 1970, county del., 1966, 68, 70; mem. Minn. Environ. Conservation Control Agy.; bd. dirs. Met. Council Task Force Computer Utility. Mem. ALA, Minn. Library Assn. (council mem. 1967-71), ACLU, Citizens League, Minn. Computer Soc. (bd. dirs.). Home: 7414 W 22d St # 303 St Louis Park MN 55426 Office: 830 Winnetka N Golden Valley MN 55427

WALDEN, JAMES WILLIAM, accountant, educator; b. Jellico, Tenn., Mar. 5, 1936; s. William Evert and Bertha L. (Faulkner) W.; B.S., Miami U., Oxford, Ohio, 1963; M.B.A., Xavier U. Cin., 1966; m. Eva June Selvia, Jan. 16. 1957; 1 son, James William. Tchr. math. Middletown (Ohio) City Sch. Dist., 1963-67, Fairfield (Ohio) High Sch., 1967-69; instr. accounting Sinclair Community Coll., Dayton, Ohio, 1969-72, asst. prof., 1972-75, asso. prof., 1975—; cons., pub. accountant. Active C.A.P. Served with USAF, 1954-59. Mem. Butler County Torch Club, Pub. Accountants Soc. Ohio (pres. S.W. chpt. 1972-73), Nat. Soc. Pub. Accountants, Greater Hamilton Estate Planning Council, Beta Alpha Psi. Home: 187 Westbrook Dr Hamilton OH 45013 Office: Sinclair Community Coll 444 W 3d St Dayton OH 45402

WALDENMYER, DALE RICHARD, real estate exec.; b. Butler, Pa., Mar. 3, 1924; s. John Elmer and Evelyn Mae (Eshenbaugh) W.; student Pa. State U., 1941-42, U. Pitts., 1943; m. Norma Dee Rufener, Dec. 28, 1955; 1 son, William Bradford. Owner, Home Engrng. Co., Dover, Ohio, 1952-68; pres. D. Waldenmyer, Inc., builder homes and apts., 1958—; pres. D. & N. Devel., Inc., developer residential subdivs., 1960—; pres. Waldenmyer Realty, Inc., residential and comml. sales, 1965—. Mem. Community Improvement Corp., 1970—; mem. Tuscarawas County Planning Commn., 1966—, chmn. subdiv. commn., 1967-71; vice chmn. Stark County Apt. Council, 1975, chmn., 1976. Bd. dirs. YMCA, 1958-59. Named Boss of the Year, Dover Jr. C. of C., 1971, Realtor Year Tuscanawas County, 1972. Mem. Nat. Assn. Home Builders (nat. dir. 1965, 69), Ohio Home Builders Assn. (exec. adv. com. 1971-72, v.p. SE region 1977), Ohio Apt. Council (vice chmn. 1977), Ohio Developers Council, Urban Land Inst., Tuscarawas County Home Builders (pres. 1962-63), Tuscarawas County C. of C. (pres. 1972), Tuscarawas County Realtors (pres. 1971). Mem. United Ch. of Christ. Mason (Shriner), Elk. Clubs: Union Country, Village Racquet, Hall of Fame Racquet (Canton, Ohio). Address: 838 Boulevard Dover OH 44622

WALDIE, WENDELL DEAN, optometrist; b. Wichita, Kans., Dec. 11, 1924; s. Robert and Eva Maye (DeVore) W.; student Wichita State U., 1942-43, 46; D. Optometry, Ill. Coll. Optometry, 1949; m. Methyl Ardyl Davis, May 31, 1947; children—David Lloyd, Jana Renee, Marc Robert. Optometric practice, Wichita, 1949—; v.p., treas. Waldie Farms, Inc., 1968—. Treas., Kans. Pub. Vision League, 1965-75, Kans. Optometric Found., 1963-75, Kan. Optometric Assn., 1957-75. Mem. alumni council Ill. Coll. Optometry, 1973—, v.p., 1975-77. Bd. dirs. Kans. Low Vision Clinic, 1971-75. Served with AUS, 1943-46. Decorated 2 Bronze Star medals. Mem. Am. Optometric Assn. (chmn. exec. com. adminstrv. div. 1972-75, trustee 1975-77, sec.-treas. 1977—), Wichita Optometric Soc., Am. Pub. Health Assn., Am. Optometric Found., Better Vision Inst., Tomb and Key, Beta Sigma Kappa. Republican. Methodist (finance chmn. 1970-72). Club: Wichita Volleyball (treas., bus. mgr. 1968-74). Home: 3111 Aloma Wichita KS 67211 Office: 2823 E Douglas Wichita KS 67211

WALDINGER, MARTIN HARRIS, constrn. co. exec.; b. Des Moines, July 5, 1938; s. Mose and Bess (Duitch) W.; B.B.A., U. Iowa, 1961; m. Beth Perlmutter, Dec. 26, 1965; children—Richard Neal, Wendy Beth. Vice-pres., Cash Credit Corp., Denver, 1964-67; with Waldinger Corp., Des Moines, 1961-64, 67—, sec., dir., 1971—; dir. Janus Fund, Inc. Commnr., Des Moines Human Rights Commn., 1974—. Bd. govs. Jewish Welfare Fedn.; bd. dirs. Orchard Place. Served with AUS, 1961. Mem. Am. Soc. Personnel Adminstrs. Democrat. Jewish. Home: 5015 Country Club Blvd Des Moines IA 50312 Office: 2601 Bell Ave Des Moines IA 50321

WALDMAN, IRVING, paper co. exec.; b. St. Paul, Aug. 13, 1913; s. Nathan Jeremy and Naomi (Kaplan) W.; B.B.A., U. Minn., 1934; m. Cecelia Rose, May 26, 1940; children—Jeremy N., Eugene M., Barbara Eve Liebo. Salesman, Kaplan Paper Box & Minn. Envelope Co., St. Paul, 1935-60; gen. mgr., prodn. mgr. Minn. Envelope Co., St. Paul, 1960-63, sales mgr., 1963—, v.p., 1970—, gen. sales mgr., 1971—; mdse. mgr. Lang Industries, Mpls., 1945-46. Co-founder, dir. Herzl Camp Assn., Webster, Wis. Mason. Home: 2084 Bayard Ave St Paul MI 55116 Office: 23 E Fairfield Ave St Paul MN 55107

WALDMAN, MAURICE, psychiatrist; b. Wachock, Poland, July 18, 1926; s. Joseph and Pauline (Tskowitch) W.; Bach., Lycee, Paris, France, 1947; M.D., Ecole de Medecine, Paris, 1954; m. Magdalena Lazar, Aug. 20, 1959. Came to U.S., 1957, naturalized, 1962. Intern, Mt. Sinai Hosp., Chgo., 1958-59; resident Mt. Sinai Hosp., also Chgo. Med. Sch., 1959-62; dir. psychiat. clinics Mt. Sinai Hosp., Chgo., 1962-71; dir. in-patient psychiat. unit Fox River Hosp., Chgo., 1971-76; asst. prof. psychiatry Chgo. Med. Sch., 1966-73, asso. prof., 1973-76. Home: 6007 N Sheridan St Chicago IL 60660 Office: 2553 W Peterson Chicago IL 60659

WALDO, C(HARLES) IVES, JR., lawyer; b. Chgo., July 23, 1911; s. C. Ives and Marian (Wade) W; B.A., Yale, 1933; J.D., Northwestern U., 1936; m. Marie Elizabeth Sergardi, Sept. 14, 1940; children—C. Ives III, Elizabeth S., Pamela W. Admitted to Ill. bar, 1936; pvt. practice Chgo., 1936-38, 40-42; atty. SEC, Washington, N.Y.C., Cleve., 1938-40; dir. investigation and research Alien Property Custodian, Chgo., 1942-44; mem. firm Hopkins, Sutter, Mulroy, Davis & Cromartie, Chgo., 1944-49, partner, 1949—. Mem. Am., Ill., Chgo., 7th Fed. Circuit bar assns., Northwestern U. Law Alumni Assn. (pres. 1962-64, Service award 1965), Chgo. Acad. Scis. (trustee), Phi Beta Kappa. Congregationalist (trustee). Clubs: Indian Hill Country (Winnetka, Ill.); University, Law, Mid-day, Legal (Chgo.). Home: 1320 Edgewood Ln Northbrook IL 60062 Office: 1 1st Nat Plaza Chicago IL 60603

WALDREN, TERRY EDWARD, counselor; b. Dodge City, Kans., Sept. 2, 1946; s. Lloyd Edward and Eunice Mary (McLeish) W.; B.S., Kans. State U., 1968, M.S., 1970; m. Donna Kristine Randel, Sept. 12, 1972. Mem. staff residence hall counseling service Kans. State U., 1967-69, fin. aids counselor, 1968-69; psychologist Larned (Kans.) State Hosp., 1969; substitute tchr. Greeley County (Kans.) High Sch., 1972; resident counselor Mich. Tech. U., Houghton, 1972—; v.p. Dial Help, Houghton, 1973, pres., 1973-75; pres. Univ. Task Force Alcohol Awareness, 1977—; condr. workshops. Mem. Am. Personnel and Guidance Assn., Am. Coll. Personnel Assn., Copper Country Council Service Agys. Baptist. Address: Coed Hall Mich Tech U Houghton MI 49931

WALDRON, BECKY JOHNSTON, realtor; b. Mpls., Feb. 24, 1920; d. Josiah U. and Myrtle (Harlan) Johnston; student Vassar Coll., 1937-39; B.A., Iowa U., 1941; m. Charles Philip Waldron, Dec. 10, 1941; children—Wendy Churchill Waldron Brandow, Charles Philip. Psychometrist, psychology dept. Iowa State U., Ames, 1945-47; realtor Neil Adamson Co., Inc., Des Moines, 1965-75; realtor, pub. relations dir. Iowa Realty Co. Inc., Des Moines, 1975—. Recipient Americanism award and medal Jewish War Vets., 1962. Mem. Nat. Assn. Real Estate Bds., Am. Jr. League Assn., Nat. Soc. Colonial Dames Am., Kappa Kappa Gamma, Psi Chi. Republican. Episcopalian. Clubs: Wakonda, Embassy, Proteus (Des Moines). Home: 25 35th St Des Moines IA 50312 Office: 2405 Ingersoll Des Moines IA 50312

WALDRON, KENNETH LYNN, lawyer; b. Cape Girardeau, Mo., Oct. 18, 1941; s. Leonard Vernal and Edna Marion (Baskerville) W.; student Westminster Coll., 1959-61; B.S., Mo. U., 1963, J.D., 1966; m. Norma Kay Norwood, Mar. 25, 1967; 1 son, Leonard Andrew. Salesman, Nat. Biscuit Co., 1963-66; admitted to Mo. bar, 1966; asso. firm Buerkle and Lowes, Jackson, Mo., 1966-71; practiced in Jackson, Mo., 1971—; mem. firm Waldron & Lichtenegger; city atty. Jackson, Mo., dir. Stonewall Enterprises, Inc., Charleston Foods, Inc., Sikeston Foods, Inc., Chaffee Foods, Inc., A & V Foods, Inc., Yamnitz Foods, Inc., Rivermines Super Market, Inc., Manassa Sound Systems, Inc., Asso. Inventory Specialists, Inc. Active Boy Scouts Am. Bd. dirs. Southeast Mo. Med. Center, Inc. Served to capt. AUS, 1966-68. Mem. Am. Trial Lawyers Assn., Mo. Claimants Attys. Assn., The Mo. Bar, Nat. Inst. Municipal Legal Officers, Jackson Jaycees (past state and regional legal counsel, dir.), Am. Legion (legal counsel). Rotarian. Home: 957 Shady Ln Jackson MO 63755 Office: 128 W Main St Jackson MO 63755

WALDSTEIN, SHELDON SAUL, physician, educator; b. Chgo., June 23, 1924; s. Herman S. and Sophia (Klapper) W.; student Harvard, 1941-43; M.D., Northwestern U., 1947; m. Jacqueline Sheila Denbo, Apr. 2, 1952; children—Sara Jean, Peter Denbo, David John. Intern, Cook County Hosp., 1947-48, resident in internal medicine, 1948-51, chief Northwestern Med. Service, 1954-62, exec. dir. dept. medicine, 1962-64, chmn. dept. medicine, 1964-69; exec. dir. N. Suburban Assn. Health Resources, 1969-72; instr., asso., asst. prof. Northwestern U., 1954-61, asso. prof. medicine, 1961-66, prof. medicine, 1966—, asso. dean health services, 1974-77, dir. Northwestern U. Med. Assos., 1974-77; exec. dir., asso. dean Cook County Grad. Sch. Medicine, 1977—. Served to capt. M.C., AUS, 1952-54. Diplomate Am. Bd. Internal Medicine. Mem. AMA, Chgo. Med. Soc., Central Soc. for Clin. Research, Endocrine Soc., Am. Fedn. for Clin. Research, Am. Assn. for Study Liver Disease, AAAS, Inst. Medicine Chgo., Chgo. Soc. Internal Medicine, Sigma Xi, Alpha Omega Alpha. Contbr. articles to med. jours. Home: 265 Walden Dr Glencoe IL 60022 Office: 222 E Superior St Chicago IL 60611

WALES, CHARLES ATHERTON, JR., chem. co. exec.; b. Attleboro, Mass., July 26, 1920; s. Charles Atherton and Marion Lucille (Howes) W.; B.S., Mass. Inst. Tech., 1941, M.S., 1946; m. Leslie Vivian Leavitt, Nov. 1, 1945; children—Margaret (Mrs. Allen Alberti), Cynthia (Mrs. Charles Tischer), Diane. Engr., Union Carbide Corp., Texas City, Tex., 1946-56, asst. plant mgr., 1956-60, plant supt., Bound Brook, N.J., 1960-62, mgr. indsl. fabricated products dept., N.Y.C., 1963-66, mgr. investment utilization, 1966-68, plant mgr., Marietta, Ohio, 1969—. Pres. LaMarque (Tex.) Sch. Bd., 1958-59. Served to capt. AUS, 1942-46. Decorated Bronze Star medal. Mem. Am. Inst. Chem. Engrs., Ohio C. of C. (dir. 1977—), Sigma Xi, Alpha Chi Sigma. Episcopalian. Mason (Shriner), Rotarian. Club: Marietta Country. Home: 122 Seneca Dr Marietta OH 45750 Office: PO Box 446 Marietta OH 45750

WALHOUT, JOHN ROBERT, city ofcl.; b. Muskegon, Mich., Mar. 5, 1925; s. Thomas and Ann (Witt) W.; student Muskegon Jr. Coll., 1943, Fenn Coll., 1943-44; B.S., Ferris State Coll., 1948; LL.B., LaSalle Extension U., 1973; m. Beverly Jean Kroeze, Oct. 22, 1948; children—Susan Beth, Ross Robert. Staff accountant Maihofer, Moore & DeLong, C.P.A.'s, Muskegon, 1948-56; v.p. fin. Challenge Stamping & Porcelain Co. and Puffer-Hubbard Refrigerator Co., Grand Haven, Mich., 1956—. Vice pres. Tri-Cities YMCA, 1963-64, pres., 1965. City councilman, Grand Haven, 1965-72, mayor, 1971—; mem. Grand Haven-Spring Lake Sewer Authority, 1970—. Pres. bd. dirs. Grand Haven Christian Sch., 1962-64. Tri-Cities United Fund, 1964; bd. dirs. Mich. United Fund. Served with USAAF, 1943-46. Mem. Am. Inst. C.P.A.'s, Mich. Assn. C.P.A.'s (dir. 1976—), Fin. Execs. Inst., Tri-Cities C. of C. (pres. 1968-69, dir.). Clubs: Spring Lake Country, Economic of Detroit. Mem. Christian Reformed Ch. Rotarian. Home: 1505 Pine Ridge Dr Grand Haven MI 49417

WALI, MOHAN KISHEN, educator; b. Kashmir, India, Mar. 1, 1937; s. Jagan Nath and Somavati (Wattal) W.; came to U.S., 1969, naturalized, 1975; B.Sc., U. Jammu and Kashmir (India), 1957; M.Sc., U. Allahabad (India), 1960; Ph.D., U. B.C. (Can.), 1970; m. Sarla Safaya, Sept. 25, 1960; children—Pamela, Promod. Lectr. S.P. Coll., Srinagar, Kashmir, India, 1963-65; research fellow U. Copenhagen (Denmark), 1965-66; grad. fellow U. B.C., Vancouver, 1967-69; asst. prof. U. N.D., Grand Forks, 1969-73, asso. prof. biology, 1973—, Hill research prof., summer 1973, dir. Forest River Biology Area Field Sta., 1970—; staff ecologist Grand Forks (N.D.) Energy Research Lab., U.S. Dept. Interior, part-time, 1974-75; dir. Project Reclamation, U. N.D., 1975—, asst. to pres. univ., 1977—. Recipient Outstanding Research award, Sigma Xi-U. N.D., 1975; B.C. Gamble Distinguished Service award, 1977. Mem. Ecol. Soc. Am., British Ecol. Soc., Canadian Bot. Assn. (dir. ecology sect. 1976-79), Torrey Bot. Club, AAAS, Am. Soc. Agronomy, Am. Inst. Biol. Sci., Internat. Assn. Ecology, Sigma Xi. Contbr. articles to profl. jours. Editor: Some Environmental Aspects of Strip-Mining in North Dakota, 1973; Prairie: A Multiple View, 1975; Practices and Problems of Land Reclamation in Western North America, 1975; sr. editor Reclamation Rev. Home: 3412 6th Ave N Grand Forks ND 58201

WALINSKI, RICHARD S., lawyer; b. Toledo, May 1, 1943; s. Thaddeus N. and Genevieve E. (Stempnik) W.; B.A. magna cum laude, U. Toledo, 1965; postgrad. Duquesne U., 1965-66; J.D. cum laude, 1969. Admitted to Ohio bar, 1969; practiced in Toledo, 1969—; partner firm Hayward, Cooper, Straub, Walinski & Cramer, 1969-76; asst. public defender, 1969-71. Instr. U. Toledo Coll. Law, 1974-75; spl. counsel to Atty. Gen. State Ohio, 1975-76, chief counsel, 1976—. Mem. Am., Ohio, Toledo bar assns. Republican. Home: 5415 Yorkshire Dr Columbus OH 43227 Office: State Office Tower Columbus OH 43215

WALK, LLOYD FRANKLIN, surgeon, bus. exec.; b. New Albany, Ind., Nov. 16, 1927; s. Frank Hobart and Helen Catherine (Flynn) W.; B.S., U. Louisville, 1947, M.D., 1951; m. Doris Ann Hohm, May 24, 1952; 1 son, Kevin Douglas. Intern, St. Louis City Hosp., 1951-53, resident in surgery, 1955-59; practice gen. surgery, 1959—; pres. staff Meml. Hosp., Belleville, 1968, St. Elizabeth's Hosp., Belleville, 1976—; pres. Belleville Med. Bldg., Inc., Apartrents, Inc., Belleville; owner, operator The Outdoor Store, Belleville; cons. Dive-Med Internat. Served with U.S. Army, 1953-55. Diplomate Am. Bd. Surgery. Fellow A.C.S.; mem. AMA, So. Med. Assn., Am. Assn. Automotive Medicine, Ill. State, St. Louis, St. Clair County med. socs., St. Louis Surg. Soc., Sports Car Club Am., Nat. Rifle Assn. Roman Catholic. Clubs: Eighteen sixty-five, Elks. Home: 45 Kimberlin Ln Belleville IL 62221 Office: 301 W Lincoln St Belleville IL 62220

WALKER, ALICE GATES, real estate broker; b. Ill., Feb. 20, 1921; d. Clarence Thomas and Lela (Chenoweth) Gates; student Eastern Ill. U., 1938-41, Rutgers U., 1950; grad. Realtors Inst. Ill., 1973. Sec. to chmn. Civil Service, Rock Island, Ill. and N.Y.C., 1941 Fred Laifer, atty., Newark, 1946-48; exec. sec. to pres. and gen. mgr. Best Mfg. Co., Irvington, N.J., 1948-50; with Glaser-Steers Corp., Newark, 1950-59; real estate sales asso. Anne Sylvester's Realty Corner, Springfield, N.J., 1960-64; real estate broker Robert Carlisle, realtor, Charleston, Ill., 1965-74; owner, mgr. Alice Walker, Realtor, Charleston, 1974—. Bd. dirs. Charleston Community Theatre, 1976—. Mem. Nat., Ill. assns. realtors, Coles County Bd. Realtors (pres. 1977—), Women's Council Realtors, Charleston Bus. and Profl. Woman's Club (legis. chmn. 1977—), Am. Bus. and Profl. Women's Club. Republican. Clubs: Zonta, Women of the Moose. Home and Office: 1408 Division St Charleston IL 61920

WALKER, DANIEL, former gov. Ill., lawyer; b. Washington, Aug. 6, 1922: s. Lewis W. and Virginia (Lynch) W.: B.S., U.S. Naval Acad., 1945: J.D., Northwestern U., 1950: L.H.D., Carroll Coll., 1969; m. Roberta M. Dowse, Apr. 12, 1947: children—Kathleen, Daniel, Julie Ann, Charles, Roberta Sue, Margaret Ann, Will. Admitted to Ill. bar, 1950: law clk. Chief Justice Fred N. Vinson, U.S. Supreme Ct., 1950-51: dep. chief commr. U.S. Ct. Mil. Appeals, 1951-52: adminstrv. asst. to Gov. Adlai E. Stevenson, Ill., 1952: partner firm Hopkins, Sutter, Owen, Mulroy, Wentz & Davis, Chgo., 1954-66: v.p., sec., gen. counsel, dir. Montgomery Ward & Co., Inc., Chgo., 1966-71, v.p. gen. counsel Marcor, Inc. Chgo. 1968-71: gov. state of Ill., 1973-77; partner firm Walker, Gende, Hatcher, Berz & Giamanco, 1977—; dir. Pioneer Trust & Savs. Bank, Chgo., 1967-71. Mem. acting chmn. Ill. Pub. Aid Commn., 1962-63: mem. Regional Export Expansion Council, Dept. Commerce, 1962-63: pres. Chgo. Crime Commn., 1967: dir. Leadership Council for Met. Open Communities, Chgo., 1966-67, Chgo. study term Nat. Commn. on Causes and Prevention Violence, 1968; pres. Met. Housing Devel. Corp., 1968. Served with USNR, 1939-46, 51-52. Recipient Roger Baldwin award, 1968; Civic award Chgo. Newspaper Guild, 1969. Mem. Chgo., Ill., Am. bar assns., Bar Assn. of 7th Fed. Circuit, Am. Soc. Internat. Law. Order of Coif, Northwestern U. Law Alumni Assn. (pres. 1969). Clubs: Law, Legal (mem. exec. com. 1969). Mid-Am. (all Chgo.). Author: Rights in Conflict, 1968. Home: 1211 W 22d St Suite 620 Oak Brook IL 60521 Office: One IBM Plaza Suite 3613 Chicago IL 60611

WALKER, DAVID BROOKS, osteo, dermatologist; b. Fall River, Mass., Sept. 24, 1935; s. H. Brooks and Mary (Pendlebury) W.; B.A., Wesleyan U., Middletown, Conn., 1957; D.O., Kirksville Coll. Osteo. Medicine, 1963; m. Lois Toner, Jan. 1958; children—Karen Sue., Douglas Brooks, Wesley Todd, Nancy Howland, Michael Howland. Intern, Normandy Osteo. Hosps., St. Louis, 1963-64, mem. staff, 1964—, vice chief staff, 1972-73, chief staff, 1975, 76, 77, cons. dermatologist, 1967—; resident in dermatology Detroit Osteo. Hosp. Group, 1964-67; practice osteo. medicine specializing in dermatology, St. Louis, 1967—; asso. clin. prof. dermatology Kirksville Coll. Osteo. Medicine, 1967—. Mem. Adv. Bd. for Osteo. Specialists, 1972—, mem. examining bd. dermatology, 1972—. Trustee Normandy Osteo. Hosps., 1976—. Diplomate Am. Osteo. Bd. Dermatology. Fellow Am. Osteo. Coll. Dermatology (pres. 1974); mem. Am. Osteo. Assn., Mo., St. Louis (sec. 1972—) assns. osteo. physicians and surgeons, Delta Kappa Epsilon. Episcopalian. Club: Nantucket Yacht. Contbr. articles to profl. jours. Home: 12669 Ladue Rd St Louis MO 63141 also 10 Walsh St Nantucket MA 02554 Office: 11245 St Charles Rock Rd Bridgeton MO 63044

WALKER, ELVA MAE DAWSON, soap co. exec.; b. Everett, Mass., June 29, 1914; d. Charles Edward and Mary Elizabeth (Livingston) Dawson; R.N., Peter Bent Brigham Hosp., Boston, 1937; student Simmons Coll., 1935, U. Minn., 1945-48; m. Walter Willard Walker, Dec. 16, 1939 (div. 1969). Supr. nursery Wesson Maternity Hosp.,

Springfield, Mass., 1937-38; asst. supr. out-patient dept. Peter Bent Brigham Hosp., Boston, 1938-40; supr. surgery out-patient dept. Univ. Hosps., Mpls., 1945. Chmn. Gov.'s Citizens Council on Aging, Minn., 1960-66, acting dir., 1962-66, Econ. Opportunity Com. Hennepin County, 1964-68; cons. on aging to Minn. Dept. of Pub. Welfare, 1962-67; mem. nat. adv. Council for Nurse Training Act, 1965-69; dir. Nat. Council on the Aging, 1963-67, sec., 1965-67; v.p., treas., Nat.-Purity Soap & Chem. Co., now chmn. bd. Dir. Planning Agy. for Hosps. of Met. Mpls., 1963-69, United Hosp. Fund of Hennepin County, 1955—, Nat. Council Social Work Edn., 1966-68; vice chmn. Hennepin County Gen. Hosp. Adv. Bd., 1965-67; chmn. bd. dirs. Am. Rehab. Found., 1962-68; pres. bd. trustees Northwestern Hosp., 1956-59; pres. bd. trustees Children's Hosp. of Mpls., 1961-65; dir. Twin Cities Internat. Program for Youth Leaders and Social Workers, Inc., 1965-67; mem. Def. Adv. Com. Status Women, 1967-71; mem. bd. United Fund and Council Am., 1967—, Candidate for Congress, Third Dist., Minn., 1966. Trustee Macalester Coll., Archie D. and Bertha H. Walker Found.; pres. U. Minn. Sch. Nursing Found., 1958-72. Mem. Am. Pub. Welfare Assn., Soap and Detergent Assn. (dir., chmn. indsl. and institutional div. steering com.), Minn. League for Nursing (pres.), Mpls. Med. Research Found., Jr. League of Mpls., Nat. Assn. State Units on Aging (v.p. 1967). Democrat. Presbyterian. Home: 3655 Northome Rd Wayzata MN 55391 Office: 110 5th Ave SE Minneapolis MN 55414

WALKER, FRANK BANGHART, pathologist; b. Detroit, June 14, 1931; s. Roger Venning and Helen Frances (Reade) W.; B.S., Union (N.Y.) Coll., 1951; M.D., Wayne State U., 1955, M.S., 1962; m. Virginia Elinor Granse, June 18, 1955; children—Nancy Anne, David Carl, Roger Osborne, Mark Andrew. Intern Detroit Meml. Hosp., 1955-56; resident Wayne State U. and affiliated hosps., Detroit, 1958-62; asso. pathologist Detroit Meml. Hosp. and Cottage Hosp., Grosse Pointe, Mich., 1962—; pathologist South Macomb Hosp., Warren, Mich., 1966—; pathologist, dir. labs. Jennings Meml. and Alexander Blain Hosps., Detroit, 1971—. Partner Langston, Walker & Assos., profl. corp., Grosse Pointe, 1968—. Instr. pathology Wayne State U. Med. Sch., Detroit, 1962-72, asst. clin. prof., 1972—. Pres. Mich. Assn. Blood Banks, 1969-70; mem. med. adv. com. Mich. Blue Cross, 1970—, ARC, 1972—; mem. Mich. Higher Edn. Assistance Authority, 1975-77. Trustee Alexander Blain Meml. Hosp., Detroit, 1974—, Detroit-Macomb Hosp. Assn., 1975—; bd. dirs. Wayne State Fund, 1971—. Served to capt., M.C., AUS, 1956-58. Diplomate Am. Bd. Pathology. Mem. Wayne State U. Alumni Assn. (bd. govs. 1968-71), Wayne State U. Med. Alumni Assn. (pres. 1969, trustee 1970-75, distinguished alumni award 1974), Coll. Am. Pathologists, Am. Soc. Clin. Pathologists (sec. 1971-77, v.p. 1977-78), Econ. Club Detroit, AMA, Am., Mich. assns. blood banks, Phi Gamma Delta, Nu Sigma Nu, Alpha Omega Alpha. Republican. Episcopalian. Clubs: Detroit Athletic, Lochmoor; Mid-America (Chgo.). Home and office: 47 DePetris Way Grosse Pointe Farms MI 48236

WALKER, JAMES, auto parts co. exec.; b. Cleve., Dec. 7, 1920; s. James and Katherine Irene (Kellie) W.; B.A., Baldwin-Wallace Coll., 1947; M.B.A., Western Res. U., 1951; m. Jean Ann Motter, Sept. 16, 1950; children—James D., William W., Scott A. Asst. mgr. Ernst & Ernst, Cleve., 1950-63; v.p. finance Columbus Auto Parts Co., Columbus, Ohio, 1963—; dir. Auan SAIC, Argentina; lectr. accounting Western Res. U., Wittenberg U. Village clerk, Broadview Heights, Ohio, 1956-57; mem. Washington Local Sch. Dist. Bd. Edn., Franklin County, Ohio, 1974—. Served with USNR, 1942-45. C.P.A., Ohio. Mem. Am. Inst. C.P.A.'s. Home: 5655 Indian Hill Rd Dublin OH 43017 Office: Hudson St. at N Freeway St Columbus OH 43211

WALKER, JAMES ADAMS, educator, artist; b. Connersville, Ind., Jan. 24, 1921; s. Stanley Irving and Goldia (Adams) W.; B.S., Western Mich. U., 1946; postgrad. U. Mich., 1947-48; M.A., Columbia, 1949, profl. diploma, 1958; M.F.A., Mich. State U., 1961. Critic tchr. art East Carolina U., 1949-56; art tchr. Flint (Mich.) No. Community High Sch., 1956-66; asso. prof. art Warren (Ohio) Campus, Kent State U., 1966—. Mem. faculty summer Nat. Music Camp, Interlochen, Mich., 1963; exhibited in one-man shows Greenville (N.C.) Art Gallery, Tidewater Artists' Gallery, Norfolk (Va.) Mus. Arts and Scis., 1953, Sculpture Assos., Inc., Flint, Mich., 1962, Wilmington (N.C.) Coll., 1962, Jersey City State Coll., 1962, Art League Daytona Beach, 1964, Flint Inst. Arts, 1964, Central Mich. U., 1964, Kellogg Community Coll., 1965, Western Mich. U., 1965, Henry Ford Community Coll., Dearborn, Mich.; exhibited group shows 8th Annual National Art Competition, Hendersonville, N.C., 1950, Creative Gallery, N.Y.C., 1953, Annual Nat. Competition, U.S. Nat. Mus., Washington, 1953, 54, 56, Am. Color Print Soc., Phila., 1961, May Arts Festival Nat. Print Competition Olivet (Mich.) Coll., 1961, 19th Nat. Competition of Prints, Library Congress, Washington, 1963; Dulin Gallery Art (Knoxville, Tenn.), Mich. Acad. Scis., Arts and Letters, Flint Inst. Arts, Sheldon Swope Art Gallery (Terre Haute, Ind.), Grand Rapids Art Mus., others; various other competitive exhibitions. Recipient various art awards and prizes. Represented in permanent collections including Albion Coll., Davidson Coll., Flint Inst. Arts, Grand Rapids Art Gallery, Mich. Acad. Sci., Arts and Letters, Sheldon Swope Art Gallery, Western Mich. U., Canton Art Inst., Butler Inst. Am. Art. Mem. Mich. Acad. Sci., Arts and Letters (chmn. fine arts sect. 1965-67), Trumbull Art Guild (trustee 1969—). Contbr. articles to profl. jours. Home: 8778 Gull Rd Richland MI 49083 Office: 4314 Mahoning Ave NW Warren OH 44483

WALKER, JAMES LEROY, ednl. adminstr.; b. Platte, S.D., June 11, 1932; s. Lynn and Phoebe (Halligan) W.; B.S., So. State Coll., Springfield, S.D., 1959; postgrad. U. S.D., summer 1965; M.Ed., S.D. State U., 1966; m. Audrey June Forgey, Nov. 28, 1952; children—Cindy June Severson, Randy James, Kelli Patrice. Rural sch. tchr., Iona, S.D., 1951-53; acting postmaster, Iona, 1956; elementary and jr. high prin., Ft. Pierre, S.D., 1959-62; jr. high tchr., Brookings, S.D., 1962-63; elementary and jr. high prin., Miller, S.D., 1963-67; coll. tchr. Huron (S.D.) Coll., summer 1965-66; supt schs., Platte, 1967—. Dir., S.E. Ednl. Service Center, Sioux Falls, S.D., 1968-70; mem. S.D. Gov.'s Vocat. Edn. Adv. Council, 1970—. Served with Signal Corps, AUS, 1953-55. Mem. NEA (life), S.D. Edn. Assn. (dir. 1966-71), Platte Tchrs. Assn., Am., S.D. assns. sch. adminstrs. Methodist. Mason. Home: Box 363 Platte SD 57369

WALKER, JAMES LESLIE, obstetrician, gynecologist; b. Memphis, July 27, 1935; s. John Knox and Virginia LaNieve W.; B.A. cum laude, Vanderbilt U., 1957; M.D., U. Tenn., 1960; m. Mary Johanna Wachter, June 14, 1958; children—Mary Elisabeth, Lucy LaNieve, James Leslie, Nelle Ewing. Intern, Barnes Hosp., St. Louis, 1961, resident in obstetrics and gynecology, 1962-65; practice medicine specializing in obstetrics and gynecology, St. Louis, 1965—; asst. prof. clin. obstetrics and gynecology Washington U. Med. Sch.; mem. Central Eastern Mo. Peer Rev. Orgn. Corp. Served to lt. comdr. USNR, 1966-68. Diplomate Am. Bd. Obstetrics and Gynecology. Fellow Am. Coll. Obstetrics and Gynecology; mem. AMA, Mo. Med. Assn. (del. 1977—), St. Louis Med. Soc. (past editor bull.), St. Louis Gynecol. Soc., Christian Med. Soc. (dir.), St. Louis Regional Maternal and Child Health Council. Presbyterian. Clubs: Algonquin Golf, Tenn. Soc. St. Louis. Home: 170 Pinehurst Estates Dr Creve Coeur MO 63141 Office: 522 N New Ballas Rd Creve Coeur MO 63141

WALKER, JAMES SCOTT, otolaryngologist; b. Indpls., Feb. 7, 1916; s. Theodore and Ruth Lydia (Shea) W.; B.S., Ind. U., 1937, M.D., 1939; m. Ida Jane Worsham, Sept. 13, 1941; children—James Scott, Sarah Jane. Rotating intern Indpls. Gen. Hosp., 1939-40, resident, 1940-41; resident otolaryngologist Johns Hopkins Hosp., 1946-47; practice medicine specializing in otolaryngology, Carle Clinic Assn., Urbana, Ill., 1947—, head dept. otolaryngology, 1947—; mem. staffs Carle Found. Hosp., Urbana, U. Ill. McKinley Hosp., Urbana. Lecr. speech and hearing dept. U. Ill., Urbana, 1947—. Mem. exec. com. Carle Found., 1968—. Served to maj. AUS, 1941-46. Decorated Bronze Star. Fellow A.C.S.; mem. Am. Acad. Eye, Ear, Nose and Throat, Am. Broncho Esophagological Assn., Johns Hopkins Med. and Surg. Assn., Ill. Soc. Ophthalmology and Otolaryngology (pres. 1977), Am. Laryngol. Rhinol. and Otol. Soc. Contbr. articles to profl. pubs. Home: 1905 Golfview Dr Urbana IL 61801 Office: 602 W University St Urbana IL 61801

WALKER, JERRY LEE, educator; b. St. Joseph, Mo., Oct. 10, 1929; s. James Speir and Hazel Irene (Speer) W.; B.A., Wayne State U., 1952, M.Ed., 1959, Ed.D., 1964; m. Shirley Marie Simpson, Jan. 9, 1954; children—Kimberly (Mrs. Keith Pillischafske), Kip Kevin. Tchr. English, Detroit Pub. Schs., 1955-59; instr. English edn., Wayne State U., Detroit, 1959-62; faculty U. Ill., Urbana, 1962—, prof. secondary edn., 1969—; prof. U. Hawaii, Honolulu, summers 1970, 71, Hunter Coll., N.Y., summer 1968; cons. sch. dists., orgns. Served with AUS, 1953-55. Mem. Nat. Council Tchrs. English (chmn. several nat. coms.), Conf. English Edn. (program chmn. nat. conf. 1969), Phi Delta Kappa. Author: (with W.H. Evans) New Trends in Teaching English in Secondary Schools, 1959; Literature of America, 1959; Responding: Two, 1973. Contbr. articles to profl. publs. Office: 380 Edn Bldg U Ill Urbana IL 61801

WALKER, JESSICA LEE, portrait painter; b. Kansas City, Mo., May 22, 1930; d. Jesse Boone and Mildred (Trueblood) Walker; student San Jose State Coll., 1947-49, Dallas Mus. Fine Arts Sch., 1949-51. Asst. to portrait painter Matteo Sandona, San Francisco, 1952-54; free lance portrait painter, San Jose, Calif., 1955-59, Chgo., 1964—; med. illustrator Consol. Lithograph Co., San Jose, 1960-63; instr. adult art classes, Dallas, 1950-52; painter portraits James Boccardo and family, 1959, Melvin Belli, 1960; represented in collections U.S. and abroad. Winner scholarship Dallas Mus. Fine Arts Sch., 1946. Mem. Am. Soc. Artists. Home: 1730 N McVicker Ave Chicago IL 60639

WALKER, JESSIE, writer; b. Milw.; d. Stuart Richard and Loraine (Freuler) Walker; B.S., M.S., Medill Sch. Journalism, Northwestern U. First major feature article appeared in the Am. Home mag., 1950, since contbr. numerous articles in nat. mags. including Better Homes and Gardens, House Beautiful, McCall's, House and Garden, Good Housekeeping, Parent's, Sphere, others; now contbg. editor Better Homes & Gardens. Recipient Dorothy Dawes award as best freelance writer Home Furnishing, 1975, 76. Mem. Nat. Home Fashion League, Am. Inst. Interior Designers, Women in Communication. Author: How to Make Window Decorating Easy, 1969; How to Create Your Own Beautiful Window Treatments, 1972; Good Design-What Makes It Last?, 1973; Nature Decorating, 1975. Address: 241 Fairview Rd Glencoe IL 60022

WALKER, KENNETH ANDREW, farmer; b. Hoople, N.D., Sept. 6, 1924; s. Thomas M. and Linnea (Larson) W.; student Concordia Coll., Moorhead, Minn., 1947-48; m. Delores H. Gullinsrud, Nov. 2, 1949; children—Robert, Lynn, David, Mary Kay. Farmer, 1948—; pres., dir. Hoople Farmers Grain Co., 1971—. Mem. Dundee Sch. Bd., 1956—; pres. Dundee Elementary Dist., 1956-63, 65-68, 70—; treas. Dundee Twp., 1956-74. Pres., Walsh County Sch. Officers Assn., 1966-70; mem. N.D. Sch. Bds. Legis. Policy Com., 1968-70. Lutheran (sec. ch. 1969—, supt. Sunday sch. 1957-58). Home and office: Hoople ND 58243

WALKER, MAURICE ANDREW, surgeon; b. Columbus, Kans., Jan. 4, 1904; s. Stephen Lorenzo and Minnie Belle (Mayhew) W.; B.S., Kans. State Tchrs. Coll., Pittsburg, 1923; M.A., U. Kans., 1925; M.D., U. Chgo., 1928; M.S., U. Minn., 1932; m. Marguerite Lescher, Nov. 10, 1928; children—Charles Stephen, Judith Ann. Intern, St. Margaret's Hosp., Kansas City, Kans., 1927-28; resident Trinity Luth. Hosp., Kansas City, 1928; fellow in surgery Mayo Found., 1929-32, U. Kans. St. Margaret's Hosp., 1932-34; gen. practice surgery, Kansas City, 1932—; attending surgeon Bethany Hosp.; cons. in surgery Community Med. Center, Gardner, Kans. Commr. and chmn. or vice-chmn. Urban Renewal Agency of Kansas City, 1955-76; mem. overall devel. plan com. Wyandotte County and Kansas City, 1977. Served. to col. M.C., U.S. Army, 1942-46. Diplomate Am. Bd. Surgery; recipient Community Citizenship citation C. of C. of Kansas City, 1974. Fellow A.C.S.; mem. AMA, Kansas City S.W. Clin. Soc., Mayo Alumni Assn., Kans. (emeritus), Wyandotte County (hon., award of merit 1972) med. socs., Sigma Xi, Phi Chi. Republican. Methodist. Clubs: Masons, Shriners. Contbr. articles to profl. jours. Home: 1417 S 37th St Kansas City KS 66106 Office: 3214 Strong Ave Kansas City KS 66106

WALKER, ROBERT GLENN, banker; b. Belsano, Pa., Aug. 18, 1923; s. Glenn E. and Ethel H. (Richardson) W.; student Washington and Lee U., 1941-43; B.A., Baldwin-Wallace Coll., 1949; B. Fgn. Trade, Am. Inst. for Fgn. Trade, 1950, Stonier Grad. Sch. Banking, 1966; m. Rebecca Jean Carey, Sept. 18, 1948; children—Rebecca (dec.), Elizabeth. Supr. export sales adminstrn. Harry Ferguson, Inc., Detroit, 1950-51; partner Chamberlin-Walker Clothing Co., Geneva, Ohio, 1951-58; asst. v.p. Geneva Savs. & Trust Co., 1959-61; asst. v.p. Northeastern Onio Nat. Bank, Ashtabula, 1961-62, v.p., 1962-69, exec. v.p., 1969-71, pres., 1971-76, chmn., chief exec. officer, 1976—, also dir. Dir. Aitken Products Inc. Trustee Ashtabula County Indsl. Devel. Inc., 1968—; trustee Meml. Hosp. of Geneva, Ashtabula Indsl. Corp., Ashtabula Urban Renewal Corp. Served with USNR, 1943-46. Mem. Sigma Alpha Epsilon, Delta Phi Epsilon. Republican. Methodist. Kiwanian. Clubs: Madison Country (North Madison, Ohio); Ashtabula Country. Home: 260 Pepperidge Dr Geneva OH 44041 Office: 4366 Main Ave Ashtabula OH 44004

WALKER, THEODORE DELBERT, landscape architect, educator; b. Tremonton, Utah, Feb. 17, 1933; s. Delbert Stevenson and Geneve Cutler W.; B.S., Utah State U., 1957; M. Landscape Architecture, U. Ill., 1967; m. Doris Lamar Jenkins, June 4, 1957; children—Steven, Alan, Dahn, Jayne. Landscape architect Office of Leon Frehner, Salt Lake City, 1957-60; site planner Brigham Young U., Provo, Utah, 1960-66; pvt. practice landscape architecture, Provo, 1960-66, West Lafayette, Ind., 1967—; faculty Purdue U., West Lafayette, 1967—, asso. prof. landscape architecture, 1972—; pres. Walker-Harris Assos. Inc., cons. landscape architects, site planners, West Lafayette, 1973—. Active Boy Scouts Am. Mem. Am. Soc. Landscape Architects (trustee 1972—), sec.-treas. North Central States chpt. 1970-72). Mem. Ch. of Jesus Christ of Latter-Day Saints (high priest). Author: Perception and Environmental Design, 1971; Perspective Sketches, 1972; (with others) Plants in the Landscape, 1975; Plan Graphics, 1975; Site Design and Construction Detailing, 1977. Home: 1200 S Sharon Chapel Rd West Lafayette IN 47906

WALKER, THOMASENIA, guidance counselor; b. St. Louis, Dec. 27; d. Frank and Lelia (Palmer) Hauck; B.S., Fla. A. and M. U., 1947; M.S., So. Ill. U., 1964; children—Irene, Henrietta. Tchr., St. Louis pub. schs., 1955-59, Spl. Sch. Dist. St. Louis County, 1959-67; asst. prof. edn. Tuskegee Inst., summers 1965-66, Lincoln (Mo.) U., falls 1965-66, 72-77; counselor East St. Louis Sch. Dist. 189, 1968—; mem. faculty So. Ill. U., summers 1968-76; dir. tutorial program Kinloch-Mo. U. project, 1966; dir. remedial reading program Sch. Dist. 189, East St. Louis, 1968-72. Mem. Am. Personnel and Guidance Assn., AAUW, Nat. Assn. Negro Women, NAACP, Delta Sigma Theta, Phi Delta Kappa. Roman Catholic. Address: 8400 Redfir Dr Berkeley MO 63134

WALKER, WALLACE LEE, chemist; b. Vincennes, Ind., June 27, 1930; s. Lee Rush and William Ann (Wallace) W.; A.A., Vincennes U., 1950; B.S., Evansville U., 1953; m. Betty June Smiley, June 21, 1953; Chemist, Naval Weapons Support Center, Crane, Ind., 1955-57, supr. chemist, quality evaluation lab., 1957-61, acting br. head, environ. br., 1961-62, asst. head sci. br., 1962-76, chemist, safety dept., 1976—; cons. explosives, pyrotechnics and hazardous materials. Served with AUS, 1953-55. Recipient Outstanding award Dept. Navy, 1962, Superior Accomplishment award, 1968. Mem. Am. Chem. Soc., AAAS, Am. Def. Preparedness Assn. Club: Mason, Shriners. Office: Dept Safety Naval Weapons Support Center Crane IN 47522

WALKER, WALLIS DEAN, architect; b. Burlington, Iowa, Oct. 8, 1940; s. Harold Atchison and Bertha Marie (Heinecke) W.; B. Archtl. Engring., Chgo. Tech. Coll., 1962; m. Sandra Lee Ward McComb, Oct. 19, 1968; 1 dau., Kimberley Lee. Archtl. engr., specifications writer The Austin Co., Chgo., 1962-67; specifications writer Mid-Am. Engrs., Chgo., 1967-68; dir. specifications Holabird & Root, architects/engrs., Chgo., 1968-73, asso., 1973—. Served with AUS, 1963-64. Registered architect, Ill. Mem. AIA, Constrn. Specifications Inst. (dir. Chgo. chpt. 1970-73, 1st v.p. 1974-75, Outstanding Vice President's award 1974, pres. 1975-76, 77-78). Home: 17626 Stonebridge Hazel Crest IL 60429 Office: 300 W Adams St Chicago IL 60606

WALKER, WALTER LADARE, lawyer; b. nr. Granby, Mo., Oct. 6, 1927; s. Walter Joseph and Mae (Patterson) W.; grad. Joplin Jr. Coll., 1946; J.D., U. Mo., 1953; m. Marilyn Louise Land, June 24, 1951; children—Marcia Lynn, Charlotte Ann. Admitted to Mo. bar, 1953, since practiced in Neosho; admitted to Western Dist. U.S. Dist. Ct., 1955; gen. counsel Crowder Coll.; municipal judge City of Neosho, 1957-66. Pres., dir. Masonic Home of Mo., 1972-73; charter mem. Crowder Coll. Found. Served with AUS, 1946-47, 50-51. Decorated Purple Heart. Mem. Nat. Assn. Coll. and Univ. Attys., Am. Judicature Soc., Newton-McDonald County Bar Assn. (pres. 1957-59), Neosho C. of C., Am. Legion, D.A.V. (life), Delta Theta Phi. Mason (32 deg., grand master Mo. 1973-74; K.T., Shriner), Lion (pres. 1971-72). Republican. Mem. Christian Ch. Home: 1301 Benton Ave Neosho MO 64850 Office: PO Box 487 Neosho MO 64850

WALKER, WALTER WILLARD, real estate and investments exec.; b. Mpls., Dec. 4, 1911; s. Archie Dean and Bertha Willard (Hudson) W.; B.A., Princeton U., 1935; M.D., Harvard U., 1940; postgrad. U. Minn., 1942-48; m. Elva Mae Dawson, Dec. 16, 1939 (div. Oct. 1969); m. Elaine Barbatsis, Mar. 17, 1972. Teaching fellow pathology U. Minn., 1942-48; left medicine, went into bus., 1948; dir. Shasta Forest Co., Redding, Calif., 1951-71, treas., 1954-66, v.p., 1966-71; sec., dir. Barlow Realty Co., Mpls., 1954-67, pres., 1967-77, chmn., 1977—; sec., dir. Walker Pence Co., 1950-72; sec. Penwalk Investment Co., 1958-72, dir., 1943-72; dir. Craig-Hallum Corp., Mpls., 1956—; adv. bd. Lincoln office Northwestern Nat. Bank, Mpls., 1957-74. Bd. dirs. T.B. Walker Found., 1953-76, v.p., 1954-76; bd. dirs. Minn. Opera Co., 1968-73, Archie D. and Bertha H. Walker Found., 1953—, Mpls. Found., 1962—, Walker Art Center, 1954-76, United Fund, 1966-72; trustee Abbott-Northwestern Hosp., 1969-77; trustee Childrens Health Center, Inc., 1968-73, treas., 1969-73; pres. Found. Services, 1967-73; bd. dirs., exec. com. Minn. Charities Review Council, 1965-74; mem. Hennepin County Capital Budgeting Task Force, 1973-74. Mem. Sigma Xi, Nu Sigma Nu. Methodist. Clubs: Minneapolis; Woodhill Country; Princeton (N.Y.C.); U. Minn. Alumni. Home: 1900 Knox Ave S Minneapolis MN 55403 Office: 1121 Hennepin Ave Minneapolis MN 55403

WALKUP, GERALD ARTHUR, assn. exec., lab. technician; b. Cedar Rapids, Iowa, June 12, 1924; s. Perry and Alcie Beatrice (Baker) W.; ed. Area Community Coll., Iowa City. m. Donna Mae Moss, Mar. 27, 1954; children—Constance, Robert, Dennis. Lab. technician U. Iowa, 1964—; pres. Nat. Trappers Assn., Inc., Iowa City, 1969-77; wildlife cons. Served with USNR, 1942-45. Mem. Izaak Walton League, Nat. (asso.), Ill. wildlife fedns., Iowa Trappers Assn. Editor Voice of the Trapper, 1970—. Home and Office: Rt 2 Iowa City IA 52240

WALL, ARTHUR EDWARD PATRICK, editor; b. Jamestown, N.Y., Mar. 12, 1925; s. George Herbert and Doris (Olmstead) W.; student pub. schs.; m. Marcella Joan Petrine, Nov. 5, 1954; children—John Wright, Marie Ann, David Arthur Edward. Copy editor Worcester (Mass.) Telegram, 1958; Sunday editor Hawaii Island Corr., Honolulu Star-Bull., 1958-60; editor Hilo (Hawaii) Tribune-Herald, 1960-63; Sunday editor Honolulu Advertiser, 1963-65, mng. editor, 1971-72; mng. editor Cath. Rev., 1965-66, editor, 1966-71; editor-in-chief Nat. Cath. News Service, Washington, 1972-76; editor, gen. mgr. The New World (name changed to Chgo. Catholic 1977), Chgo., 1976—. Dir. bur. info. Archdiocese Balt., 1965-66; mem. council Internat. Cath. Union of Press, Geneva, Switzerland, 1972—, v.p., 1974—. Chmn., Govs. Com. Ednl. TV, Honolulu, 1964-65; regent Chaminade Coll., Honolulu, 1959-65, chmn., 1963-65; trustee St. Mary's Sem. and Univ., Balt., 1975-76; mem. spiritual renewal and devel. com. 41st Internat. Eucharistic Congress, Phila., 1975-76. Named Young Man of Year, Hilo, Hawaii, 1960; recipient St. Francis de Sales award Cath. Press Assn., 1977; Father of Year, Honolulu C. of C., 1964. Mem. Internat. Fedn. Cath. Press Agys. (pres. 1974—), Internat. Fedn. Cath. Journalists (pres. 1977—), Sigma Delta Chi (past chpt. pres.). Roman Catholic. Club: Nat. Press (Washington). Author: The Big Wave, 1960. Editor: Origins and Catholic Trends, 1972-76. Contbr. articles to mags. Office: Chicago Catholic 155 E Superior St Chicago IL 60611

WALL, DORIS JANE, educator, counselor; b. Sorento, Ill., Feb. 20, 1935; d. Vivian Henry and Pauline Evelyn (Randle) Bentley; B.S. in Edn., So. Ill. U., 1972, M.S. in Edn., 1975, Edn. Specialist in Counselor Edn., 1978; m. Harry E. Wall, Jr., Jan. 23, 1954; children—Harry Lynn, Larry Gene. Bookkeeper, clk. Citizens Coach Co., Alton Ill., 1953-54; phys. therapist to physician, Alton, Ill., 1955-56; credit mgr. Utlaut Meml. Hosp., Greenville, Ill., 1960-62; sec. to counselors Bond County Community Unit 2 Schs., Greenville, Ill., 1966-69, tchr. English, 1972—, counselor, 1972—; dir. gifted program drama Pocahontas (Ill.) Jr. High Sch., 1974—. Mem. Nat., Ill., Greenville edn. assns., Am. Personnel and Guidance Assn., Ill. Assn. Tchrs. English. Baptist. Club: Eastern Star.

WALL, FRED GRAHAM, diversified mfg. exec.; b. New Burlington, Ohio, May 15, 1934; s. George Robert and Helen Marie (Graham) W.; B.S., Miami U., 1956; m. Shirley A. Schoenherr, June 30, 1956; children—Tami Lyn, Scott Devin, Wendy Lee. With Ernst & Ernst, Dayton, Ohio, 1959-65, supr., 1963-65; asst. to pres. Robbins & Myers, Inc., Springfield, Ohio, 1965-68, v.p., 1968-70, exec. v.p., 1970-72, pres., 1972—, also dir.; dir. 1st Nat. Bank of Springfield, Sweet Mfg. Co., Ponderosa System, Inc.; instr. accounting Wright State U., 1963-64, Wittenburg U., 1961-63. Trustee, Robbins and Myers Found.; bd. dirs. Wittenberg U., Met. YMCA, United Way. Served with AUS, 1957-59. Mem. Am. Inst. C.P.A.'s, Ohio Soc. C.P.A.'s, Springfield Mgmt. Assn., Springfield C. of C. (dir. 1971—, v.p. 1974—), Delta Upsilon. Republican. Clubs: Springfield Country, Van Dyke, Dayton Racquet, Rotary, Masons. Home: 2800 Cottonwood Dr Springfield OH 45504 Office: 1345 Lagonda Ave Springfield OH 45501

WALL, PAUL S., city ofcl.; b. Athens, Tex., Apr. 28, 1908; s. William Henry and Nettie (Schneider) W.; B.Arch., Kans. U., 1931; m. Violet Lucile Myers, July 20, 1935; 1 dau., Paula Mae (Mrs. Walter Hughes). Engr., Kans. Hwy. Commn., 1935-42, Army Air Forces, Dodge City, Kans., 1942-44; engring. instr. USAF Post Engrs. Tng. Sch., Denver, 1944-47; prin. instr. utilities schs. USAF Tng. Command, Cheyenne, Wyo., 1947-54; dep. civil engr. staff officer USAF Schilling AFB, Kans., 1954-66; gen. mgr. Salina Airport Authority, Salina, Kans., 1966—. Recipient many outstanding awards as civilian engr. for USAF; Outstanding award Kans. Engring. Soc., 1960. Registered profl. engr., Kans. Mem. C. of C. (aviation, transp. coms. 1967—), Kans. Engring. Soc. (pres. Smoky Valley chpt.), Kans. Nat. (dir.) socs. prof. engrs., Am. Assn. Airport Execs. Methodist (dir.). Home: 2056 Quincy St Salina KS 67401 Office: Salina Airport Indsl Center Salina KS 67401

WALL, WILLIAM LLOYD, educator; b. Cleve., Dec. 25, 1930; s. Lloyd J. and Mildred (Newman) W.; B.Ed., Ohio State U., 1953, M.A., 1955; postgrad. Ind. U., 1957, Utah U., 1968; m. Patricia Wilder, Sept. 6, 1958; children—Cynthia Ann, William Scott. Tchr., asst. football, basketball coach Summit Station (Ohio) High Sch., 1953-55; tchr., coach Grandview High Sch., Columbus, Ohio, 1955; instr. phys. edn., coach Ripon Coll., 1956; prof., dir. athletics, phys. edn., head basketball coach MacMurray Coll., 1957-75. Mem. U.S. Olympic Basketball Exec. Com., 1968-72; exec. sec. Nat. Collegiate Baseball Found., 1963-66; mem. Internat. Basketball Bd. U.S.A., 1969-72; exec. dir. Amateur Basketball Assn. U.S.A. Trustee Basketball Hall of Fame, Springfield, Mass. Served with A.C. USNR. Named Nat. Assn. Intercollegiate Athletics Dist. 20 Basketball Coach of Year, 1960-61. Mem. Nat. Assn. Basketball Coaches (2 v.p. 1969, chmn. All-Am. com. 1966-71, pres. 1971-72, exec. sec. 1973-75), Internat. Platform Assn., AAHPER, Phi Gamma Delta, Phi Epsilon Kappa. Home: 1604 Mound St Jacksonville IL 62650

WALLAART, JOHANNES PETRUS, mfg. engr., educator; b. Amsterdam, Netherlands, Jan. 6, 1927; s. Kors Willem and Corneelia (Corneelissen) W.; came to U.S., 1957, naturalized, 1962; Middenstand diploma, Amsterdamsche Techniese Sch., 1949; m. Ybeltje Hukema, Nov. 14, 1947; children—John Petrus, Sonja. Tool and die apprentice Werkspoor Naamloos Vennootschap, Amsterdam, 1941-45, tool and die mgr., 1948-57; foreman Erie Magnetics Co. (Pa.), 1957-66; tool and die instr. Nat. Tool and Die, Precision Machining Assn., Washington, 1966-68; apprentice mgr. Anson Tool & Gage Co., Erie, 1968-69; asst. prof. engring. tech. in mech. and indsl. engring. tech. Kent State U., Ashtabula, Ohio, 1969-73, instr., 1973-76, asst. prof., 1976—. Square and round dance instr./caller, 1958—. Mem. Soc. Mfg. Engrs. (certified, sr.), Am. Soc. Engring. Edn., Sets in Order (charter), Nat. Ret. Tchrs. Assn. Republican. Home: 3115 W 13th St Ashtabula OH 44004 Office: Kent State U 3325 W 13th St Ashtabula OH 44004

WALLACE, DOUGLASS STUART, cons. engr.; b. Topeka, Kans., Feb. 9, 1935; s. Thomas William and Fay (Ritchie) W.; B.S. in Mech Engring., U. Kans., 1957; m. Virginia Ann Vogel, June 10, 1955; children—Anne Denice, Todd Vogel, Marc Douglass. With Kans. Power & Light Co., 1955-70, plant engr. Lawrence Power plant, 1955-61, plant engr. Tecumseh Power plant, 1961, asst. plant supt., 1961-66, plant supt., 1966-70; with Burgess, Latimer and Miller, engrs., Topeka, 1970-75; v.p., sec. Latimer, Miller, Sommers & Wallace, P.A., engrs., Topeka, 1975—; pres. Energy Mgmt. and Control Corp., 1977—; v.p., treas. PIA, Inc., 1977—. Mem. Topeka Civic Symphony Soc.; bd. dirs., 1st v.p. Topeka Community Concert Assn. Registered profl. engr., Kans., Mo. Mem. Kans. Engring. Soc., Soc. Am. Value Engrs., ASME, Pi Tau Sigma, Theta Tau. Methodist (adminstrv. bd., trustee, chmn. music com.). Home: 1939 Belle St Topeka KS 66604 Office: 634 Harrison St Suite A Topeka KS 66603

WALLACE, FRANKLIN SHERWOOD, lawyer; b. Bklyn., Nov. 24, 1927; s. Abraham Charles and Jennie (Etkin) Wolowitz; student U. Wis., 1943-45; B.S. cum laude, U.S. Mcht. Marine Acad., 1950; LL.B., J.D., U. Mich., 1953; m. Eleanor Ruth Pope, Aug. 23, 1953; children—Julia Diane, Charles Andrew. Admitted to Ill. bar, 1954, since practiced in Rock Island; partner firm Winstein, Kavensky, Wallace & Doughty; asst. state's atty. Rock Island County, 1967-68. Bd. dirs. Tri City Jewish Center. Mem. Am., Ill. (jud. adv. polls com.), Rock Island County bar assns., Am., Ill. trial lawyers assns., Nat. Assn. Criminal Def. Lawyers Assn., Am. Judicature Soc., Internat. Platform Assn. Democrat. Jewish. Home: 3405 20th St Ct Rock Island IL 61201 Office: Rock Island Bank Bldg Rock Island IL 61201

WALLACE, JAMES DUNCAN, utility co. exec.; b. Topeka, Kans., Apr. 10, 1914; s. Thomas William and Fay Aleen (Ritchie) W.; B.S. in Elec. Engring., U. Kans., 1936; m. Harriet Elizabeth Johnson, Sept. 5, 1938; 1 son, Douglass William. Jr. engr. Kans. Power & Light Co., 1939-44, div. supt., 1946-52, system elec. engr., 1952-62, mgr. electric ops., 1962-64, v.p. electric ops., 1964—. Served with USNR, 1944-46. Registered prof. engr., Kans. Mem. Am. Rifle Assn., U. Kans. Alumni Assn., Kansas City St. Andrew's Soc., Kans., Topeka chambers commerce, Nat. Soc. Profl. Engrs., Kans. Engring. Soc., Clan Wallace Soc. (v.p.), Nat. Trust for Scotland. Home: 706 Grandview St Topeka KS 66606 Office: 818 Kansas Ave Topeka KS 66612

WALLACE, JANE YOUNG (MRS. DONALD H. WALLACE), editor; b. Geneseo, Ill., Feb. 17, 1933; d. Worling R. and Margaret C. (McBroom) Young; B.S. in Journalism, Northwestern U., 1955, M.S. in Journalism, 1956; m. Donald H. Wallace, Aug. 24, 1959; children—Robert, Julia. Editor House organ Libby McNeill & Libby, Chgo., 1956-58; prodn. editor Instns. Mag., Chgo., 1958-61, food editor, 1961-65, mng. editor, 1965-68, editor-in-chief, 1968—; editorial dir. Service World Internat. Mag., Foodservice Distributor Salesman. Cons. Nat. Restaurant Assn. Mem. U.S. Dept. Edn. Com. Investigation Vocational Needs for Food Service Tng., 1969—; mem. advisory com. hospitality edn. Ill. Dept. Edn., 1976—, cons. Nat. Inst. Foodservice Industry; pres. Instnl. Food Editors' Conf., 1967. Recipient Jesse H. Neal award for best bus. press editorial, 1969, 72, 73, 76. Fellow Am. Inst. Interior Designers; mem. Soc. for Advancement Food Service Research (dir.), Women in Communications (v.p. Chgo. 1957-58), Internat. Foodservice Mfrs. Assn. (planning com.), Nat. Assn. Foodservice Equipment Mfrs., Gamma Phi Beta, Kappa Tau Alpha. Republican. Editor: The Professional Chef, 1962; The Professional Chefs Book of Buffets, 1965; Food Service Trends, 1975; American Quantity Cooking, 1976; contbr. chpt. on restaurants to World Book Ency. Home: 186 Signal Hill Rd Barrington IL 60010 Office: 5 S Wabash Ave Chicago IL 60603

WALLACE, JOHN EDWARD, artist, educator; b. St. Louis, Dec. 29, 1929; s. John Edward and Blanche (Beck) W.; B.F.A., Washington U., 1953; M.F.A., Ind. U., 1957; student Skowhegan Sch. Painting and Sculpture, 1953; m. Margaret Whitehurst Grimes, May 30, 1964; children—Carolyn Rose, Bernard A. Hulce, Jerome M. Hulce. Exhibited one-man shows, Ind. U., 1953, 54, Decatur (Ill.) Art Mus., 1954, Ark. State Coll. Art Center, 1956, St. Louis Artists' Guild, 1959, Claude Linn Gallery, St. Louis, 1968, Roswell (N.Mex.) Mus. and Art Center, 1968, Alverno Coll., 1974, Left Bank Gallery, Wellfleet, Mass., 1977; exhibited group shows City Art Mus. St. Louis, 1950, 52, 54, Pa. Acad. Fine Arts, Phila., 1952; Denver Mus. Fine Arts, 1952, Bklyn. Mus., 1953, Cin. Art Mus. (3d prize), 1955, Dallas Mus. Fine Arts, 1955, Ill. Inst. Tech. Inst. Design, 1954, USIA traveling exhbn., 1957-59, Skowhegan Annual Exhbn., N.Y.C., 1966, 67, 68, 69, New Art Assn. Exhbn., Chgo., 1971, Bertrand Russell Centenary Exhbn., Nottingham, Eng., 1973; represented in mus., pvt. collections; executed mural South Solon (Maine) Meeting House, 1954; sculpture panel in bronze Aquatic House St. Louis Zool. Gardens, 1959; prof. fine arts Prairie State Coll., Chicago Heights, Ill., 1968—, chmn. art dept., 1971-74; vis. artist Governors State U., Park Forest South, Ill., summers, 1973, 74; instr. Fresco Mural Painting, Truro Center for the Arts, Castle Hill, Cape Cod, Mass., summers, 1976—; organizer, co-chmn. New Directions for Studio Teaching 59th Ann. Coll. Art Assn. Am., 1971. Recipient City Art Mus. St. Louis Purchase award in painting, 1950, in printmaking, 1952, Spl. Purchase award, painting, 1954; Cin. Mus. Interior Valley Exhbn. 3d prize, 1955; Margaret Tiffany Blake fellowship in Mural Painting, Skowhegan Sch. Painting and Sculpture, 1954; resident fellowship in painting Huntington Hartford Found., 1960; artist-in-residence fellowship grant Roswell Mus. and Art Center, 1968. Mem. Coll. Art Assn. Am., Midwest Coll. Art Conf. Address: PO Box 362 Truro MA 02666

WALLACE, JOHN WALTER, ednl. rehab. adminstr.; b. Steubenville, Ohio, Apr. 17, 1931; s. John M. and Janet (Pipkin) W.; A.B., Asbury Coll., 1955; M.S.W., U. Pitts, 1964; m. Doris Waugh, Dec. 16, 1952; children—Debra Jo, Jan Marie, Jonna Sue, Jeffery Jay. Tchr., Escambia County schs., 1955-57, chief dep. Pensacola Beach Police, 1958; tchr., coach Wintersville (Ohio) Jr. High, 1958-60; juvenile parole officer State Ohio, 1960-62, 62-64; social worker Ohio Youth Commn., 1964-66, group life dir., 1966-67; supt. Maumee (Ohio) Youth Camp, a correctional inst. for delinquent boys, 1967-70; cons. Columbus (Ohio) Pub. Schs., 1970-75; dir. New Hope Boys Ranch, 1975—. Active Boy Scouts Am. Mem. Nat. Assn. Social Workers, Acad. Certified Social Workers, Nat. Assn. Christians in Social Work, Ohio Probation and Parole Assn., Ohio Welfare Conf., Nat. Assn. Juvenial Agys. and Tng. Schs., Am. Ministerial Assn., Ohio Edn. Assn., Am. Assn. Pub. Adminstrn., Sertoma Club, U.N. Assn. Methodist. Home: 674 Queensway Dr Grove City OH 43123 Office: New Hope Boys Ranch 8869 National Rd SW Pataskala OH 43062

WALLACE, LELAND MORRIS, JR., mfrs. rep.; b. St. Louis, June 15, 1922; s. Leland Morris and Frances I. (Juliuson) W.; B.S., Washington U., St. Louis, 1943; m. Betty J. Elbrecht, Oct. 11, 1947; children—Leland Morris III, Jonathan, Christine, Barbara. Sales engr. Dow Chem. Co., St. Louis, 1946-48; with lamp div. Westinghouse Electric Corp., St. Louis, 1948-57, regional engr., dist. sales mgr., apparatus div., St. Louis, 1957-60; gen. sales mgr. Revere Electric Mfg. Co., Chgo., 1960-65, Joseph Goder, Inc., Chgo., 1966-72; mfrs. rep., 1972—; regional mgr. Kinney-Reese Assos., Inc., N.Y.C., 1975—; Midwest mgr. Energy Appraisal Assos., Inc., Rolling Meadows, Ill., 1975—; asso. Standards Internat., Inc., Chgo., 1975—; Midwest asso. Timelapse, Inc., Mountain View, Calif., 1976—; asso. Cons. Service Assos., Evanston, Ill., 1977—. Served to 1st lt. AUS, 1943-45. Decorated Purple Heart. Mem. Air Pollution Control Assn., Sigma Chi. Baptist. Home: 1138 Terrace Ln Glenview IL 60025

WALLACE, LEON HARRY, lawyer, educator; b. Terre Haute, Ind., Jan. 24, 1904; s. Harry Seymour and Leona A. (Wagoner) W.; student U. Ill., 1921-23; A.B., Ind. U., 1925, J.D., 1933; m. Anna Ruth Haworth, Aug. 21, 1926; children—Harry L., Susan J., Leona A. Prodn. mgr. Rand McNally & Co., San Francisco, 1927-30; admitted to Ind. bar, 1933, Supreme Ct. bar, 1950; mem. firm Wallace, Randel & Wallace, 1933-44, Randel & Wallace, Terre Haute, 1944-45; asso. prof. law Ind. U., 1945-47, prof., 1947-66, acting dean, 1951-52, dean sch. law, 1952-66, Charles McGuffey Hepburn prof. law, 1966-74, dean and Hepburn prof. emeritus, 1974—. Cons. Ind.-Ky. boundary State Ind., 1966—; spl. hearing officer U.S. Dept. Justice, 1964-68; spl. master U.S. Dist. Court, No. Dist. Ind., 1969-72; gov.'s rep. Ind. Constl. Revision Commn., 1967-69. Bd. dirs., treas. Ind. Continuing Legal Edn. Forum, 1967—; sec.-treas., dir. Ind. Bar Found. Mem. Am. (chmn. sect. local govt. law), Ind. (mem. council local govt. law) bar assns., Am. Judicature Soc., Am. Acad. Social and Polit. Sci., Acad. Polit. Sci., Inst. Jud. Adminstrn., Am. Law Inst., Order of Coif, Phi Beta Kappa, Phi Delta Phi (pres. 1949-51), Sigma Delta Chi, Delta Tau Delta. Democrat. Presbyterian. Author work on legal subjects. Contbr. articles to profl. publs. Home: 939 S High St Bloomington IN 47401

WALLACE, PAUL, polit. scientist; b. Los Angeles, July 21, 1931; s. Raymond and Goldie (Singer) W.; A.B., U. Calif., Berkeley, 1953, M.A., 1957, Ph.D., 1966; m. Robin Alison Remington, Jan. 4, 1976; children—Steven Paul, Lisa Nathalie. Supr. reference unit Asia Found., San Francisco, 1957-60; asst. prof. polit. sci. U. Mo., Columbia, 1964-69, asso. prof., 1969—, dir. South Asia Lang. and Area Center, 1966-69, 73—. Served with U.S. Army, 1953-55. Am. Inst. Indian Studies fellow, 1963-64; Fulbright-Hays sr. research fellow, 1972. Mem. Am., Mo. polit. sci. assns., Assn. Asian Studies (dir. South Asia regional council 1977—). Democrat. Author: (with N.G. Barrier) Punjab Press, 1880-1905, 1970; contbr. articles to profl. publs.; editorial bd. Asian Survey, 1974—. Home: 1707 University Ave Columbia MO 65201 Office: Dept Polit Sci U Mo Columbia MO 65201

WALLACE, ROBERT DEAN, biochemist, nutrition researcher; b. Watertown, Wis., July 7, 1939; s. Elden Robert and Dorothy (Hurd) W.; B.S., U. Wis. at Whitewater, 1967; M.S., U. Colo., 1971; m. Patti Rae Plautz, June 18, 1966. Chemist Armour Pharm. Co., Kankakee, Ill., 1967-68; mgr. Nutrition Research Lab., Gerber Products Co., Fremont, Mich., 1971—. Served with USN, 1958-62. Mem. Am. Soc. Microbiology, AAAS, Beta Beta Beta. Lutheran. Home: 6326 Lakeview St Fremont MI 49412 Office: Research-Gerber Products Fremont MI 49412

WALLACE, SHERWOOD LEE, financial public relations exec.; b. Chgo., Jan. 25, 1940; s. Paul and Jerry (Crown) W.; B.A. in Journalism and Pub. Relations, State U. Iowa, 1962; postgrad. pub. relations No. Ill. U., 1971-72; m. Lois Terri Takiff, Aug. 9, 1975. Copywriter, Ekco Products Co., Chgo., 1962; polit. reporter Lerner Newspapers, Chgo., 1962; dir. pub. relations Sta. WYNR, Chgo., 1963; account exec. Bud Solk & Assos., Inc., Chgo., 1964-65, Aaron D. Cushman & Assos., Inc., Chgo., 1966-67; sr. v.p. Financial Relations Bd., Chgo., 1967—; lectr. pub. relations and investor relations to colls. and industry groups. Co-organizer Nat. Orgn. for Non-Parents, 1971, hon. dir., 1971—; mem. Big Bros. of Met. Chgo., 1974—. Recipient awards for ann. report excellence Fin. World Mag. Mem. Pub. Relations Soc. Am., Publicity Club Chgo. (Golden Trumpet award 1966, 75, 76, certificate of merit 1969), Chgo. Film Council, State U. Iowa Alumni Assn. (life), Cousteau Soc. Jewish. Home: 1165 County Line Highland Park IL 60035 Office: 150 E Huron St Chicago IL 60611

WALLACE, THOMAS FERDINAND, mgmt. cons.; b. Cin., Nov. 15, 1935; s. Raymond Joseph and Marie (Madlener) W.; B.S., Marquette U., 1957; M.B.A., Xavier U., 1966; m. Evelyn Marie Ennis, May 30, 1961; children—David, Anne Marie, Mary Clare. Various positions with Procter & Gamble, 1960-61, Gen. Motors Corp., 1961-64, Brunswick Corp., 1964-66, Richardson-Merrell Co., 1966-72; with W.G. Seinsheimer & Assos., Cin., 1972-75, v.p., 1973-75; partner Klekamp-Wallace & Co., mgmt. cons., Cin., 1976—; speaker to various profl. and tech. socs. Co-founder, pres. Montessori Center Rooms, 1966-69; area coordinator Charter Com. of Cin., 1975-76. Served to lt. (j.g.) USNR, 1957-60. Mem. Assn. for Systems Mgmt., Am. Prodn. and Inventory Control Soc. (pres. Cin. chpt. 1969-70), ACLU, Common Cause. Democrat. Roman Catholic. Contbg. editor APICS Dictionary of Prodn. and Inventory Mgmt. Terminology. Home: 7342 Gracely Dr Cincinnati OH 45233 Office: 1730 Madison Rd Cincinnati OH 45206

WALLACE, WAYNE ORRIN, physician; b. Kansas City, Kans., Oct. 16, 1912; s. Gus and Orill Lena (Postlethwaite) W.; A.B., U. Kans., 1934; M.D., 1937; m. Ruth Louise Kieffer, Aug. 18, 1934; children—Wayne Orrin, Frederick Richard, David Bruce, Charles Leland, Paul William (dec.). Intern, St. Joseph Hosp., Kansas City, Mo., 1937-38; practice medicine specializing in family practice, Atchison, Kans., 1938—; chief staff Atchison Hosp., 1971; mem. staff St. Joseph Hosp., Kansas City; sr. med. examiner FAA, Atchison, 1968—; coroner Atchison County and Dist., 1965-69; med. officer Mo. Pacific R.R. Mem. Kaw Valley Heart Assn., 1954—; dir., 1956-62, pres., 1961, chmn. bd., 1962. Vice-pres. Bd. Edn. Dist. 409, 1958-68. Served from lt. to maj., AUS, 1943-45. Fellow Am. Acad. Family Practice; mem. Am. Assn. Physicians and Surgeons, AMA, Kans. (house dels. 1953—, dist. counselor 1969-75), Atchison County (pres. 1959, 71) med. socs., Flying Physicians Assn., Am. Legion, V.F.W., Am. Bonanza Soc. Presbyterian (elder 1946-50, trustee 1950-64). Mason (K.T., Shriner), Kiwanian (pres. 1966). Club: Bellevue Country. Home: 1415 Riverview Dr Atchison KS 66002 Office: 1301 N 3d St Atchison KS 66002

WALLACE, WILLIAM THOMAS (TOM), utility co. exec.; b. St. Charles, Ill., Jan. 28, 1937; s. William Thomas and Fern E. (Putt) W.; B.A., Monmouth Coll., 1958; M.B.A., Northwestern U., 1972; postgrad. in counseling psychology, George Williams Coll., 1972-74; children—Scott, Stephen, Mark. Mgmt. trainee Ill. Bell Telephone Co., Chgo., 1959-61, security investigator, 1962-64, security supr., 1964-67, personnel mgr., 1967-68, support services mgr., 1968-70, corporate claims mgr., 1970—. Vice pres., treas. Gestalt Inst. Chgo. Served with U.S. Army, 1960-62. Recipient Theodore N. Vail award, 1959; Fredrick Law Olmstead award, 1977. Mem. Assn. Personnel and Guidance Counselors, Casualty Adjusters Assn. Chgo. (pres.), Bell Telephone Credit Union (pres.). Home: 1838 N Orleans St Chicago IL 60614 Office: 212 W Washington Blvd HQ 2H Chicago IL 60606

WALLACE, WILLIAM WARREN, pub. relations exec.; b. Steele, Mo., Nov. 28, 1922; s. Joseph Atlas and Minnie Elizabeth (Pounds) W.; student Dartmouth Coll., 1944-45; Certificate in Profl. Photography, N.Y. Inst. Photography, 1948; m. Marjorie Ruth Clifford, June 10, 1945; children—Patricia (Mrs. Dale W. Birkhead), William Warren, Joseph A., Mary Beth. Pub. relations counsel Thomas W. Parry & Assos., St. Louis, Mo., 1954-56; corp. info. mgr. Falstaff Brewing Corp., St. Louis, 1956-72; with Carl Byoir & Assos., St. Charles, Mo., 1972-74; corp. mgr. pub. info. ACF Industries, Inc., 1974—. Bd. dirs. Kingdom House, St. Louis, 1963-65. Served as chief journalist USNR, 1942-54. Mem. Pub. Relations Soc. Am., Mo. Numis. Soc. (publicity chmn. 1970-71), Nat. Amateur Press Assn., Mo. Press Assn., Amal. Printers Assn. Club: Press of Metropolitan St. Louis (bd. dirs. 1969-72). Contbr. articles in field to jours. Home: 304 Elmhurst St St Charles MO 63301 Office: 620 N 2d St St Charles MO 63301

WALLACH, PHILIP, mfg. co. exec.; b. N.Y.C., May 29, 1928; s. Morris and Lilian (Levy) W.; B.S., U.S. Mcht. Marine Acad., 1950; postgrad. N.C. State Grad. Sch. Engring., N.Y. U. Grad. Sch. Bus.; m. Florence O'Neil, Apr. 8, 1951; children—Ruth, Sandra, Louis, David. Sales engr., regional mgr. Nordberg Mfg. Co., 1955-67; v.p. mktg., pres. Engine div. Fairbanks Morse subs. Colt Industries, Inc., Beloit, Wis., 1967-71, corporate v.p., group exec., 1971, group v.p., 1972—; pres. Colt Industries Internat., Inc. Served to lt. USNR, 1953-55. Recipient Outstanding Profl. Achievement award U.S. Mcht. Marine Acad., Marine Man of the Yr. award. Mem. Am. Soc. Naval Engrs., Soc. Naval Architects and Marine Engrs. Club: Economic (N.Y.C.). Home: 3211 Montlake Dr Rockford IL 61111 Office: 701 Lawton Ave Beloit WI 53511

WALLBROWN, FRED HAROLD, cons. psychologist; b. Spencer, W.Va., June 4, 1937; s. Amos G. and Ruth (McMillan) W.; B.S. in Edn., Ohio U., 1959, M.Ed., 1961; Ph.D., Ohio State U., 1971; m. Jane C. Downs, July 6, 1973; children—Fred Harold, Franklin, Grace, Amelia Sheldon. Tchr., Harrison, Ohio, 1960-61; counselor, Hemlock, Ohio, 1961-62; counselor Yellow Springs (Ohio) pub. schs., 1962-64; elementary counselor South-Western City schs., Grove City, Ohio, 1964-65; evaluation specialist Ohio State U., Columbus, 1965-67, vis. asst. prof., 1975-76; sch. psychologist, pub. schs. Columbus, Ohio, 1967-75; asst. prof. Wichita State U., 1976—. Pvt. practice psychol. counseling, Columbus, 1970-76, Wichita, 1976—. Licensed psychologist, Kans., Ohio. Mem. Am., Brit. psychol. assns., Am. Philatelic Soc., Soc. Philatelic Ams., Nat. Philatelic Soc., Am. Topical Assn., Am. Ednl. Research Assn., Council Exceptional Children, Nat. Assn. Sch. Psychologists, Am. Personnel and Guidance Assn., Phi Alpha Theta, Pi Gamma Mu, Psi Chi, Kappa Delta Pi. Contbr. articles to profl. jours. Home: 910 N Yale Wichita KS 67208 Office: 1845 Fairmount Wichita KS 67208

WALLBROWN, JANE DOWNS (MRS. FRED HAROLD WALLBROWN), psychologist; b. New Brunswick, N.J., Sept. 27, 1935; d. Eulius Sheldon and Gladys Minor (Hall) Downs; B.A., Coll. Wooster, 1957; M.A., Ohio State U., 1959, Ph.D., 1972; m. Fred Harold Wallbrown, Aug. 6, 1973; 1 son (by previous marriage), Laurence Dean Rupp; stepchildren—Grace Marie, Amelia Ruth, Frank Frederick; 1 son, Eulius Sheldon Downs. Tchr. pub. schs., Sterling, Ohio, 1957-58, Columbus, Ohio, 1958-59; counselor jr. high sch., Weston, Mass., 1959-62; dormitory dir. Boston U., 1963-65; counselor elementary schs., Columbus, 1969-71; intern sch. psychologist Columbus Pub. Sch. System, 1971-72; sch. psychologist pub. schs., Worthington, Ohio, 1972-76; lectr. Ohio State U., Columbus, 1972-76; pvt. practice as psychologist, Columbus, 1972-76; psychologist Wichita (Kans.) Pub. Schs. Mem. Council for Exceptional Children, Nat. Assn. Sch. Psychologists. Am. Psychol.

Assn., Phi Delta Kappa. Contbr. articles to profl. jours. Home: 910 N Yale St Wichita KS 67208 Office: 640 N Emporia Wichita KS 67214

WALLEDOM, JOHN CHRISTIAN, camp exec.; b. Albert Lea, Minn., Feb. 21, 1932; s. John Christian and Ragna Camila (Egeland) W.; B.A., St. Olaf Coll., 1954; postgrad. U. Minn., 1956-57; m. Mary Ann Martello, Nov. 8, 1974; children from previous marriage—John Christian, Shelly. Social group worker Elliot Park Neighborhood House, Mpls., 1955-59; youth dir. 1st Lutheran Ch., Sioux Falls, S.D., 1959-63; sales mgr. Dayton Hudson Co., Mpls., 1963-64; dir. camping services River Trails council Girl Scouts Am., 1963-70, camp adminstr. South Cook County Girl Scouts, Harvey, Ill., 1971-74; dir. Luther Park Bible Camp, Chetek, Wis., 1974—. Active camp YMCA, 1969-70. Bd. dirs. Good Earth Bible Camp, Rochester, Minn., 1968-70. Mem. Am. Camping Assn., Group Work and Recreation Soc. Home: Route 2 Chetek WI 54728 Office: Luther Park Bible Camp Route 2 Chetek WI 54728

WALLER, RICHARD EVAN, cosmetic co. exec.; b. St. Louis, July 2, 1937; s. Gilbert Raymond and Clarice P. (Hamar) W.; student U. Ill.; m. Mary A. Erb, Dec. 5, 1959; children—Jeffrey A., Deborah A. Vice pres., dir. Knox Assos., Inc., Oak Brook, Ill., 1965-70; partner, pres., chief exec. officer Cons. Assos., Inc., Urbana, Ill., 1970-71; exec. v.p., pres. Spencer div. Berger Bros. Co., New Haven, 1971-75; v.p., gen. mgr. Skin Care Products, Inc., Lima, Ohio, 1975—; former dir. Berger Bros. Co., mem. exec. com. Served with Army N.G., 1959. Mem. Direct Selling Assn. (dir. 1973-74, dir. hospitality com.). Methodist. Contbr. articles to profl. jours. Home: 3425 London Dr Lima OH 45805 Office: 715 W Vine St Lima OH 45805

WALLER, RUSSELL BLISS, publisher; b. St. Paul, May 21, 1907; s. Elza Russell and Grace Evelyn (Bliss) W.; B.A., U. Minn., 1935; m. Mildred Pratt, Jan. 24, 1941; children—Pamela, Dennis, Thomas, Steven, John. Sports reporter St. Paul Pioneer Press, 1925-26; city editor Bemidji (Minn.) Daily Pioneer, 1929-30; news editor Ortonville (Minn.) Ind., 1930-31; pub. Algona (Iowa) Pub. Co., 1932—; pres. Midwest Printing & Lithographing Inc., Algona, 1966—. Served with USNR, 1941-45. Mem. Nat., Minn. newspaper assns., Iowa Press Assn., Ret. Officers Assn., Beta Theta Pi, Sigma Delta Chi, V.F.W., Am. Legion. Club: Masons. Home: 100 E Oak St Algona IA 50511 Office: Algona Pub Co 111 E Call St Algona IA 50511

WALLIN, JACK IRVING MELHUS, bus. mgmt. co. exec.; b. Ames, Iowa, Dec. 7, 1946; s. Jack R. and Janet M. (Melhus) W.; ed. Iowa State U., 1965-69; m. Constance Manos, July 13, 1976. Agy. mgr. Bus. Men's Clearing House, Omaha, 1973-75; pres. Bus. Mgmt. Opportunities, Omaha, 1975—, Dyna-Mohv Systems, Omaha, 1978—. Certified profl. employment cons., 1975. Mem. Nat. Employment Assn., Nebr. Placement Services Assn., Omaha C. of C. Presbyterian. Club: Rotary. Home: 4806 81st St Omaha NE 68134 Office: 10407 Devonshire Circle Suite 132 Omaha NE 68114

WALLIN, STEVEN CRAIG, civil engr.; b. Milw., Jan. 2, 1949; s. Elmore Frederick and Marilyn Dorothy (Myrland) W.; B.S. in Civil Engring., U. Ill., 1972. Project engr. Clyde E. Williams & Assoc., Terre Haute, Ind., 1972-74, Clark, Dietz & Assoc., Urbana, Ill., 1974—. Registered profl. engr., Ill. Mem. Am. Soc. C.E., Water Pollution Control Fedn., Sigma Phi Epsilon. Home: 295 Cambridge Dr Urbana IL 61801 Office: 211 N Race St Urbana IL 61801

WALLMAN, CHARLES JAMES, money handling products co. exec.; b. Kiel, Wis., Feb. 19, 1924; s. Charles A. and Mary Ann (Loftus) W.; student Marquette U., 1942-43, Tex. Coll. Mines, 1943-44; B.B.A., U. Wis., 1949; m. Charline Marie Moore, June 14, 1952; children—Stephen, Jeffrey, Susan, Patricia, Andrew. Sales promotion mgr. Brandt, Inc., Watertown, Wis., 1949-65, v.p., 1960-70, exec. v.p., 1970—, also dir.; v.p., dir. Brandt Mfg. Co., Inc., Pell City, Ala.; v.p. Brandt Money Handling Systems, Ltd., Toronto, Ont., Can.; exec. v.p., dir. Brandt-PRA, Cornwell Heights, Pa., Brandt Nat. Service Corp., Watertown, Wis. Exec. bd. Potawatomi council Boy Scouts Am., former v.p. Trustee Joe Davies Scholarship Found. Served with armored inf. AUS, 1943-45; ETO. Decorated Bronze Star medal. Mem. Am. Legion, E. Central Golf Assn. (past pres.), Wis. Alumni Assn. (local past pres.), Phi Delta Theta. Republican. Roman Catholic. Elk. Club: Watertown Country (past dir.). Home: 700 Clyman St Watertown WI 53094 Office: 705 S 12th St Watertown WI 53094

WALLNER, MARY (MRS. FRANK WALLNER), Democratic nat. committeewoman. Art tchr., pub. schs.; mgr. Dem. Hdqrs. Polit. Campaigns, S.D., 1958, 60; mem. S.D. Dem. Central Com.; Dem. nat. committeewoman from S.D., 1965—. Treas. S.D. Arts Council. Bd. dirs. Sioux Falls Civic Fine Arts Center, Am. Cancer Soc. Mem. St. Mary's Altar Soc. Address: 2605 Poplar Dr Sioux Falls SD 57105

WALLS, RICHARD JEROME, plastics co. exec.; b. Binghamton, N.Y., Oct. 1, 1931; s. Daniel W. and Edna T. (Taylor) W.; B.S., Wheaton (Ill.) Coll., 1954; m. Marjorie R. Clark, Aug. 27, 1954; children—David, Timothy, Julie. With Nelson's Auto Service, Wheaton, 1955-56; operator Dick's Texaco Service, Geneva, Ill., 1956-62; pres. Arrem Plastics Co., Addison, Ill., 1962—. Alderman, Geneva, 1967—. Mem. Ill. Engring. Soc., Soc. Plastics Engrs. Baptist (chmn. bd. deacons). Home: 908 Garden Ave Geneva IL 60134 Office: 502 Vista Ave Addison IL 60101

WALSH, BEATRICE PASSAGE, club woman; b. Schnectady, Mar. 6, 1917; d. William Riley and Jessamine (Littlefield) Passage; student Western Res. U., 1941-42; m. Thomas Joseph Walsh, July 12, 1941; 1 dau., Joan Beatrice Walsh Waltz. Vol. worker A.R.C., 1941-46, 47-53: leader council Cleve. Beachwood (Ohio) Girl Scouts, 1952-57; vol. worker Community Chest, 1947-50; mem. women's com. Cleve. Orch., 1962—; ladies program chmn. Am. Chem. Soc., 1960, Am. Inst. Chem. Engrs., 1961, ladies program conv. com., 1969; mem. Orange Community Arts Council, 1969—, Pepper Pike Civic League, 1966—; ladies program co-chmn. Nat. Heat Transfer Conf., 1964; mem. Shaker Heights League Women Voters, Case Faculty Wives (pres. 1958-59), Western Res. Republican Women's Club, D.A.R. (Shaker chpt., corr. sec. 1962-64, registrar 1964-69, publicity chmn. 1968-70, chaplain 1969—, del. state conv. 1963, 64, 66, 69, chmn. reception del. nat. conv. 1964, regent 1974—), Daus. Am. Colonies, Suburban Garden Club. Presbyterian. Clubs: The Hugenot Society (Ohio), Blackbrook Country, Landerhaven Golf, Moreland Hills Golf, Landerwood Swim. Home: 32555 Creekside Dr Pepper Pike Cleveland OH 44124

WALSH, EDMUND CARROLL, III, mfg. co. exec.; b. Clinton, Iowa, Mar. 25, 1913; s. Edmund Carroll and Hazel Marie (Hill) W.; grad. Phillips Exeter Acad., 1931; A.B., Harvard U., 1935, postgrad. law, 1935-36; m. Miriam M. Holleran, Sept. 1, 1937; children—Judith (Mrs. William P. Houley), David E. With Johns-Manville Corp., Chgo., 1937-52; with Steel Parts Corp., Tipton, Ind., 1952—, pres., 1965—; dir. City Machine Tool & Die, Hawthorne Metals. Trustee Little Sisters of the Poor; bd. dirs. St. Vincent Hosp. Found., Health Systems Agency, Inc. Served with USNR, 1943-45. Clubs: Woodstock (dir., pres.), University, Players, Indianapolis Athletic, Harvard, Economic (Indpls.); Recess (Detroit). Home: 7475 Holliday Dr E Indianapolis IN 46260 Office: Berryman Pike Tipton IN 46072

WALSH, JAMES PATRICK, JR., ins. cons., actuary; b. Ft. Thomas, Ky., Mar. 7, 1910; s. James Patrick and Minnie Louise (Cooper) W.; comml. engr. degree, U. Cin., 1933; m. Evelyn Mary Sullivan, May 20, 1939. Accountant, Firestone Tire & Rubber Co., also Gen. Motors Corp., 1933-36; rep. ARC, 1937, A.F. of L., 1938-39; dir. Ohio div. minimum wages, Columbus, 1939-42; asst. sec.-treas. union label trades dept. AFL, Washington, 1946-53; v.p. Pension and Group Cons., Inc., Cin., 1953—. Mem. President's Commn. Jud. and Congl. Salaries, 1953, Gov. Ohio Commn. Employment of Negro, 1940, Hamilton (Ohio) County Welfare Bd., 1957—, council long term illness and rehab. Cin. Pub. Health Fedn., 1957-68. Bd. dirs. U. Cin., 1959-67; bd. govs. St. Xavier High Sch., Cin., 1953-65; trustee Newman Fund, Brown Fund; mem. Internat. Found. Employee Benefit Plans, Inc. Served to lt. col. AUS, 1942-46; col. Res. Named Ky. col., 1958, also Ky. adm., 1967; recipient Insignis award St. Xavier High Sch., Cin., 1973, Distinguished Alumni award U. Cin. Mem. Res. Officers Assn., Am. Legion (life), Q.M. Assn., V.F.W., Nat. Football Found. and Hall of Fame, Mil. Order World Wars, Am. Fedn. State, County and Employees Union, Internat. Alliance Theatrical Stage Employees (past sgt. at arms), Internat. Hodcarriers, Bldg. and Common Laborers Union, Ins. Workers Internat. Union, Office Employees Internat. Union, Cooks and Pastry Cooks Local, Friendly Sons St. Patrick (past pres.), Covington Latin Sch. Alumni Assn. (past pres.), Soc. for Advancement Mgmt., Def. Supply Assn., Ancient Order Hibernians (past pres.), Assn. U.S. Army, Cursillio, Cin. Council World Affairs, Nat. Hist. Soc., Am. Ordnance Assn., Soc. Am. Mil. Engrs., Order of Alhambra, Allied Constrn. Industries, U. Cin. Alumni Assn. (life), Internat. Assn. Health Underwriters, Health Ins. Council S.W. Ohio, Scabbard and Blade, Greater Cin. Indsl. Relations Research Assn., Zoo Soc., Nat. Council Catholic Men, Am. Public Welfare Assn., Millcreek Valley Assn., Nat. Hist. Soc., Ret. Officers Assn. (past pres. Cin.), Am. Assn. Ret. Persons, Mem. of Milford, CATS, Smithsonian Assos., Inter Am. Soc., Germania Soc., Am. Soc. Pension Actuaries, Alpha Kappa Psi. Catholic. K.C. (4 deg.), Elk. Clubs: Cuvier Press, C, St. Antoninus Athletic, Green Township Republican, Republican of Hamilton County, War Veterans Republican, Newman (Cin.), Cincinnati (past pres.), Queen City, Nat. Travel, American-Irish, Insiders, U.C. Boosters, Xavier U. Musketeer, Bengals Touchdown, Global Sportsman, Military. Home: 5563 Julmar Dr Cincinnati OH 45238 Office: 6 E 4th St Cincinnati OH 45202

WALSH, JOHN PHILIP, optometrist; b. Evanston, Ill., June 17, 1925; s. Martin Joseph and Susan Bernice (Smith) W.; B.S., Northwestern U., 1949; B.S., D. Optometry, Ill. Coll. Optometry, 1951; m. Vivian Caroline Lindeen, Sept. 12, 1952; children—Heather Lynne, Marilinda, John Philip. Individual practice optometry, Wilmette, Ill., 1951—. Served with AUS, 1944-46. Decorated Bronze Star with oak leaf cluster. Named Lion of Year, Wilmette Lions Clubs, 1970. Mem. Ill. Optometric Assn. (v.p. 1959-63). Lion (dep. dist. gov. 1960-62). Editor: Illinois Optometric Assn. Jour., 1963-66. Office: 1137 Central Ave Wilmette IL 60091

WALSH, KENNETH ALBERT, chemist; b. Yankton, S.D., May 23, 1922; s. Albert Lawrence and Edna (Slear) W.; B.A., Yankton Coll., 1942; Ph.D., Iowa State U., 1950; m. Dorothy Jeanne Thompson, Dec. 22, 1944; children—Jeanne K., Kenneth Albert, David Bruce, Rhonda Jean, Leslie Gay. Asst. prof. chemistry Iowa State U., Ames, 1950-51; staff mem. Los Alamos Sci. Lab., 1951-57; supr. Internat. Minerals & Chems. Corp., Mulberry, Fla., 1957-60; mgr. Brush Beryllium Co., Elmore, Ohio, 1960-72; asso. dir. tech. Brush Wellman Inc., Elmore, 1972—. Democratic precinct chmn., Los Alamos, 1956. Mem. Am. Chem. Soc. (sect. treas. 1956), Am. Soc. for Metals, Am. Ceramic Soc., AAAS, Toastmasters Internat., Theta Xi, Phi Lambda Upsilon. Methodist. Patentee in field. Home: 2624 Fangboner Rd Fremont OH 43420 Office: Brush Wellman Inc Elmore OH 43416

WALSH, RITA, ophthalmologist; b. Caguas, P.R., June 11, 1920; d. Clarence Joseph and Mercedes (Chiques) Walsh; B.S., U. P.R., 1939; B.S., Columbia U., 1943; M.D., Loyola U., Chgo., 1950. Clin. fellow, then instr. physiologic optics Dartmouth Eye Inst., Hanover, N.H., 1943-45; intern Hollywood Presbyn. Hosp., Los Angeles, 1950-51; preceptorship ophthalmology Gailey Eye Clinic, Bloomington, Ill., 1951-54, staff ophthalmologist, 1954—; mem. staff Mennonite Hosp. Mem. AMA, Am. Acad. Ophthalmology, Panam. Assn. Ophthalmologists, Internat., Am. colls. surgeons, McLean County (past pres.), Ill. med. socs. Republican. Roman Catholic. Club: Bloomington Country. Contbr. med. jours. Home: 815 N Prairie St Bloomington IL 61701 Office: 1008 N Main St Bloomington IL 61701

WALSH, ROBERT JOSEPH, surgeon; b. Chgo., Dec. 22, 1934; s. Joseph Michael and Iverne Lucille (Griffin) W.; A.B. cum laude, Loyola U. at Chgo., 1957, M.D. cum laude, 1961; m. Catherine Ellen Andersen, June 4, 1960; children—Kevin, Brian, Martin, Carin. Intern, U. Chgo., 1961-62, resident, 1963-66; resident U. Iowa, 1966; practice medicine specializing in orthopedic surgery, Chgo., 1967-71, Arlington Heights, Ill., 1971—; instr. U. Chgo., 1965-66, Northwestern U., 1967—. Chmn. troop com. Boy Scouts Am., 1975. Served to maj., M.C., AUS, 1968-70. Fellow A.C.S.; mem. Chgo., Ill. med. socs., AMA, Am. Acad. Orthopedic Surgeons, Chgo. Com. on Trauma, Chgo., Ill. orthopedic socs., Blue Key, Alpha Sigma Nu. Club: Michigan Shores. Office: 1430 N Arlington Heights Rd Arlington Heights IL 60004

WALSH, THOMAS J(OSEPH), chem. engr., educator; b. Troy, N.Y., July 17, 1917; s. Thomas Joseph and Anna (Sharp) W.; B.S., Rensselaer Poly. Inst., 1939, M.S., 1941; Ph.D., Case Inst. Tech., 1949; m. Beatrice Metcalfe Passage, July 12, 1941; 1 dau., Joan Beatrice. Chem. engr. Standard Oil Co. Ohio, 1941-47; prof. Case Inst. Tech., 1947-61; engr. Lewis Flight Propulsion Lab. NACA, 1951-55; cons. Thompson Ramo Wooldridge, 1955-61, sr. staff specialist, requirements mgr. research applications equipment labs. division, 1961-66; process specialist corp. engring. dept. Glidden-Durkee div. SCM Corp., Cleve., 1966-68, mgr. process engring., from 1968, now mgr. environ. conservation; cons. Glascote Products Co., 1954-61. Pres. Northeastern Ohio Science Fair, Inc. Recipient Junior Tech. award Cleve. Tech. Soc. Council, Merit award Cleve. Chem. Profession. Fellow Am. Inst. Chem. Engrs.; mem. AAAS, Am. Chem. Soc. (trustee), Am. Soc. E.E., AAUP, Cleve. Tech. Socs. Council (past pres.), Am. Inst. Aeros and Astronautics, Cleve. Engring. Soc. (gov.). Home: 32555 Creekside Dr Pepper Pike OH 44124 Office: Union Commerce Bldg Cleveland OH 44115

WALSH, THOMAS PATRICK, county ofcl.; b. Ottawa, Ill., Apr. 16, 1937; s. Thomas Pearce and Louise R. (Rude) W.; student pub. schs., Ottawa; m. Margaret Wheatland, June 19, 1971; children—Gregory, Kathleen, Thomas, Patrick. Funderal dir. Gladfelter Chapel, Ottawa, Ill., 1958-65; mgr. Bailey-Walsh Funeral Home, Ottawa, 1965-67; asst. chemist Ill. Nitrogen Corp., Marseilles, Ill., 1967-69; mgr. Sierra Leasing Inc., Ottawa, Ill., 1969-72; county clk. La Salle County, Ottawa, 1972—. Mem. Ill. Assn. of County Clks. and Recorders, Election Ofcls. and Treasurers. Democrat. Roman Catholic. Clubs: Eagles, Moose, K.C., Sons of Norway. Home: 1129 Paul St Ottawa IL 61350 Office: La Salles and Main Streets Ottawa IL 61350

WALSH, WILLIAM ARTHUR, II, realtor; b. Chgo., June 13, 1930; s. William Arthur and Ada Mary (Ruffner) W.; student Northwestern U., 1948-66; m. Dawn Etta Wilson, Feb. 11, 1950; children—Beverly Ann, Carol Sue, Patricia Lynn. Office mgr. George T. Schmidt Inc., Niles, Ill., 1946-66; v.p., Koenig & Strey Inc., realtors, Glenview, Ill., 1966—. Pres. Evanston-North Shore Bd. Realtors, 1975; lectr. in field. Mem. Ill. Assn. Realtors (dir. 1975-77, legis. chmn. 1977), Nat. Inst. Real Estate Brokers (membership chmn. Ill. 1975), Glenview C. of C. (dir. 1972-73), Nat. Assn. Realtors (legis. com. 1977). Presbyterian (past deacon ch.). Clubs: Masons (32 deg.), Shrine. Home: 328 Harlem Ave Glenview IL 60025 Office: 1009 Waukegan Rd Glenview IL 60025

WALSTROM, JOHN ALBERT JAMES, educator; b. Ramsey, Ill., Apr. 25, 1937; s. Gusta Albin and Mary Louise (Dobbs) W.; B.S., Eastern Ill. U., 1960, M.S., 1963; postgrad. North Tex. State U., 1968-69, 71; Ph.D., U. Nebr., 1976; m. Phyllis Kay Peabody, Dec. 21, 1958; children—Kent Alan, Scott Gregory, Brian James. Dir. data processing Eastern Ill. U., 1960-68; prof. data processing Western Ill. U., 1969—; vis. instr. computer sci. U. Nebr., 1974. Cubmaster Cub Scouts Am., 1970-72. Certified data processor. Mem. Data Processing Mgmt. Assn. (dir. exec. bd. East Central Ill. chpt. 1965-68, sec. 1966-68, individual performance award 1968), Assn. Computing Machinery, Ill. Assn. Data Processing Instrs., Soc. Data Educators, Beta Gamma Sigma, Sigma Iota Epsilon, Phi Delta Kappa. Home: 313 S Verzel Dr Macomb IL 61455

WALTER, JAMES TREAT, hosp. adminstr.; b. St. Paul, June 15, 1939; s. Clarence William and Bessie Irene (Treat) W.; B.A., Grinnell Coll., 1961; M.A., State U. Iowa, 1963; m. Donna Louise Wheaton, Aug. 26, 1961; children—David William, Deborah Louise. Adminstrv. asst., resident Decatur (Ill.) Hosp., 1962-64; asst. adminstr. Reid Meml. Hosp., Richmond, Ind., 1964-65; asst. adminstr. Allen Meml. Hosp., Waterloo, Iowa, 1965-68, exec. dir., 1968—. Pres. bd. N.E. Iowa Health Planning Council, 1971-72; chmn. joint council Health Planning Council Iowa, 1971; bd. dirs. United Way, 1975—, Blue Shield of Iowa, 1977—. Named Outstanding Young Religious Leader, Waterloo, 1973. Mem. Am. Coll. Hosp. Adminstrs., Iowa Hosp. Assn. (dir. 1977—). Presbyterian. Club: Rotary. Home: 3368 Mt Vernon Dr Waterloo IA 50701 Office: 1825 Logan Ave Waterloo IA 50703

WALTER, RICHARD DALE, aircraft co. ofcl.; b. Tonkawa, Okla., Jun 24, 1922; s. Robert Richard and Mabel Hanna (Davis) W.; student Braman (Okla.) pub. shcs.; m. Maryella Jackson, Mar. 9, 1946; children—Terri Dale Walter Seals, Richard Ray. With Beech Aircraft Corp., Wichita, Kans., 1950—, mgr. target missile flight services, 1960-68, mgr. aerospace product support services, 1968—; gen. mgr. Beech Aerospace Services, Inc. Served with U.S. Army, 1942-45; ETO. Democrat. Club: Masons. Home: 1441 N Rock Rd Apt 1201 Wichita KS 67206 Office: Beech Aircraft 9709 E Centeral St Wichita KS 67201

WALTER, RICHARD HARRY, cons. civil engr.; b. Manitowoc, Wis., Mar. 23, 1926; s. Earl Ferdinand and Martha Bertha (Wiesmann) W.; student Central Mich. U., 1944-45, Iowa State U., 1945-46; B.S., Carroll Coll., 1948; B.S. in Civil Engring., U. Mich., 1951; m. June Ruth Chadwick, Sept. 14, 1951; children—Richard Earl, Gregory James. Project engr. Kaiser-Frazer Co., Ypsilanti, Mich., 1951-52, Kaiser Engrs., Oakland, Calif., 1952-57; field engr. Portland Cement Assn., Milw., 1957-69; exec. dir., cons. engr. Concrete Masonry Industries, Thiensville, Wis., 1969—; lectr. Marquette U., Milw., 1960-69, Wis. State U., Platteville, 1960-69, U. Wis., Madison, 1960-69; mem. Spl. Wis. Study Com. on Energy Conservation, 1975. Served with USNR, 1944-46. Registered profl. engr., Wis. Mem. Nat., Wis (pres. Milw. N. chpt.) socs. profl. engrs., Nat., Wis., Chgo. socs. assn. execs., Constrn. Specifications Inst., Wis. Concrete Products Assn. (exec. dir. 1974—). Contbr. articles to profl. jours. Address: 512 Alta Loma Dr Thiensville WI 53092

WALTER, RODERICH, educator; b. Darmstadt, West Germany, July 16, 1937; s. Kurt and Hildegard (Huuck) W.; B.S., Justus Liebig U. (West Germany), 1961; Ph.D., U. Cin., 1964; m. Eve Walter. Asso., Cornell Med. Coll., N.Y.C., 1964-65, Mt. Sinai Hosp., N.Y.C., 1965-66; research collaborator Brookhaven Nat. Lab., Upton, N.Y., 1965—; asso. prof. physiology Mt. Sinai Sch. Medicine, City U. N.Y., 1966-71, prof., 1971-74; prof., chmn. U. Ill. Med. Center, Chgo., 1974—. USPHS grantee 1969—. Fellow N.Y. Acad. Sci.; mem. AAAS, Am. Chem. Soc., Am. Physiol. Soc., Am. Soc. Biol. Chemists, Soc. Exptl. Biology and Medicine, Biophys. Soc., Soc. Applied Spectroscopy, Harvey Soc., Endocrine Soc., Am. Peptide Symposium, Assn. Chairmen Depts. Physiology, Smithsonian Assos., Sigma Xi. Editor: Neurophysins: Carriers of Peptide Hormones, 1975; Peptides: Chemistry, Structure and Biology, 1975. Mem. editorial bds. various sci. jours. Contbr. articles to profl. jours. Home: 990 Lake Shore Dr Chicago IL 60611 Office: Dept Physiology and Biophysics U Ill Med Center Chicago IL 60612

WALTER, TERRY LYNN, cons. psychol. firm exec.; b. Great Bend, Kans., Dec. 23, 1928; s. Clifton William and Helen Naudia (Rusco) W.; B.S., Kans. State U., 1952; M.Edn., U. Mo., 1969; m. Evelyn Margaret Evans, July 3, 1949; children—Marcia Jeanne, Sandra Alice, Michael Kent, Steven Craig. Chemist, Halliburton Oil Well Cement Co., Great Bend, 1945-47; research asst. U.S. Dept. Agr., Kans. State U., Manhattan, 1948-52; math. and sci. tchr. U. Md. Extension div., Eng., 1953-54; grade sch. tchr. Fairview Sch., Norton, Kans., 1955-56, cons. engr. Walter Cons. Engring. Service, Tribune, Kans., 1954—; exec. v.p. Asso. Personnel Technicians, Inc., cons. psychologists; owner, operator Mineral Exploration and Devel. Unltd., 1975—; grad. adminstrv. asst. dir. counseling bur. U. Mo., Columbia, 1968-69, counselor for testing, 1969—, instr. extension div., 1968—; asso. dir. Greeley Coop. Assn., Tribune, 1966-68. Bd. dirs. Wichita Guidance Center; chmn. bd. Christian Community Services, Inc.; bd. dirs. Am. Bapt. Conv. Served with USAF, 1952-54. Registered profl. engr., Kans. Mem. Am. Personnel and Guidance Assn., Am. Coll. Personnel Assn., Kans. Profl. Engrs., Am. Mgmt. Soc., Am. Soc. Personnel Adminstrs. Alpha Kappa Lambda. Baptist (dir. Kans. conv. 1962-67). Patentee in field. Home: 6700 Abbotsford Pl Wichita KS 67206

WALTERS, EVERETT, univ. adminstr.; b. Bethlehem, Pa., Apr. 4, 1915; s. Raymond and Elsie (Rosenberg) W.; A.B., U. Cin., 1936; M.A., Columbia U., 1940, Ph.D., 1947; D.H.L., Mass. Coll.; m. Jane C. Schrader, Apr. 23, 1938; children—Diane Colley (Mrs. Patrick B. Hearne), Everett Garrison. Instr., Finch Jr. Coll., 1940-43; rep. U.S. CSC, 1943-44; instr. history Ohio State U., 1946-48, asst. prof., 1948-54, asso. prof., 1954-63, asst. dean Grad. Sch., 1954-55, acting dean, 1956-57, dean, 1957-63, chmn. editorial bd. Ohio State U. Press; v.p. acad. affairs Boston U., 1963-69, sr. v.p., dean faculties, 1969-71 dean faculties U. Mo., St. Louis, 1971-72, 73-75, v.p. community affairs, 1975—, interim chancellor, 1972-73; vis. prof. Whittier Coll., summer 1950; dir. grad. fellowship program U.S. Office Edn., 1962-63. Chmn., Grad. Conf. on Grad. Study and Research, 1961-62. Bd. dirs., vice chmn. Sta. KETC-TV. Served as lt. USNR, 1944-46, 1950-52. Recipient Ohio State U. Centennial award, 1974. Mem. Am. Hist. Assn., Ohio Hist. Soc. (trustee 1960-63), Assn. Grad. Schs. (sec.-treas. 1960-61), St. Louis Council World Affairs (chmn. bd.

dirs.), Bach Soc. St. Louis (pres.), Phi Delta Theta. Episcopalian. Club: Cosmos. Author: Joseph Benson Foraker: An Uncompromising Republican, 1948. Editor, contbg. author: Graduate Education Today, 1965-. Editor, Jour. Proceedings of Assn. Grad. Schs., 1959-63. Contbr. articles hist., ednl. jours. Home: 3 Fair Oaks St St Louis MO 63124 Office: 8001 Natural Bridge St Louis MO 63121

WALTERS, GOMER WINSTON, patent atty.; b. Johnstown, Pa., Sept. 24, 1937; s. Philip Thomas and Margaret Elizabeth (Peat) W.; B.Engring., Yale U., 1960; J.D. with honors, George Washington U., 1965; m. Jean Mary Jester, June 13, 1964; children—Bruce Joseph, Matthew Howel, Melinda Jean. Engring. trainee Gen. Electric Co., Syracuse N.Y. and Lynchburg, Va., 1960-61; patent engr. Patent Atty. Tng. Program, Washington, 1961-65; admitted to Ill. bar, 1965; asso. firm Kirkland & Ellis, Chgo., 1965-69, partner, 1970-72; patent atty. Westinghouse Electric Corp., Pitts., 1972-73; asso. firm Walsh, Case & Coale, Chgo., 1973-75; asso. firm Haight, Hofeldt, Davis & Jambor, Chgo., 1975-77, partner, 1977—. Mem. Am., Chgo. bar assns., Am., Pitts. patent law assns., Patent Law Assn. Chgo., Seventh Circuit Bar Assn., Am. Judicature Soc. Republican. Home: 538 Meadow Rd Winnetka IL 60093 Office: 55 E Monroe St Chicago IL 60603

WALTERS, HAROLD WALLACE, assn. exec.; b. Amarillo, Tex., Apr. 17, 1929; s. Leslie A. and Nellie (Jackson) W.; B.S., Purdue U., 1955; m. Marilyn Hull, June 13, 1953; children—Michael, David, Cynthia. With Nat. Assn. Mut. Ins. Cos., Indpls., 1955—, exec. v.p., gen. mgr., 1967-72, pres., 1972—. Mem. ins. adv. com. U. Tex., 1962-69; sec.-treas. Crop Ins. Research Bur., Inc., 1964—. Bd. dirs. Hoosier Travel Service; bd. govs. Internat. Ins. Seminars; bd. electors Ins. Hall Fame. Served with USMC, 1946-51. Mem. Ind. Soc. Assn. Execs. (pres. 1964, dir. 1963-68), Am. Soc. Assn. Execs., Chartered Assn. Execs. (dir. 1963—), Conf. Mut. Casualty Cos. Mem. Christian Ch. Home: 6219 N Parker Ave Indianapolis IN 46220 Office: 7931 Castleway Dr Indianapolis IN 46250

WALTERS, HARVEY EUGENE, adminstrv. counselor; b. Bloomington, Ind., Dec. 30, 1928; s. Alpha Lee and Nova Aleen (Cornwell) W.; A.B. cum laude, Franklin (Ind.) Coll., 1951; M.S., Ind. U., Bloomington, 1956, Ed.D., 1966; m. Charlotte Jane Boltinghouse, July 3, 1949; 1 dau., Kimberly Jane. Tchr. sci. F.J. Reitz High Sch., Evansville, Ind., 1951-52, 54-60, counselor, 1961-65; vis. prof. Ind. U., 1965-66; dir. guidance Binford Middle Sch., Bloomington, 1966—; cons. Gen. Elec. Workshops, summers 1972-77. Served with AUS, 1952-54. Recipient award for research paper Am. Sch. Counselors Assn., 1970-71. Mem. NEA (life), Ind. Tchrs. Assn., Monroe County Edn. Assn., Am. Personnel and Guidance Assn., Am. Sch. Counselors Assn., Am. Legion, Phi Delta Kappa. Clubs: Elks, Masons, Shriners. Home: 333 S Meadowbrook Ave Bloomington IN 47401 Office: 600 S Roosevelt Ave Bloomington IN 47401

WALTERS, JEFFERSON BROOKS, musician, real estate broker; b. Dayton, Ohio, Jan. 22, 1922; s. Jefferson Brooks and Mildred Frances (Smith) W.; student U. Dayton, 1947; m. Mary Elizabeth Espey, Apr. 6, 1963; children—Dinah Christine Basson, Jefferson Brooks. Composer, cornetist Dayton, 1934—; real estate broker, Dayton, 1948—; founder Am. Psalm Choir, 1965. Served with USCGR, 1942-45; PTO, ETO. Mem. S.A.R., Greater Dayton Antique Study Club (past pres.), Dayton Art Inst., Montgomery County Hist. Soc. Presbyn. Mason (32 deg.). Club: Dayton Country. Condr., composer choral, solo voice settings of psalms and poetry Alfred Lord Tennyson; composer Crossing the Bar (meml. performances U.S. Navy band), 1961. Home: 400 Ridgewood Ave Dayton OH 45409 Office: Classics Realty 53 Park Ave Dayton OH 45419

WALTERS, JOHN DENNIS, constrn. co. exec.; b. Manhattan, Kans., Feb. 11, 1944; s. John Austin and Mary Margaret (O'Laughlin) W.; B.S. in Geology, U. Notre Dame, 1966, B.S. in Civil Engring., 1967; M.S., U. Ill., 1971; m. Cheryl Elaine Dow, June 17, 1967. Geol. engr. Kans. Hwy. Commn., Topeka, 1966; commd. 1st lt., U.S. Air Force, 1967, advanced through grades to capt., 1973, ret., 1973; constrn. mgr. The Law Co., Wichita, Kans., 1973-76; cost engring. mgr. Hosp. Bldg. & Equipment Co., St. Louis, 1977—. Decorated Bronze Star medal, U.S. Air Force Commendation medal. Registered profl. engr., Kans., Pa. Mem. Nat. Soc. Profl. Engrs., Kans. Engring. Soc. Republican. Roman Catholic. Co-author: Modeling and Analysis of Construction Delays, 1971; Nondestructive Pavement Evaluation, 1973. Home: 1719 Claymont Estates Dr St Louis MO 63011 Office: 717 Office Pkwy St Louis MO 63141

WALTERS, SUMNER JUNIOR, lawyer; b. Van Wert, Ohio, Oct. 4, 1916; s. Sumner E. and Kittie (Allen) W.; J.D., Ohio No. U., 1940; m. Marjorie Acheson, May 22, 1948; 1 son, Sumner E. Admitted to Ohio bar, 1940; mem. firm Walters & Koch, 1941-42, Stroup & Walters, 1946-68; pvt. practice, Van Wert, 1969-71; mem. firm Walters, Young & Walters, 1971—; asst. pros. atty. Van Wert County, 1946-48, pros. atty., 1948-60; acting judge Van Wert Municipal Ct., also asst. city solicitor City of Van Wert, 1962; village solicitor Middle Point, 1960—; dir. Peoples Bank & Trust Co., Van Wert. Pres., Van Wert Indsl. Devel. Corp., 1966-76, Humane Soc., 1963—, YMCA, 1962-63; mem. council Camp Fire Girls, 1965-72. Pres. bd. trustees Van Wert County United Fund, 1959-60; trustee United Health Found., Van Wert County Hosp., Van Wert County Found, Marsh Found., Van Wert. Served with Mil. Police, C.I.C., AUS, 1942-45; ETO. Named Outstanding Citizen of Year, Van Wert Jr. C. of C., 1965. Mem. Ohio, Northwestern Ohio (pres. 1957-58), Van Wert County (pres. 1953-55) bar assns., Am. Legion, V.F.W., Sigma Phi Epsilon. Methodist (chmn. ofcl. bd. 1963-64, lay del. Ohio West conf. 1967—, conf. sec. 1970-71, mem. bd. hosps. and homes). Mason (32 deg., Shriner, K.T.), Rotarian (pres. 1966-67). Home: Rt 2 Ohio City OH 45874 Office: 121 S Washington St Van Wert OH 45891

WALTERS, THOMAS CHARLES, asst. supt. schs.; b. Dover, Ohio, June 2, 1933; s. Charles Henry and Mary Margaret (Kurtz) W.; B.S., Kent State U., 1957, M.Ed., 1965; certificate adminstrn., Youngstown State U., 1975; m. Betty Shepherd, Aug. 10, 1957; 1 dau., Kathleen Helen. Head football coach Portage S.E. High Sch., Portage County, Ohio, 1954-62, Jefferson area schs., Ashtabula, Ohio, 1962-65, Minerva (Ohio) High Sch., 1965-74; asst. supt. Minerva pub. schs., 1974—. Chmn. Minerva Bicentennial Com., 1975, chmn. Bicentennial Park Com., 1974—. Served with AUS, 1953-55. Named Coach of the Year, Minerva High Sch., 1973. Mem. Ohio Football Coaches Assn., NEA, Ohio Edn. Assn., Buckeye Assn. Sch. Adminstrs. Methodist. Lion. Home: 813 Allan St Minerva OH 44657

WALTH, ERWIN GOTTLEIB, real estate broker; b. Hosmer, S.D., June 5, 1918; s. Martin and Josephine (Hieb) W.; student Minn. Sch. Bus., 1943-44; m. Josephine Mary Ann Farone, Nov. 26, 1949; 1 son, Daniel Erwin. Circulation mgr. Mpls. Star and Tribune, 1946-47; partner H&W Equipment franchised dealer Internat. Harvester, New Prague, Minn., 1947-65; salesman Ford Anderson Realty Agy., Rochester, Minn., 1965-66, sales mgr., 1966-72; owner, broker Walth Agy., real estate, Rochester, 1972—. Vice-pres., pres. Rochester Bd. Realtors, 1974-75; edn. chmn. Rochester Multiple Listing Service, 1974. Served with AUS, 1941-44; PTO. Mem. New Prague Bus. and Profl. Assn. (pres. 1962), Rochester C. of C., Am. Legion, V.F.W. Lutheran (pres. ch. bd.). Rotarian (pres. New Prague 1965), Elk, Mason (Shriner). Home: 2215 17th Ave NW Rochester MN 55901 Office: 2222 E Frontage Rd Hwy 52N Rochester MN 55901

WALTHER, RICHARD EDWARD, wholesale co. exec.; b. Moline, Ill., Mar. 22, 1937; s. Edward Ruckman and Edith Viola (Swensen) W.; B.S., Augustana Coll., 1958; m. Karna Ann Johnson, Dec. 6, 1958; children—Michael, Todd, Lisa, Mark. Various accounting positions McKesson & Robbins, Omaha, 1958-66; comptroller McPike, Inc., Kansas City, Mo., 1966-68, treas., 1968—. Bd. govs. Am. Royal, 1977. Mem. C. of C., Rho Nu Delta. Lutheran (treas. 1967-71, 73-77). Club: Sherwood Forest. Home: 3714 NE 46th St Kansas City MO 64117 Office: 1315 N Chouteau St Kansas City MO 64120

WALTKE, ALFRED GEORGE, optometrist; b. Pickrell, Nebr., Feb. 1, 1933; s. Chris W. and Lena H. (Schmidt) W.; student U. Nebr., 1956-57; student Midland Coll., 1959-61; B.S., O.D., Ill. Coll. Optometry, 1964; m. Marilyn M. Holtmeier, June 9, 1957; children—Kelly, Tracy, Leslie. Practice optometry, Waukesha, Wis., 1964—. Bd. dirs. Waukesha Symphony; bd. dirs., pres. Halfway House of Waukesha; chmn. bd. dirs. Health Mgmt. Corp. Served with AUS, 1953-56. Mem. Am., Wis. (dir.) optometric assns., Kettle Moraine Optometric Soc., Am. Optometric Found., Nat. Eye Research Found. Republican. Lutheran. Lion. Club: Nagawicka Lake Yacht. Home: 912 Oak St Delafield WI 53018 Office: 411 N Grand Ave Waukesha WI 53186

WALTON, CLAUDE ALEX, park adminstr.; b. Denver, Aug. 1, 1913; s. Claude and Jennie Vera (Woolridge) W.; B. Music, U. Colo., 1937; postgrad. George Williams Coll., Chgo., 1949; m. Darwin McBeth, Sept. 2, 1950; children—Claudette, John. Instr. phys. edn. Chgo. Park Dist., 1950-54, playground supr., 1954-59, park supr., 1959-64, asst. dir. employee activities, 1964-67, dir. employee activities, 1967-70, asso. supt., 1970—. Staff mem. Colo. Inst. on Leisure Time, 1973. Recipient Alumni Recognition award U. Colo., 1975. Mem. Central Amateur Athletic Union, Alpha Phi. Office: Chgo Park Dist 425 McFetridge Dr Chicago IL 60605

WALTON, CRAIG CARLTON, dentist; b. Columbus, Ohio, Feb. 14, 1930; s. Lemmar S. and Blanche Bell (Blackburn) W.; B.S. in Music Edn., Ohio State U., 1952, D.D.S., 1959; m. Gwendolyn Jane Norton, July 5, 1952; children—Steven, Susan, Scott, Shawn. Practice dentistry, Columbus, 1959—; asst. prof. crown and bridge dept. Ohio State U., Columbus, 1959-71. Served to 1st lt. AUS, 1952-54. Mem. Am., Ohio, Columbus dental assns., Columbus Dental Vets. (pres. 1970, mem. bd. 1965-70), Am. Heart Assn., Nat. Ski Patrol, Phi Mu Alpha, Alpha Tau Omega, Psi Omega, Kappa Kappa Psi. Republican. Home: 3799 Chevington Rd Columbus OH 43220 Office: 3090 Olentangy River Rd Columbus OH 43202

WALTON, HERBERT WILSON, dist. judge; b. Anaconda, Mont., Apr. 9, 1929; s. George Myrick and Neola (Wilson) W.; student U. Kans., 1948-50; A.B., U. Mo. at Kansas City, 1955, J.D., 1957; grad. Nat. Coll. State Trial Judges, 1966; m. Barbara Lavon Pratt, Aug. 13, 1949; children—Michael Eugene, Constance Lynn, Herbert Steven, Cynthia Diane. Admitted to Kans. bar, 1957; asst. county atty. Johnson County (Kans.), 1957-60, county probate and juvenile judge, Olathe, 1960-65; judge div. 1, 10th Jud. Dist., Olathe, 1965—; instr. bus. law U. Kans. extension, 1963-72; mem. Regional Health and Welfare Council, 1963-65; founding pres. Johnson County Scholarship Found., bd. advisers Johnson County Welfare Dept., 1963-65. Trustee law sch. found. U. Mo. at Kansas City, 1963-65. Served with USNR, 1947-48, 51-52. Named hon. life mem. Kans. Congress PTA. Mem. Kans. Probate Judge Assn. (sec., treas. 1965), Kans., Am. Johnson County (sec. 1958) bar assns., Kans. Dist. Judges Assn. (pres. 1973), U. Mo. at Kansas City Alumni Assn. (pres. 1973), Kans. Judicial Council, Phi Alpha Delta. Optimist. Home: 405 Normandy Dr Olathe KS 66061 Office: Courthouse Olathe KS 66061

WALTON, ROBERT EUGENE, agrl. co. exec.; b. Shattuck, Okla., Jan. 15, 1931; s. Lonnie J. and Marguerite (Rose) W.; B.S., Okla. State U., 1952, M.S., 1956; postgrad. Royal Agrl. Coll., Sweden, 1952-53; Ph.D. (Danforth fellow 1956), Iowa State U., 1961; m. Janice Carolyn Graning, Sept. 5, 1959; children—Cynthia Claire, Robert Eugene, John Randolph. Mgr., Westhide Farms, Hereford, Eng., 1953-54; asst. prof. U. Ky., Lexington, 1958-62; geneticist Am. Breeders Service, Inc., DeForest, Wis., 1962-65, dir. marketing and breeding div., 1965-67, exec. v.p., 1967-68, pres., chief exec. officer, 1968—; pres., dir. Simmental Valley, Inc., Walton Bros., Inc.; dir. 1st Wis. Nat. Bank. Bd. dirs. World Dairy Expo, Wis. Agri-Bus. Council, Meth. Hosp., Madison. Mem. Am. Dairy Sci. Assn., Am. Soc. Animal Sci., Biometric Soc., Nat. Assn. Animal Breeders (pres., dir.), Farmhouse frat., Sigma Xi, Omicron Delta Kappa, Alpha Zeta (chancellor 1951). Republican. Methodist. Rotarian. Home: Route 2 DeForest WI 53532 Office: Am Breeders Service Inc DeForest WI 53532

WAMBO, JOHN MACK, obstetrician, gynecologist; b. Richmond, Ind., May 15, 1937; s. Herman C. and Vera E.C. (Weber) W.; A.B., Ind. U., 1959, M.D., 1962; m. Catherina M. Kousbroek, Nov. 10, 1965; children—Henry Clay, Carissa Maria. Intern, Orange County (Calif.) Gen. Hosp., 1962-63, resident in obstetrics gynecology U. Calif. at Irvine/Orange County Med. Center, 1967-70; gen. practice medicine, Richmond, Ind., 1966-67, specializing in obstetrics and gynecology, 1970—; sec.-treas. GYN Ltd., Richmond, 1971—; coroner Wayne County (Ind.), 1977—. Served with M.C., USN, 1963-65. Diplomate Am. Bd. Obstetrics and Gynecology. Fellow Am. Coll. Obstetricians and Gynecologists; mem. Ind. Bd. Health (perinatal tech. adv. com.). Republican. Lutheran. Home: 2600 Wernle Rd Richmond IN 47374

WAMPLER, LLOYD CHARLES, lawyer; b. Spencer, Ind., Nov. 4, 1920; s. Charles and Vivian (Hawkins) W.; A.B., Ind. U., 1942, J.D., 1947; m. Joyce Ann Hoppenrath, Sept. 28, 1950 (dec. 1954); 1 dau., Natalie Gay; m. 2d, Esther S. Powers, July 18, 1969. Admitted to Ind. bar, 1947, U.S. Supreme Ct. bar, 1971; instr. bus. law U. Kans., 1947-49; dep. atty. gen. Ind., 1949-50; mem. legal com. Interstate Oil Compact Commn., 1950; asst. pub. counselor Ind., 1950-53; mem. law firm Stevens, Wampler, Travis & Fortin, Plymouth, 1953—. Democratic nominee for judge Ind. Supreme Ct., 1956. Served with USNR, 1942-46. Mem. Am., Ind., Marshall County bar assns., Ind. Acad. Sci., Ind. Def. Lawyers Assn. (dir. 1967—, v.p. 1969-70, pres. 1970-71), Ind., Marshall County (dir. 1969—) hist. socs., Assn. Ins. Attys. U.S. and Can., Am. Legion, Phi Delta Phi, Delta Sigma Pi, Elk, Moose. Home: 400 South Michigan St Plymouth IN 46563 Office: 119 West Garro St Plymouth IN 46563

WAMPLER, ROBERT JOSEPH, lawyer; b. Greensboro, Ind., Mar. 3, 1936; s. Cruden V. and Mary Louise (James) W.; B.A., Yale U., 1959; J.D., Ind. U., 1963; div.; 1 son, Eric James. Admitted to Ind. bar, 1963; atty. to sr. partner Kightlinger, Young, Gray & DeTrude, Indpls., 1963—; lectr. products liability law. Mem. Am., Ind., Indpls., 7th Circuit bar assns., Comml. Law League, Order of Coif, Phi Delta Phi. Clubs: Masons, Columbia (Indpls.). Home: 5939 Cape Cod Ct Indianapolis IN 46250 Office: Market Sq Center Suite 660 Indianapolis IN 46204

WAMPLER, WESLEY EARL, accountant, state ofcl.; b. Bicknell, Ind., Dec. 2, 1922; s. H. Earl and Madeline (Stoelting) W.; B.S. in Accounting, Ind. U., 1944; m. Marjorie L. Stiles, Jan. 5, 1944; children—Linda Lou, Vicki Ann. Accountant, Ind. U., Bloomington, 1946-48; accountant, auditor Ind. Bd. Accounts, Indpls., 1949—. Treas., Bloomfield Council of Chs., 1961-63. Served to 1st lt. AUS, 1944-46. C.P.A., Ind. Mem. Ind. Bd. Accounts Field Examiners Assn. (pres. 1963-65), Ind. U. Alumni Club Greene County (pres. 1968-69). Democrat. Methodist (chmn. ofcl. bd., ch. sch. supt.). Mason. Home: 31 N Park Ln Bloomfield IN 47424 Office: State Office Bldg Room 912 Indianapolis IN 46204

WANG, EDWARD DEFORD, communications systems co. exec.; b. Shanghai, China, May 15, 1935; s. Po-Chun and Elizabeth (Pao) W.; came to U.S., 1951, naturalized, 1962; B.M.E., Syracuse U., 1956, M.B.A., 1971; m. Karin M. Seumenicht, Mar. 19, 1972; children—Aaron, Andrea, Kimberly. Mgr. advance product devel. SCM Corp., Syracuse, N.Y., 1957-64; corporate dir. new market devel. Olivetti Corp., Italy, 1964-69; dir. market devel. div. Olivetti Corp. Am., N.Y.C., 1969-71; pres. computer div., corporate v.p. for bus. devel., pres. Victor Bus. Products group Victor Comptometer Corp., Chgo., 1971-75; pres., chmn. Infolink Corp., Northbrook, Ill., 1976—; cons. fin. instns. Mem. Am. Mgmt. Assn., Am. Mktg. Assn. Methodist. Club: Economic (Chgo.). Patentee battery-operated portable electric typewriter; contbr. articles in field to profl. jours. Home: 565 Drexel Ave Glencoe IL 60022 Office: 1925 Holste Rd Northbrook IL 60062

WANG, JOSEPH YUAN, thermal energy engr.; b. Chengtu, China, Dec. 25, 1916; s. E.Y. and Kao (Kao) W.; came to U.S., 1945, naturalized, 1955; B.S., Tsin-Hua U., Peiping, China, 1938; M.S., U. Mich., 1945; m. Ming-Hung Ling, Nov. 11, 1944; children—Don L., Tom L., David L. Asst. to chmn. Chinese Supply Commn., Washington, 1946; project engr. Giffels & Rosseti, Detroit, 1950-58; dep. head dept. A.M. Kinney Inc., Cin., 1958-77; engr. thermal energy Procter & Gamble Co., Cin., 1977—. Served to capt. Chinese Army, 1939-40. Registered profl. engr., Mich., Ohio. Mem. Profl. Engrs. Soc. Detroit, Chinese-Am. Assn. Cin. (pres. 1977). Home: 12012 Cantrell Dr Cincinnati OH 45240 Office: Spring Grove and June Sts Cincinnati OH 45217

WANG, WAYNE LUNG, nuclear physicist, nuclear engr.; b. I-Lan City, Taiwan, Jan. 24, 1944; s. Tien-Hai and Ah-Lung (Yu) Wang; m. Ling L. Wang, Oct. 7, 1967; children—Sherman, Morlie. Diploma, Taipei Inst. Tech., Taiwan, 1964; student U. N.H., 1965-66, Rensselaer Poly. Inst., 1966-67; Ph.D., Mass. Inst. Tech., 1971. Research physicist Carnegie-Mellon U., 1971-73; research physicist Lawrence Berkeley Lab., 1973-75; asst. nuclear engr. Argonne (Ill.) Nat. Lab., 1975—. Mem. Am. Phys. Soc., Am. Nuclear Soc., Sigma Xi. Contbr. articles to profl. jours. Home: 1034 Park Crest Dr Darien IL 60559 Office: Reactor Analysis and Safety Div Argonne Nat Lab Argonne IL 60439

WANGELIN, HARRIS KENNETH, judge; b. Des Moines, Ia., May 10, 1913; s. Fred G. and Pearl Clymer (Harris) W.; grad. Iberia Acad. and Jr. Coll., 1932; student Drury Coll., 1932-33; LL.B., U. Mo., 1936; m. Freda Alice Buffington, June 27, 1939; 1 dau. Judith Arleen. Admitted to Mo. bar, 1936, since practiced in Poplar Bluff; judge U.S. Dist. Ct., St. Louis, 1970—. Trustee U. Mo. Law Sch. Found., 1972—. Mem. Mo. Republican State Com., 1952-66, chmn., 1957-62, chmn. Butler County Central Com., 1950-58; sec. treas. Rocky Mountain Midwest Rep. State Chmns. Assn., 1958-62; vice chmn. Mo. Senatorial Re-districting Commn., 1965. Served as lt. USNR, 1942-45. Decorated Silver Star. Mem. Am., Mo. bar assns., V.F.W., Amvets, Am. Legion, Delta Theta Phi. Conglist. Home: 10374 Chimney Rock Dr Creve Coeur MO 63141 Office: US Court and Custom House 12th and Market Sts St Louis MO 63101

WANGSNESS, WAYNE ROGER, farmer, banker; b. Decorah, Iowa, June 20, 1941; s. Elmer Melvin and Hazel (Orleans) W.; Tech. Agr. Degree, Iowa State U., 1965; B.A. in Economics, Lutheran Coll., 1968; M.A. in Economics (Fellow), U. Iowa, 1971; postgrad. (Rotary Found. fellow) Trinity Coll., Dublin, Ireland, 1969-70; m. Cheryl Ann Lee, Feb. 9, 1974; 1 dau., Amy Lee. Farmer, cattle raiser, Decorah; dir., chmn. Decorah Fed. Land Bank; mem. Agrl. Stblzn. Conservation Twp. Com. Home and Office: Rural Route 1 Decorah IA 52101

WANIEWICZ, IGNACY, broadcasting exec.; b. Cracow, Poland, Dec. 21, 1925; s. Moses David and Rachela (Ziegler) Weinberg; diploma Higher Sch. Polit. Sci. U. Warsaw, 1954; M.Ed., U. Toronto (Ont., Can.), 1974; m. Wilma V. Basser, 1970; children—Janina, Julia, Rebecca. Journalist, editor newspapers, Poprostu, Trybuna Ludu, Warsaw, Poland, 1948-57; dir., editor-in-chief, ednl. broadcasting Polish TV, Warsaw, 1957-63, 65-68; program specialist dept. mass communication UNESCO, Paris, 1963-65; dir. office of planning devel. Ont. Ednl. Communications Authority, Toronto, 1969—; dir. Canadian Communications Research Info. Centre; cons. UNESCO, OAS; guest lectr. U. Warsaw, U. Toronto; producer, dir. TV series How To Look at Art, 1958-63; founder, chief project officer Polish TV Polytechnic, 1965-68. Author: Broadcasting for Adult Education: A Guidebook to World-Wide Experience, 1972; Demand for Part-Time Learning in Ontario, 1976. Home: 11 Burmont Rd Toronto ON M6B 3E2 Canada Office: 2180 Yonge St Toronto ON M4S 2B1 Canada

WANKE, RONALD LEE, lawyer; b. Chgo., June 22, 1941; s. William Fred and Lucille Doris (Kleinwachter) W.; B.S. in Elec. Engring., Northwestern U., 1964; J.D., DePaul U., Chgo., 1968; m. Barbara Ruth Marquard, June 20, 1970. Admitted to Ill. bar, 1968, U.S. Patent Office, 1965; patent agt., firm Wegner, Stellman, McCord, Wiles & Wood, Chgo., 1965-68, asso., 1968-70, partner, 1971—; lectr. Northwestern Law Sch. seminar, 1970. Mem. Am. (chmn. copyright protection for computer software sub com. 1976-77), Chgo. bar assns., Am., Chgo. (vice chmn. govt. relations com. 1971-72, chmn. inventor services com. 1976) patent law assns., Eta Kappa Nu. Mem. staff DePaul Law Rev., 1967-68. Home: 1920 N Clark St Chicago IL 60614 Office: 20 N Wacker Dr Chicago IL 60606

WANNAMAKER, MARY LYMAN, guidance cons.; b. Ft. Collins, Colo., July 29, 1922; d. Jerry Albert and Daisy B. (Burington) Lyman; Mus.B., Colo. State U., 1944; M.A. in Musicology, U. Minn., 1949, M.A. in Ednl. Psychology, 1967; m. John Samuel Wannamaker, Sept. 7, 1946; children—Lois Marie, Daisy Ruth Wannamaker Van Valkenburg. Tchr., Des Moines Pub. Schs., 1958-65; instr., counselor U. Minn., 1966-67; guidance counselor Urbandale (Iowa) Pub. Schs., 1967-75; guidance cons. Area Edn. Agy. XI, Ankeny, Iowa, 1975—; counselor, mem. personnel advisory bd. Drake U., 1974—; pres. career planning service YWCA, 1973-74. Nat. Vocat. Guidance grantee, 1966. Mem. Am., Iowa (pres. chpt. 5) personnel and guidance assns., NEA, Am. Sch. Counselors Assn., AAUW, Profl. Women's League (pres. 1973-74), Royal Neighbors Am., P.E.O. (chmn. chpt. ednl. loan fund), Alpha Delta Kappa, Phi Kappa Phi, Delta Omicron. Club: Altrusa (dir.). Editor: Iowa Personnel and Guidance Bull., 1976—; contbr. articles to profl. jours. Home: 3907 29th St Des Moines IA 50310 Office: 1932 SW 3d St Ankeny IA 50021

WANZEK, ROBERT PAUL, univ. adminstr.; b. Bismark, N.D., June 26, 1931; s. August and Anna (Schultz) W.; B.A., St. Francis Coll., 1953; M.A., U. N.D., 1968, Ph.D., 1972; m. Judith Hendricks, Aug. 10, 1970; children—Jennifer, Jeanne. Secondary sch. adminstr. St. James High Sch., Grand Forks, N.D., 1957-67; chaplain St. Michael Hosp., Grand Forks, 1968-70; adminstr. No. Ill. U., DeKalb, 1970—; cons. Mental Health Center, Grand Forks, 1968-70; asst. dir. adult edn. Eastern Half N.D., 1965-67. No. Ill. U. grantee, 1974. Mem. Am. Personnel and Guidance Assn., Am. Coll. Personnel Assn., Nat. Assn. Fin. Aid Adminstrs., Nat. Orientation Dirs. Assn., Nat. Assn. Student Personnel Adminstrs, Phi Delta Kappa. Club: Kishwaukee Country. Contbr. articles in field to profl. jours.; author: Training Manual for Student Orientation Staff, 1976. Home: 924 S 2d St DeKalb IL 60115 Office: 105 Lowden Hall DeKalb IL 60115

WARD, ADDIS THOMPSON, mcht.; b. Bancroft, Nebr., Oct. 11, 1923; s. Clement Leroy and Florence Emaline (Thompson) W.; student Coll. City N.Y., 1943; B.Sc. in Bus. Adminstrn., U. Nebr., 1949; m. Beverly Ann Sutton, Aug. 22, 1947; children—Nancy, Marcus, Thompson, Susan, Matthew. Sales clk. Miller & Paine Inc., Lincoln, Nebr., 1949-51, dept. mgr., 1951-74, div. mdse. mgr., 1974—. Sr. warden Holy Trinity Episcopal Ch., 1977—. Served to 1st lt. AUS, 1943-46; col. Res. Mem. Lincoln C. of C., Mil. Order World Wars, (comdr. 1973-75), Res. Officers Assn., Sigma Phi Epsilon (pres. Alpha chpt. alumni 1958-74). Republican. Clubs: Executive (pres. 1974), Country of Lincoln (Lincoln). Home: 3039 Stratford Ave Lincoln NE 68502 Office: 1229 O St Lincoln NE 68501

WARD, ALAN JOSEPH, clin. psychologist; b. Boston, May 2, 1936; s. Joseph S. and Rebecca (Myrick) W.; A.B., Brandeis U., 1958; A.M., Temple U., 1960; Ph.D., State U. N.Y., Buffalo, 1965. Caseworker Boston Pub. Welfare Dept., 1959-60; USPHS psychology intern Psychology Clinic, State U. N.Y. at Buffalo, 1960-62; VA psychology intern Neuro-Psychiat. Service, VA Hosp., Buffalo, 1962-64; USPHS postdoctoral fellow in research and clin. psychology Michael Reese Hosp., Psychosomatic and Psychiat. Inst., Chgo., 1964-66; supervising clin. psychologist Eastern State Sch. and Hosp., Trevose, Pa., 1966-70, acting chief psychologist, 1970-71, chief psychologist, 1971-75, dir. autistic children's treatment, tng. and research service, 1966-75; instr. Pa. State U., 1967-68; instr., asso. prof. dept. ednl. psychology Temple U., Phila., 1968-70; pvt. practice psychology, Phila., 1966-75, Chgo., 1975—; instr. dept. psychiatry, children and youth program Jefferson Med. Sch., Phila, 1969—; mem. Gov's. Adv. Task Force on Mental Health of Children and Youth, 1971-75; dir. Henry Horner Children's Center, Chgo.-Read Mental Health Center, 1975—; chmn. subcom. on children and adolescents, Region 2 Orgnl. Change Task Force, Dept. Mental Health, 1975—, rep. to Consortium Children's Services Ill., 1976—, mem. Region 2 Diagnostic Standards of Day Treatment Centers Task Force, 1976—; instr. dept. psychiatry Abraham Lincoln Sch. Medicine, U. Ill., Chgo., 1976—, State U. N.Y. at Buffalo fellow, 1962-63, N.Y. State scholar, 1961-64. Fellow Soc. Projective Techniques, Pa. Psychol. Assn.; mem. AAAS, Am. Soc. Clin. Hypnosis, Am. Assn. Psychiat. Services for Children (mem. program com.), Psychologists Interested in Advancement of Psychotherapy, Am., Midwestern, Eastern, Ill. psychol. assns., Mental Health Assn. Southeastern Pa., Phila. Soc. Clin. Hypnosis (mem. exec. bd.), Phila. Soc. Clin. Psychologists (editor newsletter 1968-71, mem. exec. bd. 1970-73), Sigma Xi. Author: Childhood Autism and Structural Therapay, 1976; contbr. articles to profl. jours. Home: Park Tower-Edgewater Plaza 5415 N Sheridan Rd Apt 4301 Chicago IL 60640 Office: 6500 Irving Park Rd Chicago IL 60634

WARD, ALICE MARIE, civic worker; b. New London, Ohio; d. Clyde Eugene and Daisy (White) Ward; B.A., Ohio Wesleyan U., 1932. Sec., asst. treas. C.E. Ward Co., New London, 1937-72, also dir. Mem. Huron County Republican Women's Club. Recipient Rotary Community Service award, 1975; named to Ohio Wesleyan Sports Hall of Fame, 1977. Mem. New London Bus. and Profl. Women's Club (pres. 1967-68, 72—), U.S. Lawn Tennis Assn., Mortar Board, Alpha Xi Delta. Clubs: Medalist, Southwood Tennis. Methodist. Mem. Order Eastern Star. Composer songs In the Swim, 1959; Tennis for Everyone, 1963; I Hear a Bird Singing, 1963. Home: 139 E Main St New London OH 44851

WARD, ALVA JOHN, mgmt. cons.; b. Evanston, Ill., Apr. 22, 1921; s. Cyril Lyon and Francis (Fisher) W.; B.S. in Elec. Engring., Northwestern U., 1943, postgrad., 1947-50; m. Jean Skillen, Dec. 18, 1943; children—John L., Jay R., James A. Project engr. Sargent & Lundy, Chgo., 1946-50; asst. sales mgr. S & C Electric Co., Chgo., 1950-54; product mgr. Reliance Electric Co., Cleve., 1954-57; div. mgr. Warner Electric Co., South Beloit, Ill., 1957-58; mgr. mktg. services Sundstrand Corp., Rockford, Ill., 1958-61; sr. cons. A.T. Kearney & Co., Chgo., 1961-64; pres. Mgmt. Research & Planning, Inc., Evanston, Ill., 1964—; cons. industry devel. U.S. Dept. State, ICA, AID, 1960-63. Trustee, chmn. planning com. Village of Golf (Ill.), 1975-79. Served with Signal Corps, AUS, 1946. Recipient Recognition awards for mgmt. edn. Am. Mgmt. Assn., 1966, Japan Mktg. Assn., 1959, Sales Execs. of Mexico, 1960, Bolivia Mgmt. Assn., 1965. Mem. Nat. Assn. Bus. Economists, Inst. Mgmt. Scis., Am. Mktg. Assn., Acad. Mgmt., Eta Kappa Nu, Pi Mu Epsilon. Contbr. articles to bus. jours. Home: 28 Park Ln Golf IL 60029 Office: 820 Davis St Evanston IL 60201

WARD, DANIEL P., state judge; b. Chgo., Aug. 30, 1918; s. Patrick and Jane (Convery) W.; student St. Viator Coll., 1936-38; J.D., DePaul U., 1941, D.H.L., 1976; LL.D., John Marshall Law Sch., 1972; m. Marilyn Corleto, June 23, 1951; children—Mary Jane, John, Susan, and Elizabeth Ward. Admitted to Fed. bar, Ill. bar; asst. prof. law Southeastern U., Washington, 1941-42; pvt. practice of law, 1945-48; asst. U.S. atty. No. Dist. of Ill., 1948-54, chief criminal div., 1951-54; with Eardley & Ward, Chgo., 1954-55; dean Coll. Law, DePaul U., 1955-60; states atty., Cook County, Ill., 1960-66; judge Supreme Ct. Ill., 1966—, chief justice, 1976—. Chmn. Ill. Courts Commn., 1969-73. Served with AUS, 1942-45. Mem. Am., Fed., Ill., Chgo. bar assns. Roman Catholic. 11000 Kingston Ave Westchester IL 60153

WARD, DONALD EARL, educator; b. Hammond, Ind., Nov. 30, 1946; s. Earl Robert and Dorothy Helen (Foster) W.; B.A. (Edward Rector scholar), DePauw U., 1969; M.S. (NDEA fellow), Purdue U., 1970, Ph.D., 1973; m. Susan Jane Gordon, Nov. 27, 1971. Asst. prof., counseling psychologist Ball State U., Muncie, Ind., 1973-76; asst. prof. dept. psychology and counselor edn., counselor Pittsburg (Kans.) State U., 1976—, dir. Inst. for Career Devel. with The Non-Coll. Bound, 1977. Mem. Am., Kans. personnel and guidance assns., Am., Kans. assns. counselor educators and suprs., Kans. Vocat. Guidance Assn., Am. Ednl. Research Assn. Home: 411 1/2 E 8th St Pittsburg KS 66762 Office: 134 Russ Hall Pittsburg State U Pittsburg KS 66762

WARD, DONALD MAXWELL, dentist; b. Detroit, Dec. 21, 1917; s. Harold Bliss and Gertrude Ruth (Wood) W.; student Flint Jr. Coll., 1935-36, Wayne State U., 1936-37; B.A., U. Mich., 1940, D.D.S., 1944; postgrad. Northwestern U., 1958, U. Mich., 1960-72; children—Jacquelyn (Mrs. Hugh Wygmans), Wendy (Mrs. Gregory List), Cindy (Mrs. Robert Wickham), Bradley, Wayne. Pvt. practice dentistry, Detroit, 1946-47, Saginaw, Mich., 1947—. Prosthodontist, sec. bd. Saginaw Gen. Hosp. Cleft Palate Team, 1956-67. Sec., Pit and Balcony Inc., Saginaw, Mich., 1949-51. Trustee, sec. Saginaw Twp. Bd. Edn., 1961-62. Served with Dental Corps, USNR, 1944-46. Mem. Saginaw County (past pres.), Saginaw Valley Dist. dental socs., Mich. Assn. Professions, Am., Mich. dental assns., Am. Cleft Palate Assn. (hon. life), Saginaw Bus. and Profl. Men (mem. Goodwill Tour Team to USSR, Czechoslovakia 1959), U. Mich. Union (life), Am. Sunbathing Assn. (life), Mich. United Conservation Clubs, Nat. Wildlife Fedn., Smithsonian Assos., Inter Pacific, Nat. Geog. Soc., Delta Sigma Delta (life). Presbyn. Elk (life). Clubs: Saginaw Ski, Germania, Colony, Knife and Fork, Saginaw Field and Stream. Home: 3548 Doncaster Ct S Saginaw MI 48603 Office: 3422 Davenport St Saginaw MI 48602

WARD, EVELYN SVEC (MRS. WILLIAM E. WARD), artist: b. Solon, Ohio, Aug. 15, 1921; d. Charles and Lydia (Pravda) Svec; B.A., Otterbein Coll., 1943; postgrad. Sorbonne, Paris, France, summer 1952; m. William E. Ward. Nov. 12, 1952; 1 dau., Pamela. Asst. in textiles Cleve. Mus. Art, 1944-54; stitchery exhibited Cleve. Mus. of Art, 1955-76, Chagrin Valley Artists Ann. Exhbns., 1955-64, Carriage Barn Gallery, Oglebay Park, W.Va., 1955, Ohio Crafts Exhbn. Columbus Gallery Fine Art, 1962, 66, 68, 70, Artists of Chagrin Valley, Chatauqua, N.Y., 1958, Women's City Club Cleve., 1965, 69, Bloomfield Art Assn., Birmingham Mich., 1966, Foresta Hodgson Meml., Scarborough Sch., 1966, Park Synagogue Art Festival, Cleve., 1966, Mus. Contemporary Crafts, N.Y., 1967, Solon Pub. Library, 1968, 70, Oneonta (N.Y.) Community Art Center, 1969, Textile Arts Club, Cleve., 1969, 70, 71, 72, 73, 74, 75, Grand Rapids (Mich.) Art Mus., 1970, Boundless Limitations Exhbn., 1970, Ohio Designer-Craftsman Exhbn., 1971, 72, 2d Ann. All-Ohio Exhbn., 1971, Beaux-Arts Designer-Craftsman Exhbn., 1972, Ball State U., 1972; exhibited one-woman shows Ross Widen Gallery, Cleve., 1973, Ashtabula (Ohio) Arts Center, 1974, Ohio Craft Invitational, Mansfield Art Center, 1975, Carnegie Inst. Mus. Art, Pitts., 1976; represented in permanent collections including Cleve. Mus. Art. Trustee Textile Arts Club of Cleve. Mus. Art. Recipient Air Maze award Chagrin Valley Artists Exhbn., 1957; Second prize Cleve. Mus. Art, 1957. Mem. Cleve. Mus. Art (mem. jr. council 1962—, 3d vice chmn. 1971-72, 76-77, sec. 1973-74), Cleve. Inst. Art, Cleve. Soc. Contemporary Art, Print Club of Cleve., Am. Craftsmens Council. Club: Women's City of Cleve. (mem. visual arts com., 1961-70). Home: 27045 Solon Rd Solon OH 44139

WARD, HENSEL OWEN, psychologist; b. Columbus, Ohio, Jan. 24, 1921; s. Thomas Kay and Ada Alma (Owen) W.; m. Alma Louise Strader, Apr. 21, 1946; children—Hensel, Owen, Jenny Yvonne (Mrs. Steven Neil Veigel), Justin Derek. Student, Baldwin Wallace Coll., 1943-44, Notre Dame U., 1944; B.A., Ohio State U., 1947, M.A., 1948, Ph.D., 1959. Intern, Ohio State U., Columbus 1949-51, Jackson Assos., Columbus, 1959-61; asso. Ohio State U., Columbus 1950-51, fellow, 1951-54; research psychologist CAA Med. Research Lab., Columbus, 1954-58; pres. Midwestern Psychol. Services, Inc., Columbus, 1961—; cons. Ford Motor Co., Dearborn, Mich., 1960-61, N.Am. Aviation Corp., 1961-62; dir. Alfred Willson Children's Center, Columbus, 1962-65, Ednl. Skills Tng. Center, 1965—. Served to lt. J.G., USNR, 1943-46. Mem. Am., Ohio, Central Ohio psychol. assns., AAAS. Club: Athletic (Columbus). Home: 1829 Baldridge Rd Columbus OH 43221 Office: 1188 W 5th Ave Columbus OH 43212

WARD, HOWARD NELSON, hematologist, oncologist; b. Mt. Vernon, Ill., Dec. 30, 1937; s. Harry Seborn and Jenny Willana (Jeffries) W.; student U. Ill., 1955-58; B.S., Northwestern U., 1959, M.D. with distinction, 1962; m. Marilyn Jean Strobel, July 13, 1958; children—Martha Lyn, Howard Jeffries. Intern Chgo. Wesley Meml. Hosp., 1962-63; resident Barnes Hosp., St. Louis, 1963-66, chief resident, 1968-69; fellow in hematology, 1964-65; practice medicine specializing in hematology and oncology, St. Louis, 1969, Topeka, 1969—; mem. staffs Stormont-Vail Hosp., St. Francis Hosp., Meml. Hosp. (all Topeka, Kans.); instr. medicine Washington U., 1968, instr. clin. medicine, 1969; asst. prof. medicine U. Kans., 1973—; faculty Menninger Sch. Psychiatry, 1975—. Trustee 1st United Meth. Ch., Topeka, 1973-74. Served with USAF, 1966-68. Diplomate Am. Bd. Internal Medicine. Fellow A.C.P.; mem. Am. Soc. Clin. Oncology, Am., Internat. socs. hematology, Kans., Shawnee County med. socs., AMA, Alpha Omega Alpha, Omega Beta Pi. Republican. Methodist. Club: Masons. Contbr. articles to med. jours. Home: 3126 W 15th St Topeka KS 66604 Office: 901 Garfield Topeka KS 66606

WARD, JAMES RAYMOND, physician; b. Canton, Ohio, Jan. 27, 1926; s. J. Ray and Evelyn (Volzer) W.; student Kenyon Coll., 1943-44; M.D., Johns Hopkins U., 1948; m. Peggy L. Solenberger, Aug. 21, 1945; children—Kristina, Suzanne, Andrew Curtis, Pamela. Intern, Johns Hopkins Hosp., Balt., 1948-49; resident internal medicine Cin. Gen. Hosp., 1949-52, research and clin. fellow gastroenterology, 1952-54; chief of gastroenterology, asst. chief medicine Wm. Beaumont Army Hosp., El Paso, Tex., 1954-56; practice medicine, specializing in internal medicine and gastroenterology, Canton, 1956—; mem. active staff Aultman Hosp.; mem. cons. staff Molly Stark Hosp. Active Aultman Hosp. Bldg. Fund, 1956-70, United Fund, 1956-70. Served to capt. U.S. Army, 1954-56. Diplomate Am. Bd. Internal Medicine. Fellow A.C.P. Republican. Presbyterian. Contbr. articles to profl. jours. Home: 2304 Glenmont St NW Canton OH 44708 Office: 214 Dartmouth St SW Canton OH 44710

WARD, JAMES SHERIDAN, physician; b. Chgo., Apr. 9, 1929; s. William Morgan and Lillian Edna (Sheridan) W.; B.S., State U. Iowa, 1951, M.D., 1956; m. Barbara Jane Jacobs, Nov. 17, 1956; children—Elizabeth, James, Michael, Stephen, Rebecca, Carolyn. Intern, Queen of Angels Hosp., Los Angeles, 1956-57; resident Lafayette Clinic, Detroit, 1957-60; asst. prof. psychiatry U. Iowa, 1962-65; supt. Zeller Zowe Center, Peoria, Ill., 1965-76; pvt. practice psychiatry, Peoria, 1976—; regional adminstr. Ill. Dept. Mental Health, 1971-76. Served to lt. cmdr. USN, 1960-62. Recipient Walter Baer award Illinois Valley Mental Health Assn., 1976. Fellow Am. Psychiat. Assn.; mem. A.C.P., AMA, Inst. Phys. Medicine and Rehab. (dir.). Republican. Roman Catholic. Home: 123 E Coventry St Peoria IL 61614 Office: 515 NE Glen Oak St Peoria IL 61603

WARD, JOHN LANGDON, physician; b. Medford, Mass., Apr. 6, 1908; s. Paul Theodore Bliss and Helen (Ashton Ward) W.; B.A., Amherst Coll., 1929; M.D., Harvard U., 1933; m. Grace Pomeroy Porter, June 23, 1933; children—Mary Richards Ward Gover, Samuel Porter, Alice Brewer Ward Trotter. Intern, Mass. Gen. Hosp., Boston, 1934-35; practice medicine specializing in internal medicine, Medford, 1935-42, Lake Bluff, Ill., 1946—; mem. staff Lake Forest Hosp.; cons. VA Hosp., N. Chicago; clin. asso. prof. medicine Chgo. Med. Sch., 1974—. Moderator, Union Ch. of Lake Bluff. Served to lt. comdr., M.C, USN, 1943-46. Diplomate Am. Bd. Internal Medicine. Mem. Lake County, Ill. med. socs., AMA. Home and Office: 600 Scranton Ave Lake Bluff IL 60044

WARD, PATRICIA SPAIN, historian; b. Davenport, Iowa, Nov. 28, 1931; d. Marceda Ligouri and Nola Ardel (Lensch) Spain; B.A., U. Colo., 1954; M.A., Johns Hopkins U., 1963; m. Robert F. Ward, Aug. 18, 1956, (div. 1973); 1 dau., Lydia. Asst. editor Isis: Internat. Rev. Devoted to History of Sci. and Its Cultural Influences, 1961; mem. academic staff U. Wis., Dept. of History of Medicine, 1976-77, Maurice Richardson fellow, 1976—. Recipient Research grant, Nat. Inst. Mental Health, 1958-61, Nat. Library Medicine Research grant, 1974-77; Johns Hopkins Centennial Scholar, 1976. Mem. Am. Hist. Assn., Orgn. Am. Historians, Soc. Health and Human Values, Am. Assn. for History of Medicine, Am. Inst. History of Pharmacy. Contbr. med. articles to Notable Am. Women, 1971, Dictionary Am. Biography, 1973, 74. Home: 2334 W Lawn Av Madison WI 53711 Office: 1305 Linden Dr Madison WI 53706

WARD, SYLVAN DONALD, educator, music conductor; b. Rock Springs, Wyo., July 7, 1909; s. Samuel and Hannah (Davis) W.; B.Mus., Chgo. Mus. Coll., 1931, M.Mus., 1932; M.S. in Edn., Northwestern U., 1934, M.Edn., 1946; D.Mus. Edn., Chgo. Mus. Coll., 1954; m. Beatrice Dorrell Stackhouse, June 27, 1936; children—Dorrell Deen (Mrs. Gordon H. Williams), Susan Diane (Mrs. William D. Johnston), Jill Dawn (Mrs. George Manderino), Jack Donald, Nancy Deborah. Advt. mgr. Edn. Music mag., Chgo., 1931-36, asso. editor edn., 1937-43; asst. gen. mgr. edn. Music Bur., 1936-37; tchr. instrumental and vocal music Farragut High Sch., Chgo., 1936-49; instr. music Chgo. Mus. Coll., 1946-51, Chgo. Tchrs. Coll., 1949-58, Wilson Jr. Coll., part-time, 1951-63, also Crane Jr. Coll. and Loop Jr. Coll., 1965; vis. prof. U. Ill., summers 1959-61; prof. music Chgo. State U., 1958-77, chmn. dept. music, 1958-72; dir. Chgo. Regional Mormon Choir, 1935—; condr., mus. dir. Chgo. Business Men's Orch., 1963-68, 77; mem. Chgo. State U. String Quartet, 1952-77, Chgo. String Trio, 1960—, stage orch. Chgo. Lyric Opera Co., 1960-69; tchr. Vandercook Coll. Music, 1975—. Served with USAAF, 1943-45. Mem. NEA, Music Educators Nat. Conf., Ill. Music Educators Assn., Music Tchrs. Nat. Assn., Am. Choral Dirs. Assn., Am. Fedn. Musicians, Am. String Tchr. Assn. (pres. Ill. unit 1959-63; editor Scroll 1961-63), Phi Mu Alpha. Mem. Ch. of Jesus Christ Latter Day Saints (bishop 1963-72, mem. high council Chicago Heights Stake 1972-73). Author books, articles in field. Home: 2131 W 107th St Chicago IL 60643

WARD, THOMAS GENE, ednl. adminstr.; b. Saginaw, Mich., Aug. 9, 1932; s. Cletus Alphonsus and Bernice Margaret (LaFayette) W.; A.A., Bay City Jr. Coll., 1953; B.A., Mich. State U., 1955; M.Ed., Wayne State U., 1961; m. Therese Ann Solosky, Aug. 6, 1960; children—Thomas M., Jonathan J., Douglas Allan. Profl. actor, 1957; tchr. elementary and secondary schs., Detroit, 1958-69, Saginaw, 1969-70, Meridian, Mich., 1970-74; mem. supportive services div. Meridian Pub. Schs., Sanford, Mich., 1974—, Title I dir., 1976—, spl. edn., dir., 1974—. Mem. Midland County Spl. Edn. Advisory Council; speech cons. Head Start Project, Detroit. Served with USNR, 1955-57. Mem. Am., Mich. speech and hearing assns., NEA, Mich., Meridian (pres.) edn. assns., Council for Exceptional Children, Mich. Reading Assn., Mich. Assn. Adminstrs. in Spl. Edn. Roman Catholic. Home: 2112 Wilmington Dr Midland MI 48640 Office: 3361 N M-30 Sanford MI 48657

WARD, VELMA LEWIS, biochemist; b. Columbus, Ohio, Dec. 27, 1932; foster dau. John Franklin and Anna Clara (Robinson) Lewis; student U. Mich., 1947-49; B.S., Wayne State U., 1953, M.S., 1961; 1 son, Broderick Lewis. Jr. med. technologist Detroit Gen. Hosp., 1953-54; research technologist, dept. medicine Coll. Medicine Wayne State U., 1954-55; supr. med. lab., biochemistry dept. Lafayette Clinic, Detroit, 1956-69, research asso. biochemistry dept., chief clin. lab., 1960—. Bd. dirs. Detroit Met. Black Arts. Fellow Am. Inst. Chemists; mem. Am. Chem. Soc., Am. Soc. Clin. Pathologists (affiliate mem., registered med. technologist), Am. Soc. Med. Tech., N.Y. Acad. Scis., Detroit Physiol. Soc., Sigma Xi, Alpha Delta Theta, Alpha Kappa Alpha. Contbr. articles in field to profl. jours. Home: 18500 Littlefield St Detroit MI 48235 Office: 951 E Lafayette St Detroit MI 48207

WARD, VERNON GRAVES, internist; b. Palisade, Nebr., Mar. 5, 1928; s. Charles Bennett and Mildred Belle (Graves) W.; A.B., Nebr. Wesleyan U., 1948; M.D., U. Nebr., 1954; m. Eleanore Mae Farstveet, Aug. 28, 1952; children—Margo, Alison, Barry. Instr. anatomy Columbia U. Coll. Physicians and Surgeons, N.Y.C., 1948-50; intern, resident U. Wis. dept. medicine, Madison, 1954-58, 1961-62; fellow in neurophysiology and psychosomatic medicine U. Okla., Oklahoma City, 1960-61; asso. prof. U. Nebr. Coll. Medicine, Omaha, 1969—; Nebr. Heart Assn. grantee, 1975. Served with USN, 1958-60. Diplomate Am. Bd. Internal Medicine. Mem. AMA, Nebr. Med. Assn., Omaha Med. Soc., A.C.P. (Hutton traveling scholar 1965), Am. Psychosomatic Soc., Am. Rheumatism Assn. Republican. Lutheran. Clubs: Lions (Omaha). Home: 302 N 54th St Omaha NE 68132 Office: 309 Doctors Bldg Omaha NE 68131

WARD, WILLIAM EDWARD, museum exhibition designer; b. Cleve., Apr. 4, 1922; s. Edward and Lura Dell (Eckelberry) W.; B.S., Western Res. U., 1947, M.A., 1948; diploma Cleve. Inst. Art, 1947; postgrad. Columbia U., 1950; m. Evelyn Svec, Nov. 12, 1952; 1 dau., Pamela. Mem. staff edn., Oriental depts. Cleve. Mus. Art, 1947—, designer, 1957—; instr. Calligraphy and watercolor Cleve. Inst. Art, 1960—; cons. graphic and installation exhbn. Exhibited in numerous exhbns.; designer George Gund Collection of Western Art Mus., 1972; Firemen's Meml., Cleve., sculpture design, 1968; designer ofcl. seals Case Western Res. U., also Sch. Medicine, 1969; curator Culcon exhbn. Masterpieces of World Art from Am. Museums, Tokyo and Kyoto, Japan, 1976. Mem. Internat. Design Conf., Aspen, 1959—; mem. Fine Arts Adv. Com. City Cleve., 1966—; mem. mayor's com. for selection of ofcl. seal City of Cleve., 1973. Served with Terrain Intelligence, AUS, 1942-45; CBI. Recipient commn. award City Canvis competition Cleve. Area Arts Council, 1975. Mem. Cleve. Soc. Contemporary Art, Print Club Cleve. Club: Rowfant (Cleve.). Home: 27045 Solon Rd Solon OH 44139 Office: Cleve Mus Art 11150 E Boulevard Cleveland OH 44106

WARD, WILLIAM GATES, journalist, photographer, educator; b. Hanley, Sask., Can., Mar. 4, 1929 (parents Am. citizens); s. Edward G. and Lucie E. (Gates) W.; B.S., Mankato State Coll., 1953, M.S., 1958; m. Juliana de Francois. Tchr., coach, Grove City, Minn., 1953-55, Glendive, Mont., 1955-57, Rochester, Minn., 1960-63; journalist Free Press, Mankato, 1947-50, 53, 63-64, Sun-Telegram San Bernardino, Calif., 1958-59, Mpls. Tribune, 1960; asst. prof. Syracuse (N.Y.) U., 1964-66; asso. prof. journalism Nev. U., Reno, 1966-69; prof., dir. journalism So. Ill. U., 1969—. Bd. judges Asso. Collegiate Press, 1964—, adv. editor to Scholastic Editor, 1966—. Served with AUS 1951-53. Named one of Journalism Tchrs. of Years, Newspaper Fund, Inc., 1963; named Pioneer in Journalism Edn., Nat. Scholastic Press Assn., 1970. Mem. Nat. Press Photographers Assn., Assn. for Edn. in Journalism, Kappa Tau Alpha, Sigma Delta Chi. Author: A Text for Scholastic Journalism, 1967; The Student Journalist and Creative Writing, 1967; 4 texts about editorial leadership, 1969; Common Story Assignments, 1970; The Student Press, 1971, 73; Depth Reporting, 1971; Writing in Journalism, 1971; My Kingdom for Just One Strackeljahn, 1972; The Photographer as Reporter, 1974; Creative Photography, 1976; The Student Journalist as an Editor, 1977. Contbr. essays, review, articles, photographs to mags.; co-editor: The Journalism Educator, 1969. Home: Box 347 Hamel IL 62046 Office: Journalism Dept Southern Ill U Edwardsville IL 62025

WARD, WILLIS WESLEY, mktg. cons.; b. South Bend, Ind., July 14, 1923; s. Charles C. and Grace (Showalter) W.; A.B., DePauw U., 1947; M.B.A., Miami U., 1949; M.A., U. Va., 1951; m. Mary Jane Altman, Nov. 3, 1951; 1 dau., Marsha Jane. Instr., Miami U., 1948-49; extension drama specialist U. Va., 1949-51; mktg. researcher Davee-Koehnlein-Keating, Chgo., 1951-53; merchandising specialist Altman's Cash Feed Stores, Pitts., 1953-56; asst. mgr. Altman Feed Mills, Troy, O., 1956-65; media and research Northlich Stolley, Cin., 1965-71; v.p. research dir. Fahlgren & Ferriss, Inc., 1971-76; mktg. cons., 1976—; lectr., Wright State U., 1966-68, Edison State Coll., 1976-77. Pres., Troy Bd. Edn., 1963-65; Sesquicentennial narrator, 1963; dir. Troy Civic Theatre. Served with AUS, 1943-46. Mem. Am. Mktg. Assn. (pres. Cin. chpt. 1973-74), Phi Beta Kappa, Lambda Chi Alpha, Phi Eta Sigma, Beta Gamma Sigma, Delta Sigma Rho. Presbyterian (elder). Home: 1131 Fairway Rd Troy OH 45373 Office: PO Box 255 Troy OH 45373

WARDLOW, ERVIN E., retail co. exec.; b. 1921. With S.S. Kresge Co., Detroit, 1939—, store mgr., 1951-55, supt. stores, 1955-58, asst. sales dir., 1958-61, sales dir., gen. merchandise mgr., 1961-68, v.p. sales, 1968-70, exec. v.p. mdse., 1970-72, pres., 1972—, also dir. Office: 3100 W Big Beaver Rd Troy MI 48084

WARE, RICHARD ANDERSON, found. exec.; b. N.Y.C., Nov. 7, 1919; s. John Sayers and Mabelle (Anderson) W.; B.A., Lehigh U., 1941; M. Pub. Adminstrn., Wayne State U., 1943; m. Lucille Henney, Mar. 20, 1942 (div. 1972); children—Alexander W., Janet M., Bradley J., Patricia E.; m. Beverly G. Mytinger, Dec. 22, 1972. Research asst. Detroit Bur. Govt. Research, 1941-42; personnel technician Lend-Lease Adminstrn., Washington, 1942-43; research asso. to asst. dir. Citizens Research Council, Detroit, 1946-56; sec. Earhart and Relm Founds., Ann Arbor, Mich., 1956-70, trustee, pres., 1970—; (on leave) prin. dep. asst. sec. def. Internat. Security Affairs, Washington, 1969-70, cons. Office Asst. Sec. Def., 1970-73. Dir. Ann Arbor Trust Co. Vice pres. Ann Arbor United Fund and Community Services, 1968, pres., 1969; asst. dir. Mich. Joint Legis. Com. on State Reorgn., 1950-52; sec. Gov.'s Com. to Study Prisons, 1952-53; com. to chmn. Ann Arbor City Planning Commn., 1958-67; mem. Detroit Com. on Fgn. Relations, 1971; mem. adv. council Woodrow Wilson Internat. Center for Scholars, 1973—. Polit. analyst Republican Nat. Com., Washington, 1964. Trustee Greenhills Sch., 1973—; mem. vis. com. Div. Social Scis. U. Chgo., 1977—; mem. adv. com. The Citadel, 1977—. Served with USAAF, 1943-46. Recipient Civilian Meritorious Service medal Dept. Def., 1970. Mem. Govtl. Research Asso. (trustee, v.p. 1955-56), Am. Polit. Sci. Assn., Am. Soc. Pub. Adminstrn., Mont Pelerin Soc., Phi Beta Kappa, Phi Alpha Theta. Conglist. Clubs: Ann Arbor; Barton Hills Country, Cosmos (Washington). Home: 16 Haverhill Ct Ann Arbor MI 48105 Office: 904 First Nat Bldg Ann Arbor MI 48108

WARFORD, JOHN HOWARD, II, orthodontist; b. Milaca, Minn., Mar. 9, 1946; s. John Howard and Ruthine S. (Berg) W.; B.A., U. Minn., 1968, B.S. with distinction, 1968, D.D.S., 1971; M.S. in Orthodontics, Northwestern U., 1973; m. Jennifer Jo Held, June 19, 1971; children—John Howard, Andrew Held. Practice dentistry specializing in orthodontics, Bismarck, N.D., 1973—; cons. orthodontics Crippled Children's Services, N.D., 1973; lectr. Normandale Community Coll., 1973-74; chmn. Children's Dental Health Week, Bismarck, 1976. Fund raiser YMCA, Bismarck, 1975-76; trustee St. Ann's Ch., Bismarck, 1977—. Named All Am., High Sch. Basketball, 1964; Williams scholar, U. Minn., 1968; recipient Orthodontic award Minn. Soc. Orthodontists, 1973. Mem. ADA, Minn., N.D. dental assns., Am., Minn., N.D. socs. orthodontists. Republican. Roman Catholic. Club: Apple Creek Country. Home: 1302 Northview Ln Bismarck ND 58501 Office: 314 E Thayer Ave Bismarck ND 58501

WARINNER, DOUGLAS KEITH, research engr.; b. Little Falls, Minn., Jan. 20, 1941; s. Royal Henry and Lorraine Geraldine (Stolhanske) W.; student U. Colo., 1964, Sacramento City Coll., 1961-62; B.S. in Elec. Engring., U. Calif. at Davis, 1965, M.S. in Mech. Engring., 1968; Ph.D. in Mech. Engring. (David Ross fellow), Purdue U., 1973; m. Kathleen Tin-Ling Tam, May 28, 1967; children—Derek Keith, Sonja Anne. Surveyor, Oreg. Hwy. Dept., Brookings, 1958-59; party chief Western Engring. Cons., Eugene, Oreg., 1959-61, Norman Glover, Surveyor, Woodland, Calif., 1961; div. surveyor Pacific Gas and Electric Co., Sacramento, 1961-62; party chief Laugenour & Meikle Civil Engrs., Woodland, 1962-64; teaching asst. U. Calif. at Davis, 1965-67; aerodynamicist Naval Weapons Center, China Lake, Calif., 1967-68; research asst., teaching asst. Purdue U., West Lafayette, Ind., 1968-71; asst. prof. ocean engring. Fla. Atlantic U., Boca Raton, 1971-75; research engring. analyst Argonne (Ill.) Nat. Lab., 1975—; adj. asso. prof. Ill. Inst. Tech., 1977—; cons. McGraw-Hill Pub. Co., 1973—. Asst. voter registrar Tippecanoe County, Lafayette, Ind., 1970; elections judge, DuPage County, Ill., 1976—. Registered profl. engr., Fla. Mem. Am. Soc. Engring. Edn., Am. Soc. Mech. Engrs., Am. Inst. Aeros. and Astronautics, Sigma Xi. Home: 8 S 237 Winwood Way Downers Grove IL 60515 Office: 9700 S Cass St Argonne IL 60439

WARM, JOEL SEYMOUR, educator; b. Bklyn., Sept. 28, 1933; s. Abraham and Stella (Kaplan) W.; B.S., City Coll. of City U. N.Y., 1956, M.S., 1958; Ph.D., U. Ala., 1966; m. Frances Goldberg, July 31, 1966; children—Eric Jay, Ellen Sue. Research asst. U.S. Army Med. Research Lab., Fort Knox, Ky., 1958-60; instr. psychology U. Bridgeport, 1963-64; adj. asst. prof., research asso. U. Louisville, 1964-67; asst. prof. pschology U. Cin., 1967-72, asso. prof., 1972-75, prof., 1975—; participant NATO Symposium on Vigilance, 1976. Served with AUS, 1958-60. Mem. Am. Psychol. Assn., AAAS, Psychonomic Soc., So. Soc. Philosophy and Psychology, N.Y. Acad. Sci., Midwestern Psychol. Assn., Sigma Xi, Psi Chi. Contbr. articles to profl. jours. Home: 936 Finney Trail Cincinnati OH 45224

WARMBROD, JAMES ROBERT, educator; b. Belvidere, Tenn., Dec. 13, 1929; s. George Victor and Anna Sophia (Zimmerman) W.; B.S., U. Tenn., 1952, M.S., 1954; Ed.D., U. Ill., 1962; m. Catharine P. Phelps, Jan. 30, 1965. Instr. edn. U. Tenn., Knoxville, 1956-57; tchr. high sch. Winchester, Tenn., 1957-59; asst. to asso. prof. U. Ill., Urbana, 1961-67; prof. Ohio State U., Columbus, 1968—; vis. prof. Pa. State U., 1970, U. Minn., 1971, Ia. State U., 1974. Served with USAF, 1954-56. U. Ill. fellow, 1959-60; recipient Ohio State U. Alumni award distinguished teaching, 1972; distinguished service award Am. Assn. Tchrs. Educators in Agr., 1974; Ohio State U. Gamma Sigma Delta teaching award, 1977. Mem. Am. Vocat. Assn., Am. Ednl. Research Assn. (chmn. spl. interest group on vocat. edn. 1972), Am. Vocat. Edn. Research Assn. (pres. 1976), Am. Assn. Tchr. Educators in Agr., Nat. Soc. for Study Edn. Author: Review and Synthesis of Research on the Economics of Vocational Education, 1968; The Liberalization of Vocational Education, 1974. Editor: Agrl. Edn. Mag., 1968-71. Home: 3867 Mountview Rd Columbus OH 43220

WARNE, KEITH WARNELL, librarian; b. Hetland, S.D., Nov. 3, 1919; s. James Clyde and Margaret Maude (Wilcox) W.; B.A., Yankton Coll., 1943; M.A., U. S.D., 1949; M.A., U. Minn., 1953. Tchr. high sch., S.D., 1947-52; asst. librarian U. Nebr., Lincoln, 1953-55; reference librarian Rochester (Minn.) Public Library, 1956; documents librarian N.D. State U., Fargo, 1957-63; asst. librarian No. State Coll., Aberdeen, 1963-69, asso. librarian, 1969-73, asso. dir. library, 1973—. Served with AUS, 1943-45. Mem. Am., S.D. (pres. 1972) library assns., N.Y Shavians, Blue Key, Phi Delta Kappa. Elk. Home: 1223 S Main St Aberdeen SD 57401 Office: Northern State College Aberdeen SD 57401

WARNE, RALPH DICK, ins. co. exec.; b. Hillsboro, Ohio, Dec. 16, 1923; s. James Roy and Mary Jane (Dick) W.; B.S. in Bus. Adminstrn., Ohio State U., 1947; m. Dorothy Louis Brandeberry, June 30, 1957; children—Jane Lynn, Joyce Kay. State agent Hartford Accident Indemnity Co., Pitts., 1947-51; state mgr. Mass. Bonding and Ins. Co., Columbus, 1951-53; pres., C.E.O. Conva Indemnity Co., Columbus, Ohio, 1969—; pres., C.E.O. R.D. Warne & Assocs., Columbus, 1956—; cons. Ohio Hosp. Assn. Mem. areawide project review com. Mid-Ohio Health Planning Fedn., 1976—. Mem. Ohio Health Care Assn., Columbus C. of C., Ohio State Univ. Alumna Club, Upper Arlington Civic Assn. Lutheran. Clubs: Columbus University, Scioto Country. Home: 1287 Darcann Dr Columbus OH 43220 Office: 2100 Tremont Center Columbus OH 43221

WARNER, DENNIS EUGENE, mech. engr.; b. Piqua, Ohio, Dec. 23, 1949; s. Ralph Emerson and Margaret Lucille (Layer) W.; B.S. in Aero. Engring., Purdue U., 1973, M.S. Engring. (Gen. Motors fellow), 1976; m. Mary Jane Harrold, Aug. 22, 1970; children—Carrie Leigh, Gretchen Lynn. Coop. edn. participant Detroit Diesel Allison div. Gen. Motors Corp., at Purdue U., 1969-72, control systems engr., Indpls., 1973-76, advanced control systems engr., 1976—. Democrat. Mem. Ch. of Brethren. Club: Westwood Country. Contbr. articles to profl. jours. Home: 2519 Philwood Dr Speedway IN 46224 Office: PO Box 894 Speed Code T4 Indianapolis IN 46202

WARNER, DON LEE, geol. engr., educator; b. Norfolk, Nebr., Jan. 4, 1934; s. Donald A. and Cleo V. (Slagel) W.; Geol. Engr., Colo. Sch. Mines, 1956, M.S. (fellow), 1961; Ph.D., U. Calif. at Berkeley, 1964; m. Patricia Ann Walker, Feb. 24, 1957; children—Mark J., Scott Lee. Various positions industry, govt., univs., 1956-64; research geologist, engr. USPHS, Cin., 1964-67; chief earth scis., Ohio Basin Region, Fed. Water Pollution Control Adminstrn., Cin., 1967-69; asso. prof. geol. engring. U. Mo.-Rolla, Rolla, 1969-72, prof., 1972—; cons. in field. Spl. award scholar Colo. Sch. Mines, 1951-56; research fellow U. Calif., 1962-64. Certified profl. geol. scientist. Fellow Geol. Soc. Am.; mem. Am. Assn. Petroleum Geologists, Assn. Profl. Geol. Scientists. Assn. Engring. Geologists, Nat. Water Well Assn., Am. Inst. Mining Engrs., Sigma Alpha Epsilon. Contbr. articles to tech. publs. Home: PO Box 781 Rolla MO 65401

WARNER, GORDON J., steel co. exec.; b. Spalding, Nebr., Feb. 15, 1937; s. Joy J. and Ruth Lorraine (Baker) W.; B.S. in Civil Engring. with distinction, U. Nebr., 1959; m. Frances Joan Luginbill, June 12, 1960; children—Bradley J., Dustin J. Engr. trainee Pitts.-Des Moines Steel Co., 1959-62, project engr. on St. Louis (Mo.) arch, 1962-64, plant mgr., Clive, Iowa, 1964-70, constrn. mgr., Central U.S., Des Moines, 1970—; instr. constrn. safety; dir. Lazy Ike Corp. Elder, Sunday Sch. tchr. Presbyterian Ch.; b. dirs. YMCA; membership leader Cub Scouts and Webelos; asst. scoutmaster Boy Scouts Am., inst. rep. Explorer Post. Served with U.S. Army, 1959. Named hon. adm. Nebr. Navy, 1958. Mem. ASCE, Des Moines C. of C., Nat. Assn. of Constrn. Boilermaker Employers, Am. Welding Soc., Sigma Xi, Chi Epsilon. Republican. Clubs: Des Moines Art Center, Des Moines Community Playhouse, Masons, Shriners. Home: 3812 Greenbranch Dr West Des Moines IA 50265 Office: PO Box 1596 Des Moines IA 50306

WARNER, WALLACE ERNEST, judge; b. Edinburg, N.D., Oct. 9, 1916; s. Leo Arthur and Cordelia (Eikeness) W.; B.A., U. N.D., 1936, LL.B., 1938, J.D., 1969; m. Cora A. Loken, June 16, 1939; children—Colleen (Mrs. Michael Donnelly), Coralee (Mrs. W. R. Caspers), Russell. Admitted to N.D. bar, 1938; states atty. Walsh County, Grafton, 1940-48; N.D. atty. gen., 1949-51; gen. practice, Wahpeton, 1954-65; state securities commr., N.D., 1965-68; judge and justice Richland County, 1968-72; judge 3d Dist. N.D., 1972—. First chmn. N.D. Parole Bd.; mem. adv. com. Nat. Rivers and Harbors Congress, 1961—; mem. N.D. Cancer Soc., N.D. Mental Health Assn. Del., N.D. Constl. Conv., 1971-72. Mem. Am., N.D. bar assns., United Comml. Travelers, N.D. Peace Officers Assn. Mason (Shriner), Eagle, Elk, Kiwanian. Home: Wahpeton ND 58075 Office: Richland County Courthouse Wahpeton ND 58075

WARNHOLTZ, WERNER ERNST, lawyer; b. Chgo., Aug. 6, 1918; s. Paul A.F. and Frances Franciska (Wagner) W.; B.S. in Geology, Northwestern U., 1940, postgrad. Sch. Law, 1940-41, J.D., 1948; m. Herty Ida Stutzel, Dec. 31, 1950; children—Margo, M. Heidi, Marilyn. Admitted to Ill. bar, 1948; atty. Warnholtz & Warnholtz, Chgo., 1948-51; atty. Chgo. Dist. Army Engrs., 1951-54; legal counsel, dir., sec., treas. Wings & Wheels Express, Inc., Chgo., 1954-56; title officer Jackson County Title Co., Medford, Oreg., 1957-62; practice law Humphrey, Warnholtz & Sullivan, Chgo., 1962—; lectr., Ill. Inst. for Continuing Legal Edn., 1970, 72, 75. Mem. Medford United Crusade, 1957-58. Served to capt. AUS, 1941-45. Decorated Bronze Star. Mem. Ill. State Bar Assn., Technischer Verein Chgo., Phi Kappa Sigma, Phi Delta Phi. Conglist. (moderator 1973-75). Clubs: Forest Glen Community (pres. 1954, 68, dir.); Germania (Chgo.). Home: 5325 N Lawler St Chicago IL 60630 Office: 111 W Washington St Chicago IL 60602

WARPEHA, RAYMOND LEONARD, surgeon, clin. dir., educator; b. Mpls., Dec. 5, 1934; s. Frank Joseph and Sophie Helen (Fryzlewicz) W.; B.S., U. Minn., 1956, D.D.S., 1958; M.D., Northwestern U., 1965, Ph.D., 1966; m. Ivy Kloth, Aug. 15, 1975; children—Katherine, John, Joseph. Instr. anatomy Northwestern U., Chgo., 1963-65, resident in plastic surgery, Med. Sch., 1970-72, professorial lectr. anatomy, 1972—; intern Cook County Hosp., Chgo., 1965-66, resident in surgery, 1966-70; practice medicine specializing in plastic surgery, Maywood, Ill., 1972-75; asst. prof. surgery and anatomy Loyola U. Med. Sch., Maywood, 1972-75, chmn. div. plastic surgery, 1975—, asso. prof., 1975—; dir. burn unit Foster McGaw Hosp., Maywood, 1973—; attending physician Hines (Ill.) VA Hosp., 1972-76, cons. surgery, 1977; chmn. Ill. burn surgeons adv. group Ill. Div. Emergency Med. Services, 1974—; chmn. burn adv. group HEW, 1975—. Diplomate Am. Bd. Surgery, Am. Bd. Plastic Surgery. Fellow A.C.S. Roman Catholic. Contbr. articles to med. jours. Office: Loyola Univ Medical School 2160 S 1st Ave Maywood IL 60153

WARPEHA, WALTER STANLEY, prosthodontist; b. Mpls., Sept. 16, 1912; s. Frank Joseph and Sophia (Fryzlewicz) W.; D.D.S., U. Minn., 1938; m. Florence Malayne Nalezny, Sept. 2, 1939; children—Rita, Rosalie, Margaret, Walter Stanley, Paul. Pvt. practice dentistry, Mpls., 1938-43, 1946—. Clin. prof. prosthodontics U. Minn. Sch. Dentistry, 1964—; cons. Minn. Crippled Children's Service, 1960—, maxillo-facial Panel Sch. Dentistry. Bank dir., 1948—; treas. Minn. Dental Found., 1964-69. Served to lt. Dental Corps, USNR, 1943-46. Diplomate Am. Bd. Prosthodontics. Fellow Am. Coll. Dentists, Internat. Coll. Dentists, Am. Coll. Prosthodontists; mem. Am. Dental Assn., Am. (pres. 1968), Minn. (pres. 1961-62) prosthodontics socs., Midwest Acad. Prosthodontics (dir.), Minn. Acad. Restorative Dentistry (pres. 1954-55), Minn. Dental Alumni Assn. (pres. 1968), Omicron Kappa Upsilon. K.C. (4 deg.). Club: Athletic (Mpls.). Home: 10304 Mississippi Blvd Coon Rapids MN 55433 Office: 1312 2d St NE Minneapolis MN 55413

WARREN, CLAUDE MARION, lawyer; b. Marshall, Ind., Jan. 4, 1918; s. Bradford and Marcella (Isaacs) W.; A.B., Ind. U., 1938, LL.B., 1941, J.D., 1967; m. Nina Jean Davidson, Aug. 27, 1939; children—Lawrence Alan, Claude Marion, Bradford L., Barbara Jean Warren McAlister, William D., R. Kent. Admitted to Ind. bar, 1941, since practiced in Indpls.; asso. firm Goodrich & Campbell, 1942-52, partner Goodrich, Campbell & Warren, 1952-62, Goodrich & Warren, 1962-74, Warren, Snider, Koeller & Warren, 1974-76, Warren, Snider & Warren, 1976—; v.p., gen. counsel, dir. Herff Jones Co., Indpls., 1964-73; gen. counsel, dir. United Telephone Co. Ind., Warsaw, 1962—; dir. Landeco, Inc., Brektal Corp. Mem. Am., Ind., Indpls. bar assns., Indpls. Lawyers Club, Bar 7th Circuit Fed. Ct. Appeals, Ind. U. Alumni Assn. (pres. 1967-68). Clubs: Highland Golf and Country, Indpls. Press (Indpls.). Home: 3704 Delaware Common N Dr Indianapolis IN 46220 Office: Suite 2110 3500 Depauw Blvd Indianapolis IN 46268

WARREN, FRANCIS EUGENE, humanist; b. Craig, Colo., Oct. 3, 1941; s. George William and Frances Elizabeth (Wilson) W.; B.A., Kans. State Coll.-Emporia, 1966, M.A., 1967; m. Rosalee Cecelia Bazil, Jan. 19, 1963; children—Cynthia Louise, Matthew Richardson, Timothy Thomas, Jennifer Elizabeth. Instr. English, U. Mo.-Rolla, 1967-73, asst. prof., 1973—; lectr. in field. Recipient 1st place poetry Evang. Press Assn., 1975. Mem. Conf. Christianity and Lit., N.Y. C.S. Lewis Soc., Fine Arts Fellowship. Poetry editor Christianity and Lit., 1975—; author: (poetry) Christographia, 1973; Rumors of Light, 1974; Christographia 1-32, 1977; contbg. editor For the Time Being, 1975. Home: 300 W 3d St Rolla MO 65401 Office: Dept Humanities U Mo at Rolla Rolla MO 65401

WARREN, JAMES VAUGHN, physician; b. Columbus, Ohio, July 1, 1915; s. James Halford and Lucile (Vaughn) W.; m. Gloria Kicklighter, May 27, 1954; B.A., Ohio State U., 1935; M.D., Harvard U., 1939; D.Sc. (hon.), Emory U. Med. Sch., 1974; med. house officer Peter Bent Brigham Hosp., 1939-41, asst. resident medicine, 1941-42. Diplomate Am. Bd. Internal Medicine (sec.-treas. 1970-71, vice chmn. 1971-72). Research fellow medicine Harvard U., 1941-42; med. investigator problems shock and vascular injuries OSRD, 1942-46; instr. medicine Emory U. Med. Sch., 1942-46, asso. prof. medicine, prof. physiology, chmn. dept. physiology, 1947-51, prof. medicine, 1951-52; asst. prof. medicine Yale Med. Sch., 1946-47; prof. medicine Duke Sch. Medicine, 1952-58; prof. medicine, chmn. dept. internal medicine U. Tex. Sch. Medicine, 1958-61; prof., chmn. dept. medicine Ohio State U. Med. Sch., 1961—. Master A.C.P.; mem. AMA (chmn. sect. internal medicine 1964-65), Assn. Profs. Medicine (pres. 1967-68), Am. Clin. and Climatol. Assn., Soc. Univ. Cardiologists, Am. Heart Assn. (pres. 1962-63, Gold Heart award, Herrick award), Am. Soc. Clin. Physiology, Soc. Exptl. Biology and Medicine, Assn. Am. Physicians, Nat. Acad. Medicine-Inst. Medicine, So., Central socs. clin. research, Sigma Xi, Alpha Omega, Cosmos Club, Explorers Club. Author: (with others) Pre-Eclamptic and Exlamptic Toxemia of Pregnancy, 1941; Methods in Medical Research, vol. VII; mem. Harvard editorial bd. Am. Heart Jour., 1971; contbr. numerous articles to profl. publs. Home: 5526 Ashford Rd Dublin OH 43017 Office: 410 W 10th Ave Columbus OH 43210

WARREN, JOE ELLISON, state senator; b. Silverdale, Kans., Sept. 17, 1912; s. James Edman and Phoebe (Harkbroad) W.; student pub. schs. Arkansas City, Kans.; m. Pauline Goff, Sept. 4, 1931; children—James, Helen Jane. Treas., Spring Creek Twp., 1952-56; senator, State of Kans., 1956—, chmn. soil conservation dist., 1956—, minority caucus chmn. Senate, 1964-72, chmn. livestock subcom. Senate Com. on agr., 1968-72, vice chmn. legislative facilities com., 1972—, now asst. minority leader, caucus chmn.; farmer, rancher, Maple City, Kans., 1932—. Mem. sch. bd., Common Sch. Dist., Kans., 1936-57; mem. exec. Council Extension Cowley County, Kan., 1956-58; mem. fed. adv. council Bur. Employment Security, U.S. Dept. Labor; mem. Kans. Legislative Council; mem. Gov.'s Com. on Criminal Adminstrn. Address: Route 1 Maple City KS 67102

WARREN, ROSS WINSTON, dentist; b. Marshall, Ind., Nov. 7, 1923; s. Bradford and Marcella Pearl (Isaacs) W.; D.D.S., Ind. U., 1945; m. Lyndall Jo Hoopingarner, Dec. 16, 1955; 1 dau., Stacey Ann. Pvt. practice dentistry, Rockville, Ind., 1945-51, Crawfordsville, Ind., 1957—. Instr., Ind. U. Sch. Dentistry, Indpls., 1966-73. Bd. dirs. Sugar Creek Playhouse, Crawfordsville, 1970-73, chmn. bd., 1970-71. Served with AUS, 1943-44, 51-57, now col. Ind. N.G. Mem. Am., Ind. dental assns., Acad. Gen. Dentistry, Am. Equiliibration Soc. (mem. editorial rev. com. 1970-71, Ben Hur Dental Soc. (pres. 1958-59, 64-65), fellow, Am. Coll. of Dentists, 1976, Delta Sigma Delta, Delta Tau Delta. Republican. Presbyn. (deacon 1961, trustee 1967-70). Mason. Club: Ouiatenon (Crawfordsville). Home: 126 S Davis St Crawfordsville IN 47933 Office: 408 W Market St Crawfordsville IN 47933

WARRES, HERBERT LEONARD, urologist; b. Bklyn., Mar. 26, 1919; s. Israel and Bertha (Spiegelman) W.; B.S., Columbia U., 1939; M.D., Med. Coll. Va., 1943; m. Betty Byrl Clark, July 7, 1946; children—Edward C., Charlene M., Charles L. (dec.), Byrl Ann. Intern, N.Y. Med. Coll., N.Y.C., 1943; resident L.I. Coll. Medicine, N.Y.C., 1944-45, Grad. Sch. Medicine U. Pa., Phila., 1947-48, Presbyn. Hosp., Phila., 1948-49, Master Med. Sch., U. Pa., Phila., 1951; urologist Med. and Surg. Clinic, Laredo, Tex., 1949-53, Thompson-Brumm-Knepper Clinic, St. Joseph, Mo., 1953-63, practice medicine specializing in urology, Springfield, Mo., 1963-73; pres. Warres Urol. Assos., Inc., Springfield, 1973—; clin. asso. prof. surgery U. Mo., Columbia, 1971—; cons. Med. Center Fed. Prisoners, 1965—; asso. Mo. State Crippled Children Services, 1963—, Ellis Fischel State Cancer Hosp., 1965—; med. adviser Bur. Hearings and Appeals, Social Security Adminstrn., 1965—. Served with AUS, 1945-47. Recipient T. Leon Howard award South Central sect. Am. Urol. Assn., 1951. Diplomate Am. Bd. Urology. Fellow A.C.S. (liaison cancer officer Mo. area IV), Soc. Pediatric Urology, Am. Geriatric Soc.; mem. Sigma Zeta. Baptist. Contbr. articles to profl. jours. Home: 2614 S Inglewood Rd Springfield MO 65804 Office: 609 Cherry St Springfield MO 65806

WARRICK, PATRICIA SCOTT, educator; b. La Grange, Ind., Feb. 6, 1925; d. Ross B. and DeEtte L. (Ulman) Scott; B.S. in Biochemistry, Ind. U., 1946; B.A. in English, Goshen Coll., 1964; M.A., Purdue U., 1965; Ph.D., U. Wis., Milw., 1977; children—Scott, David, Kristin. Mem. staff bldg. and devel. program L.I. U., Bklyn., 1946-48; dir. technicians med. lab. St. Elizabeth Hosp., Indpls., 1948-52; instr. English, Lawrence U., Appleton, Wis., 1965-66; prof. English U. Wis., Fox Valley, Menasha, 1966—, chmn. English dept., 1976—, dir. 21st century studies, 1977—. Nat. Endowment Humanities fellow, 1973-74; U. Wis. grantee, 1975. Mem. Nat. Council Tchrs. English, Modern Lang. Assn., World Future Soc., Sci. Fiction Research Assn. Contbr. articles in field to profl. jours.; editor numerous works in field. Home: 1925 N McDonald St Appleton WI 54911 Office: U Wis Center Menasha WI 54952

WARSHAW, MARTIN RICHARD, educator; b. N.Y.C., Sept. 17, 1924; s. Irving Gregg and Adelaide (Klein) W.; A.B., Columbia U., 1947; M.B.A., U. Mich., 1957, Ph.D., 1960; m. Alice M. Present, Mar. 28, 1948; children—Gregg, Mark, Lynn, Laurie. Salesman, Daniels Jewelry Co., Battle Creek, Mich., 1947-50, store mgr., 1950-55, v.p., dir., Lansing, Mich., 1955-64; instr. bus. adminstrn. U. Mich., 1957-60, asst. prof., 1960-64, asso. prof., 1964-67, prof. mktg., 1967—, chmn. mktg. faculty, 1973—; asso. Mgmt. Analysis Center, Cambridge, Mass., 1970—. Served with C.E., U.S. Army, 1943-46. Mem. Am. Mktg. Assn. (past pres. Detroit chpt.). Author: (with Rewoldt and Scott) Introduction To Marketing Management, 3d edit., 1977; (with Engel and Wales) Promotional Strategy, 3d edit., 1975. Home: 2279 Mershon Dr Ann Arbor MI 48103 Office: 720 Business Adminstrn U Michigan Ann Arbor MI 48109

WARSTLER, IRVIN SAMUEL, ret. automotive co. exec.; b. South Bend, Ind., May 11, 1910; s. Sylvanius Irvin and Agnes Isabelle (Reid) W.; grad. Internat. Corr. Schs., 1931; m. Delouris Frances Kouder, Nov. 21, 1931; 1 dau., Lois J. (Mrs. John M. Ruffner). Foreman die shop Studebaker Corp., South Bend, 1943-49, die engr., 1949-53, mgr. die div., 1953-64; gen. mgr. Richard Bros. Die & Prototype, Hillsdale, Mich., 1964-76. Chmn. United Fund Campaign Hillsdale, 1971; mem. City of Hillsdale Bd. Pub. Utilities, 1973—. Home: 118 Orchard Ridge Hillsdale MI 49242

WASHBURN, JOST BRAINARD, clergyman; b. St. Louis, Nov. 23, 1916; s. Frank William and Frieda Emma (Geisel) W.; A.B., Elmhurst Coll., 1941; B.D., Eden Theol. Sem., 1944; postgrad. Lancaster Theol. Sem., 1959; m. Gladys Louisa Augusta Haase, Dec. 29, 1942; children—Yvonne R., Henry B., Diane L. Ordained to ministry Evang. and Reformed Ch., 1944; minister St. Paul's Church, Corpus Christi, Tex., 1944-51, Bethany Evang. and Reformed Ch., New Orleans, 1951-55, Bethlehem United Church of Christ, Buffalo, N.Y., 1955-70, Congl. Ch., Dwight, Ill., 1970-72; Mont Clare Congl. Ch., Chgo., 1972—. Vice pres. San Antonio Dist. of Tex. Synod, 1946-48; pres. Evang. Union of New Orleans, 1952-54. Named Hon. Citizen and recipient key to city, New Orleans, 1952. Mem. Am. Schs. Oriental Research, Nat. Geog. Soc., Soc. Bibl. Lit. and Exegesis. Mason. Assisted in translation of American Standard Version of Bible. Home: 6945 W Medill Ave Chicago IL 60635 Office: 6935 W Medill Ave Chicago IL 60635

WASHBURN, PAUL ARTHUR, bishop; b. Aurora, Ill., Mar. 31, 1911; s. Eliot A. and Lena (Buhrnsen) W.; B.A., N. Central Coll., Naperville, Ill., 1936, L.H.D., 1970; B.D., Evang. Theol. Sem., 1938; D.D., Ind. Central Coll., 1954; D.Cn.L., Westmar Coll., 1972; D.D., Wiley Coll., 1975; m. Kathryn E. Fischer, Jan. 12, 1937; children—Mary (Mrs. R. Smith), Jane (Mrs. Edwin Eigenbrodt), Fred, John. Teller, bookkeeper First Nat. Bank, Aurora, Ill., 1929-32; ordained to ministry Evang. Ch., 1938; pastor Eppards Point Evang. Ch., Chenoa, Ill., 1934-39, St. John's Evang. United Brethren Ch., Rockford, Ill., 1939-52; lectr. religion Rockford Coll., 1947-52; pastor First Evang. United Brethren Ch., Naperville, Ill., 1952-64; exec. sec. Commn. on Ch. Union, Evang. United Brethren Ch., 1964-68; bishop Minn. area United Meth. Ch., Mpls., 1968-72, Chgo. area, 1972—. Directed union of The Meth. Ch. and The Evang. United Brethren Ch.; pres. Bd. Global Ministries, United Meth. Ch., 1972-76. Trustee N. Central Coll., Naperville, 1963—, Garrett-Evang. Theol. Sem., Evanston, Ill., 1954—, Northwestern Meml. Hosp., Chgo., 1972—. Author: The United Methodist Primer. Home: 413 Parkway Dr Wheaton IL 60187 Office: 77 W Washington St Chicago IL 60602

WASMUTH, DUANE LEE, mfg. co. exec.; b. Midland, Mich., Jan. 2, 1939; s. Ralph and Midge Winifred (Mathewson) W.; B.S.E. in Mech. Engring., U. Mich., 1962, M.S.E. in Indsl. Engring., 1963, M.B.A., 1964; m. Gwendolyn Beatrice McKay, Aug. 10, 1963; children—Lisa Anne, Jeffrey Duane. Supt. mfg. Chevrolet Motor Div., General Motors Corp., Detroit, 1964-70; v.p. mfg. Rectrans, Inc., Brighton, Mich., 1970-71; pres. U-Tune, Inc., Madison Heights, Mich., 1971-75; pres. Internat. Husky, Inc., Bloomfield, Hills, Mich., 1972-77; v.p. Key Internat., Inc., Southfield, Mich., 1977—; dir. Mills Products, Inc.; Internat. Husky, Inc., IHRRCO, Inc. U.S. Automation Co; cons. Riverside Metal Products Co. Inst. Labor and Indsl. Relations grad. fellow, 1962-63; grad. sch. bus. admni. fellow U. Mich., 1963-64. Mem. Rotary, U. Mich. Alumni Assn., Econic Club Detroit, N. Am. Soc. for Corp. Planning, Tau Beta Pi, Pi Tau Sigma, Alpha Pi Mu, Phi Delta Theta. Republican. Presbyterian. Club: Birmingham Athletic, Bloomfield Hills Country, U. Mich. Pres.'s, U. Mich. Victors. Home: 979 Sandhurst St Bloomfield Hills MI 48013 Office: PO Box 232 Southfield MI 48037

WASSERMAN, GERALD STEWARD, educator; b. Bklyn., Nov. 22, 1937; s. Julius and Bessie (Weissman) W.; m. Louise Janet Mund, June 17, 1962; children—Mark Daniel, Rachel Lynn; B.A., N.Y.U., 1960; Ph.D. (USPHS fellow), Mass. Inst. Tech., 1965. Postdoctoral fellow NIH, 1965-67; asst. prof. U. Wis., Madison, 1967-70, asso. prof., 1970-75; prof. psychobiology Purdue U., West Lafayette, Ind., 1975—. Prin. investigator NSF grant, 1969-73, NIH grant, 1975—. Mem. AAAS, Assn. for Research in Vision and Ophthalmology, GUV (gov. 1974-77), Midwestern Psychol. Assn., Optical Soc. Am., Soc. for Neurosci., Psychonomic Soc. Author: Color Vision, 1978. Editorial bd. Color Research and Application, 1977—. Contbr. articles to profl. jours. Home: 3512 Capilano Dr West Lafayette IN 47906 Office: 1291 Cumberland Ave West Lafayette IN 47906

WASSERMAN, RODGER DEAN, transp.-computer systems cons. co. exec.; b. Detroit, Jan. 14, 1946; s. Alvin and Edith Lorraine (Kavieff) W.; M.A., Mich. State U., 1968; m. Aug. 3, 1969; children—Amy Briar, Kurt Nicholas, Songwriter, pub. Charrington Music Co., Detroit and Notable Music, Inc., N.Y., 1967-69; v.p. Allied Indsl. Contractors, Inc., Detroit, 1969-72; pres. Abacus Corp., Detroit, 1972—; dir. Allied Delivery System, Am. Delivery System, Rodger Wasserman & Partners (all Detroit); cons. v.p. Allied Iron Co., Detroit; cons. computerization and design transp. systems Gen. Motors Parts div. Upjohn Co., Signal Delivery. Jewish. Club: Bloomfield Open Hunt. Designed and developed one of first mini-computer bus. systems in U.S., 1972, first computer system capable performing 100% freight routing, billing, and control, 1974, first commercially feasable computerization of freight rating, 1976. Home: 582 Puritan St Birmingham MI 48009 Office: 300 E Seven Mile Rd Detroit MI 48203

WASSERMAN, STEPHEN MILES, pub. relations exec.; b. Chgo., Apr. 26, 1945; s. Samuel Isreal and Rayna (Krassner) W.; B.A., Bradley U., 1968; postgrad. No. Ill. U., 1972-77: m. Faye Samuelson, Oct. 17, 1971; children—Rayna, Alyssa. Sports editor Glen News Publs., 1967-68; pub. relations asso. No. Ill. Gas Co., 1968-71; account exec., asst. office mgr. Mayer & O'Brien, Chgo., 1971-72; editor internal publs., pub. relations staff asst. Chgo. Title & Trust Co., 1972-76, pub. relations officer, 1976—. Chmn. Municipal Relations Commn., Wheeling, Ill., 1975-76. Mem. Internat., Chgo. assns. bus. communicators, Pub. Relations Soc. Am., Publicity Club Chgo., Headline Club Chgo., Chgo. Assn. Bus. Communicators (pres. 1977-78), Sigma Delta Chi. Home: 1187 Devonshire Buffalo Grove IL 60090 Office: Chicago Title & Trust Co 111 W Washington St Chicago IL 60602

WASSON, BARBARA HICKAM (MRS. AUDLEY JACKSON WASSON), pianist, educator; b. Spencer, Ind., Feb. 12, 1918; d. Hubert and Ruth (Moffett) Hickam; student DePauw U., 1937-38; B.A., Vassar Coll., 1939; Mus. M., Chgo. Musical Coll., 1944; student Ind. U., summers 1963, 64; Music Asso., Wright State U., 1975; m. Audley Jackson Wasson, Aug. 29, 1942; children—Carol Ruth (Mrs. Anthony A. Pasquale, Jr.), Steven. Tchr. piano Tudor Hall Sch., Indpls., 1940-41, Chgo. Musical Coll., 1942-44, Cedarville Coll., 1971-72; founder, co-dir. Wasson Piano Studio, Dayton, Ohio, 1946—; piano tchr., workshops in Miss., Ohio, 1964—; music asso. Wright State U., 1975—; piano soloist Dayton Philharmonic. 1953, Dayton Philharmonic Tng. Orch., 1957. Mem. Nat. Guild Piano Tchrs. (judge 1965—), Ohio Music Tchrs. Assn. (chmn. western dist.), Nat. Assn. Music Tchrs. (Recognition award), Ohio Ind. Music Tchrs. Forum (chmn. 1976—), Mu Phi Epsilon, Kappa Kappa Gamma. Club: Dayton Music (v.p., 1968-70). Home: 5797 Paddington Rd Centerville OH 45459 Office: 1175 Reibold Bldg Dayton OH 45402

WASSON, WILLIAM ELWOOD, educator; b. Coweta, Okla., June 13, 1920; s. William Henry and Cora Anna (Myers) W.; B.S., Okla. State U., 1969, M.S., 1970; postgrad. So. Ill. U., 1971—; m. Betty Rosamond Main, Dec. 26, 1945. Lab. technician Shell Oil Co., Wood River, Ill., 1942-58; owner, operator residential constrn. firm, Birghton, Ill., 1958-67; tchr. constrn. trades Sparta Community Unit Dist. 140, 1970—; condr. workshops; participant U.S. Senate Hearing Com. on Status and Needs of Vocat. Edn., 1976. Served with USAAF, 1943-46; PTO. Mem. Am. Personnel and Guidance Assn., Nat., Am., Ill. vocat. assns., Ill. Vocat. Guidance Assn., Ill. Edn. Assn., Ill. Indsl. Edn. Assn., Vocat. Indsl. Clubs Am., Iota Lambda Sigma. Baptist. Club: Masons. Home: 1812 Swanwick St Chester IL 62233 Office: 200 W Hood St Sparta IL 62286

WASYLUKA, RAY GERALD, metals co. exec.; b. Madison, Ill., Oct. 30, 1935; s. Stanley and Ann (Prestly) W.; B.S., U. Mo., 1956; M.B.A., Harvard U., 1965. Accountant firm Ernst & Ernst, St. Louis, 1956-60, Peat, Marwick, Mitchell & Co., St. Louis, 1960-62; v.p. Vestal Labs. div. W.R. Grace Co., St. Louis, 1968-72; corp. v.p. finance Diversified Industries, Inc., Clayton, Mo., 1972—; instr. indsl. engring. Washington U., St. Louis, 1969-72. Served with AUS, 1957. Mem. Beta Gamma Sigma. K.C. Clubs: Mo. Athletic, Harvard (St. Louis). Contbr. articles to profl. jours. Home: 8665 Old Towne Dr University City MO 63132 Office: 123 Byassee Rd Hazelwood MO 63042

WATANABE, MARK, orthodontist; b. Santa Cruz, Calif., Sept. 3, 1919; s. Walter Kuma and Terese Tsugi (Ishikawa) W.; student San Jose State U., 1940-42, Northwestern U., 1947-49; D.D.S., U. Ill., 1953, M.S., 1955. Practice dentistry specializing in orthodontics, River Forest, Ill., 1955—. Asst. prof. orthodontics U. Ill. Grad. Sch. Orthodontics, 1955-57, 70-72, orthodontic cons. dept. pedodontics, 1970-72. Served with AUS, 1944-47. Mem. Ill. Soc. Orthodontics (sec.- treas. 1968-69), Am. Assn. Orthodontists, U. Ill. Alumni Assn., Delta Sigma Delta. Contbr. to profl. publs. in field. Home: 410 Ashland Ave River Forest IL 60305 Office: 7777 Lake St River Forest IL 60305

WATERBURY, JACKSON DEWITT, advt. agy. exec.; b. Evanston, Ill., Feb. 4, 1937; s. Jackson D. and Eleanor (Barrows) W.; A.B. Brown U., 1959; m. Suzanne Butler, Aug. 27, 1958 (div. Jan. 1970); children— Jackson D. III, Arthur Barrows; m. 2d, Lynn Hardin, Mar. 17, 1971; 1 son, Timothy Bradford. Account exec. D'Arcy Advt. Co., St. Louis, 1958-63, Batz-Hodgson-Neuwoehner, Inc., St. Louis, 1963-66; exec. v.p., sec., dir. Lynch, Phillips & Waterbury, Inc., St. Louis, 1966-68; pres. Jackson Waterbury & Co., St. Louis, 1968-73; v.p., partner Vinyard & Lee & Partners, St. Louis, 1973-74; pres. Jackson Waterbury, Inc., 1975-76; pres. Waterbury Kiem Royle Inc., St. Louis, 1977—; dir. Alice Blake, Inc. Football coach Mo. High Sch. All-Stars, 1966-67, St. Louis U., 1968-70. Mem. Ducks Unlimited, Am. Motorcycle Assn., Nat. Rifle Assn., Beta Theta Pi. Episcopalian. Clubs: Creve Coeur Racquet, Strathalbyn Farms. Home: 43 Lake Forest St Louis MO 63117 Office: 7777 Bonhomme St Louis MO 63105

WATERS, WILLIAM BAXTER, lawyer, former state senator; b. Lathrop, Mo., Apr. 26, 1916; s. Baxter and Ruth (Myers) W.; A.B., William Jewell Coll., Mo., 1937; LL.B., U. Mo., 1941; m. Ellen Bower Nesbitt, May 15, 1943 (dec.); m. Marjorie C. Nesbitt, July 15, 1975. Admitted to Mo. bar, 1941; practiced in Liberty, 1941—; asso. firm Lawson & Hale, 1941-47; judge Probate Ct. Clay County, 1947-55; partner firm Hale, Kincaid, Waters & Allen, 1955—; mem. Mo. Senate, 1956-77, majority leader, 1965-69. Mem. Mo. Democratic State Com., 1951-56. Served with CIC, AUS, 1942-46; ETO. Named Most Valuable Mem. Mo. Legislature, St. Louis Globe Democrat. 1963, 65. Mem. Am., Mo., Clay County bar assns., Mo. Probate Judges Assn. (past pres.), Am. Legion, V.F.W., 40 and 8, Phi Gamma Delta. Lion. Home: 735 N Fairview St Liberty MO 64068 Office: 17 W Kansas St Liberty MO 64068

WATERS, WILLIAM ROLAND, economist; b. Balt., Feb. 5, 1920; s. William Lee and Loretta (Moylan) W.; A.B., Loyola Coll., 1942; Ph.D. in Econs., Georgetown U., 1953; m. Regina F. Trimp, Aug. 19, 1950; children—Gerard, Karen, Patricia, Marc. Faculty DePaul U., Chgo., 1950—, prof. econs., 1960—, head behavioral-social scis. div., 1966-77, chmn. dept. econs., 1977—. Mem. Am. Econ. Assn., Assn. Social Economy, AAUP, Econ. History Assn. Democrat. Roman Catholic. Editor Rev. Social Economy, 1965—. Contbr. articles to profl. jours. Home: 2222 N Dayton St Chicago IL 60614 Office: 25 E Jackson Blvd Chicago IL 60604

WATKINS, DANIEL JOSEPH, cons. civil engr.; b. Albia, Iowa, Dec. 18, 1923; s. Thomas Joseph and Theresa Alice (O'Connor) W.; B.S., Iowa State U., 1947; m. Barbara Lorraine Van Cleve, Sept. 9, 1946; children—Daniel Lawrence, Robert Edward, Alice Elizabeth (Mrs. A.J. Scherzberg), John Vincent, Marianne, Jeanne Marie (Mrs. Gene Schinstock), Thomas Joseph, James Patrick, Barbara Susan, William Franklin, Margaret Mary, Paul Gerard (dec.), Frances Theresa, David Christopher, Patrick Anthony. Design engr., dept. head Howard, Needles, Tammen & Bergendoff, cons. engrs., architects, planners, Kansas City, Mo., 1947-70, partner, 1970—; incorporator Citizens State Bank, Shawnee Mission, Kans., 1973. City councilman Prairie Village (Kans.), 1965-71. Bd. dirs. Mayor Kansas City (Mo.) Corps Progress, 1972—; lay adv. bd. St. Joseph's Hosp., Kansas City, Mo.; mem. Civil Engring. Advisory Bd. Iowa State U. Served to lt. (j.g.), USNR, 1944-46; PTO. Named councilman of year Prairie Village, 1970. Fellow ASCE, Am. Cons. Engrs. Council; mem. Nat., Mo. (pres. Western chpt. 1965, chmn. state profl. conduct com. 1967-70) socs. profl. engrs., Cons. Engrs. Council Mo. (v.p. 1971-72), Am. Pub. Works Assn., Am. Roadbuilders Assn., Internat. Bridge, Tunnel and Turnpike Assn., Transp. Research Bd., Tau Beta Pi. Roman Catholic. Rotarian. Home: 3511 W 73d St Prairie Village KS 66208 Office: Howard Needles Tammen & Bergendoff 1805 Grand Ave Kansas City MO 64108

WATKINS, DAVID HYDER, surgeon; b. Denver, Nov. 26, 1917; s. David Milroy and Mary Rose (Hyder) W.; A.B., U. Colo., 1937, M.D., 1940; M.S. in Surgery, U. Minn., 1947, Ph.D., 1949; m. Lucile Maxine Pingel, Sept. 27, 1941; children—John David Hyder, Bryan David Pingel. Intern, U. Iowa Hosps., Iowa City, 1940-41; resident Mayo Clinic, Rochester, Minn., 1942-44, asst. surg. staff, 1945-49; instr. surgery Ohio State U., Columbus, 1949-50; asso. prof. surgery U. Colo., Denver, 1951-56, prof., 1956-67; dir. surg. services Denver Gen. Hosp., 1951-67; cons. Fitzsimmons Army Hosp., Denver, 1954-67, cons. emeritus, 1967—; clin. prof. surgery U. Iowa, Iowa City, 1967—; cons. surg. service VA Hosp., Des Moines, 1968—; mem. surg. staff Iowa Meth. Hosp., Des Moines, 1967—; attending staff Broadlawns Hosp., Des Moines, 1968—. Diplomate Am. Bd. Surgery, Am. Bd. Thoracic Surgery. Fellow A.C.S.; mem. Am. Assn. for Thoracic Surgery, Central, Western surg. assns., S.W. Surg. Congress, Soc. U. Surgeons, Societe Internationale de Chirugie, Am. Heart Assn., Am. Coll. Cardiology, Am. Coll. Chest Physicians, Am. Fedn. for Clin. Research, Am. Geriatrics Soc., Am. Soc. for Artificial Internal Organs., Phi Beta Kappa, Sigma Xi, Alpha Omega Alpha. Club: University (Denver). Contbr. articles to profl. jours. Home: 6039 N Waterbury Rd Des Moines IA 50312 Office: 1407 Woodland Ave Des Moines IA 50309

WATKINS, DEAN EDWARD, city ofcl.; b. Akron, Ohio, July 18, 1946; s. Edward David and Audrey Mae (Ritzman) W.; B.A., U. Cin., 1969, M.A., 1971, postgrad., 1972—; m. Helen Virginia McCoy, June 13, 1970; 1 son, John Gregory. Salesman, Oscar Mayer & Co., Cleve., 1968; research, teaching asst., computer programmer U. Cin., 1969-72; instr. sociology Coll. of Mt. St. Joseph, Cin., 1971; program evaluator Cin. Police Div., 1972-76, supervising mgmt. analyst City of Cin., 1976—. Mem. research task group Urban Appalachian Council, 1974—. Bd. dirs. Ravine Street Child Care Center, 1971-73. Recipient Danforth award, 1964. Mem. Am. Sociol. Assn., Population Assn. Am., Ops. Research Soc. Am., Inst. Mgmt. Scis., Internat. City Mgrs. Assn., Common Cause. Home: 1026 Egan Hills Dr Cincinnati OH 45229 Office: 801 Plum St Cincinnati OH 45202

WATKINS, DONALD RICHARD, mfg. co. exec.; b. St. Cloud, Minn., May 31, 1936; s. Richard Perry and Evelyn A. (Wicklund) W.; student St. Cloud State Coll., 1954-58; m. Janet Catherine Donaldson, Sept. 7, 1957; children—Beth, Jill, Pamela, Jon. With Zapp Abstract Co., St. Cloud, 1957-60; with Tanner Systems, Inc., Sauk Rapids, Minn., 1960—, pres., 1966—, dir. 1960—; dir. Tanner Systems of Canada Ltd. Pres., Steams County Cancer Soc., 1969-71; v.p. Central Minn. council Boy Scouts Am.; mem. exec. bd., pres.'s council St. Cloud State Coll. Mem. nat right to work com. Republican party, 1964, mem. state central com., 1969-70. Trustee Mpls.-St. Paul Sanitary Dist., 1970; bd. dirs., v.p. St. Cloud Area YMCA; pres. Central Minn. council Boy Scouts Am.; bd. dirs. Pres.'s Club St. Cloud State U. Served with Minn. Army N.G., 1954-62. Recipient award outstanding service to coll. St. Cloud State Coll., 1969. Mem. N.A.M., Minn. Employers Assn., C. of C. (bd. v.p. 1967-68). Elk, Rotarian (pres. 1967-68). Home 2004 13th St S Saint Cloud MN 56301 Office: Tanner Systems Inc PO Box 87 Sauk Rapids MN 56379

WATKINS, RAYMOND CARL, farmer; b. Dederick, Mo., Dec. 8, 1924; s. William Earl and Fredericka Elizabeth (Klumpp) W.; ed. pub. schs., El Dorado Springs, Mo.; m. Sena Lou Woodruff, Nov. 5, 1950; 1 son, William, Scott. Farmer, El Dorado Springs, 1958—; operator jack hammer, explosive supr. Sac Osage Electric Contractor, El Dorado Springs, 1951; machinist Witt Engring Co., El Dorado Springs, 1957-58. Assessor Virgil Twp. of Vernon County, 1956-73; mem. Agrl. Stblzn. and Conservation Com., 1967-75; mem. R-2 El Dorado Springs Sch. Bd., 1969-75; clk. Virgil Twp. Bd., 1956-73; active 4-H Club. Served with AUS, 1945-47. Mem. D.A.V. (post comdr. 1954-55), Nat. Farmers Orgn., Mo. Farmers Assn., Nat., Mo. sch. bd. assns., Mem. Christian Ch. (Sunday sch. supt. 1942-45, 52-56, 58-64 elder). Address: Box 66 Rural Route 1 El Dorado Springs MO 64744

WATNAAS, GENE GAYLORD, bus. exec.; b. Vining, Minn., June 16, 1930; s. Gunder G. and Edith Grace (Thompson) W.; student Land O'Lakes Mgmt. Sch., 1959-70; m. Kathryn Avon Gaarsland, Nov. 7, 1953; children—Linda, Debra, Gregory, Todd, Tracey, Kristine, Aric. Bookkeeper, Fergus Falls Nat. Bank (Minn.), 1947-49; farmer (with father) nr. Vining, 1950-53; bookkeeper Vining Coop. Creamery, 1956-58; bookkeeper Farmers Coop. Creamery, Pease, Minn., 1959-60, mgr., 1961-65; mgr. Starbuck Creamery Co. (Minn.), 1965—. Clk. sch. bd. Dist. 265, 1950-53; twp. assessor Twp., 1949-53; village assessor Vining Village, 1957-58, mem. village council, 1962-65, 68-77, village mayor, 1970-77. Bd. dirs. Starbuck Area Devel. Corp., 1973—. Served with AUS, 1954-56. Named hon. chpt. farmer Future Farmers Am., 1964. Mem. C. of C. (pres. 1968-69, 77-78), Sons of Norway. Lion (pres. 1970-71, dep. dist. gov. 1975-77). Home Starbuck MN 56381 Office: Starbuck Creamery Co Starbuck MN 56381

WATSON, BEN CHARLES, chemist; b. Mobile, Ala., Oct. 3, 1944; s. Ben and Bessie (Turner) Watson; m. Mae Johnson, Jan. 31, 1970. B.S., Morehouse Coll., 1967; M.S., Ill. Inst. Tech., 1974. Chemist Applied Research dept. The Sherwin-Williams Co., Chgo., 1968, sr. chemist, 1968-71, group supr., 1971-74, sect. supr., project coordinator, 1974-77, mgr. applied research, 1977—. Mem. Young Businessmen's Assn., Chgo., 1975-76; mem. Community Devel. Com., 1976. Mem. Am. Chem. Soc., Electrochem. Soc., Chgo. Soc. for Coatings Tech. Recipient Outstanding Scientist Yr. award, State of Ga., 1966. Home: 5201 S Cornell Ave Chicago IL 60615 Office: 10909 S Cottage Grove Ave Chicago IL 60628

WATSON, C. GORDON, dental assn. exec.: b. Rexburg, Idaho, July 2, 1921: grad. Ricks Coll., Rexburg, Brigham Young U.: D.D.S., Northwestern U., 1946: postgrad. U. Chgo., U. Santa Clara: m. 3 sons. Formerly practiced dentistry, San Diego; exec. dir. So. Calif. Dental Assn., 1964-69: exec. dir. Am. Dental Assn., 1970—. Served with Dental Corps, USNR, capt. Res. Recipient Merit award Northwestern U. Alumni Assn. 1972; Key award Am. Soc. Assn. Execs., 1972. Mem. Am., Internat. colls. dentists, Am. Pub. Health Assn., Inst. Medicine of Nat. Acad. Sci., French Dental Assn. (hon.), Am. Assn. Dental Editors, Am. Soc. Assn. Exec., Alpha Omega, Omicron Kappa Upsilon, Xi Psi Phi (life). Home: 990 Lake Shore Dr Apt E6 Chicago IL 60611 Office: 211 E Chicago Ave Chicago IL 60611

WATSON, EVERETT DONALD, mgmt. cons., mobile-modular housing park developer; b. Elgin, Ill., Jan. 26, 1931; s. Everett Glen and Helen (Knop) W.; Ph.B., Ill. Wesleyan U., 1953; M.B.A., Ind. U., 1956; m. Barbara Catlin, June 13, 1953; children—Barbara Lynn, Mark Everett. Chief quality control engr., Louis Allis Co. div. Litton Industries, Milw., 1956-59, mfg. supt., 1959-62; mgr. mfg. small motor div., 1962-65, mgr. mfg. medium motor div., 1965-66, mgr. mfg. large motor div., 1967-70; exec. v.p. House of Harmony, Inc., Reedsburg, Wis., 1970-71; pres. Everett D. Watson & Assos., Milw., 1971—, Fountainwood Recreational Center, 1974—. Mem. plant mgmt. adv. com. U. Wis. Milw., 1969; conf. leader exec. devel. program, 1968—. Asso. campaign chmn. United Fund Greater Milw., 1965—. Bd. dirs. Family Service Agy., Waukesha, Wis., 1969—. Served with AUS, 1953-55. Mem. Toastmasters Internat. (dir. 1967-69, named Mr. T 1967). Lutheran (pres. 1959, chmn. bd. edn. 1969—). Home: 5952 Kurtz Rd Hales Corners WI 53130 Office: 1840 N Farwell Dr Suite 205 Milwaukee WI 53202

WATSON, GLENN ROY, indsl. engr.; b. Alliance, Ohio, Sept. 3, 1912; s. Roy A. and Bertha Eve (Klotz) W.; student pub. schs., Ashland, Ohio; m. Helen Viola Mack, Jan. 23, 1937; children—Ronald G., Gerald R., Kenneth R., James D. Stockroom attendant Eagle Rubber Co., Ashland, 1931-34; foreman Improved Mfg. Co., Ashland, 1934-42; with Ideal Electric Co., Mansfield, Ohio, 1942—, now indsl. engr. Home: 1028 Reed Rd Mansfield OH 44903 Office: 330 E 1st St Mansfield OH 44903

WATSON, HOWARD MONROE, cons. deaf and hearing impaired; b. Bloomington, Ind., Apr. 3, 1942; s. Fred Monroe and Jane (Staudt) W.; B.A. (scholar), Gallaudet Coll., 1966; M.Ed. (fellow), U. Md., 1971. Counselor for deaf Md. Dept. Vocat. Rehab., Rockville, 1967-71; dir. Community Service Agy. for Deaf, Indpls., 1971-74; cons. to deaf and hearing impaired Western Mich. Vocat. Rehab. Services, Grand Rapids, 1974-77; unit leader Div. Vocat. Rehab. Mich. Dept. Edn., Detroit, 1977—. Chmn. workshops for interpreters of deaf, 1971-74; coordinator Grand Rapids Deaf Sign Lang. Continuing Edn. Program, 1974-77; lectr. sign lang. Ind. U. Grad. Sch. Social Work; mem. Ind. Gov.'s Com. on Handicapped, 1971-74; mem. Adv. Bd. Physically and Otherwise Health Impaired of Grand Rapids; mem. Mich. Registry of Interpreters, 1974; mem. Concerned Citizens for a Commn. for Deaf, Mich., 1975-76. Trustee, Indpls. Club for Deaf, 1972-74. Mem. Nat., Mich. (chmn. by-laws com. 1977), Grand Rapids assns. of deaf, Nat. Rehab. Assn., Profl. Rehab. Workers for Adult Deaf, Interpreters of Deaf (v.p. Ind. chpt. 1972-73), Mich. Rehab. Counselor Assn. (Counselor of Year-Elkins award 1976; dir.), Porsche Clubs. Am. Lion (1st v.p. Indpls. 1973-74). Home: 27600 Franklin Rd Apt 701 Southfield MI 48034 Office: 3132 Trumbull Detroit MI 48216

WATSON, JAMES WILLIAM, ret. automobile sales exec.; b. Marietta, Ohio, June 22, 1900; s. Archibald Jefferson and Anna Kuntz Poole W.; B.S. in Econs., U. Pa., 1922; postgrad. Northwestern U., 1942; m. Louise Lansley, Oct. 8, 1925. Salesman, trainee, spl. traveling service rep. Franklin Automobile Co., Syracuse, N.Y., 1915-23; successively retail salesman, wholesale sales rep., wholesale mgr., retail and wholesale sales mgr. Belt Franklin Co., Columbus, Ohio, 1923-30; spl. rep. Midland Corp., Cleve., 1930-31; sales mgr. Dowd-Feder, Inc., Columbus, 1931-32, Walter B. Zimmerman, Inc., 1932, Orr S. Zimmerman, Inc., 1932-33; spl. rep. Chrysler Corp., 1933-35; asst. sales promotion mgr. Oldsmobile div. Gen. Motors Corp., Lansing, Mich., 1935-36, asst. mgr. Chgo. zone, 1936-45; successively staff of v.p. in charge sales, eastern regional mgr., asst. gen. sales mgr., eastern sales mgr., gen. sales mgr. Nash Motors div. Nash-Kelvinator Corp., Detroit, 1945-54; with Am. Motors Corp., 1954-66, successively asst. dir. dealer devel. Nash Motors div. asst. sales mgr. Hudson div., spl. asst. on staff of v.p. automotive distbn. and marketing, 1954-56, sales mgr. Metropolitans, 1956-62, spl. assignments for mgmt., 1962-65. Mem. Automotive Old Timers, Western Srs. Golf Assn., Sigma Nu, Beta Gamma Sigma. Clubs: Athletic (Columbus); Marietta Country (Marietta); Parkersburg (W.Va.) Country. Home: 317 Elm Terr Marietta OH 45750

WATSON, ROBERT GORDON, printing and bldg. maintenance cos. exec.; b. St. Louis, Nov. 9, 1923; s. Gordon Lawrence and Clara Florence (Arthur) W.; B.S., Washington U., St. Louis, 1948; m. Leah Pauline Stroud, May 20, 1950; children—Kenneth, Diane, Nancy. Engr., AT&T, St. Louis, 1948-49; engr. Bell Telephone Labs., N.Y.C., 1950-51; comml. supr. AT&T, St. Louis, San Francisco, Los Angeles, 1952-56, div. accountant, Chgo., 1957-59, staff statistician, N.Y.C., 1959-61; pres. Watson Directory Corp. Mo., Kansas City, 1962—; pres. Ralston Bldg. Maintenance Inc., Kansas City, 1972—; gen. partner Antioch Gardens Club and Apts., Merriam, Kans., 1975—. Chmn. Kansas City Area, Young Life, 1976—. Served with U.S. Army, 1943-46. Mem. Kansas City C. of C., Nat. Assn. Printers and Lithographers, Baptist. Clubs: Brookridge Country, Homestead Country. Home: 6400 Granada St Prairie Village KS 66208 Office: 325 E 31st St Kansas City MO 64108

WATT, GARLAND WEDDERICK, judge; b. Elizabeth City, N.C., Feb. 10, 1932; s. Robert L. and Bessie Moore (Wesley) W.; A.B. magna cum laude, N.C. Central U., 1952; postgrad. Harvard, 1952-54; J.D. with honors, DePaul U., 1961; m. Gwendolyn LaNita Canada, Nov. 23, 1958; 1 dau., Marsha. Admitted to Ill. bar, 1961, also U.S. Dist. Ct., No. Dist. Ill., U.S. Ct. Appeals bars; partner firm Turner, Cousins, Gavin & Watt, 1961-65, Cook & Watt, 1965-67, Rivers, Watt & Lockhart, 1967-70, Watt & Holland, Chgo., 1970-74; judge Circuit Ct. Cook County, Chgo., 1975—; mem. hearing bd., atty. registration and disciplinary com. Supreme Ct. Ill., 1973-75. Mem. bd. advisers Supreme Life Ins. Co. Am., 1971-75. Bd. dirs. Mid-Am. chpt. ARC, 1972-76, Chgo. Hearing Soc., 1970-73, Joint Negro Appeal, 1965-75, Southside Chgo. br. NAACP, 1965-75. Recipient Richard E. Westbrooks award Cook County Bar Assn., 1972, Judicial award, 1975. Mem. Am., Ill., Chgo., Cook County, Nat. bar assns., Chgo. Mortgage Attys. Assn., Am. Arbitration Assn., Omega Psi Phi, Alpha Kappa Mu. Democrat. Mem. United Ch. of Christ (dir.). Mason (32 deg.). Clubs: Union League, Economic, Royal Coterie of Snakes, Chgo. Assembly, Harvard of Chgo. Home: 9655 S Calumet Ave Chicago IL 60628 Office: Chicago Civic Center Chicago IL 60602

WATTENBERG, JOAN LOUISE DILLON (MRS. CARL A. WATTENBERG, JR.), lawyer; b. Melrose Park, Ill., Feb. 18, 1941; d. Harold Vincent and Gilberta (Bond) Dillon; B.S., Washington U., 1963, J.D., 1966; m. Carl A. Wattenberg, Jr., June 5, 1965; children—Carl A. III, Elizabeth B. Admitted to Mo. bar, 1967; trademark atty. Ralston Purina Co., St. Louis, 1966-72; with firm Klamen, Summers, Wattenberg & Compton, St. Louis, 1972-76; corporate atty. The Brown Group, Inc., St. Louis, 1976—. Mem. Am., Mo. bar assns., U.S. Trademark Assn., Internat. Trademark Com., U.S. Capitol, Mo. hist. socs., Mo. Bot. Gardens, St. Louis Art Museum, Alpha Chi Omega. Club: Zonta (St. Louis). Home: 7235 Creveling Dr St Louis MO 63130 Office: 8400 Maryland Av St Louis MO 63105

WATTLES, JOHN CHARLES, banker; b. South Bend, Ind., Jan. 6, 1931; s. Charles P. and Carmen (Irvin) W.; B.B.A., Western Mich. U., 1955; m. Helen Statler Fischer, Feb. 26, 1955; children—Charles, Sara, Katie. Trust officer, v.p. First Nat. Bank & Trust Co. of Mich., Kalamazoo, 1957-69; pres. W.J. Upjohn Mgmt. Co., Kalamazoo, 1969-75; sr. v.p., trust officer Indsl. State Bank & Trust Co., Kalamazoo, 1975—; dir. APM, Inc., FCF, Inc., Wells Mfg. Corp., Wells-Index Corp. Bd. dirs. Lakeside Children's Home, Inc.; trustee YMCA, Barbour Hall Found., Howe Mil. Sch., Civic Auditorium Trustee Corp. Served as 1st lt., Q.M.C., U.S. Army, 1955-57. Mem. Investments Analyst Soc. Chgo., Western Mich. U. Alumni Assn. (dir.). Presbyterian. Club: Park. Office: 151 S Rose St Kalamazoo MI 49007

WATTS, CHARLES HERBERT, pub. offender treatment center exec.; b. Danville, Ind., July 7, 1937; s. Herbert and Harriet LaVada (Scott) W.; M.A. in Human Services, Webster Coll., 1976; m. Anna May Cale, June 5, 1959; 1 son, Charles Blair. Program dir. Westside YMCA, Oklahoma City, 1962-67; exec. dir. South County YMCA, St. Louis, 1967-72, Greater St. Louis Alliance for Shaping a Safer Community, 1972-74; residence dir. Magdala Found., St. Louis, 1974—; part-time instr. corrections Forest Park Community Coll., 1977—; pvt. practice reality therapy. Certified alcohol counselor, Mo. Mem. Am. Correctional Assn., Am. Personnel, Guidance Assn., Internat. Halfway House Assn. Democrat. Mem. Christian Ch. (Disciples of Christ). Saint Louis MO

WATTS, HENRY BRYAN, pharm. co. exec.; b. Mexico, Mo., May 26, 1942; s. Tony Bryan and Nannie Belle (Moss) W.; B.S. in Bus. Adminstrn., U. Mo., Columbia, 1964; m. Glenda Rae Garner, Nov. 26, 1975; children by previous marriage—Kathy Lynn, Karen Rae, Michael Bryan. Accountant, Peat, Marwick, Mitchell & Co., Kansas City, Mo., 1964-68; with Marion Labs. Inc., Kansas City, 1968—, corp. controller, 1970—. Bd. dirs., chmn. spl. gifts div. Jackson County br. Am. Cancer Soc., 1973-75, crusade chmn. West Met. Mo. area, 1976-77. C.P.A., Kans. Mem. Am. Soc. C.P.A.'s, Nat. Assn. Accountants (pres. Kansas City chpt. 1974-75), Fin. Execs. Inst., Am. Accounting Assn. Presbyterian. Home: 4722 W 80th St Prairie Village KS 66208 Office: PO Box 9627 Kansas City MO 64134

WATZKE, JAMES NORMAN, clergyman, psychologist; b. Chgo., July 7, 1936; s. Frank R. and Margaret M. (Murray) W.; B.A., U. Notre Dame, 1959, M.A., 1965; S.T.B., Gregorian U., Rome, 1961, S.T.L., 1963; Ph.D., Harvard U., 1972. Joined Congregation Holy Cross, later ordained priest Roman Catholic Ch.; student chaplain, counsellor U. Notre Dame, 1963-65; asst. prof. sociology Universidad Catolica de Santiago (Chile), tchr. St. George Coll., Santiago, 1965-67; teaching asst. dept. sociology Harvard U., 1968-69; lectr. dept. sociology Loyola U., Chgo., 1969-71; research asst. Nat. Opinion Research Inst., Chgo., 1969-71; clin. intern, social sci. analyst Brockton (Mass.) VA Hosp., 1970-71; psychologist, dir. day hosp. psychiat. program WestSide VA Hosp., Chgo., 1971—; asst. prof. dept. psychiatry Med. Sch., U. Ill., 1971—; pvt. practice psychotherapy, Chgo. and Oak Forest, Ill., 1975—. Mem. Am. Psychol. Assn., Am. Sociol. Assn., Am. Assn. Pastoral Counsellors, Internat. Assn., Applied Psychology, Am. Orthopsychiat. Assn., C.G. Jung Analytical Psychology Assn. (v.p., dir. 1975-77). Club: Harvard (Chgo.). Home: 1635 E 53d St Apt 1W Chicago IL 60615 Office: 5320 W 159th St Suite 203 Oak Forest IL 60452 also Day Hosp Room 116A2 WestSide VA Hosp 820 S Damen Ave Chicago IL 60680

WAUGH, MARY HESTER, hosp. adminstr.; b. Dighton, Kans., June 29, 1931; d. Harry Oscar and Lulu May (Morgan) Glenn; student Garden City Community Coll.; m. Vernon Robert Waugh, May 13, 1951; children—Vernon Robert, Sally Ann, Jack Lee, Mary Louise. Operator, United Telephone Co., Dighton, 1949-51; dep. county clk. Lane County, Kans., 1955-58; with Lane County Hosp., Dighton, 1960-75, adminstr., 1968-75; patient account mgr. St. Catherine Hosp., Garden City, Kans., 1975—. Sec. Far SW Comprehensive Health Planning Council, 1973; chmn. planning com. S.W. region Kans. Regional Med. Program, 1970, vice chmn., 1970-71; mem. Citizens Adv. Com. Lane County; adv. com., phys. therapy dept. Wichita (Kans.) State U., 1973-74. Mem. Kans. Hosp. Assn. (chmn. dist. 8 1972-73, mem. council manpower 1972-75), Kans. Assn. Hosp. Edn. and Tng. Coordinators (chmn. 1973-74), Dighton C. of C. Home: 544 W Long St Dighton KS 67839 Office: 608 N 5th St Garden City KS 67846

WAXLER, WILLIAM LORNE, ret. educator; b. Olney, Ill., Feb. 14, 1910; s. Harry L. and Sara Florence (Pilchard) W.; B.S., U. Ill., 1932, M.S., 1943; m. Helen Mae Eisnaugle, July 6, 1935; children—Sandra Lee Waxler Shanklin, Sue Lynn Waxler Fewell. Tchr., adminstr. various Ill. high schs., 1933-43; asst. chief chemist St. Louis Steel Casting Co., 1943-44; asst. chief research chemist Velsicol Corp., Marshall, Ill., 1944-45; prof. chemistry Stephens Coll., Columbia, Mo., 1945-75, head dept., 1960-75; vis. prof. chemistry U. Mo., Columbia, summers 1947-50, 53-54, 56-58, 60-62, 64-70, 74. Fellow Am. Inst. Chemists; mem. Am. Chem. Soc., AAUP. Republican. Presbyterian (deacon). Mason, Kiwanian (pres. 1963, dist. gov. 1969, internat. chmn. achievement 1970-71). Home: 308 Westridge Dr Columbia MO 65201

WAXMAN, JOSEPH HARRY, utility co. exec.; b. Warsaw, Poland, July 3, 1906; s. Sigmond and Mary Anna (Stehen) W.; came to U.S., 1908, naturalized, 1915; B.S., Coll. Advanced Traffic, 1944, M.S., 1946; postgrad. Purdue U., 1946, Ind., U., 1947. With No. Ind. Pub. Service Co., Hammond, 1923—, traffic mgr., 1941—, purchasing agt., 1957—. Lectr. Coll. Advanced Traffic, Chgo., 1946-50, Ind. U., Gary, also East Chicago, 1960-72, St. Joseph's Coll., East Chicago, 1972, Calumet Coll., Hammond, Ind., 1974. Mem. ICC Practitioners Assn. Mason (Shriner). Traffic editor Utility Purchasing Stores Mag. Home: 1828 Mansard Blvd Griffith IN 46319 Office: 5265 Hohman Ave Hammond IN 46320

WAYMAN, FRANK DONOVAN, real estate broker; b. Adair County, Mo., Oct. 3, 1931; s. Donovan E. and Virgie Maurine (Mikel) W.; B.S. in Bus. Adminstrn., N.E. Mo. State U., 1953; m. Mary Ann Funk, Jan. 10, 1954. Real estate broker, Kirksville, Mo., 1955—. Served with AUS, 1953-55. Mem. Mo. Real Estate Assn. (dir. 1964-65), N.E. Mo. Bd. Realtors (pres. 1963, 67), Mo. Assn. Realtors, Nat. Assn. Real Estate Bds. Mason (Shriner). Home: 2510 W Michigan Rd Kirksville MO 63501 Office: 1408 N Green St Kirksville MO 63501

WAYMAN, NORBURY LANSING, historian; b. Washington, Aug. 14, 1912; s. Edgar Hunt and Bertha Margaret (Lansing) W.; m. Amy Alice Penn, Oct. 1, 1937; student Hadley Tech. Sch., St. Louis, 1930-33, Washington U., St. Louis, 1934. Comml. artist, St. Louis, 1934-41; illustrator Curtiss-Wright Corp., 1942-45; plan technician Harland, Bartholomew & Assos., 1945-50, St. Louis Housing Authority, 1950-55; planner City Plan Commn., St. Louis, 1955-75; historian Community Devel. Agy., St. Louis, 1975—; represented in permanent collections of paintings at Boatmans Nat. Bank, Mo. Hist. Soc., hist. maps at St. Louis Pub. Library, Library of Congress, Washington. Mem. Mo., St. Louis hist. socs., Landmarks Assn. St. Louis, Nat. Trust for Historic Preservation, Sons and Daus. of Pioneer Rivermen, Marietta, Ohio. Author: A Pictorial History of St. Louis, 1968; History of the Physical Growth of St. Louis, 1969; Life on the River, 1971. Home: 8137 Park Ridge Dr St Louis MO 63123 Office: 1015 Locust St St Louis MO 63101

WAYT, WILLIAM ALLEN, educator, economist; b. Moundsville, W. Va., Feb. 20, 1921; s. William Blaine and Margaret (Allen) W.; B.S. in Agr., W. Va. U., 1943; M.S. in Agrl. Econs., Ohio State U., 1947, Ph.D., 1956; m. Gladys Ballard, July 28, 1945. Instr. agr. econs. Ohio State U., Columbus, 1948-56, asst. prof., 1956-61, asso. prof., 1961-66, prof., 1966—. Head dept. agrl. econs. and bus. Coll. Agr., Haile Selassie I U., Ethiopia, 1961-63; research officer Nairobi, Kenya, 1966-67; adviser U. Udaipur, India, 1969; mem. research team Uganda, 1970. Active Am. Red Cross Blood Bank, 1963—. Served with AUS, 1943-45. Recipient Distinguished Internat. Service award Okla. State U., 1969. Mem. Am. Agrl. Econs. Assn., AAUP, Internat. Conf. Agrl. Econs., AAAS, Alpha Zeta, Gamma Sigma Delta. Contbr. articles to profl. jours. Home: 187 E Northwood Ave Columbus OH 43201

WEATHERUP, ROBERT ALEXANDER, aerospace engr.; b. Champion, N.Y., Dec. 19, 1916; s. Garfield Edward and Pearl Rose (McDonald) W.; B.S., U.S. Naval Acad., 1940; B.S. in Aero. Engring., U.S. Naval Postgrad. Sch., 1948; M.S., Calif. Inst. Tech., 1949; m. Kathryn Crites Hesser, Jan. 27, 1943; children—Ann Kathryn, Roy Garfield, John Robert. Commd. ensign U.S. Navy, 1940, advanced through grades to comdr., 1951; comdg. officer Air Antisubmarine Squadron 892, 1951; comdg. officer U.S.S. Burton Island, 1959; ret., 1961; exec. adviser Douglas Aircraft Co., Long Beach, Calif., 1961-69; sr. group engr. McDonnell Aircraft Co., St. Louis, 1970—. Mem. Rolling Hills Estates (Calif.) Planning Commn., 1966-69. Deocrated D.F.C. with cluster, Air medal with 3 clusters, Purple Heart. Asso. fellow Am. Inst. Aeros. and Astronatuics; mem. Mil. Ops. Research Soc., Nat. Security Indsl. Assn. Methodist. Contbr. articles to profl. pubis. Patentee in field. Home: 883 Parma Dr Manchester MO 63011 Office: McDonnell Aircraft Co Box 516 St Louis MO 63166

WEAVER, ALLEN DALE, physicist, educator; b. Galesburg, Ill., Nov. 15, 1911; s. Harry Dale and Grace Fidelia (Allen) W.; B.S., Knox Coll., Galesburg, Ill., 1933; M.S., U. Mich., 1947; Ph.D., N.Y. U., 1954; m. Irene Fraser, June 27, 1940; children—James Allen, Peggy (Mrs. Thomas Larry Nix). Tchr. sci., math. Rio (Ill.) High Sch., 1935-37, Aledo (Ill.) Jr. High Sch., 1937-40; instr. physics and phys. sci. Md. State Tchrs. Coll., Salisbury, 1947-55; asso. prof. physics No. Ill. U., DeKalb, 1955-60, prof., 1960—. Vice-chmn. Citizens for Better Govt., DeKalb, 1958-59; pres. DeKalb-Ogle County Central Labor Council, 1972-74, sec., 1974—; mem. citizens adv. com. DeKalb Bd. Edn., 1959-75; mem. DeKalb Human Relations Commn., 1975-78. Served to capt., AUS, 1941-46. Mem. AAUP (pres. Ill. conf. 1965-68), Am. Fedn. Tchrs. (pres. local 1673 1968-70), Nat. Assn. Research in Sci. Teaching, Nat. Sci. Tchrs. Assn., Am. Assn. Physics Tchrs., Sch. Sci. and Math. Assn., ACLU, Phi Delta Kappa. Author: (with James F. Glenn) Experiments in Physical Science, 1958. Home: 591 Garden Rd DeKalb IL 60115

WEAVER, ARTHUR LAWRENCE, physician; b. Lincoln, Nebr., Sept. 3, 1936; s. Arthur J. and Harriet Elizabeth (Walt) W.; B.S. (Regents scholar) with distinction, U. Nebr., 1958; M.D., Northwestern U., 1962; M.S. in Medicine, U. Minn., 1966; m. Frances Jensen, June 18, 1959; children—Arthur Jensen, Anne Christine. Intern U. Mich. Hosps., Ann Arbor, 1962-63; resident Mayo Grad. Sch. Medicine, Rochester, Minn., 1963-66; practice medicine specializing in rheumatology and internal medicine, Lincoln, 1968—; mem. staff Bryan Meml. Hosp., chmn. dept. rheumatology, 1976—; mem. courtesy staff St. Elizabeths Hosp., Lincoln Gen. Hosp.; mem. cons. staff VA Hosp.; chmn. Juvenile Rheumatoid Arthritis Clinic, 1970—; asso. prof. dept. internal medicine U. Nebr., Omaha, 1976—; med. dir. Lincoln Benefit Life Ins. Co., Nebr., 1972—. Bd. dirs. Nebr. chpt. Arthritis Found., 1969—; trustee U. Nebr. Found., 1974—. Served to capt., M.C., U.S. Army, 1966-68. Recipient Outstanding Nebraskan award U. Nebr., 1958, also C.W. Boucher award; Philip S. Hench award Rheumatology, Mayo Grad. Sch. Medicine, 1966; diplomate Am. Bd. Internal Medicine. Fellow A.C.P.; mem. Am., Nebr. socs. of internal medicine, Am. Rheumatism Assn., Nebraska Rheumatism Assn., Lancaster County Med. Soc., Mayo Grad. Sch. Medicine Alumni Assn., Phi Beta Kappa, Sigma Xi, Alpha Omega Alpha, Pi Kappa Epsilon, Phi Rho Sigma. Republican. Presbyterian. Contbr. articles in field to med. jours. Home: 2626 S 24th St Lincoln NE 68502 Office: 1512 First National Bank Lincoln NE 68508

WEAVER, FLOYD EDWARD, surgeon; b. Dewey, Ill., Jan. 21, 1922; s. Avery Thomas and Magdalena (Ingold) W.; A.B., Goshen Coll., 1954; B.S., Med. Sch., U. Ill., M.D., 1958; m. Edna Mae Stalter, Dec. 22, 1951; children—Sharon Renee, Galen Floyd. Intern, Decatur (Ill.) Gen. Hosp., 1958-59; resident in surgery Hines (Ill.) VA Hosp., 1961-65; chief of staff, St. James Hosp., Pontiac, Ill., 1975-76, chief of surgery, 1968—; surg. cons. Children's Center, Fairburg Hosp.; clin. asso. basic sci. U. Ill. Elder, Mennonite Ch., 1968; regent Winston Churchill Coll., 1968-69; bd. Mental Health Assn., 1970, TB Assn., 1966-70. Diplomate Am. Bd. Surgery. Fellow A.C.S.; mem. Ill. Med. Soc., Ill., Pan-Am., Charles B. Paustow surg. socs., Soc. Abdominal Surgeons, Am. Geriatric Soc., Royal Soc. Physicians. Republican. Contbr. article to profl. jour. Home: 8 Dixie Lane Pontiac IL 61764 Office: 612 E Water St Pontiac IL 61764

WEAVER, GLENN MORRISON, psychiatrist; b. Huntington, W.Va., July 23, 1921; s. John Stanley and Margaret Love (Wallingford) W.; B.S., U. Cin., 1943, M.D., 1945; m. Mary Ellen Roberts, June 22, 1945; children—Pamela Ruth, Margaret Ellen. Intern, St. Louis City Hosp., 1945-46; resident in pathology Cin. Gen. Hosp., 1948-49, in psychiatry Longview State Hosp., 1949-50, Christ Hosp., 1950-51, Cin. Gen. Hosp., 1951-52; practice medicine specializing in psychiatry, Cin., 1952—; mem. staff, dir. dept. neurology and psychiatry Christ Hosp., Cin., 1965—; instr. psychiatry U. Cin., 1952-73, clin. asst. prof., 1973—; cons. AEC, 1952—, Hamilton County Probate Ct., 1956—; mem. Hamilton County Mental Health and Rehab. Bd., 1975—. Served to capt. U.S. Army, 1946-48. Recipient Physician's Recognition award AMA, 1976. Fellow Am. Psychiat. Assn.; mem. Am., Ohio State med. assns., Am. Acad. Psychiatry and Law, Acad. Legal Medicine, Ohio Psychiat. Assn., Cin. Soc. Neurology and Psychiatry, Cin. Acad. Medicine, Keeneland Assn. Presbyterian. Clubs: Univ. (Cin.), Masons, Shriners. Author: Considerations of Multiple Personality, 1965; contbr. articles to med. jour. Home: 323 Warren Ave Cincinnati OH 45220 Office: 250 Wm Howard Taft Rd Cincinnati OH 45219

WEAVER, JOHN C(ARRIER), univ. pres. emeritus, educator; b. Evanston, Ill., May 21, 1915; s. Andrew Thomas and Cornelia Myrta (Carrier) W.; A.B., U. Wis., 1936, A.M., 1937, Ph.D., 1942; LL.D., Mercer U., 1972; L.H.D., Drury Coll., 1973; Litt.D., St. Scholastica Coll., 1973; m. Ruberta Louise Harwell, Aug. 8, 1940; children—Andrew Bennett, Thomas Harwell. Mem. editorial and research staff Am. Geog. Soc. of N.Y., 1940-42; mem. research staff Office of Geographer, U.S. Dept. State, 1942-44; asst. prof. dept. geography U. Minn., 1946-47, asso. prof., 1947-48, prof., 1948-55; prof. geography, dean college arts and sciences Kans. State U., 1955-57; prof. geography, dean Grad. Coll., U. Nebr., 1957-61; prof. geography, v.p. research and dean Grad. Coll., State U. Iowa, 1961-64; prof. geography, v.p. for acad. affairs, dean faculties Ohio State U., 1964-66; prof. geography, pres. U. Mo., 1966-70; prof. geography U. Wis.-Madison, Milw., Green Bay; pres. U. Wis. System, 1971-77. Vis. prof. U. Oreg., summer 1951, Harvard U., summer 1954; Distinguished vis. prof. U. S.C., 1977-78. Research cons. Midwest Barley Improvement Assn. of Milw., 1946-50; expert cons. to Com. on Geophysics and Geography, Research and Devel. Bd., Washington, 1947-53; mem. adv. com. on geography Office Naval Research, NRC, 1949-52, chmn., 1951-52; cons. editor McGraw-Hill series in geography, 1951-67; Carnegie Found. adminstrv. fellow, 1957-58; mem. adv. com. to Sec. HEW, 1958-62, to Commr. of Edn., 1965-66; Wilton Park fellow Brit. Fgn. Office, 1965, 67, 70, 74, 76; Riecker Meml. lectr. U. Ariz., 1965. Chmn. Council Grad. Schs. U.S., 1961-62; pres. Assn. Grad. Schs. in Assn. Am. Univs., 1963-64; chmn. council acad. affairs Assn. State Univs. and Land-Grant Colls., 1965-66; mem. Com. for Inter-Instl. Cooperation, 1962-66, chmn., 1964-66; mem. commn. on policies and goals in higher edn. Am. Council on Edn., 1966-69; mem. bd. commrs. Nat. Commn. on Accrediting, 1966-76; mem. adv. council presidents Assn. Governing Bds. Univs. and Colls., 1968-71; sponsor Atlantic Council U.S., 1967—; mem. Mo. Commn. Higher Edn., 1966-70; mem. adv. bd. Mo. Assn. Retarded Children, 1968-70; mem. commn. adminstrv. affairs

Am. Council on Edn., 1969-72; mem. nat. selection com. Woodrow Wilson Fellow. Found., 1961-68; mem. sci. info. council NSF, 1968-70; mem. Edn. Commn. States, 1971-77. Trustee, Argonne Universities Assn., 1966-70, Am. Univs. Field Staff, 1971-76, Johnson Found., 1971-77; bd. dirs. Nat. Merit Scholarship Corp., 1971-77. Served as Arctic intelligence officer USNR, 1944-46; Office of Chief of Naval Operations, Washington. Recipient Vilas medal U. Wis., 1936; Letter Commendation from Chief of Naval Operations, 1946; citation for outstanding contbn. to geography Assn. Am. Geographers, 1955). Fellow Am. Geog. Soc. N.Y., A.A.A.S.; mem. Assn. Am. Geographers (mem. council 1949-51), Am. Pharm. Assn. (hon.), Am. Council on Pharm. Edn., Nat. Council on Edn. (dir. 1973-76), Am. Geophys. Union, Arctic Inst. N.A. (charter asso.), Am. Polar Soc., Sigma Xi, Phi Beta Kappa, Phi Kappa Phi, Delta Sigma Rho, Phi Eta Sigma, Chi Phi, Beta Gamma Sigma. Conglist. Rotarian. Author: Ice Atlas of the Northern Hemisphere, 1946; American Barley Production; A Study in Agricultural Geography, 1950; The American Railroads, 1958; (with Fred E. Lukerman) A World Statistical Survey of Commercial Production: A Geographical Sourcebook, 1950, World Resources Statistics, 1953; Quiet Thoughts, 1971; also articles in books and profl. periodicals. Cons. editor Geog. Rev., 1955-72. Home: Rural Route 1 Oostburg WI 53070

WEAVER, KENNARD RAY, lawyer; b. Fremont, Ohio, Mar. 27, 1940; s. Dr. Carl H. and Vera (Anderson) W.; B.A., Mich. State U., 1962; J.D., Harvard U., 1965; m. Judith Ann Westie, Sept. 16, 1961; children—Carla Louise, Lesley Elizabeth. Admitted to Wis. bar, 1965, Ind. bar, 1967, U.S. Supreme Ct. bar, 1973, Mich. bar, 1977; asso. Brady, Tyrrell & Bruce, 1965-66; with Office of Gen. Counsel of Small Bus. Adminstrn., 1966-67; partner firm Church, Meteiver & Weaver, Elkhart, Ind., 1967—. Dir. Vemco Builders, Inc. Bd. dirs. Assn. Disabled Elkhart County, Urban League. Rotarian. Clubs: Summit, Elcona Country. Home: 23255 Greenleaf Blvd Elkhart IN 46154 Office: Box 817 400 St Joseph Valley Bank Bldg Elkhart IN 46514

WEAVER, KENNETH RONALD, hosp. exec.; b. Cass County, Mich., Sept. 19, 1926; s. Clyde D. and Alma L. (Price) W.; B.S., Ball State U., 1953; m. Sharon Kay Kimble, June 15, 1957; children—Laurie Ruth, Jeffrey Kent, Gregory Scott, Michael Gerald. State editor News-Sentinel, Ft. Wayne, Ind., 1953-58; editor Tri-City Progress, Warren, Mich., 1958-60; news editor The Eccentric, Birmingham, Mich., 1960-61, mng. editor, 1961-67; mng. editor Wabash (Ind.) Plain Dealer, 1967-69; mng. editor Community-News-Macomb Group, East Detroit, Mich., 1969-71; publs. editor William Beaumont Hosp., Royal Oak, Mich., 1971, asst. dir. pub. relations, 1971—. Mem. Ball State Devel. Council, 1954-57. Served with AUS, 1945-46. Recipient Distinguished Service award Ball State U. Alumni, 1967. Mem. Southeastern Mich. (sec. 1973-74), Mich. hosp. pub. relations assns., Assn. Bus. Communicators/Detroit, C. of C. Kiwanian. Contbr. articles to mags. Home: 641 Redruth Blvd Clawson MI 48017 Office: William Beaumont Hosp Royal Oak MI 48072

WEAVER, KENNETH VERNON, farmer; b. Mpls., May 13, 1944; s. Elmer Vernon and Clarinda (Brown) W.; student Dakota Bus. Coll., Fargo, N.D., 1962-64, Lake Region Jr. Coll., Devils Lake, N.D., 1966-68; m. Sandra Corleen Weaver, Nov. 14, 1964; children—Kurt Kenneth, Craig Vernon, Joni Kay. Various positions bookkeeping, sales Midland Hosp. Supply Co., Fargo, 1964-66; lineman Research Industries, St. Paul, 1968-69; parts man, motor pool Pan Am., Nekoma, N.D., 1975—, dir. Masterpiece Products Inc. Farmer Munich, N.D., 1966—. Chmn. N.D. Dist. Amateur Athletic Union, 1969-74. Mem. N.D. Weight Lifting Club (pres. 1969-74). Methodist (chmn. bd.). Address: Route 1 Munich ND 58352

WEAVER, L. RUTH RUNDLE (MRS. C.H. WEAVER), lawyer; b. St. Joseph, Mo.; d. Charles Vail and Anna (Wist) Rundle; B.A., Kearney State Coll., 1923; J.D., Akron U. Coll. Law, 1955; m. Clyde Hulbert Weaver, Feb. 28, 1931 (dec. June 1951). Tchr., Chase County High Sch., Imperial, Nebr., 1923-24, Biwabik (Minn.) High Sch., 1924-25, Child High Sch., Edgerton, Wis., 1925-28, Central High Sch., Akron, Ohio, 1928-30; supr. personnel record sect. Goodyear Tire and Rubber Co., Akron, 1942-47; teller Evans Savs. Assn., Akron, 1951-56; admitted to Ohio bar, 1956, since in practice, Akron. Named Woman of Year, Summit chpt. Am. Bus. Women's Assn., 1961. Mem. Am. Judicature Soc. Fedn. Women's Clubs, Am. (mem. com. cooperation state and local bar groups, taxation sect., 1956-62, com. estate and gift taxes 1962-66, 67-68, gen. practice sect., real property and trust sect., family com. gen. practice sect. 1974-75), Ohio, Akron (mem. pub. relations com. 1958—, chmn. speakers bur. com. 1965-66, mem. entertainment com. 1965-66, mem. ethics com. 1969—, mem. probate court com. 1967-69, mem. inquiry com. 1967—, chmn. welfare and necrology com. 1973-76) bar assns., Ohio Acad. Trial Lawyers, Am. Trial Lawyers Assn., Cuyahoga Falls League Women Voters, Am. Bus. Women's Assn., Nat. Trust Historic Preservation, Western Res. Hist. Soc., Akron Dist. Golf Assn. (tournament chmn. 1939-41, pres. 1941-49), Phi Delta Delta (chpt. pres. 1967-70). Clubs: Quota (membership com. 1961-62, parliamentarian 1962-66, chmn. community service, 1964-65), Woman's City (1st vice chmn. six-thirty sect. 1967-68), Business Women's Current Events (pres. 1964-66). Home: 2453 16th St Cuyahoga Falls OH 44223 Office: United Bldg Akron OH 44308

WEAVER, RICHARD ALVIN, automotive supply co. exec.; b. Flint, Mich., Mar. 22, 1939; s. Thomas A. and Frances M. (Ray) W.; B.A., Mich. State U., 1963; m. Jean Mary Benson, May 29, 1965; children—Kelly, Richard, Diane. Indsl. engr., mfg. foreman Chevrolet div. Gen. Motors Corp., Bay City, Mich., 1963-67; plant mfg. engr., staff mfg. engr. Ford Motor Co., Rawsonville, Mich., 1967-69; plant mgr. Eaton Corp., Saginaw, Mich., 1969—. Bd. dirs. Saginaw Gen. Hosp., 1977—; chmn. bd. dirs. Bay County Social Intervention Service, 1977—: bd. dirs. Jr. Achievement, Saginaw, 1976—, Saginaw United Way, 1974—. Served with USN, 1961-63. Mem. Soc. Automotive Engrs., Saginaw C. of C. (bd. dirs. 1974—). Republican. Roman Catholic. Clubs: Bay City Country, Elks. Home: 3059 W Riverview Dr Bay City MI 48706 Office: 1000 Rust St Saginaw MI 48601

WEAVER, R(ICHARD) DONALD, clergyman; b. St. Louis, Mar. 25, 1926; s. Robert Raymond and Ada Viola (Holz) W.; B.S.C., St. Louis U., 1949; M.Div., Garrett Theol. Sem., 1952; postgrad U. Chgo., 1951-53; M.A., Scarritt Coll., 1978. Ordained to ministry United Methodist Ch., 1951; pastor, Lizton and Salem (Ind.) Meth. Chs., 1951-53, Centenary Meth. Ch., Veedersburg, Ind., 1954-58, Indiana Harbor United Meth. Ch., East Chicago, Ind., 1958-73, 1st United Meth. Ch., Hobart, Ind., 1973—; lectr. Calumet Coll., Whiting, Ind., 1967—. Pres., United Way, 1974, Twin Cities Community Services, 1970, Lake County Mental Health Assn., 1963, 64; v.p. Referral and Emergency Services, 1977; bd. dirs. No. Ind. Health Systems Agy., 1976—; mem. East Chicago Housing Commn., 1965. Served with AUS, 1944-46; ETO. Recipient Community Leadership award Twin City Community Services, 1971. Mem. AAUP, Am. Soc. Ch. History, Assn. Sociology of Religion, Hymn Soc. Am., Insts. Religion, Religious Edn. Assn. U.S. and Can., Religious Research Assn., Soc. Sci. Study Religion, Hobart Ministerial Assn. Home: 654 E 4th St Hobart IN 46342 Office: 658 E 4th St Hobart IN 46342

WEBB, CHARLES HAIZLIP, univ. dean; b. Dallas, Feb. 14, 1933; s. C.H. and Marion E. (Gilker) W.; m. Kenda McGibbon; children—Mark, Kent, Malcolm, Charles; B.A., So. Meth. U., 1955, Mus.M., 1955; Mus.D., Ind. U., 1964. Asst. to dean Sch. Music, So. Meth. U., 1957-58; asso. instr. piano Ind. U., Bloomington, 1958-60, instr. music, mgr. musical attractions, 1960-64, asst. prof. music, 1964-67, asso. prof., 1967, asst. dean, asso. dean Sch. Music, 1964-73, dean, 1973—; dir. Indpls. Symphonic Chorus; chmn. adv. bd. Internat. Festivals, Inc.; commr. Ind. Arts Commn.; adv. panel Music Found.; evaluator challenge grant program Nat. Endowment for Arts; mem. recommendation bd. Avery Fisher Prize Program. Organist, First Meth. Ch., Bloomington, 1959—. Mem. Pi Kappa Lambda, Phi Mu Alpha. Author editor music publs. Home: 648 Woodscrest Dr Bloomington IN 47401

WEBB, EDWARD FRANCIS, physician, ophthalmologist; b. Freeport, Ill., Dec. 5, 1915; s. Eddie D. and Mildred (Byrne) W.; B.S., U. Ill., 1935, M.D., 1939; m. June Marie Kelm, Apr. 18, 1942; children—Terrence B., Robert E. Intern, St. Luke's Hosp., Chgo., 1939-41; cons. Internat. Harvester, Western Electric Corp., Libby Foods, 1940-42; preceptorship with dr., Chgo., 1941-42, 46-48; physician-ophthalmologist St. Lukes Clinics, 1946-48, Bethesda, Henrotin hosps., others, 1946—; clin. instr. Mercy Hosp., 1954-60; asst. prof. Stritch Sch. Medicine, 1960—. Lectr. ophthalmology, 1947-54, Mulago Hosp., Makerere U., Kampala, Uganda; chief service eye sect. Skokie Valley Community Hosp. Ophthalmic cons. U.S., allied olympic teams, Mexico, 1968. Served with M.C., AUS, 1942-46. Fellow Am. Acad. Ophtalmology, Internat. Coll. Surgeons; mem. Am., Pan-Am. assns. ophthalmology, AMA, Ill., Chgo. med. socs., Chgo. Ophthalmology Soc., Internat. Eye Found., Soc. Eye Surgeons. Club: Adventurers (treas. Chgo. 1966-68, v.p. 1969, pres. 1970-71, dir.). Republican. Episcopalian. Field collector botany, entomology, geology Field Mus. Natural History. Home: 1332 Sanford Ln Glenview IL 60025 Office: 5112 Oakton St Skokie IL 60076

WEBB, JAMES R., economist; b. Granite City, Ill., Apr. 5, 1947; s. Gene and Lucille (Arney) W.; B.S., No. Ill. U., 1972, M.B.A., 1974, postgrad., 1974—. Expediter, Hydroline Mfg. Co., Rockford, Ill., 1967, corr. inside sales, 1967-69, engring. coordinator, 1969-76; analyst corporate systems finance div. Parker Pen Corp., Janesville, Wis., 1976; grad. teaching asst. econs. U. Ill., Urbana-Champaign, 1976—. Mem. AAUP, Am. Econ. Assn., Am. Fin. Assn., Am. Sociol. Assn., Am. Statis. Assn., Assn. M.B.A. Execs., Bertrand Russell Soc., other orgns. Home: 2108 W White St Apt 143 Champaign IL 61820 Office: Box 14 Room 7 David Kinley Hall U Ill Urbana IL 61801

WEBB, J(ESSE) EDGAR, educator, theatre dir.; b. Lubbock, Tex., July 11, 1929; s. Joe Edgar and Jessie Joy (Stewart) W.; student Abilene Christian Coll., 1947-50, Pratt Inst., 1948-49; B.A., N. Tex. State U., 1956; postgrad Am. Theatre Wing., 1956-58; M.A., Tex. Tech. U., 1964; Ph.D. in Theatre Arts, Ind. U., 1967; m. Dorothy Louise Beck, Aug. 13, 1967; 1 dau., Jessica Elizabeth. Tchr., Corpus Christi (Tex.) Pub. Schs., 1959-64; dir. theatre, asst. prof. theatre arts U. Corpus Christi, 1964-65; lectr. Ind. U., Indpls., 1967—; asst. prof. theatre arts Ind. U.-Purdue U., Indpls., 1967-77, asso. prof., 1977—, dir. theatre, 1967—; judge No. Ind. region Am. Coll. Theatre Festival, 1974—, head judge, 1977—. Served with USAF, 1950-54. Mem. Am. (governing bd. region 1977—), Ind. (sec. 1976—), theatre assns., Speech Communications Assn., Actor's Equity Assn. Mem. Ch. of Christ. Home: 404 E 55th St Indianapolis IN 46220 Office: 902 N Meridian St Indianapolis IN 46204

WEBB, LANCE, bishop; b. Boaz, N.Mex., Dec. 10, 1909; s. John Newton Shields and Della (Lance) W.; B.A. with highest honors, McMurry Coll., Abilene, Tex., 1931, D.D., 1948; B.D., So. Meth. U., 1934, M.A., 1934; summer student Union Theol. Sem., 1939, 47; D.D., Ohio Wesleyan, U., 1960, MacMurray Coll., 1967, McKendree Coll., 1970; L.H.D., Ill. Wesleyan U., 1966; LL.D., So. Meth. U., 1966; D.Lit., Morningside Coll., 1977; m. Mary Elizabeth Hunt, June 30, 1933; children—Gloria Jeanne (Mrs. David B. Davis), Mary M. (Mrs. Lee Edlund), Ruth Elizabeth (Mrs. Allan Lindstrom). Ordained to ministry Meth. Ch., 1935; pastor McCullough-Harrah Meth. Chs., Pampa, Tex., 1934-37; chaplain prof. religion McMurry Coll., Abilene, 1937-38; pastor, Shamrock, Tex., 1938-40, Eastland, Tex., 1940-41, University Park Meth. Ch., Dallas, 1941-52, North Broadway Meth. Ch., Columbus, O., 1953-64; bishop Meth. Ch., 1964—, resident bishop Ill. area, 1964-76, Iowa area, 1976—. Chmn. com. on worship Meth. Ch., 1964-72, mem. gen. and jurisdictional coms., co-chmn. world Meth. com. worship and liturgy, 1966-71, exec. vice-chmn., 1971-76, chmn., 1976—; mem. World Meth. Council, 1966—; mem. bd. higher edn. and ministry United Meth. Ch., 1972—; episcopal visitation to S.Am., 1965, to Africa, 1970, to Philippines, 1974; conducted good-will tours Middle East and Round the World, 1961, 63; Nat. Council Chs. interchange preacher in Britain, 1959; chancellor Disciplined Order of Christ, 1964—. Mem. Columbus Mayor's Com. on Human Relations, 1953-64; chaplain Ohio Senate, 1963; internat. chaplain Civitain Internat., 1951; chmn. Grain Belt Consultation on World Hunger, 1976. Trustee Meth. Sch. Theology in Ohio, Garrett Evang. Theol. Sch., Evanston, Ill., McKendree Coll., Lebanon, Ill., Ill. Wesleyan U., MacMurray Coll., 1964-76; chmn. bd. Wesley Found., U. Ill., 1964-76, Iowa Wesleyan U., 1976—, also Cornell Coll., Morningside Coll., Westmar Coll., Simpson Coll. Mason (33). Club: Torch (Columbus). Author: Conquering the Seven Deadly Sins, 1955; Discovering Love, 1959; Point of Glad Return, 1960; Art of Personal prayer, 1962; On the Edge of the Absurd, 1965; When God Comes Alive, 1968; Disciplines for Life in the Age of Aquarius, 1971; God's Surprises, 1976. Home: 3005 Patricia Dr Des Moines IA 50322 Office: 1019 Chestnut St Des Moines IA 50309

WEBB, LESLIE RICHARD, physician; b. Bethany, Mo., June 13, 1916; s. Leslie Richard and Clare (Darr) W.; A.B. cum laude, Dartmouth Coll., 1938; M.D., Harvard U., 1942; m. Mary Belle Shultz, Sept. 11, 1942; children—Lesley Darr, Carol Ann. Intern, Peter Bent Brigham Hosp., Boston, 1942-43, asst. resident, 1946-48; fellow Lahey Clinic, Boston, 1948-49; practice medicine specializing in gastroenterology, Springfield, Mo., 1949-74; physician Med. Center for Fed. Prisoners, Springfield, 1974—, chief of medicine, 1975-76, chief of staff, 1976—. Served with USNR, 1943-46. Decorated Bronze Star. Diplomate Am. Bd. Internal Medicine. Fellow A.C.P.; mem. Phi Beta Kappa, Alpha Omega Alpha. Home: 1243 E Loren St Springfield MO 65804 Office: 1900 W Sunshine St Springfield MO 65804

WEBB, PAUL BENEDICT, JR., physician; b. St. Louis, June 28, 1925; s. Paul Benedict and Adela Katherine (Glosemeyer) W.; M.D., St. Louis U., 1952; postgrad. Washington U., 1953-54; m. Bessie Marie Brenneisen, May 2, 1953; children—Paul Benedict III, David, Diane, Steven, Richard, Timothy, Matthew, Kevin, Patricia. Intern St. John's Hosp., 1952-53; resident ophthalmology Ind. U., 1954-56; pvt. practice ltd. to ophthalmology, St. Louis, 1956—; asst. prof. St. Louis U. Merit badge dir. pub. service group Boy Scouts Am. Served with AUS, 1943-46. Diplomate Am. Bd. Ophthalmology. Mem. AMA, Am. Acad. Ophthalmology and Otolaryngology, St. Louis Ophthalmol. Soc., Mo. Med. Assn., St. Louis Med. Soc., Mo. Ophthalmol. Soc. Home: 6207 Itaska St St Louis MO 63109 Office: 6651 Chippewa St St Louis MO 63109

WEBB, THELMA ELIZABETH, librarian; b. Bethlehem, Pa., Mar. 24, 1914; d. Ernest and Beatrice Maud (Elwell) Hooper; B.A. cum laude, Baldwin-Wallace Coll., 1936; postgrad. Pestalozzi-Froebel Sch., Chgo., 1962, Concordia Tchrs. Coll., River Forest, 1974-76; M.A. in L.S., Rosary Coll., River Forest, Ill., 1969; m. Harold W. Webb, Sept. 14, 1940; children—Paul Kent, Margaret Eileen Webb St. John. Tchr. pub. schs., Wellington, Ohio, 1936-40, Lincoln Sch., Maywood, Ill., 1961-63; tchr., librarian Jane Addams Sch., Melrose Park, Ill., 1963-74; supr. library media dist. 89 Ill., 1975—. Sec. Irving Sch., Maywood, 1960-61; fin. officer, mgr. Mid-Am. chpt. ARC, 1942-43. Mem. Nat., Ill. edn. assns., ALA, Ill. Library Assn., Am. Assn. Sch. Librarians, Bus. and Profl. Women's Club (chpt. treas.), Oak Park (Ill.) PTA (life), Gamma Sigma (treas. 1938-40), Alpha Phi Gamma (v.p. 1939-40), Pi Gamma Mu, Phi Kappa Delta. Baptist (sec., tchr. Sunday sch.). Home: 913 N 9th Ave Maywood IL 60153 Office: 1133 S 8th Ave Maywood IL 60153

WEBBE, SCOTSON, mfg. exec.; b. Chgo., July 18, 1917; s. Albion Scotson and Margaret (White) W.; student Harvard Bus. Sch., 1940-41; B.A., Williams Coll., 1938; m. Margery Michelson, Mar. 7, 1941; children—Scotson Lindsay, Richard White, Margaret Dalie. Salesman, Quaker Oats Co., North Platte, Nebr., 1938-40; with Curtis Pub. Co., Chgo. and Phila., 1946-61, advt. sales mgr., 1957-61; mktg. cons., 1962-64; v.p. mktg. Handgards, Inc., Wilmette, Ill., 1964-66, pres., 1966—, also dir.; pres., dir. Guard Corp., Wilmette, 1973—; v.p., dir. Cortez Cattle Co., Tucson, 1974—. Served to lt. comdr. USNR, 1940-45. Mem. A.I.M. (mem. pres.'s council 1968—), Chi Psi, Delta Sigma Rho. Republican. Congregationalist. Clubs: Indian Hill Country (Winnetka, Ill.); University (Chgo.); Middlefork Tennis (Northfield, Ill.). Home: 2112 Middlefork Rd Northfield IL 60093 Office: Edens Exec Center Wilmette IL 60091

WEBBER, EVERARD LELAND, museum dir.; b. Chgo., Jan. 27, 1920; s. Leland Bacon and Harriet Gaylord (Peck) W.; B.B.A., U. Cin., 1942; C.P.A., U. Ill., 1949: m. Ellen Gowen Duer, Mar. 30, 1946 (dec. 1974); children—Leland Duer, James Randall, Ellen Robinson; m. 2d, Joan Wray Malloch, Sept. 6, 1975. With Proctor & Gamble Co., Cin., 1939-42, Ernst & Ernst, C.P.A.'s, Chgo., 1945-50; with Field Museum of Natural History, 1950—, exec. asst. to dir., 1951-60, asst. dir., 1960-62, dir., 1962—, pres., 1976—, also trustee. Bd. dirs. Ill. State Mus., 1966-69; bd. govs. Ill. State Colls. and Univs., 1967-75; mem. Nat. Council on Arts, 1970-76, Nat. 4-H Service Com., 1972-76. Served to lt. (s.g.) USNR, 1942-45. Mem. AAMS, Am. Assn. Museums (v.p. 1966-70), Beta Theta Pi. Episcopalian. Clubs: Tavern, University, Economic, Caxton, Mich. Shores Arts. Home: 1224 Elmwood Ave Wilmette IL 60091 Office: Field Museum of Natural History Roosevelt Rd and Lake Shore Dr Chicago IL 60605

WEBBER, GENE FRANKLIN, furniture mfr.; b. Lisabeula, Wash., Apr. 19, 1925; s. James Harrison and Lillian (Breitigam) W.; B.S. in M.E., U. Wash., 1945; postgrad. Northwestern U., 1946-48; m. Lois Edith Okerberg, Oct. 31, 1946; children—Lawrence Alan, William Scott. Cons., Booz, Allen & Hamilton, Chgo., 1956-58; gen. sales mgr. E.R. Wagner Mfg. Co., Milw., 1959-65; gen. mgr. Housewares div. GSW Ltd., Montreal, 1966-72; pres. Korth Furniture Industries, Warsaw, Ind., 1972—, also v.p., chief operating officer Thompson Mfg. Co., Algood, Tenn., 1976—; v.p. Dorset Corp. (Louisville); cons. Union Ch. (Hinsdale, Ill.). Served with USNR, 1943-46. Mem. Nat. Assn. Furniture Mfrs., Warsaw C. of C. (dir. indsl. div. 1973-76). Republican. Presbyterian. Clubs: Tippecanoe Lake Country, Rotary. Patentee elec. ignition system for gas appliances. Home: RR 1 Box 167 Leesburg IN 46538 Office: Korth Furniture Industries Box 898 Warsaw IN 46580

WEBBER, WARREN LORAINE, univ. ofcl.; b. Cedar, Iowa, May 16, 1927; s. Curtis Raymond and Elsie (Cosby) W.; student William Penn Coll., 1946-47; B.A., B.Mus., Central Coll., 1949; M.Mus. Edn., Drake U., 1954; Ph.D., Ohio State Univ., 1966; m. Ardeth Joanne Woodard, May 31, 1949; children—Carol Lynne, David Leroy, Allen Leigh, Bonny Lanel. Tchr. pub. schs., New Sharon, Iowa, 1949-51, dir. band, Monroe, Iowa, 1951-56; prof. music, chmn. div. fine arts Cedarville (Ohio) Coll., 1956-71; dir. instl. research and planning Central State U., Wilberforce, Ohio, 1971—. City councilman, Cedarville, 1962—, pres. village council, 1967-71, chmn. street com., 1962-66, chmn. utilities com., 1967-74, chmn. finance com., 1975—. Mem. Soc. Coll. and Univ. Planning, Ohio Music Edn. Assn., Music Educators Nat. Conf., Nat. Soc. for Study Edn. Am. Assn. Higher Edn. Baptist (organist). Home: 168 Walnut St PO Box 31 Cedarville OH 45314 Office: Central State Univ Wilberforce OH 45384

WEBEL, JAMES BUELL, mfg. co. exec.; b. Ft. Sill, Okla., Nov. 23, 1923; s. Magee James and Ida May (Millican) W.; M.B.A. with high distinction, Harvard, 1956; M.A. in Internat. Relations, George Washington U., 1963; grad. Nat. War Coll., 1963; m. Ramona K. Peterson, Sept. 7, 1942; children—Katherine Lee (Mrs. William Welch), Paula Jo (Mrs. James A. Albring). Joined U.S. Army, 1939, advanced through grades to col., 1966; ret., 1966; with Owens-Corning Fiberglas Corp., N.Y.C., 1966-67, v.p. corporate planning, Toledo, 1968-71, v.p., gen. mgr. archtl. products div., 1971-74, v.p., office of pres., 1975—; v.p. adminstrn. bldg. materials group, 1976, v.p. engineered systems div., 1976—. Decorated D.S.C., Silver Star, Legion of Merit, Bronze Star with cluster, Purple Heart with Cluster; grand comdr. Royal Order of Phoenix (Greece). Mem. SNAME, Producers' Council. Club: Toledo. Home: 4109 Stonehenge Dr Sylvania OH 43560 Office: Owens-Corning Fiberglas Fiberglas Tower Toledo OH 43659

WEBER, A(DOLPH) CARL, bank exec., steel co. cons.; b. St. Louis, Apr. 3, 1909; s. Harry Carl and Caroline E. (Holthaus) W.; B.S. in Archtl. Engring., Washington U., St. Louis, 1930; C.E., Sch. Mines and Metallurgy, 1953; m. Edna Maia Crusius, Apr. 4, 1934; children—Janet Carolyn (Mrs. Alvin D. Vitt), Harry Carl. With Laclede Steel Co., St. Louis, 1930—, research engr., 1943-50, dir. research and engring., 1950-64, v.p., research-engring., 1964-70; v.p. Mark Twain Bancshares, Inc., 1970—; chmn. bd. Midwestern Joists, Inc., Washington, Mo., 1972—; Chmn. adv. bd. Washington U. Engring. Sch., 1951-52, pres. Research Found., 1949; mem. St. Louis County Traffic Commn., 1964-68; exec. bd. Salvation Army, 1960-66; mem. Univ. City Park Bd., 1940-52, pres., 1949-50; mem. Lutheran Council for Higher Edn., 1962—; mem. St. Louis County Bus. and Indsl. Devel. Commn. Bd. dirs. Luth. Hosp. St. Louis. Mem. Am. Concrete Inst. (dir. 1964—, bldg. code com.), Steel Joist Inst. (pres. 1965), Engrs. Club St. Louis (dir. 1947-50, treas. 1963), Am. Soc. Testing and Materials (chmn. reinforcement com.), Washington U. Alumni Assn. (pres. 1946), St. Louis C. of C. (chmn. sports com. 1954-64, bd. dirs. 1966-67, chmn. civic devel. com., 1967-70, chmn. St. Louis Fall Festival 1970-71), Wire Reinforcement Inst., Concrete Reinforcing Steel Inst., Am. Iron and Steel Inst., ASCE, Advt. Club St. Louis, Rail Steel Bar Assn. (pres. 1951-55), Archaeol. Soc. of St. Louis, Soc. Am. Mil. Engrs., Mo., Nat. (Engr. of Year 1959) socs. profl. engrs., Searab, Kaabah, Sigma Chi Chi Epsilon. Lutheran (pres. bd. 1950-51). Rotarian (pres. 1960). Clubs: Mo. Athletic (v.p. 1952), Old Warson Country; Woodsmill Racquet, St. Louis. Research on steel joists, steel reinforcements, wire, composite joist constrn. devel. Home: 840 Pebble Lake Dr Woodsmill Village Ballwin MO 63011 Office: 2000 W Main St Washington MO 63090

WEBER, ALBAN, lawyer, assn. exec.; b. Chgo., Jan. 29, 1915; s. Joseph A. and Anna (von Placheck) W.; A.B., Harvard U., 1935, LL.B., 1937; m. Margaret Kenny, Dec. 29, 1951; children—Alban III, Peggy Ann, Gloria, Brian. Admitted to Ill. bar, 1938, mem. firm Weber & Weber, 1937-41, with State Dept., 1946; trust officer Lake Shore Nat. Bank, Chgo., 1952-55; univ. counsel Northwestern U., Evanston Ill., 1955-70; pres. Fedn. Ind. Ill. Colls. and Univs., Evanston, 1971—, Benjamin Franklin Fund, Inc., 1965—, Northwestern U. Press, Inc., 1965-70. Pres. Northeast Ill. Council Boy Scouts Am., 1970-71. Alderman, City of Chgo., 1947-51. Served to comdr. USNR, 1941-45, rear adm. Res. ret., 1970. Mem. Nat. Assn. Coll. and Univ. Attys. (pres. 1962), Navy League (pres. Evanston council 1967-70, State of Ill. 1970-71), Univ. Ins. Mgrs. (pres.). Kiwanian (lt. gov.). Clubs: Harvard, Execs., Chgo. Yacht, White Lake Golf, White Lake Yacht. Home: 1286 Cascade Ct Lake Forest IL 60045 Office: 990 Grove St Evanston IL 60201

WEBER, ALDEN ORISON, banker; b. nr. Abilene, Kans., July 15, 1909; s. William Henry and Margaret Katherine (Rohrer) W.; A.B., U. Kans., 1931, A.M. (univ. fellow), 1932; Ph.D. (Sage scholar), Cornell U., 1936; m. Adelaide Magdalen Kaiser Chamberlin, Apr. 7, 1945. Asst. Sage Sch. Philosophy, Cornell U., Ithaca, N.Y., 1934-36, instr., 1937-39; v.p. Am. State Bank, Osawatomie, Kans., 1940-50, exec. v.p., 1950-56, pres., 1956-73, chmn. bd., 1973—. Mem. exec. bd. Kaw council Boy Scouts Am., 1971-74; trustee Miami County Hosp., Paola, Kans., 1958-74, chmn., 1960-64. Mem. Am. Philos. Assn., Phi Beta Kappa, Sigma Xi. Democrat. Methodist. Elk, Rotarian. Contbr. articles to philos. and psychol. jours. Home: 1112 Parker Ave Osawatomie KS 66064 Office: 6th and Brown Sts Osawatomie KS 66064

WEBER, ARTHUR RUDOLPH, steel co. exec.; b. St. Louis, Mar. 18, 1925; s. Rudolph C. and Minnie (Breitenbach) W.; B.S., U. Mo., 1947; m. Marian T. Stock, June 16, 1956; children—Susan A., Carol A. Engr., estimator Victor Iron Works, St. Louis, 1947—, pres., 1963—. Bd. dirs. Concordia Gymnastic Soc., 1963-71. Served with USNR, 1944-46; ETO. Registered profl. engr., Mo. Mem. ASCE, Mo. Soc. Profl. Engrs., St. Louis Area Iron and Steel Fabricators Welfare Assn. (sec.), St. Louis C. of C., St. Louis Camera Club (pres. 1972-74), Pi Kappa Alpha, Tau Beta Pi, Chi Epsilon, Pi Mu Epsilon. Home: 12434 Cinema Ln St Louis MO 63127 Office: 2415 S 7th St St Louis MO 63104

WEBER, CHARLES AUGUST, savs. and loan exec.; b. Dublin, Ohio, June 23, 1923; s. Louis Walter and Katie (Thomas) W.; student Ohio State U., 1941-42, 48, Pa. State U., 1942-43, Ohio Savs. and Loan Acad., 1966; m. Betty Joan Walker, Aug. 26, 1950; children—Scott, Richard, Lynn Dee, Karen. With Ohio Fed. Savs. & Loan Assn., 1953—, v.p., Columbus, 1961-63, exec. v.p., 1963-65, pres., 1965—. Mem. Bd. Realtors. Mem. Washington Local Bd. Edn., Dublin, 1967-73; mem. Franklin County Hosp. Commn., 1968—; mem. Gov.'s Task Force on Tax Reform, 1971; mem. Task Force on Lending Fed. Home Loan Bank, 1970-72. Trustee Mercy Hosp. Columbus. Served with USMCR, 1943-47, 50-52. Mem. U.S., Ohio (past pres.) savs. and loan leagues, Columbus Mortgage Bankers. Mason (Shriner). Clubs: Columbus Athletic, Maennorchor (Columbus). Home: 6650 Coffman Rd Dublin OH 43017 Office: 90 N High St Columbus OH 43215

WEBER, C(HARLES) EDWARD, educator; b. Chgo., Feb. 21, 1930; s. Edward W. and Augusta (Lonk) W.; student Marquette U., 1948-50; B.A., U. Ill., 1952, M.A. in Labor and Indsl. Relations, 1953; M.A. in Econs. (Hicks fellow), Princeton, 1954, Ph.D. in Econs., 1958; m. Suzanne Brodseller, Sept. 6, 1952; children—Paul Andrew, Mark Francis. Mem. research staff Princeton, 1954-56; from instr. to asso. prof. bus. U. Pitts., 1956-66, research asso. adminstrv. sci., 1961-63, acting dir. Adminstrv. Sci. Center, 1963-66; prof. policy and mgmt. studies U. Wis.-Milw., 1966—, dean Sch. Bus. Adminstrn., 1966-76. Cons. Arthur D. Little, 1964-66; field reader U.S. Office Edn., 1966—. Co-chmn. com. to advise on reorgn. Milw. City Govt., 1968-70; commr. pub. debt. City of Milw., 1976—; mem. Wis. Council Econ. Edn., Gov.'s Council Econ. Edn. Ford Found. fellow, 1959-60, 62-63. Mem. Inst. Mgmt. Sci., Am. Econ. Assn., Indsl. Relations Research Assn., Coll. on Orgns (sec.-treas. 1963-65), Acad. Mgmt., Met. Milw. Assn. Commerce (vice chmn. com. on legislation), Beta Gamma Sigma. Author: Management Action: Models of Adminstrative Decision, 1969; also articles. Home: 3453 N Hackett Ave Milwaukee WI 53211

WEBER, CHARLES THEODORE, JR., found. exec.; b. Dayton, Ohio, Apr. 25, 1924; s. Charles T. and Lenora (Keuping) W.; B.S. summa cum laude, Xavier U., 1945; M.S.S.W. Boston Coll., 1956. Auditor, C. T. Weber & Assos., Dayton, 1945-54; asst. exec. dir. Broome County United Fund, Binghamton, N.Y., 1956-60; dir. found. and fed. relations, dir. estate planning Xavier U. Cin., 1960-69; dir. devel. Cin. Symphony Orch., 1969-71; exec. dir. Kidney Found. Greater Cin., 1971-76; field cons. Nat. Kidney Found., 1976—. Active program and allocations div. Cin. Community Chest; mem. region III council Nat. Kidney Found. Trustee Council on Aging. Mem. Nat. Kidney Found. Profl. Staff Assn. (governing council). Home: 418 Torrence Ct Cincinnati OH 45202 Office: 3914 Miami Rd Suite 302 Cincinnati OH 45227

WEBER, FRANK EARL, periodontist; b. New Albany, Ind., Aug. 30, 1932; s. Frank H. and Elizabeth (Weber) W.: student Ind. U., 1950-52; postdoctorate splty. Sch. Dentistry, 1962-64; B.A., U. Louisville, 1954, D.M.D., 1962; postgrad. U. Ky., 1954; children—Gregory Kurt, Frank Henry II. Practice gen. dentistry and periodontics, Indpls., 1964—. Served from 2d lt. to capt. USAF, 1955-58. Recipient Award of Merit, Am. Acad. Dental Medicine, 1962. Fellow Royal Soc. Health; mem. Am. Acad. Gen. Dentistry, Indpls. Dist. Dental Soc., ADA, Student Clinicians ADA (3d award 1961), Am. Endodontic Soc., Police League Ind., Fraternal Order Police, Internat. Platform Assn., Nat. Fedn. Ind. Bus., Sigma Phi Epsilon (life), Delta Sigma Delta (worthy master 1961, 62, life), Phi Delta (pres. 1961-62), Beta Delta, Phi Kappa Phi, Omicron Kappa Upsilon, Omicron Delta Kappa. Home: 5428 Scarlet Dr Indianapolis IN 46224 Office: 3500 Lafayette Rd Indianapolis IN 46222

WEBER, GEORGE RUSSELL, microbiologist; b. Novinger, Mo., Dec. 29, 1911; s. William and Celia Iciphene (Helton) W.; B.S., U. Mo., 1935; Ph.D., Iowa State Coll., 1940; spl. evening student George Washington U., 1944-45, U. Cin., 1948-49; m. Margaret Carrington Cable, Apr. 19, 1947; children—Jeanine Marie, Michael Elwin. Asst. chemist, expt. sta. U. Mo., 1935-36; teaching fellow in bacteriology Iowa State Coll., 1936-38, asst., 1938-39, teaching asst., 1939-40, instr., 1940-42; bacteriologist USPHS, 1946, sr. asst. scientist, 1947, scientist, 1949, chief, sanitizing agents unit, 1949-53; research microbiologist Nat. Distillers & Chem. Corp., 1953-63, research project leader, 1963-73, sr. research microbiologist, 1973-75, research asso., 1975, ret., 1977; lectr. in biology U. Cin., 1969-70. Dir. Ky. br. Nat. Chinchilla Breeders of Am., 1955-57, research chmn., 1958-64; pres. Greater Cin. Chinchilla Breeders Assn., 1957-58, 63-64. Served from 1st lt. to maj. AUS, 1942-46; lt. col. AUS (ret.). Recipient War Dept. citation for control of food poisoning and infection, 1946. Fellow Am. Pub. Health Assn., Royal Soc. Health (Eng.); mem. AAAS, Am. Soc. Microbiology, Am. Inst. Biol. Scis., Ohio Acad. Sci., New York Acad. Scis., Am. Soc. Profl. Biologists (v.p. 1957-58), Smithsonian Assos., Inst. Food Technologists, Research Soc. Am., Res. Officers Assn. U.S. (exec. council Cin. chpt. 1963-65, chpt. pres. 1966-67), Ret. Officers Assn., others. Patentee animal feed, biol. metal corrosion control. Home: 1525 Burney Ln Cincinnati OH 45230 Office: 1275 Section Rd Cincinnati OH 45237

WEBER, GEORGE W., JR., lawyer; b. Cin., Apr. 17, 1904; s. George W. and Rosa M. (Ollier) W.; A.B., U. Cin., 1926, LL.M., 1933; J.D., Harvard U., 1929; m. Eleanor M. Kilby, Nov. 24, 1934 (dec. 1954); children—David Ollier, Stephen Kilby, Anne Marchant; m. 2d, Matilda Willis, Mar. 1957. Admitted to Ohio bar, 1930; asso. firm Decamp, Sutphin & Brumleve, 1930-36; asso. with other lawyers, 1936-42; chief rent atty. OPA, 1942, area rent dir., 1943-44, chief litigation atty., 1944; with firm Taft, Stettinius & Hollister, 1944-46; partner firm Schmidt, Effron, Josselson & Weber, Cin., 1946—. Lectr. bus. law U. Cin., 1947, conflict of laws, 1948-49, 53. Pres., Children's Heart Assn., 1946-55; pres. Hamilton County Good Government League, 1946-47, Civic Club Cin., 1939-40; v.p. Cin. Club, 1962-63. Hon. trustee Children's Heart Assn.; chmn. bd. S.W. chpt. Am. Heart Assn., 1952-53, 58-59, now hon. trustee. Mem. Am., Ohio, Cin. bar assns., Am. Judicature Soc., Lawyers Club Cin., Harvard Law Sch. Assn., Estate Planning Council, Phi Beta Kappa. Clubs: Cincinnati, Harvard of Cincinnati. Home: 2901 Utopia Pl Cincinnati OH 45208 Office: Atlas Bank Bldg Cincinnati OH 45202

WEBER, GERTRUDE CHRISTINA, musician; b. Mildmay, Ont., Can., Dec. 23, 1934; d. William Frederick and Lillian (Tegler) Hill; student Royal Conservatory of Music, Toronto, Ont., Can.; m. Eldon Weber, June 30, 1954; children—Karen, Brenda, Brian, Kevin. Organist, Mildmay (Ont.) Ch., 1951-60; asst. organist Walkerton (Ont.) Lutheran Ch., 1956—, Hanover (Ont.) Luth. Ch., 1967—; piano accompanist Hanover Ballet Sch., 1970—; pvt. practice music instruction piano, organ, violin, guitar, theory, Walkerton, Ont., 1955—; piano soloist. Rep. Grey-Blue Arts Council; dir. Grey County Kiwanis Music Festival. Mem. Ont. Registered Music Tchrs. Assn., Hanover, Walkerton music tchrs. assns. Lutheran. Clubs: Kinette of Walkerton, Lutheran Ch. Women's, Walkerton Lawn Bowling. Home and Office: 11 Park St Walkerton ON N0G 2V0 Canada

WEBER, GREGOR AUGUST, banker; b. Appleton, Minn., Sept. 21, 1923; s. Peter Leo and Anna Elizabeth (Reuther) W.; grad. high sch.; m. Dorothy Marion Erickson, Nov. 9, 1946; children—Timothy, Julie, Peggy, Kathleen, Craig, Suzan, Anita, Jack, Jeff. With Union State Bank, Montevideo, Minn., 1947-49, Citizens State Bank, Echo, 1949-62; with First Nat. Bank, Philip, S.D., 1962—, v.p., 1963-72, cashier, dir., 1963—, exec. v.p., 1972—. Owner, operator small cattle range, Philip, S.D., 1970—. Mayor, Echo, Minn., 1958-62; vol. savs. bond chmn., Haakon County. Served with AUS, 1943-45. Mem. S.D. Bankers Assn., C. of C. Republican. Roman Catholic. K.C. Club: Roping (Philip). Address: Philip SD 57567

WEBER, HARM ALLEN, coll. pres.; b. Pekin, Ill., Sept. 28, 1926; s. Harm Allen and Hilda (Meyer) W.; B.A., Bethel Coll., St. Paul, 1950; B.D., Bethel Sem., 1954; M.R.E., Christian Theol. Sem., Indpls., 1959; postgrad. Ball State U., Muncie, Ind., 1961-62; D.D., Judson Coll., Elgin, Ill., 1964; m. Arlene Olson, Dec. 18, 1948; children—Jan Christine, Harm Allen III, Matthew Karl. Ordained to ministry Baptist Ch., 1953; pastorates at Isle (Minn.) Bapt. Ch., 1950-53, Central Bapt. Ch., Indpls., 1954-60, First Bapt. Ch., Muncie, 1960-64, Covenant Bapt. Ch., Detroit, 1964-69; pres. Judson Coll., 1969—, also vice chmn. bd. trustees, 1963-69. Mem. Gov.'s Multiple Sclerosis Bd. Ind., 1957-60; chmn. evangelism Detroit Council Chs., 1967-69; chmn. Indpls. Fedn. Chs., 1955-59; pres. Delaware County Council Chs., 1963-64; mem. state exec. bd. Vols. of Am., 1976—. Bd. dirs. Camp Isongal, Delaware County Crippled Childrens Assn.; chmn. bd. Galloway Meml. Youth Camp, Wahkon, Minn.; v.p. Am. Bapt. Home Mission Soc.; mem. exec. com. Midwest Commn. on the Ministry. Mem. Elgin C. of C. (dir. 1975—). Rotarian. Address: 1151 N State St Elgin IL 60120

WEBER, HARRIETTE B. SKLADD, real estate broker and appraiser; b. Detroit; d. Alexander and Victoria (Lesnik) Skladd; student Wayne U., 1937-39, U. Mich., 1950-52; m. E. George Weber. Real estate broker H. B. Weber, Realtor, Detroit, 1953—; fee appraiser, per diem appraiser FHA, Detroit, 1958—. Mem. Detroit Real Estate Bd., Nat. Assn. Real Estate Bds., Internat. Platform Assn., Founders Soc. Detroit, Inst. Arts. Club: Detroit Yacht. Inventor beaute specs, turkey jackets. Home: 18230 Ten Mile Rd East Detroit MI 48021 Office: 14427 E Seven Mile Rd Detroit MI 48205

WEBER, JOSEPH JAMES, psychologist, instnl. adminstr.; b. Lorain, Ohio, Aug. 12, 1942; s. Joseph Sylvester and Loyola Ruth (Oberst) W.; B.S., Bowling Green U., 1964, M.A., 1966; m. Joanne Carol Kenagy, Oct. 18, 1975; 1 son by previous marriage, Shane Jack. Mental health counselor, dept. mental health Meyer Center, Decatur, Ill., 1968-70; pvt. practice psychology, Decatur, 1969-76; supt. Dept. Corrections Youth Center, Vocat., Academic and Social Tng., Decatur, 1975—. Served with U.S. Army, 1966-68. Mem. Am. Psychol. Assn., Am. Correctional Assn., Moreno Inst. Group Psychotherapy and Psychodrama. Home: 1525 Noble Dr Mount Zion IL 62549 Office: 2310 E Mound Rd VAST Program Decatur IL 62549

WEBER, MILADA (PAUKOVA), librarian; b. Brno, Czechoslovakia, Mar. 2, 1911; Dipl. Kons., Konsularakademie, Vienna, Austria, 1933; LL.D., Masaryk U., Brno, 1939; postgrad. U. Parana (Brazil), 1949; M.S. in L.S., L.I.U., 1964; m. Josef Weber. Czechoslovakian diplomat, Prague, 1945-46, attache, legation, Rio De Janeiro, Brazil, 1946-48; sec. consulate gen. of Venezuela, Houston, 1955-58; library asst. Poly. Prep. Country Day Sch., Bklyn., 1962-63; cataloguer Elmont (N.Y.) Pub. Library, 1963-65; cataloguer Hofstra U., 1965-68; head cataloguer Northwestern U. Law Sch. Library, 1968—. Mem. Am., Chgo. assns. law libraries. Home: 8842 Lavergne Ave Skokie IL 60076

WEBER, MILAN GEORGE, ret. army officer, mgmt. cons.; b. Milw., Oct. 15, 1908; s. Adam George and Frances (Lehrbaumer) W.; B.S., U.S. Mil. Acad., 1931; grad. Coast Arty. and Air Defense Sch., 1938, Nat. War Coll., 1952; m. Mary Agness Keller, Sept. 2, 1931; 1 son, Milan George. Commd. 2nd lt. U.S. Army, 1931, advanced through grades to col., 1944; various army command and staff exec. positions, Philippine Islands, 1932-36, Hawaii, 1938-41, Ft. Monroe, Va., 1936-38; anti-aircraft exec., hdqrs. armies, U.S., Europe, 1943-45; mem. Gen. Patton's staff, 1944, War Dept. Gen. staff, 1945-48; mil. adviser to Argentine govt., 1949-51; global strategic planner Joint Chiefs of Staff, 1952-54; comdr. Missile Defense of Norfolk and Hampton Roads, 1954-55; chief of staff advisory group, Japan, 1955-58; dept. comdr. Air Def. Region, Ft. Meade, Md., 1958-60, ret., 1960; mgr. electronic counter measures Loral Electronics Corp., N.Y.C., 1960-62; product mgr. electronic counter measures Hallicrafters Corp. (name changed to Northrop Corp.), Chgo., 1962-64; partner Weber Assos., Mgmt. Cons., Deerfield, Ill., 1964-69; pres. dir. Milan G. Weber Associates, Inc., Deerfield, 1969—; mgmt. cons. to various bus. firms, 1964—; acquisitions and mergers cons. to various corps., 1969—. Chmn. Great Lakes Ecology Assn. Ill., 1974—; chmn. Citizens Com. Honesty in Govt.; mem. Ill. Drivers Safety Adv. Com., 1975—; mem. Deerfield Library Bd., 1976—. Decorated Legion of Merit, Bronze Star. Mem. Assn. of Old Crows, West Point Soc. of Chgo., Assn. of Graduates U.S. Mil. Acad., Electronic Counter Measures Assn., Great Lakes Ecology Assn. of the Mil. Clubs: Ambassadors, Admirals, Army Navy, Army Navy Country. Contbr. articles on anti-aircraft arty., air defense and mil. strategy to profl. publs. author of joint strategic capabilities plan. Home: 611 Colwyn Terrace Deerfield IL 60015 Office: PO Box 81 Deerfield IL 60015

WEBER, NORBERT JOSEPH, physician; b. Defiance, Ohio, Mar. 21. 1923; s. Frank J. and Helen S. (Goller) W.; B.A., Cath. U. Am., 1945; B.S. in Chemistry, Defiance (Ohio) Coll., 1947, B.S. in Edn., 1947; M.D., Stritch Sch. Medicine, Loyola U., Chgo., 1951; m. Mary Kuksta, Sept. 29, 1951; children—Laura Jane, John Joseph. Intern, Mercy Hosp., Toledo, 1951-52; resident in surgery, Indpls. Gen. Hosp., 1955-59; practice medicine specializing in surgery, Chgo., 1960—; attending surgeon Holy Cross Hosp., Chgo., 1960—, chmn. dept. surgery, 1972. Served to capt. M.C., AUS, 1953-55. Mem. AMA, Ill., Chgo. med. socs. Roman Catholic. Club: Elks. Home: 10604 S Kolin Ave Oak Lawn IL 60453 Office: 6132 S Kedzie Ave Chicago IL 60629

WEBER, PAUL EGON, physicist, optics engr.; b. Jena, Thurungia, Ger., Nov. 8, 1913; s. Paul Alwin and Barbara B. (Bouffier) W.; came to U.S., 1953, naturalized, 1958; Ingenieur, Höhere Technische Staatslehranstalt, Frankfurt/Main, Germany, 1935; m. Johanna Kuhlich, Oct. 30, 1937 (div. 1945); children—Barbara Johanna, Elfriede Margaretha; m. 2d, Gertrud Brüningsen, Nov. 1, 1947; children—Norbert Paul, Dieter Erich; Lab. dir. J.D. Moeller Optical Works, Wedel/Holst, Ger., 1941-45; cons. in optical radiation, Hamburg, Germany, 1945-46, Glucksburg, Ger., 1946-48; physicist H. Steinmetz & Sohn, K.G., Northeim, Hannover, Ger., 1950-53; devel. engr. Am. Optical Co., Buffalo, 1953-54; research engr., Wollensak Optical Co., Rochester, N.Y., 1954-57; physicist Stromberg-Carlson, Rochester, N.Y. 1957-58; staff engr. Avco-Grosley, Cin., 1958-59; prin. engr. Bendix Corp., South Bend, Ind., 1959-60, staff engr. of Bendix Systems Div., Ann Arbor, Mich., 1960-61; scientist Trion Instruments, Inc., Ann Arbor, Mich., 1961-62; mgr. IR Lear Siegler, Inc., Ann Arbor, 1963-65; cons. in optical radiation, Ypsilanti, Mich., 1965-66; physicist Bell & Howell Co., Chgo., 1966—. Mem. Am. Phys. Soc., Optical Soc. Am., Deutsche Gesellschaft für angewandte Optik. Contbr. articles in optical physics to sci. jours.; patentee optical instruments. Home: 921 Bartlet Terr Libertyville IL 60048 Office: 6800 McCormick Rd Chicago IL 60645

WEBER, PEARL ALICE, pharmacist; b. Highland Park, Mich., Dec. 3, 1936; d. John Joseph and Muryel (Spedding) Weber; B.S. in Pharmacy, Ferris Inst. Sch. of Pharmacy, 1961; m. James D. Anderson, Aug. 14, 1976. Pharmacy intern Johnson Drug Store, Ishpeming, Mich., 1961, Johnson Pharmacy, Marquette, 1961-62, pharmacist, 1962-69, Morgan Heights San., Marquette, 1967-68; registered pharmacist, asst. mgr. City Drug Store, Ishpeming, 1969-70; staff pharmacist Johnson Drugs of Ishpeming, 1970-77. Mem. Am., Mich. (Upper Peninsula div. treas. 1967-78) pharm. assns., Mich. Assn. of Professions, Nat. Assn. Retail Druggists, Acad. Gen. Practice of Pharmacy, Lambda Kappa Sigma. Methodist (ofcl. bd. 1967-72, commn. stewardship and finance 1968-69, commn. on edn. 1967-68, ch. treas. 1969-72, rec. sec. ch. adminstrv. bd. Home: 2829 Birchwood Ave Trenton MI 48183

WEBER, RALPH EDWARD, historian; b. St. Cloud, Minn., Apr. 19, 1926; s. Andrew A. and Kathryn (Desmond) W.; student Minot State Coll., 1944-45, Iowa State Coll., 1945-46; A.B., St. John's U., 1948; Ph.D., U. Notre Dame, 1956; m. Rosemarie Hoyt, Aug. 23, 1952; children—Mary, Elizabeth, Ralph A., Anne, Catherine, Neil, Thomas, Therese, Andrew. Instr. history U. Notre Dame, 1953-54; asst. to dean Coll. Liberal Arts, Marquette U., 1954-57, registrar and dir. admissions, 1957-61, asst. prof., 1956-63, asso. prof., 1963-69, prof., 1969—; cons. Ednl. Testing Services, 1973—. Active Boy Scouts Am. Served with USNR, 1944-46. Marquette U. fellow, 1967, 73, U. Notre Dame fellow, 1950-52. Mem. Soc. Historians Am. Fgn. Relations, Am. Catholic Hist. Assn. (exec. council 1971-74), Orgn. Am. Historians, Conf. on Peace Research (exec. council 1971-77). Author: Notre Dame's John Zahm, 1961; (with James Arnold) Admission to College, 1964; United States Diplomatic Codes and Ciphers 1775-1938, 1978; editor: As Others See Us, 1972; co-editor: Voices of Revolution, 1972. Office: History Dept Marquette U Milwaukee WI 53233

WEBER, ROBERT CLAUDE, educator; b. Benham, Ind., Jan. 2, 1924; s. George Edward and Clara Emily (Benham) W.; student Ball State U., 1942-43, 47-48; B.S., Purdue U., 1947; M.S., U. Mich., 1955; m. Mary Janet Holtmeyer, Aug. 23, 1958. With U.S. Forest Service, Idaho, 1945, Tex., 1946, Calif., 1948; tchr. botany and biology South Side High Sch., Fort Wayne, Ind., 1948—. Dir. Acres Inc., Huntertown, Ind., 1960—, pres., 1972—; directing naturalist Fox Island Nature Study area Allen County, Ind., 1974—. Active YMCA, Fort Wayne, Ind., 1948—. Recipient Leadership Citation, YMCA, 1964. Mem. United Teaching Profession, Nat. Assn. Biology Tchrs., Ind. Acad. Sci., Alpha Zeta, Xi Sigma Pi. Unitarian Universalist. Home: 3649 Algonquin Pass Fort Wayne IN 46809 Office: 1802 Chapman Rd Huntertown IN 46748

WEBER, ROBERT FREDERICK, motor transp. co. exec.; b. La Crosse, Wis., Dec. 2, 1930; s. Arnold E. and Leona L. (Bartz) W.; B.S. in Accounting, U. Wis., 1953; m. Lorraine Ikert, Dec. 27, 1952; children—Robert Frederick, Sandra Kay. Auditor, Baumann, Finney & Co., C.P.A.'s, Chgo., 1953-58; supr. audit group Peat, Marwick, Mitchell & Co., C.P.A.'s, Chgo., 1958-67; fin. v.p., treas. Fruit Belt Motor Service, Inc., Forest Park, Ill., 1967-68; v.p. adminstrn., treas. Signal Delivery Service, Inc., Hinsdale, Ill., 1969—. C.P.A., Ill. Mem. Am. Inst. C.P.A.'s, Ill. Soc. C.P.A.'s, Am. Trucking Assn. (dir. nat. accounting and fin. council), Fin. Execs. Inst., Lutheran Laymen's Movement. Club: Masons. Home: 529 S Madison Ave La Grange IL 60525 Office: 201 E Ogden Ave Hinsdale IL 60521

WEBER, RUSSELL WRIGHT, newspaper pub. editor; b. Aurora, Nebr., Oct. 2, 1917; s. William Robert and Gladys (Hickman) W.; B.A., U. Nebr., 1939; m. Leah Showalter, Oct. 21, 1940; children—Gregory Keith, Kurt Jeffrey. Advt. salesman Kern Herald, Bakersfield, Calif., 1939-40, S.W. Wave, Los Angeles, 1940; wire editor Beatrice (Nebr.) Daily Sun, 1940-47, Yakima (Wash.) Daily Republic, 1947; mng. editor The Fremont (Nebr.) Tribune, 1948-59, asst. to pub., 1959-60, editor, 1960-70, publisher, 1969—; v.p. Fremont Newspapers, Inc., 1967-69, pres., 1969—. Served with USNR, 1943-46. Mem. Sigma Delta Chi, Kappa Tau Alpha, Pi Delta Epsilon. Mem. Christian Ch. Rotarian. Home: 2022 E 7th St Fremont NE 68025 Office: 135 N Main St Fremont NE 68025

WEBER, VICTOR BLAINE, II, educator; b. Seattle, Dec. 4, 1939; s. Bryle Davis and Inez Evangeline (Savage) W.; B.A., Yale U., 1961, M.A., 1962, Ph.D., 1971; m. Vida Jane Bull, Dec. 22, 1962. Dir. Yale Freshman Glee Club, New Haven, 1967-69; asst. prof. music, dir. choruses The Coll. Wooster (Ohio), 1969-72; asst. prof. music, dir. choral activities U. Ill., Chgo. Circle, 1972-77. Choral condr. various pub. performances, 1967—; choral-vocal clinician Episcopal Diocese

Chgo., 1974—; judge All-City Choral Festival, Chgo., 1974, 75; dir. music Ch. of Ascension, Chgo., 1976—. Contbg. editor The Diapason mag., 1973—. Home: 4100 N Marine Dr Chicago IL 60613

WEBER, WALTER JACOB, JR., educator; b. Pitts., June 16, 1934; s. Walter Jacob and Anne Mae (Chando) W.; B.Sc., Brown U., 1956; M.S., Rutgers U., 1959; M.A., Harvard U., 1961, Ph.D., 1962; children—Wendilyn Ruth, Elizabeth Anne, Pamela Jean, Linda Lorraine. Engr., Caterpillar Tractor Co., Peoria, Ill., 1956-57; instr. Rutgers U., New Brunswick, N.J., 1957-59; engr. Soil Conservation Service, New Brunswick, N.J., 1957-59; research and teaching asso. Harvard, Cambridge, Mass., 1959-63; asst. prof. U. Mich., Ann Arbor, 1963-65, asso. prof., 1965-68, prof., 1968—, chmn. water resources program, 1968—. Internat. cons. to industry and govt. Recipient Distinguished Faculty award U. Mich., 1967, Faraday lectr., 1970; named Engr. of Distinction, Engrs. Joint Council, 1973. Registered profl. engr., R.I., Mich. Diplomate Am. Acad. Environ. Engrs. Mem. Am. Chem. Soc. (certificate of merit 1962), Am. Inst. Chem. Engrs., ASCE, Am. Water Works Assn., Assn. Environmental Engring. Profs. (Distinguished Faculty award 1968), Nat. Soc. Profl. Engrs., Water Pollution Control Fedn. (John R. Rumsey Meml. award 1975), Sigma Xi, Tau Beta Pi, Chi Epsilon, Delta Omega. Author: (with K.H. Mancy) Analysis of Industrial Wastewaters, 1971; Physicochemical Processes for Water Quality Control, 1972; editor-author (with E. Matijevic) Adsorption from Aqueous Solution, 1968. Contbr. numerous articles to tech. and profl. jours. and books. Home: 1700 S Grove Rd Ypsilanti MI 48197 Office: Water Resources Program Coll Engring U Mich Ann Arbor MI 48109

WEBSTER, JAMES RANDOLPH, JR., pulmonary physician, clin. adminstr.; b. Chgo., Aug. 25, 1931; s. James Randolph and Ruth (Burtis) W.; B.S., Northwestern U., 1952, M.S., M.D., 1956; m. Joan Burchfield, Dec. 28, 1954; children—Susan, Donovan, John. Intern, Phila. Gen. Hosp., 1956-57; resident in medicine Wesley Meml. Hosp., Northwestern U., Chgo., 1957-60, chief of medicine Northwestern Meml. Hosp., 1973, prof. Northwestern U. Med. Sch., 1977—; USPHS fellow, 1962-64. Served with M.C., U.S. Army, 1960-62. Recipient research award Chgo. Lung Assn., 1966. Mem. A.C.P., Am. Lung Assn., Am. Thoracic Soc., Am. Fedn. Clin. Research. Home: 2530 Kenilworth Ave Wilmette IL 60091

WEBSTER, MILDRED ESTHER, ret. educator; b. Webster, N.D., Oct. 16, 1908; d. David E. and Petra Gelena (Lenes) Webster; A.B., Jamestown Coll., 1929; M.A., U. N.D., 1936; postgrad. U. Chgo., summer, 1941, Middlebury Coll., Vt., 1947, (scholarship grantee) Linguistics Inst. Mich. State U., 1965. Tchr. English pub. high schs., Webster, N.D., 1929-31, Tolna, N.D., 1933-35, Clyde, N.D., 1936-38, Luther L. Wright High Sch., Ironwood, Mich., 1938-43; tchr., head dept. English St. Joseph (Mich.) High Sch., 1943-73; guest lectr. Mich. State U., Benton Harbor, 1962-63; instr. evening sch. Lake Mich. Coll., Benton Harbor, 1968-69; mem. exec. bd. of Midwest English Conf., 1952-74; curriculum cons. on English programs, 1968-73. Mem. Nat. (dir. 1946-70, mem. com. on publs. 1968-70, council), Mich. (Charles Carpenter Fries award 1976, Distinguished Service citation 1972, pres. 1950-51, exec. sec. 1964-69) councils of tchrs. English, NEA, Mich. Edn. Assn., Nat. Ret. Tchrs. Assn., Delta Kappa Gamma, AAUW. Mem. Congregational Ch. Contbg. author: Literature of the Americas, 1957; contbr. articles on teaching of English to profl. jours. Address: 3105 Kevin St St Joseph MI 49085

WEBSTER, ROBERT BYRON, lawyer; b. Detroit, Mar. 9, 1932; s. Don Byron and Glennie Elizabeth (Cole) W.; A.B., U. Mich., 1955, J.D., 1957; m. Marilyn Dee Hey, July 18, 1959; children—Anne Elizabeth, Allison Dee, Peter Hey, James Byron. Admitted to Mich. bar, 1958; law clk. to U.S. Dist. Judge Ralph Freeman, 1957-59; asso., partner Reitz, Tait, Oetting & Webster, 1959-69, Hill, Lewis, Adams, Goodrich & Tait, Detroit, 1969-73; circuit judge Oakland County, Mich., 1973—; alt. pres. judge Oakland Circuit Ct., 1974-76, chief judge, 1976—. Chmn. Supreme Ct. Com. to Revise and Consolidate Mich. Ct. Rules. Mem. Oakland Community Mental Health Bd., 1972. Chmn. Oakland County Republican Com., 1969-71; del. Rep. Nat. Conv., 1972. Bd. dirs. Family and Children Services of Oakland County. Served with USAF, 1951-53; maj. Res. Mem. Am., Mich., Fed., Detroit, Oakland bar assns., Econs. Club Detroit, Thomas M. Cooley Club, Barristers Soc., U. Mich. Lawyers Club (pres. 1956-57), Phi Gamma Delta, Phi Alpha Delta. Unitarian. Club: Red Run Golf (Royal Oak, Mich.). Home: 21050 W 14 Mile Rd Birmingham MI 48010 Office: 1200 N Telegraph Rd Pontiac MI 48053

WEBSTER, ROBERT TRICE, chem. co. exec.; b. Detroit, Oct. 19, 1936; s. Clyde I. and Barbara A. (Trice) W.; B.B.A., U. Mich., 1958; J.D., Detroit Coll. Law, 1961; m. Sue Ann Woodside, Aug. 4, 1962; children—Tiffany, Brandon. New product mgr. Park Chem. Co., Detroit, 1965-66, exec. v.p., 1966-71, pres., 1971—. Served to capt., AUS, 1961-65. Mem. Mich. Bar Assn., Am. Soc. Metals, Young Pres.'s Orgn., Sigma Nu. Rotarian. Club: Detroit Athletic. Office: 8074 Military Ave Detroit MI 48204

WECLEW, THADDEUS VICTOR, dentist; b. Chgo., Oct. 7, 1906; s. Victor Thomas and Mary Mae (Tadrowski) W.; D.D.S., U. Ill., 1930; m. Marguerite Helene Pfister, Jan. 1931 (dec. Jan. 1954); 1 dau., Marilyn (Mrs. Vernon W. Storm); m. 2d, Priscilla Joan Glenicki, Jan. 2, 1965. Pvt. dental practice, Chgo., 1930—; prof. U. Ill. Dental Coll.; founder Acad. Gen. Dentistry. Dir. Ill. Good Govt. Inst., 1950—. Served with USCG, 1945. Named distinguished alumnus, U. Ill., 1969; decorated officeur Order Palmes Academiques (France). Fellow Acad. Gen. Dentistry (mastership, pres. emeritus 1965), Am. Coll. Dentistry, Internat. Coll. Dentistry; hon. fellow Acad. Dentistry Internat.; mem. Am. Dental Assn., Ill. Good Govt. Inst., U. Ill. Dental Alumni Assn. (pres. 1967), Chgo. Dental Soc. (dir. 1969-73), Psi Omega, Omicron Kappa Upsilon. Roman Catholic. Founder, editor Acad. Gen. Dentistry Jour., 1952-73, editor emeritus, 1973—, exec. dir., 1965-69. Contbr. articles to profl. jours. Home: 6423 N Nokomis St Chicago IL 60646 Office: 6007 N Sauganash Ave Chicago IL 60646

WEDDING, DONALD KEITH, lawyer, educator; b. Louisville, Ky., Oct. 28, 1934; s. Joseph Hilmon and Caroline Louise (Stamler) W.; B. Chem. Engring., U. Louisville, 1957; J.D., Am. U., 1963; M.B.A., U. Toledo, 1968; M.E., U. Louisville, 1974; m. Mary Ellen Karwacki, June 14, 1962; children—Carol Ann Marie, Donald Keith II, Mary Ellen Victoria, Daniel Keith. Admitted to Pa. bar, 1964, D.C. bar, 1966, Ohio bar, 1967; patent examiner U.S. Patent Office, Washington, 1961-63; patent atty. U.S. and abroad, 1964—; legal counsel, asst. sec. Owens-Ill., Inc., 1966—; asst. prof. adminstrn. and personnel U. Toledo, 1968—. Dir. Phoenician Galley Corp., Toledo. Named Ky. Col. Mem. Am., Pa., Allegheny County, Ohio, Toledo bar assns., Am., Pitts., Toledo patent law assns., Patent Office Soc., Am. Chem. Soc., IEEE, Soc. Information Displ y, Am. Mktg. Assn., Am. Mgmt. Assn., Am. Bus. Law Assn., A.C.L.U. (chmn. Northwest Ohio 1974-75, dir. Ohio 1971-77), AAAS, Am. Inst. Decision Scis., Ky., West Central Ky. hist. socs., Filson Club Ky., Archeol. Inst. Am., Am. Mus. Natural History, Sigma Xi, Sigma Nu Phi, Theta Tau, Alpha Kappa Psi, Alpha Tau Omega. Mason. Contbr. articles to profl. publs. Research on pyramid mktg., macro-tech., product liability, sex discrimination. Home: 4533 Wedgewood Ct Toledo OH 43615 Office: PO Box 7308 Toledo OH 43615

WEDDON, EDWARD RENFROE, physician; b. Chgo., Feb. 12, 1924; s. Carl Washington and Isabel Mina (Forner) W.; A.A., U. Chgo., 1946; postgrad. Kalamazoo Coll., 1946-47; M.D., U. Mich. 1951; m. Willah Mary Skinner, Sept. 19, 1942; children—Todd E., Bradley C., Patrice I., Alex R., Amy F. Intern St. Joseph Mercy Hosp., Ann Arbor, Mich., 1951-52; gen. practice medicine, Stockbridge, Mich., 1952—; mem. state bd. Mich. Drs. Polit. Action Com., 1968—. Mem. Stockbridge Community Schs. Bd. Edn., 1958-69, sec., 1959-69. Mem. Am., Mich. (del. 1971-74, 77—, regional peer rev. bd. 1970) med. assns., Jackson County Med. Soc. (pres. 1975-77, exec. bd. 1971—), Am. Legion, VFW. Club: Masons. Writer, Rural Health column Mich. Farmer mag., 1976—. Home: 4891 Dexter Trail Stockbridge MI 49285 Office: 100 Rice St Stockbridge MI 49285

WEDER, DONALD ERWIN, mfg. co. exec.; b. Highland, Ill., Aug. 18, 1947; s. Erwin Henry and Florence Louise (Graham) W.; student U. Ill., 1965-66; B.S. summa cum laude, Bradley U., 1969; m. Phyllis Ann Styron; children—Erwin Michael, Andrew Styron. Pres. Highland Supply Corp. (Ill.), 1969-70; exec. v.p. Highland Mfg. & Sales Co., 1970—, also dir.; dir. Seven W Enterprises, Highland Mfg. & Sales Corp. Served to capt., inf. AUS, 1969-71. Mem. Zeta Phi, Phi Kappa Phi. Republican. Kiwanian. Home: 1304 Washington St Highland IL 62249 Office: 1111 6th St Highland IL 62249

WEDER, ERWIN HENRY, corp. exec.; b. Highland, Ill., Dec. 13, 1904; s. August and Julia (Brunner) W.: student pub. schs.: m. Florence Louise (Graham), July 19, 1938: children—Mary Kay, Dona Lee, Donald Erwin, Wanda May, Janet Marie. Office work Highland Dairy Farms, 1923-25: detective Fla. East Coast Hotel Co., 1927-29: auto salesman, broker L.E. Anderson Co., 1930-32: salesman Metal Goods Corp., 1933-41: product devel., sales mgr., pres., Highland Supply Corp., 1941—: pres., sales and products mgr. Highland Products, Inc., 1948—: pres., sales and products mgr. Highland Mfg. Co., 1944—; mng. partner, sales and products mgr. Highland Mfg. & Sales Co., 1952—: pres. Weder Farms, Inc., 1950—, Quality Motors, Inc., 1946—: sr. partner Seven W. Enterprises, 1958—: owner, operator Six Bar X ranch, Jorden, Mont. Republican. Mason. Clubs: Mo. Athletic, Capitol Hill, OX-5. Home: 1304 Washington St Highland IL 62249 Office: 6th and Zschokke St Highland IL 62249

WEDGE, WESLEY ERNEST, constrn. equipment mfg. co. exec.; b. Modesto, Calif., Sept. 15, 1933; s. Ernest Joseph and Adeline Lillian (Bispo) W.; B.A. in Econs., Stanford U., 1955, M.B.A., 1959; m. Janet Louise Tucker, June 21, 1959; children—Jacqueline Elizabeth, Ann Jennifer. Br. mgr. Omark Industries Inc., San Diego, 1960-61, Chgo., 1961-63; mfr. saw chain, power actuated tools Indsl. Diamond Products, Chgo.; sales mgr. constrn. products div., Super Cut Inc., 1963-68; pres. Wedge Co., pres. Wedge Co., Des Plaines, Ill., 1968—; dir. James-Wedge Inc., Griffin, Ga. Coach football, track Menlo (Calif.) Sch. and Coll., 1957-59. Served to capt., USMCR, 1955-57. Mem. Am. Mgmt. Assn. (program chmn. 1964-66), Am. Concrete Paving Assn. (nat. membership chmn. 1976-77), Am. Rental Assn., Asso. Equipment Distbrs., Saw Mfrs. Inst., Concrete Sawing and Drilling Assn., Constrn. Industry Mfrs. Assn., Delta Tau Delta. Developer Diesel-Hydraulic spansaw for paving industry, 1972; specialist devel. diamond saw blades for constrn. industry. Home: 5310 N Chester St Chicago IL 60656 Office: 110 River Rd Des Plaines IL 60016

WEDGEWORTH, ROBERT, JR., assn. exec.; b. Ennis, Tex., July 31, 1937; s. Robert and Jimmie (Johnson) W.; A.B., Wabash Coll., 1959; M.S., U. Ill., 1961; Litt. D., Park Coll., 1973; m. Chung Kyun, July 28, 1972; 1 dau., Cicely Veronica. Cataloger, Kansas City Pub. Library, 1961-62; asst. librarian, acting librarian Park Coll., Parkville, Mo., 1962-64; librarian Maramec Community Coll., Kirkwood, Mo., 1964-66; acquisitions librarian Brown U. Library, 1966-69; asst. prof. Rutgers U., 1971-72; exec. dir. A.L.A., Chgo., 1972—. Mem. exec. com. Nat. Book Coms. Bd., Franklin Books Program; mem. Nat. Commn. on New Technol. Uses of Copyrighted Works, 1975—; mem. biomed. library rev. com. Nat. Library Medicine, 1975—. Council on Library Resources fellow, 1969. Mem. Am. Soc. Information Sci. Editor, Library Resources and Tech. Services, 1971-73. Home: 2626 N Lakeview Chicago IL 60614 Office: 50 E Huron Chicago IL 60611

WEED, BYRON ELLSWORTH, II, real estate broker; b. Ann Arbor, Mich., June 18, 1938; s. Cecil Max and Hannah (Chappell) W.; B.S., Eastern Mich. U., 1961, M.A., 1963; children—Dalana S., Anissa E. Tchr. high sch. Dearborn Heights, Mich., 1961-63; partner Paige-Weed Realty, Ann Arbor, 1964-69; owner Weed Realty, Ann Arbor, 1969—. Lectr., instr. U. Mich., Ann Arbor, 1968—. Served with USNR, 1954-63. Mem. C. of C., Ann Arbor Bd. Realtors (dir., sec. 1973-74), Real Estate Securities and Syndication (dir. 1973), Real Estate Alumni Mich., Phi Sigma Epsilon. Author: Papermaking: A New Process, 1963. Home: 2817 Laurel Hill Ann Arbor MI 48103 Office: 1300 S Main St Ann Arbor MI 48103

WEED, HERMAN ROSCOE, educator; b. Union City, Pa., Aug. 5, 1922; s. Roscoe Conklin and Leta Venettie (Bryner) W.; B.S. in Elec. Engring., Pa. State U., 1945; M.S. in Elec. Engring, Ohio State U., 1948; m. Sylvia Kathryn Yearick, Apr. 20, 1946; children—David Herman, Douglas Leonard, Kathryn Marie. Instr. elec. engring. Pa. State U., 1943-46; instr. dept. elec. engring. Ohio State U., Columbus, 1946-49, asst. prof., 1949-55, asso. prof., 1955-59, prof., 1959—, dir., chmn. bio-med. engring center, 1971—; cons. in field. Recipient Top 10 Engring. Achievement award Nat. Soc. Profl. Engrs., 1971. Registered profl. engr., Ohio. Mem. IEEE, Am. Soc. Engring. Edn., Internat. Fedn. Automatic Control (mem. systems com., chmn. bio-med. engring com.), Am. Automatic Control Council (chmn. bio-med. engring. com.), Ohio Acad. Sci., Sigma Xi, Eta Kappa Nu (distinguished teaching award 1965), Phi Kappa Phi, Tau Beta Pi (Robert M. Critchfield award for meritorious service). Author: (with W.L. Davis) Industrial Electronic Engineering, 1953, German edit., 1955, Fundamentals of Electronic Devices and Circuits, 1959, Asian edit., 1959, German edit., 1964. Asso. editor: Automatica. Patentee in field. Home: 425 E Kanawha Ave Columbus OH 43214

WEED, MARY THEOPHILOS, psychologist, educator; b. Miami, Fla., Nov. 11, 1928; d. John George and Elizabeth Gundhill (Sodegren) Theophilos; A.B., U. Miami (Fla.), 1953; M.A., U. Chgo., 1960; m. Perry Lewis Weed, Mar. 29, 1963 (div.); 1 dau., Heather. Psychologist, Chgo. Bd. Edn., 1960-62; asst. prof. psychology Chgo. City Colls., also Kennedy King Coll., 1962—; pvt. psychologist, Chgo. Cath. Sch. Bd., 1962—, Ill. Bd. Vocat. Edn. and Rehab., 1969—. Registerd psychologist, Ill. Mem. Am., Ill. psychol. assns. Home and office: 5534 S Harper Ave Chicago IL 60637

WEEDALL, ROBERT SCOTT, clin. psychologist, psychotherapist; b. Chgo., May 22, 1940; s. Andrew and Florence (Lott) W.; foster son Howard and Marjorie (Merton) Pett; B.S. in Psychology with honors, Carroll Coll., 1963; M.A., Bowling Green (Ohio) State U., 1965; Ph.D., U. Toledo, 1970; m. Suzanne J. Bortle, Apr. 16, 1966; children—Michael Scott, Crystal Ann, Kaaren Jean. Psychologist, Mental Hygiene Clinic, Toledo, 1965-74, pvt. practice clin. psychology psychotherapy, Toledo, 1970—; cons. in field. Mem. Am., Ohio, Northwest Ohio, Midwestern psychol. assns., Delta Rho Upsilon Alumni Assn. Home: 7141 Gillingham Ct Sylvania OH 43560 Office: 6600 Sylvania Ave Sylvania OH 43560

WEEDE, HILDA MARIAN SAWYER, counselor; b. Ladysmith, Wis., July 6, 1927; d. Frederick Dudley and Alice Helen (Fisher) Sawyer; B.S.E., No. Mo. State U., Kirksville, 1960, M.A., 1964; m. Gerald Duff Weede, Mar. 4, 1949; children—Larry Dale, Lorraine Dawn, Willard Warren (dec.), Charles Frederick. Tchr. pub. schs. Davis County, Bloomfield, Iowa, 1947-49, 54-72, elementary guidance counselor, 1972-77, counselor middle sch., 1972-77; tchr., chmn. bd. Bloomfield Christian Ch.; bd. dirs. H.E.D.C. Corp. emotionally disturbed children. Mem. Am. Legion Aux., PEO, NEA, Iowa Edn. Assn., No. Mo. State U. Alumni Assn., Am., Iowa personnel and guidance assns., Delta Kappa Gamma. Republican. Clubs: Bloomfield Country, Order Eastern Star. Home: 405 N Columbia St Bloomfield IA 52537 Office: Davis County Middle Sch 500 NE Bloomfield IA 52537

WEEDEN, ALFRED JOHN, educator; b. Waupaca, Wis., Aug. 11, 1932; s. Donald Smith and Maude Stella (Kuhr) W.; B.S., U. Wis. at Oshkosh, 1959, M.S., 1967; postgrad. U. Wis. at Milw., 1970; m. Florence Marion Taggart, Nov. 24, 1952; children—Donald Robert, Katherine Mae, Susan Ann, John William. Tchr. social sci., Wisconsin Rapids, Wis., 1959-63, New London, Wis., 1963—. Pres. bd. dirs. United Fund of New London, 1968-70; dir. Salvation Army of New London; troup leader Boy Scouts Am., 1965-67; dir. New London Little League, 1969. Mem. New London City Council, 1971; candidate for mayor, New London, 1972; mem. New London Planning Commn., 1972—. Served with AUS, 1953-55. Mem. Wisconsin Rapids (v.p. 1962-63), New London (pres. 1965-66), Wis. edn. assns., Internat. Platform Assn. Methodist (trustee). Home: 318 E Spring St New London WI 54961 Office: 1000 W Washington St New London WI 54961

WEEKS, JOHN LEONARD, physician; b. Bath, Eng., May 10, 1926; s. Leonard Cowling and Irene Emma (Evans) W.; M.B., B.S., U. London, 1953, M.D., 1975; diploma Royal Coll. Obstetrics and Gynecology, 1954; D.I.H., Royal Coll. Surgeons, 1957; L.M. C.C., Med. Council Can., 1961; m. Lotten Mari-Ann Rosenquist, Apr. 23, 1952; children—Annika, Kristin, John-Anders, Elisabeth, Bjorn. Intern, St. Thomas Hosp., Eng., 1953-54, St. Helier Hosp., 1954-55; med. officer London Transport Exec., 1955-58, Govt. of Nfld., 1958-60, Inco, Can., 1960-62; dir. health and safety div. Atomic Energy of Can., Ltd., Pinawa, Man., Can., 1962—; hon. prof. U. Man. Mem. permanent Internat. Commn. Occupational Health. Served to capt., Indian Army, 1943-47. Mem. Soc. Occupational Medicine. Contbr. articles to profl. jours. Home: 24 Prescott Pl Pinawa MB Canada Office: Whiteshell Nuclear Research Establishment Pinawa MB Canada

WEEKS, MARY CATHERINE, librarian; b. Hampton, Iowa, Sept. 23, 1925; d. Uzziel William and Mary (O'Connor) Weeks; B.A., U. No. Iowa, 1946; M.A., U. Wis., 1952; postgrad. U. Iowa, Iowa State U., U. No. Iowa. Tchr., Britt, Iowa, 1946-48, Colfax, Ia., 1946-50; library asst. Mason City Pub. Library, 1950-51; sch. librarian Long Beach, Calif., 1952-53; reference librarian Kans. State U., 1953-56; library coordinator Iowa Falls Pub. Schs. and Ellsworth Coll., 1956-68, chief librarian Ellsworth Coll., 1956—. Mem. Am., Iowa library assns., Nat., Iowa edn. assns., Bread for the World, Ellsworth Coll. Faculty Assn., Delta Kappa Gamma, Kappa Delta Pi, Pi Gamma Mu. Democrat. Roman Catholic. Club: Parchment. Home: 116 Meadow Lane Iowa Falls IA 50126 Office: Ellsworth Coll Iowa Falls IA 50126

WEEKS, SOLAN WILLIAM, city ofcl.; b. Detroit, Feb. 2, 1930; s. Otto William and Vera Wanda (Zeller) W.; B.A., Wayne State U., 1953, M.Ed., 1960; m. Patricia Kathryn Dolby, May 28, 1954; children—Douglas William, Kathleen Marie, Cynthia Mae. Curator indsl. history Detroit Hist. Mus., 1955-60; dir. Mich. State Hist. Mus., Lansing, 1960-66; asst. to pres., asso. dir. devel. Old Sturbridge (Mass.) Village, 1967-70, now overseer; dir. hist. dept. City of Detroit, coordinating dir. Detroit Hist. Soc., 1970—. Co-chmn. heritage com. Detroit Bicentennial Commn., 1974-76; treas. Detroit Adventure, 1973—; mem. Detroit Historic Designation Advisory Bd. Trustee Detroit Ednl. TV Found. Mem. Hist. Soc. Mich. (v.p. 1974-76), Midwest Mus. Conf. (v.p. 1966, 71), Mich. Museums Assn., Am. Assn. Museums, Am. Assn. for State and Local History, Nat. Trust for Hist. Preservation, Abraham Lincoln Civil War Round Table, Univ. Cultural Center Assn. (treas. 1977—), Gt. Lakes Maritime Inst., Vet. Motor Car Club Am., Assn. for Study Afro Am. Life and History. Rotarian. Clubs: Torch, Prismatic, Algonquin. Home: 16196 Shaftsbury Detroit MI 48219 Office: 5401 Woodward Ave Detroit MI 48202

WEENINK, MARY ETHEL LYNNE CRANDALL (MRS. GEORGE WEENINK), perfumer; b. Cherry Valley, Ill., Aug. 12, 1907: d. Jay Ellis and Mary Evalena (Johnson) Crandall; grad. Cleve. Acad. Cosmetic Therapy and Electrolysis, 1954; m. George Weenink, Apr. 14, 1934. Clk., teller Forest City Nat. Bank, Rockford, Ill., 1926-30; sec.-treas. Equitable Life Ins. Co., 1929-30; sec. to Capt. Lynn Harrison Pasadena (Calif.) Police Motor Squad, Chief Kelly Pasadena Police Dept., sec. Tournament Roses, 1930-35; sec., supplementary nutritionist. Cleve., 1935; lectr. Romance of Perfume, 1951—; founder Mary Lynne Cosmetics & Perfumes, Cleve., 1952; owner Mary Lynne Salon of Beauty, Cleve., 1952-59; co-owner, instr. Charm Acad., Cleve., 1959-63; owner Mary Lynne Charm Shoppe, Silver Spur Ranch, Ravenna, Ohio, 1963—. Recipient certificate of merit England, 1968; named one of 2000 Women of Achievement, 1969. Mem. D.A.R., Internat Platform Assn. Mem. Order Eastern Star, Ladies Oriental Shrine N. Am. Clubs: Silver Spur Ranch, Junior Tuesday (Ravenna, O.); Elks Ladies (Cleve.); Wimodausis (New Castle, Pa.). Address: Silver Spur Ranch 5497 Newton Falls Rd RD 2 Ravenna OH 44266

WEERTS, RICHARD KENNETH, educator; b. Peoria, Ill., Oct. 7, 1928; s. Gerhard Nicholas and Ellen (Lindeburg) W.; B.S. cum laude U. Ill., 1951; M.A., Columbia, 1956, Ed.D., 1960; m. Joan Elizabeth Metzger, Dec. 22, 1956; children—Lawrence Richard, Lynn Marie, Andrew Edward, Christie Ann; m. 2d, Mary Frances Perry, June 1, 1976; Tchr. instrumental music Lyndhurst (N.J.) Pub. Schs., 1956-57; dir. instrumental music Scotch Plains-Fanwood (N.J.) Pub. Schs., 1957-61; prof., chmn. instrumental music com. N.E. Mo. State U., Kirksville, 1961-70, chmn. music edn. faculty, 1970—. Served with AUS, 1951-55. Mem. Music Educators Nat. Conf., Nat. Assn. Am. Composers and Condrs., Nat. Assn. Coll. Wind and Percussion Instrs. (editor jour. 1968—, exec. sec. 1971—), Phi Mu Alpha Sinfonia, Kappa Delta Pi, Phi Delta Kappa. Methodist (chmn. commn. on worship 1965-66, choir dir. 1970—). Author: Original Manuscript Music for Wind and Percussion Instruments, 1964, 2d edit, 1973; Handbook for Woodwinds, 1966; Developing Individual Skills for the High School Band, 1969; How to Develop and Maintain a Successful Woodwind Section, 1972; Handbook of Rehersal Techniques for the Highschool Band, 1976. Asso. editor Woodwind World, 1965-69, contbg. editor Woodwind World—Brass & Percussion, 1970—, double reed editor, 1976-78, asso. editor, 1978—. Home: 520 W Hildreth Kirksville MO 63501 Office: Div of Fine Arts Northeast Missouri State U Kirksville MO 63501

WEESE, BENJAMIN HORACE, architect; b. Evanston, Ill., June 4, 1929; s. Harry Ernest and Marjorie (Mohr) W.; B. Arch., Harvard, 1951, M. Arch., 1957; m. Cynthia Rogers, July 5, 1963; children—Daniel Peter, Catharine Mohr. Past pres., Harry Weese and Assos., Ltd., architects, Chgo.; pres. Weese Seegers Hickey Weese Ltd., Architects, Chgo.; co-founder, past pres. Chgo. Sch. Arch. Found., Glessner House, Chgo., 1966—. Recipient certificate Ecole Des Beaux Arts, Fontainebleau, France, 1956. Fellow AIA; mem. Nat. Council Archtl. Registration Bds. Club: Cliff Dwellers (Chgo.). Home: 2133 N Hudson Ave Chicago IL 60614 Office: 230 E Ohio St Chicago IL 60611

WEESE, CARLISLE, dentist; b. Chgo., Oct. 15, 1919; s. Jacob and Minnie (Steinberg) W.; student Lewis Inst., 1937-39; D.D.S., Northwestern U., 1942; m. Florence Lorayne Kales, Dec. 27, 1942; children—William Curtis, James Leighton, Debra Ellyn Weese-Mayer. Pvt. practice dentistry, Chgo., 1946-64, Oak Park, Ill., 1964—. Served to lt. comdr. USNR, 1943-46. Fellow Acad. Gen. Dentistry, Am. Coll. Dentists; mem. Am. Dental Assn., Ill., Chgo. (dir.) dental socs., Alpha Omega. Home: 640 N Oak Park Ave Oak Park IL 60302 Office: 1011 Lake St Oak Park IL 60301

WEG, JOHN GERARD, physician; b. N.Y.C., Feb. 16, 1934; s. Leonard and Pauline M. (Kanzleiter) W.; A.B. cum laude, Coll. Holy Cross, Worcester, Mass., 1955; M.D., N.Y. Med. Coll., 1959; m. Mary Loretta Flynn, June 2, 1956; children—Diane Marie, Kathryn Mary, Carol Ann, Loretta Louise, Veronica Susanne, Michelle Celeste. Intern, Walter Reed Gen. Hosp., Washington, 1959-60; resident in internal medicine Wilford Hall USAF Hosp., Lackland AFB, Tex., 1960-63; clin. dir. pulmonary disease div. Jefferson Davis Hosp., Houston, 1967-71; asst. prof. medicine Baylor U. Coll. Medicine, Houston, 1967-71, asso. prof., 1971; asso. prof. internal medicine U. Mich., Ann Arbor, 1971-74, prof., 1974—, physician-in-charge pulmonary div., 1971—; cons. physician Meth. Hosp., Houston, 1968-71; med. adv. com. for asso. degree program in health scis. S. Tex. Jr. Coll., Houston, 1968-71; cons. to Nat. Tb and Respiratory Disease Assn. film on TB, 1971-73; cons. physician in internal medicine Wayne County Gen. Hosp., Eloise, Mich., 1973—. Adv. bd. Washtenaw County Health Dept., 1973—; mem. human relations com. Tappan Jr. High Sch., Ann Arbor, 1972. Served with M.C., USAF, 1963-67. Traveling fellow Nat. Tb and Respiratory Disease Assn., 1971; recipient Aesculapius award Tex. Med. Assn., 1971, pulmonary academic award Nat. Heart and Lung Inst., 1972-77; prof.-in-residence Am. Coll. Chest Physicians, 1972—. Diplomate Am. Bd. Internal Medicine. Fellow Am. Coll. Chest Physicians, A.C.P.; mem. AMA, Am. Thoracic Soc., AAAS, Am. Fedn. Clin. Research, Air Force Soc. Internists and Allied Specialists, Internat. Union Against Tb, Mich. Thoracic Soc. (pres. 1976—), Mich. (dir. 1976—, profl. edn. com. 1973—), Am. Lung Assn., Research Club Univ. Mich., Assn. Advancement Med. Instrumentation, Central Soc. Clin. Research, Alpha Omega Alpha. Reviewer for profl. publs. in field, VA Med. Research Programs; editorial bd. Chest; contbr. articles, abstracts, book chpts., audiovisual publs. Home: 3060 Exmoor St Ann Arbor MI 48104 Office: 1405 E Ann St Ann Arbor MI 48109

WEGENER, FREDERICK FREEMEN, architect, planner; b. Chgo., Feb. 3, 1932; s. Erwin John and Gladys Myrtle (Fingel) W.; B.Arch., U. Ill., 1958; m. Martha Georgene Carey, June 30, 1957; children—Leslie Patricia, Inger Ann, Carey Leigh. Architect, John J. Flad & Assos., Madison, Wis., 1961-65; project architect Bur. Engring., State of Wis., Madison, 1965-67, chief archtl. design, 1967-69, planner Bur. Capital Devel., 1969-73, dir. HSR Planning, 1973-75, project mgr. Bur. Facilities Mgmt., 1975—. Mem. Zoning Bd. of Appeals, Madison, 1966-69. Trustee Taychopera Found., Inc. Served with AUS, 1953-55. Home: 211 N Spooner St Madison WI 53705 Office: 1 W Wilson St Madison WI 53702

WEGENKE, GARY LEE, sch. adminstr.; b. South Bend, Ind., Feb. 27, 1938; s. Edward S. and Blanche M. (Flowers) W.; A.B., DePauw U., 1961; M.S., Ind. U., 1964; Ph.D., Ohio State U., 1971; m. Sandra S. Gard, Aug. 17, 1963; children—Bart, Bret, Blake. Tchr. secondary sch. math. South Bend Community Schs., 1961-69; research asso. Evaluation Center Ohio State U., Columbus, 1969-71; dir. Statewide Library Planning and Evaluation Project Ohio State U. and U.S. Office Edn., Columbus, 1971-72, adj. prof., 1971-72; prin. Hill Community High Sch., Lansing, Mich., 1972-76; dir. adminstrv. services Lansing Sch. Dist., 1976—; staff urban sch. adminstrn. Mich. State U., East Lansing, fall 1974; mem. various com. Mich. Dept. Edn., 1972; lectr. various insts., convs. Recipient Lansing Jr. C. of C. Concerned Citizen award, 1972. Mem. Mich. Assn. Secondary Prins., Mich. Sch. Bus. Ofcls., Am. Assn. Sch. Adminstrs., Phi Delta Kappa, Phi Gamma Delta. Methodist. Home: 2139 Northampton Way Lansing MI 48912 Office: 519 W Kalamazoo Lansing MI 48933

WEGGENMANN, NORMAN EDWARD, ins. agt.; b. Washington, Mo., Sept. 18, 1927; s. Paul Francis and Annetta (Vick) W.; m. Evelyn Louise Andriot, June 7, 1947; children—Gene Paul, Lynn Ann. Active bus.; ins. agt. Catholic Knights Am., St. Louis, 1976—, mem. advisory bd., 1977—, v.p., 1977—. Served with U.S. Army, 1946-47. Roman Catholic. Home: 14528 Bantry Ln Chesterfield MO 63017 Office: 3525 Hampton Ave St Louis MO

WEGMILLER, DONALD CHARLES, health services adminstr.; b. Cloquet, Minn., Sept. 25, 1938; s. Harold Charles and Mary (Karp) W.; B.A. magna cum laude, U. Minn. at Duluth, 1960; M.H.A., U. Minn., 1962; m. Janet Ann Listerud, Apr. 27, 1957; children—Katherine, Mark, Dean. Orderly St. Luke's Hosp., Duluth, 1958-60; adminstrv. resident Fairview Hosp., Mpls., 1961-62, adminstrv. asst., 1962-65; asst. adminstr. Fairview-Southdale Hosp., Edina, Minn., 1965-66, adminstr., 1966-76; sr. v.p. Health Central, Inc., Mpls., 1976—; staff asst. to Pres. U.S., 1972-76; lectr. hosp. adminstrn. U. Minn.; speaker, mem. faculty insts. and seminars. Dir. Richfield Bank & Trust Co., Community Hosp. Linen Service, Inc.; mem. com. econs. Mpls. Health Dept. and Minn. Dept. Health, 1964-65. Dir. Mpls. Aquatennial, 1968, Jr. Achievement, 1968, ARC, 1968; mem. exec. com. Minn. Golf Classic, 1968, Mayor's Com. Employment of Handicapped, 1962-67; asso. dir. Hennepin County United Fund, 1962-67; dir. Mpls. War Meml. Blood Bank, 1969-75; mem. Mayor's Council Youth Opportunity, 1968-72; dir. Respiratory Disease Assn. Hennepin County, 1969-74; bd. dirs. Met. Mpls. YMCA, 1972—; bd. mgmt. Southdale YMCA, 1972—, chmn., 1976-77; mem. house com. U.S. Women's Open Golf Tournament, 1977; cons. div. med. services Dept. State, 1975. Mem. Richfield (Minn.) Bd. Edn., 1970—, chmn. 1971-74; mem. Gov.'s Adv. Commn. on Community Schs., 1970—. Mem. adv. com. Normandale Jr. Coll., Bloomington, Minn. Named one of outstanding young men of Am., Outstanding Ams. Found., 1968, outstanding young hosp. adminstrs. in U.S., Am. Coll. Hosp. Adminstrs., 1969, outstanding pres. of year, Minn. Jr. C. of C., 1969, outstanding young man, Richfield Jr. C. of C., 1970, outstanding young man, Mpls. Jr. C. of C., 1970, one of 10 outstanding young men of Minn., Minn. Jr. C. of C., 1971. Mem. Am. Coll. Hosp. Adminstrs., Am., Minn., Twin City hosp. assns., Minn. League for Nursing, Mpls. Jr. C. of C. (pres. 1968-69, dir., 1964-69), Greater Southdale Area C. of C. (v.p. 1970), Greater Edina C. of C. (pres. 1971). Rotarian (Edina). Contbr. articles to profl. jours. Home: 7029 Bloomington Ave S Richfield MN 55423 Office: 2810 57th Ave N Minneapolis MN 55430

WEGNER, ROBERT ERNST, educator; b. Cleve., Mar. 1, 1929; s. Ernst Robert and Esther Marie (Strebelow) W.; B.A. with honors, Mich. State U., 1950; M.A., Case Western Reserve U., 1952, Ph.D., 1959; postgrad. State U. Iowa, 1952-53; m. Phyllis Jean Larimer, Jan. 14, 1950; children—Gregory, Julie, Mark. Asst. prof. English, Wilmington (Ohio) Coll., 1955-57; asst. prof. English, Alma (Mich.) Coll., 1957-63, asso. prof. 1963-69, prof., 1969—. Vis. prof. Augustana Coll., Rock Island, Ill., fall 1968; leader fiction workshop Saginaw Valley Coll., 1970. Named to roll of honor The Best American Short Stories, 1971. Mem. Modern Lang. Assn., Mid-Western Modern Lang. Assn. Clubs: Sierra (Alma, Mich.). Author: The Poetry and Prose of E.E. Cummings, 1965. Author of several revs., poems and short stories in mags. including Esquire, Epoch and Carleton Miscellany; story included in The Age of Anxiety, 1972. Home: Route 1 Pine Grove Rd Vestaburg MI 48891

WEGNER, WALDO WILBERT, univ. adminstr.; b. Everly, Iowa, Jan. 17, 1913; s. Ernest Frederick and Amanda Christina (Thiessen) W.; B.S., Iowa State U., 1935; postgrad. U. Chgo., 1936; m. Harriett Genevieve Olson, July 5, 1938; children—Ann Wegner Adams. Asst. city engr. City of Cedar Falls (Iowa), 1937-41; asst. city engr. City of Mason City (Iowa), 1941-42, city engr., 1945-48; city engr., city mgr. City of Chariton (Iowa), 1948-49; field engr. Portland Cement Assn., Cedar Rapids, 1949-56; v.p., civil engr. Loomis Bros., Cedar Rapids, 1956-61; chief engr., gen. mgr. Johnson Ready Mix Co., Omaha, 1961-62; dir. pub. works, city engr. City of Edina (Minn.), 1962-63; dir. Center for Indsl. Research and Service, Iowa State U., Ames, 1963—. Mem. planning commn. City of Cedar Rapids, 1950-56, bldg. code commn., 1957-59, airport commn., 1960-62. Served with USNR, 1942-45. Registered profl. engr., Iowa, Minn. Fellow ASCE; mem. Nat. Soc. Profl. Engrs. (v.p. 1961-63), Iowa Engring. Soc. (v.p. 1957-58), Cedar Rapids Engring. Club (pres. 1958-59), Iowa State U. Alumni Assn. (exec. com. 1950-53, Nat. Univ. Extension Assn. (dir. 1974-76), Mid-Continent Research and Devel. Council (chmn. 1976-77), U.S. Navy League, Res. Officers Assn., Tau Beta Pi, Sigma Pi. Lutheran. Mason, Rotarian (pres. 1957-58, 66-67). Home: 132 Broadmoor Circle Ames IA 50010 Office: Room 201 Bldg E Iowa State U Ames IA 50011

WEHLER, RICHARD HARRIS, lawyer; b. Pocahontas, Iowa, Dec. 28, 1924; s. Irvin F. and Roleen (Wearanga) W.; A.B., Wittenberg U., 1949; J.D. U. Mich., 1952; m. Jeanette Novotny, July 12, 1952; children—David O., Jon R. Admitted to Ohio bar, 1952; dir. law dept. City Springfield, 1952-59, acting city mgr., 1959; partner firm Schwer, Taggart, Wehler & Emerich, Springfield, 1960—. Mem. Springfield Charter Revision Com., 1960-66; asst. council commr. Tecumseh council Boy Scouts Am., 1966-67, dist. commr., 1968; mem. Bd. Mental Retardation Clark County, 1967—, Clark County Bd. Mental Retardation and Mental Health, 1967-74, Clark County Zoning Study Com., 1968-70, citizens adv. com. New Carlisle-Bethel Local Sch. Dist., 1970, Clark County Jail Adv. Com., 1972-75. Trustee Clark County Council Retarded Children; trustee Ohio Assn. Retarded Children; 1958-70, pres., 1968-70; trustee Nat. Assn. Retarded Citizens, 1976—. Mem. Springfield Bar and Law Library Assn., Ohio (exec. com. 1968-71), Am. bar assns. Presbyterian. Clubs: University (Springfield), Rotary. Home: 725 S Tecumseh Rd Springfield OH 45506 Office: PO Box 1406 Springfield OH 45501

WEHNER, MERLE ERNEST, physician: b. Cooks, Mich., Apr. 5, 1914: s. Paul A. and Effie (Prater) W.: B.A., Andrews U., 1940: M.D., Loma Linda U., 1944: m. Laura Mae Crawford, Dec. 8, 1934: children—Nicholas M., Karen A. Intern, Edward Sparrow Hosp., Lansing, Mich., 1943-44; practice medicine Manistique, Mich., 1947—; mem. staff Schoolcraft Meml. Hosp. Dir. First Nat. Bank, Manistique. Pres., Manistique Indsl. Devel. Corp., 1960—. Bd. dirs. Mich. div. Am. Cancer Soc., 1966—. Served with AUS, 1945-47. Fellow Am. Soc. Abdominal Surgeons: mem. AMA, World. Mich., Schoolcraft County med. assns., Am. Geriatric Soc., Am. Acad. Gen. Practice. Republican. Mem. Seventh-day Adventist Ch. Lion (dist. gov. 1957-58), Elk. Home: 101 Lake St Manistique MI 49854 Office: Med Cental Center Manistique MI 49854

WEHRER, CHARLES SIECKE, educator, author, mgmt. tng. cons.; b. Norfolk, Nebr., July 13, 1914; s. Charles C. and Ella (Augusta) W.; B.A., Nebr. State Tchrs. Coll., 1940; M.A. in Sch. Adminstrn., U. Nebr., 1950; postgrad. U. So. Calif., 1954-55, Columbia U., 1950, U. Nebr., 1950, Ohio State U., 1960-61; L.H.D., Sioux Empire Coll., 1967. Grad. asst. in edn. U. Nebr., 1949-50, U. So. Calif., 1954-55, Ohio State U., 1960-61; tchr., producer ednl. TV, dir. guest relations NBC, Los Angeles, 1951-53; tchr. pub. schs., Paramount, Calif., 1953-54, Excelsior Adult Sch., Norwalk, Calif., 1953-57; coach, supt. schs., Wood Lake, Nebr., 1947-49; prin. Scottsbluff (Nebr.) Jr. High Sch., 1950-51; asso. prof. edn., supr. student teaching program Ohio No. U., Ada, 1958-60; asso. prof., supr. elementary student teaching Capital U., Columbus, 1961-62; prof. edn., dir. student affairs, asst. to pres. Grand View Coll., Des Moines, 1962-64; prin. Jr. High Sch., Norwalk, Iowa, 1962-63; youth, TV, ednl. programming, Des Moines, 1965; prof. edn. and psychology S.W. Community Coll., Creston, Iowa, 1967; chmn. edn., psychology depts., athletic dir., coach, acad. dean Sioux Empire Coll., Hawarden, Iowa, 1967-69; exec. dir. govt. program, Webster City, Iowa, 1969-70; chmn. dept. edn. and psychology, dir. tchr. edn. J.F. Kennedy Coll., Wahoo, Nebr., 1970-71; producer, emcee youth TV program Let's Listen to Youth, moderator programs for youth KOLN-TV, Lincoln, Neb., 1971—; ednl. TV program moderator, 1971-73; prof. edn. Concordia Tchrs. Coll., Seward, Nebr., 1973; cons. to mgmt., 1973—; cons. tng. programs, adminstrn., personnel plans and procedures State Nebr., 1973—; lectr. on youth, ednl. and tng. problems and programs, 1973—. Counselor and adviser to Nebr. Boys' State, 1949-50; spl. youth cons. radio program Art Linkletter House Party, Calif., 1952. Phys. dir. YMCA, Norfolk, 1934-36, McCook, Nebr., 1937-38, Los Angeles Downtown Y, 1940-41; Neb. del. White House Conf. on Children and Youth, 1950; mem. Gov.'s Com. on Youth, Calif., also Nebr. dir. spl. project Iowa Dept. Health, 1965-66; contbr. to Congl. sub-com. on poverty-youth programs, 1964-65; spl. guest Mike Douglas TV Show; lectr. on youth and ednl. topics. Served from pvt. to capt. USAAF, 1941-45; Africa, ETO. Decorated Bronze Star; named Most Popular Tchr. by various groups; recipient numerous awards for teaching and youth work including Nat. Am. Legion Aux. award for youth radio programs in Ia. Mem. NEA, AAUP, Assn. for Higher Edn., Nat. Assn. Sch. Adminstrs., Nat. Soc. for Study Edn., Internat. Platform Assn. (spl. speaker conv. 1970), Congress Parents and Tchrs. (state chmn. Jr. high-high sch. youth com.), Delta Sigma Phi, Phi Delta Kappa, Sigma Tau Delta. Kiwanian (pres. Saunders County 1972-73). Clubs: Iowa Town and Country Saddle (pres. Des Moines), Wahoo Saddle, Lions (officer). Author: Keep in Touch—My Students, 1966. Contbr. articles on youth and edn. to various publs. Address: 2932 S 93d Plaza Apt 8 Omaha NE 68124

WEHRING, BERNARD WILLIAM, nuclear engr.; b. Monroe, Mich., Aug. 3, 1937; s. Bernard Albert and Alma Christina (Graf) W.; m. Margaret Mary (Robinson), Sept. 5, 1959; children—Mary Ann, James, Susan, Barbara. B.S.E. in Physics, U. Mich., 1959, B.S.E. in Math, 1959; M.S. in Physics, U. Ill., 1961, Ph.D., 1966. Asst. prof. nuclear engring. U. Ill., Urbana, 1966-70, asso. prof., 1970-77, prof., 1977—. Mem. Am. Soc. Engring. Edn., Am. Nuclear Soc., Am. Phys. Soc. Contbr. articles to profl. jours. Home: 1720 Bellamy Dr Champaign IL 61820 Office: 104 Nuclear Radiation Lab Urbana IL 61801

WEHRLY, RALPH E., real estate exec.; b. Ft. Wayne, Ind., Mar. 28, 1926; s. Wilfred R. and Lillian R. (Smith) W.; B.S., Purdue U., 1951; children—Linda (Mrs. Michael Sherman), Sandra (Mrs. Theodore Agness), Jack, Janet, Teresa. Engr., Magnavox, Ft. Wayne, 1951-55; prodn. supr. ITT, Ft. Wayne, 1955-58; partner Wehrly Real Estate, Ft. Wayne, 1958-69, Roth, Wehrly, Heiny Inc., Ft. Wayne, 1970—. Active Boy Scouts Am., civic, charitable orgns. Mem. Am., Ind., Ft. Wayne assns. realtors, Am. Inst. E.E. Elk, K.C. Clubs: Park Forest, Olympia. Home: 3004 Kingsley Dr Fort Wayne IN 46805 Office: 230 E Berry St Fort Wayne IN 46802

WEHRMACHER, WILLIAM HENRY, cardiologist; b. Waterloo, Iowa, May 17, 1921; s. William H. and Lulu Ella (Wahlmann) W.; student Wartburg Coll., 1939-41; B.A., State U. Iowa, 1943, M.D., 1945; m. Berdella Larsen; children—William, James, Karen, John, Charles. Intern, U.S. Naval Hosp., Norfolk, Va., 1946; resident VA Hosp. and Wayne U. Med. Sch., Detroit, 1948-50; practice medicine specializing in cardiology, 1950—; instr. Wayne U., 1948-50, State U. Iowa, 1950-51; asso. in medicine Northwestern U., 1951-71; clin. prof. medicine Loyola U., Chgo., 1971—, adj. prof. physiology, 1975—; mem. staffs Loyola, Columbus, St. Joseph hosps., Chgo., Skokie Valley Hosp. Served to lt. comdr. M.C., USN, 1942-44. Diplomate Am. Bd. Internal Medicine. Fellow A.C.P., Am. Coll. Cardiology; mem. Am. Fedn. Clin. Research, Am. Heart Assn., AMA, Am. Med. Soc. Vienna, Am. Med. Writers Assn., Chgo. Heart Assn., Chgo. Med. Soc., Chgo. Soc. Internal Medcine, Ill. Med. Soc., Inst. Medicine Chgo., Pan Am. Med. Assn., Soc. Med. History in Chgo., Alpha Kappa Kappa, Alpha Omega Alpha, Sigma Xi. Lutheran. Contbr. articles and chpts. to med. jours. and texts. Home: 5706 Capulina Morton Grove IL 60053 Office: 670 N Michigan Ave Chicago IL 60611

WEI, LUN-SHIN, educator; b. Taiwan, China, Jan. 14, 1929; s. Ya and Wu-Chen (Chu) W.; came to U.S., 1953, naturalized, 1969; B.A., Taipei Tchr's. Coll., Taiwan, 1946; B.S., Nat. Chuong-Hsing U., Taiwan, 1951; M.S., U. Ill., Urbana, 1955, Ph.D., 1958; m. Tam Thi Dang, Aug. 18, 1955; children—Michael, Max, Manuel, Aline. Tchr., Hou-long Central Elementary Sch., Taiwan, 1946-47, Bur. Commodity Inspection and Quarantine, Taiwan, 1951-52; research asst. U. Ill., 1954-56, sci. analyst, 1956-59, research asso., 1959-64, asst. prof., 1964-69, asso. prof. food sci., 1969-76, prof., 1976—. Cons. Kibun Co. Ltd., Tokyo, Japan. Recipient Ednl., Research award Land of Lincoln Soybean Assn., 1974. Mem. Am. Chem. Soc., Inst. Food Technologists, AAAS, AAUP, Cosmopolitan Club of U. Ill., Formasn Club in U.S.A. (pres. 1957), Sigma Xi, Gamma Sigma Delta. Research, publs on soybean foods. Patentee in field. Home: 309 McHenry St Urbana IL 61801

WEICKER, JACK EDWARD, educator; b. Woodburn, Ind., June 23, 1924; s. Monald Henry and Helen Mae (Miller) W.; A.B., Ind. U., 1947, M.A. (James Albert Woodburn fellow, All U. fellow), 1951; m. Janet Kathryn Thompson, May 29, 1946; children—John H., Kathryn Ann, Jane Elizabeth, Emily Jo. Tchr. history and English, Harrison Hill Sch., Ft. Wayne, Ind., 1947-48, South Side High Sch., Ft. Wayne, 1951-61; counselor, asst. prin. South Side High Sch., 1961-63, prin., 1963—. Mem. Ind. State Scholarship Commn., 1969-77; mem. exec. com. Midwest regional assembly Coll. Entrance Exam. Bd., 1974-77, chmn. nominating com., 1976-77. Mem. Ft. Wayne Prins. Assn., Nat. Assn. Secondary Sch. Prins., Ind. Assn. Jr. and Sr. High Sch. Prins., PTA (life), Phi Beta Kappa, Phi Delta Kappa, Phi Alpha Theta. Mem. Disciples of Christ Ch. (moderator of bd. trustees 1975—). Rotarian (bd. dirs. 1973-76). Author: (with others) Indiana: The Hoosier State, 1959, 63; Due Process and Students Rights/Responsibilities: Two Points of View, 1975; Back to Basics: Language Arts, 1976. Home: 5200 N Washington Rd Fort Wayne IN 46804 Office: 3601 S Calhoun St Fort Wayne IN 46807

WEIDEMANN, JOSEPH EDWARD, sales exec.; b. Tampa, Fla., Oct. 3, 1941; s. Joseph Edward and June Elizabeth (Ayer) McGlamery, Jr.; student U. Ill., 1959-63; m. Elisabeth Sue Rowand, July 27, 1963; 1 son, Edward James. Comptroller R. H. Bishop Co., Champaign, Ill., 1961-62; controller Airflex Corp., Champaign, 1962-68, gen. mgr., 1968-73; sales engr. Swanson Co., Champaign, 1973-75; nat. sales mgr., v.p. Brandt-Airflex Corp., Champaign, 1975-77; exec. v.p. WMW Enterprises, Inc., Champaign, 1977—. Mem. Sch.-Industry Relations Com. Mem. Constrn. Specifications Inst., Am. Soc. Heating, Refrigeration and Air Conditioning Engrs., Champaign Jr. C. of C. Kiwanian. Research and design solar heating. Home: Box 202 Rural Route 1 Fairmount IL 61841 Office: 3402 N Mattis St Champaign IL 61820

WEIDEMANN, WAYNE E(RWIN), pub. transp. planner; b. Belleville, Ill., July 31, 1945; s. Alvin Christian and Esther Marie (Berthold) W.; B.A., So. Ill. U., 1967, M.A., 1969. Urban transp. planner East-West Gateway Coordinating Council, St. Louis, 1969-74; transp. planner Bi-State Devel. Agency, St. Louis, 1974—. NSF trainee, 1967-69. Mem. Am. Soc. Planning Ofcls., Am. Inst. Planners (asso., exec. com. St. Louis sect. 1973). Author articles, reports on regional devel., transp. and transit Greater St. Louis area. Home: 7705 Woodcliffe Dr Belleville IL 62223 Office: 3869 Park Ave St Louis MO 63110

WEIDENTHAL, DANIEL TILLES, physician; b. Chgo., Aug. 29, 1932; s. Clarence Milton and Anne (Tilles) W.; B.A., Dartmouth Coll., 1954; M.D., Western Res. U., 1958; m. Judith Weinberg, June 22, 1958; children—David, Jeffrey. Intern, Mt. Sinai Hosp., Cleve., 1958-59; resident ophthalmology Kresge Eye Inst. and Detroit Receiving Hosp., 1959-62; fellow retina service Mass. Eye & Ear Infirmary, Boston, 1963-64; practice medicine specializing in retinal detachment surgery and diseases of retina, Cleve., 1964—; mem. staff St. Luke's Hosp., dir. AMA approved fellowship in retinal surgery and retinal vascular disease, also head sect. retinal surgery, 1968—; Mt. Sinai, Cleve. Met.-Gen. hosps.; asst. clin. prof. Case Western Res. U. Sch. Medicine, 1970—. Fellow A.C.S.; mem. Retina Soc. (charter), AMA, Phi Delta Epsilon. Clubs: Cleveland Racquet, Oakwood. Contbr. to books, articles in field. Home: 10 Pepper Creek Dr Pepper Pike OH 44124 Office: 11201 Shaker Blvd Cleveland OH 44104

WEIDER, DONNABETH, cleaning products co. exec.; b. North Platte, Nebr., Mar. 4, 1936; d. Edgar Don and Elizabeth (Giltz) Weider; student Park Coll., 1954-56; grad. Alexander Hamilton Inst., 1970. With Faultless Starch Co., Kansas City, Mo., 1962—, product mgr., 1967-72, dir. mktg. services, 1972-75, Eastern regional sales mgr., 1976—. Leader, Camp Fire Girls, Kansas City, Kans., 1958-63; chmn. women's council Better Bus. Bur., 1972—, bd. dirs., mem. exec. com., 1975—; chmn. Jr. Achievement Sales Seminar, 1971. Mem. Sales and Mktg. Execs. Assn. (officer 1972—), Women's C. of C. (consumer edn. com. 1970-72, co-chmn. 1971-72). Presbyn. Home: 5804 W 78th St Prairie Village KS 66208 Office: 1025 W 8th St Kansas City MO 64101

WEIDMAN, MARGARET LILLIAN, ednl. adminstr.; b. Bedford, Ind., Jan. 13, 1913; d. Martin Hubbard and Arla Louise (Wagner) Inman; student Ind. U., 1931-33, Butler U., 1937-38, Quincy Coll., 1951-52; B.S., Culver Stockton Coll., 1953; Ed.M., U. Ill., 1955; postgrad. Seton Hall U., 1958, Newark State Coll., 1958, West Mich. U., 1968, Nat. Coll. Ed., 1972; m. Gilbert Louis Weidman, June 14, 1937; children—Linda Weidman Schurman, Larry. Tchr. elementary sch., Hillsdale, Ind., 1933-34, St. Bernice, Ind., 1934-37; tchr. mentally handicapped classes Emerson and Franklin Schs., Quincy, Ill., 1952-57, Edison Sch., West Orange, N.J., 1957-58, Washington Sch., Montclair, N.J., 1958-60, Stevenson and Melrose Park (Ill.) schs., 1960-64; supr. mentally retarded Proviso Twp., Maywood, Ill., 1964—. Instr. Culver Stockton Coll., Canton, Mo., 1966; student tchr. counselor No. Ill. U., DeKalb, 1972-74. Mem. Ill. Council for Exceptional Children, Ill. Adminstrs. Spl. Edn., Alpha Delta Kappa. Mem. Christian Ch. Home: 617 N Taylor Ave Oak Park IL 60302 Office: 1000 Van Buren St Maywood IL 60153

WEIGAND, GEORGE ROBERT, internat. trade exec.; b. Wittenberge, Germany, June 16, 1928; s. Kurt Aenderly and Eleonore W.; Canadian citizen; student Bismarck Coll., Germany, 1946-53; diploma bus. mgmt. Centre d'Etudes Industrielles, Geneva, Switzerland, 1964; m. Margarete Bannuscher, Nov. 1, 1955; 1 son, Benjamin. With Plasser Am., Chesapeake, Va., 1964-67; exec. v.p. Ramco/Nationwide Industries, Evanston, Ill., 1967-70; pres. Fedesco, Chgo., 1971—; pres. Lukas American, Inc., Downers Grove, Ill., 1971—; cons. Welt Internat., Frieseke & Hoepfner, W. Germany, Metallwerk Boxdorf, W. Germany. Mem. Am. Railway Engring. Assn., Am. Transit Assn. Home: 353 Huntington Way Bolingbrook IL 60439 Office: 5201 Thatcher Rd Downers Grove IL 60515

WEIGAND, ROBERT EUGENE, mktg. scientist, educator; b. Terre Haute, Ind., Aug. 13, 1930; s. Arthur Alphonsus and Nora L. (Epler) W.; student Eastern Ill. State U.; B.S., U. Notre Dame, 1952; M.S., U. Ill., 1956, Ph.D., 1961. Faculty, De Paul U., Chgo., 1959-69, chmn. dept., 1960-65; vis. asso. prof. marketing U. Ill., Urbana, 1967-68; prof. U. Ill., Chgo. Circle, dept. head, 1969—; cons. in field. Mem. Chgo. Council Fgn. Relations, Internat. Visitor's Center. Served with Signal Corps, AUS, 1952-54. Mem. Am., So. mktg. assns., Am. Econ. Assn., Acad. Internat. Bus., Acad. Advt. Author: (with others) Basic Retailing. Contbr. articles to profl. publs. on internat. bus. Home: 5455 Sheridan Rd Chicago IL 60640

WEIGEL, JOHN WILLIAM, urologist; b. Manhattan, Kans., Jan. 15, 1929; s. Paul and Martha Marie (Coons) W.; student U. Kans., 1946-49; B.S., Kans. State U., 1950, M.D., 1954; m. Mary Lou Van Blarcum, Aug. 10, 1953; children—Vicki Sue, John Randall, Teresa Jane. Intern St. Mary's Hosp., Kansas City, Mo., 1954-55; resident in radiology Fitzsimons Army Med. Center, Denver, 1957-58, asst. chief, urology, Fitzsimons Gen. Hosp., 1971-72, chief, urology, 1972-75; resident in gen. surgery DeWitt Army Hosp., Ft. Belvoir, Va., 1961-62; resident in urology Brook Gen. Hosp., San Antonio, Tex., 1962-65; asst. clin. prof. urology, U. Colo., Denver, 1972-75; asst. prof. urology U. Kans., Kansas City, 1975—; chief sect. urology VA Hosp., Kansas City, Mo., 1975—, acting chief surgery, 1976—; practice medicine specializing in urology, Kansas City, Kans., 1975—. Summerfield scholar, 1946. Served with M.C., U.S. Army, 1956-75. Diplomate Am. Bd. Urology. Mem. Am. Urol. Assn. (local chmn. sci. exhibits S. Central sect. 1974), A.C.S., AMA, Assn. Mil. Surgeons, Rocky Mountain Urol. Soc., Western Trauma Assn., Soc. Univ. Urologists, Kansas City Urol. Soc., Beta Theta Pi, Nu Sigma Nu. Decorated Meritorious Service Medal, Order Golden Nephros, Legion of Merit. Contbr. articles to profl. publs. Republican. Presbyterian. Home: 23 Mohawk St Lake Quivara Kansas City KS 66106 Office: 39th and Rainbow Blvd Kansas City KS 66103

WEIGEL, PAUL, architect; b. N.Y.C., Aug. 5, 1889; s. Friederich Wilhelm and Wilhelmine (Mueller) W.; B.Arch. (scholar), Cornell U., 1912; m. Martha Marie Coons, June 6, 1926; children—John William, Paul David. Mem. faculty Sch. Architecture, Kans. State U., prof. emeritus, 1954, head Sch. Architecture, 1924-54; past pres. Collegiate Schs. Architecture; cons. archtl adviser in planning Ataturk U., Turkey, 1957-59; archtl. design staff Panama Canal, 1913-17. Past mem. Manhattan (Kans.) Planning Bd. Served as lt. F.A., U.S. Army, World War I. Hon. fellow emeritus AIA. Presbyterian. Home: 8110 Sagamore Rd Leawood KS 66206

WEIH, JACK EVANS, physician; b. Clinton, Iowa, Apr. 23, 1919; s. Elmer Paul and Grace (Evans) W.; student Lake Forest (Ill.) Coll., 1937-38, U. Iowa, 1939; M.D., Loyola U., Chgo., 1943; postgrad. U. Iowa, 1945-56, 48-50; m. Sarah Virginia Wallace, June 10, 1945; children—John Wallace, Susie Evans. Intern, Mercy Hosp., Chgo., 1944; practice medicine, ltd. to ophthalmology, Traverse City, Mich., 1950—; mem., past pres. med. staff Munson Hosp. Dir. Mich. Children's Aid Soc., Traverse City, 1960-64. Served from lt. to capt. M.C., AUS, 1946-48. Diplomate Am. Bd. Ophthalmology and Otolaryngology. Fellow A.C.S.; mem. Am. Acad. Ophthalmology, Assn. Research Ophthalmology, Pan Am. Assn. Ophthalmology, AMA, Mich., Grand Traverse med. socs. (past pres.), Mich., Chgo. ophthal socs. Elk. Home: 6203 Peninsula Dr Traverse City MI 49684 Office: 1105 E Front St Traverse City MI 49684

WEIKEL, ROBERT CHARLES, civil engr.; b. Cleve., Apr. 16, 1926; s. Daniel Irving and Ethel May (Fishel) W.; B.S., Ind. Tech. Coll., 1952; m. Marilyn Sue Pressler, Apr. 16, 1949; children—David S., Diana S. Field foreman, engr., gen. supt., corp. sec. Weikel Constrn. Co., Inc., Ft. Wayne, Ind., 1952-73; structural estimator, project engr. Cebor Constrn. Co., Inc., Ft. Wayne and Australia, 1973-77; with Ind. Constrn. Co., Inc., Ft. Wayne, 1977—. Served with USAAF, 1943-48. Decorated Air medal. Mem. Northeastern Ind. Marksmanship Assn. (dir.). Mason (32 deg., Shriner), Rotarian. Club: Khyber Rifle Gun and Pistol (past pres.) (Ft. Wayne). Address: 5109 Hickory Ln Fort Wayne IN 46825

WEIKER, OSCAR JAMES, former mayor, farmer; b. Republic, Ohio, Nov. 14, 1893; s. Levi and Jane (Schoerger) W.; student Ohio State U., 1914-18; m. Norma Mae Hoppes, June 18, 1919; children—James, Adda Jane, Joan, Eloise. Mgr., U.S. Commn. Upper Sandusky, 1923-37; field rep. Keystone Steel Wire Co., No. Ohio, 1937-63; farmer, 1973—; dir. Elevator Mut. Ins. Assn., 1938-72, pres., 1958-72; incorporator Ohio Farmers Grain Assn., Fostoria, Ohio, 1933, dir., 1937-52. Treas. United Church Home, Upper Sandusky, 1938-64; mayor, Upper Sandusky, 1968-75; mem. com. merger Evang. and Ref. Ch. and Congregational Ch. in Ohio; mem. com. farming NW Assn. United Ch. of Christ in Ohio, moderator ch., 1968, del. gen. synod, 1961, 63, 65. Named Pioneer Cooperator Ohio, 1975. Mem. Ohio Grain and Feed Dealer Assn. Mem. United Ch. Christ. Republican. Clubs: Rotary, Masons (32 deg.), Shrine, Elks. Home: 351 W Johnson St Upper Sandusky OH 43351 Office: 351 W Johnson St Upper Sandusky OH 43351

WEIL, DAVID MAXWELL, packaging co. exec.; b. Chgo., Apr. 23, 1912; s. Joseph and Blanch (Falter) W.; B.A. magna cum laude, Harvard U., 1933; m. Aase Pedersen, Feb. 28, 1950; children—Lise Weil, Greta Weil, Kari. Chmn. bd. Cromwell Paper Co.; chmn. bd. Thomas Tape Co., 1968—; fgn. editor Chgo. Jour. Commerce, 1939-42; book reviewer Chgo. Sun-Times, 1946-48; consul ad honorem El Salvador, 1940-42, 46—; fin. adviser Royal Embassy of Yugoslavia. Gov. mem. Library Internat. Relations; sponsor Chgo. Council Fgn. Relations. Served with AUS, 1942-45. Decorated comdr. Order St. Sava (Yugoslavia); officer Order Homayoun (Iran); Order Merit 1st class (Iran). Mem. Alliance Franciase, Pan Am. Soc., Phi Beta Kappa. Clubs: Adventurers, Arts, Lake Shore Country, Standard (Chgo.); Harvard (Chgo. and N.Y.C.). Home: 1540 N Lake Shore Dr Chicago IL 60610 Office: 35 E Wacker Dr Chicago IL 60601

WEIL, HERMAN, prof. emeritus; b. Reglshelm, Alsace Lorraine. Dec. 15, 1905; Ph.D. In Psychology, U. Marburg (German), 1929, state exam. In math., chemistry, physics, 1929, state exam. In edn., Kassel, Germany, 1931; m. Bertha Weller, July 26, 1931; 1 son, Gunther M. Came to U.S., 1938, naturalized, 1944. Instr., Realgymnasium for Giris, Hersfeld, Germany, 1931-33; Instr., studienrat Philanthropin Realgymnasium, Frankfurt on Main, Germany, 1933-38; postdoctoral scholar U. Ia., 1939; prof. scl. Neb. Central Coll., 1939-40; prof. Milw. Sch. Engring., 1940-43; prof. edn. and psychology, head dept. Wis. State Coll., Milw., 1943-56; prof. psychology U. Wis.-Milw., 1956-76, prof. emeritus, 1976—, chmn. dept., 1956-61, chmn. honors program superior students Coll. Letters and Scis., 1960-74, asso. dean, 1967-71, faculty retirement counselor, 1973-75; Distinguished scholar-in-residence Milw. Jewish Community Center, 1977—; vis. prof. Northwestern U., summers 1947, 48, 51; cons. Human Relations Workshop, U. Mich., summers 1952-56; dir. Workshops on Human Relations, Wis. State Coll., summers 1952-56; lectr. Milw. Downer Coll., 1943-47; cons. Dept. of State, also U.S. Office Edn., Jugenheim, Germany, 1954. Co-chmn. Wis. region Nat. Conf. Christians and Jews, 1952-72, mem. commn. on ednl. orgns., 1955-60, mem. nat. bd., 1977—; nat. co-chmn. schs. and colls. com. observance of Brotherhood Week, 1957; mem. Gov.'s Commn. on Human Rights, 1953-56; counselor Milw. B'nai B'rith Hillsl Found., 1950-60; pres. New Home Club, Inc., 1940-57, hon. pres., 1977—; pres. Milw. chpt. Am. Jewish Com., 1973-75, mem. nat. exec. com., 1973—. Recipient citation of merit for work in human relations Milw. B'nal B'rith Councils, 1952, Brotherhood award Wis. region Nat. Conf. Christians and Jews, 1959, Citation award Internat. Inst. Milw. County, 1960, Distinguished Merit citation Nat. Conf. Christians and Jews, 1973; Distinguished Merit citation Wis. Soc. for Jewish Learning, 1973, Distinguished Service award U. Wis.-Milw. chpt. A.A.U.P., 1975, Distinguished Merit citation Coll. Letters and Sci., U. Wis., Milw., 1976; Distinguished Service fellow Temple Emanu-El B'ne Jeshurun, Milw., 1976—. Mem. A.A.U.P. (pres. Wis. conf. 1973-74), Wis. Soc. for Jewish Learning (past pres.), Wis. (past pres.), Milw. County (past pres.) psychol. assns., Nat. Collegiate Honors Council (mem. exec. com. 1972-73), Ret. Faculty Assn. U. Wis.-Milw. (pres. 1977—), Phi Kappa Phi (hon.). Jewish religion (past v.p., trustee temple). Author: In Quest of Excellence, 1975; Faculty Retirement Guidebook, 1975, 2d edit, 1976. Contbr. chpts. and sects. to books on psychol. subjects. Home: 2027 E Lake Bluff Blvd Milwaukee WI 53211

WEIL, LOUIS ARTHUR, JR., newspaper pub.; b. Port Huron, Mich., June 26, 1905; s. Louis Arthur and Blanche (Granger) W.; B.A., U. Mich., 1927; m. Kathryn Ann Halligan, Oct. 20, 1934; children—Mary Kay (Mrs. James C. Shook), Elizabeth Lee (Mrs. John A. Sheridan), Louis Arthur III. Reporter, Flint (Mich.) Jour., Grand Rapids (Mich.) Herald, 1929-34; pub. Grand Rapids Herald, 1947-58; pub. Lafayette (Ind.) Jour. and Courier, 1954-62; editor, pub. Lansing (Mich.) State Jour., 1962-70; pres. Federated Publs., Inc.; v.p., dir. Gannett Co., Rochester, N.Y. Recipient award for distinguished service to journalism U. Minn., 1960. Mem. Am. Newspaper Pubs. Assn., Inland Daily Press Assn., Sigma Delta Chi. Republican. Roman Catholic. Home: 21 Ash Ct Lafayette IN 47905

WEIL, OSCAR ARNOLD, union exec.; b. Belleville, Ill., Aug. 13, 1925; s. Oscar and Clara (Perschbacher) W.; B.A., McKendree Coll., 1955; M.A., Washington U., 1960; m. Martha Jane Wylie, Mar. 29, 1956; children—Kent Allyn, Laura May. Farmer, Lebanon, Ill., 1941-44; tchr., Roxana (Ill.) High Sch., 1955-63, Bellville Area Coll., 1961-63; mem. exec. bd. Southwestern area council Ill. Fedn. Tchrs., Springfield, 1959-63, exec. dir., 1963-75, legislative dir., 1975—; chmn. com. state fedn. officers Am. Fedn. Tchrs., 1964-66, pres. Union Tchr. Press Assn., 1967-75; mem. Gov's. Commn. on Labor-Mgmt. Relations, 1966-67; mem. Com. on Reorgn., Ill. Office Edn., 1975. Served with U.S. Army, 1944-47, 50-52; PTO. Recipient Gen. Excellence award Union Tchr. Press Assn., 1967-68, 71-75, Award of Merit, Internat. Labor Press Assn., 1967, 73. Mem. Am. Fedn. Tchrs., Fund for the Republic. Methodist. Editor, Ill. Union Tchr., 1963-75, Capitol News Roundup, 1963—; contbr. articles to profl. jours. Home: 500 S Walnut St Rochester IL 62563 Office: 914 E Capitol St Springfield IL 62701

WEIL, PAUL PERES, lawyer; b. Evansville, Ind., Jan. 30, 1936; s. Henry A. and Clarice Emy (Peres) W.; student U. Pa., 1953-55; B.S., Washington U., 1959, J.D., 1959; m. Barbara Ann Podell, July 19, 1959; children—Cynthia Marie, Leslie Renee. Admitted to Mo. bar, 1960; asso. firm Thomas, Busse, Weiss, Cullen & Godfrey, 1959-68; partner firm Thomas, Busse, Cullen, Clooney, Weil & Ottsen, St. Louis, 1968-72, Bryan, Cave, McPheeters & McRoberts, 1973—. Chmn. Mid-Am. Tax Conf., 1971; lectr. Mem. Am., Mo., St. Louis bar assns., Bar Assn. Met. St. Louis (v.p., treas.), Beta Gamma Sigma, Zeta Beta Tau. Republican. Jewish. Clubs: Mo. Athletic, Noonday; Media. Home: 110 Ladue Pines St Louis MO 63141 Office: 500 N Broadway St Louis MO 63102

WEIL, ROLF ALFRED, univ. pres.; b. Pforzheim, Germany, Oct. 29, 1921; s. Henry and Lina (Landauer) W.; m. Leni Metzger, Nov. 3, 1945; children—Susan Linda, Ronald Alan; came to U.S., 1936; B.A., U. Chgo., 1942, Ph.D., 1950; D. Hebrew Letters, Coll. Jewish Studies, 1967; L.H.D. (hon.), Loyola U., 1970. Research asst. Cowles Commn. Research in Econs., 1942-44; research analyst Ill. Dept. Revenue, 1944-46; faculty Roosevelt U., Chgo., 1946—, prof. finance and econs., chmn. dept. finance, 1954-65, dean Coll. Bus. Adminstrn., 1957-65, acting pres., 1965-66, pres., 1966—. Mem. bd. Edward A. Filene Good Will Fund and Internat. House, U. Chgo., Beth Emet Synagogue, Evanston, Ill.; pres. Selfhelp Home for Aged. Mem. Investment Analysts Soc. Chgo., Fedn. Ind. Ill. Colls. Univs. (exec. com.), Chgo. Rotary Club, Cliff Dwellers Club, University Club of Chgo., Mid-Am. Club. Contbr. articles to profl. jours. Home: 3015 Simpson St Evanston IL 60201 Office: Roosevelt U 430 S Michigan Ave Chicago IL 60605

WEILAND, STEVEN EDWARD, computer cons.; b. Chgo., Feb. 27, 1947; s. Jack Nathan and Adeline (Rosenburg) W.; B.S. in Mktg., No. Ill. U., 1969; postgrad. Am. U., 1970-71; M.B.A., No. Ill. U., 1972; m. Pamela Ruth Wolin, Aug. 12, 1973; 1 dau., Karyn Eileen. Computer cons. computer services dept. No. Ill. U., DeKalb, 1972—, instr. bus. edn. and adminstrv. services dept., 1976—; advisor No. Ill. Jewish Community Center Youth Group, 1974-77. Served with U.S. Army, 1969-71. Mem. Am. Mktg. Assn., Assn. for Computing Machinery, Assn. of M.B.A. Execs. Democrat. Jewish. Home: 843 Crane Dr Apt 402 DeKalb IL 60115 Office: Northern Illinois University Computing Services DeKalb IL 60115

WEINBAUM, BARBARA HYMAN, psychologist; b. Balt., Dec. 23, 1925; d. Emanuel A. and Beatrice (Schwartzman) Hyman; A.B., Goucher Coll., 1946; M.S., Ind. State U., 1972, Ph.D., 1976; m. Jack Gerald Weinbaum, June 16, 1946; children—Marc Eliot, Betty Susan. Med. technologist Terre Haute (Ind.) Med. Lab., 1957-69; instr. psychology Ind. State U., 1972-73, asst. prof., 1973; counselor-cons. Vigo County Sch. Corp., Terre Haute, 1974-75; counselor Student Counseling Center, Ind. State U., Terre Haute, 1975-76; program dir. continuing edn. Katherine Hamilton Mental Health Center, Terre Haute, 1976-77, co-ordinator adult/aging services, 1977—. Founder, pres. Vol. Tutors, Vigo County Sch. Corp., 1965-69; v.p. Nat. Sch. Vol. Program, 1969-71; bd. dirs. Friends of Cunningham Meml. Library, Ind. State U., 1976—, co-chmn., 1976-77; bd. dirs. Vigo County Mental Health Assn., 1970—, Terre Haute Symphony Bd. Mem. Am. Assn. Behavior Therapy, Internat. Assn. Behavior Therapists, Am. Psychol. Assn., Am. Personnel and Guidance Assn., ACLU, Ind. Civil Liberties Union (dir.), Women's Polit. Caucus (dir.), League Women Voters, NAACP. Jewish. Home: 2705 Oak St Terre Haute IN 47803 Office: 2931 Ohio Blvd Terre Haute IN 47803

WEINBERG, JACK, physician; b. Kiev, Russia, Jan. 18, 1910; s. Morris M. and Gunia (Geichman) W.; came to U.S., 1924, naturalized, 1937; B.S., U. Ill., 1934, M.D., 1936; m. Ruth S. Skidelsky, Aug. 14, 1935; 1 son, Daniel R. Intern St. Elizabeth's Hosp., Chgo., 1936-37; tng. in psychiatry U. Ill. Med. Sch. and Hosps., 1938-39, Chgo. Inst. Psychoanalysis, 1941-43, 47-48; asst. mng. dir. Chgo. State Hosp., 1938-40; psychiatrist-in-chief Chgo. Community Clinic, 1942-43; asso. dir. residency tng. program Michael Reese Hosp. and Med. Center, Chgo., 1946-50; practice medicine specializing in psychiatry, Chgo., 1950-64; clin. dir. Ill. State Psychiat. Inst., 1964-75, dir., 1975—; adminstr. Ill. Mental Insts., 1975—; prof. psychiatry Abraham Lincoln Sch. Medicine, U. Ill., Chgo., 1962—, mem. com. grad. med. edn., 1972—; prof. psychiatry Rush Med. Coll., Chgo., 1972—; vis. prof. Geront. Inst., U. So. Calif., 1969—; lectr. Indsl. Relations Center, U. Chgo., 1955—; sr. attending psychiatrist Psychosomatic and Psychiat. Inst., Michael Reese Hosp. and Med. Center, 1955—; cons. in field, mem. numerous coms. on aging and elderly. Bd. dirs. Council Jewish Elderly, Chgo., 1971—, Jewish Family and Community Services, 1969—. Served to maj. M.C., USAF, 1943-46. Diplomate Am. Bd. Psychiatry and Neurology. Life fellow Am. Psychiat. Assn. (pres. 1977-78), Ill. Psychiat. Soc.; mem. Am. Geront. Soc. (Donald P. Kent award 1974), Am. Geriatric Soc. (Edward B. Allen award 1970), AMA, Group Advancement Psychiatry, AAAS. Jewish. Contbr. articles to med. jours. Home: 434 Greenleaf Ave Glencoe IL 60022 Office: 1601 W Taylor St Chicago IL 60612

WEINBERG, SYLVAN L., physician; b. Nashville, June 14, 1923; s. Abraham J. and Beatrice (Kottler) W.; B.S., Northwestern U., 1945, B.M., 1946, M.D., 1947; m. Joan Hutzler, Jan. 29, 1956; children—Andrew Lee, Leslie Dee. Intern, resident, fellow cardiovascular research Michael Reese Hosp., Chgo., 1947-51; practice medicine specializing in cardiology and internal medicine, Dayton, Ohio, 1953—; chief cardiology sect., dir. coronary care unit, trustee Good Samaritan Hosp.; clin. prof. medicine, co-dir. cardiology Wright State U., Dayton. Served to capt. M.C., AUS, 1951-53. Diplomate Am. Bd. Internal Medicine. Fellow A.C.P., Am. Coll. Chest Physicians, Am. Coll. Cardiology (past v.p., trustee and chmn. bd. govs.); mem. AMA, Am., Ohio (past trustee) socs. internal medicine, Council Biology Editors. Editor, Heart and Lung; editorial bd. Archives Internal Medicine, Chest; contbr. articles to profl. jours. in field of cardiology. Research on cold injury, Korea. Home: 400 W Nottingham Rd Dayton OH 45405 Office: 33 W 1st St Dayton OH 45402

WEINBLATT, ALAN WILLIAM, lawyer; b. St. Paul, Apr. 24, 1943; s. Louis Arthur and Ida (Schwartz) W.; B.A., U. Minn., 1965, LL.B. cum laude, 1968; m. Gloria Ellen Goldstein, Mar. 17, 1968; children—Melinda Beth, Tanya Jill, Adam Eric. Admitted to Minn. bar, 1968; law clk. U.S. Fed. Ct., 1968-69; pvt. practice law, mem. firm Leonard & Weinblatt, St. Paul, 1971—. Appeal agt., mem. Selective Service, 1970-72; pres. Ramsey County Legal Assistance, 1973-76. Chmn. Young Men's Div. United Jewish Fund, 1975; mem. B'nai B'rith Anti-Defamation League. Mem. Am., Minn., Ramsey County bar assns., Am. Judicature Soc. Jewish religion (v.p. temple brotherhood 1970-72). Home: 754 Upper Colonial Dr St Paul MN 55118 Office: 2302 Am Nat Bank Bldg St Paul MN 55101

WEINE, FRANKLIN SCOTT, dentist; b. Chgo., Mar. 5, 1934; s. Herman and Bertha (Levy) W.; B.S., U. Ill., 1953, D.D.S., 1957; M.S.D., Ind. U., 1966; m. Dorothy Ann Strohs, July 7, 1957; children—Perry N., Kenneth M., Allan D. Gen. practice dentistry, Dolton, Ill., 1959-64, ltd. to endodontics, Chgo., 1966—; asst. prof. Ind. U., also prof. Loyola U., 1970—; dir. endodontics Michael Reese Hosp.; minority owner Chgo. White Sox Baseball Club. Served with USNR, 1957-59. Diplomate Am. Bd. Endodontics. Fellow Am. Coll. Dentists, Internat. Coll. Dentists, Am. Coll. Stomatological Surgeons (pres. elect 1977); mem. E.D. Coolidge (pres. 1972), H.J. Healey (pres. 1971) endodontic study clubs, Odontographic Soc. Chgo. (treas. 1972). Author: Endodontic Therapy, 1972, 2d edit., 1976. Home: 20737 Alexander St Olympia Fields IL 60461 Office: 30 N Michigan Ave Chicago IL 60602

WEINEL, RONALD BLAIR, mfg. co. exec.; b. New Kensington, Pa., Apr. 3, 1936; s. Wilmer Blair and Velma (Fennell) W.; B.S., Lebanon Valley Coll., 1958; M.B.A., N.Y. U., 1962; m. Dorothy Ann Elliott, June 15, 1957; children—Jeffrey Blair, David Wesley. With Price Waterhouse & Co., N.Y.C., 1958-64, Pitts., 1964-70, tax mgr., 1965-70; asst. treas. taxes Bendix Corp., Southfield, Mich., 1970—; dir. Master Data Center, Inc., Southfield, Mich. Vice chmn. bd dirs. Franklin Twp. Municipal San Authority, Murrysville, Pa., 1969-70; trustee Lebanon Valley Coll., Annville, Pa. C.P.A., N.Y., Pa. Mem. Am., Pa. insts. C.P.A.'s, N.Y. State Soc. C.P.A.'s, Tax Execs. Inst. (chpt. dir.), U.S. C. of C. (tax com. 1973-77), Tax Council Washington, Tax Council of Machinery and Allied Products Inst. Methodist (chmn. finance com. Murrysville, 1967-70, auditor, finance com. Lynbrook, N.Y., 1962-64). Office: Bendix Corp Bendix Center Southfield MI 48076

WEINER, LAWRENCE MYRON, educator; b. Milw., May 21, 1923; s. Walter J. and Anna (Rottman) W.; B.A., U. Wis., 1947, M.S., 1948, Ph.D., 1951; m. Shirley Schiff, May 14, 1944; children—Nancy Ann, Carol Ann. Research asso. U. Wis., 1951; instr. dept. microbiology Wayne State U. Sch. Medicine, Detroit, 1951-55, asst. prof., 1955-59, asso. prof., 1959-65, chmn. dept., 1963-64, 70-72, prof., 1965—, asso. dean, 1970-72, dep. dean, 1972—. Cons. St. John Hosp., Detroit, Sinai Hosp., Detroit, Holy Cross Hosp., Detroit, Detroit Gen. Hosp. Pres. Mich. State Bd. Examiners in Basic Scis., 1962-68. Served to lt. (j.g.) USNR, 1942-46. NATO fellow, 1962. Mem. Am. Soc. Microbiology Soc. Exptl. Biology and Medicine, Detroit Physiol. Soc. (pres. 1960), Sigma Xi. Club: Standard City (Detroit). Contbr. articles to profl. jours. Home: 4955 Malibu Dr Bloomfield Hills MI 48013

WEINER, LEWIS PHILLIP, plastics co. exec.; b. Cin.; s. Samuel and Molly (Moel) W.; B.S., Purdue U., 1928, M.E., 1936; m. Kathryn R.; 1 dau., Ellen Stephanie (Mrs. William C. Wright). Plant engr. Am.

Products Co., 1928-32, plant supt., 1932-33; spl. engr. Spaulding Fibre Co., 1930; asst. sec., supt. Joseph S. Finch & Co., Schenley, Pa., 1933-35; distillery supt., gen. supt. Hiram Walker & Sons, Inc., Peoria, Ill., 1935-45; v.p. Pebble Springs Distilling Co., 1945-48; supt. processes and procedures Pabst Brewing Co., 1948-52, ops. mgr., 1952-53, v.p. prodn., 1953-59, v.p., gen. mgr. indsl. products div., 1959-64, gen. mgr. indsl. products div., v.p. sub. Premier Malt Products, Inc., 1964-70; v.p., gen. mgr. Lemco Plastics, Inc., 1970-76; owner, operator Lew Weiner Assos., Plastics, Milw., 1976—. Mem. Soc. Plastics Engrs., Am. Inst. Chem. Engrs. (mem. emeritus), ASME (life). Clubs: University, Athletic (Milw.). Contbr. articles to tech. jours. Office: 5645 N Green Bay Rd Milwaukee WI 53209

WEINER, MURRAY, physician; b. N.Y.C., April. 18, 1919; s. Samuel O. and Gussie (Begun) W.; B.S., Coll. City N.Y., 1939; M.S., N.Y.U., 1943, M.D., 1943; m. Marilyn Rose Greenberg, Jan. 14, 1951 (dec. Mar. 1973); children—Eve Gail, George Jay, Joan Sally; m. 2d, Helen Jane Dodd, June 15, 1976. Intern Sinai Hosp. Balt., 1944; resident, research fellow Goldwater Meml. Hosp., 1946-50; practice medicine specializing in intern medicine N.Y.C., 1948-71, Plainview, N.Y., 1953-59; mem. staffs U. Hosp., N.Y.C., Goldwater Meml. Hosp., N.Y.C., Belleview Hosp., N.Y.C., Cin. Gen. Hosp., C. Holmes Hosp., Cin.; cons. Geigy Pharms., 1953—, v.p. biol. research, 1967-71; v.p. research Merrell Nat. Labs., 1972—; prof. clin. medicine U. Cin., 1972—; asst. prof. clin. medicine N.Y. U. Coll. Medicine, 1954—. Mem. com. on biochemistry in drug safety NRC, 1966-69; chmn. Gordon Conf. in Medicinal Chemistry, 1968. Served to capt. AUS, 1944-46. Mem. A.C.P., Am. Soc. Pharm. and Exptl. Therapy, Am. Physiologic Soc., Internat. Hematological Soc., Pharm. Mfrs. Assn. (chmn. research and devel. sect.), Soc. Exptl. Biology and Medicine, Sigma Xi. Author: Coagulation, Thrombosis and Dicumarol, 1949. Contbr. articles to profl. jours. Home: 8915 Spooky Ridge Ln Cincinnati OH 45242

WEINFURTER, ROBERT WAYNE, soil testing service co. exec.; b. Appleton, Wis., May 17, 1928; s. George John and Esther Rose (Kumbier) W.; B.S., Lawrence U., 1953, postgrad. 1956; m. Cathryn Janice Masterson, June 20, 1953; children—Erich, Kurt, Karl, Hans. With Bechtel Corp., San Francisco, 1956-59; engr.-in-charge for O'Hare Field Project Soil Testing Services, Inc., Chgo., 1959-62; pres. Soil Testing Services Wis., Green Bay, 1962-70; adminstrv. v.p. Soil Testing Services Inc., Chgo., 1970-74; exec. v.p. Soil Testing Services Iowa, Cedar Rapids, 1974—, also dir.; pres. Soil Testing Services Kans., Wichita, 1975—, dir., 1962—; pres. Soil Testing Services Mo., Kansas City, 1977—, also dir. Mem. chancellor's bldg. adv. bd. U. Wis., Green Bay, 1968-70. Served with USAF, 1946-49. Registered profl. engr., Nev., Wis. Mem. Soc. Mining Engrs. Am. Inst. Metall. Engrs., Am. Concrete Inst., ASTM, Wis. Soc. Profl. Engr., Assn. Engring. Geologists, Wis. Assn. Professions, Iowa Engring. Soc., Am. Inst. Profl. Geologists, Phi Delta Theta. Republican. Presbyn. (ch. trustee 1967-70, deacon 1973-74). Home: 603 E Post Rd SE Cedar Rapids IA 52403 Office: 5855 Harnischfeger Dr SE Cedar Rapids IA 52406

WEINGARD, MARVIN ALLEN, paper co. exec.; b. Chgo., Nov. 17, 1934; s. Leo and Celia (Brook) W.; student Wright Jr. Coll., 1952-54; B.S.C., Roosevelt U., 1956; m. Renee Benkiel, Aug. 9, 1964; children—Jeffrey, Kenneth, Mitchell. Accountant, auditor Robert Heinsimer & Co., C.P.A.'s, Chgo., 1956-60; accountant, auditor Sayre Krako & Co., C.P.A.'s, Chgo., 1960-64; internal auditor, plant controller, regional controller Consol. Packaging Corp., Chgo., 1964-67; v.p., controller Rockford Paper Mills, Inc., Rosemont, Ill., 1967—. Home: 6620 N Richmond St Chicago IL 60645 Office: 7000 N Mannheim Rd Rosemont IL 60018

WEINGART, MAURICE ALEXANDER, ins. agy. exec.; b. St. Louis, Aug. 14, 1922; s. Joseph and Anna (Greenfield) W.; student Ohio U., 1943-44; m. Freida Dubman, Jan. 12, 1947; children—Sandra Weingart Hertzberg, Sherry. Broker Joseph Weingart Ins. Agy., University City, Mo., 1947-50, partner, 1950—. Mem. Met. Youth Commn., St. Louis and St. Louis County, 1963-65; hon. commr. Mo. Am. Revolution Bicentennial, 1974-76; treas. Creve Coeur-West County Bicentennial Commn., 1974—. Republican committeeman Creve Coeur (Mo.) Twp., 1967-74; chmn. Mo. 2nd Congl. Dist. Rep. Com., 1970-72; mem. Mo. Rep. State Com., 1972-74. Trustee St. Louis County Retirement Plans, 1967-69, 69-72, 72-75, 76—; regional adv. bd. Anti-Defamation League, 1973—; v.p., bd. dirs. New Mt. Sinai Cemetery Assn., 1974—; trustee Central Agy. for Jewish Edn., 1972-75; chmn. Personnel Code Com. City of Creve Coeur, 1976-77. Served to sgt., AUS, 1942-46. Mem. St. Louis Fedn. Reform Temples (pres. 1967), Soc. Chartered Property and Casualty Underwriters (chpt. pres. 1963-64), Jewish War Vets. U.S.A., Creve Coeur Twp. Rep. Men's Club (pres. 1964-65). Jewish religion (pres. congregation 1962-65). Home: 11710 Tarrytown St Creve Coeur MO 63141 Office: 8505 Delmar St University City MO 63124

WEINHARDT, CARL J., JR., museum dir.; b. Indpls., Sept. 22, 1927; s. Carl J. and Helen Irene (Rost) W.; A.B. magna cum laude, Harvard, 1948, MA., 1949, M.F.A., 1955; H.H.D., Christian Theol. Sem., 1967; m. Annetta E. Hubon, May 1, 1954; children—Carl Rost, Seth Henry, Lucia Rost. Lectr., Boston Archtl. Center, 1954-55; mem. staff Met. Mus., 1955-60, asso. curator, 1958-60; lectr. fine arts Columbia, 1958-60; dir. Mpls. Inst. Arts, 1960-62; formerly dir. Gallery of Modern Art, N.Y.C.; dir. Art Assn. (Herron Mus. Art-Herron Sch. of Art), Indpls.; now dir. Indpls. Mus. Art. Bd. dirs. Olana Preservation, Inc. Mem. Coll. Art Assn., Assn. Art Mus. Dirs., Soc. Archtl. Historians, Am. Fedn. Arts, Nat. Soc. Arts and Letters, Harvard Mus. Assn., Downtown Council Mpls., Beacon Hill Assn., Assn. Am. Mus. Dirs., Penrod Soc., Festival Music Soc. (trustee), Phi Beta Kappa. Episcopalian. Clubs: Portfolio; Literary of Indianapolis. Author: Architectural of Beacon Hill, 1957; also articles. Home: 4883 N Meridian St Indianapolis IN 46208 Office: 1200 W 38th St Indianapolis IN 46208

WEINKAUF, MARY LOUISE STANLEY (MRS. ALAN DALE WEINKAUF), educator; b. Eau Claire, Wis., Sept. 22, 1938; d. Joseph Michael and Marie (Holzinger) Stanley; B.A. in Secondary Edn. magna cum laude, Wis. State U., 1961; M.A., U. Tenn., 1962, Ph.D., 1966; m. Alan Dale Weinkauf, Oct. 12, 1962; children—Stephen Alan, Xanthippe Elizabeth. Organist, St. Johns Luth. Ch., Eau Claire, Wis., 1957-61; mem. faculty U. Tenn., Knoxville, 1961-66; asst. prof. English, Adrian (Mich.) Coll., 1966-69; asso. prof., chmn. dept., English, Dakota Wesleyan U., Mitchell, S.D., 1969-71, prof., 1971—, also chmn. Div. Humanities. Mem. Mitchell (S.D.) Community Arts Council. Mem. Tenn. State Rep. Com., 1965-66. Mem. Modern Lang. Assn. Am., AAUW, Sci. Fiction Research Assn., S.D. Council Tchrs. English, Midwest Modern Lang. Assn., Milton Soc. Am., Nat. Council Tchrs. English, Mich. Coll. English Assn., Sigma Pi Kappa, Phi Kappa Phi, Sigma Tau Delta, Pi Kappa Delta, Kappa Delta Pi, Delta Kappa Gamma. Lutheran. Author: Early Poems by A Late Beginner, 1976. Home: 914 University Blvd Mitchell SD 57301

WEINKAUF, WILLIAM CARL, instructional media co. exec.; b. Fond du Lac, Wis., Apr. 7, 1934; s. Carl Alfred and Erma Gertrude (Lueck) W.; B.A., Ripon Coll., 1955; postgrad. U. Wis., 1954, 57-58, Holy Cross Coll., 1971-73; m. Carole Jean Hill, May 3, 1958; children—Carl William, Mary Gretchen, Donald Hill. Dir. Wis. Central Lumber Co., 1959-63; with Carlton Films, Beloit, Wis., 1965-68; founder, pres. IMCO Inc., Green Lake, Wis., 1968—. Cons. Bd. Holy Cross Coll., 1972—. Chmn. council Cub Scouts Am., 1968-69. Mem. county exec. com. Republican party, 1970-71. Served to maj. AUS, 1955-57. Mem. Nat. Audio Visual Assn. (chmn. legis. com. Wis. 1975—), U.S. Res. Officers Assn. (chpt. pres. 1966-70), C. of C., Sigma Nu. Mem. United Ch. Christ. (bd. trustees 1965-66). Mason (32 deg., K.T.). Home: 596 Illinois Ave Green Lake WI 54941 Office: 506-510 Mill St Green Lake WI 54941

WEINLANDER, ALBERTINA ABRAMS (MRS. MAX M. WEINLANDER), educator; b. Mecosta, Mich., July 21, 1919; d. Edward and Albertina (Mantai) Abrams; B.S., Central Mich. U., 1942; M.A., U. Mich., 1947; Ph.D., 1955; m. Max M. Weinlander, June 4, 1945; children—Bruce, Annette. Tchr., prin. Mecosta (Mich.) High Sch., 1942-46; tchr. Sherman Twp. Rural Agrl. Sch., Weidman, Mich., 1946-48; instr., asst. prof. edn. and integrated studies Miami U., 1948-55, lectr. extension service, 1955-56; asst. prof. Wittenberg U., Springfield, Ohio, 1956-59, asso. prof. edn., 1960-68, prof. edn., 1968—. Mem. AAAS, Nat. Writers Club, NEA, Ohio Edn. Assn., AAUW (pres. Springfield br. 1962-64), Pi Lambda Theta, Kappa Delta Epsilon, Kappa Delta Pi. Clubs: Springfield Women's Zonta (pres. Springfield 1967-69). Author: Your Child in a Scientific World, 1959; How to Prepare for the National Teacher Examination, 1968; How to Prepare for the Graduate Record Examination, Advanced Education Test, 1969; How to Prepare for the National Teachers Examinations: Education in the Elementary Sch., 1970; Victim or Aggressor, 1973; The Choice, 1973; also articles in profl. jours. Home: 290 Ridge Mall Springfield OH 45504

WEINLANDER, MAX MARTIN, psychologist; b. Ann Arbor Mich., Sept. 9, 1917; s. Paul and Emma Carol (Lindemann) W.; B.A., Eastern Mich. Coll., 1940; M.A., U. Mich., 1942; M.A., Wayne U., 1951; Ph.D., U. Mich., 1955; m. Albertina Adelheit Abrams, June 4, 1945; children—Bruce, Annette. Psychometrist VA Hosp. Dearborn, Mich., 1947-51; sr. staff psychologist, Ohio Div. Corrections, London, 1954-55; lectr. Dayton and Piqua Centers, Miami U., Oxford, Ohio, 1955-62; chief clin. psychologist, Child Guidance clinic, Springfield, Ohio, 1956-61, acting director, 1961-65; clin. psychologist VA Center, Dayton, Ohio, 1964—; cons. div. mental hygiene State Ohio; summer guest prof. Miami U., 1957, 58, Wittenberg U., 1958; adj. prof. Wright State U., Dayton, 1975—; cons. State Ohio Bur. Vocat. Rehab., Oesterlen Home Emotionally Disturbed Children. Pres. Clark County Mental Health Assn., 1960, Clark County Health and Welfare Club, 1961; mem. Community Welfare Council Clark County, 1964; chmn. Comprehensive Mental Health Planning Com. Clark County, 1964; trustee United Appeals Fund, 1960—. Mem. citizens adv. council Columbus Psychiat. Inst., Ohio State U. Served as sgt. AUS, 1942-46. Fellow Ohio Psychol. Assn. (chmn. com. on utilization of pscyhologists; treas., exec. bd. 1968-71); mem. Am. Psychol. Assn., Pi Kappa Delta, Pi Gamma Mu, Phi Delta Kappa. Lutheran. Clubs: Kiwanis; Mitchell Hills Contry. Contbr. articles to psychology jours. Home: 290 Ridge Mall Springfield OH 45504 Office: VA Center Dayton OH 45428

WEINMAN, IRVIN ABRAHAM, clin. social worker, educator; b. N.Y.C., Mar. 6, 1922; s. Jacob and Minnie (Feinberg) W.; student U. Ill., 1945, Columbia, 1948; B.S., U. Wis., 1950; M.S.W., U. Denver, 1952; postgrad. Inst. Psychoanalysis, certificate child therapy, 1962; m. Miriam Kniaz, June 4, 1950; children—Natalie Zoe, Richard, Michael (dec.). Caseworker, Jewish Family and Children's Services, Milw., 1952-55, casework supr., 1955-67; lectr. to asst. prof. social welfare U. Wis.-Milw., 1967-71; pvt. practice marriage and family counseling Milw., 1967—; lectr., cons. in field. Bd. dirs. Hope Day Care Center, Elm Grove, Wis., 1970-71. Served with AUS, 1944-46. Mem. Acad. Certified Social Workers, Am. Acad. Psychotherapists, Am. Assn. Marriage and Family Counselors, Wis. Soc. Clin. Social Workers. Mem. B'nai B'rith. Home: 8641 N Servite Dr Milwaukee WI 53223 Office: 6815 W Capital Dr Milwaukee WI 53216

WEINSTEIN, DAVID, coll. pres.; b. Boston, June 26, 1927; s. Herman and Fanny (Katzoff) W.; B.A., Mass. State Coll., 1950; B.H.L., Hebrew Tchrs. Coll., 1950, M.H.L., 1953; M.Ed., Harvard U., 1952, Ed.D., 1956; m. Sandra Bargad, June 29, 1958; 1 son, Noah. Registrar, Hebrew Tchrs. Coll., 1957-61, prof. lang. edn., 1961-64; pres. Spertus Coll. of Judaica, Chgo., 1964—; cons. Lang. Research Inst., Harvard U., 1954-64; lang. coordinator Brussels Internat. Fair, 1958; field dir. Harvard U. Lang. Program, Israel, 1959-64. Served in U.S. Army, 1945-47. Author: Essential Hebrew by Examples, 196; 1964; Modern Jewish Educational Thought, 1964; co-author: Hebrew Through Pictures, 1954; First Steps in Reading Hebrew, 1955; Hebrew-English/English-Hebrew Pocket Dictionary, 1961. Office: Spertus Coll Judaica 618 S Michigan Ave Chicago IL 60605*

WEINSTOCK, FRANK JOSEPH, physician; b. Newark, Apr. 21, 1933; s. Michael Benjamin and Marguerite (Grosman) W.; student Rutgers U. at Newark, 1952-53; B.Sc., Allegheny Coll., 1955; postgrad. U. Lausanne, 1955-58; M.D., State U. N.Y. at Syracuse, 1960; m. Saragale Reinglass, May 20, 1962; children—Michael Barnett, Jill Marguerite, Jeffrey David. Intern, Mt. Sinai Hosp., Cleve., 1960-61; resident ophthalmology Western Res. U., 1961-64; cons. ophthalmology USPHS, Washington, 1964-66; pvt. practice ltd. to ophthalmology, Canton, Ohio, 1966—; instr. George Washington U., 1965-66; clin. instr. ophthalmology Ohio State U., 1967-74, clin. asst. prof. ophthalmology, 1974—; instr. Am. Acad. Ophthalmology and Otolaryngology, 1965—. Dir. Jewish Community Center of Canton, 1971—; cons. Project Headstart, 1965-69; mem. Local Bd. Edn., 1978—; adv. com. Nat. Assn. Visually Handicapped, Am. Intra-Ocular Implant Soc. Diplomate Am. Bd. Ophthalmology. Mem. Am. Acad. Ophthalmology and Otolaryngology, Am. Assn. Ophthalmology (chmn. com. on child health devel.), AMA, Ohio, Stark County med. assns., Cleve. Ophthalmology Soc., Contact Lens Assn. Ophthalmologists, Soc. Eye Surgeons, Ohio Soc. Prevention of Blindness (dir., chmn. med. adv. com.), Canton Acad. Medicine (pres. 1973-74), Cleve. Opthalmology Soc. (v.p. 1971-72). Club: Canton Lions (dir. 1969-71). Contbr. articles to profl. jours. Home: 4668 Yale Ave NW Canton OH 44709 Office: 214 Dartmouth Ave SW Canton OH 44710

WEINSTOCK, HENRY ROBERT, educator; b. Vienna, Austria, Dec. 13, 1930; s. Fred S. and Hilda (Kolber) W.; came to U.S., 1939, naturalized, 1954; B.S., U. Tampa, 1956; M.A. (NSF fellow), U. Ga., 1963, Ed.D., 1965; children—Katheryn Louise, Mary Elizabeth, Timothy Robert. Tchr. physics Tampa (Fla.) Pub. Schs., 1956-62; asst. prof. edn. Kan. State U., 1965-67; asso. prof. edn. U. Mo., St. Louis, 1967-71, prof. edn., 1971—. Served with AUS, 1951-52; lt. USNR (ret.). Mem. Am. Assn. Physics Tchrs., Philosophy Edn. Soc., Am. Ednl. Research Assn., Southwestern Philosophy Edn. Soc., A.A.U.P., Phi Kappa Phi, Phi Delta Kappa. Home: 5719 Bermuda Rd Normandy MO 63135

WEIS, JACK FRANK, ret. mfg. exec.; b. Columbus, Ohio, Apr. 1, 1902; s. Benjamin and Rose (Wallach) W.; B.S. in Elec. Engring., Ohio State U., 1926. Plant engr. Alloy Steel Casting & Comml. Steel Casting Cos., 1926-29; asst. chief elec. engr. Marion Power Shovel Co., 1929-39; chief elec. engr., 1939-57, chief engr. intermediate and large machines, 1957-67, v.p., 1968-74, cons., 1971-75, ret. Area agt. Ohio State U. Devel. Fund; pres. YMCA Endowment Fund. Mem. Am. Inst. E.E., Ohio State Profl. Engring Soc., Nat. Engring. Soc. Contbr. articles to profl. jours. Home: 758 King Ave Marion OH 43302

WEISBERG, SEYMOUR WILLIAM, physician; b. Chgo., Aug. 5, 1910; s. Isaac and Eda (Provus) W.; B.S., U. Chgo., 1932; M.D., Rush Med. Coll., 1936; m. Ella Sperling, Oct. 16, 1949; children—Gerald, Louise. Intern Michael Reese Hosp.; resident Cook County Hosp., Chgo.; practice medicine specializing in internal medicine, Chgo., 1940—; asso. prof. medicine U. Ill. Coll. Medicine, Chgo.; asso. attending physician Cook County Hosp., 1940-44; chief resident tng. unit Chgo. Regional Office VA; mem. attending staffs Michael Reese Hosp., Chgo., Louis A. Weiss Meml. Hosp., Chgo. Served with AUS, 1944-47. Diplomate Am. Bd. Internal Medicine. Mem. AMA, Ill. Med. Soc., Phi Beta Kappa, Alpha Omega Alpha. Office: 55 E Washington St Chicago IL 60602

WEISE, R. ERIC, educator; b. Charleston, W.Va., Jan. 30, 1933; s. Harry Edward and Millie Ann (Miller) W.; A.B., U. Cin., 1954, M.A., 1963; Ph.D., Ind. U., 1966; m. Betty Miller, Dec. 19, 1959; children—Rebecca Lynn, Michelle Renee, Michael Joseph. Mem. Research staff Cin. Milling Machine, Inc., 1956-59; owner Ins. Assos., Inc., 1959-62; faculty U. Cin., 1964—; chmn. Robert A. Taft Inst. Govt., 1965-68; acting dir. U.S. Fgn. Policy Inst., 1969; on leave as campaign dir. U.S. Senator Robert Taft, Jr., 1970. Cons. Inst. Govtl. Research, Cin. Pub. Sch. Task Force; v.p., dir. Ohio poll Ohio Inst. Pub. Opinion, syndicated newspaper column, 1973-76. Mem. Pres.'s Commn. White House Fellowships, 1976-78. Served with AUS, 1954-56. Mem. Am., Midwest polit. sci. assns., Am. Fgn. Service Assn., AAUP, Cincinnatus Assn., Sigma Phi Epsilon (pres. nat. bd. 1971-73, Order Golden Heart), Republican. Presbyn. Author: the Kenwood Study, 1965; Old Government-New People: Readings for New Politics, 1971; Eight Branches: American Government Today, 1975. Contbr. articles to profl. jours. Home: 2517 Fleetwood Cincinnati OH 45211

WEISER, JOHN CONRAD, educator; b. St. Paul, Jan. 7, 1922; s. George C. and Irene (Anderson) W.; student No. Mich. Coll. Edn., 1940-42; B.A., U. Iowa, 1948, M.A., 1949; Ph.D., Western Res. U., 1961; m. Lenora May Brewster, June 11, 1947; children—John David, Michael Allen, James Richard. Radio announcer, newsman WDMJ, Marquette, Mich., 1940-42, WCUE, Akron, Ohio, 1951-53; mem. faculty Kent (Ohio) State U., 1949—, mgr. radio station, 1951-73, asst. prof., 1953-62, asso. prof., 1962-69, prof., 1969—, Danforth asso., 1963—, dir. lecture artist series, 1964-68, coordinator telecommunications, 1975—. Served with USMCR, 1942-45. Mem. Speech Assn. Am., Ohio Speech Assn., Nat. Assn. Ednl. Broadcasters, Broadcast Edn. Assn., Ohio Assn. Broadcasters, Alpha Psi Omega, Theta Chi. Contbr. articles to speech jours. Home: 319 Valley View St Kent OH 44240

WEISER, JOHN EDWIN, supply co. exec.; b. Wooster, Ohio, May 8, 1928; s. John Edwin and Loanda O. (Day) W.; student Ohio Inst. Bus., 1949, Akron U., 1951; m. Judy Ann Jennings, Feb. 17, 1967. Employer in various sales positions; dist. mgr. Phila. Quartz Co., Cin., 1967-74; div. mgr. So. Chem. Co., Charleston, W.Va., 1974-76; gen. mgr. Hubman Supply Co., sanitation chems., Columbus, Ohio, 1976—. Served with USNR, 1946-48. Mem. Internat. San. Supply Assn., Internat. Fin. Inst. Club: Sertoma. Home: 5414 Pheasant Dr Orient OH 43146 Office: 1123 W Goodale Blvd Columbus OH 43212

WEISMAN, MORTON PHILIP, publishing co. exec.; b. Chgo., Dec. 12, 1933; s. Philip and Rose (Beskin) W.; student U. Ill., 1951-53; B.S. in Bus. Asminstrn., Roosevelt U., 1955; m. Judith Rose Ades, Feb. 26, 1956; chilfren—Jordan Weisman, Maya Weisman. Employed with Allied Radio Corp., Chgo., 1955; v.p. Harrison Corrugated Box Co., 1955-61; exec. v.p., sec. A.C. McClurg & Co., Chgo., 1961-67; pres., 1967-68; v.p. dir. Merc. Industries, Inc., Chgo.; pub., pres. The Swallow Press, Inc., Chgo., 1969—. Asso. exec. dir. Independent Precinct Orgn. Served with AUS, 1956-58. Mem. Tau Epsilon Phi. Club: Cliff Dwellers (award of merit 1971) (Chgo.). Home: 811 Junior Terr Chicago IL 60613 Office: 1139 S Wabash Ave Chicago IL 60605

WEISS, HERMAN, lawyer; b. Crystal, N.D., June 4, 1921; s. Herman Otto and Anna C. (Schulz) W.; student St. Olaf Coll., 1939-41; J.D., U. N.D., 1949; m. Donna M. Ovind, Sept. 4, 1943; children—Donald, Robert, Elizabeth, Jean. Admitted to N.D. bar, 1949; with Hjellum, Weiss, Nerison, Jukkala & Vinje, Jamestown, N.D., 1949—, partner, 1953—; admitted to U.S. Dist. Ct. bar, 1958, 8th Circuit Ct. bar, 1959, 9th Circuit Ct. bar, 1969; asst. states atty., Stutsman County, N.D., 1949-50; city atty. Jamestown, 1959-74; v.p. Farmers & Mchts. Bank, Wimbledon, N.D., 1956—, also chmn. Bd. Edn. Crippled Children's Sch., Jamestown, 1959—, pres., 1974—; 2d vice-chmn., bd. dirs. Lutheran Hosps. and Homes Soc. Am. Fargo, 1963; trustee Selma Alexander Found., Jamestown Civic Center Found. Served to lt., USNR, 1942-45; PTO. Decorated D.F.C. with star, Air medal with five stars. Fellow Am. Coll. Probate Council, Am. Bar Found., Mem. Jamestown C. of C. (pres. 1955-56), Am. Legion (post comdr. 1952-53, dist. dep. 1953-54), Stutsman County Bar (pres. 1953-54), 4th Judicial Dist. (pres. 1961-63), Am., N.D. State (pres. 1969-70) bar assns., V.F.W., Order of Coif, Phi Alpha Delta. Lutheran. Republican. Elk, Lion (pres. Jamestown 1960-61), Mason. Club: Jamestown Country. Del. at large N.D. to White House Conf. Aging, 1971. Home: 522 1st Ave N Jamestown ND 58401 Office: Suite 200 Jamestown Mall PO Box 1560 Jamestown ND 58401

WEISS, JULIUS SEYMOUR, editor, columnist; b. St. Louis, Apr. 7, 1922; s. Isadore and Bertha (Weisz) W.; student Western Res. U., 1941-43. Columnist, Linn's Weekly Stamp News, Sidney, Ohio, 1956-63; writer for Airpost Jour., Philatelic mag. Am. Airmail Soc., Albion, Pa., 1956-59, The Philatelic Trader, 1957—, The Philatelic mag., 1957—, The Holy Land Philatelist, Israel, 1958-61, El Eco Filatelico, Pamplona, Spain, 1959—, Filatelia Italiana, Rome, Italy, 1962-67; columnist Numis. News, 1965-67, Cleve. Press, 1967-70, Nat. Stamp News, Anderson, S.C.; editor, columnist Weiss Philatelic-Numis.-Features; contbr. articles to stamp and coin mags., newspapers, U.S. and fgn. pubs. Mgr., Bertha Weisz Philatelic-Numismatic Journalism Award. Chmn. amateur radio sect. People To People Program. Asso. editor: Weekly Philatelic Gossip, 1958-60. Club: Philatelic Press of N.Y. Address: 16000 Terrace Rd Cleveland OH 44112

WEISS, MARK LAWRENCE, anthropologist, educator; b. Bklyn., Nov. 1, 1945; s. Arthur Aaron and Ruth Esther (Heilbrunn) W.; B.A. with honors, Harpur Coll., 1966; M.A., U. Calif. at Berkeley, 1968, Ph.D., 1969; m. Sandra Eve Steiner, Dec. 28, 1969; 1 son, Evan. Asst. prof. anthropology Wayne State U., Detroit, 1969-73, asso. prof., 1973—. Fellow Am. Anthrop. Assn.; mem. Am. Assn. Phys. Anthropologists, Sigma Xi. Author: (with A. Mann) Human Biology and Behavior, 1975. Office: Dept Anthropology Wayne State U Detroit MI 48202

WEISSBLATT, ROBERT LEWIS, computer co. exec.; b. N.Y.C., May 22, 1944; s. Norman P. and Gertrude Van Dam (Young) W.; B.B.A., Pace U., 1968; M.E., Bklyn. Coll., 1970; m. Catherine Gabriel, Aug. 22, 1970; 1 dau., Maryl Lynn. Products mgr. marketing Dunn

& Bradstreet, N.Y.C., 1970-72; sales rep. Hyland Labs., N.Y., 1972-73, sales specialist, 1973-75, regional mgr., 1975-76; nat. sales mgr., v.p. The Computer Pl., Brooklyn Heights, Ohio, 1976—, also dir. Mem. Computer Dealers Assn., Internat. Word Processing Assn., Data Processing Mgmt. Assn., Small Businessmen's Assn., Nat. Fedn. Ind. Bus. Office: 4650 Spring Rd Brooklyn Heights OH 44131

WEISSE, GUENTER, adminstrv. mech. and sales engr.; b. Reutlingen, W.Ger., May 22, 1935; s. Kurt and Maria (Haug) W.; came to U.S., 1971; Mech. Engring. Degree, Stuttgart, W.Ger., 1959; m. Solveig Stuetz, Jan. 8, 1971; 1 son, Marcus. Design engr., turbo charger, J. Eberspaeher, W.Ger., 1959-61; design engr., turbocharger and fuel injection, Simms Motor Co., Eng., 1961-63; test engr. tech sales, mgr. tech. sales fuel injection systems Robert Bosch Gmbh, Stuttgart, 1963-71, v.p. sales and application engring. R. Bosch Corp., Broadview, Ill., 1971—. Mem. Soc. Automotive Engrs. Home: 21W545 Glen Valley Dr Glen Ellyn IL 60137 Office: 2800 S 25th Ave Broadview IL 60153

WEISSENBURGER, JASON TICKNOR, JR., research co. exec., city ofcl.; b. Wheeling, W. Va., Dec. 11, 1932; s. Jason Ticknor and Annabelle (Bauerle) W.; B.S. in Mech. Engring., Washington U., 1955, M.S. in Applied Mechanics, 1959, D.Sc. in Applied Mechanics (Ford Found grantee), 1966; m. Patricia Lynn Gast, Dec. 22, 1954; 1 dau., Dale Ellen. Stress engr. Emerson Electric Co., St. Louis, 1957-58; tech. specialist McDonnell Aircraft Co., St. Louis, 1959-66; prin. engring. cons. McDonnell Automation Co., St. Louis, 1967-69; pres., founder Engring. Dynamics Internat., St. Louis, 1970—. Lectr., affiliate prof. applied mechanics Washington U., St. Louis, 1955-69, tchr. div. Continuing Profl. Edn., 1970—; lectr. Grad. Engring. Center, U. Mo.-Rolla, St. Louis, 1970. Mem. traffic commn. University City, Mo., 1968-69, mem. city council, 1970—; co-founder Midwest Noise Council, St. Louis, 1972—, pres., 1974—. Registered profl. engr., Mo., Ill., Wis. Mem. ASME, Mo., Nat. socs. profl. engrs., Acoustical Soc. Am. (shock and vibration tech. com. 1975—) Engrs. Club St. Louis (dir. 1972-74), Univ. City Charter Assn. (pres. 1969), Pi Tau Sigma, Sigma Nu. Contbr. articles on noise and vibration to profl. jours. Home: 7931 Gannon St University City MO 63130 Office: 8420 Delmar Blvd St Louis MO 63124

WEISSLER, ARNOLD MERVIN, physician, educator; b. Bklyn., May 13, 1927; s. Solomon F. and Dora (Hocheiser) W.; B.A., N.Y. U., 1948; M.D., State U. N.Y. Downstate Med. Center, 1953; m. Gloria Diane Lazarus, June 22, 1953; children—Suzanne Robin, Mark Douglas, Leslie Ann, Jonathan Scott. Intern Maimonides Hosp., Bklyn., 1953-54; jr. asst. resident, Duke Hosp., Durham, N.C., 1954-55, Am. Heart Assn. research fellow, 1955-57, sr. asst. resident, 1957-58, chief resident, 1958-59; chief cardiovascular sect. Durham VA Hosp., 1959-60; asst. prof. medicine U. Tex., Galveston, 1960-61; asst. prof. medicine Ohio State U., Columbus, 1961-63, asso. prof., 1963-67, prof., 1967-71, Gustav Hirsch Meml. prof., 1969-71; dir. div. cardiology and Cardiovascular Core Facility for Research and Tng., Ohio State U. Hosp., Columbus, 1965-71; chief dept. medicine Harper Hosp., Detroit, 1971—; prof., chmn. dept. medicine Wayne State U. Sch. Medicine, Detroit, 1971—; mem. cardiovascular disease subsplty. examining bd. Am. Bd. Internal Medicine, chmn., 1975—; USPHS research career awardee, 1961-68. Served with USNR, 1944-45. Recipient Dudley Meml. medal in surgery. Diplomate Am. Bd. Internal Medicine. Fellow A.C.P., Am. Coll. Cardiology (gov. Mich. sect.); mem. Am. Heart Assn. (fellow council clin. cardiology), Assn. Profs. Medicine, AAUP, Assn. Am. Physicians, Am. Soc. Clin. Investigation, Assn. Profs. Medicine, Assn. Univ. Cardiologists, Detroit Heart Club, Central Soc. Clin. Research (exec. council), AAAS, Am. Soc. Clin. Pharmacology and Exptl. therapeutics, Am. Soc. Pharmacology and Exptl. therapeutics Phi Beta Kappa, Sigma Xi, Alpha Omega Alpha. Author: (with B.H. Marks) Basic and Clinical Pharmacology of Digitalis, 1972; Noninvasive Cardiology, 1974. Editor-in-chief Am. Jour. Medical Sciences, 1967-70; mem. editorial bd. Am. Jour. Cardiology, Am. Jour. Med. Circulation, Coeur et Med. Interne. Contbr. articles to profl. publs. Home: 999 Glengarry Circle Birmingham MI 48010 Office: 3990 John R St Detroit MI 48201

WEISSMAN, RICHARD MAYER, electronic engr.; b. Chgo., Apr. 18, 1917; s. David Hyman and Bertha (Mironoff) W.; B.S. in Elec. Engring., Ill. Inst. Tech., 1946, M.S., 1951; m. Leticia Guingona Fuentes, Oct. 5, 1966. Spl. research project engr. Bell & Howell Corp., Chgo., 1954-58; sr. project engr. Lab. for Astrophysics and Space Research, Enrico Fermi Inst., Chgo., 1958-69; cons. electronic engring. Chgo., 1969-72; project engr. Bally Mfg. Corp., Chgo., 1972-76; sr. project engr. EMI Med., Northbrook, Ill., 1977—; engring. cons. Mem. IEEE (sr., 1st. prize tech. paper 1953). Contbr. articles to profl. jours. Patentee in field. Home: 7318 N Greenview Ave Chicago IL 60626 Office: 2640 W Belmont Ave Chicago IL 60618

WEISSTEIN, ULRICH WERNER, educator; b. Breslau, Germany, Nov. 14, 1925; s. Rudolf and Berta (Wende) W.; student Goethe-Universität, Frankfurt, 1947-50, 1951-52, U. Ia., 1950-51; M.A., Ind. U., 1953, Ph.D., 1954; m. Judith Schroeder, May 9, 1964; children—Cristina, Cecily, Eric Wolfgang, Anton Edward. Came to U.S., 1950, naturalized, 1959. Instr., asst. prof. Lehigh U., Bethlehem, Pa., 1954-58; asst. prof. of English and comparative lit., Ind. U., Bloomington, 1959-62, asso. prof., 1962-66, prof., 1966—, prof. German and comparative lit., 1966—; vis. prof. comparative lit. U. Wis., Madison, summer 1966; vis. prof. German, Middlebury Coll. Summer Sch., 1970; vis. prof. comparative lit. U. Hamburg (Germany), 1971, U. Vienna, 1976. Modern Lang. Assn. Am. grantee, 1958-59; Guggenheim fellow, 1974-75. Mem. Modern Lang. Assn. Am., Am. Assn. Tchrs. German, Am. and Internat. Comparative Lit. Assn., Internat. Brecht Soc. Author: Heinrich Mann, 1962; The Essence of Opera, 1964; Max Frisch, 1967; Einführung in die Vergleichende Literaturwissenschaft, 1968 (English version: Comparative Literature and Literary Theory, 1973). Editor: German sect, Twayne World Authors series, 1964—, Yearbook of Comparative and General Literature, 1960—, Brecht-Jahrbuch, 1970—, Expressionism as an International Literary Phenomenon, 1973. Co-editor: Texte und Kontexte: Festschrift für Norbert Fuerst, 1973. Translator: The Grotesque in Art and Literature (W. Kayser), 1963. Home: 2204 Queens Way Bloomington IN 47401

WEITZEL, WILLIAM FREDERICK, JR., educator; b. Balt., Aug. 4, 1936; s. William Frederick and Margaret Anna (Roeder) W.; A.B., Wheaton Coll., 1961; A.M., U. Ill., 1963; Ph.D., Wayne State U., 1966; m. Pauline Elizabeth Nesmith, Aug. 9, 1957; children—William Frederick III, Reta Louise. Instr. Wayne State U., Detroit, 1963-66; asst. prof. U. Minn., Mpls., 1966-71, asso. prof., 1973-76, 77—; vis. prof. N. European Mgmt. Inst., Oslo, 1976-77; orgn. devel. dir. Target Stores, Inc., Mpls., 1971-72, v.p. human resources, 1972-73. Indsl. relations analyst Ford Motor Co., Detroit, 1964; cons. to bus. and govt. 1966-71, 73—. Served with USNR, 1954-57. Mem. Am., Midwestern psychol. assns., Acad. Mgmt. Home: 4832 Sheridan Ave S Minneapolis MN 55410

WELANDER, ROBERT ELDER, veterinarian; b. Belmond, Iowa, Nov. 18, 1943; s. Norman Raymond and Jean Katherine (Elder) W.; D.V.M., Iowa State U., 1967; m. Barbara Sue Taylor, Nov. 27, 1966. Pvt. practice vet. medicine, Mt. Pleasant, Iowa, 1967—; pres. Mt. Pleasant Vet. Clinic, 1974—, Woodside Properties, Inc., 1973—. County alumni chmn. Iowa State U., 1968—, S.E. Iowa legis. contact, 1968—. Bd. dirs. Fine Arts Assn., 1969—, treas., 1969; bd. dirs. County 4-H Com., 1969, S.E. Iowa council Boy Scouts Am., 1970. Mem. Am., Iowa, Eastern Iowa (dir. 1967—, pres. 1978-79), S.E. Iowa (pres. 1967—) vet. med. assns., Am. Small Animal Hosp. Assn., Iowa Acad. Vet. Practice (pres. 1974-75), Alpha Gamma Rho. Republican. Presbyterian. (ruling elder 1968). Elk. Rotarian (dir. 1967—, pres. 1977-78). Home: Route 4 Box 66 Mount Pleasant IA 52641 Office: Route 3 Box 21 Mount Pleasant IA 52641

WELBORN, WILLIAM CALVERT, JR., lawyer; b. Evansville, Ind., Aug. 2, 1937; s. William Calvert and Georgine Lillydale (Koser) W.; A.B., U. Evansville, 1963; J.D., Ind. U., 1966; m. Mary Elizabeth Jones, Dec. 24, 1956; children—Kathy, William C. III, Dawn, Elizabeth. TV dir. WEHT, WTVW, Evansville, Ind., 1955-59; WFBM, Indpls., 1959-60; admitted to Ind. bar, 1966, since practiced in Evansville; asso. firm Merrill Schroeder & Johnson, 1966-67; partner firm Merrill Schroeder, Johnson, Evans & Welborn, 1967-73, Caine & Welborn, 1973—; dep. prosecutor, Evansville, 1970-72. Mem. communications and command Civil Air Patrol, Evansville, Ind., 1951-61, 72—; dir. Conrad Baker Found., Evansville, 1967-72. Mem. Ind. State, Evansville (James Bethal Greslam award, 1970, mem. TV com. 1972, v.p. 1974, mem. spl. ct. study com. 1975) bar assns., Mil. Affilaiate Radio Service, Order of Coif. Democrat. Methodist. Editor: Indiana Law Jour., 1965-66, Note in Law Journal, 1966; (with W. Statham, H. Songer, W. Fitzgerald, J. Stone) Crime Study Commission, 1967-69. Home: Route 1 Box 49 Newburgh IN 47630 Office: 2221 W Franklin St Evansville IN 47712

WELBOURN, DALE KENNETH, veterinarian; b. Shelby, Iowa, Apr. 25, 1926; s. Maurice and Edna Myrtle (Sigler) W.; D.V.M., Iowa State U., 1954; m. Norma Jean Harris, Aug. 31, 1957; children—Lona Marie, Nancy Jean. Pvt. practice vet. medicine, Thompson, Iowa, 1954-59, Neola, Iowa, 1959—. Chmn. park bds., Thompson, 1957-58, Neola, 1960-61. Served with AUS, 1946-47. Mem. Am., Iowa, Shelby County vet. med. assns. Republican. Presbyterian. Patentee in toy, recreation fields. Home: 310 Bardsley St Neola IA 51559 Office: 2d St Neola IA 51559

WELBOURN, JOHN THROP, engring. cons.; b. Union City, Ind., Apr. 10, 1907; s. Reno Bayless and Anna (Throp) W.; student Carnegie Inst. Tech., 1924-31, Chgo. Acad. Fine Arts, 1928-29, U. Pitts., 1941-44, Pa. State Coll. Extension, 1943. Engineer, Owens-Ill. Can Co., Toledo, 1941-44; x-ray field engr. Westinghouse Electric Corp., Pitts., 1944-46; gen. engr. USAF, Wright-Patterson AFB, O., 1948-64; engring. cons., Xenia, O., 1964—. Mem. Ohio Acad. Sci., Am. Inst. Biol. Scis., AAAS, Archaeol. Soc. Am., Am. Geog. Soc., Photog. Soc. Am., Arctic Inst. N.Am., Inst. Solar Energy Soc., Sierra Club, Royal Canadian Geog. Soc., Astron. Soc. Pacific, Am. Hort. Soc., Am. Forestry Assn., Nat. Audubon Soc., Nat. Trust for Hist. Preservation. Patentee in field. Address: 8 Sexton Dr Xenia OH 45385

WELCH, JACK WYMAN, physician, surgeon; b. Lewiston, Ill., Nov. 2, 1918; s. Alan Richard and Mabel Lee Hinkle W.; A.B. cum laude, Bradley U., 1941; D.D.S., Northwestern U., 1944; M.D., U. Kans., 1951; m. Jane Chesky, Nov. 18, 1944; children—Susan Welch (Mrs. Greg Ruder), Sara, Alan Richard, Joan. Pvt. practice dentistry Lewistown, 1947; instr. U. Kans., Lawrence, 1947-48; intern Kansas City (Mo.) Gen. Hosp., 1951-52; resident surgery Halstead (Kans.) Hosp., 1952-57; staff surgeon Hertzler Clinic, Halstead, 1957—, chmn. bd. dirs., 1960—; practice medicine and surgery, Halstead, 1957—. Mem. Kans. Med. Polit. Action Com. Mem. Halstead City Commn., 1964—, pres., 1973-75; mem. Republican precinct com., 1965-67. Bd. dirs. Hertzler Research Found., Kans. Health Mus., Halstead Indsl. Found. Served to capt., Dental Corps, AUS, 1944-47; PTO. Recipient Gold medal Guffey award U. Kans., 1962, Distinguished Service award Am. Soc. Surgeons, 1964. Mem. Kans. Assn. Med. Practice Groups (dir. 1970—), Halstead C. of C., Xi Psi Phi, Nu Sigma Nu, Pi Gamma Mu. Presbyterian. Republican. Elk. Clubs: Halstead Golf (dir. 1973-75); Wichita; Prairie Dunes Country. Home: 326 Spruce St Halstead KS 67056 Office: 4th and Chestnut St Halstead KS 67056

WELCH, JOHN WILEY, home mfg. co. exec.; b. LaCrosse, Wis., June 29, 1928; s. Ralph Oliver and Dorothy Abbott (Tessman) W.; B.S., U. Wis., LaCrosse, 1955; m. Jann Deen Witt, June 21, 1958; children—Kendra Deen, Brent John, James Allen. With Trane Lab., LaCrosse, 1955-56; partner Consol. Builders Supply, LaCrescent, Minn., 1956-68; pres. CBS Homes div., 1968—; owner Brookhill Apts. Chmn., LaCrescent Pool Referendum, 1972, LaCrescent Swimming Pool Com., 1973, LaCrescent Auction and Rummage, 1973-74. Del. Republican State Conv. 1968. Bd. dirs. LaCrescent City Recreational Bd., 1974—; bd. dirs. LaCrescent Apple Festival, 1974—, pres., 1976-77. Served with Army Airborne, 1950-52. Mem. Nat. Assn. Home Builders, N.W. Lumbermans Assn., Nat. Assn. Bldg. Mfrs., LaCrosse Area Home Builders Assn. (charter; Assn. of Year 1976), Houston County Home Builders (sec. 1961, dir.), Am. Legion (bldg. com. 1969), Internat. Platform Assn., La Crescent C. of C. (pres. 1960, dir. 1960-61), LaCrosse Bus. and Profl. Couples Club (chmn. 1974-76), Lambda Tau Gamma, Eta Phi Alpha. Mem. Bethany Evang. Free Ch. Mason (32 deg., Shriner, K.T.). Clubs: Gopher Sportsman, LaCrescent Ski. Home: 713 Welshire Dr LaCrescent MN 55947 Office: 184 Main St LaCrescent MN 55947

WELCH, LESTER HAYDEN, elec. coop. exec.; b. Beaver Dam, Wis., Mar. 4, 1906; s. Arthur and Margaret A. (Snowden) W.; student pub. schs.; m. Loretta Fay Achterberg, June 25, 1924; children—Darlene (Mrs. James Schmitt). Car salesman Fox Lake Auto Co. (Wis.), also Graafsma Ford, Randolph, Wis., 1956-69; farmer nr. Beaver Dam, Wis., 1956—; sales mgr. South Randolph Sales & Service, Inc., (Wis.), 1969—; sec.-treas., dir. Columbus Rural Electric Coop. (Wis.), 1948—; v.p., dir. Westford Mut. Fire Ins. Co., Fox Lake, 1961—. Town clk. Town of Westford (Wis.), 1938-71. Presbyterian (elder 1971—). Home: Route 3 Beaver Dam WI 53916

WELCH, LYNDON, architect; b. Boston, Apr. 17, 1923; s. Joseph Nye and Judith Hampton (Lyndon) W.; B.A., Harvard U., 1943; M.S., Mass. Inst. Tech., 1948; m. Angela Dobson, July 27, 1946; children—Judith (Mrs. John R. Landecker), Angela (Mrs. William E. Lenz), Joseph. With Smith, Hinchman & Grylls, architects and engrs., Detroit, 1948-49; instr. U. Mich., Ann Arbor, 1949-50; with H.E. Beyster Asso. & Victor Gruen Asso., architects and engrs., Detroit, 1951-54; with Eberle M. Smith Assos., Inc., architects and engrs., Detroit, 1954—, pres., 1965—. Mem. Ann Arbor Housing Commn., 1965-69. Served with USNR, 1943. Mem. AIA, Am. Concrete Inst. Rotarian. Home: 2220 Glendaloch St Ann Arbor MI 48104 Office: 950 W Fort St Detroit MI 48226

WELCH, MARTHA JEAN, psychologist, nurse, educator; b. Birmingham, Ala., Nov. 20, 1933; d. Bowman Lavert and Martha Orene (Carpenter) W.; B.S., U. Ala., 1957; M.S., Case Western Res. U., 1968, Ph.D., 1973; M.S., Emory U., 1962. Instr., Univ. Hosp. Sch. Nursing, Birmingham, Ala., 1957-62; instr. Emory U. Sch. Nursing, Atlanta, 1963-66; psychologist Mental Devel. Center, Cleve., part time 1969-75; asst. prof. nursing So. Ill. U., Edwardsville, 1975—; pvt. practice psychology, Cleve., 1972-75, Collinsville, Ill., 1976—. USPHS fellow, 1966-73. Mem. Am., Ill., Ohio psychol. assns., Gestalt Inst. Cleve., Soc. Research in Child Devel., Am. Nurses Assn., Sigma Theta Tau. Home: 5 Manor Dr Collinsville IL 62234 Office: Sch Nursing So Ill Univ Edwardsville IL 62026

WELCH, ROBERT ETIENNE, farmer, twp. ofcl.; b. Bismarck, N.D., Nov. 23, 1923; s. Robert McKinley and Cecelia Marietta (Doppler) W.; grad. high sch.; m. Patricia Ann Dosch, Feb. 14, 1962; children—Timothy John, Jason Alain. Carpenter, Menoken, N.D., 1946—; farmer Menoken, 1936—. Active 4-H. Agrl. Stabilization and Conservation committeeman Menoken, 1953—; assessor Boyd Twp., 1968—; mem. Menoken Sch. Bd., 1970—. Served with USNR, World War II; PTO. Mem. Nat. Farmers Orgn. Roman Catholic. Elk, K.C., Eagle. Home and Office: Menoken ND 58558

WELCH, WILLIE F., artist; b. Steele, Mo., July 2, 1948; s. James L. and Ora Walker) W.; student pub. schs. Caruthersville, Mo.; m. Katherine Marie Weemes, Feb. 6, 1971; children—Tremal Jevon, Marty LaMar. Comml. artist, AGS & R Studios, Fort Wayne, 1968-72, Royal Lace Paper div. Standard Packaging Corp., Fort Wayne, 1972-73; tech. illustrator Magnavox Govt. and Indsl. Electronics Co., Fort Wayne, 1973—; pvt. instrn. art. Mem. Fort Wayne Artist Guide (past pres.), Indspl. Art Museum, Indpsl. Art League, Lakeland Art Assn. Home: 2709 Winch St Fort Wayne IN 46803 Office: 2131 S Coliseum Blvd Fort Wayne IN 46803

WELD, HIRAM CHESTER, clergyman, ret. educator, real estate exec.; b. Chgo., Feb. 18, 1912; s. Chester Harry and Lillie Christine (Lude) W.; A.B., Simpson Coll., 1934, D.D., 1949; A.M., Boston U., 1936, S.T.B., 1937, Ph.D., 1944; G.R.I., Ohio State U., 1973; m. Mary Elizabeth Williams, June 13, 1936; children—Wayne Robert, Devereaux Chester. Ordained to ministry United Methodist Ch., 1936; asso. prof. philosophy and psychology Baker U., Baldwin, Kans., 1940-44; minister Elm Park Methodist Ch., Scranton, Pa., 1944-51, North Methodist Ch., Indpls., 1951-59, Bexley Methodist Ch., Columbus, Ohio, 1959-71; clin. pastoral educator Riverside and Columbus State hosps., 1971-72; adj. prof. philosophy and religion Park Coll., Columbus, 1973-76; regional corp. relations dir. Century 21 Real Estate Corp. Central and So. Ohio, 1976—; cons. in field. Am. del. World Methodist Conf., 1951; Methodist del. Nat. Council Churches, 1960-66. Bd. dirs. Scranton (Pa.) Pub. Library, 1944-51, Maternal Health Clinic Scranton, 1944-51; trustee De Pauw U., 1957-60, Mt. Union Coll., 1964—, Internat. Found. for Ewah Woman's U., Seoul, Korea, 1969-71. Charterpatron Bexley Hist. Soc., 1974—. Traveling fellow Boston U., 1938-39; vis. fellow Ohio State U., 1971. Mem. Ohio Pastors Convocation (life), Ohio, Am. philos. assns., Assn. Clin. Pastoral Edn., Nat. Assn. Realtors, Ancient and Honorable Arty. Co. Mass., Nat. Jogging Assn. Mason (Shriner). Clubs: Columbus Athletic; Appalachian Mountain. Contbg. author, contbr. articles to profl. publs. Home: 364 N Ardmore Rd Columbus OH 43209 Office: Century 21 Executive House 6827 N High St Worthington OH 43085

WELDON, HOWARD GEORGE, accountant; b. Milw., Sept. 21, 1922; s. Howard John and Jennie Marguerite (Laitsch) W.; student in accounting Internat. Accountants Soc., Inc., 1948; m. Erma E. Kainz Schaub, Dec. 21, 1959 (div. June 1964); 1 son, Howard George, Jr. Clk. controller office Milw. Vocat. Sch., 1941; with Loewi & Co., Milw., 1941—, chief accountant, 1955-68, asst. controller, 1968-74, asst. treas., 1974-77, v.p., 1977—, also dir.; treas. Loewi & Co. Found., Inc., 1970—. Cubmaster Boy Scouts Am., Milw., 1969-75, recipient Scouter's Key, 1973. Served with AUS, 1943-46; ETO. Lutheran. Home: 3531 S 87th St Milwaukee WI 53228 Office: 225 E Mason St Milwaukee WI 53202

WELKER, BRUCE MARVIN, career counselor; b. Chgo., Apr. 18, 1939; s. Marvin Frederick and Clara Marion (Peterson) W.; B.Ed., No. Ill. U., 1960; M.Ed., Wash. State U., 1967; m. Beth Lynnell Schlaf, June 17, 1961; children—Kimberly Louise, Kevin Bruce. Tchr. sci., math. Hale Sch., Stillman Valley, Ill., 1961-63; tchr. sci. Lincoln Jr. High Sch., Skokie, Ill., 1963-66; counselor Jason Lee Jr. High Sch., Tacoma, Wash., 1967-68; counselor, tchr. Hillside (Ill.) Sch., 1968-69; career counselor James B. Conant High Sch., Hoffman Estates, Ill., 1969—; resource person counselor edn. courses for career edn. Northeastern Ill. U., also No. Ill. U., 1975—. Dist. chmn. Arlington Heights (Ill.) Crusade of Mercy, 1975. Mem. Am., Ill., Northwest Suburban Chpt. personnel and guidance assns., Nat., Suburban, Ill. (bd. govs. 1976—), vocat. guidance assn., NEA, Northwest Suburban Assn. Commerce and Industry, Ill. Sch. Counselors Assn., Dist. 211 Edn. Assn. Methodist. Club: United Methodist Mens. Home: 1162 N Hickory St Arlington Heights IL 60004 Office: 700 E Cougar Trail Hoffman Estates IL 60194

WELLBANK, HARRY LAURENCE, indsl. psychologist; b. Phila., Aug. 10, 1922; s. Harry Aloysius and Hilda Rachel (Greenfield) W.; B.S., Northwestern U., 1948, M.A., 1949, Ph.D., 1951; m. Margaret Mary Williams, Sept. 5, 1942; children—Melinda (Mrs. Eugene M. Ostap), Dianne (Mrs. Michael T. Foster), Jennifer (Mrs. William R. Baudin), Harry, Christopher. Tchr., Cleveland Sch., Skokie, Ill., 1947-48; instr., lectr. edn. Northwestern U., Evanston, Ill., 1948-51; asst. prof. edn. Loyola U. at Chgo., 1950-53; various personnel assignments Sears, Roebuck & Co., Chgo., 1953-57, nat. dir. tng. and devel., 1957-77, dir. human resources, 1977—; lectr. U. Ill., Urbana, 1949-50, now adj. prof. bus. adminstrn. Chmn. Ill. Curriculum Council, 1967-73; chmn. facilities and maintenance com. Gov.'s Sch. Bus. Mgmt. Task Force, 1973-74; chmn. com. of Mayor's Council of Manpower and Econ. Advisers, 1974-75. Vice-pres. U. Chgo. Cancer Research Found., 1967, pres., 1969-73, chmn. bd., 1973-74; bd. regents Ill. Regency Univs. Served with AUS, 1943-46. Recipient award Ill. Curriculum Council, 1973. Mem. Am., Ill. psychol. assns., Nat. Soc. Performance and Instrn., Chgo. Assn. Commerce, Ill. C. of C., Editor The School in Modern Society, 1949. Research on tchr.'s problems, attitudes, motives, effect of corr. courses on behavior. Home: 997 N Shore Dr Crystal Lake IL 60014 Office: Sears Tower Chicago IL 60684

WELLENKOTTER, HARRY WILLIAM, JR., telephone co. exec.; b. Janesville, Wis., Sept. 1, 1929; s. Harry William and Evelyn B. (Wilhelm) W.; grad. Internat. Accountants Soc. Corr. Sch., 1954; m. Nancy J. Dickinson, Nov. 25, 1961; children—Theresa Ann, Bart Win, Sara Lyn. Accountant, H.G. Siepert & Co., C.P.A.'s, Beloit, Wis., 1952-60; controller North-West Telephone Co., Tomah, Wis., 1960-73, asst. sec., asst. treas., 1971-73, v.p., sec., treas., 1973-76, exec. v.p., treas., dir., 1976—; dir. North-West Services Corp. C.P.A., Wis. Mem. Am., Wis. insts. C.P.A.'s. Home: PO Box 22 Tomah WI 54660 Office: 901 Kilbourn St Tomah WI 54660

WELLER, DONALD MATTHIAS, optical co. exec.; b. Watkins, Minn., Nov. 25, 1918; s. Xavier J. and Margaret (Arens) W.; grad. high sch.; m. Mardell Florine Engels, Sept. 9, 1939; children—Mariette A. (Mrs. James C. DeMorett), Verdell M. (Mrs. Lawrence A. Rudolph), Florine K., Roberta D. (Mrs. Dennis E. Heitzman), Lynette J. (Mrs. Rex C. Routh), Mark R. Mgr. Lantz Lenses, St. Cloud, Minn., 1936-55; dept. head. Visionease Corp., St. Cloud, 1955-58; owner, pres. Minoco Lens Co., St. Cloud, 1958-73; v.p. Lens div. Presicion Cosmet, St. Cloud, 1973—; pres. bd. dirs. Minoco Lens Co., Inc., St. Cloud, 1963-73. Served with AUS,

1944-46. Mem. Serra Club, Am. Legion, V.F.W. Roman Catholic. K.C. (4 deg., faithful navigator 1970-71), Elk, Eagle, Lion. Home: Big Fish Lake Rural Route 2 Box 144 Cold Spring MN 56320 Office: PO Box 114 Saint Cloud MN 56301

WELLER, EDWARD FRANK, JR., automotive co. exec.; b. Balt., Nov. 30, 1919; s. Edward Frank and Margaret Ruth (Hohman) W.; E.E., U. Cin., 1943; m. Mary E. Rourke, Sept. 18, 1943; children—Edward, Stephen, Geoffrey. Research engr. physics and instrumentation dept. Gen. Motors Research Labs., Warren, Mich., 1946-52, asst. head, 1952-62, head electronics and instrumentation dept., 1962-74, head electronics dept., 1974—. Mem. Engrs. Council Profl. Devel., 1969-75. Served with Signal Corps., AUS, 1943-46. Named Distinguished Alumnus U. Cin., 1973. Fellow IEEE, mem. Engring. Soc. Detroit, Sigma Xi. Editor: Ferroelectricity, 1967. Contbr. articles in field to profl. jours. Patentee in field. Home: 3790 Lakecrest Bloomfield Hills MI 48013 Office: Gen Motors Research Labs 12 Mile and Mound Rds Warren MI 48090

WELLER, RICHARD FRANKLIN, motel exec., restauranteur; b. Mitchell, S.D., Sept. 28, 1932; s. Sam F. and Edna D. (Braase) W.; student Stanford, 1950-52; B.S., U. Nebr., 1954; M.B.A., U. Pa., 1955; m. Derrolynn Dianne McCardle, Dec. 1, 1974; children by previous marriage—Cindy Lynn, Steven Mark, Jason Charles. Asso. Weller Co., Mitchell, 1957—; gen. mgr., franchise holder Holiday Inn, Mitchell, S.D., 1969—, innkeeper, franchise holder, No. Black Hills, S.D., 1973-75; mem. reservations com. Holiday Inn system worldwide, 1974-77; owner Pyrenees II Restaurant, 1976—; dir. Mitchell Home Savs. & Loan Assn., 1964—. Chmn. civic devel. commn. City of Mitchell, 1967-68. Sec. Young Republicans, Davison County, 1960. Mem. adv. bd. St. Joseph Hosp., 1965-68. Served with USAF, 1955-57. Recipient Henry Geisenberg award outstanding local Jaycee pres. for state of S.D., 1962; Distinguished Service award Mitchell Jaycees, 1963-64. C.L.U. Mem. Mitchell Life Underwriters (pres. 1961-62), Bd. of Realtors (pres. 1968-69), S.D. Chartered Life Underwriters (chpt. pres. 1963), S.D. Innkeepers Assn. (dir., v.p. 1973). Episcopalian. Elk. Clubs: Mitchell Country (dir. 1966-69); Mr. and Mrs. Club (pres. 1964-65). Home: 1525 W Havens St Mitchell SD 57301 Office: Box 458 Mitchell SD 57301

WELLS, BEN HARRIS, beverage co. exec.: b. Saginaw, Mich., June 11, 1906: s. Dr. Ben W. and Florence (Harris) W.: student Ind. U., 1922-25: A.B., U. Mich., 1929, M.A., 1931: m. Katherine Gladney, June 17, 1938: children—Katherine Graves, Ben Gladney. Tchr. John Burroughs Sch., St. Louis Co., 1929-31, 1933-38: critic tchr., sch. edn. U. Mich., 1931-33: copy writer, sales promotion mgr., sales mgr. Seven-Up Co., St. Louis, 1938-43, v.p. sales and advt., 1943-65, pres., chief exec. officer, 1965-74, chmn., 1974—. Bd. dirs. St. Louis council Boy Scouts Am., United Way, Blue Cross-Blue Shield, Civic Progress, Inc.; bd. dirs. St. Louis Symphony Soc., pres., 1970—: chmn. Consumers Research Inst., 1970—: trustee John Burrough Sch., 1954-61. Mem. N.A.M., Grocery Mfrs. Am., Phi Beta Kappa, Sigma Chi, Rotarian. Clubs: Media, Bellerive Country, Bogey, Noonday, University, Racquet, Saint Louis. Home: 35 Westmoreland Pl St Louis MO 63108 Office: 121 S Meramec St Louis MO 63105

WELLS, CHARLES K., physician; b. Waltonville, Ill., Jan. 1, 1920; s. James Walter and Melissa Ann (Kirkpatrick) W.; A.B., U. Ill., 1941, M.D., 1944; m. Margaret Katherine Kettel, May 12, 1958; children—Charlotte, Jane. Intern, Cook County Hosp., Chgo., 1944-45; resident U. Ill. Research and Edn. Hosp., Chgo., 1948; gen. practice medicine, Mt. Vernon, Ill., 1948—; house physician Meth. Children's Home, Mt. Vernon, 1949—; med. dir. Jeffersonian Nursing Home, Mt. Vernon, 1973—; staff Good Samaritan Hosp., Mt. Vernon, 1948—, pres. staff 1954, 58, 65, 75, also trustee. Served with AUS, USAF, 1945-47. Mem. Ill. (trustee 1964-72), Jefferson-Hamilton County (pres. 1958-65) med. socs., Am. Med. Assn. (del. 1972—). Elk, Rotarian, Mason. Author: History of Medicine Jefferson County, Ill., 1818-1968, 1968. Home: 701 Pavey St Mt Vernon IL 62864 Office: 117 N 10th St Mt Vernon IL 62864

WELLS, EUGENE RALPH, dentist, farmer; b. Hutchinson, Kans., Nov. 5, 1929; s. Ralph H. and Margaret (Crawley) W.; student Hutchinson Jr. Coll., 1947-49, Wichita U., 1949-51; D.D.S., U. Kansas City, 1960; m. Carlene Sturgis, Oct. 16, 1952; children—Melinda, Pam, Julia, Randal, Elizabeth. With Standard Oil Co., 1951-52, N.Y. Life Ins. Co., 1954-56; gen. practice dentistry, Hutchinson, 1960—. Owner, proprietor cattle ranch and farm, Hutchinson, 1963—; partner K.C. Cattle Co.; pres. Dental Center, Inc.; dir. MOD, Inc., Central State Bank, Hutchinson, Shaw Investment Corp. County co-chmn. Harmon for Gov. com. 1968. Bd. dirs. Hutchinson YMCA, 1970—. Served with AUS, 1952-54. Mem. Kan. Dental Assn. (del.). Elk, Mason (Shriner). Home: 75 Prairie Dr Hutchinson KS 67501 Office: 200 E 30th St Hutchinson KS 67501

WELLS, LAMAR OLIVER, optometrist; b. Dixon, Ill., Dec. 28, 1917; s. Grove G. and Winifred Grace (Strouss) W.; student Ill. Coll. Optometry, 1945-47; m. Ethel Lena Trotter, Dec. 31, 1947; children—Joanne Lynne, Jeffrey Lane. Pvt. practice optometry, Dixon, 1947—. Pres., Heritage Investments, Inc., Dixon, 1967—, Dixlee Devel. Corp., 1968—, Three Star Investment Co., 1964—; mem. Dixon Devel. Corp., 1965—. Mem. Nat. Eye Research Found. Served with AUS, 1942-45. Mem. C. of C. (pres. 1966), Am., Ill. (1st v.p. 1962-67) optometric assns., No. Ill. Optometric Soc. (pres. 1956-58), Am. Optometric Found., Am. Legion, Escondido C. of C., Smithsonian Assos., Vol. Optometric Services to Humanity, San Diego Zool. Soc. Mem. Christian Ch. Elk. Clubs: Dixon Country, Rancho Bernado Country. Home: 310 Heather Lane Dixon IL 61021 also 17144 Ruette Campana Rancho Bernardo San Diego CA 92128 Office: 511 Palmyra Ave Dixon IL 61021

WELLS, LARRY EUGENE, rehab. counselor; b. Flint, Mich., July 9, 1953; s. Homer Alan and Della Mae (Housley) W.; B.A., U. Mich., 1975, M.A., 1976. Youth counselor Genesee County Juvenile Facility, 1971-72; engring. clk. Chevrolet Co., Flint, Mich., 1972-73; vocat. rehab. counselor Mich. Dept. Edn., Pontiac, 1976—. Counselor 2d Bapt. Ch. Antabuse Program. Mem. Am. Personnel and Guidance Assn., Am. Rehab. Counselors Assn., Nat. Rehab. Assn.

WELLS, LEE EDWIN, lawyer; b. Canalou, Mo., Nov. 17, 1930; s. Leland Ershall and Louise K. (King) W.; B.B.A., U. Mo., 1952; LL.B., U. Kan. City, 1957; m. Judith A. Jones, July 15, 1966; children—Edward Lee, Elizabeth Ellen. Admitted to Mo. bar, 1957, since practiced in Kansas City; asso. firm Deacy & Deacy, 1957-63; partner McKenzie, Williams, Merrick, Beamer & Wells, 1964—. Bd. dirs. Walnut Ridge Devel. Co., also sec. Served with AUS, 1952-54. Mem. Mo., Kansas City bar assns., Lawyer's Assn., West Mo. Def. Council, Internat. Assn. Ins. Counsels, Phi Alpha Delta, Phi Kappa Alpha. Methodist. Club: Exchange. Home: 13001 E 58th St Kansas City MO 64133 Office: 2100 Bryant Bldg 1102 Grand St Kansas City MO 64106

WELLS, MARIAN RYDER (MRS. HAROLD ARTHUR WELLS), coll. dean; b. Oshkosh, Wis., Apr. 13, 1917; d. Alexander William and Erna (von Roenitz) Ryder; B.A., Principia Coll., 1938; m. Harold Arthur Wells, Aug. 9, 1941; children—Sallie Ryder, Stephen Ryder. Dean of women Principia Coll., Elsah, Ill., 1963—. Mem. AAUW, Nat., Ill. assns. women deans and counselors, Am. Assn. Higher Edn., League Women Voters, Hist. Elsah Soc., Nat. Orgn. for Women. Republican. Christian Scientist. Address: Principia Coll Elsah IL 62028

WELLS, NORMAN EDGAR, newspaper editor; b. Paoli, Ind., June 4, 1936; s. Norman Banks and Emma LaRue (Almand) W.; student pub. schs., Paoli; m. Patricia Kay Bennett, June 29, 1967; children—Norman Anthony, Thomas Eric. Newsman, Register Publs., Lawrenceburg, Ind., 1969-71, editor, 1971—. Named Nat. Blue Ribbon Newspaper Editor, 1974. Mem. Ind. Republican Editorial Assn. (Best Front Page 1973, 75, 76). Home: Box 397B Rural Route 2 Aurora IN 47001 Office: 414 3d St Aurora IN 47001

WELLS, RALPH MADISON, JR., pub. relations exec.; b. Cleve., Dec. 18, 1935; s. Ralph Madison and Ada (Malone) W.; B.S., Bowling Green U., 1957; postgrad. Case Western Res. U., 1963, Northwestern U., 1964; m. Sari Ann Horne, Nov. 7, 1958; children—Lynda Deanne, Laura Elizabeth, Michael Scott. With Cleve. Press, 1957-59, Berea (Ohio) News, 1959-61; Edward Howard & Co., Cleve., 1962-63; Am. Hosp. Supply Corp., Evanston, Ill., 1963-65; with Morton Internat., Inc., Chicago, 1965-71, dir. pub. relations, 1969-71; regional mgr. Ins. Info. Inst., Chgo., 1971-73; dir. pub. relations A.T. Kearney, Inc., 1973—. Chmn. office pub. relations Mid-Am. chpt. ARC, 1974-76. Bd. dirs. Northbrook Civic Found., 1974—. Served with AUS, 1958, 61-62. Mem. Pub. Relations Soc. Am. (accredited; bd. dirs. 1975—, treas. 1978), Pub. Relations Clinic Chgo. (pres. 1977-78), Publicity Club Chgo. (bd. dirs. 1970-71, 73-77, pres. 1975-76). Presbyterian (elder 1970-72, deacon 1966-70). Club: Union League (Chgo.). Home: 2218 Crabtree Ln Northbrook IL 60062 also The Highlands Lake Geneva WI 53147

WELLS, RAY MARSHALL, personnel exec., mgmt. cons.; b. New Haven, Mo., May 23, 1915; s. Ray Marshall and Annie Laurie (Thurmon) W.; student Central Coll., 1933-34, U. Mo., 1934-35; B.S., Central Mo. State U., 1943; m. Laura Lakin, Aug. 15, 1937 (dec. 1966); children—Barbara Wells Burns, Gary, Carolyn Wells Fischer, Patricia Wells Rootes; m. 2d, Huba McCroskey, June 30, 1967. Pub. sch. tchr., New Haven and Stanton, Mo., 1937-39; supt. schs., Gerald, Mo., 1939-44; field agt. State Conservation Dept., Jefferson City, Mo., 1944-55, chief field service; 1955-58, personnel officer, 1958-75; now mgmt. and personnel devel. cons. Prin. Tng. and Devel. Dynamics, Centertown, Mo., 1975—; personnel cons. for pvt. and pub. sector orgns. Vice pres. bd. dirs. United Way, Jefferson City, 1971, 74, mem. budget rev. com., 1966-69; mem. Jefferson City Mayor's city salary study com., 1968, 74. Mem. Adminstrv. Mgmt. Soc. (chpt. pres. 1968-69, area dir. 1971-73), Am. Soc. for Tng. and Devel. (dir. 1973—), Internat. Transactional Analysis Assn., Jefferson City Personnel Mgmt. Assn. Christian Ch. (chmn. bd. dirs. 1970-71). Address: Route 1 Centertown MO 65023

WELLS, ROBERT FRANCIS, guidance counselor; b. Lincoln, Nebr., Aug. 19, 1936; s. Francis Joseph and Ruth Luella (Mills) W.; student Hastings Coll., 1954-57; B.A. in Edn., Nebr. Wesleyan U., 1959; postgrad. U. No. Colo., Greeley, 1964; M.S. in Guidance, U. Nebr., 1968; postgrad. U. Nebr., Omaha, 1975-76, Lincoln, 1977—; m. C. Ann Maguire, Dec. 23, 1962; 1 dau., Jane Elizabeth. Tchr., Fairbury (Nebr.) High Sch., Jr. Coll., 1959-62; counselor, tchr. Fremont (Nebr.) Sr. High Sch., 1962-75; counselor Fremont Jr. High Sch., 1975—. Served with N.G., Nebr., 1958-64, active duty, 1959. Mem. NEA, Nebr. State Edn., Fremont edn. assns., Nebr., Am. personnel and guidance assns., Am. Sch. CoOnselors Assn. Republican. Methodist. Clubs: Masons, Shriners. Home: 1916 Cuming St Fremont NE 68025 Office: 935 Broad St Fremont NE 69025

WELLS, ROBERT MANVILLE, psychologist; b. Grand Rapids, Mich., Dec. 20, 1929; s. Clifford Charles and Henrietta (Chase) W.; grad. Davenport Inst., 1949; A.Commerce, Grand Rapids Jr. Coll., 1957; B.S., Western Mich. U., 1958, M.A., 1963; m. Isabelle Kathleen Parkhurst, June 14, 1957; children—David Alan, Cynthia Jean. Sch. psychologist Branch County Sch. Dist., Coldwater, Mich., 1961-66; sch. psychologist Ingham Intermediate Sch. Dist., Mason, Mich., 1966—, chmn. profl. staff, 1971-72, bd. dirs., 1976-77; trainer intern psychologists Mich. State U., East Lansing, 1966-75. Bd. dirs. local Cub Scouts Am., Leslie, Mich., 1968-69. Served with USAF, 1950-54. Mem. Am., Canadian psychol. assns., Mich. Assn. Sch. Psychologists. Club: Oakpark Athletic. Home: 3007 Tuttle Rd Mason MI 48854 Office: 2630 Howell Rd Mason MI 48854

WELLS, WILLARD JAMES, JR., environ. engr.; b. West Point, Nebr., Feb. 20, 1932; s. Willard James and Mabel (Goodwin) W.; B.S., U. Nebr., 1954; M.S., U. Mich., 1958; m. Paula Marie Broady, June 19, 1955; children—Kimberly, Martin, Douglas, Tracy, Alison. Design engr. Fulton & Cramer, Cons. Engrs., Lincoln, Nebr., 1956-57; san. engr. Kirkham, Michael & Assos., Omaha, 1958-66, chief san. design sect., 1966-68; v.p., partner Bell, Galyardt and Wells, Omaha, 1969—. Mem. Nebr. Bd. Health, 1973-76. Served with C.E., AUS, 1954-56. Mem. Profl. Engrs. Nebr. (state dir. 1964-66, v.p. 1968-69, treas. 1970-71, pres. 1973-74), Nebr. Water Pollution Control Assn. (dir. 1961-63, sec.-treas. 1965-67, pres. 1970), Am. Acad. Environ. Engrs., Am. Water Works Assn. (sec.-treas. 1975-77). Home: 2421 S 97th Ave Omaha NE 68124 Office: 5634 S 85th St Omaha NE 68127

WELLSO, CHARLES GEORGE, psychiatrist; b. Oshkosh, Wis., May 8, 1928; s. George Ervin and Esther Maria (Dehring) W.; student Wis. State Coll., 1945-46; B.S., U. Wis., 1949; M.D., George Washington U., 1953; m. Carolyn Louise Knapp, June 13, 1959; children—John, Charles, Elizabeth, Amy. Intern, Michael Reese Hosp., Chgo., 1953-54; resident psychiatry Topeka (Kans.) State Hosp., 1954-55, 57-59; fellow Menninger Sch. Psychiatry, Topeka, 1954-55, 57-59; practice medicine specializing in psychiatry, Los Angeles, 1959-60, Cedar Rapids, Iowa, 1960—; staff psychiatrist Rest Haven Hosp., Los Angeles, 1959-60; staff physician St. Luke's Meth. Hosp., Cedar Rapids, 1960—; courtesy staff Mercy Hosp., Cedar Rapids, 1960—; clin. asst. dept. psychiatry U. Calif. at Los Angeles, 1960; cons. Pacific Lodge Boys Home, Los Angeles, 1959-60, Linn County (Iowa) Mental Health Center, 1960-62, 74—, Cornell Coll., 1962-70. Bd. dirs. Jane Boyd Community House, Cedar Rapids, 1966-70, Cedar Rapids Art Center, 1969-71, Cedar Rapids Symphony, 1970-74. Served to capt. M.C. AUS, 1955-57. Diplomate in psychiatry Am. Bd. Psychiatry and Neurology. Fellow Am. Psychiatric Assn.; mem. Iowa Med. Soc., Linn County Med. Soc., Iowa Psychiat. Soc. Methodist (mem. ch. bd. 1966-67). Home: 345 Woodland Dr SE Cedar Rapids IA 52403 Office: 717 A Ave NE Cedar Rapids IA 52401

WELPER, FRANCIS EUGENE, educator; b. Hillsdale, Mich., July 4, 1919; s. Floyd Eugene and Neva (Post) W.; B.S., Eastern Mich. U., 1957, M.A., 1959; postgrad. U. So. Calif., 1962, Lehigh U., 1963; m. Janis Gill, Feb. 11, 1939; children—Francis Eugene II, Wendell Bruce, Charlotte Marie. Aircraft instr. Briggs Mfg. Co., Detroit, 1940-42, liaison engr., 1942-45; tchr. math. Britton (Mich.)-Macon High Sch., 1945-59; asst. prof. math. Eastern Mich. U., 1959-67, coordinator tech. services, asst. prof., 1967-69; now tchr. math., researcher religious studies. County del. Republican State Conv., 1967. Mem. Mich., Nat. edn. assns., Phi Delta Kappa, Kappa Delta Pi. Conglist. Mason. Home: 772 Beecher Rd Osseo MI 49266 Office: Pittsford High Sch Pittsford MI 49271

WELSH, DAVID JOHN, educator; b. London, Eng., Sept. 15, 1920; s. William and Ada Minnie (Russell) W.; B.A. (honors), U. London, 1954, D.Phil., 1967; M.A., U. Liverpool, 1962. Came to U.S., 1961. Prof. Slavic langs. and lits. Brit. Embassy, Warsaw, Poland, 1951-52; lang. supr. BBC, London, 1956-60; prof. Slavic dept. U. Mich., Ann Arbor, 1961—. Served with Brit. Army, 1939-46. Recipient Jurzykowski Found. award, 1968; Wyspianski award Assn. Polish-Am. Cultural Clubs, 1969, ann. award Polish Writers' Assn., 1971. Author: Russian Comedy 1765-1823, 1966; Adam Mickiewicz, 1966; Ignacy Krasicki, 1969; Jan Kochanowski, 1974. Translator: Dreambook for Our Time (T. Konwicki), 1969, The Doll, 1972, Black Torrent, 1969, Cloak of Illusion, 1969, others. Contbr. articles to profl. jours. Home: 3026 Modern Lang Bldg Ann Arbor MI 48109

WELTE, MAURICE DANIEL, chem. co. exec.; b. Danbury, Iowa, Dec. 20, 1932; s. Daniel John and Josephine (Collins) W.; B.A., Loras Coll., 1954; m. Gloria M. Bindner, Nov. 23, 1956; children—Ann, Karen, Lynn, Donald, Renee. Auditor, Dept. of Air Force, South Bend, Ind., 1955-56, auditor, Mpls., 1956-57, asst. resident auditor, Peru, Ind., 1957-59; owner grain and livestock farm, Danbury, 1959—; owner Welte Accounting & Tax Service, 1959—; tax. cons. Chmn. Woodbury Dist. Soil Conservation Commrs., 1965-70. Mem. State Policy Advisory Com. Iowa Dept. Environ. Quality, 1976—. K.C. Clubs: Maple Vale Country, Danbury Community. Home: Rural Route 1 Danbury IA 51019 Office: Danbury IA 51019

WELTER, CLARENCE JOSEPH, pharm. co. exec.; b. Tiffin, Ohio, June 11, 1932; s. Clarence John and Marie B. (Buchman) W.; B.S. cum laude, King's Coll., 1954; M.S. magna cum laude (teaching asst., NIH grantee), U. Notre Dame, 1956; Ph.D. (teaching asst.), Mich. State U., 1959; m. Doris Marie Bialek, June 6, 1955; children—Mark, Lisa, Amy Jo. Vice-pres. Research Diamond Labs., Des Moines, 1959-74; pres. Ambico, Inc., Dallas Center, Iowa, 1974—. Mem. U.S. Animal Health Assn., Am. Soc. Parasitology, Am. Soc. Microbiology, Tissue Culture Assn., Conf. of Research Workers, Am. Mgmt. Assn., Serra Club. Contbr. articles in microbiology to jours. Patentee in field. Home: 1606 Evans St Des Moines IA 50315 Office: Ambico Inc Rt 2 Dallas Center IA 50063

WELTY, QUENTIN WILBUR, advt. co. exec.; b. Apple Creek, Ohio, Mar. 27, 1925; s. Evan Edgar and Cloyva Mae (Blosser) W.; student Ohio U., 1943, Oberlin Coll., 1946-47; A.B. cum laude, Baldwin-Wallace Coll., 1948; M.A. cum laude, Northwestern U., 1949; m. Gloria Joan Ash, June 21, 1948; children—Laurel Renee (Mrs. Michael Coleman), Sharon, Russell, Dana. Instr., U. N.D., 1949-50; gen. mgr. Sta. WMVO, Mt. Vernon, Ohio, 1950-51; gen. sales mgr. WWST-WWST-FM, Wooster, Ohio, 1951-65, mgr., 1965-69; dir. Miss Ohio Pageant, 1953-58; gen. mgr. Jamboree U.S.A., Inc., WWVA, Wheeling, W.Va., 1969-71; mgmt. cons. WKNT-WKNT-FM, Kent, Ohio, 1971; pres. B-W Music, Inc., Wooster, 1963-71; mgr. Welty Advt. Agy., 1972—; regional account exec. Susquehanna Broadcasting Corp., Akron, Ohio; instr. Kent State U., 1969—; dir. Peppermint Prodns., Youngstown, Ohio. Bd. dirs. Wayne County chpt. Nat. Found., 1955-68; bd. govs. Wooster Community Hosp. Served with Signal Corps, AUS, 1943-46. Recipient Diamond key Pi Kappa Delta, 1948, Dayton C. Miller Honor award, 1948, Tex Ritter Pres.'s award Country Music Assn., 1964. Mem. Country Music Assn., Nat. Acad. Recording Arts and Scis., Wooster Jr. C. of C. (v.p.). Author: Writing and Selling the Popular Song, 1959. Contbr. articles to profl. publs. Home: 754 Fairview Dr Wooster OH 44691 Office: PO Box 561 Wooster OH 44691

WENDEL, SYLVESTER WENDELINE, architect, civil engr.; b. Kansas City, Mo., Aug. 3, 1906; s. Henry J. and Mary K. (Wendel) W.; student Washburn Coll., 1925-28; B.Arch., U. Kans., 1936; m. Clara H. Hallock, Feb. 18, 1938; children—Madelyn K. (Mrs. C. Edward Regan), Carol Anne, (Mrs. Charles Christ). Robert W., Richard H. Civil engr. Santa Fe R.R., 1928-32; archtl. engr. pvt. practice, govt. agys., 1936-48; atomic engr. projects Black & Veatch, 1948-50; engr. Central Air Def. Communications 1950-54; owner, architect Sylvester W. Wendel & Asso., Kansas City, Kans., 1954-67; architect advisor FAA (13 states) 1954-67; chief plans, program div. U.S. Army Chief Engr. Housing, Staff Coll., Ft. Leavenworth, Kans., 1967-74. Mem. Kaw council Boy Scouts Am., 1954-64; mem. Neighborhood Com., 1964-75; Cath. Com. Scouting, Kans. Mem. Credit Union League (pres. Eastern chpt. Kans.), Parish Credit Union (pres. bd. dirs. 1950-65). Registered architect, Kans., Mo.; registered civil engr. Fellow Am. Registered Architects (state pres. 1962-64, regent 5 state area); mem. Am. Mil. Engrs., Nat. Soc. Profl. Engrs. (life mem.), Kans. Engr. Soc. (pres. Eastern chpt. 1961-62), Nat. Asso. Ret. Fed. Employees (legis. chmn.), Eastern Chpt. Ret. Employees, Crown Heights Neighbors of U.S. Community Devel. Program (pres.), Am. Asso. Ret. Persons, U. Kans. Alumni Assn. (life mem.), Smithsonian Assos., C. of C. (chmn. aviation com. 1949-54). Roman Catholic. Club: K.C. Home: 2502 Lafayette Ave Kansas City KS 66104

WENDELBURG, NORMA RUTH, composer, pianist, educator; b. Stafford, Kans.; d. Henry and Anne (Moeckel) Wendelburg; Mus.B., Bethany Coll., 1943; Mus.M., U. Mich., 1947; Mus.M., Eastman Sch. Music, 1951, postgrad., 1964-65, 66-67, Ph.D. in Composition, 1969; postgrad. Mozarteum, 1953-54, Vienna Acad. Music, 1955. Asst. prof. music edn., piano Wayne (Nebr.) State Coll., 1947-50, Bethany Coll., Lindsborg, Kan., 1952-53, State Coll., Cedar Falls, Ia., 1956-58; asst. prof. composition, theory, piano Hardin-Simmons U., Abilene, Tex., 1958-66, chmn. grad. com. Sch. Music, 1960-66, founder ann. univ. festival contemporary music, 1959, chmn., 1959—; asso. prof. music Dallas Bapt. Coll., 1973-75; research asst. to dir. grad. studies Eastman Sch. Music, 1966-67; former asso. prof., chmn. dept. theory, composition Southwest Tex. State U.; appeared as pianist various solo recitals, festivals. Composition scholar Composers' Conf. Middlebury (Vt.), 1950, Berkshire Center, 1953; Fulbright award, 1953-55; Residence fellow Huntington Hartford Found., 1955-56, 58, 61; MacDowell Colony, 1958, 60, 70. Mem. Music Tchrs. Nat. Conf., Am. Music Center, MacDowell Colonists, ASCAP, Am. Soc. Univ. Composers, Am. Women Composers, Sigma Alpha Iota. Composer numerous works including Symphony, 1967, Suite for Violin and Piano, 1965, Song Cycle for Soprano, Flutes, Piano, 1974. Address: Rural Route 2 Stafford KS 67578

WENDELL, FRANCIS LEE HIGGINSON, mgmt. cons; b. Boston, Jan. 14, 1916; s. Barrett, Sr. and Barbara (Higginson) W.; student Harvard Coll., 1936; student Bus. Sch., U. Chgo., 1936-38; m. Joan Monroe, Feb. 11, 1961; children—Nathalie (Mrs. Andrew H. Thomas), Peter H. Mgmt. cons. McKinsey Wellington & Co., Chgo., 1936-38; salesman Sunbeam Corp., Chgo., 1938-42, field sales mgr., 1945-48, Eastern sales mgr., 1948-51; with A.T. Kearney Co., internat. mgmt. cons., Chgo., 1951-73, v.p., 1955-73. Mem. Chgo. Crime Commn., 1970—, pres.'s com. Lyric Opera, Chgo., 1969—. Served with USNR, 1942-45. Mem. U.S., Ill. chambers of commerce, Chgo. Assn. Commerce and Industry, Nat. Multiple Sclerosis Soc. (chmn. Chgo. chpt. 1969, mem. nat. bd. 1969—), Harvard Club Chgo. (pres. 1958), Assoc. Harvard Clubs (regional v.p. 1959), Mus. Natural

History, Art Inst. Chgo. Clubs: Chicago; Attic; Wayfarers; Brook (N.Y.C.); Onwentsia (Lake Forest) Country. Elk. Home: 1002 Woodbine Pl Lake Forest IL 60045 Office: 100 S Wacker Dr Chgo IL 60606

WENDLING, DIETER, physician; b. Mainz, W. Germany, July 8, 1928; came to U.S., 1954, naturalized 1957; s. Alois and Clara (Nuedling) W.; A.B., Humanistisches Gymnasium, Mainz, 1947; D.D.S., Johannes Gutenberg U., Mainz, 1952, M.D. 1954; m. Eva Renate Braun, May 9, 1963; children—Alexander, Richard Karen Kristina, Tanya Ingrid, Barbara Ellen, Peter Roman. Intern in otolaryngology Harper Hosp., also affiliated hosps., Detroit, 1954-55, resident, 1955-58; practice medicine specializing in otolaryngology Birmingham, Mich., 1958; asst. prof. otolaryngology Med. Sch., Wayne State U., Detroit, 1960—; chief otolaryngology service Oakland Med. Center, Pontiac State Hosp., Mich., 1970-76; attending surgeon St. Joseph Hosp., Mt. Clemens, Mich., 1976—; chmn. div. otolaryngology William Beaumont Hosp., Royal Oak, Mich., 1970—. Diplomate Am. Bd. Otolaryngology. Fellow Am. Acad. Ophthalmology and Otolaryngology, A.C.S.; mem. Am. Council Otolaryngology, Pan Pacific Surg. Assn., Internat. Soc. Macillofacial Surgery, Detroit Surg. Assn., Detroit Otolaryn. Soc., Centurion Club of Deafness Research Found. Home: 3501 Lakecrest Dr Bloomfield Hills MI 48009 Office: 14 Belleview Mount Clemens MI 48043

WENDORF, MELVIN JAMES, city ofcl.; b. Schofield, Wis., June 1, 1929; B.B.A., U. Wis., 1958; m. Ruth Margaret Newbauer, Feb. 7, 1959; children—Christine Ann, Laura Lynn. Asst. state auditor Wis. Dept. State Audit, Madison, 1958-67; spl. agt., supr. intelligence div. IRS, St. Paul, 1967-74; partner Anderson, Johnson, Kramer & Wendorf, C.P.A.'s, Anoka, Minn., 1974-76; asst. comptroller-treas. City of Mpls., 1976—. Served with AUS, 1951-54. C.P.A., Minn., Wis. Mem. Am. Inst. C.P.A.'s, Assn. U.S. Army, Res. Officers Assn. U.S., Travelers Protective Assn. Am., Minn. Soc. C.P.A.'s, U. Wis. Alumni Assn., Municipal Finance Officers Assn., Am. Legion. Lutheran (v.p., trustee 1963-67, pres., elder, treas. 1968—). Home: 3162 Shorewood Dr St Paul MN 55112 Office: 331 City Hall Minneapolis MN 55415

WENDT, ARTHUR JOHN, photographer; b. Dodge County, Wis., Aug. 14, 1928; s. Arthur August and Hilda Emma (Rossow) W.; student Winona Sch. Photography, 1949, 68, 70; m. Eileen F. Trestrail, Aug. 19, 1950; children—David L., Beth L. Owner A.J. Wendt Studio, Stoughton, Wis., 1952—. Mem. Profl. Photographers Am. (master), Wis. Profl. Photographers Assn. (dir. 1958, 68), South Central Photographers Assn. (pres. 1957), Am. Soc. Photographers, South Central Wis. Geneaology Soc., Southgton Hist. Soc. (dir. 1973-77). Lutheran (ch. treas. 1969-77). Home: 411 N Harrison St Stoughton WI 53589 Office: 183 E Main St Stoughton WI 53589

WENDT, GEORGE R., real estate co. exec.; b. Chgo., Jan. 8, 1923; s. William Henry and Katherine (Crowley) W.; B.S., U. Notre Dame, 1943; m. Loretta M. Howard, Feb. 23, 1946; children—Kathryn (Mrs. Daniel Sudeikis), George Robert, Loretta (Mrs. Gregory Jolivette), Martha (Mrs. Edward Muldoon), Nancy (Mrs. William Healy), Thomas, Paul. With William H. Wendt, Inc., Chgo., 1946—, pres., gen. mgr., dir., 1965—; pres., dir. 1814 Corp., Chgo., 1962—; dir. Beverly Bank Chgo.; mem. Chgo. Real Estate Bd., 1967—. Trustee Little Co. of Mary Hosp., St. Frances de Sales High Sch., Mother McAuley Liberal Arts High Sch.; bd. dirs. Beverly Art Assn. Served to capt. USNR, World War II. Recipient Silver Anvil award Pub. Relations Soc. Am., 1959. Mem. Navy League U.S. (Ill. pres. 1964, 65, nat. dir.), Naval Res. Assn. (nat. dir., dist. pres. 1957-60). Clubs: Beverly Country, Tavern, Chgo. Athletic (Chgo.). Home: 9201 S Bell Ave Chicago IL 60620 Office: 9933 S Western Ave Chicago IL 60643

WENDT, HAROLD JOHN, food co. exec.; b. Pender, Nebr., Apr. 7, 1919; s. Martin August and Anna A. (Moeller) W.; ed. pub. schs., Nebr., 1925-37; m. Lois Rose Wendte, Feb. 10, 1946; children—Karen, Debra. Accounting clk. Ocoma Foods Co., Omaha, 1946-47, office mgr., 1947-49, purchasing agt., 1949-53, br. mgr., Berryville, Ark., 1953-55, prodn. mgr., Omaha, 1955-59, v.p. prodn., 1959-70, v.p. procurement, 1970-71; asst. to pres. Gooch Foods, Inc., Lincoln, Nebr., 1971-72, exec. v.p., 1972-73, pres., 1973—. Bd. dirs. Lutheran Med. Center, Omaha, 1967-71. Served with U.S. Army, 1940-46, 50-53. Mem. Nat. Macaroni Assn., Poultry Hist. Soc. (life). Republican. Lutheran. Clubs: Hilcrest Country, Lincoln U. Home: 7300 Old Post Rd #12 Lincoln NE 68506 Office: 510 South St Lincoln NE 68502

WENDT, LLOYD, newspaper editor, lectr.; b. Spencer, S.D., May 16, 1908; s. Leo L. and Marie (Nylen) W.; student Sioux Falls Coll., 1928-29; S.B., Northwestern U., 1931, S.M., 1934; m. Helen Sigler, June 16, 1932; 1 dau., Bette Joan. Reporter, later columnist drama reviewer, Sioux Falls (S.D.) Press, 1927-28; state publicity dir. S.D. Democratic Central Com., 1928; reporter Daily Argus-Leader, 1929, telegraph editor, 1932-33; also tchr. journalism. Sioux Falls Coll.; joined staff Chgo. Tribune, 1934, reporter, spl. feature writer mag. sect. later editor of Grafic mag., Sunday editor; editor, pub. Chicago Today newspaper, 1961-74; asso. editor Chgo. Tribune, 1974—; lectr. fiction writing Northwestern U., 1946, chmn. fiction div. Medill Sch. Journalism, 1950-53. Served as lt. comdr. USNR, 1942-46. Author: (with Herman Kogan) Lords of the Levee, 1943, Bet a Million, Give the Lady What She Wants, 1952, Big Bill of Chicago, 1953. Chicago: A Pictorial History, 1958; Gunners Get Glory, 1944; Bright Tomorrow, 1945. Office: 435 N Michigan Ave Chicago IL 60611

WENIG, PHILLIP WAYNE, research bur. exec.; b. Oak Park, Ill., Feb. 20, 1928; s. Henry Wayne and Grace Evelyn (Carlton) W.; B.S. (bronze table student), U. Ill., 1950, M.A., 1952; m. Mary Grinter, Aug. 24, 1949; children—Constance Lynn, Janet Grace, Robert Wayne, Susan Ann. Pres. data div. Standard Rate and Data Service, N.Y.C., 1959-67; v.p., dir. mktg. services D'Arcy Advt., Chgo., 1967-72; dir. Midwest ops. Chilton Pub. Co., Chgo., 1972-73; mgr. corp. mktg. research Internat. Harvester Co., Chgo., 1973-77; v.p., dir. client services Axiom Mktg. Research Bur., N.Y.C., 1977—; cons., lectr. advt. and advt. research nat. advertisers and agys., 1959-75. Served with USMCR, 1945-46. Mem. Newcomen Soc. N.Am., Am. Mktg. Assn., Am. Psychol. Assn., Chgo. Athletic Assn. Home: 201 W Station St Barrington IL 60010 Office: 401 N Michigan Ave Chicago IL 60606

WENNEKER, JAMES EMMETT, publishing exec.; b. Quincy, Ill., Aug. 1, 1935; s. Jacob Emmett and Trula Lurlene (Brockschmidt) W.; student Quincy Coll., 1953-55, LaSalle Extension U., 1967-73; m. Joyce Ann Anderson, Sept. 15, 1956 (div. July 1973); children—Julie Lee, Jeri Ellen. TV dir., TV and radio announcer WGEM AM-FM TV, Quincy, 1953-61; gen. mgr. WZOE-AM, Princeton, Ill.; 1961-67; store mgr. Montgomery Ward, Princeton, Ill., 1967-69; TV dir. WQAD-TV, Moline, Ill., 1969-70; gen. mgr. KSIM-AM Radio, Sikeston, Mo., 1970-76; creative adviser Delta Projects, Inc., Sikeston, 1976—; self-employed piano technician, 1976—. Mem. adv. com. Health Occupations Sikeston pub. schs., 1975—; chmn. Sikeston Bicentennial Commn., 1974-76. Bd. dirs. Ret. Sr. Vol. Program, Scott County, Mo., 1973-76, Sikeston Little Theater, 1970—, Sikeston Council on the Arts, 1973-76. Served with Ill. N.G., 1955-63. Baptist. Mason (32 deg.). Contbg. author Big Bureau and Bright Prairies-History of Bureau County, Ill., 1968. Home: 1911 Oklahoma St Sikeston MO 63801 Office: Sikeston MO 63801

WENNER, HERBERT ALLAN, physician, educator; b. Drums, Pa., Nov. 14, 1912; s. Herbert C. and Verna (Walp) W.; B.S., Bucknell U., 1933; M.D., U. Rochester, 1939; m. Ruth I. Berger, June 27, 1942; children—Peter W., James M., Susan T., Thomas H. Intern pathology U. Colo. Sch. Medicine, Denver, 1939-40, pediatrics Yale Sch. Medicine, 1940-41, asst. resident in pediatrics, 1941-42, instr. preventive medicine, 1944-46; NRC fellow Yale U.-Johns Hopkins U., 1942-43; asst. prof. pediatrics and bacteriology U. Kans. Sch. Medicine, 1946-49; asso. prof. pediatrics and bacteriology U. Kans., 1949-51, research prof. pediatrics, 1951-69, adj. prof., 1975—; Joyce C. Hall Distinguished prof. pediatrics U. Mo., Children's Mercy Hosp., 1969—, adj. prof. Sch. Dentistry, 1970—. Civilian cons. epidemiology Kans. Bd. of Health, USPHS. Recipient Research Career award NIH, 1962. Diplomate Am. Bd. Microbiology, Am. Bd. Pediatrics. Fellow AAAS, Am. Pub. Health Assn., Am. Acad. Pediatrics; mem. Soc. Pediatric Research, Am. Pediatric Soc., Soc. Exptl. Biology and Medicine, Biometrics Soc., Mo. State Med. Assn. AMA, Royal Soc. Health, AAUP, N.Y. Acad. Scis., Am. Epidemiology Soc., Infectious Diseases Soc. Am. Episcopalian. Asso. editor Am. Jour. Epidemiology; editorial bd. Intervirology; mem. editorial advisory bd. Archives Virology; contbr. articles to profl. books, jours. Home: 9711 Johnson Dr Merriam KS 66203 Office: Children's Mercy Hosp 24th at Gillham Rd Kansas City MO 64108

WENSINK, DELMAR DAVID, mfg. co. exec.; b. Thompson, N.D., June 3, 1893; s. Ira B. and Ida (Stolper) W.; A.B., Ripon Coll., 1916; m. Erma Shoemaker, Nov. 15, 1919; children—Carolyn (Mrs. David Ullman)(dec.), Mary Ann (Mrs. Lloyd A. Gerlach). With Stolper Industries, Inc., and predecessor firms, 1919—, pres., gen. mgr., 1933-65, chmn. bd., 1965—; dir. No. Bank, Milw. Pres. Wauwatosa (Wis.) Bd. Vocat. and Adult Edn., 1945-48; mem. Four County Hosp. Area Planning Commn., 1960-65. Bd. dirs. Southeastern Wis. Area Jr. Achievement, 1952-57; trustee Milw. Boys' Club, 1962-72, Ripon Coll., 1953-56; mem. adv. bd. Wis. Found. Ind. Colls., 1957-72. Served as lt. Signal Corps, U.S. Army, 1918-19. Mem. Wis. Mfrs. Assn. (v.p. 1960-67). Congregationalist. Mason, Kiwanian. Clubs: Wisconsin (Milw.); Blue Mound Country (Wauwatosa); Deerfield Country (Fla.). Home: 1245 Overhill Rd Elm Grove WI 53122 Office: Box 190 Menomonee Falls WI 53051

WENTHE, EUGENE EDWARD, constrn. co. exec.; b. Effingham, Ill., July 10, 1914; s. Fred Christopher and Mabel Catherine (Jenkins) W.; student U. Ill., 1932-35; m. Beulah Catherine Newman, Mar. 6, 1936; children—Philip K., Deborah Ann, Pamela Catherine, Eugene Edward. Asst. to P.K. Wrigley, Wm. Wrigley Jr. Co., Chgo., 1936-39; pres. Wenthe Bros. Co. Bldg. Center, Effingham, 1952—. City commr., Effingham, 1943-51, mayor, 1951-55, pres. water bd., 1955-64, mem. indsl. commn., 1964-77; dir. Ill. Guarantee Savs. and Loan. Recipient Distinguished Service award City of Effingham, 1956, Mayor's Key to City, 1973. Mem. Effingham C. of C., Ill. Lumber and Material Dealers Assn. Presbyterian. Clubs: Rotary, Elks. Home: 109 N Long St Effingham IL 62401 Office: 314 W Jefferson St Effingham IL 62401

WENTWORTH, RICHARD LEIGH, editor; b. Concord, N.H., July 6, 1930; s. Leigh Mayhew and Yvonne Regina (Wilcott) W.; B.A., U. Okla., 1956; m. Marlene McClenning, June 9, 1950; children—Douglas, John, Elizabeth, James. Editorial asst. U. Okla. Press, 1957-58; asst. editor U. Wis. Press, 1958-59; mgr. sales and promotion La. State U. Press, 1959-62, asst. dir., 1962-63, dir., 1963-70; asso. dir., editor U. Ill. Press, Urbana, 1970—. Served with USAF, 1948-52. Mem. Assn. Am. Univ. Presses (dir. 1966, 77—), Orgn. Am. Historians. Democrat. Elk. Contbr. articles to profl. and sports jours. Home: 808 W Springfield St Champaign IL 61820 Office: Univ Illinois Press Urbana IL 61801

WENTZEL, ARNOLD WILLIAM, found. adminstr.; b. St. James, Minn., Sept. 18, 1927; s. William Henry and Melinda Augusta (Becker) W.; B.S.Ed., Luther Coll., New Ulm, Minn., 1950; M.B.A., Dallas State U., 1969; Ph.D. in Metaphysics (hon.), Universal Life Ch. Coll., Phoenix, 1969; m. Dorothea Martha Schramm, July 18, 1948; children—Paul Arnold, Lenice (Mrs. Larry Vaught), John William, David Luther, Philip Al. Youth leader Luth. Elementary and Jr. High Sch. 1950-71, dir. choir, 1956-66, organist, 1950-71, coach, 1950-71, tchr., 1950-56, prin., 1950-71, supt., 1950-71; mgr. Camp CILCA, Cantrall, Ill., 1972-76; adminstr. Lincoln Meml. Garden Found., 1976—. Served with AUS, 1946-48; PTO. Mem. Luth. Laymens League. Address: 1819 S Lincoln Ave Springfield IL 62704

WENTZEL, PHILIP ROBERT, coll. adminstr.; b. Eau Gallie, Fla., July 30, 1939; s. Philip August and Elizabeth (Muller) W.; B.S., C.W. Post Coll., 1962; M.A., L.I. U., 1965; m. Carole Joy Walsh, June 29, 1968; children—Philip Hugh, Elizabeth Lynley. Asst. dean students C.W. Post Coll., Greenvale, N.Y., 1966-68, dean students, 1968-72, asso. coordinator student affairs, 1972-74; dean students Webster Coll., St. Louis, 1974—. Named Man of Year, C.W. Post Coll., 1968. Mem. Am. Coll. Personnel Assn., Am. Assn. U. Adminstrs., Am. Assn. Higher Edn., Nat., L.I. Coll. (sec. 1972-73) assns. student personnel adminstrs. Home: 7464 Amherst Ave St Louis MO 63130 Office: 470 E Lockwood St Louis MO 63119

WENZEL, FREDERICK JOSEPH, biochemist; b. Marshfield, Wis., Aug. 5, 1930; s. Rudolph Eric and Theresa A. (Kaholka) W.; B.S., Wis. State U., Stevens Point, 1956; postgrad. U. Wis., 1962, 70-71; m. Mary Ann Rasmussen, Sept. 6, 1952; children—Ann Frances, Paul Frederick, Ellen Therese, Jane Marie, Thomas Richard, Mary Margaret. Research asst. St. Joseph's Hosp., Marshfield, 1950-53; dir. labs. Marshfield Clinic, 1953-65, exec. dir. clinic, 1976—; exec. dir. Marshfield Med. Found., 1965—; dir. Central State Bank, Marshfield, 1973—. Chmn. North Central area Health Planning Assn. regional tech. com. on phys. health, Marshfield, 1973—, mem. health policy council, research and devel. com., 1974—; mem. com. on drug and alcohol abuse, Clinic, Hosp., Found., Marshfield, 1971—, edn. com., 1969—; mem. gov.'s council for snowmobile recreation, 1971—. Chmn. bd. dirs. Mid-State Vocational, Tech. and Adult Edn. Dist., Marshfield, 1968—, exec. com., 1973—; chmn. adv. council St. Joseph's Hosp. Sch. Nursing, Marshfield, 1970-73; bd. dirs. U. Wis. Stevens Point Found., 1973—. Recipient Distinguished Service award, Marshfield Jr. C. of C., 1963, First Ann. Distinguished Service award, 1971; citation Wis. Jr. Acad. Sci., 1970, Spl. citation, 1972; Grand award Wis. affiliate Am. Heart Assn., 1977. Mem. Assn. Community Coll. Trustees, Wis. Heart Assn. (chmn. bd. dirs. 1974—, chmn. research com. 1971-74), Am. Chem. Soc., Am. Inst. Chemists, Am. Fedn. Clin. Research, N.Y. Acad. Scis., Wis. Acad. Sci., Arts and Letters, Am. Assn. Med. Clinics Found. (dir. 1973—). Roman Catholic (bd. edn. 1967-73). Elk, Rotarian. Contbr. numerous articles to profl. jours. Home: 610 S Sycamore St Marshfield WI 54449 Office: 1000 N Oak Ave Marshfield WI 54449

WENZLER, WILLIAM PAUL, architect; b. Milw., Feb. 9, 1929; s. Paul C. and Bertha R. (Froemming) W.; student U. Wis., 1947-48; B.S. in Archtl. Engring., U. Ill., 1952; m. Dolores A. Rahn, June 17, 1950; children—Edward, Deborah, John, Joan. Draftsman H. C. Haeuser, Architect, Milw., 1952, A.H. Siewert, Architect, Milw., 1952-54; designer Brust & Brust, Architects, 1954-55; pvt. practice architecture, Milw., 1955—; pres. William Wenzler & Assos., Architects, Inc., 1966—. Recipient Francis J. Plym fellow U. Ill., 1958; Ford Found. grantee U. Wis., 1961; named one of Wis. 5 Outstanding Young Men, Wis. Jr. C. of C., 1961; Gov.'s award for creativity in the arts, 1967; various awards for archtl. works. Registered architect, Wis., Ill., Iowa, Mo., Mass., Calif., Mich., Pa. Fellow AIA; mem. Am. Concrete Inst., Guild for Religious Architecture, Gargoyle, Tau Beta Pi. Mem. United Ch. of Christ. Prin. works include: Germantown (Wis.) Elementary Sch., 1956, St. Edmunds Episcopal Ch., Elm Grove, Wis., 1957, Zion Evangel. and Ref. Ch., Milw., 1958, 1st Congl. Ch., Mukwonago, Wis., 1959, Goldendale (Wis.) Elementary Sch., 1959, Bradford Terrace-Milw. Protestant Home for Aged, Milw., 1962, Our Shepherd Luth. Ch., Greendale, Wis., 1963, Gerald H. Nickoll residence, Fox Point, Wis., 1963, Inland Steel Factory and Office Bldg., Milw., 1966, Brookfield (Wis.) Evang. Luth. Ch., 1966, Luth. Social Services Wis. and Upper Mich. Hdqrs., Milw., 1967, Lloyd A. Gerlach residence, Elm Grove, 1967, Eden Theol. Sem.-Library, Webster Groves, Mo., 1968, Luth. Ch. Living Christ, Germantown, Wis., 1969, Grace Epis. Ch., Galesburg, 1970, Calvary Bapt. Ch., Milw., 1970, Fine Arts Complex Wis. State U., Stevens Point, 1971, Northridge Lakes Community Devel., Milw., 1971-73, Phys. Edn. Facility, U. Wis.-Parkside, Kenosha, Wis., 1972, renovation Jewish Vocat. Services, Milw., 1974, theater and anthropology bldg. Beloit Coll., 1975, Elm-Brook Ch., Brookfield, Wis., 1975, Dubuque (Iowa) Theol. Library, 1976; also numerous exhbns. of work. Home: 2823 N Shepard Ave Milwaukee WI 53211 Office: 205 W Highland Ave Milwaukee WI 53203

WERBEL, JAMES PHILLIP, advt. agy. exec.; b. Marion, Ohio, Dec. 23, 1946; s. John Charles and Dorothy Jane (Hyams) W.; B.A., Ohio Wesleyan U., 1968; M.B.A., Ohio State U., 1970. Health services field rep. Roche Labs., Nutley, N.J., 1970-73; prof. bus. adminstrn. Wittenberg U., Springfield, Ohio, 1973-74; advt. account exec. Lord, Sullivan & Yoder, Inc., Marion, 1974—; prof. mktg. Marion Tech. Coll., 1977—. Mem. Career Placement Commn., Wittenberg U., 1974; publicity chmn. Marion County Heart Assn., 1975-76, campaign chmn., 1978—; publicity com. Central Ohio Heart Assn., 1976—. Recipient Award of Excellence in Achievement, Central Ohio Heart Assn., 1976. Mem. Am. Mktg. Assn., Am. Mgmt. Assn., Central Ohio Indsl. Marketers, Marion Advt. Fedn., Tau Pi Phi, Tau Kappa Epsilon (bd. control Alpha Mu chpt. 1978—). Republican. Methodist. Club: Active 20-40. Contbr. articles to profl. jours. Office: 196 S Main St Marion OH 43302

WERGOWSKE, WILLIAM GARY, accountant; b. Cin., Sept. 6, 1941; s. William Leslie and Thelma Leah (Clemons) W.; B.B.A., U. Cin., 1963; M.B.A., Xavier U., 1971; m. Mary Helen Kemper, June 7, 1975. Mem. staff Pension Group Cons.'s, Inc., Cin., 1957-63; methods analyst Western and So. Life Ins. Co., Cin., 1965-73; mgr. mgmt. services and accounting services Main Lafrentz and Co., Cin., 1973-77; pvt. practice accounting, Cin., 1977—. Treas. home aid service Cin. Community Chest, 1975-77. Served with Signal Corp. U.S. Army, 1963-65. C.P.A., Ohio. Mem. Nat. Assn. Accountants (v.p. 1976—), Ohio Soc. C.P.A.'s, Am. Inst. C.P.A.'s, EDP Auditors Assn. Roman Catholic. Club: Cincinnati (trustee 1977—). Home: 5519 Lucenna Dr Cincinnati OH 45238 Office: 1958 Anderson Ferry Rd Cincinnati OH 45238

WERLING, MICHAEL MARION, food service dir.; b. Tiffin, Ohio, Sept. 18, 1949; s. Edward Joseph and Iretha Rose (Taylor) W.; student Ind. Central Coll., 1967-72. Asst. mgr. vending ARA Services, Inc., Kearney (Nebr.) State Coll., 1973-74, asst. food service dir. Concordia Tchrs. Coll., Seward, Nebr., 1974-76, food service dir. Columbus (Nebr.) Community Hosp., 1976—. Mem. Am. Soc. Hosp. Food Service Adminstrs. (Iowa-Nebr. chpt.), Am. Humanics, Alpha Phi Omega (life mem.). Democrat. Roman Catholic. Clubs: Columbus Optimists. Home: 2504 15th St Columbus NE 68601 Office: 3111 19th St Columbus NE 68601

WERMUTH, JOHN MARLOWE, diversified mfg. co. exec.; b. Henrietta, N.Y., Jan. 25, 1928; s. William John and Elvira Lorena (Hanson) W.; A.B. with highest distinction, U. Rochester, 1950; M.B.A., Harvard, 1952; m. Marilyn Ann McCuskey, Jan. 30, 1954; children—Robert A., Bruce M., Douglas J., Andrew G., Ann M. Credit mgr. Warner-Lambert Pharm. Co., N.Y.C., 1952-55; asst. treas. Acheson Industries Inc., chem. mfg., Pt. Huron, Mich., 1955-58; treas. Applied Power Industries, mfr. hydraulic equipment, Milw., 1958-68; v.p., sec., treas. Wehr Corp., Milw., 1968—. Past trustee Village Elm Grove (Wis.); trustee Layton Sch. Art, Milw.; bd. dirs. Day Care Services for Children, Citizens Govtl. Research Bur. Served with USN, 1946-48. Sherman fellow, 1950. Recipient Am. Legion Citizenship award, 1943. Mem. Financial Execs. Inst. (bd. dirs.), Harvard Club Wis. (dir.), Harvard Bus. Sch. Club Milw. (dir., past pres.), Phi Beta Kappa, Psi Upsilon. Methodist (adminstrv. bd.). Rotarian. Clubs: University, Westmoor Country, Brook (Milw.). Home: 915 Katherine Dr Elm Grove WI 53122 Office: 10201 W Lincoln Ave Milwaukee WI 53227

WERNER, BURTON KREADY, ins. exec.; b. St. Louis, Apr. 24, 1933; s. Elmer L. and Helen (Kready) W.; A.B. cum laude, Amherst Coll., 1954; M.B.A., Wharton Grad. Sch., U. Pa., 1958; m. Joanna Catherine Hill, Oct. 17, 1959; children—Lisa Anne, Cynthia Catherine, Bradford Kready. Sec., Insurers Service Corp., St. Louis, 1958-65, exec. v.p., 1965-75, pres., 1975—, also dir.; v.p. Safety Mut. Casualty Corp., 1958-75, exec. v.p., 1975-76, pres., 1976—, also dir.; underwriting mem. Lloyds of London; dir. Seven-Up Bottling Co. St. Louis. Mem. Arts and Edn. Council of St. Louis, Landmarks Assn. St. Louis. Served to capt. USAF, 1954-56. Mem. C.P.C.U., Nat. Assn. Safety and Claims Orgns. (sec. 1966, 67, pres. 1968-71, dir. 1967-71), Mo. Bot. Garden St. Louis, St. Louis Zoo Assn., Better Bus. Bur. St. Louis, St. Louis Symphony Soc., McDonnell Planetarium, City Art Mus. St. Louis, St. Louis Municipal Opera Assn., Backstoppers, Delta Kappa Epsilon. Episcopalian. Clubs: Indian Lake (Fla.); Racquet (St. Louis); Sugartree, University. Home: 14 Clermont Lane St Louis MO 63124 Office: 1034 S Brentwood Blvd St Louis MO 63117

WERNER, CHARLES GEORGE, editorial cartoonist; b. Marshfield, Wis., Mar. 23, 1909; s. George J. and Marie (Tippelt) W.; student Oklahoma City U., Northwestern U.; m. Eloise R. Werner, Oct. 5, 1935; children—David, Jean Louise, Stephen. Artist, photographer, Springfield, Mo., 1930-35; art dept., editorial cartoonist Daily Oklahoman, Oklahoma City, 1936-41; chief editorial cartoonist Chgo. Sun, 1941-47; editorial cartoonist Indpls. Star, 1947—. Mem. Ind. Natural Resources Commn. Recipient Pulitzer prize for cartoons, 1938; 1st place award Sigma Delta Chi, 1943, Nat. Headliners Club, 1951, Nat. Found. Hwy. Safety, 1965. Mem. Assn. Am. Editorial Cartoonists, N.Y. Cartoonists Soc. Republican. Episcopalian. Clubs: Hillcrest Country, Indpls. Athletic, Shriners. Home: 4445 Brown Rd Indianapolis IN 46226 Office: Indianapolis Star Indianapolis IN 46204

WERNER, CHRISTIAN THOR, engr.; b. Chgo., Mar. 25, 1916; s. Thor Christian and Anna Hedvig (Engstrom) Rothstein; B.S. in Aero. Engring., Aero. U., Chgo., 1937; m. Barbara Ruth Schneck, July 20, 1957; 1 dau., Diane Werner Zink. Aero. engr. Boeing Aircraft Co., Seattle, 1938-43; aerodynamicist Republic Aviation Corp.,

Farmingdale, N.Y., 1944-46, sr. aerodynamicist, 1946-48; contract aerodynamics cons. Naval Air Devel. Center, Johnsville, Pa., 1949-50; systems engr. Bendix Missile Systems Div., Mishawaka, Ind., 1951-57, sr. sytems engr., 1958-67; sr. mech. engr. Sparton Electronics Div., Jackson, Mich., 1968—, prin. mech. engr., 1969—, mgr. fluid mechanics analysis and design lab., 1970-71, staff engr., 1972—; instr. Swedish, Jackson Community Coll., 1976—. Fellow Am. Inst. Aeros. and Astronautics (asso.); mem. Am. Def. Preparedness Assn., Engrs. Club St. Joseph Valley. Home: 313 Tecumseh St Brooklyn MI 49230 Office: Sparton Electronics Div 2400 E Ganson St Jackson MI 49202

WERNER, ELMER LOUIS, JR., ins. co. exec.; b. St. Louis, Nov. 21, 1927; s. Elmer Louis and Helen M. (Kready) W.; A.B., Princeton U., 1948; B.S., Washington U., St. Louis, 1950, LL.B., 1952, J.D., 1952; m. Sandra M. Johnston, Dec. 3, 1966; children—Louis, Eric, Matthew. Admitted to Mo. bar, 1952, U.S. Ct. Mil. Appeals bar, 1963, U.S. Supreme Ct. bar, 1963; asst. v.p. Insurers Service Corp., St. Louis, 1955-59, v.p., gen. counsel, 1959-76, chmn. bd., 1976—; asst. sec. Safety Mut. Casualty Corp., St. Louis, 1955-59, sec.-treas., gen. counsel, 1959-76, exec. v.p., gen. counsel, 1976—. Bd. dirs. Playgoers of St. Louis, Inc., Better Bus. Bur., St. Louis, Asso. Industries of Mo. Served with JAGC, U.S. Army, 1952-55; ret. col. USAR. Mem. Am. Soc. Charter Property Casualty Underwriters (dir.), Res. Officers Assn. (dir.), Fed. (dir.), Mo. (dir.), St. Louis (dir.) bar assns., Nat. Assn. Safety, Claims Orgns. (dir.), Asso. Industries Mo. Presbyterian. Clubs: Mo. Athletic, St. Louis, Forest Hills Country, Ambassadors. Home: 7 Barclay Woods Dr Saint Louis MO 63124 Office: Univ Club Tower 1034 S Brentwood Blvd Saint Louis MO 63117

WERNER, JOHN CLIFFORD, mfg. co. exec.; b. Jamestown, N.D., July 9, 1920; s. Fern C. and Bessie C. (Nord) W.; A.A., Santa Monica City Coll., 1941; m. Persis V. Hite, Oct. 18, 1947; children—William J., Wendy P. Production control mgr. Cherry Rivet Co., Los Angeles, 1947-51; supr. tool and production control Bendix Aviation Corp., North Hollywood, Calif., 1951-58; tooling mgr. Cannon Electric Co., Los Angeles, 1959-61; facilities mgr. Martin Marietta Corp., Vandenberg AFB, Calif., 1961-65; production control mgr. Jostens, Inc., Attleboro, Mass., 1965-67; dir. indsl. ops. Performance Tech. Corp., Los Angeles, 1967-70; corporate staff cons. Sunstrand Corp., Rockford, Ill., 1970—; cons. ops. mgmt., cost accounting. Cons. Ill. Gov.'s Commn. on Schs., 1972. Served with USAF, 1942-45; to maj. Res., ret., 1970. Decorated Air medal; certified comml. and multi-engine pilot, USAF, Dept. Transp. Mem. Am. Inst. Indsl. Engrs. (sr. certification, past chpt. dir.), Indsl. Mgmt. Soc., Exptl. Aircraft Assn., Am. Ex-Prisoners of War. Author: Administrative Value Analysis Implementation Program, 1973; Operations Control for Productivity Improvement, 1976; Administrative Planning and Training (APT) Program, 1976; Zero Base Budgeting for Production Oriented Industry, 1977; contbr. Dept. Def. Program Management Criteria, 1967. Home: 4906 Braewild Rd Rockford IL 61107 Office: 4751 Harrison Ave Rockford IL 61101

WERNER, PETER JULIUS, mining co. exec.; b. Milw., July 27, 1925; s. Peter Julius and Helen Katherine (Sobczak) W.; B.S., Marquette U., 1949; postgrad. U. Calif. at Los Angeles, 1956; grad. Stanford Exec. Program, 1970; m. Tomasina Louise Smith, June 11, 1972; children from previous marriage—Kevin Morgan, Kerry Jo; stepchildren—Julia Melinda, Eric Randolph. Sales engr. Westinghouse Electric Corp., East Pittsburgh, Pa., 1947-51; apparatus specialist Westinghouse Electric Supply Co., Sacramento, 1951-52; asso. engr. A.V. Norberg Cons. Elec. Engr., Sacramento, 1952; prodn. mgr. A. Teichert & Son, Inc., Sacramento, 1952-73; v.p. Oak Creek Developers, Inc., Sacramento, 1969-70, France Stone Co., Toledo, Ohio, 1973—. Served with USAAF, 1944-45. Registered profl. engr., Calif. Mem. Nat. Sand and Gravel Assn. (mem. engr. and research com. 1968-73). Republican. Presbyn. Rotarian. Patentee in field. Home: 5504 Radcliffe Rd Sylvania OH 43560 Office: PO Box 1928 Toledo OH 43603

WERRELL, TERRY SHERMAN, mfg. engr.; b. Janesville, Wis., Mar. 5, 1936; s. Daniel and Vivian Virginia (Sherman) W.; m. Sandra Ethel Samuelson, July 6, 1957; children—Daniel David, Diana Dawn, Linda Louise, Pamela Leigh. Process engr. Fisher Body Co., Janesville, Wis., 1959-65; process Engr., Fisher Body div. Gen. Motors Corp., Lordstown, Ohio, 1965, sr. prodn. engr., 1966-70, maintenance shift supt., 1970-71, Gen. Motors Assembly div., 1971-72, maintenance supt. Vega plant, 1972-74, Vega and Van plants, 1974-76; dir. facilities and processing DeLorean Motor Co., Bloomfield Hills, Mich., 1976—; cons. in field. Mem. Gen. Mototrs Alumni Assn. Lutheran. Mason. Home: 723 Foxhall Rd Bloomfield Hills MI 48013 Office: PO Box 427 Bloomfield Hills MI 48013

WERT, ALICE LEOLA HECK (MRS. WILLIAM GRAU WERT), librarian; b. Monroe, Mich., Mar. 29, 1922; d. Edward Godfrey and Winifred Marie (Knisely) Heck; B.S., Eastern Mich. U., 1943; M.A. in L.S., U. Mich., 1949; m. William Grau Wert, June 24, 1944; children—Thomas Grau, Barbara Lynn, William Paul. Tchr. Denton (Mich.) elementary sch., 1943-44, Fairfield Sch., Baton Rouge, 1944-45; librarian USAAF Post Library, Avenger Field, Tex., 1945, Willow Run (Mich.) Pub. Sch. Library, 1945-48, 52-53; city librarian, Bellaire, Tex., 1955-58; elementary sch. librarian Vigo County Sch. Corp., Terre Haute, Ind., 1961-63, 64-66; library supr. Inst. Material Center, 1966-67, 69-72, acting coordinator, 1967-68; librarian Univ. Elementary Sch. Ind. U., Bloomington, 1963-64; adminstrv. asst. Higher Edn. Act Inst., Purdue U., Lafayette, Ind., 1968-69; reference librarian Vigo County Pub. Library, Terre Haute, 1972-74, coordinator tech. processing, 1974—. Chmn., Gov.'s Conf. on Libraries and Info. Services for Ind., 1978. Mem. Ind. Sch. Librarians Assn. (1st v.p. 1969-70, pres. 1970-71), Ind. Library Assn., Audio Visual Dirs. Ind., Delta Kappa Gamma. Presbyn. Contbr. articles to profl. jours. Home: 406 S Brown Ave Terre Haute IN 47803 Office: 222 N 7th St Terre Haute IN 47807

WERT, WILLIAM GRAU, educator; b. Cin., Mar. 11, 1921; s. Horace N. and Lottie (Grau) W.; student Eastern Ky. U., 1941-42; B.S., Eastern Mich. U., 1949; M.S., U. Mich., 1951; postgrad. Ohio State U. (NSF grantee), 1958-59; postgrad. Purdue U., 1968-69, Ed.S., 1970, B.S.C.S., Inst. for Supervising Tchrs., Wayne State U., 1969; m. Alice Leola Heck, June 24, 1944; children—Thomas Grau, Barbara Lynn, William Paul. Tchr., Willow Run, Mich., 1951-52; supr. tng. Willow Run Bomber Plant, 1952-53; agt. Met. Life Ins. Co., Houston, 1953-55; high sch. tchr., Pasadena, Tex., 1955-60; prof. biology Ind. State U., Terre Haute, 1960—. Bd. dirs. Wabash Valley Sci. Fair, 1968. Served with USAAF, 1943-46. Mem. Am. Assn. U. Profs. (local pres. 1962-63), Am. Inst. Biol. Sci., Nat. Sci. Tchrs. Assn., Ind. Acad. Sci., Audubon Soc., Nat. Assn. Biology Tchrs. Contbr. to Readings in Science Education (Hans Andersen), 1969. Home: 406 S Brown Ave Terre Haute IN 47803

WERTH, CARL HENRY, SR., machine tool mfg. exec.; b. Saginaw, Mich., Oct. 31, 1908; s. Charles Henry and Harriet Lowe (Bennett) W.; m. Ruth Marie Roosa, Mar. 22, 1929; children—Billie, Carl Henry, Rodney, Susan. Coremaker, Chevrolet Foundry, 1925-36; design engr. Baker Perkins Co., 1936-41; chief engr. Chapman Machine Co., 1941-45, Hoern & Dilts, Inc., Saginaw, Mich., 1945-55; chief engr. Bridgeport (Mich.) div. New Britain Co., 1955-60; founder mgr. Werth Engring. Inc., Bridgeport, 1960-78, pres., 1978—. Mem. Nat. Roster Sci. and Specialized Personnel, 1942—. Republican. Baptist. Clubs: Germania (Saginaw); Judson Coll. Pres. (Elgin, Ill.). Patentee various machines and tools. Home: 818 Thurman St Saginaw MI 48602 Office: 4480 Marlea Dr Bridgeprot MI 48722

WERTH, RICHARD GEORGE, educator; b. Markesan, Wis., Feb. 5, 1920; s. George William and Lillie (Luethe) W.; B.A., Wartburg Coll., 1942; M.S., U. Wis., 1948, Ph.D., 1950; m. Wilma Margaret Lauer, June 2, 1943; 1 son, Gerald Richard. Jr. chemist E.I. duPont de Nemours & Co., Niagara Falls, N.Y., 1942-44, 46; prof. chemistry Concordia Coll., Moorhead, Minn., 1950—, chmn. dept., 1961-69, 74-77; vis. fellow Cornell U., Ithaca, N.Y., 1970-71. Served with USNR, 1944-46. Fellow A.A.A.S., Am. Inst. Chemists; mem. Am. Chem. Soc. (councilor 1964—, com. on chem. edn. 1971-76), Midwest Assn. Chemistry Tchrs. in Liberal Arts Colls., Soc. Applied Spectroscopy, Minn., N.D. acads. sci., Am. Radio Relay League, Sigma Xi, Phi Lambda Upsilon. Home: 1207 S 7th St Moorhead MN 56560 Office: Dept Chemistry Concordia College Moorhead MN 56560

WERTHEIMER, FREDERICK WILLIAM, dentist, educator; b. Saginaw, Mich., May 21, 1925; s. Frederick and Hazel (Sanor) W.; D.D.S., U. Mich., 1949; M.S.D., Northwestern U., 1954; M.S., Georgetown U., 1960; m. Marjorie Ruth Spence, Oct. 19, 1956; children—David, Karen, Eric. Individual practice dentistry, Lansing, Mich., 1952-53, in periodontics, Lansing, 1954-58; resident oral pathology NIH, Bethesda, Md., 1958-60; sr. asso. dentistry Henry Ford Hosp., Detroit, 1962-68; prof., chmn. dept. pathology U. Detroit Dental Sch., 1968—; adj. asso. prof. dept. pathology Wayne State U. Sch. Medicine. Cons. oral pathology VA Hosp., Allen Park, Mich., 1968—, also Detroit Gen. Hosp. Served to lt. Dental Corps., USNR, 1949-52. Decorated UN, Korean service ribbons. Diplomate Am. Bd. Periodontology, Am. Bd. Oral Pathology. Fellow Am. Coll. Dentists, Internat. Coll. Dentists, A.A.A.S., Am. Acad. Oral Pathology; mem. Am. Dental Assn., Mich. Soc. Periodontists (pres. 1971—), Am. Acad. Periodontology, Internat. Assn. Dental Research, Mich. Soc. Pathologists, Sigma Xi. Contbr. articles to jours. Home: 28976 Kendallwood Dr Farmington Hills MI 48018 Office: 2985 E Jefferson St Detroit MI 48207

WERTZ, KENNETH EUGENE, tool and die co. exec.; b. Wooster, Ohio, Dec. 7, 1930; s. Earl O. and Glenna M. Siegfried W.; B.S. in Bus. Adminstrn., Kent (Ohio) State U., 1952, M.B.A., 1968; m. Nancy Ann Barton, Aug. 3, 1957; 1 son, Eric. Accountant Colonial Machine Co., Kent, 1949-52, sec.-treas., 1952-61, pres., 1961—. Divisional chmn. Portage County United Fund, 1974. C.P.A., Ohio Mem. Ohio Socs. C.P.A.'s, Am. Inst. C.P.A.'s, Portage County Personnel Mgrs. (pres. 1974), Kent Area C. of C., Delta Sigma Pi, Beta Alpha Psi, Beta Gamma Sigma. Methodist (ofcl. bd.). Rotarian (pres. Kent 1973-74). Home: 3529 Dayton Ave Kent OH 44240 Office: Colonial Machine Co Mogadore and Cherry Sts Kent OH 44240

WERTZ, ROBERT ARTHUR, dentist; b. Chgo., Apr. 9, 1931; s. Frank Arthur and Bernice (Burke) W.; D.D.S., U. Ill., 1955, M.S., 1966; m. Eleanor Hensley, July 27, 1957; children—Carrie, Robert H., Martha, Joseph, Stephen, David. Resident in orthodontics U. Ill., Chgo., 1959; individual practice orthodontics, Kankakee, Ill., 1959—. Lectr. in orthodontics U. Ill., 1964—. Served to capt., USAF, 1955-57. Diplomate Am. Bd. Orthodontics. Mem. Edward H. Angle Soc., Ill. Soc. Orthodontists (past pres.), Am. Dental Assn., Am. Assn. Orthodontists, Found. for Orthodontic Research, Ill. Orthodontic Alumni Assn. (pres.), Sigma Xi, Delta Sigma Delta, Omicron Kappa Upsilon. Clubs: Kankakee Country, Olympia Fields (Ill.) Country. Research involving orthopedic effects of orthodontic treatment and nasal respiratory changes incident to rapid maxillary expansion, also skeletal effects of midpalatal suture opening. Home: 877 S Chgo Ave Kankakee IL 60901 Office: 401 S Dearborn Ave Kankakee IL 60901

WESCOTT, PHILIP CHARLES, brake mfg. co. exec.; b. Pitts., Oct. 28, 1943; s. Louis S. and Genevieve T. (Flynn) W.; B.A., Wabash Coll., 1965; M.A., Ind. U., 1970; m. Carol Lee Hocker, June 11, 1966; children—Kimberly, Kristen, Philip C. Field pub. relations Gen. Motors Corp., New Eng. States and N.Y., 1965-66; grad. asst. Ind. U., Bloomington, 1969-70; mgr. advt. and promotion Mead Johnson Labs., Evansville, Ind., 1970-73; account supr. Rumrill-Hoyt Advt. Agency, Rochester, N.Y., and Manhattan, N.Y., 1973-74; v.p. adminstrn. Hooker Power Brake Co., Evansville, Ind., 1974—; lectr. in field. Served with Adj. Gen.'s Corp, U.S. Army, 1966-69. Mem. Res. Officers Assn. U.S., Automotive Wholesalers Inst., Sigma Delta Chi (v.p. chpt. 1974-76). Roman Catholic. Clubs: Central Turners, Evansville Kennel, Optimists, Toastmasters Internat. Home: Rural Route 1 POB 603 Newburgh IN 47630 Office: POB 117 Evansville IN 47701

WESENBERG, JOHN HERMAN, assn. exec.; b. Davenport, Iowa, Jan. 16, 1927; s. Herman B. and Nell (Watterson) W.; student Iowa State U., 1944-45, 47, Amherst Coll., 1946; B.A., U. Iowa, 1951, M.A., 1952; postgrad. Northwestern U., 1952-55, Mich. State U., 1956-67; m. Alice Jane McMahill, Sept. 10, 1949; children—Anne, John, Sue James. Research asso. Bur. Bus. and Econ. Research, U. Iowa, 1949-52; asst. mgr. Danville (Ill.) C. of C., 1952-54; exec. v.p. Belleville (Ill.) C. of C., 1954-57; sec. Retail Mchts. and Central Bus. Dist. Bur., Des Moines, 1957-62; exec. v.p. Greater Des Moines C. of C., 1963—, sec. Greater Des Moines Com., 1963—. Lectr., Inst. for Orgn. Mgmt., Mich. State U., 1959-67, 69-70, mem. bd. regents, 1962-67, chmn. bd. regents, 1965-66; co-chmn. Mail Users Council, Des Moines, 1963-67; lectr. U. Colo., 1970, 75, Tex. Christian U., 1971, Syracuse U., 1971, U. Ga., 1973, Del. U., 1973-76, Mills Coll., 1976, So. Meth. U., 1975-76. Sec., Greater Des Moines Devel. Corp., 1963—, Des Moines Industries Trustees, 1963—, Baseball, Inc., 1963—, Community Improvement, Inc., 1970—, Greater Des Moines Community Found., 1970—, Greater Des Moines, Inc., 1973—; treas. Greater Des Moines Shippers Assn., 1972—; trustee Fringe Benefit, Inc. Mem. Iowa adv. council SBA, 1973—. Bd. dirs. YMCA, 1974-76, Iowa State Fair, 1977—; bd. regents Inst. Orgn. Mgmt., U. Colo., 1977—. Served with USAAF, 1944-46. Mem. Am. C. of C. Execs. (dir. 1965-68, v.p. 1968-69, pres.-elect 1970-71, pres. 1971-72), Iowa C. of C. Execs. (dir. 1960-66, pres. 1964, v.p. 1963), Am. Retail Assn. Execs. (dir. 1961-67), So. div. Ill. Mfrs. Assn. (exec. com. 1955-57), St. Louis Indsl. Council (v.p. 1957), Am. Arbitration Assn., Nat. Assn. Housing and Redevel. Ofcls., Internat. Downtown Exec. Assn., Iowa Bd. Internat. Edn., Beta Theta Pi (gen. sec., trustee 1974—). Clubs: Des Moines, Wakonda Country. Home: 1169 Columbine Ct Norwalk IA 50211 Office: 800 High St Des Moines IA 50307

WESLEY, GLORIA MAY WALKER (MRS. CLEO WESLEY), social worker; b. Rochester, N.Y., May 21, 1928; d. Spencer Malcolm and Blossom (Pye) Walker; B.A., Fisk U., 1950; M.S.W., Loyola U., 1959; m. Cleo Wesley, Feb. 11, 1961; children—Eric Jerome, Lia Cherise. Girls counselor Lake County Children's Home, Gary, Ind., 1952-53; social worker Lake County Dept. Pub. Welfare, Child Placement and Family Service, 1953-60, Schs. City Gary, 1960-70, 74-77; coordinator out patient services Gary Community Health Center, 1977—; Lake County Assn. Retarded Children, 1963; Norman Beatty Hosp., Westville, Ind., 1964, Lake County Mental Health Clinic, Gary, 1965; pvt. practice social work, Gary, 1962—, coordinator social services and day care Gary Income Maintenance Experiment, Ind. U. N.W., Gary, 1970-74; prof. social work Valparaiso U., 1970—, fieldwork supr. undergrad. students in social work Valparaiso U., 1963-70; interim dir. Campbell Friendship House, 1969; social work cons. Planned Parenthood Assn. N.W. Ind., 1969-70; cons. Green's Geriatric Health Center, Gary, 1964—; cons., resource person Maternal and Child Health Project for Model Cities program Gary, 1968-69. With Semanon Civic and Social Clubs, Gary, 1960-68, treas., 1965-66; pres. County and Municipal Employees, Gary, 1956-58; sponsor St. Timothy Community Chs. Youth Usher Bd., 1963-66, sponsor children and youth choirs, 1971—; adv. bd. Green's Geriatric Health Center, 1967—, Hidden Talent Search, 1971—, Urban League N.W. Ind., 1972; bd. dirs. Campbell Friendship House, 1969-73; adv. council Sch. City Gary Presch. Handicapped Children, 1971—; bd. dirs. Gary Neighborhood Services, 1971-75; bd. dirs., treas. Gary Community Mental Health Center, 1974—; v.p. Tots and Teens, 1971—; adv. bd. div. gen. and tech. services Ind. U. N.W., 1971-74, adv. bd. spl. services, 1972-75. Mem. Nat. Assn. Social Workers (chmn. nominating com. 1967-68, budget com. 1968-69), Internat. Tri-State assns. pupil personnel workers, Ind. State Conf. Social Welfare (program chmn. 1964-65, membership chmn. 1963-64). Home: 3373 W 20th Pl Gary IN 46404 Office: 610 E 10th Pl Gary IN 46402

WESLEY, THEODORE PERRY, newspaper editor; b. Casey County, Ky., June 29, 1905; s. Enoch Arden and Lillie (De Bord) W.; student Western Ky. State Tchrs. Coll., 1926-27, U. Mich., 1928; m. Aline Powers, June 2, 1928 (dec. Aug. 1959); 1 dau., Betty Joanne (Mrs. Raymond Dale Blunk); m. 2d, Helen Cato Emerson, Oct. 21, 1960. Radio singer WHAS, WLAP, Louisville, WFDF, Flint, Mich., 1926-27; editor Seymour (Ind.) Tribune, 1930-43, Nat. Rural Letter Carrier Mag., Washington, 1943-45, Bicknell (Ind.) News, 1945-48; editor, publisher Spencer (Ind.) World, 1948-60, editor, 1960—. Spl. agt. U.S. Treasury Dept., 1928-29. Mem. Ind. Mental Health Adv. Council; mem. Gov.'s Com. to study and revise Ind. Mental Health Laws, 1973—; chmn. adv. bd. Bloomington (Ind.) Hosp., 1973-75, bd. dirs., 1975—. Mem. Ind. State Democratic Platform Com., 1956, 58, 60, 62, 64, sec., 1964. Mem. Ind. Dem. Editorial Assn. (past pres.), Spencer C. of C. (dir., 1959-60). Methodist. Clubs: Elks, Lions (dist. gov. Ind. 1948-49); Indianapolis Press. Advt. mgr. Hoosier Ann., 1962, 63. Home: 680 E North St Spencer IN 47460 Office: care Spencer World Spencer IN 47460

WESLOH, FERDINAND JOSEPH, priest, ednl. adminstr.; b. St. Louis, Dec. 23, 1938; s. Ferdinand Joseph and Theresa Catherine (Wohlschlaeger) W.; A.B., Cardinal Glennon Coll., 1960; M.Ed., St. Louis U., 1967. Ordained priest Roman Catholic Ch., 1964; guidance dir. Duchesne High Sch., St. Charles, Mo., 1966-74, Mercy High Sch., University City, Mo., 1974-77; adminstr. St. John's High Sch., St. Louis, 1977—; asso. pastor St. Peter Ch., St. Charles, 1964-74, St. Clement Ch., Des Peres, Mo., 1974-77, St. John's Ch., St. Louis, 1977—. Mem. Am., Mo. personnel and guidance assns., Nat. Cath. Guidance Conf. (bd. dirs. 1973-77, sec. 1977-78), St. Louis Cath. Guidance Conf. Clubs: K.C. (chaplain Mo. 1972-74, scholarship and loan chmn. Mo., 1976-78). Editor Nat. Cath. Guidance Newsletter 1973-76. Home: 4200 Delor St Saint Louis MO 63116 Office: 5021 Adkins St Saint Louis MO 63116

WESOLEK, JOHN STEVEN, vocat. rehab. dir.; b. Stevens Point, Wis., June 9, 1945; s. Stephen Joseph and Rose (Kluz) W.; B.S. in Indsl. Tech., U. Wis., 1967, M.S. in Vocat. Rehab., 1968; m. Deborah Joy Douglas, July 26, 1969; children—Brant John, Mark Douglas, Pamela Joy. Instr., evaluator, Coop. Sch. Rehab. Center, Minnetonka, Minn., 1968-69; vocat. evaluator, Evaluation Tng. Center, U. Wis., Menomonie, 1969-71, dir. Evaluation Tng. Center, 1971-73, dir. Vocat. Devel. Center, 1973—; mem. advisory bd. Goal Program, Wis. Indianhead Tech. Inst.; regional tech. cons. Rehab. Service Adminstrn., Chgo. Mem. Nat., Wis. (v.p.) assns. rehab., Vocat. Evaluation Work Adjustment Assn. Home: 604 Sunset Dr Menomonie WI 54751

WESOLOWSKI, STANLEY PETER, physician; b. Warwick, N.Y., Dec. 30, 1914; s. John Paul and Mary Ann (Zagorski) W.; B.S., Fordham U., 1938; M.D., Stritch Sch. Medicine, 1942; m. Ruth E. Swenson, Apr. 8, 1946; children—Patricia Wesolowski Casey, Theresa, Jeanne Wesolowski Darsie, Mary Wesolowski Grebinowski, John, Anne. Intern, St. Francis Hosp., Jersey City, 1942-43; fellow, resident anesthesiology U. Minn., 1946-47; practice medicine, specializing in anesthesiology, Mpls., 1947—; clin. instr. anesthesiology U. Minn. Hosp., 1947-54; chief dept. anesthesiology St. Marys Hosp., 1947-71. Served to capt., M.C., AUS, 1943-46; ETO. Decorated Silver Star medal, D.S.C. Mem. Am. Soc. Anesthesiology, A.M.A., Internat. Anesthesia Research Soc., Minn. Med. Assn., Hennepin County Med. Soc. Roman Catholic. Home: 999 S Fairview Ave St Paul MN 55116 Office: 606 24th Ave S Minneapolis MN 55454

WESSEL, GILBERT ROLAND, obstetrician, gynecologist; b. Ft. Dodge, Iowa, Apr. 25, 1937; s. Roland Henry and Edna Louise (Folkerts) W.; B.A., Wartburg Coll., 1959; M.D., U. Iowa, 1963; m. Mary Alice Reiff, June 23, 1963; children—Susan Ann, James Edward. Intern Hurley Hosp., Flint, Mich., 1963-64; resident in obstetrics and gynecology U. Iowa, Iowa City, 1964-67; individual practice medicine, specializing in obstetrics and gynecology Menasha, Wis., 1969-72, Cedar Rapids, Iowa, 1972—; asso. Riverside Clinic, Menasha, 1969-72; partner Ob-Gyn Assos., Cedar Rapids, 1972—, sec., 1973—; lectr. in field; staff St. Luke's-Mercy Hosp., Cedar Rapids. Served to capt., USAF, 1967-69. Fellow Am. Coll. Obstetricians and Gynecologists; mem. AMA, Iowa, Linn County med. socs., Iowa Alumni Obstet.—Gynecol. Soc. (exec. com. 1976—). Lutheran. Club: Cedar Rapids Country. Home: Rural Route 3 Cedar Rapids IA 52401 Office: 1030 5th Ave SE Cedar Rapids IA 52403

WESSELS, ARDWIN GILBERT, bus. services co. exec.; b. Clinton, Iowa, Mar. 20, 1933; s. Joseph Bernard and Anna Mary (Dettermann) W.; student pub. schs., Beloit, Wis.; m. Joyce Mary Poupart, Oct. 10, 1953; children—Dominic W., Daniel J., David H., Donald M., Denice J., Dennis J., Darrel A. Service technician Addressograph-Multigraph, Rockford, Ill., 1955-61; asst. supr. printing Beloit Corp., 1961-65, supr., 1965-75, mgr. copy services, 1975—. Pres. bd. dirs. Colt League, 1963, 64, Pony League, 1968, Boys Baseball Beloit, 1977. Served with USAF, 1951-55. Mem. Assn. Records Mgmt. and Adminstrs., Word Processing Soc. Am., In-Plant Printing Mgmt. Assn. Roman Catholic. Home: 1733 Avon Ct Beloit WI 53511 Office: 1 Saint Lawrence Ave Beloit WI 53511

WESSLER, WILLIAM ERNEST, clergyman; b. Collinsville, Ill., Jan. 8, 1914; s. William H. and Bertha (Washer) W.; grad. St. Pauls Coll. (Concordia, Mo.), 1934; B.D., Concordia Theol. Sem. (St. Louis), 1938; M.A., Washington U., St. Louis, 1948; m. Gertrude C. Henke, June 16, 1940; children—Judith Karen, William Lynn. Ordained to ministry Lutheran Ch., 1939; founding pastor St. Paul's Luth. Ch., Fairview Heights, Ill., 1939-43, Messiah Luth. Ch., Alton, Ill., 1943-51; pastor Trinity Luth. Ch., Gary, Ind., 1951-61; dir. ch. relations Valparaiso (Ind.) U., 1961-68; asst. dir. dept. pub. relations Lutheran Ch.-Mo. Synod, St. Louis, 1968-70, asso. counselor stewardship dept., 1970—. Chmn. editorial commn. for ofcl.

periodicals Luth. Ch.-Mo. Synod, 1959-69, pres. Council Luth. Ministries, 1964-68, Calumet Luth. Mission Assn., 1955-60. Pres., Lake County (Ind.) Assn. for Mental Health, 1957-59; mem. bd. Ind. Assn. for Mental Health. Mem. Luth. Acad. for Scholarship. Editor: Calumet Luth., 1949-51; LutheraNews, 1945-51. Home: 3 Kenstone Ct Florissant MO 63033 Office: 500 N Broadway St Louis MO 63102

WESSMAN, COLLEEN PATRICIA, food co. exec.; b. Charleroi, Pa., Oct. 17, 1936; d. Paul and Alexandra (Los) Lapcevic; B.S., Carnegie-Mellon U., 1958; M.S., Harvard U., 1971; m. Clarence Wessman, Oct. 3, 1958; children—Scott, Patrick, Cathy. Therapeutic dietitian Letterman Hosp., San Francisco, 1958-60; dir. food service Castro Valley Sch. Dist., Calif., 1960-62, Youth Devel. Center, Waynesburg, Pa., 1966-69, also instr. of nutrition; dir. food service Thera-Care Corp., Boston, 1969-72; chief dietitian St. Joseph Hosp., Elgin, Ill., 1972-74; mgr. product evaluation Quaker Oats Co. Research Center, Barrington, Ill., 1974—; cons. in nutrition, 1972-75. Den mother N.W. Suburban council Cub Scouts Am., 1972-73; pres. PTA, Ellsworth, Pa., 1967-68. Served with Med. Specialists Corps, U.S. Army, 1958-60. Named Outstanding Young Dietitian, Am. Dietetic Assn., 1961. Mem. Inst. Food Technologists, Am. Assn. Cereal Chemists, Am. Dietetic Assn., ASTM. Roman Catholic. Home: 812 Oceola Dr Algonquin IL 60102 Office: 617 W Main St Barrington IL 60010

WEST, DON EDWIN, wood products mfg. exec.; b. Canton, Ohio, June 10, 1928; s. Forest J. and Grace E. (Latimer) W.; B.A., Mt. Union Coll., 1948; postgrad. William McKinley Sch. Law, 1948-51; m. Louise H. Welsbacher, Aug. 29, 1948; children—Shelly Ann, Don Edwin. With Harter Bank & Trust Co., 1948-52; sales mgr. Republic Steel Kitchens div. Republic Steel Corp., Youngstown, Ohio, 1952-69; v.p. mktg. Yorktowne div. Wickes Corp., Red Lion, Pa., 1969-75; pres. Riviera Products div. Evans Products Co., St. Paul, 1975—. Mem. Nat. Kitchen Cabinet Assn. (bd. dirs.). Home: 127 Birnamwood Dr Burnsville MN 55337 Office: 1960 Seneca Rd Saint Paul MN 55122

WEST, GEORGE RUSSELL, architect; b. Indpls., Mar. 28, 1923; s. Frank B. and Tillie (Miller) W.; B.S. in Architecture, U. Cin., 1949; m. Rita A. Reynolds, Nov. 17, 1951; children—Steven Reynolds, Jonathan Reynolds. With McGuire Shook Corp., architects, engrs., planners, 1941—, v.p., 1963-70, pres., 1970-72, now sec., treas.; with Mid-Am. Devel. Corp. Mem. Nat. Council Archtl. Registration Bds., Bd. Wrecking Contractors Examiners. Served with inf. AUS, 1943-46. Decorated Silver Star. Mem. Ind. Soc. Architects, AIA, Scarab, Delta Phi Delta, Alpha Tau Omega. Club: Optimist (pres. Indpls.). Home: 110 Bayley Circle Noblesville IN 46060 Office: Cranbrook Center 7440 N Shadeland Indianapolis IN 46250

WEST, JAMES EDWARD, counselor; b. Jackson, Miss., Sept. 30, 1934; s. J. Leslie and Cordelia (Moore) W.; B.S., Tougaloo Coll., 1955; M.Ed., U. Mo. St. Louis, 1971; M.S. (Minority fellow), So. Ill. U., 1976; 1 son, James E. Caseworker, Mo. State Dept. Welfare, St. Louis, 1965-66; counselor Mo. State Employment Security, St. Louis, 1966-71; counselor Narcotics Service Council, St. Louis, 1973-74, So. Ill. U., Carbondale, 1976—. Served with USAF, 1955-59. Certified rehab. counselor. Mem. Am. Assn. Sex Educators and Counselors, Assn. Non-White Concerns, Am., St. Louis, Mo., Ill. personnel and guidance assns., Am. Psychol. Assn. (asso.), Nat. Rehab. Assn., Kappa Delta Pi, Alpha Phi Alpha. Home: Gen Delivery Cambria IL 62915 Office: Psychology Dept So Ill U Carbondale IL 62901

WEST, JOSEPH WARREN, physician; b. Binghamton, N.Y., Mar. 6, 1921; s. Norman Luther and Jane Katherine (Dutcher) W.; student St. Petersburg Coll., 1939-40; M.D., Duke, 1944; m. Jane A. McCay, Oct. 13, 1946; children—Louis J., Robert T., Frederick N., Daniel A. Intern Md. Gen. Hosp., Balt., 1944-45; resident Grady Meml. Hosp., Atlanta, 1945-46, Washington U., St. Louis, 1948-51; practice medicine specializing in otorhinolaryngology, St. Louis, 1951—; dir. otolaryngology service Homer G. Phillips Hosp., St. Louis, 1957—; clin. asso. prof. dept. otolaryngology, Washington U., St. Louis, 1967—; dir. dept. otolaryngology St. Louis Labor Health Inst., 1961—; lectr., demonstrator surgery of nose Holland, France, Jugoslavia, Mexico, Chile, Brazil, Honduras, U.S.A. Served in Army splty. tng. program, 1943-44, USAF, 1946-48. Fellow A.C.S.; mem. A.M.A., Mo. State Med. Assn., Am. Acad. Ophthalmology and Otolaryngology, Am. Rhinologic Soc. (pres. 1975-76), Am. Triological Soc., St. Louis Ear, Nose and Throat Club (pres. 1969-70), Internat. Assn. Eye, Ear, Nose and Throat Secs. (pres. 1972-73), Am. Soc. Ophthal. and Otolaryn. Allergy, Kirkwood Physicians and Surgeons, Inc. (pres. 1968-74). Presbyn. (pres. adult social group). Home: 215 N Dickson St Kirkwood MO 63122 Office: 135 W Adams Kirkwood MO 63122

WEST, LLOYD MARVIN, producer, dir., educator; b. McLeansboro, Ill., May 9, 1922; s. Elisha Phillip and Ruth Helen (Wilson) W.; B.F.A., Goodman Theatre, Art Inst. Chgo., 1943, M.F.A., 1947. Actor, dir. Cleve. Play House, 1945-51; dir., producer John B. Rogers Producing Co., U.S. and Can., 1951-55; asso. CBS-TV, Chgo., 1955-59; tchr. speech and theatre City Colls. Chgo., 1959-61, asst. dean Crane Coll., 1961-66, producer, 1966-71, asst. dean Learning Resources Lab. and TV Coll., 1971-73, dean, 1973—; producer series Radio Sta. WIND, 1965-67, Am. Community Coll. series, 1969; exec. producer, narrator Man and His Art, 1970; producer, host The Open Door, Sta. WTTW-TV, 1972-73. Recipient fellowship Art Inst. Chgo., 1943. Mem. Nat. Assn. Ednl. Broadcasters, Speech Assn. Am., AFTRA, Nat. Acad. Arts and Scis., Am. Nat. Theatre Assn., Nat. Acad. TV Arts and Scis. (bd. govs.), Ill. Speech Assn. Author: Effective Communications, 1968. Home: 4863 W Gregory St Chicago IL 60630 Office: 3400 N Austin Ave Chicago IL 60634

WEST, NORMAN DUDLEY, psychiatrist; b. Avoca, Iowa, July 24, 1918; s. Grant Durfee and Lulu Marie (Pittman) W.; B.S. in Medicine, Creighton U., 1940, M.D., 1943; m. Virginia Irene Hall, Aug. 5, 1955; children—Allen M., Roger D., Robert J. Intern, Northwestern Hosp., Mpls., 1943; gen. practice medicine, Avoca, 1946-65; resident Nebr. Psychiat. Inst., Omaha, 1965-68, staff psychiatrist, 1968—, chief liaison service, 1971—. Served to maj. AUS, 1944-46. Diplomate Am. Bd. Neurology and Psychiatry. Fellow Am. Psychiat. Assn.; mem. A.M.A. (recognition award, 1972). Mason. Clubs: Community, Quarterback (Avoca). Contbr. to profl. jours. Home: 110 E Taylor St Avoca IA 51521 Office: 602 S 45th St Omaha NE 68106

WEST, RICHARD IRVING, financial exec.; b. Racine, Wis., Feb. 10, 1929; s. Byron S. and Ruth (Wilson) W.; B.S., Wis. State U., 1957; M.B.A., Northwestern U., 1966; m. Virginia M. Hansen, Mar. 16, 1957; children—Ruth Ellen, Sharon Marie, David Richard, Benjamin Thomas. Asst. to dir. finance Ill. Agrl. Assn., Chgo., 1957-60; asst. v.p. Chgo. Med. Sch., 1960-63; treas., bus. mgr. George Williams Coll., Downers Grove, Ill., 1963-70; controller Mayer, Brown & Platt, Chgo., 1970—. Served with AUS, 1946-49, USAAF, 1950-51. Mem. Downers Grove C. of C. (dir.), Northwestern U. Grad. Bus. Assn. Home: 826 Birch St Downers Grove IL 60515 Office: 231 S La Salle St Chicago IL 60604

WEST, ROBERT PATTON, orthodontist; b. St. Louis, Feb. 2, 1944; s. Robert Vincel and Naomi Lucille (Patton) W.; student U. Kansas City, 1962-64; D.D.S., U. Mo., 1968; M.S., U. W. Va., 1973; m. Sally L. Blitch, 1973. Pvt. practice gen. dentistry, Windsor, Mo., 1970; resident orthodontics W.Va. U., 1971-73; pvt. practice dentistry specializing in orthodontics, Independence, Mo., 1973—. Instr. clin. dentistry U. Mo. Sch. Dentistry, Kansas City, 1970-71. Counselor, Y-Pals program, Kansas City, Mo., 1971; mem. Kansas City Crime Commn., 1975—. Served with AUS, 1968-70. Decorated Army Commendation medal. Mem. Am., Mo. dental assns., Greater Kansas City Dental Soc., Am. Assn. Orthodontists, Midwest Soc. Orthodontists, Psi Omega. Methodist (mem. M.Y.F. council western Mo. conf. 1961). Club: Lions. Home: 314 Locust Lee's Summit MO 64063 Office: 13905 E 39th St Independence MO 64055

WEST, SAM, refrigeration co. exec.; b. Glen Ullen, N.D., Jan. 6, 1916; s. Avedis M. and Jessie (Harris) W.; A.B., State Tchrs. Coll., Mayville, N.D., 1938; M.C.S., Tuck Sch. of Dartmouth, 1947; grad. econ mblzn. course Indsl. Coll. Armed Forces, 1953; m. Ruth Driskill, Aug. 27, 1948; children—Gay Anne West Trottier, Sara Elizabeth West Azarnia, Linda Lee. Instr. comml. subjects schs., McIntosh, Minn., 1938-40, Wadena, Minn., 1941; with Tyler Refrigeration Corp., Niles, Mich., 1947-55, asst. sales mgr., 1955-70, dir. mktg., 1971-76; pres. Tyler Refrigeration Internat., 1977—. Served with USAAF, 1941-45; CBI. Mem. Kappa Sigma. Republican. Presbyterian. Club: Lions. Home: 532 Cedar St Niles MI 49120 Office: 1329 Lake St Niles MI 49120

WEST, SANDRA ARLINE, city ofcl.; b. Detroit, Sept. 15, 1940; d. Walter Ernest and Arlie (Thomas) W.; B.J. (David Wilkie scholar, Inez Robb scholar), Wayne State U., 1963. Classified ad writer Detroit Free Press, 1963-66; feature writer Gary (Ind.) Post-Tribune, 1966; reporter UPI, Detroit, 1966-67; publicist City Detroit Pub. Info. Dept., 1967-73, supervising publicist, 1973—. Mem. Mayor's Com. to keep Detroit Beautiful, 1968—; pub. relations rep. Detroit Hist. Soc., 1968-70. Mem. Women in Communications, Assn. Municipal Profl. Women, Wayne State Alumni, Detroit Women's Econ. Club, Women of Wayne. Episcopalian. Home: 930 E Lafayette Apt 301 Detroit MI 48207 Office: 608 City County Bldg Detroit MI 48226

WEST, WALTER SCOTT, econ. geologist; b. Fayette, Wis., Mar. 12, 1912; s. Frank Edgar and Margaret (Scott) W.; A.B., Cornell Coll., 1934; B.E., Wis. State U., 1935; postgrad. Wis. Inst. Tech., 1935-36; M.S., U. Tenn., 1937; postgrad. U. Iowa, 1938-39, (fellow) U. N.C., 1939-40; m. Dorothy Janet Block, Aug. 30, 1940; children—Walter Scott, Janet Margaret, George LaVergne. Prin. high. sch., Wakenda, Mo., 1937-38; instr. geology N.C. U., 1940-42; engring. aide, cartographer U.S. Geol. Survey, Washington, 1942-46, geologist Alaskan geology br., 1946-54, geologist, sec. geologic names com., 1954-67, geologist and chief Wis. zinc-lead project Eastern mineral resources br., geologic div., Platteville, 1966—; dir. Citizens Nat. Bank, Darlington, Wis. Bd. dirs. Union Grove Cemetery. Recipient awards D.C. Recreation Dept.; 30-Year Service award U.S. Geol. Survey, 1972. Mem. Am. Inst. Mining Engrs., Arctic Inst. N.Am., Washington Acad. Scis., Washington Geol. Soc., Soc. Econ. Geologists, Inst. Lake Superior Geologists, Tri-State Geol. Soc. Contbr. articles to govt. publs. and profl. jours. Home: 601 E Louisa St Darlington WI 53530 Office: US Geol Survey Gardner Hall U Wis Platteville WI 53818

WEST, WILLIAM FRANCIS, JR., educator; b. Fort Smith, Ark., Dec. 18, 1921; s. William Francis and Medora Dixie (McLaughlin) W.; B.S., U. Ark., 1943; M.A., Northwestern U., 1949; Ph.D., U. Mo., 1964; m. Marian Frances Schueppert, Mar. 24, 1951; children—Laurence Francis, Lisa Ann. Announcer, prodn. mgr. Radio sta. KFPW, Ft. Smith, 1945-46; actor, dir. Clare Tree Maj. Theatrical Prodns., Inc., Crosstown Players, off-Broadway, N.Y.C., 1946-47; instr. Henderson State Coll., Arkadelphia, Ark., 1947-48, Christian Coll., Columbia, Mo., 1950-52; actor, tchr., dir. Stephens Coll., Columbia, 1952-61, chmn. dept. theatre arts, dir. Stephens Playhouse, artistic dir. Okoboji Summer Theater, 1961—. Dir. Trail Playhouse, Toledo, summers 1952-54; vis. prof. U. Wash., Seattle, 1966-67; guest dir. Contemporary Theatre, Seattle, 1967, 72, 74. Served with AUS, 1943-45. Fulbright grantee, U.K., 1949-50. Mem. Am. Theatre Assn. (dir. 1968-70), AAUP, Actors' Equity Assn. Presbyn. Editor Summer Theatre Directory, 1968-71. Home: 200 E Briarwood Lane Columbia MO 65201

WESTBURG, JOHN EDWARD, county ofcl., polit. scientist, pub.; b. Des Moines, Mar. 24, 1918; s. Lawrence Ray and Harriett May (Hewett) W.; B.A., U. S.C., 1949, M.A., 1951; M.F.S., U. So. Calif., 1954, M.A., 1956, Ph.D., 1958; m. Mildred Helen Westaway, Jan. 29, 1933; children—Donna Lee, Martial Racine, Gregory Gaius. With U.S. Civil Service, Washington, and Trinidad, B.W.I., 1940-42; owner Westburg Distbrs., Columbia, S.C., 1950-51; teaching asst. dept. polit. sci. U. So. Calif., 1951-53; research asst. Nev. Legis. Counsel Bur., 1953-56; instr. U. Ala., 1956-57; asso. prof. East Central Okla. State Coll., 1957-58; asso. prof. Pan Am. Coll., 1958-60; exec. sec. San Diego Fedn. Tchrs., 1960-62; prof., dir. div. pub. adminstrn. Bir Zeit Coll., Kingdom of Jordan, 1962-63; asso. prof. St. Ambrose Coll., Davenport, Iowa, 1963-68; acting postmaster, Davenport, 1969; asso. prof. polit. sci. U. Wis.-Platteville, 1969-72, asso. Inst. Pub. Affairs, 1969-72, mng. editor Forum on Pub. Affairs, 1967-72; dir. Legis. Reference Bur., City Milw., 1973-74; pub. John Westburg & Assos., Conesville, Iowa, also Westburg Assos. Pubs., Fennimore, Wis., 1964—. Mem. Citizens Study Com. Poverty, Scott County, Iowa, 1967-68; mem. spl. com. zoning and devel., permanent sec. city records com., project dir. Common Council study Milw. Police Dept., project dir. city recodification project (all Milw.), 1973-74; dir. Grant County (Wis.) Title VII projects, 1974—. State del. Iowa Democratic Party Conv., 1968. Served with AUS, 1942-49; ETO. Author: Public Health Adminstration in Nevada, 1954; North American Mentor Anthology of Poems, 1965; Politics the Queenly Art and the Model Constitution, 1966; Everyman's Life of the Buddha, 1966; An Anthology of Mentor Poetry for the Sixtees, 1966; Milwaukee Historical and Comparative Analysis of Local Court Systems, 1973; The Socio-Political Matrix of the Milwaukee Police Department, 1973. Editor: Classroom Teacher, 1960-62; North Am. Mentor Mag., 1964—; Ambrosian Rev., 1965; General Politics Quar., 1967; World Garden, An Anthology of Poetry (James R. Hurst), 1974; Wilderness and Gardens, An American Lady's Prospect (Margaret L. Been), 1974. Moderator, Ambrosian News Weekly, 1964-68. Home: 1745 Madison Ave Fennimore WI 53818 Office: Grant County Court House Lancaster WI 53813

WESTBURY, JUNE ALWYN (MRS. PETER WILLOUGHBY ALLEN WESTBURY), city ofcl.; b. Hamilton, New Zealand, July 26, 1925; d. Philip William and Doris Myrtle (Halcrow) Cantwell; student Brain's Coll., Auckland, N.Z., 1939-40; m. Peter Willoughby Allen Westbury, Oct. 22, 1949; children—Sheila, Pamela June, Jennifer Doris. Sec., Auckland Savs. Bank (New Zealand), 1941-46, Gt. Am. Ins. Co., Winnipeg, Man., Can., 1948-49, Lowry & Co., ins., Winnipeg, 1949-53; alderman, City of Winnipeg, 1970-71, councillor, 1971—, chmn. health and welfare com., 1971; mem. Winnipeg Police Commn., 1974-76. Sec. Liberal Party of Man., 1968-69; pres. Women's Liberal Fedn. Man., 1969-70; v.p. Liberal Party of Can., 1970-73; mem. Nat. Capital Commn., Ottawa, 1976—. Bd. dirs. Winnipeg Municipal Hosps., 1970—, chmn., 1971-75, vice chmn., 1976—; bd. dirs. Children's Aid Soc., 1972—, Canadian Council Christians and Jews, 1972—; adv. bd. YWCA, 1972—, Age and Opportunity Centers, 1973-77; bd. dirs. Man. Health Orgn., 1973-76. Mem. Internat. Platform Assn. Mem. Anglican Ch. Home: 227 Montgomery Ave Winnipeg MB R3L 1T1 Canada

WESTCOTT, ROBERT FREDERICK, mgmt. cons. co. exec.; b. Detroit, Sept. 22, 1922; s. Edgar C. and Lois G. (Strongman) W.; B.S. in Agr., Mich. State U., 1948; M.B.A., U. Detroit, 1953; children—Mark A., Robert F., Douglas K., Craig M. Cons., Booz Allen & Hamilton, Inc., Chgo., 1955-59; v.p. Spencer Stuart & Assos., Chgo., 1959-66, also dir.; pres. Westcott Assos. Inc., Chgo., 1966—. Served with U.S. Army, 1943-45. Clubs: Union League, Monroe. Office: 135 S LaSalle St Chicago IL 60603

WESTDALE, LEONARD LLOYD, real estate co. exec.; b. near LaGrange, Ind., Aug. 30, 1922; s. Fred and Edith (Loy) W.; B.B.A. with honors, U. Mich., 1948; certified residential broker Nat. Inst. Real Estate Brokers, 1970; m. June Chrisman, May 30, 1942; children—Leonard L., Jr., Candyce (Mrs. Philip Smith), Mark E. Statistician Am. Motors, Grand Rapids, Mich., 1948-53; sales mgmt. Albert Realtors, Grand Rapids, 1953-57; organize, pres. Westdale Co., Grand Rapids, 1958—; pres., chmn. bd. Wolverine Timber Corp., Ala., 1964-73. Pres. Grand Rapids Real Estate Bd., 1971; dir. Nat. Inst. Real Estate Brokers, 1970-76. Active in Jr. Achievement. Served with AUS, 1942-46. Mem. Sales and Mktg. Execs. (pres. 1971-72), Mich. Real Estate Assn. (dir. 1962-72, 77), Real Estate Polit. Action Com. (centurion), Sales and Mktg. Execs. Internat. Home: 300 N Honey Creek Ada MI 49301 Office: 3435 Lake Eastbrook Blvd SE Grand Rapids MI 49506

WESTEN, ANN PATRICIA, social worker; b. Ft. Worth, July 24, 1944; d. John Coleman and Ann Miriam (Storm) Radcliffe; A.B., Webster Coll., St. Louis, 1966; M.Ed. in Counseling Edn., U. Mo., St. Louis, 1971; m. David Edward Westen, Jan. 22, 1971. Social worker St. Louis div. Children's Services, 1966-68, Jewish Center Aged, St. Louis, 1968-71; clin. caseworker St. Louis State Hosp., 1971-72; dir. social service St. Joseph Hosp., Kirkwood, Mo., 1972—; cons. social worker Clayton House, St. Louis, 1973—; social work cons. St. Sophia Geriatric Center, 1974-75; grad. practicum instr. George Warren Brown Sch. Social Work, Washington U., St. Louis, 1972—. Mem. Nat. Assn. Social Workers, Am. Personnel and Guidance Assn., Am. Hosp. Assn. Soc. Hosp. Social Work Dirs., Soc. Hosp. Social Work Dirs. Greater St. Louis, Mo. Assn. Social Welfare. Republican. Roman Catholic. Home: 55 Heather Dr St Louis MO 63123 Office: 525 Couch Ave Kirkwood MO 63122

WESTENBERG, ROBERT WILLIAM, pub. co. exec.; b. Chgo., Mar. 30, 1933; s. William Frederick and Catherine Elizabeth (Lackner) W.; B.A., U. Ill., 1955; m. Carol Mae Godey, May 17, 1933; children—Bruce R., Mark A., Lynn C., Lawrence J. Advt. mgr. All-Pets mag., Fond du Lac, Wis., 1957-60; asst. advt. mgr. Can-Pro Corp., Fond du Lac, 1960-62; sales rep. J & K Printing, Winona, Minn., 1962-63; advt. mgr. David C. Cook Pub. Co., Elgin, Ill., 1963-73; pres. Robert W. Westenberg & Co., Inc., pub. Church Mail Market, 1973—, also Catholic Ch./Sch. Market, 1977—. Free-lance writer, advt. cons. Served as 1st lt. AUS, 1955-57. Recipient Leader award Direct Mail Advt. Assn., 1968, 69, 70, 72, Dartnell Corp. gold medal award for excellence in bus. letter writing, 1969. Mem. Direct Mail Advt. Assn. Author: The Portfolio of Bank Letters, 1974. Home: PO Box 426 Elgin IL 60120 Office: 565 River Bluff Rd Elgin IL 60120

WESTENDORP, FLOYD, physician, educator; b. Jenison, Mich., Mar. 2, 1932; s. John and Bertha (Polma) W.; A.B., Calvin Coll., 1953; M.D., U. Mich., 1957; postgrad U. Minn., 1958-61; m. Clarice Josine Baas, June 11, 1954; children—David, Douglas, Jayne, Jewell. Intern, St. Mary's Hosp., Duluth, Minn., 1957-58; resident Mpls. VA Hosp., U. Minn., 1958-61, founder, dir. adolescent unit Pine Rest Christian Hosp., Grand Rapids, Mich., 1961-69; dir. Ottawa County Community Mental Health Service, 1969-74; prof. psychiatry Mich. State U., East Lansing, 1974—, also dir. grad. edn. Lectr. Hope Coll., Holland, Mich., 1966-74; cons. Bldgett Homes for Children; cons., bd. dirs. Wedgewood Acres Christian Youth Home, Grand Rapids, 1963-69. Mem. Christian Assn. Psychol. Studies (dir. 1967-69), A.M.A., Mich. Med. Assn., Am., Mich., Western Mich. (pres. 1968-69) psychiat. assns., Am., Mich. (pres. 1969-70, dir. 1972-74) socs. for study adolescents, Inst. Religion and Health, Am. Assn. Dirs. Psychiatry Residency Tng. Mem. Christian Reform Ch. (elder 1959-60, 64-67, 71-74). Home: 2645 Capilane Dr Grand Rapids MI 49506 Office: 220 Cherry St SE Grand Rapids MI 49503

WESTENFELDER, GRANT ORVILLE, physician; b. Chgo., Jan. 12, 1940; s. Orville L. and Eleanor Jean (Langley) W.; student U. Mich., 1957-60; B.S., Northwestern U. 1961, M.D., 1964; m. Constance H. Genenz, July 7, 1960; children—Mark, Bruce, Natalie. Intern, Evanston (Ill.) Hosp., 1964-65, now sr. attending physician, resident in internal medicine Northwestern U. McGaw Med. Center, 1965-68, fellow in infectious diseases, 1968-70, mem. infectious diseases sect. Med. Sch., 1970—, asst. prof. clin. medicine Northwestern U., 1974—; sr. attending physician, head div. infectious diseases Glenbrook Hosp., Glenview, Ill. Bd. deacons Trinity Luth. Ch., Evanston, 1970-71. Diplomate Am. Bd. Internal Medicine. Fellow A.C.P., Am. Coll. Chest Physicians; mem. Am. Soc. Microbiology, Am. Fedn. Clin. Research, AMA, Chgo. Soc. Internal Medicine, Alpha Kappa Kappa. Office: 2500 Ridge Ave Evanston IL 60201

WESTERBERG, WESLEY MAGNUS, cons.; b. Taylor, Tex., July 2, 1912; s. Thor Julius and Thyra (Ekedahl) W.; B.A., Northwestern U., 1934; M.Div., Yale, 1938, S.T.M., 1945; D.D., Ill. Wesleyan U., 1962; postgrad. Scandinavian Sch. Theology, Sweden, 1934-35, Drew Theol. Sem., 1935-36; m. Lorraine J. Larson, Jan. 24, 1942; children—Kermit, Kurt, Kristine. Ordained to ministry Methodist Ch., 1932; minister Methodist chs., Ansonla, Conn., 1936-39, Cicero, Ill., 1939-40, Evanston, Ill., 1939-44, Naperville, Ill., 1944-54; pres. Kendall Coll., 1954-72, chancellor, 1972-73; dir. Am. Swedish Inst., Mpls., 1973-77. Cons.-examiner N. Central Assn. Colls. and Secondary Schs., 1966-72; pres. Nat. Council of Ind. Jr. Colls., 1969-71; bd. dirs. Am. Assn. Jr. Colls., 1971-73, v.p., 1972-73. Hon. fellow Union Scandinavian Sch. Theology, Sweden, 1966. Recipient Brotherhood award Evanston Human Relations Council, 1958; decorated knight Royal Order of North Star (Sweden), 1971. Mem. Soc. Advancement of Scandinavian Studies, Swedish Pioneer Hist. Soc. (pres. 1967-73), Swedish Council Am. (sec. 1972-77). Kiwanian. Contbr. articles to profl. jours. Home: 2730 Central St Evanston IL 60201

WESTERHAUS, CATHERINE FRANCES (MRS. GEORGE H. WESTERHAUS), social worker; b. Corydon, Ind., Oct. 13, 1910; d. Anthony J. and Permelia Ann (Mathes) Kannapel; B. Music Edn., Kans. U., 1934; M.S.W., Loyola U., Chgo., 1949; m. George H. Westerhaus, Apr. 15, 1950. Social worker Harvey County Welfare Dept., Newton, Kans., 1934-38, 40—, welfare dir., 1941-74, regional supr. adult services, 1974-75; social worker Lyon County Welfare Dept., Emporia, Kans., 1938-39. Mem. adv. com. Sch. Social Work, Kan. U., Lawrence, 1966—; mem. adv. com. to homemaker service demonstration project, dept. family econs. Kans. State U., Manhattan, 1968-71. Served with USNR, 1945-46. Recipient Outstanding Service to People award Wichita chpt. Nat. Assn. Social Workers, 1975. Mem. Acad. Certified Social Workers, Kans. Conf. Social Workers, Am. Legion (dist. child welfare chmn. 1964-71), Daus. Isabella (regent 1966, 67). Home: 613 N Plum St Newton KS 67114

WESTERHOLD, RUTH ELIZABETH, psychologist; b. Youngstown, Ohio, Aug. 4, 1926; d. Samuel Gordon and Grace Elizabeth (Green) Meadows; B.S. in Edn., Youngstown U., 1946; Ph.D., U. Ill. and So. Ill. U., 1978; m. Walter Charles Westerhold, June 1, 1949; children—Marsha Lynn, Carl Eric. Chief psychologist Alton State Hosp., Ill., 1949-55; sch. psychologist St. Louis City Spl. Sch. dist., 1963-68; chief sch. psychologist Kaskaskia Spl. Edn. Dist., Centralia, Ill., 1968—; pvt. practice clin. psychology, Centralia, 1974-78. Mem. Am., Southern Ill., Psychol. Assn., AAAS, Orton Soc., Mensa, Psi Chi. Home: PO Box 68 Hoyleton IL 62803

WESTERVELT, ROBERT ELLSWORTH, stock broker; b. Baldwin, N.Y., Apr. 27, 1929; s. Floyd Edgar and Frances Ida (Doremus) W.; B.B.A., U. Wis., 1950; m. Lucille M. Offerdahl, Apr. 25, 1953; children—Scott, Bruce, Susan. Sec., treas., v.p., pres. Bell & Farrell, Inc., Madison, Wis., 1950-65; v.p., dir. Marshall Co., Inc., Madison, 1965-73; v.p. Harris, Upham & Co., Inc., Madison, 1973-75; v.p. Smith Barney, Harris Upham & Co., 1976—. Mem. Midwest Stock Exchange; owner Madison Racquet Club. Treas., bd. dirs. Madison YMCA; bd. dirs., v.p., exec. com. Adult Christian Edn. Found.; trustee, pres. Bethel Luth. Ch. Endowment Found. Recipient Know Your Madisonian award, 1970. Mem. Nat., Wis. (vice chmn.) assns. securities dealers, Milw. Bond Club, Madison U. Wis. Alumni Club (pres., dir.), Chi Phi. Lutheran (pres., treas.). Clubs: Madison, Advocates (pres.), Madison Tennis (treas., dir.), Blackhawk Country. Home: 4817 Fond du Lac Trail Madison WI 53705 Office: 244 W Washington Ave Madison WI 53703

WESTFALL, DAVID ERNEST, cons. engr.; b. Oneonta, N.Y., Sept. 13, 1934; s. Ernest David and Carolyn Ella (Crandal) W.; Asso. Applied Sci., Westchester Community Coll., 1954; B.S. in Civil Engring., U. Mo., 1959; M.S. in Civil Engring., Pa. State U., 1962; m. Gail Irene Nettleton, June 11, 1955; children—Martin David, Jennifer Anne. Hydrodynamic test engr. Naval Ordnance Research Lab., Pa. State U., University Park, 1959-60, instr. civil engring., 1960-62; hydraulic engr. Harza Engring. Co., Chgo., 1962-66; engr. sewer design, coordinating engr. City of Chgo. Dept. Pub. Works, 1966-74; v.p. Keifer & Assos., Inc., Chgo., 1974—. Vestryman, St. John's Episcopal Ch., Naperville, Ill., 1965-68; vestryman, warden Episcopal Ch. of the Resurrection, 1971-76; pres. PTA, Sch. Dist. 90, Naperville, Ill., 1963-64; active Boy Scouts Am. Served with U.S. Army, 1955-57. Recipient Dist. award of merit Boy Scouts Am., 1974. Mem. ASCE (chmn. research com. hydraulics div.), Sigma Xi, Chi Epsilon. Episcopalian. Registered profl. engr., Ill., Conn., Mass., Vt., Mich. Home: 30 W 125 Bruce Ln Naperville IL 60540 Office: 20 N Wacker Dr Chicago IL 60606

WESTFALL, RALPH LIBBY, univ. adminstr.; b. Ft. Collins, Colo., Dec. 21, 1917; s. Alfred Rensellaer and Dorothy (Towne) W.; B.S., Colo. State U., 1939; M.B.A., Northwestern U., 1940, Ph.D., 1952; m. Charlotte Elizabeth Spengler, Feb. 23, 1946; children—Janice Lisbeth, James Samuel, Teresa Ann. Market analyst Standard Oil Co. of Ind., Chgo., 1946; asst. prof. mktg. Northwestern U., Evanston, 1946-52, asso. prof., 1952-56, prof. mktg., 1956-75, asso. dean Grad. Sch. Mgmt., 1965-75; dean Coll. Bus., U. Ill. at Chgo. Circle Campus, 1975—; Ford Found. cons. to India, 1957, Egypt, 1961-62; dir. United Wire Craft, Mgmt. Research & Planning. Served with AUS, 1940-45. Decorated Bronze Star with oak leaf cluster. Mem. Am. Mktg. Assn., Am. Econs. Assn. Democrat. Presbyterian. Club: Univ. Author: Marketing Research: Text and Cases, 1956, 4th edit., 1977; Cases in Marketing Strategy, 1958; Cases in Marketing Management, 1961. Home: 2043 Ewing St Evanston IL 60201 Office: PO Box 4348 U Ill Chicago IL 60680

WESTFIELD, JACQUELYN BADEN (MRS. MONTE WESTFIELD), home economist; b. Kalamazoo, Mich., June 21, 1940; d. Cornelius and Fran (Milliman) Baden; B.S., Western Mich. U., 1962; m. Monte Westfield, Jan. 29, 1966; children—Stephen M., J. Scott. With Consumers Power Co., Battle Creek, 1964-67; mgr. consumer services Mich. Consol. Gas Co., Muskegon, 1967—. Mem. women's div. Muskegon Area Devel. Council, 1969—. Mem. Am. Gas Assn., Am., Mich. home econs. assns., Central Mich. Home Economists in Bus. (chmn. 1971-72), Muskegon Area C. of C. (pres. women's div. 1977-78). Home: 14135 Osner Dr Grand Haven MI 49417 Office: 372 Morris Ave Muskegon MI 49440

WESTIN, HAROLD JOSEPH, engr.; b. St. Paul, May 6, 1920; s. Joseph Anders and Elsie Karen (Hagstrom) W.; B.C.E., U. Minn., 1943; B.S.L., St. Paul Coll. Law, 1950; m. Dolores Marian Swanson, May 15, 1943; children—DeeAnne Karen (Mrs. Robert Nelson), Cynthia Jannine (Mrs. Neil Smith Johnson), Rosemary Denise (Mrs. John T. McCall), AmyJo Elisabeth. Pres. Harold J. Westin and Assos., Inc., architects and engrs., St. Paul, 1958, Harold J. Westin Constructors, Inc., profl. constrn. mgrs., St. Paul, 1956, Constrn. Engring Co., Inc., St. Paul, 1954—. Lectr. in engring. Law Inst. Tech. and Grad. Sch., U. Minn., St. Paul, 1957—; pres. Nilcon U.S.A.; chmn. Nilcon Minn., Inc.; cons. constrn. problems, hosps., colls., govt. agys., St. Paul, 1956—. Dir. Hillcrest State Bank; chmn. bd. Interstate Yachts, Inc., Am. Structural Cons., Inc. Served as gunboat exec. officer USNR, Amphibious Forces, World War II; PTO. Registered profl. engr., Minn. and other states. Fellow Am. Soc. C.E.; mem. Nat. Honor Soc., Nat., Minn. (Engr. of Year 1971, chmn. com. Minn. Engring. Center 1972—) profl. engrs., U. Minn. Alumni Orgn. Republican. Lutheran (trustee, deacon, vice-chmn. bd. adminstrn.). Club: St. Paul Athletic, University. Author: Legal Insights for Architects, Engineers, and Contractors, 1969; An Engineer Looks at the Law, 1972; An Engineer Applies the Law, 1973. Devel. of Harold J. Westin System Concept of coordinated profl. responsibility for design and constrn. mgmt. Home: 4 Manitou Island White Bear Lake MN 55110 Office: 45 E Eighth St St Paul 55101

WESTLAKE, LEIGHTON DANIS, JR., civil engr.; b. St. Louis, July 14, 1946; s. Leighton Danis and Kathleen Harriett (Corbet) W.; B.S. in Civil Engring., Carnegie-Mellon U., 1968, M.S. in Civil Engring., 1970; m. Darlene Marie Bieber, Aug. 16, 1969; children—Anne Marie, Scott Louis. Dir. pub. works City of Berkeley, Mo., 1975-77; cons. engr., 1977—. Served with C.E., U.S. Army, 1968-75. Registered profl. engr., Mo., Pa. Mem. ASCE, Nat., Mo. socs. profl. engrs. Republican. Lutheran. Club: Lions. Home and Office: 3480 Santiago Dr Florissant MO 63033

WESTMAN, ROY HERMAN, newspaper exec.; b. Duluth, Minn., Apr. 26, 1913; s. Gustav E. and Henny (Hoglund) W.; B.A., U. Minn., 1938; m. Violet Marie Forsberg, Nov. 12, 1938; children—Karen Shirley (Mrs. David N. Carlson), Linda Marie (Mrs. Calvin Johnson). Advt. salesman Eau Claire (Wis.) News, 1938-39, Evening Telegram, Superior, Wis., 1939-43; advt. mgr. Mesabi Daily News, Virginia, Minn., 1943-50, gen. mgr., 1950-64; gen. mgr. Evening Telegram Co., Superior, 1964-71, exec. v.p., dir., 1971—; sec.-treas. Hibbing (Minn.) Tribune, 1967—; dir. Mesabi Pub. Co., Virginia, Minn., 1958—, v.p., 1969—; sec.-treas., dir. Ashland (Wis.) Pub. Co., 1965—; treas., dir. Wis. Bldg. Co., Superior, 1965—; sec.-treas., dir. Dunedin (Fla.) Times, 1966—, dir. Gulf Sentinel Corp., Largo, Fla., 1967—, West Coast Pub. Co., Pinellas Park, Fla., 1967—, Seminole (Fla.) Pub. Co., 1970—; dir. Apple Valley Broadcasting Co., Yakima, Wash., First Nat. Bank, Virginia, Minn., Nat. Bank of Commerce, Superior, Duluth Sci. Instruments. Chmn., East Range Red Cross, 1960; active Superior Douglas County Devel. Assn., 1966-72, Superior Douglas County United Fund, 1972—. Served with USNR, 1943-46. Mem. Superior C. of C. (pres. 1970), Wis. C. of C. (dir.), N.W. Daily Press Assn. (pres. 1960), Wis. Daily Newspaper League (v.p. 1972-73), V.F.W., Am. Legion. Mason (Shriner). Clubs: Minnesota Press; Kitchi Gammi (Duluth). Home: 2 Highgate St Superior WI 54880 Office: 1226 Ogden Ave Superior WI 54880

WESTRAN, ROY ALVIN, ins. co. exec.; b. Taft, Oreg., Apr. 30, 1925; s. Carl A. and Mae E. (Barnhardt) W.; B.B.A., Golden Gate Coll., 1955, M.B.A., 1957; m. Dawn M. Oeschger, Oct. 18, 1952; children—Denise, Thomas, Harold, Michael, Dawna. Mem. sales staff C.A. Westran Agy., Taft, 1946-49; underwriter Fireman's Fund Group, San Francisco, ins. mgr. Kaiser Aluminum Chem. Oakland, 1952-65; pres. Citizens Ins. Co. Am., Howell, Mich., 1967—, Beacon Mut. Indemnity Co., Columbus, Ohio, 1969—, Am. Select Risk Ins. Co., Columbus, 1967—; v.p. Hanover Ins. Co.; dir. Worcester Mut. Ins. Co. (Mass.), 1st Nat. Bank, Howell; dir. Oakland Kaiser Fed. Credit Union, 1957-60. Mem. ins. adv. council Salvation Army, San Francisco, 1957-60; chmn. drive United Fund, 1970. Bd. dirs., exec. com. Portage Trails council Boy Scouts Am., 1970-72; bd. dirs. McPherson Health Center; trustee Traffic Safety Assn. Detroit, 1967, Traffic Safety for Mich., 1967; trustee, exec. com. Child and Family Services Mich., 1975. Served with AUS, 1943-46, C.P.C.U. Mem. Ins. Inst. Am., Mich. C. of C. (dir. 1968-71), Am. Soc. Ins. Mgmt. (pres. 1960-62), Soc. C.P.C.U. (nat. pres. 1968-69). Home: 5835 Griffith Dr Brighton MI 48116 Office: 645 W Grand River Howell MI 48843

WETHERHOLT, DOUGLAS JIVIDEN, realtor; b. Gallipolis, Ohio, Aug. 7, 1929; s. Harold Watts and Coell (Jividen) W.; B.S.J., Ohio U., 1951, M.S., 1954; m. Janet Brown, June 15, 1952. Asst. city editor, photographer Gallipolis Daily Tribune, 1952-53; photographer, asst. editor Ohio Alumnus, Ohio U., Athens, 1954-55; photographer Marietta (Ohio) Daily Times, 1955-56; dir. pub. relations Morris Harvey Coll., Charleston, W.Va., 1956-59; health info. specialist W.Va. Dept. Health, Charleston, 1959-60; copy editor Charleston Daily Mail, 1960-61; asst. dir. info. services Ind. State U., Terre Haute, 1961-65; asst. adminstr. Holzer Clinic, Gallipolis, 1965-67; salesman Baird Realty Co., Gallipolis, 1967-69; pres. Ohio River Realty Inc., Gallipolis, 1969—. Vice pres. Gallipolis City Commn., 1974—. Mem. Southeastern Ohio Bd. Realtors (pres. 1974), Sigma Nu, Sigma Delta Chi. Methodist. Mason. Home: 226 1st Ave Gallipolis OH 45613 Office: 452 2d Ave Gallipolis OH 45631

WETNIGHT, ROBERT, ednl. adminstr.; b. Springfield, Ohio, Mar. 11, 1923; s. Frank Mantz and Romaine (Byers) W.; Ph.B., U. Toledo, 1947, M.B.A., 1958; m. Helen Fulton, Sept. 27, 1947; children—Susan, Kathryn, Barbara. With Arthur Young & Co., Toledo, 1947-51; asso. prof. accounting Western Mich. U., 1951-57, head dept., 1957-62, comptroller, 1962-65, v.p. finance, 1965—. C.P.A., Ohio. Mem. Nat. Assn. Accountants (bd. dirs. Kalamazoo 1952, pres. 1958-59, nat. bd. dirs. 1959-60, mem. nat. research project com. on practical applications of direct costing 1960), Am. Inst. C.P.A.'s, Am. Accounting Assn., Nat. Assn. Coll. and Univ. Bus. Officers, Kalamazoo Accounts Assn., Omicron Delta Kappa, Delta Sigma Phi, Alpha Kappa Psi, Beta Alpha Psi. Club: Kalamazoo Country. Home: 703 Weaver Circle Kalamazoo MI 49007

WETTER, BENJAMIN FENTON, dentist; b. Canton, Ohio, Jan. 26, 1935; s. Benjamin F. and Margaret (Treese) W.; B.S., Ashland Coll., 1957; D.D.S., Western Res. U., 1961; m. Maye Althea Johnson, Dec. 19, 1959; children—Martha Lynn, Cynthia Anne, Bruce Fredrick, Laura Ruth. Practice dentistry, Seville, Ohio, 1963—. Chief coordinator Seville Sesquicentennial, 1966; mem. Medina County Bd. Edn., 1968-74, pres., 1970—; v.p. Medina County Joint Vocational Bd. Edn., 1971, pres., 1972, mem., 1971-74. Served to capt. USAF, 1961-63. Mem. Am. Dental Assn., Ohio, Akron dental socs., Seville C. of C. (past v.p.). Mason (Shriner); mem. Order Eastern Star. Home: 124 W Main St Seville OH 44273 Office: 10 W Main St Seville OH 44273

WETTERSTROM, EDWIN, engr.; b. Oak Park, Ill., Dec. 20, 1919; s. Frank and Alma (Ekstrom) W.; bus. diploma Wright Coll., 1940; B.S. in Mech. Engring., Ill. Inst. Tech., 1944; M.S. in Engring. Mechanics, Purdue U., 1947, Ph.D., 1951; m. Betty Barbara Chase. Engr., devel. dept. Continental Can Co., 1944-45; staff mem. engring. mechanics dept. Purdue, 1945-51; analytical research engr. research and devel. dept. Graver Tank & Mfg. Co., 1951, cons., 1952—; asst. prof. civil engring. U. Mo., 1952-55; asso. prof. applied mechanics Mich. State U., 1955-57; prof. mech. engring. N.D. State U., 1957-67, U. Toledo, 1967-70, Ind. Inst. Tech., 1970-72, Tuskegee Inst., 1972-74; sr. analytical engr. Westinghouse Air Brake Co., 1974—. Mem. Am. Soc. M.E., Am. Soc. Engring. Edn., Sigma Xi. Lutheran. Contbr. articles tech. press. Home: PO Box 165 Washington IL 61571

WETZEL, DEAN ELTON, paper packaging mfg. co. exec.; b. Norfolk, Nebr., June 24, 1925; s. Dewey F. and Norah E. (Rodgers) W.; B.E.E., with distinction, U. Minn., 1946, postgrad. (Inst. Tech. fellow), Sch. Bus., 1947; m. Jo Ann Mergens, Nov. 25, 1966; children—Dena Ann, Tara Lee. Sales engr. packaging machinery Gen. Mills, Inc., Mpls., 1948-49; sales v.p. corrugated div. Waldorf Corp., St. Paul, 1950-66, v.p., gen. mgr. consumer packaging div. Hoerner-Waldorf Corp., 1966—, corporate v.p. consumer packages div., 1975-76, sr. v.p. consumer packages div. Hoerner Waldorf-Champion Internat. Corp., 1976—. Served with USNR, 1943-46. Mem. St. Paul C. of C., Eta Kappa Nu, Tau Beta Pi. Clubs: Decathlon Athletic (Bloomington, Minn.); Midway Civic (St. Paul). Home: 6260 Ridge Rd Excelsior MN 55331 Office: PO Box 3260 St Paul MN 55165

WETZEL, STUART ALAN, cons. co. mgmt. cons., merger specialist; b. St. Louis, Oct. 1, 1930; s. Stuart A. and Kathryn M. W.; A.B., U. Mo., 1952; m. Sheryl Ann, Sept. 25, 1971; children—Richard, Kathryn, Robert, Timothy. Pres., Wetzel Lumber Co., Inc., St. Louis, 1956-59, Wetzel Assos., Inc., Des Peres, Mo., 1959—; pres., partner Rainbow Investments Co., 1975—. Served with USNR, 1953-56. Mem. Greek Lit. Soc. (dir.). Clubs: Greenbriar Hills Country, Dorsett Racquet, Woods Mill. Home: 12315 Ballas Ln Town-Country MO 63131 Office: 12015 Manchester Rd Des Peres MO 63131

WEVER, HILBERT EMANUEL, welding alloy corp. exec.; b. Martinsburg, W.Va., Jan. 2, 1929; s. Hilbert Allen and Mary Josephine (Triggs) W.; B.S., U. Ill., 1958; m. Virginia Mae Gruenberg, Mar. 5, 1970; children—Karen, Irene, Diane, Wayne, Steven. With Chgo. Northwestern R.R., 1952-58; various sales positions, 1958-67; pres. Indsl. Alloys Co., Chgo., 1967-72, Dorsey Reynolds Internat. Inc., Beecher, Ill., 1972—. Served with USNR, 1945-46. Home: Rural Route 2 Box 16B Beecher IL 60401 Office: PO Box 1136 Beecher IL 60401

WEXLER, BERNARD CARL, med. research dir., educator; b. Boston, May 1, 1923; s. William and Dora (Gerson) W.; student Dartmouth Coll., 1941; B.A., U. Oreg., 1946; M.A., U. Calif., Berkeley, 1947; Ph.D., Stanford, 1952; m. Jean Alice Berkel, Sept. 3, 1946; children—Nancy, Helen, William. Responsible investigator AEC, Stanford Research Inst., Menlo Park, Calif., 1952; lectr. Dominican Coll., San Rafael, Calif., 1952; dir. endocrine and pathology dept. Baxter Lab., Morton Grove, Ill., 1953-56; Merrel scholar gerontology, 1956; research asso. May Inst. Med. Research of Jewish Hosp., Cin., 1956-64, dir., 1964—; asst. prof. exptl. medicine and pathology U. Cin. Coll. Medicine, 1956-62, asso. prof. 1962-75, asso. prof. exptl. medicine, 1971-75, prof. exptl. medicine and pathology, 1975—; mem. med. staff Jewish Hosp. Cons. NSF. Served with AUS, 1942-46. Recipient Career Devel. award Nat. Heart Inst., NIH, 1962, 72. Am. Heart Assn. fellow, 1960-62. Fellow Gerontol. Soc., Internat. Coll. Angiology; mem. Acad. Medicine Cin., Am. Psychosomatic Soc., Am. Assn. U. Profs., A.A.A.S., Am. Assn. Lab. Animals Sci., Am. Assn. Pathology and Bacteriology, Am. Diabetes Assn., Biol. Stain Commn., Diabetes Assn. Cin., Internat. Soc. Study Cardiac Metabolism, Internat. Soc. Cardiology (mem. council on arteriosclerosis and ischaemic heart disease), N.Y. Acad. Sci., Am. Soc. Exptl. Pathology, Am. Med. Coll. Am. Heart Assn. (mem. councils on arteriosclerosis, basic scis., cerebrovascular disease, high blood pressure research), Endocrine Soc., Soc. Exptl. biol. and Medicine, Soc. Study Reprodn., U. Cal. Hon. Soc., Sigma Xi. Western Hemisphere editor The Arterial Wall. Home: 7640 DeMar Rd Cincinnati OH 45243 Office: 421 Ridgeway Ave Cincinnati OH 45229

WEXNER, LESLIE HERBERT, retail co. exec.; b. Dayton, Ohio, Sept. 8, 1937; s. Harry Louis and Bella (Cabakoff) W.; B.S., Ohio State U., 1959, postgrad. Law Sch., 1959-61. Founder, pres. Ltd. Stores, Inc., fashion chain, Columbus, Ohio, 1963—. Founder Orphan's Day at Ohio State Fair. Bd. dirs. Hillel Found.; trustee United Jewish Fedn., 1972, St. Anthony's Hosp., Agudas Achim Synagogue, Council, 1972, Heritage House-Columbus Jewish Home for Aged, 1972; mem. Ohio State U. Bus. Adminstrn. Adv. Council. Named 1 of 10 Outstanding Young Men Columbus, Columbus Jaycees, 1971; Man of Yr., Am. Mktg. Assn. Mem. Young Presidents Orgn., Columbus Area C. of C., Nat. Retail Mchts. Assn., Sigma Alpha Mu. Jewish. Mem. B'nai B'rith. Office: 4661 E Main St Columbus OH 43213

WEYLS, JOHN LAWRENCE, chem. co. exec.; b. Cleve., Oct. 18, 1934; s. W.L. and Emily E. (Lue) W.; student Baldwin Wallace Coll., 1956-68; m. Barbara Ann Wheeler, June 7, 1958; children—John Lawrence, Erik W., Mark T., Daniel C. With R.O. Hull & Co. subsidiary Lubrizol Corp., Cleve., 1955—, exec. v.p., 1966-77, pres., 1977—. Mem. Am. Electroplaters Soc. Republican. Mason (Shriner). Home: 4166 State Rd Medina OH 44256 Office: 3203 W 71st St Cleveland OH 44102

WEYRENS, JOHN JOSEPH, judge, lawyer; b. St. Cloud, Minn., Jan. 27, 1935; s. Peter Matthew and Julia (Frank) W.; A.A., Itasca Jr. Coll., 1955; B.S., St. John's U., 1957; LL.B., William Mitchell Coll. Law, 1964; m. Catherine Joanne Kugler, Oct. 2, 1965; children—Mary Catherine, John Alexis, David Andrew. Admitted to Minn. bar, 1964; practice law, Dawson, 1966-72, Lac Qui Parle County court judge, Madison, Minn., 1973—; chmn. judge 8th Jud. Dist. Minn. County Ct. Judges, 1976—. Mem. Lac Qui Parle County Draft Bd., 1970-72; mem. 19 County Countryside Council, chmn., 1974-75; bd. dirs. Lac Qui Parle County Day Activity Center, Dawson Housing for the Elderly. Served with U.S. Army, 1957-60. Mem. Minn. State Bar Assn. K.C. Home: 829 3d Ave Madison MN 56256 Office: Courthouse Madison MN 56256

WHALEN, CHARLES WILLIAM, JR., congressman, educator; b. Dayton, Ohio, July 31, 1920; s. Charles W. and Colette (Kelleher) W.; B.S. in Bus. Adminstrn., U. Dayton, 1942; M.B.A., Harvard, 1946; LL.D. (hon.), Central State U., 1966; m. Mary Barbara Gleason, Dec. 27, 1958; children—Charles E., Daniel D., Edward J., Joseph M., Anne Elizabeth, Mary Barbara. Vice pres. Dayton Dress Co., Dayton, 1946-52, Whalen Investment Co., 1953—; asso. prof. retailing U. Dayton, 1952-61, prof. retailing, 1961-63, prof. econs., 1963-66; mem. Ohio Ho. Reps., 1955-60, Ohio Senate, 1961-66; mem. 90th-95th congresses from 3d Ohio Dist. Served from pvt. to 1st lt. AUS, 1943-46. Named outstanding Young Man of Dayton, 1956, Ohio, 1956 by Dayton and also Ohio jr. chambers commerce. Mem. Am. Legion, Eta Mu Pi. Home: 228 Beverly Pl Dayton OH 45419

WHALER, VAN GEORGE, city planner; b. Springfield, Ohio, Sept. 25, 1945; s. George Howard and Chellamae (Morris) W.; B.A., Miami U., 1967; M.A., U. Akron, 1972; Ph.D., U. Okla., 1976; m. Jill Verleny, Sept. 1, 1971; 1 dau., Kelly Michelle. County planner Carroll V. Hill & Assos. Ltd., Columbus, Ohio, 1967; regional planner Tri-County Regional Planning Commn., Akron, Ohio, 1970-72; project planner Floyd G. Browne & Assos. Ltd., Canton, Ohio, 1972-74; environ. planner Dalton-Dalton-Little-Newport, Cleve., 1974-76; city planner City of Springfield, 1976—; guest, vis. prof. U. Akron, Wittenberg U. Mem. devel. com. Springfield City Schs., 1976-77; mem. Clark County Overall Economic Devel. Plan Com., 1976—. Served with U.S. Army, 1967-70. Decorated Bronze Star medal. Mem. Am. Geog. Soc., Am. Inst. Planners, Am. Soc. Planning Ofcls., Assn. Am. Georgraphers, Nat. Geog. Soc., Ohio Hist. Soc., Ohio Planning Conf., Urban Land Inst. Methodist. Home: 818 Torrence Dr Springfield OH 45503 Office: 117 S Fountain Ave Springfield OH 45502

WHALLON, EVAN ARTHUR, JR., orch. condr.; b. Akron, Ind., July 24, 1923; s. Evan Arthur and Katharine (Kistler) W.; Mus.B., Eastman Sch. Music, U. Rochester, 1948, Mus.M., 1949; Mus.D. (hon.), Denison U., 1963, Otterbein U., 1969, Ohio Dominican Coll., 1970; m. Jean Pawley Borgman, Aug. 28, 1948; children—Paul Evan, Eric Andrew. Debut with Phila. Orch., 1948; condr. opera The Consul (Menotti), 1950; condr. Springfield Symphony, 1951-56; condr. Columbus (Ohio) Symphony, 1956—; condr. Chautauqua Opera, 1967—; guest condr. Rochester (N.Y.) Opera Under the Stars, N.Y.C. Opera, Spoleto (Italy) Festival, Cleve. Orch., Buffalo Philharmonic, Boston Arts Festival, Budapest Symphony, Prague Symphony. Served to lt. (j.g.) USNR, 1943-46. Clubs: Torch, Rotary. Home: 2993 Shadywood Rd Columbus OH 43221 Office: 101 E Town St Columbus OH 43215

WHARTON, CLIFTON REGINALD, JR., univ. pres.; b. Boston, Sept. 13, 1926; B.A., Harvard, 1947; M.A., Johns Hopkins, 1948, LL.D., 1970; M.A., U. Chgo., 1956, Ph.D. in Econs., 1958; LL.D., U. Mich., 1970, Wayne State U., 1970; D.Pub. Service, Central Mich. U., 1970; L.H.D., Oakland U., 1971; m. Dolores Duncan, 1950; children—Clifton 3d, Bruce. Exec. trainee Am. Internat. Assn. Econs. and Social Devel., 1948-49, program analyst, 1949-51, head reports and analysis, 1951-53; research asst. econs. U. Chgo., 1953-56, research asso., 1956-57; exec. asso. Agrl. Devel. Council, 1957-58; asso. Singapore region, 1958-64, dir. Am. univ. research program, 1964-67, v.p., 1967-70; pres. Mich. State U., 1970—; vis. prof. U. Malaya, Singapore, 1958-60, U. Malaya, 1960-64, Stanford, 1964-65. Mem. Presdl. Task Force Agr. in Vietnam, 1966, Presdl. Mission to Latin Am., 1969; adv. panel E. Asia and Pacific, State Dept., 1966-69,

U.S. Latin Am. Commn., 1974—; chmn. bd. for internat. food and agrl. devel. U.S. Dept. State, 1976—. Dir. Equitable Life Assurance Soc., Ford Motor Co., Burroughs Corp. Bd. dirs. or trustees Asia Soc., Rockefeller Found., Carnegie Found., Overseas Devel. Council, Agrl. Devel. Council. Named Man of Year, Boston Latin Sch., 1970; recipient Amistad award Am. Missionary Soc., 1970; Alumni Profl. Achievement award U. Chgo., 1971. Mem. Agrl. Econs. Assn., Am. Econs. Assn., Assn. Asian Studies, Nat. Acad. Edn., Soc. for Internat. Devel., Council on Fgn. Relations, Internat. Assn. Agrl. Econs. Clubs: Econ. of Detroit; University of N.Y. Author: The U.S. Graduate Training of Asian Agricultural Economics, 1959; Research on Agricultural and Economic Development in Southeast Asia, 1965; (with others) Patterns for Lifelong Learning, 1973. Author articles. Editor: Subsistence Agriculture and Economic Development, 1968. Address: Office of Pres Mich State East Lansing MI 48824

WHATLEY, DAVID THOMAS, army officer; b. Pampa, Tex., Aug. 11, 1936; s. Calvin Thomas and Jewel Annabelle (Burt) W.; B.M. Ed., W. Tex. State U., 1959, M.Ed., 1969; Ednl. Specialist, George Washington U., 1972; grad. Army Gen. Staff Coll., 1969; m. Cynthia Ray Thompson, Jan. 29, 1960. Commd. 2d lt. U.S. Army, 1960, advanced through grades to lt. col. 1975; staff officer Office of Army Chief of Staff, Washington, 1970-72, staff, faculty Def. Systems Mgmt. Coll., Fort Belvoir, Va., 1972-74; dept. dir. Gen. Edn. Devel. Program, Europe, 1974-77; prof. mil. sci. No. Ill. U., DeKalb, 1977—. Decorated Bronze Star, Meritorious Service medal, Joint Service Commendation medal, Army Commendation medal, recipient award Big Bend Community Coll., 1977. Mem. Am. Assn. for Higher Edn., Am. Assn. for Community and Jr. Colls., Soc. Profs. Higher Edn., Adult Edn. Assn. U.S.A., Am. Personnel and Guidance Assn., Phi Delta Kappa. Home: 1606 Carlisle Ln DeKalb IL 60115 Office: Dept Military Science Northern Illinois U DeKalb IL 60115

WHEALEY, ROBERT HOWARD, historian; b. Freeport, N.Y., May 16, 1930; s. Howard Edgar and Ethel Ann (Rooney) W.; student Bates Coll., 1948-50; B.A., U. Del., 1952; M.A., U. Mich., 1954, Ph.D., 1963; postgrad. Oxford U., 1956-57; m. Lois Elizabeth Deimel, July 2, 1954; children—Richard W., David J., Alice A. Teaching fellow history U. Mich., 1958-59; instr. history U. Maine, Orono, 1961-64, U. Del., summer 1963; asst. and asso. prof. history Ohio U., Athens, 1964—; editor for univ. press. Press sec. and polit. advisor Congressional candidates, 1974, 76; press sec. 10th Dist. Dem. Action Club, 1976—; candidate for Congress, 1972; bd. dirs. Community Action Agy. Served with U.S. Army, 1955-56. Mem. Am. Hist. Assn., Conf. Peace Research, Soc. Spanish and Portuguese Historians, Phi Kappa Phi. Democrat. Unitarian. Contbr. articles in field to profl. jours. and chpts. to books. Home: 14 Oak St Athens OH 45701 Office: Dept History Bentley Hall Ohio U Athens OH 45701

WHEATLEY, JOSEPH EDWIN, mobile home co. exec.; b. Vine Grove, Ky., Mar. 19, 1915; s. Wilford E. and Beatrice Helen (Buckman) W.; student St. Josephs Coll., 1929-33; m. Martha N. Bowlin, Nov. 19, 1938; children—Stephen B., Jane A. (Mrs. David P. Eaton). Distbn. mgr. Shell Americax Petroleum Co., Kokomo, Ind., 1947-53; area mgr. Mobil Oil Co., Indpls., 1953-58; v.p. dealer relations Schult Mobile Homes, Elkhart, Ind., 1960—. Democrat. Roman Catholic. Elk. Home: 2421 E Broadway St Logansport IN 46947 Office: PO Box 151 Middlebury IN 46540

WHEATLEY, THOMAS JOSEPH, JR., educator; b. Cleve., Apr. 29, 1951; s. Thomas Joseph and Hilda Alice (Webb) W.; B.S., Mt. Union Coll., Alliance, Ohio, 1973; M.A. in Mathematics, Kent State U., Ohio, 1977. Tchr. pub. schs., Canton, Ohio, 1973—. Recipient Carl Math. award Mt. Union Coll., 1970, Ullman Math. Award, 1973. Mem. Math. Assn. Am., Ohio Council Tchrs. Math., NEA. Roman Catholic. Home: 11537 Wm Penn St Hartville OH 44632

WHEATON, BURDETTE CARL, educator; b. Mankato, Minn., July 3, 1938; s. Burdette Willard and Elsa (Gramentz) W.; B.S., Mankato State U., 1959; M.A., U. Ia., 1961, Ph.D., 1965; m. Margaret Ann Ehlbeck, June 16, 1968; children—Timothy, Michael John, Julie Ann. Grad. asst. U. Ia., Iowa City, 1959-63; asst. prof. Western Ill. U., Macomb, 1963-65; prof. math. Mankato (Minn.) State U., 1965—. Mem. Nat. Council Tchrs. Math., Am. Math. Soc., Math. Assn. Am., Sigma Xi, Sigma Zeta. Lutheran. Home: 326 Floral Ave Mankato MN 56001 Office: Mankato State U Mankato MN 56001

WHEATON, ROBERT DONALD, microbiologist; b. Jackson, Mich., Feb. 19, 1926; s. Roy Melville and Ethel Jane (Green) W.; student Jackson Jr. Coll., 1946-48; A.B., Albion (Mich.) Coll., 1950; M.S., Mich. State U., 1952; m. Helen May Smith, Aug. 14, 1948; children—Kenneth R., Kathryn Ann. Chemist Budlong Pickle Co., Chgo., 1952-56; food technologist Swift & Co., Chgo., 1956-57; microbiologist Upjohn Co., Kalamazoo, 1957—. Served with USNR, 1944-46. Mem. Am. Soc. Microbiology, Sigma Xi (asso.). Home: 1025 Pasma Ave Kalamazoo MI 49002 Office: Upjohn Co 7171 Portage Rd Kalamazoo MI 49001

WHEATON, ROLLAND ZELBERT, educator; b. Petoskey, Mich., Nov. 27, 1922; s. Warner A. and Lucy V. (Bacon) W.; B.S., Mich. State U., 1954, M.S., 1959; Dr.E., U. Cal. at Davis, 1963; m. Lorna Carol Notestine, Nov. 8, 1946; children—Keith Brian, Holly Louise. Instr. Mich. State U., 1955-60; research fellow U. Cal. at Davis, 1960-63; instr. Mich. State U., 1963-66; asso. prof. Tex. Tech. U., 1966-69; asso. prof. soil and water engring. Purdue U., 1969—; cons. Univ. Federal of Vicosa, Brazil, 1973. Troop committeeman, Harrison Trails council Boy Scouts Am., 1971-73. Served with AUS, 1943-45. Recipient NSF Faculty fellowship, 1962-63. Mem. Am. Soc. Agrl. Engrs., Sprinkler Irrigation Assn., Sigma Xi, Tau Beta Pi, Phi Kappa Phi, Alpha Epsilon, Gamma Sigma Delta. Home: 104 Mohawk St West Lafayette IN 47906 Office: Agrl Engring Dept Purdue U Lafayette IN 47907

WHEBY, FRANK TOMAS, cons. engr.; b. Beckley, W.Va., Sept. 7, 1930; s. Albert and Katherine (Hall) W.; B.S. in Geology, Mass. Inst. Tech., 1952; B.S. in Civl Engring., W.Va. U., 1956; M.S. in Civil Engring., Northwestern U., 1961; m. Judith May Oeftering, Apr. 25, 1964; children—Christopher, Jonathan. Geotech. engr. Aluminum Co. of Am., Pitts., 1956, Maryville, Tenn., 1957, Paramaribo, Surinam, S.Am., 1958-59; asso. Harza Engring. Co., Chgo., 1960-61, Lahore, Pakistan, 1965, Athens, Greece, 1966, Chgo., 1967-73; dept. head R.W. Beck & Assos., Seattle, 1962-64; pvt. practice cons. geotech. engr., Evanston, Ill., 1974—; mem. U.S. Nat. Com. on Tunnelling Tech., 1972-77. Mem. Lakefront Recreation Mall Com., Evanston, 1970-72, Environ. Control Bd., Evanston, 1973-74, Pollution and Flood Control Com., Evanston, 1974. Served to 1st lt. U.S. Army, 1952-54. Registered profl. engr., 9 states; certified Nat. Council Engring. Examiners. Mem. ASCE, Assn. Engring. Geologists, Assn. Profl. Geol. Scientists, Nat. Soc. Profl. Engrs. Club: Rotary. Contbr. articles to profl. jours. Home: 1319 Grant St Evanston IL 60201 Office: 1604 Chicago Ave Evanston IL 60201

WHEELER, ADADE MITCHELL, educator; b. Duluth, Minn., July 20, 1910; d. Charles Sumner and Rizpah Rowena (de Laittre) Mitchell; student Principia Coll., 1928-30; B.A., Carleton Coll., 1932; M.A., Washington U., St. Louis, 1940; postgrad. various univs.; m. Frederick Barclay Wheeler, Oct. 23, 1942; children—Frederick Barclay, Ann Mitchell. Sec., tchr. Principia Coll., 1933-39; with Marshall Field & Co., Chgo., 1940-42; operating dir. Blecker's, 1942-45; tchr. Franklin Jr. High Sch., Wheaton, Ill., 1958-64, North High Sch., Wheaton, 1964-67; mem. faculty Coll. of DuPage, Wheaton, 1967—, prof. history, 1977—. Recorder, historian Ill. coordinating com. Internat. Women's Year.; chmn. Ill. Com. Concerned with Women's History and Archives; mem. faculty Inst. of Women Today. Mem. Am. Hist. Assn., Orgn. Am. Historian (com. on status of women), Chgo. Hist. Soc., Ill. Labor History Soc., League Women Voters, AAUW, NOW. Author: (with Marlene Wortman) The Roads They Made, Women in Illinois History, 1977. Home: 628 W Jefferson St Wheaton IL 60187 Office: Coll of DuPage Rd Glen Ellyn IL 60137

WHEELER, CHARLES EUGENE, assn. exec.; b. Pawhuska, Okla., Jan. 6, 1926; s. Eugene Laurenz and Lillian (Rees) W.; student Tex. A. and M. U., 1943, U. Mo., 1943-44, U. Ark., 1944-48; B.S. in Civil Engring., U. N.Mex., 1956; m. JoAnne Virginia Towers, Sept. 24, 1949. Mgr., C. of C., Pawhuska, Okla., 1962-65; dir. indsl. devel. Neb. Dept. Econ. Devel., Lincoln, 1965-72; dir. indsl. devel. Greater Springfield (Ill.) C. of C., 1972—. Served with AUS, 1943-44. Registered profl. civil engr., Okla. Mem. Am. Indsl. Devel. Council, Ill Assn. C. of C. Execs., Internat. Mgmt. Council, Ill. Soc. Assn. Execs., Great Lakes Area (v.p.), Ill. devel. councils. Home: 128 Greencastle Springfield IL 62703 Office: Myers Bldg Springfield IL 62701

WHEELER, CLARENCE JOSEPH, JR., physician; b. Dallas, Sept. 25, 1917; s. Clarence Joseph and Sadie Alice (McKinney) W.; B.S. in Math., So. Meth. U., 1941, B.A. in Psychology, 1946; M.D., Johns Hopkins, 1950; m. Alice Mary Freels, Dec. 6, 1942 (dec.); children—Stephen Freels, Clarence Joseph III, Robert McKinney, Thomas Michael, David Ritchey; m. 2d, Jean Grant Faucett, Mar. 2, 1968. Intern, Johns Hopkins Hosp., Balt., 1950-51; resident surgery Barnes Hosp., St. Louis, 1951-54; thoracic surgery fellow U. Wis. Hosps., Madison, 1954-55; instr. surgery, 1955-56; practice medicine specializing in gen. and thoracic surgery, Houston, 1956-75, Peoria, Ill., 1975—; clin. instr. surgery Baylor Coll. Medicine, Houston, 1957-75; lectr. surgery U. Tex. Postgrad. Med. Sch., Houston, 1957—; mem. active staff Herman Hosp., Houston, 1958-75, mem. cardio-vascular research team, 1960-75; mem. active staff St. Luke's Hosp., Houston, 1958-75, St. Joseph's Hosp., Houston, 1958-75, Meml. Hosp., Houston, 1959-75, Tex. Children's Hosp., Houston, 1960-75, Meth. Hosp., 1960-75, Ben Taub City-County Hosp., Jefferson Davis Hosp.; later chief of surgery, attending active staff Lewisburg (Tenn.) Community Hosp.; dir. emergency med. dept. Methodist Hosp., Peoria, Ill., 1975—, also dir. med. edn. emergency services; sr. med. office Thua Thien Province, South Vietnam, 1968-70; chief surgery Hue Central Hosp., S. Vietnam, 1968-70; mem. courtesy staff all peripheral outlying hosps.; sr. attending staff Lindley Hosp., Duncan, Okla. Treas. Samuel Clark Ree Sch., P.T.A., Houston, 1959-61; mem. bd. Salvation Army Boys Club, Houston. Served to capt. USMCR, 1942-45; PTO. Decorated D.F.C. (3), Air medal (8), Purple Heart, Navy Commendation medal, Bronze Star, Vietnamese Medal of Health, Vietnamese Medal of Social Welfare. Diplomate Am. Bd. Surgery. Fellow A.C.S., Am. Coll. Chest Phsyicians, Royal Soc. Medicine; mem. Am., Tex., So., Indsl., Middle Tenn. med. assns., Harris County, St. Louis, Marshall County (pres.) med. socs., Am., Tex. thoracic socs., Nat. Tb Assn., Am. Assn. History Medicine, Am. Soc. Contemporary Medicine and Surgery, Am., Tex., Houston, Tenn., Middle Tenn. heart assns., AAAS, Johns Hopkins Med. and Surg. Soc., Southeastern, Southwestern surg. congresses, Tex. Anti-Tb Assn., Houston Gastroent. Soc., Houston Surg. Soc., Postgrad Med. Assemlby South Tex., Am. Cancer Soc., Am. Coll. Angiology, Am. Soc. Abdominal Surgeons, Internat. Acad. Proctology, Internat. Coll. Gastroenterology, Tenn. Thoracic Assn., Internat. Coll. Surgeons, Marshall County C. of C., Common Cause, Duck River Humane Soc., Marine Corps, Naval res. officers assns., Nat. Geog. Soc., Kappa Sigma, Phi Chi, Phi Eta Sigma, Kappa Mu Epsilon, Psi Chi. Episcopalian. Rotarian. Club: International. Home: 516 Allyn Ct Creve Coeur East Peoria IL 61611 Office: Dept Emergency Medicine Methodist Hosp Peoria IL 61603

WHEELER, DAVID GENE, dentist; b. Coulterville, Ill., Nov. 26, 1929; s. Ernie Winford and Lucille (Sisk) W.; grad. Belleville Jr. Coll., 1955; student McKendree Coll., 1954-55; D.D.S., St. Louis U., 1960; m. Carol Jean Stevenson, June 23, 1950; children—Cynthia, John David, Steven, Angela, Anthony, Jacqueline Susanne. Individual practice dentistry, Belleville, Ill., 1960—; dental supr. Union Electric Light & Power Co., St. Louis, 1962-63; pres. dental staff St. Elizabeth Hosp., Belleville, 1965-66. Mem. Belleville Grade Sch. Bd. Edn., 1965-75; pres. Mental Health Center, Belleville, 1963-65. Served with USAF, 1951-55. Mem. Belleville C. of C. (pres. ednl. com. Belleville area 1970-72). Baptist (dir. adult class 1971-72). Elk. Home: 17 Berrywood Dr Belleville IL 62223 Office: 4401 W Main St Belleville IL 62223

WHEELER, GERRIDEE STENEHJEM, Republican nat. committeewoman; b. Arnegard, N.D., May 29, 1927; d. Martin S. and Emma (Bjornstad) Stenehjem; A.A., Stephens Coll.; B.A., U. N.D.; m. Ronald Wheeler, Sept. 5, 1948; children—Mary Beth Wheeler Brandborg, Kim Wheeler Collins, Lisa Wheeler DeLapp, Jennifer, Jo Ann, Pamela, Kathy, Fredrick. Legis. chmn. N.D. Mental Health Assn., 1965, bd. dirs., 1965-70, 72-75, pres. 1967-71; pres. Bismarck (N.D.) Regional Metnal Health Assn., 1966; chmn. bd. Meml. Mental Health and Retardation Center, 1966-70, personnel, bldg., program coms., 1971-73; mem. pub. policy com. Nat. Assn. Mental Health, 1969-72, bd. dirs., 1969—, exec. com., 1971-73, roles and representation com., 1971, regional v.p., 1972-73, com. community mental health centers, 1972, organizational com., 1972-73, pres., 1975; mem. Nat. Adv. Council Comprehensive Health Planning and Program Devel., 1971-73; bd. dirs. N.D. South Central Health Planning, 1971-75; v.p. Nat. Commn. for Prevention of Child Abuse, 1975—; mem. Pres.'s Commn. on Observance of Internat. Women's Yr.; mem. Sec. of HEW Adv. Council on Rights and Responsibilities of Women, 1976—. Mem. Republican Nat. Com. for N.D., 1972—, mem. nominating com., 1972, platform com., 1972; del. Rep. nat. conv., 1972, 76, mem. nat. platform com., 1972-76; chmn. N.D. Delegation Women's Conf.; mem. N.D. platform com., 1973; campaign chmn. Elkin for Congress. Named Pub. Health Worker of Year, N.D. Pub. Health Assn., 1966; Woman of Decade, N.D. Mental Health Assn., 1970, Woman of Year, 1975; N.D. Girls' State named city in her honor; Outstanding Stephens Coll. Alumnae, 1976; recipient Nat. Achievement award Bismarck Area C. of C., 1976. Mem. U. N.D. Alumni Assn. (Bismarck regional chmn.), N.D. Women's Coalition (adviser, named Outstanding Woman in Govt. and Politics 1975), Nat. Women's Polit. Caucus, N.D. Council Edn. (pres. 1971—), Kappa Alpha Theta. Lutheran. Club: Fortnightly (past pres.). Home: 1231 E Highland Acres Rd Bismarck ND 58501

WHEELER, HARRY KELLEY, JR., oil co. exec.; b. Mpls., Mar. 3, 1922; s. Harry Kelley and Ann M. (MacGeever) W.; B.Chem. Engring., U. Cin., 1944; m. Etta Jean Leeker, June 24, 1944; children—Thomas Craig, William Allen, Robert Mark. With Standard Oil Co. of Ind., Chgo., 1944—, process design engr., 1944-48, asst. dept. head. mfg., 1948-54, asst. refinery mgr., 1954-58, mgr. tech. service, 1958-61, mgr. project evaluation, 1967—. Commr. Deerfield (Ill.) Boys Baseball Assn., 1963-64; chmn. Deerfield Village Caucus, 1970-71. Recipient Most Outstanding Young Man award Eldorado Jr. C. of C., 1955. Mem. Am. Inst. Chem. Engrs., Sigma Alpha Epsilon. Patentee petroleum refining processes. Home: 22 Ct of Greenway Northbrook IL 60062 Office: 200 E Randolph St Chicago IL 60601

WHEELER, JAMES ERNEST, veterinarian; b. Elgin, N.D., Apr. 1, 1935; s. Benjamin Joseph and Irene (Brinkman) W.; student Dickenson State Tchrs. Coll., 1953; B.S., U. Minn., 1961, D.V.M., 1963; m. Valerie Patricia Horst, Oct. 16, 1955; children—Kathleen M., James J., Susan J., Paul B. Practice vet. medicine, Bismarck, N.D., 1963—; sec. Midway Vet. Clinic, 1970—; attending veterinarian Dakota Zoo, 1965—. Bd. dirs. Mo. Valley Family YMCA, 1975—, pres., 1977. Served with AUS, 1954-56. Mem. Am., N.D. vet. med. assns., Am. Assn. Zoo Veterianarians, Dakota Zool. Soc. (dir. 1965—, pres. 1973-74), Nat. Campers and Hikers Assn. (field dir. 1973-74). Clubs: Dakota Drifters (v.p. 1970-71), Y's Mens (pres. 1969-71). Home: 815 Mandan St Bismarck ND 58501 Office: Box 911 Bismarck ND 58501

WHEELER, JAMES HAMILTON, ecologist; b. Chico, Calif., June 20, 1942; s. Alfred Orin and Laura Wilhelmina (Schlegel) W.; B.A., Calif. State U. at Chico, 1967, M.A., 1968; m. Christina Margaret Gould, Dec. 21, 1973. Cons. algal ecology Res. Mining Co., Silver Bay, Minn., 1972-73; mgr. lab. services WAPORA, Inc., Charleston, Ill., 1974-78; cons. aquatic ecology, 1978—. NSF research fellow, 1968. Mem. Phycol. Soc. Am., Brit. Phycol. Soc., Am. Inst. Biol. Scis., Am. Soc. Limnology and Oceanography, ASTM, Soc. Economic Botany, Ecol. Soc. Address: 1680 University Dr Charleston IL 61920 also 202 E Colusa St Orland CA 95963

WHEELER, JOHN DEE, mgt. cons.; b. Milford Center, Ohio, Jan. 7, 1921; s. Elmer Edmund and Lela Belle (King) W.; B.S., U. Kans., 1959; m. Dorothy Louise Nicholas, Aug. 5, 1945; 1 son, Michael Terrence; m. 2d, Jean Carolyn Johnson, Sept. 3, 1955; 1 son, John Robert. Production mgr. Pacific Jewelry Mfg. Co., Santa Monica, Calif., 1946-50, 52; sr. cons., prin. v.p. Richard Muther & Assos., Kansas City, Mo., 1959-65; mgr. contract div. Barry Wehmiller Co., exec. v.p. Faircraft Mfg. Co., St. Louis, 1966-69; owner, prin. cons. Wheeler & Assos., St. Louis, 1969—. Served with AUS, 1942-45, USAF, 1950-51, 53-56. Decorated D.F.C., Air Medal with 4 oak leaf clusters. Mem. Inst. Mgmt. Cons. (certified), Am. Inst. Indsl. Engrs., Am. Production and Inventory Control Soc. (certified), Soc. Mfg. Engrs., U. Kans. Alumni Assn., Beta Gamma Sigma. Republican. Clubs: Claymont Bath and Tennis, Castle Oak Tennis. Home and office: 513 Antioch Ln Ballwin MO 63011

WHEELER, MARY FRANCES, educator; b. Chgo., Mar. 16, 1913; d. Francis L. and Mary (West) Wheeler; A.B., U. Mo., 1935, B.S. in Edn., 1937; M.A., Tchrs. Coll., Columbia, 1952; postgrad. U. Wis., 1945-47. Tchr. pub. schs., Salisbury, Mo., 1936-37, Clifton Hill, Mo., 1937-38, Maplewood, Mo., 1938-46, Madison, Wis., 1946-52; dean women Neb. State Tchrs. Coll., Chadron, 1952-53; head resident counselor So. Ill. U., 1953-55; dir. residence Wayland Acad., Beaver Dam, Wis., 1955-56; asst. dean students MacMurray Coll., Jacksonville, Ill., 1955-57; counselor, Webster Groves, Mo., 1957-68, Pompano Beach (Fla.) Jr. High Sch., 1968-69. Parkway East Jr. High Sch., Creve Coeur, Mo., 1969—. Mem. Mo. (pres. 1973-75), Nat. (nominations com. 1970-72, mem. exec. bd. 1965-67, mem. commn. on profl. employment practices 1972-75) assns. women deans and counselors, Mo. State (ho. of dels. 1975—), Parkway Ind. (exec. bd. 1973-75), Greater St. Louis (ho. of dels. 1975—), tchrs. assns., Delta Gamma. Democrat. Mem. Christian Ch. Home: 13527 Coliseum Dr Chesterfield MO 63017 Office: 181 Coeur de Ville Dr Creve Coeur MO 63141

WHEELER, ROBERT CORDELL, historian, assn. adminstr.; b. Columbus, Ohio, Aug. 5, 1913; s. Carl and Caroline Gertrude (Cordell) W.; B.S. in Edn., Ohio State U., 1938; m. Ardis May Hillman, June 9, 1939; children—Kristi, Jonathan. Newspaper librarian Ohio Hist. Soc., 1942-50; asst. dir. Ohio Sesquicentennial, 1950-53; field rep. Ohio Hist. Soc., 1954-57; asst. dir. Minn. Hist. Soc., St. Paul, 1957-64, asso. dir., 1964—; chmn. adv. council Underwater Archaeology, 1969-75; dir. Forest History Center, Grand Rapids, Minn., 1971—. Served with C.E., U.S. Army, 1942-45. Mem. Am. Assn. State and Local History, Soc. Hist. Archaeology. Unitarian. Author: Ohio Newspapers, a Living Record, 1950; Voices from the Rapids: An Underwater Search for Fur Trade Artifacts, 1975. Home: 2183 Payne Ave Saint Paul MN 55117 Office: 690 Cedar St Saint Paul MN 55101

WHELAN, GERALD T., lt. gov. Nebr.; b. Hastings, Nebr., May 14, 1925; student Creighton U., U. Colo.; LL.B., U. Nebr.; m. Sept. 8, 1948. Admitted to Nebr. bar, practice in Hastings; lt. gov. Nebr., Lincoln, 1975—. Sec. Hastings Centennial Commn. Mem. Nebr. State Bd. Edn., 1970-74. Bd. dirs. Adams County (Nebr.) ARC, Adams County Fair Assn., Hastings Community Chest. Mem. Adams County Bar Assn. (past pres.). Roman Catholic (chmn. ch.). Club: Lochland Country. Home: Lochland Village Hastings NE 68901 Office: Office of Lt Gov State Capitol Lincoln NE 68509*

WHELAN, JOSEPH L(EO), neurologist; b. Chisholm, Minn., Aug. 13, 1917; s. James Gorman and Johanna (Quilty) W.; student Hibbing Jr. Coll., 1935-38; B.S., U. Minn., 1940, M.B., 1942, M.D., 1943; m. Gloria Ann Rewoldt, June 12, 1948; children—Joseph William, Jennifer Ann. Intern, Detroit Receiving Hosp., 1942-43; fellow neurology U. Pa. Hosp., Phila., 1946-47; resident neurology U. Minn. Hosps., Mpls., 1947-49; chief neurology service VA Hosp., Mpls., 1949; spl. fellow electroencephalography Mayo Clinic, Rochester, Minn., 1951; practice medicine specializing in neurology, Detroit, 1949-73, Petoskey, Mich., 1973—; chief neurology services Grace, St. John's, Bon Secour hosps., Detroit; cons. neurologist Burns Clinic, Little Traverse Hosp., Lockwood-MacDonald Hosp., all Petoskey. Instr. U. Minn. Med. Sch., 1949; asst. prof. Wayne State U., 1957-63; cons. USPHS, Detroit Bd. Edn.; founder, mem. ad hoc Com. to Force Lawyers Out of Govt. Served to capt. AUS, 1943-46. Fellow Am. Acad. Neurology (treas. 1955-57), Am. Electroencephalography Soc.; mem. Assn. Research Nervous and Mental Diseases, Soc. Clin. Neurogists, Mich. Neurol. Assn. (sec.-treas. 1967—), Am., Mich. med. assns., No. Mich. Med. Soc. Club: Grosse Pointe (Mich.). Contbr. to profl. publs. in field. Home: Oxbow Rural Route 2 Mancelona MI 49659 Office: 820 Arlington Dr Petoskey MI 49770

WHINERY, DOROTHY COOKE (MRS. JAMES C. WHINERY), assn. exec.; b. Louisville; d. Thomas and Abigail (Latimer) Cooke; B.S. in Music, Drake U., 1935; m. James Curtis Whinery, Oct. 9, 1938 (dec. Oct. 1955); 1 dau., Janet (Mrs. Jock Evan Thompson). Tchr. music pub. schs. Somers, Iowa, 1935-38; asst. buyer Younkers, Inc., Des Moines, 1941-45; nat. exec. sec. Sigma Alpha Iota, Des Moines, 1957—, nat. exec. bd., 1957—. Bd. dirs. Des Moines Civic Music Assn., 1950-53, exec. sec., 1953-65. Recipient Sword Honor, 1950, Rose Honor, 1962, Ring Excellence, 1968, all Sigma Alpha Iota. Mem. Am. Bus. Women's Assn., Nat. Trust Historic Preservation, Smithsonian Instn. Home: 1447 57th St Des Moines IA 50311 Office: 4119 Rollins Ave Des Moines IA 50312

WHINERY, ROBERT DON, physician; b. Sioux City, Iowa, Nov. 15, 1931; s. Vern Robert and Hathor Clara (Hunt) W.; B.S. (Phi Beta Kappa), U. Iowa, 1954, M.D. (Mosby award, Alpha Kappa Kappa), 1957; m. Joyce Linduski, Feb. 9, 1953; children—Robert D., Jr., Susan, Steve, Lisa, Tom. Intern Hurley Hosp., Flint, Mich., 1957-58; resident in ophthalmology U. Iowa, 1958-62, now clin. lectr. Coll. Medicine; practice medicine specializing in ophthalmology, Iowa City, Iowa, 1962—; pres. Mercy Hosp., 1977-78, chief surgery, 1973. Mem. admissions com. U. Iowa Med. Coll., Iowa City, 1972-76. Chmn. bd. dirs. Iowa Med. Polit. Action Com. Diplomate Am. Bd. Ophthalmology. Mem. Am. Acad. Ophthalmology and Otolaryngology, A.C.S., Internat. Coll. Surgeons, AMA (alt. del. Iowa 1976-79), Soc. Eye Surgeons. Rotarian (bd. dirs. 1972-73). Home: 2 Glendale Circle Iowa City IA 52240 Office: 2409 Towncrest Dr Iowa City IA 52240

WHIPKEY, KENNETH LEE, educator; b. Cortland, Ohio, June 5, 1932; s. Charles Leigh and Marjorie Opal (Hefner) W.; student Youngstown U., 1950-52; A.B., Kent State U., 1953, M.A., 1958; student French Ministry Edn., summer 1954; student U. Colo., summers 1955, 59, Mich. State U., 1960, Mo. Sch. Mines, 1963; Ph.D., Case Western Res. U., 1969; postgrad. Ariz. State U., 1975, Oxford (Eng.) U., 1975; m. Mary Nell Glaser, Mar. 2, 1962. Instr. math, physics Vernon High Sch., Kinsman, Ohio, 1954-57, asst. prin., 1955-57,; asst. statistician Mallory Sharon Titanium Corp., Niles, O., summer 1955; grad. asst. math. Kent (Ohio) State U., 1957-58; instr. math. Youngstown (Ohio) U., 1957-60, asst. prof., 1960-67; instr. NSF-In-Service Year Inst. Tchrs. Youngstown, 1964-67; workshop instr. Holt, Rinehart & Winston, Youngstown and Canton, Ohio, 1965-66; asst. prof. math. Westminster Coll., New Wilmington, Pa., 1968-69, asso. prof., 1969-76, prof., 1976—. Mem. Danforth Assn., Nat. Council Tchrs. Math., Am. Math. Soc., Math. Assn. Am., Am. Numis. Assn., Kappa Mu Epsilon, Pi Mu Epsilon. Author: The Power of Calculus, 1972, 75; The Power of Mathematics, 1978; The Power of Basic Math, 1977. Home: 456 Bradley Ln Youngstown OH 44504 also Mt View Club RD 2 Brandon Vt 05733 Office: Westminster Coll New Wilmington PA 16142

WHIPPLE, FRANK HALL, real estate appraiser and developer; b. Chgo., Oct. 8, 1927; s. George Albert and Stella (Tuthill) W.; student Denison U., 1945-48; B.S., Utah State U., 1950; m. Anne E. Pabst, Sept. 28, 1957; children—Carolyn, David. Sr. staff appraiser Real Estate Research Corp., Chgo., 1959-63; sr. mortgage negotiater Dovenmuehle Inc., Chgo., 1963-69; propr. F.H. Whipple Assos., Northfield, Ill., 1969—; chmn. bd. Real, Search Ltd., Northfield, 1971—. Served with Finance Corps, AUS, 1951-53. Mem. Sigma Chi. Conglist. (chmn. bd., trustee). Club: Rotary (dir.). Home: 1339 Trapp St Winnetka IL 60093 Office: 550 Frontage St Northfield IL 60093

WHIPPLE, WALTER LEIGHTON, elec. engr.; b. Washington, D.C., June 23, 1940; s. Walter Jones and Marian Katharine (Leighton) Whipple; m. Jean Ewer, Sept. 10, 1965; children—Kathryn, Sara. B.S., Harvey Mudd Coll., 1962; postgrad. U. Calif. at Berkeley, 1965-66; M.S.E., U. Mich., 1974, postgrad., 1974—. Registered profl. elec. engr. Calif., Mass., Mich.; registered bus. programmer. Teaching asst., research asst. U. Mich., Ann Arbor, 1973-75; engring. aide Vidya div. Itek Corp., Palo Alto, Calif., 1961; field service rep. ordnance div. Gen. Electric Co., Pittsfield, Mass., 1962-65; resident insp. Welker & Assos., Marietta, Ga., 1966-67; asso. engr. space and info. systems div. Raytheon Co., Sudbury, Mass., 1967-68, engr., 1968-69; program analyst Control Data Corp., Waltham, Mass., 1969-71, sr. program analyst, 1971—; pvt. practice engring., Ann Arbor, 1973—. Resident mgr. Broadview Apts., Ann Arbor, 1973-74; owner The Secretariat, Ann Arbor, 1974—; notary pub. Washtenaw County, Mich., 1975—. Mem. Nat., Mich. and Profl. Socs. engrs. in pvt. practice of Nat. Soc. Profl. Engrs., So. Calif. Computing Soc., Computer and Power Engring. Soc., IEEE (sr.), Assn. Computing Machinery, Eta Kappa Nu, Nat. Notary Assn. Club: Univ. (U. Mich.). Asso. editor Simuletter, 1972-73; chmn. simulation sessions. Home: 812 S State St Ann Arbor MI 48104

WHIPPLE, WILLIAM PERRY, found. exec.; b. Cedar Rapids, Iowa, Nov. 1, 1913; s. Milo Robert and Jeanette Louise (Fry) W.; B.A. (cum laude, trustee), Coe Coll., 1935; m. Gayle Leota Schroeder, Sept. 18, 1937; children—John William, Robert Milo. Owner Whipple Ins. Agy., 1935; pres. Whipple Winterberg & Shepard, Inc., Cedar Rapids, Iowa, 1955-74, chmn. bd., 1968-74; v.p., exec. dir. Hall Found., Inc., Cedar Rapids, 1974—. Adv. dir. Am. Fed. Savs. & Loan of Iowa, 1955—. Pres. Linn County (Iowa) Chpt. ARC, 1945. Bd. dirs. YMCA, pres. 1958; trustee Wick Found., Cedar Rapids Met. YMCA, Meth Wick Manor. Mem. Iowa (state dir. 1945-47) Cedar Rapids (pres. 1938-39) assns. ins. agts. Republican. Presbyn. Elk. Home: 100 1st St NE Apt 2602 Cedar Rapids IA 52401 Office: 1200 Mchts Nat Bank Bldg Cedar Rapids IA 52401

WHIPPS, EDWARD FRANKLIN, lawyer; b. Columbus, Ohio, Dec. 17, 1936; s. Rusk Henry and Agnes Lucille (Green) W.; B.A., Ohio Wesleyan U., 1958; LL.B., Ohio State U., 1961, J.D., 1968; children—Edward Scott, Rusk Huot, Sylvia Louise, Rudyard Christian. Admitted to Ohio bar, 1961; asso. firm George, Greek, King & McMahon, Columbus, 1961-66; partner firm George, Greek, King, McMahon & McConnaughey, Columbus, 1966—; pres. Creative Living Inc., Columbus, 1975—, Community Services Inc., Columbus, 1965—. Mem. Upper Arlington Bd. Edn., 1972—, v.p., 1975, pres., 1976; bd. alumni dirs. Ohio Wesleyan U., 1975—. Mem. Columbus (chmn. municipal ct. com. 1973—), Am., Ohio bar assns., Assn. Trial Lawyers Am., Ohio Acad. Trial Lawyers, Franklin County Trial Lawyers Assn., Am. Judicature Soc., Tri-Village C. of C. Republican. Methodist. Clubs: Lawyers Columbus, Barristers Columbus, Columbus Athletic, Delta Tau Delta (nat. v.p. 1974-76). Home: 3771 Lyon Dr Columbus OH 43220 Office: 100 E Broad St Columbus OH 43215

WHISLER, ROBERT DANIEL, chem. co. exec.; b. Atlanta, Ind., Nov. 4, 1921; s. Lawrence A. and Marie Margaret (Ploch) W.; B.S., Ind. U., 1942; M.B.A., Harvard Grad. Sch. Bus. Adminstrn., 1947; m. Virginia Anne Taylor, Sept. 20, 1947; children—Robert Daniel, Nancy, Debra, William. Staff accountant S.C. Johnson & Son, Inc., Racine, Wis., 1947-58, systems and audit mgr., 1959-64, internat. controller, 1965—, dir. overseas finance, 1972—, v.p., controller overseas ops., 1977—. Treas. Racine Sch. Bd., 1954-59. Trustee Village of Elmwood, Wis., 1960-66. Served with AUS, 1943-47. Mem. Inst. Internal Auditors (internat. pres. 1962-63). Mason. Home: 3516 Gifford Rd Franksville WI 53126 Office: 1525 Howe St Racine WI 53403

WHISNANT, JACK PAGE, neurologist; b. Little Rock, Oct. 26, 1924; s. John Clifton and Zula I. (Page) W.; B.S., U. Ark., 1948, M.D., 1951; M.S., U. Minn., 1955; m. Patricia Anne Rimmey, May 12, 1944; children—Elizabeth Anne, John David, James Michael. Intern, Balt. City Hosp., 1951-52; resident in medicine and neurology Mayo Grad. Sch. Medicine, Rochester, Minn., 1952-55, instr. neurology, 1956-60, asst. prof., 1960-64, asso. prof., 1964-69, prof., 1969—, chmn. dept. neurology Mayo Clinic, Mayo Med. Sch., Mayo Grad. Sch. Medicine, 1971—; cons. in neurology Mayo Clinic, 1955—, head sect. neurology, 1964-69; dir. Mayo Cerebrovascular Clin. Research Center, 1975—. Bd. dirs. YMCA Rochester. Served with U.S. Army, 1942-45. Decorated Air medal; NIH grantee, 1958, 76. Fellow Am. Heart Assn., Am. Acad. Neurology; mem. AAUP Neurology, Am. Neurol. Assn., Zumbro Valley Med. Soc., Minn. State Med. Assn., Alumni Assn. Mayo Found., Minn. Soc. Neurol. Scis. Mem. Minn. Democratic-Farm-Labor Party. Presbyterian. Contbr. articles on neurology and cerebrovascular disease to profl. jours. Home: 1005 7th Ave NE Rochester MN 55901 Office: Dept Neurology Mayo Clinic Rochester MN 55901

WHITAKER, WALTER MERRILL, pediatrician; b. Bucyrus, Kans., June 13, 1903; s. Robert O. and Emma (Cooper) W.; student U. Kans., 1921-23; M.D., Washington U., St. Louis, 1927; m. Mary Leona Harding, Jan. 2, 1929; 1 dau., Delores Ann Whitaker Crossland. Intern, Barnes Hosp., St. Louis, 1927-29; resident fellow in pediatrics East London (Eng.) Hosp. for Children, 1929, Royal Hosp. for Sick Children, Glasgow, Scotland, 1929; pediatrician cardiologist Van Ravensway Clinic, Booneville, Mo., 1930-31; practice medicine specializing in pediatrics and cardiology, Quincy, Ill., 1931-36; co-founder, partner, Quincy Clinic, 1936—; mem. adv. hosp. council Ill. Dept. Pub. Health, 1951-63; med. adviser Adams County (Ill.) Draft Bd., 1941—. Served from lt. comdr. to comdr. M.C., USNR, 1943-46. Recipient editorial award Hosp. Mgmt. Mag., 1959; Shell Oil Co. exchange fellow, 1929. Diplomate Am. Bd. Pediatrics. Mem. Am. Acad. Pediatrics (pres. Ill. chpt. 1966-68), Ill. Heart Assn. (dir.) Alpha Omega Alpha. Republican. Congregationalist. Contbr. articles to med. jours. Home: 2003 Jersey St Quincy IL 62301 Office: 1416 Maine St Quincy IL 62301

WHITCOMB, EDGAR D., former gov. Ind., lawyer; b. Hayden, Ind., Nov. 6, 1917; s. John W. and Louise (Doud) W.; LL.B., Ind. U., 1950, LL.D. (hon.), 1973; m. Patricia Dolfuss, May 20, 1951; children—Patricia, Linda, Shelley, Alice, John. Admitted to Ind. Bar. 1952, practiced in Seymour, Ind., Indpls., 1952-66; mem. Ind. Senate, 1951-54; asst. U.S. atty. for So. Dist. Ind., Indpls., 1955-56; sec. state Ind., 1966-68; gov. of Ind., 1969-73; dir. World Trade Center, Indpls., 1973—. Chmn. Great Lakes Commn., 1965, 66; bd. dirs. U.S. Auto Club, 1973—. Served to col. USAF, ret. Mem. Phi Delta Phi. Methodist. Author: Escape from Corregidor, 1958. Home: 636 Poplar St Seymour IN 47274 Office: 1 Indiana Sq Indianapolis IN 46204

WHITE, ALEXANDER PATRICK, lawyer, govt. ofcl.; b. Chgo., Mar. 30, 1932; s. Alexander Patrick and Eleanore Marion (White) W.; B.S. in Finance, No. Ill. U., 1959; J.D. with honors, Chgo. Kent Coll. Law, 1964; LL.M., John Marshall Law Sch., 1976; m. Marilyn Karin Samuelsen, Aug. 23, 1958; children—Bradley J., Christy Lynn, Laura S., Julie K. Admitted to Ill. bar, 1964, Ill. Supreme Ct., 1964, U.S. Dist. Court, 1964, U.S. Ct. Appeals, 1966, U.S. Ct. Mil. Appeals, 1968, U.S. Supreme Ct., 1968; law clk. Ill. Appellate Ct., 1964-67; asso. Moses, McGarr, Gibbons, Abramson & Fox, Chgo., 1964-66; legislative coordinator Cook County Bd. Commrs., 1966-69; adminstrv. asst. to pres. bd., 1966-69; instr. Chgo. Kent Coll. Law, 1969—; mil. aide to gov. State of Ill., 1969-73, asst. to gov., extradition sec. for gov., 1969-70; adminstrv. asst. to U.S. Senator Ralph Tyler Smith, 1969-70; chmn. Ill. Indsl. Commn., 1970-73; regional dir. Dept. Labor, 1973-77, mem. fed. regional council, 1973-77. Fed. defender U.S. Dist. Ct., No. Dist. Ill., 1966—; counsel for indigents Ct. Appeals, 7th Circuit, 1966-68, Circuit Ct. Cook County, 1968-70. Exec. dir. Non-Partisan Citizens Com. for Improvement of Cook County Jail, 1968; sec. Cook County com. Ill. Sesquicentennial, 1968. Chmn. Cook County Young Republicans, 1964; 6th Congl. dist. gov. Ill. Young Rep. Orgn., 1964-66. Served with USMCR, 1954-58; now col. Res. Mem. Am., Il., Chgo. bar assns., Am. Judicature Soc., Bar Assn. 7th Fed. Circuit, Fed Bar Assn. (sec. 1976—), Judge Advocates Assn. (dir. 1976—), Chgo. Kent Coll. Alumni Assn. (treas. 1976—), Marine Corps Res. Officers Assn. (1st v.p. 1969-72), Marine Corps Assn., Marine Corps League, Navy League. Res. Officers Assn., Phi Delta Phi. Home: 7201 Wilson Terr Morton Grove IL 60053 Office: 10 S LaSalle St Chicago IL 60002

WHITE, ALLEN E., metal stamping co. exec.; b. Anderson, Ind., Oct. 12, 1926; s. Edgar Guy and Ila Marie (Kyte) W.; student aircraft and engine mechanics Lincoln (Neb.) Aviation Inst., 1947; m. Pauline M. Buonomo, June 27, 1947; children—Alice Anne, Paula Jeanne. Machine operator Caterpillar Tractor Co., Peoria, Ill., 1949; welder Meyer Furnace Co., Peru, Ill., 1950-51; gen. mgr. Triple A Sign Co., LaSalle, Ill., 1951-53, Jiffy Metal Products Co., Chgo., 1953-66; pres. Animated Mfg. Co., South Holland, Ill., 1966—, chmn. bd., 1972—. Mem. bus. advisory group Congressman Martin A. Russo, 3d Ill. Dist. Served with USAAF, 1945. Mem. South Suburban C. of C. of Ind., Ill., U.S. c's. of C. Club: Kiwanis (pres. South Holland club 1972). Home: 621 E 158th St South Holland IL 60473 Office: 106 W 154th St South Holland IL 60473

WHITE, CHARLES EDGAR, coll. adminstr.; b. Woodruff, Ark., Jan. 25, 1943; s. Charles Austin and Creasie (Gladney) W.; B.B.A., Cleary Coll., 1967; M.A., U. Mich., 1975; M.B.A., U. Detroit, 1977; m. Sandra Yvonne Ricks, Sept. 7, 1968; children—LaTanya, Charles. Payroll supr. Bendix Corp., Southfield, Mich., 1967-68, accountant, 1968-70, sr. accountant, 1970-72; sr. staff analyst Mich. Consol. Gas Co., Detroit, 1972-73; dir. accounting Wayne County Community Coll., Detroit, 1973-75, controller, 1975—. Treas., Inkster Bd. Edn., 1977—; bd. dirs. Franklin Wright Settlement, 1976—. Served with U.S. Army, 1960-63. Mem. Nat. Assn. Accountants, Nat. Assn. Black Accountants, Mich. Assn. Sch. Adminstrs., Mich. Bus. Ofcls. Assn., Nat. Small Bus. Assn. Mem. Ch. of God. Home: 1449 Wellesley Dr Inkster MI 48141 Office: 4612 Woodward Ave Detroit MI 48201

WHITE, CHARLES MCKINLEY, dentist; b. Mercer County, Pa., Oct. 30, 1896; s. James A. and Mary Elizabeth (Roberts) W.; D.D.S., Case Res. U., 1918; m. Letha Jane Moon, Oct. 28, 1920; children—Jean Louise White Markell, Robert C., Richard A. Resident dentist Gen. Electric Co., Warren, Ohio, 1919-27; practice dentistry, Warren, 1919—. Bd. dirs. Salvation Army, Warren, 1962—. Served with U.S. Army, World War I. Mem. ADA, Ohio State Dental Soc., Am. Assn. Dentists, Am. Soc. Dentistry for Children, Am. Endodontic Soc., Fedn. Dentaire Internat., Warren C. of C., Am. Legion. Republican. Presbyterian. Clubs: Shriners, Masons, Trumbull Country. Author: Your Dentist and You, 1958; The Miracle of Dentistry, 1974. Home: 3210 E Market St Warren OH 44483 Office: 350 N Park Ave Warren OH 44481

WHITE, CHARLOTTE ARLENE BUCHER (MRS. NORBERT WILLIAM WHITE), social worker; b. New Philadelphia, Ohio, Dec. 18, 1928; d. Adam Guy and Addie Mae (Collins) Bucher; student Cleve., 1947, Wittenburgh Coll., summer 1949, Ill. Inst. Tech., 1950-53; Asso. in govt. studies, Kent State U., 1974; m. Norbert William White, Mar. 17, 1954 (dec. Apr. 1960); 1 dau., Charl-Norene. Office mgr. Pepsi-Cola Bottling Co., Dover, New Philadelphia, 1957-64; city auditor New Philadelphia, 1964-68; caseworker Tuscarawas County Welfare Dept.; spl. rep. Frontier Attractions, musical bookings. Program chmn. PTA Council, New Philadelphia; past pres. Tuscarawa Ave. PTA; now v.p. Democratic Central Exec. Com., 1965-68; co-chmn. Dem. Campaign, 1964; sec. Young Dem. Club. Mem. DAR (sec. 1961), 1966-67. Mem. Internat. Platform Assn., Country Music Assn., Acad. Country and Western Music. Clubs: Moose, Eagles. Home: 139 Front Ave SW New Philadelphia OH 44663 Office: 154 2d St NE New Philadelphia OH 44663

WHITE, D. JERRY, realtor; b. Springfield, Ill., Nov. 21, 1937; s. George C. and Margaret B. (Kiely) W.; student Springfield Jr. Coll., 1955-56, Northwestern U., 1957-58; B.S., Loyola U., Chgo., 1960; m. Mary Ellen Bahl, June 11, 1960; children—Lynn Ann, Karyn Marie, Mark Jerry. Radio Announcer, account exec., disc jockey Radio Sta. WCVS, Springfield, 1954-56; engaged in real estate bus., 1960—; owner Jerry White & Co., Springfield, 1961—. Mem. Chgo. dist. adv. council SBA, 1974—. Commr., Springfield Airport Authority, 1971-72, chmn. land acquisition com., 1971-72; chmn. nat. airlines com. Springfield Airport Authority, 1971-72; commr. Springfield-Sangamon County Regional Plan Commn., 1972—, chmn., 1975-76; nominee Ill. Senate from 49th Senatorial Dist., 1966. Bd. dirs. Sangamon County His. Soc., 1961-64, v.p., 1961-62; bd. dirs. Sangamon County Sr. Citizens, 1974—; mem. UN Day Com., recipient Distinguished Service award UN ambassador, 1975. Recipient Loyolan award Loyola U., 1960; certificate of Merit Springfield Airport Authority, 1972. Mem. Springfield Greater C. of C., Nat. Assn. Real Estate Bds., Nat. Inst. Real Estate Appraisers, Springfield Bd. Realtors, Springfield Art Assn. Roman Catholic. Elk, Eagle. Clubs: Sangamo, Island Bay Yacht. Home: 2420 S Glenwood Springfield IL 62704 Office: 1800 S MacArthur Blvd Springfield IL 62704

WHITE, EUGENE ELLSWORTH, banker; b. Chgo., Apr. 6, 1928; s. Ellsworth M. and Julia (Morse) W.; A.B., Brown U., 1951; m. Jane Craven Beaver, May 1, 1954; children—Miles, Paisley. With Beaver Assos., Inc. (merger Am. City Bur. 1962, name now Am. City Bur.-Beaver Assos.), Chgo., 1955-72, v.p., 1960-61, exec. v.p., treas., 1961-62, v.p., dir., 1962-66, sr. v.p., mem. exec. com., 1966-68, exec. v.p., mem. exec. com., 1968-70, pres., mem. exec. com., 1970-72; chmn. bd. Bank of Clarendon Hills, Bank of Northfield, Bank of Wheaton Bank of Winfield, 1972—; pres. Wheaton Bancorp., Inc. (named changed to Charter Bancorporation, Inc.), Northfield Bancorp., Inc. (name changed to Charter Financial Corp.), Charter Group, Inc., Charter Clarendon Bancorp. Inc., Charter Bancshares, Inc., Charter Group Life Ins. Co., Charter Agy. Inc. Trustee George Williams Coll., Hadley Sch. for Blind, Chgo. Council Community Services. Served to 1st lt. USAF, 1951-55. Clubs: Sunset Ridge Country; University, Economic (Chgo.). Home: 5 Country Ln Northfield IL 60093 Office: 400 Central Ave Northfield IL 60093

WHITE, FREDERICK ARTHUR, univ. adminstr. emeritus; b. Adelphi, Ohio, July 8, 1907; s. Fred Arthur and Flora Roberta (Swinehart) W.; B.A., Otterbein Coll., 1928, LL.D., 1971; LL.D., Wright State U., 1973; m. Ruth Sims, June 21, 1931 (dec.); children—Robert F., Stephen S. High sch. prin., Adelphi, 1932-36; supt. schs., Van Wert County, Ohio, 1936-42; asst. mgr. materials Allison-Aeroproducts div. Gen. Motors Corp., Vandalia, Ohio, 1942-62; bus. mgr. to v.p., treas., dir. devel. Wright State U., Dayton, Ohio, 1962—, acting pres., 1972-73, sr. v.p. emeritus, 1973—. Bd. trustees Tipp City Pub. Library, Tipp Monroe Community Services, 1976—; bd. dirs. Jr. Achievement of Dayton; past pres., trustee Dayton Council on World Affairs, 1976—; chmn. citizens adv. programming com. Univ. Region Broadcasting, Channels 14 and 16, 1976—; mem. Great Miami Corridor Com.; trustee Community Health Plan West Central Ohio. Mem. Am. Soc. Pub. Adminstrs. (pres. Miami Valley chpt., named Outstanding Pub. Adminstr. 1967). Lutheran. Clubs: Dayton Engineers, Dayton Executives. Home: 230 W Main St Tipp City OH 45371 Office: Wright State U Dayton OH 45435

WHITE, GEOFFERY LEE, advt. exec.; b. Milw., Jan. 12, 1950; s. Frank A. and Sally D. W.; student pub. schs., Whitefish Bay, Wis.; m. Lucinda M. Hansen, Sept. 6, 1975. Account exec. Naegele Advt. Co., Mpls., 1970-72, Hansen Advt., Milw., 1972-74; gen. mgr. White Advt., La Crosse, Wis., 1974-77; v.p. Skoglund Communications, La Crosse, 1977—. Republican. Mem. C. of C. Clubs: Rotary, Elks, Eagles. Home: 304 N 22nd St La Crosse WI 54601 Office: 2517 South Ave La Crosse WI 54601

WHITE, HAROLD EDGAR, JR., newspaper editor and publisher; b. Bangalore, India, Nov. 11, 1913; s. Harold Edgar and Fannie Alice (Fowler) W.; came to U.S., 1915, naturalized, 1941; B.A., North Central Coll., 1935, LL.D., 1977; m. Eva M. Anderson, July 23, 1937. Editor, pub. Naperville (Ill.) Sun, 1936—; pub. Lisle Twp. (Ill.) Sun, 1947—; pres. Naperville Sun Inc., 1954—, Sun Printing Co., 1977—; founder, sec.-treas. Naperville Airport, 1956—; pres. Sun Bldg. Corp., Naperville, 1977—; dir. Naperville Savs. & Loan Assn., 1954—; pub. Warrenville (Ill.) News, 1958-61. Chmn. S.E. Fox Valley Emergency Med. Services Council, 1975—. Named outstanding alumnus North Central Coll., 1975. Mem. Ill. (dir.), DuPage County (treas. 1963-69) press assns., Nat. Newspaper Assn., Naperville C. of C., DuPage Pubs. Assn., Sigma Delta Chi. Republican. Methodist. Clubs: Cress Creek Country; Lions (pres. Naperville 1976), Moose. Home: 9 S 281 Aero Dr Naperville IL 60540 Office: 9 W Jackson Ave Naperville IL 60540

WHITE, HARRIET ELIZABETH, intergroup relations specialist; b. Hillsdale, N.J., Feb. 13, 1920; d. Albert T. and Laura C. (Price) White; A.B., Bates Coll., 1941; M.A., Ohio U., 1943. Indsl. relations aide Eastman Kodak Co., 1943-44; asst. house dir., employee counselor U.S. Govt., 1944-46; asst. dean of women Bucknell U., 1946-47; instr. edn. Ind. U., 1947-49; young adult program dir. Young Women's Christian Assn., Detroit, 1949-51, dir. Woodlawn Center YWCA, Chgo., 1951-56; program dir. Nat. Conf. Christians and Jews, Chgo., 1956-68; pub. relations supr. Ill. Bell Telephone Co., 1968-70, personnel supr., 1970-74, corporate equal employment mgr., 1974—; community relations coordinator Chgo. Police Dept., 1965-66. Recipient Good Am. award, Chgo. Com. of One Hundred, 1962. Mem. Delta Sigma Rho. Club: Executives (Chgo.). Home: 403 Chanticleer St Hinsdale IL 60521 Office: 225 W Randolph St Chicago IL 60606

WHITE, HUGH ERWIN, farmer; b. Hutchinson, Kans., Mar. 8, 1905; s. David Clinton and Sadie Belle (Doles) W.; B.S., Kans. State U., 1929, M.S. in Agrl. Engring. (grad. research asst. experiment sta.), 1940; m. Gladys Lucile Black, Aug. 25, 1929; children—David, Myron, Janis (Mrs. James Peter Lindsay), Sharon (Mrs. Michael Shelor). Instr. in agrl. engring. N.D. State U., Fargo, 1940-43; farmer, rancher, 1943—; pres. Kingsdown Coop. Oil Co., Kans., 1944-47, Coop. Exchange, 1948-52. Chmn. bd. trustees Dodge City Community Coll., Kans., 1965—; vice-chmn. Ford County Red Cross, Dodge City chpt. ARC, 1950-53. Trustee D.C. White trust. Recipient Bankers award for soil conservation, Ford County Bankers Assn., 1967. Mem. Ford County Meal Habitat Assn. (chmn.), Am. Soc. Agrl. Engrs., Master Farmer Assn., Flying Farmers Assn., Kans. State U. Alumni Assn., Phi Kappa Tau. Republican. Presbyn. (mem. United Presbyn. Found. Kans., chmn. Men's Work). Lion. Research on traction characteristics of tractor tires. Home and office: Route 1 Kingsdown KS 67858

WHITE, JAMES PATRICK, educator; b. Iowa City, Iowa, Sept. 29, 1931; s. Raymond Patrick and Besse (Kanak) W.; B.A., State U. Iowa, 1953, J.D., 1956; LL.M., George Washington U., 1959; m. Anna R. Seim, July 2, 1964. Teaching fellow George Washington U. Law Sch., 1958-59; asst. prof. U. N.D. Law Sch., Grand Forks, 1959-62, asso. prof., acting dean, 1962-63, asso. dean, 1963-67, dir. agrl. law research program; prof. law, Ind. U. Law Sch., Indpls., 1967—, also dir. urban legal studies program, 1971-74, univ. dean acad. devel. and planning, spl. asst. to the chancellor; cons. on legal edn. Am. Bar Assn., 1974—. Admitted to Iowa bar, 1956, D.C. bar, 1959, U.S. Supreme Ct. bar, 1959; commr. Uniform State Laws, N.D., 1961-66; Young Democratic nat. committeeman, Iowa, 1952-54. Served as 1st lt. Judge Adv. Gen., USAF, 1956-58. Carnegie postdoctoral fellow U. Mich. Center for Study Higher Edn., 1964-65. Fellow Am. Bar Found.; mem. Am., Ind., Indpls., N.D., Iowa bar assns., Am. Judicature Soc., Am. Law Inst., Order of Coif. Roman Catholic. Contbr. papers to tech. lit. Home: 7707 N Meridian St Indianapolis IN 46260

WHITE, JAMES STEPHEN, data processing exec.; b. Pitts., Dec. 17, 1940; s. Alfred Butler and Mary Ruth (Gibbens) W.; student U. Minn., 1962; B.E.E., Marquette U., 1966; m. Elaine Carol Pionke, June 10, 1967; children—Donald, Remi. Programmer VA Hosp., Wood, Wis., 1961-62; computer facility supr. Mayo Clinic, Rochester, Minn., 1962-64; computer operations mgr. Marquette U., Milw., 1964-67; data and systems mgr. Durant Digital Instruments, Watertown, Wis., 1967—. Cons. Principal Cybernation Services, Watertown, 1970—. Mem. St. Bernards Bd. Edn., Watertown, 1972-74. State dir. Minn. Young Republicans, 1963-64. Mem. Honeywell Users Group (dir. 1970-71, treas. 1971-72). Author: Your Home Computer, 1977. Reviewer: Computing Reviews, 1968-75. Home: 1202 Riverview Ln Watertown WI 53094 Office: 901 S 12 St Watertown WI 53094

WHITE, JAMES WILLIAM, library dir., b. Cedar Rapids, Iowa, May 5, 1935; s. James Barton and Caroline Catherine (Schnepf) W.; student Iowa State U., 1953-55; B.A., U. Iowa, 1960-63, M.A., 1968; m. Dorothy Jean Henderson, Nov. 10, 1956; children—Cathy Jean, Christy Lee, William Barton, Carol Anne. Tool designer Allis-Chalmers, Cedar Rapids, 1955-56; design draftsman Collins Radio, Cedar Rapids, 1956-58; statistician Square D, Cedar Rapids, 1958-60; tchr., counselor Linn-Mar Community Schs., Marion, Iowa, 1963-67; library dir. Musser Pub. Library, Muscatine, Iowa, 1968-76; library and systems dir. La Crosse (Wis.) Pub. Library, 1976—. Del. to NEA, 1965. Chmn. Emergency and Disaster Com., Cedar Rapids, 1955-57; dir. ch. choirs, Cedar Rapids, 1962-67; pres., dir. Muscatine Community Theatre, 1970—. Bd. dirs. Office Econ. Opportunity, Iowa East Central TRAIN; v.p. Western Wis. Regional Arts; adv. bd. Salvation Army; mem. Wis. Council on Certificates and Standards. Served with AUS, 1957. Recipient Community Leader of Am. award, 1969. Mem. NEA, Linn County Edn. Assn. (pres. 1966-68), Am. (councilor state Iowa 1972—), Iowa (legislative com. 1969—) library assns., Soc. Preservation and Encouragement Barbershop Quartet Singing in Am. (life), Internat. Platform Assn., Iowa Alumni Assn. (life). Home: 1309 State St LaCrosse WI 54601 Office: 800 Main St La Crosse WI 54601

WHITE, JOE, JR., mfg. co. exec.; b. Union City, Ind., Oct. 12, 1930; s. Joe I. and Ruby G. (Ralston) W.; student Ind. Bus. Coll., 1949-50; m. Ruth Anne Lininger, Aug. 19, 1956; children—Terry, Jeffrey, Melody. Time clk. Anchor Hocking Glass Corp., Winchester, Inc., 1951-52; bookkeeper Winchester Union Stockyards (Ind.), 1952-57; with Overmyer Corp., Winchester, 1957—, corp. controller, 1968—; controller Overmyer Mould Co. Pa., Greensburg, Overmyer Mould Co. Cal., Downey. C.P.A., Ind. Mem. Am. Inst. C.P.A.'s, Ind. Assn. C.P.A.'s. Lion. Home: Box 12 Rural Route 1 Lynn IN 47355 Office: 117 Railroad Ave Winchester IN 47394

WHITE, JOHN HENRY, photographer; b. Lexington, N.C., Mar. 18, 1945; s. Reid Ross and Ruby Mae (Leverett) W.; Asso. Applied Sci., Central Piedmont Coll., 1966; m. Emily Lee Miller, May 29, 1966; children—Deborah, Angela, Ruby, John Henry. Photographer, Marine Corps, Quantico, Va., 1966-68; photo lab-technician Tom Walters Photography, Charlotte, N.C., 1968-69; press photographer Chgo. Daily News, 1969—. Vol. tchr. photography South Side Art Center, Chgo., 1970—; photographer movie Young, Gifted and Black, 1971. Trustee Bishop William J. Walls Found., Yongers, N.Y. Winner contests Nat. Press Photo, 1970, World Press Photo, 1971, A.P., U.P.I., Nat. Fire Fighters Contest, Nat. Constrn. Contest, 1972, So. Photo-of-Year Contest, 1969, Marshall Field award, 1976, 1st place Edward Steichen award, 1976; named Ill. Photographer of Year, Ill. Press Photographers Assn., 1971, Chgo. Press Photographer of Year, 1976; numerous other awards. Mem. Nat., Ill., Chgo. press assns., Ill. A.P. (pres. 1972—), Chgo. Press Photography Assn. (Chgo. Photographer of Year 1972, 73, dir.). Mem. A.M.E. Ch. (sec. bd. trustees 1971—, dir. edn. 1970—). Spl. photo story of Pres. Carter's last days in Plains, Ga. and through inauguration. Home: 623 E 33d Pl Chicago IL 60616 Office: 401 N Wabash Av Chicago IL 60611

WHITE, JOHN JOSEPH, III, physicist; b. Arlington, Mass., Apr. 24, 1939; s. John Joseph and Ruth Edith (Madden) W.; B.S., Coll. William Mary, 1960; Ph.D., U. N.C., Chapel Hill, N.C., 1965; m. Marian Patricia Wagner; children—John, Edmund. Asst. prof. dept. physics astronomy U. Ga., Athens, 1967-73; sr. engr., applied sci. dept. BDM Corp., Vienna, Va., 1973-74; research scientist, Columbus (Ohio) Labs. Battelle Meml. Inst., 1974-78, prin. research scientist, 1978—; mem. design rev. panel landing vehicle assault USN; dir. Ga. Sci. Engring. Fair, 1973; cons. tank-automotive tech.; specialist material properties and applications. Served to capt., applied physicist, U.S. Army, 1965-67. Fulbright grantee, 1973. Mem. Ga. Acad. Sci. (chmn. physics engring. sect. 1971), Am. Phys. Soc., Nat. Soc. Profl. Engrs. (chpt. program chmn. 1977), ASME, Am. Soc. Metals, Sigma Xi. Registered profl. engr., Ohio. Contbr. articles to physics jours. Home: 4865 Arthur Pl Columbus OH 43220 Office: 505 King Ave Columbus OH 43201

WHITE, KATHY ANN, educator; b. Indpls., Aug. 13, 1944; d. Paul Edwards and Anna Marie (Dziewas) White; B.S., Ball State U., 1966; M.S., Ind. U., 1968. Substitute tchr. Indpls. pub. schs., 1968; mem. faculty of Ind. U.-Purdue U., Indpls., 1970-76; tchr. of bus. edn. North Central High Sch., Washington Twp., Indpls., 1968—; sec. Meth. Hosp., Indpls., summers 1963, 64, 65, 66. Rental gallery day chmn. of Indpls. Mus. of Art, 1974—. Mem. Am., Ind. vocat. assns., Adminstrv. Mgmt. Soc., Nat. Secs. Assn., Indpls. Bus. Edn. Council, North Central Bus. Edn. Assn., Internat. Word Processing (v.p. central Ind. chpt. 1978—). Mem. Zions United Ch. of Christ. Clubs: Ind. Univ. Alumni, Ball State Alumni. Contbr. articles on bus. edn. to profl. publs. Home: 3025 N Meridian 804 Indianapolis IN 46208

WHITE, LARRY CURTIS, osteo. physician; b. Decatur, Ill., May 1, 1941; s. Gerald Curtis and Elizabeth Jane (Moore) W.; B.S., U. Ill., 1963; D.O., Kirksville Coll. Osteo. Medicine, 1970; m. Mary Ann Savage, Aug. 21, 1965; children—Mark, Michelle, Gerald. Intern, Riverside Osteo. Hosp., Trenton, Mich., 1970-71; practice osteo. medicine Romeo (Mich.) Clinic, 1971—, pres., 1971—; staff, mem. med. exec. com. Crittenton Hosp., 1977—, chmn. med. records com., 1977, vice chmn. dept., family practice, 1977—. Diplomate Am. Bd. Family Practice. Mem. Am. Osteo. Assn., Mich. Assn. Osteo. Physicians and Surgeons, Am. Acad. Family Physicians, Am. Assn. Family Practice, U. Ill. Alumni Assn., Psi Sigma Alpha, Alpha Phi Omega, Sigma Sigma Phi, Theta Psi, Alpha Kappa Lambda. Methodist. Clubs: Masons, Shriners, K.T. Home: 2250 E Gunn Rd Rochester MI 48063 Office: 241 N Main St Romeo MI 48065

WHITE, MARY WINIFRED LEE, counselor; b. N.Y.C., Jan. 18, 1926; d. Charles Henry Jr. and Luella (Simpson) Lee; B.S., Wilberforce U., 1947; M.S., Purdue U., 1974; m. John P. White, Aug. 18, 1946; children—John P., E. Denis White West, Dale E., Leslie L., II. Various clerical positions, 1948-52; caseworker St. Louis Welfare Dept., 1954-56; social worker Catholic Charities, St. Louis, 1956-57; classroom tchr. St. Louis pub. schs., 1957-71; elementary sch. tchr. Michigan City (Ind.) Area Schs. Corp., 1971-74, sch. counselor, 1974—. Trustee Michigan City Pub. Library, 1972-75. Mem. Am., Ind. personnel and guidance assns., Am. Sch. Counselors Assn., AAUW, LaPorte County Mental Health Assn., Friends of Alfred Adler Inst., Festival Players Guild. Alpha Kappa Alpha, Alpha Delta Kappa. Democrat. Roman Catholic. Home: 322 Kenwood Pl Michigan City IN 46360 Office: 301 Detroit St Michigan City IN 46360

WHITE, MICHAEL THOMAS, lawyer, county ofcl.; b. Brookfield, Mo., Oct. 10, 1940; s. Ernest and Harriett Clyde (Wine) W.; grad. cum laude Kansas City Jr. Coll., 1958-60; B.A. with distinction, U. Kansas City, 1962; postgrad. U. Mich., 1962; J.D. with honors U. Mo., 1966; m. Cynthia Jean Van Zandt, Jan. 20, 1968 (div. 1976); 1 dau., Jennifer Sherrell; m. 2d, Marie Vondelle Rossello, Aug. 14, 1976. Admitted to Mo. bar, 1966; partner Sheridan, Sander, Carr, White & Mason, Kansas City, 1966—; mem. Jackson County Legislature, 1973—; chmn. Little Blue Valley Sewer Dist.; county exec., 1975—. Adult specialist Mo. Youth for Environmental Quality, 1972; instr. youth tng. and leadership conf. A.R.C., 1972. Served with AUS, 1966-70. Mem. Am. Trial Lawyers Assn., Mo. Assn. Trial Attys., Mo. Bar, Kansas City Bar Assn., Am. Civil Liberties Union (Wester Mo. dir. 1966-70, legal counsel 1968-69, Friends of Earth, Wilderness Soc., Am. Fedn. Musicians, Phi Alpha Delta. Unitarian. Club: Toastmasters. Home: 6856 Edgevale Rd Kansas City MO 64113 Office: 414 E 12th St Kansas City MO 64106

WHITE, PAUL WILLIAM, state justice; b. Mitchell, S.D., Feb. 12, 1911; s. George W. and Mary G. (Barney) W.; A.B. with honors, U. Nebr., 1930, LL.B., 1932; m. Carol M. Gillan, Oct. 31, 1942; 1 son, Mark W. Admitted to Nebr. bar, 1932; practice in Lincoln, 1932-53; acting judge Lincoln Municipal Ct., 1949-53; dist. judge 3d Jud. Dist., Lancaster County, Nebr., 1953-63, presiding judge, 1955, 59, 61; chief justice Supreme Ct. Nebr., 1963—; asst. county atty., Lancaster County, 1941-47; spl. hearings exam. Nebr. Bd. Ednl. Lands and Funds, 1950-52. Charter mem. Nebr. Gov.'s Com. for Youth, 1954; chmn. Am. Legion Boys' State, 1951-54; incorporator, charter mem. Lincoln Youth Project of Woods Charitable Fund, 1956; active other civic activities. Bd. dirs. Nebr. Boy's State. Served to capt. AUS, 1942-46. Mem. Nebr. Dist. Ct. Judges Assn. (pres.), Am., Nebr., Lincoln bar assns., Am. Judicature Soc., Nat. Center State Cts., Conf. Chief Justices, Am. Interprofl. Inst., Am. Legion 40 and 8, Vets. Fgn. Wars. Methodist. Mason (32 deg., Shriner), Elk, K.P. Club: Lincoln Barristers (past pres.) (Lincoln). Home: 2741 Scott Ave Lincoln NE 68506 Office: Supreme Ct of Nebraska Lincoln NE 68509

WHITE, RAYMOND GENE, veterinarian; b. Elana, W. Va., Oct. 10, 1930; s. Curtis Roy and Ora Mae (Coen) W.; student U. W. Va., 1956; B.S., Okla. State U., 1958, D.V.M., 1960; M.S., U. of Nebr., 1970; m. Donna Jean Wilmoth, Mar. 25, 1952; children—Janice Leah Richter, Keith Alan White. Private veterinary practice, Springfield, Mo., 1960-64; research veterinarian Chemagro Corp., Kansas City, Mo., 1964-68; extension research veterinarian U. of Nebr., 1969-76, dist. dir. N. Platte Sta. (Nebr.), 1976—; pres. Cattle Growers Inc., 1972—, cons. in field. Served with U.S. Army, 1951-54. Mem. Nebr. Veterinarian Med. Assn. (1969—), AVMA (1960—), Am. Assn. Extension Veterinarians, Am. Assn. Bovine Practitioners, C. of C. Lodges: Masons, York Rite. Home: Route 2 Box 176 North Platte NE 69101 Office: Box 429 North Platte NE 69101

WHITE, ROBERT MYRON, banker; b. Springfield, Mo., July 3, 1942; s. Myron J. and Leona Mae (Blume) W.; A.B., Drury Coll., 1964, M.B.A., 1968; m. Suzanne Carol Dischbein, July 9, 1966; children—Jamison Brett, Ashley Lynn. Systems analyst St. Louis-San Francisco R.R., Springfield, Mo., 1966-70; sr. systems rep. Burroughs Corp., Springfield, 1970-74; v.p. data processing Empire Bank, Springfield, 1974—; tchr. S.W. Mo. State U., 1968-69; chmn. Greene County Computer Advisory Com., 1977—. Fin. chmn. Girl Scouts U.S.A., 1977. Mem. Data Processing Mgmt. Assn. (pres. local chpt. 1977-78). Clubs: Lions, Shriner, Masons. Home: 3847 Camber St Springfield MO 65804 Office: 1800 S Glenstone St Springfield MO 65804

WHITE, ROGER DEAN, anesthesiologist; b. Ontonagon, Mich., July 29, 1939; s. Ellard Archie and Esther Ann (Niemi) W.; student Suomi Coll., 1957-58; M.D., U. Mich., 1964; m. Priscilla Mary Cane, Oct. 3, 1964; children—Roger Mark, Linda Jean. Intern, Henry Ford Hosp., Detroit, 1964-65; resident Mayo Grad. Sch. Medicine, Rochester, Minn., 1965-66, resident in anesthesiology, 1968-70; cons. anesthesiology Mayo Clinic, Rochester, 1970—, instr. Mayo Med. Sch., 1972-75, asst. prof., 1975—; med. dir. Gold Cross Ambulance Inc., 1970—, various awards. Bd. dirs. Nat. Registry Emergency Med. Technicians, 1975—. Served with AUS, 1966-68. Named Physician of Year, Ambulance Assn. Am., 1974. Diplomate Am. Bd. Anesthesiology. Fellow Am. Coll. Anesthesiologists, Am. Coll. Cardiology; mem. Am. Soc. Anesthesiologists, Internat. Anesthesia Research Soc., Acad. Anesthesiologists, Assn. Cardiac Anesthesiologists, Am. Coll. Emergency Physicians, Minn. Heart Assn. (chmn. com. cardio pulmonary resuscitation, 1974-76), Am. Heart Assn., Alpha Omega Alpha. Contbr. articles to profl. jours. Home: 502 16th St SW Rochester MN 55901 Office: 200 1st St SW Rochester MN 55901

WHITE, SIDNEY SHAW, JR., chemist; b. Woodville, Miss., Nov. 25, 1943; s. Sidney Shaw and Doris (Duck) W.; Ph.D., Tex. Christian U., 1970; m. Elizabeth Jane Morgan, Aug. 27, 1965; children—Laurie Lynnette, Marissa Michelle. Analytical chemist Allied Chem. Corp., Baton Rouge, 1965; research chemist, capt. U.S. Army, Edgewood Arsenal, Md., 1970-71; sr. chemist Cin. Milacron Chems., Reading, Ohio, 1971-74, group leader, 1974—. Served with U.S. Army, 1970-71. Tex. Christian U. Research Found. fellow, 1965-66, NASA fellow, 1966-70. Mem. Am. Chem. Soc., Union Twp. Jr. C. of C. (treas. 1974-75), Sigma Xi, Alpha Chi Sigma. Patentee in field. Home: 8461 Coachman Dr West Chester OH 45069 Office: West St Reading OH 45215

WHITE, THEODORE WILLIAM, optometrist; b. Gallup, N.Mex., Nov. 6, 1938; s. John Washington and Leonel Elizabeth (Cunningham) W.; B.S. in Indsl. Tech., Kans. State Coll., 1960; student West Point, 1960-61; O.D., (fellow to study developmental vision aspects), U. Houston, 1965; m. Myrna Y. Capps, Apr. 25, 1961; children—Theodore, Jr., Tiffany Lynn, Ryan Burton. Practice optometry, Aurora, Mo., 1965—. Park bd. chmn., Aurora, 1969—; chmn. United Fund, Aurora, 1968-71. Republican county chmn. Aurora, 1969—. Served with AUS, 1970; Mem. Aurora C. of C. (bd. mem. 1968-69), Aurora Jr. C. of C., Am. Mo. (chmn on inter-profl. relations 1969-70), optometric assns., Heart of Am. Contact Lens Soc., Methodist. Mason (Shriner), Rotarian (pres. 1968-69.) Home: Route 2 Box 679 Aurora MO 65605 Office: 9 W Olive St Aurora MO 65605

WHITE, THOMAS LESTER, cons. engr.; b. Youngstown, Ohio, May 30, 1903; s. William Lester and Ethel Mary (Jackson) W.; m. Marion Elizabeth Evans, Sept. 24, 1930; 1 dau., Harrietellen White McKendrick. Tool designer, engr. Comml. Shearing Inc., Youngstown, 1924-26, chief engr., 1926-51, cons. engr., 1951-68, 68—; cons. engr. coal mines, metal mines, hwy., railroad and subway tunnels, Belgium, Portugal, India, Australia, S.Am., Can., others. Fellow ASME (past chmn. petroleum div.); mem. Am. Ry. Engring. Assn., Mahoning Valley Tech. Soc. (named outstanding person 1973). Baptist. Clubs: Kiwanis, Shriners, Masons. Author: (with R.V. Proctor and Karl Terzaghi) Rock Tunneling with Steel Supports, 1946, Earth Tunneling with Steel Supports, 1946; Earth Tunneling with Steel Supports, 1977. Contbr. articles to profl. jours. Address: 721 W Warren Ave Youngstown OH 44511

WHITE, VIRGINIA KNOX, occupational therapist; b. Auburn, N.Y., Sept. 4, 1921; d. Fred C. and Faye (Foote) Knox; B.S. in Occupational Therapy, Wayne State U., 1968; M.A., Mich. State U., 1974; m. Sydney William White, Dec. 26, 1972; children by previous marriage—Jack Gajewski, Judy Nyman, Nancy Kronberg, Suzanne Mayer, Richard Gajewski. Dir. occupational therapy dept., children's psychiat. div. Clinton Valley Hosp., Pontiac, Mich., 1969-71; dir. occupational therapy Cottage Hosp., Grosse Pointe Farms, Mich., 1971-72; cons. and instr. Mich. Assn. Retarded Citizens, 1973-74, Mich. Health Facilities Assn., 1973-74; cons. Mich. State U. In-service Tng. Project, 1974-77, Mich. State Dept. Mental Health, 1976; dir. workshops Mich. State U., 1976; pvt. practice occupational therapy, East Lansing, Mich., 1972—. Certified rehab. counselor, Mich. Mem. Am., Mich. (pres. 1977—), Lansing occupational therapy assns., Am. Personnel and Guidance Assn., Am. Assn. Mental Deficiency, Am. Rehab. Counselors Assn., Eaton County Assn. Retarded Citizens, Pi Theta. Address: 133 Kenberry Dr East Lansing MI 48823

WHITE, WILLIAM ADRIAN, environmental engring. co. exec.; b. Omaha, Aug. 31, 1922; s. John P. and Helene (Adrian) W.; B.S. in Mech. Engring., Iowa State Coll., 1946; m. Phyllis Moyers, Feb. 2, 1946; children—Sherilyn (Mrs. Joseph R. Sutton III), William Adrian, James Richard. Sales engr. Murphy-Miller, Inc., 1948-58; self employed cons. engr., 1958-62; engring. cons. Chrysler Airtemp, Northlake, Ill., 1962-70; v.p. W-T Engring. Inc., Schaumberg, Ill., 1970-74; self-employed as cons. engr. as W.A. White Assos., Elmhurst, Ill., 1974—. Served with USNR, 1943-45. Recipient citation of merit Chgo. chpt. AIA and Chgo. Assn. Commerce and Industry, 1962. Registered profl. engr. Minn., Iowa, Wis., Ill., Ky., Ind., Mich., Ohio, Ariz., Ala. Mem. Ill. Soc. Profl. Engrs. Home: 804 Laramie St Wilmette IL 60091 Office: WA White Assos Cons Engrs Elmhurst IL 60126

WHITE, WILLIAM ALAN, wholesale co. exec.; b. Rapid City, S.D., Sept. 20, 1946; s. Gordon Lee and Agnes Gweneythe (Donahoe) W.; B.S. in Bus. Adminstrn., U. Denver, 1968; m. Cynthia Lear Hamilton, Sept. 5, 1970; 1 son, Alexander Mundt. Stockbroker, Dean Witter & Co., Inc., Mpls., 1970-71; stockbroker Shearson Hammill & Co., Inc., Denver, 1971-72; v.p. Hills, Brake & Equipment Co. Inc., Rapid City, 1972—. U. Denver scholar, 1964. Mem. Rapid City C. of C., Truck Equipment and Body Distbrs. Assn., U.S. Indsl. Council, Western South Dakota Devel. Crp. Republican. Roman Catholic. Clubs: Hardrock, Denver Athletic. Home: 1018 Clark St Rapid City SD 57701 Office: PO Box 80 St Patrick I-90 Rapid City SD 57709

WHITE, WILLIAM FRANCIS, newspaper exec.; b. Winona, Minn., Oct. 25, 1923; s. Maxwell H. and Ellnora (Parks) W.; student Carleton Coll., 1941-42, Cornell U., 1942-43; B.A. in Journalism, U. Minn., 1949; m. Dare Lamberton, July 8, 1950; children—Angus, Dana, Andrea. Joined Winona Daily News, 1949, mgr. 1950-61, pub., 1961—; pres. Republican & Herald Pub. Co., 1961—. Mem. Winona City Planning Commn.; campaign chmn. Winona Community Chest; pres. Winona Indsl. Devel. Assn. Bd. dirs. Winona Goodfellows. Served to capt., 148th Inf. Regt., AUS, 1943-46; PTO; lt. col. Res. Decorated Bronze Star medal, Combat Infantryman's badge. Mem. Winona C. of C. (dir.), Northwest Daily Press Assn. (chmn. bd.), Minn. Heart Assn. (dir.), Graphic Arts Industry Inc. Mpls. (dir.), Minn. Alumni Assn. (dir.), Episcopalian. Clubs: Winona (Minn.) Country; Minn. Press, Minneapolis, Minnesota Alumni (Mpls.); International (Chgo.). Home: Drumnadrochit Box 70 Winona MN 55987 Office: 601 Franklin St Winona MN 55987

WHITE, WILLIAM LETCHER, food co. exec.; b. Manchester, Ky., Feb. 8, 1918; s. D. Taylor and Laura (Wilson) W.; B.A., Berea Coll., 1941; grad Exec. Devel. Program, Cornell U., 1968; m. Dessie Lee Riddle, June 2, 1941; children—William Letcher, James Taylor. Mgr. merchandising Montgomery Ward & Co., Chgo., 1941-46; sr. marketing analyst Swift & Co., Chgo., 1946-54, mgr. consumer research sect., 1955-60, div. mgr. comml. research dept. 1960-64, gen. mgr. marketing research dept., 1965—. Treas. troop Chgo. council Boy Scouts Am., 1970-74. Mem. Comml. Research Found. Chgo. (pres. 1968-75), Am. Marketing Assn. Presbyn. (elder). Contbr. sect. Role of Marketing Research in the Evolution of Marketing Strategy to book, 1964. Home: 24 Country Squire Rd Palos Heights IL 60463 Office: 115 W Jackson Blvd Chicago IL 60604

WHITEAKER, STANLEY CYRIL, accountant; b. Hurdland, Mo., Nov. 24, 1918; s. Roscoe E. and Marie (Surry) W.; evening student Rockhurst U., 1955-58; m. Justine M. Warford, Dec. 25, 1938; 1 dau., Linda J. Accountant Mo. Pub. Service Commn., 1942-51; utility cons., 1951-58; partner Troupe Kehoe, Whiteaker & Kent, C.P.A., offices in Kansas City, Kans. and Mo., 1958—; cons. Kans. Corp. Commn., Mo. Pub. Service Commn., Nat. Energy Bd. Can., and maj. industries in midwest on natural gas usage, also U.S. Air Force; dir. Tele Serve, Inc., T.K.W. Supply Co., Inc., Westboro Builders, Inc., Bichelmeyer Meat Co. Mem. exec. council Greater Kansas City Council on Alcoholism; mem. accounting com. Fed. Power Commn. Served as sgt. USNR, 1943-45. Mem. C. of C., Kans. State Bd. Accountancy, Am. Inst. C.P.A. (chmn. fed. regulated industries com.), Kans. Soc. C.P.A., Nat. Assn. Pub. Accountants, Internat. Platform Assn., Eastern Kans. Estate Planning Council (v.p.), Odd Fellow Clubs: Kansas City, Country of Mo., Milburn Golf and Country. Author articles on utility rate making. Home: 6008 W 86th Terr Overland Park KS 66104 Office: Power and Light Bldg Kansas City MO 64105

WHITEFORD, EMMA MAY BRITTIN, educator; b. Lowder, Ill.; d. George and Katharine (Riley) Brittin: B.S. in Home Econs., N.D. State U., 1938; diploma Pa. Hosp., 1939; M.S., U. Ill., 1951, Ed.D., 1955; m. Clay Pennington Whiteford, July 2, 1940; children—William McConkey, Mary Katharine. Adminstrv. dietitian York (Pa.) Hosp., 1939-40; acting chmn. home econs. Ill. Wesleyan U., Bloomington, 1949-50; dir. homemaking and sch. lunch, Bloomington (Ill.) pub. schs., 1950-53; part-time instr., U. Ill., 1953-55; chmn. dept. home econs. Bowling Green (Ohio) State U., 1955-57; head home econs. edn. dept. Fla. State U., 1957-59; dir. Sch. Home Econs. U. Cin., 1959-66; vis. prof., research asso. U. Ill., 1966-67, prof., chmn. dept. home economics edn. U. Minn., St. Paul, 1967-71, prof., 1971—. Active ARC. Mem. Am., Minn. home econs. assns., Am., Minn. dietetic assns., Am., Minn. vocational assns., Am. Assn. U. Women, Am. Sociol. Soc., Nat. Council on Family Relations, D.A.R., Ill. Sch.

Food Service Assn. (regional v.p. 1953-54), PTA, Nat. Minn. edn. assns., Adult Edn. Assn., Am. Assn. U. Profs., Assn. for Higher Edn., Assn. for Student Teaching, Higher Edn. Assn., Council Adminstrs. Home Econs, (treas. 1965-68), Panhellenic, Alpha Phi Gamma, Pi Lambda Theta, Alpha Gamma Delta, Delta Kappa Gamma, Kappa Delta Pi, Omicron Nu, Zonta. Presbyn. Club: Woman's (Cin.). Home: 740 River Dr St Paul MN 55116

WHITEHEAD, JOHN C., judge; b. Loup City, Nebr., Mar. 4, 1939; s. Cyrus C. and Regina (Costello) W.; A.B. in History, St. Benedict's Coll., 1961; LL.B., Washburn U., 1964, J.D., m. Linda L. Lykins, Sept. 11, 1965; children—Sarah, Amy. Admitted to Nebr. and Kans. bars, 1964; mem. firm Snell & Whitehead, Columbus, Nebr., 1965-66, Walker Luckey & Whitehead, Columbus, 1966-71, Walker, Luckey, Whitehead & Sipple, Columbus, 1971-77; judge U.S. Dist. Ct., 1977—; dep. county atty. Platte County, 1965-67; atty. Columbus City, 1967-72. Bd. dirs. Lower Loup Natural Resource Dist., vice chmn., 1975; bd. dirs. Columbus Family Y, 1976—, v.p., 1977-78, pres., 1978—; bd. dirs. Platte County Playhouse, 1972—. Mem. Columbus Optimist Club (pres. 1971-72, lt. gov. Nebr. dist. 1972-73, new club bldg. chmn. 1974-75), Columbus Toastmaster's Club (pres. 1968), Columbus Jr. C. of C. (sec. 1966, dir. 1967), Columbus C. of C. (dir. 1977—), Nebr., Platte County (treas. 1965-68, pres. 1976—) bar assns. Roman Catholic (pres. St. Bonaventure Holy Name Soc. 1966). Elk, K.C. (3rd and 4th deg.). Home: 3069 25th Ave Columbus NE 68601 Office: Platte County Court House Columbus NE 68601

WHITEHILL, JAMES GIRARD, mktg. co. exec.; b. Santa Ana, Calif., Oct. 26, 1943; s. Eben C. and Mary F. (Girard) Boright; B.Mus., Yankton Conservatoire of Music., 1966; M.B.A., Case Western Res. U., 1969. Nat. sales mgr. Hammond Organ Co., 1969-70; asst. to exec. v.p., dir. mktg. Baxter Lab., Deerfield, Ill., 1970-71; v.p. Microwave Instrument Co., Corona del Mar, Calif., 1971-74; gen. mgr., nat. sales mgr., dir. electronics, v.p. M.I. Fin. Co., Norlin Corp., Lincolnwood, Ill., 1974—. Mem. Am. Mktg. Assn. Patentee in field. Home: 200 N Ridge St Apt 1A Evanston IL 60202 Office: Norlin Corp 7373 N Cicero Lincolnwood IL 60646

WHITEHOUSE, GEORGE EDWARD, communications scientist, educator; b. Holstein, Iowa, Oct. 22, 1929; s. George Edward and Jessie Evelyn (Fish) W.; B.S., U. So. Miss., 1971, M.S., 1972, Ph.D., 1974; m. Janice Kay Bresee, Feb. 7, 1961; 1 dau., Laura Lee. Enlisted U.S. Air Force, 1948, advanced through grades to master sgt., 1960; communications and tng. specialist, worldwide, 1948-68; broadcaster, engr. Sta. WPCF, U.S. Govt., Panama City, Fla., 1958-62; master instr. U.S. Air U., 1957-68; ret., 1968; dir. communications U. So. Miss., Hattiesburg, 1968-73; prof. telecommunications Stephens Coll., Columbia, Mo., 1974—; broadcast engr. FCC; chmn. cable TV commn., Columbia; cons. Miss. ETV Authority, Mo. ITV Council; producer, dir. numerous TV and film programs. Author textbooks and manuals in field. Home: 309 Tracy Dr Columbia MO 65201 Office: Stephens Coll Columbia MO 65201

WHITEHOUSE, WILLIAM ARTHUR, naturalist; b. Youngstown, Ohio, Oct. 9, 1935; s. William Reginald and Rose Marie (Takach) W.; student DePauw U., 1953-54; A.B., Youngstown State U., 1966; children—Frank Wayne, Raymond Alan, Phillip Glenn. Mus. attendant Mill Creek Park, Youngstown, 1952-54, asst. park naturalist, 1954-70, park naturalist and dir. Ford Nature Edn. Center, 1970—. Cons. Elementary Sci. Field Experiences, a grad. course for tchrs., Sch. Edn., Yo ngstown State U., 1974—. Merit badge counselor Boy Scouts Am., Youngstown, 1969—. Served with AUS, 1959-60. Mem. Assn. Interpretive Naturalists, Youngstown Nature Club, Grant M. Cook Bird Club. Contbr. to Mill Creek Park Bull., 1970—. Home: 4031 Glenwood Ave Apt 13 Youngstown OH 44512 Office: 816 Glenwood Ave Youngstown OH 44502

WHITEMAN, WESTON KIMBALL, banker; b. Evanston, Ill., Nov. 18, 1927; s. Edward Charles and Ruth (Kimball) W.; B.S., Northwestern U., 1948; m. Joan McCarthy, Sept. 16, 1950; children—Donald Kimball, Ruth Kimball. Trainee, Am. Hosp. Supply Corp., Evanston, 1949-50; with 1st Nat. Bank, Chgo., 1952—, asst. cashier, 1958-63, asst. v.p., 1963-67, v.p., 1967—. Past pres. North Shore Country Day Sch. Parents Assn., 1968-70; vice chmn. sustaining com. Ravinia Festival Assn., 1965-74; chmn. Pine Manor Jr. Coll. Parents Assn., 1975-76. Served with AUS, 1948-49, USAF, 1950-52. Clubs: Glen View, University (Chgo.). Home: 1205 Hill Rd Winnetka IL 60093 Office: 1 1st National Plaza Chicago IL 60670

WHITESIDE ALBA LEA, JR., judge; b. Lilly Chapel, Ohio, Feb. 22, 1928; s. Alba Lea and Lucille (Truitt) W.; B.A., Ohio State U., 1952, J.D., 1954; grad. Nat. Coll. State Trial Judges, 1969, Appellate Judges Seminar, N.Y. U., 1972; m. Virginia Ayres, July 12, 1958; 1 dau., Elizabeth Anne. Admitted to Ohio bar, 1954; practiced in Cleve., 1954-55, Columbus, 1955—; with firm Grossman, Schlessing & Carter, Cleve., 1954-55; right of way atty., contract atty. Ohio Turnpike Commn. Columbus, 1955-56; asst. city atty., Columbus, 1956-69; chief counsel City Columbus, 1962-69; judge Ct. Common Pleas, Franklin County, Ohio, 1969-70, 10th Dist. Ct. Appeals, 1970—. Sec. Capital City Republican Club, 1959-60; chmn. 1963 Ohio Young Rep. Conv.; del. Ohio Rep. Conv., 1964, 1966; trustee Buckeye Rep. Club; mem. Franklin County Rep. Central Com., Franklin County Rep. Exec. Com., 1963-69. Pres. Columbus Symphony Youth & Cadet Orch. Assn., 1976-77; pres. Bexley Music Parents, 1977-78. Served with U.S. Army, 1945-48; MTO. Mem. Am., Ohio, Columbus bar assns., Ohio Municipal League (chmn. annexation com. 1967, mem. legis. com.), Am. Judicature Soc., Ohio Municipal Attys. Assn., Ohio Jud. Conf., Ohio Common Pleas Judges Assn. (sec. 1970), Order of Coif, Phi Beta Kappa. Methodist. Club: Columbus Civitan (sec. 1964, 66). Author: Whiteside's Appellate Practice. Asso. editor: Crowley's Municipal Law. Contbr. to profl. publs.; lectr. in field. Home: 361 S Columbia Ave Bexley OH 43209 Office: Franklin County Hall of Justice 369 High St Columbus OH 43215

WHITESIDE, PHILIP ELRAY, scholastic jewelry and graphics mfg. co. exec.; b. Weldon, Ill., Nov. 10, 1935; s. William Rice and Hazel (Parr) W.; B.S., U. Ill., 1959; M.B.A., U. Minn., 1971; m. Nancy Jane Seal, Dec. 28, 1957; children—Cynthia Lea, Craig Alan. Indsl. engr. McCulloch Corp., Mpls., 1959-61; mfg. cost analyst Collins Radio Co. Cedar Rapids, Iowa, 1962-63; prodn. inventory control mgr. Control Data Corp., Mpls., 1963-70; systems analyst Jostens Inc., Mpls., 1970-71, mgr. jewelry research, Owatonna, Minn., 1971-76, mgr. scholastic purchasing, 1976—. Chmn. fin. dr. United Fund, 1967; chmn. fin. Methodist Ch. Served with Q.M.C., U.S. Army, 1957, 61-62. Recipient Boss of Year award Roseville (Minn.) Jr. C. of C., 1969-70. Mem. Nat. Assn. Purchasing Mgrs., Am. Inst. Indsl. Engrs. (chpt. pres. 1969-70). Republican. Club: Rotary (dir.). Office: 148 Broadway E Owatonna MN 55060

WHITE-WARE, GRACE ELIZABETH, educator; b. St. Louis, Oct. 5, 1921; d. James Eathel, Sr. and Madree (Penn) White; B.A. in Edn., H.B. Stowe Tchrs. Coll., 1943; divorced; 1 son, James Otis Ware II (Oyekunle Adeyemon). Mgr. advt. Superior Press, St. Louis, 1935-39; tri-owner, v.p. Carolina Oil Co., St. Louis, 1938-42; with pub. relations Triangle Press, St. Louis, 1939-47, sales promotion, 1939-47; account supr. overtime payroll Bell Tel. Labs., Inc., N.Y.C., 1943-46; tchr. Dunbar Elementary Sch., St. Louis, 1946-47, Newberry Elementary Sch., Chgo., 1949, Betsy Ross Elementary Sch., Chgo., 1951, Lincoln Sch., Richmond, Mo., 1951, Dunbar Sch., Kinlock, Mo., 1952, Gladstone Elementary Sch., Cleve., 1954-61, Quincy Elementary Sch., Cleve., 1961—, head tchr. Head Start program, 1965; adult edn. tchr. Cleve. Bd. Edn., 1965—; tchr. TV Tonight Sch., lessons for adults, Cleve., 1972; tri-owner, v.p., social editor Style mag., St. Louis, 1947-49; owner/mgr. Wentworth Record Distbrs., Chgo., 1947-51; supr. accounts receivable div. Spiegel, Inc., Chgo., 1947-52; radio panelist Calling All Americans, Cleve., 1957-58; sec. bd. dirs. Hough Pub. Co., also Hough Area Devel. Corp., Cleve., 1968-69. Mem. child devel. parent bd. Greater Cleve. Neighborhood Centers Assn.; mem. fund raising com. Food First Program, co.-chmn. woman's aux. Black Econ. Union, Cleve.; vice chmn. Cleve. com. Youth for Understanding Teenage Program; mem. Cleve. Council Human Relations; mem. Cleve. chpt. Congress Racial Equality; charter mem., financial sec. Tots and Teens, Inc.; treas. Jr. Women's Civic League; mem. Cleve. bd. Afro-Am. Cultural and Hist. Soc.; women's aux. bd. Talbert Clinic and Day Care Center, Cleve.; adv. bd. Langston Hughes Library; mem. Forest City Hosp. Aux. Bd., also Women's Aux. Com. Forest City Hosp.; scholarship com. Women's Allied Arts Assn. Greater Cleve., 1972-74. Named Most Outstanding Vol. of Year, N.Y. Fedn. Settlements, 1944, Leading Tchr. of Community, Cleve. Call and Post, weekly newspaper, 1958; recipient Martha Holden Jennings scholar award Martha Holden Jennings Found., Cleve., 1966-67, Spl. Outstanding Tchrs. award, 1973; Outstanding Service award Black Econ. Union, 1970; certificate appreciation City Cleve., 1973. Mem. Ohio, Cleve. edn. assns., Nat. Assn. Pub. Sch. Adult Edn., NAACP, Phillis Wheatley Assn., Moreland Community Assn., Nat. Council Negro Women, Internat. Platform Assn., Eta Phi Beta, Phi Delta Kappa (1st v.p. Cleve. 1971-73, Outstanding Achievement award 1975), Delta Sigma Theta (pres. Cleve. 1969-73). Democrat. Club: Novelette Bridge (pres. Cleve. 1973-77). Home: 14701 Milverton Rd Cleveland OH 44120

WHITFIELD, ALLEN, lawyer; b. Ruthven, Iowa, Jan. 26, 1904; s. George and Sara (Allen) W.; B.S., Iowa State U., 1924; J.D., Harvard U., 1927; student Drake U., 1928; m. Irma L. Cowan, Aug. 18, 1927; children—Lura Mae Whitfield Johnson, Harley Allen. Admitted to Fla. bar, 1928, D.C. bar, 1961; practice law, Brandenton, Fla., 1927-28; sr. partner firm Whitfield, Musgrave, Selvy, Kelly & Eddy, Des Moines, 1928—; dir. Valley Nat. Bank, Hawkeye Security Ins. Co., United Security Ins. Co., Northeastern Ins. Co., Hartford Fin., Fin. Security Group, Internat. Bank. Lay leader Iowa-Des Moines Conf. Meth. Ch., 1951-55; chmn. Vets. Meml. Auditorium Commn., Des Moines, 1946-58; former co-chmn. Iowa Crusade of Freedom; mem. commn. Chaplains and Related Ministries of United Meth. Ch., 1968-74; mem. United Meth. Bd. Publ., 1965-68; hon. trustee Morningside Coll., Simpson Coll. Served to lt. col. U.S. Army, 1942-45. Mem. Am., Iowa, Polk County, Fla. bar assns., Assn. Ins. Counsel, Fedn. Ins. Counsel, Des Moines Jr. C. of C. (pres. 1931), Iowa Jr. C. of C. (pres. 1934), U.S. Jr. C. of C. (pres. 1935-36), Des Moines C. of C. (pres. 1949), Greater Des Moines C. of C. (dir.), C. of C. U.S. (dir. 1963-69, 72—, treas. 1969-72), Iowa State U. Alumni Assn. (past pres.), Iowa State U. Alumni Achievement Fund (past chmn. bd. trustees), Iowa State U. Found. (bd. govs.), Greater Des Moines Community Found., AMVETS, VFW, Am. Legion, Sigma Delta Chi, Delta Sigma Rho, Kappa Sigma. Republican. Clubs: Des Moines, Okoboji Yacht, Masons, Shriners, Za-Ga-Zig. Home: Apt 802 The Park Fleur 3131 Fleur Dr Des Moines IA Office: 1400 Central Nat Bank Bldg Des Moines IA 50309

WHITFIELD, GEORGE POLK, educator; b. Vesta, Nebr., May 11, 1924; s. William Russell and Mary (Ellenberger) W.; student Pa. Mil. Coll., 1943-44, Iowa State Coll., 1944, 49; Mus.B., Eastman Sch. Music, 1948, Mus.M., 1950; Doctor Mus. Arts, U. Mich., 1963; m. Mary Rose Lantz, May 26, 1951 (dec. Aug. 1969); children—Stacy Anne, Lantz David, Stephanie Ellen, Kevin Crispin; m. 2d, Laila Mary Tassava Hansen, July 11, 1970; stepchildren—Michael Douglas Hansen, David Martin Hansen, Andrew Peter Hansen, Robert Gordon Hansen. Grad. asst. Eastman Sch. Music, Rochester, N.Y., 1948-50; mem. faculty Kearney (Nebr.) State Coll., 1950-63, asso. prof. music, 1959-63, mem. ensemble, 1950-63; asso. prof. music No. Mich. U., Marquette, 1963-71, prof. music, 1971—. Music contest adjudicator; dir. piano clinics; soloist, accompanist. Treas. St. Michael's Sch. Bd., Marquette, 1966-67; cub scout leader Boy Scouts Am., Marquette, 1967-68. Served with AUS, 1943-44. Mem. Nat., Mich. assns. higher edn., Marquette Community Concert Assn. (v.p. 1970-71), AAUP, Phi Mu Alpha, Sinfonia. Home: 520 Cherry Creek Rd Marquette MI 49855

WHITFIELD, RUSSELL LEE, gas co. exec.; b. Detroit, May 2, 1931; s. Emerson Laurie and Ivy E. (Hopps) W.; B.B.A., U. Mich., 1953, M.B.A., 1957; m. Rosemary Keller, June 21, 1952; children—Jeffrey, John, Chris, Terra. Sr. auditor Lyons Teetzel Wyllie & Borland, C.P.A.'s, Detroit, 1954-57, Vickers, Inc., Detroit, 1957-62, Troy, Mich., 1957-62; supr. Computer Activities Vickers, Inc., Detroit, 1959-62; data processing mgr. Nat. Twist Drill & Tool Co., Rochester, Mich., 1962-72, controller, 1972-74; gen. auditor Am. Natural Service Co., Detroit, 1974—; instr. Oakland U., Rochester, 1965—, Wayne State U., Detroit, 1965—. Scoutmaster Boy Scouts Am., Rochester, 1971—. Mem. Mich. Assn. C.P.A.'s, Am. Inst. C.P.A.'s, Data Processing Mgrs. Assn., Phi Sigma. Republican. Conglist. (deacon). Elk. Contbr. articles in field to profl. assns. Home: 550 Clair Hill Dr Rochester MI 48063 Office: 1 Woodward Ave Detroit MI 48226

WHITHAM, EDWARD CHARLES, motel owner; b. Burlington, Iowa, Aug. 16, 1939; s. Edward Charles and Margaret Montana (Bopp) W.; B.S., Bradley U., 1961; m. Marsha Catherine Williams, Aug. 20, 1960; children—Julie Catherine, David Bradley. Mgr. Lincolnville Motel, Burlington, 1961—, owner, 1964—. Chmn. sustaining membership drive Boy Scouts Am., 1970; active ann. fund drives Community Chest. Mem. Burlington City Planning Commn., 1970—, Burlington Bd. Edn., 1971—. Bd. dirs. Burlington Steamboat Days, 1968—, gen. chmn., 1968, pres., 1969; pres. YMCA, 1969—. Named Outstanding Young Man, Burlington Jr. C. of C., 1969. Mem. Burlington C. of C. (conv. chmn. 1969-70), Lambda Chi Alpha. Lutheran (pres. 1970, 71, 74, 75; mem. bd. 1966-71). Mason, Elk, Rotarian (dir. 1970—, pres. 1972). Home: 2716 Clearview Dr Burlington IA 52601 Office: 1701 Mt. Pleasant St Burlington IA 52601

WHITLOW, TYREL EUGENE, artist; b. Lynn, Ark., Aug. 1940; s. James Albert and Sara Syble (Howard) W.; B.S.E., Ark. State U., 1965; M.F.A., Instituto Allende, Mexico, 1968. One man shows So. Bapt. Coll., 1968, Vincent Price Gallery, Chgo., 1968, Ill. Valley Community Coll., Oglesby, 1973; exhibited in group shows Memphis Art Gallery, 1968, Masur Mus. Art, Monroe, La., 1968, Ark. Arts Center, Little Rock, 1968, No. Ill. U., 1971, Butler Inst. Am. Art, Youngstown, O., 1973, Nat. Cape Coral Art Exhbn., Fort Meyers, Fla., 1976, also numerous colls. and univs.; two nat. touring shows; represented in permanent collection Pulaski Fed. Savs. and Loan Assn. Religious Collection, Little Rock. Instr. art Ill. Valley Community Coll., 1968—. Recipient Top award Contemporary So. Art Exhibit, Memphis, 1968, Purchase award Ark. Art Festival, 1968, Watercolor award Ark. Watercolor Exhbn., 1968. Mem. Am. Fedn. Arts, Rockford Art Assn., Soc. Art Historians. Home: 1528 Argle Rd LaSalle IL 61301 Office: Dept Art Ill Valley Community Coll Oglesby IL 61348

WHITMIRE, PAUL THOMAS, chem. co. exec.; b. Dennison, Ohio, Aug. 10, 1921; s. William Jackson and Virginia Horatius (Sarbaugh) W.; B.S., Ohio State U., 1943; postgrad. Cornell U., 1967, U. Mich., 1972; m. Georgia Mae Hammel, May 15, 1943; children—Paul Thomas, Steven Hammel, Gregg Alan. Shift chemist B. F. Goodrich Chem. Co., Akron, Ohio, 1946, shift tech. man, 1947-49, shift foreman, 1949-52, process control supr., 1952-55, gen. foreman, 1955-60, maint. supt., 1960-63, prodn. mgr., 1963-67, plant mgr., 1967—. Pres., Lake Buckhorn Owners Assn., Millersburg, Ohio, 1975—. Served to capt., AUS, 1943-46. Decorated Purple Heart. Mem. Am. Inst. Chem. Engrs., Am. Chem. Soc., B.F. Goodrich Foremans Club. Republican. Methodist (trustee 1964-74, chmn. pastor parish com.). Mason (32 deg.). Home: 524 Parkway Blvd Norton OH 44203 Office: PO Box 2170 Akron OH 44309

WHITMORE, ALICE ELIZABETH EMMERT, poet; b. Dixon, Ill., Dec. 8, 1918; d. Howard Elmer and Ruth Ella (McClanahan) Emmert; student Northwestern U., Rockford (Ill.) Coll.; 1 son, Michael Robert Wadsworth. Books of poetry: A Garland of Leis, 1971, Our Singing States, 1973; author plays; contbr. numerous poems and short stories to lit. and popular publs.; writing judge for grade sch. contest. Mem. Ill. Fedn. Woman's Clubs (chmn. drama Dixon br.), Rockford Art Assn., Burpee Museum, Mendelssohn Music Club, Nat. League Am. Pen Women, Internat. Platform Assn., Centro Studi E Scambi Internat. (Rome) (hon. v.p. 1976-77).

WHITMORE, BERTHA HARPER, educator; b. Penfield, Ill., June 21, 1923; d. Edward and Lula Josephine (Holt) Harper; B.S., Ill. State U., 1945; M.S., U. Ill., 1946; postgrad., George Peabody Coll. for Tchrs., 1947, Ohio State U., 1951-53; m. Edward Hugh Whitmore, June 11, 1949; children—Stephen Harper, Ann Elizabeth. Instr. math. Metamora (Ill.) Twp. High Sch., 1945; sci. instr. Hall Twp. High Sch., Spring Valley, Ill., 1946-47; instr. phys. scis. Ill. State U., Normal, 1947-51; instr. chemistry West Sr. High Sch., Columbus, Ohio, 1951-54; instr. sci. Mt. Pleasant (Mich.) Jr. High Sch., 1966—, chmn. dept. sci., 1968—. Cons. Gifted Child Program, San Bruno, Calif., 1960-65. Pres. Lab. Sch. P.T.A., Mt. Pleasant, 1966-67, Crestmoor P.T.A., San Bruno, 1961-62; chmn. March of Dimes, San Bruno, 1960-65, City Book Fair, San Bruno, 1961-63; sec. Com. for Better Schs., San Bruno, 1963; chmn. Profl. Study Com., Mt. Pleasant pub. schs., 1970-73, chmn. com. on academically talented students, 1973—, chmn. gifted child com., 1972-76, chmn. profl. study com., 1976—. Recipient Outstanding Sci. Tchr. award Ohio Acad. Sci., 1954. Mem. Nat., Ohio, Mich. sci. tchrs. assns., Ill. Chemistry Tchrs. Assn. (v.p. 1948), Nat., Mich., edn. assns., Nat., Calif. congresses parents and tchrs. (hon. life), Kappa Delta Pi, Kappa Mu Epsilon, Kappa Delta Epsilon, Delta Kappa Gamma. Asst. editor Sci. Tchr., 1948-50. Home: 1105 N Fairfield Mount Pleasant MI 48858 Office: 440 S Bradley Rd Mount Pleasant MI 48858

WHITNER, ROBERT EDWARD, mktg. exec.; b. Allentown, Pa., Feb. 25, 1935; s. Stanley A. and Esther M. (Wimmer) W.; B.S., Lehigh U., 1956; M.B.A., Harvard, 1962; m. Barbara J. Trainor, May 24, 1968; children—Sara Rhoades, Douglas Edward. N.Y. sales mgr. Honeywell Information Systems, N.Y.C., 1962-66; dir. marketing Optical Scanning Corp., Newtown, Pa., 1966-68; pres. Photo Horizons div. Horizons Research, Inc., Cleve., 1968-74; v.p. Omni Securities Inc., Valley Forge, Pa., 1974—; dir. Neoterics Inc., Cleve., 1968—; partner Cambridge Research, Westport, Conn., 1963—; founder Computer Investors Group Inc., Automated Health Systems, San Francisco, Cal., 1969, dir. 1969-71. Served with USCG, 1957-58. Clubs: Harvard Club (Cleve.); Harvard Bus. Sch. (Cleve.). Home: 8232 Chagrin Mills Rd Chagrin Falls OH 44022 Office: 139 Bell St Chagrin Falls OH 44022

WHITNEY, ALBERT GAYLE, realtor; b. Chgo., Aug. 3, 1926; s. Albert Gayle and Edna Lucille (Gayle) W.; student Mich. State U., 1944-45, U. Mich., 1946-47; m. Elaine Shirley VanKampen, June 19, 1948; children—Gregory Steven, Scott Richard, James Walter, Jennifer Lynn. Mem. sales staff Beesley Realty & Mfg. Co., Inc., Chgo., 1957-62; partner Whitney Real Estate, Barrington, Ill., 1962-76, owner, 1977—; pres. Royal House, Ltd., 1976—. Mem. real estate adv. com. William Rainey Harper Coll., Palatine, Ill., 1972-76. Served with USAAF, 1945-46. Recipient Best Trade award Chgo. Real Estate Bd., 1961. Mem. N.W. Suburban Bd. Realtors (dir. 1968-69), Barrington Bd. Realtors (dir. 1971, 74, pres. 1973). Christian Scientist (dir. 1961-63, chmn. 1962). Home: 235 Thorn Hill Ct Barrington IL 60010 Office: 203 W Northwest Hwy Barrington IL 60010

WHITNEY, CLARENCE W., steel co. exec.; b. Garrison, Kans., July 20, 1925; s. John and Ada (Williams) W.; B.S., Emporia State Tchrs. Coll., 1949; M.A., Columbia U., 1953; children—Robert, Teres, Sarah, Clarisa. Instr. pub. schs., Great Bend, Kans., 1949-53, Shawnee Mission, Kans., 1953-56; dept. chief Western Electric Co., Chgo., 1956-63; dir. systems Interlake, Inc., Chgo., 1963—. Served with USNR, 1943-46. Mem. Steel Industry Systems Assn. (pres. 1974-75), Assn. Systems Mgmt. Club: Masons. Office: Interlake Inc 135th and Perry Sts Chicago IL 60627

WHITNEY, EMERSON CALHOUN, lawyer; b. Guymon, Okla., Apr. 15, 1910; s. Ralph E. and Florence May (Houston) Whitney; B.S.L., Northwestern U., 1931, J.D., 1932; m. Eileen Holmberg, Dec. 29, 1953; children—Emerson B., Kent R., Cynthia, Richard, Carolyn. Admitted to Ill. bar, 1932, since practiced in Chgo.; master in chancery Superior Ct. Cook County, Ill., 1941; gen. counsel Ill. Dept. Registration and Edn., 1931-42. Chmn. bd., pres. William F. Klemp Steel Co.; chmn. bd. Aragon, Inc.; pres. Hexarmor Co., Tacoma Town Houses, Inc., Tex. Town Houses, Inc., Klemp Steel of Tex., Emerson Whitney Steel Products, Whitney-Pacific Oil Co., Mercedes, Tex., Corpus Christi Corp.; owner Bagdad on the Biscayne Apt. Hotel, Miami Beach, Fla.; dir. Bank of Chgo.; mem. Branand & Whitney; partner. Mem. President's Adv. Com. on Nat. Rivers, Harbors and Waterways. Dir. Iron League Chgo. Republican nominee state senator, 1942; ward committeeman 1940-44. Served with AUS, 1943-46. Comdr., Chgo. Post Am. Vets., World War II. Pres., N. Shore Hamilton League, 1934-44. Mem. Am., Ill., Chgo. bar assns. Republican. Club: Union League. Author: Sweet Land of Liberty; On Trial in Old Mexico; Life Begins in 1940; Freedom of Thought; Judgements Don't Mean a Thing; Practicing in Podunk; Verdicts Necessity for Consistency. Office: 6007 N Sheridan Rd Chicago IL 60660 also 515-555 S Ohio St PO Box 355 Mercedes TX 78570

WHITNEY, JOHN FREEMAN, JR., city ofcl., educator; b. Balt., Feb. 14, 1944; s. John Freeman and Agnese (Taliaferro) W.; B.A., Baylor U., 1967; M.S., Tex. A. and I. U., 1968; postgrad. Fla. State U., 1971; m. Carolyn Elizabeth Nordyke, Aug. 5, 1966; children—Cristina, Freeman, William. Instr. polit. sci. Lamar U., Beaumont, Tex., 1970, Lincoln Land Coll., Springfield, Ill., 1971—. Parade dir., adminstrv. asst. to state fair mgr. Ill. State Fair Agy., 1973-77; cons. election central NBC News, 1972-74. Campaign mgr. and co-ordinator, various polit. campaigns, 1971—; mem. Ill. Gov.'s Transition Task Force, 1972; alt. del. Democratic Nat. Conv., 1976;

mayor City of Chatham (Ill.), 1977—. Fla. Ford. Found. legis. staff intern, Senate Health, Welfare and Instns. Com., 1970; Fla. State U. fellow, 1969. Mem. Am. Polit. Sci. Assn., Midwest, So., Southwestern polit. sci. assns., Pi Sigma Alpha, FDR Club. Baptist. Contbr. to profl. publs. Home: 18 Pheasant Run Dr Chatham IL 62629 Office: Lincoln Land College Springfield IL 62708

WHITNEY, JOHN JOSEPH, lawyer; b. Phila., Mar. 7, 1926; s. Joseph J. and Margaret (Kelly) W.; A.B., Oberlin Coll., 1947; LL.B., Western Res. U., 1950; m. Joan Durand, July 3, 1948; children—Susan E. (Mrs. Timothy Baab), John Joseph, Nancy C., Laura J. Atty., Goodyear Aircraft Corp., 1950-51; practiced law, Cleve., 1953; mem. firm Ford, Whitney, Crump & Schulz, 1953—; dir. law City of Berea, Ohio, 1966-68, 72. Gen. chmn. Berea chpt. ARC Fund Campaign, 1958; mem. subcom. on water system Berea Civic Com., 1959; mem. Berea Citizens Adv. Com. on Urban Renewal, 1962-65, Berea Bd. Bldg. Code Appeals, 1962-65; chmn. subcom. on profl. personnel Berea City Sch. Dist. Study Com., 1963-64; mem. adv. com. Deaconess Hosp. Served to lt. USNR, 1946-47, 51-53. Mem. Am., Ohio, Cleve. bar assns., Berea, Ohio, Cleve. chambers commerce. Conglist. Home: 445 S Rocky River Dr Berea OH 44017 Office: Williamson Bldg Cleveland OH 44114

WHITSITT, FRANK CASEY, editor; b. Kansas City, Mo., Sept. 22, 1927; s. Garland B. and Mary Catherine (Casey) W.; student Kansas City Jr. Coll., 1946, Mo. Valley Coll., 1947; B.J., U. Mo., 1949; m. Helen Virginia Townsend, Nov. 6, 1949; children—Christine Jill, Marsha Dell, Paul Kirk. Reporter, copyreader Evansville (Ind.) Courier, 1949-50; reporter Lubbock (Tex.) Avalanche Jour., 1950-51; reporter, copy editor Kansas City Star, 1951-60, state editor, 1965; with Farmland Industries, Kansas City, Mo., 1966—, editor Farmland News, 1969—. Dir. press room World Congress on Evangelism, Berlin, 1966. Served with AUS, 1946. Common Market study grantee, 1975. Mem. Coop. Edit. Assn. (dir. 1974—), Am. Agrl. Editors Assn. (1st place writing award 1974, 75), Coop. Edit. Assn. (1st place writing awards 1971, 73, 74). Republican. Baptist. Home: 3608 NE 49th St Kansas City MO 64119 Office: 3315 N Oak Trafficway Kansas City MO 64116

WHITTAKER, HOWARD, musician; b. Lakewood, Ohio, Dec. 19, 1922; s. Louis Howard and Ruth (Dornberger) W.; Mus.B., Cleve. Inst. Music, 1943; Mus.M., Oberlin Coll., 1947; m. Donna Moorhead, Jan. 13, 1945; children—Dwight, Katherine, John. Dir. Cleve. Music Sch. Settlement, 1948—; exec. producer Lake Erie Opera Theatre, Cleve., 1964-70; mus. condr. Orpheus Male Chorus, Cleve., 1961-63. Cons. on cultural affairs to Vice Pres. U.S.; cons. to v.p. Pres.'s Council on Youth Opportunity, 1968; mem. Ohio Arts Council, 1972-74. Pres. bd. trustees Cleve. Womens Orch., 1956-57; dir. Cleve. Summer Arts Festival, 1967-70. Served with AUS, 1943-45. Recipient Mendlesohn Glee Club award, N.Y., 1953, Cleve. Fine Arts award Women's City Club, 1963, Towne Crier award Press Club of Cleve. Mem. Cleve. Soc. for Aesthetics (past. chmn.), Cleve. Composer's Guild, Cleve. Fedn. Settlements (past pres.), Mus. Arts Assn., Nat. Guild Community Music Schs. (past pres.). Composer mus. compositions. Home: Berkshire Rd Gates Mills OH 44040 Office: 11125 Magnolia Dr Cleveland OH 44106

WHITTAKER, STANLEY WARD, electric co. exec.; b. Waupun, Wis., Aug. 29, 1920; s. Harry Ward and Katherine Leah (Allan) W.; m. Hazel Joan Berkel, Nov. 16, 1955; children—Harry W., S. Craig, Marjorie L., Mary Susan, Lisa K. With C.W.C. Foundry Co., Muskegon, Mich., 1939-42, Jones Electric Co., 1942-49; pres. Whittaker Electric Co., Muskegon, 1949—; pres. Tabor Electric Co., Benton Harbor, Mich.; dir. Alloyed Grairon Co., Computer Process Utility, Ceneast Engring. Co.; vocational and mgmt. cons. Trustee Muskegon Gen. Hosp. Served with USNR, 1942-45. Home: 609 2d St N Muskegon MI 49445 Office: 1850 Park St Muskegon MI 49443

WHITTED, JACK JOHNSON, educator; b. Danville, Ill., May 16, 1926; s. John Wesley and Sarah Elizabeth (Johnson) W.; student U. Ill., 1944; B.S., Eastern Ill. U., 1950; M.S., Washington U., 1963; m. Mildred Mason, Aug. 19, 1956. With Ill. State Tng. Sch. Boys, St. Charles, Ill., 1951-55; coach Hughes-Quinn Jr. High Sch., E. St. Louis, Ill., 1955-57; coach Rock Jr. High Sch., 1957-68, also athletic dir.; varsity track coach So. Ill. U., Edwardsville, Ill., 1968—; city recreation dir. City E. St. Louis. Served with USN, 1944-46. Mem. Ill., Mo. ofcls. assns., Ill-Mo. Ofcls. Assn. (pres. 1974), Ill. Coll. Track Coaches Assn., U.S. Track Coaches Assn., Harry S. Truman Library Inst., Ill. Phys. Edn., Health and Recreation Assn., Am. Legion., Alpha Phi Alpha. (named Midwestern Man of Year 1966). Club: Elks, Toastmasters. Home: 8140 Tulane St University City MO 63130 Office: So Ill U Edwardsville IL 62025

WHITTINGTON, LLOYD ROBERT, rubber and plastics co. exec.; b. Lima, Ohio, Dec. 24, 1917; s. Thomas and Mabel Walker (Ballard) W.; B.S., Ohio State U., 1939; m. Ruby R. Hosfeld, Jan. 4, 1941; children—Martha (Mrs. John W. Davis), Thomas Lloyd. Supt. Fredericksburg Pottery Co. (Ohio), 1940-41; supt. Coventry Metal Castings, Barberton, Ohio, 1941-48, v.p., 1948-53; v.p., sec. Nat. Latex Products Co., Ashland, Ohio, 1953—. Mem. Soc. Plastics Engrs. (recipient President's Cup 1963, contbg. editor for plastics engring. to jour.), ASTM (sec. subcom. on plastics industry terms). Mason. Author: Whittington's Dictionary of Plastics, 1968; Survey of Literature and Patents Concerning PVS Technology, 1963. Editor Urethane Abstracts. Patentee in field. Home: 402 Katherine Ave Ashland OH 44805 Office: Nat Latex Products Co 246-8 E Fourth St Ashland OH 44805

WHITWORTH, HALL BAKER, forest products co. exec.; b. St. Paul, N.C., Feb. 15, 1919; s. A. Frederick and Maude Ethel (Baker) W.; student Miss. So. Coll. 1942, U. N.C., 1957; m. Mary Margaret Mease, May 18, 1946; children—Hall Baker, Laura Ellen, David Allen. With Champion Internat., Canton, N.C., 1936-62, mgr. materials, 1956-62, dir. materials packages div., Chgo., 1962-65; dir. purchases U.S. Plywood-Champion Papers, Inc. (now Champion International Corp.), Hamilton, Ohio, 1965-68, dep. dir. corporate materials services, 1966, v.p., dir. purchases, 1968-75, v.p. materials, 1975—, also dir.; dir. Pathfork-Harlan Coal Co. Served with AUS, 1942-46. Recipient Thomas award Carolina-Va. Purchasing Agts. Assn., 1963. Mem. Am. Paper Inst. (chmn. energy subcom.), Am. Mgmt. Assn. (v.p. purchasing, transp. and phys. distbn. div. council, trustee). United Methodist (trustee). Elk, Lion (past treas., v.p.). Club: Canton Toastmasters (founder, 1st pres.). Home: 554 Chisholm Trail Cincinnati OH 45215 Office: Knightsbrige Hamilton OH 45011

WHITWORTH, WILLIAM OMAN, realtor; b. Mattoon, Ill., Aug. 27, 1946; s. Oman and Mary Dora Irene (Shadow) W.; grad. Utterback's Bus. Coll., 1966, Realtors Inst. Ill., 1971; A. Bus. Adminstrn., Lake Land Coll., 1974; m. Marianne Gardner, Dec. 30, 1964; 1 son, Douglas Neil. With Kenneth E. Gardner, realtors, Mattoon, Ill., 1967—, ins. broker, 1968—, realtor, 1970—. Instr. real estate Lake Land Coll., Mattoon, 1974—. Active United Fund, 1968, 69. Mem. Ind. Ins. Agts. Tri Counties (pres. 1971-72), Coles County Bd. Realtors (pres. 1973-74), Ill. Assn. Realtors, Nat. Assn. Realtors, East Central Ill. Ind. Ins. Agts. Assn., Ind. Ins. Agts. Assn. Ill., Nat. Assn. Ind. Ins. Agts. Elk, Moose. Home: 1121 Lafayette Ave Mattoon IL 61938 Office: 415 S 17th St Mattoon IL 61938

WHOLEBEN, BRENT EDWARD, counseling services adminstr., psychologist; b. Olean, N.Y., July 7, 1946; s. Bernard E. and Mildred F. (Camp) W.; B.S. in Math., St. Bonaventure U., 1968; M.Ed. in Psychology, U. Hawaii, 1972, M.Ed. in Adminstrn., 1974; certificate Mental Health Tng. Inst., 1972; m. Judith Ann Braun, June 22, 1968. Tchr. math. Aliamanu Inter Sch., Honolulu, 1970-73, coordinator student activities, 1971-73; dir. guidance services Mililani High Sch., Mililani Town, Hawaii, 1973-75; supr. Family Tng. Center, Glasgow AFB, Mont., 1975-77; research and devel. project asst. U. Wis.-Madison, 1977—. Served with arty., AUS, 1968-70; Vietnam. Mem. Am. Psychol. Assn., Am., Mont. personnel and guidance assns. Democrat. Roman Catholic. Contbr. articles in field to profl. publs. Home: 3109 Portage Ave Madison WI 53704 Office: Dept Ednl Adminstrn 1025 W Johnson St U Wis Madison WI 53706

WHYTE, PAUL COURTRIGHT, optometrist; b. Kimberly, Idaho, Jan. 4, 1914; s. John Joseph and Mary Della (Courtright) W.; student N.D. State U., 1931-34; D. Optometry, No. Ill. Coll. Optometry, 1940; grad. Advanced AUS Mil. Govt. Career Course, Ft. Gordon, Ga., 1956; B.S., U. Wis., 1972; m. Betty Jane Ripley, July 31, 1949; children—Daniel Paul, Deborah Jane (Mrs. Bruce Reed Hibma), Dallas Courtright, Darcy Dell (Mrs. Charles McGraw), Diana Dee. Salesman, Lever Bros. Co., Cambridge, Mass., 1937-38; Practice optometry, Oshkosh, Wis., 1940—. Minister Ch. of Humanitarians, 1975—. Pres. Oshkosh Swimpool, Inc., 1958-59; exec. dir. Trautmann-Lee Natural Foods Fund, Oshkosh, 1963—; sec. City-County Taxpayers Union Oshkosh, 1972—. Chmn., Winnebago Democratic Com., Oshkosh, 1964. Served with AUS, World War II; lt. col. Res. ret. Mem. Internat. Optometric Fellowship (v.p. 1972—), Oshkosh Res. Officers Assn. (v.p.), Ft. Sheridan (Ill.) Retiree Council. Clubs: Toastmasters (founding pres. 1955), Optimist (founding pres. 1948). Author: A 21st Century Philosophical Handbook for Living, 1973. Contbr. articles to various jours. Address: 317 Waugoo Ave Oshkosh WI 54901

WICK, ROBERT EDWARD, internat. trade exec.; b. Chgo., May 17, 1921; s. Lorenz Henry and Frances Martha (Meine) W.; M.B.A., U. Chgo., 1953; postgrad. Wharton Sch., 1959; M.E., Ill. Inst. Tech., 1946; m. Gladys Eleanor Hanan, June 29, 1952; children—Robert, David, Christopher. Dir. mktg. research Earle Ludgin & Co., Chgo., 1955-60; dir. comml. product devel. Land-Air Corp., Chgo., 1960-66; prin. Robert E. Wick & Asso., Oak Park, Ill., 1963-76; dir. internat. ops. Chgo. Dynamic Industries, 1973-76; pres. Insured Income Plans, Oak Park, 1966—; pres. Internat. Market Devel. Co., Oak Park, 1974—; instr. mech. engring. Am. Sch. Pres. Village Youth Band, Oak Park, 1977—; pres. Acorn council Boy Scouts Am.; pres. PTA Council. Recipient Distinguished Service award Hoover Commn., 1954. Mem. Fin. Analysts Fedn., Am. Inst. Mech. Engrs., Am. Mktg. Assn., Am. Mgmt. Assn., Am. Soc. for Metals, Internat. Trade Club, Internat. Assn. Execs., Chgo. Council on Fgn. Relations. Lutheran. Clubs: Exchange, Bond, Mid Day, Lake Shore. Home: 423 Greenfield St Oak Park IL 60302 Office: 205 W Wacker Dr Room 1122 Chicago IL 60606

WICKERSHAM, BEVERLY HORNER, educator; b. Des Moines, Dec. 14, 1943; d. Wendell J. and Vivian (Young) B.; B.E., Drake U., 1965, M.Ed., 1968; Ph.D., U. Iowa, 1974; m. Bill Wickersham, Apr. 6, 1975; children—Bryan, Barbara. Tchr. phys. edn. pub. schs., Urbandale, Iowa, 1965-66; counselor pub. schs., Iowa City, 1971-73; instr. U. Iowa, Iowa City, 1973-74; asst. prof. edn. So. Ill. U., Carbondale, 1974—. Mem. Ill. (treas.), Am. personnel and guidance assns., Futures Soc., AAUP, Phi Delta Kappa. Home: 10 Mockingbird Ln Carterville IL 62918 Office: Dept Guidance and Ednl Psychology So Ill U Carbondale IL 62901

WICKMAN, JOHN EDWARD, library exec.; b. Villa Park, Ill., May 24, 1929; s. John E. and Elsie (Voss) W.; A.B., Elmhurst Coll., 1953; M.A., Ind. U., 1958, Ph.D., 1964; m. Shirley Jean Swanson, Mar. 17, 1951; children—Lisa Annette, Eric John. Instr. English, history Hanover (Ind.) Coll., 1959-62; instr. history Ind. U., Jeffersonville, 1962; asst. prof. history N.W. Mo. State Coll., Maryville, 1962-64; faculty fellow Nat. Center Edn. in Politics, 1964-65; asst. prof. history Purdue U., Fort Wayne, Ind., 1965-66; dir. Dwight D. Eisenhower Library, Abilene, Kans., 1966—. Personal asst. to Gov. Kans., 1964-65. Served with AUS, 1953-55. Congl. fellow, Washington, 1975-76. Mem. Oral History Assn. (past pres.), Am. Soc. Pub. Adminstrn., Western History Assn. (council 1972-75), Am., Kans. State (bd. dirs., past pres.) hist. socs. Office: Dwight D Eisenhower Library Abilene KS 67410

WICKRAMASEKERA (WICKRAM), IAN EDWARD, psychologist; b. Colombo, Ceylon, Oct. 23, 1938; s. Henry Stanley and Maude (Robinson) W.; came to U5., 1959, naturalized, 1964; student London (Eng.) U., 1955-57; B.A., Friend's U., 1961; M.A., Roosevelt U., 1966; Ph.D., U. Ill., 1969; m. Sally McLaughlin, June 18, 1965; children—Melissa, Edward. Intern East Moline (Ill.) State Hosp., 1964-65, staff psychologist, 1965-66; research asst. Children's Research Center, U. Ill., Urbana, 1966-68; staff psychologist Peoria (Ill.) Mental Health Clinic, 1968—; pvt. practice psychology, Peoria, 1969—; clin. asso. U. Ill. Coll. Medicine, Peoria, 1971-75, asst. prof. psychiatry, 1975—. Cons. Inst. for Phys. Medicine, Peoria, 1972-73; provider workshops and tng. nationally and locally; clin. dir. Tri-County Suicide Prevention Center, Peoria, 1969-71; lectr. Internat. Congress Psychosomatic Medicine, Rome, 1975, Max Planck Inst. Psychiatry, Munich, Germany, 1975. Bd. dirs. Ill. Assn. Maternal and Child Welfare, 1973-75. Diplomate in hypnosis Ill. Biofeedback Soc. (pres. 1976-77); clin. fellow Behavior Therapy and Research Soc.; mem. AAAS, Assn. for Advancement of Behavior Therapy. Author: Biofeedback, Behavior Therapy and Hypnosis, 1976. Cons. editor Jour. of Abnormal Psychology, 1974-75; Psychol. Bull., 1973-74; Internat. Jour. of Experimental and Clin. Hypnosis, 1974-75. Office: Suite 303B 300 E War Memorial Dr Med Bldg Peoria IL 61603

WICZER, BERNARD, lawyer; b. Chgo., June 5, 1937; s. Morris Milton and Leona (Krupp) W.; B.S., Northwestern U., 1959; J.D., U. Chgo., 1962; m. Lois Diane Malmed, Aug. 23, 1959; children—Lisa Jennifer, Elliot Scott, Laura Joy. Admitted to Ill. bar, 1962; accountant Katz, Wagner & Co., Chgo., 1958-60; asso. law firm Pennish, Steele & Rockler, Chgo., 1962-63; asso. firm Norville, Walsh & Case, Chgo., 1963-68, mem. firm, 1968; mem. firm Caffarelli & Wiczer, Ltd., Chgo., 1969-74, Bernard Wiczer, profl. corp., 1975—. Dir. Life Assurance Co. Am. Tchr. accounting Northwestern U., 1958-59. Pres., Marionette Manor Home Owners Assn., 1965-67. C.P.A., Ill. Mem. Ill., Chgo. (com. on fed. income taxation 1971-73) bar assns., U.S. Power Squadron, Ill. Soc. C.P.A.'s. Jewish (pres. synagogue 1974-75). Clubs: Chgo. Yacht, Columbia Yacht (Chgo.). Home: 1348 Heatherhill Crescent Flossmoor IL 60426 Office: 104 S Michigan Ave Chicago IL 60603

WIDDIFIELD, DUANE ALDEN, clin. hypnotherapist; b. Fort Wayne, Ind., Apr. 5, 1934; s. Clarence Eugene and Madge Dolores (Graves) W.; grad. Lincoln Chiropractic Coll., 1959; LL.B., Blackstone Law Sch., 1969; D.D. (hon.), Ridgedale Theol. Sem., 1972, M.Th., 1975; B.S. in Psychology, State U. N.Y. at Albany, 1977; M.A. in Psychology, Calif. Western U., 1977, Ph.D. in Psychology, 1977; m. Marlene LaVonne Brown, Mar. 7, 1958; children—Mark Duane, Susan Marlene, Erik Michael, Janice LaVonne. Pres., Indpls. Art Craft, 1958-59; tech. asst. to physician, Indpls., 1962-66, bus. mgr., 1966-69; pvt. practice clin. psychotherapy, Indpls., 1969—. V.p., dir. Medi-Style Inc., Indpls., 1970—; dir. Inst. Clin. Hypnosis, 1977—. Served with U.S. Army, 1959-62. Diplomate Am. Psychotherapy Assn. Recipient various art awards, ordained Minister Ch. of God. Fellow Am. Inst. Hypnosis (diplomat); fellow Am. Coll. Clin. Adminstrs.; mem. So. Assn. Marriage Counselors, Internat. Transactional Analysis Assn., Am. Ministerial Assn., Am. Philos. Assn., Mensa, Intertel, Assn. to Advance Ethical Hypnosis, Fraternal Order Police (asso.), Sons Am. Revolution. Contbr. to profl. jours; also poetry. Home: 2501 Redfern Dr Indianapolis IN 46227 Office: 532 Turtle Creek Dr N Indianapolis IN 46227

WIDELL, DONALD RAYMOND, housewares sales co. exec.; b. Cambridge, Minn., Dec. 15, 1931; s. Wilbur Joseph and Alveda Helen (Swenson) W.; student Mpls. Bus. Sch., 1950-52; m. Rita Geraldine Macor, Mar. 5, 1954; children—Wendy, Scott, Brenda. Salesman, Wear-Ever Co., 1950-55; pres. Cordon Bleu Co., Mpls., 1955—. Mem. Minn. Assn. Direct Sales (pres. 1968-70). Home: 6920 Dakota Trail Minneapolis MN 55435 Office: 3612 Bryant St Minneapolis MN 55409

WIDERA, GEORG ERNST OTTO, educator; b. Dortmund, West Germany, Feb. 16, 1938; s. Otto F. and Gertrude A. (Yzermann) W.; came to U.S., 1950, naturalized, 1956; B.S., U. Wis., Madison, 1960, M.S., 1962, Ph.D., 1965; m. Kristel Kornas, June 22, 1974. Instr., U. Wis., 1963-65; asst. prof. engring. mechanics U. Ill., Chgo. Circle, 1965-69, asso. prof., 1960-73, prof., 1973—; vis. prof. U. Stuttgart, 1968-69, U. Wis., Milw., 1973-74; cons. to corps. Grantee NSF, Nat. Acad. Scis., U. Ill.-Chgo. Research Bd.; grad. fellow applied mechs. U. Wis., 1961-63; NASA fellow in space systems engring., 1966; Alexander von Humboldt fellow, 1968-69. Mem. ASCE, Am. Acad. Mechs., ASME, Ill. Soc. Porfl. Engrs., Gesellschaft fuer Angewandte Mathematik und Mechanik. Contbr. articles to profl. jours. Home: 345 Greenleaf St Wilmette IL 60091 Office: University of Illinois Box 4348 Chicago IL 60680

WIDIGER, JAN STRASZHEIM, pub. relations cons.; b. Columbus, Ohio, Apr. 16, 1929; d. Robert E. and Clara Belle (Shepherd) Straszheim; B.S., Purdue U., 1949; M.B.A., Ind. U., 1953; m. Almar Widiger, Sept. 7, 1957. Publicist pub. relations dept.: The Dow Chem. Co., 1953-58; partner Promotive Arts, pub. relations agy., 1958-60, owner, 1960—. Mem. Am. Women in Radio and Television, Inc., Purdue U. (life mem.), Ind. U. (life) alumni assns., Am. Marketing Assn. (sec. Saginaw Valley chpt. 1968-69, dir. 1969-70, v.p. 1970-71, pres. 1971-73), Women in Communications. Club: Zonta of Midland (treas. 1962-63, 69-71, v.p. 1963-65, pres. 1965-67, dist. pub. relations chmn. 1969-70). Address: 12961 Linden Ln Parma OH 44130

WIDLAK, FREDERIC WALTER, educator; b. Chgo., June 28, 1940; s. Walter Frederic and Ann Alice (Krajeski) W.; B.S., Ill. Inst. Tech., 1966; M.A., Marquette U., 1971; Ph.D., Purdue U., 1978; m. Prudence Amos, Aug. 12, 1967. Teaching, research asst. Marquette U., 1966-70; research fellow Purdue U., 1970-72, teaching and research asst., 1972-73, adminstrv. asst., 1974; research fellow Northwestern U., 1975-76; instr., program evaluator Ind. U. Med. Center, Indpls., 1975-76, asst. prof., 1976—; mem. Ind.-Purdue U. Computing Adv. Com., 1976—. Counselor Crossroads of Am. council Boy Scouts Am., 1976—; mem. Indpls. Zoo Adv. Council, 1976—. Mem. Am., Midwestern psychol. assns., Am., Ind. ednl. research assns., AAUP, Nat. Council on Measurement in Edn., Midwestern Soc. Multivariate Exptl. Psychology, Lake Mich. Fedn., Conservation-Outdoor Edn. Assn. Ind. (pres. 1977—), Izaak Walton League Am. (v.p., environ. edn. chmn. 1975—), Ind.-Purdue U. Faculty Club (v.p. 1976—), Pi Kappa Phi, Sigma Xi, Psi Chi, Kappa Delta Pi, Pi Nu Epsilon. Contbr. articles to profl. jours. Office: 1100 W Michigan St NU 317 Indianapolis IN 46202

WIDMAN, PAUL EDWARD, health care exec.; b. Norwalk, Ohio, Jan. 24, 1918; s. Edward Anthony and Josephine (Brown) W.; B.S., U. Toledo, 1941; m. Rose Hoyt, June 21, 1941; children—Jerry Paul, Kathleen Ann. Asst. dir. purchasing Johns Hopkins Hosp., Balt., 1950-51; dir. purchasing Cleve. Clinic Found., 1951-69, dir. adminstrv. services, 1969-76, dir. ops., 1977—; chmn. bd. dirs. Hosp. Bur. Inc., Cleve., 1973—. Served with USNR, 1943. Certified purchasing mgr. Nat. Assn. Purchasing Mgmt. Mem. Am. Hosp. Assn. (George R. Gossett award 1967), Am. Coll. Clinic Mgrs., Am. Coll. Hosp. Adminstrs. Home: 34780 Lakeview Dr Solon OH 44139 Office: 9500 Euclid Ave Cleveland OH 44106

WIDMER, JAMES GLENN, physician; b. Wayland, Iowa, Feb. 26, 1918; s. Christian G. and Elizabeth (Rediger) W.; student Goshen Coll., 1938-41; M.D., State U. Iowa, 1944; m. Helen Yoder, June 6, 1943; children—Gwen (Mrs. Reed Estabrook), Theodore, Jane (Mrs. Frank L. Yoder), Jean (Mrs. Dan Clark), James C., Janice. Intern, U.S. Marine Hosp., Chgo., 1944-45; practice medicine specializing in family practice, Wayland, Iowa, 1946—; mem. staff Henry County Meml. Hosp., Mt. Pleasant, Iowa; dir. Wayland State Bank. Bd. dirs. Wayland Consolidated Sch., 1954-60, Henry County Sch. System, 1963—, Henry County Community Health Program. Mem. Mennonite Med. Assn. (sec. 1969-71). Address: Box 98 Wayland IA 52654

WIDMER, REUBEN BENJAMIN, physician; b. Wayland, Iowa, June 29, 1916; s. Christian G. and Elizabeth (Rediger) W.; B.A., Goshen Coll., 1940; M.D., U. Iowa, 1943; m. Annabel Raber, Aug. 1, 1939; children—Charlotte (Mrs. John Lilliedahl Jr.), Catherine (Mrs. Aarne Seck), Frederick, Philip. Tchr. one room country sch., 1934-37; intern U.S. Marine Hosp., Norfolk, Va., 1944; resident Fla. Tb Hosp., Orlando, 1946; tb control USPHS, 1946-48; practice medicine specializing in family practice, Winfield, Iowa, 1948-72; asso. prof. dept. family practice Coll. Medicine U. Iowa, Iowa City, 1972—; asso. dir. model office, dir. med. edn., family residency program Mercy Hosp., Iowa City, 1972—; dir. model office, med. edn. Oakdale (Iowa) Hosp., U. Iowa, 1973—. Partner R & W Assos.; builder Twin Island Shopping Center, 1970—. Dir. Winfield Community Sch., 1957-60, Winfield-Mt. Union Community Sch., 1961-65; state exec. com. Iowa Tb and Health Assn., 1949-56; mem. founding bd. and chmn. Winfield Community Center, 1955-58. Served with USCGR, 1944-46. Diplomate Am. Bd. Family Practice (charter mem.). Mem. AMA, Iowa, Henry County (pres. 1960-62) med. socs., Am., Iowa (family practice club com. 1969—, bd. dirs. 1972—) acads. family practice, Iowa Trudeau Soc. (pres. 1951), VFW, Am. Legion. Presbyn. (elder 1950—). Home: Rural Route 2 West Branch IA 52358 Office: Dept Family Medicine Coll Medicine Univ Hosp Iowa City IA 52240

WIDNER, RUSSELL RALPH, ophthalmologist; b. Manchester, Iowa, May 6, 1935; s. Elmer Roy and Clarrisa Marie (Nordyke) W.; B.A., U. Iowa, 1959, M.D., 1961; m. Joyce Karolyn Turner, Sept. 13, 1958; children—Gregory, Cynthia. Intern, Phila. Gen. Hosp., 1961-62; resident dept. ophthalmology Univ. Hosps., Iowa City, 1962-65, fellow dept. ophthalmology, 1966; practice medicine specializing in ophthalmology, Marshalltown, Iowa, 1968—; ophthalmologist Wolfe Eye Clinic, Marshalltown, 1968—; mem. staff Marshalltown Area Community Hosp. Bd. dirs. Wolfe Catarect Found. Served with USPHS, 1966-68. Diplomate Am. Bd.

Ophthalmology. Fellow Am. Acad. Ophthaolmology and Otolaryngology, Phi Beta Kappa, Alpha Omega Alpha. Home: Rural Route 6 Marshalltown IA 50158 Office: Wolfe Eye Clinic 309 E Church St Marshalltown IA 50158

WIEBOLDT, RAYMOND CARL, JR., real estate developer; b. Evanston, Ill., Dec. 19, 1918; s. Raymond Carl and Nydia (Huth) W.; student Rennselaer Poly. Inst., 1937-39, Northwestern Tech. Inst., 1940-42; m. Jane L. Krause, Sept. 17, 1949; children—Nancy, Raymond Carl III, Anne. Pres. R. C. Wieboldt Co., Evanston, 1952—; pres. Inland Steel Devel. Corp., 1975-76, Dearborn Park Corp., 1977—. Bd. dirs. Chgo. Lighthouse for Blind, Wieboldt Found.; trustee Ill. Children's Home and Aid Soc. Served as capt. C.E., AUS, 1942-45. Mem. Theta Chi. Clubs: Economic, Commercial (Chgo.); Glenview Golf. Office: 327 S LaSalle St Chicago IL 60604

WIECK, GARY DEAN, accountant; b. Palmer, Nebr., Sept. 9, 1941; s. Lawrence H. ahd Lucille L. (Helzer) W.; B.A. in Bus. Adminstrn., Hasting Coll., 1963; m. Nanna Jean Mc Donald, Sept. 16, 1967; children—Trevor, Heather. Accountant, Contryman & Assos., Grand Island, Nebr., 1963-70, partner, 1970—. Mem. adv. bd. electronic data processing Central Nebr. Tech. Coll., 1969—; bd. dirs. Overland Trails council Boy Scouts Am., 1969-73; bd. dirs. Grand Island United Way, 1974-77, asso. campaign chmn., 1973, 75, 77. C.P.A.; certified data processor. Mem. Nebr. Soc. of C.P.A.s (dir.), Am. Inst. of C.P.A.s, Data Processing Mgmt. Assn. (individual performance award 1976; bd. dirs. Mid-state Nebr. chpt. 1968-74, 76, pres. 1969-70). Republican. Lutheran. Club: Riverside Golf. Home: 1515 W Hagge St Grand Island NE 68801 Office: 615 W First St Grand Island NE 68801

WIED, GEORGE LUDWIG, physician; b. Carlsbad, Czeckoslovakia, Feb. 7, 1921; s. Ernst George and Anna (Travnicek) W.; M.D., Charles U., Prague, 1945; m. Daga M. Graaz, Mar. 19, 1949 (dec. Aug. 1977). Came to U.S., 1953, naturalized, 1960. Intern, County Hosp., Carlsbad, 1945, U. Chgo. Hosps., 1955; resident obstetrics, gynecology U. Munich (Germany), 1946-48; practice medicine, specializing in obstetrics, gynecology, West Berlin, 1948-53, Chgo., 1954—; asst. obstetrics, gynecology Free U., West Berlin, 1948-52; asso. chmn. dept. obstetrics, gynecology Moabit Hosp. Free U., 1953; asst. prof., dir. cytology U. Chgo., 1954-59, asso. prof., 1959-65, prof., 1965—, mem. bd. adult edn., 1964-68, prof. pathology, 1967—, Blum-Riese prof. of obstetrics and gynecology, 1968—, acting chmn. dept. obstetrics and gynecology, 1974-75; hon. dir. Chgo. Cancer Prevention Center, 1959—; chmn. advisory com. cancer control Chgo. Bd. Health, 1961-71; chmn. jury Maurice Goldblatt Cytology award, 1963—. Recipient certificate merit U.S. Surgeon Gen., 1952, Maurice Goldblatt Cytology award, 1961; George N. Papanicolaou award, 1970. Mem. Am. (pres. 1965-66), Mexican (hon.), Spanish (hon.), Brazilian (fgn. corr.), Latin-Am. (hon.), Japanese (hon.), German (hon.), socs. cytology, Internat. Acad. Cytology (pres. 1977—), Central Soc. Clin. Research, Chgo. Path. Soc., Am. Soc. Cell Biology, German, Bavarian socs. obstetrics and gynecology, German Soc. Endocrinology, Sigma Xi. Contbr. articles to profl. jours.; editor-in-chief: Acta Cytologica, 1957—, Clin. Cytology, 1965—, Introduction to Quantitative Cytochemistry, 1965—, editor: Automated Cell Identification and Cell Sorting; editor-in-chief Jour. Reproductive Medicine. Home: 1640 E 50th St Chicago IL 60615 Office: 5841 S Maryland Ave Chicago IL 60637

WIEDEMANN, GLADYS H. GARDNER, fuel co. exec.; b. Mpls.; d. Charles Henry and Delia Margaret (Blair) Gardner; student Minn. U., 1945-47, Wichita U., 1958-59; m. Karl T. Wiedemann, July 22, 1950 (dec. Jan. 1961). Sec., Pioneer Rim & Wheel Co., Mpls., 1925-35, Socony-Vacuum Oil Co., St. Paul, 1935-42, Rosemount War Plant, Minn., 1942-44, Tankar Gas, Inc., Mpls., 1944-50; v.p. Beaumont Petroleum Co., El Dorado, Kans., 1950-61, pres., 1961—; pres. K.T. Wiedemann Trust Co., El Dorado, 1961—, trustee, 1962—. Mem. research bd. Wesley Med. Center, Wichita, Kans., 1966—; mem. research bd., student nurse com. Wesley Hosp.; adv. bd. Wichita YWCA, 1968—; v.p. Wichita Symphony Inc.; pres. K.T. Wiedemann Found., Wichita; patron Wichita area Girl Scouts U.S.A. Bd. dirs. Friends U., Wichita State U. Endowment Assn., Crime Commn., Salvation Army, Booth Meml. Hosp. Mem. Wichita Art Assn. (pres.), Women's Aux. Wichita Logopedics (dir.), Wichita Petroleum Club, Wichita Hist. Mus. Assn., P.E.O., Mu Phi Epsilon. Presbyn. Clubs: Soroptimist, 20th Century, Saturday Music, Organ Aires, Wichita, Plaza, Wichita Country (Wichita); Mpls. Athletic. Home: 8615 Shannon Way Wichita KS 67206 also 4200 Estero Blvd Fort Myers Beach FL 33931 Office: 1515 W 6th St El Dorado KS 67042

WIEGAND, JOHN ANTHONY, radio-TV producer; b. Freeport, Ill., July 10, 1914; s. John P. and Antoinette (Kautenburger) W.; B.E., U. Dayton, 1941; M.Ed., Western Res. U., 1946, M.A. in History, 1948; m. Martha Joan Wolanyk, Apr. 28, 1974; TV producer Catholic Diocese Cleve., 1952-56; producer, dir. WEDU-TV, Tampa, 1961-63; producer, dir. KVZK TV, American Samoa, 1964-66, also news anchorman; research asst. Ednl. Research Council Am., Cleve., 1966-67; TV instr., adviser, Philippines, 1968-69; tchr. St. Anthony Sch., Parma, Ohio, 1971-72; pub. relations coordinator Cath. Charities Central Services, Cleve., 1972—. Served with U.S. Armed Forces, 1942-43. Recipient George Washington Honor Medal award Freedoms Found., 1976. Home: 3455 Doris Rd Cleveland OH 44111 Office: 1031 Superior Ave Cleveland OH 44114

WIEGNER, EDWARD ALEX, economist, utility co. exec.; b. Waukesha, Wis., Dec. 13, 1939; s. Roy Edward and Margaret (Kuehnlein) W.; B.B.A., U. Wis., 1961, M.S., 1965, Ph.D., 1969; m. Kathleen Marian Knapp, Dec. 17, 1960 (div.); 1 dau., Christine; m. 2d, Catherine Jean Mullens, Oct. 17, 1970; children—Carlin, Ryan. Mem. joint staff Co-ordinating Com. for Higher Edn., Madison, Wis., 1963-64; asst. to v.p. Marquette U., Milw., 1964-68, asst. prof. econs., 1965-71; vis. asso. prof. econs. U. Wis., Madison, 1973-74; sec. revenue State of Wis., 1971-74; econ. cons. 1967-69; mem. ednl. communications bd. State of Wis., 1969-71; sr. v.p. consumer, pub. and fin. affairs Wis. Power and Light Co., Madison, 1974—, also dir. Mem. adv. com. Energy Analysis div. Edison Electric Inst.; mem. com. on financial considerations Atomic Indsl. Forum. Mem. ednl. com. Wis. Legislative Council, 1968-71; city alderman, Madison, Wis., 1961-63. Office: 222 W Washington Ave Madison WI 53703

WIELAND, CLYDE LEE, physician; b. nr. Dow, Ill., Jan. 25, 1930; s. Daniel Webster and Bessie Irene McDow) W.; B.S., U. Ill., 1951, M.D., 1955; m. Virginia Irene Robertson, Sept. 5, 1954; children—Felicia, Richard, John, Melanie. Intern Cook County Hosp., Chgo., 1955-57; resident McNeal Meml. Hosp., Berwyn, Ill., 1957; practice medicine, specializing in family practice, Jerseyville, Ill., 1959—; mem. staff Jersey Community Hosp., pres., 1962-63, chief staff, 1970-71; founder McDow Meml. Med. Clinic, Jerseyville, 1973—. Pres., chmn. bd. Jersey County chpt. Am. Cancer Soc., 1968—, bd. dirs. 8th dist. Ill. div., 1972—. Served with AUS, 1957-59. Diplomate Am. Bd. Family Practice (charter mem.). Charter fellow Am. Acad. Family Physicians; mem. AMA, Ill., Jersey Calhoun (pres. 1961-68) med. socs., C. of C., Phi Rho Sigma. Republican. Presbyn. Mason (K.T.), Rotarian. Home: 806 N State St Jerseyville IL 62052 Office: McDow Meml Med Clinic Maple Summit Rd Jerseyville IL 62052

WIELAND, RALPH GAZELL, physician; b. Cleve., Dec. 25, 1930; B.A., Yale U., 1952; M.D., U. Pa., 1956; m. Ann Matlack; children—Jeffrey, Mark, Linda. Rotating intern U. Hosps. Cleve., 1956-57, asst. resident in medicine, 1957-59 asst. physician, 1963-64; asst. dir. Clin. Research Center, Ohio State U. Hosps., 1964-66, dir., 1966-67; dir. dept. medicine and div. endocrinology and metabolism St. Luke's Hosp., Cleve., 1967, dir. Core Med. Clerkship; asso. clin. prof. medicine Case Western Res. U. Sch. Medicine, 1967-72, asso. prof. medicine, 1972-74, prof., 1974—. Mem. Health Fund Greater Cleve., Cleve. Acad. Medicine, Met. Health Planning Corp., Ohio Bur. Drug Abuse, Cleve., United Torch Services. Served with USAF, 1959-61. Diplomate Am. Bd. Internal Medicine; certified Nat. Bd. Med. Examiners, 1957; USPHS fellow, 1961-64. Fellow A.C.P.; mem. Am. Diabetes Assn., AAAS, AMA, Am. Fedn. Clin. Research, Central Soc. Clin. Research, Soc. for Study of Reprodn., Enocrine Soc., Diabetes Assn. Greater Cleve. (dir., 1967, program co-chmn. 1968-69, exec. com. 1969—, 2d v.p. 1970, pres. 1972, chmn. detection and evaluation com. 1974), Physicians Peer Rev. Orgn. (continuing med. edn. com. 1976—). Contbr. numerous articles to profl. jours. Address: St Luke's Hosp 11311 Shaker Blvd Cleveland OH 44104

WIENER, PHYLLIS AMES, artist; b. Iowa City, Iowa, Sept. 17, 1921; d. Charles Louis and Loretta (Tucker) Zager; student U. Iowa, 1939-40, U. Minn., 1950-56: m. Daniel N. Wiener, Dec. 9, 1971; children—Gareth Downs, Allison Downs, Barbara Hodne, Amy Downs. Instr. art Walker Art Center, Mpls., 1960-66, U. Minn. extension, Mpls., 1962-73, Minnetonka Art Center, Wayzata, Minn., 1965-76; one-woman shows: Walker Art Center, Mpls., 1951, 56, Mpls. Art Inst., 1967, A.L. Gallery, Mpls., 1975, 77; exhibited in group shows: Denver Art Mus., 1951, 56, 68, Butler Inst., Ohio, 1965, U.S. Dept. State Traveling Show, 1962; represented in permanent collections: Walker Art Center, Mpls. Art Inst. Mem. Artists Equity Assn. Home: Box 37B East Star Route Two Harbors MN 55616 Studio: 25 University Ave SE Minneapolis MN 55414

WIENS, JOEL HENRY, banker; b. Enid, Okla., Oct. 30, 1929; s. Henry E. and Hannah Helen (Rusch) W.; B.S., Phillips U., 1951; postgrad. Nebr. State U., Colo. U., Harvard, Mo. Auction Sch.; m. Phyllis Arlene Beu, Nov. 20, 1949; children—Thomas Joel, Timothy Dane. Various positions in farming, edn., real estate, 1948-62; pres. First State Bank, Kimball, Nebr., 1963—, Kimball County Bank, 1963—, Tri-State Ins., 1963—, First Western Corp., 1953—, Rite-A-Way Industries, 1968—; chmn. bd. Centennial State Bank, Lyons, Colo., Panhandle Western Mgmt. Corp., Summit County Bank, Frisco, Colo., Western A6-Credit Corp.; founder Interstate Inn Motel Chain, 1969; owner Flying W Ranch, Kimball; dir. Forward Kimball Industries, Packers Nat. Bank, Omaha. Bd. dirs. Bd. Pub. Works, Kimball, 1963—. County chmn. Republican gubernatorial campaign, 1970, Rep. senatorial campaign. Named Adm. Nebr. Navy. Mem. Western Nebr. Bankers Assn. (pres. 1971—). Methodist. Mason (32 deg., Shriner). Kiwanian (pres. 1960-61), Rotarian, Elk. Home: 706 S Burg St Kimball NE 69145 Office: 115 S Walnut St Kimball NE 69145

WIERMAN, JAMES LEE, osteo. physician; b. Saginaw, Mich., Jan. 11, 1941; s. Glen Sherman and Margaret Isabelle (Condon) W.; student Marion Coll., 1959-61; A.B., Asbury Coll., 1963; D.O., Kirksville Coll. Osteo. Medicine, 1967; postgrad. Wayne State U., 1970-73; m. Denise Alice Borst, May 17, 1969; children—Nicole, Meredith. Intern, Flint (Mich.) Osteo. Hosp., 1967-68; mem. staff, chief of medicine Berrien Gen. Hosp., Berrien Center, Mich., 1968-69, 73—; med. missionary Hosp. Wesleyan, La Gonave, Haiti, 1969-70; resident in medicine Harper Hosp., Detroit, 1970-73. Diplomate Am. Bd. Internal Medicine. Mem. Am. Soc. Tropical Medicine, A.C.P., Christian Med. Soc. Methodist. Home: Rural Route 2 Steimle Eau Claire MI 49111 Office: 400 W Division St Dowagiac MI 49047

WIERSUM, QUINTIN EUGENE, elec. contact mfg. co. exec.; b. Kenosha, Wis., Dec. 26, 1922; s. Charles and Maria Wilhelmina (Balk) W.; grad. in accounting Kenosha Coll. Commerce, 1945-47; postgrad. Northwestern U. Bus. Sch., 1949-50; m. Jean Marie Niederprim, Apr. 28, 1945; 1 son, Richard. Test cell supr. Nash Motors, Kenosha, 1943-45; mail clk. U.S. Post Office, Kenosha, 1945-48; cost estimator Fansteel Metall. Corp., North Chicago, 1948-51; with Deringer Mfg. Co., Mundelein, Ill., 1951—, purchasing agt., 1960—. Mem. Indsl. Assn. Skokie Valley (chmn. purchasing group 1967-68). Home: 7723 33d Ave Kenosha WI 53140 Office: 1250 Town Line Rd Mundelein IL 60060

WIERWILLE, DONALD ERNST, ednl. adminstr.; b. Lima, Ohio, Aug. 11, 1940; s. Victor Paul and Dorothea Sarah (Kipp) W.; B.Edn., U. Wis.-Whitewater, 1966; M.S. in Edn., No. Ill. U., 1968; postgrad. in ednl. adminstrn. U. Kans.; m. Wanda May Strohschein, Apr. 14, 1962; children—Laurinda, Ralph, Kristina. Tchr. elementary schs. Winnebago County, Ill., 1962-66; reading specialist pub. schs. Rockton, Ill., 1966-69; elementary prin. schs. Clinton, Wis., 1969-74; v.p. adminstrn., dean Way Coll. of Emporia (Kans.), 1974—; v.p., bd. trustees The Way Internat., New Knoxville, Ohio, 1977—. Mem. NEA, Wis. Elementary Prins., Phi Delta Kappa. Home: 1300 W 12th Ave Emporia KS 66801 Office: PO Box 328 New Knoxville OH 45871

WIERWILLE, VICTOR PAUL, clergyman; b. New Knoxville, Ohio, Dec. 31, 1916; s. Ernst Henry and Emma (Rehn) W.; A.B., Lakeland Coll., 1938; B.D., Mission House Sem., Sheboygan, Wis., 1941; M.Th., Princeton, 1941; Th.D., Pikes Peak Sem., 1958; postgrad U. Chgo., 1938-40; m. Dorothea Sarah Kipp, July 2, 1937; children—Donald Ernst, Karen Ruth (Mrs. James Kirby Martin), Mary Ellen (Mrs. John Thomas Somerville), Sara Kathryn, John Paul. Ordained to ministry Evang. and Ref. Ch., 1941; pastor Evang. and Ref. Ch., Payne, Ohio, 1941-42, Van Wert, Ohio, 1943-57; founder The Way Internat., bibl. research and teaching center, New Knoxville, O., 1958—, also pres. and founder, The Way Internat. Fine Arts and Hist. Center, Sidney, Ohio, 1974; founder The Way mag., 1945—. Pres. bd. trustees The Way Coll., Emporia, Kans., 1974—; pres. bd. trustees The Way Coll. of Bibl. Research Ind. Campus, Rome City, 1975—. Author: Victory Through Christ, 1945; Receiving the Holy Spirit Today, 1955, 6th ed., 1972; Power for Abundant Living, 1971; The Bible Tells Me So, 1971; The New, Dynamic Church, 1971; The Word's Way, 1971; Are the Dead Alive Now?, 1971; Jesus Christ is NOT God, 1975; God's Magnified Word, 1977. Address: PO Box 328 New Knoxville OH 45871

WIERZBICKI, ANTHONY JEROME, city ofcl.; b. Detroit, Nov. 24, 1917; s. Joseph Anthony and Margaret (Oleksy) W.; B.B.A., U. Detroit, 1943; m. Anna Glaza, June 21, 1941 (dec.); children—Cecelia, Barbara, Mary Margaret, Paul, Joseph, Susan, Gerald; m. 2d, Marie Carey, Dec. 29, 1973. With City of Detroit, 1936—, councilman, 1962-65, 68-73, dep. auditor gen., 1973-76. Pres. Polish Daily News, Inc., 1964-67, Am. Pub. Corp., 1966-75, Pol-Am. Pub. Co., 1968-70. USNR, 1942-46; PTO. Decorated Bronze Star medal. Mem. Municipal Finance Officers Assn., Inst. Internal Auditors, Govtl. Accountants and Analysts Assn., Polish Am. C. of C. of Mich., Am. Legion, V.F.W., Amvets, Polish Legion Am. Vets. K.C. Office: City-County Bldg Detroit MI 48226

WIESER, CHARLES EDWARD, financial cons.; b. St. Marys, Ohio, Apr. 18, 1929; s. Lawrence F. and Rose (Danaher) W.; B.S., Ohio State U., 1951, M.B.A., 1953; m. Anne Esper, Dec. 1, 1962; children—Lawrence, Carolyn, Mark, Charles T. Staff accountant Touche, Ross, Bailey &Smart, 1954-59, supr. audit, 1959-62, mgr. audit, 1962-67, adminstrv. mgr. Detroit office, 1967-68; mgr. corporate finance dept. Manley, Bennett, McDonald & Co., Detroit, 1968-70; v.p. finance Whitehead & Kales Co., Detroit, 1970—. Instr. accounting Ohio State U., 1954. Served to 2d lt. AUS, 1951-53, C.P.A., Mich. Mem. Financial Execs. Inst., Am. Inst. C.P.A.'s, Mich. Assn. C.P.A.'s, Nat. Assn. Accountants, Am. Accounting Assn., Ohio State U. Alumni Assn., Beta Alpha Psi. Club: State U. Alumni Assn. Club: Economic (Detroit). Home: 24525 Emerson St Dearborn MI 48124 Office: 58 Haltiner St River Rouge MI 48218

WIEST, EDWARD FREDERICK, state ofcl.; b. Wyoming Twp., Mich., Feb. 26, 1917; s. John J. and Mary (Rebone) W.; student Davenport Bus. Coll., 1936-37; m. Margaret M. Fehsenfeld, Nov. 20, 1941; children—Thomas, Robert, Mary Ann, Edward Frederick, Nancy, James, Margaret Mary. Office mgr. Firestone & Rubber Co., 1941-45, mgr., 1945-47; owner Wiest Sales & Service, Grand Rapids, Mich., 1947-68; asst. mgr. Decker-Davies-Jean and Mackey Ins. Agy., 1968-70; mayor, Wyoming, Mich., 1963-69; commr. Mich. Liquor Control Commn., 1970—. Recipient St. George award Boy Scouts Am., 1961. K.C. (past grand knight). Club: Am. Businessmen (charter pres. 1959—). Home: 917 Cricklewood Dr SW Wyoming MI 49509

WIEST, WALTER GIBSON, educator; b. Price, Utah, Feb. 16, 1922; s. Walter Emil and Irma Annette (Gibson) W.; A.B., Brigham Young U., 1948; M.S., U. Wis. at Madison, 1951, Ph.D., 1952; m. Myrlene Romney, June 4, 1948; children—David, Karen (Mrs. Brian Anderson), Walter, Richard, Barton, Allyson, Jennifer. From instr. to asso. prof. U. Utah, Salt Lake City, 1952-64; asso. prof. endocrinology, dept. obstetrics and gynecology Washington U. Med. Sch., St. Louis, 1964-68, prof., 1968—. Bishop, Ch. of Jesus Christ of Latter-day Saints, 1957-60, mem. high council St. Louis Stake, 1965-69, 2d counsellor presidency, 1969-74, stake patriarch, 1974—. Served with USMCR, 1944-50. USPHS spl. postdoctoral fellow, 1960-61; Population Council fellow U. Cologne (Germany), 1960-61. Mem. Am. Soc. Biol. Chemists, Endocrine Soc., Soc. Gynecologic Investigation, AAAS, Sigma Xi. Contbr. to profl. jours. Home: 13154 D'Artagnan Ct Creve Coeur MO 63141 Office: Dept Obstetrics and Gynecology Med Sch Washington Univ St Louis MO 63110

WIETERS, IVAN L., coop. co. exec.; b. Barnes, Kans., Apr. 23, 1926; s. Albert L. and Elsie (Boda) W.; grad. Clark's Bus. Coll., 1961; m. Valera Hermena Harz, July 31, 1949; owner trucking bus., 1946-47; farmer, rancher, Greenleaf, Kan., 1948-59; accountant, office mgr. Farmers Coop Elevator Assn., Greenleaf, 1961-65, sec., gen. mgr., treas., 1966-75; dist. mgr. Far-Mar-Co. Inc., Hutchinson, Kans., 1975-77, dir. info. and mem. services, 1977—. Pres. dist. 2 Kan. Coop. Council, 1969-71, pres. state bd., Kans. Coop. Council, 1971-72; mem. planning com. Nat. Council Farmer Coops., Phoenix, 1972. Served with USNR, 1944-46. Mem. adv. bd. Cloud County Community Jr. Coll., Concordia, Kans. Mem. Nat. Soc. Accountants for Coops. (stewardship chmn. 1967-69), Future Farmers Am. (mem. adv. bd., dist. 22, Washington, Kans.; hon. mem.), Internat. Platform Assn., Coop. Editorial Assn. Lutheran (chmn. 1973—). Lion (pres. 1967-68, zone chmn. 1968-69, dep. dist. gov. 1969-70). Editor Coop News and Views, 1966-75. Home: 701 Loch Lommond Dr Hutchinson KS 67501 Office: Far-Mar-Co Inc Hutchinson KS 67501

WIETERS, NELSON EDGAR, coll. adminstr.; b. St. Louis, Aug. 30, 1927; s. Henry Nelson and Myrtle Mable (Ringer) W.; B.A., William Jewell Coll., 1951; M.S., George Williams Coll., 1961; m. Velta Isora Stout, May 4, 1951; children—Robin, Julie, Jane, Fredrick. Dir. camping services City of Kansas City (Mo.), 1951-57, dist. dir. recreation, 1957-58, acting supt. recreation, 1958-59; chmn. dept. leisure and environmental resources George Williams Coll., Downers Grove, Ill., 1959—. Vice pres., Camp Orgn. & Planning Assos., Chgo.; founder Man and His Land expdns., 1959-75; mem. future of our nat. parks study com. Conservation Found., 1972. Bicentennial Commn., 1973; del. White House Conf. on Children, 1970. Trustee Fund for Advancement Camping, 1974—. Served with USNR, 1946-47. Mem. Am. Camping Assn. (dean Midwest Inst. for Tng. 1967—), nat. pres. 1972-74), Explorers Club N.Y.C., Nat. Parks and Conservation Assns., Nat. Forestry Assn., Nat. Recreation and Parks Assn., Smithsonian Assos., Nat. Geog. Soc. Contbr. articles to profl. jours. Home: 2526 Hobson Rd Downers Grove IL 60515

WIETHOFF, CLIFFORD ALLEN, surgeon; b. Seymour, Ind., May 12, 1920; s. Clifford Henry and Mary Elizabeth (Rothrock) W.; A.B. in Anatomy, Ind. U., 1942, M.D., 1944; m. Mary Lou Ferguson, June 20, 1943; children—Janet Sue, Richard Allen, Barbara Joanne, John Clifford. Intern U.S. Naval Hosp., Key West, Fla., 1944-45; resident in pathology Ind. U. Med. Center, 1946-47; resident in surgery Indpls. Gen. Hosp., 1947-49; practice medicine specializing in gen. surgery, Seymour, 1950—; me. staffs Jackson County Hosp., Seymour, 1950—, Washington County Hosp., Salem, Ind., 1950—, Bartholomew County Hosp., Columbus, Ind., 1950—; asst. in surgery, surg. pathology Ind. Med. Center, 1950-51; dir. Fidelity Fed. Savs. and Loan, Seymour, Am. Security Co., Seymour. Bd. dirs. Seymour Girls Club, 1953-56. Served to lt. USNR, 1944-46. Diplomate Am. Bd. Surgery. Fellow A.C.S.; mem. Am., Ind. State, Pan-Am. med. assns., Jackson County Med. Soc., Pan-Pacific Surg. Assn., Am. Legion, Seymour C. of C. (dir. 1952-55), Beta Theta Pi, Nu Sigma Nu. Republican. Methodist. Clubs: Seymour Country (dir. 1962-68, pres. 1965), Rotary (pres. 1956) (Seymour); Lake and Forest (Brownstown, Ind.), Elks, Masons, Eagles. Contbr. articles to med. jours. Home: 615 West Dr Sunset Pkwy Seymour IN 47274 Office: 1131 Medical Pl Seymour IN 47274

WIGEN, JORIS ODIN, state ofcl.; b. Hettinger, N.D., May 5, 1917; s. J.O. and Gea (Sether) W.; B.A., St. Olaf Coll., 1939; m. Phyllis G. Vevle, July 4, 1943; children—M. Richard, Joan, Ann. Ins. adjuster Western Adjustment & Inspection Co., Chgo., 1940-41; adjuster Western Adjustment & Inspection Co., Fargo, N.D., 1945-51, mgr., Dickinson, N.D., 1951, mgr., Bismarck, N.D., 1951-57; owner, mgr. Noble Adjustment Co., Bismarck, 1957-68; N.D. ins. commr., Bismarck, 1969-77; pres. Kwiki Car Wash. Inc., Bismarck, 1965—. Treas. N.D. Republican Central Com., 1965-67. Bd. dirs., sec. Mo. Slope Lutheran Nursing Home. Bismarck, 1960-68. Served to capt. AUS, 1941-45; ETO. Decorated Air medal with two oak leaf clusters. Mem. Bismarck C. of C. (dir., mem. exec. com. 1965-68). Lutheran. Home: 1255 W Highland Acres Rd Bismarck ND 58501 Office: 411 N 4th St Bismarck ND 58501

WIGGINS, ARTHUR WILLIAM, physicist; b. South Bend, Ind., Mar. 5, 1938; s. Donald A. and Miriam (Zurbuch) W.; B.S., U. Notre Dame, 1960; M.S., U. Mich., 1965: m. Regina M. Ritter, Feb. 4, 1961; children—Ann M., John P. Asso. research aerophysicist Bendix Systems div., Ann Arbor, 1960-64; sect. head, flight dynamics div., aero physics dept. Conductron Corp., Ann Arbor, 1964-68; research asso. Systems Research Lab. U. Mich., 1968-69,; asso. prof. physics Oakland Community Coll., Farmington Hills, Mich., 1969—, head dept. phys. scis., 1977—. Mem. Am. Assn. Physics Tchrs., Mich. Edn.

Assn., NEA. Author: Physical Science with Environmental Applications, 1974. Office: Dept Physical Sciences Oakland Community Coll Farmington Hills MI 48018

WIGGINTON, JAMES CHARLES, financial exec.; b. Detroit, Feb. 23, 1949; s. Jerry Wayne and Rosemary Adele (Hatfield) W.; B.B.A., Eastern Mich. U., 1973, M.B.A., 1976; m. Nancy Marie Lucas, May 4, 1968; children—Brent, Jeffrey, Krista. Gen. auditor Security Bank & Trust Co., Lincoln Park, Mich., 1966-68; asst. controller Diners/Fugazy, Detroit, 1968-70; sr. accountant Allen & Robson C.P.A.'s, Wayne, Mich., 1970-72; asst. controller Everlock Detroit, Inc., Sterling Heights, Mich., 1972-73; corp. controller Indsl. Fuels Corp., Southfield, Mich., 1973-76; chief fin. officer officer Gt. Lakes Container Corp., Detroit, 1976-77; v.p., controller Veratex div. W.R. Grace, Troy, Mich., 1977—; dir. Mueller Tool & Mfg. Co., Detroit, 1973—. Served with USMCR, 1967-73. C.P.A., Mich. Mem. Am. Inst. C.P.A.'s, Mich. Assn. C.P.A.'s, Am. Mgmt. Assn., Nat. Assn. Accountants. Home: 19260 Jeffrey Ln Southfield MI 48075

WIJNHOLDS, HEIKO DE BEAUFORT, educator; b. Amsterdam, Netherlands, Dec. 9, 1940; s. Heiko Wijnholds and Benudina Maria (de Beaufort) W.; B.Com. cum laude, U. Pretoria, 1962; D.Com., U. South Africa, 1970; children—Monique Constance, Heiko Aernout. Vis. prof. mktg. San Diego State U., 1970-71; asst. prof. dept. bus. adminstrn. U. South Africa, 1964-68, asso. prof. dept. bus. adminstrn., 1969-70, head mktg., 1971-74, prof., 1970-74; asso. prof. mktg. U. N.D., 1975-77, chmn. mktg. dept., 1975—, prof., 1977—. Internat. Edn. scholarship, 1964; Univ. Council Pretoria scholarship, 1962; Nat. Cash Register scholarship, 1960, 61; State N.D. grant, 1977. Mem. Am. Mktg. Assn., Midwest Bus. Adminstrn. Assn., Acad. Mktg. Sci., Acad. Internat. Bus. Co-author (with C. de Coning, N.J. Swart) Marketing Management: A South African Approach, 1968. Home: 914 N 39th St Grand Forks ND 58201 Office: Marketing Dept U ND Grand Forks ND 58202

WIKELUND, HAROLD NORMAN, engring. sales co. exec.; b. Chgo., June 2, 1907; s. Harold Norman and Josephine Elizabeth (Larson) W.; grad. pub. schs.; m. Margaret Grace Atwell, Oct. 25, 1930; children—Norma Jean, Dawn Joy, Roberta Jill. Sales engr. Celotex Corp., Des Moines, Iowa, 1945-48; pres. H. N. Wikelund Co., Des Moines, 1948-59; div. mgr. Barber-Colman Co., Rockford, Ill., 1958-60; pres., sec.-treas. Hydronics, Inc., Brookfield, Wis., 1960—. Mem. Am. Soc. Heating, Refrigerating and Air Conditioning Engrs. Methodist. Mason (Shriner), Rotarian. Patentee hydraulic operated bleachers and basketball backstops. Home: 14305 Watertown Plank Rd Elm Grove MI 53122 Office: 13960 W North Ave Brookfield WI 53005

WIKIERA, EDWARD STANLEY, physician; b. Detroit, Dec. 16, 1918; s. Stanley and Bernice (Kubik) W.; B.S., Wayne State U., 1940, M.D., 1944; m. Josephine Warchol, June 14, 1942. Intern, Woman's Hosp., Detroit, 1944-45; gen. resident Detroit Receiving Hosp., 1947, resident in dermatology, 1949-51; resident dermatology VA Hosp., Detroit, 1948; pvt. practice dermatology, Detroit, 1952-56, Dearborn, Mich., 1956—; cons. dermatology Oakwood Hosp., Alexander Blain Hosp., Annapolis Hosp., Wayne, Mich., Delray Gen. Hosp., Outer Drive Hosp., Ford Motor Co. Mem. Nat. Com. for Immigration Reform, 1966, President's Com. on Immigration Reform. Served to capt. AUS, 1945-47. Diplomate Am. Bd. Dermatology and Syphilology, PanAm. Med. Assn. Fellow Am. Acad. Dermatology and Syphilology, Am. Geriatrics Soc.; mem. AMA, Mich., Wayne County med. socs., N.Y. Acad. Scis., N.Am. Clin. Dermatol. Soc., Internat. Soc. Tropical Dermatology, Assn. Am. Med. Colls., Mich. Assn. Professions, Nat. Med. and Dental Assn. Am., Med. Dental Arts Club, Wayne State Alumni Assn., Phi Beta Pi, Alumni Phi Beta Pi. Clubs: Great Dane of America (Conn.); Deutche-Doggen of Germany; Great Dane of Gt. Britain. Home: 17400 West Outer Dr Dearborn Heights MI 48127 Office: 15120 Michigan Av Dearborn MI 48126

WIKOFF, VIRGIL CORNWELL, state legislator; gen. contractor, b. Decatur, Ill., Feb. 6, 1927; s. Virgil L. and Grace (Cornwell) W.; B.S., U. Ill., 1951; m. Ruth Helen Moore, Aug. 23, 1947; children—Terrill Joanne (Mrs. Robert G. Bolduc), Patricia Suzanne (Mrs. Gregory D. Bolton). Formed Lyman-Wikoff, Inc., Gen. contractors, Champaign, Ill., 1952, pres., 1952—, owner, 1965—; mem. Ill. Ho. of Reps. from 52d dist., 1977—. Former chmn. adv. council Ill. Dept. Local Govt. Affairs; former mem. Ill. Law Enforcement Tng. Bd. Mem. Champaign City Council, 1963-67, mayor, 1967-75; chmn. Ill. Mayors for Re-election Pres. Nixon, 1972; mem. Cities and Villages Municipal Problems Commn. of Ill. Served with USNR, 1945-46, 51-52. Named Outstanding Jaycee in Ill., 1959, Outstanding Jaycee State Dir., 1960, 1 of 10 Outstanding Young Men in Community, 1961, Outstanding Jaycee Nat. Dir., 1963. Mem. Central Ill. Builders Assn. (v.p.), Ill. Municipal League (v.p. 1968-71, pres. 1972-73, chmn. com. implementation new constn.), Central Ill. Mayors Assn. (treas. 1968, pres. 1970-71), Jr. Chamber Internat. (life), Champaign-Urbana Jr. C. of C. (life), Champaign C. of C. (v.p. 1965), Am. Arbitration Assn. (panelist), Urban League. Mem. Christian Ch. Clubs: Hi-12 (Champaign-Urbana); Masons, Shriners, Moose, Kiwanis, Elks. Home: 2120 Noel Dr Champaign IL 61820 Office: PO Box 781 Champaign IL 61820

WILBANKS, GEORGE DEWEY, obstetrician, gynecologist, med. coll. adminstr.: b. Gainesville, Ga., Feb. 24, 1931; s. George Dewey and Ruth Lucille (Chamblee) W.; A.B., Duke, 1953, M.D., 1956; m. Evelyn Freeman Rivers, July 31, 1954; children—George Rivers, Wayne Freeman. Resident instr. Duke U. Med. Center, Durham, N.C., 1961-62, asso., 1964-65, asst. prof., 1965-70, asso. prof., 1970—, dir. div. gynecol. oncology, 1968-70; clin. instr. Okla. Sch. Medicine, Oklahoma City, 1963-64; prof., chmn. Rush Med. Coll. Rush Presbyn. St. Lukes Med. Center, Chgo., 1970—; pres. Womens Health Cons. Mem. Assn. Chgo. Gynecol. Oncologists (pres. 1975-77), Am. Soc. Colposcopy Colpomicroscopy (pres. 1975-77), Am., Chgo. gynecol. socs., Soc. Gynecol. Oncologists, Soc. Pelvic Surgeons, Am. Assn. Obstetricians Gynecologists, Am. Coll. Obstetricians Gynecologists, A.C.S. Home: 39 E Elm St Chicago IL 60611 Office: Rush Presbyterian St Lukes Medical Center 1753 W Congress Pkwy Chicago IL 60612

WILBORN, JAMES CHRISTIAN, grain broker; b. Oak Park, Ill., June 16, 1947; s. Stanley Lowell and Marian Laura (Stokburger) W.; B.A., Northwestern U., 1970; m. Raylene Louise Monette, July 20, 1975. Account exec., Coop. Futures Co., Chgo., 1970-73, Clayton Brokerage Co., Chgo., 1974; ind. grain broker, Chgo., 1974—. Served with U.S. Army, 1968, Ill. N.G., 1969-74. Mem. Chgo. Bd. Trade, Cook County Farm Bur. Republican. Clubs: Univ. Chgo., Shriners. Home: 4917 Lawn Ave Western Springs IL 60558 Office: 141 W Jackson Blvd Chicago IL 60604

WILBORN, LARRY DEAN, dentist; b. Danville, Ill., Mar. 18, 1938; s. Clifford Harding and Alice Darlene (Wood) W.; student U. Ill., 1956-58, Eastern Ill. U., 1958-60; D.D.S., Northwestern U., 1964; m. Marilyn Grace James, Oct. 23, 1965; children—James Todd, Laura Lynn. Practice dentistry, Champaign, Ill., 1965—. Head dental div. United Fund Way, Champaign, 1971—; head Champaign County dental div. Am. Cancer Soc., 1972-73, 75. Mem. Am. Dental Assn., Am. Acad. Gen. Dentistry, Chgo. Dist. Dental Soc., Psi Omega. Republican. Methodist (policy adminstrn. bd. 1970-72, 76—). Club: Lincolnshire Fields (Ill.) Country. Home: 1116 Newbury St Champaign IL 61820 Office: 1210 Lancaster Dr Champaign IL 61820

WILBUR, LOWELL ROGER, librarian; b. Cherokee, Iowa, Dec. 19, 1928; s. Alva Ray and Orpha Irene (Dean) W.; B.A., Buena Vista Coll., 1951; M.A., U. Minn., 1958; m. Maxine Joyce Watson, Aug. 25, 1957; 1 dau., Sarah Elizabeth. Tchr., hospital work, 1951-55; jr. asst. circulation dept. Des Moines Pub. Library, 1956-57; teaching asst. library sch., U. Minn., 1957-58; extension librarian Mason City (Iowa) Pub. Library, 1958-59; dir. Belleville (Ill.) Pub. Library, 1959-62, LaPorte (Ind.) City and County Library, 1962-66, Mason City (Ia.) Pub. Library, 1966—. Mem. Am., Iowa library assns., Sigma Tau Delta. Episcopalian. Rotarian. Home: 922 N Madison St Mason City IA 50401 Office: 225 2d St SE Mason City IA 50401

WILCKE, HAROLD LUDWIG, food co. exec.; b. Clinton County, Ia., Aug. 5, 1906; s. Christian H. and Emily (Peterson) W.; B.S., Ia. State U., 1927, M.S., 1932, Ph.D., 1935; m. Esther Goodwin, June 10, 1930; children—Janet Louise, Carol Esther. With Meridian (Miss.) Grain & Elevator Co., 1927-29; asst. and asso. prof. Ia. State U., Ames, 1929-36, prof., 1936-46; asst. dir. research Ralston Purina, St. Louis, 1946-61, v.p., dir. research, 1961-71, cons., 1971—; pres. Agrl. Research Inst., 1966-67; mem. agr. bd. Nat. Acad. Scis.-NRC, 1966-72. Served with U.S. Army, 1943-46. Fellow AAAS, Am. Soc. Animal Sci.; mem. Am. Inst. Nutrition, Am. Chem. Soc., Am. Oil Chemists Soc., Am. Soc. Animal Sci., N.Y. Acad. Sci., Nat. Cottonseed Products Assn., Poultry Sci., World's Poultry Sci., Sigma Xi, Phi Kappa Phi, Gamma Sigma Delta, Alpha Zeta. Home: 1114 Brookhurst Dr Kirkwood MO 63122

WILCOX, ALLAN DAGGETT, pub. co. exec.; b. Elysian Minn., May 13, 1933; s. Norbert Daggett and Irene Louisa (Harriman) W.; student Mankato State Coll., 1952-53, U. Minn., 1954-55; m. Mary Ann Novotny, July 2, 1955; children—Sheri Ann, Scot Allan. Co-owner Lake Region Life, newspaper, Waterville, Minn., 1957-66, owner, 1966—; owner Morristown Press, 1968—, Elysian Enterprise, 1966-75; co-owner Barnesville Record Review, 1969—, Lakeville Times, 1967—, Hillsboro Banner, 1972—, Enderlin Independent, 1972—, Dodge Center Star Record, 1969—, Byron Review, 1969—, Life Newspapers of N.D., 1972—, Life Newspapers of Iowa, 1974—; with Lakota Am. Publs. (N.D.), 1976—, Micronics Digital Switching Devices, 1976—. Served with USNR, 1955-57. Mem. Quad County Rotary Press (sec. 1968-71), Cannon Valley Publishers (sec. 1968-71). Home: Sakatah Box 107 Waterville MN 56096 Office: 123 3d St Waterville MN 56096

WILCOX, DAVID WILLIAM, pumps and water systems mfg. co. exec.; b. Janesville, Wis., July 5, 1948; s. Ralph William and Lucille Louise (Koehl) W.; B.B.A., U. Wis. at Whitewater, 1971; m. Carol Jean Louden, Feb. 7, 1970; children—Michael James, Rebecca Cheryl. Research and devel. engr. Borg Fabric, Delavan, Wis., 1972-74; outside salesman home improvements, plumbing and heating Montgomery Ward & Co., Janesville, Wis., 1974-75; traffic clk. Sta-Rite Industries, Inc., Delavan, Wis., 1976-77, supr. sales promotion, 1977—; tchr. Gateway Tech. Inst., Kenosha, Wis. Home: 620 Ann St Delavan WI 53115 Office: 234 S 8th St Delavan WI 53115

WILCOX, FRANCES SMILEY (MRS. COURTENAY QUAYLE WILCOX), club woman; b. Athens, Ala., June 7, 1908; d. Herschel Harvey and Margaret (Anderson) Smiley; B.A., U. Neb., 1930; m. Courtenay Quayle Wilcox, Oct. 12, 1944; 1 dau., Margaret Allie Dora. Sec. swimming com. Amateur Athletic Union. Mem. D.A.R., S.D. regent 1962-64, nat. vice chmn. mag. 1965-68, v.p. gen. nat. soc. 1964-65, nat. vice chmn. Am. Indians 1968-71, nat. vice chmn. service for vet. patients, 1971-74; mem. Nat. Vice Regents Club (sec. 1960-61, pres. 1961-62), State Vice Regent's Club (life mem.), Nat. Officers Club, Vice Pres.' Gens. Club, Gen. Fedn. Women's Clubs S.D. (literature, drama chmn. dist. I, 1956-64 state lit. and drama chmn. 1964-68, state chmn. conservation 1968-70, pres. dist. I, 1969-71), Black Hills Art Assn. (pres. 1966), Am. Assn. U. Women, Chi Omega. Dist. chmn. Black Hills council Girl Scouts U.S.A., 1959-61, bd. dirs., 1961-64, mem. program com., 1964-76; sr. chmn. Am. Indians, Children of Am. Revolution, 1965-66, sr. pres. S.D., 1971-75. Chaplain, S.D. Fedn. Republican Women, 1968-72. Recipient photography awards Black Hills Art Assn., 1964-72, S.D. State Fair, 1967-72. Mem. Bromeliad Soc., Am. Shihtzu Club, Los Angeles Internat. Fern Soc. Methodist (sec. ofcl. bd. 1956-59), Rebekah. Clubs: Woman's (pres. 1964-65) (Lead); Northern Hills Duplicate Bridge (sec. 1964-70), Mile Hi Duplicate (sec.); Rapid City Kennel, Triangle Kennel. Home: 12 Parkdale St Lead SD 57754

WILCOX, HOWARD SAMUEL, pub. relations cons.; b. Indpls., Feb. 3, 1920; s. Howard Samuel and Kathryn (Dugan) W.; A.B., Ind. U., 1942; m. Joyce; children—Howard S., Donald D., David Warren, Scott Robert. With Indpls., Advt. Agy., 1946-49; exec. dir. Ind. U. Found., Bloomington, 1949-52; dir. personnel and pub. relations Indpls. Star and News, 1952-63; gen. mgr. Ariz. Republic and Phoenix Gazette, Phoenix, 1964-66; pub. relations cons., 1966—; pres. Howard S. Wilcox, Inc., Indpls., 1966—; dir. Unified Mut. Shares, Inc., Unified Funds, Inc., Wabash Life Ins. Co.; v.p. sta. WFYI; dir. Gen. Employment Enterprise, Inc. Pres. Nat. Guard Assn. Ind., 1949-51. Trustee Ind. U., 1962-65; bd. dirs. Ind. U. Found., mem. exec. com.; bd. visitors U.S. Mil. Acad.; trustee Freedoms Found. at Valley Forge, USO; bd. dirs. Indpls. Bar Found., Ind. Forum, Indpls. Boys Clubs. Served with inf. AUS, 1942-46; maj. gen. Res. Decorated Silver Star, Legion of Merit, Bronze Star with 2 oak leaf clusters, Purple Heart; Brit. Mil. Cross. Mem. Res. Officers Assn. U.S., Nat. Newspapers Promotion and Pub. Relations Assn. (pres. 1957-58), Ind. (dir.), Indpls. (dir.) chambers commerce, Sigma Delta Chi, Alpha Tau Omega. Mason (32 deg., Shriner). Clubs: United States Auto, Indianapolis Athletic (past dir.), Columbia, Indianapolis Press, Meridian Hills Country (Indpls.); Nat. Press. Home: 5335 Whisperwood Ln Indianapolis IN 46226 Office: Bd Trade Bldg Indianapolis IN 46204

WILCOX, MARK DEAN, lawyer; b. Chgo., May 25, 1952; s. Fabian Joseph and Zeryle Lucille (Tase) W.; J.D., Northwestern U., 1976; B.B.A., U. Notre Dame, 1973. Staff asst. Nat. Dist. Attys. Assn., Chgo., 1974-75; trial asst. Cook County State's Atty.'s Office, Chgo., 1975; intern U.S. Atty.'s Office, Chgo., 1975-76; law clk. Seyfarth, Shaw, Fairweather & Geraldson, Chgo., 1975-76; admitted to Ill. bar, 1976; asso. firm Lord, Bissell & Brook, Chgo., 1976—. Active campaign James Thompson for gov. Ill., 1976. Recipient Harvard Book award, 1968, West Point Leadership award, 1969. Mem. Am., Chgo., Ill. bar assns., Coll. Life Underwriters. Episcopalian. Clubs: Execs. Chgo., Nat. Monogram Notre Dame, Chgo. Lions Rugby Football. Home: 400 N Branch Rd Glenview IL 60025 Office: 115 S LaSalle St Chicago IL 60603

WILCOX, ROGER CLARK, psychologist; b. Zanesville, Ohio, Apr. 1, 1934; s. Clark Lewis and Mildred (O'Hara) W.; B.A., Ohio State U., 1959, M.A. (Nat. Inst. Mental Health fellow), 1960; Ph.D., U. Tenn., 1968; m. Joy Ann Barr, Nov. 2, 1956; children—Beth Hartigan, Wells Lewis, Judd O'Hara. Lectr. Ohio State U., Columbus, 1959-60; instr. psychology Miami U., Oxford, Ohio, 1960-62; asst. prof. Muskingum Coll., 1965-67; U.S. Office Edn. teaching fellow Wilberforce (Ohio) U., 1967-68, asso. prof. psychology, chmn. dept., 1967-69, dir. Ednl. Resources Center, 1967-69; asso. prof., chmn. dept. Calif. State U., San Luis Obispo, 1969-70; prof. psychology Ohio U., Zanesville, 1970-75; dir. adminstrn. and research Muskingum Comprehensive Mental Health Center, 1975-77; pvt. practice, Zanesville, 1977—. NSF vis. scientist Kan. Univs., 1966. Trustee, United Way Am., Goodwill Industries Am. Served with AUS, 1953-56. Mem. Am., Southeastern psychol. assns., Assn. Instl. Research, Ohio Assn. Mental Health Center Dirs. (treas.), Sigma Xi. Author: The Psychological Consequences of Being a Black American. Cons. editor: Psychological Reports, Perceptual and Motor Skills. Contbr. articles to profl. jours. Home and Office: Buckingham Manse 425 Woodlawn Ave Zanesville OH 43701

WILD, MARGARET MARY LAMBUR (MRS. W. LYDON WILD), civic worker; b. Chgo.; d. George E. and Mary (McQuaid) Lambur; grad. Chgo. Tchrs. Coll., 1932; m. W. Lydon Wild, Feb. 13, 1937; 1 dau., Margery Ann (Mrs. Homer J. Livingston, Jr.). Tchr. pub. schs., 1932-36. Past pres. Chgo. Heart Woman's Council, 1963-66; founding pres. Marilac Woman's Bd., 1955—; founder, past pres., mem. bd. De Paul U. Women's Bd.; founder, past pres. Mundelein Coll. Woman's Bd.; mem. Chgo. Bd. Edn., 1964—; past pres., mem. bd. Misericordia Home; pres. Ill. Club for Catholic Women, 1958—; chmn. Chgo. Women's Welcome Com.; adv. council St. Joseph's Hosp., 1964. Co-chmn. Ill. Citizens for Kennedy-Johnson, 1960; bd. dirs. Mercy Hosp.; pres. Chgo. Heart Assn. Woman's Bd., 1964; past chmn. woman's bd. Am. Cancer Soc., 1968—; bd. dirs. Arthritis and Rheumatism Found.; mem. women's bd. Chgo. Boys Club; chmn. adv. council educators De Paul U., 1973. Recipient Almoner award, 1960, VIP in Chgo. award, 1962, Loyola Founders Day Civic award, 1970, Am. Cancer Soc. award, 1971, Chgo. Medal of Merit for Civic Contbns., 1972, Gregorian award, 1973, Operating Engrs. award, 1973, Nat. Jewish Hosp. of Denver award, 1973, others. Roman Catholic. Address: 7006 Bennett Ave Chicago IL 60649

WILDE, ALAN HUGH, orthopaedic surgeon; b. Phila., Sept. 7, 1933; s. Norman Taylor and Elizabeth (Duthie) W.; A.B., U. Pa., 1955; M.D. Hahnemann Med. Coll., 1959; m. Marilyn Jeane Meyer, June 13, 1958; children—Alan Hugh, Douglas M., Laurie Jeanne. Intern, Martin Army Hosp., Ft. Benning, Ga., 1959-60, resident, 1960-62; resident U. Pitts., 1962-65; NIH trainee Edinburgh U., Scotland, 1965; practice medicine specializing in orthopaedic surgery, Cleve., 1966—; chmn. dept. orthopaedic surgery Cleve. Clinic Found., 1976—; orthopaedic cons. United Cerebral Palsy, Cleve., 1971-76. Bd. govs. Arthritis Found., Cleve., 1972—, Cleve. Clinic Found.; trustee Arthritis Found. Northeastern O.; trustee United Cerebral Palsy Found., Cleve., 1972—, v.p. bd. trustees, 1972. Served with M.C., AUS, 1959-62. Mem. A.C.S., Am. Acad. Orthopaedic Surgeons, Am., Ohio (pres. 1971-72) rheumatism assns., Cleve. Rheumatism Soc. (pres. 1970-71), 20th Century Orthopaedic Assn. Presbyn. (pres. bd. deacons 1972). Contbr. articles to profl. jours. Home: 2368 Roxboro Rd Cleveland Heights OH 44106 Office: 9500 Euclid Ave Cleveland OH 44106

WILDE, JOHN RAMSEY, III, textile co. exec.; b. Detroit, Oct. 22, 1940; s. John Ramsey, Jr. and Katherine Eleanor (Harrigan) W.; m. Karleen M. Marxen, June 19, 1965; children—Kathleen T., Nicole D., Rachel E.; B.S. in Engring., U. Detroit, 1963; M.B.A., Stanford U., 1967. Engr., Martin Marietta Corp., Denver, 1963-65; sr. cons. Touche Ross & Co., Milw., 1967-72; v.p., gen. mgr. Wis. div. Borg Textiles Corp. subs. Bunker Ramo Co., Jefferson, Wis., 1972—; instr. capital budgeting U. Wis. Exec. Extension. Chmn. publicity com. Mukwanago Sch. Dist. Bd. Edn., 1977—. Recipient Citizenship and Scholarship award Am. Legion, 1963; Aircraft Design award Bendix Corp., 1963. Home: W331 S5224 Hood Pkwy North Prairie WI 53153 Office: 218 Wisconsin St Jefferson WI 53549

WILDE, ROBERT EUGENE, assn. exec.; b. Ames, Iowa, Nov. 4, 1923; s. Ivan C. and Dorothy H. (Tillinghast) W.; student Iowa State Tchrs. Coll., 1942, Coll. City N.Y., 1943; B.S., Iowa State U., 1949; m. Mary Elizabeth Duff, Dec. 27, 1952; children—Catherine Alice, Patricia Ann. Draftsman Iowa Transmission Co., Waterloo, 1942; asso. editor Rock Products Mag., Chgo., 1951-52; asso. editor Am. Concrete Inst., Detroit, 1949-51, mng. editor, 1952-60, asst. sec., 1960-69, dep. exec. dir., 1969—. Mem. adv. team Nat. Concrete Tech. Curriculum Project, Office Edn., HEW, 1968-75; mem. adv. group Dept. Of Def. Project LEX, Dept. Def. thesaurus, 1966-67. Served with AUS, 1943-46. Recipient Award for Outstanding Achievement, Concrete Improvement Bd. Detroit, 1967. Fellow Am. Concrete Inst.; mem. ASCE, Am. Soc. Assn. Execs., Am. Soc. for Info. Sci., Council of Engring. and Scientific Soc. Execs., Mich. Mineralogical Soc., Concrete Improvement Bd. Detroit (chmn. 1969, bd. dirs. 1959-60, 61-70), Sigma Delta Chi, Delta Upsilon. Episcopalian. Club: Masons. Author: Practical and Decorative Concrete, 1977. Home: 19242 Warwick St Birmingham MI 48009 Office: 22400 W 7 Mile Rd Detroit MI 48219

WILDENRADT, ROBERT LEWIS, realtor; b. DeKalb, Ill., June 6, 1930; s. Carl E. and Edna J. (Crockett) W.; B.S., U. Ill., 1956; m. Norma C. Sanderson, Sept. 7, 1952; children—Sandra (Mrs. Viking Engh III), Sharon (Mrs. Carl Henke), Roger. Mgr. quality control, Gen. Elec. & Appliance Motors, DeKalb, Ill., 1956-62, mgr. shop operations, 1963-64; v.p., gen. mgr. Micro Controls, St. Louis, 1964-66; realtor, Crum-Halsted & McCabe Realtors, DeKalb, Ill., 1966—. Dir. DeKalb County Devel. Assn., 1974-75. Trustee Sycamore (Ill.) Municipal Hosp.; bd. dirs. Kishwaukee Health Services Center; bd. dirs. Sycamore United Appeal. Served with USAF, 1948-52. Mem. DeKalb County Bd. Realtors (pres. 1972), Ill. Assn. Realtors (v.p. 1975). Luth. (deacon 1968-72, chmn. bldg. com. 1969-70). Rotarian. Home: 408 Somonauk St Sycamore IL 60178 Office: 120 W Hillcrest St DeKalb IL 60115

WILDER, CARL RUDOLPH, engr.; b. Cape Girardeau, Mo., Sept. 6, 1913; s. August and Martha (Kleppisch) W.; B.S.C.E., U. Mo., 1936; postgrad. in Structural Engring., U. So. Calif., Los Angeles, 1939-41; m. Marie Reuter, May 24, 1936; 1 dau., Martha Anne. Surveyman Phillips Petroleum Co., Marshall, Tex., 1936; civil engr. U.S. Corps Engrs., Mineral Wells, Tex., also Los Angeles, 1936-47; conservation engr., mgr. pub. works and transp., dir. energy and water resources, Portland Cement Assn., Chg., 1947-48, Denver, 1948-60, Los Angeles, 1960-65, Skokie, Ill., 1965—. Mem. exec. com. U.S. commn. Irrigation, Drainage and Flood Control, 1970-75. Mem. Am. Concrete Inst., ASCE, ASTM, Am. Water Works Assn., Am. Pub. Works Assn., Tau Beta Pi, Pi Mu Epsilon, Chi Epsilon. Lutheran (chmn., finance sec.). Home: 1027 White Mountain Dr Northbrook IL 60062 Office: Portland Cement Assn 5420 Old Orchard Rd Skokie IL 60076

WILDER, JOHN TIMOTHY, marketing exec.; b. Cin., Apr. 23, 1937; s. Henry C. and Dorothy I. (Carter) W.; B.S., Xavier U., 1959, M.B.A., 1965; m. Myrna C. Lower, May 31, 1958; children—Mary Beth, Scott Anthony, John Timothy. With H.C. Wilder & Assos., Inc., Cin., 1958-65, v.p., 1961-65; advt. mgr. Clopay Corp., Cin., 1965-69, dir. marketing services, 1969—. Mem. Cin. Bd. Edn. Vocational Adv. Com. Served with USCGR, 1955-63. Mem. Cin. Advertisers Club (dir.), Am. Fedn. Advertisers, Am. Marketing Assn. Home: 2830

Urwiler St Cincinnati OH 45211 Office: Clopay Sq Cincinnati OH 45214

WILDER, ULAH, librarian; b. Winslow, Ind., Feb. 18, 1916; B.A., Oakland City Coll., 1956; M.A., Ind. State U., 1959. Dormitory housemother Oakland City (Ind.) Coll., 1953-61, asst. librarian, 1956-61, head librarian, 1961—. Bd. dirs. Ind. Library Service Authority, 1976-78, Area Library Service Authority, 1976-78; sponsor Sigma Kappa Sigma, Oakland City Coll., 1976-77. Mem. Am., Ind. (vice chmn. dist. V 1967-68, chmn. dist. VII 1974-75) library assns., Gen. Bapt. Hist. Soc., Oakland City Coll., Ind. State U. alumni assns., Ohio-Wabash Valley Hist. Soc. (charter). Alpha Beta Alpha. Baptist. Club: College Women's (sec.-treas. 1957-60). Home: 218 N Clay Oakland City IN 47660

WILDS, JOHN LAWRENCE, lawyer, judge; b. Mitchell, S.D., Sept. 1, 1928; s. George Charles and Marcella (Muggli) W.; B.A., U. S.D., 1952, J.D., 1955; m. Jeanne Marie Krueger, Aug. 18, 1951; children—Jill Marie, Jaime Ann, Joan Louisa, Judith Lynn. Admitted to S.D. bar, 1955; with law dept. C. & E.I. R.R., 1955-57; mem. firm Vail & Wilds, Sioux Falls, 1958; asst. atty. gen. S.D., 1959; gen. counsel Brezina Constrn. Co., Inc., Rapid City, 1959-62; asst. U.S. dist. atty. S.D., 1962-65; partner Christopherson, Bailin, Wilds & Bailey, Sioux Falls, 1965-69; pvt. practice, Sioux Falls, 1969-73; circuit judge, 1973—, chief circuit judge, 1977—; town atty., Tea, S.D., 1966-73; mem. State Jud. Council, 1975—; del. Nat. Conf. State Trial Judges, 1976—. Pres. Democratic Forum, Sioux Falls, 1966. Served with USNR, 1946-48, to lt. AUS, 1952-53. Mem. State Bar S.D., Am., S.D. trial lawyers assns., Minnehaha County Bar Assn., S.D. Judges Assn. (pres. elect 1977), Phi Delta Phi, Delta Tau Delta. Roman Catholic. K.C. (4 deg.). Clubs: Westward Ho Country Cosmopolitan (membership chmn. 1967). Home: 101 E 35th St Sioux Falls SD 57105 Office: Circuit Court Chambers Minnehaha County Ct House Sioux Falls SD 57102

WILDSCHUT, HENRY BALDWIN, county ofcl.; b. Groningen, Holland, Aug. 1, 1909; s. Klaas and Willemtje (Feringa) W.; came to U.S., 1913, naturalized, 1922; B.S. in Civil Engring., Mich. State U., 1933; m. Anne Mileski, May 30, 1936; 1 dau., Carol. Resident engr. Greeley & Hansen, cons. engrs., 1936-46; city engr. City of Wauwatosa (Wis.), 1946-54; expressway engr. Milwaukee County, Milw., 1954-60, county hwy. commr., dir. pub. works, 1960—. Dir. Milw. Fed. Savs. & Loan Assn. Mem. Wauwatosa Planning Commn., 1960-66. Named One of Top Ten Pub. Works Men of Year, 1965. Mem. Am. Rd. Builders Assn. (dir.). Rotarian, K.C. Club: Mich. State University Alumni (Milw.). Home: 2433 N 117th St Wauwatosa WI 53226 Office: Courthouse Milwaukee WI 53233

WILES, ALBERT DONALD, II, lawyer; b. Indpls., Dec. 8, 1938; s. A. Donald and Emma Dean (Miller) W.; A.B., Princeton, 1961; LL.B. cum laude, Columbia, 1966; m. Jeannette Marie Broyhill, Aug. 27, 1965; children—Gregory Broyhill, Bradford Broyhill, Kenton Broyhill. Admitted to Ind. bar, 1966, since practiced in Indpls.; partner firm Lowe, Linder, Gray, Steele & Wiles, 1971—; pres., dir. Washington Restaurants, Inc., Indpls., 1973—, Am. Eggs, Inc., Bargersville, Ind., 1975—; dep. corp. counsel City of Indpls., 1973-76. Mem. lawyers com. Marion County Republican Central Com., 1967—. Mem. Am. Ind., Indpls. (chmn. disciplinary com. 1970-71) bar assns., Princeton Alumni Assn. Ind. (pres. 1968-71). Club: University (Indpls.). Presbyn. (elder). Mason. Home: Rural Route 4 Box 31-A Noblesville IN 46060 Office: 1 Indiana Sq Indianapolis IN 46204

WILES, DAVID KIMBALL, ednl. adminstr.; b. Tuscaloosa, Ala., Feb. 23, 1942; s. Kimball and Hilda (Long) W.; B.S., Fla. State U., 1964; M.Ed., U. Fla., Ed.D.; m. Marilyn McCall, Dec. 31, 1964; children—Corey Kimball, Matthew Alexander. Asst. prof. edn. U. Toronto (Ont., Can.), 1969-72; asso. prof. Va. Poly. Inst. and State U., Blacksburg, 1972-74; prof. ednl. adminstrn. Miami U., Oxford, Ohio, 1974—; cons. Nat. Inst. Edn., Ohio, Va., Ind., W.Va., N.Y. depts. edn., U. Mich., U. West Fla., Syracuse U., Toronto, Nashville, Cin. sch. dists. Author: Political Interpretations of Administration, 1977; Changing Perspectives of Research, 1972; editorial bd. Ednl. Forum, 1976-78; contbr. articles to profl. jours. Home: 1337 Dana Dr Oxford OH 45056 Office: Miami U 305-F McGuffey Hall Oxford OH

WILES, RICHARD CARL, communications co. exec.; b. Maryville, Mo., Aug. 4, 1949; s. Richard Walter and Marcella (Tobin) W.; ed. in mktg. Northwest Mo. State U., 1971; m. Lynette Merrill, Oct. 25, 1975. Mgmt. trainee, United Telephone Co., Jefferson City, Mo., 1971-72, adminstrv. asst., 1972-73, comml. supr., Lexington, Mo. office, 1973-75, comml. supr., Jefferson City, Mo., 1975—. Active fund raiser for United Way, Jefferson City, 1973-77; chmn. Jefferson City area Explorer Scouts Program, 1976—; campaign coordinator for re-election of senator Ike Skelton, 1974. Mem. Downtown Assn. of Jefferson City, Jefferson City C. of C., Am. Cancer Soc., Northwest Mo. State Alumni Assn., Phi Sigma Epsilon. Republican. Roman Catholic. Club: Lions (dir. 1974-75). Home: Route 7 Shepherd Hills Manor 118 Jefferson City MO 65101 Office: 319 Madison St Jefferson City MO 65101

WILES, RICHARD SAMUEL, judge; b. Omaha, Apr. 2, 1909; s. Thomas F. and Gertrude (Fletcher) W.; LL.B., Omaha Law Sch., 1935; m. Alice E. Thorin, July 16, 1932; 1 son, Richard T. Admitted to Nebr. bar, 1934; practiced in Omaha, 1935-42, Scottsbluff, Nebr., 1942-61; U.S. commr., 1952—; county judge Scottsbluff County, 1961-69; judge Workmen's Compensation Ct., 1969—. Justice of peace, Scottsbluff, 1951-52; police judge, 1952-54; city prosecutor, 1956-58. Pres. adv. com. Scotts Bluff County Assn. Mentally Retarded, 1968—; founder, organizer Scottsbluff County Juvenile Ct. Adv. Com., 1965. Trustee Nebr. Boys Ranch, Alliance, St. Christopher Child Care Center, Scottsbluff. Named Adm. Nebr. Navy. Mem. County Judge's Assn. (pres. 1967-68). Nebr. Juvenile Judge's Assn. (pres. 1968-69). Conglist. Mason (Shriner), Elk. Home: 7300 South St 6 Lincoln NE 68520 Office: State Capitol Bldg Lincoln NE 68509

WILES, THOMAS, librarian; b. Fort Myers, Fla., July 21, 1929; s. Thomas Mahlon and Ruth Muriel (Carter) W.; B.A., Doane Coll., 1951; postgrad. Ind. U., 1954-56, U. Chgo., 1956-60; M.A. in L.S., Rosary Coll., 1975. Tchr. Gary (Ind.) Pub. Schs., 1951-52, 54-56; bookmobile and br. librarian Gary (Ind.) Pub. Library, 1956-60; reference coordinator, children's coordinator Lake County (Ind.) Pub. Library, 1960-66; librarian Central YMCA High Sch., Chgo., 1966—. Served with AUS, 1952-54. Mem. ALA. Club: Chicago Library (treas. 1967-68). Home: 4980 Marine Dr Chicago IL 60640

WILEY, DOUGLAS ALAN, constrn. co. exec.; b. Cedar Rapids, Iowa, Dec. 11, 1944; s. Weldon and Lois Arlene (Patten) W.; student Iowa Wesleyan Coll., 1962-63, Coe Coll., 1966-70; m. Mary Lou Kelley, Dec. 26, 1964; children—Kelley Ann, Scott Alan. Accountant, Vivian Equipment Co., Ames, Iowa, 1964-66, Harnishfeger Corp., Cedar Rapids, 1968-70; salesman Kelleys Inc., Cedar Rapids, 1966-68; treas. Larsen Olson Co. Iowa, Cedar Rapids, 1970-73; v.p. Hiawatha Garden Center, Inc. (Iowa), 1973-74; controller Nelson Mfg. Co., Cedar Rapids, 1974-75; pres. Wiley Constrn. Inc., Cedar Rapids, 1975—. Mem. Office Edn. Adv. Bd. Kirkwood Community Coll., 1971-74; trustee Kenwood Park Presbyterian Ch., 1977—; mem. wills emphasis team Eastern Iowa Presbytery. Mem. Cedar Rapids Area Theater Organ Soc. (dir.-at-large 1977—, sec. 1978—), Hiawatha Jr. C. of C. Presbyterian. (deacon 1967—, elder 1972—, chmn. NE Iowa Presbytery family fin. and money mgmt. team 1975—). Home: Route 1 Marion IA 52302

WILEY, GEORGE LOUIS, architect; b. Kokomo, Ind., Aug. 17, 1928; s. Chester Lloyd and Priscilla Maria (King) W.; student Purdue, Indpls. campus, 1952-53; archtl. registration Ind., 1967; m. Jean Leslie, Sept. 13, 1949; children—Jon Mark, Michael Leslie, Timothy Louis. Plant engring. Bryant Heater Corp., Indpls., 1950-51, Stewart-Warner, 1951-53; with Dorste & Pantazi, architects, 1954-56; Lennox, Matthews, Simmons & Ford, architects and engrs., 1956-57; designer Garns & Moore, architects and engrs., 1957-66; project architect Geupel Architects & Engineers, Indpls., 1966-71; architect Wolner Assos., Indpls., 1971—; exec. v.p. Wolner Corp.; v.p. Oxford Devel. Corp. Chmn. Com. for Environmental Pollution Control, Indpls., 1969-71. Served with USAF, 1947-50. Registered architect, Mich., Ohio, Ky., Ga., Ala., Ill. Mem. A.I.A., Ind. Soc. Architects (chpt. sec. 1971—, state sec. 1972), Am. Assn. for Contamination Control. Mason, Lion. Home: 4134 W 79th St Indianapolis IN 46268 Office: Wolner Assos 3935 Meadows Dr Indianapolis IN 46205

WILEY, GUILFORD MITCHELL, JR., investment banker; b. LaCrosse, Wis., Apr. 8, 1924; s. Guilford M. and Beulah (Arnold) W.; B.B.A., U. Wis., 1955; m. Helen Lois Nash, Sept. 5, 1946; children—Douglas, Michael. With Robert W. Baird & Co., Inc., mem. N.Y. Stock Exchange, Milw., 1955—, v.p., dir. Oshkosh (Wis.) office, 1962—. Chmn. Winnebago County Republican Party, 1963. Bd. dirs. Oshkosh Community YMCA, Mercy Med. Center, Oshkosh. Served with AUS, 1943-45. Decorated Purple Heart with oak leaf cluster, Bronze Star medal with oak leaf cluster. Mem. Phi Beta Kappa, Phi Kappa Phi, Beta Gamma Sigma. Home: 1608 Menominee Dr Oshkosh WI 54901 Office: 1st Wis Nat Bank Bldg Oshkosh WI 54901

WILEY, JAY WILSON, economist, educator; b. St. Paul, Aug. 24, 1913; s. Guy Edson and Grace Estelle (Wilson) W.; A.B., Lawrence Coll., 1935, A.M., 1936; Ph.D., U. Ill., 1948; m. Eleanor Breemes, June 7, 1941; 1 son, Jay Wilson. Instr. Purdue U., West Lafayette, Ind., 1938-47, asst. prof., 1947-52, asso. prof., 1952-57, prof. economics, 1957—, dir. research and grad. adminstrn. Krannert Grad. Sch. Mgmt., 1964—, acting asso. dean, 1972-73. Vis. prof. Escola de Sociologia y Politica de Sao Paulo (Brazil), 1956, U. Colo., Boulder, 1967; vis. asso. London (Eng.) Sch. Econs. and Polit. Sci., 1971, 72; cons. Ga. Inst. Tech., 1968, Miami U., 1968-69, various bus. firms, Dept. State, 1961-62. Served to lt. comdr. USNR, 1943-46. Mem. Am., Midwest (pres. 1966) econ. assns., AAUP, Ind. Acad. Social Scis. (dir. 1958-65). Rotarian. Author: (with M.B. Ogle and L. Schneider) Power, Order and the Economy, 1954; (with R.K. Davidson and V.L. Smith) Economics: An Analytical Approach, 1958, 2nd. edit. 1962. Home: 908 N Grant St West Lafayette IN 47906

WILGARDE, RALPH L., hosp. adminstr.; b. Phila., Jan. 8, 1928; B.A., U. Pa., 1949, M.B.A., 1954; M.Pub. Adminstrn., Cornell U., 1960. Adminstrv. asst. Jefferson Hosp., Phila., 1956-58; asst. adminstr. Frankford Hosp., 1960-64; adminstr. Irvington (N.J.) Gen. Hosp., 1964-66, Cottage Hosp., Grosse Pointe, Mich., 1966—. Served with AUS, 1950-52. Mem. Am. Hosp. Assn., Am. Coll. Hosp. Adminstrn. Home: 1217 Bishop Rd Grosse Pointe MI 48230 Office: 159 Kercheval St Grosse Pointe MI 48236

WILHARM, WILLIAM WAYNE, assn. exec.; b. Waterloo, Iowa, Feb. 5, 1922; s. Richard Edward and Emily Victoria (Aitken) W.; grad. high sch.; children by previous marriage—William Wayne, Bruce Edward, Beverly Jean, Brian Lee; m. Betty Marie Prahm, Feb. 25, 1969. Fireman, Waterloo, 1951-65; mem. labor staff United Way of Black Hawk County, Waterloo, 1965-69; exec. dir. ARC, Mason City, Iowa, 1969-71; exec. dir. United Way of Mason City, 1971—. Cons. on disaster Midwest ARC, 1960-64; sec. Fire Fighters Local #66, Waterloo, 1952-65; mem. exec. bd. Black Hawk County Union Council, 1954-65. Mem. exec. bd. N.E. Iowa Muscular Dystrophy, 1951-64. Bd. dirs. Black Hawk Community Services Com., 1958-64. Served with USNR, 1942-45. Mem. Ia. Assn. Profl. Fire Fighters (v.p. 1963-65), Internat. Assn. Fire Fighters Local #66 (life), Mason City Sertoma Club (Sertoman of Year 1972). Implemented priorities of services for allocation of United Way Contbns. Home: 510 11th St NE Mason City IA 50401 Office: PO Box 1465 Mason City IA 50401

WILHELM, JOSEPH EDWARD, engring. co. exec.; b. Cleve., Jan. 31, 1913; s. Jesse Everett and Ellen (Morris) W.; B.M.E., Case Inst. Tech., 1935; m. Rita Marie Jusko, Feb. 2, 1937; children—Jerome E., Donette A., Lynette A. Estimator, Mpls.-Honeywell Co., Cleve., 1935-36; with Avery Engring. Co., Cleve., 1936—, pres., 1957—, treas., chief exec. officer, 1969—. Trustee, mem. exec. com. Goodwill Industries of Cleve. Mem. Elec. League Cleve. (pres. 1977-78), Cleve. Engring. Soc., Am. Soc. Heating, Refrigerating and Air Conditioning Engrs. Republican. Roman Catholic. Clubs: Cleveland Athletic, Acacia Country, Midday. Home: 25 Fircrest Ln Chagrin Falls OH 44022 Office: 1455 E Schaaf Rd Cleveland OH 44131

WILHELMY, BETTY ROLLINS, univ. adminstr.; b. Cin., Dec. 15, 1920; d. Otmer William and Anne Laura (Lawrence) Rollins; B.A., U. Cin., 1942; M.A., Tchrs. Coll., Columbia U., 1943; postgrad. Ohio State U., 1969-70: m. Odin Wilhelmy, Jr., Nov. 23, 1945; children—Ann Leslie, Margaret Linn, Janet Lee. Asst. to head of residence Finch Jr. Coll., N.Y.C., 1942-43; asst. to counselor women Cornell U., Ithaca, N.Y., 1943-45, asst. to dean of students, 1945-47; mem. staff personnel dept. Ohio State U. Hosp., Columbus, 1970-72; acad. counselor to graduating srs., pre-theology students Coll. Arts Scis. Ohio State U., Columbus, 1972—. Volunteer worker Columbus State Mental Hosp., 1960-70. Vice pres. Ch. Women United, Columbus and Franklin County, 1968-70; mem. Women's Assn. Columbus Symphony Orch., 1960-70; ruling elder Presbyterian Ch. Recipient certificate in adult edn. Ohio Council of Chs. Mem. Am. Personnel and Guidance Assn., Am. Coll. Personnel Assn., Smithsonian Assn., Ohio Geneal. Soc., Zeta Tau Alpha, Phi Beta Kappa, Alpha Kappa Delta, Kappa Delta Pi. Clubs: Faculty Women's, Ohio State U. Faculty. Home: 2942 N Star Rd Columbus OH 43221 Office: Rm 128 Denney Hall 164 W 17th Ave Columbus OH 43210

WILHITE, DAVID EARL, lawyer; b. Springfield, Mo., Jan. 22, 1937; s. Ernest Wayne and Harriet Josephine (Hale) W.; B.A., S.W. Mo. State U., 1964; J.D., Mo. U., 1966; m. Mary Lou Ezard, May 17, 1963; 1 dau., Terri Michelle. Admitted to Mo. bar, 1966; asso. Donnelly & Donnelly, 1966-67; partner Donnelly Baldwin & Wilhite, Lebanon, Mo., 1967—; city atty. City of Lebanon, 1970-72; mayor Corkery (Mo.), 1976—. Mem. bar com. 126th Jud. Circuit Mo., 1975—, chmn., 1976—. Publicity chmn. Laclede County Cancer Crusade, 1967; v.p. Lebanon Jr. C. of C., 1968-71. Mem. Am., S. Central Mo., Laclede County (pres.) bar assns., Lebanon C. of C. (dir.), Kappa Alpha. Republican. Mem. Christian Ch. (deacon). Kiwanian. Home: 449 Sunset Dr Lebanon MO 65536 Office: 112 N Madison St Lebanon MO 65536

WILHITE, JEFFREY ALLEN, psychotherapist; b. Seattle, Jan. 5, 1951; s. Charles Joseph and Frances Ruth (Boyer) W.; B.A., Ind. U., 1973; M.A., Goddard Coll., 1976. Psychotherapist, videotherapist Quinco Cons. Center, Columbus, Ind., 1973—. Bd. dirs. Regional Arts Council, Columbus, Ind., 1972-74. Home: Rural Route 9 Columbus IN 47201 Office: 2075 Lincoln Park Dr Columbus IN 47201

WILHOIT, G(ROVER) CLEVELAND, JR., educator; b. Albemarle, N.C., Aug. 4, 1939; s. Grover Cleveland and Ruth Alberta (Hopkins) W.; A.B., U. N.C., 1961, M.A., 1963, Ph.D., 1967; m. Frances Goins, Aug. 31, 1963; children—Hannah Ruth, Peter Francis. News reporter, announcer, copywriter radio sta. WABZ, Albemarle, N.C., (part time, full time in summers) 1955-61; field researcher U. N.C. Inst. for Research in Social Scis., Chapel Hill, summer 1964; asso. prof. journalism Ind. U., Bloomington, 1967—, also asso. dir. Bur. Media Research. NSF Found. fellow NSF Mass Polit. Communication Research Inst., Ohio U., summer 1971; vis. research fellow Dutch Broadcasting Found., Hilversum, Netherlands, 1975; mem. nat. steering com. Am. Newspaper Pubs. Assn. News Research Center, 1976—. Served with USAF, 1962. Mem. Assn. for Edn. in Journalism, AAUP, Kappa Tau Alpha. Unitarian-Universalist. Office: Sch Journalism Pyle Hall Ind U Bloomington IN 47401

WILINKIN, EDWARD MAURICE, optometrist; b. Chgo., Mar. 26, 1923; s. Lee William and Mollie (Pearlman) W.; student Rose Poly. Inst., 1943-44; D.Optometry, No. Ill. Coll. Optometry, 1949; m. Wanda Lee Hall, July 22, 1950. Practice optometry, Chgo., 1950-58, House Contacts, Inc., Oak Park, Ill., 1958-72; pvt. practice, Chgo., 1972—. Served with AUS, 1943-46. Fellow Internat. Soc. Orthokeratology; mem. Better Vision Inst., Nat. Eye Research Found. Clubs: Masons, Moose. Address: 3024 S Pulaski Rd Chicago IL 60623

WILK, CLIFFORD MERRILL, dentist; b. Chgo., Oct. 12, 1926; D.D.S., Loyola U., 1949; div.; children—James, David, Merrill Beth. Pvt. practice dentistry, Chgo., 1949—; cons. in field. Mem. health planning com. Welfare Council Met. Chgo., 1962-68, chmn. com. on community dental programs, 1964-70; mem. dental adv. com. Chgo. Bd. Health, 1964-67, rev. com., 1965-67; vice chmn. Adv. Bd. for Early Detection of Oral Cancer for Met. Chgo., 1962-68; mem. med. com. operation Headstart, 1965-67. Vice chmn. Loyola U. Dental Sch. Bldg. Fund, 1964-66. Served with Dental Corps, AUS, 1952-54. Recipient citations and awards Am. Dental Assn. and Chgo. Dental Soc., 1960-70; Milestone award Loyola U., 1968. Fellow Royal Soc. Health, Inst. Medicine Chgo. (chmn. com. on liaison with med. and dental profl. socs. 1965-68, mem. membership com. 1972—), Ill. Dental Soc.; mem. Am. Dental Assn., Chgo. Dental Soc., Federation Dentaire Internationale, Am. Soc. Preventive Dentistry, Art Inst. Chgo. (life). Presbyn. (elder). Club: Internat. Sporting Club (U.K.). Home: 900 Lake Shore Dr Chicago IL 60611 Office: 30 N Michigan Ave Chicago IL 60602

WILK, THEODORE BROOKS, indsl. furnace mfg. co. exec.; b. Cleve., Sept. 11, 1930; s. Harry and Celia (Brooks) W.; B.S., Purdue U., 1952; postgrad. Case Inst. Tech., 1953; m. Marjorie Ann Kalnitz, June 15, 1952; children—Jonathan B., Robin F., Scott D. Metall. engr. Cleve. Pneumatic Tool Co., 1952-53; metall. engr., cons. Superior Foundry Co., Cleve., 1953-54; self-employed as mfrs. rep. and sales engr., Cleve., 1954-57; sales engr. A.F. Holden Co., Milford, Mich., 1957-63, sales mgr., 1963-67, v.p., 1967—, also dir. Cons. indsl. furnaces, heat treating, energy conservation, occupational health and safety. Bd. dirs. Alberta Park Homeowners Assn., 1958-63. Mem. Am. Soc. Metals (speakers bur.), Am. Inst. Mining, Metall. and Petroleum Engrs., Assn. Iron and Steel Engrs. Jewish (dir. brotherhood 1970-73). Home: 5755 Alberta Dr Lyndhurst OH 44124 Office: 2195 S Milford Rd Milford MI 48042

WILKERSON, CARNIE CLYDE, mfg. co. exec.; b. Wetumka, Okla., Oct. 12, 1935; s. Roy Clyde and Daisy Pearl (Wesson) W.; B.S., Okla. State U., 1958; m. Velma Jane Moose, May 25, 1963; children—Ronald Barry, Tammie Denise. Engr., John Deere Harvester Works, East Moline, Ill., 1958-63; engr. John Deere Zweibrucken Works (Germany), 1963-64, chief engr., 1964-68; sr. div. engr. John Deere East Moline Works, 1968-69; dir. service Deere & Co., Moline, 1969-71; mgr. product engring. dept. John Deere Plow & Planter Works, Moline, 1971—. Mem. Am. Soc. Agrl. Engrs., Soc. Automotive Engrs. Methodist (trustee 1972-76, chmn. stewardship commn. 1971). Club: New Windsor (Ill.) Sportsmen's. Home: 163 Oakwood Pl Geneseo IL 61254 Office: 501 3d Ave Moline IL 61265

WILKERSON, JEROME FRANCES, priest: b. St. Louis, June 8, 1924; s. Jerome A. and Mary Grace (Mead) W.; B.A., Cath. U. Am., 1945, M.A., 1946, Ph.D., 1963. Ordained priest Roman Catholic Ch., 1950; asso. pastor Visitation and Our Lady of Lourdes parishes, St. Louis, 1950-57; dir. Cath. Info. and Counseling Center, St. Louis, 1957-61; dir. Newman Center, Med. Campus Washington U., St. Louis, 1963—; dir. campus ministry St. Louis Diocese, 1976—; ethics cons. VA Hosp. St. Louis, Reproductive Biology Research Found. Mem. citizens adv. com. Washington U. Med. Center Redevel. Corp., 1975. Mem. Archdiocese of St. Louis Commn. on Religious Edn., 1969-73, Clergy Conf. Commn. on Continuing Edn., 1972-75, Commn. on Ecumenism, 1969-70; cons. Midwest regional meeting Cath. Commn. on Ch. in the Am. Univ., 1966. Bd. dirs. The Center, Christian Art and Book Assn., St. Louis, 1949-63, Pastoral Counseling Inst., St. Louis, 1974—, nat. campus ministry advisory bd. U.S. Cath. Conf., 1977—; 1949-63; mem. central com. Park Forest Spring Jubilee, 1972-73. Mem. Mo. Assn. Social Welfare (dir. 1972-75), Cath. Campus Ministry Assn., Nat. Inst. Cath. Ministries, Coll. Theology Soc., Nat. Assn. Cath. Chaplains, Archdiocesan Chaplains Council (pres. 1978), Soc. Health and Human Values, Inst. Soc., Ethics and the Life Scis. (asso.), Nat. Assn. Coll. and Univ. Chaplains and Dirs. Religious Life, Inst. Theol. Encounter with Sci. and Tech. Contbr. articles to religious and hosp. jours.; contbg. author: Ethical Isues in Sex Therapy and Research (Masters and Johnson), 1977. Home and Office: 225 S Euclid Ave Saint Louis MO 63110

WILKERSON, STIEFEL JUNIOR, city ofcl.; b. Novelty, Mo., Dec. 18, 1925; s. Josiah Stiefel and Flossie Maurita (Murray) W.; grad. high sch.; m. Mary Kathryn Carney, May 29, 1949; children—Terri Rena, Carroll Wayne. With Knox County (Mo.) Rd. Dept., 1947; with constrn. co., Novelty, 1948-49; postmaster U.S. Postal Service, Novelty, 1950—. Treas. Novelty Community Club, 1975—. Served with USAAF, 1945-46. League Postmasters, 1973. Mem. Am. Legion, Knox County Hist. Soc. (pres. 1974-75), Nat. League Postmasters (v.p. 1973-75, Postmaster Pub. Service Commendation award 1973), PTA. Mem. Christian Ch. (deacon 1965-75, treas. 1965-75). Home: Novelty MO 63460

WILKES, DELANO ANGUS, architect; b. Panama City, Fla., Jan. 25, 1935; s. Burnice Angus and Flora Mae (Scott) W.; B.Arch., U. Fla., 1958; m. Dona Jean Murren, June 25, 1960. Designer, Perkins & Will Partnership, Chgo., 1960-63; designer, job capt. Harry Weese, Ltd., Chgo., 1963-66; project architect Fitch Larocca Carrington, Chgo., 1967-69; architect Mittelbusher & Tourtelot, Chgo., 1970-71; asso. Bank Bldg. Corp., Chgo., 1972-75; sr. asso. Charles Edward Stade & Assos., Park Ridge, Ill., 1975-77; sr. architect Consoer Morgan, Architect, Chgo., 1977—. Design cons. Chamlin & Assos., Peru, Ill., 1969—; guest lectr., field trip guide Coll. DuPage, Glen Ellyn, Ill.,

1970—; guest architect med. adv. com. to Pres.'s Com. for Handicapped, 1977. Mem. Businessmen for Pub. Interest, Folsom Family Assn. Am. (v.p.), SAR, AIA, Soc. Colonial Wars, Gargoyle. Editor Folsom Bull. Home: 4040 Harvey Ave Western Springs IL 60558 Office: 819 Busse Hwy Park Ridge IL 60068

WILKES, HAROLD LLOYD, clergyman, tool products co. exec.; b. Haskell, Okla., July 9, 1934; s. J.J. and Daisy L. (Williams) W.; student Langston U., 1951-53; M.B.A., U. Mo., 1976; certificate U. Colo., 1970; B.S. in Theology, Midwest Sem., 1969; D.D., Am. Christian Coll., 1969; m. Mary Helen Handy, Oct. 22, 1956; children—Patrician L., Cyndy Marie, Jeffrey V. Salesman, Wilkes Music Center, Kansas City, Mo., 1963-65; exec. dir., founder Wilkes & Assos., Inc., Kansas City, Mo., 1969-77; propr., mgr. Midwest K.C. Fastner Co., Kansas City, Mo., 1973—; ordained to ministry Ch. of God, 1965; pastor, Kansas City, 1965-74, 74—; pres. Midwestern Dist. Bishop's and Ministers' Council, Ch. of the Living God, Ky., Ind., Ill., Mo., Kans., 1973-76; dir. Ill. Econ. Opportunity Corp., 1977—. Served with U.S. Army, 1957-59. Mem. Nat. Small Bus. Assn., Am. Mgmt. Assn., Nat. Urban League, World Council Chs., Nat. Assn. Community Devel., NAACP, Concerned Citizens Assn. (pres. 1977), Columbia Alumni Assn. Democrat. Home: 2820 W 90th St Leawood KS 66209 Office: 8120 Holmes Rd Kansas City MO 64131

WILKINS, ESTELLA HARMEL, lawyer; b. Christian County Mo., Sept. 12, 1891; d. Paul Louis and Julia (Marten) Harmel; LL.B., Ill. Wesleyan U., 1921. Admitted to Ill. bar, 1921, since practiced in Peoria; sr. mem. firm Wilkins & Hosafros, Peoria, Ill. Pres., dir. Tazewell County Title & Abstract Co. Mem. Ill. Wesleyan U. Counselors; bd. dirs. Vis. Nurses Assn., Peoria: v.p. bd. dirs. South Side Mission, Peoria. Mem. Am., Ill. (counsellor), Peoria bar assns., Peoria Assn. of Commerce Nat. Grange. League Women Voters, Nat., Ill. fedns. bus. and profl. women's clubs, Peoria County Bus. and Profl. Women's Club, Nat. Assn. Accountants, Peoria Bd. Realtors, Legal Secs. Assn. (hon. mem. Peoria chpt.). Republican. Methodist. Clubs: Pilot, Women's (Peoria). Home: Peoria Hilton Hotel 501 Main St Peoria IL 61602 Office: First Nat Bank Bldg Peoria IL 61602

WILKINS, FRANK EDWARD, banker; b. Mpls., July 5, 1924; s. Floyd Emmet and Gertrude Amanda (Rex) W.; B.S., Mankato State Coll., 1950; grad. Nat. Comml. Lending Sch., U. Okla., 1976; m. Phyllis Ruth Moeller, June 17, 1950; children—Steven, Suzanne, Rebecca, Jennifer. With Comml. Credit Corp., 1950-53, First Nat. Bank, Mankato, Minn., 1954; with First Nat. Bank of Willmar (Minn.), 1955—, v.p., 1963—. Served with AUS, 1943-45. Decorated Bronze Star medal, Purple Heart. Recipient award Am. Inst. Banking, 1962. Mem. Willmar C. of C. (pres. 1972), Am. Legion (post comdr. 1967), V.F.W. Mason, Elk (exalted ruler 1965). Home: 1221 Westwood Ct Willmar MN 56201 Office: Box 898 Willmar MN 56201

WILKINS, GEORGE THOMAS, educator; b. Anna, Ill., Jan. 16, 1905; s. B. Frank and Nellie Mae (Hileman) W.; B.Ed., Southern Ill. Normal U., 1937; A.M., U. of Ill., 1940; LL.D., McKendree College, 1959; m. Mary Alice Treece, July 4, 1926; 1 son, George T. Teacher pub. sch., Barringer, Ill., 1923-24; teacher and coach pub. sch., Lence, Ill., 1924-29; prin. and coach high sch., Wolf Lake, Ill., 1929-37; supt. pub. schs., Wolf Lake, Ill., 1937-39, Thebes, Ill., 1939-43; superintendent schools, Madison, Ill., 1943-47; county supt. schools, Madison Co., Edwardsville, Ill., 1947-59; supt. pub. instrn., Ill., 1959-63; prof. So. Ill. U., Edwardsville Campus, 1963-71, emeritus, 1971—, asso. dir. Communications-media services div., 1967-69, also coordinator area sch. services. Dir. Nathan Hale Life Ins. Co., Nathan Hale Investment Corp., Vernon Fire & Casualty Co., Vernon Investment Corp. Past president Madison City Post-War Planning Commn.; past pres. Madison-Venice dist. Boy Scouts Am., past pres. Cahokia Mound council. Mem. Illinois School Problems Commn.; mem. Silver Century Club Found., So. Ill. U. Edwardsville. Recipient Silver Beaver award Boy Scouts of America. Mem. Ill. Congress PTA (life). Mem. Ill. Edn. Assn., Am. Fedn. Tchrs., Am. Assn. Sch. Adminstrs., NEA (life). Council Chief State Sch. Officers, Granite City C. of C., Ill. Assn. Sch. Adminstrs., U. Ill. (life), So. Ill. U. (life, past pres.) alumni assns., Phi Delta Kappa (pres. Gateway East chpt. 1975-76), Kappa Phi Kappa. Mason (Shriner); mem. Order Eastern Star. Clubs: Rotary (past dist. gov.) Men's. Author: School Building Construction, 1968; The School Law, 1968. Home: 2611 Cleveland Blvd Granite City IL 62040

WILKINS, GEORGE THOMAS, JR., pediatrician; b. Union County, Ill., Oct. 6, 1932; s. George T. and Mary Alice (Treece) W.; B.S., U. Ill., 1953, M.D., 1957; m. Frances Dee Calvert, Dec. 18, 1955; children—George Thomas III, Geoffrey Todd, Elizabeth Ann, Cheryl Renee. Intern, Presbyn.-St. Luke's Hosp., Chgo., 1957-58; jr. resident Milw. Childrens Hosp., 1958-59, sr. resident, 1959-60; practice medicine specializing in pediatrics, Decatur, Ill., 1962-65, Granite City, Ill., 1965—; chief of staff, St. Elizabeth Hosp., 1970-76; pediatric vis. staff St. Louis Childrens Hosp., 1965—; mem. nursery staff St. Louis Maternity Hosp., 1965—; mem. courtesy nursery staff Jewish Hosp., St. Louis, 1968 and after; mem. staff Anderson Hosp., Maryville, Ill., 1975—; asst. instr. in pediatrics Med. Sch. of Wis., Milw., 1958-60; instr. in pediatrics U. Miami (Fla.) Sch. of Medicine, 1960-62; asso. prof. pediatrics Washington Sch. of Medicine, St. Louis, 1977—. Served with M.C., USAF, 1960-62. Named Outstanding Young Man of Year, Granite City Jaycees, 1967; diplomate Am. Bd. Pediatrics. Mem. Am. Acad. of Pediatrics, Ill. (pres. 1977-78), Tri-City (pres. 1972-75), Madison County, Macon County med. socs., AMA (alt. del. 1975—), Am. Coll. Sports Physicians, St. Louis, Central Ill. pediatric socs., Alpha Chi Rho, Alpha Kappa Kappa. Presbyterian. Home: 1204 27th St Granite City IL 62040 Office: 3165 Myrtle St Granite City IL 62040

WILKINS, RAYMOND EDWIN, rubber co. exec.; b. Versailles Boro, Pa., Dec. 7, 1921; s. Richard and Martha M. (Shriver) W.; B.S., Washington and Jefferson Coll., 1943; postgrad. Harvard, 1943, Mass. Inst. Tech., 1943; m. Elizabeth Osborne, Aug. 7, 1948; children—G. Mead, Elizabeth (Mrs. Bruce Kieffer). With Corning GlassWorks, 1945-51; with Firestone Tire & Rubber Co., Akron, Ohio, 1952—, dir. corporate research and planning, 1969—. Pres. East Akron Community House, 1957-61; vice chmn. Summit County Children Services Bd.; bd. dirs. Nat. Fedn. Settlement Houses, 1959-61; mem. planning div. United Way, 1968—; adv. bd. U. Akron, 1969-76. Served with USMCR, 1942-45. Mem. Ohio C. of C. (dir. 1972—), Am. Mktg. Assn., Internat. Bus. Council. Club: Firestone Country (Akron). Home: 2367 Amesbury Rd Akron OH 44313 Office: 1200 Firestone Pkwy Akron OH 44317

WILKINSON, JOHN ERCY, lawyer; b. Cherryvale, Kans., July 28, 1931; s. Alva Edward and Virgie Velma (Persinger) W.; A.A., Independence Jr. Coll., 1951; B.S., U. Kans., 1953, J.D., 1958; m. Marianne Anderson, Mar. 30, 1957; children—Thomas Martin, George Edward, Daniel John. Admitted to Kans. bar, 1958; research atty. Kans. Supreme Court, Statehouse, Topeka, 1959-62; sr. law clk., Fed. Judge George Templer, Topeka, 1962-67; partner Colmery, McClure, Funk, Letourneau & Wilkinson, Topeka, Kans., 1967-77, Wilkinson & Graves, Topeka, 1977—; franchisee Burger King Corp., 1976—. Land commr. Fed. Dist. Court, Topeka, 1968—; lectr. appellate practice Washburn U., Topeka, 1967-73. Chmn. Topeka Housing Authority, 1973. Bd. dirs. Channel 11 Club, 1971-74. Served with AUS, 1953-55. Mem. Am., Topeka bar assns., Bar Assn. State of Kans. (mem. tenure, discipline and retirement of dist. judges com. 1969-74), Phi Delta Phi, Delta Sigma Pi. Lutheran. Mason (Shriner). Home: 1278 Collins St Topeka KS 66604 Office: 1000 First National Bank Bldg Topeka KS 66603

WILKINSON, WILLIAM CHAPIN, ophthalmologist; b. Detroit, Dec. 30, 1932; s. Arthur Paul and Helen (Feetham) W.; M.D., U. Mich., 1957, M.S. in Ophthalmology, 1961; m. Mary June Foster, June 17, 1961; children—Scott, Susan, John, Julie, Sarah. Intern, University Hosp., Ann Arbor, 1957-58, resident, 1958-61; practice medicine, specializing in ophthalmology, Pontiac, Mich.; chief eye St. Joseph Mercy Hosp., Pontiac, 1973. Head Lions Club Eye Bank, Pontiac, 1964-73. Mem. Am. Med. Assn., Mich., Oakland County med. socs., Mich. Ophthalmology Soc., Detroit Ophthalmology Club. Lion. Methodist (dir. 1972-74). Home: 545 Suffield St Birmingham MI 48009 Office: 880 Woodward St Pontiac MI 48053

WILKOF, ERVIN, steel co. exec.; b. Canton, Ohio, Sept. 10, 1918; s. Louis and Eva (Friedman) W.; student Ohio State U., 1936-38; m. Marie Viverette, July 21, 1945; children—JoAnne (Mrs. Clifford Ensley), Ronald Shawn, Vicki Lynn. Pres., Wallick Coal, Inc., Strasburg, Ohio, 1968-72; sec. Wallick Mining Co., Strasburg, 1968-72; pres. Wilkof Steel & Supply Co., Canton, 1955—; pres. Wilkof Indsl. Supply Co., Turner Quick- Lift Corp., Jerved Realty Corp.; v.p. TWM Mfg. Corp.; partner Wilkof Indsl. Devel. Corp.; exec. v.p. Needs Inc., Tampa, Fla.; dir. Wilkof-Morris Steel Corp. Served as 1st lt. AUS, 1942-45. Mem. Ret. Army Officers Assn., Jewish War Vets., Sigma Alpha Mu. Mem. B'nai Brith. Home: 900 24th St NE Canton OH 44714 Office: 1060 Warner Rd SE Canton OH 44701

WILKS, LOUIS PHILIP, chem. co. exec.; b. Dayton, Ohio, June 28, 1913; s. David H. and Rebecca (Gibson) W.; B.S. cum laude, U. Dayton, 1935; certificate mgmt. devel. U. Chgo., 1960; m. Helen Claire Patterson, Oct. 23, 1938; children—Eleanore Wilks Michels, Ricki Wilks Levenberg, David. Instr. chemistry U. Dayton, 1935; research chemist Thomas & Hochwalt Lab., Dayton, 1935-38; with Velsicol Chem. Corp., Chgo., 1938—, v.p., 1956-66, dir. new product devel., 1956-63, dir. long range planning, 1963—. Mem. AAAS, Am. Chem. Soc., Comml. Devel. Assn. Club: B'nai B'rith. Patentee in field. Home: 9530 Lamon Pl Skokie IL 60076 Office: 341 Ohio St E Chicago IL 60601

WILLANDER, DUANE ALFRED, orthopaedic surgeon; b. Chgo., Feb. 26, 1923; s. Alfred Arthur and Lillian Sedalia (Broman) W.; B.S., Northwestern U., 1944, B.Medicine, 1946, M.D., 1947; m. Lee Hogrefe, Aug. 22, 1946; children—William, Susan, Jane. Intern Evanston (Ill.) Hosp., 1946; resident VA Hosp., Lincoln, Nebr., 1949-50, 51-52; children's Hosp., Los Angeles, 1950-51; practice medicine specializing in orthopaedic surgery San Diego, 1952-54, Springfield, Ill., 1954-56, San Jose (Calif.) Clinic, 1956-60, Galesburg, Ill., 1960—; mem. staff Cottage Hosp., Galesburg, chief of staff, 1974-76; asst. prof. orthopaedic surgery Rush Med. Coll., Chgo.; clin. asso. in orthopaedic surgery U. Ill., Peoria. Served to capt. U.S. Army, USMC, 1947-49. Fellow A.C.S., Internat. Coll. Surgeons; mem. Am. Acad. Orthopaedic Surgeons, AMA, Ill., Central Ill. orthopaedic socs., Knox County Med. Soc., Phi Beta Kappa. Republican. Presbyterian. Club: Soangetha Country (Galesburg). Contbr. articles to med. jours. Home: 390 Fair Acres Dr Galesburg IL 61401 Office: 575 N Kellogg Galesburg IL 61401

WILLARD, JOHN ELA, chemist; b. Oak Park, Ill., Oct. 31, 1908; s. Wallace Watson and Mary Hazeltine (Ela) W.; B.S., Harvard U., 1930; Ph.D., U. Wis., 1935; m. Adelaide Ela, June 12, 1937; children—Ann Willard Bozdogan, Mark, David, Robert. Faculty, Avon Old Farms Sch. (Conn.), 1930-32, Haverford (Pa.) Coll., 1935-37; faculty U. Wis., Madison, 1937-42, 46—, prof. chemistry, 1948—, dean grad. sch., 1958-63, chmn. chemistry dept., 1970-72, Vilas research prof. chemistry, 1963—; asso. sect. chief plutonium chemistry sect. Metall. Lab., U. Chgo., 1943-44; area supr. Hanford Engr. Works, E. I. duPont de Nemours Co., Inc., 1944-45: dir. reactor chemistry div. Metall. Lab., U. Chgo., 1945-46; mem. vis. com. phys. chemistry div. Nat. Bur. Standards, 1968-71, chmn., 1968-70, phys. chem. panel, Office of Naval Research, 1948-50; plutonium prodn. survey com., AEC, 1949, isotope distbn. adv. com., 1953-57; adv. bd. Gordon Research Conf., 1955-61; vis. com. chem. div. Brookhaven Nat. Lab., 1956-59; chmn. div. phys. chem. Am. Chem. Soc., 1957; vis. prof., Japan, 1977. Mem. Am. Chem. Soc. (policy com. 1957, award 1959), Am. Phys. Soc., Radiation Research Soc., AAAS, AAUP, Sigma Xi. Congregationalist. Asso. editor Chem. Revs., 1955-58, Radiation Research, 1965-68. Home: 2306 Hollister Ave Madison WI 53705 Office: 1101 University Ave Madison WI 53706

WILLARD, RICHARD DEWAINE, physician; b. Fountantown, Ind., July 4, 1936; s. Ray Edward and Wilma Jesse (Miller) W.; B.A., Ind. U., 1961, M.D., 1964; m. Joyce Maxine Bulmer, July 16, 1954; children—Bret Alan, Vicki Sue, Bart Travis, Cathy Marie. Intern, St. Vincent's Hosp., Indpls., 1964-65; practice of medicine, Bluffton, Ind., 1965-69, Howe, 1970—; mem. staffs various hosps. Founder Success Unltd.; v.p. ANANTA Found.; founder, pres. Mind Sci. Research Found.; bd. dirs. Inst. Med. Hypnosis. Served with USAF, 1954-58. Mem. AMA, Ind. Med. Assn. (commn. vol. health agys. 1966—), Soc. Med. Hypnoanalysts (pres. 1975-77), Soc. Clin. Hypnosis, Biofeedback Research Soc., Ind. Biofeedback Soc. (dir.), Am. Acad. Family Practice. Republican. Methodist. Home: Box 96B Howe IN 46746

WILLEY, ROY EDWARD, real estate broker; b. Clarence, Mo., Mar. 6, 1920; s. Joseph Bash and Lucy Wellman (Hagan) W.; student U. Mo., 1942-43; m. Mable Irene Eyer, July 13, 1941; 1 dau., Elizabeth Ann. Parts mgr., bookkeeper Community Motor Co., Clarence, Mo., 1941-49; gen. mgr. Noll Motors Inc., Moberly, Mo., 1949-55; sales mgr. Nathe Chevrolet, Inc., Columbia, Mo., 1955-60; realtor, partner E.S. Miner, Realtor, Columbia, 1961-67; pres., broker Roy Willey, Inc., Columbia, Mo., 1967—. Instr. Mo. Assn. Realtors, Columbia, 1967—. City councilman Moberly, Mo., 1954-55, Columbia, 1961-63; mem. Columbia Finance Study Com., 1974—. Pres. Columbia Police and Firemen's Pension Fund, 1974-76, trustee, 1964-70, 74—; v.p., bd. dirs. Eye Research Found. Mo., 1973-76, pres., 1977—. Served to maj., USAF, 1943-45. Named Outstanding Young Man, Jr. C. of C., 1955; recipient Distinguished Citizen Award, City of Moberly (Mo.), 1955. Mem. Columbia Bd. Realtors (dir. 1964-71), Mo. Assn. Realtors (dir. 1968—, pres. 1972, Realtor of Year 1975), Nat. Assn. Realtors (dir. 1974—, vice chmn. membership com. 1977—), Columbia C. of C. (dir. 1957-59), Nat. Inst. Farm and Land Brokers (chpt. v.p. 1972), Realtors Nat. Mktg. Inst. (Mo. membership chmn. 1974-75, region mktg. dir. 1977—), Am. Legion (post comdr. 1969-70, comdr. 8th dist. dept. Mo. 1972-74). Kiwanian, Elk, Mason (Shriner). Home: 224 E Parkway Columbia MO 65201 Office: PO Box 595 Forum Shopping Center Columbia MO 65201

WILLIAMS, ALBERT HAROLD, real estate broker; b. Bonnie, Ill., May 11, 1913; s. Albert and Iva Mae (Peavler) W.; grad. high sch.; m. Mabel Bonidean Dodson, Mar. 7, 1930; 1 son, Dennis Harold. With Internat. Shoe Co., Mt. Vernon, Ill., 1930-42; owner, broker A. Harold Williams Real Estate, Mt. Vernon, Ill., 1946—. Housing adviser Greater Egypt (Ill.) Planning Commn., 1973. Served with USNR, 1942-46. Named Mr. Toastmaster, Toastmaster's Club, 1963; recipient weekly community service award WMCL, 1976. Mem. Egyptian Bd. Realtors (pres. 1961-62), Ill. Assn. Realtors (dist. v.p. 1962, 73), C. of C. (dir. 1960-63). Clubs: Kiwanis (pres. 1960, 65), Masons, Shriners. Home and Office: 315 S 10th St Mt Vernon IL 62864

WILLIAMS, ARBOR WAYNE, JR., accountant; b. Cleve., Oct. 22, 1942; s. Arbor Wayne and Jean Eloise (Wilson) W.; B.A., Kent State U., 1965; M.B.A., Case Western Res. U., 1976; m. Susan Jane Lippert, May 7, 1966. Cost analyst Cleve. div. Lamson & Sessions, 1966-70, mgr. cost accounting Bedford Heights div., 1970-76, sr. accountant Bedford Heights div., 1976—; owner Speed Freak Auto Specialties, Cleve., 1976—. Pres. Warner-Turney Area Residents Council, 1973-74, finance dir., 1974—. Home: 4620 E 85th St Garfield Heights OH 44125 Office: 5185 Richmond Rd Bedford Heights OH 44146

WILLIAMS, BILLY JOE, microbiologist; b. Reed, Okla., May 16, 1924; s. Hosea Clinton and Agnes Eugene (Curtis) W.; B.A., Northeastern Okla. State Coll., 1949; M.S., U. Ark., 1952; m. Billie Jean Bonner, Oct. 5, 1972; children—Paul Howard, Kim A. Clouse. Microbiologist bacteriol. warfare div. Chem. Corps, Dept. of Army, Pine Bluff Arsenal, Ark., 1952-56, E. and J. Gallo Winery, Modesto, Cal., 1956-59, Okla. State Dept. Health, Oklahoma City, 1959-61, Children's Meml. Hosp. U. Okla. Med. Center, Oklahoma City, 1961-62, poultry diagnostic lab. and field research center Charles Pfizer & Co. Inc., Springdale, Ark., 1962-67; microbiologist animal health research dept., Terre Haute, Ind., 1967—; lectr. in field. Served with USNR, 1942-45. Mem. Am. Soc. Microbiology, Inst. Food Tech., Am. Soc. Enologists, Am. Assn. Analytical Chemists, Phi Sigma. Researcher etiology animal diseases, microbiol. assays antibiotics in feeds, synergistic activity antibiotics, other fields. Home: Rural Route 22 Box 595 Terre Haute IN 47802 Office: Pfizer Inc Terre Haute IN 47808

WILLIAMS, CHARLES THOMAS, assn. exec.; b. Charleston, Mo., May 4, 1941; B.S., Western Mich. U., 1965; M.A., U. Mich., 1970, Ph.D., 1971; m. Janet E McLaughlin, July 17, 1976; children from previous marriage—Robin, Tracey. Tchr., pub. schs. Detroit, 1965-68; counselor, supr. U. Mich. Fresh Air Camp, 1970; ednl. cons. Mich. Edn. Assn., East Lansing, 1971-73, asso. exec. sec. for minority affairs div., 1973-76, asso. exec. dir. profl. devel. and human rights div., 1976—. U.S. Office Edn. fellow, U. Mich., 1969-71. Mem. Mich. Assn. Emotionally Disturbed Children, Council Exceptional Children, Nat. Council Social Studies, Assn. Study Afro Am. Life and History, Am. Personnel Guidance Asn., Nat. Alliance Black Sch. Educators, Urban League, NAACP, Phi Delta Kappa. Home: 1935 Mendota St East Lansing MI 48823 Office: 1216 Kendale Blvd East Lansing MI 48823

WILLIAMS, DAN ARTHUR, assn. exec.; b. Lincoln, Nebr., Jan. 31, 1915; s. Terry A. and Sarah Jane (Bodley) W.; B.A. magna cum laude, U. Nebr., 1938; grad. Rochdale Inst., 1939; m. Janet Lawrence, Oct. 20, 1941; 1 son, Garrett A. Partner, Williams-Robertson Co., Lincoln, 1930-37; exec. sec. Lincoln Group Health Assn., 1937-38; asst. state dir., Workers Service Program, Lincoln, 1938-39; field rep., Nat. Farmers Union, Denver, 1939, Nationwide Ins., Columbus, Ohio, 1939-40; dir. consumer div., personnel dir. Mid-Eastern Coops., Inc., N.Y.C., 1941-60; v.p., exec. dir. Assn. for Middle Income Housing, Inc., N.Y.C., 1961-67, also dir.; dir. personnel tng. Palmer First Nat. Bank and Trust Co. of Sarasota, 1967-68; supr. central midwest dist. office Cominco-Am., Inc., Lincoln, 1968—. Faculty, Rochdale Inst., N.Y.C., 1941-45; teaching asst. U. Nebr., Lincoln, 1960-61; v.p. 6th Ave. Credit Union, N.Y.C., 1962—; dist. rep. Cominco-Am. Fed. Credit Union, 1971—. Mem. N.Y.C. Planning Bd., 1963—, Lincoln Vol. Bur. Trustee Rochdale Inst.; bd. dirs. Lincoln-Lancaster Assn. for Mental Health, 1974—. Mem. Coop. Inst. Assn. (v.p. 1949-56), Am., Nebr. civil liberties unions, Fellowship of Reconciliation, Coop. League U.S.A. (mem. pub. relations com. 1950—), Wider Quaker Fellowship, Phi Beta Kappa. U.P. (life elder). Home: 1121 Sumner St Lincoln NE 68502 Office: 3808 Normal Blvd Lincoln NE 68506

WILLIAMS, EDGAR GENE, educator, univ. ofcl.; b. Posey County, Ind., May 4, 1922; s. Noley Wesley and Anna Lena (Wilsey) W.; A.B., Evansville Coll., 1947; M.B.A., Ind. U., 1948, D.B.A., 1952; m. Joyce Ellen Grigsby, May 7, 1944; children—Cynthia Ellen Williams Mahigian, Thomas Gene. Instr. Ind. U., Bloomington, 1948-52, asst. prof., 1952-55, asso. prof., 1955-58, prof., 1958—, asso. dean, 1965-69, v.p., 1974—. Pres. Bus. and Community Services, Inc., Bloomington, Ind., 1970—. Bd. dirs. Found. for Sch. Bus., Ind. U., Bloomington, 1966—. Served with AUS, 1943-46. Mem. Am. Soc. for Personnel Adminstrn., Am. Mgmt. Assn., Beta Gamma Sigma. Democrat. Methodist. Mason. Clubs: Indpls. Athletic; Bloomington (Ind.) Country. Home: 1126 E 1st St Bloomington IN 47401

WILLIAMS, EDWARD DONALD, airline exec.; b. Chgo., Feb. 5, 1925; s. Edward Joseph and Ann Pauline (Jochum) W.; student Loyola U., Chgo., 1946-48; Ph.B. in Journalism, Marquette U., 1950; M.S. in Journalism, Northwestern U., 1951; m. Dorothy Elizabeth Schroepel, Sept. 18, 1948; children—Lee, Marc, Gregg, Faith, Joy. Reporter-photographer Sheboygan (Wis.) Press, 1951-52; reporter Chgo. Daily News, 1952-58; reporter Chgo.'s Am., 1958-61; reporter-aviation writer Milw. Jour., 1961-74; news bur. rep., dept. pub. relations United Airlines, Chgo., 1974—. Served with USMC, 1942-46. Decorated Air medal, D.F.C. Recipient awards Air Force Assn., 1967, 71, Wis. Wing CAP, 1968, Res. Officers Assn., 1968, Air Force Res., 1973, Wis. Aviation Trades Assn., 1968, Wis. Council on Aeros., 1974. Mem. Headline Club, Chgo. Press Vets., Exptl. Aircraft Assn. (awards 1967, 69), Nat. Pilots Assn., Aircraft Owners and Pilots Assn., Aviation/Space Writers Assn. Contbr. articles to aviation jours. and popular mags.; part-time asso. editor Vintage Airplane Mag. Home: 713 Eastman Dr Mount Prospect IL 60056 Office: Pub Relations Dept United Airlines PO Box 66100 Chicago IL 60666

WILLIAMS, FRANK EUGENE, supt. schs.; b. Madison, S.D., Jan. 18, 1921; s. Fred Milton and Orval Marie (Sparks) W.; B.S., Dakota State Coll., 1948; M.S., S.D. State Coll., 1956; m. Joan Piper, May 30, 1947; children—Thomas, Jolynn, David, Bradley. Coach, tchr. social studies pub. schs., Lennox, S.D., 1948-51, McGregor, Minn., 1952-55; faculty Wayne (Nebr.) State Tchrs. Coll., 1955-62; prin. Wisner, Nebr., 1962-66; supt. schs., Gresham, Nebr., 1966-71, St. Edward (Nebr.) Pub. Schs., 1971—. Served with AUS, 1940-45. Presbyn. Mason; mem. Order Eastern Star. Address: St Edward NE 68660

WILLIAMS, FRED E., librarian, educator; b. Jamieson, Fla., Mar. 22, 1927; student Emory U., 1944-48; B.S. in Zoology, Fla. State U., 1949, M.A. in L.S., 1952; Ed.D., Ind. U., 1961; m. Catherine Vaughn. Tchr. Wakulla County Schs., Crawfordville, Fla., 1949-51; film librarian Ball State U., 1952-54; lectr. edn. Ind. U., 1956-59; dir. audiovisual service Bowling Green State U., 1959-65, mem. edn. faculty, 1959—, prof., chmn. dept. library and ednl. media, 1974—. Mem. ALA, Assn. Ednl. Communications and Tech., Ohio Ednl.

Library Media Assn. Address: 212 Williams St Bowling Green OH 43402

WILLIAMS, G. MENNEN, justice; b. Detroit, Feb. 23, 1911; s. Henry Phillips and Elma Christina (Mennen) W.; A.B., Princeton, 1933; J.D., Mich. Law Sch., 1936; LL.D., Wilberforce U., Mich. State U., U. Liberia, U. Mich., Aquinas Coll., Ferris Inst., St. Augustine's Coll., Western Mich. U.; H.H.D., Lawrence Inst. Tech.; m. Nancy Lace Quirk, June 26, 1937; children—Gerhard Mennen, Nancy Quirk (Mrs. Ketterer), Wendy Stock (Mrs. Burns). Atty., Social Security Bd., 1936-38; asst. atty. gen., Mich., 1938-39; exec. asst. to U.S. atty. gen., 1939-40; with criminal div. Dept. Justice, 1940-41; deputy dir. Mich. O.P.A., 1946-47; liquor control commr., Mich., 1948; gov. of Mich., 1949-60; asst. sec. state for African affairs, 1961-66; ambassador to Republic of Philippines, 1968-69; justice Mich. Supreme Ct., 1971—. Served from lt. (j.g.) to lt. comdr. USNR, overseas, 1942-46. Decorated Legion of Merit with Combat V; grand officer Order of Orange Nassau (Netherlands); grand comdr. Royal Order of Phoenix (Greece); Humane Band of African Redemption (Liberia); Polonia Restituta (Polish govt. in exile). Democrat. Author: Africa for the Africans, 1969. Address: Law Bldg Lansing MI 48901 also 1425 Lafayette Bldg Detroit MI 48226

WILLIAMS, HAROLD MILTON, trade assn. exec.; b. Lemmon, S.D., Oct. 10, 1907; s. William Daniel and Lillian (Jackson) W.; B.A., U. Wis., 1929; M.B.A., U. Chgo., 1947; m. Alice Rosamond Fox, Jan. 20, 1931; children—Rosemary M. Williams DeMore, Martha E., Maudie G. Williams Bremer, David H., Daniel J. With Swift & Co., Chgo., 1929-31, Williams Packing Co., Chgo., 1931-43; plant mgr. Hofhers Meat Co., Chgo., 1943-44; v.p. Fox De Luxe Foods, Inc., Chgo., 1944-57; pres., dir. Inst. Am. Poultry Industries, Chgo., 1958-71, Inst. Am. Poultry Industries Internat., 1968—; pres. Poultry and Egg Inst. Am. Chgo., 1971—; dir. Poultry and Egg Nat. Bd., 1959—; treas. Asso. Poultry and Egg Industries, 1967-69; mem. U.S. Pres.'s Food for Peace Com., 1962—; adminstr. coop. program between Fgn. Agr. Service of U.S. Dept. Agr. and Inst. Am. Poultry Industries, 1958; del. European Am. Symposium on Agr. Trade, Amsterdam, Holland, 1963; del. White House Conf. on Food and Nutrition, 1969; del., speaker Nat. Symposium on Salmonella, 1964. Named hon. citizen Kansas City, Mo., 1963, New Orleans, 1968. Mem. U.S. Livestock San. Assn., Inst. Food Technologists, Assn. Food and Drug Ofcls. U.S., Def. Supply Assn. Inst. Sanitation Mgmt., Food Packaging Council (gov.), Chgo. Assn. Commerce and Industry, Phi Kappa Phi. Clubs: Serra of North Shore, Executive, Lake Shore (Chgo.); Univ. (Washington); Exec. Program (U. Chgo.). Home: 2842 W Chase Ave Chicago IL 60645 Office: 29 E Madison St Chicago IL 60603

WILLIAMS, HAROLD ROGER, economist; b. Arcade, N.Y., Aug. 22, 1935; s. Harry A. and Gertrude A. Scharf W.; B.A., Harpur Coll., State U. N.Y., Binghamton, 1961; M.A., Pa. State U., 1962; Ph.D., U. Nebr., Lincoln, 1966; postdoctoral Harvard U., Cambridge, Mass., 1969-70; m. Dorothy Preuschoff, Apr. 23, 1955; children—Theresa Lynne, Mark Roger. Instr., Pa. State U., 1962-63, U. Nebr., Lincoln, 1965-66; asst. prof. econs. Kent (Ohio) State U., 1966-68, asso. prof., 1968-72, prof., 1972—, chmn. dept. econs., 1974—. Served with M.I., AUS, 1954-57. Recipient excellence in teaching recognition Kent State U., 1970-71; NSF sci. faculty fellow, 1969-70; NDEA fellow, 1963-65, 65; recipient research grants Kent State U., 1967, 72. Mem. Internat., Am., Midwest (v.p. 1969-70), So. econ. assns., Soc. Advancement Mgmt., Assn. Evolutionary Econs., Acad. Internat. Bus., Midwest Fin. Assn., Omicron Delta Epsilon, Beta Gamma Sigma, Pi Gamma Mu. Contbr. articles to profl. jours. Home: 415 Suzanne Dr Kent OH 44240 Office: Dept Econs Kent State U Kent OH 44242

WILLIAMS, HARRY WOOLERY, ins. co. exec.; b. Aurora, Nebr., Mar. 17, 1917; s. Ed M. and Jenny Irene (Woolery) W.; B.S., U. Nebr., 1939, LL.B., 1941; m. Winifred Evelyn Hyland, June 16, 1940; children—Richard J., Jack H. Adjuster Crocker Claims Service, Omaha, 1941, br. mgr., Lincoln, Nebr., 1942-43, claims mgr., Norfolk, Nebr., 1946-49; claims mgr. Motor Club Ins. Assn., Omaha, 1949-51, gen. mgr., 1951—. Bd. govs. Nebr. Automobile Ins. Plan, 1973-75. Served with AUS, 1943-46. Recipient Man of the Year award, Omaha Bus. Men's Assn., 1968. Mem. Nat. Assn. Independent Insurers (dir. 1957-75, exec. com. bd. dirs. 1965-75), Nebr. Ins. Fedn. (dir. 1967-75), Omaha Bus. Men's Assn. (dir. 1954-75, v.p. 1965-66). Home: 7915 Shirley St Omaha NE 68124 Office: 5011 Capitol Ave Omaha NE 68132

WILLIAMS, HUGH ALEXANDER, JR., mech. engr.; b. Spencer, N.C., Aug. 18, 1926; s. Hugh Alexander and Mattie Blanche (Megginson) W.; B.S. in Mech. Engring., N.C. State U., 1948, M.S. in Diesel Engring. (Norfolk So. R.R. fellow), 1950; m. Ruth Ann Gray, Feb. 21, 1950; children—David Gray, Martha Blanche. Jr. engr.-field service engr. Baldwin-Lima Hamilton Corp., Hamilton, Ohio, 1950-52, project engr., 1953-55; project engr. Electro-Motive div. Gen. Motors Corp., La Grange, Ill., 1955-58, sr. project engr., 1958-63, supr. product devel. engine design sect., 1963—. Trustee Downers Grove (Ill.) San. Dist., 1965—, pres., 1974—; pres. Ill. Assn. San. Dists., 1976-77; mem. statewide policy advisory com. Ill. EPA; ruling elder 1st United Presbyn. Ch., Downers Grove. Served with USAAC, 1945. Registered profl. engr., Ill. Mem. ASME (Diesel and Gas Engine Power Div. Speaker award 1968, Div. citation 1977), Soc. Automotive Engrs. Republican. Club: Masons. Editor: So. Engr., 1947-48. Contbr. articles to profl. jours. Patentee in field. Home: 1119 Blanchard St Downers Grove IL 60515

WILLIAMS, JACK RAYMOND, civil engr.; b. Barberton, Ohio, Mar. 14, 1923; s. Charles Baird and Mary (Dean) W.; student Colo. Sch. Mines, 1942-43, Purdue U., 1944-45; B.S., U. Colo., 1946; m. Mary Berneice Jones, Mar. 5, 1947 (dec.); children—Jacqueline Rae, Drew Alan. Gravity and seismograph engr. Carter Oil Co., Western U.S. and Venezuela, 1946-50; with Rock Island R.R., Chgo., 1950—, structural designer, asst. to engr. bridges, asst. engr. bridges, 1950-63, engr. bridges system, 1963—. Served with USMCR, 1943-45. Fellow ASCE; mem. Am. Concrete Inst., Am. Ry. Bridge and Bldg. Assn. (past pres.), Am. Ry. Engring. Assn. Home: 293 Minocqua St Park Forest IL 60466 Office: 745 S LaSalle St Chicago IL 60605

WILLIAMS, JASPER FLEMMING, physician; b. El Paso, Tex., Feb. 8, 1918; s. Jasper B. and Clara B. (Drisdale) W.; B.S., Tuskegee Inst., 1940; postgrad. N.Mex. State U., 1947-49; M.D., Creighton U., 1953; postgrad. Harvard, 1958; m. Margaret M. Butler, June 7, 1944; children—Carolyn Joyce, Jasper F., Theodore K. Intern, Provident Hosp., Chgo., 1953-54; resident, 1954-57, chmn. div. gynecology, 1961; clin. asst. Gynecology Clinics, Cook County Hosp., 1959; obstetrician and gynecologist Williams Clinic, Chgo., 1960; cons. obstetrics St. Bernard's Hosp., 1961—, chief staff, 1973—; cons. Jackson Park Hosp., Provident Hosp., Ill. Masonic Hosp., Tabernacle Hosp. Dir. Seaway Nat. Bank; chmn. bd. Midwest Aircraft Sales Corp., TAHF. Mem. Gov.'s adv. com. State of Ill.; med. examiner FAA. Bd. dirs. Chgo. Urban League, Interaction, Inc., Ill. Social Hygiene League; trustee Tuskegee Inst. Diplomate Am. Bd. Obstetrics and Gynecology. Fellow A.C.S., Internat. Coll. Surgeons, Am. Coll. Obstetricians and Gynecologists; mem. Nat. Med. Assn. (pres., mem. council hosps. and med. edn.), Chgo. Med. Soc. (mem. ethical relations com.), Am. Hosp. Assn. (mem. com. on physicians); Ill. Med. Soc., Chgo. Human Relations Council, Chgo. Assn. Commerce and Industry, Alpha Omega Alpha, Phi Beta Pi. Home: 5012 S Woodlawn Ave Chicago IL 60615 Office: 408 E Marquette Rd Chicago IL 60637

WILLIAMS, JERRY RUTH, high sch. counselor; b. Bogalusa, La., Sept. 5, 1936; d. Charlie and Procula Marian (Norris) W.; Hutcherson; B.A. magna cum laude, So. U., 1957; M.Ed., U. Mo., St. Louis, 1969; m. Robert P. Williams, Jan. 25, 1959; 1 dau., Michelle Yvette. Tchr. English, New Orleans pub. schs., 1957-59; case worker Mo. Dept. Welfare, St. Louis, 1960-61; tchr. St. Louis pub. schs., 1961-66; counselor Normandy Sch. Dist., St. Louis, 1969—, dir. alt. learning program, 1975-76; staff trainer Title IX Workshop, 1977. Mem. Am. Personnel and Guidance Assn., Assn. Non-White Concerns, Normandy Tchrs. Assn. (exec. com.), Nat., Mo. edn. assns., Suburban Guidance Assn., Phi Delta Kappa, Alpha Kappa Alpha, Kappa Delta Pi, Alpha Kappa Mu. Methodist. Home: 1967 Willow Lake Dr Chesterfield MO 63017 Office: 6701 St Charles Rock Rd St Louis MO 63133

WILLIAMS, JOHN COBB, lawyer; b. Chgo., June 11, 1930; s. Ralph Milton and Mary (Cobb) W.; B.A., Wesleyan U., 1951; LL.B., Yale, 1954; m. Helen Grace Gilbert, Aug. 19, 1955; children—Helen Boyce, Nancy, Sarah Mason. Admitted to Ill. bar, 1955, Fla. bar, 1974; asso. firm Sidley & Austin, Chgo., 1954-63, partner, 1964—. Trustee Village of Northbrook, Ill., 1965-69, village pres., 1969-73; mem. plan commn. and zoning bd. appeals, Village of Northbrook, 1965-69. Bd. dirs. N. Suburban Assn. for Health Resources, 1973, pres., 1974-75; bd. dirs. N. Suburban Blood Center. Fellow Am. Coll. Probate Counsel (Ill. chmn. 1974—); mem. Am., Ill. (chmn. com. on legislation 1975-76), Chgo. (chmn. of the legislative com. 1969-71, chmn. com. on probate practice 1972-73), bar assns., Clubs: Skokie Country (Glencoe, Ill.); University, Economic, Law, Legal. Home: 486 Greenleaf Ave Glencoe IL 60022 Office: One First Nat Plaza Chicago IL 60603

WILLIAMS, JOHN PERSHING, brass co. exec.; b. Bluefield, W.Va., July 25, 1919; s. Deck C. and Zeora M. (Brocklehurst) W.; B.S., U. Mich., 1951; m. Ruth E. Davis, Sept. 10, 1947; 1 dau., Jeanne. With King-Seeley Thermos Co., Ann Arbor, Mich., 1950-63, labor relations mgr., 1956-58, indsl. relations mgr., 1958-63; personnel mgr. Butler Mfg. Co., Kansas City, Mo., 1963-65, indsl. relations mgr., 1965-66; dir. indsl. relations Mueller Brass Co., Port Huron, Mich., 1966-69, v.p. indsl. relations, 1969—. Cons. indsl. relations Fed. Pacific Electric Co., others. Dir. Blue Cross-Blue Shield Mich. Pres. Perry Nursery Sch., 1957; chmn, indsl. div. Ann Arbor United Fund, 1954; del. Republican State Conv., 1961; bd. dirs. Ann Arbor Family Service, 1956-57; mem. parents council Adrian (Mich.) Coll. Served with USCG, 1940-46; ETO, PTO. Mem. Am. Soc. Personnel Adminstrs., Indsl. Relations Research Assn., Indsl. Relations Assn. Detroit, Copper Devel. Assn. (labor adv. com. 1967—, chmn. indsl. relations adv. com.). Ann Arbor Mfrs. Assn. (pres. 1961), Am. Compensation Assn. Methodist. Home: 2212 Brandywine Ln Port Huron MI 48060 Office: 1925 Lapeer St Port Huron MI 48060

WILLIAMS, JOHN TROY, librarian, educator; b. Oak Park, Ill., Mar. 11, 1924; s. Michael Daniel and Donna Marie (Shaffer) W.; B.A., Central Mich. U., 1949; M.A. in Library Science, U. Mich., 1951, M.A., 1954; Ph.D., Mich. State U., 1973. Reference librarian U. Mich., Ann Arbor, 1955-59; instr. Bowling Green (Ohio) State U., 1959-60; reference librarian Mich. State U., East Lansing, 1960-62; 1st asst. reference dept. Flint (Mich.) Pub. Library, 1962-65; head reference services, Purdue U., West Lafayette, Ind., 1965-72; head pub. services No. Ill. U., Dekalb, 1972-75; asst. dean, asst. univ. librarian Wright State U., Dayton, Ohio, 1975—; cons. in field. Served with U.S. Army, 1943-46. Mich. State fellow, 1963-64; HEW fellow, 1971-72. Mem. Am. Library Assn., Spl. Libraries Assn., Genessee County Hist. Soc. (dir.), Am. Soc. for Info. Sciences, Am. Sociol. Assn., AAUP, Council on Fgn. Relations. Contbr. articles to profl. jours. Home: 26 E Hebble Fairborn OH 45324

WILLIAMS, JOHN WALTER OLDING, data processing adminstr.; b. Nanking, China, Sept. 3, 1936; s. Walter Henry and Kathryn Elizabeth (Tesack) W.; came to U.S., 1947, naturalized, 1956; student U. Wash., 1954-56, U. Md., 1957-58; B.S., Ariz. State U., 1963; postgrad. U. Okla., 1970; M.B.A., Central Mo. State U., 1975; 1 dau., Erika Anne. Enlisted in USAF, 1956, commd. 2nd lt., 1963, advanced through grades to capt., 1967; mgr. data processing ops. Tan Son Nhut Air Base, Vietnam, 1971-72, F.E. Warren AFB, Wyo., 1972-73, Whiteman AFB, Mo., 1973-76; ret., 1976; mgr. data processing ops. Med. Mutual of Cleve., 1977; asst. to pres. Leichtung Inc., 1978—. Chmn. base voting registration drive Whiteman AFB, 1974; treas. combined fed. campaign, Warren AFB, 1972. Decorated Bronze Star. Clubs: Silver Plume Samoyed (pres. 1967-68), K Bar L Saddle (dir., pub. chmn. 1975-76). Home: 4610 Brainard Rd Chagrin Falls OH 44022

WILLIAMS, KENNETH R., educator; b. Saxton, Pa., Feb. 14, 1935; s. Kenneth R. and Marian A. (Hunter) W.; A.B., Pa. State U., 1959, M.A., 1961, Ph.D., 1964; m. Linda A. Lane, Mar. 31, 1961; children—Kenneth R. III, Christopher Joel. Instr. humanities and speech Pa. State U., University Park, 1962-64; asst. prof. speech U. R.I., Kingston, 1964-66, U. Md., College Park, 1966-67; asso. prof. Ohio U., Athens, 1967-77; prof., chmn. dept. communication, U. Wis., Stevens Point, 1977—; founder, prin. coordinator Human Development Resources, Inc., Athens, 1973-77. Served with U.S. Army, 1955-57. Recipient distinguished teaching award Ohio U., 1974-75, research grantee, 1972; certified Gold Seal Flight Instr., comml. instrument rated for single and multi-engine landplanes. Mem. Internat., Wis. communication assns., Creative Edn. Found., Speech Communication Assn., Wis. Acad. Arts, Letters, and Scis., Central States Speech Assn., Nat. Assn. Flight Instrs. Contbr. articles in fields communications, semantics, sociology. Home: 1234-A Northpoint Dr Stevens Point WI 54481 Office: Dept Communication U Wisconsin at Stevens Point Stevens Point WI 54481

WILLIAMS, LANSING EARL, plant pathologist; b. Spencer, W.Va., Aug. 8, 1921; s. Harry Earl and Nora (Hickman) W.; B.S. summa cum laude, Morris Harvey Coll., 1950; M.S., Ohio State U., 1952, Ph.D., 1954; m. Mildred Juanita Hill, May 9, 1946; children—Patricia Marie, Lansing Earl. Faculty Ohio Agrl. Research and Devel. Center, Wooster, also Ohio State U., Columbus, 1954—, prof. plant pathology, asso. chmn., 1968—, prof. gen. botany Mansfield campus, 1959-65. IRI Research Inst. cons. on wheat virus problems to Brazil, 1968. Pres., Kean Sch. PTA. Served with USMCR, 1942-46. Mem. Am. Inst. Biol. Scis., AAAS, Ohio Acad. Sci. (sec.-treas. N. Central div.), Sigma Xi (pres. Wooster club), Chi Beta Phi. Methodist (chmn. missions commn. 1967-68, mem. nominating com.). Lion. Contbr. articles to profl. jours. Home: 2580 Christmas Run Wooster OH 44691 Office: Ohio Agrl Research and Devel Center Wooster OH 44691

WILLIAMS, LLOYD DEE, banker; b. Morgan County, July 9, 1933; s. Harlan Francis and Marguerite Irene Lawrence W.; student Ohio U., 1958, Am. Inst. Banking, 1963, Kent State U., 1965; m. Martha Jean Giles, June 26, 1955; children—Elaine Kay, Randel D. With Citizens Nat. Bank, McConnelsville, Ohio, 1955—, cashier, 1965-76, v.p., 1973-76, exec. v.p., 1976—, also dir. Sec. Four County Devel. Council, 1965, rep., 1960—; treas. Morgan County Heart Assn., 1968—, McConnelsville Bus. Assn., 1970—; sec.-treas. McConnelsville Cemetery Assn., 1958—, trustee, 1958—; treas. Cub Scout Pack, McConnelsville, 1969-75. Served with AUS, 1953-55. Mem. Ohio (group sec. 1973—), Morgan County (treas. 1966—, rep. to state assn. 1972—, treas. 1973—) bankers assns., Am. Legion, Malta-McConnelsville C. of C. (sec. 1960-65, 71, pres. 1970). Republican. Methodist. Mason. Clubs: Malta-McConnelsville Kiwanis (sec. 1964-70), Morgan County Coin. Home: 560 N 8th St McConnelsville OH 43756 Office: 100 E Main St McConnelsville OH 43756

WILLIAMS, LUTHER STEWARD, biologist; b. Sawyerville, Ala., Aug. 19, 1940; s. Roosevelt and Mattie B. (Wallace) W.; B.A. magna cum laude, Miles Coll., 1961; M.S., Atlanta U., 1963; Ph.D. (NIH fellow), Purdue U., 1968; m. Constance Marie Marion, Aug. 23, 1963; children—Mark Steward, Monique Marie. NSF lab. asst. Spelman Coll., 1961-62; NSF lab. asst. Atlanta U., 1962-63, instr. biology, faculty research grantee, 1963-64, asst. prof. biology, 1969-70; grad. teaching asst. Purdue U., West Lafayette, Ind., 1964-65, grad. research asst., 1965-66, asst. prof. biology, 1970-73, asso. prof., 1973—, NIH Career Devel. awardee, 1971-75, asst. provost, 1976; Am. Cancer Soc. postdoctoral fellow State U. N.Y., Stony Brook, 1968-69; asso. prof. biology Mass. Inst. Tech., 1973-74; chmn. rev. com. MARC Program, Nat. Inst. Gen. Med. Scis., NIH, 1972-76; grant reviewer NIH, 1971-73, 76, NSF, 1973, 76, Med. Research Council of N.Z., 1976. Mem. Am. Soc. Microbiology, Am. Chem. Soc., Am. Soc. Biol. Chemists, AAAS. Contbr. sci. articles to profl. jours. Home: 831 Sparta St West Lafayette IN 47906 Office: B 228 Lilly Hall Life Scis Purdue U West Lafayette IN 47907

WILLIAMS, MARY GOSHORN, psychologist; b. Kansas City, Mo., Aug. 1, 1917; d. John Franklin and Myrtle Ann (Newman) Goshorn; Ph.D., U. Kans., 1958; m. Charles C. Williams, Sept. 2, 1937; 1 son, Geoffrey John; stepdau., Kathryn Williams Sargent. Psychologist, psychiat. unit Jackson County Juvenile Ct., Kansas City, Mo., 1948-52, United Jewish Social Service, Kansas City, 1952-55, Florence Crittenton Home, Kansas City, 1955-58, Menorah Med. Center, Kansas City, 1959-65; pvt. practice psychology, Kansas City, 1965-73, 76—; cons. Rural Mental Health Center, Independence, Kans., 1973-75; postdoctoral Kansas City VA Hosp., 1975-76. Mem. Women's Polit. Caucus, NOW. Certified psychologist, Kans., Mo. Mem. Am., Kans., Mo. psychol. assns., Am. Sociol. Assn., Am. Group Therapy Assn. Home: 1510 Brush Creek St Kansas City MO 64110

WILLIAMS, MEZELL LOUIS, JR., ednl. counselor; b. Chgo., Oct. 16, 1948; s. Mezell Louis and Rosiland Matilda (Lockett) W.; B.A. in History, Upper Iowa U., 1967-71; M.S., DePaul U., 1977; m. Vida Bernadette Dyson, June 14, 1975. Scheduling supr. Montgomery Wards, Chgo., 1971-72; drug abuse worker II, Chgo. Dept. Mental Health, 1972, mental health worker II, 1973; counselor II, Dept. Human Services, Chgo., 1975—. Mem. Am. Personnel and Guidance Assn., Nat. Assn. for Community Devel., Chgo. Urban League, Alpha Phi Alpha. Baptist. Office: 3952 W Jackson St Chicago IL 60624

WILLIAMS, MILTON, optometrist; b. Monessen, Pa., Apr. 25, 1918; s. Morris and Lena (Katz) W.; D. Optometry, Ill. Coll. Optometry, 1940; m. Betty Abraham, July 22, 1945; 1 dau., Meris Margot. Partnership practice optometry, Streator, Ill., 1946—. Pres. LaSalle County Easter Seals Center, 1958-59. Bd. dirs. Sheltered Work Shop for Handicapped, 1965-73. Served with USNR, 1943-45. Mem. Am., Ill. optometric assns., Nat. Eye Research, Little City Found. for Retarded Children. Elk, Lion (pres. 1971-72, Lion of Yr. 1969). Home: 628 Boys St Streator IL 61364 Office: 125 S Vermillion St Streator IL 61364

WILLIAMS, MORRIS ODDMAN, accountant, tax cons.; b. Texarkana, Ark.; s. Edward and Izora (Burns) W.; student Wilberforce U., 1938; B.S., Wayne State U., 1940; postgrad. U. Detroit, 1975-76. Accountant, Detroit Housing Commn., 1941-47; accountant, tax cons., Detroit, 1948—; enrolled agt. IRS, 1977—; pres., founder Morris O. Williams & Co., 1977—. Mem. bd. mgmt. Fisher YMCA, 1976-77. Served with U.S. Army, 1943. Mem. Nat. Soc. Pub. Accountants, Ind. Accountants Assn. Mich. (past state treas.), NAACP, Omega Psi Phi. African Methodist Episcopal. Office: 2101 W Grand Blvd Detroit MI 48208

WILLIAMS, NED, educator; b. Laurel, Miss., May 21, 1917; s. Walter Asbury and Georgia (Carr) W.; student Holmes (Miss.) Jr. Coll., 1937-39; B.S. in Commerce, U. Miss., 1947; M.S., Columbia, 1949, Ph.D. (univ. grantee), 1965; m. Mary Elizabeth Boykin, Dec. 19, 1947; 1 dau., Sally Mae. Instr., U. Miss., 1947-48, asst. prof. to prof., 1949-69; prof. mgmt. Sch. Bus., Eastern Ill. U., Charleston, 1969—. Partner, Oxford Research Assos. (Miss.), 1960-65; v.p., dir. Lafayette Enterprises, Oxford, 1967-69. Served with AUS, 1942-45. Recipient Gen. Motors competition award, 1953. So. Fellowships Found. grantee, 1962-63. Mem. Acad. Mgmt., Am. Econ. Assn., Am. Inst. Decision Scis., Am. Mgmt. Assn., Am. Prodn. and Inventory Control Soc., Am. Statis. Assn., Beta Gamma Sigma, Alpha Iota Delta, Alpha Tau Omega. Methodist. Editor: Mississippi's Business, 1951. Home: 2249 Cortland Dr Charleston IL 61920

WILLIAMS, NELLIE ELLIS BATT, educator; b. Nashville; d. Ivan C. and Lottie B. (Phillips) James; A.B., Stowe Coll., 1942; M.S., U. Ill., 1945; postgrad. Ill. Inst. Tech., 1959, 64, Oberlin U., 1965, St. Louis U., 1962, 63, 67, 68, Rockhurst Coll., 1972; m. Napoleon Williams, July 21, 1973; 1 son by previous marriage, Charles W. Batt, Jr. Tchr. Sumner High Sch., St. Louis, 1949-54, Handly High Sch., 1954-63; tchr., head mathematics dept. Northwest High Sch., St. Louis, 1963-76; instr., dept. head, Acad. Mathematics and Sci., St. Louis, 1976—; instr. nights Harris Teacher Coll., Forest Park Community Coll. Active NAACP, YWCA. NSF grantee 1959, 62-65, 67, 72. Mem. Mathematics Club of Greater St. Louis, Math. Assn. Am., Assn. of Women in Mathematics. Methodist. Club: Delta Theta (edn. com.). Home: 7584 Amherst St Saint Louis MO 63130

WILLIAMS, NELSON WHEAT, petroleum engr.; b. Lamesa, Tex., Apr. 12, 1916; s. James Rainey and Nellirene (Haney) W.; B.A., U. Tex., Austin, 1938; m. Louella M. Woodworth, Apr. 19, 1941; 1 dau., Sarah Lou. With Core Labs., Inc., Dallas, 1939-50, chief reservior engr., 1949-50; with James A. Lewis Engring. Inc., Evansville, Ind., 1950-56, v.p., 1952-56; pres., treas. Nelson W. Williams & Co., Inc., Evansville, Ind., 1956—. Home: 808 Riverside Dr SE Evansville IN 47713 Office: PO Box 3089 Evansville IN 47730

WILLIAMS, PAUL ALLAN, physician; b. Rensselaer, Ind., Aug. 19, 1933; s. Roy David and Mary Ellen (Fitzgerald) W.; M.D., Tulane U., 1958; m. Joan Marie Congelosi, May 3, 1952; children—Paul Allan, Deni, Thane, Troy, Avery, Gabrielle. Intern, Saginaw (Mich.) Gen. Hosp., 1958-59; pvt. practice medicine specializing in family medicine, Rensselaer, 1959—; physician St. Joseph's Coll., 1960—; chief of staff Jasper County Hosp., 1970-71; faculty St. Joseph Coll., 1960—, Ind. U. Sch. Medicine, 1973—. Bd. edn. St. Augustine Sch. 1966-72. Vice pres. Stath Office Supply, Inc., 1960—, Grow Fams, Inc., 1965—, Grow Land & Cattle, 1967—, Costa-Ana Cattle Co.

Ltd., Banc Tara, Inc., 1970—. Fellow St. Joseph Coll. Diplomate Am. Bd. Family Practice. Mem. Am. Med. Polit. Action Com., Rensselaer C. of C., Ind. Acad. Family Physicians (athletic injury com. 1969—, bd. dirs., pres. elect), Ind. Intercollegiate Athletic Assn., AMA, Ind. (athletic injury com.), Jasper County med. assns. (pres. 1965, 70-71), Am. Acad. Family Physicians (com. on cancer), Royal Soc. Health, Am. Orthopaedic Soc. for Sports Medicine, Phi Chi, Pi Kappa Alpha. Clubs: Romwell Fox Hounds, Am. Foxhound Assn., Irish Wolf Hound of Am., K.C. Home: 402 N Weston St Rensselaer IN 47978 Office: 1103 E Grace St Rensselaer IN 47978

WILLIAMS, PHILIP COPELAIN, physician; b. Vicksburg, Miss., Dec. 9, 1917; s. John Oliver and Eva (Copelain) W.; B.S. magna cum laude, Morehouse Coll., 1937; M.D., U. Ill., 1941; m. Constance Sheila Rhetta, May 29, 1943; children—Philip, Susan Carol, Paul Rhetta, Intern, Cook County Hosp., Chgo., 1942-43, resident in obstetrics and gynecology, 1946-48; resident in gynecology U. Ill., 1948-49; practice medicine specializing in obstetrics and gynecology, Chgo., 1949—; mem. staff St. Joseph Hosp., Augustana Hosp., Cook County Hosp., Mc Caw Hosp.; clin. prof. Med. Sch. Loyola U., Chgo. Bd. dirs. Am. Cancer Soc. Chgo. unit and Ill. div. Served with U.S. Army, 1943-45. Recipient Civic award Loyola U., 1970; diplomate Am. Bd. Obstetrics and Gynecology. Fellow A.C.S., Internat. Coll. Surgeons; mem. Chgo., Ill. med. socs., AMA, Chgo., Ill. med. socs., AMA, Chgo. Gynecol. Soc. (treas. 1975-78), Am. Fertility Soc., Inst. Medicine, N.Y. Acad. Scis., AAAS, Presbyn. Clubs: Ill. Athletic, Carleton, Plaza. Contbr. articles to profl. jours. Home: 1040 N Lake Shore Dr Chicago IL 60611 Office: 200 E 75th St Chicago IL 60619

WILLIAMS, RICHARD DALE, advt. exec.; b. Mitchell, S.D., Jan. 17, 1938; s. Dale Lester and Georgia Belle (Frye) W.; grad. Madison (Wis.) Bus. Coll., 1960; m. Janet Louise Vorpahl, Aug. 5, 1961; children—Ted Steven, Anne Louise. Salesman, Walker Mfg. Co., Racine, Wis., 1960-66; sales engr. Racine Hydraulics Co., 1966-68; sales promotion mgr. Modine Mfg. Co., Racine, Wis., 1968-76; advt. and sales promotion mgr. Barber-Colman Co., Rockford, Ill., 1977—. Mem. Soc. of Automotive Engrs., Automotive Service Industries Assn. (dist. dir. 1970-72), Rockford Ad Club, U.S. Auto Club. Home: 2734 Soland Dr Rockford IL 61111 Office: 1300 Rock St Rockford IL 61101

WILLIAMS, ROBERT LEO, architect, educator; b. Athens, Ohio, May 29, 1926; s. Wilbur Leo and Frances Lenore (Rice) W.; B.F.A., Ohio U., 1947; M. Arch., Harvard, 1955; m. Ruth Alice Wright, Sept. 11, 1948; children—Peter Wright, Stephen Rice, Ellen Belinda. Instr. architecture U. Fla., 1947-48; draftsman Asso. Architects, Columbus, Ohio, 1948-49; draftsman Dan A. Carmichael, Columbus, 1949-51; designer, draftsman Shepley, Bulfinch, Richardson & Abbott, Boston, 1952-54; project architect A.M. Kinney Assos., Cin., 1955-62; asso. architect Pistler-Brown Architects/H.M. Garriott, Cin., 1962-70; sr. v.p., dir. Architekton, Inc., Cin., 1970—; asso. prof. architecture U. Cin., 1962—, asst. dean Coll. Design, Architecture & Art, U. Cin., 1970-75. Mem. troop com. Boy Scouts Am., 1967-72; mem. Greater Hyde Park Community Council, 1969-74. Mem. AIA, Architects Soc. Ohio (sec. Cin. chpt. 1976-77), Assn. Collegiate Schs. Architecture, Am. Assn. U. Profs., Delta Tau Delta. Republican. Methodist (nat. bd. edn. 1968). Home: 3300 Observatory Ave Cincinnati OH 45208 Office: 700 Walnut St Cincinnati OH 45202

WILLIAMS, ROGER WILLIAM, educator; b. Alton, Mo., Jan. 26, 1938; s. William Anderson and Beulah Viola (Patton) W.; B.S., U. Mo., 1960; postgrad. Southwest Mo. State U., 1963, 64, 66; m. Eleanor Rose Adrian, Sept. 1, 1957; children—Elizabeth Anna, John Mark, Josephine Rose, Alice Dale. Tchr. biology and chemistry Koshkonong, Mo., 1963-65, Alton, Mo., 1966-69; high sch. prin. Koshkonong, Mo., 1965-66, 69-70, 70-71; tchr. agr. to adults, Alton (Mo.) High Sch., 1971—. Owner beef farm, Koshkonong, 1961—; mem. extension council U. Mo., Columbia, 1965-68. Republican committeeman Highland Twp. (Mo.), 1964—; mem. Oregon County (Mo.) Fair Bd., 1968—, Oregon County Soil and Water Conservation Bd., 1976; chmn. Bicentennial Com. for History of Oregon County, 1976, Oregon County Farmers for Danforth Com., 1976. Named Mo. State Fair Family for Oregon County, 1973. Mem. Alton PTA, Alton, Mo. tchrs. assns., Mo., Am. vocat. assns., Nat. Vocational Agrl. Tchrs. Assn., Oregon County Livestock Assn., Oregon County Pork Producers Assn., Alpha Tau Alpha. Baptist (deacon 1964—). Clubs: Lions, Elks. Home: Route 1 Koshkonong MO 65692 Office: Alton High Sch Alton MO 65606

WILLIAMS, STANLEY, malting co. exec.; b. Greensboro, N.C., Sept. 16, 1913; s. Oscar Page and Sally (Ingram) W.; B.A., Princeton U., 1934; m. Katharine Varick Elwell Noyes, Dec. 28, 1972; children—Fielding, Bolton, Jocelyn, Antoinette, Haskell. Trainee, Esmond Mills, N.Y.C., 1934-36, mng. dir. Esmond Mills (U.K.) Ltd., London, 1937-39; asst. treas. Wilkes Barre Mfg. Co. (Pa.), 1940-41; contract gen. mgr. Mandel Bros., Chgo., 1946-53; pres. Wis. Malting Co., Milw., 1953-74; chmn. bd. Kurth Malting Corp., Milw., 1974—; dir. NN Corp. Mem. Greater Milw. Com., 1963—; pres. Milw. Symphony Orch., 1959-62. Served to lt. USNR, 1941-46. Recipient Pro Urbe award Mt. Mary Coll., 1963. Mem. Milw. Assn. Commerce (pres. 1962-64, dir.), Barley Malt Inst. (pres. 1973-75), U.S. Brewers Assn. (dir. 1960—), Malting Barley Assn. (treas.). Republican. Episcopalian. Clubs: Milw. Country, Milw. Univ. Home: 8207 Santa Monica St Milwaukee WI 53217 Office: 2100 S 43d St Milwaukee WI 53219

WILLIAMS, STEVE EUGENE, banker; b. Grove, Okla., Jan. 25, 1944; s. Edgar Roger and Mildred Alberta W.; asso. degree, Northeastern Okla. A. and M. Jr. Coll., 1964; B.S. in Mktg., Okla. State U., 1966, postgrad., 1967-68; m. Sharon Joyce Roberts, Sept. 7, 1963; children—Casey Joe, Stephanie Jo, Leslie Rebecca. Trainee, First Nat. Bank and Trust Co., Joplin, Mo., 1968-69, discount teller's supr., then credit dept. mgr., then personal, comml. and agrl. lending officer, 1969—; bd. dirs. Basic Sch. of Banking. Recipient Gen. Dynamics Leadership award, 1964, Okla. City Purchaser's Assn. award, 1966, Hon. Legion of Honor award, Order of DeMolay, 1977. Mem. Am. Inst. Banking (asso. councilman), Am., Mo. (chmn. edn. com.) bankers assns., Mo. Cattlemen's Assn. Democrat. Baptist. Club: Masons. Home: Rural Route 1 Box 149 Sarcoxie MO 64862 Office: PO Box 55 4th and Main Sts Joplin MO 64801

WILLIAMS, THOM ALBERT, ins. and retail exec.; b. St. Louis, Dec. 31, 1941; s. Thom Reid and Martha Ann (Ruth) W.; B.B.A., Washington U., 1962, postgrad., 1963-64; m. Susan M. Raemdonck, Nov. 26, 1966; 1 son, Thom Raemdonck. With Norris Grain Co., St. Louis, 1960, Crane Co., St. Louis and Chgo., 1961-63, VW Mid Am. and VW Ins. Co., St. Louis, 1964-67; sr. partner Williams Group Cons., St. Louis, 1967-68; pres. Williams Group Cos., Wood River, Ill., 1969—; pres., dir. Reese-Wood River Drug Stores, Wood River, 1972—; pres., chmn. bd. Van's Stores & Supermarkets, Inc., Belleville, Ill., 1972—; div. mgr. adminstrn. and devel. Marsh & McLennan ins., St. Louis, 1970-76, mgr. fin. and adminstrn., 1976, v.p., 1977—; pres., dir. Washington Connection investment syndicate, St. Louis, 1970-71; v.p., dir. Remy Distbrs. Co., Highland, Ill., 1971—; chmn. bd. Soulard W., Inc., St. Louis, 1977—. Republican primary candidate Mo. Ho. of Reps., 1968. Mem. C. of C. (dir.), Am. Mgmt. Assn., Pres.'s Assn., Nat. Retail Mchts. Assn. Clubs: Lake Shore (Chgo.); Univ., Mo. Athletic, Bath and Tennis (St. Louis). Home: 1019 Hampton Dr St Louis MO 63117 Office: 515 Olive St St Louis MO 63101

WILLIAMS, THOMAS JAMES, retailer; b. Grand Rapids, Mich., July 14, 1938; s. James Sweeny and Flora Marie (Ellis) W.; B.S., Stanford U., 1959; m. Rochelle Linda See, Feb. 6, 1960; children—Pamela Jean, Brenda Lynn. Engr., Western Electric Co., 1956-59; mgr. Steketee's Radio Shop, Grand Rapids, 1959-65; buyer Allied Stores, Grand Rapids, 1965-67; pres. Williams-Magnavox Home Entertainment Center, 1967—. Chmn. exec. com. Grand Rapids Better Bus. Bur., 1973-76. Recipient award City of Grand Rapids 1973. Methodist. Office: 4280 Plainfield St NE Grand Rapids MI 49505

WILLIAMS, THOMAS KAY, counselor; b. Milw., May 16, 1930; s. James Thomas and Pearl June (Ward) W.; B.S., B.A., Andrews U., 1959, M.A., 1960; Ed.D., Western Mich. U., 1970; m. Audrey Eunice Kaatz, June 12, 1955; children—Teresa Kay, Thomas LaMont, Tonyce Ann. Tchr., prin. parochial elementary sch., 1955-57; pastor Seventh-day Adventist Chs., Wis., 1961-62; chaplain Battle Creek (Mich.) Sanitarium, 1962-66; dir. substance abuse services Battle Creek Sanitarium Hosp., 1964—; asso. prof. counseling, dir. splty. program in alcohol and drug abuse Western Mich. U., 1973-78; pres. Sapports, Inc., 1977—; adj. prof. Andrews U. Bd. dirs. Goodwill Industries; mem. State of Mich. Substance Abuse Adv. Com. Served with USN, 1948-52. Mem. Alcohol and Drug Problems Assn. Am., Am. Protestant Hosp. Assn., Am. Personnel and Guidance Assn., Mich. Alcoholism and Addiction Assn., Midwestern Area Alcohol Edn. and Tng. Program, Inc (dir., exec. com. 1974-77). Author: Winning the Bottle Battle, 1969; co-editor: Basic Curriculum for Substance Abuse Counselors, 1977. Home and Office: 5270 E Halbert Rd Battle Creek MI 49017

WILLIAMS, THOMAS RHYS, educator, anthropologist; b. Martins Ferry, Ohio, June 13, 1928; s. Harold K. and Dorothy (Lehew) W.; B.A., Miami U., Oxford, Ohio, 1951; M.A., U. Ariz., 1956; Ph.D., Syracuse U., 1956; m. Margaret Martin, July 12, 1952; children—Rhys, Ian, Tom. Asst. prof., asso. prof. anthropology Calif. State U., Sacramento, 1956-65; prof. anthropology Ohio State U., Columbus, 1965—, chmn. dept., 1967-71, mem. athletic council, 1968-74, chmn., 1973-74, grad. council, 1969-72; vis. asso. prof. anthropology U. Calif., Berkeley, 1962; vis. prof. anthropology Stanford U., 1976. Mem. United Democrats for Humphrey, 1968, Citizens for Humphrey, 1968. Served with USN, 1946-48. Recipient basic research grants NSF, 1958, 62, Am. Council Learned Socs.-Social Sci. Research Council, 1959, 63, S.E. Asia basic research grant Ford Found., 1974, 76. Fellow Am. Anthrop. Assn., Royal Anthrop. Int. Gt. Britain; mem. AAUP, AAAS, Sigma Xi. Author: The Dusun: A North Borneo Society, 1965; Field Methods in the Study of Culture, 1967; A Borneo Childhood: Enculturation in Dusun Society, 1969; Introduction to Socialization: Human Culture Transmitted, 1972. Editor, contbr. Psychol. Anthropology, 1975; Socialization and Communication in Primary Groups, 1975. Contbr. articles to profl. jours. Home: Box 386 New Albany OH 43054 Office: Dept Anthropology Lord Hall 124 W 17th Ave Ohio State U Columbus OH 43210

WILLIAMS, VEIRL RICHARD, dentist; b. Winchester, Ind., Jan. 10, 1929; s. V. Richard and Geneva Marie (Cage) W.; B.S., Ind. U., 1953, D.D.S., 1955; m. Marilyn Simpson, Jan. 31, 1954; children—Susan, Robert, John, Kate. Pvt. practice dentistry, Winchester, 1957—. Mem. Winchester City Council, 1964-68. Served with USNR, 1955-57. Fellow Internat. Coll. Dentistry; mem. Am. Dental Assn., Ind. (del. 1965), E. Central (pres. 1967-68) dental socs., Ind. Council on Dental Edn., Acad. Gen. Dentistry. Mason. Club: Columbia (Indpls.). Home: Rural Route 2 Winchester IN 47394 Office: 457 Elm St Winchester IN 47394

WILLIAMS, WALLACE PETER, securities dealer; b. Columbus, Ohio, Feb. 5, 1929; s. William Wallace and Marion (Fulton) W.; B.A., Cornell U., 1951; m. Sarah Burba, Aug. 1, 1951; children—Andrew, Timothy, Rebecca. Treas. W.W. Williams Co., Columbus, 1954-61, dir., 1956—; pres. Thermolite, Inc., Worthington, O., 1961-67; partner McDonald & Co., Columbus, 1968-73; v.p. the Chgo. Corp., 1973—. Served as lt. AUS, 1953-54. Decorated Bronze Star medal. Mem. Delta Tau Delta. Episcopalian (trustee 1969-71). Clubs: Columbus, Columbus Country. Home: 269 Ashbourne Pl Columbus OH 43209 Office: 88 E Broad St Suite 1740 Columbus OH 43215

WILLIAMS, WAYNE WATSON, civil engr.; b. Powersville, Mo., Dec. 14, 1922; s. Charles and Hattie (Watson) W.; B.S., Iowa State U., 1951, M.S., 1953; m. Mary F. Mette (dec.); children—Marilyn (Mrs. Kenneth Rolls), Wayne II, Charles, Fred, Michael; m. 2d, Beverly Block, Mar. 16, 1961; children—Christopher, Sheryl Joy. Instr., Math. Inst. Cambria (Iowa) High Sch., 1944-45; gauger Sinclair Oil Co., Sinclair, Wyo. Refinery, 1945-46; insp. Iowa Hwy. Commn., Ottumwa, 1946-48; soils insp. U.S. Bur. Reclamation, Riverton, Wyo., 1948-49; research asst. Iowa Engring. Expt. Sta., Ames, 1951-53; geologist Lechner Engring. Co., Ames, 1953-55; owner Williams Exploration Co., Des Moines, 1955-65; with H.R. Green Engring. Co., Cedar Rapids, Iowa, summer 1966; prof. civil engring. Kans. State U., Manhattan, 1965—. Cons., Ill., Iowa, Kans., Tex., La., Okla. Served with USAAF, 1941-44. Mem. ASTM, Internat. Assn. Housing Sci., Phi Kappa Phi, Chi Epsilon, Tau Beta Pi. Mason. Contbr. articles to profl. jours. Home: 1615 Fairchild Dr Manhattan KS 66502

WILLIAMS, WENDELL STERLING, physicist; b. Lake Forest, Ill., Oct. 27, 1928; s. Sterling Price and Mary Eleanor (Simpson) W.; B.A., Swarthmore Coll., 1951; Ph.D., Cornell U., 1956; m. Dorothy Ellen Watt, June 28, 1952; children—Jennifer Anne, Laura Kathleen. Physicist, Leeds & Northrup Co., Phila., 1951; research physicist Union Carbide Corp., Parma, Ohio, 1956-67; sr. research visitor dept. metallurgy Cambridge (Eng.) U., 1965-66; asso. prof. physics and ceramic engring. U. Ill., Urbana, 1967-69, prof., physics, ceramic engring. and bioengring., 1969—; task coordinator energy related gen. research NSF, Washington, 1974-75, sect. head metallurgy and materials div. materials research, 1977-78. Founder, condr. Southwest Messiah Chorale, Parma, 1960-67; condr. Unitarian-Universalist Ch. choir, Urbana, 1968-73. Recipient grants NSF, ERDA. Fellow Am. Phys. Soc.; mem. Am. Ceramic Soc., AAAS, Am. Inst. Mech. Engrs., Sigma Xi. Club: Cosmos (Washington). Contbr. articles to sci. jours. Home: 501 E Mumford Dr Urbana IL 61801 Office: 106 Materials Research Lab Univ Ill Urbana IL 61801

WILLIAMS, WESLEY CORRIGAN, rare book curator; b. Cleve., June 19, 1940; s. Charles Wesley and Margaret (Corrigan) W.; B.A., Johns Hopkins U., 1963; M.Phil., Yale U., 1968; m. Janet Elizabeth Sandiford, Mar. 18, 1967; children—Geoffrey Brian Corrigan, Lara Trenerry. Lectr., Loyola Coll., Balt., 1964-65; curator history of sci. collection Case Western Res. U., Cleve., 1968-73, curator spl. collections, 1973—, lectr. history of sci., 1968—; asso. curator rare books, mem. advisory council Cleve. Museum Natural History; trustee Glen Oak Sch., Gates Mills, Ohio, 1970—; pres. bd. trustees Print Club Cleve.; adv. council Univ. Sch. Mem. bibliog. socs. Am. (life), London (life), AAAS (life), ALA, Manuscript Soc., Soc. Bibliography Natural History (London), Bibliog. Soc. U. Va. Republican. Episcopalian. Clubs: Rowfant, Grolier (N.Y.C.); Philos. (pres. 1977-78) (Cleve.). Editor: (with Robert E. Schofield) Man and the Frame of Nature, 1973; advisory com. Letters of Charles Darwin. Home: 2214 Demington Dr Cleveland Heights OH 44106 Office: 11161 East Blvd Cleveland Heights OH 44106

WILLIAMS, WILFRED, mfg. co. exec., engr.; b. Toledo, Aug. 29, 1911; s. Leon and Rose (Markowitz) W.; B.S. in Mech. Engring., U. Mich., 1936; m. Freida B. Baron, July 3, 1938; children—Paula (Mrs. Alfred Tobocman), Leon M., Ralph B., Deborah A. (Mrs. David Perlmutter). Tool and die engr. A.C. Spark Plug div. Gen. Motors, Flint, Mich., 1936-38; sales mgr. Acklin Stamping Co. Toledo, 1938-52; v.p., treas. Midwest Stamping & Mfg. Co., Bowling Green, Ohio, 1952-68, pres., treas., 1968-75, chmn. bd., 1975—, also dir.; chmn. bd. Mid-Am. Nat. Bank & Trust, Bowling Green, 1969—; pres. Bowling Green Investment Co. Trustee Jewish Community Center Toledo, Midwest Stamping Profit Sharing Plan & Trust. Registered profl. engr., Ohio. Mem. Am. Metal Stamping Assn. (nat. pres. 1965-66), Engring. Soc. Toledo, Soc. Automotive Engrs., Bowling Green C. of C., Tau Beta Pi. Jewish. Rotarian; mem. B'nai Brith. Clubs: Glengarry Country, Twin Oaks. Home: 4150 Stonehenge Rd Sylvania OH 43560 also Bayshore I Apt 305 100 Oakmont Ln Belleair FL 33516 Office: Napoleon and Manville Sts Bowling Green OH 43402

WILLIAMS, WILLIAM JOSEPH, holding co. exec.; b. Cin., Dec. 19, 1915; s. Charles F. and Elizabeth (Ryan) W.; student Georgetown Prep. Sch., Garret Park, Md.; A.B., Georgetown U., 1937; student Harvard Bus. Sch., 1938; m. Helen Mary DeCourcy, May 26, 1941, children—Mary F., William Joseph, Richard, Carol, Sharon, Thomas. Agy. dept. Western & Southern Life Ins. Co., Cin., 1938-41, v.p., 1939-54, now dir.; pres. N. Am. Mgmt. and Devel. Co., Inc., personal holding co., Cin., 1954—, Western Industries; sec., dir. Reading Rock Concrete Products Co.; dir. Am. Alarm Co., Cin. Equitable Ins. Co., Cin. Bengals; dir., v.p. Cin. Reds, Inc. Bd. dirs. Cin. Community Chest, 1953-55; dir. fund campaign Hamilton County chpt. Nat. Found. Infantile Paralysis, chmn. 1953 camp; bd. dirs. Cin. Boys Club; trustee Good Samaritan Hosp., Lady of Mercy Hosp. (Cin.); bd. regents Sisters of Mercy; bd. dirs. Xavier U., Cin., Cin. Zool. Soc., Childrens Home, Childrens Heart Assn. Served as capt. AUS, 1941-45. Decorated Knight of Malta, Knight Holy Sepulchre.. Mem. Cin. Zool. Soc. Clubs: Camargo Queen City, Cincinnati Country (Cin.). Home: 7801 Ayres Rd Cincinnati OH 45230 Office: Citizens Bldg 211 E 4th St Cincinnati OH 45202

WILLIAMS, WILLIE SAMUEL, psychologist, educator; b. Prattsville, Ala., May 8, 1932; s. Eddie and Iona (Scott) Williams; B.A., U. Wichita, 1958; M. Edn., Xavier U., 1960; Ph.D., Mich. State U., 1970; Kepner-Trego, Govt. Mgmt. Seminar, 1973; diploma Harvard U. Grad. Sch. of Bus. Adminstrn., 1976; m. Marva Flowers, Aug. 22, 1959; children—Kevin, Keith, Karla. Lic. psychologist, Ohio. Sr. counselor and asst. prof. psychology U. Cin., 1970-71; asst. chief psychol. research and training programs NIMH-HEW, Rockville, Md., 1971-74; asso. dean student affairs Case Western Reserve U. Sch. of Medicine, Cleve., 1974—; psychologist Cin. Police Dept., 1970-71. Mem. Am. Personnel and Guidance Assn. (senator), Assn. of Black Psychologists (treas.), Am. Psychol. Assn., Phi Delta Kappa. NSF fellowship, 1961; recipient Merit award, NIMH-HEW, 1972-74. Home: 2690 Green Rd Shaker Heights OH 44122 Office: 2119 Abington Rd Cleveland OH 44106

WILLIAMS-ASHMAN, HOWARD GUY, educator, scientist; b. London, Eng., Sept. 3, 1925; s. Edward Harold and Violet Rosamund (Sturge) Williams-A.; B.A., U. Cambridge, 1946; Ph.D., U. London, 1949; m. Elisabeth Bachli, Jan. 25, 1959; children—Anne Clare, Christian, Charlotte, Geraldine. Came to U.S., 1950, naturalized, 1962. From asst. prof. to prof. biochemistry U. Chgo., 1953-64; prof. pharmacology and exptl. therapeutics, also prof. reproductive biology Johns Hopkins Sch. Medicine, 1964-69; prof. biochemistry Ben May Lab. for Cancer Research, U. Chgo., 1969—, Maurice Goldblatt prof., 1973—. Recipient Research Career award USPHS, 1962-64. Fellow Am. Acad. Arts and Scis. (recipient Amory prize 1975); mem. Am. Soc. Biol. Chemists, Soc. Exptl. Biology and Medicine, Soc. Study Fertility. Author numerous articles in field. Home: 5421 S Cornell Ave Chicago IL 60615 Office: Ben May Lab for Cancer Research U Chgo Chicago IL 60637

WILLIAMSON, BEARL WAYNE, food processing co. exec.; b. Covington, Ky., Feb. 20, 1946; s. James William and Alice Elizabeth (Hamilton) Emerson; student Eastern Wash. State U., 1964-65, U. P.R., 1966, InterAm. U., 1967; m. Karen Lee Woods, Oct. 13, 1974; 1 dau., Ann Marie. Mgr. retail sales Army and Air Force Exchange Serivce, Ft. Benjamin Harrison, Ind., 1968-71; asst. beverage mgr. Netherland & Terrace Hilton, Cin., 1971-72; delicatessan and bakery specialist Kroger Food Stores, Cin., 1972-75; mgr. mgmt. devel. Peter Eckrich & Sons, Ft. Wayne, Ind., 1975—; cons. to retail food industry. Served in USAF, 1964-68. Mem. Am. Mktg. Assn. (v.p.), Am. Soc. Tng. and Devel., World Future Soc. Republican. Baptist. Home: 1253 Lake Ave Fort Wayne IN 46805

WILLIAMSON, JAMES REID, JR., found. exec.; b. Bridgeport, Conn., Feb. 3, 1935; s. James Reid and Emma Eunice (Harper) W.; A.B. in Am. Studies, Yale, 1956; m. Katharine Wentworth Glendinning, Feb. 7, 1959 (div. Nov. 1972); children—James Reid III, Robert G. Asst. sales mgr. Great Dane Trailers, Savannah, Ga., 1959-62; asst. exec. dir. Savannah Dist. Authority, 1962-64; exec. v.p. Dekalb C. of C., Atlanta, 1964-66; exec. v.p. Historic Savannah Found., 1966-73; exec. dir. Historic Landmarks Found. Ind., Indpls., 1974—; cons., lectr. historic preservation local, state and regional groups, 1968—. Episcopalian. Clubs: Oglethorpe, Savannah Yacht; Ind. Athletic (Indpls.). Home: 2505 Riley Towers 225 E North St Indianapolis IN 46204 Office: 3402 Boulevard Pl Indianapolis IN 46208

WILLIAMSON, JOE, JR., cons. engr.; b. St. Louis, Mar. 27, 1906; s. Joseph and Florence E. (Burton) W.; student Wash. U., 1924-26; B.S. Civil Engring., Mo. U., Rolla, 1929; m. LaVerne Nimmo, May 28, 1953. U.S. surveyman Miss. River Commn., 1926-27; prin. cons. Russell and Axon, cons. engrs., St. Louis, 1929-39, in charge Fla. office, 1939-51; owner Williamson & Assos., St. Louis, 1951—. Registered profl. engr., Mo., Ill., Fla., Calif., Tex., Va., W.Va., N.C., S.C., Ga., Ala., Miss., Tenn. Diplomate Am. Acad. Environ. Engrs. Fellow Am. Cons. Engrs. Council; mem. ASCE, Mo. Cons. Engrs. Council, Nat. Soc. Profl. Engrs., Water Pollution Control Fedn., Am. Water Works Assn., Am. Pub. Works Assn. Clubs: Masons, Shriners. Home: 6747 High Circle St Louis MO 63109 Office: 6731 Manchester Ave St Louis MO 63139

WILLIAMSON, JOHN PRITCHARD, utility exec.; b. Cleve., Feb. 22, 1922; s. John and Jane (Pritchard) W.; B.S., Kent State U., 1945; postgrad. U. Toledo, 1953-56, U. Mich., 1956; m. Helen Morgan, Aug. 3, 1945; children—John Morgan, James Russell, Wayne Arthur. Sr. Accountant Arthur Andersen & Co., Detroit and Cleve., 1945-51; dir. methods and procedures Toledo Edison Co., 1951-59, asst. treas. 1956-60, sec., 1960-62, sec.-treas., 1962-65, v.p. finance, 1965-68, sr. v.p., 1968-72, pres., chief exec. officer, 1972—, dir., 1962—; chmn. 1st Nat. Bank, Toledo, 1974-75, now dir. emeritus; dir. Toledo Trust Co.,

Ohio Valley Electric Co. Chmn. Downtown Toledo Devel. Com., 1974-75; gen. campaign chmn. Toledo United Appeal, 1971; pres. Toledo Community Chest, 1972; bd. dirs. Edison Electric Inst., Toledo Mus. Art, Ohio Electric Utility Inst., Toledo Hosp.; bd. dirs. United Way of Lucas, Wood and Ottawa Counties, pres., 1976. Recipient Echo award Boys Clubs, 1974; named Outstanding Alumnus, Kent State U., 1974, Outstanding Citizen of Toledo, 1976; C.P.A., Ohio. Mem. Am. Inst. C.P.A.'s, Toledo Area C. of C. (pres. 1970), Ohio C. of C. (v.p.), Financial Analysts Soc. Toledo (pres. 1968-69), Systems and Procedures Assn. (internat. treas. 1960), Inst. Pub. Utilities (chmn. exec. com. 1970), Kent State U. Alumni Assn. (pres. 1971-72), Blue Key, Delta Sigma Pi, Beta Alpha Psi, Delta Upsilon, Republican. Clubs: Toledo, Inverness (gov.), Toledo Kiwanis (pres. 1966); Rockwell Springs. Home: 4517 Brittany Rd Toledo OH 43615 Office: 300 Madison Ave Toledo 43652

WILLIAMSON, LAWRENCE L., computer programmer; b. Chgo., June 11, 1941; s. Harley O. and Mildred L. (Ozment) W.; student South Bend Coll. of Commerce, 1963-64, Ind. U., 1975—, IBM Programming courses, 1970—; m. Lottie B. Smith, Feb. 23, 1968; 1 dau., Diana. With automobile rental dept. Hertz Rent-A-Car, South Bend, Ind., 1963-64; computer operator, programmer LaSalle Liquor Corp., South Bend, 1964-72; computer programmer, asst. mgr. data processing Radio Distbg. Co., South Bend, 1973-77, data processing mgr., 1977—. Served with USAF, 1959-63. Home: 520 W Lowell St Mishawaka IN 46544 Office: 1915 N Bendix Dr South Bend IN 46614

WILLINGHAM, EDWARD BACON, JR., clergyman, religious broadcasting exec.; b. St. Louis, July 27, 1934; s. Edward B. and Harriet (Sharon) W.; B.S. in Physics, U. Richmond, 1956, postgrad. U. Rochester, 1958-59; M.Div., Colgate Rochester Divinity Sch., 1960; m. Angeline Walton Pettit, June 14, 1957; children—Katherine Angeline, Carol Walton. Chief engr. Radio-TV Center, Am. Bapt. Assembly, Green Lake, Wis., summers, 1952-56; various positions WVET-TV, Rochester, N.Y., 1956-60. Ordained to ministry Am. Baptist Ch., 1960; minister Christian edn. Delaware Av. Bapt. Ch., Buffalo, 1960-62; dir. radio and TV Met. Detroit Council Chs., 1962-75, exec. dir. Christian communication council, 1975—. Broadcast cons. Mich. Council Chs., 1965—; Fed. Republic Germany guest cons. religious broadcasting, 1968; mem. Interfaith Broadcasting Commn. Greater Detroit, 1968—, disc jockey weekly religious mus. show WXYZ, Detroit, 1963-75; mem. cable TV study com. city of Detroit; producer nationally syndicated TV series Choice. Instl. rep. Detroit Ednl. Television Found. Bd. mgrs., exec. com. Broadcasting and Film Commn. Nat. Council of Chs., 1965-73. Recipient Gabriel award UNDA-U.S.A., 1972. Mem. Nat. Assn. Council Broadcast Execs. (pres. 1969-71), World Assn. Christian Communications (chmn. steering com. N. Am. broadcasting sect. 1970-71, bus. mgr. 1972—, mem. central com. 1973—), Broadcast Edn. Assn., Detroit Press Club, Phi Gamma Delta, Sigma Pi Sigma. Home: 21440 Lathrup Southfield MI 48075 Office: 600 Palms Bldg Detroit MI 48201

WILLIS, CLIFFORD LEON, engring. co. exec.; b. Chanute, Kans., Feb. 20, 1913; s. Arthur Edward and Flossie Duckworth (Fouts) W.; B.S., U. Kans., 1939; Ph.D., U. Wash., 1950; m. Serreta Margaret Thiel, Aug. 21, 1947; 1 son, David Gerard. Asst. prof. geology U. Wash., 1950-54; chief geologist Harza Engring Co., Chgo., 1954-67, v.p., 1967—. Cons. geologist. Served to lt. USCG, 1942-46. Recipient Haworth distinguished alumnus award U. Kans., 1963. Fellow Geol. Soc. Am., Geol. Soc. London; mem. Am. Soc. Petroleum Geologists, Assn. Engring. Geologists, Am. Inst. Mining Metall. and Petroleum Engrs., Internat. Soc. Soil Mechanics and Found. Engring., Internat. Soc. Rock Mechanics, Sigma Xi, Tau Beta Pi, Sigma Tau, Theta Tau. Roman Catholic. Home: 16 Briar Rd Golf IL 60029 Office: 150 S Wacker Dr Chicago IL 60606

WILLIS, DAVID EDWIN, geophysicist; b. Cleve., Mar. 13, 1926; s. Russell E. and Eleanor Marie (Himebaugh) W.; B.S., Case Western Res. U., 1950; M.S., U. Mich., 1957, Ph.D., 1968; m. Martha Louise Mumma, Jan. 3, 1948; children—Karen, Mark, Marta, Seth. Party chief, asst. supr. Keystone Exploration Co., Houston, 1950-55; research geophysicist, geophysics lab. head U. Mich., Ann Arbor, 1955-70, asso. prof., 1968-70; prof. U. Wis., Milw., 1970—, chmn. dept. geol. scis., 1972-76; v.p. Geo-Aid Corp., 1975—. Served with USN, 1944-46. U. Mich. Engring. Research Inst. fellow, 1956-57; grantee NSF, Air Force Office Sci. Research, AEC, ERDA. Mem. Seismol. Soc. Am., Geol. Soc. Am., Am. Geophys. Union, Soc. Exploration Geophysicists, Sigma Xi, Phi Beta Kappa. Contbr. articles to profl. jours. Home: 4958 N Cumberland Blvd Whitefish Bay WI 53217 Office: Dept Geol Scis U Wis Milwaukee WI 53201

WILLIS, DAVID L., lawyer; b. Santa Monica, Calif., July 22, 1943; s. Bernard L. and Margaret Ann (Brodie) W.; A.B., Grinnell Coll, 1965; J.D., U. Iowa, 1968; m. Marilyn C. Price, June 30, 1967; children—Laura Lea, Jonathan L. Admitted to Iowa bar, 1968, Ohio bar, 1969; law clk. U.S. Ct. Appeals, 8th Circuit, Sioux City, Ia., 1968-69; asso. Squires, Sanders & Dempsey, Cleve., 1969-70; partner Willis & Willis, Lake City, Iowa, 1970—; city atty. City of Lake City, 1971—. Dir. Lake City Savs. & Loan Assn. Mem. Lake City C. of C., Lake City Devel. Assn. Presbyn. (ruling elder 1971—). Kiwanian. Home: 909 W Madison St Lake City IA 51449 Office: 107 W Main St Lake City IA 51449

WILLIS, FRANK NEAL, JR., psychologist; b. Kansas City, Mo., Dec. 13, 1930; s. Frank N. and Mable M. (Bolton) W.; children—Cynthia, Mary, Frank, Amanda. B.A., U. Kansas City, 1956, M.A., 1957; Ph.D., U. Mo., Columbia, 1961; intern Fulton (Mo.) State Hosp., 1957-59. Asst. prof. psychology U. Mo., Kansas City, 1963-67, asso. prof., 1967-70, prof., 1970—, chmn. psychology dept., 1973-75; research asso. dept. psychiatry U. Kans. Med. Center, 1969—. Mem. Am., Western, Southeastern psychol. assns., Animal Behavior Soc., Psychonomic Soc. Author: The Coronary Patient-Hospital Care and Rehabilitation, 1964; contbr. articles to profl. jours. Home: 2019 W 86th Terr Leawood KS 66206 Office: Dept Psychology U Mo 5301 Holmes Kansas City MO 64110

WILLIS, HAROLD ROBERT, psychologist, educator, biorhythm scientist; b. Trenton, Mo., Mar. 26, 1910; s. Arthur Robert and Myra Elizabeth (Stitt) W.; A.A., San Diego Jr. Coll., 1949; A.B., George Washington U., 1952, postgrad., 1957; M.A., Jackson Coll., 1954, M.S., 1955; Ph.D. candidate, Washington U., 1961; m. Pamela W. Willcox, Feb. 14, 1976; 1 son, David Andrew; children by previous marriage—Joe Robert, Harold Robert, Carol Lee, Shirley Jean Willis Bell, Richard Bryan. Joined, U.S. Navy, 1927, advanced through grades to comdr., 1955, ret., 1957; sr. ops. analyst McDonnell Aircraft Corp., St. Louis, 1957-61; sr. human factors engr. Martin Co., Denver, 1961-66, Lockheed Ga., Marietta, 1966-68; sr. engr. Ling Temco Vought, Dallas, 1968-69; asst. prof. psychology Mo. So. State Coll., Joplin, 1970—; head NJROTC unit Carl Junction High Sch., 1977-78; dir. Biorhythm Clinic. Vice pres. Van Schwartz Engr. & Mgmt. Cons. Corp., Denver, 1969-70; NASA fellow Geo. C. Marshall Space Flight Center, Huntsville, Ala., 1968. Community rep. Head Start Program, Joplin, Mo., 1973—. Recipient George Washington Honor Medal, Freedoms Found., 1964; named Ideal Father of Year, Washington Post, 1951. Mem. Ret. Officers Assn. (chpt. pres. 1963, 70, 71), Mo. Council Ret. Officers (chpt. pres. 1971), AAUP, Midwest Human Factors Soc. (dir. 1959), Am. Rocket Soc., I.R.E., Phi Delta Kappa. Clubs: Exchange (dir. 1972) (Iowa, Mo.); Masons, Shriners. Contbr. articles to profl. jours. Author: Sovietized Education, 1964. Home: Route 6 Box 653 Joplin MO 64801

WILLIS, HENRY EDWARD, publishing co. exec.; b. Angola, Ind., Apr. 25, 1912; s. Edward Dickinson and Olive Matilda (Rempis) W.; A.B., Wabash Coll., 1934; Litt.D., Tri-State U., 1975; m. Anna May Endicott, June 27, 1935 (dec. June 1976); children—Cynthia Anne Willis Pinkerton, Mary Josephine Willis Affolter, Victoria Jane. News reporter Steuben Printing Co., Inc., Angola, 1934-37, advt. mgr., 1937-41, prodn. mgr., 1946-49, gen. mgr., 1949, sec., 1950-56, sec.-treas., 1956-62, pres., treas., 1962—, chief exec. officer, 1962—, also dir.; dir. Angola State Bank. Mem. State of Ind. Law Enforcement Tng. Bd., 1975—; mem. James Whitcomb Riley Meml. Assn., 1968—; mem. Gov.'s Council on Edn. Beyond High Sch. and Council's Steering Com., 1956-58; mem. Ind. Regional Airport Commn., 1968-70; chmn. Steuben County Red Cross, 1949-50; council mem. Anthony Wayne council Boy Scouts Am.; mem. Ind. state platform com. Republican party, 1970-72, 74; trustee, vice-chmn. exec. com. Tri-State U.; mem. bd. govs. Asso. Colls. Ind. Served to lt. col. U.S. Army, 1941-46. Decorated Army Commendation medal; recipient award Ind. State Republican Central Com., 1958; Sagamore of Wabash award Gov. Ind., 1975. Mem. Nat. Newspaper Assn., Hoosier State Press Assn. (pres. 1965-66), Ind. Rep. Editorial Assn. (pres. 1957-58), Indpls. Press Club, Navy League U.S., Am. Legion, Angola C. of C. (pres. 1948-49), Pi Delta Epsilon, Alpha Phi Gamma, Phi Delta Theta. Congregationalist (trustee 1956-68, moderator 1965-68). Clubs: Lake James Country (Angola); Copper (Indpls.); Masons (33 deg.), Shriners, Rotary, Moose. Home: 605 S Darling St Angola IN 46703 Office: 12 Monument Pl PO Box 180 Angola IN 46703

WILLIS, JOHN FRISTOE, optometrist; b. St. Louis, Jan. 27, 1910; s. Prior Fristoe and Elva Cora (Moss) W.; A.B., Washington U., St. Louis, 1932, postgrad., 1934; postgrad. U. So. Calif., 1938, Am. Conservatory Music, Chgo., 1952-55; Dr. Optometry, No. Ill. Coll. Optometry, 1948; m. Alice Alvana Overbay, Aug. 31, 1943; 1 son, John Thomas. Violinist-soloist, stations KWK, WIL, KSD, KMOX, St. Louis, 1927-32; supr. music Prosser (Wash.) Pub. Schs., 1935-36; prof. violin Fla. State Sch. for Deaf and Blind, 1937; violin soloist So. Cal. Symphony Orch., 1939, concertmaster, 1939-41; pvt. practice optometry, Villa Park, Ill., 1955—. Violin soloist Chgo. Bus. Men's Symphony, 1956-61, 71-72, concertmaster, 1956—. Bd. dirs. Chgo. Bus. Men's Orch., 1972-74. Served with USNR, 1942-45. Recipient Albert Coates Masterly Violinist award, 1939. Mem. Am., Ill. optometric assns., SAR (Ill. soc.), VFW. Lion (chmn. Save Our Sight program 1975, chmn. finance com. 1974-75). Home: 106 E Kenilworth St Villa Park IL 60181 Office: 4 W Central St Villa Park IL 60181

WILLIS, MAURICE EARL, psychiatrist; b. Burlington, Ky., May 12, 1920; s. Albert Gaines and Izora Mae (Aylor) W.; M.D., Wayne State U., 1945; m. Lorraine E. Awes, May 24, 1949; children—Joan Willis Lee, Donna Christine, Maurice Clark. Intern, Mt. Carmel Mercy Hosp., Detroit, 1945-46; resident, U.S. Army, 1946-48, Pontiac (Mich.) State Hosp., 1948-51; pvt. practice gen. medicine, Detroit, 1946; practice medicine, specializing in psychiatry, Pontiac, 51—; gen. staff Pontiac Gen. Hosp., 1961—, chief psychiatry, 1964, 65, 70, 71, 72. Served to capt. AUS, 1946-48. Diplomate Am. Bd. Psychiatry and Neurology. Mem. Am. Med. Assn., Mich., Oakland County med. socs., Am. Psychiatric Assn., Mich. Psychiat. Soc., Am. Contract Bridge Assn. Home: 4406 Knightsbridge West Bloomfield MI 48033 Office: 500 W Huron St Pontiac MI 48053

WILLIS, ROBERT LUTHER, JR., radiologist; b. Toledo, Ohio, Aug. 29, 1927; s. Robert Luther and Eva Tong (Powell) W.; student Kenyon Coll., 1944-47; M.D., Wayne State U., 1951; m. Patricia Jackson, Sept. 7, 1973. Intern, Harper Hosp., Detroit, 1951-52, resident in radiology, 1952-57; practice medicine specializing in radiology Luth. Hosp., Ft. Wayne, Ind.; radiologist Beaumont Hosp., Royal Oak, Mich., 1957-62, Harper Hosp., Detroit, 1962-68, Lutheran Hosp., Fort Wayne, Ind., 1968—; asst. prof. Wayne State U. Coll. Medicine, Detroit, 1962-68. Served with USAF, M.C., 1953-55. Diplomate Am. Bd. Radiology. Fellow Am. Coll. Radiology; mem. AMA, Radiol. Soc. N. Am., Ind. State Med. Soc. Republican. Presbyn. Clubs: Fort Wayne Country, Plum Hollow Country (Detroit), LaGorce Country, Palm Bay, Jockey, Cricket (Miami, Fla.). Home: 4701 Covington Rd Fort Wayne IN 46804 Office: 2828 Fairfield Ave Fort Wayne IN 46807

WILLIS, SHELBY KENNETH, cons. engr.; b. Alton, Ill., June 9, 1924; s. Thomas Shelby and Mary Sigel (Worsham) W.; B.S., U. Ill., 1945, M.S., 1947; m. Ruth Marie Buchanan, Nov. 8, 1945; children—Jan Merry (Mrs. J. Randal Long), Jill Marie (Mrs. Eric K. Meyer), James Shelby. Civil engr. Western Electric Corp., Duluth, 1947, Howard, Needles, Tammen & Bergendoff, Kansas City, Mo., 1947-57; partner Bucher & Willis, cons. engrs., planners and architects, Salina, Kans., Kansas City, Mo., 1957—; pres. Kancen Printing Co., Salina, 1961—, Kancen Advt., Salina, 1966—; v.p., sec. Anilas, Inc., Salina, 1960—. Served to lt. (j.g.) USNR, 1942-46. Registered profl. engr., Ala., Ariz., Ark., Colo., Ill., Iowa, Kans., La., Mo., Miss., Nebr., N.Mex., N.D., Ohio, Okla., Pa., Tex., Wis., Wyo. Mem. ASCE, Nat. Soc. Profl. Engrs., Kans. Engrs. Soc., Am. Concrete Inst., ASTM, Am. Soc. Photogrammetry, Am. Cons. Engrs. Council (nat. v.p. 1977-79), Am. Congress Land Surveyors, Salina C. of C. Presbyterian. Elk. Club: Optimist (Salina). Home: 840 Millwood Dr Salina KS 67401 Offices: 605 W North St Salina KS 67401 also 6183 Paseo Kansas City MO 64110

WILLIS, THOMAS CREIGHTON, music critic; b. Flat Rock, Ill., Apr. 24, 1928; s. Albert and Alice (Creighton) W.; Mus.B., Northwestern U., 1949, Ph.D., 1966; postgrad. (scholar) Yale, 1949-52; m. Mildred Drefs, June 17, 1949; children—Deborah Sue, Christopher Lee. Asst. prof. music Sweet Briar (Va.) Coll., 1953-54; with Chgo. Tribune, 1957-77, copy editor, 1959, asst. theater and music reviewer, 1960-65, music critic, 1966-68, 74-77, music and art editor, 1968-74; vis. lectr. Northwestern U., Evanston, Ill., 1967-77, asso. prof. music, lit. and history, concert mgr., 1977—. Mem. commn. on ch. papers Lutheran Ch. in Am., 1966-72. Republican. Bd. dirs. Am. Mus. Digest, 1968-69, chmn. 1970-71; bd. dirs. Music Critics Assn., 1971-73, treas., 1973-74, 2d v.p., 1975-77. Contbg. editor Chicago mag., 1977—. Home: 1011 Crain St Evanston IL 60202 Office: 1977 Sheridan Rd Evanston IL 60201

WILLIS, WILLIAM HENRY, otolaryngologist; b. St. Louis, Aug. 1, 1940; s. William Thomas and Faye Irene (White) W.; student St. Louis Coll. Pharmacy, 1958-59, DePauw U., 1959-61; M.D., U. Ill., 1965; m. Jane Rueger, July 6, 1963; children—Peter, Penny. Intern, Henry Ford Hosp., Detroit, 1965-66; resident in gen. surgery Hutzel Hosp., Detroit, 1966-67, resident in otolaryngology N.Y. Eye and Ear Infirmary, N.Y.C., 1967-70, chief resident, 1969-70; practice medicine specializing in otolaryngology Toledo Otolaryngology Group, Inc., 1970—; active staff otolaryngologist St. Vincent's Hosp., Toledo, 1970—, Toledo Hosp., 1970—; trustee Toledo Hearing and Speech Center, 1971-77; cons. to Parents Hearing Edn. Assn. Toledo Pub. Schs., 1976—. Community health commr., Toledo, 1973-76; council mem. Glenwood Luth. Ch., 1973-76. Diplomate Am. Bd. Otolaryngology. Mem. AMA (recipient Physicians' Recognition award 1977-80), Toledo and Lucas County Acad. Medicine, Am. Acad. Ophthalmology and Otolaryngology, Am. Council Otolaryngology, Deafness Research Found., Pan-Am. Assn. Otorhinolaryngology and Bronchoesophagology, Mich. Otolaryngological Soc. Clubs: Centurion, Toledo. Contbr. articles in field to med. jours. Office: 2743 W Central Ave Toledo OH 43606

WILLISON, GEORGE WYMAN, physician; b. Dale, Ind., Mar. 28, 1910; s. George McClellan and Ida Belle (Mottweiler) W.; A.B., DePauw U., 1930; M.D., Ind. U., 1934; m. Mary Allison Hinkle, Nov. 23, 1940; children—Elizabeth Willison Bennett, Jane Willison Madison, George R. Intern, Phila. Gen. Hosp., 1934-36; field rep. ARC, 1936-37; fellow in internal medicine Lahey Clinic, Boston, 1937-38; practice medicine specializing in internal medicine, Evansville, Ind., 1938—; bd. dirs. Ind. Blue Shield Ins., 1960-72. Diplomate Am. Bd. Internal Medicine. Fellow A.C.P.; mem. Vanderburgh County Med. Soc., AMA, Ind. State Med. Assn., Am., Ind. (pres.) socs. internal medicine. Republican. Methodist. Home: 605 Saint Marys Dr Evansville IN 47715 Office: 3700 Bellemeade Ave Evansville IN 47715

WILLMAN, JOE IRVIN, pathologist; b. Indpls., June 8, 1934; s. Floyd I. and Juanita I. (Cornwell) W.; A.B., Ind. U., 1960, M.A., 1961, M.D., 1966; m. Barbara Ellen Beery, Dec. 26, 1961; children—Maria, Joseph, John, Marta. Resident, Ind. U. Med. Center, Indpls., 1966-69, Ball Meml. Hosp., Muncie, Ind., 1969-70; asso. pathologist Ball Meml. Hosp., 1973—; asst. clin. prof. pathology Ind. U. Pres., Delaware County Cancer Soc., 1976, 77. Served with USNR, 1957, 58. Mem. Delaware County, Ind. State med. socs., AMA, Am. Soc. Clin. Pathologists, Coll. Am. Pathologists, Internat. Acad. Pathology. Republican. Methodist. Club: Elks. Home: Rural Route 1 Gaston IN 47342 Office: 2401 University St Muncie IN 47303

WILLMAN, WARREN PAGE, dentist; b. Kankakee, Ill., Aug. 15, 1903; s. Arthur Charles and Phoebe Ann (Bollman) W.; student Millikin U., 1921-23; B.S. in Medicine, Loyola U., Chgo., 1926; D.D.S., Chgo. Coll. Dental Surgery, 1927, M.S., 1935; m. Marguerite Susan Dietrich, Feb. 3, 1940; children—Warren Walton, Denise (Mrs. Thomas Pelham Curtis), Nancy (Mrs. John Harry Shaulis). Pvt. practice dentistry, Chgo., 1927—; instr. crown and bridge prosthesis Chgo. Coll. Dental Surgery, 1927-28, instr. periodontics, 1928-30, instr. operative dentistry, 1930-32, asst. prof., 1932-38, asso. prof., 1938-41, prof., chmn. dept., 1941-51. Life mem. Art Inst. Chgo.; mem. Orchestral Assn. Mem. Am. Dental Assn., Ill., Chgo. dental socs., Federation Dentaire Internationale, Internat. Assn. Dental Research, Odontographic Soc. Chgo., Blue Key, Omicron Kappa Upsilon, Delta Sigma Delta. Mason. Club: Chicago Camera. Author: Periodontia, 1938. Editor The Bur, Jour. of Alumni Assn., 1944-50. Contbr. articles to profl. jours. Home: 629 Fair Oaks Ave Oak Park IL 60302 Office: 55 E Washington St Chicago IL 60602

WILLMES, FRANCIS EDWIN, wholesale grocery co. exec.; b. Hancock, Mich., Jan. 12, 1929; s. Elmer Francis and Hilda Elvira (Erickson) W.; B.B.A., U. Detroit, 1960; m. Carol Lois Lauffer, May 27, 1961; children—Karen Leigh, Gary Francis, David Eric. Dir. purchasing Mchts. Wholesale Service Co., Detroit, 1951-64; mdse. mgr. Herst-Allen Co., Chgo., 1964-65; with Spartan Stores, Inc., Grand Rapids, Mich., 1965—, v.p. gen. merchandise, 1971—. Served with AUS, 1951-52. Mem. Western Mich. Marketing Assn. (dir. 1968-74, 77), Gen. Mdse. Distbrs. Council (pres. 1970, 71, dir. 1970-75), Housewares Club Detroit (pres. 1963). Presbyn. Mason. Club: Grand Rapids Ski. Home: 1540 Woodlawn SE Grand Rapids MI 49506 Office: 850 76th St SW PO Box 8700 Grand Rapids MI 49508

WILLMOT, ROBERT JOSEPH, publishing and chem. co. exec.; b. Cleve., Feb. 21, 1928; s. Edward Joseph and Laura Mary (Berlyoung) W.; B.S., Kent State U., 1952, M.A., 1958; postgrad Ohio State U., 1964; m. Mary Guerra, Aug. 13, 1955; children—Lorraine, Mary Ellen, Karen. Tchr., audiovisual dir., dir. pub. relations Massillon (Ohio) Bd. Edn., 1952-65; dir. info., conv. mgr. Nat. Sch. Bds. Assn., Evanston, Ill., 1965-70; dir. pub. relations Carus Corp., La Salle, Ill., 1970—. Bd. dirs. Ill. Valley United Way, 1971—, pres., 1973-74; bd. dirs. Ill. Valley YMCA, 1976—. Served with U.S. Navy, 1946-48. Mem. Mfg. Chemists Assn. (pub. realtions com.), Pub. Relations Soc. Am. (accredited), Nat. Sch. Pub. Relations Assn. (accredited), Ednl. Press Assn. Am., Edn. Writers Assn., Chgo., N.Y.C. publicity clubs, Ill. Valley Area C. of C. (dir. 1973—, pres. 1975). Clubs: Rotary Internat. (pres. 1975-76), LaSalle, Elks. Home: 2704 Plum St Peru IL 61354 Office: 1500 8th St La Salle IL 61301

WILLSON, BARBARA JEAN, psychologist; b. Walnut, Iowa, Oct. 29, 1927; d. Harry August and Harriet Evelyn (Halden) Burmeister; B.A., U. Nebr., Omaha, 1966, M.A., 1968; m. Philip James Willson, Aug. 24, 1968; children—Victoria Howe, David Hicks. Instr. U. Nebr., Omaha, 1967-70; psychologist Pottawattamie County schs., Council Bluffs, Iowa, 1970-75; pres. Tin Pan Alley, Inc., 1975—; bd. dirs., pres. River Bluffs Mental Health Center; bd. dirs. Omaha, Council Bluffs Family Services Agy. Certified psychologist, Iowa. Mem. Am., Midwest, Iowa (licensed psychologist) psychol. assns., Midlands Mall Merchant's Assn. (bd. dirs.), Council Bluffs C. of C. Democrat. Unitarian. Contbr. articles to profl. jours. Home: 548 Cogleywood Ln Council Bluffs IA 51501 Office: 176 Midlands Mall Council Bluffs IA 51501

WILMOTH, CLARENCE HAROLD, real estate broker; b. Belington, W. Va., Sept. 6, 1929; s. Boyd D. and Bertha S. (Haak) W.; student Hammel Actual Bus. Sch., 1955-56; m. Dolores A. Fumea, Nov. 4, 1956; children—Rosalind, Sheila, James, Timothy, Terri, Patti. With Roadway Express, Akron, Ohio, 1955-56; office mgr. A. Schulman Inc., Akron, 1956-66; real estate broker C. Wilmoth Inc., Cuyahoga Falls, Ohio, 1964—, pres., chmn. bd. dirs., 1969—; pres., dir. C. Wilmoth Builders Inc., Cuyahoga Falls, 1972—, C. Wilmoth Ins. Agy., Inc., Cuyahoga Falls, 1972—; chmn. bd., pres. C. Wilmoth Developers, Inc. Served with USNR, 1946-53. Mem. Akron Area Bd. Realtors. Home: 852 Ashmun Ave Tallmadge OH 44278 Office: 1912 Portage Trail Cuyahoga Falls OH 44223

WILNER, FREEMAN MARVIN, hematologist, oncologist; b. Detroit, Mich., June 14, 1926; s. Jack B. and Bell G. (Goldberg) W.; B.S., Wayne State U., 1950, M.D., 1953; m. Marjorie Louise Tewkesbury, Aug. 29, 1948; children—Jeffrey, Robert, Paul, Laura. Intern and resident in internal medicine and hematology Detroit Gen. Hosp., 1953-57, chief med. resident, 1957; staff mem. VA Hosp., Dearborn, Mich., 1957-58; practice medicine specializing in hematology and oncology, Southfield, Mich., 1958—; chmn. dept. internal medicine Providence Hosp., Southfield, 1963-66; chief sect. hematology-oncology William Beaumont Hosp., Royal Oak, Mich.; clin. asso. prof. medicine Wayne State U. Sch. Medicine; pres. Hematology Assos., Southfield. Served with USAAF, 1944-47. Fellow A.C.P. (counselor Mich. br.); mem. Internat., Am. socs. hematology, Mich. Cancer Found., Am. Soc. Clin. Oncology, Mich. State, Wayne County, Oakland County med. socs., AMA, Alpha Omega Alpha. Contbr. articles to profl. jours. Office: 20905 Greenfield Rd Suite 501 Southfield MI 48075

WILSMAN, JAMES MICHAEL, lawyer; b. Port Huron, Mich., Oct. 7, 1939; s. Leo George and Fay Viola (Peterman) W.; B.A., Hiram Coll., 1961; J.D., U. Mich., 1964; m. Sandra Keith, July 28, 1962; children—Sarah, David. Admitted to Ohio bar; mem. firm Squire, Sanders & Dempsey, Cleve., 1964-66; mem. firm Parks, Eisele, Bates & Wilsman, Cleve., 1966-69, partner, 1969—. Trustee Citizens League Greater Cleve., 1970-76, v.p., 1972-74, pres., 1974-76; mem. pres.'s forum Hiram Coll., 1970—; chmn. Gov.'s Task Force on Commn. Rev. Mem. Am. (chmn. Ohio com. to provide legal assistance to families of P.O.W.'s/M.I.A.'s 1971—), Ohio (mem. unauthorized practice of law com. 1971-76), Cleve. (trustee 1972-75, chmn. justice center dedication, chmn. merit selection judges) bar assns., Hiram Coll. Alumni Assn. (pres. 1971-73). Congregationalist. Clubs: Cleveland Athletic, Shaker Heights Country. Home: 3139 Montgomery Rd Shaker Heights OH 44122 Office: 1100 Illuminating Bldg Cleveland OH 44113

WILSON, AARON AUBREY, JR., lawyer; b. Puxico, Mo., May 11, 1924; s. Aaron Aubrey and Louise Marguerite (Cruchon) W.; B.A., U. Kans., 1949, LL.B., 1950. Admitted to Mo., Kans. bars, 1950, Fla. bar, 1966; asst. city counselor St. Joseph, Mo., 1950-51; pvt. practice, law, Kansas City, Mo., 1951-65; dep. city atty. Kansas City, Mo., 1965-69, city atty., 1970—. Served with USNR, 1943-46. Mem. Am. Bar Assn. (vice chmn. intergovtl. relations com. 1974-75), Am. Trial Lawyers Assn., Nat. Cities Attys. Assn. (Mo. state chmn. 1970-71, regional v.p. 1972-73, trustee 1974-75, 2d v.p. 1977—, Distinguished Pub. Service award 1977), Phi Delta Phi, Sigma Chi. Home: 121 W 48th St Kansas City MO 64112 Office: City Hall 414 E 12th St Kansas City MO 64106

WILSON, ALBERT ERLE, ins. co. exec.; b. Indpls., Aug. 26, 1917; s. Charles Erle and Vada (Southall) W.; student pub. schs.; children—Robert E., Suzanne M., Mary E., Margaret E. Asst. sec. Fidelity Mut. Ins. Co., Indpls., 1946-58; comptroller Wabash Fire & Casualty Ins. Co., Indpls., 1958-60; self-employed as mgmt. cons., Indpls., 1960-61; data processing mgr. Kiefer-Stewart Wholesale Drug, Indpls., 1961-63; comptroller Crown Ins. Co. W.Va., Clayton, Mo., 1963-64; asst. comptroller, data processing mgt. Central Nat. Ins. Group Omaha, 1964-73; exec. v.p., comptroller Gt. Plains Ins. Co., Omaha, 1973—. Cons., spl. examiner Ind. Ins. Dept., 1956-60. Mem. Assn. for Systems Mgmt., Assn. Computing Machinery, Ins. Accounting and Statis. Assn. (chpt. v.p. 1952-53, 59-60). Republican. Club: Omaha Press. Contbr. to ins. and data processing jours. Home: 604 S 22d St Apt 916 Omaha NE 68102 Office: 3001 Douglas St Omaha NE 68131

WILSON, ALDEN PEABODY, librarian; b. Oberlin, Ohio, Aug. 28, 1924; s. Paul Andrew and Halloween (Peabody) W.; A.B., Fenn Coll., 1948; M.S. in L.S., Western Res. U., 1949; m. Bernice M. Franz, Sept. 24, 1949; children—Anne Elizabeth, Philip Stewart. Asst. reference librarian Dearborn (Mich.) Pub. Library, 1949-51; head librarian Berkley (Mich.) Pub. Library, 1951-57, St. Joseph (Mo.) Pub. Library, 1957-62, Park Ridge (Ill.) Pub. Library, 1962—. Served with C.E., AUS, 1943-46. Mem. ALA, Ill. Library Assn. Lion. Home: 2800 Habberton Ave Park Ridge IL 60068 Office: 515 Touhy Ave Park Ridge IL 60068

WILSON, CHARLES AUGUSTINE, mgmt. cons.; b. N.Y.C., Sept. 12, 1938; s. Charles Augustine and Anne D. (Feddern) W.; B.A., L.I. U., 1960, postgrad. 1960-62; certificate in ins. brokerage, Bklyn. Coll., 1961; certificate in exec. devel., Wabash Coll., 1968; m. Ann Marie Teahan, Sept. 19, 1959; children—Charles Augustine III, James J., Bernadette M., Anne Marie, Michael P., Timothy J. Tchr., officer recreation Bur. Community Edn., N.Y.C., 1958-60; adjuster Hartford Accident and Indemnity, N.Y.C., 1950-61; pres. Kelson Co., N.Y.C., 1961-62; staff cons. Alexander Proudfood Co., Chgo., 1962-63, Anthony B. Cassedy & Assos., Ridgefield, Conn., 1963; engr. Wofac Corp., Moorsetown, N.J., 1963-64, ops. mgr., Fort Wayne, Ind., 1964-65, gen. ops. mgr., 1965—, div. v.p., 1969, v.p. mktg., 1970, div. v.p., 1971, group v.p., 1973-75, sr. v.p., 1975—; chmn. bd. Corson, Inc., Fort Wayne, 1976; pres. Personalized Sportswear, Fort Wayne, 1977—. Dir. Work Factor Assos. Midwest, Chgo., 1975—. Mem. Indsl. Mgmt. Assn., Econ. Soc., Tau Epsilon Phi. K.C. Home: 1416 Woodmoor Dr Fort Wayne IN 46804 Office: 1810 S Anthony Blvd Fort Wayne IN 46803

WILSON, CHARLES STEPHEN, cardiologist; b. Geneva, Nebr., June 14, 1938; s. Robert Butler and Naoma Luella (Norgren) W.; B.A. cum laude, U. Nebr., 1960; M.D., Northwestern U., 1964; m. Linda Stern Walt, Aug. 21, 1960; children—Michael Scott, Amy Lynn, Cynthia Lee. Intern, Fitzsimons Gen. Hosp., Denver, 1964-65; fellow in internal medicine and cardiology Mayo Grad. Sch. Medicine, Rochester, Minn., 1968-72; practice medicine specializing in Cardiology, Lincoln, Nebr., 1972—; attending staff, Bryan Meml. Hosp., Lincoln, 1972—, chmn. cardiology, 1976—; asst. prof. medicine and cardiology, U. Nebr. Med. Center, Omaha; mem. Mayor's Council on Emergency Med. Services, Lincoln, 1974—; med. dir. Lincoln Mobile Heart Team, 1977—. Served as major, M.C., USAR, 1963-68. Diplomate Am. Bd. Internal Medicine, Subspecialty bd. cardiovascular disease, Nat. Bd. Med. Examiners; recipient Gen. Motors Nat. Scholarship, 1956-60, Nat. Found. Med. Scholarship, 1960-64, Mead Johnson scholarship A.C.P., 1968-71. Fellow A.C.P., Am. Coll. Cardiology, Am. Coll. Chest Physicians, Am. Heart Assn.; mem. Am. Coll. Echocardiography, Nebr. Cardiovascular Soc., Nebr. (bd. dirs., 1973-77, pres., 1976-77), Lincoln (bd. dirs., 1972-75, pres., 1974-75) heart assns., Nebr. Med. Assn., Lancaster County Med. Soc., Am. Soc. Internal Medicine, Phi Beta Kappa, Alpha Omega Alpha, Phi Delta Theta (pres. Nebr. Alpha chpt. 1959-60). Congregationalist. Club: Elks Contbr. numerous articles in field; editorial cons. Chest, 1975-76. Home: 1425 Imperial Dr Lincoln NE 68506 Office: 1512 1st National Bank Lincoln NE 68508

WILSON, CHESTER HUMPHREY, geologist; b. Detroit, Sept. 9, 1939; s. Chester H. and Mary E. (Humphrey) W.; M.S., Mich. State U., 1967, Ph.D., 1975; m. Anne Cascaddan, Apr. 26, 1970. Instr., Mott Coll., Flint, Mich., 1967—; dir. geol. studies Omega Inst. Geol. Research, Flint, 1968-77. Registered geologist, Calif. Mem. Am. Geophys. Union, Geol. Soc. Am., Soc. Exploration Geophysicists, Michigan Basin Geol. Soc., Sigma Xi, Phi Kappa Phi, Sigma Gamma Epsilon. Author: Geology of Genesee County, 1972. Home: Box 18 Flushing MI 48433 Office: 1401 E Court St Flint MI 48503

WILSON, CLIFFORD D., JR., mfg. co. exec.; b. Conrad, Iowa, Dec. 25, 1928; s. Clifford D. and Jimma Lou (Nicely) W.; grad. high sch.; m. Maxine Phyllis Buss, Nov. 12, 1950; children—Connie, Denise, Curtis Nancy, Scott. With Ritchie Industries, Inc., Conrad, 1955, exec. v.p., 1970—, dir., 1955—; dir. 1st State Bank, Conrad. Mem. Library Bd., Conrad, 1968—. Bd. dirs. Wilson Found., Judson Coll. Served with AUS, 1951-53. Baptist. Home: 406 S Main St Conrad IA 50621 Office: Conrad IA 50621

WILSON, DAVID DUCE, lawyer, judge; b. West Union, Ohio, Jan. 5, 1932; s. Charles H. and Mary K. (Theis) W.; student Ohio Wesleyan U., 1950-51, Ohio No. U., 1954-59; m. Fern Dee Cooper, Jan. 24, 1951; children—Teresa Wilson, Charles T., Mary J., David D. Admitted to Ohio bar, 1959; gen. practice Wilson, Wilson & Wilson, West Union, 1959—; judge Adams County Ct., 1961—. Dir., officer Farmers Bank, West Union, Adams County Bldg. and Loan, West Union. Active Boy Scouts Am.; v.p. West Union Local Sch. Dist. Bd. Edn., 1960-69. Pres., Adams County Young Republican Club. Served with USCGR, 1951-54. Mem. Am., Ohio bar assns., West Union C. of C. (sec.-treas.). Presbyn. (trustee). Lion. Home: Rural Route 3 West Union OH 45693 Office: 108 E Mulberry West Union OH 45693

WILSON, DAVID JOHN, lawyer; b. Meade, Kans., Apr. 10, 1904; s. James and Cora McGaffin) W.; J.D., U. Kans., 1930; m. Ann L. Fuller, May 8, 1948. Admitted to Kans. bar, 1930, since practiced in Meade. Dir., Kans. Television Corp., Dodge City. Mem. Supreme Ct. Nominating Com., 1959-64. Pres., Meade unit Salvation Army, 1950—. Meade County chmn. Republican party, 1952-54; atty. Meade County, 1931-35. Mem. Am., S.W. Kans. (pres.) bar assns., Bar Assn. State Kans., Order of Coif. Presbyn. Mason. Home: 320 S Blain St Meade KS 67864 Office: 148 N Fowler St Meade KS 67864

WILSON, DON WHITMAN, city ofcl., library adminstr.; b. Clay Center, Kans., Dec. 17, 1942; s. Donald J. and Lois M. (Sutton) W.; A.B., Washburn U., 1963; M.A., U. Cin., 1964, Ph.D. (NDEA fellow), 1972; m. Gayle Lynn Gibson, Aug. 30, 1964; children—Todd Whitman, Jeffrey Scott. Archivist, Kans. State Hist. Soc., Topeka, 1967-69; historian Dwight D. Eisenhower Library, Abilene, Kans., 1969-74, dep. dir., 1974—; commr. City of Abilene, 1977—; instr. of U.S. history Washburn U., Topeka, 1967-69; lectr. in U.S. history Marymount Coll., Salina, Kans., 1974, Kans. State U., 1975. Mem. Abilene Library Bd., 1974—. Recipient Outstanding Performance award Nat. Archives and Records Service, 1977, Gen. Serivces Adminstrn. Pub. Serivce award, 1973. Mem. Kans. State Hist. Soc., Kans. Mus. Assn., Am. Assn. for State and Local History, Kans. History Tchrs. Assn., Abilene Jaycees (pres. 1972), Phi Alpha Theta. Republican. Methodist. Clubs: Elks, Optimist Internat., Abilene Country. Contbr. articles on Am. history to scholarly publs. Home: 615 NW 3d St Abilene KS 67410 Office: Dwight D Eisenhower Library Abilene KS 67401

WILSON, DONALD EDWARD, physician, educator; b. Worcester, Mass., Aug. 28, 1936; s. Rivers Rivo and Licine (Bradshaw) W.; A.B., Harvard U., 1958; M.D., Tufts U., 1962; 1 son, Jeffrey D.E. Intern, St. Elizabeth Hosp., Boston, 1962-63; resident and research fellow in medicine VA Hosp., Lamuel Shattuck Hosp., Boston, 1963-66; asso. chief gastroenterology Bklyn. Hosp., 1968-71; dir. div. gastroenterology U. Ill. Hosp., Chgo., 1971-73, chief of gastroenterology, 1973—, physician-in-chief, 1976—; instr. medicine State U. N.Y. Downstate Med. Center, Blkyn., 1968-71; asst. prof. medicine U. Ill., Chgo., 1971-73, asso. prof., 1973-75, prof., 1975—, acting head dept. medicine, 1976-77; vis. prof. medicine U. London, Kings Coll. Med. Sch., 1977-78. Active Art Inst., Chgo., Chgo. Zool. Soc. Served to capt. M.C., USAF, 1966-68. Recipient Research awards HEW, 1971, 74, John A. Hartford Found., Inc., Distilled Spirits Council of U.S., VA; diplomate Am. Bd. Internal Medicine. Fellow A.C.P.; mem. Am. Gastroenterol. Assn., Am. Fedn. Clin. Research, Central Soc. Clin. Research, Central Research Club, Am. Assn. Study Liver Diseases, Chgo. Soc. Gastroenterology, Digestive Disease Found. Clubs: Harvard (Chgo.), Midwest Gut. Contbr. numerous articles to profl. jours. Home: 20 E Cedar St Chicago IL 60611 Office: 840 S Wood St Chicago IL 60612

WILSON, DONALD LEE, govt. ofcl.; b. Covington, Ky., Sept. 23, 1933; s. Charles and Harriet Eleanor (Vogt) W.; B.S., Asso. in Chem. Engring., U. Cin., 1965; m. Maltha Geraldean Knight, June 26, 1965; 1 dau., Jennifer Lee. Editorial clk. Cin. Post, 1951-56; chem. technician Nat. Lead Co. Ohio, Fernald, 1956-65; formulating chemist Interchem. Corp., Cin., 1965; with EPA., Cin., 1965—, phys. scientist Indsl. Environ. Research Lab., 1973—. Mem. Am. Chem. Soc., Am. Inst. Chem. Engrs. Republican. Contbr. articles to profl. jours. Home: 6724 Menz Ln Cincinnati OH 45238 Office: EPA 5555 Ridge Ave Cincinnati OH 45268

WILSON, DORIS VIVIAN, social worker; b. Pitts., Aug. 20, 1920; d. John W. and I. Roberta (Taylor) Wilson; B.S., Tuskegee Inst., 1942; M.A., Union Theol. Sem. at Columbia, 1946; M.S., Western Res. U., 1964. Program asso. G.F.S. of U.S.A., N.Y.C., 1946-49; nat. student sec. Nat. bd. YWCA, Rocky Mountain, Kan. and So. Atlanta, 1951-59; exec. dir. Univ. YWCA, Los Angeles, 1959-62, asso. exec., 1965-69; exec. dir. YWCA of Met. Chgo., 1969-77. Dir., Wednesdays in Miss. Project, Nat. Council of Negro Women, Jackson, Miss., 1964. Mem. Nat. Assn. Social Workers, Acad. Certified Social Workers. Home: 3001 S King Dr Chicago IL 60616

WILSON, FLOYD W., ins. co. exec.; b. Cedar, Iowa, Oct. 29, 1921; s. John Peter and Elva Bell (Wilson) Funck; student Rockhurst Coll., 1942-43; B.C.S., Am. Inst. Bus., 1948; material damage estimate certificate, Vale Tech. Inst., 1954; student Dale Carnegie, 1954; m. Beverly Rose Yeary, Sept. 22, 1946. Claims adjuster Farm Bur. Mut. Ins. Co., Des Moines, 1948-54, material damage supr., 1954-56; fleet mgr. Farm Bur. Life Ins. Co., Des Moines, 1956—. Served with USAAF, 1942-46. Mem. Nat. Assn. Fleet Adminstrs. (co-organizer, chpt. chmn. Mid-West chpt. 1977—), Phi Theta Phi. Methodist. Mason (Shriner). Home: 5424 SW 20th St Des Moines IA 50315 Office: 5400 University Ave West Des Moines IA 50265

WILSON, FRANCIS SERVIS, JR., securities dealer; b. Chgo., Oct. 7, 1906; s. Francis Servis and Caroline (Seigfried) W.; student Dartmouth Coll., 1925-26; Ph.B., U. Chgo., 1930; m. Kathryn A. Wilson, June 1, 1945; children—Grace E., Francis Servis III, John G., William P., Thomas S. With investment firms, 1930-40; v.p. War Dept., Washington, 1942-43; analyst Standard & Poors Corp., Chgo., 1943-53; chief analyst Bache & Co., Chgo., 1954-63; exec. v.p. Woolard & Co., Chgo., 1963—; dir. McIntosh Corp., Chgo., Dynatech Corp., Boston, Data Disc Corp., Sunnyvale, Calif., CIC Fin. Corp., Chgo., Energy Absorption Systems, Chgo. Mem. Delta Kappa Epsilon. Episcopalian. Clubs: Univ., Tavern, Attic (Chgo.); Chikaming Country (Lakeside, Mich.); Everglades, Bath and Tennis (Palm Beach, Fla.). Home: 199 E Lake Shore Dr Chicago IL 60611 Office: 135 S La Salle St Chicago IL 60603

WILSON, GEORGE MCCONNELL, religious orgn. exec.; b. Churchs Ferry, N.D., Oct. 19, 1913; s. Clarence McNair and Mary Belle (McConnell) W.; grad. Northwestern Coll., Mpls., 1936; Litt.D. (hon.), Houghton (N.Y.) Coll., 1962; LL.D., Gordon Coll., Wenham, Mass., 1969; m. Helen Josephine Bjorck, Sept. 3, 1940; children—Jean Elizabeth (Mrs. Ralph Bertram Greener), Judith (Mrs. Larry Grimes), Janet (Mrs. Steve Hanks). Owner Wilson Press, also Northwestern Book and Bible House, 1940-49; asst. to pres. Northwestern Coll., also mng. editor N.W. Pilot Mag., bus. mgr. Northwestern Coll., 1947-50; bus. mgr. Billy Graham Evangelistic Assn., 1950—, sec.-treas., 1950-62, exec. v.p., treas., 1962-69, exec. v.p., 1969—; mng. editor Decision mag., 1960—; sec.-treas., dir. World Wide Pictures, Hollywood, Calif.; sec.-treas. Blue Ridge Broadcasting Corp., Black Mountain, N.C.; v.p., dir. Christian Broadcasting Assn., Honolulu; sec.-treas., bd. dirs. Billy Graham Evangelistic Assn. Ltd., London, Eng., sec.-treas. The Hour of Decision, Sydney, Australia and Paris, France; dir. Global Concern, Mpls. Bank and Trust Co., 1967—; pres. World Wide Publs., Grason Co. Founder, dir. Mpls. Youth for Christ, 1944-54; sec., dir. Youth for Christ Internat., 1944-49; bd. dirs. Goodwill Industries Mpls., 1973—. Recipient Direct Mail award, 1973. Mem. Direct Mailers Assn., Nat. Religious Publicity Council, Nat. Assn. Evangelicals (named layman of year 1969). Nat. Soc. Fund raisers. Baptist. Kiwanian (past pres., past sec. Mpls.). Clubs: Minneapolis Athletic (Mpls.); Minn. Press; Six O'Clock; Decathlon. Author: Words of Wisdom, 20 Years Under God. Home: 3113 Humboldt Ave S Minneapolis MN 55408 Office: 1300 Harmon Pl Minneapolis MN 55403

WILSON, GEORGE PICKET, JR., educator; b. Nelson, Va., July 14, 1918; s. George Picket and Helen (Leeson) W.; M.A., U. N.C., 1941; Ph.D., Columbia U., 1958; m. Margaret Fordham, Dec. 19, 1942; children—Anne, George, Edeard, Robert, Thomas, Patsy, James. Ednl. dir. WBIG, Greensboro, N.C., 1941-42; dir. radio La Poly. Inst., Ruston, 1942-45; chmn. dept. speech and drama U. Va., Charlottesville, 1958-61, dir. radio TV film div. extension, 1961-62; dir. telecommunicative arts Iowa State U., Ames, 1962—, prof., 1962—; chmn. adv. com. programming and gen. policy for Iowa Ednl. Broadcasting Network, 1976-77. Pres., Venable PTA, 1959-60, 60-61, Charlottesville. Mem. Speech Communication Assn., Broadcast Edn. Assn., Univ. Film Assn., Nat. Assn. Broadcasters, Soc. Motion Picture TV Engrs., Central States Speech Assn., AAUP, Phi Kappa Phi. Clubs: Actors, Playmakers. Editor Newsletter Nat. Assn. Ednl. Broadcasters, 1974-77. Home: 135 Hazel St N Ames IA 50010 Office: Exhibit Hall Iowa State Univ Ames IA 50011

WILSON, GEORGE PORTER, III, veterinarian, educator; b. Flint, Mich., Nov. 10, 1927; s. George Porter and Eva Harris (Spencer) W.; B.S., U. Ill., 1951; V.M.D., (Phi Zeta scholar), U. Pa., 1955; M.S., Ohio State U., 1959; children—George Anderson, Todd Spencer, Amy Patricia, Laurie Beth. Intern Angell Mem. Animal Hosp., 1955-56; instr. Coll. Vet. Medicine, Ohio State U., 1956-60, asst. prof., 1960-63, asso. prof., 1963-69, prof., 1969—, also asso. prof. Coll. Biol. Scis., Dept. Microbiology, 1967—, chmn. Coll. Curriculum Residency, 1968—, chmn. grad. com. Vet. Clin. Scis. Dept., 1968—; vis. scientist epidemiology div. Nat. Cancer Inst., 1978. Served with USN, 1945-46. Mem. AVMA, Am. Coll. Vet. Surgeons, Ohio Vet. Med. Assn., AAAS, Acad. Sci., Sigma Psi, Phi Zeta, Omega Tau Sigma. Episcopalian (vestryman 1967-69). Contbr. articles to profl. jours. Home: Veterinary Clinical Sciences Ohio State University 1935 Coffey Rd Columbus OH 43210

WILSON, HARRY HOWARD, JR., ednl. products co. exec.; b. Blue Island, Ill., Dec. 30, 1926; s. Harry H. and Kathryn Anne (Nicola) W.; B.S., Western Ill. U., 1950; m. Doris Ann Flanary, July 6, 1948; children—Kimberly, Kyle Ann, Kacy. Radio sportscaster WKAI, Macomb, Ill., 1948-50; with Container Corp. Am., Chgo., 1950-52; sales mgr. audio-visual and photog. products Radiant Mfg. Corp., Chgo., 1952-59; pres. H. Wilson Corp., mfg. ednl. audiovisual-products, pub. ednl. materials, South Holland, Ill., 1959—; dir. James Metal Products, Chgo. Served with AUS, 1946-47. Mem. Dept. Audio-Visual Instrn., Nat. Audio-Visual Assn. (dir. 1966, chmn. S/S/mgmt. inst.), Nat. Sch. Supply Assn. (dir. 1966-68, exec. com. 1967-68), Am. Soc. Curriculum DIrs., Phi Delta Kappa, Sigma Tau Gamma. Club: Chicago Heights (Ill.) Country. Patentee in field. Home: 651 E Steger Rd Chicago Heights IL 60411 Office: 555 Taft St South Holland IL 60473

WILSON, JACKIE BYRON, telephone co. exec.; b. Houston, Jan. 7, 1952; s. Artie and Eva Jeanette Wilson; B.S., Prairie View A. and M. Coll., 1974; M.S., Stanford U., 1976; m. Mary Catherine Washington, June 19, 1976. With Exxon Corp., Houston, 1970-73; elec. engr. tech. staff Bell Telephone Lab., Naperville, Ill., 1974—. Rockwell scholar, 1972-74; C.J. Wrightman fellow, 1973-74. Mem. IEEE, Soc. Black Scientists and Engrs., NAACP, Tau Beta Pi, Pi Mu Epsilon, Eta Kappa Nu, Phi Beta Sigma. Baptist. Home: Apt 3A 4675 Lake Trail Dr Lisle IL 60532 Office: Room 2A-231 Warrenville-Naperville Rd Naperville IL 60540

WILSON, JAMES ROBERT, pediatrician; b. Silver Creek, N.Y., Aug. 1, 1897; b. Henry Davidson and Cora E.M.(Thompson) W.; B.S., Syracuse U., 1922, M.D., 1921; m. Anna May Caldwell, June 29, 1929; children—Robert C., Janet B., Virginia C., Yribia. Margaret E. Koeller. Intern, Syracuse U., 1922; resident in pediatric pathology, Harvard U., 1922-23, resident in pathology, 1923-24; instr. pediatrics Cornell U., 1924-29; asso. prof. pediatrics Syracuse (N.Y.) U., 1929-46; exec. sec. Council on Foods and Nutrition AMA, Chgo., 1946-57; cons. to food processors, Winnetka, Ill., 1957-66; med. dir. Colo. State Home and Tng. Sch., Grand Junction, Colo., 1967-70; dir. pub. health Mesa County, Colo., 1970-73; clin. asso., pediatrics So. Ill. U., Springfield, 1973—; cons. in field: individual practice medicine, specializing in pediatrics Springfield, 1978—; vis. prof. pediatrics Mass. Inst. Tech., 1949-51, Columbia U., 1951—. Bd. dirs. Food Law Inst., 1948-54; mem. Food and Nutrition Research Adv. Bd. U.S. Dept. Agr., 1959-61. Served as pvt., U.S. Army, 1918. Recipient Pub. Service award City of Syracuse, 1946, Mayor Daley's Hall of Fame award Chgo., 1963. Diplomate Am. Bd. Pediatrics, Am. Bd. Human Nutrition. Mem. Soc. Pediatric Research (founding), Inst. Nutrition, Am. Acad. Pediatrics, Inst. Food Technologists, AMA, Nat. Rehab. Assn., Sigma Xi, Alpha Omega Alpha, Phi Kappa Phi. Presbyterian. Contbr. articles to profl. publs.; pioneered pathological description vitamin A deficiency disease, 1923. Home: Apt 101 W Canedy St Springfield IL 62704 Office: State Office Bldg 1st and Washington Sts Springfield IL 62701

WILSON, JOHN CLARK, organist; b. East Liverpool, Ohio, May 19, 1957; s. John Richard and Donna Jean (Richards) W.; grad. high sch. Organist, Anderson and Orchard Grove Ch., East Liverpool, 1973-76; asst. organist First United Meth. Ch., East Liverpool, 1971—; builder pipe organs Schantz Organ Co., Orrville. Mem. Am. Theatre Organ Soc., Thespian Internat., Key Club Internat. Republican. Methodist. Home: 1029 Ambrose Ave East Liverpool OH 43920 Office: 311 S Main St Orrville OH 44667

WILSON, JOHN DAVID, physician; b. Evansville, Ind., Nov. 24, 1922; s. Noble Lincoln and Mary Kathryn (Levi) W.; A.B., Ind. U., 1943, M.D., 1945; m. Mary Bernadine Fuchs, May 5, 1943; children—John David, Mary Kathryn (Mrs. Robert Andersen), Brian Henry, Lynn Bernadine. Intern San Diego (Cal.) Naval Hosp., 1945-46; resident Deaconess Hosp., Evansville, Ind., 1948-49; practice of medicine, Evansville, 1949—; mem. staffs Deaconess Hosp., Evansville, St. Mary's Hosp., Evansville. Pres. Evansville (Ind.) Med. Arts Bldg., 1963-67, dir., 1955—. Active Boy Scouts Am. Bd. dirs. Vanderburgh County Cancer Soc., Vanderburgh County Rehab. Center, Evansville; mem. alumni council Ind. U. Med. Sch. Served with USNR, 1945-48. Diplomate Am. Bd. Family Practice. Mem. Am., Ind. (pres. 1966-67) acads. family physicians, AMA, Ind. State Med. Assn., Vanderburgh County Med. Soc. (pres. 1970-71), Nu Sigma Nu, Alpha Phi Omega, Delta Upsilon. Republican. Methodist. Club: Evansville Country. Home: 921 Colony Rd Evansville IN 47715 Office: 3700 Bellemeade St Evansville IN 47715

WILSON, (JOHN) ROGER, physiol. psychologist; b. Boone, Iowa, Feb. 1, 1944; s. John Raymond and Marjorie Theola (Hiatt) W.; M.S., Kans. State U., 1969; Ph.D., Kent State U., 1973; m. Linda Gail Morrissey, Sept. 14, 1969. NIH predoctoral trainee Kans. State U., Manhattan, 1966-69; predoctoral fellow in psychology Kent (Ohio) State U., 1969-72; NIMH postdoctoral fellow in neurosci. U. Mich.

Med. Sch., Ann Arbor, 1972-74, advanced research asso. in psychiatry, 1974-77; asst. prof. psychology U. Man. (Can.), Winnipeg, 1977—. Mem. Neurosci. Soc., Am. Physiol. Soc., AAAS, Am., Midwestern psychol. assns., Psychophysiol. Research Soc., Sigma Xi, Psi Chi. Contbr. articles to profl. jours. Research on brain mechanisms in hypertension, stress, thermoregulation. Office: Dept Psychology U Manitoba Winnipeg MB R3T 2N2 Canada

WILSON, JOHN TODD, univ. pres.; b. Punxsutawney, Pa., Mar. 7, 1914; s. Clark Hayes and Alice (Haire) W.; A.B. with distinction, George Washington U., 1941; M.A., State U. Iowa, 1942; Ph.D., Stanford, 1948; m. Ann B. Camilli, Nov. 23, 1939. Asst. exec. sec. Am. Psychol. Assn., 1948-49; asst. prof. psychology George Washington U., 1949; head personnel and tng. res. br. Office Naval Research, 1949-52; program dir. for psychology NSF, 1952-55, asst. dir. for biol. and med. sci., 1955-61; prof. psychology U. Chgo., 1961—, spl. asst. to pres., 1961-63, v.p., dean faculties, 1968-69, provost, 1969-75, provost, acting pres., 1975, pres., 1975—. Served from ensign to lt. comdr. USNR, 1942-46. Mem. AAAS, Phi Beta Kappa, Sigma Xi. Home: 5555 S Everett Ave Chicago IL 60637

WILSON, KEITH, JR., lawyer; b. Independence, Mo., Mar. 3, 1928; s. Keith and Elizabeth (Baxter) W.; B.A., U. Kans., 1949, LL.B., 1951; m. Yvonne Camille Josserand, June 30, 1951; 1 dau., Leslie Yvonne. Admitted to Mo. bar, 1951, Kans. bar, 1951, also U.S. bars; practiced in Kansas City, Mo., 1951—, Independence, 1955—; asso. firm Stinson, Mag. Thomson, McEvers & Fizzell, Kansas City, 1951-54; prin. firm Keith Wilson and Assos. and predecessor firms, Independence, 1955-67; city mgr. of Independence, 1967-68; spl. city counselor, Independence, 1967—; lectr. U. Kans. Sch. Law, Lawrence, 1953. Pres. P. B. Wilson, Inc., Independence, 1953—; vice pres. Burlington Mfg. Co., 1965-72; v.p., sec. Luzier, Inc., 1977—. Founding dir. Big Bros. of Greater Kansas City, Inc. Election Commr., Jackson County, Mo., 1954-60; asst. atty. gen. State Mo., 1961; city counselor, Kansas City, Mo., 1961-63; commr. Jackson County Redevel. Authority, 1976—. Bd. dirs. Jackson County Hist. Soc., Starlight Theatre Assn. Trustee Kansas City Coll. Osteo. Medicine. Served to maj., inf. AUS, 1949-55. Mem. Mil. Order World Wars, Am. Kansas City, Independence bar assns., Lawyer's Assn. Kansas City. Internat. City Mgrs. Assn., Nat. Municipal League, Nat. Inst. Municipal Law Officers (v.p. 1962-64, chmn. com. on civil liberties), Phi Gamma Delta Alumni Assn. (pres.), Phi Gamma Delta, Omicron Delta Kappa, Phi Delta Phi, Delta Sigma Rho. Mason (32 deg., K.T., Shriner, Jester). Clubs: Carriage, Kansas City. Author: Search and Seizure, 1951; Whither Weather, 1951; The Origin of the Antitrust Cause of Action, 1953; also articles law jours. Home: 1215 W 63d St Terr Kansas City MO 64113 Office: Chrisman-Sawyer Bank Bldg Independence MO 64050

WILSON, LAWRENCE FRANCIS, cons. engr.; b. Delbarton, W.Va., May 21, 1933; s. John Henry and Crete (Thompson) W.; B.C.E., Ohio State U., 1960; postgrad. Toledo U., 1961-62; m. Mary June Salmons, Dec. 20, 1952; children—Gerald Anthony, Timothy Dean, Teresa Diane. Rodman Norfolk & Western Ry. Co., Williamson, W.Va. and Portsmouth, Ohio, 1951-53, 55-56; furnace engr. LOF Co., Toledo Tech. Center, 1960-65; mfg. engr. Permaglass Co., Woodville, Ohio, 1965-68; pvt. practice cons. engr., Oregon, Ohio, 1968-75; chief engr. Toledo Testing Lab., 1970-72; v.p. engring., Tryco Steel Corp., Novi, Mich., 1974—; pres., chief exec. officer Lawrence F. Wilson Assos., Inc., Oregon, 1975—, Product Analysis & Structural Testing, Inc., 1976—; pres. Product Analysis & Structural Testing Inc., Oregon and Luling, La., 1976—. Served with Signal Corps, U.S. Army, 1953-55. Registered profl. engr., Ohio, W.Va., Pa., Mich., La., S.D., Ind. Mem. ASCE, Nat., Ohio socs. profl. engrs. Republican. Baptist. Club: East Toledo. Patentee device for drawing sheet glass. Home and office: 3504 Worden Rd Oregon OH 43616

WILSON, MALCOLM AARON, state ofcl.; b. Manhattan, Kans., June 30, 1932; s. Charley James and Alys Emaline (Scofield) W.; B.S., Kans. State U., 1953. News editor Rush County News, La Crosse, Kans., 1953-54; placement officer Kans. Employment Service, Manhattan, 1954-56; pub. relations dir. Employment Security Div., Kan. Dept. Labor, Topeka, 1956-60; asst. sec. state for elections and legislative matters State of Kans., Topeka, 1960-66; asst. sec. State of Kans., Topeka, 1966-70; dir. legislative reference State of Kans., 1970—. Cons. election com. Kans. legislature, 1961-70. Bd. dirs. Kans. Heart Assn., Sec., 1971—. Mem. Kans. Assn. Pub. Employees (dir. 1963-66), Am. Soc. for Pub. Adminstrn., Internat. Assn. Employees in Employment Security, Sigma Delta Chi. Home: 105 N Courtland St Topeka KS 66612 Office: State House Topeka KS 66612

WILSON, MARY CARTER, guidance counselor; b. St. Louis, May 5, 1917; d. Hannibal Cleveland and Rose Belle (Cooper) Carter; A.B., Harris-Stowe Coll., 1937; M.A., Washington U., 1960; m. Albert Wayne Wilson, June 25, 1943 (dec.); 1 dau., Marilyn Wilson Hayes. Tchr., St. Louis Bd. Edn., 1938-44, 48-61, guidance counselor Turner Middle Sch., 1961—; coordinator, cons. scholarship program to Eastern and St. Louis County prep. schs., 1963—. Mem. Am., St. Louis personnel and guidance assns., Am. Sch. Counselors Assn., Mo. St. Louis guidance assns., Pupil Personnel Services Assn., Delta Sigma Theta, Kappa Delta Pi. Roman Catholic. Established first guidance dept. in St. Louis elementary schools, 1961. Home: 5220 Lexington Ave St Louis MO 63115 Office: Turner Middle Sch 2615 Pendleton Ave St Louis MO 63113

WILSON, MYRON ROBERT, JR., psychiatrist; b. Helena, Mont., Sept. 21, 1932; s. Myron Robert and Constance (Bultman) W.; B.A. in Humanities, Stanford U., 1954, M.D., 1957. Rotating intern U. Wis. Hosps., Madison, 1957-58; fellow Grad. Sch. Medicine, Mayo Clinic, Rochester, Minn., 1960-65, cons. psychiatry, 1965-72; prof. psychiatry Carleton Coll., Northfield, Minn., 1970; pres., psychiatrist-in-chief Constance Bultman Wilson Center Edn. and Psychiatry, Faribault, Minn., 1971—; attending staff Rice County Dist. I Hosp., Faribault; courtsey staff United Hosps., St. Paul; prof., cons. psychiatry Antioch Coll., Yellow Springs, Ohio. Served with M.C., USNR, 1958-60. Diplomate Am. Bd. Psychiatry and Neurology. Mem. Am. Psychiat. Assn., Am. Soc. Adolescent Psychiatry, Am. Coll. Health Assn., Pan Am., Minn., Zumbro Valley med. assns., Am. Acad. Med. Dirs., N.Y. Acad. Scis., Minn. Psychiat. Soc., St. Paul Soc. Psychiatry and Neurology, S.A.R., Sigma Xi. Episcopalian. Contbr. med. jours. Address: Box 917 Faribault MN 55021

WILSON, NEIL BRYAN, food co. exec.; b. Chgo., May 12, 1932; s. Ellis D. and Rose (Friedman) W.; B.S., La. Poly. Inst., 1954; M.S., U. Mo., 1956; m. Marlene Seeley, Jan. 22, 1956; children—Diane, Kenneth, Kurtis. Instr., U. Mo., 1954-55; marketing services mgr. Rath Packing Co., Waterloo, Iowa, 1956-63; mgr. new food products Archer Daniels Midland Co., Mpls., 1963-64; various marketing Libby, McNeill & Libby, Chgo., 1964-68, v.p., 1968-73; v.p. Stokely Van Camp, Inc., Indpls., 1973—. Mem. Am. Marketing Assn., Am. Mgmt. Assn. Clubs: Chicago Athletic., Executive, University, Ind. Athletic, Econs. Home: 7630 Cape Cod Circle Indianapolis IN 46250 Office: 941 N Meridian Indianapolis IN 46206

WILSON, NOEL AVON, educator; b. Weiser, Idaho, Feb. 10, 1914; s. William T. and Winifred Mae (Cutright) W.; B.A., U. Idaho, 1938; M.A., U. Mo., 1960; Ph.D., U. Ill., 1968; m. Geraldine Vaughan Pope, Aug. 15, 1965; children—Linda Ellen Stevenson. Free lance writer, editor, mgr. weekly and sml. daily newspapers, Idaho, Mont., Wyo., Colo., 1938-41, 46-56; instr. Tex. So. U., Houston, 1958-60, asst. prof., head dept. journalism, 1960-66; instr. dept. journalism Lincoln U., Jefferson City, Mo., 1956-58, asst. prof., 1966-68, asso. prof., 1968—. Served with inf., AUS, 1941-46. Mem. Am. Acad. Advt., Assn. Edn. in Journalism, AAUP, Mo. Polit. Sci. Assn., Sigma Delta Chi (nat. profl. devel. com. 1973—). Methodist. Author: The Urbanization of Man, 1972; Say It with Pictures, 1972; A Journalists Guide to Graphic Design and Planning, 1975. Home: 1311 Kolb Dr Jefferson City MO 65101

WILSON, PENTON JEAN, osteo. physician and surgeon; b. Swainsboro, Ga., Nov. 29, 1915; s. Penton W. and Rosalie (Bell) W.; student N. Ga. Coll., 1934-36, Emory U., 1938, U. Ga., 1937; D.P., Kansas City Coll. Osteopathy and Surgery, 1942; m. Bonnie Dean Riddle, Nov. 6, 1954. Intern Conley Clin. Hosp., 1941; resident pediatrics Gibson Hosp., Kansas City, 1952-53; practice medicine, Linneus, Mo., and Eminence, Mo.; county physician, health officer Linn County (Mo.), 1952-59; county physician, health officer, coroner Shannon County (Mo.), 1964—. Recipient Eagle Scout award Boy Scouts Am., 1930. Mem. Alpha Phi Omega. Address: Hwy 206-West Eminence MO 65466

WILSON, QUENTIN CHALMER, optometrist; b. Eldorado, Ill., Sept. 30, 1919; s. George F. and M. Aileen (Goldman) W.; student So. Ill. U., 1936-39; D.Optometry, Ill. Coll. Optometry, 1941, D.Optometric Sci., 1942; m. E. Louise Wallace, Jan. 27, 1944; children—George Q., Nancy Lou, Chloe Ann. Pvt. practice optometry, Eldorado, 1946—; optometrist Ill. Eye and Ear Infirmary, So. Ill. Clinics, 1951-64. Chief, Fire Dept., Eldorado, 1952—; dir. Civil Def., Eldorado, 1963—; mem. Eldorado-Raleigh Park Bd., 1964—. Served with AUS, 1943-46. Mem. Ill. Optometric Assn. (exec. council 1954-59), So. Ill. Optometric Soc. (pres. 1960), C. of C. (pres. 1961, 70-72), V.F.W. (post comdr. 1947). Baptist. Mason, Elk, Rotarian. Home: 1113 3d St Eldorado IL 62930 Office: 1420 Locust St Eldorado IL 62930

WILSON, REX HAMILTON, physician; b. Hendrysburg, Ohio, Aug. 22, 1909; s. Harvey Hoyt and Margaret Maude (Hamilton) W.; A.B., Ohio Wesleyan, 1931; M.D., Ohio State U., 1935; m. Maribel McDaniel, Apr. 11, 1936; 1 son, Peter McDaniel. Intern Presbyn. Hosp., Chgo., 1935-36, resident in medicine, 1936-37; pvt. practice internal medicine, Akron, O., 1937-42; cons. medicine Goodyear Tire & Rubber Co., 1938-42; med. dir., v.p. The B. F. Goodrich Co., 1946-75; bd. dirs., v.p., med. dir. Summit Nat. Life Ins. Co.; past chmn. utilization com., sr. staff medicine Akron City Hosp.; staff Children's St. Thomas hosps., Akron; mem. hon. med. staff Akron Gen. Hosp.; mem. Summit Portage County Comprehensive Health Planning Agy.; mem. environmental health com. Ohio Comprehensive Health Planning Agy. Speaker 11th Internat. Congress Indsl. Medicine, Naples, 1954. Former v.p., trustee, mem. exec. com. United Found. of Akron, Inc.; mem. adv. com. Arthritis and Rheumatism Found. of Akron; founder, trustee, past pres. Rehab. Center, Summit Co.; med. com. Chlorine Inst.; mem. Com. Workmen's Compensation-Ohio State Med. Served as major, M.C., AUS, 1942-46, PTO, 1945-46. Troop counselor Boy Scouts Am. Past chmn. health com., rubber sect., mem. exec. and adv. coms. Nat. Safety Council; mem. pres. com. on safety. Recipient citation for excellence in med. authorship Am. Assn. Indsl. Physicians and Surgeons, 1948. Diplomate Am. Bd. Internal Medicine, Am. Bd. Preventive Medicine (founders group occupational medicine). Fellow Am. Coll. Preventive Medicine, A.M.A., A.C.P., Am. Acad. Occupational Medicine, Assn. Mil. Surgeons U.S., Indsl. Med. Assn. (dir. 1955-57); mem. Indsl. Med. Assn., World Med. Assn., Internat. Congress Indsl. Medicine (past pres. Pitts.), Akron Internat. Med. Soc. (past pres.), Nat. Med. Dirs. Forum, Aerospace Med. Assn., Pan Am. Med. Assn., Am. Rheumatism Assn., Am. Medical Writers Assn., Nat. Air Pollution Control Assn., Nat. Rehab. Assn., Am. Assn. Physicians and Surgeons, Med. Round Table, Ramazzini, Ohio Med. Assn. (ex-chmn. sect. indsl. medicine; chmn. com. environmental and pub. health), Summit County Med. Soc. (chmn. hosp. laision com.), Rubber Mfrs. Assn. (chmn. environmental health com.), Am. Soc. Internal Medicine, Phi Rho Sigma, Alpha Tau Omega. Methodist. Mason (32 deg.). Clubs: Rotary (past pres.), Portage Country. Former asso. editor Indsl. Medicine and Surgery, Jour. of Occupational Medicine, (column) Tips to Better Health. Contbr. articles to profl. journals Speaker before med. orgns. Home: 401 Inverness Rd Akron OH 44313

WILSON, RICHARD FORREST, instrument co. exec.; b. Fort Wayne, Ind., Sept. 9, 1931; s. Forrest Frazier and Helen Hazel (Miller) W.; B.S., Butler U., 1955; m. Patricia A. Mc Comb, Oct. 22, 1959; children—Peter C., Sarah E. With Honeywell Co., 1957-62; pres. Pyromation Inc., Fort Wayne, Ind., 1962—; v.p. W.C. Grant Co., Ft. Wayne, Ind., 1967-76. Pres., Aboite Township Assn., 1969-70; mem. parent's bd. S.W. Allen County Schs. Served with U.S. Army, 1955-57. Mem. Instrument Soc. Am., Am. Soc. Metals, Fortnightly Hist. Soc. Republican. Clubs: Summit, Tennis. Home: 4225 W Hamilton Rd Fort Wayne IN 46804 Office: 5211 Industrial Rd Fort Wayne IN 46804

WILSON, ROBERT WOOD, newspaper publisher; b. Centerville, Iowa, Mar. 29, 1935; s. Robert McClary and Bertha Belle (Wood) W.; B.S. in Bus. Adminstrn., U. Mo., Columbia, 1959; m. Marilyn K. McMillan, July 2, 1976; 1 dau., Kimberly Ann. With Milan (Mo.) Standard, 1959—, editor, publisher, 1964—; publisher Green City (Mo.) Press, 1966—; co-pub. Marceline (Mo.) Press, 1968-77; pres. Wilson Pub. Co.; sec. bd. Modern Devel. Co. Chmn., Milan Planning Commn.; sec. bd. Sullivan County (Mo.) Indsl. Corp. Mem. NE Mo. Press Assn. (pres.). Home: 431 E 2d St Milan MO 63556 Office: 105 S Market St Milan MO 63556

WILSON, SLOAN JACOB, physician; b. Dallas, Jan. 22, 1910; s. Jacob Resor and Estella (Cherrie) W.; A.B., U. Wichita, 1931, M.S., 1932; B.S. In Medicine, U. Kans., 1934, M.D., 1936; m. M. June Bowles, June 14, 1959; children—Sloan Richard, Charles Rook, Nancy Joan, Mark Samuel. Intern Ohio State U. Hosp., Columbus, 1936-37, resident, 1937-40; practice medicine specializing in internal medicine 1940—; instr. U. Wichita, 1933-34; Ohio State U., 1940; asst. prof. medicine U. Kans., 1946-53, asso. prof., 1954-61, prof., 1962—, chief exec. officer, dept. medicine, treas. Med. Assn. Chartered, 1962—; trustee Mutrusco, 1968-71; cons. in field.; bd. dirs. Community Blood Bank Greater Kans City (Kans.), 1956-59. Mem. Friends of Art, Nelson Gallery of Art, Kansas City, Kans. Served to lt. col. M.C. U.S. Army, 1940-46. Named hon. curator Japanese Art, U. Kans.; recipient Distinguished Service award, dept. medicine, 1976. Diplomate Am. Bd. Internal Medicine. Fellow A.C.P. (gov. Kans., nat. bd. govs. 1964-70), Central Soc. for Clin. Research, N.Y. Acad. Sci., Fin. Analysts Fedn., Kansas City Soc. Fin. Analysts, Japan Am. Soc., SAR, Delta Tau Delta, Phi Beta Pi. Presbyterian. Clubs: Homestead Country, Masons. Author: Public Participation in the Stock Market, 1962; The Speculator and the Stock Market, 1962; Introduction to Stock Market Credit Analysis, 1965, Borrowed Money and Stock Market Trends, 1975; Hematology, Basic Rev., 1975; Hematology, Advanced, Rev., 1975; Hematology, Pediatric, Rev., 1975; contbr. articles to profl. jours. Home: 5618 W 62d St Shawnee Mission KS 66202 Office: 39th & Rainbow Blvd Kansas City KS 66103

WILSON, SLOAN RICHARD, lawyer; b. Columbus, Ohio, Oct. 2, 1939; s. Sloan Jacob and Edna Eleanora (Ora) W.; B.A., Baker U., 1962; J.D., Boston U., 1965; m. Carolyn Kay Leeper, June 20, 1969. Admitted to Mo. bar, 1965, U.S. Dist. Ct. for Western Dist. Mo. bar, 1965, U.S. Ct. Appeals for 8th and 10th Circuit bars, 1974, U.S. Supreme Ct. bar, 1974; atty., criminal div. Legal Aid and Defender Soc. Kansas City, 1965-67; fellow forensic psychiatry Mo. Div. Mental Diseases, Western Mo. Mental Health Center, Kansas City, 1967-68; partner Collet & Wilson, Kansas City, Mo., 1968-72; individual practice, Kansas City, 1972-73; partner firm Hill, McMullin & Wilson, Kansas City, 1973-75, McMullin, Wilson & Schwarz, 1975—. Mem. Am. (natural resources sect. 1970-73, gen. practice sect. 1970-73, criminal law sect. 1973—, ins. sect. 1973—), Mo. (internat. relations com. 1967-68, eminent domain com. 1969-72), Kansas City (pre-paid legal services com. 1975) bar assns., Am. Judicature Soc., ACLU (dir. Western Mo. 1971-72), SAR. Home: 2101 W 50th St Shawnee Mission KS 66205 Office: 1125 Grand Av Suite 1510 Kansas City MO 64106

WILSON, TERRY C., lumber co. exec.; b. Little Falls, N.Y., Sept. 4, 1947; s. Charles A. and Shirley Mae (Crocker) W.; B.B.A., U. Miami, Coral Gables, Fla., 1971; M.A., U. South Fla., 1973; Ph.D., Mich. State U., 1976. Asst. prof. mktg. Mich. State U., East Lansing, 1973-76, Central Mich. U., Mt. Pleasant, 1976-77; dir. mktg. research Wickes Lumber Co., Saginaw, Mich., 1977—. Mem. Am. Mktg. Assn., Mt. Pleasant C. of C. Office: 515 Washington St N Saginaw MI 48607

WILSON, THOMAS BURRELL, welder mfg. co. exec.; b. Milw., May 16, 1920; s. John Crosier and Helen Lovisa (Stone) W.; student Cornell U., 1941; m. Virginia Gray Campbell, May 27, 1950; children—Bruce, Elizabeth, John, Steve. Sales trainee Kearney & Trecker Corp., 1941-42; with Acro Welder Mfg. Co., Milw., 1946—, v.p. sales, sec., 1965-77, pres., 1977—. Mem. Whitefish Bay Village Plan Commn., 1972-75; v.p. Glendale Bus. Council, 1973-75, pres., 1975-77. Served with USAF, 1942-46. Mem. Am. Welding Soc. (dir. Milw. sect., 1962-65). Episcopalian. Clubs: The Town (bd. dirs. 1970—, v.p. 1976-77), Cornell of Milwaukee (pres. 1950-53). Home: 6135 N Bay Ridge Ave Milwaukee WI 53217 Office: 2900 W Green Tree Rd Milwaukee WI 53209

WILSON, WILLIAM FALCONER, econ. devel. exec.; b. Broxbourne, Eng., May 25, 1911; s. George and Jean (Robertson) W.; B.S., Washington U., 1950; m. Betty Anne Wilson, Aug. 13, 1949; children—Pamela Gail, Penelope Anne, Peter Craig, Victoria Lynn, Valerie Sue. Salesman, Wilson Shops, St. Louis, 1928-40; supervising engr. City of University City, Mo., 1952-54; city mgr. Vassar, Mich., 1954-60, Buchanan, Mich., 1960-63; exec. mgr. Operation Action-Upper Peninsula, Marquette, Mich., 1963-75; officer, dir. Solartran Corp.; dir., sec. Upper Gt. Lakes Timber, Inc., Marquette, 1968-73; dir. Am. Timber Homes, Inc., Escanaba, Mich. Mem. Mich. Gov.'s Adv. Task Force to Upper Gt. Lakes Regional Commn., 1967-72; mem. adv. council Mich. dist. SBA, 1971—; city commr. Marquette, 1977—. Mem. Marquette City Charter Commn.; chmn. Marquette Transit Authority, 1973. Served with AUS, 1944-46, 50-52. Mem. Mich. Profl. Indsl. Devel. Assn., Mich. Muncipal League (mem. legislative com. 1957-63), Internat. City Mgrs. Assn. (v.p. Mich. chpt. 1959-60), Mich. Soc. Planning Ofcls., Soc. Indsl. Archeology, Mich. Forest Assn., Newcomen Soc. N.Am. Presbyterian (elder). Club: Rotary. Home: 501 E Arch St Marquette MI 49855

WILSON, WILLIAM VICTOR, appliance mfg. exec.; b. N.Y.C., Oct. 16, 1912; s. Maurice and Caroline (Wissemann) W.; B.S. in Electrical Engring., N.Y. U., 1936; m. Mary Rose Vinci, May 16, 1942; children—Carolyn (Mrs. Carl J. Johnson), Victor W. Guide Elec. & Gas Assn., N.Y.C., 1936-39; various positions Ordnance Dept. U.S. War Dept., 1940-43; asst. chief buyer Remington Arms Co., Bridgeport, Conn., 1943-44, Denver, 1944-45; with The Maytag Co., Newton, Iowa, 1946—, dir. purchases, 1968—. Recipient Silver Beaver award Boy Scouts Am., 1960. Mem. Purchasing Mgrs. of Central Iowa (pres. 1966-67). Elk. Address: 518 E 2d St South Newton IA 50208

WILT, WILLIAM LEWIS, accountant; b. Shelbina, Mo., Jan. 5, 1928; s. Lewis Craig and Willa Mae (Heathman) W.; B.S., U. Mo., 1956, postgrad. 1956; m. Mary Elizabeth Taylor, Sept. 23, 1951; children—Ann Renee, Sandra Kay. Traveling sec. to gen. mgr. CB&Q R.R., 1948-51; staff auditor Arthur Young & Co., Kansas City, Mo., 1956-59; with Wilt & Garrison, pub. accountants, Brookfield, Mo., 1959—, sr. partner, 1963—. Dir., treas. Brookfield Land Corp., 1969—. Treas. A.R.C., Brookfield, 1959-65; auditor Boy Scouts Am., Brookfield, 1972—. Served with USN, 1945-47, 51-53. C.P.A., Mo. Mem. Independent Accountants Soc. Mo. (dir. 1965-75, pres. 1972-73), Nat. Soc. Pub. Accountants, C. of C., Am. Legion, V.F.W. Mem. Christian Ch. (elder 1967—, chmn. bd. 1976-77). Lion (pres. 1966-67), Elk. Club: Brookfield Country (pres. 1963-64). Contbr. articles to profl. jours. Editor Mo. Independent Accountant, 1967—. Editorial com. Nat. Pub. Accountant, 1972—, vice chmn., 1976-77. Home: 19 Markham Estates Brookfield MO 64628 Office: 108 N Main St Brookfield MO 64628

WILTON, WILLIAM EVERETT, mfg. exec.; b. East St. Louis, Ill., May 23, 1916; s. Lane E. and Nettie May (Lukey) W.; A.B. in Econs., Ill. Coll., 1939; m. Ruth Jean Campbell, June 4, 1916; children—Douglas H., Kent R. Mfg. technician Jasper Blackburn Corp., St. Louis, 1939-47, works mgr., 1947-53, v.p. engring. and mfg., 1953-61, exec. v.p., 1961-67, pres., 1967—, pres. ITT Blackburn Co. div. Internat. Tel. & Tel. Corp., 1968—; gen. mgr. utility products Internat. Tel. & Tel. Corp., 1972—; dir. Boatmen's Nat. Bank of St. Louis, Debron Corp. Chmn. bd. mgrs. YMCA, Webster Groves, Mo., 1959—; trustee Ill. Coll., Jacksonville, Deaconess Hosp., 1975—; bd. dirs. Jr. Achievement. Mem. Am. Electric Mfg. Corp. (pres. 1969-72), Pres.'s Assn., Am. Mgmt. Assn., St. Louis Elec. Bd. Trade. Conglist. (chmn. endowment trust, chmn. bd. trustees). Club: Engineers (St. Louis). Home: 321 Planthurst Rd Webster Groves MO 63119 Office: 1525 Woodson Rd St Louis MO 63114 also 320 Park Ave New York City NY 10022

WILTSE, GLADYS GARNER (MRS. DORR N. WILTSE, SR.), educator, social worker; b. Vassar, Mich., July 2, 1908; d. Norman J. and Alice (Levis) Garner; B.A., Eastern Mich. U., 1948; postgrad. U. Mich.; m. Dorr N. Wiltse, Sr., Nov. 11, 1932; children—Dorr Norman, Sharon Christine. Tchr. Mayville (Mich.) High Sch., 1927-30, Vassar (Mich.) high schs., 1930-33; social worker Tuscola County Bur of Social Aid, Caro, Mich., 1937-40, supr., 1940-44; area rep. Mich. State Dept. Social Welfare, Thumb Area, 1944-48; tchr. Caro High Sch., 1955-73, founder, sponsor history club, 1958-73. Vice chmn. Tuscola County Social Services Bd., 1952—. Active Nat. Found. Mem. Planning Commn. of Village of Caro, Mich., 1951; Tuscola County chmn. graves registration com. Mich. Civil War

Centennial Observance Commn. Mem. Mich. Hist. Soc., Saginaw Valley Hist. Society, Archaeol. Soc. Mich., Saginaw Valley Archaeol. Soc., Saginaw Geneal. Soc., D.A.R., Watrousville-Caro Hist. Soc. and Mus. (charter mem., co-founder 1972), Cass River Gem and Mineral Soc., Colonial Daus. of Seventeenth Century, Nat. Soc. Magna Charta Dames, Huguenot Soc. Mich., Nat. Soc. Dames of Ct. Honor, Nat. Soc. Women Desc. Ancient and Honorable Arty. Co., Alpha Xi Delta. Democrat. Presbyn. Clubs: Caro Garden (pres.), Twentieth Century (past pres.), Fuddy-Duddy (co-founder and co-standing chmn. 1955—), Indianfields Questers (past pres.). Home: 708 W Sherman St Caro MI 48723

WINAKOR, BESS RUTH, journalist; b. Springfield, Ill., Mar. 17, 1942; d. Arthur H. and Annette (Wright) Winakor; B.A., Northwestern U., 1963, M.S. in Journalism, 1964. Interviewer Creative Research Workshop of Leo Burnett Co., Chgo., 1963-64; research analyst Post-Keyes-Gardner Advt., Chgo., 1964-65; account exec. Daniel J. Edelman & Assos., Chgo., 1965-67; Chgo. corr. Fairchild Publs. Women's Wear Daily, also broadcaster Capital Cities Broadcast, 1967-74; commentator channel 32 WFLD-TV, Chgo., 1975-76; chtbg. editor Architectural Digest, Chgo., 1975—; columnist and feature writer Chgo. Sun-Times, 1976—. Mem. Am. Home Econs. Assn., Home Economists in Bus., Chgo. Council Fgn. Relations, Women in Communications. Home: 111 E Chestnut Chicago IL 60611 Office: 401 N Wabash Ave Chicago IL 60611

WINBINGER, CHARLES LEE, ednl. adminstr.; b. Cuba, Kans., July 26, 1934; s. Leon L. and Frances Ann (Baxa) W.; B.A. in Sociology, Creighton U., 1966, M.S. in Guidance, 1970; m. Kathleen E. Bracht, Feb. 8, 1969; children—Beth, Deborah, Matthew, Kristine, Amy. Youth counselor, Father Flanagan's Boys Town (Nebr.), 1963-71, head counselor, 1971-73, tchr. high sch., 1973-77; dir. edn. Nebr. Credit Union League, Omaha, 1977—. Mem. Nat. Personnel Guidance Assn. Roman Catholic. Home: 3404 Augusta Ave Omaha NE 68144

WINBLAD, JAMES NORMAN, surgeon; b. Lindsborg, Kans., May 27, 1927; s. Hjalmar and Nora W.; student Bethany Coll., 1944-45, U.S. Mil. Acad., 1945-46; A.B., U. Kans., 1948; M.A., Kans. U., 1951, M.D., 1953; m. Gloria Danielson, Aug. 16, 1950; children—James Kent, John Mark, Kristin, Ingrid, Sonja. Intern, USPHS Hosp., San Francisco, Detroit, 1954-55, resident Indian Hosp., Phoenix, 1955-56, resident, New Orleans, 1956-62; practice medicine specializing in surgery, Winfield, Kans., 1962—; asso. Snyder Clinic., Winfield, 1962-71; mem. staff William Newton Hosp., Arkansas City (Kans.) Meml. Hosp. Diplomate Am. Bd. Surgery. Fellow Am. Coll. Surgeons, Southwestern Surg. Assn., Pan-Am. Surg. Assn.; mem. AMA, Kans., Cowley County med. socs. Episcopalian. Home: 1604 E 12th St Winfield KS 67156 Office: 1211 E 5th St Winfield KS 67156

WINBUSH, LEROY, design cons.; b. Memphis, Dec. 7, 1915; s. LeRoy and Alberta (Mebane) W.; grad. high sch.; m. Frances Robinson, June 28, 1948. Art dir. Goldblatt Bros. Dept. Stores, Chgo., 1938-45, Consol. Mfg. Co., Chgo., 1945-51, Ebony Mag., Chgo., 1945-54; pres. Winbush Assos., Inc., Chgo., 1957-68; owner, pres. Winbush Design Inc., Chgo., 1967—. Instr. skin and scuba 20 Fathom Club, 1966—; asst. prof. graphic design Art Inst. Chgo., 1967—; v.p. Slvart Corp., Chgo. Adv. dir. Our World-Underwater. Exhibit chmn. A.R.C., Chgo., 1962—; v.p. YMCA Met. Council Skin and Scuba Divers. Bd. dirs. spl. events, design dir. Ill. Sesquicentennial, 1968. Recipient several awards Art Dirs. Club, Chgo., 1948-49, 52, 55, 57, Nat. Shoe Fair, 1956, Chgo. Federated Advt. Club, Lawson Knight, 1966; named Diver of Year, YMCA, 1970, others. Fellow Chgo. Defender Round Table of Commerce; mem. Nat. (treas. 1968), Chgo. socs. communicating arts, Soc. Typographic Arts (award 1956), Am. Inst. Graphic Arts (award 1952), Federated Advt. Club, Artists Guild Chgo., Underwater Soc. Am. (v.p.). Clubs: 20 Fathom (pres.); Art Directors (Chgo., pres. 1966). Home: 400 E Randolph St Chicago IL 60601 Office: 540 N Lake Shore Dr Chicago IL 60611

WINCHESTER, VERNON LARRY, grain co. exec.; b. Denton, Kans., Jan. 18, 1937; s. Vernon Francis and Ruby Mae (Lange) W.; student pub. schs., Denton; children—Michael Zane, Randy Kirk, Larry Scott, Rhonda Diane. With Winchester Grain Co., Inc., Denton, 1954—, v.p., 1961-68, pres., 1968—. Bd. dirs. Kaw Valley Heart Assn. Mem. Kans. Grain and Feed Dealers Assn., Kans. Assn. Commerce and Industry. Republican. Methodist. Clubs: Elks, Eagles. Home and Office: Railroad St Denton KS 66017

WINDELL, VIOLET BRUNER, artist; b. DePauw, Ind., Nov. 1, 1922; d. Emory David and Audra Belle (White) Bruner; A.B., U. Louisville, 1943, M.A., 1958; m. Charles Lester Windell, May 22, 1943; children—Norma Helen, Eugene Kinsey, Lester Ann. Mem. staff advt. dept. Stewart Dry Goods Co., Louisville, 1944-46; instr. English, Ind. U., Jeffersonville, 1958-60; tchr. art North Harrison Schs., Ramsey, Ind., 1965-70; artist in residence Squire Boone Caverns, Corydon, Ind., 1973—; one-woman show: Port-o-Call Gallery, Louisville, 1965; group shows: State Art Festival, French Lick, Ind., 1966; Salute to Arts Week, Louisville, 1966; Lincoln Hills Ann. Shows, 1966, 77; represented in permanent collection: rare books U. Louisville Library. Mem. Lincoln Hills Arts Crafts Assn. (pres. 1973-74), DAR (regent 1968-69, 71-73), Bus. and Profl. Women, Am. Humanist Assn., Retired Tchrs. Assn. Ind. (asso.). Republican. Mem. Soc. Friends. Club: Spencer Extension Home Makers. Author: The Fairy Bells Tinkle Afar, family biography, 1968; Rainbows and Daisies, 1972. Home: Rt 1 Box 108 Ramsey IN 47166 Office: Squire Boone Caverns Rt 1 Box 35A Mauckport IN 47142

WINEGARDNER, CARL NORMAN, diversified co. exec.; b. East Lynne, Mo., July 13, 1931; s. Carl and Thelma Olene (Schmoll) W.; student Central Coll., Fayette, Mo., 1950, U. Ark., 1950-51; B.S., U. Mo., 1955; postgrad. So. Ill. U., 1968-69; m. Rose Mary Barco, July 23, 1954; children—Laura Helen, Thelma Rose, Jacob Harrison. Mgmt. trainee Nat. Dairies, Peoria, Ill., 1955-56; mgr. prodn. control Bendix Corp., Kansas City, Mo., 1956-63; dir. prodn. control Fabri-Tek, Inc., Mpls., 1963-66; sr. marketing analyst Doane Agrl. Service, St. Louis, 1966-68; with Walnut Grove Products div. W.R. Grace & Co., Atlantic, Iowa, 1969-74, mgr. 1969-74; dir. marketing and econ. analysis marketing planning Lockwood Corp., Gering, Nebr., 1974—. Instr. U. Iowa Inst. Pub. Affairs in Bus. Mgmt., 1969-74; mem. constrn. adv. bd. Iowa Office Comprehensive Health Planning. Pres. Fact Found., Atlantic, 1971-74. Served with USCGR, 1948-49, AUS, 1952-54. Recipient Best Pub. Relations Performance award Midwest Feed Mfrs. Assn., 1972. Mem. Am. Mktg. Assn. (chmn. agrl. com. 1967-70), Am. Mgmt. Assn., Am. Feed Mfrs. Assn. (mem. market research com. 1969-74), Am., Nebr. socs. farm mgrs. and rural appraisers. Rotarian, Elk. Home: 1655 M St Gering NE 69340 Office: PO Box 160 Gering NE 69341

WINEMAN, JEFFRY STERN, ins. brokerage co. exec.; b. Chgo., Nov. 9, 1938; s. John S. and Katherine S. (Stern) W.; B.A., Colgate U., 1961; m. Doris Nathan, Mar. 17, 1963; children—Jeffry Stern, Jill Susan. Vice pres. Wineman Bros., Inc., Chgo., 1961-68, Marsh & McLennan, Inc., 1968—. Co-chmn. ins. div. Jewish United Fund; mem. sustaining com. Ravinia Festival Assn. Clubs: Standard (officer, dir.), Tavern; Lake Shore Country (Glencoe, Ill.). Home: 935 Forest Glen E Winnetka IL 60093 Office: 222 S Riverside Plaza Chicago IL 60606

WINEMAN, JOHN HENRY, psychologist; b. Detroit, Aug. 4, 1941; s. Henry Cameron and Betty Sue (Cockrall) W.; B.A., Calif. State Coll., 1967, M.A., 1970; Ph.D. (NIH fellow), U. Utah, 1973; m. Sheila Ann Brooks, Aug. 17, 1968. Cottage supr. Boys and Girls Aid Soc., San Diego, 1964-65; data analyst U.S. Navy Neuropsychiat. Research Unit, San Diego, 1965-66; research asst. U.S. Navy Project SeaLab II, San Diego, summer 1966; student probation officer San Diego County Probation Dept., San Diego, part time, 1966; tchr. aide Westminster (Calif.) Sch. Dist., 1966-67, Seal Beach (Calif.) Sch. Dist., 1967; social worker Los Angeles County Dept. Pub. Social Services, 1967-68; project leader Mental Health Assn. Los Angeles, Long Beach, Calif., 1969-70; instructional aide Los Angeles County Sch. Dist., 1969-70; psychology intern Children's Center, Salt Lake City, part time, 1970-71; psychologist Granite Sch. Dist., Salt Lake City, 1971-74; psychologist Lucas County Children's Services Bd., Maumee, Ohio, 1974—. Served with USAF, 1960-63. Mem. Am., Ohio psychol. assns., Phi Delta Kappa, Alpha Phi Omega, Psi Chi. Contbr. articles to profl. jours. Home: 4113 Vogel Dr Toledo OH 43613 Office: 2500 River Rd Maumee OH 43537

WINEMILLER, JAMES D., accountant; b. Sullivan, Ind., July 22, 1944; s. Floyd Maurice and Doris Marie (Lone) W.; A.S., Vincennes U., 1964; B.S., Ind. U., 1966, M.B.A., 1967; m. Nancy Kay Walters, Aug. 10, 1963; 1 dau., Nancy Marie. Accountant Peat, Marwick, Mitchell & Co., C.P.A.'s, Honolulu, 1967-71; with Blue & Co., C.P.A.'s, Indpls., 1971—, partner-in-charge, 1974-76, mng. partner, 1977—. Grad. teaching asst. Dept. Accounting, Ind. U., Bloomington, 1966-67; instr. accounting Coll. Gen. Studies, U. Hawaii, Honolulu, 1968-69; dir. Poland State Bank (Ind.), 1974-75. Recipient Gold Medal for highest grades in state on C.P.A. examination, State Ind., 1966; Elizah Watt Sells Nat. Honorable Mention award, 1966. C.P.A., Ind., Hawaii. Mem. Am. Inst. C.P.A.'s, Ind. Assn. C.P.A.'s, Hawaii Soc. C.P.A.'s, Nat. Assn. Accountants, Am. Accounting Assn., Ind. U. Alumni Assn., Ind. U. Varsity-Hoosier Hundred, Vincennes U. Alumni Assn. Presbyterian. Clubs: Rotary (Ind. dir. 1973-75, pres. 1974-75), Indpls. Columbia. Home: 9242 Whitehall Ct Indianapolis IN 46256 Office: 5546 Shorewood Dr Indianapolis IN 46220

WINET, HOWARD, biophysicist, physiologist; b. Chgo., Sept. 13, 1937; s. Maurice and Lillian (Silver) W.; B.S., U. Ill., 1959; M.A., U. Calif. at Los Angeles, 1962, Ph.D., 1969; m. Carol Katherine Kasper, Nov. 23, 1969; children—Evan Darwin, Wendy Lynn. Master tchr. Los Angeles City Schs., 1962-66; NSF postdoctoral research fellow Calif. Inst. Tech., Pasadena, 1969-73; biophysicist, 1973-76; asst. research physiologist U. Calif. at Los Angeles Med. Sch., 1976-77; asso. prof. physiology So. Ill. U., Carbondale, 1977—; adviser Com. Advanced Sci. Tng., 1971; mem. natural sci. adv. panel Calif. State Commn. on Tchr. Preparation and Licensing, 1972-77. NIH trainee, 1967-69. Mem. Am. Physiol. Soc., Am. Soc. Andrology, Am. Soc. Cell Biologists, Biophys. Soc., Brit. Biophys. Soc., Soc. Exptl. Biology, Soc. Gen. Physiologists, Center Study Democratic Instns., Internat. Soc. Biorheology, Soc. Study Reprodn., Sigma Xi. Contbr. articles to sci. publs. Home: 813 S University Ave Carbondale IL 62901

WINETEER, RONALD ROYAL, educator; b. Chadron, Nebr., Oct. 1, 1944; s. Royal Rodney and Shirley Jean (Naylor) W.; B.S. in Edn., Chadron State Coll., 1967; postgrad. Minot State Coll., 1972, 77; m. Linda Susan Fellows, Oct. 11, 1969. Instr., Gering (Nebr.) Pub. Schs., 1967-69; tutor Hiram Scott Coll., 1969; instr. Minot (N.D.) Pub. Schs., 1969—. Dir. theatre Sawmill Playhouse, 1972-76, bd. dirs., 1974-76; mem. resident co. Minot State Coll. Summer Mus. Amphitheatre, 1966—, dir., 1976; tenor Minot Chamber Chorale Assn., Inc., 1969—, bd. dirs., 1973—, pres., 1973-75, v.p., 1975-78. Tech. dir. Miss Minot Pageant, 1971-72, N.D. Jr. Miss Pageant, 1974—. Mem. NEA, Internat. Thespian Soc., Minot C. of C. (cultural affairs com.), Tau Kappa Epsilon, Phi Mu Alpha Sinfonia. Episcopalian. Home: 908 2d St NE Minot ND 58701 Office: 1100 11th Ave SW Minot ND 58701

WING, ANNE MARIE HINSHAW (MRS. LEONARD WILLIAM WING), writer, artist, naturalist; b. Chgo., Oct. 28, 1901; d. William Wade and Anna T. (Williams) Hinshaw; B.A., U. Mich., 1923, M.A., 1931, M. in Landscape design, 1937, life certification edn., 1929; m. Leonard W. Wing, Mar. 18, 1936; children—William Hinshaw, Thomas Leonard Hinshaw, Anne (Mrs. Robert Bruce Petters), George Clyde. Landscape design asst. Wash. State Coll. (now U.), Pullman, 1943-44; author illustrator nature conservation articles Ypsilanti (Mich.) Press, 1957, Ann Arbor (Mich.) News, series 1958-64, various other newspapers, mags. Chmn. Ann Arbor Garden Club conservation com., Washtenaw Roadside Council, Ann Arbor, 1931-35; mem. Superior Twp. (Mich.) Citizens' Adv. Com., 1967; pres. Superior Twp. Civic Assn., 1959. Mem. D.A.R. (chmn. chpt. conservation com. 1960, 77—), P.E.O., Nat. League Am. Penwomen, Ann Arbor Art Assn., Mich. Audubon Soc., Am. Ornithologists Union, Wilson Ornithol. Soc., Assn. Interpretive Naturalists, Sierra Club, Federated Gard Clubs Mich. (mem. roadside devel. com. 1933-34), U. Mich. Alumni Assn., AAAS, Am. Forestry Assn., Nat. Soc. New Eng. Women, Washtenaw Hist. Soc., Mich. Hist. Soc., Wilderness Soc., Alpha Phi. Episcopalian. Club: Ann Arbor Women's City, Research and publs. on musical aspects of bird song. Home: Ann Arbor Woods Apts 2129 Medford Rd Ann Arbor MI 48104

WINGER, HOWARD WOODROW, educator; b. Marion, Ind., Oct. 29, 1914; s. Joseph Pendleton and Amanda Ellen (Shoemaker) W.; A.B., Manchester Coll., 1936, LL.D., 1975; B.S., George Peabody Coll., 1945; M.S., U. Ill., 1948, Ph.D., 1953; m. Helen Margaret Gray, Dec. 25, 1941; children—John, Michael, Philip, Elizabeth, Robert. Tchr. Swayzee (Ind.) High Sch., 1936-37; copy writer Crowell Pub. Co., Springfield, O., 1937-38; tchr. Jefferson Twp. High Sch., Warren, Ind., 1940-42; asst. librarian U. Ill. at Urbana, 1945-50; asst. prof. U. Wis.-Madison, 1950-53; asst. prof. Grad. Library Sch., U. Chgo., 1953-59, asso. prof., 59-68, prof. 1968—, dean, 1972-77. Bd. library dirs. Park Forest (Ill.) Pub. Library, 1955-61. Served to cpl. AUS, 1942-44. Mem. ALA (mem. council 1956-60), Assn. of Am. Library Schs. (sec. 1953-56), Beta Phi Mu (internat. pres. 1977-78), Phi Kappa Rho. Mem. United Protestant Ch. (chmn. bd. elders 1966-68). Clubs: Quadrangle (Chgo.). Author: Iron Curtains and Scholarship, 1959; Seven Questions About the Profession of Librarianship, 1962; The Medium Sized Public Library, 1964; Area Studies and the Library, 1966; Deterioration and Preservation of Library Materials, 1970; American Library History, 1876-1976, 1976; Printers' and Publishers' Devices, 1976; At This Point in Time (poems), 1976. Mng. editor: Library Quarterly, 1962-72. Home: 121 Walnut St Park Forest IL 60466 Office: 1100 E 57th St Chicago IL 60637

WINGERSON, GEORGE EDGAR, dentist; b. Terril, Iowa, Jan. 29, 1927; s. Henry Ray and Edna May (Glover) W.; A.A., City Coll., San Francisco, 1955; student U. Calif. at Berkeley, 1955-57; D.D.S., U. St. Louis, 1961; m. Alvera Margaret Hessenius, Dec. 1, 1946; children—Mark (dec.), Monty, Robin, Daron. Apprentice plasterer G.H. & C. Martinelli, San Francisco, 1946-50; journeyman plasterer Dante Bertocchini, San Francisco, 1950-57; pvt. practice dentistry, Hartley, Iowa, 1961—; mem. staff Community Meml. Hosp., Hartley, Baum-Harmon Hosp., Primghar. Mem. Am., Iowa, Northwest Iowa dental assns., C. of C. (dir. 1961-67, pres. 1965, 66), Psi Omega. Lutheran. Kiwanian (pres. 1972-73). Home: 111 S 1st Ave E Hartley IA 51346 Office: 111 E 1st Ave S Hartley IA 51346

WINITZ, HARRIS, speech pathologist; b. White Plains, N.Y., Mar. 4, 1933; s. Israel and Ann (Weinshank) W.; B.A., U. Vt., 1954; M.A., U. Iowa, 1956, Ph.D., 1956; m. Shevie Schuman, Feb. 26, 1961; children—Flora Sue, Simeon, Jennifer. Research asso. U. Kans. at Lawrence, 1959-63; asst. prof. Western Res. U., Cleve., 1963-65; prof. U. Mo., Kansas City, 1965—. Recipient Career Devel. award NIH, 1968-73. Mem. Am. Psychol. Assn., Am. Speech and Hearing Assn., Linguistic Soc. Am., Acoustical Soc. Am. Jewish. Author: Articulatory Acquisition and Behavior, 1969; From Syllable to Conversation, 1975. Home: 607 W Montcrew Dr Kansas City MO 64114 Office: Dept Psychology U Mo Kansas City MO 64110

WINKLE, WILLIAM ALLAN, educator; b. Rapid City, S.D., Oct. 1, 1940; s. Curtis Powell and June Ada (Alexander) W.; B.Mus., Huron Coll., 1962; M.A. in Music, U. Vt., 1971; postgrad. Morehead State U., 1966; D.Arts in Music U. No. Colo., 1976; m. Carola Kay Croll, June 16, 1968; 1 dau., Brenda Jane. Dir. instrumental music Arlington (S.D.) High Sch., 1962-64, DeSmet (S.D.) High Sch., 1964-67; music coordinator Huron (S.D.) pub. schs., 1967-69; head, instrumental music, mus. dir. Huron Coll., 1969-71; dir. bands Chadron (Nebr.) State Coll., 1971—. Profl. tuba and bassoon player Huron Symphony, 1957-69, Huron Municipal Band, 1953-62, U. Vt. Faculty Orch., 1964-70, S.D. Wind Arts Quintet, 1967-69, Nebr. Panhandle Symphony, 1971-77, Am. Youth Symphony Chamber Orch., 1973—; judge, condr. music festivals S.D., Nebr., Tex., Pa., N.D., Wyo., Vt. Chmn. Chadron Fine Arts League, 1974—; dist. chmn. Boy Scouts Am., Chadron, 1972-74. Bd. dirs. Huron Community Concert Assn., 1959-71; bd. dirs. Huron Symphony League, 1965-67, pres., 1955-69; bd. dirs. Am. Youth Symphony and Chorus European Tours, 1967-77. Recipient Freedom Found. award for Am. Youth Symphonic Band Concert Tour Head Condr., 1971; Sousa Band award, 1958; Distinguished Citation in Applied Music, Huron Coll., 1962. Chadron State Coll. research grantee, 1975—. Mem. Tuba Universal Brotherhood Assn. for S.D., Nebr., N.D. (dist. chmn. 1973-77), Chadron C. of C., Nebr. Bandmasters, Chadron State Coll. Edn. Assn. (pres. elect, chmn. Band Day-Homecoming), Music Educators Nat. Conf., Nat. Assn. Jazz Educators, Nat. Band Assn., Coll. Band Dirs. Nat. Assn., NEA, Coll. Music Soc., Nat. Assn. Coll. Wind and Percussion Instrs., Kappa Kappa Psi (life), Kappa Delta Pi, Phi Beta Mu. United Ch. of Christ (campus ministry bd. 1974—, chmn. bd. deacons 1974—). Clubs: Elks, Rotary. Home: 318 Ann St Chadron NE 69337 Office: 10th and Main St Chadron State Coll Chadron NE 69337

WINKLER, HELEN HUTULA, physician; b. Covington, Mich., Jan. 20, 1939; d. Charles August and Dagmar (Kaura) Hutula; student Mich. Tech. U., 1956-57; B.A., Mich. State U., 1959; M.D., Wayne State U., 1963; m. William S. Powell, Mar. 1, 1968; children—Tanya Marie, Michael Randall. Intern Wayne County Gen. Hosp., Eloise, Mich., 1963-64; instr. anatomy Wayne State U., Detroit, 1964-65; resident in internal medicine Henry Ford Hosp., Detroit, 1965-68; practice medicine specializing in internal medicine, Detroit, 1968-69, 74—; internist Blain Clinic, Detroit, 1971-74. Diplomate Am. Bd. Internal Medicine. Mem. Am. Occupational Med. Assn., Mich. Indsl. Med. Assn., Mich., Wayne County med. socs., AMA, Am. Med. Women's Assn., A.C.P., Mich. Heart Assn., Finnish Center Assn., Alpha Omega Alpha, Phi Mu, Phi Kappa Phi. Unitarian. Clubs: Eastpointe Racquet, Grosse Pointe Hunt. Home: 445 Neff St Grosse Pointe MI 48230 Office: 14638 E Seven Mile St Detroit MI 48205

WINKLER, RAYMOND S., publishing co. exec.; b. Chgo., Oct. 15, 1945; s. S. W. and H. J. (Budyn) W.; B.S., No. Ill. U., 1968; M.B.A., DePaul U., 1973; m. Truletta Jean Stunkel, Oct. 14, 1972; 1 son, Todd Jeffery. Market analyst Admiral Corp., 1969-70; mgr. mktg. services Kiver Publs., Inc., Chgo., 1970-74; mgr. research Hitchcock Pub. Co., Wheaton, Ill., 1974—. Mem. Am. mktg. Assn. Home: 214 Aspen Ct Bolingbrook IL 60439 Office: Hitchcock Pub Co Hitchcock Bldg Wheaton IL 60187

WINN, MAURICE EDWARD, hobby mfg. co. exec.; b. Lucerne, Ind., Oct. 8, 1927; s. Chester B. and Hazel (Kistler) W.; B.S., Purdue U., 1950; postgrad. Butler U., 1951-52; M.A., Acadamia Hispano Americano, San Miquel De Allende, Guanajuato, Mexico, 1964; m. Mary L. Cline, Jan. 3, 1954; children—Lauren A., M. Douglas. Salesman, Davidsons Lumber Co., Indpls., 1950-52; gen. mgr. Keystone Distbrs., Inc., Indpls., 1952-63; pres. Twinn-K, Inc., Indpls., 1964—; chmn. bd. Twinn-K Internat. Inc., Indpls.; instr. English, Instituto Allende, 1963-64. Served with AUS, 1945-46. Recipient Merit award Gen. Hobby Corp., Phila., 1966-68. Mem. Hobby Industry Assn. Am. (dir. model racing div. 1967—), Nat. Competition Com. (sec. 1969—). Republican. Lion (pres. Indpls. 1961), Elk. Clubs: Columbia, Highland Country, World Trade (Indpls.). Contbr. numerous articles to trade mags. Home: 430 S Center St Plainfield IN 46168 Office: 10296 W Washington St PO Box 31228 Indianapolis IN 46231

WINN, RHONDA LEE, psychologist; b. Williamsport, Pa., July 23, 1946; d. James Branch and Juanita Blanche (Dennis) Skeen; A.B., Morris Harvey Coll., 1968; M.A., W.Va. U., 1971; postgrad. Northwestern U., 1976—. Tchr., Kanawha County Pub. Schs., Charleston, W.Va., 1968-74; counseling psychologist Job Corps, U.S. Dept. Labor, Charleston, 1974-76; part-time faculty evening div. Morris Harvey Coll., 1969. Certified tchr., W.Va. Mem. Am. Personnel and Guidance Assn., NEA, NOW (editor chpt. newsletter Charleston 1973-75). Home: 136 Main St Evanston IL 60202

WINN, ROBERT CHEEVER, air force officer; b. N.Y.C., Apr. 11, 1939; s. Richard Wilkens and Ella Jane (MacKenzie) W.; B.A., U. Bridgeport, 1962; M.A., Ball State U., 1975; student Squadron Officer's Sch., 1966, Air Command Staff Coll., 1972, Indsl. Coll. Armed Forces, 1976; m. Margery Ellen Irwin, Dec. 22, 1962; children—Elizabeth Jane, Margaret Ruth, Nancy Louise. Commd. 2nd lt. U.S. Air Force, 1963, advanced through grades to maj., 1974; aircraft maintenance officer Brookley AFB, Mobile, Ala., 1964-65, spl. project officer, 1965-66, McClellan AFB, Sacramento, Calif., 1966; officer in charge maintenance support div. Tan Son Nhut Air Base, Saigon, Vietnam, 1967-68; job control officer Beale AFB, Marysville, Calif., 1968-69, officer in charge, 1968-71; officer in chief of maintenance control br. RAF Mildenhall, Eng., 1971-74, dep. chief of maintenance, 1974-75; squadron comdr. Minot (N.D.) AFB, 1975-76, maintenance supr., 1976-77, maintenance control officer, 1977; integrated logistics support officer, acquisition logistics br. Hdqrs. SAC, 1977—. Active PTA, 1972-74, exec. com. chmn., 1972; church council mem., 1973, usher, 1972-77, Sunday sch. leader, 1973-74, lay leader, 1976-77, counselor, 1978. Decorated Bronze Star. Mem. Am. Personnel Guidance Assn., Smithsonian Assos., Air Force Assn. Republican. Presbyterian. Home: 4915 Dumfries Dr Omaha NE 68157 Office: HQ SAC/LGXX Offutt AFB NE 68113

WINN, WESLEY WAYNE, ednl. adminstr.; b. Detroit, Mar. 10, 1945; s. Harry David and Lillian Mildred (Dunsmore) W.; B.A., Eastern Mich. U., 1967; M.A., Northwestern U., 1968; Ph.D., 1974; m. Nancy Ellen Bishop, May 4, 1968; children—Wesley Wayne, Paul

Jarret. Counselor, Tech. Inst. Northwestern U., Evanston, Ill., 1969-71; asso. dir. admissions Olivet (Mich.) Coll., 1974-75; dean student affairs, dir. career planning and placement Marygrove Coll., Detroit, 1975—, instr. div. continuing edn., 1975—. Served to 1st lt. U.S. Army, 1971-73. Recipient Spoke Award U.S. Jaycees, 1977; NDEA fellow, 1967-70. Mem. Am., Mich. personnel and guidance assns., Am., Mich. coll. personnel assns., Nat. Vocat. Guidance Assn., Nat. Assn. Student Personnel Adminstrs., Midwest Coll. Placement Assn., Delta Sigma Phi (Nat. Certificate of Merit 1967), Phi Delta Kappa. Clubs: Foresters. Editor Mich. Coll. Personnel Assn. newsletter, 1977—. Contbr. articles to Jour. Coll. Student Personnel. Home: 29304 Rose St Madison Heights MI 48071

WINNICK, COLONEL NORBERT, dentist; b. Muskegon, Mich., July 7, 1927; s. Nicholas and Stephania (Boydunik) W.; student Muskegon Jr. Coll., 1948, 49; B.S., U. Detroit, 1952, D.D.S., 1957; m. Patricia Ann Boyer, May 29, 1954; children—Leslie Ann, Todd Christopher. Pvt. practice dentistry, Muskegon, 1957—. Served with USNR, 1945-47, 50-51. Mem. Am., Mich. dental assns., Muskegon Dist. Dental Soc. (pres. 1971-72). Elk, Rotarian. Club: Muskegon Country. Home: 4082 Nobhill Dr Muskegon MI 49441 Office: 4461 Grand Haven Rd Muskegon MI 49441

WINQUIST, ALAN HANSON, educator; b. Astoria, N.Y., June 7, 1942; s. Emil Nils and Gertrude Eleanor (Enborg) W.; A.B., Wheaton (Ill.) Coll., 1964; M.A. in Teaching, Northwestern U., 1965; postgrad U. Stockholm, 1965-66; Ph.D., N.Y. U., 1976. Tchr. social studies schools, Northbrook, Ill., 1964-65, Port Washington, N.Y., 1966-67; tchr. history Martin Luther High Sch., Maspeth, N.Y., 1967-69; instr. dept. history Nassau Community Coll., Garden City, N.Y., 1970-74; asso. prof. European history Taylor U., Upland, Ind., 1974—, also acting chmn. dept. history. Ford Found. scholar: N.Y. U. Travel grantee, 1974; Assn. Swedish Industries grantee. Mem. Am. Hist. Assn., African Studies Assn., Soc. Advancement of Scandinavian Studies, Conf. Faith and History. Presbyterian. Contbr. articles in field to profl. jours. Home and Office: Taylor University Upland IN 46989

WINSLOW, ALFRED AKERS, govt. ofcl.; b. Gary, Ind., June 16, 1923; s. Harry Wendell and Lenora (Allen) W.; A.A., Wilson Jr. Coll., 1964; B.B.A., Northwestern U., 1969; m. Maud Esther Franklin, Jan. 15, 1954. With Chgo. Post Office, 1947-66; with U.S. Postal Service, Chgo. Central Region, 1967—, dir. Office Employee Relations, 1973—. Partner Winslow's Apparel Shop, Chgo., 1954-66. Mem. adv. com. on human relations City of Chgo., 1969-73; pres. Cheryl Condominium, Chgo., 1965-67, Evans-Langley Neighborhood Club, Chgo., 1960-64; chmn. Post Office Bd. U.S. Civil Service Examiners Ill., Mich., 1967-71. Served with USCGR, 1943-46. Recipient Outstanding Achievement award, Chgo. Assn. Commerce and Industry, 1969, 70, 68; Great Guy award, Radio Sta. WGRT, 1969. Mem. Northwestern U. Bus. Honor Soc., NAACP bd. dirs. 1968-71), Soc. Personnel Adminstrn., Indsl. Relations Assn. Chgo., Am. Legion, Field Mus. Natural History, Chgo. Art Inst., Chgo. Ednl. TV Assn., Northwestern U. Alumni Assn.

WINSLOW, DONALD REXFORD, educator; b. Sanford, Maine, Mar. 12, 1923; s. Rexford R. and Glenna (Swett) W.; A.B., Ind. U., 1951, M.S., 1953; m. Frances D. Thomason, Sept. 4, 1949; 1 son, Donald Rexford II. Tchr. Metro Sch. Dist., Martinsville, Ind., 1953-57; head sci. dept., div. university schs., Ind. U., Bloomington, 1958-70, asst. prof. edn., 1970—, regional campus adminstr. Office of Research and Devel., 1973—. Exec. sec. Sch. Sci. and Math. Assn., 1966-72. Served with USNR, 1942-46, 51-52. Recipient Outstanding Biology Tchr. award Nat. Assn. Biology Tchrs., 1964. Fellow Ind. Acad. Sci. (chmn. youth activities); mem. Ind. Jr. Acad. Sci. (dir. 1964-71), Conservation-Outdoor Edn. Assn. Ind. (pres. 1977). Asso. editor American Biology Teacher, 1965-69. Contbr. articles to profl. jours. Home: 1210 Elliston Dr Bloomington IN 47401 Office: 204 Education Bldg Indiana University Bloomington IN 47401

WINSLOW, EDWARD BYRON, educator, physician; b. London, Ont., Can., Apr. 1, 1942; s. Edward Thompson and Barbara Jean (Knowles) W.; M.D., U. B.C., Can., 1966; m. Rosemarie van Eyck, Apr. 26, 1969; children—Edward Byron, Robert Douglas. Intern, Cook County Hosp., Chgo., 1966-67; resident, cardiology fellow U. Ill. Hosp., 1967-71, asst. prof. medicine 1973-77, asso. prof. clin. medicine, 1977—; dir. coronary care unit VA West Side Hosp., Chgo., 1971-73; dir. med. and coronary care units Ill. Masonic Med. Center, 1973—. Fellow Royal Coll. Physicians, Am. Coll. Cardiology, Am. Coll. Chest Physicians, A.C.P.; mem. Am. Fedn. Clin. Research, Am. Heart Assn. Home: 914 Sheridan Rd Wilmette IL 60091 Office: 836 Wellington St Chicago IL 60657

WINSTEIN, BRUCE DARRELL, physicist, educator; b. Los Angeles, Sept. 25, 1943; s. Saul and Sylvia (Levin) W.; B.A., U. Calif., Los Angeles, 1965; Ph.D., Calif. Inst. Tech., 1970; grad. Erhard Seminars Tng. (EST), 1976. Research physicist, Max Planck Inst. Physics Astrophysics, Munich, Germany, 1970-72; sr. research asso. Enrico Fermi Inst., U. Chgo., 1972-76, Arthur H. Compton lectr., 1976, asst. prof. physics, 1976—. NSF grantee, 1976—. Mem. Am. Phys. Soc., Sigma Pi Sigma. Home: 5521 S University Ave Chicago IL 60637 Office: 5630 Ellis Ave Chicago IL 60637

WINSTON, HAROLD RONALD, lawyer; b. Atlantic, Iowa, Feb. 7, 1932; s. Louie D. and Leta B. (Carter) W.; B.A., U. Ia., 1954, J.D., 1958; m. Carol J. Sundeen, June 11, 1955; children—Leslie Jane, Lisa Carol, Laura Louise. Admitted to Iowa bar, 1958, U.S. Supreme Ct. bar, 1969; trust officer United Home Bank & Trust Co., Mason City, Iowa, 1958-59; individual practice law, Mason City; mem. firm Winston Schroeder & Reuber, Mason City, 1973—; police judge, Mason City, 1961-73. Dir. Damons's, Inc. Active local charitable orgns. Active worker Rep. party. Bd. dirs. Mason City United Way, Mason City YMCA. Served with USAF, 1955-57. Mem. Am., Iowa, Cerro Gordo County bar assns., Am. Coll. Probate Counsel, Am. Trial Lawyers Assn. Mason (32 deg.), Kiwanian. Clubs: Mason City Country; Euchre and Cycle, Executive (Mason CIty). Home: 118 Linden Dr Mason City IA 50401 Office: 119 2d St Mason City IA 50401

WINSTON, WARREN DEE, pharmacist, historian, writer, preservationist; b. Quincy, Ill., 1940; s. Hazan Churchill and Bessie Martha Rosalyn (Large) W.; B.S., St. Louis Coll. Pharmacy, 1963. Pharmacist, Aldrich Pharmacy, Pittsfield, Ill., 1963-67; owner Winston's Pharmacy (restored to 1880 vintage), Pittsfield, 1967—. Mem. Pike County Hist. Soc., 1958—, chmn., pres., v.p., trustee, 1963—; leader Pittsfield Explorer Post, Boy Scouts Am., 1964-71, organizer, lectr. Drug Abuse Prevention Program, 1972; chmn. Pittsfield Planning Commn., 1966-67, Ill. Gov.'s Citizens Involvement Council of Pike County, 1971-72, East Sch. Preservation Com., 1967, Pittsfield Hist. Sites Commn., 1968-69, Com. for 76, 1974; chmn. People-to-People Orgn., 1967. Named Outstanding Young Person, Ill. Jr. C. of C., 1975; Ill. recipient Nat. Bowl of Hygeia award, 1976; semifinalist White House Fellows Competition, 1975, finalist, 1976. Mem. Am. (policy com. on pub. affairs, speaker conv. 1976), Ill. (lectr. on drug abuse, pub. relations com. 1976—) pharm. assns., Pittsfield Jr. C. of C., Pittsfield Theater Guild. Lion. Author: The Great Triumvirate, 1958; Historic Pittsfield, 1958; Pike-Lincoln Trail, 1960; Air Contamination Analysis: A study of St. Louis Hospitals, 1961; Pittsfield's Historic Area Preservation Ordinance, 1969; The Sam Wade Farm-A Historic District, 1976. Developer concept of computerized pharmacy; featured in articles profl. publs., newspapers; active preservation campaign to re-route 4-lane hwy., 1976. Home: 231 S Jackson St Pittsfield IL 62363 Office: 103 N Madison St Pittsfield IL 62363

WINSTROM, WILLIS LEE, chem. mfg. co. exec.; b. Omaha, Apr. 17, 1933; s. Reuben William and Clara (Anderson) W.; B.S., Grinnell Coll., 1954; m. Sydney Joyce Marshall, June 11, 1955; children—Andrew Lee, Clair C. With Pennfield Oil Co., Omaha, 1954—, v.p., 1968; pres. Vitamin Premixers of Omaha, Inc., 1968—. Mem. Am. Petroleum Inst., Am. Feed Mfrs. Assn., C. of C. Co-inventor vitamin stblzn. process. Home: 9126 Shirley St Omaha NE 68124 Office: 4444 S 76th St Omaha NE 68127

WINTER, FRANCIS DONALD, pathologist; b. Hinton, Iowa, Sept. 19, 1922; s. Francis Dietrich and Lydia 8Jensen) W.; M.D., U. Louisville, 1946; m. Margaret Lola Smith, May 26, 1945; children—Susan A., John D., Carol L., James A. Intern, Broadlawns Hosp., Des Moines, 1947; resident in pathology Mercy Hosp., Des Moines, 1948, 49, Charity Hosp., New Orleans, 1950; dir. pathology and nuclear medicine Community Hosps. SE Iowa and W. Central Ill. (central offices in Burlington, Iowa and Macomb, Ill.), 1950-76. Served with USAAF, 1943; USAF, 1955-56. Diplomate Am. Bd. Pathology, Am. Bd. Nuclear Medicine. Fellow Am. Soc. Clin. Pathology, Coll. Am. Pathologists; mem. AMA, Ill., Iowa med. socs., Ill. Path. Soc., Am. Coll. Nuclear Medicine, Am. Coll. Nuclear Physicians, Am. Assn. Blood Banks, Am. Assn. Physicians and Surgeons. Episcopalian. Home: 13 Cascade Terr Burlington IA 52601

WINTER, MAX, profl. football team exec.; b. Ostrava, Austria, June 29, 1904; s. Jacob and Bertha (Ruker) W.; came to U.S., 1913, naturalized, 1920; student Hamline U., 1925-26, U. Chgo., 1927: m. Helen Horovitz, Dec. 5, 1939; children—Susan (Mrs. Robert Diamond), Nancy (Mrs. Dennis Ditlove), Diane (Mrs. Richard Cohen). Co-owner, gen. mgr. Mpls. Lakers Basketball Team, 1947-56; originator Minn. Vikings (Nat. Football League), Mpls., 1960, pres., 1960—; chmn. bd., dir. Viking Enterprises; pres. Max Winter Enterprises, Max Winter Enterprises Hawaii; dir. Downtown Bank St. Paul, Bank of Mpls. Mem. County Park Bd., 1959-64; chmn. Muscular Dystrophy, 1961; mem. Gov.'s Bus. Adv. Com., 1965; chmn. Nat. Govs. Conf., 1965. Recipient Hon. Scout award, 1946, 47, 48. Mem. Mpls. C. of C. (v.p.). Jewish. Clubs: Optimists; Minneapolis Athletic; Oak Ridge Country, Wacalae Country, Outrigger (Honolulu): Rotary. Author: Sports Books for Children, 1957. Home: 3412 Oak Ridge Rd Minneapolis MN 55343 Office: 5200 W 74th St Minneapolis MN 55435

WINTER, RICHARD ALLEN, internat. mgmt. cons.; b. Chgo., Mar. 25, 1914; s. D. Allen and Lillian (Mees) W.; B.S. in Econs. and Indsl. Psychology, Northwestern U., 1936; postgrad. Detroit Coll. Law, 1938; m. Emily Elisabeth Young, Oct. 23, 1942; children—Barbara Jean, William Richard. Salesman A.B. Dick Co., Chgo., 1936-38, Nebr. Salesbook Co., Chgo., 1938-42; v.p. Fed. Tool Corp., Chgo., 1945-60; chmn. bd. Winter-Kahn-Nielsen-Ross & Buckwalter, Inc., Lake Forest, Ill., 1957—; now pres. Richard/Allen/Winter, Ltd., Lake Forest; dir. ServiceMaster Industries Inc., AMC Corp., Electronic Periodicals, Inc., Programs Internat., Inc., Mgmt. Consultants Publishers, Inc.; chmn. Results-Assured Mgmt., Inc. Bd. dirs. Chgo. Internat. Program for Youth Leaders and Social Workers, Inc., 1969—. Mem. Chgo., Lake Forest chambers commerce. Soc. Plastics Industry, Nat. Housewares Mfrs. Assn., Soc. Profl. Mgmt. Consultants, Nat. Assn. Exec. Consultants, Inc. (pres. 1970-71), Am. Mgmt. Assn., Nat. Police Res. Assn., Ill. Security Chiefs Assn., Assn. Mgmt. Cons., Assn. Sch. Bus. Ofcls., Am. Soc. Indsl. Security, Direct Mail Advt. Assn., Internat. Assn. Hosp. Security, Internat. Platform Assn., Ducks Unltd., Audubon Soc., Chgo. Zool. Soc. Home: 885 Waveland Rd Lake Forest IL 60045 Office: 222 Wisconsin Ave Suite 303 Lake Forest IL 60045

WINTER, WALLACE EDWARD, ins. co. exec.; b. Wausau, Wis., May 20, 1930; s. Edward Julius and Angeline Anastatia (Herback) W.; B.B.A., U. Wis., 1952; student DePaul U., 1949-50; m. Barbara Mae Beaumont, June 20, 1953; children—Kathryn Beau, Rebecca Lynn. With Employers Ins. Wausau, 1954-68, Kansas City, Mo., 1956-58, River Forest, Ill., 1958-60, sales rep., Kansas City, Mo., 1960-63, field sales mgr., 1963-66, Omaha, Neb., 1966-68; v.p. regional sales Am. Mutual Reins. Co., Chgo., 1968-73, pres., chief exec. officer, 1973-76, dir., 1973-76; sr. v.p. Intere Intermediaries, Inc., Chgo., 1976—. Councilman City of Merriam (Kan.), 1961-66. Served with USMCR, 1952-54. Mem. Reins. Assn. Am. (dir. 1973-76), Soc. Chartered Property and Casualty Underwriters, Chgo. Athletic Assn. Clubs: Metropolitan; Execs. (Chgo). Home: ON 282 Peter Rd Winfield IL 60190 Office: 125 S Wacker Dr Chicago IL 60606

WINTER, WILLIAM EARL, beverage co. exec.; b. Granite City, Ill., Sept. 21, 1920; s. William Martin and Ada Maude (Compton) W.; A.B., U. Ill., 1942; m. Mildred E. Stiebel, Mar. 18, 1977; children—William C., Douglas E. With The Seven-Up Co., St. Louis, 1946—, mgr. sales promotion, 1952-65, marketing mgr., 1965-68, dir. marketing, 1968-72, exec. v.p., 1972-74, pres., 1974—, dir., 1972—, chief exec. officer, 1976—; dir. Warner-Jenkinson Co., St. Louis, Ventura Coastal Co. (Calif.), Seven-Up Can., Ltd., Toronto, Ont., Seven-Up Internat. Inc., Bank Bldg. Corp., St. Louis, First Nat. Bank St. Louis. Vice chmn. YMCA of Greater St. Louis; nat. v.p. Muscular Dystrophy Assn. Served with USAAF, 1942-46. Mem. Am. Marketing Assn., Sales and Marketing Execs., Premium Advt. Assn. Am., Phi Beta Kappa. Baptist. Mason. Home: 12310 Boothbay Ct Creve Coeur MO 63141 Office: 121 S Meramec St St Louis MO 63105

WINTERS, PETER LEE, dermatologist; b. Lockport, N.Y., Dec. 19, 1938; s. Earl Lloyd and Ruby Josephine (Gilmer) W.; B.S., Allegheny Coll., 1960; M.D., Temple U., 1965; m. Christine L. Wells, June 5, 1976; children by previous marriage—Christopher L., Jonathan B. Intern, Meth. Hosp., Indpls., 1965-66, resident in family medicine, 1966-68; resident in dermatology Skin and Cancer Hosp., Phila., 1968-71; practice medicine specializing in dermatology, Indpls., 1971—; instr. dermatology clinic Meth. Hosp. Served to lt. USNR, 1966-68. Recipient physician's recognition award, 1971-73, 73-76, 76-79. Am. Bd. Dermatology, Nat. Bd. Med. Examiners. Mem. AMA, Ind. Med. Soc., Am. Acad. Dermatology, Soc. for Investigative Dermatology. Republican. Methodist. Clubs: Riveria Swim, West Indy Racquet. Home: 6969 Warwick Rd Indianapolis IN 46220 Office: 8402 Harcourt Rd Suite 305 Indianapolis IN 46260

WINTHER, DONN ERNST, radio-TV exec.; b. Phila., Mar. 21, 1933; s. Ernst and Ruth (Temple) W.; grad. high sch.; m. Nancy Kohler, July 18, 1953 (div. 1975); children—Kristen, Donn Gregory; m. 2d, Phyllis Walker, May 24, 1975. Announcer, actor, dir. various radio, tv shows, 1950-53; with WFIL-TV, Phila., 1957-60, WBZ-TV, Boston, 1960-63, ABC, N.Y.C., 1963-67; sales exec. Blair Radio-TV, Chgo., 1967-76, RKO Radio, Chgo., 1976-77; gen. mgr. Selcom, Inc., Chgo., 1977—. Mem. Chgo. Art Inst.; bd. dirs. League of Thought; pres. Direction One. Served with AUS, 1953-55. Recipient Promotion award NBC, 1961; citation Leukemia Found., 1963; Art award TV Guide, 1962. Mem. Broadcast Pioneers. Clubs: Chicago Broadcast Advertisers; Milline (Chgo.). Contbr. articles, short stories to mags. Home: 10 Mayland Villa Mundelein IL 60060 Office: 400 N Michigan Ave Suite 702 Chicago IL 60601

WINTON, JEFFREY BLAKE, arbitrator; b. Chgo., Feb. 16, 1945; s. Stanley A. and Phyllis R. (Levin) W.; B.S., U. Ill., 1966, M.S., 1968. With Midwest Stock Exchange, Chgo., 1968-70; asst. to state sch. supt. for tchr. negotiations (Ill.), 1970-73; pres. Radionic Industries, Inc. (formerly Radionic Transformers Corp.), Chgo., 1973—; pres. Jeffrey B. Winton & Assos., Chgo., 1972—. Lectr. labor relations and mgmt. Northwestern U., 1974-75. Campaign aide Senator Adlai E. Stevenson, III, 1966, 70, 74, mediator, arbitrator Edn. Employment Relations Bd., State of Ind., 1974—; fact finder, mediator, arbitrator Iowa Pub. Employment Relations Bd., also Wis. Pub. Employment Relations Bd. Recipient Gold Key to City of Champaign, Ill., 1968. Mem. Am. Arbitration Assn. (labor panel), Am. Civil Liberties Union, Chgo. Assn. Commerce, Ams. for Democratic Action. Contbr. articles to profl. publs. Home: 832 Forest Evanston IL 60202 Office: 2525 W Moffat Chicago IL 60647

WINTZER, FREDERICK STONE, rendering co. exec.; b. Wapakoneta, Ohio, Aug. 19, 1923; s. Carl Frederick and Edith Muriel (Link) W.; A.B., Mt. Union Coll., Alliance, Ohio, 1944; m. Mary Alice Spar, Oct. 1, 1950; children—Gustave S., Christopher L., William James, Carl C. Pres., G.A. Wintzer & Son Co., Wapakoneta, 1947—; chmn. bd. 1st Nat. Bank Wapakoneta, 1969—. Chmn. Fats and Proteins Research Found., Inc., Des Plaines, Ill., 1975—. Mem. Bd. Edn., Wapakoneta, 1955-62. Councilman-at-large, Wapakoneta, 1949-50; pres. Auglaize County Regional Planning Commn., 1970-72; dir. Auglaize County Republican Finance Orgn., 1974—. Bd. dirs. devel. council Med. Coll. Ohio, Toledo; trustee Mt. Union Coll. Served to lt. (j.g.), USNR, 1943-46. Patentee bulk hauling vehicle, gas pressure tankage press. Home: Rural Route 3 Glynwood Rd Wapakoneta OH 45895 Office: 5 N Blackhoof St Wapakoneta OH 45895

WION, JESSE LLOYD, lawyer; b. St. Louis, Oct. 7, 1916; s. James Frederick and Angie Margaret (Sigmund) W.; LL.B., City Coll. Law and Finance, St. Louis, 1941; m. Clarice E. Hoeffner, Sept. 11, 1938; children—James E., Clarice (Mrs. Dennis Mertz), Walter L., Marilynn B. (Mrs. Gary Hartmann). Admitted to Mo. bar, 1941; individual practice law, St. Louis also Clayton, Mo.; city judge City of Overland (Mo.), 1972—, city of Pagedale, 1969-74. Served with AUS, 1943-45. Mem. Assn. Ins. Attys. (nat. sec. 1968—), Am., Met., St. Louis, St. Louis County bar assns., Mo. Bar, Internat. Assn. Ins. Counsel. Mason. Home: 12760 Whispering Hills Ln St Louis MO 63141 Office: 110 S Central Ave Clayton MO 63105

WIRICK, BETTY JO, welfare adminstr.; b. Bedford, Ind., Jan. 28, 1930; d. Walter Samuel and Mary Edna (Swango) Smith; student Gary (Ind.) Pub. Schs.; m. George Wirick, Sept. 28, 1951; children—Stephen, Paula, Donald. Clk. typist Lake County (Ind.) Welfare Dept., Gary, from 1949, adminstrv. asst., 1968—. Mem. Data Processing Mgmt. Assn., Am. Pub. Welfare Assn., Delta Theta Tau. Lutheran. Home: 9404 Arthur St Crown Point IN 46307 Office: 800 Massachusetts St Gary IN 46402

WIRT, MICHAEL DEAN, educator; b. Saginaw, Mich., Aug. 30, 1938; s. Malcolm Lewis and Ethel Lenore (Honeywell) W.; student Kalamazoo Coll., 1956-57; B.S., Western Mich. U., 1962, M.A., 1965; Ph.D. (NDEA fellow), U. Mich., 1975; m. Karen E. Egly, Jan. 30, 1960; children—Michael Dean II, Andrew C. Grad. asst. Western Mich. U., 1964-66; social worker Mich. Crippled Children Commn., 1963-64; counselor Ferris State Coll., Big Rapids, Mich., 1966-68; research asst. Ednl. Resources Info. Center, Ann Arbor, Mich., 1969-71; counselor U. Alaska, Fairbanks, 1971-72; tchr. cons. Ann Arbor (Mich.) Pub. Schs., 1972-73; counselor Mich. Technol. U., Houghton, 1973—. Vice pres. Copper Country Jr. Hockey Assn., 1975-76. Mem. Am., Mich. personnel and guidance assns., Assn. for Counselor Edn. and Supervision. Club: Portage Lake Golf (v.p. 1974-76). Home: 30 Peepsock Circle Houghton MI 49931 Office: Mich Technol U Houghton MI 49931

WIRT, ROBERT DUANE, educator; b. Whittler, Calif., Apr. 28, 1924; s. Duane Arthur and Helen (Brennan) W.; A.A., Los Angeles City Coll., 1942; B.A., U. Calif. at Berkeley, 1948; M.A., Stanford U., 1951, Ph.D., 1952; m. Anne Louise Antelman, Feb. 19, 1955 (div. May 1972); 1 dau., Elizabeth Anne. Asst. dir., instr. psychol. clinic Stanford U., Palo Alto, Calif., 1952-53; asst. prof. psychology, child devel., psychiatry U. Minn., Mpls., 1954-58; asso. prof., 1958-61, prof., 1961—, dir. tng. clin. child psychology, 1954-71, dir. clin. psychology tng. program, 1963-71, dir. div. health care psychology, 1971—, coordinator edn. in psychiatry Health Scis. Center, 1971—; dir. Center Personality Research, Mpls., 1959-61; chief psychologist Twin Cities Psychiat. and Psychol. Services, Mpls., 1958—; cons. Minn. Dept. Corrections, St. Paul, 1959—, Minn. Depts. Edn. and Pub. Welfare, St. Paul, 1954—, Minn. VA, Mpls., 1955—, Mpls. pub. schs., 1953—. Chmn. Minn. Mental Health Adv. Council, 1964—; mem. Gov.'s Crime Commn., 1967—. Served from pvt. to capt., USMCR, 1942-47, 1951-52. Diplomate Bd. Examiners Profl. Psychology. Fellow Am. Psychol. Assn. (council reps. 1970-73), AAAS; mem. Minn. Psychol. Assn. (exec. com.), Soc. Research Child Development, Sigma Xi. Author: (with W. E. Broen) Personality Inventory for Children, 1958; (with W. Simon) Differential Treatment and Prognosis in Schizophrenia, 1959; (with James L. Jacobson) The Men in Prison in Minnesota, 1966. Contbr. articles to profl. jours. Home: 2615 Irving Ave S Minneapolis MN 55408 Office: Health Sciences Center Univ of Minn Minneapolis MN 53455

WIRTH, RICHARD MARVIN, educator; b. Grosse Pointe, Mich., Aug. 26, 1929; s. Marvin Oscar and Marion (Maxfield) W.; B.Sc., Wayne State U., 1950, M.A., 1952; postgrad. U. Wis., Western State Coll. Colo., Ball State Tchrs. Coll. Tchr., Warren (Mich.) Consol. Schs., 1951—. Organist and choir dir. St. John's Evangelical United Church of Christ. Mem. scholastic writing awards adv. com. S.E. Mich. Named Vol. of Week, United Found., 1963; recipient Distinguished Educator award Mich. State Fair, 1964, Silver Beaver award Boy Scouts Am., 1962; Distinguished Tchr. award Mich. Assn. Classroom Tchrs., 1969. Mem. Mich. (pres. dept. classroom tchrs., Tchr. of Year 1962, dir. area 6, parliamentarian 1972—, dir.), Ky. (parliamentarian 1974), Kans., Warren (editor Harbinger, past pres., sr. trustee) edn. assns., Speech Assn. Am., Nat. Council Tchrs. of English, Mich. League Credit Unions, Delta Sigma Rho. Editor of ednl. publs. Contbr. articles to profl. jours. Home: 9212 Bishop St Detroit MI 48224 Office: 5460 Arden St Warren MI 48092

WIRTJES, LARRY ALLAN, pattern co. exec.; b. Buffalo Center, Iowa, Aug. 17, 1942; s. Wilbur and Margaret Grace (Johnson) W.; welding diploma Hawkeye Inst. Tech., Waterloo, Iowa, 1971; m. Susan Elizabeth Ruelbach, June 20, 1969; children—Sean Michael, Jill Susan, Ryan Joseph. Apprentice patternmaker Manning Pattern Co., Waterloo, 1959-68, journeyman patternmaker, 1970-74; owner Woodland Pattern Co., Waterloo, 1974—. Bd. dirs. Waterloo Youth Hockey Assn., 1976—; mem. Am. Legion X Aux. Police Unit, 1966-68. Served in U.S. Army, 1968-70; Vietnam. Recipient Indsl. Arts award Ford Motor Co., 1960; certificate completion of apprenticeship U.S. Dept. Labor, 1970. Mem. Am. Foundrymen's Soc., Patternmakers League N.Am. (exec. bd. 1971-74). Office: 848 Rainbow Dr Waterloo IA 50701

WIRTZ, ARTHUR M(ICHAEL), real estate and corp. exec.; b. Chgo., Jan. 23, 1901; s. Fredrick C. and Leona (Miller) W.; B.A., U. Mich., 1922; m. Virginia Wadsworth, Mar. 1, 1926; children—Cynthia Wirtz MacArthur, William W., Arthur Michael, Elizabeth V. Founder, 1927, and since chmn., chief exec. officer Wirtz Corp., Chgo.; founder, chmn., chief exec. officer Consol. Enterprises, Inc.; chmn. bd., chief exec. officer Am. Furniture Mart, Chgo.; chmn. Consol. Broadcasting Corp., operators Stas. WEMP and WNUW, Milw., Bismarck Hotel Co., Chgo., Chgo. Stadium Corp., Chgo. Blackhawk Hockey Team, Inc., Wirtz Prodns. Ltd., Ice Follies, Inc., Holiday on Ice, Inc., Forman Realty Corp., Chgo., First Nat. Bank of So. Miami (Fla.), Standard Theatres, Inc., Milw.; dir., chmn. exec. com. Chgo. Milw. Corp.; brought Sonja Henie to U.S., 1936, originator, producer Sonja Henie-Hollywood Ice Revue. Pres., Chgo. Urban Transp. Dist.; dir. Met. Fair and Expn. Authority, Chgo. Mem. Hockey Hall of Fame; named Man of Year, Chgo. Boys Club, 1977. Presbyterian. Clubs: Racquet, Chgo. Athletic, Saddle and Cycle, Chgo. Yacht, Tavern (Chgo.); Knollwood Country. Home: 1420 Lake Shore Dr Chicago IL 60610 Office: 666 Lake Shore Dr Chicago IL 60611

WIRTZ, DWIGHT C., orthopaedic surgeon; b. Boone, Iowa, May 7, 1902; s. William E. and Carrie (Wickersheim) W.; M.D., U. Iowa, 1928; m. Dorothy M. Edwards, Sept. 4, 1937; children—Paul E., Peter D., Ann M. Intern, Fairview Hosp., Mpls., 1928-29; resident in orthopaedics Gillette State Hosp., St. Paul, 1929-30; practice medicine specializing in orthopaedic surgery, Des Moines, 1930—; pres. Des Moines Med. Center; chief staff Broadlawns Hosp., Des Moines, 1949-53; chief staff Luth. Hosp., Des Moines, 1959, organizer 1st pvt. polio Kenney treatment clinic in U.S., 1942; dir. 1st Fed. State Bank. Trustee United Campaign, 1952-61. Served to capt. USNR, 1942-46. Mem. A.C.S., AMA, Iowa Orthopaedic Soc. (pres. 1949-50), Polk County Med. Soc. (trustee 1948-52, pres. 1953), Iowa Clin. Surgical Soc. (pres. 1963-64), Mid-Central States Orthopaedic Soc. (pres. 1963-64). Republican. Episcopalian. Clubs: Des Moines, Des Moines Golf and Country, Masons, Shriners. Home: 4130 River Oaks Dr Des Moines IA 50312 Office: 3716 Ingersoll St Des Moines IA 50312

WIRTZ, PETER GEORGE, ednl. adminstr.; b. New Ulm, Minn., Aug. 13, 1940; s. Edward Francis and Dorothy Mildred (Streukens) W.; B.S., Mankato State Coll., 1962, M.S., 1966; Ed.D., U. Nebr., 1970; m. Marilyn Lee Schugel, Aug. 18, 1962; children—Terri Lee, Toni Marie, Danny Peter. Resident advisor Mankato (Minn.) State Coll., 1960-62; tchr.-coach secondary schs. El Rancho Unified Sch. Dist., Pico Rivera, Calif., 1962-64; tchr.-coach-counselor secondary schs. Central High Sch., Marshall, Minn., 1964-66; student affairs asst., coordinator students, dir. recreation, asst. prof. U. Nebr., Lincoln, 1966-73; dir. student activities-services, asst. prof. U. Iowa, Iowa City, 1974—. Bd. dirs. Lincoln Community Concert Assn., 1971-73, Iowa City Vol. Bur., 1974-77; pres., lifetime mem. PTA, 1972; pres. Regina High Sch. Home-Sch. Assn., 1976-78; bd. dirs. Jr. Achievement Program, Iowa City, 1977—, Far Horizons Improvement Inc.; candidate Iowa City Catholic Sch. Bd., 1976. Mem. NEA, Am., Nebr. personnel and guidance assns., Iowa Student Personnel Assn., Am. Coll. Personnel Assn. (chairperson commn. IV 1976-78), Nat. Assn. Student Personnel Adminstrs., Phi Delta Kappa. Democrat. Roman Catholic. Clubs: Univ. Athletic, Iowa, Fairview Golf. Contbr. articles to profl. jours. Home: 917 Fairway Ln Iowa City IA 52240 Office: Student Activities Center Iowa City IA 52242

WIRTZ, VIRGINIA WADSWORTH (MRS. ARTHUR M. WIRTZ), civic worker; b. Cleve., Jan. 30, 1903; d. Charles and Anna (Doyle) Wadsworth; student U. Colo., 1920-21; B.S., Northwestern U., 1924; m. Arthur Michael Wirtz, Mar. 1, 1926; children—Cynthia Wirtz MacArthur, William Wadsworth, Arthur Michael, Jr., Elizabeth Virginia. Mem. Presbyn.-St. Luke's Hosp. Women's Bd., 1926—; mem. women's council Chgo. div. Am. Heart Assn.; women's com. Mental Health Soc. Chgo.; mem. women's bd. Am. Cancer Soc.; trustee Ill. Children's Home and Aid Soc., Am. Opera Soc.; trustee Fourth Presbyterian Ch. Mem. Mortar Bd., Pi Beta Phi. Clubs: Women's Athletic, Saddle and Cycle, Racquet, Arts; Knollwood Country. Home: 1420 Lake Shore Dr Chicago IL 60610 (summer) Ivanhoe Farm Route 60 Mundelein IL 60060

WIRTZ, WAYNE HENRY, pathologist; b. Mandan, N.D., Feb. 21, 1948; s. John and Colleen (Hermanson) W.; B.S. in Chemistry, U. N.D., 1970, B.S. in Chem. Edn., 1971, B.S. in Medicine, 1975; M.D., Rush Med. Coll., 1975. Intern, Ill. Masonic Med. Center, Chgo., 1975-76, resident in pathology, 1976-77, chief pathology resident, 1977-78; asst. in pathology U. Ill., Chgo., 1976—; instr. med. tech. Ill. Masonic Med. Center, 1976—; co-dir. labs. Mile Sq. Health Center, Chgo., 1977—. NSF grantee in chemistry, 1969. Mem. Chgo. Path. Soc., AMA, Ill. Med. Soc. Home: 657 Melrose St Chicago IL 60657 Office: Ill Masonic Hosp 836 Wellington St Chicago IL 60657

WIRTZ, WILLIAM WADSWORTH, corp. exec.; b. Chgo., Oct. 5, 1929; s. Arthur Michael and Virginia (Wadsworth) W.; A.B., Brown U., 1950; m. Joan Roney, Dec. 15, 1950; children—William R., Gail W., Karen K., Peter R., Alison M. Pres. Am. Furniture Mart, Chgo., 1965—, Chgo. Blackhawk Hockey Team, Inc., 1966—, Chgo. Stadium Corp., 1966—, Consol. Enterprises, Inc., Chgo., 1966—. First Security Trust and Savs. Bank, Elmwood Park, Ill., 1960—, Forman Realty Corp., Chgo., 1965—, 333 Building Corp., Chgo., 1966—, Wirtz Corp., Chgo., 1964—. Clubs: Saddle and Cycle, Racquet, Mid-America (Chgo.); Fin and Feather (Elgin, Ill.). Home: Winnetka IL Office: 666 Lake Shore Dr Chicago IL 60611

WISCHMEIER, WALTER HENRY, soil erosion cons.; b. Lincoln, Mo., Jan. 18, 1911; s. August and Sophia Magdalene (Maas) W.; B.S., U. Mo., 1953; M.S., Purdue U., 1957; m. Marjorie Scheurer, Oct. 25, 1947; children—Joyce Ann (Mrs. Michael Plantenga), Dennis Walter. Tchr., Golden Sch., Ionia, Mo., 1928-29, Feaster Sch., Warsaw, Mo., 1933-37; salesman Farmers Merc. Co., Lincoln, 1929-32, S.F. Baker Co., Lincoln, 1932-33; office mgr. State Social Security Commn., Kansas City, Mo., 1937-39; statis. and adminstrv. clk. Soil Conservation Service, U.S. Dept. Agr., Columbia, Mo., 1940-53; erosion investigations leader Agrl. Research Service, U.S. Dept. Agr., Purdue U., West Lafayette, Ind., 1954-76; prof. emeritus Purdue, 1976—; soil erosion cons., 1976—. Served with AUS, 1943-46. Recipient Superior Service award U.S. Dept. Agr., 1959, 73. Fellow Soil Conservation Soc. Am. (nat. erosion and sedimentation com. 1964-72); mem. Am. Soc. Agronomy, Soil Sci. Soc. Am., Am. Soc. Agrl. Engrs. Contbr. articles to profl. jours. Home: 2009 Indian Trail Dr West Lafayette IN 47906 Office: Agrl Engring Dept Purdue U West Lafayette IN 47907

WISE, BETTY JEAN DAVIS (MRS. EUGENE EDWARD WISE, JR.), social worker, educator; b. Covington, Ky., Apr. 27, 1932; d. John Henry and Anna (Asher) Davis; B.S., Central State U. (Ohio), 1954; M.S., U. Conn., 1956; m. Eugene Edward Wise, Jr., Dec. 18, 1955; children—Eugene Edward III, Lauren Ann, Roland Walter. Dir. social services dept. Catherine Booth Maternity Home and Hosp., Cin., 1958-59, psychiat. social worker, Spokane, 1959-60; case analyst for study Wash. State Dept. of Pub. Assistance, Greenleigh Assos., Inc., Spokane, 1964; adult edn. instr. USAF, Fairchild AFB, Wash., 1962-64; tchr. 6th grade gen. curriculum Hamilton Local Sch. Dist., Lockbourne, Ohio, 1966-69; social planner, div. urban renewal Dept. Devel., Columbus, Ohio, 1969; asst. dean students Wilmington (Ohio) Coll., 1969-71; counselor Counseling Center, Capital U., Columbus, 1972—, part-time instr., 1973-76; leader Expt. in Internat. Living; core faculty Univ. Without Walls of Ohio. Trustee Children's Mental Health Center, Columbus. Registered clin. social worker. Mem. Royal Soc. Health (London, Eng.), Nat. Assn. Social Workers (charter), League of Women Voters, Nat. Council Negro Women (life mem.), Acad. Certified Social Workers Alumni Assn. U. Conn. Sch. Soc. Work, Central State U. Alumni Assn. (life, nat. trustee), Alpha Kappa Alpha. Democrat. Baptist. Club: Columbus Metro (charter). Home: 2650 Halleck Dr Columbus OH 43209

WISE, HENRY SEILER, U.S. judge; b. Mt. Carmel, Ill., July 16, 1909; A.B., LL.B., Washington U., St. Louis, 1933; m. G. Louise Hawkins, Dec. 10, 1938; children—H. Michael, Patricia (Mrs. Stephen Satre), N. Susanne (Mrs. Robert Lang), Marilyn (Mrs. Gerald L. Furnish), David. Admitted to Mo. bar, 1933, Ill. bar, 1934; practice in Danville, Ill., 1934—; mem. firms Jinkins & Jinkins, 1934-37, Meeks & Lowenstein, 1937-42, Meeks & Wise, 1942-51, Graham, Wise, Meyer, Young & Welsch, 1951-66; judge U.S. Dist. Ct., Eastern Dist. Ill., Danville, 1966—. Commr., Ill. Ct. of Claims, 1949-53; mem. Ill. Parole and Pardon Bd., 1961-66. County chmn. Dem. party, 1948-54; del. Dem. nat. conv., 1952, 56, 60, 64. Mem. Am., Ill., Vermilion (Ill.) County bar assns., Am. Judicature Soc., Danville C. of C. K.C. (4), Elk. Club: Danville Country. Home: 507 Chester Ave Danville IL 61832 Office: US Dist Ct Danville IL 61832

WISE, JOHN AUGUSTUS, JR., lawyer; b. Detroit, Mar. 30, 1938; s. John Augustus and Mary Blanche (Parent) W.; A.B. cum laude, Coll. Holy Cross, 1959; student U. Vienna, 1957-58; J.D., U. Mich., 1962; postgrad. (Ford Found. grantee) U. Munich, 1962-63; m. Helga M. Bessin, Nov. 27, 1965; children—Monique, John Eric. Admitted to Mich. bar, 1963; asso. firm Dykema, Wheat, Spencer, Goodnow & Trigg, Detroit, 1962-64; asst. to pres. Internat. Econ. Policy Assn., Washington, 1964-66; practiced in Detroit, 1967-70; partner Ziegler, Dykhouse & Wise, Detroit, 1970—. Dir. Peltzer & Ehlers Am. Corp., Columbian Am. Friends, Inc. Vice pres., treas. Hyde Park Co-op., 1974-77. Mem. Am., Mich., Detroit bar assns. Roman Catholic. Clubs: Detroit Athletic, Detroit Economic. Home: 1221 Yorkshire St Grosse Pointe Park MI 48230 Office: 3000 Book Bldg Detroit MI 48226

WISE, LEW EDGAR, educator; b. Washington, Ind., Nov. 5, 1931; s. Wilbur Roscoe and Emma Elsie (Hart) W.; B.S., Ind. State U., 1957; M.S., Ind. U., 1959, Ed.D., 1969; m. Peggy Ruth Warfield, Nov. 22, 1951; children—Elizabeth Ann, Bret Warfield, Steven Wilbur. Tchr., Paoli, Ind., 1957-59; instr. Ind. U. Lab. Sch., Bloomington, 1959-69; asst. prof. edn. Ind. U., Ft. Wayne, 1969—. Cons. workshops in sci. and outdoor edn. Bd. dirs. Fox Island Alliance. Served with AUS, 1952-54. HEW grantee, 1974. Mem. Conservation-Outdoor Edn. Assn., Assn. Tchr. Educators, Nat. Sci. Tchrs. Assn., Hoosier Assn. Sci. Tchrs., Phi Delta Kappa. Contbr. articles to profl. publs. Home: 5616 Dartmouth Dr Fort Wayne IN 46825

WISE, VIRGIL JAY, educator; b. Washington, Ind., May 7, 1917; s. Adrian J. and Ethel Mae (McCracken) W.; B.S., Ind. State U., 1940; M.S., Butler U., 1949; Ed.D., Ind. U., 1959; m. Lilly Mae Byrum, May 30, 1941; children—Jeanie Renee, Virgil Jay II. Tchr. city schs., Frankfort, Ind., 1940-42, Indpls., 1946-50; prin. DeWitt Sch., Indpls., 1952-60, Buck Sch., Indpls., 1960-65; asso. prof. lang. arts edn. U. Wis., Whitewater, 1968—. Vis. lectr. grad. sch. Butler U., summers 1960, 61, Miami U. Grad. Sch., 1962-63; chmn. lang. arts curriculum com. Indpls. Pub. Schs., 1956-58; mem. com. Tchr. Preparation in Wis., 1968-70. Served with USNR, 1942-46, 50-52. Mem. NEA (life), Nat., Wis. councils tchrs. English, Assn. Supervision and Curriculum Devel., Phi Delta Kappa. Mason, Rotarian. Home: 15 Riggert Rd Rural Route 4 Box 155 Fort Atkinson WI 53538

WISEMAN, MAXINE CLAIRE SCHRADER (MRS. ERLOW WILLIAM WISEMAN), educator, assn. exec.; b. Mount Vernon, S.D., Jan. 13, 1906; d. Henry Louis and Augusta (Wagner) Schrader; student Gen. Beadle State Coll., 1923-24; B.A., Dakota Wesleyan U., 1931; postgrad. U. Wis., summer 1933, Grand Island Bus. Coll., summers 1935-39; M.S., S.D. State U., 1960; m. Erlow William Wiseman, June 18, 1941. Tchr. S.D. pub. schs., Mount Vernon, 1924-69; instr. English Dakota Wesleyan U., 1969-75, asst. prof. English, 1975—. Mem. Order Eastern Star, 1944—, holder various offices, 1945—, Worthy Matron, 1949; mem. state treas. S.D. Press Women, 1953—; mem. and treas. Nat. Fedn. Press Women, 1956-58, editorial bd., 1960—; state sec.; treas. S.D. Trapshooting Assn., 1959-65. Bd. dirs. Mount Vernon Cemetery Assn. Named woman of year, S.D. Press Assn., 1966; recipient Achievement award, Delta Kappa Gamma, 1958, award for contbns. Dakota Wesleyan U., 1974. Mem. Nat. (life), S.D. (life) edn. assns., League Am. Pen Women, Delta Kappa Gamma, Phi Kappa Phi, Pi Gamma Mu, Sigma Delta Chi. Address: Box 71 Mount Vernon SD 57363

WISINSKI, STANLEY JOSEPH, III, real estate broker; b. Grand Rapids, Mich., Sept. 10, 1940; s. Stanley Joseph, Jr. and Mary Stella (Goleniewski) W.; student Aquinas Coll., Grand Rapids, 1958-60; certificate real estate U. Mich., 1972; m. Phyllis June White, Aug. 29, 1968; step-children—Steve Glupner, Sue Glupker, Carol Gluper; 1 dau., Maryanne. With Westdale Co., Grand Rapids, 1960—, mgr. comml. dept., 1968-72, successively v.p., gen. mgr. comml. investment div., pres., 1972—. Mem. adv. bd. Marywood Acad., Grand Rapids, 1973—. Served with N.G., 1964-65. Recipient Distinguished Sales award Sales and Mktg. Exec. Club Grand Rapids, 1971. Mem. Nat. Assn. Realtors (highest comml. investment designation 1974), Soc. Indsl. Realtors (highest indsl. designation 1976), Grand Rapids C. of C. Home: 8080 Wilderness Lake Trail NE Ada (Grand Rapids) MI 49301 Office: 3435 Lake Eastbrook Blvd SE Grand Rapids MI 49506

WISNESKI, KENNETH THOMAS, newspaper editor; b. Cloquet, Minn., May 20, 1933; s. Stanley Paul and Lynda (Niemi) W.; B.A., U. Minn., 1958; m. Susan Jane Hinkens, Mar. 16, 1959; children—Joseph S., Victoria Ann, Patrick H. Newswriter, Sta. KSTP-TV, St. Paul, 1963-64; reporter UPI, Mpls., 1959; editor Sausalito (Calif.) News, 1959-60, Suburban Life, St. Paul, 1960-63; mng. editor N. Suburban Newspapers, St. Paul, 1963-66; exec. editor and v.p. Sun Newspapers, Inc., Mpls., St. Paul, 1966—; tchr. journalism Lakewood Jr. Coll., White Bear Lake, Minn., 1965-66. Bd. dirs. N.W. Br. YMCA, 1964-68, Mpls. United Fund, 1968-74. Served with USAR, 1955-62. Josephine L. Miriam scholar, 1951; recipient Feature Writing award U.S. Suburban Press Found., 1966. Mem. Roseville C. of C., Minn. Newspaper Assn. Club: Midland Country. Home: 1025 W County Rd G2 Saint Paul MN 55112 Office: 8801 W 78th St Edina MN 55438

WISNIEWSKI, CHARMAINE, bus. exec.; b. Chgo., May 19, 1952; d. Edmund Henry and Regina Anne (Trzybinski) Wisniewski; B.S. in Engring. Physics, U. Ill., 1974; M.B.A. in Mktg., Xavier U., 1976—. Mfg. supr. Procter & Gamble, Chgo., 1974-76, project eng., Cin., 1976, asst. tech. brand mgr., 1976-77, tech. brand mgr., 1978—. Mem. Soc. of Women Engrs., Internat. Microwave Power Inst. Club: Cin. Ski. Home: 15 N Applewood Ct Fairfield OH 45014 Office: 6071 Center Hill Rd Cincinnati OH 45224

WISSLER, ROBERT WILLIAM, physician, educator; b. Richmond, Ind., Mar. 1, 1917; s. William O. and Muriel (Thomas) W.; A.B., Earlham Coll., 1939, D.Sc. (hon.), 1959; Ph.D., U. Chgo., 1946, M.D. with honors, 1948; M.D. (hon.), U. Heidelberg (Germany), 1973; m. Elizabeth Anne Polk, 1940; children—Barbara, Mary, David, John. Intern USPHS, Chgo. Marine Hosp., 1949-50; instr. pathology U. Chgo., 1943-47, asst. prof., 1947-52, asso. prof., 1952-57, prof., chmn. dept. pathology, 1957-72, Donald N. Pritzker prof., 1972—, Distinguished Service prof., 1977—, cancer coordinator, 1962-74. Nutritional and immunologic research Army and Navy, 1941-45; cons. pathology study sect. Surg. Gen. USPHS, 1957-61; com. pathology Nat. Acad. Scis.-NRC, 1958, chmn. com., 1962-69; cons. Armed Forces Inst. Pathology, 1962-72, chmn. sci. adv. com., 1965-66; adv. com. Ill. Bd. Higher Edn.; mem. pathol. tng. grant com. NIH, 1963-67; organizing sec., program chmn. 2d Internat. Symposium Atherosclerosis, Chgo., 1969; mem. pathology adv. com. VA, 1970—, sci. adv. com. Lankenau Hosp., 1970—, nat. adv. com. Nat. Center Primate Biology, 1970-72, Selection com. Stouffer prize, 1971-73. Trustee Earlham Coll., 1968-71, 76—. Recipient David Worth Dennis award for excellence in chem. Earlham Coll., 1939, Howard Taylor Ricketts grad. student award for outstanding research pathology and bacteriology, 1947, Joseph A. Capps prize Chgo. Inst. Medicine, 1951, award of merit Am. Heart Assn., 1971. Diplomate Nat. Bd. Med. Examiners (chmn. path. test com. 1962-64), Am. Bd. Pathology (trustee 1968—, sec. 1974—). Mem. Am. Soc. Exptl. Pathology (pres. 1961-62), Am. Soc. Cell Biology, Reticuloendothelial Soc., Soc. Exptl. Biology and Med., Am. (council arteriosclerosis, sec. 1964, chmn. 1966, com. internat. programs 1968—), Chgo. (gov. 1962-66, pres. 1972-73), heart assns., Am. Cancer Soc. (chmn. research com. 1966-70, chmn. med.-sci. com. 1970-71, Ill. div.), European Atherosclerosis Group, Am. Assn. Pathologists and Bacteriologist (council 1963—, v.p. 1967, pres. 1968), Am. Vet. Med. Assn. (hon.), Am. Soc. Clin. Pathology, Internat. Acad. Path., Am. Assn. Immunologists, A.M.A., Am. Assn. Cancer Research Coll. Am. Pathologists (sec. acad sect. 1960, mem. assembly 1966) N.Y. Acad. of Scis., Am. Assn. of Chmn. Med. Sch. Depts. Pathology (pres. 1967). Univs. Assn. for Research and Edn. in Pathology (v.p. dir., pres. 1969-71), Am. Assn. Accreditation on Lab. Animal Care (trustee 1967—, pres. 1971—), Sigma Xi (pres. Chgo. 1961), Alpha Omega Alpha, Gamma Alpha. Unitarian (chmn. bd. trustees 1962-63). Contbr. numerous sci. papers in field. Asso. editor Metabolism, 1953-58; Nutrition Revs., 1954-63; editorial bd. Recent Results in Cancer Research. Editor: Endogenous Factors Influencing Host-Tumor Balance, 1967; Pathogenesis of Atherosclerosis, 1972. Home: 5532 S Lake Shore Dr Chicago IL 60637

WITHAM, GLENN WINTON, JR., retailer; b. Pine River, Minn., Mar. 22, 1934; s. Glenn Winton and Marvina Christine (Breiland) W.; B.S., Bemidji State Coll., 1959; m. Donna Mae Nemic, Dec. 17, 1955; children—Kim, Keely, Kari, Karla. Owner Witham Concrete Products, Hackensack Lumber and Hardware (Minn.), 1959—; real estate broker Chippewa Realty, Hackensack, 1966—. Commr. Cass County, 1975—. Bd. dirs. Walker-Hackensack Sch. Bd., 1966-74, vice chmn., 1974. Served with AUS, 1953-55. Recipient Meritorious Service award Cass County 4-H, 1974. Mem. Cass County Bd. Realtors (pres. 1973, 74), Hackensack C. of C. (dir. 1962-69), Nat. Pilots Assn., VFW, Nat., Minn. assns. realtors. Lutheran (treas. 1965-67, elder 1970-73). Lion (3d v.p. 1975). Home: Hackensack MN 56452

WITHERS, CARL RAYMOND, lawyer; b. Reading, Pa., Jan. 26, 1924; s. Stuart Schnable and Edith (Garman) W.; A.B., Wittenberg U., 1950; LL.B., U. Mich., 1953; m. Jenny Constance Cory, Sept. 2, 1950; children—Wren Alice, Jill Cory, Bradford John. Admitted to Ohio bar, 1954; since practiced in Cleve.; with firm Van Aken, Bond, Withers & Asman. Precinct committeeman Republican party, 1964—, dist. leader, 1972—; pres. Shaker Heights Rep. Club, 1973-75. Served to 1st lt. USAAF, 1942-46. Mem. Cleve., Ohio bar assns., Am. Legion (past comdr.), Cleve Grays, Ohio Curling Assn. (treas., trustee), Beta Theta Pi, Delta Theta Phi. Presbyn. Club: Cleveland Skating (trustee). Home: 17501 Shaker Blvd Shaker Heights OH 44120 Office: Nat City Bank Bldg Cleveland OH 44114

WITHERSPOON, VIVAION MAUDIETTE, educator; b. Waldo, Ark., Aug. 23, 1941; d. Bert and Narvell (Jamerson) Porter; B.S., Western Mich. U., 1972, M.A., 1976; postgrad. U. Mich., 1976—; m. Henry James Witherspoon, July 31, 1965. Caseworker, Muskegon (Mich.) Social Service, 1966-67; attendance officer Muskegon Heights (Mich.) pub. schs., 1967-71, tchr., 1971—. Pres. Woodcliffe Neighborhood Assn., Muskegon Heights, 1970-77. Mem. Nat., Mich. edn. assns., Mich. Assn. Middle Sch. Edn., Mich. Assn. Sch. Curriculum Devel. Club: Masons. Home: 3020 Woodcliffe Dr Muskegon Heights MI 49444 Office: Peck and Sherman Sts Muskegon Heights MI 49444

WITHERSPOON, WILLIAM, investment economist; b. St. Louis, Nov. 21, 1909; s. William Conner and Mary (Houston) W.; student Washington U. Evening Sch., 1928-47; m. Margaret Telford Johanson, June 25, 1938; children—James Tomlin, Jane Witherspoon Peltz, Elizabeth Witherspoon Vodra. Research dept. A. G. Edwards & Sons, 1928-31; pres. Witherspoon Investment Co., 1931-34; head research dept. Newhard Cook & Co., 1934-43; chief price analysis St. Louis Ordnance Dist., 1943-45; head research dept. Newhard Cook & Co., 1945-53; owner Witherspoon Investment Counsel, 1953-64; ltd. partner Newhard Cook & Co., economist, investment analyst, 1965-68; v.p., researcher Stifel, Nicolaus & Co., 1968—; lectr. on investments Washington U., 1948-67. Mem. Clayton Bd. of Edn., 1955-68, pres., 1966-67; mem. Clayton Park and Recreation Commn., 1959-60; trustee Ednl. TV, KETC, 1963-64; mem. investment com. Gen. Assembly Mission Bd. Presbyterian Ch. U.S., Atlanta, 1976—. Served as civilian Ordnance Dept., AUS, 1943-45. Chartered fin. analyst. Mem. St. Louis Soc. Fin. Analysts (pres. 1949-50). Home: 6401 Ellenwood Clayton MO 63105 Office: 500 N Broadway St Louis MO 63102

WITHEY, JOSEPH ANTHONY, educator; b. N.Y.C., Nov. 1, 1918; s. Percy Harding and Mary Genevieve (Craven) W.; A.B., State U. N.Y. at Albany, 1941; M.A., Cornell U., 1947, Ph.D., 1953; m. Gertrude Elizabeth Wilson, Apr. 14, 1942; children—Mark, David. Instr. speech and drama Kan. State Tchrs. Coll., Emporia, 1947-49; instr. drama Utica (N.Y.) Coll. of Syracuse U., 1949-51; prof. English, East Carolina U., Greenville, N.C., 1953-62; prof. speech and drama Hanover (Ind.) Coll., 1962-66, prof. Asian studies 1966—. Served with Signal Corps, AUS, 1942-46. Fulbright research scholar to U. Mandalay (Burma), 1960-61, Fulbright-Hays Faculty Research Study grantee U. Chgo., 1969-70. Mem. Assn. Asian Studies, Am. Assn. U. Profs., Am. Theatre Assn. (chmn. Afro-Asian theatre project 1966-68, chmn. film/tape selection com. 1971-73), Asia Soc (mem. Burma council 1963—). Author: (with Kenneth Sein) The Great PO Sein: A Chronicle of the Burmese Theater, 1965; Theater As A Fine Art,

1965; An Annotated Bibliography of the Theatre of Southeast Asia to 1971, 1974. Home: Faculty Rd Hanover IN 47243

WITHINGTON, JOSEPH GARDNER, machine shop exec.; b. Pine Lawn, Mo., Jan. 27, 1925; s. Joseph Gardner and Margarette Mary (Watts) W.; student Washington U., St. Louis, 1946-49, intermittently, 1956-62, Mo. U., 1967; m. Evelyn Jule Nieman, Aug. 14, 1948; children—Joseph Scott, Kurt Steven. With U.S. Govt. Civil Service, 1951-60; with Withington Typewriter & Supply Co., Inc., St. Louis, 1958—, pres., 1960—; sec., dir. Am. Fed. Savs. & Loan Co., Sullivan, Mo., 1964—; with Nieman Tool & Machine Co., 1950—, pres. Nieman Machine Co., Inc., Tempe, Ariz., 1964—. Bd. dirs. Crawford County (Mo.) Civil Def., 1971—; active Boy Scouts Am. Served with AUS, 1943-46. Mem. Am. Ordnance Assn. Home: 414 Hillcrest Dr Sullivan MO 63080 Office: 406 Ramsey St Sullivan MO 63080

WITT, COLEMAN BOYD, physician; b. Richmond, Ky., July 14, 1930; s. Boyd Burnam and May Coleman (Wallace) W.; B.S. cum laude, Eastern Ky. U., 1952; M.D., U. Louisville, 1956; m. Anna Frances Wylie, Aug. 12, 1951; children—Patricia May, Michael Burnam, Kevin Boyd. Intern St. Elizabeth Med. Center, Dayton, 1956-57; employee with physician, Dayton, 1957-59; partner med. practice, Dayton, Ohio, 1959-67; pres. Brandt Med. Assos., Inc., 1967—; pres. Brandt Med. Center, Inc.; mem. staff St. Elizabeth Med. Center, Children's Med. Center, Miami Valley Hosp., Good Samaritan Hosp. Diplomate Am. Acad. Family Practice. Mem. Ohio, Montgomery County med. socs., AMA, Am., Ohio acads. family practice, C. of C. Republican. Mem. Christian Ch. Club: Optimist (pres. 1968-69) (East Dayton, Ohio). Home: 1208 Hidden Oaks Dr Dayton OH 45459 Office: 5173 Brandt Pike Dayton OH 45424

WITT, S. LEE, educator; b. Golden, Ill., May 13, 1923; s. Samuel Oliver and Ruth (Johnson) W.; A.B., Carthage Coll., 1947; M.S., Western Ill. U., 1960; postgrad. U. Wis., No. Ill. U.; m. Bette Carroll, May 1, 1945; children—Karen Lynn, Harold Lee. Basketball coach Monroe Center (Ill.) High Sch., 1947-51; county orgn. dir. Adair County Farm Bur., Greenfield, Ia., 1951-55; head basketball coach Carthage (Ill.) High Sch., 1955-60, sci. tchr., 1969-73; head basketball coach Aurora (Ill.) East High Sch., 1960-67; athletic dir., basketball coach Waubonsee Coll., Aurora, 1967-68; basketball coach Belvidere (Ill.) High Sch., 1973—. Pres. Hancock County Heart Assn., Carthage, 1971-72. Served with USAAF, 1943-45. Mem. NEA, Ill. Edn. Assn., AAHPER, Alpha Mu Gamma, Beta Beta Beta. Episcopalian (mem. ch. bd. 1957-60). Mason. Home: 7769 Bel-Mar Dr Belvidere IL 61008 Office: 1500 East Ave Belvidere IL 61008

WITTCOFF, CONSTANCE CYNTHIA CLEIN, educator, psychologist counselor; b. Seattle, Nov. 12, 1931; d. Norman Ward and Therese Cynthia (Budwig) Clein; B.A., Stanford U., 1952; M.A.Ed., Counseling Psychology, Washington U., St. Louis, 1977; m. Raymond H. Wittcoff, June 25, 1958; children—Mark Raymond, Caroline Cynthia. Writer, San Francisco Chronicle, 1953-55; dir. Am. Assn. UN, St. Louis, 1956-60; lectr., program developer St. Louis Art Mus., 1960-71; producer Sta. KETC-TV, pub. broadcasting, St. Louis, 1973-75; instr. dept. edn., counselor for women U. Mo., St. Louis, 1976—; researcher, clin. asst. dept. psychiatry Med. Sch., Washington U., 1977—; cons. Danforth Found., Am. Cancer Soc.; bd. dirs. Adult Edn. Council of Greater St. Louis, 1977—, Com. for Arts and Sr. Citizens, St. Louis. Bd. dirs. women's aux. St. Louis Symphony, 1959-63, Dance Concert Soc., St. Louis, 1974-77; mem. exec. com. Contemporary Art Soc., St. Louis, 1965-70. Recipient numerous pub. service honors for cultural and civic contbns. Mem. Am. Personnel and Guidance Assn., Am. Vocat. Guidance Assn., Assn. Counselor Edn. and Supervision, Nat. Assn. Ednl. Broadcasters, Am. Soc. Tng., Devel., Assos. Mus. Modern Art, St. Louis Art Mus. (life), Stanford Alumni Assn. (life). Clubs: Stanford of St. Louis, Whittimore House-Washington U. Faculty. Author: Effective Learning Skills, 1977; What is Treatment?, 1977; writer, producer, dir. film: Women and Money: Myths and Realities, 1976. Home: 50 Randelay Dr St Louis MO 63124 Office: Dept Psychiatry Washington U Med Sch Jewish Hospital St Louis MO 63110

WITTEMANN, HENRY, cosmetic co. exec.; b. N.Y.C., Mar. 20, 1930; s. Henry and Emilie Julie (Preuss) W.; B.S. in Commerce, N.Y.U., 1962; m. Marilyn Bobinsky, May 18, 1968. Account exec. Ogilvy & Mather, Inc., N.Y.C., 1950-63; v.p., account supr. Compton Advt., Chgo., 1963-65; v.p. advt. Alberto Culver Co., 1965—. Served with AUS, 1954-56. Home: 6 Sheffield Ln Oak Brook IL 60521 Office: 2525 W Armitage Melrose Park IL 60160

WITTICH, JOHN JACOB, coll. adminstr.; b. Huntley, Ill., Nov. 13, 1921; s. John and Eva (Karl) W.; B.A., DePauw U., 1943, LL.D., 1971; M.A., U. N.Mex., 1949; Ph.D., Stanford, 1952; m. Leah Glynn, Apr. 2, 1944; children—Karen Ann, Jane Ellen, John Elliott. Grad. asst. U. N.Mex., Albuquerque, 1947-48; tchr. Albuquerque High Sch., 1948-49; teaching asst. Stanford, 1949-51; asst. prof. psychology Coll. of Pacific, Stockton, Calif., 1951-52; dean of admissions, dir. scholarships, asso. prof. DePauw U., Greencastle, Ind., 1952-61; dir. Coll. Center of Finger Lakes, Corning, N.Y., 1961-63; exec. dir. Coll. Student Personnel Inst., Claremont, Calif., 1963-68; vis. lectr. Claremont Grad. Sch., 1963-68; pres. MacMurray Coll., Jacksonville, Ill., 1968—. Mem. exec. com. Div. Higher Edn., Central Ill. Conf. of United Meth. Ch., 1968—; mem. exec. com. Fedn. Ind. Ill. Colls. and Univs., Asso. Colls. Ill.; mem. non-pub. adv. com. Ill. Bd. Higher Edn., 1973—. Trustee Lincoln Acad. Ill., 1968—. Served with USMCR, 1943-46. Mem. Am. Psychol. Assn., Am. Coll. Personnel Assn., AAUP, Assn. Coll. Admissions Counselors (exec. bd.), Central States Coll. Assn. (exec. com. 1969—, treas. 1970, 71, sec.-treas. 1972—), DePauw U. So. Calif. Alumni Assn. (pres. 1966-68), Sigma Chi. Methodist. Rotarian. Contbr. articles to popular and profl. jours. Home: 339 E State St Jacksonville IL 62650

WITTMUSS, HOWARD DALE, educator, b. Papillion, Nebr., July 15, 1922; s. Albert Emil and Ella Mae (Zeisler) W.; B.S., U. Nebr., 1947, M.S., 1950, Ph.D., 1956; m. Mildred Lucille Schlaphoff, Aug. 5, 1950; children—Jane Marie, Steven Howard, Lynne Ellen. Research asst., dept. agrl. engring. U. Nebr., Lincoln, 1952-56, asst. prof., 1956-58, asso. prof., 1958—. Product evaluator Western Irrigation Valve Corp., Des Moines, Iowa, 1969—. Served as lt. (j.g.) USNR, 1943-46, lt., 1950-52. Names Engr. of Distinction, Engrs. Joint Council N.Y.C., 1970. Mem. Am. Soc. Agrl. Engrs. (regional dir. 1968-70), Soil Conservation Soc. Am., Sigma Xi. Methodist. Kiwanian. Home: 1808 Morningside Dr Lincoln NE 68506 Office: Dept Agrl Engring U Nebraska Lincoln NE 68503

WOCKENFUSS, JAMES HAROLD, performing arts dir., educator; b. Fond du Lac, Wis., Jan. 14, 1930; s. Harold Frederick and Florence Marie (Hanisch) W.; B.A., U. Wis., 1953; m. Lena May Sewell, May 27, 1961; children—Erica Lynn, Kirsten Lee. Theatre mgr. Wis. Union Theater, U. Wis., Madison, 1954-63; dir. La. State U. Union Theater, Baton Rouge, 1963-70; dir. Hancher Auditorium, coordinator Ia. Center for Arts, U. Iowa, Iowa City, 1970—, prof. speech and dramatic arts, arts mgmt. program, 1975—. Mem. Urban Renewal Design Com., 1974—; mem. music task force com. Iowa Arts Council, 1974-77. Mem. Assn. Coll., Univ. and Community Arts Adminstrs. (pres. 1972-74), Assn. Coll. Unions Internat. (chmn. com. on performing and visual arts 1971-73), Omicron Delta Kappa. Rotarian. Home: 1409 E Davenport St Iowa City IA 52240

WODLINGER, MARK LOUIS, radio station exec.; b. Jacksonville, Fla., July 13, 1922; s. Mark H. and Beatrice May (Boney) W.; B.S., U. Fla., 1943; m. Constance J. Bates, May 3, 1974; children—Kevin, Michael, Stephen, Jacqueline, Mark. Salesman, WQUA Radio, Moline, Ill., 1948; sales mgr., mgr. radio WOC Am/FM and TV, Davenport, Iowa, 1949-58; pres. Community Telecasting Corp., Moline, 1958-62; v.p., gen. mgr. WZZM TV, Grand Rapids, Mich., 1962, KMBC-TV, Kansas City, Mo., 1963-69; pres. Intermedia, Inc., Kansas City, 1969-72; pres., owner, gen. mgr. KBEQ, Inc., Kansas City, 1972—. Active Civic Council, YMCA, Art Inst., Am. Royal (bd. govs.). Served with USN, 1943-46. Mem. Nat. Assn. Broadcasters, Advt. Club, Broadcast Pioneers, Mo. Broadcast Assn. Clubs: Kansas City, Univ., Carriage, Masons, Rotary. Home: 6439 Wenonga Rd Mission Hills KS 66208 Office: 3100 Broadway #111 Kansas City MO 64111

WOELLHOF, LAWRENCE RAY, social worker; b. Clay Center, Kans., Nov. 28, 1922; s. Jacob F. and Laura M. (Hahn) W.; B.S., Emporia (Kans.) State U., 1949, M.S., 1954; m. Eldene Cook, Sept. 21, 1962; 1 son, Jeffrey. Tchr., Meade (Kans.) Pub. Schs., 1949-53; prin. Lakin (Kans.) Grade Sch., 1953-59; instr. Emporia State U., 1960-63; counselor supr. Kans. State Employment Service, Topeka, 1965-67, asst. mgr., 1967-70; ednl. dir. Kans. Neurol. Inst., Topeka, 1970-72; dir. Foster Grandparent Project, Topeka, 1972; bd. dirs. Community Resources Council, Topeka, 1972—, chmn. aging sect., 1973-74, 77—; mem. Older Citizens Info. Center, Topeka, 1973—, pres. bd. dirs., 1977; dir. Kans. Citizens Council on Aging, Topeka, 1975—; mem. adv. council Shawnee County (Kans.) Community Mental Health Corp., 1971-72; chmn. Topeka Area Manpower Adv. Planning Council, 1968. Mem. Am. Personnel and Guidance Assn., Nat. Employment Counselors Assn., NEA, Nat. Ret. Tchrs. Assn. Home: 4432 Twilight Dr Topeka KS 66614

WOEPPEL, KAREN ALCORN, social services agy. adminstr.; b. Hagerstown, Md., Dec. 4, 1950; d. Alfred Cloyd and Alberta Grace (Glasgow) Alcorn; B.A., George Washington U., 1972; M.S., So. Ill. U., 1973; m. James Joseph Woeppel, May 11, 1974. Speech pathologist Appalachian Regional Council Head Start, Washington County, Md., 1973-74; speech pathologist Clark County Council for Retarded Children, Jeffersonville, Ind., 1975-77, Floyd County Council for Retarded, New Albany, Ind., 1976-77; dir. Children's Services, Clark County Council for Retarded Children, 1977—. lectr. speech Ind. U. Southeast, New Albany. Licensed Speech Pathologist, Ind. Mem. Am., Ind. speech and hearing assns. Council Exceptional Children. Democrat. Club: Ind. U. Southeast Women. Home: 509 Drawbrook Circle New Albany IN 47150 Office: 725 S Wall St Jeffersonville IN 47130

WOERNER, EARL LAVERN, dentist; b. Vandalia, Ill., Apr. 30, 1934; s. Earl Arling and Ruby Opal (Johnson) W.; student Blackburn Coll., 1952-55; D.D.S., Washington U., St. Louis, 1959; m. Marilyn Jean Stonecipher, Sept. 17, 1967; 1 son, Barclay. Rotating intern Jewish Hosp., St. Louis, 1959-60, now mem. staff, cons. home care dept., 1966—; pvt. practice dentistry, St. Louis, 1961—; dentist Amber Ridge Sch. for Handicapped, Ballwin, Mo., 1967—; chief St. Louis Dental Clinic, United Cerebral Palsy Assn., 1968-73; clin. asst. prof. prosthodontics So. Ill. U., Edwardsville, 1976—. Mem. ADA, Am. Soc. Dentistry for Children, Am. Assn. Hosp. Dentists, Internat. Platform Assn. Methodist. Home: 13135 Weatherfield Dr Creve Coeur MO 63141 Office: 8631 Delmar Blvd University City MO 63124

WOERPEL, DWAYNE RAYMOND, oil co. exec.; b. Madison, Wis., Mar. 29, 1939; s. Raymond Arnold and Carol Margaret (Hoyt) W.; B.S., U. Wis., 1962; m. Elizabeth Edwards Easley Hendrickson, Aug. 3, 1968; children—Robert T. Hendrickson, Diane Elizabeth. Advtg. sales Superior (Wis.) Evening Telegram, 1962-63; pub. relations and sales promotion dir. Ojibway Press, Inc., Duluth, Minn., 1963-64; field supr. Tau Kappa Epsilon Fraternity, Indpls., 1964-66, alumni dir., 1966-71; asst. v.p., dir. communications Roosevelt Nat. Investment Co., Springfield, Ill., 1971-76; pub. communications asso. The Standard Oil Co. (Ohio) Cleve., 1976—. Founder, chmn. Alpha Leadership Group, North Olmsted, Ohio, 1972—; precinct committeeman, Lawrence, Ind., 1969-71; active Boy Scouts Am. Chmn., bd. dirs. Teke Ednl. Found., Inc.; bd. dirs. Tau Kappa Epsilon, Inc. Mem. Internat. Platform Assn., Pub. Relations Soc. Am., Success Leaders Speakers Bur., Nat. Speakers Network. Republican. United Methodist. Home: 4632 Carsten Ln North Olmsted OH 44070 Office: 1760 Guildhall Bldg Cleveland OH 44115

WOFFORD, THEODORE JOHN, architect; b. St. Louis, Sept. 1, 1931; s. George Henry and Dorothy (Ferguson) W.; B.Arch., Washington U., St. Louis, 1953; m. Phyllis Ann Horn, July 31, 1954; children—Kathleen, Michael, Stephen, Ellen, Jonathan. Architect Murphy & Mackey, Inc., St. Louis, 1955-70; partner Murphy Downey Wofford & Richman, 1970—. Cons. designing library bldgs., equipment, instructional spaces, ednl. theatre. Mem. adv. commn. AMTRAK. Served to 1st lt. AUS, 1953-55. Recipient 2d place award St. Louis Gateway Mall Competition. Mem. AIA, (chmn. com. for preservation of hist. resources), Landmarks Assn. of St. Louis, Soc. Archtl. Historians, Nat. Trust Historic Preservation, Mo. Adv. Council Historic Preservation. Prin. archtl. projects include John M. Olin Library, Washington U., Fed. Office Bldg., St. Louis, Loretto Hilton Performing Arts Center, Sangamon State U., Springfield, Ill., architect-in-charge restoration Mo. Exec. Mansion. Contbr. to profl. publs. Home: 941 Dougherty Ferry Rd Kirkwood MO 63122 Office: 6124 Enright St St Louis MO 63112

WOGAMAN, MAURICE AARON, cons., ret. supt. schs.; b. Clayton, Ohio, July 29, 1916; s. Edward R. and Nellie (Garverick) W.; B.S., Ohio State U., 1939, M.A., 1947; Ed.D., Ind. U., 1955; m. Louise Wright, Apr. 16, 1943; 1 dau., Sue Ann. Tchr., Jefferson Twp. schs., Montgomery County, Ohio, 1939, Kettering schs., 1940-49; asst. prin. Van Buren Jr. High, 1949-54; asst. supt. city schs., Kettering, Ohio, 1954-75; vis. instr. Toledo U., 1956, Ohio State U., 1959, U. Dayton, 1957—, Miami U., 1962—, also Wright State U. Treas. Montgomery County Child Guidance Center, 1962-74, bd. dirs., 1955-74. Bd. dirs. Dayton Childrens Psychiat. Hosp. Served from 2d lt. to capt., AUS, 1942-45. Mem. Ohio Sch. Counselors (past pres.), Am. Personnel and Guidance Assn., Nat., Ohio edn. assns., Nat. (charter) Ohio (charter, past pres.) assns. pupil personnel adminstrs. Office: 3742 Benfield Dr Kettering OH 45429

WOHLFEIL, PAUL FREDERICK, psychologist; b. Saginaw, Mich., Aug. 28, 1934; s. Herman Frederick and Rose Elizabeth (Kueffner) W.; B.A., Mich. State U., 1962; M.A., Eastern Mich. U., 1966; Ph.D., Ind. U. Mo.; m. Shirley Jean Setzer, July 20, 1976; children—Paul John, Ondria Rose. Psychologist, Whaley Home for Disturbed Children, Flint, Mich., 1963-67; asst. dir., psychologist Shiawasee Mental Health Clinic, Owosso, Mich., 1967-68; psychologist Bay County Mental Health Clinic, Bay City, Mich., 1968-74; psychologist, Salman Psychiat. Clinic, Bay City, 1974—; mem. faculty Delta Coll., 1976-77, Central Mich. U., 1969-71. Chmn. bd. Bay County Half Way House for Alcoholics. Served with AUS, 1954-56. Recipient grant Rutgers U., 1974; recipient awards Mich. Assn. Child Agys., 1964, Mich. AP, 1973. Mem. Am., Mich. psychol. assns., Acad. Psychologists in Marital Counseling, Mich. Sch. Psychologists. Lutheran. Club: Riverview Rod and Gun. Author: If I Go See A Shrink Does It Mean I'm Crazy?, 1977. Home: 3102 Sharon Rd Midland MI 48640 Office: 2117 16th St Bay City MI 48706

WOHLGEMUTH, EDWARD WARREN, publishing co. exec.; b. Cin., Dec. 24, 1915; s. Albert Joseph and Francis Louise (Bell) W.; A.B. in Lit., U. Mich., 1937; M.B.A., Harvard, 1939; m. Virginia Nulsen Balke, Nov. 29, 1940; children—Virginia N. (Mrs. Gary Fritts), Barbara B. (Mrs. Edward Blaine), Edward Warren. Salesman Nat. Underwriter Co., Cin., 1938; salesman The Rough Notes Co., Inc., Indpls., 1939—, mgr. circulation dept., 1940-41, mgr. pictorial div., 1945-58, dir., sec., 1950-59, pres., 1959—; dir. John C. Nulsen Investment Co., St. Louis, RN-AAA Co., Inc., Indpls., Ronaco Realty Co., Indpls. Served from pvt. to capt., AUS, 1941-45. Mem. Phi Delta Theta. Presbyn. Kiwanian. Home: 180 E 71st St Indianapolis IN 46220 Office: 1200 N Meridian St Indianapolis IN 46204

WOITO, ROBERT SEVERIN, ednl. orgn. exec.; b. Sioux Falls, S.D., Dec. 13, 1937; s. Harold August and Lois Louise (Severin) W.; B.A., Grinnell Coll., 1960; M.A., U. Calif., Berkeley, 1965, Ph.D., 1976; m. Linda Newman, Aug. 26, 1961; children—Katrina, Andrea, Brian; m. 2d, Jacky Phillips, Oct. 26, 1974; step-children—Jengis, Aaron. With Turn Toward Peace, Berkeley, Calif., 1964-67; dir. publs. World Without War Council, Berkeley, 1967-72, publs. and asso. dir., Chgo., 1972-77, co-dir. Midwest, 1977—; instr. YMCA Community Coll. Mem. fgn. policy com. Ind. Voters of Ill., 1976-77. Served as info. officer USAF, 1960-63. Recipient first prize short story contest, Air Defense Command, 1961. Mem. Am. Hist. Assn., Conf. on Peace Research in History. Clubs: UN Assn. Greater Chgo. and Ill. (bd. dirs.). Co-author: To End War, 1971; editor: Vietnam Peace Proposals, Modern Classics of Peace Series, World Hunger Crisis Kit, World Disarmament Kit, Internat. Human Rights Kit. Home: 5441 S Ridgewood Ct Chicago IL 60615 Office: 67 E Madison St Suite 1417 Chicago IL 60603

WOJCIK, CASS, florist supply co. exec., former city ofcl.; b. Rochester, N.Y., Dec. 3, 1920; s. Emil M. and Casimira C. (Krawiecz) W.; student Lawrence Inst. Tech., 1941-43, Yale, 1943-44, U.S. Sch. for European Personnel, Czechoslovakia, 1945; m. Lilliam Leocadia Lendzion, Sept. 25, 1948; 1 son, Robert Cass. Owner Nat. Florists Supply Co., Detroit, 1948—; owner Nat. Decorative, Detroit, 1950—; co-owner Creation Center, Detroit, 1955-60; cons.-contractor hort.-bot. design auto show displays, TV producers, designers and decorators. Mem. Regional Planning and Evaluation Council, 1969—; city-wide mem. Detroit Bd. Edn., 1970-75; commr. Detroit Pub. Schs. Employees Retirement Commn., until 1975; mem. Area Occupational Ednl. Commn., Ednl. Task Force; chmn., grand marshall Ann. Gen. Pulaski Day Parade, Detroit, 1970, 71, chmn. Pulaski Day Citizens Award Com.; mem. Boys Towns of Italy. Served with AUS, 1944-46. Decorated Bronze Star; recipient citation Polish-Am. Congress, 1971. Mem. S.E. Mich. Council Govts. (exec. com.), Friends of Belle Isle Task Force, Founders Soc. Detroit Inst. Arts, Mich. State Heritage Groups Council, Nat. Small Bus. Assn., Nat. Conf. Am. Ethic Groups, DAV, Central Citizens Com. Detroit, Internat. Platform Assn., Nat. Geog. Soc. Roman Catholic. Clubs: Univ. of Ann Arbor, Polish Century (Detroit). Home: 451 Lodge Dr Detroit MI 48214

WOJCIK, JAMES JOSEPH, univ. exec.; b. Detroit, Nov. 23, 1942; s. Mitchell J. and Anne A. (Kulpa) W.; B.S. in Edn., Central Mich. U., 1965, M.A. in Journalism, 1968; m. Carol L. Humm, June 11, 1966; children—Mark William, Scott James. Dir. sports info. Central Mich. U., Mt. Pleasant, 1966-68, instr. journalism, 1968-69, asst. dir. devel., 1971-72, dir. student publs., 1972—; news editor Daily Times-News, Mt. Pleasant, 1968, editor, 1968-71. Rep. of profl. journalism bd. student publs. Central Mich. U. Trustee Central Mich. Community Hosp. Mem. U.S. Basketball Writers Assn., Nat. Sportswriters and Sportscasters, Mt. Pleasant C. of C. (dir.), Nat. Assn. Publs. Advisers, Sigma Delta Chi. Roman Catholic. Club: Optimist Internat. (Mt. Pleasant). Home: 1207 Glenwood Dr Mt Pleasant MI 48858 Office: Anspach Hall Room 8 Central Mich Univ Mt Pleasant MI 48858

WOJTA, GERALD CHARLES, pharm. co. exec.; b. Manitowoc, Wis., Aug. 17, 1930; s. Charles J. and Agnes (Stefl) W.; student U. Wis., 1948-51; children—Pamela, Jerold, Daniel, James, Ann, Kimberly, Melissa. Salesman, Dorsey Labs., Inc., Lincoln, Neb., 1953-55, asst. sales mgr., 1956, sales mgr., 1957-61; dir. marketing Philips Roxane Lab., Inc., Columbus, Ohio, 1962-64, v.p., gen. mgr., 1965, pres., 1967—; also dir.; pres., dir. Alliance Labs., Inc., 1967—; dir. Mediplex, Inc. Trustee Coll. Osteo. Medicine and Surgery, Des Moines. Fellow Am. Coll. Osteo. Obstetricians and Gynecologists; mem. Am., Ohio pharm. assns., Drug Chem. and Allied Trades Assn., Am. Assn. Mil. Physicians. Clubs: Scioto Country, Columbus Athletic. Office: 330 Oak St Columbus OH 43216

WOLCOTT, ROGER LODGE, assn. exec., inventor; b. Kent, Ohio, May 19, 1912; s. Duncan Brewster and Evelyn Daisy (Lodge) W.; B.S., Kent State U., 1935; m. Dorothy May Kenty, Aug. 15, 1936; children—Vange Elene (Mrs. Charles L. Firestone), Kent Edward, Janet Louise (Mrs. Carter B.W. Meyers). Tchr. pub. schs., various Ohio cities, 1935-36; with Taylorcraft Aviation Corp., Alliance, 1936-46, chief insp., 1943-46; specialist aeromech. research and devel. engring. dept. Goodyear Aerospace Corp., Akron, 1946-71, zoning insp., 1971-77; balloon pilot for TV and movies; charter mem., treas. Balloon Flyers of Akron, 1956-59, v.p., 1960, pres., 1961-62; charter mem. Lighter Than Air Soc., Akron, pres., 1952-54, 55-57, v.p., 1959-61, also rec. sec. Recipient leadership awards Kent State U., 1933, 34, 35; Richard Pollard trophy award Wingfoot sect., 1963, Ward T. Van Orman Thermal Balloon trophy; named Pilot of Year Balloon Flyers Akron, 1961. Mem. Balloon Fedn. Am. (v.p. 1961, charter and founding mem.), OX5 Aviation Pioneers, Soc. Exptl. Stress Analysis, Smithsonian Assos., Am. Assn. Ret. Persons, Portage County Farm Bur., Akron Area Pilots' Assn., Assn. Balloon and Airship Constructors, Portage County Assn. Twp. Trustees and Clks., USCG Aux. (life), Airplane Model League Am., Western Res. Engring. Assn., Goodyear Foremen's Club (life), Kent Jaycees, Balloon Flyers Akron, Lighter Than Air Soc., Taylor Young Flying Club (founding mem., past pres.), Randolph Hayseed Club (past pres.), Am. Balloon Corps Vets. (asso.), Goodyear 25 Year Club (life). Patentee in field including inflatable airplane, automatic airplane fuel pump system for inflatable airplane, also double-Y multiple wall attachment. Home: 4796 Waterloo Rd Atwater OH 44201

WOLF, ADOLPH, mfg. exec.; b. Galecia, Austria, June 17, 1913; s. Phillip and Katherina (Baisch) W.; student Austin Jr. Coll., 1933-36, Lewis Inst., 1937-39, Northwestern U., 1940-41; m. L. Bernice Anderson, May 29, 1938; children—Suzanne A. (Mrs. William Marrs), Sandra R. (Mrs. Ronald Jensen), Pamela J. (Mrs. Michael Marrs), Philip C. Supt., Buick Motors, Melrose Park, Ill., 1940-44, Poole Bros., Chgo., 1944-48; v.p. mfg. Makatoy, Inc. Chgo., 1948-52; v.p. mfg. Webcor, Inc., Chgo., 1952-59, adminstrv. asst. to works mgr. Zenith Radio, Chgo., 1959-61; exec. v.p., dir. Electro-Voice, Inc., Buchanan, Mich., 1961-71, pres., 1972-73, chmn. bd., 1973—; v.p. mfg. South Bend Range Co. (Ind.), 1973-77; dir. Electro-Voice of

Korea, Electro-Voice of Brazil, E/V of Can.; mfg. mgmt. cons., Niles, Mich., 1977—. Mem. pres.'s council Valparaiso U., 1969. Republican. Lutheran. Home: 2709 Riverside Rd Niles MI 49120 Office: 2709 Riverside Rd Niles MI

WOLF, ANNE L. MCCAUGHERTY (MRS. DONALD MYLES WOLF), civic worker; b. Omaha, Aug. 26, 1937; d. Lloyd Ernest and Helen (Bosley) McCaugherty; B.A., Cornell U., 1959; postgrad. Harvard, 1959-60, Northwestern U., 1961-63; m. Donald Myles Wolf, Aug. 11, 1963; children—Mark, Linda. Research asst. Glore Forgan, Wm. R. Staats, Inc., Chgo., 1960-61, securities analyst, 1961-67, sec.-treas. Carriage Way, Inc., Hinsdale, Ill.; asst. comptroller Carriage Way West, Darien, Ill., 1976-77. Regional council mem. Cornell U., 1969-75; Benefit chmn. Ill. Childrens Home and Aid Soc.-Hinsdale Aux., 1969-70, publicity chmn., 1970-71, sec., 1971-72, v.p., 1972-73, pres., 1973-74; mem. Council of Bds., 1972-73, sec., 1973-75, benefit chmn., 1975-77. Clubs: Cornell Womens (pres. 1969-71, sec. 1971-72) (Chgo.); Salt Creek (women's tennis chmn. 1975), Oak Brook Racquet. Co-author: (cookbook) Measures of Love. Home: 161 Carriage Way Hinsdale IL 60521

WOLF, EARL DANIEL, veterinarian; b. Xenia, Ohio, July 28, 1943; s. Elmer Marcus and Wanda Jeanne (Hess) W.; D.V.M., Ohio State U., 1968; m. Phyllis Jean DeRose, June 8, 1968. Chmn. dept. radiology Bevlab Vet. Med. Center, Blue Island, Ill., 1968-72; practice vet. ophthalmology, Berwyn, Ill., 1972—; researcher U. Ill., 1972—. Diplomate Am. Coll. Vet. Ophthalmology. Mem. Am., Ill., Ohio, Chgo. vet. med. assns., Acad. Vet. Cardiology, Am. Vet. Radiology Soc. Home: 15007 S Kildare Ave Midlothian IL 60445 Office: 2845 S Harlem Ave Berwyn IL 60402

WOLF, FRANCES LORETA SMITH (MRS. MILTON HARRY WOLF), banker, civic worker; b. Cleve., Sept. 3, 1917; d. Francis William and Laura (Barrett) Smitha; grad. Sch. Pub. Relations and Mktg., 1965; m. Milton Harry Wolf, Feb. 14, 1935 (dec. Aug. 1954); children—Henry George II, Jacqueline Jeanne (Mrs. Ralph Matthew Gruenewald). Writer, visuals, asst. to producer comml. films Ray Waters Inc., 1950-55; adminstrv. asst. to Willard Johnson, NCCJ, 1955-57; craft stylist Chgo. Printed String Co., 1956-59; free lance advt., pub. relations, commls., 1959-60; dir. pub. relations Ave. State Bank (now Ave. Bank & Trust Co. Oak Park), Oak Park, Ill., 1961-68, asst. cashier, pub. relations and advt., 1968-71, asst. v.p. pub. relations, 1971-75, dir. dept. community services, 1975—. Co-chmn. publicity Santa Claus Event, Oak Park, 1961-69; publicity chmn. Frank Lloyd Wright Festival, Oak Park-River Forest, 1969, chmn. pub. relations com. Frank Lloyd Wright Home and Studio Found., 1974-77; chmn. pub. relations Oak Park-River Forest Antique Show and Sales, 1967-70; bd. mem. Oak Park-River Forest Symphony, 1965-67; incorporator Cultural Arts Center, Oak Park, 1970. Bd. dirs. Sr. Citizens' Oak Park-River Forest; bd. dirs., mem. exec. bd. Thatcher Woods council Boy Scouts Am., 1977—; mem. Camp Shin-Go-Beck Fire Dept., Amundsen Park Community Council, N.W. Austin Community Council. Recipient fund raising award Thatcher Woods council Boy Scouts Am., 1976. Mem. Nat. Assn. Bank Women, Hist. Soc. Oak Park and River Forest (1st v.p., program chmn. 1973-78), Women in Communications (chmn. Jacob Scher awards 1977), Ave.-Lake Plaza Assn. (pres. 1969-70, v.p., treas. 1970-77), 1973—), Woman's Advt. Club Chgo. (pub. relations com. mem. 1969—), Oak Park-River Forest C. of C. (co-chmn. ann. dinner 1963—), Chgo. Zool. Soc., Art Inst. Chgo., Publicity Club Chgo. (dir. 1975-77), Zonta Internat. (dir. Oak Park chpt. 1976-77, chmn. community affairs 1976-77), 19th Century Woman's Club Assn. (spl. events com. 1969-70). Clubs: Chgo. Press, Suburban Press, Zonta. Home: 151 N Kenilworth Ave Oak Park IL 60301 Office: 104 N Oak Park Ave Oak Park IL 60303

WOLF, JOHN PHILLIP, univ. adminstr; b. Cleve., Oct. 27, 1940; s. Elden Laufer and Mildred (Pursell) W.; B.A., U. Kans., 1962, M.A., 1966. Instr. philosophy U. Kans.; vis. prof. philosophy Universidad Nacional Autonoma de Honduras, Centro Universitario de Estudios Generales, Tegucigalpa, Honduras, C.A.; regional program prof. philosophy U.S. AID, U.S. Agy. for Internat. Devel., San Jose, Costa Rica, C.A., 1966-68; asst. dir. Corbin Coll., U. Kans., 1968-71, asst. to dean and budget officer Coll. Liberal Arts and Scis., 1969-74, lectr. philosophy, 1970—, dir. adminstrv. services, asst. to dean div. continuing edn., 1974—. Mem. AAUP, Nat. Univ. Ext. Assn., Am. Radio Relay League. Home: 435 Maine St Lawrence KS 66044 Office: Div Continuing Edn U Kans Lawrence KS 66045

WOLF, MARLANE LOUISE, marketing exec.; b. St. Paul, June 20, 1945; d. Robert Earl and Natalie Dora (Lethert) Ayers; B.A., U. Minn., 1968; m. Thomas J. Wolf, Jan. 28, 1977. Mktg. research analyst Batten, Barton, Durstine & Osborn Advt., Mpls., 1969-71, mktg. research dir., 1971-75, account exec., 1975-76; dir. mktg. Fisher Nut Co., St. Paul, 1976—. Mem. Minn. Advt. Fedn., Am. Mktg. Assn. (chpt. dir. 1972-73). Home: 15 S First St Apt A1619 Minneapolis MN 55401 Office: 2327 Wycliff St Saint Paul MN 55114

WOLF, RAYMOND BERNARD, chem. co. exec.; b. Cin., Aug. 26, 1923; s. Charles and Margaret (Herrmann) W.; B. Chem. Engring., U. Cin., 1950, MB. A., 1974; m. Bernice M. Fix, Aug. 29, 1948; children—Randall K., Bradley R., Leslie R. Prodn. supr. Nat. Lead Co. of Ohio, Cin., 1951-66; engring. supr. Maumee Chem. Co., Cin., 1966-69; prodn. mgr. Sherwin Williams Chem. Co., Cin., 1970-74, plant mgr., Coffeyville, Kan., 1974—. Served with USCG, 1942-46. Registered profl. engr., Ohio, Kans. Mem. Am. Inst. Chem. Engrs., Nat. Soc. Profl. Engrs., Kans. Engring. Soc., Kan. Assn. Commerce and Industry, U.S., Coffeyville chambers commerce, Am. Legion, VFW. Rotarian. Club: Coffeyville Country. Home: 602 Overlook St Coffeyville KS 67337 Office: PO Box 855 Coffeyville KS 67337

WOLF, SY L., wine co. exec.; b. Chgo., May 12, 1921; s. Charles K. and May (Lando) W.; student Coll. of Pacific; LL.B., Northwestern U.; m. Ellie Schreiber, Oct. 28, 1945; children—Susan, Stephen, Charles. Rep. liquor sales, regional divisional mgr. Meier's Wine Cellar, Silverton, Ohio, 1976; v.p. Selected Brands, Northfield, Ill., 1976—, Ceramic World Ltd., Northfield, Villa Salceda Condominium Assn., Northfield. Active City of Hope; Constable, justice of peace Niles Ill. Twp. Served with U.S. Army, 1942-45. Clubs: Midlane Country. Home: 2245 Vista Ct Northbrook IL 60062 Office: 550 Frontage Rd Northfield IL 60093

WOLF, WALTER AUGUST, mfg. co. exec.; b. Logansport, Ind., Mar. 23, 1918; s. Daniel G. and Lucy P. (Brenneke) W.; grad. high sch.; m. Gertrude Figley, June 6, 1941; children—Robert, Michael. Toolmaker, Bendix Corp., South Bend, 1939-43; with Switches, Inc., Logansport, Ind., 1947—, gen. mgr., 1947—, pres., 1949—. Bd. dirs. Jr. Achievement. Served with USAAF, 1943-46. Mem. Soc. Automotive Engrs. Elk. Patentee in field. Office: 516 High St Logansport IN 46947

WOLF, WAYNE STANLEY, ret. supermarket and dept. store exec.; b. Canton, Ohio, Jan. 18, 1919; s. Jack M. and Marion (Perskey) W.; student U. Wis., 1936-39; D.D.S., Northwestern U., 1942; m. Anita Manheim, Dec. 28, 1941; children—Fredric M., JoAnn. Pvt. practice dentistry, Canton, also Alliance, Ohio, 1942-50; pres. Persky's Inc., 1958—, Super Centers, Inc., 1962—; pres. Tusco Grocers, 1960-64; pres. Quik Shop Food Marts, Inc., 1965-72; pres. Persky & Wolf Inc., to 1978; now cons.; dir. Alliance Devel. Corp. Lectr., cons. dept. food mktg. Ohio State U., 1962-66; lectr. Purdue U.; mem. Midwest Food Dealers and Distbrs. People to People Delegation, Europe, Soviet Union, 1964. Mem. adv. bd., chmn. site selection com. and fund raising Stark County br. Kent State U.; chmn. Mayor's Adv. Com. Alliance on Urban Affairs, 1968-72. Bd. dirs., vice chmn. Better Bus. Bur.; bd. dirs. United Fund Alliance, pres., 1965.; bd. dirs. Canton Civic Opera Assn., 1977—. Served from lt. (j.g.) to lt. comdr. USNR, 1943-46. Recipient Distinguished Service award Kent State U., 1967. Mem. Am. Legion, Stark County Dental Soc., Alliance Area C. of C. (pres. 1964-65, dir.), Pi Lambda Phi. Jewish (dir. temple 1955-58, 70—). Clubs: Arrowhead Country (dir. 1947-57, 70—, pres. 1954); Alliance Country, Shrine Rotary (dir. 1966-69) (Alliance); Lakeview Country (Morgantown, W.Va.); Masons (32 deg.), Shriners, Odd Fellows. Lectr. on travels. Home: 2111 Applegrove NW North Canton OH 44720 Office: 1918 S Union Alliance OH 44601

WOLFE, BARD ALTON, mfg. co. exec.; b. Ripley, W. Va., May 14, 1940; s. Boyd Alton and Kathleen (Carder) W.; student W.Va. U., 1958-59, Marietta (Ohio) Coll., 1959-62; children—Bradley, Russell. Regional sales mgr. GTE Info. Systems, Cleve., 1969-72; applications engr. Tektronix, Inc., Cleve., 1972-75; nat. sales mgr. Magnavox Display Systems, Ft. Wayne, Ind., 1975—; cons. in field. Mem. Nat. Mgmt. Assn. Roman Catholic. Home: 744 Candlelite Ct Fort Wayne IN 46807 Office: 2131 Coliseum Blvd Fort Wayne IN 46803

WOLFE, CHARLES JAMES, counselor; b. Boston, Dec. 4, 1947; s. Sumner and Helen (Hanock) W.; B.A. in Psychology, Northeastern U., 1971, Ed.M. with honors, 1972; m. Barbara Dean Greif, Oct. 26, 1968; 1 dau., Jennifer Nan. Counselor, Heath Elementary Sch., Brookline, Mass., 1971-72, Washington Jr. High Sch., Dubuque, Iowa, 1972-75, Fulton Pub. Sch., also Holy Ghost Elementary Sch., Dubuque, 1975-77, Jefferson Jr. High Sch., Dubuque, 1977—; instr. Clarke Coll., Dubuque, 1977—, U. Dubuque, 1978—, U. No. Iowa, 1973; human relations cons. to schs., social service agys., businesses, parent orgns. Mem. Am. Personnel and Guidance Assn., Iowa, Dubuque edn. assns., NEA, Assn. of Socialists in Group Work, Kappa Delta Pi. Home: PO Box 120 Rural Route 1 Durango IA 52039 Office: 1105 Althauser Dubuque IA 52001

WOLFE, ESTEMORE ALVIS, ins. co. exec.; b. Crystal Springs, Miss., Dec. 29, 1929; s. Henry and Vinia (Crump) W.; B.S., Jackson State U., 1947; student Fla. Meml. Coll., 1948-49, N.Y. U., 1952-53; M.Ed., Wayne State U., 1951; M.A., Purdue U., 1953; D.Ed., Boston U., 1958; L.H.D., Wilberforce U., 1959; Litt.D., Creighton U., 1961; L.H.D., Syracuse U., 1963; postgrad. Purdue U., 1964; divorced. Dir. med. technicians Detroit Tb Sanitorium, 1947-48; ednl. cons., mass media specialist Detroit Bd. Edn., 1948—; v.p., sec. Wright Mut. Ins. Co., Detroit, 1955—; mem. internat. adv. Hamilton Funding Corp.; dir. Ind. Prodns. Corp., also chmn. nat. edn. com. for educators. Lectr., guest prof. Gt. Lakes Coll., Assumption Coll. (Can.), Wayne U., 1953-56, Jackson State U., Bethany Coll., U. Detroit, Wis. State U., Stevens Point, So. U. (La.); writer column Detroit Times; cons. to pres. P. Lenud & Co. Mem. White House Conf. of Children and Youth, 1960; mem. Council on Aging, 1965-66; founder, pres. Detroit chpt. Friends of AMISTAD, 1972—, nat. pres., chmn. bd., 1974—. Chmn. bd. trustees Detroit Met. Symphony Orch.; sec., trustee Teen Power Service, Inc., Detroit; trustee Jackson State U. Devel. Fund, campaign chmn. fund drive, 1970-71, mem. univ. centennial commn., 1973—; trustee Nat. Negro Archives Mus., Washington, Mich. council Arts, Scis. and Letters, Bethany (W.Va.) Coll.; mem. nat. alumni bd. Boston U., 1976. Served with AUS, 1942-46. Recipient Nat. Human Relations award Clark U., 1969, citation Am. Airlines in recognition of contbns. to devel. air transp. and nat. air power, 1969, Presidential citation for performance beyond call of duty, 1945, Hutchins award, 1973; plaques Delta Airlines, 1976, Jackson State U., 1975, 76, Kiwanis Internat., 1976; other awards. Mem. NAACP, Nat. Soc. for Visual Edn., Nat. Geog. Soc., Am. Acad. Social and Polit. Sci., Nat. Ins. Assn., Detroit Fedn. Tchrs., Detroit Assn. Film Tchrs. (plaque 1976), Detroit Reading Assn., Detroit Assn. Radio and TV, Internat. Platform Assn., Detroit Schoolmens Club, Detroit Roundtable, Nat. Congress Parents and Tchrs., Orgn. Grad. Alumni Assn. Wayne State U. (pres.), Jackson State U. Nat. Alumni Assn. (pres. 1976—, Midwest regional dir. 1974—). Democrat. Methodist (trustee ch.). Office: 2995 E Grand Blvd Detroit MI 48202

WOLFE, GENE HENRY, printing co. exec.; b. Calumet City, Ill., May 18, 1936; s. Henry L. and Sue (Goreski) Wojciechowski; B.S. (Univ. fellow 1958-60), U. Ill., 1958, M.S, 1959, postgrad., 1959-60; m. Elaine Marie Mateja, Aug. 27, 1960; children—Lynn Marie, Lisa Ann, Eugene Michael, Karen Sue, Kimberly Ann, Amy Lynn. Research asso. Argonne (Ill.) Nat. Lab., 1959; asst. physicist Ill. Inst. Tech. Research Inst., Chgo., 1960-62, asso. physicist, 1962-64; creative engr. R.R. Donnelley & Sons, Chgo., 1964—. Counselor, Jr. Achievement, Chgo., 1964-65. Am. Optical Soc., Am. Phys. Soc., Tau Beta Pi. Republican. Roman Catholic. K.C. Contbr. tech. articles to profl. jours. Inventor method automatically inspecting books at high speeds, camera for taking 3-D pictures, methods and devices for electrostatic printing. Home: 1309 Buffalo St Calumet City IL 60409 Office: 2223 S King Dr Chicago IL 60616

WOLFE, GOLDIE BRANDELSTEIN, realtor; b. Linz, Austria, Dec. 20, 1945; d. Albert and Regina (Sandman) Brandelstein; student U. Ill., 1963-64; B.S. in Bus. Adminstrn. cum laude, Roosevelt U., 1967; postgrad. U. Chgo. Grad. Sch. Bus., 1969; 1 dau., Alicia Danielle Schuyler. Account research mgr., research dept. J. Walter Thompson Advt., Chgo., 1967-71, asso. account exec., 1971-72; account exec. Needham, Harper & Steers Advt., Inc., Chgo., 1972; real estate broker, office leasing dept. Arthur Rubloff & Co., Chgo., 1972—, asst. v.p., 1975-77, v.p. office leasing, 1977—; tchr. bus. Evanston Twp. High Sch. Chmn. services group Channel 11 TV Auction, 1974-75; bd. dirs. realty div. Jewish United Fund, 1976-77. Mem. Am. Mktg. Assn., Ill., Nat. assns. realtors, Chgo. Real Estate Bd., Chgo. Council Fgn. Relations. Clubs: Execs., Jr. Women's Advt. (Chgo.); Glen View Country (Golf, Ill.). Home: 1555 N Sandburg Terrace Apt 401 Chicago IL 60610 Office: 69 W Washington St Chicago IL 60602

WOLFE, JAMES RICHARD, lawyer, railroad exec.; b. Hannibal, Mo., Nov. 7, 1929; s. James Edward and Grace (Kirn) W.; student Georgetown U., 1947-49; B.S., Loyola U., 1951; J.D., DePaul U., 1953; m. Helen Lorraine Rosedale, Dec. 29, 1951; children—Yvonne Marie Bazar, Mary Lorraine, Theresa Eileen, James E., Michaela Ann, Kathleen Grace, Lorraine Helene. Admitted to Ill. bar, 1953, U.S. Ct. Mil. Appeals bar, 1957, U.S. Supreme Ct. bar, 1961; practiced in Chgo., 1953—; atty. Burlington R.R., Chgo., 1953-55, 58-59; mem. Nat. R.R. Adjustment Bd., Chgo., 1959-63; counsel U.S. R.R.'s, Nat. Labor Cases, 1959-65; gen. atty. Nat. Ry. Labor Conf., 1965-67, gen. counsel, 1967-68; v.p. labor relations Chgo. and Northwestern Transp. Co., 1968-73, v.p. operations, 1973-76, pres., chief operating officer, chief exec. officer, 1976—, also dir., trustee; dir. No. Ill. Gas Co. Trustee DePaul U. Served as 1st lt. AUS, 1955-58; capt. Res. Mem. Assn. Am. Railroads (dir. 1976—), Western Ry. Assn. (dir.), Internat. Wine and Food Soc. Chgo. Clubs: Hinsdale Golf; Chicago, Mid-Am., Carlton. Home: 422 S Oak St Hinsdale IL 60521 Office: 400 W Madison St Chicago IL 60606

WOLFE, JOHN BINNIE, banker; b. Macomb, Ill., Feb. 25, 1907; s. Edward Clark and Eleanor (Binnie) W.; B.S., Knox Coll., 1930; postgrad. Northwestern U., 1931-32; m. Sara Kramer, Aug. 15, 1936 (dec. Aug. 1969); 1 dau., Mary Eleanor (Mrs. John Satter); m. 2d, Alice Findley Reno, Aug. 22, 1970. Asst. examiner FDIC, 1933-34; bookkeeper, teller Citizens Nat. Bank of Macomb, 1935-36, asst. cashier, 1936-38, cashier, 1938-50, exec. v.p., 1950-51, pres., 1951-73, chmn. bd. dirs., 1966—, also dir. Bd. dirs. Western Ill. U. Found., 1944—, pres., 1973—; bd. dirs. Western Ill. Arts Council, 1971-73; bd. dirs. McDonough County chpt. Nat. Found., 1938—, treas., 1938—. Recipient award of recognition for service to community and univ. Macomb C. of C.-Western Ill. U. Coll. Bus., 1975. Mem. Macomb C. of C. (dir. 1956-59). Rotarian. Club: Macomb Country. Home: 646 Lincoln Dr Macomb IL 61455 Office: 127 South Side Square Macomb IL 61455

WOLFE, WARREN DWIGHT, lawyer; b. Boston, July 30, 1926; s. Louis Julius and Rose (Daniels) W.; B.S. in Journalism, Northwestern U., 1949; M. Internat. Affairs, Columbia U., 1951; J.D. with high honors, U. Toledo, 1959; m. Caroline M. DuMont, Dec. 29, 1973. Reporter, Wilmington (Del.) Record, 1951-52; Sunday editor, asst. news editor Middletown (Ohio) Jour., 1952-55; copy reader, sect. editor Toledo Blade, 1955-60; admitted to Ohio bar, 1959, Mich. bar, 1960; asso. Bugbee & Conkle, Toledo, 1960-64, partner, 1964—. Pres. Health Planning Assn. Northwest Ohio, 1970-73; mem. Comprehensive Health Planning Adv. Council to Ohio Dept. Health, 1972-75; mem. Ohio Gov.'s Task Force on Health, 1973-74. Trustee Toledo Legal Aid Soc., 1968—, pres., 1973-75; trustee Toledo Animal Shelter Assn., 1962-75; trustee Lucas County unit Am. Cancer Soc., 1964—, v.p., 1976—, trustee Ohio div., 1969-74. Served with USNR, 1944-46. Mem. Am., Ohio, Lucas County (pres. 1966), Toledo (exec. com. 1969-75) bar assns., State Bar Mich., Am. Trial Lawyers Assn., Law Alumni Assn. U. Toledo Coll. Law (pres. 1965), Sigma Delta Chi. Mason. Club: Toledo Ski (treas. 1972-75, pres. 1975-76). Home: 4562 Westbourne Toledo OH 43623 Office: 1301 Toledo Trust Bldg Toledo OH 43604

WOLFE, WAYNE WENDELL, automotive co. exec.; b. Akron, Ohio, June 30, 1950; s. Merritt W. and Catharine Elizabeth (Wimmer) W.; B.A., Malone Coll., 1972. Indsl. designer Goodyear Tire & Rubber Co., Akron, 1972-76, sales rep. indsl. products, 1974-76; sales mgr. central region E-T Mags., Benicia, Calif., 1976; mem. racing crew Holley Carburetor Co. div. of Colt Industries, Warren, Mich., 1976-77; sales rep., 1977—. Mem. Nat. Hot Rod Assn., Nat. Council of Corvette Clubs. Home: 2234 Woodview Rd Apt 352 Ypsilanti MI 48197 Office: 11955 E Nine Mile Rd Warren MI 48090

WOLFENBARGER, FLOYD ORSON, architect; b. Winkler, Kans., Nov. 29, 1904; student Kan. State U., 1924-27. With firm F.O. Wolfenbarger & Assos., Manhattan, Kans., 1934-69; prin. firm Wolfenbarger & McCulley, Manhattan, 1968—; works include Lee Elementary Sch., Manhattan, 1952, Manhattan High Sch., 1957, Convent and Hosp. Sisters St. Joseph, Manhattan; home econs. bldg., phys. sci. bldg., auditorium vet. medicine tng. bldg., clin. sci. and pathology bldg., all Kans. State U., Mem. Kan. State Registration and Exam. Bd. Architects, 1949-66. Recipient Regional Silver medal Tau Sigma Delta, 1970. Registered architect, Ill., Kans., Nebr. Fellow AIA (mem. com. hosp. architecture 1965-66, pres. Kan. chpt. 1949, dir. Central States Region 1969-73). Home: 731 Humboldt St Manhattan KS 66502 Office: 800 Poyntz Ave Manhattan KS 66502

WOLFERT, RICHARD JEROME, librarian; b. Chgo., Oct. 18, 1929; s. Jerome and Emma (Awe) W.; M.A., U. Chgo., 1959; m. Ann Zaslavsky, Feb. 11, 1953; children—Jenny Ann, Emily Ann. Tech. services librarian Municipal Reference Library, City Hall, Chgo., 1957-60; head, tech. services dept. Racine (Wis.) Pub. Library, 1960-64; dir. Wis. State Reference and Loan Library, Madison, 1965-67; city librarian Bismarck (N.D.) Pub. Library, 1967-69; dir. N.D. State Library Commn., 1970—. Author: The Government of the City of Chicago, 1960; The North Dakota Constitutional Convention, 1971-72: A Newspaper Account, 1974. Editor N.D. Library Notes, 1970—. Home: 523 Ave A West Bismarck ND 58501 Office: State Library Bismarck ND 58501

WOLFF, AARON SIDNEY, lawyer, arbitrator; b. Chgo., May 9, 1930; s. Joseph S. and Esther (Nadell) W.; B.S., Northwestern U., 1951, J.D., 1954; m. Arlene Gottlieb, Aug. 10, 1952; children—Elizabeth, Peter. Admitted to Ill. bar, 1955; asso. Alex Elson, 1955, Elson and Lassers, Chgo., 1960; partner Elson, Lassers & Wolff, Chgo., 1963; spl. arbitrator Bd. Arbitration, U.S. Steel and U.S. Steelworkers, Pitts., 1969—. Mem. Am., Ill., Chgo. bar assns, Chgo. Council Lawyers, Am. Arbitration Assn. Author: (with Elson and Lassers), Civil Practice Forms - Illinois and Federal, 1965. Home: 591 Broadview Highland Park IL 60035 Office: 11 S LaSalle St Chicago IL 60603

WOLFF, GUNTHER ARTHUR, phys. chemist; b. Essen, Germany, Mar. 31, 1918; s. Joseph and Anna (Breidecker) W.; B.S., Berlin U., 1944, M.S., 1945; Sc.D., Berlin Tech. U., 1948; m. Gertrude Anna Stolte, Feb. 27, 1945; children—Christine, Francis, Came to U.S., 1953, naturalized, 1958. Research asso. Fritz Haber Inst., Berlin, 1944-50, sci. head, asst., dep. chief crystal kinetics dept., 1950-53; cons. sr. scientist, team leader U.S. Army Signal Corps Research and Devel. Lab., Fort Monmouth, N.J., 1953-60; sr. group leader material research Harshaw Chem. Co., Cleve., 1960-63; dir. material research Erie Tech. Products (Pa.), 1963-64; prin. scientist Tyco Labs., Inc., Waltham, Mass., 1964-70; cons. chemist Lamp Phenomena Research Lab., Lamp Envelope Materials Research Lab., Gen. Electric Co., Cleve., 1970—. Chmn., Gordon Research Conf. on Chemistry and Metallurgy of Semiconductors, 1965; mem. crystal growth com. Internat. Union Crystallography, 1967-75, mem. Am. com. for crystal growth, 1967-72. Fellow Am. Inst. Chemists, Mineral. Soc. Am.; mem. Am. Phys. Soc., Am. Chem. Soc., Electrochem. Soc., Am. Crystallographic Assn., Am. Ceramic Soc. Home: 3776 Northampton Rd Cleveland OH 44121 Office: Lamp Envelope Materials Research Lab Gen Electric Co Nela Park Cleveland OH 44112

WOLFF, MILLIE BENDER, author, civic worker; b. Mt. Pleasant, Pa.; d. Ben and Ruth (Murstein) Bender; student Ohio State U., 1936-37, Akron U., 1940-41, Washington U., 1958-60; B.A. in Mass Communications, Webster Coll., 1974; children—Mack Bender Shaw, Henry Stephen Shaw, Alvin Wolff. TV chmn., pub. relations chmn., v.p. Akron League Women Voters, 1946-54; community relations dir. Family Service Soc., Akron, 1954-55; author column Family Counselor, Akron Beacon Jour., 1955; dir. spl. events GEM Internat., 1961; tv, radio chmn. Leagues Women Voters Met. St. Louis, 1956-63; bd. dirs. League Women Voters Mo., 1964; dir. People's Art Center, 1958-61, JCCA, 1956—; columnist Palm Beach Daily News; author-free lance acticles. Pub. relations dir. Gateway Theatre, 1964—; pub. relations cons., also producer Armchair Critic, Edn. Council Greater St. Louis. Mem. Press Women of Mo., Nat. Press Women, St. Louis Writer's Guild, Writer's Guild Am., Women in Communications. Home: 10374 Chimney Rock St St Louis MO 63141

WOLFF, PAUL GEORGE, ophthalmologist; b. Chester, Ill., June 26, 1915; s. Frank B. and Alma S. (Ebers) W.; B.S., U. Chgo., 1942, M.D., 1944; m. Mary J. Prather, Oct. 24, 1942; children—Paul George II, Alma (Mrs. Raymond K. Mueller). Intern, U. Chgo. Clinics, 1944-45, resident, 1946-48, instr. surgery, 1948-49; practice medicine, specializing in ophthalmology, Cape Girardeau, Mo., 1949—; pres. staff St. Francis Hosp., Cape Girardeau, 1957, Southeast Mo. Hosp., Cape Girardeau, 1964; cons. VA Hosp., Poplar Bluff, Mo., 1950-60, Ill. Security Hosp., Menard, 1955—, Perry County Hosp., Perryville, Mo., 1965—; guest lectr. U. Mo., Columbia, 1964. Bd. dirs. Mo. Blue Cross-Blue Shield, 1965-68. Served as lt. (j.g.) USNR, 1944-46. Diplomate Am. Bd. Ophthalmology. Fellow A.C.S., Am. Acad. Ophthalmology and Otolaryngology, Assn. for Research in Vision and Ophthalmology, AAAS; mem. Am. Assn. Ophthalmology (dir. 1962-63, 71-73), Mo. Ophthal. Soc. (co-founder 1963, pres. 1972-73, Gold medallion 1975), Cape Girardeau County Med. Soc. (pres. 1958), Pan Am. Assn. Ophthalmology, Eye Study Club. Home: 90 E Cape Rock Dr Cape Girardeau MO 63701 Office: 1819 Broadway Cape Girardeau MO 63701

WOLFF, ROBERT ADOLPH, mfg. co. exec.; b. Chgo., May 26, 1931; s. Robert Adolph and Ruth Elizabeth (Head) W.; B.S. in Elec. Engring., Ill. Inst. Tech., 1959; m. Marlene June Sande, May 22, 1951; children—Katharine, Brian. Mgr. advance engring. Admiral group Rockwell Internat., Chgo., 1959—. Recipient Engr. of Yr. award Rockwell Internat., 1976. Mem. IEEE, Profl. Group on Consumer Electronics. Patentee in field. Home: 21 W 281 Briar Cliff Rd Lombard IL 60148 Office: 1925 N Springfield St Chicago IL 60647

WOLFF, ROBERT EUGENE, electronic engr.; b. South Haven, Minn., Aug. 24, 1931; s. Walter Frederick and Evalyn Mary (Holmes) W.; B.S., U. Minn., 1959, M.B.A., 1974; m. Jacquelyn Bertha George, Sept. 25, 1952; children—Frederick, Sharon, William, Thomas. Devel. engr. Mpls. Honeywell, Mpls., 1959-61; v.p. operations Diginamics Corp., Mpls., 1961-63; computer applications supr. Minn. Mining & Mfg. Co., St. Paul, 1963—. Served with USAF, 1950-54. Mem. IEEE, Eta Kappa Nu. Home: 4405 Fondell Dr Edina MN 55435 Office: 3M Center St. Paul MN 55101

WOLFF, ROBERT SAMUEL, dentist, real estate, developer; b. Springfield, Ill., Feb. 13, 1932; s. Jack A. and Anna (Sherman) W.; student U. Colo., 1949; D.D.S., Washington U., St. Louis, 1955; m. Nancy Merkadeau, Dec. 19, 1954; children—Steven Mark, Brett David, Julie Lynne. Practice dentistry, St. Louis, 1957-59, East Alton, Ill., 1958—; pres. Wolff Devel., Inc., East Alton, 1969—. Served with USAF, 1955-57. Mem. Am. Dental Assn., Zeta Beta Tau, Alpha Omega. Mason (32 deg., Shriner). Home: 4 Colonial Hills Dr Creve Coeur MO 63141 Office: 707 Berkshire Blvd East Alton IL 62024

WOLFORD, DONOVAN SEMLER, structural engr., steel co. exec.; b. Indpls., June 5, 1912; s. Emory Charles and Martha (Semler) W.; student U. Cin., 1930-31; B.Mech. Engring., Ohio State U., 1934, M.E., 1944; m. Dorothy Evelyn Jordan, July 21, 1951: children—James Jordan, Elizabeth Ann. Weight control engr. Waco Aircraft Co., Troy, Ohio, 1934-35; research staff Armco Steel Corp., Middletown, Ohio, 1935—, supervising research mech. engr., 1958-70, prin. research asso., 1970—, prin. research structural engr., 1975-77, ret., 1977; cons. cold-formed steel, 1977—. Mem. Hwy. Research Bd. Mem. ASCE, Theta Tau. Republican. Lutheran. Author: (with Paul S. Buker) Light Steel Design and Construction, 1967, 76; also articles. Home: 1804 Schirm Dr Middletown OH 45042

WOLFSON, ALBERT, educator; b. N.Y.C., Feb. 3, 1917; s. Sigmund and Pauline (Segall) W.; B.S., Cornell U., 1937; Ph.D., U. Calif. at Berkeley, 1942; m. Dorothy Duke, June 19, 1937 (dec. Mar. 1971); children—Linda Jean (Mrs. Rostrom), Robert Neal; m. 2d, Sylvia Holland Mayer, Dec. 1971; children—Jan Alynn (Mrs. Robert L. Walker), Diane Lee (Mrs. Laurence Istvan), Gary Arthur. Instr. U. Calif. at Berkeley, 1942-44; mem. faculty Northwestern U., 1944—, instr., asst. prof., asso. prof., 1944-57, prof., 1957—, mem. steering com. Biol. Scis. Curriculum Study Com., 1961-65, Alumni Fund lectr., 1964; lectr. Am. Inst. Biol. Scis., 1959-61; research asso. Field Mus., Chgo. Cons. adv. panel on environmental biology NSF, 1965-67; mem. adv. com. for biotron U. Wis., Madison. Active Boy Scouts Am., 1957-67. Recipient Phi Sigma medal in biology U. Calif., 1941; sr. postdoctoral fellow NSF, U. Tokyo (Japan), 1961-62. Fellow AAAS, Am. Ornithologists' Union (sec. 1951-53, recipient Brewster Meml. medal and award for research on birds 1962); mem. Am. Soc. Naturalists, Brit. Ornithologists Union, Endocrine Soc., Am. Soc. Zoologists, Chgo. Acad. Scis. (1st v.p. 1975—), Phi Beta Kappa. Sigma Xi, Phi Kappa Phi. Author: The Human, The Earthworm, The Frog (all 1955); also articles World Book Ency., Ency. Brit., profl. jours. Editor: Avian Biology, 1955. Research on migration and breeding cycles in birds, reproductive physiology and neuroendocrinology. Home: 1260 Sherwood Rd Highland Park IL 60035

WOLIN, HAROLD DAVID, office supply co. exec.; b. Chgo., Mar. 25, 1930; s. Irving and Fannie (Orange) W.; student U. Ill., 1949; m. Merle Olenick, Feb. 17, 1951; children—Richard, Beth Ann, Nancy Susan, Robert Jay. With sales dept. Better Office Supply Co., Chgo., 1953-69; owner, operator Ram Industries, Chgo., 1969—. Served with U.S. Army, 1951-53. Club: Cavendish. Home: 640 Laramie Ln Glenview IL 60025 Office: 3510 N Elston Ave Chicago IL 60618

WOLKIN, JULIUS, neurosurgeon; b. Newark, Dec. 19, 1910; s. James and Mary (Danzis) W.; B.S., City Coll. of N.Y. 1932; M.S., U. Iowa, 1933, M.D., 1937; m. Hazel Mae Brogan, Feb. 28, 1942; children—David L., Robert S., Philip C., Steven E. Intern, Newark Beth Israel Hosp., 1937-39; resident Univ. Hosps., Iowa City, 1939-42; instr. neurosurgery U. Iowa, Iowa City, 1941-42; chief neurosurgeon Mt. Sinai Hosp., Cleve., 1947; practice medicine specializing in neurosurgery, Cleve., 1947—; asso. clin. prof. neurosurgery Case Western Reserve U., 1975—. Trustee, Free Clinic, 1972—. Served to capt. M.C., AUS, 1944-46. Diplomate Am. Bd. Neurosurgery. Fellow A.C.S.; mem. Sigma Xi, Alpha Omega Alpha. Contbr. articles to med. jours. Home: 2667 Wicklow St Shaker Heights OH 44120 Office: 11811 Shaker Blvd Cleveland OH 44120

WOLL, DAVID LAWRENCE, state ofcl.; b. Olney, Ill., Oct. 25, 1948; s. Albert and Pearl (Loeb) W.; B.A., Washington U., 1970; M. in Urban Planning, Columbia, 1972; spl. student Sch. for Social Research, 1970; M. in Pub. Affairs, Ind. U.-Purdue U., Indpls., 1975, postgrad. in law, 1976—. Community organizer Cambridge (Mass.) Settlement Houses, summer 1969; supr. children's program Cambridge Neighborhood House, summer 1970; tchr., curriculum developer Comprehensive Ednl. Center, Park East High Sch., N.Y.C., 1907-71; intern in planning Southwestern Ind.-Ky. Regional Council Govts., Evansville, Ind., summer 1971; legis. aide to Ind. state senator, Indpls., fall 1972; asst. to Ind. lt. gov., Indpls., 1972, 73; asst. dir. for local planning assistance Ind. Planning Services Agy., Indpls., spring, 1973, asst. dir. for local and regional planning assistance, spring 1974—. Mem. Am. Soc. Planning Officials, Am. Soc. Pub. Adminstrn., Anti-Defamation League (bd. dirs. local chpt. 1975—), Ind. Community Devel. Soc., Ind. Soc. Chgo., Ind. U. Alumni Assn., Indpls. Econ. Club, Indpls. Jewish Community Relations Council, Nat. Assn. Housing and Redevel. Ofcls., Zionist Orgn. Am. Republican. Jewish. Clubs: Broadmoor Country, Columbia, Optomists (v.p. local chpt.). Home: 3225 Fall Creekway E Indianapolis IN 46205 Office: 143 W Market St Indianapolis IN 46205

WOLL, ROBERT HENRY, mcht., banker; b. San Jose, Ill., Sept. 7, 1900; s. Henry and Catherine (Neikirk) W.; grad. San Jose High Sch., 1920; m. Amanda Williams, Dec. 25, 1925; 1 son, Robert Nicholas. With N. Woll & Co. (established 1867), San Jose, 1920—, mgr., 1928-38, sole owner, 1938-69, partner, 1969—; sr. v.p. San Jose Tri-County Bank, 1944-75, pres., 1975—; mem. adv. com. Happy Hour Stores, 1947-53; treas. Green Hill Cemetery Assn., 1938-56; established Amanda's Antique Shop, 1959. Sch. dir., 1937-40; Boy Scout committeeman, 1920-46; Community Council, Mason County Pub. Welfare Com., Mason County Planning Commn.; chmn. Mason County Housing Bd., 1959—; committeeman Salvation Army. Mem. adv. bldg. com. Sch. Dist. 122; auditor Allen Grove Tup., Ill., 1973—. Sec., treas. Green Hill Cemetery Assn. Mem. Am. Legion, Ill. Hist. Soc., Ill. Retail Grocers Assn., Farm Bur., Nat. Assn. Housing and Redevel. Ofcls., Nat. C. of C. Republican. Methodist (trustee 1938-66, pres. bd. 1959-62, hon. trustee 1966—, trustee sustaining fund; treas., sec. Meth. Men). Address: San Jose IL 62682

WOLL, ROBERT NICOLAS, educator; b. San Jose, Ill., Aug. 3, 1936; s. Robert Henry and Amanda Kathryn (Williams) W.; B.S., Western Ill. U., 1962; M.S., No. Ill. U., 1972, certificate of advanced study in ednl. curriculum and supervision, 1976. Physicist, So. Ill. U., Carbondale, 1961-63; research technician Argonne (Ill.) Nat. Lab., 1963-69; mem. faculty No. Ill. U., DeKalb, 1969—, faculty asst. allied health professions, 1977—; asso. prof. electronics tech., program coordinator Moraine Valley Coll., Palos Hills, Ill., 1972-77; prin. N. Woll & Co., San Jose, 1955—; engr. Anaconda Co., Sycamore, Ill., 1970-71; tech. tng. cons. to industry and schs. Mem. curriculum adv. com. various orgns. and instns. Post adviser Explorer Scouts Am., 1974—. Certified Electronics technician, 1973. Mem. IEEE, Ill. Acad. Sci. (mem. exec. council 1976—), Ill. Indsl. Edn. Assn., Ill. Soc. for Med. Research, Midwest Bio-Med. Soc., Ill. Assn. Elec. and Electronic Educators (pres. 1972-74), Aircraft Owners and Pilots Assn., Exptl. Aircraft Assn., Flying Huskies No. Ill. U. (pres. 1969-70), Sigma Pi Sigma. Republican. Lutheran. Club: Toastmasters (charter mem. Argonne chpt.). Home: N Woll & Co San Jose IL 62682 Office: Dept Industry and Technology No Ill U DeKalb IL 60115

WOLLMAN, HARVEY, lt. gov. S.D.; b. May 14, 1935: B.A., Huron Coll.; m. Dec. 30, 1958; 3 children. Farmer; mem. S.D. Senate, 1968-75; lt. gov. S.D., Pierre, 1975—. Chmn. Spink County (S.D.) Democratic party; chmn. State Midwest Conf. Council State Govts., mem. nat. adv. bd.: mem. S.D. Constl. Revision Commn. Served with U.S. Army, 1958-60. Mem. Phi Kappa Delta. Mem. Mennonite Brethren Ch. Address: Office of Lt Gov State Capitol Pierre SC 57501*

WOLLMAN, ROGER LELAND, state justice; b. Frankfort, S.D., May 29, 1934; s. Edwin and Katherine Wollman; B.A., Tabor Coll., Hillsboro, Kans., 1957; J.D. magna cum laude, U. S.D., 1962; LL.M., Harvard, 1964; m. Diane Marie Schroeder, June 21, 1959; children—Steven James, John Mark, Thomas Roger. Admitted to S.D. bar, 1964, practiced in Aberdeen, 1964-71; asso. justice S.D. Supreme Ct., 1971—; states atty. Brown County, Aberdeen, 1967-71. Served with AUS, 1957-59. Home: 1516 E Sunset Dr Pierre SD 57501 Office: SD Supreme Ct Pierre SD 57501

WOLLMANN, WILLIS JAMES, dentist, mayor; b. Yankton, S.D., May 10, 1925; s. Joseph A. and Elisabeth B. (Ewert) W.; student Bethel Coll., 1943-44, Freeman Jr. Coll., 1946-47, U. S.D., 1947-48; D.D.S., Washington U., St. Louis, 1952; m. Naomi Marie Tiezen, Sept. 9, 1951; children—Wayne Joseph, Janet Marie, Jean Elizabeth, Wilma Joyce, Marilyn Sue. Pvt. practice dentistry, Moundridge, Kans., 1952—. Mem. Moundridge City Council, 1957—, mayor, 1962-65, 77—; mem. McPherson County Airport Bd., 1964—, chmn., 1967-73; chmn. Moundridge City Airport Bd., 1971—, Moundridge Housing Authority, 1968-77. Mem. Kans. (exec. council 1971—), 7th Dist (pres. 1970-71) dental socs. Mem. Mennonite Ch. (deacon 1962—). Club: Lions (pres. 1964). Address: Moundridge KS 67107

WOLLNEY, JOHN LOWELL, dentist; b. Portland, Maine, Feb. 4, 1942; s. Arthur Edward and Kathleen Harper (Hudson) W.; B.A., Tulane U., 1963; D.D.S., Loyola U., New Orleans, 1967; children by previous marriage—Kathryn Ann, John Lowell, Elizabeth Giltner. Practice dentistry specializing in orthodontics, 1971—; orthodontic asso. of M. Braun, Olympia Fileds, Ill., 1970-72, J.R. Thompson and A. Venezia, Flossmoor, Ill., 1974-76; clin. instr. orthodontics Loyola U. Dental Sch., Maywood, Ill., 1976—. Sunday sch. instr. Presbyn. Ch. of Libertyville (Ill.), 1976—, deacon, 1977—. Served to capt. U.S. Army, 1967-69. Mem. Ill. Soc. Orthodontists, Am. Dental Assn., Chgo. Dental Soc., Am. Orthodontic Assn., C. of C. Republican. Presbyterian. Club: Lions. Home: 11 Oak Creek Dr Buffalo Grove IL 60090 Office: 109 W Maple Ave Libertyville IL 60048

WOLLSTEIN, DONALD GUSTAV, mgmt. cons., tax specialist, accountant; b. Chgo., May 28, 1923; s. Gustav Herman Henry and Anna Millicent (Hoffmann) W.; grad. Northwestern U., 1953; M.A., Internat. Graphoanalysis Soc., 1964; m. Florence Edith Ellis, Oct. 10, 1953. Field rep. for mortgage closings Hammond Mortgage Co., 1941-44; with cashier's dept. Paul H. Davis & Co., 1945-48; supr. cashier's dept. Kleins Sporting Goods Co., 1948-51; mem. statis. staff Millar Coffee Co., Chgo., 1951-54; owner, operator Donald Wollstein Enterprises, Kenosha, Wis., 1954—. Certified and master graphoanalyst. Mem. Internat. Graphoanalysis Soc., Assn. Research and Enlightenment, Allemande Sq. Dance Club (Kenosha). Home and Office: 9901 8th Ave Carol Beach Estates Kenosha WI 53140

WOLNAK, BERNARD, biochemist, cons.; b. Chgo., Dec. 30, 1918; s. Max and Bessie (Kaplan) W.; B.S., U. Chgo., 1939, M.S., 1940; Ph.D., Ind. U., 1943; m. Frances R. Knoblauch, Aug. 27, 1943; children—Eve K. (Mrs. Ronald Bremen), Laurie R. (Mrs. Craig Steadman). Research chemist Miner Labs., Chgo., 1946-54; pres. Midwest Labs., Chgo., 1954-63, B. Wolnak & Assos., Chgo., 1963—. Mem. Am. Chem. Soc., AAAS, Am. Soc. Microbiology, Inst. Food Technologists. Home: 6101 Sheridan Rd E Chicago IL 60660 Office: 75 E Wacker Dr Chicago IL 60601

WOLPERT, EDWARD ALAN, psychiatrist; b. Chgo., Apr. 22, 1930; s. Sol and Dorothy (Greenwald) W.; B.A., U. Chgo., 1950, M.A. in Psychology, 1954, Ph.D. in Psychology, 1959, M.D., 1960; m. Gloria Adele Yanoff, Mar. 23, 1958; children—Seth I., Andrew O., Edward G. Intern U. Ill. Research and Ednl. Hosp., Chgo., 1960-61; resident in psychiatry Inst. for Psychosomatic and Psychiat. Research and Tng., Michael Reese Hosp. and Med. Center, Chgo., 1961-64, dir. clin. services, 1966—; grad. Inst. for Psychoanalysis, 1973; practice medicine specializing in psychiatry, Chgo., 1964—; clin. asso. prof. psychiatry Pritzker Sch. Medicine, U. Chgo., 1972-76, clin. prof., 1976—; faculty mem. continuing edn. program for psychiatrists, Chgo. Inst. for Psychoanalysis, 1974—. Served with USNG, 1948-51. Diplomate Am. Bd. Neurology and Psychiatry. Fellow Am. Psychiat. Assn.; mem. AMA, Chgo., Ill. State med. socs., Ill. State Psychiat. Soc., Am. Psychol. Assn., Assn. for Psychophysiol. Study of Sleep, AAAS, N.Y. Acad. Sci., George S. Klein Meml. Psychoanalytic Research Forum, Center for Study of Psychosocial Problems (mem. organizing group), Am. Soc. for Clin. Pharmacology and Therapeutics, Chgo., Am. psychoanalytic assns., Am. Psychosomatic Soc., Wis. Acad. Arts, Letters, and Scis., Sigma Xi, Alpha Omega Alpha. Home: 727 Elmwood St Wilmette IL 60091 Office: 2959 S Ellis Ave Chicago IL 60616

WOLPERT, HENRY WILLIAM, automotive mfg. co. exec.; b. Wuerzburg, Germany, July 4, 1926; s. Wilhelm G. and Paula (Dieterich) W.; Ph.D., U. Munich, 1952; m. Mary Anne Watkins, Sept. 12, 1953; children—William H., Gregory G. Came to U.S., 1952, naturalized, 1956. Research dir. Opinion Research Corp., Princeton, N.J., 1952-62; market research mgr. European sales and assembly operations Ford Motor Co., Dearborn, Mich., 1962-66, overseas marketing research mgr., marketing staff, 1966-70, car marketing research mgr., product planning group N.Am. operation, 1970-72, marketing research mgr., 1972—. Mem. faculty, Wayne State U. Sch. Bus. Adminstrn., 1968-71. Mem. Am. Psychol. Assn. Home: 7299 Old Mill Rd Birmingham MI 48010 Office: American Rd Dearborn MI 48121

WOLSEY, WILLIAM JEROME, steel fabricating and equipment mfg. co. exec.; b. South Milwaukee, Wis., Mar. 17, 1931; s. William Franklyn and Helen Mary (Kaczanowski) W.; student U. Wis., Marquette U., 1950-56; m. Dolores Mildred Hartz, Aug. 22, 1959; children—Kathleen, Brian, Lisa, Craig. Estimating engring. checker Ladish Co., Cudahy, Wis., 1955-S8; sales engr. Internstate Drop Forge Co., Milw., 1958-66, v.p., 1973—, div. mgr. H.P. Norling Co., 1971—. Served with U.S. Army, 1952-54. Mem. Forging Industry Assn. Roman Catholic. Club: Tuckaway Country. Home: 301 Parkway Dr South Milwaukee WI 53172 Office: 4051 27th St N Milwaukee WI 53216

WOLSKY, MILTON LABAN, advt. agy. exec., artist; b. Omaha, Jan. 23, 1916; s. Samuel Soloman and Agnes (Horwich) W.; student U. Omaha, 1932-34, Art Inst. Chgo., 1934, Art Students League, 1946, also pvt. tchrs. Illustration and art dir. Bozell & Jacobs, Omaha, 1970—; instr. painting Joslyn Art Mus., 1959-62. One-man shows Joslyn Art Mus., 1961; exhibited group shows Joslyn Midwest, 1938, Am. Watercolor Soc., 1947, U.S. Air Force Art Exhbn., 1960, Smithsonian Inst., 1960, Walker Biennial, 1962; represented permanent collection Air Force Hist. Found. Served with AUS, 1942-46; ETO. Recipient award Council Neb.'s Cultural Resources, 1962. Mem. Am. Watercolor Soc., Soc. Illustrators. Author: Basic Elements of Painting; Rock People. Contbr. editorial and advt. illustration to popular mags. Home and studio: 5804 Leavenworth St Omaha NE 68106

WOLTERS, PAUL HENRY, educator; b. Steeleville, Ill., Mar. 25, 1932; s. August Henry and Anna Sophia Maria (Kothe) W.; Mus.B., So. Ill. U., 1957, Mus. M., 1958; postgrad. U. Ill., 1970-71; m. Marianna Henrietta Dirks, June 6, 1970; children—David Paul, Kristi Ann Kimberly. Grad. asst. So. Ill. U., Carbondale, 1957-58; dir. music Webber Twp. High Sch., Bluford, Ill., 1958-60; orchestra dir. Rantoul (Ill.) City Schs., 1960-62; supr. music, 1962—. Bd. dirs. Rantoul Community Concert Assn., 1962-70, pres. 1968-70. Served with AUS, 1954-56. Mem. Nat., Ill. edn. assns., Music Educator's Nat. Conf., Ill. Music Educators Assn., Rantoul City Schs. Edn. Assn. (pres. 1971-72), Ill. Elementary Sch. Assn. (mem. music com. 1965—), Phi Mu Alpha. Lutheran. Home: 1529 Gleason Dr Rantoul IL 61866 Office: 400 E Wabash Ave Rantoul IL 61866

WOLTZ, FRANK EARL, JR., chemist; b. Bethlehem, Pa., Nov. 29, 1916; s. Frank Earl and Mary Rose (Meyer) W.; B.S., Bethany Coll., 1938; M.S., W.Va. U., 1940, Ph.D., 1943; M.S., Ohio U., 1970; m. Jean Marie Lawrence, Oct. 12, 1947; children—Frank Earl, Lois Ann. Materials engr. Westinghouse Electric Corp., Pitts., 1942-44; lab. mgr. Goodyear Synthetic Rubber Corp., Akron, Ohio, 1944-47; research chemist, rubber compounder Goodyear Tire & Rubber Co., Akron, 1947-53; supr. ops. analysis Goodyear Atomic Corp., Piketon, Ohio, 1953-67, supt. engring. devel., 1967—; mem. faculty Ohio U., also Shawnee State Coll., Portsmouth, Ohio. Mem. Waverly (Ohio) Village Council, 1956-59; clk. Village of Waverly, 1959-64. Mem. Am. Nuclear Soc. Presbyterian. Home: 400 E 3d St Waverly OH 45690 Office: PO Box 628 Piketon OH 45661

WOLZ, ROBERT CHARLES, dentist; b. St. Louis, June 15, 1931; s. Frederick Robert and Bertha Ethel (Hammer) W.; D.D.S., St. Louis U., 1956; m. Ludeane Jeanette Fowler, Dec. 28, 1952; children—Jay Frederick, Robert Russell. Pvt. practice dentistry, Chester, Ill., 1956-57, 59—; mem. staff Meml. Hosp., Chester, St. Clements Hosp., Red Bud, Ill., Sparta (Ill.) Community Hosp., St. Genevieve (Mo.) Hosp.; owner Viking Sauna Midstates, Chester, 1971—; asso. prof. U. Ill. Coll. Dentistry. Liaison officer, ofcl. rep. of admissions officer U.S. Air Force Acad., 1971—. Served with USAF, 1957-59. Mem. ADA, Ill., St. Clair, Greater St. Louis dental socs., Aircraft Owners and Pilots Assn., Nat. Aero. Assn., Res. Officers Assn. United Methodist (pres. ofcl. bd. ch. 1973). Mason (Shriner), Elk. Club: Chester Country. Home: 1214 Henrietta St Chester IL 62233 Office: 1101 Opdyke St Chester IL 62233

WOMBLE, GEORGE EDWIN, farm equipment mfg. co. exec.; b. Parsons, Kan., Jan. 9, 1924; s. David Hubbard and Una Hazel (Woodward) W.; B.S., Kan. State U., 1949; m. Betty Lou Arnold, Sept. 4, 1945; children—James R., Thomas L., Timothy A. With Avco-New Idea, Coldwater, Ohio, 1949-60, J.I. Case, Rockford, Ill., 1960-64; with Kewanee Machinery div. Chromalloy Am. Corp., 1964—, now v.p. engring. Served with USAAF, 1942-45. Recipient Engr. of Yr. award Farm and Indsl. Equipment Inst., 1974. Mem. Am. Soc. Agrl. Engrs. (sr.), Soc. Automotive Engrs. Mason, Elk, Kiwanian (dir. 1970-72). Club: Midland Country (Kewanee). Patentee in field. Home: 231 Hillside Dr Kewanee IL 61443 Office: 1516 Burlington St Kewanee IL 61443

WOMELDORFF, PORTER JOHN, elec. engr.; b. Milw., Feb. 26, 1933; s. Virgil Leslie and Leorra (Porter) W.; B.S. in Elec. Engring., U. Ill., 1954; m. Marilyn P. Sapp, Jan. 7, 1966; children—John Porter, Michael Wayne. Elec. engr. Ill. Power Co., Decatur, 1954-59, results supr., 1959-60, instrumentation engr., 1960-73, supr. system planning, 1973-75, mgr. planning, 1975—. Mem. Mid Am. Interpool Network Engring. Com.; mem. system planning com. Edison Electric Inst. Trustee Wesley Found. Served to lt., C.E., AUS, 1955-57. Decorated Army Commendation medal. Mem. Instrument Soc. Am. (v.p. 1971-73), IEEE, ASME, U. Ill. Elec. Engring. (dir.), U. Ill. (dir.) alumni assns., Phi Kappa Phi, Tau Beta Pi, Sigma Tau, Eta Kappa Nu. Alpha Kappa Lambda. Methodist (lay mem. Central Ill. Ann. Conf., 1968—, lay leader, 1976—, lay mem. N.Central Jurisdictional Conf., 1972—, lay mem. Gen. Conf. 1976—). Pioneered magnetic tape for utility billing. Home: 433 S Westdale Decatur IL 62522 Office: 500 S 27th St Decatur IL 62525

WOMER, FRANK BURTON, psychologist; b. South Bend, Ind., Sept. 25, 1921; s. William A. and Ruth (Boal) W.; B.A., U. Colo., 1948; M.A., U. Mich., 1951, Ph.D., 1956. Tchr. math. high sch., Alamosa, Colo., 1948-50; test editor Houghton Mifflin Co., 1954-56; dir. Nat. Assessment Ednl. Progress, Edn. Commn. of the States, Denver,

1967-71; mem. faculty Sch. Edn. U. Mich., Ann Arbor, 1956—, asso. prof. ednl. psychology, 1962-67, prof., 1967—. Mem. Am. Personnel and Guidance Assn. (dir. 1975-78, exec. com. 1977-78), Am. Ednl. Research Assn., Assn. Measurement and Evaluation in Guidance (pres. 1973-74), Nat. Council Measurement in Edn. (pres. 1969-70), Ednl. Records Bur. (dir. 1972-76). Home: 1020 Bruce St Ann Arbor MI 48103 Office: 401 4th St S Ann Arbor MI 48109

WONER, JOHN WILLIAM, physician; b. Sullivan County, Apr. 22, 1910; s. James Irwin and Esther Urania (Moore) W.; M.D. Ind. U., 1933; postgrad. Cook County Postgrad. Sch. Surgery, 1946, Gynecology, 1955, Proctology 1963; m. Marie Willis, July 6, 1934; children—James E. Julia Ann (dec.). Pvt. practice medicine, Sullivan County, Ind., 1933-40, Linton, Ind., 1940—. Del. Ind. Republican Conv., 1950-52. Served with inf. AUS, 1941-45. Recipient Distinguished Hoosier award Franklin Coll. Football Team, 1970; named to Franklin Coll. Athletic Hall of Fame, 1976. Mem. AMA, Ind. Med. Soc., Am. Fracture Assn., 29th Div. Assn. (nat. comdr. 1971-72, Philadelphia award 1973), OX 5 Pioneers Aviation, Chi Gamma Tau, Theta Kappa Pi. Republican. Methodist. Elk. Club: Columbia (Indpls.). Home: Rural Route 3 Linton IN 47441 Office: 390 NE A St Linton IN 47441

WONG, ALFONSO YAN, physician; b. Zamboanga City, Philippines, Mar. 16, 1939; s. Pedro F. and Maxima (Yan) W.; came to U.S., 1967; B.S., U. Philippines, 1961; M.D., U. of the East, 1966; m. Elisa See Keh, July 26, 1975; 1 son, Jason Scott. Intern, Youngstown (Ohio) Hosp. Assn., 1967-68; resident Cook County Hosp., Chgo., 1968-71, asso. attending anesthesiologist, 1971-72, attending anesthesiologist div. pediatric anesthesia, 1972-74, chmn. div. pediatric anesthesia, 1974—, asso. dir. pediatric intensive care unit, 1977; asst. prof. clin. anesthesiology Loyola U., Stritch Sch. Medicine, 1975. Diplomate Am. Bd. Anesthesiologists. Fellow Am. Coll. Anesthesiology; mem. Am., Ill. socs. anesthesiologists, Ill. State, Chgo. med. socs., Internat. Anesthesia Research Soc., Chgo. Soc. Anesthesia, AMA. Office: 1835 W Harrison Chicago IL 60612

WONG, HERMAN HOY, systems engr.; b. Canton, China, Apr. 15, 1938; s. Edward Gooey and Ellen Gooey (Lee) W.; came to U.S., 1949; B.S. in Math. with distinction, San Diego State U., 1962, M.S. in Math., 1964; M.S. in Indsl. and Systems Engring., Ohio State U., 1975; m. Carol Young, Aug. 6, 1966; 1 dau., Debra Anne. Instr. math. Clarkson Coll. Tech., Potsdam, N.Y., 1964-67; asst. prof. math. Ohio No. U., Ada, 1969-72; systems engr. Ohio Dept. Mental Health, Columbus, 1975—. NSF study grantee, 1972. Mem. Ops. Research Soc. Am., Math. Assn. Am., Ohio Acad. Sci., Am. Inst. Indsl. Engrs., Alpha Pi Mu. Club: Lions. Methodist. Contbr. articles to math. jours. Home: 906 Havendale Dr Columbus OH 43220 Office: 30 E Broad St 12th Floor Columbus OH 43215

WONG, JIMMY PAN, restaurant exec.; b. Canton, China, Oct. 10, 1914; s. Jaw and Toy (Shee) W.; came to U.S., 1923, naturalized, 1923; student pub. schs., Ellensburg, Wash.; m. Cynthia Chan, June 6, 1956; children—Ella, Rosalind, Lisa. Partner, Nan Yan Restaurant, Chgo., 1947-50, owner, mgr., 1950—; owner, mgr. Jimmy Wong's Restaurant, Chgo., 1959—, Jimmy Wong's North, Chgo., 1965—; dir. Bank of Chgo. Adviser Chinese Overseas Commn., Republic China, Taiwan, 1973-74, 75-77; developer Chgo.'s New Chinatown. Served with USAAF, W.W. II; ETO. Recipient award recognition Ann. Nat. Restaurant Conv., 1962; Man of Year award Ill. Combined Vets Assn., 1971-72. Mem. Nat. Hip Sing Benevolence Assn. (asst. chmn.), Chew Lun Benevolence Assn. (past Midwest pres.), Am. Vets. Press Assn., VFW (life). Club: Chinese Passenger (pres.) (Chgo.). Home: 9217 N Kenton St Skokie IL 60076 Office: 426 S Wabash Ave Chicago IL 60605

WONNENBERG, KENNETH RAY, county extension agt.; b. Burke, S.D., Aug. 24, 1945; s. William and Alvina Freda (Lindwarm) W.; B.S., S.D. State U., 1970; m. Diane Kay Broekemeier, Dec. 31, 1971; children—Daniel Ray, Brenda Kay, Kimberly Joy. Asst. county extension agt. Brown County, S.D. State U., U.S. Dept. Agr. Extension Service, Aberdeen, 1970-71, Lyman county extension agt., Kennebec, 1971—. Raiser angus cattle, Presho, S.D. Served with AUS, 1968-69. Decorated Commendation medal, Combat Infantryman's badge; recipient Jr. Achievement award Nat. County Agts., 1974. Mem. VFW, Child Evangelism Fellowship (com. mem., sec. South Central dist. 1975—), S.D. County Agts. Assn., Am. Angus Assn. Mem. Bible Ch. (Sunday sch. supt. 1974-75, chmn. bd. 1975-76). Lion. Home: PO Box 119 Presho SD 57568 Office: PO Box 68 Kennebec SD 57544

WOOD, ARTHUR MACDOUGALL, corp. exec.; b. Chgo., Jan. 27, 1913; s. R. Arthur and Emily (Smith) W.; A.B., Princeton U., 1934, LL.D. (hon.), 1976; LL.B., Harvard U., 1937; m. Pauline Palmer, Nov. 17, 1945; children—Pauline, Arthur MacDougall. Admitted to Ill. bar, 1937; atty. Bell, Boyd & Marshall, Chgo., 1937-41; atty. Sears, Roebuck & Co., 1946-52, sec., 1952-56, v.p., 1956-68, dir., 1959—, comptroller, 1960-62, v.p. charge Pacific Coast terr., 1962-67, v.p. Midwest terr., 1967, pres. 1968-72, chmn., 1973-77; dir. Quaker Oats, Homart Devel. Co., Allstate Ins. Co., Continental Ill. Corp., Simpsons Sears Ltd. Trustee Art Inst. Chgo., Rush-Presbyn.-St. Lukes Med. Center. Served from pvt. F.A., AUS to lt. col. USAAF, 1941-45. Decorated Legion of Merit. Mem. Bus. Council, Bus. Roundtable. Address: Sears Roebuck & Co Sears Tower Chicago IL 60684

WOOD, BRUCE DEAN, indsl. relations cons.; b. Vermillion, SD., Dec 15, 1928; s. Edward Athey and Helen Lee (Patton) W.; B.S. in Bus., U. Mo., 1952; m. Jeanne D. Wood, Aug. 19, 1950; children—Edward, Deborah. Personnel mgr. Mpls. Honeywell Corp., Phila., 1960-62, mgr. indsl. relations, 1962-66; v.p. indsl. relations Conductron Corp., Ann Arbor, Mich., 1966-67, KMS Industries, Ann Arbor, 1967-70; pres. Mgmt. Edn. Center, Whitmore Lake, Mich., 1970—. Republican. Author. publs. in field. Home: 700 Lans Way Ann Arbor MI 48103 Office: 7038 Whitmore Lake Rd Whitmore Lake MI 48189

WOOD, CHARLES RICHARD, mfg. co. exec.: b. Middleboro, Mass., Aug. 20, 1933; s. Raymond H. and Ernestine Thelma (Brigham) W.: B.S. in Bus. Adminstrn., Boston U., 1957; m. Roswitha E. Bauer, Apr. 3, 1974; children—Charles R., Diane M. Salesman, Wood Conversion Co., Chgo., 1957-59, Dayton Rubber Co., 1959-60; dist. mgr. Vanant Co., Chgo., 1960-61; pres. Republic Packaging Corp., Chgo., 1961—. Mem. bd. Village of Palos Park (Ill.), 1966-69. Mem. Young Pres.'s Orgn. Club: Union League. Home: 203 Hilltop St Mokena IL 60448 Office: 9160 S Green St Chicago IL 60620

WOOD, EARL HOWARD, physiologist, physician; b. Mankato, Minn., Jan. 1, 1912; s. William Clark and Inez (Goff) W.; B.A. summa cum laude, Macalester Coll., St. Paul, 1934, D.Sc. (hon.), 1950; B.S., U. Minn., 1939, M.S., 1940, M.D., 1941, Ph.D., 1941; m. Ada Peterson, Dec. 20, 1936; children—Phoebe Wood Busch, Mark Goff, Guy Harland, Earl Andrew. Teaching fellow dept. physiology U. Minn., 1936-37, instr., 1939-40; NRC fellow, dept. pharmacology U. Pa. Med. Sch., 1940-41; instr. pharmacology Harvard U. Med. Sch., 1942; research asst. physiology Acceleration Lab., Mayo Aeromed. Unit, 1942-46; sci. cons. to surg. gen. USAF Aeromed. Center, Heidelberg, Germany, 1946; asst. prof. physiology Mayo Grad. Sch., 1943-47, asso. prof., 1947-51; prof. physiology and medicine Mayo Med. Sch., Rochester, Minn., 1951—; cons. physiology Mayo Clinic and Mayo Found., 1946-76; career investigator Am. Heart Assn., 1962—; vis. prof. Physiology Inst., U. Bern, Switzerland, 1965-66; hon. research fellow dept. physiology Univ. Coll., London, 1972-73; chmn. biophys. scis. Unit Mayo Found., 1974-76, sr. cons., biodynamics research unit, 1977—; mem. Pres.'s Sci. Adv. Com., 1962-66; dir. Def. Research and Engring. Adv. Panel on Med. Biol. Scis., 1962-67; mem. ad hoc med. adv. panel NASA SPAMAG, 1964-65; cons. Aerospace Corp., 1964-65; mem. biomed. subcom. sci. and tech. adv. com. NASA, 1967—; mem. med. adv. group USAF Manned Orbital Lab., 1969-74. Mem. Am. Physiol. Soc. (Travel award Internat. Congress Physiology, Oxford, Eng. 1947), Biomed. Engring. Soc., Soc. for Exptl. Biology and Medicine (chmn. Minn. sect. 1963), Soc. for Clin. Investigation, Central Soc. for Clin. Research, Aerospace Med. Assn., Minn. Acad. Sci., AAAS, Am. Physiology Soc. (chmn. circulatory group 1963-64, Carl J. Wiggers award 1968), Cardiac Muscle Soc., Am. Inst. Biol. Scis., Nat. Acad. Sci., Am. (Research Achievement award 1973), Minn. (research com. 1962-65) heart assn., Sigma Xi, Alpha Omega Alpha, Pi Phi Epsilon. Recipient AMA award, 1962, Eric Liljencrantz award, 1963, Modern Medicine award, 1963, Alumni award Phi Beta Kappa, 1970, Distinguished Citizen award Macalester Coll. Alumni, 1974; Distinguished lectr. Am. Coll. Chest Physicians, 1974; contbr. articles to med. jours. Home: 1147 2d St NW Rochester MN 55901 Office: 200 1st St NW Rochester MN 55901

WOOD, EDWARD ALBERT, optical mfg. co. exec.; b. Vandalia, Ill., May 2, 1933; s. Edward Albert and Agnes (Sheehan) W.; B.S., Marquette U., 1955; m. Jean Harmer, Jan. 29, 1955; children—Mary, Lawrence, Kathleen, Susan. Ill. rep. Amerock Cabinet Hardware, 1955-63; marketing mgr. Varo Optical Inc., 1963-69; v.p., dir. FJW Industries, Mt. Prospect, Ill., 1969—. Pres. parish sch. bd., 1970-72. Pres., Addison (Ill.) Twp. Young Republicans, 1964-65; Rep. committeeman, 1965-72; mem. DuPage Co. Rep. Bd., 1970-72. Mem. planning commn. village Addison, 1972—. Mem. Optical Soc. Am., Soc. Photog. Instrumentation Engrs., Soc. Photog. Scientists and Engrs. Elk, K.C., Moose. Club: Itasca (Ill.) Country. Home: 116 Adams Dr Addison IL 60101 Office: 215 E Prospect St Mt Prospect IL 60056

WOOD, GEORGE MICHAEL, real estate broker; b. Weaubleau, Mo., Feb. 27, 1951; s. George Lewis and Helen Lucile (Dietz) W.; student Reisch Auction Sch., Mason City, Ia., 1971. Propr. G. Michael Wood, auction co., Wheatland, Mo., 1971—; real estate broker Wood Realtors, Wheatland, 1972—; self-employed contractor, Wheatland, 1974—; ins. agt., 1976—. Notary Public, 1973—. Recipient State Farmer award Future Farmers Am., 1969. Mem. Ozarks Bd. Realtors (pres. 1977—). Home: Quincy MO 65735 Office: Weaubleau MO 65774

WOOD, GORDON R., real estate and ins. exec.; b. Mattoon, Ill., Jan. 24, 1934; s. Forrest W. and Phyllis E. (Harshman) W.; B.A., Trinity Coll., Hartford, Conn., 1956; m. Sandra S. Locklar, Dec. 21, 1957; children—Gordon R., Laura L., Gerald R. Commd. 2d lt. USAF, 1956, advanced through grades to capt., 1963; pilot tng., Hondo, Tex., 1957; student Single Engine Jet Pilot Sch., Laredo, Tex., 1957, Weapons Controller Sch., Panama City, Fla., 1958, Squadron Officer Sch., Montgomery, Ala., 1962; resigned, 1963; with Wood Ins. Agy., Inc., Sullivan, Ill., 1964—, pres., 1972—. Counselor, Lincoln Trails council Boy Scouts Am., 1967—; bd. dirs. Moultrie County United Way, pres., 1977-78; trustee Sullivan Fire Protection Dist., 1977, Sullivan Ambulance Dist., 1977. Mem. Nat. Assn. Real Estate Bds., Nat., Ill. assns. ind. agts., Central Ill. Bd. Realtors, Sullivan C. of C., Illini Quarterback Club (dir.), Moultrie County Area Christian Men's Assn. (past pres. bd.), Kaskaskia Valley Assn. (dir.), Moultrie County Flying Club (sec.-treas.). Methodist (past pres. bd.). Clubs: Sullivan Country (past pres. bd.), Sullivan Sno-N-Go Snowmobile (sec.-treas. 1977), Lions (past pres.), Masons, Shriners. Home: Box 157 Sullivan IL 61951 Office: 7 W Harrison St Sullivan IL 61951

WOOD, JAMES NOWELL, museum ofcl.; b. Boston, Mar. 20, 1941; s. Charles H. and Helen N. (Nowell) W.; diploma Universita per Stranieri, Perugia, Italy, 1962; B.A., Williams Coll., Williamstown, Mass., 1963; M.A. (Ford Mus. Tng. fellow), N.Y.U., 1966; m. Emese Forizs; children—Lenke Hancock, Rebecca Noel. Asst. to dir. Met. Mus., N.Y.C., 1967-68, asst. curator dept. 20th Century art, 1968-70; curator Albright-Knox Art Gallery, Buffalo, 1970-73, asso. dir., 1973-75; adj. prof. dept. art history State U. N.Y., 1972-75; dir. St. Louis Art Mus., 1975—. Mem. Intermuseum Conservation Assn. (pres.). Office: 6665 Delmar Blvd Saint Louis MO 63130

WOOD, JOSEPHINE GREEN (MRS. NEAL S. WOOD), preservationist; b. St. Louis, July 5, 1907; d. Allen Percival and Josephine (Brown) Green; student pvt. sch., Tarrytown, N.Y.; D.P.A., Westminster Coll., 1969; m. Neal Shackleford Wood, Sept. 1, 1928; children—Neal Shackleford, Josephine (Mrs. George Ochoa), Robert Alexander, Mem. historic com. Mo. Bot. Garden; mem. St. Louis County Hist. Sites Bd. Decorative Arts Commn. of St. Louis Art Mus. Bd. dirs. St. Louis Woman's Exchange, Friends of Winterthur Museum; bd. regents Kenmore, Fredericksburg, Va., Gunston Hall, Lorton, Va., bd. of overseers Old Sturbridge Village, Mass.; bd. dirs. Mo. Mansion Preservation, St. Louis Art Mus. Named Woman Achievement, 1966. Mem. Nat. Soc. Colonial Dames America (chmn. museum house) Mo. Hist. Soc. (dir.), Soc. Descendants Knights Order of the Garter, Huguenot Soc. of S.C., Colonial Order of Crown, Nat. Soc. Magna Charta Dames, St. Louis Garden Club. Republican. Presbyterian. Clubs: Colony, St. Louis, St. Louis Country, Sulgrave. Home: 816 S Hanley Rd Ladue MO 63105 also 35 Colonia Miramonte Scottsdale AZ 85253

WOOD, KATHLEEN ANN STUDT, educator; b. Lansing, Mich., Aug. 20, 1943; d. Robert E. and Georgia (Preston) Studt; B.A., Trevecca Nazarene Coll., 1966; M.A., Wayne State U., 1972; M.Ed., U. Detroit, 1974; children—Elizabeth, David. Tchr., Southfield (Mich.) Christian Sch., 1972-75; child therapist Met. Guidance Center, Farmington, Mich., 1975-76; instr. John Wesley Coll., Farmington, also dir. lab. sch. for early learners; asst. prof. early childhood edn. Mt. Vernon (Ohio) Nazarene Coll., 1976; dir. day nurseries and kindergartens, Hazel Park Ferndale, 1969-72; presenter workshops seminars, 1969—. Mem. Am. Assn. Colls. for Tchrs. Edn., Ohio Assn. Colls for Tchr. Edn., Columbus Assn. Edn. Young Children, Nat. Assn. Edn. Young Children, Council Exceptional Children, Am. Personnel and Guidance Assn., Nazarene Assn. Tchr. Edn. Home: 12 Craig Dr Mt Vernon OH 43050 Office: Mt Vernon Nazarene Coll Mt Vernon OH 43050

WOOD, KENNETH HAROLD, mfg. engr.; b. Eau Galle, Wis., Jan. 4, 1927; s. Lyle Forest and Ellen Marie (Frederickson) W.; student Coyne Elec. Sch., 1949-50, Chgo. Tech. Sch., 1954-55; Asso. Prodn. Tech., Rock Valley Coll., 1972-75; m. Barbara Ann Johnson, July 3, 1954; 1 dau., Nancy Ann. Process planner Gen. Electric Co., DeKalb, Ill., 1956-61, Rockford, Ill., 1964-69; indsl. engr. Sundstrand Corp., Rockford, 1961-64, Barber-Colman Co., Rockford, 1969—. Precinct committeeman Republican Party, 1964-66. Served with U.S. Army, 1945-48, USAF, 1950-52; Germany, Korea. Mem. Soc. Mfg. Engrs. (certified), Am. Inst. Indsl. Engrs., PTA, Parent-Tchr. Orgn., VFW, Am. Legion. Home: 5599 Dorchester Dr Rockford IL 61108 Office: Barber-Colman Co Clifford Ave Loves Park IL 61111

WOOD, LAWRENCE EDWARD, investment banker; b. Kansas City, Kans., Nov. 23, 1935; s. Lawrence E. and Agnes (Gordon) W.; A.A., U. Ark., 1955; B.A., U. Kans., 1957; m. Jaye Eddie, June 7, 1958; children—Sara, Elisabeth. With Stern Bros. & Co., Kansas City, Mo., 1959—, v.p., 1962—; pres., dir. Asso. Mgmt. Service, Inc., Kansas City, Mo., 1972—; owner L.E. Wood and Assos. dir. Comfort Equipment Co., Holden, Mo. Bd. govs., trustee Kansas City Philharmonic, 1970-73; bd. dirs. Wood Found., 1958-74. Named to Aviation Hall of Fame, Dayton, Ohio. Fellow Am. Acad. Police Sci.; mem. Am. Mgmt. Assn., Inst. Certified Photographers Nat. Bus. Aircraft Assn., C. of C., Real Estate Bd. Home: 7215 Eby Dr Shawnee Mission KS 66204 Office: 9 W 10th St PO Box 13486 Kansas City MO 64199 also 2330 Commerce Tower Bldg Kansas City MO 64199

WOOD, LESLIE ALFRED, educator; b. Huntington, Ind., June 13, 1930; s. Ralph W. and Roxie (Kerns) W.; student Olivet Coll., 1948-50; B.S. in Social Sci., Ball State U., 1952; M.A. in Econ., Case Western Res. U., 1957; Ed.D., Stanford, 1962; m. Ruth Elaine Baker. Aug. 1, 1954; children—Jeffrey, Pamela, Sara. Tchr. pub. schs., Ind., Ohio, Cal., 1952-53, 55-59; instr., dir. student teaching Stanford, 1959-62; dir. student field experiences U. Toledo, 1962-65; asso. prof. Ind. U., Bloomington, 1965-70; prof., dir. secondary edn. Ind. U., Indpls., 1970—. Cons. pub. schs. Nat. Council Social Studies. Mem. Assn. Supervison and Curriculum Devel, Nat. Council Social Studies (chmn. publs. com. 1969-70), NEA, Am. Assn. U. Profs., Phi Delta Kappa, Pi Gamma Mu. Author: Characteristics of Teacher Education Students in the British Isles and United States, 1965; A Guide to Human Rights Education, 1969; Comtemporary Strategies in Teaching Social Studies, 1969. Editor: Cal. Social Sci. Rev., 1961-62. Home: 4140 Melbourne Rd Indianapolis IN 46208 Office: 902 N Meridian St Indianapolis IN 46204

WOOD, MILDRED H., ednl. cons.; b. Alta, Iowa, Apr. 19, 1920; d. Jesse L. and Hazel E. (David) Fisher; B.A., U. No. Iowa, 1956, M.A., 1962, Ed.S., 1963; Ed.D., Ind. U., 1970; m. William O. Wood, June 23, 1940; children—Larry Allan, Donald David. Tchr. pub. schs., Rowley, Iowa, 1939-42; speech and hearing therapist Black Hawk County (Iowa) Sch., 1956-60; tchr. Price Lab. Sch., U. No. Iowa, 1965, instr. spl. edn. dept. edn. and psychology, 1962-65; ednl. cons. and diagnostician Area Edn. Agency Iowa, 1965-69, 70—; chmn. state adv. com. on speech and hearing, 1956-60. Mem. Housing and Community Devel. Task Force, Cedar Falls, 1975—; v.p. Human Devel. Commn., Cedar Falls, 1975—; mem. Family Service League exec. bd. Black Hawk County, 1976—; bd. dirs. Cedar Arts Forum, 1977. Mem. Council Exceptional Children, Iowa Council Exceptional Children (v.p. 1975), Iowa Assn. Retarded Children (chmn. 1960-64), Assn. Children with Learning Disabilities, Am. Speech and Hearing Assn., Am. Assn. Mental Defiency, Internat. Reading Assn., Assn. Supervision and Curriculum Devel., NSF, Delta Kappa Gamma, Pi Lambda Theta. Baptist. Author 2 books; contbr. articles to profl. jours. Home: 1825 Iowa St Cedar Falls IA 50613 Office: 3712 Cedar Heights Dr Cedar Falls IA 50613

WOOD, NEAL SHACKLEFORD, ret. refractories co. exec.; b. St. Louis, Sept. 21, 1902; s. Nathaniel Scudder and Lulie (Schackleford) W.; student Westminster Coll., 1920-22 LL.D., 1946; B.S.C., Washington U., St. Louis, 1924; m. Josephine Green, Sept. 1, 1928; children—Neal Shackleford, Josephine Wood Altamirano, Robert A. Sec., treas. N.S. Wood, Inc. real estate, St. Louis, 1934-50; dir. A.P. Green Refractories Co., 1934-67, v.p., 1945-67; real estate cons., 1967-70. Sr. fellow, chmn. bd. govs. Winston Churchill Meml. and Library U.S.A., Fulton, Mo. Trustee St. Louis Children's Hosp., pres. 1969, chmn., 1970-72; bd. dirs. Jefferson Nat. Assn.; trustee Westminster Coll., Fulton, 1933—, chmn., 1942-46; commr. Mus. Sci. and Natural History, St. Louis. Decorated officer Order of Brit. Empire. Mem. Beta Theta Pi. Republican. Presbyterian. Clubs: Noonday (St. Louis); St. Louis Country, Bogey (Ladue, Mo.); Saint Louis (Clayton, Mo.). Home: 43 Glen Eagles Dr Ladue MO 63124

WOOD, PAUL FLETCHER, assn. exec.; b. Lockport, N.Y., Dec. 7, 1935; s. Dwight Edward and Sarah Frances (Fletcher) W.; B.A. with honors (Peter Witt scholar), Case Western Res. U., 1959, Ph.D., 1975; M.A., Kent State U., 1968; m. Kathleen Frances Stretton, May 27, 1957; children—Paul, Richard. Comdg. officer Salvation Army, Cleve., Elyria, Canton, O., 1956-67; divisional youth sec. Western N.Y. State, Buffalo, 1967; asso. exec. dir. United Fund, Stark County, Ohio, 1967-70; exec. dir. United Way Tuscarawas County, New Philadelphia, Ohio, 1970—; owner, cons. Community Services . Assos., Canton, Ohio, 1970—. Instr. Walsh Coll., Canton, 1974—. Vice pres. Stark County Mental Health Found. Bd. dirs. Alcoholism Program Tuscarawas County. Club: Atwood Yacht (Dellroy, Ohio). Home: 2585 Hyacinth Dr NE North Canton OH 44720 Office: 2886 Whipple Ave NW Canton OH 44708

WOOD, RICHARD DONALD, pharm. co. exec.; b. Brazil, Ind., Oct. 22, 1926; s. Howard T. and Dorothy F. (Norfolk) W.; B.S., Purdue U., 1948, LL.D., 1973; M.B.A., U. Pa., 1950; D.Sc., Butler U., 1974; LL.D., DePauw U., 1972, Phila. Coll. Pharmacy and Sci., 1975; m. Billie Lou Carpenter, Dec. 29, 1951; children—Catherine Ann, Marjorie Elizabeth. Gen. mgr. ops. in Argentina, Eli Lilly & Co., 1961, dir. ops., Mex. and Central Am., 1962-70, pres. Eli Lilly Internat. Corp., 1970-72; pres. Eli Lilly & Co., Indpls., 1972-73, chmn. bd., chief exec. officer, dir., 1973—, also dir.; dir. Elizabeth Arden, Inc., Chem. N.Y. Corp. & Chem. Bank, Standard Oil Co. (Ind.). Trustee Park-Tudor Sch.; bd. dirs. Lilly Endowment, Inc., Ind. State Symphony Soc., Indpls. Mus. Art; trustee DePauw U., Am. Enterprise Inst.; bd. govs. Asso. Colls. Ind. Mem. Pharm. Mfrs. Assn. (dir.), Council on Fgn. Relations, Com. for Econ. Devel., Internat. C. of C. (trustee U.S. council), Indsl. Conf. Bd. Presbyterian. Clubs: Links (N.Y.C.); Indianapolis Athletic, Meridian Hills Country (Indpls.). Home: 5715 Sunset Ln Indianapolis IN 46208 Office: 307 E McCarty St Indianapolis IN 46206

WOOD, THOMAS MICHAEL, ins. co. exec.; b. Detroit, June 20, 1935; s. Alfred Waller and Merle (Hobgood) W.; student Alma Coll., 1953-54, U. Mich., 1954-55; m. Jaqueline Koenes, Jan. 7, 1956; 1 dau., Lisa Michelle. Underwriter Aetna Casualty & Surety Co., 1956-57; insp. sr. insp. Wis. Compensation Rating Bur., 1957-60; owner ins. agy., Milw., 1960-62; v.p. underwriting Accredited Hosp. & Life Ins. Co., St. Louis, 1962-68, exec. v.p., 1968-69, pres., 1969-76, dir., 1968—; pres. KIAGA, Inc., 1968-76, Am. Gen. Agy., 1968-76; chmn. bd., chief exec. officer Accredited Premium Acceptance Corp.; dir., mem. exec. com. Mo. State Bank & Trust; v.p., dir., mem. exec. com. Lincoln Heritage Life, 1974-76; asst. sec. West State Ins. Co., 1975-76. Mayor City of Manchester, Mo., 1966-68. Bd. dirs. West County YMCA, 1965-66. Mem. Home Office Underwriters Assn., Claim Adjusters Assn., Delta Gamma Tau. Mason; Order DeMolay (chmn. bd. Lafayette chpt. 1968-70). Home: 1134 Foxworth Ct Manchester MO 63011 Office: PO Box 21684 St Louis MO 63109

WOOD, WILLIAM JEROME, lawyer; b. Indpls., Feb. 14, 1928; s. Joseph Gilmore and Anne Cecelia (Morris) W.; student Butler U., 1945-46; A.B. with honors, Ind. U., 1950, J.D. with distinction, 1952; m. Joann Janet Jones, Jan. 23, 1954; children—Steven, Matthew,

Kathleen, Michael, Joseph, James, Julie, David. Admitted to Ind. bar, 1952; mem. firm Wood Tuohy Gleason & Mercer, formerly Schortemeier, Eby, & Wood, Indpls., 1952—; dir. Am. Income Life Ins. Co., Waco, Tex., Grain Dealers Mut. Ins. Co., Indpls. Gen. counsel Ind. Realtors Assn., Ind. Cath. Conf., Ind. Assn. Osteo. Physicians and Surgeons; city atty. Indpls., part-time 1959-60; instr. Ind. U. Sch. Law, part time 1960-62. Mem. Ind. Corp. Survey Commn., 1963—, chmn., 1977—. Past bd. dirs. Alcoholic Rehab. Center, Indpls., Indpls. Lawyer's Commn., Community Service Council Indpls., Indpls. Bar Found. Served with AUS, 1946-48. Recipient Brotherhood award Ind. region NCCJ, 1973. Mem. Am., Ind. (award 1968, sec. 1977-78), Indpls. (pres. 1972-73) bar assns., St. Thomas More Legal Soc. (pres. 1970), Nat. Audubon Soc. Democrat. Roman Catholic. K.C. Clubs: Indpls. Literary (pres. 1973-74), Indpls. Athletic. Home: 7265 Merriam Rd Indianapolis IN 46240 Office: 1930 Indiana Tower Indianapolis IN 46204

WOODARD, PAUL ELON, hearing aid co. exec.; b. Marshalltown, Iowa, Feb. 24, 1933; s. Harold and Frances W.; B.A., Bethany (W.Va.) Coll., 1954; B.D., Tex. Christian U., 1959; m. Betty A. Turner, June 12, 1955; children—Bruce P., Dale A., Dawn M. Minister, Christian Ch. (Disciples of Christ), Van Alstyne, Tex., 1957-59, Princeton, Mo., 1959-62; salesman Prudential Ins. Co., Maryville, Mo., 1962-65; mgr. ins. agency Occidental Life of Calif., Chillicothe, Mo., 1965-67; regional supt. agencies Farmers and Bankers Life Ins. Co., Wichita, Kans., 1967-68; salesman Acousticon Woodard Co., Des Moines, 1969-74, pres., 1974—. Scoutmaster, Boy Scouts Am. Mem. Nat. Hearing Aid Soc. (certified hearing aid audiologist), Iowa Hearing Aid Soc., Am. Audiology Soc. Republican. Methodist. Home: 8801 Boston Ave Des Moines IA 50322 Office: 303 Securities Bldg Des Moines IA 50309

WOODBURY, FRANKLIN BENNETT WESSLER, metall. engr.; b. Joplin, Mo., Dec. 11, 1937; s. Samuel and Pauline Patricia (Bennett) W.; A.S., Joplin Jr. Coll., 1963; B.S. in Metall. Engring., U. Mo., Rolla, 1966. Asso. engr. Mallinckrodt Chem. Works, St. Charles, Mo., 1964; research fellow Gen. Motors Research Lab., Warren, Mich., 1966; asst. instr. metall. engring. U. Mo., Rolla, 1968-71; research metall. U.S. Bur. Mines, Twin Cities (Minn.) Metallurgy Research Center, 1971—; bd. dirs. Scientists and Engrs. Tech. Assessment Council, Inc., sec., treas., 1976-77, v.p., 1978; chmn. Minn. Engring. Socs. Joint Task Com. on Engring. Edn., 1977-78; mem. ad hoc sci. and tech. com. Minn. Legis. Sci. and Tech. Project, 1977—. Served with USAF, 1957-61. NDEA fellow, 1968-70; registered profl. metall. engr., Minn., Mo. Mem. Am. Inst. Mining, Metall. and Petroleum Engrs., Am. Soc. Metals, Nat. (chmn. nat. mgmt. study task com., gov. profl. engrs. in govt.), Minn. (chmn. edn. com., gov. profl. engrs. in govt.). Roman Catholic. Clubs: K.C. Devel. device for monitoring taconite slurry compositions. Home: 1368 High Site Dr Eagan MN 55121 Office: PO Box 1660 Twin Cities MN 55111

WOODCOCK, LEONARD, ambassador, ret. labor ofcl.; b. Providence, Feb. 15, 1911; s. Ernest and Margaret (Freel) W.; student Wayne State U., 1928-30, Walsh Inst. Accountancy, Detroit, 1928-30; 8 hon. degrees; m. Loula Martin, May 28, 1941; children—Leslie, Janet, John. Staff rep. United Automobile Workers, 1940-46, adminstrv. asst. to pres., 1946-47, regional dir., 1947-55, internat. v.p., 1955-70, pres., 1970-77, pres. emeritus, 1977—; dynomometer operator Continental Aviation & Engring. Co., 1947; chief of mission U.S. Liaison office, People's Republic China, 1977—. Bd. govs. Wayne State U., 1959-70; Mem. ACLU, NAACP (dir.). Office: 8000 E Jefferson St Detroit MI 48214

WOODEN, HOWARD EDMUND, III, clin. psychologist; b. Balt., Sept. 20, 1944; s. Howard Edmund and Virginia Irene (Burkert) W.; A.B., Wabash Coll., 1966; M.S., Ind. State U., 1969; Ph.D., U. So. Miss., 1972; m. Elizabeth Ann Smith, Oct. 18, 1967; 1 dau., Sarah Elizabeth. Dir. social scis., St. Benedict's Sch., Evansville, Ind., 1967-68; psychology intern, Warren G. Murray Hosp., Centralia, Ill., 1968-69, staff psychologist, 1969-70; clin. psychologist, Katherine Hamilton Mental Health Center, Terre Haute, Ind., 1972—; dir. psychology sect. women's external degree program, St. Mary of the Woods Coll., Terre Haute, 1974—; adj. asst. prof. psychology, Ind. State U., Terre Haute, 1972—. Pres., bd. dirs. Vigo County Assn. Retarded Citizens, 1975-76; bd. dirs. Ind. Assn. Retarded Citizens, 1975—; treas. Thornton Sch. Parent-Tchr. Orgn., 1976—. Research grantee, prin. investigator Sandoz Pharms., 1976-78; certified pvt. practice in psychology, Ind. Mem. Am., Ind., Southeastern Psychol. Assn., Phi Delta Kappa, Lambda Chi Alpha. Episcopalian. Contbr. articles to profl. jours. Home: 2726 Wilson Dr Terre Haute IN 47803 Office: 620 8th Ave Terre Haute IN 47804

WOODHAMS, BERTHOLD, ins. exec.; b. Aurora, Ill., Feb. 28, 1894; s. Herbert and Amelia (Degenhardt) W.; student pub. schs.; LL.D. (hon.), Ferris Inst., Big Rapids, Mich.; m. Florence M. Legg, June 29, 1921; children—Carolyn W. Woodhams Jones, Frederick B. Claims adjuster Citizens' Mut. Automobile Ins. Co., Howell, Mich., 1920-26, v.p., 1926-50, dir. 1932—, pres., 1950-63, chmn. bd., 1963-65, hon. chmn., 1965—; dir. First Nat. Bank, Howell; pres. Conf. Mut. Casualty Cos., 1955. Pres., Bd. Edn. Howell, mayor, 1943-49; chmn. bd. govs., treas. Mich. Ins. Info. Service. Clubs: Masons, K.T., Rotary (past pres.). Author of Man-to-Man and Dad-to-Daughter good driving agreements distributed by safety orgns., automobile clubs. Home: 1108 Burns Dr Howell MI 48843 Office: Citizens' Mut Automobile Ins Co 1108 Burns Dr Howell MI 48843

WOODMAN, WILLIAM E., theatre dir.; b. N.Y.C., Oct. 1, 1932; s. William E. and Ruth Pond (Cornwall) W.; B.A., Hamilton Coll., 1954; M.F.A., Columbia U., 1959; m. Elizabeth Roberts, June 5, 1971. Mem. prodn. staff Am. Shakespeare Festival, Stratford, Conn., 1957-60; co-producar, dir. Robin Hood Theatre, Ardentown, Del., 1961-64; free lance dir. at resident profl. theatres throughout U.S., 1965-67; mem. directing faculty Juilliard Sch. Drama div. Lincoln Center, 1968-72; artistic dir. Goodman Theatre Center, Chgo., 1973—. Mem. Arts Club Chgo., Chgo. Council on Fine Arts, Ill. Arts Council. Home: 1350 Lakeshore Dr Chicago IL 60610 Office: Goodman Theatre Center 200 S Columbus Dr Chicago IL 60603

WOODRING, DEWAYNE STANLEY, clergyman, ch. ofcl.; b. Gary, Ind., Nov. 10, 1931; s. J. Stanley and Vera Luella (Brown) W.; B.S. with distinction, Northwestern U., 1954, postgrad.; M.Div., Garrett Theol. Sem., 1957; Dr. Humane Letters Mt. Union Coll., 1967; D.D., Salem Coll., 1970; m. Donna Jean Wishart, June 15, 1957; children—Judith Lynn, Beth Ellen. YMCA Youth dept. staff, Gary, 1946-50, asso. youth dir., 1950-55; staff mem. radio services dept. Second Assembly, World Council of Chs., Evanston, Ill., 1954; minister edn. Griffith Meth. Ch., Ind., 1955-57; minister adminstrn. and program 1st Meth. Ch., Eugene, Oreg., 1957-59; dir. pub. relations Dakotas Area Meth. Ch., 1959-60, Ohio Area, 1960-64; adminstrv. asst. to bishop, Ohio E. Area, 1964-77; asst. gen. sec. Gen. Council on Fin. and Adminstrn., United Meth. Ch., Evanston, Ill., 1977—; bd. mgrs. United Meth. Bldg., Evanston. Exec. sec. Ohio Meth. TV, Radio and Film Commn., 1960-72; del. World Meth. Conf., London, Eng., 1966, Dublin, Ireland, 1976; mem. mass communications com. Meth. N-Central Jurisdiction, 1964-68; chmn. commn. on communications Ohio Council Chs., 1961-65; mem. div. interpretation United Meth. Ch., 1969-72, mem. commn. on gen. conf., 1972—, bus. mgr., 1976—, mem. program com. N. Central Jurisdictional Conf., 1968—, chmn., 1972-76, mem. council on ministries, 1972-76; exec. com. Assn. United Meth. Founds., 1968-72; participant U.S. Dept. Def. Joint Civilian Orientation Conf., 1970; lectr., cons. on fgn. travel. Trustee, v.p. Ohio East Area United Meth. Found, 1967-76; pres. Guild Travel Assos.; trustee, v.p. Copeland Oaks Retirement Center Sebring, Ohio, 1969-76. Mem. Pub. Relations Soc. Am., Meeting Planners Internat., Religious Conv. Mgrs. Assn. Def. Orientation Conf. Assn. (dir.). Contbr. to religious periodicals, Editor Ohio East Area News, 1964-73. Home: 205 Enid Ln Northfield IL 60093 Office: 1200 Davis St Evanston IL 60201

WOODRUFF, CHRISTINE LIPPS, psychologist; b. Phila., July 14, 1929; d. Willard F. and Christine Louis (Staab) Lipps; B.A., Lawrence U., 1951; postgrad. Yale U., 1951-52; M.S., U. Pitts., 1958, Ph.D., 1967; m. Neal Woodruff, Aug. 30, 1952; children—Susan Barnes, David Presley. Instr. psychology U. Pitts., 1967-68; asst. prof. psychology Cornell Coll., 1968-69, Coe Coll., 1969-72; asso. prof. psychology Mt. Mercy Coll., Cedar Rapids, Iowa, 1972-78, prof., 1978—, chmn., 1972-76. Mem. Cedar Rapids Human Rights Commn., 1973, vice chmn., 1974-76, chmn., 1977—. Andrew Mellon predoctoral fellow, 1963-65, NDEA fellow, 1965-67, Lawrence Coll. prize fellow, 1947-51. Mem. AAUP, Am., Midwestern psychol. assns., Phi Beta Kappa, Phi Sigma Iota, Mortarboard. Home: 218 15th St NE Cedar Rapids IA 52402 Office: Mount Mercy Coll Cedar Rapids IA 52402

WOODRUFF, PHILLIP STEVEN, mgmt. exec., aircraft co. exec.; b. McLeansboro, Ill., May 8, 1944; s. Max Eugene and Gladys Marguerite (Bell) W.; diploma De Vry Inst. Tech., Chgo., 1966; B.S. in Aviation Mgmt., Embry Riddle Aero. U., 1970; postgrad. Fla. Atlantic U., 1970-71, U. S.C., 1971-72, Okla. State U., 1974-75, Johns Hopkins Sch. Advanced Internat. Studies, 1976; m. Betty Sue Allen, Sept. 24, 1966; 1 son, Michael Andrew. Asst. in Coll. Aviation Mgmt., Embry Riddle Aero. U., Daytona Beach, Fla., 1968-71; various engring. and tech. positions in Midwest and So. U.S., Am. Tel. & Tel. Co., 1966-68, 71-72; mgr. aviation edn. div. Cessna Aircraft Co., Wichita, Kans., 1972-74, mgr. Africa and Middle East Div., 1974-77, mgr. Internat. Marketing Div., Far East and Pacific, 1977—; mng. partner Aviation Investment Assos., 1973—; tchr. aviation in grad. workshops at various colls. and univs., 1972-75. Trustee Embry Riddle Aero. U. Served with U.S. Army, 1961-64. Recipient Aircraft Distbrs. Mfrs. award, 1975. Mem. Air Force Assn., Nat. Aerospace Edn. Assn. (dir. 1972-73), Gen. Aviation Mfrs. Assn. (chmn. 1974-75), Am. Inst. Aeros. and Astronautics, Aircraft Owners and Pilots Assn., Exptl. Aircraft Assn., Nat. Geog. Soc., Smithsonian Instn., Alfa Eta Rho (hon. life). Republican. Contbr. articles on aviation edn. to profl. publs. Home: 6517 Beachy St Wichita KS 67206

WOODRUFF, REGINALD DOW, printing co. exec.; b. Lincoln, Nebr., Dec. 23, 1895; s. Lorenzo Dow and Rose (Wahlbridge) W.; student U. Nebr., 1913-15; m. Lucile Foster, Oct. 10, 1917; children—Suzanne Woodruff Batten, Marcia Woodruff Russell (dec.), Foster. Pres., mgr. Woodruff Printing Co., Lincoln, 1919—. Mem. Lincoln C. of C. (life mem., past dir.), Am. Legion, Phi Kappa Psi. Republican. Presbyterian. Clubs: Masons, Shriners, Elks, Lions (pres. 1946), Lincoln Country (past dir.), Red Deer Hunting (sec.-treas.), Nebraska, University. Office: PO Box 81157 Lincoln NE 68501

WOODS, CHARLES HARRISON, chemist; b. Kirwan Heights, Pa., Dec. 10, 1934; s. Leroy Homer and Julia (Voinovich) W.; student Carnegie Inst. Tech., 1952, Muskingum Coll., 1957; m. Ruth Ann Gildea, Oct. 20, 1956; children—Tamara Sue, Charles K., Cyrstal, David. Chief chemist John M. Sherry Labs., Muncie, Ind., 1961-64; chief spectroscopist Vanadium Corp. Am., Cambridge, Ohio, 1965-68; analytical chemist, lab. supr. Foote Mineral Co., Exton, Pa., 1968-70; corporate dir. analytical chemistry Ohio Ferro-Alloys Corp., Philo, Ohio, 1970—. Mem. citizens adv. com. Ohio EPA Muskingum River Basin; judge sci. fairs, high sch. Mem. Am. Chem. Soc., Am. Soc. Metals, Nat. Mgmt. Assn. Democrat. Lutheran. Home: 3655 Sunset Circle Zanesville OH 43701 Office: PO Box 158 Philo OH 43771

WOODS, FLOYD WAYNE, optometrist; b. Chgo., June 13, 1927; s. Otis Clifford and May (Leeds) W.; D. Optometry, Ill. Coll. Optometry, 1951; M.Ed., Loyola U., Chgo., 1973; m. Dorothy Mae Barker, Mar. 15; children—Cheryl, Douglas, Andrew. Pvt. practice optometry, Oak Lawn, Ill., 1952—. Tchr. reading Central YMCA Coll., Chgo., 1972—; vision cons. various pub. and parochial schs., 1964—; sec. Ill. Optometry Examining Com., 1968-76. Del. White House Conf. on Children, 1970. Mem. bd. edn. Oak Lawn-Hometown Schs., 1962-69. Asst. dir. G.N. Getman Found., 1968-72. Served with USNR, 1944-46. Mem. Am., Ill. optometric assns. Kiwanian (lt. gov. 1962). Home: 9701 Cook Ave Oak Lawn IL 60453 Office: 5511 W 95th St Oak Lawn IL 60453

WOODS, GEORGE THEODORE, vet. microbiologist, educator; b. Tyro, Kans., Aug. 21, 1924; s. Samuel Branchford and Harriett (Crawford) W.; D.V.M., Kans. State U., 1946; M.P.H., U. Calif. at Berkeley, 1959; M.S., Purdue U., 1960; m. Helen Louise Jordan, June 20, 1948; children—David, Jeffrey, Linda. Field veterinarian Ill. Dept. Agr., Danville, 1946-47; gen. supr. lab. animals Northwestern U. Med. Sch., Chgo., 1947-48; pvt. practice vet. medicine Shelbyville, Ill., 1948-49; extension veterinarian U. Ill., Urbana, 1949-59, faculty, 1959—, prof. vet. microbiology, 1965—; cons. in field. Chmn. ednl. com. Champaign County (Ill.) Health Dept., 1960-62. USPHS trainee 1958-59. Served with AUS, 1943-44, USAF, 1954-56. Mem. Eastern Ill. (pres. 1964-65), Ill. (exec. com. 1970-72), Am. vet. med. assns., Ill. Pub. Health Assn., Am. Pub. Health Assn., Am. Assn. Food Hygiene Veterinarians, Am. Assn. Tchrs. Vet. Pub. Health and Preventive Medicine (pres. 1970-71), Am. Acad. Vet. Preventive Medicine, Phi Kappa Phi, Gamma Sigma Delta, Phi Zeta. Contbr. articles to profl. publs. Office: 63 Vet Medicine U Ill at Urbana-Champaign Urbana IL 61801

WOODS, JOHN WARREN, educator, author; b. Martinsville, Ind., July 12, 1926; s. Jefferson Blount and Doris (Underwood) W.; B.S., Ind. U., 1949, M.A. in Teaching, 1955; m. Emily Carol Newbury, Dec. 1, 1951; children—David Warren, Richard William. Faculty Western Mich. U., Kalamazoo, 1955—, prof. English, 1965—. Vis. prof. U. Calif. at Irvine, 1967-68, Purdue U., 1975. Served with USAAF, 1945-46. Author: The Deaths at Paragon, Indiana, 1955; On the Morning of Color, 1961; The Cutting Edge, 1966; Keeping Out of Trouble, 1968; Turning to Look Back: Poems, 1955-1970, 1972; Alcohol, 1973; Bone Flicker, 1973; Voyages to the Inland Sea, 1972; Striking the Earth, 1976; Thirty Years on the Force, 1977. Home: 6411 Hampton St Portage MI 49081 Office: English Dept Western Mich U Kalamazoo MI 49008

WOODS, KENNETH REGINALD, architect; b. Chgo., Apr. 14, 1925; s. Otis Clifford and May (Leeds) W.; B.S., Northwestern U., 1948; m. Betty Jane Seline, Sept. 20, 1946; children—Geoffrey Scott, Candace Lynn, Steven Alan. Pres. Woods & Assos., Inc., Naperville, Ill., 1960—. Mem. Naperville City Council, 1967-71. Served with A.C., USNR, 1943-47. Mem. AIA, Nat. Soc. Profl. Engrs., Am. Congress for Surveying and Mapping, Ill. Registered Land Surveyors Assn. Clubs: Moose, Lions. Home: 721 Hillside Rd Naperville IL 60540

WOODS, PAUL EDWARD, ednl. adminstr.; b. East St. Louis, Ill., Oct. 31, 1921; s. William J. and Mary (Scates) W.; B.A., McKendree Coll., 1953; M.Ed., St. Louis U., 1955; L.H.D., Sioux Empire Coll., 1966; m. Martha Pizzini; children—Gina, Paul Edward, John, Robert. Pres., East St. Louis Fedn. Tchrs., 1956-59; v.p. Ill. Fedn. Tchrs., 1959, exec. sec., 1959-63; dir. title III Nat. Def. Edn. Act, 1963-71; dir. curriculum State of Ill., Springfield, 1971-73; sch. facilities specialist Ill. Office Edn., Springfield, 1973—. Served with AUS, 1942-46, 51-52. Mem. Am. Assn. Adminstrs., Ill. Fedn. Tchrs., Ill. Assn. Adminstrs., VFW. Home: 12 Lake Knolls Dr Chatham IL 62629 Office: Ill Office Edn 100 N 1st St Springfield IL 62702

WOODS, RICHARD DEAN, editor, pub.; b. Verdigree, Nebr., Jan. 11, 1941; s. Charles Curtis and Edna Mildred (Hopkins) W.; student pub. schs.; m. Shirley Maxine Wade, Jan. 8, 1966; children—Mistie Dee, James Richard, Brian Thomas. With Palmer (Nebr.) Jour., 1953—, pressman, 1956-58, foreman, 1959-64, editor, pub., 1964—, owner, 1964—; founder, editor, pub. Twin City Post, 1971; foreman Crane (Tex.) News, 1964. Instl. rep. Boy Scouts Am., 1965-71. Bd. dirs. Mid-Nebr. adv. bd. Juvenile Delinquency, 1970-71; pres. Christian Builders Assn., 1967-71, dir., 1965-67. Mem. Lone Tree, Mid-States rodeo assns., Loup Valley Roping Club (treas. 1976—). Mem. Ch. of Christ (elder). Address: Palmer NE 68864

WOODS, THOMAS COCHRANE, JR., communications co. exec.; b. Lincoln, Nebr., May 4, 1920; s. Thomas Cochrane and Sarah (Ladd) W.; B.A., U. Nebr., 1943; m. Marjorie Jane Jones, June 1, 1943; children—Thomas Cochrane III, Avery Ladd. Asst. advt. mgr. Addressograph-Multigraph Corp., Cleve., 1947-58; pres. Lincoln Tel. & Tel. Co., 1958—, chmn. exec. com., 1958—; pres. Nellewood Corp., Lincoln, 1961—, T-V Transmission, Inc., Lincoln, 1966-75; v.p. Lincoln Devel. Co., 1958—, W.K. Realty Co., Lincoln, 1958—; pres. Woods Charitable Fund, Inc., 1968—; dir. Sahara Coal Co., Chgo., Woodmen Accident & Life Co., Lincoln.; dir., mem. exec. com., mem. trust com. First Nat. Bank & Trust Co., Lincoln. Mem. State Bldg Commn., Lincoln, 1962—. Mem. exec. com. Bryan Meml. Hosp., 1962-66. Mem. Lincoln City Park and Recreation Adv. Bd., 1962-72. Bd. dirs. Lincoln Center Devel. Assn., 1967—; trustee Nebr. Human Resources Research Found., 1968—, U. Nebr. Found., 1961—, Joslyn Liberal Arts Soc., Omaha, 1964—, Nebr. Ind. Coll. Found., 1965-73. Served to 1st lt. F.A., AUS, 1943-46. Mem. C. of C. of U.S., Lincoln C. of C., SAR. Conglist. Clubs: Lincoln University, Lincoln Country, Nebraska (Lincoln). Home: 2540 Woodscrest Ave Lincoln NE 68502 Office: 1440 M St PO Box 81309 Lincoln NE 68501

WOODS, WILLIAM CRAIG, physician; b. Baker, Mont., Nov. 1, 1922; s. William S. and Beth C. (Conser) W.; student Milw. State Tchrs. Coll., 1940-43; M.D., Marquette U., 1952; m. Esther Alma Glaser, Mar. 14, 1944; children—Barbara (Mrs. John Olsen), William Craig, Tom, John, Patricia, Kevin, Deborah, Lisa. Intern, St. Joseph Hosp., Milw., 1952-53; gen. practice medicine and surgery, Delavan, Wis., 1953—; chief of staff Lakeland Hosp., 1964-68. Pres. St. Andrews Sch. Bd., 1970—. Served with AUS, 1943-46. Mem. AMA, Wis. Med. Assn., Walworth County Med. Soc. (past pres.), Alpha Omega Alpha. Home: 594 Laurel Heights Dr Delavan WI 53115 Office: 915 Geneva St Delavan WI 53115

WOODS, WILLIAM EDWARD, librarian; b. Chgo., Jan. 21, 1928; s. William Edward and Pearl Cecelia (Gordon) W.; B.E., Chgo. Tchrs. Coll., 1951, M.Ed., 1958; M.A., U. Chgo., 1965; m. Margaret Louise Byrnes, Aug. 16, 1952; children—Larry, Elisabeth, Daniel, Timothy, Thomas, Margaret, Jennifer, Andrew. Tchr., tchr. librarian Chgo. Pub. Schs., 1951-59; head circulation dept. Chgo. Tchrs. Coll.-Wilson Jr. Coll. Library, 1960-65, librarian materials center, 1965-67; br. librarian Kennedy-King Coll., Chgo., 1967-69, coordinator library tech. program, 1968—, Richard J. Daley Coll., Chgo., 1972—; pres. Woods Library Pub. Co., Chgo., 1968—. Mem. Ill. State Library Adv. Com. on Continuing Edn., 1974—. Served with AUS, 1945-47. Recipient fellowship Innovations Center, Chgo. City Colls., 1968. Mem. Am., Ill. library assns., Cook County Coll. Tchrs. Union-AFT Local 1600, Kappa Mu Epsilon. Clubs: Chgo. Library. Devel. the Woods cross reference card system, 1967. Contbr. articles to profl. jours. Home: 9159 Clifton Park Evergreen Park IL 60642 Office: 7500 S Pulaski Rd Chicago IL 60652

WOODSON, JAMES WARREN, paper products co. exec.; b. Chattahoochee, Fla., Oct. 5, 1945; s. George Wilson and Clara Louise (Williams) W.; B.S., Phila. Coll. Textiles and Sci., 1967; M.B.A., Wharton Bus. Sch., 1972; m. Mildred Virginia Arnold, Mar. 2, 1968; 1 son, James Warren. Research asst. DuPont Corp., Wilmington, Del., 1966-67; prodn. chemist Gen. Tire & Rubber Co., Lawrence, Mass., 1967-68; analyt. chemist Shell Chem. Co., Princeton, N.J., 1968-70; tech. dir. Scott Paper Co., Detroit, 1971—. Bd. dirs. West Branch Y.M.C.A. Certified Waste Treatment Plant Operator. Mem. TAPPI, Pulp and Paper Industry Mgmt. Assn., Water Pollution Control Fedn. Democrat. Baptist. Home: 14019 Mansfield St Detroit MI 48227 Office: 9125 W Jefferson St Detroit MI 48209

WOODSON, RILEY DONALD, thoracic and cardiovascular surgeon; b. Winfield, Kans., Dec. 24, 1931; s. Riley Delma and Ruth Philena (Benedict) W.; B.A., U. Kans., 1953, M.D., 1956; m. Donna Louise Ailport, Nov. 30, 1968; children—Riley David, Wade Clinton. Intern, Parkland Meml. Hosp., Dallas, 1956-57, resident in surgery U. Minn. Hosp., Mpls., 1957-63; fellow in cardio-thoracic surgery U. Oreg. Hosp., Portland, 1965-67; mem. staff U. Ill. Hosp., Chgo., 1967-68; asst. prof. surgery U. Ill., Chgo., 1967-68; asso. prof. surgery Med. Coll. Ohio, Toledo, 1969—. Sec. bd. trustees Regional Emergency Med. Services of NW Ohio, 1975—. Served to capt., M.C., USNR, 1963-77. Diplomate Am. Bd. Surgery, Am. Bd. Thoracic Surgery. Fellow A.C.S., Am. Coll. Cardiology, Am. Coll. Chest Physicians; mem. AMA, Pan Am., Undersea med. assns., Soc. Thoracic Surgeons, Am. Thoracic Soc., Internat. Cardiovascualr Soc., Soc. Vascular Surgery, Am. Assn. Surgery of Trauma, Am. Trauma Soc., Assn. Mil. Surgeons, Profl. Assn. Diving Instrs., NW Ohio Heart Assn. (trustee, chmn. emergency cardiac care 1975—), Beta Theta Pi, Omicron Delta Kappa, Phi Kappa Phi. Contbr. articles on thoracic and cardiovascular surgery, physiology, diving physiology to profl. jours. Office: 6005 Monclova Rd Maumee OH 43537

WOODWARD, ADDISON ELY, JR., psychologist; b. Montclair, N.J., Apr. 30, 1940; s. Addison Ely and Lucy (Copeland) W.; B.A. summa cum laude, C.W. Post Coll., 1964; M.A., Conn. Coll., 1966; Ph.D. (NRC fellow), U. Toronto, 1968; m. Jocelyn Lyman, Dec. 19, 1974; children—Susan, Addison Ely. Asst. prof. Albion Coll., 1968-72; mem. faculty Governors State U., Park Forest South, Ill., 1972—, coordinator behavioral studies, 1974-76, prof. psychology, 1977—. Mem. Am., Midwestern psychol. assns., Psychonomic Soc., Am. Fedn. Tchrs. (sec. local 3500, 1976-77), Sigma Xi. Home: 1605 Euclid St Chicago Heights IL 60411 Office: Governors State U Park Forest South IL 60466

WOODWARD, FREDERICK ROBERT, JR., newspaper pub., broadcaster; b. Dubuque, Iowa, Oct. 26, 1936; s. Frederick Robert and Mary Jeanne (Glab) W.; student Brown U., 1955-57; B.A., Drake U.,

1959; m. Barbara Jo Sullivan, July 2, 1971; children—Frederick Robert III, Mona Jeanne, John Duncan, Anne-Marie. Feature-photo editor Ft. Dodge (Iowa) Messenger, 1959-60; reporter radio sta. KDTH, Dubuque, 1960-62, asst. gen. mgr., 1962-63, gen. mgr., 1963-70; v.p. Telegraph Herald, Inc., Dubuque, 1965—. Mem. exec. com. Dubuque Community Services Survey Com., 1965; fin. chmn. Dubuque Child Care Center, 1972; mem. U. Dubuque Devel. Council, 1968, Clarke Coll. Devel. Council, 1968. Bd. dirs Dubuque Indsl. Bur., 1965-68, Boys' Club, 1964, Dubuque County Hist. Soc.; chmn. bd. United Way, 1969-70, mem. exec. com., 1966; trustee YMCA, 1972; bd. dirs. N.E. Iowa council Boy Scouts Am., 1972. Mem. Iowa Press Photographers Assn., C. of C. (dir. 1962-65, chmn. community renewal com. 1963-65), Dubuque Childbirth and Parent Edn. Assn. (v.p. 1973-75), Inland Daily Press Assn. (dir.), Aircraft Owners and Pilots Assn., Sports Car Club Am., Sigma Delta Chi. Rotarian. Contbr. articles and photographs to various mags., including Road and Track. Home: 240 Fremont St Dubuque IA 52001 Office: PO Box 688 Dubuque IA 52001

WOODWARD GARNITA CAROL, guidance counselor, educator, coach; b. Kirksville, Mo., July 8, 1952; d. Owen Lester and Marybelle (Ashby) Woodward; B.S. in Edn., No. Mo. State U., 1973, M.A., 1978; m. Philip Paul Knoche, July 30, 1977. Tchr. phys. edn. Dallas City (Ill.) High Sch., 1974-76, head girls jr. high athletics, 1974-76, head girls softball, volleyball, basketball and track, 1974-76; now substitute tchr. Mem. Am. Personnel and Guidance Assn., Assn. for Non-White Concerns in Personnel and Guidance, Sigma Kappa. Baptist. Address: 16 Windy Ct Warsaw IL 62379

WOODWARD, HARRY HASTINGS, JR., health and welfare cons.; b. Augusta, Ga., Apr. 14, 1933; s. Harry Hasting and Almena (Preacher) W.; A.B. in Polit. Sci., U. S.C., 1955; M.A., U. Chgo., 1960; m. Violeta Janina Pabarcius, Sept. 9, 1966. Exec. dir. North River Commn., Chgo., 1964, Chgo. So. Center, 1964-65, pres., 1968—. Dir. center Chgo. Com. Urban Opportunity, 1965-67; dir. correctional programs Stone-Bandel Center, Chgo., 1967-70, dir. correctional programs W. Clement and Jessie V. Stone Found., Chgo., 1970-73; exec. dir. Spl. Services Center, Lewis U., 1975-77; pvt. cons. in health and welfare field, 1977—; pres. World Correction Service Center for Community and Social Changes. Bd. dirs. John Howard Assn. Chgo. Served with USNR, 1956-57. Mem. Nat. Assn. Social Workers, Kappa Alpha. Baptist. Clubs: Cliff Dwellers, Pres. Author: Southern White Migrant in Lakeview, 1962. Home: 2849 W 71st St Chicago IL 60629

WOODWARD, HERBERT NORTON, sci. co. exec.; b. Altadena, Calif., Dec. 16, 1911; s. Arthur Herbert and Edith May (Norton) W.; B.A., Cornell U., 1933; J.D., U. Chgo., 1936; D.C.L., Blackburn Coll., 1972; m. Nancy Thomas, Oct. 2, 1948; children—Cynthia Woodward King, James L., Deborah Woodward Leach. Admitted to Ill. bar, 1937: individual practice law, Chgo., 1937-41; asst. to pres. Intermatic Inc. (formerly Internat. Register Co.), Chgo., 1941-43, dir., 1946—, vice-chmn. bd., 1968-73, chmn. bd., 1973—; with DK Mfg. Co., Batavia, Ill., 1946-68, chmn. bd., 1958-68; chmn. bd. Dunbar Kapple Inc., Chgo., 1968-71, Printing Plate Supply Co., Chgo., 1968-76; pres. Internat. Sci. Industries Inc., Chgo., 1968-76, chmn. bd., 1976—; dir. Vaughan-Jacklin Corp., Astron Dental Corp., Programming Techs. Inc., Ideal Roller & Graphics Co. Trustee Blackburn Coll., 1958—, chmn. bd., 1973—. Served to lt. USNR, 1943-45. Clubs: Univ., Lit. (Chgo.); Indian Hill (Winnetka, Ill.)(pres. 1975-76). Author: Illinois Tax Rate Objections, 1937; The Human Dilemma, 1971; Capitalism Can Survive in a No-Growth Economy, 1976. Home: 4 Golf Ln Winnetka IL 60093 Office: 100 W Monroe St Chicago IL 60603

WOODWARD, RAYMOND BERNARD, lawyer; b. Louisville, July 2, 1923; s. Lewis Carl and Loraine Frances (Neff) W.; J.D., U. Louisville, 1948; postgrad. Notre Dame U., John Carroll U., Ind. U.; m. Edna Jean Bowers, Feb. 16, 1946; children—Ronald Lee, Diane (Mrs. Millard Allen Hudson), Gloria. Admitted to Ind. bar, 1948; dep. atty. gen. State of Ind., 1950; dep. prosecutor, Floyd County, Ind., 1955-56; city atty. City of New Albany, Ind., 1956-63; practice law, 1948—, justice of peace New Albany Twp., 1963-76. Trustee Raymond B. Woodward Scholarship Found., 1966-76; bd. dirs. Ind. Masonic Home, 1961-62. Served with USNR, 1943-45, 50-54. Mem. Floyd County Bar Assn. (pres. 1958-59), VFW, Am. Legion (comdr. 1966-76), World Conf. on Local Govts. (U.S. del. 1961), Nat. Soc. Pub. Poets. Mason. Contbr. articles to profl. jours. Home: 2804 Charleston Rd New Albany IN 47150 Office: 155 E Main St New Albany IN 47150

WOODWARD, SIDNEY LEE, lawyer, farmer; b. Danville, Ill., Oct. 24, 1948; s. Ralph M. and Winifred E. (Thompson) W.: B.S. in Agrl. Econs., Purdue U., 1970; J.D., Ind. U., 1973; m. Rebecca Jane Hurst, Aug. 26, 1971. Admitted to Ind. bar, 1973; mem. firm Bedwell, Springer and Woodward, Sullivan, Ind., 1977—; partner Middlefork, Inc., Springwood, Ind. Served with USN, 1973-76. Mem. Am., Ind., Sullivan County bar assns. Democrat. Office: Box 526 15 S Main St Sullivan IN 47882

WOODYARD, OMAR REECE, JR., funeral dir.; b. Waterford, Ohio, Jan. 28, 1928; s. Omar Reece and Celia M. (Bell) W.; student Ind. State Tchrs. Coll., 1945, Stevens Inst. Tech., 1946; grad. Pitts. Inst. Mortuary Sci., 1949; m. Sally Ann Stout, June 1, 1951; children—Dean Alan, Pamela Ann. Asso., corporate officer O.R. Woodyard Co. Funeral Dirs., Columbus, Ohio, 1950-61; owner, operator Woodyard East Chapel Funeral Dirs., Columbus, 1961—. Vice pres. Columbus Legal Aid and Pub. Defender Soc. Bd., 1965—; chmn. bd. mgmt. South Side YMCA Columbus. Exhibited watercolors Bexley Area Art Guild, 1964, Central Ohio Watercolor Soc., 1965, Candidate for mayor, Bexley, 1967. Bd. dirs. Stelios M. Stelson Found. Served with USNR, 1945-46. Mem. Central Ohio Watercolor Soc. Mason (Shriner), K.P. Club: Eastern Sertoma (Distinguished Pres. award 1965-66, past pres., Columbus). Address: 2300 E Livingston Ave Columbus OH 43209

WOOLARD, GEORGE SWARTZ, accountant; b. Newark, Ohio, May 29, 1910; s. Marion Edgar and Susie Anna (Swartz) W.; grad. Newark Coll. Commerce, 1929; grad. Internat. Accountants Soc. Corr. Sch., 1948; m. Emma Margaret Wheeler, May 25, 1940. Numerous positions, Bates & Rogers Constrn. Co., Chgo., 1929-35; supt. Engleside Prefabricated House Co., Newark, 1935-37; budget supr., bus. mgr. Owens Corning Fiberglas Labs., Newark, 1937-54; staff assignments Owens Corning Fiberglas, Newark, 1954-58; pub. accountant, Newark, 1958—. Pres. Harbor Hills Civic Assn., 1947-52. Mem. Nat. Assn. Accountants, Nat. Soc. Pub. Accountants. Club: Newark Kiwanis (chmn. fin. com. 1960-67). Home: 6124 Jacksontown Rd SE Route 5 Newark OH 43055 Office: 200 Maholm St Newark OH 43055

WOOLF, HOWARD LEONARD, obstetrician, gynecologist; b. Chgo., Nov. 28, 1922; s. Harry and Jeannette (Singer) W.; M.D., Loyola U., Chgo., 1946; m. Honette Fidelman, Dec. 24, 1944; children—Jay Steven, Robert Harris, Mark Gary. Practice medicine specializing in obstetrics and gynecology, Skokie, Ill.; v.p. Winer & Woolf, M.D., S.C., Skokie; sec. med. staff Skokie Valley Community Hosp. Served to capt., M.C. AUS, 1947-49. Mem. Am. Coll. Obstetricians and Gynecologists, Chgo. Gynecol. Soc., AMA. Jewish. Office: 8424 Skokie Blvd Skokie IL 60076

WOOLF, PRESTON G., lawyer; b. Indpls., Oct. 10, 1906; s. Merritt Edgar and Bertha E. (Stone) W.; B.S., U. Fla., 1928; LL.B., Ind. U., 1932; grad. in material resources Indsl. Coll. Armed Forces; m. Pheobe Ann Cummins, Nov. 9, 1937. Export mgr. Hurty-Peck & Co., Indpls., 1932-36, asst. sec., 1936-47, sec., 1947-77; asst. sec. Universal Flavors of Cal., Santa Ana, 1942-46, sec., 1946-77; pres. Am. Beverage and Supply Corp., Indpls. 1945-77, chmn., 1977—; pres. Universal Flavors, London, Eng., until 1977; sec. Costa Rican Devel. Co., San Jose, Universal Flavors of N.J., Somerset, Blanke-Baer Co., St. Louis, Gt. Am. Trading Corp., St. Louis, Mfrs. Fin. Corp., Indpls., until 1977; v.p. Lucky Club Corp., St. Louis, until 1977; sec., dir. Universal Flavor Corp., Indpls., Universal Green Corp., Houston, RemiFoods, Schiller Park, Ill., Bowey-Krimko Chocolate Co., Bensonville, Ill., Flavorol Corp., Aromix Corp. (both Franklin Park, Ill.), Air Age Realty Corp., Indpls., until 1977; chmn. Woolf Internat., Ltd., Hong Kong, Woolf Internat., Tokyo; spl. fgn. corr. Indpls. Star. 1959—; columnist chain South Am. newspapers, 1960-76. Mem. world trade adv. com. U.S. Dept. Commerce, 1958-60, mem. Midwest regional com., 1960-67; leader Republican polit. study mission to Arabian world, 1966; leader Ind. Bankers and Indsl. Leaders study tour around world, 1967, to Africa, 1968; cons. on Oriental affairs; mem. Trade Missions subcom., Council Fgn. Relations; mem. Ind. Fgn. Lang. Adv. Com.; leader numerous trade study missions, Africa, Middle East, USSR, Far East, China, 1968—. Pres. Indpls. Council World Affairs, 1958-60; dir. Internat. Bldg., Ind. State Fair, 1958-60; chmn. Ind. Peoples World Affairs Com., 1965—; dir. Internat. Sch. Bus., Ind. U., 1961-67; mem. adv. council State Ind. Fgn. Lang. Program; 1st v.p. Ind. Econ. Edn. Found., 1965-70; dir. Citizen's Com. for Free Cuba, 1965-69. Mem. bd. strategy Episcopal Diocese Indpls., 1961-66. Decorated Gold Cross Merit, 1st class (Fed. Republic West Germany); recipient citation Indpls. C. of C., 1960; Rabbi Stephen S. Wise Meml. citation Am. Jewish Congress, 1959; named Indiana's Ambassador to World, 1976, hon. Lt. Gov. Ind., 1976. Mem. English-Speaking Union, Japan Soc., Asia Soc., C. of C. U.S. (World trade com.), Pan Am. Soc., AIM, Am. Bar Assn., Am. Security Council Chgo., Inter-Am. Lawyers Assn. (founder 1935, pres. 1935-38), Am. Legion, Indpls. C. of C. (leader trade missions, Orient 1963, Latin Am. 1965), Delta Chi, Sigma Delta Chi, Sigma Delta Kappa. Republican. Episcopalian. Mason (32 deg.), Elk. Clubs: Rotary (dir.; chmn. internat. contacts com.), Athletic, Press, Literary (Indpls.); Overseas Press (N.Y.C.); American (Hong Kong, Singapore); Foreign Correspondents (Tokyo, Japan). Home: 14825 Allisonville Rd Noblesville IN 46060 Office: 5700 W Raymond St Indianapolis IN 46241

WOOLFOLK, IDA GOODWIN (MARTIMA), counselor, educator; b. Dallas, Nov. 19, 1943; d. Beamenty Wendell and Myrtle Elizabeth (Perdue) Goodwin; B.A., Harris Tchrs. Coll., 1965; M.Ed., St. Louis U.; 1 dau., Sarah Myrtle. Guidance counselor, 1967—; cons. and lectr. in field; workshop and seminar leader; adjunct faculty mem. Harris Tchrs. Coll., Webster Coll., Wash. U. Family living specialist YMCA; pub. relations chairperson Dr. Martin Luther King Jr. Holiday Observance. Named Outstanding Citizen of Year Nat. Assn. Univ. Women St. Louis Br., 1969. Mem. Am., St. Louis (trustee) personnel, guidance assns., Mo. Guidance Assn., St. Louis Pub. Schs. Guidance Assn. (past pres.), Delta Sigma Theta. Mem. Ch. of God in Christ. Producer radio talk show: An Evening with Ida. Contbr. articles to profl. jours. Home: 3438 C Laclede St Saint Louis MO 63103

WOOLSEY, WILLIAM STOVER, printing co. exec.; b. Chgo., Dec. 22, 1917; s. William Robert and Grace (Peck) W.; B.S. in Mech. Engring., U. Mich., 1939, M.S., 1940; m. Doris Marie Neely, Jan. 5, 1946; children—Robert, Mary Woolsey Porter, Carolyn. Engr., Commonwealth Edison Co., Chgo., 1940-55; exec. Neely Printing Co., Chgo., 1955-60, pres., dir., 1960—; pres., dir. Dayanite Corp., Chgo., 1957—, Franklin Offset Litho Co., Chgo., 1960—, N.B.L. Corp., Chgo., 1960—, 917 Bldg. Corp., Chgo., 1960—. Trustee Pressman Pension Fund, Pressman Sch. Fund, Feeder Pension Fund; chmn. Lithographer Health and Welfare Fund. Served to lt. col. USAAF, 1940-45. Decorated Bronze Star. Mem. Western Soc. Engrs., Printing Industry of Ill. (pres.), Union Employers Assn. (exec. bd.) Chgo. Lithographers Bd., Franklin Assn. (dir.), Printing Industry Am. (exec. bd. union employers sect.). Clubs: Westmoreland Country; Swedish. Home: 1500 Sheridan Rd Wilmette IL 60091 Office: 871 N Franklin St Chicago IL 60610

WOOLSON, ALLEN MICHAEL, psychiatrist; b. Newark, Ohio, Dec. 13, 1934; s. Robert Eugene and Lucille M. (Cassidy) W.; B.A., U. Mich., 1956, M.D., 1964; postgrad. U. Mich. Neuropsychiat. Inst., 1965-68; m. Kathleen Mary Merkel, June 3, 1971; children—Martha Ann, Michael Keith, Robert Keith. Intern Oakwood Hosp., Dearborn, Mich., 1965-68; resident U. Mich. Neuropsychiat. Inst., Ann Arbor, Mich., ward psychiatrist VA Hosp., Ann Arbor, 1968-69; practice medicine specializing in psychiatry, Midland, Mich., 1969-71, Lincoln Park, Mich., 1969-72, Dearborn, 1972—; clin. instr. psychiatry U. Mich. Med. Sch., 1969—; psychiatrist-in-charge Crisis Walk-in-Clinic, Washtenaw County Community Mental Health Center, 1969-70; chief psychiatrist Downriver Child Guidance Clinic, Lincoln Park, 1969-72; asst. dir. med. edn. psychosomatic medicine Oakwood Hosp., Dearborn, Mich., 1972—; clin. asst. prof. psychiatry U. Mich. Med. Sch., Ann Arbor, 1974—; psychiat. cons. Ann Arbor Police Dept., 1968—, Midland-Gladwin Community Health Center, 1969-71, Wyandotte (Mich.) Sch. System, 1971—, Dearborn Pub. Schs., 1976. Bd. dirs. Washtenaw County Cath. Social Services, 1968—. Served to lt. (j.g.) USN, 1952-60. Diplomate Am. Bd. Psychiatry and Neurology. Office: 15350 Commerce Dr North Dearborn MI 48120

WOOLSON, JOHN RANSOM, editor; b. Page County, Iowa, Mar. 19, 1939; s. George D. and Lucile Mae (Ransom) W.; B.J., Mo. U., 1961; m. Elizabeth Ann Slinkerd, July 9, 1960; children—John Ransom, Anne Elizabeth, Paul Reese. News writer Clarinda (Iowa) Herald Jour., 1955—, sports writer, 1955-70, photographer, 1953—, news editor, 1961-69, mng. editor, 1969—. Pres., Clarinda: Town of Tomorrow; Republican precinct committeeman, 1969-74. Mem. C. of C. (pres. 1971-72), Omicron Delta Kappa, Kappa Tau Alpha, Sigma Delta Chi, Jaycees (pres. 1963, Iowa editor 1963-68, senator). Methodist (dist. council chmn. 1969-72). Home: 300 N 18th St Clarinda IA 51632 Office: Box 298 Clarinda IA 51632

WOOLUM, MAX TERRY, real estate broker; b. Alexandria, Ky., July 10, 1935; s. Letcher Earnest and Lena (Amstutz) W.; B.S. in Agr., U. Ky., 1957; m. Norma Lee Hoeferkamp, Oct. 24, 1959; children—Jeffery Earl, Steve Wade, Michael Terry. Salesman, Internat. Minerals and Chems., Skokie, Ill., 1958-63; appraiser Fed. Land Bank Louisville, 1963-68; sales engr. Ohio Red Products, Versailles, Ind., 1968-72; self-employed real estate broker, Versailles, 1972—; farmer, Versailles, 1966—. Mem. sch. bd. South Ripley Community Schs. Mem. Southeastern Ind. Bd. Realtors (v.p. 1975), Ind. Soc. Farm Mgrs. and Rural Appraisers, Versailles C. of C. (v.p. 1956), Alpha Gamma Rho. Baptist (deacon 1972-75). Club: Lions (pres. 1977). Address: PO Box 391 Versailles IN 47042

WOOLUMS, LARRY LEE, instrument and control engr.: b. Ottumwa, Iowa, Nov. 15, 1935; s. Loren Edward and Neva Adeline (Michael) W.; A.A.S., DeVry Tech. Inst., 1958; m. Delores Ellen Lee, May 27, 1956; children—Sheri Lynn, Lesa Kay, Kristin Lea, Michael Loren. Asso. engr. instrumentation sect. Sundstrand Corp., Rockford, Ill., 1958-62; design engr. instrument and control sect. Central Engring. Center, Am. Can Co., Neenah, Wis., 1962-66; sr. process control engr. process equipment engring. dept. Fair Lawn Engring. Center, Am. Can Co. (N.J.), 1966-68; task force engr. new pulp and paper mill, Halsey, Oreg., 1968; engring. supr. elec. and instrumentation Halsey Pulp and Paper Mill, Am. Can Co., 1969-77; process control systems mgr. process tech. dept. Am. Can Co., Greenwich, Conn., 1977—. Licensed 1st class radio telephone operator FCC. Mem. Instrument Soc. Am. (sr. mem., 1st pres., organizer Pacific Cascade sect.). Contbg. author to Instrumentation in the Process Industries, 1973. Home: 788 Brookwood Circle Oneida WI 54155 Office: 916 Willard Dr Green Bay WI 54305

WOON, PAUL SAM, paper co. scientist; b. Shanghai, China, July 1, 1942; s. Ramon and Rita (Wu) W.; came to U.S., 1959, naturalized, 1968; B.S., U. Iowa, Iowa City, 1965, M.S., 1968; Ph.D. (Indsl. fellow), U. Akron, 1974; m. Lin-Sun Rwan, Dec. 7, 1973; 1 dau., Audrey Hui. Research chemist Clin. Research Center, U. Iowa, Iowa City, 1965-68, PPG Industries, Barberton, Ohio, 1968-71; instr. chemistry Cuyahoga Coll., Cleve., 1972-73; staff research asso. Appleton Papers div. Nat. Cash Register, Appleton, Wis., 1974-76; project leader Kimberly-Clark Corp., Neenah, Wis., 1976—. Fellow Am. Inst. Chemists; mem. Am. Chem. Soc. Contbr. articles to profl. jours.; patentee. Office: Kimberly-Clark Corp W 2100 Winchester Rd Neenah WI 54956

WOOSLEY, SHIRLEY MATHIS, designer, retail trade co. exec.; b. Du Quoin, Ill., Sept. 1, 1933; d. John A. and Thelma (Atwood) Mathis; Asso. in Architecture, So. Ill. U., 1966, B.S., 1976; m. Frank Phillip Woosley, Oct. 11, 1952; children—John C., Frank K., Carol P. Various sales and adminstrv. positions Woosley Lumber Co., Pinckneyville, Ill., 1962-75; propr., mgr. The Cupboard Shop, Pinckneyville, 1975—; kitchen designer, 1973—; instr. interior design Rend Lake Jr. Coll., 1976. Pres., Dist. 50 PTA, 1967. Mem. Am. Inst. Kitchen Dealers (dir. 1978—), Pinckneyville C. of C. (v.p. 1977, pres. 1978). Republican. Home: 304 W Saint Louis Ave Pinckneyville IL 62274 Office: 111 S Walnut Pinckneyville IL

WOOSTER, GEORGE FREDERICK, librarian; b. Fort Johnson, N.Y., Mar. 12, 1923; s. George Henry and Lillian Aurora (Fleisch) W.; A.B., magna cum laude, U. Rochester, 1949; M.A., Ohio State U., 1950, Ph.D. in Psychology, 1953; M.L.S., U. Mich., 1973; m. R. Jane Hamilton, Feb. 1, 1953; 1 son, Douglas M. Asst. coordinator student personnel, asst. prof. psychology Ohio State U., Columbus, 1952-60, asst. prof. edn., 1955-60, dir. Counseling Center, 1963-71, div. Vets. Center, asst. dir. student fin. aids, 1971-72; dir. counseling and testing bur., asso. prof. counselor edn. U. Toledo (Ohio), 1960-63; asst. librarian Ashland (Ohio) Pub. Library, 1973-77, librarian, 1977—. Chmn. bd. dirs. Univ. Area Pastoral Counseling Center, Columbus, 1971-72; chmn. bd. trustees Drug Crisis Center, Columbus, 1970-72. Served with U.S. Army, 1942-45. Mem. Am., Ohio library assns., Am., Ohio psychol. assns., Am. Personnel and Guidance Assn., Nat., Ohio edn. assns., Library Sci. Alumni Soc. U. Mich., Phi Beta Kappa, Phi Kappa Phi, Beta Phi Mu, Sigma Xi. Mem. Ch. of Christ. Club: Kiwanis. Author: Teaching in Indiana and Ohio, 1958. Home: 703 Ohio St Ashland OH 44805 Office: Ashland Public Library 224 Claremont Ave Ashland OH 44805

WOOTTEN, GEORGE SIMMONS, JR., mgmt. cons.; b. Evanston, Ill., Oct. 1, 1930; s. George Simmons and Mildred (Knisple) W.; B.S. in Bus. Adminstrn., Northwestern U., 1951; m. Patricia A. Beach; children—George III, Stephanie Lynn. With Union Tank Car Co., Chgo., 1951-60; mgmt. cons. William Kordsiemon & Assos., Chgo., 1960-63; dir. data processing and communications Marquette Cement Co., Chgo., 1966-74; sr. partner Wootten & Assos., Glenview, Ill., 1974-76; mgr. info. systems Kinkead Industries, Chgo., 1976—; dir., v.p. Leo G. Lauzen Co., Aurora, Ill., 1957-72, Waterloo Ideas Co. (Iowa), 1963-66. Served with USN, 1948-50. Mem. Assn. Computer Machinery, Internat. Communication Assn., Armed Forces Communications and Electronic Assn., Assn. Systems Mgmt. Mason. Club: Executives (Chgo.). Home: 4200 W Lake Ave Glenview IL 60025

WOOTTON, MICHAEL DUANE, dentist; b. Columbus, Ohio, Feb. 11, 1941; s. Verne Brokaw and Shirley Ann (Tice) W.; D.D.S., Ohio State U., 1965; m. Maureen Ann Roach, Dec. 26, 1965; children—Ross, Tommy. Individual practice dentistry, Athens, Ohio, 1967—; mem. staff O'Bleness Meml. Hosp., Athens. Served with USMCR, 1958-59; served as capt. Dental Corps, AUS, 1965-67. Mem. Am., Ohio dental assns., Hocking Valley Dental Soc. Club: Athens Downtown Kiwanis. Home: 19 Ball Dr Athens OH 45701 Office: Blue Line Dr Athens OH 45701

WORACHEK, JOHN EDWARD, supt. schs.; b. Casco, Wis., May 22, 1921; s. Frank J. and Mary (Jazwinski) W.; B.A., St. Norbert Coll., 1943; M.A., U. Wis., 1952. Instr. chemistry, math. St. Norbert Coll., West De Pere, Wis., 1943-44; psychometrist, counselor St. Nobert VA Guidance Center, Green Bay, Wis., 1946-50; sch. adminstr. Reedsville (Wis.) Pub. Schs., 1953—. Organizer, bd. dirs. Reedsville Indsl. Devel. Corp., 1957—, pres. bd. dirs., 1960—; chmn. Reedsville Christmas Seal campaign, 1953—; bd. dirs. Vocat. Dist., Lakeshore Tech. Dist.; bd. dirs., vice chmn. Manitowoc County Handicapped Children's Assn., 1969; chmn. Reedsville Housing Authority, 1965. Served to lt. USNR, 1944-46; 50-52; PTO. Mem. Nat. Guidance Assn., Nat. Roster Sci. and Specialized Personnel, Wis. Assn. Sch. Adminstrs. (dir.). Lion (past pres. Reedsville). Home: Reedsville WI 54230

WORDEN, GEORGE JEROME, pub. relations and devel. exec.; b. Cadillac, Mich., Mar. 2, 1936; s. H. Lee and Loraine (Raak) W.; B.A., Hope Coll., Mich., 1959; m. Merry Kate Samuelson, Dec. 27, 1959; 1 dau., Kathryn Lynn. Newsman-announcer Midwestern Broadcasting Co., Traverse City, Mich., 1959-60; dist. mgr. Robert E. Brittan & Asso., 1960-61; newsman-sales Ottawa Broadcasting Co., 1961-62; dir. admissions Interlochen (Mich.) Arts Acad., 1962-65; pub. relations dir. Dallas County United Fund, Dallas, pub. relations dir. asst. prof. speech Wichita (Kans.) State U., 1967-70; nat. dir. devel. Elmer Fox & Co., Wichita, 1970-72; v.p. Trans Am. Investment Properties, Inc., Wichita, 1971-72; dir. devel. and pub. relations Interlochen (Mich.) Center for Arts, 1972—. Recipient Distinguished Service award Wichita Jaycees, 1970; named one of three outstanding young men of Kans., Kans. Jaycees, 1970. Rotarian. Republican. Office: Interlochen Center for Arts Interlochen MI 49643

WORKMAN, GEORGE HENRY, engring. cons.; b. Muskegon, Mich., Sept. 18, 1939; s. Harvey Merton and Bettie Jane (Meyers) W.; Asso. Sci., Muskegon Community Coll., 1960; B.S.E., U. Mich., 1966, M.S.E., 1966, Ph.D., 1969; m. Vicki Sue Hanish, June 17, 1967; children—Mark, Larry. Prin. engr. Battelle Meml. Inst., Columbus, Ohio, 1969-76; pres. Applied Mechanics Inc., Columbus, 1976—; instr. dept. civil engring. Ohio State U., 1973. Served with USN, 1961-64. Named Outstanding Undergrad. Student, Engring.

Mechanics dept. U. Mich., 1965-66, Outstanding Grad. Student, Civil Engring. dept., 1968-69. Registered profl. engr., Ohio. Mem. Am. Acad. of Mechanics, ASME, ASCE, Sigma Xi, Chi Epsilon, Phi Kappa Phi, Phi Theta Kappa. Congregationalist. Contbr. tech. papers to nat. and internat. confs. Home and office: 2121 Mc Coy Rd Columbus OH 43220

WORKMAN, LLOYD E., food co. exec.; b. Minn., July 16, 1914; s. Frank S. and Minnie (Eppler) W.; ed. U. Minn.; m. Dorothy T., Sept. 17, 1938; children—Peter, Dena, Sarah. With Casualty Ins. Co., 1938-42; purchasing mgr. Internat. Multifoods Corp., Mpls., 1946—, successively plant mgr., personnel mgr., gen. mgr. Eagle Roller Mills, 1946-76; v.p., gen. mgr. U.S. Flour div., also vice chmn. bd. Served with USAAF, 1942-46. Clubs: Minneapolis, Lafayette. Home: 19680 Lakeview Ave Excelsior MN 55331 Office: 1540 Shelard Tower Minneapolis MN 55426

WORLEY, MARVIN GEORGE, JR., architect; b. Oak Park, Ill., Oct. 10, 1934; s. Marvin George and Marie Hyancinth (Donahue) W.; B.Arch., U. Ill., 1958; m. Maryalice Ryan, July 11, 1959; children—Michael Craig, Carrie Ann, Alissa Maria. Project engr. St. Louis area Nike missile bases U.S. Army C.E., Granite City, Ill., 1958-59, architect N.Central div. U.S. Army C.E., Chgo., 1960; architect Yerkes & Grunsfeld, architects, Chgo., 1961-65, asso., 1965; asso. Grunsfeld & Assos., architects, Chgo., 1966—. Dist. architect Oak Park Elementary Schs. Dist. 97, 1973—. Mem. Oak Park Community Improvement Commn., 1973-75; mem. exec. bd. Oak Park Council PTA, 1970-73, pres., 1971-72. Served with AUS, 1959. Mem. AIA (corporate), Chgo. Assn. Commerce and Industry. Home: 811 N Ridgeland Ave Oak Park IL 60302 Office: 520 N Michigan Ave Chicago IL 60611

WORRELL, FREDERICK MARQUIS, educator; b. Akron, Ohio, Feb. 11, 1929; s. William Roy and Grace Ilo (Cring) W.; B.A., Kent State U., 1952, M.A., 1958; postgrad. U. Del., 1959; m. Lois Jean Gardner, June 12, 1953; children—Pamela Rae, Frederick Marquis. Community service dir. Wilmington (Del.) YMCA, 1956-59; exec. dir. Town and Country YMCA, Canton, 1959-62; dir. Canton community schs., 1962-64; asso. dir. United Fund Stark County, 1964-66; asst. prof. sociology and social work Kent State U., 1966-73, asso. prof., 1975—; dir. Canton-Stark-Wayne Manpower Consortium, Canton, 1973-75; cons. in field. Chmn. Stark County Comprehensive Health Planning Com., 1973—, United Fund Stark County, 1966—; chmn. social disabilities task force Gov. Ohio Conf. Vocat. Rehab., 1967-69, manpower task force 7 County Health/Planning Council, 1973—. Bd. dirs. Interfaith Campus Ministry, Kent State U., 1966—, Referral and Info. Sers. of Vol. Action Center, 1972—, Canton and Case Western Res. U. Social Work Program. Served with AUS, 1953-55. Mem. Am. Sociol. Assn., North Canton Heritage Soc., Pi Gamma Mu, Alpha Kappa Delta. Presbyn. (trustee). Home: 940 Lindy Ln North Canton OH 44720 Office: 6000 Frank Ave NW Canton OH 44702

WORRELL, MARY THORA LEWIS, pub. affairs exec.; b. Montreal, Que., Can., July 8, 1932; d. Samuel Reinhardt and Rose Elizabeth (St. Louis) Lewis; B.A., Sir George Williams U., Montreal, 1957; m. Henry G. Worrell, July 18, 1953 (div.); children—Jaime M. Lewis, H. Geoffrey, John Craig. Sec. to dean medicine McGill U., Montreal, 1950-51; sec. to headmaster Sir George Williams U., 1051-55, lectr., 1963-74; mgr. info. services Descon/Concordia Systems, Ltd., 1970-71; adminstr., info. specialist Alcan Aluminium Ltd., Montreal, 1972-74; mgr. pub. affairs research B.F. Goodrich Co., Akron, Ohio, 1974-77; pub. affairs cons. Chmn. human rights panel Action Can. Conv., 1971; panelist seminar human rights Nat. Parliamentary Prayer Breakfast, Ottawa, Ont., Can., 1972; speaker bicentennial program Ashland Coll., 1976. Former trustee Pointe Claire (Que.) Municipal Library; trustee Family and Children's Service Soc. for Summit County, also rep. United Way bd., 1975—; trustee Western Res. council Girl Scouts U.S., Akron. Mem. Am. Soc. Info. Sci. (pub. affairs com., speaker bicentennial conf. 1976), Am. Mgmt. Assn., World Future Soc. (adv. com. for speakers), World Population Soc., Soc. for Internat. Devel. Home: 3631 Kenwood Dr Uniontown OH 44685

WORRELL, WILLIAM JAMES, rubber co. exec.; b. Akron, Ohio, Feb. 16, 1920; s. William Roy and Ilo Grace (Cring) W.; student U. Akron, 1940-41; m. Camella B. Bonkrude, July 14, 1945; children—William P., Jamelle E., Janice H., Susan J., Merrie J., Beverly J. With chem. engring. dept. Goodyear Tire & Rubber Co., Akron, 1939-41; in charge govt. sales Amerace Akron, 1945-51; in charge sales Ace Rubber Co., Akron, 1951-54; v.p. sales, gen. mgr. Bearfoot Airway & Sole Co., Wadsworth, Ohio, 1954-68, exec. v.p., 1968—; pres. Rubber Mixing Industries, Inc., Dispersed Materials, Inc. (both Akron); dir. Bearfoot Sole Co., Inc., Wadsworth, Bearfoot Airway Corp., Inc., Wadsworth; founder, dir. Pilgrim Book Soc., Inc., Akron. Mem. Gov. Council Libraries, 1964—, program com. chmn., 1973—; pres. Friends of Library, 1963-67. Served to capt. AUS, 1941-45. Decorated Bronze Star (2); Croix de Guerre (France); Order of Leopold (Belgium). Mem. Am., Ohio library assns., Am. Mgmt. Assn. Mason (32 deg., Shriner). Home: 82 Pembroke Rd Akron OH 44313 Office: 1st and Water Sts Wadsworth OH 44280

WORSEK, ERNEST DAVID, real estate cons.; b. Chgo., Dec. 31, 1926; s. Milton M. and Caroline (Fantus) W.; U. Ill., 1944, Roosevelt Coll., 1947; student in real estate, Central YMCA Community Coll., 1948; m. Thelma Lou Serlin, Mar. 3, 1948; children—Judith (Mrs. William Bashkin), Lynn (Mrs. Gary Gagerman), Warren. Engaged in family real estate bus., Milton Worsek & Co., Chgo., 1947-72; pres. Urban Am. Property Counselors, Inc., Chgo., 1972—; mgmt., sales agt. Fed. Savs. and Loan Ins. Corp., VA, FHA; receiver Circuit Ct. Cook County, 1970—; instr. real estate mgmt. Central YMCA Community Coll., 1970—; nat. lectr. real estate mgmt. Served with USNR, 1944-46. Mem. Chgo. Real Estate Bd. (past chmn. renting and mgmt. div.), Ill., Northwest Side, North Side (treas.) real estate bds., Nat. Assn. Realtors, Nat. Inst. Real Estate Brokers, Inst. Real Estate Mgmt. (Mgr. of Year award Chgo. chpt., 1973; past pres.), Chgo. Bd. Underwriters, North River Commn., Jewish Chautauqua Soc. (life). Jewish (past pres. temple brotherhood). Home: 6101 N Sheridan Rd E Chicago IL 60660 Office: 3557 W Peterson Ave Chicago IL 60659

WORTH, RICHARD LEE, real estate appraiser, broker; b. Indpls., July 2, 1927; s. Lee Roy and Edna Josephine (Rohrbaugh) W.; B.S., Ind. State U., 1949; postgrad. Ind. U., 1954-56, Ball State U., Muncie, Ind., 1963, Kans. State U. (Community Devel. grantee), 1967; m. Lavina Loretta Reynolds, Nov. 22, 1956; 1 son, Keith Marshall. With Greer Steel Co., Anderson, Ind., 1951-63; asst. dir. redevel., Anderson, 1963-65; exec. dir. Urban Renewal Agy. and Housing Authority, Salina, Kans., 1965-76; head Worth Appraisal Service and Dick Worth Realty, 1976—; vis. prof. community and regional devel., 1968; lectr. in field; cons., appraiser, 1968—. Vice pres. Saline County (Kans.) Mental Health Assn., 1968-69; treas. Central Kans. Alcoholic Found., 1966—. Mem. Nat., Kans. (legis. chmn. 1973—) rifle assns., Nat. Wild Life Fedn., Hunter Safety Instrs., Nat. Assn. Realtors, Farm and Land Inst., Am. Soc. Planning Ofcls., Kans. Soc. Farm Mgrs. and Rural Appraisers, Central Kans. Humane Assn. Episcopalian (bishop's com. 1973-76). Mason, Lion. Club: Saline County Rod and Gun (legis. chmn. 1969—). Home: 611 Max Ave Salina KS 67401 Office: PO Box 503 Salina KS 67401

WORTH, ROBERT MARSHALL, JR., indsl. buyer; b. Indpls., Oct. 17, 1943; s. Robert Marshall and Dorothy (McDuffee) W.; student U. Dayton, 1962-63, Purdue U., Indpls., 1968-73; m. Carol Jean Laird, Nov. 26, 1965; children—Robert Charles, Joseph Marshall. Quality analyst Prestolite Co., Toledo, 1964-67; ins. underwriter Ind. Lumberman's Ins. Co., Indpls., 1967-68; buyer, expeditor Mallory Distbr. Co. div. P.R. Mallory, Indpls., 1968-72, buyer Mallory Timers Co. div., 1972-76, sr. buyer, 1977—. Pres., bd. dirs. Woodruff Place Civic League, 1967-70. Mem. Nat. Mgmt. Assn., Mallory Mgmt. Club (dir., chmn. pub. relations 1968-73), Key Clubs Internat. (life). Club: Indpls. Jaycees (dir. 1970, chmn. pub. relations 1969-70, Outstanding Service award 1970). Author application essay for nomination of Woodruff Place to be registered as nat. hist. site, 1970. Home: 4032 Arquette Dr Indianapolis IN 46236 Office: 3029 E Washington St Indianapolis IN 46201

WORTHAM, JAMES CALVIN, educator; b. Oconee County, Ga., Sept. 12, 1928; s. James Notley and Effie (Cross) W.; B.A., U. Akron, 1957; M.A. (NSF Scholar), Ohio State U., 1969; m. Mary Helena Shelley, Dec. 23, 1953; children—Sharon Elaine, Marilyn Kay, Deborah Louise, James Donald. Tchr. high sch. Akron Pub. Schs., 1956-62, tchr. sr. high sch., 1962-66; math. curriculum specialist Akron (Ohio) Pub. Schs., 1966—; instr. math. U. Akron, 1966—. Served with USAF, 1951-55. Mem. NEA, Ohio Edn. Assn., Math. Assn. Am., Nat., Ohio councils tchrs. of math., Nat. Council Suprs. of Math., Pi Mu Epsilon. Republican. Mem. Ch. of Nazarene. Home: 1665 Wiltshire Rd Akron OH 44313 Office: 70 N Broadway Akron OH 44308

WORTHINGTON, JAMES NORMAN, physicist; b. Seattle, Jan. 25, 1945; s. Robert Edger and Janet Main (Izett) W.; B.S., U. Wash., Seattle, 1967. Sci. asst. Argonne (Ill.) Nat. Lab., Physics div., 1967-74, sci. asso., originator div.'s tech. support group, 1974—; cons. in field. Mem. Downers Grove (Ill.) CD Com., 1968-69. Mem. Am. Inst. Chem. Engrs. Presbyterian. Contbg. author books; contbr. articles to profl. publs. Home: 3455 Regan Rd Joliet IL 60435 Office: 9700 S Cass Ave Argonne IL 60439

WORTHINGTON, LORNE RAYMOND, ins. co. exec.; b. Penticton, B.C., Can., June 14, 1938; s. Paul A. and Alice (Marsland) W.; student State U. Iowa, 1960-61; B.A. cum laude, Graceland Coll., 1964; m. Veneta Faye Snethen, May 30, 1959; children—Penelope, Deborah, Suzanne, Michael, Jonathan. Office mgr. Lamoni Sales Corp. (Iowa), 1961-64; auditor State of Iowa, Des Moines, 1965-66, commr. of ins., 1967-71; v.p. planning and devel. Preferred Risk Mut. Ins. Co., West Des Moines, Iowa, 1971-76, sr. v.p., 1976-77, pres., 1978—, also dir.; dir. Scandia Savs. & Loan, Midwest Mut. Ins. Co. Treas., Am. Indian Devel. Center, 1971-74; bd. dirs. Native Am. Project on Alcohol, 1977—; mem. Iowa Ho. of Reps., 1962-64; asst. chmn. Iowa Dem. party, 1972-74. Mem. Lamoni C. of C. (pres. 1964), Nat. Assn. Ins. Commrs. (pres. 1971). Mem. Reorganized Ch. of Jesus Christ of Latter-day Saints (elder). Home: 1215 20th Pl West Des Moines IA 50265 Office: 1111 Ashworth Rd West Des Moines IA 50265

WORTLEY, CHARLES ALLEN, civil engr.; b. St. Joseph, Mo., May 21, 1934; s. Cabray C. and Janet (Olmsted) W.; B.S., Antioch Coll., 1956; M.S. in Civil Engring., Calif. Inst. Tech., 1957; m. Ardale Dorothy Broch, Aug. 20, 1955; children—Marguerite, Caroline. Partner, Lorenzi, Dodds & Gunnill, cons. engrs., Pitts., 1957-66; v.p., chief engr. Warzyn Engring. Co., cons. engrs., Madison, Wis., 1966-74; asst. prof. engring. U. Wis., Madison, 1974—. Registered profl. engr., Wis. Mem. Wis. Soc. Profl. Engrs. (engr. of year in pvt. practice, 1972, engr. of year Southwest chpt. 1974), Nat. Soc. Profl. Engrs., Am. Soc. Engring. Edn., Am. Water Works Assn. Contbr. articles to profl. jours. Home: 206 Everglade Dr Madison WI 53717 Office: 432 Lake St N Madison WI 53706

WOUTILA, NORMAN EMERSON, engine components mfg. co. exec.; b. Spokane, Wash., Sept. 15, 1926; s. John Nels and Roberta (Eckley) W.; student U. Wis., 1950-51, bus. adminstrn. and mech. engring. Purdue U., 1960-65, cost accounting Butler U., 1963; m. Beverly Rose Pokora, Nov. 27, 1947; children—Pamela, Patricia. Gen. mgr. Jeffboat, Inc., Jeffersonville, Ind., 1965-68; asst. plant mgr. Erbrich Products, Inc., Indpls., 1968-69; plants engr. Stark-Wetzel, Inc., Indpls., 1969-70; plant mgr. FRP, Inc., Indpls., 1970; plant mgr. Schwitzer div. Wallace-Murray Corp., Elwood, Ind., 1970—. Served with USN, 1944-52. Mem. Soc. Plastic Engrs., Soc. Design Engrs., Ethyl Corp., VFW. Home: 703 Elmwood Circle Noblesville IN 46060 Office: 926 N 9th St Elmwood IN 46036

WOYCZYNSKI, WOJBOR ANDRZEJ, educator; b. Czestochowa, Poland, Oct. 24, 1943; s. Eugeniusz and Otylia Sabina (Borkiewicz) W.; came to U.S., 1976; M.Sc. in Elec. Engring., Wroclaw Tech. U., 1966, Ph.D. in Math., 1968; m. Alexandra Krasna, May 25, 1976. Teaching asst. Inst. of Math., Wroclaw U., 1966-68, asst. prof., 1968-72, asso. prof., 1972-76, vice dir. sci. affairs, 1975-76; fellow Carnegie-Mellon U., Pitts., 1970-71; asso. prof. math. U. Wis., 1976, Northwestern U., 1976-77; prof. math. Cleve. State U., 1977—. NSF grantee, 1970, 71, 76. Mem. Am. Math. Soc., Inst. Math. Statistics, Polish Math. Soc. (Great prize 1972). Roman Catholic. Author: Gometry and Martingales in Banach Spaces, 1975. Editor: (with Z. Ciesielski and K. Urbanik) Winter School on Probability, 1975. Dep. editor-in-chief Annals of Polish Math. Soc., 1973—. Home: 1725 Orrington Ave Evanston IL 60201 Office: Math Dept Northwestern U Evanston IL 60201

WOZENCRAFT, MARIAN, educator; b. McConnelsville, Ohio; d. John George and Marian (Leitch) Wozencraft; B.A., U. Chgo., 1941; M.A., U. Ill., 1950; Ph.D., Western Res. U., 1957. Elementary tchr. Dupage County, (Ill.) pub. schs., 1937-41; cost engr. Johns-Manville Co., Waukegan, Ill., 1942-49; elementary supr. Paris (Ill.) pub. schs., 1950-51; instr. Ind. State Tchrs. Coll., 1951-52; asst. prof. Fenn Coll., Cleve., 1952-59; prof. N.Y. State U. Coll., Geneseo, 1959—; guest lectr. Eastern Ill. U., 1969-70, 71-72, Northeastern Ill. U., 1971, Case Western Res. U., U. Vt. Mem. AAUP, Internat. Reading Assn., Nat. Council Tchrs. English (nat. com. jr. memberships 1960-63), AAUW (legis. chmn. Geneseo br., v.p. Geneseo br. 1975-77), United Univ. Profession, League Women Voters, Kappa Delta Pi, Phi Delta Kappa, Delta Kappa Gamma. Contbr. articles to profl. jours. Home: 1219 Monroe St Charleston IL 61920

WOZNIAK, SAM, engring. exec.; b. Timblin, Pa., Mar. 6, 1931; s. John and Fenyi (Fedasz) W.; student Carnegie Inst. Tech., 1948-50; B.S., U. Tulsa, 1971, M.B.A., 1972; m. Shirley J. Johnson, Dec. 28, 1961; children—Susan Rae, John David. Elec. engr. Douglas Aircraft Corp., Long Beach, Calif., 1955; supr. Bell Aircraft Corp., Cleve., 1955-58; supr. and research scientist N.Am. Aviation, Downey, Calif., 1958-61; engring. mgr. Rockwell Internat., Tulsa, 1964-74; dir. div. engring. Brunswick Corp., Skokie, Ill., 1974-76, dir. engring., 1976—; adj. prof. U. Tulsa, 1971-73; spl. adviser to USAF, 1971-74. Vice chmn. YMCA, Tulsa, 1968-70. Served with USAF, 1951-55. Mem. Am. Mgmt. Assn., IEEE, Electric Def. Assn., AAAS, Assn. MBA Execs., Am. Inst. Aeros. and Astronautics, Delta Sigma Pi, Pi Sigma Epsilon, Sigma Iota Epsilon. Republican. Presbyterian. Club: Rotary. Author: (with others) Guided Missiles Fundamentals, 1953, Radar Systems Manual, 1954, Highly Integrated Defensive Electromagnetic Systems Manual, 1967, Manufacturing Methods for Radar Materials, 1969, Radar Camouflage Benefits, 1975, Army Camouflage Net System, 1975. Home: 2806 Farmington Rd Northbrook IL 60062 Office: 1 Brunswick Plaza Skokie IL 60076

WRAGE, JOHN RUSSEL, psychologist, mgmt. cons.; b. Oshkosh, Wis., Aug. 17, 1907; s. John Henry and Mercedes (Fisher) W.; B.S., Oshkosh State Tchrs. Coll., 1932; M.S., U. Wis., 1942, Ph.D., 1949; m. Florence Elizabeth Hayes, Nov. 4, 1932; 1 dau., Judith Ann Wrage Bunge. Machine operator J. I. Case Co., Racine, Wis., 1929-31; tool maker Gisholt Machine Co., 1941-44, safety dir., 1944-63, apprentice trainer, 1945-62, dir. exec. devel., 1946-64, personnel mgr., 1947-63, v.p., 1963-64; owner, mgr. Indsl. Mgmt. Cons., Inc. and John Wrage Employment Service, Madison, Wis., 1964—; prin., tchr. Abrams (Wis.) State Graded Sch., 1932-35, Mazomanie, Wis., 1935-37; supr. tchrs. East Dane County, Sun Prairie, Wis., 1937-41; prof. LaCrosse Tchrs. Coll., 1941. Mem. Gov.'s Commn. Human Rights, Employ the Handicapped, 1942-55; chmn. survey Child and Family Welfare Services, Madison, 1941—; pres. exec. bd. Wesley Found., 1950-51; chmn. indsl. com. ARC, 1950-51; chmn. labor mgmt. com. Local 1404, United Steel Workers, CIO, 1942-44. Mem. NAM, Wis. Edn. Assn. (del.), Wis. Indsl. Tng. Dirs. Assn. (pres.), Oconto County (pres.), West Dane County tchrs. assns., Madison Personnel Assn. (pres.), Madison Safety Assn. (pres. exec. bd.)., Alpha Kappa Psi, Pi Kappa Delta, Phi Delta Kappa. Club: Masons, Rotary, Downtown. Home: 5301 Coney Weston Pl Madison WI 53711 Office: 25 W Main St Madison WI 53703

WRANGELL, LEWIS JOSEPH, chemist; b. Milw., July 30, 1914; s. Ludvig H. and Anna (Jirachek) W.; B.S., Marquette U., 1936, M.S., 1939; m. Eunice Mae Park, Sept. 28, 1940; 1 son, James L. Head chemist John Graf Co., Milw., 1937-42; analytical chemist, research div. Allis Chalmers Mfg. Co., West Allis, Wis., 1942-45, chemist in charge, 1945-59, research chemist, 1959-68, quality assurance engr., product assurance dept., process engr. in prodn. and product testing dept. advanced products div., Greendale, Wis., 1969; chief engring. chemistry and sci. George J. Meyer Mfg. Co., 1969-70; cons. analytical chemist, Wauwatosa, Wis., 1970-72; sr. chemist reduction systems div. Allis Chalmers Corp., West Allis, 1972—. Cubmaster Milwaukee County council Boy Scouts Am., 1953-54, scoutmaster, 1933-46, committeeman, 1946-64, recipient Silver Beaver award, 1956. Fellow Am. Inst. Chemists; mem. Am. Chem. Soc. Conglist. Contbr. articles to profl. jours. Patentee in field. Home: 2325 80th St N Wauwatosa WI 53226 Office: PO Box 512 Milwaukee WI 53201

WRAY, BETH E., coll. adminstr.; b. Hutchinson, Kans., Oct. 19, 1942; d. Clifford Warren and Marian Ruth (McFadden) W.; B.S., Pittsburg (Kans.) State U., 1964, M.S., 1966; Ed.D., U. Kans., 1972. Tchr., Lakeside Jr. High Sch., Pittsburg, 1964-67; asso. dean students No. State Coll., Aberdeen, S.D., 1969—. Sec. Northeastern Mental Health Center, 1973-76, treas., 1977—; pres. Aberdeen Area Vol. Bur., 1975-76, Aberdeen Arts Council, 1976—; v.p. Aberdeen Sr. Center, 1977. Named Adminstr. of Year No. State Coll., 1974, 1st Lady of Aberdeen, 1976. Mem. Aberdeen City Panhellenic Assn. (pres. 1975-76), AAUW (v.p. Aberdeen br. 1976—), Aberdeen Bus. and Profl. Women (pres. 1972-74), No. State Coll. Faculty and Adminstrv. Women (pres. 1970-71), S.D. Fedn. Bus. and Profl. Women's Clubs (pres. 1977-78), Nat., S.D. assns. women deans, adminstrs. and counselors, Am., S.D. coll. personnel assns., Nat. Assn. Student Personnel Adminstrs., Am., S.D. personnel and guidance assns. Home: 1112 S Washington St Aberdeen SD 57401 Office: Box 742 No State Coll Aberdeen SD 57401

WRIGHT, ALFRED GEORGE JAMES, educator; b. London, Eng., June 23, 1916; s. Alfred Francis and Elizabeth (Chapman) W.; B.A., U. Miami (Fla.), 1937, M.Ed., 1947; m. Bertha Marie Farmer, Aug. 6, 1938; children—Adele Marie (Mrs. George Ronald Needham), Cynthia Elaine (Mrs. Lawrence Williams); m 2d, Gladys Violet Stone, June 28, 1953. Dir. music Miami Sr. High Sch., 1938-54; prof., head dept. bands Purdue U., Lafayette, Ind., 1954—; condr. Purdue U. Symphony Orch., 1971—. Mem. nat. bd. control Nat. Interscholastic Music Activities Commn., 1952, pres., 1958; bd. advisers Music Jour. Mag., 1964-67; condr. Am. Youth Band European Tours, 1966-67; pres. Internat. Music Tours, Inc., 1975; founder, condr. U.S. Coll. Wind Band Tours, 1971, 72, 73, 74, 75, 76; dir. prerace pageant Indpls. 500 Mile Automobile Race, 1957—; mem. adv. council Performing Arts Abroad, 1972—; chmn. N.Am. Band Dirs. Coordinating Commn., 1974-75; chmn. Nat. High Sch. Honors Band, 1975-76, 77—. Bd. dirs. 500 Festival Assos., 1961—. Mem. Am. (dir. 1952, 72—), Ind. bandmasters assns., Nat. Band Assn. (pres. 1960-63, sec.-treas. 1965-68), Coll. Band Dirs. Nat. Assn., Am. Sch. Band Dirs. Nat. Assn., Japan Marching Band Assn. (dir. 1971—), Big Ten Band Dirs. Assn. (pres. 1977), Nat. Acad. Wind and Percussive Arts (chmn. 1971—), Phi Mu Alpha, Kappa Kappa Psi, Phi Beta Mu. Author: The Show Band, 1957; Marching Band Fundamentals, 1963; Bands of the World, 1970. Marching band editor Instrumentalist Mag., 1953—. Contbr. articles to profl. mags., jours. Home: 344 Overlook Dr Lafayette IN 47906

WRIGHT, BEVERLY RUTH, ednl. adminstr.; b. Hillsdale, Mich., Nov. 3, 1938; d. Jim Franklin and Ruth Harriet (Perkins) Wilson; B.S., Western Mich. U., 1961, postgrad., 1962-63; m. Philip A. Wright, Jr., July 29, 1972; children—James Walter, Juddson. Tchr., Otsego (Mich.) Pub. Schs., 1961-63, Homer (Mich.) Pub. Schs., 1963; model Wright Modeling Agency, Columbus, 1970, asst. dir., 1972, tng. dir. finishing sch., 1970-73, advt. dir., 1973—. Mem. Modeling Assn. Am. Internat., Columbus Convention Bur., Columbus Area C. of C., Columbus Advt. Fedn. (bd. dirs.), Zonta (bd. dirs. 1976-78). Home: 1408 Westshire Rd Columbus OH 43214 Office: 4100 N High St Columbus OH 43214

WRIGHT, CELIA S., advt. exec.; b. Des Moines, June 18, 1936; d. John L. and Harriet (Bolon) Wright; B.A., U. Denver, 1958. Tchr. Newton (Iowa) Community Schs., 1958-61; journalist, advt.-pub. relations Ia. Power & Light Co., Des Moines, 1961-64; tchr. Englewood (Colo.) Pub. Schs., 1964-67; radio and TV supr., acct. exec. Lessing-Flynn Advt. Co., Des Moines, 1967-74; v.p., media dir. Fultz, LaCasse & Assos., Inc., Advt., Des Moines, 1974-76, v.p., 1976—. Pub. Info. and publicity dir. Polk County Crime Alert, 1968—; publicity chmn. Polk County Cancer Soc., 1971—; mem. Iowa Advt. Rev. Bd., 1975—. Bd. dirs. Des Moines Drama Workshop, 1974-76. Named Des Moines Advt. Woman of Yr., 1970. Mem. Advt. Fedn. of Des Moines (pub. service chmn. 1969-70, 1st v.p. 1970-71, pres. 1971-72, 75-76), Am. Women in Radio and TV, Am. Advt. Fedn. (named 1973 Advt. Woman of Year by 9th Dist.), Des Moines Advt. Club. Republican. Presbyn. Home: Apt 301 5012 Ingersoll St Des Moines IA 50312 Office: PO Box 4807 Des Moines IA 50306

WRIGHT, CHARLES HOWARD, physician; b. Dothan, Ala., Sept. 20, 1918; s. Willie P. and Laura (Florence) W.; B.S., Ala. State Coll., 1939; M.D., Meharry Med. Coll., 1943; m. Louise L. Lovett, Feb. 11, 1950; children—Stephanie Jeanne, Carla Louise. Intern, Harlem Hosp., N.Y.C., 1943-45; asst. resident in pathology Cleve. City Hosp., Cleve., 1945; resident in obstetrics and gynecology Harlem Hosp.,

N.Y.C., 1950-53; gen. practice medicine Detroit, 1946-50, specializing in obstetrics and gynecology, Detroit, 1953—; attending physician Southwest Detroit Hosp.; asst. Grace Hosp., 1954—; attending physician Womans Hosp., Detroit, 1953—; chmn. dept. obstetrics and gynecology Highland Park (Mich.) Gen. Hosp. 1972-75. Founders, chmn. bd. trustees Afro-Am. Mus. of Detroit, Inc. Pres., African Med. Edn. Fund. Trustee U. Detroit, until 1975, WTVS. Named Omega Man of the Year, by Omega Psi Phi fraternity, 1965; recipient Certificate Commendation, Mich. Med. Soc., 1967. Diplomate Am. Bd. Obstetrics and Gynecology. Fellow A.C.S., Am. Coll. Obstetricians and Gynecologists; mem. NAACP. Author articles in field pub. profl. jours. Author, producer: (mus. drama) Were You There?, 1963; exec. producer; (film) This Bank is Open to You, 1969, producer TV spls.: Were You There?, 1972; Venereal Disease, 1973; writer, narrator radio documentaries: Paul Robeson, 1970; Rosa Parks, 1971; (book) Robeson, Labor's Forgotten Champion, 1975. Exec. dir. (med. recruitment film) You Can Be A Doctor, 1968. Home: 1342 Nicolet Pl Detroit MI 48202

WRIGHT, DAVID BURTON, newspaper pub. co. exec.; b. Fowler, Ind., Agu. 29, 1933; s. Claude Matthew and Rosa Ellen (Lavelle) W.; A.B., Wabash Coll., 1955; postgrad. Ind. U., 1958-59; m. Geraldine F. Gray, May 9, 1964; children—David Andrew, Anne Kathleen. With George S. Olive & Co., C.P.A.'s, Indpls., 1958-65, mgmt. cons. supr., 1963-65; with Herff Jones Co., Indpls., 1965-71, corp. controller, asst. sec., 1970-71; with Indpls. Newspapers Inc., 1971—, asst. bus. mgr., 1973-77, bus. mgr., 1977—, asst. sec., asst. treas., 1976—. Served with AUS, 1956-58. C.P.A., Ind. Mem. Am. Inst. C.P.A.'s, Ind. Assn. C.P.A.'s, Inst. Newspaper Controllers and Fin. Officers, Indpls. C. of C., Indpls. Mus. Art. Roman Catholic. Club: Indpls. Athletic. Home: 658 Mellowood Dr Indianapolis IN 46217 Office: 307 N Pennsylvania St Indianapolis IN 46204

WRIGHT, DONALD CARLYLE, economist, educator; b. Ft. Dodge, Iowa, Sept. 28, 1923; s. Burr Clayton and Gladys Leah (Root) W.; student Dartmouth, 1943-44; B.S., U. Iowa, 1948, M.S., 1949, postgrad., 1958-60; m. Anna Margaret Beebe, July 28, 1946; children—Jacalyn G., Bradley C. Instr. econs. and bus. adminstrn. Washburn U., Topeka, 1949-51, asst. prof., 1951-55, asso. prof., 1955-68, prof., 1968—; mgmt. and govt. cons., 1960—. Mediator Kans. Dept. Labor, 1964. Served with USNR, 1942-45. Mem. Am. Soc. Pub. Adminstrn. (v.p. Kaw Valley chpt. 1974-75), Am., S.W. acads. mgmt., Kans. Econ. Assn., Beta Gamma Sigma, Pi Gamma Mu, Phi Kappa Phi, Delta Sigma Pi. Home: 3719 Munson St Topeka KS 66604

WRIGHT, DONALD EUGENE, librarian; b. Boulder, Colo., July 25, 1930; s. Kelley E. and Iva (Winkle) W.; B.A., U. Colo., 1952; M.A., U. Denver, 1953; m. Verna Venetta Vorpahl, June 18, 1953; children—Sara Jane, Amy Louise, John Kelley. Library asst. Denver Pub. Library, 1953; reference asst. Ft. Wayne (Ind.) Pub. Library, 1953-55, Detroit Pub. Library, 1953-56; librarian North Platte (Nebr.) Pub. Library, 1956-58; cons. Nebr. Pub. Library Commn., Lincoln, 1958-60; asst. dir. Lincoln City Libraries, 1960-61; dir. small libraries project ALA, Chgo., 1961-63; exec. sec. reference service div. ALA, also ALA. Am. Library Trustee Assn., Chgo., 1963-64; chief bur. library services Conn. Dept. Edn., Hartford, 1964-65; chief library devel., asso. state librarian Ill. State Library, Springfield, 1965-67; librarian Evanston (Ill.) Pub. Library, 1967—; co-chmn. Ill. White House Conf. on Library and Info. Services. Mem. ALA (life mem.; pres. elect library adminstrn. div. 1977-78), Ill. Library Assn. (pres. 1971-72). Clubs: Caxton, University, Rotary (pres. 1978—) (Evanston). Home: 1715 Chancellor St Evanston IL 60201 Office: 1703 Orrington Ave Evanston IL 60201

WRIGHT, DORIS JEAN, coll. adminstr.; b. Independence, Kans., June 7, 1952; d. Lawrence G. and Betty E. (Pruitt) Wright; B.S. in Psychology, Kans. State U., 1974, M.S.Edn., 1976; postgrad. in Counseling Psychology (Am. Psychol. Assn. Minority fellow) U. Nebr., 1975—. Tutor-counselor Center for Student Devel., Kans. State U., Manhattan, 1971-73, grad. asst., 1974-75; grad. advising asst. U. Nebr. Coll. Arts and Scis., 1976-77; student affairs program asst. Doane Coll., 1977—; intern U.S. Congress, Washington, summer 1977. Mem. Am. Psychol. Assn., Am., Nebr. personnel and guidance assns., Am. Coll. Personnel Assn., Kans. State U. Alumni Assn., Smithsonian Assos., Phi Delta Kappa, Phi Delta Gamma, Pi Lambda Theta. Democrat. Methodist. Home: 2445 E St Apt 1 Lincoln NE 68510 Office: Dean of Students Office Doane Coll Crete NE 68333

WRIGHT, EDWARD BENTON, JR., journalist; b. Cleve., Nov. 21, 1938; s. Edward Benton and Marian (Tissot) W.; student Ohio U., 1957-61; m. Barbara Jean Rita, June 24, 1967. With Procter & Gamble Co., Cin., 1957-60; editor, v.p. Forest Hills Jour., Cin., 1961-70; editor, v.p. Forest Hills Jour. and Community Jour., Cin., 1970—. Mem. Ohio Citizens Com. to Study State Legislature. Sec., Ohio U. Circle K. 1958-59. Bd. dirs. Cin. area chpt. ARC, 1974-77, Clermont County unit Am. Cancer Soc. Mem. Nat. Newspaper Assn., Buckeye Press Assn. (treas. 1970, v.p., sec. 1971), Eastern Hills Jaycees (chmn. pub. relations), Anderson Twp. C. of C. (rec. sec.), Sigma Delta Chi (sec. Cin. chpt. 1971-72). Home: 6945 Moorfield Dr Cincinnati OH 45230 Office: 564 Batavia Pike Cincinnati OH 45244

WRIGHT, ELDON MILLARD, lawyer; b. North Manchester, Ind., June 14, 1912; s. Glen Ellis and Grace E. (Wine) W.; A.B., Manchester Coll., 1934; J.D., Valparaiso U., 1939; H.H.D., Kingstown U.; m. Frances Ada Gibble, Oct. 16, 1954; children—Renee Carmen, Glen Eldon. Admitted to Ind. bar, 1939; gen. practice law, Wabash County, 1939—; nat. claims mgr. Secured Casualty Ins. Co., Indpls., 1947-49; owner, mgr. Wright Realty Co., North Manchester, Ind., 1954—; municipal judge, North Manchester, 1971—. Trustee Town of North Manchester, 1964—, chmn. bd., 1965—; mem. North Manchester Planning Commn. Served with AUS, 1942-45. Named Ky. col. Mem. Ind., Wabash County bar assns. Republican. Mem. Christian Fellowship Ch. Mason. Home: 405 W 6th St Manchester IN 46962 Office: 116 E Main St North Manchester IN 46962

WRIGHT, GEORGE FOREST, surgeon; b. Johnstown, Pa., Apr. 16, 1933; s. George Arthur and Vivian Allene (Miller) W.; student Pa. State U., 1951-54; M.D., Temple U., 1958; m. Eva Lynne Best, June 12, 1959; children—George Forest, III, Wendy Ann, Craig Ashley. Intern, Conemaugh Valley Meml. Hosp., Johnstown, 1958-59; resident in gen. surgery Temple U. Med. Center, 1959-63; dep. chief surgery Gallup (N.Mex.) USPHS Indian Hosp., 1964-64; chief of surgery Shiprock (N.Mex.) USPHS Indian Hosp., 1964-65; practice medicine specializing in surgery, Hanover, Pa., 1965-66, Cleve., 1966—; mem. staff Euclid (Ohio) Gen. Hosp., 1966—, chief of surgery, 1973—; mem. staff Hanover Gen. Hosp., 1965-66; mem. courtesy staff. St. Vincent Charity Hosp.; bd. dirs. Euclid Clinic Found. Served with USPHS, 1963-65. Diplomate Am. Bd. Surgery. Mem. A.C.S., Am., Ohio med. assns., Acad. Medicine of Cleve., Cleve. Surg. Assn., Cleve. Vascular Soc. (founding). Republican. Methodist. Clubs: N.E. Yacht (Cleve.); Masons. Home: 19801 Edgecliff Dr Euclid OH 44119 Office: 18599 Lake Shore Blvd Cleveland OH 44119

WRIGHT, HARRY SMITH, JR., county ofcl.; b. Aurora, Ill., Oct. 16, 1931; s. Harry Smith and Mary Emma (Iftner) W.; B.S., U. Ill., 1957, M.S., 1969; m. Helen Elizabeth Hower, Aug. 8, 1953; children—Harry Smith, John Franklin, Peter Charles. With U. Ill., U.S. Dept. Agr. Extension Service, Fulton County, Ill., 1957-64, sr. extension adviser Region 5, specialized livestock adviser Pike County, Pittsfield, Ill., 1964—; co-founder Pike County Pork Producers, 1968—. Cons. in agr. to Two Rivers Resource Conservation and Devel. Area, 1971—, Title V project area Western Ill., 1973—; disaster chmn. Pike County, 1967—. Active Pike County chpt. ARC, 1964—. Served with USAF, 1951-55. Recipient Nat. Distinguished Service award Nat. Assn. County Agts., 1973. Mem. Ill. Extension Advisers Assn. (dir. 1971-73), Am. Legion, Ill. Dairy Goat Assn. Methodist. Mason (K.T.), Moose, Rotarian (pres. Pittsfield 1969-70). Home: Route 3 Pittsfield IL 62363

WRIGHT, HELEN KENNEDY, editor; b. Indpls., Sept. 23, 1927; d. William Henry and Ida Louise (Crosby) Kennedy; B.A., Butler U., 1945, M.S., 1950; M.S., Columbia U., 1952; m. Samuel A. Wright, Sept. 5, 1970; 1 son, Carl F. Prince II. Reference librarian N.Y. Pub. Library, N.Y.C., 1952-53, Bklyn. Pub. Library, 1953-54; cataloger U. Utah, 1954-57; librarian Chgo. Pub. Library; asst. dir. pub. dept. ALA, Chgo., 1958—, now subscription books coordinator, editor Reference and Subscription Books Revs. Mem. Phi Kappa Phi, Kappa Delta Phi, Sigma Gamma Rho. Roman Catholic. Home: 1138 W 111th St Chicago IL 60643 Office: 50 E Huron Chicago IL 60611

WRIGHT, JAMES LYNN, savs. and loan co. exec.; b. Springfield, Ill., Sept. 22, 1940; s. Glenn LaRue and Freida Pearl (Bloomfield) W.; B.S., Ill. Coll., 1963; M. Accounting Sci., U. Ill., 1965, postgrad., 1969-71; m. Karen Ann Barber, Nov. 24, 1976; 1 son, Jeffrey Michael. Staff auditor Arthur Young & Co., Chgo., 1965-66, 68-69; teaching asst. accounting U. Ill., Urbana, 1969-70; instr. accounting Ill. State U., Normal, 1970-71; accountant Bloomington (Ill.) Fed. Savs. & Loan Assn., 1972, asst. treas., 1972-73, dir. data processing, 1974-76, v.p., 1976—, comptroller, 1976—. Served with U.S. Army, 1966-68. Home: 308 Vista Dr Bloomington IL 61701 Office: 115 E Washington St Bloomington IL 61701

WRIGHT, JAMES MERCER, securities broker; b. Rockford, Ill., June 6, 1912; s. Isaac and Elizabeth Louisa (Anderson) W.; grad. high sch.; m. Mildred Lundine, Dec. 2, 1933; children—Richard Douglas, Gary Randall. With U.S. Postal Dept., 1929-45; owner confectionary store, Rockford, 1945-58; real estate salesman, Rockford, 1959-61; registered rep. stock and bonds, Rockford, 1962-70; owner, pres. Paul Conrads & Co., Inc., Rockford, 1970-76; v.p. Bridegan, Conrads & Co. Inc., Rochford, 1976—. Mason (33 deg., Shriner). Club: Forest Hills Country. (Rockford). Home: 3930 Guilford Rd Rockford IL 61107 Office: 1111 S Alpine Rd Rockford IL 61108

WRIGHT, JOHN LESLIE, orthopaedic surgeon: b. Normal, Ill., Jan. 8, 1920; s. Frank and Ruth (Bramwell) W.; B.S., Ill. Wesleyan U., 1943; M.D., U. Ill., 1945; m. Shirley Jean Barr, May 13, 1943; children—Judy Lee, Barbara Jean, Patricia Ann, John L., Gretchen Sue. Intern, St. Mary's Mercy Hosp., Gary, Ind., 1945-46; resident VA Hosp., Alexandria, La., 1946-48, La. Meth. Hosp., Peoria, Ill., 1948-49; practice medicine, Minier, Ill., 1949-54; resident in orthopaedics Oschner Found. Hosp. and Clinic, New Orleans, 1954-57; practice medicine specializing in orthopaedics, Bloomington, Ill., 1957—; mem. staffs Mennonite and St. Joseph's hosps., Bloomington, Brokaw Hosp., Normal; clin. asso. Sch. Basic Med. Scis., U. Ill., Urbana-Champaign, 1971—; adviser Am. Assn. Med. Assts., 1975, chmn. adv. bd. Ill. Soc., 1973. Served with U.S. Army, M.C., 1946-48. Mem. Ill. Soc. Am. Assn. Med. Assts. (hon.), McLean County, Ill. State med. socs., AMA, Am. Acad. Orthopaedic Surgeons, A.C.S., Oschner Found. Assn., Am. Fracture Assn., Tulane Caldwell Orthopaedic Club, Ill. Mid-State Orthopaedic Surgery Club. Methodist. Clubs: Aviation Owners and Pilots Assn., Bloomington, Masons. Contbr. articles to profl. jours. Home: 1112 N Fell Ave Bloomington IL 61701 Office: 2416 E Washington St Suite A Bloomington IL 61701

WRIGHT, JOHNSON KENT, dermatologist; b. Cleve., Sept. 8, 1924; s. J. Kent and Gwendolyn (Santo) W.; B.A., U. Mich., 1948; M.D., Temple U., 1952; m. Katherine Rogan, Dec. 20, 1950; children—Johnson Kent III, Marilyn Kay, James Kevin. Intern, Univ. Hosp., Ann Arbor, Mich., 1952-53, 1953-56; practice medicine specializing in dermatology, Traverse City, Mich.; chief of dermatology Munson Med. Center, Traverse City, 1956-72; cons. staff Grand Traverse Med. Care Facility, Benzie Med. Care Facility, Traverse City State Hosp. Served with USNR, 1943-45. Diplomate Am. Bd. Dermatology. Mem. AMA, Acad. of Dermatology, Mich. Med. Soc., Grand Traverse-Leelanau-Benzie Med. Soc. Republican. Clubs: Traverse City (Mich.) Golf and Country; Elks. Home: 1236 Randall Ct Traverse City MI 49684 Office: 1105 E Front St Traverse City MI 49684

WRIGHT, JOSEPH WILLIAM, JR., physician; b. Indpls., Oct. 30, 1916; s. Joseph William and Ethel (Woodard) W.; A.B., U. Mich., 1938, M.D., 1942; children (by previous marriage)—Joseph William III, Michael Wynne; m. 2d, Verna Roberta Miller, Jan. 3, 1965; children—Joseph Bruce, Lisa Marie, Andrew Woodard. Intern, U. Mich., Ann Arbor, 1942-43; mem. AAF residency tng. program Buckley Field, Denver, 1943-46; resident otorhinolaryngology Ind. U. Med. Center, Indpls., 1946-48; fellow fenestration surgery Northwestern Med. Sch., Chgo., 1955-56; practice medicine specializing in otology, Indpls., 1948—; asso. prof. otology Ind. U. Med. Sch., 1948—; med. dir. Wright Inst. Otology, Indpls., 1964—. Mem. Ind. State Hearing Commn., 1955—, chmn., 1955-59; mem. adv. com. on hearing aids Dealers Ind. Bd. Health, 1967—; mem. adv. bd. Crossroads Rehab. Center, 1958—, hearing and speech Ind. State Vocat. Rehab., 1975; trustee Community Hosp., Indpls. Served form lt. to maj. M.C., USAAF, 1943-46. Recipient Appreciation certificates Gov. Ind., 1960, 64, 68. Mem. AMA, Ind. Acad. Ophthalmology and Otolaryngology (pres. 1973-74), Ind., Indpls. med. socs., Trilogical Soc., Inc. Indpls. otol. and otolaryngol. socs., Ind. Med. Fedn. (sec.-treas. 1974-75). Author: Polytomography of the Temporal Bone, 1973. Contbr. articles to profl. jours. Home: 4220 Knollton Rd Indianapolis IN 46208 Office: 5506 E 16th St Indianapolis IN 46218

WRIGHT, KATHERYN THORNE, civic worker; b. Ravenswood, Ill., Sept. 19, 1895; d. Albert H. and Sarah (Chapman) Wright; A.B., Mather Coll. (now Western Res. Coll.), 1917, A.M., Case Western Res. U., 1927. Substitute tchr. Cleve. pub. schs., 1917-18; sec. First Meth. Ch., Cleve., 1920; sec. clk.'s office Cleveland Heights (Ohio) Bd. of Edn., 1921-22; sec. Squire, Sanders & Dempsey, Cleve., 1924-62, ret.; also free-lance writer, 1962—. Vol. ARC, Am. Cancer Soc., Cleve. Psychiat. Inst. Recipient Cleve. Vol. Year award, 1969. Mem. Cleve. Coll. Writers Club, Nat. Secs. Assn. (charter mem.), Greater Cleve. Orchid Soc., D.A.R. (Western Res. chpt.), Women's Assn. for Continuing Edn. Episcopalian (lay reader 1973—). Clubs: Quota (charter mem.), College. Home: 2543 Derbyshire Rd Cleveland OH 44106

WRIGHT, KAY MORROW, hosp. exec.; b. Baytown, Tex., Sept. 28, 1942; d. Morris Robinson and Martha (Whiteman) Morrow; B.A. in Mathematics, U. Tex., 1964; m. Terry Frank Wright, June 4, 1966; children—Stephanie Lynn, Stacie Cole. Programmer, The Bankers Life, Des Moines, 1966-68; programmer analyst Enjay Fibers and Laminates Co., Odenton, Md., 1968-69; dir. data processing Mercy Hosp., Des Moines, 1969-75, dir. computer planning and info. services, 1975—. Bd. dirs. Iowa Soc. for the Prevention of Blindness, 1977-79; benefit chmn. Flip for Sight, 1977. Mem. Data Processing Mgmt. Assn. (Des Moines chpt.), Electronic Computing Health Oriented. Democrat. Methodist. Clubs: Delta Zeta Alumnae, Young Attys. Wives. Office: 6th and University Ave Des Moines IA 50314

WRIGHT, MARK LESLIE, trucking co. exec.; b. Chgo., Feb. 8, 1953; s. Louis and Diane (Friedlander) W.; student Chgo. Acad. Fine Arts, 1970-71, Oakton Community Coll., 1971-72; m. Rochelle Ilene Schuman, Feb. 22, 1976. Spl. asst. to comptroller Wright Industries, Inc., Summit, Ill., 1970, v.p., 1976—; salesman Edward J. Meyers Co., Summit, 1971-73, gen. mgr., 1973-75, pres., 1975—. Co-chmn. chem. div. Israel Bond Drive, 1974; sec. Ad Hoc Labor Adv. Com., 1977. Mem. Chgo. Cartage Exchange, Cicero-Clearing Traffic Club, City of Hope Found. (trucking div.), Am. Mgmt. Assn., Ill. Trucking Assn., 100 Club of Cook County. Office: 7665 Lawndale Ave Summit IL 60501

WRIGHT, MICHAEL STEVENSON, univ. adminstr.; b. Cleve., Mar. 13, 1947; B.S., Kent State U., 1975, M.Ed., 1976. Counselor student devel. program Cleve. State U., 1976-77, adminstr., asst. dir. student activities and placement services, 1977—, dir. campus child care center. Served with USAF, 1966-70. Mem. Am. Personnel and Guidance Assn., Alpha Pi Sigma, Kappa Alpha Psi. Democrat. Home: 3736 E 147th St Cleveland OH 44120 Office: 25444 Harvard Rd Warrensville OH

WRIGHT, PETER HENRY, rec. co. exec.; b. Chgo., July 31, 1935; s. William Joseph and Marie (Tansor) W.; grad. high sch.; m. Dolores Joyce O'Black, Sept. 21, 1957; children—Lisa Gabrielle, Christian Adam, Maria Danielle. Pres. Peter H. Wright Assos., 1960-69; pres. Audio Talent, Inc., Chgo., 1969—; pres. Bedno-Wright Assos., 1969—; pres. Twinight Records, Inc., Program Data Sales, Inc., Quill Records, Inc.; Served with U.S. Army, 1956-59. Mem. Nat. Acad. Rec. Arts and Scis. (bd. govs. 1968-71). Home: 6523 N Longmeadow St Lincolnwood IL 60646 Office: 233 E Erie St Chicago IL 60611

WRIGHT, RAYMOND CLIFFORD, librarian; b. Winnipeg, Man., Can., May 4, 1917; s. Pearce Vancouver and Maud (Lipsett) W.; B.A., U. Man., 1939; B.L.S., McGill U., 1947; m. Eileen Patricia Collins, Aug. 22, 1942; children—Robert Clifford, Terry Eileen. Librarian, Provincial Library, 1947-55, U. Man. Extension Library, 1955-61; chief librarian U. Winnipeg, 1961-71, dir. libraries, 1971—. Served with RCAF, 1941-45. Mem. Man. Library Assn. (pres. 1966, 67). Home: 488 Queenston St Winnipeg MB R3N 0X2 Canada Office: 515 Portage Ave Winnipeg MB R3B 2E9 Canada

WRIGHT, ROBERT LEE, accountant; b. Des Moines, July 20, 1932; s. Kenneth A. and Thelma Pauline (Brooks) W.; B.S., Drake U., 1958; m. Donna Mae Mattis; children—Michelle, Kimberly, Melanie, Robin, Melinda, Robert Lee. Accountant, Peat, Marwick Mitchell & Co., 1958-62; instr., lectr. Drake U., Des Moines, 1962-71; owner, mgr. Wright & Co., C.P.A.'s, Des Moines, 1962-72; prin. Robert L. Wright fin. cons., West Des Moines, 1972—; dir. Investors Fin. Corp., Warehouse Systems Ltd., Parkview Care Center, Inc., others. Bd. dirs. West Des Moines Girls Softball Assn., West Suburban YMCA basketball program. Served with U.S. Army, 1951-54. Mem. Am. Inst. C.P.A.'s, Iowa Soc. C.P.A.'s, Nat. Assn. Accountants, Alpha Kappa Psi, Omicron Delta Kappa, Beta Gamma Sigma. Mem. Ch. of Christ. Home: 2108 Center St West Des Moines IA 50265 Office: PO Box 127 West Des Moines IA 50265

WRIGHT, ROBERT OREN, city mgr.; b. Chgo., Jan. 19, 1922; s. Oren Henry and Chloe (Stoneking) W.; A.B. in Polit. Sci., U. Chgo., 1942; M.P.A., Syracuse U., 1947; m. Marilyn E. Leonard, Dec. 12, 1942; children—Alan L., Carolyn G. (Mrs. Alan Batten). Adminstrv. asst. to city mgr., Pontiac, Mich., 1947-50; city mgr., Clawson, Mich., 1950-59, Aurora, Colo., 1959-69, Peoria, Ill., 1970—. Instr. U. Colo., 1966-67. Chmn. Inter-County Regional Planning Commn., Denver, 1961-62; mem. Oakland County (Mich.) Bd. Suprs., 1950-59; mem. Denver Regional Council Govts., 1959-69, chmn., 1961-62; mem. Southeast Oakland County Water Authority, 1952-59, Southeast Oakland County Garbage and Rubbish Authority, 1951-59; mem. Tri-County Planning Commn., Peoria, Woodford and Tazewell counties, 1971—, mem. exec. com., 1973—; mem. Peoria City Beautiful, 1972—, Urban Affairs Inst., Bradley U., 1973—; chmn. Regional Intergovtl. Coordinating Group, Peoria, 1970—. Served to 2d lt. Med. Adminstrn. Corps, AUS, 1942-46. Mem. Am. Acad. Polit. Sci., Am. Soc. Pub. Adminstrn. (pres. Central Ill. chpt. 1973-74, exec. bd. chpt. 1974—), State Assn. City Mgrs. (past v.p. Mich. chpt., past pres. Colo. chpt.), Internat City Mgmt. Assn. Presbyn. (trustee). Kiwanian (v.p., dir.). Club: Clawson Exchange (charter mem.). Home: 2522 N Woodbine Terr Peoria IL 61604 Office: 419 Fulton St Peoria IL 61602

WRIGHT, ROBERT RICHARD, educator; b. Indpls., May 12, 1942; s. Herbert Harold and Kathleen Elizabeth (Hayworth) W.; A.B., Butler U., 1964; M.S., Ohio State U., 1967, Ph.D., 1975; m. Alice Jane Mc Laughlin, Dec. 30, 1972. Planetarium lectr., asst. to dir. J.I. Holcomb Obs. and Planetarium, Indpls., 1962-64; guest investigator Snow Telescope, Mt. Wilson Obs., Calif., 1964; planetarium lectr., instr. The Center of Sci. and Industry of Columbus, Ohio, 1966; physics and astronomy lectr. Ohio Dominican Coll., 1969-73; vis. prof. dept. mathematics Ohio Wesleyan U., 1976-77; lectr. dept. math. The Ohio State U., 1973—; cons. mathematics and sci. editor Collegiate Publishing, Inc., Columbus, Ohio, 1971—. Recipient James E. Hughes scholarship, 1962-64; NDEA fellow, 1964-67. Mem. Am. Astronom. Soc., Ohio Acad. Sci., AAAS, Am. Inst. Physics, Math. Assn. Am., Nat. Council Teachers of Math. Republican. Co-author (with W. R. Klinger) Basic Algebra, 1972; collaborator: The Professor, 1974; contbr. articles to profl. jours. Home: 174 W Aldrich Rd Columbus OH 43214 Office: Dept Mathematics Ohio State U Columbus OH 43210

WRIGHT, ROBERT W(ILLIAMS), lawyer; b. Elgin, Ill., May 31, 1928; s. Robert Williams and Caroline (Chapman) W.; S.B., Mass. Inst. Tech., 1950; LL.B., Harvard, 1954; m. Nancy Campbell Tucker, Oct. 30, 1954; children—Patricia Jane, Katherine Elizabeth, Robert Tucker. Indsl. engr. Inland Steel Co., East Chicago, Ind., 1950-51; admitted to Ill. bar, 1954, since practiced Chgo.; with firm Keck, Cushman, Mahin & Cate, 1954—, partner, 1964—. Mem. Am., Ill., Chgo. bar assns., Law and Legal Clubs Chgo., Delta Kappa Epsilon. Club: Mid-Day (Chgo.). Home: 122 Kenilworth Ave Kenilworth IL 60043 Office: 233 S Wacker Dr Chicago IL 60606

WRIGHT, RODNEY HUGH, architect; b. Valparaiso, Ind., June 2, 1931; s. George Edward and Lena May (Cahoon) W.; grad. high sch.; m. Sydney Sullivan Goelitz, Feb. 16, 1966; children by previous marriage—Weston, Julie; step-children—Louise Goelitz, Ann Goelitz, Thomas Goelitz. With various archtl. firms, 1953-60; individual archtl. practice, 1960—; architect, pres. Hawkweed Group, Ltd., specializing in solar and alt. energy, Chgo.; lectr. Northwestern U., 1971. Bd. dirs. Lake County Urban League, 1961-69, chmn.,

1961-65, Uptown Devel. Center, Chgo. Served with AUS, 1950-53. Design fellow Nat. Endowment for Arts, 1975. Mem. AIA (chpt. dir. 1971, co-chmn. task force 1 1969-72, mem. nat. com. community devel. centers 1970-72). Address: 4643 N Clark St Chicago IL 60640

WRIGHT, RUSSELL BARRY, drug store chain exec.; b. Maywood, Ill., Aug. 31, 1941; s. Jennings Bryan and Anne Esther (Barry) W.; student DePaul U., 1960-62; B.S., No. Ill. U., 1963; postgrad., U. Chgo., 1964-66, Stanford, 1977; m. Mary Theresa Traub, Aug. 12, 1961; children—Michael, Keith, Mark, Matthew. Gen. mgr. drug and personal care Turnstyle, div. Jewel Co., 1969—73, v.p. gen. mgr., 1973—74, v.p. drug and personal care procurement Osco Drug div. Jewel Co., 1974—76, v.p. mktg., 1976—. Village trustee, Green Oaks, Ill., 1975—77. Mem. Nat. Assn. Chain Drug Stores. Office: 1818 Swift Dr Oakbrook IL 60521

WRIGHT, TED BYRON, architect; b. Linneus, Mo., Feb. 6, 1937; s. Jesse Hughes and Martha Irlene (Slaughter) W.; B.Arch., U. Nebr., 1967, M.Arch., 1973; Ph.D., 1976; m. Delivee L. Cramer, Mar. 10, 1961; children—Jessica L., Ted M. Supr. community planning Extension Service, U. Nebr., 1967-74, dir. Community Resource and Research Center, 1974—. Pres.-elect Nebr. Planning and Zoning Assn. Mem. Nat. U. Extension Assn. (chmn.-elect community devel. div. adminstrv. com.), Sigma Tau, Tau Sigma Delta. Home: 3500 Stockwell St Lincoln NE 68506 Office: Community Resource and Research Center Coll Architecture U Nebr Lincoln NE 68508

WRIGHT, WALTER BARTLETT, univ. dean; b. Ottumwa, Iowa, Apr. 6, 1919; s. Clifton O. and Tina (Frazier) W.; A.B., U. Iowa, 1942; M.B.A., U. Kans., 1960; postgrad. Washington U., 1961; m. Ruth May Hogan, Jan. 10, 1943; children—Thomas C., James B., Sharon M. Pres., chmn. bd. Food Brokerage Corp., 1945-58; asst. prof. bus. adminstrn. U. Mo., Kansas City, 1960-64, dir. div. continuing edn., 1963-65, asso. prof. bus. adminstrn., 1964-71, dean continuing edn. and extension, 1965—, prof. bus. adminstrn., 1971—; mktg. cons. pvt. firms; cons. to univs. on continuing edn. and extension; breeder, exhibitor Arabian show horses. Mem. program com. Gov.'s Conf. on Aging, 1966-70; mem. tech. adv. com. Human Resources Corp., 1967; mem. Mayor's Council on Youth Opportunity, 1968-70; mem. U.S. Office Edn. 1st Nat. Consultation on Adult Basic Edn., 1965; mem. adv. com. Harry S. Truman Center for Govtl. Affairs, 1969—; founder, mem. Mo. Com. for Humanities, 1970-77, chmn., 1972-73; mem. Nat. Com. on Continuing Edn. for Women, 1970. Bd. dirs. troop Kaw council Boy Scouts Am., Overland Park, Kans., Milhaven Homes Assn., Johnson County, Kan. Served to capt. AUS, 1942-45. Mem. Am. Mktg. Assn. (dir. Kansas City chpt. 1960-62), Nat. U. Extension Assn. (chmn. region 4 1970-71, govt. relations com. 1970-71, chmn. resolutions com. 1970-71, dir. 1972-76), Internat. Arabian Horse Assn., Delta Upsilon, Beta Gamma Sigma. Editor: NUEA Spectator, 1971-76. Home: 6620 Dearborn Dr Mission KS 66202 Office: 5100 Rockhill Rd Kansas City MO 64110

WRIGHT, WILBUR E., orgn. exec.; b. July 23, 1933; B.S. in Sociology, St. Peter's Coll., 1955; M.S.S. in Psychiat. Social Work, Fordham U., 1958; married, 4 children. Family counselor United Family and Children's Soc., Plainfield, N.J., 1958-59; sr. med. social worker U. Calif., San Diego County Hosp., 1965-66; dir. social worker Scripps Meml. Hosp., LaJolla, Calif., 1966-68; dir. service and rehab. Calif. div. Am. Cancer Soc., San Francisco, 1968-72; cons., dir. resource devel. Orgn. for Bus., Edn., and Community Advancement, Cath. Charities, Archdiocese of San Francisco, 1972-73: dep. head dept. social work dept. preventive and social medicine Alfred-Monash U. Hosp., Fawkner Park Community Health Center, Prahran, Victoria, Australia, 1973-74; head dept social work Royal Perth Hosp., Western Australia, 1974-75; exec. dir. Community Mental Health Bd. Central Fla., Inc., Orlando, 1975-78; dep. sec. gen. Council Internat. Programs, Cleve., 1978—; mem. internat. case com. San Diego-Tijuana (Mexico) Health Council, Pan-Am. Health Orgn., 1966-68; mem. stroke com. Regional Med. Program, U. Calif., San Diego, 1967-68; mem. Richmond fellowship bd. Community Devel. Center, Western Australia Dept. Mental Hygiene, 1974-75; mem. task force on emotionally disturbed children and adolescents Fla. Dept. Health and Rehabilitative Services, 1976-78; mem. advisory com. Fla. Mental Health/ Health Systems Tng. Program, 1977-78. Commr. Marinwood (Calif.) Community Service Dist., 1971-73; rep. So. region Australian Assistance Plan, Melbourne, 1973-74; mem. Prahran Social Action Com., 1973-74; mem. Blue Ridge Inst., So. Community Services Exec., 1977. Served with M.C., U.S. Army, 1959-62, USPHS, 1962-65. Fellow Am. Pub. Health Assn., Royal Soc. Health (U.K.); mem. Nat. Assn. Social Workers (chmn. health council San Diego chpt. 1968), Am. Acad. Polit. and Social Sci., Assn. Mental Health Adminstrs., Am. Soc. Pub. Adminstrn., Internat. Health Soc., Fla. Assn. Dist. Mental Health Bds. (exec. dir. rep. 1976-77). Address: 18502 Lynton Rd Shaker Heights OH 44122

WRIGHT, WILLIAM EDWARD, educator; b. Fairfield, Ala., Nov. 5, 1926; s. Cecil Augustus and Leila Myrtle (Greer) W.; student Long Beach City Coll., 1947-49; B.S., U. Colo., 1951, M.A., 1953, Ph.D., 1957; postgrad. U. Vienna, 1954-55; m. Norma Louise Lacy, Sept. 2, 1950; 1 dau., Mariellen Lacy. Instr. dept. history U. Minn., Mpls., 1957-59, asst. prof., 1959-62, asso. prof., 1962-73, prof., 1973—, dir. center for immigration studies, 1964-67, asso. dean internat. programs, 1969-70, asso. to v.p. internat. programs, 1970-76, dir. Center for Austrian Studies, 1977—. Democratic Farmer Labor candidate Minn. Senate, 1966, chmn. legis. task force, 1966-67, campaign mgr. Congressman Donald Fraser, 1968; mem. campaign com. Gov. Wendell Anderson, 1970. Served with AUS, 1945-47. Recipient awards McKnight Found., 1961, Phi Alpha Theta, 1967; Fulbright fellow, 1954-55, 62-63, Mem. AAUP, Am. Hist. Assn., Am. Assn. Advancement Slavic Studies, Am. Soc. 18th Century Studies, Mpls. Soc. Fine Arts, Mpls. Citizens League. Mem. Democratic-Farmer-Labor party. Author: Serf, Seigneur, and Sovereign: Agrarian Reform in Eighteenth-Century Bohemia, 1966. Home: 18200 Honeysuckle Ln Deephaven MN 55391 Office: 715 Social Sci Bldg U Minn Minneapolis MN 55455

WRIGLEY, WILLIAM, corp. exec.; b. Chgo., Jan. 21, 1933; s. Philip Knight and Helen (Atwater) W.; B.A., Yale, 1954; m. Alison Hunter, June 1, 1957 (div.); children—Alison, Philip, William; m. 2d, Joan Fischer, Mar. 26, 1970. With Wm. Wrigley Jr. Co., Chgo., 1956—, dir., 1960—, pres., chief exec. officer, 1961—; pres., dir. Wrigley Espana S.A. (Spain); dir. Wm. Wrigley, Jr. Co., Ltd. (Can.), The Wrigley Co. Ltd. (U.K.), The Wrigley Co. Pty. Ltd. (Australia), The Wrigley Co. (N.Z.) Ltd., New Zealand, Wrigley Philippines, Inc., Wrigley S.A. (France), Wrigley Co. (H.K.) Ltd. (Hong Kong), Wrigley & Co. Ltd., Japan, Wrigley Co. (East Africa) Ltd., Nat. Blvd. Bank Chgo., (Kenya), Wrigley N.V. (Netherlands); dir., mem. salary and auditing coms., com. non-mgmt. dirs. and spl. com. non-mgmt. dirs. Texaco, Inc.; dir., v.p., chmn. exec. com. Santa Catalina Island Co.; dir., chmn. exec. com. Chgo. Nat. League Ball Club. Bd. dirs. Wrigley Meml. Garden Found, Northwestern Meml. Hosp. Served from ensign to lt. (j.g.) USNR, 1954-56, lt. comdr. Res. Mem. Chgo. Hist. Soc., Field Mus. Natural History, Art Inst. Chgo., Navy League U.S., Wolf's Head Soc., Santa Catalina Island Conservancy (benefactor mem.), Nat. League Profl. Baseball Clubs, USC Oceanographic Assos., Delta Kappa Epsilon. Clubs: Chicago Yacht, Racquet, Saddle and Cycle, Tavern, Commercial (Chgo.); Lake Geneva (Wis.) Country, Lake Geneva Yacht; Brook (N.Y.C.); Catalina Island Yacht (hon. life). Office: 410 N Michigan Ave Chicago IL 60611

WROBLEY, RALPH GENE, lawyer; b. Denver, Sept. 19, 1935; s. Matthew B. and Hedvig (Lyon) W.; B.A., Yale, 1957; J.D., U. Chgo., 1962; m. Madeline C, Kearney, June 13, 1959; children—Kirk Lyon, Eric Lyon. With Bell Telephone Co. Pa., Phila., 1957-59; admitted to Mo. bar, 1962; mem. firm Stinson, Mag, Thomson, McEvers & Fizzell, Kansas City, Mo., 1962—, partner, 1965—; sec., dir. Gordon Johnson Industries, Inc., 1976—. Dir. Human Resources Corp., 1971; chmn. Pub. Housing Authority Kansas City, 1971-74; vice chmn. Mayor's Adv. Commn. on Housing, Kansas City, Mo., 1971-74; bd. govs. Citizens Assn., 1965—, mem. adv. com., 1966-69, 75—, mem. exec. com., 1969-75, vice chmn., 1971-75; mem. Council on Edn., 1975—, v.p., 1977—; bd. dirs., pres. Sam E. and Mary F. Roberts Found., 1974—. Recipient Outstanding Mem. award Yale club Kansas City, 1967. Mem. Am. Bar Assn., Mo. Bar, Lawyers Assn. Kansas City. Republican. Presbyterian (deacon). Clubs: Yale (pres. 1969-71), Carriage (Kansas City, Mo.). Home: 6242 Valley Rd Kansas City MO 64113 Office: 10 Main Center Kansas City MO 64105

WRONA, BERNARD JOHN, materials engr.; b. Joliet, Ill., Oct. 2, 1937; s. Paul P. and Mary Ann (Mechon) W.; B.S. in Metall. Engring., Ill. Inst. Tech., 1972, M.S., 1974; m. Janet L. Judnick, May 23, 1964; children—James, Paul, Kristi. Materials engr., materials sci. div. Argonne (Ill.) Nat. Lab., 1962—, prin. investigator in devel. of direct elec. heating apparatus, 1972—. Mem. Am. Nuclear Soc. Clubs: University. Contbr. articles in field to profl. jours. Home: 512 Tana Ln Joliet IL 60435 Office: 9700 S Cass Ave Argonne IL 60439

WRONE, DAVID ROGER, historian; b. Clinton, Ill., May 15, 1933; s. Harold and Esther (Matthews) H.; B.S., U. Ill., Urbana, 1959, A.M., 1960, Ph.D., 1964; m. Elaine Alley, Aug. 25, 1964; children—Elizabeth M., David A. Mem. faculty U. Wis., Stevens Point, 1964—, prof. history, 1975—; bd. dirs. Nancy McElroy Davis Fund History. Served with AUS, 1954-55. Mem. Hegelian Soc. Am., Orgn. Am. Historians, Wis. State Hist. Soc., Ill. Hist. Soc. Co-author: Who's the Savage: A Documentary History of the Mistreatment of the Native North Americans, 1973; also articles, chpts. in books. Home: 1518 Blackberry Ln Stevens Point WI 54481 Office: Hist Dept U Wis Stevens Point WI 54481

WROOLIE, MELVIN SIMON, mus. curator; b. Delaven, Minn., July 22, 1892; s. Simon S. and Margit S. (Scarvie) W.; student Luth. Normal Sch., Madison, Minn., 1914, also A.E.F. U., Beaune, France; B.A., St. Olaf Coll., 1922; postgrad. U. Minn., 1923. Tchr. rural schs., Minn., 1914-16; supt. schs., Bearsley, Minn., 1922-27, Lac qui Parle County, Minn., 1928-67; curator Lac qui Parle County Mus., Madison, Minn., 1967—; sec. Lac qui Parle County Hist. Soc., 1948—. Chmn., County Territorial Centennial, 1949, Minn. Statehood Centennial, 1958; bd. dirs. Madison Hosp. Served with AEF, World War I. Honored at Minn. State Fair Sch. Adminstrs. Recognition Day, 1955; recipient awards Order of North Star, 1958, 35 years or more as Sch. Adminstr., 1964, Christmas Seal Orgn., 1965, Good Neighbor award, 1966; named Outstanding Sr. Citizen Lac qui Parle County, 1967, Grand Marshall Centennial Parade, 1972. Mem. Am. Legion (Fifty Year award 1968), VFW. Lutheran. Kiwanian (lt. gov.; Shield award 1973). Home: 408 Park Ave Apt 2 Madison MN 56256 Office: County Mus S Hwy 75 Madison MN 56256

WU, HARRY PAO-TUNG, librarian; b. Chinan, Shantung, China, May 1, 1932; s. James Ching-Mei and Elizabeth Hsiao (Lu) W.; B.A., Nat. Taiwan U., Taipei, 1959; student Ohio State U., 1962; M.L.S., Kent State U., 1966; m. Irene I-Len Sun, June 23, 1961; children—Eva Pei-Chen, Walter Pei-Liang. Came to U.S., 1960. Archive and library asst. Taiwan Handicraft Promotion Center, Taipei, 1959-60; student asst. Kent State U. Library, 1960-61; reference librarian Massillon (Ohio) Pub. Library, 1964-65, acting asst. dir., 1965, asst. dir., head adult services, 1966; dir. Flesh Pub. Library, Piqua, Ohio, 1966-68; dir. St. Clair County Library System, Port Huron, Mich., 1968—; founder, dir. Blue Water Library Fedn., Port Huron, 1974—; pres. Mich. Library Film Circuit, Lansing, 1977—. Mem. Am., Mich. (chmn. library systems roundtable 1974-75) library assns., Detroit Suburban Librarians Roundtable. Clubs: Port Huron Internat., Rotary (dir. 1972-74). Home: 1518 Holland Ave Port Huron MI 48060 Office: 210 McMorran Blvd Port Huron MI 48060

WU, HSIN-HSIUNG, physician; b. Taiwan, China, Dec. 9, 1938; s. Seng Ping and Wang Yen (Wang) W.; came to U.S., 1967; M.D., Kaeshiung Med. Coll., Taiwan, China, 1964; m. Sally Hsimei, Jan. 1, 1966; children—Richard, Andrew. Intern Columbus-Cuneo Med. Center, Chgo., 1967-68; resident in anesthesiology U. Ill., Chgo., 1970-72; fellow in anesthesiology Rush Med. Coll., Chgo., 1972; instr. anesthesiology Med. Coll. of Va., Richmond, 1973-74; anesthesiologist, Annapolis Hosp., Wayne, Mich., 1974—. Diplomate Am. Bd. Anesthesiology. Fellow Am. Coll. Anesthesiologists; mem. Am. Soc. Anesthesiology. Buddhist. Contbr. numerous articles to profl. publs. Office: Dept Anesthesiology Annapolis Hosp Wayne MI 48184

WU, KENNETH KUN-YU, physician; b. Taiwan, July 6, 1941; s. Chuan and Chin-Piau (Yeh) W.; came to U.S., 1967, naturalized, 1976; M.D., Nat. Taiwan U., 1966; M.S. (Research fellow 1967—68), Yale U., 1968; m. Lung-Chin Shih, Mar. 29, 1969; children—Stanley, David. Intern, Bridgeport (Conn.) Hosp., 1968—69; in internal medicine U. Iowa, Iowa City, Washington U., St. Louis, 1969—71; NIH fellow in hematology U. Iowa, 1971—73, asst. prof. medicine, 1974-76; chief and attending physician coagulation and throbosis unit Rush-Presbyn.-St. Lukes Med. Center, Chgo., 1976—; asso. prof. Rush Med. Coll., 1976—. Served to 2d lt. Republic of China Army, 1966—67. Fellow A.C.P.; mem. Am. Soc. Hematology, Am. Assn. Immunologists, AAAS, Internat. Soc. Hematology, Internat. Soc. Thrombosis and Hemostasis, Cental Soc. Clin. Research, Am. Fedn. Clin. Research. Presbyn. Club: Room 600. Contbr. articles to profl. jours. Home: 1642 Robin Ln Glenview IL 60025 Office: 1753 W Congress Pky Chicago IL 60612

WU, TAI TE, educator; b. Aug. 2, 1935; M.B., B.S., U. Hong Kong, 1956; B.S. in Mech. Engring., U. Ill., Urbana, 1958; M.S. in Applied Physics, Harvard, 1959, Ph.D. in Engring. (Gordon McKay fellow) 1961; m. Anna Fang. Research fellow in structural mechanics Harvard, 1961-63, research fellow in biol. chemistry Med. Sch., 1964, research asso., 1965-66; research scientist Hydronautics, Inc., Rockville, Md., 1962; asst. prof. engring. Brown U., Providence, 1963-65; asst. prof. biomath. Grad. Sch. Med. Scis., Cornell U. Med. Coll., N.Y.C., 1967-68, asso. prof., 1968-70; asso. prof. physics and engring. scis. Northwestern U., Evanston, Ill., 1970-73, chmn. com. on biophysics, 1972—, acting chmn. dept. engring. scis., 1973, prof. physics and engring. scis., 1973-74, prof. biochemistry and molecular biology and engring. scis., 1974—. Mem. AAAS, Am. Phys. Soc., Am. Soc. Biol. Chemists, Soc. Microbiology, Biophys. Soc., Chgo. Assn. Immunology, N.Y. Acad. Scis., Soc. Indsl. and Applied Math., Sigma Xi, Tau Beta Pi, Pi Mu Epsilon. Recipient Progress award Chinese Engrs. and Scientists Assn. So. Calif., Los Angeles, 1971, Research Career Devel. award USPHS, NIH, 1974-79; C.T. Loo scholar China Inst., N.Y.C., 1959-60; Author: (with E.A. Kabat and H. Bilofsky) Variable Regions of Immunoglobulin Chains, 1976. Contbr. articles to profl. jours. Office: Dept Biochemistry and Molecular Biology Northwestern U Evanston IL 60201

WULF, GEORGE RICHARD, geologist, oil co. exec.; b. Clinton, Iowa, May 6, 1930; s. Richard Lyle and Bernice Margaret (Thomsen) W.; B.S., S.D. Sch. Mines, 1951, M.S., 1955; Ph.D., U. Mich., 1959, LL.B., 1964; m. Janis Marie Burrows, June 3, 1955; 1 dau., Jennifer. Geophysicist, Mobil Oil Co., Tripoli, Libya, 1955-63; sr. operating geologist Amoco, Casper, Wyo., 1963-64; cons. geologist, Casper, 1964-74; pres., chmn. bd. Wulf Oil Corp., Chadron, Nebr., 1974—. Served with M.I., U.S. Army, 1952-54. Mobil Oil scholar, 1954; U. Mich. research fellow, 1957-59. Certified profl. geologist. Fellow Geol. Soc. Am.; mem. Am. Assn. Petroleum Geologists, AAAS, Soc. Econ. Paleontologists and Mineralogists, Sigma Xi, Sigma Tau. Democrat. Lutheran. Clubs: Rotary, Elk. Editor Wyo. Geol. Soc. Guidebook, 1968. Contbr. articles on petroleum geology, stratigraphy to profl. publs. Home: 475 Cedar St Chadron NE 69337 Office: PO Box 946 Chadron NE 69337

WURFEL, DAVID OMER DRURY, educator; b. Seattle, May 22, 1929; s. Seymour W. and Violet Elizabeth (Mark) W.; student U. Philippines, 1947-48; B.A., San Diego State Coll., 1950; M.A., U. Calif., Berkeley, 1953; Ph.D. (Ford Found. fellow), Cornell U., 1960; m. Katherine M. Watada, June 6, 1964; children—Mark, Julia, Chris. Asst. prof. polit. sci. Internat. Christian U., Tokyo, 1959-62; asso. prof. polit. sci. U. Mo., Columbia, 1962-68; prof. polit. sci. U. Windsor (Ont.), Can., 1968—; vis. lectr. U. Singapore, 1964-65; vis. asso. prof. U. Mich., Ann Arbor, 1966-67. Mem. Boone County (Mo.) Com. for McCarthy, 1968; bd. dirs. Iona Coll., U. Windsor, 1970—. Served with U.S. Army, 1953-55. Can. Council grantee, 1970, 74, 75-76; Social Sci. Research grantee, 1961. Mem. Assn. Asian Studies (dir. 1973-75), Can. Soc. Asian Studies (exec. council 1974—), Can. Council Southeast Asian Studies (founding chmn. 1973-74), Can. Inst. Internat. Affairs (chmn. Windsor br. 1972-73). Mem. United Ch. of Canada. Contbr. to Government and Politics of Southeast Asia, 1964; U.S. and the Philippines, 1966; editor: Japan's Centennial, 1971; author: Philippine Government and Politics; contbr. articles on polit. sci. to profl. jours. Home: Rural Route 1 Harrow ON Canada Office: Dept Political Science U Windsor Windsor ON Canada

WUTZ, FRANKLIN CHARLES, nursing home adminstr.; b. Buffalo, Apr. 7, 1918; s. Frank Adam and Minnie (Lindeke) W.; student Woffard Coll., 1943-44, student Miami-Dade U., 1965-68; M.H.A., George Washington U., 1968; m. Vera Martha Sass, May 9, 1944; children—Nancy Wutz Snyder, Barry Keith. Adminstr. Fair Havens, Miami, Fla., 1964-73, Good Samaritan Home, Flanagan, Ill., 1973-74; adminstr. Lutheran. Sr. City, Columbus, Ohio, 1974—. Bus. adminstr. Christ Luth. Ch., N. Miami, Fla., 1958-62; bd. dirs. Friends, Miami, 1959-61. Served with AUS, 1941-45. Nat. Council Chs. grantee, 1964-65. Mem. Miami Council Chs. (dir. 1962-64), Ohio Nursing Home Assn. (preceptor 1976—), 72), Nat. Council on Aging, Gerontol. Soc., Nat. Geriatrics Soc., Am. Nursing Home Assn., Am. Assn. Homes for Aging, Am. Coll. Nursing Home Adminstrs., C. of C. Lutheran (pres. council 1966, 71). Office: 977 N Parkview Blvd Columbus OH 43219

WYATT, M(ELAINE) MILDRED, pub. relations cons.; b. Gary, Ind., Aug. 11, 1922; d. Mark E. and Stella (Wuletich) Wajagich; A.B., Ind. U., 1946. Reporter, night editor Logansport (Ind.) Pharos-Tribune, 1946-52; news supr., pub. relations dept. Ill. Inst. Tech. and IIT Research Inst., 1953-58; asso. editor Purchasing News & Elec./Electronic Procurement, 1958-60; mng. editor Indsl. Research mag., 1960-61; account exec. Donald Young Assos., 1961-63, Fulton-Morrissey Co., advt. and pub. relations, 1964-65, Griswold-Eshleman Co., advt. and pub. relations, 1965-68; v.p., dir. pub. relations K & A Advt., Inc., Chgo., 1968-69; pres., owner Wyatt Communications, Chgo., 1969—; guest lectr. indsl. pub. relations Roosevelt U., 1968—. Mem. pub. info. conf. com. Nat. Safety Council, 1973-75; mem. pub. relations com. Girl Scouts of Chgo., 1959-61; bd. dirs. Met. Chgo. YWCA, 1969-70, NCCJ, 1976—. Mem. Pub. Relations Soc. Am. (chmn. counselors sect.), Women's Advt. Club Chgo., Women in Communications (chpt. pres.), Publicity Club Chgo., Agrl. Editors Assn. (asso.). Author: How to Relate with Youth Various Publics, 1974. Office: One IBM Plaza Suite 4515 Chicago IL 60611

WYLIE, CHALMERS PANGBURN, congressman; b. Norwich, Ohio, Nov. 23, 1920; s. Chalmer C. and Margaret (Pangburn) W.; student Otterbein Coll., 1939-40, Ohio State U., 1940-43; LL.B., Harvard, 1948; m. Marjorie Ann Siebold, Sept. 19, 1964; children—Jacquelyn, Bradley. Admitted to Ohio bar, 1948; asst. atty. gen. State of Ohio, 1948; asst. atty. City of Columbus (Ohio), 1949-50, city atty., 1953-57; adminstr. Ohio Bur. Workmen's Compensation, 1957; 1st asst. to gov. Ohio, 1957-58; formerly partner firm Gingher & Christensen, Columbus; mem. Ohio Ho. of Reps., 1961-67; mem. 90th to 95th Congresses from 15th Ohio Dist. Past trustee Blue Cross Central Ohio, Inc. Served from pvt. to 1st lt. AUS, World War II. Decorated Silver Star, Bronze Star, Purple Heart, Croix de Guerre (France), Belgian Fouragier. Named One of 10 Men of Year, Columbus Citizen Jour., One of 5 Outstanding Young Men of Ohio, Nat. Jr. C. of C.; recipient Distinguished Service award Columbus Jr. C. of C., 1955. Mem. Ohio, Columbus bar assns., Am. Legion. Republican. Methodist (past trustee). Mason (33 deg.), Kiwanian. Home: 1019 Spring Grove Ln Columbus OH 43085 Office: House of Reps Washington DC 20515

WYMAN, AUSTIN LOWELL, lawyer; b. Chgo., July 14, 1899; s. Vincent Delwin and Ida (Phelps) W.; degree Harvard U., 1920; LL.B., Chgo. Kent Coll. Law, 1922; m. Helen Dorothy Smock, July 16, 1922; children—Patricia (Mrs. R.F. Thurrell), Roberta Gay (Mrs. John G. Lynch), Austin Lowell, Carol (Mrs. Norman Rosen), Ritchey Wyman Helpingstine (dec.). Admitted to Ill. bar, 1922, since practiced in Chgo.; mem. firm Cummings & Wyman, 1922-73; chmn. bd. S.E. Nat. Bank Chgo., 1960—. Mem. Ill. State Toll Hwy. Commn, 1955—, chmn., 1955-70; mem. Ill. Bldg. Authority, 1967-71; pres. Village of Glencoe (Ill.), 1960-68. Served with U.S. Army, World War I. Mem. Chgo. Bar Assn. (gov.), Law Club Chgo. (pres. 1964-65). Clubs: Executives, Economic, Commercial, Mid Day (Chgo.); Skokie Country (Glencoe). Home: 558 Glencoe Rd Glencoe IL 60022 Office: 69 Washington St Chicago IL 60602

WYMAN, MARVIN EUGENE, nuclear engr., educator; b. North Branch, Minn., Apr. 9, 1921; s. Einar Olaf and Clara (Swanson) W.; B.S. in Physics, St. Olaf Coll., Northfield, Minn., 1942; M.S. in Physics, U. Ill., 1943, Ph.D., 1950; m. Betty Louise Sexton, Mar. 12, 1955; children—Christina, Dorcas. Grad. teaching asst. physics U. Ill., 1942-44, 46-49; asst. prof. physics St. Olaf Coll., 1949-52, asso. prof., 1952-53; mem. staff Los Alamos Sci. Lab., 1953-58; prof. nuclear engring. and physics U. Ill. at Urbana, 1958-75, chmn. nuclear engring. program, 1965-75, asst. to dean engring. for long range planning, 1975—; cons. for UN at Mexican Nuclear Energy Commn., 1963. Served to lt. (j.g.) USNR, World War II. Mem. com. nuclear sci. Nat. Acad. Sci.-NRC, 1965-70, chmn. su com. research reactors, 1965-70; mem. fellowship bd. AEC, 1965-68, chmn., 1967-68. Fellow Am. Phys. Soc., Am. Nuclear Soc.; mem. Am. Soc. Engring. Edn.

(chmn. nuclear engring. div. 1967-68), Am. Inst. Physics, Sigma Xi, Tau Beta Pi. Home: 605 E Harding Dr Urbana IL 61801

WYMAN, PAUL BARTRAM, lawyer; b. Three Rivers, Mich., Oct. 8, 1913; s. Charles Bartram and Bertha (Gesaman) W.; student Kalamazoo Coll., 1932-35; LL.B., Duke U., 1938; m. Louise Cabell Warren, June 10, 1940; children—Warren Bartram, Michael Louis. Admitted to Colo. bar, 1939, Mich. bar, 1943; gen. law practice in Colo., 1939-42; pros. atty, Kalkaska County, Mich., 1943-55; spl. asst. atty. gen. Mich., 1950; asst. pros. atty. Wexford County, Mich., 1955-57, spl. pros. atty., 1962; city atty., City of Cadillac (Mich.), 1959-64; friend of ct. 28th Jud. Circuit of Mich., 1948—. Pres., Kalkaska Sch. Bd., 1943-46; exec. bd. Scenic Trails council Boy Scouts Am. Mem. Am., Mich., Wexford-Missankee (past pres.) bar assns., Am. Judicature Soc., Am. Rifle Assn., Mich. Assn. Professions, Mich. Friends of Ct. Assn. (exec. bd. 1977—). Clubs: Rotary (pres. 1958-59), Cadillac, Caberfce Ski, Masons (32 deg.). Contbr. articles to profl. publs. Home: 426 Crippen St Cadillac MI 49601 Office: Court House Annex Cadillac MI 49601

WYMAN, WILLIAM ARTHUR, musician, educator; b. Pitts., May 19, 1942; s. William Harper and Marian Kathern (Bode) W.; B.A., Bethany Coll., 1964; M.Mus., W.Va. U., 1967, D.Mus. Arts, 1971; postgrad. Westminster Choir Coll., 1974. Admissions counselor Bethany (W.Va.) Coll., 1964-66; tchr. vocal music North Hills Sch. Dist., Pitts., 1967-68; dir. Children's Opera Theater, W.Va. U., Morgantown, 1969-71; dir. choral activities Otterbein Coll., Westerville, Ohio, 1971-75; dir. choral activities Nebr. Wesleyan U., Lincoln, 1975—; dir. music Worthington (Ohio) United Presbyterian Ch., 1971-75, Christ United Methodist Ch., Lincoln, 1976—. Bd. dirs. Lincoln Community Concert Assn. NDEA fellow, 1966-67. Mem. Am. Choral Dirs. Assn., Music Educators Nat. Conf., Am. Guild Mus. Artists, AAUP, Alpha Sigma Phi. Home: 3941 Bel-Ridge Dr Lincoln NE 68521

WYMORE, JOHN BENJAMIN, realtor; b. Liberty, Mo., Dec. 7, 1925; s. Harold L. and Dora B. (Gray) W.; student pub. schs., Liberty; m. Carlida Breckenridge, Dec. 24, 1954; children—Ann B., Thomas G. Owner, mgr. Wymore & Son Co., Liberty, 1946-52, The JBW Co., Liberty, 1953—; founder, owner, mgr. Jesse James Bank Mus., Liberty, 1966—; lectr. on Jesse James to museums, hist. socs., clubs, orgns., 1966-71. Mem. Clay County (Mo.) Hist. Mus., 1965-75, bd. dirs., 1965-67; mem. Mo. Bicentennial Com., 1974-75, Lewis and Clark Trail Com., Clay County, 1968-73, Liberty Bicentennial Commn., 1976, Clay County Jail Com., 1976; past mem. bd. govs. Agrl. Hall of Fame. Served with AUS, 1944-46. Mem. Liberty C. of C. (dir. 1948-49), State Hist. Soc. of Mo. Methodist (chmn. ofcl. bd. 1969-71). Author: Good Bye, Jesse James, 1967; co-author Heritage of Liberty. Home: 741 Ridgeway Dr Liberty MO 64068 Office: 104 E Franklin St Liberty MO 64068

WYNN, GEORGE ALLAN, ednl. devel. specialist; b. Youngstown, Ohio, Sept. 9, 1945; s. Rudolph George and Marian Eleanor (Repko) W.; student U. Calif., Berkeley, 1963-65, U.S. Mil. Acad., 1965-66; B.S., Ohio State U., 1970, M.A., 1974; m. Helen Jeanette McGhee, Sept. 12, 1970. Instr. drafting and math. Columbus (Ohio) Tech. Coll., 1966-68, asst. to v.p., 1968-73; research asso., asso. project dir. Center for Vocat. Edn., Ohio State U., Columbus, 1973-77; exec. dir. Community Organizational Vocat. Ednl. Devel. Group, Columbus, 1976—; asso. dir. Sch. Studies Council of Ohio, Columbus, 1977—; sr. ednl. devel. specialist, tng. and curriculum expert Appalachia Ednl. Labs., Charleston, W.Va., 1977. Mem. Am. Ednl. Research Assn., Am. Personnel and Guidance Assn., Am. Coll. Personnel Assn., Ohio Chpt. Instructional Tech., Porsche Club Am. (pres. Mid-Ohio region). Designer, developer mgmt. assessment seminars. Home: 2315 Woodbrook Circle N Suite B Columbus OH 43223 Office: Room 143 Arps Hall 1945 N High St Columbus OH 43210

WYNN, WILLIAM THOMAS, constrn. co. exec.; b. Hartville, Mo., May 26, 1922; s. William Thomas and Tina Bertha (Russell) W.; B.S., Washington U., 1948; m. Rose E. Walker, Oct. 23, 1940; children—Cynthia (Mrs. James William Essman), Alison (Mrs. Steven Roy Wallis). With Brining & Co., C.P.A.'s, St. Louis, 1948-57, jr. partner, 1951-57; audit mgr. Arthur Young & Co., C.P.A.'s, St. Louis, 1957-63; with Bank Bldg. and Equipment Corp. Am., St. Louis, 1963—, controller, 1968-71, v.p., treas., 1971—. Served with 94th Inf. Div., AUS, 1942-45. C.P.A., Mo. Mem. Nat. Assn. Accountants, Am. Inst. C.P.A.'s, Mo. Soc. C.P.A.'s, Fin. Execs. Inst. Home: 13011 Tiger Lily Ct St Louis MO 63141 Office: 1130 Hampton Ave St Louis MO 63139

WYSE, HAROLD GABRIELE, elec. products mfg. co. exec.; b. Dayton, Ohio, June 3, 1918; s. James H. and Estella J. (Office) W.; student Sinclair Coll., 1936-37, Miami U., 1937-38, 39-40, U. Dayton, 1938-39; m. Alice E. Reck, May 8, 1943; children—Pamela Gay, Alicia Joy, Harold Gary. Project engr. Globe Industries, 1940-41; process engr. Aero Products div. Gen. Motors, 1941; v.p., gen. mgr. Wyse Labs., 1941-47; v.p., gen. mgr. Gad Jets Inc., 1947-53, pres., 1953—; v.p. Projects Unlimited, 1954-66; pres. Hed Realty, 1954—; pres. Asso. Tenical Sales, 1954—; chmn. bd. Automated Plastic Products, Inc. Dist. chmn. Republican Party. Bd. dirs. Grandview Hosp. Mem. IEEE, Dayton Engrs. Club, Sigma Alpha Epsilon. Mason (Shriner). Rotarian. Club: Miami Valley Golf. Patentee in field. Home: 5970 Frederick Rd Dayton OH 45414 Office: 3629 N Dixie Dr Dayton OH 45414

WYSLOTSKY, IHOR, engring. co. exec.; b. Kralovane, Czechoslovakia, Dec. 22, 1930: s. Ivan and Nadia (Alexiew) W.; came to U.S., 1958, naturalized, 1961; M.E., Advanced Sch. Aeros., Buenos Aires, Argentina, 1955; m. Maria Czechut, Nov. 22, 1958; children—Katria, Bohdan. Design engr. Kaiser Industries, Buenos Aires, Argentina, 1955-58; cons. design engr., Newark, 1959-64; chief engr. Universal Tool Co., Chgo., 1964-69; pres. CBC Devel Co., Inc., Chgo., 1969-74; pres. Thermoplastics Engring. Co., Chgo., 1972—; engring. adviser to bd. dirs. Biosystems Assos., Inc., La Jolla, Calif. Trustee Ukrainian Studies Dept., U. Ill. Mem. Brit. Engring. Assn. Plate River, Soc. Mfg. Engrs., Am-Israeli C. of C., Modern Plastics Inst. (mgmt. adv. panel), Package Inst./U.S.A. Club: Burnham Harbor Yacht. Patentee in field. Home: 3311 Montmartre Ave Hazel Crest IL 60429 Office: 14823 McKinley Posen IL 60469

WYSONG, WALTER LEE, mgmt. cons.; b. Dayton, Ohio, Feb. 20, 1929; s. William Walter and Elsie Lee (McCormick) W.; B.S., Ohio U., 1952, postgrad., 1954-56; m. Judith Ann Betts, July 13, 1952; children—Walter Mark, Shelley Ann, Jeffrey Lee, Tricia Marie. Successively indsl. engr., prodn. foreman, personnel asst., safety dir. Union Carbide Corp., Nat. Carbon Co., Fostoria, Ohio and Cleve., 1956-63; personnel dir. Am. Shipbldg., Cleve., 1963-66; v.p. Search Assos., Inc., Cleve., 1966-72, pres., chmn., 1972—; pres. W.L. Wysong Assos., Lakewood, Ohio, 1972—. Counselor, Montgomery County council Boy Scouts Am., 1942, com. chmn. Cleve. council, 1965-70; instr. YMCA, 1945—; pres. Jr. Achievement Co., 1945-47; bd. dirs. steering com. Cath. Hosp. Nurses Sch., Lorain, Ohio, 1965-66. Served with AUS, 1952-54. Mem. Theta Ki. Presbyn. (deacon, elder). Home: 26747 Russell Rd Bay Village OH 44140 Office: 12700 Lake Ave Lakewood OH 44107

WYSZYNSKI, RICHARD CHESTER, orgn. exec.; b. Chgo., Feb. 15, 1933; s. John Ignatius and Victoria (Gerlich) W.; Mus.B., Northwestern U., 1955, B. Music Edn., 1955; pupil Marcel Moyse, 1961-65; postgrad. U. So. Cal, 1965-66. Charter mem. Consol. Athletic Commn., Chgo., 1948, editor Sportrecord, 1948, exec. dir. commn., 1950—, liaison officer in charge exchange of data with Found. for Research on Nature of Man, 1968-70; producer, announcer Interplay radio sta. WHPK-FM, Chgo., 1973-76; mem. faculty DeLaSalle Inst., Chgo., 1952-56; chmn. music dept. Adult Edn. Centers, Chgo., 1957-60; mem. faculty Exptl. Coll., U. So. Calif., Los Angeles, 1972, Central YMCA Community Coll., Chgo., 1976, MONACEP, 1977—; solo flutist N.C. Symphony Orch., 1960-61, Shreveport (La.) Symphony Orch., 1961-62; asst. condr. nat. cos. Man of La Mancha, 1967-70; mus. dir. Cardinal Chamber Orch., Chgo., 1971—; mus. condr. Lincolnwood (Ill.) Community Theater. Mus. compositions dedicated in his honor. Rockefeller Found. grantee for music criticism, 1965. Mem. Am. Fedn. Musicians, Visual Spectrum Research Inst. (research mem.). Editor: Interplay mag., Chgo., 1951-54; music critic, columnist Old Town Voice, Chgo., 1962-65. Address: 851 N Leavitt St Chicago IL 60622

WYTE, WILLIAM C., surgeon; b. Detroit, Sept. 19, 1918; s. Konstatin Paul and Pauline (Kavalevich) W.; B.S. in Physics, Wayne State U., 1938, B.M., 1942. M.D., 1943; m. Geraldine M. Bird, June 17, 1944; children—William Constantine Jr., Collette Marie. Intern, Grace Hosp., Detroit, 1943, resident in surgery, 1947-50; surg. resident Gulfport Army Air Force Sta. Hosp., Gulfport, Miss., 1943-44; physician Packard Motor Car Co., 1943, Cadillac Motor Car Co., 1946-47; practice medicine specializing in gen. surgery, Mt. Clemens, Mich., 1950—; mem. active staff, sr. attending surgeon, former chmn. dept. surgery St. Joseph Hosp.; surg. cons. Selfridge AFB Hosp., Almont Community Hosp. Pres., Wyte Investment Corp., Mt. Clemens, 1962—; pres. BGW Investment Fund, Mt Clemens Surg. Assos. Bd. dirs. Macomb div. Am. Cancer Soc., 1955-60, pub. speaker, 1955—; asso. dir. Mich. Cancer Found., 1960—. Served from 1st lt. to capt., M.C., AUS, 1943-46. Fellow Am. Soc. Abdominal Surgeons, A.C.S., Am. Coll. Gastroenterologists; mem. AMA, Mich., Macomb County (pres. 1973-74) med. socs., Digestive Disease Found. (founder), Cath. Physicians Guild Detroit, Am. Geriatrics Soc., Mt. Clemens C. of C., Am. Vets., Wayne State U. Coll. Medicine Alumni Assn. (regional rep.), Detroit Cancer Club (founder). Phi Beta Pi. Roman Catholic. K.C., (4 deg.), Kiwanian (founder, 1st v.p. Mt. Clemens-L'Anse Creuse 1958). Home: 38616 Lakeshore Dr Mt Clemens MI 48045 Office: 236 S Gratiot St Mt Clemens MI 48043

WYTRWAL, JOSEPH ANTHONY, sch. adminstr.; b. Detroit, Oct. 24, 1924; s. Joseph and Nellie (Kadlof) W.; Ph.B., U. Detroit, 1949, M.Ed., 1950; M.Ed. (Beta Sigma Phi fellow), Wayne State U., 1954, B.A., 1957; M.A., U. Mich., 1955, Ph.D., 1958. Tchr., Cleveland Jr. High Sch., Detroit, 1952-54, Eastern High Sch., Detroit, 1954-60; tchr. Chadsey High Sch., Detroit, 1960-63, counselor, 1963-70, prin. evening sch., 1968-70; asst. prin. Mumford Sr. High Sch., Detroit, 1970-73; prin. Wilson Jr. High Sch., Detroit, 1973—; mem. faculties U. Detroit, 1956-59, Wayne State U., 1959-62; dir. Southeastern Mich. Regional Ethnic Heritage Studies Center, 1968-75; coordinator Wayne County Community Coll., 1968-70; columnist Polish Daily News, English edit., 1974—. Mem. citizens' adv. com. selection gen. supt. Detroit Pub. Schs., 1970; commr. Detroit Commn. on Community Relations, 1969-74; v.p. Polish Am. Congress, 1969-72, recipient certificate of Achievement Mich. div., 1971. Precinct del. 16th Democratic Dist. Orgn., 1971. Served with USNR, 1943-46. Recipient Coe Fellowship award U. Wyo., 1958. Mem. Polish Nat. Alliance, Polish Roman Catholic Union, Assn. Sons Poland, Polish Falcons, Polish Black Conf. (exec. v.p. 1971-72), Alliance Poles in Am., Polish Hungarian World Fedn., Smithsonian Instn., Schoolmen's Club, Polish Am. Hist. Assn., Phi Delta Kappa, Delta Tau Kappa. Author: America's Polish Heritage (Am. Heritage award), 1961; Poles in American History and Tradition, (Am. Heritage award), 1969; Poles in America, 1969; Behold! The Polish Americans, 1977. Editor-pub. Endurance Press, 1962—; asst. editor Polish American Studies, 1959-62. Home: 5695 Lumley St Detroit MI 48210 Office: 7735 Lane Detroit MI 48209

YACKEL, JOHN PETER, ednl. publishing co. exec.; b. Sanborn, Minn., Apr. 20, 1932; s. Ewald William and Marie Ernestine (Heydlauff) Y.; B.B.A., U. Minn., 1958; m. Eleanor Ruth Goehring, Aug. 4, 1956; children—Margaret, Peter, Carl, Jean. Incorporator, Am. Guidance Service, Inc., Mpls., 1957, gen. mgr., 1958-69, v.p., 1969-71, pres., 1971—; dir., sec. Psycan Ltd., Willowdale, Ont., Can., 1970—. Spl. adviser Nat. Forum Found. for Am. Edn., 1971—. Mem. Assn. for Supervision and Curriculum Devel., Am. Ednl. Research Assn., Nat. Council on Measurement in Edn. Lutheran. Patentee in field. Office: Am Guidance Service Inc Publishers Bldg Circle Pines MN 55014

YACKTMAN, VICTOR, publishing, real estate, utility cos. exec.; b. N.Y.C., July 14, 1905; s. Ignatz and Victoria (Darocha) Y.; student U. So. Cal., 1925-26; m. Pauline Matsoukas, Dec. 31, 1948; children—Donald Arthur, Eugenia Valerie, William Allen. Salesman various reference book, mag. pubs., Los Angeles, 1922-26; sales mgr., Butterick Publ. Co., Los Angeles, 1928, dist. mgr., Denver, 1929-30, regional mgr., Cleve., 1931-34; nat. sales mgr. Curtis Pub. Co., Cin., 1935-38; pres. Victill Corp., Glenview, Ill., 1939-74; real estate developer Glenview, 1954—; developer, owner Domestic Utility Services Co., Glenview, 1956—. Mem. Nat. Pub. Assn. (dir. central registry 1955-63), Chgo. Assn. Commerce and Industry. Clubs: Execs. of Chgo., Variety Internat. (life patron), Post and Paddock. Home: 133 Washington Rd Glenview IL 60025 Office: 2640 Golf Rd Glenview IL 60025

YAFFE, DOROTHY ANNE, speech pathologist; b. Omaha, Feb. 25, 1918; d. Harry and Fannie (Tatelman) Camel; B.S. in Edn., U. Omaha, 1962; M.S. in Speech Pathology, U. Neb., Omaha, 1968; m. Sol Yaffe, Apr. 7, 1943; children—Robert, Jane. Speech pathologist Omaha Pub. Schs., 1968; dir. speech and hearing dept. Neb. Meth. Hosp., Omaha, 1968—; founder, adviser Omaha Stroke Club; mem. cleft palate team Children's Hosp.; cons. speech and hearing Shared Services System. Mem. Council Jewish Women, Omaha. Mem. Am. Speech, Hearing Assn., Neb. Heart Assn. (dir. Douglas-Sarpy div.). Club: Highland Country. Home: 224 S 85th St Omaha NE 68114

YAGELLO, VIRGINIA ELIZABETH, librarian; b. Cleve., Sept. 10, 1919; d. John Adolph and Louise Sophy (Midura) Y.; A.B., Western Res. U. (now Case Western Res. U.), 1944; M.L.S., Carnegie Tech. Library Sch., 1950. Young adult librarian, Enoch Pratt Free Library, Balt., 1950-54; librarian U.S. Army Europe Spl. Services, France, Germany, Italy, 1954-59, command librarian Hdqrs. So. European Task Force, 1959-61; asst. to supr. dept. libraries Ohio State U., Columbus, 1961-63, head chemistry and physics libraries, asst. prof. library adminstrn., 1967-72, asso. prof., 1972—. Mem. Spl. Libraries Assn. (chpt. pres. 1971-72, chmn. chemistry div. 1974—, dir.), Am. Soc. Info. Sci. (chmn. membership and nominating com., 1970-71), Franklin County Library Assn. (v.p. 1970-71), Am. Women in Sci. (chpt. nominating com. 1977), Am. Chem. Soc. (Patterson-Crane award com. 1976—). Contbr. to publs. in field. Home: 3677 N High St Columbus OH 43214 Office: 140 W 18th Ave Columbus OH 43210

YAKURA, THELMA PAULINE MASTICOLA (MRS. JAMES N. YAKURA), librarian; b. Wilmington; d. Michael J. and Bertha (Blansfield) Masticola; B.A., U. Del., 1945; B.S. in L.S., Drexel Inst. Tech., 1946; m. James N. Yakura, Nov. 18, 1950; children—James Peter, Kristie. Reference asst. U. Pitts. Library, 1946; head, engring. library Carnegie Inst. Tech., 1947-51; children's librarian, head adult bookmobile Cuyahoga County Pub. Library, Cleve., 1952-55; asst. head bookmobile dept. Westwood Br., Dayton Pub. Library, 1956-57, head librarian, 1957-64; dir. Wright Library, Oakwood (Dayton), Ohio, 1964—. Mem. ALA, Ohio Assn. Sch. Librarians, Ohio Library Assn. (sec., coordinator library adminstrs' div. 1968-69, 73-75, chmn. staff orgns. round table 1970-71), Miami Valley Library Orgn. (steering com. 1972—), Oakwood Hist. Soc. (pres.), Phi Kappa Phi. Home: 1327 Carlwood Dr Miamisburg OH 45342 Office: 1776 Far Hills Ave Dayton OH 45419

YAMMINE, RIAD NASSIF, oil co. exec.; b. Hammana, Lebanon, Apr. 12, 1934; s. Nassib Nassif and Emilie (Daou) Y.; came to U.S., 1952, naturalized, 1963; B.S. in Petroleum Engring., Pa. State U., 1956; postgrad. Advanced Mgmt. Program, Harvard U., 1977; m. Beverly Ann Hosack, Sept. 14, 1954; children—Kathleen, Cynthia, Michael. Engr., Trans-Arabian Pipe Line Co., Saudi Arabia, 1956-61; with Marathon Pipe Line Co., 1961-75, mgr. Western div., Casper, Wyo., 1971-74, mgr. Eastern div., Martinsville, Ill., 1974-75; with Marathon Oil Co., 1975—, mgr. div. mktg. ops. Findlay, Ohio, 1975—, also officer, dir. various subs. Mem. ch. council, mem. finance com. First Luth. Ch., Findlay. Registerd profl. engr., Ohio. Mem. ASME, Am. Petroleum Inst. Republican. Club: Findlay Country. Patentee in field. Home: 624 Winterhaven St Findlay OH 45840 Office: 539 S Main St Findlay OH 45840

YANG, EASHY, elec. engr.; b. Republic of China, Mar. 4, 1941; s. Tsing-Liu and Lin-Yee (Chang) Y.; came to U.S., 1967; naturalized, 1977; m. Jeane C. Chen, Sept. 4, 1970; children—Angela, Jennifer. Research and devel. electronics engr. Engring. System Inc., Omaha, 1970-71; corp. elec. engr. Wilson Concrete Co., Omaha, 1972-74; sr. elec. engr. Hydrocarbon Transp. Inc., Omaha, 1974—. Registered profl. engr., Nebr. Mem. IEEE, Nat. Soc. Profl. Engrs., Sigma Xi. Contbr. articles to profl. jours. Home: 3223 S 130th Ave Omaha NE 68144 Office: 2223 Dodge St Omaha NE 68102

YANG, EUGENE LI CHUN, mech. engr.; b. Foochow, China, Feb. 13, 1935; s. Hsin Pao and Jean (Hwang) Yang; m. Cynthia Chang, June 12, 1960; children—Keegan, Kyle. B.M.E., Ohio State U., 1957, M.Sc., 1958, Ph.D., 1967. Registered profl. engr., Ohio, Staff engr. RCA Corp., Meadow Lands, Pa., 1966-70; prin. design engr. Bell & Howell Co., Chgo., 1970-72; engring. mgr. Addressograph Multigraph Corp., Cleve., 1973—. Sec. Cubscout Com., Northeast Ohio council Boy Scouts Am., 1975—. Mem. Audio Engring. Soc., Soc. Photographic Scientists and Engrs., ASME, Solid State Investment Club (pres. 1969), Phi Eta Sigma, Pi Tau Sigma, Tau Beta Pi, Pi Mu Epsilon. Benjamin Lamme scholar, 1956-57; Stillman Robinson fellow, 1958-59; Am. Contract Bridge League Nat. Master, 1975. Patentee audiovisual and reprographics products. Home: 8201 Westhill Dr Chagrin Falls OH 44022 Office: 19701 S Miles Rd Warrenville OH 44128

YANG, PATRICK YUHMIN, elec. engr.; b. Taiwan, China, Jan. 2, 1948; s. Ching-Tsung and A-Fong Yang; came to U.S., 1970, M.S. in Elec. Engring., U. Cin., 1972; Ph.D., Ohio State U., 1975; m. Shu-O Wu, Aug. 19, 1971; 1 son, Dennis Ted. Research asso. Ohio State U., 1972-75; project mgr./prin. engr. Life Systems, Inc., Cleve., 1975—. Mem. IEEE. Club: Toastmasters Internat. Home: 1724 Gladwin Dr Mayfield Heights OH 44124 Office: 24755 Highpoint Rd Cleveland OH 44122

YANKOSKI, JOHN JOSEPH, paper co. exec.; b. Shenandoah, Pa., Aug. 25, 1936; s. John Anthony and Helen Cecilia (Brochman) Y.; student Goldey Beacom Bus. Coll., 1958-60; B.S., Drexel U., 1965, M.B.A., 1967; m. Mary Louise Gicas, Aug. 30, 1959 (div. Aug. 1974); children—Melanie Ann, Carla Marie. Cost accountant Ludlow Mfg. Co., Del., 1960-62; chief div. accountant Nat. Vulcanized Fibre, paper products, Del., 1962-63; asst. contracts adminstr. All Am. Engring. Co., related aircraft products, Del., 1963-67; mgr. mktg. services Fox River Paper Co., Appleton, Wis., 1967—. Served with USMC, 1954-57. Mem. Am. Mktg. Assn., Direct Mail Mktg. Assn. (Silver Mailbox award 1973). Contbr. articles to profl. jours. Home: 2217 Sunrise Dr Appleton WI 54911 Office: 401 S Appleton St Appleton WI 54911

YANTIS, DANIEL LEE, credit union exec.; b. Kansas City, Mo., May 28, 1949; s. Harry Glen and Arlene Elizabeth (Roberts) Y.; student U. Mo., 1968-71; m. Kathleen Marie Mascal, May 6, 1972; children—Patricia Anne, Mary Anne. Treas., gen. mgr. Vendo Corp. Credit Union, Kansas City, Mo., 1971—. Bd. dirs. NoValEa YMCA. Mem. Credit Union Exec. Soc., Mo. Credit Union League (dir. 1976—), Mo. Central Credit Union (dir. 1974—). Club: Kiwanis. Home: 2700 NE 39th Terr Kansas City North MO 64117 Office: 10500 Barkley St Overland Park KS 66212

YANTIS, ETHEL MAY BEATY (MRS. NORVAL K. YANTIS), ednl. adminstr.; b. nr. Howard, Kans., Oct. 1, 1903; d. John S. and Margaret (Patterson) Beaty; B.A., Southwestern Coll., 1959; m. Norval K. Yantis, Apr. 4, 1923; children—John, Sharolyn Kay Yantis Lager. Tchr. elementary schs., Elk County, Kans., 1922-56, supt. schs., 1956-68, dir. sch. dist., dir. fed. projects, 1965-70. Mem. adoption com. Kans. State Reading Circle, 1960-61. Named Kans. Master Tchr., Kans. State Tchrs. COll., 1965. Mem. S.E. Kans. (pres. 1964-67), Kans. . Past (sec.-treas. 1969) county supts. assns., Howard C. of C., N.E.A., Kans. State Tchrs. Assn., Elk County Edn. Assn., P.E.O. (chpt. pres. 1964-66), Delta Kappa Gamma. Republican. Methodist (Sunday Sch. supt. 1940-50). Address: 853 Jefferson St Howard KS 67349

YANTIS, JOHN AUBREY, lawyer; b. Shelbyville, Ill., Apr. 11, 1927; s. Aubrey Leon and Josephine Headstrom (Frawley) Y.; B.A., Colo. U., 1950; J.D., U. Colo., 1952; m. Dorothy MacNiall Tomlinson, June 15, 1950; children—Margaret (Mrs. A.W. Fathauer), Robert T., Elizabeth F. (Mrs. T.E. Schafer). Admitted to Ill. bar, 1952, U.S. Dist. Ct. for Eastern Ill., 1961; mem. firm Yantis & Yantis, Shelbyville, 1952-73, Yantis & Freeman, Shelbyville, 1975—; states atty., Shelby County, 1956-60; former asst. atty. gen. State of Ill.; Atty. Lake Land Coll., Mattoon, Ill., 1966—. Vice pres. Lincoln Trails council Boy Scouts Am., 1968—, Silver Beaver award; bd. dirs. ARC, 1955-65, Shelby County Meml. Hosp., 1967—. Served with USNR, 1945-46. Fellow Am. Acad. Matrimonial Lawyers; Am. Coll. Probate Counsel; mem. Am., Ill. (bd. govs. 1963-69, 75-77, mem. assembly 1970-77), Shelby County (pres., sec.) bar assns., Ill. Bar Found. (dir. 1973-76, v.p. 1975-78), Shelbyville C. of C., Phi Delta Phi, Beta Theta Pi. Methodist (chmn. bd. 1963-65). Kiwanian (dist. lt. gov. 1970-71). Home: 207 N Washington St Shelbyville IL 62565 Office: 304 E Main St Shelbyville IL 62565

YANTIS, JOHN THOMAS, ednl. adminstr.; b. Winfield, Kans., Nov. 13, 1936; s. Norval K. and Ethel Mae (Beaty) Y.; B.S. in Edn., Kans. State Coll. at Pittsburg, 1959, M.S., 1962; Ed.D. in Ednl. Adminstrn., U. Wyo., 1968; m. Lois Jane Kirk, June 27, 1959;

children—Cynthia Sue, Deborah Kay. Prin. elementary sch. Grenola, Kans., 1959-60, Moline, Kans., 1960-62, Winfield, Kans., 1963-65; vice prin. high sch. Winfield, Kans., 1965-67; asso. prof. Central Mich. U., Mt. Pleasant, 1968-72, dir. Inst. Personal and Career Devel., 1972—. Named Adviser of Year, Mich. Student Edn. Assn., 1970. Mem. NEA (pres. local chpt. 1961, 64), Nat. Univ. Extension Assn., Phi Delta Kappa (pres. local chpt. 1974), Kappa Delta Pi (pres. local chpt. 1967), Sigma Tau Gamma. Contbr. articles to profl. jours. Home: 607 S Main St Mt Pleasant MI 48858 Office: Rowe Hall Central Michigan University Mt Pleasant MI 48858

YAO, JOSEPH HUNG, phys. therapist; b. Hanchu, China, Jan. 8, 1935; s. Stephen C. and Pei-Hsing (Shen) Y.; came to U.S., 1958, naturalized, 1969; B.A., Tamkang Coll., Republic of China, 1955; postgrad. U. Madrid (Spain), 1955-56, U. Barcelona (Spain), 1956-58; B.A., Loras Coll., 1961; certificate phys. therapy U. Iowa Sch. Medicine, 1963; certificate acupuncture China Med. Coll., Republic of China, 1973; m. Jessie Lee Collingsworth, Dec. 26, 1964; children—Dana, David, E. Stephen. Staff phys. therapist Univ. Hosps., Iowa City, 1963-64; chief phys. therapist St. Mary's Hosp., Streator, Ill., 1964-66; dir. phys. therapy dept. St. Therese Hosp., Waukegan, Ill., 1966-70; staff phys. therapy dept. VA Hosp., North Chicago, Ill., 1970—, dir. phys. therapy dept., 1974—; clin. instr. Northwestern U. Med. Sch., 1975—, Chgo. Med. Coll., 1975—; lectr. on acupuncture to univs., various civic groups; past chmn. and bd. dirs. Internat. Study Group for Acupuncture and Related Energy Based Therapeutics. Mem. Am. Phys. Therapy Assn., Nat. Soc. Crippled Children and Adults, Am. Center Chinese Medicine, Acupuncture Research Inst., Am. Acupuncture Assn. Author: The Selected Acupuncture Points, 1972. Home: 2249 N Sheridan Rd Waukegan IL 60085 Office: Phys Therapy Dept VA Hosp North Chicago IL 60064

YAP, CHONG-BUN, neurologist; b. Amoy, Fukien, China, Apr. 2, 1930; s. Chin-Chay and Ben-Chu (Chua) Y.; came to U.S., 1959, naturalized, 1973; M.D. cum laude, U. Santo Tomas, 1958; m. Le-Kheng Chua, July 6, 1958; children—Renee Mei, Eric Wei. Intern, Santo Tomas U. Hosp., Manila, Pilippines, 1957-58; resident in neurology U. Louisville Hosp., 1959-62; neurology fellow, Montreal (Que., Can.) Neurol. Inst., 1962-64; instr., Louisville U., 1964-65; asst. prof., Northwestern U., Chgo., 1965-75; chmn. dept. medicine, Henrotin Hosp., 1976-77, pres. med. staff, 1978; dir. EEG dept. Swedish Covenant, Bethesda Hosps. Diplomate Am. Bd. Neurology. Certified Am. Bd. of Qualification in Electroencephalography, Inc. Fellow Am. Acad. Neurology; mem. AMA, Am. Assn. Electromyography and Electrodiagnosis, Am. Epilepsy Soc. Contbr. articles to med. jours. Home: 245 Sheridan Rd Kenilworth IL 60043 Office: 9701 Kenton Dr Skokie IL 60076

YAP, ENRIQUE TAN, surgeon; b. San Fernando, P.I., Oct. 9, 1937; s. Intong and Romana Rodriguez (Tan) Y.; A.A., U. Santo Thomas (Manila), 1948, B.S., 1950, M.D., 1953; m. Bette Limestahl, Jan. 27, 1956; children—Elizabeth Ann, Enrique Louis, Mary Leslie. Intern St. Laurence Hosp., Lansing, Mich., 1960-61, resident Maumee Valley Hosp., Toledo, 1955-58, Mo. State Sanitorium, Mt. Vernon, 1958-59, Galesburg (Ill.) Research Hosp., 1960; group practice Hoopeston (Ill.) Med. Center, 1961; practice medicine specializing in surgery, Metropolis, Ill., 1962—; mem. staff Massac Meml. Hosp., Hoopeston, pres. med. staff, 1969, 75; mem. staff Western Bapt. Hosp., Lourdes Hosp., Paducah, Ky. Bd. dirs. Massac Mental Health Center, Quadricounty Dept. Pub. Health. Diplomate Am. Bd. Surgery. Fellow A.C.S., Internat. Coll. Surgeons; mem. So. Ill. Surg. Soc., Massac County Med. Soc. (pres. 1968), C. of C., Tau Mu Sigma Phi. Republican. Roman Catholic. Elk, Rotarian (v.p. 1968, pres. 1969-70). Club: Metropolis Country. Home: Rural Route 2 Metropolis IL 62960 Office: 510 W 10th St Metropolis IL 62960

YASHON, DAVID, educator; b. Chgo., May 13, 1935; s. Samuel and Dorothy (Cutler) Y.; B.S., in Medicine, U. Ill., 1958, M.D., 1960; m. Myrna D. Foreman, Dec. 29, 1957; children—Jaclyn, Lisa, Steven. Intern, U. Ill., 1961, resident, 1961-64, asst. in neuroanatomy, 1960; clin. instr. neurosurgery, U. Chgo., 1965-66; asso. attending neurosurgeon Cook County Hosp., Chgo., 1965-66; asst. prof. neurosurgery, Case-Western Reserve U., Cleve., 1966-69; asso. prof. neurosurgery Ohio State U., Columbus, 1969-74, prof., 1974—, co-investigator Acute Spinal Cord Injury Center, asst. dir. postdoctoral tng. in neurol. surgery; cons. Med. Research and Devel. Command U.S. Army; mem. Nat. Paraplegia Found., Neurology B. Study Sect. NIH. Served to capt. USAR, 1961-67. Diplomate Am. Bd. Neurol. Surgery. Fellow Royal Coll. Surgeons Can. (certified), A.C.S.; mem. AMA, Am. Physiol. Soc., Congress Neurol. Surgeons, Am. Assn. Anatomists, Ohio State Med. Soc., Ohio State, Canadian Neurosurg. Socs., Am. Assn. Neurol. Surgeons, Research Soc. Neurol. Surgeons, Acad. of Medicine of Columbus and Franklin County, Columbus Surg. Soc., Soc. for Neurosci., Soc. Univ. Surgeons, Am. Acad. Neurology, Assn. for Academic Surgery, Am. Acad. Neurol. Surgery, Am. Assn. for the Surgery of Trauma, Central Surg. Soc., Sigma Xi. Contbr. articles to publs. Home: 5735 Saranac Dr Columbus OH 43227 Office: 410 W 10th Ave Columbus OH 43210

YASSIN, ROBERT ALAN, art mus. dir.; b. Malden, Mass., May 22, 1941; s. Harold Benjamin and Florence Gertrude (Hoffman) Y.; B.A., Dartmouth Coll., 1962; M.A., U. Mich., 1964; postgrad. Yale U., U. Mich.; m. Marilyn Kramer, June 9, 1963; children—Frederic Giles, Aaron David. Asst. to dir. U. Mich. Mus. Art, 1964-65, asst. to dir., 1971-73, asso. and acting dir., 1973; Ford fellow Yale U. Art Gallery, 1966-68; instr. art history U. Mich., 1970-73; chief curator Indpls. Mus. Art, 1973-75, acting dir., 1975, dir., 1975—; adj. prof. Herron Sch. Art, Ind. U., 1976—. Adv. council Internat. Center Indpls.; mem. bd. Indpls. Consortium for Urban Edn., 1976—, Ensemble Music Soc., Indpls., 1976—. Samuel H. Kress Found. fellow, 1968-70. Mem. Am. Assn. Museums, Assn. Art Mus. Dirs., Am. Assn. State and Local History, Midwest Mus. Assn., Am., Midwest coll. art assns., Nat. Trust Historic Preservation. Club: Rotary (Indpls.). Editor Yale U. Art Gallery Bull., 1966-68, U. Mich. Mus. Art Bull., 1970-73; editor: Durer's Cities, Nuremberg and Venice, 1971; Art and the Excited Spirit, 1972. Home: 2525 Blue Grass Dr Indianapolis IN 46208 Office: 1200 W 38th St Indianapolis IN 46208

YATES, CURTIS HUNTER, savs. and loan exec.; b. Water Valley, Ky., Jan. 25, 1913; s. Sherman Curtis and Grace Willie (Weaks) Y.; grad. Detroit Bus. Inst., 1939; student Detroit Inst. Tech., 1946; postgrad. Ind. U., 1951-53; m. Evaline D. Smith, Nov. 5, 1972; children—Linda Christine, Ronald Curtis, Constance Kay, Sally Ann, John Thomas. Messenger, file clerk Surety Fed. Savs. & Loan Assn., Detroit, 1939-41, teller, 1941-42, asst. v.p., 1949-56, asst. sec.-treas., 1956-57, sec.-treas., 1957-68, pres., mng. officer, 1968—, also dir. Served with AUS, 1942-45. Mem. Soc. Real Estate Appraisers, Constrn. Industries Credit Group, United N.W. Realty Assn., Mortgage Bankers Assn. Mich., Builders Assn. Met. Detroit, Greater Detroit C. of C. Presbyn. (trustee 1968—). Rotarian. Home: 31805 Westlady Rd Birmingham MI 48010 Office: 27255 Lahser Rd Southfield MI 48034

YATES, SIDNEY R(ICHARD), congressman, lawyer; b. Chgo., Aug. 27, 1909; s. Louis and Ida (Siegel) Y.; Ph.B., U. Chgo., 1931; J.D., 1933; m. Adeline Holleb, June 24, 1935; 1 son, Stephen R. Admitted to Ill. bar, 1933; asst. atty. for Ill. State Bank Receiver, 1935-37; asst. atty. gen. attached to Ill. Commerce Commn. as traction atty., 1937-40; mem. 81st to 87th, 89th to 95th Congresses from 9th Ill. Dist. U.S. del. UN Trusteeship Council with rank of ambassador, 1963-64. Served to USNR, 1944-46. Mem. Am. Ill., Chgo. bar assns., Decalogue Soc. Laws. Democrat. Jewish. Clubs: City, Bryn Mawr Country. Home: 3500 Lake Shore Dr Chicago IL 60657 Office: 219 S Dearborn Chicago IL 60604

YATES, WILLIAM MILLER, lawyer; b. Chgo., Feb. 26, 1913; s. William Henry and Eleanor Adelaide (Miller) Y.; student So. Meth. U., 1929-30; B.S. in Chem. Engring., Washington U., St. Louis, 1933, M.S. in Chemistry, 1935; m. Dorothy LaVerne Langdon, Oct. 7, 1939; children—Susan G. (Mrs. Henry B.R. Beale), Thomas V., Samuel L. Asst. instr. Washington U., St. Louis, 1933-35; admitted to Mich. bar 1943; with Dow Chem. Co., Midland, Mich., 1935—, metallurgist, 1943-45, patent lawyer, 1945-55, dir. patent dept., 1955-72, gen. patent counsel, 1972—. Mem. Family Service Agy., 1942-45; v.p. Midland Symphony Orch. Soc., 1970-74; mem. Mich. Orch. Assn., chmn. lawyers campaign Midland Hosp. 1970; bd. fellows Saginaw Valley State Coll., 1968—. Recipient Engring. Alumni prize Washington U., 1933. Mem. U.S. Supreme Ct. Bar, State Bar Mich., Am., Midland County (pres. 1948-49) bar assns., Am., Mich. (nat. councilman 1968-69) patent law assns., Assn. Corp. Patent Counsel, Am. Judicature Soc., Am. Arbitration Assn., Am. Chem. Soc., Am. Inst. Chemists, Glen Lake Assn., Sigma Xi, Tau Beta Pi. Presbyn. (elder, trustee 1946-55). Clubs: Midland Country, Saginaw Valley Torch (pres. 1973-74). Contbr. articles to profl. jours. Home: 27 Lexington Ct Midland MI 48640 Office: 2030 Dow Center Midland MI 48640

YAU, STEPHEN SIK-SANG, educator; b. Wusei, Kiangsu, China, Aug. 6, 1935; s. Pen-Chi and Wing-Chun (Shum) Y.; B.S., Nat. Taiwan U., 1958; M.S., U. Ill. at Urbana, 1959, Ph.D., 1961; m. Vickie Liu, June 14, 1964; children—Andrew, Philip. Came to U.S., 1958, naturalized, 1968. Asst. prof. elec. engring. Northwestern U., 1961-64, asso. prof., 1964-68, prof., 1968-70, prof. elec. engring. and computer scis., 1970—, chmn. dept. computer scis., 1972-77, chmn. dept. elec. engring. and computer sci., 1977—. Trustee Nat. Electronics Conf., 1965-68; mem. Joint Computer Conf. Bd., 1972-73; gen. chmn. Nat. Computer Conf. and Expn., Chgo., 1974. Fellow IEEE (conf. chmn. 1st ann. computer conf. 1967, gen. chmn. 1st internat. conf. on computer software and applications 1977), Franklin Inst. (life; Louis E. Levy medal 1963); mem. IEEE Computer Soc. (pres. 1974-75, chmn. confs. and meeting com. 1970, mem. governing bd. 1967-76), Am. Fedn. Info. Processing Socs. (dir. 1972—, mem. nominations com. 1973-75, mem. exec. com. 1974-76), Assn. Computing Machinery, Soc. Indsl. and Applied Math., AAAS, Am. Soc. Engring. Edn., Sigma Xi, Eta Kappa Mu, Pi Mu Epsilon. Contbr. numerous articles to profl. jours. Patentee in field. Home: 2609 Noyes St Evanston IL 60201 Office: Dept Elec Engring and Computer Sci Northwestern U Evanston IL 60201

YAW, PETER BARNETT, surgeon, educator; b. Cin., July 31, 1937; s. Owen Foley and Margaret Emelia (Hack) Y.; B.S., Ohio U., 1959; M.D., U. Cin., 1963; m. Marlene Marie Bura, Feb. 3, 1962; children—Rebecca Lynn, Michelle Emelia. Intern, U. Cin., 1963-64, resident surgery, 1964-68, 69-71; asso. prof. surgery Ind. U., Indpls., 1971—; pvt. practice surgery Indpls., 1972—; treas. Glover & Assos., Indpls., 1973—. Served with M.C., AUS, 1968-69. Decorated Bronze Star. Diplomate Am. Bd. Surgery, Am. Bd. Thoracic Surgery. Fellow A.C.S. (chmn. com. trauma Ind. div. 1975); mem. Am. Trauma Soc. (pres. Ind. div. 1974—), AMA, Am. Thoracic Soc., Phi Beta Kappa, Alpha Omega Alpha, Pi Kappa Epsilon, Sigma Chi. Club: Indpls. Athletic. Office: 960 Locke St Indianapolis IN 46204

YAW, WILLIAM HARVEY, agrl. economist; b. Iowa Falls, Iowa, Feb. 3, 1921; s. Harvey Edwin and Margaret (Wyss) Y.; grad. Ellsworth Jr. Coll., Iowa Falls, 1940; B.S. in Agrl. Econs., Iowa State U., 1943; grad. USAF Statis. Control Sch., Harvard U., 1945; M.Agrl. Econs., Purdue U., 1948; m. Genevieve Edith Ries, June 11, 1943; children—William, Stephen, Robert, Richard, Randall. Owner, Farm Clinic, Galesburg, Ill., 1948—. Mem. Galesburg City Planning Commn., 1968-71. Served as 1st lt. USAAF, 1943-45. Mem. Am. Simmental Assn. (founding trustee, chmn. 1st rules com.), Nat. Planning Assn. (agr. com., nat. land use subcom., rural devel. subcom.), Common Cause, Am. Farm Econ. Assn., Am. Soc. Agrl. Engrs., Soil Conservation Am., Nat. Economists Club, Farm House Frat. Presbyn. Rotarian. Address: 207 Hill Arcade Galesburg IL 61401

YEATES, CHARLES HERBERT, hosp. adminstr.; b. Chichester, Sussex, Eng., July 8, 1916; s. Charles and Amy (Yates) Y.; student London (Eng.) U., 1934-38; m. Esther Hagen, Sept. 27, 1975; children—Penelope Ann, Alan Hugh. Came to U.S., 1951, naturalized, 1958. Adminstrv. asst., local govt. service, Chichester, 1938-39; adminstr. Devizes Hosp., Wilts, Eng., 1948-51; accountant Allis Chalmers Mfg. Co., La Porte, Ind., 1951-55; adminstr. Paul Oliver Meml. Hosp., Frankfort, Mich., 1955-64, Allegan (Mich.) Gen. Hosp., 1964-75; health care cons., 1975—. Vice chmn. West Mich. Comprehensive Health Planning Unit. Commr. Sleeping Bear Nat. Lakeshore Adv. Commn.; mem. Frankfort City Council, 1962-64, mayor pro-tem, 1963-64; chmn. Crippled Children's Commn., Mich.; mem. adv. council heart, stroke and cancer Mich. State U. Sch. Medicine. Chmn. Benzie County Republican Party, 1958-64; chmn. Allegan County Republican Com., 1966-73; del. Rep. Nat. Conv., 1968. Served to capt. med. service Brit. Army, 1939-48. Fellow Am. Coll. Hosp. Adminstrs., Faculty of Bldg. (Eng.); mem. Inst. Hosp. Adminstrs. Eng., Mich. Hosp. Assn. (v.p. 1961-62, trustee 1962-65, treas. 1969-74, chmn. legislative com.), Frankfort C. of C. (past pres.), Internat. Platform Assn. Mason (Shriner), Rotarian (past pres. Allegan and Frankfort, dist. gov.). Home: 1436 Roxburgh Ave East Lansing MI 48823 Office: 505 Stoddard Bldg Lansing MI 48933

YEE, TEODORICO CHIONG, pharm. co. mktg. exec.; b. Madridejos, Cebu, Philippines, June 30, 1933; s. Lucio Ah and Mena Montano (Chiong) Y.; came to U.S., 1973; B.B.A., U. East, Manila, Philippines, 1955; m. Elsa Galvez, Jan. 4, 1975. Fin. analyst Mobil Oil Co., Manila, Philippines, 1959-63; coordinator U. East C.P.A. Rev. Sch., 1963-65; asst. budget supr. Iligan Integrated Steel Mills Inc., Manila, 1965-66; asst. to treas. Colgate-Palmolive Co., Manila, 1966-68; finance mgr. Tupperware div. Rexall Inc., Manila, 1968-69; v.p., gen. mgr. G. D. Searle Inc., Manila, 1969-73, mgr. mktg. adminstrn. G.D. Searle Internat. Co., Skokie, Ill., 1973—; asst. prof. accounting Coll. Bus. Adminstrn. U. East, 1963—. C.P.A., Philippines. Mem. Philippine Inst. C.P.A.'s., Am. Mgmt. Assn. Clubs: Rotary, Toastmasters News editor Dawn, U. East, 1953-55. Home: 1715 Queensbury Circle Hoffman Estates IL 60172 Office: G D Searle Internat Co 4711 Golf Rd Skokie IL 60076

YEH, PAI TAO, educator; b. Canton, China, Feb. 5, 1920; s. Yun Sun and Shu Yen (Tsai) Y.; came to U.S., 1948, naturalized, 1961; B.S., Nat. Checkiang U., China, 1943; M.S., Purdue U., 1949, Ph.D., 1953; m. Ching Siang Tang, Aug. 12, 1951; children—Sophia, Shirley. Asst. engr. Checkiang Waterway Engring. Office, 1943-44; engr. Kwok Wah Engring. Devel. Co., Kuming-Shanghai, China, 1944-48; research engr. Purdue U., West Lafayette, Ind., 1953—, asst. prof., 1959-65, asso. prof. 1965—; cons. Photog. Interpretation Research Div. U.S. Army, Terrestrial Scis. Center, 1969—, J.W. Sih & Assos., Inc., 1970—, U.S. Army C.E., 1977—. Bd. dirs. Midwest Chinese Student and Alumni Service. Mem. Am. Mil. Engrs., Am. Photogrammetry Engring., AAAS, Am. Soc. for Engring. Edn., Am. Soc. Profl. Engrs., Sigma Xi. Methodist. Producer various engring. maps. Home: 1718 Sheridan Dr West Lafayette IN 47906

YELLAND, WAYNE DOUGLAS, chemist; b. Negaunee, Mich., Sept. 4, 1929; s. Arnold Edwin and Pearl Mae (Burrows) Y.; A.B., No. Mich. U., 1951; postgrad. Northwestern U. Dental Sch., 1951-53; m. Winifred Jayne Van Luvender, Dec. 24, 1959; children—Brian Harry, Stephen Paul, Gregory Andrew, Elizabeth Jayne, Richard Wayne. With Dearborn Chem. Co., Chgo., 1953-60; new products office mgr., salesman, chemist Inland Chem., Ft. Wayne, Ind., 1960-65; field chemist, salesman, project engr. Kellermeyer Chem., Toledo, 1965-72; self-employed water chemist, Gwinn, Mich., 1973—. Active in youth program, Ft. Wayne, 1964-65; adult leader, committeeman Boy Scouts Am., Toledo, 1966-68; mem. Forsyth Singers, Negaunee City Band, Gwinn Community Band; precinct worker Republican party, West Toledo, 1965-70. Fellow Am. Inst. Chemists; mem. Am. Chem. Soc., Universal Council Engrs., Toledo Tech. Soc. Episcopalian. Mason (32 deg., Shriner). Address: Rural Route Box 94 Mehl Lake Gwinn MI 49841

YEN, SHING IE, orthopedic surgeon; b. Taiwan, China, July 17, 1939; s. Hsin H. and Pau Z. (Lo) Y.; came to U.S., 1968; naturalized, 1977; M.D., Kaohsiung (Taiwan) Med. Coll., 1965; m. Shu L. Su, Dec. 23, 1966; children—Esmond, Judia, Eugene. Practice medicine specializing in orthopedic surgery, Blue Island, Ill., 1973—; owner partner Pronger-Smith Clinic, Blue Island, 1975—; mem. active staff St. Francis Hosp., Blue Island, Ill., 1977—; orthopedic cons. Oak Forest (Ill.) Hosp. Diplomate Am. Bd. Orthopedic Surgery. Fellow Internat. Coll. Surgeons, A.C.S., Am. Acad. Orthopedic Surgery. Home: 12303 S Oak Park Ave Palos Heights IL 60463

YENERICH, GEORGE WESLEY, ednl. adminstr., fund raising cons.; b. Ashton, Ill., June 6, 1926; s. Wesley H. and Minnie (Krug) Y.; B.A. cum laude, North Central Coll., Naperville, Ill., 1947; M.B.A., U. Wis., 1955; m. Jeanne A. Callagan, June 5, 1947; children—Ann (Mrs. T.E. Essig), Alan, Barbara (Mrs. R.A. Stengard, Jr.), Beth. Statis. clk. Hotpoint div. Gen. Electric Co., Chgo., 1947-49, supr. statis. sect., 1949-51, supr. accounting, Milw., 1951-55, mgr. gen. accounting, Chgo., 1955-59, mgr. budgets and measurements, 1959-61; dir. pub. affairs and devel., North Central Coll., Naperville, Ill., 1961-71; cons. Ill. Sch. Cons. Service, Naperville, 1971-72; dir. devel. George Williams Coll., Downers Grove, Ill., 1972—; pres. Rich Rustic Homes, Three Lakes, Wis.; chmn. bd. Yenerich's Food Store Inc. (Al's Super Valu), Three Lakes. Commr. Park Dist., 1967-71; pres. Naperville Community Fund., 1965-66; bd. dirs. Naperville YMCA, pres. 1970. Named Outstanding local Jaycee of Ill., 1959-60. Mem. Naperville Jr. C. of C. (pres. 1960-61), Naperville C. of C. (pres. 1964-65), Council for Advancement and Support of Edn., Men's Assn. North Central Coll. (dir., sec.). N. Central Coll. Alumni Assn. (dir. 1960-63), Pub. Relations Soc. Am. (accredited), Pi Gamma Mu. Republican. United Methodist (supt. ch. sch., rep. Naperville Council Chs., pres. 1963-64). Lion (pres. 1968-69). Club: Y's Mens (charter pres. 1965) (Naperville). Home: 625 Thornwood Dr Naperville IL 60540 also Route 1 Three Lakes WI 54562 Office: 555 31st St Downers Grove IL 60540 also 625 Superior St Three Lakes WI 54562

YESNER, MICHAEL ALAN, advt. and mktg. exec.; b. Chgo., Aug. 12, 1943; s. Sol J. and Sophie (Saidel) Y.; B.A., U. Chgo., 1965, M.B.A., 1967; m. Donna Carol Kaufman, Aug. 20, 1967; children—Staci Dyan, Stephen Jerome. Brand asst. Procter & Gamble Co., Cin., 1967-68; v.p., dir. research Images, Inc., Cin., 1968-69; project dir. Sears Roebuck Co., Chgo., 1969-71, sr. project dir., 1972-73, asso. dir. advt. research, 1974-75; v.p. G.M. Feldman & Co., Chicago, 1975-77; v.p. and gen. mgr. Chgo. office Marc & Co., 1978—; instr. advt. continuing edn. program, 1971—. Named outstanding v.p. Chgo. Jaycees, 1973, outstanding state chmn. Ill. Jaycees, 1974. Mem. Am. Mktg. Assn., Chgo. Jaycees (v.p. 1973-74, dir. 1971-72), Ill. Jaycees (chmn. criminal justice 1973-77), Delta Upsilon (pres. Chgo. alumni 1975-77). Democrat. Jewish. Club: B'nai B'rith (past pres. local chpt.). Home: 9384 Home Circle Des Plaines IL 60016 Office: 444 N Michigan Ave Chicago IL 60611

YESSIK, MICHAEL JOHN, physicist; b. Worcester, Mass., Nov. 22, 1941; s. Joseph and Alyce (Trotsky) Y.; B.A., Williams Coll., 1962; Ph.D., Syracuse U., 1966; M.A., U. Cambridge (U.K.), 1967. Research scientist Sci. Lab., Ford Motor Co., Dearborn, Mich., 1968-75; mgr. process devel. Photon Sources, Inc., Livonia, Mich., 1975—. NSF grad. fellow, 1964-66, NATO postdoctoral fellow, 1966-67, NSF postdoctoral fellow, 1967-68. Mem. Am. Phys. Soc., IEEE, Am. Soc. Metals, Fedn. Am. Scientists, AAAS, Sigma Xi, Phi Beta Kappa. Contbr. articles to profl. jours. Home: 29220 Pointe Woods Pl Southfield MI 48034 Office: 37100 Plymouth Rd Livonia MI 48150

YOCK, GORDON AUGUST, telephone co. exec.; b. Clara City, Minn., Aug. 10, 1907; s. Emil Ernest and Wilhamina (Buethe) T.; student St. Olaf Coll., 1925-26, U. So. Calif., 1929-30; m. Hedwig E. Kumpf, Feb. 12, 1933; children—Marjorie Ann (Mrs. John Willingham), Karen Marie (Mrs. Vernon Bigalk), Laird Gay. Founder, chmn. bd. VCS, Inc., Clara City, from 1939; formerly founder and pres. or officer Internat. V. Stores, Star Fin. Co., Variety Furniture Co., Variety Bldg. Co., Village Dept. Stores, Northwest Stores, Inc., Variety Foods, Inc. (all Clara City, Minn.); pres., dir. Clara City Telephone Co., Citizens Telephone Co., Maynard, Minn.; v.p., dir. Sacred Heart Telephone Co. (Minn.); dir. Starbuck Telephone Co. (Minn.); chmn. bd., pres. WHAM, Inc., Memphis, 1973-74, dir., 1970—. Mem. Clara City Sch. Bd., 1940-42; mem. Minn. Adv. Council on Vocat. Edn., 1960-69; former mem. Pres.'s Com. Small Bus.; mem. bd. Viking council Boy Scouts Am., 1950-69, v.p., 1958-67, mem. nat. bd., 1958-67, recipient Silver Beaver award, 1961. Chmn. Republican County Com., 1950-54, state chmn., 1954-55. Bd. regents Augustana Coll., Sioux Falls, S.D., 1963-75; mem. devel. bd. Wartburg Coll., 1954-64. Recipient I Care award Republican party, 1965; Distinguished Service award Minn. Retail Fedn., 1966; honored by Clara City for contbns. to welfare of his community with Gordon Yock Day, 1967; named Man of Yrs., V. Stores, 1967. Mem. Clara City C. of C. (past pres.). Lion (past pres. and zone chmn.). Home: North Shore Green Lake Spicer MN 56288 Office: VSC Inc Clara City MN 56222

YODER, FREDERICK FLOYD, assn. exec.; b. Wilkinsburg, Pa., Oct. 7, 1935; s. Floyd Elvin and Mary Viola (Stahl) Y.; B.S. in Journalism, Ohio U., 1957. Mem. hdqrs. staff Sigma Chi Fraternity, Evanston, Ill., 1957—, coordinator chpt. visitation and installations program, 1964-72, leadership tng. adminstr., 1962-76, editor Mag. of Sigma Chi and Sigma Chi publs., 1972—. Mem. Coll. Fraternity Editors Assn. (past pres.), Am. Soc. Assn. Execs., Pub. Relations Soc. Am., Chgo. Headline Club, Sigma Chi, Sigma Delta Chi, Omicron Delta Kappa. Editor: The Norman Shield, 1973; Sigma Chi Membership Directory, 1977. Contbr. articles to interfraternity jours. Home: 2603 Sheridan Rd Evanston IL 60201 Office: 1714 Hinman Ave Box 469 Evanston IL 60204

YOEST, DONALD DEANE, real estate exec.; b. California, Mo., Jan. 17, 1941; s. Andrew John and Agnes Elizabeth (Hartman) Y.; B.S., U. Mo., 1965; m. Marilyn Kay Null, Sept. 18, 1965; children—Scott, Kent, Joel. Field editor Rural Electric Missourian, Jefferson City, Mo., 1965-68, asso. editor, 1968-69, mng. editor, 1969-72, editor, 1972-77; br. mgr. Strout Realty, Inc., Tipton, Mo., 1977—. Mem. Mid-Mo. Comprehensive Health Care Com., 1972-74. Recipient George W. Haggard Meml. Journalism award Nat. Rural Elec. Co-op Assn., 1972. Mem. Nat. Electric Co-op. Editorial Assn. (pres. 1974-75), Co-op. Editorial Assn. (pres. 1973-74). Home: Route 2 Tipton MO 65081 Office: Strout Realty PO Box 154 Hwy 5 S Tipton MO 65081

YOHE, RICHARD ROYAL, roofing mfg. co. exec.; b. Canton, Ohio, Dec. 4, 1927; s. Royal Keith and Laura Odessa (Deckerd) Y.; B.S., Miami U. at Oxford, 1948; m. Marlene Lucille White, Oct. 30, 1948; children—Dennis Michael, Melinda Sue. Sales rep. Berger div. Republic Steel Corp., Canton, 1949-51; sales rep. Tremco Mfg. Co., Cleve., 1951-60, dist. mgr., Mpls., 1960-64, Chgo., 1964-67, nat. dist. mgr. Cleve., 1967-70; founder, mgr. Maco Coatings Inc., Chgo., 1970—, Gravel Vac Inc., Chgo., 1973—, Tenn. Coatings Co., Memphis, 1977—; instr. pres.'s assn. Am. Mgmt. Assn., N.Y. Mem. Nat. Roofers Contractors Assn. Republican. Lutheran. Clubs: Masons, Shriners, Toastmasters. Home: 14 Hawley Ct Grayslake IL 60030 Office: 225 Industrial Ln Wheeling IL 60090

YOHO, ROBERT OSCAR, pub. health adminstr.; b. Solsberry, Ind., Sept. 29, 1913; s. Oscar and Ola (Cox) Y.; M.A., Ind. U., 1939, D.Health Sci., 1957; m. Jeanette Slinkard, Oct. 13, 1935; children—Jon Lance, Helen Roberta, Michael Blaine. Tchr., athletic coach pub. sch. Solsberry and Mt. Vernon, Ind., 1935-41; dir. div. health and phys. edn. Ind. Bd. Health, Indpls., 1941-60, dir. Bur. Health Edn., Records and Statistics, 1946-68, asst. state health commr., 1968-75, dep. state health commr., 1975—; instr. Ind. U. Sch. Medicine, 1951—, Butler U., 1964-73. Pres., Ind. Partners of Alliance, AID, 1966-77; nat. health chmn. Nat. Congress of Parents and Tchrs., 1964-68; chmn. profl. adv. com. Indpls. Sr. Citizens Center, 1960-76; pres. Ind. Heart Assn., 1960-61; mem. med. and sci. com. Ind. unit Am. Cancer Soc., 1966-72. Fellow Am. Acad. Phys. Edn. Home: 2318 N Fisher St Speedway IN 46224 Office: 1330 W Michigan St Indianapolis IN 46206

YOKOM, RICHARD ASHTON, wholesale trade exec.; b. Marshalltown, Iowa, Nov. 21, 1926; s. George Ashton and Esther (Sommer) Y.; B.S., Omaha U., 1950; m. Barbara Jean Haynes, Aug. 30, 1947; children—Marilyn Kay, Marcia Leigh. Controller, Howard Mfg. Corp., Council Bluffs, Iowa, 1950-57; chief internal auditor Cryovac Co. div. W.R. Grace & Co., Cambridge, Mass., 1957-61; auditor Peat, Marwick, Mitchell & Co., Omaha, 1961-64; controller Harding Glass Industries, Inc., Omaha, 1964-65; controller S. Riekes & Sons, Inc., Omaha, 1965—, v.p. fin., 1973—, dir., 1965-75, treas., 1974-75. Served with USMC, 1944-47. C.P.A., Nebr. Mem. Am. Inst. C.P.A.'s, Nebr. Soc. C.P.A.'s, Inst. Internal Auditors. Republican. Methodist. Home: 1230 Pine Rd Omaha NE 68144 Office: 1818 Leavenworth St Omaha NE 68102

YOMINE, DANIEL JOSEPH, mfg. co. exec.; b. Chgo., Sept. 22, 1921; s. Nicholas D. and Josephine (Ciancio) Y.; student Northwestern U., 1943-45, Am. U., 1951-53; m. Helen Mable Douzanis, Jan. 30, 1943; 1 son, Daniel Frank. Tool engr. No. Tool and Die Co., 1944-50; products engr. ACF Ind., Riverdale, Md., 1950-55; mfg. engring. mgr. Bell and Howell Co., Chgo., 1955-59, gen. mgr., dir., Japan, 1959-62; dir., chmn. exec. com. Tomoika Optical Co., Japan, 1959-62; asst. corp. sec., div. operations mgr., v.p. mfg. Ampex Corp., Redwood City, Calif., 1962-71; v.p. Internat. Video Corp., Sunnyvale, Calif., 1971-72, sr. v.p., 1973; pres., chief exec. officer, dir. Consol. Video Systems, Inc., Santa Clara, Calif., 1973-75; pres., treas. Convid Internat., Santa Clara, 1974-75; pres., owner Mfrs. Mgmt. Cons., Northbrook, Ill., 1975—; group v.p., corp. v.p. Bell & Howell, 1977—; dir. Carter Assos., Computer Image Corp. Mem. Mfrs. Engrings. Soc., Ill. C. of C., Am. Arbitration Assn., Am. Mgmt. Assn., Western Electronic Mfrs. Assn., Peninsula Mfrs. Assn. (dir.). Republican. Presbyterian. Clubs: Mission Hill Country, Exec. Club, Commonwealth (San Francisco). Patentee in field. Home: 263 Onwentsia Rd Lake Forest IL 60045

YON, WYATT SCHALLER, ins., real estate exec.; b. Chgo., May 14, 1932; s. Wyatt L. and Catherine (Schaller) Y.; B.S. in Bus. Adminstrn., Northwestern U., 1954; m. Lola D. Kelsey, June 22, 1958; children—Wyatt K., Catherine M. Partner, Wyatt Yon Agy., Storm Lake, Iowa, 1956—; pres. Yon Co., Inc., Storm Lake, 1974—; dir. 1st Nat. Co., Storm Lake. Mem. Storm Lake Library Bd., 1969-75, pres., 1973—; mayor Storm Lake, 1975-76; mem. adv. council Job Service Iowa, 1977—. Served with AUS, 1954-56. Recipient Distinguished Service award Storm Lake Jr. C. of C., 1966. Mem. Storm Lake C. of C. (pres. 1965). Presbyterian (elder). Clubs: Elks, Masons, Shriners. Home: 302 Lake Ave Storm Lake IA 50588 Office: 541 Cayuga Storm Lake IA 50588

YORDE, BETTY SMITH, coll. counselor; b. Cleve., Feb. 22, 1925; d. Chester Arthur and Mary Emeline (Rockey) Smith; B.S. in Edn., Ohio U., 1969, M.A., 1974, Ph.D., 1977; m. Richard Eugene Yorde Sr., May 9, 1947; children—Richard Eugene, William Myron. Various secretarial positions, Cleve. and Columbus, Ohio, 1943-59; sec. Dunbar, Kienzle & Murphey, law firm, Columbus, 1959-61; tchr. Nelsonville-York High Sch., Nelsonville, Ohio, 1969-73; instr. oral interpretation, group dynamics, biofeedback Ohio U., Athens, 1973-77; coll. counselor Rio Grande Coll./Community Coll., Rio Grande, Ohio, 1977—; cons., lectr. in field. Mem. Am. Assn. Biofeedback Clinicians, Am. Psychol. Assn., Am. Personnel and Guidance Assn., Am., Ohio biofeedback socs., Phi Delta Kappa, Order Eastern Star. Home: PO Box 29 Nelsonville OH 45764 Office: Box 876 Rio Grande Coll Rio Grande OH 45674

YORK, JOSEPH RUSSELL, film co. exec.; b. Royal Center, Ind., Oct. 19, 1940; s. William Russell and Naomi (Wellman) Y.; A.B., Olivet Nazarene Coll., 1965; m. Teresa Luanne Ping, June 15, 1963; children—Sherra JoAnn, Kerra SuzAnn, Darren Joseph, Terra LeAnn. Photojournalist, Danville (Ill.) Comml. News, 1961-62, Kankakee (Ill.) Daily Jour., 1963; motion picture dir.-editor Calvin Prodns., Inc., Kansas City, Mo., 1965-71, Communico, Inc., St. Louis, 1971-73; editing supr. Premier Film & Rec. Co., Inc., St. Louis, 1973—; owner, operator Trinity Prodns., St. Louis, 1963—. Recipient 1st Pl. award U.S. Indsl. Film Festival, 1972; 2d Pl. award Festival of Ams.-V.I., 1977. Mem. Profl. Photographers Am. Home: 2120 Mullanphy Rd Florissant MO 63031 Office: 3033 Locust St St Louis MO 63103

YORK, WILLIE RAY, city ofcl.; b. Artemus, Ky., Nov. 17, 1933; s. Howard Kelley and Emily Elizebeth (Wilson) Y.; student Union Coll., Barbourville, Ky., 1954-55, Otterbein Coll., 1961-63; Columbus (Ohio) Tech. Inst., 1973-74; m. Mary M. Mackley, Oct. 25, 1959. Plant insp. Western Electric Co., Columbus, 1959—; real estate salesman Forman Realtor, Sunbury, Ohio, 1972—. Mayor, chmn. zoning bd. City of Galena (Ohio), 1972—; mem. Delaware County Regional Planning Commn., 1972—; mem. exec. com. Delaware County Democratic Party, 1972—; trustee Big Walnut Bicentennial. Served with USNR, 1951-54. Recipient award for support and dedication to Galena Police Dept., 1974. Mem. Am. Legion, Amvets. Mason, Odd Fellow. Home: 46 Columbus St Galena OH 43021 Office: 6200 E Broad St Columbus OH 43213

YOST, CHARLES EDWARD, librarian; b. Pitts., May 4, 1932; s. Edward Joseph and Mary Cecelia (Becker) Y.; B.A., Sacred Heart Monastery Coll., 1955, B.A. in Theology, 1959; S.T.L., Catholic U. Am., 1960, M.S., 1961. Ordained priest Roman Catholic Ch., 1958; librarian, prof. liturgy and patristic theology Sacred Heart Sch. Theology, 1964—, dir. student affairs, 1976; retreat dir. Sacred Heart Monastery, Hales Corners, Wis., 1964—, superior, 1977—; prof. pastoral theology St. John Coll. Gisting, Lampung, Sumatra, Indonesia, 1962-64. Mem. Am., Cath. library assns., Am. Cath. Hist. Soc. Author: Notes for Advent Homilies, 1972; Exegetical and Homily Notes for Lent, 1973; Preaching to the Sick, 1974. Editor: Liturgical Pubs. of the Priests of the Sacred Heart, 1964—. Home: Sacred Heart Monastery 7335 S Lovers Lane Rd Hales Corners WI 53130

YOST, WILLIAM KENT, lawyer; b. Massillon, Ohio, June 27, 1912; s. William Kent and Anna Laura (Silk) Y.; ed. Ohio Wesleyan U., 1930-31, Ohio No. U., 1932-36; J.D., Western Res. U., also LL.M.; m. Marguerite Trimble, Apr. 21, 1937; children—Stephen T., Ann T. (Mrs. James Luther Binge). Admitted to Ohio bar; practiced law, Massillon. Bd. dirs. First Nat. Bank, Massillon, Massillon Mus. Found.; mem. Massillon Mus., Served to capt. AUS, 1943-46; PTO. Fellow Ohio Bar Assn.; mem. Am., Stark County (pres. 1962-63) bar assns., Am. Judicature Soc., Sigma Phi Epsilon, Alpha Phi Gamma, Delta Theta Phi. Republican. Episcopalian. Mason. Clubs: Canton; Massilon. Author publs. in field. Home: 1718 10th St NE Massillon OH 44646 Office: 108 3d St NE Massillon OH 44646

YOUAKIM, MAURICE YACOUB, elec. engr.; b. Jerusalem, Palestine, Sept. 10, 1938; s. Yacoub Abdul-Ahad and Angele (Mascovich) Y.; came to U.S., 1963, naturalized, 1974; B.S. in E.E., U. Ill., 1967, M.S., 1968, Ph.D., 1970; m. Cathleen Julie Gannon, June 24, 1967; children—Jacques Antoine, Marie Angelique, Theresa Helen, Laila Alexandra, Charles Ghassan. Lectr., U. Lyvia, Tripoli, 1971; research asso. U. Ill., Urbana, 1972-73; owner, mgr. MYY Systems Co., Champaign, Ill., 1973-76; project engr. FMC Corp., Mpls., 1976—. U. Ill. scholar, 1966-67; recipient UN award, 1967. Mem. IEEE, Am. Phys. Soc. Roman Catholic. Contbr. articles to tech. jours. Home: 10657 Wren St NW Coon Rapids MN 55453 Office: No Ordnance Div 48th and NE Marshall Minneapolis MN 55421

YOUEL, DAVID BRUCE, physician, educator; b. Parsons, Kans., Oct. 20, 1937; s. Donald Bruce and Burnette Luthera (Ash) Y.; B.A., Mankato State Coll., 1958; M.D., U. Minn., 1963; m. Kathryn Carole Johnson, Sept. 29, 1962; children—Steven Scott, Michael Todd, Sandra Jo, Barbara Lynn. Intern, Pontiac (Mich.) Gen. Hosp., 1964, resident in internal medicine, 1965-68, dir. edn. internal medicine, 1970-74; ednl. program coordinator for internal medicine Southwestern Mich. Area Health Edn. Center, Kalamazoo, 1974—; acting asst. dean acad. affairs Kalamazoo campus Mich. State U., 1977—; individual practice medicine, specializing in internal medicine, Pontiac, 1970-74; cons. in field. Served to lt. comdr., M.C., USNR, 1968-70. Named tchr. of yr. Pontiac Gen. Hosp., 1972-74, Mich. State U., 1976; recipient physicians recognition award AMA, 1973-76. Diplomate Am. Bd. Internal Medicine. Mem. Assn. Am. Med. Colls., AMA, Assn. Hosp. Med. Edn., Mich. Assn. Med. Edn., Phi Rho Sigma. Republican. Presbyterian. Club: Rotary. Home: 2203 Crosswind Dr Kalamazoo MI 49008 Office: 252 E Lovell St Kalamazoo MI 49006

YOULE, (JOHN) CLINTON, writer, financial cons., investment banker; b. Chgo., Apr. 4, 1916; s. John Wilbur and Sadie (Muench) Y.; A.B., Wheaton (Ill.) Coll., 1939. Editor NBC, 1940-50; TV westher commentator, 1949-59; syndicated newspaper columnist, 1952-53; pub. 5 Ill. newspapers, 1949-59; asso. Lehman Bros., investment bankers, 1959-66; v.p., dir. Donald R. Booz & Assos., Inc., 1966-67; pvt. financial cons., 1967—; dir. Safety-Kleen Corp., Madison Kipp Corp. Mem. Ill. Ho. of Reps., 1964-66; mem. vis. com. Div. Sch. and Grad. Sch. Edn., U. Chgo. With USAF Intelligence, 1942-46. Mem. Am. Meteorol. Soc. Clubs: Chicago; Executives (pres. 1959-60); Dunham Woods Riding (Wayne, Ill.); University. Inventor and mfr. automatic stock gates. Home and Office: Box 187 Scales Mound IL 61075

YOULIOS, JAMES, elec. engr.; b. Patterson, N.J., Mar. 23, 1923; s. Stephen and Catherine (Actipis) Y.; B.S., Newark Coll. Engring., 1960; m. Angela Colonias, Oct. 11, 1953; children—Stephan James, athy Margot, George Dennis. Asso. mem. tech. staff Bell Labs., Murray Hill, N.J., 1954-60; project engr. ITT Labs., Nutley, N.J., 1960-67; regional mgr. Western Union Data Services, Chgo., 1967-74; pres. Jay Assos., Oak Brook, Ill., 1974-76; regional mgr. Codex Corp. div. Motorola, Rosemont, Ill., 1976—. Served with USNR, 1942-45. Mem. IEEE. Greek Orthodox. Clubs: Masons, AHEPA. Home: 9 Lambeth Ct Oak Brook IL 60521 Office: 10600 W Higgins Rd Suite 224 Rosemont IL 60018

YOUNG, ARTHUR LEROY, food co. exec.; b. St. Louis, Nov. 22, 1928; s. Arthur LeRoy and LaVerne (Young) Y.; B.S., Northwestern U., 1950; M.B.A., U. Chgo., 1969; m. Shirley Ann Newcomer, May 8, 1954; children—Scott, John. Account supr. J. Walter Thompson Co., Chgo., 1950-65; dir. mktg. Food Service Systems div. Armour & Co., Chgo., 1965-71; pres. food service div. Green Giant Co., Mpls., 1971-77; pres. Diversified Human Services, Mpls., 1977—. Mem. Northbrook caucus com., candidates selection com. Sch. Bd., 1970-71. Mem. Am. Assn. Radio and TV Artists, Internat. Foodservice Mfrs. Assn. (dir.), Chi Psi. Episcopalian (fin. chmn. ch. vestry 1965-69). Clubs: Thunderbird Sportsman (McHenry, Ill.); Wild Outdoors, Sportsman (Prior Lake, Minn.); Hazeltine Nat. Golf. Editorial bd. Instl. Mgmt. Home: 6517 Ridgeview Circle Edina MN 55435 Office: 7710 Computer Ave Minneapolis MN 55435

YOUNG, CLYDE WILLIAM, musicologist; b. Springfield, Mo., Aug. 14, 1919; s. Clyde Anton and Rose Marie (Kiefer) Y.; student Drury Coll., 1937-38; B.S. with high distinction in Edn., diploma in Organ, S.W. Mo. State Coll., 1941; Mus.M. in Organ, U. Mich., 1949; Ph.D. in Musicology, U. Ill., 1957, M.L.S., 1958; postgrad. Union Theol. Sem., 1949; m. Helen Nancy Dinge, Dec. 29, 1962; children—Martha Rose, Anne Marie. Clk., St. Louis-San Francisco Ry., Springfield, Mo. and St. Louis, 1941-47; teaching asst., fellow dept. music U. Mich., Ann Arbor, 1947-53; dormitory counselor, library asst. U. Ill., Urbana, 1954-58; asst. prof. music State U. N.Y., Cortland, 1958-60; asst. prof. library sci. U. Nebr., Lincoln, 1960-61; asst., then asso. prof. music Nebr. Wesleyan U., Lincoln, 1961-64; asso. prof. Wayne State U., Detroit, 1965-73, prof., 1973—. Mem. Am. Musicol. Soc. Mem. United Ch. of Christ. Contbr. articles in field of Renaissance music to profl. jours., Die Musik in Geschichte und Gegenwart, Grove's Dictionary of Music and Musicians, 6th edit.; editor mus. texts. Home: 498 Barrington Rd Grosse Pointe Park MI 48230 Office: Dept Music Wayne State U Detroit MI 48202

YOUNG, DONALD E., business equipment co. exec.; b. Pitts., July 23, 1920; s. William P. and Helen (Bollenberg) Y.; B.A., George Washington U., 1948; M.B.A., Harvard, 1951; m. Pauline Schloesser; children—Leigh, Anna Dey, Lance. Spl. agt. FBI, 1948-49; with Office Spl. Investigations, 1951-53; asst. to pres. G.H. Packwood Co., 1953; asst. to v.p. and treas., bank sales rep. regional bank mgr. Todd Co., 1956; asst. to v.p. mktg. Burroughs Corp., Detroit, then exec. asst. to pres., 1960-61, asst. v.p.-gen., 1961-66, v.p. corporate communications, 1966-76, sr. v.p., 1976—; dir. Mich. Nat. Bank of Detroit, Blue Cross and Blue Shield of Mich.; Mem. Wayne County Republican Fin. Com.; bd. dirs. Detroit Conv. Bur., Boys Clubs Met. Detroit, Police Athletic League; bd. govs. Nat. Invest-in-Am., Greater Mich. Found.; bd. mems. Mich. Coll. Found.; trustee Met. Fund, Founders Soc. Detroit Inst. Arts, William Beaumont Hosp., Detroit Renaissance, Served to capt. USAF, 1941-46; ETO. Decorated D.F.C. with oak leaf cluster, Air medal with 5 oak leaf clusters. Mem. Soc. Former Spl. Agts. FBI, Mich. C. of C. (charter), Econ. Club Detroit (v.p.). Clubs: Detroit, Detroit Athletic, Harvard Bus. Sch. (Detroit); Harvard (N.Y.C.); Adcraft; Bloomfield Hills Country (dir.). Home: 376 Dunston Rd Bloomfield Hills MI 48013 Office: Burroughs Corp Detroit MI 48232

YOUNG, GARY EDWARD, clergyman; b. Marshall, Mo., June 12, 1943; s. Herbert Hadley and Ruby Evelyn (McCall) Y.; B.S. in Edn., Central Mo. State U., 1965; postgrad. Gen. Theol. Sem., N.Y.C., 1965-67; M.Div., Va. Theol. Sem., 1968; spl. studies, Sweden, 1967. Tchr., St. John's Sch., Salina, Kans., summers 1965-66, Grace Sch., N.Y.C., 1966-67; ordained to ministry Protestant Episcopal Ch., 1968; asst. rector Trinity Episc. Ch., Independence Mo., 1968-69; vicar Christ Episc. Ch., Lexington, Mo., 1969—. Mem. Lexington Planning and Zoning Commn., 1972—; bd. dirs. United Fund, Lexington Library and Hist. Assn., Arrow Rock Lyceum. Mem. English Speaking Union, SAR, Nat. Trust for Historic Preservation. Democrat. Lectr., writer on Mo. decorative arts. Home: PO Box 307 Lexington MO 64067 Office: 1300 Franklin Ave Lexington MO 64067

YOUNG, GEORGE GORDON, educator, camp dir.; b. Canton, Ohio, Feb. 22, 1929; s. George Warren and Ivy (Johnson) Y.; B.S., Mich. State U., 1954; M.A., Wayne State U., 1964; m. Mary Christine Finlayson; children—Mark Gordon, Terrie (Mrs. James McNeiece), Scott Allen. Phys. edn. tchr., head football coach, head wrestling coach South Redford (Mich.) Sch. Dist., 1954-57, dist. dir. phys. edn., health and recreation, head football coach, 1957-66, counselor, 1966-70, attendance counselor, 1970—, work experience dir., 1974—; owner, dir. pvt. co-ednl. camp for boys and girls Camp Upper Peninsula, Mich., 1970—; co-ordinator job placement service South Redford, 1975—. Mem. Nat. Thespian Soc., Phi Epsilon Kappa. Mason. Home: 855 Scott Northville MI 48167

YOUNG, GERALD, ins. co. exec.; b. Grand Rapids, Mich., Sept. 4, 1933; s. Clarence Leon and Mamie Mary (Karsten) Y.; student Grand Rapids Jr. Coll., 1952-54; B.B.A., Western Mich. U., 1957; m. Maxine Kathryn VanderVeen, July 3, 1954; children—Kathleen Jo, Derk Alan, Daryl Evan. Sr. accountant Scovell, Wellington & Co., Niles, Mich., 1957-61; internal auditor Central Soya Co., Inc., Ft. Wayne, Ind., 1961-66; div. controller Memcor, Inc., Huntington, Ind., 1966; 2d v.p., tax mgr. Lincoln Nat. Life Ins. Co., Ft. Wayne, 1966—; partner Young & Co., C.P.A.'s, dir. Universal Mdse. Co., Inc. Pres. Ludwig Circlee Community Assn., 1967; mem. precinct election bd., 1964, 68; treas. Anthony Wayne Rehab. Center. C.P.A., Ind. Mem. Am. Inst. C.P.A.'s, Ind. Assn. C.P.A.'s, Tax. Execs. Inst., Izaak Walton League (chpt. treas. 1964-66). Home: 8026 Manor Dr Fort Wayne IN 46825 Office: 1300 S Clinton St Fort Wayne IN 46801

YOUNG, H. EDWIN, univ. adminstr.; b. Bonne Bay, Nfld., Can., May 3, 1917; s. William and Anne (McKenzie) Y.; B.S., U. Maine, 1940, M.A., 1942; Ph.D., U. Wis., 1950; m. Phyllis Smart, Feb. 14, 1941; children—Jill, John, Dorothy, Nathan, Barbara. Instr., U. Maine, 1942-47; became mem. faculty U. Wis., 1947, successively instr., asst. prof., asso. prof., 1947-55, prof. dept. econs., 1955, chmn. dept., 1953-61, dean Coll. Letters and Sci., 1961-65; pres. U. Maine Orono, 1965-68; v.p., chancellor U. Wis., Madison, 1968-77; pres. U. Wis. System, Madison, 1977—; coordinator Wis.-Gadjah Mada (Indonesia) Project. Mem. Indsl. Relations Research Assn. (pres. 1965-66). Editor: (with M. Derber) Labor and the New Deal, 1957. Address: 6021 S Highlands Ave Madison WI 53705

YOUNG, HAROLD CHESTER, library adminstr.; b. Cambridge, Mass., Oct. 26, 1932; s. Louie Clarence and Gertrude Edna (Eyers) Avery; A.B., Boston U., 1958; M.L.S. (Library Service scholar), U. Mich., 1960, M.B.A., 1966, Ph.D. (HEW grantee), 1974; m. Margaret Labash, June 7, 1958; children—Jeffery Avery, Amy Margaret. Jr. asst. librarian Cambridge Pub. Library, 1946-58; jr. archivist Fairlane Archives, Ford Motor Co., Dearborn, Mich., 1959-60, road show mgr., 1960-62; reference librarian U. Mich., Dearborn, 1962-65; dir. learning resource center Washtenaw (Mich.) Community Coll., 1965-68; editorial cons. Gale Research Co., Detroit, 1960-75; asst. dir. pub. services U. Minn., Mpls., 1975—; research editor Ency. of Assns., 1965-69; asso. editor Library Congress Nat. Union Catalog Author List, 1942-62; co-editor Directory Spl. Libraries and Info. Centers, 1974, Subject Directory Spl. Libraries and Info. Centers, 1975. Served as sgt. AUS, 1953-55. Mem. ALA, Assn. Coll. Research Libraries (chmn. jr. coll. library bibliog. com. 1967-68), Spl. Libraries Assn. (co-editor Mich. chpt. Bull. 1967-68). Author: Planning, Programming, Budgeting Systems in Academic Libraries, 1975. Home: 313 Farmdale Rd Hopkins MN 55343 Office: U Minn Wilson Library Minneapolis MN 55455

YOUNG, JOHN HARLEY, elec. engr.; b. Springfield, Mo., May 10, 1944; s. Louis L. and Clarinda Elizabeth (Kelly) Y.; A.B., Drury Coll., 1966; M.S., Purdue U., 1975; m. Pamela Sue Larkin, Aug. 10, 1965; 1 son, John Edward. Broadcast engr. Ind. Broadcasters Inc., Springfield, Mo., 1964-67; tchr. Springfield Pub. Schs., 1966-67; with Magnavox G & I Electronics Co., Ft. Wayne, Ind., 1967—, sr. engr., 1974—. Mem. IEEE, Nat. Mgmt. Assn., Internat. Soc. Hybrid Microcircuits, Automatic Test Equipment Assn., Creation Research Soc., Phi Alpha Beta, Phi Eta Sigma. Baptist. Home: 7022 Strawberry Dr Ft Wayne IN 46825 Office: 1313 Production Rd Ft Wayne IN 46808

YOUNG, JOHN PAUL, librarian; b. Cranberry Creek, N.Y., July 31, 1942; s. Fred E. and Sue K. (Shellhammer) Y.; B.A., William Jewell Coll., 1964; M.L.S., U. Denver, 1967; M.P.A., U. Mo., Kansas City, 1974. m. Patricia O'Bryan, May 30, 1964; children—Bryan Dale, Jay Patrick, James Edward. Mem. library circulation and periodicals staff Curry Library, William Jewell Coll., Liberty, Mo., 1964-67, reference librarian, 1967-68, acting dir., 1968-69, dir., 1969—. Mem. ALA, Mo. Library Assn. Home: 121 Avondale St Liberty MO 64068

YOUNG, KENT ALAN, clin. psychologist; b. Tulsa, Dec. 28, 1940; s. Wilson and Naomi (Smyth) Y.; A.B., Oberlin Coll., 1964; postgrad. New Sch. for Social Research, 1964-65; M.A., Western Res. U., 1967, Ph.D., 1972; m. Joan Moore, July 5, 1969; children—Kimberly Allison, Justin Michael, Kevin Matthew. Staff psychologist Lake County Mental Health Center, Mentor, Ohio, 1971-72, coordinator research, 1972-73, asso. dir., 1973—; pvt. practice clin. psychology,

Mentor, 1973—; cons. Lake County Ct. Common Pleas, 1976—. Mem. Lake County Mental Retardation Bd., 1977—. Mem. Am., Midwestern, Ohio (legis. com. 1973—, ins. com. 1974—, trustee 1975—), Cleve. (chmn. profl. affairs com. 1974—) psychol. assns., Cleve. Acad. Cons. Psychologists (trustee 1974—, pres. 1976-77, pres. elect 1977-78). Home: 8872 Edgehill Rd Mentor OH 44060 Office: Mentor Profl Center 8925 Mentor Ave Mentor OH 44060

YOUNG, LAMAR LEWIS, JR., audiologist, educator; b. Shelby, N.C., Oct. 3, 1942; s. Lamar L. and Eugenia Lee (Harrill) Y.; B.A., Wake Forest U., 1964; Ed.M., U. Va., 1969; Ph.D., Northwestern U., 1973; m. Florida Truitt Love, Apr. 8, 1965; children—Brenton Lewis, Frank Kevin. Asst. prof. of speech Northwestern U., Evanston, Ill., 1974-76, asst. dir. of Auditory Research Lab., 1974-76; asso. prof. of speech and hearing scis. Ind. U., Bloomington, 1976—, dir. of Auditory Research Lab., 1976—. Mem. Acoustical Soc. of Am., Am. Speech and Hearing Assn., Sci. Research Soc. of N.Am., Sigma Xi. Democrat. Baptist. Contbr. numerous articles on audiology to profl. jours. Home: 1903 Chelsey Ct Bloomington IN 47401 Office: Dept of Speech and Hearing Sciences Indiana Univ Bloomington IN

YOUNG, MICHAEL KENNETH, bus. equipment mfg. co. rep.; b. Cozad, Nebr., Feb. 20, 1955; s. Kenneth M. and Edith (Walters) Y.; B.S., Chadron State Coll., 1977. Asst. mgr. Round Up Motel, Chadron, 1974-75; adminstrv. asst. Exec. Office of Bd. Trustees, Nebr. State Colls., 1975-76; asst. mgr. Fireside Inn, Chadron, 1976; mktg. rep. Burroughs Corp., Omaha, 1977—. Mem. Nat. Umpires Assn., Nat. Baseball Congress, Phi Beta Lambda. Home: 7766 Highland St Omaha NE 68127 Office: 101 N 31st St Omaha NE 68131

YOUNG, MILTON R., U.S. senator; b. Berlin, N.D., Dec. 6, 1897; s. John Young and Rachel (Zimmerman) Y.; student N.D. State Agr. Coll. and Graceland Coll., Lamoni, Iowa; m. 2d, Patricia M. Byrne, Dec. 27, 1969; children by previous marriage-Wendell M., Duane C., John M. Mem. N.D. Ho. of Reps., 1933-34, N.D. Senate, 1935-45; U.S. Senator from N.D., 1945—, sec. to Senate Republican Conf. Com., 1946-71, ranking Rep. on Senate Appropriations Com., 1967—. Home: La Moure ND 58458 Office: US Senate Bldg Washington DC 20510

YOUNG, PEGGY MARIE SANBORN, psychologist; b. Painesville, Ohio, Aug. 25, 1926; d. Philip Harold and Josephine (Masters) Sanborn; B.S. in Edn., Baldwin-Wallace Coll., 1955; Ph.D., Kent State U., 1977; M.A. in Ednl. Psychology, Western Res. U., 1963; divorced; children—Philip Harold, Timothy Mark, Don Sanborn. Tchr. various schs., 1956-58, 60-61; vocat. counselor Booth Meml. Hosp., Cleve., 1961-62; intern psychologist Willoughby (Ohio)-Eastlake Schs., 1962-63; sch. psychologist Fairless and Tuslaw schs., Stark County, 1965-67; sch. psychologist Mentor (Ohio) Pub. Schs., 1963-65, chief. sch. psychologist, 1967-77, coordinator regional classes for orthopedic children, 1970-74, coordinator psychol. services and spl. edn., 1977—; workshop dir. Lake Erie Region Project Breakthrough; mem. advisory bd. East Shore Center for Handicapped Children, 1969-75; supr. sch. psychology interns John Carroll U., 1968-77, Case Western Res. U., 1968-70, Cleve. State U., 1973-74, Kent State U., 1967-75; mem. advisory bd. Family Service, Painesville, 1968-70, chmn. edn. com., 1969-70; mem. advisory bd. Lake County Soc. Crippled Children, 1963-65. Teaching fellow Kent State U., 1973-74. Mem. Am., Ohio, Cleve. psychol. assns., Nat. Council Exceptional Children (legis. com. 1969-70), Ohio Sch. Psychologists Assn., Cleve. Area (chmn. 1968-69), Kent Area sch. psychologists, Gestalt Inst. Cleve. Home: 9956 Johnnycake Ridge Painesville OH 44077

YOUNG, RICHARD EMERSON, educator; b. Owosso, Mich., July 12, 1932; s. William Charles and Katherine Marie (Middaugh) Y.; B.A. with honors, U. Mich., 1954, Ph.D., 1964; M.A., U. Conn., 1956; m. Ann Elizabeth Albert, Aug. 29, 1953; children—Jonathan Field, Lynn Mikell, David Thurston. Instr. English, U. Mich., 1956-64, asst. prof., 1964-67, asso. prof., 1967-71, prof., 1971—, chmn. dept. humanities, 1971-76, research asso. Center for Research on Lang. and Lang. Behavior, 1965-69; cons. NDEA Insts., 1965-68, Edn. Professions Devel. Act Insts., 1968-70; dir. summer seminar Nat. Endowment for Humanities, 1976. Recipient Distinguished Service award Coll. Engring., U. Mich., 1968; research grantee Nat. Endowment for Humanities, 1971, program planning grantee, 1974. Mem. Nat. Council Tchrs. English (com. on tech. and sci. writing), Modern Lang. Assn., Conf. Coll. Composition and Communication (exec. com. 1966-69), Rhetoric Soc. Am. (dir. 1969-71, 76-78), Delta Upsilon. Author: (with A. L. Becker and K. L. Pike) Rhetoric: Discovery and Change, 1970. Home: 1309 Fountain St Ann Arbor MI 48103

YOUNG, ROBERT ANTON, Congressman: b. St. Louis, Nov. 27, 1923; s. Melvin A. and Margaret (Degnan) Y.; student pub. schs., St. Louis; m. Irene Slawson, Nov. 27, 1947; children—Anne Young Lewis, Robert A., Margaret Mary. Mem. 95th Congress from 2d Mo. Dist., mem. Pub. Works and Transp. Com., Sci. and Tech. Com.; Democratic committeeman Airport Twp., St. Louis County, 1952-77; mem. Mo. Ho. of Reps., 1956-62; mem. Mo. Senate, 1962-76. Mem. Pipefitters Union, Am. Legion, VFW (post comdr.), Amvets (life). Club: St. Ann Lions. Recipient awards for meritorious service St. Louis Globe Democrat, 1972, 74, 76. Home: 4154 Cypress Rd Saint Ann MO 63074 Office: 1315 Longworth Bldg Washington DC 20515

YOUNG, ROBERT ARTHUR, coal co. exec.; b. Waterloo, Iowa, Sept. 23, 1910; s. J. Arthur and Gertrude M. (Lukhart) Y.; B.S., U. Iowa, 1932; m. Edith Van Houten, Feb. 3, 1932; children—Robert Arthur, James Van. Partner, Young Coal Co., Waterloo, 1932—; pres. Young Lumber Co., Waterloo, 1964—; partner Young Plumbing & Heating Co., Waterloo, 1950-60; v.p. Artificial Ice & Cold Storage, Waterloo, 1960—; dir. Waterloo Savs. Bank, Black Hawk Broadcasting Co., Coca Cola Bottling Co., Keller Apex Loan Co. Mem. Iowa Devel. Commn., 1969-73; mem. Republican Central Com., 1972—; trustee Waterloo Auditorium Commn., 1969-73, Mus. History and Sci., 1969—; chmn. bd. trustees Waterloo YMCA, 1950-76; mem. bd. control athletics U. Iowa, 1966—. Mem. Sigma Alpha Epsilon, Beta Gamma Sigma. Congregationalist (chmn. bd. trustees 1945-76). Clubs: Masons, Shriners, Elks, Rotary. Home: 135 Pershing Rd Waterloo IA 50701 Office: 430 W 1st St Waterloo IA 50704

YOUNG, ROBERT LAWRENCE, ophthalmologist; b. Harlem, Mont., Oct. 25, 1918; s. Morris Davis and Esther Rae (Urkov) Yampolsky; B.S., U. Ill., 1940, M.D., 1943; m. Roberta Sternberg, Oct. 10, 1943; children—Fredric, Barbara, James, Michael. Intern, Michael Reese Hosp., Chgo., 1944, resident, 1949-50; resident U. Ill. Hosp., 1948-49, Aspinwall VA Hosp., Pitts., 1950; practice medicine specializing in ophthalmology, Gary, Ind., 1951—; mem. staff, pres. St. Mary of Mercy Hosp., Gary; sr. staff Meth. Hosp., Ind. U. Hosp., both Gary, Community Hosp., Munster, Ind.; mem. adv. com. Ind. U. N.W. br. Med. Sch. Bd. dirs. Munster Community Hosp. Served to capt. M.C., AUS, 1946-48. Diplomate Am. Bd. Ophthalmology. Fellow Internat. Coll. Surgeons; mem. AMA, Assn. Research in Ophthalmology, World Med. Assn., Am. Acad. Ophthalmology, Ind., N.W. Ind., Chgo. ophthalmology socs., AAAS, Ind., Munster chambers commerce, Tau Delta Phi, Phi Delta Epsilon. Democrat. Jewish (temple mens' club). Club: B'nai B'rith. Home: 8809 Crestwood Munster IN 46321 Office: 1646 45th Ave Munster IN 46321

YOUNG, ROXEY CHESTER, architect; b. East St. Louis, Ill., Mar. 19, 1921; s. Roxey Emmett and Mary Jeanette (Stofiel) Y.; B.Arch., Washington U., St. Louis, 1954; m. Jeanette L. Clark, Apr. 1946; children—Mark C., Patrice J.; m. 2d, Marie Zoder-Johnston, Sept. 25, 1965; stepson, Jerry Mac-Johnston. Pvt. practice architecture, Springfield, Mo., 1957—; partner Designer Assos., Interior Designers & Decorators, 1964—; lectr. interior design and architecture Drury Coll.; lectr. S.W. Mo. State U. Bd. dirs., set designer Springfield Little Theatre, 1956-60, 1976—. Served with AUS, 1943-46, 47-48. Mem. AIA (dir. Springfield chpt. 1970-72, treas. 1977-78). Clubs: Exchange (pres. 1964—), Univ. (Springfield).

YOUNG, SUMNER BACHELER, lawyer; b. Marion, Mass., Aug. 14, 1898; s. Frank Linnaeus and Minnie Ella (Jones) Y.; A.B., Harvard U., 1920, J.D., 1927; m. Sidney Washburn, Aug. 19, 1925; children—Elisabeth W. Young Krueger, Rosamond, Sidney Young Wear, Sumner S., Jeremiah O'B. Admitted to Minn. bar, 1927, U.S. Supreme Ct. bar, 1950; trainee Frank L. Young Co., Boston, 1920-24, then dir.; with law office Prendergast & Flannery, Mpls., 1928-31; partner Prendergast, Flannery & Young, 1931-37; with law dept. Cargill, Inc., Mpls., 1937-60, asst. sec., 1937-61, v.p., dir., 1961-63, ret., 1963, spl. counsel to exec. com. bd. dirs., 1949-61, with adminstrn. div., 1960-63; counsel Cargill Securities Co., to 1963, now ret. Mayor, Village of Woodland (Minn.), 1949-53. Served as elec. 2/c (R) and elec. 1/c (R) USNRF, 1917-19. Mem. IEEE, Minn. Bar Assn., Am. Radio Relay League, Am. Polar Soc., Kappa Sigma. Club: Wayzata (Minn.) Country. Contbr. articles to radio mag. Home: 2600 Maplewood Circle East Wayzata MN 55391

YOUNG, SUMNER SULLIVAN, bus. exec.; b. Mpls., Sept. 17, 1932; s. Sumner Bacheler and Sidney (Washburn) Y.; A.B., Brown U., 1955; m. Eris Lundin, Nov. 10, 1962; children—Katherine Dianne, Jennifer Eris. Account exec. Pidgeon Savage Lewis, Inc., 1957-60; advt. and market planning mgr. boat div. Brunswick Corp., 1960-62; account exec. Batten, Barton, Durstine & Osborn, N.Y.C., 1963; v.p. Erle Savage Co., Mpls., 1963-67, pres., 1967-72; chmn. bd. Larson Industries, Inc., Mpls., 1972-76; chmn., chief exec. officer Gen. Boats, Inc., Mpls., 1976—. Served to capt. USAF, 1955-57. Mem. N. Central Marine Assn. (dir., pres.), Young Pres.'s Orgn., Minn. Execs. Orgn., Phi Gamma Delta. Clubs: Mpls.; Wayzata (Minn.) Yacht. Home: 2600 Maplewood Circle E Wayzata MN 55391 Office: 1110 Baker Bldg Minneapolis MN 55402

YOUNG, VERNA JEAN, market research analyst; b. St. Louis, Mo., Sept. 26, 1938; d. Robert Lee and Ivy (Kenzie) Thompson; B.L.S., U. Okla., 1961; m. Kenneth B. Young, June 23, 1972; children—Robbie Maria, Kevin Andre. Supply mgmt. analyst U.S. Aviation Systems Command, St. Louis, 1963-72; computer programmer Blue Cross, Omaha, 1974-75; market research analyst Blue Cross/Blue Shield, of Nebr., Omaha, 1975—; condr. corp. tng. sessions. Mem. Nebr., Internat. assns. of bus. communicators, Am. Mktg. Assn., Am. Mgmt. Assn. Clubs: Jack and Jill of Am., Inc. Editor: The Market Place, 1975-76; writer and dir. play: Journey to Calvary, 1976; dir. and choreagrapher many stage productions. Home: 5616 Willit St Omaha NE 68152 Office: 7261 Mercy Rd Omaha NE 68180

YOUNG, VERNON EUGENE, bus. cons.; b. Springfield, Ohio, Aug. 13, 1917; s. Jesse Melvin and Florence Helen (Hare) Y.; student pub. schs., Springfield; m. Bonnie Mae Larson, Feb. 21, 1945; children—Ronnie, Cyndie, Randy. Buyer, Wright Patterson AFB, Ohio, 1948-56, contracting officer, 1956-61; dept. dir. procurement and prodn. Def. Electronics Supply Center, Dayton, 1961-77; bus. cons., electronics firms, New Carlisle, Ohio, 1977—. Served to col. USAF, 1942-46, 51-56. Republican. Home and Office: 621 Bischoff Rd New Carlisle OH 45344

YOUNG, WILLIAM GEORGE, ednl. adminstr.; b. Stambaugh, Mich., Aug. 21, 1936; s. William John and Esther (Wickman) Y.; student Pa. State U., 1954-56, Northwestern U., 1956-58; B.S., No. Mich. U., 1960, M.A., 1961; m. Joan Carole Hansen, Aug. 25, 1962; 1 dau., Cara Elizabeth. Lab. asst. Chgo. Fire Brick Co., 1956-58; tchr. Greenhill Sch., Dallas, 1961-66, head, Middle Sch., 1966-69, head Upper Sch., 1969-72; headmaster Park-Tudor Sch., Indpls., 1972—, also bd. dirs. Chmn. pvt. sch. div. United Way, 1972-75; bd. dirs. Indpls. Children's Bur. Mem. Nat. Assn. Coll. Admissions Counselors, Nat. Assn. Secondary Sch. Prins., Middle W. Assn. Schs. for Girls (pres.), Ind. Schs. Assn. Central States (dir.), Council Advancement and Support Edn. Episcopalian. Address: 7200 N College Indianapolis IN 46240

YOUNGBERG, HOLGER RAY, cons. energy conservation; b. Indpls., Apr. 15, 1930; s. Holger Raymond and Eva Boyd (Carr) Y.; B.E.E., Ill. Inst. Tech., 1968; m. Beatrice Fern Pope, Oct. 6, 1956; children—Denise Ray, Rick Alan. Asst. chief engr. electric products div. Ferro Corp., Chgo., 1957-67; process design engr. comml. div. Honeywell Inc., Morton Grove, Ill., 1967-68; chief facilities plant engr. Hawley Products div. Armco Corp., St. Charles, Ill.,1968-73; prin. protect elec. engr., energy systems div. Air Resources, Inc., Palatine, Ill., 1973-75; adminstr. dir. environ. services, facilities engr. Good Samaritan Hosp. and Health Center, Dayton, Ohio, 1975-78; corporate energy mgr. Philips Industries Inc., Dayton, 1978—. Served with AUS, 1953-55. Mem. Am. Inst. Plant Engrs., Am. Soc. Hosp. Engrs., Nat. Fire Protection Assn., Soc. Preservation and Encouragement Barbershop Quartet Singing in Am. Republican. Home: 6353 Freeport Dr Dayton OH 45415 Office: 4801 Springfield St Dayton OH 45401

YOUNGBERG, MANLEY DONALD, audio-visual co. exec.; b. New Richland, Minn., May 25, 1917; s. Reuben Theophil and Elsie (Goodlund) Y.; B.E.E., U. Minn., 1940; postgrad. U. Chgo., 1943, Mass. Inst. Tech., 1944; m. Mildred Jacobson, June 14, 1941; children—Susan Youngberg Johnson, Sally, Jane, Laura, Donald. Engr., Commonwealth Edison Co., Chgo., 1940-44, 46-47; sr. design engr. E.F. Johnson Co., Waseca, Minn., 1947-54; pres., gen. mgr. Audio Visual Research Co., Waseca, 1954—; instr. coll. physics night sch. North Park Coll., 1946-47. Chmn. Waseca County chpt. ARC, 1960-66, treas., 1969—; pres. Bob Hodgson Student Loan Fund, 1969-71; chmn. bd. edn. Waseca Pub. Schs., 1961-62, clk., 1962-65, treas., 1965-68. Served to lt. (s.g.) USNR, 1944-46. Mem. Waseca C. of C. (edn. com. 1969-71), Eta Kappa Nu. Lutheran (chmn. 1966). Clubs: Toastmasters, Rotary (Waseca). Home: 1305 8th St SE Waseca MN 56093 Office: 1317 8th St SE Waseca MN 56093

YOUNGBERG, ROBERT STANLEY, sch. adminstr.; b. Chgo., Apr. 21, 1932; s. Holger Ray and Eva Boyd (Carr) Y.; B.S., U. Ill., 1954; M.Ed., Wayne State U., 1959, postgrad., 1959-65; Ph.D., U. Mich., 1975; m. Catherine Jane Fitzpatrick, June 19, 1954; children—Kevin Robert, Melissa Catherine, Margo Sarah, Brian Fitzpatrick. Tchr. pub. schs., Detroit, 1956-62, counselor jr. high sch., 1962-67, counselor sr. high sch., swim coach, 1967-70; prin. Novi (Mich.) Middle Sch., 1970—; insp. U.S. Customs and Immigration Service, Detroit, 1961-64; mgr., dir. summer camps, Wis., Mich., 1965-70; standards visitor summer camps, Mich., 1972—. Mem. Detroit Citizens' Adv. Com. on Sch. Bldgs., 1958; bd. dirs. Brightmoor Community Center, Detroit, 1962. Served with AUS, 1954-56. Mem. Oakland County Curriculum Council, Nat., Mich. assns. secondary sch. prins., Am. Camping Assn., Mich. Assn. of the Professions, Assn. Supervision and Curriculum Devel., Phi Delta Kappa. Presbyterian. Contbr. article to ednl. jour. Home: 36757 Sherwood St Livonia MI 48154 Office: 25299 Taft Rd Novi MI 48050

YOUNGBLOOD, JOHN L., elec. engr.; b. Elkhart, Tex., Mar. 14, 1941; s. J. Douglas and Hessie B. (Caffy) Y.; B.S., U. Tex., Arlington, 1963; M.S., Okla. State U., 1965, Ph.D. (NDEA fellow), 1967; m. Larri Sharon Doyle, Aug. 31, 1963; children—John Scott, Jennifer Lynn, Stacy D'Ann, Jay David. Research asst. Okla. State U., Stillwater, 1965-66; project aerosystem engr. Ft. Worth div. Gen. Dynamics, 1966-69, group engr., 1969-72, project mgr. 1972-75, dir. corporate devel., St. Louis, 1975—. Mem. staff elec. engring. U. Tex., Arlington, 1969-70. Mem. IEEE, Eta Kappa Nu, Phi Kappa Phi, Tau Beta Pi, Pi Mu Epsilon. Home: 741 Crab Thicket Ln Saint Louis MO 63131 Office: Pierce Laclede Center Saint Louis MO 63105

YOUNGREN, RALPH PARK, architect; b. Cloquet, Minn., Dec. 26, 1924; s. Andrew Frederick and Eunice (Park) Y.; A.B., Harvard U., 1948, M.Arch., 1950; m. Ann Henderson, June 28, 1962; children—Todd Park, Malcolm Park. Asso. partner, sr. designer Skidmore, Owings & Merrill, Chgo., 1950-67; with Metz Train Olson & Youngren, Inc., Chgo., 1967—, prin. charge design, 1962—; archtl. adviser Chgo. Dept. Urban Renewal, 1962—; design critic, lectr. U. Ill., 1962-67. Mem. men's council Art Inst. Chgo., 1966-72, aux. bd., 1973—; trustee Chgo. Sch. Architecture Found., 1969—, pres., 1972-73, hon. pres., 1974, bd. dirs., 1975—; dir. Soc. Contemporary Art, 1966-69, Arts Club Chgo., 1968—; archtl. advisory com. Ill. Sec. State, 1973—. Served with U.S. Army, 1944-46. Recipient Citation of Merit, Chgo. Assn. Commerce and Industry, 1963, also Chgo. chpt. AIA, 1973; R. S. Reynolds Meml. award Air Force Acad. chapel, 1964; Distinguished Bldg. award Chgo. chpt. AIA, 1972, 75. Fellow AIA. Clubs: Cliff Dwellers', Saddle and Cycle, Harvard (Chgo.). Prin. archtl. works include U.S. Air Force Chapel, U.S. Air Force Acad.; Grover M. Hermann Hall, Ill. Inst. Tech.; Joseph Regenstein Library, U. Chgo.; Dormitories and Academic Complex Lake Forest Acad.; Westinghouse Research Labs., Rush-Presbyn.-St. Luke's Med. Center, Chgo.; Osco Drug Hdqrs. Office Bldg., Oak Brook, Ill. Home: 1958 N Mohawk Chicago IL 60614 Office: One E Wacker Dr Chicago IL 60601

YOUNGREN, WAYNE ALFRED, mfg. co. exec.; b. Duluth, Minn., Aug. 20, 1923; s. Alfred and Winifred Winnete (McCandless) Y.; B.S., U. Minn., 1950; m. Queneth Arlowynne Carleton, Aug. 25, 1944; children—Laurel Lee Youngren Lufholm, Cynthia Ann Youngren Kuklis, Sandra Lynn Youngren Drennan. Engr., Duluth Steel Fabricators, Inc., 1950-59, sec., treas., 1959-64, pres., 1964—; dir. Duluth Builders Exchange, 1970-73, Western Nat. Bank, Duluth, 1966—. Mem. bd. edn. Hermantown Sch., 1957-63. Served to capt. USMC, 1942-46. Decorated Air medals. Mem. Nat., Minn. (pres. 1967) socs. profl. engrs., ASCE, U.S. Power Squadron, C. of C. (dir. 1968-70). Club: Rotary. Home: 3311 Morris Thomas Rd Duluth MN 55811 Office: 59th Ave West and Main St Duluth MN 55807

YOUNGS, VERNON LEROY, chemist; b. Roseglen, N.D., Oct. 1, 1924; s. Frank E. and C. Florence (Doble) Y.; B.S., Jamestown Coll., 1948; M.S., N.D. State U., 1963, Ph.D., 1965; m. Helen L. Buck, July 31, 1948; children—Deborah Lynn, Victor Lee. High sch. sci. instr., Columbus, N.D., 1948-55; instr. chemistry N.D. Sch. Forestry, Bottineau, 1955-60; research asst. N.D. State U., Fargo, 1960-65, research chemist U.S. Dept. Agr. and asst. prof. univ., 1965-70, chemist in charge Nat. Oat Quality Lab., U.S. Dept. Agr. and prof. U. Wis., 1970—. Served with USNR, 1943-46. Fellow Am. Inst. Chemists; mem. Am. Chem. Soc., AAAS, Am. Assn. Cereal Chemists, Am. Soc. Agronomy, Sigma Xi. Methodist. Contbr. articles to profl. jours. Home: 6018 Piping Rock Rd Madison WI 53711 Office: Nat Oat Quality Lab Dept Agronomy U Wis Madison WI 53706

YOUSSEF, TAWFIK KARAM, radiologist; b. Fayoum, Egypt, Sept. 8, 1935; s. Allam Fowzi and Asma (Bollis) Y.; came to U.S., 1969; naturalized, 1975; M.B.CH.B., Eln Shams U., 1960; m. Aida Nakhla, Sept. 2, 1965; children—Sam, Andrew. Gen. surgeon Egyptian Ministry of Health Hosps., Egypt, 1961-68; resident in surgery Peterbourough Meml. Hosp., Peterbourough, Eng., and Sutton Gen. Hosp., Eng., 1968-69; intern, resident in gen. surgery Englewood (N.J.) Hosp., 1969-71, resident in radiology, 1971-74; radioiogist Good Samaritan Hosp., Mt. Vernon, Ill., 1974-75; cons. radiologist Washington County Hosp., 1974-75, Fairfield (Ill.) Meml. Hosp., 1974-75, Highland (Ill.) St. Joseph Hosp., 1974-75, St. Francis Hosp., Washington, Mo., 1974-75; radiologist Harrisburg (Ill.) Med. Center, 1975—, Pearce Hosp. Found., Eldorado, Ill., 1975—; clin. instr. Mallinkhrodt Inst. Radiology, Washington U., St. Louis, Mo., 1975—. Diplomate Royal Coll. Physicians and Surgeons of Can., Am. Bd. Radiology, Am. Bd. Nuclear Medicine. Mem. Royal Coll. Radiologists of Eng., Can. Assn. of Radiologists, Radiol. Soc. of N. Am., Am. Coll. Radiologists, Am. Soc. Nuclear Medicine. Roman Catholic. Contbr. articles in field. Home: 8 Peachtree Pl Harrisburg IL 62946 Office: 203 N Vine St Harrisburg IL 62946

YOUSSI, FRANCIS EDWARD, lawyer; b. Menominie, Wis., July 11, 1923; s. Edward G. and Wandah (Hendrickson) Y.; B.S., Aurora Coll., 1948; J.D., DePaul U., 1950; m. Frances June Gittleson, Mar. 15, 1952; children—Debra Joan, Cathy Lynn. Admitted to Ill. bar, 1950; pvt. practice law, Batavia, Ill., 1950—; city atty. Batavia, 1954-63; instr. bus. law Aurora Coll., 1952-61; dir. Batavia Savs. & Loan Assn. Served with USAAF, 1943-45. Decorated Air medal. Mem. Kane County Bar Assn. (pres. 1968-69). Lutheran. Home: 405 S Forest Ave Batavia IL 60510 Office: Batavia Profl Bldg Batavia IL 60510

YOVICICH, GEORGE STEVEN JONES, civil engr.; b. Belgrade, Yugoslavia, June 2, 1927; s. Steven and Draginja (Djurdjevic) Y.; B.C.E., High Tech. Sch., Belgrade; M.C.E., U. Darmstadt (Germany), 1956; Ph.D. in Bus. and Adminstrn., Northwestern U., 1958; Ph.D. (hon.) in Bus. and Adminstrn., U. Fla.; Ph.D. (hon.) in Civil Engring., Hamilton State U.; m. Sofija Sekulic, Feb. 3, 1960; 1 son, Steven. Civil engr. Hollabird & Root, Chgo., 1956-58; bridge engr. Div. Hwys., Ill. Dept. Transp., Chgo., 1958-70; v.p.-project mgr. Arcadia Internat. & Co., Skokie, Ill., 1956-70, chmn. bd., pres., 1970—; prof. structural engring. Northwestern U.; prof. math. and structural engring. U. Ill. at Chgo. and Urbana. Legis. asst., mem. hwys. com., mem. traffic safety com., utilities com., r.r. and aviation com., welfare com. Ill. Ho. of Reps., 1970—; bd. dirs. Oakton Community Coll., Skokie, Sch. Dist. #68, Skokie. Served to capt. AUS, 1954-56. Registered profl. engr., Ill., others. Mem. ASCE, Registered Profl. Engrs. Soc. Home: 5309 Arcadia St Skokie IL 60076 Office: PO Box 712 Skokie IL 60026

YOWELL, DONALD LEE, dentist; b. Delphos, Kans., Jan. 1, 1931; s. Wayne Archie and Doris (Shroyer) Y.; student Kans. Wesleyan U., 1948-51; D.D.S., U. Mo., 1955; m. JoAnn Klein, Sept. 6, 1953; children—Ann, Donalea, Janelle, Glenn. Individual practice dentistry, Minneapolis, Kans., 1955, Delphos, Kans., 1957—. Council mem. City of Delphos, 1961-67; asst. scoutmaster Coronado Area council Boy Scouts Am., 1957-60, scoutmaster, 1960-62, neighborhood commr., 1963—, cub scoutmaster, 1968-70, asst.

scoutmaster, 1970-73; hunter safety instr., 1973. Served with USNR, 1955-57. Mem. ADA, Kans. Dental Assn., Saline County Dental Soc., Am. Legion, Nat. (life), Kans. (life) rifle assns., Am., Kans. trapshooters assns., Kans. Bowhunters Assn. Clubs: Lions, Elks. Home: 301 Main St Delphos KS 67436 Office: PO Box 327 Delphos KS 67436

YOWELL, GEORGE KENT, lawyer; b. St. Louis, May 12, 1927; s. John Jasper and Helen (Callahan) Y.; B.A., U. Colo., 1949; J.D., Northwestern U., 1952; m. Joyce McCallum, Sept. 8, 1951; children—John Jasper, Susan Kent, Margaret Ann, Helen Elizabeth. Admitted to Ill. bar, 1952; asst. U.S. atty. No. Dist. Ill., 1954-57; practice in Chgo., 1957—, mem. firm Littlejohn, Glass & Yowell; village prosecutor Glencoe (Ill.), 1963—, village atty., 1970—; commr. character and fitness com. Supreme Ct. Ill., 1961-71, chmn., 1970-71; mem. joint com. Ill. State and Chgo. Bar Assn. on Jud. Article, 1961-62. Served with JAGC, AUS, 1952-54. Mem. Am., Ill. State, Chgo. bar assns., Am. Judicature Soc., Phi Kappa Psi, Phi Delta Phi. Mem. Union Ch. (chmn. bd. trustees 1969). Clubs: Univ., Legal, Law (Chgo.). Home: 400 Lincoln Ave Glencoe IL 60022 Office: 899 Skokie Blvd Northbrook IL 60062 also 135 S LaSalle St Chicago IL 60603

YU, FERMIN TONG, surgeon; b. Lianga, Surigao, Philippines, Aug. 23, 1934; s. Huan Tee and Song Tong Y.; came to U.S., 1964, naturalized, 1972; A.A., U. San Carlos, Cebu City, Philippines, 1956; M.D. cum laude, U. Santo Tomas, Manila, 1962; m. Carol Ann Swartz, July 15, 1967; children—Christopher, Michael. Rotating intern St. Elizabeth Hosp., Youngstown, Ohio, 1964-65, resident gen. surgery, 1965-69; house physician in surgery St. Joseph Hosp., Warren, Ohio, 1969-70; practice medicine specializing in surgery, Warren, 1970—; pres. Emergency Physicians Assos. Inc., Warren, 1974. Diplomate Am. Bd. Surgery. Fellow A.C.S.; mem. Trumbull Med. Soc., Ohio, Am. med. assns. Home: 8528 Carriage Hill Dr Warren OH 44484 Office: 1446 Parkman Rd Warren OH 44485

YUENGER, DAVID ANTHONY, newspaper exec.; b. Marinette, Wis., Aug. 21, 1914; s. John Francis and Evelyn (Laury) Y.; B.A., St. Norbert Coll., 1936; m. Carol J. Haines, Sept. 3, 1938; children—James, Kay Yuenger Wisneski, David, John, Mary Ellen Yuenger Barbeau, Mark, Ann, Julie. Instr. English, St. Norbert Coll., West De Pere, Wis., 1936-42; reporter Green Bay (Wis.) Press-Gazette, 1942-54, city editor, 1954-60, mng. editor, 1960-66, editor, 1966—; dir. Green Bay Newspaper Co., 1963—, v.p., 1966—. Pres., Brown County United Fund, 1966-68, Green Bay Curative Workshop, 1963-65. Mem. Wis. AP Assn. (pres. 1965-66), Sigma Delta Chi. Home: 1236 Cherry St Green Bay WI 54301 Office: Box 430 Green Bay WI 54305

YUN, SUK KOO, physicist, educator; b. Seoul, Korea, Nov. 10, 1930; s. IllSun and Young Sook (Cho) Y.; came to U.S., 1955, naturalized, 1968; B.S., Seoul Nat. U., 1955; M.S., U. Chgo., 1957; Ph.D., Boston U., 1967; m. Chung Hei Kim, July 20, 1957; children—Stephen Tae-Young, Elise Hae-Ryung, Christina Ae-Ryung. Instr. of physics, Clarkson Coll. of Tech., Potsdam, N.Y., 1959-63; teaching fellow Boston U., 1963-66, research asso., 1966-67; research asso. Syracuse (N.Y.) U., 1967-69; asst. prof. physics Saginaw Valley Coll., University Center, Mich., 1969-71, asso. prof., 1971—, chmn. natural sci. div., 1972-74, chmn. dept. physics, 1977—; vis. prof. U. Mich., Ann Arbor, summers, 1974, 75, Harvard U., Cambridge, Mass., 1975, summer, 1976. Am.-Korean Found. grantee 1955-56. Mem. Am. Phys. Soc. (mem. particles and fields div. 1970—), Sigma Xi. Methodist. Author: Laboratory Manual for General Physics, 1971, A Vision of Beauty in Order, 1972, Readings in the Interaction of Science and Society, 1973; contbr. articles in high energy physics to sci. jours. Home: 714 Columbia Rd Midland MI 48640 Office: Saginaw Valley State College University Center MI 48710

YUNG, R. DALE, state ofcl.; b. Sesser, Ill., Oct. 29, 1931; s. Roy E. and Leola E. (Allen) Y.; B.S. with honors, U. Ill., 1953, J.D., 1955; m. Anita Jean Tull, Feb. 7, 1953; children—Linda Marie, Michael Roy, Valarie Ann. Admitted to Ill. bar, 1955; asso. firm Olsen & Cantrill, Springfield, Ill., 1955-57; legis. draftsman Ill. Legis. Reference Bur., Springfield, 1957-64; adminstrv. asst. Ill. sec. state, Springfield, 1964; legal adviser, asst. to gov., 1964-69; exec. sec. Ill. Property Tax Appeal Bd., Springfield, 1969-70; legal counsel Ill. Dept. Local Govt. Affairs, Springfield, 1970—; chmn. adv. com. Midwest Govs.' Conf., 1967-68. Mem. Ill., Sangamon County bar assns., U. Ill. Alumni Assn., Ill. State Employees Assn. Clubs: Elks, K.C., Rotary. Home: 2401 S 8th St Springfield IL 62703 Office: 303 E Monroe St Springfield IL 62706

YURK, GERALD JOHN, architect; b. Flint, Mich., Jan. 18, 1941; s. John C. and Mary M. (Brug) Y.; B.Arch. (Dean's scholar), Lawrence Inst. Tech., 1966; postgrad. Wayne State U., 1966-67; m. Elaine Joyce Friesorger, Aug. 12, 1961; 1 son, Scott Gerald. Architect for firm T. Neel Eubank, architect, Flint, 1966-67; architect Tomblinson, Harburn, Hanoute & Assos., Inc., Flint, 1967-70, prin., 1970-75; prin. Tomblinson, Harburn, Yurk & Assos., Inc., Flint, 1976—; U.S. rep. to Pan Am. Congress Student Architects, 1966; gen. partner Wilderness Resorts, owners Lost Valley Campground, Lupton, Mich., 1971—. Mem. Urban Coalition Flint, 1973-74, 76-77; chmn. Flint Planning Commn., 1973-74; mem. Flint City Council, 1970-73, chmn. water and sewer com., 1970-73, chmn. govt. ops. com., 1970-73; adv. bd. Tall Pine council Boy Scouts Am., 1973-74. Registered architect, Mich., Fla. Mem. AIA, Mich. Soc. Architects, Greater Flint Jaycees, Flint C. of C. (govtl. affairs com. 1971—), Lambda Iota Tau. Major works: Lost Valley Resort, Reigle Sunrise Chapel, Flint, Marlette Homes Inc. (Mich.), YMCA addition, Owosso, Mich., Pioneer State Mut. Ins. Co., Flint, Doyle Neighborhood Redevel., Genesee Twp. Municipal Center, Flint. Home: 3829 Craig Dr Flint MI 48506 Office: 705 Kelso St Flint MI 48506

ZABECKI, DAVID TADEUSZ, quality engr.; b. Springfield, Mass., Aug. 8, 1947; s. Julian Tadeusz and Virginia Charlotte (Luthgren) Z.; B.A., Xavier U., 1972, M.A., 1973; M.S., Fla. Inst. Tech., 1976; m. Christin Ann Hellkamp, July 29, 1972; 1 son, Konrad Josef. Patrolman, Xavier U. Campus Police, Cin., 1972-74; specialist quality assurance Rock Island (Ill.) Arsenal, 1974-77; quality engr. Deere & Co., Moline, Ill., 1977—; adj. instr. Fla. Inst. Tech., 1977—; lectr. in field. Served with U.S. Army, 1966-69; 1st lt. Ill. N.G. Decorated Combat Infantryman's Badge. Mem. Am. Soc. Quality Control (certified quality and reliability engr.), Res. Officers Assn., Am. Soc. Internat. Law, Am., German philatelic socs., V.F.W., Alpha Sigma Nu. Author in field. Home: 29 Oak Ln Davenport IA 52803 Office: Plow and Planter Works John Deere & Co Moline IL 61265

ZABLOCKI, CLEMENT JOHN, Congressman; b. Milw., Nov. 18, 1912; s. Mathew and Mary (Jankowski) Z.; Ph.B., Marquette U., 1936, LL.D. (hon.), 1966; LL.D., Alverno Coll., 1969, Sogang U., Seoul, Korea, 1974, Alliance Coll., 1975, Jagiellonian U., Cracow, Poland, 1975; m. Blanche Janic, May 26, 1937; children—Joseph, Jane. High sch. tchr., 1938-39; organist, choir dir., 1932-48; mem. Wis. Senate, 1942-48; mem. 81st to 95th Congresses from 4th Wis. Dist., chmn. internat. relations com., chmn. subcom. internat. security and sci. affairs; mem. spl. congressional study mission to West Europe, 1951, S. Asia and Far East, 1953, 54, 63, Poland, 1961; U.S. del. 14th Gen. Assembly UN, 1959; mem. adv. council Center for Strategic Studies, Georgetown U.; congressional adviser U.S. del. Philippine U.S. Commn. Study Vets. Problems; mem. Commn. on Orgn. Govt. for Conduct Fgn. Policy. Mem. Father Marquette Tercentenary Commn. Mem. Cath. Order of Foresters, St. Vincent Conf., Polish Nat. Alliance, Fedn. Polish Assn. Am., Holy Name Soc. Democrat. Roman Catholic. Home: 3245 W Drury Ln Milwaukee WI 53215 Office: House Office Bldg Washington DC 20515

ZACHARIAH, MATHEW, sociologist, educator; b. Kerala, India, Feb. 17, 1930; s. George and Elizabeth (George) Z.; B.A., U. Madras (India), 1952; M.A. in Sociology, U. Kerala, 1965; M.A., U. Minn., 1966, Ph.D., 1968; m. Kunjamma Thomas, Jan. 7, 1957; children—Elizabeth, Georgie. Research asst. U. Minn., Mpls., 1965-67, teaching asst., 1967-68; asst. prof. sociology Marquette U., Milw., 1968-70; asso. prof. dept. sociology U. Wis. at Whitewater, 1970—; lectr. sociology U. Kerala, 1965; lectr., edn. officer Windsor Coll., Mauritius, 1958-63; secondary sch. tchr., Singapore, 1955-58; tchr. higher secondary sch., Malaysia, 1953-55. Recipient Padmanabha Menon Meml. award U. Madras, 1951. Mem. Sociol. Soc. India (life), Am., Wis., Midwest sociol. assns., Alpha Kappa Delta. Asso. editor Internat. Jour. Comparative and Applied Criminal Justice, 1976—. Office: Dept Sociology U Wis Whitewater WI 53190

ZACHER, PETER MICHAEL, publishing co. exec.; b. Milw., Mar. 23, 1935; s. William F. and Ruth M. (Mohegan) Z.; B.B.A., Babson Coll., 1957; m. Constance S. Neff, Feb. 5, 1958; children—Wendy, Andrea. Sales rep. Cleworth Pub. Co., Cleve., 1960-66; sales mgr. Plastics World Mag., Cahners Pub. Co., Cleve., 1966-71; co-founder Industry Media, Cleve., 1971—; dir. Erico Product Corp. Served to lt. j.g. USNR, 1957-60. Mem. Soc. Plastics Engrs., Soc. Plastics Industry, Am. Bus. Press. Republican. Roman Catholic. Clubs: Hermit (dir.), Cleve. Racquet. Home: 15875 Shaker Blvd Shaker Heights OH 44120 Office: 24500 Chagrin Blvd Cleveland OH 44122

ZACKS, SHELEMYAHU, mathematician, statistician; b. Tel Aviv, Israel, Oct. 15, 1932; s. Yechezkiel and Dvora (Kolemoitzev) Z.; came to U.S., 1965, naturalized, 1972; Ph.D., Columbia U., 1962; m. Hanna A. Bilik, Oct. 15, 1955; children—Yuval J., David N. Research asso., Stanford (Calif.) U., 1962-63; sr. lectr. Technion-Israel, 1962-65; prof., Kans. State U., Manhattan, 1965-68, U. N. Mex., Albuquerque, 1968-70; prof. mathematics and statistics, Case Western Res. U., Cleve., 1970-74, prof., dept. chmn. 1974—; cons. program in logistics, George Washington U., 1967—. Served with Israel Defense Force, 1950-52. NSF research grantee, 1966-76, research contracts, Office of Naval Research, 1970—. Fellow Inst. Math. Statistics, Am. Statis. Assn.; mem. Internat. Statis. Inst. Jewish. Author: The Theory of Statistical Inference, 1971; contbr. articles to profl. jours. Home: 2340 Milton Rd Cleveland OH 44115 Office: University Circle Cleveland OH 44106

ZADEK, ROBERT LAWRENCE, automotive co. exec.; b. Oak Park, Ill., Apr. 26, 1940; s. Robert Frank and Marie Edna (Jindra) Z.; student So. Ill. U., 1958-59, Walton Sch. Commerce, 1960-71, Contract Mgmt. Inst., Washington, 1969; m. Jacqueline Louise Braun, Apr. 29, 1961; children—Pamela Marie, Robert Lawrence. With First Nat. Bank, Chgo., 1959-61; cost accountant Rockwell Mfg. Co., Chgo., 1961-64; chief cost accountant Aircraft Gear Corp., Chgo., 1964-71; sec.-treas. Rockford Acromatic Co. (ill.), 1971—; sec.-treas. Diemax Products Co., Rockford, 1971—, also dir. Mem. exec. bd., com. chmn. YMCA Indian Guides, 1973; active Rockford United Fund, 1972-74; trustee, treas. D.A.O. Found., Rockford Acromatic Profit-Sharing and Retirement Fund; bd. dirs. Civic League Rockford, 1974—. Served with USCGR, 1959-67 Mem. Rockford Area C. of C. (grad. leadership sch. 1973), Ill. Mfrs. Assn., Fin. Mgmt. Assn. (com. mem., dir. 1974—). Presbyterian. Home: 1960 Honeysuckle Ln Rockford IL 61107 Office: Rockford Acromatic 611 Beacon St Rockford IL 61111

ZADROZNY, MITCHELL GEORGE, geographer; b. Chgo., Dec. 23, 1923; s. John and Jeanette (Ulick) Z.; B.S., Ill. State Normal U., 1947; S.M., U. Chgo., 1949, Ph.D., 1956. Geographer analyst Dept. Army, Tokyo, 1950-52; lectr. U. Chgo. Downtown Coll., 1953-55; dir. research Cambodia-Laos Project, Human Relations Area Files, Inc., 1954-55; tchr. Chgo. City Jr. Coll., Wright br., 1955-63, asst. prof., 1963-65, asso. prof., 1965-69, prof., 1969—; vis. asso. prof. econ. geography N.Y. U., 1958; research asso. Mississippi Valley investigations So. Ill. U., 1955-62; mem. Pres.'s Water Pollution Control Adv. Bd., 1972-75. Served as 2d lt, USAAF, 1942-45. Mem. Assn. Am. Geographers, Chgo., Ill., Am. geog. socs., Ill. Edn. Assn., Société des Etudes Indochinoises. Author: Water Utilization in the Middle Mississippi Valley, 1956; editor: Cambodia Handbook 1955; contbr. to Laos Handbook, 1956. Home: 4158 N McVicker Ave Chicago IL 60634 Office: 3400 N Austin Ave Chicago IL 60634

ZAHN, BERT CHARLES, artist, author; b. Milw., Sept. 11, 1896; s. August and Alma (Ries) Z.; student U. Toronto, 1917; m. Wilma Jirousek, Dec. 10, 1938; children—Lorraine Zahn Loeb, Harold, Florence Zahn Schwartz, Bert W. Jr., Bert Charles. Artist, graphic arts mgr. Sherwin Williams Co., Glidden Co., Cleve., 1940-62; past tech. adviser Craftint Mfg. Co.; exec. sec. Associated Sign Industry of Ohio. Councilman, Bedford, Ohio, 1956, vice mayor, 1957. Served with U.S. Army, USMC, Royal Flying Corps, 1914-18. Recipient Ed. G. Voight award Graphic Arts Edn. Soc.; Parmelee award Screen Printing Assn. Mem. Acad. Screen Printing Tech., Internat. Sign Assn. (organizer; exec. v.p. 1958-65), Screen Process Printing Assn. (organizer assn.; founder Acad. Screen Printing Tech. 1973), Mark Twain Soc. (hon. life), Eugene Field Soc. Authors and Journalists, Am. Legion (life). Author books on silk screen printing. Developed screen process printing; intial work now in Smithsonian Instn. Home: 253 Ledge Rd Northfield OH 44067

ZAK, EDWARD JOSEPH, bus. exec.; b. Oak Park, Ill., Apr. 13, 1940; s. Edward Joseph and Mildred (Korous) Z.; student U. Ill., Urbana, 1958-59; A.A., Morton Coll., 1965; m. Helen Eileen Novy, Oct. 7, 1961; children—Michael Edward, Thomas Eric. Data processing mgr. Pelam, Inc., Hinsdale, Ill., 1967-68, Assn. Ancilla Domini Hosps., Chgo., 1969-71; dir. hosp. info. systems U. Chgo. Hosps. and Clinics, 1971-77; dist. mgr. HBO & Co., Des Plaines, Ill., 1977—. cons. to hosps.; former instr. adult edn. Morton Coll., Cicero, Ill. Chmn. Community Caucus Riverside-Brookfield (Ill.) High Sch. Dist., 1976—, Riverside July Fourth Com., 1974, Riverside Centennial Parade Com.; twp. chmn. Cancer Soc., 1975; mem. Riverside Plan Commn., 1975—. Mem. Electronic Computing Health Oriented, Assn. Ill. Med. Systems (past pres.), Lyric Opera Chgo., Riverside-North Riverside Jaycees (pres. 1974-75), Phi Theta Kappa. Clubs: Riverside Swim, Foresters. Home: 190 Woodside Rd Riverside IL 60546 Office: 2700 River Rd Des Plaines IL 60018

ZAKON, SAMUEL JOSEPH, physician; b. Russia, 1898; M.D., Eclectic Med. Coll., Cin., 1925. Intern, Washington Park Community Hosp., 1925-27; postgrad. dermatology Gen. Hosp., Vienna, Austria, 1930-31; attending dermatologist Mt. Sinai Hosp., Chgo.; cons. dermatologist Franklin Blvd. Hosp., Schwab Rehab. Hosp., Park View Home for Aged, Columbus-Cuneo Med. Center; prof. emeritus dermatology Northwestern U., 1967—. Diplomate AM. Bd. Dermatology. Mem. Am. Acad. Dermatology (hon.), AMA, Am. Soc. Investigative Dermatology, Am. Assn. History Medicine, Chgo. Inst. Medicine, Noah Worcester Dermatol. Soc. Address: 25 E Washington St Chicago IL 60602

ZAKS, MISHA S., clin. psychologist; came to U.S., 1950, naturalized, 1970; student U. Chgo., 1950-54; M.A., Roosevelt U., 1954; Ph.D., Ill. Inst. Tech., 1959; m. Sonia Resnik, 1946; Asso. prof. dept. psychiatry Northwestern U. Med. Sch., Chgo., 1963—, asso. staff clin. psychologist, Northwestern Meml. Hosp., 1960—; asso. prof. health sci., clin. psychologist, research cons., U. Ill., Chgo., 1962—. Registered psychologist, Ill. Mem. Am., Midwestern, Ill. psychol. assns., AAUP, AAAS., Sigma Xi. Contbr. articles on psychol. aspects of med. diseases, test devel. and problems of addictions to profl. jours. Office: Northwestern Meml Hosp Wesley Pavilion 251 E Chicago Ave Chicago IL 60611

ZALBA, SERAPIO RICHARD, cons., educator; b. San Francisco, July 16, 1927; s. Serapio and Agueda (Arribas) Z.; B.A., U. Calif. at Berkeley, 1951, M.S.W., 1956; Ph.D., Case Western Res. U., 1971; m. Patricia Ellen Pool, July 20, 1954; children—Elisa Anne, David William, Anthony Serapio. Social service worker San Francisco Welfare Dept., 1952-54; probation and parole officer Wis. Dept. Corrections, Janesville, 1956-57; supr., exec. dir. No. Calif. Service League, San Mateo County, 1958-62; dir. Children of Women Prisoners Project, Calif. Depts. Corrections and Pub. Welfare, Corona, 1962-64; dir. agy. effectiveness project, faculty Case Western Res. U., Cleve., 1965-69, chmn., prof. urban studies and applied social scis., 1975—; chmn., prof. social service dept. Cleve. State U., 1969-73; partner Zalba/Hirsch Assos., Chagrin Falls, Ohio, 1973-74; cons. Nat. Study Service, N.Y.C., 1963-64, Youth Study Center, U. So. Calif., 1963-64, VA Hosp., Cleve., 1970, Adminstrn. Justice Com., Cleve., 1971-75, Jr. League Cleve. 1974-75. Precinct chmn. Democratic party, Chagrin Falls, 1974; trustee Belmont (Calif.) Sch. Dist., 1959-62; trustee Greater Cleve. Neighborhood Centers Assn., Chagrin Falls Park Community Center. Served with USNR, 1945-46. NIMH fellow, 1964-66, Career tchr. fellow, 1966. Mem. Nat. Assn. Social Workers (pres. Cleve. chpt. 1973-75), Calif. Social Workers Orgn. (v.p. 1961), Nat. Council Crime and Delinquency, Cleve. Council Corrections (dir. 1970-72). Author: Women Prisoners and Their Families, 1964; (with Herman Stein) Assessing Agency Effectiveness, 1969; editor: (with William Schwartz) The Practice of Group Work, 1971. Home: 240 S Franklin St Chagrin Falls OH 44022

ZALETEL, JOE HENRY, clin. chemist; b. Pueblo, Colo., June 25, 1918; s. John Frank and Mary (Mezan) Z.; B.S., Colo. State U., 1939; M.S., Iowa State U., 1950; m. Myrtle D. Bunch, June 15, 1946; children—Joe Henry, Mary K. Zaletel Colacino, John D., Edward T., Cora Anne. Chemist, Nat. Broom Mfg. Co., Pueblo, Colo., 1939-40, Colo. Fuel & Iron Corp., Pueblo, 1940-42; research asso. Iowa State U., Ames, 1950-53; clin. chemist Mercy Hosp., Des Moines, 1953-73, research asso. cancer research 1973—. Served with M.C., AUS, 1942-46. Mem. Am. Assn. Clin. Chemists, Am. Chem. Soc., Am. Soc. Clin. Pathology, Iowa Acad. Sci., Sigma Xi. Democrat. Roman Catholic. Club: K.C. Contbr. articles to profl. jours. Home: 4212 Leonard Pl Des Moines IA 50310 Office: Mercy Hospital 6th and University Des Moines IA 50314

ZAMPA, VICTOR MICHAEL, architect; b. Valetta, Malta, Mar. 3, 1931; s. Michael Leon and Mary Stella (Bugeja) Z.; came to U.S., 1947, naturalized, 1952; B.Archtl. Engring., U. Detroit, 1953, M.B.A., 1963; m. Sylvia M. Taylor, Oct. 19, 1968; children—Kerry Margaret, Julie Marisa. Job capt. Earl Confer, Architect, Detroit, 1957-59; architect Eero Saarinen Asso., Hamden, Conn., 1959-64; office mgr. Sanford Rossen Architects, Detroit, 1964-67; partner, project adminstr. Harley Ellington Pierce Yee Asso., Southfield, Mich., 1967—. Served with AUS, 1953-55. Mem. AIA, Mich. Soc. Architects (health environment com., constrn. mgmt. com.), Am. Assn. Hosp. Planning, Tau Beta Pi, Beta Gamma Sigma. Home: 920 S Glenhurst Birmingham MI 48009 Office: 26111 Evergreen St Southfield MI 48076

ZANDER, HENRY EDWARD, bank exec.; b. Cross Plains, Wis., Dec. 6, 1926; s. Henry L. and Loretta I. (Kerl) Z.; student Madison Bus. Coll.; grad. Wis. Sch. Banking, 1968; m. Geraldine M. Knipschield, Apr. 21, 1951; children—Debra, Diane, Linda, Lori, Lisa. Cashier, Bank of Waunakee (Wis.), 1957-75, pres., 1975—. Pres. Centennial Corp., Civic Club; mem. ch. bd.; treas. Fire Dept.; active Waunakee Arts Council, Waunakee Hist. Soc. Served to master sgt. U.S. Army, 1945-51. Named Boss of Year, 1975, Bus. Man of Year, 1977. Mem. Ind., Am., Wis. bankers assns., Nat. Bank Auditors Assn., Am. Legion. Club: Rotary. Home: 501 Holiday Dr Waunakee WI 53597 Office: 500 W Main St Waunakee WI 53597

ZANGER, LARRY MARTIN, lawyer; b. Bklyn., July 10, 1946; s. Mark Henry and Lillian (Cohen) Z.; B.S., Northwestern U., 1967, J.D., 1970; m. Bonnie Agnes Zanger, June 8, 1975; 1 dau., Laura. Admitted to Ill. bar, 1970; asso. firm McDermott, Will & Emery, Chgo., 1970-72; partner firm Zanger & Looney, Medinah, Ill., 1972-75; adj. prof. law U. Ill. Chgo. Circle Campus, 1972—; partner firm McHugh, Zanger, Bromberg & Lang, Chgo., 1975—. Chgo. Title & Trust Co. scholar, 1969-70. Mem. Am. Inst. C.P.A.'s (Elijah Watts Sell award 1968), Am., Ill., Chgo., Du Page County bar assns., Beta Alpha Psi. Home: 265 Adelia St Elmhurst IL 60126 Office: 10 S La Salle St Chicago IL 60603

ZANGRANDO, JOANNA SCHNEIDER, educator; b. Hastings, Minn., June 13, 1939; d. Russel Philip and Sophia Elizabeth (Mayer) Schneider; B.A., Wayne State U., 1961, M.A., 1963; Ph.D., George Washington U., 1974; m. Robert Lewis Zangrando, Mar. 29, 1969. Research asst. hist. office AEC, Washington, 1964-66; legis. asst. U.S. Office Edn., Washington, 1966-67; predoctoral fellow Smithsonian Inst., Washington, 1968-69; instr. Am. history U. Hartford (Conn.), 1970-71; museum cons., 1972-74; vis. asst. prof. Am. studies George Washington U., 1974-76; asst. prof. Am. studies Skidmore Coll., Saratoga Springs, N.Y., 1976—; cons. mus. and women's studies; co-sec., editor newsletter Coordinating Com. Women in Hist. Profession, 1970-76; mem. bd. Nat. Am. Studies Faculty, 1974-77; mem. grant panel Eleanor Roosevelt Inst. (grantee, 1974-75), F.D.R. Library, Hyde Park, 1977—; project proposal panelist Nat. Endowment for Humanities, 1976—. Smithsonian Inst. fellow. Mem. Am. Studies Assn. (council 1973—, nat. coordinator women's com. 1973—), Ohio Acad. History, Am. Hist. Assn., Orgn. Am. Historians, Am. Assn. State and Local History. Author numerous publs. in field. Home: 501 Mineola Ave Akron OH 44320 Office: Am Studies Dept Skidmore Coll Saratoga Springs NY 12866

ZANGWILL, WILLARD IRA, educator; b. Pitts., Mar. 18, 1940; s. Bernard Louis and Lillian Ruth (Abel) Z.; A.B., Columbia U., 1959; M.S., Stanford U., 1963, Ph.D., 1965; children—Richard Michael, Monica Laurie. Prof., U. Calif. at Berkeley, 1965-69; dir. edn. evaluation HEW, Washington, 1969-71; pres. Sullivan Edn. Systems, Palo Alto, Calif., 1972-73; spl. asst. to commr. ednl. tech. U.S. Office Edn., Washington, 1971-73; prof. mgmt. sci. U. Ill., Urbana, 1973—; prof. Am. U., 1972-73; vis. prof. U. Chgo., 1977. NSF fellow. Mem. Ops. Research Soc., Inst. Mgmt. Sci. Author: Nonlinear Programming: A Unified Approach, 1969; Success With People:

Theory Z, 1976. Deptl. editor Mgmt. Sci.; contbr. articles to profl. jours. Home: 2505 Sheridan Dr Champaign IL 61820

ZAPP, HANS ROLAND, elec. engr.; b. Germany, July 3, 1941; s. Ludwig and Alma (Schafer) Z.; B.S., Mass. Inst. Tech., 1963, M.S., 1965; Ph.D., Stanford U., 1969; m. Roberta Grace Mark, June 12, 1965; children—Alisa Ruth, Jonathan Mark. Mem. tech. staff Lincoln Lab., Mass. Inst. Tech., Lexington, 1968-74, liaison officer aerospace and space and missile systems, San Bernadino, Calif., 1970-71, mem. staff research radar site, Kwajalein, Marshall Islands, 1971-74; asst. prof. elec. engring. and systems sci. Mich. State U., E. Lansing, 1974—; mem. sr. staff Central Solar Energy Research Corp., Detroit, 1977—. Den leader local Cub Scouts, 1976—; Sunday sch. tchr. United Presbyn. Ch., Okemos, Mich., 1976—. Mem. IEEE, Internat. Solar Energy Soc., Sigma Xi, Eta Kappa Nu, Tau Beta Pi. Contbr. articles to profl. jours. Home: 3617 E Arbutus Okemos MI 48864 Office: Dept Elec Engring and Systems Sci Mich State U East Lansing MI 48824

ZAPPOLA, PETER CHARLES, pipe products co. exec.; b. Cleve., Apr. 27, 1952; s. Charles Biagio and Rose Josephine (Drago) Z.; m. Linda Martucci, Aug. 2, 1974; A.A., Lakeland Community Coll., 1973; B.S. in Mktg., Lake Erie Coll., 1976. Waterline products mgr. Allied Pipe Products, Inc., Cleve., 1974—. Mem. Am. Mktg. Assn., Am. Water Works Assn. U.S.A. Leadership finalist, 1969-70. Home: 326 St Lawrence Blvd Eastlake OH 44094 Office: 23880 Broadway Cleveland OH 44146

ZARET, MATTHEW ELIAS, acoustical cons.; b. N.Y.C., Sept. 13, 1909; s. Elias A. and Fanny (Burgunker) Z.; B.S., City U. N.Y., 1931; M.Sc., N.Y. U., 1936, Ph.D., 1967; m. Lillian Diamond, May 25, 1937; children—Peter, Philip, Eli. Electroacoustic research engr. Sonotone Corp., Elmsford, N.Y., 1941-46; project engr. Poly. Research & Devel. Corp., Bklyn., 1946-47; asst. prof. elec. engring. Newark Coll. Engring., 1947-51; asso. prof. Cooper Union, N.Y.C., 1951-60; dir. engring. Dyna Magnetic Devices Co., Hicksville, N.Y., 1960-63; asso. prof. Suffolk Coll., Selden, N.Y., 1963-66; prof., chmn. dept. elec. engring. Western New Eng. Coll., Springfield, Mass., 1966-75; acoustical cons., Ann Arbor, Mich., 1976—. Lectr. Wayne State U., Detroit, Mich., 1978—. Ednl. cons. N.Y. Telephone Co., 1957-63. Pres., double bass player Huntington (N.Y.) Symphony Orch., 1960-66. Recipient Founders Day award N.Y. U., 1967; NSF research participant, 1965, 72. Fellow AAAS, Radio Club Am.; mem. IEEE (sr., chmn. S.E. Mich. sect. student activities com., nat. edn. com. 1952-57), Acoustical Soc. Am., Soc. Engring. Edn., Audio Engring. Soc. (charter), Friends of Opera (U. Mich.). Author: Electroacoustics, 1949; Electromagnetic Theory, 1966; Environmental Noise and Vibration Control, 1975; contbr. articles to Jour. Acoustical Soc. Am., Jour. Chem. Edn., Engring. Edn. Home and Office: 511 Benjamin Ann Arbor MI 48104

ZARICZNYJ, BASILIUS, orthopaedic surgeon; b. Ukraine, Aug. 31, 1924; s. Alex and Maria (Kostiw) Z.; arrived in U.S., 1951, naturalized, 1956; M.D., U. Bonn, Germany, 1951; m. Stefania Pidbirny, Aug. 21, 1954; children—Marta, Stephanie Christine, Andrea Maria, Mark B. Intern, Little Co. Mary Hosp., Chgo., 1953-54; resident in orthopaedic surgery St. Luke's Hosp., Chgo., 1954-55, Univ. Hosp., Oklahoma City, 1955-56; orthopaedic fellow Northwestern U., Chgo., 1957; asst. prof. orthopaedic surgery U. Okla. Sch. Medicine, 1957-58; practice medicine specializing in orthopaedic surgery, Springfield, Ill., 1958—; clinical prof. orthopaedic surgery, So. Ill. U. Sch. Medicine, Springfield, 1976—. Mem. Bd. Orthopaedic Surgeons, AMA, Ill. Med. Soc., Am. Acad. Orthopaedic Surgeons, Internat. Soc. Orthopaedic Surgery and Traumatology. Roman Catholic. Clubs: Illini Country. Contbr. articles in field to profl. jours. Home: 125 Oakmont St Springfield IL 62704 Office: 901 W Jefferson St Springfield IL 62702

ZARIF, ABBAS, pathologist; b. India, Mar. 15, 1942; s. Tayebbhai Mohammedali and Zainebbai (Sabuwala) Z.; came to U.S., 1967, naturalized, 1977; M.B.B.S., Calcutta Med. Coll., 1964; m. Mehrunnisa A. Dalal, May 30, 1967; 1 son, Adil. Intern, Christ Hosp., Oak Lawn, Ill., 1967-68; resident in pathology Cook County Hosp., Chgo., 1968-72; asso. pathologist Oak Park (Ill.) Hosp., 1972—; pres. A & M Med. Service Co., Ltd. Fellow Am. Coll. Pathology, Am. Soc. Clin. Pathologists; mem. AMA, Chgo. Med. Soc. Home: 10600 Dorchester St Westchester IL 60153 Office: 520 S Maple St Oak Park IL 60304

ZARING, PHILIP BREWER, historian; b. Soda Springs, Idaho, July 29, 1932; s. Byron K. and Florence A. (Brewer) Z.; A.B., Ind. U., 1955; M.A., Yale U., 1959, Ph.D., 1966; m. Jane M. Thomas, Aug. 6, 1966; children—David, Noah. Instr. history Iowa State U., Ames, 1966-68, asst. prof., 1968—. Served with U.S. Army, 1956-58. Mem. Am. Hist. Assn., Conf. Brit. Studies. Home: 1955 Meadow Glen St North Ames IA 50010 Office: 603 Ross Hall Iowa State U Ames IA 50011

ZARISH, JOSEPH FREDERICK, furniture mfg. co. exec.; b. Chgo., Mar. 13, 1919; s. Michael and Ursula (Petrick) Z.; B.S. in Mktg. Distbn., U. Ill., 1940; postgrad. Northwestern U., Havana Bus. U.; m. Jane Butler, June 21, 1952; children—Janet Ann, Karen Patricia, Barbara Beth, Jeffrey Frederick. Set up export co., Havana, Cuba, 1946; salesman Salmanson & Co., N.Y.C., 1946-48, mgr. Chgo. office, 1947, asst. to pres., 1948; nat. sales and merchandising mgr. Sealy, Inc., Chgo., 1948-53; exec. dir. Spring Air Co., 1953, exec. v.p., 1953-56; became v.p. merchandising Schnadig Corp. and subs.'s, Internat., Karpen, 1956; v.p. mktg. Schnadig Corp., 1958-60, Storkline Corp., 1961-62; pres. Chamberlain Metal Products Co., Frankfort, Mich., 1962-64, also dir.; pres. Canterbury House, Inc., Peru, Ind., 1964—; pres. Flagship Enterprises, 1950-65; dir. Sandymac Corp., Buelah, Mich., 1961-63; pres. Award Exhibits, Inc., 1956-62; cons. in field. Mem. savs. bond div. U.S. Sec. Treasury Staff, 1943-48; steering com. NCCJ; sec. community council Grissom Air Base, 1976, 1st v.p., 1977; treas. Peru United Fund, 1974; membership chmn. Mississinewa Reservoir Devel. Assn., 1965-68; chmn. Miami County Heart Fund; bd. dirs. Clarence Darrow Community Center, Hull House, 1969-74, hon. mem. bd., 1974—; bd. dirs. United Fund, Peru, 1966-67; bd. dirs., mem. exec. com. Chgo. chpt. Am. Diabetic Assn.; treas. Am. Diabetic Assn. Greater Chgo. and N. Affiliates, bd. dirs., chmn. nat. audit com., 1975—; chmn. indsl. div. Heart Fund, 1971-74, chmn. Ind. div., 1975. Served from pvt. to maj. Signal Corps, U.S. Army, 1941-46. Recipient Kimberly Clark Promotional award, 1953. Mem. AIM, Res. Officers Assn., Soc. Gen. Semantics, Peru Circus, Peru C. of C., Nat. Assn. Bedding Mfrs., Am. Legion (post chaplain), Nat. Sales Execs. Assn., Furniture Club Am. (pres. 1962), Alpha Kappa Psi, Delta Phi (trustee). Clubs: Elks, Execs. Author promotional booklets, articles in sales jours. Home: 1275 Warwick Ct Deerfield IL 60015 Office: 217 E Canal St Peru IN 46970

ZAROSLINSKI, JOHN FELIX, pharm. co. exec.; b. Chgo., Sept. 12, 1925; s. Frank S. and Sophie (Pietrowicz) Z.; Ph.B., U. Chgo., 1951; Ph.D., Loyola U., 1965; m. Beryl Edith Kitchen, June 17, 1951; children—John Ross, Jennifer Ann. Chemist, Armour Labs., Chgo., 1951-53; sr. pharmacologist Baxter Labs., Morton Grove, Ill., 1953-58; sci. dir. Arnar Stone Labs., Mt. Prospect, Ill., 1958-65, v.p. research and devel., 1965-76, v.p. sci. liaison and planning, worldwide, 1976—; lectr. pharmacology Stritch Sch. Medicine, Loyola U., Chgo., 1966—. Served with AUS, 1943-46. Mem. N.Y. Acad. Sci., AAAS, Am. Pharm. Assn., Acad. Pharm. Scis., Am. Soc. Pharmacology and Exptl. Therapeutics, Brit. Pharmacol. Soc., Am. Chem. Soc., Midwest Pharm. Group. Home: 1202 Norman Ln Deerfield IL 60015 Office: 601 E Kensington Rd Mount Prospect IL 60056

ZARSE, LEIGH BRYANT, architect, archtl. engr.; b. Wauwatosa, Wis., Sept. 26, 1930; s. Alfred Henry and Cecile (Moreau) Z.; student U. Wis., Milw., 1948-50, Ohio State U., 1950-52; B. Archtl. Engring., U. Ill., 1954; m. Hannelore Schilling, June 30, 1973. Partner, Zarse & Zarse, Inc., Milw., 1957—, pres., 1967—; mem. municipal planning com. City Club of Milw., 1965—, sec. bd. dirs., 1971. Served to maj. USAFR, 1954-57. Registered architect and profl. engr., Wis.; certified multi-disaster design protection specialist CD Preparedness Agy. Mem. AIA (Top Honor award 1963), ASCE, Am. Concrete Inst., Engrs. and Scientists of Milw., Aircraft Owners Pilots Assn., Alpha Rho Chi, Sigma Delta Omega (pres. local chpt. 1949-50). Designer numerous local, state and fed. govt. bldgs., including: 1500 seat amphitheater for Gen. McCormack, Lackland AFB, San Antonio, 1954, 40 schs. in S.E. Wis., 1957—, Kenosha (Wis. City Hall, 1971, St. Francis (Wis.) City Hall, 1963, Hales Corners (Wis.) City Hall, 1968, FAA and Weather Bur. Bldg. at Gen. Billy Mitchell Field, Milw., 1970. Home: 1812 Mountain Ave Wauwatosa WI 53213 Office: 1201 N Prospect Ave Milwaukee WI 53202

ZAUN, ROBERT LEROY, real estate broker; b. Evanston, Ill., Jan. 4, 1940; s. Franklin LeRoy and Marion Gladys (Paulsen) Z.; B.A., Valparaiso U., 1962; m. Karin Nedra Kamlin, July 6, 1963; children—Stacy Carlene, Gregory LeRoy. Real estate salesman Homefinders Realtors, Palatine, Ill., 1967-68, owner, 1969-76, treas., 1969-70, v.p., 1970-72, pres., 1972-76; pres. ERA-Behrens & Zaun, Inc., Realtors, Palatine, 1976—, ERA of No. Ill., 1976—; tchr. Harper Coll., 1971, 72, 73, mem. real estate adv. bd., 1971—. Served to capt. USAF, 1963-67. Mem. N.W. Suburban (v.p. 1974-75), Lake County, McHenry County bds. realtors, Delta Theta Phi. Office: 235 N Northwest Hwy Palatine IL 60067

ZAVALA, DONALD CHARLES, physician, research scientist, educator; b. El Centro, Calif., Nov. 1, 1923; s. Michael Joseph and Effie Delores (McElyea) Z.; B.A., Wooster Coll., 1944; M.D., U. Cin., 1948; m. Julia Frances Hart, Nov. 23, 1946; children—Catherine Anne, Rebecca Anne, Donald Charles, Jr. Intern, U. Iowa Hosp., Iowa City, 1948-49, resident, 1949-52; pvt. practice medicine specializing in internal medicine, El Centro, Calif., 1952-69; fellow in pulmonary disease U. Iowa, 1969-70; instr. pulmonary disease U. Iowa Hosps., Iowa City, 1970-71, asst. prof., 1971-73, asso. prof. 1973-76, prof. medicine, 1976—. Served to pvt., M.C., U.S. Army, 1944; with Army N.G., 1949-67. Career research awardee Am. Lung. Assn. Iowa.; grantee Iowa, Nat. Tb and respiratory diseases assns.; licensed physician Ohio, Iowa, Calif.; diplomate Am. Bd. Internal Medicine. Fellow A.C.P.; mem. Am. Thoracic Soc., Am. Lung. Assn., Am. Fedn. Clin. Research, Central Soc. Clin. Research, Am. Coll. Chest Physicians, Am. Broncho-Esophagological Assn., Iowa Thoracic Soc. (pres., 1975-76). Author: Flexible Fiberoptic Bronchoscopy—A Training Handbook, 1978; contbr. articles to med. jours. and books. Home: 1630 Derwen Dr Iowa City IA 52240 Office: U Iowa Hospitals Iowa City IA 52242

ZAWORSKI, BERNARD EDWARD, surgeon; b. Joliet, Ill., Dec. 1. 1923; s. Walter and Regina M. (Plewa) Z.; M.D., Loyola U., Chgo.; m. Marjorie R. Huston, Dec. 29, 1951; children—Bernard, Regina, Phillip, Suzanne, Richard, Thomas, Rebecca, James. Intern, Cook County Hosp., Chgo., 1951-53, resident in obstetrics and gynecology, 1956-59; practice gen. medicine, 1953-56; practice medicine, specializing in obstetrics and gynecology, Joliet, 1959—; chmn. dept. obstetrics Silver Cross Hosp., 1976-78. Served in U.S. Army, 1943-46. Diplomate Am. Bd. Obstetrics and Gynecology. Mem. AMA, Ill. Med. Soc., Am. Coll. Obstetricians and Gynecologists, Am. Fertility Soc., Am. Geriatrics Soc., Am. Interprofl. Inst. Roman Catholic. Home: 610 Manhattan Rd Joliet IL 60433 Office: 1000 W Jefferson St Joliet IL 60435

ZECH, ARTHUR CONRAD, agronomist; b. Julian, Nebr., Aug. 24, 1927; s. Hellmut William and Erna Clara (Thomas) Z.; B.S., U. Nebr., 1958; M.S., Kans. State U., 1959, Ph.D., 1962; m. Emma Loyce Betterton, Mar. 21, 1959; 1 dau., Agnes Fern Zech Newman. Sr. agronomist Farmland Industries, Inc., Kansas City, Mo., 1961-65, research scientist, 1965-69, mgr. agrl. sci. research, 1960-75, mgr. plant scis. research, 1975—. Served with AUS, 1950-52. Decorated Bronze Star. Mem. Alpha Gamma Sigma, Alpha Zeta, Alpha Tau Alpha, Gamma Sigma Delta, Sigma Xi. Home: Route 2 PO Box 197 Plattsburg MO 64477 Office: 3315 N Oak Trafficway Kansas City MO 64116

ZEHNDER, WILLIAM J., JR., restaurant exec.; b. Frankenmuth, Mich., Apr. 6, 1919; s. William and Amelia (Bickel) Z.; grad. high sch.; m. Dorothy Hecht, May 2, 1943; children—Judith Ann, William Albert, Roxie Jean. Asst. mgr. Zehnder's Restaurant, 1937-41, mgr., 1941-45; owner, mgr. Zehnder's Farms, Frankenmuth, 1938—, Frankenmuth Hauling Service, 1938—, Zehnder's Slaughterhouse, 1944-55, Frankenmuth Bavarian Inn, 1955—; v.p. Zehnder's Corp., Frankenmuth, 1955-64, pres., 1964—; owner, mgr. Frankenmuth Cheese Haus, 1968—, Frankenmuth Schnitzelbank Shop, 1967—; dir., v.p. Star of West Milling Co. Bd. dirs. Saginaw County Jr. Achievement Assn., 1965—; mem. adv. bd. Boy Scouts Am., 1959-72; life mem. Hist. Assn.; chmn. ops. com. Frankenmuth Mus., 1972—; mem. City Meml. Park Assn.; mem. pres.'s council Concordia Luth. Jr. Coll.; mem. bd. County Democratic Com., 1967-68; mem. Mich. Central Dem. Com., 1952—, Saginaw County Donkey Club, 1952—. Recipient awards Nat. Restaurant Assn., Progress award C. of C., 1965, 66, U.S. Distinguished Service award Jr. C. of C., 1966; Mich. Embassy Tourism award, 1974. Mem. Frankenmuth C. of C. (dir. 1972-76), Nat., Mich., Saginaw Valley restaurant assns., Conservation Club, East Mich. Tourist Assn. (Beaver award 1973), Saginaw County Farm Bur., Mich. Simmental Assn. (pres.), United Comml. Travelers, Luth. Laymen's League. Lutheran (ch. extension United Comml. Travelers, Luth. Laymen's League. Lutheran (ch. extension bd. Mich. dist. Mo. Synod 1957-70, bd. dirs. Mo. Synod 1971-75). Clubs: Saginaw Valley Knife and Fork, Frankenmuth Homing Pigeon. Home: 1038 S Main St Frankenmuth MI 48734 Office: 713 S Main St Frankenmuth MI 48734

ZEHRING, JOHN WILLIAM, coll. adminstr.; b. Phila., Sept. 9, 1947; s. C. Ruth (Ackleson) Z.; B.A., Eastern Coll., 1969; M.A., Princeton Theol. Sem., 1971; M.A., Rider Coll., 1971; postgrad. R.I. Coll. and Earlham Sch. Religion, 1971-78; m. Donna Taber, Aug. 3, 1968; children—Micaela Ruth, Jeremiah Donald. Dir. career planning and placement, asst. dean students Barrington (R.I.) Coll., 1971-75; dir. career planning and placement, lectr. in edn. Earlham Coll., Richmond, Ind., 1975—; cons. to govt., higher edn., religious orgns.; lectr. in field; instr. Sch. Christian Living, Richmond, 1977—. Mem. Coll. Placement Council, Midwest Coll. Placement Assn., Am. Personnel and Guidance Assn., Am. Coll. Personnel Assn., Nat. Vocat. Guidance Assn. Democrat. Presbyterian. Club: St. Davids Christian Writers's Conf. Author: Get Your Career in Gear: How to Find or Change Your Lifework, 1976; contbr. articles in field to religious, popular and profl. mags.; co-editor: Career Information for College Graduates, 1976. Home: 425 S W 16th St Richmond IN 47374 Office: PO Box 166 Earlham Coll Richmond IN 47374

ZEIGLER, EARLE FREDERICK, educator; b. N.Y.C., Aug. 20, 1919; s. Clarence Mattison and Margery Christina (Beyerkohler) Shinkle; A.B., Bates Coll., 1940; A.M., Yale U., 1944, Ph.D., 1951; LL.D., U. Windsor, 1975; m. Bertha M. Bell, June 25, 1941; children—Donald H., Barbara A. Asso. phys. dir., aquatic dir. Bridgeport (Conn.) YMCA, 1941-43; instr. German, U. Conn., Storrs, 1943-47; coach, instr. phys. edn. Yale U., New Haven, 1943-49; asst. prof. U. Western Ont. (Can.), London, 1949-50, prof., chmn. dept. phys., health and recreation edn., 1950-56; asso. prof. Sch. Edn., supr. phys. edn. and athletics U. Mich., Ann Arbor, 1956-63, chmn. dept. phys. edn. Sch. Edn., 1961-63; prof. dept. phys. edn. for men Coll. Phys. Edn., U. Ill., Urbana, 1963-72, head dept. phys. edn. for men, chmn. grad. dept., 1964-68; prof. dept. phys. and health edn. U. Western Ont., London, 1971—, dean faculty phys. edn., 1972-77. Fellow Am. Acad. Phys. Edn.; mem. Philosophy Edn. Soc.; mem. Internat. Assn. Profl. Schs. Phys. Edn., Am. Recreation Soc., AAHPER (Alliance scholar 1977-78), Can. Assn. Health, Phys. Edn. and Recreation (honor award 1975), Am. Philos. Assn., Coll. Phys. Edn. Assn., N.Am. Soc. Sport History (life), Philosophic Soc. for Study Sport (pres. 1974-75), Canadian Profl. Schs. Conf. (pres. 1953-55), Ont. Recreation Assn. (v.p., dir. 1955-56), Soc. Municipal Recreation Dirs. Ont. (Honor award 1956), Phi Epsilon Kappa. Unitarian-Universalist (religious edn. com. 1965—). Author: Administration of Physical Education and Athletics, 1959; Philosophical Foundations for Physical, Health, and Recreation Education, 1964; (with H. J. VanderZwaag) Physical Education: Progressivism or Essentialism?, 1968; Problems in the History and Philosophy of Physical Education and Sport, 1968; (with M. L. Howell and M. Trekell) Research in the History, Philosophy and Comparative Aspects of Physical Education and Sport, 1971; A History of Sport and Physical Education to 1900, 1973; Administrative Theory and Practice in Physical Education and Athletics, 1975; A History of Physical Education and Sport in the United States and Canada, 1975; Professing Physical Education and Sport Philosophy, 1975; Physical Education and Sport Philosophy, 1977; contbr. articles to profl. jours. Home: 25 Berkshire Ct London ON N6J 3N8 Canada

ZEIMET, EDWARD JOSEPH, biologist; b. Madison, Wis., Jan. 16, 1925; s. Anthony Joseph and Stella Mary (Orlowicz) Z.; B.A., U. Wis., 1948, M.S., 1950, Ph.D., 1970; m. Frances Ann Ward, May 29, 1954; children—Edward, Stephanie, Ann, Thomas, Symantha. Biology tchr. Ft. Atkinson (Wis.) High Sch., 1948-49; biologist Holtzman-Rolfsmeyer Co., Madison, 1949-52; salesman Oscar Mayer Co., Madison, 1952-54; project asst. endocrine research U. Wis. at Madison, 1954-61, zoology specialist, 1964-70; tech. rep. Spinco div. Beckman Industries, Palo Alto, Calif., 1961-64; prof. ednl. media dept. U. Wis. at LaCrosse, 1970— community care orgn. cons. Mem. budget rev. bd. United Way, LaCrosse, 1974; campus coordinator Gene McCarthy for Pres., 1972, state alternate del., 1972; campus coordinator Alvin Baldus for U.S. Congress, 1974, 76. Served with AUS, 1943-46; PTO. Mem. Assn. Ednl. Communication Tech., Wis. Audio Visual Assn., Phi Sigma. Democrat. Author: College Biology II, 1969; The Microslide Viewer, 1969; College Biology I, 1970; Trigger Tapes: A Tool for Teacher Education, 1975; asst. editor Wis. Audiovisual Dispatch, 1975-76. Home: 445 S 19th St LaCrosse WI 54601

ZEISSLER, RENATE HARE, physician; b. Zwickau, Germany; d. Martin N. and Eva A. (Hempel) Z.; came to U.S., 1956, naturalized, 1961; M.D., U. Giessen, 1955; children—Geoffrey Hare, Sylvia H., Detlev D.H. Intern, St. Joseph's Hosp., Phoenix, 1958-59; resident in phys. medicine and rehab. Case-Western Res. U. Affiliated Hosp., Cleve., 1963-64, 66-69; staff physiatrist Cleve. Clinic, 1970-73, Cuyahoga County Hosp., Cleve., 1973-74, Kinderzentrum, U. Munich (W.Ger.), 1974-75; asso. chief rehab. medicine service Cleve. VA Hosp., 1975—; sr. instr. dept. medicine Case Western Res. U., Cleve. Recipient Jobst award for med. research Am. Congress Rehab. Medicine, 1971; Physician's Recognition award AMA, 1969, 72. Fellow Am. Acad. Phys. Medicine and Rehab.; mem. Internat. Med. Rehab. Assn., Ohio Soc. Phys. Medicine and Rehab., Cleve. Acad. Medicine. Contbr. articles to profl. jours. Office: Cleve VA Hosp 10701 East Blvd Cleveland OH 44106

ZEITINGER, ROBERT CARL, SR., advt. agy. exec.; b. St. Louis, Aug. 10, 1927; s. Fred Carl and Florence May (Theby) Z.; student Ohio U., 1945; student U. Mo., 1947-48, B.J., 1955; m. Jacquelyn Lillian Read, May 9, 1953; children—Robert Carl, Janice Read. With Moloney Electric Co., St. Louis, 1951, 53, Hebert-Robinson, Inc., 1955-56; with Batz Hodgson Neuwoehner, Inc., St. Louis, 1956—, v.p., 1968—, also dir. Vice chmn. camping com. St. Louis Area council Boy Scouts Am., 1954-65, mem. Sea Explorer com., 1953-62. Served with USNR, 1945-46, 52-53. Mem. Pub. Utility Communicators Assn., Nat., Mo. (dir.) pilots assns., Bus./Profl. Advertisers Assn. (gov., regional dir.), Delta Tau Delta. Contbr. articles on Boy Scouts to nat. mags. Home: 620 Gaslite Ln Kirkwood MO 63122 Office: 411 N 10th St Saint Louis MO 63101

ZEITNER, C. ALBERT, museum curator; b. Avon, S.D., June 12, 1901; s. Gottleib B. and Ida (Fuerniss) Z.; student Northwestern Coll., 1918-20; m. June Culp, June 25, 1941; 1 son, Charles M. Postmaster, Mission, S.D., 1922-30; owner Mission Hardware & Lumber Co., 1941-50; mayor City of Mission, 1945-48; owner, curator Zeitner Geol. Mus., Mission, 1951—; judge, lectr. Nat. Mineral Convs., 1952—. Mem. Mission City Bd., 1940-50; treas. Todd County Sch. Bd., 1936-48; committeeman Republican Com., 1924-30. Mem. Soc. Vertebrate Paleontology, Am. Geol. Inst., Lakota Glacier Mineral Club, Rio Grande, Sioux Falls gem and mineral socs., Rosebud Geol. Soc., West River Earth Soc., Midwest Fedn. Mineral. Socs. (exec. com. 1967-69), Tropical Trail Gemorama (dir. 1972), Tri-County Mineral Soc., Des Moines Lapidary Soc., Corn Palace Rock Club. Republican. Lutheran (bd. treas. 1947-51). Club: Lions. Address: PO Drawer 69 Mission SD 57555

ZEKMAN, PAMELA LOIS, journalist; b. Chgo., Oct. 22, 1944; d. Theodore Nathan and Lois Jane (Bernstein) Zekman; B.A., U. Calif. at Berkeley, 1965; m. James B. Zagel, Mar. 8, 1970 (div.); m. 2d, Fredric Soll, Nov. 29, 1975. Social worker Dept. Public Aid Cook County, Chgo., 1965-66; reporter City News Bur., Chgo., 1966-70; reporter Chgo. Tribune, 1970-75, mem. task force on vote fraud investigation; reporter Chgo. Sun-Times, 1975—. Recipient Pulitzer Prize for gen. local reporting on vote fraud series, 1976; Community Service award for vote fraud series UPI, 1972; Feature Series award for nursing home abuses series AP, 1971; Pub. Service award for slumlord series UPI, 1973, Newswriting award AP, 1973; In Depth Reporting award for police brutality series AP, 1974, Investigative Reporting award Inland Daily Press Assn., 1974; Investigative Reporting award for series on city waste AP, 1975; Pulitzer Prize for pub. service for series on hosp. abuses, 1976, Investigative Reporting award for series on baby selling, 1976; Pub. Service award for series on currency exchange abuses UPI, 1976, Investigative Reporting award for series on abuses in home for retarded children AP; Edward Scott Beck award for outstanding journalistic performance, 1974.

Mem. Sigma Delta Chi. Office: 438 N Michigan Ave Chicago IL 60611

ZELASKO, THEODORE EDWARD, dir. engring.; b. Chgo., Oct. 7, 1921; s. Andrew and Antoinette (Chrobak) Z.; B.S. in Civil Engring., Purdue U., 1948; m. Irene Mary Leggo, Oct. 6, 1974; children by a previous marriage—Ronald, Mark, Thea, Andrea, Gary. Estimator, Cook County (Ill.) Hwy. Dept., 1948-51; successively field engr., project engr., tech. office engr., chief engr., dir. engring. Kenny Constrn. Co., Wheeling, Ill., 1951—. Served with USAF, 1942-45. Deocrated Air medal, D.F.C. Mem. ASCE, Purdue Alumni Assn. Roman Catholic. Club: Purdue Club of Chgo. Home: 318 W Noyes St Arlington Heights IL 60005 Office: 250 N 12th St Wheeling IL 60090

ZELIN, ROBERT EDWARD, corp. exec.; b. Chgo., Apr. 16, 1922; s. Edward Joseph and Augustine (Doles) Z.; B.S., Ill. Inst. Tech., 1943; m. Evelyn Margaret Finn, Sept. 20, 1947; children—Roberta, Barbara. Div. head engring. dept. Todd Ship Yards, Tacoma, 1943-44; with Economy Plumbing & Heating Co., Inc., Chgo., 1946-63, v.p., 1952-63; v.p. Jupiter Corp., Chgo., 1963-72, also dir.; pres. Kenosha Auto Transport Corp. (Wis.), 1969-71, also dir.; v.p. Urban Investment & Devel. Corp., Chgo., 1972-74; v.p. House of Vision, Inc., Chgo., 1974—; dir. Fed. Bake Shops, Testor Corp. Served with USNR, 1944-46. Roman Catholic. Club: Edgewood Valley Country (LaGrange, Ill.). Home: 2 S 703 Ave La Tour Oak Brook IL 60521 Office: 137 N Wabash Ave Chicago IL 60602

ZELINKOFF, MILTON ARNOLD, mfg. co. exec.; b. Denver, Oct. 18, 1906; s. Samuel Max and Jean (Katz) Z.; grad. U. Colo., 1928; m. Beatrice Besse Le Vin, July 10, 1930; children—Sandra Maxine Zelinkoff Rosenblum and Sonya Marlene Zelinkoff Simon (twins). Vice pres. Zelinkoff Co., Wichita, Kans., 1920-31, owner, gen. mgr., 1931—; mem. adv. council U.S. SBA, 1970—. Mem. Wichita Mfrs. Club (v.p.), Internat. San. Supply Assn. (pres. 1970-71), Mfrs. Club, Zeta Beta Tau. Republican. Clubs: Masons, Shriners. Patentee in field. Home: 4 Lakeside Blvd Eastborough Village Wichita KS 67207 Office: PO Box 1115 Wichita KS 67201

ZELKOWITZ, LEO, oncologist, hematologist; b. Bklyn., May 11, 1934; s. Max Herman and Ray (Gorbaty) Z.; B.S. cum laude, U. Pitts., 1956, M.D., 1960; m. Patricia Simon, Aug. 1, 1959; children—Marlyn Lee, Leslie Beth. Intern, Presbyterian-U. Hosp., Pitts., 1960-61, resident in medicine, 1963-64; resident Montefiore Hosp., Pitts., 1964-65, chief med. resident, 1965-66; fellow in hematology U. Miami (Fla.), 1966-68; asst. prof. medicine U. Ill., 1968-71; attending physician U. Ill. Hosp., 1968-71; attending hematologist VA W. Side, U. Ill. hosps., 1968-71; lectr. hematology Cook County (Chgo.) Postgrad. Sch. Medicine, 1971-72; asst. clin. prof. Mich. State U., 1975—, Cancer Center Adv. Council, 1976—, Cancer Center Search Com. for Dir., 1976—, Cancer Center Task Force, 1976—, Cancer Edn. Grant Adv. Council, 1976—, Cancer Center Outreach Program Chmn., 1976—; teaching staff Bronson Methodist Hosp., Kalamazoo, 1971—, asso. staff, 1971-72, active staff, 1972—; teaching staff Borgess Hosp., Kalamazoo, 1971—, chmn. edn. com., 1972-74, dir. med. edn., 1972-73, asso. staff, 1971-72, active staff, 1972—, chief of medicine, 1977—; bd. dirs. SW Mich. Area Health Edn. Center, Kalamazoo, 1973-74, 1976-77, resident com., 1973-74, Adv. and Rev. Bd., 1976-77; practice medicine specializing in oncology and hematology, Kalamazoo, 1971—; pres. Chgo. Blood Club, 1969-71. Bd. dirs. Little Long Lake Assn., Richland, Mich. Served with USPHS, 1961-63. Diplomate Am. Bd. Internal Medicine. Fellow A.C.P., Am. Soc. Hematology; mem. Am. Fed. Clin. Research, AMA, AAAS, Children's Leukemia Found. (med. adv. bd. 1975—), Kalamazoo Acad. Medicine (Kalamazoo Blood Adv. Com. and Pub. Health Com. for Cancer Control), Mich. State Med. Soc., Kalamazoo Mammary Study Group, SW Oncology Group (asso. 1972-74), Mich. State U. Cancer Center. Club: Gull Lake Country. Contbr. numerous articles to profl. jours. Office: 252 E Lovell St Kalamazoo MI 49006

ZELLER, GERALD LEROY, mgmt. exec.; b. Watseka, Ill., Oct. 7, 1935; s. Leroy Edward and Verna (Swanson) Z.; B.S in Bus. Adminstrn., Western Ill. U., 1961; m. Marilyn Cornish, Aug. 15, 1959; children—Scott L., Heidi Ann, Holly Jo. Sales and service supr. Pillsbury Co., Mpls., 1961-63; with Spencer Turbine Co., 1963—, regional mgr., Chgo., 1966-70; exec. v.p. Process Systems, Inc., 1970-72; pres. Advanced Indsl. Design, Addison, Ill., also Pitts., 1972—; dir. Hemox Med. Co., Lake Bluff, Ill., Indsl. Mktg. Assos., Milw.; producers Council liaison officer State of Ill. to Ill. AIA, 1967. Budget dir. Gorton Community Center, Lake Forest, Ill.; asst. dir. Nat. Ski Patrol, 1975—; mem. campaign staff state rep. Ron Griksheimer, 1972, 74, 76. Served with AUS, 1954-56. Named Nat. Sales Leader, Spencer Turbine Co., 1967. Mem. Nat. Ski Patrol, Navy League (v.p. Ill., sec. Lake County council, Midwest awards chmn. 1973—), Am. Legion, Phi Sigma Epsilon. Presbyterian. K.P. Club: Lake Bluff Yacht. Home: 131 Indian Rd Lake Bluff IL 60044 Office: 24 E Lake St Addison IL 60101

ZELLER, JOHN PAUL, assn. exec.; b. Snyder, Okla., Aug. 26, 1950; s. John Herman and Velma Lorene (Branson) Z.; B.S. in Agrl. Econs., Okla. State U., 1972; m. Barbara Ellen Mudge, Apr. 26, 1975. Trainee, Security State Bank, Wewoka, Okla., 1972-73, Fed. Intermediate Credit Bank, Wichita, 1973; field rep. Chanute (Kans.) Prodn. Credit Assn., 1973-74; v.p. Greensburg (Kans.) Prodn. Credit Assn., 1974-75; pres. Chanute Prodn. Credit Assn., 1975—; sec. 9th Farm Credit Dist. Credit Com., 1976—. Mem. Chanute C. of C., Kans. Prodn. Credit Assn. Pres.'s Assn. (sec.). Mem. Ch. Christ. Home: 1217 W 14th Ct Chanute KS 66720 Office: Box 516 Chanute KS 66720

ZEMEL, LOU, retail food exec.; b. Lagow, Poland, Feb. 19, 1918; s. Morris and Dora (Spiegel) Z.; came to U.S., 1923, naturalized, 1942; student YMCA Coll., Northwestern U.; m. Lita Hernreich, May 28, 1950; children—Dean Bruce, Gale Sue, Ellen Renee, Jeffrey Howard. With Zemel Bros. Grocery, Chgo., 1938-41; treas. Morris Zemel & Co., Chgo., 1946; pres. Riverside Farm Foods, Ft. Atkinson, Wis., 1947—. Served with U.S. Army, 1941-45. Home and Office: Riverside Dr Fort Atkinson WI 53538

ZEMJANIS, RAIMUNDS, veterinarian; b. Peterhoff, Russia, Sept. 16, 1918; s. Jean and Lucy (Akis) Z.; came U.S., 1952, naturalized, 1957; D.V.M., Royal Vet. Coll. of Sweden, 1948; Ph.D., U. Minn., 1957; m. Helene Mitucls, Apr. 11, 1942; children—Ilze, John Paul, Sylvia, Pvt. vet. practice, Sweden, 1948-51, Minn., 1952-53; with U. Minn., 1953—, prof., head dept. reproductive physiology and pathology of animals, 1959-73, prof., dir. Nat. Animal Prodn. Research Inst., Ahmadu Bello U., Nigeria, 1973—, asso. dean Coll. Vet. Medicine, 1975—; AID and WHO cons. to S.Am. and Central Am. countries, Mexico and Jamaica. Mem. bd. PTA; pres. Latvian Evang. Lutheran Ch.; leader Boy Scouts Am.; chmn. bd. Latvian Youth Center, Three Rivers, Mich. NIH sr. postdoctoral fellow, 1968-69; recipient HIH, state and found. grants; recipient excellence awards for ednl. films and videotapes, 1974-75. Mem. Am. Coll. Theriogenologists, Am., Minn. vet. med. assns., Soc. Theriogenology, N.Y. Acad. Scis., Am. Assn. Vet. Med. Colls., Sigma Xi, Alpha Psi, Phi Zeta, Sigma Delta. Author: Diagnostic Techniques in Animal Reproduction, 1970; Cattle Infertility, 1966. Contbr. chpts. in books; creator ednl. films. Home; 2080 Rosewood Ln S St Paul MN 55113 Office: College of Veterinary Medicine University of Minnesota St Paul MN 55108

ZEMLICKA, JIRÍ, chemist, educator; b. Prague, Czechoslovakia, July 31, 1933; s. Vojtech and Otilie (Hummelova) Z.; came to U.S., 1968; R.N. Dr.(M.S.) summa cum laude, Charles U., Prague, 1956; postgrad. Inst. Organic Chemistry and Biochemistry, Czechoslovakia, 1956-59, Ph.D., 1959; m. Helena Zvárová, Mar. 30, 1961; children—Helena, Jirí. Research scientist Inst. Organic Chemistry and Biochemistry, Czechoslovak Acad. Scis., Prague, 1959-69; vis. scientist Mich. Cancer Found., Detroit, 1968-69, research scientist, 1969—; asso. prof. biochemistry in oncology Wayne State U. Sch. Medicine, Detroit, 1971—; prin. investigator NIH, Bethesda, Md., 1972—. Mem. Am. Chem. Soc., Czechoslovak Soc. Arts and Scis. in Am. Author: Molecular Rearrangements, 1962; (with J. Novák) Acid-catalyzed Syntheses, 1962; contbg. author Vitamins, Chemistry and Biochemistry, 1964; contbr. articles on organic chemistry and biochemistry to profl. jours. Patentee in field. Home: 2025 Common Rd Warren MI 48092 Office: 110 E Warren St Detroit MI 48201

ZENI, BETTY JOY WAGNER, retail co. exec.; b. Chgo., Mar. 3, 1926; d. Percy E. and Elizabeth Cecelia (McGeeney) Wagner; student U. Chgo., 1942-44; B.A., Vassar Coll., 1947; postgrad. U. Zurich, 1947, Katharine Gibbs Sch., 1947-48; m. Ferdinand Joseph Zeni, Nov. 16, 1974. With Marshall Field & Co., Chgo., 1950—, mem. real estate div., 1950-72, mgr. corp. ins., 1972—. Dir. dist. Republican assembly; asst. sec. ward Rep. Orgn., 1964—; sec. dist. state central com., 1968—; pres. Women's Nat. Rep. Club, Chgo., 1976—. alternate del. Rep. Nat. Conv., 1968; bd. dirs. Lake Shore Condominium Assn., 1975—; advisory bd. Civic Fedn., 1975—. Recipient Leadership certificate Women in Met. Chgo., YWCA, 1973. Mem. Vassar Alumnae Assn., Vassar Club Chgo., Katharine Gibbs Alumnae Assn. (past pres.), Am. Soc. Ins. Mgmt. (dir. Chgo. chpt.), Risk and Ins. Mgmt. Soc. (dir. 1974-77). Pewter Collectors Club Am., Midwest Pewter Collectors Club. Home: 1440 N Lake Shore Dr Chicago IL 60610 Office: 25 E Washington St Chicago IL 60602

ZENTZ, LARRY ERVIN, assn. exec.; b. Council Bluffs, Iowa, Sept. 8, 1942; s. Ervin and Verna Lee (Stowell) Z.; B.A., Calif. State U., Chico, 1963; M.A., U. No. Colo., 1964; m. Jacqueline B. Olson, June 17, 1962; children—Randy Jon, Stephanie Lynn. Dean students, dir. admissions Rockmont Coll., Denver, 1964-67; dean students, dir. alumni affairs Trinity Coll. and Trinity Evang. Div. Sch., Deerfield, Ill., 1967-71; adminstrv. asst. to v.p.-dean of students Loyola U., Chgo., 1971-72; dir. pub. awareness, dir. development Met. Chgo. YMCA, 1972-74; dir. devel., asst. exec. dir. Chgo. Lung Assn., 1974-76; managing dir. Am. Lung Assn. Ind., Indianapolis, 1976—. Bd. dirs. Memomonee Club Boys Girls, 1974-76, Logos Bookstore, 1974-76, Chgo. Ballet Assos. N., 1975-76. Episcopalian. Home: 4305 56th St Indianapolis IN 46220 Office: 30 E Georgia St Indianapolis IN 46204

ZEOLI, WILLIAM JUDSON, motion picture exec.; b. Phila., Sept. 25, 1932; s. Anthony and Elizabeth (Hoffman) Z.; student Phila. Coll. Bible, 1950-53; B.A., Wheaton Coll., 1955; D.R.E. (hon.), Greenville (Ill.) Coll., 1973; m. Marilyn Brock, Oct. 15, 1955; children—Stephen Anthony, David Andrew, Patricia. Exec. dir. Indpls. Youth for Christ, 1955-60; v.p. Youth Films, Inc., Muskegon, Mich., 1960-62; exec. v.p. Gospel Films, Inc., Muskegon, 1962-64, pres., 1964—, dir., 1955—; exec. sec. Billy Graham Crusade in Greater Indpls., 1958-59. Bd. dirs. Radio Bible House, 1957—, Ch. Centered Evangelism, 1958—, Teen Crusades, Inc., 1967—. Recipient Spl. Service award U.S. Air Force, 1961, Meritorious Service award Army Chaplain Bd., 1966, Community Achievement award, Indpls., 1959, Outstanding Achievement award State of Ind., 1959, Ind. Boys Schs., 1959, Key to City of Tacoma, 1960, Key to State of Wash., 1960, spl. achievement award for audio-visuals Nat. Film Found. Club: Indpls. Athletic. Author: Tom Landry and the Dallas Cowboys; Supergoal; numerous articles. Home: 944 Rosalie Dr Grand Rapids MI 49504 Office: PO Box 455 Muskegon MI 49443

ZEPF, THOMAS HERMAN, physicist; b. Cin., Feb. 13, 1935; s. Paul A. and Agnes J. (Schulz) Z.; B.S., Xavier U., 1957; M.S. (NSF research fellow), St. Louis U., 1960, Ph.D., 1963. Asst. prof. physics Creighton U., Omaha, 1962-67, acting chmn. dept., 1963-66, chmn. dept., 1966-73, asso. prof., 1967-75, prof., 1975—, coordinator advising for pre-health scis. students, 1976—; vis. prof. St. Louis U., 1973-74. Chmn. physics judging com. Greater Nebr. Sci. and Engring. Fair, 1973—; moderator Explorer post Mid-Am. council Boy Scouts Am., 1971-73. Mem. Am. Assn. Physics. Tchrs. (pres. Nebr. sect. 1977-78), Am. Phys. Soc., Nebr. Acad. Scis., AAAS, Albertus Magnus Guild, Sigma Xi, Sigma Pi Sigma. Club: K.C. Contbr. articles to profl. jours. Home: 3316 S 54th St Omaha NE 68106 Office: 2500 California St Omaha NE 68178

ZERBI, PAUL GENOESE, thoracic and cardiovascular surgeon; b. Italy, Aug. 2, 1933; s. Domenico Genoese and Rose (Contestabile) Z.; came to U.S., 1962, naturalized, 1972; M.D., U. Modena (Italy), 1960; m. Mary Martha Berring, Jan. 11, 1964; children—Paula, Jayne, Dominic. Intern U. Hosp., U. Modena, 1960; physician with U.S. Army, Germany, 1961; resident in surgery Aultman Hosp., Canton, Ohio, 1962-63, Mercy Hosp., Canton, 1963-65, Columbus Hosp., N.Y.C., 1965-66; resident in thoracic and cardiovascular surgery Emory U. Hosps., Atlanta, 1966-68; chief surgery Central State Hosp., Milledgeville, Ga., 1968-70; practice medicine specializing in thoracic and cardiovascular surgery, Warren, Ohio, 1970—; chief thoracic and cardiovascular surgery Trumbull Meml. Hosp., 1973—. Diplomate Am. Bd. Surgery, Am. Bd. Thoracic Surgery. Fellow A.C.S., Am. Coll. Chest Physicians; mem. Am., Ohio State med. assns., Trumbull County Med. Soc., Cleve. Surg. Soc., Soc. Thoracic Surgeons, Am. Heart Assn. Roman Catholoic. Home: 1734 Coventry Dr Warren OH 44483 Office: 3843 E Market St Warren OH 44484

ZIBELL, DONALD FREDERICK, lawyer, accountant; b. St. Paul, Feb. 13, 1937; s. Otto Ernest and Anna (Schroeder) Z.; student St. Olaf Coll., 1955-57; B.A., U. Minn., 1959; J.D. cum laude, William Mitchell Coll. Law, 1962; m. Luella Louise Lepisto, Oct. 14, 1967; 1 dau., Deanne. Tax accountant Boulay & Co., C.P.A.'s, Mpls., 1959-67, tax mgr., 1964-67; partner, tax mgr. Boulay, Heutmaker, Zibell & Co., C.P.A.'s, Mpls., 1967—; gen. partner Roseville Profl. Center, 1969—; dir. Roseville State Bank; chmn. Minn. C.P.A. Tax Conf. Com., 1972-73. Bd. dirs. The Residence, Inc. (for retarded citizens), 1972—, treas., 1972—. Named one of Minn.'s Ten Outstanding Young Men, Minn. Jr. C. of C., 1971; C.P.A., Minn. Mem. Am. Bar Assn., Am. Inst. C.P.A.'s, Minn. Soc. C.P.A.'s, Mpls. C.P.A. Tax Roundtable (chmn. 1975-76), Phi Alpha Delta. Republican. Lutheran. Club: Rotary. Home: 3061 N Hamline Ave Roseville MN 55113 Office: 6800 France Ave S Minneapolis MN 55435

ZICHEK, MELVIN EDDIE, clergyman, educator; b. Lincoln, Nebr., May 5, 1918; s. Eddie and Agnes (Varga) Z.; A.B., Nebr. Central Coll., 1942; M.A., U. Nebr., 1953; D.Litt., McKinley-Roosevelt Ednl. Inst., 1955; m. Dorothy Virginia Patrick, May 28, 1942; 1 dau., Shannon Elaine. Ordained to ministry Christian Ch., 1942; minister Christian chs., Brock, Nebr., 1941, Ulysses, Nebr., 1942-43, Elmwood, Nebr., 1943-47, Central City, Nebr., 1947—; rural tchr., Merrick County, Nebr., 1937-40; prin. Alvo (Nebr.) Consol. High Sch., 1943-47; supt. Archer (Nebr.) Pub. Schs., 1948-57; head dept. English and speech Central City (Nebr.) High Sch., 1957-63; supt. Marquette (Nebr.) Consol. Schs., 1963—. Served as chaplain's asst. AUS, 1942. Mem. Nebr., Hamilton County edn. assns., Nebr. Sch. Adminstrs. Assn., Internat. Platform Assn., Merrick County Ministerial Assn., Disciples of Christ Hist. Soc., Nat. Sch. Adminstrs. Assn. Home: 1621 15th Ave Central City NE 68826

ZICK, LEONARD O., mfg. exec., financial cons.; b. St. Joseph, Mich., Jan. 16, 1905; s. Otto J. and Hannah (Heyn) Z.; student Western State Coll., Kalamazoo; m. Anna Essig, June 27, 1925 (dec. May 1976); children—Rowene Zick Neidow, Arlene Zick Anton, Constance Mae Zick Snell, Shirley Ann Zick Vander Ley (dec.). Sr. partner firm Zick, Campbell & Rose, C.P.A.'s, South Bend, Ind., 1928-48; sec.-treas. C. M. Hall Lamp Co., Detroit, 1948-51, pres. 19S1-54, chmn. bd., 1954-56; pres., treas., dir. Allen Electric & Equipment Co., Kalamazoo, 1954-56; pres., dir., treas. The Lithibar Co., Holland, Mich., 1956-61; v.p., treas. Crampton Mfg. Co., 1961-63; mgr. corporate fin. dept. Manley, Bennett, McDonald & Co., Detroit, 1963-68; mgr. Leonard O. Zick & Assos., Holland, 1968—; chmn. fin. com., dir. Eberhard's Foods, Inc., Grand Rapids; dir. Kandu Industries. Former mem. Mich. Republican Central Com. Mem. Nat. Assn. Accountants (past nat. v.p., dir.), Fin. Execs. Inst., Stuart Cameron McLeod Soc. (past pres.). Lutheran. Clubs: E. Bay Country (Fla.); Detroit Athletic; Peninsular (Grand Rapids); Holland Country; Union League (Chgo.); Rotary. Home: 849 Brook Village Holland MI 49423 Office: 21 W 16th St Holland MI 49423

ZICK, THOMAS RUSSELL, accountant; b. Kalamazoo, Mich., June 26, 1948; s. Thomas Russell and Margaret Ellen (Soper) Z.; B.B.A., Eastern Mich. U., 1970, M.B.A., 1975; m. Marilyn Lou Boyce, Jan. 26, 1968; children—Melissa Lynn, Angela Marie. Audit sr. Peat, Marwick, Mitchell & Co., Detroit, 1970-72; audit supr. Young, Stutt & Breitenwischer, Jackson, Mich., 1972-74; instr. accounting Eastern Mich. U., Ypsilanti, 1975; partner Robertson & Zick, Rose City, Mich., 1976—. Treas., Johannesburg-Lewiston Area Sch. Bd., 1976—. C.P.A. Mem. Am. Inst. C.P.A.'s, Mich. Assn. C.P.A.'s, Lewiston C. of C. Lion. Office: 103 E Main St Rose City MI 48654

ZIEBARTH, ROBERT CHARLES, mgmt. cons.; b. Evanston, Ill., Sept. 12, 1936; s. Charles Alvin and Marian (Miller) Z.; A.B., Princeton U., 1958; M.B.A., Harvard U., 1964; m. Patience Arnold Kirkpatrick, Aug. 28, 1971; children—Dana Kirkpatrick, Scott Kirkpatrick, Christopher, Nicholas. Mgr. fin. analysis Bell & Howell Co., Chgo., 1964, mgr. fin. planning, 1965-68, controller photo products group, 1968-69, treas., chief fin. exec., 1969-73; mgmt. cons. Ziebarth Co., Chgo., 1973—; mem. dirs. adv. bd. Arkwright Boston Ins. Co., 1969—; dir. Corp Resources Inc., Telemedia, Inc. Asso., Community Renewal Soc., 1969—; trustee Choate Sch., Wallingford, Conn., Latin Sch., Chgo.; bd. dirs. Harvard Bus. Sch. Fund, Gateway House Citizens' Council; mem. Ill. Bd. Higher Edn., Ill. Joint Edn. Commn. Served to lt. USNR, 1959-62. Mem. Naval Hist. Found., Chgo. Hist. Soc., Art Inst., Mus. Modern Art. Clubs: Mid Am., Econ., Execs., Racquet, Saddle and Cycle. Office: 1500 Lake Shore Dr Chicago IL 60610

ZIEGLER, DUANE HERBERT, elec. engr.; b. Richardton, N.D., July 27, 1944; s. Herbert Raymond and Dorthea Anna (Bergstedt) Z.; B.S. in Elec. Engring., N.D. State U., 1967; m. Carol Louise Kragnes, June 15, 1968; children—Melanie Marie, Christopher Duane. Engr., John Deere Harvester Works, East Moline, Ill., 1967—. Dir., sec. and v.p. E. Moline-Silvia Jaycees. Recipient Presdl. award of honor, Jaycees, 1972. Republican. Lutheran. Holder patent for harvester shaft speed monitoring system, automatic height control system. Home: 1109 Melody Ln Level Acres Colona IL 61241 Office: 1100 13th Ave East Moline IL 61244

ZIEMELIS, ANDRIS, psychologist; b. Rezekne, Latvia, Mar. 16, 1943; s. Bruno and Brunhilde (Klepper) Danisevskis; came to U.S., 1949, naturalized, 1955; A.B., Ind. U., 1966, M.S., 1967, Ed.D., 1971; m. Luise Caroline Schull, June 8, 1968. Counselor-psychometrist, Indpls. Goodwill Industries, 1968-69; staff psychologist Hot Springs (Ark.) Rehab. Center, 1969-70; counseling psychologist, asso. prof. U. Wis. at LaCrosse, 1970—; psychol. cons. Ouachita Regional Counseling and Mental Health Center, Hot Springs, 1969-70; asst. dir. program analysis and assessment Cath. Social Service, LaCrosse, 1972-76. Mem. Am. Psychol. Assn., Am. Personnel and Guidance Assn., Am. Rehab. Counseling Assn., AAUP, Coulee Region Psychologists, Phi Delta Kappa. Lutheran. Home: Route 1 Brownsville MN 55919 Office: U Wis LaCrosse WI 54601

ZIEN, BURT, mech. contracting co. exec.: b. Milw., Nov. 2, 1912; s. Herman and Florence Z.; B.S.M.E., U. Wis., 1935; m. Betty Segal, Mar. 10, 1946; 1 son, Jim. Clk., TVA, Knoxville, 1935-38; investigator unemployment compensation div. Tenn. Dept. Labor, 1938-40; mgr. East Tenn. office wage and hour div. U.S. Dept. Labor, 1940-42, 46-48; mgr. East Tenn. office NLRB, Knoxville, 1948-50; gen. mgr., chmn. bd. Zien Plumbing and Heating Co., Milw., 1950—; treas., exec. bd. Zien Sheet Metal Co. V.p. Wis. Bd. Vocat., Tech. and Adult Edn., co-chmn. inter-agency com. correctional instns.; mem. County Exec.'s Advisory Com. Manpower and Employment; mem. subcom. minority enterprise Gov.'s Task Force on Commerce and Industry; bd. dirs., exec. com. Am.-Israel Pub. Affairs Com., Milw. Jewish Council; bd. dirs. Mt. Sinai Med. Center; del. Democratic Nat. Conv., 1968, 72, 76; mem. Dem. Nat. Platform Com., 1972, 76. Served as capt. USAAF, 1942-46. Recipient Human Rights award Milw. B'nai B'rith, 1971; Distinguished Service award Opportunities Industrialization Center (inner city tng. program), 1971; Internat. citation Internat. Assn. Personnel in Employment Security, 1977. Mem. NAACP, Milw. Urban League, Met. Milw. Assn. Commerce, U. Wis. Alumni Assn. Democrat. Jewish. Club: River Oaks Country. Home: 501 East Lake Terr Whitefish Bay WI 53217 Office: 4450 N Oakland Ave Milwaukee WI 53211

ZIEN, HWA MING, mech. engr.; b. Shanghai, China, Jan. 28, 1937; s. Vicent and Wen Tsen (Tao) Z.; came to U.S., 1962, naturalized, 1974; B.S., Nat. Taiwan U., 1960; M.S., U. Rochester (N.Y.), 1964, Ph.D., 1965; m. Cherry Chi, Aug. 12, 1967; children—Jason Y., Harvey Y. Research asso., dept. mech. and aerospace scis. U. Rochester (N.Y.), 1965-69; research specialist Babcock & Wilcox Co., Alliance (Ohio) Research Center, 1969—; co-owner Alliance Data Processing; researcher magneto hydrodynamic stabilities; developer computer programs for analysis advanced composite structures, analyst stress and vibration of structures. Mem. Sigma Xi. Contbr. tech. papers to profl. jours. Home: 2052 Crestview Ave Alliance OH 44601 Office: Babcock Wilcox Co 1562 Beeson St Alliance OH 44601

ZIENTY, FERDINAND BENJAMIN, chem. co. exec.; b. Chgo., Mar. 21, 1915; s. Albert Frank and Rose Cecelia (Przypyszny) Z.; B.S., U. Ill., 1935; M.S., U. Mich., 1936, Ph.D., 1938; m. Claylain Lorraine Cawiezell, Apr. 14, 1945; children—Jane Zienty Wheeler, Donald Ferd. Research chemist organic chems. div. Monsanto Co., St. Louis, 1938-40, research group leader, 1940-47, asst. dir. research,

1947-50, asso. dir. research, 1950-56, dir. research, 1956-60, dir. advanced organic chems. research, 1960-64, mgr. research and devel., 1964—; v.p. research George Lueders & Co. subs. Monsanto Co., St. Louis, 1968-70. Recipient Hodel, Saltiel, Hodel Prize for scholarship, 1935, Sesquicentennial award U. Mich., 1967; Fairchild scholar, 1935, Frederick Stearns fellow, 1936-37. Fellow AAAS, N.Y. Acad. Scis.; mem. Am. Chem. Soc., Am. Inst. Chem. Engrs., Am. Pharm. Assn., Inst. Food Technologists, Mo. Acad. Sci., Soc. Chem. Industry (London), Soc. Cosmetic Chemists. Club: Triple A Country. Contbr. articles to profl. jours. Patentee in field. Home: 850 Rampart Dr Warson Woods MO 63122 Office: 800 N Lindbergh Blvd Saint Louis MO 63166

ZIGERELL, JAMES JOSEPH, educator; b. Monaca, Pa., June 12, 1920; s. Otto and Catherine (Howe) Z.; A.B., Loyola U., Chgo., 1940, A.M., 1948; Ph.D. in English Lang. and Lit., U. Chgo., 1962; m. Rosamond Carney, June 27, 1949; 1 dau., Joan Marie. Adminstrv. asst. Chgo. City Jr. Coll., 1962—, prof. English, 1947—, dean, 1965—, exec. dean learning resources, 1971, asst. vice chancellor, 1976—; translator with occupation forces, Europe, 1945-46; lectr. on uses TV in edn., 1962—. Served with AUS, 1942-45. Mem. Nat. Council Tchrs. English, Modern Lang. Assn., AAUP, NEA, Nat. Assn. Edn. Broadcasters. Contbr. articles and revs. to profl. and lit. jours. Office: 11th Floor 180 N Michigan Ave Chicago IL 60601

ZIKE, VICTOR MILTON, psychologist; b. Westfield, Iowa, Sept. 1, 1920; s. Floyd Milton and Stella Murl (Randall) Z.; B.S., Simpson Coll., 1948; M.S., U. Ill., 1951; postgrad. Drake U., 1955-56, Iowa State U., 1965, U. Colo., 1973; m. Rosalene Annette Corbus, Nov. 26, 1947; children—Carole Ann Zike Custer, Susan Marie Zike White. Dir. social services dept. Clarinda (Iowa) Mental Hosp., 1948; head psychology dept. Glenwood (Iowa) State Sch., 1951-56; dir. spl. edn. Greene County Bd. Edn., Jefferson, Iowa, 1956-66; sch. psychologist Perry (Iowa) Community Schs., 1966-68, Jefferson Community Schs., 1968-69, Urbandale (Iowa) Community Schs., 1969—; mem. adv. bd. Iowa Mental Retardation Assn., 1952-55; mem. Iowa Gov's. Adv. Bd. on Mental Retardation, 1961. Leader, 4-H, 1964-70; mem. County 4-H County Bd., 1967-70. Served with USAAC, 1942-46. Mem. Am. Assn. Mental Retardation, Am., Iowa psychol. assns., Phi Beta Kappa, Pi Gamma Mu. Methodist (ednl. bd. bd. 1958-61). Home: 1424 Otley Perry IA 50220 Office: 8100 Airline St Urbandale IA 50322

ZILLES, LELAND CARL, veterinarian; b. Fremont, Ohio, Mar. 11, 1937; s. Earl Raymond and Marian Elizabeth (Reed) Z.; D.V.M., Ohio State U., 1961; m. Joyce Ann Titsch, Aug. 27, 1960; 1 son, Earl Raymond. Resident veterinarian Marlu Farm, Lincroft, N.J., 1961-63; pvt. practice veterinary medicine specializing in bovine medicine, West Liberty, Ohio, 1963—; pres. Big Ten Pen's Inc., Cable, Ohio, 1971—. Mem. West Liberty-Salem Bd. Edn., 1968—, pres., 1969, 73. Recipient Alumni award 4-H, Sandusky County, Ohio, 1973. Mem. Am., Ohio veterinary med. assns., Am. Assn. Bovine Practioners (charter). Club: Lions (pres. West Liberty 1967-68). Home: McClain Rd West Liberty OH 43357 Office: Box 543 West Liberty OH 43357

ZILLMAN, ROY STUART, social scientist, educator; b. Batavia, N.Y., Mar. 28, 1932; s. Stuart Edward and Winifred Nancy (Dery) Z.; A.B., U. Miami, 1958; M.A. (Falk fellow), U. Calif. at Los Angeles, 1964; Ph.D. (Ford Found. grantee, univ. research grantee), U. Calif. at Riverside, 1971; m. Anne Reymond, Dec. 28, 1972. Vis. research prof. U. Chile, Santiago, 1967-69; asst. prof. polit. sci. Ind. State U., Terre Haute, 1969—, coordinator Latin Am. studies program, 1974—; pres. Calif. Investments, Los Angeles, 1962-64, Internat. Mgmt. Consultants, 1976—. Served with USAF, 1952-56. U. Chile at Santiago research grantee, 1968. Mem. Inter-Am. Soc., Am. Polit. Sci. Assn., Latin Am., Mid-West Latin Am. studies assns. Home: Box 11 Bowling Green IN 47833

ZILLMANN, ROBERT EDWARD, fin. exec.; b. Evanston, Ill., Mar. 16, 1929; s. Emil R. and Daisy (Greenland) Z.; student Lake Forest Coll., 1948-49; B.S., Northwestern U., 1952; m. Marie Frances Vranicar, May 24, 1953; children—Barbara Marie, Eric Robert. Pub. accountant H. C. Goettsche & Co., Chgo., 1952-57; fin. exec. Abbott Labs., Chgo., 1957-61; ops. mgr. Abbott Labs,, S.A.R.L., Montreaux, Switzerland, 1962-63; corp. controller G.D. Searle & Co., Chgo., 1964-68; treas. Marsteller, Inc., Chgo., 1968-70, fin. v.p., 1970-73; asst. treas. APECO Corp., Evanston, Ill., 1973, corp. controller, 1974; comptroller Nat. Assn. Realtors, Chgo., 1974, staff v.p. fin. and adminstrn., 1975—. Served with AUS, 1946-48. C.P.A., Ill. Mem. Ill. Soc. C.P.A.'s, Am. Inst. C.P.A.'s, Fin. Execs. Inst., Controllers Inst. Home: 2235 Central Park Ave Evanston IL 60201 Office: 430 N Michigan Ave Chicago IL 60611

ZILM, KARL MILLER, mathematician; b. Carlinville, Ill., Feb. 22, 1948; s. Henry George and Mary Augusta (Loehr) Z.; B.A., Blackburn Coll., 1970; M.S., Purdue U., 1972. Teaching asst., math. dept. Purdue U., West Lafayette, Ind., 1970-72; prof. statistics Blackburn Coll., Carlinville, 1973-74; instr. math. Lewis Clark Community Coll., Godfrey, Ill., 1973—. Recipient Bierd Sr. Honor prize, math. prize Blackburn Coll., 1970. Mem. Math. Assn. Am., Ill. Math. Assn. Community Colls. Lutheran. Home: 241 Woodbury St Alton IL 62002 Office: Lewis Clark Community Coll Godfrey Rd Godfrey IL 62035

ZILVERSMIT, ARTHUR, historian, coll. adminstr.; b. The Hague, Netherlands, July 5, 1932; s. Marcus and Marianne (deKorte) Z.; B.A., Cornell U., 1954; M.A., Harvard U., 1955; Ph.D., U. Calif. at Berkeley, 1962; came to U.S., 1939, naturalized, 1943; m. Charlotte Perlman, Dec. 26, 1955; children—Marc Jonathan, Karen Janny. Instr., asst. prof. history Williams Coll., Williamstown, Mass., 1961-66; asst. prof. Lake Forest (Ill.) Coll., 1966-68, asso. prof., 1968-73, prof., 1973—, dir. grad. and continuing edn., 1977—. Hon. fellow Shelby Cullom David Center, Princeton U., 1972-73. Mem. Am. Hist. Assn., Orgn. Am. Historians, Inst. Early Am. History, History of Edn. Soc. Author: The First Emancipation, 1966; Lincoln on Black and White, 1972. Home: 320 Spruce Ave Lake Forest IL 60045 Office: Lake Forest Coll Lake Forest IL 60045

ZIMA, WILLARD JAMES, JR., sign co. exec.; b. Gary, Ind., Apr. 2, 1941; s. Willard James and Helen Hazel (Wilson) Z.; student Ind. U., El Camino Coll., Calif. Inst. Tech.; m. Martha Frances Shipp, Dec. 15, 1967; 1 son, Willard James. Foreman, supr., asst. to v.p., gen. mgr. Arcata Data Mgmt. Co., Hawthorne, Calif., 1964-73; div. mgr. Neon Products Signs, S. El Monte, Calif., 1973-75; v.p., gen. mgr. Zima and Co., Inc. (formerly Ad-Craft Sign Co.), Portage, Ind., 1977—. Mem. Am. Mgmt. Assn. Home: 6467 Portage Ave Portage IN 46368 Office: 7215 Industrial Ave Portage IN 46368

ZIMBERG, HARVEY, photographer; b. Winnipeg, Man., Can., July 19, 1941; s. Joseph and Rose (Okil) Z.; student United Coll., 1962-63. Electronics technician RCAF, Winnipeg, 1963-66; photographer Canadian Grain Commn., Winnipeg, 1966—. Mem. Am., Minn. profl. photographers assns., Winona Sch. Profl. Photography Alumni Assn., Winnipeg (v.p. 1973-76, pres. 1977—), Man. bowling assns. Club: Bel Acres Golf and Country (dir. 1977—). Home: 611 1030 Grant St Winnipeg MB R3M 2A2 Canada Office: 1404-303 Main St Winnipeg MB R3C 3G9 Canada

ZIMMER, JOHN H., lawyer; b. Sioux Falls, S.D., Dec. 30, 1922; s. John Francis and Veronica (Berke) Z.; student Augustana Coll., Sioux Falls, 1941-42, Mont. State Coll., 1943; LL.B., U. S.D., 1948; m. Deanna Langner, 1976; children by previous marriage—June, Mary Zimmer Levine, Robert Joseph, Judith Maureen. Admitted to S.D. bar, 1948; practice law, Turner County, S.D., 1948—; partner firm Zimmer, Richter & Duncan, Parker, S.D.; states atty. Turner County, 1955-58, 62-64; asst. prof. med. jurisprudence; minority counsel S.D. Senate Armed Services Com. on Strategic and Critical Materials Investigation, 1962-63; chmn. Southeastern Council Govts., 1973-75; mem. U. S.D. Law Sch. adv. council, 1973—. Chmn. Turner County Republican Com., 1955-56; mem. S.D. Rep. adv. com., 1959-60; alt. del. Rep. Nat. Conv., 1968. Served with AUS, 1943-46; PTO. Decorated Bronze Star, Philippine Liberation ribbon. Mem. Am., Fed., S.D. (commr. 1954-57) bar assns., Am., S.D. (pres. 1967-68) trial lawyers assns., VFW, Am. Legion, Phi Delta Phi. Roman Catholic. Club: Elks. Home: Parker SD 57053 Office: Law Bldg Parker SD 57053

ZIMMER, KARL R., JR., flexible packaging co. exec.; b. Kalamazoo, Sept. 5, 1926; s. Karl Raymond and Lorena (Hunter) Z.; A.B., U. Chgo., 1951; postgrad. U. Copenhagen, 1951-52; m. Barbara Jean Evans, Mar. 19, 1949; children—Kaarina Ann, Karl R., Erik Hunter. Columnist, Danish and Am. newspapers, 1950-56; asst. sales mgr. Ballantine Books, Inc., N.Y.C., 1952-56; columnist Syosset (N.Y.) Advance, 1953-56; European dir. Feffer & Simons, Inc., The Hague, Netherlands, 1956-63, v.p., N.Y.C., 1963-64; pres. Zimmer Paper Products, Inc., Indpls. and San Francisco, 1964—; pres. Indy Enterprises, Inc. Chmn., Syosset Stevenson-for-Pres. Com., 1956. Served with USNR, 1944-46. Mem. Packaging Inst., TAPPI, Sports Car Club Am., Indpls. Mus. Art., Ind. State Symphony Soc. Home: 140 E 77th St Indianapolis IN 46240 Office: 1450 E 20th St Indianapolis IN 46218

ZIMMER, ROBERT CULVER, assn. exec.; b. Ft. Wayne, Ind., Apr. 11, 1924; s. Ford Culver and Tressa B. (Culver) Z.; B.A., De Pauw U., 1950; M.A., Ohio State U., 1951; certificate Inst. Orgnl. Mgmt., Mich. State U., 1956; m. Ethel Eva Ford, Aug. 21, 1948; children—Teri Lou. With Columbus (Ohio) C. of C., 1953—, pub. monthly mag., 1965-66, v.p.-adminstrn., 1966—. Served in U.S. Army, 1943-46; ETO. Mem. Nat. Assn. Membership Dirs. (past pres.), C. of C. Execs. Ohio (past dir.), C. of C. Execs. U.S. Methodist. Club: Kiwanis (dir.) (Columbus). Home: 5174 Northcliff Loop E Columbus OH 43229 Office: PO Box 1527 Columbus OH 43216

ZIMMERLY, ISAAC PRESTON, constrn. co. exec.; b. McClusky, N.D., July 17, 1906; s. Jacob Truman and Josephine Blanche (Preston) Z.; B.C.E., U. Ill., 1927; m. Lola Jeanette Muns, Dec. 1, 1963. Pres. Zimmerly Ready Mix Co., Paris, Ill., also pres. Zimmerly Constrn. Co. Bd. dirs. YMCA. Mem. MW, Nat. ready mixed concrete assns. Presbyterian. Clubs: Elks, Masons, Shriners, Rotary. Home: Sulphur Springs Rd Paris IL 61944 Office: 1604 Marshall St Paris IL 61944

ZIMMERMAN, DAVID NEAL, clin. pharmacist; b. Detroit, Jan. 25, 1950; s. Milton J. and Helen K.; B.S. in Pharmacy, Ferris State Coll., 1973; m. Judith Richman, May 19, 1974; 1 son, Steven. Owner, operator Astro Pharmacy, Gratiot Pharmacy, Medco Pharmacy, Metro Pharmacy, and others, Detroit, and D.O.H. Pharmacy, Highland Park, Mich. Certified fitter surg. appliances. Fellow Am. Coll. Apothecaries; mem. Am., Mich. pharm. assns. Home and office: 6193 Wynford Dr West Bloomfield MI 48033

ZIMMERMAN, DELANO ELMER, physician; b. Fond du Lac, Wis., Mar. 21, 1933; s. Elmer Herbert and Agatha Angeline (Freund) Z.; B.S., U. Wis., 1961, M.D., 1965; m. Nancy Margaret Garry, Aug. 13, 1966; children—Kate, Joseph, Nick. Intern, Hennepin County Hosp., Mpls., 1965; physician, surgeon Winnebago (Wis.) State Hosp., 1966-67; gen. practice medicine, Neenah, Wis., 1966-73; emergency room physician Community Emergency Services, Appleton, 1973-77, Meml. Med. Center, Springfield, Ill., 1977—; faculty So. Ill. U. Sch. Medicine, Springfield, 1977—. Served with USN, 1951-56. Mem. AMA, Am. Coll. Emergency Physicians, Sangamon County Med. Soc. Roman Catholic. Home: 5 Beacon Ridge Dr Springfield IL 62707 Office: Meml Med Center 1st and Miller Sts Springfield IL 62702

ZIMMERMAN, DONALD LEE, photographer; b. Covington, Ohio, Aug. 8, 1935; s. Leslie Loy and Wauneta Waveline (Gephardt) Z.; B.F.A., Ohio U., 1957; postgrad. Ind. U., 1974—, M. Photography; m. Patricia Ann Fanning, Apr. 20, 1957; children—Sandra Lynne, Susan Elaine, Stacey Carol. Photographer, Cromer Photos, Covington, 1957-58; studio mgr., photographer Krider Studios, Inc., Lawrenceburg, Ind., 1958-62; photographer Alderman Studios, Inc., High Point, N.C., 1962-67; dir. photography, v.p. H.G. Peters/Format, Indpls., 1967-76; pres. Foto-Graphics, Inc., Indpls., 1976—. Mem. Profl. Photographers Am., Am. Soc. Profl. Photographers. Club: Masons. Home: 5821 Bywood Dr E Indianapolis IN 46220 Office: 2402 N Shadeland Ave Indianapolis IN 46219

ZIMMERMAN, GEORGE HERBERT, banker, fin. cons.; b. N.Y.C., Sept. 10, 1895; s. George Henry and Jessie (Browne) Z.; B.C.S., N.Y. U., 1921; D.Sc. (hon.), Assumption U., Windsor, Ont., Can., 1961; m. Mary Helen Campion, July 7, 1926; children—Doris Zimmerman Bato, Elaine Zimmerman Peck, Jessie Zimmerman Hitchens, Georgia Zimmerman Loftus, Louis. Employee N.Y. Edison Co., 1911-16, Guaranty Securities Corp., N.Y.C. and Montreal, 1916-18, Gen. Motors Acceptance Corp., N.Y.C. and Chgo., 1919-26; v.p. Comml. Credit Co., Balt., 1926-28; exec. v.p. Universal Credit Corp., 1928-41; v.p. Universal C.I.T. Credit Corp., Detroit, 1941-50; chmn. bd., pres., dir. Mich. Bank, Detroit, 1944-50; organizer, G. H. Zimmerman Co., bus. and fin. cons., 1950; surveyed econ. and fin. conditions in Australia and New Zealand, 1956; dir. C.I.T. Fin. Corp. (N.Y.C.); cons. Dearborn Motors Credit Corp. (Birmingham, Mich.), Ford Motor Co. Can., Ltd. (Windsor, Ont.); fin. cons. Gar Wood Industries, Inc., Wayne, Mich. Dir., Met. Detroit Bdg. Found., 1954; pres., trustee Friends Assumption Found., 1955-60. Chmn. fin. com. bd. regents Assumption U., Windsor, Ont., Can., 1953. Chmn. bldg. com. St. Paul Sch. and Convent, Grosse Pointe, Mich., 1950-51. Served with 30th CAC, World War I; war chest Met. Detroit, 1942; U.S. Treasury Dept. war fin. com. for Mich., 1944-45. Recipient Assumption U. Alumni award, 1959. Mem. A.I.M. (charter mem. pres.'s council 1951-56), Fin. Analysts Soc. Detroit, Albert Gallatin Assos. of N.Y. U., N.Y. U. Alumni Detroit (organizer, 1st pres.), Delta Sigma Pi (life). Catholic. Clubs: Grosse Point, Detroit Athletic, Detroit Country, Grosse Pointe Yacht (Detroit); Century (Chgo.); N.Y. University; Surf (Miami Beach, Fla.). Home: 125 Kenwood Rd Grosse Pointe Farms MI 48236 Office: 150 Bagley Ave Detroit MI 48226

ZIMMERMAN, GEORGE RUDOLPH, physician; b. Amana, Iowa, Jan. 7, 1923; s. Karl Henry and Helen (Pecher) Z.; M.D., U. Iowa, 1951; m. Vivian Earp, Sept. 2, 1946 (div. Jan. 1977); children—Karl L., Kent G., Jess K. Intern, resident U. Iowa, 1951-54; resident Gorgas Hosp., C.Z., 1954-55; practice medicine specializing in pathology and nuclear medicine, Iowa City; staff U. Iowa Hosps.; asso. dept. pathology U. Iowa, 1955-56, asst. prof., 1956-61, asso. prof., 1961-68, prof., 1968-70; mem. adv. com. state commr. health Med. Examiner Law, 1962-68. Bd. dirs. Iowa Med. Service. Served with USAAF, 1943-45. Mem. Am. Soc. Exptl. Pathology, Am. Assn. Pathologists and Bacteriologists, Soc. Exptl. Biology and Medicine, AAAS, Coll. Am. Pathologists, Am. Soc. Clin. Pathologists, AMA, Johnson County Med. Soc. (sec.-treas. 1966, pres. 1970), Iowa Assn. Pathologists (exec. council 1965-68), Sigma Xi. Address: 424 North St Burlington IA 52601

ZIMMERMAN, HENRY ABRAM, II, cardiologist; b. Holsopple, Pa., May 8, 1915; s. Henry A. and Mary E. (Plough) Z.; B.S., U. Pitts., 1937; B.M., U. Cin., 1940, M.D., 1941; m. Mary McClaren, Apr. 5, 1952; children—Henry Abram, Jane. Intern, U. Cin. Gen. Hosp., 1940-41; resident U. Iowa Hosp., 1941-42, Cleve. City Hosp., 1945-47; teaching fellow Western Reserve U., Cleve., 1947-50; practice medicine specializing in cardiology, Cleve., 1950—; dir. cardiovascular lab. Cleve. City Hosp., 1947-50, hosp. physician, 1948-50; chief cardiovascular service St. Vincent Charity Hosp., 1950—, chief of medicine, 1960-62, dir. Marie L. Coakley Cardiovascular Lab., 1950—; cons. in cardiovascular disease St. Alexis Hosp., Cleve., St. John's Hosp., Cleve., Marymount Hosp., Cleve., Geauga Community Hosp., Chardon, Ohio; mem. exec. com. Cleve. Zool. Bd., 1968—; mem. med. and surg. cons. bd. Cleve. Police and Fire Depts., 1968—. Trustee Gilmour Acad. for Boys. Served to capt., M.C., USAAF, 1942-45; MTO. Decorated Purple Heart, Air medal; recipient Angel award Cleve. Fire Fighters Union, 1962; Susan and Theodore Cummings Humanitarian award; diplomate Am. Bd. Internal Medicine. Fellow A.C.P., Am. Coll. Chest Physicians, Am. Coll. Angiology, Am. Coll. Cardiology (v.p. 1966), Am. Therapeutic Soc.; mem. Am. Fedn. Clin. Research, Am. Soc. Internal Medicine, N.Y. Acad. Sci., Internat. Cardiovascular Soc., AAAS, Sociedade Brasileira de Cariologia, SAR, AMA, Am. Heart Assn., Ohio Med. Assn., Cleve. Acad. Medicine, Sigma Xi. Methodist. Clubs: Rolling Rock, Hermit, Hunting Valley Gun, Beaver Creek Hunt. Author: The Auricular Electrocardiogram, 1968; Intravascular Catheterization, 1959; contbr. numerous articles on cardiovascular disease to med. jours.; cons. editor Am. Heart Jour., 1970-75, Catheterization and Cardiovascular Diagnosis, 1974—; pioneer in cardiovascular catheterization. Home: 33851 Old Kinsman Rd Chagrin Falls OH 44022 Office: 1610 Hanna Bldg Cleveland OH

ZIMMERMAN, JERRY LEE, psychologist; b. Lansing, Mich., May 2, 1944; s. Howard David and Elizabeth Margaret (Shirey) Z.; B.A. with high honors, Mich. State U., 1966; M.S. (fellow), Ohio U., 1970, Ph.D., 1973; m. Sephanie Naomi Meyersburg, June 8, 1968; 1 son, Gregory Scott. Intern, Upstate Med. Center, State U. N.Y. at Syracuse, 1970-71; clin. psychologist N.W. Community Mental Health Center, Lima, Ohio, 1971-76; pvt. practice clin. psychology, Lima, 1973—. Pres., Social Service Council Greater Lima, 1973-75; cons. Allen County Children's Services Bd., 1971-75, Cerebral Palsy Clinic, 1973-76. Mem. Am., Ohio psychol. assns., Allen County, Auglaize County mental health assns. Home: 839 Westerly Dr Lima OH 45805 Office: 1000 W Market St Lima OH 45805

ZIMMERMAN, MARY ANN, civil engr.; b. Washington, Apr. 22, 1945; d. Robert James and Anna Catherine (Hyland) Z.; B.S. in Civil Engring., Purdue U., 1966, M.S., 1968. Grad. research asst. Purdue U., 1966-68; staff engr. Am. Pub. Works Assn., Chgo., 1968-70; traffic engr. III, City of Chgo., 1970-73; tech. specialist-environ., then group leader performance engring. Cummins Engine Co., Columbus, Ind., 1973-76, mgr. program mgmt., 1977-78, mgr. product environ. mgmt., 1978—; mem. engring. vis. com. Purdue U., 1977—; career guidance cons., 1967—. Mem. Columbus Elected Ofcls. Salary Com., 1974, Mayor Columbus Task Force Status Women, 1974—; chmn. vol. newsletter com., chmn. nat. conv. com. Operation PUSH, 1971-73; com. chmn. Black Expo, Chmn. vol. div. com. So. Christian Leadership Conf., Chgo., 1969-71; mem. Columbus Transit Adv. Com., 1976, Columbus Transp. Adv. Com., 1976—; acting chmn. Columbus Women's Center, 1975. Recipient Spl. recognition award, young engr. competition Chgo. chpt. Ill. Soc. Profl. Engrs., 1971; named Ill. Outstanding Young Woman of Year, 1973. Registered profl. engr., Ill., Ind. Mem. Am. Pub. Works Assn., ASCE, Inst. Traffic Engrs., Nat. Soc. Profl. Engrs. (chpt. sec. 1971-73, chpt. pres. 1977—, Ind. dir.-at-large 1976—), Soc. Women Engrs. (sect. vice chmn. 1972-73; established Purdue Engring. Scholarship for Women 1967), AAUW (dir. Columbus 1975-76; chpt. award of merit 1966), League Women Voters (dir. Columbus 1975-76; chpt. award of merit 1966), League Women Voters (dir. Columbus 1974-76), Mortar Bd., Chi Epsilon, Tau Beta Sigma, Sigma Kappa. Democrat. Roman Catholic. Club: Columbus Zonta (v.p. 1977—). Home: 1811 Pennsylvania Columbus IN 47201 Office: 1000 5th St Columbus IN 47201

ZIMMERMAN, MARY HELEN CAMPION, lawyer; b. St. Louis, July 22, 1901; d. George Henry and Mary (McNamara) Campion; J.D., DePaul U., Chgo., 1926, L.H.D., 1971. LL.D., Assumption U., Windsor, Can., 1957; m. George Herbert Zimmerman, July 7, 1926; children—Doris Zimmerman Bato, Elaine Zimmerman Peck, Jessie Zimmerman Hitchens, Georgia Zimmerman Loftus, Louis. Admitted to Md. bar, 1927, Mich. bar, 1933, U.S. Supreme Ct. bar, 1950; practice law, Md., 1927-28, Detroit and Grosse Pointe, Mich., 1933—. Mem. tax com. Detroit Bd. Commerce, 1945-51; mem. adv. bd. Marygrove Coll., Detroit, 1960-65; bd. dirs. Inter Am. Bar Found., 1949-63, trustee, 1963—. Fellow Am. Bar Found.; mem. Women's Assn. Detroit Symphony, League Catholic Women, Cath. Daus. Am., Nat. Assn. Women Lawyers (past pres.), Inter-Am. (council dels. 1951-63), Internat. (dep. Ho. of Deps. London 1950, Madrid 1952), Am. (resolutions com. 1952-55), Mich., Detroit bar assns,, Am. Judicature Soc., Women Lawyers Assn. Mich. (past pres,) Internacional Federation de Abogades, Mich. State Bar Found. (trustee, pres. 1972-74), Kappa Beta Pi. Republican. Roman Catholic. Clubs: Nat. Lawyers (Washington); Pardi (pres. 1947-48, 59-60, 75-76), Republican Women's (Grosse Pointe). Editor Kappa Beta Pi Quar., 1961-63, Hon., Lambda Chi, 1966. Home: 125 Kenwood Rd Grosse Pointe Farms MI 48236

ZIMMERMAN, WILLIAM, polit. scientist; b. Washington, Dec. 26, 1936; s. William and Isabel Edith (Ryan) Z.; B.A. with honors, Swarthmore Coll., 1958; M.A., George Washington U., 1959; Ph.D., Columbia U., 1965; m. Barbara Marshall Lamar, Feb. 7, 1959; children—W. Frederick, Carl L., Alice R. Lectr. polit. sci. U. Mich., Ann Arbor, 1963-64, asst. prof., 1964-69, asso. prof., 1969-74, prof., 1974—, asso. chmn. dept., 1971, dir. Center for Russian and E. European Studies, 1972—; cons. in field; mem. academic council Kennan Inst. Advanced Russian Studies, Woodrow Wilson Center, 1975—. Fgn. Area Tng. fellow Ford Found., 1961-62, William Bayard Cutting traveling fellow, 1962-63, Inter-Univ. Com. Travel Grants fellow, 1956-66. Mem. Am. Polit. Sci. Assn. (Helen Dwight Reid award 1966, Pi Sigma Alpha award 1974), Am. Assn. Slavic Studies (chmn. research and devel. 1976—), Phi Kappa Phi. Author: Soviet Perspectives on International Relations; contbr. articles to profl. publs. Office: 208 Lane Hall U Mich Ann Arbor MI 48109

ZINAM, OLEG, educator; b. Kharkov, Ukraine, Sept. 29, 1918; s. Nicolas and Maria-Regina (Yantovsky de Tolli) Cinamzgwarow; came to U.S., 1952, naturalized, 1957; B.S., Belgrade Mil. Acad., 1939; B.S. in Econs., Xavier U., 1956, M.B.A., 1958; Ph.D., U. Cin., 1963. Instr. math. Secondary Sch., Displaced Persons Camp,

Salzburg, Austria, 1945-46; registrar, chief clk. Prep. Commn. Internat. Refugee Orgn., Klagenfurt, Austria, 1947-50; translator, editor Lutch, Salzburg, 1950-52; clk. Central Trust Co., Cin., 1952-56; accountant, research analyst Proctor & Gamble Co., Cin., 1956-65; adj. asst. prof. dept. econs. U. Cin., 1963-65, asst. prof., 1965-68, asso. prof., 1968-74, prof. econs., 1974—; tchr. Russian lang. Xavier U., 1958—. Served with Yugoslav Army, 1936-45. Grantee-in-aid Taft Meml. Fund, U. Cin., 1971-72. Mem. Internat. Soc. Comparative Study Civilization, World Population Soc., Am. Econ. Assn., Am. Acad. Polit. and Social Sci., Royal Econ. Soc., Assn. Evolutionary Econs., Canadian Assn. Slavists, Am. Assn. Advancement Slavic Studies, Delta Tau Kappa (internat. v.p. 1973—). Office: Dept Econs 1209 Crosley Tower U Cin Cincinnati OH 45221

ZINGALE, FRANK LEE, diversified industry exec.; b. St. Louis, Sept. 6, 1932; s. Frank George and Elizabeth Virginia (Curtin) Z.; B.A. cum laude, Princeton U., 1954; student Med. Sch. Washington U., St. Louis, 1954-57; m. Barbara Anne Whittemore, Feb. 17, 1956 (div.); 1 dau., Laureson Whittemore. Stockbroker, G.H. Walker & Co., St. Louis, 1958-62; advt.-media group supr. Gardner Advt. Co., St. Louis, 1962-68; dir. media Ralston Purina Co., St. Louis, 1968—; exec. v.p., Checkerboard Advt. Co., St. Louis, 1968—; cons. in field. Mem. Assn. Nat. Advertisers. Home: 490 N Berry Rd St Louis MO 63122 Office: Ralston Purina Co Checkerboard Sq St Louis MO 63188

ZINN, LARRY ORLAN, rehab. orgn. exec.; b. Piqua, Ohio, Feb. 14, 1936; s. Arthur LeRoy and Nellie Irene (Henderson) Z.; B.S., Miami U., Oxford, Ohio, 1958, M.Ed., 1965; m. Charlene Welch, June 21, 1959; children—Jeffrey Todd, Bradley Troy, Duerk Edward. Speech and hearing therapist Cin. Pub. Schs., 1958-69; exec. dir. Stepping Stones Center for Handicapped, Cin., 1969—; tchr. U. Cin., 1970-75. Bd. dirs. Spl. Olympics for Mentally Retarded. Recipient Manpower award for outstanding achievement in community betterment Manpower Inc. Summer Action, 1973. Home: 938 Avondale St Cincinnati OH 45229 Office: 5650 Given Rd Cincinnati OH 45243

ZINNEMAN, HORACE HELMUT, physician, educator; b. Frankfurt/Main, Ger., Oct. 10, 1910; s. Lazar Ludeig and Lea (Margulies) Z.; came to U.S., 1938, naturalized, 1942; M.D., U. Vienna, 1937; m. Ruth May York, Oct. 10, 1941. Intern Lincoln (Nebr.) Gen. Hosp., 1939-40; practice medicine specializing in internal medicine, Lincoln, 1940-42, 46-50; postgrad. resident in internal medicine U. Minn. Med. Sch., 1951-52, mem. faculty, 1952—, prof. medicine, 1968—; mem. staff Mpls. VA Hosp., 1952—. Served with AUS, 1943-46. Decorated Bronze Star. Diplomate Am. Bd. Internal Medicine. Fellow A.C.P.; mem. Am. Assn. Immunologists, Central Soc. Clin. Research, Soc. Exptl. Biology and Medicine, Minn. Med. Assn. Author research papers, chpts. in books. Asso. editor Minn. Medicine, 1970—. Address: 1826 Beechwood Ave St Paul MN 55116

ZINSCHLAG, EDWARD NIEHOFF, surgeon; b. Beckemyer, Ill., June 2, 1914; s. Edward August and Emma Jane (Niehoff) Z.; M.D., St. Louis U., 1939; m. Mary Louise Godfrey, June 22, 1940; children—Edward G., Thomas L. Practice medicine, specializing in surgery, Mattoon, Ill., 1946—; mem. surg. staff Mattoon Meml. Hosp., Charleston (Ill.) Community Hosp.; chief of staff Sarah Bush Lincoln Health Center, cons. St. Anthony Meml. Hosp., Effingham, Ill.; co-founder, surgeon Link Clinic, Mattoon, 1946—; mem. faculty St. Louis U., U. Ill.; med. dir. Mattoon Lamp Plant, Gen. Electric Co., 1946—, Blaw Knox Co., 1955—, R.R. Donnelley & Sons, 1970—, Asso. Spring Corp., 1965—; dir. First Nat. Bank, Mattoon; pres. Lake Land Volkswagen-Am. Motors Dealership, Mattoon, 1958—. Chmn. Physicians' com. ARC Bloodbank, Mattoon; commr., chmn. Coles County Airport Authority, 1958—; bd. dirs. Civil Def., Mattoon, 1955-60; pres. Ill. Pub. Airports Assn., 1976—. Served to maj. M.C., AUS, 1940-45; ETO. Decorated Silver Star. Fellow A.C.S.; mem. AMA, World, Aerospace, Civil Aviation med. assns., Flying Physicians Assn., Ill., Coles County med. socs., St. Louis, Pan Am. surg. socs., Am. Fracture Assn., Pan Pacific Surg. Soc., Mattoon Assn. Commerce (dir.), Am. Trauma Assn. (dir. Ill. chpt.), Alpha Kappa Kappa. Republican. Roman Catholic. Home: 21 Elm Ridge Mattoon IL 61938 Office: 1710 Wabash Ave Mattoon IL 61938

ZIPF, ROBERT EUGENE, JR., pathologist; b. Dayton, Ohio, Sept. 18, 1940; s. Robert Eugene and Meriam (Murr) Z.; B.A., DePauw U., Greencastle, Ind., 1962; M.D., Ohio State U., 1966; m. Nancy Jane Gaskell, Sept. 11, 1965; children—Karin Lorene, Marjorie Kristine. Intern Miami Valley Hosp., Dayton, 1966-67; dir. forensic pathology Duke Med. Center, 1967-72; dir. radioisotope pathology Riverside Hosp., Columbus, Ohio, 1972—; clin. asst. prof. Ohio State U. Coll. Medicine, 1972—; med. examiner Durham County, 1970-72; dep. coroner, forensic pathologist Franklin County, Ohio, 1974—. Served to maj. M.C., USAF, 1972-74. Diplomate Am. Bd. Pathology (forensic and radioisotope pathology). Mem. Am. Soc. Clin. Pathologists, Acad. Forensic Scientists, Am. Coll. Nuclear Medcine, Franklin County Acad. Medicine. Contbr. med. jours. Home: 2230 Hadleigh Rd Columbus OH 43220 Office: 3535 Olentangy River Rd Columbus OH 43214

ZISHKA, RONALD LOUIS, clergyman, educator; b. Sheldon, Iowa, Mar. 27, 1935; s. Louie Frank and Wilma M. (Plautz) Z.; B.A., Capital U., 1958, M.Div., 1962; M.A., Case Western Res. U., 1965; Ph.D., Ohio State U., 1973; children—Mary L., John L., Cathy A. Ordained to ministry Lutheran Ch., 1962; clergyman Am. Luth. Ch., various cities in Ohio, 1961-71; instr. Ohio U., Lancaster, 1967-73, asst. prof. sociology, 1973—; pvt. practice marriage and family counselor, Columbus, Ohio, 1973—; co-dir. Eastland Psychol. Center, Columbus, 1975—; cons. Ohio Youth Commn., 1969-71; mem. exec. bd., chmn. family services Luth. Social Services Central Ohio, 1965-70; asst. state dir. Community Contact Programs Ohio, 1969-71; founder Life Enrichment, Inc., 1974. Named Outstanding Profl. in Human Services, Am. Acad. Human Services, 1974-75. Mem. Am. Sociol. Assn., Nat. Council Family Relations, Soc. Sci Study Social Problems, Am. Assn. Marriage and Family Counselors, North Central Sociol. Assn., Alpha Kappa Delta. Home: 1080 Beechwood Dr Lancaster OH 43130

ZISKA, RICHARD FRANCIS, acoustical contractor; b. Cleve., Oct. 2, 1929; s. Anthony John and Mary (Komarek) Z.; B.S., Ohio U., 1952; m. Marjorie L. Cornish, May 16, 1953; children—Richard Francis, Robin Lynn, Susan Lorraine. Salesman, estimator The Myron Cornish Co., Dayton, Ohio, 1954-60, pres., chmn. bd., Columbus, Ohio, 1960—. Employer trustee Carpenters Health, Welfare & Pension Funds; past pres. Builders Exchange of Columbus; chmn. Construction Div. Heart Fund Central Ohio. Served with U.S. Army, 1952-54. Decorated Commendation ribbon. Mem. Bldg. Trades Employers Assn. Central Ohio (past pres.), Columbus Regional Constrn. Industry Adv. Council of Am. Arbitration Assn., Am. Subcontractors Assn. (past dir. Central Ohio chpt.). Clubs: Scioto Country, The Mercator (past dir.). Home: 1707 Sundridge St Columbus OH 43221 Office: 2800 Fisher St Columbus OH 43204

ZITZ, MARTIN, advt. agy. exec.; b. Hammond, Ind., Feb. 6, 1916; s. John Theadore and Nowicki Veronica (Bittner) Z.; B.A., Yankton Coll., 1939; m. Lucille Lippenberger, Aug. 13, 1942; children—Carol, Joan, Janet. Writer radio plays; corr. Sioux City Jour., Sioux Falls Argus Leader, 1937-39; own accountant bus., 1939-40; merchandising exec. Wieboldt Stores, Inc., Chgo., 1940-46; mktg. dir. Elgin American, Elgin, Ill., 1946-50; v.p., merchandising exec. Henri, Hurst & McDonald, Chgo., 1950-54, became pres., 1954; chmn. bd. Roche, Rickerd, Henri, Hurst, Inc., 1962; sr. v.p. N.W. Ayer & Son, Inc., 1965—; spl. feature contbr. book rev. Chgo. Tribune. Bd. govs. Elmhurst Hosp.; trustee, mem. corp. bd. Yankton Coll. Congregationalist (trustee). Home: 722 Bittersweet Ln Hinsdale IL 60521 Office: 111 E Wacker Dr Chicago IL 60601

ZIZES, PETER ANTONIOS, chemist, quality control engr.; b. Steubenville, Ohio, June 24, 1924; s. Antonios Peter and G. (Mavrikis) Z.; B.A., West Liberty State Coll., 1948; M.A., Kent State U., 1955; m. Wanda Iola Macri, July 26, 1948; children—Adriann Gilda, Antonios Peter. Instr., Northwestern Mil. and Naval Acad., Lake Geneva, Wis., 1948-53; tchr. Ravenna (Ohio) High Sch., 1953-55; process control chemist Gen. Tire & Rubber Co., Mogodore, Ohio, 1955-59, quality control chemist mgr., Akron, Ohio, 1959-76, quality control staff engr., Akron, 1975—; tchr. statis. quality control Akron U. Active pub. relations and speakers bur. United Fund, 1962-76, named Mr. Good Guy, 1972. Certified quality engr. Mem. Am. Chem. Soc., Am. Soc. Quality Control, Akron Council Engring. and Sci. Socs., Canton Joint Engring. Council, Internat. Platform Assn., Am. Hellenic Ednl. and Progressive Assn., Pan-Icarian. Democrat. Greek Orthodox. Club: Toastmasters. Home: 2682 Fairview Pl Cuyahoga Falls OH 44221 Office: 1144 E Market St Akron OH 44316

ZOBEL, HERBERT LAWRENCE, educator; b. Chgo., Nov. 17, 1924; s. Herbert E. and Marie P. (Fett) Z.; A.A., U. Chgo., 1947; B.S., Ill. State U., 1948, M.S., 1949; M.A., Northwestern U., 1955; Ph.D., U. Mich., 1964; children—Priscilla M. Zobel Brandlehner, Patricia M., Zobel Valek. Substitute tchr. Chgo. Pub. Sch. System, 1949-50; asst. prof. Western Ill. Coll., Macomb, 1953-54; unified studies tchr. Cleveland Sch., Skokie, Ill., 1954-55; instr. Joliet Twp. (Ill.) High Sch. and Jr. Coll., 1955-57; asst. prof. Eastern Mich. U., Ypsilanti, 1957-64; research asso. Ednl. Research Council Am., Cleve., 1964-66; asso. prof. geography Kent (Ohio) State U., 1966—; vis. prof. Cleve. State U., 1966, Case Western Res. U., Cleve., 1967-69; cons., writer Grolier Soc., Inc., 1963-64, Ginn & Co., 1962-63. Sec., Hudson (Ohio) Ecumenical Council, 1973, asst. chmn., 1974-75; mem. Council Ministries, 1974-76; co-chmn. UnCoupled Club Hudson, 1973-75; trustee Homeowner's Assn., 1972-75. Served with USAAF, 1944-46. Fellow Nat. Council Geog. Edn. (exec. bd. 1972-75), AAUP, Ohio Acad. Sci. (v.p. geography sect. 1968-69), Ill. Geog. Soc. (pres. 1957-58), Mich. Schoolmasters' Club (chmn. geography 1959-60), Profl. Men's Club Cleve., Sigma Xi, Kappa Delta Pi, Phi Delta Kappa, Gamma Theta Upsilon, Sigma Zeta. Annotator tchrs. edit. World Geography, 1964. Author: Mid-America Panorama, 1969; contbr. chpt. on Mich., New Book of Knowledge, 1967. Home: 1575 S Lincoln St Kent OH 44240 Office: Dept Geography Kent State U Kent OH 44242

ZOBEL, MILTON MILFORD, contracting and bldg. co. exec.; b. Ida Grove, Iowa, Jan. 22, 1922; s. Louis G. and Anna (Schwenk) Z.; m. Frieda Reuscher, May 20, 1947; 1 dau., Carol Ann. Pres., United Builders, Inc., Ida Grove, 1962—. Served with USAAF, 1942-46. Mem. Master Builders Iowa (pres. 1973), C. of C., Am. Legion. Republican. Lutheran. Clubs: Kiwanis (pres. 1977-78), Med. Arts-Rec. (dir. 1977—). Home: Valley View Dr Ida Grove IA 51445 Office: 200 2d St Ida Grove IA 51445

ZOBENICA, RONALD MILAN, veterinarian; b. Grand Rapids, Minn., Sept. 18, 1940; s. Milan I. and Marilyn Marie (Sutich) Z.; student Mich. Tech. U., 1958-60; B.S. in Indsl. Engring., Iowa State U., 1963, D.V.M., 1975; m. Sandra Jean Strauss, June 8, 1963; children—Haidee, Jon. Sales engr., instruments and life support div. Bendix Corp., Davenport, Iowa, 1968-70; veterinarian Virginia (Minn.) Pet Clinic, 1975—, East Range Pet Clinic, Aurora-Hoyt Lakes, Minn., 1975—. Served to capt. USMC, 1963-68. Mem. Am., Minn., Arrowhead veterinary med. assns., Am. Animal Hosp. Assn. (asso.), Greater Virginia C. of C., Phi Zeta, Gamma Sigma Delta. Mem. Serbian Eastern Orthodox Christian Ch. Home: Route 1 Box 109H Mountain Iron MN 55768 Office: Virginia Pet Clinic Midway Gardens Virginia MN 55792

ZOELLER, GILBERT NORBERT, dentist; b. St. Louis, Sept. 30, 1931; s. Conrad Phillip and Opal (Miller) Z.; B.S., St. Louis U., 1953, D.D.S., 1957; m. Jeanne Helen Gieselmann, Sept. 5, 1953; children—Scott Conrad, Krista Meriel, Christopher Clark. Dental practice, St. Louis, 1957—; instr. pedodontics St. Louis U., 1957-60, dental anatomy, operative dentistry, 1960-62, mem. grad. faculty, 1966—, asso. prof. prosthodontics, 1969—; dir. clinics Sch. Dental Medicine, So. Ill. U.; lectr. various orgns. Recipient Certificate of Merit, Am. Soc. Dentistry for Children, 1957. Mem. ADA, Mo., St. Louis, Ill. (affiliate) dental socs., Internat. Assn. Dental Research, Omicron Kappa Upsilon (alumni mem.), Psi Omega. Contbr. articles to profl. jours. Office: 10004 Kennerly Rd Saint Louis MO 63128

ZOELLNER, WELDON JOSEPH, real estate broker; b. Perryville, Mo., Apr. 20, 1927; s. Louis William and Albertie Mary (Renaud) Z.; grad. high sch.; m. Virginia Lee Smith, Oct. 28, 1950; children—Beverly Zoeliner Groneck, Cynthia Zoeliner Banta, Weldon P. Journeyman, St. Louis Plasterers Union Local No. 3, 1945-49, Cement Masons Local No. 1, St. Louis, 1949-54; sales mgr. Insul-Air Aluminum Products, St. Louis, 1954; partner, J & J Window Sales, St. Louis, 1955-58; pres. W. J. Wildow Sales, St. Louis, 1959-69, Superior Color Reception, St. Louis, 1965—, Denner Food Products, St. Louis, 1966-67, W. J. Zoellner Realty Co., St. Louis, 1969—. Recipient Distinguished Service award Bridgeton Kiwanis Club, 1970. Mem. Nat. Farm and Land Inst. (chmn. pub. relations Mo. chpt. 1974-75, Distinguished award 1975, 2d v.p. 1977), Nat. Assn. Real Estate Bds., Ind. Fee Appraisers, Nat. Market Inst., Am. Investment Counselors (exec. v.p. 1974, pres. 1975), St. Louis Real Estate Exchange (pres. 1975). Democrat. Roman Catholic. Clubs: K.C., Kiwanis. Patentee in field. Home: 10955 Ridgecrest St Saint Ann MO 63074 Office: 11545 Saint Charles Rock Rd Bridgeton MO 63044

ZOGLIO, MICHAEL ANTHONY, JR., research pharmacist; b. Providence, June 27, 1936; s. Michael Anthony and Levatina (Greco) Z.; B.Sc., U. R.I., 1958; Ph.D., U. Minn., 1966; m. Arlene Marie Lania, Aug. 22, 1959; children—Michael Anthony III, Robert Steven, David Louis. Mgr. pharmacy research Sandoz Inc., Hanover, N.J., 1964-70; dir. pharm. devel. Hoechst Pharm. Co., Somerville, N.J., 1970-72; dir. Pharm. research and devel. Merrell Nat. Lab., Cin., 1972—; adj. asst. prof. biopharmaceutics U. Cin., 1974—; vis. prof. U. Wis. extension, 1976, 77. Served with U.S. N.G., 1956-62. Registered pharmacist, Minn. Fellow Acad. Pharm. Scis.; mem. Am. Pharm. Assn., AAAS, Am. Assn. Colls. Pharmacy, Midwest Pharm. Group. Contbr. articles to profl. jours. Patentee in pharmaceuticals. Home: 6835 Stonington Rd Cincinnati OH 45230 Office: Merrell Nat Lab 110 Amity Rd E Cincinnati OH 45215

ZOLD, EDWIN JOSEPH, engr.; b. Chgo., Dec. 2, 1927; s. John Joseph and Helen (Kudelas) Z.; B.E.E., Chgo. Tech. Coll., 1951; postrad. Northwestern U., 1951-55; m. Eleanor Margaret Keegan, June 27, 1953; children—David, Kathleen, Mary Elizabeth, Jennifer. New products engr. Synchro-Start Products Co., Skokie, Ill., 1950-55, purchasing agt., 1955-56; chief engr. LaMarche Mfg. Co., Des Plaines, Ill., 1956-76, v.p., dir. engring., 1976—; mem. industry adv. com. Underwriters Labs., Northbrook Ill. Served with USNR, 1946-47. Mem. IEEE, Nat. Elec. Mfrs. Assn. (chmn. utility battery charger standards com., indsl. truck charger com.). Home: 410 N Maple St Prospect Heights IL 60070

ZONDERVAN, MARY SWIER, pub. co. exec.; b. Grand Rapids, Mich., Aug. 18, 1913; d. Walter and Susan (Muller) Swier; grad. high sch.; m. Peter John Zondervan, May 21, 1934; children—Robert Lee, Patricia Lucille, William J., Mary Beth. Dir., Zondervan Pub. House, Grand Rapids, 1972—, Zondervan Family Book Stores Am., Inc., Grand Rapids, 1972—. Mem. Aux. Gideons Internat. (life). Mem. Ref. Ch. Clubs: Blythefield Country (Belmont, Mich.); Peninsular (Grand Rapids). Home: 545 Lakeside Dr SE Grand Rapids MI 49506 Office: 1415 Lake Dr Grand Rapids MI 49506

ZONDERVAN, PETER (PAT) JOHN, publisher, religious orgn. exec.; b. Paterson, N.J., Apr. 2, 1909; s. Louis and Nellie Petronella (Eerdmans) Z.; student Christian and pub. schs.; D.Litt. (hon.), John Brown U., 1969; Litt.D., Lee Coll., Cleveland, Tenn., 1972; m. Mary Swier, May 21, 1934: children—Robert Lee, Patricia Lucille, William J., Mary Beth. Co-founder, chmn. bd. Zondervan Pub. House, Grandville, Mich., 1931, Grand Rapids, Mich., 1932—; pres. Zondervan Music Pubs., Grand Rapids, 1955, also Singspiration Inc.; dir. Mich. Nat. Bank, Grand Rapids. Pres., Grand Rapids Camp of Gideons, 1947-48, 1962-74, chaplain, 1944-46, internat. trustee, 1950-52, v.p. Gideons Internat., 1952-55, pres., 1956-59, chaplain, 1969-71, internat. treas., 1972-75, internat. chaplain, 1975—: bd. dirs. Christian Nats. Evangelism Com., San Jose, Calif.; bd. dirs. Winona Lake Christian Assembly, Ind., 1937—, sec., 1961-65; organizer, 1st chmn. Christian Businessmen's Com., Grand Rapids, 1942; chmn. com. for city-wide Evangelistic meeting, 1946. Mem. Internat. Platform Assn. Club: Lotus (pres. 1949, 65-67) (Grand Rapids). Home: 545 Lakeside Dr SE Grand Rapids MI 49506 Office: 1415 Lake Dr SE Grand Rapids MI 49506 also 4145 Kalamazoo St SE Grand Rapids MI 49508

ZONIA, DHIMITRI, artist; b. St. Louis, June 12, 1921; s. Ligor and Polixenna (Rucho) Z.; student pub. schs., St. Louis; m. Margaret Carolina Wieland, Apr. 20, 1947; children—Margaret Elizabeth, Susan Catherine, Carolynn Louise, Laura Elaine. Engraver, Pulitzer Pub. Co., St. Louis, 1951-58, color specialist, 1957-61; tchr. art Hanley High Sch., St. Louis, 1961-63, Artist Guild of Potosie, Mo., 1963-64, of St. Genevieve, Mo., 1963-65, of Festus, Mo., 1964-65; artist-in-residence Albrecht Art Museum, St. Joseph, Mo., 1975; instr. Jewish Community Center's Assn., St. Louis, 1976-77; one-man shows: St. Louis Artist's Guild, 1962, Brooks Meml. Mus., Memphis, 1964, Albrecht Art Mus., St. Joseph, 1971; group shows: Okla. Art Center, 1975, Bicentennial Invitational, Paris, 1976-77; represented in permanent collections: Ark. Art Center, Little Rock, Del Mar Coll., Butler Inst. Am. Art, Youngstown, Ohio, Albrecht Art Mus.; ceiling murals: St. Michael's Ch., St. Louis, Oak Grove Mausoleum, St. Louis; lectr., demonstrator of painting, drawing. Served with USAAF, 1942-45; ETO. Recipient 1st prize St. Louis Artist's Guild Regional Portrait Competition, 1968, Best Book of Year award for Stepka and the Majik Fire, Cath. Press Assn., 1975, Best Book award for Arise My Love, Nat. Printing Inst., 1975, Best Book in Mid-West award for Arise My Love, U. Ky., 1976, Best in Show, Chattanooga Nat., 1977, Trustees First award Harlin Mus., W. Plains, Mo., 1977; 1st prize St. Louis Artists Guild, 1977. Mem. St. Louis Artist's Guild, Graphic Artist's Guild Am. Eastern Orthodox. Author: (with Dorothy Van Woerkom) Stepka and the Magic Fire, 1974, Journey to Bethlehem, 1974; Some Thoughts on Book Illustrating, 1975; co-author: Arise My Love, 1975. Home and Office: 4680 Karamar Dr Saint Louis MO 63128

ZOOK, ELVIN GLENN, plastic surgeon, educator; b. Huntington County, Ind., Mar. 21, 1937; s. Glenn Hardman and Ruth (Barton) Z.; B.A., Manchester Coll., 1959; M.D., Ind. U., 1963; m. Sharon Kay Neher, Dec. 11, 1960; children—Tara E., Leigh A., Nicole L. Intern, Meth. Hosp., Indpls., 1963-64; resident in gen. and thoracic surgery Ind. U. Med. Center, Indpls., 1964-69, resident in plastic surgery Ind. U. Hosp., Indpls., 1969-71, asst. prof. plastic surgery, 1971-73; asso. prof. surgery So. Ill. U., Springfield, 1973-75, prof., 1975—, chmn. div. plastic surgery, 1973—; mem. staff Meml. Med. Center, St. John's Hosp., Springfield; cons. Marion (Ill.) VA Hosp. Chmn. program com. So. Ill. U. Sch. Medicine Explorer Scouts, Boy Scouts Am. Diplomate Am. Bd. Surgery, Am. Bd. Thoracic Surgery, Am. Bd. Plastic Surgery. Mem. Assn. Acad. Surgery, Shumacker Surg. Soc., AMA, Am. Soc. Plastic and Reconstructive Surgeon, Midwestern Soc. Plastic and Reconstructive Surgery, A.C.S., Sangamon County Med. Soc., Am. Cleft Palate Assn., Am. Assn. Plastic Surgery, Plastic Surgery Research Council, Am. Burn Assn., Ill. Surg. Soc., Am. Soc. Surgery of the Hand, Am. Soc. Aesthetic Plastic Surgery. Presbyterian. Clubs: Sangamo, Springfield Med., Island Bay Yacht. Contbr. articles to profl. jours. Home: 42 Hazel Dell Springfield IL 62707 Office: 200 W Dodge St Springfield IL 62702

ZOOK, ROBERT LOUIS, cons. engring. geologist, geotech. engr.; b. Ft. Scott, Kans., Mar. 9, 1942; s. Robert Benjamin and Lena Mary Curtis (Carl) Z.; B.S., U. Mo., Kansas City, 1964; postgrad. Brigham Young U., 1964-66; m. Ruth Ann Stewart, Mar. 10, 1967; children—Robert Louis, Zabrina Ann. Tchr. earth sci. Whitesboro (N.Y.) Jr. High Sch., 1966-67; geologist Woodward-Clyde Consultants, Kansas City, Mo., 1967-69; chief engring. geologist and geotech. engr. L. Robert Kimball, Ebensburg, Pa., 1969-74; sr. engring. geologist Bechtel, Inc., Norwalk, Calif., 1974-75; sr. engring. geologist NFS/Nat. Soil Services, Inc., Dallas, 1975; soils, geol. engr. N.Am. Coal Corp., Cleve., 1975—. Elder, Ch. of Jesus Christ of Latter-day Saints. Registered profl. geologist, Del., Ga., Maine. Mem. Assn. Engring. Geologists, Geol. Soc. Am., Assn. Profl. Geol. Scientists, Am. Inst. Mining Engrs., Nat. Water Well Assn., Sigma Gamma Epsilon. Contbr. articles to profl. jours. Home: 5914 Kimberly Dr Bedford Heights OH 44146 Office: 12800 Shaker Blvd Cleveland OH 44120

ZOPF, DAVID EDWARD, business exec.; b. Lansing, Mich., July 14, 1941; s. Edward Jay and Eva Mae (Bauer) Z.; B.A., Mich. State U., 1963; m. Donna Marie Thompson, May 13, 1967; children—David Edward, Amy Marie, Mary Katherine. Purchasing agt. Hager Fox Home Center, Lansing, 1964-66, Ren Plastics, Lansing, 1966-72; founder, pres. Abacus Enterprises, Lansing, 1972—; co-founder, pres. Complete Bus. Services, 1974—; initiated and taught 1st purchasing courses Lansing Community Coll., 1974. Served with AUS, 1964-70. Named Alumnus of Year, Alpha Kappa Psi, 1968. Mem. Purchasing Mgmt. Assn. Central Mich. (pres. 1971). Home: 2216 Marilyn Plaza Lansing MI 48910 Office: 121 W Mount Hope Lansing MI 48910

ZORN, TIMOTHY JOHN, veterinarian; b. Saginaw, Mich., Nov. 20, 1951; s. Donald George and Sally Ann Z; B.S. with honors, Mich. State U., 1973, D.V.M. with honors, 1974. Veterinarian Braeutigam-Luhring Veterinary Clinic, Frankenmuth, Mich. Mem. Saginaw Valley, Mich., Am. veterinary med. assns., Am. Animal Hosp. Assn., Am. Assn. Equine Practitioners, Am. Assn. Bovine

Practitioners, Mich. State U. Alumni Assn. Republican. Lutheran. Clubs: Centurion, Mich. State U. Office: 141 Churchgrove St Frankenmuth MI 48734

ZORNOW, HARRY BENJAMIN, broker; b. Columbus, Ohio, Aug. 9, 1928; s. Harry Benjamin and Gladys Myrtle (Bogle) Z.; B.A., Oberlin Coll., 1950; M.B.A., U. Mich., 1951; m. Shirley Ruth Barco, May 14, 1955; children—Harry Benjamin, Peter David, Gregory Lee, Steven John. Regional rep. McDonald & Co., Cleve., 1953-55, Hamilton, Ohio, 1955-69; partner Harrison & Co., Hamilton, 1969—; adv. prof. fin. Miami U., Oxford, Ohio, 1965-67; v.p. Permanent Savs. and Loan Assn., Hamilton, 1969—, also dir. Investment adv. bd. Hamilton YMCA, 1972—, bd. dirs. Hamilton West YMCA, 1970-76; treas. Presbyn. Ch., Hamilton, 1976—. Served with USMCR, 1951-53. Republican. Club: Lions (v.p. Hamilton). Home: 1630 Sunset Dr Hamilton OH 45013 Office: 401 2d Nat Bank Bldg Hamilton OH 45011

ZORNOW, WILLIAM FRANK, educator; b. Cleve., Aug. 13, 1920; s. William Frederick Emil and Viola (Schulz) Z.; A.B., Western Res. U., 1942, A.M., 1944, Ph.D., 1952. Vice pres., treas. Glenville Coal & Supply Co., Real Value Coal Corp., Zornow Coal Corp., 1941-45; dep. clk. Probate Ct., Cuyahoga County, Ohio, 1941-43; prodn. planning engr. Hickok Elec. Instrument Co., Cleve., 1943-46; teaching asst. Western Res. U., 1944-47; instr. U. Akron, 1946-47, Case Inst. Tech., 1947-50, Washburn U., 1950-51; lectr. Cleve. Coll., 1948-49; asst. prof. Kans. State U., 1951-58; asst. prof. Kent (Ohio) State U., 1958-61, asso. prof., 1961-66, prof. history, 1966—; collection corr. for Berkshire Loan & Fin. Co., Painesville, Ohio, Security Credit Acceptance Corp., Mentor, Ohio, 1951-60; cons. Karl E. Mundt Library Dakota State Coll., Madison, S.D. Mem. Am. Acad. Polit. and Social Sci., Am. Assn. State and Local History (award of merit 1958), Am. Hist. Assn., Orgn. Am. Historians, Ohio Acad. History (chmn. awards com.), Ohio Hist. Soc. (library adv. com. 1969—), Ohio Soc. N.Y., Delta Tau Delta, Pi Gamma Mu, Phi Alpha Theta, Phi Delta Kappa. Author: Lincoln and the Party Divided, 1954, 72; Kansas: A History of the Jayhawk State, 1957; America at Mid-Century, 1959; contbr. to Abraham Lincoln: A New Portrait, 1959, Kansas: The First Century, 1956; also articles to encys., profl. jours.; editor: Shawnee County (Kans.) Hist. Bull., 1950-51. Home: 7893 Middlesex Rd Mentor OH 44060 Office: Kent State U Kent OH 44242

ZRIM, MARION JOHN, first aid co. exec.; b. Vleje, Yugoslavia, Aug. 11, 1950; s. Ernest and Mary (Legeza) Z.; came to U.S., 1955, naturalized, 1962; student Ohio U., 1969-75; m. Gloria Jean Pluth, Sept. 28, 1974. Foreman, Grosel Landscaping Co., Euclid, Ohio, 1967-70; floater Wells Nat. TV Services Corp., Beachwood, Ohio, 1970-75; pres. Will Johnston Co., Inc., Willoughby, Ohio, 1976—; dir. Midland Moor Co., Willoughby. Mem. Smithsonian Assn., Nat. Hist. Soc., Am. Museum Natural History, Nat. Geog. Soc., Nat. Audubon Soc., Found. Econ. Edn., Woodrow Wilson Internat. Center for Scholars. Club: Acacia Mutual Life. Home: 25450 Marsdon Ave Euclid OH 44132 Office: 4982 Campbell St Willoughby OH 44094

ZSIGMOND, ELEMÉR KALMAN, physician; b. Budapest, Hungary, May 16, 1930; s. Elemér Zeykvary and Terez (Kartori) Z.; came to U.S., 1956, naturalized, 1966; M.D., U. Budapest, 1955; m. Kathryn Fogarasi, Oct. 19, 1953; 1 son, Zoltan William. Intern, Med. Clinics, U. Budapest, 1954-55; intern Allegheny Gen. Hosp., Pitts., 1960-61, resident anesthesiology, 1961-63; resident internal medicine Hosp. Sztalinvaros and Cardiac Sanatorium, Balatonfured, Hungary, 1955-56; practice medicine specializing in anesthesiology; cardiologist, dir. lab. Cardiologic Inst., Balatonfured, 1956-57; dir. anesthesia research lab. Mercy Hosp., Pitts., 1957-60; clin. research fellow anesthesiology Allegheny Gen. Hosp., 1963-66, clin. anesthesiologist dir. anesthesiology research labs., 1966-68; prof. anesthesiology U. Mich. Med. Sch., 1968—. Diplomate Am. Bd. Anesthesiology. Fellow Am. Coll. Anesthesiologists, Am. Coll. Clin. Pharmacologists; mem. Am. Soc. Anesthesiologists, Internat. Anesthesia Research Soc., N.Y. Acad. Scis., AAAS, AMA, Mich., Washtenaw County med. socs. Research and publs. in anesthesiology, neuropharmacology, pulmonary physiology. Home: 2265 Delaware Ann Arbor MI 48103 Office: U Mich Med Center Ann Arbor MI 48109

ZUBROFF, LEONARD SAUL, surgeon; b. Minersville, Pa., Mar. 27, 1925; s. Abe and Fannie (Freedline) Z.; B.A., Wayne State U., 1945, M.D., 1949. Intern Garfield Hosp., Washington, 1949-50, resident in surgery, 1951-55, chief resident surgery, 1954-55; practice medicine specializing in surgery, 1958-76; med. dir. Chevrolet Gear and Axle Plant, Chevrolet Forge Plant, Gen. Motors Corp., Detroit, 1977—; mem. staff Hutzel Hosp., Sinai Hosp., Detroit Meml. Hosp. Served with USAF, 1956-58. Diplomate Am. Bd. Surgery. Fellow A.C.S.; mem. AMA, Mich. State, Wayne County med. socs., Acad. Surgery Detroit, Pan Am. Med. Soc., Am. Soc. Abdominal Surgeons, Am., Mich. occupational med. assns., Detroit Surg. Soc., NAACP, Phi Lambda Kappa. Jewish. Club: Masons (33 deg.). Home: 8701 Kingswood Detroit MI 48221 Office: 1840 Holbrook St Detroit MI 48212

ZUCKER, ADELE HABER, journalist; b. Chambersburg, Pa., Apr. 7, 1932; d. Ira and Caroline (Reiner) Haber; B.S., Ohio U., 1954; m. Henry J. Zucker, Sept. 2, 1956; children—Clifford A., JoAnn Sue. Program editor TV Guide mag., Cleve., 1954-56; editor internal publ. Blue Cross of N.E. Ohio, Cleve., 1956-58; suburban reporter Cleve. Plain Dealer, 1967-74; Cleve. rep. for cotton promotions Nat. Cotton Council, N.Y.C., 1969-71; advt. layouts Cleve. Jewish News, 1976—; freelancer; partner The Flappers, 1974—. Recipient citation for work in Northeastern Ohio Indsl. Editors Assn., 1958. Mem. Women in Communications, Womens Am. ORT (chpt. pres. 1973-75), Hadassah, Parent Vol. Assn. for Retarded Children, Nat. Council Jewish Women. Home: 2461 Claver Rd University Heights OH 44118

ZUCKER, ROBERT LOUIS, hosp. adminstr.; b. Portsmouth, Ohio, 1910; s. Louis Andrew and Elizabeth (Wright) Z.; B.A., Ohio State U., 1933; student Franklin Law Coll., 1934-37; m. Marguerite Dryden Smithson, Sept. 2, 1939; 1 dau., Suzanne. With auditor's dept. State of Ohio, Columbus, 1933-42; mem. staff Benjamin Franklin Hosp., Columbus, 1942-45, Aultman Hosp., Canton, Ohio, 1945-48, Union Hosp., Dover, Ohio, 1948-50; v.p., dir. devel. Massillon City Hosp. (Ohio), 1950-75; mem. Ohio Bd. Examiners Nursing Home Adminstrs., hosp cons. Iran Ministry Social Welfare, Tehran, 1975. Pres., Washington High Sch. chpt. Am. Field Service, 1966-68; bd. dirs. YMCA, Massillon, 1955-58, Salvation Army, Massillon, 1955, Massillon Family Counseling Service, 1975—, Stark-Wayne Lung Assn., 1954—. Mem. Am. Coll. Hosp. Adminstrs., Am., Ohio (trustee 1965-67) hosp. assns., Ohio Bd. Examiners Nursing Home Admistrs., Massillon C. of C., Ohio Lung Assn., Delta Chi. Clubs: Masons, Kiwanis (pres. 1960), Massillon. Home: 3266 Trillium NW Canton OH 44708

ZUCKERBERG, HARVEY DAVID, health assn. exec.; b. Detroit, Nov. 23, 1934; s. Max and Esther (Kaplan) Z.; student U. Mich., 1953-55, U. Wis., summer 1954; A.B., Wayne State U., 1957; m. Irma Pape, Aug. 11, 1973; children by previous marriage—Matthew, Andrew. Reporter, The Detroit News, 1955-56; med. editor The Pontiac (Mich.) Press, 1956-60, city editor The Detroit Jewish News, 1960-63; asst. dir. pub. relations Ill. State Med. Soc., Chgo., 1963-65; asso. exec. Ill. Assn. for Mentally Retarded, Chgo., 1965-70; exec. dir. Mich. Assn. for Retarded Children, 1970—; mem. Mich. Gov.'s Adv. Council on Developmental Disabilities; mem. adv. com. Inst. Study of Mental Retardation. Mem. Am. Assn. Mental Deficiency, Orgn. Mich. Health and Service Agy. Execs. (past pres.). Contbr. articles to profl. jours. Home: 501 Rampart Way East Lansing MI 48823 Office: Mich Nat Tower Lansing MI 48933

ZUCKERMAN, STUART, psychiatrist; b. Syracuse, N.Y., Feb. 18, 1933; s. George and Cassie (Kolsan) Z.; student U. Kans., 1950-51; B.S., U. Ala., 1954; D.O., Phila. Coll. Osteo. Medicine, 1958. Rotating intern Hosp. Phila. Coll. Osteo. Medicine, 1958-59; psychiat. fellow, resident Phila. Mental Health Clinic, 1959-62; chief resident Psychoanalytic Studies Inst., Phila., 1961-62; chief div. neuropsychiatry Grandview Hosp., Dayton, Ohio, 1962-65; asst. med. dir., chief children's and adolescent's unit N.J. State Hosp., Ancora, 1967-70; sect. treas. v.p. med. staff, 1968-70; chief outpatient dept. Atlantic City, Ancora Psychiat. Hosp., 1970-72; mem. faculty U. Pa. Sch. Medicine, dept. psychiatry, 1972-76, Phila. Coll. Osteo. Medicine 1971-76; prof., chmn. dept. psychiatry Ohio U., Athens, 1976—; past asst. dir. Reception Center; attending psychiatrist Phila. Gen. Hosp.; attending psychiatrist Atlantic City, Shore Meml., Keesler Meml., Washington Meml., Atlantic County Mental hosps.; cons. child study, spl. services. Chmn. profl. adv. com. Atlantic County Mental Health Bd., 1969-71; mem. nominating com. Mental Health Assn. Atlantic County, 1972-75; mem. hosp. inspection team Am. Osteo. Assn., 1971—; examining psychiatrist South Jersey Police Depts., Fire Depts., Sch. Systems. Bd. dirs. Family Services Assn. Atlantic County, Cape May County Drug Abuse Council. Diplomate Am. Osteo. Bd. Neurology and Psychiatry. Fellow Royal Soc. Health; mem. Am. Osteo. Assn., Am. Coll. Neuropsychiatrists, Am. Coll. Emergency Physicians, Am. Acad. Psychotherapists, Am. Assn. Suicidology, Am. Pub. Health Assn., Am. Assn. Mental Deficiency, Acad. Psychosomatic Medicine, Am. Assn. Social Psychiatry, N.J. Assn. Osteo. Physicians and Surgeons, N.J. Hosp. Assn., N.J. Welfare Council, N.J. Pub. Health Assn., Am. Vocat. Assn., N.J. Soc. Med. Edn. and Research, Atlantic County Osteo. Med. Soc. (pres. 1970-72), Am. Med. Writers Assn., Am. Soc. Criminology, AAUP, Am. Assn. Cin. Pharmacology and Therapeutics, Am. Assn. Group Therapy, Am. Assn. Mental Health Adminstrs., Am. Physicians Fellowship. Clubs: Elks, Rotary. Asso. editor Bull. Am. Coll. Neuropsychiatrists, 1963-70. Contbr. articles to profl. jours. Office: Dept Psychiatry Ohio U Athens OH 45701

ZUMHAGEN, VERNON EUGENE, metal products co. exec.; b. Oconomowoc, Wis., Feb. 15, 1923; s. Fred Herman and Hazel Gene (Young) Z.; student Beloit Coll., 1946; B.S., Ball State U., 1952; postgrad. Ind. U., 1952; m. Doris Jean Wilkison, Sept. 24, 1945; children—Caryl Zumhagen Baringer), Mark, Paul. Controller, J.L. Clark Mfg. Co., Rockford, Ill., 1952—. Bd. dirs. Woodside YMCA, 1964-67, Rockford Pub. Library, No. Ill. Library System, Rockford Day Nursery. Served with USNR, 1942-45; ETO. Mem. Nat. Assn. Accountants (pres. Rockford chpt. 1966, nat. dir. 1971-72, nat. v.p. 1975—, exec. com. 1975—). Club: Ind. U. Alumni (pres. Rockford 1969). Home: 3407 Guilford Rd Rockford IL 61107 Office: 2300 6th St Rockford IL 61101

ZUMKEHR, CHARLES EUGENE, lawyer; b. Canton, Ohio, July 26, 1938; s. Albert F. and Lucille (Egger) Z.; A.B., Ohio U., 1961; J.D., Case Western Res. U., 1964; m. Phyllis D. Donley, Jan. 30, 1960; children—Jennifer Lynn, Chad Phillip. Admitted to Ohio bar, 1964; since practiced in Kent, mem. firm Williams, Purtill, Zumkehr & Welser, 1968-73, 75—; asso. firm Kelley, McCann & Livingstone, Cleve., 1973-75; dir. Huntington Bank, Kent, other local corps. Mayor, Village of Sugarbush Knolls, 1975-77; chmn. Franklin Twp. Bd. Zoning Appeals, 1966-68; bd. dirs. profl. div. Kent United Fund, 1968; pres. Library Bd. Trustees Kent, 1972—; bd. advisers Robinson Meml. Hosp., Ravenna, Ohio, 1971-75. Recipient Distinguished Service award and named Outstanding Young Man, City of Kent, 1972. Mem. Portage County (sec. 1964-71), Am., Ohio, Cleve., Akron, Portage County bar assns., Kent Jaycees (v.p. 1967-68), Kent Area C. of C., Portage County Law Library Assn. (pres. 1971-73), Delta Tau Delta, Phi Delta Phi. Episcopalian (past vestryman). Clubs: Rotary (dir. Kent 1972-73), Kent State U. Booster (sec. 1971-76), Twin Lakes Country. Home: 1323 Lake Roger Dr Kent OH 44240 Office: Huntington Bank Bldg 117 E Main St Kent OH 44240

ZUNG, THOMAS TSE-KWAI, architect; b. Shanghai, China, Feb. 8, 1933; s. Bate and Rose Yu-Sun (Fong) Z.; came to U.S., 1937, naturalized, 1954; student Drew U., 1950-51, (Rose scholar) Va. Poly. Inst., 1951-53, Columbia U., 1955-57; B.Arch., U. Mich., 1960; m. Carol Ann Williams, Dec. 28, 1963; 1 son, Thomas Ba-Tse. Project architect Edward Durell Stone, architect, N.Y.C., 1958, 60-65; architect, Cleve., 1967—; prin. archtl. works include City Cleve. Pub. Utilities Bldg., world's 1st elongated geodesic dome Cleve. State U., Mayfran, Inc., Sawmill Creek Lodge, U. Akron Guzzetta Hall, music, speech and theater arts center, Alumni Center Bowling Green State U., U. Akron Master Plan-West, City of East Cleveland, Superior Euclid beautification plan, student recreation center at Bowling Green State U. Task force chmn. Greater Cleve. Growth Assn., 1970; mem. Council Human Relations, 1972, Leadership Cleve. Class '77; cubmaster local Boy Scouts Am., 1977-78; trustee Pace Assn., 1970-73, Karamu House, 1974-78. Served with Signal Corps, AUS, 1953-55. Recipient Design award Cleve. chpt. AIA, 1972; Anicka Design award U. Mich., 1959, Sr. design prize, 1960. Mem. AIA (dir. Cleve. chpt. 1978), Am. Soc. Planning Ofcls., English Speaking Union (trustee 1972-75), Ohio Soc. Architects. Clubs: Rotary, Hermit, City of Cleve. (dir. 1972-74, v.p. 1974) (Cleve.). Home: Echo Glen Gates Mills OH 44040 Office: 808 The Arcade Cleveland OH 44114

ZUNKEL, VIRGIL LEE, sav. and loan assn. exec.; b. Ogden, Iowa, Mar. 21, 1932; s. Galard Roland and Beulah Isabel (Ray) Z.; B.S., Iowa State U., 1957; m. Roberta Joanne Robertson, Oct. 18, 1953; children—Christene Leone, Virgil Lee, Jennifer Lynn. Telegrapher, So. Pacific R.R., West Tex., 1951, 53-54; teller Boone State Bank & Trust Co. (Iowa), 1958-60; sec.-treas. Ames Bldg. and Loan Assn. (Iowa), 1960-65; pres. Windom Fed. Savs. & Loan Assn. (Minn.), 1965—. Mem. Windom City Council, 1969-72. Served with USNR, 1951-53; Korea. Mem. Windom C. of C. (pres. 1968). Club: Kiwanis. Home: 677 Fuller Dr Box 383 Windom MN 56101 Office: PO Box 338 Windom MN 56101

ZWACK, CLARENCE ANTON, constrn. co. exec.; b. Ossian, Iowa, July 16, 1899; s. Anton and Susan (Waldbillig) Z.; B.Archtl. Engring., U. Notre Dame, 1922. Vice pres. Anton Zwack, Inc., Dubuque, Iowa, 1923-58, pres., 1958—. Mem. Asso. Gen. Contractors Am., Master Builders Iowa, Am. Legion. Roman Catholic. Club: Elks. Home: 2542 Stafford Ave Dubuque IA 52001 Office: 1330 White St Dubuque IA 52001

ZYDLO, STANLEY MATHEW, physician; b. Chgo., Dec. 15, 1933; s. Stanley Mathew and Estelle Helen (Tubilewicz) Z.; B.A., Westminster Coll., 1956; M.D., Loyola U., Chgo., 1960; m. Joyce M. Reid, Aug. 29, 1976; children—Kristi La Ree, Sheryl Anne, Scott, Mathew, Mark Alan. Intern, St. Francis Hosp., Evanston, Ill., 1960-61; gen. practice medicine, Wabash, Ind., 1963-69; emergency physician, pres. Med. Emergency Service Assos., Chgo., 1969—; founder, co-owner Vernon Manor, home for retarded children, Wabash, 1968—; dir. mobile intensive care unit system N.W. Community Hosp., Arlington Heights, Ill.; med. cons. Nat. Registry Emergency Med. Technicians, 1975—; del. AMA Commn. Emergency Med. Services. Served with USAF, 1961-63. Mem. Am. Coll. Emergency Physicians (chmn. bd. dirs. Ill. 1971—, past chmn. emergency med. systems com.), Am., Ind. med. assns., Wabash County, Chgo. med. socs., Aerospace Med. Assn., Am. Inst. Aeros. and Astronautics, Air Force Assn., Soc. Flight Surgeons, Am. Profl. Practice Assn., Am. Assn. Physicians and Surgeons, Isaac Walton League, Frat. Order Police. Clubs: Elks, Optimists (charter). Developer, dir. 1st multicommunity mobile intensive care emergency system in 12 N.W. Chgo. suburbs with paramedic level emergency aid. Home: 108 Chicory Ct Rolling Meadows IL 60008 Office: 800 W Central Rd Arlington Heights IL 60005

Who'sWho in America
Biographees of the Midwest

The following biographees of the Midwestern region have sketches appearing in the 40th edition of *Who's Who in America*.

Aaron, Charles
Abbey, George Marshall
Abbott, Douglas Eugene
Abbott, Gardner
Abbott, John David
Abbott, Lyle Charles
Abboud, A. Robert
Abboud, Francois Mitry
Abegg, Martin G.
Abel, Clarence, Jr.
Abel, Harold
Abel, Miles Leroy
Abele, Homer E.
Abell, David Robert
Abell, Murray Richardson
Abelson, Lester Sidney
Abelson, Richard D.
Abernathy, Kenneth Brooks
Abert, Donald Byron
Abraham, John Milton
Abraham, Paul Leslie
Abrahams, John Hambleton
Abrahamson, Shirley Schlanger (Mrs. Seymour Abrahamson)
Abramoff, Peter
Abramowicz, Alfred L.
Abrams, Alan Michael
Abrams, Irwin
Abrams, Talbert
Abramson, David Irvin
Abts, Henry William
Abu-Lughod, Ibrahim Ali
Acheson, Allen Morrow
Acker, Duane Calvin
Ackerman, Eugene
Ackerman, James Nils
Ackerman, James Waldo
Ackerman, John Henry
Ackerman, Lennis Campbell
Ackerman, Ora Ray
Ackermann, William Carl
Ackert, Paul Herman
Ackley, Clark Russell
Ackley, (Hugh) Gardner
Adair, Edwin Ross
Adair, John Douglas
Adams, Albert Willie, Jr.
Adams, Algalee Pool
Adams, Arthur Eugene
Adams, Beatrice
Adams, Benjamin Cullen, Jr.
Adams, Bernard Schroder
Adams, Charles Francis
Adams, Cyrus Hall, III
Adams, David Kenneth
Adams, Edward, Jr.
Adams, George Rodgers
Adams, George Worthington
Adams, Jack Ashton
Adams, James Carlton
Adams, John Richard
Adams, Joseph Elkan
Adams, Mark Hanna
Adams, Paul Lincoln
Adams, Philip Rhys
Adams, Robert McCormick
Adams, Robert McLean
Adams, Thomas Brooks
Adams, Thomas Hammond
Adams, Walter
Adamson, John Friece
Adamson, Oscar Charles, II
Adawi, Ibrahim Hasan
Addison, Robert Arthur
Addy, Frederick Seale
Ade, Walter Frank Charles
Adelman, R. J.
Adelson, Joseph Bernard
Adesko, Thaddeus Vincent
Adkins, Howard Eugene
Adkins, Richard Eugene
Adler, Aaron
Adler, Arthur M., Jr.
Adler, Eugene Max
Adler, Felix T.
Adler, Jacob Henry
Adler, Mortimer Jerome
Adler, Philip
Adler, Robert
Adolfson, Lorentz Henning
Adrian, Walter Frederick
Aeschbacher, William Driver
Agase, Alex A.
Agee, William M.
Agnew, Dwight Luther
Agnew, Spiro Theodore
Agnew, William George
Agranoff, Bernard William
Ahern, John Joseph
Ahlberg, Clark David
Ahlbrand, Russell Lowell, Jr.
Ahlem, Lloyd Harold
Ahlgren, Gilbert Harold
Ahlgren, Henry L.
Ahlschwede, Arthur Martin
Ahlstrom, Richard Mather
Ahmann, John Stanley
Ahner, Alfred Fredrick
Ahnquist, Elwyn Theodore
Ahrenholz, H(erman) William
Aikawa, Masamichi
Aikman, Charles David
Aines, Philip Deane
Aird, Kenneth
Aitay, Victor
Aitken, William Inglis
Akcasu, Ziyaeddin Ahmet
Akers, John
Akin, Paul B.
Akin, Wallace Elmus
Akos, Francis
Al-Ani, Salman Hassan
Alberding, Charles Howard
Albert, Ethel Mary
Albert, John George
Alberti, John Robert
Alberts, Warren Ebel
Albon, Ross K.
Albrecht, Erich August
Albrecht, Frederick Ivan
Albrecht, Richard Eugene
Albrecht, William Price
Albright, Edwin Carter
Albright, Justin W.
Albright, Malvin Marr
Albright, Penrose Strong
Alden, (Howel) Henry
Alden, Raymond Macdonald
Aldridge, Alfred Owen
Aldridge, Gordon James
Aldridge, John Watson
Alexander, Arvin J.
Alexander, Benjamin Harold
Alexander, Leonard Clayton
Alexander, Leroy Elbert
Alexander, Quentin
Alexander, Richard Dale
Alexander, Robert Baldwin
Alexander, William Henry
Alexis, Marcus
Alfonso, Robert John
Alford, John William
Alfred, Theodore Mark
Alger, Chadwick Fairfax
Alig, Cornelius O., Jr.
Allaben, Fred Roland
Allard, Jean (Mrs. Robert Allard)
Allbritten, Frank F., Jr.
Allemang, Paul Vernon
Allen, Carl E.
Allen, Charles Joseph, II
Allen, Charles Richard
Allen, Darryl Frank
Allen, David Donald
Allen, David Frank
Allen, Durward Leon
Allen, Edward Switzer
Allen, Francis Alfred
Allen, Garland Edward
Allen, George Whitaker
Allen, Harold Byron
Allen, Harold G.
Allen, Harry Lee
Allen, Henry Ellsha
Allen, James Norman
Allen, Lucius Oliver, Jr.
Allen, Maurice Bartelle, Jr.
Allen, Richard Blose
Allen, Robert Eugene
Allen, Robert Hutton
Allen, Spencer Turner
Allen, Wilburn Ray
Allen, William Arthur
Alley, William Edward
Alley, William J.
Allinsmith, Wesley
Allison, James Ralph
Allison, Marvin Lawrence (Larry)
Alloway, James Alexander
Alloway, R(upert) Brooke
Allred, Albert Louis
Allred, George Edward
Allrich, Robert William
Alltop, James Howard
Almy, Gerald Marks
Alnes, Ellis Stephen
Alpaugh, Walter George, Jr.
Alpern, Mathew
Alpert, Daniel
Alschuler, Sam
Alsdorf, James William
Alsop, Donald Douglas
Alspach, Philip Halliday
Alspaugh, Robert Odo
Alston, Walter Emmons
Altbach, Chaim
Altemeier, William Arthur
Altenbernd, A(ugust) Lynn
Altheimer, Alan J.
Alton, Ralph Taylor
Altschul, Alfred Samuel
Alverson, William H.
Alvord, William Howard
Al Yasiri, Kahtan Abbass
Alyea, Ethan Davidson, Jr.
Amann, Peter Henry
Amaya, Rene D.
Ambuel, John Philip
Amdahl, Byrdelle John
Amendola, Anthony Joseph
Ames, Alfred Campbell
Ames, Bruce Charles
Ames, Donald Paul
Ames, John Dawes
Ames, Van Meter
Amick, Charles L(orayne)
Ammon, James Brown
Ammons, Edsel Albert
Amos, James Lawrence
Amstadter, Laurence
Amudson, Duane Melvin
Anagnost, Catherine Cook
Anagnostopoulos, Constantine Efthymios
Ancker-Johnson, Betsy
Andelman, Samuel Louis
Anderhalter, Oliver Frank
Anders, Edward
Andersen, Elmer L.
Andersen, Harold Wayne
Andersen, Kenneth Benjamln
Anderskow, Ralph Anthony
Anderson, Albert Esten
Anderson, Carl Wilson
Anderson, Carlyle Elmer
Anderson, Charles Arner
Anderson, Charles Arnold
Anderson, Corliss Doran
Anderson, Dale Kenneth
Anderson, Donald Edward
Anderson, Donald George
Anderson, Edwin John
Anderson, Elmer Ebert
Anderson, Ernest W.
Anderson, Ernest Washington
Anderson, Eugene I.
Anderson, Eugenie Moore
Anderson, Fred Woodrow Wilson
Anderson, Frederic Ducey
Anderson, Gaylord West
Anderson, George Lee (Sparky)
Anderson, Glenn Richard
Anderson, Gordon Caldwell
Anderson, Harold Albert
Anderson, Harold H.
Anderson, Harry Frederick, Jr.
Anderson, Herbert Adolph
Anderson, Herbert Lawrence
Anderson, Herschel Vincent
Anderson, Hurst Robins
Anderson, Iain Mair
Anderson, J. D.
Anderson, James Frederick
Anderson, James Keith
Anderson, Jerry Maynard
Anderson, John Adolph
Anderson, John Stephen
Anderson, Joseph Norman
Anderson, Joseph Tomlinson
Anderson, Karl Walter
Anderson, Kenneth Eugene
Anderson, LaVerne Eric
Anderson, Leland Dale
Anderson, Lyle Arthur
Anderson, Marquard John
Anderson, Milton Henry
Anderson, Odin Waldemar
Anderson, Oscar Alfred
Anderson, Paul F.
Anderson, Richard Lee
Anderson, Richard Paul
Anderson, Robert Ferdinand
Anderson, Robert Morris, Jr.
Anderson, Robert Theodore
Anderson, Roger E.
Anderson, Rudolph Emil
Anderson, Sigurd
Anderson, Stefan Stolen
Anderson, Theodore Robert
Anderson, Thomas Harold
Anderson, Truman Oliver, Jr.
Anderson, Victor Elving
Anderson, Virgil Lee
Anderson, Wilbert Seth, Jr.
Anderson, Willard Victor
Anderson, William Ernest
Anderson, William Eugene
Anderson, William Gain
Anderson, William Otis
Anderson, William Summers
Anderson, Woodrow S.
Andes, John Wilbur
Andre, Camille Desmoulins
Andre, Paul Dean
Andreano, Ralph Louis
Andreas, John Louis, Jr.
Andreas, Lowell Willard
Andress, Samuel Coe
Andrew, Gwen
Andrew, Warren
Andrews, Clarence Adelbert
Andrews, David Kneeland
Andrews, Fletcher Reed
Andrews, Frank Meredith
Andrews, Frederick Newcomb
Andrews, George William
Andrews, James Frederick
Andrews, James Newton
Andrews, Mark
Andrews, Richard Vincent
Andrews, Wayne
Andrews, William Henry
Andrus, Elwin A.
Andrus, John Emory, III
Andry, E. Robert
Anello, John David
Ang, Alfredo Hua-Sing
Angell, Richard Bradshaw
Angell, Robert Cooley
Angelo, Frank
Angevine, Daniel Murray
Angland, Dennis Warren
Angst, John Edward
Anixter, Alan B.
Anjard, Ronald Paul
Ankeny, DeWalt Hosmer, Jr.
Ankrum, William Dean
Annear, Paul Richard
Ansfield, Fred Joseph
Anthes, Jacob
Anthony, E. James
Anthony, Michael Joseph
Anthony, Robert L.
Anton, William John
Antonsen, Elmer Harold
Anvaripour, M.A.
Apostle, Hippocrates George
Appel, William Frank
Appelman, Evan Hugh
Appl, Fredric Carl
Apple, Walter Eugene
Applebaum, Hy
Appleberry, James Bruce
Applegate, Douglas
Appleman, Jean
Applequist, Douglas Einar
Appleton, Arthur Ivar
Aprison, Morris Herman
Aram, Nathan Walter
Arbogast, Zollie O., Jr.
Archambault, Bennett
Archer, John Dale
Archer, Lawrence Harry
Archibald, Kalman Dale
Arden, Eugene
Ardery, James Donald
Areen, Gordone E.
Arehart, Robert Arthur
Arena, Angelo Richard
Arey, Leslie Brainerd
Arey, Mary Edith
Argento, Dominick
Argersinger, William John, Jr.
Aries, Leon Judah
Aring, Charles Dair
Aris, Rutherford
Arkush, Arthur Spencer
Arling, Leonard Swenson
Armbruster, John Henry
Armbruster, Kernel Lantin
Armerding, Hudson Taylor
Armington, Raymond Q.
Armitage, Richard
Armor, Raymond Hughes
Armour, Laurance Hearne, Jr.
Armour, Norbert Fred
Armour, T. Stanton
Armsey, James William
Armstrong, Arthur James
Armstrong, Arthur Soper
Armstrong, Charles Harry
Armstrong, Frank Goodell
Armstrong, John Alexander
Armstrong, John Henry
Armstrong, Jon Stephen
Armstrong, Neil A.
Armstrong, Neill
Armstrong, Robert Bradley
Armstrong, Robert Eugene
Armstrong, W(allace) D(avid)
Armstrong, William H.
Arnall, Paul McGrew
Arneson, Axel Norman
Arneson, George Stephen
Arnett, Harold Edward
Arnett, Judd
Arnheim, Rudolf
Arnoff, E. Leonard
Arnold, Arthur Olof
Arnold, Chester A.
Arnold, David Clement
Arnold, Duane
Arnold, Everett John
Arnold, Harry Bartley
Arnold, John Phillip
Arnold, Melvin Chester
Arnold, Paul Beaver
Arnold, Ralph Moffett
Arnold, Richard Eugene
Arnold, Richard Thomas
Arnold, William H.
Arnott, Struther
Arnstein, Walter Leonard
Aronberg, Ronald Jerry
Arpe, John Edwin
Arquilla, Robert
Arrington, William Russell
Arsem, Alvan Donald
Arthos, John
Arthur, Max
Arthur, Robert Milton
Artis, Jay William
Artz, Frederick Binkerd
Arvey, Jacob M.
Aschaffenburg, Walter Eugene
Aschauer, Charles Joseph, Jr.
Ash, Philip
Ashbrook, Charles Garner
Ashby, Donald Wayne, Jr.
Ashby, Robert Samuel
Ashcroft, John
Ashenhurst, Robert Lovett
Asher, Frederick
Asher, Raymond Matthais
Ashfield, George McLain
Ashford, James Knox
Ashin, Mark
Ashley, Benedict
Ashley, Robert Paul, Jr.
Ashmore, James
Ashton, Sister Mary Madonna
Ashworth, John Lawrence
Asman, Robert Joseph
Asmuth, Anton William, Jr.
Asp, William George
Aspis, Samuel Louis
Asplin, Edward William
Assell, Leo Nicholas
Astrin, Marvin H.
Athow, Kirk Leland
Atkin, J. Myron
Atkin, Rupert Lloyd
Atkins, Stanley Hamilton
Atkinson, Arthur John
Atkinson, Hugh Craig
Atkinson, John William
Atkinson, Milton Anson, Jr.
Atteberry, William Duane
Atwater, Horace Brewster, Jr.
Atwell, Robert James
Atwood, Donald Jesse, Jr.
Atwood, Harry Erwin
Auer, James Matthew
Auerbach, Boris
Auerbach, Carl Abraham
Auerbach, Robert
Aufmuth, Raymond Berton
Aughenbaugh, Nolan Blaine
August, Robert Olin
Ault, Phillip H.
Aurand, Calvin William, Jr.
Aurbach, Lester Phillip
Ausmus, James Tipton
Austin, Allan Stewart
Austin, Alvin Edward
Austin, Edwin Charles
Austin, James Augustus
Austin, Kenneth Ralph
Austin, Richard Henry
Austin, Ruben Vargas
Austin, Sam M.
Austin, Spencer Peter
Austin, Whitley
Austin, William Lamont
Autry, James Arthur
Auwers, Stanley John
Avedisian, Armen G.
Averill, Lloyd James, Jr.
Averill, Paul Neal
Avery, James Knuckey
Avery, Noyes Latham, Jr.
Avery, William Herbert
Avischious, Raymond
Avriel, Ehud
Axeen, Marina Esther
Axel, Peter
Axelrad, Norman David
Axelrod, Bernard
Axelrod, Solomon Jacob
Axelson, Charles Frederic, Jr.
Axelson, Joseph Allen
Axelson, Robert Richard
Axford, Roy Arthur
Axley, Ralph Emerson
Aydelotte, Myrtle Kitchell
Aydelotte, William Osgood
Ayers, Donald Walter
Ayers, John Carr
Ayers, Thomas G.
Aylward, Ronald Lee
Aymond, Alphonse Henry
Ayres, John Samuel
Ayres, Lyman S.
Azrael, Jeremy Richard
Azrin, Nathan Harold
Babcock, Charles Luther
Babcock, David Edward
Babcock, Michael Joseph
Babcock, Richard Felt
Babillis, Alexander
Babler, Wayne E.
Bach, David Rudolph
Bach, Fritz Heinz
Bach, Jan Morris
Bachert, Raymond Paul
Bachman, John Walter
Bachman, Nathan Dulaney, IV
Bachmeyer, Robert Wesley
Backes, James Glenn
Backlund, Brandon Haze
Bacon, Charles Langston
Bacon, Roger Victor
Bacon, Vinton Walker
Bacon, Wallace Alger
Baddeley, D. Jeffrey
Bader, Arno Lehman
Bader, Kenneth Leroy
Bader, Robert Smith
Badger, Edward William
Badskey, Lorin Justin
Baer, Eric
Baer, George Robert
Baer, Joseph Winslow
Baer, Julius Arthur, II
Baer, Robert Jacob
Baer, Robert Joseph
Baerreis, David Albert
Baerwald, John Edward
Baeumer, Max Lorenz
Baeumler, Walter Ludwig
Baffes, Thomas Gus
Bagby, Frederick Lair, Jr.
Bahn, Robert Carlton
Bail, Philip Milo
Bailar, John Christian, Jr.
Bailey, Bart Dean
Bailey, Cecil Dewitt
Bailey, Charles Waldo, II
Bailey, Dudley
Bailey, Harold Stevens, Jr.
Bailey, Herbert George, Jr.
Bailey, Herman Tracy
Bailey, J. Harold
Bailey, John Turner
Bailey, Joseph T.
Bailey, Merritt Elton, Jr.
Bailey, Orville Taylor
Bailey, Reeve Maclaren
Bailey, Richard Paul
Bailey, Robert Marland
Bailey, Sturges Williams
Bailey, Virginia Long
Bailey, William Rufus
Baillif, Ernest Allen
Bain, Jack Mainsfield
Bain, Wilfred Conwell

Bair, Edward Jay
Baird, George Henry
Baird, James Abington
Baird, John Pierson
Baird, Joseph Arthur
Baird, Roger Allen
Baird, Russell Miller
Baird, Warner Green
Baisler, Albert Wilford
Baisley, James Mahoney
Bakalar, John Stephen
Bakalis, Michael John
Baker, A.B.
Baker, Bernard Robert, II
Baker, Burton Lowell
Baker, Chester Bird
Baker, Clifton Earl
Baker, Crowdus
Baker, David Nathaniel, Jr.
Baker, Donald Arthur
Baker, Earl DeWitt
Baker, Edward Martin
Baker, George Robert
Baker, Hollis MacClure
Baker, James Edward
Baker, Michael Harry
Baker, Newell Alden
Baker, Norman Henderson
Baker, Richard Southworth
Baker, Robert Lewis
Baker, Robert Thomas
Baker, Rollin Harold
Baker, Russell
Baker, Sheridan Warner, Jr.
Baker, Stannard Luther
Baker, Warren Edward
Baker, William Wallace
Bakken, Earl Elmer
Bakken, Glenn P.
Bakrow, William John
Bakula, J. Stewart
Bakwin, Edward Morris
Balbach, Stanley Byron
Balcer, Charles Louis
Balch, Clyde Wilkinson
Balch, John Nethercot
Baldwin, Benjamin Harrison
Baldwin, Ira Lawrence
Baldwin, Ralph Belknap
Baldwin, Robert Edward
Baldwin, Rosecrans
Baldwin, William Howard
Balentine, Conrad James
Balester, Raymond James
Balfour, William Mayo
Balk, Eugene Norman
Balke, Victor H.
Ball, Edmund Ferdinand
Ball, Richard Edward
Ball, Stuart Scoble
Ballantyne, Victor Adolphus, Jr.
Ballar, Benjamin Franklin
Ballard, John Stuart
Ballard, John William, Jr.
Ballard, Larry Coleman
Ballard, Russell Ward
Ballenger, William Sylvester, Jr.
Ballinger, Walter Francis
Ballis, William Belcher
Ballmann, Donald Lawrence
Ballou, Mildred Oralee Tesdahl (Mrs. Philip E. Ballou)
Balogh, Joseph Kenneth
Baloun, John Charles
Balyo, John Gabriel
Bamberg, Robert Douglas
Bamert, Matthias
Banchero, Julius Thomas
Bancroft, Theodore Alfonso
Bando, Salvatore Leonard (Sal)
Bane, Charles Arthur
Bank, Theodore Paul, Jr.
Banker, Gilbert Stephen
Banker, Oscar H.
Banks, Ernest (Ernie)
Banks, Lloyd J.
Banks, Seymour
Banks, William Venoid
Bannon, Edmond Joseph
Bannon, John Francis
Banser, Henry P.
Banta, George, III
Banzhaf, Clayton Harris
Barach, Philip G.
Barbash, Jack
Barber, George Cullen
Barber, Henry P. C. W.
Barber, Hollis William
Barber, Willard Frame, Jr.
Barber, William Lee
Barbero, Giulio John
Barbier, Guy Hubert
Barbour, Ian Graeme
Barclay, William Robert
Barcome, Donald Francis
Bardeen, John
Barden, Horace George
Bardes, Paul Metzner
Bardgett, John E.
Bardis, Panos Demetrios
Barger, Cecil Edwin
Barger, Vernon Duane
Barker, Gregson Leard
Barker, Harold Kenneth
Barker, Hugh Alton
Barker, Richard L.
Barker, William Shirmer, II
Barkin, Ben
Barkofske, Francis Lee
Barksdale, Clarence Caulfield
Barloon, Marvin John
Barlowe, Raleigh
Barmann, Lawrence Francis
Barnard, Harry
Barner, Charles Wilbur
Barnes, Charles Andrew
Barnes, George Elton
Barnes, James Milton
Barnes, James Woodrow
Barnes, Peter Crain
Barnes, Richard George
Barnes, Robert Marshall
Barnes, Russell
Barnes, Wallace Ray
Barnes, Wilfred Eaton
Barnes, Zane Edison
Barnett, Anthony Allen
Barnett, George Leonard
Barnett, Harold Joseph
Barnett, Howard Albert
Barnett, John Vincent
Barnett, Joseph H.
Barnett, Max George
Barney, Charles Richard
Barney, Frederick William
Barney, Lemuel Jackson (Lem)
Barnhart, Hugh Arthur
Barnothy, Jeno Michael
Barnothy, Madeleine Forro
Barnstone, Willis (Robert)
Barone, Paul Louis
Barr, John Andrew
Barr, Kenneth John
Barr, Martin
Barrell, Charles Alden
Barrett, Charles Clayton
Barrett, Charles Marion
Barrett, Frank Joseph
Barrett, James Madison, Jr.
Barrett, Richard Wichgar
Barris, Ivan Edward
Barron, George Francis
Barron, Harold Sheldon
Barrow, Charles Herbert
Barrows, Marjorie
Barrus, Clyn Dee
Barry, Colman James
Barry, David George
Barry, Fred, Jr.
Barsanti, John Richard, Jr.
Barschall, Henry Herman
Barstow, Roland J.
Barta, Wesley James
Bartell, Gerald Aaron
Bartell, Harry Robert, Jr.
Bartell, Lawrence Sims
Bartelt, Louis Franklin, Jr.
Barth, Earl E.
Barth, Frank R.
Barthelmas, Ned Kelton
Bartholomay, William Conrad
Bartholomew, Harland
Bartholomew, Lloyd Gibson
Bartholomew, Robert H.
Bartimo, Alex Victor
Bartlett, Donald Elton
Bartlett, Francis Wayland
Bartlett, Paul Dana, Jr.
Bartlett, Robert Carrick
Bartoletti, Bruno
Barton, Evan Mansfield
Barton, Thomas Frank, Sr.
Bartone, Francis Frederick
Bartunek, Robert Richard
Bartz, Edward F., Jr.
Barzan, Leonard Angelo
Bash, James Francis
Bash, Philip Edwin
Basile, William Basil
Baska, James Louis
Baskett, Thomas Sebree
Basolo, Fred
Bass, Frank Myron
Bass, Robert Olin
Bass, Wesley Edward, Jr.
Bassett, Leslie Raymond
Bassett, Robert Cochem
Bassie, V Lewis
Bast, William Herbert
Batch, John Martin
Batchelder, Mildred Leona
Batchelder, William George, Jr.
Bateman, Barry Lynn
Bateman, John Jay
Bateman, Paul Trevier
Bates, Henry Elmer, Jr.
Bates, Hubert Bissell
Bates, Richard Oliver
Batt, James Robert
Batten, John Henry, III
Batten, John Marshall
Battey, Charles Wheaton, Jr.
Battison, John Henry
Batts, Warren Leighton
Bauer, Ludwig
Bauer, Richard Max
Bauer, Robert Paul
Bauer, Walter Emil
Bauer, William Joseph
Bauers, Eloi
Baughman, Gene Knox
Baughman, Lewis Edwin
Baughman, Millard Dale
Bauhof, Rudolf
Baum, Bernard Helmut
Baum, Harry A.
Baum, Werner A.
Bauman, George Duncan
Bauman, Harold Ernest
Bauman, Howard Eugene
Bauman, John Duane
Baumann, Carl A.
Baumann, Edward Robert
Baumgardner, Robert Lorain
Baumgartner, Norman Bernard
Baumhart, Raymond Charles
Baur, Werner Heinz
Baustian, Robert Frederick
Bavor, Herbert John
Baxter, James Phinney, 4th
Baxter, John Wallace
Baxter, Maurice Glen
Baxter, Neal Edward
Baxter, Reginald Robert
Baxter, William Lester
Bay, Alfred Paul
Bayer, Frank Calvin
Bayliss, George Vincent
Baylor, Hugh Murray
Bayman, Benjamin Frank
Bayne, David Cowan
Bayrd, Edwin Dorrance
Bays, Karl Dean
Bays, Robert Earl
Bazant, Zdenek Pavel
Beaber, James Duane
Beach, P. Goff
Beadle, George Wells
Beadle, John Grant
Beadle, Muriel McClure Barnett (Mrs. George Wells Beadle)
Beadles, Thomas Harvey
Beahrs, Oliver Howard
Beal, John M.
Beall, George Brooke
Beam, Alvin Wesley
Beaman, Berry Nelson
Beamer, Parker Reynolds
Beams, Harold William
Bean, Atherton
Bean, John William
Beard, David Breed
Bearden, Henry Joe
Beardsley, Richard King
Beardsley, Walter Raper
Beare, Gene Kerwin
Bearinger, Van William
Beasley, Robert Power
Beatie, Bruce Alan
Beattie, Orville Carl
Beatty, Lloyd Edward
Beaudine, Frank Richard
Beavers, Wiley Iaeger
Bebout, John William
Becher, Paul Ronald
Becht, Arno Cumming
Bechtel, Paul Moyer
Beck, Anatole
Beck, Axel John
Beck, Charles Beverley
Beck, George William
Beck, Joan Wagner
Beck, John Matthew
Beck, Paul Adams
Beck, Samuel Jacob
Beck, Warren
Beckenstein, Myron
Becker, Arthur Peter
Becker, Donald Eugene, Sr.
Becker, Dwight Lowell
Becker, Gary Stanley
Becker, George J.
Becker, George Roth
Becker, Hayward Charles
Becker, Jason Charles
Becker, Rex Louis
Becker, Richard Charles
Becker, Samuel
Becker, Samuel Leo
Becker, William Henry
Beckett, Theodore Charles
Beckman, John Stephen
Beckner, Harry Gene
Beckwith, Albert Edwin
Bedard, Bernard John
Bedell, George Noble
Bedell, Ralph Clairon
Bedford, Bruce Paul
Bedford, Norton Moore
Beebe, Raymond Mark
Beech, Olive Ann Mellor
Beecher, William John
Beeler, John Watson
Beeler, Thomas Joseph
Beelke, Ralph Gilbert
Beeman, William Waldron
Beering, Steven Claus
Beermann, Allen Jay
Beers, Bertram Robert
Beers, John Mason
Beers, William O.
Beeson, William Malcolm
Beeton, Alfred Merle
Beets, Freeman Haley
Begando, Joseph Sheridan
Beggs, James Montgomery
Behlen, Herbert Peter
Behlen, Walter Dietrich
Behnke, Wallace Blanchard, Jr.
Behnke, William Alfred
Behrendt, David Frogner
Behrens, Alfred J.
Behrens, Roland Conrad
Behrman, Edward Joseph
Behrman, Richard Elliot
Behrman, Samuel Jan
Beichner, Paul Edward
Beierwaltes, William Henry
Beil, Gary Milton
Beile, Harold Mathew
Beilfuss, Bruce F.
Beilke, James Ernest
Beimford, Louis Armstead
Beisel, Ervin Eugene
Beitler, Samuel Reid
Bekkum, Owen D.
Belin, David William
Beljan, John Richard
Bell, Daniel Long, Jr.
Bell, James Duncan
Bell, Robert Paul
Bell, William Joseph
Bella, Salvatore Joseph
Bellamy, James Andrew
Bellamy, Peter
Bellinson, Leonard Edward
Bellow, Saul
Bellows, Carole Kamin
Bellows, Charles Sanger
Bellows, John
Belmore, Frederick Martin
Belshe, Francis Bland
Belt, William Alvin
Beltaire, Mark Anthony, III
Belthuis, Lyda Carol
Beltz, Herbert Allison
Beltz, LeRoy Duane
Belzer, Folkert Oene
BeMiller, James Noble
Benade, Arthur Henry
Benbow, John Robert
Bench, Johnny Lee
Benda, Sister Ludmilla
Bender, Myron Lee
Bender, Paul Junior
Bender, Ralph Edward
Bendixen, Harold A.
Benecchi, Roy J.
Benedict, Clarence Corwin
Benedict, Donald LaVerne
Beneke, Everett Smith
Benenson, Walter
Benes, Louis Henry
Benfield, Warren Abraham
Benforado, David M.
Benford, Harry Bell
Bengtson, John Robert
Benjaminov, Benjamin Samuel
Benkeser, Robert Anthony
Bennett, Edward Herbert, Jr.
Bennett, Emmett Leslie, Jr.
Bennett, Granville Allison
Bennett, James Edward
Bennett, James Eugene, Jr.
Bennett, Jerome
Bennett, John F(rederic)
Bennett, John William
Bennett, Kenneth Herbert
Bennett, Lerone, Jr.
Bennett, Otes, Jr.
Bennett, Rainey
Bennett, Richard Marsh
Bennett, Robert Barclay
Bennett, Robert Frederick
Bennett, Russell Hoadley
Bennett, Russell Odbert
Benninghoff, William Shiffer
Benninghoven, Edward Daniel
Bennington, Neville Lynne
Bennington, Ronald Kent
Bensinger, Benjamin Edward
Bensinger, David August
Benson, Donald Warren
Benson, Ellis Starbranch
Benson, James DeWayne
Benson, Keith Stone
Benson, Kenneth Victor
Benson, Lawrence Paul
Benson, Paul
Benson, William Henry
Benson, Winston Willard
Bent, Henry Edward
Bent, Robert Demo
Bentley, Charles Harry
Bentley, Charles Raymond
Bentley, Orville George
Benton, John Hemingway
Benton, Robert Austin, Jr.
Benton, Robert Dean
Benton, William Pettigrew
Bentz, Carl Ellsworth
Bentz, Frederick Jacob
Benward, Bruce Charles
Berardi, Anthony Charles, Jr.
Berberian, Ara
Bercher, Harry Oldham
Berdahl, Clarence Arthur
Berdich, Vera
Bere, James Frederick
Beresford, Hobart
Berg, Eugene Paulsen
Berg, Glen Virgil
Berg, John Robert
Berg, Norbert Raymond
Berg, Norman Walter
Berg, Rodney Kenneth
Berg, Sherwood Olman
Bergendoff, Conrad John Immanuel
Berger, Sydney L.
Bergerson, J. Steven
Berggren, Ronald Bernard
Berghoff, Robert Anderson, Sr.
Bergland, Bob Selmer
Bergman, Edwin Alfred
Bergman, Melvin Robert
Bergmann, Fredrick Louis
Bergmann, Gustav
Bergren, Gustav Walter
Bergstrom, Dedric Waldemar
Bergstrom, Richard Norman
Bergstrom, Robert William
Bergwall, Evan Harold
Berick, James Herschel
Berk, Roger G.
Berkenkamp, Fred Julius
Berkman, Irving Jay
Berkman, Louis
Berkovitz, Leonard David
Berkowitz, Leonard
Berland, Abel Edward
Berlin, Nathaniel Isaac
Berlin, Stanton Henry
Berman, Abraham S.
Berman, Bennett I.
Berman, David Theodore
Berman, Jerome Richard
Berman, Russell Richard
Bernard, J. Pierre
Bernard, Lowell Francis
Bernard, Paul Peter
Bernardin, Joseph Louis
Berney, Joseph Henry
Bernhagen, Lillian Flickinger
Bernhagen, Ralph John
Bernhard, John Torben
Berninghausen, David Knipe
Bernotas, Ralph Joseph
Bernstein, Barry
Bernstein, Eugene Merle
Bernstein, Robert
Bernstein, Seymour
Bernstein, Sidney Ralph
Bernthal, Harold George
Berrey, Robert Forrest
Berry, Brewton
Berry, Donald Stilwell
Berry, Helen Janice
Berry, Jack
Berry, James Frederick
Berry, John William
Berry, Leonidas Harris
Berry, Lloyd Eason
Berry, Loren Murphy
Berry, Richard Stephen
Berry, William Martin
Berryman, Robert Glen
Berssenbruegge, Ruth Elizabeth
Bertelson, Arthur Robards
Berthoff, Rowland Tappan
Berthrong, Donald John
Bertram, Harry Edward
Bertrand, Joseph Gustaus
Bertsch, Frank Henry
Berwald, Helen Dorothy
Beshears, James Keith
Besse, Ralph Moore
Bessey, William Higgins
Best, Elmer Richard
Best, John Stevens
Bettinghaus, Erwin Paul
Betts, Charles Julius
Betts, Edward
Betts, George Cornelius
Betts, Henry Brognard
Betts, Howard M.
Betts, Jackson Edward
Betz, Charles W.
Betz, Eugene William
Beuerlein, Sister Juliana
Beutler, Frederick Joseph
Bever, Ellis Dorwin
Beveridge, Thomas Robinson
Bevington, David Martin
Beyer, Werner William
Beyerl, Merrill Charles
Beyler, Roger Eldon
Bezanson, Peter Floyd
Bhargava, Triloki Nath
Bialek, Thaddeus Richard
Bianco, Joseph Paul, Jr.
Bible, H(enry) Harold
Bibler, Lester David
Bibo, Franz
Bickford, George Percival
Bidelman, William Pendry
Bidlack, Russell Eugene
Bidwell, Bennett E.
Bidwell, Seth Roland
Biebel, Lawrence Burton
Biederman, Lester Martin
Biegelmeier, Frank
Bien, David Duckworth
Bienemann, William Joseph
Bierce, Harley R.
Bierley, Paul Edmund
Bieser, Irvin Gruen
Bieter, Raymond Nicholas
Bigelow, Leonard
Biggar, James McCrea
Biggs, Clifford Earl
Biggs, J.O.
Biggs, John H.
Biggs, Robert Mitchell
Biggs, Robert Wilder
Bigley, James Philip
Bilandic, Michael
Bilheimer, Robert Sperry
Billingsly, Leon C.
Bilsing, David Charles
Bilsky, Manuel
Bincer, Adam Marian
Binder, Leonard
Bindner, Harry L.
Bing, Karl Roger
Binger, Charles Robert
Binger, Eugene Thomas
Binger, James Henry
Bingham, William John, Jr.
Binkerd, Gordon Ware
Binnion, John Edward
Binz, Leo
Birckhead, Oliver William, Jr.
Bird, Robert Byron
Birdzell, Samuel Henry
Birkeland, Charles John
Birkenhauer, Henry Francis
Birkerts, Gunnar
Birnbaum, Eugene Albert
Birnbaum, Howard Kent
Birnbaum, Robert
Birnkrant, Norman Howard
Bishop, Albert Bentley, III
Bishop, David Wakefield
Bishop, John H.
Bishop, Robert W.
Bishop, Warner Bader
Bishop, William Warner, Jr.
Biskup, George Joseph
Bisplinghoff, Raymond Lewis
Bissell, Cushman Brewer
Bisson, Edmond Emile
Bitker, Bruno Voltaire
Bitondo, Domenic
Bitzer, Donald Lester
Bivens, Gordon Ellsworth
Bixby, Frank Lyman
Bixby, Harold Glenn
Bixby, Joseph R.
Bixler, Paul (Howard)
Bjoraker, Walter Thomas
Bjork, Alton Joseph
Bjorklund, Frederick
Blaber, Leo Bernard, Jr.
Black, Charles Allen
Black, Henry Montgomery
Black, John Wilson
Black, Neal Francis
Black, Richard Bruce
Black, Roger Antrim
Black, Samuel Paul West
Blackburn, Norman
Blackburn, William F.
Blacklidge, Richard Henry
Blackmar, Charles Blakey
Blackshear, Perry Lynnfield, Jr.
Blackwell, Harold Richard
Blackwell, Menefee Davis
Blackwell, Richard Joseph
Blaedel, Walter John
Blaes, Emmet Andrew
Blair, Bowen
Blair, Claude Maclary
Blair, Edward McCormick
Blair, Herbert Arthur
Blair, John Morris
Blair, Walter
Blair, William McCormick
Blair, Wren Alvin
Blake, Emmet Reid
Blake, H. William
Blake, Martin Irving
Blake, William Henry
Blakefield, William Henry
Blakely, Robert John
Blakeslee, William Sherman, Jr.
Blanch, Edward James
Blanchar, Carroll Henry
Blanchard, Converse Herrick
Blanchard, Townsend Eugene
Blanchette, Romeo Roy
Blank, Jonas LeMoyne
Blank, Sheldon Haas
Blanksten, George Irving
Blasingame, Francis James Levi
Blasius, Donald Charles
Blass, Gerhard Alois
Blatnik, John A.
Blau, Henry Hess
Blauvelt, Fowler
Blaylock, William Curtis
Blazey, Thomas William
Blecker, Harry Herman
Blecker, Michael Paulin
Blee, Thomas Joseph
Blenkinsopp, Joseph
Blessing, Charles Alexander
Blettner, Edward Frederick
Blewitt, Thomas Hugh
Bleznick, Donald William
Blinder, Seymour Michael
Bliss, Charles Melbourne
Bliss, George William
Bliss, Ray Charles
Bliven, Charles Watson
Bloch, Henry Wollman
Bloch, Herman Samuel
Bloch, Richard A.
Block, Joseph L.
Block, Kenneth LeRoy
Block, Melvin August
Block, Paul, Jr.
Block, Philip D., Jr.
Block, Stanley Marlin
Blodgett, Frank Caleb
Blodgett, Omer William
Blodi, Frederick Christopher
Blommers, Paul J.
Bloodgood, Don Evans
Bloodworth, J. M. Bartow, Jr.
Bloom, Herbert
Bloom, Myron
Bloomer, Henry Harlan
Bloomfield, Coleman
Bloomfield, Daniel Kermit
Blosser, Henry Gabriel
Blotner, Joseph Leo
Bluefarb, Samuel Mitchell
Bluestein, Paul Harold
Blum, Anna Ottillia
Blum, John Leo
Blum, Lawrence Philip
Blum, Robert Joseph
Blum, Virgil Clarence
Blum, Walter J.
Blume, Louis John
Blumenthal, Leonard Mascot
Blumer, James William
Blunt, Stanhope Eccleston, Jr.
Blutter, Joan Wernick
Bly, Robert Elwood
Blythe, Jack Gordon
Boardman, Eugene Powers
Boardman, Thomas Leslie
Boardman, W. Wade
Boas, Ralph Philip, Jr.
Boast, Warren Benefield
Bobbitt, Archie Newton
Bobbitt, Vernon Leroy
Bobinette, Charles Kenneth
Bobosky, W. Brand
Bobulski, Edward
Bock, Edward John
Bock, Robert Howard
Bock, Robert M.
Bockhoff, Frank James
Bockhop, Clarence William
Bockius, George Hamlin
Bodanszky, Miklos

Cain, Howard Bruce
Cain, James Clarence
Cairns, Earle Edwin
Cairns, James Robert
Cairns, Stewart Scott
Calamaras, Louis Basil
Calame, Don L.
Calandra, Joseph Carl
Calapai, Letterio
Calbert, Harold Edward
Caldecott, Richard Stanley
Calderon, Alberto Pedro
Caldwell, James Edward
Caldwell, Lynton Keith
Caldwell, Oliver Johnson
Caldwell, Philip
Caldwell, Robert Graham
Caldwell, Warren W.
Caldwell, Will M.
Caldwell, William Virgil
Calef, Wesley Carr
Caley, Earle Radcliffe
Calfee, John Beverly
Calhoun, Daniel Fairchild
Calhoun, Donald Eugene, Jr.
Cali, Lloyd William
Caliri, Joseph Louis
Calkins, Hugh
Calkins, Kingsley Mark
Callahan, Carroll Bernard
Callahan, Joseph Murray
Callahan, Raymond Eugene
Callahan, William Edward
Callaway, John Douglas
Callis, Robert
Callison, Charles Hugh
Calloway, Earl
Calloway, Jean Mitchener
Calvert, Jack George
Cameron, Alister
Cameron, Eugene Nathan
Cameron, George Glenn
Cameron, Gordon Brent
Cameron, John Roderick
Cameron, Marlyn Glen
Campaigne, Ernest Edwin
Campbell, Albert Angus
Campbell, Ann Morgan
Campbell, Donald Broughton
Campbell, Donald Thomas
Campbell, Douglas
Campbell, Edward Fay, Jr.
Campbell, Hayward, Jr.
Campbell, Jackson Justice
Campbell, James Arthur
Campbell, Kenneth Nielsen
Campbell, Margaret Anne Linger
Campbell, Paul Barton
Campbell, Richard John
Campbell, Richard Rice
Campbell, Robert Bruce
Campbell, Robert Erle
Campbell, Robert James
Campbell, Robert Wellington
Campbell, Wendell Jerome
Campbell, Willard Donald
Campbell, William Edward
Campbell, William J.
Campbell, William Murray
Campion, Frank Davis
Campoli, Cosmo Pietro
Camras, Marvin
Canary, Sumner
Candela, Felix
Canepa, John Charles
Canever, Victor William
Canfield, Delos Lincoln
Canfield, Earle Lloyd
Canfield, Francis Xavier
Canisia, Sister Mary
Cann, William Franklin
Cannell, Charles Frederick
Canning, Lee (Leonard)
Cannon, William Bernard
Cantelon, John Edward
Cantlon, John Edward
Cantor, Bernard Jack
Cantrall, Irving J(ames)
Capehart, Homer Earl, Jr.
Capel, Charles Edward
Caplan, Benjamin Bernard
Caples, William Goff
Caplice, William Francis
Capolongo, James Anthony
Caponigri, Aloysius Robert
Cappon, Alexander Patterson
Cappon, Lester Jesse
Capps, John Grierson, Jr.
Capps, Richard Huntley
Capps, Wilbur Dean
Caray, Harry Christopher
Carberry, James John
Carberry, John J.
Carbon, Max William
Carbone, Paul Peter
Cardwell, Alvin Boyd
Cardwell, John James
Carew, Rodney Cline
Carey, Archibald J., Jr.
Carey, Bruce Douglas
Carey, Frederick Arthur
Carey, John Leo
Carey, Tom Max
Carl, Ralph Fletcher
Carlander, Kenneth Dixon
Carlen, Sister Claudia
Carlen, Raymond Nils
Carleton, Jim G.
Carley, L. David
Carlin, Donald Walter
Carlin, Edward Augustine
Carlin, John William
Carlin, Leo Joseph
Carlin, Thomas L.
Carlson, Bille Chandler
Carlson, Curtis LeRoy
Carlson, Dean Bernard
Carlson, Gustaf Harry
Carlson, Gustav Gunnar
Carlson, Jerry Alan
Carlson, LeRoy Theodore Sheridan
Carlson, Milton Charles
Carlson, Oscar Norman
Carlson, Robert John
Carmin, Robert Leighton
Carnahan, Brice
Carney, Charles J.
Carney, Frank L.
Carney, Robert Alfred
Carozzi, Albert Victor
Carpenter, Allan
Carpenter, Anna-Mary Passier
Carpenter, Charles Colcock Jones
Carpenter, David Bailey
Carpenter, Edward Lester
Carpenter, John Marland
Carpenter, Noble Olds
Carpenter, Paul Leonard
Carpenter, Robert Beach
Carpenter, Russell Phelps
Carr, Charles William
Carr, David Turner
Carr, Frank Charles
Carr, Franklin David
Carr, Gilbert Randle
Carr, Harold Noflet
Carr, Jay Phillip
Carr, Robert Kenneth
Carracio, George Victor
Carrara, Arthur Alfonso
Carrier, Warren Pendleton
Carriuolo, Christopher Wilfred
Carroll, Daniel Thuering
Carroll, Grayson
Carroll, Lester Edward
Carroll, Michael Adrian
Carroll, Robert Lloyd
Carroll, Robert Wayne
Carroll, Wallace Edward
Carron, Malcolm
Carson, Bruce Lynn
Carson, Gordon Bloom
Carson, Harry Albert
Carson, Samuel Goodman
Carter, Byrum Earl
Carter, Claude I.
Carter, Collins L.
Carter, Donald Patton
Carter, Earl Thomas
Carter, Elton Stewart
Carter, Everitt A.
Carter, Frederick Elbe
Carter, Jaine Marie
Carter, John Coles
Carter, John Robert
Carter, Ovie
Carter, Robert Eldred
Carter, Roy Ernest, Jr.
Carter, Thomas Smith, Jr.
Carter, William Lee
Cartmill, George Edwin, Jr.
Carton, John Hazelton
Carton, Laurence Alfred
Cartwright, David Philip
Cartwright, Dorwin Philip
Carty, Ricardo Adolfo Jacobo
Carus, Milton Blouke
Carver, Norman F., Jr.
Carver, Richard E.
Carver, Roy James
Cary, William Sterling
Casado, Antonio Francisco
Casagrande, Joseph Bartholomew
Cascino, Anthony Elmo
Case, Weldon Wood
Caseley, Donald Joseph
Caserio, Martin Joseph
Casey, Edmund C.
Casey, Edward Paul
Casey, Genevieve Mary
Casey, Samuel Brown, Jr.
Casey, Warren Peter
Cash, Paul Thalbert
Cashman, John W.
Cashman, Robert J.
Caskey, John Langdon
Casmey, Howard Birdwell
Cassady, Edwin Leonald
Cassady, John Mac
Cassara, Frank
Cassell, Frank Hyde
Cassell, Martin Leroy
Cassell, Ray E.
Cassels, Donald Ernest
Cassidy, Claudia
Cassidy, Frederic Gomes
Cassidy, Harold Gomes
Cassidy, Hélène Monod
Cassill, Herbert Carroll
Castaneda, Hector-Neri
Casteel, John Laurence
Castle, Herbert
Castle, Latham
Cathcart, Silas Strawn
Cation, Paul Curtis
Catlett, George Roudebush
Catlin, Karl Aydelotte
Caton, Charles Edwin
Cattell, Raymond B.
Caudill, Rebecca (Mrs. James Ayars)
Caughran, Roy Willard
Cauley, Frank William
Cavanagh, Jerome Patrick
Cavanaugh, Francis P.
Cavanaugh, Ward Arthur
Cave, Alfred Alexander
Cavert, Henry Mead
Cavin, William Brooks, Jr.
Cayce, Eldred A.
Ceccato, Aldo
Cecil, Lawrence Keith
Cecil, Lester LeFevre
Cederberg, Elford Albin
Cederquist, Dena Caroline
Ceithaml, Joseph James
Celebrezze, Anthony J.
Celeste, Frank Palm
Celeste, Richard F.
Cena, Lawrence
Cernica, John N.
Cernugel, William John
Cerny, Robert George
Cerrone, Warren Edward
Cervenak, Edward David
Cesari, Lamberto
Chadbourne, Joseph Humphrey, Jr.
Chadwick, John Lloyd
Chafetz, Sidney
Chait, William
Challoner, David Reynolds
Chalmers, Edwin Laurence, Jr.
Chalmers, John
Chamberlain, Charles James
Chamberlain, Joseph Miles
Chamberlin, Thomas Wilson
Chambers, Clarke Alexander
Chambers, Curtis Allen
Chambers, David Laurance, Jr.
Chambers, Maurice Ripley
Chambers, Merritt Madison
Chambers, Stanley W.
Chambers, William Nisbet
Champlin, Keith Schaffner
Chandler, B.J.
Chandler, Harry Edgar
Chandler, Marvin
Chandrasekhar, Subrahmanyan
Chaney, William Albert
Chang, William Shen Chie
Changnon, Stanley A., Jr.
Chao, Bei Tse
Chao, Kwang-Chu
Chapin, Bradley
Chapin, Richard Earl
Chapin, Roy Dikeman, Jr.
Chaplin, Hugh, Jr.
Chapman, Arthur Barclay
Chapman, Dave
Chapman, Douglas Kenneth
Chapman, Helen (Mrs. Theodore Stillman Chapman)
Chapman, Reid Gillis
Chapman, William Paul
Chappell, Roy Mack
Chard, Chester Stevens
Charfoos, Lawrence Selig
Charfoos, Samuel
Charles, Bertram
Charles, John Fredrick
Charlson, Chauncey Rudolph, Jr.
Charnley, Mitchell Vaughn
Chase, Lucius Peter
Chase, William Rowell
Chavez, Simon Joseph
Cheek, King Virgil, Jr.
Chen, Kun-Mu
Chen, Kuo-Tsai
Chen, Paul E.
Chenea, Paul Franklin
Cheney, Thomas Ward
Cherney, Colburn George
Cherniack, Neil Stanley
Cherrington, Homer Virgil
Cherry, Robert Earl Patrick
Cheskin, Louis
Chesser, Al H.
Chesteen, John Saffell
Chester, William Merrill, Jr.
Cheverie, Carroll LeRoy
Chiappetta, Michael
Chiarulli, Peter
Chicoine, Lionel Mason
Chih, Yu-Ju
Childe, John Edward
Childs, Homer A.
Childs, James William
Childs, Robert Edward
Chilton, Arthur Bounds
Chitwood, Julius Richard
Choate, Robert Alden
Choka, Allen Dale
Chollar, Robert Ganun
Cholvin, Neal Robert
Chon, Myron Edward
Chope, Henry Roy
Chou, Shelley Nien-chun
Chover, Joshua
Chow, Tse-Tsung
Chow, Ven Te
Christensen, Albert Kent
Christensen, Clyde Martin
Christensen, George Curtis
Christensen, Halvor Niels
Christensen, John William
Christensen, Keith Lavar
Christensen, Paul Walter
Christensen, Paul Walter, Jr.
Christenson, Donald Dee
Christian, John Edward
Christian, Joseph Ralph
Christian, Richard Carlton
Christiansen, Kenneth Allen
Christiansen, Robert Lester
Christianson, Robert James
Christie, Robert Wayne
Christ-Janer, Arland Frederick
Christman, Luther Parmalee
Christoph, James Bernard
Christoph, John Ronald
Christopherson, Fred Carl
Christopherson, Paul
Christopherson, Weston
Chroust, Anton-Hermann
Chu, Kuang-Han
Chung, Paul Myungha
Chung, Young-iob
Church, C. Howard
Church, Marguerite Stitt
Church, Robert LeValley
Churchill, James Paul
Churchill, Mac Milo
Churchill, Ruel Vance
Churchill, Ruth Dietz
Cianciolo, Pauline Anne
Cifelli, John Louis
Cisler, Walker Lee
Citron, Stephen Joel
Claar, John Bennett
Claflin, Robert Malden
Clagett, Oscar Theron
Claggett, William Morgan
Clapper, Lyle Nielsen
Clapsaddle, Gerald Leon
Clare, Carl Peter
Clare, Stewart
Clark, Alice Thompson
Clark, Allan Hersh
Clark, Carl Arthur
Clark, Carroll D.
Clark, David Louis
Clark, David Willard
Clark, Donald Cameron
Clark, Donald Robert
Clark, Edward Ferdnand
Clark, Elmer J.
Clark, Emery T.
Clark, Glynn Alden
Clark, Glynn E.
Clark, Helen Edith
Clark, James Gordon
Clark, John Alden
Clark, John Lewis
Clark, John Scott
Clark, John Whitcomb
Clark, Larry Dale
Clark, Leland Charles, Jr.
Clark, Montague Graham, Jr.
Clark, Peter Bruce
Clark, Robert Arthur
Clark, Russell Gentry
Clark, Samuel Ingalls
Clark, Sherman Edward
Clark, Thomas Barron
Clark, Thomas Garis
Clark, Thomas McKinstry
Clark, Truman Brouse
Clark, Vincent Hendrix
Clark, Walter Hill
Clark, William George
Clarke, Alfred Carpenter
Clarke, Allen Bruce
Clarke, Jack Alden
Clarke, John P.
Clarke, Owen Frederick
Clarke, Philip Ream, Jr.
Clarkson, James
Clatworthy, Harry William, Jr.
Clawson, John Addison
Clay, George Harry
Clay, William Lacy
Clayson, David Barringer
Clayton, Charles Curtis
Clayton, Glenn Lowell
Clayton, Robert Allen
Clayton, Robert Norman
Cleary, Catherine Blanchard
Cleary, John Joseph
Cleary, John Washington
Cleary, Russell George
Cleghorn, Reese
Cleland, George L.
Cleland, Sherrill
Clelland, Rod
Clement, Howard Wheeler
Clement, James Wheeler
Clement, Richard Francis
Clements, George Harold
Clevenger, Raymond Charles
Clewett, Richard Monroe
Clifford, Sister Adele
Clifford, Sylvester
Clifford, Thomas John
Clifton, James Albert
Clinard, Marshall Barron
Clinch, John Houstoun McIntosh
Cline, Richard Gordon
Clingerman, John Rufus
Clink, Stephen H.
Clinton, Lawrence Martin
Cloak, Frank Theodore
Clodius, Robert LeRoy
Close, Elizabeth Scheu
Close, Gordon Ralph
Close, Winston Arthur
Closs, Gerhard Ludwig
Clotfelter, Beryl Edward
Clouse, Roger Roy
Cluxton, Harley Ernest, Jr.
Clymer, Wayne Kenton
Cmich, Stanley A.
Coakley, John A(loysius), Jr.
Coakley, Joseph Charles
Coase, Ronald Harry
Coates, Clarence Leroy, Jr.
Coates, James Otis
Cobb, Jacob Ernest
Cobble, James William
Coberly, Camden Arthur
Cobey, Ralph
Cochran, John Daniel
Cochrane, Eric
Cochrane, Willard Wesley
Coder, Samuel Maxwell
Cody, John Cardinal
Coerver, Harrison F.
Coffee, James Frederick
Coffelt, John J.
Cogswell, Glenn Dale
Cohan, George Sheldon
Cohan, Leon Sumner
Cohen, Albert
Cohen, Allen Richard
Cohen, Benjamin Bernard
Cohen, Bernard Cecil
Cohen, Calvin James
Cohen, Charles L.
Cohen, Donald Panama
Cohen, Gabriel Murrel
Cohen, Jerome
Cohen, Jerome Bernard
Cohen, Jozef
Cohen, Lawrence
Cohen, Leonard Arlin
Cohen, Maynard Manuel
Cohen, Melvin Samuel
Cohen, Milton Howard
Cohen, Morrel Herman
Cohen, Peter Jacob
Cohen, Philip Pacy
Cohen, Raymond
Cohen, Ronald
Cohen, Seymour
Cohen, Seymour Jay
Cohen, Wilbur Joseph
Cohn, Avern Levin
Cohn, Bernard Samuel
Cohn, Earl
Cohn, Norman Stanley
Cohn, Robert Jay
Cohn, Ronald Ira
Cohodas, Sam Myron
Cohodes, Eli Aaron
Colás, Antonio Espada
Colasurd, Richard Michael
Colbert, Marvin Jay
Colborn, Theodore Reynolds
Colburn, Irving Walker
Colclaser, H. Alberta
Cole, Bruce Herman
Cole, Charles Chester, Jr.
Cole, Clifford Adair
Cole, David Harris
Cole, Douglas
Cole, Edward N.
Cole, Franklin Alan
Cole, Ira William
Cole, James F.
Cole, John W.
Cole, Joseph Edmond
Cole, Richard
Coleman, Clarence
Coleman, Delbert William
Coleman, E. Thomas
Coleman, James Samuel
Coleman, Lester Earl
Coleman, Mary Stallings
Coleman, Paul Dare
Coleman, Sheldon
Coleman, William Luther
Coles, Embert Harvey, Jr.
Colescott, Warrington Wickham
Collett, Wallace Tibbals
Collier, David Charles
Collier, Donald
Collier, Donald Walter
Collin, Robert Emanuel
Collings, John Kempthorne, Jr.
Collins, Cardiss Robertson
Collins, Carvel
Collins, Charles Joseph
Collins, Dennis Alphonsus
Collins, Edmund Martin
Collins, George Bernard
Collins, Harker
Collins, Jack Dorr
Collins, James Daniel
Collins, Julien H.
Collins, Orell Tex
Collins, Terrance Alfred
Collinson, John Theodore
Collinson, William Robert
Collinsworth, Even Thomas, Jr.
Colloton, John William
Colman, John Charles
Colt, Thomas Clyde, Jr.
Colwell, Arthur Ralph, Sr.
Combs, Clarence Murphy
Combs, Thomas Neal
Combs, William Hobart
Come, Donald Robert
Comey, David Dinsmore
Comfort, Thomas Edwin
Commoner, Barry
Comparin, Robert Anton
Compere, Clinton Lee
Compton, Norma Haynes
Compton, Robert Dale
Compton, W. Dale
Compton, Walter Ames
Comstock, Lyndon Davis
Comstock, Ralph Ernest
Conant, Howard Rosset
Conard, Alfred Fletcher
Concepcion, David Ismael
Condit, Carl Wilbur
Condon, Arnold Clarion
Condon, Edward Maurice
Condon, Justin Jerome
Cone, Fairfax Mastick
Cone, Spencer Burtis
Conerly, Richard Pugh
Confer, Ogden Palmer
Conforti, James Anthony
Congdon, Richard Tower
Conklin, Thomas William
Conley, Charles Cameron
Conley, Eugene Allen
Conley, James Daniel
Conley, Lois Ruth Ramseth
Conlin, Roxanne Barton
Conn, Arthur Leonard
Conn, Howard James
Connable, Alfred Barnes
Connaughton, James Francis
Connell, Alastair McCrae
Conner, Gabel Henry
Connolly, J. Wray
Connor, James Richard
Connor, Lawrence Stanton
Connors, Dorsey (Mrs. John E. Forbes)
Connors, Gerald Anthony
Connors, James (Jimmy) Scott
Connors, Jeanne Louise
Conover, Donald P.
Conrad, Edwin
Conrad, Lary Allyn
Conroy, Jack
Conroyd, W. Daniel
Conser, Eugene Poole
Considine, Frank William
Considine, John Joseph
Constantino, Jerry Raymond
Conte, Richard Nicholas
Conte, Samuel Daniel
Conterato, Bruno Paul
Contie, Leroy John, Jr.
Contreras, Phillip Angel
Converse, Philip E(rnest)
Conway, James Francis
Conway, Thomas James
Conway, William Ignatius
Conyers, Nathan George
Cook, Addison Gilbert
Cook, David Charles, III
Cook, Davy Clay
Cook, Donald Jack
Cook, Elton Straus
Cook, Fred S.
Cook, Howard Carl
Cook, Louis
Cook, Robert Edward
Cook, Robert James
Cook, Sam B.
Cook, Stanton R.
Cook, Thomas G.
Cooke, Strathmore Ridley Barnott
Cooke, William Bridge
Cooley, Nancy Colver (Mrs. Rome G. Arnold, II)
Cooling, William Peter
Coombe, V. Anderson
Coomes, Edward Arthur
Coon, Charles Edward
Coon, Minor Jesser
Cooney, George Augustin
Cooney, Thomas Michael
Cooper, Carl Major
Cooper, George Robert
Cooper, Richard Quinten
Cooper, Wesley Paul
Cope, Betty
Cope, David Howell
Cope, Harold Cary
Copeland, S. Bruce
Coppel, Harry Charles
Copps, Chandler Vincent
Copps, Donald William
Copps, Timothy James
Corbally, John Edward
Corbato, Charles Edward
Corbett, Cletus John
Corbett, Frank Joseph
Corbett, J. Ralph
Corbett, John Dudley
Corbin, David Chenault
Corboy, Philip Harnett
Corcoran, Tom
Cordes, Donald Wesley
Cordes, Eugene Harold
Cordes, Loverne Christian
Cordier, Hubert Victor
Corey, Gordon Richard
Corlett, Allen N.
Corley, Francis Joseph
Cormier, Ramona Theresa
Cornatzer, William Eugene
Cornelius, Francis duPont
Cornelius, John Church
Cornelius, William Edward
Cornell, Richard Garth
Cornell, Robert John
Cornelsen, Paul Frederick
Corner, David Nelson
Cornfeld, Dave Louis
Corning, Duane Leonard
Cornish, Dudley Taylor
Cornwell, Charles Daniel
Cornwell, David George
Corp, Robert W.
Corrigan, Fredric H.
Corrigan, James Joseph Patrick
Corrigan, John Edward, Jr.
Corrigan, Robert Willoughby
Corrington, Louis Earle, Jr.
Corso, Gaspare Alan
Corson, Thomas Harold
Cortelyou, John R.
Cortright, Edgar Maurice, Jr.
Corwin, David Rothe
Corwin, Swift Churchill
Cosand, Joseph Parker, Jr.
Cosgrove, Robert Carver
Cosper, Russell A.
Costello, Lawrence Ronald
Costigan, Edward John
Costill, David Lee
Costin, Frank
Coston, Bessie Ruth
Cota, John Francis
Cothran, Tilman Christopher
Cotsonas, Nicholas John, Jr.
Cottam, Grant
Cotter, Patrick William

Cottingham, John Elmer
Cottingham, William Brooks
Cotton, Eugene
Couey, Duane Emerson
Coughlin, Richard William
Coulson, John Selden
Coulter, Glenn Monroe
Coulter, Llewellyn Legrande
Coulter, Thomas Henry
Coultrap, James Will
Counen, Michael Nicholas
Counsell, Raymond Ernest
Countryman, Dayton Wendell
Courtney, William Francis
Cousens, Frances Reissman
Cousineau, Lawrence Henry
Cousins, William, Jr.
Cousins, William Edward
Couts, Charles Raymond
Coutts, John Wallace
Covault, Lloyd R., Jr.
Cover, John Higson
Covey, Alan Dale
Covington, Clarence Allen, Jr.
Covington, John Ralph
Covington, Joseph Ethridge
Cowan, William Maxwell
Cowen, James Laurence
Cowen, Martin Lindsey
Cowgill, Donald Olen
Cowles, John
Cowles, John, Jr.
Cowperthwaite, Lowery LeRoy
Cox, Allan James
Cox, Earl Glenn
Cox, Frederick Kingsley
Cox, Harry Seymour
Cox, James Charles
Cox, Jerome Rockhold, Jr.
Cox, Lester Lee
Cox, Robert Gene
Coye, Robert Dudley
Coyne, Frank Holder
Cozad, James William
Cozier, J. Kenneth
Crabbe, John Roth
Craddock, Campbell
Craddock, Joseph Douglas
Craft, Alfred Thomas
Craft, Edward Oliver
Crafts, Roger Conant
Cragg, Ernest Elliott
Craib, Donald Forsyth, Jr.
Craig, Bernard Duffy
Craig, Eugene W.
Craig, George Brownlee, Jr.
Craig, Harald Franklin
Craig, J. William, Jr.
Craig, John William
Craig, Robert Charles
Craighead, Rodkey
Craigmile, David Francis
Crain, Mrs. G.D.
Craine, John Pares
Cramblett, Henry Gaylord
Cramer, Clarence Henley
Cramer, Fred
Cramer, Robert Vern
Crampton, James Mylan
Crandall, Arthur Bert
Crane, Allan Chandler
Crane, Arnold Herman
Crane, Carlson Eldridge
Crane, Douglas Pratt
Crane, Edward J.
Crane, Frank Harrison
Crane, Horace Richard
Crane, Louis Arthur
Crawford, Bryce Low, Jr.
Crawford, Charles Merle
Crawford, Leonard Kenneth
Crawford, Richard (Arthur)
Crawford, Thomas James
Crawford, William Basil, Jr.
Crawford, William F.
Creamer, Andrew Gates
Creel, Herrlee Glessner
Creese, Walter Littlefield
Crehan, Joseph Edward
Creigh, Thomas, Jr.
Crewe, Albert Victor
Cribari, Samuel Lewis
Cribbet, John Edward
Crile, George, Jr.
Cripe, Nicholas McKinney
Crocker, Jack J.
Crockett, Campbell
Crockett, Richard Calwell
Croft, William Crosswell
Croghan, Harold Heenan
Croker, Richard James
Cromie, Robert Allen
Crompton, Louis William
Cromwell, Norman Henry
Cronin, James Watson
Cronin, Joseph Marr
Cronon, Edmund David, Jr.
Cronson, Robert Granville
Crooks, Edwin William
Croonquist, David G.
Cropp, Frederick William, III
Crosby, Fred McClellan
Cross, Aureal Theophilus
Cross, John Richard
Cross, Leslie (Frank)
Cross, Ralph Emerson
Cross, Richard Clayton
Cross, Richard Eugene
Cross, Robert Clark
Crosson, Frederick James
Crosson, James D.
Croteau, John Tougas
Crotty, Harold Clifford
Crotty, Leo Alan
Crouch, Fordyce William
Crow, Browning
Crow, James Franklin
Crow, Paul Abernathy, Jr.
Crowe, James Joseph
Crowe, Robert William
Crowell, Edward Prince
Crowell, Prince Sears, Jr.
Crowley, George Charles
Crowley, Jerome Joseph
Crowley, John Powers
Crowley, Joseph B.
Crowley, William James
Crown, Henry
Crown, Lester
Croxton, Frank Cutshaw
Cruickshank, William Mellon
Cruikshank, John W., III
Crumpacker, Shepard J., Jr.
Cruse, Harold
Crutsinger, Robert Keane
Cruz, Jose Bejar
Cryderman, William Dale
Cuber, John Frank
Cudd, Herschel Herbert
Cudlip, William Byrnes
Cugell, David Wolf
Cuisinier, Francis Xavier
Culbert, Taylor
Culbertson, John Mathew
Culhane, Frank James
Cullers, Vincent Terry
Cullinan, Harry Thomas, Jr.
Cullity, Bernard Dennis
Culmer, Marjorie Mehne
Culp, Ormond Skinner
Culvahouse, Jack Wayne
Culver, Dwight Wendell
Culverwell, Anna Belle (Columba) Krebs
Cummings, Edward McLean
Cummings, Frederick James
Cummings, Herbert Kellert
Cummings, Larry Lee
Cummings, Richard Howe
Cummings, Tilden
Cummings, Walter J.
Cummins, Alfred Byron
Cummins, Kenneth Burdette
Cuneo, John F.
Cunion, Earl Eugene
Cunnane, James Joseph
Cunningham, Clark Edward
Cunningham, David
Cunningham, Floyd Franklin
Cunningham, Glenn Clarence
Cunningham, Harry Blair
Cunningham, James Gerald, Jr.
Cunningham, Luvern Lee
Cunningham, Marcus Eddy
Cunningham, Marilyn Alice Eneix
Cunningham, Maurice Patrick
Cunningham, Paul Millard
Cunningham, R. John
Cunningham, Robert Cyril
Cunningham, Robert Maris, Jr.
Cunnyngham, Jon Spurgeon
Curatolo, Alphonse Frank
Curcio, Louis Leroy
Cure, Charles William
Curfman, Lawrence Everett
Curl, Rane Locke
Curley, Ronald Franklin
Curran, John Charles, Jr.
Curran, Michael Walter
Current, Wayne Gast
Curreri, Anthony Rudolph
Currie, Allan Baldwin
Currie, Leonard James
Currie, William Richard
Curry, Ella Adams
Curry, Howard Millard
Curry, Robert Lee
Curti, Merle Eugene
Curtin, David Yarrow
Curtin, John William
Curtis, Ellwood F.
Curtis, Hugh Everett, Jr.
Curtis, Isaac Fisher
Curtis, Jerome Nathaniel
Curtis, John Kimberly
Curtis, Kenneth Stewart
Curtis, Mary Lou
Curtis, Philip James
Curtis, Richard Kenneth
Curtis, Samuel Ralston, Jr.
Curtis, Thomas Bradford
Curtis, William Hall
Curtiss, Charles Francis
Curtiss, Paul Herbert, Jr.
Cusack, Anne Millicent
Cusack, John Francis
Cushman, Aaron D.
Cushman, Edward L.
Cushman, Lewis Arthur, Jr.
Cushman, Martelle Loreen
Cuthbert, Marvin Peare
Cuthbertson, George Raymond
Cutinella, Joseph R.
Cutler, Hugh Carson
Cutler, Richard Woolsey
Cutler, Warren Gale
Cutlip, Randall Brower
Cutright, Phillips
Cutting, Philip Francis
Cutts, Charles Eugene
Cyphert, Frederick Ralph
Czarnecki, Richard Edward
Daane, Adrian Hill
Dabney, Seth Mason, III
Dacey, Timothy John, Jr.
Dagenais, Elmer Arthur
Daggett, Walter Hans
Dagley, Stanley
Dagnese, Joseph Martocci
Dahl, Erno Joyce
Dahl, Harry Waldemar
Dahlberg, LeRoy Waldo
Dahler, John Spillers
Dahlgren, George
Dahlgren, Lawrence Jungblom
Dahlin, David Carl
Dahling, Louis Ferdinand
Dailey, Donald Earl
Daily, James Wallace
Daken, James Benard
Dakin, Allin Winston
Dale, Edgar
Dale, Thomas Randall
Dale, Wesley John
d'Alelio, Gaetano Francis
D'Alexander, William Joseph
Daley, Arthur James
Daley, Richard Joseph
Dallmayr, Winfried (Fred) Reinhard
Dallos, Peter John
Dalrymple, Charles, Jr.
Dalrymple, Ruth
Dalrymple, Thomas Lawrence
Daly, Hugh Collins
Daly, John Francis
Daly, Maggie (Mrs. Arthur Bazlen)
Daly, Robert Frederic
Dam, Kenneth W.
Damman, James Joseph
D'Amour, Robert Arthur
Dampeer, John Lyell
Dancey, Charles Lohman
Danco, Léon Antoine
Danenbarger, William Fowler
Danenberg, Emil Charles
Danforth, David Newton
Danforth, George Edson
Danforth, John Claggett
Danforth, Joseph D.
Danforth, William Henry
Dangel, Robert Frederick
Daniel, David Logan
Daniel, Ralph Dudley
Daniel, Robert Woodham
Daniel, Walter Clarence
Daniels, Derick January
Daniels, Edward Bernard
Daniels, John Hancock
Daniels, Melvin Joe
Daniels, Robert Sanford
Danielson, Andrew William
Danielson, Gordon Charles
Danielson, John Oswald
Danielson, Lee Erle
Danilevicius, Zenonas
Danilov, Victor Joseph
Danis, Peter Godfrey
Danly, James C.
Danner, Patsy (Pat) Ann
Dante, Harris Loy
Dapples, Edward Charles
Darack, Arthur J.
Darbo, Howard Helseth
Darby, Edwin Wheeler
Darby, Harry
Darby, William Leonard
D'Arcy, John, Jr.
Darden, Sperry Eugene
Dargusch, Carlton Spencer
Dark, Philip John Crosskey
Darland, Raymond Winston
Darley, John Gordon
Darling, Frank Clayton
Darling, Stephen Foster
Darlington, Oscar Gilpin
Darnton, Thomas Edward
Darr, John Walker
Darr, Milton Freeman, Jr.
Dart, Donald Edward
Daughaday, William Hamilton
Daugherty, Paul John
Daum, Oscar Robert, Jr.
Dauphinais, George Arthur
Dautel, Charles Shreve
Davenport, Fred Marshall
Davenport, Horace Willard
Davenport, William Kirk
Davey, George Albert
Davidow, Leonard S.
Davids, Lewis Edmund
Davids, Richard Carlyle
Davidsohn, Israel
Davidson, Charles Henry
Davidson, Donald Herbert
Davidson, Eugene Arthur
Davidson, John Allan
Davidson, John Lefler, Jr.
Davidson, Louis Gordon
Davidson, Robert Laurenson Dashiell
Davidson, Sidney
Davidson, William
Davidson, William Robert
Davies, Dennis Russell
Davies, Elam
Davies, Paul Ewing
Davies, Robert Holborn
Davies, Ronald N.
Davies, Walter Henry, Jr.
Davis, A. Arthur
Davis, Allison
Davis, Alva Leroy
Davis, Arleigh
Davis, Benjamin Bernard
Davis, Britton Anthony
Davis, Charles Alexander
Davis, Charles L.
Davis, Chester R., Jr.
Davis, Curtis Woodward
Davis, David, IV
Davis, Dwight M.
Davis, Earle Rosco
Davis, Gale Elwood
Davis, Gene Carlton
Davis, Harry Rex
Davis, Herbert Haywood, Jr.
Davis, Howard Ted
Davis, Hubert Eugene
Davis, Ilus Winfield
Davis, Jacob Erastus
Davis, James (Othello)
Davis, John Bradford, Jr.
Davis, John Dwelle
Davis, Jonathan Farr
Davis, Julius E.
Davis, Laurence Laird
Davis, Loyal
Davis, M. Edward
Davis, Muller
Davis, Nelson Vincent
Davis, Pearce
Davis, Ralph Lanier
Davis, Richard Josef
Davis, Robert S.
Davis, Roger Edwin
Davis, Roy William
Davis, S. Robert
Davis, Samuel Spencer
Davis, Victoria (Vicky)
Davis, William Harry
Davis, William Robert
Davison, Francis Mackey
Davitt, Thomas Edward
Dawes, Irving Hemphill
Dawn, Clarence Ernest
Dawson, Clayton Leroy
Dawson, Horace
Dawson, John Albert
Dawson, John Frederick
Dawson, John Harper
Dawson, Martha Eaton
Dawson, William Ryan
Day, Cecil LeRoy
Day, Emerson
Day, Harry Gilbert
Day, John Sidney
Day, Lewis Israel
Day, Mahlon Marsh
Day, Sister Mary Agnita Claire
Day, Ralph Lewis
Day, Roland Bernard
Dayton, Bruce Bliss
Dayton, Donald Chadwick
Dayton, George Draper, II
Dayton, Kenneth Nelson
Deacy, Thomas Edward, Jr.
Deahl, Warren Anthony
Deale, Henry Vail, Jr.
Deam, Edward Lee
Dean, Burton Victor
Dean, Donald Stewart
Dean, Howard Frederick
Dean, John Clement
Dean, John Ladd
Dean, Leland Wilbur
Dean, Robert Hal
Dearden, Douglas Morey
Dearden, John Francis
Dearth, Robert Alfred
Deasy, Mary Margaret
Deatherage, Fred E.
DeAtley, Lindley Shafer
Deaver, Darwin Holloway
DeBardeleben, Arthur
De Bartolo, Edward J., Jr.
Debelak, William F.
De Bloom, Carl George, Jr.
DeBow, Russell Robinson
DeBruler, Roger O.
De Bruyn, Peter Paul Henry
De Bruyn, Robert L.
de Bruyn Kops, Julian
Debus, Allen George
de Chasca, Edmund
Decio, Arthur Julius
Decker, Bernard Martin
Decker, David Garrison
Decker, Freeman Bernard
Decker, Robert David
Decker, Wayne Leroy
de Coningh, Edward Hurlbut
DeCosta, Edwin J.
DeCoster, Cyrus Cole
DeCrane, Raymond Edward
Dederick, Robert Gogan
Dedmon, Emmett
Deeb, Gary James
Deegan, James Wayne
Deep, Ira Washington
Defoe, Thomas Joseph
Defoe, William Martin
De Gaetano, Armand Leonard
De George, Richard Thomas
Degnan, Thomas Leonard
DeGraaf, Donald Earl
de Gravelles, William Decatur, Jr.
DeGroot, Don Ferdinand
DeGroot, Leslie Jacob
DeGuire, Frank C.
DeGuisti, Dominic Lawrence
DeHaan, Norman Richard
Deikel, Theodore
Dein, Raymond Charles
De Jong, Meindert
DeJong, Russell Nelson
DeKemper, Herman Franklin
Dekovic, Gene
De Lacey, J. Gibson
Delakas, Daniel Liudviko
De Lancey, William John
DeLapp, George Leslie
Delforge, Ralph Henry
del Greco, Francesco
Delhey, John Donald
Delleur, Jacques William
Dellow, Reginald Leonard
Delor, Camille Joseph
DeLorean, John Zachary
De Lorenzo, Anthony George
DeLuca, Hector Floyd
De Marco, Thomas Joseph
De Marinis, Frank
DeMars, Richard Bruce
DeMascio, Robert Edward
Dember, William Norton
Dembo, Lawrence Sanford
Dembowski, Peter Florian
Dementis, Gilbert X.
Demerath, Nicholas Jay
Demetrion, James Thomas
Demetrios, Bishop (Demetrios Makris)
Demetriou, Angelo John
De Mets, Pierre Austin
DeMicheal, Donald Anthony
Demoff, Samuel Louis
DeMong, Vance Clyde
Demorest, Robert Steele
Demos, James Thomas
DeMoss, Ralph Dean
Dempsey, Frank Joseph
Dempsey, James Howard, Jr.
Dempsey, John Cornelius
Dempsey, Louis Francis, III
Dempsey, Thomas L.
Denavit, Jacques
Denise, Malcolm Lawrence
Denisen, Ervin Loren
Denkhoff, Elizabeth
Denler, William Harris
Dennen, David Warren
Denney, Robert Vernon
Dennig, Louis Schaefer, Jr.
Dennis, Charles Leslie
Denniston, Joseph Charles
Denny, James McCahill
Denny, Wayne Belding
Denov, Sam
DeNovo, John August
Denslow, John Stedman
Dent, Louis Linton
Denton, Eugene Harold
Depew, Charles Gardner
dePeyster, Frederic Augustus
DePiero, Nicholas G.
De Pree, Willard Ames
Deramus, William Neal, III
Derber, Milton
Derby, Stanley Kingdon
Derge, David Richard
Derk, Richard George
Derlacki, Eugene L(ubin)
Derse, Philip Henry
Derwinski, Edward Joseph
De Santis, Anthony
De Santis, Vincent Paul
Desch, Theodore Edward
DeSchweinitz, Karl, Jr.
Desloge, Taylor Stith
Despres, Leo Arthur
Despres, Leon Mathis
Deters, James Raymond
Detlefsen, Guy-Robert
deTreville, Robert Treat Paine
Dettmer, Roger Christian
Detuno, Joseph Edward
Detweiler, Joseph Hall
Detzer, Karl William
Deusing, Murl
Deutsch, Alfred Leonard
Deveau, Thomas C.
Devenow, Chester
Devereux, Lawrence Hackett
Devereux, Timothy Edward
Devinatz, Allen
Devine, Daniel John
DeVine, Joseph Lawrence
Devine, Vaughan P. (Bing)
Devitt, Edward James
DeVos, Richard Marvin
De Voursney, Andrew Merle
De Vries, Adriaan
DeVries, Bernard Jerin
Dew, Charles Burgess
Dewald, Ernest Leroy
DeWald, Franklin Kenneth
DeWall, Richard Allison
Dewar, Robert Earl
DeWeese, Marion Spencer
Dewey, Ernest Wayne
Dewey, Horace William
Dewey, Lewis William, Jr.
Dewhurst, Harold A.
de Windt, Edward Mandell
DeWitt, Jesse R.
DeWitt, William Orville
DeWolfe, John Chauncey, Jr.
DeWolfe, John Chauncey, III
DeWoody, Charles Ownby
Dexter, Richard Norman
Dhanak, Amritlal Maganlal
Diamant, Alfred
Diamond, Seymour
D'Ianni, James D(onato)
Dible, William Trotter
Di Chiera, David
Dick, Albert Blake, III
Dick, Edison
Dick, Raymond Dale
Dick, Ross Melvin
Dickason, John Hamilton
Dicke, Robert Jerome
Dickerson, Earl Burrus
Dickerson, Frederick Reed
Dickhoner, William Harold
Dickie, George Thomas
Dickie, Helen Aird
Dickinson, Martin Brownlow, Jr.
Dickinson, Richard Donald Nye
Dickinson, William Harold
Dickinson, William Reynolds
Dickmann, Dale Sidney
Dickson, George Edmond
Dicus, Clarence Howard, Jr.
Dicus, John Carmack
DiDio, Liberato John Alphonse
Diebold, Robert Ernest
Diefenbach, Allan Berleman
Diefenbach, Viron Leroy
Diehl, Harvey
Dieker, Charles Wayne
Dienner, John Astor
Diercks, Chester William, Jr.
Dierks, Richard Ernest
Dietch, Henry Xerxes
Dieterle, Donald Lyle
Dietrich, Joseph Jacob
Dietrich, Marion Clarence
Dietrich, William Allen
Dietrich, William Gale
Dietz, Charlton Henry
Dietz, David Henry
DiFederico, Mario A.
Difford, Winthrop Cecil
DiGangi, Frank Edward
Diggs, Matthew O'Brien, Jr.
DiGirolamo, Joseph
Dille, Earl Kaye
Dille, John Flint, Jr.
Dille, Roland Paul
Diller, Theodore Craig
Dilliard, Irving
Dillin, Samuel Hugh
Dilling, Lawrence Sheridan
Dillman, L. Thomas
Dillon, George Chaffee
Dillon, John Joseph
Dillon, Merton Lynn
Dillon, Neal
Dillon, Paul Washington
Dillon, Ray Earnest
Dillon, Ray Earnest, Jr.
Dillon, Richard Wayne
Dillon, W. Martin
Diman, Ezra Sampson
Dimling, James Sledge
Dimmerling, Harold J.
Dimond, Edmunds Grey
Dimond, Robert Edward
Dineen, Thomas L.
Ding, Gar Day
Dingeman, James Herbert
Dingman, Maurice J.
Dingman, Reed Othelbert
Dingman, William Ellsworth
Dinielli, Nicholas Anthony
Dinitz, Simon
Dinkines, Flora
Dinkins, Paul Newton
Dinsmore, Ray Putnam
Diotte, Alfred Peter
Di Pasquale, Pasquale, Jr.
Dirks, Lee Edward
Discher, Charles Dale
Dishman, Leonard I.
Dittrich, Raymond Joseph
Divall, Robert Keith
Dively, George Samuel
Divertie, Matthew Burgess
Divine, Thomas Francis
Dixit, Padmakar Kashinath
Dixon, Alan John
Dixon, Arthur George John
Dixon, George Hall
Dixon, John James
Dixon, Robert Galloway, Jr.
Dixon, Stewart Strawn
Dixon, Wendell Lowell
Dixon, Wesley Moon, Jr.
Doan, Charles Austin
Doan, Herbert Dow
Doan, Miles J.
Doane, John Philip
Dobkin, Irving Bern
Dobler, William O.
Doblin, Jay
Dobrovolny, Jerry Stanley
Dobson, William David
Dobyns, Brown McIlvaine
Docking, Robert Blackwell
Doctoroff, Martin Myles
Dodd, Edwin Dillon
Dodd, James Robert
Dodd, Robert Bruce
Dodge, John Vilas
Dodge, Philip Rogers
Dodrill, Forest Dewey
Dodson, Clifford Lowel
Dodson, Oscar Henry
Dodson, Raymond M.
Doe, Richard Philip
Doelz, Paul Rudolph
Doering, Grace Bernardina (Mrs. John W. McCord)
Doermann, Humphrey
Doermer, Richard T.
Dohnal, William Edward
Doisy, Edward Adelbert
Dolan, Thomas James
Dolch, William Lee
Dolibois, John Ernest
Dolin, Albert Harry
Dollahon, James Clifford
Dolland, Joseph Frank
Dolph, Charles Laurie
Dominik, Jack Edward
Domino, Edward Felix
Domke, Clifford Howard
Domke, Herbert Reuben
Don, Daniel Arthur
Donabedian, Avedis
Donachie, James Ross
Donagan, Alan
Donahue, Daniel Jackson
Donahue, Phil
Donahue, Russell B.
Donahue, Thomas Michael
Donald, Larry Watson
Donaldson, Ethelbert Talbot

Donaldson, Frank Arthur, Jr.
Donaldson, Joseph Bruce
Donaldson, Richard Miesse
Donath, Fred Arthur
Doner, Mary Frances
Doner, Wilfred B.
Dongus, Gustav Herman
Donley, Harvey Edward
Donnell, Edward S.
Donnell, Forrest C.
Donnell, James C., II
Donnell, John Randolph
Donnelley, Elliott
Donnelley, Gaylord
Donnelly, Charles Francis
Donnelly, Kenneth Gerald
Donnelly, Robert True
Donnem, Roland William
Donohue, Carroll John
Donovan, Frank William
Donovan, John Anthony
Donovan, Paul V.
Doob, Joseph Leo
Doody, John Raymond
Dooley, Donald John
Dooley, James A.
Dooley, William Grover
Doolittle, Robert Frederick
Doran, Madeleine
Doran, Robert C.
Doremus, Robert Barnard
Dorfman, Albert
Dorfman, Henry S.
Dorfman, Isaiah S.
Dorfman, Leon Monte
Dorfman, Saul
Dorfmeyer, Robert Edward
Dorman, Linneaus Cuthbert
Dorn, Charles Meeker
Dorner, Peter Paul
Dorr, John A., Jr.
Dorschel, Querin Peter
Dorsey, Gray Lankford
Dorsey, John Michael
Dorsey, John Morris
Dorsey, Peter
Dorsey, Thomas Andrew
Dorson, Richard M.
Dortch, Carl Raymond
Dorweiler, John P.
Doss, Lawrence Paul
Dott, Robert Henry, Jr.
Dotts, Harold William
Doubet, Earl Wesley
Douce, Wayne Richard
Doudna, Quincy Von Ogden
Dougan, Arthur Lewis
Dougherty, Charles Joseph
Douglas, Bruce Lee
Douglas, James Henderson, Jr.
Douglas, John Harold
Douglas, Kenneth Jay
Douglas, Murray Alanson
Douglas, Paul Louis
Douglas, Robert Ellis
Douglass, Bruce E.
Douglass, Kingman, Jr.
Doumas, John J.
Dourlet, Ernest Francis
Dovenmuehle, George Henry
Dovre, Paul John
Dow, Alden Ball
Dow, Dorothy Minerva
Dow, James Wilson
Dow, William Gould
Dowling, James Hamilton
Downey, Glanville
Downey, John Charles
Downey, Joseph Francis
Downie, Dana
Downing, Bruce Theodore
Downing, Joan Forman
Downing, Reginald Horton
Downs, James Chesterfield, Jr.
Downs, John A.
Downs, Robert Bingham
Downs, Thomas Joseph
Doyle, Bertram Wilbur
Doyle, James Alexander
Doyle, James Edward
Doyle, John Vincent
Drago, Russell Stephen
Drake, Carl Bigelow, Jr.
Drake, John Warren
Drake, Robert Tucker
Drake, William Depue
Drane, Walter Harding
Drange, Robert Oyloe
Dranoff, Joshua Simon
Draper, Maurice Lee
Draper, Norman Richard
Dray, Sheldon
Drebin, Allan Richard
Dreher, Thomas Haller
Dreifke, Gerald Edmond
Dreiske, John
Dressel, Paul Leroy
Drevs, Robert M.
Dreyer, John Edward
Dreyfus, Lee Sherman
Drick, John Edward
Drickamer, Harry George
Driggs, H. Perry, Jr.
Driker, Eugene
Drimmer, Melvin
Drinko, John Deaver
Driscoll, Glen Robert
Driscoll, Hugh MacPherson
Driscoll, Justin Albert
Driscoll, Robert Edward, Jr.
Drossin, Julius
Drott, Edward
Drown, Gary Kidd
Drucker, Daniel Charles
Druhot, Theodore Joseph
Drummond, Edward Joseph

Drury, Charles Edwin
Drury, Robert Edward
Drury, Robert Merrill
Drushal, John Garber
Dubin, Alvin
Dubin, Arthur Detmers
Dubin, Martin David
DuBois, Philip Hunter
Du Brul, Ernest Lloyd
DuCanto, Joseph N.
Duchen, Charles
Duckworth, T.A.
Duckworth, Winston Howard
Ducoff, Howard S.
Duddy, Frank Edward, Jr.
Due, John Fitzgerald
Duff, Cloyd Edgar
Duff, Ivan Francis
Duffy, Edward William
Duffy, Francis Ryan
Du Flon, Henry A.
Dugan, Patrick Raymond
Dugan, Richard Taylor
Duggan, Jerome Timothy
Duggan, John Michael
Dugger, Robert Wellford
Duke, Wayne
Dulany, Elizabeth Gjelsness
Dulin, Jacques (James) Matagne
Duncan, Carl Porter
Duncan, Charles Howard
Duncan, Charles William
Duncan, Clarence Avery, Jr.
Duncan, Donald Pendleton
Duncan, Hearst Randolph
Duncan, James Herbert Cavanaugh
Duncan, Kent Whitney
Duncan, Louis Charles
Duncan, Robert Morton
Duncan, Walter
Dunham, Allison
Dunham, Clive Fleeming
Dunham, Douglas
Dunham, Katherine
Dunham, Meneve
Dunhill, John Stokes
Dunklau, Rupert Louis
Dunkle, William Earl
Dunlap, Charles Lee
Dunlap, Leslie Whittaker
Dunleavy, Gareth Winthrop
Dunlop, Douglas Wayne
Dunlop, Ralph Gordon
Dunmore, Albert Jonathan
Dunn, Elwood
Dunn, Floyd
Dunn, Francis G.
Dunn, Francis John
Dunn, James Everett
Dunn, Leon J.
Dunn, Marvin Irvin
Dunn, Samuel Watson
Dunn, William Lewis
Dunne, George W.
Dunoyer, Philippe
Duprey, Wilson Gilliland
Duram, Arthur E.
Durand, Loyal, III
Duren, Peter Larkin
Durenberger, David Ferdinand
Durham, Charles William
Durham, Robert Gregory
Durrenberger, William John
Durtsche, Sheldon Vernon
DuShane, James William
Dutcher, James Duane
DuTemple, Octave Joseph
Dutmers, Raymond M.
Dutt, James Lee
Dutton, Clarence Benjamin
Dutton, Frederic Booth
Duvick, Donald Nelson
Duvin, Robert Phillip
Dvorak, Raymond Francis
Dwight, Donald Rathbun
Dwinger, Philip
Dworschak, Baldwin
Dwyer, Gregg Allan
Dwyer, John William
Dye, James D.
Dyer, William Allan, Jr.
Dykema, John Russel
Dykes, Archie Reece
Dykes, Charles Edwin
Dykhouse, David Jay
Dykstra, Robert Rozeboom
Dysinger, Wendell Stuart
Dziewiatkowski, Dominic Donald
Dziuba, Henry Frank
Eady, Carol Murphy (Mrs. Karl Ernest Eady)
Eagan, Emmett Edward
Eager, Henry Ide
Eagleton, Richard Ernest
Eagleton, William Lester, Jr.
Eakin, Thomas Capper
Ealy, Robert Phillip
Eames, S. Morris
Earl, Lewis Harold
Earle, David Prince, Jr.
Earley, Arthur Edsel
Earley, Ernest Benton
Early, Bert Hylton
Early, Robert Paul
Earnhart, Don Brady
Easley, Eddie Vee
Easley, John Allen, Jr.
Easlick, David Kenneth
Easlick, Kenneth A(lexander)
Easterling, Marion Rex
Eastham, William Kenneth
Eastman, Anthony Dey
Eastman, John Richard

Eastman, Richard Morse
Easton, David
Easton, Loyd David
Eastwick, Rawlins Jackson, III
Eastwood, Clyde William
Eastwood, Douglas William
Eaton, Alvin Kane
Eaton, Andrew Jackson
Eaton, Cyrus Stephen
Eaton, Cyrus Stephen, Jr.
Eaton, Henry Felix
Eaton, Leonard Kimball
Ebel, Marvin Emerson
Eberhardt, John Fowler
Eberhart, Wilbur Lyle
Eberle, August William
Ebersold, Charles Waldemar, Jr.
Ebert, Harvey Harry
Ebert, Lynn John
Ebert, Robert Alvin
Ebert, Roger Joseph
Ebinger, Robert Frederick
Ebner, Kurt Ewald
Eby, Cecil DeGrotte
Eccles, Elisabeth Norris
Eccles, Mark
Echols, Roy C.
Eckenhoff, James Edward
Eckert, Allan W.
Eckert, Ernst R. G.
Eckert, Roger E(arl)
Eckhardt, Richard Dale
Eckler, John Alfred
Eckley, Robert Spence
Eckley, Wilton Earl, Jr.
Ecklund, Glenn Algot
Ecklund, LeRoy A.
Eckman, James Russell
Ecksel, Meyer M.
Eckstein, John William
Eddy, Gerald Ernest
Eddy, John Paul
Eddy, William Crawford
Edelman, Alvin
Edelman, Daniel Joseph
Edelman, Joel
Edelman, Murray Jacob
Edelson, David
Edens, Robert Luther, Jr.
Edgar, Earl Eugene
Edgell, Walter Francis
Edgren, Carl Hobart
Edie, James M.
Edison, Allen Ray
Edison, Bernard
Edison, Irving
Edison, Julian Irving
Edlund, Roscoe Claudius
Edmonds, Harold Frederick
Edmondson, Frank K.
Edmondson, Keith Henry
Edmunds, Palmer Daniel
Edson, Charles Farwell, Jr.
Edwards, Benjamin Franklin, III
Edwards, David Olaf
Edwards, Donald Mervin
Edwards, Edward Everett
Edwards, Esther G.
Edwards, George
Edwards, Jesse Efrem
Edwards, John Allen
Edwards, John S.
Edwards, Joseph Castro
Edwards, Joshua Leroy
Edwards, Julius Howard
Edwards, Lucille Winters
Edwards, Robert Hazard
Edwards, Wallace Winfield
Edwards, Wilbur Shields
Egan, Richard Leo
Egbert, Robert Lindsay
Egekvist, W. Soren
Egertson, Darrell Jerlow
Eggan, Fred Russell
Eggen, Donald Tripp
Eggen, John Archer
Eggertsen, Claude Andrew
Ehlers, Henry James
Ehrenfeld, John Henry
Ehrenhaft, Johann Leo
Ehrle, Elwood Bernhard
Ehrmann, Winston Wallace
Eicher, Joanne Bubolz
Eichman, Peter Liebert
Eicoff, Alvin Maurey
Eidam, John Edward
Eidson, O. Bain
Eidson, Richard Irwin
Eigel, Edwin George, Jr.
Eigenbrodt, Harold John
Eiger, Norman Nathan
Eiges, Herbert M.
Eimers, Howard Gordon
Einsweiler, Robert Charles
Eiseman, Paul James
Eisemann, Carl, Jr.
Eisenberg, Leonard Sterling
Eisenberg, M. Michael
Eisenberg, Marvin
Eisenberg, Robert Shim
Eisenberg, Stephen Paul David
Eisenberger, Gary D.
Eisenstadt, William Sawyer
Eisley, Joe Griffin
Eisner, Robert
Eiteman, Wilford J.
Ekberg, Carl Edwin, Jr.
Ekman, William Elvin
El-Abiad, Ahmed Hanafy
Elam, James O.
Elam, John Carlton
Elberson, Elwood L.
Elder, Joseph Walter
Elder, William Hanna

Eldersveld, Samuel James
Eldredge, Charles Child, III
Eley, Lommen Donald
Eley, Lynn W.
Elges, George Robert
Elgood, William Richard
Eliade, Mircea
Eliason, Frans Robert
Eliot, Robert Salim
Elken, John Haynes
Elkin, Stanley Lawrence
Elkind, Mortimer Murray
Eller, John Clinton
Ellett, Alan Sidney
Ellingboe, Albert Harlan
Ellingson, Harold Victor
Elliot, Willard Somers
Elliott, Carl Hartley
Elliott, Daniel Whitacre
Elliott, Howard
Elliott, John Alfred
Elliott, John L.
Ellis, E. Frank
Ellis, Elmer
Ellis, Gilbert R.
Ellis, Harold Bernard
Ellis, Howard Woodrow
Ellis, Paul Niemeier
Ellis, Pierce George
Ellis, Richard Winfield
Ellis, Wade
Ellison, Lorin Bruce
Ellmann, William Marshall
Ellson, Douglas George
Ellwood, Paul Murdock, Jr.
Ellwood, William Prescott
Elmblad, Thomas Robert
Elmendorf, William Welcome
Else, Gerald Frank
Elsila, David August
Elslager, Edward Faith
Elsman, James Leonard, Jr.
Elsner, Sidney Edgar
Elson, Alex
Elson, Sam
Elston, Wilbur Evans
El-Wakil, Mohamed
Elwell, Kenneth Ray
Elworthy, Robert William
Ely, Albert Love, Jr.
Emanuelson, James Robert
Embry, Wayne Richard
Emerson, Thomas Edward, Jr.
Emery, Alden Hayes, Jr.
Emery, Guy Trask
Emery, John Murray
Eminian, Sarkis Joseph
Emlen, John Thompson, Jr.
Emmons, Ardath Henry
Emmons, Richard Conrad
Emont, Milton David
Emorey, Howard Omer
Emrick, Terry Lamar
Enarson, Harold L.
Endicott, Frank Simpson
Endress, Richard Roy
Enersen, Lawrence Albert
Eng, Bjarne Reidar
Engbretson, William Earl
Engdahl, Richard Bott
Engebretson, Milton Benjamin
Engebretson, Oscar Edwin
Engel, Albert Joseph
Engel, Joseph Henry
Engel, Tala
Engelbart, Roger William
Engelbert, Arthur Ferdinand
Engelhardt, LeRoy A.
Engelhardt, Thomas Alexander
Engelman, Robert S.
Engelmann, Hugo Otto
Engels, Norbert Anthony
Enggas, Carl E.
Engin, Ali Erkan
England, Joseph Walker
Engle, Donald Edward
Engle, Donald Leroy
Engle, Paul Hamilton
Engle, Shirley H.
Engles, William Norbert
Engley, Frank B., Jr.
English, Charles Brand
English, Earl Franklin
English, John Edward
Enlund, E. Stanley
Ennis, Thomas Michael
Enns, Mark Kynaston
Enouen, William Albert
Enright, John Joseph
Ensign, William James
Entenza, John Dymock
Entzeroth, Robert Elleard
Enyedy, Gustav, Jr.
Ephraim, Max, Jr.
Epley, Dean George
Epp, Eldon Jay
Eppelsheimer, Daniel Snell
Eppenberger, Fred Arnold
Eppler, Heinz
Eppley, George Edward
Epps, Edgar Gustavus
Epsteen, Casper Morley
Epstein, Alvin
Epstein, Dena Julia
Epstein, Leon David
Epstein, Ralph Jerome
Epstein, Raymond
Epstein, Samuel Stanley
Epstein, Sidney
Epton, Bernard Edward
Epton, Saul Arthur
Erb, Donald
Erbe, Norman Arthur
Erber, Thomas
Erich, John Bernhardt
Erickson, Ellworth Vincent

Erickson, Ernst Walfred
Erickson, Frank William
Erickson, Harold Lewis
Erickson, Homer Theodore
Erickson, Luther Eugene
Erickson, Richard Ames
Erickson, Robert Arlen
Erickson, Roy Frederick, Jr.
Erickson, Roy Lydeen
Erickstad, Ralph John
Ericson, James Donald
Ericson, William Arnold
Ericsson, William G.
Eriksen, Charles Walter
Eriksen, John George
Ernest, Robert C.
Ernst, Edward Willis
Ernst, William Theodore
Ersted, Robert Stephen
Ervin, John, Jr.
Erwin, Albert Rich
Erwin, James Otis
Erwin, William Walter
Esbjornson, Robert Glendon
Esch, I. Lynd
Eschbach, Jesse Ernest
Eschman, Donald Frazier
Eshelman, Raymond Harry
Eslick, Leonard James
Esmay, Merle Linden
Espelie, Ernest Marvin
Espenshade, Edward Bowman, Jr.
Esposito, Anthony James
Essex, Martin Walker
Estee, Charles Remington
Estep, Samuel D.
Estes, Elliott M.
Estlow, Edward Walker
Esworthy, Raymond W.
Etcheson, A. Thomas
Ethington, Ivan Claire
Ethington, James William
Ethridge, James Merritt
Etken, Edward Henry
Etter, David Pearson
Ettinger, Cecil Ray
Etzkorn, K. Peter
Etzwiler, Donnell Dencil
Eubanks, Ernest Morris
Eustis, John Norman
Evans, Arthur Thompson
Evans, Austin James
Evans, Bruce Haselton
Evans, Daniel Fraley
Evans, Donald F.
Evans, Earl Alison, Jr.
Evans, Ellsworth E.
Evans, Evelyn Corinne
Evans, Franklin Bachelder
Evans, Frederick Harris
Evans, Harold Edward
Evans, Howard Vernon
Evans, John Erik
Evans, Joseph Patrick
Evans, Mari
Evans, Medford Stanton
Evans, Nicholas Monsarrat
Evans, Richard Virdin
Evans, Rupert Nelson
Evanson, Robert Verne
Even, Francis Alphonse
Everett, Ardell Tillman
Everett, C. Curtis
Everett, Warren Sylvester
Everhart, David Leslie
Everingham, Lyle J.
Everitt, George Bain
Everly, Robert Edward
Evers, Walter
Evert, Ray Franklin
Ewell, James Marvin
Ewert, Marvin Henry
Ewigleben, Robert Leon
Ewing, Benjamin Baugh
Ewing, Gordon Richardson
Ewing, Robert Paul
Ewing, Sidney Alton
Exley, Charles Errol, Jr.
Exon, John James
Eye, Glen Gordon
Eye, John David
Eyerly, Frank Rinehart
Eyerly, Jeannette Hyde
Eyler, William Ross
Eyman, Earl Duane
Fabian, Donald Leroy
Faches, William George
Fackler, John Paul, Jr.
Fackler, Walter David
Fadell, Edward Richard
Faerber, Louis Joseph
Fagan, John Paul
Fahey, Leslie J.
Fahrer, George William, Jr.
Fahs, Charles Burton
Failing, George Edgar
Faiman, Robert Neil
Fain, Haskell
Fainstat, Theodore
Fair, Jean Everhard
Fair, Robert James
Fairbanks, Richard Monroe
Fairchild, Clem William
Fairchild, Mahlon Lowell
Fairhurst, Charles
Fairweather, Owen
Falberg, Weaver Emmanuel
Falk, Carl Anton
Falk, Louis Wahl
Falk, Marshall Allen
Falk, Ralph, II
Falke, Lee Charles
Falkner, Frank Tardrew
Fallon, Jerome Francis
Falls, Joseph Francis

Falsgraf, Wendell Albert
Falstein, Eugene I.
Fama, Eugene F.
Fambrough, Don Preston
Fan, Hsu Yun
Fan, Liang-tseng
Fane, Irvin
Fano, Ugo
Fanta, Donald Charles
Fanta, Paul Edward
Farber, Isadore E.
Farber, Lester Joseph
Farber, Marvin
Farber, Robert Holton
Farber, William Ogden
Farbman, Aaron Abraham
Farison, James Blair
Farkas, Philip Francis
Farley, James Thomas
Farlow, David Raymond
Farmer, Richard Neil
Farnsworth, Norman Robert
Farrall, Arthur W.
Farran, Charles
Farrar, Frank Leroy
Farrar, Martin Wilbur
Farrell, David Coakley
Farrell, Frank Samuel
Farrell, Paul Harry
Farris, Charles Lowell
Farris, Hansford White
Farris, Paul Leonard
Faruki, Mahmud Taji
Farwell, Elwin D.
Farwell, Loring Chapman
Fassel, Velmer Arthur
Fateley, William Gene
Fathauer, George Harry
Fatzer, Harold Ralph
Faucett, Philip Matson, Jr.
Faucett, Thomas Richard
Faulhaber, Robert William
Faulkner, Edwin Jerome
Faulkner, John Arthur
Faulkner, Virginia Louise
Faure, Gunter
Fauri, Fedele Frederick
Faverty, Frederic Everett
Fawcett, Henry Mitchell
Fawcett, Novice G.
Fawcett, Robert James
Fawcett, Sherwood Luther
Faxon, Jack
Fay, Robert Jesse
Fayle, Harlan Downing
Fazio, Carl
Fazio, John
Feather, William
Feck, Luke Matthew
Fedor, George Edward
Fee, Walter R.
Feeley, John Paul
Feenberg, Eugene
Fehr, Kenneth Manbeck
Fehskens, Kenneth Paul
Feickert, Carl William
Feiffer, Jules
Feikens, John
Feinberg, David Erwin
Feinberg, Leonard
Feinsinger, Nathan Paul
Feinstein, Irwin Keith
Feirer, John Louis
Feitler, Robert
Fejer, Andrew Akos
Feld, Lipman Goldman
Feldman, Burton Gordon
Feldman, Oscar Henry
Feldstein, Joel Robert
Felknor, Bruce Lester
Fell, Robert Todd
Fellin, Phillip Alexander
Fellman, David
Felmer, Andrew Robert
Felson, Benjamin
Felten, John Charles
Feltes, Robert Edward
Felton, Dean Russell
Fenn, Howard Nathan
Fennessey, John Joseph, Jr.
Fenninger, Leonard Davis
Fensterbusch, Jack Alvin
Fenton, Robert Leonard
Ferber, Robert
Ferer, Harvey Dean
Ferguson, Daniel Cuthbert
Ferguson, Donald John
Ferguson, Francis Eugene
Ferguson, Gary Warren
Ferguson, Homer
Ferguson, James A.
Ferguson, John Marshall
Ferguson, William McDonald
Fermi, Laura
Fernández, Oscar
Fernandez-Moran, Humberto
Fernstrom, Henry Allen
Ferrara, V(ernon) Peter
Ferris, John Byron
Ferris, John Orland
Ferris, Richard J.
Ferris, Virginia Rogers
Ferriss, David Platt
Ferry, John Douglass
Fess, Philip Eugene
Fetler, Paul
Fetridge, William Harrison
Fett, Eugene Werner
Fetter, Richard Elwood
Fetzer, John Earl
Feuer, Henry
Feuer, Paula Berger
Feuerwerker, Albert
Fibich, Howard Raymond
Fickinger, Wayne Joseph
Fidrych, Mark Steven

Gilbert, Richard Geoffrey
Gilbert, William James
Gilchrist, Richard Kennedy
Gil de Lamadrid, Jesús
Giles, Warren Crandall
Giles, William Bliss
Giles, William Elmer
Gilfillen, George C., Jr.
Gill, Bernard Ives
Gill, John Glanville
Gill, John Kermode, Jr.
Gillam, Basil Early
Gille, Frank Hugo
Gillen, Albert John
Gillespie, David Joseph
Gillespie, Harold Stanley
Gillett, George Nield, Jr.
Gillette, E. Genevieve
Gillette, Edward Scranton
Gillham, Mary Mewborn
Gillis, Frank James
Gillis, Marvin Bob
Gillmor, Paul Marshall
Gilman, Henry
Gilmore, Artis
Gilmore, Donald Sherwood
Gilmore, Durward Wilson
Gilmore, George Norman
Gilmore, James Stanley, Jr.
Gilmore, Joseph Patrick
Gilmore, Robert Eugene
Gilmore, Roger
Gilmour, Allan Dana
Giltner, Thomas A.
Gimmestad, Victor Edward
Ginger, Leonard George
Gingerich, Vernon Jason
Gingiss, Benjamin Jack
Gingrich, Newell Shiffer
Ginn, Robert Martin
Ginn, Rosemary Lucas (Mrs. Milton Stanley Ginn)
Ginsberg, Donald Maurice
Ginsberg, Edward
Ginsburg, Norton Sydney
Giovacchini, Peter Louis
Giovanello, William P.
Giroux, Robert J.
Gislason, Sidney Payson
Gist, Noel Pitts
Gisvold, Ole
Givan, Richard Martin
Givens, James Wallace, Jr.
Givens, Paul Ronald
Givens, William Phillip
Glaab, Charles Nelson
Gladders, Glenn Warren
Glagov, Seymour
Glagovy, Alfred Robinson, III
Glander, Charles Emory
Glanton, John Floyd
Glascock, David Grover
Glasgow, James Hersman
Glasoe, Paul Kirkwold
Glasser, James Jay
Glasser, Melvin Allan
Glauch, Alden Glenwood
Glaviano, Vincent Valentino
Glavin, John Edmund
Glazer, Edward
Gleason, Douglas
Gleason, Eliza Atkins
Gleason, James Arthur
Gleason, Thomas Daues
Gleisser, Marcus David
Glendon, Thomas Herbert
Glenister, Brian Frederick
Glenn, John Herschel, Jr.
Glickman, Carl Davis
Glickman, Louis
Glidden, Robert Burr
Glidden, Robert T.
Glockner, Maurice
Glomset, Daniel Anders
Glossbrenner, Alfred Stroup
Glotfelty, Philip Rutherford, Jr.
Glover, Gleason
Glower, Donald Duane
Glueck, Helen Iglauer
Glynn, Joseph William
Glynn, Thomas Joseph
Gnat, Raymond Earl
Gobin, Leo Calvin
Gockenbach, Harold Conrad
Goddard, William Paul
Godfrey, James Edwin
Godfrey, Joseph Edward
Goebel, William Mathers
Goehring, Luther Waldemar
Goelz, George William, Jr.
Goetsch, Gerald D.
Goetz, Charles Albert
Goetz, John Bullock
Goetz, John Richard
Goetzinger, Robert James
Goffman, William
Goggin, Joseph Robert
Goggin, William Charles
Going, William Thornbury
Gold, Aaron Michael
Gold, Bela
Gold, Gerald Seymour
Gold, Ike
Gold, Norman Myron
Goldberg, Arthur Lewis
Goldberg, Bertrand
Goldberg, John Edward
Goldberg, Lawrence Irwin
Goldberg, Robert
Goldberger, Arthur Stanley
Goldblatt, Louis
Goldblatt, Stanford Jay
Golden, Max
Goldenberg, Edie Nan
Goldenhersh, Joseph Herman
Goldenstein, Erwin Harmon
Goldfarb, Bernard Sanford
Goldhammer, Keith
Goldhammer, Paul
Goldhor, Herbert
Goldiamond, Israel
Goldin, Sol
Golding, Brage
Goldman, Bernard Marvin
Goldman, Jay
Goldman, Nathan
Goldring, Norman Max
Goldsborough, Robert Gerald
Goldsholl, Mildred
Goldsmith, Julian Royce
Goldsmith, Myron
Goldsmith, Robert Holloway
Goldsmith, William M.
Goldstein, Bernard
Goldstein, Jerome
Goldstein, Norman Philip
Goldstein, Richard Jay
Goldstein, Robert
Goldwasser, Edwin Leo
Goldwasser, Eugene
Golightly, Lena Mills
Golightly, Trueman Harlan
Golomski, William Arthur
Golter, Robert Andrew
Gomberg, Henry Jacob
Gomer, Robert
Gonge, John Foster
Gonzalez, Richard Florentz
Good, Clarence Allen
Good, Don LaDoyt
Good, James William, Jr.
Good, John Ehrmin
Good, Robert Crocker
Goodall, Leonard Edwin
Goodger, John Verne
Goodheart, Clyde Raymond
Goodman, Bernard
Goodman, Elliott Irvin
Goodman, Harold S.
Goodman, Oscar R.
Goodman, Robert Norman
Goodman, Stanley Joshua
Goodman, William I.
Goodnight, Clarence James
Goodnow, Nathan Brooks
Goodrich, Henry Calvin
Goodrich, John Bernard
Goodrich, Paul W.
Goodrich, Robert Edward, Jr.
Goodson, Louis Hoffman
Goodwin, John Mitchell
Goodwin, Louis Payne
Goostree, Robert Edward
Goran, Morris
Gordon, Arnold Mark
Gordon, Bernard
Gordon, Burgess Lee
Gordon, Edgar George
Gordon, Edward
Gordon, Ezra
Gordon, George Longan, Jr.
Gordon, Howard Scott
Gordon, John Lutz
Gordon, Marjorie
Gordon, Myron Lee
Gordon, Paul
Gordon, Paul John
Gordon, Robert Dyas
Gordon, Robert Edward
Gordon, William Glenn
Gordon, William Jones, Jr.
Gordon, William Livingston
Gore, Jerome Sidney
Goren, Seymour Bernard
Gorguze, Vincent Thomas
Gorham, Eville
Gorham, Sidney Smith, Jr.
Gorisek, Albin Anthony
Gorlin, Robert James
Gorman, Joseph Tolle
Gorman, Patrick Emmet
Gornick, Alan Lewis
Gorske, Robert Herman
Gorski, Jack
Gorsuch, John Wilbert
Gorton, Thomas Arthur
Goschi, Nicholas Peter
Goslee, George Fisher
Gosline, Robert Bradley
Gosman, Albert Louis
Gosman, James Hubert
Gosselin, John William
Gossett, William Thomas
Gotesky, Rubin
Gottier, Richard Chalmers
Gottlieb, Jacques S.
Gottlieb, Manuel
Gottschalk, Alfred
Gough, Harry Patterson
Gould, Benjamin Z.
Gould, Chester
Gould, Edwin Sheldon
Gould, Fredrick G.
Gould, Ira A., Jr.
Gould, John Philip, Jr.
Gouldner, Alvin Ward
Goulet, Charles Ryan
Goulet, Thomas John
Gousha, Richard Paul
Gove, Roger Madden
Gove, Samuel Kimball
Govindjee
Gowan, Arthur Mitchell
Grabau, Richard Fred
Graber, Doris Appel
Graber, Thomas M.
Grabner, George John
Grace, Richard Edward
Gradison, Willis David, Jr.
Gradwohl, Bernard Sam
Graebel, William Paul
Graessley, William Walter
Graettinger, John Sells
Graf, Donald Lee
Graf, Paul Luther
Graff, George Stephen
Graff, Maurice Otto
Graff, Roland William
Graham, Albert Bruce
Graham, Bruce Douglas
Graham, Bruce John
Graham, Charles John
Graham, David Tredway
Graham, Edward Henry
Graham, Elmer Albert
Graham, Erwin Herman
Graham, Evarts Ambrose, Jr.
Graham, Frances Keesler (Mrs. David Tredway Graham)
Graham, Jarlath John
Graham, John Dalby
Graham, Kenneth L.
Graham, Robert Leslie
Graham, Walker Ryan Allen
Graham, William B.
Graham, William Butterworth
Graham, William Hugh
Grainger, David William
Gralla, Eugene
Grambsch, Paul Victor
Grampp, William Dyer
Granberg, Charles Boyd
Grangaard, Bernhard Clarence
Grangaard, Donald R.
Granger, William Woodard, Jr.
Granick, David
Grant, Barry Marvin
Grant, Edward
Grant, Evva H.
Grant, Patrick Allan
Grant, Robert Allen
Grant, Robert McQueen
Grant, Virgil Vesco
Grant, William Downing
Graser, Clarence Francis
Grassmuck, George Ludwig
Grau, Albert A.
Graven, David Lauren
Gravenstein, Joachim Stefan
Graves, Gerald William
Graves, Robert Lawrence
Graves, Wallace Billingsley
Gray, Allen Gibbs
Gray, Donald Joseph
Gray, Elisha, II
Gray, Franklin Dingwall
Gray, Hamilton
Gray, Helen Theresa Gott
Gray, John Delbert
Gray, Milton Hefter
Gray, Richard George
Gray, Robert Lee
Gray, Walter Franklin
Gray, William Ashley, Jr.
Grayhack, John Thomas
Grayson, Richard Carl
Greathouse, Joe Stephen, Jr.
Greco, Salvatore J.
Gredys, Daniel Nestor
Greek, Darold I.
Greeley, Andrew Moran
Greeley, John Bernard, III
Greeley, Joseph May
Greeley, Samuel Sewall
Green, Arthur George
Green, Ben Charles
Green, Charles Edward
Green, Chester R.
Green, Clinton
Green, David Ezra
Green, David O.
Green, Edward
Green, Edward Fairchild
Green, Elmer Ellsworth
Green, Ernest
Green, Hal Keith
Green, Harry Edward
Green, James Leonard
Green, Jay Patrick, Sr.
Green, Marguerite
Green, Meyer H.
Green, Morris
Green, Orville Cronkhite, III
Green, Oscar Underwood
Green, Richard Harold
Green, Robert Smith
Green, Robert Thomas
Green, Warren Harold
Green, Winfield Rush
Greenberg, Ben Norton
Greenberg, Bernard
Greenberg, Edward
Greenberg, Frank
Greenberg, Martin Gary
Greenberg, Richard Aaron
Greenberger, Ernest
Greenberger, Norton Jerald
Greene, Anthony Storm
Greene, Bruno H.
Greene, Charles Cassius
Greene, Laurence Francis
Greene, Robert Bernard, Jr.
Greene, Wesley Hammond
Greenfield, George B.
Greenfield, Norman Samuel
Greenfield, Sanford Raymond
Greenkorn, Robert Albert
Greenleaf, Elizabeth Adele
Greenlee, Delbert O.
Greenman, Martin Allen
Greenspan, Donald
Greenwald, Joseph Adolph
Greenwalt, Harlan Edward
Greenwood, Donald Theodore
Greer, Carl Crawford
Greer, Gordon Gregory
Greer, Scott A.
Greer, Thomas Hoag
Gregg, Duane Lawrence
Gregory, Gustav Robinson
Gregory, Ian Walter
Gregory, Ross
Gregory, Ruth Wilhelmene
Greiber, Clarence Leonard
Greig, Walter
Greiner, Edward David
Grenell, James Henry
Greteman, Frank Henry
Grether, Henry Moroni, Jr.
Gribbin, John Hawkins
Gribbs, Roman S.
Griebenow, George William
Griem, Melvin Luther
Gries, John Paul
Grieve, Pierson MacDonald
Griffeth, Paul Lyman
Griffin, Claibourne Eugene
Griffin, Clare Elmer
Griffin, James Bennett
Griffin, Jerald Lee
Griffin, Leland Milburn
Griffin, Mary
Griffin, Richard Thomas
Griffin, William Lester Hadley
Griffing, Joseph Bruce
Griffith, Calvin Robertson
Griffith, David William
Griffith, Donald Raymond
Griffith, Frank Wells
Griffith, Garth Ellis
Griffith, Lynn B.
Griffith, Richard Eugene
Griffith, Robert Wilson
Griffiths, George Findley
Griffiths, Henry Joseph
Griffiths, Martha Wright
Griggs, James Henry
Griggs, Richard Leslie
Grignon, Ro Duane
Grigsby, John Lambert
Grim, Eugene Donald
Grimes, Alden
Grimes, Burton Piper
Grimes, Irvin Lorenzo
Grimes, John R.
Grimm, Carl Hugo
Grimm, Edith Rambar
Grimm, Harold John
Grimm, Reinhold
Grimm, Richard Seaton
Grimm, Wilbur Winfield
Grinker, Roy Richard, Jr.
Grinker, Roy Richard, Sr.
Grinnell, Ernest Doane, Jr.
Grip, Carl Manfred, Jr.
Griskey, Richard George
Grissinger, James Adams
Grissom, Donald Bauer
Grissom, Joseph Carol
Grissom, Robert Leslie
Griswold, Bruce
Griswold, Ralph Esty
Groble, George William
Grobman, Arnold Brams
Grobman, Hulda Gross (Mrs. Arnold B. Grobman)
Groebli, Werner Fritz (Mr. Frick)
Groening, William Andrew, Jr.
Groennert, Charles Willis
Groff, John Robert
Grogan, Hugh
Grogan, Steven James
Grollmes, Eugene E.
Grommesh, Donald Joseph
Gronvall, John Arnold
Groom, John Miller
Grosh, Richard Joseph
Gros Louis, Kenneth Richard Russell
Gross, Calvin Edward
Gross, Carl Henry
Gross, John Arthur
Gross, Seymour Lee
Gross, William Joseph
Grosse, Eduard
Grossman, Burton Jay
Grossman, Jerome Barnett
Grossman, Joel Barry
Grossman, Richard
Grossman, Sebastian Peter
Grossweiner, Leonard Irwin
Grove, William Johnson
Grover, William Luther
Groves, Franklin Nelson
Groves, Ray John
Growe, Joan Anderson
Grube, Gerald George
Gruber, Elbert Egidius
Gruber, John Balsbaugh
Gruber, William Paul
Gruberg, Martin
Grubert, Carl
Gruenewald, Wendell LeRoy
Gruenisen, Allan George
Gruenwald, George Henry
Grueser, Robert J.
Grulee, Clifford Grosselle, Jr.
Gruman, Robert Clayton
Grumme, Fred J.
Grummitt, Oliver Joseph
Grundstein, Nathan David
Grundy, Kenneth William
Grutka, Andrew Gregory
Guastafeste, Joseph Robert
Guba, Egon Gotthold
Gubbrud, Archie
Gubow, Lawrence
Guendel, Thomas Joseph
Guenther, Charles John
Guenzel, Paul Walter
Guerri, William G.
Guest, Judith Ann
Guetzkow, Harold
Guffey, James Roger
Guggenheim, Richard E.
Guidrey, Joseph James
Guilford, Richard Griswold
Guillery, Rainer Walter
Guin, Russell Lowell
Guindon, William G.
Guinn, Leslie Wayne
Guinther, Harry Philip
Guion, Robert Morgan
Gullen, George Edgar, Jr.
Gulley, Halbert Edison
Gullickson, Glenn, Jr.
Gum, Moy Fook
Gumbiner, Julian Lee
Gummere, Walter Cooper
Gundersen, James Novotny
Gundersen, Roy Melvin
Gunderson, Harvey Jones
Gunkler, Carl Andrew, Jr.
Gunnemann, Louis Herman
Gunnerson, James Howard
Gunness, Robert Charles
Gunsalus, Irwin Clyde
Gunts, Robert Felton
Gupta, Hem Chander
Gupta, Suraj Narayan
Guralnick, Sidney Aaron
Gurd, Frank Ross Newman
Gurdjian, Elisha Stephens
Guren, Sheldon Bruce
Gurganus, William Ray
Gurney, Clifford William
Gurnham, C(harles) Fred(erick)
Gurr, Ted Robert
Gurtner, Wendell Jones
Gusewelle, Charles Wesley
Gushman, John Louis
Guskin, Alan Edward
Gustad, John Wilbert
Gustafson, Elmer T.
Gustafson, James M.
Gustafson, John Emil
Gustafson, Winthrop Adolph
Gustavson, Carl Gustav
Gutchë, Gene
Guterbock, Hans Gustav
Gutfeld, Norman E.
Guth, John Elias, Jr.
Guth, Sylvester Karl
Guthrie, Frank Albert
Guthrie, George Ralph
Guthrie, Louis Charles
Guthrie, Mearl Raymond, Jr.
Guthrie, William Nelson
Guthrie, William Stone
Gutknecht, Paul Herbert
Gutmann, Max
Gutowsky, Herbert Sander
Gutsche, Carl David
Gutschick, Raymond Charles
Gutwirth, Samuel William
Guy, Ralph B., Jr.
Guy, William Lewis
Guyer, Gordon Earl
Guyon, John Carl
Guze, Samuel Barry
Guzzetta, Dominic James
Gwinn, Robert P.
Gysbers, Norman Charles
Haack, William Burger
Haag, Everett Keith
Haag, Richard Herman
Haakenstad, Otto
Haas, Felix
Haas, Howard Green
Haas, Leonard Clarence
Haas, Robert Green
Haase, Carl Alvin
Haase, William Xavier
Haass, Erwin Herman
Haayen, Richard Jan
Habeck, Irwin John
Haber, William
Haberman, Frederick William
Habermann, Philip Sanford
Haberstroh, Chadwick John
Habig, Thomas Louis
Hachten, William Andrews
Hackel, Emanuel
Hacker, Hilary Baumann
Hackett, James Wallace
Hackett, John Thomas
Hackett, Roger Fleming
Hackler, John Byron, III
Haddad, George Ilyas
Haddock, Aubura Glen
Haddox, Benjamin Edward
Hadley, Elbert Hamilton
Hadley, Marlin LeRoy
Haeberli, Willy
Haelterman, Edward Omer
Haenicke, Diether Hans
Haensel, Vladimir
Haenszel, William Manning
Haferbecker, Gordon Milton
Haffner, Charles Christian, Jr.
Haffner, Charles Christian, III
Hagan, Paul Wandel
Hagedorn, Robert Harry
Hagelman, Charles William, Jr.
Hagen, Charles William, Jr.
Hagenah, William John, Jr.
Hager, Carl
Hager, Helen Lucille
Hager, Joseph Arthur
Hager, Lowell Paul
Haggard, Forrest Deloss
Haggard, J.D.
Haggerty, Lawrence George
Haglund, E(dward) James
Haglund, Gerhard Oscar
Hagman, Harlan Lawrence
Hagstrom, Warren Olaf
Hagstrum, Jean Howard
Hague, James Edward
Hague, Robert Worst
Hahn, Arvin William
Hahn, Donna Nicholas
Hahn, George LeRoy
Hahn, Jack Albert Louis
Hahn, Lewis Edwin
Hahn, Richard Ferdinand
Hahn, Samuel Wilfred
Hahn, Walter Frederick
Haigh, George Whylden
Haight, Edward Allen
Haight, Gilbert Pierce, Jr.
Haile, H. G.
Hailstones, Thomas John
Haiman, Franklyn Saul
Haiman, Irwin Sanford
Haimann, Theo
Haimo, Deborah Tepper
Hainey, Richard Willis
Hainline, Forrest Arthur, Jr.
Hakeem, Michael
Hakimi, S. Louis
Halas, George Stanley
Halas, George Stanley, Jr.
Halcrow, Harold Graham
Hale, Frank Wilbur, Jr.
Hale, Hamilton Orin
Hale, Mark Pendleton
Hale, Merle Leroy
Hale, Phale Dophis
Haley, George
Hall, Albert Leander, Jr.
Hall, Asaph Hale
Hall, Bernard
Hall, Charles Rudolph
Hall, David Goodsell, III
Hall, Donald Joyce
Hall, Ernest LeRoy
Hall, E(ugene) Raymond
Hall, Frederick Leonard
Hall, Harry Benjamin
Hall, J. Frank
Hall, Jack H.
Hall, John Walton
Hall, Joseph Bates
Hall, Joyce Clyde
Hall, Marion Trufant
Hall, Philip Barton
Hall, Robert Latané
Hall, Thomas Munroe
Hall, Thomas Steele
Hall, William Delaney
Hall, William Edward, Jr.
Hall, William Joel
Halladay, Henry Earnest
Hallberg, Owen Kenneth
Halleck, Charles A.
Hallene, Alan Montgomery
Haller, Archibald Orben
Hallerberg, Arthur Edward
Halliday, William James, Jr.
Hallman, George Harlan
Halloran, William Frank
Haloftis, Timothy
Halom, James Tibor
Halpern, Jack
Halpern, Norman Gerald
Halpern, Sheldon William
Halporn, James Werner
Halstead, Georgia
Halverson, Wendell Quelprud
Halvorson, Newman Thorbus
Hamady, Jack Ameen
Hamand, Lavern Marshall
Hamann, John Rial
Hambleton, Chalkley Jay
Hamblin, Clifford William
Hambrick, George Walter, Jr.
Hamburger, Viktor
Hamby, Alonzo Lee
Hamelberg, William
Hamermesh, Bernard
Hamermesh, Morton
Hamerow, Theodore Stephen
Hamil, Harold
Hamill, William Henry
Hamilton, Bryce Leland
Hamilton, Charles Owen
Hamilton, Clarence Otis
Hamilton, Earl Jefferson
Hamilton, Jerald
Hamilton, Robert Earl
Hamilton, Robert Snyder
Hamilton, Stuart
Hamlin, Richard Eugene
Hammar, Lester Everett
Hammel, Richard Frank
Hammer, Charles Lawrence
Hammer, Preston Clarence
Hammes, George Albert
Hammett, Ralph Warner
Hammink, Niles H.
Hammond, Charles Taylor
Hammond, James Wright
Hammond, Joe Phil
Hamp, Eric Pratt
Hampson, Robert Joseph
Hampton, Kent Bronson
Hampton, Leroy
Hamrock, Bernard John
Han, Seong Soo
Hanawalt, Joseph Donald
Hancock, John Coulter
Hancock, Robert Spencer
Hancock, Thomas
Hand, Avery Chapman, Jr.
Handler, Jerome Sidney
Handler, Paul
Haney, Paul Dunlap
Hanford, William James
Hangen, John, Jr.
Hanifin, John William
Hanigan, John Leonard
Hanink, Dean Kneale

Hanke, Oscar August
Hankin, Bernard Jacob
Hanley, Charles
Hanley, John Thomas
Hanley, John Weller
Hanley, Leo B.
Hanley, Marshall Edward
Hanlin, Hugh Carey
Hanlon, C. Rollins
Hanna, Gordon
Hannah, John Donald
Hannah, Larry Joseph
Hannan, Frank P.
Hannan, James MacClymont
Hannon, Bruce M.
Hannon, Joseph P.
Hanold, Terrance
Hanrahan, Robert Paul
Hanratty, Thomas Joseph
Hans, Robert John
Hansen, Albert Martin
Hansen, Arthur Gene
Hansen, Charles
Hansen, Connor Theodore
Hansen, Francis Eugene
Hansen, Frederick Jacob
Hansen, Grover J.
Hansen, James Roger
Hansen, Kermit Read
Hansen, Leroy C.
Hansen, Marc Frederick
Hansen, Robert Suttle
Hansen, Robert Wayne
Hanson, Dick Vincent
Hanson, Eugene Nelson
Hanson, Howard Grant
Hanson, John Bernard
Hanson, Lester Eugene
Hanson, Lyle Eugene
Hanson, Richard Stephen
Hanson, Robert Alfred
Hanson, Robert Arthur
Hanson, Robert Warren
Hanson, Roger James
Hanson, Walter Edmund
Hanson, William C.
Harary, Frank
Harbage, Mary
Harberger, Arnold Carl
Harbourt, Cyrus Oscar
Hard, Walter Leon
Harden, Edgar Lawrence
Harden, Norman Eugene
Hardenbrook, Harry Junior
Hardesty, Hiram Haines
Hardin, Clifford Morris
Hardin, Robert Calvin
Harding, James Warren
Harding, Thomas Spencer
Harding, Victor Mathews
Hardman, Harold Francis
Hardy, John Edward
Hardy, L. Martin
Hardy, Walter Lincoln
Hare, Robert Yates
Harger, Arthur James
Harger, Chester Arthur
Hargis, Billy James
Hargrave, Robert Webb
Hargrave, Victoria Elizabeth
Hargreaves, Robert
Harju, Onni Rudolph
Harkins, Paul William
Harkins, William Blake
Harkness, Bruce
Harlan, Jack Rodney
Harman, John Royden
Harmet, A(rnold) Richard
Harmon, Albert John
Harmon, Laurence George
Harmon, Patrick
Harmon, Reuel Durkee
Harned, Malcolm Stuart
Harness, Don Kenneth
Harness, Edward Granville
Harnett, Joseph Durham
Harnischfeger, Henry
Harnish, James Lester
Haro, John Calvin
Harper, Alfred Edwin
Harper, Charles Little
Harper, Charles Michel
Harper, Edward O'Neil
Harper, Ramey Wilson
Harper, Roy W.
Harrell, Everett Richard, Jr.
Harrell, Samuel M.
Harrell, Samuel Runnels
Harrelson, Allen McRae, Jr.
Harries, Lyndon Pritchard
Harriman, Gerald Eugene
Harringer, Olaf Carl
Harrington, David Van
Harrington, Fred Harvey
Harrington, Harry Francis
Harrington, Jeremy Thomas
Harrington, Robert Warren
Harris, Charles Elmer
Harris, Chauncy Dennison
Harris, David John
Harris, David William
Harris, Edgar Starr, Jr.
Harris, Everette Bagby
Harris, George Taylor
Harris, Irving Brooks
Harris, Isaac Henson
Harris, John Edward
Harris, John William
Harris, John William
Harris, Julian Earle
Harris, K. David
Harris, L. Julian
Harris, Louis Kenneth
Harris, Neison
Harris, Philip Brewer
Harris, Richard Lee
Harris, Stanley Gale, Jr.
Harris, Sydney Justin
Harris, Wayne Webster
Harris, Whitney Robson
Harrison, Carter Ridgely
Harrison, Earle
Harrison, Edward James
Harrison, E(rnest) Frank(lin)
Harrison, Henry Stuart
Harrison, Jim (James Thomas)
Harrison, Michael Jay
Harrison, Paul Melvin Dale
Harrison, Waldo Maurice
Harrison, Ward Duncan
Harrison, William Henry
Harrod, Scott
Harrold, Bernard
Harsha, Wayne V.
Harsha, William Howard
Harsha, William Newcomb, Jr.
Hart, Alvin Leroy
Hart, Augustin Snow, Jr.
Hart, Buddy Warren
Hart, Craig C.
Hart, Don LeRoy
Hart, James Austin
Hart, James Warren
Hart, John Fraser
Hart, John Lewis
Hart, William Milton
Hartenberg, Richard
Scheunemann
Harth, Phillip
Hartigan, Neil F.
Hartje, Robert George
Hartley, Richard Glendale
Hartman, Alexander Paul
Hartman, Clinton W.
Hartman, Glen Junior
Hartman, John Jacob
Hartman, Kenath
Hartman, Robert S.
Hartmann, Henrik Anton
Hartmeyer, John
Hartnett, James Patrick
Hartnett, Robert Clinton
Hartsaw, William O.
Hartsuch, Paul Jackson
Hartung, Theodore Eugene
Harvey, Dorothy May
Harvey, John Henry
Harvey, Lashley Grey
Harvey, Paul
Harvey, Peter Robert
Harvey, Robert Duncan
Harwood, John Henry
Harza, Richard Davidson
Hasbrouck, Wilbert Roland
Haselkorn, Robert
Haselmayer, Louis August
Haskin, Larry Allen
Hasler, Arthur Davis
Hasler, Wyndham
Hass, Firman Henry
Hassan, Ihab Habib
Hassel, Milton John
Hasselblad, Oliver William
Hassett, Paul Elliot
Hast, Malcolm Howard
Hastings, Elizabeth Thomson
Hastings, John Simpson
Hastings, John Thomas
Hatch, Arthur Joel
Hatch, Henry Reynolds, III
Hatcher, Gordon Merrell
Hatcher, Harlan Henthorne
Hatcher, Richard G.
Hathorne, Robert S.
Hathway, Clifford Newton
Hatie, George Daniel
Hatmaker, George Edward
Hatten, William Seward
Hattin, Donald Edward
Haugan, Randolph Edgar
Haugen, Rolf Eugene
Haughton, James Gray
Haughton, Ronald Waring
Haugland, John Clarence
Haun, James William
Haunz, Edgar Alfred
Hauptmann, (Phyllis) Maxine
Haurowitz, Felix
Hausberg, William
Hauser, Crane Cheshire
Hauser, Gayelord (Hauser,
Helmut Eugene Benjamin
Gellert)
Hauser, Jon William
Hauser, Philip Morris
Hauserman, William Foley
Hausman, Jerome Joseph
Hausman, William
Hausmann, Frank William, Jr.
Hausser, Robert Louis
Havdala, Henri Salomon
Haven, Thomas Kenneth
Havens, Dwight Bowles
Haverkamp, Harold Judson
Haverstick, Edward Everett,
Jr.
Havighurst, Robert J.
Hawkins, Donald Merton
Hawkins, Eugene Palmer
Hawkins, George Andrew
Hawkins, John Clinton
Hawkins, Robert Bruce
Hawkinson, John
Hawkinson, Robert Wayne
Hawkland, William Dennis
Hawley, Don Carlton
Hawley, John Blackstock, Jr.
Hawthorn, Horace Boles
Hawthorne, Bower
Hawthorne, Joseph Campbell
Hay, George Edward
Hay, William Henry
Hay, William Walter
Hayashi, Teru
Hayashi, Tetsumaro
Hayden, Joseph Page, Jr.
Hayden, Martin Scholl
Haydon, Harold Emerson
Hayes, Albert McHarg
Hayes, Douglas Anderson
Hayes, Frank N.
Hayes, John Cornelius
Hayes, John Daniel
Hayes, John W.
Hayes, Marvin LeRoy
Hayes, Milton John
Hayes, Nevin William
Hayes, Reginald Carroll
Hayes, Richard Johnson
Hayes, William Aloysius
Hayes, Woody (Wayne
Woodrow)
Haygreen, John Grant
Haynes, Eugene, Jr.
Haynes, Sherwood Kimball
Hays, Kathryn
Hays, Robert L.
Hayt, William Hart, Jr.
Hayter, Earl Wiley
Haythorne, Robert E.
Hayton, Jacob William
Hayward, Edward Beardsley
Haywood, Bruce
Haywood, Clarence Robert
Hazard, Willis Gilpin
Hazel, David William
Hazen, Arlon Giberson
Hazen, Stanley Phillip
Hazen, Wayne Eskett
Hazlett, James Arthur
Heaberlin, Fred S.
Headlee, Richard Harold
Headley, Sherman Knight
Heady, Earl Orel
Heald, James Eudean
Heald, Morrell
Healey, George
Healey, Harry Joseph
Heaney, Gerald William
Heaney, Robert Proulx
Heaphy, John Merrill
Heard, Arthur Bernard
Hearnes, Warren Eastman
Heartney, Matthew Joseph, Jr.
Heath, Edward Charles
Heath, John Clovis
Heath, Thomas Doran
Heather, George Gail
Heavenrich, Robert Maurice
Hebbard, Frederick Worthman
Hebel, Anthony Jerome
Hechter, Oscar Milton
Heck, Charles Voisin
Heck, James Baker
Heckel, Richard Wayne
Hecker, Lewis J.
Hecker, Robert Levi
Heckman, Russell Frederick
Heckmann, Irvin Lee
Hedden, Russell Alfred
Heddens, Barret Spencer, Jr.
Heddesheimer, Walter Jacob
Hedges, Harry George
Hedrick, Frank Edgar
Heerman, William Robert
Heffern, Gordon Emory
Heffernan, Nathan Stewart
Heffley, Linda Anne
Heffner, Grover Chester
Hefner, Harry Simon
Hefner, Hugh Marston
Hegener, Mark Paul
Heggers, John Paul
Heggie, Robert James
Hegre, Theodore A.
Hehemann, Robert Frederick
Hehmeyer, Alexander
Heidel, Charles MacLeish
Heidenheim, Roger Stewart
Heil, Joseph Frank
Heilman, Charles George
Heim, Leo Edward
Heimberg, Murray
Heimlich, Henry Jay
Heimsch, Charles
Hein, Lawrence Bert
Heindl, Warren Anton
Heineman, Mrs. Ben W.
Heineman, Ben Walter
Heineman, Paul Lowe
Heinen, Paul A.
Heiney, John Weitzel
Heinicke, Herbert Raymond
Heinkel, Fred Victor
Heinrich, Ross Raymond
Heins, Allison Edward
Heins, Arthur James
Heinzerling, Lynn Louis
Heise, George Armstrong
Heise, Richard Allen
Heiser, Charles Bixler, Jr.
Heisler, John Columbus
Heiss, Richard Walter
Heistad, Gordon Thomas
Heitler, George
Heitmann, Fred William, Jr.
Heitner, Robert Richard
Heitz, Glenn Edward
Heitzmann, Alfred Otto
Hejna, William Frank
Hekhuis, Gerrit Leverne
Helbert, Clifford L.
Helgeland, Glenn Bernard
Helgeson, Arlan Clayton
Heller, Alfred
Heller, Erich
Heller, Francis Howard
Heller, John Lewis
Heller, Paul
Heller, Robert Leo
Heller, Walter Wolfgang
Hellmuth, George Francis
Helman, Alfred Blair
Helmer, Hugh Joslin
Helmsing, Charles Herman
Helmsworth, James Alexander
Helstad, Orrin LaVerne
Helstein, Ralph L.
Hemenway, Robert
Hemond, Roland
Henderson, James Alan
Henderson, John Warren
Henderson, John Wayne
Henderson, John William, Jr.
Henderson, John Woodworth
Henderson, LaVell Merl
Henderson, Lowell Lawrence
Henderson, Paul Audine
Henderson, Robert Arthur
Henderson, William L.
Hendricks, John Burke
Hendrickson, Bruce Carl
Hendrickson, Frank Rogers
Hendrickson, Marshall David
Hendrix, Herschel J.
Henebry, John Philip
Heneman, Herbert Gerhard, Jr.
Hengen, William Lincoln
Hengst, Raymond Guthrie
Henken, Willard John
Henle, Robert John
Henley, Fred Louis
Henley, Keith Stuart
Hennessey, Mary Agnes
Hennessy, John Leonard
Hennessy, William Joseph, II
Henning, Harold Walter
Henning, Valerian John
Henninger, John George
Henny, Fred Alfred
Henrickson, Eiler Leonard
Henry, Charles Joseph, Jr.
Henry, Charles R.
Henry, Hugh Fort
Henry, Nelson Robert
Henshall, James Arthur, Jr.
Henson, Albert Lee
Henson, Paul Harry
Hentschell, Charles Joseph
Hepler, James William
Hepler, John Chislett
Hepp, K. Kevin
Hepp, Maylon Harold
Herbert, James Hall
Herbert, Kevin Barry John
Herbert, Michael Kinzly
Herbert, Ralph
Herbert, Thomas M.
Herbert, Victor James
Herbst, Arthur Lee
Herbster, Ben Mohr
Herfindahl, Lloyd Manford
Herget, Paul
Herleman, William Nicholas
Herlihy, Horace Murray
Herman, David Theodore
Herman, Edith Carol
Herman, Harold Wilcox
Herman, Harry A.
Herman, Robert
Herman, Stephen Mark
Hermann, Paul David
Hermann, Philip J.
Hermes, Thomas Joseph
Herndon, Charles Harbison
Herndon, Vernon Edward
Herpich, Wiliam Arthur
Herr, Dan
Herrell, Wallace Edgar
Herrick, Allan Adair
Herrin, Moreland
Herring, James P.
Herring, Wilfred Ernest
Herrinton, John Peter
Herrmann, Arthur Dominey
Herrmann, Edward J.
Herron, Frank Leon, Jr.
Herron, Orley Rufus
Herseth, Lorna B.
Hershey, Daniel
Hershey, Falls Bacon
Herson, Lawrence J. R.
Herstein, Israel Nathan
Hertz, David Ralph
Hertz, Richard Cornell
Hertzberg, Paul Stuart
Hertzberg, Stuart Earl
Herweg, John Courtright
Herzog, Donald Roswell
Herzog, Dorrel Norman Elvert
(Whitey)
Herzog, Fred F.
Herzog, Raymond Harry
Hesburgh, Theodore Martin
Hess, Eckhard Heinrich
Hess, Evelyn Victorine (Mrs.
Michael Howett)
Hess, Howard Martin
Hess, Sidney J., Jr.
Hesse, Don
Hesseltine, Henry Close
Hessert, Paul Bernard
Hessler, Robert Roamie
Hesterberg, Gene Arthur
Hettinger, Edward G.
Heubaum, William Lincoln
Heuer, Gerald Arthur
Heuer, Michael Alexander
Heuerman, Richard Arnold
Heuermann, Laura Hall
Heuertz, Matt E.
Heumann, Ralph Lewis
Hewitt, Barnard
Hewitt, William Alexander
Hexter, Robert Maurice
Heydt, Richard Gordon
Heyman, Ralph Edmond
Heymann, Walter
Heymann, Walter M.
Heyse, Margaret Farr
Heytow, Eugene Perry
Hickam, Hubert
Hickam, Willis
Hicken, Victor
Hickey, Edward Hutchins
Hickey, James Aloysius
Hickey, John Thomas
Hickey, Joseph James
Hickey, Lawrence Thomas
Hickey, Matthew Joseph, III
Hickey, Thomas Philip, Jr.
Hicks, Allan Charles
Hicks, Allen Morley
Hicks, Charles Robert
Hicks, Clifford Byron
Hicks, Clifford Milton
Hicks, Edwin Hugh
Hicks, Irle Raymond
Hickson, John LeFever
Hiett, Edward Emerson
Higdon, John Kenneth
Higginbotham, William Henry
Higgins, Edward Aloysius
Higgins, Hugh Richard
Higgins, Ruth Loving
Higuchi, Takeru
Hildebrand, Kenneth Norman
Hildebrand, Roger Henry
Hilder, Frazer Frost
Hilding, Anderson Cornelius
Hildreth, Clifford
Hildreth, R(oland) James
Hilker, Robert Reuben John
Hill, Alwyn Spencer
Hill, Delmas Carl
Hill, James Stanley
Hill, John Paul
Hill, Knox Calvin
Hill, L. Draper
Hill, Lewis Warren
Hill, Luther Lyons, Jr.
Hill, Owen L.
Hill, Ralph Jay
Hill, Reuben Lorenzo, Jr.
Hill, Richard Earl
Hill, Richard J.
Hill, Stephen Van
Hill, Theodore Albert
Hill, Winfred Farrington
Hillberry, Ben(ny) M(ax)
Hillegass, Clifton Keith
Hillenbrand, Barry Richard
Hiller, Gerald Lee
Hilliard, John Evelyn
Hilliard, William Alexander
Hillila, Bernhard Hugo Paul
Hillis, Margaret
Hillman, Arthur
Hillman, John Wesley
Hillman, Jordan Jay
Hillman, Stanley Eric Gordon
Hills, George Burkhart, Jr.
Hills, Roderick M.
Hiltner, William Albert
Himmelright, Robert John, Jr.
Hinchliff, James Donohue
Hind, Joseph Edward, Jr.
Hine, Daryl
Hine, Jack
Hine, Maynard Kiplinger
Hiner, Robert L.
Hines, Harold H., Jr.
Hines, Herbert Waldo
Hines, James Rodger
Hines, Norman William, Jr.
Hines, Roderick Ludlow
Hinkle, B. J.
Hinkle, John Elmer, Jr.
Hinkley, Don Raymond
Hinnendael, John Joseph
Hinrichsen, John James Luett
Hinshaw, Virgil Goodman, Jr.
Hinsvark, Inez Genieve
Hinton, Claude Willey
Hinton, Warren S.
Hintz, Robert Louis
Hinz, Gerald Emil
Hipke, Gilbert Jacob
Hipp, Urban
Hirsch, Edwin Walter
Hirsch, Jerome Charles
Hirsch, Jerry
Hirsch, Robert William
Hirschboeck, Herbert C.
Hirschfelder, Joseph Oakland
Hirschhorn, Austin
Hirschmann, Hans
Hirsh, Ira Jean
Hirshler, Eric Ernest
Hirshman, George White
Hirth, John Price
Hisaka, Don M.
Hitchcock, Claude Raymond
Hitchcock, John Thayer
Hite, James Tillman, III
Hite, Samuel Charles
Hitt, John Charles, Jr.
Hixon, Carl Kilmer, Jr.
Hjalmarson, Gordon Ross
Hjelle, John Orlo
Hjellum, John
Hlavacek, Roy George
Hoad, John G.
Hoag, Leverett Paddock
Hoagland, Karl King, Jr.
Hoagland, Laurance
Redington, Jr.
Hoak, John Charles
Hoare, Richard David
Hobàn, George Savre
Hobart, Edward A.
Hobbs, James Allen
Hobbs, Lewis Mankin
Hobbs, Mary Monteuese
Hobgood, Burnet McLean
Hoblitzelle, George Knapp
Hobson, Henry Wise, Jr.
Hoch, Lambert Anthony
Hochberg, Joel Morton
Hochgurtel, Jerome Leo
Hochwald, Werner
Hochwalt, Carroll Alonzo
Hockaday, Irvine O., Jr.
Hockeimer, Henry Eric
Hocker, Lon
Hocking, Fred Girvin
Hocking, John Gilbert
Hodapp, Leroy Charles
Hodder, William Alan
Hoddy, George Warren
Hoddy, Raymond Arthur
Hodes, Arthur William
Hodes, Marion Edward
Hodes, Scott
Hodge, James Campbell
Hodges, Elmer Burkett
Hodges, Lawrence Turnour
Hodges, Mary Doris
Hodges, Robert Manley
Hodgkins, Earl Warner
Hodgkinson, Charles Paul
Hodgson, Charles Arthur
Hodgson, Corrin Haley
Hodgson, Voigt Ralph
Hodson, Alexander Carlton
Hoebel, Edward Adamson
Hoeflin, Ruth Merle
Hoeflinger, Norman Charles
Hoekstra, William George
Hoenig, William Charles
Hoerner, Richard Norris, Jr.
Hoerr, Stanley Obermann
Hofeldt, John W.
Hoffer, Joe Ralph
Hoffer, Robert M.
Hoffman, Alfred John
Hoffman, Gene
Hoffman, James Harvey
Hoffman, Julius J.
Hoffman, Lois Wladis
Hoffman, Paul Richard
Hoffman, Richard Wagner
Hoffman, Richard William
Hoffman, Warren Eugene
Hoffmann, Charles Wesley
Hoffmann, Donald
Hoffmann, Jack Curtis
Hoffmann, Oswald Carl Julius
Hoffmann, Robert Frederick
Hoffmann, Thomas Russell
Hoffmeister, Donald Frederick
Hoffmeister, Harold Maxwell
Hofstad, Ralph Parker
Hofstatter, Leopold
Hofstede, Albert John
Hofstetter, Henry W.
Hogan, Coleman Francis
Hogan, Joseph Charles
Hogan, Philip Jerome
Hogan, Timothy S.
Hogben, Charles Adrian
Michael
Hoge, James Fulton, Jr.
Hogg, Robert Vincent, Jr.
Hoglund, John H.
Hognestad, Eivind
Hogrefe, Pearl
Hogue, Lillian Genevieve
Hohnstedt, Leo Frank
Hokenstad, Merl Clifford, Jr.
Hokin, Edwin E.
Hokin, Lowell Edward
Holabird, John Augur, Jr.
Holaday, Allan Gibson
Holbrook, Clyde Amos
Holck, Frederick H. George
Holden, Arthur Stone, Jr.
Holden, William Douglas
Holder, Cale James
Holder, Thomas Martin
Holdren, John Richard
Holdt, Roy Howard
Hole, William Edward, Jr.
Hole, William Edward, Sr.
Holiday, Harry, Jr.
Holland, Eugene, Jr.
Holland, Eugene Paul
Holland, Israel Irving
Hollenhorst, George Donald
Hollenhorst, Robert William
Hollett, Byron Pierce
Holley, Jack Karl
Holley, Jerry
Holliday, Barbara Miriam
Brooks Gregg
Holliday, John Moffitt
Hollington, Richard Rings
Hollis, Everett Loftus
Hollis, Virgil A.
Hollister, John Baker
Hollon, William Eugene
Holloway, Robert J.
Holm, Wilton Robert
Holman, Ralph Theodore
Holmberg, Lawrence Oscar
Holmes, Arthur Frank
Holmes, Colgate Frederick
Holmes, James Clifford
Holmes, Melvin Charles
Holmes, Reed M.
Holmes, Robert William
Holmgren, Marvin Edward
Holmgren, Robert Bruce
Holmquist, William Axel
Holonyak, Nick, Jr.
Holroyd, Harry James

Holroyd, Louis Vincent
Holschuh, John David
Holsen, Robert Charles
Holshouser, Don Franklin
Holsinger, George Robert, Jr.
Holt, Donald Edward, Jr.
Holt, Ivan Lee, Jr.
Holter, Don Wendell
Holthaus, Joseph Michael
Holthusen, Hans E.
Holton, Ira James
Holtz, Henry John
Holtzclaw, Henry Fuller, Jr.
Holtzer, Alfred Melvin
Holyoke, Thomas Campbell
Holzer, Edwin
Hong, Howard Vincent
Hong, Richard
Honigman, Jason Lester
Hoobler, Sibley Worth
Hood, Robert Chambers
Hook, John Burney
Hooper, Bayard
Hooper, Blake Howard
Hooper, Emmet Thurman, Jr.
Hoopman, Harold Dewaine
Hoover, Charles M.
Hoover, Dwight Wesley
Hoover, Joseph Schiltz
Hoover, William Jay
Hope, Quentin Manning
Hopkins, Frederick Mercer, Jr.
Hopp, Ralph H.
Hopp, William Beecher
Hopping, Louis Melbert
Hopps, Howard Carl
Hord, Stephen Y.
Horgan, James Donald
Horn, Charles Lilley
Hornbruch, Frederick William, Jr.
Hornby, Lesley (Twiggy)
Horner, James Melvin
Horner, John Edward
Horner, Richard Elmer
Horner, Richard William
Horns, Howard Lowell
Hornsby, Roger Allen
Hornung, Paul Andrew
Horr, William Henry
Horsbrugh, Patrick
Horsman, Reginald
Horst, Bruce Everett
Horton, John Tod
Horvath, Ian
Horvay, Frank Dominic
Horwich, Herbert F.
Horwitz, Donald Paul
Horwitz, Irwin D.
Hosford, William Fuller
Hosler, Russell John
Hotchkiss, Eugene, III
Hotchkiss, Sanford Norman
Hotz, Alfred Julius
Hotze, Charles Wayne
Houck, George Clarence
Hougas, Robert Wayne
Hougen, Olaf Andreas
Hough, Hugh Frederick
Hough, John E.
Hough, Richard T.
Houghton, David Drew
Houk, Ralph George
Houle, Cyril Orvin
Hountras, Peter Timothy
House, Frank Owen
House, Roy C.
Houser, Robert Norman
Housh, Charles Leighton
Houston, Ernest James, Jr.
Houston, John Albert
Hovde, Frederick Lawson
Hoving, John Hannes Forester
Hovnanian, Armen
Hovorka, Frank
Howard, Bion Bradbury
Howard, Edward Allen
Howard, Giles William John
Howard, Harold Hill
Howard, Howell Hoffman
Howard, John Addison
Howard, Nathaniel Richardson
Howard, Robert Bruce
Howdle, John Clayton
Howe, David Leonard
Howe, Harold
Howe, Herbert Marshall
Howe, Joseph Warner
Howe, Lawrence
Howe, Robert Hsi Lin
Howe, Stanley Merrill
Howell, George Bedell
Howell, Robert Wayne
Howell, Sidney Charles
Howell, William Smiley
Howells, John Andrew
Howery, Bill Nelson
Howery, Victor Irving
Howland, Richard Henry
Howlett, Carolyn Svrluga
Howlett, William Porter
Howley, Lee Christopher
Howsam, Robert Lee
Hoyer, Harvey Conrad
Hoyman, Howard Stanley
Hoyme, Chad Earl
Hoyt, Clark Freeland
Hoyt, Elton, III
Hoyt, Lester Harold
Hoyt, Ralph Melvin
Hrones, John Anthony
Hruby, Frank M.
Hruby, Norbert Joseph
Hruska, Roman Lee
Hsu, Francis Lang Kwang
Hubachek, Frank Brookes

Hubata, Joseph Allen
Hubay, Charles Alfred
Hubbard, Jesse Donald
Hubbard, Orville Liscum
Hubbard, Philip Gamaliel
Hubbard, Robert Elbert
Hubbard, Stanley Stub
Hubbard, William Neill, Jr.
Hubbell, Ernest
Hubbell, James Windsor, Jr.
Hubbs, Ronald M.
Hubenka, Lloyd John
Huber, Sister Alberta
Huber, Robert Frederick
Huber, Robert James
Hubert, Alfred William
Huck, John Wenzel
Hucker, Charles Oscar
Hudnut, Robert Kilborne
Hudnut, William Herbert, III
Hudson, Jack Kenneth
Hudson, Jerry E.
Hudson, Joseph Lowthian, Jr.
Hudson, Roy Davage
Hudson, Thomas Philip
Hudson, William Burchell, Jr.
Hueg, William Frederick, Jr.
Huegli, Albert George
Huegli, Richard Frederick
Hueter, Ernest Boyd
Huff, David Jerome
Huff, George Charles
Huff, Stanley Eugene
Huffer, Dan Leigh
Huffman, Horace McKee, Jr.
Huffman, John William
Hugel, Charles Emil
Hugghins, Ernest Jay
Huggins, Charles
Huggins, Rollin Charles, Jr.
Hughes, Earl Mulford
Hughes, Fred
Hughes, George Robert
Hughes, James A.
Hughes, James John
Hughes, John Russell
Hughes, Mary Ruth Browne
Hughes, Parker Kellum
Hughes, Paul Lester
Hughes, William Franklin, Jr.
Hughes, William Nolin
Hughey, M. Stanley
Huizenga, Charles B.
Huizenga, Peter H.
Hulbert, Lucius Gaylord
Hulbert, Marshall Brandt
Hulburt, Hugh McKinney
Hulett, Charles Wilbur
Hulett, James Edward, Jr.
Hulings, Albert DeWayne
Hull, Dennis William
Hull, Harvard Leslie
Hull, James Richard
Hull, John Daniel, Jr.
Hull, Robert Glenn
Hull, William Henry
Hulley, Clair Montrose
Hulsebosch, Charles Joseph
Hulsen, Robert Bennard
Hulsman, Carl Henry
Humbard, Rex Emmanuel
Humensky, John Joseph
Hummel, Gene Maywood
Hummer, Donal
Humphrey, Edward William
Humphrey, Edwin Murray
Humphrey, Gilbert Watts
Humphrey, John W.
Humphrey, Robert Clayton
Humphreys, Henry Sigurd
Humphreys, Lloyd Girton
Hungate, William Leonard
Hungerford, Herbert Eugene
Hungerford, Lester Bailie
Hunt, Andrew Dickson
Hunt, Carlton Cuyler, Jr.
Hunt, Charles Brownlow, Jr.
Hunt, E. George
Hunt, Howard Beeman
Hunt, James Calvin
Hunt, James Robert
Hunt, J(oseph) McVicker
Hunt, Lamar
Hunt, Robert M.
Hunt, Roger Schermerhorn
Hunt, William Alvin
Hunter, Charles Axtell, Jr.
Hunter, Charles David
Hunter, Donald H.
Hunter, Elmo Bolton
Hunter, Jack Corbett
Hunter, Jack Duval
Hunter, James Alexander
Hunter, Lee
Hunter, Norman L.
Hunter, Robert E.
Hunter, Thom Hugh
Hunter, William Andrew
Hunting, David Dyer
Huntington, David Mack Goode
Huntington, James Cantine, Jr.
Huntress, Keith Gibson
Huntzicker, Harry Noble
Hunzeker, Hubert La Von
Hupp, Robert Paul
Hurd, James Braddock
Hurley, Frank House
Hurley, Samuel Clay, III
Hurley, William Joseph
Hursh, Merritt Hutton
Hurst, Charles Gaines, Jr.
Hurst, James Willard
Huskins, William Everett, Jr.
Husovsky, Ivan
Huss, Alvin J.

Husseini, Sufian Yunis
Hussey, Keith Morgan
Husted, Ralph Waldo
Huston, Beatrice Louise
Huston, John Lewis
Huston, Margo
Huston, Marvin L.
Huston, Norman Earl
Huston, Thomas Scott, Jr.
Hutchens, John Oliver
Hutcheson, Harold Leo
Hutchings, Harold Emerson
Hutchinson, Edward
Hutchinson, John L.
Hutchinson, Melvin J.
Hutchison, Clyde Allen, Jr.
Hutchison, Stanley Philip
Hutson, Thomas Raymond
Huttenlocher, Janellen
Hutton, Edward Luke
Hutton, Robert John
Hutton, William
Huzar, Eleanor Goltz
Hyatt, Gerhardt Wilfred
Hyatt, Guy William
Hyde, Frederick Wright, Jr.
Hyde, Henry John
Hyde, Lawrence Henry, Jr.
Hyland, Robert Francis, Jr.
Hynek, Josef Allen
Hyneman, Charles S.
Hynes, Thomas Charles
Iacocca, Lido Anthony (Lee)
Ibele, Warren Edward
Iben, Icko, Jr.
Ibers, James Arthur
Ice, Harry Treese
Ichord, Richard Howard
Iffland, Don Charles
Igasaki, Masao, Jr.
Igleski, Thomas Robert
Ihde, Aaron John
Ilie, Paul
Iltis, Hugh Hellmut
Imesch, Joseph Leopold
Imholte, John Quinn
Imirie, John Frederick, Jr.
Immel, Vincent Clare
Inbau, Fred Edward
Inch, Morris Alton
Inger, Robert Frederick
Ingersoll, Robert Stephen
Inghram, Mark Gordon
Ingle, Dwight Joyce
Ingle, Lester
Ingram, John Watson
Ingram, Robert Palmer
Ingram, Walter Robinson
Ingram, William
Inhorn, Stanley Lee
Inman, William Peter
Inskeep, Patricia Ruth
Instone, Frank Donald
Int-Hout, Dan, Jr.
Inzer, William Henry
Ionescu Tulcea, Cassius
Ireland, George Martin
Ireland, Herbert Orin
Ireland, James Duane
Ireland, Ralph Leonard
Ireland, Robert Ebel
Ireland, W(illiam) Byron
Irion, Arthur Lloyd
Irmen, Thomas Leo
Irminger, Eugene Herman
Irons, Lester
Irrgang, William
Irrmann, Robert Henry
Irving, Donald J.
Irving, Frank Dunham
Irving, Gordon Ernest
Irwin, Glenn Ward, Jr.
Irwin, H. William
Irwin, Hale S.
Irwin, Joseph James
Irwin, Malcolm Robert
Irwin, Richard Dorsey
Isaac, Sol Morton
Isaacs, Gerald William
Isaacs, Lawrence Martin
Isaacs, Roger David
Isaacson, William James
Isbin, Herbert Stanford
Isham, James Livingston
Israelievitch, Jacques Herbert
Itkin, Bella
Ito, Rikuma
Ittmann, Marjorie McCullough
Ivan, Thomas Nathaniel
Iverson, Robert Lester
Ives, David Homer
Ivey, Ellis Murphy, Jr.
Iwasaki, Iwao
Iz, Fahir
Jabara, Francis Dwight
Jache, Albert William
Jackamonis, Edward George
Jackisch, Frederick Frank
Jackman, Albert Havens
Jackson, Billy Morrow
Jackson, Clarence Evert
Jackson, Constance Burts
Jackson, Curtis Maitland
Jackson, Frederick Herbert
Jackson, George Gee
Jackson, Graham H., Jr.
Jackson, Herbert Cooper
Jackson, Horace Dwight
Jackson, Jacqueline Dougan
Jackson, James Sidney
Jackson, Jesse Louis
Jackson, John Howard
Jackson, John Mathews
Jackson, Lewis Albert
Jackson, Marion LeRoy
Jackson, Mark Evan

Jackson, Philip Wesley
Jackson, Reginald Sherman
Jackson, Richard Hewell
Jackson, Robert Lawrence
Jackson, William Vernon
Jackson, Willis Carl
Jacob, Charles Waldemar, Jr.
Jacob, Herbert
Jacob, Richard Joseph
Jacob, Thomas Bernard
Jacobi, Peter Paul
Jacobs, Burleigh Edmund
Jacobs, Carl Bearse
Jacobs, Donald P.
Jacobs, Harvey Collins
Jacobs, John Edward
Jacobs, Joseph Maurice
Jacobs, Louis Sullivan
Jacobs, Norman G(abriel)
Jacobs, Norman Joseph
Jacobs, Richard Matthew
Jacobs, Robert
Jacobs, Robert
Jacobs, William Bruce
Jacobsen, James Conrad
Jacobsen, Theodor Lincoln
Jacobsmeyer, Vincent Paul
Jacobsohn, David Henry
Jacobson, Albert Hillman
Jacobson, Edmund
Jacobson, Eugene Donald
Jacobson, Harold Karan
Jacobson, Jerome Joseph
Jacobson, Leon Orris
Jacobson, Norman Leonard
Jacobson, Samuel David
Jacobson, William Orville
Jacoby, George Alonzo
Jacoby, Peter Ramsey
Jacoby, Sidney Bernhard
Jaeschke, Walter Henry
Jaffe, Hans H.
Jaffe, Leonard Sigmund
Jagow, Elmer
Jahn, Helmut
Jaicks, Frederick G.
Jakowatz, Charles V.
Jakstas, Alfred John
Jambor, Robert Vernon
James, Arthur Giangiacomo
James, Byron Elfed
James, Charles D.
James, Francis Edward, Jr.
James, Harold Arthur
James, Henry Thomas
James, Hubert Maxwell
James, John William
James, Lee Morton
James, Sydney Vincent
Jamieson, John Calhoun
Jamieson, Robert Arthur
Jamieson, Robert Wallace
Jamrich, John Xavier
Jandacek, George Warren
Janke, Otto M.
Janklow, William John
Janning, Mary Bernadette
Janovy, David Lee
Janowitz, Morris
January, Lewis Edward
Janzow, Walter Theophilus
Jarc, Frank Robert
Jaroch, Francis Anthony (Randy)
Jarratt, William Robert
Jarrett, Jerry Vernon
Jarrett, Vernon D.
Jaumot, Frank Edward, Jr.
Javid, Hushang
Javid, Manucher J.
Jaworowski, Jan Wlodzimierz
Jay, Burton Dean
Jaye, David Robert, Jr.
Jeannero, Douglas M.
Jebsen, Robert Harry
Jeffay, Henry
Jeffers, Dean W.
Jeffers, Donald E.
Jefferson, Thomas Bradley
Jeffery, Edwin T.
Jeffrey, Balfour Silliman
Jeffrey, Walter Leslie
Jelinek, John Peter
Jelinek, Richard C.
Jend, William, Jr.
Jenkins, Harold Richard
Jenkins, Harry Mack
Jenkins, James Allister
Jenkins, Orville Wesley
Jenkins, Thomas Llewellyn
Jenks, Downing Bland
Jenks, Major B.
Jenks, William Furness
Jenner, Albert Ernest, Jr.
Jenness, Robert
Jennett, William Armin
Jennings, Burgess Hill
Jennings, Frank Lamont
Jennings, Leander Warren
Jennings, Lee Byron
Jensen, Adolph Robert
Jensen, Dick Leroy
Jensen, Don Arlen
Jensen, Elwood Vernon
Jensen, Erling N.
Jensen, George Albert
Jensen, Harold Sherwood
Jensen, Ivan Raymond
Jensen, James Robert
Jensen, Jay Walbourne
Jensen, Merrill Monroe
Jensen, Paul
Jensen, Reuben Rolland
Jenson, Theodore Joel
Jerger, Edward William
Jerison, Meyer

Jernigan, Kenneth
Jerrard, Richard Patterson
Jerrick, Stephen Joseph
Jessup, Paul Frederick
Jeuck, John Edward
Jewson, Ruth Hathaway (Mrs. Vance Jewson)
Joachim, Harold
Joanis, John Weston
Jobe, Morris Butler
Johannes, Wilfred Clemens
Johannsen, Robert Walter
Johanson, Sven Lennart
John, Edward Clarence
Johns, William Davis, Jr.
Johnsen, Gordon Norman
Johnson, Albert William
Johnson, Alton Cornelius
Johnson, Alvin Carl
Johnson, Alyn William
Johnson, Andrew N.
Johnson, Arthur Gerald
Johnson, Arthur Gilbert
Johnson, Benjamin Edgar
Johnson, Carl Edwin
Johnson, Cecil August
Johnson, Charles Harold
Johnson, Charles Raymond
Johnson, Chauncey Paul
Johnson, Clifford Francis
Johnson, Clifford R.
Johnson, Curtis Lee
Johnson, David Butler
Johnson, David Gale
Johnson, David Pierce
Johnson, Dennis Lester
Johnson, Donald Edward
Johnson, Donald James
Johnson, Donald McEwen
Johnson, Earl Gilius
Johnson, Earl Mortimer
Johnson, Earle Bertrand
Johnson, Eldon Lee
Johnson, Falk Simmons
Johnson, George Robert
Johnson, Gerald Edwin
Johnson, Glenn Thompson
Johnson, Grant Lester
Johnson, H. Arvid
Johnson, Hal Harold Gustav
Johnson, Harrison Foster
Johnson, Harry Morton
Johnson, Jack Thomas
Johnson, James
Johnson, James Lawrence
Johnson, James Leslie
Johnson, James Noel
Johnson, James Robert
Johnson, James Winston
Johnson, Jean Elaine
Johnson, Jerry A.
Johnson, John Arthur
Johnson, John H.
Johnson, John Irwin, Jr.
Johnson, John Prescott
Johnson, Joseph Stuart
Johnson, Josephine Winslow (Mrs. Grant G. Cannon)
Johnson, Keach
Johnson, Leland Parrish
Johnson, Lester Elwin
Johnson, Lorand Victor
Johnson, Marjorie Carroll (Mrs. Owen M. Johnson)
Johnson, Marvin Joyce
Johnson, Millard Wallace, Jr.
Johnson, Milton Axel
Johnson, Monte Charles
Johnson, Paul Cornelius
Johnson, Paul Oren
Johnson, Philip D.
Johnson, Ralph Haakon
Johnson, Richard Louis
Johnson, Richard Merrill
Johnson, Richard Walter
Johnson, Robert Allan
Johnson, Robert Bruce
Johnson, Robert Edward
Johnson, Robert Eugene
Johnson, Robert Ivar
Johnson, Robert Norman
Johnson, Robert Willard
Johnson, Roy Ragnar
Johnson, Royal Kenneth
Johnson, Russell Melvin
Johnson, Samuel Curtis
Johnson, Sidney Malcolm
Johnson, Stephen Carl
Johnson, Van Charles
Johnson, Victor
Johnson, Vincent Hadar
Johnson, Virgil Allen
Johnson, Virginia Eshelman (Mrs. William H. Masters)
Johnson, Walter Conrad
Johnson, Walter Heinrich, Jr.
Johnson, Walter Kline
Johnson, Warren C.
Johnson, Warren Donald
Johnson, William Benjamin
Johnson, William Howard
Johnson, William Roy
Johnson, Willis Hugh
Johnstad, Errol Loy
Johnston, Benjamin Burwell, Jr.
Johnston, John Andrew
Johnston, John Clifford, Jr.
Johnston, Percy Walker, Jr.
Johnston, Richard Fourness
Johnston, Scott Doran
Joiner, Charles Wycliffe
Jolliffe, Elwin Tebbitt
Jolly, Bruce Dwight
Jonas, John, Jr.
Jondahl, Donald Edward

Jones, Alexander Elvin
Jones, Alfred Welwood
Jones, Archer
Jones, Butler Alfonso
Jones, Charles Edward
Jones, Charles Richard
Jones, Clara Araminta Stanton (Mrs. Albert D. Jones)
Jones, Clifton Clyde
Jones, Curtis Harvey
Jones, David Charles
Jones, Donald Edward
Jones, Donald S.
Jones, E(ben) Bradley
Jones, Edgar Wagstaff
Jones, Edward Cole
Jones, Edwin S.
Jones, Ernest Albin
Jones, Frances Downey (Mrs. Vern B. Jones)
Jones, Frank Garfield
Jones, Fred Eugene
Jones, Helen Hart
Jones, Howard Robert
Jones, James Victor
Jones, John Sills
Jones, Joseph Frech
Jones, Kensinger
Jones, Landon Y.
Jones, Larry Richard
Jones, Lawrence Campbell
Jones, Lawrence Marion
Jones, Lawrence William
Jones, Mark Elmer, Jr.
Jones, Maurice Frank
Jones, Peter d'Alroy
Jones, Philip Newton
Jones, Phillip Sanford
Jones, Robert Huhn
Jones, Robert Leon
Jones, Robert Russell
Jones, Roderic Miller
Jones, Scott
Jones, Sidney Arlington, Jr.
Jones, Theodore W.
Jones, Tom Bard
Jones, Trevor Owen
Jones, Walter Clyde, Jr.
Jones, Walter Heath
Jones, Wilbur Boardman, Jr.
Jones, William Catron
Jones, William Hugh
Jones, William Marcellus
Jonte, John Haworth
Joravsky, David
Jordan, Charles Morrell
Jordan, Edward Conrad
Jordan, Kenneth Allan
Jordan, Philip Dillon
Jordan, Richard Charles
Jordan, Roy Wilcox
Jordan, William Burnap, III
Jorgenson, Donald Van
Joseph, Burton M.
Joseph, Daniel Donald
Joseph, David J., Jr.
Joseph, James Alfred
Joseph, John J.
Joseph, Jules K.
Josetta, Sister Mary
Joslyn, Jay Thomas
Joslyn, Robert Bruce
Josselson, Jack Bernard
Jossem, Edmund Leonard
Jourdian, George William
Joyce, Edmund Patrick
Joyce, James Neal
Joyce, Patrick Vincent
Juckem, Wilfred Philip
Judd, Edward Starr
Judd, Robert Carpenter
Judd, William Edward
Judd, William Robert
Judge, John Emmet
Judis, Joseph
Judkins, Donald Ward
Judson, Lyman Spicer Vincent
Judson, Robert Drake
Judy, John Wayne, Jr.
Judy, Paul Ray
Juergens, William George
Juettner, Thomas Richard
Juhl, John Harold
Juniper, Kerrison, Jr.
Justice, Donald Rodney
Justis, Guy R.
Justus, Roy Braxton
Kachru, Braj Behari
Kadish, Mortimer Raymond
Kaesler, Roger LeRoy
Kaess, Frederick William
Kafarski, Mitchell I.
Kagan, Sioma
Kagin, Arthur Meyer
Kahane, Henry
Kahler, Herbert Frederick
Kahn, Henry Sidney
Kahn, Herta Hess (Mrs. Howard Kahn)
Kahn, Journet David
Kahn, Mark Leo
Kahrl, Stanley J.
Kaiser, Emil Thomas
Kaiser, Leo Max
Kalamaros, Edward Nicholas
Kales, Robert Gray
Kaley, Arthur Warren
Kallio, Reino Emil
Kalman, Andrew
Kalp, Karl Rex
Kamerick, John Joseph
Kamisar, Yale
Kamm, Herbert
Kamm, Jacob Oswald
Kammermeyer, Karl
Kammholz, Theophil Carl

Lambeth, Jennings Renick
Lambros, Thomas Demetrios
Lamey, William Lawrence, Jr.
Lammers, Delmar Richard
LaMore, George Edward, Jr.
Lamoreux, Frederick Holmes
Lamothe, William Edward
Lampen, Sister Mary Joel
Lamphier, Thomas Joseph
Lampl, Jack Willard, Jr.
Lampman, Robert James
Lance, Dowe Jefferson
Landau, Richard L.
Landau, William Milton
Landecker, Werner Siegmund
Landers, Ann (Mrs. Jules Lederer)
Landers, Frank Michael
Landes, Kenneth Knight
Landis, Elwood Winton
Landis, Fred
Landis, Jacob
Landon, Alfred Mossman
Lands, William Edward Mitchell
Landsman, Herbert Samuel
Landuyt, Bernard Francis
Lane, Burl Spencer
Lane, Harold Edwin
Lane, James Lee
Lane, William James
Laner, Richard Warren
Lanford, Luke Dean
Lang, Francis Harover
Lang, Gordon
Lang, H. Jack
Lang, Hans Joachim
Lang, William Charles
Langdon, Herschel Garrett
Langdon, William Mondeng
Lange, Charles Henry
Langell, Jerome Edwin
Langenheim, Ralph Louis, Jr.
Langer, Lawrence Marvin
Langer, Robert Adolph
Langevin, Thomas Harvey
Langford, Anna Riggs
Langford, James Rouleau
Langham, Michael
Langhaug, Woodrow Pershing
Langius, Adrian Nelson
Langs, John Frank
Langsam, Walter Consuelo
Langsdorf, Alexander, Jr.
Langsley, Donald Gene
Langston, Hiram Thomas
Langston, Ira Wright
Langworthy, Robert Burton
Lanham, Frank Bristol
Lanier, Robert Jerry, Jr.
Lanigan, Robert J.
Lanners, Fred Thomas, Jr.
Lano, Charles Jack
Lanterman, Joseph Barney
Lanyon, Ellen (Mrs. Roland Ginzel)
Lapensky, M. Joseph
Lapick, Frank Paul
Lapides, Jack
LaPidus, Jules Benjamin
Lapwing, Leo John
Larabee, Byron Hanly
Lardner, Henry Petersen
Lardner, Thomas Joseph
Lardy, Henry Arnold
Larkin, Arthur Edward, Jr.
Larkin, Emmet
Larkin, John Day
Larmon, William Alexander
LaRoche, Robert Eugene
Laronge, Marvin Joseph
Laros, Gerald Snyder, II
Larrowe, Charles Patrick
Larsen, Arthur Hoff
Larsen, Edwin Merritt
Larsen, Harold Cecil
Larsen, Joseph Reuben
Larsen, Wesley Bernard
Larson, Carl Theodore
Larson, Curtis Luverne
Larson, Earl Richard
Larson, Frank Clark
Larson, Henrietta Melia
Larson, John David
Larson, Leland Albert
Larson, Roy
Larson, Thurston Eric
Larson, Ward Jerome
Larson, Wilfred Joseph
Lasansky, Mauricio
Lasater, Donald E.
Laseski, Wesley John
Lash, Kenneth
Lashly, Paul Webster
Lasker, Gabriel
Laskin, Daniel M.
Laskin, Sylvester
Laskowski, Michael, Jr.
Lassers, Willard J.
Laster, Howard Joseph
Latshaw, John
Latz, G. Irving, II
Latzer, Thomas Franklin
Lauchner, Julian Hawthorne
Lauck, Anthony Joseph
Laudeman, Randolph Douglass
Lauff, George Howard
Laughren, Terry
Lauhoff, Howard Joseph
Laun, Harold George
Launstein, Howard Cleveland
Lauritzen, John Ronnow
Laushey, Louis McNeal
Lauterbach, Henry Sebastian
Lavatelli, Leo Silvio
LaVelle, Arthur
Lavidge, Robert James
Lavin, Bernice E.
Lavin, David J.
Lavin, Leonard H.
Law, Bernard Francis
Law, Cursey Shelby
Law, Edward
Lawhorn, Donald Samuel
Lawler, Edmund G.
Lawler, Gordon Joseph
Lawlor, William James, Jr.
Lawrence, Charles Harris
Lawrence, Charles Seely, III
Lawrence, Merle
Lawrence, Thomas Hoel
Lawrence, Willard Earl
Lawrence, William Joseph, Jr.
Lawrie, Roy Thomas
Lawroski, Stephen
Lawshe, Charles Hubert
Lawson, Donald Elmer
Lawson, Ernest Thomas
Lawson, Warren Robert
Lawton, Richard Graham
Laxson, Russell William
Lay, Donald Pomeroy
Layde, Durward Charles
Layman, Emma McCloy (Mrs. James W. Layman)
Layton, Emmet John
Layton, Wilbur Leslie
Lazarus, A(rnold) L(eslie)
Lazarus, Charles Yondorf
Lazarus, David
Lazarus, Fred, III
Lazarus, Mell
Lazarus, Monte
Lazarus, Ralph
Lea, Merlyn Dean
Lea, William Sentelle
Leabo, Dick Albert
Leach, David Goheen
Leach, James Albert Smith
Leader, Robert Wardell
League, Max A.
Leahy, Thomas Richard
Leak, David Keith
Lean, Arthur Edward
Lear, John
Leasure, John Keith
Leban, Michael Eugene
Lebeck, Warren Wells
Lebedow, Aaron Louis
Lebor, John F(rancis)
LeBoutillier, Philip, Jr.
Lebovitz, Harold Paul
Lebowitz, Albert
Lecker, Abraham
Ledder, Edward John
Ledecky-Janecek, Emanuel V.A.
Ledford, Frank Finley, Jr.
Lee, Ausby Eugene
Lee, Carl E.
Lee, Carl Qualley
Lee, Don L. (Haki R. Madhubuti)
Lee, E. Bruce
Lee, George Hamor
Lee, Harley Clyde
Lee, Jack (Jim Sanders Beasley)
Lee, Laurence Raymond
Lee, Leroy William
Lee, Ronald Barry
Lee, Sherman Emery
Lee, Sook
Lee, William Marshall
Leech, Charles Russell, Jr.
Leedy, Paul Francis
Leenhouts, Willis Cornelius
Leeson, Charles Roland
Leestamper, Robert Eugene
Leet, Richard Hale
Leete, Edward
Lefebvre, Arthur Henry
LeFevre, Fay Atkinson
LeFevre, Perry Deyo
Leffel, Charles Poague
Lefkowitz, Irving
Leggett, Glenn
LeGrand, Clay
Lehiste, Ilse
Lehman, John Howard
Lehman, Kieffer Ross
Lehman, Ralph Malcolm
Lehman, Richard Leroy
Lehman, Warren Winfred
Lehmann, Charles Frederick
Lehmann-Haupt, Hellmut E.
Lehnhoff, Sheppard
Lehrman, Edgar Harold
Lehrman, Nat
Leibham, John Albert
Leibman, Morris Irwin
Leibowitz, Irving
Leichliter, Van Handlin
Leidner, Harold Edward
Leighton, George Neves
Leighton, Leroy George
Leimkuhler, Ferdinand Francis
Lein, Malcolm Emil
Leinbach, Frederick Harold
Leinbach, Samuel Packard
Leinfelder, Placidus Joseph
Leinfellner, Werner Hubertus
Leith, Emmett Norman
Leith, W(illiam) Gordon
Leja, Stanislaw
Leland, Austin Porter
Lelyveld, Arthur Joseph
LeMay, William Edward
Lemberger, August Paul
Lemcoe, M. Marshall
Lemlich, Robert
Lempert, Richard Owen
Lenard, Andrew
Lenardon, Robert Joseph
Lenkoski, Leo Douglas
Lennon, Sister Mary Isidore
Lenon, Richard Allen
Lens, Sidney
Lentz, Harold Herbert
Lentz, James Eugene
Leon, Bruno
Leonard, Eugene Albert
Leonard, George Adams
Leonard, Henry Siggins, Jr.
Leonard, John Walter
Leonard, Nelson Jordan
Leonard, Richard
Leontis, Thomas Ernest
Leopold, Richard William
Le Page, Frank Albright
Lepper, Mark Hummer
Lerchen, Edward Hodson
Lerner, Eugene Max
Lerner, Harry Jonas
LeRoy, George Veach
Leroy, Robert Pierre
Lesar, Hiram Henry
Leslie, John Hampton
Leslie, Robert Wendell
Leslie, Royal Conrad
Lesly, Philip
Lesner, Samuel Joel
Less, Clifford Michael
Lesselyoung, Nicholas Jacob, III
Lessiter, Frank Donald
Lester, Wilbur Rufus
Letsinger, Robert Lewis
Lett, Austin Sherwood, Jr.
Levandowski, Donald William
Leven, Charles Louis
Leventhal, Howard
Levi, Albert William
Levi, Edward Hirsch
Levi, Kurt
Levin, Bertram
Levin, Charles Leonard
Levine, Edwin Burton
Levine, Myron
Levine, Norman Dion
Levis, Larry Patrick
Levi-Setti, Riccardo
Levitt, Aaron Louis
Levitt, LeRoy Paul
Levitt, Richard Sander
Levy, Edward Charles, Jr.
Levy, Jack I.
Levy, John David
Levy, Sidney Jay
Levy, Solomon E.
Levy, Willard Linz
Lewert, Robert Murdoch
Lewine, Sidney
Lewis, Ben William
Lewis, Benjamin Morgan
Lewis, Carl Chandler, Jr.
Lewis, Cary Blackburn, Jr.
Lewis, Charles John
Lewis, Darrell L.
Lewis, David Lanier
Lewis, David Sloan, Jr.
Lewis, Donald S.
Lewis, Edward Earl
Lewis, Edwin Henderson
Lewis, Gene Dale
Lewis, James Kirtley
Lewis, James Mose
Lewis, L(eo) Rhodes
Lewis, Philip
Lewis, Phillip Harold
Lewis, Ramsey Emanuel, Jr.
Lewis, Robert Burns
Lewis, Robert Lawrence
Lewis, Voyle Herbert
Lewis, Welbourne Walker, Jr.
Lewis, William Edward
Leymaster, Glen R.
Li, Peter Joseph Ta
Li, Tien-yi
Li, Ting Yi
Liberman, Lee Marvin
Liberman, Myron Mandell
Lichstein, Herman Carlton
Lichtenberg, Don Bernett
Lichtenstein, David Benjamin
Lichter, Edward Arthur
Lichtin, J. Leon
Lichtmann, Samuel Arthur
Lick, Wilbert James
Lidbetter, Ward Pritchard
Liddell, Leon Morris
Lieb, Ernest Horst
Liebelt, Robert Arthur
Lieberman, Laurence J.
Lieberman, Leonard
Lieblein, Seymour
Liebman, William Lewis
Liener, Irvin Ernest
Lienert, Robert Marcellus
Lietz, Fred Edgar
Lifton, Donald Brian
Liggett, Thomas Jackson
Liggett, William N.
Light, Kenneth B.
Lightburn, William Charles
Liipfert, Otto Edworth
Liljegren, Frank Sigfrid
Lillehei, Clarence Walton
Lillehei, Richard Carlton
Lilly, David Maher
Lilly, Eli
Lim, Henry Chol
Limbaugh, Rush Hudson
Lin, Yukweng Michael
Linck, Lawrence J.
Lincoln, James Helme
Lind, Chester Carl
Lind, Levi Robert
Lindberg, Howard Avery
Lindell, Edward Albert
Lindemer, Lawrence Boyd
Linden, Henry Robert
Lindenbusch, John Henry
Lindesmith, Alfred Ray
Lindgren, Bernard William
Lindgren, Richard Thomas
Lindner, Carl H.
Lindner, Kenneth Edward
Lindner, Robert David
Lindquist, Emory Kempton
Lindquist, Everet Franklin
Lindsay, Charles Rogers, III
Lindsay, Edward Emerson
Lindsay, George Clayton
Lindsay, Robert Blake Theodore (Ted)
Lindsell, Harold
Lindstrom, David Edgar
Lindstrom, Ernest Algot
Lindstrom, Kenneth Albert
Ling, Cyril Curtis
Lingl, Friedrich Albert
Lingoes, James Charles
Link, Arthur A.
Link, David Thomas
Link, Edward Richard, Jr.
Link, Robert Allen
Link, Roger Paul
Linnell, Albert Paul
Linnenburger, Ralph Leroy
Linowes, David Francis
Linsalata, Frank Natale
Linse, Eugene W., Jr.
Linsky, Leonard
Linster, John Edward
Linton, Margaret Reynolds
Linton, Rodney Curtis
Linton, Roy Nathan
Lipford, Rocque Edward
Lipham, James Maurice
Lipman, David
Lippe, Melvin Karl
Lippincott, Benjamin Evans
Lipton, Martha
Lira, Emil Patrick
Lis, Edward Francis
Lischer, Ludwig Frederick
Lison, James J., Jr.
Littell, James Elmer
Little, Alan Brian
Little, Bernard Harold
Little, Robert Andrews
Little, Robert William
Littlefair, Duncan Elliot
Littler, Mark Dunham
Littner, Ner
Litzsinger, Paul Richard
Liu, Ben-chieh
Liu, Benjamin Young-hwai
Liu Vi-Cheng
Lively, Edwin Lowe
Livesay, Jackson Edward
Livingood, Clarence S.
Livingston, Ellis N.
Livingston, Henry Lucion
Livingston, Robert Louis
Livingstone, Frank Brown
Llewellyn, Ralph Alvin
Lloyd, Fredric Reynolds
Lloyd, John A.
Lloyd, John Henry, Jr.
Lloyd, Marion Musser
Lloyd, Russell G.
Lo, Irving Yucheng
Loach, Paul Allen
Lobeck, Charles Champlin
Lober, Donald Warring, Jr.
Lober, Paul Hallam
Lo Chiano, Rocco
Locke, Charles Stanley
Lockhart, James Blakely
Lockhart, John Mallory
Lockhart, William Raymond
Lockridge, Ernest Hugh
Lockwood, Ralph Harold
Loder, Dwight Ellsworth
Lodwick, Gwilym Savage
Loebl, Jerrold
Loechler, Leon Paul
Loeffler, Frank Joseph
Loesch, Harrison
Loeschner, Ray B.
Loess, Henry Bernard
Loew, Cornelius Richard
Loewenberg, Gerhard
Loft, Abram
Lofton, John Marion
Loftsgard, Laurel Duane
Logan, David Reid
Logan, Frederick Manning
Logan, Henry Vincent
Logan, James C.
Logan, James Kenneth
Logan, John Alexander
Logan, John O.
Logsdon, Thomas Allen
Loh, Jerome Wei-Ping
Lohman, Victor John (Gus)
Lohman, Walter Rearick
Lohr, Donald Russell
Lohr, Mary Margaret
Lohrman, John J.
Lohwater, A.J.
Loken, Merle Kenneth
Lolich, Mickey Stephen
Lomas, Anna Cochrane
Lomas, Bernard Tagg
Lomason, William Keithledge
Lombardi, Cornelius Ennis, Jr.
Lombardo, Lawrence James
Long, Alvin William
Long, Archie Merrill
Long, Charles Franklin
Long, Clarence William
Long, Forrest Edwin
Long, Helen Halter
Long, Herbert Strainge
Long, Howard Rusk
Long, Isaac Adelbert
Long, Robert Eugene
Long, Scott
Long, Theodore Dixon
Longe, Patricia O'Donnell
Longhorn, Milton
Longmire, John Robinson
Longo, Michael Joseph
Longone, Daniel Thomas
Lonnecker, Paul Leroy
Lonning, Joseph E.
Lonnquist, John Hall
Loofbourrow, Alan G.
Loomis, Bernard
Loomis, Wesley Horace, III
Looney, Marvin Olen
Looper, Joseph Henry
Loory, Stuart Hugh
Lopata, Helena Znaniecki (Mrs. Richard Stefan Lopata)
Loppnow, Milo Alvin
LoPrete, James Hugh
Lorand, Laszlo
Lord, Charles Austin
Lord, Frank Harmon
Lord, John Solon
Lord, Miles Welton
Lore, John Samuel
Lorentzsen, Norman Martin
Lorenz, Hugo Albert
Lorenz, Paul Francis
Lorie, James Hirsch
Lorincz, Allan Levente
Lottes, John William
Loucks, Terry Lee Anton
Loucks, Vernon Reece
Loucks, Vernon Reece, Jr.
Loud, Warren Simms
Louis, John Jeffry
Lourenco, Ruy Valentim
Love, J. Grafton
Love, Rodney Marvin
Lovejoy, David Sherman
Lovejoy, Robert Carr
Lovelace, Eldridge Hirst
Loving, Hamilton Elwyn
Lovinger, Warren Conrad
Lovre, Curtis A.
Low, William Hugh
Lowe, Henry Thomas
Lowe, William Henry
Lowe, William Stewart
Lowenstine, Maurice Richard, Jr.
Lowery, Percival C.
Lowinsky, Edward Elias
Lowrie, Jean Elizabeth
Lowry, Gary William
Lowry, H. J.
Lowry, Oliver Howe
Lowry, Robert James
Lowry, Robert James
Lowther, Gerald Halbert
Lubbers, Arend Donselaar
Lubin, Bernard
Lucas, John Kenneth
Lucas, John Wayne
Lucas, Lawrence Newton
Lucas, Robert Elwood
Luchs, Fred E.
Luck, John Virgil
Luckenbach, Carl Frederick
Lucker, Raymond Alphonse
Luckey, Thomas Donnell
Luckmann, William Henry
Lucow, Milton
Ludgin, Earle
Ludlow, Charles Henry
Ludvigsen, Elliot Leon
Ludwig, Harvey Allen
Ludwig, Richard Joseph
Luedtke, Kurt Mamre
Luerssen, Frank Wonson
Lueth, Harold Charles
Luffler, Ralph Raymond
Luisada, Aldo A.
Luke, Hugh D.
Lukens, Donald E. Buz
Lumry, Rufus Worth, II
Lund, Bert Oscar, Jr.
Lund, Sister Candida
Lund, Kenneth Wilhelm
Lund, Lois Ann
Lund, Lowell Dale
Lundahl, Arthur Brown
Lundberg, James Thomas
Lundegard, John Thomas
Lunden, Laurence Raymond
Lundgren, Robert Wayne
Lundin, Bruce Theodore
Lundin, Oscar Alexis
Lunding, Franklin Jerome
Lundquist, Carl Harold
Lundy, Joseph Edward
Luneburg, William V.
Lura, Loren Elroy
Lurie, Melvin
Lurie, Nancy Oestreich
Lurton, H. William
Lurtsema, Robert Ross
Lush, Jay Laurence
Lusk, William Edward
Luskin, Bert L.
Luther, Clark Edward
Lutwak, Leo
Lutz, Adeline Louise
Lutz, Arthur Leroy
Lutz, Carl Freiheit
Lutz, James
Lutz, Joseph Graham
Lutz, Norman Emil
Lutz, Walter Frederick
Lydolph, Paul Edward
Lyjak, Robert Fred
Lykos, Peter George
Lykoudis, Paul S.
Lyman, Margaret Morner (Peggy)
Lyman, Richard Randall
Lynch, Benjamin Leo
Lynch, Beverly Pfeifer
Lynch, David William
Lynch, Frederick, Jr.
Lynch, Henry Thomson
Lynch, Ray Joseph
Lynch, Russell George
Lynch, William Walmsley, Jr.
Lynn, Arthur Dellert, Jr.
Lynn, Donald Justin
Lynn, Edward Earl
Lynn, Janet (Janet Lynn Nowicki)
Lynn, Michael Edward, III
Lynn, Robert Athan
Lynn, Robert Wood
Lyon, Harvey William
Lyon, John Alexander Melvin
Lyon, Philip Schuyler
Lyon, Wayne Barton
Lyons, Frederick William, Jr.
Lyons, James David
Lyons, M. Arnold
Lysaught, J. Donald
Maas, Duane Harris
Maazel, Lorin
Mabley, Jack
MacAlister, Paul Ritter
MacAllister, Jack Alfred
MacCarty, Collin Stewart
MacChesney, (Alfred) Brunson, III
MacCorquodale, Kenneth
MacDonald, Caleb Alan
MacDonald, David Robert
MacDonald, John Angus
MacDonald, Kenneth
Macdonald, Peter McIntyre
Macdonald, Ray Woodward
MacDonald, Reynold Coleman
MacDonald, Roderick
MacDonald, Walter Howard
MacDonnell, Wilfred Donald
MacDougall, Curtis Daniel
Macfarlane, Malcolm Harris
MacFie, Clyde Allen
Machol, Robert E.
Macht, Carol Malisoff
MacIver, John Kenneth
Mack, Clifford Glenn
Mack, Clifton Eugene
Mack, Eugene Kevin
Mack, John Wilfred
Mack, Raymond Wright
Mack, Walter Noel
Mackal, Roy Paul
Mackall, Henry Clinton
MacKendrick, Paul Lachlan
Mackenzie, Donald Matthew
Mackenzie, Fred Theodore
MacKenzie, Louis Augustine
Mackie, Frederick David
Mackie, Robert Joseph
MacLane, Saunders
MacLaughlin, Harry Hunter
MacLean, John Allan
MacMaster, Daniel Miller
MacMurray, Charles Gaylord
MacNaughton, Alexander Douglas
MacNider, Jack
MacQueen, James Robert
Mac Veigh, Joseph Gibbs
MacWatters, Virginia
Maddocks, Robert Allen
Madgett, Naomi Long
Madison, Robert P.
Madsen, Charles Clifford
Madsen, Donald George
Mag, Arthur
Magad, Samuel
Magath, Thomas Byrd
Magen, Myron Shimin
Magill, Robert Francis
Maginn, Raymond Graham
Magnuson, Keith Arlen
Magnuson, Richard H.
Magnuson, Warren Roger
Magrath, C. Peter
Magrish, Alfred E.
Maguire, James Francis
Maguire, John Patrick
Magyar, Gabriel
Mahaffey, Maryann
Mahan, Harold Dean
Mahard, Richard Harold
Maher, Frank Thomas
Maher, Philip Brooks
Maher, Robert Francis
Maher, Trafford Patrick
Mahin, Charles Boyd
Mahler, Henry Ralph
Mahoney, Daniel Joseph, Jr.
Mahoney, Edward Maurice
Mahoney, William Patrick
Mahowald, Mark Edward
Maibach, Ben C., Jr.
Maickel, Roger Philip
Maidenburg, Ben
Maier, Henry W.
Maier, Irwin
Maier, Jack Craig
Maier, Norman Raymond Frederick
Maier, Robert Jules
Mainous, Bruce Hale
Major, Coleman Joseph
Major, John Keene

Metcalf, Lawrence Eugene
Metcalf, Robert Clarence
Metcalf, Robert Lee
Metcalf, Terrance Randolph (Terry)
Method, Harold Lambert
Mettler, Ruben Frederick
Metzenbaum, Howard Morton
Metzler, Dwight Fox
Meuser, Fredrick William
Meyer, Adolphe Erich
Meyer, Alex Alfred
Meyer, Alfred George
Meyer, Alfred Herman Ludwig
Meyer, Alvin Earl
Meyer, August Christopher
Meyer, August Christopher, Jr.
Meyer, Axel
Meyer, Brud Richard
Meyer, Charles Appleton
Meyer, Charles Edward
Meyer, Daniel Joseph
Meyer, Donald Gordon
Meyer, Duane Gilbert
Meyer, George Herbert
Meyer, Karl William
Meyer, Leonard Herman
Meyer, Maynard William
Meyer, Ovid Otto
Meyer, Peter
Meyer, Raymond Joseph
Meyer, Robert Anthony
Meyer, Roland Kenneth
Meyer, Russel William, Jr.
Meyer, Samuel James
Meyerhoff, Arthur Edward
Meyerhoff, Jack Fulton
Meyers, Arthur Christian, Jr.
Meyers, Cal Yale
Meyers, Gerald Carl
Meyers, Philip Mitchell
Mezera, James Allen
Micali, Thomas Agatino
Michael, Donald Nelson
Michael, Floyd Donald
Michael, I. E.
Michael, John William
Michael, Lloyd Styers
Michael, R. Keith
Michaelides, Constantine Evangelos
Michaud, Howard Henry
Michel, Robert Henry
Micheli, Frank James
Michelson, Irving
Michelson, Richard Albert
Michener, Charles Duncan
Mickelson, Arnold Rust
Mickelson, Merlyn Francis
Miechur, Thomas Frank
Miedema, Sylvia Ann
Mielke, Donald Craig
Mihalik, Emil John
Mihanovich, Clement Simon
Mikita, Stanley
Mikva, Abner Joseph
Miles, Arthur Parker
Miles, John Bruce
Miles, Wendell A.
Mileti, Nick James
Miley, George Hunter
Milford, Howard
Milgrim, Franklin Marshall
Milholland, James, Jr.
Milic, Louis Tonko
Militzer, Walter Ernest
Milivojevich, Dionisije
Miller, Allan John
Miller, Anna Blair
Miller, Arthur LaRue
Miller, Arthur Leonard
Miller, Barry
Miller, C(harles) Phillip, Jr.
Miller, Charles Williams
Miller, Clarence Harvey
Miller, Daniel Weber
Miller, David Hewitt
Miller, Donald Calvin
Miller, Edward B.
Miller, Elfer Buel
Miller, Elizabeth Cavert
Miller, Eugene
Miller, Eugene Albert
Miller, Ewing Harry
Miller, Florence Lowden (Mrs. C. Phillip Miller)
Miller, Francis Marion
Miller, Frank
Miller, Frank William
Miller, Freeman Devold
Miller, Fritz Henry
Miller, George W.
Miller, Gertrude Nevada
Miller, Glenn Leroy
Miller, Harry George
Miller, Herbert Chauncey
Miller, Howard C.
Miller, Irving Franklin
Miller, Ivan Lawrence
Miller, J. Duane
Miller, James Alexander
Miller, James Alvin
Miller, James Edwin, Jr.
Miller, James Franklin
Miller, James Roscoe
Miller, James William
Miller, Jean Roger
Miller, John Frederick
Miller, John Oscar
Miller, John Pearse
Miller, John William, Jr.
Miller, Joseph Irwin
Miller, Kenneth Edward
Miller, Lavern Archie
Miller, Leslie Haynes
Miller, Leslie Raymond
Miller, Lester David
Miller, Lloyd Daniel
Miller, Lloyd Ivan
Miller, Louis Gerard
Miller, Lynn Harvey
Miller, Sister Mary Aquin
Miller, Max
Miller, Melvin Hull
Miller, Merle Hamilton
Miller, Merton Howard
Miller, Morris Folsom
Miller, Pleasant Voorhees, Jr.
Miller, Ralph Paul
Miller, Richard Nathan
Miller, Robert Branson
Miller, Robert Carl
Miller, Robert Fred
Miller, Robert LaVelle
Miller, Robert Richey Conklin
Miller, Roland Drew
Miller, Russell Harold
Miller, Shelby Alexander
Miller, Stanford
Miller, Thomas Goss
Miller, Thomas Milton
Miller, Thomas Williams
Miller, Victor Charles
Miller, Wilbur Casteel
Miller, William Jesse, Jr.
Miller, William Johnson
Miller, William Peter
Miller, Wilmer Glenn
Millichap, Joseph Gordon
Milligan, Floyd Wilmer
Milligan, Francis Joseph, Jr.
Milligan, John Thomas
Milliken, William Grawn
Millikin, Severance Allen
Millis, John Schoff
Millor, William James
Mills, Barriss
Mills, Charles Bright
Mills, Donald Calvin
Mills, John Welch
Mills, Paul Gerald
Mills, Ralph Joseph, Jr.
Mills, Rilla Dean
Mills, Robert Laurence
Mills, Russell Clarence
Millstone, Isadore Erwin
Milne, Donald George
Milne, George Davidson
Milne, William Gordon
Milner, Harold William
Milner, Ned Edward
Milone, Charles Robert
Minahan, Roger Copp
Minahan, Victor Ivan
Minar, Edwin LeRoy, Jr.
Mindlin, Richard Barnett
Miner, Earl Howard
Miner, Horace Mitchell
Miner, Paul Virgil
Minko, Philip Peter
Minner, Robert Schermerhorn
Minor, Charles Daniel
Minor, Robert Walter
Minow, Josephine Baskin
Minow, Newton Norman
Minshall, Drexel David
Minter, Thomas Frederic
Mints, Thomas M., Jr.
Minty, George James
Mintz, Harry
Mintz, Loren Alexander
Mintzer, David
Miossi, Alfred F.
Mirabito, Paul S.
Miranda, Constancio Fernandes
Miron, William L.
Miroyiannis, Stanley Demetrius
Misch, Herbert Louis
Mischakoff, Mischa
Mischke, Charles Russell
Mischke, Frederick Charles
Mischler, Harland Louis
Mischler, James Jolly
Mischley, Walter Anthony
Missar, Richard Rudolph
Mitau, G. Theodore
Mitby, Norman Peter
Mitchell, Bryan Henry
Mitchell, Clifford Robert
Mitchell, Irving Eugene
Mitchell, John Francis
Mitchell, Marvin George
Mitchell, Roger Lowry
Mitchell, Virgil Allen
Mitchell, Wallace MacMahon
Mitchell, William George
Mitchell, William Hamilton
Mitchell, William LeRoy
Mithun, Ray Otis
Mitseff, Carl
Mnich, William Richard
Moate, Lester Thomas
Moberg, David Oscar
Modell, Arthur B.
Modersohn, Robert John, III
Modic, Stanley John
Modrey, Joseph
Moe, John Howard
Moede, Gustave Herman, Jr.
Moeller, Arnold Henry
Moeller, Carl William
Moeller, Leslie G.
Moellering, Alfred William
Moersch, Herman John
Moeser, James Charles
Moesta, Rodman Charles
Mogk, John Edward
Mohlenbrock, Robert Herman, Jr.
Mohler, Orren Cuthbert
Mohlman, Robert Henry
Mohr, Roger John
Mohs, Frederic Edward
Moirano, Hugo John
Mokodean, Michael John
Molenaar, Harry
Moline, Jon Nelson
Molitor, Sister Margaret Anne
Moll, Kenneth Leon
Moller, Hans Stern, Jr.
Mollison, Clarence Longman
Molloy, Julia Sale
Moloney, Sister Margaret Mary
Moltz, Howard
Monasee, Charles Arthur
Monat, William Robert
Monek, Francis Herman
Monk, Albert Herschel
Monroe, Clarence Webster
Monroe, James Walter
Monson, Forrest Truman
Monson, Karen Ann
Montgomery, Charles Howard
Montgomery, Charles Raymond
Montgomery, Donald Joseph
Montgomery, Henry Close, Jr.
Montgomery, James Winchester
Montgomery, Leo Raymond
Montgomery, Max Malcolm
Montgomery, Robert Lausen
Monypenny, Phillip
Moo, Paul Richard
Moody, Blair, Jr.
Moody, Peter Richard
Moody, Richard
Moody, Tom
Moon, Gordon Ames, II
Mooney, Edward Joseph, Jr.
Mooney, Robert Phillip
Moore, Dan Tyler
Moore, Douglas Ross
Moore, Edward Carter
Moore, Edward Forrest
Moore, Edwin Charles
Moore, Fred L., Jr.
Moore, George Emerson, Jr.
Moore, Harry Clare
Moore, Harry T.
Moore, Hobert Charles
Moore, Hollis Andrew, Jr.
Moore, Horace Duff
Moore, Hugh Ramsay
Moore, John Cordell
Moore, John Duain
Moore, John Raymond
Moore, Kenneth Edwin
Moore, Kenneth Thompson
Moore, Mechlin Dongan
Moore, Richard Albert
Moore, Richard Kerr
Moore, Robert Etheridge
Moore, Robert S.
Moore, Ruth
Moore, Thomas P.
Moore, William Grover, Jr.
Moore, Willis
Moos, Malcolm Charles
Moran, James Byron
Moran, John Vincent
Moran, Thomas Joseph
Moran, William Edward
Morch, Ernst Trier
Mordy, Wendell Allen
Morehead, Dwight Hoyt
Morel, Paul Maurice
Morem, Neil Roderick
Morgan, David Page
Morgan, Graham James
Morgan, J. Alan
Morgan, Joe Leonard
Morgan, John Allen
Morgan, John Bruce
Morgan, June P.
Morgan, Lee Laverne
Morgan, Leger James, Jr.
Morgan, Raleigh, Jr.
Morgan, Robert Dale
Morgan, Robert Edward
Morgan, Samuel Huntington
Morgan, William T., Jr.
Morgan, William Wilson
Moriarty, Robert Michael
Morin, Carlton Paul
Morin, Robert Edgar
Moritz, Alan Richards
Moritz, Edward, Jr.
Moritz, Timothy Bovie
Morkovin, Mark Vladimir
Morley, Harry Thomas, Jr.
Morlock, Carl Grismore
Morrill, James Frederick
Morrill, John Rhodes
Morrill, Thomas Clyde
Morris, Allen Ray
Morris, Alvin Eugene
Morris, Donald Charles
Morris, Donald Fraser
Morris, Doyle Sterling
Morris, Earl Franklin
Morris, Edward Lawrence
Morris, George Bader, Jr.
Morris, Harry Leland
Morris, Joan Clair
Morris, Kenneth Rex
Morris, Norval
Morris, Thomas James, Jr.
Morrison, Clinton
Morrison, John Herbert
Morrison, John Washburn
Morrison, Karl Frederick
Morrison, Keith Anthony
Morrison, Paul Leslie
Morrison, Robert Stanley
Morrison, William Angus
Morrissette, Bruce Archer
Morrow, George Lester
Morrow, Ralph Ernest
Morse, Cynthia Brown
Morse, Erskine Vance
Morse, Grant Wesley
Morse, Henry Ladd
Morse, Kenneth Pratt
Mortensen, James Merwin
Morter, Raymond Lione
Mortimer, Edward Albert, Jr.
Mortland, Max Merle
Morton, Joseph Neil
Morton, Walter Albert
Mosby, Wade Hamilton
Moscona, Aron Arthur
Moscowitz, Albert Joseph
Moseley, George Boswell
Moseley, Ray Benjamin Franklin
Moseley, Ray Neal
Moses, Leon Nathan
Mosher, Charles Adams
Mosier, Jacob Eugene
Mosier, Paul George
Moskos, Charles C., Jr.
Moskow, Michael H.
Moss, Charles Malcolm
Moss, Cruse Watson
Moss, James Herbert
Moss, Leonard Wallace
Moss, Robert Drexler
Mosse, Baskett Pershing
Mosse, George L.
Most, Woodrow Lloyd
Mostert, Paul Stallings
Mouat, Malcolm Palmer
Moulder, James William
Moulton, Benjamin
Moulton, Edward Quentin
Moulton, Phillips Prentice
Moulton, Ralph Eugene
Mounce, Donald Malind
Mount, John Thomas
Mount, Richard Carl
Mountjoy, Paul Tomb
Mourek, Joseph Edward
Moutoussamy, John Warren
Mowery, Bob Lee
Mowrer, George Edwin
Mowrer, Orval Hobart
Moy, Richard Henry
Moyer, Frederick Weaver, Jr.
Moyer, Sheldon
Muchnic, William Henry
Mudge, Lewis Seymour
Muedeking, George Herbert
Muehling, Arthur James
Muelder, Milton E.
Mueller, Alvin William
Mueller, Harald Charles
Mueller, Harold
Mueller, Herbert A.
Mueller, Jack William
Mueller, John Alfred
Mueller, Kate Hevner
Mueller, Willard Fritz
Muessig, Raymond Henry
Muhammad, Wallace D.
Muhlenbruch, Carl W.
Mulder, Donald William
Muldoon, John William
Mulheim, Joseph Elbert
Mullaney, Paul Lynch
Mullen, Januarius Arthur
Mullen, William Charles
Mullenbach, Philip
Muller, Herbert Joseph
Mulligan, James Anthony
Mulligan, James Joseph
Mulligan, Robert William
Mulliken, Robert Sanderson
Mullikin, Thomas Wilson
Mullin, Gail Edward
Mulrow, Patrick Joseph
Mulroy, Thomas Robert
Mulvihill, Edward Robert
Mumaw, James Webster
Mundie, William Lade
Mundinger, Donald Charles
Mundt, Donald Keith
Munger, Elmer Lewis
Munger, Paul Francis
Munk, Arthur William Philip
Munro, William Delmar
Munsell, Claude Edward
Munsick, Robert Alliot
Munson, Thomas Lewis
Muntyan, Miodrag
Muntz, Ernest Gordon
Munzer, Cynthia Brown
Murch, Boynton Daggett
Murchison, Elisha P.
Murdock, Charles William
Murdock, John Carey
Murdock, Stuart Laird
Murphey, Rhoads
Murphy, Charles Francis
Murphy, Charles Francis, Jr.
Murphy, Charles Theophilus
Murphy, Glenn
Murphy, Gordon John
Murphy, Harry Crisman
Murphy, Irene Ellis
Murphy, John Arthur
Murphy, John Carey
Murphy, John Price
Murphy, John Thomas
Murphy, Margaret Nesbitt
Murphy, Robert Brady Lawrence
Murphy, Robert Ward
Murphy, Terrence J.
Murphy, Thomas Aquinas
Murphy, Thomas T.
Murphy, William A.
Murphy, William Celestin
Murphy, William Thomas
Murray, Charles Emerson
Murray, Dolor Patrick, Jr.
Murray, Donald Alan
Murray, George Rathell
Murray, Haydn Herbert
Murray, Hugh Vincent
Murray, James Nigel, Jr.
Murray, John Francis Thomas
Murray, John Joseph
Murray, Leonard Hugh
Murray, Peter Bryant
Murray, Raymond Gorbold
Murray, Thomas Dwight
Murray, William Frederic
Murtfeldt, Frederick Harold
Murthy, Varanasi Rama
Muschenheim, William Emil
Muse, William Van
Musial, Stan (Frank)
Musselman, Peter Rogers
Mussio, John King
Musson, Noverre
Mydland, Gordon James
Myers, Allen
Myers, Daniel Wilbur
Myers, David N.
Myers, Frances
Myers, Franklin Lewis, II
Myers, Fred Arthur
Myers, Fredrick Sames
Myers, George Vincent
Myers, Harry J., Jr.
Myers, James William
Myers, Jay Arthur
Myers, Joe Crawford
Myers, John Humbird
Myers, John Thomas
Myers, Kenneth Ellis
Myers, Kenneth Melvin
Myers, Phillip Samuel
Myers, Phillip Ward
Myers, Ray Franklin
Myers, Raymond Reever
Myers, Richard Gordon
Myers, Robert Durant
Myers, Robert Gilbert
Myers, Theodore Ash
Myers, William Graydon
Myklebust, Helmer Rudolph
Mylod, Robert Joseph
Myra, Harold Lawrence
Nachtrieb, Norman Harry
Nachtsheim, Edward Ernest
Nadel, Eli Maurice
Nader, Robert Alexander
Nadler, Henry Louis
Nadler, Myron Jay
Naeve, Milo Merle
Naftalin, Arthur
Nagel, Stuart Samuel
Nagy, Andrew Francis
Nagy, Charles Franklin
Najarian, John Sarkis
Nakhnikian, George
Nambu, Yoichiro
Nance, James J.
Nangle, John Francis
Nantz, Thomas Benton
Nara, Harry Raymond
Nartker, Raymond Henry
Nasatir, Maimon
Nash, Curtis Eliot
Nash, Jay Robert, III
Nash, John Arthur
Nash, Manning
Nash, Robert Fred
Nason, Howard King
Nason, Philip Hathaway
Nater, James Ronald
Nathanson, Don Paul
Nathanson, Nathaniel Louis
Natvig, Paul
Naugle, Thomas Earl
Nault, William Henry
Naumann, Oscar John
Naumann, William Louis
Naunton, Ralph Frederick
Navin, Louis Edmond
Nawoj, Edward John
Naylor, Arch Waugh, III
Naylor, James Charles
Nazette, Richard Follett
Neal, Phil Caldwell
Nease, Stephen Wesley
Neathery, Wayne Dwight
Neavoll, George Franklin
Nebenzahl, Kenneth
Nebergall, Roger Ellis
Nederlander, Robert Elliott
Neece, Robert Frederic
Neel, James Van Gundia
Neely, Earl Fisher
Neff, Frederick Clifton
Neff, Robert Carl
Neff, William Duwayne
Negley, Harold Hoover
Neidhardt, Frederick Carl
Neidhardt, Paul Woodrow
Neill, Robert
Neill, Wayne Kenneth
Neinas, Charles Merrill
Neitzert, Howard
Nellor, John Ernest
Nelson, Alvie Charles
Nelson, Bernard Andrew
Nelson, C. Hjalmar
Nelson, Charles Edmund
Nelson, Charles Ellsworth
Nelson, David Aldrich
Nelson, David Leonard
Nelson, Don Nichols
Nelson, Donald Eugene
Nelson, Edwin Clarence
Nelson, Gordon Leon
Nelson, Grant Steel
Nelson, Harold Lewis
Nelson, Harry J.
Nelson, John
Nelson, John Monninger
Nelson, John Thilgen
Nelson, John Wilton
Nelson, Katherine Greacen
Nelson, Lawrence Evan
Nelson, LeRoy
Nelson, Obert K.
Nelson, Oliver Evans
Nelson, Randall Hylman
Nelson, Raymond John
Nelson, Robert Hartley
Nelson, Ronald Harvey
Nelson, Stanley R.
Nelson, Walter Gerald
Nelson, Werner Lind
Nelson, Wilbur Clifton
Nelson, William Clarence
Nemerov, Howard
Nemeth, Peter John
Nemmers, Erwin Esser
Nequist, John Leonard
Nerlinger, John William
Nerlove, Marc L.
Nesbitt, Cecil James
Nester, William Raymond, Jr.
Netsch, Walter Andrew, Jr.
Nettl, Bruno
Netzer, Donald Leo
Netzer, Lanore Agnes
Neu, Arthur Alan
Neubauer, Charles Frederick
Neubauer, Joseph
Neubeck, Gerhard
Neubert, Theodore John
Neuce, Edwin Olando
Neuenschwander, Frederick Phillip
Neugarten, Bernice Levin
Neuhaus, Otto Wilhelm
Neuman, Donald Bernard
Neuman, Howard Jay
Neumann, Forrest Karl
Neuschel, Robert Percy
Neusner, Milton Michael
Nevid, Norbert
Nevill, William Albert
Neville, James Morton
Neville, Margaret Mary
Nevin, John Joseph
Nevins, Albert J.
Nevins, Francis Michael, Jr.
Nevitt, Michael Vogt
Newberg, John Myron
Newbrough, Edgar Truett
Newcomb, Eldon Henry
Newcombe, Leo Raymond
Newell, Frank William
Newell, Sterling, Jr.
Newhard, Harry Wallace
Newlin, John Robert
Newman, Bruce Lee
Newman, Eric Pfeiffer
Newman, Gerald
Newman, Leon Theophane
Newman, Louis Benjamin
Newman, M.W.
Newman, Max Karl
Newman, Melvin Spencer
Newman, Ralph Geoffrey
Newmark, Nathan Mortimore
Newsom, Lionel Hodge
Newton, George Addison
Newton, John Edward
Newton, John Skillman
Newton, Michael
Newton, Robert Chaffer
Newton, Roger Gerhard
Nexon, Hubert Henry
Nichol, Fred Joseph
Nicholas, Arthur Soterios
Nichols, Donald Richardson
Nichols, Frederick Adams
Nichols, George A.
Nichols, Hugh Conklin
Nichols, John Alden
Nichols, Marie Hochmuth
Nichols, Miller
Nichols, Owen Harvey
Nichols, Raymond Francis
Nichols, Roy Elwyn
Nichols, Stephen Robert
Nichols, William Curtis, Jr.
Nicholson, Donald Grant
Nicholson, George Albert, Jr.
Nicholson, Morris Emmons, Jr.
Nicholson, Robert Arthur
Nickelson, Harry Edward
Nickerson, John Lester
Niefeld, Jaye Sutter
Niehm, Bernard Frank
Nielsen, Arthur Charles
Nielsen, Arthur Charles, Jr.
Nielsen, Ernest D.
Niemann, William Lovekamp
Niemeyer, Gerhart
Nier, Alfred Otto Carl
Niezer, Louis Fox
Niles, Thomas McMaster
Nims, John Frederick
Nipson, Herbert
Nisbet, Jerry J.
Niswonger, Clifford Rollin
Nitsche, Johannes Carl Christian
Nix, Edmund Alfred
Nixon, Raymond Blalock
Nixon, Robert Pleasants
Noback, Richardson Kilbourne
Noble, David Watson
Noble, Donald Edgar

Pierson, Donald
Pierson, George Allen
Pierson, John Theodore, Jr.
Pikarsky, Milton
Pike, Albert Raymond
Pike, Kenneth Lee
Pike, Randall Leslie
Pilafian, Suren
Pile, Robert Bennett
Pilliod, Charles Jule, Jr.
Pillsbury, Frederick Hobart
Pillsbury, George Sturgis
Pillsbury, John Sargent, Jr.
Pillsbury, Philip Winston
Pincus, Howard Jonah
Pine, Irving
Pines, David
Pines, Herman
Ping, Charles Jackson
Pingel, John Spencer
Pings, Vern Matthew
Pinken, Bernard H.
Pinkerton, Henry
Pinsof, Nathan
Pipal, Faustin A.
Piper, Harry C., Jr.
Piper, Henry Dan
Piper, Howard
Piper, Mark Harry
Piper, Robert Johnston
Pirie, John T., Jr.
Pirsig, Robert Maynard
Pisciotta, Anthony Vito
Pitkin, Milo James
Pitot, Henry Clement
Pittenger, Reid Maurice
Pitts, Guy Harvey
Pitts, Henry LaRue
Plagenz, George Richard
Plager, Sheldon Jay
Plambeck, Herbert Henry
Planje, Theodore John
Plank, Betsy Ann (Mrs. Sherman V. Rosenfield)
Plank, Raymond
Plant, Marcus Leo
Planting, Charles Oliver
Plath, David William
Platou, Carl Nicolai
Platt, Joseph Swan
Platts, John H.
Platzman, George William
Player, Gary Jim
Pletsch, George Burgess
Pletz, Francis Gregory
Plews, George Montague
Ploeser, Walter Christian
Plonsey, Robert
Plonus, Martin Algirdas
Plotnick, Harvey Barry
Plotnik, Arthur
Plucker, Orvin Lowell
Plum, Charles Walden
Plumb, Valworth Rice
Plunkett, Robert
Poboisk, Donald Paul
Pochyly, Donald Frederick
Pocock, John William
Podesta, Robert Angelo
Poe, Bryce, II
Poelker, John Henry
Pohl, John Florian
Poinier, Arthur Best
Poinsett, Alexander Caesar
Polasek, Theo Louis
Polesky, Herbert Fred
Polizzi, Salvatore Emmanuel
Polk, George
Polk, Louis Frederick
Polk, Ralph Lane
Polk, Ralph Lane, Jr.
Pollack, Gerald Leslie
Pollack, Norman
Pollard, Braxton
Pollard, Darrell Henry
Pollard, Harry
Pollard, Herman Marvin
Pollard, James Edward
Pollard, Morris
Polley, Howard Freeman
Polley, Ira
Pollock, George Howard
Pomerantz, Louis
Pomeroy, Benjamin Sherwood
Pomeroy, Lawrence Hitchcock
Pomeroy, William Tamplin
Pommerening, Edwin Carlton
Pompey, Maurice Dale
Pomroy, Jesse Herbert, Jr.
Pond, Alonzo William
Ponseti, Ignacio Vives
Pont, John
Poole, John Bayard
Poorman, Paul Arthur
Poovey, William Arthur
Popham, Arthur Cobb, Jr.
Popham, Richard Allen
Popham, Wayne Gordon
Poplinger, Louis L.
Poppelbaum, Wolfgang Johann
Porile, Norbert Thomas
Poropat, Anthony Richard
Porter, Arthur Reno
Porter, Barry Lavon
Porter, David Stewart
Porter, Donald James
Porter, Helen Viney (Mrs. Lewis M. Porter, Jr.)
Porter, John Roger
Porter, John Willard
Porter, John Wilson
Porter, Philip Wayland
Porter, Rutherford B.
Porter, Walter Arthur
Porter, William Lee
Porth, Donald Lester
Porthouse, Cyril Routledge
Portoghese, Philip Salvatore
Posnick, Adolph
Potchen, Edward James
Pott, Herman Theodore
Potter, Charles Steele
Potter, David Samuel
Potter, Donald Albert
Potter, Van Rensselaer
Potts, Robert Henderson
Pound, Glenn Simpson
Pounds, Ralph Linnaeus
Pour-El, Marian Boykan
Poust, John G.
Povish, Kenneth Joseph
Povolny, Mojmir
Powell, Edmund William
Powell, George Everett, Jr.
Powell, James Lawrence
Powell, Robert Nicholas
Powell, William Andrew
Power, Aloysius Francis
Power, Eugene Barnum
Power, Fremont Alvin
Power, Philip Harwick
Powers, Anne
Powers, Arthur Jay
Powers, Dudley
Powers, Odell Eugene
Powers, Philip Nathan
Powers, Raymond Edwin, Jr.
Powers, Robert Throop
Powers, Ronald Clair
Powers, Ronald Dean
Pozzatti, Rudy Otto
Prager, David
Prager, Stephen
Prall, Bert R.
Prange, Henry Carl
Pranses, Anthony Louis
Prasad, Ananda Shiva
Pratt, Edward Lowell
Pratt, Joseph Hyde, Jr.
Pratt, Philip
Pray, Lloyd Charles
Preckshot, George William
Preer, John Randolph, Jr.
Prell, Arthur Ely
Prendergast, Charles J., Jr.
Prentice, Dixon Wright
Press, Charles
Preston, David Michael
Preus, David Walter
Preus, Herman Amberg
Preus, Jacob Aall Ottesen
Preuss, Roger E(mil)
Preves, Milton
Prewitt, Carl Kenneth, Jr.
Price, Charles Morgan
Price, Dalias Adolph
Price, Donald Albert
Price, Edwin Farrow
Price, Griffith Baley
Price, Harry Steele, Jr.
Price, Jacob Myron
Price, Melvin
Price, Paxton (Pate)
Price, Raymond Glenn
Pride, Armistead S.
Priest, Paul Edward
Priestley, James Taggart, II
Priestley, William Turk
Primm, Alexander Timon, III
Primm, James Neal
Prince, Aaron Erastus
Prince, Albert Irving
Prince, Kenneth C.
Prince, Robert Mason
Prince, Thomas Richard
Prince, William Henry Wood
Pringle, Kenneth George
Pringle, Oran Allan
Prior, John Alan
Pritchard, Harold Wayne
Pritchard, Walter Herbert
Pritikin, Roland I.
Pritsker, A.B.
Pritzker, Jack Nicholas
Pritzker, Jay Arthur
Pritzker, Robert Alan
Prochnow, Herbert Victor
Proctor, Alvin Horace
Proctor, Barbara Gardner
Proctor, Lorne Douglas
Proctor, Paul Dean
Proctor, William Zinsmaster
Proffer, Ellendea Catherine
Proffitt, Roy Franklin
Prokopoff, Stephen S.
Propp, Leslie B.
Prosser, Clifford Ladd
Prosser, Franklin Pierce
Proud, G. O'Neil
Prout, Charles Henry, Jr.
Prouty, Chilton Eaton
Provost, Wally (Wallace B.)
Proxmire, William
Pruis, John J.
Pruitt, Gregory Donald
Pruitt, Malcolm Everett
Pruter, Karl Hugo
Pryor, John Carlisle
Przemieniecki, Janusz Stanislaw
Pucinski, Roman C.
Pugh, Roderick Wellington
Pugh, Samuel Franklin
Pulitzer, Emily S. Rauh (Mrs. Joseph Pulitzer, Jr.)
Pulitzer, Joseph, Jr.
Pulliam, Eugene Smith
Pulliam, Nina Mason (Mrs. Eugene C. Pulliam)
Pulte, William John
Punzo, Vincent Christopher
Purcell, Dale
Purdy, Charles Robert
Purdy, Harold Wayne
Puri, Madan Lal
Purintun, Orin
Purse, James Nathaniel
Purves, Alan Carroll
Puscas, George
Putka, Andrew Charles
Putman, Dale Cornelius
Putman, Paul
Putnam, Allan Ray
Putnam, Calvin Richard
Putnam, Frank William
Putnam, Leon Joseph
Putnam, Robert E.
Putzell, Edwin Joseph, Jr.
Pyle, Everett Gustav
Pyle, Francis Johnson
Pytell, Robert Henry
Quaal, Ward Louis
Quackenbush, Austin Joseph, Jr.
Quackenbush, Forrest Ward
Quade, Quentin Lon
Quail, John Joseph
Qualey, Carlton Chester
Quarles, Albert Merold
Quarton, William Barlow
Quayle, Calvin King
Quayle, Dan
Quayle, Thomas James
Queller, Donald Edward
Quellmalz, Frederick
Quick, Armand James
Quie, Paul Gerhardt
Quigley, Jack Allen
Quigley, Joseph Milton
Quinlan, Joseph Edward
Quinlan, Sterling Carroll
Quinn, Bayard Elmer
Quinn, James Hockley McKee
Quinn, James Leland, III
Quinn, Robert J.
Quinn, William John
Quintana, Ricardo Beckwith
Rabb, George B.
Rabinovitsj, Max
Rabjohn, Norman
Rachie, Cyrus
Radaker, Byron Claire
Radcliffe, Robert Lane
Radell, Nicholas John
Rademacher, Richard Joseph
Radock, Michael
Rae, Wesley Dennis
Raether, Howard Charles
Rafelson, Max Emanuel, Jr.
Raffel, Leroy B.
Rafferty, Keen Alexander, Jr.
Ragan, Roy Allen
Ragone, David Vincent
Rahl, James Andrew
Rahman, Aneesur
Rahman, Yueh-Erh
Rahn, Alvin Albert
Railsback, Thomas F.
Raimondi, Anthony John
Rainsford, George Nichols
Raitt, Cecil Gerald
Raitt, David Harris
Raizes, Maurice Philip
Raju, Poolla Tirupati
Rakel, Robert Edwin
Rakestraw, Warren Vincent
Rakita, Louis
Raley, Donald William
Rall, Owen
Ramachandran, Gopalasamudram Narayana
Ramage, Edwin Stephen
Ramaley, Judith Aitken
Rambo, James Edmondson
Ramey, Madison Louie
Ramlow, Donald Eric
Rammelkamp, Charles Henry, Jr.
Ramsey, Paul Willard
Ramsey, William Lee
Rand, Charles Clinton
Rand, Leon
Rand, Norfleet Hale
Rand, Sidney Anders
Randall, Dudley Felker
Randall, James Edwin
Randall, Walter Clark
Randall, William Seymour
Randolph, John Wilson
Raney, Edward Thomas
Raney, Leon
Rankin, Alan Carson
Rankin, (B.) Don
Rankin, Robert
Rannells, Will
Ranney, George Alfred
Ranz, John Haynes
Ranz, William Edwin
Rao, Narahari Kandarpa
Raper, Charles Albert
Raper, Kenneth Bryan
Raphaelson, Joel
Rapp, Gerald Duane
Rapp, John Cyril
Rappaport, Earle Samuel, Jr.
Rappaport, Roy Abraham
Rapson, Ralph
Rash, Jesse Keogh
Rasin, Rudolph Stephen
Raskind, Leo Joseph
Raskosky, Edward J.
Rasmus, Robert Nelson
Rasmusen, Roger Ward
Rasmussen, Harold Theodore
Rasmussen, Wallace N.
Ratcliffe, Myron Fenwick
Rath, Gustave Joseph
Rathbone, Donald Earl
Rathmann, Franz Heinrich
Ratigan, William O.
Ratliff, Eugene Field
Ratner, Gerald
Ratner, Lazarus Gershon
Ratnoff, Oscar Davis
Raubinger, Frederick Melton
Rauch, George Washington
Rauen, Arnold John
Rauh, John David
Rauma, John Gunnar
Raun, Earle Spangler
Raushenbush, Walter Brandeis
Raven, Peter Hamilton
Ravin, Arnold Warren
Rawley, James Albert
Rawlings, Maurice Edward
Rawson, Catharine Grote
Rawson, Merle R.
Ray, Ben T.
Ray, David Eugene
Ray, Kenneth C.
Ray, Robert D.
Ray, Robert D.
Ray, Robert Frederick
Ray, Roy Fremont
Rayman, Warren Samuel
Raymond, Robert Hugh
Raynor, John Patrick
Razak, Charles Kenneth
Read, John Conyers
Read, Willard Oliver
Reardon, John Edward
Reardon, Robert Horman
Reavis, John Wallace
Rebenack, John Henry
Rechin, Carl Leon
Rechtschaffen, Allan
Reck, W(aldo) Emerson
Rector, Gail Wesley
Redden, Jack Allison
Reddig, Edward Sterling
Reder, Robert Paul
Redman, William Charles
Redmond, Robert Francis
Redmond, William Aloysius
Redstone, Louis Gordon
Redwine, Jack Theodore
Reece, Glenn Albert
Reed, A(lfred) Byron
Reed, Charles Allen
Reed, Charles Emmett
Reed, Darwin Cramer
Reed, David Wooderson
Reed, John Frederick
Reed, John Shedd
Reed, John Wesley
Reed, Marcus George
Reed, Ronald Swain, Jr.
Reed, Ruddell, Jr.
Reed, William Earl
Reeder, Clifton Lee
Reeder, Howard Chandler
Reeder, Lee
Reeder, Pearl Ann
Reedy, George Edward
Reedy, Jerry Edward
Reedy, John Louis
Rees, Warren James
Reese, Anne Catherine Ohlson (Mrs. Edwin Lee Reese)
Reese, Bruce Alan
Reese, Everett D.
Reese, Francis Edward
Reese, Harry Browne
Reese, John Gilbert
Reese, Raymond Castle
Reeve, John Paxton
Reeves, Charles Howell
Reeves, Floyd Wesley
Reeves, Norman Pennington
Reeves, Robert Grier LeFevre
Refior, Everett Lee
Regenburg, Bernard H.
Regensteiner, Else Friedsam (Mrs. Bertold Regensteiner)
Regnery, Henry
Regula, Ralph Straus
Reh, Carl William
Reh, Francis Frederick
Rehark, Russell John
Rehn, Henry Joseph
Rehnstrom, Vernley Rae
Reich, David Lee
Reich, Edgar
Reich, Jack Egan
Reich, Peter Maria
Reichart, Walter Albert
Reichert, Jack Frank
Reichert, Norman Vernon
Reichman, Owen Howard
Reickert, Frederick Arthur
Reid, Bryan Seaborne, Jr.
Reid, Francis P.
Reid, George Williams
Reid, James Sims
Reid, James Sims, Jr.
Reid, John Edward
Reid, Loren Dudley
Reid, Morris William
Reid, William Hill
Reidenbaugh, Lowell Henry
Reidy, John Joseph
Reif, Myles William
Reiffel, Leonard
Reilly, James Dunn
Reimers, Arthur John
Reims, Clifford Waldemar
Reindel, John Donald
Reine, Francis Joseph
Reiner, Irving
Reinert, Carl M.
Reinert, Paul Clare
Reinert, Raymond Edward
Reingold, Haim
Reinhardt, Siegfried Gerhard
Reinhold, Meyer
Reinke, John Henry
Reinke, Ralph Louis
Reisner, Ensworth Thayer
Reissig, Merle Harris
Reiten, Palmer James
Reiter, Stanley
Reitman, Robert Stanley
Reizen, Maurice S.
Remak, Henry Heymann Herman
Rembolt, Raymond Ralph
Remer, Vernon Ralph
Remington, Richard Delleraine
Remini, Robert Vincent
Remsberg, Bonnie Kohn
Remsberg, Charles Andruss
Renda, Randolph Bruce
Reneker, Robert William
Renfroe, Earl Wiley
Renken, Henry Algernon
Renko, Steve, Jr.
Reno, Roger
Renshaw, Charles Clark, Jr.
Replogle, Frederick Allen
Requarth, William Henry
Resch, Glenn Allan
Reshotko, Eli
Resnekov, Leon
Rettaliata, John Theodore
Retzler, Kurt Egon
Reusche, Robert Frederick
Reuss, Henry S.
Reuss, Robert Pershing
Reusswig, Frederick Webster
Reuter, George Edward
Reutzel, Emil William, Jr.
Revzin, Marvin E.
Reynold, Gordon E.
Reynolds, A. William
Reynolds, Albert Eugene
Reynolds, Don L.
Reynolds, Earl
Reynolds, Ellsworth Galbraith
Reynolds, Ernest West
Reynolds, Fred Curtis
Reynolds, Frederick James
Reynolds, Jame H.
Reynolds, John Todd
Reynolds, John W.
Reynolds, Maynard Clinton
Reynolds, Samuel Williams
Reynolds, Thomas F.
Reynolds, Warren Gene
Reynolds, Warren Lind
Reynoldson, Walter Ward
Rezler, Julius
Reznick, Morris Martin
Rhind, James Thomas
Rhoden, Elmer Carl
Rhodes, George
Rhodes, Irwin Seymour
Rhodes, James Allen
Rhodes, Richard Lee
Rhodes, Vilas James
Riccardo, John Joseph
Rice, Arthur Louis, Jr.
Rice, Clarence Irwin
Rice, Edwin Stevens
Rice, Ernest F., Jr.
Rice, (Ethel) Ann
Rice, H. LaMarr
Rice, Harold R.
Rice, James Grundy
Rice, John Rischard
Rice, Joseph David
Rice, Raymond Main
Rice, Stuart Alan
Rich, Michael James
Rich, Willis Frank, Jr.
Richard, Calvin Aird
Richards, Gilbert Francis
Richards, Hugh Taylor
Richards, John Noble
Richards, Riley Harry
Richards, Robert Benjamin
Richards, Roger Claude
Richards, William Frederick
Richardson, Ambrose Madison
Richardson, Dean Eugene
Richardson, Donald F.
Richardson, Douglas Winslow
Richardson, Frank Charles
Richardson, Harold Wellington
Richardson, Irvine
Richardson, John Thomas
Richardson, Lloyd Merritt
Richardson, Orville Willcott
Richardson, Ransom Lloyd
Richardson, Sylvia Onesti
Richart, Frank Edwin, Jr.
Richey, Herbert Southall
Richey, Robert William
Richey, Thomas Adam
Richman, Harold Alan
Richman, John Marshall
Richman, Sumner
Richter, Earl Edward
Rickbeil, Raymond Earl
Ricketts, John Adrian
Rickey, Martin Eugene
Ricks, Michael Theodore
Riddell, Matthew Donald Rutherford
Ridder, Bernard Herman, Jr.
Riddle, Donald Husted
Rideout, Walter Bates
Ridley, Elton Taft
Riedel, Marcus Eric John
Riedy, John K.
Riegle, Donald Wayne, Jr.
Rielly, John Edward
Ries, Herman Elkan, Jr.
Rieselbach, Leroy N(ewman)
Rigdon, Vernon Drew
Righter, Richard Scott
Righter, Walter Cameron
Rikhoff, John Lawrence
Riley, David Clyde
Riley, Harold Marvin
Riley, Patrick James
Riley, Richard A.
Riley, Robert Bartlett
Riley, Warren Barbour
Rill, Michael
Rilling, John William
Rinaldo, John Beach
Rinder, George Greer
Rinder, Irwin Daniel
Rinehart, Kenneth Lloyd, Jr.
Rinehart, Raymond George
Ringel, Robert Lewis
Ringelberg, Harold Adrian
Ringenberg, Lawrence Albert
Ringer, Alexander Lothar
Ringer, Robert Kosel
Ringer, Walter Marden
Ringler, Ira
Ringler, William Andrew, Jr.
Ringness, Thomas Alexander
Rink, George Albrecht
Rink, Susan
Rinker, Carl Daniel
Rinker, George, Jr.
Riordan, Timothy James
Ripken, John Frederick
Ripley, Randall Butler
Ris, Hans
Rising, Jesse David
Risk, J. Fred
Rissler, Herbert J.
Rist, Leslie Vernon
Ristine, Richard Osborne
Ritchie, Alexander Buchan
Ritchie, Richard Lee
Rittenhouse, Joseph Wilson
Ritter, George William
Rittmaster, Robert
Ritts, Roy Ellot, Jr.
Ritz, Gordon Herron
Ritzenthaler, Arthur Bernard
River, Louis Philip
Rivette, Gerard Bertram
Rivkin, Ellis
Roach, Francis Vinson
Roach, John Robert
Roach, Thomas Adair
Robb, James Harry
Robbins, Burr L.
Robbins, Frederick Chapman
Robbins, Glaydon Donaldson
Robbins, Henry Zane
Robbins, Ray Charles
Robel, Robert Joseph
Robenalt, John Alton
Roberts, Arthur
Roberts, Bruce Everett
Roberts, Burnell Richard
Roberts, Charles Corwin
Roberts, Edwin Albert, Jr.
Roberts, Edwin George
Roberts, Harry Vivian
Roberts, James Herbert
Roberts, Kline Leslie
Roberts, Maurice A.
Roberts, Rosalee Ann
Roberts, S.M.
Roberts, Shepherd McGregor
Roberts, Theodore Harris
Roberts, Thomas Humphrey, Jr.
Roberts, William B.
Roberts, William John
Robertson, Bruce Manson
Robertson, Donald Jackson
Robertson, Edwin Wales, II
Robertson, George Leven
Robeson, Mark D.
Robin, Sidney Leon
Robins, Eli
Robinson, Alexander Cochrane, III
Robinson, Arthur Howard
Robinson, David Weaver
Robinson, Donald Keith
Robinson, Frank D.
Robinson, George Wayne
Robinson, Herbert Edwin
Robinson, James Kenneth
Robinson, John Edmund
Robinson, John Hamilton
Robinson, Paul Heron, Jr.
Robinson, Paul Minnich
Robinson, Richard Earl
Robinson, Richard Norman
Robinson, S. Benton
Robinson, Stanley Clay
Robinson, Thomas Bullene
Robinson, William Dodd
Robinson, William Ingraham
Robson, Edwin Albert
Robson, John Edwin
Roby, Frank Helmuth
Rocek, Jan
Roche, Burke Bernard
Roche, George Charles, III
Roche, James M.
Roche, Thomas Francis
Rock, William Ray
Rockwell, Perry Jack, Jr.
Rod, Donald Olaf
Rodeck, Willard Martin
Rodenberg, Sidney Dan
Rodman, George Bush
Rodman, Hugh Burgess
Rodman, Thomas D.
Roe, Jerrold Melvin
Roebuck, Carl Angus
Roeder, Robert Gayle
Roelofs, Vernon William
Roemer, James A.
Roeming, Robert Frederick

Seidel, Glenn Ernest
Seidlin, Oskar
Seidner, Frederic Jay
Seifert, George
Seifert, Ralph Louis (Edwin)
Seifert, Thomas Lloyd
Seikel, Oliver Edward
Seiler, Robert Eldridge
Seils, William George
Seitz, Reynolds C.
Sejnost, Richard Leonard
Selby, John Douglas
Selfridge, George Dever
Selig, Allan H. (Bud)
Selkurt, Ewald Erdman
Selleck, Robert W.
Sellers, James McBrayer
Sellon, William Arthur
Selonick, Edward Henry
Seltzer, Leon Zee
Selzer, Charles Louis
Sember, Michael Daniel
Seminoff, Serje Geoffrey
Semkow, Jerzy Georg
Semler, Bernard Henry
Semple, Robert Baylor
Semrow, Harry H.
Semsrott, William Henry
Sendak, Theodore Lorraine
Sengelaub, Mary Maurita
Sengstacke, John Herman Henry
Sernett, Richard Patrick
Serrin, James Burton
SerVaas, Beurt Richard
SerVaas, Cory Synhorst (Mrs. Beurt R. SerVaas)
Sesker, Monte Neil
Sesonske, Alexander
Sessions, Paul Stanley
Sessions, William Crighton
Sethna, Patarasp Rustomji
Seulberger, Ferdinand George
Sevcik, John George
Severa, Gordon
Severino, Dominick Alexander
Seward, Harry Paul
Seward, Matthew Allen
Sewell, Daniel Keith
Sewell, Jack Vincent
Sewell, William Hamilton
Sexton, Thomas Mackin
Seymour, Arthur Hallock
Seymour, Frank Marcellous
Seymour, James Owens
Seymour, Lyle Eugene
Seymour, Thaddeus
Shabat, Oscar E.
Shackelford, Donald Bruce
Shaddy, Raymond William
Shafer, B. Lyle
Shafer, Everett Earl
Shafer, Stephen John
Shafer, William Gene
Shaffer, Charles Elwood
Shaffer, Dale Eugene
Shaffer, Paul E.
Shaffer, Robert Howard
Shaffer, Thomas Eugene
Shaffer, Wayne Eugene
Shafter, Albert Jene, Jr.
Shaheen, Michael George
Shain, Irving
Shake, Curtis Grover
Shakespeare, Walter Samuel
Shambaugh, George E., Jr.
Shanahan, Elwill Mattson
Shane, Harold Gray
Shank, Howard Cortland
Shank, Robert Ely
Shank, Stephen George
Shank, William O.
Shanker, Morris Gerald
Shankland, Robert Sherwood
Shanks, Merrill Edward
Shanley, James Lyndon
Shannahan, John Henry Kelly
Shannon, Iris Reed
Shannon, Lyle William
Shannon, Michael Edward
Shapey, Ralph
Shapiro, Burton Leonard
Shapiro, Fred David
Shapiro, Harold Benjamin
Shapiro, Henry
Shapiro, Henry
Shapiro, Milton
Shapiro, Samuel Harvey
Shapiro, Sherman
Shapleigh, Warren McKinney
Shaplin, Judson Tiffany
Shappirio, David Gordon
Sharfman, Robert Jay
Sharkey, Thomas Palmer
Sharp, Allen
Sharp, Robert Weimer
Sharpe, Robert Francis
Shartle, Carroll Leonard
Shattuck, Charles Harlen
Shaver, John Rodney
Shaver, Robert Harold
Shaw, Donald Hardy
Shaw, George Robert
Shaw, James Howard
Shaw, John Harrison
Shaw, Joseph Thomas
Shaw, Kenneth Alan
Shaw, Lee Charles
Shaw, Leroy Robert
Shaw, Michael Allan
Shaw, Paul Dale
Shaw, Raymond Kenneth
Shawaker, Wayne Edward
Shay, Arthur
Shea, Donald Richard
Shea, Francis Raymond
Shea, Francis Xavier
Shea, George Beverly
Shealy, Clyde Norman
Shearer, Sybil
Shearman, Robert William
Sheatsley, Paul Baker
Sheehan, Daniel Eugene
Sheehan, Dennis William
Sheehan, John Francis
Sheehy, Howard Sherman, Jr.
Sheerin, Harry John
Sheets, George Henkle
Sheetz, Richard Smedley
Shefchik, Thomas Joseph, Jr.
Sheffield, Horace Lindsey
Sheldahl, Leon DeVere
Sheldon, John William
Sheldon, Victor Lawrence
Shell, Claude Irving, Jr.
Shelton, James Reid
Shemin, David
Shenk, John Christian, Jr.
Shennan, James Grierson
Shepard, Earl Emanuel
Shepard, Horace Armor
Shepard, Merrill
Shepard, Roger Bulkley, Jr.
Shepard, Trent Allen
Shepherd, Alan J.
Shepherd, John Calvin
Shepherd, John Herbert
Shepherd, John Thompson
Shepherd, William Gerald
Shepley, Ethan Allen Hitchcock, Jr.
Sheppard, Robert Blair
Shera, Jesse Hauk
Sheran, Robert Joseph
Sherbo, Arthur
Shere, Dennis
Shere, Louis
Sheridan, Edward Philip
Sheridan, Harriet Waltzer
Sheridan, James
Sheridan, James Edward
Sheridan, Martin
Sherman, Charles Edwin
Sherman, Saul S.
Sherman, Seymour
Sherman, Thomas Monroe
Sherman, Vernon Wesley
Shermoen, Richard Eugene
Sherry, Peter Joseph
Sherry, Richard
Shertzer, Bruce Eldon
Shervheim, Lloyd Oliver
Sherwin, John
Sherwood, Bernath Pardee, Jr.
Shetler, Richard Louis
Shewalter, Charles Ellis
Shewmon, Paul Griffith
Shideman, Frederick Earl
Shield, Richard Thorpe
Shield, Wilbur Lee, Jr.
Shields, Allen Lowell
Shields, Charles Daniel
Shields, Clifford Dale
Shields, Thomas William
Shimkin, Demitri Boris
Shindell, Sidney
Shine, Neal James
Shiner, Vernon Jack, Jr.
Shipley, George Edward
Shipley, James Ross
Shipman, E. F.
Shipman, James Johnston
Shipman, Robert Jack
Shipp, Joseph Calvin
Shirk, Charles Albert
Shive, Thomas M.
Shlyen, Ben
Shoch, David Eugene
Shoemaker, William Hutchinson
Shoenhofen, Leo H., Jr.
Sholander, Marlow Canon
Shontz, Patricia Jane (Mrs. Peter M. Shontz, Jr.)
Shoquist, Joseph William
Short, Ray Everett
Short, Robert Earl
Shouldice, Kenneth James
Shoup, Harold Arthur
Shoup, Robert John
Shrader, Erwin Fairfax
Shriver, Garner Edward
Shriver, Phillip Raymond
Shronts, John Frank
Shryock, Gerald Duane
Shryock, Russell Webster
Shubik, Philippe
Shughart, Donald L.
Shull, Franklin Buckley
Shull, Harrison
Shull, Willard Charles, III
Shumacker, Harris B, Jr.
Shuman, Nicholas Roman
Shurman, Michael Mendelsohn
Shutz, Byron Christopher
Shutz, Byron Theodore
Shwayder, David Samuel
Shy, John Willard
Shy, Paul Russel
Sibley, Willis Elbridge
Sicherman, Marvin Allen
Sick, Theodore Alfred
Sick, Wilson William, Jr.
Sickman, Laurence Chalfant Stevens
Sickmiller, Edward Paul
Sieben, Harry Albert, Jr.
Sieben, James George
Siebenthaler, Harold Jacob
Sieber, Roy
Siebers, Jack Alan
Siebring, Barteld Richard
Siegel, Jeffrey
Siegel, Sid
Sieger, Robert R.
Siegert, Arnold John Frederick
Siekman, William August
Sieling, Vernon Erwin
Siemers, William Frederick
Siert, Harry Henry
Siess, Chester Paul
Sigel, Bernard
Sigler, LeRoy Walter
Sih, Charles John
Sih, Julius Wei Wu
Sikking, Arthur Leland, Jr.
Sikorovsky, Eugene Frank
Sikula, Andrew Frank
Silets, Harvey Marvin
Silha, Otto Adelbert
Sill, Webster Harrison, Jr.
Silliman, James Orwell
Sills, Budd
Silver, David Mayer
Silver, Donald
Silver, Gerald
Silver, Howard
Silver, Melvin J.
Silver, Ralph David
Silverman, Albert A.
Silverman, Albert Jack
Silverman, Sol Richard
Silverman, Theodore N.
Silverman, William Joseph
Silverstein, Abe
Silverstein, Adolph Traub
Silverstein, Shelby (Shel)
Silverstein, Theodore
Silvoso, Joseph Anton
Sim, John Cameron
Simmons, Charles Edward Phillip
Simmons, Edward Dwyer
Simmons, John Edwards
Simmons, John William
Simmons, Ralph Oliver
Simms, Kenneth Lee
Simokaitis, Frank Joseph
Simon, Jack Aaron
Simon, John Bern
Simon, Julian Lincoln
Simon, Mordecai
Simon, Paul
Simon, Ralph
Simon, Rita James (Mrs. Julian Simon)
Simon, Seymour F.
Simon, Todd
Simon, Werner
Simon, William John
Simonet, John Thomas
Simons, Dolph Collins
Simons, Dolph Collins, Jr.
Simons, Leonard Norman Rashall
Simonton, Wesley Clark
Simpkin, Lawrence James
Simpkins, Joe
Simpkins, John Edward
Simpson, Donald James
Simpson, Ernest Clifford
Simpson, John Alexander
Simpson, John McLaren
Simpson, Lyle Lee
Simpson, Oliver Cecil
Simpson, Richard Howard
Simpson, Robert Whiteside
Simpson, Vinson Raleigh, Jr.
Simpson, Wayne
Simpson, Wilbur Herman
Sims, John LeRoy
Sims, Melvin Earl
Sims, Richard Lee
Singer, Marcus George
Singer, Marcus Joseph
Singer, Milton Borah
Singer, Ronald
Sinkula, William Joseph
Sinnema, John Ralph
Sinnott, Maurice Joseph
Sinor, Denis
Sinsabaugh, Art (Arthur Reeder)
Sinykin, Gordon
Siragusa, Charles
Siragusa, Ross David
Sisson, Everett Arnold
Sisson, George Allen
Sisson, Jacqueline Demorest
Sisson, Joseph Andrew
Sittler, Joseph
Sitton, Fred Monroe
Siu, Paul Chan-Paang
Sivage, Gerald Albert
Skadden, Donald Harvey
Skaggs, Harvey Teague
Skaggs, Lester S.
Skeels, Jack William
Skeggs, Leonard Tucker
Skeldon, Philip Cass
Skelton, Isaac Newton, IV
Skernick, Abraham
Skidmore, Howard Franklyn
Skidmore, Louis Thomas
Skidmore, Roger Wayne
Skidmore, Thomas Elliott
Skilling, Raymond Inwood
Skillman, Thomas Grant
Skilton, Robert Henry
Skinner, David Bernt
Skinner, Gordon Sweetland
Skinner, Kenneth Barnes
Skinner, Lloyd Edward
Skinner, Robert Glenn
Skirving, John Lionel
Skok, Richard Arnold
Skolrood, Robert Kenneth
Skoog, Folke Karl
Skoog, Ralph Edward
Skove, Thomas Malcolm
Skram, Joseph E.
Skramstad, Harold Kenneth, Jr.
Skrebneski, Victor
Skrowaczewski, Stanislaw
Skutt, Vestor Joseph
Slade, Gerald Jack
Slade, Hutton Davison
Slade, Llewellyn Eugene
Slade, Roy
Sladek, Ronald John
Slagle, L. Orin
Slane, Henry Pindell
Slater, John Greenleaf
Slattery, James Joseph (Joe Slattery)
Slaughter, William Edward, Jr.
Slawecki, Tadeusz Karol
Slaybaugh, David James
Slettebak, Arne
Sletto, Raymond Franklin
Slezak, John
Slichter, Charles Pence
Slife, Harry G.
Sligh, Charles Robert, Jr.
Sloan, Edward William, Jr.
Sloan, William
Slominski, Leo Frank
Sloss, Laurence Louis
Slosson, Preston William
Slotkin, Edward James
Slough, Major Carl
Slowinski, Emil John
Slowter, Edward Eugene
Smale, John Gray
Small, Burrell Leslie
Small, LaVerne Doreyn
Small, Stanton Harrison
Smalley, Donald Arthur
Smart, Jackson Wyman, Jr.
Smelser, Marshall
Smiley, Floyd Franklin, Jr.
Smiley, Robert William
Smiley, Saul Charles
Smith, A. Anthes
Smith, Allan Frederick
Smith, Allen Elmer
Smith, Arthur James Marshall
Smith, Bardwell Leith
Smith, Barnard Elliot
Smith, Bruce Harry
Smith, C. Kenneth
Smith, Carl Sylvester
Smith, Carleton
Smith, Charles Henry, Jr.
Smith, Charles Oliver
Smith, Charles Roger
Smith, Charles Wallace
Smith, D. Richard
Smith, Dale Copic
Smith, Daniel Clayton
Smith, Daniel Richard
Smith, Darwin Eatna
Smith, David Waldo Edward
Smith, Denton Henry
Smith, Donald Cameron
Smith, Donald Edward
Smith, Donald Kliese
Smith, Donald McEwen
Smith, Earl William
Smith, Eberle Minard
Smith, Edward Byron
Smith, Edward Kenneth
Smith, Edwin Burrows
Smith, Eldred Reid
Smith, Elsdon Coles
Smith, Elton Robert
Smith, Ephraim Philip
Smith, Eric Wilburn, Jr.
Smith, Eugene Preston
Smith, Everett Dale
Smith, Everett Ware
Smith, F. Alan
Smith, Frank Arthur Cushing
Smith, Frank Earl
Smith, Frank Edward
Smith, Fred George, Jr.
Smith, Frederick Coe
Smith, Geoffrey F. N.
Smith, George Baxter
Smith, Gerald Allen
Smith, Glenn Sanborn
Smith, Goff
Smith, Gordon Howell
Smith, Haddon Hartung
Smith, Harold Albert
Smith, Harold Byron, Jr.
Smith, Harold L.
Smith, Harold Philip
Smith, Hartman William
Smith, Henry Charles, 3d
Smith, J. Thomas
Smith, Jack Francis
Smith, Jackie Larue
Smith, J(ames) E(verett) Keith
Smith, James Hammond
Smith, James John
Smith, James R.
Smith, Jane Farwell
Smith, Jay Alfred
Smith, Jerome Irving
Smith, John Burnside
Smith, John Francis
Smith, John J.
Smith, Jonathan Zittell
Smith, Joseph Earl, Jr.
Smith, Joseph Victor
Smith, Karl Ulrich
Smith, Kenneth
Smith, Kenneth Byrant
Smith, Lacey Baldwin
Smith, Leo Emmet
Smith, Leonard Bingley
Smith, Leonard Charles
Smith, Linn Charles
Smith, Lloyd Bruce
Smith, Malcolm Norman
Smith, Marion Leroy
Smith, Mary Louise
Smith, Maryann
Smith, Matthew Joseph
Smith, Mervin George
Smith, Mowry
Smith, Neal Austin
Smith, Otis M.
Smith, Paul David
Smith, Paul Francis
Smith, Peter Alan Somervail
Smith, Philip George
Smith, Philip Richter
Smith, Raymond G.
Smith, Raymond Lloyd
Smith, Raymond Thomas
Smith, Raymond Thomas
Smith, Richard Griffiths
Smith, Richard Harry
Smith, Richard Lee
Smith, Richey
Smith, Robert Burns
Smith, Robert Drake
Smith, Robert Lee
Smith, Robert Nelson
Smith, Roger Bonham
Smith, Roger Dean
Smith, Roy Emerson
Smith, Seymour Alfred
Smith, Shelby
Smith, Sherman Allen
Smith, Stephen Cory
Smith, Stewart Gene
Smith, Stewart Worland, Jr.
Smith, Thomas Ross
Smith, Thomas Stevenson
Smith, Thomas Timothy
Smith, Thomas William, Jr.
Smith, Victor Earle
Smith, Virginia Dodd (Mrs. Haven Smith)
Smith, Ward
Smith, Waverly Graves
Smith, William Lewis
Smith, William P.
Smith, William Wallace
Smith, Worthington LeHuray
Smoot, Joseph Grady
Smoot, Thurlow Bergen
Smucker, Paul Highnam
Smucker, Richard Kim
Smudski, James William
Smyth, Charles Edward
Smyth, Glen Miller
Snedaker, Robert Hume, Jr.
Snelham, Thomas
Snell, John Raymond
Snider, Delbert Arthur
Snider, Lawrence K.
Snider, Robert Joe
Snider, Robert Larry
Snitzer, Martin Harry
Snively, William Daniel, Jr.
Snook, John Orla
Snortland, Howard Jerome
Snowbarger, Willis Edward
Snyder, Charles Royce
Snyder, George Edward
Snyder, Gerald Curlee
Snyder, Harold Ray
Snyder, James Newton
Snyder, John William
Snyder, Leon Carleton
Snyder, Leonard Wayne
Snyder, Lewis Emil
Snyder, Melvin Harold
Snyder, Milo F.
Snyder, Rachel Frances
Snyder, Richard Carlton
Snyder, Robert Harvey
Snyder, Robert Owen
Sobel, Walter Howard
Soelter, Robert Richard
Soffer, Alfred
Sofield, Harold Augustus
Soglin, Paul Richard
Soine, Taito Olaf
Soladay, Charles W.
Solberg, Archie Norman
Solberg, Oscar
Solberg, Winton Udell
Solinsky, Robert S.
Sollars, Benjamin Kemp
Sollo, Eugene Donald
Solomon, Izler
Solomon, Jack Avrum, Jr.
Solomon, Samuel Randolph
Solomonson, Charles D.
Soloway, Albert Herman
Solti, Georg
Soltow, James Harold
Somers, Gerald George
Sommer, Charles H.
Sommer, Howard Ellsworth
Sommer, John Robert
Sommerness, Martin Duane
Sommers, Lawrence Melvin
Sonderegger, John Forster
Sonkowsky, Robert Paul
Sonneborn, Harry Lee
Sonneborn, Tracy Morton
Sonnecken, Edwin Herbert
Sonnedecker, Glenn Allen
Sonnenschein, Hugo, Jr.
Sons, Raymond William
Soper, LaVern Gerald
Sopkin, George
Soraug, Francis Joseph
Sorby, Donald Lloyd
Sorensen, Clarence Woodrow
Sorensen, Leif Boge
Sorensen, Philip Chaikin
Sorkin, Cylvia Aaron
Sorkin, Leonard
Sorling, Carl Axel
Sornson, Helen Henrietta
Soshnik, Joseph
Sosin, Sidney
Sosnovksy, George
Sotak, Joseph Edward
Soth, Lauren Kephart
Sott, Herbert
Souder, Paul Clayton
Souers, Loren Eaton
Soules, Jack Arbuthnott
Souris, Theodore
Southall, Geneva Handy
Southern, Darrell Baker
Southgate, Marie Therese
Southgate, Wyndham Mason
Southwick, Harry Webb
Sovik, Edward Anders
Sowada, Alphonse Augustus
Sowers, Wesley Hoyt
Sowers, William Vance
Sowle, Claude Raymond
Spaeth, Raymond Julius
Spahn, Glen J.
Spahr, Charles Eugene
Spain, James Dorris, Jr.
Spalding, Vernon Benjamin
Spangle, Clarence Wilbur
Spann, Meno Hans
Spannaus, Warren Richard
Spanton, William Floyd
Spargo, Benjamin H.
Sparks, Earl Edwin
Sparks, Jack David
Sparks, John C.
Sparks, Robert Dean
Sparling, Edward James
Sparrow, Ephraim Maurice
Speaks, Donald Wesley
Spear, Louis Lawrence
Spector, Norman Bernard
Spector, Stanley
Speer, David James
Speer, George Scott
Speidel, George
Speirs, Neil P.
Spellman, James Walter
Speltz, George Henry
Spence, Clark Christian
Spence, John Daniel
Spence, Robert Dean
Spencer, Harry Arthur
Spencer, John Franklin
Spencer, Lewis Douglas
Spencer, Robert C.
Spencer, William Courtney
Spengler, William Frederick, Jr.
Sperandio, Glen Joseph
Sperlich, Harold Keith
Sperti, George Speri
Speyer, A. James
Speziale, Angelo John
Spiegel, Edwin John, Jr.
Spiegel, Modie Joseph, Jr.
Spiegelberg, Herbert
Spieker, Edmund Maute
Spier, Robert Forest Gayton
Spiller, Robert Earl
Spina, Tony J.
Spingola, Joseph Peter
Spink, Charles Claude Johnson
Spink, Wesley W.
Spinner, Frank Kenneth
Spiotta, Raymond Herman
Spitzbart, Abraham
Spitzer, John Brumback
Spivey, Charles Samuel, Jr.
Spohn, Charles L.
Spokes, Ernest Melvern
Spoor, William Arthur
Spoor, William Howard
Sprague, Austin Dever
Sprague, George Frederick
Sprague, Philip Allcock
Sprague, Randall George
Sprayregen, Joel Jay
Sprecher, Melvin
Sprecher, Robert Arthur
Sprenger, Gordon Merril
Sprenkle, Case Middleton
Spriestersbach, Duane Caryl
Springer, Georg Ferdinand
Springer, George
Springer, Gerald Norman
Springer, William Lee
Sprinkel, Beryl Wayne
Sproger, Charles Edmund
Sprowl, Charles Riggs
Sprugel, George, Jr.
Sprunger, Meredith Justin
Spulber, Nicolas
Spurway, Harold R.
Squires, James Radcliffe
Srail, George William
Sroge, Maxwell Harold
Sroka, Francis Theodore
Staba, Emil John
Stack, James Keane
Stacy, Rufus David
Stade, Charles Edward
Stadelman, William Jacob
Stadtler, Beatrice Horwitz
Stagl, John Matthew
Stagner, Ross
Stahl, Henry George
Stahmann, Mark Arnold
Staley, Delbert Cleo
Staley, Henry Mueller
Staley, Oren Lee
Staley, Wayne Daniel
Stallard, Richard Elgin
Stallknecht, Newton Phelps
Stalnaker, Armand Carl
Stalnaker, John Marshall

Stamler, Jeremiah
Stamos, John James
Stanczak, Julian
Standen, Charles Raymond
Stander, Richard Wright
Standish, Samuel Miles
Stanek, Jerome Hamata
Stangeland, Arlan Inghart
Stanhope, E. Raymond
Stanistic, Milomir Mirkov
Stanley, Arthur Jehu, Jr.
Stanley, C. Maxwell
Stanley, Cecil Eugene
Stanley, Justin Armstrong
Stanley, Lawrence Delaney
Stanley, Paul Elwood
Stanley, Richard Holt
Stanton, Frank D.
Stanton, Gerald Elroy
Stanton, James Vincent
Stanton, John William
Stanton, Robert Lee
Stanton, Roger
Stanton, Thomas Mitchell
Stapert, John Charles
Staples, Jack Robison
Stapleton, Harvey James
Stapleton, Patrick James
Stark, Camille Rene
Starker, Janos
Starkey, Paul Edward
Starr, Bryan Bartlett (Bart)
Starr, Chester G.
Starr, Maurice Kenneth
Starrs, John Richard
Stasheff, Edward
Staub, Daniel Joseph (Rusty)
Staub, E. Norman
Staub, Milton
Staudenbaur, Craig Anthony
Stauder, William Vincent
Stauderman, Bruce Ford
Stauffacher, Charles B.
Stauffer, Oscar Stanley
Stauffer, Paul Stephen
Stauffer, Stanley Howard
Stauffer, Thomas George
Stauffer, William Albert
Stavitsky, Abram Benjamin
Steadman, Jack W.
Steans, Harrison Irwin
Stearns, Martin
Steck, Norman Martin
Steck, Robert Carl
Steckel, Matthew
Stecklein, John Ellsworth
Steckler, William Elwood
Steeg, Carl Worth, Jr.
Steele, Betty Louise
Steele, Robert Michael
Steele, William Frank
Steer, Max David
Stefancic, Emil Joseph
Stefaniak, Norbert John
Steffel, Victor Lawrence
Steffes, Arnold Michael
Steffey, Albert O.
Steffy, David Louis
Stegemeier, Henri
Steger, Byron Ludwig
Stehli, Francis Greenough
Steiger, William Albert
Steigerwalt, Albert Kleckner
Stein, Bernard Alvin
Stein, Elliot H.
Stein, Eric
Stein, Gertrude Emilie
Stein, Herman David
Stein, Leon
Stein, Marvin Leonard
Stein, Richard Paul
Stein, Sydney, Jr.
Stein, Walter
Steinbicker, Paul George
Steinbrenner, George Michael, III
Steinbrink, Paul M.
Steiner, Donald Frederick
Steiner, Erich Ernst
Steiner, Peter Otto
Steiner, Wilfred Joseph
Steinhauser, Fredric Robert
Steinhoff, William Richard
Steinmann, Frederick Roger
Steinmetz, Alexander William
Steinmeyer, Robert Henry
Stella, Charles Guy, Jr.
Stelly, Matthias
Stempel, John Emmert
Stenehjem, Leland Manford
Stenger, R. G.
Stensvaag, John Monrad
Stenvig, Charles S.
Stepan, Alfred Charles, Jr.
Stepan, Frank Quinn
Stephan, Edmund Anton
Stephan, Robert Downs
Stephanopoulos, Robert George
Stephens, Donald Emmons
Stephens, Norval Blair, Jr.
Stephenson, Charles Bruce
Stephenson, Harold F.
Stephenson, Hugh Edward, Jr.
Stephenson, Roy L.
Stepto, Robert Charles
Sterling, Chandler Winfield
Sterling, Henry Somers
Stern, Clarence Ames
Stern, Edward M.
Stern, Gerald Joseph
Stern, James Lawrence
Stern, Joseph Smith, Jr.
Stern, Louis William
Stern, Richard Gustave
Stern, Richard Jay
Stern, Robert Louis
Sternberg, Paul
Sternberg, Vernon Arthur
Sterne (LeFevre), Richard Stephen
Sterner, Frank Maurice
Stevens, David Harrison
Stevens, Donald Gage
Stevens, Dwight Marlyn
Stevens, Harvey Alonzo
Stevens, Mark Chancellor
Stevens, Paul Edward
Stevens, Robert Gene
Stevens, Robert Jay
Stevens, Rolland Elwell
Stevens, Roy W.
Stevens, William Foster, III
Stevenson, Ernest Vail
Stevenson, George Franklin
Stevenson, Harold William
Stewart, Charles Leslie
Stewart, Chester Larry
Stewart, Donald Charles
Stewart, Donald Edwin
Stewart, Gathings
Stewart, Jarvis Anthony
Stewart, Melbourne George, Jr.
Stewart, Robert Murray, Jr.
Stewart, Robert Wayne
Stewart, Warren Earl
Stewart, Wellington Buel
Stichnoth, Dean Roger
Stichter, Wayne Edwin
Stickney, James Minott
Stieber, Jack
Stiers, Robert Archer
Stievater, James Edward
Stigler, George Joseph
Stiles, John Stephen
Stiles, Lindley Joseph
Stiles, Martin
Still, Ray
Stillinger, Jack Clifford
Stillings, Frank Stuart
Stillman, Donald Dennis
Stillwell, Henry Sheldon
Stine, Leo Clair
Stines, Fred, Jr.
Stipanowich, Joseph Jean
Stipher, Karl Joseph
Stipp, John Edgar
Stippes, Marvin Clifford
Stivender, Donald Lewis
Stock, Gregg Francis
Stocklen, Joseph Bernard
Stockmeyer, C. Boyd
Stocks, William George
Stockton, Jack Jenks
Stockwell, Richard E.
Stoddard, Burdett Clark
Stoddard, Charles Hatch
Stodnick, Gregory John
Stoelting, Vergil Kenneth
Stokely, Alfred Jehu
Stokes, William Forrest
Stokley, Donald Laverne
Stokley, James
Stokowski, Eugene Edward
Stokstad, Marilyn Jane
Stoll, Robert Roth
Stoll, Wilhelm
Stolle, John Fred
Stolley, Alexander
Stollman, Israel
Stolper, Warren Herbert
Stolper, Wolfgang Friedrich
Stolte, Sidney Lloyd
Stoltz, Charles Edward
Stolz, Benjamin Armond
Stolz, Robert George
Stone, Clement
Stone, Fred Dalzell
Stone, Frederick Hamilton
Stone, Gregory Prentice
Stone, Harry H.
Stone, Irving I.
Stone, Jerome H.
Stone, Loyal Russell
Stone, Marguerite Beverley
Stone, Marvin N.
Stone, Morris Samuel
Stone, Morton Joseph
Stone, Robert Frederick
Stone, Robert Joseph
Stone, Roger Warren
Stone, Sidney L.
Stone, Thomas S.
Stone, W. Clement
Stone, William Harold
Stoneburner, John Grant, Jr.
Stonecipher, Eldo Hugh
Stonehill, Robert Berrell
Stoner, Richard Burkett
Stormont, Robert Tulloch
Storry, Junis Oliver
Storvick, Truman Sophus
Stotter, David W.
Stousland, Charles Eugene, Jr.
Stout, Alan Burrage
Stout, Bill A.
Stout, John Willard
Stout, William Jewell
Stover, Harry Manning
Stover, John Ford
Stover, William Ruffner
Stowe, Leland
Strable, Edward George
Strachan, Donald M.
Strachota, Bernard Arthur
Stranberg, Don Frederick
Strandness, Theodore Benson
Strang, Charles Daniel
Strang, Marian Boundy
Strang, Ruth Hancock
Strasburger, Joseph Julius
Strasser, Edwin Francis
Strassmeyer, Mary
Straumfjord, Jon Vidalin, Jr.
Strauss, Bernard S.
Strauss, Karl Martin
Strauss, Walter Adolf
Strauss, Willis Addison
Strawbridge, Herbert Edward
Strecker, Ignatius J.
Street, John Charles
Streeter, Robert Eugene
Streeter, Victor Lyle
Streetman, John William, III
Strehlow, Roger Albert
Streichler, Jerry
Strickland, Hugh Alfred
Strickland, William Alexander, Jr.
Strickler, Ivan K.
Stright, I. Leonard
Strnad, James John
Strodel, Robert Carl
Strohl, Clarence Orville
Strohm, John Louis
Strom, Everald Hanson
Strom, Lyle Elmer
Stromberg, Melvin Willard
Stronach, William Charles
Strong, Carter Bruce
Strong, Frederick Smith, Jr.
Strong, Merle Edward
Strong, William Augustus
Strong, William Lee
Strother, George B.
Strothman, Maurice Henry, Jr.
Strotz, Robert Henry
Stroud, Joe Hinton
Stroud, Malcolm Herbert
Stroup, Atlee LaVere
Strubbe, John Lewis
Strubbe, Thomas R.
Struchen, J Maurice
Struever, Stuart McKee
Struggles, John Edward
Strunk, Norman
Stryker, Clinton Everett
Stryker, Sheldon
Stuart, Joseph Martin
Stuart, Robert
Stuart, Robert Douglas, Jr.
Stuart, Thomas Joseph
Stuart, William Corwin
Stubbins, James Burnside
Stubbs, Francis Leon
Stucky, Kenneth Joseph
Stucky, Marvin Wayne
Studden, William J.
Studer, William Joseph
Studier, Martin Herman
Studsgaard, Anker Christian
Stuebner, Erwin August
Stuehr, John Edward
Stuit, Dewey Bernard
Stull, Richard John
Stull, William DeMott
Stults, Allen Parker
Stundza, Thomas John
Sturdivant, Frederick David
Sturges, Richard Barrett
Styan, John Louis
Styles, William Brewster
Stynes, Stanley Kenneth
Suchors, William James
Sudler, Louis Courtenay
Suerth, John Charles
Sugar, Oscar
Sugarman, Nathan
Sugihara, James Masanobu
Suhre, Walter Anthony, Jr.
Sullivan, Bolton
Sullivan, Francis Copeland
Sullivan, Frank E.
Sullivan, George Raymond
Sullivan, James Francis
Sullivan, James Hall
Sullivan, Jeremiah David
Sullivan, John, Jr.
Sullivan, John Joseph
Sullivan, John W.
Sullivan, Joseph B.
Sullivan, Joseph Patrick
Sullivan, R. E.
Sullivan, Richard Eugene
Sullivan, Richard Thomas
Sullivan, Robert Emmett, Sr.
Sullivan, Robert Francis
Sullivan, Thomas Patrick
Sullivan, William Albert, Jr.
Sullivan, William James
Sullivant, Robert Scott
Suloway, Irwin Jerome
Sultan, Paul Edward
Summers, Hollis
Summitt, (William) Robert
Sundaram, Swaminatha
Sundberg, R. Dorothy
Sundquist, Wesley Burton
Sunukjian, Helen
Super, Robert Henry
Surdam, Robert McClellan
Suriano, Raffaele
Sursa, Charles David
Suskind, Raymond Robert
Sussman, Alfred Sheppard
Sussman, Sidney X.
Sutera, Salvatore Philip
Sutherland, Donald Wayne
Sutherland, Ronald Roy
Suthers, Roderick Atkins
Sutphin, Samuel Reid
Sutton, Albert Alton
Sutton, David B.
Sutton, George Edwin
Sutton, Robert Mize
Suzuki, Michio
Swain, Frederick Morrill, Jr.
Swain, Henry Huntington
Swain, O.E.
Swan, James Wesley
Swan, Joyce Alonzo
Swaney, Russel Alger
Swank, Ben R.
Swank, Emory Coblentz
Swanson, A. Herbert
Swanson, Alfred Bertil
Swanson, Bernet Steven
Swanson, Carroll Arthur
Swanson, Charles Elroy
Swanson, Don Richard
Swanson, Donald Frederick
Swanson, Dwight Harold
Swanson, Lloyd Oscar
Swanson, Robert Draper
Swanson, Robert Killen
Swanson, Roy Arthur
Swanson, Roy Paul
Swanson, Vernon Andrew
Swarthout, Herbert Marion
Swartz, Donald Everett
Swartzendruber, Dale
Swearingen, John Eldred
Sweeney, Asher William
Sweeney, (Charles) Leo
Sweeney, James Raymond
Sweeney, James Thomas, Jr.
Sweeney, Leo Patrick Augustine
Sweet, Bernard
Sweet, Cody
Sweet, Philip W.K., Jr.
Sweet, Waldo Earle
Sweeting, George
Swenson, Birger
Swenson, Clayton A.
Swenson, George Warner, Jr.
Swenson, Lowell Theodore
Swenson, Melvin John
Swibel, Charles Robert
Swift, A. Dean
Swift, Edward Foster, III
Swift, George Hastings, Jr.
Swift, Hewson Hoyt
Swigert, James Mack
Swihart, James Calvin
Swing, Gael Duane
Swinyard, Alfred Wilbur
Swisher, Scott Neil
Swope, Harold Roy
Swygert, Luther Merritt
Sykes, Weathers York
Sylvester, George Howard
Sylvester, Norbert A.
Symes, Arthur Lee
Symon, Keith Randolph
Syndergaard, Parley Rex
Synhorst, Melvin D.
Syse, Glenna Marie Lowes
Sytsma, John Frederick
Syverson, Aldrich
Szabo, Joseph Charles
Szathmáry, Louis István, II
Szesko, Lenore Rundle
Szoka, Edmund Casimir
Szybalski, Waclaw
Szymanski, Frederick John
Taaffe, Edward James
Taaffe, James Griffith
Taaffe, Robert Norman
Tabacchi, Fred Lawrence
Tabakoff, Widen
Tabin, Julius
Tachdjian, Mihran O.
Tack, Peter Isaac
Tacker, Willis Arnold, Jr.
Taeuber, Karl E(rnst)
Taft, Charles Phelps
Taft, Dudley Sutphin
Taft, Frederick Lovett
Taft, Robert, Jr.
Taft, William Howard
Taggart, Ross Edgar
Taibleson, Mitchell Herbert
Taibleson, W.B.
Taira, Koji
Tait, James M.
Tajo, Italo
Takacs, Lajos Ferenc
Talbert, Ernest William
Talbott, Nelson Strobridge
Talkington, Robert Van
Tall, William Elmer, Jr.
Tallchief, Maria
Talley, Warren Dennis Rick
Talmadge, Robert Louis
Talso, Peter J.
Tamarkin, Robert Allen
Tamraz, Lincoln Samuel
Tanaka, Tomoyasu
Tangerman, Margaretta Sackville
Tankin, Richard Samuel
Tankus, Harry
Tannenbaum, Stanley Irving
Tanselle, Donald William
Taoka, George Mazumi
Tappan, William Richard
Tappen, Neil Campbell
Taren, James Arthur
Tarkenton, Francis Asbury
Tarlov, Alvin Richard
Tarr, Curtis W.
Tarr, David William
Tarzian, Mary (Mrs. Sarkes Tarzian)
Tatz, Paul Henry
Taussig, James Thomas
Tavard, George Henry
Tave, Stuart Malcolm
Taw, Dudley Joseph
Tax, Sol
Taylor, Ardell Nichols
Taylor, C. James
Taylor, Charles Edwin
Taylor, Daniel John
Taylor, D(arl) Coder
Taylor, David George
Taylor, Donald Arthur
Taylor, Edwin William
Taylor, Fred Rankin
Taylor, George Allen
Taylor, Henry Longstreet
Taylor, Herbert John
Taylor, Howard Roy
Taylor, James Stewart
Taylor, Jay Eugene
Taylor, John B.
Taylor, John Clyde, Jr.
Taylor, John Frank Adams
Taylor, John Richard
Taylor, John Wilkinson
Taylor, Joseph Thomas
Taylor, Kenneth Nathaniel
Taylor, Phillip Seyfang
Taylor, Robert Cooper
Taylor, Robert James
Taylor, Robert William
Taylor, Ross McLaury
Taylor, Ryland Arthur (Riley)
Taylor, Thomas Norwood
Taylor, William James
Teach, Gordon L.
Teare, Wallace Gleed
Teasdale, Joseph Patrick
Tecklenburg, Harry
Teece, Robert Dayton, Sr.
Teegarden, Kenneth Leroy
Teichroew, Daniel
Teitelbaum, Philip
TeKolste, Dale
Telfer, Bruce Thomas
Telleen, John Martin
Telling, Edward Riggs
Telser, Lester Greenspan
Temin, Howard Martin
Tempas, Cornelius John
Templar, George
Temple, Wayne Calhoun
Templin, Robert Earl
Tendam, Donald Jan
Tenenbaum, Michael
Teninga, Walter Henry
Tennant, Donald George
Tenney, Merrill Chapin
Terkel, Studs Louis
Terkhorn, Henry K.
Terpstra, William Cornelius
Terra, Daniel James
Terrell, Richard L.
Terry, Clifford Lewis
Terry, Frank Reilly
Terry, Joseph Guilford
Terwilliger, Herbert Lee
Tesauro, Dominic Aloysius
Teschner, Richard Rewa
Test, Charles Edward
Tester, John Robert
Testolin, Reno Joseph
Tetrick, Elbert Lain
Thaden, Edward Carl
Thalacker, Arbie Otto
Thalberg, Irving, Jr.
Tharp, Carter B.
Thatcher, John Sherman
Thayer, Harold Eugene
Theil, Henri
Theis, Francis William
Theis, Frank Gordon
Thelen, Herbert Arnold
Thelin, Calvin Blaine
Theodoroff, B. James
Theuer, Fred George
Thibault, John Crowell
Thiede, Wilson Bickford
Thiemann, Charles Lee
Thieme, Walter Irving
Thierry, John Adams
Thistlethwaite, Robert Lee
Thoburn, David Mills
Thodos, George
Thoele, Charles Edward
Thomas, Beth Eileen Wood (Mrs. Raymond O. Thomas)
Thomas, Bruce Wallace
Thomas, Charles Allen
Thomas, Charles Franklin
Thomas, Christopher Yancey
Thomas, Edwin John
Thomas, Elmer Marshall
Thomas, Frank Almerine, Jr.
Thomas, Frederick W.
Thomas, George Sloan
Thomas, James Gladwyn
Thomas, James Samuel
Thomas, John Joseph
Thomas, Joseph Harruff
Thomas, Lawrence Bruce
Thomas, Llywelyn Murray
Thomas, Mark Stanton
Thomas, Morgan Irwyn
Thomas, Norman Carl
Thomas, O. Pendleton
Thomas, Payne Edward Lloyd
Thomas, Philip Stanley
Thomas, R. David
Thomas, Richard L.
Thomas, Robert Jay
Thomas, Robert Wilburn
Thomas, Russell
Thomas, Todd Edwin
Thomas, William J.
Thomas, William Kernahan
Thomforde, Clifford John
Thompson, Allen Paul
Thompson, Barbara Storck
Thompson, Bert Allen
Thompson, Blair Harris
Thompson, Clarence Miles, Jr.
Thompson, Craig Snover
Thompson, Dale Moore
Thompson, Dudley
Thompson, Edward Charles, Jr.
Thompson, Era Bell
Thompson, Everett Steven
Thompson, Glenn
Thompson, Hannis Woodson, Jr.
Thompson, Hugh Lee
Thompson, James Robert
Thompson, Jettie King
Thompson, John Douglas
Thompson, John Leslie
Thompson, John S.
Thompson, Joseph Earl
Thompson, Karl Frederick
Thompson, Larry Clark
Thompson, Louis Milton
Thompson, M. B.
Thompson, Manley Hawn, Jr.
Thompson, Maynard
Thompson, Milton Douhan
Thompson, Morley Punshon
Thompson, Morris Milholland
Thompson, Richard Horner
Thompson, Richard Neil
Thompson, Thomas Henry
Thompson, Thomas Miller
Thompson, Thomas Sanford
Thompson, Tyler
Thompson, Wayne Edward
Thompson, Willard Linn
Thompson, William Franklin
Thompson, William Hayton
Thomsen, Ib
Thomsen, John G.
Thomson, Bruce Randolph
Thomson, Harry Pleasant, Jr.
Thomson, James Campbell
Thorelli, Hans B.
Thoresen, Asa Clifford
Thorfinnson, Ross Lawrence
Thorkelson, Willmar
Thornberry, David Ritchie
Thorndal, Herbert Louis
Thorne, Marlowe Driggs
Thornton, Frank Eberle
Thornton, Gerald DeWayne
Thorpe, James Franklin
Thorshov, Roy Norman
Thorson, Gerald Howard
Thorson, Oswald Hagen
Thorson, Ralph Edward
Thorson, Reuben
Thorson, Thomas Bertel
Thrall, Arthur Alvin
Thrash, Patricia Ann
Thrasher, Jack Rall
Threlkeld, James LeRoy
Throckmorton, Lynn Hiram
Throckmorton, Robert Bentley
Throckmorton, Tom D.
Throdahl, Monte Corden
Thuleen, Roland Howard
Thurber, Cleveland
Thurber, Cleveland, Jr.
Thurber, Donald MacDonald Dickinson
Thurlow, Willard Rowand
Thurman, Christa Charlotte Mayer
Thurman, John Royster, III
Thurmond, Nate
Thurston, George Riley, Jr.
Thurston, Marlin Oakes
Thyen, James Conrad
Tideman, Philip Lundsten
Tidrick, Robert Thompson
Tiedeman, David Valentine
Tieken, Theodore David
Tietjen, John Henry
Tigerman, Stanley
Tigges, Kenneth Edwin
Tigrak, Mehmet Faut
Tillman, Frank Aubrey
Tillmann, George Lloyd
Tillstrom, Burr
Tilmon, James Alphonso, Sr.
Ting, Tsuan Wu
Tinstman, Dale Clinton
Tipton, Clyde Raymond, Jr.
Tiscornia, Lester Clinton
Tisdale, Stuart Williams
Titsworth, John Valentine
Toalson, Nathan Augustus
Tober, Lester Victor
Tobias, Russell Stuart
Tobin, Richard Thomas
Tocco, James
Todd, Alva Cress
Todd, Harry Williams
Todd, John Joseph
Todd, Lee John
Todd, Paul Harold, Jr.
Todd, Thomas Carmel
Todd, William Lewis
Todd, William Miller
Todd, Zane Grey
Toepfer, Louis Adelbert
Toland, James Alfred Lewis
Toles, Edward Bernard
Tolin, Cecil Alvin
Toll, Daniel Roger
Tolle, Donald James
Tomanek, Gerald Wayne
Tomasek, Henry John
Tomes, James Steel
Tomes, Mark Louis
Tomlin, Eugene Bernard
Tompkins, Willis Lynn
Tone, Kenneth Edward
Tone, Philip Willis
Tongue, William Walter
Tonsor, Stephen John
Tooill, Kenneth du Vall
Topper, Joseph Ray

Toppin, Clare Thomas
Topping, Peter (William)
Torchiana, Donald Thornhill
Torchinsky, Abe
Torda, T. Paul
Tordoff, Harrison Bruce
Torgersen, Torwald Harold
Torgerson, Truman
Torley, John Frederic
Tormey, John L.
Tornabene, Charles A.
Torrace, William G.
Torres, Fernando
Torrielli, Andrew Joseph
Torrington, William Paul
Torrison, Mandt
Totman, Conrad Davis
Toulmin, Stephen Edelston
Touloukian, Yeram Sarkis
Tourlentes, Thomas Theodore
Toussaint, Wayne E.
Tow, Clarence Wesley
Tower, Lucia Elizabeth (Mrs. Edward P. Troy)
Tower, Raymond Camille
Towers, Kenneth Dale
Towner, Lawrence William
Townsend, Burt Allison
Townsend, Earl Cunningham, Jr.
Townsend, Lynn Alfred
Townsend, Paul Henson
Townsend, Ronald Dee
Tracy, Eugene Arthur
Tracy, Theodore James
Trahman, Carl Richard
Train, Jack Durkee
Travers, Robert Morris William
Travers, Thomas Joseph
Travis, Dempsey Jerome
Traxler, Bob
Treadway, Lyman Hambright, III
Trebilcott, James Joseph
Treckelo, Richard M.
Trecker, Francis Julius
Tredway, John Thomas
Treffert, Darold Allen
Treiman, Edward
Tremayne, Bertram William, Jr.
Tremonti, Joseph Benjamin
Trenkmann, Richard J.
Treon, William Cornelius
Treumann, William Borgen
Treves, Samuel Blain
Trezevant, John Gray
Triandis, Harry Charalambos
Trichel, Gervais William
Trienens, Howard Joseph
Trifa, Valerian D.
Trigg, Paul Reginald, Jr.
Trimble, George Simpson
Trimble, Marsh Paul
Trimble, Paul Edwin
Trinkaus, Charles Edward, Jr.
Trippet, Byron Kightly
Trotter, Donald McLean
Trotter, John Ellis
Trova, Ernest Tino
Trow, Robert Charles
Trowbridge, Calvin D.
Trowbridge, Charles Lambert
Trowbridge, Frederick Newell
Trowbridge, Roy Post
Truby, John Louis
Truce, William Everett
Trudeau, Garry B.
Trueblood, David Elton
Trued, Constantine
Trufant, Samuel Adams
Truman, Bess Wallace (Mrs. Harry S. Truman)
Trump, Alfred George, Jr.
Trump, Robert M.
Trump, Ross Myron
Trussell, Albert Clyde
Truxell, Robert W.
Trytten, Merriam Hartwick
Tsou Tang
Tsuchiya, Henry Mitsumasa
Tuatay, Hulusi
Tuchman, Joseph
Tucker, Daniel Eugene
Tucker, Don Eugene
Tucker, Robert C.
Tucker, Robert L.
Tucker, Thomas Allen
Tuckey, John Sutton
Tuerkheimer, Frank Mitchel
Tull, E. Don
Tullio, Peter A.
Tullis, Richard Barclay
Tully, Richard Lowden
Tulsky, Alex Sol
Tunks, Frederick Edward
Tuohy, John Joseph
Turben, Claude Franklin
Turcotte, Jeremiah George
Turk, Leonard Gerald
Turkevich, Anthony Leonid
Turnbull, Charles Vincent
Turnbull, Don Mason
Turnbull, Robert George
Turner, Almon Richard
Turner, Arthur Edward
Turner, Basil Sidney
Turner, Darwin Theodore Troy
Turner, Edward Clark
Turner, Fred L.
Turner, Harry Edward
Turner, Harry Morris
Turner, Hester Hill
Turner, John Elliot
Turner, Larry Eugene

Turner, Lynn Warren
Turner, Lynne Alison (Mrs. Paul H. Singer)
Turner, Othel DeVoice
Turner, Peter Merrick
Turner, Richard Clark
Turner, Robert Kean, Jr.
Turner, Sol
Turner, W. B.
Turner, Walter James
Turner, William Steele
Turnquist, Nels Ernest
Turquette, Atwell Rufus
Tusken, Roger Anthony
Tussing, Robert Theodore
Tutt, Charles Leaming, Jr.
Tuttle, Jay Forrester
Tuttle, Sherwood Dodge
Twarog, Leon Ignace
Tweedie, Earl Robert
Twersky, Victor
Twiss, Page Charles
Twyman, Robert Wickliffe
Tyce, Francis Anthony
Tye, Joseph Claire
Tyer, Travis Earl
Tyler, David Malcolm
Tyler, Frederick Clifford, Jr.
Tyler, Leslie J.
Tyler, Ralph Sargent, Jr.
Tyler, Varro Eugene
Tylman, Stanley Daniel
Tyner, Neal Edward
Tyree, Alan Dean
Tyree, Donald Andrew
Tyrrell, Richard Hanlon
Tyson, Remer Hoyt, Jr.
Ubbelohde, Carl William
Uber, Lowell Donald
Uelner, Roy Walter
Uhl, Kenneth Paul
Uhlenhopp, Harvey Harold
Uhlenhuth, Eberhard Henry
Uhr, Leonard Merrick
Uhrig, Daniel James
Uihlein, Robert August, Jr.
Ulevich, Neal Hirsh
Ullestad, Harold Norman
Ulrich, Benjamin Harrison, Jr.
Ulrich, Myron Wilbur
Ulrich, Roger Elwood
Ulry, Orval Lee
Ulstrom, Robert Alger
Ultan, Lloyd
Ultmann, John Ernest
Underkofler, James Russell
Underwood, Benton J.
Underwood, Robert Charles
Undlin, Charles Thomas
Ungar, Frank
Unger, Leonard Howard
Unger, Sherman Edward
Unklesbay, Athel Glyde
Unna, Klaus Robert Walter
Unser, Bobby
Uotila, Urho Antti Kalevi
Upjohn, Everett Gifford
Upshaw, Harry Stephan
Urbanek, James Frank
Urbom, Warren Keith
Uretz, Robert Benjamin
Urry, Wilbert Herbert
Urse, Vladimir George
Useem, John Hearld
Utley, Charles Bland
Utrecht, James C.
Utt, Glenn S., Jr.
Uttal, William R(eichenstein)
Utter, Merton Franklin
Uyeki, Eugene Shigemi
Vacano, Wolfgang
Vail, Herman Lansing
Vail, Thomas Van Husen
Vainstein, Rose
Vaisrub, Samuel
Valdman, Albert
Valk, Robert Earl
Valk, William Lowell
Valley, Doris Lorraine
Van Aken, William Russell
Van Allen, James Alfred
Van Andel, Jay
Van Arsdale, Talman Walker, Jr.
Van Arsdell, Paul Marion
Van Atta, Robert Ernest
Van Bergen, Frederick Hall
Van Brunt, Constance
Van Brunt, Constance
van Buitenen, Johannes Adrian Bernard
Vance, Elbridge Putnam
Vance, Graham Alexander
Vance, James
Vance, Joseph Anderson, Jr.
Vance, Lee
Vandamme, Jacques Marie
Van den Akker, Johannes Archibald
Vandenburgh, Edward Clinton, III
Van der Eb, Henry Gerard
Vanderlind, Merwyn Ray
Vandermolen, Mimi Willemina
Van der Poel, Cornelius J.
Vanderstappen, Harrie Albert
Vander Veen, Richard Franklin
Vander Velde, John Christian
Vanderwicken, Edwin Pierce
Vanderwier, Constance Jean
Van Deventer, William Carlstead
Vande Visse, Orie John
Van De Weghe, Raymond Francis
Van Doren, Charles

Van Dusen, Richard Campbell
Van Duyn, Mona Jane
Van Dyke, Vernon Brumbaugh
Van Elderen, Marlin James
Van Gorkom, Jerome William
VanHagen, George Ely, III
VanHandel, Ralph Anthony
Van Hauer, Robert
VanHeukelom, Raymond Richard
Van Hoefen, Hari
Van Hoek, Robert
Van Housen, Edward Irvin
Vanik, Charles A.
Van Leeuwen, Gerard
Van Lier, Norm
Van Mell, Herman Teufel
Van Meter, Abram DeBois
Van Meter, Craig
VanMeter, Theodore
Van Ness, James Edward
Van Nice, Clement
Van Oostenburg, Gordon
Van Oosterhout, Martin D.
VanOrdstrand, Howard Scott
Van Pelt, Robert
Van Praag, Alex, Jr.
Van Schooneveld, Cornelis Hendrik
Vanselow, Neal Arthur
Van Sickle, Bruce Marion
Van Tassel, David Dirck
Van Tassel, Karl Raymond
Van Til, William
Van Valkenburg, Mac Elwyn
Van Valkenburg, Paul
Van Vlack, Lawrence Hall
Van Vlissingen, Arthur
Van Wylen, Gordon John
Van Zante, Shirley Mae
Van Zanten, Frank Veldhuyzen
VanZelst, Theodore William
van Zwoll, Cornelius
Varco, Richard Lynn
Varga, Richard Steven
Varner, Barton Douglas
Varner, Durward Belmont
Vass, Guy Boyd
Vaughan, Alfred Leland
Vaughan, Herbert Edward
Vaughan, James Herbert, Jr.
Vaughan, James Samson
Vaughan, Richard Henry
Vaughn, Charles Melvin
Vaughn, Dorris Weldon
Vaughn, Robert Allen
Veale, Tinkham, II
Vecoli, Rudolph John
Vedder, Blair
Vedder, Byron Charles
Veeck, William Louis
Veeder, Nicholas Phipps
Veis, Arthur
Veit, Fritz
Velardo, Joseph Thomas
Velicer, Leland Frank
Velt, Werner
Veltman, Peter
Velzen, Bernard Henry
Venema, Maynard Peter
Veneman, Gerard Earl
Ventura, Frank Robert
Venzke, Walter George
Veraldi, Lewis Carmen
Verber, Richard William
Verbrugge, Frank
Verdeyen, Joseph Thomas
Verdier, Leonard D'Ooge, Jr.
Verduin, Jacob
Vereen, Robert Charles
Verger, Don Marshall
Verity, Calvin William, Jr.
Verma, Manindra Kishore
Vermeil, Stanley Mario
Vermeulen, Cornelius W.
Vernier, Robert Lawrence
Vernon, David Harvey
Verschoor, Curtis Carl
Ver Steeg, Clarence Lester
Vertes, Victor
Vespa, Ned Angelo
Vesselinovitch, Stan D.
Vestling, Carl Swensson
Vey, Ebenezer
Veys, Albert Louis
Veysey, Arthur Ernest
Vick, Homer Jerome
Vilter, Richard William
Vincent, Dietrich Hermann
Vincent, Howard Paton
Vincze, Tibor
Vining, Richard Alfred
Vinograde, Bernard
Virdon, William Charles
Virzi, Richard A.
Visek, Willard James
Viskanta, Raymond
Visotsky, Harold Meryle
Visser, John Evert
Vitale, Philip H.
Vivas, Eliseo
Vivian, Weston Edward
Vivrett, Walter Koellein
Vlasin, Raymond Daniel
Vodovnik, Raymond Frank
Vodrey, William Henry
Voegelin, Charles Frederick
Voelker, John Donaldson (Robert Traver)
Vogel, Arthur Anton
Vogel, Charles Joseph
Vogel, Cyril J.
Vogel, Manfred Henry
Vogel, Robert
Vogel, William Dickerman
Vogt, John Henry

Voigt, Adolf Frank
Voigt, Keith Marion
Voigt, Stuart Alan
Voit, Richard Louis
Voldseth, Edward Victor
Volk, Garth William
Volkober, John Anton
Voll, Bernard John
Vollen, Robert Jay
Volwiler, Ernest Henry
Vonesh, Raymond James
von Glahn, Gerhard Ernst
Von Hoffmann, George
von Lang, Frederick William
Von Tersch, Lawrence Wayne
von Wyss, Marc Robert
Voorhees, Alan Manners
Voris, Harold Cornelius
Vormelker, Rose
Vorys, Arthur Isaiah
Voss, Jack Donald
Voss, Jerrold Richard
Voss, Omer Gerald
Voth, Melvin H.
Vowles, Donald DeForest
Vowles, Richard Beckman
Voxman, Himie
Voysey, Frank Ernest
Vrablik, Edward Robert
Vrba, William Henry
Vredenburg, Dwight Charles
Vredenburgh, John Culloden
Waas, David Asher
Wachowski, Theodore John
Wacker, Frederick Glade, Jr.
Wada, Harry Nobuyoshi
Waddles, Charleszetta Lina Campbell
Wade, Harry Van Nuys
Wade, James Francis
Wade, Jay Paul
Wade, John Edward
Wade, John William
Wade, Richard Gene
Wadlin, George Knowlton, Jr.
Wadsworth, George Leland
Wadsworth, Homer Clark
Waetjen, Walter Bernhard
Wagenknecht, Robert Edward
Waggoner, George Ruble
Waggoner, Raymond Walter
Waggoner, William Comer
Wagman, Frederick Herbert
Wagner, Durrett
Wagner, Edward Frederick
Wagner, Everett Frank
Wagner, Harvey Arthur
Wagner, Howard Otto
Wagner, John A.
Wagner, John Addington, Jr.
Wagner, John Garnet
Wagner, Leonard George
Wagner, Ralph Charles
Wagner, Richard
Wagner, Richard
Wagner, Robert Wayne
Wagner, Thomas Herman
Wagner, Warren Herbert, Jr.
Wagner, Wienczyslaw Joseph
Wagner, William Charles
Wagoner, Kenneth Shrout
Wagonseller, James Myrl
Wagstaff, Robert Wilson
Wahl, Arthur Charles
Wahl, Eberhard Wilhelm
Wahlen, Edwin Alfred
Wahlert, Robert Henry
Wahlke, John Charles
Wahlstrom, Lawrence Ferdinand
Wahoski, Helen Isabel
Waite, Daniel Elmer
Wakefield, Benton McMillin, Jr.
Wakefield, Howard
Wakefield, Theodore Dunmore
Wakeley, John Halbert
Wakim, Khalil Georges
Walaszek, Edward Joseph
Walbot, Virginia
Walch, W. Stanley
Walden, Robert Edison
Waldman, Bernard
Waldo, Ralph Emerson
Waldron, Charles Marcian
Waldstein, Sheldon Saul
Walgenbach, Paul Henry
Walgreen, Charles Rudolph, Jr.
Walgreen, Charles Rudolph, III
Waling, Joseph Lee
Walinski, Nicholas Joseph
Walker, Albert Lyell
Walker, Bruce Edward
Walker, Daniel
Walker, Donald B.
Walker, Duard Lee
Walker, E. Jerry
Walker, Everette Leroy
Walker, Francis Gene
Walker, George Herbert, III
Walker, Harold Blake
Walker, Howard
Walker, Jerald Carter
Walker, Pinkney Calvin
Walker, Richard Harold
Walker, Richard Winfrey
Walker, Robert Alander
Walker, Robert Mowbray
Walker, Ronald Edward
Walker, Russell T.
Walker, Waldo Sylvester
Walkonen, Helvi Esther
Wall, Arthur Edward Patrick
Wall, Fred Graham
Wall, (Hermon) Duncan
Wall, James McKendree

Wall, Joseph Frazier
Wallace, Donald Gordon
Wallace, Dwane L.
Wallace, Hugh Donald
Wallace, James Brevard
Wallace, James Donald
Wallace, Jane Young (Mrs. Donald H. Wallace)
Wallace, John Francis
Wallace, John Malcolm
Wallace, Leon Harry
Wallace, Ralph Howes
Wallace, Robert Francis
Wallace, William Douglas
Wallach, Don H.
Wallach, Luitpold
Wallach, Philip
Waller, George Macgregor
Waller, John Oscar
Waller, Richard Conrad
Wallerstedt, Robert W.
Wallerstein, David B.
Wallin, Franklin Whittelsey
Wallin, Winston Roger
Walsh, Chad
Walsh, James Clement
Walsh, James Patrick, Jr.
Walsh, John Charles
Walsh, Loren Melford
Walster, Elaine Catherine (Mrs. G. William Walster)
Walster, George William
Walt, Dick K.
Walter, Frank Sherman
Walter, Paul William
Walter, Robert Irving
Walters, Donald E.
Walters, Everett
Walters, Waltman
Walters, William LeRoy
Walther, Don Herman
Walton, Alan George
Walton, Charles Whitney, III
Walton, Lloyd Barker
Walton, William C.
Waltz, Jon Richard
Waltzer, Herbert
Walzl, Florence LeDuc Litchfield (Mrs. Edward McColgan Walzl)
Wambach, Edward John
Wanamaker, Robert Joseph
Wanda, Dimitry
Wanderone, Rudolf Walter (Minnesota Fats)
Wandmacher, Cornelius
Wang, L. Edwin
Wangaard, Arthur Carl, Jr.
Wangelin, Harris Kenneth
Wankelman, Willard Fred
Wanous, Edward Elmer
Wanvig, Chester Odin, Jr.
Ward, Daniel P.
Ward, Donald Butler
Ward, Donovan Frederick
Ward, Dudley Avery
Ward, Elmer L.
Ward, George Henry
Ward, Mrs. John Harris (Mary Van Etten)
Ward, Louis Emmerson
Ward, Louis Larrick
Ward, Richard Guerin
Ward, Robertson, Jr.
Ward, Sylvan Donald
Ward, Thomas Nelson
Ward, Wallace Dixon
Ward, Warren Hayden
Warden, Gail Lee
Wardlow, Ervin Eugene
Ware, Karl Ellis
Ware, Mitchell
Ware, Richard Anderson
Warfield, Gerald Alexander
Warfield, Paul Dryden
Warfield, William Caesar
Warin, Edward George
Waring, Edward Graham, Jr.
Waring, Walter Weyler
Warkany, Josef
Warmack, John Lee
Warner, Eldon Dezelle
Warner, Emory Dean
Warner, George Swift
Warner, Harry Hathaway
Warner, Huber Richard
Warner, James Daniel
Warner, Robert Mark
Warner, William Hamer
Warns, Raymond H.
Warren, Gerald Emery
Warren, James Caldwell
Warren, James Vaughn
Warren, Kenneth Austin
Warren, L.D.
Warren, Louis Austin
Warren, Richard M.
Warren, Robert Willis
Warriner, Charles King
Warrington, John Wesley
Wartell, C. Robert
Warwick, Ronald Eugene
Wasan, Darsh Tilakchand
Washa, George William
Washburn, Paul
Wasiolek, Edward
Wasmuth, Edmund Max
Watchman, William Surtess, Jr.
Waterhouse, John Percival
Waters, Muddy (McKinley Morganfield)
Watkins, Daniel Joseph
Watkins, George Harold
Watkins, Glenn Elson
Watkins, Hays Thomas
Watkins, Lloyd Irion

Watrel, Albert Adam
Watrous, David Gapen
Watrous, James Scales
Watson, C. Gordon
Watson, Catherine Elaine
Watson, Cecil James
Watson, Dennis Wallace
Watson, Jack McLaurin
Watson, James A.
Watson, Roy
Watson, Thomas Albert
Watson, Thomas Sturges
Watt, Andrew J.
Watt, Dean Day
Watt, James Arthur
Watt, Richard Frye
Wattenberg, Albert
Watters, David Jerome
Watters, James I(saac)
Watters, Loras Joseph
Watterson, Ray Leighton
Watts, Amos Holston
Watts, David Alden
Waud, Morrison
Wawzonek, Stanley
Waymire, Joseph Oliver
Wean, Raymond John
Weaner, Karl Hull
Weary, Daniel Croft
Weaver, David Andrew
Weaver, Guy Carroll
Weaver, J. Edward
Weaver, John Carrier
Weaver, Lawrence Clayton
Webb, Charles Haizlip, Jr.
Webb, George Henry
Webb, Harold Vernon
Webb, Howard William, Jr.
Webb, James Okrum, Jr.
Webb, Jervis Campbell
Webb, Lance
Webb, Neil John
Webb, Richard Gilbert
Webb, Tessa Sweazy
Webb, Thompson
Webb, William Duncan
Webber, Cletus Harlan
Webber, Everard Leland
Webber, Howard Rodney
Weber, Alvin Francis
Weber, Arthur
Weber, Bertram Anton
Weber, Charles Edward
Weber, Delbert Dean
Weber, Gregorio
Weber, Harm Allen
Weber, James Harold
Weber, Morton M.
Weber, Philip Joseph
Weber, Robert Collins
Weber, Ronald Gilbert
Weber, Roy Edwin
Weber, Walter Jacob, Jr.
Weber, Walter Peter
Weber, Wendell William
Webster, Augusta
Webster, James Carson
Webster, Leslie Tillotson, Jr.
Webster, Shirley Alton
Webster, William Hedgcock
Webster, Willis Harry
Weclew, Thaddeus Victor
Wedgeworth, Robert, Jr.
Weed, Ithamar Dryden
Weeks, Francis William
Weeks, LeRoy Gilbert
Weeks, Robert Walker
Weeks, Walter LeRoy
Weening, Richard William, Jr.
Weertman, Johannes
Weerts, C. Harris
Weese, Benjamin Horace
Weese, Harry M.
Weg, John Gerard
Wegener, Charles William
Weger, Eric
Weger, James Edward
Wegman, Myron Ezra
Wegner, Helmuth Adalbert
Wegner, Herbert Gaird
Wegner, Karl Heinrich
Wegria, Rene William Edward
Wehner, William E.
Wehrenberg, Robert Henry
Wehrle, Leroy Snyder
Wehrli, Roger Russel
Wehrwein, Austin Carl
Weichlein, William Jesset
Weick, Paul Charles
Weidenaar, Reynold Henry
Weidenbaum, Murray Lew
Weidenthal, Maurice (Bud) David
Weidner, Edward William
Weidner, Steven Arthur
Weihaupt, John George
Weil, Herman
Weil, Louis Arthur, Jr.
Weil, Myron
Weil, Rolf Alfred
Weil, Roman Lee
Weil, William Bachrach, Jr.
Weiler, Emanuel Thornton
Weimer, Arthur Martin
Weinberg, Arthur
Weinberg, Eugene David
Weinberg, Joseph Lewis
Weinberg, Lila Shaffer
Weinberg, Max Hess
Weinberg, Michael, Jr.
Weinberg, Saul S.
Weinberger, Hans Felix
Weinberger, Jerome A.
Weinel, John Philip
Weiner, Egon
Weiner, Irving Bernard

Zemmer, Joseph Lawrence, Jr.
Zeoli, William Judson
Zeps, Valdis Juris
Zerby, Lewis Kenneth
Ziebarth, E. William
Ziebarth, Robert Charles
Ziegler, Jesse H.
Ziegler, John Augustus, Jr.
Zierdt, John Graham
Zieve, Leslie

Zigman, Robert S.
Zilli, Harry Angelo, Jr.
Zillmann, Robert Edward
Zilly, Margaret Bernice
Zimmer, Hans Willi
Zimmer, William H., Jr.
Zimmerman, Anne Katherine
Zimmerman, Austin Manlove
Zimmerman, Edward John
Zimmerman, George Herbert

Zimmerman, Howard Elliot
Zimmerman, Leo M.
Zimmerman, Mary Helen
  Campion
Zimmerman, Mortimer
  William
Zimmerman, Paul Albert
Zimmerman, Robert Earl
Zimmerman, Robert Kuhlthau
Zimmerman, Thomas Fletcher

Zimmerman, Willard Paul
Zimmermann, Gerhardt
Zintel, Harold Albert
Ziolkowski, Korczak
Zion, Roger H.
Ziperski, James Richard
Zissis, George John
Zitz, Martin
Zmeskal, Otto
Zobrist, Benedict Karl

Zobrist, George Winston
Zolik, Edwin Stanislaus
Zollinger, Robert Milton
Zoltai, Tibor Zoltan
Zondervan, Peter John (Pat)
Zotter, Walter James
Zuck, Fred Hecker
Zuckerman, Stuart
Zumwalt, Donald Dean
Zumwalt, Elmo Russell, Jr.

Zumwalt, Glen Wallace
Zung, Joseph Tranvan
Zurheide, Charles Henry
Zuspan, Frederick Paul
Zwers, John Bernard
Zwettler, John Edward